PRESENTED TO

BY

ON

The fruit of the Spirit is love, joy, peace,
patience, kindness, goodness, faithfulness,
gentleness and self-control.

GALATIANS 5:22

NEW INTERNATIONAL VERSION

A One Year Study for Cultivating a Fruitful Life

GENERAL EDITOR
CALVIN MILLER

ZondervanPublishingHouse
Grand Rapids, Michigan, 49530, U.S.A.

Requests for information should be addressed to
The Zondervan Corporation
Grand Rapids, Michigan 49530

Library of Congress Catalog Card Number 99-131352

Published by Zondervan Publishing House
Grand Rapids, Michigan 49530, U.S.A.
http://www.zondervan.com

Printed in the United States of America

00 01 02 03 04 05 8 7 6 5 4 3 2 1

RRD-C

You will be pleased to know that a portion of the purchase price of your new NIV Bible has been provided to International Bible Society to help spread the gospel of Jesus Christ around the world!

TABLE OF CONTENTS

OLD TESTAMENT

NEW TESTAMENT

Books of the Bible

in Alphabetical Order

The books of the New Testament are in *italic.*

INTRODUCTION

The Fruit of the Spirit Bible

ON LIVING IN THE SPIRIT

So I say, live by the Spirit, and you will not gratify the desires of the sinful nature. For the sinful nature desires what is contrary to the Spirit, and the Spirit what is contrary to the sinful nature.

The acts of the sinful nature are obvious: sexual immorality, impurity and debauchery; idolatry and witchcraft; hatred, discord, jealousy, fits of rage, selfish ambition, dissentions, factions and envy; drunkenness, orgies and the like. I warn you, as I did before, that those who live like this will not inherit the kingdom of God.

But the fruit of the Spirit is love, joy, peace, patience, kindness, goodness, faithfulness, gentleness and self-control. Against such things there is no law. Those who belong to Christ Jesus have crucified the sinful nature with its passions and desires (Galatians 5:16–17,19–24).

VIEWING THE BIBLE AS THE FRUIT BASKET

Christian publishers and leaders point out that there appears to be a nearly universal interest in the Christian community in the "fruit of the Spirit." The passage listing the fruit of the Spirit is found in Galatians 5:22–23, but as you read through the entire Bible, you will notice people who embody love, joy and peace. You will encounter people who profile patience and kindness. You will read passages about goodness, faithfulness, gentleness and self-control. *The Fruit of the Spirit Bible* highlights the fruit of the Spirit as it is presented throughout the entire Bible, leading you to greater understanding of each quality and challenging you to cultivate that quality in your own life.

THE FRUIT OF THE SPIRIT BIBLE

This Bible has been developed as an aid toward pursuing these indispensable qualities of the committed Christian life. The layout and helps have been designed to help those who long to move on in their Christian walk to maturity in Christ. To assist the reader in accomplishing this level of maturity, this Bible strives to do two things: First, our hope is that you will begin thinking about the fruit of the Spirit in a way that will daily renew your mind and invigorate your spirit. Thinking straight results in living straight, and the mind is the battleground upon which most of our spiritual battles are ultimately won or lost. Paul wrote to the Philippians, "Finally, brothers, whatever is true, whatever is noble, whatever is right, whatever is pure, whatever is lovely, whatever is admirable—if anything is excellent or praiseworthy—think about such things" (Philippians 4:8).

Second, we must act out our faith before the theater of a watching world. Merely thinking about the fruit of the Spirit will not impress or impact the world. Our thoughts must coach and control our behavior. Paul wrote, "I urge you, brothers, in view of God's mercy, to offer your bodies as living sacrifices, holy and pleasing to God—this is your spiritual act of worship. Do not conform any longer to the pattern of this world, but be transformed by the renewing of your mind" (Romans 12:1–2). Acting out the values known as the fruit of the Spirit will indeed transform our hearts and forge our characters.

Desiring to embody the fruit of the Spirit makes us inwardly like Christ.
Acting out the fruit of the Spirit convinces and converts a needy world.

HOW TO OWN THE FRUIT OF THE SPIRIT

The fruit of the Spirit are not merely characteristics that we aspire to own. They are glorious graces that must characterize all those who pursue a Christlike character. There are nine fruit of the Spirit listed in Galatians 5:22–23. This is a catalog of the cardinal virtues of the Christian faith. The notes of this Bible focus on those virtues and offer guidance as to how we can make them a part of our lives. But there are no "how to's" in this Bible. Incorporating the fruit of the Spirit into our lives is not the result of personal effort or direct discipline. Love, joy, peace, patience, kindness, goodness, faithfulness, gentleness and self-control are not personality traits achieved by repetition and rehearsal. Rather these beautiful qualities of Christlikeness are added to our lives as the by-product of an indirect focus. Those who seek Christ that they may "know [him] and the power of his resurrection and the fellowship of sharing in his sufferings" (Philippians 3:10) are possessed of a passion that produces a Christlike spirit. The spiritual hunger that causes us to want to be more like Jesus will in time be satisfied. At that point the fruit of the Spirit will inevitably characterize our lives—because our focus will permit no other culmination to our love affair with Jesus Christ.

HOW TO USE THE FRUIT OF THE SPIRIT BIBLE

1. Turn to the first "Journey Into Christlikeness" home page (Genesis 1:29, page 5) and begin your study with "Day One."
2. At the end of your first day's study, turn to the next designated passage and place your marker at the passage for the next day's study. Hold your place at the home page with a different marker. Follow the Day Two through Day Five prompts to complete your week's study. Note that you will read a short commentary on each of Days Two through Five on the Home Page, followed by the longer reading to which you are referred.
3. On Friday of your first week, look to the bottom of the home page for direction to the next week's study.
4. If you prefer to focus on one particular fruit of the Spirit until you have moved through all the relevant passages, simply look up that fruit in the "Home Page Contents" (page xi) and follow the readings as designated.
5. If you're looking for insights into other topics that might pertain to more than one fruit of the Spirit, consider using the Topical Index at the back of the Bible, page 1548.

FEATURES OF THE FRUIT OF THE SPIRIT BIBLE

This Bible uses the New International Version, the world's most widely read and best-loved translation. As you seek to use this Bible as a tool to become increasingly conformed to Christ, you will find that the gripping and convicting words of Scripture, rather than the ancillary notes, provide the real impetus for the transformation in your life. Nonetheless, the notes have been written with the greatest possible care in the hope that they may link their encouragement with that of the Biblical text, helping to make your life and witness a real force for the Kingdom of God.

Study System

The main study system of the *Fruit of the Spirit Bible* centers around 52 home pages, each of which will guide you through a five-day study of what God says in his Word about a fruit of the Spirit. Each week addresses a different principle related to the fruit being discussed.

Each of the 52 home pages is located near a Bible passage that relates specifically to the particular aspect of the fruit of the Spirit to be considered for that week. The Day 1 study can be found on the home page itself. After the first day's study, the home page provides you with prompts to direct your study for Day Two through Day Five. Each of these "journey into Christlikeness" study paths will guide you to different passages in the Bible that address the principle being discussed.

The home pages are designed to lead your study in the following manner:

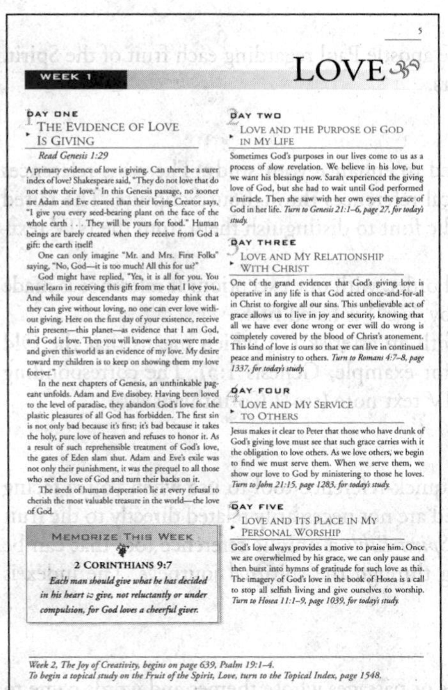

5

LOVE

WEEK 1

DAY ONE
THE EVIDENCE OF LOVE IS GIVING

Read Genesis 1:29

A primary evidence of love is giving. Can there be a surer index of love? Shakespeare said, "They do not love that do not show their love." In this Genesis passage, no sooner are Adam and Eve created than their loving Creator says, "I give you every seed-bearing plant on the face of the whole earth . . . They will be yours for food." Human beings are barely created when they receive from God a gift: the earth itself!

One can only imagine "Mr. and Mrs. First Folks" saying, "No, God—it is too much! All this for us?"

God might have replied, "Yes, it is all for you. You must learn in receiving this gift from me that I love you. And while your descendants may someday think that they can give without loving, no one can ever love without giving. Here on the first day of your existence, receive this present—this planet—as evidence that I am God, and God is love. Then you will know that you were made and given this world as an evidence of my love. My desire toward my children is to keep on showing them my love forever."

In the next chapters of Genesis, an unthinkable pageant unfolds. Adam and Eve disobey. Having been loved to the level of paradise, they abandon God's love for the plastic pleasures of all God has forbidden. The first sin is not only bad because it's first; it's bad because it takes the holy, pure love of heaven and refuses to honor it. As a result of such reprehensible treatment of God's love, the gates of Eden slam shut. Adam and Eve's exile was not only their punishment, it was the prequel to all those who see the love of God and turn their backs on it.

The seeds of human desperation lie at every refusal to cherish the most valuable treasure in the world—the love of God.

MEMORIZE THIS WEEK

2 CORINTHIANS 9:7

Each man should give what he has decided in his heart to give, not reluctantly or under compulsion, for God loves a cheerful giver.

DAY TWO
LOVE AND THE PURPOSE OF GOD IN MY LIFE

Sometimes God's purposes in our lives come to us as a process of slow revelation. We believe in his love, but we want his blessings now. Sarah experienced the giving love of God, but she had to wait until God performed a miracle. Then she saw with her own eyes the grace of God in her life. *Turn to Genesis 21:1–6, page 27, for today's study.*

DAY THREE
LOVE AND MY RELATIONSHIP WITH CHRIST

One of the grand evidences that God's giving love is operative in any life is that God acted once-and-for-all in Christ to forgive all our sins. This unbelievable act of grace allows us to live in joy and security, knowing that all we have ever done wrong or ever will do wrong is completely covered by the blood of Christ's atonement. This kind of love is ours so that we can live in continued peace and ministry to others. *Turn to Romans 4:7–8, page 1337, for today's study.*

DAY FOUR
LOVE AND MY SERVICE TO OTHERS

Jesus makes it clear to Peter that those who have drunk of God's giving love must see that such grace carries with it the obligation to love others. As we love others, we begin to find we must serve them. When we serve them, we show our love to God by ministering to those he loves. *Turn to John 21:15, page 1283, for today's study.*

DAY FIVE
LOVE AND ITS PLACE IN MY PERSONAL WORSHIP

God's love always provides a motive to praise him. Once we are overwhelmed by his grace, we can only pause and then burst into hymns of gratitude for such love as this. The imagery of God's love in the book of Hosea is a call to stop all selfish living and give ourselves to worship. *Turn to Hosea 11:1–9, page 1039, for today's study.*

Week 2, The Joy of Creativity, begins on page 639, Psalm 19:1–4.
To begin a topical study on the Fruit of the Spirit, Love, turn to the Topical Index, page 1548.

Day One: Fruit Introduction
The initial study introduces the fruit and the topic to which it relates and provides Biblical background. All the following days expand on this introductory study—a particular aspect or employment of the fruit of the Spirit. Note once again that the brief entries for Days Two through Five on the home page serve as prompts or "teasers" to lead you to the more lengthy discussions found elsewhere in Scripture.

Day Two: Fruit and God's Purpose in My Life
This second study inspires you to manifest this fruit in a particular context, both as a response to, and a working out of, God's grand design for your life.

Day Three: Fruit and My Relationship With Christ
Day Three demonstrates ways to exercise this fruit to enhance and deepen the quality of your relationship with Jesus Christ.

Day Four: Fruit and My Service to Others
The fourth day study points out a specific application of this fruit for the benefit of others whom you are striving to serve.

Day Five: Fruit and Its Place in My Personal Worship
This final study discusses a facet or utilization of this fruit as it relates to your personal worship experience.

Each of the Day Two through Day Five Bible studies ends with a note that will direct you back to the home page for the week. And at the end of the week's study, you'll find a note that will direct you to the next study.

Book Introductions

Each book of the Bible begins with an introduction designed to help the reader understand the themes and motifs of that particular book, to identify the author and to set the book within its historical context.

Inspirational Notes

Epigrams are included at varioius points of the Scriptural text. They are tied to a specific text and written in order to highlight the relationship of the passage to the overall Biblical theme of the fruit of the Spirit.

Character Profiles

Character profiles are scattered throughout the Bible to spotlight Bible characters and describe how each serves as a positive—or negative—example of a particular fruit of the Spirit. The profiles contain encouragement for the reader to cultivate each fruit of the Spirit in his or her daily quest for Christlikeness. A complete list of these character profiles is contained in the "Character Profile Index," page 1547.

Jesus Speaks Out on the Fruit of the Spirit

Nine special, full-page articles, in which Jesus himself comments on each of the fruit of the Spirit, appear at various locations throughout the Bible. These passages are gleaned from the four Gospels and from the book of Revelation.

Paul Speaks Out on the Fruit of the Spirit

Nine special, full-page articles offer commentary from the apostle Paul regarding each fruit of the Spirit. These insights are gleaned from his New Testament letters.

NIV Side-Column Reference System

The NIV side-column reference system has been included to enhance your study. The cross-references link words or phrases in the NIV text with related Biblical references throughout Scripture. The raised letters denoting these cross-references are set in a light italic font to distinguish them from the NIV text-note letters, which use a Roman typeface.

The list of references for a particular verse is in Biblical order, with one exception: If reference is made to a verse within the same chapter, that verse (indicated by "ver") is listed first.

In the Old Testament, some references are marked with an asterisk (*), which means that the Old Testament verse is quoted in the New Testament (see, for example, Genesis 1:3). The corresponding information is provided in the New Testament by the NIV text note (see 2 Corinthians 4:6).

Topical Index

The Topical Index for this Bible has been designed as a quick-reference tool to use when you're facing everyday challenges and opportunities, and the topics listed are not necessarily related directly to the fruit of the Spirit. This Topical Index makes *The Fruit of the Spirit Bible* a unique reference tool that can be of continued use long after your initial year of traveling through the spiritual journeys. The index is found on page 1548.

Concordance

The concordance is a helpful tool for locating those verses or passages whose themes and words come to mind but whose citations may not. This concordance targets key words throughout Scripture and will serve as a lifelong resource to enhance your Bible study. The concordance begins on page 1564.

HOME PAGE CONTENTS

This page is provided to give you a perspective on the different fruit of the Spirit addressed in The Fruit of the Spirit Bible. *The various fruits are addressed in the 52 weekly home pages. These "Journey Into Christlikeness" study passages form the main framework for this Bible's many study features. While these "Journey Into Christlikeness" articles are placed throughout the text in Biblical order, this list is in alphabetical order under the nine fruit of the Spirit listed in Galatians 5:22–23.*

LOVE

JOY

PEACE

PATIENCE

KINDNESS

Home Page Contents

GOODNESS

FAITHFULNESS

GENTLENESS

SELF-CONTROL

PREFACE TO THE NIV

THE NEW INTERNATIONAL VERSION is a completely new translation of the Holy Bible made by over a hundred scholars working directly from the best available Hebrew, Aramaic and Greek texts. It had its beginning in 1965 when, after several years of exploratory study by committees from the Christian Reformed Church and the National Association of Evangelicals, a group of scholars met at Palos Heights, Illinois, and concurred in the need for a new translation of the Bible in contemporary English. This group, though not made up of official church representatives, was transdenominational. Its conclusion was endorsed by a large number of leaders from many denominations who met in Chicago in 1966.

Responsibility for the new version was delegated by the Palos Heights group to a self-governing body of fifteen, the Committee on Bible Translation, composed for the most part of biblical scholars from colleges, universities and seminaries. In 1967 the New York Bible Society (now the International Bible Society) generously undertook the financial sponsorship of the project—a sponsorship that made it possible to enlist the help of many distinguished scholars. The fact that participants from the United States, Great Britain, Canada, Australia and New Zealand worked together gave the project its international scope. That they were from many denominations—including Anglican, Assemblies of God, Baptist, Brethren, Christian Reformed, Church of Christ, Evangelical Free, Lutheran, Mennonite, Methodist, Nazarene, Presbyterian, Wesleyan and other churches—helped to safeguard the translation from sectarian bias.

How it was made helps to give the New International Version its distinctiveness. The translation of each book was assigned to a team of scholars. Next, one of the Intermediate Editorial Committees revised the initial translation, with constant reference to the Hebrew, Aramaic or Greek. Their work then went to one of the General Editorial Committees, which checked it in detail and made another thorough revision. This revision in turn was carefully reviewed by the Committee on Bible Translation, which made further changes and then released the final version for publication. In this way the entire Bible underwent three revisions, during each of which the translation was examined for its faithfulness to the original languages and for its English style.

All this involved many thousands of hours of research and discussion regarding the meaning of the texts and the precise way of putting them into English. It may well be that no other translation has been made by a more thorough process of review and revision from committee to committee than this one.

From the beginning of the project, the Committee on Bible Translation held to certain goals for the New International Version: that it would be an accurate translation and one that would have clarity and literary quality and so prove suitable for public and private reading, teaching, preaching, memorizing and liturgical use. The Committee also sought to preserve some measure of continuity with the long tradition of translating the Scriptures into English.

In working toward these goals, the translators were united in their commitment to the authority and infallibility of the Bible as God's Word in written form. They believe that it contains the divine answer to the deepest needs of humanity, that it sheds unique light on our path in a dark world, and that it sets forth the way to our eternal well-being.

The first concern of the translators has been the accuracy of the translation and its fidelity to the thought of the biblical writers. They have weighed the significance of the lexical and grammatical details of the Hebrew, Aramaic and Greek texts. At the same time, they have striven for more than a word-for-word translation. Because thought patterns and syntax differ from language to language, faithful communication of the meaning of the writers of the Bible demands frequent modifications in sentence structure and constant regard for the contextual meanings of words.

A sensitive feeling for style does not always accompany scholarship. Accordingly the Committee on Bible Translation submitted the developing version to a number of stylistic consultants. Two of them read every book of both Old and New Testaments twice—once before and once after the last major revision—and made invaluable suggestions. Samples of the translation were tested for clarity and ease of reading by various kinds of people—young and old, highly educated and less well educated, ministers and laymen.

Concern for clear and natural English—that the New International Version should be idiomatic but not idiosyncratic, contemporary but not dated—motivated the translators and consultants. At the same time, they tried to reflect the differing styles of the biblical writers. In view of the international use of English, the translators sought to avoid obvious Americanisms on the one hand and obvious Anglicisms on the other. A British edition reflects the comparatively few differences of significant idiom and of spelling.

As for the traditional pronouns "thou," "thee" and "thine" in reference to the Deity, the translators judged that to use these archaisms (along with the old verb forms such as "doest," "wouldest" and "hadst") would violate accuracy in translation. Neither Hebrew, Aramaic nor Greek uses special pronouns for the persons of the Godhead. A present-day translation is not enhanced by forms that in the time of the King James Version were used in everyday speech, whether referring to God or man.

For the Old Testament the standard Hebrew text, the Masoretic Text as published in the latest editions of *Biblia Hebraica*, was used throughout. The Dead Sea Scrolls contain material bearing on an earlier stage of the Hebrew text. They were consulted, as were the Samaritan Pentateuch and the ancient scribal traditions relating to textual changes. Sometimes a variant Hebrew reading in the margin of the Masoretic Text was followed instead of the text itself. Such instances, being variants within the Masoretic tradition, are not specified by footnotes. In rare cases, words in the consonantal text were divided differently from the way they appear in the Masoretic Text. Footnotes indicate this. The translators also consulted the more important early versions—the Septuagint; Aquila, Symmachus and Theodotion; the Vulgate; the Syriac Peshitta; the Targums; and for the Psalms the Juxta Hebraica of Jerome. Readings from these versions were occasionally followed where the Masoretic Text seemed doubtful and where accepted principles of textual criticism showed that one or more of these textual witnesses appeared to provide the correct reading. Such instances are footnoted. Sometimes vowel letters and vowel signs did not, in the judgment of the translators, represent the correct vowels for the original consonantal text. Accordingly some words were read with a different set of vowels. These instances are usually not indicated by footnotes.

The Greek text used in translating the New Testament was an eclectic one. No other piece of ancient literature has such an abundance of manuscript witnesses as does the New Testament. Where existing manuscripts differ, the translators made their choice of readings according to accepted principles of New Testament textual criticism. Footnotes call attention to places where there was uncertainty about what the original text was. The best current printed texts of the Greek New Testament were used.

There is a sense in which the work of translation is never wholly finished. This applies to all great literature and uniquely so to the Bible. In 1973 the New Testament in the New International Version was published. Since then, suggestions for corrections and revisions have been received from various sources. The Committee on Bible Translation carefully considered the suggestions and adopted a number of them. These were incorporated in the first printing of the entire Bible in 1978. Additional revisions were made by the Committee on Bible Translation in 1983 and appear in printings after that date.

As in other ancient documents, the precise meaning of the biblical texts is sometimes uncertain. This is more often the case with the Hebrew and Aramaic texts than with the Greek text. Although archaeological and linguistic discoveries in this century aid in understanding difficult passages, some uncertainties remain. The more significant of these have been called to the reader's attention in the footnotes.

In regard to the divine name *YHWH*, commonly referred to as the *Tetragrammaton*, the translators adopted the device used in most English versions of rendering that name as LORD in capital letters to distinguish it from *Adonai*, another Hebrew word rendered "Lord," for which small letters are used. Wherever the two names stand together in the Old Testament as a compound name of God, they are rendered "Sovereign LORD."

Because for most readers today the phrases "The LORD of hosts" and "the God of hosts" have little meaning, this version renders them "the LORD

Almighty" and "God Almighty." These renderings convey the sense of the Hebrew, namely, "he who is sovereign over all the 'hosts' (powers) in heaven and on earth, especially over the 'hosts' (armies) of Israel." For readers unacquainted with Hebrew this does not make clear the distinction between *Sabaoth* ("hosts" or "Almighty") and *Shaddai* (which can also be translated "Almighty"), but the latter occurs infrequently and is always footnoted. When *Adonai* and *YHWH Sabaoth* occur together, they are rendered "the Lord, the LORD Almighty."

As for other proper nouns, the familiar spellings of the King James Version are generally retained. Names traditionally spelled with "ch," except where it is final, are usually spelled in this translation with "k" or "c," since the biblical languages do not have the sound that "ch" frequently indicates in English—for example, in *chant*. For well-known names such as Zechariah, however, the traditional spelling has been retained. Variation in the spelling of names in the original languages has usually not been indicated. Where a person or place has two or more different names in the Hebrew, Aramaic or Greek texts, the more familiar one has generally been used, with footnotes where needed.

To achieve clarity the translators sometimes supplied words not in the original texts but required by the context. If there was uncertainty about such material, it is enclosed in brackets. Also for the sake of clarity or style, nouns, including some proper nouns, are sometimes substituted for pronouns, and vice versa. And though the Hebrew writers often shifted back and forth between first, second and third personal pronouns without change of antecedent, this translation often makes them uniform, in accordance with English style and without the use of footnotes.

Poetical passages are printed as poetry, that is, with indentation of lines and with separate stanzas. These are generally designed to reflect the structure of Hebrew poetry. This poetry is normally characterized by parallelism in balanced lines. Most of the poetry in the Bible is in the Old Testament, and scholars differ regarding the scansion of Hebrew lines. The translators determined the stanza divisions for the most part by analysis of the subject matter. The stanzas therefore serve as poetic paragraphs.

As an aid to the reader, italicized sectional headings are inserted in most of the books. They are not to be regarded as part of the NIV text, are not for oral reading, and are not intended to dictate the interpretation of the sections they head.

The footnotes in this version are of several kinds, most of which need no explanation. Those giving alternative translations begin with "Or" and generally introduce the alternative with the word preceding it in the text, except when it is a single-word alternative; in poetry quoted in footnote a slant mark indicates a line division. Footnotes introduced by "Or" do not have uniform significance. In some cases two possible translations were considered to have about equal validity. In other cases, though the translators were convinced that the translation in the text was correct, they judged that another interpretation was possible and of sufficient importance to be represented in a footnote.

In the New Testament, footnotes that refer to uncertainty regarding the original text are introduced by "Some manuscripts" or similar expressions. In the Old Testament, evidence for the reading chosen is given first and evidence for the alternative is added after a semicolon (for example: Septuagint; Hebrew *father*). In such notes the term "Hebrew" refers to the Masoretic Text.

It should be noted that minerals, flora and fauna, architectural details, articles of clothing jewelry, musical instruments and other articles cannot always be identified with precision. Also measures of capacity in the biblical period are particularly uncertain (see the table of weights and measures following the text).

Like all translations of the Bible, made as they are by imperfect man, this one undoubtedly falls short of its goals. Yet we are grateful to God for the extent to which he has enabled us to realize these goals and for the strength he has given us and our colleagues to complete our task. We offer this version of the Bible to him in whose name and for whose glory it has been made. We pray that it will lead many into a better understanding of the Holy Scriptures and a fuller knowledge of Jesus Christ the incarnate Word, of whom the Scriptures so faithfully testify.

The Committee on Bible Translation

June 1978
(Revised August 1983)

Names of the translators and editors may be secured from the International Bible Society, translation sponsors of the New International Version, 1820 Jet Stream Drive, Colorado Springs, Colorado 80921-3696 U.S.A.

OLD TESTAMENT

GENESIS

AUTHORSHIP AND DATE

Moses

c. 1450 B.C., to c. 1410 B.C.

KEY THEMES

The first phrase of the book of Genesis is from the Hebrew word *bereshith* or "in the beginning." The Greek word for this first phrase is *geneseos*, which can mean "genealogy," "history of origin" or "beginning." Genesis falls into two distinct segments. Chapters 1–11 deal with creation and the fall, and chapters 12–50 explain the earliest roots of the Hebrew people. In Genesis, the origins of the following important ideas are explored:

1. The origin of the universe and, particularly, the human race
2. How sin came to be and the results of human disobedience
3. The beginnings of the nation of Israel through the coming of the patriarch Abraham into the land of Canaan
4. An explanation of Israel in Egypt

FRUIT OF THE SPIRIT IN GENESIS

Love: The love of God is evident as God created, led, redeemed and moved through the lives of the first people, as well as the covenant people of Israel.

Joy: Joy was manifested in the personal satisfaction God derived from creation. As he created, he daily observed that each of the creative acts was "good." Joy was part of Rebekah's life when her obedience to God's will led her to a husband and family. Joy was the result of Joseph's life as he saved his family from famine.

Peace: Peace is the natural corollary of covenant. When God gave Noah his covenant, peacefulness settled on the entire earth as the floodwaters soaked into the ground and plants grew. The promise of "never again" is a central theme in God's will and is a promise by God for all people throughout time.

Patience: While we wait, patience makes the time seem shorter and sweeter. Abraham waited for an heir, and while he waited, he obeyed God.

Kindness: If faithfulness leads to obedience, kindness indicates the spirit in which we obey. Both Abraham and Joseph illustrate a willing desire to obey God. Kindness means that we obey

God out of love, with joyous compliance, and we serve others without resentment. Kindness always wears a spirit of servanthood, which our egos gladly assume whenever we come face-to-face with God.

Goodness: From the very beginning of time, God's holiness and his intolerance for sin have been obvious. Genesis describes how people learned about God's goodness and his desire that atonement be made for sin. God required that all people deal seriously with the problem of sin in their lives. Every altar that was built displayed the roots of the sacrificial system and made it clear that goodness was God's agenda.

Faithfulness: Abraham became the model of how God esteems those who obey him, whether or not they understand the consequences of what he requires. Again and again Abraham trusted and obeyed God. He was asked to leave his homeland in Ur and go to Canaan; he was asked to believe that he would be the father of a great nation; he was asked to wait for a son; he was asked to sacrifice that son on Mount Moriah. Abraham obeyed. There was no requirement too stringent or too demanding for Abraham to accept.

Gentleness: Gentleness is God's manner when disclosing himself to his people. Think of his walks with Adam and Eve in the garden. God's requirements are firm, but his approach to those whom he will use is so often gentle. Where his manner is more austere and demanding, this stance is necessary to get the attention of those to whom he would reveal himself.

Self-Control: Self-control is expressed when we set aside our own agendas and life plans in order to follow God's will. Many of the patriarchs and matriarchs described in this book followed God's will and became honored for their choices.

The Beginning

1:1 [a]Jn 1:1-2 [b]Job 38:4; Ps 90:2; Isa 42:5; 44:24; 45:12,18; Ac 17:24; Heb 11:3; Rev 4:11

1 In the beginning[a] God created
the heavens and the earth.[b] 2Now
the earth was[a] formless and empty,[c]
darkness was over the surface of
the deep, and the Spirit of God[d]
was hovering over the waters.

LOVE

GOD LOVED THE WORLD BEFORE HE MADE IT

Genesis 1:1

Every world was in God's mind before it came to occupy his sky. God created and all things came into existence; Jesus came and all things acquired new significance.

1:2 [c]Jer 4:23 [d]Ps 104:30
1:3 [e]Ps 33:6,9; 148:5; Heb 11:3 [f]2Co 4:6*
1:5 [g]Ps 74:16
1:6 [h]Jer 10:12

3And God said,[e] "Let there be light,"
and there was light.[f] 4God saw that
the light was good, and he separated the light from the darkness.
5God called the light "day," and
the darkness he called "night."[g]
And there was evening, and there
was morning—the first day.
6And God said, "Let there be an expanse[h] between the waters to separate water from water." 7So God
made the expanse and separated
the water under the expanse from
the water above it.[i] And it was
so. 8God called the expanse "sky."
And there was evening, and there
was morning—the second day.
9And God said, "Let the water under
the sky be gathered to one place,[j]
and let dry ground appear." And
it was so. 10God called the dry
ground "land," and the gathered
waters he called "seas." And God
saw that it was good.
11Then God said, "Let the land
produce vegetation:[k] seed-bearing
plants and trees on the land that
bear fruit with seed in it, according to their various kinds." And it
was so. 12The land produced vegetation: plants bearing seed according to their kinds and trees bearing
fruit with seed in it according to
their kinds. And God saw that it
was good. 13And there was evening, and there was morning—the
third day.

1:7 [i]Job 38:8-11, 16; Ps 148:4
1:9 [j]Job 38:8-11; Ps 104:6-9; Pr 8:29; Jer 5:22; 2Pe 3:5
1:11 [k]Ps 65:9-13; 104:14

14And God said, "Let there be lights[l]
in the expanse of the sky to separate the day from the night, and
let them serve as signs[m] to mark
seasons[n] and days and years, 15and
let them be lights in the expanse of
the sky to give light on the earth."
And it was so. 16God made two
great lights—the greater light to
govern[o] the day and the lesser light
to govern[p] the night. He also made
the stars.[q] 17God set them in the

1:14 [l]Ps 74:16 [m]Jer 10:2 [n]Ps 104:19
1:16 [o]Ps 136:8 [p]Ps 136:9 [q]Job 38:7, 31-32; Ps 8:3; Isa 40:26

[a]2 Or possibly *became*

DAY 5 FIVE

JOY AND ITS PLACE IN MY PERSONAL WORSHIP

Read Genesis 1:1–5

During the first week of the world's existence, God created the heavens and the earth. And on the first day of that week—there in the middle of dark chaos—God created light. What a wonder! Light! Splitting dead nothingness like a laser instrument, driving malignant darkness from the universe. Light! Traveling at 186,000 miles per second at the very command of God. Light! Bringing things that could not be seen to eyes as yet uncreated. God breathed the words *fiat lux* and smiled at this phenomenon of both science and grace. God smiled because he knew that the power of his glorious first light would in time make vision possible.

He created light so that a cold world could orbit a distant sun and find its silver track warm enough to sustain life. He created light so that lasers, super-novae and galaxies could all proclaim themselves. He created light to warm and illuminate all things cold and dark.

But light isn't merely a physical energy form. Light represents the spirituality of God. He created light because darkness is hopeless stuff. He created light so that despair will have no place to hide. When God said, "Let there be light," the angels must have broken into glad *hallelujahs*. For when there is light, the natural response of all who behold it is joy. Joy cannot survey the marvels of anything God has created and keep silent.

To begin a study on the topic of The Joy of Creativity, turn to the home page on page 639.

1:18 [r]Jer 33:20,25

expanse of the sky to give light on the earth, 18 to govern the day and the night,[r] and to separate light from darkness. And God saw that it was good. 19 And there was evening, and there was morning—the fourth day.

20 And God said, "Let the water teem with living creatures, and let birds fly above the earth across the expanse of the sky." 21 So God created the great creatures of the sea and every living and moving thing with which the water teems,[s] according to their kinds, and every winged bird according to its kind. And God saw that it was good. 22 God blessed them and said, "Be fruitful and increase in number and fill the water in the seas, and let the birds increase on the earth."[t] 23 And there was evening, and there was morning—the fifth day.

1:21 [s]Ps 104:25-26

1:22 [t]ver 28; Ge 8:17

24 And God said, "Let the land produce living creatures according to their kinds: livestock, creatures that move along the ground, and wild animals, each according to its kind." And it was so. 25 God made the wild animals[u] according to their kinds, the livestock according to their kinds, and all the creatures that move along the ground according to their kinds. And God saw that it was good.

1:25 [u]Jer 27:5

26 Then God said, "Let us[v] make man in our image,[w] in our likeness, and let them rule[x] over the fish of the sea and the birds of the air, over the livestock, over all the earth,[a] and over all the creatures that move along the ground."

1:26 [v]Ps 100:3 [w]Ge 9:6; Jas 3:9 [x]Ps 8:6-8

GOODNESS

GOD'S MORAL MIRROR

Genesis 1:26

It was a high compliment to human beings when God made us his moral mirror. It was an even higher compliment when God, in Christ, assumed a human form to repair that broken mirror.

The human renovation
Was a costly thing indeed.
Who knew that God could suffer?
Who knew that God could bleed?

27 So God created man in his own image,[y]
in the image of God he created him;
male and female[z] he created them.

1:27 [y]1Co 11:7 [z]Ge 5:2; Mt 19:4*; Mk 10:6*

28 God blessed them and said to them, "Be fruitful and increase in number; fill the earth[a] and subdue it. Rule over the fish of the sea and the birds of the air and over every living creature that moves on the ground."

1:28 [a]Ge 9:1,7; Lev 26:9

29 Then God said, "I give you every seed-bearing plant on the face of the whole earth and every tree that has fruit with seed in it. They will be yours for food.[b] 30 And to all the beasts of the earth and all the birds of the air and all the creatures that move on the ground—everything that has the breath of life in it—I give every green plant for food.[c]" And it was so.

1:29 [b]Ps 104:14

1:30 [c]Ps 104:14,27; 145:15

31 God saw all that he had made,[d] and it was very good.[e] And there was evening, and there was morning—the sixth day.

1:31 [d]Ps 104:24 [e]1Ti 4:4

2 Thus the heavens and the earth were completed in all their vast array.

2 By the seventh day God had finished the work he had been doing; so on the seventh day he rested[b] from all his work.[f] 3 And God blessed the seventh day and made it holy,[g] because on it he rested from all the work of creating that he had done.

2:2 [f]Ex 20:11; 31:17; Heb 4:4*

2:3 [g]Lev 23:3; Isa 58:13

Adam and Eve

4 This is the account of the heavens and the earth when they were created.

When the LORD God made the earth and the heavens— 5 and no shrub of the field had yet appeared on the earth[c] and no plant of the field had yet sprung up,[h] for the LORD God had not sent rain on the earth[c][i] and there was no man to work the ground, 6 but streams[d] came up from the earth and watered the whole surface of the ground— 7 the LORD

2:5 [h]Ge 1:11 [i]Ps 65:9-10

[a] *26* Hebrew; Syriac *all the wild animals* [b] *2* Or *ceased*; also in verse 3 [c] *5* Or *land*; also in verse 6 [d] *6* Or *mist*

LOVE

WEEK 1

1 DAY ONE ✓

▸ THE EVIDENCE OF LOVE IS GIVING

Read Genesis 1:29

A primary evidence of love is giving. Can there be a surer index of love? Shakespeare said, "They do not love that do not show their love." In this Genesis passage, no sooner are Adam and Eve created than their loving Creator says, "I give you every seed-bearing plant on the face of the whole earth . . . They will be yours for food." Human beings are barely created when they receive from God a gift: the earth itself!

One can only imagine "Mr. and Mrs. First Folks" saying, "No, God—it is too much! All this for us?"

God might have replied, "Yes, it is all for you. You must learn in receiving this gift from me that I love you. And while your descendants may someday think that they can give without loving, no one can ever love without giving. Here on the first day of your existence, receive this present—this planet—as evidence that I am God, and God is love. Then you will know that you were made and given this world as an evidence of my love. My desire toward my children is to keep on showing them my love forever."

In the next chapters of Genesis, an unthinkable pageant unfolds. Adam and Eve disobey. Having been loved to the level of paradise, they abandon God's love for the plastic pleasures of all God has forbidden. The first sin is not only bad because it's first; it's bad because it takes the holy, pure love of heaven and refuses to honor it. As a result of such reprehensible treatment of God's love, the gates of Eden slam shut. Adam and Eve's exile was not only their punishment, it was the prequel to all those who see the love of God and turn their backs on it.

The seeds of human desperation lie at every refusal to cherish the most valuable treasure in the world—the love of God.

> **MEMORIZE THIS WEEK**
>
> **2 CORINTHIANS 9:7**
>
> ***Each man should give what he has decided in his heart to give, not reluctantly or under compulsion, for God loves a cheerful giver.***

2 DAY TWO ✓

▸ LOVE AND THE PURPOSE OF GOD IN MY LIFE

Sometimes God's purposes in our lives come to us as a process of slow revelation. We believe in his love, but we want his blessings now. Sarah experienced the giving love of God, but she had to wait until God performed a miracle. Then she saw with her own eyes the grace of God in her life. *Turn to Genesis 21:1–6, page 27, for today's study.*

3 DAY THREE

▸ LOVE AND MY RELATIONSHIP WITH CHRIST

One of the grand evidences that God's giving love is operative in any life is that God acted once-and-for-all in Christ to forgive all our sins. This unbelievable act of grace allows us to live in joy and security, knowing that all we have ever done wrong or ever will do wrong is completely covered by the blood of Christ's atonement. This kind of love is ours so that we can live in continued peace and ministry to others. *Turn to Romans 4:7–8, page 1337, for today's study.*

4 DAY FOUR

▸ LOVE AND MY SERVICE TO OTHERS

Jesus makes it clear to Peter that those who have drunk of God's giving love must see that such grace carries with it the obligation to love others. As we love others, we begin to find we must serve them. When we serve them, we show our love to God by ministering to those he loves. *Turn to John 21:15, page 1283, for today's study.*

5 DAY FIVE

▸ LOVE AND ITS PLACE IN MY PERSONAL WORSHIP

God's love always provides a motive to praise him. Once we are overwhelmed by his grace, we can only pause and then burst into hymns of gratitude for such love as this. The imagery of God's love in the book of Hosea is a call to stop all selfish living and give ourselves to worship. *Turn to Hosea 11:1–9, page 1039, for today's study.*

Week 2, The Joy of Creativity, begins on page 639, Psalm 19:1–4.
To begin a topical study on the Fruit of the Spirit, Love, turn to the Topical Index, page 1548.

God formed the man[a] from the dust[j] of
the ground[k] and breathed into his nostrils the breath[l] of life,[m] and the man
became a living being.[n]
8Now the LORD God had planted
a garden in the east, in Eden;[o] and
there he put the man he had formed.
9And the LORD God made all kinds
of trees grow out of the ground—trees
that were pleasing to the eye and good
for food. In the middle of the garden
were the tree of life[p] and the tree of the
knowledge of good and evil.[q]
10A river watering the garden flowed
from Eden; from there it was separated
into four headwaters. 11The name of
the first is the Pishon; it winds through
the entire land of Havilah, where there
is gold. 12(The gold of that land is
good; aromatic resin[b] and onyx are also
there.) 13The name of the second river
is the Gihon; it winds through the entire land of Cush.[c] 14The name of the
third river is the Tigris;[r] it runs along
the east side of Asshur. And the fourth
river is the Euphrates.
15The LORD God took the man and
put him in the Garden of Eden to work
it and take care of it. 16And the LORD
God commanded the man, "You are
free to eat from any tree in the garden;
17but you must not eat from the tree
of the knowledge of good and evil, for
when you eat of it you will surely die."[s]
18The LORD God said, "It is not
good for the man to be alone. I will
make a helper suitable for him."[t]
19Now the LORD God had formed
out of the ground all the beasts of the
field[u] and all the birds of the air. He
brought them to the man to see what
he would name them; and whatever the
man called each living creature,[v] that
was its name. 20So the man gave names
to all the livestock, the birds of the air
and all the beasts of the field.
But for Adam[d] no suitable helper was
found. 21So the LORD God caused the
man to fall into a deep sleep; and while
he was sleeping, he took one of the man's
ribs[e] and closed up the place with flesh.
22Then the LORD God made a woman
from the rib[f][w] he had taken out of the
man, and he brought her to the man.
23The man said,

"This is now bone of my bones
and flesh of my flesh;[x]
she shall be called 'woman,[g]'
for she was taken out of man."

24For this reason a man will leave his
father and mother and be united[y] to
his wife, and they will become one
flesh.[z]
25The man and his wife were both
naked,[a] and they felt no shame.

2:7 [j]Ge 3:19 [k]Ps 103:14 [l]Job 33:4 [m]Ac 17:25 [n]1Co 15:45*
2:8 [o]Ge 3:23,24; Isa 51:3
2:9 [p]Ge 3:22,24; Rev 2:7; 22:2,14,19 [q]Eze 47:12
2:14 [r]Da 10:4
2:17 [s]Dt 30:15,19; Ro 5:12; 6:23; Jas 1:15
2:18 [t]1Co 11:9
2:19 [u]Ps 8:7 [v]Ge 1:24
2:22 [w]1Co 11:8, 9,12
2:23 [x]Ge 29:14; Eph 5:28-30
2:24 [y]Mal 2:15 [z]Mt 19:5*; Mk 10:7-8*; 1Co 6:16*; Eph 5:31*
2:25 [a]Ge 3:7,10-11

The Fall of Man

3 Now the serpent[b] was more crafty
than any of the wild animals the
LORD God had made. He said to the
woman, "Did God really say, 'You must
not eat from any tree in the garden'?"
2The woman said to the serpent, "We
may eat fruit from the trees in the garden, 3but God did say, 'You must not
eat fruit from the tree that is in the
middle of the garden, and you must not
touch it, or you will die.' "
4"You will not surely die," the serpent said to the woman.[c] 5"For God
knows that when you eat of it your eyes
will be opened, and you will be like
God,[d] knowing good and evil."
6When the woman saw that the fruit
of the tree was good for food and pleasing to the eye, and also desirable[e] for
gaining wisdom, she took some and ate
it. She also gave some to her husband,
who was with her, and he ate it.[f] 7Then
the eyes of both of them were opened,
and they realized they were naked; so
they sewed fig leaves together and made
coverings for themselves.
8Then the man and his wife heard
the sound of the LORD God as he was
walking[g] in the garden in the cool of
the day, and they hid[h] from the LORD
God among the trees of the garden.
9But the LORD God called to the man,
"Where are you?"
10He answered, "I heard you in the
garden, and I was afraid because I was
naked; so I hid."
11And he said, "Who told you that
you were naked? Have you eaten from
the tree that I commanded you not to
eat from?"
12The man said, "The woman you

3:1 [b]2Co 11:3; Rev 12:9; 20:2
3:4 [c]Jn 8:44; 2Co 11:3
3:5 [d]Isa 14:14; Eze 28:2
3:6 [e]Jas 1:14-15; 1Jn 2:16 [f]1Ti 2:14
3:8 [g]Dt 23:14 [h]Job 31:33; Ps 139:7-12; Jer 23:24

[a]*7* The Hebrew for *man (adam)* sounds like and may be related to the Hebrew for *ground (adamah)*; it is also the name *Adam* (see Gen. 2:20). [b]*12* Or *good; pearls* [c]*13* Possibly southeast Mesopotamia [d]*20* Or *the man* [e]*21* Or *took part of the man's side* [f]*22* Or *part* [g]*23* The Hebrew for *woman* sounds like the Hebrew for *man.*

put here with me—she gave me some fruit from the tree, and I ate it."

[13]Then the LORD God said to the woman, "What is this you have done?"

The woman said, "The serpent deceived me,[i] and I ate."

3:13 [i]2Co 11:3; 1Ti 2:14

[14]So the LORD God said to the serpent, "Because you have done this,

"Cursed[j] are you above all the
 livestock
 and all the wild animals!
You will crawl on your belly
 and you will eat dust[k]
 all the days of your life.
[15]And I will put enmity
 between you and the woman,
 and between your offspring[a][l] and
 hers;[m]
he will crush[b] your head,[n]
 and you will strike his heel."

3:14 [j]Dt 28:15-20 [k]Isa 65:25; Mic 7:17

3:15 [l]Jn 8:44; Ac 13:10; 1Jn 3:8 [m]Isa 7:14; Mt 1:23; Rev 12:17 [n]Ro 16:20; Heb 2:14

PATIENCE

WHAT DAMAGE, ADAM?

Genesis 3:15

What damage, Adam, have you done to injure God's great dream?
"I sinned and left the
Race dying just outside of paradise,"
replied Adam.
Come, God, and shred the gates of
paradise, and with the timbers make
the world a cross, and Eden shall be open
once again.

[16]To the woman he said,

"I will greatly increase your pains in
 childbearing;
 with pain you will give birth to
 children.
Your desire will be for your husband,
 and he will rule over you.[o]"

3:16 [o]1Co 11:3; Eph 5:22

[17]To Adam he said, "Because you listened to your wife and ate from the tree about which I commanded you, 'You must not eat of it,'

"Cursed[p] is the ground because
 of you;
 through painful toil you will eat
 of it
 all the days of your life.[q]
[18]It will produce thorns and thistles
 for you,
 and you will eat the plants of the
 field.[r]
[19]By the sweat of your brow
 you will eat your food[s]
 until you return to the ground,
 since from it you were taken;
 for dust you are
 and to dust you will return."[t]

3:17 [p]Ge 5:29; Ro 8:20-22 [q]Job 5:7; 14:1; Ecc 2:23

3:18 [r]Ps 104:14

3:19 [s]2Th 3:10 [t]Ge 2:7; Ps 90:3; 104:29; Ecc 12:7

[20]Adam[c] named his wife Eve,[d] because she would become the mother of all the living.

[21]The LORD God made garments of skin for Adam and his wife and clothed them. [22]And the LORD God said, "The man has now become like one of us, knowing good and evil. He must not be allowed to reach out his hand and take also from the tree of life[u] and eat, and live forever." [23]So the LORD God banished him from the Garden of Eden[v] to work the ground[w] from which he had been taken. [24]After he drove the man out, he placed on the east side[e] of the Garden of Eden cherubim[x] and a flaming sword[y] flashing back and forth to guard the way to the tree of life.[z]

3:22 [u]Rev 22:14

3:23 [v]Ge 2:8 [w]Ge 4:2

3:24 [x]Ex 25:18-22 [y]Ps 104:4 [z]Ge 2:9

Cain and Abel

4 Adam[c] lay with his wife Eve, and she became pregnant and gave birth to Cain.[f] She said, "With the help of the LORD I have brought forth[g] a man." [2]Later she gave birth to his brother Abel.[a]

Now Abel kept flocks, and Cain worked the soil. [3]In the course of time Cain brought some of the fruits of the soil as an offering to the LORD.[b] [4]But Abel brought fat portions[c] from some of the firstborn of his flock.[d] The LORD looked with favor on Abel and his offering,[e] [5]but on Cain and his offering he did not look with favor. So Cain was very angry, and his face was downcast.

[6]Then the LORD said to Cain, "Why are you angry? Why is your face downcast? [7]If you do what is right, will you not be accepted? But if you do not do what is right, sin is crouching at your door;[f] it desires to have you, but you must master it.[g]"

[8]Now Cain said to his brother Abel,

4:2 [a]Lk 11:51

4:3 [b]Nu 18:12

4:4 [c]Lev 3:16 [d]Ex 13:2,12 [e]Heb 11:4

4:7 [f]Nu 32:23 [g]Ro 6:16

[a]*15* Or *seed* [b]*15* Or *strike* [c]*20,1* Or *The man* [d]*20 Eve* probably means *living.* [e]*24* Or *placed in front* [f]*1 Cain* sounds like the Hebrew for *brought forth* or *acquired.* [g]*1* Or *have acquired*

"Let's go out to the field."[a] And while
4:8 [b]Mt 23:35; 1Jn 3:12 they were in the field, Cain attacked his
brother Abel and killed him.[b]
9Then the LORD said to Cain,
"Where is your brother Abel?"
"I don't know," he replied. "Am I my
brother's keeper?"
10The LORD said, "What have you
done? Listen! Your brother's blood cries
4:10 [i]Ge 9:5; Nu 35:33; Heb 12:24; Rev 6:9-10 out to me from the ground.[i] 11Now you
are under a curse and driven from the
ground, which opened its mouth to receive your brother's blood from your
hand. 12When you work the ground, it
will no longer yield its crops for you.
You will be a restless wanderer on the
earth."
13Cain said to the LORD, "My punishment is more than I can bear. 14Today
you are driving me from the land, and
4:14 [j]2Ki 17:18; Ps 51:11; 139:7-12; Jer 7:15; 52:3 [k]Ge 9:6; Nu 35:19,21,27,33 I will be hidden from your presence;[j] I
will be a restless wanderer on the earth,
and whoever finds me will kill me."[k]
15But the LORD said to him, "Not
so[b]; if anyone kills Cain[l], he will suffer
vengeance seven times over.[m]" Then the
4:15 [l]Eze 9:4,6 [m]ver 24; Ps 79:12 LORD put a mark on Cain so that no
one who found him would kill him.
16So Cain went out from the LORD's
presence and lived in the land of Nod,[c]
4:16 [n]Ge 2:8 east of Eden.[n]
17Cain lay with his wife, and she became pregnant and gave birth to Enoch.
Cain was then building a city, and he
4:17 [o]Ps 49:11 named it after his son[o] Enoch. 18To
Enoch was born Irad, and Irad was the
father of Mehujael, and Mehujael was
the father of Methushael, and Methushael was the father of Lamech.
19Lamech married two women, one
named Adah and the other Zillah.
20Adah gave birth to Jabal; he was the
father of those who live in tents and
raise livestock. 21His brother's name was
Jubal; he was the father of all who
play the harp and flute. 22Zillah also
had a son, Tubal-Cain, who forged all
kinds of tools out of[d] bronze and iron.
Tubal-Cain's sister was Naamah.
23Lamech said to his wives,

"Adah and Zillah, listen to me;
wives of Lamech, hear my words.
4:23 [p]Ex 20:13; Lev 19:18 I have killed[e][p] a man for wounding
me,
a young man for injuring me.
4:24 [q]Dt 32:35 [r]ver 15 24If Cain is avenged[q] seven times,[r]
then Lamech seventy-seven times."

25Adam lay with his wife again, and
she gave birth to a son and named him
Seth,[f][s] saying, "God has granted me an- 4:25 [s]Ge 5:3 [t]ver 8
other child in place of Abel, since Cain
killed him."[t] 26Seth also had a son, and
he named him Enosh.
At that time men began to call on[g] 4:26 [u]Ge 12:8; 1Ki 18:24; Ps 116:17; Joel 2:32; Zep 3:9; Ac 2:21; 1Co 1:2
the name of the LORD.[u]

From Adam to Noah

5 This is the written account of
Adam's line.
When God created man, he made 5:1 [v]Ge 1:27; Eph 4:24; Col 3:10
him in the likeness of God.[v] 2He created
them male and female[w] and blessed
them. And when they were created, he 5:2 [w]Ge 1:27; Mt 19:4; Mk 10:6; Gal 3:28
called them "man."[h]
3When Adam had lived 130 years, he
had a son in his own likeness, in his
own image;[x] and he named him Seth. 5:3 [x]Ge 1:26; 1Co 15:49
4After Seth was born, Adam lived 800
years and had other sons and daughters.
5Altogether, Adam lived 930 years, and
then he died.[y] 5:5 [y]Ge 3:19
6When Seth had lived 105 years, he
became the father[i] of Enosh. 7And after he became the father of Enosh, Seth
lived 807 years and had other sons and
daughters. 8Altogether, Seth lived 912
years, and then he died.
9When Enosh had lived 90 years,
he became the father of Kenan. 10And
after he became the father of Kenan,
Enosh lived 815 years and had other
sons and daughters. 11Altogether, Enosh
lived 905 years, and then he died.
12When Kenan had lived 70 years, he
became the father of Mahalalel. 13And
after he became the father of Mahalalel,
Kenan lived 840 years and had other
sons and daughters. 14Altogether, Kenan lived 910 years, and then he died.
15When Mahalalel had lived 65 years,
he became the father of Jared. 16And
after he became the father of Jared,
Mahalalel lived 830 years and had other
sons and daughters. 17Altogether, Mahalalel lived 895 years, and then he
died.

[a]*8* Samaritan Pentateuch, Septuagint, Vulgate and Syriac; Masoretic Text does not have *"Let's go out to the field."* [b]*15* Septuagint, Vulgate and Syriac; Hebrew *Very well* [c]*16 Nod* means *wandering* (see verses 12 and 14). [d]*22* Or *who instructed all who work in* [e]*23* Or *I will kill* [f]*25 Seth* probably means *granted.* [g]*26* Or *to proclaim* [h]*2* Hebrew *adam* [i]*6 Father* may mean *ancestor*; also in verses 7-26.

DAY 3 THREE

GOODNESS AND MY RELATIONSHIP WITH CHRIST

Read Genesis 5:21–24

Enoch only lived to be 365 years old, a mere youth compared to Methuselah, who lived to be 969 years old. The walk was Enoch's thing! He loved God. He liked walking with God. He loved it so much that he ultimately walked right into God's presence, and "he was no more."

Our relationship with Christ is also a walk. How good are you at it? Is there anything that Enoch could teach you?

A little girl once described how it was that Enoch got into heaven without the necessity of death:

"God and Enoch decided to go on a walk. It was nice being together, and so they walked. Enoch really loved God, but on this walk he didn't say so. God really loved Enoch, but he didn't say so either. It was one of those kinds of walks that neither of them wanted to hurry. They weren't walking to get any place. They were just walking to be together.

"Finally they had walked so far that Enoch didn't recognize where they were any longer. 'Now where are we, God?' asked Enoch.

"God just nodded—he knew where they were—and if God knew, Enoch didn't need to. When they had walked even farther, Enoch couldn't see the sun.

" 'Know where the sun is?' asked Enoch. God just smiled. He knew, and if God knew, Enoch didn't need to. It never gets dark where God is anyway, and so they walked some more. Enoch said, 'You know what time it is, God?' God knew and didn't seem to care, so Enoch didn't care either.

"They just kept walking until finally God, who hadn't said a thing all day, said, 'Well, Enoch, we've walked a long way—it's closer to my house than yours . . . Let's go to my house.' So they did, and nobody ever saw Enoch again."

To begin a study on the topic of Goodness, the Result of Imitating Christ, turn to the home page on page 1409.

18When Jared had lived 162 years, he
became the father of Enoch.[z] 19And after he became the father of Enoch, Jared lived 800 years and had other sons
and daughters. 20Altogether, Jared lived
962 years, and then he died.
21When Enoch had lived 65 years, he
became the father of Methuselah. 22And
after he became the father of Methuselah, Enoch walked with God[a] 300
years and had other sons and daughters.
23Altogether, Enoch lived 365 years.
24Enoch walked with God;[b] then he
was no more, because God took him
away.[c]

5:18 [z]Jude 1:14

5:22 [a]ver 24; Ge 6:9; 17:1; 48:15; Mic 6:8; Mal 2:6

5:24 [b]ver 22 [c]2Ki 2:1,11; Heb 11:5

SELF-CONTROL

A SHORTCUT TO HEAVEN

Genesis 5:24

There are two ways to get into heaven: One is to die in faith. The other is to walk with God so closely that dying is unnecessary. Enoch practiced the discipline of holiness and found that heaven was much nearer than he had supposed.

25When Methuselah had lived 187
years, he became the father of Lamech.
26And after he became the father of Lamech, Methuselah lived 782 years and
had other sons and daughters. 27Alto-
gether, Methuselah lived 969 years, and
then he died.
28When Lamech had lived 182 years,
he had a son. 29He named him Noah[a]
and said, "He will comfort us in the
labor and painful toil of our hands
caused by the ground the LORD has
cursed.[d]" 30After Noah was born, Lamech lived 595 years and had other
sons and daughters. 31Altogether, Lamech lived 777 years, and then he
died.
32After Noah was 500 years old, he
became the father of Shem, Ham and
Japheth.

5:29 [d]Ge 3:17; Ro 8:20

The Flood

6 When men began to increase in
number on the earth[e] and daughters were born to them, 2the sons of
God saw that the daughters of men
were beautiful, and they married any of
them they chose. 3Then the LORD said,

6:1 [e]Ge 1:28

[a]29 *Noah* sounds like the Hebrew for *comfort.*

6:3 "My Spirit will not contend with[a] man
[f]Isa 57:16 forever,[f] for he is mortal[b];[g] his days will
[g]Ps 78:39 be a hundred and twenty years."
6:4 4 The Nephilim[h] were on the earth in
[h]Nu 13:33 those days—and also afterward—when
the sons of God went to the daughters
of men and had children by them.
They were the heroes of old, men of renown.
5 The LORD saw how great man's
wickedness on the earth had become,
and that every inclination of the
6:5 thoughts of his heart was only evil all
[i]Ge 8:21; the time.[i] 6 The LORD was grieved[j]
Ps 14:1-3 that he had made man on the earth,
6:6 and his heart was filled with pain.
[j]1Sa 15:11,35; Isa 63:10 7 So the LORD said, "I will wipe mankind, whom I have created, from the
face of the earth—men and animals,
and creatures that move along the
ground, and birds of the air—for I am
grieved that I have made them." 8 But
Noah found favor in the eyes of the 6:8 [k]Ge 19:19;
LORD.[k] Ex 33:12,13,17;
Lk 1:30;
9 This is the account of Noah. Ac 7:46

Noah was a righteous man, blameless 6:9
among the people of his time,[l] and he [l]Ge 7:1; Eze 14:14,20;
walked with God.[m] 10 Noah had three Heb 11:7; 2Pe 2:5
sons: Shem, Ham and Japheth.[n] [m]Ge 5:22
11 Now the earth was corrupt in God's
sight and was full of violence.[o] 12 God 6:10 [n]Ge 5:32
saw how corrupt the earth had become,
for all the people on earth had corrupted 6:11 [o]Eze 7:23; 8:17
their ways.[p] 13 So God said to Noah, "I
am going to put an end to all people, 6:12 [p]Ps 14:1-3
for the earth is filled with violence because of them. I am surely going to 6:13 [q]ver 17;
destroy both them and the earth.[q] 14 So Eze 7:2-3
make yourself an ark of cypress[c] wood;[r] 6:14 [r]Heb 11:7; 1Pe 3:20

[a]3 Or *My spirit will not remain in* [b]3 Or *corrupt*
[c]14 The meaning of the Hebrew for this word is uncertain.

NOAH

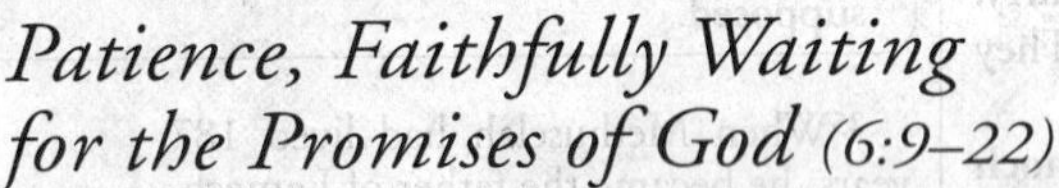

Patience, Faithfully Waiting for the Promises of God (6:9–22)

Patience is not just the ability to keep from hurrying. Patience is a willingness to surrender your private agenda and proceed at the exact pace that God has ordained for you to walk. Noah was given an assignment to build a huge seagoing vessel, and he was told that his family would be the entire construction crew. Obviously, it was not an assignment that could be accomplished quickly. Such an instruction was similar to giving a hammer and saw to a single worker in the Southampton shipyards and saying, "Go thou and build the Queen Mary." It would take him many long years. Noah may not have known how long this task would take, but he did know God's requirements and agreed to abide by God's schedule (6:22).

We are not told how Noah dealt in the short term with his long-term calling. But patience is not patience if it frets over time. Patience rises each day, picks up its hammer and saw, faces the heavens and says, "God, this day is yours. I may not finish the ship before lunch, but I will drive each nail on schedule."

Patience holds no resentment. It never forgets that the finished product will be a boat built God's way, by God's timetable. The best masons never merely cut stones; they build cathedrals. What if the cathedral is still unfinished when they die? There is no need to worry—they have been training their apprentices. Like the mason, the apprentice must never waste a day haphazardly chipping granite; every moment must serve the final dream.

Noah found grace in the eyes of the Lord. He served God's dream. He was a good steward of every second. The boat would be finished when God's plans were completed, and that plan was Noah's focus every day for 120 years. In the meantime, he dabbed the tar and sawed the timbers and looked to heaven. He saved his life one confident day at a time.

To do anything great is a matter of waking each morning and learning to bless the timetables of God. Patience is that inner peace that comes from accepting that God, who has all the time in the world, cannot be hurried. Working in God's good time and enjoying God while you labor are the keys to patience.

6:14 [s]Ex 2:3 make rooms in it and coat it with pitch[s]
inside and out. 15This is how you are
to build it: The ark is to be 450 feet
long, 75 feet wide and 45 feet high.[a]
16Make a roof for it and finish[b] the ark
to within 18 inches[c] of the top. Put a
door in the side of the ark and make
lower, middle and upper decks. 17I am
going to bring floodwaters on the earth
to destroy all life under the heavens,
every creature that has the breath of life
6:17 [t]Ge 7:4, 21-23; 2Pe 2:5 in it. Everything on earth will perish.[t]
18But I will establish my covenant with
6:18 [u]Ge 9:9-16 [v]Ge 7:1,7,13 you,[u] and you will enter the ark[v]—you
and your sons and your wife and your
sons' wives with you. 19You are to bring
into the ark two of all living creatures,
male and female, to keep them alive
6:20 [w]Ge 7:15 with you. 20Two[w] of every kind of bird,
of every kind of animal and of every
kind of creature that moves along the
ground will come to you to be kept
alive. 21You are to take every kind of
food that is to be eaten and store it
away as food for you and for them."
22Noah did everything just as God
6:22 [x]Ge 7:5,9,16 commanded him.[x]

7 The LORD then said to Noah, "Go
into the ark, you and your whole
7:1 [y]Mt 24:38; 1Pe 3:20; 2Pe 2:5 family,[y] because I have found you righ-
[z]Ge 6:9; Eze 14:14 teous[z] in this generation. 2Take with
you seven[d] of every kind of clean[a] ani-
mal, a male and its mate, and two of
7:2 [a]ver 8; Ge 8:20; Lev 10:10; 11:1-47 every kind of unclean animal, a male
and its mate, 3and also seven of every
kind of bird, male and female, to keep
their various kinds alive throughout the
earth. 4Seven days from now I will send
rain on the earth for forty days and forty nights, and I will wipe from the face
of the earth every living creature I have
made."
5And Noah did all that the LORD
7:5 [b]Ge 6:22 commanded him.[b]
6Noah was six hundred years old
when the floodwaters came on the earth.
7And Noah and his sons and his wife
and his sons' wives entered the ark to
escape the waters of the flood. 8Pairs
of clean and unclean animals, of birds
and of all creatures that move along
the ground, 9male and female, came to
Noah and entered the ark, as God had
commanded Noah. 10And after the sev-
en days the floodwaters came on the
earth.
11In the six hundredth year of Noah's
life, on the seventeenth day of the second month—on that day all the springs
of the great deep[c] burst forth, and the 7:11 [c]Eze 26:19 [d]Ge 8:2
floodgates of the heavens[d] were opened.
12And rain fell on the earth forty days
and forty nights.[e] 7:12 [e]ver 4
13On that very day Noah and his
sons, Shem, Ham and Japheth, together with his wife and the wives of his
three sons, entered the ark. 14They had
with them every wild animal according
to its kind, all livestock according to
their kinds, every creature that moves
along the ground according to its kind
and every bird according to its kind,
everything with wings. 15Pairs of all
creatures that have the breath of life
in them came to Noah and entered
the ark.[f] 16The animals going in were 7:15 [f]Ge 6:19
male and female of every living thing,
as God had commanded Noah. Then
the LORD shut him in.
17For forty days[g] the flood kept com- 7:17 [g]ver 4
ing on the earth, and as the waters increased they lifted the ark high above
the earth. 18The waters rose and increased greatly on the earth, and the
ark floated on the surface of the water.
19They rose greatly on the earth, and
all the high mountains under the en- 7:19
tire heavens were covered.[h] 20The wa- [h]Ps 104:6
ters rose and covered the mountains
to a depth of more than twenty
feet.[e,f] 21Every living thing that moved
on the earth perished—birds, livestock,
wild animals, all the creatures that
swarm over the earth, and all mankind.[i] 7:21 [i]Ge 6:7,13
22Everything on dry land that had the
breath of life[j] in its nostrils died. 23Ev- 7:22 [j]Ge 1:30
ery living thing on the face of the
earth was wiped out; men and animals
and the creatures that move along the
ground and the birds of the air were 7:23 [k]Mt 24:39; Lk 17:27; 1Pe 3:20; 2Pe 2:5 [l]Heb 11:7
wiped from the earth.[k] Only Noah was
left, and those with him in the ark.[l]
24The waters flooded the earth for a
hundred and fifty days.[m] 7:24 [m]Ge 8:3

8 But God remembered[n] Noah and 8:1 [n]Ge 9:15; 19:29; Ex 2:24; 1Sa 1:11,19 [o]Ex 14:21
all the wild animals and the live-
stock that were with him in the ark,
and he sent a wind over the earth,[o] and
the waters receded. 2Now the springs of

[a] *15* Hebrew *300 cubits long, 50 cubits wide and 30 cubits high* (about 140 meters long, 23 meters wide and 13.5 meters high) [b] *16* Or *Make an opening for light by finishing* [c] *16* Hebrew *a cubit* (about 0.5 meter) [d] *2* Or *seven pairs*; also in verse 3 [e] *20* Hebrew *fifteen cubits* (about 6.9 meters) [f] *20* Or *rose more than twenty feet, and the mountains were covered*

the deep and the floodgates of the heavens[p] had been closed, and the rain had stopped falling from the sky. 3The water receded steadily from the earth. At the end of the hundred and fifty days the water had gone down, 4and on the seventeenth day of the seventh month the ark came to rest on the mountains of Ararat. 5The waters continued to recede until the tenth month, and on the first day of the tenth month the tops of the mountains became visible.

6After forty days Noah opened the window he had made in the ark 7and sent out a raven, and it kept flying back and forth until the water had dried up from the earth. 8Then he sent out a dove to see if the water had receded from the surface of the ground. 9But the dove could find no place to set its feet because there was water over all the surface of the earth; so it returned to Noah in the ark. He reached out his hand and took the dove and brought it back to himself in the ark. 10He waited seven more days and again sent out the dove from the ark. 11When the dove returned to him in the evening, there in its beak was a freshly plucked olive leaf! Then Noah knew that the water had receded from the earth. 12He waited seven more days and sent the dove out again, but this time it did not return to him.

13By the first day of the first month of Noah's six hundred and first year, the water had dried up from the earth. Noah then removed the covering from the ark and saw that the surface of the ground was dry. 14By the twenty-seventh day of the second month the earth was completely dry.

15Then God said to Noah, 16"Come out of the ark, you and your wife and your sons and their wives.[q] 17Bring out every kind of living creature that is with you—the birds, the animals, and all the creatures that move along the ground—so they can multiply on the earth and be fruitful and increase in number upon it."[r]

18So Noah came out, together with his sons and his wife and his sons' wives. 19All the animals and all the creatures that move along the ground and all the birds—everything that moves on the earth—came out of the ark, one kind after another.

20Then Noah built an altar to the LORD[s] and, taking some of all the clean animals and clean[t] birds, he sacrificed burnt offerings[u] on it. 21The LORD smelled the pleasing aroma[v] and said in his heart: "Never again will I curse the ground[w] because of man, even though[a] every inclination of his heart is evil from childhood.[x] And never again will I destroy all living creatures,[y] as I have done.

22"As long as the earth endures,
seedtime and harvest,
cold and heat,
summer and winter,
day and night
will never cease."[z]

God's Covenant With Noah

9 Then God blessed Noah and his sons, saying to them, "Be fruitful and increase in number and fill the earth.[a] 2The fear and dread of you will fall upon all the beasts of the earth and all the birds of the air, upon every creature that moves along the ground, and upon all the fish of the sea; they are given into your hands. 3Everything that lives and moves will be food for you.[b] Just as I gave you the green plants, I now give you everything.

4"But you must not eat meat that has its lifeblood still in it.[c] 5And for your lifeblood I will surely demand an accounting. I will demand an accounting from every animal.[d] And from each man, too, I will demand an accounting for the life of his fellow man.[e]

6"Whoever sheds the blood of man,
by man shall his blood be shed;[f]
for in the image of God[g]
has God made man.

7As for you, be fruitful and increase in number; multiply on the earth and increase upon it."[h]

8Then God said to Noah and to his sons with him: 9"I now establish my covenant with you[i] and with your descendants after you 10and with every living creature that was with you—the birds, the livestock and all the wild animals, all those that came out of the ark with you—every living creature on earth. 11I establish my covenant[j] with you: Never again will all life be cut off

[a]21 Or *man, for*

8:2 [p]Ge 7:11
8:16 [q]Ge 7:13
8:17 [r]Ge 1:22
8:20 [s]Ge 12:7-8; 13:18; 22:9 [t]Ge 7:8; Lev 11:1-47 [u]Ge 22:2,13; Ex 10:25
8:21 [v]Lev 1:9,13; 2Co 2:15 [w]Ge 3:17 [x]Ge 6:5; Ps 51:5; Jer 17:9 [y]Ge 9:11,15; Isa 54:9
8:22 [z]Ge 1:14; Jer 33:20,25
9:1 [a]Ge 1:22
9:3 [b]Ge 1:29
9:4 [c]Lev 3:17; 17:10-14; Dt 12:16, 23-25; 1Sa 14:33
9:5 [d]Ex 21:28-32 [e]Ge 4:10
9:6 [f]Ge 4:14; Ex 21:12,14; Lev 24:17; Mt 26:52 [g]Ge 1:26
9:7 [h]Ge 1:22
9:9 [i]Ge 6:18
9:11 [j]ver 16; Isa 24:5

by the waters of a flood; never again will
9:11 [k]Ge 8:21; Isa 54:9 — there be a flood to destroy the earth.[k]"
12And God said, "This is the sign of
9:12 [l]ver 17; Ge 17:11 — the covenant[l] I am making between me
and you and every living creature with
you, a covenant for all generations to
come: 13I have set my rainbow in the

DAY 5 FIVE

PEACE AND ITS PLACE IN MY PERSONAL WORSHIP

Read Genesis 9:8–17

There is no way to comprehend Genesis 9 without first understanding Genesis 6:5–8. It grieved God that human beings, whom he had created, had become evil, and that everything in their imagination was only evil continually. In Genesis 6, God resolved to wipe humankind from the planet.

But a man named Noah was faithful to God. God saved him and his family from the judgment of water. After the judgment, God called a truce with the earth and confirmed the deal with a promise and a sign. The promise "never again" (Genesis 9:11), and the sign was a rainbow (vv. 12–13).

The truce God made with Noah and his children was sealed by very powerful words: "never again" and "for all generations to come" (vv. 11–12). When God establishes his covenants, they stand forever, through all time.

God offered a truce to the world—a covenant—just so people will know they do not have to live in terror of a worldwide flood ever again. With such a promise, Noah and his family were free to leave their boat on Mount Ararat and live in bright security for the rest of their lives. They were liberated to praise God and worship him in hope and joy.

But these same words, "never again" and "for all generations to come," also pertain to the Christian life. Jesus died and ended our estrangement to God. Never again do we need to fear that Christ will abandon us. The cross, like the rainbow, is God's seal and image of peace. We can only erupt in grand worship in response to God's great gift.

To begin a study on the topic of Peace, a Truce With God to End My Alienation From Him, turn to the home page on page 1353.

clouds, and it will be the sign of the
covenant between me and the earth.
14Whenever I bring clouds over the
earth and the rainbow appears in the
clouds, 15I will remember my covenant[m] — 9:15 [m]Ex 2:24; Lev 26:42,45; Dt 7:9; Eze 16:60
between me and you and all living crea-
tures of every kind. Never again will
the waters become a flood to destroy all
life. 16Whenever the rainbow appears in
the clouds, I will see it and remember — 9:16 [n]ver 11; Ge 17:7, 13,19; 2Sa 7:13; 23:5
the everlasting covenant[n] between God
and all living creatures of every kind on
the earth."

GENTLENESS

COVENANT COLORS

Genesis 9:16

Consider the rainbow. Its simple colors reveal God's truce of gentleness with humankind. He used mere sun and mist to sign his name across the skies—a promise in a prism.

17So God said to Noah, "This is the — 9:17 [o]ver 12; Ge 17:11
sign of the covenant[o] I have established
between me and all life on the earth."

The Sons of Noah

18The sons of Noah who came out of
the ark were Shem, Ham and Japheth.
(Ham was the father of Canaan.)[p] — 9:18 [p]ver 25-27; Ge 10:6,15
19These were the three sons of Noah,
and from them came the people who
were scattered over the earth.[q] — 9:19 [q]Ge 10:32
20Noah, a man of the soil, proceeded[a]
to plant a vineyard. 21When he drank
some of its wine, he became drunk and
lay uncovered inside his tent. 22Ham,
the father of Canaan, saw his father's
nakedness and told his two brothers
outside. 23But Shem and Japheth took
a garment and laid it across their shoulders; then they walked in backward and
covered their father's nakedness. Their
faces were turned the other way so that
they would not see their father's nakedness.
24When Noah awoke from his wine
and found out what his youngest son
had done to him, 25he said,

"Cursed be Canaan![r] — 9:25 [r]ver 18 [s]Ge 25:23; Jos 9:23
The lowest of slaves
will be he to his brothers.[s]"

[a]20 Or *soil, was the first*

[26]He also said,

"Blessed be the LORD, the God of
Shem!
May Canaan be the slave of Shem.[a]
[27]May God extend the territory of
Japheth[b];
may Japheth live in the tents of
Shem,
and may Canaan be his[c] slave."

[28]After the flood Noah lived 350
years. [29]Altogether, Noah lived 950
years, and then he died.

LOVE

LONG LIFE TO ALL

Genesis 9:29

Poor Noah. Poor Methusaleh. A thousand years of life—so short a time! Jesus pitied the brevity of human life so much that he rose from the dead, obliterating the temporal. Where the tomb stood open, the average life span took a leap. When Jesus put his Easter footprint in the dust outside his tomb, it was one giant step for God *and* one giant step for humankind.

The Table of Nations

10:1 [t]Ge 2:4 **10** This is the account[t] of Shem,
Ham and Japheth, Noah's sons,
who themselves had sons after the
flood.

The Japhethites

10:2 [u]Eze 38:6 [v]Eze 38:2; Rev 20:8 [w]Isa 66:19 [2]The sons[d] of Japheth:
Gomer,[u] Magog,[v] Madai, Javan,
Tubal,[w] Meshech and Tiras.
[3]The sons of Gomer:
10:3 [x]Jer 51:27 [y]Eze 27:14; 38:6 Ashkenaz,[x] Riphath and Togarmah.[y]
[4]The sons of Javan:
10:4 [z]Eze 27:12,25; Jnh 1:3 Elishah, Tarshish,[z] the Kittim
and the Rodanim.[e] [5](From these
the maritime peoples spread out
into their territories by their
clans within their nations, each
with its own language.)

The Hamites

[6]The sons of Ham:
10:6 [a]ver 15; Ge 9:18 Cush, Mizraim,[f] Put and Canaan.[a]
[7]The sons of Cush:
Seba, Havilah, Sabtah, Raamah
and Sabteca.
The sons of Raamah:
Sheba and Dedan.

[8]Cush was the father[g] of Nimrod,
who grew to be a mighty warrior on
the earth. [9]He was a mighty hunter before the LORD; that is why it is said,
"Like Nimrod, a mighty hunter before
the LORD." [10]The first centers of his
kingdom were Babylon,[b] Erech, Akkad 10:10 [b]Ge 11:9 [c]Ge 11:2
and Calneh, in[h] Shinar.[i][c] [11]From that
land he went to Assyria,[d] where he built 10:11 [d]Ps 83:8; Mic 5:6 [e]Jnh 1:2; 4:11; Na 1:1
Nineveh,[e] Rehoboth Ir,[j] Calah [12]and
Resen, which is between Nineveh and
Calah; that is the great city.

[13]Mizraim was the father of
the Ludites, Anamites, Leha-
bites, Naphtuhites, [14]Pathru- 10:14 [f]Ge 21:32,34; 26:1,8
sites, Casluhites (from whom the
Philistines[f] came) and Caphtorites.
[15]Canaan[g] was the father of 10:15 [g]ver 6; Ge 9:18 [h]Eze 28:21 [i]Ge 23:3,20
Sidon[h] his firstborn,[k] and of the
Hittites,[i] [16]Jebusites,[j] Amorites, 10:16 [j]1Ch 11:4
Girgashites, [17]Hivites, Arkites,
Sinites, [18]Arvadites, Zemarites
and Hamathites.

10:18 [k]Ge 12:6; Ex 13:11
Later the Canaanite[k] clans scattered
[19]and the borders of Canaan[l] reached 10:19 [l]Ge 11:31; 13:12; 17:8 [m]ver 15
from Sidon[m] toward Gerar as far as Gaza,
and then toward Sodom, Gomorrah,
Admah and Zeboiim, as far as Lasha.
[20]These are the sons of Ham by their
clans and languages, in their territories
and nations.

The Semites

[21]Sons were also born to Shem, whose
older brother was[l] Japheth; Shem was 10:21 [n]ver 24; Nu 24:24
the ancestor of all the sons of Eber.[n]

[22]The sons of Shem: 10:22 [o]Jer 49:34 [p]Lk 3:36
Elam,[o] Asshur, Arphaxad,[p] Lud
and Aram.
[23]The sons of Aram: 10:23 [q]Job 1:1
Uz,[q] Hul, Gether and Meshech.[m]

[a]*26* Or *be his slave* [b]*27 Japheth* sounds like the Hebrew for *extend.* [c]*27* Or *their* [d]*2 Sons* may mean *descendants* or *successors* or *nations*; also in verses 3, 4, 6, 7, 20-23, 29 and 31. [e]*4* Some manuscripts of the Masoretic Text and Samaritan Pentateuch (see also Septuagint and 1 Chron. 1:7); most manuscripts of the Masoretic Text *Dodanim* [f]*6* That is, Egypt; also in verse 13 [g]*8 Father* may mean *ancestor* or *predecessor* or *founder*; also in verses 13, 15, 24 and 26. [h]*10* Or *Erech and Akkad—all of them in* [i]*10* That is, Babylonia [j]*11* Or *Nineveh with its city squares* [k]*15* Or *of the Sidonians, the foremost* [l]*21* Or *Shem, the older brother of* [m]*23* See Septuagint and 1 Chron. 1:17; Hebrew *Mash*

[24]Arphaxad was the father of[a] Shelah,
10:24 [r]ver 21 and Shelah the father of Eber.[r]
[25]Two sons were born to Eber:
One was named Peleg,[b] because
in his time the earth was divided; his brother was named
Joktan.
[26]Joktan was the father of
Almodad, Sheleph, Hazarmaveth, Jerah, [27]Hadoram, Uzal,
Diklah, [28]Obal, Abimael, Sheba, [29]Ophir, Havilah and Jobab.
All these were sons of Joktan.
[30]The region where they lived stretched
from Mesha toward Sephar, in the eastern hill country.
[31]These are the sons of Shem by their
clans and languages, in their territories
and nations.

[32]These are the clans of Noah's sons,[s]
10:32 [s]ver 1 according to their lines of descent, with-
[t]Ge 9:19 in their nations. From these the nations
spread out over the earth[t] after the
flood.

The Tower of Babel

11 Now the whole world had one
language and a common speech.
[2]As men moved eastward,[c] they found a
11:2 [u]Ge 10:10 plain in Shinar[d][u] and settled there.
11:3 [3]They said to each other, "Come, let's
[v]Ex 1:14 make bricks[v] and bake them thorough-
[w]Ge 14:10 ly." They used brick instead of stone,
and tar[w] for mortar. [4]Then they said,
"Come, let us build ourselves a city, with
11:4 [x]Dt 1:28; 9:1 a tower that reaches to the heavens,[x] so
[y]Ge 6:4 that we may make a name[y] for ourselves
[z]Dt 4:27 and not be scattered over the face of the
whole earth."[z]
11:5 [a]ver 7; [5]But the LORD came down[a] to see the
Ge 18:21; city and the tower that the men were
Ex 3:8; building. [6]The LORD said, "If as one
19:11,18,20 people speaking the same language they
have begun to do this, then nothing
they plan to do will be impossible for
11:7 [b]Ge 1:26 them. [7]Come, let us[b] go down and con-
[c]Ge 42:23 fuse their language so they will not understand each other."[c]
[8]So the LORD scattered them from
11:8 [d]Ge 9:19; there over all the earth,[d] and they
Lk 1:51 stopped building the city. [9]That is why
11:9 [e]Ge 10:10 it was called Babel[e][e]—because there the
LORD confused the language of the
whole world. From there the LORD
scattered them over the face of the
whole earth.

From Shem to Abram

[10]This is the account of Shem.

Two years after the flood, when Shem
was 100 years old, he became the father[f] of Arphaxad. [11]And after he became the father of Arphaxad, Shem
lived 500 years and had other sons and
daughters.
[12]When Arphaxad had lived 35 years, 11:12
he became the father of Shelah.[f] [13]And [f]Lk 3:35
after he became the father of Shelah,
Arphaxad lived 403 years and had other
sons and daughters.[g]
[14]When Shelah had lived 30 years,
he became the father of Eber. [15]And after he became the father of Eber, Shelah
lived 403 years and had other sons and
daughters.
[16]When Eber had lived 34 years, he
became the father of Peleg. [17]And after
he became the father of Peleg, Eber
lived 430 years and had other sons and
daughters.
[18]When Peleg had lived 30 years,
he became the father of Reu. [19]And after he became the father of Reu, Peleg
lived 209 years and had other sons and
daughters.
[20]When Reu had lived 32 years, he 11:20
became the father of Serug.[g] [21]And af- [g]Lk 3:35
ter he became the father of Serug, Reu
lived 207 years and had other sons and
daughters.
[22]When Serug had lived 30 years, he
became the father of Nahor. [23]And after
he became the father of Nahor, Serug
lived 200 years and had other sons and
daughters.
[24]When Nahor had lived 29 years, he 11:24
became the father of Terah.[h] [25]And af- [h]Lk 3:34
ter he became the father of Terah, Na-
hor lived 119 years and had other sons
and daughters.
[26]After Terah had lived 70 years, he

[a]*24* Hebrew; Septuagint *father of Cainan, and Cainan was the father of* [b]*25* *Peleg* means *division.* [c]*2* Or *from the east*; or *in the east* [d]*2* That is, Babylonia [e]*9* That is, Babylon; *Babel* sounds like the Hebrew for *confused.* [f]*10* *Father* may mean *ancestor*; also in verses 11-25. [g]*12,13* Hebrew; Septuagint (see also Luke 3:35, 36 and note at Gen. 10:24) *35 years, he became the father of Cainan. [13]And after he became the father of Cainan, Arphaxad lived 430 years and had other sons and daughters, and then he died. When Cainan had lived 130 years, he became the father of Shelah. And after he became the father of Shelah, Cainan lived 330 years and had other sons and daughters*

WEEK 7 FAITHFULNESS

1 DAY ONE
GOD'S BLESSING ON FAITHFULNESS

Read Genesis 12:1–5

We don't know much about Abram and Sarai when God called them to be the parents of the Jewish nation. We only know they were old, and we can guess that they were pagans like the Chaldean world from which they came. Some scholars have suggested that they were moon worshipers, serving some celestial set of gods and goddesses.

Then suddenly into their comfortable pagan world comes a voice unheard before. It is the voice of a God much mightier than those they have worshiped. It is the voice of *the* God. This unknown God speaks to them and says, "Leave your country, your people and your father's household and go to the land I will show you." And with this brief summons, Abram and Sarai, old in years—some would say too old to make such a pilgrimage—set out to obey God.

In so simple a way Judaism was born. An old man and woman obeyed God in a manner that went unnoticed in its day. It went unmarked, for few believed it remarkable at the time. Yet this is the way God works. He often begins great things through events that seem of no historical importance. A baby in a stable, an old couple doddering out of the moon temples of the Tigris Valley: such things comprise the methodology of God.

In such ordinary things comes the roar of God. The quaking world is reborn in the name of nameless people who obeyed the extraordinary claim God held on their lives. They were faithful, and in following their faithfulness, they were swallowed whole by God's blessings.

Did you once hear a whisper of simplicity? Did it seem an unimportant thing? Did it seem unreasonable? Listen up! God waits to bless you. He longs to bless you. All you have to do is say, "Yes, Lord, I will!" Then act upon the whisper.

2 DAY TWO
FAITHFULNESS AND THE PURPOSE OF GOD IN MY LIFE

When Deuteronomy was written, 400 years had passed since God had made promises to the old man and woman in Genesis. But centuries do not destroy the pending promises of God. A half-millennium later, all is coming to pass. The nation whose citizens would be as the sand of the sea is already being born. Its people are exiles from Egypt when this book is written, but they are en route to an area of the world that will belong to them forever. *Turn to Deuteronomy 10:20–22, page 214, for today's study.*

3 DAY THREE
FAITHFULNESS AND MY RELATIONSHIP WITH CHRIST

Jesus clearly indicates in this passage that when the end times approach, things are going to get rough for believers. Christians are going to be severely persecuted. But the mark of the true believer is that he or she will remain true throughout the persecution. Notice that the blessing attached to the faithfulness is the blessing of eternal salvation. Those who endure to the end will be saved. *Turn to Matthew 24:9–13, page 1155, for today's study.*

4 DAY FOUR
FAITHFULNESS AND MY SERVICE TO OTHERS

Christianity is never intentionally near-sighted. There is a world of hurt that exists beyond us. In Matthew 25, the King (who is Jesus) rewards or condemns people merely on the basis of what they have done to bless or curse others. Those who have served others are called blessed by the Father. Faithfulness is not just a fruit of the Spirit. It is a world-view—the basis of our eternal rewards. *Turn to Matthew 25:31–40, page 1158, for today's study.*

5 DAY FIVE
FAITHFULNESS AND ITS PLACE IN MY PERSONAL WORSHIP

A Christian woman I once knew got up early every morning of the week and went to worship. Snow, rain or heat could not impede her attendance. I found myself struck by her faithfulness, but more than that, I could not help but wonder how God must have loved her persistence in praise and prayer. Surely heaven must pay special attention to those worshipers who cannot be lulled into a comfortable selfishness that never feels a need to worship the Creator. *Turn to Hebrews 11:8–12, page 1472, for today's study.*

MEMORIZE THIS WEEK

REVELATION 2:10

Be faithful, even to the point of death, and I will give you the crown of life.

Week 8, Gentleness, the Approachable Life, begins on page 306, Ruth 2:19–22.
To begin a topical study on the Fruit of the Spirit, Faithfulness, turn to the Topical Index, page 1548.

11:26 [i]Lk 3:34 [j]Jos 24:2 became the father of Abram,[i] Nahor[j]
and Haran.
27This is the account of Terah.
Terah became the father of Abram,
11:27 [k]ver 31; Ge 12:4; 14:12; 19:1; 2Pe 2:7 Nahor and Haran. And Haran became
the father of Lot.[k] 28While his father
Terah was still alive, Haran died in Ur
11:28 [l]ver 31; Ge 15:7 of the Chaldeans,[l] in the land of his
birth. 29Abram and Nahor both mar-
ried. The name of Abram's wife was
11:29 [m]Ge 17:15 [n]Ge 22:20 Sarai,[m] and the name of Nahor's wife
was Milcah;[n] she was the daughter of
Haran, the father of both Milcah and
Iscah. 30Now Sarai was barren; she had
11:30 [o]Ge 16:1; 18:11 no children.[o]
31Terah took his son Abram, his grandson Lot son of Haran, and his daughter-
11:31 [p]Ge 15:7; Ne 9:7; Ac 7:4 [q]Ge 10:19 in-law Sarai, the wife of his son Abram,
and together they set out from Ur of
the Chaldeans[p] to go to Canaan.[q] But
when they came to Haran, they settled
there.
32Terah lived 205 years, and he died
in Haran.

The Call of Abram

12 The LORD had said to Abram,
12:1 [r]Ac 7:3*; Heb 11:8 "Leave your country, your people and your father's household and go
to the land I will show you.[r]
12:2 [s]Ge 15:5; 17:2,4; 18:18; 22:17; Dt 26:5 [t]Ge 24:1,35 2"I will make you into a great nation[s]
and I will bless you;[t]
I will make your name great,
and you will be a blessing.
3I will bless those who bless you,
12:3 [u]Ge 27:29; Ex 23:22; Nu 24:9 [v]Ge 18:18; 22:18; 26:4; Ac 3:25; Gal 3:8* and whoever curses you I will
curse;[u]
and all peoples on earth
will be blessed through you.[v]"
4So Abram left, as the LORD had told
him; and Lot went with him. Abram
was seventy-five years old when he set
12:4 [w]Ge 11:31 out from Haran.[w] 5He took his wife Sa-
12:5 [x]Ge 14:14; 17:23 rai, his nephew Lot, all the possessions
they had accumulated and the people[x]
they had acquired in Haran, and they
set out for the land of Canaan, and they
12:6 [y]Heb 11:9 [z]Ge 35:4; Dt 11:30 [a]Ge 10:18 arrived there.
6Abram traveled through the land[y] as
far as the site of the great tree of Moreh[z]
at Shechem. At that time the Canaan-
12:7 [b]Ge 17:1; 18:1; Ex 6:3 [c]Ge 13:15,17; 15:18; 17:8; Ps 105:9-11 [d]Ge 13:4 ites[a] were in the land. 7The LORD appeared to Abram[b] and said, "To your
offspring[a] I will give this land."[c] So he
built an altar there to the LORD,[d] who
had appeared to him.

8From there he went on toward the
hills east of Bethel[e] and pitched his 12:8 [e]Ge 13:3
tent, with Bethel on the west and Ai on
the east. There he built an altar to the
LORD and called on the name of the
LORD. 9Then Abram set out and continued toward the Negev.[f] 12:9 [f]Ge 13:1,3

Abram in Egypt

10Now there was a famine in the
land, and Abram went down to Egypt
to live there for a while because the
famine was severe. 11As he was about
to enter Egypt, he said to his wife Sarai, "I know what a beautiful woman
you are. 12When the Egyptians see you,
they will say, 'This is his wife.' Then
they will kill me but will let you live.
13Say you are my sister,[g] so that I will 12:13 [g]Ge 20:2; 26:7
be treated well for your sake and my life
will be spared because of you."
14When Abram came to Egypt, the
Egyptians saw that she was a very beautiful woman. 15And when Pharaoh's
officials saw her, they praised her to
Pharaoh, and she was taken into his
palace. 16He treated Abram well for her
sake, and Abram acquired sheep and
cattle, male and female donkeys, menservants and maidservants, and camels.
17But the LORD inflicted serious dis- 12:17 [h]1Ch 16:21
eases on Pharaoh and his household[h]
because of Abram's wife Sarai. 18So Pharaoh summoned Abram. "What have
you done to me?"[i] he said. "Why didn't 12:18 [i]Ge 20:9; 26:10
you tell me she was your wife? 19Why
did you say, 'She is my sister,' so that I
took her to be my wife? Now then, here
is your wife. Take her and go!" 20Then
Pharaoh gave orders about Abram to
his men, and they sent him on his way,
with his wife and everything he had.

Abram and Lot Separate

13 So Abram went up from Egypt
to the Negev,[j] with his wife and 13:1 [j]Ge 12:9
everything he had, and Lot went with
him. 2Abram had become very wealthy
in livestock and in silver and gold.
3From the Negev he went from place
to place until he came to Bethel,[k] to the 13:3 [k]Ge 12:8
place between Bethel and Ai where his
tent had been earlier 4and where he had
first built an altar.[l] There Abram called 13:4 [l]Ge 12:7
on the name of the LORD.
5Now Lot, who was moving about

[a]7 Or *seed*

DAY 5 FIVE

Patience and Its Place in My Personal Worship

Read Genesis 13:1–4

The wait is the relationship. The wait is the remembrance. Abraham had previously built an altar at Bethel (Genesis 12:8). Now he returned to that place where he had entered Canaan and he rebuilt the altar. It was there that Abraham had met with God and followed his covenant course of patience. It was there, again, that he renewed it for the future.

Abraham must have meditated at Bethel on the why's and wherefore's of covenant faith. God had called him, and he had followed in obedience and patience. But the question "why" must have dogged him constantly. "Why me, God? Why, of all people in the world, should I be so central to your saving dreams for all humankind?"

Joseph Bayley wrote about the wonderment of call when he pondered Palm Sunday:

King Jesus
why did you choose
a lowly ass
to carry you
to ride in your parade?
Had you no friend
who owned a horse
—a royal mount with spirit
fit for a king to ride? . . .
King Jesus
why did you choose
me
a lowly unimportant person
to bear you
in my world today?
I'm poor and unimportant
trained to work
not carry kings
—let alone the King of kings
and yet you've chosen me
to carry you in triumph
in this world's parade.

To begin a study of the topic Patience, the Wait for What God Promises, turn to the home page on page 1201.

with Abram, also had flocks and herds
and tents. 6But the land could not support them while they stayed together,
for their possessions were so great that
they were not able to stay together.[m]
7And quarreling[n] arose between Abram's
herdsmen and the herdsmen of Lot.
The Canaanites and Perizzites were also
living in the land[o] at that time.
8So Abram said to Lot, "Let's not
have any quarreling between you and
me,[p] or between your herdsmen and
mine, for we are brothers.[q] 9Is not the
whole land before you? Let's part company. If you go to the left, I'll go to the
right; if you go to the right, I'll go to
the left."
10Lot looked up and saw that the
whole plain of the Jordan was well watered, like the garden of the LORD,[r] like
the land of Egypt, toward Zoar.[s] (This
was before the LORD destroyed Sodom and Gomorrah.)[t] 11So Lot chose for
himself the whole plain of the Jordan
and set out toward the east. The two
men parted company: 12Abram lived
in the land of Canaan, while Lot lived
among the cities of the plain[u] and
pitched his tents near Sodom.[v] 13Now
the men of Sodom were wicked and
were sinning greatly against the
LORD.[w]
14The LORD said to Abram after Lot
had parted from him, "Lift up your
eyes from where you are and look north
and south, east and west.[x] 15All the
land that you see I will give to you
and your offspring[a] forever.[y] 16I will
make your offspring like the dust of
the earth, so that if anyone could count
the dust, then your offspring could be
counted. 17Go, walk through the length
and breadth of the land,[z] for I am giving it to you."
18So Abram moved his tents and went
to live near the great trees of Mamre[a] at
Hebron,[b] where he built an altar to the
LORD.[c]

Abram Rescues Lot

14 At this time Amraphel king of
Shinar,[b][d] Arioch king of Ellasar, Kedorlaomer king of Elam and Tidal king of Goiim 2went to war against
Bera king of Sodom, Birsha king of

13:6 mGe 36:7
13:7 nGe 26:20,21 oGe 12:6
13:8 pPr 15:18; 20:3 qPs 133:1
13:10 rGe 2:8-10; Isa 51:3 sGe 19:22,30 tGe 14:8; 19:17-29
13:12 uGe 19:17, 25,29 vGe 14:12
13:13 wGe 18:20; Eze 16:49-50; 2Pe 2:8
13:14 xGe 28:14; Dt 3:27
13:15 yGe 12:7; Gal 3:16*
13:17 zver 15; Nu 13:17-25
13:18 aGe 14:13,24; 18:1 bGe 35:27 cGe 8:20
14:1 dGe 10:10

a*15* Or *seed;* also in verse 16 b*1* That is, Babylonia; also in verse 9

WEEK 12

PEACE

1 DAY ONE

PEACE AND THE PRINCE OF PEACE

Read Genesis 14:17–20

The cryptic king of Salem, Melchizedek, holds for most of us a spellbinding sense of mystery. Who he is and what he means carries an intrigue for all of us. Called the "king of peace" in the book of Hebrews, Melchizedek suddenly appears to bless Abram and then just as suddenly disappears. The mystery of his priesthood, dedicated to the Most High God, seems to make him an archetype of Christ.

Hebrews calls Jesus a priest forever after the order of Melchizedek. The passage says that Jesus, like Melchizedek, became a high priest forever, not on the basis of his ancestry but on "the basis of the power of an indestructible life" (7:16). One of the functions of a priest is intercession. Jesus himself is our high priest, according to this passage and another passage in Romans 8:34, always living and ever interceding for us.

Jesus the priest—the constantly interceding priest—is our hope. He continues interceding when we think we've grown too busy to pray. Always at his post, Jesus prays for us. Life becomes manageable—not always because we have been faithful, but because Jesus is our priest—our always interceding priest—our priest forever after the order of Melchizedek.

Have you any turmoil in your life? Let it go. Are you afraid that your personality is so flawed that God might never really accept you? Rejoice! You have a continually interceding priest, Jesus Christ the Righteous. He won peace for you on a bloody hill. And even as he died, he secured your right to immediate access to the Father. Best of all, his sacrifice was so sufficient that you never need fear that any of your sins can prevent your entrance into heaven, nor can your moral weaknesses bar you from his eternal peace.

2 DAY TWO

PEACE AND THE PURPOSE OF GOD IN MY LIFE

This brief verse tells us that God has ordained that each of us become peacemakers who sow in peace and produce a harvest of righteousness. What is God's purpose in your life? Isn't it to publish to all of those who feel alienated from God a sense of his perfect peace? The world is at enmity with God, and Paul says in 2 Corinthians 5:18 that all Christians have been called to a ministry of reconciliation. *Turn to James 3:18, page 1486, for today's study.*

3 DAY THREE

PEACE AND MY RELATIONSHIP WITH CHRIST

Once again we arrive back at the image of Melchizedek, this mysterious "king of peace"—without parents, without beginning or end, without genealogy. In this passage, Christ is compared to Melchizedek. Like Melchizedek, Christ has come to plunge us into the kind of peace that he mediates day and night for us, cleansing turbulence from our lives and giving us peace. *Turn to Hebrews 7:1–3, page 1466, for today's study.*

4 DAY FOUR

PEACE AND MY SERVICE TO OTHERS

Peter encourages us to make every effort to be blameless and to live at peace with Christ. We are to live so much in the center of Christ's peace that we exude that same peace, and it becomes for those around us a haven from their own turbulence. We are to create peace for others by living in it ourselves. Those who try to preach peace while embroiled in their unresolved anxieties cannot make Christ appear much of a solution in a jittery world. *Turn to 2 Peter 3:14, page 1502, for today's study.*

5 DAY FIVE

PEACE AND ITS PLACE IN MY PERSONAL WORSHIP

There is joy in the hearts of those who promote peace. Our personal quiet time in the presence of the Savior ought to be approached, enjoyed and concluded on a note of quiet and untroubled love. Yet sometimes we hurry into his presence terribly troubled, spout off our intercessory lists and then hurry off still troubled. Worrying in the presence of God is not prayer. Certainly, worrying in his presence cannot promote real peace in the Christian's life. *Turn to Proverbs 12:20, page 746, for today's study.*

MEMORIZE THIS WEEK

ISAIAH 53:5

But he was pierced for our transgressions,
he was crushed for our iniquities;
the punishment that brought us peace was upon him,
and by his wounds we are healed.

Week 13, Patience Brings the Blessing of God, begins on page 1476, Hebrews 11:35–40.
To begin a topical study on the Fruit of the Spirit, Peace, turn to the Topical Index, page 1548.

Gomorrah, Shinab king of Admah, Shemeber king of Zeboiim,[e] and the king of Bela (that is, Zoar).[f] 3All these latter kings joined forces in the Valley of Siddim (the Salt Sea[a][g]). 4For twelve years they had been subject to Kedorlaomer, but in the thirteenth year they rebelled.

5In the fourteenth year, Kedorlaomer and the kings allied with him went out and defeated the Rephaites[h] in Ashteroth Karnaim, the Zuzites in Ham, the Emites[i] in Shaveh Kiriathaim 6and the Horites[j] in the hill country of Seir,[k] as far as El Paran[l] near the desert. 7Then they turned back and went to En Mishpat (that is, Kadesh), and they conquered the whole territory of the Amalekites, as well as the Amorites who were living in Hazazon Tamar.[m]

8Then the king of Sodom, the king of Gomorrah,[n] the king of Admah, the king of Zeboiim[o] and the king of Bela (that is, Zoar) marched out and drew up their battle lines in the Valley of Siddim 9against Kedorlaomer king of Elam, Tidal king of Goiim, Amraphel king of Shinar and Arioch king of Ellasar—four kings against five. 10Now the Valley of Siddim was full of tar pits, and when the kings of Sodom and Gomorrah fled, some of the men fell into them and the rest fled to the hills.[p] 11The four kings seized all the goods of Sodom and Gomorrah and all their food; then they went away. 12They also carried off Abram's nephew Lot and his possessions, since he was living in Sodom.

13One who had escaped came and reported this to Abram the Hebrew. Now Abram was living near the great trees of Mamre[q] the Amorite, a brother[b] of Eshcol and Aner, all of whom were allied with Abram. 14When Abram heard that his relative had been taken captive, he called out the 318 trained men born in his household[r] and went in pursuit as far as Dan.[s] 15During the night Abram divided his men to attack them and he routed them, pursuing them as far as Hobah, north of Damascus. 16He recovered all the goods and brought back his relative Lot and his possessions, together with the women and the other people.

17After Abram returned from defeating Kedorlaomer and the kings allied with him, the king of Sodom came out

14:2 [e]Ge 10:19 [f]Ge 13:10
14:3 [g]Nu 34:3,12; Dt 3:17; Jos 3:16; 15:2,5
14:5 [h]Ge 15:20; Dt 2:11,20 [i]Dt 2:10
14:6 [j]Dt 2:12,22 [k]Dt 2:1,5,22 [l]Ge 21:21; Nu 10:12
14:7 [m]2Ch 20:2
14:8 [n]Ge 13:10; 19:17-29 [o]Dt 29:23
14:10 [p]Ge 19:17,30
14:13 [q]ver 24; Ge 13:18
14:14 [r]Ge 15:3 [s]Dt 34:1; Jdg 18:29

to meet him in the Valley of Shaveh (that is, the King's Valley).[t]

18Then Melchizedek[u] king of Salem[c][v] brought out bread and wine. He was priest of God Most High, 19and he blessed Abram,[w] saying,

"Blessed be Abram by God Most High,
Creator[d] of heaven and earth.[x]
20And blessed be[e] God Most High,[y]
who delivered your enemies into your hand."

Then Abram gave him a tenth of everything.[z]

GOODNESS

MELCHIZEDEK FOREVER!

Genesis 14:18

Jesus is a high priest forever, in the order of Melchizedek. This priest was of old, yet young in every age. He was a symbol of the sinless Christ, who met our sinfulness, washed us in holiness and blessed us with relationship.

Melchizedek, who were you?
A nomad cleric on the go?
You remind us down the years
Of a carpenter we know.

21The king of Sodom said to Abram, "Give me the people and keep the goods for yourself."

22But Abram said to the king of Sodom, "I have raised my hand[a] to the LORD, God Most High, Creator of heaven and earth,[b] and have taken an oath 23that I will accept nothing belonging to you,[c] not even a thread or the thong of a sandal, so that you will never be able to say, 'I made Abram rich.' 24I will accept nothing but what my men have eaten and the share that belongs to the men who went with me—to Aner, Eshcol and Mamre. Let them have their share."

God's Covenant With Abram

15 After this, the word of the LORD came to Abram[d] in a vision:

"Do not be afraid,[e] Abram.
I am your shield,[f][f]
your very great reward.[g]"

[a]3 That is, the Dead Sea [b]13 Or *a relative*; or *an ally* [c]18 That is, Jerusalem [d]19 Or *Possessor*; also in verse 22 [e]20 Or *And praise be to* [f]1 Or *sovereign* [g]1 Or *shield; / your reward will be very great*

14:17 [t]2Sa 18:18
14:18 [u]Ps 110:4; Heb 5:6 [v]Ps 76:2; Heb 7:2
14:19 [w]Heb 7:6 [x]ver 22
14:20 [y]Ge 24:27 [z]Ge 28:22; Dt 26:12; Heb 7:4
14:22 [a]Ex 6:8; Da 12:7; Rev 10:5-6 [b]ver 19
14:23 [c]2Ki 5:16
15:1 [d]Da 10:1 [e]Ge 21:17; 26:24; 46:3; 2Ki 6:16; Ps 27:1; Isa 41:10, 13-14 [f]Dt 33:29; 2Sa 22:3,31; Ps 3:3

2But Abram said, "O Sovereign
LORD, what can you give me since I
remain childless[g] and the one who will
inherit[a] my estate is Eliezer of Damascus?" 3And Abram said, "You have giv-
en me no children; so a servant[h] in my
household will be my heir."
4Then the word of the LORD came
to him: "This man will not be your
heir, but a son coming from your own
body will be your heir.[i]" 5He took
him outside and said, "Look up at
the heavens and count the stars[j]—if
indeed you can count them." Then
he said to him, "So shall your offspring be."[k]
6Abram believed the LORD, and he
credited it to him as righteousness.[l]
7He also said to him, "I am the
LORD, who brought you out of Ur of
the Chaldeans to give you this land to
take possession of it."
8But Abram said, "O Sovereign
LORD, how can I know[m] that I will
gain possession of it?"
9So the LORD said to him, "Bring
me a heifer, a goat and a ram, each
three years old, along with a dove and a
young pigeon."
10Abram brought all these to him,
cut them in two and arranged the halves
opposite each other;[n] the birds, however, he did not cut in half.[o] 11Then
birds of prey came down on the carcasses, but Abram drove them away.

[a]2 The meaning of the Hebrew for this phrase is uncertain.

15:2 [g]Ac 7:5
15:3 [h]Ge 24:2,34
15:4 [i]Gal 4:28
15:5 [j]Ps 147:4; Jer 33:22 [k]Ge 12:2; 22:17; Ex 32:13; Ro 4:18*; Heb 11:12
15:6 [l]Ps 106:31; Ro 4:3*, 20-24*; Gal 3:6*; Jas 2:23*
15:8 [m]Lk 1:18
15:10 [n]ver 17; Jer 34:18 [o]Lev 1:17

ABRAHAM

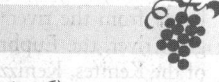

Faithfulness, Unwavering Fidelity (15:1–6)

Faithfulness trusts even when the final form of our circumstances cannot be foreseen. God promised Abraham that he would father a great nation. But the promise was given to an old man whose wife was well past the years for having children. The child was to be born in a land far from Abraham's homeland. Faithfulness was Abraham's confidence that all God's promises would occur—even though his age and circumstances made this seem impossible.

Hebrews 11:8–19 lists nine qualities of Abraham's life of faithfulness:

1. He followed God, even though he did not know where God was leading (v. 8). Faith follows through the mists of uncertain destinies.

2. He lived in tents as a foreigner (v. 9). Being a foreigner is hard work, for one is constantly seeking a home.

3. He was looking forward to a city, a kingdom that would rise silhouetted against the horizon (v. 10). Little did he know that the city would be called Zion, and that his own descendants would build it in the generations to come. God's greatest dreams are owned only by those who can see beyond the frail years of their own lifetime.

4. He counted on God's promise that, even as an old man, he would become a father (v. 11).

5. Abraham considered God faithful—One who did not make idle promises (v. 11).

6. Abraham saw God as faithful in a time beyond his own (v. 13). All that God promised would eventually come to pass.

7. Abraham longed for the coming of a wonderful kingdom (v. 16). People of faith believe that this wonder—the glorious wonder of God—is ever on the way.

8. Abraham was so faithful that he did not refuse to give God his only beloved son when God asked for his son's life—all that was most precious to him (v. 17). In this act of sacrifice, the faithfulness of Abraham is a picture of the faithfulness of God, who would later give his only Son to redeem the world.

9. Abraham's faith was so great that he was confident that, even if he killed his own son at God's request, God could raise the boy from the dead (v. 19). Faithfulness always sees that nothing is impossible for God.

Abraham remains the Bible's premier example of faithfulness, and from such faithfulness the Israelite nation came to be.

15:12 12As the sun was setting, Abram
pGe 2:21 fell into a deep sleep,[p] and a thick
and dreadful darkness came over him.
13Then the LORD said to him, "Know
for certain that your descendants will
be strangers in a country not their own,
15:13 qEx 1:11 and they will be enslaved[q] and mistreat-
rver 16; ed four hundred years.[r] 14But I will
Ex 12:40; Ac 7:6,17 punish the nation they serve as slaves,
15:14 sAc 7:7* and afterward they will come out[s] with
tEx 12:32-38 great possessions.[t] 15You, however, will
go to your fathers in peace and be bur-
15:15 uGe 25:8 ied at a good old age.[u] 16In the fourth
generation your descendants will come
15:16 v1Ki 21:26 back here, for the sin of the Amorites[v]
has not yet reached its full measure."
17When the sun had set and darkness had fallen, a smoking firepot with
a blazing torch appeared and passed be-
15:17 wver 10 tween the pieces.[w] 18On that day the
LORD made a covenant with Abram and
15:18 xGe 12:7 said, "To your descendants I give this
yNu 34:5 land,[x] from the river[a] of Egypt[y] to the
great river, the Euphrates— 19the land
of the Kenites, Kenizzites, Kadmonites,
20Hittites, Perizzites, Rephaites, 21Am-
orites, Canaanites, Girgashites and Jebusites."

Hagar and Ishmael

16 Now Sarai, Abram's wife, had
16:1 zGe 11:30; borne him no children.[z] But she
Gal 4:24-25 aGe 21:9 had an Egyptian maidservant[a] named
Hagar; 2so she said to Abram, "The
LORD has kept me from having children. Go, sleep with my maidservant;
16:2 perhaps I can build a family through
bGe 30:3-4, 9-10 her."[b]
Abram agreed to what Sarai said. 3So
16:3 cGe 12:5 after Abram had been living in Canaan[c]
ten years, Sarai his wife took her Egyp-
tian maidservant Hagar and gave her to
her husband to be his wife. 4He slept
with Hagar, and she conceived.
When she knew she was pregnant,
she began to despise her mistress. 5Then
Sarai said to Abram, "You are responsible for the wrong I am suffering. I put
my servant in your arms, and now that
she knows she is pregnant, she despises
me. May the LORD judge between you
16:5 dGe 31:53 and me."[d]
6"Your servant is in your hands,"
Abram said. "Do with her whatever you
think best." Then Sarai mistreated Ha-
16:7 eGe 21:17; gar; so she fled from her.
22:11,15; 7The angel of the LORD[e] found Ha-
31:11 gar near a spring in the desert; it was
the spring that is beside the road to 16:7
Shur.[f] 8And he said, "Hagar, servant of fGe 20:1
Sarai, where have you come from, and
where are you going?"
"I'm running away from my mistress
Sarai," she answered.
9Then the angel of the LORD told
her, "Go back to your mistress and submit to her." 10The angel added, "I will
so increase your descendants that they 16:10
will be too numerous to count."[g] gGe 13:16; 17:20
11The angel of the LORD also said to
her:

"You are now with child
and you will have a son.
You shall name him Ishmael,[b]
for the LORD has heard of your
misery.[h] 16:11 hEx 2:24; 3:7,9
12He will be a wild donkey of a man;
his hand will be against everyone
and everyone's hand against him,
and he will live in hostility 16:12
toward[c] all his brothers.[i]" iGe 25:18

13She gave this name to the LORD
who spoke to her: "You are the God
who sees me," for she said, "I have now
seen[d] the One who sees me."[j] 14That 16:13 jGe 32:30
is why the well was called Beer Lahai
Roi[e]; it is still there, between Kadesh
and Bered. 16:15
15So Hagar bore Abram a son,[k] and kGal 4:22
Abram gave the name Ishmael to the
son she had borne. 16Abram was eighty-
six years old when Hagar bore him Ishmael.

The Covenant of Circumcision

17 When Abram was ninety-nine
years old, the LORD appeared
to him and said, "I am God Almighty[f];[l] 17:1 lGe 28:3; Ex 6:3
walk before me and be blameless.[m] 2I mDt 18:13
will confirm my covenant between me 17:2
and you[n] and will greatly increase your nGe 15:18
numbers."
3Abram fell facedown, and God said 17:4 oGe 15:18
to him, 4"As for me, this is my cov- pver 16; Ge 12:2
enant with you:[o] You will be the father 35:11; 48:19
of many nations.[p] 5No longer will you 17:5
be called Abram[g]; your name will be qver 15; Ne 9:7
Abraham,[h][q] for I have made you a fa- rRo 4:17*
ther of many nations.[r] 6I will make you 17:6
very fruitful;[s] I will make nations of sGe 35:11

[a]*18* Or *Wadi* [b]*11 Ishmael* means *God hears.* [c]*12* Or *live to the east / of* [d]*13* Or *seen the back of* [e]*14 Beer Lahai Roi* means *well of the Living One who sees me.* [f]*1* Hebrew *El-Shaddai* [g]*5 Abram* means *exalted father.* [h]*5 Abraham* means *father of many.*

you, and kings will come from you.[t] **7**I will establish my covenant as an everlasting covenant between me and you and your descendants after you for the generations to come, to be your God[u] and the God of your descendants after you.[v] **8**The whole land of Canaan,[w] where you are now an alien,[x] I will give as an everlasting possession to you and your descendants after you;[y] and I will be their God."

17:6 [t]Mt 1:6
17:7 [u]Ex 29:45,46 [v]Ro 9:8; Gal 3:16
17:8 [w]Ps 105:9,11 [x]Ge 23:4; 28:4; Ex 6:4 [y]Ge 12:7

PATIENCE

BLESS ME NOW, BLESS ME LATER

Genesis 17:7

The promises of God are never hurried. His blessings sit atop the centuries, watching the years dawdle by. God's covenant has snared us in its four-millennium web of truth, still making peace with us.

9Then God said to Abraham, "As for you, you must keep my covenant, you and your descendants after you for the generations to come. **10**This is my covenant with you and your descendants after you, the covenant you are to keep: Every male among you shall be circumcised.[z] **11**You are to undergo circumcision,[a] and it will be the sign of the covenant[b] between me and you. **12**For the generations to come every male among you who is eight days old must be circumcised,[c] including those born in your household or bought with money from a foreigner—those who are not your offspring. **13**Whether born in your household or bought with your money, they must be circumcised. My covenant in your flesh is to be an everlasting covenant. **14**Any uncircumcised male, who has not been circumcised in the flesh, will be cut off from his people;[d] he has broken my covenant."

15God also said to Abraham, "As for Sarai your wife, you are no longer to call her Sarai; her name will be Sarah. **16**I will bless her and will surely give you a son by her.[e] I will bless her so that she will be the mother of nations;[f] kings of peoples will come from her."

17Abraham fell facedown; he laughed[g] and said to himself, "Will a son be born to a man a hundred years old? Will Sarah bear a child at the age of ninety?" **18**And Abraham said to God, "If only Ishmael might live under your blessing!"

17:10 [z]ver 23; Ge 21:4; Jn 7:22; Ac 7:8; Ro 4:11
17:11 [a]Ex 12:48; Dt 10:16 [b]Ro 4:11
17:12 [c]Lev 12:3 Lk 2:21
17:14 [d]Ex 4:24-26
17:16 [e]Ge 18:10 [f]Ge 35:11; Gal 4:31
17:17 [g]Ge 18:12; 21:6

19Then God said, "Yes, but your wife Sarah will bear you a son,[h] and you will call him Isaac.[a] I will establish my covenant with him[i] as an everlasting covenant for his descendants after him. **20**And as for Ishmael, I have heard you: I will surely bless him; I will make him fruitful and will greatly increase his numbers.[j] He will be the father of twelve rulers,[k] and I will make him into a great nation.[l] **21**But my covenant I will establish with Isaac, whom Sarah will bear to you by this time next year."[m] **22**When he had finished speaking with Abraham, God went up from him.

23On that very day Abraham took his son Ishmael and all those born in his household or bought with his money, every male in his household, and circumcised them, as God told him. **24**Abraham was ninety-nine years old when he was circumcised,[n] **25**and his son Ishmael was thirteen; **26**Abraham and his son Ishmael were both circumcised on that same day. **27**And every male in Abraham's household, including those born in his household or bought from a foreigner, was circumcised with him.

17:19 [h]Ge 18:14; 21:2 [i]Ge 26:3
17:20 [j]Ge 16:10 [k]Ge 25:12-16 [l]Ge 21:18
17:21 [m]Ge 21:2
17:24 [n]Ro 4:11

The Three Visitors

18 The LORD appeared to Abraham near the great trees of Mamre[o] while he was sitting at the entrance to his tent in the heat of the day. **2**Abraham looked up and saw three men[p] standing nearby. When he saw them, he hurried from the entrance of his tent to meet them and bowed low to the ground.

3He said, "If I have found favor in your eyes, my lord,[b] do not pass your servant by. **4**Let a little water be brought, and then you may all wash your feet[q] and rest under this tree. **5**Let me get you something to eat,[r] so you can be refreshed and then go on your way—now that you have come to your servant."

"Very well," they answered, "do as you say."

6So Abraham hurried into the tent to Sarah. "Quick," he said, "get three

18:1 [o]Ge 13:18; 14:13
18:2 [p]ver 16,22; Ge 32:24; Jos 5:13; Jdg 13:6-11; Heb 13:2
18:4 [q]Ge 19:2; 43:24
18:5 [r]Jdg 13:15

[a]19 *Isaac* means *he laughs.* [b]3 Or *O Lord*

seahs[a] of fine flour and knead it and
bake some bread."
7Then he ran to the herd and selected a choice, tender calf and gave it to a
servant, who hurried to prepare it. 8He
then brought some curds and milk and
the calf that had been prepared, and set
18:8 [s]Ge 19:3 these before them.[s] While they ate, he
stood near them under a tree.
9"Where is your wife Sarah?" they
asked him.
"There, in the tent," he said.
10Then the LORD[b] said, "I will surely return to you about this time next
year, and Sarah your wife will have a
18:10 [t]Ro 9:9* son."[t]
Now Sarah was listening at the entrance to the tent, which was behind
him. 11Abraham and Sarah were already
18:11 [u]Ge 17:17 [v]Ro 4:19 old and well advanced in years,[u] and
Sarah was past the age of childbearing.[v]
18:12 [w]Ge 17:17; 21:6 [x]1Pe 3:6 12So Sarah laughed[w] to herself as she
thought, "After I am worn out and my
master[c][x] is old, will I now have this
pleasure?"
13Then the LORD said to Abraham,
"Why did Sarah laugh and say, 'Will I
really have a child, now that I am old?'
18:14 [y]Jer 32:17,27; Zec 8:6; Mt 19:26; Lk 1:37; Ro 4:21 14Is anything too hard for the LORD?[y] I
will return to you at the appointed time
next year and Sarah will have a son."
15Sarah was afraid, so she lied and
said, "I did not laugh."
But he said, "Yes, you did laugh."

Abraham Pleads for Sodom

16When the men got up to leave, they
looked down toward Sodom, and Abraham walked along with them to see
them on their way. 17Then the LORD
18:17 [z]Am 3:7 [a]Ge 19:24 said, "Shall I hide from Abraham[z] what
I am about to do?[a] 18Abraham will sure-
18:18 [b]Gal 3:8* ly become a great and powerful nation,[b]
and all nations on earth will be blessed
18:19 [c]Dt 4:9-10; 6:7 [d]Jos 24:15; Eph 6:4 through him. 19For I have chosen him,
so that he will direct his children[c] and
his household after him to keep the way
of the LORD[d] by doing what is right
and just, so that the LORD will bring
about for Abraham what he has promised him."
20Then the LORD said, "The outcry
against Sodom and Gomorrah is so
great and their sin so grievous 21that I
18:21 [e]Ge 11:5 will go down[e] and see if what they have
done is as bad as the outcry that has
reached me. If not, I will know."

22The men turned away and went to- 18:22 [f]Ge 19:1
ward Sodom,[f] but Abraham remained
standing before the LORD.[d] 23Then
Abraham approached him and said:
"Will you sweep away the righteous 18:23 [g]Nu 16:22
with the wicked?[g] 24What if there are
fifty righteous people in the city? Will
you really sweep it away and not spare[e]
the place for the sake of the fifty righteous people in it?[h] 25Far be it from 18:24 [h]Jer 5:1
you to do such a thing—to kill the
righteous with the wicked, treating the
righteous and the wicked alike. Far be
it from you! Will not the Judge[f] of all
the earth do right?"[i] 18:25 [i]Job 8:3,20; Ps 58:11; 94:2; Isa 3:10-11; Ro 3:6
26The LORD said, "If I find fifty
righteous people in the city of Sodom,
I will spare the whole place for their
sake.[j]" 18:26 [j]Jer 5:1
27Then Abraham spoke up again:
"Now that I have been so bold as to
speak to the Lord, though I am noth- 18:27 [k]Ge 2:7; 3:19; Job 30:19; 42:6
ing but dust and ashes,[k] 28what if the
number of the righteous is five less than
fifty? Will you destroy the whole city
because of five people?"
"If I find forty-five there," he said, "I
will not destroy it."
29Once again he spoke to him, "What
if only forty are found there?"
He said, "For the sake of forty, I will
not do it."
30Then he said, "May the Lord not
be angry, but let me speak. What if only
thirty can be found there?"
He answered, "I will not do it if I
find thirty there."
31Abraham said, "Now that I have
been so bold as to speak to the Lord,
what if only twenty can be found
there?"
He said, "For the sake of twenty, I
will not destroy it."
32Then he said, "May the Lord not
be angry, but let me speak just once 18:32 [l]Jdg 6:39 [m]Jer 5:1
more.[l] What if only ten can be found
there?"
He answered, "For the sake of ten,[m]
I will not destroy it."
33When the LORD had finished
speaking with Abraham, he left, and
Abraham returned home.

[a]*6* That is, probably about 20 quarts (about 22 liters) [b]*10* Hebrew *Then he* [c]*12* Or *husband* [d]*22* Masoretic Text; an ancient Hebrew scribal tradition *but the LORD remained standing before Abraham* [e]*24* Or *forgive*; also in verse 26 [f]*25* Or *Ruler*

Sodom and Gomorrah Destroyed

19:1 **19** The two angels arrived at Sod-
[n]Ge 18:22 om[n] in the evening, and Lot was
[o]Ge 18:1 sitting in the gateway of the city.[o] When
he saw them, he got up to meet them
and bowed down with his face to the
ground. 2“My lords,” he said, “please
19:2 turn aside to your servant’s house. You
[p]Ge 18:4; can wash your feet[p] and spend the night
Lk 7:44 and then go on your way early in the
morning.”
“No,” they answered, “we will spend
the night in the square.”
3But he insisted so strongly that they
did go with him and entered his house.
19:3 He prepared a meal for them, baking
[q]Ge 18:6 bread without yeast, and they ate.[q] 4Be-
fore they had gone to bed, all the men
from every part of the city of Sodom—
both young and old—surrounded the
house. 5They called to Lot, “Where are
the men who came to you tonight?
Bring them out to us so that we can
19:5 have sex with them.”[r]
[r]Jdg 19:22; Isa 3:9; 6Lot went outside to meet them[s] and
Ro 1:24-27 shut the door behind him 7and said,
19:6 “No, my friends. Don’t do this wicked
[s]Jdg 19:23 thing. 8Look, I have two daughters who
have never slept with a man. Let me
bring them out to you, and you can
do what you like with them. But don’t
do anything to these men, for they
have come under the protection of my
19:8 roof.”[t]
[t]Jdg 19:24 9“Get out of our way,” they replied.
And they said, “This fellow came here
as an alien, and now he wants to play
19:9 the judge![u] We’ll treat you worse than
[u]Ex 2:14; Ac 7:27 them.” They kept bringing pressure on
Lot and moved forward to break down
the door.
10But the men inside reached out and
pulled Lot back into the house and shut
the door. 11Then they struck the men
who were at the door of the house,
19:11 young and old, with blindness[v] so that
[v]Dt 28:28-29; 2Ki 6:18; Ac 13:11 they could not find the door.
12The two men said to Lot, “Do
you have anyone else here—sons-in-
19:12 law, sons or daughters, or anyone else
[w]Ge 7:1 in the city who belongs to you?[w] Get
them out of here, 13because we are going to destroy this place. The outcry to
the LORD against its people is so great
19:13 [x]1Ch 21:15 that he has sent us to destroy it.”[x]
14So Lot went out and spoke to his
sons-in-law, who were pledged to marry[a] his daughters. He said, “Hurry and
get out of this place, because the LORD
is about to destroy the city![y]” But his 19:14 [y]Nu 16:21
sons-in-law thought he was joking.[z] [z]Ex 9:21; Lk 17:28
15With the coming of dawn, the an-
gels urged Lot, saying, “Hurry! Take
your wife and your two daughters who
are here, or you will be swept away[a] 19:15 [a]Nu 16:26
when the city is punished.[b]” [b]Rev 18:4
16When he hesitated, the men
grasped his hand and the hands of his
wife and of his two daughters and led
them safely out of the city, for the
LORD was merciful to them. 17As soon
as they had brought them out, one of
them said, “Flee for your lives![c] Don’t 19:17 [c]Jer 48:6
look back,[d] and don’t stop anywhere in [d]ver 26
the plain! Flee to the mountains or you
will be swept away!”
18But Lot said to them, “No, my
lords,[b] please! 19Your[c] servant has found
favor in your[c] eyes, and you[c] have
shown great kindness to me in sparing
my life. But I can’t flee to the mountains; this disaster will overtake me, and
I’ll die. 20Look, here is a town near
enough to run to, and it is small. Let
me flee to it—it is very small, isn’t it?
Then my life will be spared.”
21He said to him, “Very well, I will
grant this request too; I will not overthrow the town you speak of. 22But flee
there quickly, because I cannot do anything until you reach it.” (That is why
the town was called Zoar.[d])
23By the time Lot reached Zoar, the
sun had risen over the land. 24Then
the LORD rained down burning sulfur
on Sodom and Gomorrah[e]—from the 19:24 [e]Dt 29:23; Isa 1:9; 13:19
LORD out of the heavens.[f] 25Thus he [f]Lk 17:29; 2Pe 2:6; Jude 7
overthrew those cities and the entire
plain, including all those living in the
cities—and also the vegetation in the 19:25
land.[g] 26But Lot’s wife looked back,[h] [g]Ps 107:34; Eze 16:48
and she became a pillar of salt.[i]
27Early the next morning Abraham 19:26 [h]ver 17
got up and returned to the place where [i]Lk 17:32
he had stood before the LORD.[j] 28He 19:27
looked down toward Sodom and Go- [j]Ge 18:22
morrah, toward all the land of the plain,
and he saw dense smoke rising from the 19:28
land, like smoke from a furnace.[k] [k]Rev 9:2; 18:9
29So when God destroyed the cities of
the plain, he remembered Abraham, and 19:29
he brought Lot out of the catastrophe[l] [l]2Pe 2:7

[a]*14* Or *were married to* [b]*18* Or *No, Lord*; or *No, my lord* [c]*19* The Hebrew is singular. [d]*22* *Zoar* means *small.*

SELF-CONTROL

MRS. LOT

Genesis 19:26

Poor Sodom; it never seemed to understand that brimstone always buries cultures that lose their need for God.

What makes a culture die?
Mrs. Lot instructs us all.
Those who worry too much about being a pillar in society
May, in time, become a pillar of salt.

that overthrew the cities where Lot had
lived.

Lot and His Daughters

30Lot and his two daughters left Zoar
19:30 [m]ver 19 and settled in the mountains,[m] for he
was afraid to stay in Zoar. He and his
two daughters lived in a cave. 31One
day the older daughter said to the younger, "Our father is old, and there is no
man around here to lie with us, as is
the custom all over the earth. 32Let's get
our father to drink wine and then lie
with him and preserve our family line
through our father."
33That night they got their father
to drink wine, and the older daughter
went in and lay with him. He was not
aware of it when she lay down or when
she got up.
34The next day the older daughter
said to the younger, "Last night I lay
with my father. Let's get him to drink
wine again tonight, and you go in and
lie with him so we can preserve our
family line through our father." 35So
they got their father to drink wine that
night also, and the younger daughter
went and lay with him. Again he was
not aware of it when she lay down or
when she got up.
36So both of Lot's daughters became
pregnant by their father. 37The older
daughter had a son, and she named him
19:37 [n]Dt 2:9 Moab[a]; he is the father of the Moabites[n]
of today. 38The younger daughter also
had a son, and she named him Ben-
19:38 [o]Dt 2:19 Ammi[b]; he is the father of the Ammonites[o] of today.

Abraham and Abimelech

20:1 [p]Ge 18:1 **20** Now Abraham moved on from
there[p] into the region of the
Negev and lived between Kadesh and
Shur. For a while he stayed in Gerar,[q] 20:1 [q]Ge 26:1,6,17
2and there Abraham said of his wife
Sarah, "She is my sister.[r]" Then Abim- 20:2 [r]ver 12; Ge 12:13; 26:7
elech king of Gerar sent for Sarah and
took her.[s] [s]Ge 12:15
3But God came to Abimelech in a
dream[t] one night and said to him, "You 20:3 [t]Job 33:15; Mt 27:19
are as good as dead because of the wom- [u]Ps 105:14
an you have taken; she is a married
woman."[u]
4Now Abimelech had not gone near
her, so he said, "Lord, will you destroy
an innocent nation?[v] 5Did he not say 20:4 [v]Ge 18:25
to me, 'She is my sister,' and didn't she
also say, 'He is my brother'? I have done
this with a clear conscience and clean
hands."
6Then God said to him in the dream,
"Yes, I know you did this with a clear
conscience, and so I have kept[w] you 20:6 [w]1Sa 25:26,34
from sinning against me. That is why I
did not let you touch her. 7Now return
the man's wife, for he is a prophet, and 20:7 [x]ver 17; 1Sa 7:5; Job 42:8
he will pray for you[x] and you will live.
But if you do not return her, you may
be sure that you and all yours will die."
8Early the next morning Abimelech
summoned all his officials, and when
he told them all that had happened,
they were very much afraid. 9Then
Abimelech called Abraham in and said,
"What have you done to us? How have
I wronged you that you have brought
such great guilt upon me and my kingdom? You have done things to me that
should not be done.[y]" 10And Abime- 20:9 [y]Ge 12:18; 26:10; 34:7
lech asked Abraham, "What was your
reason for doing this?"
11Abraham replied, "I said to myself,
'There is surely no fear of God[z] in this 20:11 [z]Ge 42:18; Ps 36:1
place, and they will kill me because of [a]Ge 12:12; 26:7
my wife.'[a] 12Besides, she really is my
sister, the daughter of my father though
not of my mother; and she became my
wife. 13And when God had me wander
from my father's household, I said to
her, 'This is how you can show your
love to me: Everywhere we go, say of
me, "He is my brother." ' "
14Then Abimelech brought sheep and
cattle and male and female slaves and
gave them to Abraham,[b] and he re- 20:14 [b]Ge 12:16
turned Sarah his wife to him. 15And
Abimelech said, "My land is before you;
live wherever you like."[c] 20:15 [c]Ge 13:9

[a]37 *Moab* sounds like the Hebrew for *from father.*
[b]38 *Ben-Ammi* means *son of my people.*

16To Sarah he said, "I am giving your
brother a thousand shekels[a] of silver.
This is to cover the offense against you
before all who are with you; you are
completely vindicated."
17Then Abraham prayed to God,[d] 20:17 [d]Job 42:9
and God healed Abimelech, his wife
and his slave girls so they could have
children again, 18for the LORD had
closed up every womb in Abimelech's
household because of Abraham's wife
Sarah.[e] 20:18 [e]Ge 12:17

The Birth of Isaac

21 Now the LORD was gracious 21:1 [f]1Sa 2:21
to Sarah[f] as he had said, and [g]Ge 8:1; 17:16,21;
the LORD did for Sarah what he had Gal 4:23
promised.[g] 2Sarah became pregnant and
bore a son[h] to Abraham in his old age,[i] 21:2 [h]Ge 17:19
at the very time God had promised [i]Gal 4:22;
him. 3Abraham gave the name Isaac[b][j] Heb 11:11
to the son Sarah bore him. 4When his 21:3 [j]Ge 17:19
son Isaac was eight days old, Abraham
circumcised him,[k] as God commanded 21:4 [k]Ge 17:10,12;
him. 5Abraham was a hundred years old Ac 7:8
when his son Isaac was born to him.
6Sarah said, "God has brought me
laughter,[l] and everyone who hears about 21:6 [l]Ge 17:17;
this will laugh with me." 7And she add- Isa 54:1
ed, "Who would have said to Abraham
that Sarah would nurse children? Yet I
have borne him a son in his old age."

GOODNESS

GOD'S GOOD HUMOR

Genesis 21:6

Sarah laughed at the promise that she would have a child, so her son was named *Isaac,* which means "he laughs." Out of such folly comes hope. From such lunacy, in time, flow rivers of redemption.

Hagar and Ishmael Sent Away

8The child grew and was weaned,
and on the day Isaac was weaned Abraham held a great feast. 9But Sarah saw
that the son whom Hagar the Egyptian 21:9 [m]Ge 16:15
had borne to Abraham[m] was mocking,[n] [n]Gal 4:29
10and she said to Abraham, "Get rid of
that slave woman and her son, for that
slave woman's son will never share in 21:10 [o]Gal 4:30*
the inheritance with my son Isaac."[o]
11The matter distressed Abraham 21:11 [p]Ge 17:18
greatly because it concerned his son.[p]
12But God said to him, "Do not be
so distressed about the boy and your

[a]*16* That is, about 25 pounds (about 11.5 kilograms)
[b]*3* *Isaac* means *he laughs.*

DAY 2 TWO

LOVE AND THE PURPOSE OF GOD IN MY LIFE

Read Genesis 21:1–6

God's giving love is signed and sealed in grace. In fact, the glory of Sarah's life can be summed up in Genesis 21:1–2, "The LORD was gracious to Sarah . . . and the LORD did for Sarah what he had promised. Sarah became pregnant." Here then is the odd, irrational schedule of God's giving love. When Sarah is past the age of having children, when she is physically incapable of pregnancy, God acts in her life. God gives Sarah a son. Sarah, the old one, had once laughed at the notion of late-in-life motherhood, and so the name of her firstborn son, *Isaac,* is "Laughter." She found that God's promises may sleep awhile, but they are never silent forever.

Now at an age when other women gaze back across the years to the infancies of their grandchildren, Sarah holds her firstborn. She can see that God is love. She can see that God's heart of love compels him to give. And she can understand what God has revealed to all humanity: The words *grace* and *gracious* are related, and grace in its best reduction means *gift.*

If we say "grace" before a meal, we are thanking God for his gifts. If we say a ballerina has grace, we mean she has been given the gifts of poise, balance and interpretation. If we say that God is gracious, or full of grace, we mean that God gives gifts to his children—gifts not deserved, but given to enrich us and establish our knowledge of God's giving love in the center of our souls. At the moment of this insight, we are changed forever.

So then how are we to view the purpose of God in our lives? God desires that our bodies be the emissaries of communicating his love. Our feet are to carry his message. Our hands are to break his living bread. Our minds are to hold his vision. Our hearts are to beat with his compassion. All of this is to be done in the name of love.

To begin a study of the topic of The Evidence of Love is Giving, turn to the home page on page 5.

maidservant. Listen to whatever Sarah
tells you, because it is through Isaac that
21:12 your offspring[a] will be reckoned.[q] 13I
[q]Ro 9:7*; Heb 11:18* will make the son of the maidservant
21:13 into a nation[r] also, because he is your
[r]ver 18 offspring."
14Early the next morning Abraham
took some food and a skin of water and
gave them to Hagar. He set them on
her shoulders and then sent her off with
the boy. She went on her way and wan-
21:14 dered in the desert of Beersheba.[s]
[s]ver 31,32 15When the water in the skin was
gone, she put the boy under one of the
bushes. 16Then she went off and sat
down nearby, about a bowshot away,
for she thought, "I cannot watch the
boy die." And as she sat there nearby,
she[b] began to sob.
21:17 17God heard the boy crying,[t] and
[t]Ex 3:7 the angel of God called to Hagar from
heaven and said to her, "What is the
matter, Hagar? Do not be afraid; God
has heard the boy crying as he lies there.
18Lift the boy up and take him by the
hand, for I will make him into a great
21:18 nation.[u]"
[u]ver 13 19Then God opened her eyes[v] and
21:19 [v]Nu 22:31 she saw a well of water. So she went and
filled the skin with water and gave the
boy a drink.
21:20 20God was with the boy[w] as he grew
[w]Ge 26:3,24; 28:15; up. He lived in the desert and became
39:2,21,23 an archer. 21While he was living in the
Desert of Paran, his mother got a wife
21:21 [x]Ge 24:4,38 for him[x] from Egypt.

The Treaty at Beersheba

22At that time Abimelech and Phicol the commander of his forces said to
Abraham, "God is with you in every-
21:23 thing you do. 23Now swear[y] to me here
[y]ver 31; Jos 2:12 before God that you will not deal falsely with me or my children or my de-
scendants. Show to me and the country
where you are living as an alien the
same kindness I have shown to you."
24Abraham said, "I swear it."
25Then Abraham complained to
21:25 Abimelech about a well of water that
[z]Ge 26:15,18, 20-22 Abimelech's servants had seized.[z] 26But
Abimelech said, "I don't know who has
done this. You did not tell me, and I
heard about it only today."
27So Abraham brought sheep and cat-
21:27 [a]Ge 26:28,31 tle and gave them to Abimelech, and
the two men made a treaty.[a] 28Abra-
ham set apart seven ewe lambs from the

flock, 29and Abimelech asked Abraham,
"What is the meaning of these seven
ewe lambs you have set apart by themselves?"
30He replied, "Accept these seven 21:30
lambs from my hand as a witness[b] that [b]Ge 31:44,47,
I dug this well." 48,50,52
31So that place was called Beersheba,[c][c] 21:31
because the two men swore an oath [c]Ge 26:33
there.
32After the treaty had been made at
Beersheba, Abimelech and Phicol the
commander of his forces returned to
the land of the Philistines. 33Abraham
planted a tamarisk tree in Beersheba,
and there he called upon the name of 21:33
the LORD,[d] the Eternal God.[e] 34And [d]Ge 4:26 [e]Dt 33:27
Abraham stayed in the land of the Phi-
listines for a long time.

Abraham Tested

22 Some time later God tested[f] 22:1
Abraham. He said to him, "Abra- [f]Dt 8:2,16; Heb 11:17;
ham!" Jas 1:12-13
"Here I am," he replied. 22:2
2Then God said, "Take your son[g], [g]ver 12,16;
your only son, Isaac, whom you love, Jn 3:16; Heb 11:17;
and go to the region of Moriah.[h] Sac- 1Jn 4:9 [h]2Ch 3:1
rifice him there as a burnt offering on
one of the mountains I will tell you
about."
3Early the next morning Abraham
got up and saddled his donkey. He took
with him two of his servants and his
son Isaac. When he had cut enough
wood for the burnt offering, he set out
for the place God had told him about.
4On the third day Abraham looked up
and saw the place in the distance. 5He
said to his servants, "Stay here with the
donkey while I and the boy go over
there. We will worship and then we will
come back to you."
6Abraham took the wood for the
burnt offering and placed it on his son 22:6
Isaac,[i] and he himself carried the fire [i]Jn 19:17
and the knife. As the two of them went
on together, 7Isaac spoke up and said to
his father Abraham, "Father?"
"Yes, my son?" Abraham replied.
"The fire and wood are here," Isaac
said, "but where is the lamb[j] for the 22:7
burnt offering?" [j]Lev 1:10
8Abraham answered, "God himself

[a]*12* Or *seed* [b]*16* Hebrew; Septuagint *the child*
[c]*31 Beersheba* can mean *well of seven* or *well of the oath.*

DAY 2 TWO

GOODNESS AND THE PURPOSE OF GOD IN MY LIFE

Read Genesis 22:1–2,6–14

Let's look again at the life of Abraham. His goodness and righteousness are celebrated later in the Bible. He is held up to all believers as a model of faithfulness. What does God work in Abraham's life? What purposes are there for us to examine?

When God demands of Abraham the ultimate sacrifice of his son, Abraham obeys. Even if Abraham feels the requirement too severe, he does not condemn the request. So he and his son make the long trip to the region of Moriah.

Isaac is no fool. He has no doubt accompanied his father on other sacrificial pilgrimages, but this time he has noticed that they are taking no sacrificial animal with them. So his obvious question is: "Where is the sacrifice?"

Abraham answers Isaac's queries: "God will provide a sacrifice."

Abraham is right. And he is spared the very price that God himself would later pay. When Jesus was nailed to the cross, there was no ram caught in the thicket to take his place. Jesus was the perfect sacrifice. He entered the tabernacle as the high priest—not a high priest who offered a sacrifice, but a high priest who *was* a sacrifice. (see Hebrews 9:12).

What was it that Jesus actually accomplished? In Romans 3:21 Paul says that we now can enjoy a righteousness apart from the law. What is this righteousness? It is a perfect moral standing before God, but one that we do not gain by being good. We can claim this righteousness from God because Jesus lived perfectly and died perfectly, and because God has taken his flawless morality and placed it in the center of our lives.

We are free to do the work that God has determined for us because we are made good through Christ. When God asks the "impossible" of us, like Abraham we can follow him without fear, knowing that his plan encompasses the ultimate good for our lives.

To begin a study on the topic of Goodness Implanted Into Our Lives Through Christ, turn to the home page on page 1484.

will provide the lamb for the burnt offering, my son." And the two of them
went on together.
9When they reached the place God
had told him about, Abraham built an
altar there and arranged the wood on it.
He bound his son Isaac and laid him on
the altar,[k] on top of the wood. 10Then
he reached out his hand and took the
knife to slay his son. 11But the angel of
the LORD called out to him from heav-
en, "Abraham! Abraham!"
"Here I am," he replied.
12"Do not lay a hand on the boy," he
said. "Do not do anything to him. Now
I know that you fear God,[l] because you
have not withheld from me your son,
your only son.[m]"

22:9 [k]Heb 11:17-19; Jas 2:21
22:12 [l]1Sa 15:22; Jas 2:21-22 [m]ver 2; Jn 3:16

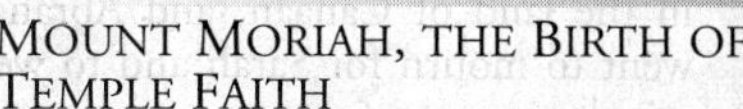

FAITHFULNESS

MOUNT MORIAH, THE BIRTH OF TEMPLE FAITH

Genesis 22:9–12

Was the great temple of God built here on Mount Moriah? On this very spot? Probably. The place where fathers offer up their sons to God is a place of love strong enough to form the foundations of enduring faith.

13Abraham looked up and there in
a thicket he saw a ram[a] caught by its
horns. He went over and took the ram
and sacrificed it as a burnt offering instead of his son.[n] 14So Abraham called
that place The LORD Will Provide. And
to this day it is said, "On the mountain
of the LORD it will be provided.[o]"
15The angel of the LORD called to
Abraham from heaven a second time
16and said, "I swear by myself,[p] declares
the LORD, that because you have done
this and have not withheld your son,
your only son, 17I will surely bless you
and make your descendants[q] as numerous as the stars in the sky[r] and as the
sand on the seashore.[s] Your descendants
will take possession of the cities of their
enemies,[t] 18and through your offspring[b]
all nations on earth will be blessed,[u] because you have obeyed me."[v]
19Then Abraham returned to his

22:13 [n]Ro 8:32
22:14 [o]ver 8
22:16 [p]Lk 1:73; Heb 6:13
22:17 [q]Heb 6:14* [r]Ge 15:5 [s]Ge 26:24; 32:12 [t]Ge 24:60
22:18 [u]Ge 12:2,3; Ac 3:25*; Gal 3:8* [v]ver 10

[a]*13* Many manuscripts of the Masoretic Text, Samaritan Pentateuch, Septuagint and Syriac; most manuscripts of the Masoretic Text *a ram behind him* [b]*18* Or *seed*

servants, and they set off together for
Beersheba. And Abraham stayed in Beersheba.

Nahor's Sons

20Some time later Abraham was told,
22:20 "Milcah is also a mother; she has borne
[w]Ge 11:29 sons to your brother Nahor:[w] 21Uz the
firstborn, Buz his brother, Kemuel (the
father of Aram), 22Kesed, Hazo, Pildash,
22:23 Jidlaph and Bethuel." 23Bethuel became
[x]Ge 24:15 the father of Rebekah.[x] Milcah bore
these eight sons to Abraham's brother
Nahor. 24His concubine, whose name
was Reumah, also had sons: Tebah, Ga-
ham, Tahash and Maacah.

The Death of Sarah

23 Sarah lived to be a hundred
23:2 and twenty-seven years old. 2She
[y]Jos 14:15 died at Kiriath Arba[y] (that is, Hebron)[z]
[z]ver 19; Ge 13:18 in the land of Canaan, and Abraham
went to mourn for Sarah and to weep
over her.
3Then Abraham rose from beside his
dead wife and spoke to the Hittites.[a]
23:4 He said, 4"I am an alien and a stranger[a]
[a]Ge 17:8; 1Ch 29:15; among you. Sell me some property for
Ps 105:12; a burial site here so I can bury my
Heb 11:9,13 dead."
5The Hittites replied to Abraham,
23:6 6"Sir, listen to us. You are a mighty
[b]Ge 14:14-16; prince[b] among us. Bury your dead in
24:35 the choicest of our tombs. None of us
will refuse you his tomb for burying
your dead."
7Then Abraham rose and bowed
down before the people of the land, the
Hittites. 8He said to them, "If you are
willing to let me bury my dead, then
listen to me and intercede with Ephron
23:8 [c]Ge 25:9 son of Zohar[c] on my behalf 9so he will
sell me the cave of Machpelah, which
belongs to him and is at the end of his
field. Ask him to sell it to me for the
full price as a burial site among you."
10Ephron the Hittite was sitting
among his people and he replied to
Abraham in the hearing of all the Hit-
23:10 tites who had come to the gate[d] of his
[d]Ge 34:20-24; Ru 4:4 city. 11"No, my lord," he said. "Listen
23:11 to me; I give[b][e] you the field, and I give[b]
[e]2Sa 24:23 you the cave that is in it. I give[b] it to
you in the presence of my people. Bury
your dead."
12Again Abraham bowed down before the people of the land 13and he
said to Ephron in their hearing, "Listen
to me, if you will. I will pay the price
of the field. Accept it from me so I can
bury my dead there."
14Ephron answered Abraham, 15"Listen to me, my lord; the land is worth
four hundred shekels[c] of silver,[f] but 23:15 [f]Eze 45:12
what is that between me and you? Bury
your dead."
16Abraham agreed to Ephron's terms
and weighed out for him the price he
had named in the hearing of the Hit- 23:16
tites: four hundred shekels of silver,[g] ac- [g]Jer 32:9;
cording to the weight current among Zec 11:12
the merchants.
17So Ephron's field in Machpelah
near Mamre[h]—both the field and the 23:17 [h]Ge 25:9;
cave in it, and all the trees within the 49:30-32;
borders of the field—was deeded 18to 50:13; Ac 7:16
Abraham as his property in the presence
of all the Hittites who had come to the
gate of the city. 19Afterward Abraham
buried his wife Sarah in the cave in the
field of Machpelah near Mamre (which
is at Hebron) in the land of Canaan.
20So the field and the cave in it were
deeded[i] to Abraham by the Hittites as a 23:20 [i]Jer 32:10
burial site.

Isaac and Rebekah

24 Abraham was now old and well
advanced in years, and the
LORD had blessed him in every way.[j] 24:1 [j]ver 35
2He said to the chief[d] servant in his
household, the one in charge of all
that he had,[k] "Put your hand under 24:2 [k]Ge 39:4-6
my thigh.[l] 3I want you to swear by the [l]ver 9; Ge 47:29
LORD, the God of heaven and the God
of earth,[m] that you will not get a wife 24:3 [m]Ge 14:19
for my son[n] from the daughters of the [n]Ge 28:1; Dt 7:3
Canaanites,[o] among whom I am living, [o]Ge 10:15-19
4but will go to my country and my own
relatives[p] and get a wife for my son 24:4 [p]Ge 12:1 28:2
Isaac."
5The servant asked him, "What if
the woman is unwilling to come back
with me to this land? Shall I then take
your son back to the country you came
from?"
6"Make sure that you do not take my
son back there," Abraham said. 7"The
LORD, the God of heaven, who brought
me out of my father's household and
my native land and who spoke to me
and promised me on oath, saying, 'To

[a]3 Or *the sons of Heth*; also in verses 5, 7, 10, 16, 18 and 20 [b]11 Or *sell* [c]15 That is, about 10 pounds (about 4.5 kilograms) [d]2 Or *oldest*

your offspring[a][q] I will give this land'[r]—he will send his angel before you[s] so that you can get a wife for my son from there. 8If the woman is unwilling to come back with you, then you will be released from this oath of mine. Only do not take my son back there." 9So the servant put his hand under the thigh[t] of his master Abraham and swore an oath to him concerning this matter.

10Then the servant took ten of his master's camels and left, taking with him all kinds of good things from his master. He set out for Aram Naharaim[b] and made his way to the town of Nahor. 11He had the camels kneel down near the well[u] outside the town; it was toward evening, the time the women go out to draw water.[v]

12Then he prayed, "O LORD, God of my master Abraham,[w] give me success today, and show kindness to my master Abraham. 13See, I am standing beside this spring, and the daughters of the townspeople are coming out to draw water. 14May it be that when I say to a girl, 'Please let down your jar that I may have a drink,' and she says, 'Drink, and I'll water your camels too'—let her be the one you have chosen for your servant Isaac. By this I will know[x] that you have shown kindness to my master."

15Before he had finished praying,[y] Rebekah[z] came out with her jar on her shoulder. She was the daughter of Bethuel son of Milcah,[a] who was the wife of Abraham's brother Nahor.[b] 16The girl was very beautiful,[c] a virgin; no man had ever lain with her. She went down to the spring, filled her jar and came up again.

17The servant hurried to meet her and said, "Please give me a little water from your jar."

18"Drink,[d] my lord," she said, and quickly lowered the jar to her hands and gave him a drink.

19After she had given him a drink, she said, "I'll draw water for your camels too,[e] until they have finished drinking." 20So she quickly emptied her jar into the trough, ran back to the well to draw more water, and drew enough for all his camels. 21Without saying a word, the man watched her closely to learn whether or not the LORD had made his journey successful.[f]

22When the camels had finished drinking, the man took out a gold nose ring[g] weighing a beka[c] and two gold bracelets weighing ten shekels.[d] 23Then he asked, "Whose daughter are you? Please tell me, is there room in your father's house for us to spend the night?"

24She answered him, "I am the daughter of Bethuel, the son that Milcah bore to Nahor.[h]" 25And she added, "We have plenty of straw and fodder, as well as room for you to spend the night."

26Then the man bowed down and worshiped the LORD,[i] 27saying, "Praise be to the LORD,[j] the God of my master Abraham, who has not abandoned his kindness and faithfulness[k] to my master. As for me, the LORD has led me on the journey[l] to the house of my master's relatives."[m]

28The girl ran and told her mother's household about these things. 29Now Rebekah had a brother named Laban,[n] and he hurried out to the man at the spring. 30As soon as he had seen the nose ring, and the bracelets on his sister's arms, and had heard Rebekah tell what the man said to her, he went out to the man and found him standing by the camels near the spring. 31"Come, you who are blessed by the LORD,"[o] he said. "Why are you standing out here? I have prepared the house and a place for the camels."

32So the man went to the house, and the camels were unloaded. Straw and fodder were brought for the camels, and water for him and his men to wash their feet.[p] 33Then food was set before him, but he said, "I will not eat until I have told you what I have to say."

"Then tell us," ⌊Laban⌋ said.

34So he said, "I am Abraham's servant. 35The LORD has blessed my master abundantly,[q] and he has become wealthy. He has given him sheep and cattle, silver and gold, menservants and maidservants, and camels and donkeys.[r] 36My master's wife Sarah has borne him a son in her[e] old age,[s] and he has given him everything he owns.[t] 37And my master made me swear an oath, and said, 'You must not get a wife for my son from the daughters of the

[a] *7* Or *seed* [b] *10* That is, Northwest Mesopotamia
[c] *22* That is, about 1/5 ounce (about 5.5 grams)
[d] *22* That is, about 4 ounces (about 110 grams)
[e] *36* Or *his*

24:7 [q]Gal 3:16* [r]Ge 12:7; 13:15 [s]Ex 23:20,23
24:9 [t]ver 2
24:11 [u]Ex 2:15 [v]ver 13; 1Sa 9:11
24:12 [w]ver 27,42,48; Ge 26:24; Ex 3:6,15,16
24:14 [x]Jdg 6:17,37
24:15 [y]ver 45 [z]Ge 22:23 [a]Ge 22:20 [b]Ge 11:29
24:16 [c]Ge 26:7
24:18 [d]ver 14
24:19 [e]ver 14
24:21 [f]ver 12
24:22 [g]ver 47
24:24 [h]ver 15
24:26 [i]ver 48,52; Ex 4:31
24:27 [j]Ex 18:10; Ru 4:14; 1Sa 25:32 [k]ver 49; Ge 32:10; Ps 98:3 [l]ver 21 [m]ver 12,48
24:29 [n]ver 4; Ge 29:5, 12,13
24:31 [o]Ge 26:29; Ru 3:10; Ps 115:15
24:32 [p]Ge 43:24; Jdg 19:21
24:35 [q]ver 1 [r]Ge 13:2
24:36 [s]Ge 21:2,10 [t]Ge 25:5

24:37 [u]ver 3 Canaanites, in whose land I live,[u] 38but
go to my father's family and to my own
24:38 [v]ver 4 clan, and get a wife for my son.'[v]
39"Then I asked my master, 'What if the
24:39 [w]ver 5 woman will not come back with me?'[w]
40"He replied, 'The LORD, before
whom I have walked, will send his an-
24:40 [x]ver 7 gel with you[x] and make your journey a
success, so that you can get a wife for
my son from my own clan and from
my father's family. 41Then, when you
go to my clan, you will be released from
my oath even if they refuse to give her
to you—you will be released from my
24:41 [y]ver 8 oath.'[y]
42"When I came to the spring today,
I said, 'O LORD, God of my master
Abraham, if you will, please grant suc-
24:42 [z]ver 12 cess[z] to the journey on which I have
come. 43See, I am standing beside this
24:43 [a]ver 13 [b]ver 14 spring;[a] if a maiden comes out to draw
water and I say to her, "Please let me
drink a little water from your jar,"[b]
44and if she says to me, "Drink, and I'll
draw water for your camels too," let her
be the one the LORD has chosen for my
master's son.'
45"Before I finished praying in my
24:45 [c]1Sa 1:13 [d]ver 15 [e]ver 17 heart,[c] Rebekah came out, with her jar
on her shoulder.[d] She went down to the
spring and drew water, and I said to
her, 'Please give me a drink.'[e]
46"She quickly lowered her jar from
24:46 [f]ver 18-19 her shoulder and said, 'Drink, and I'll
water your camels too.'[f] So I drank, and
she watered the camels also.
47"I asked her, 'Whose daughter are
24:47 [g]ver 23 [h]ver 24 [i]Eze 16:11-12 you?'[g]
"She said, 'The daughter of Bethuel
son of Nahor, whom Milcah bore to
him.'[h]
"Then I put the ring in her nose
and the bracelets on her arms,[i] 48and I
24:48 [j]ver 26 [k]ver 27 bowed down and worshiped the LORD.[j]
I praised the LORD, the God of my
master Abraham, who had led me on
the right road to get the granddaughter of my master's brother for his son.[k]
24:49 [l]Ge 47:29; Jos 2:14 49Now if you will show kindness and
faithfulness[l] to my master, tell me; and
if not, tell me, so I may know which
way to turn."
50Laban and Bethuel answered, "This
24:50 [m]Ps 118:23 [n]Ge 31:7,24,29,42 is from the LORD;[m] we can say nothing
to you one way or the other.[n] 51Here is
Rebekah; take her and go, and let her
become the wife of your master's son, as
the LORD has directed."

52When Abraham's servant heard
what they said, he bowed down to the
ground before the LORD.[o] 53Then the 24:52 [o]ver 26
servant brought out gold and silver jewelry and articles of clothing and gave
them to Rebekah; he also gave costly
gifts[p] to her brother and to her mother. 24:53 [p]ver 10,22
54Then he and the men who were with
him ate and drank and spent the night
there.

When they got up the next morning,
he said, "Send me on my way[q] to my 24:54 [q]ver 56,59
master."
55But her brother and her mother replied, "Let the girl remain with us ten
days or so; then you[a] may go."
56But he said to them, "Do not detain me, now that the LORD has granted success to my journey. Send me on
my way so I may go to my master."
57Then they said, "Let's call the girl
and ask her about it." 58So they called
Rebekah and asked her, "Will you go
with this man?"
"I will go," she said.
59So they sent their sister Rebekah
on her way, along with her nurse[r] and 24:59 [r]Ge 35:8
Abraham's servant and his men. 60And
they blessed Rebekah and said to her,

"Our sister, may you increase
to thousands upon thousands;[s] 24:60 [s]Ge 17:16 [t]Ge 22:17
may your offspring possess
the gates of their enemies."[t]

61Then Rebekah and her maids got
ready and mounted their camels and
went back with the man. So the servant
took Rebekah and left.
62Now Isaac had come from Beer La-
hai Roi,[u] for he was living in the Negev.[v] 24:62 [u]Ge 16:14; 25:11 [v]Ge 20:1
63He went out to the field one evening
to meditate,[b][w] and as he looked up, 24:63 [w]Ps 1:2; 77:12; 119:15,27,48, 97,148; 143:5; 145:5
he saw camels approaching. 64Rebekah
also looked up and saw Isaac. She got
down from her camel 65and asked the
servant, "Who is that man in the field
coming to meet us?"
"He is my master," the servant answered. So she took her veil and covered herself.
66Then the servant told Isaac all he
had done. 67Isaac brought her into the
tent of his mother Sarah, and he mar-
ried Rebekah.[x] So she became his wife, 24:67 [x]Ge 25:20 [y]Ge 29:18,20 [z]Ge 23:1-2
and he loved her;[y] and Isaac was com-
forted after his mother's death.[z]

[a]55 Or *she* [b]63 The meaning of the Hebrew for this word is uncertain.

The Death of Abraham

25 Abraham took[a] another wife,
whose name was Keturah. 2She
bore him Zimran, Jokshan, Medan,
Midian, Ishbak and Shuah.[a] 3Jokshan
was the father of Sheba and Dedan;
the descendants of Dedan were the As-
shurites, the Letushites and the Leum-
mites. 4The sons of Midian were Ephah,
Epher, Hanoch, Abida and Eldaah. All
these were descendants of Keturah.
5Abraham left everything he owned
to Isaac.[b] 6But while he was still living,
he gave gifts to the sons of his concubines[c] and sent them away from his son
Isaac[d] to the land of the east.
7Altogether, Abraham lived a hundred and seventy-five years. 8Then Abraham breathed his last and died at a good
old age,[e] an old man and full of years;
and he was gathered to his people.[f] 9His
sons Isaac and Ishmael buried him[g] in
the cave of Machpelah near Mamre,
in the field of Ephron son of Zohar
the Hittite,[h] 10the field Abraham had
bought from the Hittites.[b][i] There Abraham was buried with his wife Sarah.
11After Abraham's death, God blessed
his son Isaac, who then lived near Beer
Lahai Roi.[j]

Ishmael's Sons

12This is the account of Abraham's
son Ishmael, whom Sarah's maidservant,
Hagar[k] the Egyptian, bore to Abraham.[l]

13These are the names of the sons
of Ishmael, listed in the order of their
birth: Nebaioth the firstborn of Ishmael, Kedar, Adbeel, Mibsam, 14Mishma,
Dumah, Massa, 15Hadad, Tema, Jetur,
Naphish and Kedemah. 16These were
the sons of Ishmael, and these are the
names of the twelve tribal rulers[m] according to their settlements and camps.
17Altogether, Ishmael lived a hundred
and thirty-seven years. He breathed his
last and died, and he was gathered to
his people.[n] 18His descendants settled
in the area from Havilah to Shur, near
the border of Egypt, as you go toward
Asshur. And they lived in hostility toward[c] all their brothers.[o]

Jacob and Esau

19This is the account of Abraham's
son Isaac.

25:2 [a]1Ch 1:32,33
25:5 [b]Ge 24:36
25:6 [c]Ge 22:24 [d]Ge 21:10,14
25:8 [e]Ge 15:15 [f]ver 17; Ge 35:29; 49:29,33
25:9 [g]Ge 35:29 [h]Ge 50:13
25:10 [i]Ge 23:16
25:11 [j]Ge 16:14
25:12 [k]Ge 16:1 [l]Ge 16:15
25:16 [m]Ge 17:20
25:17 [n]ver 8
25:18 [o]Ge 16:12

Abraham became the father of Isaac,
20and Isaac was forty years old[p] when
he married Rebekah[q] daughter of Bethuel the Aramean from Paddan Aram[d]
and sister of Laban[r] the Aramean.
21Isaac prayed to the LORD on behalf of his wife, because she was barren.
The LORD answered his prayer,[s] and his
wife Rebekah became pregnant. 22The
babies jostled each other within her,
and she said, "Why is this happening
to me?" So she went to inquire of the
LORD.[t]
23The LORD said to her,

"Two nations[u] are in your womb,
and two peoples from within you
will be separated;
one people will be stronger than the
other,
and the older will serve the
younger.[v]"

24When the time came for her to
give birth, there were twin boys in her
womb. 25The first to come out was red,
and his whole body was like a hairy garment;[w] so they named him Esau.[e] 26Af-
ter this, his brother came out, with his
hand grasping Esau's heel;[x] so he was
named Jacob.[f][y] Isaac was sixty years old
when Rebekah gave birth to them.
27The boys grew up, and Esau became a skillful hunter, a man of the
open country,[z] while Jacob was a quiet
man, staying among the tents. 28Isaac,
who had a taste for wild game,[a] loved
Esau, but Rebekah loved Jacob.[b]
29Once when Jacob was cooking some
stew, Esau came in from the open
country, famished. 30He said to Jacob,
"Quick, let me have some of that red
stew! I'm famished!" (That is why he
was also called Edom.[g])
31Jacob replied, "First sell me your
birthright."
32"Look, I am about to die," Esau
said. "What good is the birthright
to me?"
33But Jacob said, "Swear to me first."
So he swore an oath to him, selling his
birthright[c] to Jacob.
34Then Jacob gave Esau some bread

25:20 [p]ver 26; Ge 26:34 [q]Ge 24:67 [r]Ge 24:29
25:21 [s]1Ch 5:20; 2Ch 33:13; Ezr 8:23; Ps 127:3; Ro 9:10
25:22 [t]1Sa 9:9; 10:22
25:23 [u]Ge 17:4 [v]Ge 27:29,40; Mal 1:3; Ro 9:11-12*
25:25 [w]Ge 27:11
25:26 [x]Hos 12:3 [y]Ge 27:36
25:27 [z]Ge 27:3,5
25:28 [a]Ge 27:19 [b]Ge 27:6
25:33 [c]Ge 27:36; Heb 12:16

[a]*1* Or *had taken* [b]*10* Or *the sons of Heth*
[c]*18* Or *lived to the east of* [d]*20* That is, Northwest
Mesopotamia [e]*25 Esau* may mean *hairy*; he was
also called Edom, which means *red.* [f]*26 Jacob*
means *he grasps the heel* (figuratively, *he deceives*).
[g]*30 Edom* means *red.*

and some lentil stew. He ate and drank, and then got up and left.

So Esau despised his birthright.

Isaac and Abimelech

26 Now there was a famine in the land[d]—besides the earlier famine of Abraham's time—and Isaac went to Abimelech king of the Philistines in Gerar.[e] 2The LORD appeared[f] to Isaac and said, "Do not go down to Egypt; live in the land where I tell you to live.[g] 3Stay in this land for a while,[h] and I will be with you and will bless you.[i] For to you and your descendants I will give all these lands[j] and will confirm the oath I swore to your father Abraham. 4I will make your descendants as numerous as the stars in the sky[k] and will give them all these lands, and through your offspring[a] all nations on earth will be blessed,[l] 5because Abraham obeyed me[m] and kept my requirements, my commands, my decrees and my laws." 6So Isaac stayed in Gerar.

7When the men of that place asked him about his wife, he said, "She is my sister,[n]" because he was afraid to say, "She is my wife." He thought, "The men of this place might kill me on account of Rebekah, because she is beautiful."

8When Isaac had been there a long time, Abimelech king of the Philistines looked down from a window and saw Isaac caressing his wife Rebekah. 9So Abimelech summoned Isaac and said, "She is really your wife! Why did you say, 'She is my sister'?"

Isaac answered him, "Because I thought I might lose my life on account of her."

10Then Abimelech said, "What is this you have done to us?[o] One of the men might well have slept with your wife, and you would have brought guilt upon us."

11So Abimelech gave orders to all the people: "Anyone who molests[p] this man or his wife shall surely be put to death."

12Isaac planted crops in that land and the same year reaped a hundredfold, because the LORD blessed him.[q] 13The man became rich, and his wealth continued to grow until he became very wealthy.[r] 14He had so many flocks and herds and servants[s] that the Philistines envied him.[t] 15So all the wells[u] that his father's servants had dug in the time of his father Abraham, the Philistines stopped up,[v] filling them with earth.

16Then Abimelech said to Isaac, "Move away from us; you have become too powerful for us.[w]"

17So Isaac moved away from there and encamped in the Valley of Gerar and settled there. 18Isaac reopened the wells[x] that had been dug in the time of his father Abraham, which the Philistines had stopped up after Abraham died, and he gave them the same names his father had given them.

19Isaac's servants dug in the valley and discovered a well of fresh water there. 20But the herdsmen of Gerar quarreled with Isaac's herdsmen and said, "The water is ours!"[y] So he named the well Esek,[b] because they disputed with him. 21Then they dug another well, but they quarreled over that one also; so he named it Sitnah.[c] 22He moved on from there and dug another well, and no one quarreled over it. He named it Rehoboth,[d] saying, "Now the LORD has given us room and we will flourish[z] in the land."

23From there he went up to Beersheba. 24That night the LORD appeared to him and said, "I am the God of your father Abraham.[a] Do not be afraid,[b] for I am with you; I will bless you and will increase the number of your descendants[c] for the sake of my servant Abraham."[d]

25Isaac built an altar[e] there and called on the name of the LORD. There he pitched his tent, and there his servants dug a well.

26Meanwhile, Abimelech had come to him from Gerar, with Ahuzzath his personal adviser and Phicol the commander of his forces.[f] 27Isaac asked them, "Why have you come to me, since you were hostile to me and sent me away?[g]"

28They answered, "We saw clearly that the LORD was with you;[h] so we said, 'There ought to be a sworn agreement between us'—between us and you. Let us make a treaty with you 29that you will do us no harm, just as we did not molest you but always treated you

[a]4 Or *seed* [b]20 *Esek* means *dispute.* [c]21 *Sitnah* means *opposition.* [d]22 *Rehoboth* means *room.*

26:1 [d]Ge 12:10 [e]Ge 20:1
26:2 [f]Ge 12:7; 17:1; 18:1 [g]Ge 12:1
26:3 [h]Ge 20:1; 28:15 [i]Ge 12:2; 22:16-18 [j]Ge 12:7; 13:15; 15:18
26:4 [k]Ge 15:5; 22:17 Ex 32:13 [l]Ge 12:3; 22:18; Gal 3:8
26:5 [m]Ge 22:16
26:7 [n]Ge 12:13; 20:2,12; Pr 29:25
26:10 [o]Ge 20:9
26:11 [p]Ps 105:15
26:12 [q]ver 3; Job 42:12
26:13 [r]Pr 10:22
26:14 [s]Ge 24:36
26:14 [t]Ge 37:11
26:15 [u]Ge 21:30 [v]Ge 21:25
26:16 [w]Ex 1:9
26:18 [x]Ge 21:30
26:20 [y]Ge 21:25
26:22 [z]Ge 17:6; Ex 1:7
26:24 [a]Ge 24:12; Ex 3:6 [b]Ge 15:1 [c]ver 4 [d]Ge 17:7
26:25 [e]Ge 12:7,8; 13:4,18; Ps 116:17
26:26 [f]Ge 21:22
26:27 [g]ver 16
26:28 [h]Ge 21:22

well and sent you away in peace. And
26:29 [i]Ge 24:31; Ps 115:15 now you are blessed by the LORD."[i]
30 Isaac then made a feast[j] for them,
26:30 [j]Ge 19:3 and they ate and drank. 31 Early the
next morning the men swore an oath[k]
26:31 [k]Ge 21:31 to each other. Then Isaac sent them on
their way, and they left him in peace.
32 That day Isaac's servants came and
told him about the well they had dug.
They said, "We've found water!" 33 He
26:33 [l]Ge 21:14 called it Shibah,[a] and to this day the
name of the town has been Beersheba.[b][l]
26:34 [m]Ge 25:20 34 When Esau was forty years old,[m]
he married Judith daughter of Beeri the
Hittite, and also Basemath daughter of
Elon the Hittite.[n] 35 They were a source 26:34 [n]Ge 28:9; 36:2
of grief to Isaac and Rebekah.[o] 26:35 [o]Ge 27:46

Jacob Gets Isaac's Blessing

27 When Isaac was old and his eyes
were so weak that he could no
longer see,[p] he called for Esau his older 27:1 [p]Ge 48:10; 1Sa 3:2 [q]Ge 25:25
son[q] and said to him, "My son."
"Here I am," he answered.
2 Isaac said, "I am now an old man

[a]33 *Shibah* can mean *oath* or *seven.* [b]33 *Beersheba* can mean *well of the oath* or *well of seven.*

JACOB

Self-Control, an Agenda for Achievement (27:1–29)

Jacob is not a person we can turn to in order to point out sterling character. From the time he was born, he was named the *Supplanter* or *Heel Grabber*. Jacob was born the second of twins. He came out of the womb grabbing the heel of Esau, trying to pull Esau back in so that he could be the firstborn himself (Genesis 25:24–26). From that point on, Jacob led a rather devious life. Still these things must be remembered: He was the father of the 12 tribes of Israel and was, therefore, critically involved in Abraham's lineage. He was at the center of God's plan to bless the whole world through the Abrahamic covenant.

Jacob must be credited as a good businessman—at least good at achieving his goals—even if he was not as honest as he should have been. There are four evidences that he was a man of self-control, the kind of self-control that creates its own agenda for achievement.

First, he stole his brother's blessing (27:1–29). Rebekah obviously favored Jacob over Esau, his twin. She decided to help Jacob convince Isaac that Jacob was Esau—thereby stealing the blessing. So Rebekah and Jacob contrived through an elaborate plan to do just that. Only a thoughtless son would deceive his old, blind father. But Jacob followed through on his plan seemingly without remorse.

Second, after Jacob fled to Paddan Aram, he went to work for Laban and worked seven years to win the hand of Rachel in marriage. But his father-in-law was as devious as Jacob was. When Jacob woke up on the morning after his wedding, he found he had been married to Leah, the heavily-veiled sister of Rachel. So he worked another seven years for the woman he had been denied the first time around (29:15–30).

Third, Jacob devised a stratagem to multiply his own flocks and herds at his father-in-law's expense (30:25–32,37–43). Jacob had earlier asked that the mottled animals in Laban's herd be his, and Laban had agreed. Jacob then found a way to swindle Laban out of the stronger animals, while Laban retained the weaker, more sickly livestock. In this way Jacob "grew exceedingly prosperous and came to own large flocks, and maidservants and menservants, and camels and donkeys" (30:43).

Fourth, Jacob fled away while Laban had his back turned, thus appropriating all he could at Laban's expense (31:17–21). Jacob was a schemer and most devious, but he knew how to press his ambitions through obdurate self-control to get what he wanted out of life.

Self-control must be exercised for godly reasons and, in this, Jacob failed. But if we can see that our own dreams for achievement can be given to God, then surely self-control—handed over to God and sanctified by the Spirit—is the path to becoming resourceful, even as we give those very resources to God for his use.

27:2 [r]Ge 47:29 and don't know the day of my death.[r]
3Now then, get your weapons—your
quiver and bow—and go out to the
27:3 open country[s] to hunt some wild game
[s]Ge 25:27 for me. 4Prepare me the kind of tasty
27:4 food I like and bring it to me to eat, so
[t]ver 10,25,31; Ge 49:28; that I may give you my blessing[t] before
Dt 33:1; Heb 11:20 I die."
5Now Rebekah was listening as Isaac
spoke to his son Esau. When Esau left
for the open country to hunt game and
bring it back, 6Rebekah said to her son
27:6 [u]Ge 25:28 Jacob,[u] "Look, I overheard your father
say to your brother Esau, 7'Bring me
some game and prepare me some tasty
food to eat, so that I may give you my
blessing in the presence of the LORD
27:8 before I die.' 8Now, my son, listen care-
[v]ver 13,43 fully and do what I tell you:[v] 9Go out
to the flock and bring me two choice
young goats, so I can prepare some tasty
food for your father, just the way he
likes it. 10Then take it to your father to
eat, so that he may give you his blessing
before he dies."
11Jacob said to Rebekah his mother,
27:11 "But my brother Esau is a hairy man,[w]
[w]Ge 25:25 and I'm a man with smooth skin.
27:12 12What if my father touches me?[x] I
[x]ver 22 would appear to be tricking him and
would bring down a curse on myself
rather than a blessing."
27:13 13His mother said to him, "My son,
[y]Mt 27:25 let the curse fall on me.[y] Just do what I
[z]ver 8 say;[z] go and get them for me."
14So he went and got them and
brought them to his mother, and she
prepared some tasty food, just the way
his father liked it. 15Then Rebekah took
27:15 [a]ver 27 the best clothes[a] of Esau her older son,
which she had in the house, and put
them on her younger son Jacob. 16She
also covered his hands and the smooth
part of his neck with the goatskins.
17Then she handed to her son Jacob
the tasty food and the bread she had
made.
18He went to his father and said, "My
father."
"Yes, my son," he answered. "Who
is it?"
19Jacob said to his father, "I am Esau
your firstborn. I have done as you told
me. Please sit up and eat some of my
game so that you may give me your
27:19 [b]ver 4 blessing."[b]
20Isaac asked his son, "How did you
find it so quickly, my son?"

"The LORD your God gave me success,"[c] he replied. 27:20 [c]Ge 24:12
21Then Isaac said to Jacob, "Come
near so I can touch you,[d] my son, to 27:21 [d]ver 12
know whether you really are my son
Esau or not."
22Jacob went close to his father Isaac,
who touched him and said, "The voice
is the voice of Jacob, but the hands are
the hands of Esau." 23He did not recognize him, for his hands were hairy like
those of his brother Esau;[e] so he blessed 27:23
him. 24"Are you really my son Esau?" he [e]ver 16
asked.
"I am," he replied.
25Then he said, "My son, bring me
some of your game to eat, so that I may
give you my blessing."[f] 27:25 [f]ver 4
Jacob brought it to him and he
ate; and he brought some wine and
he drank. 26Then his father Isaac said
to him, "Come here, my son, and kiss
me."
27So he went to him and kissed him.[g] 27:27
When Isaac caught the smell of his [g]Heb 11:20 [h]SS 4:11
clothes,[h] he blessed him and said, [i]Ps 65:9-13

"Ah, the smell of my son
is like the smell of a field
that the LORD has blessed.[i]
28May God give you of heaven's 27:28
dew[j] [j]Dt 33:13
and of earth's richness[k]— [k]ver 39
an abundance of grain and new [l]Ge 45:18; Nu 18:12; Dt 33:28
wine.[l]
29May nations serve you 27:29
and peoples bow down to you.[m] [m]Isa 45:14, 23; 49:7,23
Be lord over your brothers, [n]Ge 9:25; 25:23; 37:7
and may the sons of your mother [o]Ge 12:3;
bow down to you.[n] Nu 24:9;
May those who curse you be cursed Zep 2:8
and those who bless you be
blessed.[o]"

30After Isaac finished blessing him
and Jacob had scarcely left his father's
presence, his brother Esau came in from
hunting. 31He too prepared some tasty
food and brought it to his father. Then
he said to him, "My father, sit up and
eat some of my game, so that you may 27:31
give me your blessing."[p] [p]ver 4
32His father Isaac asked him, "Who
are you?"[q] 27:32 [q]ver 18
"I am your son," he answered, "your
firstborn, Esau."
33Isaac trembled violently and said,
"Who was it, then, that hunted game
and brought it to me? I ate it just be-

fore you came and I blessed him—and
27:33 [r]ver 29; Ge 28:3,4; Ro 11:29 indeed he will be blessed![r]"
[34]When Esau heard his father's words,
he burst out with a loud and bitter cry[s]
27:34 [s]Heb 12:17 and said to his father, "Bless me—me
too, my father!"
[35]But he said, "Your brother came
27:35 [t]Jer 9:4; 12:6 deceitfully[t] and took your blessing."
[36]Esau said, "Isn't he rightly named
27:36 [u]Ge 25:26 Jacob[a]?[u] He has deceived me these two
[v]Ge 25:33 times: He took my birthright,[v] and
now he's taken my blessing!" Then he
asked, "Haven't you reserved any blessing for me?"
[37]Isaac answered Esau, "I have made
him lord over you and have made all
27:37 his relatives his servants, and I have sus-
[w]ver 28 tained him with grain and new wine.[w]
So what can I possibly do for you, my
son?"
[38]Esau said to his father, "Do you
have only one blessing, my father? Bless
27:38 me too, my father!" Then Esau wept
[x]Heb 12:17 aloud.[x]
[39]His father Isaac answered him,

"Your dwelling will be
away from the earth's richness,
27:39 [y]ver 28 away from the dew[y] of heaven
above.
[40]You will live by the sword
27:40 [z]2Sa 8:14 [a]Ge 25:23 and you will serve[z] your brother.[a]
But when you grow restless,
[b]2Ki 8:20-22 you will throw his yoke
from off your neck.[b]"

Jacob Flees to Laban

27:41 [c]Ge 37:4 [d]Ge 32:11 [41]Esau held a grudge[c] against Jacob[d]
[e]Ge 50:4,10 because of the blessing his father had
[f]Ob 1:10 given him. He said to himself, "The days
of mourning[e] for my father are near;
then I will kill my brother Jacob."[f]
[42]When Rebekah was told what her
older son Esau had said, she sent for
her younger son Jacob and said to him,
"Your brother Esau is consoling himself
27:43 with the thought of killing you. [43]Now
[g]ver 8 then, my son, do what I say:[g] Flee at
[h]Ge 24:29 [i]Ge 11:31 once to my brother Laban[h] in Haran.[i]
27:44 [44]Stay with him for a while[j] until your
[j]Ge 31:38,41 brother's fury subsides. [45]When your
27:45 brother is no longer angry with you and
[k]ver 35 forgets what you did to him,[k] I'll send
word for you to come back from there.
Why should I lose both of you in one
day?"
[46]Then Rebekah said to Isaac, "I'm
disgusted with living because of these

Hittite women. If Jacob takes a wife
from among the women of this land,
from Hittite women like these, my life
will not be worth living."[l] 27:46 [l]Ge 26:35

28 So Isaac called for Jacob and
blessed[b] him and commanded
him: "Do not marry a Canaanite
woman.[m] [2]Go at once to Paddan Aram,[c] 28:1 [m]Ge 24:3
to the house of your mother's father
Bethuel.[n] Take a wife for yourself there, 28:2 [n]Ge 25:20
from among the daughters of Laban,
your mother's brother. [3]May God Al-
mighty[d][o] bless you and make you fruit- 28:3 [o]Ge 17:1
ful[p] and increase your numbers until [p]Ge 17:6
you become a community of peoples.
[4]May he give you and your descen- 28:4
dants the blessing given to Abraham,[q] [q]Ge 12:2,3
so that you may take possession of the [r]Ge 17:8
land where you now live as an alien,[r]
the land God gave to Abraham." [5]Then
Isaac sent Jacob on his way, and he
went to Paddan Aram,[s] to Laban son 28:5 [s]Hos 12:12
of Bethuel the Aramean, the brother of [t]Ge 24:29
Rebekah,[t] who was the mother of Jacob
and Esau.
[6]Now Esau learned that Isaac had
blessed Jacob and had sent him to Paddan Aram to take a wife from there, and
that when he blessed him he commanded him, "Do not marry a Canaanite
woman,"[u] [7]and that Jacob had obeyed 28:6 [u]ver 1
his father and mother and had gone
to Paddan Aram. [8]Esau then realized
how displeasing the Canaanite women[v] 28:8 [v]Ge 24:3
were to his father Isaac;[w] [9]so he went [w]Ge 26:35
to Ishmael and married Mahalath, the
sister of Nebaioth[x] and daughter of Ish- 28:9 [x]Ge 25:13
mael son of Abraham, in addition to [y]Ge 26:34
the wives he already had.[y]

Jacob's Dream at Bethel

[10]Jacob left Beersheba and set out
for Haran.[z] [11]When he reached a cer-
tain place, he stopped for the night be- 28:10 [z]Ge 11:31
cause the sun had set. Taking one of
the stones there, he put it under his
head and lay down to sleep. [12]He had
a dream[a] in which he saw a stairway[e] 28:12 [a]Ge 20:3
resting on the earth, with its top reach- [b]Jn 1:51
ing to heaven, and the angels of God
were ascending and descending on it.[b]
[13]There above it[f] stood the LORD,[c] and 28:13 [c]Ge 12:7;
he said: "I am the LORD, the God of 35:7,9; 48:3

[a]*36 Jacob* means *he grasps the heel* (figuratively, *he deceives*). [b]*1* Or *greeted* [c]*2* That is, Northwest Mesopotamia; also in verses 5, 6 and 7 [d]*3* Hebrew *El-Shaddai* [e]*12* Or *ladder* [f]*13* Or *There beside him*

your father Abraham and the God of Isaac.[d] I will give you and your descendants the land[e] on which you are lying. 14Your descendants will be like the dust of the earth, and you[f] will spread out to the west and to the east, to the north and to the south.[g] All peoples on earth will be blessed through you and your offspring.[h] 15I am with you[i] and will watch over you[j] wherever you go, and I will bring you back to this land. I will not leave you[k] until I have done what I have promised you."[l]

16When Jacob awoke from his sleep, he thought, "Surely the LORD is in this place, and I was not aware of it." 17He was afraid and said, "How awesome is this place![m] This is none other than the house of God; this is the gate of heaven."

18Early the next morning Jacob took the stone he had placed under his head and set it up as a pillar[n] and poured oil on top of it.[o] 19He called that place Bethel,[a] though the city used to be called Luz.[p]

20Then Jacob made a vow,[q] saying, "If God will be with me and will watch over me[r] on this journey I am taking and will give me food to eat and clothes to wear 21so that I return safely[s] to my father's house, then the LORD[b] will be my God[t] 22and[c] this stone that I have set up as a pillar will be God's house,[u] and of all that you give me I will give you a tenth.[v]"

28:13 [d]Ge 26:24 [e]Ge 13:15; 35:12
28:14 [f]Ge 26:4 [g]Ge 13:14 [h]Ge 12:3; 18:18; 22:18; Gal 3:8
28:15 [i]Ge 26:3; 48:21 [j]Nu 6:24; Ps 121:5,7-8 [k]Dt 31:6,8 [l]Nu 23:19
28:17 [m]Ex 3:5; Jos 5:15
28:18 [n]Ge 35:14; [o]Lev 8:11
28:19 [p]Jdg 1:23,26
28:20 [q]Ge 31:13; Jdg 11:30; 2Sa 15:8 [r]ver 15
28:21 [s]Jdg 11:31 [t]Dt 26:17
28:22 [u]Ge 35:7,14 [v]Ge 14:20; Lev 27:30

Jacob Arrives in Paddan Aram

29 Then Jacob continued on his journey and came to the land of the eastern peoples.[w] 2There he saw a well in the field, with three flocks of sheep lying near it because the flocks were watered from that well. The stone over the mouth of the well was large. 3When all the flocks were gathered there, the shepherds would roll the stone away from the well's mouth and water the sheep. Then they would return the stone to its place over the mouth of the well.

4Jacob asked the shepherds, "My brothers, where are you from?"

"We're from Haran,[x]" they replied.

5He said to them, "Do you know Laban, Nahor's grandson?"

"Yes, we know him," they answered.

6Then Jacob asked them, "Is he well?"

"Yes, he is," they said, "and here comes his daughter Rachel with the sheep."

7"Look," he said, "the sun is still high; it is not time for the flocks to be gathered. Water the sheep and take them back to pasture."

8"We can't," they replied, "until all the flocks are gathered and the stone has been rolled away from the mouth of the well. Then we will water the sheep."

9While he was still talking with them, Rachel came with her father's sheep,[y] for she was a shepherdess. 10When Jacob saw Rachel daughter of Laban, his mother's brother, and Laban's sheep, he went over and rolled the stone away from the mouth of the well and watered his uncle's sheep.[z] 11Then Jacob kissed Rachel and began to weep aloud.[a] 12He had told Rachel that he was a relative[b] of her father and a son of Rebekah. So she ran and told her father.[c]

13As soon as Laban[d] heard the news about Jacob, his sister's son, he hurried to meet him. He embraced him and kissed him and brought him to his home, and there Jacob told him all these things. 14Then Laban said to him, "You are my own flesh and blood."[e]

Jacob Marries Leah and Rachel

After Jacob had stayed with him for a whole month, 15Laban said to him, "Just because you are a relative of mine, should you work for me for nothing? Tell me what your wages should be."

16Now Laban had two daughters; the name of the older was Leah, and the name of the younger was Rachel. 17Leah had weak[d] eyes, but Rachel was lovely in form, and beautiful. 18Jacob was in love with Rachel and said, "I'll work for you seven years in return for your younger daughter Rachel."[f]

19Laban said, "It's better that I give her to you than to some other man. Stay here with me." 20So Jacob served seven years to get Rachel, but they seemed like only a few days to him because of his love for her.[g]

29:1 [w]Jdg 6:3,33
29:4 [x]Ge 28:10
29:9 [y]Ex 2:16
29:10 [z]Ex 2:17
29:11 [a]Ge 33:4
29:12 [b]Ge 13:8; 14:14,16 [c]Ge 24:28
29:13 [d]Ge 24:29
29:14 [e]Ge 2:23; Jdg 9:2; 2Sa 19:12-13
29:18 [f]Hos 12:12
29:20 [g]SS 8:7; Hos 12:12

[a] *19 Bethel* means *house of God.* [b] *20,21* Or *Since God . . . father's house, the LORD* [c] *21,22* Or *house, and the LORD will be my God,* [22]*then* [d] *17* Or *delicate*

21Then Jacob said to Laban, "Give
me my wife. My time is completed, and
29:21 [h]Jdg 15:1 I want to lie with her.[h]"
22So Laban brought together all the
people of the place and gave a feast.[i]
29:22 [i]Jdg 14:10; 23But when evening came, he took his
Jn 2:1-2 daughter Leah and gave her to Jacob,
and Jacob lay with her. 24And Laban
gave his servant girl Zilpah to his daughter as her maidservant.
25When morning came, there was
Leah! So Jacob said to Laban, "What is
29:25 [j]Ge 12:18 this you have done to me?[j] I served you
[k]Ge 27:36 for Rachel, didn't I? Why have you deceived me?[k]"
26Laban replied, "It is not our custom here to give the younger daughter
in marriage before the older one. 27Fin-
29:27 [l]Jdg 14:12 ish this daughter's bridal week;[l] then
we will give you the younger one also,
in return for another seven years of
work."
28And Jacob did so. He finished the
week with Leah, and then Laban gave
him his daughter Rachel to be his
wife. 29Laban gave his servant girl Bil-
29:29 [m]Ge 30:3 hah[m] to his daughter Rachel as her
[n]Ge 16:1 maidservant.[n] 30Jacob lay with Rachel
29:30 also, and he loved Rachel more than
[o]ver 16 Leah.[o] And he worked for Laban an-
[p]Ge 31:41 other seven years.[p]

Jacob's Children

29:31 31When the LORD saw that Leah
[q]Dt 21:15-17 was not loved,[q] he opened her womb,[r]
[r]Ge 11:30; 30:1; but Rachel was barren. 32Leah became
Ps 127:3 pregnant and gave birth to a son. She
29:32 named him Reuben,[a] for she said, "It is
[s]Ge 16:11; because the LORD has seen my misery.[s]
31:42; Ex 4:31; Surely my husband will love me now."
Dt 26:7; Ps 25:18 33She conceived again, and when she
gave birth to a son she said, "Because
the LORD heard that I am not loved,
29:33 he gave me this one too." So she named
[t]Ge 34:25; 49:5 him Simeon.[b][t]
34Again she conceived, and when she
gave birth to a son she said, "Now at
last my husband will become attached
29:34 [u]Ge 30:20; to me,[u] because I have borne him three
1Sa 1:2-4 [v]Ge 49:5-7 sons." So he was named Levi.[c][v]
35She conceived again, and when she
gave birth to a son she said, "This time
29:35 I will praise the Lord." So she named
[w]Ge 49:8; Mt 1:2-3 him Judah.[d][w] Then she stopped having
children.
30:1 [x]Ge 29:31; 1Sa 1:5-6 **30** When Rachel saw that she was
not bearing Jacob any children,[x]
[y]Lev 18:18 she became jealous of her sister.[y] So she
said to Jacob, "Give me children, or I'll
die!"
2Jacob became angry with her and
said, "Am I in the place of God, who
has kept you from having children?"[z] 30:2 [z]Ge 16:2;
3Then she said, "Here is Bilhah, 20:18; 29:31
my maidservant. Sleep with her so
that she can bear children for me and
that through her I too can build a fam- 30:3
ily."[a] [a]Ge 16:2
4So she gave him her servant Bilhah
as a wife.[b] Jacob slept with her,[c] 5and 30:4 [b]ver 9,18
she became pregnant and bore him a [c]Ge 16:3-4
son. 6Then Rachel said, "God has vin- 30:6
dicated me;[d] he has listened to my plea [d]Ps 35:24;
and given me a son." Because of this 43:1; La 3:59
she named him Dan.[e][e] [e]Ge 49:16-17
7Rachel's servant Bilhah conceived
again and bore Jacob a second son.
8Then Rachel said, "I have had a great
struggle with my sister, and I have 30:8
won."[f] So she named him Naphtali.[f][g] [f]Hos 12:3-4 [g]Ge 49:21
9When Leah saw that she had stopped 30:9
having children, she took her maidser- [h]ver 4
vant Zilpah and gave her to Jacob as a
wife.[h] 10Leah's servant Zilpah bore Jacob
a son. 11Then Leah said, "What good
fortune!"[g] So she named him Gad.[h][i] 30:11 [i]Ge 49:19
12Leah's servant Zilpah bore Jacob a
second son. 13Then Leah said, "How 30:13
happy I am! The women will call me[j] [j]Ps 127:3
happy."[k] So she named him Asher.[i][l] [k]Pr 31:28; Lk 1:48
14During wheat harvest, Reuben went [l]Ge 49:20
out into the fields and found some 30:14
mandrake plants,[m] which he brought to [m]SS 7:13
his mother Leah. Rachel said to Leah,
"Please give me some of your son's mandrakes."
15But she said to her, "Wasn't it
enough[n] that you took away my hus- 30:15 [n]Nu 16:9,13
band? Will you take my son's man-
drakes too?"
"Very well," Rachel said, "he can
sleep with you tonight in return for
your son's mandrakes."
16So when Jacob came in from the
fields that evening, Leah went out to
meet him. "You must sleep with me,"
she said. "I have hired you with my

[a]*32 Reuben* sounds like the Hebrew for *he has seen my misery*; the name means *see, a son.*
[b]*33 Simeon* probably means *one who hears.*
[c]*34 Levi* sounds like and may be derived from the Hebrew for *attached.* [d]*35 Judah* sounds like and may be derived from the Hebrew for *praise.*
[e]*6 Dan* here means *he has vindicated.* [f]*8 Naphtali* means *my struggle.* [g]*11* Or *"A troop is coming!"*
[h]*11 Gad* can mean *good fortune* or *a troop.*
[i]*13 Asher* means *happy.*

son's mandrakes." So he slept with her
that night.
30:17 [17]God listened to Leah,[o] and she be-
[o]Ge 25:21 came pregnant and bore Jacob a fifth
son. [18]Then Leah said, "God has rewarded me for giving my maidservant
to my husband." So she named him
30:18 Issachar.[a][p]
[p]Ge 49:14 [19]Leah conceived again and bore Jacob a sixth son. [20]Then Leah said,
"God has presented me with a precious gift. This time my husband will
treat me with honor, because I have
30:20 borne him six sons." So she named him
[q]Ge 35:23; 49:13; Zebulun.[b][q]
Mt 4:13 [21]Some time later she gave birth to a
daughter and named her Dinah.
30:22 [22]Then God remembered Rachel;[r] he
[r]Ge 8:1; 1Sa 1:19-20 listened to her and opened her womb.[s]
[s]Ge 29:31 [23]She became pregnant and gave birth
30:23 to a son[t] and said, "God has taken
[t]ver 6 [u]Isa 4:1; away my disgrace."[u] [24]She named him
Lk 1:25 Joseph,[c][v] and said, "May the LORD add
30:24 to me another son."[w]
[v]Ge 35:24; 37:2; 39:1; 49:22-26 [w]Ge 35:17

Jacob's Flocks Increase

[25]After Rachel gave birth to Joseph,
30:25 Jacob said to Laban, "Send me on my
[x]Ge 24:54 way[x] so I can go back to my own home-
30:26 [y]Ge 29:20,30; land. [26]Give me my wives and children,
Hos 12:12 for whom I have served you,[y] and I will
be on my way. You know how much
work I've done for you."
[27]But Laban said to him, "If I have
found favor in your eyes, please stay.
30:27 I have learned by divination that[d] the
[z]Ge 26:24; LORD has blessed me because of you."[z]
39:3,5 [28]He added, "Name your wages,[a] and I
30:28 will pay them."
[a]Ge 29:15 [29]Jacob said to him, "You know how
30:29 I have worked for you[b] and how your
[b]Ge 31:6 [c]Ge 31:38-40 livestock has fared under my care.[c]
[30]The little you had before I came has
increased greatly, and the LORD has
blessed you wherever I have been. But
30:30 now, when may I do something for my
[d]1Ti 5:8 own household?[d]"
[31]"What shall I give you?" he asked.
"Don't give me anything," Jacob replied. "But if you will do this one thing
for me, I will go on tending your flocks
and watching over them: [32]Let me go
through all your flocks today and remove from them every speckled or spot-
30:32 ted sheep, every dark-colored lamb and
[e]Ge 31:8,12 every spotted or speckled goat.[e] They
will be my wages. [33]And my honesty
will testify for me in the future, whenever you check on the wages you have
paid me. Any goat in my possession
that is not speckled or spotted, or any
lamb that is not dark-colored, will be
considered stolen."
[34]"Agreed," said Laban. "Let it be as
you have said." [35]That same day he
removed all the male goats that were
streaked or spotted, and all the speckled or spotted female goats (all that
had white on them) and all the dark-
colored lambs, and he placed them in
the care of his sons.[f] [36]Then he put a 30:35
three-day journey between himself and [f]Ge 31:1
Jacob, while Jacob continued to tend
the rest of Laban's flocks.
[37]Jacob, however, took fresh-cut
branches from poplar, almond and plane
trees and made white stripes on them by
peeling the bark and exposing the white
inner wood of the branches. [38]Then he
placed the peeled branches in all the
watering troughs, so that they would be
directly in front of the flocks when they
came to drink. When the flocks were in
heat and came to drink, [39]they mated
in front of the branches. And they bore
young that were streaked or speckled or
spotted. [40]Jacob set apart the young of
the flock by themselves, but made the
rest face the streaked and dark-colored
animals that belonged to Laban. Thus
he made separate flocks for himself and
did not put them with Laban's animals. [41]Whenever the stronger females
were in heat, Jacob would place the
branches in the troughs in front of
the animals so they would mate near
the branches, [42]but if the animals were
weak, he would not place them there.
So the weak animals went to Laban
and the strong ones to Jacob. [43]In this
way the man grew exceedingly prosperous and came to own large flocks,
and maidservants and menservants, and 30:43
camels and donkeys.[g] [g]ver 30; Ge 12:16; 13:2; 24:35; 26:13-14

Jacob Flees From Laban

31 Jacob heard that Laban's sons
were saying, "Jacob has taken
everything our father owned and has
gained all this wealth from what belonged to our father." [2]And Jacob no-

[a]*18 Issachar* sounds like the Hebrew for *reward.* [b]*20 Zebulun* probably means *honor.* [c]*24 Joseph* means *may he add.* [d]*27* Or possibly *have become rich and*

ticed that Laban's attitude toward him
was not what it had been.
31:3 [b]ver 13; Ge 32:9 [i]Ge 21:22; 26:3; 28:15 3 Then the LORD said to Jacob, "Go
back[b] to the land of your fathers and to
your relatives, and I will be with you."[i]
4 So Jacob sent word to Rachel and
Leah to come out to the fields where
his flocks were. 5 He said to them, "I see
that your father's attitude toward me is
31:5 [j]Ge 21:22; 26:3 not what it was before, but the God
of my father has been with me.[j] 6 You
know that I've worked for your father
31:6 [k]Ge 30:29 with all my strength,[k] 7 yet your father
has cheated me by changing my wages
31:7 [l]ver 41; Job 19:3 [m]ver 52; Ps 37:28; 105:14 ten times.[l] However, God has not allowed him to harm me.[m] 8 If he said,
'The speckled ones will be your wages,'[n]
then all the flocks gave birth to speck-
31:8 [n]Ge 30:32 led young; and if he said, 'The streaked
ones will be your wages,' then all the
flocks bore streaked young. 9 So God
has taken away your father's livestock
31:9 [o]ver 1,16; Ge 30:42 and has given them to me.[o]
10 "In breeding season I once had a
dream in which I looked up and saw
that the male goats mating with the
flock were streaked, speckled or spot-
31:11 [p]Ge 16:7; 48:16 ted. 11 The angel of God[p] said to me
in the dream, 'Jacob.' I answered, 'Here
I am.' 12 And he said, 'Look up and
see that all the male goats mating with
the flock are streaked, speckled or spotted, for I have seen all that Laban has
31:12 [q]Ex 3:7 been doing to you.[q] 13 I am the God
of Bethel,[r] where you anointed a pillar
31:13 [r]Ge 28:10-22 [s]ver 3; Ge 32:9 and where you made a vow to me. Now
leave this land at once and go back to
your native land.[s]' "
14 Then Rachel and Leah replied, "Do
we still have any share in the inheritance of our father's estate? 15 Does he
not regard us as foreigners? Not only
has he sold us, but he has used up what
31:15 [t]Ge 29:20 was paid for us.[t] 16 Surely all the wealth
that God took away from our father
belongs to us and our children. So do
whatever God has told you."
17 Then Jacob put his children and
31:18 [u]Ge 35:27 [v]Ge 10:19 his wives on camels, 18 and he drove all
his livestock ahead of him, along with
all the goods he had accumulated in
31:19 [w]ver 30,32, 34-35; Ge 35:2; Jdg 17:5; 1Sa 19:13; Hos 3:4 Paddan Aram,[a] to go to his father Isaac[u]
in the land of Canaan.[v]
19 When Laban had gone to shear his
sheep, Rachel stole her father's house-
31:20 [x]Ge 27:36 [y]ver 27 hold gods.[w] 20 Moreover, Jacob deceived[x]
Laban the Aramean by not telling him
he was running away.[y] 21 So he fled with

all he had, and crossing the River,[b] he
headed for the hill country of Gilead.[z] 31:21 [z]Ge 37:25

Laban Pursues Jacob

22 On the third day Laban was told
that Jacob had fled. 23 Taking his relatives with him, he pursued Jacob for
seven days and caught up with him
in the hill country of Gilead. 24 Then
God came to Laban the Aramean in a
dream at night and said to him,[a] "Be 31:24 [a]Ge 20:3; Job 33:15 [b]Ge 24:50
careful not to say anything to Jacob, ei-
ther good or bad."[b]
25 Jacob had pitched his tent in the
hill country of Gilead when Laban overtook him, and Laban and his relatives
camped there too. 26 Then Laban said
to Jacob, "What have you done? You've 31:26 [c]Ge 27:36 [d]1Sa 30:2-3
deceived me,[c] and you've carried off my
daughters like captives in war.[d] 27 Why
did you run off secretly and deceive
me? Why didn't you tell me, so I could
send you away with joy and singing to 31:27 [e]Ex 15:20 [f]Ge 4:21
the music of tambourines[e] and harps?[f]
28 You didn't even let me kiss my grandchildren and my daughters good-by.[g] 31:28 [g]ver 55
You have done a foolish thing. 29 I have
the power to harm you;[h] but last night 31:29 [h]ver 7 [i]ver 53
the God of your father[i] said to me, 'Be
careful not to say anything to Jacob,
either good or bad.' 30 Now you have
gone off because you longed to return
to your father's house. But why did you 31:30 [j]ver 19; Jdg 18:24
steal my gods?[j]"
31 Jacob answered Laban, "I was
afraid, because I thought you would
take your daughters away from me by
force. 32 But if you find anyone who
has your gods, he shall not live.[k] In the 31:32 [k]Ge 44:9
presence of our relatives, see for your-
self whether there is anything of yours
here with me; and if so, take it." Now
Jacob did not know that Rachel had
stolen the gods.
33 So Laban went into Jacob's tent and
into Leah's tent and into the tent of the
two maidservants, but he found nothing. After he came out of Leah's tent,
he entered Rachel's tent. 34 Now Rachel had taken the household gods and
put them inside her camel's saddle and 31:34 [l]ver 37; Ge 44:12
was sitting on them. Laban searched[l]
through everything in the tent but
found nothing.
35 Rachel said to her father, "Don't be

[a] *18* That is, Northwest Mesopotamia [b] *21* That is, the Euphrates

angry, my lord, that I cannot stand up
31:35 [m]Ex 20:12; in your presence;[m] I'm having my peri-
Lev 19:3,32 od." So he searched but could not find
the household gods.
36Jacob was angry and took Laban to
task. "What is my crime?" he asked Laban. "What sin have I committed that
you hunt me down? 37Now that you
have searched through all my goods,
what have you found that belongs to
your household? Put it here in front of
31:37 [n]ver 23 your relatives[n] and mine, and let them
judge between the two of us.
38"I have been with you for twenty
years now. Your sheep and goats have
not miscarried, nor have I eaten rams
from your flocks. 39I did not bring you
animals torn by wild beasts; I bore the
loss myself. And you demanded payment from me for whatever was stolen
31:39 by day or night.[o] 40This was my situ-
[o]Ex 22:13 ation: The heat consumed me in the
daytime and the cold at night, and sleep
fled from my eyes. 41It was like this for
the twenty years I was in your household. I worked for you fourteen years
31:41 [p]Ge 29:30 for your two daughters[p] and six years
[q]ver 7 for your flocks, and you changed my
wages ten times.[q] 42If the God of my
31:42 [r]ver 5; father,[r] the God of Abraham and the
Ex 3:15; 1Ch 12:17 Fear of Isaac,[s] had not been with me,[t]
[s]ver 53; you would surely have sent me away
Isa 8:13 [t]Ps 124:1-2 empty-handed. But God has seen my
[u]Ge 29:32 hardship and the toil of my hands,[u] and
last night he rebuked you."
43Laban answered Jacob, "The wom-
en are my daughters, the children are
my children, and the flocks are my
flocks. All you see is mine. Yet what
can I do today about these daughters
of mine, or about the children they
have borne? 44Come now, let's make a
31:44 [v]Ge 21:27; 26:28 covenant,[v] you and I, and let it serve as
[w]Jos 24:27 a witness between us."[w]
45So Jacob took a stone and set it
31:45 [x]Ge 28:18 up as a pillar.[x] 46He said to his relatives, "Gather some stones." So they
took stones and piled them in a heap,
and they ate there by the heap. 47La-
ban called it Jegar Sahadutha,[a] and Jacob called it Galeed.[b]
48Laban said, "This heap is a witness
between you and me today." That is
why it was called Galeed. 49It was also
31:49 [y]Jdg 11:29; called Mizpah,[c][y] because he said, "May
1Sa 7:5-6 the LORD keep watch between you and
me when we are away from each other.
50If you mistreat my daughters or if you
take any wives besides my daughters,
even though no one is with us, remem- 31:50
ber that God is a witness[z] between you [z]Jer 29:23;
and me." 42:5
51Laban also said to Jacob, "Here is
this heap, and here is this pillar[a] I have 31:51 [a]Ge 28:18
set up between you and me. 52This heap
is a witness, and this pillar is a witness,[b] 31:52 [b]Ge 21:30
that I will not go past this heap to your [c]ver 7; Ge 26:29
side to harm you and that you will not
go past this heap and pillar to my side
to harm me.[c] 53May the God of Abra-
ham[d] and the God of Nahor, the God 31:53 [d]Ge 28:13
of their father, judge between us."[e] [e]Ge 16:5 [f]Ge 21:23,27
So Jacob took an oath[f] in the name [g]ver 42
of the Fear of his father Isaac.[g] 54He offered a sacrifice there in the hill country
and invited his relatives to a meal. After they had eaten, they spent the night
there.
55Early the next morning Laban
kissed his grandchildren and his daugh- 31:55 [h]ver 28
ters[h] and blessed them. Then he left [i]Ge 18:33;
and returned home.[i] 30:25

Jacob Prepares to Meet Esau

32 Jacob also went on his way, and
the angels of God[j] met him. 32:1 [j]Ge 16:11;
2When Jacob saw them, he said, "This 2Ki 6:16-17; Ps 34:7;
is the camp of God!"[k] So he named that 91:11;
place Mahanaim.[d][l] Heb 1:14
3Jacob sent messengers ahead of him 32:2 [k]Ge 28:17
to his brother Esau[m] in the land of [l]2Sa 2:8,29
Seir, the country of Edom.[n] 4He in-
structed them: "This is what you are to 32:3 [m]Ge 27:41-42
say to my master Esau: 'Your servant Ja- [n]Ge 25:30; 36:8,9
cob says, I have been staying with La-
ban and have remained there till now.
5I have cattle and donkeys, sheep and
goats, menservants and maidservants.[o] 32:5 [o]Ge 12:16;
Now I am sending this message to my 30:43 [p]Ge
lord, that I may find favor in your 33:8,10,15
eyes.[p]'"
6When the messengers returned to
Jacob, they said, "We went to your
brother Esau, and now he is coming to
meet you, and four hundred men are
with him."[q] 32:6 [q]Ge 33:1
7In great fear[r] and distress Jacob divided the people who were with him 32:7 [r]ver 11
into two groups,[e] and the flocks and
herds and camels as well. 8He thought,

[a]47 The Aramaic *Jegar Sahadutha* means *witness heap.*
[b]47 The Hebrew *Galeed* means *witness heap.*
[c]49 *Mizpah* means *watchtower.* [d]2 *Mahanaim* means *two camps.* [e]7 Or *camps;* also in verse 10

"If Esau comes and attacks one group,[a]
the group[a] that is left may escape."
[9]Then Jacob prayed, "O God of my
32:9 [s]Ge 28:13; 31:42 [t]Ge 31:13 father Abraham, God of my father
Isaac,[s] O LORD, who said to me, 'Go
back to your country and your relatives, and I will make you prosper,'[t] [10]I
32:10 [u]Ge 24:27 am unworthy of all the kindness and
faithfulness[u] you have shown your servant. I had only my staff when I crossed
this Jordan, but now I have become
two groups. [11]Save me, I pray, from
the hand of my brother Esau, for I am
32:11 [v]Ps 59:2 [w]Ge 27:41 afraid he will come and attack me,[v] and
also the mothers with their children.[w]
32:12 [x]Ge 22:17 [y]Ge 28:13-15; Hos 1:10; Ro 9:27 [12]But you have said, 'I will surely make
you prosper and will make your descen-
dants like the sand[x] of the sea, which
cannot be counted.[y]'"
[13]He spent the night there, and from
32:13 [z]Ge 43:11,15, 25,26; Pr 18:16 what he had with him he selected a gift[z]
for his brother Esau: [14]two hundred fe-
male goats and twenty male goats, two
hundred ewes and twenty rams, [15]thirty
female camels with their young, forty
cows and ten bulls, and twenty female
donkeys and ten male donkeys. [16]He
put them in the care of his servants,
each herd by itself, and said to his servants, "Go ahead of me, and keep some
space between the herds."
[17]He instructed the one in the lead:
"When my brother Esau meets you and
asks, 'To whom do you belong, and
where are you going, and who owns all
these animals in front of you?' [18]then
you are to say, 'They belong to your
32:18 [a]Ge 18:3 servant[a] Jacob. They are a gift sent to
my lord Esau, and he is coming behind
us.'"
[19]He also instructed the second, the
third and all the others who followed
the herds: "You are to say the same thing
to Esau when you meet him. [20]And be
sure to say, 'Your servant Jacob is coming behind us.'" For he thought, "I will
pacify him with these gifts I am sending
32:20 [b]Ge 33:10; Pr 21:14 on ahead; later, when I see him, perhaps he will receive me."[b] [21]So Jacob's
gifts went on ahead of him, but he himself spent the night in the camp.

Jacob Wrestles With God

[22]That night Jacob got up and took
his two wives, his two maidservants and
32:22 [c]Dt 2:37; 3:16; Jos 12:2 his eleven sons and crossed the ford of
the Jabbok.[c] [23]After he had sent them
across the stream, he sent over all his
possessions. [24]So Jacob was left alone,
and a man[d] wrestled with him till day- 32:24 [d]Ge 18:2
break. [25]When the man saw that he
could not overpower him, he touched
the socket of Jacob's hip so that his hip[e] 32:25 [e]ver 32
was wrenched as he wrestled with the
man. [26]Then the man said, "Let me go,
for it is daybreak."
But Jacob replied, "I will not let you
go unless you bless me."[f] 32:26 [f]Hos 12:4

LOVE

LOVE, A LONGING AFTER GOD

Genesis 32:26

Jacob wrestled with God at Jabbok, a tiny desert stream that separated his past and his future. Jabbok is the river of our needy present. Like Jacob, we must have God's blessing in the moment, for yesterday's blessings will not suffice and tomorrow's are uncertain.

[27]The man asked him, "What is your
name?"
"Jacob," he answered.
[28]Then the man said, "Your name
will no longer be Jacob, but Israel,[b][g] be- 32:28 [g]Ge 17:5; 35:10; 1Ki 18:31
cause you have struggled with God and
with men and have overcome."
[29]Jacob said, "Please tell me your 32:29 [h]Jdg 13:17 [i]Jdg 13:18 [j]Ge 35:9
name."[h]
But he replied, "Why do you ask my
name?"[i] Then he blessed[j] him there.
[30]So Jacob called the place Peniel,[c]
saying, "It is because I saw God face to 32:30 [k]Ge 16:13; Ex 24:11; Nu 12:8; Jdg 6:22; 13:22
face,[k] and yet my life was spared."
[31]The sun rose above him as he passed
Peniel,[d] and he was limping because of
his hip. [32]Therefore to this day the Israelites do not eat the tendon attached
to the socket of the hip, because the
socket of Jacob's hip was touched near
the tendon.

Jacob Meets Esau

33 Jacob looked up and there was
Esau, coming with his four hun-
dred men;[l] so he divided the children 33:1 [l]Ge 32:6
among Leah, Rachel and the two maid-
servants. [2]He put the maidservants and
their children in front, Leah and her
children next, and Rachel and Joseph
in the rear. [3]He himself went on ahead

[a]8 Or *camp* [b]28 *Israel* means *he struggles with God.*
[c]30 *Peniel* means *face of God.* [d]31 Hebrew *Penuel,*
a variant of *Peniel*

33:3 [m]Ge 18:2; and bowed down to the ground[m] seven
42:6 times as he approached his brother.
4But Esau ran to meet Jacob and embraced him; he threw his arms around
his neck and kissed him. And they
33:4 wept.[n] 5Then Esau looked up and saw
[n]Ge 45:14-15 the women and children. "Who are
these with you?" he asked.
Jacob answered, "They are the chil-
33:5 dren God has graciously given your ser-
[o]Ge 48:9; Ps 127:3; vant.[o]"
Isa 8:18 6Then the maidservants and their
children approached and bowed down.
7Next, Leah and her children came
and bowed down. Last of all came Joseph and Rachel, and they too bowed
down.
8Esau asked, "What do you mean by
33:8 [p]Ge 32:14-16 all these droves I met?"[p]
[q]Ge 24:9; 32:5 "To find favor in your eyes, my
lord,"[q] he said.
9But Esau said, "I already have plenty, my brother. Keep what you have for
yourself."
10"No, please!" said Jacob. "If I have
found favor in your eyes, accept this
33:10 gift from me. For to see your face is like
[r]Ge 16:13 seeing the face of God,[r] now that you
[s]Ge 32:20 have received me favorably.[s] 11Please ac-
33:11 [t]1Sa 25:27 cept the present[t] that was brought to
[u]Ge 30:43 you, for God has been gracious to me[u]
and I have all I need." And because Jacob insisted, Esau accepted it.
12Then Esau said, "Let us be on our
way; I'll accompany you."
13But Jacob said to him, "My lord
knows that the children are tender and
that I must care for the ewes and cows
that are nursing their young. If they are
driven hard just one day, all the animals
will die. 14So let my lord go on ahead of
his servant, while I move along slowly
at the pace of the droves before me and
that of the children, until I come to my
33:14 [v]Ge 32:3 lord in Seir.[v]"
15Esau said, "Then let me leave some
of my men with you."
"But why do that?" Jacob asked. "Just
33:15 let me find favor in the eyes of my
[w]Ge 34:11; 47:25; lord."[w]
Ru 2:13 16So that day Esau started on his way
33:17 back to Seir. 17Jacob, however, went to
[x]Jos 13:27; Succoth,[x] where he built a place for
Jdg 8:5,6,8, 14,14-16, himself and made shelters for his live-
15,16; Ps 60:6 stock. That is why the place is called
Succoth.[a]
33:18 18After Jacob came from Paddan
[y]Ge 25:20; 28:2 Aram,[b][y] he arrived safely at the[c] city of
Shechem[z] in Canaan and camped with- 33:18 [z]Jos 24:1;
in sight of the city. 19For a hundred Jdg 9:1
pieces of silver,[d] he bought from the
sons of Hamor, the father of Shechem,[a] 33:19
the plot of ground[b] where he pitched [a]Jos 24:32 [b]Jn 4:5
his tent. 20There he set up an altar and
called it El Elohe Israel.[e]

Dinah and the Shechemites

34 Now Dinah,[c] the daughter Leah 34:1 [c]Ge 30:21
had borne to Jacob, went out
to visit the women of the land. 2When
Shechem son of Hamor the Hivite, the
ruler of that area, saw her, he took her
and violated her. 3His heart was drawn
to Dinah daughter of Jacob, and he
loved the girl and spoke tenderly to her.
4And Shechem said to his father Hamor, "Get me this girl as my wife."
5When Jacob heard that his daughter Dinah had been defiled, his sons
were in the fields with his livestock; so
he kept quiet about it until they came
home.
6Then Shechem's father Hamor went 34:6
out to talk with Jacob.[d] 7Now Jacob's [d]Jdg 14:2-5
sons had come in from the fields as
soon as they heard what had happened.
They were filled with grief and fury, because Shechem had done a disgraceful 34:7
thing in[f] Israel[e] by lying with Jacob's [e]Dt 22:21; Jdg 20:6;
daughter—a thing that should not be 2Sa 13:12
done.[f] [f]Jos 7:15
8But Hamor said to them, "My son
Shechem has his heart set on your
daughter. Please give her to him as his
wife. 9Intermarry with us; give us your
daughters and take our daughters for
yourselves. 10You can settle among us;[g] 34:10
the land is open to you.[h] Live in it, trade[g] [g]Ge 47:6,27 [h]Ge 13:9;
in it,[i] and acquire property in it." 20:15
11Then Shechem said to Dinah's fa- [i]Ge 42:34
ther and brothers, "Let me find favor in
your eyes, and I will give you whatever 34:12
you ask. 12Make the price for the bride[j] [j]Ex 22:16; Dt 22:29;
and the gift I am to bring as great as 1Sa 18:25
you like, and I'll pay whatever you ask
me. Only give me the girl as my wife."
13Because their sister Dinah had been
defiled, Jacob's sons replied deceitfully
as they spoke to Shechem and his father

[a]*17 Succoth* means *shelters.* [b]*18* That is, Northwest Mesopotamia [c]*18* Or *arrived at Shalem, a* [d]*19* Hebrew *hundred kesitahs*; a kesitah was a unit of money of unknown weight and value. [e]*20 El Elohe Israel* can mean *God, the God of Israel* or *mighty is the God of Israel.* [f]*7* Or *against* [g]*10* Or *move about freely*; also in verse 21

Hamor. 14They said to them, "We can't
do such a thing; we can't give our sister
34:14 [k]Ge 17:14; Jdg 14:3
to a man who is not circumcised.[k] That
would be a disgrace to us. 15We will
give our consent to you on one condi-
34:15 [l]Ex 12:48
tion only: that you become like us by
circumcising all your males.[l] 16Then we
will give you our daughters and take
your daughters for ourselves. We'll settle among you and become one people
with you. 17But if you will not agree
to be circumcised, we'll take our sister[a]
and go."
18Their proposal seemed good to Hamor and his son Shechem. 19The young
man, who was the most honored of
all his father's household, lost no time
34:19 [m]ver 3
in doing what they said, because he
was delighted with Jacob's daughter.[m]
20So Hamor and his son Shechem went
34:20 [n]Ru 4:1; 2Sa 15:2
to the gate of their city[n] to speak to
their fellow townsmen. 21"These men
are friendly toward us," they said. "Let
them live in our land and trade in it;
the land has plenty of room for them.
We can marry their daughters and they
can marry ours. 22But the men will
consent to live with us as one people
only on the condition that our males
be circumcised, as they themselves are.
23Won't their livestock, their property
and all their other animals become ours?
So let us give our consent to them, and
they will settle among us."
24All the men who went out of the
34:24 [o]Ge 23:10
city gate[o] agreed with Hamor and his
son Shechem, and every male in the
city was circumcised.
25Three days later, while all of them
were still in pain, two of Jacob's sons,
34:25 [p]Ge 49:5 [q]Ge 49:7
Simeon and Levi, Dinah's brothers, took
their swords[p] and attacked the unsuspecting city, killing every male.[q] 26They
put Hamor and his son Shechem to the
sword and took Dinah from Shechem's
house and left. 27The sons of Jacob
came upon the dead bodies and looted
the city where[b] their sister had been
defiled. 28They seized their flocks and
herds and donkeys and everything else
of theirs in the city and out in the fields.
29They carried off all their wealth and
all their women and children, taking as
plunder everything in the houses.
30Then Jacob said to Simeon and
Levi, "You have brought trouble on me
34:30 [r]Ex 5:21; 1Sa 13:4
by making me a stench[r] to the Canaanites and Perizzites, the people living in
34:30 [s]Ge 13:7 [t]Ge 46:27; 1Ch 16:19; Ps 105:12
this land.[s] We are few in number,[t] and
if they join forces against me and attack me, I and my household will be
destroyed."
31But they replied, "Should he have
treated our sister like a prostitute?"

Jacob Returns to Bethel

35:1 [u]Ge 28:19 [v]Ge 27:43
35 Then God said to Jacob, "Go
up to Bethel[u] and settle there,
and build an altar there to God, who
appeared to you when you were fleeing
from your brother Esau."[v]
35:2 [w]Ge 18:19; Jos 24:15 [x]Ge 31:19 [y]Ex 19:10,14
2So Jacob said to his household[w] and
to all who were with him, "Get rid of
the foreign gods[x] you have with you,
and purify yourselves and change your
clothes.[y] 3Then come, let us go up to
Bethel, where I will build an altar to
God, who answered me in the day of
35:3 [z]Ge 32:7 [a]Ge 28:15,20-22; 31:3,42
my distress[z] and who has been with me
wherever I have gone.[a]" 4So they gave
Jacob all the foreign gods they had and
35:4 [b]Jos 24:25-26
the rings in their ears, and Jacob buried them under the oak at Shechem.[b]
5Then they set out, and the terror of
35:5 [c]Ex 15:16; 23:27; Jos 2:9
God[c] fell upon the towns all around
them so that no one pursued them.
35:6 [d]Ge 28:19; 48:3
6Jacob and all the people with him
came to Luz[d] (that is, Bethel) in the
land of Canaan. 7There he built an altar, and he called the place El Bethel,[c]
35:7 [e]Ge 28:13
because it was there that God revealed
himself to him[e] when he was fleeing
from his brother.
35:8 [f]Ge 24:59
8Now Deborah, Rebekah's nurse,[f]
died and was buried under the oak
below Bethel. So it was named Allon
Bacuth.[d]
9After Jacob returned from Paddan
35:9 [g]Ge 32:29
Aram,[e] God appeared to him again
and blessed him.[g] 10God said to him,
35:10 [h]Ge 17:5
"Your name is Jacob,[f] but you will no
longer be called Jacob; your name will
be Israel.[g]"[h] So he named him Israel.
11And God said to him, "I am God
35:11 [i]Ge 17:1; Ex 6:3 [j]Ge 28:3; 48:4 [k]Ge 17:6
Almighty[h];[i] be fruitful and increase in
number. A nation[j] and a community of
nations will come from you, and kings
will come from your body.[k] 12The land
I gave to Abraham and Isaac I also give
to you, and I will give this land to your

[a]*17* Hebrew *daughter* [b]*27* Or *because* [c]*7 El Bethel* means *God of Bethel.* [d]*8 Allon Bacuth* means *oak of weeping.* [e]*9* That is, Northwest Mesopotamia; also in verse 26 [f]*10 Jacob* means *he grasps the heel* (figuratively, *he deceives*). [g]*10 Israel* means *he struggles with God.* [h]*11* Hebrew *El-Shaddai*

35:12 [l]Ge 13:15; descendants after you.[l]"[m] 13 Then God
28:13 went up from him[n] at the place where
[m]Ge 12:7; 26:3 he had talked with him.
14 Jacob set up a stone pillar at the
35:13 [n]Ge 17:22 place where God had talked with him,
and he poured out a drink offering on
it; he also poured oil on it.[o] 15 Jacob
called the place where God had talked
35:14 [o]Ge 28:18 with him Bethel.[a][p]
35:15 [p]Ge 28:19

The Deaths of Rachel and Isaac

16 Then they moved on from Bethel.
While they were still some distance
from Ephrath, Rachel began to give
birth and had great difficulty. 17 And as
she was having great difficulty in childbirth, the midwife said to her, "Don't
35:17 [q]Ge 30:24 be afraid, for you have another son."[q]
18 As she breathed her last—for she
was dying—she named her son Ben-
Oni.[b] But his father named him Benjamin.[c]
19 So Rachel died and was buried on
the way to Ephrath (that is, Bethle-
35:19 [r]Ge 48:7; Ru 1:1,19; Mic 5:2; Mt 2:16 hem[r]). 20 Over her tomb Jacob set up a
pillar, and to this day that pillar marks
Rachel's tomb.[s]
21 Israel moved on again and pitched
35:20 [s]1Sa 10:2 his tent beyond Migdal Eder. 22 While
Israel was living in that region, Reuben
35:22 [t]Ge 49:4; 1Ch 5:1 [u]Ge 29:29; Lev 18:8 went in and slept with his father's concubine[t] Bilhah,[u] and Israel heard of it.

Jacob had twelve sons:
23 The sons of Leah:
35:23 [v]Ge 46:8 [w]Ge 29:35 [x]Ge 30:20 Reuben the firstborn[v] of Jacob,
Simeon, Levi, Judah,[w] Issachar
and Zebulun.[x]
24 The sons of Rachel:
35:24 [y]Ge 30:24 [z]ver 18 Joseph[y] and Benjamin.[z]
25 The sons of Rachel's maidservant
Bilhah:
35:25 [a]Ge 30:8 Dan and Naphtali.[a]
26 The sons of Leah's maidservant
Zilpah:
35:26 [b]Ge 30:11 [c]Ge 30:13 Gad[b] and Asher.[c]
These were the sons of Jacob, who
were born to him in Paddan Aram.

35:27 [d]Ge 13:18; 18:1 [e]Jos 14:15 27 Jacob came home to his father Isaac
in Mamre,[d] near Kiriath Arba[e] (that
is, Hebron), where Abraham and Isaac
35:28 [f]Ge 25:7,20 had stayed. 28 Isaac lived a hundred and
35:29 [g]Ge 25:8; 49:33 [h]Ge 15:15 [i]Ge 25:9 eighty years.[f] 29 Then he breathed his
last and died and was gathered to his
people,[g] old and full of years.[h] And
his sons Esau and Jacob buried him.[i]

Esau's Descendants

36 This is the account of Esau (that
is, Edom).[j] 36:1 [j]Ge 25:30
2 Esau took his wives from the
women of Canaan:[k] Adah daugh- 36:2 [k]Ge 28:8-9 [l]Ge 26:34 [m]ver 25
ter of Elon the Hittite,[l] and Ohol-
ibamah daughter of Anah[m] and
granddaughter of Zibeon the Hivite— 3 also Basemath daughter of
Ishmael and sister of Nebaioth.
4 Adah bore Eliphaz to Esau, Bas-
emath bore Reuel,[n] 5 and Oholiba- 36:4 [n]1Ch 1:35
mah bore Jeush, Jalam and Korah.
These were the sons of Esau, who
were born to him in Canaan.
6 Esau took his wives and sons
and daughters and all the members of his household, as well as his
livestock and all his other animals
and all the goods he had acquired
in Canaan,[o] and moved to a land 36:6 [o]Ge 12:5
some distance from his brother Ja-
cob. 7 Their possessions were too
great for them to remain together;
the land where they were staying
could not support them both be-
cause of their livestock.[p] 8 So Esau[q] 36:7 [p]Ge 13:6; 17:8; 28:4
(that is, Edom) settled in the hill
country of Seir.[r] 36:8 [q]Dt 2:4 [r]Ge 32:3

9 This is the account of Esau the father of the Edomites in the hill country
of Seir.

10 These are the names of Esau's
sons:
Eliphaz, the son of Esau's wife
Adah, and Reuel, the son of
Esau's wife Basemath.
11 The sons of Eliphaz:[s] 36:11 [s]ver 15-16; Job 2:11 [t]Am 1:12; Hab 3:3
Teman,[t] Omar, Zepho, Gatam
and Kenaz.
12 Esau's son Eliphaz also had a
concubine named Timna, who
bore him Amalek.[u] These were 36:12 [u]Ex 17:8,16; Nu 24:20; 1Sa 15:2 [v]ver 16
grandsons of Esau's wife Adah.[v]
13 The sons of Reuel:
Nahath, Zerah, Shammah and
Mizzah. These were grandsons
of Esau's wife Basemath.
14 The sons of Esau's wife Oholibamah daughter of Anah and granddaughter of Zibeon, whom she
bore to Esau:
Jeush, Jalam and Korah.

[a] *15 Bethel* means *house of God.* [b] *18 Ben-Oni* means *son of my trouble.* [c] *18 Benjamin* means *son of my right hand.*

36:15 [w]Ex 15:15 [x]Job 2:11

15 These were the chiefs[w] among Esau's descendants:

The sons of Eliphaz the firstborn of Esau:
Chiefs Teman,[x] Omar, Zepho, Kenaz, 16 Korah,[a] Gatam and Amalek. These were the chiefs descended from Eliphaz in Edom; they were grandsons of Adah.[y]

36:16 [y]ver 12

17 The sons of Esau's son Reuel:[z]

36:17 [z]1Ch 1:37

Chiefs Nahath, Zerah, Shammah and Mizzah. These were the chiefs descended from Reuel in Edom; they were grandsons of Esau's wife Basemath.

18 The sons of Esau's wife Oholibamah:
Chiefs Jeush, Jalam and Korah. These were the chiefs descended from Esau's wife Oholibamah daughter of Anah.

19 These were the sons of Esau (that is, Edom),[a] and these were their chiefs.

36:19 [a]Ge 25:30

20 These were the sons of Seir the Horite,[b] who were living in the region:

36:20 [b]Ge 14:6; Dt 2:12,22; 1Ch 1:38

Lotan, Shobal, Zibeon, Anah, 21 Dishon, Ezer and Dishan. These sons of Seir in Edom were Horite chiefs.

22 The sons of Lotan:
Hori and Homam.[b] Timna was Lotan's sister.

23 The sons of Shobal:
Alvan, Manahath, Ebal, Shepho and Onam.

24 The sons of Zibeon:
Aiah and Anah. This is the Anah who discovered the hot springs[c] in the desert while he was grazing the donkeys of his father Zibeon.

25 The children of Anah:
Dishon and Oholibamah daughter of Anah.

26 The sons of Dishon[d]:
Hemdan, Eshban, Ithran and Keran.

27 The sons of Ezer:
Bilhan, Zaavan and Akan.

28 The sons of Dishan:
Uz and Aran.

29 These were the Horite chiefs:
Lotan, Shobal, Zibeon, Anah, 30 Dishon, Ezer and Dishan. These were the Horite chiefs, according to their divisions, in the land of Seir.

The Rulers of Edom

31 These were the kings who reigned in Edom before any Israelite king[c] reigned[e]:

36:31 [c]Ge 17:6; 1Ch 1:43

32 Bela son of Beor became king of Edom. His city was named Dinhabah.

33 When Bela died, Jobab son of Zerah from Bozrah[d] succeeded him as king.

36:33 [d]Jer 49:13,22

34 When Jobab died, Husham from the land of the Temanites[e] succeeded him as king.

36:34 [e]Eze 25:13

35 When Husham died, Hadad son of Bedad, who defeated Midian in the country of Moab,[f] succeeded him as king. His city was named Avith.

36:35 [f]Ge 19:37; Nu 22:1; Dt 1:5; Ru 1:1,6

36 When Hadad died, Samlah from Masrekah succeeded him as king.

37 When Samlah died, Shaul from Rehoboth on the river[f] succeeded him as king.

38 When Shaul died, Baal-Hanan son of Acbor succeeded him as king.

39 When Baal-Hanan son of Acbor died, Hadad[g] succeeded him as king. His city was named Pau, and his wife's name was Mehetabel daughter of Matred, the daughter of Me-Zahab.

40 These were the chiefs descended from Esau, by name, according to their clans and regions:

Timna, Alvah, Jetheth, 41 Oholibamah, Elah, Pinon, 42 Kenaz, Teman, Mibzar, 43 Magdiel and Iram. These were the chiefs of Edom, according to their settlements in the land they occupied.

This was Esau the father of the Edomites.

[a] *16* Masoretic Text; Samaritan Pentateuch (see also Gen. 36:11 and 1 Chron. 1:36) does not have *Korah.* [b] *22* Hebrew *Hemam,* a variant of *Homam* (see 1 Chron. 1:39) [c] *24* Vulgate; Syriac *discovered water;* the meaning of the Hebrew for this word is uncertain. [d] *26* Hebrew *Dishan,* a variant of *Dishon* [e] *31* Or *before an Israelite king reigned over them* [f] *37* Possibly the Euphrates [g] *39* Many manuscripts of the Masoretic Text, Samaritan Pentateuch and Syriac (see also 1 Chron. 1:50); most manuscripts of the Masoretic Text *Hadar*

Joseph's Dreams

37 Jacob lived in the land where his father had stayed,[g] the land of Canaan.[h]

[2]This is the account of Jacob.

Joseph, a young man of seventeen, was tending the flocks[i] with his brothers, the sons of Bilhah[j] and the sons of Zilpah,[k] his father's wives, and he brought their father a bad report[l] about them.

[3]Now Israel loved Joseph more than any of his other sons,[m] because he had been born to him in his old age;[n] and he made a richly ornamented[a] robe[o] for him. [4]When his brothers saw that their father loved him more than any of them, they hated him[p] and could not speak a kind word to him.

[5]Joseph had a dream,[q] and when he told it to his brothers, they hated him all the more. [6]He said to them, "Listen to this dream I had: [7]We were binding sheaves of grain out in the field when suddenly my sheaf rose and stood upright, while your sheaves gathered around mine and bowed down to it."[r]

[8]His brothers said to him, "Do you intend to reign over us? Will you actually rule us?"[s] And they hated him all the more because of his dream and what he had said.

[9]Then he had another dream, and he told it to his brothers. "Listen," he said, "I had another dream, and this time the sun and moon and eleven stars were bowing down to me."

[10]When he told his father as well as his brothers,[t] his father rebuked him and said, "What is this dream you had? Will your mother and I and your brothers actually come and bow down to the ground before you?"[u] [11]His brothers were jealous of him,[v] but his father kept the matter in mind.[w]

37:1 [g]Ge 17:8 [h]Ge 10:19
37:2 [i]Ps 78:71 [j]Ge 35:25 [k]Ge 35:26 [l]1Sa 2:24
37:3 [m]Ge 25:28 [n]Ge 44:20 [o]2Sa 13:18-19
37:4 [p]Ge 27:41; 49:22-23; Ac 7:9
37:5 [q]Ge 20:3; 28:12
37:7 [r]Ge 42:6,9; 43:26,28; 44:14; 50:18
37:8 [s]Ge 49:26
37:10 [t]ver 5 [u]ver 7; Ge 27:29
37:11 [v]Ac 7:9 [w]Lk 2:19,51

Joseph Sold by His Brothers

[12]Now his brothers had gone to graze their father's flocks near Shechem, [13]and Israel said to Joseph, "As you know, your brothers are grazing the flocks near Shechem. Come, I am going to send you to them."

"Very well," he replied.

[14]So he said to him, "Go and see if all is well with your brothers and with the flocks, and bring word back to me." Then he sent him off from the Valley of Hebron.[x]

When Joseph arrived at Shechem, [15]a man found him wandering around in the fields and asked him, "What are you looking for?"

[16]He replied, "I'm looking for my brothers. Can you tell me where they are grazing their flocks?"

[17]"They have moved on from here," the man answered. "I heard them say, 'Let's go to Dothan.'"[y]

So Joseph went after his brothers and found them near Dothan. [18]But they saw him in the distance, and before he reached them, they plotted to kill him.[z]

[19]"Here comes that dreamer!" they said to each other. [20]"Come now, let's kill him and throw him into one of these cisterns[a] and say that a ferocious animal devoured him. Then we'll see what comes of his dreams."[b]

[21]When Reuben heard this, he tried to rescue him from their hands. "Let's not take his life," he said.[c] [22]"Don't shed any blood. Throw him into this cistern here in the desert, but don't lay a hand on him." Reuben said this to rescue him from them and take him back to his father.

[23]So when Joseph came to his brothers, they stripped him of his robe—the richly ornamented robe he was wearing— [24]and they took him and threw him into the cistern. Now the cistern[d] was empty; there was no water in it.

[25]As they sat down to eat their meal, they looked up and saw a caravan of Ishmaelites coming from Gilead. Their camels were loaded with spices, balm and myrrh,[e] and they were on their way to take them down to Egypt.[f]

[26]Judah said to his brothers, "What will we gain if we kill our brother and cover up his blood?[g] [27]Come, let's sell him to the Ishmaelites and not lay our hands on him; after all, he is our brother,[h] our own flesh and blood." His brothers agreed.

[28]So when the Midianite[i] merchants came by, his brothers pulled Joseph up out of the cistern and sold him for

37:14 [x]Ge 13:18; 35:27
37:17 [y]2Ki 6:13
37:18 [z]1Sa 19:1; Mk 14:1; Ac 23:12
37:20 [a]Jer 38:6,9 [b]Ge 50:20
37:21 [c]Ge 42:22
37:24 [d]Jer 41:7
37:25 [e]Ge 43:11 [f]ver 28
37:26 [g]ver 20; Ge 4:10
37:27 [h]Ge 42:21
37:28 [i]Ge 25:2; Jdg 6:1-3

[a]3 The meaning of the Hebrew for *richly ornamented* is uncertain; also in verses 23 and 32.

twenty shekels[a] of silver to the Ishmaelites, who took him to Egypt.[j]

29When Reuben returned to the cistern and saw that Joseph was not there, he tore his clothes.[k] 30He went back to his brothers and said, "The boy isn't there! Where can I turn now?"[l]

31Then they got Joseph's robe,[m] slaughtered a goat and dipped the robe in the blood. 32They took the ornamented robe back to their father and said, "We found this. Examine it to see whether it is your son's robe."

33He recognized it and said, "It is my son's robe! Some ferocious animal[n] has devoured him. Joseph has surely been torn to pieces."[o]

34Then Jacob tore his clothes,[p] put on sackcloth[q] and mourned for his son many days[r]. 35All his sons and daughters came to comfort him, but he refused to be comforted. "No," he said, "in mourning will I go down to the grave[b][s] to my son." So his father wept for him.

36Meanwhile, the Midianites[c] sold Joseph in Egypt to Potiphar, one of Pharaoh's officials, the captain of the guard.[t]

37:28 [j]Ge 45:4-5; Ps 105:17; Ac 7:9
37:29 [k]ver 34; Ge 44:13; Job 1:20
37:30 [l]ver 22; Ge 42:13,36
37:31 [m]ver 3,23
37:33 [n]ver 20 [o]Ge 44:20,28
37:34 [p]ver 29 [q]2Sa 3:31 [r]Ge 50:3, 10,11
37:35 [s]Ge 42:38; 44:22,29,31
37:36 [t]Ge 39:1

Judah and Tamar

38 At that time, Judah left his brothers and went down to stay with a man of Adullam named Hirah. 2There Judah met the daughter of a Canaanite man named Shua.[u] He married her and lay with her; 3she became pregnant and gave birth to a son, who was named Er.[v] 4She conceived again and gave birth to a son and named him Onan. 5She gave birth to still another son and named him Shelah. It was at Kezib that she gave birth to him.

6Judah got a wife for Er, his firstborn, and her name was Tamar. 7But Er, Judah's firstborn, was wicked in the LORD's sight; so the LORD put him to death.[w]

8Then Judah said to Onan, "Lie with your brother's wife and fulfill your duty to her as a brother-in-law to produce offspring for your brother."[x] 9But Onan knew that the offspring would not be his; so whenever he lay with his brother's wife, he spilled his semen on the ground to keep from producing offspring for his brother. 10What he did was wicked in the LORD's sight; so he put him to death also.[y]

11Judah then said to his daughter-in-law Tamar, "Live as a widow in your father's house until my son Shelah grows up."[z] For he thought, "He may die too, just like his brothers." So Tamar went to live in her father's house.

12After a long time Judah's wife, the daughter of Shua, died. When Judah had recovered from his grief, he went up to Timnah,[a] to the men who were shearing his sheep, and his friend Hirah the Adullamite went with him.

13When Tamar was told, "Your father-in-law is on his way to Timnah to shear his sheep," 14she took off her widow's clothes, covered herself with a veil to disguise herself, and then sat down at the entrance to Enaim, which is on the road to Timnah. For she saw that, though Shelah[b] had now grown up, she had not been given to him as his wife.

15When Judah saw her, he thought she was a prostitute, for she had covered her face. 16Not realizing that she was his daughter-in-law,[c] he went over to her by the roadside and said, "Come now, let me sleep with you."

"And what will you give me to sleep with you?" she asked.

17"I'll send you a young goat[d] from my flock," he said.

"Will you give me something as a pledge[e] until you send it?" she asked.

18He said, "What pledge should I give you?"

"Your seal[f] and its cord, and the staff in your hand," she answered. So he gave them to her and slept with her, and she became pregnant by him. 19After she left, she took off her veil and put on her widow's clothes[g] again.

20Meanwhile Judah sent the young goat by his friend the Adullamite in order to get his pledge back from the woman, but he did not find her. 21He asked the men who lived there, "Where is the shrine prostitute[h] who was beside the road at Enaim?"

"There hasn't been any shrine prostitute here," they said.

22So he went back to Judah and said, "I didn't find her. Besides, the men who lived there said, 'There hasn't been any shrine prostitute here.' "

[a]*28* That is, about 8 ounces (about 0.2 kilogram)
[b]*35* Hebrew *Sheol* [c]*36* Samaritan Pentateuch, Septuagint, Vulgate and Syriac (see also verse 28); Masoretic Text *Medanites*

38:2 [u]1Ch 2:3
38:3 [v]ver 6; Ge 46:12; Nu 26:19
38:7 [w]ver 10; Ge 46:12; 1Ch 2:3
38:8 [x]Dt 25:5-6; Mt 22:24-28
38:10 [y]Ge 46:12; Dt 25:7-10
38:11 [z]Ru 1:13
38:12 [a]ver 14; Jos 15:10,57
38:14 [b]ver 11
38:16 [c]Lev 18:15; 20:12
38:17 [d]Eze 16:33 [e]ver 20
38:18 [f]ver 25
38:19 [g]ver 14
38:21 [h]Lev 19:29; Hos 4:14

[23]Then Judah said, "Let her keep
what she has, or we will become a
laughingstock. After all, I did send her
this young goat, but you didn't find
her."
[24]About three months later Judah was
told, "Your daughter-in-law Tamar is
guilty of prostitution, and as a result
she is now pregnant."
38:24 Judah said, "Bring her out and have
[i]Lev 21:9; Dt 22:21,22 her burned to death!"[i]
[25]As she was being brought out, she
sent a message to her father-in-law. "I
am pregnant by the man who owns
these," she said. And she added, "See if
you recognize whose seal and cord and
38:25 [j]ver 18 staff these are."[j]
38:26 [26]Judah recognized them and said,
[k]1Sa 24:17 "She is more righteous than I,[k] since I
[l]ver 11 wouldn't give her to my son Shelah.[l]"
And he did not sleep with her again.
[27]When the time came for her to
38:27 give birth, there were twin boys in her
[m]Ge 25:24 womb.[m] [28]As she was giving birth, one
of them put out his hand; so the mid-
wife took a scarlet thread and tied it
on his wrist and said, "This one came
out first." [29]But when he drew back
38:29 his hand, his brother came out, and
[n]Ge 46:12; she said, "So this is how you have
Nu 26:20,21; broken out!" And he was named Perez.[a][n]
Ru 4:12,18; 1Ch 2:4; [30]Then his brother, who had the scarlet
Mt 1:3 thread on his wrist, came out and he
38:30 [o]1Ch 2:4 was given the name Zerah.[b][o]

Joseph and Potiphar's Wife

39 Now Joseph had been taken down
to Egypt. Potiphar, an Egyptian
who was one of Pharaoh's officials, the
39:1 [p]Ge 37:36 captain of the guard,[p] bought him from
[q]Ge 37:25; Ps 105:17 the Ishmaelites who had taken him
there.[q]
[2]The LORD was with Joseph[r] and he
39:2 [r]Ge 21:20,22; Ac 7:9 prospered, and he lived in the house
of his Egyptian master. [3]When his mas-
39:3 ter saw that the LORD was with him[s]
[s]Ge 21:22; 26:28 and that the LORD gave him success
[t]Ps 1:3 in everything he did,[t] [4]Joseph found favor in his eyes and became his atten-
dant. Potiphar put him in charge of his
household, and he entrusted to his care
39:4 [u]ver 8,22; Ge 24:2 everything he owned.[u] [5]From the time
he put him in charge of his household
and of all that he owned, the LORD
39:5 blessed the household of the Egyptian
[v]Ge 26:24; 30:27 because of Joseph.[v] The blessing of the
LORD was on everything Potiphar had,
both in the house and in the field. [6]So
he left in Joseph's care everything he
had; with Joseph in charge, he did not
concern himself with anything except
the food he ate.
Now Joseph was well-built and hand- 39:6
some,[w] [7]and after a while his master's [w]1Sa 16:12
wife took notice of Joseph and said, 39:7
"Come to bed with me!"[x] [x]2Sa 13:11; Pr 7:15-18
[8]But he refused.[y] "With me in
charge," he told her, "my master does 39:8 [y]Pr 6:23-24
not concern himself with anything in
the house; everything he owns he has
entrusted to my care. [9]No one is greater 39:9
in this house than I am.[z] My master has [z]Ge 41:33,40
withheld nothing from me except you, [a]Ge 20:6; 42:18;
because you are his wife. How then 2Sa 12:13
could I do such a wicked thing and sin
against God?"[a] [10]And though she spoke
to Joseph day after day, he refused to go
to bed with her or even be with her.
[11]One day he went into the house to
attend to his duties, and none of the
household servants was inside. [12]She 39:12
caught him by his cloak[b] and said, [b]Pr 7:13
"Come to bed with me!" But he left his
cloak in her hand and ran out of the
house.
[13]When she saw that he had left his
cloak in her hand and had run out of
the house, [14]she called her household
servants. "Look," she said to them, "this
Hebrew has been brought to us to make
sport of us! He came in here to sleep 39:14
with me, but I screamed.[c] [15]When he [c]Dt 22:24,27
heard me scream for help, he left his
cloak beside me and ran out of the
house."
[16]She kept his cloak beside her until
his master came home. [17]Then she told
him this story:[d] "That Hebrew slave 39:17 [d]Ex 23:1,7;
you brought us came to me to make Ps 101:5
sport of me. [18]But as soon as I screamed
for help, he left his cloak beside me and
ran out of the house."
[19]When his master heard the story
his wife told him, saying, "This is how
your slave treated me," he burned with
anger.[e] [20]Joseph's master took him and 39:19 [e]Pr 6:34
put him in prison,[f] the place where the
king's prisoners were confined. 39:20
But while Joseph was there in the [f]Ge 40:3; Ps 105:18
prison, [21]the LORD was with him; he
showed him kindness and granted him 39:21
favor in the eyes of the prison warden.[g] [g]Ex 3:21
[22]So the warden put Joseph in charge

[a]*29 Perez* means *breaking out.* [b]*30 Zerah* can mean *scarlet* or *brightness.*

WEEK 6

GOODNESS

DAY ONE

GOODNESS, CARING HOW GOD FEELS ABOUT MY MORALITY

Read Genesis 39:1–10

Genesis 39:6 makes the statement that Joseph was "well-built and handsome." But Joseph's spirituality was even more rugged than his physique, and so when Potiphar's wife seeks to lure him into a sexual entanglement, Joseph answers her out of a sense of his own moral goodness. "My master does not concern himself with anything in the house; everything he owns he has entrusted to my care . . . How then could I do such a wicked thing and sin against God?"

Goodness is that fruit of the Spirit that does not hesitate to label all immorality for what it is—sin. Goodness never allows categories of sin and righteousness to become fuzzy by using more acceptable definitions of sin like *goof-ups, no-no's*, or *indiscretions*. Joseph knew immorality for what it was and was not willing to widen his definitions of sin to the point that he could call any kind of evil *good*. Goodness is the art of measuring ethical values with ethical norms. Goodness never excuses immorality by seeing it in some new and broader way.

So in the character of Joseph we see a man whose goodness rises higher than those around him. Some scholars think of Joseph as the Jesus of the Old Testament. He was not perfect, as Christ was, for Joseph was a mere man. But sinful people can live a righteous life, and Joseph was very much like Jesus in that he sought the pleasure of God with a life that never confused the categories of good and evil.

DAY TWO

GOODNESS AND THE PURPOSE OF GOD IN MY LIFE

Sinai became the mountain where Israel learned the idea of goodness. Morality was ever to be God's requirement for his people. Moses climbed Sinai to bring back the Decalogue. There, written in stone by the very "finger of God" was Israel's way of righteousness. Recorded for Israel as well as for us were ten rules that would define for the whole Judeo-Christian tradition exactly what it means to "be good." But in this passage is laid out an even simpler key to being good: loving God. *Turn to Deuteronomy 11:1, page 215, for today's study.*

DAY THREE

GOODNESS AND MY RELATIONSHIP WITH CHRIST

Loving good is possible by loving God. Good people are created by their affections. Those who love God become good without having to focus on it very much. Their righteousness comes from loving Christ, the only one who was ever wholly righteous. *Turn to Jeremiah 4:22, page 876, for today's study.*

DAY FOUR

GOODNESS AND MY SERVICE TO OTHERS

When the young Isaiah is called into the service of the Lord, he protests that he is not morally worthy: "I am a man of unclean lips, and I live among a people of unclean lips." Isaiah took his call to ministry seriously. He understood that moral goodness is an important component of the life of a servant. *Turn to Isaiah 6:1–7, page 797, for today's study.*

DAY FIVE

GOODNESS AND ITS PLACE IN MY PERSONAL WORSHIP

The words of John the Baptist must have blistered those who came to hear him. But John merely made the point that to come into the presence of God to worship should not be a casual thing. Indeed we should desire that we be cleaned up and made ready for holiness. We should not artificially try to create our own aura of holiness, but we should allow his cleansing power to "scrub us up" until our renewed lives allow us to approach his utter righteousness. *Turn to Luke 3:7–9, page 1203, for today's study.*

MEMORIZE THIS WEEK

JAMES 4:17

Anyone, then, who knows the good he ought to do and doesn't do it, sins.

Week 7, God's Blessing on Faithfulness, begins on page 16, Genesis 12:1–5.
To begin a topical study on the Fruit of the Spirit, Goodness, turn to the Topical Index, page 1548.

of all those held in the prison, and he
was made responsible for all that was
39:22 done there.[b] 23The warden paid no at-
hver 4 tention to anything under Joseph's care,
39:23 because the LORD was with Joseph and
iver 3 gave him success in whatever he did.[i]

The Cupbearer and the Baker

40:1 **40** Some time later, the cupbearer[j]
jNe 1:11 and the baker of the king of
Egypt offended their master, the king
40:2 kPr 16:14,15 of Egypt. 2Pharaoh was angry[k] with his
two officials, the chief cupbearer and
the chief baker, 3and put them in custody in the house of the captain of the
40:3 lGe 39:20 guard,[l] in the same prison where Joseph was confined. 4The captain of the
40:4 guard assigned them to Joseph,[m] and he
mGe 39:4 attended them.

After they had been in custody for
some time, 5each of the two men—the
cupbearer and the baker of the king
of Egypt, who were being held in pris-
40:5 on—had a dream the same night, and
nGe 41:11 each dream had a meaning of its own.[n]

6When Joseph came to them the next
morning, he saw that they were dejected. 7So he asked Pharaoh's officials
who were in custody with him in his
master's house, "Why are your faces so
40:7 sad today?"[o]
oNe 2:2 8"We both had dreams," they answered, "but there is no one to interpret
40:8 them."[p]
pGe 41:8,15 qGe 41:16; Then Joseph said to them, "Do not
Da 2:22, interpretations belong to God?[q] Tell me
28,47 your dreams."

9So the chief cupbearer told Joseph
his dream. He said to him, "In my
dream I saw a vine in front of me, 10and
on the vine were three branches. As
soon as it budded, it blossomed, and its
clusters ripened into grapes. 11Pharaoh's
cup was in my hand, and I took the
grapes, squeezed them into Pharaoh's
cup and put the cup in his hand."

40:12 12"This is what it means,[r]" Joseph
rGe 41:12, 15,25; said to him. "The three branches are
Da 2:36; 4:19 three days. 13Within three days Pharaoh
will lift up your head and restore you to
your position, and you will put Pharaoh's cup in his hand, just as you used
40:14 to do when you were his cupbearer.
sLk 23:42 14But when all goes well with you, re-
tJos 2:12; member me[s] and show me kindness;[t]
1Sa 20:14,42; 1Ki 2:7 mention me to Pharaoh and get me out
40:15 of this prison. 15For I was forcibly car-
uGe 37:26-28 ried off from the land of the Hebrews,[u]
and even here I have done nothing to
deserve being put in a dungeon."

16When the chief baker saw that Joseph had given a favorable interpretation, he said to Joseph, "I too had a
dream: On my head were three baskets
of bread.[a] 17In the top basket were all
kinds of baked goods for Pharaoh, but
the birds were eating them out of the
basket on my head."

18"This is what it means," Joseph 40:18
said. "The three baskets are three days.[v] vver 12
19Within three days Pharaoh will lift
off your head[w] and hang you on a 40:19
tree.[b] And the birds will eat away your wver 13
flesh."

20Now the third day was Pharaoh's
birthday,[x] and he gave a feast for all his 40:20 xMt 14:6-10
officials.[y] He lifted up the heads of the yMk 6:21
chief cupbearer and the chief baker in
the presence of his officials: 21He restored the chief cupbearer to his position, so that he once again put the cup 40:21
into Pharaoh's hand,[z] 22but he hanged[c] zver 13
the chief baker,[a] just as Joseph had said 40:22
to them in his interpretation.[b] aver 19 bPs 105:19

23The chief cupbearer, however, did 40:23
not remember Joseph; he forgot him.[c] cJob 19:14;
Ecc 9:15

Pharaoh's Dreams

41 When two full years had passed,
Pharaoh had a dream:[d] He was 41:1 dGe 20:3
standing by the Nile, 2when out of the
river there came up seven cows, sleek
and fat,[e] and they grazed among the 41:2
reeds.[f] 3After them, seven other cows, ever 26 fIsa 19:6
ugly and gaunt, came up out of the Nile
and stood beside those on the river-
bank. 4And the cows that were ugly and
gaunt ate up the seven sleek, fat cows.
Then Pharaoh woke up.

5He fell asleep again and had a second
dream: Seven heads of grain, healthy
and good, were growing on a single
stalk. 6After them, seven other heads
of grain sprouted—thin and scorched
by the east wind. 7The thin heads of
grain swallowed up the seven healthy,
full heads. Then Pharaoh woke up; it
had been a dream.

8In the morning his mind was
troubled,[g] so he sent for all the magi- 41:8
cians[h] and wise men of Egypt. Pharaoh gDa 2:1,3; 4:5,19
told them his dreams, but no one could hEx 7:11,22;
interpret them for him. Da 1:20; 2:2,27; 4:7

[a]16 Or *three wicker baskets* [b]19 Or *and impale you on a pole* [c]22 Or *impaled*

9 Then the chief cupbearer said to
Pharaoh, "Today I am reminded of my
shortcomings. 10 Pharaoh was once an-
41:10 [i]Ge 40:2 gry with his servants,[i] and he impris-
[j]Ge 39:20 oned me and the chief baker in the
house of the captain of the guard.[j]
11 Each of us had a dream the same
41:11 night, and each dream had a meaning
[k]Ge 40:5 of its own.[k] 12 Now a young Hebrew
was there with us, a servant of the captain of the guard. We told him our
dreams, and he interpreted them for us,
giving each man the interpretation of
41:12 his dream.[l] 13 And things turned out ex-
[l]Ge 40:12 actly as he interpreted them to us: I was
41:13 restored to my position, and the other
[m]Ge 40:22 man was hanged.[a][m]"
41:14 14 So Pharaoh sent for Joseph, and he
[n]Ps 105:20; was quickly brought from the dungeon.[n]
Da 2:25 When he had shaved and changed his
clothes, he came before Pharaoh.
15 Pharaoh said to Joseph, "I had a
dream, and no one can interpret it.
But I have heard it said of you that
41:15 when you hear a dream you can inter-
[o]Da 5:16 pret it."[o]
16 "I cannot do it," Joseph replied to
41:16 Pharaoh, "but God will give Pharaoh
[p]Ge 40:8; the answer he desires."[p]
Da 2:30; Ac 3:12; 17 Then Pharaoh said to Joseph, "In
2Co 3:5 my dream I was standing on the bank
of the Nile, 18 when out of the river
there came up seven cows, fat and sleek,
and they grazed among the reeds. 19 After them, seven other cows came up—
scrawny and very ugly and lean. I had
never seen such ugly cows in all the
land of Egypt. 20 The lean, ugly cows
ate up the seven fat cows that came up
first. 21 But even after they ate them, no
one could tell that they had done so;
they looked just as ugly as before. Then
I woke up.
22 "In my dreams I also saw seven
heads of grain, full and good, growing
on a single stalk. 23 After them, seven
other heads sprouted—withered and
thin and scorched by the east wind.
24 The thin heads of grain swallowed up
the seven good heads. I told this to the
41:24 magicians, but none could explain it to
[q]ver 8 me.[q]"
25 Then Joseph said to Pharaoh, "The
dreams of Pharaoh are one and the
41:25 same. God has revealed to Pharaoh
[r]Da 2:45 what he is about to do.[r] 26 The seven
41:26 good cows[s] are seven years, and the sev-
[s]ver 2 en good heads of grain are seven years;
it is one and the same dream. 27 The
seven lean, ugly cows that came up afterward are seven years, and so are the
seven worthless heads of grain scorched
by the east wind: They are seven years
of famine.[t] 41:27 [t]Ge 12:10;
28 "It is just as I said to Pharaoh: God 2Ki 8:1
has shown Pharaoh what he is about
to do. 29 Seven years of great abundance[u] are coming throughout the land 41:29
of Egypt, 30 but seven years of famine[v] [u]ver 47
will follow them. Then all the abun- 41:30
dance in Egypt will be forgotten, and [v]ver 54; Ge 47:13
the famine will ravage the land.[w] 31 The [w]ver 56
abundance in the land will not be remembered, because the famine that follows it will be so severe. 32 The reason
the dream was given to Pharaoh in two
forms is that the matter has been firmly 41:32
decided[x] by God, and God will do it [x]Nu 23:19;
soon. Isa 46:10-11
33 "And now let Pharaoh look for
a discerning and wise man[y] and put 41:33
him in charge of the land of Egypt. [y]ver 39
34 Let Pharaoh appoint commissioners
over the land to take a fifth[z] of the har- 41:34 [z]1Sa 8:15
vest of Egypt during the seven years of [a]ver 48
abundance.[a] 35 They should collect all
the food of these good years that are
coming and store up the grain under
the authority of Pharaoh, to be kept in
the cities for food.[b] 36 This food should 41:35 [b]ver 48
be held in reserve for the country, to be
used during the seven years of famine
that will come upon Egypt,[c] so that the 41:36
country may not be ruined by the fam- [c]ver 56
ine."
37 The plan seemed good to Pharaoh
and to all his officials.[d] 38 So Pharaoh 41:37 [d]Ge 45:16
asked them, "Can we find anyone like
this man, one in whom is the spirit of
God[b]?"[e] 41:38
39 Then Pharaoh said to Joseph, [e]Nu 27:18; Job 32:8;
"Since God has made all this known to Da 4:8,8-9,
you, there is no one so discerning and 18; 5:11,14
wise as you. 40 You shall be in charge
of my palace, and all my people are 41:40
to submit to your orders.[f] Only with [f]Ps 105:21-22;
respect to the throne will I be greater Ac 7:10
than you."

Joseph in Charge of Egypt

41 So Pharaoh said to Joseph, "I here- 41:41
by put you in charge of the whole land [g]Ge 42:6; Da 6:3
of Egypt."[g] 42 Then Pharaoh took his 41:42
signet ring[h] from his finger and put it [h]Est 3:10

[a]*13* Or *impaled* [b]*38* Or *of the gods*

on Joseph's finger. He dressed him in
robes of fine linen and put a gold chain
41:42 [i]Da 5:7,16,29 around his neck.[i] 43He had him ride in
a chariot as his second-in-command,[a]
41:43 [j]Est 6:9 and men shouted before him, "Make
way[b]!"[j] Thus he put him in charge of
the whole land of Egypt.
44Then Pharaoh said to Joseph, "I am
Pharaoh, but without your word no one
41:44 [k]Ps 105:22 will lift hand or foot in all Egypt."[k] 45Phar-
aoh gave Joseph the name Zaphenath-
Paneah and gave him Asenath daughter
of Potiphera, priest of On,[c] to be his
41:45 [l]ver 50; Ge 46:20,27 wife.[l] And Joseph went throughout the
land of Egypt.
41:46 [m]Ge 37:2 46Joseph was thirty years old[m] when
[n]1Sa 16:21; Da 1:19 he entered the service[n] of Pharaoh king
of Egypt. And Joseph went out from
Pharaoh's presence and traveled throughout Egypt. 47During the seven years
of abundance the land produced plen-
tifully. 48Joseph collected all the food
produced in those seven years of abundance in Egypt and stored it in the cities. In each city he put the food grown
in the fields surrounding it. 49Joseph
stored up huge quantities of grain, like
the sand of the sea; it was so much that
he stopped keeping records because it
was beyond measure.
50Before the years of famine came,
two sons were born to Joseph by As-
41:50 [o]Ge 46:20; 48:5 enath daughter of Potiphera, priest of
On.[o] 51Joseph named his firstborn[p] Ma-
41:51 [p]Ge 48:14, 18,20 nasseh[d] and said, "It is because God has
made me forget all my trouble and all
my father's household." 52The second
41:52 [q]Ge 48:1,5; 50:23 son he named Ephraim[e][q] and said, "It
[r]Ge 17:6; 28:3; 49:22 is because God has made me fruitful[r] in
the land of my suffering."
53The seven years of abundance in
Egypt came to an end, 54and the seven
41:54 [s]ver 30; Ps 105:11; Ac 7:11 years of famine began,[s] just as Joseph
had said. There was famine in all the
other lands, but in the whole land of
41:55 [t]Dt 32:24 [u]ver 41 Egypt there was food. 55When all Egypt
began to feel the famine,[t] the people
cried to Pharaoh for food. Then Pharaoh told all the Egyptians, "Go to Joseph and do what he tells you."[u]
56When the famine had spread over
the whole country, Joseph opened the
storehouses and sold grain to the
41:56 [v]Ge 12:10 Egyptians, for the famine[v] was severe
throughout Egypt. 57And all the coun-
tries came to Egypt to buy grain from
41:57 [w]Ge 42:5; 47:15 Joseph,[w] because the famine was severe
in all the world.

Joseph's Brothers Go to Egypt

42 When Jacob learned that there
was grain in Egypt,[x] he said to 42:1 [x]Ac 7:12
his sons, "Why do you just keep look-
ing at each other?" 2He continued, "I
have heard that there is grain in Egypt.
Go down there and buy some for us, so
that we may live and not die."[y] 42:2 [y]Ge 43:8
3Then ten of Joseph's brothers went
down to buy grain from Egypt. 4But
Jacob did not send Benjamin, Joseph's
brother, with the others, because he was
afraid that harm might come to him.[z] 42:4 [z]ver 38
5So Israel's sons were among those who
went to buy grain,[a] for the famine was 42:5 [a]Ge 41:57
in the land of Canaan also.[b] [b]Ge 12:10; Ac 7:11
6Now Joseph was the governor of the
land,[c] the one who sold grain to all its 42:6 [c]Ge 41:41
people. So when Joseph's brothers ar- [d]Ge 37:7-10
rived, they bowed down to him with
their faces to the ground.[d] 7As soon as
Joseph saw his brothers, he recognized
them, but he pretended to be a stranger
and spoke harshly to them.[e] "Where do 42:7 [e]ver 30
you come from?" he asked.
"From the land of Canaan," they replied, "to buy food."
8Although Joseph recognized his
brothers, they did not recognize him.[f] 42:8 [f]Ge 37:2
9Then he remembered his dreams[g]
about them and said to them, "You are 42:9 [g]Ge 37:7
spies! You have come to see where our
land is unprotected."
10"No, my lord," they answered.
"Your servants have come to buy food.
11We are all the sons of one man. Your
servants are honest men, not spies."
12"No!" he said to them. "You have
come to see where our land is unprotected."
13But they replied, "Your servants
were twelve brothers, the sons of one
man, who lives in the land of Canaan.
The youngest is now with our father,
and one is no more."[h] 42:13 [h]Ge 37:30,33; 44:20
14Joseph said to them, "It is just as
I told you: You are spies! 15And this
is how you will be tested: As surely
as Pharaoh lives,[i] you will not leave 42:15 [i]1Sa 17:55
this place unless your youngest brother
comes here. 16Send one of your number
to get your brother; the rest of you will

[a]43 Or *in the chariot of his second-in-command*; or *in his second chariot* [b]43 Or *Bow down* [c]45 That is, Heliopolis; also in verse 50 [d]51 *Manasseh* sounds like and may be derived from the Hebrew for *forget.* [e]52 *Ephraim* sounds like the Hebrew for *twice fruitful.*

be kept in prison, so that your words
may be tested to see if you are telling
42:16 [j]ver 11 the truth.[j] If you are not, then as surely
as Pharaoh lives, you are spies!" 17And
42:17 [k]Ge 40:4 he put them all in custody[k] for three
days.
18On the third day, Joseph said to
them, "Do this and you will live, for
42:18 [l]Ge 20:11; Lev 25:43 I fear God:[l] 19If you are honest men,
let one of your brothers stay here in
prison, while the rest of you go and
take grain back for your starving households. 20But you must bring your youn-
42:20 [m]ver 15,34; Ge 43:5; 44:23 gest brother to me,[m] so that your words
may be verified and that you may not
die." This they proceeded to do.

21They said to one another, "Surely
we are being punished because of our
brother.[n] We saw how distressed he was 42:21 [n]Ge 37:26-28 [o]Hos 5:15
when he pleaded with us for his life,
but we would not listen; that's why this
distress[o] has come upon us."
22Reuben replied, "Didn't I tell you
not to sin against the boy?[p] But you 42:22 [p]Ge 37:21-22 [q]Ge 9:5 [r]1Ki 2:32; 2Ch 24:22; Ps 9:12
wouldn't listen! Now we must give an
accounting[q] for his blood."[r] 23They did
not realize that Joseph could understand them, since he was using an interpreter.
24He turned away from them and began to weep, but then turned back and
spoke to them again. He had Simeon

JOSEPH

Goodness, Living Beyond Vengeance (46:6–24)

Goodness is that moral quality that sets virtue as a premium. Goodness does not always result in a hunger to be like God, but a hunger to be like God always results in goodness. People who seek goodness often become so moral that they do not fit into a sinful, self-excusing world. Thus, they are often misunderstood.

Joseph may indeed have been such a misunderstood man. In Genesis 37 we see how his nearness to God may have produced a visionary life. In his dreams Joseph envisioned a time when his family would bow down before him (vv. 5–11). It may be that what Joseph stated as a simple truth, his brothers came to see as a kind of arrogance.

Joseph's brothers began to experience a simmering resentment because their father seemed to dote on Joseph. Finally, they plotted against their younger brother and sold him into slavery. This might easily have forged within Joseph a long-term resentment. But that was not the case. Joseph pursued nobility of character. Those who are bent on goodness never allow themselves to be resentful because resentment never destroys those it resents. Rather, resentfulness works like acid in the soul of its keeper, eating away at the soul from the inside out. Joseph's brothers would later be amazed that Joseph's goodness would be their keeper at a season of their lives when they would have perished without it (chs. 42–45).

We also witness Joseph's goodness in his dealings with the wife of Potiphar, his master (ch. 39). Potiphar's wife wanted to seduce Joseph into immorality, but Joseph, enticed by a secret tryst, would not even allow himself the luxury of one secret immorality. And in the face of her accusations, Joseph did not give himself to the belittling task of getting even. Naturally, he was punished with imprisonment, but even in prison Joseph seems to have found God's favor—even during his darkest days—and finally his visionary life came to be of service to Pharaoh himself.

Goodness treasures virtue.

It never seeks to win the approval of those who are less good.

It won't sell out ideals to gain the nearest way to self-esteem.

It will not lower itself to return envy for envy, nor vengeance for vengeance.

It looks into the hellish heart of evil and celebrates the purpose of God, even when it seems as though God might not take notice.

It smiles upon those who have mistreated it and asks:

"Am I in the place of God? You intended to harm me, but God intended it for good" (50:19–20).

taken from them and bound before
42:24 [s]ver 13; their eyes.[s]
Ge 43:14,23; 25 Joseph gave orders to fill their bags
45:14-15 with grain,[t] to put each man's silver
42:25 [t]Ge 43:2 back in his sack,[u] and to give them pro-
[u]Ge 44:1,8 visions for their journey.[v] After this was
[v]Ro 12:17, 20-21 done for them, 26 they loaded their grain
on their donkeys and left.
27 At the place where they stopped for
the night one of them opened his sack
42:27 [w]Ge 43:21-22 to get feed for his donkey, and he saw
his silver in the mouth of his sack.[w]
28 "My silver has been returned," he said
to his brothers. "Here it is in my sack."
Their hearts sank and they turned to
42:28 each other trembling and said, "What
[x]Ge 43:23 is this that God has done to us?"[x]
29 When they came to their father Jacob in the land of Canaan, they told
him all that had happened to them.
They said, 30 "The man who is lord over
42:30 the land spoke harshly to us[y] and treat-
[y]ver 7 ed us as though we were spying on the
land. 31 But we said to him, 'We are
42:31 [z]ver 11 honest men; we are not spies.[z] 32 We
were twelve brothers, sons of one fa-
ther. One is no more, and the youngest
is now with our father in Canaan.'
33 "Then the man who is lord over the
land said to us, 'This is how I will know
whether you are honest men: Leave one
of your brothers here with me, and take
food for your starving households and
42:33 [a]ver 19,20 go.[a] 34 But bring your youngest brother
to me so I will know that you are not
spies but honest men. Then I will give
your brother back to you, and you can
42:34 [b]Ge 34:10 trade[a] in the land.[b]' "
35 As they were emptying their sacks,
there in each man's sack was his pouch
of silver! When they and their father
saw the money pouches, they were
42:35 [c]Ge 43:12, frightened.[c] 36 Their father Jacob said to
15,18 them, "You have deprived me of my
children. Joseph is no more and Simeon
is no more, and now you want to take
42:36 [d]Ge 43:14 Benjamin.[d] Everything is against me!"
37 Then Reuben said to his father,
"You may put both of my sons to death
if I do not bring him back to you. Entrust him to my care, and I will bring
him back."
38 But Jacob said, "My son will not
go down there with you; his brother
42:38 [e]Ge 37:33 is dead[e] and he is the only one left.
[f]ver 4 If harm comes to him[f] on the journey
[g]Ge 37:35 you are taking, you will bring my gray
[h]Ge 44:29,34 head down to the grave[b][g] in sorrow."[h]

The Second Journey to Egypt

43 Now the famine was still severe 43:1
in the land.[i] 2 So when they had [i]Ge 12:10; 41:56-57
eaten all the grain they had brought from
Egypt, their father said to them, "Go
back and buy us a little more food."
3 But Judah said to him, "The man
warned us solemnly, 'You will not see
my face again unless your brother is 43:3 [j]Ge 42:15;
with you.'[j] 4 If you will send our brother 44:23
along with us, we will go down and buy
food for you. 5 But if you will not send
him, we will not go down, because the
man said to us, 'You will not see my
face again unless your brother is with 43:5 [k]Ge 42:15;
you.[k]' " 2Sa 3:13
6 Israel asked, "Why did you bring
this trouble on me by telling the man
you had another brother?"
7 They replied, "The man questioned
us closely about ourselves and our fam-
ily. 'Is your father still living?'[l] he asked 43:7 [l]ver 27
us. 'Do you have another brother?'[m] We [m]Ge 42:13
simply answered his questions. How
were we to know he would say, 'Bring
your brother down here'?"
8 Then Judah said to Israel his father,
"Send the boy along with me and we
will go at once, so that we and you and 43:8
our children may live and not die.[n] 9 I [n]Ge 42:2;
myself will guarantee his safety; you can Ps 33:18-19
hold me personally responsible for him.
If I do not bring him back to you and
set him here before you, I will bear the 43:9 [o]Ge 42:37;
blame before you all my life.[o] 10 As it is, 44:32;
if we had not delayed, we could have Phm 1:18-19
gone and returned twice."
11 Then their father Israel said to
them, "If it must be, then do this:
Put some of the best products of the
land in your bags and take them down
to the man as a gift[p]—a little balm[q] 43:11 [p]Ge 32:20;
and a little honey, some spices[r] and Pr 18:16
myrrh, some pistachio nuts and al- [q]Ge 37:25; Jer 8:22
monds. 12 Take double the amount of [r]1Ki 10:2
silver with you, for you must return
the silver that was put back into the
mouths of your sacks.[s] Perhaps it was a
mistake. 13 Take your brother also and 43:12 [s]Ge 42:25
go back to the man at once. 14 And may
God Almighty[c][t] grant you mercy be- 43:14 [t]Ge 17:1;
fore the man so that he will let your 28:3; 35:11
other brother and Benjamin come back [u]Ge 42:24
with you.[u] As for me, if I am bereaved, [v]Est 4:16
I am bereaved."[v]

[a]*34* Or *move about freely* [b]*38* Hebrew *Sheol*
[c]*14* Hebrew *El-Shaddai*

15So the men took the gifts and double the amount of silver, and Benjamin also. They hurried[w] down to Egypt and presented themselves[x] to Joseph. 16When Joseph saw Benjamin with them, he said to the steward of his house,[y] "Take these men to my house, slaughter an animal and prepare dinner;[z] they are to eat with me at noon."

17The man did as Joseph told him and took the men to Joseph's house. 18Now the men were frightened[a] when they were taken to his house. They thought, "We were brought here because of the silver that was put back into our sacks the first time. He wants to attack us and overpower us and seize us as slaves and take our donkeys."

19So they went up to Joseph's steward and spoke to him at the entrance to the house. 20"Please, sir," they said, "we came down here the first time to buy food.[b] 21But at the place where we stopped for the night we opened our sacks and each of us found his silver—the exact weight—in the mouth of his sack. So we have brought it back with us.[c] 22We have also brought additional silver with us to buy food. We don't know who put our silver in our sacks."

23"It's all right," he said. "Don't be afraid. Your God, the God of your father, has given you treasure in your sacks;[d] I received your silver." Then he brought Simeon out to them.[e]

24The steward took the men into Joseph's house,[f] gave them water to wash their feet[g] and provided fodder for their donkeys. 25They prepared their gifts for Joseph's arrival at noon, because they had heard that they were to eat there.

26When Joseph came home, they presented to him the gifts[h] they had brought into the house, and they bowed down before him to the ground.[i] 27He asked them how they were, and then he said, "How is your aged father you told me about? Is he still living?"[j]

28They replied, "Your servant our father is still alive and well." And they bowed low to pay him honor.[k]

29As he looked about and saw his brother Benjamin, his own mother's son, he asked, "Is this your youngest brother, the one you told me about?"[l] And he said, "God be gracious to you,[m] my son." 30Deeply moved[n] at the sight of his brother, Joseph hurried out and looked for a place to weep. He went into his private room and wept[o] there.

31After he had washed his face, he came out and, controlling himself,[p] said, "Serve the food."

32They served him by himself, the brothers by themselves, and the Egyptians who ate with him by themselves, because Egyptians could not eat with Hebrews,[q] for that is detestable to Egyptians.[r] 33The men had been seated before him in the order of their ages, from the firstborn to the youngest; and they looked at each other in astonishment. 34When portions were served to them from Joseph's table, Benjamin's portion was five times as much as anyone else's.[s] So they feasted and drank freely with him.

A Silver Cup in a Sack

44 Now Joseph gave these instructions to the steward of his house: "Fill the men's sacks with as much food as they can carry, and put each man's silver in the mouth of his sack.[t] 2Then put my cup, the silver one, in the mouth of the youngest one's sack, along with the silver for his grain." And he did as Joseph said.

3As morning dawned, the men were sent on their way with their donkeys. 4They had not gone far from the city when Joseph said to his steward, "Go after those men at once, and when you catch up with them, say to them, 'Why have you repaid good with evil?[u] 5Isn't this the cup my master drinks from and also uses for divination?[v] This is a wicked thing you have done.'"

6When he caught up with them, he repeated these words to them. 7But they said to him, "Why does my lord say such things? Far be it from your servants to do anything like that! 8We even brought back to you from the land of Canaan the silver we found inside the mouths of our sacks.[w] So why would we steal silver or gold from your master's house? 9If any of your servants is found to have it, he will die;[x] and the rest of us will become my lord's slaves."

10"Very well, then," he said, "let it be as you say. Whoever is found to have it will become my slave; the rest of you will be free from blame."

11Each of them quickly lowered his

43:15 [w]Ge 45:9,13 [x]Ge 47:2,7
43:16 [y]Ge 44:1,4,12 [z]ver 31; Lk 15:23
43:18 [a]Ge 42:35
43:20 [b]Ge 42:3
43:21 [c]ver 15; Ge 42:27,35
43:23 [d]Ge 42:28 [e]Ge 42:24
43:24 [f]ver 16 [g]Ge 18:4; 24:32
43:26 [h]Mt 2:11 [i]Ge 37:7,10
43:27 [j]ver 7
43:28 [k]Ge 37:7
43:29 [l]Ge 42:13 [m]Nu 6:25; Ps 67:1
43:30 [n]Jn 11:33,38
43:30 [o]Ge 42:24; 45:2,14,15; 46:29
43:31 [p]Ge 45:1
43:32 [q]Gal 2:12 [r]Ge 46:34; Ex 8:26
43:34 [s]Ge 37:3; 45:22
44:1 [t]Ge 42:25
44:4 [u]Ps 35:12
44:5 [v]Ge 30:27; Dt 18:10-14
44:8 [w]Ge 42:25; 43:21
44:9 [x]Ge 31:32

sack to the ground and opened it. 12Then the steward proceeded to search, beginning with the oldest and ending with the youngest. And the cup was found in Benjamin's sack.[y] 13At this, they tore their clothes.[z] Then they all loaded their donkeys and returned to the city.

14Joseph was still in the house when Judah and his brothers came in, and they threw themselves to the ground before him.[a] 15Joseph said to them, "What is this you have done? Don't you know that a man like me can find things out by divination?[b]"

16"What can we say to my lord?" Judah replied. "What can we say? How can we prove our innocence? God has uncovered your servants' guilt. We are now my lord's slaves[c]—we ourselves and the one who was found to have the cup.[d]"

17But Joseph said, "Far be it from me to do such a thing! Only the man who was found to have the cup will become my slave. The rest of you, go back to your father in peace."

18Then Judah went up to him and said: "Please, my lord, let your servant speak a word to my lord. Do not be angry[e] with your servant, though you are equal to Pharaoh himself. 19My lord asked his servants, 'Do you have a father or a brother?'[f] 20And we answered, 'We have an aged father, and there is a young son born to him in his old age.[g] His brother is dead,[h] and he is the only one of his mother's sons left, and his father loves him.'[i]

21"Then you said to your servants, 'Bring him down to me so I can see him for myself.'[j] 22And we said to my lord, 'The boy cannot leave his father; if he leaves him, his father will die.'[k] 23But you told your servants, 'Unless your youngest brother comes down with you, you will not see my face again.'[l] 24When we went back to your servant my father, we told him what my lord had said.

25"Then our father said, 'Go back and buy a little more food.'[m] 26But we said, 'We cannot go down. Only if our youngest brother is with us will we go. We cannot see the man's face unless our youngest brother is with us.'

27"Your servant my father said to us, 'You know that my wife bore me two sons.[n] 28One of them went away from me, and I said, "He has surely been torn to pieces."[o] And I have not seen him since. 29If you take this one from me too and harm comes to him, you will bring my gray head down to the grave[a] in misery.'[p]

30"So now, if the boy is not with us when I go back to your servant my father and if my father, whose life is closely bound up with the boy's life,[q] 31sees that the boy isn't there, he will die. Your servants will bring the gray head of our father down to the grave in sorrow. 32Your servant guaranteed the boy's safety to my father. I said, 'If I do not bring him back to you, I will bear the blame before you, my father, all my life!'[r]

33"Now then, please let your servant remain here as my lord's slave[s] in place of the boy,[t] and let the boy return with his brothers. 34How can I go back to my father if the boy is not with me? No! Do not let me see the misery that would come upon my father."[u]

Joseph Makes Himself Known

45 Then Joseph could no longer control himself[v] before all his attendants, and he cried out, "Have everyone leave my presence!" So there was no one with Joseph when he made himself known to his brothers. 2And he wept[w] so loudly that the Egyptians heard him, and Pharaoh's household heard about it.[x]

3Joseph said to his brothers, "I am Joseph! Is my father still living?"[y] But his brothers were not able to answer him,[z] because they were terrified at his presence.

4Then Joseph said to his brothers, "Come close to me." When they had done so, he said, "I am your brother Joseph, the one you sold into Egypt![a] 5And now, do not be distressed[b] and do not be angry with yourselves for selling me here,[c] because it was to save lives that God sent me ahead of you.[d] 6For two years now there has been famine in the land, and for the next five years there will not be plowing and reaping. 7But God sent me ahead of you to preserve for you a remnant[e] on earth and to save your lives by a great deliverance.[b][f]

[a]29 Hebrew *Sheol;* also in verse 31 [b]7 Or *save you as a great band of survivors*

44:12 [y]ver 2
44:13 [z]Ge 37:29; Nu 14:6; 2Sa 1:11
44:14 [a]Ge 37:7,10
44:15 [b]ver 5; Ge 30:27
44:16 [c]ver 9; Ge 43:18 [d]ver 2
44:18 [e]Ge 18:30; Ex 32:22
44:19 [f]Ge 43:7
44:20 [g]Ge 37:3 [h]Ge 37:33 [i]Ge 42:13
44:21 [j]Ge 42:15
44:22 [k]Ge 37:35
44:23 [l]Ge 43:5
44:25 [m]Ge 43:2
44:27 [n]Ge 46:19
44:28 [o]Ge 37:33
44:29 [p]Ge 42:38
44:30 [q]1Sa 18:1
44:32 [r]Ge 43:9
44:33 [s]Ge 43:18 [t]Jn 15:13
44:34 [u]Est 8:6
45:1 [v]Ge 43:31
45:2 [w]Ge 29:11 [x]ver 16; Ge 46:29
45:3 [y]Ac 7:13 [z]ver 15
45:4 [a]Ge 37:28
45:5 [b]Ge 42:21 [c]Ge 42:22 [d]ver 7-8; Ge 50:20; Ps 105:17
45:7 [e]2Ki 19:4, 30,31; Isa 10:20,21; Mic 4:7; Zep 2:7 [f]Ex 15:2; Est 4:14; Isa 25:9

8“So then, it was not you who sent
me here, but God. He made me father[g]
to Pharaoh, lord of his entire household and ruler of all Egypt.[h] 9Now hurry back to my father and say to him,
‘This is what your son Joseph says:
God has made me lord of all Egypt.
Come down to me; don’t delay.[i] 10You
shall live in the region of Goshen[j] and
be near me—you, your children and
grandchildren, your flocks and herds,
and all you have. 11I will provide for
you there,[k] because five years of famine are still to come. Otherwise you and
your household and all who belong to
you will become destitute.’
12“You can see for yourselves, and
so can my brother Benjamin, that it is
really I who am speaking to you. 13Tell
my father about all the honor accorded
me in Egypt and about everything you
have seen. And bring my father down
here quickly.[l]”
14Then he threw his arms around his
brother Benjamin and wept, and Benjamin embraced him, weeping. 15And he
kissed[m] all his brothers and wept over
them. Afterward his brothers talked
with him.[n]
16When the news reached Pharaoh’s
palace that Joseph’s brothers had come,[o]
Pharaoh and all his officials were
pleased. 17Pharaoh said to Joseph, “Tell
your brothers, ‘Do this: Load your animals and return to the land of Canaan,
18and bring your father and your families back to me. I will give you the best
of the land of Egypt[p] and you can enjoy
the fat of the land.’[q]
19“You are also directed to tell them,
‘Do this: Take some carts[r] from Egypt
for your children and your wives, and
get your father and come. 20Never mind
about your belongings, because the best
of all Egypt will be yours.’ ”
21So the sons of Israel did this. Joseph
gave them carts, as Pharaoh had commanded, and he also gave them provisions for their journey.[s] 22To each of
them he gave new clothing, but to Benjamin he gave three hundred shekels[a]
of silver and five sets of clothes.[t] 23And
this is what he sent to his father: ten
donkeys loaded with the best things of
Egypt, and ten female donkeys loaded
with grain and bread and other provisions for his journey. 24Then he sent his
brothers away, and as they were leaving

45:8 [g]Jdg 17:10 [h]Ge 41:41
45:9 [i]Ge 43:10
45:10 [j]Ge 46:28,34; 7:1
45:11 [k]Ge 47:12
45:13 [l]Ac 7:14
45:15 [m]Lk 15:20 [n]ver 3
45:16 [o]Ac 7:13
45:18 [p]Ge 27:28; 46:34; 47:6,11,27; Nu 18:12,29 [q]Ps 37:19
45:19 [r]Ge 46:5
45:21 [s]Ge 42:25
45:22 [t]Ge 37:3; 43:34

he said to them, “Don’t quarrel on the
way!”[u]
25So they went up out of Egypt and
came to their father Jacob in the land
of Canaan. 26They told him, “Joseph
is still alive! In fact, he is ruler of all
Egypt.” Jacob was stunned; he did not
believe them.[v] 27But when they told
him everything Joseph had said to them,
and when he saw the carts[w] Joseph had
sent to carry him back, the spirit of
their father Jacob revived. 28And Israel
said, “I’m convinced! My son Joseph is
still alive. I will go and see him before
I die.”

Jacob Goes to Egypt

46 So Israel set out with all that
was his, and when he reached
Beersheba,[x] he offered sacrifices to the
God of his father Isaac.[y]
2And God spoke to Israel in a vision
at night[z] and said, “Jacob! Jacob!”
“Here I am,”[a] he replied.
3“I am God, the God of your father,”[b]
he said. “Do not be afraid to go down
to Egypt, for I will make you into a
great nation[c] there.[d] 4I will go down to
Egypt with you, and I will surely bring
you back again.[e] And Joseph’s own hand
will close your eyes.[f]”
5Then Jacob left Beersheba, and Israel’s sons took their father Jacob and
their children and their wives in the
carts[g] that Pharaoh had sent to transport him. 6They also took with them
their livestock and the possessions they
had acquired in Canaan, and Jacob and
all his offspring went to Egypt.[h] 7He
took with him to Egypt his sons and
grandsons and his daughters and grand-
daughters—all his offspring.[i]

8These are the names of the sons of
Israel[j] (Jacob and his descendants) who
went to Egypt:

Reuben the firstborn of Jacob.
9The sons of Reuben:[k]
Hanoch, Pallu, Hezron and Car-
mi.
10The sons of Simeon:[l]
Jemuel,[m] Jamin, Ohad, Jakin,
Zohar and Shaul the son of a
Canaanite woman.

[a] *22* That is, about 7 1/2 pounds (about 3.5 kilograms)

45:24 [u]Ge 42:21-22
45:26 [v]Ge 44:28
45:27 [w]ver 19
46:1 [x]Ge 21:14; 28:10 [y]Ge 26:24; 28:13; 31:42
46:2 [z]Ge 15:1; Job 33:14-15 [a]Ge 22:1; 31:11
46:3 [b]Ge 28:13 [c]Ge 12:2; Dt 26:5 [d]Ex 1:7
46:4 [e]Ge 28:15; 48:21; Ex 3:8 [f]Ge 50:1,24
46:5 [g]Ge 45:19
46:6 [h]Dt 26:5; Jos 24:4; Ps 105:23; Isa 52:4; Ac 7:15
46:7 [i]Ge 45:10
46:8 [j]Ex 1:1; Nu 26:4
46:9 [k]1Ch 5:3
46:10 [l]Ge 29:33; Nu 26:14 [m]Ex 6:15

46:11 [n]Ge 29:34; 11The sons of Levi:[n]
Nu 3:17 Gershon, Kohath and Merari.
46:12 12The sons of Judah:[o]
[o]Ge 29:35 Er, Onan, Shelah, Perez and Ze-
[p]1Ch 2:5; rah (but Er and Onan had died
Mt 1:3 in the land of Canaan).
The sons of Perez:[p]
Hezron and Hamul.
46:13 13The sons of Issachar:[q]
[q]Ge 30:18 Tola, Puah,[a][r] Jashub[b] and Shim-
[r]1Ch 7:1 ron.
46:14 [s]Ge 30:20 14The sons of Zebulun:[s]
Sered, Elon and Jahleel.
15These were the sons Leah bore to
Jacob in Paddan Aram,[c] besides his
daughter Dinah. These sons and daughters of his were thirty-three in all.

46:16 [t]Ge 30:11 16The sons of Gad:[t]
[u]Nu 26:15 Zephon,[d][u] Haggi, Shuni, Ez-
46:17 bon, Eri, Arodi and Areli.
[v]Ge 30:13; 17The sons of Asher:[v]
1Ch 7:30-31 Imnah, Ishvah, Ishvi and Beriah.
Their sister was Serah.
The sons of Beriah:
Heber and Malkiel.
18These were the children born to Ja-
46:18 [w]Ge 30:10 cob by Zilpah,[w] whom Laban had given
[x]Ge 29:24 to his daughter Leah[x]—sixteen in all.

46:19 19The sons of Jacob's wife Rachel:
[y]Ge 44:27 Joseph and Benjamin.[y] 20In
46:20 Egypt, Manasseh[z] and Ephraim[a]
[z]Ge 41:51 [a]Ge 41:52 were born to Joseph by Asenath
daughter of Potiphera, priest of
On.[e]
46:21 21The sons of Benjamin:[b]
[b]Nu 26:38- Bela, Beker, Ashbel, Gera, Naa-
41; 1Ch 7:6-12; man, Ehi, Rosh, Muppim, Hup-
8:1 pim and Ard.
22These were the sons of Rachel who
were born to Jacob—fourteen in all.

23The son of Dan:
Hushim.
24The sons of Naphtali:
Jahziel, Guni, Jezer and Shillem.
25These were the sons born to Jacob
46:25 [c]Ge 30:8 by Bilhah,[c] whom Laban had given to
[d]Ge 29:29 his daughter Rachel[d]—seven in all.

26All those who went to Egypt with
Jacob—those who were his direct
descendants, not counting his sons'
46:26 [e]ver 5-7; wives—numbered sixty-six persons.[e]
Ex 1:5; 27With the two sons[f] who had been
Dt 10:22 born to Joseph in Egypt, the members
46:27 of Jacob's family, which went to Egypt,
[f]Ac 7:14 were seventy[g] in all.[f]

28Now Jacob sent Judah ahead of him
to Joseph to get directions to Goshen.[g] 46:28 [g]Ge 45:10
When they arrived in the region of Go-
shen, 29Joseph had his chariot made
ready and went to Goshen to meet his
father Israel. As soon as Joseph appeared
before him, he threw his arms around 46:29 [h]Ge 45:14-15;
his father[h] and wept for a long time.[h] Lk 15:20
30Israel said to Joseph, "Now I am
ready to die, since I have seen for myself that you are still alive."
31Then Joseph said to his brothers
and to his father's household, "I will
go up and speak to Pharaoh and will
say to him, 'My brothers and my father's household, who were living in 46:31
the land of Canaan, have come to me.[i] [i]Ge 47:1
32The men are shepherds; they tend
livestock, and they have brought along
their flocks and herds and everything
they own.' 33When Pharaoh calls you
in and asks, 'What is your occupation?'[j] 46:33 [j]Ge 47:3
34you should answer, 'Your servants
have tended livestock from our boy-
hood on, just as our fathers did.' Then
you will be allowed to settle in the re- 46:34
gion of Goshen,[k] for all shepherds are [k]Ge 45:10 [l]Ge 43:32;
detestable to the Egyptians.[l]" Ex 8:26

47

Joseph went and told Pharaoh,
"My father and brothers, with
their flocks and herds and everything
they own, have come from the land of 47:1
Canaan and are now in Goshen."[m] 2He [m]Ge 46:31
chose five of his brothers and presented
them before Pharaoh.
3Pharaoh asked the brothers, "What
is your occupation?"[n] 47:3 [n]Ge 46:33
"Your servants are shepherds," they
replied to Pharaoh, "just as our fathers
were." 4They also said to him, "We 47:4
have come to live here awhile,[o] because [o]Ge 15:13;
the famine is severe in Canaan[p] and Dt 26:5 [p]Ge 43:1
your servants' flocks have no pasture. [q]Ge 46:34
So now, please let your servants settle in
Goshen."[q]
5Pharaoh said to Joseph, "Your father
and your brothers have come to you,
6and the land of Egypt is before you;

[a] *13* Samaritan Pentateuch and Syriac (see also 1 Chron. 7:1); Masoretic Text *Puvah* [b] *13* Samaritan Pentateuch and some Septuagint manuscripts (see also Num. 26:24 and 1 Chron. 7:1); Masoretic Text *Iob* [c] *15* That is, Northwest Mesopotamia [d] *16* Samaritan Pentateuch and Septuagint (see also Num. 26:15); Masoretic Text *Ziphion* [e] *20* That is, Heliopolis [f] *27* Hebrew; Septuagint *the nine children* [g] *27* Hebrew (see also Exodus 1:5 and footnote); Septuagint (see also Acts 7:14) *seventy-five* [h] *29* Hebrew *around him*

settle your father and your brothers in
47:6 [r]Ge 45:18 the best part of the land.[r] Let them live
[s]Ex 18:21,25 in Goshen. And if you know of any
47:7 among them with special ability,[s] put
[t]ver 10; them in charge of my own livestock."
2Sa 14:22 7Then Joseph brought his father
Jacob in and presented him before
Pharaoh. After Jacob blessed[a] Pharaoh,[t]
8Pharaoh asked him, "How old are
you?"
9And Jacob said to Pharaoh, "The
47:9 years of my pilgrimage are a hundred
[u]Ge 25:7; and thirty.[u] My years have been few and
[v]Heb 11:9,13 difficult,[v] and they do not equal the
[w]Ge 35:28 years of the pilgrimage of my fathers.[w]"
47:10 10Then Jacob blessed[b] Pharaoh[x] and
[x]ver 7 went out from his presence.
11So Joseph settled his father and his
brothers in Egypt and gave them prop-
47:11 erty in the best part of the land, the dis-
[y]Ex 1:11; trict of Rameses,[y] as Pharaoh directed.
12:37 12Joseph also provided his father and
his brothers and all his father's house-
47:12 hold with food, according to the num-
[z]Ge 45:11 ber of their children.[z]

Joseph and the Famine

13There was no food, however, in the
whole region because the famine was
47:13 severe; both Egypt and Canaan wasted
[a]Ge 41:30; away because of the famine.[a] 14Joseph
Ac 7:11 collected all the money that was to be
found in Egypt and Canaan in payment
47:14 for the grain they were buying, and he
[b]Ge 41:56 brought it to Pharaoh's palace.[b] 15When
the money of the people of Egypt and
Canaan was gone, all Egypt came to
Joseph and said, "Give us food. Why
47:15 should we die before your eyes?[c] Our
[c]ver 19; Ex 16:3 money is used up."
16"Then bring your livestock," said
Joseph. "I will sell you food in exchange
for your livestock, since your money is
gone." 17So they brought their livestock
47:17 to Joseph, and he gave them food in ex-
[d]Ex 14:9 change for their horses,[d] their sheep and
goats, their cattle and donkeys. And he
brought them through that year with
food in exchange for all their livestock.
18When that year was over, they came
to him the following year and said, "We
cannot hide from our lord the fact that
since our money is gone and our livestock belongs to you, there is nothing
left for our lord except our bodies and
our land. 19Why should we perish before your eyes—we and our land as
well? Buy us and our land in exchange
for food, and we with our land will be
in bondage to Pharaoh. Give us seed so
that we may live and not die, and that
the land may not become desolate."
20So Joseph bought all the land in
Egypt for Pharaoh. The Egyptians, one
and all, sold their fields, because the
famine was too severe for them. The
land became Pharaoh's, 21and Joseph
reduced the people to servitude,[c] from
one end of Egypt to the other. 22How-
ever, he did not buy the land of the
priests, because they received a regular
allotment from Pharaoh and had food
enough from the allotment[e] Pharaoh 47:22 [e]Dt 14:28-29;
gave them. That is why they did not sell Ezr 7:24
their land.
23Joseph said to the people, "Now
that I have bought you and your land
today for Pharaoh, here is seed for you
so you can plant the ground. 24But
when the crop comes in, give a fifth[f] 47:24
of it to Pharaoh. The other four-fifths [f]Ge 41:34
you may keep as seed for the fields and
as food for yourselves and your households and your children."
25"You have saved our lives," they
said. "May we find favor in the eyes 47:25
of our lord;[g] we will be in bondage to [g]Ge 32:5
Pharaoh."
26So Joseph established it as a law
concerning land in Egypt—still in force
today—that a fifth of the produce belongs to Pharaoh. It was only the land
of the priests that did not become Phar- 47:26
aoh's.[h] [h]ver 22
27Now the Israelites settled in Egypt
in the region of Goshen. They acquired
property there and were fruitful and increased greatly in number.[i] 47:27 [i]Ge 17:6;
28Jacob lived in Egypt[j] seventeen 46:3;
years, and the years of his life were a Ex 1:7
hundred and forty-seven. 29When the 47:28
time drew near for Israel to die,[k] he [j]Ps 105:23
called for his son Joseph and said to 47:29 [k]Dt 31:14
him, "If I have found favor in your eyes, [l]Ge 24:2
put your hand under my thigh[l] and [m]Ge 24:49
promise that you will show me kindness and faithfulness.[m] Do not bury me
in Egypt, 30but when I rest with my fa-
thers, carry me out of Egypt and bury 47:30 [n]Ge 49:29-32;
me where they are buried."[n] 50:5,13; Ac 7:15-16
"I will do as you say," he said.
31"Swear to me,"[o] he said. Then Joseph 47:31 [o]Ge 21:23

[a]7 Or *greeted* [b]10 Or *said farewell to* [c]21 Samaritan Pentateuch and Septuagint (see also Vulgate); Masoretic Text *and he moved the people into the cities*

47:31 [p]Ge 24:3 [q]Heb 11:21 *fn* 1Ki 1:47

swore to him,[p] and Israel worshiped as he leaned on the top of his staff.[a][q]

Manasseh and Ephraim

48:1 [r]Ge 41:52

48 Some time later Joseph was told, "Your father is ill." So he took his two sons Manasseh and Ephraim[r] along with him. 2 When Jacob was told, "Your son Joseph has come to you," Israel rallied his strength and sat up on the bed.

48:3 [s]Ge 28:19 [t]Ge 28:13; 35:9-12
48:4 [u]Ge 17:6

3 Jacob said to Joseph, "God Almighty[b] appeared to me at Luz[s] in the land of Canaan, and there he blessed me[t] 4 and said to me, 'I am going to make you fruitful and will increase your numbers.[u] I will make you a community of peoples, and I will give this land as an everlasting possession to your descendants after you.'

48:5 [v]Ge 41:50-52; 46:20 [w]1Ch 5:1; Jos 14:4
48:7 [x]Ge 35:19

5 "Now then, your two sons born to you in Egypt[v] before I came to you here will be reckoned as mine; Ephraim and Manasseh will be mine,[w] just as Reuben and Simeon are mine. 6 Any children born to you after them will be yours; in the territory they inherit they will be reckoned under the names of their brothers. 7 As I was returning from Paddan,[c] to my sorrow Rachel died in the land of Canaan while we were still on the way, a little distance from Ephrath. So I buried her there beside the road to Ephrath" (that is, Bethlehem).[x]

8 When Israel saw the sons of Joseph, he asked, "Who are these?"

48:9 [y]Ge 33:5 [z]Ge 27:4

9 "They are the sons God has given me here,"[y] Joseph said to his father.

Then Israel said, "Bring them to me so I may bless[z] them."

48:10 [a]Ge 27:1 [b]Ge 27:27

10 Now Israel's eyes were failing because of old age, and he could hardly see.[a] So Joseph brought his sons close to him, and his father kissed them[b] and embraced them.

48:11 [c]Ge 50:23; Ps 128:6

11 Israel said to Joseph, "I never expected to see your face again, and now God has allowed me to see your children too."[c]

48:13 [d]Ps 110:1

12 Then Joseph removed them from Israel's knees and bowed down with his face to the ground. 13 And Joseph took both of them, Ephraim on his right toward Israel's left hand and Manasseh on his left toward Israel's right hand,[d] and brought them close to him. 14 But Israel reached out his right hand and put it on Ephraim's head, though he was the younger, and crossing his arms, he put his left hand on Manasseh's head, even though Manasseh was the firstborn.[e]

48:14 [e]Ge 41:51
48:15 [f]Ge 17:1 [g]Ge 49:24

15 Then he blessed[f] Joseph and said,

"May the God before whom my fathers
Abraham and Isaac walked,
the God who has been my shepherd[g]
all my life to this day,
16 the Angel who has delivered me from all harm
—may he bless these boys.[h]
May they be called by my name
and the names of my fathers
Abraham and Isaac,[i]
and may they increase greatly
upon the earth."

48:16 [h]Heb 11:21 [i]Ge 28:13
48:17 [j]ver 14

17 When Joseph saw his father placing his right hand on Ephraim's head[j] he was displeased; so he took hold of his father's hand to move it from Ephraim's head to Manasseh's head. 18 Joseph said to him, "No, my father, this one is the firstborn; put your right hand on his head."

48:19 [k]Ge 17:20; [l]Ge 25:23

19 But his father refused and said, "I know, my son, I know. He too will become a people, and he too will become great.[k] Nevertheless, his younger brother will be greater than he,[l] and his descendants will become a group of nations." 20 He blessed them that day and said,

48:20 [m]Nu 2:18 [n]Nu 2:20; Ru 4:11

"In your[d] name will Israel pronounce this blessing:
'May God make you like
Ephraim[m] and Manasseh.[n]' "

So he put Ephraim ahead of Manasseh.

48:21 [o]Ge 26:3; 46:4 [p]Ge 28:13; 50:24
48:22 [q]Ge 37:8 [r]Jos 24:32; Jn 4:5

21 Then Israel said to Joseph, "I am about to die, but God will be with you[e][o] and take you[e] back to the land of your[e] fathers.[p] 22 And to you, as one who is over your brothers,[q] I give the ridge of land[f][r] I took from the Amorites with my sword and my bow."

Jacob Blesses His Sons

49:1 [s]Nu 24:14; Jer 23:20

49 Then Jacob called for his sons and said: "Gather around so I can tell you what will happen to you in days to come.[s]

[a] *31* Or *Israel bowed down at the head of his bed*
[b] *3* Hebrew *El-Shaddai*
[c] *7* That is, Northwest Mesopotamia
[d] *20* The Hebrew is singular.
[e] *21* The Hebrew is plural.
[f] *22* Or *And to you I give one portion more than to your brothers—the portion*

49:2 [t]Ps 34:11

[2] "Assemble and listen, sons of Jacob;
listen to your father Israel.[t]

49:3 [u]Ge 29:32 [v]Dt 21:17; Ps 78:51

[3] "Reuben, you are my firstborn,[u]
my might, the first sign of my strength,[v]
excelling in honor, excelling in power.

49:4 [w]Isa 57:20 [x]Ge 35:22; Dt 27:20

[4] Turbulent as the waters,[w] you will no longer excel,
for you went up onto your father's bed,
onto my couch and defiled it.[x]

49:5 [y]Ge 34:25; Pr 4:17

[5] "Simeon and Levi are brothers—
their swords[a] are weapons of violence.[y]

49:6 [z]Pr 1:15; Eph 5:11 [a]Ge 34:26

[6] Let me not enter their council,
let me not join their assembly,[z]
for they have killed men in their anger[a]
and hamstrung oxen as they pleased.

49:7 [b]Jos 19:1,9; 21:1-42

[7] Cursed be their anger, so fierce,
and their fury, so cruel!
I will scatter them in Jacob
and disperse them in Israel.[b]

49:8 [c]Dt 33:7; 1Ch 5:2

[8] "Judah,[b] your brothers will praise you;
your hand will be on the neck of your enemies;
your father's sons will bow down to you.[c]

49:9 [d]Nu 24:9; Eze 19:5; Mic 5:8 [e]Rev 5:5

[9] You are a lion's[d] cub, O Judah;[e]
you return from the prey, my son.
Like a lion he crouches and lies down,
like a lioness—who dares to rouse him?

49:10 [f]Nu 24:17,19; Ps 60:7 [g]Ps 2:9; Isa 42:1,4

[10] The scepter will not depart from Judah,[f]
nor the ruler's staff from between his feet,
until he comes to whom it belongs[c]
and the obedience of the nations is his.[g]

[11] He will tether his donkey to a vine,
his colt to the choicest branch;
he will wash his garments in wine,
his robes in the blood of grapes.

[12] His eyes will be darker than wine,
his teeth whiter than milk.[d]

49:13 [h]Ge 30:20; Dt 33:18-19; Jos 19:10-11

[13] "Zebulun[h] will live by the seashore
and become a haven for ships;
his border will extend toward Sidon.

49:14 [i]Ge 30:18

[14] "Issachar[i] is a rawboned[e] donkey
lying down between two saddlebags.[f]

[15] When he sees how good is his resting place
and how pleasant is his land,
he will bend his shoulder to the burden
and submit to forced labor.

49:16 [j]Ge 30:6; Dt 33:22; Jdg 18:26-27

[16] "Dan[g][j] will provide justice for his people
as one of the tribes of Israel.

49:17 [k]Jdg 18:27

[17] Dan[k] will be a serpent by the roadside,
a viper along the path,
that bites the horse's heels
so that its rider tumbles backward.

49:18 [l]Ps 119:166,174

[18] "I look for your deliverance, O LORD.[l]

49:19 [m]Ge 30:11; Dt 33:20; 1Ch 5:18

[19] "Gad[h][m] will be attacked by a band of raiders,
but he will attack them at their heels.

49:20 [n]Ge 30:13; Dt 33:24

[20] "Asher's[n] food will be rich;
he will provide delicacies fit for a king.

49:21 [o]Ge 30:8; Dt 33:23

[21] "Naphtali[o] is a doe set free
that bears beautiful fawns.[i]

49:22 [p]Ge 30:24; Dt 33:13-17

[22] "Joseph[p] is a fruitful vine,
a fruitful vine near a spring,
whose branches climb over a wall.[j]

49:23 [q]Ge 37:24

[23] With bitterness archers attacked him;
they shot at him with hostility.[q]

49:24 [r]Ps 18:34 [s]Ps 132:2,5; Isa 1:24; 41:10 [t]Isa 28:16

[24] But his bow remained steady,
his strong arms[r] stayed[k] limber,
because of the hand of the Mighty One of Jacob,[s]
because of the Shepherd, the Rock of Israel,[t]

49:25 [u]Ge 28:13

[25] because of your father's God,[u] who helps you,
because of the Almighty,[l] who blesses you

[a]*5* The meaning of the Hebrew for this word is uncertain. [b]*8 Judah* sounds like and may be derived from the Hebrew for *praise.* [c]*10* Or *until Shiloh comes;* or *until he comes to whom tribute belongs* [d]*12* Or *will be dull from wine, / his teeth white from milk* [e]*14* Or *strong* [f]*14* Or *campfires* [g]*16 Dan* here means *he provides justice.* [h]*19 Gad* can mean *attack* and *band of raiders.* [i]*21* Or *free; / he utters beautiful words* [j]*22* Or *Joseph is a wild colt, / a wild colt near a spring, / a wild donkey on a terraced hill* [k]*23,24* Or *archers will attack . . . will shoot . . . will remain . . . will stay* [l]*25* Hebrew *Shaddai*

with blessings of the heavens above,
blessings of the deep that lies
below,[v]

49:25 [v]Ge 27:28

blessings of the breast and womb.
26 Your father's blessings are greater
than the blessings of the ancient
mountains,
than[a] the bounty of the age-old
hills.
Let all these rest on the head of
Joseph,
on the brow of the prince among[b]
his brothers.[w]

49:26 [w]Dt 33:15-16

27 "Benjamin[x] is a ravenous wolf;
in the morning he devours the
prey,
in the evening he divides the
plunder."

49:27 [x]Ge 35:18; Jdg 20:12-13

28 All these are the twelve tribes of Israel, and this is what their father said to them when he blessed them, giving each the blessing appropriate to him.

The Death of Jacob

29 Then he gave them these instructions:[y] "I am about to be gathered to my people.[z] Bury me with my fathers[a] in the cave in the field of Ephron the Hittite, 30 the cave in the field of Machpelah,[b] near Mamre in Canaan, which Abraham bought as a burial place from Ephron the Hittite, along with the field.[c] 31 There Abraham[d] and his wife Sarah[e] were buried, there Isaac and his wife Rebekah[f] were buried, and there I buried Leah. 32 The field and the cave in it were bought from the Hittites.[c]"

49:29 [y]Ge 50:16 [z]Ge 25:8 [a]Ge 15:15; 47:30; 50:13
49:30 [b]Ge 23:9 [c]Ge 23:20
49:31 [d]Ge 25:9 [e]Ge 23:19 [f]Ge 35:29

33 When Jacob had finished giving instructions to his sons, he drew his feet up into the bed, breathed his last and was gathered to his people.[g]

49:33 [g]ver 29; Ge 25:8; Ac 7:15

50 Joseph threw himself upon his father and wept over him and kissed him.[h] 2 Then Joseph directed the physicians in his service to embalm his father Israel. So the physicians embalmed him,[i] 3 taking a full forty days, for that was the time required for embalming. And the Egyptians mourned for him seventy days.[j]

50:1 [h]Ge 46:4
50:2 [i]ver 26; 2Ch 16:14
50:3 [j]Ge 37:34; Nu 20:29; Dt 34:8

4 When the days of mourning had passed, Joseph said to Pharaoh's court, "If I have found favor in your eyes, speak to Pharaoh for me. Tell him, 5 'My father made me swear an oath[k] and said, "I am about to die; bury me in the tomb I dug for myself[l] in the land of Canaan."[m] Now let me go up and bury my father; then I will return.' "

50:5 [k]Ge 47:31 [l]2Ch 16:14; Isa 22:16 [m]Ge 47:31

6 Pharaoh said, "Go up and bury your father, as he made you swear to do."

7 So Joseph went up to bury his father. All Pharaoh's officials accompanied him—the dignitaries of his court and all the dignitaries of Egypt— 8 besides all the members of Joseph's household and his brothers and those belonging to his father's household. Only their children and their flocks and herds were left in Goshen. 9 Chariots and horsemen[d] also went up with him. It was a very large company.

10 When they reached the threshing floor of Atad, near the Jordan, they lamented loudly and bitterly;[n] and there Joseph observed a seven-day period[o] of mourning for his father. 11 When the Canaanites who lived there saw the mourning at the threshing floor of Atad, they said, "The Egyptians are holding a solemn ceremony of mourning." That is why that place near the Jordan is called Abel Mizraim.[e]

50:10 [n]2Sa 1:17; Ac 8:2 [o]1Sa 31:13; Job 2:13

12 So Jacob's sons did as he had commanded them: 13 They carried him to the land of Canaan and buried him in the cave in the field of Machpelah, near Mamre, which Abraham had bought as a burial place from Ephron the Hittite, along with the field.[p] 14 After burying his father, Joseph returned to Egypt, together with his brothers and all the others who had gone with him to bury his father.

50:13 [p]Ge 23:20; Ac 7:16

Joseph Reassures His Brothers

15 When Joseph's brothers saw that their father was dead, they said, "What if Joseph holds a grudge against us and pays us back for all the wrongs we did to him?"[q] 16 So they sent word to Joseph, saying, "Your father left these instructions before he died: 17 'This is what you are to say to Joseph: I ask you to forgive your brothers the sins and the wrongs they committed in treating you so badly.' Now please forgive the sins of the servants of the God of your father." When their message came to him, Joseph wept.

50:15 [q]Ge 37:28; 42:21-22

18 His brothers then came and threw

[a]26 Or *of my progenitors, / as great as* [b]26 Or *the one separated from* [c]32 Or *the sons of Heth* [d]9 Or *charioteers* [e]11 *Abel Mizraim* means *mourning of the Egyptians.*

DAY 4 FOUR

LOVE AND MY SERVICE TO OTHERS

Read Genesis 50:15–21

The dying patriarch, Jacob, begs his family to forgive each other for their past sins. And mercifully they do it. This is no light matter in the history of the nation of Israel. Without Joseph's forgiveness would the nation of Israel ever have become a possibility? If Israel were to avoid becoming inconsequential in human history, it was imperative that each of Jacob's sons both grant and accept forgiveness.

When members of God's family insist on quarreling with each other, they do not reflect God's love. A fighting congregation is a slur on Calvary. It insults the forgiving heart of our heavenly Father.

What happens when we reflect God's forgiving heart? Wonderful things came about because Joseph was willing to forgive his brothers. His own sons, Ephraim and Manasseh, became heirs along with their ten uncles to the land that God was about to give them. Jacob's family would in time be forged into a great nation. Jacob's descendants would bring the world the greatest single cultural force in human history: Judaism. From Judaism—which began with the clan of the all-forgiving Joseph and his brothers—would come a force for learning, law, medicine and the mercantile that would play a role in world history out of all proportion to its size. One philosopher of our own time has said, "Of the four names that have most influenced modern history, only one of them, Charles Darwin, was not a Jew." Could it be that the whole Jewish structure of civilization was made possible by Joseph's forgiveness so long ago?

How much do others suffer when we ourselves are unforgiving within his church? Let us forgive readily, so that our service to others may be made possible. Let's show God's love and forgiveness in our actions to others.

To begin a study on the topic of Love Forgives, turn to the home page on page 1227.

themselves down before him.[r] "We are
your slaves,"[s] they said.
19But Joseph said to them, "Don't
be afraid. Am I in the place of God?[t]
20You intended to harm me,[u] but God
intended[v] it for good[w] to accomplish
what is now being done, the saving
of many lives.[x] 21So then, don't be
afraid. I will provide for you and your
children.[y]" And he reassured them and
spoke kindly to them.

50:18 [r]Ge 37:7 [s]Ge 43:18
50:19 [t]Ro 12:19; Heb 10:30
50:20 [u]Ge 37:20 [v]Mic 4:11-12 [w]Ro 8:28 [x]Ge 45:5
50:21 [y]Ge 45:11; 47:12

GOODNESS

THE OTHER SIDE OF PAIN

Genesis 50:20

So often God's goodness comes to us disguised as pain or crisis. But God is a blessed architect who sometimes fashions temples out of trials.

Where rise the marble altars, someone paid the price of pain.
Each edifice of love declares that Calv'ry lives again.
Where souls are ripped by anguish, such altar makers say,
"God builds the best tomorrows from the rubble of today!"

The Death of Joseph

22Joseph stayed in Egypt, along with
all his father's family. He lived a hundred and ten years[z] 23and saw the third
generation[a] of Ephraim's children. Also
the children of Makir[b] son of Manasseh were placed at birth on Joseph's
knees.[a]
24Then Joseph said to his brothers,
"I am about to die.[c] But God will surely come to your aid[d] and take you up
out of this land to the land[e] he promised on oath to Abraham, Isaac and
Jacob."[f] 25And Joseph made the sons
of Israel swear an oath and said, "God
will surely come to your aid, and then
you must carry my bones up from this
place."[g]
26So Joseph died at the age of a
hundred and ten. And after they embalmed him,[h] he was placed in a coffin
in Egypt.

[a]23 That is, were counted as his

50:22 [z]Ge 25:7; Jos 24:29
50:23 [a]Job 42:16 [b]Nu 32:39,40
50:24 [c]Ge 48:21 [d]Ex 3:16-17 [e]Ge 15:14 [f]Ge 12:7; 26:3; 28:13; 35:12
50:25 [g]Ge 47:29-30; Ex 13:19; Jos 24:32; Heb 11:22
50:26 [h]ver 2

EXODUS

AUTHORSHIP AND DATE

Moses

c. 1450 B.C. to c. 1410 B.C.

KEY THEMES

Exodus is a Latin word taken from the Greek word *Exodos*, which literally means "the way out." Appropriately, this book focuses on Israel's departure from Egypt. The heart of Exodus is summed up in these verses: "The LORD said, 'I have indeed seen the misery of my people in Egypt. I have heard them crying out because of their slave drivers, and I am concerned about their suffering . . . So now, go. I am sending you to Pharaoh to bring my people the Israelites out of Egypt' " (3:7,10).

FRUIT OF THE SPIRIT IN EXODUS

Love: Throughout the first five books of the Bible, God's love was often evidenced inductively. God may not have said "I love you" to Israel, but his love was evidenced by his strong desire to redeem Israel from slavery. His guidance of the nation in fire by night and cloud by day can certainly be seen as the fruit of his love. In Israel's deliverance, in the giving of the law and in dividing the waters of the Red Sea, God demonstrated his love for Israel.

Joy: Joy was expressed in its most exhilarating form after the crossing of the Red Sea when the people praised God for the victory over Egypt. Miriam led the people in dancing and anthems of praise. Her song was jubilant: "Sing to the LORD, for he is highly exalted. The horse and its rider he has hurled into the sea" (15:21).

Peace: Peace, like love, is implied in Exodus. Peace and freedom were the result of the elimination of Pharaoh's armies and the beginning of Israel's journey in the wilderness. Although there are references to fellowship offerings or peace offerings in the book of Exodus, peace results from steps of obedience to and a relationship with God.

Patience: Israel had been waiting for a deliverer for many years. But once that deliverance began, the people were unwilling to wait on God and his plan, and they erupted in criticism of Moses. The pressure felt by Moses finally led to the temper tantrum recorded in Numbers 20. Moses' loss of patience was costly: God did not allow him to enter the promised land.

Goodness: At the center of Exodus is the Law, the Ten Commandments. Its purpose was to help God's people become a people of character. Those who lived in the law and honored it would, at last, become more than good; they would become holy.

Faithfulness: The word *covenant* occurs 11 times in the book of Exodus. Covenants are agreements between two parties—in this case God and Israel—mandating that both parties be faithful to the promises stated. The heart of the Exodus covenant is stated in Exodus 34:10–11: "The LORD said: 'I am making a covenant with you. Before all your people I will do wonders never before done in any nation in all the world. The people you live among will see how awesome is the work that I, the LORD, will do for you. Obey what I command you today.'" The desired end of all great covenants is faithfulness.

Self-Control: The law is an incitement to obedience. The call for obedience is always a call for self-control. In Exodus this call was offered within the covenant of God: "Now if you obey me fully and keep my covenant, then out of all nations you will be my treasured possession. Although the whole earth is mine, you will be for me a kingdom of priests and a holy nation" (19:5–6). As the people of Israel practiced self-control, they would be of great use to God. Their ability to deny themselves the indulgences of the nations around them would bring them, at last, the direct blessing of God.

The Israelites Oppressed

1 These are the names of the sons
1:1 of Israel[a] who went to Egypt with
[a]Ge 46:8 Jacob, each with his family: 2Reuben,
Simeon, Levi and Judah; 3Issachar, Zebulun and Benjamin; 4Dan and Naphtali; Gad and Asher. 5The descendants of
Jacob numbered seventy[a] in all;[b] Joseph 1:5
was already in Egypt. [b]Ge 46:26
6Now Joseph and all his brothers and
all that generation died,[c] 7but the Israel- 1:6
ites were fruitful and multiplied greatly [c]Ge 50:26
and became exceedingly numerous,[d] so 1:7
that the land was filled with them. [d]Ge 46:3; Dt 26:5;
8Then a new king, who did not know Ac 7:17
about Joseph, came to power in Egypt.
9"Look," he said to his people, "the
Israelites have become much too nu- 1:9
merous[e] for us. 10Come, we must deal [e]Ps 105:24-25
shrewdly[f] with them or they will be- 1:10
come even more numerous and, if war [f]Ps 83:3 [g]Ac 7:17-19
breaks out, will join our enemies, fight 1:11
against us and leave the country."[g] [h]Ex 3:7
11So they put slave masters[h] over them [i]Ge 15:13; Ex 2:11; 5:4;
to oppress them with forced labor,[i] and 6:6-7
they built Pithom and Rameses[j] as store [j]Ge 47:11 [k]1Ki 9:19;
cities[k] for Pharaoh. 12But the more they 2Ch 8:4
were oppressed, the more they multi- 1:13
plied and spread; so the Egyptians came [l]Dt 4:20
to dread the Israelites 13and worked 1:14
them ruthlessly.[l] 14They made their lives [m]Ex 2:23; 6:9;
bitter with hard labor in brick and mor- Nu 20:15; Ps 81:6; Ac
tar and with all kinds of work in the 7:19
fields; in all their hard labor the Egyptians used them ruthlessly.[m]
15The king of Egypt said to the
Hebrew midwives, whose names were
Shiphrah and Puah, 16"When you help
the Hebrew women in childbirth and
observe them on the delivery stool, if
it is a boy, kill him; but if it is a girl,
let her live." 17The midwives, however, 1:17
feared[n] God and did not do what the [n]ver 21; Pr 16:6
king of Egypt had told them to do;[o] [o]Da 3:16-18; Ac 4:18-20;
they let the boys live. 18Then the king 5:29
of Egypt summoned the midwives and
asked them, "Why have you done this?
Why have you let the boys live?" 1:19 [p]Jos 2:4-6; 2Sa 17:20
19The midwives answered Pharaoh,
"Hebrew women are not like Egyptian 1:20
women; they are vigorous and give birth [q]ver 12; Pr 11:18;
before the midwives arrive."[p] Isa 3:10
20So God was kind to the midwives[q] 1:21
and the people increased and became [r]1Sa 2:35; 2Sa 7:11,
even more numerous. 21And because 27-29; 1Ki 11:38
the midwives feared God, he gave them
families[r] of their own.
22Then Pharaoh gave this order to all
his people: "Every boy that is born[b] you

[a]*5* Masoretic Text (see also Gen. 46:27); Dead Sea Scrolls and Septuagint (see also Acts 7:14 and note at Gen. 46:27) *seventy-five* [b]*22* Masoretic Text; Samaritan Pentateuch, Septuagint and Targums *born to the Hebrews*

DAY 2 TWO

Kindness and the Purpose of God in My Life

Exodus 1:15–21

Kindness in a brutal world is always as refreshing as it is surprising. The kindness shown in this passage has said its prayers and has been instilled with courage. Kindness that practices grace in a world where grace is forbidden is definitely God's sort of kindness.

Aleksandr Solzhenitsyn said that his faith in Christ came to be because one of his doctors, Doctor Kornpett, was a Christian. This doctor was so consistently caring that he at first impressed Solzhenitsyn and later inspired him to believe in Christ.

During the Cuban revolution, one of my very good friends was incarcerated for four years, during which time he ministered to his fellow inmates in extraordinary ways. One way he ministered was by taking his Spanish New Testament, the only New Testament in the prison, and tearing it into six equal parts. He then ran a surreptitious lending library of New Testament fragments from his jail cell. This kindness was illegal, of course, but the ministry it brought to his fellow believers was a kindness that endured in their memories for the rest of their lives.

Even to this day, I am baffled by my friend's courage—perhaps because he doesn't seem particularly heroic to me. And I feel sure that he doesn't seem heroic to himself. But one thing that cannot be missed is his kindness. This friend has taught me that where courage and kindness make friends, the grace of God is apt to transform the world, whether on the birthing stools of Egypt or in a Cuban prison—or, for that matter, in the center of our lives.

To begin a study on the topic of Kindness, the Approach to Grace, turn to the home page on page 343.

1:22 [s]Ac 7:19 must throw into the Nile, but let every
girl live."[s]

The Birth of Moses

2 Now a man of the house of Levi
2:1 [t]Ex 6:20; Nu 26:59 married a Levite woman,[t] 2 and she
became pregnant and gave birth to a
son. When she saw that he was a fine
2:2 [u]Ac 7:20; Heb 11:23 child, she hid him for three months.[u]
3 But when she could hide him no longer,
she got a papyrus basket for him
and coated it with tar and pitch. Then
she placed the child in it and put it
among the reeds along the bank of the
Nile. 4 His sister[v] stood at a distance to
2:4 [v]Ex 15:20; Nu 26:59 see what would happen to him.
5 Then Pharaoh's daughter went down
2:5 [w]Ex 7:15; 8:20 to the Nile to bathe, and her attendants
were walking along the river bank.[w] She
saw the basket among the reeds and
sent her slave girl to get it. 6 She opened
it and saw the baby. He was crying, and
she felt sorry for him. "This is one of
the Hebrew babies," she said.
7 Then his sister asked Pharaoh's
daughter, "Shall I go and get one of the
Hebrew women to nurse the baby for
you?"
8 "Yes, go," she answered. And the girl
went and got the baby's mother. 9 Pharaoh's
daughter said to her, "Take this
baby and nurse him for me, and I will
pay you." So the woman took the baby
and nursed him. 10 When the child grew
older, she took him to Pharaoh's daughter
and he became her son. She named
him Moses,[a] saying, "I drew him out of
the water."

Moses Flees to Midian

11 One day, after Moses had grown
2:11 [x]Ac 7:23; Heb 11:24-26 up, he went out to where his own people[x]
were and watched them at their
hard labor. He saw an Egyptian beating
a Hebrew, one of his own people.
12 Glancing this way and that and seeing
no one, he killed the Egyptian and hid
him in the sand. 13 The next day he went
out and saw two Hebrews fighting. He
asked the one in the wrong, "Why are
you hitting your fellow Hebrew?"[y]
14 The man said, "Who made you
2:13 [y]Ac 7:26 ruler and judge over us?[z] Are you thinking
2:14 [z]Ac 7:27* of killing me as you killed the
Egyptian?" Then Moses was afraid and
thought, "What I did must have become
known."
15 When Pharaoh heard of this, he
tried to kill Moses, but Moses fled from
Pharaoh and went to live in Midian,[a] 2:15 [a]Ac 7:29; Heb 11:27
where he sat down by a well. 16 Now
a priest of Midian[b] had seven daugh- 2:16 [b]Ex 3:1 [c]Ge 24:11
ters, and they came to draw water and
fill the troughs to water[c] their father's
flock. 17 Some shepherds came along
and drove them away, but Moses got up
and came to their rescue and watered
their flock.[d] 2:17 [d]Ge 29:10
18 When the girls returned to Reuel[e] 2:18 [e]Nu 10:29
their father, he asked them, "Why have
you returned so early today?"
19 They answered, "An Egyptian rescued
us from the shepherds. He even
drew water for us and watered the
flock."
20 "And where is he?" he asked his
daughters. "Why did you leave him?
Invite him to have something to eat."[f] 2:20 [f]Ge 31:54
21 Moses agreed to stay with the man, 2:21 [g]Ex 18:2
who gave his daughter Zipporah[g] to
Moses in marriage. 22 Zipporah gave
birth to a son, and Moses named him
Gershom,[b] saying, "I have become an 2:22 [h]Ex 18:3-4; Heb 11:13
alien[h] in a foreign land."
23 During that long period,[i] the king
of Egypt died. The Israelites groaned in 2:23 [i]Ac 7:30 [j]Ex 3:7,9; Dt 26:7; Jas 5:4
their slavery and cried out, and their cry[j]
for help because of their slavery went
up to God. 24 God heard their groan- 2:24 [k]Ex 6:5; Ps 105:10,42
ing and he remembered his covenant[k]
with Abraham, with Isaac and with Jacob.
25 So God looked on the Israelites 2:25 [l]Ex 3:7; 4:31
and was concerned[l] about them.

KINDNESS

KINDNESS, ONE OF GOD'S FINEST QUALITIES

Exodus 2:25

Egypt was the crying place of God. Slaves died; God cried.

He still weeps when people kill each other in their zeal for any god. There is silence in heaven whenever humanity is inhumane.

Moses and the Burning Bush

3 Now Moses was tending the flock
of Jethro[m] his father-in-law, the 3:1 [m]Ex 2:18 [n]1Ki 19:8 [o]Ex 18:5
priest of Midian, and he led the flock
to the far side of the desert and came to
Horeb,[n] the mountain[o] of God. 2 There

[a]*10 Moses* sounds like the Hebrew for *draw out.*
[b]*22 Gershom* sounds like the Hebrew for *an alien there.*

3:2 pGe 16:7 qDt 33:16; Mk 12:26; Ac 7:30 the angel of the LORD[p] appeared to
him in flames of fire from within a
bush.[q] Moses saw that though the bush
was on fire it did not burn up. 3So Moses thought, "I will go over and see this
strange sight—why the bush does not
burn up."
4When the LORD saw that he had
gone over to look, God called to him
from within the bush, "Moses! Moses!"
And Moses said, "Here I am."
5"Do not come any closer," God said.
"Take off your sandals, for the place
3:5 rGe 28:17; Jos 5:15; Ac 7:33* where you are standing is holy ground."[r]
6Then he said, "I am the God of your
father, the God of Abraham, the God
3:6 sEx 4:5; Mt 22:32*; Mk 12:26*; Lk 20:37*; Ac 7:32* of Isaac and the God of Jacob."[s] At
this, Moses hid his face, because he was
afraid to look at God.
7The LORD said, "I have indeed seen
the misery of my people in Egypt. I
have heard them crying out because of
3:7 tEx 2:25 their slave drivers, and I am concerned[t]
about their suffering. 8So I have come
3:8 uGe 50:24 vver 17; Ex 13:5; Dt 1:25 wGe 15:18-21 down[u] to rescue them from the hand
of the Egyptians and to bring them up
out of that land into a good and spacious land, a land flowing with milk
and honey[v]—the home of the Canaanites, Hittites, Amorites, Perizzites, Hivites and Jebusites.[w] 9And now the cry
of the Israelites has reached me, and
I have seen the way the Egyptians are
3:9 xEx 1:14; 2:23 oppressing[x] them. 10So now, go. I am
3:10 yMic 6:4 sending you to Pharaoh to bring my
people the Israelites out of Egypt."[y]
3:11 zEx 6:12,30; 1Sa 18:18 11But Moses said to God, "Who am
I,[z] that I should go to Pharaoh and
bring the Israelites out of Egypt?"

FAITHFULNESS

I AM, YOU ARE, HE IS . . . FOREVER

Exodus 3:14

God's *is-ness* will never be a *was-ness*. His *now-ness* will never be a *then-ness*. To say his name is to confess that he exists for all time—beyond time.

3:12 aGe 31:3; Jos 1:5; Ro 8:31 12And God said, "I will be with you.[a]
And this will be the sign to you that it
is I who have sent you: When you have
brought the people out of Egypt, you[a]
will worship God on this mountain."
13Moses said to God, "Suppose I go
to the Israelites and say to them, 'The
God of your fathers has sent me to you,'
and they ask me, 'What is his name?'
Then what shall I tell them?"
14God said to Moses, "I AM WHO I
AM.[b] This is what you are to say to the
Israelites: 'I AM[b] has sent me to you.' " 3:14 bEx 6:2-3; Jn 8:58; Heb 13:8
15God also said to Moses, "Say to the
Israelites, 'The LORD,[c] the God of your
fathers—the God of Abraham, the God
of Isaac and the God of Jacob—has sent 3:15 cPs 135:13; Hos 12:5
me to you.' This is my name[c] forever,
the name by which I am to be remembered from generation to generation.
16"Go, assemble the elders[d] of Israel 3:16 dEx 4:29
and say to them, 'The LORD, the God
of your fathers—the God of Abraham,
Isaac and Jacob—appeared to me and
said: I have watched over you and have
seen what has been done to you in
Egypt. 17And I have promised to bring
you up out of your misery in Egypt[e] 3:17 eGe 15:16; Jos 24:11
into the land of the Canaanites, Hit-
tites, Amorites, Perizzites, Hivites and
Jebusites—a land flowing with milk and
honey.'
18"The elders of Israel will listen[f] to 3:18 fEx 4:1,8,31 gEx 5:1,3
you. Then you and the elders are to go
to the king of Egypt and say to him,
'The LORD, the God of the Hebrews,
has met with us. Let us take a three-
day journey into the desert to offer sac-
rifices[g] to the LORD our God.' 19But I 3:19 hEx 4:21; 5:2
know that the king of Egypt will not
let you go unless a mighty hand[h] com- 3:20 iEx 6:1,6; 9:15 jDt 6:22; Ne 9:10; Ac 7:36 kEx 12:31-33
pels him. 20So I will stretch out my
hand[i] and strike the Egyptians with all
the wonders[j] that I will perform among
them. After that, he will let you go.[k]
21"And I will make the Egyptians fa-
vorably disposed[l] toward this people, so 3:21 lEx 12:36 mPs 105:37
that when you leave you will not go
empty-handed.[m] 22Every woman is to 3:22 nEx 11:2 oEze 39:10
ask her neighbor and any woman living
in her house for articles of silver and
gold[n] and for clothing, which you will
put on your sons and daughters. And so
you will plunder[o] the Egyptians."

Signs for Moses

4 Moses answered, "What if they do
not believe me or listen[p] to me and 4:1 pEx 3:18; 6:30
say, 'The LORD did not appear to you'?"

[a]*12* The Hebrew is plural. [b]*14* Or *I WILL BE WHAT I WILL BE* [c]*15* The Hebrew for *LORD* sounds like and may be derived from the Hebrew for *I AM* in verse 14.

2Then the LORD said to him, "What
is that in your hand?"
4:2 [q]ver 17,20 "A staff,"[q] he replied.
3The LORD said, "Throw it on the
ground."
Moses threw it on the ground and
it became a snake, and he ran from it.
4Then the LORD said to him, "Reach
out your hand and take it by the tail."
So Moses reached out and took hold
of the snake and it turned back into
a staff in his hand. 5"This," said the
4:5 [r]Ex 19:9 LORD, "is so that they may believe[r] that
the LORD, the God of their fathers—
the God of Abraham, the God of Isaac
and the God of Jacob—has appeared to
you."
6Then the LORD said, "Put your
hand inside your cloak." So Moses put
his hand into his cloak, and when he
4:6 [s]Nu 12:10; 2Ki 5:1,27 took it out, it was leprous,[a] like snow.[s]
7"Now put it back into your cloak,"
4:7 [t]Nu 12:13-15; Dt 32:39; 2Ki 5:14; Mt 8:3 he said. So Moses put his hand back
into his cloak, and when he took it
out, it was restored,[t] like the rest of his
flesh.
8Then the LORD said, "If they do
not believe you or pay attention to the
first miraculous sign, they may believe
the second. 9But if they do not believe
these two signs or listen to you, take
some water from the Nile and pour it
on the dry ground. The water you take
4:9 [u]Ex 7:17-21 from the river will become blood[u] on
the ground."
10Moses said to the LORD, "O Lord,
I have never been eloquent, neither in
the past nor since you have spoken to
4:10 [v]Ex 6:12; Jer 1:6 your servant. I am slow of speech and
tongue."[v]
4:11 [w]Ps 94:9; Mt 11:5 11The LORD said to him, "Who gave
man his mouth? Who makes him deaf
or mute? Who gives him sight or makes
him blind?[w] Is it not I, the LORD?
4:12 [x]Isa 50:4; Jer 1:9; Mt 10:19-20; Mk 13:11; Lk 12:12; 21:14-15 12Now go; I will help you speak and
will teach you what to say."[x]
13But Moses said, "O Lord, please
send someone else to do it."
14Then the LORD's anger burned
against Moses and he said, "What about
your brother, Aaron the Levite? I know
he can speak well. He is already on his
4:14 [y]ver 27 way to meet[y] you, and his heart will be
glad when he sees you. 15You shall speak
4:15 [z]Nu 23:5,12,16 to him and put words in his mouth;[z]
I will help both of you speak and will
teach you what to do. 16He will speak
to the people for you, and it will be as
if he were your mouth[a] and as if you 4:16 [a]Ex 7:1-2
were God to him. 17But take this staff[b]
in your hand so you can perform mi- 4:17 [b]ver 2 [c]Ex 7:9-21
raculous signs[c] with it."

▸ **KINDNESS**

KINDNESS: A QUALITY EMANATING FROM OBEDIENCE

Exodus 4:13

Has God asked you to do a fearsome task? Do the very thing you fear. Obey. If a job is easily done, it is likely not an assignment from God. Only if it requires the spending of the soul can you be sure the task is his.

Moses Returns to Egypt

18Then Moses went back to Jethro
his father-in-law and said to him, "Let
me go back to my own people in Egypt
to see if any of them are still alive."
Jethro said, "Go, and I wish you
well."
19Now the LORD had said to Moses
in Midian, "Go back to Egypt, for all 4:19 [d]Ex 2:15 [e]Ex 2:23
the men who wanted to kill[d] you are
dead."[e] 20So Moses took his wife and
sons, put them on a donkey and started 4:20 [f]Ex 17:9; Nu 20:8-9,11
back to Egypt. And he took the staff[f] of
God in his hand.
21The LORD said to Moses, "When 4:21 [g]Ex 3:19,20 [h]Ex 7:3,13; 9:12,35; 14:4,8; Dt 2:30; Isa 63:17; Jn 12:40; Ro 9:18
you return to Egypt, see that you per-
form before Pharaoh all the wonders[g] I
have given you the power to do. But I
will harden his heart[h] so that he will not
let the people go. 22Then say to Phar-
aoh, 'This is what the LORD says: Israel 4:22 [i]Isa 63:16; 64:8; Jer 31:9; Hos 11:1; Ro 9:4
is my firstborn son,[i] 23and I told you,
"Let my son go,[j] so he may worship
me." But you refused to let him go; so I
will kill your firstborn son.'"[k] 4:23 [j]Ex 5:1; 7:16 [k]Ex; 11:5; 12:12,29
24At a lodging place on the way, the
LORD met ⌞Moses⌟[b] and was about to
kill[l] him. 25But Zipporah took a flint 4:24 [l]Nu 22:22
knife, cut off her son's foreskin[m] and
touched ⌞Moses'⌟ feet with it.[c] "Surely 4:25 [m]Ge 17:14; Jos 5:2,3
you are a bridegroom of blood to me,"
she said. 26So the LORD let him alone.
(At that time she said "bridegroom of
blood," referring to circumcision.)
27The LORD said to Aaron, "Go into
the desert to meet Moses." So he met

[a]6 The Hebrew word was used for various diseases affecting the skin—not necessarily leprosy. [b]*24* Or ⌞*Moses' son*⌟; Hebrew *him* [c]*25* Or *and drew near* ⌞*Moses'*⌟ *feet*

4:27 [n]Ex 3:1 Moses at the mountain[n] of God and
[o]ver 14 kissed[o] him. 28Then Moses told Aaron
4:28 everything the LORD had sent him to
[p]ver 8-9,16 say,[p] and also about all the miraculous
signs he had commanded him to per-
form.
4:29 29Moses and Aaron brought togeth-
[q]Ex 3:16 er all the elders[q] of the Israelites, 30and
Aaron told them everything the LORD
had said to Moses. He also performed
4:31 the signs before the people, 31and they
[r]ver 8; believed.[r] And when they heard that
Ex 3:18 [s]Ex 2:25 the LORD was concerned[s] about them
5:1 and had seen their misery, they bowed
[t]Ex 3:18 down and worshiped.

Bricks Without Straw

5 Afterward Moses and Aaron went
to Pharaoh and said, "This is what
the LORD, the God of Israel, says: 'Let
my people go, so that they may hold a
5:2 festival[t] to me in the desert.'"
[u]2Ki 18:35; 2Pharaoh said, "Who is the LORD,[u]
Job 21:15 that I should obey him and let Israel
[v]Ex 3:19 go? I do not know the LORD and I will
not let Israel go."[v]
3Then they said, "The God of the
Hebrews has met with us. Now let us
take a three-day journey into the desert
5:3 to offer sacrifices to the LORD our God,
[w]Ex 3:18 or he may strike us with plagues[w] or
with the sword."
4But the king of Egypt said, "Moses
and Aaron, why are you taking the peo-
5:4 ple away from their labor?[x] Get back
[x]Ex 1:11 to your work!" 5Then Pharaoh said,
5:5 "Look, the people of the land are now
[y]Ex 1:7,9 numerous,[y] and you are stopping them
from working."
6That same day Pharaoh gave this order to the slave drivers and foremen in
charge of the people: 7"You are no longer to supply the people with straw for
making bricks; let them go and gather
their own straw. 8But require them to
make the same number of bricks as before; don't reduce the quota. They are
lazy; that is why they are crying out,
'Let us go and sacrifice to our God.'
9Make the work harder for the men so
that they keep working and pay no attention to lies."
10Then the slave drivers and the foremen went out and said to the people,
"This is what Pharaoh says: 'I will not
give you any more straw. 11Go and get
your own straw wherever you can find
it, but your work will not be reduced at
all.'" 12So the people scattered all over
Egypt to gather stubble to use for straw.
13The slave drivers kept pressing them,
saying, "Complete the work required
of you for each day, just as when you
had straw." 14The Israelite foremen appointed by Pharaoh's slave drivers were
beaten[z] and were asked, "Why didn't 5:14 [z]Isa 10:24
you meet your quota of bricks yesterday
or today, as before?"
15Then the Israelite foremen went
and appealed to Pharaoh: "Why have
you treated your servants this way?
16Your servants are given no straw, yet
we are told, 'Make bricks!' Your servants are being beaten, but the fault is
with your own people."
17Pharaoh said, "Lazy, that's what you 5:17
are—lazy![a] That is why you keep saying, [a]ver 8
'Let us go and sacrifice to the LORD.'
18Now get to work. You will not be
given any straw, yet you must produce
your full quota of bricks."
19The Israelite foremen realized they
were in trouble when they were told,
"You are not to reduce the number of
bricks required of you for each day."
20When they left Pharaoh, they found
Moses and Aaron waiting to meet them,
21and they said, "May the LORD look
upon you and judge you! You have
made us a stench to Pharaoh[b] and his 5:21 [b]Ge 34:30
officials and have put a sword in their [c]Ex 14:11
hand to kill us."[c]

God Promises Deliverance

22Moses returned to the LORD and
said, "O Lord, why have you brought 5:22
trouble upon this people?[d] Is this why you [d]Nu 11:11
sent me? 23Ever since I went to Pharaoh
to speak in your name, he has brought
trouble upon this people, and you have 5:23
not rescued[e] your people at all." [e]Jer 4:10

6 Then the LORD said to Moses,
"Now you will see what I will do to
Pharaoh: Because of my mighty hand[f] 6:1 [f]Ex 3:19
he will let them go;[g] because of my [g]Ex 3:20
mighty hand he will drive them out of [h]Ex 12:31,
his country."[h] 33,39
2God also said to Moses, "I am the 6:3
LORD. 3I appeared to Abraham, to Isaac [i]Ge 17:1
and to Jacob as God Almighty,[a][i] but by [j]Ps 68:4; 83:18;
my name[j] the LORD[b][k] I did not make Isa 52:6
myself known to them.[c] 4I also estab- [k]Ex 3:14

[a]3 Hebrew *El-Shaddai* [b]3 See note at Exodus 3:15.
[c]3 Or *Almighty, and by my name the LORD did I not let myself be known to them?*

lished my covenant[l] with them to give them the land of Canaan, where they lived as aliens.[m] 5Moreover, I have heard the groaning[n] of the Israelites, whom the Egyptians are enslaving, and I have remembered my covenant.

6"Therefore, say to the Israelites: 'I am the LORD, and I will bring you out from under the yoke of the Egyptians. I will free you from being slaves to them, and I will redeem[o] you with an outstretched arm[p] and with mighty acts of judgment. 7I will take you as my own people, and I will be your God.[q] Then you will know[r] that I am the LORD your God, who brought you out from under the yoke of the Egyptians. 8And I will bring you to the land[s] I swore with uplifted hand[t] to give to Abraham, to Isaac and to Jacob.[u] I will give it to you as a possession. I am the LORD.' "

6:4 [l]Ge 15:18 [m]Ge 28:4,13
6:5 [n]Ex 2:23
6:6 [o]Dt 7:8; 1Ch 17:21 [p]Dt 26:8
6:7 [q]Dt 4:20; 2Sa 7:24 [r]Ex 16:12; Isa 41:20
6:8 [s]Ge 15:18; 26:3 [t]Ge 14:22 [u]Ps 136:21-22

KINDNESS

BELONGING TO GOD

Exodus 6:6–7

God came to the slaves of Goshen and said, "I will not have you owned by Egypt, for you belong to me." God gets possessive with his children.

9Moses reported this to the Israelites, but they did not listen to him because of their discouragement and cruel bondage.

10Then the LORD said to Moses, 11"Go, tell Pharaoh king of Egypt to let the Israelites go out of his country."

12But Moses said to the LORD, "If the Israelites will not listen to me, why would Pharaoh listen to me, since I speak with faltering lips[a]?"[v]

6:12 [v]ver 30; Ex 4:10; Jer 1:6

Family Record of Moses and Aaron

13Now the LORD spoke to Moses and Aaron about the Israelites and Pharaoh king of Egypt, and he commanded them to bring the Israelites out of Egypt.

14These were the heads of their families[b]:[w]

The sons of Reuben the firstborn son of Israel were Hanoch and Pallu, Hezron and Carmi. These were the clans of Reuben.

6:14 [w]Ge 46:9

15The sons of Simeon[x] were Jemuel, Jamin, Ohad, Jakin, Zohar and Shaul the son of a Canaanite woman. These were the clans of Simeon.

16These were the names of the sons of Levi according to their records: Gershon,[y] Kohath and Merari.[z] Levi lived 137 years.

17The sons of Gershon, by clans, were Libni and Shimei.[a]

18The sons of Kohath were Amram, Izhar, Hebron and Uzziel.[b] Kohath lived 133 years.

19The sons of Merari were Mahli and Mushi.[c]

These were the clans of Levi according to their records.

20Amram married his father's sister Jochebed, who bore him Aaron and Moses.[d] Amram lived 137 years.

21The sons of Izhar[e] were Korah, Nepheg and Zicri.

22The sons of Uzziel were Mishael, Elzaphan[f] and Sithri.

23Aaron married Elisheba, daughter of Amminadab[g] and sister of Nahshon, and she bore him Nadab and Abihu,[h] Eleazar[i] and Ithamar.[j]

24The sons of Korah[k] were Assir, Elkanah and Abiasaph. These were the Korahite clans.

25Eleazar son of Aaron married one of the daughters of Putiel, and she bore him Phinehas.[l]

These were the heads of the Levite families, clan by clan.

26It was this same Aaron and Moses to whom the LORD said, "Bring the Israelites out of Egypt by their divisions."[m] 27They were the ones who spoke to Pharaoh king of Egypt about bringing the Israelites out of Egypt. It was the same Moses and Aaron.

Aaron to Speak for Moses

28Now when the LORD spoke to Moses in Egypt, 29he said to him, "I am the LORD.[n] Tell Pharaoh king of Egypt everything I tell you."

30But Moses said to the LORD, "Since

[a] *12* Hebrew *I am uncircumcised of lips*; also in verse 30 [b] *14* The Hebrew for *families* here and in verse 25 refers to units larger than clans.

6:15 [x]Ge 46:10; 1Ch 4:24
6:16 [y]Ge 46:11 [z]Nu 3:17
6:17 [a]1Ch 6:17
6:18 [b]1Ch 6:2,18
6:19 [c]Nu 3:20,33; 1Ch 6:19; 23:21
6:20 [d]Ex 2:1-2; Nu 26:59
6:21 [e]1Ch 6:38
6:22 [f]Lev 10:4; Nu 3:30
6:23 [g]Ru 4:19,20 [h]Lev 10:1 [i]Nu 3:2,32 [j]Nu ; 26:60
6:24 [k]Nu 26:11
6:25 [l]Nu 25:7,11; Jos 24:33; Ps 106:30
6:26 [m]Ex 7:4; 12:17,41,51
6:29 [n]ver 11; Ex 7:2

I speak with faltering lips,[o] why would Pharaoh listen to me?"

7 Then the LORD said to Moses, "See, I have made you like God[p] to Pharaoh, and your brother Aaron will be your prophet. 2You are to say everything I command you, and your brother Aaron is to tell Pharaoh to let the Israelites go out of his country. 3But I will harden Pharaoh's heart,[q] and though I multiply my miraculous signs and wonders in Egypt, 4he will not listen[r] to you. Then I will lay my hand on Egypt and with mighty acts of judgment[s] I will bring out my divisions, my people the Israelites. 5And the Egyptians will know that I am the LORD[t] when I stretch out my hand[u] against Egypt and bring the Israelites out of it."

6Moses and Aaron did just as the LORD commanded[v] them. 7Moses was eighty years old[w] and Aaron eighty-three when they spoke to Pharaoh.

Aaron's Staff Becomes a Snake

8The LORD said to Moses and Aaron, 9"When Pharaoh says to you, 'Perform a miracle,[x]' then say to Aaron, 'Take your staff and throw it down before Pharaoh,' and it will become a snake."[y]

10So Moses and Aaron went to Pharaoh and did just as the LORD commanded. Aaron threw his staff down in front of Pharaoh and his officials, and it became a snake. 11Pharaoh then summoned wise men and sorcerers, and the Egyptian magicians[z] also did the same things by their secret arts:[a] 12Each one threw down his staff and it became a snake. But Aaron's staff swallowed up their staffs. 13Yet Pharaoh's heart[b] became hard and he would not listen to them, just as the LORD had said.

The Plague of Blood

14Then the LORD said to Moses, "Pharaoh's heart is unyielding;[c] he refuses to let the people go. 15Go to Pharaoh in the morning as he goes out to the water. Wait on the bank of the Nile to meet him, and take in your hand the staff that was changed into a snake. 16Then say to him, 'The LORD, the God of the Hebrews, has sent me to say to you: Let my people go, so that they may worship me[d] in the desert. But until now you have not listened. 17This is what the LORD says: By this you will know that I am the LORD:[e] With the staff that is in my hand I will strike the water of the Nile, and it will be changed into blood.[f] 18The fish in the Nile will die, and the river will stink; the Egyptians will not be able to drink its water.'"[g]

19The LORD said to Moses, "Tell Aaron, 'Take your staff and stretch out your hand[h] over the waters of Egypt—over the streams and canals, over the ponds and all the reservoirs'—and they will turn to blood. Blood will be everywhere in Egypt, even in the wooden buckets and stone jars."

20Moses and Aaron did just as the LORD had commanded. He raised his staff in the presence of Pharaoh and his officials and struck the water of the Nile,[i] and all the water was changed into blood.[j] 21The fish in the Nile died, and the river smelled so bad that the Egyptians could not drink its water. Blood was everywhere in Egypt.

22But the Egyptian magicians did the same things by their secret arts,[k] and Pharaoh's heart became hard; he would not listen to Moses and Aaron, just as the LORD had said. 23Instead, he turned and went into his palace, and did not take even this to heart. 24And all the Egyptians dug along the Nile to get drinking water, because they could not drink the water of the river.

The Plague of Frogs

25Seven days passed after the LORD struck the Nile. 8 1Then the LORD said to Moses, "Go to Pharaoh and say to him, 'This is what the LORD says: Let my people go, so that they may worship[l] me. 2If you refuse to let them go, I will plague your whole country with frogs. 3The Nile will teem with frogs. They will come up into your palace and your bedroom and onto your bed, into the houses of your officials and on your people,[m] and into your ovens and kneading troughs. 4The frogs will go up on you and your people and all your officials.'"

5Then the LORD said to Moses, "Tell Aaron, 'Stretch out your hand with your staff[n] over the streams and canals and ponds, and make frogs come up on the land of Egypt.'"

6So Aaron stretched out his hand

6:30 [o]ver 12; Ex 4:10
7:1 [p]Ex 4:16
7:3 [q]Ex 4:21; 11:9
7:4 [r]Ex 11:9 [s]Ex 3:20; 6:6
7:5 [t]ver 17; Ex 8:19,22 [u]Ex 3:20
7:6 [v]ver 2
7:7 [w]Dt 31:2; 34:7; Ac 7:23,30
7:9 [x]Isa 7:11; Jn 2:18 [y]Ex 4:2-5
7:11 [z]Ge 41:8; 2Ti 3:8 [a]ver 22; Ex 8:7,18
7:13 [b]Ex 4:21
7:14 [c]Ex 8:15,32; 10:1,20,27
7:16 [d]Ex 3:18; 5:1,3
7:17 [e]Ex 5:2 [f]Ex 4:9; Rev 11:6; 16:4
7:18 [g]ver 21,24
7:19 [h]Ex 8:5-6,16; 9:22; 10:12,21; 14:21
7:20 [i]Ex 17:5 [j]Ps 78:44; 105:29
7:22 [k]ver 11
8:1 [l]Ex 3:12,18; 4:23
8:3 [m]Ex 10:6
8:5 [n]Ex 7:19

8:6 [o]Ps 78:45; over the waters of Egypt, and the frogs[o]
105:30 came up and covered the land. 7But the
8:7 magicians did the same things by their
[p]Ex 7:11 secret arts;[p] they also made frogs come
8:8 up on the land of Egypt.
[q]ver 28; Ex 8Pharaoh summoned Moses and Aar-
9:28; 10:17 [r]ver 25 on and said, "Pray[q] to the LORD to take
the frogs away from me and my people,
and I will let your people go to offer
sacrifices[r] to the LORD."
9Moses said to Pharaoh, "I leave to
you the honor of setting the time for me
to pray for you and your officials and
your people that you and your houses
may be rid of the frogs, except for those
that remain in the Nile."
10"Tomorrow," Pharaoh said.
Moses replied, "It will be as you say,
so that you may know there is no one
8:10 [s]Ex 9:14; like the LORD our God.[s] 11The frogs
Dt 4:35; will leave you and your houses, your
33:26; 2Sa 7:22; officials and your people; they will re-
1Ch 17:20; Ps 86:8; main only in the Nile."
Isa 46:9; 12After Moses and Aaron left Phar-
Jer 10:6 aoh, Moses cried out to the LORD
about the frogs he had brought on Pharaoh. 13And the LORD did what Moses
asked. The frogs died in the houses, in
the courtyards and in the fields. 14They
were piled into heaps, and the land
reeked of them. 15But when Pharaoh
saw that there was relief, he hardened
8:15 [t]Ex 7:14 his heart[t] and would not listen to Moses and Aaron, just as the LORD had
said.

The Plague of Gnats

16Then the LORD said to Moses,
"Tell Aaron, 'Stretch out your staff and
strike the dust of the ground,' and
throughout the land of Egypt the dust
will become gnats." 17They did this,
and when Aaron stretched out his hand
with the staff and struck the dust of the
8:17 [u]Ps 105:31 ground, gnats[u] came upon men and animals. All the dust throughout the land
8:18 of Egypt became gnats. 18But when the
[v]Ex 9:11; Da 5:8 magicians[v] tried to produce gnats by
[w]Ex 7:11 their secret arts,[w] they could not. And
the gnats were on men and animals.
19The magicians said to Pharaoh,
8:19 [x]Ex 7:5; 10:7; "This is the finger[x] of God." But Phar-
Ps 8:3; aoh's heart was hard and he would not
Lk 11:20 listen, just as the LORD had said.

The Plague of Flies

8:20 20Then the LORD said to Moses,
[y]Ex 7:15; 9:13 "Get up early in the morning[y] and
confront Pharaoh as he goes to the
water and say to him, 'This is what the
LORD says: Let my people go, so that 8:20
they may worship[z] me. 21If you do not [z]ver 1;
let my people go, I will send swarms Ex 3:18
of flies on you and your officials, on
your people and into your houses.
The houses of the Egyptians will be
full of flies, and even the ground where
they are.
22" 'But on that day I will deal differ- 8:22
ently with the land of Goshen, where [a]Ex 9:4,6,26;
my people live;[a] no swarms of flies will 10:23; 11:7
be there, so that you will know[b] that [b]Ex 7:5; 9:29
I, the LORD, am in this land. 23I will
make a distinction[a] between my people
and your people. This miraculous sign
will occur tomorrow.' "
24And the LORD did this. Dense
swarms of flies poured into Pharaoh's
palace and into the houses of his of-
ficials, and throughout Egypt the land 8:24 [c]Ps 78:45;
was ruined by the flies.[c] 105:31
25Then Pharaoh summoned[d] Moses 8:25 [d]ver 8;
and Aaron and said, "Go, sacrifice to Ex 9:27
your God here in the land."
26But Moses said, "That would not
be right. The sacrifices we offer the
LORD our God would be detestable to
the Egyptians.[e] And if we offer sacri- 8:26 [e]Ge 43:32;
fices that are detestable in their eyes, 46:34
will they not stone us? 27We must take
a three-day journey into the desert to
offer sacrifices[f] to the LORD our God, 8:27
as he commands us." [f]Ex 3:18
28Pharaoh said, "I will let you go to
offer sacrifices to the LORD your God
in the desert, but you must not go very
far. Now pray[g] for me." 8:28 [g]ver 8;
29Moses answered, "As soon as I leave Ex 9:28;
you, I will pray to the LORD, and 1Ki 13:6
tomorrow the flies will leave Pharaoh
and his officials and his people. Only
be sure that Pharaoh does not act
deceitfully[h] again by not letting the 8:29 [h]ver 15
people go to offer sacrifices to the
LORD."
30Then Moses left Pharaoh and 8:30
prayed to the LORD,[i] 31and the LORD [i]ver 12
did what Moses asked: The flies left
Pharaoh and his officials and his people; not a fly remained. 32But this time
also Pharaoh hardened his heart[j] and 8:32 [j]ver 8,15;
would not let the people go. Ex 4:21

[a]23 Septuagint and Vulgate; Hebrew *will put a deliverance*

The Plague on Livestock

9 Then the LORD said to Moses, "Go
to Pharaoh and say to him, 'This
is what the LORD, the God of the Hebrews, says: "Let my people go, so that
9:1 kEx 8:1 they may worship[k] me." 2If you refuse
9:3 to let them go and continue to hold
lEx 7:4 them back, 3the hand[l] of the LORD will
bring a terrible plague on your livestock
in the field—on your horses and donkeys and camels and on your cattle and
sheep and goats. 4But the LORD will
make a distinction between the live-
9:4 mver 26; stock of Israel and that of Egypt,[m] so
Ex 8:22 that no animal belonging to the Israelites will die.' "

GENTLENESS

LET MY PEOPLE GO OR LOOK OUT!

Exodus 9:1

"Let my people go" is one of the first, great civil rights cries. Whatever the Israelites sang around their campfires in Goshen, it probably sounded like:

"We shall overcome...
Deep in my heart,
I do believe,
We shall overcome someday!"

5The LORD set a time and said, "Tomorrow the LORD will do this in the
land." 6And the next day the LORD did
9:6 nver 19-21; it: All the livestock[n] of the Egyptians
Ex 11:5 oPs 78:48-50 died,[o] but not one animal belonging to
the Israelites died. 7Pharaoh sent men
to investigate and found that not even
one of the animals of the Israelites had
died. Yet his heart was unyielding and
9:7 pEx 7:14; 8:32 he would not let the people go.[p]

The Plague of Boils

8Then the LORD said to Moses and
Aaron, "Take handfuls of soot from a
furnace and have Moses toss it into the
air in the presence of Pharaoh. 9It will
become fine dust over the whole land
9:9 qDt 28:27,35; of Egypt, and festering boils[q] will break
Rev 16:2 out on men and animals throughout
the land."
10So they took soot from a furnace
and stood before Pharaoh. Moses tossed
it into the air, and festering boils broke
9:11 out on men and animals. 11The magi-
rEx 8:18 cians[r] could not stand before Moses because of the boils that were on them and
on all the Egyptians. 12But the LORD
hardened Pharaoh's heart[s] and he would 9:12
not listen to Moses and Aaron, just as sEx 4:21
the LORD had said to Moses.

The Plague of Hail

13Then the LORD said to Moses,
"Get up early in the morning, confront
Pharaoh and say to him, 'This is what
the LORD, the God of the Hebrews,
says: Let my people go, so that they
may worship[t] me, 14or this time I will 9:13
send the full force of my plagues against tEx 8:20
you and against your officials and your
people, so you may know[u] that there is 9:14
no one like[v] me in all the earth. 15For uEx 8:10
by now I could have stretched out my v2Sa 7:22;
hand and struck you and your people[w] 1Ch 17:20; Ps 86:8;
with a plague that would have wiped Isa 46:9; Jer 10:6
you off the earth. 16But I have raised 9:15
you up[a] for this very purpose,[x] that I wEx 3:20
might show you my power[y] and that 9:16
my name might be proclaimed in all xPr 16:4 yRo 9:17*
the earth. 17You still set yourself against
my people and will not let them go.
18Therefore, at this time tomorrow I
will send the worst hailstorm[z] that has 9:18
ever fallen on Egypt, from the day it zver 23 aver 24
was founded till now.[a] 19Give an order
now to bring your livestock and everything you have in the field to a place
of shelter, because the hail will fall on
every man and animal that has not been
brought in and is still out in the field,
and they will die.' "
20Those officials of Pharaoh who
feared[b] the word of the LORD hurried 9:20
to bring their slaves and their livestock bPr 13:13
inside. 21But those who ignored the
word of the LORD left their slaves and
livestock in the field.
22Then the LORD said to Moses,
"Stretch out your hand toward the sky
so that hail will fall all over Egypt—on
men and animals and on everything
growing in the fields of Egypt." 23When
Moses stretched out his staff toward
the sky, the LORD sent thunder[c] and 9:23
hail,[d] and lightning flashed down to cPs 18:13
the ground. So the LORD rained hail dJos 10:11;
on the land of Egypt; 24hail fell and Ps 78:47; 105:32;
lightning flashed back and forth. It Isa 30:30; Eze 38:22;
was the worst storm in all the land of Rev 8:7; 16:21
Egypt since it had become a nation.
25Throughout Egypt hail struck every-

a16 Or *have spared you*

thing in the fields—both men and animals; it beat down everything growing
9:25 [e]Ps 105:32-33 in the fields and stripped every tree.[e]
26The only place it did not hail was the
9:26 [f]ver 4 land of Goshen,[f] where the Israelites
[g]Ex 8:22; 10:23; 11:7; 12:13 were.[g]
27Then Pharaoh summoned Moses
and Aaron. "This time I have sinned,"[h]
9:27 [h]Ex 10:16 he said to them. "The LORD is in the
[i]2Ch 12:6; Ps 129:4; La 1:18 right,[i] and I and my people are in the
wrong. 28Pray[j] to the LORD, for we
9:28 have had enough thunder and hail. I
[j]Ex 10:17 [k]Ex 8:8 will let you go;[k] you don't have to stay
any longer."
29Moses replied, "When I have gone
9:29 [l]1Ki 8:22,38; Ps 143:6; Isa 1:15 out of the city, I will spread out my
hands[l] in prayer to the LORD. The
[m]Ex 19:5; Ps 24:1; 1Co 10:26 thunder will stop and there will be no
more hail, so you may know that the
earth[m] is the LORD's. 30But I know that
you and your officials still do not fear
9:31 [n]Ru 1:22; 2:23 the LORD God."
31(The flax and barley[n] were destroyed, since the barley had headed
and the flax was in bloom. 32The wheat
and spelt, however, were not destroyed,
because they ripen later.)
33Then Moses left Pharaoh and went
out of the city. He spread out his hands
toward the LORD; the thunder and hail
stopped, and the rain no longer poured
down on the land. 34When Pharaoh
saw that the rain and hail and thunder
had stopped, he sinned again: He and
his officials hardened their hearts. 35So
9:35 [o]Ex 4:21 Pharaoh's heart[o] was hard and he would
not let the Israelites go, just as the
LORD had said through Moses.

The Plague of Locusts

10 Then the LORD said to Moses,
"Go to Pharaoh, for I have hard-
10:1 [p]Ex 4:21 [q]Ex 7:3 ened his heart[p] and the hearts of his
officials so that I may perform these
miraculous signs[q] of mine among them
10:2 [r]Ex 12:26-27; 13:8,14; Dt 4:9; Ps 44:1; 78:4,5; Joel 1:3 2that you may tell your children[r] and
grandchildren how I dealt harshly with
the Egyptians and how I performed my
signs among them, and that you may
know that I am the LORD."
3So Moses and Aaron went to Pharaoh and said to him, "This is what
the LORD, the God of the Hebrews,
10:3 [s]1Ki 21:29; Jas 4:10; 1Pe 5:6 says: 'How long will you refuse to humble[s] yourself before me? Let my people
go, so that they may worship me. 4If
10:4 [t]Rev 9:3 you refuse to let them go, I will bring
locusts[t] into your country tomorrow.
5They will cover the face of the ground
so that it cannot be seen. They will
devour what little you have left[u] after 10:5 [u]Ex 9:32; Joel 1:4
the hail, including every tree that is
growing in your fields. 6They will fill
your houses and those of all your officials and all the Egyptians—something
neither your fathers nor your forefathers
have ever seen from the day they settled in this land till now.'" Then Moses
turned and left Pharaoh.
7Pharaoh's officials said to him, "How
long will this man be a snare[v] to us? Let 10:7 [v]Ex 23:33; Jos 23:13; 1Sa 18:21; Ecc 7:26 [w]Ex 8:19
the people go, so that they may worship
the LORD their God. Do you not yet
realize that Egypt is ruined?"[w]
8Then Moses and Aaron were
brought back to Pharaoh. "Go, wor-
ship[x] the LORD your God," he said. 10:8 [x]Ex 8:8
"But just who will be going?"
9Moses answered, "We will go with
our young and old, with our sons and
daughters, and with our flocks and
herds, because we are to celebrate a festival to the LORD."
10Pharaoh said, "The LORD be with
you—if I let you go, along with your
women and children! Clearly you are
bent on evil.[a] 11No! Have only the men
go; and worship the LORD, since that's
what you have been asking for." Then
Moses and Aaron were driven out of
Pharaoh's presence.
12And the LORD said to Moses,
"Stretch out your hand[y] over Egypt so 10:12
that locusts will swarm over the land [y]Ex 7:19
and devour everything growing in the
fields, everything left by the hail."
13So Moses stretched out his staff
over Egypt, and the LORD made an
east wind blow across the land all that
day and all that night. By morning the
wind had brought the locusts;[z] 14they 10:13 [z]Ps 105:34
invaded all Egypt and settled down in
every area of the country in great numbers. Never before had there been such 10:14
a plague of locusts,[a] nor will there ever [a]Ps 78:46; Joel 2:1-11,25
be again. 15They covered all the ground
until it was black. They devoured[b] all 10:15 [b]ver 5; Ps 105:34-35
that was left after the hail—everything
growing in the fields and the fruit on
the trees. Nothing green remained on
tree or plant in all the land of Egypt.
16Pharaoh quickly summoned Moses
and Aaron and said, "I have sinned[c] 10:16
against the LORD your God and against [c]Ex 9:27

[a]10 Or *Be careful, trouble is in store for you!*

10:17 you. 17Now forgive my sin once more
[d]Ex 8:8 and pray[d] to the LORD your God to take
this deadly plague away from me."
10:18 18Moses then left Pharaoh and prayed
[e]Ex 8:30 to the LORD.[e] 19And the LORD changed
the wind to a very strong west wind,
which caught up the locusts and carried
them into the Red Sea.[a] Not a locust
was left anywhere in Egypt. 20But the
10:20 [f]Ex 4:21; LORD hardened Pharaoh's heart,[f] and
11:10 he would not let the Israelites go.

The Plague of Darkness

21Then the LORD said to Moses,
"Stretch out your hand toward the
10:21 sky so that darkness[g] will spread over
[g]Dt 28:29 Egypt—darkness that can be felt." 22So
Moses stretched out his hand toward
10:22 the sky, and total darkness covered[h] all
[h]Ps 105:28; Rev 16:10 Egypt for three days. 23No one could
see anyone else or leave his place for
three days. Yet all the Israelites had light
10:23 [i]Ex 8:22 in the places where they lived.[i]
10:24 24Then Pharaoh summoned Moses
[j]ver 8-10 and said, "Go, worship the LORD. Even
your women and children[j] may go with
you; only leave your flocks and herds
behind."
25But Moses said, "You must allow
us to have sacrifices and burnt offerings to present to the LORD our God.
26Our livestock too must go with us;
not a hoof is to be left behind. We have
to use some of them in worshiping the
LORD our God, and until we get there
we will not know what we are to use to
worship the LORD."
27But the LORD hardened Pharaoh's
10:27 [k]ver 20; heart,[k] and he was not willing to let
Ex 4:21 them go. 28Pharaoh said to Moses, "Get
out of my sight! Make sure you do not
appear before me again! The day you
see my face you will die."
29"Just as you say," Moses replied, "I
10:29 [l]Heb 11:27 will never appear[l] before you again."

The Plague on the Firstborn

11 Now the LORD had said to Moses, "I will bring one more plague
on Pharaoh and on Egypt. After that,
he will let you go from here, and when
he does, he will drive you out completely. 2Tell the people that men and
women alike are to ask their neighbors
11:2 [m]Ex 3:21,22 for articles of silver and gold."[m] 3(The
LORD made the Egyptians favorably
11:3 disposed toward the people, and Moses
[n]Dt 34:11 himself was highly regarded[n] in Egypt
by Pharaoh's officials and by the peo-
ple.)
4So Moses said, "This is what the
LORD says: 'About midnight[o] I will 11:4 [o]Ex 12:29
go throughout Egypt. 5Every firstborn[p]
son in Egypt will die, from the firstborn 11:5 [p]Ex 4:23;
son of Pharaoh, who sits on the throne, Ps 78:51
to the firstborn son of the slave girl,
who is at her hand mill, and all the firstborn of the cattle as well. 6There will 11:6
be loud wailing[q] throughout Egypt— [q]Ex 12:30
worse than there has ever been or ever
will be again. 7But among the Israelites not a dog will bark at any man
or animal.' Then you will know that
the LORD makes a distinction[r] between 11:7 [r]Ex 8:22
Egypt and Israel. 8All these officials of
yours will come to me, bowing down
before me and saying, 'Go,[s] you and all 11:8 [s]Ex 12:31-33
the people who follow you!' After that
I will leave." Then Moses, hot with an- 11:9 [t]Ex 7:4
ger, left Pharaoh.
9The LORD had said to Moses, "Pharaoh will refuse to listen[t] to you—so
that my wonders may be multiplied in
Egypt." 10Moses and Aaron performed
all these wonders before Pharaoh, but
the LORD hardened Pharaoh's heart,[u] 11:10 [u]Ex 4:21;
and he would not let the Israelites go 10:20,27
out of his country.

The Passover

12 The LORD said to Moses and
Aaron in Egypt, 2"This month
is to be for you the first month,[v] the 12:2 [v]Ex 13:4;
first month of your year. 3Tell the whole Dt 16:1
community of Israel that on the tenth
day of this month each man is to take
a lamb[b] for his family, one for each
household. 4If any household is too
small for a whole lamb, they must share
one with their nearest neighbor, having
taken into account the number of people there are. You are to determine the
amount of lamb needed in accordance
with what each person will eat. 5The
animals you choose must be year-old
males without defect,[w] and you may 12:5 [w]Lev 22:18-21;
take them from the sheep or the goats. Heb 9:14
6Take care of them until the fourteenth
day of the month,[x] when all the peo- 12:6 [x]Lev 23:5;
ple of the community of Israel must Nu 9:1-3,5,11
slaughter them at twilight.[y] 7Then they [y]Ex 16:12;
are to take some of the blood and put it Dt 16:4,6

[a]*19* Hebrew *Yam Suph*; that is, Sea of Reeds
[b]*3* The Hebrew word can mean *lamb* or *kid*; also in verse 4.

on the sides and tops of the doorframes of the houses where they eat the lambs. 8That same night[z] they are to eat the meat roasted[a] over the fire, along with bitter herbs,[b] and bread made without yeast.[c] 9Do not eat the meat raw or cooked in water, but roast it over the fire—head, legs and inner parts. 10Do not leave any of it till morning;[d] if some is left till morning, you must burn it. 11This is how you are to eat it: with your cloak tucked into your belt, your sandals on your feet and your staff in your hand. Eat it in haste;[e] it is the LORD's Passover.[f]

12"On that same night I will pass through[g] Egypt and strike down every firstborn—both men and animals—and I will bring judgment on all the gods[h] of Egypt. I am the LORD.[i] 13The blood will be a sign for you on the houses where you are; and when I see the blood, I will pass over you. No destructive plague will touch you when I strike Egypt.

SELF-CONTROL

THE FINAL PLAGUE

Exodus 12:13

The final plague contains this truth: A choice is born of blood or death. The lamb must die, slaughtered by prescription. The blood must be daubed upon the doorframes. Then when the Lord comes with blade and plague, he will see the blood and say, "Forbear and sheathe the sword of death. Pass over these, for they have honored me."

14"This is a day you are to commemorate;[j] for the generations to come you shall celebrate it as a festival to the LORD—a lasting ordinance.[k] 15For seven days you are to eat bread made without yeast.[l] On the first day remove the yeast from your houses, for whoever eats anything with yeast in it from the first day through the seventh must be cut off[m] from Israel. 16On the first day hold a sacred assembly, and another one on the seventh day. Do no work at all on these days, except to prepare food for everyone to eat—that is all you may do.

17"Celebrate the Feast of Unleavened Bread, because it was on this very day that I brought your divisions out of Egypt.[n] Celebrate this day as a lasting ordinance for the generations to come. 18In the first month[o] you are to eat bread made without yeast, from the evening of the fourteenth day until the evening of the twenty-first day. 19For seven days no yeast is to be found in your houses. And whoever eats anything with yeast in it must be cut off from the community of Israel, whether he is an alien or native-born. 20Eat nothing made with yeast. Wherever you live, you must eat unleavened bread."

21Then Moses summoned all the elders of Israel and said to them, "Go at once and select the animals for your families and slaughter the Passover lamb.[p] 22Take a bunch of hyssop, dip it into the blood in the basin and put some of the blood[q] on the top and on both sides of the doorframe. Not one of you shall go out the door of his house until morning. 23When the LORD goes through the land to strike down the Egyptians, he will see the blood[r] on the top and sides of the doorframe and will pass over[s] that doorway, and he will not permit the destroyer[t] to enter your houses and strike you down.

24"Obey these instructions as a lasting ordinance for you and your descendants. 25When you enter the land that the LORD will give you as he promised, observe this ceremony. 26And when your children[u] ask you, 'What does this ceremony mean to you?' 27then tell them, 'It is the Passover[v] sacrifice to the LORD, who passed over the houses of the Israelites in Egypt and spared our homes when he struck down the Egyptians.'" Then the people bowed down and worshiped.[w] 28The Israelites did just what the LORD commanded Moses and Aaron.

29At midnight[x] the LORD struck down all the firstborn[y] in Egypt, from the firstborn of Pharaoh, who sat on the throne, to the firstborn of the prisoner, who was in the dungeon, and the firstborn of all the livestock[z] as well. 30Pharaoh and all his officials and all the Egyptians got up during the night, and there was loud wailing[a] in Egypt, for there was not a house without someone dead.

The Exodus

31During the night Pharaoh summoned Moses and Aaron and said, "Up!

12:8 [z]Ex 34:25; Nu 9:12 [a]Dt 16:7 [b]Nu 9:11 [c]Dt 16:3-4; 1Co 5:8
12:10 [d]Ex 23:18; 34:25
12:11 [e]Dt 16:3 [f]ver 13,21, 27,43; Dt 16:1
12:12 [g]Ex 11:4; Am 5:17 [h]Nu 33:4 [i]Ex 6:2
12:14 [j]Ex 13:9 [k]ver 17,24; Ex 13:5,10; 2Ki 23:21
12:15 [l]Ex 13:6-7; 23:15; 34:18; Lev 23:6; Dt 16:3 [m]Ge 17:14; Nu 9:13
12:17 [n]ver 41; Ex 13:3
12:18 [o]ver 2; Lev 23:5-8; Nu 28:16-25
12:21 [p]ver 11; Mk 14:12-16
12:22 [q]ver 7; Heb 11:28
12:23 [r]Rev 7:3 [s]ver 13 [t]1Co 10:10; Heb 11:28
12:26 [u]Ex 10:2; 13:8,14-15; Jos 4:6
12:27 [v]ver 11 [w]Ex 4:31
12:29 [x]Ex 11:4 [y]Ex 4:23; Ps 78:51 [z]Ex 9:6
12:30 [a]Ex 11:6

Leave my people, you and the Israel-
12:31 [b]Ex 8:8 ites! Go, worship[b] the LORD as you
12:32 have requested. 32Take your flocks and
[c]Ex 10:9,26 herds[c] as you have said, and go. And
also bless me."
33The Egyptians urged the people
12:33 to hurry and leave[d] the country. "For
[d]Ps 105:38 otherwise," they said, "we will all die!"
34So the people took their dough be-
fore the yeast was added, and carried it
on their shoulders in kneading troughs
wrapped in clothing. 35The Israelites
did as Moses instructed and asked the
12:35 Egyptians for articles of silver and gold[e]
[e]Ex 3:22 and for clothing. 36The LORD had
made the Egyptians favorably disposed
toward the people, and they gave them
12:36 what they asked for; so they plundered[f]
[f]Ex 3:22 the Egyptians.
37The Israelites journeyed from Ram-
12:37 eses to Succoth.[g] There were about
[g]Nu 33:3-5 [h]Ex 38:26; six hundred thousand men[h] on foot,
Nu 1:46; 11:13,21 besides women and children. 38Many
12:38 other people[i] went up with them, as
[i]Nu 11:4 well as large droves of livestock, both
flocks and herds. 39With the dough they
had brought from Egypt, they baked
cakes of unleavened bread. The dough
was without yeast because they had
12:39 [j]ver 31-33; been driven out[j] of Egypt and did not
Ex 6:1; 11:1 have time to prepare food for themselves.
40Now the length of time the Israelite
12:40 [k]Ge 15:13; people lived in Egypt[a] was 430 years.[k]
Ac 7:6; 41At the end of the 430 years, to the
Gal 3:17 very day, all the LORD's divisions[l] left
12:41 [l]ver 17; Egypt.[m] 42Because the LORD kept vigil
Ex 6:26 that night to bring them out of Egypt,
[m]Ex 3:10 on this night all the Israelites are to
12:42 [n]Ex 13:10; keep vigil to honor the LORD for the
Dt 16:1,6 generations to come.[n]

Passover Restrictions

43The LORD said to Moses and Aar-
12:43 [o]ver 11 on, "These are the regulations for the
[p]ver 48; Nu 9:14 Passover:[o]
"No foreigner[p] is to eat of it. 44Any
slave you have bought may eat of it af-
12:44 [q]Ge 17:12-13 ter you have circumcised[q] him, 45but a
temporary resident and a hired worker[r]
12:45 [r]Lev 22:10 may not eat of it.
46"It must be eaten inside one house;
12:46 [s]Nu 9:12; take none of the meat outside the house.
Jn 19:36* Do not break any of the bones.[s] 47The
whole community of Israel must celebrate it.
48"An alien living among you who
wants to celebrate the LORD's Passover

must have all the males in his household circumcised; then he may take
part like one born in the land.[t] No un- 12:48 [t]Nu 9:14
circumcised male may eat of it. 49The 12:49
same law applies to the native-born and [u]Nu 15:15-16,29;
to the alien[u] living among you." Gal 3:28

50All the Israelites did just what the
LORD had commanded Moses and Aaron. 51And on that very day the LORD
brought the Israelites out of Egypt by 12:51
their divisions.[v] [v]ver 41; Ex 6:26

Consecration of the Firstborn

13 The LORD said to Moses,
2"Consecrate to me every first-
born male.[w] The first offspring of every 13:2 [w]ver 12,13,15;
womb among the Israelites belongs to Ex 22:29;
me, whether man or animal." Nu 3:13; Dt 15:19;
3Then Moses said to the people, Lk 2:23*
"Commemorate this day, the day you
came out of Egypt, out of the land
of slavery, because the LORD brought
you out of it with a mighty hand.[x] Eat 13:3 [x]Ex 3:20; 6:1
nothing containing yeast.[y] 4Today, in [y]Ex 12:19
the month of Abib,[z] you are leaving. 13:4
5When the LORD brings you into the [z]Ex 12:2
land of the Canaanites, Hittites, Amo-
rites, Hivites and Jebusites[a]—the land 13:5 [a]Ex 3:8
he swore to your forefathers to give you, [b]Ex 12:25-26
a land flowing with milk and honey—
you are to observe this ceremony[b] in
this month: 6For seven days eat bread
made without yeast and on the seventh
day hold a festival[c] to the LORD. 7Eat 13:6 [c]Ex 12:15-20
unleavened bread during those seven
days; nothing with yeast in it is to be
seen among you, nor shall any yeast
be seen anywhere within your borders. 13:8
8On that day tell your son,[d] 'I do this [d]ver 14;
because of what the LORD did for me Ex 10:2;
when I came out of Egypt.' 9This ob- Ps 78:5-6
servance will be for you like a sign on
your hand and a reminder on your forehead[e] that the law of the LORD is to 13:9
be on your lips. For the LORD brought [e]ver 16; Dt 6:8; 11:18
you out of Egypt with his mighty hand. 13:10
10You must keep this ordinance[f] at the [f]Ex 12:24-25
appointed time year after year.
11"After the LORD brings you into
the land of the Canaanites and gives it
to you, as he promised on oath to you
and your forefathers, 12you are to give
over to the LORD the first offspring
of every womb. All the firstborn males

[a]40 Masoretic Text; Samaritan Pentateuch and Septuagint *Egypt and Canaan*

of your livestock belong to the LORD.[g] 13Redeem with a lamb every firstborn donkey, but if you do not redeem it, break its neck.[h] Redeem every firstborn among your sons.[i]

14"In days to come, when your son[j] asks you, 'What does this mean?' say to him, 'With a mighty hand the LORD brought us out of Egypt, out of the land of slavery.[k] 15When Pharaoh stubbornly refused to let us go, the LORD killed every firstborn in Egypt, both man and animal. This is why I sacrifice to the LORD the first male offspring of every womb and redeem each of my firstborn sons.'[l] 16And it will be like a sign on your hand and a symbol on your forehead[m] that the LORD brought us out of Egypt with his mighty hand."

Crossing the Sea

17When Pharaoh let the people go, God did not lead them on the road through the Philistine country, though that was shorter. For God said, "If they face war, they might change their minds and return to Egypt."[n] 18So God led[o] the people around by the desert road toward the Red Sea.[a] The Israelites went up out of Egypt armed for battle.[p]

19Moses took the bones of Joseph[q] with him because Joseph had made the sons of Israel swear an oath. He had said, "God will surely come to your aid, and then you must carry my bones up with you from this place."[b] [r]

20After leaving Succoth they camped at Etham on the edge of the desert.[s] 21By day the LORD went ahead of them in a pillar of cloud[t] to guide them on their way and by night in a pillar of fire to give them light, so that they could travel by day or night. 22Neither the pillar of cloud by day nor the pillar of fire by night left its place in front of the people.

14 Then the LORD said to Moses, 2"Tell the Israelites to turn back and encamp near Pi Hahiroth, between Migdol[u] and the sea. They are to encamp by the sea, directly opposite Baal Zephon. 3Pharaoh will think, 'The Israelites are wandering around the land in confusion, hemmed in by the desert.' 4And I will harden Pharaoh's heart,[v] and he will pursue them. But I will gain glory[w] for myself through Pharaoh and all his army, and the Egyptians will know that I am the LORD."[x] So the Israelites did this.

5When the king of Egypt was told that the people had fled, Pharaoh and his officials changed their minds about them and said, "What have we done? We have let the Israelites go and have lost their services!" 6So he had his chariot made ready and took his army with him. 7He took six hundred of the best chariots, along with all the other chariots of Egypt, with officers over all of them. 8The LORD hardened the heart[y] of Pharaoh king of Egypt, so that he pursued the Israelites, who were marching out boldly.[z] 9The Egyptians—all Pharaoh's horses and chariots, horsemen[c] and troops—pursued the Israelites and overtook[a] them as they camped by the sea near Pi Hahiroth, opposite Baal Zephon.

10As Pharaoh approached, the Israelites looked up, and there were the Egyptians, marching after them. They were terrified and cried[b] out to the LORD. 11They said to Moses, "Was it because there were no graves in Egypt that you brought us to the desert to die?[c] What have you done to us by bringing us out of Egypt? 12Didn't we say to you in Egypt, 'Leave us alone; let us serve the Egyptians'? It would have been better for us to serve the Egyptians than to die in the desert!"

13Moses answered the people, "Do not be afraid.[d] Stand firm and you will see[e] the deliverance the LORD will bring you today. The Egyptians you see today you will never see[f] again. 14The LORD will fight[g] for you; you need only to be still."[h]

15Then the LORD said to Moses, "Why are you crying out to me? Tell the Israelites to move on. 16Raise your staff[i] and stretch out your hand over the sea to divide the water[j] so that the Israelites can go through the sea on dry ground. 17I will harden the hearts of the Egyptians so that they will go in after them.[k] And I will gain glory through Pharaoh and all his army, through his chariots and his horsemen. 18The Egyptians will know that I am the LORD when I gain glory through Pharaoh, his chariots and his horsemen."

[a] *18* Hebrew *Yam Suph*; that is, Sea of Reeds
[b] *19* See Gen. 50:25.
[c] *9* Or *charioteers*; also in verses 17, 18, 23, 26 and 28

13:12 [g]Lev 27:26; Lk 2:23*
13:13 [h]Ex 34:20 [i]Nu 18:15
13:14 [j]Ex 10:2; 12:26-27; Dt 6:20 [k]ver 3,9
13:15 [l]Ex 12:29
13:16 [m]ver 9
13:17 [n]Ex 14:11; Nu 14:1-4; Dt 17:16
13:18 [o]Ps 136:16 [p]Jos 1:14
13:19 [q]Jos 24:32; Ac 7:16 [r]Ge 50:24-25
13:20 [s]Nu 33:6
13:21 [t]Ex 14:19,24; 33:9-10; Nu 9:16; Dt 1:33; Ne 9:12,19; Ps 78:14; 99:7; 105:39; Isa 4:5; 1Co 10:1
14:2 [u]Nu 33:7; Jer 44:1
14:4 [v]Ex 4:21 [w]Ro 9:17, 22-23
14:4 [x]Ex 7:5
14:8 [y]ver 4; Ex 11:10 [z]Nu 33:3; Ac 13:17
14:9 [a]Ex 15:9
14:10 [b]Jos 24:7; Ne 9:9; Ps 34:17
14:11 [c]Ps 106:7-8
14:13 [d]Ge 15:1 [e]2Ch 20:17; Isa 41:10, 13-14 [f]ver 30
14:14 [g]ver 25; Ex 15:3; Dt 1:30; 3:22; 2Ch 20:29 [h]Ps 37:7; 46:10; Isa 30:15
14:16 [i]Ex 4:17; Nu 20:8-9,11 [j]Isa 10:26
14:17 [k]ver 4

19 Then the angel of God, who had
been traveling in front of Israel's army,
withdrew and went behind them. The
14:19 [l]Ex 13:21 pillar of cloud[l] also moved from in
front and stood behind them, 20 com-
ing between the armies of Egypt and
Israel. Throughout the night the cloud
brought darkness to the one side and
light to the other side; so neither went
near the other all night long.
21 Then Moses stretched out his hand
over the sea, and all that night the
LORD drove the sea back with a strong
14:21 [m]Ex 15:8 [n]Ps 74:13; 114:5; Isa 63:12 east wind[m] and turned it into dry land.
The waters were divided,[n] 22 and the Is-
raelites went through the sea on dry
ground,[o] with a wall of water on their
14:22 [o]Ex 15:19; Ne 9:11; Ps 66:6; Heb 11:29 right and on their left.
23 The Egyptians pursued them, and
all Pharaoh's horses and chariots and
horsemen followed them into the sea.
24 During the last watch of the night the
LORD looked down from the pillar of
14:24 [p]Ex 13:21 fire and cloud[p] at the Egyptian army
and threw it into confusion. 25 He made
the wheels of their chariots come off[a]
so that they had difficulty driving. And
the Egyptians said, "Let's get away from
14:25 [q]ver 14 the Israelites! The LORD is fighting[q] for
them against Egypt."
26 Then the LORD said to Moses,
"Stretch out your hand over the sea so
that the waters may flow back over the
Egyptians and their chariots and horsemen." 27 Moses stretched out his hand
over the sea, and at daybreak the sea
14:27 [r]Jos 4:18 [s]Ex 15:1,21; Ps 78:53; 106:11 went back to its place.[r] The Egyptians
were fleeing toward[b] it, and the LORD
swept them into the sea.[s] 28 The water
flowed back and covered the chariots
and horsemen—the entire army of Pharaoh that had followed the Israelites into
the sea. Not one of them survived.
29 But the Israelites went through the
14:29 [t]ver 22 sea on dry ground,[t] with a wall of water
on their right and on their left. 30 That
14:30 [u]Ps 106:8,10,21 day the LORD saved[u] Israel from the
hands of the Egyptians, and Israel saw
the Egyptians lying dead on the shore.
31 And when the Israelites saw the great
power the LORD displayed against the
Egyptians, the people feared the LORD
and put their trust[v] in him and in Mo-
14:31 [v]Ps 106:12; Jn 2:11 ses his servant.

The Song of Moses and Miriam

15:1 [w]Rev 15:3 **15** Then Moses and the Israelites
sang this song[w] to the LORD:

"I will sing[x] to the LORD, 15:1 [x]Ps 106:12
for he is highly exalted.
The horse and its rider
he has hurled into the sea.
2 The LORD is my strength[y] and my 15:2 [y]Ps 59:17
song; [z]Ps 18:2,46; Isa 12:2; Hab 3:18
he has become my salvation.[z] [a]Ge 28:21
He is my God, and I will praise him, [b]Ex 3:6, 15-16; Isa 25:1
my father's God,[a] and I will exalt[b]
him.
3 The LORD is a warrior;[c] 15:3 [c]Ex 14:14; Ps 24:8; Rev 19:11
the LORD is his name.[d] [d]Ex 6:2-3,7-8; Ps 83:18
4 Pharaoh's chariots and his army[e]
he has hurled into the sea.
The best of Pharaoh's officers 15:4 [e]Ex 14:6-7
are drowned in the Red Sea.[c]
5 The deep waters have covered them; 15:5 [f]ver 10; Ne 9:11
they sank to the depths like a
stone.[f]

6 "Your right hand,[g] O LORD, 15:6 [g]Ps 118:15
was majestic in power.
Your right hand, O LORD,
shattered the enemy.
7 In the greatness of your majesty
you threw down those who
opposed you.
You unleashed your burning 15:7 [h]Ps 78:49-50
anger;[h]
it consumed them like stubble.
8 By the blast of your nostrils[i] 15:8 [i]Ex 14:21
the waters piled up.[j] [j]Ps 78:13
The surging waters stood firm like a [k]Ex 14:22
wall;[k]
the deep waters congealed in the
heart of the sea.

9 "The enemy boasted,
'I will pursue,[l] I will overtake 15:9: [l]Ex 14:5-9
them. [m]Jdg 5:30; Isa 53:12
I will divide the spoils;[m]
I will gorge myself on them.
I will draw my sword
and my hand will destroy them.'
10 But you blew with your breath,
and the sea covered them.
They sank like lead
in the mighty waters.[n] 15:10 [n]ver 5; Ex 14:27-28

11 "Who among the gods is like you,[o]
O LORD? 15:11 [o]Ex 8:10; Dt 3:24; Ps 77:13
Who is like you—
majestic in holiness,[p] [p]Isa 6:3; Rev 4:8
awesome in glory,[q] [q]Ps 8:1
working wonders?

[a]25 Or *He jammed the wheels of their chariots* (see Samaritan Pentateuch, Septuagint and Syriac)
[b]27 Or *from*
[c]4 Hebrew *Yam Suph*; that is, Sea of Reeds; also in verse 22

[12]You stretched out your right hand
and the earth swallowed them.
[13]"In your unfailing love you will
lead[r]
the people you have redeemed.
In your strength you will guide them
to your holy dwelling.[s]

15:13
[r]Ne 9:12;
Ps 77:20
[s]Ps 78:54

DAY 4 FOUR

▸ JOY AND MY SERVICE TO OTHERS

Exodus 15:19–21

It is impossible to witness the salvation of God and not experience joy. The Israelites were an unarmed and defenseless horde of slaves. They could not raise any arms nor produce an effective battle strategy against Pharaoh's mighty military. They would be lost if God did not fight for them.

Then comes the miracle! A strong east wind holds back the waters of the sea, and Israel passes through it "on dry ground" (Exodus 14:21–22). The entire army of Pharaoh is destroyed, and Israel is saved.

Miriam, caught up in the rapture of victory, begins to praise the God who defends the defenseless. And her burst of joy leads all the other women in dancing and praise. Her joy is contagious. Her response to God's work strikes a universal nerve that leads to corporate worship.

Joy erupts from all who observe the victories of God. When John Newton saw all that God was doing in his life, he sang,

Amazing grace!
How sweet the sound
That saved a wretch like me!
I once was lost, but now am found;
Was blind, but now I see.

When Miriam of Israel saw the victory of God, she sang, "Amazing grace... he is highly exalted. The horse and its rider he has hurled into the sea." When others see our worship, they too are amazed by the work of God. And their response is to join us in praising God for the evidence of his presence.

To begin a study on the topic of Joy, the Infallible Proof of the Presence of God, turn to the home page on page 1086.

[14]The nations will hear and
tremble;[t]
anguish will grip the people of
Philistia.
[15]The chiefs[u] of Edom will be
terrified,
the leaders of Moab will be seized
with trembling,[v]
the people[a] of Canaan will melt[w]
away;
[16] terror[x] and dread will fall upon
them.
By the power of your arm
they will be as still as a stone[y]—
until your people pass by,
O LORD,
until the people you bought[b][z]
pass by.
[17]You will bring them in and plant[a]
them
on the mountain[b] of your
inheritance—
the place, O LORD, you made for
your dwelling,
the sanctuary, O Lord, your hands
established.
[18]The LORD will reign
for ever and ever."

[19]When Pharaoh's horses, chariots
and horsemen[c] went into the sea,[c] the
LORD brought the waters of the sea
back over them, but the Israelites walked
through the sea on dry ground.[d] [20]Then
Miriam[e] the prophetess,[f] Aaron's sister,
took a tambourine in her hand, and all
the women followed her, with tambourines
and dancing.[g] [21]Miriam sang to
them:

"Sing to the LORD,
for he is highly exalted.
The horse and its rider
he has hurled into the sea."[h]

[a]*15* Or *rulers* [b]*16* Or *created* [c]*19* Or *charioteers*

15:14
[t]Dt 2:25
15:15
[u]Ge 36:15
[v]Nu 22:3
[w]Jos 5:1
15:16
[x]Ex 23:27;
Jos 2:9
[y]1Sa 25:37
[z]Ps 74:2
15:17
[a]Ps 44:2
[b]Ps 78:54,68
15:19
[c]Ex 14:28
[d]Ex 14:22
15:20
[e]Nu 26:59
[f]Jdg 4:4
[g]Jdg 11:34;
1Sa 18:6;
Ps 30:11;
150:4
15:21
[h]ver 1;
Ex 14:27

▸ JOY
THE TAMBOURINES OF THANKSGIVING

Exodus 15:21

We are saved! Erupt in gratitude! Over every sea of terror must float a song of praise. So let all who want to praise him take up the music. All of God's victories demand the tambourine and dance.

The Waters of Marah and Elim

22 Then Moses led Israel from the
Red Sea and they went into the Desert
of Shur. For three days they traveled
in the desert without finding water.
23 When they came to Marah, they could
not drink its water because it was bitter. (That is why the place is called
15:23 Marah.[a][i]) 24 So the people grumbled[j]
[i]Nu 33:8 against Moses, saying, "What are we to
15:24 drink?"
[j]Ex 14:12; 25 Then Moses cried out[k] to the
16:2 LORD, and the LORD showed him a
15:25 piece of wood. He threw it into the wa-
[k]Ex 14:10 ter, and the water became sweet.
[l]Jdg 3:4 There the LORD made a decree and a
law for them, and there he tested[l] them.
26 He said, "If you listen carefully to the
voice of the LORD your God and do
what is right in his eyes, if you pay attention to his commands and keep all
his decrees,[m] I will not bring on you 15:26 [m]Dt 7:12
any of the diseases[n] I brought on the [n]Dt 28:27, 58-60
Egyptians, for I am the LORD, who [o]Ex 23:25-26
heals[o] you."
27 Then they came to Elim, where
there were twelve springs and seventy 15:27
palm trees, and they camped[p] there [p]Nu 33:9
near the water.

Manna and Quail

16 The whole Israelite community
set out from Elim and came to 16:1
the Desert of Sin,[q] which is between [q]Nu 33:11,12

[a]23 *Marah* means *bitter.*

MIRIAM

Joy, the Voice of Praise (15:21)

Praise is our reflexive response to joy. When we meet God, we feel elation. When we are elated, we must praise him.

Miriam was a complex woman. She is first mentioned in Exodus 2:1–10, a passage that shows her as a young girl, watching her mother place the infant Moses into a little basket and gently nudge it into the Nile. Miriam was responsible for watching over the baby Moses—her little brother—until Pharaoh's daughter discovered him. It was then that Miriam forthrightly suggested to Pharaoh's daughter, who wanted to keep the baby, "Shall I go and get one of the Hebrew women to nurse the baby for you?" (v. 7). Pharaoh's daughter agreed, and thus Miriam arranged for Moses' own mother to be the nursemaid.

In this scene when we first meet Miriam, she appears intelligent, brave and kind. However, we also learn that Miriam could be critical. She, along with her brother Aaron, spoke against Moses because of his Cushite wife (Numbers 12:1). Why Miriam criticized Moses about this is not clear. But God was displeased with Miriam and Aaron, and Miriam was afflicted with leprosy as punishment for her critical stance.

But perhaps Miriam is best remembered for the spontaneous joy that gripped her life after the Egyptian army has been buried in the Red Sea (Exodus 15:21). The people Israel had been delivered. In many ways the crossing of the Red Sea in the Old Testament is a picture of the cross and resurrection in the New Testament. Both events represent victory and are miracles of redemption. Israel would from this time on celebrate this crossing as the time when God saved them. Today Christians celebrate the cross and resurrection as the place at which Christ saved them. Although the Israelites made this event the center of their highest praise for centuries, it was Miriam who saw the glory of the moment as it happened. Praise is glorious, and blessed are those who can seize upon a moment, see God in that moment and break into spontaneous praise.

God had acted; God had saved! History had been made! A nation had been forged! Miriam's joy was authentic, and her praise from the heart:

Sing to the LORD,
for he is highly exalted.
The horse and its rider
he has hurled into the sea.

(15:21)

Elim and Sinai, on the fifteenth day of
the second month after they had come
16:2 out of Egypt. 2In the desert the whole
[r]Ex 14:11; community grumbled[r] against Moses
15:24; 1Co 10:10 and Aaron. 3The Israelites said to them,
"If only we had died by the LORD's
hand in Egypt![s] There we sat around 16:3 [s]Ex 17:3
pots of meat and ate all the food[t] we [t]Nu 11:4,34
wanted, but you have brought us out
into this desert to starve this entire assembly to death."
4Then the LORD said to Moses, "I

MOSES

Self-Control, the Key to God's Blessing (15:22)

There are two contrasting passages describing events in the life of Moses that together demonstrate both the blessing that comes to us when we practice self-control and the consequences that can result from failure to do so. The two incidents are remarkably alike in some ways. In both instances the people were grumbling. In both instances hundreds of thousands of people were suffering from heat and thirst. In both instances the people were critical. But notice the very different ways that Moses responded to God's instruction in each of the circumstances.

First, in Exodus 15:22–27 there was water, but it was too bitter to drink. Moses cried out to the Lord, and the Lord showed him a piece of wood that he was to throw into the bitter water. Moses did this, and the water became sweet. Moses obeyed the Lord in perfect self-control and displayed no anger. The Lord said, "If you listen carefully to the voice of the LORD your God and do what is right in his eyes, if you pay attention to his commands and keep all his decrees, I will not bring on you any of the diseases I brought on the Egyptians, for I am the LORD, who heals you" (v. 26).

In the second instance, again the people complained about the lack of water. But in this case, Moses became infuriated and lost his temper. God had said to him, "Speak to that rock before their eyes and it will pour out its water" (Numbers 20:8). Unfortunately, Moses didn't faithfully follow directions: "Moses took the staff from the LORD's presence, just as he commanded him. He and Aaron gathered the assembly together in front of the rock and Moses said to them, 'Listen, you rebels, must we bring you water out of this rock?'" (vv. 9–10). Then, in a fit of temper, he struck the rock and water gushed out. All the people in Israel quenched their thirst. "But the LORD said to Moses and Aaron, 'Because you did not trust in me enough to honor me as holy in the sight of the Israelites, you will not bring this community into the land I give them'" (v. 12). Thus, because of a moment of lost self-control, Moses wandered in the desert with the Israelites for an additional 40 years, never to know the joy of entering the promised land.

We must remember that, except for that one notable failure to exercise self-control, Moses was a man whose resolve and restraint produced a quality of leadership rarely known in this world. So glorious was this man of faith that the writer of Hebrews wrote of him: "By faith Moses, when he had grown up, refused to be known as the son of Pharaoh's daughter. He chose to be mistreated along with the people of God rather than to enjoy the pleasures of sin for a short time" (Hebrews 11:24–25). This statement alone speaks of Moses as a man of self-denial, whose self-control was the key to all God's blessings.

Self-control feeds the soul, and the soul lives forever. Indulgence feeds—and often overfeeds—the body until its years are shortened, its health is gone and it weeps that it lived for years but gleaned only a few minutes for God.

God enables the person of self-control to influence the world. The person who cannot or will not channel his or her own desires is soon controlled by such massive addictions so as to be of no use to anyone. To say yes to every temptation is to become a slave to our indulgences; it is to live for the trivial objective of serving ourselves.

16:4 will rain down bread from heaven[u] for
[u]Dt 8:3; Jn 6:31* you. The people are to go out each day
and gather enough for that day. In this
way I will test them and see whether
they will follow my instructions. 5On
the sixth day they are to prepare what
16:5 they bring in, and that is to be twice[v]
[v]ver 22 as much as they gather on the other
days."
6So Moses and Aaron said to all the
Israelites, "In the evening you will know
that it was the LORD who brought you
16:6 out of Egypt,[w] 7and in the morning
[w]Ex 6:6 you will see the glory[x] of the LORD,
16:7 [x]ver 10; because he has heard your grumbling[y]
Isa 35:2; 40:5 against him. Who are we, that you
[y]ver 12; Nu 14:2, should grumble against us?"[z] 8Moses
27,28 [z]Nu 16:11 also said, "You will know that it was the
LORD when he gives you meat to eat in
the evening and all the bread you want
in the morning, because he has heard
your grumbling against him. Who are
we? You are not grumbling against us,
16:8 but against the LORD."[a]
[a]1Sa 8:7; Ro 13:2 9Then Moses told Aaron, "Say to the
entire Israelite community, 'Come be-
fore the LORD, for he has heard your
grumbling.'"
10While Aaron was speaking to the
whole Israelite community, they looked
toward the desert, and there was the
16:10 glory[b] of the LORD appearing in the
[b]ver 7; Nu 16:19 cloud.[c]
[c]Ex 13:21; 1Ki 8:10 11The LORD said to Moses, 12"I have
heard the grumbling[d] of the Israelites.
16:12 Tell them, 'At twilight you will eat meat,
[d]ver 7 and in the morning you will be filled
16:13 [e]Nu 11:31; with bread. Then you will know that I
Ps 78:27-28; 105:40 am the LORD your God.'"
[f]Nu 11:9 13That evening quail[e] came and covered the camp, and in the morning
there was a layer of dew[f] around the
camp. 14When the dew was gone, thin
16:14 flakes like frost[g] on the ground ap-
[g]ver 31; Nu 11:7-9; peared on the desert floor. 15When the
Ps 105:40 Israelites saw it, they said to each other,
"What is it?" For they did not know
what it was.
16:15 Moses said to them, "It is the bread[h]
[h]ver 4; Jn 6:31 the LORD has given you to eat. 16This is
what the LORD has commanded: 'Each
one is to gather as much as he needs.
16:16 Take an omer[a][i] for each person you
[i]ver 32,36 have in your tent.'"
17The Israelites did as they were told;
some gathered much, some little. 18And
when they measured it by the omer, he
who gathered much did not have too
much, and he who gathered little did
not have too little.[j] Each one gathered 16:18
as much as he needed. [j]2Co 8:15*
19Then Moses said to them, "No one 16:19
is to keep any of it until morning."[k] [k]ver 23; Ex 12:10;
20However, some of them paid no at- 23:18
tention to Moses; they kept part of it
until morning, but it was full of maggots and began to smell. So Moses was
angry with them.
21Each morning everyone gathered as
much as he needed, and when the sun
grew hot, it melted away. 22On the sixth
day, they gathered twice[l] as much— 16:22
two omers[b] for each person—and the [l]ver 5 [m]Ex 34:31
leaders of the community[m] came and
reported this to Moses. 23He said to
them, "This is what the LORD commanded: 'Tomorrow is to be a day of
rest, a holy Sabbath[n] to the LORD. So 16:23 [n]Ge 2:3;
bake what you want to bake and boil Ex 20:8;
what you want to boil. Save whatever is 23:12; Lev 23:3
left and keep it until morning.'"
24So they saved it until morning, as
Moses commanded, and it did not stink
or get maggots in it. 25"Eat it today,"
Moses said, "because today is a Sabbath
to the LORD. You will not find any of
it on the ground today. 26Six days you
are to gather it, but on the seventh day, 16:26
the Sabbath,[o] there will not be any." [o]Ex 20:9-10
27Nevertheless, some of the people
went out on the seventh day to gather
it, but they found none. 28Then the
LORD said to Moses, "How long will
you[c] refuse to keep my commands[p] and 16:28 [p]2Ki 17:14;
my instructions? 29Bear in mind that Ps 78:10;
the LORD has given you the Sabbath; 106:13
that is why on the sixth day he gives
you bread for two days. Everyone is to
stay where he is on the seventh day; no
one is to go out." 30So the people rested
on the seventh day.
31The people of Israel called the bread
manna.[d][q] It was white like coriander 16:31 [q]Nu 11:7-9
seed and tasted like wafers made with
honey. 32Moses said, "This is what the
LORD has commanded: 'Take an omer
of manna and keep it for the generations to come, so they can see the bread
I gave you to eat in the desert when I
brought you out of Egypt.'"
33So Moses said to Aaron, "Take a jar

[a] *16* That is, probably about 2 quarts (about 2 liters); also in verses 18, 32, 33 and 36 [b] *22* That is, probably about 4 quarts (about 4.5 liters) [c] *28* The Hebrew is plural. [d] *31 Manna* means *What is it?* (see verse 15).

16:33 [r]Heb 9:4

and put an omer of manna[r] in it. Then place it before the LORD to be kept for the generations to come."

34 As the LORD commanded Moses, Aaron put the manna in front of the Testimony,[s] that it might be kept. 35 The Israelites ate manna[t] forty years,[u] until they came to a land that was settled; they ate manna until they reached the border of Canaan.[v]

16:34 [s]Ex 25:16, 21,22; 40:20; Nu 17:4,10
16:35 [t]Jn 6:31,49 [u]Ne 9:21 [v]Jos 5:12

36 (An omer is one tenth of an ephah.)

JOY

JOY AND THE MANNA JAR

Exodus 16:31

Celebrate God's providence. Praise him for his manna in whatever form it comes! It is the bread of his abundance.

***Manna* is a Hebrew word, they say.**
It means "What is this odd stuff anyway?"
Its taste is honey wafers,
Like coriander seed.
It's what grace puts on the plate
In our wilderness of need.

Water From the Rock

17 The whole Israelite community set out from the Desert of Sin,[w] traveling from place to place as the LORD commanded. They camped at Rephidim, but there was no water[x] for the people to drink. 2 So they quarreled with Moses and said, "Give us water[y] to drink."

17:1 [w]Ex 16:1 [x]Nu 33:14
17:2 [y]Nu 20:2 [z]Dt 6:16; Ps 78:18,41; 1Co 10:9

Moses replied, "Why do you quarrel with me? Why do you put the LORD to the test?"[z]

3 But the people were thirsty for water there, and they grumbled[a] against Moses. They said, "Why did you bring us up out of Egypt to make us and our children and livestock die of thirst?"

17:3 [a]Ex 15:24; 16:2-3

4 Then Moses cried out to the LORD, "What am I to do with these people? They are almost ready to stone[b] me."

17:4 [b]Nu 14:10; 1Sa 30:6

5 The LORD answered Moses, "Walk on ahead of the people. Take with you some of the elders of Israel and take in your hand the staff with which you struck the Nile,[c] and go. 6 I will stand there before you by the rock at Horeb. Strike the rock, and water[d] will come out of it for the people to drink." So Moses did this in the sight of the elders of Israel. 7 And he called the place Massah[a] and Meribah[b][e] because the Israelites quarreled and because they tested the LORD saying, "Is the LORD among us or not?"

17:5 [c]Ex 7:20
17:6 [d]Nu 20:11; Ps 114:8; 1Co 10:4
17:7 [e]Nu 20:13,24; Ps 81:7

The Amalekites Defeated

8 The Amalekites[f] came and attacked the Israelites at Rephidim. 9 Moses said to Joshua, "Choose some of our men and go out to fight the Amalekites. Tomorrow I will stand on top of the hill with the staff[g] of God in my hands."

17:8 [f]Ge 36:12; Dt 25:17-19
17:9 [g]Ex 4:17

10 So Joshua fought the Amalekites as Moses had ordered, and Moses, Aaron and Hur[h] went to the top of the hill. 11 As long as Moses held up his hands, the Israelites were winning,[i] but whenever he lowered his hands, the Amalekites were winning. 12 When Moses' hands grew tired, they took a stone and put it under him and he sat on it. Aaron and Hur held his hands up—one on one side, one on the other—so that his hands remained steady till sunset. 13 So Joshua overcame the Amalekite army with the sword.

17:10 [h]Ex 24:14
17:11 [i]Jas 5:16

14 Then the LORD said to Moses, "Write[j] this on a scroll as something to be remembered and make sure that Joshua hears it, because I will completely blot out the memory of Amalek[k] from under heaven."

17:14 [j]Ex 24:4; 34:27; Nu 33:2 [k]1Sa 15:3; 30:17-18

15 Moses built an altar and called it The LORD is my Banner. 16 He said, "For hands were lifted up to the throne of the LORD. The[c] LORD will be at war against the Amalekites from generation to generation."

Jethro Visits Moses

18 Now Jethro, the priest of Midian[l] and father-in-law of Moses, heard of everything God had done for Moses and for his people Israel, and how the LORD had brought Israel out of Egypt.

18:1 [l]Ex 2:16; 3:1

2 After Moses had sent away his wife Zipporah,[m] his father-in-law Jethro received her 3 and her two sons.[n] One son was named Gershom,[d] for Moses said, "I have become an alien in a foreign land";[o] 4 and the other was named

18:2 [m]Ex 2:21; 4:25
18:3 [n]Ex 4:20; Ac 7:29 [o]Ex 2:22

[a]7 *Massah* means *testing.* [b]7 *Meribah* means *quarreling.* [c]16 Or *"Because a hand was against the throne of the LORD, the* [d]3 *Gershom* sounds like the Hebrew for *an alien there.*

Eliezer,[a][p] for he said, "My father's God was my helper; he saved me from the sword of Pharaoh."

5 Jethro, Moses' father-in-law, together with Moses' sons and wife, came to him in the desert, where he was camped near the mountain[q] of God. 6 Jethro had sent word to him, "I, your father-in-law Jethro, am coming to you with your wife and her two sons."

7 So Moses went out to meet his father-in-law and bowed down[r] and kissed[s] him. They greeted each other and then went into the tent. 8 Moses told his father-in-law about everything the LORD had done to Pharaoh and the Egyptians for Israel's sake and about all the hardships they had met along the way and how the LORD had saved[t] them.

9 Jethro was delighted to hear about all the good things the LORD had done for Israel in rescuing them from the hand of the Egyptians. 10 He said, "Praise be to the LORD,[u] who rescued you from the hand of the Egyptians and of Pharaoh, and who rescued the people from the hand of the Egyptians. 11 Now I know that the LORD is greater than all other gods,[v] for he did this to those who had treated Israel arrogantly."[w] 12 Then Jethro, Moses' father-in-law, brought a burnt offering and other sacrifices to God, and Aaron came with all the elders of Israel to eat bread with Moses' father-in-law in the presence[x] of God.

13 The next day Moses took his seat to serve as judge for the people, and they stood around him from morning till evening. 14 When his father-in-law saw all that Moses was doing for the people, he said, "What is this you are doing for the people? Why do you alone sit as judge, while all these people stand around you from morning till evening?"

15 Moses answered him, "Because the people come to me to seek God's will.[y] 16 Whenever they have a dispute, it is brought to me, and I decide between the parties and inform them of God's decrees and laws."[z]

17 Moses' father-in-law replied, "What you are doing is not good. 18 You and these people who come to you will only wear yourselves out. The work is too heavy for you; you cannot handle it alone.[a] 19 Listen now to me and I will give you some advice, and may God be with you.[b] You must be the people's representative before God and bring their disputes[c] to him. 20 Teach them the decrees and laws,[d] and show them the way to live[e] and the duties they are to perform.[f] 21 But select capable men[g] from all the people—men who fear God, trustworthy men who hate dishonest gain[h]—and appoint them as officials[i] over thousands, hundreds, fifties and tens. 22 Have them serve as judges for the people at all times, but have them bring every difficult case[j] to you; the simple cases they can decide themselves. That will make your load lighter, because they will share[k] it with you. 23 If you do this and God so commands, you will be able to stand the strain, and all these people will go home satisfied."

FAITHFULNESS

THE ART OF DELEGATING

Exodus 18:17–23

Moses was "hyper-faithful," killing himself with micro-management. Jethro said to him, "It is neither godly nor smart to try to do everything yourself. Become a real leader. Delegate! Quit giving the world a vacation from responsibility. Call in a little help. Relax! Rest in your pilgrimage. Share your burden. Carry less. Praise more."

24 Moses listened to his father-in-law and did everything he said. 25 He chose capable men from all Israel and made them leaders of the people, officials over thousands, hundreds, fifties and tens.[l] 26 They served as judges for the people at all times. The difficult cases they brought to Moses, but the simple ones they decided themselves.[m]

27 Then Moses sent his father-in-law on his way, and Jethro returned to his own country.[n]

At Mount Sinai

19 In the third month after the Israelites left Egypt—on the very day—they came to the Desert of Sinai. 2 After they set out from Rephidim,[o] they entered the Desert of Sinai, and

18:4 [p]1Ch 23:15
18:5 [q]Ex 3:1
18:7 [r]Ge 43:28 [s]Ge 29:13
18:8 [t]Ex 15:6,16; Ps 81:7
18:10 [u]Ge 14:20; Ps 68:19-20
18:11 [v]Ex 12:12; 15:11; 2Ch 2:5 [w]Lk 1:51
18:12 [x]Dt 12:7
18:15 [y]Nu 9:6,8; Dt 17:8-13
18:16 [z]Lev 24:12
18:18 [a]Nu 11:11, 14,17
18:19 [b]Ex 3:12 [c]Nu 27:5
18:20 [d]Dt 5:1 [e]Ps 143:8 [f]Dt 1:18
18:21 [g]Ac 6:3 [h]Dt 16:19; Ps 15:5; Eze 18:8 [i]Dt 1:13,15; 2Ch 19:5-10
18:22 [j]Dt 1:17-18 [k]Nu 11:17
18:25 [l]Dt 1:13-15
18:26 [m]ver 22
18:27 [n]Nu 10:29-30
19:2 [o]Ex 17:1

[a]4 *Eliezer* means *my God is helper.*

WEEK 37

LOVE

1 DAY ONE

LOVE, THE UNCONDITIONAL LONGING OF GOD

Read Exodus 19:3–6

God is not passive in his romance with humankind. Do you object to the word *romance* as too human and too shallow to be applied to God? It is a reasonable objection because purely human love affairs often prove to be fickle and temporary. But consider the pure energy in the word *romance*. God is in love with us, and he loves us with an active and ardent passion.

In Hungary long ago there lived a young woman named Elizabeth and a young crusader named Louis. They fell in love, and their love was so celebrated in Hungarian history that it still is remembered as one of the great love affairs of all time. Elizabeth said that her passion for Louis knew no bounds and that every moment apart from him was a moment wasted. But, over the course of time, Louis left to serve in the crusades and was lost in war, never to return to Elizabeth.

Elizabeth at first pined deeply for Louis and lived in black, somber seclusion. But God was ever near to her during her bereavement, and soon Elizabeth began to turn the romantic affections she had once held for Louis upon Christ. She never married again, but her love for Christ prompted her to become one of the greatest ministers of all time. She lived as a kind of "Mother Teresa of Hungary," bearing the Word of God in counsel, in healing and in converting the lost. Ultimately she learned that the love of God was the most superior and undeserved love in the world.

Moses understood the deep passion God has for his people. He knew, well before the time of Saint Elizabeth of Hungary, that God's great love has about it an unconditional grandeur. If God could quit loving, he would quit being God. Therefore, Moses spoke these words of God to the Israelites: "You yourselves have seen what I did to Egypt, and how I carried you on eagles' wings and brought you to myself…Although the whole earth is mine, you will be for me a kingdom of priests and a holy nation."

> **MEMORIZE THIS WEEK**
>
> **SONG OF SONGS 2:4**
>
> ***He has taken me to the banquet hall, and his banner over me is love.***

2 DAY TWO

LOVE AND THE PURPOSE OF GOD IN MY LIFE

This passage constitutes, perhaps, the highest tribute in the Bible to human love. Yet there is nothing in the verbiage that detracts from the holy love that God gives freely to us. Which of us, upon receiving the glorious love of Christ at our conversion, did not breathe words that sounded much like, "Place me like a seal over your heart…"? Christ, in a storm of redeeming love, entered our hearts and there placed his calling—our purpose: to publish the Good News that God was in Christ loving us. *Turn to Song of Songs 8:6–7, page 786, for today's study.*

3 DAY THREE

LOVE AND MY RELATIONSHIP WITH CHRIST

In the morning when first your eyes welcome the light, are you not grateful for the love of Christ, so all-powerful that it awakens you to your birthright, your true home in the kingdom of God? Isn't it amazing that we, in our sin, did nothing to prompt this unmerited, unconditional display of divine affection? All we did was show up, and there was Jesus, redeeming, loving and filling us. The divine Godhead loved us just as though we deserved it. *Turn to Romans 5:5–8, page 1338, for today's study.*

4 DAY FOUR

LOVE AND MY SERVICE TO OTHERS

Ezekiel allows us to see that God's unconditional love takes "no pleasure in the death of anyone." God has too long been seen by some as a God who stands on the brink of hell and laughs while people perish. Such a mistaken view is a terrible scar on the face of holy love! Much to the contrary, God is in love with humankind, begging us to accept new hearts, to robe ourselves in new spirits and to get dressed for his good favor. *Turn to Ezekiel 18:30–32, page 971, for today's study.*

5 DAY FIVE

LOVE AND ITS PLACE IN MY PERSONAL WORSHIP

God is gracious and compassionate. He stands astride our weeping existence crying, "Return to me!" In his pursuit of us, cried poet Francis Thompson, God is as "the hound of heaven." Our Lord will never abandon that pursuit until his love has followed us into eternity. *Turn to Joel 2:12–13, page 1047, for today's study.*

Week 38, Joy, Focusing on a Higher Reality, begins on page 413, 1 Kings 18:20–21,38–39.
To begin a topical study on the Fruit of the Spirit, Love, turn to the Topical Index, page 1548.

Israel camped there in the desert in front of the mountain.[p]

3 Then Moses went up to God, and the LORD called[q] to him from the mountain and said, "This is what you are to say to the house of Jacob and what you are to tell the people of Israel: 4 'You yourselves have seen what I did to Egypt,[r] and how I carried you on eagles' wings[s] and brought you to myself. 5 Now if you obey me fully[t] and keep my covenant,[u] then out of all nations you will be my treasured possession.[v] Although the whole earth[w] is mine, 6 you[a] will be for me a kingdom of priests[x] and a holy nation.'[y] These are the words you are to speak to the Israelites."

7 So Moses went back and summoned the elders of the people and set before them all the words the LORD had commanded him to speak. 8 The people all responded together, "We will do everything the LORD has said."[z] So Moses brought their answer back to the LORD.

9 The LORD said to Moses, "I am going to come to you in a dense cloud,[a] so that the people will hear me speaking[b] with you and will always put their trust in you." Then Moses told the LORD what the people had said.

10 And the LORD said to Moses, "Go to the people and consecrate[c] them today and tomorrow. Have them wash their clothes[d] 11 and be ready by the third day,[e] because on that day the LORD will come down on Mount Sinai in the sight of all the people. 12 Put limits for the people around the mountain and tell them, 'Be careful that you do not go up the mountain or touch the foot of it. Whoever touches the mountain shall surely be put to death. 13 He shall surely be stoned[f] or shot with arrows; not a hand is to be laid on him. Whether man or animal, he shall not be permitted to live.' Only when the ram's horn sounds a long blast may they go up to the mountain."

14 After Moses had gone down the mountain to the people, he consecrated them, and they washed their clothes. 15 Then he said to the people, "Prepare yourselves for the third day. Abstain from sexual relations."

16 On the morning of the third day there was thunder and lightning, with a thick cloud over the mountain, and a very loud trumpet blast.[g] Everyone in the camp trembled.[h] 17 Then Moses led the people out of the camp to meet with God, and they stood at the foot of the mountain. 18 Mount Sinai was covered with smoke,[i] because the LORD descended on it in fire.[j] The smoke billowed up from it like smoke from a furnace,[k] the whole mountain[b] trembled[l] violently, 19 and the sound of the trumpet grew louder and louder. Then Moses spoke and the voice[m] of God answered[n] him.[c]

20 The LORD descended to the top of Mount Sinai and called Moses to the top of the mountain. So Moses went up 21 and the LORD said to him, "Go down and warn the people so they do not force their way through to see[o] the LORD and many of them perish. 22 Even the priests, who approach[p] the LORD, must consecrate themselves, or the LORD will break out against them."[q]

23 Moses said to the LORD, "The people cannot come up Mount Sinai, because you yourself warned us, 'Put limits[r] around the mountain and set it apart as holy.'"

24 The LORD replied, "Go down and bring Aaron[s] up with you. But the priests and the people must not force their way through to come up to the LORD, or he will break out against them."

25 So Moses went down to the people and told them.

The Ten Commandments

20 And God spoke all these words:

2 "I am the LORD your God,
who brought you out of
Egypt, out of the land of
slavery.[t]

3 "You shall have no other gods before[d] me.[u]

4 "You shall not make for yourself
an idol[v] in the form of anything in heaven above or
on the earth beneath or in
the waters below. 5 You shall
not bow down to them or

19:2 [p]Ex 3:1
19:3 [q]Ex 3:4; Ac 7:38
19:4 [r]Dt 29:2 [s]Isa 63:9
19:5 [t]Ex 15:26 [u]Dt 5:2 [v]Dt 14:2; Ps 135:4 [w]Ex 9:29; Dt 10:14
19:6 [x]1Pe 2:5 [y]Dt 7:6; 26:19; Isa 62:12
19:8 [z]Ex 24:3,7; Dt 5:27
19:9 [a]ver 16; Ex 24:15-16 [b]Dt 4:12,36
19:10 [c]Lev 11:44; Heb 10:22 [d]Ge 35:2
19:11 [e]ver 16
19:13 [f]Heb 12:20*
19:16 [g]Heb 12:18-19; Rev 4:1 [h]Heb 12:21
19:18 [i]Ps 104:32 [j]Ex 3:2; 24:17; Dt 4:11; 2Ch 7:1; Ps 18:8; Heb 12:18 [k]Ge 19:28 [l]Jdg 5:5; Ps 68:8; Jer 4:24
19:19 [m]Ne 9:13 [n]Ps 81:7
19:21 [o]Ex 3:5; 1Sa 6:19
19:22 [p]Lev 10:3 [q]2Sa 6:7
19:23 [r]ver 12
19:24 [s]Ex 24:1,9
20:2 [t]Ex 13:3
20:3 [u]Dt 6:14; Jer 35:15
20:4 [v]Lev 26:1; Dt 4:15-19, 23; 27:15

[a] 5,6 Or *possession, for the whole earth is mine.* [6] *You* [b] *18* Most Hebrew manuscripts; a few Hebrew manuscripts and Septuagint *all the people* [c] *19* Or *and God answered him with thunder* [d] *3* Or *besides*

worship[w] them; for I, the
LORD your God, am a jeal-
ous God,[x] punishing the
children for the sin of the fathers to the third and fourth
generation[y] of those who
hate me, 6 but showing love
to a thousand[z] ⌞generations⌟
of those who love me and
keep my commandments.

20:5 [w]Isa 44:15,17,19 [x]Ex 34:14; Dt 4:24 [y]Nu 14:18; Jer 32:18
20:6 [z]Dt 7:9

FAITHFULNESS

ADULTERY OF THE HEART

Exodus 20:3

Faith will not allow us to divide our devotion between the living God and our petty idolatries. What do you worship besides the living God? Take care. God will have all your love or none of it. Faith is monogamy of spirit. To love two gods at once is adultery of the heart.

7 "You shall not misuse the name
of the LORD your God, for
the LORD will not hold anyone guiltless who misuses his
name.[a]
8 "Remember the Sabbath[b] day by
keeping it holy. 9 Six days
you shall labor and do all
your work,[c] 10 but the seventh day is a Sabbath to
the LORD your God. On it
you shall not do any work,
neither you, nor your son
or daughter, nor your manservant or maidservant, nor
your animals, nor the alien
within your gates. 11 For in
six days the LORD made
the heavens and the earth,
the sea, and all that is in
them, but he rested[d] on the
seventh day. Therefore the
LORD blessed the Sabbath
day and made it holy.
12 "Honor your father and your
mother,[e] so that you may live
long in the land the LORD
your God is giving you.
13 "You shall not murder.[f]
14 "You shall not commit adultery.[g]
15 "You shall not steal.[h]
16 "You shall not give false testimony against your neighbor.[i]

20:7 [a]Lev 19:12; Mt 5:33
20:8 [b]Ex 31:13-16; Lev 26:2
20:9 [c]Ex 34:21; Lk 13:14
20:11 [d]Ge 2:2
20:12 [e]Mt 15:4*; Mk 7:10*; Eph 6:2
20:13 [f]Mt 5:21*; Ro 13:9*
20:14 [g]Mt 19:18*
20:15 [h]Lev 19:11,13; Mt 19:18*
20:16 [i]Ex 23:1,7; Mt 19:18*

17 "You shall not covet[j] your neighbor's house. You shall not
covet your neighbor's wife,
or his manservant or maidservant, his ox or donkey,
or anything that belongs to
your neighbor."

18 When the people saw the thunder
and lightning and heard the trumpet[k]
and saw the mountain in smoke, they
trembled with fear. They stayed at a
distance 19 and said to Moses, "Speak to
us yourself and we will listen. But do
not have God speak to us or we will
die."[l]
20 Moses said to the people, "Do not
be afraid. God has come to test you, so
that the fear[m] of God will be with you
to keep you from sinning."[n]
21 The people remained at a distance,
while Moses approached the thick darkness[o] where God was.

20:17 [j]Ro 7:7*; 13:9*; Eph 5:3
20:18 [k]Ex 19:16-19; Heb 12:18-19
20:19 [l]Dt 5:5,23-27; Gal 3:19
20:20 [m]Dt 4:10; Isa 8:13 [n]Pr 16:6
20:21 [o]Dt 5:22

LOVE

SMOKE ON THE MOUNTAIN

Exodus 20:18

Fear God even as you love him. Do not presume that the God who roared at Sinai can be folded inside your table napkin. He is not your pet deity. To crave his intimacy is to risk living almost unbearably close to his power. Love God, but remember that his love sometimes comes dressed in severity. His fire upon the altar of your heart will sometimes warm you; at other times, consume you.

Idols and Altars

22 Then the LORD said to Moses,
"Tell the Israelites this: 'You have seen
for yourselves that I have spoken to
you from heaven:[p] 23 Do not make any
gods to be alongside me;[q] do not make
for yourselves gods of silver or gods of
gold.[r]
24 " 'Make an altar of earth for me and
sacrifice on it your burnt offerings and
fellowship offerings,[a] your sheep and
goats and your cattle. Wherever I cause
my name[s] to be honored, I will come
to you and bless[t] you. 25 If you make an
altar of stones for me, do not build it
with dressed stones, for you will defile

20:22 [p]Ne 9:13
20:23 [q]ver 3 [r]Ex 32:4,8,31
20:24 [s]Dt 12:5; 16:6,11; 2Ch 6:6 [t]Ge 12:2

[a]*24* Traditionally *peace offerings*

20:25 [u]Dt 27:5-6

it if you use a tool[u] on it. 26 And do not go up to my altar on steps, lest your nakedness be exposed on it.'

21:1 [v]Dt 4:14

21

"These are the laws[v] you are to set before them:

Hebrew Servants

21:2 [w]Jer 34:8,14

2 "If you buy a Hebrew servant, he is to serve you for six years. But in the seventh year, he shall go free,[w] without paying anything. 3 If he comes alone, he is to go free alone; but if he has a wife when he comes, she is to go with him. 4 If his master gives him a wife and she bears him sons or daughters, the woman and her children shall belong to her master, and only the man shall go free.

21:5 [x]Dt 15:16
21:6 [y]Ex 22:8-9 [z]Ne 5:5

5 "But if the servant declares, 'I love my master and my wife and children and do not want to go free,'[x] 6 then his master must take him before the judges.[a][y] He shall take him to the door or the doorpost and pierce his ear with an awl. Then he will be his servant for life.[z]

21:10 [a]1Co 7:3-5

7 "If a man sells his daughter as a servant, she is not to go free as menservants do. 8 If she does not please the master who has selected her for himself,[b] he must let her be redeemed. He has no right to sell her to foreigners, because he has broken faith with her. 9 If he selects her for his son, he must grant her the rights of a daughter. 10 If he marries another woman, he must not deprive the first one of her food, clothing and marital rights.[a] 11 If he does not provide her with these three things, she is to go free, without any payment of money.

Personal Injuries

21:12 [b]Ge 9:6; Mt 26:52
21:13 [c]Nu 35:10-34; Dt 19:2-13; Jos 20:9; 1Sa 24:4,10,18
21:14 [d]Heb 10:26 [e]Dt 19:11-12; 1Ki 2:28-34

12 "Anyone who strikes a man and kills him shall surely be put to death.[b] 13 However, if he does not do it intentionally, but God lets it happen, he is to flee to a place[c] I will designate. 14 But if a man schemes and kills another man deliberately,[d] take him away from my altar and put him to death.[e]

21:16 [f]Ge 37:28 [g]Ex 22:4; Dt 24:7
21:17 [h]Lev 20:9-10; Mt 15:4*; Mk 7:10*

15 "Anyone who attacks[c] his father or his mother must be put to death.

16 "Anyone who kidnaps another and either sells[f] him or still has him when he is caught must be put to death.[g]

17 "Anyone who curses his father or mother must be put to death.[h]

18 "If men quarrel and one hits the other with a stone or with his fist[d] and he does not die but is confined to bed, 19 the one who struck the blow will not be held responsible if the other gets up and walks around outside with his staff; however, he must pay the injured man for the loss of his time and see that he is completely healed.

21:21 [i]Lev 25:44-46

20 "If a man beats his male or female slave with a rod and the slave dies as a direct result, he must be punished, 21 but he is not to be punished if the slave gets up after a day or two, since the slave is his property.[i]

21:22 [j]ver 30; Dt 22:18-19
21:23 [k]Lev 24:19; Dt 19:21
21:24 [l]Mt 5:38*

22 "If men who are fighting hit a pregnant woman and she gives birth prematurely[e] but there is no serious injury, the offender must be fined whatever the woman's husband demands[j] and the court allows. 23 But if there is serious injury, you are to take life for life,[k] 24 eye for eye, tooth for tooth,[l] hand for hand, foot for foot, 25 burn for burn, wound for wound, bruise for bruise.

26 "If a man hits a manservant or maidservant in the eye and destroys it, he must let the servant go free to compensate for the eye. 27 And if he knocks out the tooth of a manservant or maidservant, he must let the servant go free to compensate for the tooth.

21:28 [m]ver 32; Ge 9:5
21:30 [n]ver 22; Nu 35:31
21:32 [o]Zec 11:12-13; Mt 26:15; 27:3,9

28 "If a bull gores a man or a woman to death, the bull must be stoned to death,[m] and its meat must not be eaten. But the owner of the bull will not be held responsible. 29 If, however, the bull has had the habit of goring and the owner has been warned but has not kept it penned up and it kills a man or woman, the bull must be stoned and the owner also must be put to death. 30 However, if payment is demanded of him, he may redeem his life by paying whatever is demanded.[n] 31 This law also applies if the bull gores a son or daughter. 32 If the bull gores a male or female slave, the owner must pay thirty shekels[f][o] of silver to the master of the slave, and the bull must be stoned.

33 "If a man uncovers a pit or digs one and fails to cover it and an ox or a donkey falls into it, 34 the owner of

[a]6 Or *before God* [b]8 Or *master so that he does not choose her* [c]15 Or *kills* [d]18 Or *with a tool* [e]22 Or *she has a miscarriage* [f]32 That is, about 12 ounces (about 0.3 kilogram)

the pit must pay for the loss; he must pay its owner, and the dead animal will be his.

35 "If a man's bull injures the bull of another and it dies, they are to sell the live one and divide both the money and the dead animal equally. 36 However, if it was known that the bull had the habit of goring, yet the owner did not keep it penned up, the owner must pay, animal for animal, and the dead animal will be his.

Protection of Property

22 "If a man steals an ox or a sheep and slaughters it or sells it, he must pay back[p] five head of cattle for the ox and four sheep for the sheep.

2 "If a thief is caught breaking in[q] and is struck so that he dies, the defender is not guilty of bloodshed;[r] 3 but if it happens[a] after sunrise, he is guilty of bloodshed.

"A thief must certainly make restitution, but if he has nothing, he must be sold[s] to pay for his theft.

4 "If the stolen animal is found alive in his possession—whether ox or donkey or sheep—he must pay back double.[t]

5 "If a man grazes his livestock in a field or vineyard and lets them stray and they graze in another man's field, he must make restitution from the best of his own field or vineyard.

6 "If a fire breaks out and spreads into thornbushes so that it burns shocks of grain or standing grain or the whole field, the one who started the fire must make restitution.

7 "If a man gives his neighbor silver or goods for safekeeping and they are stolen from the neighbor's house, the thief, if he is caught, must pay back double.[u] 8 But if the thief is not found, the owner of the house must appear before the judges[b][v] to determine whether he has laid his hands on the other man's property. 9 In all cases of illegal possession of an ox, a donkey, a sheep, a garment, or any other lost property about which somebody says, 'This is mine,' both parties are to bring their cases before the judges.[w] The one whom the judges declare[c] guilty must pay back double to his neighbor.

10 "If a man gives a donkey, an ox, a sheep or any other animal to his neighbor for safekeeping and it dies or is injured or is taken away while no one is looking, 11 the issue between them will be settled by the taking of an oath[x] before the LORD that the neighbor did not lay hands on the other person's property. The owner is to accept this, and no restitution is required. 12 But if the animal was stolen from the neighbor, he must make restitution to the owner. 13 If it was torn to pieces by a wild animal, he shall bring in the remains as evidence and he will not be required to pay for the torn animal.[y]

14 "If a man borrows an animal from his neighbor and it is injured or dies while the owner is not present, he must make restitution. 15 But if the owner is with the animal, the borrower will not have to pay. If the animal was hired, the money paid for the hire covers the loss.

Social Responsibility

16 "If a man seduces a virgin[z] who is not pledged to be married and sleeps with her, he must pay the bride-price, and she shall be his wife. 17 If her father absolutely refuses to give her to him, he must still pay the bride-price for virgins.

18 "Do not allow a sorceress[a] to live.

19 "Anyone who has sexual relations with an animal[b] must be put to death.

20 "Whoever sacrifices to any god other than the LORD must be destroyed.[d][c]

21 "Do not mistreat an alien[d] or oppress him, for you were aliens[e] in Egypt.

22 "Do not take advantage of a widow or an orphan.[f] 23 If you do and they cry out[g] to me, I will certainly hear their cry.[h] 24 My anger will be aroused, and I will kill you with the sword; your wives will become widows and your children fatherless.[i]

25 "If you lend money to one of my people among you who is needy, do not be like a moneylender; charge him no interest.[e][j] 26 If you take your neighbor's cloak as a pledge,[k] return it to him by sunset, 27 because his cloak is the only covering he has for his body. What else will he sleep in? When he cries out

22:1 [p]2Sa 12:6; Pr 6:31; Lk 19:8
22:2 [q]Mt 6:19-20; 24:43 [r]Nu 35:27
22:3 [s]Ex 21:2; Mt 18:25
22:4 [t]Ge 43:12
22:7 [u]ver 4
22:8 [v]Ex 21:6; Dt 17:8-9; 19:17
22:9 [w]ver 28; Dt 25:1
22:11 [x]Heb 6:16
22:13 [y]Ge 31:39
22:16 [z]Dt 22:28
22:18 [a]Lev 20:27; Dt 18:11; 1Sa 28:3
22:19 [b]Lev 18:23; Dt 27:21
22:20 [c]Dt 17:2-5
22:21 [d]Lev 19:33 [e]Dt 10:19
22:22 [f]Dt 24:6,10, 12,17
22:23 [g]Lk 18:7 [h]Dt 15:9; Ps 18:6
22:24 [i]Ps 69:24; 109:9
22:25 [j]Lev 25:35-37; Dt 23:20; Ps 15:5
22:26 [k]Dt 24:6

[a]3 Or *if he strikes him* [b]8 Or *before God;* also in verse 9 [c]9 Or *whom God declares* [d]20 The Hebrew term refers to the irrevocable giving over of things or persons to the LORD, often by totally destroying them. [e]25 Or *excessive interest*

DAY 4 FOUR

Patience and My Service to Others

Exodus 23:9

We were all at one time strangers to God. We all once needed someone to save us. But now we are rescued and called by the Savior to go and rescue others. To be effective in our callings, we must not forget what it felt like to be an alien, a stranger. It has long been noted that those who have most recently come to Christ are the most motivated to try to win others. Why? Probably because those newest in their salvation still remember what it was like to be lost.

Most of those who exclude others from their social circles have never lived as an outcast. Cherish the times you have been lonely, for such experiences have been your teachers. Their lessons were painful, but they have left you more human. When you had hurt enough, you knew you would never want one other person to have to endure what you had been through.

Here in Exodus Moses counsels the Israelites to remember that for 400 years they have been exiles and foreigners in Egypt. Surely their four-century period of bondage has softened their hearts toward the strangers in their midst. If they will remember how they lived before God rescued them in the exodus, surely they can feel compassion for all of those still living beyond the community of God.

Small wonder E. A. Robinson wrote,

He drew a circle that shut me out,
A rebel, heretic, thing to flout.
But love and I had the wit to win
We drew a circle that shut him in.

As Christians, it is our job to "shut in" those around us. When we understand that hard times are our teachers, and we bear those times with patience, we can pass along that understanding to others. We can bring others into our world and close around them the arms of love and peace that we also have experienced.

To begin a study on the topic of Patience, the Art of Waiting on God, turn to the home page on page 1500.

to me, I will hear, for I am compassionate.[l]
28"Do not blaspheme God[a][m] or curse
the ruler of your people.[n]
29"Do not hold back offerings[o] from
your granaries or your vats.[b]
"You must give me the firstborn of
your sons.[p] 30Do the same with your
cattle and your sheep.[q] Let them stay
with their mothers for seven days, but
give them to me on the eighth day.[r]
31"You are to be my holy people.[s] So
do not eat the meat of an animal torn
by wild beasts;[t] throw it to the dogs.

Laws of Justice and Mercy

23 "Do not spread false reports.[u]
Do not help a wicked man by
being a malicious witness.[v]
2"Do not follow the crowd in doing
wrong. When you give testimony in a
lawsuit, do not pervert justice[w] by siding with the crowd, 3and do not show
favoritism to a poor man in his lawsuit.
4"If you come across your enemy's
ox or donkey wandering off, be sure
to take it back to him.[x] 5If you see
the donkey[y] of someone who hates you
fallen down under its load, do not leave
it there; be sure you help him with it.
6"Do not deny justice[z] to your poor
people in their lawsuits. 7Have nothing
to do with a false charge[a] and do not
put an innocent or honest person to
death, for I will not acquit the guilty.
8"Do not accept a bribe,[b] for a bribe
blinds those who see and twists the
words of the righteous.
9"Do not oppress an alien;[c] you yourselves know how it feels to be aliens, because you were aliens in Egypt.

Sabbath Laws

10"For six years you are to sow your
fields and harvest the crops, 11but during the seventh year let the land lie
unplowed and unused. Then the poor
among your people may get food from
it, and the wild animals may eat what
they leave. Do the same with your vineyard and your olive grove.
12"Six days do your work,[d] but on
the seventh day do not work, so that
your ox and your donkey may rest and

22:27 [l]Ex 34:6
22:28 [m]Lev 24:11,16 [n]Ecc 10:20; Ac 23:5*
22:29 [o]Ex 23:15, 16,19 [p]Ex 13:2
22:30 [q]Ex 13:12; Dt 15:19 [r]Lev 22:27
22:31 [s]Lev 19:2 [t]Eze 4:14
23:1 [u]Ex 20:16; Ps 101:5 [v]Ps 35:11; Ac 6:11
23:2 [w]Dt 16:19
23:4 [x]Dt 22:1-3
23:5 [y]Dt 22:4
23:6 [z]ver 2
23:7 [a]Eph 4:25
23:8 [b]Dt 10:17; 16:19; Pr 15:27
23:9 [c]Ex 22:21
23:12 [d]Ex 20:9

[a]28 Or *Do not revile the judges* [b]29 The meaning of the Hebrew for this phrase is uncertain.

the slave born in your household, and
the alien as well, may be refreshed.
23:13 [e]1Ti 4:16 13"Be careful[e] to do everything I have
said to you. Do not invoke the names
of other gods; do not let them be heard
on your lips.

The Three Annual Festivals

23:14 [f]Ex 34:23,24 14"Three times[f] a year you are to celebrate a festival to me.

JOY

PRAISE TO BE COPIED AND PUBLISHED

Exodus 23:14

"Three times a year celebrate a festival to me," cried God. But who, in all honesty, could muzzle joy in between times? Only three times a year? No, it is too little. Let us praise him three times a day; nay, three times an hour. No, let us never cease celebrating.

15"Celebrate the Feast of Unleavened
23:15 [g]Ex 12:17 [h]Ex 34:20 Bread;[g] for seven days eat bread made
without yeast, as I commanded you.
Do this at the appointed time in the
month of Abib, for in that month you
came out of Egypt.
"No one is to appear before me
empty-handed.[h]
16"Celebrate the Feast of Harvest
23:16 [i]Ex 34:22 [j]Dt 16:13 with the firstfruits[i] of the crops you sow
in your field.
"Celebrate the Feast of Ingathering
at the end of the year, when you gather
in your crops from the field.[j]
23:17 [k]Dt 16:16 17"Three times[k] a year all the men are
to appear before the Sovereign LORD.
18"Do not offer the blood of a sacrifice to me along with anything contain-
23:18 [l]Ex 34:25 [m]Dt 16:4 ing yeast.[l]
"The fat of my festival offerings must
not be kept until morning.[m]
19"Bring the best of the firstfruits[n]
23:19 [n]Ex 22:29; Dt 26:2,10 [o]Dt 14:21 of your soil to the house of the LORD
your God.
"Do not cook a young goat in its
mother's milk.[o]

God's Angel to Prepare the Way

23:20 [p]Ex 14:19; 32:34 [q]Ex 15:17 20"See, I am sending an angel[p] ahead
of you to guard you along the way
and to bring you to the place I have
23:21 [r]Nu 14:11; Dt 18:19 prepared.[q] 21Pay attention to him and
listen[r] to what he says. Do not rebel
against him; he will not forgive your
rebellion,[s] since my Name is in him. 23:21 [s]Ps 78:8,40,56
22If you listen carefully to what he says
and do all that I say, I will be an enemy[t] 23:22 [t]Ge 12:3; Dt 30:7
to your enemies and will oppose those
who oppose you. 23My angel will go
ahead of you and bring you into the
land of the Amorites, Hittites, Periz-
zites, Canaanites, Hivites and Jebusites,[u] 23:23 [u]ver 20; Jos 24:8,11
and I will wipe them out. 24Do not
bow down before their gods or wor- 23:24 [v]Ex 20:5 [w]Dt 12:30-31 [x]Ex 34:13; Nu 33:52
ship[v] them or follow their practices.[w]
You must demolish[x] them and break
their sacred stones to pieces. 25Worship
the LORD your God,[y] and his blessing[z] 23:25 [y]Dt 6:13; Mt 4:10 [z]Dt 7:12-15; 28:1-14 [a]Ex 15:26
will be on your food and water. I will
take away sickness[a] from among you,
26and none will miscarry or be barren[b]
in your land. I will give you a full life 23:26 [b]Dt 7:14; Mal 3:11 [c]Job 5:26
span.[c]
27"I will send my terror[d] ahead of you
and throw into confusion[e] every nation 23:27 [d]Ex 15:14; Dt 2:25 [e]Dt 7:23
you encounter. I will make all your en-
emies turn their backs and run. 28I will
send the hornet[f] ahead of you to drive 23:28 [f]Dt 7:20; Jos 24:12
the Hivites, Canaanites and Hittites out
of your way. 29But I will not drive them
out in a single year, because the land
would become desolate and the wild
animals[g] too numerous for you. 30Lit- 23:29 [g]Dt 7:22
tle by little I will drive them out before
you, until you have increased enough
to take possession of the land.
31"I will establish your borders from
the Red Sea[a] to the Sea of the Philistines,[b] and from the desert to the
River.[c][h] I will hand over to you the peo- 23:31 [h]Ge 15:18 [i]Jos 21:44; 24:12,18
ple who live in the land and you will
drive them out[i] before you. 32Do not
make a covenant[j] with them or with 23:32 [j]Ex 34:12; Dt 7:2
their gods. 33Do not let them live in
your land, or they will cause you to sin 23:33 [k]Dt 7:16; Ps 106:36
against me, because the worship of their
gods will certainly be a snare[k] to you."

The Covenant Confirmed

24 Then he said to Moses, "Come
up to the LORD, you and Aar-
on, Nadab and Abihu,[l] and seventy of 24:1 [l]Ex 6:23; Lev 10:1-2 [m]Nu 11:16
the elders[m] of Israel. You are to wor-
ship at a distance, 2but Moses alone is
to approach the LORD; the others must
not come near. And the people may not
come up with him."
3When Moses went and told the people all the LORD's words and laws, they

[a]*31* Hebrew *Yam Suph*; that is, Sea of Reeds
[b]*31* That is, the Mediterranean [c]*31* That is, the Euphrates

responded with one voice, "Everything
the LORD has said we will do."[n] 4Moses
then wrote[o] down everything the LORD
had said.
He got up early the next morning
and built an altar at the foot of the
mountain and set up twelve stone pillars[p] representing the twelve tribes of
Israel. 5Then he sent young Israelite
men, and they offered burnt offerings
and sacrificed young bulls as fellowship offerings[a] to the LORD. 6Moses
took half of the blood[q] and put it in
bowls, and the other half he sprinkled
on the altar. 7Then he took the Book
of the Covenant[r] and read it to the
people. They responded, "We will do
everything the LORD has said; we will
obey."
8Moses then took the blood, sprinkled it on the people and said, "This
is the blood of the covenant[s] that the
LORD has made with you in accordance
with all these words."
9Moses and Aaron, Nadab and Abihu, and the seventy elders[t] of Israel
went up 10and saw[u] the God of Israel.
Under his feet was something like a
pavement made of sapphire,[b][v] clear as
the sky[w] itself. 11But God did not raise
his hand against these leaders of the Israelites; they saw[x] God, and they ate
and drank.
12The LORD said to Moses, "Come
up to me on the mountain and stay
here, and I will give you the tablets of
stone,[y] with the law and commands I
have written for their instruction."
13Then Moses set out with Joshua[z]
his aide, and Moses went up on the
mountain[a] of God. 14He said to the elders, "Wait here for us until we come
back to you. Aaron and Hur are with
you, and anyone involved in a dispute
can go to them."
15When Moses went up on the mountain, the cloud[b] covered it, 16and the
glory[c] of the LORD settled on Mount
Sinai. For six days the cloud covered
the mountain, and on the seventh day
the LORD called to Moses from within
the cloud.[d] 17To the Israelites the glory
of the LORD looked like a consuming
fire[e] on top of the mountain. 18Then
Moses entered the cloud as he went
on up the mountain. And he stayed
on the mountain forty[f] days and forty
nights.[g]

24:3 [n]Ex 19:8; Dt 5:27
24:4 [o]Dt 31:9 [p]Ge 28:18
24:6 [q]Heb 9:18
24:7 [r]Heb 9:19
24:8 [s]Heb 9:20*; 1Pe 1:2
24:9 [t]ver 1
24:10 [u]Mt 17:2; Jn 1:18; 6:46 [v]Eze 1:26 [w]Rev 4:3
24:11 [x]Ge 32:30; Ex 19:21
24:12 [y]Ex 32:15-16
24:13 [z]Ex 17:9 [a]Ex 3:1
24:15 [b]Ex 19:9
24:16 [c]Ex 16:10 [d]Ps 99:7
24:17 [e]Ex 3:2; Dt 4:36; Heb 12:18,29
24:18 [f]Dt 9:9 [g]Ex 34:28

Offerings for the Tabernacle

25 The LORD said to Moses, 2"Tell
the Israelites to bring me an offering. You are to receive the offering
for me from each man whose heart
prompts[h] him to give. 3These are the
offerings you are to receive from them:
gold, silver and bronze; 4blue, purple
and scarlet yarn and fine linen; goat
hair; 5ram skins dyed red and hides of
sea cows[c]; acacia wood; 6olive oil[i] for
the light; spices for the anointing oil
and for the fragrant incense; 7and onyx
stones and other gems to be mounted
on the ephod[j] and breastpiece.[k]
8"Then have them make a sanctuary[l]
for me, and I will dwell[m] among them.
9Make this tabernacle and all its furnishings exactly like the pattern[n] I will
show you.

The Ark

10"Have them make a chest[o] of acacia wood—two and a half cubits long,
a cubit and a half wide, and a cubit
and a half high.[d] 11Overlay it with pure
gold, both inside and out, and make
a gold molding around it. 12Cast four
gold rings for it and fasten them to its
four feet, with two rings on one side
and two rings on the other. 13Then
make poles of acacia wood and overlay
them with gold. 14Insert the poles into
the rings on the sides of the chest to
carry it. 15The poles are to remain in
the rings of this ark; they are not to be
removed.[p] 16Then put in the ark the
Testimony,[q] which I will give you.
17"Make an atonement cover[e][r] of pure
gold—two and a half cubits long and a
cubit and a half wide.[f] 18And make two
cherubim out of hammered gold at the
ends of the cover. 19Make one cherub on
one end and the second cherub on the
other; make the cherubim of one piece
with the cover, at the two ends. 20The
cherubim are to have their wings spread
upward, overshadowing[s] the cover with
them. The cherubim are to face each
other, looking toward the cover. 21Place
the cover on top of the ark[t] and put
in the ark the Testimony,[u] which I will

25:2 [h]Ex 35:21; 1Ch 29:5,7,9; Ezr 2:68; 2Co 8:11-12; 9:7
25:6 [i]Ex 27:20; 30:22-32
25:7 [j]Ex 28:4,6-14 [k]Ex 28:15-30
25:8 [l]Ex 36:1-5; Heb 9:1-2 [m]Ex 29:45; 1Ki 6:13; 2Co 6:16; Rev 21:3
25:9 [n]ver 40; Ac 7:44; Heb 8:5
25:10 [o]Dt 10:1-5; Heb 9:4
25:15 [p]1Ki 8:8
25:16 [q]Dt 31:26; Heb 9:4
25:17 [r]Ro 3:25
25:20 [s]1Ki 8:7; 1Ch 28:18; Heb 9:5
25:21 [t]Ex 26:34 [u]ver 16

[a]5 Traditionally *peace offerings* [b]*10* Or *lapis lazuli* [c]5 That is, dugongs [d]*10* That is, about 3 3/4 feet (about 1.1 meters) long and 2 1/4 feet (about 0.7 meter) wide and high [e]*17* Traditionally *a mercy seat* [f]*17* That is, about 3 3/4 feet (about 1.1 meters) long and 2 1/4 feet (about 0.7 meter) wide

25:22 [v]Nu 7:89; 1Sa 4:4; 2Sa 6:2; 2Ki 19:15; Ps 80:1; Isa 37:16 [w]Ex 29:42-43 give you. 22There, above the cover between the two cherubim[v] that are over
the ark of the Testimony, I will meet[w]
with you and give you all my commands for the Israelites.

GOODNESS

SINLESSNESS AND NEEDINESS

Exodus 25:13

The priests were instructed to carry the ark with poles in rings. Why? Because God's holiness must never be touched by human sinfulness. "Holy, Holy, Holy" is the anthem of the ark. "I Need Thee Every Hour" is the desperate hymn of those who carried it. Draw near to God, but respect the rings and poles that separate us from his untouchable majesty. Fear him, love him; respect him and live.

The Table

25:23 [x]Heb 9:2 23"Make a table[x] of acacia wood—
two cubits long, a cubit wide and a cubit and a half high.[a] 24Overlay it with
pure gold and make a gold molding
around it. 25Also make around it a rim
a handbreadth[b] wide and put a gold
molding on the rim. 26Make four gold
rings for the table and fasten them to
the four corners, where the four legs
are. 27The rings are to be close to the
rim to hold the poles used in carrying
the table. 28Make the poles of acacia
wood, overlay them with gold and carry
the table with them. 29And make its
plates and dishes of pure gold, as well as
its pitchers and bowls for the pouring
25:29 [y]Nu 4:7 out of offerings.[y] 30Put the bread of the
Presence[z] on this table to be before me
25:30 [z]Lev 24:5-9 at all times.

The Lampstand

25:31 [a]1Ki 7:49; Zec 4:2; Heb 9:2; Rev 1:12 31"Make a lampstand[a] of pure gold
and hammer it out, base and shaft; its
flowerlike cups, buds and blossoms shall
be of one piece with it. 32Six branches
are to extend from the sides of the lampstand—three on one side and three on
the other. 33Three cups shaped like almond flowers with buds and blossoms
are to be on one branch, three on the
next branch, and the same for all six
branches extending from the lampstand.
34And on the lampstand there are to
be four cups shaped like almond flowers with buds and blossoms. 35One bud
shall be under the first pair of branches
extending from the lampstand, a second
bud under the second pair, and a third
bud under the third pair—six branches
in all. 36The buds and branches shall
all be of one piece with the lampstand,
hammered out of pure gold.
37"Then make its seven lamps[b] and 25:37 [b]Ex 27:21; Lev 24:3-4; Nu 8:2
set them up on it so that they light the
space in front of it. 38Its wick trimmers
and trays are to be of pure gold. 39A
talent[c] of pure gold is to be used for
the lampstand and all these accessories.
40See that you make them according to
the pattern[c] shown you on the moun- 25:40 [c]Ex 26:30; Nu 8:4; Ac 7:44; Heb 8:5*
tain.

The Tabernacle

26 "Make the tabernacle with ten
curtains of finely twisted linen
and blue, purple and scarlet yarn, with
cherubim worked into them by a skilled
craftsman. 2All the curtains are to be
the same size—twenty-eight cubits long
and four cubits wide.[d] 3Join five of the
curtains together, and do the same with
the other five. 4Make loops of blue material along the edge of the end curtain
in one set, and do the same with the
end curtain in the other set. 5Make fifty
loops on one curtain and fifty loops on
the end curtain of the other set, with
the loops opposite each other. 6Then
make fifty gold clasps and use them to
fasten the curtains together so that the
tabernacle is a unit.
7"Make curtains of goat hair for the
tent over the tabernacle—eleven altogether. 8All eleven curtains are to be the
same size—thirty cubits long and four
cubits wide.[e] 9Join five of the curtains
together into one set and the other six
into another set. Fold the sixth curtain
double at the front of the tent. 10Make
fifty loops along the edge of the end
curtain in one set and also along the
edge of the end curtain in the other set.
11Then make fifty bronze clasps and put
them in the loops to fasten the tent together as a unit. 12As for the additional

[a]*23* That is, about 3 feet (about 0.9 meter) long and 1 1/2 feet (about 0.5 meter) wide and 2 1/4 feet (about 0.7 meter) high [b]*25* That is, about 3 inches (about 8 centimeters) [c]*39* That is, about 75 pounds (about 34 kilograms) [d]*2* That is, about 42 feet (about 12.5 meters) long and 6 feet (about 1.8 meters) wide [e]*8* That is, about 45 feet (about 13.5 meters) long and 6 feet (about 1.8 meters) wide

length of the tent curtains, the half curtain that is left over is to hang down
at the rear of the tabernacle. 13The tent
curtains will be a cubit[a] longer on both
sides; what is left will hang over the
sides of the tabernacle so as to cover it.
14Make for the tent a covering of ram
skins dyed red, and over that a covering
26:14 of hides of sea cows.[b][d]
[d]Ex 36:19; Nu 4:25 15"Make upright frames of acacia
wood for the tabernacle. 16Each frame
is to be ten cubits long and a cubit
and a half wide,[c] 17with two projections
set parallel to each other. Make all the
frames of the tabernacle in this way.
18Make twenty frames for the south side
of the tabernacle 19and make forty silver bases to go under them—two bases
for each frame, one under each projection. 20For the other side, the north
side of the tabernacle, make twenty
frames 21and forty silver bases—two
under each frame. 22Make six frames
for the far end, that is, the west end of
the tabernacle, 23and make two frames
for the corners at the far end. 24At
these two corners they must be double
from the bottom all the way to the
top, and fitted into a single ring; both
shall be like that. 25So there will be
eight frames and sixteen silver bases—
two under each frame.
26"Also make crossbars of acacia
wood: five for the frames on one side
of the tabernacle, 27five for those on the
other side, and five for the frames on
the west, at the far end of the tabernacle. 28The center crossbar is to extend
from end to end at the middle of the
frames. 29Overlay the frames with gold
and make gold rings to hold the crossbars. Also overlay the crossbars with
26:30 gold.
[e]Ex 25:9,40; Ac 7:44; Heb 8:5 30"Set up the tabernacle according to
the plan[e] shown you on the mountain.
31"Make a curtain[f] of blue, purple
26:31 and scarlet yarn and finely twisted lin-
[f]2Ch 3:14; Mt 27:51; Heb 9:3 [g]Ex 36:35 en, with cherubim[g] worked into it by a
skilled craftsman. 32Hang it with gold
hooks on four posts of acacia wood
26:33 overlaid with gold and standing on four
[h]Ex 40:3,21; Lev 16:2 [i]Heb 9:2-3 silver bases. 33Hang the curtain from
the clasps and place the ark of the Testi-
26:34 mony behind the curtain.[h] The curtain
[j]Ex 25:21; 40:20; Heb 9:5 will separate the Holy Place from the
Most Holy Place.[i] 34Put the atonement
26:35 cover[j] on the ark of the Testimony in
[k]Heb 9:2 the Most Holy Place. 35Place the table[k]
outside the curtain on the north side of
the tabernacle and put the lampstand[l] 26:35 [l]Ex 40:22,24
opposite it on the south side.
36"For the entrance to the tent make
a curtain of blue, purple and scarlet
yarn and finely twisted linen—the work
of an embroiderer. 37Make gold hooks
for this curtain and five posts of acacia
wood overlaid with gold. And cast five
bronze bases for them.

GOODNESS

THE HUGE, HEAVY CURTAIN

Exodus 26:33

The curtain of God's sanctity separated the Holy Place and the Most Holy Place. God dwelt in awesome splendor and holiness beyond this separating veil.

Yet now our Lord has left us free
To face the ark of mystery.
Tidal grace has split the curtain,
Making all our access certain.

The Altar of Burnt Offering

27 "Build an altar[m] of acacia wood,
three cubits[d] high; it is to be 27:1 [m]Eze 43:13
square, five cubits long and five cubits
wide.[e] 2Make a horn[n] at each of the 27:2 [n]Ps 118:27
four corners, so that the horns and
the altar are of one piece, and overlay
the altar with bronze. 3Make all its
utensils of bronze—its pots to remove
the ashes, and its shovels, sprinkling
bowls, meat forks and firepans. 4Make
a grating for it, a bronze network, and
make a bronze ring at each of the four
corners of the network. 5Put it under
the ledge of the altar so that it is halfway up the altar. 6Make poles of acacia
wood for the altar and overlay them
with bronze. 7The poles are to be inserted into the rings so they will be on
two sides of the altar when it is carried.
8Make the altar hollow, out of boards.
It is to be made just as you were shown[o] 27:8 [o]Ex 25:9,40
on the mountain.

The Courtyard

9"Make a courtyard for the tabernacle. The south side shall be a hundred

[a] *13* That is, about 1 1/2 feet (about 0.5 meter)
[b] *14* That is, dugongs
[c] *16* That is, about 15 feet (about 4.5 meters) long and 2 1/4 feet (about 0.7 meter) wide
[d] *1* That is, about 4 1/2 feet (about 1.3 meters)
[e] *1* That is, about 7 1/2 feet (about 2.3 meters) long and wide

cubits[a] long and is to have curtains of finely twisted linen, 10 with twenty posts and twenty bronze bases and with silver hooks and bands on the posts. 11 The north side shall also be a hundred cubits long and is to have curtains, with twenty posts and twenty bronze bases and with silver hooks and bands on the posts.

12 "The west end of the courtyard shall be fifty cubits[b] wide and have curtains, with ten posts and ten bases. 13 On the east end, toward the sunrise, the courtyard shall also be fifty cubits wide. 14 Curtains fifteen cubits[c] long are to be on one side of the entrance, with three posts and three bases, 15 and curtains fifteen cubits long are to be on the other side, with three posts and three bases.

16 "For the entrance to the courtyard, provide a curtain twenty cubits[d] long, of blue, purple and scarlet yarn and finely twisted linen—the work of an embroiderer—with four posts and four bases. 17 All the posts around the courtyard are to have silver bands and hooks, and bronze bases. 18 The courtyard shall be a hundred cubits long and fifty cubits wide,[e] with curtains of finely twisted linen five cubits[f] high, and with bronze bases. 19 All the other articles used in the service of the tabernacle, whatever their function, including all the tent pegs for it and those for the courtyard, are to be of bronze.

Oil for the Lampstand

20 "Command the Israelites to bring you clear oil of pressed olives for the light so that the lamps may be kept burning. 21 In the Tent of Meeting,[p] outside the curtain that is in front of the Testimony,[q] Aaron and his sons are to keep the lamps[r] burning before the LORD from evening till morning. This is to be a lasting ordinance[s] among the Israelites for the generations to come.

27:21 [p]Ex 28:43 [q]Ex 26:31,33 [r]Ex 25:37; 30:8; 1Sa 3:3; 2Ch 13:11 [s]Ex 29:9; Lev 3:17; 16:34; Nu 18:23; 19:21

The Priestly Garments

28 "Have Aaron[t] your brother brought to you from among the Israelites, along with his sons Nadab and Abihu, Eleazar and Ithamar, so they may serve me as priests.[u] 2 Make sacred garments[v] for your brother Aaron, to give him dignity and honor. 3 Tell all the skilled men[w] to whom I have given wisdom[x] in such matters that they are to make garments for Aaron, for his consecration, so he may serve me as priest. 4 These are the garments they are to make: a breastpiece,[y] an ephod, a robe,[z] a woven tunic,[a] a turban and a sash. They are to make these sacred garments for your brother Aaron and his sons, so they may serve me as priests. 5 Have them use gold, and blue, purple and scarlet yarn, and fine linen.

28:1 [t]Heb 5:4 [u]Nu 18:1-7; Heb 5:1

28:2 [v]Ex 29:5,29; 31:10; 39:1; Lev 8:7-9,30

28:3 [w]Ex 31:6; 36:1

28:3 [x]Ex 31:3

28:4 [y]ver 15-30 [z]ver 31-35 [a]ver 39

The Ephod

6 "Make the ephod of gold, and of blue, purple and scarlet yarn, and of finely twisted linen—the work of a skilled craftsman. 7 It is to have two shoulder pieces attached to two of its corners, so it can be fastened. 8 Its skillfully woven waistband is to be like it—of one piece with the ephod and made with gold, and with blue, purple and scarlet yarn, and with finely twisted linen.

9 "Take two onyx stones and engrave on them the names of the sons of Israel 10 in the order of their birth—six names on one stone and the remaining six on the other. 11 Engrave the names of the sons of Israel on the two stones the way a gem cutter engraves a seal. Then mount the stones in gold filigree settings 12 and fasten them on the shoulder pieces of the ephod as memorial stones for the sons of Israel. Aaron is to bear the names on his shoulders as a memorial before the LORD. 13 Make gold filigree settings 14 and two braided chains of pure gold, like a rope, and attach the chains to the settings.

The Breastpiece

15 "Fashion a breastpiece for making decisions—the work of a skilled craftsman. Make it like the ephod: of gold, and of blue, purple and scarlet yarn, and of finely twisted linen. 16 It is to be square—a span[g] long and a span wide—and folded double. 17 Then mount four rows of precious stones on it. In the

[a] *9* That is, about 150 feet (about 46 meters); also in verse 11 [b] *12* That is, about 75 feet (about 23 meters); also in verse 13 [c] *14* That is, about 22 1/2 feet (about 6.9 meters); also in verse 15 [d] *16* That is, about 30 feet (about 9 meters) [e] *18* That is, about 150 feet (about 46 meters) long and 75 feet (about 23 meters) wide [f] *18* That is, about 7 1/2 feet (about 2.3 meters) [g] *16* That is, about 9 inches (about 22 centimeters)

first row there shall be a ruby, a topaz and a beryl; 18in the second row a turquoise, a sapphire[a] and an emerald; 19in the third row a jacinth, an agate and an amethyst; 20in the fourth row a chrysolite, an onyx and a jasper.[b] Mount them in gold filigree settings. 21There are to be twelve stones, one for each of the names of the sons of Israel, each engraved like a seal with the name of one of the twelve tribes.

22"For the breastpiece make braided chains of pure gold, like a rope. 23Make two gold rings for it and fasten them to two corners of the breastpiece. 24Fasten the two gold chains to the rings at the corners of the breastpiece, 25and the other ends of the chains to the two settings, attaching them to the shoulder pieces of the ephod at the front. 26Make two gold rings and attach them to the other two corners of the breastpiece on the inside edge next to the ephod. 27Make two more gold rings and attach them to the bottom of the shoulder pieces on the front of the ephod, close to the seam just above the waistband of the ephod. 28The rings of the breastpiece are to be tied to the rings of the ephod with blue cord, connecting it to the waistband, so that the breastpiece will not swing out from the ephod.

29"Whenever Aaron enters the Holy Place,[b] he will bear the names of the sons of Israel over his heart on the breastpiece of decision as a continuing memorial before the LORD. 30Also put the Urim and the Thummim[c] in the breastpiece, so they may be over Aaron's heart whenever he enters the presence of the LORD. Thus Aaron will always bear the means of making decisions for the Israelites over his heart before the LORD.

28:29 [b]ver 12

28:30 [c]Lev 8:8; Nu 27:21; Dt 33:8; Ezr 2:63; Ne 7:65

Other Priestly Garments

31"Make the robe of the ephod entirely of blue cloth, 32with an opening for the head in its center. There shall be a woven edge like a collar[c] around this opening, so that it will not tear. 33Make pomegranates of blue, purple and scarlet yarn around the hem of the robe, with gold bells between them. 34The gold bells and the pomegranates are to alternate around the hem of the robe. 35Aaron must wear it when he ministers. The sound of the bells will be heard when he enters the Holy Place before the LORD and when he comes out, so that he will not die.

36"Make a plate of pure gold and engrave on it as on a seal: HOLY TO THE LORD.[d] 37Fasten a blue cord to it to attach it to the turban; it is to be on the front of the turban. 38It will be on Aaron's forehead, and he will bear the guilt[e] involved in the sacred gifts the Israelites consecrate, whatever their gifts may be. It will be on Aaron's forehead continually so that they will be acceptable to the LORD.

39"Weave the tunic of fine linen and make the turban of fine linen. The sash is to be the work of an embroiderer. 40Make tunics, sashes and headbands for Aaron's sons,[f] to give them dignity and honor. 41After you put these clothes on your brother Aaron and his sons, anoint[g] and ordain them. Consecrate them so they may serve me as priests.[h]

42"Make linen undergarments[i] as a covering for the body, reaching from the waist to the thigh. 43Aaron and his sons must wear them whenever they enter the Tent of Meeting[j] or approach the altar to minister in the Holy Place, so that they will not incur guilt and die.[k]

"This is to be a lasting ordinance[l] for Aaron and his descendants.

Consecration of the Priests

29 "This is what you are to do to consecrate them, so they may serve me as priests: Take a young bull and two rams without defect. 2And from fine wheat flour, without yeast, make bread, and cakes mixed with oil, and wafers spread with oil.[m] 3Put them in a basket and present them in it—along with the bull and the two rams. 4Then bring Aaron and his sons to the entrance to the Tent of Meeting and wash them with water.[n] 5Take the garments[o] and dress Aaron with the tunic, the robe of the ephod, the ephod itself and the breastpiece. Fasten the ephod on him by its skillfully woven waistband.[p] 6Put the turban on his head and attach the sacred diadem[q] to the turban. 7Take the anointing oil[r] and

[a]*18* Or *lapis lazuli* [b]*20* The precise identification of some of these precious stones is uncertain. [c]*32* The meaning of the Hebrew for this word is uncertain.

28:36 [d]Zec 14:20

28:38 [e]Lev 10:17; 22:9,16; Nu 18:1; Heb 9:28; 1Pe 2:24

28:40 [f]ver 4; Ex 39:41

28:41 [g]Ex 29:7; Lev 10:7 [h]Ex 29:7-9; 30:30; 40:15; Lev 8:1-36; Heb 7:28

28:42 [i]Lev 6:10; 16:4,23; Eze 44:18

28:43 [j]Ex 27:21 [k]Ex 20:26 [l]Lev 17:7

29:2 [m]Lev; 2:1,4; 6:19-23

29:4 [n]Ex 40:12; Heb 10:22

29:5 [o]Ex 28:2; Lev 8:7 [p]Ex 28:8

29:6 [q]Lev 8:9

29:7 [r]Ex 30:25 30,31; Lev; 8:12; 21:10; Nu 35:25; Ps 133:2

anoint him by pouring it on his head. 8 Bring his sons and dress them in tunics 9 and put headbands on them. Then tie sashes on Aaron and his sons.[a][s] The priesthood is theirs by a lasting ordinance.[t] In this way you shall ordain Aaron and his sons.

10 "Bring the bull to the front of the Tent of Meeting, and Aaron and his sons shall lay their hands on its head. 11 Slaughter it in the LORD's presence at the entrance to the Tent of Meeting. 12 Take some of the bull's blood and put it on the horns[u] of the altar with your finger, and pour out the rest of it at the base of the altar. 13 Then take all the fat[v] around the inner parts, the covering of the liver, and both kidneys with the fat on them, and burn them on the altar. 14 But burn the bull's flesh and its hide and its offal outside the camp.[w] It is a sin offering.

15 "Take one of the rams, and Aaron and his sons shall lay their hands on its head. 16 Slaughter it and take the blood and sprinkle it against the altar on all sides. 17 Cut the ram into pieces and wash the inner parts and the legs, putting them with the head and the other pieces. 18 Then burn the entire ram on the altar. It is a burnt offering to the LORD, a pleasing aroma,[x] an offering made to the LORD by fire.

19 "Take the other ram,[y] and Aaron and his sons shall lay their hands on its head. 20 Slaughter it, take some of its blood and put it on the lobes of the right ears of Aaron and his sons, on the thumbs of their right hands, and on the big toes of their right feet. Then sprinkle blood against the altar on all sides. 21 And take some of the blood[z] on the altar and some of the anointing oil[a] and sprinkle it on Aaron and his garments and on his sons and their garments. Then he and his sons and their garments will be consecrated.[b]

22 "Take from this ram the fat, the fat tail, the fat around the inner parts, the covering of the liver, both kidneys with the fat on them, and the right thigh. (This is the ram for the ordination.) 23 From the basket of bread made without yeast, which is before the LORD, take a loaf, and a cake made with oil, and a wafer. 24 Put all these in the hands of Aaron and his sons and wave them before the LORD as a wave offering.[c]

29:9 [s]Ex 28:40 [t]Ex 40:15; Nu 3:10; 18:7; 25:13; Dt 18:5
29:12 [u]Ex 27:2
29:13 [v]Lev 3:3,5,9
29:14 [w]Lev 4:11-12, 21; Heb 13:11
29:18 [x]Ge 8:21
29:19 [y]ver 3
29:21 [z]Heb 9:22 [a]Ex 30:25,31 [b]ver 1
29:24 [c]Lev 7:30

25 Then take them from their hands and burn them on the altar along with the burnt offering for a pleasing aroma to the LORD, an offering made to the LORD by fire. 26 After you take the breast of the ram for Aaron's ordination, wave it before the LORD as a wave offering, and it will be your share.[d]

27 "Consecrate those parts of the ordination ram that belong to Aaron and his sons:[e] the breast that was waved and the thigh that was presented. 28 This is always to be the regular share from the Israelites for Aaron and his sons. It is the contribution the Israelites are to make to the LORD from their fellowship offerings.[b][f]

29 "Aaron's sacred garments will belong to his descendants so that they can be anointed and ordained in them.[g] 30 The son[h] who succeeds him as priest and comes to the Tent of Meeting to minister in the Holy Place is to wear them seven days.

31 "Take the ram for the ordination and cook the meat in a sacred place. 32 At the entrance to the Tent of Meeting, Aaron and his sons are to eat the meat of the ram and the bread[i] that is in the basket. 33 They are to eat these offerings by which atonement was made for their ordination and consecration. But no one else may eat[j] them, because they are sacred. 34 And if any of the meat of the ordination ram or any bread is left over till morning,[k] burn it up. It must not be eaten, because it is sacred.

35 "Do for Aaron and his sons everything I have commanded you, taking seven days to ordain them. 36 Sacrifice a bull each day[l] as a sin offering to make atonement. Purify the altar by making atonement for it, and anoint it to consecrate[m] it. 37 For seven days make atonement for the altar and consecrate it. Then the altar will be most holy, and whatever touches it will be holy.[n]

38 "This is what you are to offer on the altar regularly each day:[o] two lambs a year old. 39 Offer one in the morning and the other at twilight.[p] 40 With the first lamb offer a tenth of an ephah[c] of fine flour mixed with a quarter of a hin[d] of oil from pressed olives, and a

[a]*9* Hebrew; Septuagint *on them* [b]*28* Traditionally *peace offerings* [c]*40* That is, probably about 2 quarts (about 2 liters) [d]*40* That is, probably about 1 quart (about 1 liter)

29:26 [d]Lev 7:31-34
29:27 [e]Lev 7:31,34; Dt 18:3
29:28 [f]Lev 10:15
29:29 [g]Nu 20:26,28
29:30 [h]Nu 20:28
29:32 [i]Mt 12:4
29:33 [j]Lev 10:14; 22:10,13
29:34 [k]Ex 12:10
29:36 [l]Heb 10:11 [m]Ex 40:10
29:37 [n]Ex 30:28-29; 40:10; Mt 23:19
29:38 [o]Nu 28:3-8; 1Ch 16:40; Da 12:11
29:39 [p]Eze 46:13-15

quarter of a hin of wine as a drink offering. 41 Sacrifice the other lamb at twilight with the same grain offering and
its drink offering as in the morning—a
pleasing aroma, an offering made to the
LORD by fire.
29:42 42 "For the generations to come[q] this
[q]Ex 30:8 [r]Ex 25:22 burnt offering is to be made regularly
at the entrance to the Tent of Meeting
before the LORD. There I will meet
you and speak to you;[r] 43 there also
I will meet with the Israelites, and
29:43 the place will be consecrated by my
[s]1Ki 8:11 glory.[s]
44 "So I will consecrate the Tent of
Meeting and the altar and will conse-
29:44 crate Aaron and his sons to serve me
[t]Lev 21:15 as priests.[t] 45 Then I will dwell[u] among
29:45 [u]Ex 25:8; the Israelites and be their God.[v] 46 They
Lev 26:12; Zec 2:10; will know that I am the LORD their
Jn 14:17 [v]2Co 6:16; God, who brought them out of Egypt
Rev 21:3 so that I might dwell among them. I
29:46 [w]Ex 20:2 am the LORD their God.[w]

The Altar of Incense

30:1 [x]Ex 37:25 **30** "Make an altar[x] of acacia wood
[y]Rev 8:3 for burning incense.[y] 2 It is to
30:2 be square, a cubit long and a cubit
[z]Ex 27:2 wide, and two cubits high[a]—its horns[z]
of one piece with it. 3 Overlay the top
and all the sides and the horns with
pure gold, and make a gold molding
around it. 4 Make two gold rings for
the altar below the molding—two on
opposite sides—to hold the poles used
to carry it. 5 Make the poles of acacia
wood and overlay them with gold. 6 Put
the altar in front of the curtain that
is before the ark of the Testimony—
30:6 [a]Ex 25:22; before the atonement cover[a] that is
26:34 over the Testimony—where I will meet
30:7 with you.
[b]ver 34-35; 7 "Aaron must burn fragrant incense[b]
Ex 27:21; 1Sa 2:28 on the altar every morning when he
tends the lamps. 8 He must burn incense
again when he lights the lamps at twilight so incense will burn regularly before the LORD for the generations to
come. 9 Do not offer on this altar any
30:9 other incense[c] or any burnt offering or
[c]Lev 10:1 grain offering, and do not pour a drink
30:10 offering on it. 10 Once a year Aaron shall
[d]Lev 16:18-19, 30 make atonement[d] on its horns. This annual atonement must be made with the
blood of the atoning sin offering for the
generations to come. It is most holy to
the LORD."

Atonement Money

11 Then the LORD said to Moses,
12 "When you take a census[e] of the Isra- 30:12
elites to count them, each one must pay [e]Ex 38:25; Nu 1:2,49;
the LORD a ransom[f] for his life at the 2Sa 24:1 [f]Nu 31:50;
time he is counted. Then no plague[g] will Mt 20:28
come on them when you number them. [g]2Sa 24:13
13 Each one who crosses over to those
already counted is to give a half shekel,[b]
according to the sanctuary shekel,[h] 30:13 [h]Nu 3:47;
which weighs twenty gerahs. This half Mt 17:24
shekel is an offering to the LORD. 14 All
who cross over, those twenty years old
or more, are to give an offering to the
LORD. 15 The rich are not to give more
than a half shekel and the poor are not
to give less[i] when you make the of- 30:15 [i]Pr 22:2;
fering to the LORD to atone for your Eph 6:9
lives. 16 Receive the atonement money
from the Israelites and use it for the
service of the Tent of Meeting.[j] It will 30:16 [j]Ex 38:25-28
be a memorial for the Israelites before
the LORD, making atonement for your
lives."

Basin for Washing

17 Then the LORD said to Moses,
18 "Make a bronze basin,[k] with its bronze 30:18 [k]Ex 38:8;
stand, for washing. Place it between the 40:7,30
Tent of Meeting and the altar, and put
water in it. 19 Aaron and his sons are
to wash their hands and feet[l] with wa- 30:19 [l]Ex 40:31-32;
ter[m] from it. 20 Whenever they enter the Isa 52:11 [m]Ps 26:6
Tent of Meeting, they shall wash with
water so that they will not die. Also,
when they approach the altar to minister by presenting an offering made
to the LORD by fire, 21 they shall wash
their hands and feet so that they will
not die. This is to be a lasting ordi-
nance[n] for Aaron and his descendants 30:21 [n]Ex 27:21;
for the generations to come." 28:43

Anointing Oil

22 Then the LORD said to Moses,
23 "Take the following fine spices: 500
shekels[c] of liquid myrrh,[o] half as much 30:23 [o]Ge 37:25
(that is, 250 shekels) of fragrant cin-
namon, 250 shekels of fragrant cane,
24 500 shekels of cassia[p]—all according 30:24 [p]Ps 45:8
to the sanctuary shekel—and a hin[d] of
olive oil. 25 Make these into a sacred

[a] *2* That is, about 1 1/2 feet (about 0.5 meter) long and wide and about 3 feet (about 0.9 meter) high [b] *13* That is, about 1/5 ounce (about 6 grams); also in verse 15 [c] *23* That is, about 12 1/2 pounds (about 6 kilograms) [d] *24* That is, probably about 4 quarts (about 4 liters)

anointing oil, a fragrant blend, the work
30:25 [q]Ex 37:29 [r]Ex 40:9
of a perfumer.[q] It will be the sacred
anointing oil.[r] [26]Then use it to anoint[s]
30:26 [s]Ex 40:9; Lev 8:10; Nu 7:1
the Tent of Meeting, the ark of the Testimony, [27]the table and all its articles,
the lampstand and its accessories, the
altar of incense, [28]the altar of burnt offering and all its utensils, and the basin
with its stand. [29]You shall consecrate
them so they will be most holy, and
30:29 [t]Ex 29:37
whatever touches them will be holy.[t]
[30]"Anoint Aaron and his sons and
30:30 [u]Ex 29:7; Lev 8:2,12,30
consecrate[u] them so they may serve me
as priests. [31]Say to the Israelites, 'This
is to be my sacred anointing oil for
the generations to come. [32]Do not pour
it on men's bodies and do not make
any oil with the same formula. It is sa-
30:32 [v]ver 25,37
cred, and you are to consider it sacred.[v]
[33]Whoever makes perfume like it and
whoever puts it on anyone other than
30:33 [w]ver 38; Ge 17:14
a priest must be cut off[w] from his people.' "

Incense

[34]Then the LORD said to Moses,
"Take fragrant spices—gum resin, ony-
cha and galbanum—and pure frankincense, all in equal amounts, [35]and make
a fragrant blend of incense, the work of
30:35 [x]ver 25
a perfumer.[x] It is to be salted and pure
and sacred. [36]Grind some of it to powder and place it in front of the Testimony in the Tent of Meeting, where I will
30:36 [y]ver 32; Ex 29:37; Lev 2:3
meet with you. It shall be most holy[y] to
you. [37]Do not make any incense with
this formula for yourselves; consider it
30:37 [z]ver 32
holy[z] to the LORD. [38]Whoever makes
any like it to enjoy its fragrance must be
30:38 [a]ver 33
cut off[a] from his people."

Bezalel and Oholiab

31 Then the LORD said to Moses,
[2]"See, I have chosen Bezalel[b]
31:2 [b]Ex 36:1,2; 1Ch 2:20
son of Uri, the son of Hur, of the tribe
of Judah, [3]and I have filled him with
the Spirit of God, with skill, ability and
31:3 [c]1Ki 7:14
knowledge in all kinds of crafts[c]— [4]to
make artistic designs for work in gold,
silver and bronze, [5]to cut and set stones,
to work in wood, and to engage in all
kinds of craftsmanship. [6]Moreover, I
have appointed Oholiab son of Ahisamach, of the tribe of Dan, to help him.
Also I have given skill to all the craftsmen to make everything I have com-
31:7 [d]Ex 36:8-38 [e]Ex 37:1-5
manded you: [7]the Tent of Meeting,[d] the
ark of the Testimony[e] with the atone-
ment cover[f] on it, and all the other fur- 31:7 [f]Ex 37:6
nishings of the tent— [8]the table[g] and
its articles, the pure gold lampstand[h] 31:8 [g]Ex 37:10-16 [h]Ex 37:17-24
and all its accessories, the altar of in-
cense, [9]the altar of burnt offering and
all its utensils, the basin with its stand—
[10]and also the woven garments,[i] both 31:10 [i]Ex 28:2; 39:1,41
the sacred garments for Aaron the priest
and the garments for his sons when they
serve as priests, [11]and the anointing oil[j] 31:11 [j]Ex 30:22-32
and fragrant incense for the Holy Place.
They are to make them just as I commanded you."

▸ PATIENCE

AN ARTIST IN THE WILDERNESS

Exodus 31:3

"Make me a box of gold," said God.
"A mercy seat for sinners—
A throne for ruling snakes and scorpions,
A bit of art to remind my people I will travel with them.
No pilgrimage of desolation—
But sun on gold from light unknown.
The sculpted cherubim ride high.
Your sojourn shall not be alone."

The Sabbath

[12]Then the LORD said to Moses,
[13]"Say to the Israelites, 'You must ob-
serve my Sabbaths.[k] This will be a sign[l] 31:13 [k]Ex 20:8; Lev 19:3,30 [l]Eze 20:12,20 [m]Lev 11:44
between me and you for the genera-
tions to come, so you may know that I
am the LORD, who makes you holy.[a][m]
[14]" 'Observe the Sabbath, because it
is holy to you. Anyone who desecrates
it must be put to death;[n] whoever does 31:14 [n]Nu 15:32-36
any work on that day must be cut off
from his people. [15]For six days, work[o] 31:15 [o]Ex 20:8-11 [p]Ge 2:3; Ex 16:23
is to be done, but the seventh day is
a Sabbath of rest,[p] holy to the LORD.
Whoever does any work on the Sabbath
day must be put to death. [16]The Israelites are to observe the Sabbath, celebrating it for the generations to come as a
lasting covenant. [17]It will be a sign[q] be- 31:17 [q]ver 13 [r]Ge 2:2-3
tween me and the Israelites forever, for
in six days the LORD made the heavens
and the earth, and on the seventh day
he abstained from work and rested.[r]' "
[18]When the LORD finished speaking
to Moses on Mount Sinai, he gave him
the two tablets of the Testimony, the

[a]13 Or *who sanctifies you*; or *who sets you apart as holy*

31:18 [s]Ex 24:12 [t]Ex 32:15-16; 34:1,28; Dt 4:13; 5:22 tablets of stone[s] inscribed by the finger
of God.[t]

The Golden Calf

32 When the people saw that Moses was so long in coming down
32:1 [u]Ex 24:18; Dt 9:9-12 [v]Ac 7:40* from the mountain,[u] they gathered
around Aaron and said, "Come, make
us gods[a] who will go before us. As for
this fellow Moses who brought us up
out of Egypt, we don't know what has
happened to him."[v]
2Aaron answered them, "Take off the
32:2 [w]Ex 35:22 gold earrings[w] that your wives, your
sons and your daughters are wearing,
and bring them to me." 3So all the people took off their earrings and brought
them to Aaron. 4He took what they
handed him and made it into an idol
32:4 [x]Dt 9:16; Ne 9:18; Ps 106:19; Ac 7:41 cast in the shape of a calf,[x] fashioning it
with a tool. Then they said, "These are
your gods,[b] O Israel, who brought you
up out of Egypt."
5When Aaron saw this, he built an
32:5 [y]Lev 23:2,37; 2Ki 10:20 altar in front of the calf and announced,
"Tomorrow there will be a festival[y] to
the LORD." 6So the next day the people
rose early and sacrificed burnt offerings
32:6 [z]Nu 25:2; Ac 7:41 [a]ver 17-19; 1Co 10:7* and presented fellowship offerings.[c][z] Afterward they sat down to eat and drink
and got up to indulge in revelry.[a]
32:7 [b]ver 4,11 [c]Ge 6:11-12; Dt 9:12 7Then the LORD said to Moses, "Go
down, because your people, whom you
brought up out of Egypt,[b] have become
corrupt.[c] 8They have been quick to turn
away from what I commanded them
32:8 [d]Ex 20:4 [e]Ex 22:20 [f]1Ki 12:28 and have made themselves an idol[d] cast
in the shape of a calf. They have bowed
down to it and sacrificed[e] to it and have
said, 'These are your gods, O Israel,
who brought you up out of Egypt.'[f]
9"I have seen these people," the LORD
said to Moses, "and they are a stiff-
32:9 [g]Ex 33:3,5; 34:9; Isa 48:4; Ac 7:51 necked[g] people. 10Now leave me alone
so that my anger may burn against them
and that I may destroy them. Then I
will make you into a great nation."[h]
32:10 [h]Nu 14:12; Dt 9:14 11But Moses sought the favor[i] of the
LORD his God. "O LORD," he said,
32:11 [i]Dt 9:18 [j]Dt 9:26 "why should your anger burn against
your people, whom you brought out of
Egypt with great power and a mighty
hand?[j] 12Why should the Egyptians say,
'It was with evil intent that he brought
them out, to kill them in the mountains and to wipe them off the face of
32:12 [k]Nu 14:13-16; Dt 9:28 the earth'?[k] Turn from your fierce anger; relent and do not bring disaster on
your people. 13Remember[l] your servants 32:13 [l]Ex 2:24
Abraham, Isaac and Israel, to whom [m]Ge 22:16; Heb 6:13
you swore by your own self:[m] 'I will [n]Ge 15:5; 26:4
make your descendants as numerous as [o]Ge 12:7
the stars[n] in the sky and I will give your
descendants all this land[o] I promised
them, and it will be their inheritance
forever.'" 14Then the LORD relented[p] 32:14 [p]2Sa 24:16; Ps 106:45
and did not bring on his people the di-
saster he had threatened.
15Moses turned and went down the
mountain with the two tablets of the
Testimony[q] in his hands.[r] They were 32:15 [q]Ex 31:18 [r]Dt 9:15
inscribed on both sides, front and back.
16The tablets were the work of God;
the writing was the writing of God, engraved on the tablets.[s] 32:16 [s]Ex 31:18
17When Joshua heard the noise of
the people shouting, he said to Moses,
"There is the sound of war in the
camp."
18Moses replied:

"It is not the sound of victory,
it is not the sound of defeat;
it is the sound of singing that I
hear."

19When Moses approached the camp 32:19 [t]Dt 9:16 [u]Dt 9:17
and saw the calf[t] and the dancing, his
anger burned and he threw the tablets
out of his hands, breaking them to
pieces[u] at the foot of the mountain.
20And he took the calf they had made
and burned it in the fire; then he ground
it to powder, scattered it on the water[v] 32:20 [v]Dt 9:21
and made the Israelites drink it.

FAITHFULNESS

METALLIC DRINKING WATER

Exodus 32:20
Moses ground the calf to powder,
Bid them lift their glasses high,
Toast their bogus god and drink—
Celebrate their idols and die.

21He said to Aaron, "What did these
people do to you, that you led them
into such great sin?"
22"Do not be angry, my lord," Aaron
answered. "You know how prone these
people are to evil.[w] 23They said to me, 32:22 [w]Dt 9:24
'Make us gods who will go before us.

[a] *1* Or *a god*; also in verses 23 and 31 [b] *4* Or *This is your god*; also in verse 8 [c] *6* Traditionally *peace offerings*

WEEK 27 SELF-CONTROL

DAY ONE

SELF-CONTROL, SAYING NO TO OUR APPETITES

Read Exodus 32:19–26

Golden calves! Nice idols for the self-indulgent. They require so little and promise to give us so much of what we think we want from life. But best of all, unlike the great God, idols are tangible; they are visible. We can see a golden calf, touch a golden calf. Unlike the invisible, true God, golden calves can be apprehended by all the senses. In a word, idols are sensual.

When Moses comes down from the mountain, he sees that Aaron, God's high priest, has become the high priest of idolatry. When Moses asks him why he has committed this atrocity, Aaron responds, "You know how prone these people are to evil...They gave me the gold, and I threw it into the fire, and out came this calf" (Exodus 32:22,24).

Aaron's deportment is self-excusing. He makes it sound as though the calf made itself. "All I did," Aaron might have said, "was throw the gold into the fire and presto...out came this false god. So, there you have it, Moses, it was nothing much that I did. The thing made itself!" But Moses makes no such excuse before the Lord. Moses takes sin very seriously, and says to the people, "You have committed a great sin. But now I will go up to the LORD; perhaps I can make atonement for your sin" (Exodus 32:30).

While Aaron gives excuses for the sins of the people, Moses sees that saying no to sin is the only cure for idolatry. Self-control can save the Israelites from their spiral into sin. If everyone were to obey every demand of every appetite, the world would be left in the charge of gluttons, rapists, murderers and warlords. To follow Christ is to say no to our appetites, take up our cross and follow him (Luke 9:23).

DAY TWO

SELF-CONTROL AND THE PURPOSE OF GOD IN MY LIFE

Amos the prophet blamed the secular flavor of life in eighth century B.C. Israel in part on the indulgent women of the nation. It was a sumptuous season in the life of Israel, and such good times tend to promote decadence. So the people ate and drank, denying themselves nothing. Yet Amos prophesied a time of siege and military destruction when the indulgent would surrender their decadence in chains. *Turn to Amos 4:1–2, page 1055, for today's study.*

DAY THREE

SELF-CONTROL AND MY RELATIONSHIP WITH CHRIST

It is worth noticing that just before Paul lists the fruit of the Spirit in Galatians 5:22–23, he lists the fruit of indulgence (vv. 19–21). The people who indulge themselves in these appetites are detestable in contrast to those who deny these appetites. Self-control is the only path to holiness, and holiness is the only turf on which we may build a relationship with Christ. *Turn to Galatians 5:16,19–21, page 1400, for today's study.*

DAY FOUR

SELF-CONTROL AND MY SERVICE TO OTHERS

The way we make our lives effective is to say no to our appetites. It has yet to be proved that a habitual adulterer has ever been gifted with ministry and service to others. The same thing might be said of a compulsive liar, a seasoned shoplifter, etc. We become spiritually effective only as we practice self-control. *Turn to 1 Corinthians 6:12–13, page 1362, for today's study.*

DAY FIVE

SELF-CONTROL AND ITS PLACE IN MY PERSONAL WORSHIP

Leviticus 11:44 orders us to consecrate ourselves to a life of holiness, for only then will we have enough in common to build an ongoing relationship with God. Holiness is the fruit of self-denial. Indulgence can only isolate us from a relationship with God, but if we practice a life of temperance and of faith, we will draw near to him. In his presence, mystery flows, and the mystery of godliness hallows our own forbearance. Self-control then becomes the usher that seats us down front along the center aisle of our worship, and makes the experience glorious. *Turn to Leviticus 11:44, page 128, for today's study.*

MEMORIZE THIS WEEK

1 CORINTHIANS 10:31

So whether you eat or drink or whatever you do, do it all for the glory of God.

Week 28, Love, God's Passion for His World, begins on page 1253, John 4:1–10.
To begin a topical study on the Fruit of the Spirit, Self-Control, turn to the Topical Index, page 1548.

As for this fellow Moses who brought us up out of Egypt, we don't know what has happened to him.'[x] 24 So I told them, 'Whoever has any gold jewelry, take it off.' Then they gave me the gold, and I threw it into the fire, and out came this calf!"[y]

25 Moses saw that the people were running wild and that Aaron had let them get out of control and so become a laughingstock to their enemies. 26 So he stood at the entrance to the camp and said, "Whoever is for the LORD, come to me." And all the Levites rallied to him.

27 Then he said to them, "This is what the LORD, the God of Israel, says: 'Each man strap a sword to his side. Go back and forth through the camp from one end to the other, each killing his brother and friend and neighbor.' "[z] 28 The Levites did as Moses commanded, and that day about three thousand of the people died. 29 Then Moses said, "You have been set apart to the LORD today, for you were against your own sons and brothers, and he has blessed you this day."

30 The next day Moses said to the people, "You have committed a great sin.[a] But now I will go up to the LORD; perhaps I can make atonement[b] for your sin."

31 So Moses went back to the LORD and said, "Oh, what a great sin these people have committed![c] They have made themselves gods of gold.[d] 32 But now, please forgive their sin—but if not, then blot me[e] out of the book[f] you have written."

33 The LORD replied to Moses, "Whoever has sinned against me I will blot out[g] of my book. 34 Now go, lead the people to the place[h] I spoke of, and my angel[i] will go before you. However, when the time comes for me to punish,[j] I will punish them for their sin."

35 And the LORD struck the people with a plague because of what they did with the calf[k] Aaron had made.

33 Then the LORD said to Moses, "Leave this place, you and the people you brought up out of Egypt, and go up to the land I promised on oath to Abraham, Isaac and Jacob, saying, 'I will give it to your descendants.'[l] 2 I will send an angel[m] before you and drive out the Canaanites, Amorites, Hittites, Perizzites, Hivites and Jebusites.[n] 3 Go up to the land flowing with milk and honey.[o] But I will not go with you, because you are a stiff-necked[p] people and I might destroy[q] you on the way."

4 When the people heard these distressing words, they began to mourn[r] and no one put on any ornaments. 5 For the LORD had said to Moses, "Tell the Israelites, 'You are a stiff-necked people. If I were to go with you even for a moment, I might destroy you. Now take off your ornaments and I will decide what to do with you.' " 6 So the Israelites stripped off their ornaments at Mount Horeb.

The Tent of Meeting

7 Now Moses used to take a tent and pitch it outside the camp some distance away, calling it the "tent of meeting."[s] Anyone inquiring of the LORD would go to the tent of meeting outside the camp. 8 And whenever Moses went out to the tent, all the people rose and stood at the entrances to their tents,[t] watching Moses until he entered the tent. 9 As Moses went into the tent, the pillar of cloud[u] would come down and stay at the entrance, while the LORD spoke[v] with Moses. 10 Whenever the people saw the pillar of cloud standing at the entrance to the tent, they all stood and worshiped, each at the entrance to his tent. 11 The LORD would speak to Moses face to face,[w] as a man speaks with his friend. Then Moses would return to the camp, but his young aide Joshua son of Nun did not leave the tent.

Moses and the Glory of the LORD

12 Moses said to the LORD, "You have been telling me, 'Lead these people,'[x] but you have not let me know whom you will send with me. You have said, 'I know you by name[y] and you have found favor with me.' 13 If you are pleased with me, teach me your ways[z] so I may know you and continue to find favor with you. Remember that this nation is your people."[a]

14 The LORD replied, "My Presence[b] will go with you, and I will give you rest."[c]

15 Then Moses said to him, "If your Presence does not go with us, do not send us up from here. 16 How will anyone know that you are pleased with me

32:23 [x]ver 1
32:24 [y]ver 4
32:27 [z]Nu 25:3,5; Dt 33:9
32:30 [a]1Sa 12:20 [b]Lev 1:4; Nu 25:13
32:31 [c]Dt 9:18 [d]Ex 20:23
32:32 [e]Ro 9:3 [f]Ps 69:28; Da 12:1; Php 4:3; Rev 3:5; 21:27
32:33 [g]Dt 29:20; Ps 9:5
32:34 [h]Ex 3:17 [i]Ex 23:20 [j]Dt 32:35; Ps 99:8; Ro 2:5-6
32:35 [k]ver 4
33:1 [l]Ge 12:7
33:2 [m]Ex 32:34 [n]Ex 23:27-31; Jos 24:11
33:3 [o]Ex 3:8 [p]Ex 32:9 [q]Ex 32:10
33:4 [r]Nu 14:39
33:7 [s]Ex 29:42-43
33:8 [t]Nu 16:27
33:9 [u]Ex 13:21 [v]Ex 31:18; Ps 99:7
33:11 [w]Nu 12:8; Dt 34:10
33:12 [x]Ex 3:10 [y]ver 17; Jn 10:14-15; 2Ti 2:19
33:13 [z]Ps 25:4; 86:11; 119:33 [a]Ex 34:9; Dt 9:26,29
33:14 [b]Isa 63:9 [c]Jos 21:44; 22:4

its accessories, lamps and oil for the
35:15 [l]Ex 30:1-6 light; 15the altar[l] of incense with its
[m]Ex 30:25 poles, the anointing oil[m] and the fra-
[n]Ex 30:34-38 grant incense;[n] the curtain for the doorway at the entrance to the tabernacle;
35:16 [o]Ex 27:1-8 16the altar[o] of burnt offering with its
bronze grating, its poles and all its uten-
sils; the bronze basin with its stand;
17the curtains of the courtyard with its
posts and bases, and the curtain for
35:17 [p]Ex 27:9 the entrance to the courtyard;[p] 18the
tent pegs for the tabernacle and for
the courtyard, and their ropes; 19the
woven garments worn for ministering
in the sanctuary—both the sacred gar-
35:19 ments[q] for Aaron the priest and the
[q]Ex 28:2; 31:10; 39:1 garments for his sons when they serve
as priests."
20Then the whole Israelite community withdrew from Moses' presence,
21and everyone who was willing and
whose heart moved him came and
brought an offering to the LORD for
the work on the Tent of Meeting, for
all its service, and for the sacred garments. 22All who were willing, men and
women alike, came and brought gold
jewelry of all kinds: brooches, earrings,
rings and ornaments. They all presented their gold as a wave offering to the
35:23 [r]1Ch 29:8 LORD. 23Everyone who had blue, purple or scarlet yarn[r] or fine linen, or goat
hair, ram skins dyed red or hides of
sea cows brought them. 24Those presenting an offering of silver or bronze
brought it as an offering to the LORD,
and everyone who had acacia wood for
any part of the work brought it. 25Every
35:25 [s]Ex 28:3 skilled woman[s] spun with her hands and
brought what she had spun—blue, pur-
ple or scarlet yarn or fine linen. 26And
all the women who were willing and
35:27 had the skill spun the goat hair. 27The
[t]1Ch 29:6; Ezr 2:68 leaders[t] brought onyx stones and other
gems to be mounted on the ephod and
breastpiece. 28They also brought spices
and olive oil for the light and for
the anointing oil and for the fragrant
35:28 [u]Ex 25:6 incense.[u] 29All the Israelite men and
women who were willing[v] brought to
35:29 [v]ver 21; 1Ch 29:9 the LORD freewill offerings[w] for all the
[w]ver 4-9; Ex 25:1-7; 36:3; 2Ki 12:4 work the LORD through Moses had
commanded them to do.

Bezalel and Oholiab

30Then Moses said to the Israelites,
"See, the LORD has chosen Bezalel son
of Uri, the son of Hur, of the tribe
of Judah, 31and he has filled him with
the Spirit of God, with skill, ability 35:31
and knowledge in all kinds of crafts[x]— [x]ver 35; 2Ch 2:7,14
32to make artistic designs for work in
gold, silver and bronze, 33to cut and set
stones, to work in wood and to engage
in all kinds of artistic craftsmanship.
34And he has given both him and Oho- 35:34
liab[y] son of Ahisamach, of the tribe of [y]Ex 31:6
Dan, the ability to teach[z] others. 35He [z]2Ch 2:14
has filled them with skill to do all kinds
of work[a] as craftsmen, designers, em- 35:35 [a]ver 31;
broiderers in blue, purple and scarlet Ex 31:3,6;
yarn and fine linen, and weavers—all of 1Ki 7:14
them master craftsmen and designers.

36

1So Bezalel, Oholiab and every
skilled person[b] to whom the 36:1 [b]Ex 28:3
LORD has given skill and ability to [c]Ex 25:8
know how to carry out all the work of
constructing the sanctuary[c] are to do
the work just as the LORD has commanded."
2Then Moses summoned Bezalel[d] and 36:2
Oholiab[e] and every skilled person to [d]Ex 31:2 [e]Ex 31:6
whom the LORD had given ability and [f]Ex 25:2; 35:21,26;
who was willing[f] to come and do the 1Ch 29:5
work. 3They received from Moses all
the offerings[g] the Israelites had brought 36:3 [g]Ex 35:29
to carry out the work of constructing
the sanctuary. And the people continued to bring freewill offerings morning after morning. 4So all the skilled
craftsmen who were doing all the work
on the sanctuary left their work 5and
said to Moses, "The people are bringing
more than enough[h] for doing the work 36:5
the LORD commanded to be done." [h]2Ch 24:14;
6Then Moses gave an order and they 31:10; 2Co 8:2-3
sent this word throughout the camp:
"No man or woman is to make anything else as an offering for the sanctuary." And so the people were restrained
from bringing more, 7because what they 36:7
already had was more[i] than enough to [i]1Ki 7:47
do all the work.

The Tabernacle

8All the skilled men among the workmen made the tabernacle with ten curtains of finely twisted linen and blue,
purple and scarlet yarn, with cherubim
worked into them by a skilled craftsman. 9All the curtains were the same
size—twenty-eight cubits long and four
cubits wide.[a] 10They joined five of the

[a]9 That is, about 42 feet (about 12.5 meters) long and 6 feet (about 1.8 meters) wide

curtains together and did the same with
the other five. 11Then they made loops
of blue material along the edge of the
end curtain in one set, and the same
was done with the end curtain in the
other set. 12They also made fifty loops
on one curtain and fifty loops on the
end curtain of the other set, with the
loops opposite each other. 13Then they
made fifty gold clasps and used them to
fasten the two sets of curtains together
36:13 so that the tabernacle was a unit.[j]
[j]ver 18 14They made curtains of goat hair for
the tent over the tabernacle—eleven altogether. 15All eleven curtains were the
same size—thirty cubits long and four
cubits wide.[a] 16They joined five of the
curtains into one set and the other six
into another set. 17Then they made fifty
loops along the edge of the end curtain
in one set and also along the edge of
the end curtain in the other set. 18They
made fifty bronze clasps to fasten the
36:18 tent together as a unit.[k] 19Then they
[k]ver 13 made for the tent a covering of ram
skins dyed red, and over that a covering
of hides of sea cows.[b]

20They made upright frames of acacia wood for the tabernacle. 21Each
frame was ten cubits long and a cubit
and a half wide,[c] 22with two projections
set parallel to each other. They made
all the frames of the tabernacle in this
way. 23They made twenty frames for the
south side of the tabernacle 24and made
forty silver bases to go under them—
two bases for each frame, one under
each projection. 25For the other side,
the north side of the tabernacle, they
made twenty frames 26and forty silver
bases—two under each frame. 27They
made six frames for the far end, that
is, the west end of the tabernacle, 28and
two frames were made for the corners
of the tabernacle at the far end. 29At
these two corners the frames were double from the bottom all the way to the
top and fitted into a single ring; both
were made alike. 30So there were eight
frames and sixteen silver bases—two
under each frame.

31They also made crossbars of acacia
wood: five for the frames on one side
of the tabernacle, 32five for those on the
other side, and five for the frames on
the west, at the far end of the tabernacle. 33They made the center crossbar so
that it extended from end to end at the
middle of the frames. 34They overlaid
the frames with gold and made gold
rings to hold the crossbars. They also
overlaid the crossbars with gold.

35They made the curtain[l] of blue, 36:35
purple and scarlet yarn and finely twist- [l]Ex 39:38;
ed linen, with cherubim worked into Mt 27:51;
it by a skilled craftsman. 36They made Lk 23:45; Heb 9:3
four posts of acacia wood for it and
overlaid them with gold. They made
gold hooks for them and cast their four
silver bases. 37For the entrance to the
tent they made a curtain of blue, purple and scarlet yarn and finely twisted
linen—the work of an embroiderer;[m] 36:37
38and they made five posts with hooks [m]Ex 27:16
for them. They overlaid the tops of the
posts and their bands with gold and
made their five bases of bronze.

The Ark

37 Bezalel[n] made the ark[o] of aca- 37:1
cia wood—two and a half cu- [n]Ex 31:2
bits long, a cubit and a half wide, and [o]Ex 30:6; 39:35; Dt 10:3
a cubit and a half high.[d] 2He overlaid
it with pure gold,[p] both inside and out, 37:2
and made a gold molding around it. [p]ver 11,26
3He cast four gold rings for it and fastened them to its four feet, with two
rings on one side and two rings on
the other. 4Then he made poles of acacia wood and overlaid them with gold.
5And he inserted the poles into the rings
on the sides of the ark to carry it.

6He made the atonement cover[q] of 37:6
pure gold—two and a half cubits long [q]Ex 26:34;
and a cubit and a half wide.[e] 7Then he 31:7; Heb 9:5
made two cherubim[r] out of hammered 37:7
gold at the ends of the cover. 8He made [r]Eze 41:18
one cherub on one end and the second
cherub on the other; at the two ends he
made them of one piece with the cover.
9The cherubim had their wings spread
upward, overshadowing[s] the cover with 37:9
them. The cherubim faced each other, [s]Heb 9:5
looking toward the cover.[t] [t]Dt 10:3

The Table

10They[f] made the table[u] of acacia 37:10
wood—two cubits long, a cubit wide, [u]Heb 9:2

[a] *15* That is, about 45 feet (about 13.5 meters) long and 6 feet (about 1.8 meters) wide [b] *19* That is, dugongs [c] *21* That is, about 15 feet (about 4.5 meters) long and 2 1/4 feet (about 0.7 meter) wide [d] *1* That is, about 3 3/4 feet (about 1.1 meters) long and 2 1/4 feet (about 0.7 meter) wide and high [e] *6* That is, about 3 3/4 feet (about 1.1 meters) long and 2 1/4 feet (about 0.7 meter) wide [f] *10* Or *He;* also in verses 11-29

37:11 and a cubit and a half high.[a] 11Then
[v]ver 2 they overlaid it with pure gold[v] and
made a gold molding around it. 12They
also made around it a rim a handbreadth[b] wide and put a gold molding
on the rim. 13They cast four gold rings
for the table and fastened them to the
four corners, where the four legs were.
37:14 14The rings[w] were put close to the rim
[w]ver 27 to hold the poles used in carrying the
table. 15The poles for carrying the table were made of acacia wood and
were overlaid with gold. 16And they
made from pure gold the articles for the
table—its plates and dishes and bowls
and its pitchers for the pouring out of
drink offerings.

The Lampstand

37:17 [x]Heb 9:2; Rev 1:12
17They made the lampstand[x] of pure
gold and hammered it out, base and
shaft; its flowerlike cups, buds and blossoms were of one piece with it. 18Six
branches extended from the sides of the
lampstand—three on one side and three
on the other. 19Three cups shaped like
almond flowers with buds and blossoms
were on one branch, three on the next
branch and the same for all six branches
extending from the lampstand. 20And
on the lampstand were four cups shaped
like almond flowers with buds and blossoms. 21One bud was under the first
pair of branches extending from the
lampstand, a second bud under the second pair, and a third bud under the
third pair—six branches in all. 22The
buds and the branches were all of one
piece with the lampstand, hammered
37:22 [y]ver 17; Nu 8:4 out of pure gold.[y]
23They made its seven lamps,[z] as well
37:23 [z]Ex 40:4,25 as its wick trimmers and trays, of pure
gold. 24They made the lampstand and
all its accessories from one talent[c] of
pure gold.

The Altar of Incense

37:25 [a]Ex 30:34-36; Lk 1:11; Heb 9:4; Rev 8:3 [b]Ex 27:2; Rev 9:13
25They made the altar of incense[a]
out of acacia wood. It was square, a cubit long and a cubit wide, and two cubits high[d]—its horns[b] of one piece with
it. 26They overlaid the top and all the
sides and the horns with pure gold, and
made a gold molding around it. 27They
37:27 [c]ver 14 made two gold rings[c] below the molding—two on opposite sides—to hold
the poles used to carry it. 28They made
the poles of acacia wood and overlaid 37:28 [d]Ex 25:13
them with gold.[d]
29They also made the sacred anoint- 37:29 [e]Ex 31:11 [f]Ex 30:1,25; 39:38
ing oil[e] and the pure, fragrant in-
cense[f]—the work of a perfumer.

The Altar of Burnt Offering

38 They[e] built the altar of burnt
offering of acacia wood, three
cubits[f] high; it was square, five cubits
long and five cubits wide.[g] 2They made
a horn at each of the four corners, so
that the horns and the altar were of
one piece, and they overlaid the altar
with bronze.[g] 3They made all its uten- 38:2 [g]2Ch 1:5
sils[h] of bronze—its pots, shovels, sprinkling bowls, meat forks and firepans. 38:3 [h]Ex 31:9
4They made a grating for the altar, a
bronze network, to be under its ledge,
halfway up the altar. 5They cast bronze
rings to hold the poles for the four corners of the bronze grating. 6They made
the poles of acacia wood and overlaid
them with bronze. 7They inserted the
poles into the rings so they would be
on the sides of the altar for carrying it.
They made it hollow, out of boards.

Basin for Washing

38:8 [i]Ex 30:18; 40:7 [j]Dt 23:17; 1Sa 2:22; 1Ki 14:24
8They made the bronze basin[i] and its
bronze stand from the mirrors of the
women[j] who served at the entrance to
the Tent of Meeting.

The Courtyard

9Next they made the courtyard. The
south side was a hundred cubits[h] long
and had curtains of finely twisted linen,
10with twenty posts and twenty bronze
bases, and with silver hooks and bands
on the posts. 11The north side was also
a hundred cubits long and had twenty
posts and twenty bronze bases, with silver hooks and bands on the posts.
12The west end was fifty cubits[i] wide
and had curtains, with ten posts and
ten bases, with silver hooks and bands

[a] *10* That is, about 3 feet (about 0.9 meter) long, 1 1/2 feet (about 0.5 meter) wide, and 2 1/4 feet (about 0.7 meter) high [b] *12* That is, about 3 inches (about 8 centimeters) [c] *24* That is, about 75 pounds (about 34 kilograms) [d] *25* That is, about 1 1/2 feet (about 0.5 meter) long and wide, and about 3 feet (about 0.9 meter) high [e] *1* Or *He*; also in verses 2-9 [f] *1* That is, about 4 1/2 feet (about 1.3 meters) [g] *1* That is, about 7 1/2 feet (about 2.3 meters) long and wide [h] *9* That is, about 150 feet (about 46 meters) [i] *12* That is, about 75 feet (about 23 meters)

on the posts. [13]The east end, toward the sunrise, was also fifty cubits wide. [14]Curtains fifteen cubits[a] long were on one side of the entrance, with three posts and three bases, [15]and curtains fifteen cubits long were on the other side of the entrance to the courtyard, with three posts and three bases. [16]All the curtains around the courtyard were of finely twisted linen. [17]The bases for the posts were bronze. The hooks and bands on the posts were silver, and their tops were overlaid with silver; so all the posts of the courtyard had silver bands.

[18]The curtain for the entrance to the courtyard was of blue, purple and scarlet yarn and finely twisted linen—the work of an embroiderer. It was twenty cubits[b] long and, like the curtains of the courtyard, five cubits[c] high, [19]with four posts and four bronze bases. Their hooks and bands were silver, and their tops were overlaid with silver. [20]All the tent pegs[k] of the tabernacle and of the surrounding courtyard were bronze.

38:20 [k]Ex 35:18

The Materials Used

[21]These are the amounts of the materials used for the tabernacle, the tabernacle of the Testimony,[l] which were recorded at Moses' command by the Levites under the direction of Ithamar[m] son of Aaron, the priest. [22](Bezalel[n] son of Uri, the son of Hur, of the tribe of Judah, made everything the LORD commanded Moses; [23]with him was Oholiab[o] son of Ahisamach, of the tribe of Dan—a craftsman and designer, and an embroiderer in blue, purple and scarlet yarn and fine linen.) [24]The total amount of the gold from the wave offering used for all the work on the sanctuary[p] was 29 talents and 730 shekels,[d] according to the sanctuary shekel.[q]

[25]The silver obtained from those of the community who were counted in the census[r] was 100 talents and 1,775 shekels,[e] according to the sanctuary shekel— [26]one beka per person,[s] that is, half a shekel,[f] according to the sanctuary shekel,[t] from everyone who had crossed over to those counted, twenty years old or more,[u] a total of 603,550 men.[v] [27]The 100 talents[g] of silver were used to cast the bases[w] for the sanctuary and for the curtain—100 bases from the 100 talents, one talent for each base. [28]They used the 1,775 shekels[h] to make the hooks for the posts, to overlay the tops of the posts, and to make their bands.

[29]The bronze from the wave offering was 70 talents and 2,400 shekels.[i] [30]They used it to make the bases for the entrance to the Tent of Meeting, the bronze altar with its bronze grating and all its utensils, [31]the bases for the surrounding courtyard and those for its entrance and all the tent pegs for the tabernacle and those for the surrounding courtyard.

38:21 [l]Nu 1:50,53; 8:24; 9:15; 10:11; 17:7; 1Ch 23:32; 2Ch 24:6; Ac 7:44; Rev 15:5 [m]Nu 4:28,33
38:22 [n]Ex 31:2
38:23 [o]Ex 31:6
38:24 [p]Ex 30:16 [q]Ex 30:13; Lev 27:25; Nu 3:47; 18:16
38:25 [r]Ex 30:12
38:26 [s]Ex 30:12 [t]Ex 30:13 [u]Ex 30:14 [v]Ex 12:37; Nu 1:46
38:27 [w]Ex 26:19

The Priestly Garments

39

From the blue, purple and scarlet yarn[x] they made woven garments for ministering in the sanctuary.[y] They also made sacred garments[z] for Aaron, as the LORD commanded Moses.

39:1 [x]Ex 35:23 [y]Ex 35:19 [z]ver 41; Ex 28:2

The Ephod

[2]They[j] made the ephod of gold, and of blue, purple and scarlet yarn, and of finely twisted linen. [3]They hammered out thin sheets of gold and cut strands to be worked into the blue, purple and scarlet yarn and fine linen—the work of a skilled craftsman. [4]They made shoulder pieces for the ephod, which were attached to two of its corners, so it could be fastened. [5]Its skillfully woven waistband was like it—of one piece with the ephod and made with gold, and with blue, purple and scarlet yarn, and with finely twisted linen, as the LORD commanded Moses.

[6]They mounted the onyx stones in gold filigree settings and engraved them like a seal with the names of the sons of Israel. [7]Then they fastened them on the shoulder pieces of the ephod as memorial[a] stones for the sons of Israel, as the LORD commanded Moses.

39:7 [a]Lev 24:7; Jos 4:7

[a] *14* That is, about 22 1/2 feet (about 6.9 meters)
[b] *18* That is, about 30 feet (about 9 meters)
[c] *18* That is, about 7 1/2 feet (about 2.3 meters)
[d] *24* The weight of the gold was a little over one ton (about 1 metric ton). [e] *25* The weight of the silver was a little over 3 3/4 tons (about 3.4 metric tons). [f] *26* That is, about 1/5 ounce (about 5.5 grams) [g] *27* That is, about 3 3/4 tons (about 3.4 metric tons) [h] *28* That is, about 45 pounds (about 20 kilograms) [i] *29* The weight of the bronze was about 2 1/2 tons (about 2.4 metric tons).
[j] *2* Or *He*; also in verses 7, 8 and 22

The Breastpiece

39:8 [b]Lev 8:8 8They fashioned the breastpiece[b]—
the work of a skilled craftsman. They
made it like the ephod: of gold, and
of blue, purple and scarlet yarn, and of
finely twisted linen. 9It was square—a
span[a] long and a span wide—and folded double. 10Then they mounted four
rows of precious stones on it. In the
first row there was a ruby, a topaz and a
beryl; 11in the second row a turquoise, a
sapphire[b] and an emerald; 12in the third
row a jacinth, an agate and an amethyst;
13in the fourth row a chrysolite, an
onyx and a jasper.[c] They were mounted
in gold filigree settings. 14There were
twelve stones, one for each of the names
of the sons of Israel, each engraved like
a seal with the name of one of the
39:14 [c]Rev 21:12 twelve tribes.[c]
15For the breastpiece they made
braided chains of pure gold, like a rope.
16They made two gold filigree settings
and two gold rings, and fastened the
rings to two of the corners of the breastpiece. 17They fastened the two gold
chains to the rings at the corners of
the breastpiece, 18and the other ends
of the chains to the two settings, attaching them to the shoulder pieces of
the ephod at the front. 19They made
two gold rings and attached them to
the other two corners of the breastpiece
on the inside edge next to the ephod.
20Then they made two more gold rings
and attached them to the bottom of
the shoulder pieces on the front of the
ephod, close to the seam just above
the waistband of the ephod. 21They
tied the rings of the breastpiece to the
rings of the ephod with blue cord, connecting it to the waistband so that the
breastpiece would not swing out from
the ephod—as the LORD commanded
Moses.

Other Priestly Garments

22They made the robe of the ephod
entirely of blue cloth—the work of a
weaver— 23with an opening in the center of the robe like the opening of a
collar,[d] and a band around this opening,
so that it would not tear. 24They made
pomegranates of blue, purple and scarlet yarn and finely twisted linen around
the hem of the robe. 25And they made
bells of pure gold and attached them
around the hem between the pomegranates. 26The bells and pomegranates alternated around the hem of the
robe to be worn for ministering, as the
LORD commanded Moses.
27For Aaron and his sons, they made
tunics of fine linen[d]—the work of a 39:27 [d]Lev 6:10
weaver— 28and the turban[e] of fine
linen, the linen headbands and the 39:28 [e]Ex 28:4
undergarments of finely twisted linen.
29The sash was of finely twisted linen
and blue, purple and scarlet yarn—the
work of an embroiderer—as the LORD
commanded Moses.
30They made the plate, the sacred diadem, out of pure gold and engraved on
it, like an inscription on a seal: HOLY
TO THE LORD. 31Then they fastened
a blue cord to it to attach it to the turban, as the LORD commanded Moses.

Moses Inspects the Tabernacle

32So all the work on the tabernacle,
the Tent of Meeting, was completed.
The Israelites did everything just as
the LORD commanded Moses.[f] 33Then 39:32 [f]ver 42-43;
they brought the tabernacle to Moses: Ex 25:9
the tent and all its furnishings, its clasps,
frames, crossbars, posts and bases; 34the
covering of ram skins dyed red, the
covering of hides of sea cows[e] and the
shielding curtain; 35the ark of the Testi-
mony[g] with its poles and the atonement 39:35 [g]Ex 30:6
cover; 36the table with all its articles and
the bread of the Presence; 37the pure
gold lampstand[h] with its row of lamps 39:37 [h]Ex 25:31
and all its accessories, and the oil for
the light; 38the gold altar,[i] the anointing 39:38 [i]Ex 30:1-10
oil, the fragrant incense, and the cur- [j]Ex 36:35
tain[j] for the entrance to the tent; 39the
bronze altar with its bronze grating, its
poles and all its utensils; the basin with
its stand; 40the curtains of the courtyard
with its posts and bases, and the curtain
for the entrance to the courtyard;[k] the 39:40 [k]Ex 27:9-19
ropes and tent pegs for the courtyard;
all the furnishings for the tabernacle,
the Tent of Meeting; 41and the woven
garments worn for ministering in the
sanctuary, both the sacred garments for
Aaron the priest and the garments for
his sons when serving as priests.
42The Israelites had done all the

[a] *9* That is, about 9 inches (about 22 centimeters)
[b] *11* Or *lapis lazuli* [c] *13* The precise identification of some of these precious stones is uncertain. [d] *23* The meaning of the Hebrew for this word is uncertain.
[e] *34* That is, dugongs

work just as the LORD had commanded Moses.[l] 43Moses inspected the work and saw that they had done it just as the LORD had commanded. So Moses blessed[m] them.

39:42 [l]Ex 25:9
39:43 [m]Lev 9:22,23; Nu 6:23-27; 2Sa 6:18; 1Ki 8:14,55; 2Ch 30:27

Setting Up the Tabernacle

40 Then the LORD said to Moses: 2"Set up the tabernacle, the Tent of Meeting,[n] on the first day of the first month.[o] 3Place the ark[p] of the Testimony in it and shield the ark with the curtain. 4Bring in the table and set out what belongs on it.[q] Then bring in the lampstand[r] and set up its lamps. 5Place the gold altar[s] of incense in front of the ark of the Testimony and put the curtain at the entrance to the tabernacle.

6"Place the altar of burnt offering in front of the entrance to the tabernacle, the Tent of Meeting; 7place the basin[t] between the Tent of Meeting and the altar and put water in it. 8Set up the courtyard around it and put the curtain at the entrance to the courtyard.

9"Take the anointing oil and anoint[u] the tabernacle and everything in it; consecrate it and all its furnishings, and it will be holy. 10Then anoint the altar of burnt offering and all its utensils; consecrate[v] the altar, and it will be most holy. 11Anoint the basin and its stand and consecrate them.

12"Bring Aaron and his sons to the entrance to the Tent of Meeting and wash them with water.[w] 13Then dress Aaron in the sacred garments,[x] anoint him and consecrate[y] him so he may serve me as priest. 14Bring his sons and dress them in tunics. 15Anoint them just as you anointed their father, so they may serve me as priests. Their anointing will be to a priesthood that will continue for all generations to come.[z]" 16Moses did everything just as the LORD commanded him.

17So the tabernacle[a] was set up on the first day of the first month[b] in the second year. 18When Moses set up the tabernacle, he put the bases in place, erected the frames, inserted the crossbars and set up the posts. 19Then he spread the tent over the tabernacle and put the covering over the tent, as the LORD commanded him.

20He took the Testimony[c] and placed it in the ark, attached the poles to the ark and put the atonement cover over it. 21Then he brought the ark into the tabernacle and hung the shielding curtain[d] and shielded the ark of the Testimony, as the LORD commanded him.

22Moses placed the table[e] in the Tent of Meeting on the north side of the tabernacle outside the curtain 23and set out the bread[f] on it before the LORD, as the LORD commanded him.

24He placed the lampstand[g] in the Tent of Meeting opposite the table on the south side of the tabernacle 25and set up the lamps[h] before the LORD, as the LORD commanded him.

26Moses placed the gold altar[i] in the Tent of Meeting in front of the curtain 27and burned fragrant incense on it, as the LORD commanded[j] him. 28Then he put up the curtain[k] at the entrance to the tabernacle.

29He set the altar of burnt offering near the entrance to the tabernacle, the Tent of Meeting, and offered on it burnt offerings and grain offerings,[l] as the LORD commanded him.

30He placed the basin[m] between the Tent of Meeting and the altar and put water in it for washing, 31and Moses and Aaron and his sons used it to wash their hands and feet. 32They washed whenever they entered the Tent of Meeting or approached the altar,[n] as the LORD commanded Moses.

33Then Moses set up the courtyard[o] around the tabernacle and altar and put up the curtain[p] at the entrance to the courtyard. And so Moses finished the work.

The Glory of the LORD

34Then the cloud[q] covered the Tent of Meeting, and the glory of the LORD filled the tabernacle. 35Moses could not enter the Tent of Meeting because the cloud had settled upon it, and the glory of the LORD filled the tabernacle.[r]

36In all the travels of the Israelites, whenever the cloud lifted from above the tabernacle, they would set out;[s] 37but if the cloud did not lift, they did not set out—until the day it lifted. 38So the cloud[t] of the LORD was over the tabernacle by day, and fire was in the cloud by night, in the sight of all the house of Israel during all their travels.

40:2 [n]Nu 1:1 [o]ver 17; Ex 12:2
40:3 [p]ver 21; Nu 4:5; Ex 26:33
40:4 [q]Ex 25:30 [r]ver 22-25; Ex 26:35
40:5 [s]ver 26; Ex 30:1
40:7 [t]ver 30; Ex 30:18
40:9 [u]Ex 30:26; Lev 8:10
40:10 [v]Ex 29:36
40:12 [w]Lev 8:1-13
40:13 [x]Ex 28:41 [y]Lev 8:12
40:15 [z]Ex 29:9; Nu 25:13
40:17 [a]Nu 7:1 [b]ver 2
40:20 [c]Ex 16:34; 25:16; Dt 10:5; 1Ki 8:9; Heb 9:4
40:21 [d]Ex 26:33
40:22 [e]Ex 26:35
40:23 [f]ver 4
40:24 [g]Ex 26:35
40:25 [h]ver 4; Ex 25:37
40:26 [i]ver 5; Ex 30:6
40:27 [j]Ex 30:7
40:28 [k]Ex 26:36
40:29 [l]ver 6; Ex 29:38-42
40:30 [m]ver 7
40:32 [n]Ex 30:20
40:33 [o]Ex 27:9 [p]ver 8
40:34 [q]Nu 9:15-23; 1Ki 8:12
40:35 [r]1Ki 8:11; 2Ch 5:13-14
40:36 [s]Nu 9:17-23; 10:13; Ne 9:19
40:38 [t]Ex 13:21; Nu 9:15; 1Co 10:1

LEVITICUS

AUTHORSHIP AND DATE

Moses

c. 1450 B.C. to c. 1410 B.C.

KEY THEMES

Holiness is the key theme in the book of Leviticus. Within this framework lie the issues of worship (including all matters regarding sacrifices and offerings), community sanitation and health laws, and the special duties of the Levites.

FRUIT OF THE SPIRIT IN LEVITICUS

Love: The seeds of the Golden Rule are planted in the book of Leviticus: "Do not seek revenge or bear a grudge against one of your people, but love your neighbor as yourself. I am the LORD" (19:18). This concept of loving others as ourselves is a frequent principle in the Bible. Loving our neighbors is a basic law of relationship that, if practiced, would limit all conflict.

Joy: In reading Leviticus it is easy to forget that the purpose of the festivals and ordinances was to produce a people in harmony with God. Many of these passages seem tangled and tedious to the novice. But God instituted these festivals and ordinances to produce spiritual wholeness in the nation. Whole people live in continual rejoicing before God. They fulfill what is recorded in Leviticus 23:40: "On the first day you are to take choice fruit from the trees, and palm fronds, leafy branches and poplars, and rejoice before the LORD your God for seven days." Joy is the evidence that our worship has vitality.

Peace: God was ever calling his people to peace. The fellowship offering can also be called a "peace offering," and God instituted it as a symbol of concord or peace *(shalom)* between the worshiper and God. It was a voluntary offering given with thanksgiving to celebrate the security and peace between God and people.

Goodness: Goodness and holiness are not the same thing. Goodness is what we acquire by our own resolve. Holiness is the quality of godliness that hungers for the approval of God. Holiness is a blessing of the Spirit that grows from our resolve to be accepted by God. Everyone who is holy is good, but not everyone who is good is holy. God said, "Consecrate yourselves and be holy, because I am the LORD your God. Keep my decrees and follow them. I am the LORD, who makes you holy" (20:7–8).

Faithfulness: Every call for obedience in this book was a cry for faithfulness. In every emphasis on covenant, God was soliciting faithfulness. The lists of services and offerings in the book of Leviticus were a call to obedience. Leviticus carried within its rituals and health mandates a patient summons from God to do all that he required. The book does not use the word *faithfulness*, but faithfulness is the goal of the peoples' worship and sacrifice.

The Burnt Offering

1:1 [a]Ex 19:3; 25:22 [b]Nu 7:89 **1** The LORD called to Moses[a] and
spoke to him from the Tent of
Meeting.[b] He said, 2"Speak to the Israelites and say to them: 'When any of
you brings an offering to the LORD,
1:2 [c]Lev 22:18-19 bring as your offering an animal from
either the herd or the flock.[c]

FAITHFULNESS

ALWAYS GIVING THE BEST TO GOD

Leviticus 1:2

"Bring an animal to offer," said the God of Israel. This was God's way of saying, "Let faith cost you; don't get cheap. The cost of what you bring will set the value of your faith."

In heaven is the bank where we invest on earth.

It's what we lay on altars that demonstrates our worth.

3" 'If the offering is a burnt offering
1:3 [d]Ex 12:5; Dt 15:21; Heb 9:14; 1Pe 1:19 [e]Lev 17:9 from the herd, he is to offer a male
without defect.[d] He must present it at
the entrance to the Tent[e] of Meeting so
that it[a] will be acceptable to the LORD.
4He is to lay his hand on the head[f] of
1:4 [f]Ex 29:10,15; Lev 3:2 [g]2Ch 29:23-24 the burnt offering, and it will be accepted on his behalf to make atone-
ment[g] for him. 5He is to slaughter[h] the
young bull before the LORD, and then
Aaron's sons the priests shall bring the
1:5 [h]Lev 3:2,8 [i]Heb 12:24; 1Pe 1:2 blood and sprinkle it against the altar
on all sides[i] at the entrance to the Tent
of Meeting. 6He is to skin[j] the burnt
1:6 [j]Lev 7:8 offering and cut it into pieces. 7The
sons of Aaron the priest are to put fire
1:7 [k]Lev 6:12 on the altar and arrange wood[k] on the
fire. 8Then Aaron's sons the priests shall
1:8 [l]ver 12 arrange the pieces, including the head
and the fat,[l] on the burning wood that
1:9 [m]Ex 29:18 [n]ver 13; Ge 8:21; Nu 15:8-10; Eph 5:2 is on the altar. 9He is to wash the inner
parts and the legs with water, and the
priest is to burn all of it on the altar.[m]
It is a burnt offering, an offering made
by fire, an aroma pleasing to the
LORD.[n]
10" 'If the offering is a burnt offering
1:10 [o]ver 3; Ex 12:5 from the flock, from either the sheep
or the goats,[o] he is to offer a male with-
out defect. 11He is to slaughter it at the
north side of the altar before the LORD,
and Aaron's sons the priests shall sprinkle its blood against the altar on all
sides.[p] 12He is to cut it into pieces, and 1:11 [p]ver 5
the priest shall arrange them, includ-
ing the head and the fat, on the burning wood that is on the altar. 13He is to
wash the inner parts and the legs with
water, and the priest is to bring all of
it and burn it on the altar. It is a burnt
offering, an offering made by fire, an
aroma pleasing to the LORD.
14" 'If the offering to the LORD is a
burnt offering of birds, he is to offer a
dove or a young pigeon.[q] 15The priest 1:14 [q]Ge 15:9; Lev 5:7; Lk 2:24
shall bring it to the altar, wring off the
head and burn it on the altar; its blood
shall be drained out on the side of the
altar.[r] 16He is to remove the crop with 1:15 [r]Lev 5:9
its contents[b] and throw it to the east
side of the altar, where the ashes[s] are. 1:16 [s]Lev 6:10
17He shall tear it open by the wings, not
severing it completely,[t] and then the 1:17 [t]Ge 15:10 [u]Lev 5:8
priest shall burn it on the wood[u] that
is on the fire on the altar. It is a burnt
offering, an offering made by fire, an
aroma pleasing to the LORD.

The Grain Offering

2 " 'When someone brings a grain of-
fering[v] to the LORD, his offering is 2:1 [v]Lev 6:14-18 [w]Nu 15:4
to be of fine flour. He is to pour oil[w]
on it, put incense on it 2and take it to 2:2 [x]Lev 5:11 [y]Lev 6:15; Isa 66:3 [z]ver 9,16; Lev 5:12; 6:15; 24:7; Ac 10:4
Aaron's sons the priests. The priest shall
take a handful of the fine flour[x] and oil,
together with all the incense,[y] and burn
this as a memorial portion[z] on the altar, an offering made by fire, an aroma
pleasing to the LORD. 3The rest of the
grain offering belongs to Aaron and his
sons;[a] it is a most holy part of the offer- 2:3 [a]ver 10; Lev 6:16; 10:12,13
ings made to the LORD by fire.
4" 'If you bring a grain offering baked
in an oven, it is to consist of fine flour:
cakes made without yeast and mixed
with oil, or[c] wafers made without yeast
and spread with oil.[b] 5If your grain of- 2:4 [b]Ex 29:2
fering is prepared on a griddle, it is
to be made of fine flour mixed with
oil, and without yeast. 6Crumble it and
pour oil on it; it is a grain offering. 7If
your grain offering is cooked in a pan,[c] 2:7 [c]Lev 7:9
it is to be made of fine flour and oil.
8Bring the grain offering made of these
things to the LORD; present it to the
priest, who shall take it to the altar. 9He
shall take out the memorial portion[d] 2:9 [d]ver 2

[a]3 Or *he* [b]16 Or *crop and the feathers*; the meaning of the Hebrew for this word is uncertain.
[c]4 Or *and*

from the grain offering and burn it on the altar as an offering made by fire, an aroma pleasing to the LORD.[e] 10The rest of the grain offering belongs to Aaron and his sons;[f] it is a most holy part of the offerings made to the LORD by fire.

11" 'Every grain offering you bring to the LORD must be made without yeast,[g] for you are not to burn any yeast or honey in an offering made to the LORD by fire. 12You may bring them to the LORD as an offering of the firstfruits,[h] but they are not to be offered on the altar as a pleasing aroma. 13Season all your grain offerings with salt. Do not leave the salt of the covenant[i] of your God out of your grain offerings; add salt to all your offerings.

14" 'If you bring a grain offering of firstfruits[j] to the LORD, offer crushed heads of new grain roasted in the fire. 15Put oil and incense on it; it is a grain offering. 16The priest shall burn the memorial portion[k] of the crushed grain and the oil, together with all the incense, as an offering made to the LORD by fire.

The Fellowship Offering

3 " 'If someone's offering is a fellowship offering,[a][l] and he offers an animal from the herd, whether male or female, he is to present before the LORD an animal without defect.[m] 2He is to lay his hand on the head[n] of his offering and slaughter it[o] at the entrance to the Tent of Meeting. Then Aaron's sons the priests shall sprinkle the blood against the altar on all sides. 3From the fellowship offering he is to bring a sacrifice made to the LORD by fire: all the fat[p] that covers the inner parts or is connected to them, 4both kidneys with the fat on them near the loins, and the covering of the liver, which he will remove with the kidneys. 5Then Aaron's sons[q] are to burn it on the altar on top of the burnt offering[r] that is on the burning wood, as an offering made by fire, an aroma pleasing to the LORD.

6" 'If he offers an animal from the flock as a fellowship offering[s] to the LORD, he is to offer a male or female without defect. 7If he offers a lamb, he is to present it before the LORD.[t] 8He is to lay his hand on the head of his offering and slaughter it[u] in front of the Tent of Meeting. Then Aaron's sons shall sprinkle its blood against the altar on all sides. 9From the fellowship offering he is to bring a sacrifice made to the LORD by fire: its fat, the entire fat tail cut off close to the backbone, all the fat that covers the inner parts or is connected to them, 10both kidneys with the fat on them near the loins, and the covering of the liver, which he will remove with the kidneys. 11The priest shall burn them on the altar[v] as food,[w] an offering made to the LORD by fire.

12" 'If his offering is a goat, he is to present it before the LORD. 13He is to lay his hand on its head and slaughter it in front of the Tent of Meeting. Then Aaron's sons shall sprinkle[x] its blood against the altar on all sides. 14From what he offers he is to make this offering to the LORD by fire: all the fat that covers the inner parts or is connected to them, 15both kidneys with the fat on them near the loins, and the covering of the liver, which he will remove with the kidneys. 16The priest shall burn them on the altar as food, an offering made by fire, a pleasing aroma. All the fat is the LORD's.[y]

17" 'This is a lasting ordinance for the generations to come,[z] wherever you live: You must not eat any fat or any blood.[a]' "

The Sin Offering

4 The LORD said to Moses, 2"Say to the Israelites: 'When anyone sins unintentionally[b] and does what is forbidden in any of the LORD's commands—

3" 'If the anointed priest sins, bringing guilt on the people, he must bring to the LORD a young bull[c] without defect as a sin offering[d] for the sin he has committed. 4He is to present the bull at the entrance to the Tent of Meeting before the LORD.[e] He is to lay his hand on its head and slaughter it before the LORD. 5Then the anointed priest shall take some of the bull's blood[f] and carry it into the Tent of Meeting. 6He is to dip his finger into the blood and sprinkle some of it seven times before the LORD, in front of the curtain of

[a] *1* Traditionally *peace offering*; also in verses 3, 6 and 9

2:9 [e]Ex 29:18; Lev 6:15
2:10 [f]ver 3
2:11 [g]Ex 23:18; 34:25; Lev 6:16
2:12 [h]Lev 7:13; 23:10
2:13 [i]Nu 18:19; Eze 43:24
2:14 [j]Lev 23:10
2:16 [k]ver 2
3:1 [l]Lev 7:11-34 [m]Lev 1:3; 22:21
3:2 [n]Ex 29:10,15 [o]Lev 1:5
3:3 [p]Ex 29:13
3:5 [q]Lev 7:29-34 [r]Ex 29:13, 38-42
3:6 [s]ver 1
3:7 [t]Lev 17:8-9
3:8 [u]ver 2; Lev 1:5
3:11 [v]ver 5 [w]ver 16; Lev 21:6,17
3:13 [x]Ex 24:6
3:16 [y]1Sa 2:16
3:17 [z]Lev 6:18; 17:7 [a]Ge 9:4; Lev 7:25-26; 17:10-16; Dt 12:16; Ac 15:20
4:2 [b]Lev 5:15-18; Ps 19:12; Heb 9:7
4:3 [c]ver 14; Ps 66:15 [d]Lev 9:2-22; Heb 9:13-14
4:4 [e]Lev 1:3
4:5 [f]Lev 16:14

the sanctuary. 7The priest shall then put
some of the blood on the horns of the
altar of fragrant incense that is before
the LORD in the Tent of Meeting. The
rest of the bull's blood he shall pour
out at the base of the altar[g] of burnt offering[h] at the entrance to the Tent of
Meeting. 8He shall remove all the fat[i]
from the bull of the sin offering—the
fat that covers the inner parts or is connected to them, 9both kidneys with the
fat on them near the loins, and the covering of the liver, which he will remove
with the kidneys[j]— 10just as the fat is
removed from the ox[a] sacrificed as a fellowship offering.[b] Then the priest shall
burn them on the altar of burnt offering. 11But the hide of the bull and all
its flesh, as well as the head and legs,
the inner parts and offal[k]— 12that is, all
the rest of the bull—he must take outside the camp[l] to a place ceremonially
clean,[m] where the ashes are thrown, and
burn it in a wood fire on the ash heap.

4:7 [g]ver 34; Lev 8:15 [h]ver 18,30; Lev 5:9; 9:9; 16:18
4:8 [i]Lev 3:3-5
4:9 [j]Lev 3:4
4:11 [k]Ex 29:14; Lev 9:11; Nu 19:5
4:12 [l]Heb 13:11 [m]Lev 6:11

GOODNESS

REPENTANCE IN RETROSPECT

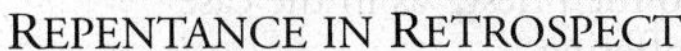

Leviticus 4:13

God requires an accounting of those sins we didn't know were sins. So when a nation sins in ignorance, someone with an up-to-date lexicon of wickedness should keep the culture abreast of all the latest definitions. The sins of a culture awaken God's summons to repentance. "God save the queen!" is no real prayer unless the queen prays it.

13" 'If the whole Israelite community
sins unintentionally[n] and does what is
forbidden in any of the LORD's commands, even though the community is
unaware of the matter, they are guilty.
14When they become aware of the sin
they committed, the assembly must
bring a young bull[o] as a sin offering[p]
and present it before the Tent of Meeting. 15The elders of the community are
to lay their hands on the bull's head[q]
before the LORD, and the bull shall be
slaughtered before the LORD. 16Then
the anointed priest is to take some of
the bull's blood[r] into the Tent of Meeting. 17He shall dip his finger into the
blood and sprinkle it before the LORD[s]
seven times in front of the curtain. 18He
is to put some of the blood on the
horns of the altar that is before the
LORD[t] in the Tent of Meeting. The rest
of the blood he shall pour out at the
base of the altar of burnt offering at the
entrance to the Tent of Meeting. 19He
shall remove all the fat[u] from it and
burn it on the altar, 20and do with this
bull just as he did with the bull for the
sin offering. In this way the priest will
make atonement[v] for them, and they
will be forgiven.[w] 21Then he shall take
the bull outside the camp and burn it
as he burned the first bull. This is the
sin offering for the community.[x]

22" 'When a leader[y] sins unintentionally[z] and does what is forbidden in any
of the commands of the LORD his God,
he is guilty. 23When he is made aware
of the sin he committed, he must bring
as his offering a male goat without defect. 24He is to lay his hand on the
goat's head and slaughter it at the place
where the burnt offering is slaughtered
before the LORD. It is a sin offering.
25Then the priest shall take some of the
blood of the sin offering with his finger and put it on the horns of the altar
of burnt offering and pour out the rest
of the blood at the base of the altar.[a]
26He shall burn all the fat on the altar as
he burned the fat of the fellowship offering. In this way the priest will make
atonement for the man's sin, and he
will be forgiven.[b]

27" 'If a member of the community
sins unintentionally[c] and does what is
forbidden in any of the LORD's commands, he is guilty. 28When he is made
aware of the sin he committed, he must
bring as his offering[d] for the sin he committed a female goat[e] without defect.
29He is to lay his hand on the head[f] of
the sin offering[g] and slaughter it at the
place of the burnt offering. 30Then the
priest is to take some of the blood with
his finger and put it on the horns of the
altar of burnt offering[h] and pour out
the rest of the blood at the base of the
altar. 31He shall remove all the fat, just
as the fat is removed from the fellowship offering, and the priest shall burn
it on the altar as an aroma pleasing to

4:13 [n]ver 2; Lev 5:2-4,17; Nu 15:24-26
4:14 [o]ver 3 [p]ver 23,28
4:15 [q]Lev 1:4; 8:14,22; Nu 8:10
4:16 [r]ver 5
4:17 [s]ver 6
4:18 [t]ver 7
4:19 [u]ver 8
4:20 [v]Heb 10:10-12 [w]Nu 15:25
4:21 [x]Lev 16:5,15
4:22 [y]Nu 31:13 [z]ver 2
4:25 [a]ver 7,18, 30,34; Lev 9:9
4:26 [b]Lev 5:10
4:27 [c]ver 2; Nu 15:27
4:28 [d]ver 23 [e]ver 3
4:29 [f]ver 4,24 [g]Lev 1:4
4:30 [h]ver 7

[a] *10* The Hebrew word can include both male and female. [b] *10* Traditionally *peace offering*; also in verses 26, 31 and 35

4:31 [i]Ge 8:21 the LORD.[i] In this way the priest will
make atonement for him, and he will
be forgiven.
32“ ‘If he brings a lamb as his sin offering, he is to bring a female without
4:32 [j]ver 28 defect.[j] 33He is to lay his hand on its
head and slaughter it for a sin offering
at the place where the burnt offering
4:33 [k]ver 29 is slaughtered.[k] 34Then the priest shall
take some of the blood of the sin of-
fering with his finger and put it on the
horns of the altar of burnt offering and
pour out the rest of the blood at the
4:34 [l]ver 7 base of the altar.[l] 35He shall remove all
the fat, just as the fat is removed from
the lamb of the fellowship offering, and
4:35 [m]ver 26,31 the priest shall burn it on the altar[m] on
top of the offerings made to the LORD
by fire. In this way the priest will make
atonement for him for the sin he has
committed, and he will be forgiven.

5 “ ‘If a person sins because he does
not speak up when he hears a pub-
5:1 [n]Pr 29:24 [o]ver 17 lic charge to testify[n] regarding something he has seen or learned about, he
will be held responsible.[o]
2“ ‘Or if a person touches anything
ceremonially unclean—whether the carcasses of unclean wild animals or of
unclean livestock or of unclean crea-
5:2 [p]Lev 11:11, 24-40; Dt 14:8 tures that move along the ground[p]—
even though he is unaware of it, he has
become unclean and is guilty.
3“ ‘Or if he touches human unclean-
5:3 [q]Nu 19:11-16 ness[q]—anything that would make him
unclean—even though he is unaware
of it, when he learns of it he will be
guilty.
4“ ‘Or if a person thoughtlessly takes
5:4 [r]Nu 30:6,8 an oath[r] to do anything, whether good
or evil—in any matter one might care-
lessly swear about—even though he is
unaware of it, in any case when he
learns of it he will be guilty.
5“ ‘When anyone is guilty in any of
5:5 [s]Lev 16:21; 26:40; Nu 5:7; Pr 28:13 these ways, he must confess[s] in what
way he has sinned 6and, as a penalty
for the sin he has committed, he must
bring to the LORD a female lamb or
5:6 [t]Lev 4:28 goat from the flock as a sin offering;[t]
and the priest shall make atonement for
him for his sin.
5:7 [u]Lev 12:8; 14:21 7“ ‘If he cannot afford[u] a lamb, he is
to bring two doves or two young pi-
geons to the LORD as a penalty for
his sin—one for a sin offering and the
other for a burnt offering. 8He is to
bring them to the priest, who shall first
offer the one for the sin offering. He
is to wring its head from its neck,[v] not 5:8 [v]Lev 1:15 [w]Lev 1:17
severing it completely,[w] 9and is to sprin-
kle some of the blood of the sin offering against the side of the altar; the rest
of the blood must be drained out at the
base of the altar.[x] It is a sin offering. 5:9 [x]Lev 4:7,18
10The priest shall then offer the other as
a burnt offering in the prescribed way[y] 5:10 [y]Lev 1:14-17 [z]Lev 4:26
and make atonement for him for the
sin he has committed, and he will be
forgiven.[z]
11“ ‘If, however, he cannot afford two
doves or two young pigeons, he is to
bring as an offering for his sin a tenth
of an ephah[a] of fine flour[a] for a sin of- 5:11 [a]Lev 2:1
fering. He must not put oil or incense
on it, because it is a sin offering. 12He is
to bring it to the priest, who shall take
a handful of it as a memorial portion
and burn it on the altar on top of the
offerings made to the LORD by fire. It
is a sin offering. 13In this way the priest
will make atonement[b] for him for any 5:13 [b]Lev 4:26 [c]Lev 2:3
of these sins he has committed, and he
will be forgiven. The rest of the offering
will belong to the priest,[c] as in the case
of the grain offering.’ ”

The Guilt Offering

14The LORD said to Moses: 15“When
a person commits a violation and sins
unintentionally in regard to any of the
LORD's holy things, he is to bring to
the LORD as a penalty[d] a ram[e] from 5:15 [d]Lev 22:14 [e]Nu 5:8 [f]Ex 30:13
the flock, one without defect and of the
proper value in silver, according to the
sanctuary shekel.[b][f] It is a guilt offering.
16He must make restitution[g] for what 5:16 [g]Lev 6:4 [h]Lev 22:14; Nu 5:7
he has failed to do in regard to the holy
things, add a fifth of the value[h] to that
and give it all to the priest, who will
make atonement for him with the ram
as a guilt offering, and he will be forgiven.
17“If a person sins and does what is
forbidden in any of the LORD's commands, even though he does not know
it,[i] he is guilty and will be held respon- 5:17 [i]ver 15; Lev 4:2
sible. 18He is to bring to the priest as
a guilt offering a ram from the flock,
one without defect and of the proper
value. In this way the priest will make
atonement for him for the wrong he

[a] *11* That is, probably about 2 quarts (about 2 liters)
[b] *15* That is, about 2/5 ounce (about 11.5 grams)

has committed unintentionally, and he
5:18 will be forgiven.[j] 19It is a guilt offer-
[j]ver 15 ing; he has been guilty of[a] wrongdoing
against the LORD."

6

The LORD said to Moses: 2"If anyone sins and is unfaithful to the
6:2 [k]Nu 5:6; LORD[k] by deceiving his neighbor[l] about
Ac 5:4; Col 3:9 something entrusted to him or left in
[l]Pr 24:28 his care[m] or stolen, or if he cheats him,
[m]Ex 22:7 3or if he finds lost property and lies
6:3 [n]Dt 22:1-3 about it,[n] or if he swears falsely, or if he
commits any such sin that people may
do— 4when he thus sins and becomes
6:4 guilty, he must return[o] what he has sto-
[o]Lk 19:8 len or taken by extortion, or what was
entrusted to him, or the lost property
he found, 5or whatever it was he swore
falsely about. He must make restitu-
6:5 tion[p] in full, add a fifth of the value to
[p]Nu 5:7 [q]Lev 5:15 it and give it all to the owner on the day
he presents his guilt offering.[q] 6And as
a penalty he must bring to the priest,
6:6 [r]Lev 5:15 that is, to the LORD, his guilt offering,[r]
a ram from the flock, one without de-
fect and of the proper value. 7In this
6:7 way the priest will make atonement[s] for
[s]Lev 4:26 him before the LORD, and he will be
forgiven for any of these things he did
that made him guilty."

The Burnt Offering

8The LORD said to Moses: 9"Give
Aaron and his sons this command:
'These are the regulations for the burnt
offering: The burnt offering is to remain on the altar hearth throughout the
night, till morning, and the fire must be
kept burning on the altar. 10The priest
shall then put on his linen clothes, with
6:10 [t]Ex 28:39-42, linen undergarments next to his body,[t]
43; 39:28 and shall remove the ashes of the burnt
offering that the fire has consumed on
the altar and place them beside the altar. 11Then he is to take off these clothes
and put on others, and carry the ashes
outside the camp to a place that is cer-
6:11 emonially clean.[u] 12The fire on the altar
[u]Lev 4:12 must be kept burning; it must not go
out. Every morning the priest is to add
firewood and arrange the burnt offering on the fire and burn the fat of the
fellowship offerings[b] on it. 13The fire
must be kept burning on the altar con-
tinuously; it must not go out.

The Grain Offering

6:14 14" 'These are the regulations for the
[v]Lev 2:1; 15:4 grain offering:[v] Aaron's sons are to bring
it before the LORD, in front of the altar.
15The priest is to take a handful of fine
flour and oil, together with all the incense on the grain offering,[w] and burn 6:15
the memorial portion[x] on the altar as [w]Lev 2:9 [x]Lev 2:2
an aroma pleasing to the LORD. 16Aar- 6:16
on and his sons[y] shall eat the rest[z] of it, [y]Lev 2:3
but it is to be eaten without yeast[a] in [z]Eze 44:29 [a]Lev 2:11
a holy place;[b] they are to eat it in the [b]Lev 10:13
courtyard of the Tent of Meeting. 17It
must not be baked with yeast; I have
given it as their share of the offerings
made to me by fire. Like the sin offering and the guilt offering, it is most
holy.[c] 18Any male descendant of Aaron 6:17 [c]ver 29;
may eat it.[d] It is his regular share of Ex 40:10;
the offerings made to the LORD by fire Nu 18:9,10
for the generations to come. Whatever 6:18
touches them will become holy.[c][e]' " [d]ver 29; Nu 18:9-10
19The LORD also said to Moses, [e]ver 27
20"This is the offering Aaron and his
sons are to bring to the LORD on
the day he[d] is anointed: a tenth of an
ephah[e][f] of fine flour as a regular grain 6:20
offering,[g] half of it in the morning and [f]Ex 16:36 [g]Ex 29:2
half in the evening. 21Prepare it with
oil on a griddle;[h] bring it well-mixed 6:21 [h]Lev 2:5
and present the grain offering broken[f]
in pieces as an aroma pleasing to the
LORD. 22The son who is to succeed
him as anointed priest shall prepare it.
It is the LORD's regular share and is to
be burned completely. 23Every grain offering of a priest shall be burned completely; it must not be eaten."

The Sin Offering

24The LORD said to Moses, 25"Say
to Aaron and his sons: 'These are the
regulations for the sin offering: The sin
offering is to be slaughtered before the 6:25
LORD[i] in the place[j] the burnt offering [i]Lev 1:3
is slaughtered; it is most holy. 26The [j]Lev 1:5,11
priest who offers it shall eat it; it is to be
eaten in a holy place,[k] in the courtyard[l] 6:26 [k]ver 16
of the Tent of Meeting. 27Whatever [l]Lev 10:17-18
touches any of the flesh will become
holy,[m] and if any of the blood is spat- 6:27 [m]Ex 29:37
tered on a garment, you must wash it in
a holy place. 28The clay pot[n] the meat 6:28
is cooked in must be broken; but if it [n]Lev 11:33;
is cooked in a bronze pot, the pot is 15:12

[a]*19* Or *has made full expiation for his*
[b]*12* Traditionally *peace offerings* [c]*18* Or *Whoever touches them must be holy*; similarly in verse 27
[d]*20* Or *each* [e]*20* That is, probably about 2 quarts (about 2 liters) [f]*21* The meaning of the Hebrew for this word is uncertain.

to be scoured and rinsed with water.
29Any male in a priest's family may eat
6:29 [o]ver 18 it;[o] it is most holy.[p] 30But any sin of-
[p]ver 17 fering whose blood is brought into the
Tent of Meeting to make atonement in
6:30 [q]Lev 4:18 the Holy Place[q] must not be eaten; it
[r]Lev 4:12 must be burned.[r]

The Guilt Offering

7 " 'These are the regulations for the
guilt offering,[s] which is most holy:
7:1 [s]Lev 5:14-6:7 2The guilt offering is to be slaughtered
in the place where the burnt offering
is slaughtered, and its blood is to be
sprinkled against the altar on all sides.
7:3 [t]Ex 29:13; 3All its fat[t] shall be offered: the fat tail
Lev 3:4,9 and the fat that covers the inner parts,
4both kidneys with the fat on them
near the loins, and the covering of the
liver, which is to be removed with the
kidneys. 5The priest shall burn them
on the altar as an offering made to the
LORD by fire. It is a guilt offering. 6Any
7:6 [u]Lev 6:18; male in a priest's family may eat it,[u] but
Nu 18:9-10 it must be eaten in a holy place; it is
[v]Lev 2:3 most holy.[v]

7" 'The same law applies to both the
sin offering and the guilt offering: They
7:7 belong to the priest[w] who makes atone-
[w]Lev 6:17,26; ment with them. 8The priest who of-
1Co 9:13 fers a burnt offering for anyone may
keep its hide for himself. 9Every grain
offering baked in an oven or cooked
7:9 in a pan or on a griddle[x] belongs to
[x]Lev 2:5 the priest who offers it, 10and every
grain offering, whether mixed with oil
or dry, belongs equally to all the sons of
Aaron.

The Fellowship Offering

11" 'These are the regulations for
the fellowship offering[a] a person may
present to the LORD:

12" 'If he offers it as an expression
of thankfulness, then along with this
7:12 [y]ver 13,15 thank offering[y] he is to offer cakes of
[z]Lev 2:4; bread made without yeast and mixed
Nu 6:15 with oil, wafers[z] made without yeast
and spread with oil, and cakes of fine
flour well-kneaded and mixed with oil.
13Along with his fellowship offering of
thanksgiving he is to present an offering
7:13 [a]Lev 23:17; with cakes of bread made with yeast.[a]
Am 4:5 14He is to bring one of each kind as an
offering, a contribution to the LORD;
it belongs to the priest who sprinkles
the blood of the fellowship offerings.
15The meat of his fellowship offering of
thanksgiving must be eaten on the day
it is offered; he must leave none of it till
morning.[b] 7:15 [b]Lev 22:30

16" 'If, however, his offering is the result of a vow or is a freewill offering,
the sacrifice shall be eaten on the day he
offers it, but anything left over may be
eaten on the next day.[c] 17Any meat of 7:16
the sacrifice left over till the third day [c]Lev 19:5-8
must be burned up. 18If any meat of the
fellowship offering is eaten on the third
day, it will not be accepted.[d] It will not 7:18 [d]Lev 19:7
be credited[e] to the one who offered it, [e]Nu 18:27
for it is impure; the person who eats
any of it will be held responsible.

19" 'Meat that touches anything ceremonially unclean must not be eaten; it
must be burned up. As for other meat,
anyone ceremonially clean may eat it.
20But if anyone who is unclean eats any
meat of the fellowship offering belonging to the LORD, that person must be 7:20
cut off from his people.[f] 21If anyone [f]Lev 22:3-7
touches something unclean[g]—whether 7:21
human uncleanness or an unclean ani- [g]Lev 5:2;
mal or any unclean, detestable thing— 11:24,28
and then eats any of the meat of the
fellowship offering belonging to the
LORD, that person must be cut off from
his people.' "

Eating Fat and Blood Forbidden

22The LORD said to Moses, 23"Say to
the Israelites: 'Do not eat any of the fat 7:23
of cattle, sheep or goats.[h] 24The fat of [h]Lev 3:17;
an animal found dead or torn by wild 17:13-14
animals[i] may be used for any other pur- 7:24 [i]Ex 22:31
pose, but you must not eat it. 25Any-
one who eats the fat of an animal from
which an offering by fire may be[b] made
to the LORD must be cut off from his
people. 26And wherever you live, you 7:26
must not eat the blood[j] of any bird [j]Ge 9:4
or animal. 27If anyone eats blood,[k] that 7:27
person must be cut off from his peo- [k]Lev
ple.' " 17:10-24;
Ac 15:20,29

The Priests' Share

28The LORD said to Moses, 29"Say
to the Israelites: 'Anyone who brings a
fellowship offering to the LORD is to
bring part of it as his sacrifice to the
LORD. 30With his own hands he is to
bring the offering made to the LORD
by fire; he is to bring the fat, together

[a]*11* Traditionally *peace offering*; also in verses 13-37
[b]*25* Or *fire is*

with the breast, and wave the breast
7:30 [l]Ex 29:24; Nu 6:20 before the LORD as a wave offering.[l]
31The priest shall burn the fat on the al-
tar, but the breast belongs to Aaron and
7:31 [m]ver 34 his sons.[m] 32You are to give the right
thigh of your fellowship offerings to the
7:32 [n]ver 34; Lev 9:21; Nu 6:20 priest as a contribution.[n] 33The son of
Aaron who offers the blood and the fat
of the fellowship offering shall have the
right thigh as his share. 34From the fellowship offerings of the Israelites, I have
taken the breast that is waved and the
7:34 [o]Lev 10:15 [p]Ex 29:27; Nu 18:18-19 thigh[o] that is presented and have given
them to Aaron the priest and his sons[p]
as their regular share from the Israelites.' "
35This is the portion of the offerings
made to the LORD by fire that were
allotted to Aaron and his sons on the
day they were presented to serve the
LORD as priests. 36On the day they
7:36 [q]Ex 40:13,15; Lev 8:12,30 were anointed,[q] the LORD commanded
that the Israelites give this to them as
their regular share for the generations
to come.

37These, then, are the regulations for
7:37 [r]Lev 6:9 [s]Lev 6:14 [t]ver 1,11 the burnt offering,[r] the grain offering,[s]
the sin offering, the guilt offering, the
ordination offering[t] and the fellowship
offering, 38which the LORD gave Moses on Mount Sinai on the day he commanded the Israelites to bring their
7:38 [u]Lev 1:2 offerings to the LORD,[u] in the Desert
of Sinai.

The Ordination of Aaron and His Sons

8 The LORD said to Moses, 2"Bring
Aaron and his sons, their garments,
8:2 [v]Ex 30:23-25, 30 [w]Ex 29:2-3 the anointing oil,[v] the bull for the sin
offering, the two rams and the basket
containing bread made without yeast,[w]
8:3 [x]Nu 8:9 3and gather the entire assembly[x] at the
entrance to the Tent of Meeting." 4Mo-
ses did as the LORD commanded him,
and the assembly gathered at the entrance to the Tent of Meeting.
5Moses said to the assembly, "This
is what the LORD has commanded to
be done." 6Then Moses brought Aaron
8:6 [y]Ex 29:4; 30:19; Ps 26:6; Ac 22:16; 1Co 6:11; Eph 5:26 and his sons forward and washed them
with water.[y] 7He put the tunic on Aar-
on, tied the sash around him, clothed
him with the robe and put the ephod
on him. He also tied the ephod to him
8:7 [z]Ex 28:4 by its skillfully woven waistband; so
it was fastened on him.[z] 8He placed
the breastpiece on him and put the
Urim and Thummim[a] in the breast- 8:8 [a]Ex 28:30
piece. 9Then he placed the turban on
Aaron's head and set the gold plate, the
sacred diadem,[b] on the front of it, as 8:9 [b]Ex 28:36
the LORD commanded Moses.
10Then Moses took the anointing oil[c] 8:10 [c]ver 2 [d]Ex 30:26
and anointed[d] the tabernacle and every-
thing in it, and so consecrated them.
11He sprinkled some of the oil on the
altar seven times, anointing the altar
and all its utensils and the basin with
its stand, to consecrate them.[e] 12He 8:11 [e]Ex 30:29
poured some of the anointing oil on
Aaron's head and anointed[f] him to con- 8:12 [f]Lev 21:10,12 [g]Ex 30:30
secrate him.[g] 13Then he brought Aaron's
sons forward, put tunics on them, tied
sashes around them and put headbands
on them, as the LORD commanded
Moses.
14He then presented the bull[h] for the 8:14 [h]Lev 4:3 [i]Ps 66:15; Eze 43:19
sin offering,[i] and Aaron and his sons
laid their hands on its head. 15Moses
slaughtered the bull and took some of
the blood, and with his finger he put
it on all the horns of the altar[j] to pu- 8:15 [j]Lev 4:7 [k]Heb 9:22 [l]Eze 43:20
rify the altar.[k] He poured out the rest
of the blood at the base of the altar.
So he consecrated it to make atonement for it.[l] 16Moses also took all the
fat around the inner parts, the covering
of the liver, and both kidneys and their
fat, and burned it on the altar. 17But the
bull with its hide and its flesh and its 8:17 [m]Lev 4:11 [n]Lev 4:12
offal[m] he burned up outside the camp,[n]
as the LORD commanded Moses.
18He then presented the ram[o] for the 8:18 [o]ver 2
burnt offering, and Aaron and his sons
laid their hands on its head. 19Then
Moses slaughtered the ram and sprinkled the blood against the altar on all
sides. 20He cut the ram into pieces and
burned the head, the pieces and the fat.
21He washed the inner parts and the
legs with water and burned the whole
ram on the altar as a burnt offering, a
pleasing aroma, an offering made to the
LORD by fire, as the LORD commanded Moses.
22He then presented the other ram,
the ram for the ordination,[p] and Aar- 8:22 [p]ver 2
on and his sons laid their hands on its
head. 23Moses slaughtered the ram and
took some of its blood and put it on the
lobe of Aaron's right ear, on the thumb
of his right hand and on the big toe
of his right foot. 24Moses also brought
Aaron's sons forward and put some of

the blood on the lobes of their right
ears, on the thumbs of their right hands
and on the big toes of their right feet.
Then he sprinkled blood against the
8:24 altar on all sides.[q] 25He took the fat,
[q]Heb 9:18-22 the fat tail, all the fat around the inner
parts, the covering of the liver, both kidneys and their fat and the right thigh.
26Then from the basket of bread made
without yeast, which was before the
LORD, he took a cake of bread, and
one made with oil, and a wafer; he put
these on the fat portions and on the
right thigh. 27He put all these in the
hands of Aaron and his sons and waved
them before the LORD as a wave offering. 28Then Moses took them from
their hands and burned them on the altar on top of the burnt offering as an
ordination offering, a pleasing aroma,
an offering made to the LORD by fire.
29He also took the breast—Moses' share
8:29 of the ordination ram[r]—and waved it
[r]Lev 7:31-34 before the LORD as a wave offering, as
the LORD commanded Moses.
30Then Moses took some of the
anointing oil and some of the blood
from the altar and sprinkled them on
8:30 [s]Ex 28:2 Aaron and his garments[s] and on his
[t]Nu 3:3 sons and their garments. So he consecrated[t] Aaron and his garments and his
sons and their garments.

PEACE

PEACE, THE COMPULSION OF GOD

Leviticus 8:30

As priest, Aaron brought peace between God and humankind. Our own priesthood must also serve the cause of peace in a world estranged from God.

It is time to lay down our cold philosophies and
our thumb-worn arguments,
take up the olive branch,
and become obsessed with eradicating hate.

31Moses then said to Aaron and his
sons, "Cook the meat at the entrance
to the Tent of Meeting and eat it there
with the bread from the basket of ordination offerings, as I commanded,
saying,[a] 'Aaron and his sons are to eat
it.' 32Then burn up the rest of the meat
and the bread. 33Do not leave the entrance to the Tent of Meeting for seven
days, until the days of your ordination
are completed, for your ordination will
last seven days. 34What has been done
today was commanded by the LORD[u] 8:34
to make atonement for you. 35You must [u]Heb 7:16
stay at the entrance to the Tent of Meeting day and night for seven days and do
what the LORD requires,[v] so you will 8:35 [v]Nu 3:7; 9:19;
not die; for that is what I have been Dt 11:1;
commanded." 36So Aaron and his sons 1Ki 2:3;
did everything the LORD commanded Eze 48:11
through Moses.

The Priests Begin Their Ministry

9 On the eighth day[w] Moses sum- 9:1
moned Aaron and his sons and [w]Eze 43:27
the elders of Israel. 2He said to Aaron,
"Take a bull calf for your sin offering
and a ram for your burnt offering, both
without defect, and present them before the LORD. 3Then say to the Israelites: 'Take a male goat for a sin offering,
a calf and a lamb—both a year old and
without defect—for a burnt offering,
4and an ox[b] and a ram for a fellowship
offering[c] to sacrifice before the LORD,
together with a grain offering mixed
with oil. For today the LORD will ap- 9:4
pear to you.[x]'" [x]Ex 29:43
5They took the things Moses commanded to the front of the Tent of
Meeting, and the entire assembly came
near and stood before the LORD. 6Then
Moses said, "This is what the LORD has
commanded you to do, so that the glory
of the LORD[y] may appear to you." 9:6
7Moses said to Aaron, "Come to the [y]ver 23;
altar and sacrifice your sin offering and Ex 24:16
your burnt offering and make atone-
ment for yourself and the people; sacrifice the offering that is for the people
and make atonement for them, as the
LORD has commanded."[z] 9:7
8So Aaron came to the altar and [z]Heb 5:1,3; 7:27
slaughtered the calf as a sin offering[a] for 9:8
himself. 9His sons brought the blood to [a]Lev 4:1-12
him,[b] and he dipped his finger into the 9:9
blood and put it on the horns of the al- [b]ver 12,18
tar; the rest of the blood he poured out [c]Lev 4:7
at the base of the altar.[c] 10On the altar
he burned the fat, the kidneys and the
covering of the liver from the sin offering, as the LORD commanded Moses;

[a]31 Or *I was commanded:* [b]4 The Hebrew word can include both male and female; also in verses 18 and 19. [c]4 Traditionally *peace offering*; also in verses 18 and 22

9:11 [d]Lev 4:11 [e]Lev 4:12; 8:17

11the flesh and the hide[d] he burned up
outside the camp.[e]
12Then he slaughtered the burnt offering. His sons handed him the blood,
and he sprinkled it against the altar on
all sides. 13They handed him the burnt

DAY 5 FIVE

▸ JOY AND ITS PLACE IN MY PERSONAL WORSHIP

Leviticus 9:22–24

Let us examine the order of the events that led to the people's praise. First, Aaron, the high priest, makes an offering for their sins *(which for Christians happened when Jesus paid the price for our sins on the cross)*. Second, the Israelites gather in the place of public assembly *(which for Christians is equal to the church)*. Third, Aaron blesses all the people *(which for Christians means Christ's unforsaking presence)*. Fourth, the glory of the Lord appeared in real fire and devoured the sacrifice *(which for Christians signifies the guaranteed living presence of the Holy Spirit in our lives whenever we meet together)*. Finally, all the people fall on their faces in joyous praise and worship God with their whole hearts.

What is the cumulative effect of all this collective adoration? Unity. Worship not only brings God to the people; it also brings the people into oneness. They are united into one body, functioning as a single organism of praise. Unity allows those rough edges of separateness to be smoothed away, and we draw together with others to praise God and draw close to him.

Isn't this our great hunger of heart as believers? We long to be connected with others just as we long to be brought into a closer relationship with God. We sing "Draw Me Nearer" as an expression of our hearts, for we are tired of our separateness. We long to be one with Jesus, and when we enter into praise, a wonderful phenomenon begins to happen. Gradually, the hard, fast lines that have separated us from God begin to disappear, and we, like these ancient Israelites, fall face down before him. He unites with us, and enfolded in his Glory, we experience the great values of human existence.

To begin a study on the topic of Joy, a Positive Attitude, turn to the home page on page 358.

offering piece by piece, including the
head, and he burned them on the altar.[f]
14He washed the inner parts and the
legs and burned them on top of the
burnt offering on the altar.
15Aaron then brought the offering
that was for the people.[g] He took the
goat for the people's sin offering and
slaughtered it and offered it for a sin offering as he did with the first one.
16He brought the burnt offering and
offered it in the prescribed way.[h] 17He
also brought the grain offering, took a
handful of it and burned it on the altar in addition to the morning's burnt
offering.[i]
18He slaughtered the ox and the ram
as the fellowship offering for the people.[j]
His sons handed him the blood, and
he sprinkled it against the altar on all
sides. 19But the fat portions of the ox
and the ram—the fat tail, the layer of
fat, the kidneys and the covering of the
liver— 20these they laid on the breasts,
and then Aaron burned the fat on the
altar. 21Aaron waved the breasts and the
right thigh before the LORD as a wave
offering,[k] as Moses commanded.
22Then Aaron lifted his hands toward
the people and blessed them.[l] And having sacrificed the sin offering, the burnt
offering and the fellowship offering, he
stepped down.
23Moses and Aaron then went into
the Tent of Meeting. When they came
out, they blessed the people; and the
glory of the LORD[m] appeared to all
the people. 24Fire[n] came out from the
presence of the LORD and consumed
the burnt offering and the fat portions
on the altar. And when all the people
saw it, they shouted for joy and fell
facedown.[o]

The Death of Nadab and Abihu

10 Aaron's sons Nadab and Abihu[p]
took their censers, put fire in
them[q] and added incense; and they
offered unauthorized fire before the
LORD, contrary to his command.[r] 2So
fire came out from the presence of the
LORD and consumed them,[s] and they
died before the LORD. 3Moses then
said to Aaron, "This is what the LORD
spoke of when he said:

"'Among those who approach me[t]
I will show myself holy;[u]

9:13 [f]Lev 1:8
9:15 [g]Lev 4:27-31
9:16 [h]Lev 1:1-13
9:17 [i]Lev 2:1-2; 3:5
9:18 [j]Lev 3:1-11
9:21 [k]Ex 29:24,26; Lev 7:30-34
9:22 [l]Nu 6:23; Dt 21:5; Lk 24:50
9:23 [m]ver 6
9:24 [n]Jdg 6:21; 2Ch 7:1 [o]1Ki 18:39
10:1 [p]Ex 24:1; Nu 3:2-4; 26:61 [q]Lev 16:12 [r]Ex 30:9
10:2 [s]Nu 3:4; 16:35; 26:61
10:3 [t]Ex 19:22 [u]Ex 30:29; Lev 21:6; Eze 28:22

10:3 [v]Isa 49:3

in the sight of all the people
I will be honored.[v]' "

Aaron remained silent.

10:4 [w]Ex 6:22 [x]Ex 6:18 [y]Ac 5:6,9,10

4Moses summoned Mishael and
Elzaphan,[w] sons of Aaron's uncle Uzziel,[x]
and said to them, "Come here; carry
your cousins outside the camp,[y] away
from the front of the sanctuary." 5So
they came and carried them, still in

10:5 [z]Lev 8:13

their tunics,[z] outside the camp, as Moses ordered.

GOODNESS

TAINTED GOODNESS

Leviticus 10:1

Thoreau wrote that there is no odor so bad as that which arises from tainted goodness. Good and bad religion can walk side by side and look alike to the untrained eye.

Religious hype is pseudo-fire.
It looks as though the flame's intense.
But it's a bogus, icy heat
Whose heart is arctic with pretense.

6Then Moses said to Aaron and his
sons Eleazar and Ithamar, "Do not let

10:6 [a]Lev 21:10 [b]Nu 1:53; 16:22; Jos 7:1; 22:18; 2Sa 24:1

your hair become unkempt,[a][a] and do
not tear your clothes, or you will die
and the LORD will be angry with the
whole community.[b] But your relatives,
all the house of Israel, may mourn for
those the LORD has destroyed by fire.
7Do not leave the entrance to the Tent
of Meeting or you will die, because the
LORD's anointing oil[c] is on you." So

10:7 [c]Ex 28:41; Lev 21:12

they did as Moses said.
8Then the LORD said to Aaron, 9"You
and your sons are not to drink wine[d] or

10:9 [d]Hos 4:11 [e]Pr 20:1; Isa 28:7; Eze 44:21; Lk 1:15; Eph 5:18; 1Ti 3:3; Tit 1:7

other fermented drink[e] whenever you
go into the Tent of Meeting, or you
will die. This is a lasting ordinance for
the generations to come. 10You must
distinguish between the holy and the
common, between the unclean and the

10:10 [f]Lev 11:47; 20:25; Eze 22:26

clean,[f] 11and you must teach[g] the Israelites all the decrees the LORD has given

10:11 [g]Mal 2:7 [h]Dt 24:8

them through Moses.[h]"
12Moses said to Aaron and his remaining sons, Eleazar and Ithamar,
"Take the grain offering left over from
the offerings made to the LORD by fire
and eat it prepared without yeast beside

10:12 [i]Lev 6:14-18; 21:22

the altar,[i] for it is most holy. 13Eat it in a
holy place, because it is your share and
your sons' share of the offerings made
to the LORD by fire; for so I have been
commanded. 14But you and your sons
and your daughters may eat the breast
that was waved and the thigh that was
presented. Eat them in a ceremonially
clean place;[j] they have been given to
you and your children as your share
of the Israelites' fellowship offerings.[b]

10:14 [j]Ex 29:24, 26-27; Lev 7:31,34; Nu 18:11

15The thigh[k] that was presented and the
breast that was waved must be brought

10:15 [k]Lev 7:34

with the fat portions of the offerings
made by fire, to be waved before the
LORD as a wave offering. This will be
the regular share for you and your children, as the LORD has commanded."
16When Moses inquired about the
goat of the sin offering[l] and found that
it had been burned up, he was angry

10:16 [l]Lev 9:3

with Eleazar and Ithamar, Aaron's remaining sons, and asked, 17"Why didn't
you eat the sin offering[m] in the sanctuary area? It is most holy; it was given to

10:17 [m]Lev 6:24-30

you to take away the guilt of the community by making atonement for them
before the LORD. 18Since its blood was
not taken into the Holy Place,[n] you
should have eaten the goat in the sanc-

10:18 [n]Lev 6:26,30

tuary area, as I commanded."
19Aaron replied to Moses, "Today
they sacrificed their sin offering and
their burnt offering[o] before the LORD,

10:19 [o]Lev 9:12

but such things as this have happened
to me. Would the LORD have been
pleased if I had eaten the sin offering
today?" 20When Moses heard this, he
was satisfied.

Clean and Unclean Food

11 The LORD said to Moses and
Aaron, 2"Say to the Israelites:
'Of all the animals that live on land,
these are the ones you may eat:[p] 3You

11:2 [p]Ac 10:12-14

may eat any animal that has a split
hoof completely divided and that chews
the cud.
4" 'There are some that only chew the
cud or only have a split hoof, but you
must not eat them. The camel, though
it chews the cud, does not have a split
hoof; it is ceremonially unclean for you.
5The coney,[c] though it chews the cud,
does not have a split hoof; it is unclean
for you. 6The rabbit, though it chews
the cud, does not have a split hoof; it is

[a]6 Or *Do not uncover your heads* [b]14 Traditionally *peace offerings* [c]5 That is, the hyrax or rock badger

11:7 [q]Isa 65:4; 66:3,17 unclean for you. 7And the pig,[q] though
it has a split hoof completely divided,
does not chew the cud; it is unclean for
you. 8You must not eat their meat or
touch their carcasses; they are unclean
11:8 [r]Isa 52:11; Heb 9:10 for you.[r]
9" 'Of all the creatures living in the
water of the seas and the streams, you
may eat any that have fins and scales.
10But all creatures in the seas or streams
that do not have fins and scales—
whether among all the swarming things
or among all the other living creatures
11:10 [s]Lev 7:18 in the water—you are to detest.[s] 11And
since you are to detest them, you must
not eat their meat and you must detest
their carcasses. 12Anything living in the
water that does not have fins and scales
is to be detestable to you.
13" 'These are the birds you are to detest and not eat because they are detestable: the eagle, the vulture, the black
vulture, 14the red kite, any kind of black
kite, 15any kind of raven, 16the horned
owl, the screech owl, the gull, any kind
of hawk, 17the little owl, the cormorant, the great owl, 18the white owl,
the desert owl, the osprey, 19the stork,
any kind of heron, the hoopoe and the
bat.[a]
20" 'All flying insects that walk on
11:20 [t]Ac 10:14 all fours are to be detestable to you.[t]
21There are, however, some winged crea-
tures that walk on all fours that you
may eat: those that have jointed legs
for hopping on the ground. 22Of these
11:22 [u]Mt 3:4; Mk 1:6 you may eat any kind of locust,[u] ka-
tydid, cricket or grasshopper. 23But all
other winged creatures that have four
legs you are to detest.
24" 'You will make yourselves unclean
by these; whoever touches their carcasses
will be unclean till evening. 25Whoever
picks up one of their carcasses must
11:25 [v]Lev 14:8, 47; 15:5 [w]ver 40; Nu 31:24 wash his clothes,[v] and he will be unclean till evening.[w]
26" 'Every animal that has a split hoof
not completely divided or that does not
chew the cud is unclean for you; whoever touches ⌞the carcass of⌟ any of them
will be unclean. 27Of all the animals
that walk on all fours, those that walk
on their paws are unclean for you; whoever touches their carcasses will be unclean till evening. 28Anyone who picks
up their carcasses must wash his clothes,
and he will be unclean till evening.
They are unclean for you.

29" 'Of the animals that move about
on the ground, these are unclean for
you: the weasel, the rat,[x] any kind of 11:29 [x]Isa 66:17
great lizard, 30the gecko, the monitor
lizard, the wall lizard, the skink and the
chameleon. 31Of all those that move
along the ground, these are unclean for
you. Whoever touches them when they
are dead will be unclean till evening.
32When one of them dies and falls on
something, that article, whatever its use,
will be unclean, whether it is made of
wood, cloth, hide or sackcloth.[y] Put it 11:32 [y]Lev 15:12
in water; it will be unclean till evening,
and then it will be clean. 33If one of
them falls into a clay pot, everything in
it will be unclean, and you must break
the pot.[z] 34Any food that could be eat- 11:33 [z]Lev 6:28; 15:12
en but has water on it from such a pot
is unclean, and any liquid that could
be drunk from it is unclean. 35Anything
that one of their carcasses falls on becomes unclean; an oven or cooking pot
must be broken up. They are unclean,
and you are to regard them as unclean.
36A spring, however, or a cistern for collecting water remains clean, but anyone who touches one of these carcasses
is unclean. 37If a carcass falls on any
seeds that are to be planted, they remain clean. 38But if water has been put
on the seed and a carcass falls on it, it is
unclean for you.
39" 'If an animal that you are allowed
to eat dies, anyone who touches the carcass will be unclean till evening. 40Any-
one who eats some of the carcass must
wash his clothes, and he will be unclean
till evening.[a] Anyone who picks up the 11:40 [a]Lev 17:15; 22:8; Eze 44:31
carcass must wash his clothes, and he
will be unclean till evening.
41" 'Every creature that moves about
on the ground is detestable; it is not to
be eaten. 42You are not to eat any creature that moves about on the ground,
whether it moves on its belly or walks
on all fours or on many feet; it is de- 11:43 [b]Lev 20:25
testable. 43Do not defile yourselves by
any of these creatures.[b] Do not make 11:44 [c]Ex 6:2,7; Isa 43:3; 51:15
yourselves unclean by means of them
or be made unclean by them. 44I am [d]Lev 20:7
the LORD your God;[c] consecrate your- [e]Ex 19:6
selves[d] and be holy,[e] because I am holy.[f] [f]Lev 19:2; Ps 99:3; Eph 1:4; 1Th 4:7; 1Pe 1:15,16*
Do not make yourselves unclean by
any creature that moves about on the

[a] *19* The precise identification of some of the birds, insects and animals in this chapter is uncertain.

DAY 5 FIVE

Self-Control and Its Place in My Personal Worship

Leviticus 11:44

"Consecrate yourselves," said Moses. What he really meant was, "Say no to those appetites that God forbids in your life." The result will be that we will be able to come into God's presence, and our adoration of him will be sweet.

But what is God really trying to accomplish with these kosher taboos of Leviticus? Is God trying to restrict his people to a killjoy life in which they will always be on the lookout for sin and never really enjoy a single day of positive living? Of course not. Every taboo that God asks us to honor is given for our own sake and for the sake of the kingdom of God. Take the Ten Commandments: Are they intended to regiment and restrict our freedom? It is not their constraint that is so important. At the center of every *you shall not* is a glorious liberty—not a coercion. What kind of world would we have if everybody went around lying, stealing, murdering and committing adultery at will? It is only when we honor these constrictions that we become truly free—and the world along with us.

The result of our honoring of God's commandment, says this verse in Leviticus, is that we are truly free. We have been set free by our own desire for holiness and in the practice of self-control. By entering into God's holiness, our worship becomes glorious. For great worship sets us free from ourselves just as self-control ensures that we stay in charge of our lives.

To begin a study on the topic of Self-Control, Saying No to Our Appetites, turn to the home page on page 105.

ground. 45 I am the LORD who brought
11:45 [g]Lev 25:38,55; Ex 6:7; 20:2 [h]Ge 17:7 [i]Ex 19:6; 1Pe 1:16* you up out of Egypt[g] to be your God;[h]
therefore be holy, because I am holy.[i]
46 "'These are the regulations concerning animals, birds, every living thing
that moves in the water and every creature that moves about on the ground.
47 You must distinguish between the unclean and the clean, between living creatures that may be eaten and those that
11:47 [j]Lev 10:10 may not be eaten.'"[j]

Purification After Childbirth

12 The LORD said to Moses, 2 "Say
to the Israelites: 'A woman who
becomes pregnant and gives birth to
a son will be ceremonially unclean for
seven days, just as she is unclean during
her monthly period.[k] 3 On the eighth 12:2 [k]Lev 15:19; 18:19
day the boy is to be circumcised.[l] 4 Then
the woman must wait thirty-three days
to be purified from her bleeding. She 12:3 [l]Ge 17:12; Lk 1:59; 2:21
must not touch anything sacred or go
to the sanctuary until the days of her
purification are over. 5 If she gives birth
to a daughter, for two weeks the woman will be unclean, as during her period. Then she must wait sixty-six days to
be purified from her bleeding.
6 "'When the days of her purification
for a son or daughter are over,[m] she is to 12:6 [m]Lk 2:22 [n]Ex 29:38; Lev 23:12; Nu 6:12,14; 7:15 [o]Lev 5:7
bring to the priest at the entrance to the Tent of Meeting a year-old lamb[n] for a burnt offering and a young pigeon or a
dove for a sin offering.[o] 7 He shall offer
them before the LORD to make atonement for her, and then she will be ceremonially clean from her flow of blood.
"'These are the regulations for the woman who gives birth to a boy or a
girl. 8 If she cannot afford a lamb, she
is to bring two doves or two young
pigeons,[p] one for a burnt offering and 12:8 [p]Ge 15:9; Lev 14:22 [q]Lev 5:7; Lk 2:22-24* [r]Lev 4:26
the other for a sin offering.[q] In this way the priest will make atonement for her, and she will be clean.[r]'"

Regulations About Infectious Skin Diseases

13 The LORD said to Moses and
Aaron, 2 "When anyone has a
swelling[s] or a rash or a bright spot[t] on 13:2 [s]ver 10,19,28,43 [t]ver 4,38,39; Lev 14:56 [u]ver 3,9,15; Ex 4:6; Lev 14:3,32; Nu 5:2; Dt 24:8 [v]Dt 24:8
his skin that may become an infectious skin disease,[a][u] he must be brought to Aaron the priest[v] or to one of his sons[b]
who is a priest. 3 The priest is to examine the sore on his skin, and if the hair in the sore has turned white and the sore appears to be more than skin 13:3 [w]ver 8,11,20,30; Lev 21:1; Nu 9:6
deep,[c] it is an infectious skin disease. When the priest examines him, he shall pronounce him ceremonially unclean.[w]
4 If the spot[x] on his skin is white but 13:4 [x]ver 2
does not appear to be more than skin

[a]2 Traditionally *leprosy*; the Hebrew word was used for various diseases affecting the skin—not necessarily leprosy; also elsewhere in this chapter. [b]2 Or *descendants* [c]3 Or *be lower than the rest of the skin*; also elsewhere in this chapter

deep and the hair in it has not turned white, the priest is to put the infected person in isolation for seven days.[y] 5On the seventh day[z] the priest is to examine him,[a] and if he sees that the sore is unchanged and has not spread in the skin, he is to keep him in isolation another seven days. 6On the seventh day the priest is to examine him again, and if the sore has faded and has not spread in the skin, the priest shall pronounce him clean;[b] it is only a rash. The man must wash his clothes,[c] and he will be clean.[d] 7But if the rash does spread in his skin after he has shown himself to the priest to be pronounced clean, he must appear before the priest again.[e] 8The priest is to examine him, and if the rash has spread in the skin, he shall pronounce him unclean; it is an infectious disease.

9"When anyone has an infectious skin disease, he must be brought to the priest. 10The priest is to examine him, and if there is a white swelling in the skin that has turned the hair white and if there is raw flesh in the swelling, 11it is a chronic skin disease[f] and the priest shall pronounce him unclean. He is not to put him in isolation, because he is already unclean.

12"If the disease breaks out all over his skin and, so far as the priest can see, it covers all the skin of the infected person from head to foot, 13the priest is to examine him, and if the disease has covered his whole body, he shall pronounce that person clean. Since it has all turned white, he is clean. 14But whenever raw flesh appears on him, he will be unclean. 15When the priest sees the raw flesh, he shall pronounce him unclean. The raw flesh is unclean; he has an infectious disease.[g] 16Should the raw flesh change and turn white, he must go to the priest. 17The priest is to examine him, and if the sores have turned white, the priest shall pronounce the infected person clean;[h] then he will be clean.

18"When someone has a boil[i] on his skin and it heals, 19and in the place where the boil was, a white swelling or reddish-white[j] spot[k] appears, he must present himself to the priest. 20The priest is to examine it, and if it appears to be more than skin deep and the hair in it has turned white, the priest shall pronounce him unclean. It is an infectious skin disease[l] that has broken out where the boil was. 21But if, when the priest examines it, there is no white hair in it and it is not more than skin deep and has faded, then the priest is to put him in isolation for seven days. 22If it is spreading in the skin, the priest shall pronounce him unclean; it is infectious. 23But if the spot is unchanged and has not spread, it is only a scar from the boil, and the priest shall pronounce him clean.[m]

24"When someone has a burn on his skin and a reddish-white or white spot appears in the raw flesh of the burn, 25the priest is to examine the spot, and if the hair in it has turned white, and it appears to be more than skin deep, it is an infectious disease that has broken out in the burn. The priest shall pronounce him unclean; it is an infectious skin disease.[n] 26But if the priest examines it and there is no white hair in the spot and if it is not more than skin deep and has faded, then the priest is to put him in isolation for seven days.[o] 27On the seventh day the priest is to examine him,[p] and if it is spreading in the skin, the priest shall pronounce him unclean; it is an infectious skin disease. 28If, however, the spot is unchanged and has not spread in the skin but has faded, it is a swelling from the burn, and the priest shall pronounce him clean; it is only a scar from the burn.[q]

29"If a man or woman has a sore on the head[r] or on the chin, 30the priest is to examine the sore, and if it appears to be more than skin deep and the hair in it is yellow and thin, the priest shall pronounce that person unclean; it is an itch, an infectious disease of the head or chin. 31But if, when the priest examines this kind of sore, it does not seem to be more than skin deep and there is no black hair in it, then the priest is to put the infected person in isolation for seven days.[s] 32On the seventh day the priest is to examine the sore,[t] and if the itch has not spread and there is no yellow hair in it and it does not appear to be more than skin deep, 33he must be shaved except for the diseased area, and the priest is to keep him in isolation another seven days. 34On the seventh day the priest is to examine the itch,[u] and if it has not spread in the skin and

13:4 [y]ver 5,21,26, 33,46; Lev 14:38; Nu 12:14,15; Dt 24:9
13:5 [z]Lev 14:9 [a]ver 27,32, 34,51
13:6 [b]ver 13,17,23, 28,34; Mt 8:3; Lk 5:12-14 [c]Lev 11:25 [d]Lev 11:25; 14:8,9,20,48; 15:8; Nu 8:7
13:7 [e]Lk 5:14
13:11 [f]Ex 4:6; Lev 14:8; Nu 12:10; Mt 8:2
13:15 [g]ver 2
13:17 [h]ver 6
13:18 [i]Ex 9:9
13:19 [j]ver 24,42; Lev 14:37 [k]ver 2
13:20 [l]ver 2
13:23 [m]ver 6
13:25 [n]ver 11
13:26 [o]ver 4
13:27 [p]ver 5
13:28 [q]ver 2
13:29 [r]ver 43,44
13:31 [s]ver 4
13:32 [t]ver 5
13:34 [u]ver 5

appears to be no more than skin deep,
the priest shall pronounce him clean.
He must wash his clothes, and he will
13:34 [v]Lev 11:25 be clean.[v] 35But if the itch does spread
in the skin after he is pronounced clean,
36the priest is to examine him, and if
the itch has spread in the skin, the priest
does not need to look for yellow hair;
13:36 [w]ver 30 the person is unclean.[w] 37If, however, in
his judgment it is unchanged and black
hair has grown in it, the itch is healed.
He is clean, and the priest shall pronounce him clean.
38"When a man or woman has white
spots on the skin, 39the priest is to examine them, and if the spots are dull
white, it is a harmless rash that has
broken out on the skin; that person is
clean.
40"When a man has lost his hair and
13:40 [x]Lev 21:5; 2Ki 2:23; Isa 3:24; 15:2; 22:12; Eze 27:31; 29:18; Am 8:10; Mic 1:16 is bald,[x] he is clean. 41If he has lost his
hair from the front of his scalp and has
a bald forehead, he is clean. 42But if
he has a reddish-white sore on his bald
head or forehead, it is an infectious disease breaking out on his head or forehead. 43The priest is to examine him,
and if the swollen sore on his head or
forehead is reddish-white like an infectious skin disease, 44the man is diseased
and is unclean. The priest shall pronounce him unclean because of the sore
on his head.
45"The person with such an infec-
13:45 [y]Lev 10:6 [z]Eze 24:17,22; Mic 3:7 [a]Lev 5:2; La 4:15; Lk 17:12 tious disease must wear torn clothes,[y]
let his hair be unkempt,[a] cover the lower
part of his face[z] and cry out, 'Unclean!
Unclean!'[a] 46As long as he has the infec-
tion he remains unclean. He must live
13:46 [b]Nu 5:1-4; 12:14; 2Ki 7:3; 15:5; Lk 17:12 alone; he must live outside the camp.[b]

Regulations About Mildew

47"If any clothing is contaminated
with mildew—any woolen or linen clothing, 48any woven or knitted material of
linen or wool, any leather or anything
made of leather— 49and if the contamination in the clothing, or leather, or
woven or knitted material, or any leather article, is greenish or reddish, it is a
13:49 [c]Mk 1:44 spreading mildew and must be shown
to the priest.[c] 50The priest is to exam-
13:50 [d]Eze 44:23 ine the mildew[d] and isolate the affected
article for seven days. 51On the sev-
13:51 [e]ver 5 enth day he is to examine it,[e] and if
the mildew has spread in the clothing,
or the woven or knitted material, or
the leather, whatever its use, it is a de-
structive mildew; the article is unclean.[f] 13:51 [f]Lev 14:44
52He must burn up the clothing, or the
woven or knitted material of wool or
linen, or any leather article that has the
contamination in it, because the mildew is destructive; the article must be
burned up.[g] 13:52 [g]ver 55,57
53"But if, when the priest examines
it, the mildew has not spread in the
clothing, or the woven or knitted material, or the leather article, 54he shall
order that the contaminated article be
washed. Then he is to isolate it for another seven days. 55After the affected
article has been washed, the priest is to
examine it, and if the mildew has not
changed its appearance, even though it
has not spread, it is unclean. Burn it
with fire, whether the mildew has affected one side or the other. 56If, when
the priest examines it, the mildew has
faded after the article has been washed,
he is to tear the contaminated part out
of the clothing, or the leather, or the
woven or knitted material. 57But if it
reappears in the clothing, or in the woven or knitted material, or in the leather article, it is spreading, and whatever
has the mildew must be burned with
fire. 58The clothing, or the woven or
knitted material, or any leather article
that has been washed and is rid of the
mildew, must be washed again, and it
will be clean."
59These are the regulations concerning contamination by mildew in wool-
en or linen clothing, woven or knitted
material, or any leather article, for pro-
nouncing them clean or unclean.

Cleansing From Infectious Skin Diseases

14 The LORD said to Moses,
2"These are the regulations for
the diseased person at the time of 14:2 [h]Mt 8:2-4; Mk 1:40-44; Lk 5:12-14; 17:14
his ceremonial cleansing, when he is
brought to the priest:[h] 3The priest is to
go outside the camp and examine him.[i] 14:3 [i]Lev 13:46
If the person has been healed of his in-
fectious skin disease,[b] 4the priest shall 14:4 [j]ver 6,49,51,52; Nu 19:6; Ps 51:7
order that two live clean birds and some
cedar wood, scarlet yarn and hyssop be
brought for the one to be cleansed.[j]

[a]45 Or *clothes, uncover his head* [b]3 Traditionally *leprosy*; the Hebrew word was used for various diseases affecting the skin—not necessarily leprosy; also elsewhere in this chapter.

[5]Then the priest shall order that one of the birds be killed over fresh water in a clay pot. [6]He is then to take the live bird and dip it, together with the cedar wood, the scarlet yarn and the hyssop, into the blood of the bird that was killed over the fresh water.[k] [7]Seven times he shall sprinkle[l] the one to be cleansed of the infectious disease and pronounce him clean. Then he is to release the live bird in the open fields.

[8]"The person to be cleansed must wash his clothes,[m] shave off all his hair and bathe with water;[n] then he will be ceremonially clean.[o] After this he may come into the camp,[p] but he must stay outside his tent for seven days. [9]On the seventh day he must shave off all his hair; he must shave his head, his beard, his eyebrows and the rest of his hair. He must wash his clothes and bathe himself with water, and he will be clean.

[10]"On the eighth day[q] he must bring two male lambs and one ewe lamb a year old, each without defect, along with three-tenths of an ephah[a] of fine flour mixed with oil for a grain offering,[r] and one log[b] of oil.[s] [11]The priest who pronounces him clean shall present both the one to be cleansed and his offerings before the LORD at the entrance to the Tent of Meeting.

[12]"Then the priest is to take one of the male lambs and offer it as a guilt offering,[t] along with the log of oil; he shall wave them before the LORD as a wave offering.[u] [13]He is to slaughter the lamb in the holy place[v] where the sin offering and the burnt offering are slaughtered. Like the sin offering, the guilt offering belongs to the priest;[w] it is most holy. [14]The priest is to take some of the blood of the guilt offering and put it on the lobe of the right ear of the one to be cleansed, on the thumb of his right hand and on the big toe of his right foot.[x] [15]The priest shall then take some of the log of oil, pour it in the palm of his own left hand, [16]dip his right forefinger into the oil in his palm, and with his finger sprinkle some of it before the LORD seven times. [17]The priest is to put some of the oil remaining in his palm on the lobe of the right ear of the one to be cleansed, on the thumb of his right hand and on the big toe of his right foot, on top of the blood of the guilt offering. [18]The rest of the oil in his palm the priest shall put on the head of the one to be cleansed and make atonement for him before the LORD.

[19]"Then the priest is to sacrifice the sin offering and make atonement for the one to be cleansed from his uncleanness. After that, the priest shall slaughter the burnt offering [20]and offer it on the altar, together with the grain offering, and make atonement for him, and he will be clean.[y]

[21]"If, however, he is poor[z] and cannot afford these,[a] he must take one male lamb as a guilt offering to be waved to make atonement for him, together with a tenth of an ephah[c] of fine flour mixed with oil for a grain offering, a log of oil, [22]and two doves or two young pigeons,[b] which he can afford, one for a sin offering and the other for a burnt offering.

[23]"On the eighth day he must bring them for his cleansing to the priest at the entrance to the Tent of Meeting, before the LORD.[c] [24]The priest is to take the lamb for the guilt offering,[d] together with the log of oil,[e] and wave them before the LORD as a wave offering.[f] [25]He shall slaughter the lamb for the guilt offering and take some of its blood and put it on the lobe of the right ear of the one to be cleansed, on the thumb of his right hand and on the big toe of his right foot.[g] [26]The priest is to pour some of the oil into the palm of his own left hand,[h] [27]and with his right forefinger sprinkle some of the oil from his palm seven times before the LORD. [28]Some of the oil in his palm he is to put on the same places he put the blood of the guilt offering—on the lobe of the right ear of the one to be cleansed, on the thumb of his right hand and on the big toe of his right foot. [29]The rest of the oil in his palm the priest shall put on the head of the one to be cleansed, to make atonement for him before the LORD.[i] [30]Then he shall sacrifice the doves or the young pigeons, which the person can afford,[j] [31]one[d] as a sin offering and the other as a burnt offering,[k]

14:6 [k]ver 4
14:7 [l]2Ki 5:10,14; Isa 52:15; Eze 36:25
14:8 [m]Lev 11:25; 13:6 [n]ver 9 [o]ver 20 [p]Nu 5:2,3; 12:14,15; 2Ch 26:21
14:10 [q]Mt 8:4; Mk 1:44; Lk 5:14 [r]Lev 2:1 [s]ver 12,15, 21,24
14:12 [t]Lev 5:18; 6:6-7 [u]Ex 29:24
14:13 [v]Ex 29:11 [w]Lev 6:24-30; 7:7
14:14 [x]Ex 29:20; Lev 8:23
14:20 [y]ver 8
14:21 [z]Lev 5:7; 12:8 [a]ver 22,32
14:22 [b]Lev 5:7
14:23 [c]ver 10,11
14:24 [d]Nu 6:14 [e]ver 10 [f]ver 12
14:25 [g]ver 14; Ex 29:20
14:26 [h]ver 15
14:29 [i]ver 18
14:30 [j]Lev 5:7
14:31 [k]ver 22; Lev 5:7; 15:15,30

[a]*10* That is, probably about 6 quarts (about 6.5 liters) [b]*10* That is, probably about 2/3 pint (about 0.3 liter); also in verses 12, 15, 21 and 24
[c]*21* That is, probably about 2 quarts (about 2 liters)
[d]*31* Septuagint and Syriac; Hebrew *[31]such as the person can afford, one*

together with the grain offering. In this way the priest will make atonement before the LORD on behalf of the one to be cleansed.[l]"

32These are the regulations for anyone who has an infectious skin disease[m] and who cannot afford the regular offerings[n] for his cleansing.

Cleansing From Mildew

33The LORD said to Moses and Aaron, 34"When you enter the land of Canaan,[o] which I am giving you as your possession,[p] and I put a spreading mildew in a house in that land, 35the owner of the house must go and tell the priest, 'I have seen something that looks like mildew in my house.' 36The priest is to order the house to be emptied before he goes in to examine the mildew, so that nothing in the house will be pronounced unclean. After this the priest is to go in and inspect the house. 37He is to examine the mildew on the walls, and if it has greenish or reddish[q] depressions that appear to be deeper than the surface of the wall, 38the priest shall go out the doorway of the house and close it up for seven days.[r] 39On the seventh day[s] the priest shall return to inspect the house. If the mildew has spread on the walls, 40he is to order that the contaminated stones be torn out and thrown into an unclean place outside the town.[t] 41He must have all the inside walls of the house scraped and the material that is scraped off dumped into an unclean place outside the town. 42Then they are to take other stones to replace these and take new clay and plaster the house.

43"If the mildew reappears in the house after the stones have been torn out and the house scraped and plastered, 44the priest is to go and examine it and, if the mildew has spread in the house, it is a destructive mildew; the house is unclean.[u] 45It must be torn down—its stones, timbers and all the plaster—and taken out of the town to an unclean place.

46"Anyone who goes into the house while it is closed up will be unclean till evening.[v] 47Anyone who sleeps or eats in the house must wash his clothes.[w]

48"But if the priest comes to examine it and the mildew has not spread after the house has been plastered, he shall pronounce the house clean,[x] because the mildew is gone. 49To purify the house he is to take two birds and some cedar wood, scarlet yarn and hyssop.[y] 50He shall kill one of the birds over fresh water in a clay pot.[z] 51Then he is to take the cedar wood, the hyssop,[a] the scarlet yarn and the live bird, dip them into the blood of the dead bird and the fresh water, and sprinkle the house seven times.[b] 52He shall purify the house with the bird's blood, the fresh water, the live bird, the cedar wood, the hyssop and the scarlet yarn. 53Then he is to release the live bird in the open fields[c] outside the town. In this way he will make atonement for the house, and it will be clean.[d]"

54These are the regulations for any infectious skin disease,[e] for an itch, 55for mildew[f] in clothing or in a house, 56and for a swelling, a rash or a bright spot,[g] 57to determine when something is clean or unclean.

These are the regulations for infectious skin diseases and mildew.[h]

Discharges Causing Uncleanness

15 The LORD said to Moses and Aaron, 2"Speak to the Israelites and say to them: 'When any man has a bodily discharge,[i] the discharge is unclean. 3Whether it continues flowing from his body or is blocked, it will make him unclean. This is how his discharge will bring about uncleanness:

4" 'Any bed the man with a discharge lies on will be unclean, and anything he sits on will be unclean. 5Anyone who touches his bed must wash his clothes[j] and bathe with water,[k] and he will be unclean till evening.[l] 6Whoever sits on anything that the man with a discharge sat on must wash his clothes and bathe with water, and he will be unclean till evening.

7" 'Whoever touches the man[m] who has a discharge[n] must wash his clothes and bathe with water, and he will be unclean till evening.

8" 'If the man with the discharge spits[o] on someone who is clean, that person must wash his clothes and bathe with water, and he will be unclean till evening.

9" 'Everything the man sits on when riding will be unclean, 10and whoever touches any of the things that were un-

14:31 [l]ver 18,19
14:32 [m]Lev 13:2 [n]ver 21
14:34 [o]Ge 12:5; Ex 6:4; Nu 13:2 [p]Ge 17:8; 48:4; Nu 27:12; 32:22; Dt 3:27; 7:1; 32:49
14:37 [q]Lev 13:19
14:38 [r]Lev 13:4
14:39 [s]Lev 13:5
14:40 [t]ver 45
14:44 [u]Lev 13:51
14:46 [v]Lev 11:24
14:47 [w]Lev 11:25
14:48 [x]Lev 13:6
14:49 [y]ver 4; 1Ki 4:33; ver 4
14:50 [z]ver 5
14:51 [a]ver 6; Ps 51:7 [b]ver 4,7
14:53 [c]ver 7 [d]ver 20
14:54 [e]Lev 13:2,30
14:55 [f]Lev 13:47-52
14:56 [g]Lev 13:2
14:57 [h]Lev 10:10
15:2 [i]ver 16,32; Lev 22:4; Nu 5:2; 2Sa 3:29; Mt 9:20
15:5 [j]Lev 11:25 [k]Lev 14:8 [l]Lev 11:24
15:7 [m]ver 19; Lev 22:5 [n]ver 16; Lev 22:4
15:8 [o]Nu 12:14

der him will be unclean till evening;
15:10 whoever picks up those things[p] must
[p]Nu 19:10 wash his clothes and bathe with water,
and he will be unclean till evening.
11“ ‘Anyone the man with a discharge
touches without rinsing his hands with
water must wash his clothes and bathe
with water, and he will be unclean till
evening.
15:12 [q]Lev 6:28 12“ ‘A clay pot[q] that the man touches
[r]Lev 11:32 must be broken, and any wooden article[r]
is to be rinsed with water.
13“ ‘When a man is cleansed from his
15:13 [s]Lev 8:33 discharge, he is to count off seven days[s]
[t]ver 5 for his ceremonial cleansing; he must
wash his clothes and bathe himself with
fresh water, and he will be clean.[t] 14On
the eighth day he must take two doves
15:14 [u]Lev 14:22 or two young pigeons[u] and come before the LORD to the entrance to the
Tent of Meeting and give them to the
priest. 15The priest is to sacrifice them,
15:15 [v]Lev 5:7 the one for a sin offering[v] and the other
[w]Lev 14:31 [x]Lev 14:18,19 for a burnt offering.[w] In this way he
will make atonement before the LORD
for the man because of his discharge.[x]
16“ ‘When a man has an emission of
15:16 [y]ver 2; semen,[y] he must bathe his whole body
Lev 22:4; with water, and he will be unclean till
Dt 23:10 [z]ver 5; evening.[z] 17Any clothing or leather that
Dt 23:11 has semen on it must be washed with
water, and it will be unclean till evening. 18When a man lies with a woman and there is an emission of semen,[a]
15:18 [a]1Sa 21:4 both must bathe with water, and they
will be unclean till evening.
19“ ‘When a woman has her regular
flow of blood, the impurity of her
15:19 [b]ver 24; monthly period[b] will last seven days,
Lev 12:2 and anyone who touches her will be
unclean till evening.
20“ ‘Anything she lies on during her
period will be unclean, and anything
she sits on will be unclean. 21Whoever
touches her bed must wash his clothes
and bathe with water, and he will be un-
15:21 [c]ver 27 clean till evening.[c] 22Whoever touches
anything she sits on must wash his
clothes and bathe with water, and he
will be unclean till evening. 23Whether
it is the bed or anything she was sitting
on, when anyone touches it, he will be
unclean till evening.
24“ ‘If a man lies with her and her
15:24 [d]ver 19; monthly flow[d] touches him, he will be
Lev 12:2; unclean for seven days; any bed he lies
18:19; 20:18; Eze 18:6 on will be unclean.
25“ ‘When a woman has a discharge
of blood for many days at a time other
than her monthly period[e] or has a dis- 15:25
charge that continues beyond her peri- [e]Mt 9:20; Mk 5:25;
od, she will be unclean as long as she Lk 8:43
has the discharge, just as in the days of
her period. 26Any bed she lies on while
her discharge continues will be unclean,
as is her bed during her monthly period, and anything she sits on will be unclean, as during her period. 27Whoever
touches them will be unclean; he must
wash his clothes and bathe with water,
and he will be unclean till evening.
28“ ‘When she is cleansed from her
discharge, she must count off seven
days, and after that she will be ceremonially clean. 29On the eighth day she
must take two doves or two young pigeons[f] and bring them to the priest at 15:29
the entrance to the Tent of Meeting. [f]Lev 14:22
30The priest is to sacrifice one for a sin
offering and the other for a burnt offering. In this way he will make atone- 15:30
ment for her before the LORD for the [g]Lev 5:10; 14:20,31;
uncleanness of her discharge.[g] 18:19;
31“ ‘You must keep the Israelites sep- 2Sa 11:4; Mk 5:25;
arate from things that make them un- Lk 8:43
clean, so they will not die in their 15:31
uncleanness for defiling my dwelling [h]Lev 20:3; Nu 5:3;
place,[a][h] which is among them.’ ” 19:13,20;
32These are the regulations for a man 2Sa 15:25; 2Ki 21:7;
with a discharge, for anyone made un- Ps 33:14; 74:7; 76:2;
clean by an emission of semen,[i] 33for Eze 5:11; 23:38
a woman in her monthly period, for a 15:32
man or a woman with a discharge, and [i]ver 2
for a man who lies with a woman who 15:33
is ceremonially unclean.[j] [j]ver 19,24,25

The Day of Atonement

16 The LORD spoke to Moses after the death of the two sons of
Aaron who died when they approached
the LORD.[k] 2The LORD said to Moses: 16:1
“Tell your brother Aaron not to come [k]Lev 10:1
whenever he chooses[l] into the Most 16:2 [l]Ex 30:10;
Holy Place[m] behind the curtain in front Heb 9:7
of the atonement cover on the ark, or [m]Heb 9:25; 10:19
else he will die, because I appear[n] in the [n]Ex 25:22
cloud[o] over the atonement cover. [o]Ex 40:34
3“This is how Aaron is to enter the
sanctuary area:[p] with a young bull for 16:3
a sin offering and a ram for a burnt [p]Heb 9:24,25
offering. 4He is to put on the sacred
linen tunic, with linen undergarments
next to his body; he is to tie the linen
sash around him and put on the linen

[a]*31* Or *my tabernacle*

turban.[q] These are sacred garments;[r] so he must bathe himself with water[s] before he puts them on. **5**From the Israelite community[t] he is to take two male goats[u] for a sin offering and a ram for a burnt offering.

6"Aaron is to offer the bull for his own sin offering to make atonement for himself and his household.[v] **7**Then he is to take the two goats and present them before the LORD at the entrance to the Tent of Meeting. **8**He is to cast lots for the two goats—one lot for the LORD and the other for the scapegoat.[a] **9**Aaron shall bring the goat whose lot falls to the LORD and sacrifice it for a sin offering. **10**But the goat chosen by lot as the scapegoat shall be presented alive before the LORD to be used for making atonement[w] by sending it into the desert as a scapegoat.

11"Aaron shall bring the bull for his own sin offering to make atonement for himself and his household,[x] and he is to slaughter the bull for his own sin offering. **12**He is to take a censer full of burning coals[y] from the altar before the LORD and two handfuls of finely ground fragrant incense[z] and take them behind the curtain. **13**He is to put the incense on the fire before the LORD, and the smoke of the incense will conceal the atonement cover above the Testimony, so that he will not die.[a] **14**He is to take some of the bull's blood[b] and with his finger sprinkle it on the front of the atonement cover; then he shall sprinkle some of it with his finger seven times before the atonement cover.[c]

15"He shall then slaughter the goat for the sin offering for the people[d] and take its blood behind the curtain[e] and do with it as he did with the bull's blood: He shall sprinkle it on the atonement cover and in front of it. **16**In this way he will make atonement[f] for the Most Holy Place because of the uncleanness and rebellion of the Israelites, whatever their sins have been. He is to do the same for the Tent of Meeting, which is among them in the midst of their uncleanness. **17**No one is to be in the Tent of Meeting from the time Aaron goes in to make atonement in the Most Holy Place until he comes out, having made atonement for himself, his household and the whole community of Israel.

16:4 [q]Ex 28:39 [r]Ex 28:42 [s]ver 24; Heb 10:22
16:5 [t]Lev 4:13-21 [u]2Ch 29:23
16:6 [v]Lev 9:7; Heb 5:3; 7:27; 9:7,12
16:10 [w]Isa 53:4-10; Ro 3:25; 1Jn 2:2
16:11 [x]Heb 7:27; 9:7
16:12 [y]Lev 10:1 [z]Ex 30:34-38
16:13 [a]Ex 28:43; Lev 22:9
16:14 [b]Lev 4:5; Heb 9:7,13,25 [c]Lev 4:6
16:15 [d]Heb 9:7,12 [e]Heb 9:3
16:16 [f]Ex 29:36

18"Then he shall come out to the altar[g] that is before the LORD and make atonement for it. He shall take some of the bull's blood and some of the goat's blood and put it on all the horns of the altar.[h] **19**He shall sprinkle some of the blood on it with his finger seven times to cleanse it and to consecrate it from the uncleanness of the Israelites.[i]

20"When Aaron has finished making atonement for the Most Holy Place, the Tent of Meeting and the altar, he shall bring forward the live goat. **21**He is to lay both hands on the head of the live goat and confess[j] over it all the wickedness and rebellion of the Israelites—all their sins—and put them on the goat's head. He shall send the goat away into the desert in the care of a man appointed for the task. **22**The goat will carry on itself all their sins[k] to a solitary place; and the man shall release it in the desert.

23"Then Aaron is to go into the Tent of Meeting and take off the linen garments he put on before he entered the Most Holy Place, and he is to leave them there.[l] **24**He shall bathe himself with water in a holy place and put on his regular garments.[m] Then he shall come out and sacrifice the burnt offering for himself and the burnt offering for the people, to make atonement for himself and for the people. **25**He shall also burn the fat of the sin offering on the altar.

26"The man who releases the goat as a scapegoat must wash his clothes[n] and bathe himself with water; afterward he may come into the camp. **27**The bull and the goat for the sin offerings, whose blood was brought into the Most Holy Place to make atonement, must be taken outside the camp;[o] their hides, flesh and offal are to be burned up. **28**The man who burns them must wash his clothes and bathe himself with water; afterward he may come into the camp.

29"This is to be a lasting ordinance for you: On the tenth day of the seventh month you must deny yourselves[b][p] and not do any work—whether native-born or an alien living among you— **30**because on this day atonement will be

16:18 [g]Lev 4:7 [h]Lev 4:25
16:19 [i]Eze 43:20
16:21 [j]Lev 5:5
16:22 [k]Isa 53:12
16:23 [l]Eze 42:14; 44:19
16:24 [m]ver 3-5
16:26 [n]Lev 11:25
16:27 [o]Lev 4:12,21; Heb 13:11
16:29 [p]Lev 23:27,32; Nu 29:7; Isa 58:3

[a]8 That is, the goat of removal; Hebrew *azazel*; also in verses 10 and 26 [b]29 Or *must fast*; also in verse 31

made for you, to cleanse you. Then, before the LORD, you will be clean from all your sins.[q] 31It is a sabbath of rest, and you must deny yourselves;[r] it is a lasting ordinance. 32The priest who is anointed and ordained to succeed his father as high priest is to make atonement. He is to put on the sacred linen garments[s] 33and make atonement for the Most Holy Place, for the Tent of Meeting and the altar, and for the priests and all the people of the community.[t]

34"This is to be a lasting ordinance for you: Atonement is to be made once a year[u] for all the sins of the Israelites."

And it was done, as the LORD commanded Moses.

16:30 [q]Jer 33:8; Eph 5:26
16:31 [r]Isa 58:3,5
16:32 [s]ver 4; Nu 20:26,28
16:33 [t]ver 11,16-18
16:34 [u]Heb 9:7,25

FAITHFULNESS

HONEST TO GOD... CONSISTENTLY

Leviticus 16:34

The Day of Atonement was annual catch-up time for the faithful. On that day people faced all their sins and begged the God of truth for cleansing. Purity of heart must center on one thing: a seeking of the kingdom, a loving of the King.

Eating Blood Forbidden

17 The LORD said to Moses, 2"Speak to Aaron and his sons and to all the Israelites and say to them: 'This is what the LORD has commanded: 3Any Israelite who sacrifices an ox,[a] a lamb or a goat in the camp or outside of it 4instead of bringing it to the entrance to the Tent of Meeting to present it as an offering to the LORD in front of the tabernacle of the LORD[v]—that man shall be considered guilty of bloodshed; he has shed blood and must be cut off from his people.[w] 5This is so the Israelites will bring to the LORD the sacrifices they are now making in the open fields. They must bring them to the priest, that is, to the LORD, at the entrance to the Tent of Meeting and sacrifice them as fellowship offerings.[b] 6The priest is to sprinkle the blood against the altar of the LORD[x] at the entrance to the Tent of Meeting and burn the fat as an aroma pleasing to the LORD.[y] 7They must no longer offer any of their sacrifices to the goat idols[c][z] to whom they prostitute themselves.[a] This is to be a lasting ordinance for them and for the generations to come.'

8"Say to them: 'Any Israelite or any alien living among them who offers a burnt offering or sacrifice 9and does not bring it to the entrance to the Tent of Meeting[b] to sacrifice it to the LORD—that man must be cut off from his people.

10" 'Any Israelite or any alien living among them who eats any blood—I will set my face against that person who eats blood[c] and will cut him off from his people. 11For the life of a creature is in the blood,[d] and I have given it to you to make atonement for yourselves on the altar; it is the blood that makes atonement for one's life.[e] 12Therefore I say to the Israelites, "None of you may eat blood, nor may an alien living among you eat blood."

13" 'Any Israelite or any alien living among you who hunts any animal or bird that may be eaten must drain out the blood and cover it with earth,[f] 14because the life of every creature is its blood. That is why I have said to the Israelites, "You must not eat the blood of any creature, because the life of every creature is its blood; anyone who eats it must be cut off."[g]

15" 'Anyone, whether native-born or alien, who eats anything found dead or torn by wild animals[h] must wash his clothes and bathe with water, and he will be ceremonially unclean till evening; then he will be clean. 16But if he does not wash his clothes and bathe himself, he will be held responsible.' "

Unlawful Sexual Relations

18 The LORD said to Moses, 2"Speak to the Israelites and say to them: 'I am the LORD your God.[i] 3You must not do as they do in Egypt, where you used to live, and you must not do as they do in the land of Canaan, where I am bringing you. Do not follow their practices.[j] 4You must obey my laws and be careful to follow my decrees. I am the LORD your God.[k] 5Keep my decrees and laws, for the man who obeys them will live by them.[l] I am the LORD.

17:4 [v]Dt 12:5-21 [w]Ge 17:14
17:6 [x]Lev 3:2 [y]Nu 18:17
17:7 [z]Ex 22:20; 2Ch 11:15
17:7 [a]Ex 32:8; 34:15; Dt 32:17; 1Co 10:20
17:9 [b]ver 4
17:10 [c]Ge 9:4; Lev 3:17; Dt 12:16,23; 1Sa 14:33
17:11 [d]ver 14; Ge 9:4 [e]Heb 9:22
17:13 [f]Lev 7:26; Dt 12:16
17:14 [g]ver 11; Ge 9:4
17:15 [h]Ex 22:31; Dt 14:21
18:2 [i]Ex 6:7; Lev 11:44; Eze 20:5
18:3 [j]ver 24-30; Ex 23:24; Lev 20:23
18:4 [k]ver 2
18:5 [l]Eze 20:11; Ro 10:5*; Gal 3:12*

[a]3 The Hebrew word can include both male and female. [b]5 Traditionally *peace offerings* [c]7 Or *demons*

6“ ‘No one is to approach any close relative to have sexual relations. I am the LORD.

7“ ‘Do not dishonor your father[m] by having sexual relations with your mother.[n] She is your mother; do not have relations with her.

8“ ‘Do not have sexual relations with your father's wife;[o] that would dishonor your father.[p]

9“ ‘Do not have sexual relations with your sister,[q] either your father's daughter or your mother's daughter, whether she was born in the same home or elsewhere.

10“ ‘Do not have sexual relations with your son's daughter or your daughter's daughter; that would dishonor you.

11“ ‘Do not have sexual relations with the daughter of your father's wife, born to your father; she is your sister.

12“ ‘Do not have sexual relations with your father's sister;[r] she is your father's close relative.

13“ ‘Do not have sexual relations with your mother's sister, because she is your mother's close relative.

14“ ‘Do not dishonor your father's brother by approaching his wife to have sexual relations; she is your aunt.[s]

15“ ‘Do not have sexual relations with your daughter-in-law.[t] She is your son's wife; do not have relations with her.

16“ ‘Do not have sexual relations with your brother's wife;[u] that would dishonor your brother.

17“ ‘Do not have sexual relations with both a woman and her daughter.[v] Do not have sexual relations with either her son's daughter or her daughter's daughter; they are her close relatives. That is wickedness.

18“ ‘Do not take your wife's sister as a rival wife and have sexual relations with her while your wife is living.

19“ ‘Do not approach a woman to have sexual relations during the uncleanness of her monthly period.[w]

20“ ‘Do not have sexual relations with your neighbor's wife[x] and defile yourself with her.

21“ ‘Do not give any of your children[y] to be sacrificed[a] to Molech,[z] for you must not profane the name of your God.[a] I am the LORD.

22“ ‘Do not lie with a man as one lies with a woman;[b] that is detestable.

23“ ‘Do not have sexual relations with an animal and defile yourself with it. A woman must not present herself to an animal to have sexual relations with it; that is a perversion.[c]

24“ ‘Do not defile yourselves in any of these ways, because this is how the nations that I am going to drive out before you[d] became defiled.[e] 25Even the land was defiled; so I punished it for its sin,[f] and the land vomited out its inhabitants.[g] 26But you must keep my decrees and my laws. The native-born and the aliens living among you must not do any of these detestable things, 27for all these things were done by the people who lived in the land before you, and the land became defiled. 28And if you defile the land, it will vomit you out as it vomited out the nations that were before you.

29“ ‘Everyone who does any of these detestable things—such persons must be cut off from their people. 30Keep my requirements[h] and do not follow any of the detestable customs that were practiced before you came and do not defile yourselves with them. I am the LORD your God.[i]’ ”

Various Laws

19 The LORD said to Moses, 2“Speak to the entire assembly of Israel and say to them: ‘Be holy because I, the LORD your God, am holy.[j]

3“ ‘Each of you must respect his mother and father,[k] and you must observe my Sabbaths. I am the LORD your God.[l]

4“ ‘Do not turn to idols or make gods of cast metal for yourselves.[m] I am the LORD your God.

5“ ‘When you sacrifice a fellowship offering[b] to the LORD, sacrifice it in such a way that it will be accepted on your behalf. 6It shall be eaten on the day you sacrifice it or on the next day; anything left over until the third day must be burned up. 7If any of it is eaten on the third day, it is impure and will not be accepted. 8Whoever eats it will be held responsible because he has desecrated what is holy to the LORD; that person must be cut off from his people.

[a]21 Or *to be passed through ⌊the fire⌋*
[b]5 Traditionally *peace offering*

18:7 [m]Lev 20:11 [n]Eze 22:10
18:8 [o]1Co 5:1 [p]Lev 20:11
18:9 [q]Lev 20:17
18:12 [r]Lev 20:19
18:14 [s]Lev 20:20
18:15 [t]Lev 20:12
18:16 [u]Lev 20:21
18:17 [v]Lev 20:14
18:19 [w]Lev 15:24; 20:18
18:20 [x]Ex 20:14; Lev 20:10; Mt 5:27,28; 1Co 6:9; Heb 13:4
18:21 [y]Dt 12:31 [z]Lev 20:2-5 [a]Lev 19:12; 21:6; Eze 36:20
18:22 [b]Lev 20:13; Dt 23:18; Ro 1:27
18:23 [c]Ex 22:19; Lev 20:15; Dt 27:21
18:24 [d]ver 3,27,30 [e]Dt 18:12
18:25 [f]Lev 20:23; Dt 9:5; 18:12 [g]ver 28; Lev 20:22
18:30 [h]Dt 11:1 [i]ver 2
19:2 [j]1Pe 1:16*; Lev 11:44
19:3 [k]Ex 20:12 [l]Lev 11:44
19:4 [m]Ex 20:4,23; 34:17; Lev 26:1; Ps 96:5; 115:4-7

9" 'When you reap the harvest of your
land, do not reap to the very edges of
your field or gather the gleanings of
19:9 [n]Lev 23:10, 22; Dt 24:19-22
your harvest.[n] 10 Do not go over your
vineyard a second time or pick up the
grapes that have fallen. Leave them for
the poor and the alien. I am the LORD
your God.
19:11 [o]Ex 20:15 [p]Eph 4:25
11" 'Do not steal.[o]
" 'Do not lie.[p]
" 'Do not deceive one another.
19:12 [q]Ex 20:7; Mt 5:33
12" 'Do not swear falsely by my name[q]
and so profane the name of your God.
I am the LORD.
13" 'Do not defraud your neighbor or
19:13 [r]Ex 22:15, 25-27 [s]Dt 24:15; Jas 5:4
rob him.[r]
" 'Do not hold back the wages of a
hired man overnight.[s]
14" 'Do not curse the deaf or put a
19:14 [t]Dt 27:18
stumbling block in front of the blind,[t]
but fear your God. I am the LORD.
19:15 [u]Ex 23:2,6 [v]Dt 1:17
15" 'Do not pervert justice;[u] do not
show partiality[v] to the poor or favoritism to the great, but judge your neighbor fairly.
16" 'Do not go about spreading slan-
19:16 [w]Ps 15:3; Eze 22:9 [x]Ex 23:7
der[w] among your people.
" 'Do not do anything that endangers
your neighbor's life.[x] I am the LORD.
17" 'Do not hate your brother in your
19:17 [y]1Jn 2:9; 3:15 [z]Mt 18:15; Lk 17:3
heart.[y] Rebuke your neighbor frankly[z]
so you will not share in his guilt.
18" 'Do not seek revenge[a] or bear a
19:18 [a]Ro 12:19 [b]Ps 103:9 [c]Mt 5:43*; 19:16*; 22:39*; Mk 12:31*; Lk 10:27*; Jn 13:34; Ro 13:9*; Gal 5:14*; Jas 2:8*
grudge[b] against one of your people, but
love your neighbor as yourself.[c] I am
the LORD.
19" 'Keep my decrees.
" 'Do not mate different kinds of animals.
" 'Do not plant your field with two
kinds of seed.[d]
19:19 [d]Dt 22:9 [e]Dt 22:11
" 'Do not wear clothing woven of two
kinds of material.[e]
20" 'If a man sleeps with a woman
who is a slave girl promised to another
man but who has not been ransomed
or given her freedom, there must be
due punishment. Yet they are not to
be put to death, because she had not
been freed. 21 The man, however, must
bring a ram to the entrance to the Tent
of Meeting for a guilt offering to the
19:21 [f]Lev 5:15
LORD.[f] 22 With the ram of the guilt offering the priest is to make atonement
for him before the LORD for the sin he
has committed, and his sin will be forgiven.
23" 'When you enter the land and
plant any kind of fruit tree, regard its
fruit as forbidden.[a] For three years you
are to consider it forbidden[a]; it must
not be eaten. 24 In the fourth year all its
19:24 [g]Pr 3:9
fruit will be holy,[g] an offering of praise
to the LORD. 25 But in the fifth year you
may eat its fruit. In this way your harvest will be increased. I am the LORD
your God.

[a]23 Hebrew *uncircumcised*

DAY 2 TWO

▸ LOVE AND THE PURPOSE OF GOD IN MY LIFE

Leviticus 19:33–34

Give Leviticus 19:34 your heart, and soon it will own your soul. This splendid verse falls out in a triptych of three panels, each speaking its own glory. "The alien living with you must be treated as one of your native-born."

In this verse God brings up a perennial problem. It's the issue of insiders and outsiders. Insiders are those who belong, outsiders are those who don't. Insiders get all the good deals; outsiders don't. Insiders control; outsiders are controlled.

As if this were not enough, there also exists a feeling among insiders that outsiders need to be further outside than they already are. If they were far enough outside, then they would never again bother any insiders. God, in this passage, is acting to clear up this tension. Aliens (outsiders as it were) must be treated just like you, who are native-born (insiders). End of argument—beginning of love.

"Love him as yourself, for you were aliens in Egypt." Here is a very novel idea: Love people in the outsider category. Why? Because you were once outsiders in Egypt. You Israelites know how rotten it feels to be an outsider. You yourselves have felt that pain. Don't ever make anyone, anywhere feel as you did.

"I am the LORD your God." This last phrase is the signature. Why should we love outsiders? Who said so? Well, we all know who said so—God said so. The Lord. If he takes such an interest in loving outsiders, it must be a good idea for everyone else to do the same.

To begin a study on the topic of Love, Permeating All We Do, turn to the home page on page 1372.

26"'Do not eat any meat with the
19:26 blood still in it.[h]
[h]Lev 17:10 "'Do not practice divination or
[i]Dt 18:10 sorcery.[i]
27"'Do not cut the hair at the sides of
your head or clip off the edges of your
19:27 beard.[j]
[j]Lev 21:5 28"'Do not cut your bodies for the
dead or put tattoo marks on yourselves.
I am the LORD.
29"'Do not degrade your daughter by
19:29 making her a prostitute,[k] or the land
[k]Dt 23:18 will turn to prostitution and be filled
with wickedness.
30"'Observe my Sabbaths and have
reverence for my sanctuary. I am the
19:30 [l]Lev 26:2 LORD.[l]
19:31 31"'Do not turn to mediums or seek
[m]Lev 20:6; out spiritists,[m] for you will be defiled by
Isa 8:19 them. I am the LORD your God.
19:32 32"'Rise in the presence of the aged,
[n]1Ti 5:1 show respect for the elderly[n] and revere
your God. I am the LORD.
33"'When an alien lives with you in
your land, do not mistreat him. 34The
alien living with you must be treated as
one of your native-born.[o] Love him as
19:34 [o]Ex 12:48 yourself, for you were aliens in Egypt.[p]
[p]Dt 10:19 I am the LORD your God.
35"'Do not use dishonest standards
when measuring length, weight or quantity. 36Use honest scales and honest
weights, an honest ephah[a] and an hon-
19:36 est hin.[b][q] I am the LORD your God,
[q]Dt 25:13-15 who brought you out of Egypt.
37"'Keep all my decrees and all my
laws and follow them. I am the
LORD.'"

Punishments for Sin

20 The LORD said to Moses, 2"Say
to the Israelites: 'Any Israelite or
any alien living in Israel who gives[c] any
of his children to Molech must be put
to death. The people of the community are to stone him. 3I will set my
face against that man and I will cut
him off from his people; for by giving
his children to Molech, he has defiled
20:3 my sanctuary[r] and profaned my holy
[r]Lev 15:31 name.[s] 4If the people of the communi-
[s]Lev 18:21 ty close their eyes when that man gives
one of his children to Molech and they
20:4 fail to put him to death,[t] 5I will set my
[t]Dt 17:2-5 face against that man and his family
and will cut off from their people both
him and all who follow him in prosti-
tuting themselves to Molech.

6"'I will set my face against the person who turns to mediums and spiritists to prostitute himself by following
them, and I will cut him off from his
people.[u] 20:6 [u]Lev 19:31
7"'Consecrate yourselves and be
holy,[v] because I am the LORD your 20:7 [v]Eph 1:4;
God. 8Keep my decrees and follow 1Pe 1:16*
them. I am the LORD, who makes you 20:8
holy.[d][w] [w]Ex 31:13
9"'If anyone curses his father or
mother,[x] he must be put to death.[y] He 20:9 [x]Dt 27:16
has cursed his father or his mother, and [y]Ex 21:17;
his blood will be on his own head.[z] Mt 15:4*; Mk 7:10*
10"'If a man commits adultery with [z]ver 11;
another man's wife[a]—with the wife of 2Sa 1:16
his neighbor—both the adulterer and 20:10 [a]Ex 20:14;
the adulteress must be put to death. Dt 5:18; 22:22
11"'If a man sleeps with his father's
wife, he has dishonored his father.[b] Both 20:11 [b]Lev 18:7;
the man and the woman must be put to Dt 27:23
death; their blood will be on their own
heads.
12"'If a man sleeps with his daughter- 20:12
in-law,[c] both of them must be put to [c]Lev 18:15
death. What they have done is a perversion; their blood will be on their own
heads.
13"'If a man lies with a man as one
lies with a woman, both of them have
done what is detestable.[d] They must be 20:13
put to death; their blood will be on [d]Lev 18:22
their own heads.
14"'If a man marries both a woman
and her mother,[e] it is wicked. Both he 20:14 [e]Lev 18:17
and they must be burned in the fire, [f]Dt 27:23
so that no wickedness will be among
you.[f]
15"'If a man has sexual relations with
an animal,[g] he must be put to death, 20:15 [g]Lev 18:23
and you must kill the animal.
16"'If a woman approaches an animal to have sexual relations with it, kill
both the woman and the animal. They
must be put to death; their blood will
be on their own heads.
17"'If a man marries his sister,[h] the 20:17
daughter of either his father or his [h]Lev 18:9
mother, and they have sexual relations,
it is a disgrace. They must be cut off
before the eyes of their people. He has
dishonored his sister and will be held
responsible.
18"'If a man lies with a woman dur-

[a]*36* An ephah was a dry measure. [b]*36* A hin was a liquid measure. [c]*2* Or *sacrifices*; also in verses 3 and 4 [d]*8* Or *who sanctifies you*; or *who sets you apart as holy*

20:18 [i]Lev 15:24; ing her monthly period[i] and has sexual
18:19 relations with her, he has exposed the
source of her flow, and she has also uncovered it. Both of them must be cut
off from their people.
19"'Do not have sexual relations with
the sister of either your mother or your
20:19 father,[j] for that would dishonor a close
[j]Lev 18:12-13 relative; both of you would be held responsible.
20:20 20"'If a man sleeps with his aunt,[k]
[k]Lev 18:14 he has dishonored his uncle. They will
be held responsible; they will die childless.
21"'If a man marries his brother's
20:21 wife,[l] it is an act of impurity; he has dis-
[l]Lev 18:16 honored his brother. They will be childless.

DAY 3 THREE

▸ GOODNESS AND MY RELATIONSHIP WITH CHRIST

Leviticus 20:26

Craving holiness is searching for the nearest way to God. The hunger for holiness is insatiable in the souls of those who want a deepening relationship with God. How shall we have enough of him of whom we have had too little? We must have more. "More, more about Jesus," runs the hymn, "More of His saving fullness see, More of His love Who died for me." The hunger for holiness.

Holy Spirit breathe on me
Until my heart is clean;
Let sunshine fill its inmost part
With not a cloud between.

It is like the old missionary who, in seeking to teach a new convert a hunger for Jesus, held his newly immersed disciple under the water long past the ending of the baptismal formula. Finally the convert was struggling to come up for air but still the missionary held him under. At last he let his gasping convert through the surface to gulp in greedy wafts of air. "Now," he told him, "when you want God as much as you just wanted air, you shall have all of him you crave."

To begin a study on the topic of Goodness and the Desire for Holiness, turn to the home page on page 790.

22"'Keep all my decrees and laws and 20:22
follow them, so that the land[m] where I [m]Lev 18:25-
am bringing you to live may not vom- 28
it you out. 23You must not live according to the customs of the nations[n] I 20:23
am going to drive out before you.[o] Be- [n]Lev 18:3
cause they did all these things, I ab- [o]Lev 18:24, 27,30
horred them. 24But I said to you, "You
will possess their land; I will give it to
you as an inheritance, a land flowing
with milk and honey."[p] I am the LORD 20:24
your God, who has set you apart from [p]Ex 3:8; 13:5; 33:3
the nations.[q] [q]Ex 33:16
25"'You must therefore make a distinction between clean and unclean animals and between unclean and clean
birds.[r] Do not defile yourselves by any 20:25
animal or bird or anything that moves [r]Lev 11:1-47;
along the ground—those which I have Dt 14:3-21
set apart as unclean for you. 26You are
to be holy to me[a] because I, the LORD,
am holy,[s] and I have set you apart from 20:26
the nations to be my own. [s]Lev 19:2
27"'A man or woman who is a medium or spiritist among you must be put
to death.[t] You are to stone them; their 20:27
blood will be on their own heads.'" [t]Lev 19:31

Rules for Priests

21 The LORD said to Moses,
"Speak to the priests, the sons of
Aaron, and say to them: 'A priest must
not make himself ceremonially unclean
for any of his people who die,[u] 2except 21:1 [u]Eze 44:25
for a close relative, such as his mother or
father, his son or daughter, his brother,
3or an unmarried sister who is dependent on him since she has no husband—for her he may make himself
unclean. 4He must not make himself
unclean for people related to him by
marriage,[b] and so defile himself.
5"'Priests must not shave their heads
or shave off the edges of their beards[v] 21:5 [v]Eze 44:20
or cut their bodies.[w] 6They must be [w]Lev 19:28;
holy to their God and must not pro- Dt 14:1
fane the name of their God.[x] Because 21:6 [x]Lev 18:21
they present the offerings made to the [y]Lev 3:11
LORD by fire,[y] the food of their God,
they are to be holy.
7"'They must not marry women de-
filed by prostitution or divorced from 21:7 [z]ver 13,14
their husbands,[z] because priests are holy
to their God.[a] 8Regard them as holy,[b] 21:8 [a]Eze 44:22
because they offer up the food of your [b]ver 6

[a]26 Or *be my holy ones* [b]4 Or *unclean as a leader among his people*

God. Consider them holy, because I
the LORD am holy—I who make you
holy.[a]
9"'If a priest's daughter defiles herself
by becoming a prostitute, she disgraces
her father; she must be burned in the
21:9 fire.[c]
[c]Ge 38:24; 10"'The high priest, the one among
Lev 19:29 his brothers who has had the anointing oil poured on his head and who
has been ordained to wear the priestly
21:10 garments,[d] must not let his hair be-
[d]Lev 16:32 [e]Lev 10:6 come unkempt[b] or tear his clothes.[e]
21:11 11He must not enter a place where there
[f]Nu 19:11, is a dead body.[f] He must not make
13,14 himself unclean,[g] even for his father or
[g]Lev 19:28 mother, 12nor leave the sanctuary of his
God or desecrate it, because he has been
21:12 dedicated by the anointing oil[h] of his
[h]Ex 29:6-7; Lev 10:7 God. I am the LORD.
21:13 13"'The woman he marries must be a
[i]Eze 44:22 virgin.[i] 14He must not marry a widow,
a divorced woman, or a woman defiled
by prostitution, but only a virgin from
his own people, 15so he will not defile
his offspring among his people. I am
the LORD, who makes him holy.[c]'"
16The LORD said to Moses, 17"Say
to Aaron: 'For the generations to come
none of your descendants who has a defect may come near to offer the food of
21:17 [j]ver 6 his God.[j] 18No man who has any de-
21:18 fect[k] may come near: no man who is
[k]Lev 22:19-25 blind or lame, disfigured or deformed;
19no man with a crippled foot or hand,
20or who is hunchbacked or dwarfed,
or who has any eye defect, or who has
festering or running sores or damaged
21:20 testicles.[l] 21No descendant of Aaron the
[l]Dt 23:1; Isa 56:3 priest who has any defect is to come
near to present the offerings made to
the LORD by fire. He has a defect; he
must not come near to offer the food
of his God. 22He may eat the most
21:22 holy food of his God,[m] as well as the
[m]1Co 9:13 holy food; 23yet because of his defect,
he must not go near the curtain or approach the altar, and so desecrate my
sanctuary. I am the LORD, who makes
them holy.[d]'"
24So Moses told this to Aaron and his
sons and to all the Israelites.

22 The LORD said to Moses, 2"Tell
Aaron and his sons to treat with
respect the sacred offerings the Israelites
consecrate to me, so they will not profane my holy name. I am the LORD.
3"Say to them: 'For the generations
to come, if any of your descendants
is ceremonially unclean and yet comes
near the sacred offerings that the Israelites consecrate to the LORD, that person must be cut off from my presence.[n] 22:3
I am the LORD. [n]Lev 7:20,21; Nu 19:13
4"'If a descendant of Aaron has an 22:4
infectious skin disease[e] or a bodily dis- [o]Lev 14:1-32;
charge,[o] he may not eat the sacred of- 15:2-15 [p]Lev 11:24-
ferings until he is cleansed. He will also 28,39
be unclean if he touches something defiled by a corpse[p] or by anyone who has
an emission of semen, 5or if he touches 22:5
any crawling thing[q] that makes him un- [q]Lev 11:24-28,43
clean, or any person[r] who makes him [r]Lev 15:7
unclean, whatever the uncleanness may
be. 6The one who touches any such
thing will be unclean till evening. He
must not eat any of the sacred offerings
unless he has bathed himself with water. 7When the sun goes down, he will
be clean, and after that he may eat the 22:7
sacred offerings, for they are his food.[s] [s]Nu 18:11
8He must not eat anything found dead[t] 22:8
or torn by wild animals,[u] and so be- [t]Lev 11:39
come unclean[v] through it. I am the [u]Ex 22:31; Lev 17:15
LORD. [v]Lev 11:40
9"'The priests are to keep my requirements so that they do not become 22:9
guilty and die[w] for treating them with [w]ver 16;
contempt. I am the LORD, who makes Ex 28:43
them holy.[f]
10"'No one outside a priest's family
may eat the sacred offering, nor may
the guest of a priest or his hired worker
eat it. 11But if a priest buys a slave with
money, or if a slave is born in his house- 22:11
hold, that slave may eat his food.[x] 12If [x]Ge 17:13;
a priest's daughter marries anyone other Ex 12:44
than a priest, she may not eat any of the
sacred contributions. 13But if a priest's
daughter becomes a widow or is divorced, yet has no children, and she returns to live in her father's house as in
her youth, she may eat of her father's
food. No unauthorized person, however, may eat any of it.
14"'If anyone eats a sacred offering
by mistake, he must make restitution
to the priest for the offering and add

[a]*8* Or *who sanctify you*; or *who set you apart as holy* [b]*10* Or *not uncover his head* [c]*15* Or *who sanctifies him*; or *who sets him apart as holy* [d]*23* Or *who sanctifies them*; or *who sets them apart as holy* [e]*4* Traditionally *leprosy*; the Hebrew word was used for various diseases affecting the skin—not necessarily leprosy. [f]*9* Or *who sanctifies them*; or *who sets them apart as holy*; also in verse 16

a fifth of the value to it.[y] 15 The priests must not desecrate the sacred offerings the Israelites present to the LORD[z] 16 by allowing them to eat the sacred offerings and so bring upon them guilt requiring payment.[a] I am the LORD, who makes them holy.' "

22:14 [y]Lev 5:15
22:15 [z]Nu 18:32
22:16 [a]ver 9

Unacceptable Sacrifices

17 The LORD said to Moses, 18 "Speak to Aaron and his sons and to all the Israelites and say to them: 'If any of you—either an Israelite or an alien living in Israel—presents a gift[b] for a burnt offering to the LORD, either to fulfill a vow or as a freewill offering, 19 you must present a male without defect[c] from the cattle, sheep or goats in order that it may be accepted on your behalf. 20 Do not bring anything with a defect,[d] because it will not be accepted on your behalf. 21 When anyone brings from the herd or flock a fellowship offering[a][e] to the LORD to fulfill a special vow or as a freewill offering, it must be without defect or blemish to be acceptable. 22 Do not offer to the LORD the blind, the injured or the maimed, or anything with warts or festering or running sores. Do not place any of these on the altar as an offering made to the LORD by fire. 23 You may, however, present as a freewill offering an ox[b] or a sheep that is deformed or stunted, but it will not be accepted in fulfillment of a vow. 24 You must not offer to the LORD an animal whose testicles are bruised, crushed, torn or cut.[f] You must not do this in your own land, 25 and you must not accept such animals from the hand of a foreigner and offer them as the food of your God.[g] They will not be accepted on your behalf, because they are deformed and have defects.' "

26 The LORD said to Moses, 27 "When a calf, a lamb or a goat is born, it is to remain with its mother for seven days.[h] From the eighth day on, it will be acceptable as an offering made to the LORD by fire. 28 Do not slaughter a cow or a sheep and its young on the same day.[i]

29 "When you sacrifice a thank offering[j] to the LORD, sacrifice it in such a way that it will be accepted on your behalf. 30 It must be eaten that same day; leave none of it till morning.[k] I am the LORD.

22:18 [b]Lev 1:2
22:19 [c]Lev 1:3
22:20 [d]Dt 15:21; 17:1; Mal 1:8,14; Heb 9:14; 1Pe 1:19
22:21 [e]Lev 3:6; Nu 15:3,8
22:24 [f]Lev 21:20
22:25 [g]Lev 21:6
22:27 [h]Ex 22:30
22:28 [i]Dt 22:6,7
22:29 [j]Lev 7:12; Ps 107:22
22:30 [k]Lev 7:15

31 "Keep[l] my commands and follow them. I am the LORD. 32 Do not profane my holy name.[m] I must be acknowledged as holy by the Israelites.[n] I am the LORD, who makes[c] you holy[d] 33 and who brought you out of Egypt to be your God.[o] I am the LORD."

22:31 [l]Dt 4:2,40; Ps 105:45
22:32 [m]Lev 18:21 [n]Lev 10:3
22:33 [o]Lev 11:45

23

The LORD said to Moses, 2 "Speak to the Israelites and say to them: 'These are my appointed feasts,[p] the appointed feasts of the LORD, which you are to proclaim as sacred assemblies.[q]

23:2 [p]ver 4,37,44; Nu 29:39 [q]ver 21,27

The Sabbath

3 " 'There are six days when you may work,[r] but the seventh day is a Sabbath of rest,[s] a day of sacred assembly. You are not to do any work; wherever you live, it is a Sabbath to the LORD.

23:3 [r]Ex 20:9 [s]Ex 20:10; 31:13-17; Lev 19:3; Dt 5:13; Heb 4:9,10

The Passover and Unleavened Bread

4 " 'These are the LORD's appointed feasts, the sacred assemblies you are to proclaim at their appointed times: 5 The LORD's Passover begins at twilight on the fourteenth day of the first month.[t] 6 On the fifteenth day of that month the LORD's Feast of Unleavened Bread begins; for seven days you must eat bread made without yeast. 7 On the first day hold a sacred assembly[u] and do no regular work. 8 For seven days present an offering made to the LORD by fire. And on the seventh day hold a sacred assembly and do no regular work.' "

23:5 [t]Ex 12:18-19; Nu 28:16-17; Dt 16:1-8
23:7 [u]ver 3,8

Firstfruits

9 The LORD said to Moses, 10 "Speak to the Israelites and say to them: 'When you enter the land I am going to give you and you reap its harvest, bring to the priest a sheaf[v] of the first grain you harvest. 11 He is to wave the sheaf before the LORD[w] so it will be accepted on your behalf; the priest is to wave it on the day after the Sabbath. 12 On the day you wave the sheaf, you must sacrifice as a burnt offering to the LORD a lamb a year old without defect, 13 together

23:10 [v]Ex 23:16,19; 34:26
23:11 [w]Ex 29:24

[a]*21* Traditionally *peace offering* [b]*23* The Hebrew word can include both male and female. [c]*32* Or *made* [d]*32* Or *who sanctifies you;* or *who sets you apart as holy*

with its grain offering[x] of two-tenths of an ephah[a] of fine flour mixed with oil—an offering made to the LORD by fire, a pleasing aroma—and its drink offering of a quarter of a hin[b] of wine. 14You must not eat any bread, or roasted or new grain, until the very day you bring this offering to your God.[y] This is to be a lasting ordinance for the generations to come,[z] wherever you live.

23:13 [x]Lev 2:14-16; 6:20
23:14 [y]Ex 34:26 [z]Nu 15:21

Feast of Weeks

15" 'From the day after the Sabbath, the day you brought the sheaf of the wave offering, count off seven full weeks. 16Count off fifty days up to the day after the seventh Sabbath,[a] and then present an offering of new grain to the LORD. 17From wherever you live, bring two loaves made of two-tenths of an ephah of fine flour, baked with yeast, as a wave offering of firstfruits[b] to the LORD. 18Present with this bread seven male lambs, each a year old and without defect, one young bull and two rams. They will be a burnt offering to the LORD, together with their grain offerings and drink offerings—an offering made by fire, an aroma pleasing to the LORD. 19Then sacrifice one male goat for a sin offering and two lambs, each a year old, for a fellowship offering.[c] 20The priest is to wave the two lambs before the LORD as a wave offering, together with the bread of the firstfruits. They are a sacred offering to the LORD for the priest. 21On that same day you are to proclaim a sacred assembly[c] and do no regular work.[d] This is to be a lasting ordinance for the generations to come, wherever you live.

22" 'When you reap the harvest[e] of your land, do not reap to the very edges of your field or gather the gleanings of your harvest.[f] Leave them for the poor and the alien. I am the LORD your God.' "

23:16 [a]Nu 28:26; Ac 2:1
23:17 [b]Ex 34:22; Lev 2:12
23:21 [c]ver 2 [d]ver 3
23:22 [e]Lev 19:9 [f]Lev 19:10; Dt 24:19-21; Ru 2:15

Feast of Trumpets

23The LORD said to Moses, 24"Say to the Israelites: 'On the first day of the seventh month you are to have a day of rest, a sacred assembly commemorated with trumpet blasts.[g] 25Do no regular work,[h] but present an offering made to the LORD by fire.' "

23:24 [g]Lev 25:9; Nu 10:9,10; 29:1
23:25 [h]ver 21

Day of Atonement

26The LORD said to Moses, 27"The tenth day of this seventh month[i] is the Day of Atonement.[j] Hold a sacred assembly[k] and deny yourselves,[d] and present an offering made to the LORD by fire. 28Do no work on that day, because it is the Day of Atonement, when atonement is made for you before the LORD your God. 29Anyone who does not deny himself on that day must be cut off from his people.[l] 30I will destroy from among his people[m] anyone who does any work on that day. 31You shall do no work at all. This is to be a lasting ordinance for the generations to come, wherever you live. 32It is a sabbath of rest for you, and you must deny yourselves. From the evening of the ninth day of the month until the following evening you are to observe your sabbath."

23:27 [i]Lev 16:29 [j]Ex 30:10 [k]Nu 29:7
23:29 [l]Ge 17:14; Nu 5:2
23:30 [m]Lev 20:3

Feast of Tabernacles

33The LORD said to Moses, 34"Say to the Israelites: 'On the fifteenth day of the seventh month the LORD's Feast of Tabernacles[n] begins, and it lasts for seven days. 35The first day is a sacred assembly; do no regular work. 36For seven days present offerings made to the LORD by fire, and on the eighth day hold a sacred assembly[o] and present an offering made to the LORD by fire. It is the closing assembly; do no regular work.

37(" 'These are the LORD's appointed feasts, which you are to proclaim as sacred assemblies for bringing offerings made to the LORD by fire—the burnt offerings and grain offerings, sacrifices and drink offerings[p] required for each day. 38These offerings are in addition to those for the LORD's Sabbaths[q] and[e] in addition to your gifts and whatever you have vowed and all the freewill offerings you give to the LORD.)

39" 'So beginning with the fifteenth day of the seventh month, after you have gathered the crops of the land, celebrate the festival to the LORD for

23:34 [n]Ex 23:16; Dt 16:13; Ezr 3:4; Ne 8:14; Zec 14:16; Jn 7:2
23:36 [o]2Ch 7:9; Ne 8:18; Jn 7:37
23:37 [p]ver 2,4
23:38 [q]Eze 45:17

[a]*13* That is, probably about 4 quarts (about 4.5 liters); also in verse 17 [b]*13* That is, probably about 1 quart (about 1 liter) [c]*19* Traditionally *peace offering* [d]*27* Or *and fast*; also in verses 29 and 32 [e]*38* Or *These feasts are in addition to the LORD's Sabbaths, and these offerings are*

23:39 ʳEx 23:16; Dt 16:13 seven days;[r] the first day is a day of
rest, and the eighth day also is a day of
rest. 40 On the first day you are to take
choice fruit from the trees, and palm
23:40 ˢNe 8:14-17 fronds, leafy branches and poplars,[s] and
rejoice before the LORD your God for
seven days. 41 Celebrate this as a festival to the LORD for seven days each
year. This is to be a lasting ordinance
for the generations to come; celebrate it
23:42 ᵗNe 8:14-16 in the seventh month. 42 Live in booths[t]
for seven days: All native-born Israelites
are to live in booths 43 so your descen-
23:43 ᵘDt 31:13; Ps 78:5 dants will know[u] that I had the Israelites live in booths when I brought them
out of Egypt. I am the LORD your
God.'"

44 So Moses announced to the Israelites the appointed feasts of the LORD.

Oil and Bread Set Before the LORD

24 The LORD said to Moses,
2 "Command the Israelites to
bring you clear oil of pressed olives for
the light so that the lamps may be kept
burning continually. 3 Outside the curtain of the Testimony in the Tent of
Meeting, Aaron is to tend the lamps before the LORD from evening till morning, continually. This is to be a lasting
ordinance for the generations to come.
4 The lamps on the pure gold lamp-
24:4 ᵛEx 25:31; 31:8 stand[v] before the LORD must be tended continually.

5 "Take fine flour and bake twelve
24:5 ʷEx 25:30 loaves of bread,[w] using two-tenths of
an ephah[a] for each loaf. 6 Set them in
two rows, six in each row, on the table
24:6 ˣEx 25:23-30; 1Ki 7:48 of pure gold[x] before the LORD. 7 Along
each row put some pure incense as
a memorial portion[y] to represent the
24:7 ʸLev 2:2 bread and to be an offering made to
the LORD by fire. 8 This bread is to be
24:8 ᶻNu 4:7; 1Ch 9:32; 2Ch 2:4 set out before the LORD regularly,[z] Sabbath after Sabbath,[a] on behalf of the
ᵃMt 12:5 Israelites, as a lasting covenant. 9 It be-
24:9 ᵇLev 8:31; Mt 12:4; Mk 2:26; Lk 6:4 longs to Aaron and his sons,[b] who are
to eat it in a holy place, because it is
a most holy part of their regular share
of the offerings made to the LORD by
fire."

A Blasphemer Stoned

10 Now the son of an Israelite mother
and an Egyptian father went out among
the Israelites, and a fight broke out in
the camp between him and an Israelite. 11 The son of the Israelite woman
blasphemed the Name[c] with a curse; so 24:11 ᶜEx 3:15
they brought him to Moses. (His moth-
er's name was Shelomith, the daughter
of Dibri the Danite.) 12 They put him
in custody until the will of the LORD
should be made clear to them.[d] 24:12 ᵈEx 18:16; Nu 15:34

13 Then the LORD said to Moses:
14 "Take the blasphemer outside the
camp. All those who heard him are to
lay their hands on his head, and the en-
tire assembly is to stone him.[e] 15 Say to 24:14 ᵉLev 20:27; Dt 13:9; 17:5,7; 21:21
the Israelites: 'If anyone curses his God,[f]
he will be held responsible; 16 anyone
who blasphemes the name of the LORD 24:15 ᶠEx 22:28
must be put to death.[g] The entire assem-
bly must stone him. Whether an alien 24:16 ᵍ1Ki 21:10, 13; Mt 26:66
or native-born, when he blasphemes the
Name, he must be put to death.

17 "'If anyone takes the life of a hu-
man being, he must be put to death.[h] 24:17 ʰGe 9:6; Ex 21:12; Nu 35:30-31; Dt 27:24
18 Anyone who takes the life of some-
one's animal must make restitution[i]—
life for life. 19 If anyone injures his
neighbor, whatever he has done must 24:18 ⁱver 21
be done to him: 20 fracture for fracture,
eye for eye, tooth for tooth.[j] As he has 24:20 ʲEx 21:24; Mt 5:38*
injured the other, so he is to be in-
jured. 21 Whoever kills an animal must
make restitution, but whoever kills a
man must be put to death.[k] 22 You are 24:21 ᵏver 17
to have the same law for the alien[l] and
the native-born.[m] I am the LORD your 24:22 ˡEx 12:49 ᵐNu 9:14; 15:16
God.'"

23 Then Moses spoke to the Israelites,
and they took the blasphemer outside
the camp and stoned him. The Israelites
did as the LORD commanded Moses.

The Sabbath Year

25 The LORD said to Moses on
Mount Sinai, 2 "Speak to the Israelites and say to them: 'When you enter the land I am going to give you, the
land itself must observe a sabbath to the
LORD. 3 For six years sow your fields,
and for six years prune your vineyards
and gather their crops.[n] 4 But in the sev- 25:3 ⁿEx 23:10
enth year the land is to have a sabbath
of rest, a sabbath to the LORD. Do
not sow your fields or prune your vineyards. 5 Do not reap what grows of itself
or harvest the grapes of your untended
vines. The land is to have a year of rest.
6 Whatever the land yields during the
sabbath year[o] will be food for you—for 25:6 ᵒver 20

[a] 5 That is, probably about 4 quarts (about 4.5 liters)

yourself, your manservant and maidservant, and the hired worker and temporary resident who live among you,
7as well as for your livestock and the
wild animals in your land. Whatever
the land produces may be eaten.

The Year of Jubilee

8“ ‘Count off seven sabbaths of
years—seven times seven years—so that
the seven sabbaths of years amount to a
period of forty-nine years. 9Then have
25:9 [p]Lev 23:24
the trumpet[p] sounded everywhere on
the tenth day of the seventh month;
on the Day of Atonement sound the
trumpet throughout your land. 10Con-
secrate the fiftieth year and proclaim
25:10 [q]Isa 61:1; Jer 34:8, 15,17; Lk 4:19 [r]Nu 36:4
liberty[q] throughout the land to all its
inhabitants. It shall be a jubilee[r] for
you; each one of you is to return to
his family property and each to his own
clan. 11The fiftieth year shall be a jubilee for you; do not sow and do not reap
what grows of itself or harvest the untended vines. 12For it is a jubilee and
is to be holy for you; eat only what is
taken directly from the fields.
25:13 [s]ver 10
13“ ‘In this Year of Jubilee[s] everyone is
to return to his own property.
14“ ‘If you sell land to one of your
countrymen or buy any from him, do
not take advantage of each other.[t] 15You
25:14 [t]Lev 19:13; 1Sa 12:3,4
are to buy from your countryman on
the basis of the number of years since
the Jubilee. And he is to sell to you
25:15 [u]Lev 27:18,23
on the basis of the number of years[u]
left for harvesting crops. 16When the
years are many, you are to increase the
price, and when the years are few, you
25:16 [v]ver 27,51,52
are to decrease the price,[v] because what
he is really selling you is the number of
25:17 [w]Pr 22:22; Jer 7:5,6; 1Th 4:6 [x]Lev 19:14 [y]Lev 19:32
crops. 17Do not take advantage of each
other,[w] but fear your God.[x] I am the
LORD your God.[y]
18“ ‘Follow my decrees and be careful to obey my laws, and you will live
25:18 [z]Lev 26:4,5; Dt 12:10; Ps 4:8; Jer 23:6
safely in the land.[z] 19Then the land will
yield its fruit,[a] and you will eat your
fill and live there in safety. 20You may
25:19 [a]Lev 26:4
ask, “What will we eat in the seventh
year[b] if we do not plant or harvest our
25:20 [b]ver 4
crops?” 21I will send you such a blessing[c] in the sixth year that the land will
25:21 [c]Dt 28:8,12; Hag 2:19; Mal 3:10
yield enough for three years. 22While
you plant during the eighth year, you
will eat from the old crop and will con-
25:22 [d]Lev 26:10
tinue to eat from it until the harvest of
the ninth year comes in.[d]

23“ ‘The land must not be sold per-
25:23 [e]Ex 19:5 [f]Ge 23:4; 1Ch 29:15; Ps 39:12; Heb 11:13; 1Pe 2:11
manently, because the land is mine[e]
and you are but aliens[f] and my tenants. 24Throughout the country that
you hold as a possession, you must provide for the redemption of the land.
25“ ‘If one of your countrymen becomes poor and sells some of his prop-
25:25 [g]Ru 2:20; Jer 32:7 [h]Lev 27:13, 19,31; Ru 4:4
erty, his nearest relative[g] is to come and
redeem[h] what his countryman has sold.
26If, however, a man has no one to redeem it for him but he himself prospers and acquires sufficient means to
redeem it, 27he is to determine the value for the years since he sold it and re-
fund the balance to the man to whom
he sold it; he can then go back to his
own property. 28But if he does not acquire the means to repay him, what he
sold will remain in the possession of the
buyer until the Year of Jubilee. It will be
returned in the Jubilee, and he can then
25:28 [i]ver 10
go back to his property.[i]
29“ ‘If a man sells a house in a walled
city, he retains the right of redemption
a full year after its sale. During that
time he may redeem it. 30If it is not redeemed before a full year has passed,
the house in the walled city shall belong
permanently to the buyer and his descendants. It is not to be returned in the
Jubilee. 31But houses in villages without walls around them are to be considered as open country. They can be
redeemed, and they are to be returned
in the Jubilee.
25:32 [j]Nu 35:1-8; Jos 21:2
32“ ‘The Levites always have the right
to redeem their houses in the Levitical
towns,[j] which they possess. 33So the

PATIENCE

THE WAIT FOR WHAT IS BETTER

Leviticus 25:29

This odd verse came to Israel during the long wandering in the desert. Living in tents caused the Israelites to think a lot about the homes they longed to own.

When you live in tents for 40 years,
you think a lot of houses.
Sinai always dreams of Canaan,
where her wanderings are settled
and her homesickness is cured.
There the God of hard times
becomes the God of better times.

property of the Levites is redeemable—that is, a house sold in any town they hold—and is to be returned in the Jubilee, because the houses in the towns of the Levites are their property among the Israelites. 34But the pastureland belonging to their towns must not be sold; it is their permanent possession.[k]

35" 'If one of your countrymen becomes poor[l] and is unable to support himself among you, help him[m] as you would an alien or a temporary resident, so he can continue to live among you. 36Do not take interest[n] of any kind[a] from him, but fear your God, so that your countryman may continue to live among you. 37You must not lend him money at interest or sell him food at a profit. 38I am the LORD your God, who brought you out of Egypt to give you the land of Canaan and to be your God.[o]

39" 'If one of your countrymen becomes poor among you and sells himself to you, do not make him work as a slave.[p] 40He is to be treated as a hired worker or a temporary resident among you; he is to work for you until the Year of Jubilee. 41Then he and his children are to be released, and he will go back to his own clan and to the property[q] of his forefathers. 42Because the Israelites are my servants, whom I brought out of Egypt, they must not be sold as slaves. 43Do not rule over them ruthlessly,[r] but fear your God.

44" 'Your male and female slaves are to come from the nations around you; from them you may buy slaves. 45You may also buy some of the temporary residents living among you and members of their clans born in your country, and they will become your property. 46You can will them to your children as inherited property and can make them slaves for life, but you must not rule over your fellow Israelites ruthlessly.

47" 'If an alien or a temporary resident among you becomes rich and one of your countrymen becomes poor and sells himself to the alien living among you or to a member of the alien's clan, 48he retains the right of redemption after he has sold himself. One of his relatives[s] may redeem him: 49An uncle or a cousin or any blood relative in his clan may redeem him. Or if he prospers,[t] he may redeem himself. 50He and his buyer are to count the time from the year he sold himself up to the Year of Jubilee. The price for his release is to be based on the rate paid to a hired man[u] for that number of years. 51If many years remain, he must pay for his redemption a larger share of the price paid for him. 52If only a few years remain until the Year of Jubilee, he is to compute that and pay for his redemption accordingly. 53He is to be treated as a man hired from year to year; you must see to it that his owner does not rule over him ruthlessly.

54" 'Even if he is not redeemed in any of these ways, he and his children are to be released in the Year of Jubilee, 55for the Israelites belong to me as servants. They are my servants, whom I brought out of Egypt. I am the LORD your God.

Reward for Obedience

26 " 'Do not make idols[v] or set up an image or a sacred stone[w] for yourselves, and do not place a carved stone[x] in your land to bow down before it. I am the LORD your God.

2" 'Observe my Sabbaths and have reverence for my sanctuary.[y] I am the LORD.

3" 'If you follow my decrees and are careful to obey[z] my commands, 4I will send you rain[a] in its season, and the ground will yield its crops and the trees of the field their fruit.[b] 5Your threshing will continue until grape harvest and the grape harvest will continue until planting, and you will eat all the food you want[c] and live in safety in your land.[d]

6" 'I will grant peace in the land,[e] and you will lie down[f] and no one will make you afraid.[g] I will remove savage beasts[h] from the land, and the sword will not pass through your country. 7You will pursue your enemies, and they will fall by the sword before you. 8Five of you will chase a hundred, and a hundred of you will chase ten thousand, and your enemies will fall by the sword before you.[i]

9" 'I will look on you with favor and make you fruitful and increase your numbers,[j] and I will keep my covenant[k] with you. 10You will still be eating last

[a]36 Or *take excessive interest*; similarly in verse 37

25:34 [k]Nu 35:2-5
25:35 [l]Dt 24:14,15 [m]Dt 15:8; Ps 37:21,26; Lk 6:35
25:36 [n]Ex 22:25; Dt 23:19-20
25:38 [o]Ge 17:7; Lev 11:45
25:39 [p]Ex 21:2; Dt 15:12; 1Ki 9:22
25:41 [q]ver 28
25:43 [r]Ex 1:13; Eze 34:4; Col 4:1
25:48 [s]Ne 5:5
25:49 [t]ver 26
25:50 [u]Job 7:1; Isa 16:14; 21:16
26:1 [v]Ex 20:4; Lev 19:4; Dt 5:8 [w]Ex 23:24 [x]Nu 33:52
26:2 [y]Lev 19:30
26:3 [z]Dt 7:12; 11:13,22; 28:1,9
26:4 [a]Dt 11:14 [b]Ps 67:6
26:5 [c]Dt 11:15; Joel 2:19,26; Am 9:13 [d]Lev 25:18
26:6 [e]Ps 29:11; 85:8; 147:14 [f]Ps 4:8 [g]Zep 3:13 [h]ver 22
26:8 [i]Dt 32:30; Jos 23:10
26:9 [j]Ge 17:6; Ne 9:23 [k]Ge 17:7

year's harvest when you will have to move it out to make room for the new.[l] 11 I will put my dwelling place[a][m] among you, and I will not abhor you. 12 I will walk[n] among you and be your God, and you will be my people.[o] 13 I am the LORD your God, who brought you out of Egypt so that you would no longer be slaves to the Egyptians; I broke the bars of your yoke[p] and enabled you to walk with heads held high.

Punishment for Disobedience

14 "'But if you will not listen to me and carry out all these commands,[q] 15 and if you reject my decrees and abhor my laws and fail to carry out all my commands and so violate my covenant, 16 then I will do this to you: I will bring upon you sudden terror, wasting diseases and fever[r] that will destroy your sight and drain away your life.[s] You will plant seed in vain, because your enemies will eat it.[t] 17 I will set my face[u] against you so that you will be defeated by your enemies; those who hate you will rule over you,[v] and you will flee even when no one is pursuing you.[w]

18 "'If after all this you will not listen to me, I will punish you for your sins seven times over.[x] 19 I will break down your stubborn pride[y] and make the sky above you like iron and the ground beneath you like bronze.[z] 20 Your strength will be spent in vain,[a] because your soil will not yield its crops, nor will the trees of the land yield their fruit.[b]

21 "'If you remain hostile toward me and refuse to listen to me, I will multiply your afflictions seven times over,[c] as your sins deserve. 22 I will send wild animals[d] against you, and they will rob you of your children, destroy your cattle and make you so few in number that your roads will be deserted.

23 "'If in spite of these things you do not accept my correction[e] but continue to be hostile toward me, 24 I myself will be hostile toward you and will afflict you for your sins seven times over. 25 And I will bring the sword upon you to avenge the breaking of the covenant. When you withdraw into your cities, I will send a plague[f] among you, and you will be given into enemy hands. 26 When I cut off your supply of bread,[g] ten women will be able to bake your bread in one oven, and they will dole out the bread by weight. You will eat, but you will not be satisfied.

27 "'If in spite of this you still do not listen to me but continue to be hostile toward me, 28 then in my anger I will be hostile toward you, and I myself will punish you for your sins seven times over. 29 You will eat the flesh of your sons and the flesh of your daughters.[h] 30 I will destroy your high places,[i] cut down your incense altars[j] and pile your dead bodies on the lifeless forms of your idols,[k] and I will abhor you. 31 I will turn your cities into ruins and lay waste your sanctuaries,[l] and I will take no delight in the pleasing aroma of your offerings. 32 I will lay waste the land,[m] so that your enemies who live there will be appalled. 33 I will scatter you among the nations[n] and will draw out my sword and pursue you. Your land will be laid waste, and your cities will lie in ruins. 34 Then the land will enjoy its sabbath years all the time that it lies desolate and you are in the country of your enemies;[o] then the land will rest and enjoy its sabbaths. 35 All the time that it lies desolate, the land will have the rest it did not have during the sabbaths you lived in it.

36 "'As for those of you who are left, I will make their hearts so fearful in the lands of their enemies that the sound of a windblown leaf will put them to flight.[p] They will run as though fleeing from the sword, and they will fall, even though no one is pursuing them. 37 They will stumble over one another as though fleeing from the sword, even though no one is pursuing them. So you will not be able to stand before your enemies.[q] 38 You will perish among the nations; the land of your enemies will devour you.[r] 39 Those of you who are left will waste away in the lands of their enemies because of their sins; also because of their fathers' sins they will waste away.[s]

40 "'But if they will confess their sins and the sins of their fathers[t]—their treachery against me and their hostility toward me, 41 which made me hostile toward them so that I sent them into the land of their enemies—then when their uncircumcised hearts[u] are humbled and they pay for their sin, 42 I

[a] *11* Or *my tabernacle*

26:10 [l]Lev 25:22
26:11 [m]Ex 25:8; Ps 76:2; Eze 37:27
26:12 [n]Ge 3:8 [o]2Co 6:16*
26:13 [p]Eze 34:27
26:14 [q]Dt 28:15-68; Mal 2:2
26:16 [r]Dt 28:22,35 [s]1Sa 2:33 [t]Job 31:8
26:17 [u]Lev 17:10 [v]Ps 106:41 [w]ver 36,37; Dt 28:7,25; Ps 53:5
26:18 [x]ver 21
26:19 [y]Isa 25:11 [z]Dt 28:23
26:20 [a]Ps 127:1; Isa 17:11 [b]Dt 11:17
26:21 [c]ver 18
26:22 [d]Dt 32:24
26:23 [e]Jer 2:30; 5:3
26:25 [f]Nu 14:12; Eze 5:17
26:26 [g]Ps 105:16; Isa 3:1; Mic 6:14
26:29 [h]Dt 28:53
26:30 [i]2Ch 34:3; Eze 6:3 [j]Eze 6:6 [k]Eze 6:13
26:31 [l]Ps 74:3-7
26:32 [m]Jer 9:11
26:33 [n]Dt 4:27; Eze 12:15; 20:23; Zec 7:14
26:34 [o]ver 43; 2Ch 36:21
26:36 [p]Eze 21:7
26:37 [q]Jos 7:12
26:38 [r]Dt 4:26
26:39 [s]Eze 4:17
26:40 [t]Jer 3:12-15; Lk 15:18; 1Jn 1:9
26:41 [u]Eze 44:7,9; Ac 7:51

26:42 [v]Ge 22:15-18; 28:15 [w]Ge 26:5 will remember my covenant with Jacob[v]
and my covenant with Isaac[w] and my
covenant with Abraham, and I will remember the land. 43For the land will
be deserted by them and will enjoy its
sabbaths while it lies desolate without
them. They will pay for their sins because they rejected my laws and abhorred my decrees. 44Yet in spite of this,
when they are in the land of their en-
26:44 [x]Ro 11:2 [y]Dt 4:31; Jer 30:11 [z]Jer 33:26 emies, I will not reject them or abhor[x]
them so as to destroy them completely,[y]
breaking my covenant[z] with them. I am
26:45 [a]Ge 17:7 [b]Ex 6:8; Lev 25:38 the LORD their God. 45But for their
sake I will remember[a] the covenant with
their ancestors whom I brought out of
Egypt[b] in the sight of the nations to be
their God. I am the LORD.' "
46These are the decrees, the laws and
the regulations that the LORD established on Mount Sinai between himself
26:46 [c]Lev 7:38; 27:34 and the Israelites through Moses.[c]

Redeeming What Is the LORD's

27 The LORD said to Moses,
2"Speak to the Israelites and say
to them: 'If anyone makes a special
27:2 [d]Nu 6:2 vow[d] to dedicate persons to the LORD
by giving equivalent values, 3set the value of a male between the ages of twenty
and sixty at fifty shekels[a] of silver, ac-
27:3 [e]Ex 30:13; Nu 3:47; 18:16 cording to the sanctuary shekel[b];[e] 4and
if it is a female, set her value at thirty
shekels.[c] 5If it is a person between the
ages of five and twenty, set the value of
a male at twenty shekels[d] and of a female at ten shekels.[e] 6If it is a person
between one month and five years, set
27:6 [f]Nu 18:16 the value of a male at five shekels[f][f] of
silver and that of a female at three shek-
els[g] of silver. 7If it is a person sixty years
old or more, set the value of a male at
fifteen shekels[h] and of a female at ten
shekels. 8If anyone making the vow is
27:8 [g]Lev 5:11 [h]ver 12,14 too poor to pay[g] the specified amount,
he is to present the person to the priest,
who will set the value[h] for him according to what the man making the vow
can afford.
9" 'If what he vowed is an animal
that is acceptable as an offering to the
LORD, such an animal given to the
LORD becomes holy. 10He must not exchange it or substitute a good one for
a bad one, or a bad one for a good
one;[i] if he should substitute one animal
27:10 [i]ver 33 for another, both it and the substitute
become holy. 11If what he vowed is a
ceremonially unclean animal—one that
is not acceptable as an offering to the
LORD—the animal must be presented
to the priest, 12who will judge its quality as good or bad. Whatever value the
priest then sets, that is what it will be.
13If the owner wishes to redeem[j] the an- 27:13 [j]ver 15,19; Lev 25:25
imal, he must add a fifth to its value.
14" 'If a man dedicates his house as
something holy to the LORD, the priest
will judge its quality as good or bad.
Whatever value the priest then sets, so
it will remain. 15If the man who ded-
icates his house redeems it,[k] he must 27:15 [k]ver 13,20
add a fifth to its value, and the house
will again become his.
16" 'If a man dedicates to the LORD
part of his family land, its value is to be
set according to the amount of seed required for it—fifty shekels of silver to a
homer[i] of barley seed. 17If he dedicates
his field during the Year of Jubilee, the
value that has been set remains. 18But
if he dedicates his field after the Jubilee, the priest will determine the value
according to the number of years that
remain[l] until the next Year of Jubilee, 27:18 [l]Lev 25:15
and its set value will be reduced. 19If
the man who dedicates the field wishes
to redeem it, he must add a fifth to its
value, and the field will again become
his. 20If, however, he does not redeem
the field, or if he has sold it to someone
else, it can never be redeemed. 21When
the field is released in the Jubilee,[m] it 27:21 [m]Lev 25:10 [n]ver 28; Nu 18:14; Eze 44:29
will become holy, like a field devoted to
the LORD;[n] it will become the property
of the priests.[j]
22" 'If a man dedicates to the LORD
a field he has bought, which is not part
of his family land, 23the priest will determine its value up to the Year of Jubilee, and the man must pay its value
on that day as something holy to the
LORD. 24In the Year of Jubilee the field
will revert to the person from whom he
bought it,[o] the one whose land it was. 27:24 [o]Lev 25:28
25Every value is to be set according to

[a] *3* That is, about 1 1/4 pounds (about 0.6 kilogram); also in verse 16 [b] *3* That is, about 2/5 ounce (about 11.5 grams); also in verse 25 [c] *4* That is, about 12 ounces (about 0.3 kilogram) [d] *5* That is, about 8 ounces (about 0.2 kilogram) [e] *5* That is, about 4 ounces (about 110 grams); also in verse 7 [f] *6* That is, about 2 ounces (about 55 grams) [g] *6* That is, about 1 1/4 ounces (about 35 grams) [h] *7* That is, about 6 ounces (about 170 grams) [i] *16* That is, probably about 6 bushels (about 220 liters) [j] *21* Or *priest*

27:25 [p]Ex 30:13; Nu 18:16 [q]Nu 3:47; Eze 45:12
the sanctuary shekel,[p] twenty gerahs[q] to
the shekel.
26“ ‘No one, however, may dedicate
the firstborn of an animal, since the
27:26 [r]Ex 13:2,12
firstborn already belongs to the LORD;[r]
whether an ox[a] or a sheep, it is the
LORD’s. 27If it is one of the unclean
27:27 [s]ver 11
animals,[s] he may buy it back at its set
value, adding a fifth of the value to it.
If he does not redeem it, it is to be sold
at its set value.
28“ ‘But nothing that a man owns and
27:28 [t]Nu 18:14; Jos 6:17-19
devotes[b] [t] to the LORD—whether man
or animal or family land—may be sold
or redeemed; everything so devoted is
most holy to the LORD.
29“ ‘No person devoted to destruction[c] may be ransomed; he must be put
to death.
27:30 [u]Ge 28:22; 2Ch 31:6; Mal 3:8
30“ ‘A tithe[u] of everything from the
land, whether grain from the soil or
fruit from the trees, belongs to the
LORD; it is holy to the LORD. 31If a
man redeems any of his tithe, he must
add a fifth of the value to it. 32The entire tithe of the herd and flock—every
tenth animal that passes under the shep-
27:32 [v]Jer 33:13; Eze 20:37
herd’s rod[v]—will be holy to the LORD.
33He must not pick out the good from
the bad or make any substitution.[w] If 27:33 [w]ver 10
he does make a substitution, both the
animal and its substitute become holy
and cannot be redeemed.’ ”

▸ LOVE

LOVE FIRST, GIVE SECOND

Leviticus 27:33

Tithe? Me?
Why?
Will my refusal make God poorer?
No.
But keeping all we have makes us poorer—a prisoner of our own greed. Tithing says how much we love God. Refusing to tithe shows how much we love ourselves.

34These are the commands the LORD
gave Moses on Mount Sinai for the 27:34 [x]Lev 26:46; Dt 4:5
Israelites.[x]

[a]*26* The Hebrew word can include both male and female. [b]*28* The Hebrew term refers to the irrevocable giving over of things or persons to the LORD. [c]*29* The Hebrew term refers to the irrevocable giving over of things or persons to the LORD, often by totally destroying them.

NUMBERS

AUTHORSHIP AND DATE

Moses

c. 1450 B.C. to c. 1410 B.C.

KEY THEMES

The title, *Numbers,* is based on the census lists found in Numbers 1 and 26. The Hebrew title of the book is *bemidbar* or *in the desert.* Since all that occurred in the book transpired in the wilderness, the Hebrew title seems in many ways more appropriate. There are four ideas that keep resurfacing in the book:

1. The numbering of the people (the census)
2. The uprising of the rebels
3. Their wandering in the wilderness
4. Their first explorations of Canaan

FRUIT OF THE SPIRIT IN NUMBERS

Joy: The joy of God is evidenced in several places throughout this book. The optimism of Joshua and Caleb upon their return from Canaan (see 13:30) displayed a spirit of joy. Better still is the oracle of Balaam (see 24:5–25), in which Balaam offered praise to the hosts of Israel, saying, "How beautiful are your tents, O Jacob, your dwelling places, O Israel!" (v. 5). But the most beautiful of all the statements of joy is found in the blessing of Numbers 6:24–26: "The LORD bless you and keep you; the LORD make his face shine upon you and be gracious to you; the LORD turn his face toward you and give you peace."

Peace: Peace can be seen in a most interesting way in Numbers. After Phinehas drove a spear through an Israelite man and his illicit Midianite lover, God commended Phinehas for his defense of morality and honor. God then promised the priest peace: "I am making my covenant of peace with him. He and his descendents will have a covenant of a lasting priesthood, because he was zealous for the honor of his God and made atonement for the Israelites" (25:12–13). Peace is the corollary of holy obedience. When we have obeyed, we can expect the blessing of peace.

Patience: In Numbers 20 the people were again complaining about the lack of water and wishing they had died in Egypt. One wonders if Moses didn't occasionally wish that too, but his forbearance, for the most part, was equal to their complaints. Yet on this occasion, he lost his patience. God was not pleased with Moses and told him he would not enter the promised land. Some have viewed God as harsh for visiting so strict a punishment on Moses, but one thing is clear: Our unwillingness to be patient and to trust God in all he asks is a serious matter with him.

Kindness: Numbers 12:3 indicates that great leaders, like Moses, are often possessed by a spirit of kindness. Kindness doesn't mean being weak; it means having authority and power that is always kept within control. Great leaders—kind leaders—usually have the power to "lord it over" their constituencies, but they rarely do. A spirit of kindness possesses them.

Goodness: It is refreshing to find traces of gentle goodness among the often stern requirements of God. Moses invited his brother-in-law Hobab, a Midianite, to accompany the Israelites on their journey and share in their inheritance: "Come with us and we will treat you well," said Moses, "for the LORD has promised good things to Israel" (10:29). Moses' invitation was consistent with God's concern for the aliens and Gentiles (see Exodus 23:9), and it recognized that hospitality is indeed kind goodness.

Faithfulness: When devoted people faithfully preach God's Word, they are to be heeded by those who hear them. The Lord, speaking from a pillar of cloud at the door of the tabernacle, rebuked the Israelites for not following their faithful leaders: "[Moses] is faithful in all my house. With him I speak face to face, clearly and not in riddles; he sees the form of the LORD. Why then were you not afraid to speak against my servant Moses?" (12:7–8).

The Census

1:1 1 The LORD spoke to Moses in the
[a]Ex 40:2 Tent of Meeting[a] in the Desert of
[b]Ex 19:1 Sinai[b] on the first day of the second
[c]Ex 40:17 month[c] of the second year after the Israelites came out of Egypt. He said:
1:2 2“Take a census[d] of the whole Israelite
[d]Ex 30:11-16; Nu 26:2 community by their clans and families,
listing every man by name, one by one.
3You and Aaron are to number by their
divisions all the men in Israel twenty
1:3 [e]Ex 30:14 years old or more[e] who are able to serve
1:4 in the army. 4One man from each tribe,
[f]ver 16 each the head of his family,[f] is to help
[g]Ex 18:21; Dt 1:15 you.[g] 5These are the names of the men
who are to assist you:
1:5 [h]Ge 29:32; from Reuben,[h] Elizur son of Shed-
Dt 33:6; Rev 7:5 eur;
1:7 6from Simeon, Shelumiel son of
[i]Ge 29:35; Zurishaddai;
Ps 78:68 7from Judah,[i] Nahshon son of
[j]Ru 4:20; 1Ch 2:10; Amminadab;[j]
Lk 3:32 8from Issachar,[k] Nethanel son of
1:8 [k]Ge 30:18 Zuar;
9from Zebulun,[l] Eliab son of He-
1:9 [l]ver 30 lon;
10from the sons of Joseph:
1:10 [m]ver 32 from Ephraim,[m] Elishama son
of Ammihud;
from Manasseh, Gamaliel son of
Pedahzur;
11from Benjamin, Abidan son of
Gideoni;
1:12 [n]ver 38 12from Dan,[n] Ahiezer son of Ammishaddai;
1:13 [o]ver 40 13from Asher,[o] Pagiel son of Ocran;
1:14 14from Gad, Eliasaph son of
[p]Nu 2:14 Deuel;[p]
1:15 15from Naphtali,[q] Ahira son of
[q]ver 42 Enan.”
16These were the men appointed from
1:16 the community, the leaders[r] of their an-
[r]Ex 18:25 [s]ver 4; cestral tribes. They were the heads of
Ex 18:21; Nu 7:2 the clans of Israel.[s]
17Moses and Aaron took these men
whose names had been given, 18and
they called the whole community together on the first day of the second
1:18 month.[t] The people indicated their an-
[t]ver 1 cestry[u] by their clans and families, and
[u]Ezr 2:59; Heb 7:3 the men twenty years old or more were
listed by name, one by one, 19as the
LORD commanded Moses. And so he
counted them in the Desert of Sinai:
1:20 [v]Nu 26:5-11; 20From the descendants of Reuben[v] the
Rev 7:5 firstborn son of Israel:
All the men twenty years old or
more who were able to serve in
the army were listed by name,
one by one, according to the
records of their clans and families. 21The number from the
tribe of Reuben was 46,500.
22From the descendants of Simeon:[w] 1:22 [w]Nu 26:12-14;
All the men twenty years old Rev 7:7
or more who were able to serve
in the army were counted and
listed by name, one by one, according to the records of their
clans and families. 23The number from the tribe of Simeon
was 59,300.
24From the descendants of Gad:[x] 1:24 [x]Ge 30:11;
All the men twenty years old or Nu 26:15-18;
more who were able to serve in Rev 7:5
the army were listed by name,
according to the records of their
clans and families. 25The number from the tribe of Gad was
45,650.
26From the descendants of Judah:[y] 1:26
All the men twenty years old or [y]Ge 29:35;
more who were able to serve in Nu 26:19-22;
the army were listed by name, Mt 1:2; Rev 7:5
according to the records of their
clans and families. 27The number from the tribe of Judah was
74,600.
28From the descendants of Issachar:[z] 1:28
All the men twenty years old or [z]Nu 26:23-25; Rev 7:7
more who were able to serve in
the army were listed by name, 1:30
according to the records of their [a]Nu 26:26-27; Rev 7:8
clans and families. 29The num-
ber from the tribe of Issachar
was 54,400.
30From the descendants of Zebulun:[a]
All the men twenty years old or
more who were able to serve in
the army were listed by name,
according to the records of their
clans and families. 31The number from the tribe of Zebulun
was 57,400.
32From the sons of Joseph:
From the descendants of Ephraim:[b] 1:32 [b]Nu 26:35-37
All the men twenty years old or
more who were able to serve in
the army were listed by name,
according to the records of their
clans and families. 33The number

from the tribe of Ephraim was 40,500.

34From the descendants of Manasseh:[c]
All the men twenty years old or more who were able to serve in the army were listed by name, according to the records of their clans and families. 35The number from the tribe of Manasseh was 32,200.

1:34 [c]Nu 26:28-34; Rev 7:6

36From the descendants of Benjamin:[d]
All the men twenty years old or more who were able to serve in the army were listed by name, according to the records of their clans and families. 37The number from the tribe of Benjamin was 35,400.

1:36 [d]Nu 26:38-41; 2Ch 17:17; Rev 7:8

38From the descendants of Dan:[e]
All the men twenty years old or more who were able to serve in the army were listed by name, according to the records of their clans and families. 39The number from the tribe of Dan was 62,700.

1:38 [e]Ge 30:6; Nu 26:42-43

40From the descendants of Asher:[f]
All the men twenty years old or more who were able to serve in the army were listed by name, according to the records of their clans and families. 41The number from the tribe of Asher was 41,500.

1:40 [f]Nu 26:44-47; Rev 7:6

42From the descendants of Naphtali:[g]
All the men twenty years old or more who were able to serve in the army were listed by name, according to the records of their clans and families. 43The number from the tribe of Naphtali was 53,400.

1:42 [g]Nu 26:48-50; Rev 7:6

44These were the men counted by Moses and Aaron[h] and the twelve leaders of Israel, each one representing his family. 45All the Israelites twenty years old or more who were able to serve in Israel's army were counted according to their families. 46The total number was 603,550.[i]

47The families of the tribe of Levi,[j] however, were not counted[k] along with the others. 48The LORD had said to Moses: 49"You must not count the tribe of Levi or include them in the census of the other Israelites. 50Instead, appoint the Levites to be in charge of the tabernacle of the Testimony[l]—over all its furnishings and everything belonging to it. They are to carry the tabernacle and all its furnishings; they are to take care of it and encamp around it. 51Whenever the tabernacle is to move, the Levites are to take it down, and whenever the tabernacle is to be set up, the Levites shall do it.[m] Anyone else who goes near it shall be put to death. 52The Israelites are to set up their tents by divisions, each man in his own camp under his own standard.[n] 53The Levites, however, are to set up their tents around the tabernacle of the Testimony so that wrath will not fall[o] on the Israelite community. The Levites are to be responsible for the care of the tabernacle of the Testimony.[p]"

54The Israelites did all this just as the LORD commanded Moses.

1:44 [h]Nu 26:64
1:46 [i]Ex 12:37; 38:26; Nu 2:32; 26:51
1:47 [j]Nu 2:33; 26:57 [k]Nu 4:3,49
1:50 [l]Ex 38:21; Ac 7:44
1:51 [m]Nu 3:38; 4:1-33
1:52 [n]Nu 2:2; Ps 20:5
1:53 [o]Lev 10:6; Nu 16:46; 18:5 [p]Nu 18:2-4

The Arrangement of the Tribal Camps

2 The LORD said to Moses and Aaron: 2"The Israelites are to camp around the Tent of Meeting some distance from it, each man under his standard[q] with the banners of his family."

3On the east, toward the sunrise, the divisions of the camp of Judah are to encamp under their standard. The leader of the people of Judah is Nahshon son of Amminadab.[r] 4His division numbers 74,600.

5The tribe of Issachar will camp next to them. The leader of the people of Issachar is Nethanel son of Zuar.[s] 6His division numbers 54,400.

2:2 [q]Nu 1:52; Ps 74:4; Isa 31:9
2:3 [r]Nu 10:14; Ru 4:20; 1Ch 2:10
2:5 [s]Nu 1:8

GENTLENESS

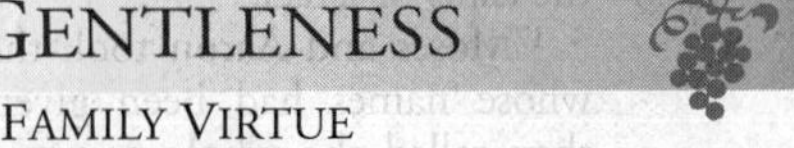

THE FAMILY VIRTUE

Numbers 2:5
Israel camped by families—a gentle way to organize in preparation for warfare. Families that bond in tough seasons are families for all seasons.

7The tribe of Zebulun will be next. The leader of the people of Zebulun is Eliab son of Helon.[t]

2:7 [t]Nu 1:9

8His division numbers 57,400.
9All the men assigned to the
camp of Judah, according to their
divisions, number 186,400. They
2:9 [u]Nu 10:14 will set out first.[u]
10On the south will be the divisions of the camp of Reuben under their standard. The leader of
the people of Reuben is Elizur son
2:10 [v]Nu 1:5 of Shedeur.[v] 11His division numbers 46,500.
12The tribe of Simeon will camp
next to them. The leader of the
2:12 [w]Nu 1:6 people of Simeon is Shelumiel
son of Zurishaddai.[w] 13His division numbers 59,300.
14The tribe of Gad will be next.
The leader of the people of Gad is
2:14 [x]Nu 1:14 Eliasaph son of Deuel.[a][x] 15His division numbers 45,650.
16All the men assigned to the
2:16 [y]Nu 10:18 camp of Reuben,[y] according to
their divisions, number 151,450.
They will set out second.
17Then the Tent of Meeting and
2:17 [z]Nu 1:53; 10:21 the camp of the Levites[z] will set
out in the middle of the camps.
They will set out in the same order
as they encamp, each in his own
place under his standard.
18On the west will be the divi-
2:18 [a]Ge 48:20; Jer 31:18-20 [b]Nu 1:10 sions of the camp of Ephraim[a] under their standard. The leader of
the people of Ephraim is Elishama
son of Ammihud.[b] 19His division
numbers 40,500.
20The tribe of Manasseh will be
next to them. The leader of the
people of Manasseh is Gamaliel
2:20 [c]Nu 1:10 son of Pedahzur.[c] 21His division
numbers 32,200.
22The tribe of Benjamin will
be next. The leader of the people
2:22 [d]Nu 1:11; Ps 68:27 of Benjamin is Abidan son of
Gideoni.[d] 23His division numbers
35,400.
24All the men assigned to the
2:24 [e]Nu 10:22 [f]Ps 80:2 camp of Ephraim,[e] according to
their divisions, number 108,100.
They will set out third.[f]
25On the north will be the divisions of the camp of Dan, under their standard. The leader of
the people of Dan is Ahiezer son
2:25 [g]Nu 1:12 of Ammishaddai.[g] 26His division
numbers 62,700.

27The tribe of Asher will camp
next to them. The leader of the
people of Asher is Pagiel son of
Ocran.[h] 28His division numbers 2:27 [h]Nu 1:13
41,500.
29The tribe of Naphtali will be
next. The leader of the people of
Naphtali is Ahira son of Enan.[i] 2:29 [i]Nu 1:15
30His division numbers 53,400.
31All the men assigned to the
camp of Dan number 157,600.
They will set out last,[j] under their 2:31 [j]Nu 10:25
standards.

32These are the Israelites, counted according to their families. All
those in the camps, by their di-
visions, number 603,550.[k] 33The 2:32 [k]Ex 38:26; Nu 1:46
Levites, however, were not count-
ed[l] along with the other Israelites, 2:33 [l]Nu 1:47; 26:57-62
as the LORD commanded Moses.
34So the Israelites did everything the
LORD commanded Moses; that is the
way they encamped under their standards, and that is the way they set out,
each with his clan and family.

The Levites

3 This is the account of the family
of Aaron and Moses[m] at the time 3:1 [m]Ex 6:27
the LORD talked with Moses on Mount
Sinai.
2The names of the sons of Aaron
were Nadab the firstborn and Abihu,
Eleazar and Ithamar.[n] 3Those were the 3:2 [n]Ex 6:23; Nu 26:60
names of Aaron's sons, the anointed
priests,[o] who were ordained to serve 3:3 [o]Ex 28:41
as priests. 4Nadab and Abihu, how-
ever, fell dead before the LORD[p] when 3:4 [p]Lev 10:2 [q]Lev 10:1 [r]1Ch 24:1
they made an offering with unauthor-
ized fire before him in the Desert of
Sinai.[q] They had no sons; so only Eleazar and Ithamar served as priests during
the lifetime of their father Aaron.[r]
5The LORD said to Moses, 6"Bring
the tribe of Levi[s] and present them to 3:6 [s]Dt 10:8; 31:9; 1Ch 15:2 [t]Nu 8:6-22; 18:1-7; 2Ch 29:11
Aaron the priest to assist him.[t] 7They
are to perform duties for him and for
the whole community at the Tent of
Meeting by doing the work[u] of the tab-
ernacle. 8They are to take care of all the 3:7 [u]Lev 8:35–Nu 1:50
furnishings of the Tent of Meeting, ful-
filling the obligations of the Israelites by
doing the work of the tabernacle. 9Give

[a]*14* Many manuscripts of the Masoretic Text, Samaritan Pentateuch and Vulgate (see also Num. 1:14); most manuscripts of the Masoretic Text *Reuel*

3:9 [v]Nu 8:19; the Levites to Aaron and his sons;[v] they
18:6 are the Israelites who are to be given
wholly to him.[a] 10Appoint Aaron and
3:10 his sons to serve as priests;[w] anyone else
[w]Ex 29:9 [x]Nu 1:51 who approaches the sanctuary must be
put to death."[x]
11The LORD also said to Moses, 12"I
3:12 [y]Mal 2:4 have taken the Levites[y] from among the
[z]ver 41; Nu 8:16,18 Israelites in place of the first male off-
[a]Ex 13:2 spring[z] of every Israelite woman. The
Levites are mine,[a] 13for all the firstborn
3:13 [b]Ex 13:12 are mine.[b] When I struck down all the
firstborn in Egypt, I set apart for myself
every firstborn in Israel, whether man
or animal. They are to be mine. I am
the LORD."
14The LORD said to Moses in the
3:15 [c]ver 39 Desert of Sinai, 15"Count[c] the Levites
[d]Nu 26:62 by their families and clans. Count every
male a month old or more."[d] 16So Mo-
ses counted them, as he was commanded by the word of the LORD.

17These were the names of the sons
3:17 [e]Ge 46:11 of Levi:[e]
[f]Ex 6:16 Gershon, Kohath and Merari.[f]
18These were the names of the Gershonite clans:
3:18 [g]Ex 6:17 Libni and Shimei.[g]
19The Kohathite clans:
Amram, Izhar, Hebron and Uz-
3:19 [h]Ex 6:18 ziel.[h]
20The Merarite clans:[i]
3:20 [i]Ge 46:11 Mahli and Mushi.[j]
[j]Ex 6:19 These were the Levite clans, according to their families.

3:21 [k]Ex 6:17 21To Gershon belonged the clans of
the Libnites and Shimeites;[k] these were
the Gershonite clans. 22The number
of all the males a month old or more
who were counted was 7,500. 23The
Gershonite clans were to camp on the
west, behind the tabernacle. 24The leader of the families of the Gershonites was
Eliasaph son of Lael. 25At the Tent of
Meeting the Gershonites were respon-
3:25 [l]Ex 25:9 sible for the care of the tabernacle[l] and
[m]Ex 26:14 tent, its coverings,[m] the curtain at the
[n]Ex 26:36; Nu 4:25 entrance[n] to the Tent of Meeting, 26the
curtains of the courtyard,[o] the curtain
3:26 [o]Ex 27:9 at the entrance to the courtyard sur-
[p]Ex 35:18 rounding the tabernacle and altar, and
the ropes[p]—and everything related to
their use.

27To Kohath belonged the clans of
the Amramites, Izharites, Hebronites
3:27 [q]1Ch 26:23 and Uzzielites;[q] these were the Kohathite clans. 28The number of all the
males a month old or more was 8,600.[b]
The Kohathites were responsible for the
care of the sanctuary. 29The Kohathite
clans were to camp on the south side[r]
of the tabernacle. 30The leader of the 3:29 [r]Nu 1:53
families of the Kohathite clans was El-
izaphan son of Uzziel. 31They were re- 3:31 [s]Ex 25:10-22
sponsible for the care of the ark,[s] the [t]Ex 25:23
table,[t] the lampstand,[u] the altars,[v] the [u]Ex 25:31
articles of the sanctuary used in minis- [v]Ex 27:1; 30:1
tering, the curtain,[w] and everything re- [w]Ex 26:33 [x]Nu 4:15
lated to their use.[x] 32The chief leader of
the Levites was Eleazar son of Aaron,
the priest. He was appointed over those
who were responsible for the care of the
sanctuary.

33To Merari belonged the clans of the
Mahlites and the Mushites;[y] these were 3:33 [y]Ex 6:19
the Merarite clans. 34The number of all
the males a month old or more who
were counted was 6,200. 35The leader
of the families of the Merarite clans was
Zuriel son of Abihail; they were to camp
on the north side of the tabernacle.[z] 3:35 [z]Nu 1:53;
36The Merarites were appointed[a] to take 2:25
care of the frames of the tabernacle, 3:36
its crossbars, posts, bases, all its equip- [a]Nu 4:32
ment, and everything related to their
use, 37as well as the posts of the surrounding courtyard with their bases,
tent pegs and ropes.

38Moses and Aaron and his sons were
to camp to the east[b] of the tabernacle, 3:38 [b]Nu 2:3
toward the sunrise, in front of the Tent [c]Nu 1:53
of Meeting.[c] They were responsible for [d]ver 7; Nu 18:5
the care of the sanctuary[d] on behalf [e]ver 10; Nu 1:51
of the Israelites. Anyone else who ap-
proached the sanctuary was to be put to
death.[e]

39The total number of Levites counted at the LORD's command by Moses
and Aaron according to their clans, including every male a month old or 3:39 [f]Nu 26:62
more, was 22,000.[f]

40The LORD said to Moses, "Count
all the firstborn Israelite males who are
a month old or more[g] and make a 3:40 [g]ver 15
list of their names. 41Take the Levites

[a]*9* Most manuscripts of the Masoretic Text; some manuscripts of the Masoretic Text, Samaritan Pentateuch and Septuagint (see also Num. 8:16) *to me* [b]*28* Hebrew; some Septuagint manuscripts *8,300*

for me in place of all the firstborn of
3:41 the Israelites,[b] and the livestock of the
[b]ver 12 Levites in place of all the firstborn of
the livestock of the Israelites. I am the
LORD."
42 So Moses counted all the firstborn
of the Israelites, as the LORD commanded him. 43 The total number of
3:43 firstborn males a month old or more,
[i]ver 39 listed by name, was 22,273.[i]
44 The LORD also said to Moses,
45 "Take the Levites in place of all the
firstborn of Israel, and the livestock of
the Levites in place of their livestock.
The Levites are to be mine. I am the
3:46 [j]Ex 13:13; LORD. 46 To redeem[j] the 273 firstborn
Nu 18:15 Israelites who exceed the number of the
3:47 Levites, 47 collect five shekels[a][k] for each
[k]Lev 27:6 [l]Ex 30:13 one, according to the sanctuary shekel,[l]
[m]Lev 27:25 which weighs twenty gerahs.[m] 48 Give
the money for the redemption of the
additional Israelites to Aaron and his
sons."
49 So Moses collected the redemption money from those who exceeded
the number redeemed by the Levites.
50 From the firstborn of the Israelites
he collected silver weighing 1,365
3:50 shekels,[b][n] according to the sanctuary
[n]ver 46-48 shekel. 51 Moses gave the redemption
money to Aaron and his sons, as he
was commanded by the word of the
LORD.

The Kohathites

4 The LORD said to Moses and
4:2 [o]Ex 30:12 Aaron: 2 "Take a census[o] of the Kohathite branch of the Levites by their
4:3 clans and families. 3 Count all the men
[p]ver 23; Nu 8:25; from thirty to fifty years of age[p] who
1Ch 23:3, 24,27; come to serve in the work in the Tent
Ezr 3:8 of Meeting.
4 "This is the work of the Kohathites
in the Tent of Meeting: the care of the
4:4 most holy things.[q] 5 When the camp is
[q]ver 19 to move, Aaron and his sons are to go
4:5 in and take down the shielding curtain[r]
[r]Ex 26:31,33 [s]Ex 25:10,16 and cover the ark of the Testimony with
4:6 it.[s] 6 Then they are to cover this with
[t]Ex 25:13-15; hides of sea cows,[c] spread a cloth of
1Ki 8:7; 2Ch 5:8 solid blue over that and put the poles[t]
4:7 in place.
[u]Ex 25:23,29; 7 "Over the table of the Presence[u] they
Lev 24:6 [v]Ex 25:30 are to spread a blue cloth and put on
it the plates, dishes and bowls, and the
jars for drink offerings; the bread that
is continually there[v] is to remain on it.
8 Over these they are to spread a scarlet
cloth, cover that with hides of sea cows
and put its poles in place.
9 "They are to take a blue cloth and
cover the lampstand that is for light,
together with its lamps, its wick trimmers and trays,[w] and all its jars for the 4:9
oil used to supply it. 10 Then they are to [w]Ex 25:31, 37,38
wrap it and all its accessories in a cover-
ing of hides of sea cows and put it on a
carrying frame.
11 "Over the gold altar[x] they are to 4:11
spread a blue cloth and cover that with [x]Ex 30:1
hides of sea cows and put its poles in
place.
12 "They are to take all the articles
used for ministering in the sanctuary,
wrap them in a blue cloth, cover that
with hides of sea cows and put them on
a carrying frame.
13 "They are to remove the ashes from
the bronze altar[y] and spread a purple 4:13
cloth over it. 14 Then they are to place [y]Ex 27:1-8
on it all the utensils used for ministering
at the altar, including the firepans, meat
forks,[z] shovels and sprinkling bowls.[a] 4:14 [z]2Ch 4:16
Over it they are to spread a covering of [a]Jer 52:18
hides of sea cows and put its poles[b] in [b]Ex 27:6
place.
15 "After Aaron and his sons have finished covering the holy furnishings and
all the holy articles, and when the camp
is ready to move, the Kohathites are to
come to do the carrying.[c] But they must 4:15 [c]Nu 7:9
not touch the holy things or they will [d]Nu 1:51;
die.[d] The Kohathites are to carry those 2Sa 6:6,7
things that are in the Tent of Meeting.
16 "Eleazar[e] son of Aaron, the priest, 4:16
is to have charge of the oil for the light,[f] [e]Lev 10:6
the fragrant incense, the regular grain [f]Ex 25:6 [g]Ex 29:41;
offering[g] and the anointing oil. He is Lev 6:14-23
to be in charge of the entire tabernacle
and everything in it, including its holy
furnishings and articles."
17 The LORD said to Moses and Aaron, 18 "See that the Kohathite tribal
clans are not cut off from the Levites.
19 So that they may live and not die
when they come near the most holy
things,[h] do this for them: Aaron and his 4:19
sons are to go into the sanctuary and as- [h]ver 15
sign to each man his work and what he
is to carry. 20 But the Kohathites must 4:20
not go in to look[i] at the holy things, [i]Ex 19:21;
even for a moment, or they will die." 1Sa 6:19

[a] *47* That is, about 2 ounces (about 55 grams)
[b] *50* That is, about 35 pounds (about 15.5 kilograms)
[c] *6* That is, dugongs; also in verses 8, 10, 11, 12, 14 and 25

The Gershonites

21 The LORD said to Moses, 22 "Take a census also of the Gershonites by their families and clans. 23 Count all the men from thirty to fifty years of age[j] who come to serve in the work at the Tent of Meeting.

24 "This is the service of the Gershonite clans as they work and carry burdens: 25 They are to carry the curtains of the tabernacle,[k] the Tent of Meeting,[l] its covering[m] and the outer covering of hides of sea cows, the curtains for the entrance to the Tent of Meeting, 26 the curtains of the courtyard surrounding the tabernacle and altar, the curtain for the entrance, the ropes and all the equipment used in its service. The Gershonites are to do all that needs to be done with these things. 27 All their service, whether carrying or doing other work, is to be done under the direction of Aaron and his sons. You shall assign to them as their responsibility all they are to carry. 28 This is the service of the Gershonite clans[n] at the Tent of Meeting. Their duties are to be under the direction of Ithamar son of Aaron, the priest.

The Merarites

29 "Count the Merarites by their clans and families.[o] 30 Count all the men from thirty to fifty years of age who come to serve in the work at the Tent of Meeting. 31 This is their duty as they perform service at the Tent of Meeting: to carry the frames of the tabernacle, its crossbars, posts and bases,[p] 32 as well as the posts of the surrounding courtyard with their bases, tent pegs, ropes, all their equipment and everything related to their use. Assign to each man the specific things he is to carry. 33 This is the service of the Merarite clans as they work at the Tent of Meeting under the direction of Ithamar son of Aaron, the priest."

The Numbering of the Levite Clans

34 Moses, Aaron and the leaders of the community counted the Kohathites[q] by their clans and families. 35 All the men from thirty to fifty years of age who came to serve in the work in the Tent of Meeting, 36 counted by clans, were 2,750. 37 This was the total of all those in the Kohathite clans[r] who served in the Tent of Meeting. Moses and Aaron counted them according to the LORD's command through Moses.

38 The Gershonites[s] were counted by their clans and families. 39 All the men from thirty to fifty years of age who

4:23 [j]ver 3; 1Ch 23:3, 24,27
4:25 [k]Ex 27:10-18; Nu 3:26 [l]Nu 3:25 [m]Ex 26:14
4:28 [n]Nu 7:7
4:29 [o]Ge 46:11
4:31 [p]Nu 3:36
4:34 [q]ver 2
4:37 [r]Nu 3:27
4:38 [s]Ge 46:11

DAY 4 FOUR

▸ PATIENCE AND MY SERVICE TO OTHERS

Numbers 4:21–28

The Gershonites performed menial tasks, and yet they were not menial themselves. They packed and carried the coverings of the portable cathedral called the tabernacle. They accepted the lot in life that God had assigned to them. And so they packed and carried. I've often wondered if someday, in an old clay jar sealed for 3,500 years, there might be found a papyrus tablet—a lost testimony of one of the Gershonites—that reads:

I am a Gershonite.
There's no use wishing I were a priest.
The priests get to wear the fine vestments, the golden ephods
And stuff like that.
We Gershonites but carried the tabernacle, a thousand, hot-sand miles
Through the Sinai wilderness.
It was not a job that made for glory or historical remembrance.
But it was a job by which God daily measured our patience.
And when we'd folded and unfolded the tabernacle of our God for a thousand times,
We rejoiced!
Our service made it possible for Israel to worship.
And if they have forgotten us,
It matters not, for God never forgets.
Especially does he love those who serve in patience.
He blesses those at every sunset
For all they've done that will never be remembered.

To begin a study on the topic of Patience, the Wait for What God Promises, turn to the home page on page 1201.

came to serve in the work at the Tent of
Meeting, 40counted by their clans and
families, were 2,630. 41This was the total of those in the Gershonite clans who
served at the Tent of Meeting. Moses
and Aaron counted them according to
the LORD's command.
42The Merarites were counted by
their clans and families. 43All the men
from thirty to fifty years of age who
came to serve in the work at the Tent of
Meeting, 44counted by their clans, were
3,200. 45This was the total of those in
4:45 the Merarite clans.[t] Moses and Aaron
[t]ver 29 counted them according to the LORD's
command through Moses.
46So Moses, Aaron and the leaders of
Israel counted all the Levites by their
clans and families. 47All the men from
4:47 thirty to fifty years of age[u] who came to
[u]ver 3 do the work of serving and carrying the
4:48 Tent of Meeting 48numbered 8,580.[v]
[v]Nu 3:39 49At the LORD's command through
Moses, each was assigned his work and
told what to carry.
4:49 Thus they were counted,[w] as the
[w]Nu 1:47 LORD commanded Moses.

The Purity of the Camp

5 The LORD said to Moses, 2"Command the Israelites to send away
5:2 from the camp anyone who has an in-
[x]Lev 13:46 fectious skin disease[a][x] or a discharge[y]
[y]Lev 15:2; Mt 9:20 of any kind, or who is ceremonially un-
[z]Lev 13:3; clean[z] because of a dead body. 3Send
Nu 9:6-10 away male and female alike; send them
outside the camp so they will not defile
their camp, where I dwell among them.[a]"
5:3 4The Israelites did this; they sent them
[a]Lev 26:12; Nu 35:34; outside the camp. They did just as the
2Co 6:16 LORD had instructed Moses.

Restitution for Wrongs

5The LORD said to Moses, 6"Say to
the Israelites: 'When a man or woman
wrongs another in any way[b] and so is
5:6 [b]Lev 6:2 unfaithful[b] to the LORD, that person
[c]Lev 5:14-6:7 is guilty[c] 7and must confess[d] the sin
5:7 he has committed. He must make full
[d]Lev 5:5; restitution[e] for his wrong, add one fifth
26:40; to it and give it all to the person he
Jos 7:19; Lk 19:8 has wronged. 8But if that person has
[e]Lev 6:5 no close relative to whom restitution
can be made for the wrong, the restitution belongs to the LORD and must
be given to the priest, along with the
5:8 ram with which atonement is made for
[f]Lev 6:6,7; 7:7 him.[f] 9All the sacred contributions the
Israelites bring to a priest will belong to
him.[g] 10Each man's sacred gifts are his 5:9 [g]Lev 6:17;
own, but what he gives to the priest will 7:6-14
belong to the priest.[h]'" 5:10 [h]Lev 10:13

The Test for an Unfaithful Wife

11Then the LORD said to Moses,
12"Speak to the Israelites and say to
them: 'If a man's wife goes astray[i] and 5:12 [i]Ex 20:14
is unfaithful to him 13by sleeping with
another man,[j] and this is hidden from 5:13
her husband and her impurity is unde- [j]Lev 18:20; 20:10
tected (since there is no witness against 5:14
her and she has not been caught in the [k]Pr 6:34; SS 8:6
act), 14and if feelings of jealousy[k] come
over her husband and he suspects his
wife and she is impure—or if he is jealous and suspects her even though she is
not impure— 15then he is to take his
wife to the priest. He must also take an
offering of a tenth of an ephah[c][l] of bar- 5:15 [l]Ex 16:36
ley flour[m] on her behalf. He must not [m]Lev 6:20
pour oil on it or put incense on it, be- [n]Eze 29:16
cause it is a grain offering for jealousy,
a reminder[n] offering to draw attention
to guilt.
16"'The priest shall bring her and
have her stand before the LORD. 17Then
he shall take some holy water in a clay
jar and put some dust from the tabernacle floor into the water. 18After the
priest has had the woman stand before
the LORD, he shall loosen her hair[o] 5:18 [o]Lev 10:6;
and place in her hands the reminder of- 1Co 11:6
fering, the grain offering for jealousy,
while he himself holds the bitter water
that brings a curse. 19Then the priest
shall put the woman under oath and
say to her, "If no other man has slept
with you and you have not gone astray[p] 5:19
and become impure while married to [p]ver 12,29
your husband, may this bitter water
that brings a curse not harm you. 20But
if you have gone astray[q] while married 5:20
to your husband and you have defiled [q]ver 12
yourself by sleeping with a man other
than your husband"— 21here the priest
is to put the woman under this curse of
the oath[r]—"may the LORD cause your 5:21
people to curse and denounce you when [r]Jos 6:26;
he causes your thigh to waste away and 1Sa 14:24;
your abdomen to swell.[d] 22May this Ne 10:29

[a]*2* Traditionally *leprosy;* the Hebrew word was used for various diseases affecting the skin—not necessarily leprosy. [b]*6* Or *woman commits any wrong common to mankind* [c]*15* That is, probably about 2 quarts (about 2 liters) [d]*21* Or *causes you to have a miscarrying womb and barrenness*

5:22 [s]Ps 109:18 [t]ver 18 [u]Dt 27:15 water[s] that brings a curse[t] enter your
body so that your abdomen swells and
your thigh wastes away.[a]"
"'Then the woman is to say, "Amen.
So be it.[u]"
23"'The priest is to write these curses
5:23 [v]Jer 45:1 on a scroll[v] and then wash them off
into the bitter water. 24He shall have
the woman drink the bitter water that
brings a curse, and this water will enter her and cause bitter suffering. 25The
priest is to take from her hands the
grain offering for jealousy, wave it be-
5:25 [w]Lev 8:27 fore the LORD[w] and bring it to the altar.
26The priest is then to take a handful
of the grain offering as a memorial offering and burn it on the altar; after
that, he is to have the woman drink the
water. 27If she has defiled herself and
been unfaithful to her husband, then
when she is made to drink the water
that brings a curse, it will go into her
and cause bitter suffering; her abdomen
will swell and her thigh waste away,[b]
5:27 [x]Isa 43:28; 65:15; Jer 26:6; 29:18; 42:18; 44:12,22; Zec 8:13 and she will become accursed[x] among
her people. 28If, however, the woman
has not defiled herself and is free from
impurity, she will be cleared of guilt
and will be able to have children.
29"'This, then, is the law of jealousy
5:29 [y]ver 19 when a woman goes astray[y] and defiles
herself while married to her husband,
30or when feelings of jealousy come over
a man because he suspects his wife. The
priest is to have her stand before the
LORD and is to apply this entire law to
her. 31The husband will be innocent of
any wrongdoing, but the woman will
5:31 [z]Lev 5:1; 20:17 bear the consequences[z] of her sin.'"

The Nazirite

6 The LORD said to Moses, 2"Speak
to the Israelites and say to them:
'If a man or woman wants to make a
6:2 [a]Ge 28:20; Ac 21:23 [b]Jdg 13:5; 16:17; Am 2:11,12 special vow[a], a vow of separation to the
LORD as a Nazirite,[b] 3he must abstain
from wine[c] and other fermented drink
and must not drink vinegar[d] made from
6:3 [c]Lk 1:15 [d]Ru 2:14; Ps 69:21; Pr 10:26 wine or from other fermented drink.
He must not drink grape juice or eat
grapes or raisins. 4As long as he is a
Nazirite, he must not eat anything that
comes from the grapevine, not even the
seeds or skins.
6:5 [e]Ps 52:2; 57:4; 59:7; Isa 7:20; Eze 5:1 [f]1Sa 1:11 5"'During the entire period of his
vow of separation no razor[e] may be used
on his head.[f] He must be holy until the
period of his separation to the LORD is
over; he must let the hair of his head
grow long. 6Throughout the period of
his separation to the LORD he must
not go near a dead body.[g] 7Even if his 6:6 [g]Lev 21:1-3; Nu 19:11-22
own father or mother or brother or sis-
ter dies, he must not make himself ceremonially unclean[h] on account of them, 6:7 [h]Nu 9:6
because the symbol of his separation to
God is on his head. 8Throughout the
period of his separation he is consecrated to the LORD.
9"'If someone dies suddenly in his
presence, thus defiling the hair he has
dedicated,[i] he must shave his head on 6:9 [i]ver 18 [j]Lev 14:9
the day of his cleansing[j]—the seventh
day. 10Then on the eighth day he must
bring two doves or two young pigeons[k] 6:10 [k]Lev 5:7; 14:22
to the priest at the entrance to the Tent
of Meeting. 11The priest is to offer one
as a sin offering and the other as a burnt
offering[l] to make atonement[m] for him 6:11 [l]Ge 8:20 [m]Ex 29:36
because he sinned by being in the pres-
ence of the dead body. That same day
he is to consecrate his head. 12He must
dedicate himself to the LORD for the
period of his separation and must bring
a year-old male lamb as a guilt offering. The previous days do not count,
because he became defiled during his
separation.
13"'Now this is the law for the Nazirite when the period of his separation
is over.[n] He is to be brought to the en- 6:13 [n]Ac 21:26
trance to the Tent of Meeting. 14There
he is to present his offerings to the
LORD: a year-old male lamb without
defect for a burnt offering, a year-old
ewe lamb without defect for a sin
offering,[o] a ram without defect for a fel- 6:14 [o]Lev 14:10; Nu 15:27
lowship offering,[c] 15together with their
grain offerings and drink offerings,[p] 6:15 [p]Nu 15:1-7 [q]Ex 29:2; Lev 2:4
and a basket of bread made without
yeast—cakes made of fine flour mixed
with oil, and wafers spread with oil.[q]
16"'The priest is to present them before the LORD and make the sin offering and the burnt offering. 17He is to
present the basket of unleavened bread
and is to sacrifice the ram as a fellowship
offering to the LORD, together with its
grain offering and drink offering.
18"'Then at the entrance to the Tent
of Meeting, the Nazirite must shave off

[a]*22* Or *body and cause you to be barren and have a miscarrying womb* [b]*27* Or *suffering; she will have barrenness and a miscarrying womb*
[c]*14* Traditionally *peace offering*; also in verses 17 and 18

DAY 4 FOUR

▸ PEACE AND MY SERVICE TO OTHERS

Numbers 6:22–26

What then is to be my service to others in the ministry of peace? Aaron and the priests blessed Israel with a benediction of peace. Benedictions of peace help each of us minister to others by seeking for them a life free of turmoil. It is godly to bless the turbulence out of our lives—flooding the world with the peace of Christ.

Jesus once drove the demons of peacelessness from the life of a man with an evil spirit. When the striving demons were dispersed, it is said that the man was once again in his right mind (Mark 5:1–20). One can view this true story as a model of what we do for others when we help them discover the indwelling Christ. Their lives of turmoil are transformed into lives characterized by peace. Thus, evangelism becomes our ministry of peace to a troubled world.

Evangelists do not merely keep people out of hell. They publish peace, and by so doing they remove the hell from the here and now. If hell were only out "there" in the future, people would scarcely give it a thought. But hell is now. Hell is here. Hell is divorce, pain, cancer, family dysfunction and job loss. Hell is neurosis, addiction, co-dependency, loss. Above all this struggle Christ offers his benediction—and we offer Christ as the healing peace-bringer.

A clergyman I know tells in one of his sermons about a Christmas Eve long ago when his father gave a dollar to a hobo. "I give you this in the name of Christ," said the father. "Thank you," said the hobo. "I accept this in the name of Christ." Blessings spread through the world in the name of peace.

What wonders would be wrought if we would say to those around us, "The LORD bless you and keep you; the LORD make his face shine upon you and be gracious to you; the LORD turn his face toward you and give you peace."

To begin a study on the topic of Peace, a Truce With God to End My Alienation From Him, turn to the home page on page 1353.

the hair that he dedicated.[r] He is to
take the hair and put it in the fire that
is under the sacrifice of the fellowship
offering.
19"'After the Nazirite has shaved off
the hair of his dedication, the priest is
to place in his hands a boiled shoulder
of the ram, and a cake and a wafer from
the basket, both made without yeast.
20The priest shall then wave them before the LORD as a wave offering; they
are holy and belong to the priest, together with the breast that was waved
and the thigh that was presented. After
that, the Nazirite may drink wine.[s]
21"'This is the law of the Nazirite
who vows his offering to the LORD in
accordance with his separation, in addition to whatever else he can afford. He
must fulfill the vow he has made, according to the law of the Nazirite.'"

The Priestly Blessing

22The LORD said to Moses, 23"Tell
Aaron and his sons, 'This is how you
are to bless[t] the Israelites. Say to them:
24"'"The LORD bless you[u]
and keep you;[v]
25the LORD make his face shine upon
you[w]
and be gracious to you;[x]
26the LORD turn his face[y] toward you
and give you peace.[z]"'
27"So they will put my name[a] on the
Israelites, and I will bless them."

Offerings at the Dedication of the Tabernacle

7 When Moses finished setting up
the tabernacle,[b] he anointed it and
consecrated it and all its furnishings.[c]
He also anointed and consecrated the
altar and all its utensils.[d] 2Then the
leaders of Israel,[e] the heads of families
who were the tribal leaders in charge of
those who were counted, made offerings. 3They brought as their gifts before
the LORD six covered carts and twelve
oxen—an ox from each leader and a
cart from every two. These they presented before the tabernacle.
4The LORD said to Moses, 5"Accept
these from them, that they may be used
in the work at the Tent of Meeting.
Give them to the Levites as each man's
work requires."
6So Moses took the carts and oxen

6:18 [r]ver 9; Ac 21:24
6:20 [s]Ecc 9:7
6:23 [t]Dt 21:5; 1Ch 23:13
6:24 [u]Dt 28:3-6; Ps 28:9 [v]1Sa 2:9; Ps 17:8
6:25 [w]Job 29:24; Ps 31:16; 80:3; 119:135 [x]Ge 43:29; Ps 25:16; 86:16
6:26 [y]Ps 4:6; 44:3 [z]Ps 29:11; 37:11,37; Jn 14:27
6:27 [a]Dt 28:10; 2Sa 7:23; 2Ch 7:14; Ne 9:10; Jer 25:29
7:1 [b]Ex 40:17 [c]Ex 40:9 [d]ver 84,88; Ex 40:10
7:2 [e]Nu 1:5-16

and gave them to the Levites. [7]He
gave two carts and four oxen to the
7:7 [f]Nu Gershonites,[f] as their work required,
4:24-26,28 [8]and he gave four carts and eight oxen
7:8 to the Merarites,[g] as their work re-
[g]Nu 4:31-33 quired. They were all under the direction of Ithamar son of Aaron, the priest.
[9]But Moses did not give any to the
Kohathites, because they were to carry
7:9 on their shoulders[h] the holy things, for
[h]Nu 4:15 which they were responsible.
[10]When the altar was anointed,[i] the
7:10 [i]ver 1 leaders brought their offerings for its
[j]2Ch 7:9 dedication[j] and presented them before
the altar. [11]For the LORD had said to
Moses, "Each day one leader is to bring
his offering for the dedication of the
altar."

[12]The one who brought his offering on
the first day was Nahshon son of Amminadab of the tribe of Judah.

[13]His offering was one silver plate
weighing a hundred and thirty
shekels,[a] and one silver sprinkling
bowl weighing seventy shekels,[b]
both according to the sanctuary
7:13 [k]Ex 30:13; shekel,[k] each filled with fine flour
Nu 3:47 mixed with oil as a grain offering;[l]
[l]Lev 2:1 [14]one gold dish weighing ten
7:14 shekels,[c] filled with incense;[m] [15]one
[m]Ex 30:34 young bull,[n] one ram and one
7:15 male lamb a year old, for a burnt
[n]Ex 24:5; 29:3; offering;[o] [16]one male goat for a
Nu 28:11 sin offering;[p] [17]and two oxen, five
[o]Lev 1:3 rams, five male goats and five male
7:16 [p]Lev 4:3,23 lambs a year old, to be sacrificed
as a fellowship offering.[d][q] This was
7:17 [q]Lev 3:1 the offering of Nahshon son of
[r]Nu 1:7 Amminadab.[r]

[18]On the second day Nethanel son of
7:18 Zuar,[s] the leader of Issachar, brought
[s]Nu 1:8 his offering.
[19]The offering he brought was one
silver plate weighing a hundred
and thirty shekels, and one silver
sprinkling bowl weighing seventy
shekels, both according to the sanctuary shekel, each filled with fine
flour mixed with oil as a grain
7:20 offering; [20]one gold dish[t] weigh-
[t]ver 14 ing ten shekels, filled with incense;
[21]one young bull, one ram and
one male lamb a year old, for a
burnt offering; [22]one male goat for
a sin offering; [23]and two oxen, five
rams, five male goats and five male
lambs a year old, to be sacrificed as

GOODNESS

"ALTAR" EGOS

Numbers 7:10

From Abraham forward in time, a thousand little, rough stone altars dotted the desert where sinners, one at a time, dealt with their sins—one at a time.

Then Christ came.

Enough, one time! One perfect life, one lifted cross!

One altar for all altars,

One losing for all loss!

a fellowship offering. This was the
offering of Nethanel son of Zuar.

[24]On the third day, Eliab son of Helon,[u] 7:24 [u]Nu 1:9
the leader of the people of Zebulun,
brought his offering.
[25]His offering was one silver plate
weighing a hundred and thirty
shekels, and one silver sprinkling
bowl weighing seventy shekels,
both according to the sanctuary
shekel, each filled with fine flour
mixed with oil as a grain offering;
[26]one gold dish weighing ten shekels, filled with incense; [27]one young
bull, one ram and one male lamb
a year old, for a burnt offering;
[28]one male goat for a sin offering;
[29]and two oxen, five rams, five
male goats and five male lambs a
year old, to be sacrificed as a fellowship offering. This was the offering of Eliab son of Helon.

[30]On the fourth day Elizur son of Shed-
eur,[v] the leader of the people of Reu- 7:30 [v]Nu 1:5
ben, brought his offering.
[31]His offering was one silver plate
weighing a hundred and thirty
shekels, and one silver sprinkling
bowl weighing seventy shekels,
both according to the sanctuary
shekel, each filled with fine flour
mixed with oil as a grain offering;
[32]one gold dish weighing ten shekels, filled with incense; [33]one young

[a] *13* That is, about 3 1/4 pounds (about 1.5 kilograms); also elsewhere in this chapter
[b] *13* That is, about 1 3/4 pounds (about 0.8 kilogram); also elsewhere in this chapter
[c] *14* That is, about 4 ounces (about 110 grams); also elsewhere in this chapter
[d] *17* Traditionally *peace offering*; also elsewhere in this chapter

Jesus Speaks Out *on the Fruit of the Spirit:* Love

Matthew 22:37

Love the Lord your God with all your heart and with all your soul and with all your mind.

Luke 6:27

I tell you who hear me: Love your enemies, do good to those who hate you.

John 13:34

A new command I give you: Love one another. As I have loved you, so you must love one another.

John 14:15

If you love me, you will obey what I command.

John 15:9

As the Father has loved me, so have I loved you. Now remain in my love.

John 15:12–13

My command is this: Love each other as I have loved you. Greater love has no one than this, that he lay down his life for his friends.

▸ The Lost Son

There was a man who had two sons. The younger one said to his father, "Father, give me my share of the estate." So he divided his property between them.

Not long after that, the younger son got together all he had, set off for a distant country and there squandered his wealth in wild living. After he had spent everything, there was a severe famine in that whole country, and he began to be in need. So he went and hired himself out to a citizen of that country, who sent him to his fields to feed pigs. He longed to fill his stomach with the pods that the pigs were eating, but no one gave him anything.

When he came to his senses, he said, "How many of my father's hired men have food to spare, and here I am starving to death! I will set out and go back to my father and say to him: Father, I have sinned against heaven and against you. I am no longer worthy to be called your son; make me like one of your hired men." So he got up and went to his father.

But while he was still a long way off, his father saw him and was filled with compassion for him; he ran to his son, threw his arms around him and kissed him.

The son said to him, "Father, I have sinned against heaven and against you. I am no longer worthy to be called your son."

But the father said to his servants, "Quick! Bring the best robe and put it on him. Put a ring on his finger and sandals on his feet. Bring the fattened calf and kill it. Let's have a feast and celebrate. For this son of mine was dead and is alive again; he was lost and is found." So they began to celebrate.

Meanwhile, the older son was in the field. When he came near the house, he heard music and dancing. So he called one of the servants and asked him what was going on. "Your brother has come," he replied, "and your father has killed the fattened calf because he has him back safe and sound."

The older brother became angry and refused to go in. So his father went out and pleaded with him. But he answered his father, "Look! All these years I've been slaving for you and never disobeyed your orders. Yet you never gave me even a young goat so I could celebrate with my friends. But when this son of yours who has squandered your property with prostitutes comes home, you kill the fattened calf for him!"

"My son," the father said, "you are always with me, and everything I have is yours. But we had to celebrate and be glad, because this brother of yours was dead and is alive again; he was lost and is found."

Luke 15:11–32

Paul Speaks Out *on the Fruit of the Spirit:* Love

Galatians 5:22

But the fruit of the Spirit is love, joy, peace, patience, kindness, goodness, faithfulness, gentleness and self-control.

Romans 12:9

Love must be sincere. Hate what is evil; cling to what is good.

Romans 13:10

Love does no harm to its neighbor. Therefore love is the fulfillment of the law.

Galatians 5:13–14

You, my brothers, were called to be free. But do not use your freedom to indulge the sinful nature; rather, serve one another in love. The entire law is summed up in a single command: "Love your neighbor as yourself."

Ephesians 5:25

Husbands, love your wives, just as Christ loved the church and gave himself up for her.

The Greatest Is Love

If I speak in the tongues of men and of angels, but have not love, I am only a resounding gong or a clanging cymbal. If I have the gift of prophecy and can fathom all mysteries and all knowledge, and if I have a faith that can move mountains, but have not love, I am nothing. If I give all I possess to the poor and surrender my body to the flames, but have not love, I gain nothing.

Love is patient, love is kind. It does not envy, it does not boast, it is not proud. It is not rude, it is not self-seeking, it is not easily angered, it keeps no record of wrongs. Love does not delight in evil but rejoices with the truth. It always protects, always trusts, always hopes, always perseveres.

Love never fails. But where there are prophecies, they will cease; where there are tongues, they will be stilled; where there is knowledge, it will pass away. For we know in part and we prophesy in part, but when perfection comes, the imperfect disappears. When I was a child, I talked like a child, I thought like a child, I reasoned like a child. When I became a man, I put childish ways behind me. Now we see but a poor reflection as in a mirror; then we shall see face to face. Now I know in part; then I shall know fully, even as I am fully known.

And now these three remain: faith, hope and love. But the greatest of these is love.

1 Corinthians 13:1–13

bull, one ram and one male lamb
a year old, for a burnt offering;
34one male goat for a sin offering;
35and two oxen, five rams, five
male goats and five male lambs a
year old, to be sacrificed as a fellowship offering. This was the offering of Elizur son of Shedeur.

36On the fifth day Shelumiel son of
7:36 [w]Nu 1:6 Zurishaddai,[w] the leader of the people
of Simeon, brought his offering.
37His offering was one silver plate
weighing a hundred and thirty
shekels, and one silver sprinkling
bowl weighing seventy shekels,
both according to the sanctuary
shekel, each filled with fine flour
mixed with oil as a grain offering;
38one gold dish weighing ten shekels, filled with incense; 39one young
bull, one ram and one male lamb a
year old, for a burnt offering; 40one
male goat for a sin offering; 41and
two oxen, five rams, five male goats
and five male lambs a year old, to
be sacrificed as a fellowship offering. This was the offering of Shelumiel son of Zurishaddai.

42On the sixth day Eliasaph son of
7:42 [x]Nu 1:14 Deuel,[x] the leader of the people of Gad,
brought his offering.
43His offering was one silver plate
weighing a hundred and thirty
shekels, and one silver sprinkling
bowl weighing seventy shekels,
both according to the sanctuary
shekel, each filled with fine flour
mixed with oil as a grain offering;
44one gold dish weighing ten shekels, filled with incense; 45one young
bull, one ram and one male lamb
a year old, for a burnt offering;
46one male goat for a sin offering;
47and two oxen, five rams, five
male goats and five male lambs a
year old, to be sacrificed as a fellowship offering. This was the offering of Eliasaph son of Deuel.

48On the seventh day Elishama son of
7:48 [y]Nu 1:10 Ammihud,[y] the leader of the people of
Ephraim, brought his offering.
49His offering was one silver plate
weighing a hundred and thirty
shekels, and one silver sprinkling
bowl weighing seventy shekels,
both according to the sanctuary
shekel, each filled with fine flour
mixed with oil as a grain offering;
50one gold dish weighing ten shekels, filled with incense; 51one young
bull, one ram and one male lamb a
year old, for a burnt offering; 52one
male goat for a sin offering; 53and
two oxen, five rams, five male goats
and five male lambs a year old, to
be sacrificed as a fellowship offering. This was the offering of Elishama son of Ammihud.[z] 7:53 [z]Nu 1:10

54On the eighth day Gamaliel son of
Pedahzur,[a] the leader of the people of 7:54 [a]Nu 1:10; 2:20
Manasseh, brought his offering.
55His offering was one silver plate
weighing a hundred and thirty
shekels, and one silver sprinkling
bowl weighing seventy shekels,
both according to the sanctuary
shekel, each filled with fine flour
mixed with oil as a grain offering;
56one gold dish weighing ten shekels, filled with incense; 57one young
bull, one ram and one male lamb a
year old, for a burnt offering; 58one
male goat for a sin offering; 59and
two oxen, five rams, five male goats
and five male lambs a year old, to
be sacrificed as a fellowship offering. This was the offering of Gamaliel son of Pedahzur.

60On the ninth day Abidan son of
Gideoni,[b] the leader of the people of 7:60 [b]Nu 1:11
Benjamin, brought his offering.
61His offering was one silver plate
weighing a hundred and thirty
shekels, and one silver sprinkling
bowl weighing seventy shekels,
both according to the sanctuary
shekel, each filled with fine flour
mixed with oil as a grain offering;
62one gold dish weighing ten shekels, filled with incense; 63one young
bull, one ram and one male lamb
a year old, for a burnt offering;
64one male goat for a sin offering;
65and two oxen, five rams, five
male goats and five male lambs a
year old, to be sacrificed as a fellowship offering. This was the offering of Abidan son of Gideoni.

66On the tenth day Ahiezer son of Am-
mishaddai,[c] the leader of the people of 7:66 [c]Nu 1:12; 2:25
Dan, brought his offering.
67His offering was one silver plate

weighing a hundred and thirty
shekels, and one silver sprinkling
bowl weighing seventy shekels,
both according to the sanctuary
shekel, each filled with fine flour
mixed with oil as a grain offering;
68 one gold dish weighing ten shekels, filled with incense; 69 one young
bull, one ram and one male lamb
a year old, for a burnt offering;
70 one male goat for a sin offering;
71 and two oxen, five rams, five
male goats and five male lambs
a year old, to be sacrificed as a
fellowship offering. This was the
offering of Ahiezer son of Ammishaddai.

72 On the eleventh day Pagiel son of
7:72 [d]Nu 1:13 Ocran,[d] the leader of the people of Asher, brought his offering.
73 His offering was one silver plate
weighing a hundred and thirty
shekels, and one silver sprinkling
bowl weighing seventy shekels,
both according to the sanctuary
shekel, each filled with fine flour
mixed with oil as a grain offering;
74 one gold dish weighing ten shekels, filled with incense; 75 one young
bull, one ram and one male lamb
a year old, for a burnt offering;
76 one male goat for a sin offering;
77 and two oxen, five rams, five
male goats and five male lambs a
year old, to be sacrificed as a fellowship offering. This was the offering of Pagiel son of Ocran.

78 On the twelfth day Ahira son of
7:78 [e]Nu 1:15; 2:29 Enan,[e] the leader of the people of Naphtali, brought his offering.
79 His offering was one silver plate
weighing a hundred and thirty
shekels, and one silver sprinkling
bowl weighing seventy shekels,
both according to the sanctuary
shekel, each filled with fine flour
mixed with oil as a grain offering;
80 one gold dish weighing ten shekels, filled with incense; 81 one young
bull, one ram and one male lamb
a year old, for a burnt offering;
82 one male goat for a sin offering;
83 and two oxen, five rams, five
male goats and five male lambs a
year old, to be sacrificed as a fellowship offering. This was the offering of Ahira son of Enan.

84 These were the offerings of the
Israelite leaders for the dedication of
the altar when it was anointed:[f] twelve 7:84 [f]ver 1,10
silver plates, twelve silver sprinkling [g]Nu 4:14
bowls[g] and twelve gold dishes.[h] 85 Each [h]ver 14
silver plate weighed a hundred and thir-
ty shekels, and each sprinkling bowl
seventy shekels. Altogether, the silver
dishes weighed two thousand four hundred shekels,[a] according to the sanctuary shekel. 86 The twelve gold dishes
filled with incense weighed ten shekels
each, according to the sanctuary shekel. Altogether, the gold dishes weighed
a hundred and twenty shekels.[b] 87 The
total number of animals for the burnt
offering came to twelve young bulls,
twelve rams and twelve male lambs a
year old, together with their grain offering. Twelve male goats were used for
the sin offering. 88 The total number of
animals for the sacrifice of the fellowship offering came to twenty-four oxen,
sixty rams, sixty male goats and sixty
male lambs a year old. These were the
offerings for the dedication of the altar
after it was anointed.[i] 7:88 [i]ver 1,10
89 When Moses entered the Tent of
Meeting to speak with the LORD,[j] he 7:89 [j]Ex 25:21,22; 33:9,11
heard the voice speaking to him from [k]Ps 80:1; 99:1
between the two cherubim above the
atonement cover[k] on the ark of the Testimony. And he spoke with him.

Setting Up the Lamps

8 The LORD said to Moses, 2 "Speak
to Aaron and say to him, 'When
you set up the seven lamps, they are
to light the area in front of the lampstand.[l] ' " 8:2 [l]Ex 25:37; Lev 24:2,4
3 Aaron did so; he set up the lamps
so that they faced forward on the lampstand, just as the LORD commanded
Moses. 4 This is how the lampstand
was made: It was made of hammered
gold[m]—from its base to its blossoms. 8:4 [m]Ex 25:18,36
The lampstand was made exactly like [n]Ex 25:9
the pattern[n] the LORD had shown
Moses.

The Setting Apart of the Levites

5 The LORD said to Moses: 6 "Take
the Levites from among the other Is- 8:6 [o]Lev 22:2;
raelites and make them ceremonially Isa 1:16;
clean.[o] 7 To purify them, do this: Sprin- 52:11

[a] *85* That is, about 60 pounds (about 28 kilograms)
[b] *86* That is, about 3 pounds (about 1.4 kilograms)

kle the water of cleansing[p] on them; then have them shave their whole bodies[q] and wash their clothes,[r] and so purify themselves. 8Have them take a young bull with its grain offering of fine flour mixed with oil;[s] then you are to take a second young bull for a sin offering. 9Bring the Levites to the front of the Tent of Meeting[t] and assemble the whole Israelite community.[u] 10You are to bring the Levites before the LORD, and the Israelites are to lay their hands on them.[v] 11Aaron is to present the Levites before the LORD as a wave offering[w] from the Israelites, so that they may be ready to do the work of the LORD.

12"After the Levites lay their hands on the heads of the bulls,[x] use the one for a sin offering to the LORD and the other for a burnt offering, to make atonement[y] for the Levites. 13Have the Levites stand in front of Aaron and his sons and then present them as a wave offering to the LORD. 14In this way you are to set the Levites apart from the other Israelites, and the Levites will be mine.[z]

15"After you have purified the Levites and presented them as a wave offering,[a] they are to come to do their work at the Tent of Meeting. 16They are the Israelites who are to be given wholly to me. I have taken them as my own in place of the firstborn, the first male offspring[b] from every Israelite woman. 17Every firstborn male in Israel, whether man or animal,[c] is mine. When I struck down all the firstborn in Egypt, I set them apart for myself.[d] 18And I have taken the Levites in place of all the firstborn sons in Israel.[e] 19Of all the Israelites, I have given the Levites as gifts to Aaron and his sons[f] to do the work at the Tent of Meeting on behalf of the Israelites[g] and to make atonement for them[h] so that no plague will strike the Israelites when they go near the sanctuary."

20Moses, Aaron and the whole Israelite community did with the Levites just as the LORD commanded Moses. 21The Levites purified themselves and washed their clothes.[i] Then Aaron presented them as a wave offering before the LORD and made atonement for them to purify them.[j] 22After that, the Levites came to do their work at the Tent of Meeting under the supervision of Aaron and his sons. They did with the Levites just as the LORD commanded Moses.

23The LORD said to Moses, 24"This applies to the Levites: Men twenty-five years old or more[k] shall come to take part in the work at the Tent of Meeting,[l] 25but at the age of fifty, they must retire from their regular service and work no longer. 26They may assist their brothers in performing their duties at the Tent of Meeting, but they themselves must not do the work. This, then, is how you are to assign the responsibilities of the Levites."

The Passover

9 The LORD spoke to Moses in the Desert of Sinai in the first month[m] of the second year after they came out of Egypt.[n] He said, 2"Have the Israelites celebrate the Passover at the appointed time. 3Celebrate it at the appointed time, at twilight on the fourteenth day of this month, in accordance with all its rules and regulations.[o]"

4So Moses told the Israelites to celebrate the Passover, 5and they did so in the Desert of Sinai at twilight on the fourteenth day of the first month.[p] The Israelites did everything just as the LORD commanded Moses.

6But some of them could not celebrate the Passover on that day because they were ceremonially unclean[q] on account of a dead body. So they came to Moses and Aaron[r] that same day 7and said to Moses, "We have become unclean because of a dead body, but why should we be kept from presenting the LORD's offering with the other Israelites at the appointed time?"

8Moses answered them, "Wait until I find out what the LORD commands concerning you."[s]

9Then the LORD said to Moses, 10"Tell the Israelites: 'When any of you or your descendants are unclean because of a dead body or are away on a journey, they may still celebrate[t] the LORD's Passover. 11They are to celebrate it on the fourteenth day of the second month at twilight. They are to eat the lamb, together with unleavened bread and bitter herbs.[u] 12They must not leave any of it till morning[v] or break any of its bones.[w] When they celebrate the Passover, they

8:7 [p]Nu 19:9,17 [q]Lev 14:9; Dt 21:12 [r]Lev 14:8
8:8 [s]Lev 2:1; Nu 15:8-10
8:9 [t]Ex 40:12 [u]Lev 8:3
8:10 [v]Ac 6:6
8:11 [w]Lev 7:30
8:12 [x]Ex 29:10 [y]Ex 29:36
8:14 [z]Nu 3:12
8:15 [a]Ex 29:24
8:16 [b]Nu 3:12
8:17 [c]Ex 4:23 [d]Ex 13:2; Lk 2:23
8:18 [e]Nu 3:12
8:19 [f]Nu 3:9 [g]Nu 1:53 [h]Nu 16:46
8:21 [i]ver 7 [j]ver 12
8:24 [k]1Ch 23:3 [l]Ex 38:21; Nu 4:3
9:1 [m]Ex 40:2 [n]Nu 1:1
9:3 [o]Ex 12:2-11, 43-49; Lev 23:5-8; Dt 16:1-8
9:5 [p]Ex 12:1-13; Jos 5:10
9:6 [q]Lev 5:3 [r]Ex 18:15; Nu 27:2
9:8 [s]Ex 18:15; Nu 27:5,21; Ps 85:8
9:10 [t]2Ch 30:2
9:11 [u]Ex 12:8
9:12 [v]Ex 12:10,43 [w]Ex 12:46; Jn 19:36*

must follow all the regulations. 13 But if
a man who is ceremonially clean and
not on a journey fails to celebrate the
Passover, that person must be cut off
9:13 from his people[x] because he did not
[x]Ge 17:14; Ex 12:15 present the LORD's offering at the appointed time. That man will bear the
consequences of his sin.
9:14 14 " 'An alien[y] living among you who
[y]Ex 12:48,49 wants to celebrate the LORD's Passover
must do so in accordance with its rules
and regulations. You must have the
same regulations for the alien and the
native-born.' "

The Cloud Above the Tabernacle

15 On the day the tabernacle, the Tent
of the Testimony, was set up, the cloud
covered it. From evening till morning
9:15 the cloud[z] above the tabernacle looked
[z]Ex 40:34 [a]Ex 13:21 like fire.[a] 16 That is how it continued to
be; the cloud covered it, and at night it
looked like fire. 17 Whenever the cloud
lifted from above the Tent, the Israelites
set out; wherever the cloud settled, the
9:17 Israelites encamped.[b] 18 At the LORD's
[b]Ex 40:36-38; Nu 10:11,12; 1Co 10:1 command the Israelites set out, and at
his command they encamped. As long
as the cloud stayed over the tabernacle,
they remained in camp. 19 When the
cloud remained over the tabernacle a
long time, the Israelites obeyed the
LORD's order and did not set out.
20 Sometimes the cloud was over the tabernacle only a few days; at the LORD's
command they would encamp, and
then at his command they would set
out. 21 Sometimes the cloud stayed only
from evening till morning, and when
it lifted in the morning, they set out.
Whether by day or by night, whenever
the cloud lifted, they set out. 22 Whether
the cloud stayed over the tabernacle for
two days or a month or a year, the Israelites would remain in camp and not
set out; but when it lifted, they would

SELF-CONTROL

THE WEATHER OF OBEDIENCE

Numbers 9:23

Following God is not just a matter of doing what he says, but doing what he says when he says to do it. Does the foul weather prevent your obedience? Is it difficult to see the column of smoke? Follow, regardless.

set out. 23 At the LORD's command they
encamped, and at the LORD's command they set out. They obeyed the
LORD's order, in accordance with his
command through Moses.

The Silver Trumpets

10 The LORD said to Moses:
2 "Make two trumpets[c] of ham- 10:2
mered silver, and use them for calling [c]Ne 12:35; Ps 47:5
the community[d] together and for hav- [d]Jer 4:5,19; 6:1; Hos 5:8;
ing the camps set out. 3 When both are Joel 2:1,15; Am 3:6
sounded, the whole community is to
assemble before you at the entrance to
the Tent of Meeting. 4 If only one is
sounded, the leaders[e]—the heads of the 10:4
clans of Israel—are to assemble before [e]Ex 18:21; Nu 1:16; 7:2
you. 5 When a trumpet blast is sounded,
the tribes camping on the east are to
set out.[f] 6 At the sounding of a second 10:5
blast, the camps on the south are to set [f]ver 14
out.[g] The blast will be the signal for set- 10:6 [g]ver 18
ting out. 7 To gather the assembly, blow
the trumpets,[h] but not with the same 10:7 [h]Eze 33:3; Joel 2:1
signal.[i] [i]1Co 14:8

8 "The sons of Aaron, the priests, are
to blow the trumpets. This is to be a
lasting ordinance for you and the generations to come.[j] 9 When you go into 10:8
battle in your own land against an en- [j]Nu 31:6
emy who is oppressing you,[k] sound a 10:9 [k]Jdg 2:18; 6:9;
blast on the trumpets. Then you will be 1Sa 10:18; Ps 106:42
remembered[l] by the LORD your God [l]Ge 8:1
and rescued from your enemies.[m] 10 Also [m]Ps 106:4
at your times of rejoicing—your ap-
pointed feasts and New Moon festi-
vals[n]—you are to sound the trumpets[o] 10:10 [n]Ps 81:3
over your burnt offerings and fellow- [o]Lev 23:24
ship offerings,[a] and they will be a memorial for you before your God. I am
the LORD your God."

The Israelites Leave Sinai

11 On the twentieth day of the second
month of the second year,[p] the cloud 10:11 [p]Ex 40:17
lifted[q] from above the tabernacle of the [q]Nu 9:17
Testimony. 12 Then the Israelites set out
from the Desert of Sinai and traveled
from place to place until the cloud came
to rest in the Desert of Paran. 13 They
set out, this first time, at the LORD's
command through Moses.[r] 10:13 [r]Dt 1:6
14 The divisions of the camp of Ju-
dah went first, under their standard.[s] 10:14 [s]Nu 2:3-9
Nahshon son of Amminadab[t] was in [t]Nu 1:7

[a] *10* Traditionally *peace offerings*

command. 15Nethanel son of Zuar was
over the division of the tribe of Issachar,
16and Eliab son of Helon was over the
division of the tribe of Zebulun. 17Then
the tabernacle was taken down, and the
Gershonites and Merarites, who carried
10:17 it, set out.[u]
uNu 4:21-32 18The divisions of the camp of Reu-
10:18 ben went next, under their standard.[v]
vNu 2:10-16 Elizur son of Shedeur was in command. 19Shelumiel son of Zurishaddai
was over the division of the tribe of
Simeon, 20and Eliasaph son of Deuel
was over the division of the tribe of
Gad. 21Then the Kohathites set out,
10:21 wNu 4:20 carrying the holy things.[w] The taber-
xver 17 nacle was to be set up before they
arrived.[x]
22The divisions of the camp of Ephra-
10:22 im[y] went next, under their standard.
yNu 2:24 Elishama son of Ammihud was in
command. 23Gamaliel son of Pedahzur
was over the division of the tribe of
Manasseh, 24and Abidan son of Gideoni was over the division of the tribe of
Benjamin.
10:25 25Finally, as the rear guard[z] for all the
zNu 2:31; Jos 6:9 units, the divisions of the camp of Dan
set out, under their standard. Ahiezer
son of Ammishaddai was in command.
26Pagiel son of Ocran was over the division of the tribe of Asher, 27and Ahira
son of Enan was over the division of the
tribe of Naphtali. 28This was the order
of march for the Israelite divisions as
they set out.
10:29 29Now Moses said to Hobab[a] son of
aJdg 4:11 bEx 2:18 Reuel[b] the Midianite, Moses' father-in-
cEx 3:1 law,[c] "We are setting out for the place
dGe 12:7 about which the LORD said, 'I will give
it to you.'[d] Come with us and we will
treat you well, for the LORD has promised good things to Israel."
10:30 30He answered, "No, I will not go;[e] I
eMt 21:29 am going back to my own land and my
own people."
31But Moses said, "Please do not
leave us. You know where we should
camp in the desert, and you can be our
10:31 eyes.[f] 32If you come with us, we will
fJob 29:15 share with you[g] whatever good things
10:32 the LORD gives us.[h]"
gDt 10:18 33So they set out[i] from the moun-
hPs 22:27-31; 67:5-7 tain of the LORD and traveled for three
10:33 days. The ark of the covenant of the
iver 12; Dt 1:33 LORD[j] went before them during those
jJos 3:3 three days to find them a place to rest.
34The cloud of the LORD was over

them by day when they set out from
the camp.[k] 10:34 kNu 9:15-23
35Whenever the ark set out, Moses
said,

"Rise up, O LORD!
May your enemies be scattered;[l] 10:35 lPs 68:1
may your foes flee before you.[m]" mDt 7:10; 32:41; Ps 68:2; Isa 17:12-14

36Whenever it came to rest, he said,

"Return,[n] O LORD, 10:36
to the countless thousands of nIsa 63:17
Israel.[o]" oDt 1:10

Fire From the LORD

11 Now the people complained
about their hardships in the hearing of the LORD, and when he heard
them his anger was aroused. Then fire
from the LORD burned among them[p] 11:1
and consumed some of the outskirts of pLev 10:2
the camp. 2When the people cried out
to Moses, he prayed to the LORD[q] and 11:2 qNu 21:7
the fire died down. 3So that place was
called Taberah,[a][r] because fire from the 11:3 rDt 9:22
LORD had burned among them.

Quail From the LORD

4The rabble with them began to crave
other food,[s] and again the Israelites 11:4
started wailing[t] and said, "If only we sEx 12:38
had meat to eat! 5We remember the fish tPs 78:18; 1Co 10:6
we ate in Egypt at no cost—also the
cucumbers, melons, leeks, onions and
garlic.[u] 6But now we have lost our ap- 11:5
petite; we never see anything but this uEx 16:3
manna!"
7The manna was like coriander seed[v] 11:7
and looked like resin.[w] 8The people vEx 16:31 wGe 2:12
went around gathering it, and then
ground it in a handmill or crushed it
in a mortar. They cooked it in a pot or
made it into cakes. And it tasted like
something made with olive oil. 9When
the dew[x] settled on the camp at night, 11:9
the manna also came down. xEx 16:13
10Moses heard the people of every
family wailing, each at the entrance to
his tent. The LORD became exceedingly angry, and Moses was troubled.
11He asked the LORD, "Why have you
brought this trouble on your servant?
What have I done to displease you that
you put the burden of all these people
on me?[y] 12Did I conceive all these peo- 11:11
ple? Did I give them birth? Why do you yEx 5:22

[a]3 *Taberah* means *burning.*

DAY 4 FOUR

▸ FAITHFULNESS AND MY SERVICE TO OTHERS

Numbers 11:10–15

"I cannot bear the burden of all these people," laments Moses. It seemed to those whom God had lately saved that the world had become negative. Those who had once been joyous over their exodus salvation now wailed in their tents.

It would be a delight to minister to others if they were to thank us for our sacrifice, but their response is usually grumbling at the door of their tent. This grumbling in the local church is a "soul beater" for the pastor who is called to lead. How often within a single year does a pastor lament like Moses, "My burdens are too great for me to bear"? How the pastors in our narcissistic society long for church members who crave obedience to God. But so often they meet only their self-indulgent flocks full of pastoral contempt and criticism.

Proposition: Why don't you determine to have a "Pastor's Day" at your church? On this day celebrate the noble men and women who seek to follow the Great Shepherd while they live out their callings as under-shepherds. In addition, your own dependency on God and your faithfulness to his calling can greatly relieve the burdens of those who lead. Your obedience can be their blessing.

If you are a leader and are feeling the burdens of your role, major on your responsibility and develop a dependency on Christ. He is faithful, and the habit of dependency is the only one that can provide a positive and continuing ministry when you feel the overwhelming burden of ministering to others.

To begin a study on the topic of Faithfulness, the Habit of Spiritual Dependency, turn to the home page on page 260.

tell me to carry them in my arms, as
11:12 [z]Isa 40:11; 49:23 [a]Ex 13:5 a nurse carries an infant,[z] to the land
you promised on oath to their fore-
fathers?[a] 13Where can I get meat for all
11:13 [b]Jn 6:5-9 these people?[b] They keep wailing to me,
'Give us meat to eat!' 14I cannot carry
11:14 [c]Ex 18:18 all these people by myself; the burden is
too heavy for me.[c] 15If this is how you
11:15 [d]Ex 32:32 are going to treat me, put me to death[d]
right now[e]—if I have found favor in 11:15 [e]1Ki 19:4; Jnh 4:3
your eyes—and do not let me face my
own ruin."
16The LORD said to Moses: "Bring
me seventy of Israel's elders who are
known to you as leaders and officials
among the people. Have them come
to the Tent of Meeting, that they may
stand there with you. 17I will come
down and speak with you there, and I
will take of the Spirit that is on you
and put the Spirit on them.[f] They will 11:17 [f]ver 25,29; 1Sa 10:6; 2Ki 2:9,15; Joel 2:28 [g]Ex 18:18
help you carry the burden of the peo-
ple so that you will not have to carry it
alone.[g]
18"Tell the people: 'Consecrate your-
selves[h] in preparation for tomorrow, 11:18 [h]Ex 19:10 [i]Ex 16:7 [j]ver 5; Ac 7:39
when you will eat meat. The LORD
heard you when you wailed,[i] "If only
we had meat to eat! We were better off
in Egypt!"[j] Now the LORD will give
you meat, and you will eat it. 19You
will not eat it for just one day, or two
days, or five, ten or twenty days, 20but
for a whole month—until it comes out
of your nostrils and you loathe it[k]—be- 11:20 [k]Ps 78:29; 106:14,15 [l]Jos 24:27; 1Sa 10:19
cause you have rejected the LORD,[l] who
is among you, and have wailed before
him, saying, "Why did we ever leave
Egypt?"'"
21But Moses said, "Here I am among
six hundred thousand men[m] on foot, 11:21 [m]Ex 12:37
and you say, 'I will give them meat to
eat for a whole month!' 22Would they
have enough if flocks and herds were
slaughtered for them? Would they have
enough if all the fish in the sea were 11:22 [n]Mt 15:33
caught for them?"[n]
23The LORD answered Moses, "Is the
LORD's arm too short?[o] You will now 11:23 [o]Isa 50:2; 59:1 [p]Nu 23:19; Eze 12:25; 24:14
see whether or not what I say will come
true for you.[p]"
24So Moses went out and told the
people what the LORD had said. He
brought together seventy of their elders
and had them stand around the Tent.
25Then the LORD came down in the
cloud[q] and spoke with him,[r] and he 11:25 [q]Nu 12:5 [r]ver 17 [s]1Sa 10:6 [t]Ac 2:17 [u]1Sa 10:10
took of the Spirit[s] that was on him and
put the Spirit on the seventy elders.[t]
When the Spirit rested on them, they
prophesied,[u] but they did not do so
again.[a]
26However, two men, whose names
were Eldad and Medad, had remained
in the camp. They were listed among

[a]25 Or *prophesied and continued to do so*

the elders, but did not go out to the Tent. Yet the Spirit also rested on them, and they prophesied in the camp. 27A young man ran and told Moses, "Eldad and Medad are prophesying in the camp."

28Joshua son of Nun, who had been Moses' aide[v] since youth, spoke up and said, "Moses, my lord, stop them!"[w]

29But Moses replied, "Are you jealous for my sake? I wish that all the LORD's people were prophets[x] and that the LORD would put his Spirit on them!" 30Then Moses and the elders of Israel returned to the camp.

31Now a wind went out from the LORD and drove quail[y] in from the sea. It brought them[a] down all around the camp to about three feet[b] above the ground, as far as a day's walk in any direction. 32All that day and night and all the next day the people went out and gathered quail. No one gathered less than ten homers.[c] Then they spread them out all around the camp. 33But while the meat was still between their teeth[z] and before it could be consumed, the anger of the LORD burned against the people, and he struck them with a severe plague.[a] 34Therefore the place was named Kibroth Hattaavah,[d][b] because there they buried the people who had craved other food.

35From Kibroth Hattaavah the people traveled to Hazeroth[c] and stayed there.

11:28 [v]Ex 33:11; Jos 1:1 [w]Mk 9:38-40
11:29 [x]1Co 14:5
11:31 [y]Ex 16:13; Ps 78:26-28
11:33 [z]Ps 78:30 [a]Ps 106:15
11:34 [b]Dt 9:22
11:35 [c]Nu 33:17

Miriam and Aaron Oppose Moses

12 Miriam and Aaron began to talk against Moses because of his Cushite wife,[d] for he had married a Cushite. 2"Has the LORD spoken only through Moses?" they asked. "Hasn't he also spoken through us?"[e] And the LORD heard this.[f]

3(Now Moses was a very humble man,[g] more humble than anyone else on the face of the earth.)

4At once the LORD said to Moses, Aaron and Miriam, "Come out to the Tent of Meeting, all three of you." So the three of them came out. 5Then the LORD came down in a pillar of cloud;[h] he stood at the entrance to the Tent and summoned Aaron and Miriam. When both of them stepped forward, 6he said, "Listen to my words:

"When a prophet of the LORD is
among you,
I reveal myself to him in visions,[i]
I speak to him in dreams.[j]
7But this is not true of my servant
Moses;[k]
he is faithful in all my house.[l]
8With him I speak face to face,
clearly and not in riddles;[m]
he sees the form of the LORD.[n]
Why then were you not afraid
to speak against my servant Moses?"

9The anger of the LORD burned against them, and he left them.[o]

10When the cloud lifted from above the Tent, there stood Miriam—leprous,[e] like snow.[p] Aaron turned toward her and saw that she had leprosy;[q] 11and he said to Moses, "Please, my lord, do not hold against us the sin we have so foolishly committed.[r] 12Do not let her be like a stillborn infant coming from its mother's womb with its flesh half eaten away."

13So Moses cried out to the LORD, "O God, please heal her!"[s]

14The LORD replied to Moses, "If her father had spit in her face,[t] would she not have been in disgrace for seven days? Confine her outside the camp[u] for seven days; after that she can be brought back." 15So Miriam was confined outside the camp for seven days, and the people did not move on till she was brought back.

16After that, the people left Hazeroth[v] and encamped in the Desert of Paran.

12:1 [d]Ex 2:21
12:2 [e]Nu 16:3 [f]Nu 11:1
12:3 [g]Mt 11:29
12:5 [h]Nu 11:25
12:6 [i]Ge 15:1; 46:2 [j]Ge 31:10; 1Ki 3:5; Heb 1:1
12:7 [k]Jos 1:1-2; Ps 105:26 [l]Heb 3:2,5
12:8 [m]Dt 34:10 [n]Ex 20:4; Ps 17:15
12:9 [o]Ge 17:22
12:10 [p]Ex 4:6; Dt 24:9 [q]2Ki 5:1,27
12:11 [r]2Sa 19:19; 24:10
12:13 [s]Isa 30:26; Jer 17:14
12:14 [t]Dt 25:9; Job 17:6; 30:9-10; Isa 50:6 [u]Lev 13:46; Nu 5:2-3
12:16 [v]Nu 11:35

Exploring Canaan

13 The LORD said to Moses, 2"Send some men to explore[w] the land of Canaan, which I am giving to the Israelites. From each ancestral tribe send one of its leaders."

3So at the LORD's command Moses sent them out from the Desert of Paran. All of them were leaders of the Israelites. 4These are their names:

from the tribe of Reuben, Shammua son of Zaccur;

13:2 [w]Dt 1:22

[a]31 Or *They flew* [b]31 Hebrew *two cubits* (about 1 meter) [c]32 That is, probably about 60 bushels (about 2.2 kiloliters) [d]34 *Kibroth Hattaavah* means *graves of craving.* [e]10 The Hebrew word was used for various diseases affecting the skin—not necessarily leprosy.

[5]from the tribe of Simeon, Shaphat son of Hori;

13:6 [a]ver 30; Nu 14:6,24; 34:19; Jdg 1:12-15

[6]from the tribe of Judah, Caleb son of Jephunneh;[a]

[7]from the tribe of Issachar, Igal son of Joseph;

[8]from the tribe of Ephraim, Hoshea son of Nun;

[9]from the tribe of Benjamin, Palti son of Raphu;

[10]from the tribe of Zebulun, Gaddiel son of Sodi;

[11]from the tribe of Manasseh (a tribe of Joseph), Gaddi son of Susi;

[12]from the tribe of Dan, Ammiel son of Gemalli;

[13]from the tribe of Asher, Sethur son of Michael;

[14]from the tribe of Naphtali, Nahbi son of Vophsi;

CALEB

Faithfulness, the Truth That God Plus One Is a Majority (13:26–33)

The dream inspired by God always requires faithfulness. If a task is easy, it's possible that God has not asked us to undertake it. It seems that only when the job requires the spending of the soul is it likely that God is really calling us to do it.

So it was with the conquest of Canaan. For generations God had told the Israelites he would give them Canaan, a land flowing with milk and honey. The proposition sounded good until the people went to pick up the gift. Then they discovered there were already people living in Canaan. The land God had said he would give them was already owned by others. Acceptance of his gift would require a great deal of Israel. It is in this same sense that we receive the gift of eternal life, only to discover that we must work out our own salvation (Philippians 2:11) and discipline ourselves with faithfulness to make our lives really count for God.

The spies came back with a majority report and a minority report. The majority (ten of the spies) pointed out the size and strength of the cities. They told Moses that the land God had promised to give them was in truth already owned by other people: "The Amalekites live in the Negev; the Hittites, Jebusites and Amorites live in the hill country; and the Canaanites live near the sea and along the Jordan" (Numbers 13:29). But worst of all was the size of the inhabitants: "The people who live there are powerful, and the cities are fortified and very large. We even saw descendants of Anak there" (v. 28). These were big people. "We can't attack those people; they are stronger than we are . . . All the people we saw there are of great size . . . We seemed like grasshoppers in our own eyes, and we looked the same to them" (vv. 31–33).

Enter the minority report: Caleb and Joshua. Caleb demonstrated faithfulness. He silenced the people and said, "We should go up and take possession of the land, for we can certainly do it" (v. 30). With God all things are possible; God and any size army form a powerful majority. So while the people moaned, "If only we had died in Egypt!" (14:2)—a "rallying cry" that lacked force for motivating conquest—Joshua had a word of faith: "The land we passed through and explored is exceedingly good. If the LORD is pleased with us, he will lead us into that land . . . Only do not rebel against the LORD" (vv. 7–9).

Faithfulness is the only response genuine believers make to the will of God. Caleb and Joshua lived long enough to dwell in that good land, and faithfulness was the key to their triumph.

Faithfulness is the energy that keeps on keeping on. It sees giants and makes no comparison with itself, for it sets giants next to God and wonders why anyone would ever be afraid. Faithfulness desires a clear word, not an easy word. Faithfulness knows that God plus one is a majority—a clear majority. Faithfulness pities those who think numbers alone constitute strength.

15 from the tribe of Gad, Geuel son of Maki.

16 These are the names of the men Moses sent to explore the land. (Moses gave Hoshea son of Nun[y] the name Joshua.)[z]

17 When Moses sent them to explore Canaan, he said, "Go up through the Negev[a] and on into the hill country.[b] 18 See what the land is like and whether the people who live there are strong or weak, few or many. 19 What kind of land do they live in? Is it good or bad? What kind of towns do they live in? Are they unwalled or fortified? 20 How is the soil? Is it fertile or poor? Are there trees on it or not? Do your best to bring back some of the fruit of the land.[c]" (It was the season for the first ripe grapes.)

21 So they went up and explored the land from the Desert of Zin[d] as far as Rehob,[e] toward Lebo[a] Hamath.[f] 22 They went up through the Negev and came to Hebron, where Ahiman, Sheshai and Talmai,[g] the descendants of Anak,[h] lived. (Hebron had been built seven years before Zoan in Egypt.)[i] 23 When they reached the Valley of Eshcol,[b] they cut off a branch bearing a single cluster of grapes. Two of them carried it on a pole between them, along with some pomegranates and figs. 24 That place was called the Valley of Eshcol because of the cluster of grapes the Israelites cut off there. 25 At the end of forty days they returned from exploring the land.

13:16 [y]ver 8 [z]Dt 32:44
13:17 [a]Ge 12:9 [b]Jdg 1:9
13:20 [c]Dt 1:25
13:21 [d]Nu 20:1; 27:14; 33:36; Jos 15:1 [e]Jos 19:28 [f]Jos 13:5
13:22 [g]Jos 15:14 [h]Jos 15:13 [i]Ps 78:12,43; Isa 19:11,13

Report on the Exploration

26 They came back to Moses and Aaron and the whole Israelite community at Kadesh in the Desert of Paran. There they reported to them[j] and to the whole assembly and showed them the fruit of the land. 27 They gave Moses this account: "We went into the land to which you sent us, and it does flow with milk and honey![k] Here is its fruit.[l] 28 But the people who live there are powerful, and the cities are fortified and very large.[m] We even saw descendants of Anak there. 29 The Amalekites live in the Negev; the Hittites, Jebusites and Amorites live in the hill country; and the Canaanites live near the sea and along the Jordan."

30 Then Caleb silenced the people before Moses and said, "We should go up and take possession of the land, for we can certainly do it."

31 But the men who had gone up with him said, "We can't attack those people; they are stronger than we are."[n] 32 And they spread among the Israelites a bad report[o] about the land they had explored. They said, "The land we explored devours[p] those living in it. All the people we saw there are of great size.[q] 33 We saw the Nephilim[r] there (the descendants of Anak[s] come from the Nephilim). We seemed like grasshoppers in our own eyes, and we looked the same to them."

13:26 [j]Nu 32:8
13:27 [k]Ex 3:8 [l]Dt 1:25
13:28 [m]Dt 1:28; 9:1,2
13:31 [n]Dt 1:28; 9:1; Jos 14:8
13:32 [o]Nu 14:36,37 [p]Eze 36:13,14 [q]Am 2:9
13:33 [r]Ge 6:4 [s]Dt 1:28

The People Rebel

14 That night all the people of the community raised their voices and wept aloud. 2 All the Israelites grumbled against Moses and Aaron, and the whole assembly said to them, "If only we had died in Egypt! Or in this desert![t] 3 Why is the LORD bringing us to this land only to let us fall by the sword? Our wives and children will be taken as plunder. Wouldn't it be better for us to go back to Egypt?" 4 And they said to each other, "We should choose a leader and go back to Egypt.[u]"

5 Then Moses and Aaron fell facedown[v] in front of the whole Israelite assembly gathered there. 6 Joshua son of Nun and Caleb son of Jephunneh, who were among those who had explored the land, tore their clothes 7 and said to the entire Israelite assembly, "The land we passed through and explored is exceedingly good.[w] 8 If the LORD is pleased with us,[x] he will lead us into that land, a land flowing with milk and honey,[y] and will give it to us. 9 Only do not rebel[z] against the LORD. And do not be afraid of the people of the land,[a] because we will swallow them up. Their protection is gone, but the LORD is with us. Do not be afraid of them."

10 But the whole assembly talked about stoning[b] them. Then the glory of the LORD[c] appeared at the Tent of Meeting to all the Israelites. 11 The LORD said to Moses, "How long will these people treat me with contempt? How long will they refuse to believe in me,[d] in spite of all the miraculous

14:2 [t]Nu 11:1
14:4 [u]Ne 9:17
14:5 [v]Nu 16:4, 22,45
14:7 [w]Nu 13:27; Dt 1:25
14:8 [x]Dt 10:15 [y]Nu 13:27
14:9 [z]Dt 1:26; 9:7,23,24 [a]Dt 1:21; 7:18; 20:1
14:10 [b]Ex 17:4 [c]Lev 9:23
14:11 [d]Ps 78:22; 106:24

[a]21 Or *toward the entrance to* [b]23 *Eshcol* means *cluster*; also in verse 24.

signs I have performed among them?
[12]I will strike them down with a plague
and destroy them, but I will make you
14:12 into a nation[e] greater and stronger than
[e]Ex 32:10 they."
[13]Moses said to the LORD, "Then
the Egyptians will hear about it! By
your power you brought these people
14:13 up from among them.[f] [14]And they will
[f]Ex 32:11-14; tell the inhabitants of this land about
Ps 106:23 it. They have already heard[g] that you,
14:14 O LORD, are with these people and
[g]Ex 15:14 [h]Ex 13:21 that you, O LORD, have been seen face
to face, that your cloud stays over them,
and that you go before them in a pillar
of cloud by day and a pillar of fire
by night.[h] [15]If you put these people to
death all at one time, the nations who
have heard this report about you will
say, [16]'The LORD was not able to bring
these people into the land he promised
them on oath; so he slaughtered them
14:16 in the desert.'[i]
[i]Jos 7:7 [17]"Now may the Lord's strength be
displayed, just as you have declared:
[18]'The LORD is slow to anger, abounding in love and forgiving sin and
14:18 rebellion.[j] Yet he does not leave the
[j]Ex 34:6; Ps 145:8; guilty unpunished; he punishes the chil-
Jnh 4:2 [k]Ex 20:5 dren for the sin of the fathers to the
third and fourth generation.'[k] [19]In ac-
14:19 cordance with your great love, forgive[l]
[l]Ex 34:9 [m]Ps 106:45 the sin of these people,[m] just as you
[n]Ps 78:38 have pardoned them from the time they
left Egypt until now."[n]
[20]The LORD replied, "I have for-
14:20 [o]Ps 106:23; given them,[o] as you asked. [21]Neverthe-
Mic 7:18-20 less, as surely as I live[p] and as surely as
14:21 the glory of the LORD fills the whole
[p]Dt 32:40; earth,[q] [22]not one of the men who saw
Isa 49:18 [q]Ps 72:19; my glory and the miraculous signs I
Isa 6:3; Hab 2:14 performed in Egypt and in the desert
but who disobeyed me and tested me
14:22 [r]Ex 14:11; ten times[r]— [23]not one of them will ever
32:1; see the land I promised on oath[s] to their
1Co 10:5 forefathers. No one who has treated me
14:23 [s]Nu 32:11 with contempt will ever see it.[t] [24]But
[t]Heb 3:18 because my servant Caleb has a different
14:24 spirit and follows me wholeheartedly,[u]
[u]ver 6-9; I will bring him into the land he went
Jos 14:8,14 [v]Nu 32:12 to, and his descendants will inherit it.[v]
[25]Since the Amalekites and Canaanites
14:25 are living in the valleys, turn[w] back to-
[w]Dt 1:40 morrow and set out toward the desert
along the route to the Red Sea.[a]"
[26]The LORD said to Moses and
Aaron: [27]"How long will this wicked
community grumble against me? I have

heard the complaints of these grum-
bling Israelites.[x] [28]So tell them, 'As sure- 14:27
ly as I live,[y] declares the LORD, I will [x]Ex 16:12
do to you the very things I heard you 14:28
say: [29]In this desert your bodies will [y]ver 21
fall[z]—every one of you twenty years old 14:29
or more[a] who was counted in the cen- [z]Nu 26:65
sus and who has grumbled against me. [a]Nu 1:45
[30]Not one of you will enter the land I
swore with uplifted hand to make your
home, except Caleb son of Jephunneh
and Joshua son of Nun. [31]As for your
children that you said would be taken
as plunder, I will bring them in to enjoy the land you have rejected.[b] [32]But 14:31
you—your bodies will fall[c] in this desert. [b]Ps 106:24
[33]Your children will be shepherds here 14:32
for forty years, suffering for your un- [c]1Co 10:5
faithfulness, until the last of your bodies
lies in the desert. [34]For forty years—
one year for each of the forty days you 14:34
explored the land[d]—you will suffer for [d]Nu 13:25
your sins and know what it is like to
have me against you.' [35]I, the LORD,
have spoken, and I will surely do these
things[e] to this whole wicked commu- 14:35
nity, which has banded together against [e]Nu 23:19
me. They will meet their end in this
desert; here they will die."
[36]So the men Moses had sent[f] to ex- 14:36
plore the land, who returned and made [f]Nu 13:4-16 [g]Nu 13:32
the whole community grumble against
him by spreading a bad report[g] about
it— [37]these men responsible for spreading the bad report[h] about the land were 14:37
struck down and died of a plague[i] be- [h]1Co 10:10
fore the LORD. [38]Of the men who went [i]Nu 16:49
to explore the land, only Joshua son
of Nun and Caleb son of Jephunneh
survived.[j] 14:38
[39]When Moses reported this to all [j]Jos 14:6
the Israelites, they mourned[k] bitterly. 14:39
[40]Early the next morning they went up [k]Ex 33:4
toward the high hill country. "We have
sinned[l]," they said. "We will go up to 14:40
the place the LORD promised." [l]Dt 1:41
[41]But Moses said, "Why are you disobeying the LORD's command? This
will not succeed![m] [42]Do not go up, 14:41
because the LORD is not with you. [m]2Ch 24:20
You will be defeated by your enemies,[n] 14:42
[43]for the Amalekites and Canaanites [n]Dt 1:42
will face you there. Because you have
turned away from the LORD, he will
not be with you and you will fall by the
sword."

[a]25 Hebrew *Yam Suph*; that is, Sea of Reeds

44Nevertheless, in their presumption they went up[o] toward the high hill country, though neither Moses nor the ark of the LORD's covenant moved from the camp.[p] 45Then the Amalekites and Canaanites who lived in that hill country came down and attacked them and beat them down all the way to Hormah.[q]

Supplementary Offerings

15 The LORD said to Moses, 2"Speak to the Israelites and say to them: 'After you enter the land I am giving you[r] as a home 3and you present to the LORD offerings made by fire, from the herd or the flock,[s] as an aroma pleasing to the LORD[t]—whether burnt offerings[u] or sacrifices, for special vows or freewill offerings[v] or festival offerings[w]— 4then the one who brings his offering shall present to the LORD a grain offering[x] of a tenth of an ephah[a] of fine flour mixed with a quarter of a hin[b] of oil. 5With each lamb for the burnt offering or the sacrifice, prepare a quarter of a hin of wine[y] as a drink offering.

6" 'With a ram[z] prepare a grain offering[a] of two-tenths of an ephah[c] of fine flour mixed with a third of a hin[d] of oil,[b] 7and a third of a hin of wine as a drink offering. Offer it as an aroma pleasing to the LORD.

8" 'When you prepare a young bull as a burnt offering or sacrifice, for a special vow or a fellowship offering[e][c] to the LORD, 9bring with the bull a grain offering of three-tenths of an ephah[f][d] of fine flour mixed with half a hin[g] of oil. 10Also bring half a hin of wine as a drink offering. It will be an offering made by fire, an aroma pleasing to the LORD. 11Each bull or ram, each lamb or young goat, is to be prepared in this manner. 12Do this for each one, for as many as you prepare.

13" 'Everyone who is native-born[e] must do these things in this way when he brings an offering made by fire as an aroma pleasing to the LORD. 14For the generations to come, whenever an alien or anyone else living among you presents an offering made by fire as an aroma pleasing to the LORD, he must do exactly as you do. 15The community is to have the same rules for you and for the alien living among you; this is a lasting ordinance for the generations to come.[f] You and the alien shall be the same before the LORD: 16The same laws and regulations will apply both to you and to the alien living among you.[g]' "

17The LORD said to Moses, 18"Speak to the Israelites and say to them: 'When you enter the land to which I am taking you 19and you eat the food of the land,[h] present a portion as an offering to the LORD. 20Present a cake from the first of your ground meal[i] and present it as an offering from the threshing floor.[j] 21Throughout the generations to come you are to give this offering to the LORD from the first of your ground meal.[k]

Offerings for Unintentional Sins

22" 'Now if you unintentionally fail to keep any of these commands the LORD gave Moses[l]— 23any of the LORD's commands to you through him, from the day the LORD gave them and continuing through the generations to come— 24and if this is done unintentionally without the community being aware of it,[m] then the whole community is to offer[n] a young bull for a burnt offering as an aroma pleasing to the LORD, along with its prescribed grain offering and drink offering, and a male goat for a sin offering.[o] 25The priest is to make atonement for the whole Israelite community, and they will be forgiven,[p] for it was not intentional and they have brought to the LORD for their wrong an offering made by fire and a sin offering. 26The whole Israelite community and the aliens living among them will be forgiven, because all the people were involved in the unintentional wrong.[q]

27" 'But if just one person sins unintentionally,[r] he must bring a year-old female goat for a sin offering. 28The priest is to make atonement before the LORD for the one who erred by sinning unintentionally, and when atonement

[a]*4* That is, probably about 2 quarts (about 2 liters) [b]*4* That is, probably about 1 quart (about 1 liter); also in verse 5 [c]*6* That is, probably about 4 quarts (about 4.5 liters) [d]*6* That is, probably about 1 1/4 quarts (about 1.2 liters); also in verse 7 [e]*8* Traditionally *peace offering* [f]*9* That is, probably about 6 quarts (about 6.5 liters) [g]*9* That is, probably about 2 quarts (about 2 liters); also in verse 10

14:44 [o]Dt 1:43 [p]Nu 31:6
14:45 [q]Nu 21:3; Dt 1:44; Jdg 1:17
15:2 [r]Lev 23:10
15:3 [s]Lev 1:2 [t]ver 24; Ge 8:21; Ex 29:18 [u]Nu 28:19,27 [v]Lev 22:18,21; Ezr 1:4 [w]Lev 23:1-44
15:4 [x]Lev 2:1; 6:14
15:5 [y]Nu 28:7,14
15:6 [z]Lev 5:15 [a]Nu 28:12 [b]Eze 46:14
15:8 [c]Lev 1:3; 3:1
15:9 [d]Lev 14:10
15:13 [e]Lev 16:29
15:15 [f]ver 29; Nu 9:14
15:16 [g]Nu 9:14
15:19 [h]Jos 5:11,12
15:20 [i]Ex 34:26; Lev 23:14; Dt 26:2,10 [j]Lev 2:14
15:21 [k]Ro 11:16
15:22 [l]Lev 4:2
15:24 [m]Lev 5:15 [n]Lev 4:14 [o]Lev 4:3
15:25 [p]Lev 4:20; Ro 3:25; Heb 2:17
15:26 [q]ver 24
15:27 [r]Lev 4:27

has been made for him, he will be
15:28 forgiven.[s] [29]One and the same law ap-
[s]Lev 4:35 plies to everyone who sins unintentionally, whether he is a native-born Israelite
or an alien.
15:30 [30]" 'But anyone who sins defiantly,[t]
[t]Nu 14:40-44; Dt 1:43; whether native-born or alien,[u] blas-
17:13; Ps 19:13 phemes the LORD, and that person
[u]ver 14 must be cut off from his people. [31]Be-
cause he has despised the LORD's word
15:31 and broken his commands,[v] that per-
[v]2Sa 12:9; Ps 119:126; son must surely be cut off; his guilt re-
Pr 13:13 [w]Lev 5:1; mains on him.[w]' "
Eze 18:20

The Sabbath-Breaker Put to Death

[32]While the Israelites were in the
desert, a man was found gathering wood
15:32 on the Sabbath day.[x] [33]Those who found
[x]Ex 31:14,15; 35:2,3 him gathering wood brought him to
Moses and Aaron and the whole assem-
bly, [34]and they kept him in custody, because it was not clear what should be
15:34 done to him.[y] [35]Then the LORD said
[y]Nu 9:8 to Moses, "The man must die.[z] The
15:35 whole assembly must stone him out-
[z]Ex 31:14,15; Dt 21:21 side the camp."[a] [36]So the assembly took
[a]Lev 20:2; him outside the camp and stoned him
24:14; Ac 7:58 to death, as the LORD commanded
Moses.

Tassels on Garments

[37]The LORD said to Moses, [38]"Speak
to the Israelites and say to them:
'Throughout the generations to come
you are to make tassels on the corners
15:38 of your garments,[b] with a blue cord on
[b]Dt 22:12; Mt 23:5 each tassel. [39]You will have these tassels to look at and so you will remem-
15:39 ber[c] all the commands of the LORD,
[c]Dt 4:23; 6:12; that you may obey them and not pros-
Ps 73:27 titute yourselves by going after the lusts
of your own hearts and eyes. [40]Then
you will remember to obey all my commands and will be consecrated to your
15:40 God.[d] [41]I am the LORD your God, who
[d]Lev 11:44; Ro 12:1; brought you out of Egypt to be your
Col 1:22; 1Pe 1:15 God. I am the LORD your God.' "

Korah, Dathan and Abiram

16:1 **16** Korah[e] son of Izhar, the son of
[e]Jude 1:11 [f]Nu 26:8; Kohath, the son of Levi, and
Dt 11:6 certain Reubenites—Dathan and Abiram, sons of Eliab,[f] and On son of
Peleth—became insolent[a] [2]and rose up
against Moses. With them were 250
Israelite men, well-known community
16:2 leaders who had been appointed mem-
[g]Nu 1:16; 26:9 bers of the council.[g] [3]They came as a
group to oppose Moses and Aaron[h] and 16:3 [h]ver 7;
said to them, "You have gone too far! Ps 106:16
The whole community is holy,[i] every [i]Ex 19:6
one of them, and the LORD is with [j]Nu 14:14
them.[j] Why then do you set yourselves [k]Nu 12:2
above the LORD's assembly?"[k]
[4]When Moses heard this, he fell face-
down.[l] [5]Then he said to Korah and 16:4 [l]Nu 14:5
all his followers: "In the morning the
LORD will show who belongs to him
and who is holy,[m] and he will have that 16:5
person come near him. The man he [m]Lev 10:3; 2Ti 2:19*
chooses[n] he will cause to come near [n]Nu 17:5; Ps 65:4
him. [6]You, Korah, and all your follow-
ers are to do this: Take censers [7]and tomorrow put fire and incense in them
before the LORD. The man the LORD
chooses will be the one who is holy. You
Levites have gone too far!"
[8]Moses also said to Korah, "Now listen, you Levites! [9]Isn't it enough for you
that the God of Israel has separated you
from the rest of the Israelite community
and brought you near himself to do the
work at the LORD's tabernacle and to
stand before the community and min-
ister to them?[o] [10]He has brought you 16:9 [o]Nu 3:6;
and all your fellow Levites near himself, Dt 10:8
but now you are trying to get the priest-
hood too.[p] [11]It is against the LORD that 16:10 [p]Nu 3:10;
you and all your followers have banded 18:7
together. Who is Aaron that you should
grumble[q] against him?[r]"
[12]Then Moses summoned Dathan 16:11 [q]1Co 10:10 [r]Ex 16:7
and Abiram, the sons of Eliab. But
they said, "We will not come! [13]Isn't it
enough that you have brought us up
out of a land flowing with milk and
honey to kill us in the desert?[s] And 16:13 [s]Nu 14:2
now you also want to lord it over us?[t] [t]Ac 7:27,35
[14]Moreover, you haven't brought us into
a land flowing with milk and honey[u] 16:14 [u]Lev 20:24
or given us an inheritance of fields [v]Ex 22:5;
and vineyards.[v] Will you gouge out the 23:11; Nu 20:5
eyes of[b] these men?[w] No, we will not [w]Jdg 16:21;
come!" 1Sa 11:2
[15]Then Moses became very angry
and said to the LORD, "Do not accept
their offering. I have not taken so much
as a donkey[x] from them, nor have I 16:15
wronged any of them." [x]1Sa 12:3
[16]Moses said to Korah, "You and all
your followers are to appear before the
LORD tomorrow—you and they and 16:16
Aaron.[y] [17]Each man is to take his cen- [y]ver 6

[a]*1* Or *Peleth—took* ⌊*men*⌋ [b]*14* Or *you make slaves of*; or *you deceive*

ser and put incense in it—250 censers
in all—and present it before the LORD.
You and Aaron are to present your censers also." 18So each man took his censer, put fire and incense in it, and stood
with Moses and Aaron at the entrance
to the Tent of Meeting. 19When Korah
had gathered all his followers in op-
16:19 [z]ver 42 [a]Ex 16:7; Nu 14:10; 20:6 position to them[z] at the entrance to
the Tent of Meeting, the glory of the
LORD[a] appeared to the entire assembly.
20The LORD said to Moses and Aaron,
21"Separate yourselves from this assembly so I can put an end to them at
once."[b]
16:21 [b]Ex 32:10 22But Moses and Aaron fell face-
16:22 [c]Nu 14:5 [d]Nu 27:16; Job 12:10; Heb 12:9 [e]Ge 18:23 down[c] and cried out, "O God, God of
the spirits of all mankind,[d] will you be
angry with the entire assembly when
only one man sins?"[e]
23Then the LORD said to Moses,
24"Say to the assembly, 'Move away
from the tents of Korah, Dathan and
Abiram.'"
25Moses got up and went to Dathan
and Abiram, and the elders of Israel
followed him. 26He warned the assembly, "Move back from the tents of these
16:26 [f]Isa 52:11 [g]Ge 19:15 wicked men![f] Do not touch anything
belonging to them, or you will be swept
away[g] because of all their sins." 27So
they moved away from the tents of Korah, Dathan and Abiram. Dathan and
Abiram had come out and were standing with their wives, children and little
ones at the entrances to their tents.
28Then Moses said, "This is how you
16:28 [h]Ex 3:12; Jn 5:36; 6:38 will know that the LORD has sent me[h]
to do all these things and that it was not
my idea: 29If these men die a natural
death and experience only what usually
happens to men, then the LORD has
16:29 [i]Ecc 3:19 not sent me.[i] 30But if the LORD brings
about something totally new, and the
earth opens its mouth and swallows
them, with everything that belongs to
them, and they go down alive into the
16:30 [j]ver 33; Ps 55:15 grave,[a][j] then you will know that these
men have treated the LORD with con-
tempt."
31As soon as he finished saying all
16:31 [k]Mic 1:3-4 this, the ground under them split apart[k]
32and the earth opened its mouth and
16:32 [l]Nu 26:11; Dt 11:6; Ps 106:17 swallowed them,[l] with their households
and all Korah's men and all their pos-
sessions. 33They went down alive into
the grave, with everything they owned;
the earth closed over them, and they

perished and were gone from the community. 34At their cries, all the Israelites
around them fled, shouting, "The earth
is going to swallow us too!"
35And fire came out from the LORD[m] 16:35 [m]Nu 11:1-3; 26:10 [n]Lev 10:2
and consumed[n] the 250 men who were
offering the incense.
36The LORD said to Moses, 37"Tell
Eleazar son of Aaron, the priest, to take
the censers out of the smoldering remains and scatter the coals some distance away, for the censers are holy—
38the censers of the men who sinned
at the cost of their lives.[o] Hammer 16:38 [o]Pr 20:2 [p]Nu 26:10; Eze 14:8; 2Pe 2:6
the censers into sheets to overlay the al-
tar, for they were presented before the
LORD and have become holy. Let them
be a sign[p] to the Israelites."
39So Eleazar the priest collected the
bronze censers brought by those who
had been burned up, and he had them
hammered out to overlay the altar, 40as
the LORD directed him through Moses.
This was to remind the Israelites that
no one except a descendant of Aaron
should come to burn incense[q] before 16:40 [q]Ex 30:7-10; Nu 1:51 [r]2Ch 26:18 [s]Nu 3:10
the LORD,[r] or he would become like
Korah and his followers.[s]
41The next day the whole Israelite
community grumbled against Moses
and Aaron. "You have killed the LORD's
people," they said.
42But when the assembly gathered in
opposition[t] to Moses and Aaron and 16:42 [t]ver 19; Nu 20:6
turned toward the Tent of Meeting,
suddenly the cloud covered it and the
glory of the LORD appeared. 43Then
Moses and Aaron went to the front of
the Tent of Meeting, 44and the LORD
said to Moses, 45"Get away from this
assembly so I can put an end to them at
once." And they fell facedown.
46Then Moses said to Aaron, "Take
your censer and put incense in it, along
with fire from the altar, and hurry to
the assembly[u] to make atonement[v] for 16:46 [u]Lev 10:6 [v]Nu 18:5; 25:13; Dt 9:22 [w]Nu 8:19; Ps 106:29
them. Wrath has come out from the
LORD; the plague[w] has started." 47So
Aaron did as Moses said, and ran into
the midst of the assembly. The plague
had already started among the people,[x] 16:47 [x]Nu 25:6-8
but Aaron offered the incense and made
atonement for them. 48He stood between the living and the dead, and the
plague stopped.[y] 49But 14,700 people 16:48 [y]Nu 25:8; Ps 106:30
died from the plague, in addition to

[a]*30* Hebrew *Sheol*; also in verse 33

16:49 [z]ver 32 those who had died because of Korah.[z]
50Then Aaron returned to Moses at the
entrance to the Tent of Meeting, for the
plague had stopped.

The Budding of Aaron's Staff

17 The LORD said to Moses,
2"Speak to the Israelites and get
twelve staffs from them, one from the
leader of each of their ancestral tribes.
Write the name of each man on his
staff. 3On the staff of Levi write Aaron's
17:3 [a]Nu 1:3 name,[a] for there must be one staff for
the head of each ancestral tribe. 4Place
17:4 them in the Tent of Meeting in front
[b]ver 7 of the Testimony,[b] where I meet with
[c]Ex 25:22 you.[c] 5The staff belonging to the man I
17:5 [d]Nu 16:5 choose[d] will sprout, and I will rid myself of this constant grumbling against
you by the Israelites."
6So Moses spoke to the Israelites,
and their leaders gave him twelve staffs,
one for the leader of each of their
ancestral tribes, and Aaron's staff was
among them. 7Moses placed the staffs
before the LORD in the Tent of the
17:7 [e]Ex 38:21; Testimony.[e]
Ac 7:44 8The next day Moses entered the
Tent of the Testimony and saw that Aaron's staff, which represented the house
of Levi, had not only sprouted but
17:8 had budded, blossomed and produced
[f]Eze 17:24; almonds.[f] 9Then Moses brought out all
Heb 9:4 the staffs from the LORD's presence to
all the Israelites. They looked at them,
and each man took his own staff.

LOVE

STAFF FLOWERS

Numbers 17:8

If love is God's name, life is God's business. Walking sticks grow flowers at God's command. Are you living in a Sinai of lost hope? Lay your dried and unproductive dreams at the feet of Christ. See! They have blossomed. There is fruit.

10The LORD said to Moses, "Put
back Aaron's staff in front of the Testimony, to be kept as a sign to the
17:10 [g]Dt 9:24 rebellious.[g] This will put an end to their
grumbling against me, so that they will
not die." 11Moses did just as the LORD
commanded him.
12The Israelites said to Moses, "We
17:12 [h]Isa 6:5 will die! We are lost, we are all lost![h]

13Anyone who even comes near the tab- 17:13
ernacle of the LORD will die.[i] Are we all [i]Nu 1:51
going to die?"

Duties of Priests and Levites

18 The LORD said to Aaron, "You,
your sons and your father's fam-
ily are to bear the responsibility for of- 18:1
fenses against the sanctuary,[j] and you [j]Ex 28:38
and your sons alone are to bear the
responsibility for offenses against the
priesthood. 2Bring your fellow Levites
from your ancestral tribe to join you
and assist you when you and your sons
minister[k] before the Tent of the Testi- 18:2
mony. 3They are to be responsible to [k]Nu 3:10
you and are to perform all the duties of
the Tent,[l] but they must not go near the 18:3
furnishings of the sanctuary or the altar, [l]Nu 1:51
or both they and you will die.[m] 4They [m]ver 7; Nu 4:15
are to join you and be responsible for
the care of the Tent of Meeting—all the
work at the Tent—and no one else may
come near where you are.
5"You are to be responsible for the
care of the sanctuary and the altar,[n] so 18:5
that wrath will not fall on the Israelites [n]Nu 16:46
again. 6I myself have selected your fel-
low Levites from among the Israelites as
a gift to you,[o] dedicated to the LORD 18:6
to do the work at the Tent of Meeting. [o]Nu 3:9
7But only you and your sons may serve
as priests in connection with everything
at the altar and inside the curtain.[p] I am 18:7
giving you the service of the priesthood [p]Heb 9:3,6
as a gift.[q] Anyone else who comes near [q]ver 20; Ex 29:9
the sanctuary must be put to death.[r]" [r]Nu 3:10

Offerings for Priests and Levites

8Then the LORD said to Aaron, "I
myself have put you in charge of the offerings presented to me; all the holy offerings the Israelites give me I give to
you and your sons as your portion and
regular share.[s] 9You are to have the part 18:8
of the most holy offerings that is kept [s]Lev 6:16; 7:6,31-34,36
from the fire. From all the gifts they
bring me as most holy offerings, wheth-
er grain[t] or sin[u] or guilt offerings,[v] that 18:9
part belongs to you and your sons. 10Eat [t]Lev 2:1
it as something most holy; every male [u]Lev 6:25 [v]Lev 5:15; 7:7
shall eat it.[w] You must regard it as holy. 18:10
11"This also is yours: whatever is set [w]Lev 6:16
aside from the gifts of all the wave offerings[x] of the Israelites. I give this to 18:11
you and your sons and daughters as [x]Ex 29:26
your regular share. Everyone in your

household who is ceremonially clean[y] may eat it.

12“I give you all the finest olive oil and all the finest new wine and grain they give the LORD as the firstfruits of their harvest.[z] 13All the land’s firstfruits that they bring to the LORD will be yours.[a] Everyone in your household who is ceremonially clean may eat it.

14“Everything in Israel that is devoted[a] to the LORD[b] is yours. 15The first offspring of every womb, both man and animal, that is offered to the LORD is yours.[c] But you must redeem[d] every firstborn son and every firstborn male of unclean animals.[e] 16When they are a month old, you must redeem them at the redemption price set at five shekels[b][f] of silver, according to the sanctuary shekel,[g] which weighs twenty gerahs.

17“But you must not redeem the firstborn of an ox, a sheep or a goat; they are holy.[h] Sprinkle their blood[i] on the altar and burn their fat as an offering made by fire, an aroma pleasing to the LORD. 18Their meat is to be yours, just as the breast of the wave offering[j] and the right thigh are yours. 19Whatever is set aside from the holy offerings the Israelites present to the LORD I give to you and your sons and daughters as your regular share. It is an everlasting covenant of salt[k] before the LORD for both you and your offspring.”

20The LORD said to Aaron, “You will have no inheritance in their land, nor will you have any share among them;[l] I am your share and your inheritance[m] among the Israelites.

21“I give to the Levites all the tithes[n] in Israel as their inheritance[o] in return for the work they do while serving at the Tent of Meeting. 22From now on the Israelites must not go near the Tent of Meeting, or they will bear the consequences of their sin and will die.[p] 23It is the Levites who are to do the work at the Tent of Meeting and bear the responsibility for offenses against it. This is a lasting ordinance for the generations to come. They will receive no inheritance[q] among the Israelites. 24Instead, I give to the Levites as their inheritance the tithes that the Israelites present as an offering to the LORD. That is why I said concerning them: ‘They will have no inheritance among the Israelites.’”

25The LORD said to Moses, 26“Speak to the Levites and say to them: ‘When you receive from the Israelites the tithe I give you[r] as your inheritance, you must present a tenth of that tithe as the LORD’s offering.[s] 27Your offering will be reckoned to you as grain from the threshing floor or juice from the winepress. 28In this way you also will present an offering to the LORD from all the tithes[t] you receive from the Israelites. From these tithes you must give the LORD’s portion to Aaron the priest. 29You must present as the LORD’s portion the best and holiest part of everything given to you.’

30“Say to the Levites: ‘When you present the best part, it will be reckoned to you as the product of the threshing floor or the winepress.[u] 31You and your households may eat the rest of it anywhere, for it is your wages for your work at the Tent of Meeting. 32By presenting the best part[v] of it you will not be guilty in this matter; then you will not defile the holy offerings[w] of the Israelites, and you will not die.’”

The Water of Cleansing

19 The LORD said to Moses and Aaron: 2“This is a requirement of the law that the LORD has commanded: Tell the Israelites to bring you a red heifer[x] without defect or blemish[y] and that has never been under a yoke.[z] 3Give it to Eleazar[a] the priest; it is to be taken outside the camp[b] and slaughtered in his presence. 4Then Eleazar the priest is to take some of its blood on his finger and sprinkle[c] it seven times toward the front of the Tent of Meeting. 5While he watches, the heifer is to be burned—its hide, flesh, blood and offal.[d] 6The priest is to take some cedar wood, hyssop[e] and scarlet wool[f] and throw them onto the burning heifer. 7After that, the priest must wash his clothes and bathe himself with water.[g] He may then come into the camp, but he will be ceremonially unclean till evening. 8The man who burns it must also wash his clothes and bathe with water, and he too will be unclean till evening.

9“A man who is clean shall gather up

[a] *14* The Hebrew term refers to the irrevocable giving over of things or persons to the LORD. [b] *16* That is, about 2 ounces (about 55 grams)

18:11 [y]Lev 22:1-16
18:12 [z]Ex 23:19; Ne 10:35
18:13 [a]Ex 22:29; 23:19
18:14 [b]Lev 27:28
18:15 [c]Ex 13:2 [d]Nu 3:46 [e]Ex 13:13
18:16 [f]Lev 27:6 [g]Ex 30:13
18:17 [h]Dt 15:19 [i]Lev 3:2
18:18 [j]Lev 7:30
18:19 [k]Lev 2:13; 2Ch 13:5
18:20 [l]Dt 12:12 [m]Dt 10:9; 14:27; 18:1-2; Jos 13:33; Eze 44:28
18:21 [n]Dt 14:22; Mal 3:8 [o]Lev 27:30-33; Heb 7:5
18:22 [p]Lev 22:9; Nu 1:51
18:23 [q]ver 20
18:26 [r]ver 21 [s]Ne 10:38
18:28 [t]Mal 3:8
18:30 [u]ver 27
18:32 [v]Lev 22:15 [w]Lev 19:8
19:2 [x]Ge 15:9; Heb 9:13 [y]Lev 22:19-25 [z]Dt 21:3; 1Sa 6:7
19:3 [a]Nu 3:4 [b]Lev 4:12,21; Heb 13:11
19:4 [c]Lev 4:17
19:5 [d]Ex 29:14
19:6 [e]ver 18; Ps 51:7 [f]Lev 14:4
19:7 [g]Lev 11:25; 16:26,28; 22:6

19:9 [h]Heb 9:13; the ashes of the heifer[h] and put them
[i]ver 13; in a ceremonially clean place outside
Nu 8:7 the camp. They shall be kept by the
Israelite community for use in the water of cleansing;[i] it is for purification
from sin. 10The man who gathers up
the ashes of the heifer must also wash
his clothes, and he too will be unclean
till evening. This will be a lasting ordinance both for the Israelites and for the
aliens living among them.
19:11 [j]Lev 21:1; 11"Whoever touches the dead body[j]
Nu 5:2 [k]Nu 31:19 of anyone will be unclean for seven
days.[k] 12He must purify himself with
the water on the third day and on the
19:12 seventh day;[l] then he will be clean.
[l]ver 19; But if he does not purify himself on
Nu 31:19 the third and seventh days, he will not
be clean. 13Whoever touches the dead
19:13 body[m] of anyone and fails to purify him-
[m]Lev 20:3; [n]Lev 15:31; self defiles the LORD's tabernacle.[n] That
2Ch 36:14 person must be cut off from Israel.[o] Be-
[o]Lev 7:20; 22:3 cause the water of cleansing has not
[p]Hag 2:13 been sprinkled on him, he is unclean;[p]
his uncleanness remains on him.
14"This is the law that applies when a
person dies in a tent: Anyone who enters the tent and anyone who is in it
will be unclean for seven days, 15and
every open container without a lid fastened on it will be unclean.
16"Anyone out in the open who
touches someone who has been killed
with a sword or someone who has died
19:16 a natural death,[q] or anyone who touches
[q]Nu 31:19 [r]Mt 23:27 a human bone or a grave,[r] will be unclean for seven days.
17"For the unclean person, put some
19:17 [s]ver 9 ashes[s] from the burned purification offering into a jar and pour fresh water
over them. 18Then a man who is cer-
19:18 [t]ver 6 emonially clean is to take some hyssop,[t]
dip it in the water and sprinkle the tent
and all the furnishings and the people
who were there. He must also sprinkle
anyone who has touched a human bone
or a grave or someone who has been
killed or someone who has died a natural death. 19The man who is clean is to
sprinkle the unclean person on the third
and seventh days, and on the seventh
19:19 day he is to purify him.[u] The person
[u]Eze 36:25; Heb 10:22 being cleansed must wash his clothes
and bathe with water, and that evening
he will be clean. 20But if a person who
is unclean does not purify himself, he
must be cut off from the community,
because he has defiled the sanctuary of
the LORD. The water of cleansing has
not been sprinkled on him, and he is
unclean. 21This is a lasting ordinance
for them.
"The man who sprinkles the water
of cleansing must also wash his clothes,
and anyone who touches the water of
cleansing will be unclean till evening.
22Anything that an unclean[v] person 19:22 [v]Lev 5:2;
touches becomes unclean, and anyone Hag 2:13,14
who touches it becomes unclean till
evening."

Water From the Rock

20 In the first month the whole
Israelite community arrived at
the Desert of Zin,[w] and they stayed at 20:1 [w]Nu 13:21
Kadesh.[x] There Miriam[y] died and was [x]Nu 33:36 [y]Ex 15:20
buried.
2Now there was no water for the
community,[z] and the people gathered 20:2 [z]Ex 17:1
in opposition[a] to Moses and Aaron. [a]Nu 16:19
3They quarreled[b] with Moses and said, 20:3
"If only we had died when our broth- [b]Ex 17:2 [c]Nu 14:2;
ers fell dead before the LORD![c] 4Why 16:31-35
did you bring the LORD's community
into this desert, that we and our live-
stock should die here?[d] 5Why did you 20:4 [d]Ex 14:11;
bring us up out of Egypt to this terrible 17:3; Nu
place? It has no grain or figs, grapevines 14:3; 16:13
or pomegranates.[e] And there is no wa- 20:5 [e]Nu 16:14
ter to drink!"
6Moses and Aaron went from the assembly to the entrance to the Tent of
Meeting and fell facedown,[f] and the 20:6 [f]Nu 14:5
glory of the LORD[g] appeared to them. [g]Nu 16:19
7The LORD said to Moses, 8"Take the
staff,[h] and you and your brother Aaron 20:8 [h]Ex 4:17,20
gather the assembly together. Speak to [i]Ex 17:6;
that rock before their eyes and it will Isa 43:20
pour out its water.[i] You will bring water
out of the rock for the community so
they and their livestock can drink."
9So Moses took the staff from the
LORD's presence,[j] just as he command- 20:9
ed him. 10He and Aaron gathered the [j]Nu 17:10
assembly together in front of the rock
and Moses said to them, "Listen, you
rebels, must we bring you water out
of this rock?"[k] 11Then Moses raised his 20:10 [k]Ps 106:32,33
arm and struck the rock twice with his
staff. Water[l] gushed out, and the com- 20:11 [l]Ex 17:6;
munity and their livestock drank. Dt 8:15;
12But the LORD said to Moses and Ps 78:16;
Aaron, "Because you did not trust in Isa 48:2; 1Co 10:4
me enough to honor me as holy[m] in 20:12
the sight of the Israelites, you will not [m]Nu 27:14

WEEK 36 SELF-CONTROL

DAY ONE

1 SELF-CONTROL, MANAGING MY MOODS

Read Numbers 20:6–13

Moses lost his cool at the rock. If he had retained a therapist, he could have made a pretty good case for why he behaved as he did. First, the people were always complaining—one of the perennial downers of leadership. Second, they were taking too long to become ready to conquer Canaan. This preparation period ultimately took 40 years, and most great leaders can't stand long, drawn-out campaigns. Moses didn't get a lot of support from other team leaders—like Aaron, who made a golden calf while Moses was away from camp (see Exodus 32:1–6). And there was Korah, who stirred up a popular rebellion against Moses' leadership (see Numbers 16). The spies said Moses' objectives were unrealistic and the whole process should be abandoned (ch. 13). Moses' sister Miriam had publicly opposed his leadership, and his brother Aaron took her side (ch. 12).

With all of this baggage to deal with, it seems understandable that Moses would lose his cool. But God reminded Moses, and us, that the failure to manage our moods doesn't only make us look foolish, it also diminishes our ability to follow the leadership of God. When evangelists become indulgent and allow their emotions to dictate their actions, people not only stop supporting their ministry, but they may also turn away from God. Our responsibility is similar to Moses' responsibility: We are to manage our moods and reflect our obedience to God in our actions.

MEMORIZE THIS WEEK

PSALM 42:11

Why are you downcast, O my soul?
Why so disturbed within me?
Put your hope in God,
for I will yet praise him.

DAY TWO

2 SELF-CONTROL AND THE PURPOSE OF GOD IN MY LIFE

King Saul let his emotions control his actions, and he lost an important and potentially beneficial relationship with David as a result. When we are faced with demons that vie for control of our souls, what will we do in response? How will we choose to live? The answer lies in self-control. *Turn to 1 Samuel 19:8–17, page 335, for today's study.*

DAY THREE

3 SELF-CONTROL AND MY RELATIONSHIP WITH CHRIST

Jesus, facing the end of his earthly ministry and his ensuing death and resurrection, sent messengers into some Samaritan villages to invite the residents to participate in the coming baptism of joy that would soon envelop the world. When the Samaritans did not welcome them, James and John lost control. Had God left heaven's thunderbolts in their keeping, they would have destroyed the Samaritans with fire. Their uncontrolled moods made God appear to be as stern as they were. *Turn to Luke 9:51–56, page 1215, for today's study.*

DAY FOUR

4 SELF-CONTROL AND MY SERVICE TO OTHERS

Acts 15:39 reveals a quarrel between two godly men: Barnabas, who had sold his farm on Cyprus and given all to Christ, and Paul, who had given up a distinguished career in Jewish law. These two spiritual giants were quarreling. No one in Scripture is so holy as to be free of human failings, but the failure to manage our moods may scar the reputation of even the most noble. *Turn to Acts 15:36–41, page 1312, for today's study.*

DAY FIVE

5 SELF-CONTROL AND ITS PLACE IN MY PERSONAL WORSHIP

Edom, the mountain fortress, would be brought low. Perched high in the mountains and carved from the rock, this nation trusted in topography as its strength and in its high and precipitous cliffs as protection. But God said Edom's self-protection encouraged its indulgence, and the nation would be brought down. *Turn to Obadiah 1–4, page 1064, for today's study.*

Week 37, Love, the Unconditional Longing of God, begins on page 89, Exodus 19:3–6.
To begin a topical study on the Fruit of the Spirit, Self-Control, turn to the Topical Index, page 1548.

GOODNESS

HOLINESS AND HUMAN EMPOWERMENT

Numbers 20:12

God is not our chummy consort. Let him be holy. Let him be separate. "What a Friend We Have in Jesus" is best sung by those who know the song "Holy, Holy, Holy."

bring this community into the land I give them."[n]

13These were the waters of Meribah,[a][o] where the Israelites quarreled[p] with the LORD and where he showed himself holy among them.

20:12 [n]ver 24; Dt 1:37; 3:27
20:13 [o]Ex 17:7 [p]Dt 33:8; Ps 95:8; 106:32

Edom Denies Israel Passage

14Moses sent messengers from Kadesh[q] to the king of Edom,[r] saying:

"This is what your brother Israel says: You know[s] about all the hardships that have come upon us. 15Our forefathers went down into Egypt,[t] and we lived there many years.[u] The Egyptians mistreated us[v] and our fathers, 16but when we cried out to the LORD, he heard our cry[w] and sent an angel[x] and brought us out of Egypt.

"Now we are here at Kadesh, a town on the edge of your territory. 17Please let us pass through your country. We will not go through any field or vineyard, or drink water from any well. We will travel along the king's highway and not turn to the right or to the left until we have passed through your territory.[y]"

20:14 [q]Jdg 11:16-17 [r]Dt 2:4 [s]Jos 2:11; 9:9
20:15 [t]Ge 46:6 [u]Ge 15:13; Ex 12:40 [v]Ex 1:11; Dt 26:6
20:16 [w]Ex 2:23; 3:7 [x]Ex 14:19
20:17 [y]Nu 21:22

18But Edom answered:

"You may not pass through here; if you try, we will march out and attack you with the sword."

19The Israelites replied:

"We will go along the main road, and if we or our livestock[z] drink any of your water, we will pay for it.[a] We only want to pass through on foot—nothing else."

20:19 [z]Ex 12:38 [a]Dt 2:6,28

20Again they answered:

"You may not pass through."

Then Edom came out against them with a large and powerful army. 21Since Edom refused to let them go through their territory, Israel turned away from them.[b]

20:21 [b]Dt 2:8; Jdg 11:18

The Death of Aaron

22The whole Israelite community set out from Kadesh and came to Mount Hor.[c] 23At Mount Hor, near the border of Edom,[d] the LORD said to Moses and Aaron, 24"Aaron will be gathered to his people.[e] He will not enter the land I give the Israelites, because both of you rebelled against my command[f] at the waters of Meribah. 25Get Aaron and his son Eleazar and take them up Mount Hor.[g] 26Remove Aaron's garments and put them on his son Eleazar, for Aaron will be gathered to his people;[h] he will die there."

27Moses did as the LORD commanded: They went up Mount Hor in the sight of the whole community. 28Moses removed Aaron's garments and put them on his son Eleazar.[i] And Aaron died there[j] on top of the mountain. Then Moses and Eleazar came down from the mountain, 29and when the whole community learned that Aaron had died, the entire house of Israel mourned for him[k] thirty days.

20:22 [c]Nu 33:37
20:23 [d]Nu 33:37
20:24 [e]Ge 25:8 [f]ver 10
20:25 [g]Nu 33:38
20:26 [h]ver 24
20:28 [i]Ex 29:29 [j]Nu 33:38; Dt 10:6; 32:50
20:29 [k]Dt 34:8

Arad Destroyed

21 When the Canaanite king of Arad,[l] who lived in the Negev,[m] heard that Israel was coming along the road to Atharim, he attacked the Israelites and captured some of them. 2Then Israel made this vow to the LORD: "If you will deliver these people into our hands, we will totally destroy[b] their cities." 3The LORD listened to Israel's plea and gave the Canaanites over to them. They completely destroyed them and their towns; so the place was named Hormah.[c]

21:1 [l]Nu 33:40; Jos 12:14 [m]Jdg 1:9,16

The Bronze Snake

4They traveled from Mount Hor[n] along the route to the Red Sea,[d] to go around Edom. But the people grew

21:4 [n]Nu 20:22

[a]*13 Meribah* means *quarreling.* [b]*2* The Hebrew term refers to the irrevocable giving over of things or persons to the LORD, often by totally destroying them; also in verse 3. [c]*3 Hormah* means *destruction.* [d]*4* Hebrew *Yam Suph*; that is, Sea of Reeds

21:4 [o]Dt 2:8; Jdg 11:18
impatient on the way;[o] 5they spoke
against God[p] and against Moses, and
21:5 [p]Ps 78:19 [q]Nu 14:2,3 [r]Nu 11:6
said, "Why have you brought us up out
of Egypt to die in the desert?[q] There is
no bread! There is no water! And we detest this miserable food!"[r]
6Then the LORD sent venomous
21:6 [s]Dt 8:15; Jer 8:17 [t]1Co 10:9
snakes[s] among them; they bit the people
and many Israelites died.[t] 7The people
came to Moses[u] and said, "We sinned
21:7 [u]Ps 78:34; Hos 5:15 [v]Ex 8:8; Ac 8:24 [w]Nu 11:2
when we spoke against the LORD and
against you. Pray that the LORD[v] will
take the snakes away from us." So Moses prayed[w] for the people.
8The LORD said to Moses, "Make a
21:8 [x]Jn 3:14
snake and put it up on a pole;[x] anyone
who is bitten can look at it and live."
9So Moses made a bronze snake[y] and
21:9 [y]2Ki 18:4 [z]Jn 3:14-15
put it up on a pole. Then when anyone
was bitten by a snake and looked at the
bronze snake, he lived.[z]

PEACE

THE HEALING SNAKES OF HUMILITY

Numbers 21:9

There is a serpent on a pole.
Look and live or turn and die!
The snakes of Sinai never are a problem
To those who can confess.
Pride is the only venom that destroys.

The Journey to Moab

10The Israelites moved on and
21:10 [a]Nu 33:43
camped at Oboth.[a] 11Then they set out
from Oboth and camped in Iye Abarim,
21:11 [b]Nu 33:44
in the desert that faces Moab[b] toward
the sunrise. 12From there they moved
21:12 [c]Dt 2:13,14
on and camped in the Zered Valley.[c]
13They set out from there and camped
21:13 [d]Nu 22:36; Jdg 11:13,18
alongside the Arnon[d], which is in the
desert extending into Amorite territory.
The Arnon is the border of Moab, between Moab and the Amorites. 14That
is why the Book of the Wars of the
LORD says:

"... Waheb in Suphah[a] and the
ravines,
the Arnon 15and[b] the slopes of the
ravines
21:15 [e]ver 28; Dt 2:9,18
that lead to the site of Ar[e]
and lie along the border of
Moab."

16From there they continued on to
21:16 [f]Jdg 9:21
Beer,[f] the well where the LORD said
to Moses, "Gather the people together
and I will give them water."
21:17 [g]Ex 15:1
17Then Israel sang this song:[g]

"Spring up, O well!
Sing about it,
18about the well that the princes dug,
that the nobles of the people
sank—
the nobles with scepters and
staffs."

Then they went from the desert to Mattanah, 19from Mattanah to Nahaliel,
from Nahaliel to Bamoth, 20and from
Bamoth to the valley in Moab where
the top of Pisgah overlooks the wasteland.

Defeat of Sihon and Og

21Israel sent messengers to say to Sihon[h] king of the Amorites:
21:21 [h]Dt 1:4; 2:26-27; Jdg 11:19-21

22"Let us pass through your
country. We will not turn aside
into any field or vineyard, or drink
water from any well. We will travel
along the king's highway until we
have passed through your territory.[i]"
21:22 [i]Nu 20:17

23But Sihon would not let Israel pass
through his territory.[j] He mustered his
21:23 [j]Nu 20:21 [k]Dt 2:32; Jdg 11:20
entire army and marched out into the
desert against Israel. When he reached
Jahaz,[k] he fought with Israel. 24Israel,
21:24 [l]Dt 2:33; Ps 135:10-11; Am 2:9 [m]Dt 2:37
however, put him to the sword[l] and
took over his land from the Arnon
to the Jabbok, but only as far as the
Ammonites,[m] because their border was
fortified. 25Israel captured all the cities
of the Amorites[n] and occupied them,
21:25 [n]Nu 13:29; Jdg 10:11; Am 2:10
including Heshbon and all its surrounding settlements. 26Heshbon was the city
of Sihon[o] king of the Amorites, who
21:26 [o]Dt 29:7; Ps 135:11
had fought against the former king of
Moab and had taken from him all his
land as far as the Arnon.
27That is why the poets say:

"Come to Heshbon and let it be
rebuilt;
let Sihon's city be restored.

28"Fire went out from Heshbon,
21:28 [p]Jer 48:45 [q]ver 15
a blaze from the city of Sihon.[p]
It consumed Ar[q] of Moab,

[a]*14* The meaning of the Hebrew for this phrase is uncertain. [b]*14,15* Or *"I have been given from Suphah and the ravines / of the Arnon [15]to*

21:28 [r]Nu 22:41; Isa 15:2

the citizens of Arnon's heights.[r]

21:29 [s]Isa 25:10; Jer 48:46 [t]Jdg 11:24; 1Ki 11:7,33; 2Ki 23:13; Jer 48:7,46 [u]Isa 15:5 [v]Isa 16:2

29 Woe to you, O Moab![s]
You are destroyed, O people of
Chemosh![t]
He has given up his sons as fugitives[u]
and his daughters as captives[v]
to Sihon king of the Amorites.

30 "But we have overthrown them;
Heshbon is destroyed all the way
to Dibon.[w]

21:30 [w]Nu 32:3; Isa 15:2; Jer 48:18,22

We have demolished them as far as
Nophah,
which extends to Medeba."

31 So Israel settled in the land of the
Amorites.

21:32 [x]Nu 32:1,3,35; Jer 48:32

32 After Moses had sent spies to Jazer,[x]
the Israelites captured its surrounding
settlements and drove out the Amorites
who were there. 33 Then they turned

21:33 [y]Dt 3:3 [z]Dt 3:4 [a]Dt 1:4; 3:1,10; Jos 13:12,31

and went up along the road toward
Bashan[y,z] and Og king of Bashan and
his whole army marched out to meet
them in battle at Edrei.[a]

34 The LORD said to Moses, "Do not
be afraid of him, for I have handed him
over to you, with his whole army and
his land. Do to him what you did to Sihon king of the Amorites, who reigned
in Heshbon.[b]"

21:34 [b]Dt 3:2

35 So they struck him down, together
with his sons and his whole army, leaving them no survivors. And they took
possession of his land.

Balak Summons Balaam

22 Then the Israelites traveled to
the plains of Moab and camped
along the Jordan across from Jericho.[a] [c]

22:1 [c]Nu 33:48

2 Now Balak son of Zippor[d] saw all
that Israel had done to the Amorites,

22:2 [d]Jdg 11:25

3 and Moab was terrified because there
were so many people. Indeed, Moab
was filled with dread[e] because of the Israelites.

22:3 [e]Ex 15:15

4 The Moabites said to the elders of
Midian, "This horde is going to lick up
everything around us, as an ox licks up
the grass of the field."

So Balak son of Zippor, who was king
of Moab at that time, 5 sent messengers
to summon Balaam son of Beor,[f] who
was at Pethor, near the River,[b] in his native land. Balak said:

22:5 [f]Dt 23:4; Jos 13:22; 24:9; Ne 13:2; Mic 6:5; 2Pe 2:15

"A people has come out of
Egypt; they cover the face of the
land and have settled next to me.
6 Now come and put a curse[g] on
these people, because they are too
powerful for me. Perhaps then I
will be able to defeat them and
drive them out of the country. For
I know that those you bless are
blessed, and those you curse are
cursed."

22:6 [g]ver 12,17; Nu 23:7, 11,13

7 The elders of Moab and Midian left,
taking with them the fee for divination.[h]
When they came to Balaam, they told
him what Balak had said.

22:7 [h]Nu 23:23; 24:1

8 "Spend the night here," Balaam said
to them, "and I will bring you back the
answer the LORD gives me.[i]" So the
Moabite princes stayed with him.

22:8 [i]ver 19

9 God came to Balaam[j] and asked,[k]
"Who are these men with you?"

22:9 [j]Ge 20:3 [k]ver 20

10 Balaam said to God, "Balak son
of Zippor, king of Moab, sent me this
message: 11 'A people that has come out
of Egypt covers the face of the land.
Now come and put a curse on them for
me. Perhaps then I will be able to fight
them and drive them away.' "

12 But God said to Balaam, "Do not
go with them. You must not put a
curse on those people, because they are
blessed.[l]"

22:12 [l]Ge 12:2; 22:17; Nu 23:20

13 The next morning Balaam got up
and said to Balak's princes, "Go back
to your own country, for the LORD has
refused to let me go with you."

14 So the Moabite princes returned
to Balak and said, "Balaam refused to
come with us."

15 Then Balak sent other princes, more
numerous and more distinguished than
the first. 16 They came to Balaam and
said:

"This is what Balak son of Zippor says: Do not let anything keep
you from coming to me, 17 because
I will reward you handsomely[m]
and do whatever you say. Come
and put a curse[n] on these people
for me."

22:17 [m]ver 37; Nu 24:11 [n]ver 6

18 But Balaam answered them, "Even
if Balak gave me his palace filled with
silver and gold, I could not do anything
great or small to go beyond the command of the LORD my God.[o] 19 Now
stay here tonight as the others did, and

22:18 [o]ver 38; Nu 23:12,26; 24:13; 1Ki 22:14; 2Ch 18:13; Jer 42:4

[a]*1* Hebrew *Jordan of Jericho*; possibly an ancient name for the Jordan River [b]*5* That is, the Euphrates

I will find out what else the LORD will
tell me.[p]"
20That night God came to Balaam[q]
and said, "Since these men have come
to summon you, go with them, but do
only what I tell you."[r]

Balaam's Donkey

21Balaam got up in the morning,
saddled his donkey and went with the
princes of Moab. 22But God was very
angry[s] when he went, and the angel of
the LORD[t] stood in the road to oppose
him. Balaam was riding on his donkey,
and his two servants were with him.
23When the donkey saw the angel of
the LORD standing in the road with a
drawn sword[u] in his hand, she turned
off the road into a field. Balaam beat
her to get her[v] back on the road.
24Then the angel of the LORD stood
in a narrow path between two vineyards, with walls on both sides. 25When
the donkey saw the angel of the LORD,
she pressed close to the wall, crushing
Balaam's foot against it. So he beat her
again.
26Then the angel of the LORD moved
on ahead and stood in a narrow place
where there was no room to turn, either
to the right or to the left. 27When the
donkey saw the angel of the LORD, she
lay down under Balaam, and he was angry[w] and beat her with his staff. 28Then
the LORD opened the donkey's mouth,[x]
and she said to Balaam, "What have I
done to you to make you beat me these
three times?[y]"
29Balaam answered the donkey, "You
have made a fool of me! If I had a
sword in my hand, I would kill you
right now.[z]"
30The donkey said to Balaam, "Am I
not your own donkey, which you have
always ridden, to this day? Have I been
in the habit of doing this to you?"
"No," he said.
31Then the LORD opened Balaam's
eyes,[a] and he saw the angel of the LORD
standing in the road with his sword
drawn. So he bowed low and fell facedown.
32The angel of the LORD asked him,
"Why have you beaten your donkey
these three times? I have come here to
oppose you because your path is a reckless one before me.[a] 33The donkey saw
me and turned away from me these
three times. If she had not turned away,
I would certainly have killed you by
now,[b] but I would have spared her."
34Balaam said to the angel of the
LORD, "I have sinned.[c] I did not realize you were standing in the road to oppose me. Now if you are displeased, I
will go back."
35The angel of the LORD said to
Balaam, "Go with the men, but speak
only what I tell you." So Balaam went
with the princes of Balak.
36When Balak heard that Balaam was
coming, he went out to meet him at the
Moabite town on the Arnon[d] border,
at the edge of his territory. 37Balak said
to Balaam, "Did I not send you an urgent summons? Why didn't you come
to me? Am I really not able to reward
you?"
38"Well, I have come to you now,"
Balaam replied. "But can I say just anything? I must speak only what God puts
in my mouth."[e]
39Then Balaam went with Balak to
Kiriath Huzoth. 40Balak sacrificed cattle
and sheep,[f] and gave some to Balaam
and the princes who were with him.
41The next morning Balak took Balaam
up to Bamoth Baal,[g] and from there he
saw part of the people.[h]

Balaam's First Oracle

23 Balaam said, "Build me seven
altars here, and prepare seven
bulls and seven rams[i] for me." 2Balak
did as Balaam said, and the two of them
offered a bull and a ram on each altar.[j]
3Then Balaam said to Balak, "Stay
here beside your offering while I go
aside. Perhaps the LORD will come to
meet with me.[k] Whatever he reveals to
me I will tell you." Then he went off to
a barren height.
4God met with him,[l] and Balaam
said, "I have prepared seven altars, and
on each altar I have offered a bull and
a ram."
5The LORD put a message in Balaam's
mouth[m] and said, "Go back to Balak
and give him this message."[n]
6So he went back to him and found
him standing beside his offering, with
all the princes of Moab.[o] 7Then Balaam[p]
uttered his oracle:[q]

[a]*32* The meaning of the Hebrew for this clause is uncertain.

22:19 [p]ver 8
22:20 [q]Ge 20:3 [r]ver 35,38; Nu 23:5,12, 16,26; 24:13; 2Ch 18:13
22:22 [s]Ex 4:14 [t]Ge 16:7; Ex 23:20; Jdg 13:3,6,13
22:23 [u]Jos 5:13 [v]ver 25,27
22:27 [w]Nu 11:1; Jas 1:19
22:28 [x]2Pe 2:16 [y]ver 32
22:29 [z]Dt 25:4; Pr 12:10; 27:23-27; Mt 15:19
22:31 [a]Ge 21:19
22:33 [b]ver 29
22:34 [c]Ge 39:9; Nu 14:40; 1Sa 15:24,30; 2Sa 12:13; 24:10; Job 33:27; Ps 51:4
22:36 [d]Nu 21:13
22:38 [e]Nu 23:5,16,26
22:40 [f]Nu 23:1,14,29; Eze 45:23
22:41 [g]Nu 21:28 [h]Nu 23:13
23:1 [i]Nu 22:40
23:2 [j]ver 14,30
23:3 [k]ver 15
23:4 [l]ver 16
23:5 [m]Dt 18:18; Jer 1:9 [n]Nu 22:20
23:6 [o]ver 17
23:7 [p]Nu 22:5 [q]ver 18; Nu 24:3,21

"Balak brought me from Aram,
the king of Moab from the eastern mountains.
'Come,' he said, 'curse Jacob for me;
come, denounce Israel.'[r]
8 How can I curse
those whom God has not cursed?[s]
How can I denounce
those whom the LORD has not denounced?
9 From the rocky peaks I see them,
from the heights I view them.
I see a people who live apart
and do not consider themselves
one of the nations.[t]
10 Who can count the dust of Jacob[u]
or number the fourth part of Israel?
Let me die the death of the righteous,[v]
and may my end be like theirs![w]"

11 Balak said to Balaam, "What have you done to me? I brought you to curse my enemies, but you have done nothing but bless them!"[x]

12 He answered, "Must I not speak what the LORD puts in my mouth?"[y]

Balaam's Second Oracle

13 Then Balak said to him, "Come with me to another place where you can see them; you will see only a part but not all of them. And from there, curse them for me." 14 So he took him to the field of Zophim on the top of Pisgah, and there he built seven altars and offered a bull and a ram on each altar.[z]

15 Balaam said to Balak, "Stay here beside your offering while I meet with him over there."

16 The LORD met with Balaam and put a message in his mouth[a] and said, "Go back to Balak and give him this message."

17 So he went to him and found him standing beside his offering, with the princes of Moab. Balak asked him, "What did the LORD say?"

18 Then he uttered his oracle:

"Arise, Balak, and listen;
hear me, son of Zippor.
19 God is not a man,[b] that he should lie,
nor a son of man, that he should change his mind.[c]
Does he speak and then not act?

23:7 [r]Nu 22:6; Dt 23:4
23:8 [s]Nu 22:12
23:9 [t]Ex 33:16; Dt 32:8; 33:28
23:10 [u]Ge 13:16 [v]Ps 116:15; Isa 57:1 [w]Ps 37:37
23:11 [x]Nu 24:10; Ne 13:2
23:12 [y]Nu 22:20,38
23:14 [z]ver 2
23:16 [a]Nu 22:38
23:19 [b]Isa 55:9; Hos 11:9 [c]1Sa 15:29; Mal 3:6; Tit 1:2; Jas 1:17

Does he promise and not fulfill?
20 I have received a command to bless;
he has blessed,[d] and I cannot change it.[e]
21 "No misfortune is seen in Jacob,[f]
no misery observed in Israel.[a][g]
The LORD their God is with them;[h]
the shout of the King[i] is among them.
22 God brought them out of Egypt;[j]
they have the strength of a wild ox.[k]
23 There is no sorcery against Jacob,
no divination[l] against Israel.
It will now be said of Jacob
and of Israel, 'See what God has done!'
24 The people rise like a lioness;[m]
they rouse themselves like a lion[n]
that does not rest till he devours his prey
and drinks the blood of his victims."

25 Then Balak said to Balaam, "Neither curse them at all nor bless them at all!"

26 Balaam answered, "Did I not tell you I must do whatever the LORD says?"

Balaam's Third Oracle

27 Then Balak said to Balaam, "Come, let me take you to another place.[o] Perhaps it will please God to let you curse them for me from there." 28 And Balak took Balaam to the top of Peor,[p] overlooking the wasteland.

29 Balaam said, "Build me seven altars here, and prepare seven bulls and seven rams for me." 30 Balak did as Balaam had said, and offered a bull and a ram on each altar.

24

Now when Balaam saw that it pleased the LORD to bless Israel, he did not resort to sorcery[q] as at other times, but turned his face toward the desert.[r] 2 When Balaam looked out and saw Israel encamped tribe by tribe, the Spirit of God came upon him[s] 3 and he uttered his oracle:

"The oracle of Balaam son of Beor,
the oracle of one whose eye sees clearly,

[a]21 Or *He has not looked on Jacob's offenses / or on the wrongs found in Israel.*

23:20 [d]Ge 22:17; Nu 22:12 [e]Isa 43:13
23:21 [f]Ps 32:2,5; Ro 4:7-8 [g]Isa 40:2; Jer 50:20 [h]Ex 29:45,46; Ps 145:18 [i]Dt 33:5; Ps 89:15-18
23:22 [j]Nu 24:8 [k]Dt 33:17; Job 39:9
23:23 [l]Nu 24:1; Jos 13:22
23:24 [m]Na 2:11 [n]Ge 49:9
23:27 [o]ver 13
23:28 [p]Ps 106:28
24:1 [q]Nu 23:23 [r]Nu 23:28
24:2 [s]Nu 11:25,26; 1Sa 10:10; 19:20; 2Ch 15:1

24:4 [t]Nu 22:20 [u]Ge 15:1

4 the oracle of one who hears the
words of God,[t]
who sees a vision from the
Almighty,[a][u]
who falls prostrate, and whose
eyes are opened:

5 "How beautiful are your tents,
O Jacob,
your dwelling places, O Israel!

6 "Like valleys they spread out,
like gardens beside a river,
like aloes[v] planted by the LORD,
like cedars beside the waters.[w]

24:6 [v]Ps 45:8 [w]Ps 1:3; 104:16

7 Water will flow from their
buckets;
their seed will have abundant
water.

"Their king will be greater than
Agag;[x]
their kingdom will be exalted.[y]

24:7 [x]2Sa 15:8 [y]2Sa 5:12; 1Ch 14:2; Ps 145:11-13

8 "God brought them out of Egypt;
they have the strength of a wild
ox.
They devour hostile nations
and break their bones in
pieces;[z]
with their arrows they pierce
them.[a]

24:8 [z]Ps 2:9; Jer 50:17 [a]Ps 45:5

9 Like a lion they crouch and lie
down,
like a lioness[b]—who dares to rouse
them?

"May those who bless you be
blessed
and those who curse you be
cursed!"[c]

24:9 [b]Ge 49:9; Nu 23:24 [c]Ge 12:3

10 Then Balak's anger burned against
Balaam. He struck his hands together[d]
and said to him, "I summoned you to
curse my enemies, but you have blessed
them[e] these three times.[f] 11 Now leave
at once and go home! I said I would reward you handsomely,[g] but the LORD
has kept you from being rewarded."
12 Balaam answered Balak, "Did I
not tell the messengers you sent me,[h]
13 'Even if Balak gave me his palace filled
with silver and gold, I could not do
anything of my own accord, good or
bad, to go beyond the command of the
LORD[i]—and I must say only what the
LORD says'?[j] 14 Now I am going back
to my people, but come, let me warn
you of what this people will do to your
people in days to come."[k]

24:10 [d]Eze 21:14 [e]Nu 23:11 [f]Ne 13:2
24:11 [g]Nu 22:17
24:12 [h]Nu 22:18
24:13 [i]Nu 22:18 [j]Nu 22:20
24:14 [k]Ge 49:1; Nu 31:8,16; Da 2:28; Mic 6:5

Balaam's Fourth Oracle

15 Then he uttered his oracle:

"The oracle of Balaam son of Beor,
the oracle of one whose eye sees
clearly,
16 the oracle of one who hears the
words of God,
who has knowledge from the Most
High,
who sees a vision from the Almighty,
who falls prostrate, and whose
eyes are opened:

17 "I see him, but not now;
I behold him, but not near.[l]
A star will come out of Jacob;[m]
a scepter will rise out of Israel.[n]
He will crush the foreheads of
Moab,[o]
the skulls[b] of[c] all the sons of
Sheth.[d]
18 Edom[p] will be conquered;
Seir, his enemy, will be conquered,
but Israel will grow strong.
19 A ruler will come out of Jacob[q]
and destroy the survivors of the
city."

24:17 [l]Rev 1:7 [m]Mt 2:2 [n]Ge 49:10 [o]Nu 21:29; Isa 15:1-16:14
24:18 [p]Am 9:12
24:19 [q]Ge 49:10; Mic 5:2

JOY

TWINKLE, TWINKLE, JACOB'S STAR

Numbers 24:17

There, in a desert place, astronomy surpassed science. There, with timeless Vega and eternal Betelgeuse, now stood a star of Jacob. For a thousand ages the sky had waited on tiptoe till the heavens birthed this star—a new sun for God's Son—a twinkle in timelessness.

Balaam's Final Oracles

20 Then Balaam saw Amalek[r] and uttered his oracle:

"Amalek was first among the nations,
but he will come to ruin at last."

21 Then he saw the Kenites[s] and uttered his oracle:

"Your dwelling place is secure,
your nest is set in a rock;

24:20 [r]Ex 17:14
24:21 [s]Ge 15:19

[a]4 Hebrew *Shaddai*; also in verse 16
[b]17 Samaritan Pentateuch (see also Jer. 48:45); the meaning of the word in the Masoretic Text is uncertain. [c]17 Or possibly *Moab, / batter* [d]17 Or *all the noisy boasters*

24:22 [t]Ge 10:22

22 yet you Kenites will be destroyed
when Asshur[t] takes you captive."

23 Then he uttered his oracle:

"Ah, who can live when God does
this?[a]

24:24 [u]Ge 10:4 [v]Ge 10:21 [w]ver 20

24 Ships will come from the shores of
Kittim;[u]
they will subdue Asshur and Eber,[v]
but they too will come to ruin.[w]"

24:25 [x]Nu 31:8

25 Then Balaam[x] got up and returned home and Balak went his own way.

Moab Seduces Israel

25:1 [y]Jos 2:1; Mic 6:5 [z]1Co 10:8; Rev 2:14 [a]Nu 31:16

25 While Israel was staying in Shittim,[y] the men began to indulge in sexual immorality[z] with Moabite women,[a] 2 who invited them to the sacrifices[b] to their gods.[c] The people ate and bowed down before these gods.

25:2 [b]Ex 34:15 [c]Ex 20:5; Dt 32:38; 1Co 10:20

3 So Israel joined in worshiping the Baal of Peor.[d] And the LORD's anger burned against them.

25:3 [d]Ps 106:28; Hos 9:10

4 The LORD said to Moses, "Take all the leaders of these people, kill them and expose them in broad daylight before the LORD,[e] so that the LORD's fierce anger[f] may turn away from Israel."

25:4 [e]Dt 4:3 [f]Dt 13:17

5 So Moses said to Israel's judges, "Each of you must put to death[g] those of your men who have joined in worshiping the Baal of Peor."

25:5 [g]Ex 32:27

6 Then an Israelite man brought to his family a Midianite woman right before the eyes of Moses and the whole assembly of Israel while they were weeping at the entrance to the Tent of Meeting. 7 When Phinehas son of Eleazar, the son of Aaron, the priest, saw this, he left the assembly, took a spear in his hand 8 and followed the Israelite into the tent. He drove the spear through both of them—through the Israelite and into the woman's body. Then the plague against the Israelites was stopped;[h] 9 but those who died in the plague[i] numbered 24,000.[j]

25:8 [h]Nu 16:46-48; Ps 106:30

25:9 [i]Nu 14:37; 1Co 10:8 [j]Nu 31:16

10 The LORD said to Moses, 11 "Phinehas son of Eleazar, the son of Aaron, the priest, has turned my anger away from the Israelites;[k] for he was as zealous as I am for my honor[l] among them, so that in my zeal I did not put an end to them. 12 Therefore tell him I am making my covenant of peace[m] with him. 13 He and his descendants will have a covenant of a lasting priesthood,[n] because he was zealous for the honor of his God and made atonement[o] for the Israelites."

25:11 [k]Ps 106:30 [l]Ex 20:5; Dt 32:16,21; Ps 78:58

25:12 [m]Isa 54:10; Eze 34:25; Mal 2:4,5

25:13 [n]Ex 29:9 [o]Nu 16:46

14 The name of the Israelite who was killed with the Midianite woman was Zimri son of Salu, the leader of a Simeonite family. 15 And the name of the Midianite woman who was put to death was Cozbi[p] daughter of Zur, a tribal chief of a Midianite family.[q]

25:15 [p]ver 18 [q]Nu 31:8; Jos 13:21

16 The LORD said to Moses, 17 "Treat the Midianites[r] as enemies and kill them, 18 because they treated you as enemies when they deceived you in the affair of Peor[s] and their sister Cozbi, the daughter of a Midianite leader, the woman who was killed when the plague came as a result of Peor."

25:17 [r]Nu 31:1-3

25:18 [s]Nu 31:16

The Second Census

26 After the plague the LORD said to Moses and Eleazar son of Aaron, the priest, 2 "Take a census[t] of the whole Israelite community by families—all those twenty years old or more who are able to serve in the army[u] of Israel." 3 So on the plains of Moab[v] by the Jordan across from Jericho,[b][w] Moses and Eleazar the priest spoke with them and said, 4 "Take a census of the men twenty years old or more, as the LORD commanded Moses."

26:2 [t]Ex 30:11-16; 38:25-26; Nu 1:2 [u]Nu 1:3

26:3 [v]Nu 33:48 [w]Nu 22:1

These were the Israelites who came out of Egypt:

5 The descendants of Reuben, the firstborn son of Israel, were:

26:5 [x]Ge 46:9 [y]1Ch 5:3

through Hanoch,[x] the Hanochite clan;
through Pallu,[y] the Palluite clan;
6 through Hezron, the Hezronite clan;
through Carmi, the Carmite clan.

7 These were the clans of Reuben; those numbered were 43,730.

8 The son of Pallu was Eliab, 9 and the sons of Eliab[z] were Nemuel, Dathan and Abiram. The same Dathan and Abiram were the community[a] officials who rebelled against Moses and Aaron and were among Korah's followers when they rebelled against the LORD.[b] 10 The earth opened its mouth and swallowed them along with Korah, whose follow-

26:9 [z]Nu 16:1 [a]Nu 1:16 [b]Nu 16:2

[a]*23* Masoretic Text; with a different word division of the Hebrew *A people will gather from the north.*
[b]*3* Hebrew *Jordan of Jericho*; possibly an ancient name for the Jordan River; also in verse 63

ers died when the fire devoured the 250 men. And they served as a warning sign.[c]
26:10 [c]Nu 16:35,38
11 The line of Korah,[d] however, did not die out.[e]
26:11 [d]Ex 6:24 [e]Nu 16:33; Dt 24:16

12 The descendants of Simeon by their clans were:
through Nemuel, the Nemuelite clan;
26:12 [f]1Ch 4:24
through Jamin,[f] the Jaminite clan;
through Jakin, the Jakinite clan;
26:13 [g]Ge 46:10
13 through Zerah,[g] the Zerahite clan;
through Shaul, the Shaulite clan.
14 These were the clans of Simeon; there
26:14 [h]Nu 1:23
were 22,200 men.[h]

15 The descendants of Gad by their clans were:
26:15 [i]Ge 46:16
through Zephon,[i] the Zephonite clan;
through Haggi, the Haggite clan;
through Shuni, the Shunite clan;
16 through Ozni, the Oznite clan;
through Eri, the Erite clan;
17 through Arodi,[a] the Arodite clan;
through Areli, the Arelite clan.
26:18 [j]Nu 1:25; Jos 13:24-28
18 These were the clans of Gad;[j] those numbered were 40,500.

19 Er and Onan were sons of Judah, but
26:19 [k]Ge 38:2-10; 46:12
they died[k] in Canaan.
20 The descendants of Judah by their clans were:
26:20 [l]1Ch 2:3 [m]Jos 7:17
through Shelah,[l] the Shelanite clan;
through Perez, the Perezite clan;
through Zerah, the Zerahite clan.[m]
21 The descendants of Perez were:
26:21 [n]Ru 4:19; 1Ch 2:9
through Hezron,[n] the Hezronite clan;
through Hamul, the Hamulite clan.
26:22 [o]Nu 1:27
22 These were the clans of Judah;[o] those numbered were 76,500.

23 The descendants of Issachar by their clans were:
26:23 [p]Ge 46:13; 1Ch 7:1
through Tola,[p] the Tolaite clan;
through Puah, the Puite[b] clan;
26:24 [q]Ge 46:13
24 through Jashub,[q] the Jashubite clan;
through Shimron, the Shimronite clan.
26:25 [r]Nu 1:29
25 These were the clans of Issachar;[r] those numbered were 64,300.

26 The descendants of Zebulun by their clans were:
through Sered, the Seredite clan;
through Elon, the Elonite clan;
through Jahleel, the Jahleelite clan.
27 These were the clans of Zebulun;[s] those numbered were 60,500.
26:27 [s]Nu 1:31

28 The descendants of Joseph by their clans through Manasseh and Ephraim were:

29 The descendants of Manasseh:
26:29 [t]Jos 17:1 [u]Jdg 11:1
through Makir,[t] the Makirite clan (Makir was the father of Gilead[u]);
through Gilead, the Gileadite clan.
30 These were the descendants of Gilead:
26:30 [v]Jos 17:2; Jdg 6:11
through Iezer,[v] the Iezerite clan;
through Helek, the Helekite clan;
31 through Asriel, the Asrielite clan;
through Shechem, the Shechemite clan;
32 through Shemida, the Shemidaite clan;
through Hepher, the Hepherite clan.
26:33 [w]Nu 27:1 [x]Nu 36:11
33 (Zelophehad[w] son of Hepher had no sons; he had only daughters, whose names were Mahlah, Noah, Hoglah, Milcah and Tirzah.)[x]
34 These were the clans of Manasseh; those numbered were 52,700.[y]
26:34 [y]Nu 1:35

35 These were the descendants of Ephraim by their clans:
through Shuthelah, the Shuthelahite clan;
through Beker, the Bekerite clan;
through Tahan, the Tahanite clan.
36 These were the descendants of Shuthelah:
through Eran, the Eranite clan.
37 These were the clans of Ephraim;[z] those numbered were 32,500.
26:37 [z]Nu 1:33

These were the descendants of Joseph by their clans.

38 The descendants of Benjamin[a] by their clans were:
26:38 [a]Ge 46:21; 1Ch 7:6
through Bela, the Belaite clan;

[a] *17* Samaritan Pentateuch and Syriac (see also Gen. 46:16); Masoretic Text *Arod* [b] *23* Samaritan Pentateuch, Septuagint, Vulgate and Syriac (see also 1 Chron. 7:1); Masoretic Text *through Puvah, the Punite*

through Ashbel, the Ashbelite clan;
through Ahiram, the Ahiramite clan;
39 through Shupham,[a] the Shuphamite clan;
through Hupham, the Huphamite clan.
40 The descendants of Bela through Ard[b] and Naaman were:
26:40 [b]Ge 46:21; 1Ch 8:3 through Ard,[b] the Ardite clan;
through Naaman, the Naamite clan.
26:41 [c]Nu 1:37 41 These were the clans of Benjamin;[c]
those numbered were 45,600.

42 These were the descendants of Dan by their clans:
26:42 [d]Ge 46:23 through Shuham,[d] the Shuhamite clan.
These were the clans of Dan: 43 All of them were Shuhamite clans; and those numbered were 64,400.

44 The descendants of Asher by their clans were:
through Imnah, the Imnite clan;
through Ishvi, the Ishvite clan;
through Beriah, the Beriite clan;
45 and through the descendants of Beriah:
through Heber, the Heberite clan;
through Malkiel, the Malkielite clan.
46 (Asher had a daughter named Serah.)
26:47 [e]Nu 1:41 47 These were the clans of Asher;[e] those
numbered were 53,400.

26:48 [f]Ge 46:24; 1Ch 7:13 48 The descendants of Naphtali[f] by their clans were:
through Jahzeel, the Jahzeelite clan;
through Guni, the Gunite clan;
49 through Jezer, the Jezerite clan;
through Shillem, the Shillemite clan.
26:50 [g]Nu 1:43 50 These were the clans of Naphtali;[g]
those numbered were 45,400.

51 The total number of the men of Israel
26:51 [h]Ex 12:37; 38:26; Nu 1:46; 11:21 was 601,730.[h]

52 The LORD said to Moses, 53 "The land is to be allotted to them as an inheritance based on the number of names.[i]
26:53 [i]Jos 11:23; 14:1; Eze 45:8 54 To a larger group give a larger inheritance, and to a smaller group a smaller one; each is to receive its inheritance according to the number[j] of those listed. 26:54 [j]Nu 33:54
55 Be sure that the land is distributed by lot.[k] What each group inherits will be 26:55 [k]Nu 34:14
according to the names for its ancestral tribe. 56 Each inheritance is to be distributed by lot among the larger and smaller groups."

57 These were the Levites[l] who were 26:57 [l]Ge 46:11; Ex 6:16-19
counted by their clans:
through Gershon, the Gershonite clan;
through Kohath, the Kohathite clan;
through Merari, the Merarite clan.
58 These also were Levite clans:
the Libnite clan,
the Hebronite clan,
the Mahlite clan,
the Mushite clan,
the Korahite clan.
(Kohath was the forefather of
Amram;[m] 59 the name of Amram's 26:58 [m]Ex 6:20
wife was Jochebed,[n] a descendant
of Levi, who was born to the 26:59 [n]Ex 2:1 [o]Ex 6:20
Levites[c] in Egypt. To Amram she bore Aaron, Moses[o] and their sister Miriam. 60 Aaron was the father of Nadab and Abihu, Eleazar
and Ithamar.[p] 61 But Nadab and 26:60 [p]Nu 3:2
Abihu[q] died when they made an 26:61 [q]Lev 10:1-2 [r]Nu 3:4
offering before the LORD with unauthorized fire.)[r]

62 All the male Levites a month old or more numbered 23,000.[s] They were not 26:62 [s]Nu 3:39 [t]Nu 1:47 [u]Nu 18:23 [v]Nu 2:33; Dt 10:9
counted[t] along with the other Israelites because they received no inheritance[u] among them.[v]

63 These are the ones counted by Moses and Eleazar the priest when they counted the Israelites on the plains of 26:63 [w]ver 3
Moab[w] by the Jordan across from Jericho. 64 Not one of them was among
those counted[x] by Moses and Aaron 26:64 [x]Nu 14:29; Dt 2:14-15; Heb 3:17
the priest when they counted the Israelites in the Desert of Sinai. 65 For
the LORD had told those Israelites they 26:65 [y]Nu 14:28; 1Co 10:5
would surely die in the desert,[y] and not

[a]*39* A few manuscripts of the Masoretic Text, Samaritan Pentateuch, Vulgate and Syriac (see also Septuagint); most manuscripts of the Masoretic Text *Shephupham* [b]*40* Samaritan Pentateuch and Vulgate (see also Septuagint); Masoretic Text does not have *through Ard.* [c]*59* Or *Jochebed, a daughter of Levi, who was born to Levi*

one of them was left except Caleb son of Jephunneh and Joshua son of Nun.[z]

Zelophehad's Daughters

27 The daughters of Zelophehad son[a] of Hepher,[b] the son of Gilead, the son of Makir,[c] the son of Manasseh, belonged to the clans of Manasseh son of Joseph. The names of the daughters were Mahlah, Noah, Hoglah, Milcah and Tirzah. They approached 2the entrance to the Tent of Meeting and stood before Moses, Eleazar the priest, the leaders and the whole assembly, and said, 3"Our father died in the desert.[d] He was not among Korah's followers, who banded together against the LORD,[e] but he died for his own sin and left no sons.[f] 4Why should our father's name disappear from his clan because he had no son? Give us property among our father's relatives."

5So Moses brought their case[g] before the LORD[h] 6and the LORD said to him, 7"What Zelophehad's daughters are saying is right. You must certainly give them property as an inheritance[i] among their father's relatives and turn their father's inheritance over to them.[j]

8"Say to the Israelites, 'If a man dies and leaves no son, turn his inheritance over to his daughter. 9If he has no daughter, give his inheritance to his brothers. 10If he has no brothers, give his inheritance to his father's brothers. 11If his father had no brothers, give his inheritance to the nearest relative in his clan, that he may possess it. This is to be a legal requirement[k] for the Israelites, as the LORD commanded Moses.' "

Joshua to Succeed Moses

12Then the LORD said to Moses, "Go up this mountain in the Abarim range[l] and see the land[m] I have given the Israelites. 13After you have seen it, you too will be gathered to your people,[n] as your brother Aaron[o] was, 14for when the community rebelled at the waters in the Desert of Zin, both of you disobeyed my command to honor me as holy[p] before their eyes." (These were the waters of Meribah[q] Kadesh, in the Desert of Zin.)

15Moses said to the LORD, 16"May the LORD, the God of the spirits of all mankind,[r] appoint a man over this community 17to go out and come in before them, one who will lead them out and bring them in, so the LORD's people will not be like sheep without a shepherd."[s]

18So the LORD said to Moses, "Take Joshua son of Nun, a man in whom is the spirit,[a][t] and lay your hand on him.[u] 19Have him stand before Eleazar the priest and the entire assembly and commission him[v] in their presence.[w] 20Give him some of your authority so the whole Israelite community will obey him.[x] 21He is to stand before Eleazar the priest, who will obtain decisions for him by inquiring[y] of the Urim[z] before the LORD. At his command he and the entire community of the Israelites will go out, and at his command they will come in."

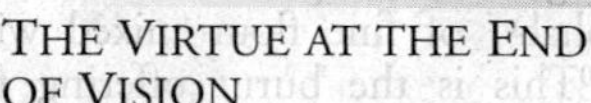

PEACE

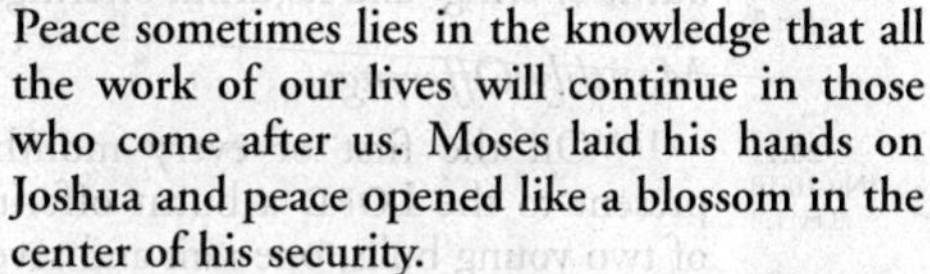

THE VIRTUE AT THE END OF VISION

Numbers 27:18

Peace sometimes lies in the knowledge that all the work of our lives will continue in those who come after us. Moses laid his hands on Joshua and peace opened like a blossom in the center of his security.

We die with dreams and grand theophanies
In debt to those who bear our legacies.

22Moses did as the LORD commanded him. He took Joshua and had him stand before Eleazar the priest and the whole assembly. 23Then he laid his hands on him and commissioned him, as the LORD instructed through Moses.

Daily Offerings

28 The LORD said to Moses, 2"Give this command to the Israelites and say to them: 'See that you present to me at the appointed time the food[a] for my offerings made by fire, as an aroma pleasing to me.' 3Say to them: 'This is the offering made by fire that you are to present to the LORD: two lambs a year old without defect, as a regular burnt offering each day.[b] 4Prepare one lamb in the morning and the other at twilight, 5together with a grain

[a] 18 Or *Spirit*

26:65 [z]Jos 14:6-10
27:1 [a]Nu 26:33 [b]Jos 17:2,3 [c]Nu 36:1
27:3 [d]Nu 26:65 [e]Nu 16:2 [f]Nu 26:33
27:5 [g]Ex 18:19 [h]Nu 9:8
27:7 [i]Job 42:15 [j]Jos 17:4
27:11 [k]Nu 35:29
27:12 [l]Nu 33:47; Jer 22:20 [m]Dt 3:23-27; 32:48-52
27:13 [n]Nu 31:2 [o]Nu 20:28
27:14 [p]Nu 20:12 [q]Ex 17:7; Dt 32:51; Ps 106:32
27:16 [r]Nu 16:22
27:17 [s]Dt 31:2; 1Ki 22:17; Eze 34:5; Zec 10:2; Mt 9:36; Mk 6:34
27:18 [t]Ge 41:38; Nu 11:25-29 [u]ver 23; Dt 34:9
27:19 [v]Dt 3:28; 31:14,23 [w]Dt 31:7
27:20 [x]Jos 1:16,17
27:21 [y]Jos 9:14 [z]Ex 28:30
28:2 [a]Lev 3:11
28:3 [b]Ex 29:38

offering of a tenth of an ephah[a] of fine
flour mixed with a quarter of a hin[b] of
oil[c] from pressed olives. 6 This is the regular burnt offering instituted at Mount
Sinai[d] as a pleasing aroma, an offering
made to the LORD by fire. 7 The accompanying drink offering[e] is to be a
quarter of a hin of fermented drink
with each lamb. Pour out the drink offering to the LORD at the sanctuary.[f]
8 Prepare the second lamb at twilight,
along with the same kind of grain offering and drink offering that you prepare in the morning. This is an offering
made by fire, an aroma pleasing to the
LORD.[g]

Sabbath Offerings

9 " 'On the Sabbath[h] day, make an offering of two lambs a year old without
defect, together with its drink offering
and a grain offering of two-tenths of
an ephah[c][i] of fine flour mixed with
oil. 10 This is the burnt offering for
every Sabbath, in addition to the regular
burnt offering[j] and its drink offering.

Monthly Offerings

11 " 'On the first of every month,[k]
present to the LORD a burnt offering
of two young bulls, one ram and seven
male lambs a year old, all without
defect.[l] 12 With each bull there is to be
a grain offering[m] of three-tenths of an
ephah[d][n] of fine flour mixed with oil;
with the ram, a grain offering of two-
tenths of an ephah of fine flour mixed
with oil; 13 and with each lamb, a grain
offering[o] of a tenth of an ephah of fine
flour mixed with oil. This is for a burnt
offering, a pleasing aroma, an offering
made to the LORD by fire. 14 With each
bull there is to be a drink offering[p] of
half a hin[e] of wine; with the ram, a
third of a hin[f]; and with each lamb, a
quarter of a hin. This is the monthly
burnt offering to be made at each new
moon[q] during the year. 15 Besides the
regular burnt offering[r] with its drink
offering, one male goat is to be presented to the LORD as a sin offering.[s]

The Passover

16 " 'On the fourteenth day of the first
month the LORD's Passover[t] is to be
held. 17 On the fifteenth day of this
month there is to be a festival; for sev-
en days[u] eat bread made without yeast.[v]

28:5 [c]Lev 2:1; Nu 15:4
28:6 [d]Ex 19:3
28:7 [e]Ex 29:41 [f]Lev 3:7
28:8 [g]Lev 1:9
28:9 [h]Ex 20:10 [i]Lev 23:13
28:10 [j]ver 3
28:11 [k]Nu 10:10 [l]Lev 1:3
28:12 [m]Nu 15:6 [n]Nu 15:9
28:13 [o]Lev 6:14
28:14 [p]Nu 15:7 [q]Ezr 3:5
28:15 [r]ver 3,23,24 [s]Lev 4:3
28:16 [t]Ex 12:6,18; Lev 23:5; Dt 16:1
28:17 [u]Ex 12:19 [v]Ex 23:15; 34:18; Lev 23:6; Dt 16:3-8

18 On the first day hold a sacred assembly and do no regular work.[w] 19 Present
to the LORD an offering made by fire, a
burnt offering of two young bulls, one
ram and seven male lambs a year old, all
without defect. 20 With each bull prepare a grain offering of three-tenths of
an ephah[x] of fine flour mixed with oil;
with the ram, two-tenths; 21 and with
each of the seven lambs, one-tenth.
22 Include one male goat as a sin offering[y] to make atonement for you.[z] 23 Prepare these in addition to the regular
morning burnt offering. 24 In this way
prepare the food for the offering made
by fire every day for seven days as an
aroma pleasing to the LORD; it is to
be prepared in addition to the regular
burnt offering and its drink offering.
25 On the seventh day hold a sacred assembly and do no regular work.

Feast of Weeks

26 " 'On the day of firstfruits,[a] when
you present to the LORD an offering of
new grain during the Feast of Weeks,[b]
hold a sacred assembly and do no regular work.[c] 27 Present a burnt offering
of two young bulls, one ram and seven
male lambs a year old as an aroma pleasing to the LORD. 28 With each bull there
is to be a grain offering of three-tenths
of an ephah of fine flour mixed with oil;
with the ram, two-tenths; 29 and with
each of the seven lambs, one-tenth.[d]
30 Include one male goat to make atonement for you. 31 Prepare these together
with their drink offerings, in addition
to the regular burnt offering[e] and its
grain offering. Be sure the animals are
without defect.

Feast of Trumpets

29 " 'On the first day of the seventh month hold a sacred assembly and do no regular work.[f] It is a
day for you to sound the trumpets. 2 As
an aroma pleasing to the LORD,[g] prepare a burnt offering of one young bull,

28:18 [w]Ex 12:16; Lev 23:7
28:20 [x]Lev 14:10
28:22 [y]Ro 8:3 [z]Nu 15:28
28:26 [a]Ex 34:22 [b]Ex 23:16 [c]ver 18; Dt 16:10
28:29 [d]ver 13
28:31 [e]ver 3,19
29:1 [f]Lev 23:24
29:2 [g]Nu 28:2

[a]5 That is, probably about 2 quarts (about 2 liters); also in verses 13, 21 and 29 [b]5 That is, probably about 1 quart (about 1 liter); also in verses 7 and 14 [c]9 That is, probably about 4 quarts (about 4.5 liters); also in verses 12, 20 and 28 [d]12 That is, probably about 6 quarts (about 6.5 liters); also in verses 20 and 28 [e]14 That is, probably about 2 quarts (about 2 liters) [f]14 That is, probably about 1 1/4 quarts (about 1.2 liters)

one ram and seven male lambs a year
29:2 [h]Nu 28:3 old, all without defect.[h] 3With the bull
prepare a grain offering of three-tenths
of an ephah[a] of fine flour mixed with
oil; with the ram, two-tenths[b]; 4and
with each of the seven lambs, one-
29:5 [i]Nu 28:15 tenth.[c] 5Include one male goat[i] as a sin
offering to make atonement for you.
29:6 [j]Nu 28:11 [k]Nu 28:3 6These are in addition to the monthly[j]
and daily burnt offerings[k] with their
grain offerings and drink offerings as
specified. They are offerings made to
the LORD by fire—a pleasing aroma.

Day of Atonement

7“ ‘On the tenth day of this seventh
month hold a sacred assembly. You must
29:7 [l]Ac 27:9 [m]Ex 31:15; Lev 16:29; 23:26-32 deny yourselves[d l] and do no work.[m]
8Present as an aroma pleasing to the
LORD a burnt offering of one young
bull, one ram and seven male lambs
a year old, all without defect. 9With
29:9 [n]ver 3,18 the bull prepare a grain offering[n] of
three-tenths of an ephah of fine flour
mixed with oil; with the ram, two-
tenths; 10and with each of the seven
29:10 [o]Nu 28:13 lambs, one-tenth.[o] 11Include one male
goat as a sin offering, in addition to the
sin offering for atonement and the reg-
29:11 [p]Lev 16:3; Nu 28:3 ular burnt offering[p] with its grain offering, and their drink offerings.

Feast of Tabernacles

12“ ‘On the fifteenth day of the sev-
29:12 [q]1Ki 8:2 [r]Lev 23:24 enth[q] month,[r] hold a sacred assembly
and do no regular work. Celebrate a
festival to the LORD for seven days.
13Present an offering made by fire as an
aroma pleasing to the LORD, a burnt
offering of thirteen young bulls, two
rams and fourteen male lambs a year
old, all without defect. 14With each of
the thirteen bulls prepare a grain offer-
29:14 [s]ver 3 ing[s] of three-tenths of an ephah of fine
flour mixed with oil; with each of the
two rams, two-tenths; 15and with each
of the fourteen lambs, one-tenth. 16In-
clude one male goat as a sin offering,
in addition to the regular burnt offering with its grain offering and drink
29:16 [t]ver 6 offering.[t]
17“ ‘On the second day[u] prepare
29:17 [u]Lev 23:36 [v]Nu 28:3 twelve young bulls, two rams and fourteen male lambs a year old, all without
defect.[v] 18With the bulls, rams and
29:18 [w]ver 9 [x]Nu 28:7 [y]Nu 15:4-12 lambs, prepare their grain offerings[w]
and drink offerings[x] according to the
number specified.[y] 19Include one male
goat as a sin offering,[z] in addition to 29:19 [z]Nu 28:15
the regular burnt offering with its grain
offering, and their drink offerings.
20“ ‘On the third day prepare eleven
bulls, two rams and fourteen male lambs
a year old, all without defect.[a] 21With 29:20 [a]ver 17
the bulls, rams and lambs, prepare their
grain offerings and drink offerings ac-
cording to the number specified.[b] 22In- 29:21 [b]ver 18
clude one male goat as a sin offering,
in addition to the regular burnt offering with its grain offering and drink offering.
23“ ‘On the fourth day prepare ten
bulls, two rams and fourteen male lambs
a year old, all without defect. 24With
the bulls, rams and lambs, prepare their
grain offerings and drink offerings according to the number specified. 25In-
clude one male goat as a sin offering,
in addition to the regular burnt offering with its grain offering and drink offering.
26“ ‘On the fifth day prepare nine
bulls, two rams and fourteen male lambs
a year old, all without defect. 27With
the bulls, rams and lambs, prepare their
grain offerings and drink offerings according to the number specified. 28In-
clude one male goat as a sin offering,
in addition to the regular burnt offering with its grain offering and drink offering.
29“ ‘On the sixth day prepare eight
bulls, two rams and fourteen male lambs
a year old, all without defect. 30With
the bulls, rams and lambs, prepare their
grain offerings and drink offerings according to the number specified. 31In-
clude one male goat as a sin offering,
in addition to the regular burnt offering with its grain offering and drink offering.
32“ ‘On the seventh day prepare sev-
en bulls, two rams and fourteen male
lambs a year old, all without defect.
33With the bulls, rams and lambs, prepare their grain offerings and drink
offerings according to the number specified. 34Include one male goat as a
sin offering, in addition to the regular
burnt offering with its grain offering
and drink offering.

[a]*3* That is, probably about 6 quarts (about 6.5 liters); also in verses 9 and 14 [b]*3* That is, probably about 4 quarts (about 4.5 liters); also in verses 9 and 14 [c]*4* That is, probably about 2 quarts (about 2 liters); also in verses 10 and 15 [d]*7* Or *must fast*

35" 'On the eighth day hold an assem-
29:35 [c]Lev 23:36 bly[c] and do no regular work. 36Present
an offering made by fire as an aroma
29:36 [d]Lev 1:9 [e]ver 2 pleasing to the LORD,[d] a burnt offering of one bull, one ram and seven
male lambs a year old,[e] all without defect. 37With the bull, the ram and the
lambs, prepare their grain offerings and
drink offerings according to the number specified. 38Include one male goat
as a sin offering, in addition to the regular burnt offering with its grain offering and drink offering.
29:39 [f]Nu 6:2 [g]Lev 23:2 [h]Lev 1:3; 1Ch 23:31; 2Ch 31:3 39" 'In addition to what you vow[f] and
your freewill offerings, prepare these for
the LORD at your appointed feasts:[g]
your burnt offerings,[h] grain offerings,
drink offerings and fellowship offerings.[a]' "
40Moses told the Israelites all that the
LORD commanded him.

Vows

30 Moses said to the heads of the
30:1 [i]Nu 1:4 tribes of Israel:[i] "This is what
the LORD commands: 2When a man
makes a vow to the LORD or takes an
oath to obligate himself by a pledge, he
must not break his word but must do
30:2 [j]Dt 23:21-23; Jdg 11:35; Job 22:27; Ps 22:25; 50:14; 116:14; Pr 20:25; Ecc 5:4,5; Jnh 1:16 2 everything he said.[j]
3"When a young woman still living
in her father's house makes a vow to the
LORD or obligates herself by a pledge
4and her father hears about her vow or
pledge but says nothing to her, then all
her vows and every pledge by which she
30:4 [k]ver 7 obligated herself will stand.[k] 5But if her
father forbids her when he hears about
it, none of her vows or the pledges by
which she obligated herself will stand;
the LORD will release her because her
father has forbidden her.
6"If she marries after she makes a
30:6 [l]Lev 5:4 vow[l] or after her lips utter a rash promise by which she obligates herself 7and
her husband hears about it but says
nothing to her, then her vows or the
pledges by which she obligated herself
30:8 [m]Ge 3:16 will stand. 8But if her husband[m] forbids
her when he hears about it, he nullifies
the vow that obligates her or the rash
promise by which she obligates herself,
and the LORD will release her.
9"Any vow or obligation taken by a
widow or divorced woman will be binding on her.
10"If a woman living with her husband makes a vow or obligates herself
by a pledge under oath 11and her husband hears about it but says nothing to
her and does not forbid her, then all her
vows or the pledges by which she obligated herself will stand. 12But if her
husband nullifies them when he hears
about them, then none of the vows or
pledges that came from her lips will
stand.[n] Her husband has nullified them, 30:12 [n]Eph 5:22; Col 3:18
and the LORD will release her. 13Her
husband may confirm or nullify any
vow she makes or any sworn pledge to
deny herself. 14But if her husband says
nothing to her about it from day to day,
then he confirms all her vows or the
pledges binding on her. He confirms
them by saying nothing to her when
he hears about them. 15If, however, he
nullifies them some time after he hears
about them, then he is responsible for
her guilt."
16These are the regulations the LORD
gave Moses concerning relationships between a man and his wife, and between
a father and his young daughter still living in his house.

Vengeance on the Midianites

31 The LORD said to Moses,
2"Take vengeance on the Midi-
anites[o] for the Israelites. After that, you 31:2 [o]Ge 25:2 [p]Nu 20:26; 27:13
will be gathered to your people."[p]
3So Moses said to the people, "Arm
some of your men to go to war against
the Midianites and to carry out the
LORD's vengeance[q] on them. 4Send into 31:3 [q]Jdg 11:36; 1Sa 24:12; 2Sa 4:8; 22:48; Ps 94:1; 149:7
battle a thousand men from each of the
tribes of Israel." 5So twelve thousand
men armed for battle, a thousand from
each tribe, were supplied from the clans
of Israel. 6Moses sent them into battle,
a thousand from each tribe, along with
Phinehas son of Eleazar, the priest, who
took with him articles from the sanctu-
ary[r] and the trumpets[s] for signaling. 31:6 [r]Nu 14:44 [s]Nu 10:9
7They fought against Midian, as the
LORD commanded Moses, and killed
every man.[t] 8Among their victims were 31:7 [t]Dt 20:13; Jdg 21:11; 1Ki 11:15,16
Evi, Rekem, Zur, Hur and Reba[u]—the
five kings of Midian.[v] They also killed
Balaam son of Beor with the sword.[w] 31:8 [u]Jos 13:21 [v]Nu 25:15 [w]Jos 13:22
9The Israelites captured the Midianite
women and children and took all the
Midianite herds, flocks and goods as
plunder. 10They burned all the towns
where the Midianites had settled, as

[a]*39* Traditionally *peace offerings*

well as all their camps.[x] 11They took all the plunder and spoils, including the people and animals,[y] 12and brought the captives, spoils and plunder to Moses and Eleazar the priest and the Israelite assembly[z] at their camp on the plains of Moab, by the Jordan across from Jericho.[a]

13Moses, Eleazar the priest and all the leaders of the community went to meet them outside the camp. 14Moses was angry with the officers of the army[a]—the commanders of thousands and commanders of hundreds—who returned from the battle.

15"Have you allowed all the women to live?" he asked them. 16"They were the ones who followed Balaam's advice[b] and were the means of turning the Israelites away from the LORD in what happened at Peor,[c] so that a plague struck the LORD's people. 17Now kill all the boys. And kill every woman who has slept with a man,[d] 18but save for yourselves every girl who has never slept with a man.

19"All of you who have killed anyone or touched anyone who was killed[e] must stay outside the camp seven days. On the third and seventh days you must purify yourselves[f] and your captives. 20Purify every garment[g] as well as everything made of leather, goat hair or wood."

21Then Eleazar the priest said to the soldiers who had gone into battle, "This is the requirement of the law that the LORD gave Moses: 22Gold, silver, bronze, iron,[h] tin, lead 23and anything else that can withstand fire must be put through the fire,[i] and then it will be clean. But it must also be purified with the water of cleansing.[j] And whatever cannot withstand fire must be put through that water. 24On the seventh day wash your clothes and you will be clean.[k] Then you may come into the camp."

Dividing the Spoils

25The LORD said to Moses, 26"You and Eleazar the priest and the family heads of the community are to count all the people[l] and animals that were captured. 27Divide[m] the spoils between the soldiers who took part in the battle and the rest of the community. 28From the soldiers who fought in the battle, set apart as tribute for the LORD[n] one out of every five hundred, whether persons, cattle, donkeys, sheep or goats. 29Take this tribute from their half share and give it to Eleazar the priest as the LORD's part. 30From the Israelites' half, select one out of every fifty, whether persons, cattle, donkeys, sheep, goats or other animals. Give them to the Levites, who are responsible for the care of the LORD's tabernacle.[o]" 31So Moses and Eleazar the priest did as the LORD commanded Moses.

32The plunder remaining from the spoils that the soldiers took was 675,000 sheep, 3372,000 cattle, 3461,000 donkeys 35and 32,000 women who had never slept with a man.

36The half share of those who fought in the battle was:

> 337,500 sheep, 37of which the tribute for the LORD[p] was 675;
> 38 36,000 cattle, of which the tribute for the LORD was 72;
> 39 30,500 donkeys, of which the tribute for the LORD was 61;
> 40 16,000 people, of which the tribute for the LORD was 32.

41Moses gave the tribute to Eleazar the priest as the LORD's part,[q] as the LORD commanded Moses.

42The half belonging to the Israelites, which Moses set apart from that of the fighting men— 43the community's half—was 337,500 sheep, 4436,000 cattle, 4530,500 donkeys 46and 16,000 people. 47From the Israelites' half, Moses selected one out of every fifty persons and animals, as the LORD commanded him, and gave them to the Levites, who were responsible for the care of the LORD's tabernacle.

48Then the officers who were over the units of the army—the commanders of thousands and commanders of hundreds—went to Moses 49and said to him, "Your servants have counted the soldiers under our command, and not one is missing.[r] 50So we have brought as an offering to the LORD the gold articles each of us acquired—armlets, bracelets, signet rings, earrings and necklaces—to make atonement for ourselves[s] before the LORD."

[a]12 Hebrew *Jordan of Jericho;* possibly an ancient name for the Jordan River

31:10 [x]Ge 25:16; 1Ch 6:54; Ps 69:25; Eze 25:4
31:11 [y]Dt 20:14
31:12 [z]Nu 27:2
31:14 [a]ver 48; Ex 18:21; Dt 1:15
31:16 [b]2Pe 2:15; Rev 2:14 [c]Nu 25:1-9
31:17 [d]Dt 7:2; 20:16-18; Jdg 21:11
31:19 [e]Nu 19:16 [f]Nu 19:12
31:20 [g]Nu 19:19
31:22 [h]Jos 6:19; 22:8
31:23 [i]1Co 3:13 [j]Nu 19:9,17
31:24 [k]Lev 11:25
31:26 [l]Nu 1:19
31:27 [m]Jos 22:8; 1Sa 30:24
31:28 [n]Nu 18:21
31:30 [o]Nu 3:7; 18:3
31:37 [p]ver 38-41
31:41 [q]Nu 5:9; 18:8
31:49 [r]Jer 23:4
31:50 [s]Ex 30:16

51 Moses and Eleazar the priest accepted from them the gold—all the crafted articles. 52 All the gold from the commanders of thousands and commanders of hundreds that Moses and Eleazar presented as a gift to the LORD weighed 16,750 shekels.[a] 53 Each soldier had taken plunder[t] for himself. 54 Moses and Eleazar the priest accepted the gold from the commanders of thousands and commanders of hundreds and brought it into the Tent of Meeting as a memorial[u] for the Israelites before the LORD.

31:53 [t]Dt 20:14
31:54 [u]Ex 28:12

The Transjordan Tribes

32 The Reubenites and Gadites, who had very large herds and flocks, saw that the lands of Jazer[v] and Gilead were suitable for livestock.[w] 2 So they came to Moses and Eleazar the priest and to the leaders of the community, and said, 3 "Ataroth,[x] Dibon, Jazer, Nimrah,[y] Heshbon, Elealeh,[z] Sebam, Nebo and Beon[a]— 4 the land the LORD subdued[b] before the people of Israel—are suitable for livestock,[c] and your servants have livestock. 5 If we have found favor in your eyes," they said, "let this land be given to your servants as our possession. Do not make us cross the Jordan."

6 Moses said to the Gadites and Reubenites, "Shall your countrymen go to war while you sit here? 7 Why do you discourage the Israelites from going over into the land the LORD has given them?[d] 8 This is what your fathers did when I sent them from Kadesh Barnea to look over the land.[e] 9 After they went up to the Valley of Eshcol[f] and viewed the land, they discouraged the Israelites from entering the land the LORD had given them. 10 The LORD's anger was aroused[g] that day and he swore this oath: 11 'Because they have not followed me wholeheartedly, not one of the men twenty years old or more[h] who came up out of Egypt will see the land I promised on oath[i] to Abraham, Isaac and Jacob[j]— 12 not one except Caleb son of Jephunneh the Kenizzite and Joshua son of Nun, for they followed the LORD wholeheartedly.'[k] 13 The LORD's anger burned against Israel[l] and he made them wander in the desert forty years, until the whole generation of those who had done evil in his sight was gone.[m]

14 "And here you are, a brood of sinners, standing in the place of your fathers and making the LORD even more angry with Israel.[n] 15 If you turn away from following him, he will again leave all this people in the desert, and you will be the cause of their destruction.[o]"

16 Then they came up to him and said, "We would like to build pens here for our livestock[p] and cities for our women and children. 17 But we are ready to arm ourselves and go ahead of the Israelites[q] until we have brought them to their place.[r] Meanwhile our women and children will live in fortified cities, for protection from the inhabitants of the land. 18 We will not return to our homes until every Israelite has received his inheritance.[s] 19 We will not receive any inheritance with them on the other side of the Jordan, because our inheritance has come to us on the east side of the Jordan."[t]

32:1 [v]Nu 21:32 [w]Ex 12:38
32:3 [x]ver 34 [y]ver 36 [z]ver 37; Isa 15:4; 16:9; Jer 48:34 [a]ver 38; Jos 13:17; Eze 25:9
32:4 [b]Nu 21:34 [c]Ex 12:38
32:7 [d]Nu 13:27-14:4
32:8 [e]Nu 13:3,26; Dt 1:19-25
32:9 [f]Nu 13:23; Dt 1:24
32:10 [g]Nu 11:1
32:11 [h]Ex 30:14 [i]Nu 14:23 [j]Nu 14:28-30
32:12 [k]Nu 14:24,30; Dt 1:36; Ps 63:8
32:13 [l]Ex 4:14 [m]Nu 14:28-35; 26:64,65
32:14 [n]ver 10; Dt 1:34; Ps 78:59
32:15 [o]Dt 30:17-18; 2Ch 7:20
32:16 [p]Ex 12:38; Dt 3:19
32:17 [q]Jos 4:12,13 [r]Nu 22:4; Dt 3:20
32:18 [s]Jos 22:1-4
32:19 [t]Jos 12:1

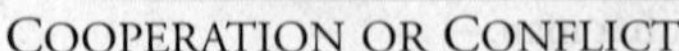

PEACE

COOPERATION OR CONFLICT

Numbers 32:18

Come, let us share the blessings of our common peace
Till all of us drink deeply of liberty.
Then none of us will boast of what we are
But all of us confess that we are free.

20 Then Moses said to them, "If you will do this—if you will arm yourselves before the LORD for battle,[u] 21 and if all of you will go armed over the Jordan before the LORD until he has driven his enemies out before him— 22 then when the land is subdued before the LORD, you may return[v] and be free from your obligation to the LORD and to Israel. And this land will be your possession before the LORD.[w]

23 "But if you fail to do this, you will be sinning against the LORD; and you may be sure that your sin will find you out.[x] 24 Build cities for your women and children, and pens for your flocks,[y] but do what you have promised.[z]"

25 The Gadites and Reubenites said to Moses, "We your servants will do as our lord commands. 26 Our children and wives, our flocks and herds will remain here in the cities of Gilead.[a] 27 But

32:20 [u]Dt 3:18
32:22 [v]Jos 22:4 [w]Dt 3:18-20
32:23 [x]Ge 4:7; 44:16; Isa 59:12
32:24 [y]ver 1,16 [z]Nu 30:2
32:26 [a]Jos 1:14

[a] 52 That is, about 420 pounds (about 190 kilograms)

your servants, every man armed for battle, will cross over to fight before the LORD, just as our lord says."

28 Then Moses gave orders about them[b] to Eleazar the priest and Joshua son of Nun and to the family heads of the Israelite tribes. 29 He said to them, "If the Gadites and Reubenites, every man armed for battle, cross over the Jordan with you before the LORD, then when the land is subdued before you, give them the land of Gilead as their possession. 30 But if they do not cross over with you armed, they must accept their possession with you in Canaan."

31 The Gadites and Reubenites answered, "Your servants will do what the LORD has said.[c] 32 We will cross over before the LORD into Canaan armed, but the property we inherit will be on this side of the Jordan."

33 Then Moses gave to the Gadites,[d] the Reubenites and the half-tribe of Manasseh son of Joseph the kingdom of Sihon king of the Amorites[e] and the kingdom of Og king of Bashan—the whole land with its cities and the territory around them.[f]

34 The Gadites built up Dibon, Ataroth, Aroer,[g] 35 Atroth Shophan, Jazer,[h] Jogbehah, 36 Beth Nimrah[i] and Beth Haran as fortified cities, and built pens for their flocks. 37 And the Reubenites rebuilt Heshbon, Elealeh and Kiriathaim, 38 as well as Nebo[j] and Baal Meon (these names were changed) and Sibmah. They gave names to the cities they rebuilt.

39 The descendants of Makir[k] son of Manasseh went to Gilead, captured it and drove out the Amorites who were there. 40 So Moses gave Gilead to the Makirites,[l] the descendants of Manasseh, and they settled there. 41 Jair, a descendant of Manasseh, captured their settlements and called them Havvoth Jair.[a][m] 42 And Nobah captured Kenath and its surrounding settlements and called it Nobah after himself.[n]

Stages in Israel's Journey

33 Here are the stages in the journey of the Israelites when they came out of Egypt[o] by divisions under the leadership of Moses and Aaron.[p] 2 At the LORD's command Moses recorded the stages in their journey. This is their journey by stages:

3 The Israelites set out from Rameses on the fifteenth day of the first month, the day after the Passover.[q] They marched out boldly[r] in full view of all the Egyptians, 4 who were burying all their firstborn, whom the LORD had struck down among them; for the LORD had brought judgment on their gods.[s]

5 The Israelites left Rameses and camped at Succoth.[t]

6 They left Succoth and camped at Etham, on the edge of the desert.[u]

7 They left Etham, turned back to Pi Hahiroth, to the east of Baal Zephon,[v] and camped near Migdol.[w]

8 They left Pi Hahiroth[b] and passed through the sea[x] into the desert, and when they had traveled for three days in the Desert of Etham, they camped at Marah.[y]

9 They left Marah and went to Elim, where there were twelve springs and seventy palm trees, and they camped[z] there.

10 They left Elim and camped by the Red Sea.[c]

11 They left the Red Sea and camped in the Desert of Sin.[a]

12 They left the Desert of Sin and camped at Dophkah.

13 They left Dophkah and camped at Alush.

14 They left Alush and camped at Rephidim, where there was no water for the people to drink.

15 They left Rephidim[b] and camped in the Desert of Sinai.[c]

16 They left the Desert of Sinai and camped at Kibroth Hattaavah.[d]

17 They left Kibroth Hattaavah and camped at Hazeroth.[e]

18 They left Hazeroth and camped at Rithmah.

19 They left Rithmah and camped at Rimmon Perez.

20 They left Rimmon Perez and camped at Libnah.[f]

[a]41 Or *them the settlements of Jair* [b]8 Many manuscripts of the Masoretic Text, Samaritan Pentateuch and Vulgate; most manuscripts of the Masoretic Text *left from before Hahiroth*
[c]10 Hebrew *Yam Suph*; that is, Sea of Reeds; also in verse 11

32:28 [b]Dt 3:18-20; Jos 1:13
32:31 [c]ver 29
32:33 [d]Jos 13:24-28; 1Sa 13:7 [e]Dt 2:26 [f]Nu 21:24; Jos 12:6
32:34 [g]Dt 2:36; Jdg 11:26
32:35 [h]ver 3
32:36 [i]ver 3
32:38 [j]ver 3; Isa 15:2; Jer 48:1,22
32:39 [k]Ge 50:23
32:40 [l]Dt 3:15; Jos 17:1
32:41 [m]Dt 3:14; Jos 13:30; Jdg 10:4; 1Ch 2:23
32:42 [n]2Sa 18:18; Ps 49:11
33:1 [o]Mic 6:4 [p]Ps 77:20
33:3 [q]Ex 13:4 [r]Ex 14:8
33:4 [s]Ex 12:12
33:5 [t]Ex 12:37
33:6 [u]Ex 13:20
33:7 [v]Ex 14:9 [w]Ex 14:2
33:8 [x]Ex 14:22 [y]Ex 15:23
33:9 [z]Ex 15:27
33:11 [a]Ex 16:1
33:15 [b]Ex 17:1 [c]Ex 19:1
33:16 [d]Nu 11:34
33:17 [e]Nu 11:35
33:20 [f]Jos 10:29

21 They left Libnah and camped at Rissah.

22 They left Rissah and camped at Kehelathah.

23 They left Kehelathah and camped at Mount Shepher.

24 They left Mount Shepher and camped at Haradah.

25 They left Haradah and camped at Makheloth.

26 They left Makheloth and camped at Tahath.

27 They left Tahath and camped at Terah.

28 They left Terah and camped at Mithcah.

29 They left Mithcah and camped at Hashmonah.

30 They left Hashmonah and camped at Moseroth.[g]

31 They left Moseroth and camped at Bene Jaakan.

32 They left Bene Jaakan and camped at Hor Haggidgad.

33 They left Hor Haggidgad and camped at Jotbathah.[h]

34 They left Jotbathah and camped at Abronah.

35 They left Abronah and camped at Ezion Geber.[i]

36 They left Ezion Geber and camped at Kadesh, in the Desert of Zin.[j]

37 They left Kadesh and camped at Mount Hor,[k] on the border of Edom.[l] 38 At the LORD's command Aaron the priest went up Mount Hor, where he died[m] on the first day of the fifth month of the fortieth year after the Israelites came out of Egypt.[n] 39 Aaron was a hundred and twenty-three years old when he died on Mount Hor.

40 The Canaanite king of Arad,[o] who lived in the Negev of Canaan, heard that the Israelites were coming.

41 They left Mount Hor and camped at Zalmonah.

42 They left Zalmonah and camped at Punon.

43 They left Punon and camped at Oboth.[p]

44 They left Oboth and camped at Iye Abarim, on the border of Moab.[q]

45 They left Iyim[a] and camped at Dibon Gad.

33:30 [g]Dt 10:6
33:33 [h]Dt 10:7
33:35 [i]Dt 2:8; 1Ki 9:26; 22:48
33:36 [j]Nu 20:1
33:37 [k]Nu 20:22 [l]Nu 20:16; 21:4
33:38 [m]Dt 10:6 [n]Nu 20:25-28
33:40 [o]Nu 21:1
33:43 [p]Nu 21:10
33:44 [q]Nu 21:11

46 They left Dibon Gad and camped at Almon Diblathaim.

47 They left Almon Diblathaim and camped in the mountains of Abarim,[r] near Nebo.

48 They left the mountains of Abarim and camped on the plains of Moab by the Jordan across from Jericho.[b][s] 49 There on the plains of Moab they camped along the Jordan from Beth Jeshimoth to Abel Shittim.[t]

50 On the plains of Moab by the Jordan across from Jericho the LORD said to Moses, 51 "Speak to the Israelites and say to them: 'When you cross the Jordan into Canaan,[u] 52 drive out all the inhabitants of the land before you. Destroy all their carved images and their cast idols, and demolish all their high places.[v] 53 Take possession of the land and settle in it, for I have given you the land to possess.[w] 54 Distribute the land by lot, according to your clans.[x] To a larger group give a larger inheritance, and to a smaller group a smaller one. Whatever falls to them by lot will be theirs. Distribute it according to your ancestral tribes.

55 " 'But if you do not drive out the inhabitants of the land, those you allow to remain will become barbs in your eyes and thorns[y] in your sides. They will give you trouble in the land where you will live. 56 And then I will do to you what I plan to do to them.' "

Boundaries of Canaan

34 The LORD said to Moses, 2 "Command the Israelites and say to them: 'When you enter Canaan, the land that will be allotted to you as an inheritance[z] will have these boundaries:[a]

3 " 'Your southern side will include some of the Desert of Zin[b] along the border of Edom. On the east, your southern boundary will start from the end of the Salt Sea,[c][c] 4 cross south of Scorpion[d] Pass,[d] continue on to Zin and go south of Kadesh Barnea.[e] Then it will go to Hazar Addar and over to

33:47 [r]Nu 27:12
33:48 [s]Nu 22:1
33:49 [t]Nu 25:1
33:51 [u]Jos 3:17
33:52 [v]Ex 23:24; 34:13; Lev 26:1; Dt 7:2,5; 12:3; Jos 11:12; Ps 106:34-36
33:53 [w]Dt 11:31; Jos 21:43
33:54 [x]Nu 26:54
33:55 [y]Jos 23:13; Jdg 2:3; Ps 106:36
34:2 [z]Ge 17:8; Dt 1:7-8; Ps 78:54-55 [a]Eze 47:15
34:3 [b]Jos 15:1-3 [c]Ge 14:3
34:4 [d]Jos 15:3 [e]Nu 32:8

[a]*45* That is, Iye Abarim [b]*48* Hebrew *Jordan of Jericho*; possibly an ancient name for the Jordan River; also in verse 50 [c]*3* That is, the Dead Sea; also in verse 12 [d]*4* Hebrew *Akrabbim*

Azmon, 5where it will turn, join the
Wadi of Egypt[f] and end at the Sea.[a]
6" 'Your western boundary will be the
coast of the Great Sea. This will be your
boundary on the west.
7" 'For your northern boundary,[g] run
a line from the Great Sea to Mount
Hor 8and from Mount Hor to Lebo[b]
Hamath.[h] Then the boundary will go
to Zedad, 9continue to Ziphron and
end at Hazar Enan. This will be your
boundary on the north.
10" 'For your eastern boundary, run
a line from Hazar Enan to Shepham.
11The boundary will go down from
Shepham to Riblah[i] on the east side of
Ain and continue along the slopes east
of the Sea of Kinnereth.[c][j] 12Then the
boundary will go down along the Jordan and end at the Salt Sea.

" 'This will be your land, with its boundaries on every side.' "

13Moses commanded the Israelites:
"Assign this land by lot as an inheritance.[k] The LORD has ordered that it
be given to the nine and a half tribes,
14because the families of the tribe of
Reuben, the tribe of Gad and the half-tribe of Manasseh have received their
inheritance.[l] 15These two and a half
tribes have received their inheritance on
the east side of the Jordan of Jericho,[d]
toward the sunrise."
16The LORD said to Moses, 17"These
are the names of the men who are to
assign the land for you as an inheritance: Eleazar the priest and Joshua[m]
son of Nun. 18And appoint one leader
from each tribe to help[n] assign the land.
19These are their names:

Caleb[o] son of Jephunneh,
from the tribe of Judah;[p]
20 Shemuel son of Ammihud,
from the tribe of Simeon;[q]
21 Elidad son of Kislon,
from the tribe of Benjamin;[r]
22 Bukki son of Jogli,
the leader from the tribe of Dan;
23 Hanniel son of Ephod,
the leader from the tribe of Manasseh son of Joseph;
24 Kemuel son of Shiphtan,
the leader from the tribe of Ephraim son of Joseph;
25 Elizaphan son of Parnach,
the leader from the tribe of Zebulun;
26 Paltiel son of Azzan,
the leader from the tribe of Issachar;
27 Ahihud son of Shelomi,
the leader from the tribe of Asher;[s]
28 Pedahel son of Ammihud,
the leader from the tribe of Naphtali."

29These are the men the LORD commanded to assign the inheritance to the
Israelites in the land of Canaan.

Towns for the Levites

35 On the plains of Moab by the
Jordan across from Jericho,[e] the
LORD said to Moses, 2"Command the
Israelites to give the Levites towns to
live in[t] from the inheritance the Israelites will possess. And give them pasturelands around the towns. 3Then they
will have towns to live in and pasturelands for their cattle, flocks and all their
other livestock.
4"The pasturelands around the towns
that you give the Levites will extend
out fifteen hundred feet[f] from the town
wall. 5Outside the town, measure three
thousand feet[g] on the east side, three
thousand on the south side, three thousand on the west and three thousand on
the north, with the town in the center.
They will have this area as pastureland
for the towns.

Cities of Refuge

6"Six of the towns you give the Levites will be cities of refuge, to which
a person who has killed someone may
flee.[u] In addition, give them forty-two
other towns. 7In all you must give the
Levites forty-eight towns, together with
their pasturelands. 8The towns you give
the Levites from the land the Israelites
possess are to be given in proportion
to the inheritance of each tribe: Take
many towns from a tribe that has many,
but few from one that has few."[v]
9Then the LORD said to Moses:
10"Speak to the Israelites and say to
them: 'When you cross the Jordan into

34:5 [f]Ge 15:18; Jos 15:4
34:7 [g]Eze 47:15-17
34:8 [h]Nu 13:21; Jos 13:5
34:11 [i]2Ki 23:33; Jer 39:5 [j]Dt 3:17; Jos 11:2; 13:27
34:13 [k]Jos 14:1-5
34:14 [l]Nu 32:33; Jos 14:3
34:17 [m]Jos 14:1
34:18 [n]Nu 1:4,16
34:19 [o]Nu 26:65 [p]Ge 29:35; Dt 33:7
34:20 [q]Ge 49:5
34:21 [r]Ge 49:27; Ps 68:27
34:27 [s]Nu 1:40
35:2 [t]Lev 25:32-34; Jos 14:3,4
35:6 [u]Jos 20:7-9; 21:3,13
35:8 [v]Nu 26:54; 33:54; Jos 21:1-42

[a]5 That is, the Mediterranean; also in verses 6 and 7
[b]8 Or *to the entrance to* [c]11 That is, Galilee
[d]15 *Jordan of Jericho* was possibly an ancient name for the Jordan River. [e]1 Hebrew *Jordan of Jericho*; possibly an ancient name for the Jordan River
[f]4 Hebrew *a thousand cubits* (about 450 meters)
[g]5 Hebrew *two thousand cubits* (about 900 meters)

35:10 [w]Jos 20:2 Canaan,[w] 11select some towns to be
your cities of refuge, to which a person
35:11 [x]ver 22-25 [y]Ex 21:13; Dt 19:1-13 who has killed someone[x] accidentally[y]
may flee. 12They will be places of refuge
from the avenger,[z] so that a person accused of murder may not die before he
35:12 [z]Dt 19:6; Jos 20:3 stands trial before the assembly. 13These
six towns you give will be your cities
of refuge. 14Give three on this side of
the Jordan and three in Canaan as cities of refuge. 15These six towns will be a
place of refuge for Israelites, aliens and
any other people living among them, so
that anyone who has killed another accidentally can flee there.

16" 'If a man strikes someone with
an iron object so that he dies, he is a
murderer; the murderer shall be put to
35:16 [a]Ex 21:12; Lev 24:17 death.[a] 17Or if anyone has a stone in
his hand that could kill, and he strikes
someone so that he dies, he is a murderer; the murderer shall be put to death.
18Or if anyone has a wooden object in
his hand that could kill, and he hits
someone so that he dies, he is a murderer; the murderer shall be put to death.
19The avenger of blood shall put the
murderer to death; when he meets him,
35:19 [b]ver 21 he shall put him to death.[b] 20If anyone
with malice aforethought shoves an-
other or throws something at him in-
35:20 [c]Ge 4:8; Ex 21:14; Dt 19:11; 2Sa 3:27; 20:10 tentionally[c] so that he dies 21or if in
hostility he hits him with his fist so
that he dies, that person shall be put to
death; he is a murderer. The avenger of
blood shall put the murderer to death
when he meets him.

22" 'But if without hostility someone
suddenly shoves another or throws
35:22 [d]ver 11; Ex 21:13 something at him unintentionally[d] 23or,
without seeing him, drops a stone on
him that could kill him, and he dies,
then since he was not his enemy and he
did not intend to harm him, 24the as-
35:24 [e]ver 12; Jos 20:6 sembly[e] must judge between him and
the avenger of blood according to these
regulations. 25The assembly must protect the one accused of murder from
the avenger of blood and send him back
to the city of refuge to which he fled.
He must stay there until the death of
the high priest, who was anointed with
35:25 [f]Ex 29:7 the holy oil.[f]

26" 'But if the accused ever goes outside the limits of the city of refuge to
which he has fled 27and the avenger of
blood finds him outside the city, the
avenger of blood may kill the accused
without being guilty of murder. 28The
accused must stay in his city of refuge
until the death of the high priest; only
after the death of the high priest may
he return to his own property.

29" 'These are to be legal require-
ments[g] for you throughout the genera- 35:29 [g]Nu 27:11
tions to come, wherever you live.

30" 'Anyone who kills a person is to
be put to death as a murderer only on
the testimony of witnesses. But no one
is to be put to death on the testimony
of only one witness.[h] 35:30 [h]ver 16; Dt 17:6; 19:15; Mt 18:16; Jn 7:51; 2Co 13:1; Heb 10:28

31" 'Do not accept a ransom for the
life of a murderer, who deserves to die.
He must surely be put to death.

32" 'Do not accept a ransom for anyone who has fled to a city of refuge and
so allow him to go back and live on his
own land before the death of the high
priest.

33" 'Do not pollute the land where
you are. Bloodshed pollutes the land,[i] 35:33 [i]Ge 9:6; Ps 106:38; Mic 4:11
and atonement cannot be made for the
land on which blood has been shed,
except by the blood of the one who
shed it. 34Do not defile the land[j] where 35:34 [j]Lev 18:24,25 [k]Ex 29:45
you live and where I dwell,[k] for I, the
LORD, dwell among the Israelites.' "

Inheritance of Zelophehad's Daughters

36 The family heads of the clan of
Gilead[l] son of Makir, the son 36:1 [l]Nu 26:29 [m]Nu 27:2
of Manasseh, who were from the clans
of the descendants of Joseph, came and
spoke before Moses and the leaders,[m]
the heads of the Israelite families. 2They
said, "When the LORD commanded
my lord to give the land as an inheritance to the Israelites by lot, he ordered you to give the inheritance of our
brother Zelophehad[n] to his daughters. 36:2 [n]Nu 26:33; 27:1,7
3Now suppose they marry men from
other Israelite tribes; then their inheritance will be taken from our ancestral
inheritance and added to that of the
tribe they marry into. And so part of
the inheritance allotted to us will be
taken away. 4When the Year of Jubilee[o] 36:4 [o]Lev 25:10
for the Israelites comes, their inheri-
tance will be added to that of the tribe
into which they marry, and their property will be taken from the tribal inheritance of our forefathers."

5Then at the LORD's command Moses gave this order to the Israelites:
"What the tribe of the descendants of

Joseph is saying is right. 6This is what
the LORD commands for Zelophehad's
daughters: They may marry anyone they
please as long as they marry within the
tribal clan of their father. 7No inheri-
36:7 [p]1Ki 21:3 tance[p] in Israel is to pass from tribe
to tribe, for every Israelite shall keep
the tribal land inherited from his forefathers. 8Every daughter who inherits
land in any Israelite tribe must marry
36:8 [q]1Ch 23:22 someone in her father's tribal clan,[q] so
that every Israelite will possess the inheritance of his fathers. 9No inheritance
may pass from tribe to tribe, for each
Israelite tribe is to keep the land it inherits."

10So Zelophehad's daughters did as
the LORD commanded Moses. 11Zelo-
phehad's daughters—Mahlah, Tirzah,
Hoglah, Milcah and Noah[r]—married 36:11 [r]Nu 26:33; 27:1
their cousins on their father's side.
12They married within the clans of the
descendants of Manasseh son of Joseph,
and their inheritance remained in their
father's clan and tribe.

13These are the commands and regu-
lations the LORD gave through Moses[s] 36:13 [s]Lev 26:46; 27:34 [t]Nu 22:1
to the Israelites on the plains of Moab
by the Jordan across from Jericho.[a][t]

[a]13 Hebrew *Jordan of Jericho*; possibly an ancient name for the Jordan River

DEUTERONOMY

AUTHORSHIP AND DATE

Moses

c. 1450 B.C. to c. 1410 B.C.

KEY THEMES

The word *Deuteronomy* is derived from *deuter* meaning "second" and *nomos* meaning "law," forming the composite word meaning "a repetition of the law." The Ten Commandments are repeated in Deuteronomy in much the same form as given in Exodus 20. The book of Deuteronomy is divided into Moses' three farewell sermons. The discussions in these sermons are a more studied and reflective examination of the law than was first revealed in Exodus. The book essentially looks at its themes within these frameworks:

Sermon #1, Deuteronomy 1:1–4:43, what God had done for Israel

Sermon #2, Deuteronomy 4:44–28:68, a focus on the law and the various kinds of relationships it engendered

Sermon #3, Deuteronomy 29:1–30:20, a summons to national commitment

Conclusion, Deuteronomy 31:1–34:12, Moses' last days and the passing of the leadership baton to Joshua

FRUIT OF THE SPIRIT IN DEUTERONOMY

Love: God was in love with Israel, and he said so in Deuteronomy. His loving-kindness toward Israel was set in juxtaposition to all he might have done had he been less merciful and more exacting. His love caused him to keep his promises, and the expectation of his love was that Israel would live in holy obedience to his covenants.

Joy: Deuteronomy teaches two things regarding joy. First, joy should be our general attitude. We are to rejoice in all good things (see 26:11). Second, we are to rejoice when we enter the house of the Lord. This joy is connected to the act of eating together. When we bring our offerings to the house of God, we are to rejoice in everything we put our hands to (see 12:7).

Goodness: The purpose of the commandments and covenants contained in the books of Moses were to guide people toward genuine holiness. Goodness comes after the foundation of holiness. When we offer our frail but good characters on the altar of God, we find that God sanctifies our moral efforts, and we are drawn to God. The result is not merely that we are made good, but we are possessed of a desire to be holy, for God is holy.

Gentleness: The three sermons that comprise Deuteronomy contain a strong—though subtle—command to care for others who are in need. Israel was to be gentle, for God himself is gentle. "He defends the cause of the fatherless and the widow, and loves the alien, giving him food and clothing. And you are to love those who are aliens, for you yourselves were aliens in Egypt" (10:18–19).

Self-Control: Deuteronomy 34:4 is perhaps the saddest verse in this book. Concerning the promised land, God said to Moses: "I have let you see it with your eyes, but you will not cross over into it." Moses was not allowed to enter the promised land because he failed to honor God. Before the eyes of the Israelites, he struck the rock in anger, and his loss of self-control had heavy consequences indeed (see Numbers 20:1–13). The loss of self-control in our own lives will likewise be costly. If we are temper-ridden in our service for God, our loss of self-control doesn't only cause people to think less of us—it may also cause them to think less of God.

The Command to Leave Horeb

1 These are the words Moses spoke
to all Israel in the desert east of the
Jordan—that is, in the Arabah—opposite Suph, between Paran and Tophel,
Laban, Hazeroth and Dizahab. 2(It takes
1:2 [a]Ex 3:1 eleven days to go from Horeb[a] to
[b]Nu 13:26; Dt 9:23 Kadesh Barnea[b] by the Mount Seir
road.)
3In the fortieth year,[c] on the first
day of the eleventh month, Moses pro-
1:3 [c]Nu 33:38 claimed[d] to the Israelites all that the
[d]Dt 4:1-2 LORD had commanded him concern-
ing them. 4This was after he had de-
1:4 [e]Nu 21:21-26 feated Sihon[e] king of the Amorites,
[f]Nu 21:25 who reigned in Heshbon,[f] and at Edrei
[g]Nu 21:33-35; Jos 13:12 had defeated Og[g] king of Bashan, who
reigned in Ashtaroth.
5East of the Jordan in the territory
of Moab, Moses began to expound this
law, saying:

1:6 6The LORD our God said to us[h] at
[h]Nu 10:13 [i]Ex 3:1 Horeb,[i] "You have stayed long enough
at this mountain. 7Break camp and ad-
vance into the hill country of the Amor-
rites; go to all the neighboring peoples
in the Arabah, in the mountains, in
1:7 the western foothills, in the Negev[j] and
[j]Jos 10:40 [k]Dt 11:24 along the coast, to the land of the Canaanites and to Lebanon,[k] as far as the
great river, the Euphrates. 8See, I have
given you this land. Go in and take
possession of the land that the LORD
1:8 swore[l] he would give to your fathers—
[l]Ge 12:7; 15:18; 17:7-8; 26:4; 28:13 to Abraham, Isaac and Jacob—and to
their descendants after them."

The Appointment of Leaders

9At that time I said to you, "You
are too heavy a burden for me to carry
1:9 [m]Ex 18:18 alone.[m] 10The LORD your God has increased your numbers so that today you
1:10 [n]Ge 15:5 are as many[n] as the stars in the sky.[o]
[o]Dt 10:22; 28:62 11May the LORD, the God of your fathers, increase you a thousand times
1:11 [p]Ge 22:17; Ex 32:13 and bless you as he has promised![p]
12But how can I bear your problems
and your burdens and your disputes all
by myself? 13Choose some wise, un-
1:13 [q]Ex 18:21 derstanding and respected men[q] from
each of your tribes, and I will set them
over you."
14You answered me, "What you propose to do is good."
1:15 [r]Ex 18:25 15So I took[r] the leading men of your
tribes, wise and respected men, and appointed them to have authority over
you—as commanders of thousands, of
hundreds, of fifties and of tens and as
tribal officials. 16And I charged your
judges at that time: Hear the disputes
between your brothers and judge fairly,[s] 1:16 [s]Dt 16:18; Jn 7:24
whether the case is between brother Is-
raelites or between one of them and [t]Lev 24:22
an alien.[t] 17Do not show partiality[u] in 1:17 [u]Lev 19:15; Dt 16:19; Pr 24:23; Jas 2:1
judging; hear both small and great alike.
Do not be afraid of any man,[v] for judgment belongs to God. Bring me any [v]2Ch 19:6
case too hard for you, and I will hear [w]Ex 18:26
it.[w] 18And at that time I told you everything you were to do.

Spies Sent Out

19Then, as the LORD our God commanded us, we set out from Horeb
and went toward the hill country of
the Amorites through all that vast and
dreadful desert[x] that you have seen, and 1:19 [x]Dt 8:15; Jer 2:2,6
so we reached Kadesh Barnea.[y] 20Then [y]ver 2; Nu 13:26
I said to you, "You have reached the
hill country of the Amorites, which
the LORD our God is giving us. 21See,
the LORD your God has given you the
land. Go up and take possession of it
as the LORD, the God of your fathers,
told you. Do not be afraid;[z] do not be 1:21 [z]Jos 1:6,9,18
discouraged."

FAITHFULNESS

THE REAL ESTATE OF GOD

Deuteronomy 1:21

The fringe benefit of faith is real estate eternal.
In our Father's house is Christ our brother.
In our Father's house is God our Father.
In our Father's house are windows laced with sunlight.
In our Father's house are porticoes of seraphim
and banisters of beauty.
In our Father's land are many zip codes—one of them is ours.

22Then all of you came to me and
said, "Let us send men ahead to spy out
the land for us and bring back a report
about the route we are to take and the
towns we will come to."
23The idea seemed good to me; so I
selected[a] twelve of you, one man from 1:23 [a]Nu 13:1-3
each tribe. 24They left and went up into
the hill country, and came to the Val-

1:24 [b]Nu 13:21-25 ley of Eshcol[b] and explored it. 25Tak-
ing with them some of the fruit of the
land, they brought it down to us and
1:25 [c]Nu 13:27 reported,[c] "It is a good land that the
LORD our God is giving us."

Rebellion Against the LORD

1:26 [d]Nu 14:1-4 26But you were unwilling to go up;[d]
you rebelled against the command of
1:27 [e]Dt 9:28; the LORD your God. 27You grumbled[e]
Ps 106:25 in your tents and said, "The LORD
hates us; so he brought us out of Egypt
to deliver us into the hands of the Amorites to destroy us. 28Where can we go?
Our brothers have made us lose heart.
They say, 'The people are stronger and
1:28 [f]Nu 13:32 taller[f] than we are; the cities are large,
[g]Nu 13:33; with walls up to the sky. We even saw
Dt 9:1-3 the Anakites[g] there.'"
29Then I said to you, "Do not be terrified; do not be afraid of them. 30The
LORD your God, who is going before
1:30 you, will fight[h] for you, as he did for
[h]Ex 14:14; Dt 3:22; you in Egypt, before your very eyes,
Ne 4:20 31and in the desert. There you saw how
the LORD your God carried[i] you, as a
1:31 [i]Dt 32:10-12; father carries his son, all the way you
Isa 46:3-4; 63:9; went until you reached this place."
Hos 11:3; 32In spite of this, you did not trust[j]
Ac 13:18 in the LORD your God, 33who went
1:32 [j]Ps 106:24; ahead of you on your journey, in fire by
Jude 1:5 night and in a cloud by day,[k] to search[l]
1:33 out places for you to camp and to show
[k]Ex 13:21; Ps 78:14 you the way you should go.
[l]Nu 10:33 34When the LORD heard what you
1:34 said, he was angry and solemnly swore:[m]
[m]Nu 14:23, 35"Not a man of this evil generation
28-30 shall see the good land[n] I swore to give
1:35 [n]Ps 95:11 your forefathers, 36except Caleb son of
Jephunneh. He will see it, and I will
give him and his descendants the land
he set his feet on, because he followed
1:36 [o]Nu 14:24; the LORD wholeheartedly."[o]
Jos 14:9 37Because of you the LORD became
1:37 angry[p] with me also and said, "You shall
[p]Dt 3:26; 4:21 not enter[q] it, either. 38But your assis-
[q]Nu 20:12 tant, Joshua[r] son of Nun, will enter it.
1:38 Encourage[s] him, because he will lead[t]
[r]Nu 14:30 [s]Dt 31:7 Israel to inherit it. 39And the little ones
[t]Dt 3:28 that you said would be taken captive,[u]
your children who do not yet know[v]
1:39 [u]Nu 14:3 good from bad—they will enter the
Isa 7:15-16 land. I will give it to them and they will
take possession of it. 40But as for you,
turn around and set out toward the des-
1:40 [w]Nu 14:25 ert along the route to the Red Sea.[a][w]"
41Then you replied, "We have sinned
against the LORD. We will go up and
fight, as the LORD our God commanded us." So every one of you put on his
weapons, thinking it easy to go up into
the hill country.
42But the LORD said to me, "Tell
them, 'Do not go up and fight, because
I will not be with you. You will be defeated by your enemies.'"[x] 1:42 [x]Nu 14:41-43
43So I told you, but you would not
listen. You rebelled against the LORD's
command and in your arrogance you
marched up into the hill country. 44The
Amorites who lived in those hills came
out against you; they chased you like
a swarm of bees[y] and beat you down 1:44 [y]Ps 118:12
from Seir all the way to Hormah. 45You
came back and wept before the LORD,
but he paid no attention to your weeping and turned a deaf ear to you. 46And
so you stayed in Kadesh[z] many days— 1:46 [z]Nu 20:1;
all the time you spent there. Jdg 11:17

Wanderings in the Desert

2 Then we turned back and set out
toward the desert along the route
to the Red Sea,[a][a] as the LORD had di- 2:1 [a]Nu 21:4
rected me. For a long time we made our
way around the hill country of Seir.
2Then the LORD said to me, 3"You
have made your way around this hill
country long enough; now turn north.
4Give the people these orders:[b] 'You are 2:4 [b]Nu 20:14-21
about to pass through the territory of
your brothers the descendants of Esau,
who live in Seir. They will be afraid of
you, but be very careful. 5Do not provoke them to war, for I will not give you
any of their land, not even enough to
put your foot on. I have given Esau the 2:5
hill country of Seir as his own.[c] 6You are [c]Ge 36:8;
to pay them in silver for the food you Jos 24:4
eat and the water you drink.'"
7The LORD your God has blessed
you in all the work of your hands. He
has watched[d] over your journey through 2:7 [d]Dt 8:2-4
this vast desert. These forty years the
LORD your God has been with you,
and you have not lacked anything.
8So we went on past our brothers
the descendants of Esau, who live in
Seir. We turned from the Arabah road,
which comes up from Elath and Ezion
Geber,[e] and traveled along the desert 2:8 [e]1Ki 9:26
road of Moab.[f] [f]Jdg 11:18
9Then the LORD said to me, "Do not

[a]*40,1* Hebrew *Yam Suph*; that is, Sea of Reeds

harass the Moabites or provoke them to
war, for I will not give you any part of
2:9 [g]Nu 21:15 their land. I have given Ar[g] to the de-
[h]Ge 19:36-38 scendants of Lot[h] as a possession."
2:10 10(The Emites[i] used to live there—a
[i]Ge 14:5 people strong and numerous, and as tall
[j]Nu 13:22,33 as the Anakites.[j] 11Like the Anakites,
they too were considered Rephaites, but
the Moabites called them Emites. 12Ho-
rites used to live in Seir, but the descendants of Esau drove them out. They
destroyed the Horites from before them
and settled in their place, just as Israel
2:12 [k]ver 22 did[k] in the land the LORD gave them as
their possession.)
13And the LORD said, "Now get up
and cross the Zered Valley." So we
crossed the valley.
14Thirty-eight years passed from the
2:14 [l]Nu 13:26 time we left Kadesh Barnea[l] until we
[m]Nu 14:29-35 crossed the Zered Valley. By then, that
[n]Dt 1:34-35 entire generation[m] of fighting men had
perished from the camp, as the LORD
had sworn to them.[n] 15The LORD's hand
was against them until he had complete-
2:15 [o]Ps 106:26 ly eliminated[o] them from the camp.
16Now when the last of these fight-
ing men among the people had died,
17the LORD said to me, 18"Today you
are to pass by the region of Moab at Ar.
2:19 [p]Ge 19:38 19When you come to the Ammonites,[p]
[q]ver 9 do not harass them or provoke them to
war, for I will not give you possession
of any land belonging to the Ammonites. I have given it as a possession to
the descendants of Lot."[q]
20(That too was considered a land
of the Rephaites, who used to live
there; but the Ammonites called them
Zamzummites. 21They were a people
strong and numerous, and as tall as the
2:21 [r]ver 10 Anakites.[r] The LORD destroyed them
from before the Ammonites, who drove
them out and settled in their place.
22The LORD had done the same for the
2:22 [s]Ge 36:8 descendants of Esau, who lived in Seir,[s]
when he destroyed the Horites from be-
fore them. They drove them out and
have lived in their place to this day.
2:23 [t]Jos 13:3 23And as for the Avvites[t] who lived in
[u]Ge 10:14 villages as far as Gaza, the Caphtorites[u]
[v]Am 9:7 coming out from Caphtor[a][v] destroyed
them and settled in their place.)

Defeat of Sihon King of Heshbon

2:24 [w]Nu 21:13-14; Jdg 11:13,18 24"Set out now and cross the Arnon
Gorge.[w] See, I have given into your
hand Sihon the Amorite, king of Heshbon, and his country. Begin to take possession of it and engage him in battle.
25This very day I will begin to put the
terror[x] and fear[y] of you on all the na- 2:25 [x]Dt 11:25
tions under heaven. They will hear re- [y]Jos 2:9,11
ports of you and will tremble[z] and be in [z]Ex 15:14-16
anguish because of you."
26From the desert of Kedemoth I sent
messengers to Sihon king of Heshbon
offering peace and saying, 27"Let us pass
through your country. We will stay on
the main road; we will not turn aside to
the right or to the left.[a] 28Sell us food 2:27 [a]Nu 21:21-22
to eat and water to drink for their price
in silver. Only let us pass through on
foot[b]— 29as the descendants of Esau, 2:28 [b]Nu 20:19
who live in Seir, and the Moabites, who
live in Ar, did for us—until we cross
the Jordan into the land the LORD our
God is giving us." 30But Sihon king of
Heshbon refused to let us pass through.
For the LORD[c] your God had made his 2:30 [c]Jos 11:20
spirit stubborn[d] and his heart obstinate [d]Ex 4:21; Nu 21:23;
in order to give him into your hands, as Ro 9:18
he has now done.
31The LORD said to me, "See, I have
begun to deliver Sihon and his country
over to you. Now begin to conquer and
possess his land."[e] 2:31 [e]Dt 1:8
32When Sihon and all his army came
out to meet us in battle[f] at Jahaz, 33the 2:32 [f]Nu 21:23
LORD our God delivered him over to us
and we struck him down,[g] together with
his sons and his whole army. 34At that 2:33 [g]Dt 29:7
time we took all his towns and com-
pletely destroyed[b][h] them—men, wom- 2:34 [h]Dt 3:6; 7:2
en and children. We left no survivors.
35But the livestock and the plunder
from the towns we had captured we
carried off for ourselves. 36From Aroer[i]
on the rim of the Arnon Gorge, and
from the town in the gorge, even as far
as Gilead, not one town was too strong
for us. The LORD our God gave[j] us all 2:36
of them. 37But in accordance with the [i]Dt 3:12;
command of the LORD our God,[k] you 4:48; Jos 13:9 [j]Ps 44:3
did not encroach on any of the land
of the Ammonites,[l] neither the land 2:37 [k]ver 18-19
along the course of the Jabbok[m] nor [l]Nu 21:24 [m]Ge 32:22;
that around the towns in the hills. Dt 3:16

Defeat of Og King of Bashan

3 Next we turned and went up along
the road toward Bashan, and Og
king of Bashan with his whole army

[a]*23* That is, Crete [b]*34* The Hebrew term refers to the irrevocable giving over of things or persons to the LORD, often by totally destroying them.

marched out to meet us in battle at
3:1 [n]Nu 21:33 Edrei.[n] 2The LORD said to me, "Do
not be afraid[o] of him, for I have handed
3:2 [o]Nu 21:34 him over to you with his whole army
and his land. Do to him what you did
to Sihon king of the Amorites, who
reigned in Heshbon."
3So the LORD our God also gave into
our hands Og king of Bashan and all
his army. We struck them down, leav-
3:3 [p]Nu 21:35 ing no survivors.[p] 4At that time we took
all his cities. There was not one of the
sixty cities that we did not take from
them—the whole region of Argob, Og's
3:4 [q]1Ki 4:13 kingdom in Bashan.[q] 5All these cities
were fortified with high walls and with
gates and bars, and there were also a
great many unwalled villages. 6We completely destroyed[a] them, as we had done
with Sihon king of Heshbon, destroy-
3:6 [r]Dt 2:24,34 ing[a] [r] every city—men, women and children. 7But all the livestock and the
plunder from their cities we carried off
for ourselves.
8So at that time we took from these
two kings of the Amorites the territory
east of the Jordan, from the Arnon
Gorge as far as Mount Hermon. 9(Her-
3:9 [s]Dt 4:48; Ps 29:6 mon is called Sirion[s] by the Sidonians;
[t]1Ch 5:23 the Amorites call it Senir.)[t] 10We took
all the towns on the plateau, and all
3:10 [u]Jos 13:11 Gilead, and all Bashan as far as Salecah[u]
and Edrei, towns of Og's kingdom in
Bashan. 11(Only Og king of Bashan was
3:11 [v]Ge 14:5 left of the remnant of the Rephaites.[v]
[w]2Sa 12:26; Jer 49:2 His bed[b] was made of iron and was
more than thirteen feet long and six
feet wide.[c] It is still in Rabbah[w] of the
Ammonites.)

Division of the Land

12Of the land that we took over at
that time, I gave the Reubenites and the
3:12 [x]Nu 32:32-38; Dt 2:36; Jos 13:8-13 Gadites the territory north of Aroer[x]
by the Arnon Gorge, including half the
hill country of Gilead, together with its
towns. 13The rest of Gilead and also
all of Bashan, the kingdom of Og, I
gave to the half tribe of Manasseh. (The
whole region of Argob in Bashan used
to be known as a land of the Rephaites.
3:14 [y]Nu 32:41; 1Ch 2:22 14Jair,[y] a descendant of Manasseh, took
the whole region of Argob as far as the
border of the Geshurites and the Maaca-
athites; it was named after him, so that
to this day Bashan is called Havvoth
3:15 [z]Nu 32:39-40 Jair.[d]) 15And I gave Gilead to Makir.[z]
16But to the Reubenites and the Gad-
ites I gave the territory extending from
Gilead down to the Arnon Gorge (the
middle of the gorge being the border)
and out to the Jabbok River,[a] which 3:16 [a]Nu 21:24
is the border of the Ammonites. 17Its
western border was the Jordan in the
Arabah, from Kinnereth[b] to the Sea of 3:17 [b]Nu 34:11; Jos 13:27
the Arabah (the Salt Sea[e] [c]), below the [c]Ge 14:3; Jos 12:3
slopes of Pisgah.
18I commanded you at that time:
"The LORD your God has given you
this land to take possession of it. But all
your able-bodied men, armed for battle,
must cross over ahead of your brother
Israelites.[d] 19However, your wives, your 3:18 [d]Nu 32:17
children and your livestock (I know
you have much livestock) may stay in
the towns I have given you, 20until the
LORD gives rest to your brothers as he
has to you, and they too have taken
over the land that the LORD your God
is giving them, across the Jordan. After
that, each of you may go back to the
possession I have given you."

Moses Forbidden to Cross the Jordan

21At that time I commanded Joshua: "You have seen with your own eyes
all that the LORD your God has done
to these two kings. The LORD will
do the same to all the kingdoms over
there where you are going. 22Do not be 3:22 [e]Dt 1:29
afraid[e] of them; the LORD your God [f]Ex 14:14; Dt 20:4
himself will fight[f] for you."

▸ KINDNESS

MIGHTY DEMONSTRATIONS BY GOD

Deuteronomy 3:24

We came to Christ and knew
That—having made us heirs of glory—
All our needs he would supply.

23At that time I pleaded with the
LORD: 24"O Sovereign LORD, you have
begun to show to your servant your 3:24
greatness[g] and your strong hand. For [g]Dt 11:2

[a]*6* The Hebrew term refers to the irrevocable giving over of things or persons to the LORD, often by totally destroying them. [b]*11* Or *sarcophagus* [c]*11* Hebrew *nine cubits long and four cubits wide* (about 4 meters long and 1.8 meters wide) [d]*14* Or *called the settlements of Jair* [e]*17* That is, the Dead Sea

3:24 what god[h] is there in heaven or on
[h]Ex 15:11; earth who can do the deeds and mighty
Ps 86:8 works[i] you do?[j] 25Let me go over and
[i]Ps 71:16,19 [j]2Sa 7:22 see the good land[k] beyond the Jordan—
3:25 [k]Dt 4:22 that fine hill country and Lebanon."
26But because of you the LORD was
3:26 angry[l] with me and would not listen to
[l]Dt 1:37; 31:2 me. "That is enough," the LORD said.
"Do not speak to me anymore about
this matter. 27Go up to the top of Pisgah and look west and north and south
and east. Look at the land with your
own eyes, since you are not going to
3:27 cross this Jordan.[m] 28But commission[n]
[m]Nu 27:12 Joshua, and encourage and strengthen
3:28 him, for he will lead this people across[o]
[n]Nu 27:18-23 [o]Dt 31:3,23 and will cause them to inherit the land
that you will see." 29So we stayed in the
3:29 [p]Dt 4:46; 34:6 valley near Beth Peor.[p]

Obedience Commanded

4 Hear now, O Israel, the decrees and
laws I am about to teach you. Fol-
4:1 low them so that you may live[q] and
[q]Dt 5:33; 8:1; 16:20; may go in and take possession of the
30:15-20; Eze 20:11; land that the LORD, the God of your
Ro 10:5 fathers, is giving you. 2Do not add[r] to
4:2 what I command you and do not sub-
[r]Dt 12:32; tract from it, but keep the commands
Jos 1:7; Rev 22:18-19 of the LORD your God that I give you.
4:3 3You saw with your own eyes what
[s]Nu 25:1-9; the LORD did at Baal Peor.[s] The LORD
Ps 106:28 your God destroyed from among you
everyone who followed the Baal of Peor,
4but all of you who held fast to the
LORD your God are still alive today.
5See, I have taught you decrees and
laws as the LORD my God commanded
me, so that you may follow them in the
land you are entering to take posses-
4:6 sion of it. 6Observe them carefully, for
[t]Dt 30:19-20; this will show your wisdom[t] and under-
Ps 19:7; Pr 1:7 standing to the nations, who will hear
[u]Job 28:28 about all these decrees and say, "Surely
this great nation is a wise and understanding people."[u] 7What other nation
4:7 is so great[v] as to have their gods near[w]
[v]2Sa 7:23 [w]Ps 46:1; them the way the LORD our God is
Isa 55:6 near us whenever we pray to him? 8And
what other nation is so great as to have
such righteous decrees and laws as this
body of laws I am setting before you
today?
9Only be careful,[x] and watch yourselves closely so that you do not forget
4:9 [x]Pr 4:23 the things your eyes have seen or let
[y]Ge 18:19; Eph 6:4 them slip from your heart as long as
[z]Ps 78:5-6 you live. Teach[y] them to your children[z]

FAITHFULNESS

THE FORGET-ME-NOTS OF THE LORD

Deuteronomy 4:9

The best of all our reveries sleeps warmly, remembering the faithfulness of God. The Christian mind is but a photo album filled with pictures of the Savior taken with the camera of obedience.

and to their children after them. 10Re-
member the day you stood before the
LORD your God at Horeb,[a] when he 4:10 [a]Ex 19:9,16
said to me, "Assemble the people be-
fore me to hear my words so that they
may learn to revere me as long as they
live in the land and may teach them
to their children." 11You came near and
stood at the foot of the mountain while
it blazed with fire[b] to the very heavens, 4:11 [b]Ex 19:18;
with black clouds and deep darkness. Heb 12:18-19
12Then the LORD spoke[c] to you out of 4:12
the fire. You heard the sound of words [c]Ex 20:22;
but saw no form; there was only a voice. Dt 5:4,22
13He declared to you his covenant,[d] the 4:13 [d]Dt 9:9,11
Ten Commandments,[e] which he com- [e]Ex 24:12;
manded you to follow and then wrote 31:18; 34:28
them on two stone tablets. 14And the
LORD directed me at that time to teach
you the decrees and laws you are to follow in the land that you are crossing the
Jordan to possess.

Idolatry Forbidden

15You saw no form[f] of any kind the 4:15
day the LORD spoke to you at Horeb [f]Isa 40:18
out of the fire. Therefore watch your- [g]Jos 23:11
selves very carefully,[g] 16so that you do
not become corrupt and make for your-
selves an idol,[h] an image of any shape, 4:16 [h]Ex 20:4-5;
whether formed like a man or a woman, 32:7; Dt 5:8;
17or like any animal on earth or any bird Ro 1:23
that flies in the air, 18or like any creature
that moves along the ground or any fish
in the waters below. 19And when you
look up to the sky and see the sun,[i] the 4:19
moon and the stars—all the heavenly [i]Dt 17:3; Job 31:26
array[j]—do not be enticed into bowing [j]2Ki 17:16; 21:3;
down to them and worshiping things Ro 1:25
the LORD your God has apportioned
to all the nations under heaven. 20But
as for you, the LORD took you and 4:20
brought you out of the iron-smelting [k]1Ki 8:51;
furnace,[k] out of Egypt, to be the people Jer 11:4 [l]Ex 19:5;
of his inheritance,[l] as you now are. Dt 9:29

[21]The LORD was angry with me[m] because of you, and he solemnly swore
that I would not cross the Jordan and
enter the good land the LORD your
God is giving you as your inheritance.
[22]I will die in this land; I will not cross
the Jordan; but you are about to cross
over and take possession of that good
land.[n] [23]Be careful not to forget the
covenant[o] of the LORD your God that
he made with you; do not make for
yourselves an idol[p] in the form of anything the LORD your God has forbidden. [24]For the LORD your God is a
consuming fire,[q] a jealous God.
[25]After you have had children and
grandchildren and have lived in the land
a long time—if you then become corrupt and make any kind of idol, doing
evil[r] in the eyes of the LORD your God
and provoking him to anger, [26]I call
heaven and earth as witnesses against
you[s] this day that you will quickly perish from the land that you are crossing
the Jordan to possess. You will not live
there long but will certainly be destroyed. [27]The LORD will scatter[t] you
among the peoples, and only a few of
you will survive among the nations to
which the LORD will drive you. [28]There
you will worship man-made gods[u] of
wood and stone, which cannot see or
hear or eat or smell.[v] [29]But if from there
you seek[w] the LORD your God, you
will find him if you look for him with
all your heart[x] and with all your soul.[y]
[30]When you are in distress and all these
things have happened to you, then in
later days[z] you will return to the LORD
your God and obey him. [31]For the
LORD your God is a merciful[a] God; he
will not abandon or destroy you or forget the covenant with your forefathers,
which he confirmed to them by oath.

The LORD Is God

[32]Ask[b] now about the former days,
long before your time, from the day
God created man on the earth;[c] ask
from one end of the heavens to the
other.[d] Has anything so great as this ever
happened, or has anything like it ever
been heard of? [33]Has any other people
heard the voice of God[a] speaking out of
fire, as you have, and lived?[e] [34]Has any
god ever tried to take for himself one nation out of another nation,[f] by testings,
by miraculous signs[g] and wonders,[h] by
war, by a mighty hand and an outstretched arm,[i] or by great and awesome
deeds,[j] like all the things the LORD
your God did for you in Egypt before
your very eyes?
[35]You were shown these things so
that you might know that the LORD
is God; besides him there is no other.[k]
[36]From heaven he made you hear his
voice[l] to discipline you. On earth he
showed you his great fire, and you
heard his words from out of the fire.
[37]Because he loved[m] your forefathers
and chose their descendants after them,
he brought you out of Egypt by his
Presence and his great strength,[n] [38]to
drive out before you nations greater and
stronger than you and to bring you into
their land to give it to you for your
inheritance,[o] as it is today.
[39]Acknowledge and take to heart this
day that the LORD is God in heaven
above and on the earth below. There is
no other.[p] [40]Keep[q] his decrees and commands, which I am giving you today,
so that it may go well[r] with you and
your children after you and that you
may live long[s] in the land the LORD
your God gives you for all time.

Cities of Refuge

[41]Then Moses set aside three cities
east of the Jordan, [42]to which anyone
who had killed a person could flee if he
had unintentionally killed his neighbor
without malice aforethought. He could
flee into one of these cities and save his
life. [43]The cities were these: Bezer in
the desert plateau, for the Reubenites;
Ramoth in Gilead, for the Gadites; and
Golan in Bashan, for the Manassites.

Introduction to the Law

[44]This is the law Moses set before the
Israelites. [45]These are the stipulations,
decrees and laws Moses gave them when
they came out of Egypt [46]and were in
the valley near Beth Peor east of the Jordan, in the land of Sihon[t] king of the
Amorites, who reigned in Heshbon and
was defeated by Moses and the Israelites as they came out of Egypt. [47]They
took possession of his land and the land
of Og king of Bashan, the two Amorite
kings east of the Jordan. [48]This land extended from Aroer[u] on the rim of the

[a]33 Or *of a god*

4:21 [m]Nu 20:12; Dt 1:37
4:22 [n]Dt 3:25
4:23 [o]ver 9,16 [p]Ex 20:4
4:24 [q]Ex 24:17; Dt 9:3; Heb 12:29
4:25 [r]2Ki 17:2,17
4:26 [s]Dt 30:18-19; Isa 1:2; Mic 6:2
4:27 [t]Lev 26:33; Dt 28:36,64; Ne 1:8
4:28 [u]Dt 28:36,64; 1Sa 26:19; Jer 16:13 [v]Ps 115:4-8; 135:15-18
4:29 [w]2Ch 15:4; Isa 55:6 [x]Jer 29:13 [y]Dt 30:1-3,10
4:30 [z]Dt 31:29; Jer 23:20; Hos 3:5
4:31 [a]2Ch 30:9; Ne 9:31; Ps 116:5; Jnh 4:2
4:32 [b]Dt 32:7; Job 8:8 [c]Ge 1:27 [d]Mt 24:31
4:33 [e]Ex 20:22; Dt 5:24-26
4:34 [f]Ex 6:6 [g]Ex 7:3 [h]Dt 7:19; 26:8
4:34 [i]Ex 13:3 [j]Dt 34:12
4:35 [k]Dt 32:39; 1Sa 2:2; Isa 45:5,18
4:36 [l]Ex 19:9,19
4:37 [m]Dt 10:15 [n]Ex 13:3,9,14
4:38 [o]Dt 7:1; 9:5
4:39 [p]ver 35; Jos 2:11
4:40 [q]Lev 22:31; Dt 5:33 [r]Dt 5:16 [s]Dt 6:3,18; Eph 6:2-3
4:46 [t]Nu 21:26; Dt 3:29
4:48 [u]Dt 2:36

4:48 Arnon Gorge to Mount Siyon[a][v] (that
[v]Dt 3:9 is, Hermon), 49and included all the Arabah east of the Jordan, as far as the Sea
of the Arabah,[b] below the slopes of Pisgah.

The Ten Commandments

5 Moses summoned all Israel and
said:
Hear, O Israel, the decrees and laws
I declare in your hearing today. Learn
them and be sure to follow them. 2The
5:2 LORD our God made a covenant[w] with
[w]Ex 19:5 us at Horeb. 3It was not with our fathers that the LORD made this cove-
nant, but with us, with all of us who are
5:3 alive here today.[x] 4The LORD spoke[y]
[x]Heb 8:9 to you face to face out of the fire on
5:4 the mountain. 5(At that time I stood
[y]Dt 4:12, 33,36 between[z] the LORD and you to declare
to you the word of the LORD, because
5:5 you were afraid[a] of the fire and did not
[z]Gal 3:19 [a]Ex 20:18,21 go up the mountain.) And he said:

6"I am the LORD your God,
who brought you out of
Egypt, out of the land of
slavery.
7"You shall have no other gods before[c] me.
8"You shall not make for yourself
an idol in the form of anything in heaven above or on
the earth beneath or in the
waters below. 9You shall not
bow down to them or wor-
ship them; for I, the LORD
your God, am a jealous God,
punishing the children for
the sin of the fathers to the
third and fourth generation
5:9 of those who hate me,[b] 10but
[b]Ex 34:7 showing love to a thousand
⌞generations⌟ of those who
love me and keep my com-
5:10 mandments.[c]
[c]Jer 32:18 11"You shall not misuse the name
of the LORD your God, for
the LORD will not hold anyone guiltless who misuses his
5:11 name.[d]
[d]Lev 19:12; Mt 5:33-37 12"Observe the Sabbath day by
keeping it holy,[e] as the LORD
5:12 your God has commanded
[e]Ex 20:8 you. 13Six days you shall labor and do all your work,
5:14 14but the seventh day[f] is a
[f]Ge 2:2; Heb 4:4 Sabbath to the LORD your
God. On it you shall not do
any work, neither you, nor
your son or daughter, nor
your manservant or maid-
servant, nor your ox, your
donkey or any of your an-
imals, nor the alien within
your gates, so that your manservant and maidservant may
rest, as you do. 15Remem-
ber that you were slaves in
Egypt and that the LORD
your God brought you out
of there with a mighty hand
and an outstretched arm.[g] 5:15 [g]Dt 4:34
Therefore the LORD your
God has commanded you to
observe the Sabbath day.
16"Honor your father and your
mother,[h] as the LORD your 5:16 [h]Ex 20:12;
God has commanded you, Lev 19:3;
so that you may live long[i] Dt 27:16; Eph 6:2-3*;
and that it may go well with Col 3:20
you in the land the LORD [i]Dt 4:40
your God is giving you.
17"You shall not murder.[j] 5:17 [j]Mt 5:21-22*
18"You shall not commit adultery.[k] 5:18
19"You shall not steal. [k]Mt 5:27-30;
20"You shall not give false testimo- Lk 18:20*; Jas 2:11*
ny against your neighbor.
21"You shall not covet your neighbor's wife. You shall not set
your desire on your neighbor's house or land, his
manservant or maidservant,
his ox or donkey, or any-
thing that belongs to your 5:21
neighbor."[l] [l]Ro 7:7*; 13:9*

22These are the commandments the
LORD proclaimed in a loud voice to
your whole assembly there on the
mountain from out of the fire, the
cloud and the deep darkness; and he
added nothing more. Then he wrote
them on two stone tablets[m] and gave 5:22 [m]Ex 24:12;
them to me. 31:18; Dt 4:13
23When you heard the voice out of
the darkness, while the mountain was
ablaze with fire, all the leading men of
your tribes and your elders came to me.
24And you said, "The LORD our God
has shown us his glory and his majesty, and we have heard his voice from
the fire. Today we have seen that a man
can live even if God speaks with him.[n] 5:24 [n]Ex 19:19

[a]*48* Hebrew; Syriac (see also Deut. 3:9) *Sirion*
[b]*49* That is, the Dead Sea [c]*7* Or *besides*

25But now, why should we die? This
great fire will consume us, and we will
die if we hear the voice of the LORD
5:25 our God any longer.[o] 26For what mor-
[o]Dt 18:16 tal man has ever heard the voice of
the living God speaking out of fire, as
5:26 we have, and survived?[p] 27Go near and
[p]Dt 4:33 listen to all that the LORD our God
says. Then tell us whatever the LORD
our God tells you. We will listen and
obey."
28The LORD heard you when you
spoke to me and the LORD said to me,
"I have heard what this people said to
5:28 you. Everything they said was good.[q]
[q]Dt 18:17 29Oh, that their hearts would be in-
5:29 clined to fear me[r] and keep all my com-
[r]Ps 81:8,13 [s]Dt 11:1; mands[s] always, so that it might go well
Isa 48:18 with them and their children forever![t]
[t]Dt 4:1,40 30"Go, tell them to return to their
5:31 tents. 31But you stay here[u] with me so
[u]Ex 24:12 that I may give you all the commands,
decrees and laws you are to teach them
to follow in the land I am giving them
to possess."
32So be careful to do what the LORD
your God has commanded you; do not
5:32 turn aside to the right or to the left.[v]
[v]Dt 17:11,20; 33Walk in all the way that the LORD
28:14; Jos 1:7; 23:6; your God has commanded you,[w] so
Pr 4:27 that you may live and prosper and pro-
5:33 long your days[x] in the land that you
[w]Jer 7:23 [x]Dt 4:40 will possess.

Love the LORD Your God

6 These are the commands, decrees
and laws the LORD your God directed me to teach you to observe in the
land that you are crossing the Jordan to
possess, 2so that you, your children and
6:2 their children after them may fear[y] the
[y]Ex 20:20; Dt 10:12-13 LORD your God as long as you live by
keeping all his decrees and commands
that I give you, and so that you may
enjoy long life. 3Hear, O Israel, and be
careful to obey so that it may go well
with you and that you may increase
6:3 greatly[z] in a land flowing with milk and
[z]Dt 5:33 [a]Ex 3:8 honey,[a] just as the LORD, the God of
your fathers, promised you.
6:4 4Hear, O Israel: The LORD our God,
[b]Mk 12:29*; 1Co 8:4 the LORD is one.[a][b] 5Love[c] the LORD
6:5 your God with all your heart and with
[c]Mt 22:37*; all your soul and with all your strength.[d]
Mk 12:30*; Lk 10:27* 6These commandments that I give you
[d]Dt 10:12 today are to be upon your hearts.[e] 7Im-
6:6 press them on your children. Talk about
[e]Dt 11:18 them when you sit at home and when

LOVE

A CREED FOR LIFE

Deuteronomy 6:4–6

Hear, O Israel:
The Lord our God is one.
Love him.
Write his words upon the doorposts;
Teach them to your children.
Celebrate his providence
And remember your salvation.

you walk along the road, when you lie
down and when you get up.[f] 8Tie them 6:7 [f]Dt 4:9;
as symbols on your hands and bind 11:19;
them on your foreheads.[g] 9Write them Eph 6:4
on the doorframes of your houses and 6:8 [g]Ex 13:9,16;
on your gates.[h] Dt 11:18
10When the LORD your God brings 6:9
you into the land he swore to your fa- [h]Dt 11:20
thers, to Abraham, Isaac and Jacob, to
give you—a land with large, flourish- 6:10
ing cities you did not build,[i] 11houses [i]Jos 24:13
filled with all kinds of good things you
did not provide, wells you did not dig,
and vineyards and olive groves you did
not plant—then when you eat and are 6:11
satisfied,[j] 12be careful that you do not [j]Dt 8:10
forget the LORD, who brought you out
of Egypt, out of the land of slavery.
13Fear the LORD[k] your God, serve 6:13
him only[l] and take your oaths in his [k]Dt 10:20 [l]Mt 4:10*;
name. 14Do not follow other gods, the Lk 4:8*
gods of the peoples around you; 15for
the LORD your God[m], who is among 6:15 [m]Dt 4:24
you, is a jealous God and his anger will
burn against you, and he will destroy
you from the face of the land. 16Do
not test the LORD your God[n] as you 6:16 [n]Ex 17:7;
did at Massah. 17Be sure to keep the Mt 4:7*;
commands of the LORD your God and Lk 4:12*
the stipulations and decrees he has giv- 6:17 [o]Dt 11:22;
en you.[o] 18Do what is right and good Ps 119:4
in the LORD's sight, so that it may go 6:18
well[p] with you and you may go in and [p]Dt 4:40
take over the good land that the LORD
promised on oath to your forefathers,
19thrusting out all your enemies before
you, as the LORD said.
20In the future, when your son asks
you,[q] "What is the meaning of the 6:20 [q]Ex 13:14
stipulations, decrees and laws the LORD

[a]4 Or *The LORD our God is one LORD*; or *The LORD is our God, the LORD is one*; or *The LORD is our God, the LORD alone*

our God has commanded you?” 21tell
him: “We were slaves of Pharaoh in
Egypt, but the LORD brought us out
of Egypt with a mighty hand. 22Before
our eyes the LORD sent miraculous
signs and wonders—great and terrible—upon Egypt and Pharaoh and his
whole household. 23But he brought us
out from there to bring us in and give
us the land that he promised on oath
to our forefathers. 24The LORD commanded us to obey all these decrees and
6:24 [r]Dt 10:12; to fear the LORD our God,[r] so that we
Jer 32:39 might always prosper and be kept alive,
[s]Ps 41:2 as is the case today.[s] 25And if we are
careful to obey all this law before the
LORD our God, as he has commanded
6:25 us, that will be our righteousness.[t]”
[t]Dt 24:13; Ro 10:3,5

Driving Out the Nations

7 When the LORD your God brings
you into the land you are entering
to possess and drives out before you
7:1 many nations[u]—the Hittites, Gir-
[u]Dt 31:3; gashites, Amorites, Canaanites, Perizz-
Ac 13:19 ites, Hivites and Jebusites, seven nations
larger and stronger than you— 2and
when the LORD your God has delivered
them over to you and you have defeated them, then you must destroy them
7:2 totally.[a] Make no treaty[v] with them, and
[v]Ex 23:32 show them no mercy.[w] 3Do not inter-
[w]Dt 13:8 marry with them.[x] Do not give your
7:3 daughters to their sons or take their
[x]Ex 34:15-16; Ezr 9:2 daughters for your sons, 4for they will
turn your sons away from following me
to serve other gods, and the LORD’s
anger will burn against you and will
7:4 quickly destroy[y] you. 5This is what you
[y]Dt 6:15 are to do to them: Break down their
altars, smash their sacred stones, cut
down their Asherah poles[b] and burn
7:5 their idols in the fire.[z] 6For you are a
[z]Ex 23:24; people holy[a] to the LORD your God.[b]
Dt 12:2-3 The LORD your God has chosen[c] you
7:6 [a]Ex 19:5-6; out of all the peoples on the face of
1Pe 2:9 [b]Ps 50:5; the earth to be his people, his treasured
Jer 2:3 [c]Dt 14:2 possession.
7The LORD did not set his affection
on you and choose you because you
were more numerous than other peoples, for you were the fewest of all
7:7 peoples.[d] 8But it was because the LORD
[d]Dt 10:22 loved[e] you and kept the oath he swore[f]
7:8 to your forefathers that he brought you
[e]Dt 10:15 out with a mighty hand and redeemed
[f]Ex 32:13 you from the land of slavery,[g] from
[g]Ex 13:14 the power of Pharaoh king of Egypt.

9Know therefore that the LORD your
God is God;[h] he is the faithful God,[i] 7:9 [h]Dt 4:35
keeping his covenant of love[j] to a thou- [i]1Co 1:9; 2Ti 2:13
sand generations of those who love him [j]Ne 1:5;
and keep his commands. 10But Da 9:4

those who hate him he will repay to
their face by destruction;
he will not be slow to repay to
their face those who hate
him.

11Therefore, take care to follow the
commands, decrees and laws I give you
today.
12If you pay attention to these laws
and are careful to follow them, then
the LORD your God will keep his covenant of love with you, as he swore
to your forefathers.[k] 13He will love you 7:12 [k]Lev 26:3-13;
and bless you[l] and increase your num- Dt 28:1-14;
bers. He will bless the fruit of your Ps 105:8-9
womb, the crops of your land—your 7:13 [l]Jn 14:21
grain, new wine and oil—the calves [m]Dt 28:4
of your herds and the lambs of your
flocks in the land that he swore to
your forefathers to give you.[m] 14You will
be blessed more than any other people; none of your men or women will
be childless, nor any of your livestock
without young.[n] 15The LORD will keep 7:14
you free from every disease.[o] He will [n]Ex 23:26
not inflict on you the horrible diseases 7:15
you knew in Egypt, but he will inflict [o]Ex 15:26
them on all who hate you. 16You must
destroy all the peoples the LORD your
God gives over to you. Do not look on
them with pity[p] and do not serve their 7:16
gods, for that will be a snare[q] to you. [p]ver 2; Ex 23:33
17You may say to yourselves, “These [q]Jdg 8:27
nations are stronger than we are. How
can we drive them out?[r]” 18But do not 7:17
be afraid[s] of them; remember well what [r]Nu 33:53
the LORD your God did to Pharaoh 7:18
and to all Egypt.[t] 19You saw with your [s]Dt 31:6 [t]Ps 105:5
own eyes the great trials, the miraculous
signs and wonders, the mighty hand
and outstretched arm, with which the
LORD your God brought you out. The
LORD your God will do the same to all 7:19
the peoples you now fear.[u] 20Moreover, [u]Dt 4:34
the LORD your God will send the hor- 7:20
net[v] among them until even the survi- [v]Ex 23:28;
vors who hide from you have perished. Jos 24:12

[a]*2* The Hebrew term refers to the irrevocable giving over of things or persons to the LORD, often by totally destroying them; also in verse 26.
[b]*5* That is, symbols of the goddess Asherah; here and elsewhere in Deuteronomy

21Do not be terrified by them, for the
7:21 [w]Jos 3:10 LORD your God, who is among you,[w]
[x]Dt 10:17; Ne 9:32 is a great and awesome God.[x] 22The
LORD your God will drive out those
7:22 [y]Ex 23:28-30 nations before you, little by little.[y] You
will not be allowed to eliminate them
all at once, or the wild animals will
multiply around you. 23But the LORD
your God will deliver them over to you,
throwing them into great confusion until they are destroyed. 24He will give
their kings into your hand, and you
will wipe out their names from under
heaven. No one will be able to stand
7:24 [z]Jos 23:9 up against you;[z] you will destroy them.
25The images of their gods you are to
7:25 [a]Ex 32:20; 1Ch 14:12 burn[a] in the fire. Do not covet[b] the
silver and gold on them, and do not
[b]Jos 7:21 [c]Jdg 8:27 take it for yourselves, or you will be en-
[d]Dt 17:1 snared[c] by it, for it is detestable[d] to the
LORD your God. 26Do not bring a de-
testable thing into your house or you,
7:26 [e]Lev 27:28-29 like it, will be set apart for destruction.[e]
Utterly abhor and detest it, for it is set
apart for destruction.

Do Not Forget the LORD

8 Be careful to follow every command I am giving you today, so
8:1 [f]Dt 4:1 that you may live[f] and increase and
may enter and possess the land that the
LORD promised on oath to your forefathers. 2Remember how the LORD your
8:2 [g]Am 2:10 God led[g] you all the way in the desert
these forty years, to humble you and to
test you in order to know what was in
your heart, whether or not you would
keep his commands. 3He humbled you,
causing you to hunger and then feeding
8:3 [h]Ex 16:12, 14,35 you with manna,[h] which neither you
nor your fathers had known, to teach
[i]Ex 16:2-3; Mt 4:4*; Lk 4:4* you that man does not live on bread
alone but on every word that comes
from the mouth of the LORD.[i] 4Your
clothes did not wear out and your feet
8:4 [j]Dt 29:5; Ne 9:21 did not swell during these forty years.[j]
5Know then in your heart that as a man
disciplines his son, so the LORD your
8:5 [k]2Sa 7:14; Pr 3:11-12; Heb 12:5-11; Rev 3:19 God disciplines you.[k]
6Observe the commands of the LORD
your God, walking in his ways and re-
8:6 [l]Dt 5:33 vering him.[l] 7For the LORD your God
is bringing you into a good land—a
land with streams and pools of water,
with springs flowing in the valleys and
8:7 [m]Dt 11:9-12 hills;[m] 8a land with wheat and barley,
vines and fig trees, pomegranates, olive
oil and honey; 9a land where bread will
not be scarce and you will lack nothing;
a land where the rocks are iron and you
can dig copper out of the hills.
10When you have eaten and are
satisfied,[n] praise the LORD your God 8:10 [n]Dt 6:10-12
for the good land he has given you.
11Be careful that you do not forget the
LORD your God, failing to observe his
commands, his laws and his decrees that
I am giving you this day. 12Otherwise,
when you eat and are satisfied, when
you build fine houses and settle down,[o] 8:12 [o]Hos 13:6
13and when your herds and flocks grow
large and your silver and gold increase
and all you have is multiplied, 14then
your heart will become proud and you
will forget[p] the LORD your God, who 8:14 [p]Ps 106:21
brought you out of Egypt, out of the
land of slavery. 15He led you through
the vast and dreadful desert,[q] that thirsty 8:15 [q]Jer 2:6
and waterless land, with its venomous [r]Nu 21:6
snakes[r] and scorpions. He brought you [s]Nu 20:11; Ps 78:15; 114:8
water out of hard rock.[s] 16He gave you
manna to eat in the desert, something
your fathers had never known,[t] to hum- 8:16 [t]Ex 16:15
ble and to test you so that in the end
it might go well with you. 17You may
say to yourself,[u] "My power and the 8:17 [u]Dt 9:4,7,24
strength of my hands have produced
this wealth for me." 18But remember
the LORD your God, for it is he who
gives you the ability to produce wealth,[v] 8:18 [v]Pr 10:22; Hos 2:8
and so confirms his covenant, which he
swore to your forefathers, as it is today.
19If you ever forget the LORD your
God and follow other gods and worship and bow down to them, I testify
against you today that you will surely
be destroyed.[w] 20Like the nations the 8:19 [w]Dt 4:26; 30:18
LORD destroyed before you, so you will
be destroyed for not obeying the LORD
your God.

Not Because of Israel's Righteousness

9 Hear, O Israel. You are now about
to cross the Jordan to go in and dispossess nations greater and stronger than
you,[x] with large cities that have walls up 9:1 [x]Dt 4:38; 11:23,31
to the sky.[y] 2The people are strong and [y]Dt 1:28
tall—Anakites! You know about them
and have heard it said: "Who can stand
up against the Anakites?"[z] 3But be as- 9:2 [z]Nu 13:22,28, 32-33
sured today that the LORD your God is
the one who goes across ahead of you[a] 9:3 [a]Dt 31:3; Jos 3:11
like a devouring fire.[b] He will destroy [b]Dt 4:24; Heb 12:29
them; he will subdue them before you.
And you will drive them out and anni-

9:3 [c]Ex 23:31; Dt 7:23-24 hilate them quickly,[c] as the LORD has
promised you.
4 After the LORD your God has driv-
en them out before you, do not say to
9:4 [d]Dt 8:17 yourself,[d] "The LORD has brought me
[e]Lev 18:21, 24-30; Dt 18:9-14 here to take possession of this land because of my righteousness." No, it is on
account of the wickedness of these nations[e] that the LORD is going to drive
them out before you. 5 It is not because
9:5 [f]Tit 3:5 of your righteousness or your integrity[f]
[g]Ge 12:7; 13:15; 15:7; 17:8; 26:4 that you are going in to take possession
of their land; but on account of the
wickedness of these nations, the LORD
your God will drive them out before
you, to accomplish what he swore[g] to
your fathers, to Abraham, Isaac and Jacob. 6 Understand, then, that it is not
because of your righteousness that the
LORD your God is giving you this good
land to possess, for you are a stiff-
9:6 [h]ver 13; Ex 32:9; Dt 31:27 necked people.[h]

The Golden Calf

7 Remember this and never forget how
you provoked the LORD your God to
anger in the desert. From the day you
left Egypt until you arrived here, you
have been rebellious against the LORD.
8 At Horeb you aroused the LORD's
wrath so that he was angry enough
9:8 [i]Ex 32:7-10; Ps 106:19 to destroy you.[i] 9 When I went up on
the mountain to receive the tablets of
stone, the tablets of the covenant that
the LORD had made with you, I stayed
on the mountain forty days and forty
nights; I ate no bread and drank no
9:9 [j]Ex 24:12, 15,18; 34:28 water.[j] 10 The LORD gave me two stone
tablets inscribed by the finger of God.[k]
9:10 [k]Ex 31:18; Dt 4:13 On them were all the commandments
the LORD proclaimed to you on the
mountain out of the fire, on the day of
the assembly.
11 At the end of the forty days and
forty nights, the LORD gave me the
two stone tablets, the tablets of the
covenant. 12 Then the LORD told me,
"Go down from here at once, because
your people whom you brought out
9:12 [l]Ex 32:7-8; Dt 31:29 of Egypt have become corrupt.[l] They
[m]Jdg 2:17 have turned away quickly[m] from what
I commanded them and have made a
9:13 [n]ver 6; Ex 32:9; Dt 10:16 cast idol for themselves."
13 And the LORD said to me, "I have
seen this people,[n] and they are a stiff-
9:14 [o]Ex 32:10 necked people indeed! 14 Let me alone,[o]
[p]Nu 14:12; Dt 29:20 so that I may destroy them and blot
out[p] their name from under heaven.
And I will make you into a nation stronger and more numerous than they."

▸ FAITHFULNESS

A BETTER LAW

Deuteronomy 9:11

After Moses fasted 40 days, he came down the mountain with the Ten Commandments. After Jesus fasted 40 days, he entered the human arena with one great reduction of all ten. Moses said, "Do good and you will please God." Jesus said, "You have but to believe to please God, for what you believe will determine what you do."

15 So I turned and went down from
the mountain while it was ablaze with
fire. And the two tablets of the covenant
were in my hands.[a][q] 16 When I looked, 9:15 [q]Ex 19:18; 32:15
I saw that you had sinned against the
LORD your God; you had made for
yourselves an idol cast in the shape of a
calf.[r] You had turned aside quickly from 9:16 [r]Ex 32:19
the way that the LORD had command-
ed you. 17 So I took the two tablets and
threw them out of my hands, breaking
them to pieces before your eyes.

▸ SELF-CONTROL

GEHENNA'S GOLDEN CALVES

Deuteronomy 9:16

Did stone sphinxes line the avenues of Egypt? Did limestone lions guard the roads to Nineveh? Yes. It is in similar ways that golden calves flank all the roads that lead to hell.

18 Then once again I fell[s] prostrate
before the LORD for forty days and for- 9:18 [s]Ex 34:28
ty nights; I ate no bread and drank no
water, because of all the sin you had
committed, doing what was evil in the
LORD's sight and so provoking him to
anger. 19 I feared the anger and wrath
of the LORD, for he was angry enough
with you to destroy you.[t] But again 9:19 [t]Ex 32:10-11, 14
the LORD listened to me.[u] 20 And the [u]Dt 10:10
LORD was angry enough with Aaron to
destroy him, but at that time I prayed
for Aaron too. 21 Also I took that sinful
thing of yours, the calf you had made,
and burned it in the fire. Then I crushed

[a] *15* Or *And I had the two tablets of the covenant with me, one in each hand*

it and ground it to powder as fine as
dust and threw the dust into a stream
that flowed down the mountain.[v]
22 You also made the LORD angry at
Taberah,[w] at Massah[x] and at Kibroth
Hattaavah.[y]
23 And when the LORD sent you out
from Kadesh Barnea, he said, "Go up
and take possession of the land I have
given you." But you rebelled against the
command of the LORD your God. You
did not trust[z] him or obey him. 24 You
have been rebellious against the LORD
ever since I have known you.[a]
25 I lay prostrate before the LORD
those forty days and forty nights because the LORD had said he would destroy you.[b] 26 I prayed to the LORD
and said, "O Sovereign LORD, do not
destroy your people, your own inheritance that you redeemed by your great
power and brought out of Egypt with
a mighty hand.[c] 27 Remember your servants Abraham, Isaac and Jacob. Overlook the stubbornness of this people,
their wickedness and their sin. 28 Otherwise, the country from which you
brought us will say, 'Because the LORD
was not able to take them into the
land he had promised them, and because he hated them, he brought them
out to put them to death in the desert.'[d]
29 But they are your people, your inheritance[e] that you brought out by
your great power and your outstretched
arm."[f]

9:21 [v]Ex 32:20
9:22 [w]Nu 11:3 [x]Ex 17:7 [y]Nu 11:34
9:23 [z]Ps 106:24
9:24 [a]ver 7; Dt 31:27
9:25 [b]ver 18
9:26 [c]Ex 32:11
9:28 [d]Ex 32:12; Nu 14:16
9:29 [e]Dt 4:20; 1Ki 8:51 [f]Dt 4:34; Ne 1:10

Tablets Like the First Ones

10 At that time the LORD said to
me, "Chisel out two stone tablets[g] like the first ones and come up
to me on the mountain. Also make a
wooden chest.[a] 2 I will write on the tablets the words that were on the first tablets, which you broke. Then you are to
put them in the chest."[h]
3 So I made the ark out of acacia
wood[i] and chiseled[j] out two stone tablets like the first ones, and I went up
on the mountain with the two tablets
in my hands. 4 The LORD wrote on
these tablets what he had written before, the Ten Commandments he had
proclaimed[k] to you on the mountain,
out of the fire, on the day of the assembly. And the LORD gave them to me.
5 Then I came back down the mountain[l] and put the tablets in the ark[m] I
had made, as the LORD commanded
me, and they are there now.[n]
6 (The Israelites traveled from the
wells of the Jaakanites to Moserah.[o]
There Aaron died and was buried, and
Eleazar his son succeeded him as priest.[p]
7 From there they traveled to Gudgo-
dah and on to Jotbathah, a land with
streams of water.[q] 8 At that time the

10:1 [g]Ex 25:10; 34:1-2
10:2 [h]Ex 25:16,21; Dt 4:13
10:3 [i]Ex 25:5,10; 37:1-9 [j]Ex 34:4
10:4 [k]Ex 20:1
10:5 [l]Ex 34:29 [m]Ex 40:20
10:5 [n]1Ki 8:9
10:6 [o]Nu 33:30-31, 38 [p]Nu 20:25-28
10:7 [q]Nu 33:32-34

[a]1 That is, an ark

DAY 2 TWO

Kindness and the Purpose of God in My Life

Deuteronomy 10:17–19

We must be careful as we read the Pentateuch that we do not see merely the "legal" side of God. Here in this passage, the Lord doesn't say, "Thou shalt not," but instead says, "Go to it." Here, instead of simply telling Israel what they must avoid doing to keep from sinning, God deals with the more subtle kinds of sin—the sins of omission. To fail to defend the cause of the orphan is sin. So is the failure to protect widows. So is the failure to help the foreigner who suffers from severe loneliness in a strange and engulfing culture.

Once when I was traveling in Spain, I was attacked by thieves. I remember the ordeal of having to go to court and listen to the proceedings being carried out in Spanish, a language I could not understand. I knew the pain of being a stranger in a strange land. I felt the odd sensation of being central in a court scene without the slightest ability to defend myself.

Christians are to look around and seek those who are lost and alone, those who are unable to defend or protect themselves. Once we find these people, we need to know that God has given us the green light; our purpose is to minister to those who are in need of a little kindness.

If we are God's children, we are to act like it. We are to look to God's kindness to us and then spread that kindness to others. God's purpose for our lives is that we model our actions and attitudes after his care for those who are in need.

To begin a study on the topic of Kindness As a Worldview, turn to the home page on page 1058.

10:8 LORD set apart the tribe of Levi[r] to
[r]Nu 3:6 carry the ark of the covenant of the
[s]Dt 18:5 LORD, to stand before the LORD to
[t]Dt 21:5 minister[s] and to pronounce blessings[t] in
his name, as they still do today. 9That is
why the Levites have no share or inheritance among their brothers; the LORD
10:9 is their inheritance,[u] as the LORD your
[u]Nu 18:20; Dt 18:1-2; God told them.)
Eze 44:28 10Now I had stayed on the mountain
forty days and nights, as I did the first
time, and the LORD listened to me at
this time also. It was not his will to de-
10:10 stroy you.[v] 11"Go," the LORD said to
[v]Ex 33:17; 34:28; me, "and lead the people on their way,
Dt 9:18-19, so that they may enter and possess the
25 land that I swore to their fathers to give
them."

Fear the LORD

12And now, O Israel, what does the
10:12 LORD your God ask of you[w] but to
[w]Mic 6:8 fear the LORD your God, to walk in
[x]Dt 5:33; 6:13; all his ways, to love him,[x] to serve the
Mt 22:37 LORD your God with all your heart[y]
[y]Dt 6:5 and with all your soul, 13and to observe
the LORD's commands and decrees that
I am giving you today for your own
good?
14To the LORD your God belong
10:14 the heavens, even the highest heavens,[z]
[z]1Ki 8:27 the earth and everything in it.[a] 15Yet the
[a]Ex 19:5 LORD set his affection on your forefathers and loved[b] them, and he chose
10:15 you, their descendants, above all the na-
[b]Dt 4:37 tions, as it is today. 16Circumcise[c] your
10:16 hearts, therefore, and do not be stiff-
[c]Jer 4:4 necked[d] any longer. 17For the LORD
[d]Dt 9:6 your God is God of gods[e] and Lord of
10:17 lords, the great God, mighty and awe-
[e]Jos 22:22; Da 2:47 some, who shows no partiality[f] and ac-
[f]Ac 10:34; Ro 2:11; cepts no bribes. 18He defends the cause
Eph 6:9 of the fatherless and the widow,[g] and
10:18 loves the alien, giving him food and
[g]Ps 68:5 clothing. 19And you are to love those
10:19 who are aliens, for you yourselves were
[h]Lev 19:34 aliens in Egypt.[h] 20Fear the LORD your
10:20 God and serve him.[i] Hold fast[j] to him
[i]Mt 4:10 and take your oaths in his name.[k] 21He
[j]Dt 11:22 is your praise;[l] he is your God, who
[k]Ps 63:11 performed for you those great and awe-
10:21 some wonders[m] you saw with your own
[l]Ex 15:2; Jer 17:14 eyes. 22Your forefathers who went down
[m]Ps 106:21-22 into Egypt were seventy in all,[n] and
10:22 now the LORD your God has made
[n]Ge 46:26-27 you as numerous as the stars in the
[o]Ge 15:5; Dt 1:10 sky.[o]

DAY 2 TWO

▸ FAITHFULNESS AND THE PURPOSE OF GOD IN MY LIFE

Deuteronomy 10:20–22

Moses reminds the Israelites that God took Israel into Egypt as a group of some 70 souls. Four hundred years later they emerged as a nation. Many of us never live long enough to see God's promises to us completely fulfilled. God made this promise of nationhood to Abram and Sarai in Genesis 12. Even at the end of Abraham's life, Israel was a very small nation, numbering only three people. But in a day long after his death, the nation numbered in the millions.

Faithfulness always serves the purposes of God in our lives, but often the mills of God grind slowly. Only from a vantage point far down the years can we really see the intentions of God come to pass. Faithfulness is the character trait Abraham exhibited to the very end of his life. But even as he died, he could not measure the extent of the promise that was to come from his faithfulness. That finished vision was perhaps a score of lifetimes away.

Still, the promises of God never sleep.

In past days, a stonecutter often handed down the work of a cathedral to his son, and he to his son, and so on down the line, until—long after the original stonecutter himself slept in the churchyard—his dreams towered above his sleeping confidence. Faithfulness instructs us on how to live with purpose, but even better than that, it is something that we can hand off to our children until—as Abraham discovered—the world is blessed because of that simple discipline called obedience.

Faithfulness is something that any of us can offer to God. And when we give it, he gives us a purpose for every morning's sunrise. We live and have great reason to live.

To begin a study on the topic of God's Blessing on Faithfulness, turn to the home page on page 16.

Love and Obey the LORD

11 Love[p] the LORD your God and 11:1
keep his requirements, his de- [p]Dt 10:12; [q]Zec 3:7
crees, his laws and his commands
always.[q] 2Remember today that your

DAY 2 TWO

▸ GOODNESS AND THE PURPOSE OF GOD IN MY LIFE

Deuteronomy 11:1

"Goodness," said Moses, "is a matter of loving." Those who love God will behave themselves. Struggling to keep God's commands while we are indifferent to loving God will produce only a mechanical obedience. That is why Augustine said, "Love God and do what you will," because love is the key to goodness. Love is the key to morality. Love is the foundation of genuine goodness.

This verse in Deuteronomy offers four categories of mandates to which love is the empowering key: God's requirements, his decrees, his laws and his commands. God's requirements are different from his laws. Exodus names the Ten Commandments as laws, but Micah lists but three moral requirements: "To act justly and to love mercy and to walk humbly with your God" (Micah 6:8). Notice that these requirements are not a part of the Ten Commandments. One might keep all of the commandments but still not love mercy or walk humbly. Yet for even the most righteous, these traits enumerated by Micah are beautiful virtues, which not only make those who wear them more beautiful, they make a relationship with God appear more inviting.

The world usually admires those who live by the Ten Commandments, but the world would be more likely to seek God if those who kept his Ten Commandments would also keep Micah's three requirements. Acting justly is that behavior that makes us treat all people fairly, regardless of social station. Loving mercy is that requirement that makes us appear gentle. Walking humbly is that approach to life that takes away every hint of pretense and arrogance.

Obeying the commandments will give us moral rectitude, but living by God's requirements will give us the best form of goodness, which is Christlikeness.

To begin a study on the topic of Goodness, Caring How God Feels About My Morality, turn to the home page on page 51.

children were not the ones who saw and
experienced the discipline of the LORD
your God:[r] his majesty, his mighty
hand, his outstretched arm; 3 the signs
he performed and the things he did in
the heart of Egypt, both to Pharaoh
king of Egypt and to his whole country; 4 what he did to the Egyptian army,
to its horses and chariots, how he overwhelmed them with the waters of the
Red Sea[a][s] as they were pursuing you,
and how the LORD brought lasting
ruin on them. 5 It was not your children
who saw what he did for you in the
desert until you arrived at this place,
6 and what he did[t] to Dathan and Abiram, sons of Eliab the Reubenite, when
the earth opened its mouth right in the
middle of all Israel and swallowed them
up with their households, their tents
and every living thing that belonged to
them. 7 But it was your own eyes that
saw all these great things the LORD has
done.

8 Observe therefore all the commands
I am giving you today, so that you may
have the strength to go in and take over
the land that you are crossing the Jordan
to possess,[u] 9 and so that you may live
long[v] in the land that the LORD swore[w]
to your forefathers to give to them and
their descendants, a land flowing with
milk and honey.[x] 10 The land you are
entering to take over is not like the land
of Egypt, from which you have come,
where you planted your seed and irrigated it by foot as in a vegetable garden.
11 But the land you are crossing the Jordan to take possession of is a land of
mountains and valleys that drinks rain
from heaven.[y] 12 It is a land the LORD
your God cares for; the eyes[z] of the
LORD your God are continually on it
from the beginning of the year to its
end.

13 So if you faithfully obey[a] the commands I am giving you today—to love[b]
the LORD your God and to serve him
with all your heart and with all your
soul— 14 then I will send rain[c] on your
land in its season, both autumn and
spring rains,[d] so that you may gather in
your grain, new wine and oil. 15 I will
provide grass[e] in the fields for your cattle, and you will eat and be satisfied.[f]
16 Be careful, or you will be enticed

a4 Hebrew *Yam Suph;* that is, Sea of Reeds

11:2 [r]Dt 5:24; 8:5
11:4 [s]Ex 14:27
11:6 [t]Nu 16:1-35
11:8 [u]Jos 1:7
11:9 [v]Dt 4:40; Pr 10:27 [w]Dt 9:5 [x]Ex 3:8
11:11 [y]Dt 8:7
11:12 [z]1Ki 9:3
11:13 [a]Dt 6:17 [b]Dt 10:12
11:14 [c]Lev 26:4; Dt 28:12 [d]Joel 2:23; Jas 5:7
11:15 [e]Ps 104:14 [f]Dt 6:11

to turn away and worship other gods
11:16 [g]Dt 8:19; and bow down to them.[g] 17Then the
29:18; LORD's anger[h] will burn against you,
Job 31:9,27 and he will shut[i] the heavens so that it
11:17 will not rain and the ground will yield
[h]Dt 6:15 no produce, and you will soon perish[j]
[i]1Ki 8:35; 2Ch 6:26 from the good land the LORD is giv-
[j]Dt 4:26 ing you. 18Fix these words of mine in
your hearts and minds; tie them as symbols on your hands and bind them on
11:18 [k]Dt 6:6-8 your foreheads.[k] 19Teach them to your
children,[l] talking about them when you
11:19 [l]Dt 6:7 sit at home and when you walk along
[m]Dt 4:9-10 the road, when you lie down and when
you get up.[m] 20Write them on the doorframes of your houses and on your
11:20 [n]Dt 6:9 gates,[n] 21so that your days and the days
of your children may be many[o] in the
11:21 [o]Pr 3:2; 4:10 land that the LORD swore to give your
[p]Ps 72:5 forefathers, as many as the days that the
heavens are above the earth.[p]
11:22 [q]Dt 6:17 22If you carefully observe[q] all these
[r]Dt 10:20 commands I am giving you to follow—
to love the LORD your God, to walk in
all his ways and to hold fast[r] to him—
23then the LORD will drive out all these
nations before you, and you will dispossess nations larger and stronger than
11:23 [s]Dt 4:38; 9:1 you.[s] 24Every place where you set your
foot will be yours:[t] Your territory will
11:24 [t]Ge 15:18; extend from the desert to Lebanon, and
Ex 23:31; from the Euphrates River to the west-
Jos 1:3; 14:9 ern sea.[a] 25No man will be able to stand
against you. The LORD your God, as he
promised you, will put the terror and
fear of you on the whole land, wherever
11:25 you go.[u]
[u]Ex 23:27; Dt 7:24 26See, I am setting before you today
a blessing and a curse[v]— 27the bless-
11:26 [v]Dt 30:1, ing[w] if you obey the commands of the
15,19 LORD your God that I am giving you
11:27 [w]Dt 28:1-14 today; 28the curse if you disobey[x] the
commands of the LORD your God and
11:28 [x]Dt 28:15 turn from the way that I command
you today by following other gods,
which you have not known. 29When
the LORD your God has brought you
into the land you are entering to possess, you are to proclaim on Mount
Gerizim the blessings, and on Mount
11:29 [y]Dt 27:12-13; Ebal the curses.[y] 30As you know, these
Jos 8:33 mountains are across the Jordan, west
of the road,[b] toward the setting sun,
11:30 [z]Ge 12:6 near the great trees of Moreh,[z] in the
[a]Jos 4:19 territory of those Canaanites living in
the Arabah in the vicinity of Gilgal.[a]
11:31 [b]Dt 9:1; 31You are about to cross the Jordan
Jos 1:11 to enter and take possession[b] of the
land the LORD your God is giving you.
When you have taken it over and are
living there, 32be sure that you obey all
the decrees and laws I am setting before
you today.

The One Place of Worship

12 These are the decrees and laws
you must be careful to follow in
the land that the LORD, the God of
your fathers, has given you to possess—
as long as you live in the land.[c] 2De- 12:1 [c]Dt 4:9-10;
stroy completely all the places on the 1Ki 8:40
high mountains and on the hills and
under every spreading tree[d] where the 12:2 [d]2Ki 16:4;
nations you are dispossessing worship 17:10
their gods. 3Break down their altars,
smash[e] their sacred stones and burn 12:3 [e]Nu 33:52;
their Asherah poles in the fire; cut down Dt 7:5;
the idols of their gods and wipe out Jdg 2:2
their names from those places.
4You must not worship the LORD
your God in their way. 5But you are to
seek the place the LORD your God will
choose from among all your tribes to
put his Name there for his dwelling.[f] 12:5 [f]ver 11,13;
To that place you must go; 6there bring 2Ch 7:12,16
your burnt offerings and sacrifices, your
tithes[g] and special gifts, what you have 12:6 [g]Dt 14:22-23
vowed to give and your freewill offer-
ings, and the firstborn of your herds and
flocks. 7There, in the presence of the
LORD your God, you and your families
shall eat and shall rejoice[h] in everything 12:7 [h]ver 12,18;
you have put your hand to, because the Lev 23:40;
LORD your God has blessed you. Dt 14:26
8You are not to do as we do here today, everyone as he sees fit, 9since you
have not yet reached the resting place

[a]*24* That is, the Mediterranean [b]*30* Or *Jordan, westward*

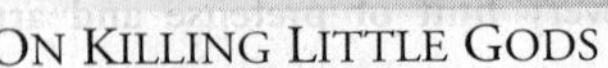

GENTLENESS

ON KILLING LITTLE GODS

Deuteronomy 12:4

End your idolatry. Show your small tin gods that you mean business. Stop giving the place of Christ to the smaller gods of your appetites.

Adore the living Christ with gentle adoration,
And be quiet about it.
Let silence in your praise confide.
Boisterous sacrifice is vain
And smacks of unsurrendered pride.

and the inheritance the LORD your
God is giving you. 10But you will cross
12:10 the Jordan and settle in the land the
iDt 11:31 LORD your God is giving[i] you as an inheritance, and he will give you rest from
all your enemies around you so that
you will live in safety. 11Then to the
place the LORD your God will choose
12:11 jver 5; as a dwelling for his Name[j]—there you
Dt 15:20; are to bring everything I command
16:2 you: your burnt offerings and sacrifices, your tithes and special gifts, and
all the choice possessions you have
vowed to the LORD. 12And there re-
12:12 kver 7 joice[k] before the LORD your God, you,
lDt 10:9; your sons and daughters, your men-
14:29 servants and maidservants, and the Levites from your towns, who have no
allotment or inheritance[l] of their own.
13Be careful not to sacrifice your burnt
offerings anywhere you please. 14Offer
them only at the place the LORD will
12:14 choose[m] in one of your tribes, and there
mver 11 observe everything I command you.
15Nevertheless, you may slaughter
your animals in any of your towns and
eat as much of the meat as you want, as
12:15 nver 20-23; if it were gazelle or deer,[n] according to
Dt 14:5; the blessing the LORD your God gives
15:22 you. Both the ceremonially unclean and
the clean may eat it. 16But you must
12:16 not eat the blood;[o] pour it out on the
oGe 9:4; Lev 7:26; ground like water.[p] 17You must not eat
17:10-12 pDt 15:23 in your own towns the tithe of your
grain and new wine and oil, or the firstborn of your herds and flocks, or whatever you have vowed to give, or your
freewill offerings or special gifts. 18In-
12:18 qDt 14:23 stead, you are to eat[q] them in the pres-
rver 5 ence of the LORD your God at the place
sver 7,12 the LORD your God will choose[r]—you,
your sons and daughters, your menservants and maidservants, and the Levites from your towns—and you are to
rejoice[s] before the LORD your God in
everything you put your hand to. 19Be
12:19 careful not to neglect the Levites[t] as
tDt 14:27 long as you live in your land.
20When the LORD your God has en-
12:20 uDt 19:8 larged your territory[u] as he promised[v]
vGe 15:18; Dt 11:24 you, and you crave meat and say, "I
would like some meat," then you may
eat as much of it as you want. 21If
the place where the LORD your God
chooses to put his Name is too far away
from you, you may slaughter animals
from the herds and flocks the LORD
has given you, as I have commanded

you, and in your own towns you may
eat as much of them as you want. 22Eat
them as you would gazelle or deer.[w] 12:22
Both the ceremonially unclean and the wver 15
clean may eat. 23But be sure you do not
eat the blood,[x] because the blood is the 12:23 xver 16;
life, and you must not eat the life with Ge 9:4;
the meat. 24You must not eat the blood; Lev 17:11,14
pour it out on the ground like water.
25Do not eat it, so that it may go well[y] 12:25
with you and your children after you, yDt 4:40; Isa 3:10
because you will be doing what is right[z] zEx 15:26; Dt 13:18;
in the eyes of the LORD. 1Ki 11:38
26But take your consecrated things
and whatever you have vowed to give,[a] 12:26
and go to the place the LORD will aver 17; Nu 5:9-10
choose. 27Present your burnt offerings[b] 12:27
on the altar of the LORD your God, bLev 1:5,9,13
both the meat and the blood. The
blood of your sacrifices must be poured
beside the altar of the LORD your God,
but you may eat the meat. 28Be careful
to obey all these regulations I am giv- 12:28
ing you, so that it may always go well[c] cver 25;
with you and your children after you, Dt 4:40
because you will be doing what is good
and right in the eyes of the LORD
your God.
29The LORD your God will cut off[d] 12:29
before you the nations you are about dJos 23:4
to invade and dispossess. But when you
have driven them out and settled in
their land, 30and after they have been
destroyed before you, be careful not to
be ensnared by inquiring about their
gods, saying, "How do these nations
serve their gods? We will do the same."
31You must not worship the LORD your
God in their way, because in worshiping their gods, they do all kinds of detestable things the LORD hates.[e] They 12:31
even burn their sons[f] and daughters in eDt 9:5
the fire as sacrifices to their gods. fDt 18:10; Jer 32:35
32See that you do all I command you; 12:32
do not add[g] to it or take away from it. gDt 4:2; Jos 1:7; Rev 22:18-19

Worshiping Other Gods

13 If a prophet,[h] or one who fore- 13:1 hMt 24:24;
tells by dreams, appears among Mk 13:22; 2Th 2:9
you and announces to you a miraculous
sign or wonder, 2and if the sign or wonder of which he has spoken takes place,
and he says, "Let us follow other gods"[i] 13:2 iver 6,13
(gods you have not known) "and let us
worship them," 3you must not listen to
the words of that prophet or dreamer.
The LORD your God is testing[j] you 13:3 jDt 8:2,16
to find out whether you love him with

all your heart and with all your soul. 4It is the LORD your God you must follow,[k] and him you must revere. Keep his commands and obey him; serve him and hold fast[l] to him. 5That prophet or dreamer must be put to death, because he preached rebellion against the LORD your God, who brought you out of Egypt and redeemed you from the land of slavery; he has tried to turn you from the way the LORD your God commanded you to follow. You must purge the evil[m] from among you.

6If your very own brother, or your son or daughter, or the wife you love, or your closest friend secretly entices[n] you, saying, "Let us go and worship other gods" (gods that neither you nor your fathers have known, 7gods of the peoples around you, whether near or far, from one end of the land to the other), 8do not yield[o] to him or listen to him. Show him no pity. Do not spare him or shield him. 9You must certainly put him to death.[p] Your hand must be the first in putting him to death, and then the hands of all the people. 10Stone him to death, because he tried to turn you away from the LORD your God, who brought you out of Egypt, out of the land of slavery. 11Then all Israel will hear and be afraid,[q] and no one among you will do such an evil thing again.

12If you hear it said about one of the towns the LORD your God is giving you to live in 13that wicked men[r] have arisen among you and have led the people of their town astray, saying, "Let us go and worship other gods" (gods you have not known), 14then you must inquire, probe and investigate it thoroughly. And if it is true and it has been proved that this detestable thing has been done among you, 15you must certainly put to the sword all who live in that town. Destroy it completely,[a] both its people and its livestock. 16Gather all the plunder of the town into the middle of the public square and completely burn the town and all its plunder as a whole burnt offering to the LORD your God.[s] It is to remain a ruin[t] forever, never to be rebuilt. 17None of those condemned things[a] shall be found in your hands, so that the LORD will turn from his fierce anger;[u] he will show you mercy, have compassion[v] on you, and increase your numbers,[w] as he promised[x] on oath to your forefathers, 18because you obey the LORD your God, keeping all his commands that I am giving you today and doing what is right[y] in his eyes.

Clean and Unclean Food

14 You are the children[z] of the LORD your God. Do not cut yourselves or shave the front of your heads for the dead, 2for you are a people holy to the LORD your God.[a] Out of all the peoples on the face of the earth, the LORD has chosen you to be his treasured possession.[b]

3Do not eat any detestable thing.[c] 4These are the animals you may eat:[d] the ox, the sheep, the goat, 5the deer, the gazelle, the roe deer, the wild goat, the ibex, the antelope and the mountain sheep.[b] 6You may eat any animal that has a split hoof divided in two and that chews the cud. 7However, of those that chew the cud or that have a split hoof completely divided you may not eat the camel, the rabbit or the coney.[c] Although they chew the cud, they do not have a split hoof; they are ceremonially unclean for you. 8The pig is also unclean; although it has a split hoof, it does not chew the cud. You are not to eat their meat or touch their carcasses.[e]

9Of all the creatures living in the water, you may eat any that has fins and scales. 10But anything that does not have fins and scales you may not eat; for you it is unclean.

11You may eat any clean bird. 12But these you may not eat: the eagle, the vulture, the black vulture, 13the red kite, the black kite, any kind of falcon, 14any kind of raven, 15the horned owl, the screech owl, the gull, any kind of hawk, 16the little owl, the great owl, the white owl, 17the desert owl, the osprey, the cormorant, 18the stork, any kind of heron, the hoopoe and the bat.

19All flying insects that swarm are unclean to you; do not eat them. 20But any winged creature that is clean you may eat.

[a] *15,17* The Hebrew term refers to the irrevocable giving over of things or persons to the LORD, often by totally destroying them. [b] *5* The precise identification of some of the birds and animals in this chapter is uncertain. [c] *7* That is, the hyrax or rock badger

13:4 [k]2Ki 23:3; 2Ch 34:31 [l]Dt 10:20
13:5 [m]Dt 17:7,12; 1Co 5:13
13:6 [n]Dt 17:2-7; 29:18
13:8 [o]Pr 1:10
13:9 [p]Dt 17:5,7
13:11 [q]Dt 19:20
13:13 [r]ver 2,6; 1Jn 2:19
13:16 [s]Jos 6:24 [t]Jos 8:28; Jer 49:2
13:17 [u]Nu 25:4 [v]Dt 30:3 [w]Dt 7:13
13:17 [x]Ge 22:17; 26:4,24; 28:14
13:18 [y]Dt 12:25,28
14:1 [z]Lev 19:28; 21:5; Jer 16:6; 41:5; Ro 8:14; 9:8; Gal 3:26
14:2 [a]Lev 20:26 [b]Dt 7:6; 26:18-19
14:3 [c]Eze 4:14
14:4 [d]Lev 11:2-45; Ac 10:14
14:8 [e]Lev 11:26-27

21 Do not eat anything you find already dead.[f] You may give it to an alien living in any of your towns, and he may eat it, or you may sell it to a foreigner. But you are a people holy to the LORD your God.[g]

Do not cook a young goat in its mother's milk.[h]

14:21 [f]Lev 17:15; 22:8 [g]ver 2 [h]Ex 23:19; 34:26

Tithes

22 Be sure to set aside a tenth[i] of all that your fields produce each year. 23 Eat the tithe of your grain, new wine and oil, and the firstborn of your herds and flocks in the presence of the LORD your God at the place he will choose as a dwelling for his Name,[j] so that you may learn[k] to revere the LORD your God always. 24 But if that place is too distant and you have been blessed by the LORD your God and cannot carry your tithe (because the place where the LORD will choose to put his Name is so far away), 25 then exchange your tithe for silver, and take the silver with you and go to the place the LORD your God will choose. 26 Use the silver to buy whatever you like: cattle, sheep, wine or other fermented drink, or anything you wish. Then you and your household shall eat there in the presence of the LORD your God and rejoice.[l] 27 And do not neglect the Levites[m] living in your towns, for they have no allotment or inheritance of their own.[n]

14:22 [i]Lev 27:30; Dt 12:6,17; Ne 10:37
14:23 [j]Dt 12:5 [k]Dt 4:10
14:26 [l]Dt 12:7-8
14:27 [m]Dt 12:19 [n]Nu 18:20

JOY

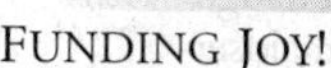

FUNDING JOY!

Deuteronomy 14:26

Tithing furnishes the party at the house of God. Giving to God funds the life of joy. And the joy it buys draws earth's disconsolate, transforming their dirges into anthems. God loves authentic parties and, like any good parent, he loves to watch his children play.

28 At the end of every three years, bring all the tithes of that year's produce and store it in your towns,[o] 29 so that the Levites (who have no allotment[p] or inheritance of their own) and the aliens,[q] the fatherless and the widows who live in your towns may come and eat and be satisfied, and so that the LORD your God may bless[r] you in all the work of your hands.

14:28 [o]Dt 26:12
14:29 [p]ver 27 [q]Dt 26:12 [r]Dt 15:10; Mal 3:10

The Year for Canceling Debts

15 At the end of every seven years you must cancel debts.[s] 2 This is how it is to be done: Every creditor shall cancel the loan he has made to his fellow Israelite. He shall not require payment from his fellow Israelite or brother, because the LORD's time for canceling debts has been proclaimed. 3 You may require payment from a foreigner,[t] but you must cancel any debt your brother owes you. 4 However, there should be no poor among you, for in the land the LORD your God is giving you to possess as your inheritance, he will richly bless[u] you, 5 if only you fully obey the LORD your God and are careful to follow[v] all these commands I am giving you today. 6 For the LORD your God will bless you as he has promised, and you will lend to many nations but will borrow from none. You will rule over many nations but none will rule over you.[w]

7 If there is a poor man among your brothers in any of the towns of the land that the LORD your God is giving you, do not be hardhearted or tightfisted[x] toward your poor brother. 8 Rather be openhanded[y] and freely lend him whatever he needs. 9 Be careful not to harbor this wicked thought: "The seventh year, the year for canceling debts,[z] is near," so that you do not show ill will[a] toward your needy brother and give him nothing. He may then appeal to the LORD against you, and you will be found guilty of sin.[b] 10 Give generously to him and do so without a grudging heart;[c] then because of this the LORD your God will bless[d] you in all your work and in everything you put your hand to. 11 There will always be poor people in the land. Therefore I command you to be openhanded toward your brothers and toward the poor and needy in your land.[e]

15:1 [s]Dt 31:10
15:3 [t]Dt 23:20
15:4 [u]Dt 28:8
15:5 [v]Dt 28:1
15:6 [w]Dt 28:12-13, 44
15:7 [x]1Jn 3:17
15:8 [y]Mt 5:42; Lk 6:34
15:9 [z]ver 1 [a]Mt 20:15 [b]Dt 24:15
15:10 [c]2Co 9:5 [d]Dt 14:29; 24:19
15:11 [e]Mt 26:11; Mk 14:7; Jn 12:8

Freeing Servants

12 If a fellow Hebrew, a man or a woman, sells himself to you and serves you six years, in the seventh year you must let him go free.[f] 13 And when you release him, do not send him away empty-handed. 14 Supply him liberally from your flock, your threshing floor and your winepress. Give to him as the

15:12 [f]Ex 21:2; Lev 25:39; Jer 34:14

LORD your God has blessed you. 15Re-
member that you were slaves[g] in Egypt
and the LORD your God redeemed
you.[h] That is why I give you this command today.
16But if your servant says to you, "I
do not want to leave you," because he
loves you and your family and is well
off with you, 17then take an awl and
push it through his ear lobe into the
door, and he will become your servant
for life. Do the same for your maidservant.
18Do not consider it a hardship to set
your servant free, because his service to
you these six years has been worth twice
as much as that of a hired hand. And
the LORD your God will bless you in
everything you do.

The Firstborn Animals

19Set apart for the LORD your God
every firstborn male[i] of your herds and
flocks. Do not put the firstborn of your
oxen to work, and do not shear the
firstborn of your sheep. 20Each year you
and your family are to eat them in the
presence of the LORD your God at the
place he will choose.[j] 21If an animal has
a defect, is lame or blind, or has any serious flaw, you must not sacrifice it to
the LORD your God.[k] 22You are to eat
it in your own towns. Both the ceremonially unclean and the clean may eat it,
as if it were gazelle or deer.[l] 23But you
must not eat the blood; pour it out on
the ground like water.[m]

Passover

16 Observe the month of Abib[n]
and celebrate the Passover of the
LORD your God, because in the month
of Abib he brought you out of Egypt by
night. 2Sacrifice as the Passover to the
LORD your God an animal from your
flock or herd at the place the LORD
will choose as a dwelling for his Name.[o]
3Do not eat it with bread made with
yeast, but for seven days eat unleavened
bread, the bread of affliction,[p] because
you left Egypt in haste[q]—so that all the
days of your life you may remember
the time of your departure from Egypt.[r]
4Let no yeast be found in your possession in all your land for seven days. Do
not let any of the meat you sacrifice on
the evening of the first day remain until
morning.[s]

15:15 [g]Dt 5:15 [h]Dt 16:12
15:19 [i]Ex 13:2
15:20 [j]Dt 12:5-7, 17,18; 14:23
15:21 [k]Lev 22:19-25
15:22 [l]Dt 12:15,22
15:23 [m]Dt 12:16
16:1 [n]Ex 12:2; 13:4
16:2 [o]Dt 12:5,26
16:3 [p]Ex 12:8,39; 34:18 [q]Ex 12:11, 15,19 [r]Ex 13:3,6-7
16:4 [s]Ex 12:10; 34:25

5You must not sacrifice the Passover
in any town the LORD your God gives
you 6except in the place he will choose
as a dwelling for his Name. There you
must sacrifice the Passover in the evening, when the sun goes down, on the
anniversary[a][t] of your departure from
Egypt. 7Roast[u] it and eat it at the place
the LORD your God will choose. Then
in the morning return to your tents.
8For six days eat unleavened bread and
on the seventh day hold an assembly[v] to
the LORD your God and do no work.

Feast of Weeks

9Count off seven weeks[w] from the
time you begin to put the sickle to the
standing grain.[x] 10Then celebrate the
Feast of Weeks to the LORD your God
by giving a freewill offering in proportion to the blessings the LORD your
God has given you. 11And rejoice[y] before the LORD your God at the place
he will choose as a dwelling for his
Name—you, your sons and daughters,
your menservants and maidservants, the
Levites[z] in your towns, and the aliens,
the fatherless and the widows living
among you. 12Remember that you were
slaves in Egypt,[a] and follow carefully
these decrees.

Feast of Tabernacles

13Celebrate the Feast of Tabernacles
for seven days after you have gathered
the produce of your threshing floor[b]
and your winepress.[c] 14Be joyful[d] at
your Feast—you, your sons and daughters, your menservants and maidservants, and the Levites, the aliens, the
fatherless and the widows who live in
your towns. 15For seven days celebrate
the Feast to the LORD your God at the
place the LORD will choose. For the
LORD your God will bless you in all
your harvest and in all the work of your
hands, and your joy[e] will be complete.
16Three times a year all your men
must appear before the LORD your
God at the place he will choose: at the
Feast of Unleavened Bread, the Feast of
Weeks and the Feast of Tabernacles.[f] No
man should appear before the LORD
empty-handed:[g] 17Each of you must
bring a gift in proportion to the way
the LORD your God has blessed you.

[a]6 Or *down, at the time of day*

16:6 [t]Ex 12:6; Dt 12:5
16:7 [u]Ex 12:8; 2Ch 35:13
16:8 [v]Ex 12:16; 13:6; Lev 23:8
16:9 [w]Ex 34:22; Lev 23:15 [x]Ex 23:16; Nu 28:26
16:11 [y]Dt 12:7 [z]Dt 12:12
16:12 [a]Dt 15:15
16:13 [b]Lev 23:34 [c]Ex 23:16
16:14 [d]ver 11
16:15 [e]Lev 23:39
16:16 [f]Ex 23:14,16 [g]Ex 34:20

Judges

16:18 [h]Dt 1:16
18 Appoint judges[h] and officials for
each of your tribes in every town the
LORD your God is giving you, and they
16:19 [i]Ex 23:2,8 [j]Lev 19:15; Dt 1:17 [k]Ecc 7:7
shall judge the people fairly. 19 Do not
pervert justice[i] or show partiality.[j] Do
not accept a bribe,[k] for a bribe blinds
the eyes of the wise and twists the words
of the righteous. 20 Follow justice and
justice alone, so that you may live and
possess the land the LORD your God is
giving you.

16:21 [l]Dt 7:5 [m]Ex 34:13; 2Ki 17:16; 21:3; 2Ch 33:3

Worshiping Other Gods

21 Do not set up any wooden Asherah
pole[a][l] beside the altar you build to the
LORD your God,[m] 22 and do not erect a
16:22 [n]Lev 26:1
sacred stone,[n] for these the LORD your
God hates.

17 Do not sacrifice to the LORD
your God an ox or a sheep that
17:1 [o]Mal 1:8,13 [p]Dt 15:21
has any defect[o] or flaw in it, for that
would be detestable to him.[p]
2 If a man or woman living among
you in one of the towns the LORD gives
you is found doing evil in the eyes of
the LORD your God in violation of his
17:2 [q]Dt 13:6-11
covenant,[q] 3 and contrary to my com-
17:3 [r]Jer 7:22-23 [s]Job 31:26
mand[r] has worshiped other gods, bowing down to them or to the sun[s] or
the moon or the stars of the sky, 4 and
this has been brought to your attention,
then you must investigate it thoroughly. If it is true and it has been proved
that this detestable thing has been done
17:4 [t]Dt 13:12-14
in Israel,[t] 5 take the man or woman who
has done this evil deed to your city gate
17:5 [u]Lev 24:14
and stone that person to death.[u] 6 On
the testimony of two or three witnesses
a man shall be put to death, but no one
shall be put to death on the testimony
17:6 [v]Nu 35:30; Dt 19:15; Jos 7:25; Mt 18:16; Jn 8:17; 2Co 13:1; 1Ti 5:19; Heb 10:28
of only one witness.[v] 7 The hands of the
witnesses must be the first in putting
him to death, and then the hands of all
the people. You must purge the evil[w]
from among you.

17:7 [w]Dt 13:5,9

Law Courts

8 If cases come before your courts that
are too difficult for you to judge—wheth-
17:8 [x]2Ch 19:10 [y]Dt 12:5; Hag 2:11
er bloodshed, lawsuits or assaults[x]—take
them to the place the LORD your God
will choose.[y] 9 Go to the priests, who
are Levites, and to the judge who is in
office at that time. Inquire of them and
17:9 [z]Dt 19:17; Eze 44:24
they will give you the verdict.[z] 10 You
must act according to the decisions they
give you at the place the LORD will
choose. Be careful to do everything they
direct you to do. 11 Act according to the
law they teach you and the decisions
they give you. Do not turn aside from
what they tell you, to the right or to the
17:11 [a]Dt 25:1
left.[a] 12 The man who shows contempt[b]
for the judge or for the priest who
17:12 [b]Nu 15:30
stands ministering there to the LORD
your God must be put to death. You
must purge the evil from Israel. 13 All
the people will hear and be afraid, and
17:13 [c]Dt 13:11; 19:20
will not be contemptuous again.[c]

The King

14 When you enter the land the LORD
your God is giving you and have taken
possession of it and settled in it, and
you say, "Let us set a king over us
17:14 [d]Dt 11:31; 1Sa 8:5,19-20
like all the nations around us,"[d] 15 be
sure to appoint over you the king the
LORD your God chooses. He must be
17:15 [e]Jer 30:21
from among your own brothers.[e] Do
not place a foreigner over you, one who
is not a brother Israelite. 16 The king,
moreover, must not acquire great num-
17:16 [f]1Ki 4:26; 10:26 [g]Isa 31:1; Hos 11:5 [h]1Ki 10:28; Eze 17:15 [i]Ex 13:17
bers of horses for himself[f] or make the
people return to Egypt[g] to get more of
them,[h] for the LORD has told you, "You
are not to go back that way again."[i]
17 He must not take many wives,[j] or his
heart will be led astray. He must not
17:17 [j]1Ki 11:3
accumulate large amounts of silver and
gold.
18 When he takes the throne of his
17:18 [k]Dt 31:22,24
kingdom, he is to write[k] for himself on
a scroll a copy of this law, taken from
that of the priests, who are Levites. 19 It
is to be with him, and he is to read it all
17:19 [l]Jos 1:8
the days of his life[l] so that he may learn
to revere the LORD his God and follow
carefully all the words of this law and
these decrees 20 and not consider himself better than his brothers and turn
17:20 [m]1Ki 15:5 [n]Dt 5:32
from the law[m] to the right or to the
left.[n] Then he and his descendants will
reign a long time over his kingdom in
Israel.

Offerings for Priests and Levites

18 The priests, who are Levites—
indeed the whole tribe of Levi—
are to have no allotment or inheritance
with Israel. They shall live on the of-
18:1 [o]Dt 10:9; 1Co 9:13
ferings made to the LORD by fire, for
that is their inheritance.[o] 2 They shall

[a]21 Or *Do not plant any tree dedicated to Asherah*

have no inheritance among their brothers; the LORD is their inheritance, as he
promised them.
3This is the share due the priests from
the people who sacrifice a bull or a
sheep: the shoulder, the jowls and the
18:3 inner parts.[p] 4You are to give them the
pLev 7:28-34 firstfruits of your grain, new wine and
oil, and the first wool from the shear-
18:4 ing of your sheep,[q] 5for the LORD your
qEx 22:29; God has chosen them[r] and their de-
Nu 18:12 scendants out of all your tribes to stand
18:5 rEx 28:1 and minister[s] in the LORD's name al-
sDt 10:8 ways.
6If a Levite moves from one of your
towns anywhere in Israel where he is living, and comes in all earnestness to the
18:6 place the LORD will choose,[t] 7he may
tNu 35:2-3 minister in the name of the LORD his
God like all his fellow Levites who serve
there in the presence of the LORD. 8He
is to share equally in their benefits, even
though he has received money from the
18:8 u2Ch 31:4; sale of family possessions.[u]
Ne 12:44,47

Detestable Practices

9When you enter the land the LORD
your God is giving you, do not learn
18:9 to imitate[v] the detestable ways of the
vDt 12:29-31 nations there. 10Let no one be found
among you who sacrifices his son or
daughter in[a] the fire, who practices div-
18:10 wDt 12:31 ination[w] or sorcery, interprets omens,
xLev 19:31 engages in witchcraft,[x] 11or casts spells,
or who is a medium or spiritist or who
consults the dead. 12Anyone who does
these things is detestable to the LORD,
and because of these detestable practices the LORD your God will drive
18:12 out those nations before you.[y] 13You
yLev 18:24; must be blameless before the LORD
Dt 9:4 your God.

The Prophet

14The nations you will dispossess listen to those who practice sorcery or
divination. But as for you, the LORD
your God has not permitted you to do
so. 15The LORD your God will raise up
for you a prophet like me from among
18:15 your own brothers.[z] You must listen to
zJn 1:21; him. 16For this is what you asked of the
Ac 3:22*; 7:37* LORD your God at Horeb on the day
of the assembly when you said, "Let us
not hear the voice of the LORD our
18:16 God nor see this great fire anymore, or
aEx 20:19; we will die."[a]
Dt 5:23-27 17The LORD said to me: "What they
say is good. 18I will raise up for them
a prophet like you from among their
brothers; I will put my words[b] in his 18:18
mouth, and he will tell them everything bIsa 51:16; Jn 17:8
I command him.[c] 19If anyone does not cJn 4:25-26;
listen to my words that the prophet 8:28; 12:49-50
speaks in my name, I myself will call
him to account.[d] 20But a prophet who 18:19 dAc 3:23*
presumes to speak in my name any-
thing I have not commanded him to
say, or a prophet who speaks in the 18:20
name of other gods,[e] must be put to eJer 14:14
death."[f] fDt 13:1-5

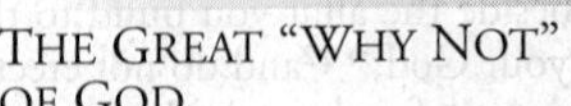

KINDNESS

THE GREAT "WHY NOT" OF GOD

Deuteronomy 18:19

Jesus is the ultimate fulfillment of Moses' prophecy. Kindness is strength that has said its prayers and followed Christ. It doesn't talk much, having made the grace of God a listening exercise.

21You may say to yourselves, "How
can we know when a message has
not been spoken by the LORD?" 22If
what a prophet proclaims in the name
of the LORD does not take place or
come true, that is a message the LORD
has not spoken.[g] That prophet has spo- 18:22 gJer 28:9
ken presumptuously.[h] Do not be afraid hver 20
of him.

Cities of Refuge

19 When the LORD your God has
destroyed the nations whose
land he is giving you, and when you
have driven them out and settled in
their towns and houses,[i] 2then set aside 19:1 iDt 12:29
for yourselves three cities centrally lo-
cated in the land the LORD your God
is giving you to possess. 3Build roads
to them and divide into three parts the
land the LORD your God is giving you
as an inheritance, so that anyone who
kills a man may flee there.
4This is the rule concerning the man
who kills another and flees there to save
his life—one who kills his neighbor
unintentionally, without malice aforethought. 5For instance, a man may go
into the forest with his neighbor to cut

a10 Or *who makes his son or daughter pass through*

wood, and as he swings his ax to fell a
tree, the head may fly off and hit his
neighbor and kill him. That man may
flee to one of these cities and save his
19:6 life. 6Otherwise, the avenger of blood[j]
[j]Nu 35:12 might pursue him in a rage, overtake
him if the distance is too great, and kill
him even though he is not deserving
of death, since he did it to his neighbor without malice aforethought. 7This
is why I command you to set aside for
yourselves three cities.
8If the LORD your God enlarges your
territory, as he promised on oath to your
forefathers, and gives you the whole
land he promised them, 9because you
carefully follow all these laws I command you today—to love the LORD
your God and to walk always in his
19:9 ways[k]—then you are to set aside three
[k]Jos 20:7-8 more cities. 10Do this so that innocent
blood will not be shed in your land,
which the LORD your God is giving
you as your inheritance, and so that
19:10 you will not be guilty of bloodshed.[l]
[l]Nu 35:33; 11But if a man hates his neighbor and
Dt 21:1-9 lies in wait for him, assaults and kills
19:11 him,[m] and then flees to one of these
[m]Nu 35:16 cities, 12the elders of his town shall
send for him, bring him back from the
city, and hand him over to the avenger
19:13 [n]Dt 7:2 of blood to die. 13Show him no pity.[n]
[o]1Ki 2:31 You must purge from Israel the guilt
of shedding innocent blood,[o] so that it
may go well with you.
14Do not move your neighbor's
boundary stone set up by your predecessors in the inheritance you receive in
the land the LORD your God is giving
19:14 [p]Dt 27:17; you to possess.[p]
Pr 22:28; Hos 5:10

Witnesses

15One witness is not enough to convict a man accused of any crime or offense he may have committed. A matter
19:15 [q]Nu 35:30; must be established by the testimony of
Dt 17:6; two or three witnesses.[q]
Mt 18:16*; Jn 8:17; 16If a malicious witness[r] takes the
2Co 13:1*; 1Ti 5:19; stand to accuse a man of a crime, 17the
Heb 10:28 two men involved in the dispute must
19:16 stand in the presence of the LORD be-
[r]Ex 23:1; Ps 27:12 fore the priests and the judges[s] who
are in office at the time. 18The judges
must make a thorough investigation,
and if the witness proves to be a liar,
19:17 [s]Dt 17:9 giving false testimony against his broth-
19:19 er, 19then do to him as he intended to
[t]Pr 19:5,9 do to his brother.[t] You must purge the
evil from among you. 20The rest of the
people will hear of this and be afraid,[u] 19:20
and never again will such an evil thing [u]Dt 17:13; 21:21
be done among you. 21Show no pity:[v]
life for life, eye for eye, tooth for tooth, 19:21 [v]ver 13
hand for hand, foot for foot.[w] [w]Ex 21:24; Lev 24:20; Mt 5:38*

Going to War

20 When you go to war against
your enemies and see horses
and chariots and an army greater than
yours,[x] do not be afraid[y] of them,[z] be- 20:1
cause the LORD your God, who brought [x]Ps 20:7; Isa 31:1
you up out of Egypt, will be with you. [y]Dt 31:6,8
2When you are about to go into battle, [z]2Ch 32:7-8
the priest shall come forward and ad-
dress the army. 3He shall say: "Hear,
O Israel, today you are going into battle
against your enemies. Do not be faint-
hearted[a] or afraid; do not be terrified or 20:3 [a]Jos 23:10
give way to panic before them. 4For the
LORD your God is the one who goes
with you to fight[b] for you against your 20:4 [b]Dt 1:30;
enemies to give you victory." 3:22;
5The officers shall say to the army: Jos 23:10
"Has anyone built a new house and not
dedicated[c] it? Let him go home, or he 20:5 [c]Ne 12:27
may die in battle and someone else may
dedicate it. 6Has anyone planted a vineyard and not begun to enjoy it? Let
him go home, or he may die in battle
and someone else enjoy it. 7Has anyone become pledged to a woman and
not married her? Let him go home,
or he may die in battle and someone
else marry her.[d]" 8Then the officers 20:7 [d]Dt 24:5
shall add, "Is any man afraid or faint-
hearted? Let him go home so that his
brothers will not become disheartened
too."[e] 9When the officers have finished 20:8
speaking to the army, they shall appoint [e]Jdg 7:3
commanders over it.
10When you march up to attack a
city, make its people an offer of peace.[f] 20:10 [f]Lk 14:31-32
11If they accept and open their gates,
all the people in it shall be subject to
forced labor[g] and shall work for you. 20:11 [g]1Ki 9:21
12If they refuse to make peace and they
engage you in battle, lay siege to that
city. 13When the LORD your God delivers it into your hand, put to the sword
all the men in it.[h] 14As for the women, 20:13 [h]Nu 31:7
the children, the livestock[i] and every-
thing else in the city, you may take these 20:14 [i]Jos 8:2; 22:8
as plunder for yourselves. And you may
use the plunder the LORD your God
gives you from your enemies. 15This is
how you are to treat all the cities that

are at a distance from you and do not belong to the nations nearby.

16However, in the cities of the nations the LORD your God is giving you as an inheritance, do not leave alive anything that breathes.[j] 17Completely destroy[a] them—the Hittites, Amorites, Canaanites, Perizzites, Hivites and Jebusites—as the LORD your God has commanded you. 18Otherwise, they will teach you to follow all the detestable things they do in worshiping their gods,[k] and you will sin[l] against the LORD your God.

20:16 [j]Ex 23:31-33; Nu 21:2-3; Dt 7:2; Jos 11:14
20:18 [k]Ex 34:16; Dt 7:4; 12:30-31 [l]Ex 23:33

19When you lay siege to a city for a long time, fighting against it to capture it, do not destroy its trees by putting an ax to them, because you can eat their fruit. Do not cut them down. Are the trees of the field people, that you should besiege them?[b] 20However, you may cut down trees that you know are not fruit trees and use them to build siege works until the city at war with you falls.

Atonement for an Unsolved Murder

21 If a man is found slain, lying in a field in the land the LORD your God is giving you to possess, and it is not known who killed him, 2your elders and judges shall go out and measure the distance from the body to the neighboring towns. 3Then the elders of the town nearest the body shall take a heifer that has never been worked and has never worn a yoke 4and lead her down to a valley that has not been plowed or planted and where there is a flowing stream. There in the valley they are to break the heifer's neck. 5The priests, the sons of Levi, shall step forward, for the LORD your God has chosen them to minister and to pronounce blessings[m] in the name of the LORD and to decide all cases of dispute and assault.[n] 6Then all the elders of the town nearest the body shall wash their hands[o] over the heifer whose neck was broken in the valley, 7and they shall declare: "Our hands did not shed this blood, nor did our eyes see it done. 8Accept this atonement for your people Israel, whom you have redeemed, O LORD, and do not hold your people guilty of the blood of an innocent man." And the bloodshed will be atoned for.[p] 9So you will purge[q] from yourselves the guilt of shedding innocent blood, since you have done what is right in the eyes of the LORD.

21:5 [m]1Ch 23:13 [n]Dt 17:8-11
21:6 [o]Mt 27:24
21:8 [p]Nu 35:33-34
21:9 [q]Dt 19:13

Marrying a Captive Woman

10When you go to war against your enemies and the LORD your God delivers them into your hands[r] and you take captives, 11if you notice among the captives a beautiful woman and are attracted to her, you may take her as your wife. 12Bring her into your home and have her shave her head,[s] trim her nails 13and put aside the clothes she was wearing when captured. After she has lived in your house and mourned her father and mother for a full month,[t] then you may go to her and be her husband and she shall be your wife. 14If you are not pleased with her, let her go wherever she wishes. You must not sell her or treat her as a slave, since you have dishonored her.[u]

21:10 [r]Jos 21:44
21:12 [s]Lev 14:9; Nu 6:9
21:13 [t]Ps 45:10
21:14 [u]Ge 34:2

The Right of the Firstborn

15If a man has two wives, and he loves one but not the other, and both bear him sons but the firstborn is the son of the wife he does not love,[v] 16when he wills his property to his sons, he must not give the rights of the firstborn to the son of the wife he loves in preference to his actual firstborn, the son of the wife he does not love.[w] 17He must acknowledge the son of his unloved wife as the firstborn by giving him a double share of all he has. That son is the first sign of his father's strength.[x] The right of the firstborn belongs to him.[y]

21:15 [v]Ge 29:33
21:16 [w]1Ch 26:10
21:17 [x]Ge 49:3 [y]Ge 25:31

A Rebellious Son

18If a man has a stubborn and rebellious son who does not obey his father and mother[z] and will not listen to them when they discipline him, 19his father and mother shall take hold of him and bring him to the elders at the gate of his town. 20They shall say to the elders, "This son of ours is stubborn and rebellious. He will not obey us. He is a profligate and a drunkard." 21Then all the men of his town shall stone him to

21:18 [z]Pr 1:8; Isa 30:1; Eph 6:1-3

[a]*17* The Hebrew term refers to the irrevocable giving over of things or persons to the LORD, often by totally destroying them. [b]*19* Or *down to use in the siege, for the fruit trees are for the benefit of man.*

death. You must purge the evil[a] from among you. All Israel will hear of it and be afraid.[b]

21:21 [a]Dt 19:19; 1Co 5:13* [b]Dt 13:11

Various Laws

22If a man guilty of a capital offense[c] is put to death and his body is hung on a tree, 23you must not leave his body on the tree overnight.[d] Be sure to bury him that same day, because anyone who is hung on a tree is under God's curse.[e] You must not desecrate[f] the land the LORD your God is giving you as an inheritance.

21:22 [c]Dt 22:26; Mk 14:64; Ac 23:29
21:23 [d]Jos 8:29; 10:27; Jn 19:31 [e]Gal 3:13* [f]Lev 18:25; Nu 35:34

LOVE

THE HILL OF LOVERS

Deuteronomy 21:23

Only grace can erase self-will and offer life to those who are willing to apologize for a certain Roman crucifixion. Love gathered itself up at Golgotha that we might be redeemed. No wonder Francis de Sales called Calvary "the hill of lovers."

22

If you see your brother's ox or sheep straying, do not ignore it but be sure to take it back to him.[g] 2If the brother does not live near you or if you do not know who he is, take it home with you and keep it until he comes looking for it. Then give it back to him. 3Do the same if you find your brother's donkey or his cloak or anything he loses. Do not ignore it.

4If you see your brother's donkey[h] or his ox fallen on the road, do not ignore it. Help him get it to its feet.

5A woman must not wear men's clothing, nor a man wear women's clothing, for the LORD your God detests anyone who does this.

6If you come across a bird's nest beside the road, either in a tree or on the ground, and the mother is sitting on the young or on the eggs, do not take the mother with the young.[i] 7You may take the young, but be sure to let the mother go, so that it may go well with you and you may have a long life.[j]

8When you build a new house, make a parapet around your roof so that you may not bring the guilt of bloodshed on your house if someone falls from the roof.

22:1 [g]Ex 23:4-5
22:4 [h]Ex 23:5
22:6 [i]Lev 22:28
22:7 [j]Dt 4:40

9Do not plant two kinds of seed in your vineyard;[k] if you do, not only the crops you plant but also the fruit of the vineyard will be defiled.[a]

10Do not plow with an ox and a donkey yoked together.[l]

11Do not wear clothes of wool and linen woven together.[m]

12Make tassels on the four corners of the cloak you wear.[n]

22:9 [k]Lev 19:19
22:10 [l]2Co 6:14
22:11 [m]Lev 19:19
22:12 [n]Nu 15:37-41; Mt 23:5

Marriage Violations

13If a man takes a wife and, after lying with her,[o] dislikes her 14and slanders her and gives her a bad name, saying, "I married this woman, but when I approached her, I did not find proof of her virginity," 15then the girl's father and mother shall bring proof that she was a virgin to the town elders at the gate. 16The girl's father will say to the elders, "I gave my daughter in marriage to this man, but he dislikes her. 17Now he has slandered her and said, 'I did not find your daughter to be a virgin.' But here is the proof of my daughter's virginity." Then her parents shall display the cloth before the elders of the town, 18and the elders[p] shall take the man and punish him. 19They shall fine him a hundred shekels of silver[b] and give them to the girl's father, because this man has given an Israelite virgin a bad name. She shall continue to be his wife; he must not divorce her as long as he lives.

20If, however, the charge is true and no proof of the girl's virginity can be found, 21she shall be brought to the door of her father's house and there the men of her town shall stone her to death. She has done a disgraceful thing[q] in Israel by being promiscuous while still in her father's house. You must purge the evil from among you.

22If a man is found sleeping with another man's wife, both the man who slept with her and the woman must die.[r] You must purge the evil from Israel.

23If a man happens to meet in a town a virgin pledged to be married and he sleeps with her, 24you shall take both of them to the gate of that town and stone them to death—the girl because she was in a town and did not scream

22:13 [o]Dt 24:1
22:18 [p]Ex 18:21
22:21 [q]Ge 34:7; Dt 13:5; 23:17-18; Jdg 20:6; 2Sa 13:12
22:22 [r]Lev 20:10; Jn 8:5

[a]9 Or *be forfeited to the sanctuary* [b]19 That is, about 2 1/2 pounds (about 1 kilogram)

for help, and the man because he violated another man's wife. You must purge the evil from among you.[s]

25But if out in the country a man happens to meet a girl pledged to be married and rapes her, only the man who has done this shall die. 26Do nothing to the girl; she has committed no sin deserving death. This case is like that of someone who attacks and murders his neighbor, 27for the man found the girl out in the country, and though the betrothed girl screamed, there was no one to rescue her.

28If a man happens to meet a virgin who is not pledged to be married and rapes her and they are discovered,[t] 29he shall pay the girl's father fifty shekels of silver.[a] He must marry the girl, for he has violated her. He can never divorce her as long as he lives.

30A man is not to marry his father's wife; he must not dishonor his father's bed.[u]

Exclusion From the Assembly

23 No one who has been emasculated by crushing or cutting may enter the assembly of the LORD.

2No one born of a forbidden marriage[b] nor any of his descendants may enter the assembly of the LORD, even down to the tenth generation.

3No Ammonite or Moabite or any of his descendants may enter the assembly of the LORD, even down to the tenth generation.[v] 4For they did not come to meet you with bread and water on your way when you came out of Egypt, and they hired Balaam[w] son of Beor from Pethor in Aram Naharaim[c] to pronounce a curse on you. 5However, the LORD your God would not listen to Balaam but turned the curse[x] into a blessing for you, because the LORD your God loves you. 6Do not seek a treaty of friendship with them as long as you live.[y]

7Do not abhor an Edomite, for he is your brother.[z] Do not abhor an Egyptian, because you lived as an alien in his country.[a] 8The third generation of children born to them may enter the assembly of the LORD.

Uncleanness in the Camp

9When you are encamped against your enemies, keep away from everything impure. 10If one of your men is unclean because of a nocturnal emission, he is to go outside the camp and stay there.[b] 11But as evening approaches he is to wash himself, and at sunset he may return to the camp.

12Designate a place outside the camp where you can go to relieve yourself. 13As part of your equipment have something to dig with, and when you relieve yourself, dig a hole and cover up your excrement. 14For the LORD your God moves[c] about in your camp to protect you and to deliver your enemies to you. Your camp must be holy,[d] so that he will not see among you anything indecent and turn away from you.

Miscellaneous Laws

15If a slave has taken refuge with you, do not hand him over to his master.[e] 16Let him live among you wherever he likes and in whatever town he chooses. Do not oppress[f] him.

17No Israelite man[g] or woman is to become a shrine prostitute.[h] 18You must not bring the earnings of a female prostitute or of a male prostitute[d] into the house of the LORD your God to pay any vow, because the LORD your God detests them both.

19Do not charge your brother interest, whether on money or food or anything else that may earn interest.[i] 20You may charge a foreigner interest, but not a brother Israelite, so that the LORD your God may bless[j] you in everything you put your hand to in the land you are entering to possess.

21If you make a vow to the LORD your God, do not be slow to pay it, for the LORD your God will certainly demand it of you and you will be guilty of sin.[k] 22But if you refrain from making a vow, you will not be guilty. 23Whatever your lips utter you must be sure to do, because you made your vow freely to the LORD your God with your own mouth.

24If you enter your neighbor's vineyard, you may eat all the grapes you want, but do not put any in your basket. 25If you enter your neighbor's grainfield, you may pick kernels with your

[a]*29* That is, about 1 1/4 pounds (about 0.6 kilogram) [b]*2* Or *one of illegitimate birth* [c]*4* That is, Northwest Mesopotamia [d]*18* Hebrew *of a dog*

22:24 [s]ver 21-22; 1Co 5:13*
22:28 [t]Ex 22:16
22:30 [u]Lev 18:8; 20:11; 18:8; Dt 27:20; 1Co 5:1
23:3 [v]Ne 13:2
23:4 [w]Nu 22:5-6; 23:7; 2Pe 2:15
23:5 [x]Pr 26:2
23:6 [y]Ezr 9:12
23:7 [z]Ge 25:26; Ob 1:10,12 [a]Ex 22:21; 23:9; Lev 19:34; Dt 10:19
23:10 [b]Lev 15:16
23:14 [c]Lev 26:12 [d]Ex 3:5
23:15 [e]1Sa 30:15
23:16 [f]Ex 22:21
23:17 [g]Ge 19:25; 2Ki 23:7 [h]Lev 19:29; Dt 22:21
23:19 [i]Ex 22:25; Lev 25:35-37
23:20 [j]Dt 15:10; 28:12
23:21 [k]Nu 30:1-2; Ecc 5:4-5; Mt 5:33

hands, but you must not put a sickle to his standing grain.[l]

24 If a man marries a woman who becomes displeasing to him[m] because he finds something indecent about her, and he writes her a certificate of divorce,[n] gives it to her and sends her from his house, 2and if after she leaves his house she becomes the wife of another man, 3and her second husband dislikes her and writes her a certificate of divorce, gives it to her and sends her from his house, or if he dies, 4then her first husband, who divorced her, is not allowed to marry her again after she has been defiled. That would be detestable in the eyes of the LORD. Do not bring sin upon the land the LORD[o] your God is giving you as an inheritance.

5If a man has recently married, he must not be sent to war or have any other duty laid on him. For one year he is to be free to stay at home and bring happiness to the wife he has married.[p]

6Do not take a pair of millstones—not even the upper one—as security for a debt, because that would be taking a man's livelihood as security.

7If a man is caught kidnapping one of his brother Israelites and treats him as a slave or sells him, the kidnapper must die.[q] You must purge the evil from among you.

8In cases of leprous[a] diseases be very careful to do exactly as the priests, who are Levites, instruct you. You must follow carefully what I have commanded them.[r] 9Remember what the LORD your God did to Miriam along the way after you came out of Egypt.[s]

10When you make a loan of any kind to your neighbor, do not go into his house to get what he is offering as a pledge. 11Stay outside and let the man to whom you are making the loan bring the pledge out to you. 12If the man is poor, do not go to sleep with his pledge in your possession. 13Return his cloak to him by sunset[t] so that he may sleep in it. Then he will thank you, and it will be regarded as a righteous act in the sight of the LORD your God.[u]

14Do not take advantage of a hired man who is poor and needy, whether he is a brother Israelite or an alien living in one of your towns.[v] 15Pay him his wages each day before sunset, because he is poor[w] and is counting on it.[x] Otherwise he may cry to the LORD against you, and you will be guilty of sin.[y]

16Fathers shall not be put to death for their children, nor children put to death for their fathers; each is to die for his own sin.[z]

17Do not deprive the alien or the fatherless of justice,[a] or take the cloak of the widow as a pledge. 18Remember that you were slaves in Egypt and the LORD your God redeemed you from there. That is why I command you to do this.

19When you are harvesting in your field and you overlook a sheaf, do not go back to get it.[b] Leave it for the alien, the fatherless and the widow, so that the LORD your God may bless[c] you in all the work of your hands. 20When you beat the olives from your trees, do not go over the branches a second time.[d] Leave what remains for the alien, the fatherless and the widow. 21When you harvest the grapes in your vineyard, do not go over the vines again. Leave what remains for the alien, the fatherless and the widow. 22Remember that you were slaves in Egypt. That is why I command you to do this.[e]

25 When men have a dispute, they are to take it to court and the judges will decide the case,[f] acquitting the innocent and condemning the guilty.[g] 2If the guilty man deserves to be beaten,[h] the judge shall make him lie down and have him flogged in his presence with the number of lashes his crime deserves, 3but he must not give him more than forty lashes.[i] If he is flogged more than that, your brother will be degraded in your eyes.[j]

4Do not muzzle an ox while it is treading out the grain.[k]

5If brothers are living together and one of them dies without a son, his widow must not marry outside the family. Her husband's brother shall take her and marry her and fulfill the duty of a brother-in-law to her.[l] 6The first son she bears shall carry on the name of the dead brother so that his name will not be blotted out from Israel.[m]

7However, if a man does not want to marry his brother's wife, she shall go to the elders at the town gate and say,

[a]*8* The Hebrew word was used for various diseases affecting the skin—not necessarily leprosy.

23:25 [l]Mt 12:1; Mk 2:23; Lk 6:1
24:1 [m]Dt 22:13 [n]Mt 5:31*; 19:7-9; Mk 10:4-5
24:4 [o]Jer 3:1
24:5 [p]Dt 20:7
24:7 [q]Ex 21:16
24:8 [r]Lev 13:1-46; 14:2
24:9 [s]Nu 12:10
24:13 [t]Ex 22:26 [u]Dt 6:25; Da 4:27
24:14 [v]Lev 25:35-43; Dt 15:12-18
24:15 [w]Jer 22:13 [x]Lev 19:13
24:15 [y]Dt 15:9; Jas 5:4
24:16 [z]2Ki 14:6; 2Ch 25:4; Jer 31:29-30; Eze 18:20
24:17 [a]Dt 1:17; 10:17-18; 16:19
24:19 [b]Lev 19:9; 23:22 [c]Pr 19:17
24:20 [d]Lev 19:10
24:22 [e]ver 18
25:1 [f]Dt 19:17 [g]Dt 1:16-17
25:2 [h]Lk 12:47-48
25:3 [i]2Co 11:24 [j]Job 18:3
25:4 [k]Pr 12:10; 1Co 9:9*; 1Ti 5:18*
25:5 [l]Mt 22:24; Mk 12:19; Lk 20:28
25:6 [m]Ge 38:9; Ru 4:5,10

“My husband’s brother refuses to carry
on his brother’s name in Israel. He will
not fulfill the duty of a brother-in-law
25:7 to me.”[n] 8Then the elders of his town
[n]Ru 4:1-2,5-6 shall summon him and talk to him. If
he persists in saying, “I do not want to
marry her,” 9his brother’s widow shall
go up to him in the presence of the el-
25:9 ders, take off one of his sandals,[o] spit in
[o]Ru 4:7-8,11 his face and say, “This is what is done
to the man who will not build up his
brother’s family line.” 10That man’s line
shall be known in Israel as The Family
of the Unsandaled.

11If two men are fighting and the
wife of one of them comes to rescue
her husband from his assailant, and she
reaches out and seizes him by his private parts, 12you shall cut off her hand.
Show her no pity.[p]

25:12 13Do not have two differing weights
[p]Dt 19:13 in your bag—one heavy, one light.[q]
25:13 [q]Lev 19:35-37; 14Do not have two differing measures
Pr 11:1; in your house—one large, one small.
Eze 45:10; 15You must have accurate and honest
Mic 6:11 weights and measures, so that you may
25:15 live long[r] in the land the LORD your
[r]Ex 20:12 God is giving you. 16For the LORD your
25:16 God detests anyone who does these
[s]Pr 11:1 things, anyone who deals dishonestly.[s]

25:17 17Remember what the Amalekites[t]
[t]Ex 17:8 did to you along the way when you
came out of Egypt. 18When you were
weary and worn out, they met you on
your journey and cut off all who were
lagging behind; they had no fear of
25:18 God.[u] 19When the LORD your God
[u]Ps 36:1; Ro 3:18 gives you rest from all the enemies
around you in the land he is giving you
to possess as an inheritance, you shall
25:19 blot out the memory of Amalek[v] from
[v]1Sa 15:2-3 under heaven. Do not forget!

Firstfruits and Tithes

26 When you have entered the land
the LORD your God is giving
you as an inheritance and have taken
possession of it and settled in it, 2take
26:2 some of the firstfruits[w] of all that you
[w]Ex 22:29; 23:16,19; produce from the soil of the land the
Nu 18:13; LORD your God is giving you and put
Pr 3:9 them in a basket. Then go to the place
[x]Dt 12:5 the LORD your God will choose as a
dwelling for his Name[x] 3and say to the
priest in office at the time, “I declare today to the LORD your God that I have
come to the land the LORD swore to
our forefathers to give us.” 4The priest
shall take the basket from your hands
and set it down in front of the altar of
the LORD your God. 5Then you shall
declare before the LORD your God:
“My father was a wandering Aramean,[y] 26:5
and he went down into Egypt with a [y]Hos 12:12
few people[z] and lived there and became [z]Ge 43:1-2; 45:7,11; 46:27;
a great nation, powerful and numerous. Dt 10:22
6But the Egyptians mistreated us and 26:6
made us suffer,[a] putting us to hard la- [a]Ex 1:11,14
bor. 7Then we cried out to the LORD,
the God of our fathers, and the LORD
heard our voice[b] and saw[c] our misery, 26:7
toil and oppression. 8So the LORD [b]Ex 2:23-25 [c]Ex 3:9
brought us out of Egypt with a mighty
hand and an outstretched arm, with
great terror and with miraculous signs 26:8
and wonders.[d] 9He brought us to this [d]Dt 4:34
place and gave us this land, a land flowing with milk and honey;[e] 10and now 26:9
I bring the firstfruits of the soil that [e]Ex 3:8
you, O LORD, have given me.” Place
the basket before the LORD your God
and bow down before him. 11And you 26:11 [f]Dt 12:7
and the Levites[f] and the aliens among [g]Dt 16:11
you shall rejoice[g] in all the good things
the LORD your God has given to you
and your household.

12When you have finished setting
aside a tenth[h] of all your produce in the 26:12 [h]Lev 27:30
third year, the year of the tithe,[i] you [i]Nu 18:24;
shall give it to the Levite, the alien, the Dt 14:28-29; Heb 7:5,9
fatherless and the widow, so that they
may eat in your towns and be satisfied.
13Then say to the LORD your God: “I
have removed from my house the sacred portion and have given it to the
Levite, the alien, the fatherless and the
widow, according to all you commanded. I have not turned aside from your
commands nor have I forgotten any of
them.[j] 14I have not eaten any of the sa- 26:13 [j]Ps 119:141,
cred portion while I was in mourning, 153,176
nor have I removed any of it while I was
unclean,[k] nor have I offered any of it 26:14
to the dead. I have obeyed the LORD [k]Lev 7:20; Hos 9:4
my God; I have done everything you
commanded me. 15Look down from
heaven,[l] your holy dwelling place, and 26:15 [l]Isa 63:15;
bless your people Israel and the land Zec 2:13
you have given us as you promised on
oath to our forefathers, a land flowing
with milk and honey.”

Follow the LORD’s Commands

16The LORD your God commands
you this day to follow these decrees
and laws; carefully observe them with

all your heart and with all your soul.[m] 17You have declared this day that the LORD is your God and that you will walk in his ways, that you will keep his decrees, commands and laws, and that you will obey him. 18And the LORD has declared this day that you are his people, his treasured possession[n] as he promised, and that you are to keep all his commands. 19He has declared that he will set you in praise, fame and honor high above all the nations[o] he has made and that you will be a people holy[p] to the LORD your God, as he promised.

The Altar on Mount Ebal

27 Moses and the elders of Israel commanded the people: "Keep all these commands that I give you today. 2When you have crossed the Jordan into the land the LORD your God is giving you, set up some large stones and coat them with plaster.[q] 3Write on them all the words of this law when you have crossed over to enter the land the LORD your God is giving you, a land flowing with milk and honey,[r] just as the LORD, the God of your fathers, promised you. 4And when you have crossed the Jordan, set up these stones on Mount Ebal,[s] as I command you today, and coat them with plaster. 5Build there an altar[t] to the LORD your God, an altar of stones. Do not use any iron tool[u] upon them. 6Build the altar of the LORD your God with fieldstones and offer burnt offerings on it to the LORD your God. 7Sacrifice fellowship offerings[a] there, eating them and rejoicing in the presence of the LORD your God. 8And you shall write very clearly all the words of this law on these stones you have set up."

Curses From Mount Ebal

9Then Moses and the priests, who are Levites, said to all Israel, "Be silent, O Israel, and listen! You have now become the people of the LORD your God.[v] 10Obey the LORD your God and follow his commands and decrees that I give you today."

11On the same day Moses commanded the people:

12When you have crossed the Jordan, these tribes shall stand on Mount Gerizim[w] to bless the people: Simeon, Levi, Judah, Issachar, Joseph and Benjamin.[x] 13And these tribes shall stand on Mount Ebal to pronounce curses: Reuben, Gad, Asher, Zebulun, Dan and Naphtali.

14The Levites shall recite to all the people of Israel in a loud voice:

15"Cursed is the man who carves an image or casts an idol[y]—a thing detestable to the LORD, the work of the craftsman's hands—and sets it up in secret."

Then all the people shall say,
"Amen!"

16"Cursed is the man who dishonors his father or his mother."[z]

Then all the people shall say,
"Amen!"

17"Cursed is the man who moves his neighbor's boundary stone."[a]

Then all the people shall say,
"Amen!"

18"Cursed is the man who leads the blind astray on the road."[b]

Then all the people shall say,
"Amen!"

19"Cursed is the man who withholds justice from the alien,[c] the fatherless or the widow."[d]

Then all the people shall say,
"Amen!"

20"Cursed is the man who sleeps with his father's wife, for he dishonors his father's bed."[e]

Then all the people shall say,
"Amen!"

21"Cursed is the man who has sexual relations with any animal."[f]

Then all the people shall say,
"Amen!"

22"Cursed is the man who sleeps with his sister, the daughter of his father or the daughter of his mother."[g]

Then all the people shall say,
"Amen!"

23"Cursed is the man who sleeps with his mother-in-law."[h]

Then all the people shall say,
"Amen!"

24"Cursed is the man who kills[i] his neighbor secretly."

Then all the people shall say,
"Amen!"

25"Cursed is the man who accepts a bribe to kill an innocent person."[j]

[a]7 Traditionally *peace offerings*

26:16 [m]Dt 4:29
26:18 [n]Ex 6:7; 19:5; Dt 7:6; 14:2; 28:9
26:19 [o]Dt 4:7-8; 28:1,13,44 [p]Ex 19:6; Dt 7:6; 1Pe 2:9
27:2 [q]Jos 8:31
27:3 [r]Dt 26:9
27:4 [s]Dt 11:29
27:5 [t]Jos 8:31 [u]Ex 20:25
27:9 [v]Dt 26:18
27:12 [w]Dt 11:29
27:12 [x]Jos 8:35
27:15 [y]Ex 20:4; 34:17; Lev 19:4; 26:1; Dt 4:16,23; 5:8; Isa 44:9
27:16 [z]Ex 20:12; 21:17; Lev 19:3; 20:9
27:17 [a]Dt 19:14; Pr 22:28
27:18 [b]Lev 19:14
27:19 [c]Ex 22:21; Dt 24:19 [d]Dt 10:18
27:20 [e]Lev 18:7; Dt 22:30
27:21 [f]Lev 18:23
27:22 [g]Lev 18:9; 20:17
27:23 [h]Lev 20:14
27:24 [i]Lev 24:17; Nu 35:31
27:25 [j]Ex 23:7-8; Dt 10:17; Eze 22:12

Then all the people shall say,
"Amen!"

26"Cursed is the man who does not uphold the words of this law by carrying them out."[k]

Then all the people shall say,
"Amen!"

Blessings for Obedience

28 If you fully obey the LORD your God and carefully follow all his commands[l] I give you today, the LORD your God will set you high above all the nations on earth.[m] 2All these blessings will come upon you[n] and accompany you if you obey the LORD your God:

3You will be blessed[o] in the city and blessed in the country.[p]
4The fruit of your womb will be blessed, and the crops of your land and the young of your livestock— the calves of your herds and the lambs of your flocks.[q]
5Your basket and your kneading trough will be blessed.
6You will be blessed when you come in and blessed when you go out.[r]

7The LORD will grant that the enemies who rise up against you will be defeated before you. They will come at you from one direction but flee from you in seven.[s]

8The LORD will send a blessing on your barns and on everything you put your hand to. The LORD your God will bless you in the land he is giving you.

9The LORD will establish you as his holy people,[t] as he promised you on oath, if you keep the commands of the LORD your God and walk in his ways. 10Then all the peoples on earth will see that you are called by the name[u] of the LORD, and they will fear you. 11The LORD will grant you abundant prosperity—in the fruit of your womb, the young of your livestock and the crops of your ground—in the land he swore to your forefathers to give you.[v]

12The LORD will open the heavens, the storehouse of his bounty, to send rain[w] on your land in season and to bless all the work of your hands. You will lend to many nations but will borrow from none.[x] 13The LORD will make you the head, not the tail. If you pay attention to the commands of the LORD your God that I give you this day and carefully follow them, you will always be at the top, never at the bottom. 14Do not turn aside from any of the commands I give you today, to the right or to the left,[y] following other gods and serving them.

27:26 [k]Jer 11:3; Gal 3:10*
28:1 [l]Ex 15:26; Lev 26:3; Dt 7:12-26 [m]Dt 26:19
28:2 [n]Zec 1:6
28:3 [o]Ps 128:1,4 [p]Ge 39:5
28:4 [q]Ge 49:25; Pr 10:22
28:6 [r]Ps 121:8
28:7 [s]Lev 26:8,17
28:9 [t]Ex 19:6; Dt 7:6
28:10 [u]2Ch 7:14
28:11 [v]Dt 30:9; Pr 10:22
28:12 [w]Lev 26:4 [x]Dt 15:3,6
28:14 [y]Dt 5:32

Curses for Disobedience

15However, if you do not obey[z] the LORD your God and do not carefully follow all his commands and decrees I am giving you today, all these curses will come upon you and overtake you:[a]

16You will be cursed in the city and cursed in the country.
17Your basket and your kneading trough will be cursed.
18The fruit of your womb will be cursed, and the crops of your land, and the calves of your herds and the lambs of your flocks.
19You will be cursed when you come in and cursed when you go out.

20The LORD will send on you curses,[b] confusion and rebuke[c] in everything you put your hand to, until you are destroyed and come to sudden ruin[d] because of the evil you have done in forsaking him.[a] 21The LORD will plague you with diseases until he has destroyed you from the land you are entering to possess.[e] 22The LORD will strike you with wasting disease, with fever and inflammation, with scorching heat and drought,[f] with blight and mildew, which will plague you until you perish.[g] 23The sky over your head will be bronze, the ground beneath you iron.[h] 24The LORD will turn the rain of your country into dust and powder; it will come down from the skies until you are destroyed.

25The LORD will cause you to be defeated before your enemies. You will come at them from one direction but flee from them in seven,[i] and you will become a thing of horror to all the kingdoms on earth.[j] 26Your carcasses will be food for all the birds of the air and the beasts of the earth, and there will be no one to frighten them away.[k] 27The LORD will afflict you with the boils of Egypt[l] and with tumors, fester-

[a]20 Hebrew *me*

28:15 [z]Lev 26:14 [a]Jos 23:15; Da 9:11; Mal 2:2
28:20 [b]Mal 2:2 [c]Isa 51:20; 66:15 [d]Dt 4:26
28:21 [e]Lev 26:25; Jer 24:10
28:22 [f]Lev 26:16 [g]Am 4:9
28:23 [h]Lev 26:19
28:25 [i]Isa 30:17 [j]Jer 15:4; 24:9; Eze 23:46
28:26 [k]Jer 7:33; 16:4; 34:20
28:27 [l]ver 60-61; 1Sa 5:6

ing sores and the itch, from which you
cannot be cured. **28**The LORD will afflict you with madness, blindness and
confusion of mind. **29**At midday you
will grope[m] about like a blind man in
the dark. You will be unsuccessful in everything you do; day after day you will
be oppressed and robbed, with no one
to rescue you.
30You will be pledged to be married
to a woman, but another will take her
and ravish her.[n] You will build a house,
but you will not live in it.[o] You will
plant a vineyard, but you will not even
begin to enjoy its fruit.[p] **31**Your ox will
be slaughtered before your eyes, but you
will eat none of it. Your donkey will be
forcibly taken from you and will not be
returned. Your sheep will be given to
your enemies, and no one will rescue
them. **32**Your sons and daughters will be
given to another nation,[q] and you will
wear out your eyes watching for them
day after day, powerless to lift a hand.
33A people that you do not know will
eat what your land and labor produce,
and you will have nothing but cruel oppression all your days.[r] **34**The sights you
see will drive you mad. **35**The LORD
will afflict your knees and legs with
painful boils[s] that cannot be cured,
spreading from the soles of your feet to
the top of your head.
36The LORD will drive you and the
king[t] you set over you to a nation unknown to you or your fathers.[u] There
you will worship other gods, gods of
wood and stone.[v] **37**You will become a
thing of horror and an object of scorn
and ridicule to all the nations where the
LORD will drive you.[w]
38You will sow much seed in the field
but you will harvest little,[x] because locusts will devour[y] it. **39**You will plant
vineyards and cultivate them but you
will not drink the wine or gather the
grapes, because worms will eat them.[z]
40You will have olive trees throughout
your country but you will not use the
oil, because the olives will drop off.[a]
41You will have sons and daughters but
you will not keep them, because they
will go into captivity.[b] **42**Swarms of locusts will take over all your trees and
the crops of your land.
43The alien who lives among you will
rise above you higher and higher, but
you will sink lower and lower.[c] **44**He
will lend to you, but you will not lend
to him.[d] He will be the head, but you
will be the tail.[e]
45All these curses will come upon
you. They will pursue you and overtake
you until you are destroyed,[f] because
you did not obey the LORD your God
and observe the commands and decrees
he gave you. **46**They will be a sign and
a wonder to you and your descendants
forever.[g] **47**Because you did not serve[h]
the LORD your God joyfully and glad-
ly[i] in the time of prosperity, **48**therefore
in hunger and thirst, in nakedness and
dire poverty, you will serve the enemies
the LORD sends against you. He will
put an iron yoke[j] on your neck until he
has destroyed you.
49The LORD will bring a nation
against you from far away, from the
ends of the earth,[k] like an eagle[l] swooping down, a nation whose language you
will not understand, **50**a fierce-looking
nation without respect for the old[m] or
pity for the young. **51**They will devour
the young of your livestock and the
crops of your land until you are destroyed. They will leave you no grain,
new wine or oil, nor any calves of your
herds or lambs of your flocks until you
are ruined.[n] **52**They will lay siege to all
the cities throughout your land until
the high fortified walls in which you
trust fall down. They will besiege all the
cities throughout the land the LORD
your God is giving you.[o]
53Because of the suffering that your
enemy will inflict on you during the
siege, you will eat the fruit of the womb,
the flesh of the sons and daughters
the LORD your God has given you.[p]
54Even the most gentle and sensitive
man among you will have no compassion on his own brother or the wife he
loves or his surviving children, **55**and
he will not give to one of them any of
the flesh of his children that he is eating. It will be all he has left because of
the suffering your enemy will inflict on
you during the siege of all your cities.
56The most gentle and sensitive[q] woman among you—so sensitive and gentle
that she would not venture to touch the
ground with the sole of her foot—will
begrudge the husband she loves and
her own son or daughter **57**the after-
birth from her womb and the children
she bears. For she intends to eat them

28:29 [m]Job 5:14; Isa 59:10
28:30 [n]Job 31:10; Jer 8:10 [o]Am 5:11 [p]Jer 12:13
28:32 [q]ver 41
28:33 [r]Jer 5:15-17
28:35 [s]ver 27
28:36 [t]2Ki 17:4,6; 24:12,14; 25:7,11 [u]Jer 16:13 [v]Dt 4:28
28:37 [w]Jer 24:9
28:38 [x]Mic 6:15; Hag 1:6,9 [y]Joel 1:4
28:39 [z]Isa 5:10; 17:10-11
28:40 [a]Mic 6:15
28:41 [b]ver 32
28:43 [c]ver 13
28:44 [d]ver 12 [e]ver 13
28:45 [f]ver 15
28:46 [g]Isa 8:18; Eze 14:8
28:47 [h]Dt 32:15 [i]Ne 9:35
28:48 [j]Jer 28:13-14
28:49 [k]Jer 5:15; 6:22 [l]La 4:19; Hos 8:1
28:50 [m]Isa 47:6
28:51 [n]ver 33
28:52 [o]Jer 10:18; Zep 1:14-16, 17
28:53 [p]Lev 26:29; 2Ki 6:28-29; Jer 19:9; La 2:20; 4:10
28:56 [q]ver 54

secretly during the siege and in the distress that your enemy will inflict on you
in your cities.
58 If you do not carefully follow all
the words of this law, which are writ-
28:58 [r]Mal 1:14 ten in this book, and do not revere[r]
[s]Ex 6:3 this glorious and awesome name[s]—the
LORD your God— 59 the LORD will
send fearful plagues on you and your
descendants, harsh and prolonged disasters, and severe and lingering illnesses.
60 He will bring upon you all the dis-
28:60 [t]ver 27 eases of Egypt[t] that you dreaded, and
they will cling to you. 61 The LORD will
also bring on you every kind of sickness
and disaster not recorded in this Book
28:61 [u]Dt 4:25-26 of the Law, until you are destroyed.[u]
62 You who were as numerous as the
28:62 [v]Dt 4:27; 10:22; Ne 9:23 stars in the sky[v] will be left but few in
number, because you did not obey the
LORD your God. 63 Just as it pleased[w]
28:63 [w]Jer 32:41 [x]Pr 1:26 [y]Jer 12:14; 45:4 the LORD to make you prosper and increase in number, so it will please[x] him
to ruin and destroy you. You will be uprooted[y] from the land you are entering
to possess.
28:64 [z]Lev 26:33; Dt 4:27 [a]Ne 1:8 64 Then the LORD will scatter[z] you
among all nations,[a] from one end of
the earth to the other. There you will
worship other gods—gods of wood and
stone, which neither you nor your fathers have known. 65 Among those nations you will find no repose, no resting
place for the sole of your foot. There the
LORD will give you an anxious mind,
eyes weary with longing, and a despair-
28:65 [b]Lev 26:16,36 ing heart.[b] 66 You will live in constant
suspense, filled with dread both night
and day, never sure of your life. 67 In the
morning you will say, "If only it were
evening!" and in the evening, "If only it
were morning!"—because of the terror
that will fill your hearts and the sights
28:67 [c]ver 34; Job 7:4 that your eyes will see.[c] 68 The LORD
will send you back in ships to Egypt on
a journey I said you should never make
again. There you will offer yourselves
for sale to your enemies as male and female slaves, but no one will buy you.

Renewal of the Covenant

29 These are the terms of the covenant the LORD commanded
Moses to make with the Israelites in
Moab, in addition to the covenant he
29:1 [d]Dt 5:2-3 had made with them at Horeb.[d]
2 Moses summoned all the Israelites
and said to them:

Your eyes have seen all that the LORD
did in Egypt to Pharaoh, to all his
officials and to all his land.[e] 3 With 29:2 [e]Ex 19:4
your own eyes you saw those great tri-
als, those miraculous signs and great
wonders.[f] 4 But to this day the LORD 29:3 [f]Dt 4:34; 7:19
has not given you a mind that under-
stands or eyes that see or ears that hear.[g] 29:4 [g]Isa 6:10; Ac 28:26-27; Ro 11:8*; Eph 4:18
5 During the forty years that I led you
through the desert, your clothes did not
wear out, nor did the sandals on your
feet.[h] 6 You ate no bread and drank no 29:5 [h]Dt 8:4
wine or other fermented drink. I did
this so that you might know that I am
the LORD your God.[i] 29:6 [i]Dt 8:3
7 When you reached this place, Si-
hon[j] king of Heshbon and Og king of 29:7 [j]Dt 2:32; 3:1 [k]Nu 21:21-24, 33-35
Bashan came out to fight against us,
but we defeated them.[k] 8 We took their
land and gave it as an inheritance to the
Reubenites, the Gadites and the half-
tribe of Manasseh.[l] 29:8 [l]Nu 32:33; Dt 3:12-13
9 Carefully follow[m] the terms of this
covenant, so that you may prosper in 29:9 [m]Dt 4:6; Jos 1:7 [n]1Ki 2:3
everything you do.[n] 10 All of you are
standing today in the presence of the
LORD your God—your leaders and
chief men, your elders and officials, and
all the other men of Israel, 11 together
with your children and your wives, and
the aliens living in your camps who
chop your wood and carry your water.[o] 29:11 [o]Jos 9:21,23,27
12 You are standing here in order to en-
ter into a covenant with the LORD your
God, a covenant the LORD is making
with you this day and sealing with an
oath, 13 to confirm you this day as his
people,[p] that he may be your God[q] as 29:13 [p]Dt 28:9 [q]Ge 17:7; Ex 6:7
he promised you and as he swore to
your fathers, Abraham, Isaac and Ja-
cob. 14 I am making this covenant,[r] with 29:14 [r]Jer 31:31
its oath, not only with you 15 who are
standing here with us today in the presence of the LORD our God but also
with those who are not here today.[s] 29:15 [s]Ac 2:39
16 You yourselves know how we lived
in Egypt and how we passed through
the countries on the way here. 17 You
saw among them their detestable images
and idols of wood and stone, of silver
and gold.[t] 18 Make sure there is no man 29:17 [t]Dt 28:36
or woman, clan or tribe among you to-
day whose heart turns away from the
LORD our God to go and worship the
gods of those nations; make sure there
is no root among you that produces
such bitter poison.[u] 29:18 [u]Dt 11:16; Heb 12:15
19 When such a person hears the

words of this oath, he invokes a blessing on himself and therefore thinks, "I will be safe, even though I persist in going my own way." This will bring disaster on the watered land as well as the dry.[a] 20The LORD will never be willing to forgive him; his wrath and zeal[v] will burn[w] against that man. All the curses written in this book will fall upon him, and the LORD will blot[x] out his name from under heaven. 21The LORD will single him out from all the tribes of Israel for disaster, according to all the curses of the covenant written in this Book of the Law.

22Your children who follow you in later generations and foreigners who come from distant lands will see the calamities that have fallen on the land and the diseases with which the LORD has afflicted it.[y] 23The whole land will be a burning waste[z] of salt[a] and sulfur—nothing planted, nothing sprouting, no vegetation growing on it. It will be like the destruction of Sodom and Gomorrah,[b] Admah and Zeboiim, which the LORD overthrew in fierce anger. 24All the nations will ask: "Why has the LORD done this to this land?[c] Why this fierce, burning anger?"

25And the answer will be: "It is because this people abandoned the covenant of the LORD, the God of their fathers, the covenant he made with them when he brought them out of Egypt. 26They went off and worshiped other gods and bowed down to them, gods they did not know, gods he had not given them. 27Therefore the LORD's anger burned against this land, so that he brought on it all the curses written in this book.[d] 28In furious anger and in great wrath the LORD uprooted[e] them from their land and thrust them into another land, as it is now."

29The secret things belong to the LORD our God, but the things revealed belong to us and to our children forever, that we may follow all the words of this law.

29:20 [v]Eze 23:25 [w]Ps 74:1; 79:5 [x]Ex 32:33; Dt 9:14
29:22 [y]Jer 19:8
29:23 [z]Isa 34:9 [a]Jer 17:6 [b]Ge 19:24,25; Zep 2:9
29:24 [c]1Ki 9:8; Jer 22:8-9
29:27 [d]Da 9:11, 13,14
29:28 [e]1Ki 14:15; 2Ch 7:20; Ps 52:5; Pr 2:22

Prosperity After Turning to the LORD

30 When all these blessings and curses[f] I have set before you come upon you and you take them to heart wherever the LORD your God disperses you among the nations,[g] 2and when you and your children return[h] to the LORD your God and obey him with all your heart and with all your soul according to everything I command you today, 3then the LORD your God will restore your fortunes[b][i] and have compassion on you and gather[j] you again from all the nations where he scattered you.[k] 4Even if you have been banished to the most distant land under the heavens, from there the LORD your God will gather you and bring you back.[l] 5He will bring[m] you to the land that belonged to your fathers, and you will take possession of it. He will make you more prosperous and numerous than your fathers. 6The LORD your God will circumcise your hearts and the hearts of your descendants,[n] so that you may love him with all your heart and with all your soul, and live. 7The LORD your God will put all these curses on your enemies who hate and persecute you.[o] 8You will again obey the LORD and follow all his commands I am giving you today. 9Then the LORD your God will make you most prosperous in all the work of your hands and in the fruit of your womb, the young of your livestock and the crops of your land.[p] The LORD will again delight in you and make you prosperous, just as he delighted in your fathers, 10if you obey the LORD your God and keep his commands and decrees that are written in this Book of the Law and turn to the LORD your God with all your heart and with all your soul.[q]

30:1 [f]ver 15,19; Dt 11:26 [g]Lev 26:40-45; Dt 28:64; 29:28; 1Ki 8:47
30:2 [h]Dt 4:30; Ne 1:9
30:3 [i]Ps 126:4 [j]Ps 147:2; Jer 32:37; Eze 34:13 [k]Jer 29:14
30:4 [l]Ne 1:8-9; Isa 43:6
30:5 [m]Jer 29:14
30:6 [n]Dt 10:16; Jer 32:39
30:7 [o]Dt 7:15
30:9 [p]Dt 28:11; Jer 31:28; 32:41
30:10 [q]Dt 4:29

The Offer of Life or Death

11Now what I am commanding you today is not too difficult for you or beyond your reach.[r] 12It is not up in heaven, so that you have to ask, "Who will ascend into heaven to get it and proclaim it to us so we may obey it?"[s] 13Nor is it beyond the sea, so that you have to ask, "Who will cross the sea to get it and proclaim it to us so we may obey it?" 14No, the word is very near you; it is in your mouth and in your heart so you may obey it.

15See, I set before you today life and prosperity, death and destruction.[t] 16For I command you today to love the LORD

30:11 [r]Isa 45:19,23
30:12 [s]Ro 10:6*
30:15 [t]Dt 11:26

[a]*19* Or *way, in order to add drunkenness to thirst."*
[b]*3* Or *will bring you back from captivity*

DAY 3 THREE

Self-Control and My Relationship With Christ

Deuteronomy 30:15–16

The self-control that bears the mark of obedience will always enhance our relationship with Christ. Moses said to Israel that there are three steps to self-control, and when these are carried out, they yield three specific rewards. The three steps to self-control listed in Deuteronomy 30:16 are these:

First, we must love the Lord our God. Loving God more than any other single force in our lives will enable us to practice self-control.

Second, we must walk in his ways. So often in Scripture our union with Christ is pictured as a journey, a walk. We walk along, and God instructs us in the inner person as we grow toward spiritual maturity. Walking with God will in every case enhance our relationship with Christ as it results in a life of self-control.

Third, we must keep his decrees and laws. His commandments define the parameters of our self-control.

The rewards of our self-control are also three: First, we will live and prosper. This particular verse is not referring to the rewards we will receive in eternity. It is God's promise that self-control will result in better life in the present. Second, we will increase. Life generally gets bigger in every way for those who learn the art of obedience. Third, we will experience the full blessing of God. This is the richest reward of all.

All in all, our walk with Christ will be as victorious as we are submissive. Our closeness to him and our degree of self-control always maintain the same happy ratio.

To begin a study on the topic of Self-Control, the Mark of Obedience, turn to the home page on page 1011.

your God, to walk in his ways, and to
keep his commands, decrees and laws;
then you will live and increase, and the
LORD your God will bless you in the
land you are entering to possess.
17But if your heart turns away and
you are not obedient, and if you are
drawn away to bow down to other
gods and worship them, 18I declare to
you this day that you will certainly be
destroyed.[u] You will not live long in the
land you are crossing the Jordan to enter and possess.
19This day I call heaven and earth as
witnesses against you[v] that I have set
before you life and death, blessings and
curses.[w] Now choose life, so that you
and your children may live 20and that
you may love[x] the LORD your God, listen to his voice, and hold fast to him.
For the LORD is your life,[y] and he will
give you many years in the land he
swore to give to your fathers, Abraham,
Isaac and Jacob.

Joshua to Succeed Moses

31 Then Moses went out and spoke
these words to all Israel: 2"I am
now a hundred and twenty years old[z]
and I am no longer able to lead you.[a]
The LORD has said to me, 'You shall
not cross the Jordan.'[b] 3The LORD your
God himself will cross[c] over ahead of
you.[d] He will destroy these nations before you, and you will take possession
of their land. Joshua also will cross[e]
over ahead of you, as the LORD said.
4And the LORD will do to them what
he did to Sihon and Og, the kings of
the Amorites, whom he destroyed along
with their land. 5The LORD will deliver[f] them to you, and you must do to
them all that I have commanded you.
6Be strong and courageous.[g] Do not be
afraid or terrified[h] because of them, for
the LORD your God goes with you;[i] he
will never leave you[j] nor forsake[k] you."
7Then Moses summoned Joshua and
said[l] to him in the presence of all Israel, "Be strong and courageous, for
you must go with this people into the
land that the LORD swore to their forefathers to give them, and you must divide it among them as their inheritance.
8The LORD himself goes before you
and will be with you;[m] he will never
leave you nor forsake you. Do not be
afraid; do not be discouraged."

The Reading of the Law

9So Moses wrote down this law and
gave it to the priests, the sons of Levi,
who carried[n] the ark of the covenant of
the LORD, and to all the elders of Israel. 10Then Moses commanded them:
"At the end of every seven years, in the
year for canceling debts,[o] during the
Feast of Tabernacles,[p] 11when all Israel

30:18 [u]Dt 8:19
30:19 [v]Dt 4:26 [w]ver 1
30:20 [x]Dt 6:5; 10:20 [y]Ps 27:1; Jn 11:25
31:2 [z]Dt 34:7 [a]Nu 27:17; 1Ki 3:7 [b]Dt 3:23,26
31:3 [c]Nu 27:18 [d]Dt 9:3 [e]Dt 3:28
31:5 [f]Dt 7:2
31:6 [g]Jos 10:25; 1Ch 22:13 [h]Dt 7:18 [i]Dt 1:29; 20:4 [j]Jos 1:5 [k]Heb 13:5*
31:7 [l]Dt 1:38; 3:28
31:8 [m]Ex 13:21; 33:14
31:9 [n]ver 25; Nu 4:15; Jos 3:3
31:10 [o]Dt 15:1 [p]Lev 23:34

31:11 [q]Dt 16:16 comes to appear[q] before the LORD your
[r]Jos 8:34-35; God at the place he will choose, you
2Ki 23:2 shall read this law[r] before them in their
hearing. 12Assemble the people—men,
women and children, and the aliens living in your towns—so they can listen
31:12 and learn[s] to fear the LORD your God
[s]Dt 4:10 and follow carefully all the words of
31:13 this law. 13Their children,[t] who do not
[t]Dt 11:2; know this law, must hear it and learn
Ps 78:6-7 to fear the LORD your God as long as
you live in the land you are crossing the
Jordan to possess."

Israel's Rebellion Predicted

14The LORD said to Moses, "Now
31:14 the day of your death[u] is near. Call
[u]Nu 27:13; Joshua and present yourselves at the
Dt 32:49-50 Tent of Meeting, where I will commission him." So Moses and Joshua came
and presented themselves at the Tent of
Meeting.

15Then the LORD appeared at the
Tent in a pillar of cloud, and the cloud
31:15 [v]Ex 33:9 stood over the entrance to the Tent.[v]
16And the LORD said to Moses: "You
are going to rest with your fathers, and
31:16 [w]Jdg 2:12 these people will soon prostitute[w] them-
[x]Jdg 10:6,13 selves to the foreign gods of the land
they are entering. They will forsake[x] me
and break the covenant I made with
them. 17On that day I will become an-
31:17 gry[y] with them and forsake[z] them; I
[y]Jdg 2:14,20 will hide[a] my face from them, and they
[z]Jdg 6:13; will be destroyed. Many disasters and
2Ch 15:2 [a]Dt 32:20; difficulties will come upon them, and
Isa 1:15; 8:17 on that day they will ask, 'Have not
[b]Nu 14:42 these disasters come upon us because
our God is not with us?'[b] 18And I will
certainly hide my face on that day because of all their wickedness in turning
to other gods.

19"Now write down for yourselves
this song and teach it to the Israelites
and have them sing it, so that it may be
a witness for me against them. 20When
I have brought them into the land flowing with milk and honey, the land I
31:20 promised on oath to their forefathers,[c]
[c]Dt 6:10-12 and when they eat their fill and thrive,
[d]Dt 32:15-17 they will turn to other gods[d] and wor-
[e]ver 16 ship them, rejecting me and breaking
my covenant.[e] 21And when many disas-
31:21 ters and difficulties come upon them,[f]
[f]ver 17 this song will testify against them, be-
[g]Hos 5:3 cause it will not be forgotten by their
descendants. I know what they are disposed to do,[g] even before I bring them
into the land I promised them on oath."
22So Moses wrote[b] down this song that 31:22
day and taught it to the Israelites. [h]ver 19

23The LORD gave this command[i] to 31:23 [i]ver 7
Joshua son of Nun: "Be strong and [j]Jos 1:6
courageous,[j] for you will bring the Israelites into the land I promised them on
oath, and I myself will be with you."

24After Moses finished writing in a
book the words of this law from beginning to end, 25he gave this command
to the Levites who carried the ark of
the covenant of the LORD: 26"Take this
Book of the Law and place it beside the
ark of the covenant of the LORD your
God. There it will remain as a witness
against you.[k] 27For I know how rebel- 31:26 [k]ver 19
lious and stiff-necked[l] you are. If you 31:27
have been rebellious against the LORD [l]Ex 32:9;
while I am still alive and with you, how Dt 9:6,24
much more will you rebel after I die!
28Assemble before me all the elders of
your tribes and all your officials, so that
I can speak these words in their hearing and call heaven and earth to testify
against them.[m] 29For I know that after 31:28
my death you are sure to become utter- [m]Dt 4:26; 30:19; 32:1
ly corrupt[n] and to turn from the way I 31:29
have commanded you. In days to come, [n]Dt 32:5;
disaster[o] will fall upon you because you Jdg 2:19 [o]Dt 28:15
will do evil in the sight of the LORD
and provoke him to anger by what your
hands have made."

The Song of Moses

30And Moses recited the words of
this song from beginning to end in
the hearing of the whole assembly of Israel:

32 Listen, O heavens,[p] and I will 32:1
speak; [p]Isa 1:2
hear, O earth, the words of my
mouth.
2Let my teaching fall like rain
and my words descend like dew,[q] 32:2
like showers[r] on new grass, [q]Isa 55:11
like abundant rain on tender [r]Ps 72:6
plants.

3I will proclaim the name of the
LORD.[s] 32:3 [s]Ex 33:19
Oh, praise the greatness[t] of our [t]Dt 3:24
God!
4He is the Rock,[u] his works are 32:4
perfect,[v] [u]ver 15,18,30
and all his ways are just. [v]2Sa 22:31
A faithful God[w] who does no wrong, [w]Dt 7:9
upright and just is he.

DAY 5 FIVE

▸ Love and Its Place in My Personal Worship

Deuteronomy 32:1–4,9–12

"Let my teaching fall like rain," cries Moses, "like abundant rain on tender plants." There follows this admonition some words of celebration of the God who finds us "in a barren and howling waste" and bears us up just as eagles catch and teach their frightened young to fly. God led us into the glorious promised land of our relationship with himself. To be saved is to be released from our commitment to things that don't matter and to develop a larger commitment to the things that do.

But following our salvation, it is those secondary issues of love that really define God. Like an eagle teaching its young to fly, God pushes us into new, exhilarating levels of flight, never allowing us to fall very far before he catches us on his wings, and we are secure during every lesson of flight. At last we soar into the fullest, loftiest relationships of love.

Moses, who uses the book of Deuteronomy as the format for his three farewell addresses to Israel, exults in praising the gracious love of God. What is the nature of this praise? It focuses on the God who rescues us and the God who keeps us. These two images are worth our celebrating, for they call to mind our own pilgrimage with God. After all, he went before us through the barren fields of our pitiful, trivial commitments. Then, right there where he met us, he saved us. But that wasn't the last we saw of him. We soon discovered that his saving grace gave way to his keeping grace. Then we could see what Paul meant in 2 Timothy 1:12 when he said, "That is why I am suffering as I am. Yet I am not ashamed, because I know whom I have believed, and am convinced that he is able to guard what I have entrusted to him for that day."

To begin a study on the topic of Love, the Definition of God, turn to the home page on page 1033.

[5]They have acted corruptly toward
him;
to their shame they are no longer
his children,
but a warped and crooked
generation.[a][x]
[6]Is this the way you repay[y] the LORD,
O foolish and unwise people?[z]
Is he not your Father,[a] your Creator,[b]
who made you and formed you?[b]
[7]Remember the days of old;
consider the generations long past.
Ask your father and he will tell you,
your elders, and they will explain
to you.[c]
[8]When the Most High gave the
nations their inheritance,
when he divided all mankind,[d]
he set up boundaries for the peoples
according to the number of the
sons of Israel.[c]
[9]For the LORD's portion[e] is his
people,
Jacob his allotted inheritance.[f]
[10]In a desert[g] land he found him,
in a barren and howling waste.
He shielded him and cared for him;
he guarded him as the apple of his
eye,[h]
[11]like an eagle that stirs up its nest
and hovers over its young,[i]
that spreads its wings to catch them
and carries them on its pinions.
[12]The LORD alone led him;
no foreign god was with him.[j]
[13]He made him ride on the heights[k] of
the land
and fed him with the fruit of the
fields.
He nourished him with honey from
the rock,
and with oil[l] from the flinty crag,
[14]with curds and milk from herd and
flock
and with fattened lambs and
goats,
with choice rams of Bashan
and the finest kernels of wheat.[m]
You drank the foaming blood of the
grape.[n]
[15]Jeshurun[d] grew fat[o] and kicked;
filled with food, he became heavy
and sleek.
He abandoned[p] the God who made
him

[a]5 Or *Corrupt are they and not his children, / a generation warped and twisted to their shame* [b]6 Or *Father, who bought you* [c]8 Masoretic Text; Dead Sea Scrolls (see also Septuagint) *sons of God* [d]*15 Jeshurun* means *the upright one*, that is, Israel.

32:5 [x]Dt 31:29
32:6 [y]Ps 116:12 [z]Ps 74:2 [a]Dt 1:31; Isa 63:16 [b]ver 15
32:7 [c]Ex 13:14
32:8 [d]Ge 11:8; Ac 17:26
32:9 [e]Jer 10:16 [f]1Ki 8:51,53
32:10 [g]Jer 2:6 [h]Ps 17:8; Zec 2:8
32:11 [i]Ex 19:4
32:12 [j]ver 39
32:13 [k]Isa 58:14 [l]Job 29:6
32:14 [m]Ps 81:16; 147:14 [n]Ge 49:11
32:15 [o]Dt 31:20 [p]ver 6; Isa 1:4,28

32:15 [q]ver 4

and rejected the Rock[q] his Savior.

32:16 [r]1Co 10:22 [s]Ps 78:58

16 They made him jealous[r] with their
 foreign gods
and angered[s] him with their
 detestable idols.
17 They sacrificed to demons, which
 are not God—

32:17 [t]Dt 28:64 [u]Jdg 5:8

gods they had not known,[t]
gods that recently appeared,[u]
gods your fathers did not fear.

32:18 [v]Isa 17:10

18 You deserted the Rock, who fathered
 you;
you forgot[v] the God who gave you
 birth.

32:19 [w]Jer 44:21-23 [x]Ps 106:40

19 The LORD saw this and rejected
 them[w]
because he was angered by his
 sons and daughters.[x]

32:20 [y]Dt 31:17,29 [z]ver 5

20 "I will hide my face[y] from them," he
 said,
"and see what their end will be;
for they are a perverse generation,[z]
 children who are unfaithful.

32:21 [a]1Co 10:22 [b]1Ki 16:13,26 [c]Ro 10:19*

21 They made me jealous[a] by what is
 no god
and angered me with their
 worthless idols.[b]
I will make them envious by those
 who are not a people;
I will make them angry by a
 nation that has no
 understanding.[c]
22 For a fire has been kindled by my
 wrath,
one that burns to the realm of

32:22 [d]Ps 18:7-8; Jer 15:14; La 4:11

 death[a] below.[d]
It will devour the earth and its
 harvests
and set afire the foundations of
 the mountains.

32:23 [e]Dt 29:21 [f]Ps 7:13; Eze 5:16

23 "I will heap calamities[e] upon them
and spend my arrows[f] against
 them.
24 I will send wasting famine against
 them,

32:24 [g]Dt 28:22 [h]Ps 91:6 [i]Lev 26:22 [j]Am 5:18-19

consuming pestilence[g] and deadly
 plague;[h]
I will send against them the fangs of
 wild beasts,[i]
the venom of vipers[j] that glide in
 the dust.
25 In the street the sword will make
 them childless;

32:25 [k]Eze 7:15 [l]2Ch 36:17; La 2:21

in their homes terror will reign.[k]
Young men and young women will
 perish,
infants and gray-haired men.[l]

32:26 [m]Dt 4:27 [n]Ps 34:16

26 I said I would scatter[m] them
and blot out their memory from
 mankind,[n]
27 but I dreaded the taunt of the
 enemy,
lest the adversary misunderstand
and say, 'Our hand has triumphed;

32:27 [o]Isa 10:13

 the LORD has not done all this.'"[o]
28 They are a nation without sense,
there is no discernment in them.
29 If only they were wise and would

32:29 [p]Dt 5:29; Ps 81:13

 understand this[p]
and discern what their end will be!
30 How could one man chase a
 thousand,
or two put ten thousand to
 flight,[q]

32:30 [q]Lev 26:8 [r]Ps 44:12

unless their Rock had sold them,
unless the LORD had given them
 up?[r]
31 For their rock is not like our Rock,
as even our enemies concede.
32 Their vine comes from the vine of
 Sodom
and from the fields of Gomorrah.
Their grapes are filled with poison,
and their clusters with bitterness.
33 Their wine is the venom of serpents,

32:33 [s]Ps 58:4

the deadly poison of cobras.[s]
34 "Have I not kept this in reserve

32:34 [t]Jer 2:22; Hos 13:12

and sealed it in my vaults?[t]
35 It is mine to avenge; I will repay.[u]

32:35 [u]Ro 12:19*; Heb 10:30* [v]Jer 23:12 [w]Eze 7:8-9

In due time their foot will slip;[v]
their day of disaster is near
and their doom rushes upon
 them."[w]
36 The LORD will judge his people
and have compassion on his

32:36 [x]Dt 30:1-3; Ps 135:14; Joel 2:14

 servants[x]
when he sees their strength is gone
and no one is left, slave or free.
37 He will say: "Now where are their
 gods,

32:37 [y]Jdg 10:14; Jer 2:28

the rock they took refuge in,[y]
38 the gods who ate the fat of their
 sacrifices
and drank the wine of their drink
 offerings?
Let them rise up to help you!
Let them give you shelter!

32:39 [z]Isa 41:4 [a]Isa 45:5 [b]1Sa 2:6; Ps 68:20 [c]Hos 6:1

39 "See now that I myself am He![z]
There is no god besides me.[a]
I put to death and I bring to life,[b]
I have wounded and I will heal,[c]

[a]22 Hebrew *to Sheol*

and no one can deliver out of my
 hand.[d]
40 I lift my hand to heaven and
 declare:
 As surely as I live forever,
41 when I sharpen my flashing sword[e]
 and my hand grasps it in
 judgment,
I will take vengeance on my
 adversaries
 and repay those who hate me.[f]
42 I will make my arrows drunk with
 blood,[g]
 while my sword devours flesh:[h]
the blood of the slain and the
 captives,
 the heads of the enemy leaders."

43 Rejoice,[i] O nations, with his
 people,[a,b]
 for he will avenge the blood of his
 servants;[j]
he will take vengeance on his
 enemies
 and make atonement for his land
 and people.[k]

44 Moses came with Joshua[c][l] son of
Nun and spoke all the words of this song
in the hearing of the people. 45 When
Moses finished reciting all these words
to all Israel, 46 he said to them, "Take to
heart all the words I have solemnly declared to you this day,[m] so that you may
command your children to obey carefully all the words of this law. 47 They
are not just idle words for you—they
are your life.[n] By them you will live
long in the land you are crossing the
Jordan to possess."

Moses to Die on Mount Nebo

48 On that same day the LORD told
Moses, 49 "Go up into the Abarim[o]
Range to Mount Nebo in Moab, across
from Jericho, and view Canaan, the
land I am giving the Israelites as their
own possession. 50 There on the mountain that you have climbed you will die[p]
and be gathered to your people, just
as your brother Aaron died on Mount
Hor and was gathered to his people.
51 This is because both of you broke
faith with me in the presence of the Israelites at the waters of Meribah Kadesh in the Desert of Zin[q] and because
you did not uphold my holiness among
the Israelites.[r] 52 Therefore, you will see
the land only from a distance;[s] you will
not enter[t] the land I am giving to the
people of Israel."

32:39 [d]Ps 50:22
32:41 [e]Isa 34:6; 66:16; Eze 21:9-10 [f]Jer 50:29
32:42 [g]ver 23 [h]Jer 46:10,14
32:43 [i]Ro 15:10* [j]2Ki 9:7 [k]Ps 65:3; 85:1; Rev 19:2
32:44 [l]Nu 13:8,16
32:46 [m]Eze 40:4
32:47 [n]Dt 30:20
32:49 [o]Nu 27:12
32:50 [p]Ge 25:8
32:51 [q]Nu 20:11-13 [r]Nu 27:14
32:52 [s]Dt 34:1-3 [t]Dt 1:37

Moses Blesses the Tribes

33 This is the blessing that Moses the man of God[u] pronounced on the Israelites before his death. 2 He said:

"The LORD came from Sinai[v]
 and dawned over them from Seir;[w]
 he shone forth from Mount
 Paran.[x]
He came with[d] myriads of holy
 ones[y]
 from the south, from his
 mountain slopes.[e]
3 Surely it is you who love[z] the people;
 all the holy ones are in your
 hand.[a]
At your feet they all bow down,[b]
 and from you receive instruction,
4 the law that Moses gave us,[c]
 the possession of the assembly of
 Jacob.[d]
5 He was king over Jeshurun[f]
 when the leaders of the people
 assembled,
 along with the tribes of Israel.

6 "Let Reuben live and not die,
 nor[g] his men be few."

7 And this he said about Judah:[e]

"Hear, O LORD, the cry of Judah;
 bring him to his people.
With his own hands he defends his
 cause.
 Oh, be his help against his foes!"

8 About Levi he said:

"Your Thummim and Urim[f] belong
 to the man you favored.
You tested him at Massah;
 you contended with him at the
 waters of Meribah.[g]
9 He said of his father and mother,[h]
 'I have no regard for them.'
He did not recognize his brothers
 or acknowledge his own children,
but he watched over your word
 and guarded your covenant.[i]

33:1 [u]Jos 14:6
33:2 [v]Ex 19:18; Ps 68:8 [w]Jdg 5:4 [x]Hab 3:3 [y]Da 7:10; Ac 7:53; Rev 5:11
33:3 [z]Hos 11:1 [a]Dt 14:2 [b]Lk 10:39
33:4 [c]Jn 1:17 [d]Ps 119:111
33:7 [e]Ge 49:10
33:8 [f]Ex 28:30 [g]Ex 17:7
33:9 [h]Ex 32:26-29 [i]Mal 2:5

[a] 43 Or *Make his people rejoice, O nations* [b] 43 Masoretic Text; Dead Sea Scrolls (see also Septuagint) *people, / and let all the angels worship him /* [c] 44 Hebrew *Hoshea,* a variant of *Joshua* [d] 2 Or *from* [e] 2 The meaning of the Hebrew for this phrase is uncertain. [f] 5 *Jeshurun* means *the upright one,* that is, Israel; also in verse 26. [g] 6 Or *but let*

10He teaches your precepts to Jacob
and your law to Israel.[j]
He offers incense before you
and whole burnt offerings on your altar.[k]
11Bless all his skills, O LORD,
and be pleased with the work of his hands.[l]
Smite the loins of those who rise up against him;
strike his foes till they rise no more."

12About Benjamin he said:
"Let the beloved of the LORD rest secure in him,[m]
for he shields him all day long,
and the one the LORD loves rests between his shoulders.[n]"

13About Joseph[o] he said:
"May the LORD bless his land
with the precious dew from heaven above
and with the deep waters that lie below;[p]
14with the best the sun brings forth
and the finest the moon can yield;
15with the choicest gifts of the ancient mountains[q]
and the fruitfulness of the everlasting hills;
16with the best gifts of the earth and its fullness
and the favor of him who dwelt in the burning bush.[r]
Let all these rest on the head of Joseph,
on the brow of the prince among[a] his brothers.
17In majesty he is like a firstborn bull;
his horns are the horns of a wild ox.[s]
With them he will gore[t] the nations,
even those at the ends of the earth.
Such are the ten thousands of Ephraim;
such are the thousands of Manasseh."

18About Zebulun[u] he said:
"Rejoice, Zebulun, in your going out,
and you, Issachar, in your tents.
19They will summon peoples to the mountain[v]
and there offer sacrifices of righteousness;[w]
they will feast on the abundance of the seas,[x]
on the treasures hidden in the sand."

20About Gad[y] he said:
"Blessed is he who enlarges Gad's domain!
Gad lives there like a lion,
tearing at arm or head.
21He chose the best land for himself;[z]
the leader's portion was kept for him.
When the heads of the people assembled,
he carried out the LORD's righteous will,[a]
and his judgments concerning Israel."

22About Dan[b] he said:
"Dan is a lion's cub,
springing out of Bashan."

23About Naphtali he said:
"Naphtali is abounding with the favor of the LORD
and is full of his blessing;
he will inherit southward to the lake."

24About Asher[c] he said:
"Most blessed of sons is Asher;
let him be favored by his brothers,
and let him bathe his feet in oil.[d]
25The bolts of your gates will be iron and bronze,
and your strength will equal your days.[e]

26"There is no one like the God of Jeshurun,[f]
who rides on the heavens to help you[g]
and on the clouds in his majesty.
27The eternal God is your refuge,[h]
and underneath are the everlasting arms.
He will drive out your enemy before you,[i]
saying, 'Destroy him!'[j]
28So Israel will live in safety alone;[k]
Jacob's spring is secure
in a land of grain and new wine,

[a]16 Or *of the one separated from*

33:10 [j]Lev 10:11; Dt 31:9-13 [k]Ps 51:19
33:11 [l]2Sa 24:23
33:12 [m]Dt 12:10 [n]Ex 28:12
33:13 [o]Ge 49:25 [p]Ge 27:28
33:15 [q]Hab 3:6
33:16 [r]Ex 3:2
33:17 [s]Nu 23:22 [t]1Ki 22:11; Ps 44:5
33:18 [u]Ge 49:13-15
33:19 [v]Ex 15:17; Isa 2:3
33:19 [w]Ps 4:5 [x]Isa 60:5,11
33:20 [y]Ge 49:19
33:21 [z]Nu 32:1-5, 31-32 [a]Jos 4:12; 22:1-3
33:22 [b]Ge 49:16
33:24 [c]Ge 49:21 [d]Ge 49:20; Job 29:6
33:25 [e]Dt 4:40; 32:47
33:26 [f]Ex 15:11 [g]Ps 104:3
33:27 [h]Ps 90:1 [i]Jos 24:18 [j]Dt 7:2
33:28 [k]Nu 23:9; Jer 23:6

DAY 2 TWO

▸ PATIENCE AND THE PURPOSE OF GOD IN MY LIFE

Deuteronomy 34:5–8

The life of Moses seems to be divisible by three. His life span of 120 years is a triad of three 40-year segments. During the first 40 years of his life, he lived as royalty in Egypt. The second 40 years he spent in the wilderness of Sinai. Then, at approximately 80 years of age, he went back to Egypt, arranged for the exodus and led the people in and around Sinai for the last 40 years of his life.

But there is something wistful about this passage. Vital for all his years, Moses does not enter Canaan. The memories of all those years must have come flooding over him all at once, and his reckoning with them must have been a study in steely patience. Perhaps he learned that God desires patience from his servants. His lapse of patience at Meribah Kadesh caused him to forfeit the right to enter Canaan (32:48–52). Then at the end of his life and career, he had to wait patiently and obediently for the Lord's final instructions to him.

The book of Deuteronomy is composed mainly of the last three farewell addresses that Moses made to Israel. Moses instructed the people to carry on without him. At the end of his final sermon he read one of his poems to the people, and it stands as a celebration of his patience—the unhurried virtue—and also as an epitaph for his life:

Remember the days of old;
consider the generations long past.
Ask your father and he will tell you,
your elders, and they will explain to you.
When the Most High gave the nations their inheritance,
when he divided all mankind,
he set up boundaries for the peoples
according to the number of the sons of Israel.

(32:7–8)

To begin a study on the topic of Patience, the Unhurried Virtue, turn to the home page on page 1146.

where the heavens drop dew.[l]
29 Blessed are you, O Israel![m]
Who is like you,[n]
a people saved by the LORD?[o]
He is your shield and helper[p]
and your glorious sword.
Your enemies will cower before you,
and you will trample down their
high places.[a] [q]"

33:28 [l]Ge 27:28
33:29 [m]Ps 144:15 [n]Ps 18:44 [o]2Sa 7:23 [p]Ps 115:9-11 [q]Dt 32:13

The Death of Moses

34 Then Moses climbed Mount
Nebo from the plains of Moab
to the top of Pisgah, across from
Jericho.[r] There the LORD showed[s] him
the whole land—from Gilead to Dan,
2 all of Naphtali, the territory of Ephraim and Manasseh, all the land of Judah
as far as the western sea,[b] [t] 3 the Negev
and the whole region from the Valley
of Jericho, the City of Palms,[u] as far
as Zoar. 4 Then the LORD said to him,
"This is the land I promised on oath[v] to
Abraham, Isaac and Jacob when I said,
'I will give it[w] to your descendants.' I
have let you see it with your eyes, but
you will not cross[x] over into it."

34:1 [r]Dt 32:49 [s]Dt 32:52
34:2 [t]Dt 11:24
34:3 [u]Jdg 1:16; 3:13; 2Ch 28:15
34:4 [v]Ge 28:13 [w]Ge 12:7 [x]Dt 3:27

▸ GENTLENESS

THE FINAL CLIMB

Deuteronomy 34:1

Moses climbed Mount Nebo at 120 years of age. Christ climbed Calvary at 33 years of age. Both of them died on the mountains they ascended. But Jesus conquered death. Remember his victory?

Count on his climb. Then begin your own.
Crucify yourself.
Is the route of your own ascent hard to keep?
Think of Jesus on his climb.
No climb since then has been too steep.

5 And Moses the servant of the LORD[y]
died[z] there in Moab, as the LORD had
said. 6 He buried him[c] in Moab, in the
valley opposite Beth Peor,[a] but to this
day no one knows where his grave is.[b]
7 Moses was a hundred and twenty years
old[c] when he died, yet his eyes were
not weak[d] nor his strength gone. 8 The
Israelites grieved for Moses in the plains
of Moab thirty days, until the time

34:5 [y]Nu 12:7 [z]Dt 32:50; Jos 1:1-2
34:6 [a]Dt 3:29 [b]Jude 1:9
34:7 [c]Dt 31:2 [d]Ge 27:1

[a]29 Or *will tread upon their bodies* [b]2 That is, the Mediterranean [c]6 Or *He buried was buried*

of weeping and mourning[e] was over.
9 Now Joshua son of Nun was filled
with the spirit[a] of wisdom[f] because Moses had laid his hands on him.[g] So the
Israelites listened to him and did what
the LORD had commanded Moses.
10 Since then, no prophet has risen
in Israel like Moses,[h] whom the LORD
knew face to face,[i] 11 who did all those
miraculous signs and wonders[j] the
LORD sent him to do in Egypt—to
Pharaoh and to all his officials[k] and to
his whole land. 12 For no one has ever
shown the mighty power or performed
the awesome deeds that Moses did in
the sight of all Israel.

[a] 9 Or *Spirit*

34:8 [e] Ge 50:3,10; 2Sa 11:27
34:9 [f] Ge 41:38; Isa 11:2; Da 6:3 [g] Nu 27:18,23
34:10 [h] Dt 18:15,18 [i] Ex 33:11; Nu 12:6,8; Dt 5:4
34:11 [j] Dt 4:34 [k] Dt 7:19

JOSHUA

▸ AUTHORSHIP AND DATE

Joshua (except for the final verses, which must have been written by an observer)

c. 1410 B.C. to c. 1390 B.C.

▸ KEY THEMES

The main themes of Joshua are leadership, the conquest of Canaan, faith in God and the manner of advance. These themes are revealed in three areas: Israel's entry into Canaan (see 1:1–5:12), Israel's conquest of the people of Canaan (see 5:13–12:24) and Israel's division of the conquered territories among the twelve tribes (see 13:1–24:33).

▸ FRUIT OF THE SPIRIT IN JOSHUA

Love: Joshua, the leader who had conquered in the power of God, gave his people this advice on two different occasions: "Be very careful to love the LORD your God" (22:5; 23:11). This was not so much a mandate as it was a plaintive and spiritual plea. Joshua, an old and tender warrior, could not imagine any sin more horrible than failing to love the God who had given Israel a national identity and a land for their eternal inheritance.

Joy: The conquest of the city of Jericho may be seen as a conquest of joy. The Israelites marched around the city in silence for seven days, and on the seventh day they followed the instructions that Joshua had given them: "Shout! For the LORD has given you the city!" (6:16). Whether it was a shout of joy or merely of godly triumph it is impossible to know, but joy and triumph are close companions.

Peace: The conquest of the land ended with a season of peace—a final peace that Moses had only dreamed of in the wilderness. At the end of the account of Israel's struggle to wage war and subdue the land was a short benediction that must have meant a lot to the people: "The land had rest from war" (11:23).

Patience: Two verses must be taken together to see a wonderful lesson of patience in the book of Joshua. Rahab the prostitute befriended and protected the Hebrew spies when they secretly came to spy out Jericho. They swore an oath to protect her when they came back to take the city. To mark her house, Rahab tied a scarlet cord in the window as a remembrance of the oath (see 2:21). Then came the season of Rahab's patient waiting for the Israelites to demonstrate faithfulness to her. When much time had passed, Rahab's patience was rewarded, and she and her family were spared. Joshua instructed those whom she had befriended, "Go into the prostitute's house and bring her out and all who belong to her, in accordance with your oath to her" (6:22).

Faithfulness: Joshua instructed the people of Israel to explain to their descendants the monument made of stones taken from the bed of the Jordan River. When children asked their parents to explain the meaning of the stones, the parent was to tell them how the warriors had gathered the stones as they passed through the Jordan. God had proven himself faithful. Just as he had done to the Red Sea, "God dried up the Jordan before you until you had crossed over" (4:23).

Self-Control: Joshua, at the close of both the book and his life, reminded Israel that the key to self-control is to fear God and to follow him in strict obedience. Joshua knew that idolatry would always be a part of the lives of those Israel had conquered, and thus idolatry would be an ever-present threat to Israel's worship. To be a people of self-control, they would have to abandon the worship of idols. So in his parting sermon, Joshua gave them this advice, "Now fear the LORD and serve him with all faithfulness. Throw away the gods your forefathers worshiped beyond the River and in Egypt, and serve the LORD" (24:14).

The LORD Commands Joshua

1 After the death of Moses the ser-
1:1 [a]Nu 12:7; Dt 34:5 [b]Ex 24:13; Dt 1:38 vant of the LORD, the LORD[a] said
to Joshua[b] son of Nun, Moses' aide:
2"Moses my servant is dead. Now then,
you and all these people, get ready to
1:2 [c]ver 11 cross the Jordan River[c] into the land
I am about to give to them—to the
Israelites. 3I will give you every place
1:3 [d]Dt 11:24 where you set your foot,[d] as I promised
Moses. 4Your territory will extend from
the desert to Lebanon, and from the
1:4 [e]Ge 15:18 [f]Nu 34:2-12 great river, the Euphrates[e]—all the Hittite country—to the Great Sea[a] on the
west.[f] 5No one will be able to stand up
1:5 [g]Dt 7:24 [h]Jos 3:7; 6:27 [i]Dt 31:6-8 against you[g] all the days of your life. As
I was with[h] Moses, so I will be with you;
I will never leave you nor forsake[i] you.
6"Be strong and courageous, because
you will lead these people to inherit
1:6 [j]Dt 31:23 the land I swore to their forefathers[j] to
give them. 7Be strong and very coura-
geous. Be careful to obey all the law my
servant Moses gave you; do not turn
1:7 [k]Dt 5:32; 28:14 [l]Jos 11:15 from it to the right or to the left,[k] that
you may be successful wherever you go.[l]
8Do not let this Book of the Law depart from your mouth; meditate on it
day and night, so that you may be care-
1:8 [m]Dt 29:9; Ps 1:1-3 ful to do everything written in it. Then
you will be prosperous and successful.[m]
9Have I not commanded you? Be strong
1:9 [n]Ps 27:1 [o]ver 7; Dt 31:7-8; Jer 1:8 and courageous. Do not be terrified;[n]
do not be discouraged, for the LORD
your God will be with you wherever
you go."[o]
10So Joshua ordered the officers of
the people: 11"Go through the camp
and tell the people, 'Get your supplies
ready. Three days from now you will
cross the Jordan here to go in and take
1:11 [p]Joel 3:2 possession[p] of the land the LORD your
God is giving you for your own.' "
1:12 [q]Nu 32:20-22 12But to the Reubenites, the Gadites
and the half-tribe of Manasseh,[q] Joshua
said, 13"Remember the command that
Moses the servant of the LORD gave
you: 'The LORD your God is giving
1:13 [r]Dt 3:18-20 you rest[r] and has granted you this land.'
14Your wives, your children and your
livestock may stay in the land that Moses gave you east of the Jordan, but all
your fighting men, fully armed, must
cross over ahead of your brothers. You
are to help your brothers 15until the
LORD gives them rest, as he has done
for you, and until they too have taken
possession of the land that the LORD
your God is giving them. After that,
you may go back and occupy your own
land, which Moses the servant of the
LORD gave you east of the Jordan toward the sunrise."[s] 1:15 [s]Jos 22:1-4
16Then they answered Joshua,
"Whatever you have commanded us we
will do, and wherever you send us we
will go. 17Just as we fully obeyed Mo- 1:17 [t]ver 5,9
ses, so we will obey you.[t] Only may
the LORD your God be with you as
he was with Moses. 18Whoever rebels
against your word and does not obey
your words, whatever you may command them, will be put to death. Only
be strong and courageous!"

Rahab and the Spies

2 Then Joshua son of Nun secretly
sent two spies[u] from Shittim.[v] "Go, 2:1 [u]Jas 2:25 [v]Nu 25:1; Jos 3:1 [w]Heb 11:31
look over the land," he said, "especially
Jericho." So they went and entered the
house of a prostitute[b] named Rahab[w]
and stayed there.
2The king of Jericho was told, "Look!
Some of the Israelites have come here
tonight to spy out the land." 3So the
king of Jericho sent this message to Rahab: "Bring out the men who came to
you and entered your house, because
they have come to spy out the whole
land."

LOVE

LOVING THE LIES OF RAHAB

Joshua 2:4

Rahab was a prostitute.
Rahab also lied.
Rahab is our sinning sister.

We are a lot more like Rahab than we would care to admit. Still, it's the nature of grace to make all sinners usable.

4But the woman had taken the two
men and hidden them.[x] She said, "Yes, 2:4 [x]2Sa 17:19-20
the men came to me, but I did not
know where they had come from. 5At
dusk, when it was time to close the city
gate, the men left. I don't know which
way they went. Go after them quickly.
You may catch up with them." 6(But

[a]*4* That is, the Mediterranean [b]*1* Or possibly *an innkeeper*

2:6 [y]Jas 2:25 [z]Ex 1:17,19; 2Sa 17:19

she had taken them up to the roof and
hidden them under the stalks of flax[y]
she had laid out on the roof.)[z] 7 So the
men set out in pursuit of the spies on
the road that leads to the fords of the
Jordan, and as soon as the pursuers had
gone out, the gate was shut.
8 Before the spies lay down for the
night, she went up on the roof 9 and
said to them, "I know that the LORD
has given this land to you and that a
great fear[a] of you has fallen on us, so
that all who live in this country are
melting in fear because of you. 10 We
have heard how the LORD dried up[b]
the water of the Red Sea[a] for you when
you came out of Egypt,[c] and what you
did to Sihon and Og,[d] the two kings of
the Amorites east of the Jordan, whom
you completely destroyed.[b] 11 When we
heard of it, our hearts melted and everyone's courage failed because of you,[e] for
the LORD your God is God in heaven
above and on the earth[f] below. 12 Now
then, please swear to me by the LORD
that you will show kindness to my family, because I have shown kindness to
you. Give me a sure sign[g] 13 that you
will spare the lives of my father and
mother, my brothers and sisters, and all
who belong to them, and that you will
save us from death."
14 "Our lives for your lives!" the men
assured her. "If you don't tell what we
are doing, we will treat you kindly and
faithfully[h] when the LORD gives us the
land."
15 So she let them down by a rope
through the window,[i] for the house she
lived in was part of the city wall. 16 Now
she had said to them, "Go to the hills

2:9 [a]Ge 35:5; Ex 23:27; Dt 2:25
2:10 [b]Ex 14:21 [c]Nu 23:22 [d]Nu 21:21,24, 34-35
2:11 [e]Ex 15:14; Jos 5:1; 7:5; Ps 22:14; Isa 13:7 [f]Dt 4:39
2:12 [g]ver 18
2:14 [h]Jdg 1:24; Mt 5:7
2:15 [i]Ac 9:25

[a] *10* Hebrew *Yam Suph*; that is, Sea of Reeds
[b] *10* The Hebrew term refers to the irrevocable giving over of things or persons to the LORD, often by totally destroying them.

RAHAB

Kindness, the Scarlet Cord of Promise (2:1–21)

It is kindness that spared Rahab the prostitute. But kindness also gave her a niche forever in Hebrew history. Kindness has the power to establish us in a place of permanence if we give it sway in our lives.

Rahab noticed the greatness of God in the movement of Israel from Egypt to the borders of Canaan. Rahab knew that the Israelites could never have escaped the clutches of Pharaoh and lived in the none-too-accommodating conditions of the Sinai desert unless their God was *the* God. "I know that the LORD has given this land to you," she told the spies (Joshua 2:9). So Rahab determined to help the spies. In the process, she helped herself and her family.

Kindness begets kindness. Rahab befriended the spies, and the spies reciprocated by promising to treat Rahab and her family kindly and faithfully after Israel had conquered Jericho. The sign was set: She was to tie a scarlet cord in her window (vv. 17–20). When the Israelites attacked Jericho, they would see the scarlet cord and would spare Rahab's entire family in the day of slaughter. The scarlet cord was the signet of kindness.

The fall of Jericho is described in Joshua 6:24–25, a passage in which Rahab's kindness to the spies is pointed out: "They burned the whole city and everything in it . . . But Joshua spared Rahab the prostitute, with her family and all who belonged to her, because she hid the men Joshua had sent as spies to Jericho—and she lives among the Israelites to this day."

Rahab and her family were not only spared from death during the fall of Jericho, but Rahab's one act of kindness eventually wound its scarlet cord into the very lineage of Christ, as Matthew 1:5 includes Rahab in the genealogy of Jesus.

Kindness pays dividends here in this life, yet it is no mere political maneuver.

It smiles to reassure the frightened.

It holds out bread to the starving.

It is an oasis in the desert of "everybody's got to make a living."

It is a banquet in the famine of "God helps those who help themselves."

KINDNESS

WEEK 14

1 DAY ONE
KINDNESS IN THE TIME OF NEED

Read Joshua 2:8–14

Here is the fascinating tale of a kind prostitute. She hid the Israelite spies and lied to the government officials to protect them. We need not investigate Rahab's integrity. She could tell the worst of lies for the best of reasons. But this passage describes Rahab with the word *kind*, and her integrity (or lack of it) was usable to God.

Kindness in a time of need may have been Rahab's motto. Notice that she has several strikes against her as an expected source of kindness. She is a prostitute, a Gentile, and...yes, a liar. Yet hidden beneath her faults was a woman capable of kindness.

One night following the derailment of an Indian train on which I was a passenger, I found myself on a cold stretch of unfamiliar highway 70 miles south of New Delhi. It was near midnight, and I did not know a single word of Hindi. After several vain attempts to flag down a cattle truck, a rather well dressed, clearly upper-caste Hindu man approached me and offered me a ride back to the city and my hotel. I was overjoyed by his kindness. On the way back to New Delhi I discovered that he was a devout Hindu and was currently celebrating the feasts of the nine goddesses. He was a reincarnationist and strongly held to caste, an abomination that I despised. Like Rahab, he was a person with lots of things "wrong" with him, but God used him to show me kindness in my time of need.

The story of Rahab reminds us that we need not be perfect to be used by God, but we do have to be willing to take a chance in doing God's will. Rahab risked her life in defying the authorities of her city and hiding the spies. Rahab did the right thing and showed kindness. Will we demonstrate the same kind of desire to help others no matter what the cost to us?

> **MEMORIZE THIS WEEK**
>
> **JEREMIAH 9:23-24**
>
> ***"Let not the wise man boast of his wisdom***
> ***or the strong man boast of his strength***
> ***or the rich man boast of his riches,***
> ***but let him who boasts boast about this:***
> ***that he understands and knows me,***
> ***that I am the LORD, who exercises kindness,***
> ***justice and righteousness on earth,***
> ***for in these I delight,"***
> ***declares the LORD.***

2 DAY TWO
KINDNESS AND THE PURPOSE OF GOD IN MY LIFE

Job suffered the loss of almost everything. His family was destroyed. His friends offered no help. Even his wife advised him to curse God and die (Job 2:9). But in spite of all this, Job perceives God as the Lord of kindness and blesses his providence. *Turn to Job 10:8–12, page 596, for today's study.*

3 DAY THREE
KINDNESS AND MY RELATIONSHIP WITH CHRIST

God is kind, and his ultimate display of kindness was the sacrifice of his Son for the sins of all people. When we fully begin to realize the great kindness of God, we respond with sorrow and contrition for our sins that brought about the greatest act of kindness the world has ever seen—Christ crucified. *Turn to Romans 2:3–4, page 1334, for today's study.*

4 DAY FOUR
KINDNESS AND MY SERVICE TO OTHERS

Christ offers a reward to all who will extend water. It is so little a gift, one wonders that it ranks so highly in Christ's estimation. He does not command us to give a "pheasant under glass dinner with a crème torte dessert." Just water—something to which everyone has access, and something almost anyone can offer. *Turn to Matthew 10:40–42, page 1134, for today's study.*

5 DAY FIVE
KINDNESS AND ITS PLACE IN MY PERSONAL WORSHIP

Isaiah, who often celebrates the grand themes of exile and restoration, uses the word *kindnesses* twice and a good many other soft, warm words like *compassion, good things* and *deeds for which he is to be praised.* The austere and all-powerful God of Sinai has come down to us in softer garments, so soft that Jesus would call him Father and make him so touchable that only the word *Immanuel* (God with us) would do. *Turn to Isaiah 63:7, page 863, for today's study.*

Week 15, Goodness and the Desire for Holiness, begins on page 790, Isaiah 1:1–6.
To begin a topical study on the Fruit of the Spirit, Kindness, turn to the Topical Index, page 1548.

so the pursuers will not find you. Hide
2:16 [j]Jas 2:25 [k]Heb 11:31
yourselves there three days[j] until they
return, and then go on your way."[k]
2:17 [l]Ge 24:8
17The men said to her, "This oath[l]
you made us swear will not be binding
on us 18unless, when we enter the land,
you have tied this scarlet cord in the
window through which you let us down,
and unless you have brought your father and mother, your brothers and all
2:18 [m]ver 12; Jos 6:23
your family[m] into your house. 19If anyone goes outside your house into the
street, his blood will be on his own
2:19 [n]Eze 33:4 [o]Mt 27:25
head;[n] we will not be responsible. As
for anyone who is in the house with
you, his blood will be on our head[o] if
a hand is laid on him. 20But if you tell
what we are doing, we will be released
from the oath you made us swear."
21"Agreed," she replied. "Let it be as
you say." So she sent them away and
they departed. And she tied the scarlet
cord in the window.
22When they left, they went into
the hills and stayed there three days, until the pursuers had searched all along
the road and returned without finding
them. 23Then the two men started back.
They went down out of the hills, ford-
ed the river and came to Joshua son
of Nun and told him everything that
had happened to them. 24They said to
Joshua, "The LORD has surely given the
2:24 [p]ver 9; Jos 6:2
whole land into our hands;[p] all the people are melting in fear because of us."

Crossing the Jordan

3 Early in the morning Joshua and
all the Israelites set out from
3:1 [q]Jos 2:1
Shittim[q] and went to the Jordan, where
they camped before crossing over. 2Af-
ter three days the officers went through-
3:2 [r]Jos 1:11
out the camp,[r] 3giving orders to the
people: "When you see the ark of the
3:3 [s]Nu 10:33 [t]Dt 31:9
covenant[s] of the LORD your God, and
the priests,[t] who are Levites, carrying
it, you are to move out from your positions and follow it. 4Then you will
know which way to go, since you have
never been this way before. But keep
a distance of about a thousand yards[a]
between you and the ark; do not go
near it."
3:5 [u]Ex 19:10,14; Lev 20:7; Jos 7:13; 1Sa 16:5; Joel 2:16
5Joshua told the people, "Consecrate
yourselves,[u] for tomorrow the LORD
will do amazing things among you."
6Joshua said to the priests, "Take up
the ark of the covenant and pass on

GOODNESS

A THOUSAND YARDS OF REVERENCE AND FEAR

Joshua 3:4

The ark symbolized the presence of the living God. The Israelites were not to get too close lest the glory of pure holiness consume them with lightning and fire. It is as though God shouted out:

Keep your distance.
I am God, astride the ark.
Come not too near my dwelling place.
Face my sanctity and power
If you would know my saving grace.

ahead of the people." So they took it up
and went ahead of them.
7And the LORD said to Joshua, "To-
day I will begin to exalt you[v] in the eyes 3:7 [v]Jos 4:14; 1Ch 29:25 [w]Jos 1:5
of all Israel, so they may know that I
am with you as I was with Moses.[w] 8Tell
the priests[x] who carry the ark of the 3:8 [x]ver 3
covenant: 'When you reach the edge of
the Jordan's waters, go and stand in the 3:10 [y]Dt 5:26; 1Sa 17:26,36; 2Ki 19:4,16; Hos 1:10; Mt 16:16; 1Th 1:9 [z]Ex 33:2; Dt 7:1
river.' "
9Joshua said to the Israelites, "Come
here and listen to the words of the
LORD your God. 10This is how you will
know that the living God[y] is among
you and that he will certainly drive
out before you the Canaanites, Hittites,
Hivites, Perizzites, Girgashites, Amo- 3:11 [a]ver 13; Job 41:11; Zec 6:5
rites and Jebusites.[z] 11See, the ark of the
covenant of the Lord of all the earth[a]
will go into the Jordan ahead of you.
12Now then, choose twelve men[b] from 3:12 [b]Jos 4:2,4
the tribes of Israel, one from each tribe.
13And as soon as the priests who carry 3:13 [c]ver 11 [d]ver 16 [e]Ex 15:8; Ps 78:13
the ark of the LORD—the Lord of all
the earth[c]—set foot in the Jordan, its
waters flowing downstream[d] will be cut
off and stand up in a heap.[e]"
14So when the people broke camp
to cross the Jordan, the priests carrying
the ark of the covenant[f] went ahead[g] 3:14 [f]Ps 132:8 [g]Ac 7:44-45
of them. 15Now the Jordan is at flood
stage[h] all during harvest. Yet as soon as 3:15 [h]Jos 4:18; 1Ch 12:15
the priests who carried the ark reached
the Jordan and their feet touched the
water's edge, 16the water from upstream 3:16 [i]Ps 66:6; 74:15
stopped flowing.[i] It piled up in a heap
a great distance away, at a town called

[a]4 Hebrew *about two thousand cubits* (about 900 meters)

3:16 [j]1Ki 4:12; 7:46 [k]ver 13 [l]Dt 1:1 [m]Ge 14:3
Adam in the vicinity of Zarethan,[j] while
the water flowing down[k] to the Sea of
the Arabah[l] (the Salt Sea[a][m]) was completely cut off. So the people crossed
over opposite Jericho. 17The priests who
carried the ark of the covenant of the
LORD stood firm on dry ground in
the middle of the Jordan, while all Israel passed by until the whole nation
had completed the crossing on dry
3:17 [n]Ex 14:22,29
ground.[n]

4:1 [o]Dt 27:2
4 When the whole nation had finished crossing the Jordan,[o] the
LORD said to Joshua, 2"Choose twelve
4:2 [p]Jos 3:12
men[p] from among the people, one from
each tribe, 3and tell them to take up
4:3 [q]ver 20 [r]ver 19
twelve stones[q] from the middle of the
Jordan from right where the priests
stood and to carry them over with you
and put them down at the place where
you stay tonight.[r]"

4So Joshua called together the twelve
men he had appointed from the Israelites, one from each tribe, 5and said
to them, "Go over before the ark of
the LORD your God into the middle
of the Jordan. Each of you is to take
up a stone on his shoulder, according
to the number of the tribes of the Israelites, 6to serve as a sign among you.
4:6 [s]ver 21; Ex 12:26; 13:14
In the future, when your children ask
you, 'What do these stones mean?'[s] 7tell
them that the flow of the Jordan was
4:7 [t]Jos 3:13 [u]Ex 12:14
cut off[t] before the ark of the covenant
of the LORD. When it crossed the Jordan, the waters of the Jordan were cut
off. These stones are to be a memorial[u]
to the people of Israel forever."

GENTLENESS

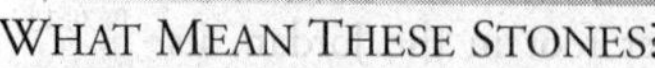

WHAT MEAN THESE STONES?

Joshua 4:6–7

What mean these stones?
These stones mean the God of grace responds
To create nations from a horde of vagabonds.

8So the Israelites did as Joshua commanded them. They took twelve stones
from the middle of the Jordan, according to the number of the tribes of the
4:8 [v]ver 20
Israelites, as the LORD had told Joshua;[v]
and they carried them over with them
to their camp, where they put them
down. 9Joshua set up the twelve stones[w]
that had been[b] in the middle of the 4:9 [w]Ge 28:18; Jos 24:26; 1Sa 7:12
Jordan at the spot where the priests
who carried the ark of the covenant had
stood. And they are there to this day.

10Now the priests who carried the
ark remained standing in the middle of
the Jordan until everything the LORD
had commanded Joshua was done by
the people, just as Moses had directed
Joshua. The people hurried over, 11and
as soon as all of them had crossed,
the ark of the LORD and the priests
came to the other side while the people
watched. 12The men of Reuben, Gad
and the half-tribe of Manasseh crossed
over, armed, in front of the Israelites,
as Moses[x] had directed them. 13About 4:12 [x]Nu 32:27
forty thousand armed for battle crossed
over before the LORD to the plains of
Jericho for war.

14That day the LORD exalted[y] Josh- 4:14 [y]Jos 3:7
ua in the sight of all Israel; and they revered him all the days of his life, just as
they had revered Moses.

15Then the LORD said to Joshua,
16"Command the priests carrying the
ark of the Testimony[z] to come up out 4:16 [z]Ex 25:22
of the Jordan."

17So Joshua commanded the priests,
"Come up out of the Jordan."

18And the priests came up out of the
river carrying the ark of the covenant
of the LORD. No sooner had they set
their feet on the dry ground than the
waters of the Jordan returned to their
place and ran at flood stage[a] as before. 4:18 [a]Jos 3:15

19On the tenth day of the first month
the people went up from the Jordan 4:19 [b]Jos 5:9
and camped at Gilgal[b] on the eastern
border of Jericho. 20And Joshua set up 4:20 [c]ver 3,8
at Gilgal the twelve stones[c] they had
taken out of the Jordan. 21He said to
the Israelites, "In the future when your
descendants ask their fathers, 'What do
these stones mean?'[d] 22tell them, 'Israel 4:21 [d]ver 6
crossed the Jordan on dry ground.'[e] 4:22 [e]Jos 3:17
23For the LORD your God dried up the
Jordan before you until you had crossed
over. The LORD your God did to the
Jordan just what he had done to the
Red Sea[c] when he dried it up before us
until we had crossed over.[f] 24He did this 4:23 [f]Ex 14:21
so that all the peoples of the earth might

[a]*16* That is, the Dead Sea [b]*9* Or *Joshua also set up twelve stones* [c]*23* Hebrew *Yam Suph*; that is, Sea of Reeds

4:24 [g]1Ki 8:42-43; 2Ki 19:19; Ps 106:8; Jer 10:7 [h]Ex 15:16; 1Ch 29:12; Ps 89:13 [i]Ex 14:31 know[g] that the hand of the LORD is
powerful[h] and so that you might always
fear the LORD your God.[i]"

Circumcision at Gilgal

5 Now when all the Amorite kings
5:1 [j]Nu 13:29 [k]Jos 2:9-11 west of the Jordan and all the Canaanite kings along the coast[j] heard
how the LORD had dried up the Jordan before the Israelites until we had
crossed over, their hearts melted[k] and
they no longer had the courage to face
the Israelites.
2At that time the LORD said to Josh-
5:2 [l]Ex 4:25 ua, "Make flint knives[l] and circumcise
the Israelites again." 3So Joshua made
flint knives and circumcised the Israelites at Gibeath Haaraloth.[a]
4Now this is why he did so: All those
who came out of Egypt—all the men
of military age—died in the desert on
5:4 [m]Dt 2:14 the way after leaving Egypt.[m] 5All the
people that came out had been circum-
cised, but all the people born in the desert during the journey from Egypt had
not. 6The Israelites had moved about in
5:6 [n]Dt 2:7 [o]Nu 14:23, 29-35; Dt 2:14 [p]Ex 3:8 the desert forty years[n] until all the men
who were of military age when they
left Egypt had died, since they had not
obeyed the LORD. For the LORD had
sworn to them that they would not see
the land that he had solemnly promised their fathers to give us,[o] a land
flowing with milk and honey.[p] 7So he
raised up their sons in their place, and
these were the ones Joshua circumcised.
They were still uncircumcised because
they had not been circumcised on the
way. 8And after the whole nation had
been circumcised, they remained where
they were in camp until they were
5:8 [q]Ge 34:25 healed.[q]
9Then the LORD said to Joshua, "Today I have rolled away the reproach of
Egypt from you." So the place has been
called Gilgal[b] to this day.
5:10 [r]Ex 12:6 10On the evening of the fourteenth
day of the month,[r] while camped at
Gilgal on the plains of Jericho, the Israelites celebrated the Passover. 11The day
after the Passover, that very day, they
5:11 [s]Nu 15:19 [t]Lev 23:14 ate some of the produce of the land:[s]
unleavened bread and roasted grain.[t]
12The manna stopped the day after[c]
they ate this food from the land; there
was no longer any manna for the Isra-
5:12 [u]Ex 16:35 elites, but that year they ate of the produce of Canaan.[u]

The Fall of Jericho

13Now when Joshua was near Jericho,
he looked up and saw a man[v] standing 5:13 [v]Ge 18:2; 32:24 [w]Nu 22:23
in front of him with a drawn sword[w] in
his hand. Joshua went up to him and
asked, "Are you for us or for our enemies?"
14"Neither," he replied, "but as commander of the army of the LORD I have
now come." Then Joshua fell facedown[x] 5:14 [x]Ge 17:3
to the ground in reverence, and asked
him, "What message does my Lord[d]
have for his servant?"
15The commander of the LORD's
army replied, "Take off your sandals,
for the place where you are standing is
holy."[y] And Joshua did so. 5:15 [y]Ex 3:5; Ac 7:33
6 Now Jericho[z] was tightly shut up
because of the Israelites. No one 6:1 [z]Jos 24:11
went out and no one came in.
2Then the LORD said to Joshua, 6:2 [a]Dt 7:24; Jos 2:9,24; 8:1
"See, I have delivered[a] Jericho into your
hands, along with its king and its fighting men. 3March around the city once
with all the armed men. Do this for six
days. 4Have seven priests carry trumpets
of rams' horns in front of the ark. On
the seventh day, march around the city
seven times, with the priests blowing
the trumpets.[b] 5When you hear them 6:4 [b]Lev 25:9; Nu 10:8
sound a long blast[c] on the trumpets,
have all the people give a loud shout;[d]
then the wall of the city will collapse 6:5 [c]Ex 19:13 [d]ver 20; 1Sa 4:5; Ps 42:4; Isa 42:13
and the people will go up, every man
straight in."
6So Joshua son of Nun called the
priests and said to them, "Take up the
ark of the covenant of the LORD and
have seven priests carry trumpets in
front of it." 7And he ordered the peo- 6:7 [e]Ex 14:15
ple, "Advance[e]! March around the city,
with the armed guard going ahead of
the ark of the LORD."
8When Joshua had spoken to the
people, the seven priests carrying the
seven trumpets before the LORD went
forward, blowing their trumpets, and
the ark of the LORD's covenant followed
them. 9The armed guard[f] marched 6:9 [f]ver 13; Isa 52:12
ahead of the priests who blew the trum-
pets, and the rear guard followed the
ark. All this time the trumpets were
sounding. 10But Joshua had commanded the people, "Do not give a war cry,

[a]3 *Gibeath Haaraloth* means *hill of foreskins.*
[b]9 *Gilgal* sounds like the Hebrew for *roll.* [c]12 Or *the day* [d]14 Or *lord*

do not raise your voices, do not say a
word until the day I tell you to shout.
6:10 Then shout![g]" 11So he had the ark of
[g]ver 20 the LORD carried around the city, circling it once. Then the people returned
to camp and spent the night there.
12Joshua got up early the next morning and the priests took up the ark of
the LORD. 13The seven priests carrying the seven trumpets went forward,
marching before the ark of the LORD
and blowing the trumpets. The armed
men went ahead of them and the rear
guard followed the ark of the LORD,
while the trumpets kept sounding. 14So
on the second day they marched around
the city once and returned to the camp.
They did this for six days.
15On the seventh day, they got up
at daybreak and marched around the
city seven times in the same manner,
6:15 except that on that day they circled the
[h]1Ki 18:44 city seven times.[h] 16The seventh time
around, when the priests sounded the
trumpet blast, Joshua commanded the
people, "Shout! For the LORD has given
6:17 you the city! 17The city and all that is
[i]Lev 27:28; Dt 20:17 in it are to be devoted[a][i] to the LORD.
[j]Jos 2:4 Only Rahab the prostitute[b] and all who
are with her in her house shall be spared,
6:18 because she hid[j] the spies we sent. 18But
[k]Jos 7:1 [l]Jos 7:12 keep away from the devoted things,[k]
[m]Jos 7:25,26 so that you will not bring about your
own destruction by taking any of them.
Otherwise you will make the camp of
Israel liable to destruction[l] and bring
6:19 trouble[m] on it. 19All the silver and gold
[n]ver 24; Nu 31:22 and the articles of bronze and iron[n] are
sacred to the LORD and must go into
his treasury."
6:20 20When the trumpets sounded,[o] the
[o]Jdg 6:34; Jer 4:21; Am 2:2 people shouted, and at the sound of the
[p]ver 5 trumpet, when the people gave a loud
[q]Heb 11:30 shout,[p] the wall collapsed; so every man
charged straight in, and they took the
6:21 city.[q] 21They devoted the city to the
[r]Dt 20:16 LORD and destroyed[r] with the sword
every living thing in it—men and wom-
en, young and old, cattle, sheep and
donkeys.
22Joshua said to the two men who
had spied out the land, "Go into the
prostitute's house and bring her out and
6:22 all who belong to her, in accordance
[s]Jos 2:14; Heb 11:31 with your oath to her.[s]" 23So the young
men who had done the spying went in
and brought out Rahab, her father and
mother and brothers and all who belonged to her.[t] They brought out her 6:23
entire family and put them in a place [t]Jos 2:13
outside the camp of Israel.
24Then they burned the whole city
and everything in it, but they put
the silver and gold and the articles of 6:24
bronze and iron[u] into the treasury of [u]ver 19
the LORD's house. 25But Joshua spared 6:25
Rahab the prostitute,[v] with her family [v]Heb 11:31
and all who belonged to her, because [w]Jos 2:6
she hid the men Joshua had sent as
spies to Jericho[w]—and she lives among
the Israelites to this day.
26At that time Joshua pronounced
this solemn oath: "Cursed before the
LORD is the man who undertakes to rebuild this city, Jericho:

"At the cost of his firstborn son
will he lay its foundations;
at the cost of his youngest 6:26
will he set up its gates."[x] [x]1Ki 16:34

27So the LORD was with Joshua,[y] and 6:27 [y]Ge 39:2;
his fame spread[z] throughout the land. Jos 1:5 [z]Jos 9:1

Achan's Sin

7 But the Israelites acted unfaithfully
in regard to the devoted things[c];[a] 7:1 [a]Jos 6:18
Achan son of Carmi, the son of Zimri,[d] [b]Jos 22:20
the son of Zerah,[b] of the tribe of Judah,
took some of them. So the LORD's anger burned against Israel.

▸ SELF-CONTROL

GIVE ME GOD AND
GIVE ME STUFF

Joshua 7:1

Achan has many children who still get rich by secret schemes. They would be rich and yet would pretend to want some poorer office in the kingdom of God. Wanting stuff and wanting God sometimes look alike. But then, the words *God* and *gold* almost look alike.

2Now Joshua sent men from Jericho 7:2
to Ai, which is near Beth Aven[e] to the [e]Jos 18:12;
east of Bethel, and told them, "Go up 1Sa 13:5; 14:23

[a] *17* The Hebrew term refers to the irrevocable giving over of things or persons to the LORD, often by totally destroying them; also in verses 18 and 21.
[b] *17* Or possibly *innkeeper*; also in verses 22 and 25
[c] *1* The Hebrew term refers to the irrevocable giving over of things or persons to the LORD, often by totally destroying them; also in verses 11, 12, 13 and 15.
[d] *1* See Septuagint and 1 Chron. 2:6; Hebrew *Zabdi*; also in verses 17 and 18.

and spy out the region." So the men
went up and spied out Ai.
3When they returned to Joshua, they
said, "Not all the people will have to go
up against Ai. Send two or three thousand men to take it and do not weary
all the people, for only a few men are
there." 4So about three thousand men
went up; but they were routed by the
7:4 [d]Lev 26:17; Dt 28:25
men of Ai,[d] 5who killed about thirty-
six of them. They chased the Israelites
7:5 [e]Lev 26:36; Jos 2:9,11; Eze 21:7; Na 2:10
from the city gate as far as the stone
quarries[a] and struck them down on the
slopes. At this the hearts of the people
melted[e] and became like water.
7:6 [f]Ge 37:29 [g]1Sa 4:12; 2Sa 13:19; Ne 9:1; Job 2:12; La 2:10; Rev 18:19
6Then Joshua tore his clothes[f] and
fell facedown to the ground before
the ark of the LORD, remaining there
till evening. The elders of Israel did
the same, and sprinkled dust[g] on their
heads. 7And Joshua said, "Ah, Sovereign LORD, why did you ever bring this
people across the Jordan to deliver us
into the hands of the Amorites to de-
7:7 [h]Ex 5:22
stroy us?[h] If only we had been content
to stay on the other side of the Jordan!
8O Lord, what can I say, now that Israel
has been routed by its enemies? 9The
Canaanites and the other people of the
country will hear about this and they
7:9 [i]Ex 32:12; Dt 9:28
will surround us and wipe out our name
from the earth.[i] What then will you do
for your own great name?"
10The LORD said to Joshua, "Stand
up! What are you doing down on your
face? 11Israel has sinned; they have vio-
7:11 [j]Jos 6:17-19 [k]Ac 5:1-2
lated my covenant,[j] which I commanded them to keep. They have taken some
of the devoted things; they have stolen, they have lied,[k] they have put them
with their own possessions. 12That is
why the Israelites cannot stand against
7:12 [l]Nu 14:45; Jdg 2:14 [m]Jos 6:18
their enemies;[l] they turn their backs
and run because they have been made
liable to destruction.[m] I will not be with
you anymore unless you destroy whatever among you is devoted to destruction.
7:13 [n]Jos 3:5; 6:18
13"Go, consecrate the people. Tell
them, 'Consecrate yourselves[n] in preparation for tomorrow; for this is what
the LORD, the God of Israel, says: That
which is devoted is among you, O Israel. You cannot stand against your enemies until you remove it.
14" 'In the morning, present yourselves tribe by tribe. The tribe that the
LORD takes shall come forward clan
by clan; the clan that the LORD takes[o] 7:14 [o]Pr 16:33
shall come forward family by family;
and the family that the LORD takes
shall come forward man by man. 15He
who is caught with the devoted things
shall be destroyed by fire, along with
all that belongs to him.[p] He has violat- 7:15 [p]1Sa 14:39 [q]ver 11 [r]Ge 34:7
ed the covenant[q] of the LORD and has
done a disgraceful thing in Israel!' "[r]
16Early the next morning Joshua had
Israel come forward by tribes, and Judah
was taken. 17The clans of Judah came
forward, and he took the Zerahites.[s] He 7:17 [s]Nu 26:20
had the clan of the Zerahites come for-
ward by families, and Zimri was taken.
18Joshua had his family come forward
man by man, and Achan son of Carmi,
the son of Zimri, the son of Zerah, of
the tribe of Judah, was taken.
19Then Joshua said to Achan, "My 7:19 [t]1Sa 6:5; Jer 13:16; Jn 9:24* [u]1Sa 14:43
son, give glory[t] to the LORD,[b] the God
of Israel, and give him the praise.[c] Tell[u]
me what you have done; do not hide it
from me."
20Achan replied, "It is true! I have
sinned against the LORD, the God of Israel. This is what I have done: 21When
I saw in the plunder a beautiful robe
from Babylonia,[d] two hundred shekels[e]
of silver and a wedge of gold weighing 7:21 [v]Dt 7:25; Eph 5:5; 1Ti 6:10
fifty shekels,[f] I coveted[v] them and took
them. They are hidden in the ground
inside my tent, with the silver underneath."
22So Joshua sent messengers, and they
ran to the tent, and there it was, hidden
in his tent, with the silver underneath.
23They took the things from the tent,
brought them to Joshua and all the Israelites and spread them out before the
LORD.
24Then Joshua, together with all Israel, took Achan son of Zerah, the silver, the robe, the gold wedge, his sons
and daughters, his cattle, donkeys and
sheep, his tent and all that he had, 7:24 [w]ver 26; Jos 15:7
to the Valley of Achor.[w] 25Joshua said,
"Why have you brought this trouble[x]
on us? The LORD will bring trouble on 7:25 [x]Jos 6:18 [y]Dt 17:5
you today."
Then all Israel stoned him,[y] and after
they had stoned the rest, they burned
them. 26Over Achan they heaped up a

[a]5 Or *as far as Shebarim* [b]19 A solemn charge to tell the truth [c]19 Or *and confess to him* [d]21 Hebrew *Shinar* [e]21 That is, about 5 pounds (about 2.3 kilograms) [f]21 That is, about 1 1/4 pounds (about 0.6 kilogram)

large pile of rocks, which remains to this day. Then the LORD turned from his fierce anger.[z] Therefore that place has been called the Valley of Achor[a] [a] ever since.

Ai Destroyed

8 Then the LORD said to Joshua, "Do not be afraid;[b] do not be discouraged.[c] Take the whole army[d] with you, and go up and attack Ai. For I have delivered[e] into your hands the king of Ai, his people, his city and his land. 2 You shall do to Ai and its king as you did to Jericho and its king, except that you may carry off their plunder and livestock for yourselves.[f] Set an ambush behind the city."

3 So Joshua and the whole army moved out to attack Ai. He chose thirty thousand of his best fighting men and sent them out at night 4 with these orders: "Listen carefully. You are to set an ambush behind the city. Don't go very far from it. All of you be on the alert. 5 I and all those with me will advance on the city, and when the men come out against us, as they did before, we will flee from them. 6 They will pursue us until we have lured them away from the city, for they will say, 'They are running away from us as they did before.' So when we flee from them, 7 you are to rise up from ambush and take the city. The LORD your God will give it into your hand.[g] 8 When you have taken the city, set it on fire.[h] Do what the LORD has commanded.[i] See to it; you have my orders."

9 Then Joshua sent them off, and they went to the place of ambush[j] and lay in wait between Bethel and Ai, to the west of Ai—but Joshua spent that night with the people.

10 Early the next morning[k] Joshua mustered his men, and he and the leaders of Israel[l] marched before them to Ai. 11 The entire force that was with him marched up and approached the city and arrived in front of it. They set up camp north of Ai, with the valley between them and the city. 12 Joshua had taken about five thousand men and set them in ambush between Bethel and Ai, to the west of the city. 13 They had the soldiers take up their positions—all those in the camp to the north of the city and the ambush to the west of it. That night Joshua went into the valley.

14 When the king of Ai saw this, he and all the men of the city hurried out early in the morning to meet Israel in battle at a certain place overlooking the Arabah.[m] But he did not know[n] that an ambush had been set against him behind the city. 15 Joshua and all Israel let themselves be driven back[o] before them, and they fled toward the desert.[p] 16 All the men of Ai were called to pursue them, and they pursued Joshua and were lured away[q] from the city. 17 Not a man remained in Ai or Bethel who did not go after Israel. They left the city open and went in pursuit of Israel.

18 Then the LORD said to Joshua, "Hold out toward Ai the javelin[r] that is in your hand,[s] for into your hand I will deliver the city." So Joshua held out his javelin[t] toward Ai. 19 As soon as he did this, the men in the ambush rose quickly[u] from their position and rushed forward. They entered the city and captured it and quickly set it on fire.[v]

20 The men of Ai looked back and saw the smoke of the city rising against the sky,[w] but they had no chance to escape in any direction, for the Israelites who had been fleeing toward the desert had turned back against their pursuers. 21 For when Joshua and all Israel saw that the ambush had taken the city and that smoke was going up from the city, they turned around and attacked the men of Ai. 22 The men of the ambush also came out of the city against them, so that they were caught in the middle, with Israelites on both sides. Israel cut them down, leaving them neither survivors nor fugitives.[x] 23 But they took the king of Ai alive[y] and brought him to Joshua.

24 When Israel had finished killing all the men of Ai in the fields and in the desert where they had chased them, and when every one of them had been put to the sword, all the Israelites returned to Ai and killed those who were in it. 25 Twelve thousand men and women fell that day—all the people of Ai.[z] 26 For Joshua did not draw back the hand that held out his javelin until he had destroyed[b] [a] all who lived in Ai.[b] 27 But

7:26 [z]Nu 25:4; Dt 13:17 [a]ver 24; Isa 65:10; Hos 2:15
8:1 [b]Dt 31:6 [c]Dt 1:21; 7:18; Jos 1:9 [d]Jos 10:7 [e]Jos 6:2
8:2 [f]ver 27; Dt 20:14
8:7 [g]Jdg 7:7; 1Sa 23:4
8:8 [h]Jdg 20:29-38 [i]ver 19
8:9 [j]2Ch 13:13
8:10 [k]Ge 22:3 [l]Jos 7:6
8:14 [m]Dt 1:1 [n]Jdg 20:34
8:15 [o]Jdg 20:36 [p]Jos 15:61; 16:1; 18:12
8:16 [q]Jdg 20:31
8:18 [r]Job 41:26; Ps 35:3 [s]Ex 4:2; 14:16; 17:9-12 [t]ver 26
8:19 [u]Jdg 20:33 [v]ver 8
8:20 [w]Jdg 20:40
8:22 [x]Dt 7:2; Jos 10:1
8:23 [y]1Sa 15:8
8:25 [z]Dt 20:16-18
8:26 [a]Nu 21:2 [b]Ex 17:12

[a] *26 Achor* means *trouble.* [b] *26* The Hebrew term refers to the irrevocable giving over of things or persons to the LORD, often by totally destroying them.

Israel did carry off for themselves the
livestock and plunder of this city, as the
8:27 [c]ver 2 LORD had instructed Joshua.[c]
8:28 28So Joshua burned[d] Ai[e] and made
[d]Nu 31:10 it a permanent heap of ruins,[f] a deso-
[e]Jos 7:2; Jer 49:3 late place to this day.[g] 29He hung the
[f]Dt 13:16; king of Ai on a tree and left him there
Jos 10:1 [g]Ge 35:20 until evening. At sunset,[h] Joshua ordered them to take his body from the
8:29 [h]Dt 21:23; tree and throw it down at the entrance
Jn 19:31 [i]2Sa 18:17 of the city gate. And they raised a large
pile of rocks[i] over it, which remains to
this day.

The Covenant Renewed at Mount Ebal

8:30 [j]Dt 11:29 30Then Joshua built on Mount Ebal[j]
[k]Ex 20:24 an altar[k] to the LORD, the God of Israel, 31as Moses the servant of the LORD
had commanded the Israelites. He built
it according to what is written in the
8:31 Book of the Law of Moses—an altar of
[l]Ex 20:25 [m]Dt 27:6-7 uncut stones, on which no iron tool[l]
had been used. On it they offered to
the LORD burnt offerings and sacrificed
fellowship offerings.[a] [m] 32There, in the
presence of the Israelites, Joshua copied
8:32 on stones the law of Moses, which he
[n]Dt 27:8 had written.[n] 33All Israel, aliens and cit-
8:33 izens[o] alike, with their elders, officials
[o]Lev 16:29 [p]Dt 31:12 and judges, were standing on both sides
[q]Dt 11:29; 27:11-14 of the ark of the covenant of the LORD,
facing those who carried it—the priests,
who were Levites.[p] Half of the people
stood in front of Mount Gerizim and
half of them in front of Mount Ebal,[q]
as Moses the servant of the LORD had
formerly commanded when he gave instructions to bless the people of Israel.
34Afterward, Joshua read all the
words of the law—the blessings and
8:34 the curses—just as it is written in the
[r]Dt 28:61; 31:11; Book of the Law.[r] 35There was not a
Jos 1:8 word of all that Moses had commanded
that Joshua did not read to the whole
assembly of Israel, including the wom-
8:35 [s]Ex 12:38; en and children, and the aliens who
Dt 31:12 lived among them.[s]

The Gibeonite Deception

9 Now when all the kings west of the
Jordan heard about these things—
those in the hill country, in the western
foothills, and along the entire coast of
9:1 [t]Nu 34:6 the Great Sea[b] [t] as far as Lebanon (the
[u]Ex 3:17; kings of the Hittites, Amorites, Canaan-
Jos 3:10 ites, Perizzites, Hivites and Jebusites)[u]—
2they came together to make war against
Joshua and Israel.
3However, when the people of Gib-
eon[v] heard what Joshua had done to 9:3 [v]ver 17;
Jericho and Ai, 4they resorted to a ruse: Jos 10:2;
They went as a delegation whose don- 2Sa 2:12; 2Ch 1:3;
keys were loaded[c] with worn-out sacks Isa 28:21
and old wineskins, cracked and mend-
ed. 5The men put worn and patched
sandals on their feet and wore old
clothes. All the bread of their food supply was dry and moldy. 6Then they
went to Joshua in the camp at Gilgal[w] 9:6 [w]Jos 5:10
and said to him and the men of Israel,
"We have come from a distant country;
make a treaty with us."
7The men of Israel said to the 9:7 [x]ver 1;
Hivites,[x] "But perhaps you live near us. Jos 11:19
How then can we make a treaty[y] with [y]Ex 23:32; Dt 7:2
you?"
8"We are your servants,[z]" they said to
Joshua. 9:8 [z]Dt 20:11;
But Joshua asked, "Who are you and 2Ki 10:5
where do you come from?"
9They answered: "Your servants have 9:9
come from a very distant country[a] be- [a]Dt 20:15 [b]ver 24;
cause of the fame of the LORD your Jos 2:9
God. For we have heard reports[b] of him:
all that he did in Egypt, 10and all that
he did to the two kings of the Amorites east of the Jordan—Sihon king of 9:10
Heshbon, and Og king of Bashan,[c] who [c]Nu 21:33
reigned in Ashtaroth.[d] 11And our el- [d]Nu 21:24,35
ders and all those living in our country
said to us, 'Take provisions for your
journey; go and meet them and say to
them, "We are your servants; make a
treaty with us."' 12This bread of ours
was warm when we packed it at home
on the day we left to come to you. But
now see how dry and moldy it is. 13And
these wineskins that we filled were new,
but see how cracked they are. And our
clothes and sandals are worn out by the
very long journey."
14The men of Israel sampled their
provisions but did not inquire[e] of the 9:14 [e]Nu 27:21
LORD. 15Then Joshua made a treaty of
peace[f] with them to let them live, and 9:15
the leaders of the assembly ratified it by [f]Ex 23:32; Jos 11:19;
oath. 2Sa 21:2
16Three days after they made the
treaty with the Gibeonites, the Israelites

[a]*31* Traditionally *peace offerings* [b]*1* That is, the Mediterranean [c]*4* Most Hebrew manuscripts; some Hebrew manuscripts, Vulgate and Syriac (see also Septuagint) *They prepared provisions and loaded their donkeys*

heard that they were neighbors, living
near them. 17So the Israelites set out
and on the third day came to their cit-
9:17 [g]Jos 18:25 [h]1Sa 7:1-2 ies: Gibeon, Kephirah, Beeroth[g] and
Kiriath Jearim.[h] 18But the Israelites did
not attack them, because the leaders
9:18 [i]Ps 15:4 [j]Ex 15:24 of the assembly had sworn an oath[i]
to them by the LORD, the God of Is-
rael.
The whole assembly grumbled[j]
against the leaders, 19but all the leaders
answered, "We have given them our
oath by the LORD, the God of Israel,
and we cannot touch them now. 20This
is what we will do to them: We will
let them live, so that wrath will not fall
on us for breaking the oath we swore
to them." 21They continued, "Let them
9:21 [k]ver 15 [l]Dt 29:11 live,[k] but let them be woodcutters and
water carriers[l] for the entire communi-
ty." So the leaders' promise to them was
kept.
22Then Joshua summoned the
Gibeonites and said, "Why did you de-
9:22 [m]ver 6 [n]ver 16 ceive us by saying, 'We live a long way[m]
from you,' while actually you live near[n]
9:23 [o]Ge 9:25 us? 23You are now under a curse:[o] You
will never cease to serve as woodcutters
and water carriers for the house of my
God."
24They answered Joshua, "Your ser-
9:24 [p]ver 9 vants were clearly told[p] how the LORD
your God had commanded his servant
Moses to give you the whole land and
to wipe out all its inhabitants from before you. So we feared for our lives because of you, and that is why we did
9:25 [q]Ge 16:6 this. 25We are now in your hands.[q] Do
to us whatever seems good and right to
you."
26So Joshua saved them from the Israelites, and they did not kill them.
27That day he made the Gibeonites
woodcutters and water carriers for the
community and for the altar of the
LORD at the place the LORD would
9:27 [r]Dt 12:5 choose.[r] And that is what they are to
this day.

The Sun Stands Still

10 Now Adoni-Zedek king of Jerusalem[s] heard that Joshua had
10:1 [s]Jdg 1:7 [t]Jos 8:1 [u]Dt 20:16; Jos 8:22 [v]Jos 9:15 taken Ai[t] and totally destroyed[a][u] it, doing to Ai and its king as he had done
to Jericho and its king, and that the
people of Gibeon had made a treaty of
peace[v] with Israel and were living near
them. 2He and his people were very
much alarmed at this, because Gibeon
was an important city, like one of the
royal cities; it was larger than Ai, and
all its men were good fighters. 3So Adoni-Zedek king of Jerusalem appealed to
Hoham king of Hebron,[w] Piram king 10:3 [w]Ge 13:18 [x]2Ch 11:9; 25:27; Ne 11:30; Isa 36:2; 37:8; Jer 34:7; Mic 1:13
of Jarmuth, Japhia king of Lachish[x] and
Debir king of Eglon. 4"Come up and
help me attack Gibeon," he said, "because it has made peace[y] with Joshua
and the Israelites."
5Then the five kings of the Amo- 10:4 [y]Jos 9:15
rites[z]—the kings of Jerusalem, Hebron,
Jarmuth, Lachish and Eglon—joined 10:5 [z]Nu 13:29
forces. They moved up with all their
troops and took up positions against
Gibeon and attacked it.
6The Gibeonites then sent word to
Joshua in the camp at Gilgal: "Do not
abandon your servants. Come up to us
quickly and save us! Help us, because all
the Amorite kings from the hill country
have joined forces against us."
7So Joshua marched up from Gilgal
with his entire army,[a] including all the 10:7 [a]Jos 8:1
best fighting men. 8The LORD said to
Joshua, "Do not be afraid[b] of them; I 10:8 [b]Dt 3:2; Jos 1:9
have given them into your hand. Not
one of them will be able to withstand
you."
9After an all-night march from Gilgal, Joshua took them by surprise. 10The
LORD threw them into confusion be- 10:10 [c]Dt 7:23 [d]Jos 16:3,5 [e]Jos 15:35
fore Israel,[c] who defeated them in a
great victory at Gibeon. Israel pursued
them along the road going up to Beth
Horon[d] and cut them down all the way
to Azekah[e] and Makkedah. 11As they
fled before Israel on the road down
from Beth Horon to Azekah, the LORD 10:11 [f]Ps 18:12; Isa 28:2,17
hurled large hailstones[f] down on them
from the sky, and more of them died
from the hailstones than were killed by
the swords of the Israelites.
12On the day the LORD gave the
Amorites[g] over to Israel, Joshua said to 10:12 [g]Am 2:9 [h]Jdg 1:35; 12:12
the LORD in the presence of Israel:

"O sun, stand still over Gibeon,
O moon, over the Valley of
Aijalon.[h]"
13So the sun stood still,[i] 10:13 [i]Hab 3:11
and the moon stopped,

[a] *1* The Hebrew term refers to the irrevocable giving over of things or persons to the LORD, often by totally destroying them; also in verses 28, 35, 37, 39 and 40.

JOY

THE STOLID SUN

Joshua 10:12

To help his children own the day, God stuck the solar system in his pocket. Triumph came to Israel. What manner of God is ours! He commanded a sphere of flaming hydrogen to stand in the corner until things got better.

till the nation avenged itself on[a] its
enemies,
10:13 [j]2Sa 1:18 as it is written in the Book of Jashar.[j]
[k]Isa 38:8 The sun stopped[k] in the middle of
the sky and delayed going down about
a full day. 14There has never been a
day like it before or since, a day when
10:14 the LORD listened to a man. Surely the
[l]ver 42; LORD was fighting[l] for Israel!
Ex 14:14; 15Then Joshua returned with all Is-
Dt 1:30; Ps 106:43; 136:24 rael to the camp at Gilgal.[m]

10:15 [m]ver 43

Five Amorite Kings Killed

16Now the five kings had fled and hidden in the cave at Makkedah. 17When
Joshua was told that the five kings
had been found hiding in the cave at
Makkedah, 18he said, "Roll large rocks
up to the mouth of the cave, and post
some men there to guard it. 19But don't
stop! Pursue your enemies, attack them
from the rear and don't let them reach
their cities, for the LORD your God has
given them into your hand."
10:20 20So Joshua and the Israelites de-
[n]Dt 20:16 stroyed them completely[n]—almost to a
man—but the few who were left reached
their fortified cities. 21The whole army
then returned safely to Joshua in the
camp at Makkedah, and no one uttered
a word against the Israelites.
22Joshua said, "Open the mouth of
the cave and bring those five kings out
to me." 23So they brought the five kings
out of the cave—the kings of Jerusalem,
Hebron, Jarmuth, Lachish and Eglon.
24When they had brought these kings
to Joshua, he summoned all the men of
Israel and said to the army command-
10:24 ers who had come with him, "Come
[o]Mal 4:3 here and put your feet[o] on the necks of
[p]Ps 110:1 these kings." So they came forward and
placed their feet[p] on their necks.
25Joshua said to them, "Do not be
10:25 [q]Dt 31:6 afraid; do not be discouraged. Be strong
and courageous.[q] This is what the LORD
will do to all the enemies you are going to fight." 26Then Joshua struck and
killed the kings and hung them on five
trees, and they were left hanging on the
trees until evening.
27At sunset[r] Joshua gave the order 10:27 [r]Dt 21:23;
and they took them down from the trees Jos 8:9,29
and threw them into the cave where
they had been hiding. At the mouth of
the cave they placed large rocks, which
are there to this day.
28That day Joshua took Makkedah.
He put the city and its king to the
sword and totally destroyed everyone in
it. He left no survivors.[s] And he did to 10:28 [s]Dt 20:16
the king of Makkedah as he had done [t]Jos 6:21
to the king of Jericho.[t]

Southern Cities Conquered

29Then Joshua and all Israel with him
moved on from Makkedah to Libnah
and attacked it. 30The LORD also gave
that city and its king into Israel's hand.
The city and everyone in it Joshua put
to the sword. He left no survivors there.
And he did to its king as he had done
to the king of Jericho.
31Then Joshua and all Israel with him
moved on from Libnah to Lachish; he
took up positions against it and attacked it. 32The LORD handed Lachish
over to Israel, and Joshua took it on the
second day. The city and everyone in
it he put to the sword, just as he had
done to Libnah. 33Meanwhile, Horam
king of Gezer[u] had come up to help La- 10:33 [u]Jos 16:3,10;
chish, but Joshua defeated him and his Jdg 1:29;
army—until no survivors were left. 1Ki 9:15
34Then Joshua and all Israel with him
moved on from Lachish to Eglon; they
took up positions against it and attacked it. 35They captured it that same
day and put it to the sword and totally
destroyed everyone in it, just as they
had done to Lachish.
36Then Joshua and all Israel with him
went up from Eglon to Hebron[v] and at- 10:36 [v]Jos 14:13;
tacked it. 37They took the city and put 15:13;
it to the sword, together with its king, Jdg 1:10
its villages and everyone in it. They left
no survivors. Just as at Eglon, they totally destroyed it and everyone in it.
38Then Joshua and all Israel with him
turned around and attacked Debir.[w] 10:38 [w]Jos 15:15;
39They took the city, its king and its Jdg 1:11
villages, and put them to the sword.

[a]*13* Or *nation triumphed over*

Everyone in it they totally destroyed.
They left no survivors. They did to
Debir and its king as they had done to
Libnah and its king and to Hebron.
[40]So Joshua subdued the whole region, including the hill country, the
10:40 [x]Ge 12:9; Jos 12:8 [y]Dt 1:7 [z]Dt 7:24 [a]Dt 20:16-17 Negev,[x] the western foothills and the
mountain slopes,[y] together with all
their kings.[z] He left no survivors. He
totally destroyed all who breathed, just
as the LORD, the God of Israel, had
10:41 [b]Ge 14:7 [c]Ge 10:19 [d]Jos 11:16; 15:51 commanded.[a] [41]Joshua subdued them
from Kadesh Barnea[b] to Gaza[c] and from
the whole region of Goshen[d] to Gibeon.
[42]All these kings and their lands Joshua conquered in one campaign, because
10:42 [e]ver 14 the LORD, the God of Israel, fought[e]
for Israel.
10:43 [f]ver 15; Jos 5:9 [43]Then Joshua returned with all Israel to the camp at Gilgal.[f]

Northern Kings Defeated

11:1 [g]Jdg 4:2,7,23 [h]ver 10; 1Sa 12:9 [i]Jos 19:15 **11** When Jabin[g] king of Hazor[h]
heard of this, he sent word to
Jobab king of Madon, to the kings
of Shimron[i] and Acshaph, [2]and to
the northern kings who were in the
11:2 [j]Jos 12:3 [k]Nu 34:11 [l]Jos 17:11; Jdg 1:27; 1Ki 4:11 mountains, in the Arabah[j] south of
Kinnereth,[k] in the western foothills and
in Naphoth Dor[a][l] on the west; [3]to the
Canaanites in the east and west; to the
Amorites, Hittites, Perizzites and Jebusites in the hill country; and to the Hi-
11:3 [m]Dt 7:1; Jdg 3:3,5; 1Ki 9:20 [n]Ge 31:49; Jos 15:38; 18:26 vites[m] below Hermon in the region of
Mizpah.[n] [4]They came out with all their
troops and a large number of horses
and chariots—a huge army, as numerous as the sand on the seashore.[o] [5]All
11:4 [o]Jdg 7:12; 1Sa 13:5 these kings joined forces[p] and made
camp together at the Waters of Merom,
11:5 [p]Jdg 5:19 to fight against Israel.
[6]The LORD said to Joshua, "Do not
11:6 [q]Jos 10:8 [r]2Sa 8:4 be afraid of them, because by this time
tomorrow I will hand all of them over[q]
to Israel, slain. You are to hamstring[r]
their horses and burn their chariots."
[7]So Joshua and his whole army came
against them suddenly at the Waters of
Merom and attacked them, [8]and the
LORD gave them into the hand of Israel. They defeated them and pursued
them all the way to Greater Sidon, to
11:8 [s]Jos 13:6 Misrephoth Maim,[s] and to the Valley
of Mizpah on the east, until no survi-
vors were left. [9]Joshua did to them as
the LORD had directed: He hamstrung
their horses and burned their chariots.
[10]At that time Joshua turned back
and captured Hazor and put its king to
the sword. (Hazor had been the head
of all these kingdoms.) [11]Everyone in
it they put to the sword. They totally
destroyed[b] them, not sparing anything
that breathed,[t] and he burned up Hazor 11:11 [t]Dt 20:16-17
itself.
[12]Joshua took all these royal cities and
their kings and put them to the sword.
He totally destroyed them, as Moses the
servant of the LORD had commanded.[u] 11:12 [u]Nu 33:50-52; Dt 7:2
[13]Yet Israel did not burn any of the
cities built on their mounds—except
Hazor, which Joshua burned. [14]The Israelites carried off for themselves all the
plunder and livestock of these cities,
but all the people they put to the sword
until they completely destroyed them,
not sparing anyone that breathed.[v] [15]As 11:14 [v]Nu 31:11-12
the LORD commanded his servant Mo-
ses, so Moses commanded Joshua, and
Joshua did it; he left nothing undone
of all that the LORD commanded 11:15 [w]Ex 34:11; Jos 1:7
Moses.[w]
[16]So Joshua took this entire land: the
hill country, all the Negev, the whole re-
gion of Goshen, the western foothills,[x] 11:16 [x]Jos 10:41
the Arabah and the mountains of Israel
with their foothills, [17]from Mount Halak, which rises toward Seir, to Baal Gad
in the Valley of Lebanon[y] below Mount 11:17 [y]Jos 12:7 [z]Dt 7:24
Hermon. He captured all their kings
and struck them down, putting them
to death.[z] [18]Joshua waged war against
all these kings for a long time. [19]Ex- 11:19 [a]Jos 9:3
cept for the Hivites living in Gibeon,[a]
not one city made a treaty of peace
with the Israelites, who took them all
in battle. [20]For it was the LORD him-
self who hardened their hearts[b] to wage 11:20 [b]Ex 14:17; Ro 9:18 [c]Dt 7:16; Jdg 14:4
war against Israel, so that he might de-
stroy them totally, exterminating them
without mercy, as the LORD had commanded Moses.[c]
[21]At that time Joshua went and de-
stroyed the Anakites[d] from the hill coun- 11:21 [d]Nu 13:22,33; Dt 9:2
try: from Hebron, Debir and Anab,
from all the hill country of Judah, and
from all the hill country of Israel. Joshua
totally destroyed them and their towns. 11:22 [e]1Sa 17:4; 1Ki 2:39; 1Ch 8:13 [f]1Sa 5:1; Isa 20:1
[22]No Anakites were left in Israelite ter-
ritory; only in Gaza, Gath[e] and Ash-
dod[f] did any survive. [23]So Joshua took 11:23 [g]Jos 21:43-45
the entire land,[g] just as the LORD had

[a] *2* Or *in the heights of Dor* [b] *11* The Hebrew term refers to the irrevocable giving over of things or persons to the LORD, often by totally destroying them; also in verses 12, 20 and 21.

directed Moses, and he gave it as an inheritance[h] to Israel according to their tribal divisions.[i]

Then the land had rest from war.[j]

List of Defeated Kings

12 These are the kings of the land whom the Israelites had defeated and whose territory they took over east of the Jordan, from the Arnon Gorge to Mount Hermon,[k] including all the eastern side of the Arabah:

[2]Sihon king of the Amorites,
who reigned in Heshbon. He ruled from Aroer on the rim of the Arnon Gorge—from the middle of the gorge—to the Jabbok River, which is the border of the Ammonites. This included half of Gilead.[l] [3]He also ruled over the eastern Arabah from the Sea of Kinnereth[a][m] to the Sea of the Arabah (the Salt Sea[b]), to Beth Jeshimoth,[n] and then southward below the slopes of Pisgah.

[4]And the territory of Og king of Bashan,[o]
one of the last of the Rephaites, who reigned in Ashtaroth[p] and Edrei. [5]He ruled over Mount Hermon, Salecah,[q] all of Bashan to the border of the people of Geshur[r] and Maacah,[s] and half of Gilead to the border of Sihon king of Heshbon.

[6]Moses, the servant of the LORD, and the Israelites conquered them. And Moses the servant of the LORD gave their land to the Reubenites, the Gadites and the half-tribe of Manasseh to be their possession.[t]

[7]These are the kings of the land that Joshua and the Israelites conquered on the west side of the Jordan, from Baal Gad in the Valley of Lebanon[u] to Mount Halak, which rises toward Seir (their lands Joshua gave as an inheritance to the tribes of Israel according to their tribal divisions— [8]the hill country, the western foothills, the Arabah, the mountain slopes, the desert and the Negev[v]—the lands of the Hittites, Amorites, Canaanites, Perizzites, Hivites and Jebusites):

[9]the king of Jericho[w] one
the king of Ai[x] (near Bethel) one
[10]the king of Jerusalem[y] one
the king of Hebron one
[11]the king of Jarmuth one
the king of Lachish one
[12]the king of Eglon one
the king of Gezer[z] one
[13]the king of Debir one
the king of Geder one
[14]the king of Hormah one
the king of Arad[a] one
[15]the king of Libnah one
the king of Adullam one
[16]the king of Makkedah one
the king of Bethel[b] one
[17]the king of Tappuah one
the king of Hepher[c] one
[18]the king of Aphek[d] one
the king of Lasharon one
[19]the king of Madon one
the king of Hazor one
[20]the king of Shimron Meron one
the king of Acshaph[e] one
[21]the king of Taanach one
the king of Megiddo one
[22]the king of Kedesh[f] one
the king of Jokneam in Carmel[g] one
[23]the king of Dor (in Naphoth Dor[c][h]) one
the king of Goyim in Gilgal one
[24]the king of Tirzah one
thirty-one kings in all.[i]

Land Still to Be Taken

13 When Joshua was old and well advanced in years,[j] the LORD said to him, "You are very old, and there are still very large areas of land to be taken over.

[2]"This is the land that remains: all the regions of the Philistines and Geshurites: [3]from the Shihor River[k] on the east of Egypt to the territory of Ekron[l] on the north, all of it counted as Canaanite (the territory of the five Philistine rulers[m] in Gaza, Ashdod, Ashkelon, Gath and Ekron—that of the Avvites);[n] [4]from the south, all the land of the Canaanites, from Arah of the Sidonians as far as Aphek,[o] the region of the Amorites,[p] [5]the area of the Gebalites[d];[q] and all Lebanon[r] to the east, from Baal Gad below Mount Hermon to Lebo[e] Hamath.

[a]3 That is, Galilee [b]3 That is, the Dead Sea [c]23 Or *in the heights of Dor* [d]5 That is, the area of Byblos [e]5 Or *to the entrance to*

11:23 [h]Dt 1:38; 12:9-10; 25:19 [i]Nu 26:53 [j]Jos 14:15
12:1 [k]Dt 3:8
12:2 [l]Dt 2:36
12:3 [m]Jos 11:2 [n]Jos 13:20
12:4 [o]Nu 21:21,33; Dt 3:11 [p]Dt 1:4
12:5 [q]Dt 3:10 [r]1Sa 27:8 [s]Dt 3:14
12:6 [t]Nu 32:29,33; Jos 13:8
12:7 [u]Jos 11:17
12:8 [v]Jos 11:16
12:9 [w]Jos 6:2 [x]Jos 8:29
12:10 [y]Jos 10:23
12:12 [z]Jos 10:33
12:14 [a]Nu 21:1
12:16 [b]Jos 7:2
12:17 [c]1Ki 4:10
12:18 [d]Jos 13:4
12:20 [e]Jos 11:1
12:22 [f]Jos 19:37; 20:7; 21:32 [g]1Sa 15:12
12:23 [h]Jos 11:2
12:24 [i]Ps 135:11; Dt 7:24
13:1 [j]Ge 24:1; Jos 14:10
13:3 [k]Jer 2:18 [l]Jdg 1:18 [m]Jdg 3:3 [n]Dt 2:23
13:4 [o]Jos 12:18; 19:30 [p]Am 2:10
13:5 [q]1Ki 5:18; Ps 83:7; Eze 27:9 [r]Jos 12:7

6“As for all the inhabitants of the
mountain regions from Lebanon to
13:6 [s]Jos 11:8 Misrephoth Maim,[s] that is, all the Sido-
[t]Nu 33:54 nians, I myself will drive them out before the Israelites. Be sure to allocate
this land to Israel for an inheritance, as
13:7 [u]Jos 11:23; I have instructed you,[t] 7and divide it as
Ps 78:55 an inheritance[u] among the nine tribes
and half of the tribe of Manasseh.”

Division of the Land East of the Jordan

13:8 [v]Jos 12:6 8The other half of Manasseh,[a] the Reubenites and the Gadites had received
the inheritance that Moses had given
them east of the Jordan, as he, the servant of the LORD, had assigned[v] it to
them.

13:9 [w]ver 16; 9It extended from Aroer[w] on the
Jdg 11:26 rim of the Arnon Gorge, and from
[x]Jer 48:8,21 the town in the middle of the
[y]Nu 21:30 gorge, and included the whole plateau[x] of Medeba as far as Dibon,[y]
10and all the towns of Sihon king
of the Amorites, who ruled in
Heshbon, out to the border of
13:10 [z]Nu 21:24 the Ammonites.[z] 11It also included Gilead, the territory of the peo-
ple of Geshur and Maacah, all of
Mount Hermon and all Bashan
13:11 [a]Jos 12:5 as far as Salecah[a]— 12that is, the
13:12 [b]Dt 3:11 whole kingdom of Og in Bashan,[b]
[c]Jos 12:4 who had reigned in Ashtaroth[c] and
[d]Ge 14:5 Edrei and had survived as one of
the last of the Rephaites.[d] Moses
had defeated them and taken over
their land. 13But the Israelites did
not drive out the people of Ge-
13:13 [e]Jos 12:5 shur[e] and Maacah,[f] so they con-
[f]Dt 3:14 tinue to live among the Israelites
to this day.

14But to the tribe of Levi he gave no
inheritance, since the offerings made by
fire to the LORD, the God of Israel,
are their inheritance, as he promised
13:14 [g]ver 33; them.[g]
Dt 18:1-2

15This is what Moses had given to the
tribe of Reuben, clan by clan:

13:16 [h]ver 9; 16The territory from Aroer[h] on the
Jos 12:2 rim of the Arnon Gorge, and from
[i]Nu 21:30 the town in the middle of the
13:17 [j]Nu 32:3 gorge, and the whole plateau past
[k]1Ch 5:8 Medeba[i] 17to Heshbon and all its
towns on the plateau, including
13:18 [l]Nu 21:23 Dibon,[j] Bamoth Baal, Beth Baal
Meon,[k] 18Jahaz,[l] Kedemoth, Meph-
aath,[m] 19Kiriathaim,[n] Sibmah, Ze- 13:18 [m]Jer 48:21
reth Shahar on the hill in the valley,
20Beth Peor,[o] the slopes of Pisgah, 13:19 [n]Nu 32:37
and Beth Jeshimoth 21—all the
towns on the plateau and the entire 13:20 [o]Dt 3:29
realm of Sihon king of the Amo-
rites, who ruled at Heshbon. Moses
had defeated him and the Midian-
ite chiefs,[p] Evi, Rekem, Zur, Hur 13:21 [p]Nu 25:15
and Reba[q]—princes allied with Si- [q]Nu 31:8
hon—who lived in that country.
22In addition to those slain in bat-
tle, the Israelites had put to the 13:22 [r]Nu 22:5;
sword Balaam son of Beor,[r] who 31:8
practiced divination. 23The boundary of the Reubenites was the bank
of the Jordan. These towns and
their villages were the inheritance
of the Reubenites, clan by clan.

24This is what Moses had given to the
tribe of Gad, clan by clan:

25The territory of Jazer,[s] all the 13:25 [s]Nu 21:32;
towns of Gilead and half the Am- Jos 21:39
monite country as far as Aroer,
near Rabbah; 26and from Hesh-
bon[t] to Ramath Mizpah and Bet- 13:26 [t]Nu 21:25;
onim, and from Mahanaim to the Jer 49:3
territory of Debir;[u] 27and in the [u]Jos 10:3
valley, Beth Haram, Beth Nim-
rah, Succoth[v] and Zaphon with the 13:27 [v]Ge 33:17
rest of the realm of Sihon king of [w]Nu 34:11
Heshbon (the east side of the Jor-
dan, the territory up to the end of
the Sea of Kinnereth[b] [w]). 28These
towns and their villages were the
inheritance of the Gadites,[x] clan 13:28 [x]Nu 32:33
by clan.

29This is what Moses had given to
the half-tribe of Manasseh, that is, to
half the family of the descendants of
Manasseh, clan by clan:

30The territory extending from
Mahanaim[y] and including all of 13:30 [y]Ge 32:2
Bashan, the entire realm of Og king [z]Nu 32:41
of Bashan—all the settlements of
Jair[z] in Bashan, sixty towns, 31half
of Gilead, and Ashtaroth and Edrei
(the royal cities of Og in Bashan).
This was for the descendants of
Makir[a] son of Manasseh—for half 13:31 [a]Ge 50:23
of the sons of Makir, clan by clan.

32This is the inheritance Moses had
given when he was in the plains of

[a]8 Hebrew *With it* (that is, with the other half of Manasseh) [b]27 That is, Galilee

Moab across the Jordan east of Jericho.
[33]But to the tribe of Levi, Moses had
given no inheritance; the LORD, the
13:33 God of Israel, is their inheritance,[b] as
[b]Nu 18:20 [c]ver 14; Jos 18:7 he promised them.[c]

Division of the Land West of the Jordan

14 Now these are the areas the Israelites received as an inheritance
in the land of Canaan, which Eleazar
the priest, Joshua son of Nun and the
14:1 heads of the tribal clans of Israel allot-
[d]Nu 34:17-18 ted to them.[d] [2]Their inheritances were
14:2 assigned by lot[e] to the nine-and-a-half
[e]Nu 26:55 tribes, as the LORD had commanded
through Moses. [3]Moses had granted the
two-and-a-half tribes their inheritance
14:3 east of the Jordan[f] but had not granted
[f]Nu 32:33 [g]Jos 13:14 the Levites an inheritance among the
14:4 rest,[g] [4]for the sons of Joseph had become
[h]Ge 41:52; 48:5 two tribes—Manasseh and Ephraim.[h]
The Levites received no share of the
land but only towns to live in, with pasturelands for their flocks and herds. [5]So
14:5 the Israelites divided the land, just as
[i]Nu 34:13; 35:2; Jos 21:2 the LORD had commanded Moses.[i]

Hebron Given to Caleb

[6]Now the men of Judah approached
14:6 Joshua at Gilgal, and Caleb son of Je-
[j]Nu 13:6; 14:30 phunneh[j] the Kenizzite said to him,
[k]Nu 13:26 "You know what the LORD said to Moses the man of God at Kadesh Barnea[k]
about you and me. [7]I was forty years old
when Moses the servant of the LORD
sent me from Kadesh Barnea to explore
14:7 the land.[l] And I brought him back a
[l]Nu 13:17 [m]Nu 13:30; 14:6-9 report according to my convictions,[m]
[8]but my brothers who went up with me
14:8 made the hearts of the people melt with
[n]Nu 13:31 fear.[n] I, however, followed the LORD my
[o]Nu 14:24 God wholeheartedly.[o] [9]So on that day
Moses swore to me, 'The land on which
your feet have walked will be your in-
14:9 heritance and that of your children[p]
[p]Nu 14:24; Dt 1:36 forever, because you have followed the
LORD my God wholeheartedly.'[a]
[10]"Now then, just as the LORD
14:10 promised,[q] he has kept me alive for
[q]Nu 14:30 forty-five years since the time he said
this to Moses, while Israel moved about
in the desert. So here I am today, eighty-
14:11 five years old! [11]I am still as strong[r] to-
[r]Dt 34:7 day as the day Moses sent me out; I'm
just as vigorous to go out to battle now
as I was then. [12]Now give me this hill
country that the LORD promised me
that day. You yourself heard then that
the Anakites[s] were there and their cities 14:12
were large and fortified,[t] but, the LORD [s]Nu 13:33 [t]Nu 13:28
helping me, I will drive them out just
as he said."

GENTLENESS

SOLID STEEL PATRIARCHS

Joshua 14:11

At 85 years of age, Caleb is still a picture of gentleness encased in steel resolve. Those who will not take a stand have no idea how God might honor them. Timidly they shirk what would have made them saints.

[13]Then Joshua blessed[u] Caleb son of 14:13
Jephunneh and gave him Hebron[v] as [u]Jos 22:6,7 [v]Jos 10:36
his inheritance.[w] [14]So Hebron has be- [w]Jdg 1:20; 1Ch 6:56
longed to Caleb son of Jephunneh the
Kenizzite ever since, because he followed
the LORD, the God of Israel, wholeheartedly. [15](Hebron used to be called
Kiriath Arba[x] after Arba,[y] who was 14:15
the greatest man among the Anakites.) [x]Ge 23:2 [y]Jos 15:13
Then the land had rest[z] from war. [z]Jos 11:23

Allotment for Judah

15 The allotment for the tribe of
Judah, clan by clan, extended 15:1
down to the territory of Edom,[a] to the [a]Nu 34:3 [b]Nu 33:36
Desert of Zin[b] in the extreme south.
[2]Their southern boundary started from the bay at the southern
end of the Salt Sea,[b] [3]crossed south
of Scorpion[c] Pass,[c] continued on 15:3 [c]Nu 34:4
to Zin and went over to the south
of Kadesh Barnea. Then it ran past
Hezron up to Addar and curved
around to Karka. [4]It then passed
along to Azmon[d] and joined the 15:4 [d]Nu 34:5
Wadi of Egypt,[e] ending at the sea. [e]Ge 15:18
This is their[d] southern boundary.
[5]The eastern boundary[f] is the 15:5 [f]Nu 34:10
Salt Sea as far as the mouth of the [g]Jos 18:15-19
Jordan.
The northern boundary[g] started from the bay of the sea at the
mouth of the Jordan, [6]went up to 15:6
Beth Hoglah[h] and continued north [h]Jos 18:19,21
of Beth Arabah to the Stone of Bo- [i]Jos 18:17
han[i] son of Reuben. [7]The bound-
ary then went up to Debir from 15:7
the Valley of Achor[j] and turned [j]Jos 7:24

[a]9 Deut. 1:36 [b]2 That is, the Dead Sea; also in verse 5 [c]3 Hebrew *Akrabbim* [d]4 Hebrew *your*

WEEK 25

FAITHFULNESS

DAY ONE

1 FAITHFULNESS, THE HABIT OF SPIRITUAL DEPENDENCY

Read Joshua 14:13–14

The best of all habits is the habit of spiritual dependency. "Trust in the LORD with all your heart and lean not on your own understanding;" says the writer of Proverbs, "in all your ways acknowledge him, and he will make your paths straight" (Proverbs 3:5–6).

Joshua blessed Caleb and gave him the city of Hebron because Caleb served the LORD "wholeheartedly." Caleb is one of those inheritors of promise who trusted God with his whole life. He only appears in Scripture exhibiting a positive spirit toward the plan of God in his life. In short, his very name stands for faithfulness.

Faithfulness simply means God can count on us. He can count on us to be positive when others are negative. He can count on us to obey when others are disobedient. He can count on us to follow when others bail out because of the steepness of the ascent. Faithfulness is the quality that honors God with obedience—joyous obedience. A faithfulness that grumbles at the requirements of God is not faithfulness at all. It is only grudging acquiescence.

Faithfulness is the habit of spiritual dependency. Caleb did not follow so that he could offer a proud example to the spiritual quitters. Caleb followed because he needed God. He depended on God's steadfast love and providence. Providence? Indeed, those who grow dependent on God have found that they must count on God, for within themselves they find only weakness. But God is their "refuge and strength." He is their "ever-present help in trouble" (Psalm 46:1). They are so dependent on God that they appear to be faithful; however, their faithfulness comes about because of their need.

DAY TWO

2 FAITHFULNESS AND THE PURPOSE OF GOD IN MY LIFE

God is a strong foundation for times like these. He is a rich storehouse of wisdom and knowledge. But how do we tap into this treasure? Isaiah says that the fear of the Lord is the key. This fear of the Lord is that awe with which we approach his almighty power. It is that unfailing respect that causes our unrighteous souls to wilt into the heart of his holiness. With such respect we learn his wisdom. *Turn to Isaiah 33:5–6, page 827, for today's study.*

DAY THREE

3 FAITHFULNESS AND MY RELATIONSHIP WITH CHRIST

Our relationship with Christ is constant—not because we're constant but because he is constant. Hebrews 13:5 says he will never leave us nor forsake us. Verse 8 says he is the same yesterday, today and forever. Is he dependable—the answer is an unqualified *Yes!* Are we dependable? The answer has many qualifiers—sometimes yes, sometimes no. But bit by bit, in time we learn dependency on him and in turn our faithfulness grows. *Turn to Hebrews 13:5–8, page 1478, for today's study.*

DAY FOUR

4 FAITHFULNESS AND MY SERVICE TO OTHERS

This passage at one time or another is the lament of all in leadership. "These people have become too heavy for me," laments Moses. Yet Moses was a faithful servant, and when the times were heavy, God was available to stand under the yoke with him. Moses unfortunately forgot to count on the ability of God and for one brief moment neglected his dependency on God. *Turn to Numbers 11:10–15, page 168, for today's study.*

DAY FIVE

5 FAITHFULNESS AND ITS PLACE IN MY PERSONAL WORSHIP

God's message to the church at Smyrna was that they were not to quail before all they were about to suffer. Rather, they were to be faithful in their worship, and then they would enter the final state of God's congratulations. Worship only because it's the thing to do, and God may not attend you; but worship when your very life is under threat, and you may be sure of his presence. *Turn to Revelation 2:10, page 1524, for today's study.*

MEMORIZE THIS WEEK

PROVERBS 3:5-6

Trust in the LORD with all your heart
and lean not on your own understanding;
in all your ways acknowledge him,
and he will make your paths straight.

Week 26, Gentleness, the Art of Ego Displacement, begins on page 1387, 2 Corinthians 10:1–6.
To begin a topical study on the Fruit of the Spirit, Faithfulness, turn to the Topical Index, page 1548.

north to Gilgal, which faces the Pass
of Adummim south of the gorge.
It continued along to the waters
of En Shemesh and came out at
15:7 [k]2Sa 17:17; En Rogel.[k] 8Then it ran up the
1Ki 1:9 Valley of Ben Hinnom along the
15:8 southern slope of the Jebusite[l] city
[l]ver 63; (that is, Jerusalem). From there it
Jos 18:16,28; climbed to the top of the hill west
Jdg 1:21; of the Hinnom Valley at the north-
19:10 ern end of the Valley of Rephaim.
9From the hilltop the boundary
15:9 headed toward the spring of the
[m]Jos 18:15 waters of Nephtoah,[m] came out at
[n]1Ch 13:6 the towns of Mount Ephron and
went down toward Baalah[n] (that is,
Kiriath Jearim). 10Then it curved
westward from Baalah to Mount
Seir, ran along the northern slope
of Mount Jearim (that is, Kes-
alon), continued down to Beth
15:10 Shemesh and crossed to Timnah.[o]
[o]Ge 38:12; 11It went to the northern slope of
Jdg 14:1 Ekron, turned toward Shikkeron,
15:11 passed along to Mount Baalah and
[p]Jos 19:33 reached Jabneel.[p] The boundary
ended at the sea.
12The western boundary is the
15:12 [q]Nu 34:6 coastline of the Great Sea.[a][q]
These are the boundaries around the
people of Judah by their clans.

13In accordance with the LORD's
command to him, Joshua gave to Caleb son of Jephunneh a portion in Judah—Kiriath Arba, that is, Hebron.
15:13 [r]Jos 14:13-15 (Arba was the forefather of Anak.)[r]
14From Hebron Caleb drove out the
15:14 [s]Nu 13:33 three Anakites[s]—Sheshai, Ahiman and
[t]Nu 13:22 Talmai[t]—descendants of Anak.[u] 15From
[u]Jdg 1:10,20 there he marched against the people living in Debir (formerly called Kiriath
15:16 Sepher). 16And Caleb said, "I will give
[v]Jdg 1:12 my daughter Acsah[v] in marriage to the
15:17 man who attacks and captures Kiriath
[w]Jdg 3:9,11 Sepher." 17Othniel[w] son of Kenaz, Caleb's brother, took it; so Caleb gave his
daughter Acsah to him in marriage.
18One day when she came to Othniel, she urged him[b] to ask her father
for a field. When she got off her donkey, Caleb asked her, "What can I do
for you?"
19She replied, "Do me a special favor.
Since you have given me land in the
Negev, give me also springs of water."
So Caleb gave her the upper and lower
springs.

20This is the inheritance of the tribe
of Judah, clan by clan:

21The southernmost towns of the tribe
of Judah in the Negev toward the
boundary of Edom were:
Kabzeel, Eder,[x] Jagur, 22Kinah, 15:21 [x]Ge 35:21
Dimonah, Adadah, 23Kedesh, Ha-
zor, Ithnan, 24Ziph,[y] Telem, Bea- 15:24 [y]1Sa 23:14
loth, 25Hazor Hadattah, Kerioth
Hezron (that is, Hazor), 26Amam,
Shema, Moladah,[z] 27Hazar Gad- 15:26 [z]1Ch 4:28
dah, Heshmon, Beth Pelet, 28Ha-
zar Shual, Beersheba,[a] Biziothiah, 15:28 [a]Ge 21:31
29Baalah,[b] Iim, Ezem, 30Eltolad,[c] 15:29 [b]ver 9
Kesil, Hormah, 31Ziklag,[d] Mad-
mannah, Sansannah, 32Lebaoth, 15:30 [c]Jos 19:4
Shilhim, Ain and Rimmon[e]—a to-
tal of twenty-nine towns and their 15:31 [d]1Sa 27:6
villages.

33In the western foothills: 15:32 [e]Jdg 20:45
Eshtaol,[f] Zorah, Ashnah, 34Za- 15:33 [f]Jdg 13:25;
noah,[g] En Gannim, Tappuah, 16:31
Enam, 35Jarmuth,[h] Adullam,[i] So-
coh, Azekah, 36Shaaraim, Adithaim 15:34 [g]1Ch 4:18;
and Gederah[j] (or Gederothaim)[c]— Ne 3:13
fourteen towns and their villages.
37Zenan, Hadashah, Migdal 15:35 [h]Jos 10:3
Gad, 38Dilean, Mizpah, Joktheel,[k] [i]1Sa 22:1
39Lachish,[l] Bozkath,[m] Eglon, 15:36 [j]1Ch 12:4
40Cabbon, Lahmas, Kitlish, 41Ge-
deroth, Beth Dagon, Naamah and 15:38 [k]2Ki 14:7
Makkedah[n]—sixteen towns and
their villages. 15:39 [l]Jos 10:3;
42Libnah, Ether, Ashan,[o] 43Iph- 2Ki 14:19
tah, Ashnah, Nezib, 44Keilah, Ac- [m]2Ki 22:1
zib[p] and Mareshah[q]—nine towns 15:41 [n]Jos 10:10
and their villages.
45Ekron, with its surrounding 15:42 [o]1Sa 30:30
settlements and villages; 46west of
Ekron, all that were in the vicin- 15:44 [p]Jdg 1:31
ity of Ashdod, together with their [q]Mic 1:15
villages; 47Ashdod,[r] its surround- 15:47 [r]Jos 11:22
ing settlements and villages; and [s]ver 4
Gaza, its settlements and villages, [t]Nu 34:6
as far as the Wadi of Egypt[s] and
the coastline of the Great Sea.[t] 15:48 [u]1Sa 30:27

48In the hill country:
Shamir, Jattir,[u] Socoh, 49Dan- 15:49 [v]Jos 10:3
nah, Kiriath Sannah (that is,
Debir[v]), 50Anab, Eshtemoh,[w] Anim, 15:50 [w]Jos 21:14
51Goshen,[x] Holon and Giloh— 15:51 [x]Jos 10:41;
eleven towns and their villages. 11:16

[a]*12* That is, the Mediterranean; also in verse 47
[b]*18* Hebrew and some Septuagint manuscripts; other Septuagint manuscripts (see also note at Judges 1:14) *Othniel, he urged her* [c]*36* Or *Gederah and Gederothaim*

15:52 52 Arab, Dumah,[y] Eshan, 53 Ja-
[y]Ge 25:14 nim, Beth Tappuah, Aphekah,
54 Humtah, Kiriath Arba (that is,
Hebron) and Zior—nine towns
15:55 and their villages.
[z]Jos 12:22 55 Maon, Carmel,[z] Ziph, Jut-
15:56 tah, 56 Jezreel,[a] Jokdeam, Zanoah,
[a]Jos 17:16 57 Kain, Gibeah[b] and Timnah—ten
15:57 towns and their villages.
[b]Jos 18:28; Jdg 19:12 58 Halhul, Beth Zur,[c] Gedor,
59 Maarath, Beth Anoth and El-
15:58 [c]1Ch 2:45 tekon—six towns and their villages.
15:60 60 Kiriath Baal (that is, Kiriath
[d]Jos 18:14 [e]Dt 3:11 Jearim[d]) and Rabbah[e]—two towns
and their villages.

61 In the desert:
Beth Arabah, Middin, Secacah,
15:62 62 Nibshan, the City of Salt and
[f]1Sa 23:29 En Gedi[f]—six towns and their
15:63 villages.
[g]Jdg 1:21 [h]2Sa 5:6 63 Judah could not[g] dislodge the Jebusites,[h] who were living in Jerusalem;
to this day the Jebusites live there with
the people of Judah.

Allotment for Ephraim and Manasseh

16 The allotment for Joseph
began at the Jordan of Jeri-
cho,[a] east of the waters of Jericho,
and went up from there through
16:1 [i]Jos 8:15; the desert[i] into the hill country of
18:12 Bethel. 2 It went on from Bethel
16:2 (that is, Luz[j]),[b] crossed over to the
[j]Jos 18:13 territory of the Arkites in Ataroth,
3 descended westward to the terri-
16:3 tory of the Japhletites as far as the
[k]2Ch 8:5 region of Lower Beth Horon[k] and
[l]Jos 10:33; 1Ki 9:15 on to Gezer,[l] ending at the sea.
4 So Manasseh and Ephraim, the de-
16:4 scendants of Joseph, received their
[m]Jos 17:14 inheritance.[m]

5 This was the territory of Ephraim, clan
by clan:
The boundary of their inheri-
16:5 [n]Jos 18:13 tance went from Ataroth Addar[n] in
the east to Upper Beth Horon 6 and
16:6 continued to the sea. From Mic-
[o]Jos 17:7 methath[o] on the north it curved
eastward to Taanath Shiloh, pass-
ing by it to Janoah on the east.
16:7 7 Then it went down from Janoah
[p]1Ch 7:28 to Ataroth[p] and Naarah, touched
Jericho and came out at the Jor-
16:8 dan. 8 From Tappuah the border
[q]Jos 17:9 went west to the Kanah Ravine[q]
and ended at the sea. This was
the inheritance of the tribe of the
Ephraimites, clan by clan. 9 It also
included all the towns and their
villages that were set aside for the
Ephraimites within the inheritance
of the Manassites.
10 They did not dislodge the Canaanites
living in Gezer; to this day the Canaanites live among the people of Ephraim
but are required to do forced labor.[r] 16:10
17 This was the allotment for the [r]Jos 17:13;
tribe of Manasseh as Joseph's Jdg 1:28-29; 1Ki 9:16
firstborn,[s] that is, for Makir,[t] Manasseh's 17:1
firstborn. Makir was the ancestor of [s]Ge 41:51 [t]Ge 50:23
the Gileadites, who had received Gilead
and Bashan because the Makirites were
great soldiers. 2 So this allotment was for
the rest of the people of Manasseh—
the clans of Abiezer,[u] Helek, Asriel, 17:2
Shechem, Hepher and Shemida. These [u]Nu 26:30; 1Ch 7:18
are the other male descendants of
Manasseh son of Joseph by their clans. 17:3
3 Now Zelophehad son of Hepher,[v] [v]Nu 27:1
the son of Gilead, the son of Makir, [w]Nu 26:33
the son of Manasseh, had no sons but
only daughters,[w] whose names were
Mahlah, Noah, Hoglah, Milcah and
Tirzah. 4 They went to Eleazar the priest,
Joshua son of Nun, and the leaders and
said, "The LORD commanded Moses
to give us an inheritance among our
brothers." So Joshua gave them an inheritance along with the brothers of
their father, according to the LORD's
command.[x] 5 Manasseh's share consisted 17:4
of ten tracts of land besides Gilead and [x]Nu 27:5-7
Bashan east of the Jordan, 6 because the
daughters of the tribe of Manasseh received an inheritance among the sons.
The land of Gilead belonged to the rest
of the descendants of Manasseh.
7 The territory of Manasseh ex- 17:7
tended from Asher to Micmethath[y] [y]Jos 16:6
east of Shechem.[z] The boundary [z]Ge 12:6; Jos 21:21
ran southward from there to in-
clude the people living at En Tappuah. 8 (Manasseh had the land 17:8
of Tappuah, but Tappuah[a] itself, [a]Jos 16:8
on the boundary of Manasseh, belonged to the Ephraimites.) 9 Then
the boundary continued south to
the Kanah Ravine.[b] There were 17:9
towns belonging to Ephraim ly- [b]Jos 16:8

[a] *1 Jordan of Jericho* was possibly an ancient name for the Jordan River. [b] *2* Septuagint; Hebrew *Bethel to Luz*

ing among the towns of Manasseh,
but the boundary of Manasseh was
the northern side of the ravine and
ended at the sea. 10On the south
the land belonged to Ephraim, on
the north to Manasseh. The territory of Manasseh reached the sea
and bordered Asher on the north
and Issachar[c] on the east.
11Within Issachar and Asher,
Manasseh also had Beth Shan,[d]
Ibleam and the people of Dor,[e]
Endor,[f] Taanach and Megiddo,[g]
together with their surrounding
settlements (the third in the list is
Naphoth[a]).
12Yet the Manassites were not able[h] to
occupy these towns, for the Canaanites were determined to live in that
region. 13However, when the Israelites
grew stronger, they subjected the Canaanites to forced labor but did not
drive them out completely.[i]
14The people of Joseph said to Joshua, "Why have you given us only one
allotment and one portion for an inheritance? We are a numerous people and
the LORD has blessed us abundantly."[j]
15"If you are so numerous," Joshua
answered, "and if the hill country of
Ephraim is too small for you, go up
into the forest and clear land for yourselves there in the land of the Perizzites
and Rephaites.[k]"
16The people of Joseph replied, "The
hill country is not enough for us, and
all the Canaanites who live in the plain
have iron chariots,[l] both those in Beth
Shan and its settlements and those in
the Valley of Jezreel."
17But Joshua said to the house of
Joseph—to Ephraim and Manasseh—
"You are numerous and very powerful.
You will have not only one allotment
18but the forested hill country as well.
Clear it, and its farthest limits will be
yours; though the Canaanites have iron
chariots[m] and though they are strong,
you can drive them out."

Division of the Rest of the Land

18 The whole assembly of the Israelites gathered at Shiloh[n] and
set up the Tent of Meeting[o] there. The
country was brought under their control, 2but there were still seven Israelite
tribes who had not yet received their inheritance.

17:10 [c]Ge 30:18
17:11 [d]1Sa 31:10; 1Ki 4:12; 1Ch 7:29 [e]Jos 11:2 [f]1Sa 28:7; Ps 83:10 [g]1Ki 9:15
17:12 [h]Jdg 1:27
17:13 [i]Jos 16:10
17:14 [j]Nu 26:28-37
17:15 [k]Ge 14:5
17:16 [l]Jdg 1:19; 4:3,13
17:18 [m]ver 16
18:1 [n]Jos 19:51; 21:2; Jdg 18:31; 21:12,19; 1Sa 1:3; 4:3; Jer 7:12; 26:6 [o]Ex 27:21

3So Joshua said to the Israelites: "How
long will you wait before you begin
to take possession of the land that the
LORD, the God of your fathers, has
given you? 4Appoint three men from
each tribe. I will send them out to make
a survey of the land and to write a description of it, according to the inheritance of each.[p] Then they will return
to me. 5You are to divide the land into
seven parts. Judah is to remain in its
territory on the south[q] and the house
of Joseph in its territory on the north.[r]
6After you have written descriptions
of the seven parts of the land, bring
them here to me and I will cast lots[s]
for you in the presence of the LORD
our God. 7The Levites, however, do not
get a portion among you, because the
priestly service of the LORD is their
inheritance.[t] And Gad, Reuben and the
half-tribe of Manasseh have already received their inheritance on the east side
of the Jordan. Moses the servant of the
LORD gave it to them.[u]"
8As the men started on their way to
map out the land, Joshua instructed
them, "Go and make a survey of the
land and write a description of it. Then
return to me, and I will cast lots for
you here at Shiloh[v] in the presence of
the LORD." 9So the men left and went
through the land. They wrote its description on a scroll, town by town, in
seven parts, and returned to Joshua in
the camp at Shiloh. 10Joshua then cast
lots[w] for them in Shiloh in the presence[x]
of the LORD, and there he distributed
the land to the Israelites according to
their tribal divisions.[y]

Allotment for Benjamin

11The lot came up for the tribe of Benjamin, clan by clan. Their allotted territory lay between the tribes of Judah and
Joseph:
12On the north side their boundary began at the Jordan, passed
the northern slope of Jericho and
headed west into the hill country,
coming out at the desert[z] of Beth
Aven.[a] 13From there it crossed to
the south slope of Luz[b] (that is,
Bethel[c]) and went down to Ataroth
Addar[d] on the hill south of Lower
Beth Horon.

[a] *11* That is, Naphoth Dor

18:4 [p]Mic 2:5
18:5 [q]Jos 15:1 [r]Jos 16:1-4
18:6 [s]Jos 14:2
18:7 [t]Jos 13:33 [u]Jos 13:8
18:8 [v]ver 1
18:10 [w]Nu 34:13 [x]ver 1; Jer 7:12 [y]Nu 33:54; Jos 19:51
18:12 [z]Jos 16:1 [a]Jos 7:2
18:13 [b]Ge 28:19 [c]Jdg 1:23 [d]Jos 16:5

14From the hill facing Beth Ho-
18:14 ron[e] on the south the boundary
[e]Jos 10:10 turned south along the western
side and came out at Kiriath Baal
(that is, Kiriath Jearim), a town of
the people of Judah. This was the
western side.
15The southern side began at
the outskirts of Kiriath Jearim on
the west, and the boundary came
18:15 out at the spring of the waters of
[f]Jos 15:9 Nephtoah.[f] 16The boundary went
down to the foot of the hill facing
the Valley of Ben Hinnom, north
18:16 of the Valley of Rephaim. It con-
[g]Jos 15:8; tinued down the Hinnom Valley[g]
2Ki 23:10 along the southern slope of the
[h]Jos 15:7 Jebusite city and so to En Rogel.[h]
17It then curved north, went to En
Shemesh, continued to Geliloth,
which faces the Pass of Adummim, and ran down to the Stone
18:17 [i]Jos 15:6 of Bohan[i] son of Reuben. 18It con-
18:18 tinued to the northern slope of
[j]Jos 15:6 Beth Arabah[a][j] and on down into
the Arabah. 19It then went to the
northern slope of Beth Hoglah and
18:19 came out at the northern bay of
[k]Ge 14:3 the Salt Sea,[b][k] at the mouth of the
Jordan in the south. This was the
southern boundary.
18:20 20The Jordan formed the bound-
[l]Jos 21:4,17; 1Sa 9:1 ary on the eastern side.[l]
These were the boundaries that marked
out the inheritance of the clans of Benjamin on all sides.
21The tribe of Benjamin, clan by clan,
had the following cities:
Jericho, Beth Hoglah, Emek
18:22 Keziz, 22Beth Arabah, Zemaraim,
[m]Jos 16:1 Bethel,[m] 23Avvim, Parah, Ophrah,
18:24 24Kephar Ammoni, Ophni and
[n]Isa 10:29 Geba[n]—twelve towns and their vil-
18:25 lages.
[o]Jos 9:3 25Gibeon,[o] Ramah,[p] Beeroth,[q]
[p]Jdg 4:5 26Mizpah,[r] Kephirah, Mozah, 27Re-
[q]Jos 9:17 kem, Irpeel, Taralah, 28Zelah,[s]
18:26 Haeleph, the Jebusite city[t] (that
[r]Jos 11:3 is, Jerusalem[u]), Gibeah[v] and Kiri-
18:28 [s]2Sa 21:14 ath—fourteen towns and their vil-
[t]Jos 15:8 [u]Jos 10:1 lages.
[v]Jos 15:57 This was the inheritance of Benjamin
for its clans.

Allotment for Simeon

19 The second lot came out for the
tribe of Simeon, clan by clan.
Their inheritance lay within the terri-
tory of Judah.[w] 2It included: 19:1 [w]ver 9; Ge 49:7
Beersheba[x] (or Sheba),[c] Mola-
dah, 3Hazar Shual, Balah, Ezem, 19:2
4Eltolad, Bethul, Hormah, 5Ziklag, [x]Ge 21:14; 1Ki 19:3
Beth Marcaboth, Hazar Susah,
6Beth Lebaoth and Sharuhen—
thirteen towns and their villages;
7Ain, Rimmon, Ether and 19:7
Ashan[y]—four towns and their [y]Jos 15:42
villages— 8and all the villages
around these towns as far as Baal- 19:8
ath Beer (Ramah in the Negev).[z] [z]Jos 10:40
This was the inheritance of the tribe of
the Simeonites, clan by clan. 9The inheritance of the Simeonites was taken 19:9
from the share of Judah,[a] because Judah's [a]Ge 49:7
portion was more than they needed. [b]Eze 48:24
So the Simeonites received their inheritance within the territory of Judah.[b]

Allotment for Zebulun

10The third lot came up for Zebulun,[c] 19:10 [c]Jos 21:7,34
clan by clan:
The boundary of their inheritance went as far as Sarid. 11Going
west it ran to Maralah, touched
Dabbesheth, and extended to the 19:11
ravine near Jokneam.[d] 12It turned [d]Jos 12:22
east from Sarid toward the sunrise
to the territory of Kisloth Tabor
and went on to Daberath and
up to Japhia. 13Then it continued
eastward to Gath Hepher and Eth 19:13
Kazin; it came out at Rimmon[e] [e]Jos 15:32
and turned toward Neah. 14There
the boundary went around on the
north to Hannathon and ended at
the Valley of Iphtah El. 15Includ-
ed were Kattath, Nahalal, Shim- 19:15
ron, Idalah and Bethlehem.[f] There [f]Ge 35:19
were twelve towns and their vil-
lages.
16These towns and their villages were 19:16
the inheritance of Zebulun,[g] clan by [g]ver 10; Jos 21:7
clan.[h] [h]Eze 48:26

Allotment for Issachar

17The fourth lot came out for Issachar,[i]
clan by clan. 18Their territory in- 19:17 [i]Ge 30:18
cluded:
Jezreel,[j] Kesulloth, Shunem,[k] 19:18 [j]Jos 15:56
19Hapharaim, Shion, Anaharath, [k]1Sa 28:4;
20Rabbith, Kishion, Ebez, 21Re- 2Ki 4:8

[a]*18* Septuagint; Hebrew *slope facing the Arabah*
[b]*19* That is, the Dead Sea [c]*2* Or *Beersheba, Sheba*; 1 Chron. 4:28 does not have *Sheba.*

meth, En Gannim, En Haddah and Beth Pazzez. 22 The boundary touched Tabor,[l] Shahazumah and Beth Shemesh,[m] and ended at the Jordan. There were sixteen towns and their villages.

19:22 [l]Jdg 4:6,12; Ps 89:12 [m]Jos 15:10

23 These towns and their villages were the inheritance of the tribe of Issachar,[n] clan by clan.[o]

19:23 [n]Jos 17:10 [o]Ge 49:15; Eze 48:25

Allotment for Asher

24 The fifth lot came out for the tribe of Asher,[p] clan by clan. 25 Their territory included:

19:24 [p]Jos 17:7

Helkath, Hali, Beten, Acshaph, 26 Allammelech, Amad and Mishal. On the west the boundary touched Carmel[q] and Shihor Libnath. 27 It then turned east toward Beth Dagon, touched Zebulun[r] and the Valley of Iphtah El, and went north to Beth Emek and Neiel, passing Cabul[s] on the left. 28 It went to Abdon,[a] Rehob,[t] Hammon[u] and Kanah, as far as Greater Sidon.[v] 29 The boundary then turned back toward Ramah[w] and went to the fortified city of Tyre,[x] turned toward Hosah and came out at the sea in the region of Aczib,[y] 30 Ummah, Aphek and Rehob. There were twenty-two towns and their villages.

19:26 [q]Jos 12:22
19:27 [r]ver 10 [s]1Ki 9:13
19:28 [t]Jdg 1:31 [u]1Ch 6:76 [v]Ge 10:19; Jos 11:8
19:29 [w]Jos 18:25 [x]2Sa 5:11; 24:7; Isa 23:1; Jer 25:22; Eze 26:2 [y]Jdg 1:31

31 These towns and their villages were the inheritance of the tribe of Asher,[z] clan by clan.

19:31 [z]Ge 30:13; Eze 48:2

Allotment for Naphtali

32 The sixth lot came out for Naphtali, clan by clan:

33 Their boundary went from Heleph and the large tree in Zaanannim, passing Adami Nekeb and Jabneel to Lakkum and ending at the Jordan. 34 The boundary ran west through Aznoth Tabor and came out at Hukkok. It touched Zebulun on the south, Asher on the west and the Jordan[b] on the east. 35 The fortified cities were Ziddim, Zer, Hammath, Rakkath, Kinnereth,[a] 36 Adamah, Ramah,[b] Hazor,[c] 37 Kedesh, Edrei,[d] En Hazor, 38 Iron, Migdal El, Horem, Beth Anath and Beth Shemesh. There were nineteen towns and their villages.

19:35 [a]Jos 11:2
19:36 [b]Jos 18:25 [c]Jos 11:1
19:37 [d]Nu 21:33

39 These towns and their villages were the inheritance of the tribe of Naphtali, clan by clan.[e]

19:39 [e]Dt 33:23; Eze 48:3

Allotment for Dan

40 The seventh lot came out for the tribe of Dan, clan by clan. 41 The territory of their inheritance included:

Zorah, Eshtaol, Ir Shemesh, 42 Shaalabbin, Aijalon,[f] Ithlah, 43 Elon, Timnah,[g] Ekron, 44 Eltekeh, Gibbethon, Baalath, 45 Jehud, Bene Berak, Gath Rimmon,[h] 46 Me Jarkon and Rakkon, with the area facing Joppa.[i]

19:42 [f]Jdg 1:35
19:43 [g]Ge 38:12
19:45 [h]Jos 21:24; 1Ch 6:69
19:46 [i]2Ch 2:16; Jnh 1:3

47 (But the Danites had difficulty taking possession of their territory,[j] so they went up and attacked Leshem,[k] took it, put it to the sword and occupied it. They settled in Leshem and named it Dan after their forefather.)[l]

19:47 [j]Jdg 18:1 [k]Jdg 18:7,14 [l]Jdg 18:27,29

48 These towns and their villages were the inheritance of the tribe of Dan,[m] clan by clan.

19:48 [m]Ge 30:6

Allotment for Joshua

49 When they had finished dividing the land into its allotted portions, the Israelites gave Joshua son of Nun an inheritance among them, 50 as the LORD had commanded. They gave him the town he asked for—Timnath Serah[c][n] in the hill country of Ephraim. And he built up the town and settled there.

19:50 [n]Jos 24:30

FAITHFULNESS

OBEY GOD AND PICK A CITY

Joshua 19:49–50

Joshua had been a faithful leader. The conquest was over and Joshua received the city of Timnath Serah as his reward. It is even as Jesus said, "Whoever can be trusted with very little can also be trusted with much" (Luke 16:10). Follow Christ and order up a crown. Obey God and pick a city.

51 These are the territories that Eleazar the priest, Joshua son of Nun and the heads of the tribal clans of Israel assigned by lot at Shiloh in the presence of the LORD at the entrance to the

[a] *28* Some Hebrew manuscripts (see also Joshua 21:30); most Hebrew manuscripts *Ebron*
[b] *34* Septuagint; Hebrew *west, and Judah, the Jordan,*
[c] *50* Also known as *Timnath Heres* (see Judges 2:9)

Tent of Meeting. And so they finished dividing the land.[o]

Cities of Refuge

20 Then the LORD said to Joshua: 2"Tell the Israelites to designate the cities of refuge, as I instructed you through Moses, 3so that anyone who kills a person accidentally and unintentionally[p] may flee there and find protection from the avenger of blood.[q]

4"When he flees to one of these cities, he is to stand in the entrance of the city gate[r] and state his case before the elders[s] of that city. Then they are to admit him into their city and give him a place to live with them. 5If the avenger of blood pursues him, they must not surrender the one accused, because he killed his neighbor unintentionally and without malice aforethought. 6He is to stay in that city until he has stood trial before the assembly[t] and until the death of the high priest who is serving at that time. Then he may go back to his own home in the town from which he fled."

7So they set apart Kedesh[u] in Galilee in the hill country of Naphtali, Shechem[v] in the hill country of Ephraim, and Kiriath Arba (that is, Hebron[w]) in the hill country of Judah.[x] 8On the east side of the Jordan of Jericho[a] they designated Bezer[y] in the desert on the plateau in the tribe of Reuben, Ramoth in Gilead[z] in the tribe of Gad, and Golan in Bashan in the tribe of Manasseh. 9Any of the Israelites or any alien living among them who killed someone accidentally could flee to these designated cities and not be killed by the avenger of blood prior to standing trial before the assembly.[a]

Towns for the Levites

21 Now the family heads of the Levites approached Eleazar the priest, Joshua son of Nun, and the heads of the other tribal families of Israel[b] 2at Shiloh[c] in Canaan and said to them, "The LORD commanded through Moses that you give us towns to live in, with pasturelands for our livestock."[d] 3So, as the LORD had commanded, the Israelites gave the Levites the following towns and pasturelands out of their own inheritance:

4The first lot came out for the Kohathites, clan by clan. The Levites who were descendants of Aaron the priest were allotted thirteen towns from the tribes of Judah, Simeon and Benjamin.[e] 5The rest of Kohath's descendants were allotted ten towns from the clans of the tribes of Ephraim, Dan and half of Manasseh.[f]

19:51 [o]Jos 14:1; 18:10; Ac 13:19
20:3 [p]Lev 4:2 [q]Nu 35:12
20:4 [r]Ru 4:1; Jer 38:7 [s]Jos 7:6
20:6 [t]Nu 35:12
20:7 [u]Jos 21:32; 1Ch 6:76 [v]Ge 12:6 [w]Jos 10:36; 21:11 [x]Lk 1:39
20:8 [y]Jos 21:36; 1Ch 6:78 [z]Jos 12:2
20:9 [a]Ex 21:13; Nu 35:15
21:1 [b]Jos 14:1
21:2 [c]Jos 18:1 [d]Nu 35:2-3

6The descendants of Gershon were allotted thirteen towns from the clans of the tribes of Issachar,[g] Asher, Naphtali and the half-tribe of Manasseh in Bashan.

7The descendants of Merari,[h] clan by clan, received twelve towns from the tribes of Reuben, Gad and Zebulun.[i]

8So the Israelites allotted to the Levites these towns and their pasturelands, as the LORD had commanded through Moses.

9From the tribes of Judah and Simeon they allotted the following towns by name 10(these towns were assigned to the descendants of Aaron who were from the Kohathite clans of the Levites, because the first lot fell to them):

11They gave them Kiriath Arba (that is, Hebron[j]), with its surrounding pastureland, in the hill country of Judah. (Arba was the forefather of Anak.) 12But the fields and villages around the city they had given to Caleb son of Jephunneh as his possession.

13So to the descendants of Aaron the priest they gave Hebron (a city of refuge for one accused of murder), Libnah,[k] 14Jattir,[l] Eshtemoa,[m] 15Holon,[n] Debir, 16Ain, Juttah[o] and Beth Shemesh,[p] together with their pasturelands—nine towns from these two tribes.

17And from the tribe of Benjamin they gave them Gibeon, Geba,[q] 18Anathoth and Almon, together with their pasturelands—four towns.

19All the towns for the priests, the descendants of Aaron, were thirteen, together with their pasturelands.

20The rest of the Kohathite clans of the Levites were allotted towns from the tribe of Ephraim:

21In the hill country of Ephraim

[a]8 *Jordan of Jericho* was possibly an ancient name for the Jordan River.

21:4 [e]ver 19
21:5 [f]ver 26
21:6 [g]Ge 30:18
21:7 [h]Ex 6:16 [i]Jos 19:10
21:11 [j]Jos 15:13; 1Ch 6:55
21:13 [k]Jos 15:42; 1Ch 6:57
21:14 [l]Jos 15:48 [m]Jos 15:50
21:15 [n]Jos 15:51
21:16 [o]Jos 15:55 [p]Jos 15:10
21:17 [q]Jos 18:24

they were given Shechem[r] (a city of refuge for one accused of murder) and Gezer, 22 Kibzaim and Beth Horon,[s] together with their pasturelands—four towns.[t]

23 Also from the tribe of Dan they received Eltekeh, Gibbethon, 24 Aijalon and Gath Rimmon,[u] together with their pasturelands—four towns.

25 From half the tribe of Manasseh they received Taanach and Gath Rimmon, together with their pasturelands—two towns.

26 All these ten towns and their pasturelands were given to the rest of the Kohathite clans.

27 The Levite clans of the Gershonites were given:

from the half-tribe of Manasseh,
Golan in Bashan[v] (a city of refuge for one accused of murder[w]) and Be Eshtarah, together with their pasturelands—two towns;

28 from the tribe of Issachar,[x]
Kishion, Daberath, 29 Jarmuth and En Gannim, together with their pasturelands—four towns;

30 from the tribe of Asher,[y]
Mishal, Abdon, 31 Helkath and Rehob, together with their pasturelands—four towns;

32 from the tribe of Naphtali,
Kedesh[z] in Galilee (a city of refuge for one accused of murder[a]), Hammoth Dor and Kartan, together with their pasturelands—three towns.

33 All the towns of the Gershonite[b] clans were thirteen, together with their pasturelands.

34 The Merarite clans (the rest of the Levites) were given:

from the tribe of Zebulun,[c]
Jokneam, Kartah, 35 Dimnah and Nahalal, together with their pasturelands—four towns;

36 from the tribe of Reuben,
Bezer,[d] Jahaz, 37 Kedemoth and Mephaath, together with their pasturelands—four towns;

38 from the tribe of Gad,
Ramoth[e] in Gilead (a city of refuge for one accused of murder), Mahanaim,[f] 39 Heshbon and Jazer, together with their pasturelands—four towns in all.

21:21 [r]Jos 17:7; 20:7
21:22 [s]Jos 10:10 [t]1Sa 1:1
21:24 [u]Jos 19:45
21:27 [v]Jos 12:5 [w]Nu 35:6
21:28 [x]Ge 30:18
21:30 [y]Jos 17:7
21:32 [z]Jos 12:22 [a]Nu 35:6; Jos 20:7
21:33 [b]ver 6
21:34 [c]Jos 19:10; 1Ch 6:77
21:36 [d]Jos 20:8
21:38 [e]Dt 4:43 [f]Ge 32:2

40 All the towns allotted to the Merarite clans, who were the rest of the Levites, were twelve.

41 The towns of the Levites in the territory held by the Israelites were forty-eight in all, together with their pasturelands.[g] 42 Each of these towns had pasturelands surrounding it; this was true for all these towns.

43 So the LORD gave Israel all the land he had sworn to give their forefathers,[h] and they took possession[i] of it and settled there.[j] 44 The LORD gave them rest[k] on every side, just as he had sworn to their forefathers. Not one of their enemies[l] withstood them; the LORD handed all their enemies[m] over to them.[n] 45 Not one of all the LORD's good promises[o] to the house of Israel failed; every one was fulfilled.

Eastern Tribes Return Home

22 Then Joshua summoned the Reubenites, the Gadites and the half-tribe of Manasseh 2 and said to them, "You have done all that Moses the servant of the LORD commanded,[p] and you have obeyed me in everything I commanded. 3 For a long time now—to this very day—you have not deserted your brothers but have carried out the mission the LORD your God gave you. 4 Now that the LORD your God has given your brothers rest as he promised, return to your homes[q] in the land that Moses the servant of the LORD gave you on the other side of the Jordan.[r] 5 But be very careful to keep the commandment[s] and the law that Moses the servant of the LORD gave you: to love the LORD your God, to walk in all his ways, to obey his commands,[t] to hold fast to him and to serve him with all your heart and all your soul.[u]"

6 Then Joshua blessed[v] them and sent them away, and they went to their homes. 7 (To the half-tribe of Manasseh Moses had given land in Bashan,[w] and to the other half of the tribe Joshua gave land on the west side[x] of the Jordan with their brothers.) When Joshua sent them home, he blessed them, 8 saying, "Return to your homes with your great wealth—with large herds of livestock,[y] with silver, gold, bronze and iron, and a great quantity of clothing—and divide[z]

21:41 [g]Nu 35:7
21:43 [h]Dt 34:4 [i]Dt 11:31 [j]Dt 17:14
21:44 [k]Ex 33:14; Jos 1:13 [l]Dt 6:19 [m]Ex 23:31 [n]Dt 7:24; 21:10
21:45 [o]Jos 23:14; Ne 9:8
22:2 [p]Nu 32:25
22:4 [q]Nu 32:22; Dt 3:20 [r]Nu 32:18; Jos 1:13-15
22:5 [s]Isa 43:22 [t]Dt 5:29 [u]Dt 6:6,17
22:6 [v]Ex 39:43
22:7 [w]Nu 32:33; Jos 12:5 [x]Jos 17:2,5
22:8 [y]Dt 20:14 [z]Nu 31:27

22:8 [a]Ge 49:27; 1Sa 30:16; Isa 9:3
with your brothers the plunder[a] from
your enemies."
[9]So the Reubenites, the Gadites and
the half-tribe of Manasseh left the Is-
22:9 [b]Nu 32:26,29
raelites at Shiloh in Canaan to return
to Gilead,[b] their own land, which
they had acquired in accordance with
the command of the LORD through
Moses.
[10]When they came to Geliloth near
the Jordan in the land of Canaan, the
Reubenites, the Gadites and the half-
tribe of Manasseh built an imposing altar there by the Jordan. [11]And when
the Israelites heard that they had built
the altar on the border of Canaan at
Geliloth near the Jordan on the Israel-
22:12 [c]Jos 18:1
ite side, [12]the whole assembly of Israel
gathered at Shiloh[c] to go to war against
them.
22:13 [d]Nu 25:7 [e]Nu 3:32; Jos 24:33
[13]So the Israelites sent Phinehas[d] son
of Eleazar,[e] the priest, to the land of
Gilead—to Reuben, Gad and the half-
tribe of Manasseh. [14]With him they
sent ten of the chief men, one for each
of the tribes of Israel, each the head
of a family division among the Israelite
22:14 [f]Nu 1:4
clans.[f]
[15]When they went to Gilead—to
Reuben, Gad and the half-tribe of
Manasseh—they said to them: [16]"The
whole assembly of the LORD says: 'How
22:16 [g]Dt 13:14 [h]Dt 12:13-14
could you break faith[g] with the God
of Israel like this? How could you turn
22:17 [i]Nu 25:1-9
away from the LORD and build yourselves an altar in rebellion[h] against him
now? [17]Was not the sin of Peor[i] enough
for us? Up to this very day we have not
cleansed ourselves from that sin, even
though a plague fell on the community
of the LORD! [18]And are you now turning away from the LORD?
"'If you rebel against the LORD to-
22:18 [j]Lev 10:6; Nu 16:22
day, tomorrow he will be angry with
the whole community[j] of Israel. [19]If the
land you possess is defiled, come over
to the LORD's land, where the LORD's
tabernacle stands, and share the land
with us. But do not rebel against the
LORD or against us by building an altar for yourselves, other than the altar
of the LORD our God. [20]When Achan
22:20 [k]Jos 7:1 [l]Ps 7:11 [m]Jos 7:5
son of Zerah acted unfaithfully regarding the devoted things,[a][k] did not wrath[l]
come upon the whole community of Israel? He was not the only one who died
for his sin.'"[m]
[21]Then Reuben, Gad and the half-

DAY 4 FOUR

▸ KINDNESS AND MY SERVICE TO OTHERS

Joshua 22:9–27

The tribes east of the Jordan had built an altar so they would never forget that even though they were separated from the tribes west of the Jordan, they celebrated the same great heritage of faith. When the tribes west of the Jordan understood the reasoning behind the building of the new altar, they were all the more ready to bless their brothers as they celebrated a common legacy of faith. The new altar's name became: "A Witness Between Us that the LORD is God" (Joshua 22:34).

In Joshua 4:20–22, Joshua built a very similar altar and told Israel that, in future years when their children asked, "What do these stones mean?" they were to give their testimony of God's grace.

Altars are sometimes reared as monuments to celebrate the kindness of God. I have never viewed the Lincoln Memorial without reflecting back on this presidential martyr. It is said that after President Lincoln was shot and killed, an African-American mother and her daughter passed the funeral bier upon which the dead president lay in state. The mother said to her daughter, "Take a good, long look at that man, Sweetie. He died for you."

Each time I have seen the Lincoln Memorial, I remember that story. It is a story of thankfulness for the kindness of others.

Altars should celebrate kindness, and they should motivate us to serve others with the virtues those monuments memorialize.

To begin a study on the topic of Kindness, Always Applying the Golden Rule, turn to the home page on page 1141.

tribe of Manasseh replied to the heads
of the clans of Israel: [22]"The Mighty 22:22 [n]Dt 10:17 [o]Ps 50:1
One, God, the LORD! The Mighty [p]1Ki 8:39; Job 10:7;
One, God,[n] the LORD![o] He knows![p] Ps 44:21;
And let Israel know! If this has been in Jer 17:10
rebellion or disobedience to the LORD,

[a]*20* The Hebrew term refers to the irrevocable giving over of things or persons to the LORD, often by totally destroying them.

do not spare us this day. 23 If we have built our own altar to turn away from the LORD and to offer burnt offerings and grain offerings,[q] or to sacrifice fellowship offerings[a] on it, may the LORD himself call us to account.[r]

24 "No! We did it for fear that some day your descendants might say to ours, 'What do you have to do with the LORD, the God of Israel? 25 The LORD has made the Jordan a boundary between us and you—you Reubenites and Gadites! You have no share in the LORD.' So your descendants might cause ours to stop fearing the LORD.

26 "That is why we said, 'Let us get ready and build an altar—but not for burnt offerings or sacrifices.' 27 On the contrary, it is to be a witness[s] between us and you and the generations that follow, that we will worship the LORD at his sanctuary with our burnt offerings, sacrifices and fellowship offerings.[t] Then in the future your descendants will not be able to say to ours, 'You have no share in the LORD.'

28 "And we said, 'If they ever say this to us, or to our descendants, we will answer: Look at the replica of the LORD's altar, which our fathers built, not for burnt offerings and sacrifices, but as a witness between us and you.'

29 "Far be it from us to rebel[u] against the LORD and turn away from him today by building an altar for burnt offerings, grain offerings and sacrifices, other than the altar of the LORD our God that stands before his tabernacle.[v]"

30 When Phinehas the priest and the leaders of the community—the heads of the clans of the Israelites—heard what Reuben, Gad and Manasseh had to say, they were pleased. 31 And Phinehas son of Eleazar, the priest, said to Reuben, Gad and Manasseh, "Today we know that the LORD is with us,[w] because you have not acted unfaithfully toward the LORD in this matter. Now you have rescued the Israelites from the LORD's hand."

32 Then Phinehas son of Eleazar, the priest, and the leaders returned to Canaan from their meeting with the Reubenites and Gadites in Gilead and reported to the Israelites. 33 They were glad to hear the report and praised God.[x] And they talked no more about going to war against them to devastate the country where the Reubenites and the Gadites lived.

34 And the Reubenites and the Gadites gave the altar this name: A Witness[y] Between Us that the LORD is God.

Joshua's Farewell to the Leaders

23 After a long time had passed and the LORD had given Israel rest[z] from all their enemies around them, Joshua, by then old and well advanced in years,[a] 2 summoned all Israel—their elders,[b] leaders, judges and officials[c]—and said to them: "I am old and well advanced in years. 3 You yourselves have seen everything the LORD your God has done to all these nations for your sake; it was the LORD your God who fought for you.[d] 4 Remember how I have allotted[e] as an inheritance for your tribes all the land of the nations that remain—the nations I conquered—between the Jordan and the Great Sea[b][f] in the west. 5 The LORD your God himself will drive them out of your way. He will push them out before you, and you will take possession of their land, as the LORD your God promised you.[g]

6 "Be very strong; be careful to obey all that is written in the Book of the Law of Moses, without turning aside to the right or to the left.[h] 7 Do not associate with these nations that remain among you; do not invoke the names of their gods or swear[i] by them. You must not serve them or bow down[j] to them. 8 But you are to hold fast to the LORD[k] your God, as you have until now.

9 "The LORD has driven out before you great and powerful nations;[l] to this day no one has been able to withstand you.[m] 10 One of you routs a thousand,[n] because the LORD your God fights for you,[o] just as he promised. 11 So be very careful to love the LORD[p] your God.

12 "But if you turn away and ally yourselves with the survivors of these nations that remain among you and if you intermarry with them[q] and associate with them,[r] 13 then you may be sure that the LORD your God will no longer drive out these nations before you. Instead, they will become snares[s] and traps for you, whips on your backs and thorns in your eyes,[t] until you perish

[a] *23* Traditionally *peace offerings*; also in verse 27
[b] *4* That is, the Mediterranean

22:23 [q]Jer 41:5 [r]Dt 12:11; 18:19; 1Sa 20:16
22:27 [s]Ge 21:30; Jos 24:27 [t]Dt 12:6
22:29 [u]Jos 24:16 [v]Dt 12:13-14
22:31 [w]Lev 26:11-12; 2Ch 15:2
22:33 [x]1Ch 29:20; Da 2:19; Lk 2:28
22:34 [y]Ge 21:30
23:1 [z]Dt 12:9; Jos 21:44 [a]Jos 13:1
23:2 [b]Jos 7:6 [c]Jos 24:1
23:3 [d]Ex 14:14
23:4 [e]Jos 19:51 [f]Nu 34:6
23:5 [g]Ex 23:30; Nu 33:53
23:6 [h]Dt 5:32; Jos 1:7
23:7 [i]Ex 23:13; Ps 16:4; Jer 5:7 [j]Ex 20:5
23:8 [k]Dt 10:20
23:9 [l]Dt 11:23 [m]Dt 7:24
23:10 [n]Lev 26:8 [o]Ex 14:14; Dt 3:22
23:11 [p]Jos 22:5
23:12 [q]Dt 7:3 [r]Ex 34:16; Ps 106:34-35
23:13 [s]Ex 23:33 [t]Nu 33:55

from this good land, which the LORD
your God has given you.
23:14 [14]"Now I am about to go the way
[u]1Ki 2:2 of all the earth.[u] You know with all
[v]Jos 21:45 your heart and soul that not one of all
the good promises the LORD your God
gave you has failed. Every promise has
been fulfilled; not one has failed.[v] [15]But
just as every good promise of the LORD
your God has come true, so the LORD
will bring on you all the evil he has
23:15 threatened, until he has destroyed you
[w]Lev 26:17; Dt 28:15 from this good land he has given you.[w]
[16]If you violate the covenant of the
LORD your God, which he commanded you, and go and serve other gods
and bow down to them, the LORD's
anger will burn against you, and you
23:16 will quickly perish from the good land
[x]Dt 4:25-26 he has given you.[x]"

The Covenant Renewed at Shechem

24 Then Joshua assembled all the
tribes of Israel at Shechem. He
24:1 summoned the elders, leaders, judges
[y]Jos 23:2 and officials of Israel,[y] and they presented themselves before God.
[2]Joshua said to all the people, "This is
what the LORD, the God of Israel, says:
'Long ago your forefathers, including
Terah the father of Abraham and Na-
24:2 hor, lived beyond the River[a] and wor-
[z]Ge 11:32 shiped other gods.[z] [3]But I took your
father Abraham from the land beyond
the River and led him throughout Ca-
24:3 [a]Ge 12:1 naan[a] and gave him many descendants.[b]
[b]Ge 15:5 I gave him Isaac,[c] [4]and to Isaac I gave
[c]Ge 21:3 Jacob and Esau.[d] I assigned the hill
24:4 country of Seir[e] to Esau, but Jacob and
[d]Ge 25:26 [e]Dt 2:5 his sons went down to Egypt.[f]
[f]Ge 46:5-6 [5]"'Then I sent Moses and Aaron,[g]
24:5 and I afflicted the Egyptians by what
[g]Ex 3:10 I did there, and I brought you out.
[6]When I brought your fathers out of
Egypt, you came to the sea, and the
24:6 Egyptians pursued them with chariots
[h]Ex 14:9 and horsemen[b][h] as far as the Red Sea.[c]
[7]But they cried to the LORD for help,
24:7 and he put darkness[i] between you and
[i]Ex 14:20 the Egyptians; he brought the sea over
[j]Ex 14:28 [k]Dt 1:46 them and covered them.[j] You saw with
your own eyes what I did to the Egyptians. Then you lived in the desert for a
long time.[k]
[8]"'I brought you to the land of the
Amorites who lived east of the Jordan.
They fought against you, but I gave
them into your hands. I destroyed them
from before you, and you took posses- 24:8
sion of their land.[l] [9]When Balak son of [l]Nu 21:31
Zippor,[m] the king of Moab, prepared to 24:9
fight against Israel, he sent for Balaam [m]Nu 22:2
son of Beor to put a curse on you.[n] [n]Nu 22:6
[10]But I would not listen to Balaam, so 24:10
he blessed you[o] again and again, and I [o]Nu 23:11; Dt 23:5
delivered you out of his hand. 24:11
[11]"'Then you crossed the Jordan[p] [p]Jos 3:16-17
and came to Jericho.[q] The citizens of Jer- [q]Jos 6:1
icho fought against you, as did also the [r]Ex 23:23; Dt 7:1
Amorites, Perizzites, Canaanites, Hittites, Girgashites, Hivites and Jebusites,
but I gave them into your hands.[r] [12]I
sent the hornet[s] ahead of you, which 24:12 [s]Ex 23:28; Dt 7:20; Ps 44:3,6-7
drove them out before you—also the
two Amorite kings. You did not do it
with your own sword and bow. [13]So I
gave you a land on which you did not
toil and cities you did not build; and
you live in them and eat from vineyards and olive groves that you did not
plant.'[t] 24:13
[14]"Now fear the LORD and serve him [t]Dt 6:10-11
with all faithfulness.[u] Throw away the 24:14
gods[v] your forefathers worshiped be- [u]Dt 10:12; 18:13; 1Sa 12:24; 2Co 1:12
yond the River and in Egypt,[w] and serve [v]ver 23
the LORD. [15]But if serving the LORD [w]Eze 23:3
seems undesirable to you, then choose
for yourselves this day whom you will
serve, whether the gods your forefathers
served beyond the River, or the gods of 24:15
the Amorites,[x] in whose land you are [x]Jdg 6:10; Ru 1:15
living. But as for me and my house- [y]Ru 1:16; 1Ki 18:21
hold, we will serve the LORD."[y]

SELF-CONTROL

THE WELCOME GUEST

Joshua 24:15

God holds the right to be the only altarpiece of your home. Lead your family to adore the Lord! Your home will change! Your country, also. Nations learn righteousness one godly family at a time.

[16]Then the people answered, "Far be
it from us to forsake the LORD to serve
other gods! [17]It was the LORD our God
himself who brought us and our fathers
up out of Egypt, from that land of slavery, and performed those great signs be-

[a]2 That is, the Euphrates; also in verses 3, 14 and 15 [b]6 Or *charioteers* [c]6 Hebrew *Yam Suph*; that is, Sea of Reeds

fore our eyes. He protected us on our entire journey and among all the nations through which we traveled. 18 And the LORD drove out before us all the nations, including the Amorites, who lived in the land. We too will serve the LORD, because he is our God."

19 Joshua said to the people, "You are not able to serve the LORD. He is a holy God;[z] he is a jealous God.[a] He will not forgive your rebellion[b] and your sins. 20 If you forsake the LORD[c] and serve foreign gods, he will turn[d] and bring disaster on you and make an end of you,[e] after he has been good to you."

21 But the people said to Joshua, "No! We will serve the LORD."

22 Then Joshua said, "You are witnesses against yourselves that you have chosen[f] to serve the LORD."

"Yes, we are witnesses," they replied.

23 "Now then," said Joshua, "throw away the foreign gods[g] that are among you and yield your hearts[h] to the LORD, the God of Israel."

24 And the people said to Joshua, "We will serve the LORD our God and obey him."[i]

25 On that day Joshua made a covenant[j] for the people, and there at Shechem he drew up for them decrees and laws.[k] 26 And Joshua recorded these things in the Book of the Law of God.[l] Then he took a large stone[m] and set it up there under the oak near the holy place of the LORD.

27 "See!" he said to all the people. "This stone will be a witness[n] against us. It has heard all the words the LORD has said to us. It will be a witness against you if you are untrue to your God."

24:19 [z]Lev 19:2; 20:26 [a]Ex 20:5 [b]Ex 23:21
24:20 [c]1Ch 28:9,20 [d]Ac 7:42 [e]Jos 23:15
24:22 [f]Ps 119:30, 173
24:23 [g]ver 14 [h]1Ki 8:58; Ps 119:36; 141:4
24:24 [i]Ex 19:8; 24:3,7; Dt 5:27
24:25 [j]Ex 24:8 [k]Ex 15:25
24:26 [l]Dt 31:24 [m]Ge 28:18

Buried in the Promised Land

28 Then Joshua sent the people away, each to his own inheritance.

29 After these things, Joshua son of Nun, the servant of the LORD, died at the age of a hundred and ten.[o] 30 And they buried him in the land of his inheritance, at Timnath Serah[a][p] in the hill country of Ephraim, north of Mount Gaash.

31 Israel served the LORD throughout the lifetime of Joshua and of the elders[q] who outlived him and who had experienced everything the LORD had done for Israel.

32 And Joseph's bones, which the Israelites had brought up from Egypt,[r] were buried at Shechem in the tract of land[s] that Jacob bought for a hundred pieces of silver[b] from the sons of Hamor, the father of Shechem. This became the inheritance of Joseph's descendants.

33 And Eleazar son of Aaron died[t] and was buried at Gibeah, which had been allotted to his son Phinehas[u] in the hill country of Ephraim.

[a]*30* Also known as *Timnath Heres* (see Judges 2:9)
[b]*32* Hebrew *hundred kesitahs*; a kesitah was a unit of money of unknown weight and value.

24:27 [n]Jos 22:27
24:29 [o]Jdg 2:8
24:30 [p]Jos 19:50
24:31 [q]Jdg 2:7
24:32 [r]Ge 50:25; Ex 13:19 [s]Ge 33:19; Jn 4:5; Ac 7:16
24:33 [t]Jos 22:13 [u]Ex 6:25

JUDGES

AUTHORSHIP AND DATE

Possibly Samuel

The exact date of the writing is unknown.

KEY THEMES

The book of Judges is a cyclical tale of people falling into sin as they fell away from God. The cycle ran in this form: Israel cried out to God at a time of national crisis, and God would send a judge to deliver them. Following their deliverance, the people seemed to live morally for a while, but then they would fall into sin and apostasy again. The judges sent by God saved Israel during a time when Israel had no king and was a loose confederacy of tribes with no real interlocking military system. The time of the judges was a time of wickedness, a time when "everyone did as he saw fit" (17:6).

FRUIT OF THE SPIRIT IN JUDGES

Love: Israel constantly offended the true love of God by serving idols. Idolatry in the Scriptures is often compared to adultery. As adultery is human unfaithfulness (one person being unfaithful to another), so idolatry is spiritual unfaithfulness (one person being unfaithful to God by choosing to serve other gods). This blasphemy against God's love is expressed many times in the book of Judges, but this single passage makes the point: "Again the Israelites did evil in the eyes of the LORD. They served the Baals and the Ashtoreths, and the gods of Aram, the gods of Sidon, the gods of Moab, the gods of the Ammonites and the gods of the Philistines" (10:6).

Joy: Joy is hard to find in the book of Judges. But Deborah and Barak managed to find joy, and they sang a song of thanksgiving to the God who had helped them defeat their enemies: "When the princes in Israel take the lead, when the people willingly offer themselves—praise the LORD! Hear this, you kings! Listen, you rulers! I will sing to the LORD, I will sing; I will make music to the LORD, the God of Israel" (5:2–3).

Goodness: Goodness, like love, is only seen in Judges through its antithesis: ingratitude. "No sooner had Gideon died than the Israelites again prostituted themselves to the Baals . . . They also failed to show kindness to the family of Jerub-Baal (that is, Gideon) for all the good things he had done for them" (8:33,35). Goodness and gratitude are never qualities inspired by false gods.

Faithfulness: Jephthah's daughter, like Isaac on Mount Moriah, played a faithful and passive role in honoring her father's pledge to the Lord. Her father had rashly made a vow to God: If God would give him victory, he would offer the first thing that ran out of his house to meet him when he returned from the war. Perhaps he supposed that it would be an animal, but it was his daughter. Jephthah kept his promise, but he could never have done so without his daughter's compliant faithfulness to his vow. " 'My father,' she replied, 'you have given your word to the LORD. Do to me just as you promised' " (11:36).

Israel Fights the Remaining Canaanites

1:1 [a]Jos 24:29 1 After the death[a] of Joshua, the Isra-
[b]Nu 27:21 elites asked the LORD, “Who will
[c]ver 27; be the first[b] to go up and fight for us
Jdg 3:1-6 against the Canaanites?[c]”
1:2 [d]Ge 49:8 2The LORD answered, “Judah[d] is to
[e]ver 4; go; I have given the land into their
Jdg 3:28 hands.[e]”
3Then the men of Judah said to the
Simeonites their brothers, “Come up
with us into the territory allotted to us,
to fight against the Canaanites. We in
turn will go with you into yours.” So
1:3 [f]ver 17 the Simeonites[f] went with them.
4When Judah attacked, the LORD
1:4 [g]Ge 13:7; gave the Canaanites and Perizzites[g] into
Jos 3:10 their hands and they struck down ten
[h]1Sa 11:8 thousand men at Bezek.[h] 5It was there
that they found Adoni-Bezek and
fought against him, putting to rout
the Canaanites and Perizzites. 6Adoni-
Bezek fled, but they chased him and
caught him, and cut off his thumbs and
big toes.
7Then Adoni-Bezek said, “Seventy
kings with their thumbs and big toes
cut off have picked up scraps under my
1:7 [i]Lev 24:19 table. Now God has paid me back[i] for
what I did to them.” They brought him
to Jerusalem, and he died there.
8The men of Judah attacked Jerusa-
1:8 [j]ver 21; lem[j] also and took it. They put the city
Jos 15:63 to the sword and set it on fire.
9After that, the men of Judah went
down to fight against the Canaanites
1:9 [k]Nu 13:17 living in the hill country,[k] the Negev[l]
[l]Nu 21:1 and the western foothills. 10They advanced against the Canaanites living
1:10 [m]Ge 13:18 in Hebron[m] (formerly called Kiriath
[n]Ge 35:27 Arba[n]) and defeated Sheshai, Ahiman
[o]Jos 15:14 and Talmai.[o]
11From there they advanced against
1:11 [p]Jos 15:15 the people living in Debir[p] (formerly
called Kiriath Sepher). 12And Caleb
said, “I will give my daughter Acsah in
marriage to the man who attacks and
captures Kiriath Sepher.” 13Othniel son
of Kenaz, Caleb’s younger brother, took
it; so Caleb gave his daughter Acsah to
him in marriage.
14One day when she came to Othniel, she urged him[a] to ask her father for
a field. When she got off her donkey,
Caleb asked her, “What can I do for
you?”
15She replied, “Do me a special favor. Since you have given me land in
the Negev, give me also springs of water.” Then Caleb gave her the upper
and lower springs.
16The descendants of Moses’ father-
in-law,[q] the Kenite,[r] went up from the 1:16 [q]Nu 10:29
City of Palms[b][s] with the men of Judah [r]Ge 15:19;
to live among the people of the Desert Jdg 4:11
of Judah in the Negev near Arad.[t] [s]Dt 34:3; Jdg 3:13 [t]Nu 21:1
17Then the men of Judah went with
the Simeonites[u] their brothers and at- 1:17 [u]ver 3
tacked the Canaanites living in Ze-

[a]*14* Hebrew; Septuagint and Vulgate *Othniel, he urged her* [b]*16* That is, Jericho

DAY 2 TWO

▸ Kindness and the Purpose of God in My Life

Judges 1:12–15

Caleb had received an inheritance in Canaan. Now he takes what he had received and passes it on to his daughter and son-in-law. How could Caleb be so kind and generous?

Caleb’s life is a study of faithfulness to God’s purposes in his life. His life was spared when all of his generation—except himself and Joshua—were condemned to die. He and Joshua together trusted God’s goodness and encouraged the people to take the land of Canaan (Numbers 14:1–9,24). God in turn promised to bless Caleb and give him part of the land. Now we see that promise being fulfilled. Caleb is given the entire area of Hebron (see Joshua 15:13).

How could one who had received so much ever be stingy? Caleb is faithful to God and trusted him, so when God blessed him, Caleb blessed others. Isn’t that the essence of the Golden Rule? When we are blessed, shouldn’t our immediate response be to share the benefits of God with those around us?

Caleb was practicing the Golden Rule hundreds of years before Jesus gave it form and words, and as a result, Caleb’s life became a witness to the ultimate triumph of kindness. When we find that God has blessed our faithfulness, we can share with others and know that we will not run out of the blessings of God.

To begin a study on the topic of Kindness, Always Applying the Golden Rule, turn to the home page on page 1141.

phath, and they totally destroyed[a] the
1:17 [v]Nu 21:3 city. Therefore it was called Hormah.[b][v]
18The men of Judah also took[c] Gaza,[w]
1:18 [w]Jos 11:22 Ashkelon and Ekron—each city with
its territory.
1:19 [x]ver 2 19The LORD was with[x] the men of
[y]Jos 17:16 Judah. They took possession of the hill
country, but they were unable to drive
the people from the plains, because
they had iron chariots.[y] 20As Moses had
promised, Hebron[z] was given to Ca-
1:20 [z]Jos 14:9; leb, who drove from it the three sons
15:13-14 of Anak.[a] 21The Benjamites, however,
[a]ver 10; failed[b] to dislodge the Jebusites, who
Jos 14:13 were living in Jerusalem;[c] to this day
1:21 [b]Jos 15:63 the Jebusites live there with the Benja-
[c]ver 8 mites.
22Now the house of Joseph attacked
Bethel, and the LORD was with them.
23When they sent men to spy out Beth-
1:23 el (formerly called Luz),[d] 24the spies saw
[d]Ge 28:19 a man coming out of the city and they
said to him, "Show us how to get into
the city and we will see that you are
treated well."[e] 25So he showed them,
1:24 and they put the city to the sword but
[e]Jos 2:12,14 spared[f] the man and his whole family.
1:25 26He then went to the land of the Hit-
[f]Jos 6:25 tites, where he built a city and called it
Luz, which is its name to this day.

FAITHFULNESS

THE PLASTER GODS

Judges 1:28

Israel's nemesis was its kindness to idolaters. In letting idolaters live, Israel fell heir to their addictions. There's a contagion in idolatry. The love of golden calves spreads like a typhus of the heart. It takes a city made for God and lines the streets with Baals.

27But Manasseh did not drive out the
people of Beth Shan or Taanach or Dor
1:27 [g]Jos 17:11 or Ibleam[g] or Megiddo and their sur-
[h]ver 1 rounding settlements, for the Canaanites[h] were determined to live in that
land. 28When Israel became strong, they
pressed the Canaanites into forced labor
but never drove them out completely.
29Nor did Ephraim drive out the Ca-
1:29 [i]1Ki 9:16 naanites living in Gezer,[i] but the Ca-
[j]Jos 16:10 naanites continued to live there among
them.[j] 30Neither did Zebulun drive out
the Canaanites living in Kitron or Na-
halol, who remained among them; but
they did subject them to forced labor.
31Nor did Asher drive out those living
in Acco or Sidon or Ahlab or Aczib[k] or 1:31
Helbah or Aphek or Rehob, 32and be- [k]Jdg 10:6
cause of this the people of Asher lived
among the Canaanite inhabitants of the
land. 33Neither did Naphtali drive out
those living in Beth Shemesh or Beth
Anath[l]; but the Naphtalites too lived 1:33
among the Canaanite inhabitants of the [l]Jos 19:38
land, and those living in Beth Shemesh
and Beth Anath became forced laborers for them. 34The Amorites[m] confined
the Danites to the hill country, not al- 1:34
lowing them to come down into the [m]Ex 3:17
plain. 35And the Amorites were determined also to hold out in Mount Heres,
Aijalon[n] and Shaalbim, but when the 1:35
power of the house of Joseph increased, [n]Jos 19:42
they too were pressed into forced labor.
36The boundary of the Amorites was
from Scorpion[d] Pass[o] to Sela and be- 1:36
yond. [o]Jos 15:3

The Angel of the LORD at Bokim

2 The angel of the LORD[p] went up 2:1
from Gilgal to Bokim[q] and said, "I [p]Jdg 6:11 [q]ver 5
brought you up out of Egypt[r] and led [r]Ex 20:2 [s]Ge 17:8
you into the land that I swore to give [t]Lev 26:42-44;
to your forefathers.[s] I said, 'I will never Dt 7:9
break my covenant with you,[t] 2and you 2:2
shall not make a covenant with the peo- [u]Ex 23:32;
ple of this land,[u] but you shall break 34:12; Dt 7:2
down their altars.[v]' Yet you have dis- [v]Ex 34:13
obeyed me. Why have you done this? 2:3
3Now therefore I tell you that I will not [w]Jos 23:13 [x]Nu 33:55
drive them out before you;[w] they will [y]Dt 7:16;
be ⌞thorns⌟[x] in your sides and their gods Jdg 3:6; Ps 106:36
will be a snare[y] to you."
4When the angel of the LORD had
spoken these things to all the Israelites,
the people wept aloud, 5and they called
that place Bokim.[e] There they offered
sacrifices to the LORD.

Disobedience and Defeat

6After Joshua had dismissed the Israelites, they went to take possession of
the land, each to his own inheritance.
7The people served the LORD throughout the lifetime of Joshua and of the
elders who outlived him and who had

[a] *17* The Hebrew term refers to the irrevocable giving over of things or persons to the LORD, often by totally destroying them. [b] *17 Hormah* means *destruction.* [c] *18* Hebrew; Septuagint *Judah did not take* [d] *36* Hebrew *Akrabbim* [e] *5 Bokim* means *weepers.*

seen all the great things the LORD had
done for Israel.
8Joshua son of Nun, the servant of
the LORD, died at the age of a hundred and ten. 9And they buried him in
the land of his inheritance, at Timnath
2:9 Heres[a][z] in the hill country of Ephraim,
zJos 19:50 north of Mount Gaash.
10After that whole generation had
been gathered to their fathers, another
generation grew up, who knew neither
2:10 the LORD nor what he had done for
aEx 5:2; Israel.[a] 11Then the Israelites did evil
1Sa 2:12; 1Ch 28:9; in the eyes of the LORD[b] and served
Gal 4:8 the Baals.[c] 12They forsook the LORD,
2:11 the God of their fathers, who had
bJdg 3:12; 4:1; 6:1; 10:6 brought them out of Egypt. They fol-
cJdg 3:7; 8:33 lowed and worshiped various gods[d] of
2:12 the peoples around them.[e] They pro-
dPs 106:36 voked the LORD to anger 13because they
eDt 31:16; Jdg 10:6 forsook him and served Baal and the
2:13 Ashtoreths.[f] 14In his anger[g] against Isra-
fJdg 10:6 el the LORD handed them over[h] to raid-
2:14 ers who plundered them. He sold them[i]
gDt 31:17 to their enemies all around, whom they
hPs 106:41 iDt 32:30; were no longer able to resist.[j] 15When-
Jdg 3:8 jDt 28:25 ever Israel went out to fight, the hand
of the LORD was against them to de-
feat them, just as he had sworn to them.
They were in great distress.
2:16 kAc 13:20 16Then the LORD raised up judges,[b][k]
lPs 106:43 who saved[l] them out of the hands of
these raiders. 17Yet they would not lis-
2:17 ten to their judges but prostituted[m]
mEx 34:15 themselves to other gods and worshiped
nver 7 them. Unlike their fathers, they quickly
turned from the way in which their fathers had walked, the way of obedience
to the LORD's commands.[n] 18When-
ever the LORD raised up a judge for
them, he was with the judge and saved
them out of the hands of their enemies as long as the judge lived; for
2:18 oDt 32:36; the LORD had compassion[o] on them
Jos 1:5 as they groaned[p] under those who op-
pPs 106:44 pressed and afflicted them. 19But when
the judge died, the people returned to
2:19 qJdg 3:12 ways even more corrupt[q] than those of
rJdg 4:1; 8:33 their fathers, following other gods and
serving and worshiping them.[r] They refused to give up their evil practices and
stubborn ways.
20Therefore the LORD was very an-
2:20 sver 14; gry[s] with Israel and said, "Because this
Jos 23:16 nation has violated the covenant that I
laid down for their forefathers and has
2:21 not listened to me, 21I will no longer
tJos 23:13 drive out[t] before them any of the nations Joshua left when he died. 22I will 2:22
use them to test[u] Israel and see wheth- uDt 8:2,16;
er they will keep the way of the LORD Jdg 3:1,14
and walk in it as their forefathers did."
23The LORD had allowed those nations
to remain; he did not drive them out at
once by giving them into the hands of
Joshua.

3 These are the nations the LORD
left to test[v] all those Israelites who 3:1
had not experienced any of the wars in vJdg 2:21-22
Canaan 2(he did this only to teach warfare to the descendants of the Israelites
who had not had previous battle expe- 3:3
rience): 3the five[w] rulers of the Philis- wJos 13:3
tines, all the Canaanites, the Sidonians,
and the Hivites living in the Lebanon
mountains from Mount Baal Hermon
to Lebo[c] Hamath. 4They were left to
test[x] the Israelites to see whether they 3:4 xDt 8:2;
would obey the LORD's commands, Jdg 2:22
which he had given their forefathers
through Moses.
5The Israelites lived[y] among the Canaanites, Hittites, Amorites, Perizzites, 3:5 yPs 106:35
Hivites and Jebusites. 6They took their 3:6
daughters in marriage and gave their zEx 34:16; Dt
own daughters to their sons, and served 7:3-4
their gods.[z]

Othniel

7The Israelites did evil in the eyes
of the LORD; they forgot the LORD[a] 3:7 aDt 4:9
their God and served the Baals and bEx 34:13;
the Asherahs.[b] 8The anger of the LORD Jdg 2:11,13
burned against Israel so that he sold[c]
them into the hands of Cushan- 3:8 cJdg 2:14
Rishathaim king of Aram Naharaim,[d]
to whom the Israelites were subject for
eight years. 9But when they cried out[d] 3:9 dver 15;
to the LORD, he raised up for them a Jdg 6:6,7; 10:10;
deliverer, Othniel[e] son of Kenaz, Caleb's Ps 106:44
younger brother, who saved them. 10The eJdg 1:13
Spirit of the LORD came upon him,[f] 3:10 fNu 11:25,29;
so that he became Israel's judge[e] and 24:2;
went to war. The LORD gave Cushan- Jdg 6:34;
Rishathaim king of Aram into the hands 11:29; 13:25;
of Othniel, who overpowered him. 11So 14:6,19; 1Sa 11:6
the land had peace for forty years, until
Othniel son of Kenaz died.

Ehud

12Once again the Israelites did evil 3:12
in the eyes of the LORD,[g] and because gJdg 2:11,14

[a] 9 Also known as *Timnath Serah* (see Joshua 19:50 and 24:30) [b] 16 Or *leaders;* similarly in verses 17-19 [c] 3 Or *to the entrance to* [d] 8 That is, Northwest Mesopotamia [e] 10 Or *leader*

they did this evil the LORD gave Eg-
3:12 [h]1Sa 12:9 lon king of Moab[h] power over Israel.
13Getting the Ammonites and Amalek-
ites to join him, Eglon came and attacked Israel, and they took possession
3:13 [i]Jdg 1:16 of the City of Palms.[a][i] 14The Israelites
were subject to Eglon king of Moab for
eighteen years.
15Again the Israelites cried out to
the LORD, and he gave them a deliv-
3:15 [j]ver 9; Ps 78:34; 107:13 erer[j]—Ehud, a left-handed man, the
son of Gera the Benjamite. The Isra-
elites sent him with tribute to Eglon
king of Moab. 16Now Ehud had made
a double-edged sword about a foot and
a half[b] long, which he strapped to his
right thigh under his clothing. 17He
presented the tribute to Eglon king of
3:17 [k]ver 12 Moab, who was a very fat man.[k] 18After
Ehud had presented the tribute, he sent
on their way the men who had carried
it. 19At the idols[c] near Gilgal he himself
turned back and said, "I have a secret
message for you, O king."
The king said, "Quiet!" And all his
attendants left him.
20Ehud then approached him while
he was sitting alone in the upper room
of his summer palace[d] and said, "I have
a message from God for you." As the
king rose from his seat, 21Ehud reached
with his left hand, drew the sword from
his right thigh and plunged it into the
king's belly. 22Even the handle sank in
after the blade, which came out his
back. Ehud did not pull the sword out,
and the fat closed in over it. 23Then
Ehud went out to the porch[e]; he shut
the doors of the upper room behind
him and locked them.
24After he had gone, the servants
came and found the doors of the upper
room locked. They said, "He must be
3:24 [l]1Sa 24:3 relieving himself[l] in the inner room of
the house." 25They waited to the point
3:25 [m]2Ki 2:17; 8:11 of embarrassment,[m] but when he did
not open the doors of the room, they
took a key and unlocked them. There
they saw their lord fallen to the floor,
dead.
26While they waited, Ehud got away.
He passed by the idols and escaped
to Seirah. 27When he arrived there, he
3:27 [n]Jdg 6:34; 1Sa 13:3 blew a trumpet[n] in the hill country of
Ephraim, and the Israelites went down
with him from the hills, with him leading them.
28"Follow me," he ordered, "for the
LORD has given Moab, your enemy,
into your hands.[o]" So they followed 3:28 [o]Jdg 7:9,15 [p]Jos 2:7; Jdg 7:24; 12:5
him down and, taking possession of the
fords of the Jordan[p] that led to Moab,
they allowed no one to cross over. 29At
that time they struck down about ten
thousand Moabites, all vigorous and
strong; not a man escaped. 30That day
Moab was made subject to Israel, and
the land had peace[q] for eighty years. 3:30 [q]ver 11

Shamgar

31After Ehud came Shamgar son of
Anath,[r] who struck down six hundred[s] 3:31 [r]Jdg 5:6 [s]Jos 23:10
Philistines with an oxgoad. He too saved
Israel.

▸ FAITHFULNESS

HONORABLE MENTION

Judges 3:31

Here's to Shamgar, who found a small place in the world's best book! He was a minor judge with major clout. His name is all but lost in the many pages of the Bible, for he holds but one verse among thousands. But God never overlooks uncompromising souls.

Deborah

4 After Ehud died, the Israelites once
again did evil[t] in the eyes of the 4:1 [t]Jdg 2:19
LORD. 2So the LORD sold them into
the hands of Jabin, a king of Canaan,
who reigned in Hazor.[u] The command- 4:2 [u]Jos 11:1
er of his army was Sisera,[v] who lived [v]ver 13,16; 1Sa 12:9; Ps 83:9
in Harosheth Haggoyim. 3Because he
had nine hundred iron chariots[w] and 4:3 [w]Jdg 1:19
had cruelly oppressed[x] the Israelites for [x]Ps 106:42
twenty years, they cried to the LORD
for help.
4Deborah, a prophetess, the wife of
Lappidoth, was leading[f] Israel at that
time. 5She held court under the Palm of
Deborah between Ramah and Bethel[y] 4:5 [y]Ge 35:8
in the hill country of Ephraim, and the
Israelites came to her to have their disputes decided. 6She sent for Barak son
of Abinoam[z] from Kedesh in Naphtali 4:6 [z]Heb 11:32
and said to him, "The LORD, the God
of Israel, commands you: 'Go, take with
you ten thousand men of Naphtali and

[a]13 That is, Jericho [b]16 Hebrew *a cubit* (about 0.5 meter) [c]19 Or *the stone quarries*; also in verse 26 [d]20 The meaning of the Hebrew for this phrase is uncertain. [e]23 The meaning of the Hebrew for this word is uncertain. [f]4 Traditionally *judging*

Zebulun and lead the way to Mount
Tabor. 7I will lure Sisera, the commander of Jabin's army, with his chariots and
4:7 [a]Ps 83:9 his troops to the Kishon River[a] and give
him into your hands.'"
8Barak said to her, "If you go with
me, I will go; but if you don't go with
me, I won't go."
9"Very well," Deborah said, "I will go
with you. But because of the way you
are going about this,[a] the honor will
not be yours, for the LORD will hand
4:9 [b]ver 21; Jdg 2:14 Sisera over to a woman." So Deborah
went with Barak to Kedesh,[b] 10where
4:10 [c]ver 14; Jdg 5:15,18 he summoned[c] Zebulun and Naphtali.
Ten thousand men followed him, and
Deborah also went with him.
11Now Heber the Kenite had left
4:11 [d]Jdg 1:16 the other Kenites,[d] the descendants of
Hobab,[e] Moses' brother-in-law,[b] and 4:11 [e]Nu 10:29
pitched his tent by the great tree in Za- [f]Jos 19:33
anannim[f] near Kedesh.
12When they told Sisera that Barak
son of Abinoam had gone up to Mount
Tabor, 13Sisera gathered together his
nine hundred iron chariots[g] and all the 4:13 [g]ver 3
men with him, from Harosheth Hag-
goyim to the Kishon River.
14Then Deborah said to Barak, "Go!
This is the day the LORD has given Sis- 4:14
era into your hands. Has not the LORD [h]Dt 9:3;
gone ahead[h] of you?" So Barak went 2Sa 5:24; Ps 68:7
down Mount Tabor, followed by ten
thousand men. 15At Barak's advance, 4:15 [i]Jos 10:10;
the LORD routed[i] Sisera and all his Ps 83:9-10

[a]9 Or *But on the expedition you are undertaking*
[b]11 Or *father-in-law*

DEBORAH

Faithfulness, the Forerunner of Praise (4:1–10)

When godly leaders were hard to find in Israel, Deborah accepted the call of God to lead the people with wisdom and trust in his guidance. Deborah judged the nation of Israel with a heart that followed God. She listened to God's direction, and when difficulties arose, she remained faithful to her calling.

Deborah judged during the time when the Israelites were under the power of the Canaanites. The commander of the Canaanite army, Sisera, was renowned for his cruelty and evil actions. God intended to free the Israelites from this oppressive regime and called Deborah to prepare someone to lead the Israelite attack. Deborah obeyed God's command and called Barak: "The LORD, the God of Israel, commands you: 'Go, take with you ten thousand men of Naphtali and Zebulun and lead the way to Mount Tabor. I will lure Sisera, the commander of Jabin's army, with his chariots and his troops to the Kishon River and give him into your hands'" (Judges 4:6–7). God's words were clear—he would give the victory to Israel. But Barak was insecure and failed to trust God's promises. He requested Deborah's presence at the battle: "If you go with me, I will go; but if you don't go with me, I won't go" (v. 8).

Deborah probably didn't want to go to battle. It would mean leaving her family and the comforts of home. Army camp probably wouldn't be comfortable for a civilian, especially a female civilian with no battle experience. But Deborah didn't let setbacks affect her faith in God. She remained faithful to her calling as God's prophetess, and she set out to accompany the army into battle.

One result of faithfulness is praise. The battle was won, just as God had promised. So Deborah and Barak sang a song of high praise after the battle, once more affirming that faithfulness to one's calling furnishes both the stamina and the joy for every crisis.

When the princes in Israel take the lead,
when the people willingly offer
themselves—
praise the LORD!
Hear this, you kings! Listen, you rulers!
I will sing to the LORD, I will sing;
I will make music to the LORD, the
God of Israel.

(5:2–3)

Faithfulness leads to song. It brings joy and peace to those who follow the call of God.

chariots and army by the sword, and Sisera abandoned his chariot and fled on foot. 16But Barak pursued the chariots and army as far as Harosheth Haggoyim. All the troops of Sisera fell by the sword; not a man was left.[j]

4:16 [j]Ps 83:9

17Sisera, however, fled on foot to the tent of Jael, the wife of Heber the Kenite, because there were friendly relations between Jabin king of Hazor and the clan of Heber the Kenite.

18Jael went out to meet Sisera and

DAY 4 FOUR

▸ PATIENCE AND MY SERVICE TO OTHERS

Judges 5:1–2

Deborah and Barak sing a long anthem in celebration of the victory over their enemies, but the first words of the song reflect the joy that emanates from seeing a whole nation wait on God:

> **When the princes in Israel take the lead,**
> **when the people willingly offer**
> **themselves—**
> **praise the LORD!**
> **(Judges 5:2)**

God's leadership in Israel was clearly dependent upon patience. Deborah was instructed by God to summon a leader to wage war against the army of Sisera. But that leader, Barak, was unwilling to act on his own. Engaging in battle with the mighty armies of Sisera was a daunting prospect. But Deborah did not give up her charge. She accompanied Barak to war, encouraging him and sharing God's wisdom with the army leader. Through her patient obedience to God's leading, Deborah in turn led others.

The details of the victorious campaign show the result of the patience that operated in Deborah's life and the patience and obedience in the lives of those who followed her instructions from God. So the promise of Deborah's song is right, "When the princes in Israel take the lead, when the people willingly offer themselves," and when all of them wait on God, victory and blessing always ensue.

To begin a study on the topic of Patience, the Slowly Acquired Virtue, turn to the home page on page 565.

said to him, "Come, my lord, come right in. Don't be afraid." So he entered her tent, and she put a covering over him.

19"I'm thirsty," he said. "Please give me some water." She opened a skin of milk,[k] gave him a drink, and covered him up.

4:19 [k]Jdg 5:25

20"Stand in the doorway of the tent," he told her. "If someone comes by and asks you, 'Is anyone here?' say 'No.' "

21But Jael, Heber's wife, picked up a tent peg and a hammer and went quietly to him while he lay fast asleep, exhausted. She drove the peg through his temple into the ground, and he died.[l]

4:21 [l]Jdg 5:26

22Barak came by in pursuit of Sisera, and Jael went out to meet him. "Come," she said, "I will show you the man you're looking for." So he went in with her, and there lay Sisera with the tent peg through his temple—dead.

23On that day God subdued[m] Jabin, the Canaanite king, before the Israelites. 24And the hand of the Israelites grew stronger and stronger against Jabin, the Canaanite king, until they destroyed him.

4:23 [m]Ne 9:24; Ps 18:47

The Song of Deborah

5 On that day Deborah and Barak son of Abinoam sang this song:[n]

5:1 [n]Ex 15:1

2"When the princes in Israel take the lead,
when the people willingly offer[o]
themselves—
praise the LORD![p]

5:2 [o]2Ch 17:16; Ps 110:3 [p]ver 9

3"Hear this, you kings! Listen, you rulers!
I will sing to[a] the LORD, I will sing;
I will make music to[b] the LORD,
the God of Israel.[q]

5:3 [q]Ps 27:6

4"O LORD, when you went out from Seir,[r]
when you marched from the land of Edom,
the earth shook, the heavens poured,
the clouds poured down water.[s]

5:4 [r]Dt 33:2 [s]Ps 68:8

5The mountains quaked[t] before the LORD, the One of Sinai,
before the LORD, the God of Israel.

5:5 [t]Ex 19:18; Ps 68:8; 97:5; Isa 64:3

[a]3 Or *of* [b]3 Or / *with song I will praise*

6 “In the days of Shamgar son of
Anath,[u]
in the days of Jael,[v] the roads[w]
were abandoned;
travelers took to winding paths.

5:6 [u]Jdg 3:31 [v]Jdg 4:17 [w]Isa 33:8

7 Village life[a] in Israel ceased,
ceased until I,[b] Deborah, arose,
arose a mother in Israel.
8 When they chose new gods,[x]
war came to the city gates,
and not a shield or spear was seen
among forty thousand in Israel.

5:8 [x]Dt 32:17

9 My heart is with Israel's princes,
with the willing volunteers[y]
among the people.
Praise the LORD!

5:9 [y]ver 2

10 “You who ride on white donkeys,[z]
sitting on your saddle blankets,
and you who walk along the road,
consider 11 the voice of the singers[c] at
the watering places.
They recite the righteous acts[a] of
the LORD,
the righteous acts of his warriors[d]
in Israel.

5:10 [z]Jdg 10:4; 12:14

5:11 [a]1Sa 12:7; Mic 6:5 [b]ver 8

“Then the people of the LORD
went down to the city gates.[b]
12 ‘Wake up,[c] wake up, Deborah!
Wake up, wake up, break out in
song!
Arise, O Barak!
Take captive your captives,[d] O son
of Abinoam.’

5:12 [c]Ps 57:8 [d]Ps 68:18; Eph 4:8

13 “Then the men who were left
came down to the nobles;
the people of the LORD
came to me with the mighty.
14 Some came from Ephraim, whose
roots were in Amalek;[e]
Benjamin was with the people
who followed you.
From Makir captains came down,
from Zebulun those who bear a
commander's staff.

5:14 [e]Jdg 3:13

15 The princes of Issachar were with
Deborah;[f]
yes, Issachar was with Barak,
rushing after him into the valley.
In the districts of Reuben
there was much searching of heart.

5:15 [f]Jdg 4:10

16 Why did you stay among the
campfires[e]
to hear the whistling for the
flocks?[g]
In the districts of Reuben
there was much searching of heart.

5:16 [g]Nu 32:1

17 Gilead stayed beyond the Jordan.
And Dan, why did he linger by
the ships?
Asher remained on the coast[h]
and stayed in his coves.

5:17 [h]Jos 19:29

18 The people of Zebulun risked their
very lives;
so did Naphtali on the heights of
the field.[i]

5:18 [i]Jdg 4:6,10

19 “Kings came[j], they fought;
the kings of Canaan fought
at Taanach by the waters of
Megiddo,[k]
but they carried off no silver, no
plunder.[l]

5:19 [j]Jos 11:5; Jdg 4:13 [k]Jdg 1:27 [l]ver 30

20 From the heavens[m] the stars fought,
from their courses they fought
against Sisera.

5:20 [m]Jos 10:11

21 The river Kishon[n] swept them away,
the age-old river, the river
Kishon.
March on, my soul; be strong!

5:21 [n]Jdg 4:7

22 Then thundered the horses'
hoofs—
galloping, galloping go his mighty
steeds.
23 ‘Curse Meroz,’ said the angel of the
LORD.
‘Curse its people bitterly,
because they did not come to help
the LORD,
to help the LORD against the
mighty.’
24 “Most blessed of women be Jael,[o]
the wife of Heber the Kenite,
most blessed of tent-dwelling
women.

5:24 [o]Jdg 4:17

25 He asked for water, and she gave
him milk;[p]
in a bowl fit for nobles she
brought him curdled milk.

5:25 [p]Jdg 4:19

26 Her hand reached for the tent peg,
her right hand for the workman's
hammer.
She struck Sisera, she crushed his
head,
she shattered and pierced his
temple.[q]

5:26 [q]Jdg 4:21

27 At her feet he sank,
he fell; there he lay.
At her feet he sank, he fell;
where he sank, there he fell—
dead.

[a]7 Or *Warriors* [b]7 Or *you* [c]11 Or *archers*; the meaning of the Hebrew for this word is uncertain. [d]11 Or *villagers* [e]16 Or *saddlebags*

28"Through the window peered Sisera's
mother;
5:28 [r]Pr 7:6 behind the lattice she cried out,[r]
'Why is his chariot so long in
coming?
Why is the clatter of his chariots
delayed?'
29The wisest of her ladies answer her;
indeed, she keeps saying to herself,
30'Are they not finding and dividing
5:30 [s]Ex 15:9; 1Sa 30:24 the spoils:[s]
a girl or two for each man,
colorful garments as plunder for
Sisera,
colorful garments embroidered,
highly embroidered garments for
my neck—
all this as plunder?'

31"So may all your enemies perish,
O LORD!
But may they who love you be like
5:31 [t]2Sa 23:4; Ps 19:4; 89:36 [u]Jdg 3:11 the sun[t]
when it rises in its strength."

Then the land had peace[u] forty
years.

Gideon

6:1 [v]Jdg 2:11 [w]Nu 25:15-18; 31:1-3 6 Again the Israelites did evil in the
eyes of the LORD,[v] and for seven
years he gave them into the hands of
the Midianites.[w] 2Because the power
6:2 [x]1Sa 13:6; Isa 8:21 [y]Heb 11:38 of Midian was so oppressive,[x] the Israelites prepared shelters for themselves
in mountain clefts, caves and strongholds.[y] 3Whenever the Israelites planted
6:3 [z]Jdg 3:13 their crops, the Midianites, Amalekites[z]
and other eastern peoples invaded the
country. 4They camped on the land and
6:4 [a]Lev 26:16; Dt 28:30,51 ruined the crops[a] all the way to Gaza
and did not spare a living thing for Isra-
el, neither sheep nor cattle nor donkeys.
5They came up with their livestock and
6:5 [b]Jdg 7:12 [c]Jdg 8:10 their tents like swarms of locusts.[b] It
was impossible to count the men and
their camels;[c] they invaded the land to
ravage it. 6Midian so impoverished the
6:6 [d]Jdg 3:9 Israelites that they cried out[d] to the
LORD for help.
7When the Israelites cried to the
LORD because of Midian, 8he sent them
a prophet, who said, "This is what the
LORD, the God of Israel, says: I brought
6:8 [e]Jdg 2:1 you up out of Egypt,[e] out of the land of
slavery. 9I snatched you from the power
of Egypt and from the hand of all your
oppressors. I drove them from before
you and gave you their land.[f] 10I said to 6:9 [f]Ps 44:2
you, 'I am the LORD your God; do not
worship[g] the gods of the Amorites,[h] in 6:10 [g]2Ki 17:35 [h]Jer 10:2
whose land you live.' But you have not
listened to me."
11The angel of the LORD[i] came and 6:11 [i]Ge 16:7 [j]Jos 17:2 [k]Heb 11:32
sat down under the oak in Ophrah that
belonged to Joash the Abiezrite,[j] where
his son Gideon[k] was threshing wheat in
a winepress to keep it from the Midian-
ites. 12When the angel of the LORD ap- 6:12 [l]Jos 1:5; Jdg 13:3; Lk 1:11,28
peared to Gideon, he said, "The LORD
is with you,[l] mighty warrior."

PEACE

MIGHTY COWARDS

Judges 6:12

Gideon, hiding in fear, was called a mighty warrior. God touched the fear within this trembling servant and displaced the fragile tissue of his soul with granite.

The saints are those whom God surprised
By touching what was paralyzed
Until they conquered worlds with power
They never saw nor realized.

13"But sir," Gideon replied, "if the
LORD is with us, why has all this happened to us? Where are all his wonders
that our fathers told[m] us about when
they said, 'Did not the LORD bring us 6:13 [m]Ps 44:1 [n]2Ch 15:2
up out of Egypt?' But now the LORD
has abandoned[n] us and put us into the
hand of Midian."
14The LORD turned to him and said,
"Go in the strength you have[o] and save 6:14 [o]Heb 11:34
Israel out of Midian's hand. Am I not
sending you?"
15"But Lord,[a]" Gideon asked, "how
can I save Israel? My clan is the weakest
in Manasseh, and I am the least in my 6:15 [p]Ex 3:11; 1Sa 9:21
family.[p]"
16The LORD answered, "I will be
with you[q], and you will strike down all 6:16 [q]Ex 3:12; Jos 1:5
the Midianites together."
17Gideon replied, "If now I have
found favor in your eyes, give me a
sign[r] that it is really you talking to me. 6:17 [r]ver 36-37; Ge 24:14; Isa 38:7-8
18Please do not go away until I come
back and bring my offering and set it
before you."
And the LORD said, "I will wait until
you return."

[a]15 Or *sir*

19 Gideon went in, prepared a young
goat, and from an ephah[a] of flour he
made bread without yeast. Putting the
meat in a basket and its broth in a pot,
he brought them out and offered them
6:19 to him under the oak.[s]
[s]Ge 18:7-8 20 The angel of God said to him,
6:20 "Take the meat and the unleavened
[t]Jdg 13:19 bread, place them on this rock,[t] and
pour out the broth." And Gideon did
so. 21 With the tip of the staff that was
in his hand, the angel of the LORD
touched the meat and the unleavened
6:21 bread.[u] Fire flared from the rock, con-
[u]Lev 9:24 suming the meat and the bread. And
6:22 the angel of the LORD disappeared.
[v]Jdg 13:16,21 22 When Gideon realized[v] that it was the
[w]Ge 32:30; angel of the LORD, he exclaimed, "Ah,
Ex 33:20; Sovereign LORD! I have seen the angel
Jdg 13:22 of the LORD face to face!"[w]
23 But the LORD said to him, "Peace!
6:23 Do not be afraid.[x] You are not going
[x]Da 10:19 to die."
24 So Gideon built an altar to the
6:24 [y]Ge 22:14 LORD there and called[y] it The LORD is
[z]Jdg 8:32 Peace. To this day it stands in Ophrah[z]
of the Abiezrites.
25 That same night the LORD said to
him, "Take the second bull from your
father's herd, the one seven years old.[b]
Tear down your father's altar to Baal
6:25 and cut down the Asherah pole[c][a] be-
[a]Ex 34:13; side it. 26 Then build a proper kind of[d]
Dt 7:5 altar to the LORD your God on the top
of this height. Using the wood of the
Asherah pole that you cut down, offer
the second[e] bull as a burnt offering."
27 So Gideon took ten of his servants
and did as the LORD told him. But because he was afraid of his family and
the men of the town, he did it at night
rather than in the daytime.
28 In the morning when the men of
6:28 the town got up, there was Baal's altar,[b]
[b]1Ki 16:32 demolished, with the Asherah pole beside it cut down and the second bull
sacrificed on the newly built altar!
29 They asked each other, "Who did
this?"
When they carefully investigated,
they were told, "Gideon son of Joash
did it."
30 The men of the town demanded of
Joash, "Bring out your son. He must
die, because he has broken down Baal's
altar and cut down the Asherah pole
beside it."
31 But Joash replied to the hostile
crowd around him, "Are you going to
plead Baal's cause? Are you trying to save
him? Whoever fights for him shall be put
to death by morning! If Baal really is a
god, he can defend himself when someone breaks down his altar." 32 So that day
they called Gideon "Jerub-Baal,[f][c]" say- 6:32 [c]Jdg 7:1;
ing, "Let Baal contend with him," be- 8:29,35;
cause he broke down Baal's altar. 1Sa 12:11
33 Now all the Midianites, Amalek- 6:33
ites and other eastern peoples[d] joined [d]ver 3
forces and crossed over the Jordan and [e]Jos 17:16
camped in the Valley of Jezreel.[e] 34 Then 6:34
the Spirit of the LORD came upon[f] [f]Jdg 3:10;
Gideon, and he blew a trumpet,[g] sum- 1Ch 12:18; 2Ch 24:20
moning the Abiezrites to follow him. [g]Jdg 3:27
35 He sent messengers throughout Manasseh, calling them to arms, and also
into Asher, Zebulun and Naphtali,[h] so 6:35
that they too went up to meet them. [h]Jdg 4:6
36 Gideon said to God, "If you will 6:36
save[i] Israel by my hand as you have [i]ver 14
promised— 37 look, I will place a wool
fleece on the threshing floor.[j] If there 6:37 [j]Ex 4:3-7
is dew only on the fleece and all the [k]Ge 24:14
ground is dry, then I will know[k] that
you will save Israel by my hand, as
you said." 38 And that is what happened. Gideon rose early the next day;
he squeezed the fleece and wrung out
the dew—a bowlful of water.
39 Then Gideon said to God, "Do not
be angry with me. Let me make just
one more request.[l] Allow me one more 6:39 [l]Ge 18:32
test with the fleece. This time make the
fleece dry and the ground covered with
dew." 40 That night God did so. Only
the fleece was dry; all the ground was
covered with dew.

Gideon Defeats the Midianites

7 Early in the morning, Jerub-Baal[m] 7:1 [m]Jdg 6:32
(that is, Gideon) and all his men [n]Ge 12:6
camped at the spring of Harod. The
camp of Midian was north of them in
the valley near the hill of Moreh.[n] 2 The 7:2 [o]Dt 8:17;
LORD said to Gideon, "You have too 2Co 4:7
many men for me to deliver Midian into
their hands. In order that Israel may not
boast against me that her own strength[o]
has saved her, 3 announce now to the

[a] *19* That is, probably about 3/5 bushel (about 22 liters) [b] *25* Or *Take a full-grown, mature bull from your father's herd* [c] *25* That is, a symbol of the goddess Asherah; here and elsewhere in Judges [d] *26* Or *build with layers of stone an* [e] *26* Or *full-grown*; also in verse 28 [f] *32 Jerub-Baal* means *let Baal contend.*

people, 'Anyone who trembles with fear
may turn back and leave Mount Gil-
7:3 ead.[p]'" So twenty-two thousand men
[p]Dt 20:8 left, while ten thousand remained.
4But the LORD said to Gideon,
7:4 "There are still too many[q] men. Take
[q]1Sa 14:6 them down to the water, and I will sift
them for you there. If I say, 'This one
shall go with you,' he shall go; but if I
say, 'This one shall not go with you,' he
shall not go."
5So Gideon took the men down to
the water. There the LORD told him,
"Separate those who lap the water with
their tongues like a dog from those who
kneel down to drink." 6Three hundred
men lapped with their hands to their
mouths. All the rest got down on their
knees to drink.
7The LORD said to Gideon, "With
the three hundred men that lapped I
will save you and give the Midianites
into your hands. Let all the other men
7:7 go, each to his own place."[r] 8So Gide-
[r]1Sa 14:6 on sent the rest of the Israelites to their
tents but kept the three hundred, who
took over the provisions and trumpets
of the others.
Now the camp of Midian lay below
him in the valley. 9During that night
the LORD said to Gideon, "Get up, go
down against the camp, because I am
7:9 going to give it into your hands.[s] 10If
[s]Jos 2:24; you are afraid to attack, go down to the
10:8; 11:6 camp with your servant Purah 11and
listen to what they are saying. Afterward, you will be encouraged to attack
the camp." So he and Purah his servant
went down to the outposts of the camp.
7:12 12The Midianites, the Amalekites[t] and
[t]Jdg 8:10 all the other eastern peoples had settled
[u]Jdg 6:5 in the valley, thick as locusts.[u] Their
[v]Jer 49:29 camels[v] could no more be counted than
[w]Jos 11:4 the sand on the seashore.[w]
13Gideon arrived just as a man was
telling a friend his dream. "I had a
dream," he was saying. "A round loaf
of barley bread came tumbling into the
Midianite camp. It struck the tent with
such force that the tent overturned and
collapsed."
14His friend responded, "This can be
nothing other than the sword of Gideon
son of Joash, the Israelite. God has giv-
en the Midianites and the whole camp
into his hands."
7:15 15When Gideon heard the dream and
[x]1Sa 15:31 its interpretation, he worshiped God.[x]

He returned to the camp of Israel and
called out, "Get up! The LORD has
given the Midianite camp into your
hands." 16Dividing the three hundred
men[y] into three companies,[z] he placed 7:16 [y]Ge 14:15
trumpets and empty jars in the hands [z]2Sa 18:2
of all of them, with torches inside.
17"Watch me," he told them. "Follow my lead. When I get to the edge of
the camp, do exactly as I do. 18When
I and all who are with me blow our
trumpets,[a] then from all around the 7:18
camp blow yours and shout, 'For the [a]Jdg 3:27
LORD and for Gideon.'"
19Gideon and the hundred men with
him reached the edge of the camp at
the beginning of the middle watch,
just after they had changed the guard.
They blew their trumpets and broke
the jars that were in their hands. 20The
three companies blew the trumpets and
smashed the jars. Grasping the torches
in their left hands and holding in their
right hands the trumpets they were to
blow, they shouted, "A sword[b] for the 7:20 [b]ver 14
LORD and for Gideon!" 21While each
man held his position around the camp,
all the Midianites ran, crying out as 7:21
they fled.[c] [c]2Ki 7:7
22When the three hundred trumpets 7:22
sounded,[d] the LORD caused the men [d]Jos 6:20
throughout the camp to turn on each [e]1Sa 14:20; 2Ch 20:23
other[e] with their swords. The army fled [f]1Ki 4:12;
to Beth Shittah toward Zererah as far as 19:16
the border of Abel Meholah[f] near Tab-
bath. 23Israelites from Naphtali, Asher 7:23
and all Manasseh were called out,[g] and [g]Jdg 6:35
they pursued the Midianites. 24Gideon
sent messengers throughout the hill
country of Ephraim, saying, "Come
down against the Midianites and seize 7:24
the waters of the Jordan[h] ahead of them [h]Jdg 3:28
as far as Beth Barah."
So all the men of Ephraim were called
out and they took the waters of the Jordan as far as Beth Barah. 25They also
captured two of the Midianite leaders, 7:25
Oreb and Zeeb.[i] They killed Oreb at [i]Jdg 8:3; Ps 83:11
the rock of Oreb,[j] and Zeeb at the [j]Isa 10:26
winepress of Zeeb. They pursued the [k]Jdg 8:4
Midianites and brought the heads of
Oreb and Zeeb to Gideon, who was by
the Jordan.[k]

Zebah and Zalmunna

8 Now the Ephraimites asked Gideon, "Why have you treated us like
this? Why didn't you call us when you

8:1 [l]Jdg 12:1 [m]2Sa 19:41 went to fight Midian?"[l] And they criticized him sharply.[m]
2But he answered them, "What have
I accomplished compared to you? Aren't
the gleanings of Ephraim's grapes better
than the full grape harvest of Abiezer?
8:3 [n]Jdg 7:25; Pr 15:1 3God gave Oreb and Zeeb,[n] the Midianite leaders, into your hands. What
was I able to do compared to you?" At
this, their resentment against him subsided.
4Gideon and his three hundred men,
exhausted yet keeping up the pursuit,
8:4 [o]Jdg 7:25 came to the Jordan[o] and crossed it. 5He
said to the men of Succoth,[p] "Give
8:5 [p]Ge 33:17 [q]Ps 83:11 my troops some bread; they are worn
out, and I am still pursuing Zebah and
Zalmunna,[q] the kings of Midian."
6But the officials of Succoth said,
"Do you already have the hands of Zebah and Zalmunna in your possession?
8:6 [r]1Sa 25:11 [s]ver 15 Why should we give bread[r] to your
troops?"[s]
7Then Gideon replied, "Just for that,
when the LORD has given Zebah and
8:7 [t]Jdg 7:15 Zalmunna[t] into my hand, I will tear
your flesh with desert thorns and
briers."
8:8 [u]Ge 32:30; 1Ki 12:25 8From there he went up to Peniel[a][u]
and made the same request of them,
but they answered as the men of Succoth had. 9So he said to the men of Pe-
8:9 [v]ver 17 niel, "When I return in triumph, I will
tear down this tower."[v]
10Now Zebah and Zalmunna were
in Karkor with a force of about fifteen
thousand men, all that were left of the
armies of the eastern peoples; a hundred and twenty thousand swordsmen
8:10 [w]Jdg 6:5; 7:12; Isa 9:4 had fallen.[w] 11Gideon went up by the
route of the nomads east of Nobah[x] and
8:11 [x]Nu 32:42 [y]Nu 32:35 Jogbehah[y] and fell upon the unsuspecting army. 12Zebah and Zalmunna, the
two kings of Midian, fled, but he pursued them and captured them, routing
their entire army.
13Gideon son of Joash then returned
from the battle by the Pass of Heres.
14He caught a young man of Succoth
and questioned him, and the young
man wrote down for him the names of
the seventy-seven officials of Succoth,
the elders of the town. 15Then Gideon
came and said to the men of Succoth,
"Here are Zebah and Zalmunna, about
whom you taunted me by saying, 'Do
you already have the hands of Zebah
and Zalmunna in your possession? Why
should we give bread to your exhaust-
ed men?'[z]" 16He took the elders of the 8:15 [z]ver 6
town and taught the men of Succoth a
lesson[a] by punishing them with desert 8:16 [a]ver 7
thorns and briers. 17He also pulled
down the tower of Peniel and killed the
men of the town.[b] 8:17 [b]ver 9
18Then he asked Zebah and Zalmunna, "What kind of men did you kill at
Tabor?"[c] 8:18 [c]Jos 19:22; Jdg 4:6
"Men like you," they answered, "each
one with the bearing of a prince."
19Gideon replied, "Those were my
brothers, the sons of my own mother.
As surely as the LORD lives, if you had
spared their lives, I would not kill you."
20Turning to Jether, his oldest son, he
said, "Kill them!" But Jether did not
draw his sword, because he was only a
boy and was afraid.
21Zebah and Zalmunna said, "Come,
do it yourself. 'As is the man, so is his
strength.'" So Gideon stepped forward
and killed them, and took the orna-
ments[d] off their camels' necks. 8:21 [d]ver 26; Ps 83:11

Gideon's Ephod

22The Israelites said to Gideon, "Rule
over us—you, your son and your grandson—because you have saved us out of
the hand of Midian."
23But Gideon told them, "I will not
rule over you, nor will my son rule[e] over 8:23 [e]Ex 16:8; 1Sa 8:7; 10:19; 12:12
you. The LORD will rule over you."
24And he said, "I do have one request,
that each of you give me an earring
from your share of the plunder." (It was
the custom of the Ishmaelites[f] to wear 8:24 [f]Ge 25:13
gold earrings.)
25They answered, "We'll be glad to
give them." So they spread out a garment, and each man threw a ring from
his plunder onto it. 26The weight of
the gold rings he asked for came to
seventeen hundred shekels,[b] not counting the ornaments, the pendants and
the purple garments worn by the kings
of Midian or the chains that were on
their camels' necks. 27Gideon made the
gold into an ephod,[g] which he placed in
Ophrah, his town. All Israel prostituted 8:27 [g]Jdg 17:5; 18:14 [h]Dt 7:16; Ps 106:39
themselves by worshiping it there, and
it became a snare[h] to Gideon and his
family.

[a] *8* Hebrew *Penuel,* a variant of *Peniel*; also in verses 9 and 17 [b] *26* That is, about 43 pounds (about 19.5 kilograms)

Gideon's Death

28Thus Midian was subdued before
the Israelites and did not raise its head
again. During Gideon's lifetime, the
8:28 ⁱJdg 5:31 land enjoyed peace[i] forty years.
29Jerub-Baal[j] son of Joash went back
8:29 ʲJdg 7:1 home to live. 30He had seventy sons[k]
8:30 of his own, for he had many wives.
ᵏJdg 9:2,5, 18,24 31His concubine, who lived in Shechem, also bore him a son, whom he
8:31 named Abimelech.[l] 32Gideon son of Jo-
ˡJdg 9:1 ash died at a good old age[m] and was
8:32 ᵐGe 25:8 buried in the tomb of his father Joash
in Ophrah of the Abiezrites.
33No sooner had Gideon died than
the Israelites again prostituted them-
8:33 ⁿJdg 2:11, 13,19 selves to the Baals.[n] They set up Baal-
ᵒJdg 9:4 Berith[o] as their god[p] and 34did not
ᵖJdg 9:27,46 remember[q] the Lord their God, who
8:34 had rescued them from the hands of all
ᵠJdg 3:7; Dt 4:9; Ps 78:11,42 their enemies on every side. 35They also
failed to show kindness to the family of
8:35 Jerub-Baal (that is, Gideon) for all the
ʳJdg 9:16 good things he had done for them.[r]

Abimelech

9:1 ˢJdg 8:31 9 Abimelech[s] son of Jerub-Baal went
to his mother's brothers in She-
chem and said to them and to all his
mother's clan, 2"Ask all the citizens of
Shechem, 'Which is better for you: to
have all seventy of Jerub-Baal's sons rule
over you, or just one man?' Remember,
9:2 ᵗGe 29:14; Jdg 8:30 I am your flesh and blood.[t]"
3When the brothers repeated all this
to the citizens of Shechem, they were
inclined to follow Abimelech, for they
said, "He is our brother." 4They gave
him seventy shekels[a] of silver from the
9:4 ᵘJdg 8:33 temple of Baal-Berith,[u] and Abimelech
ᵛJdg 11:3; 2Ch 13:7 used it to hire reckless adventurers,[v]
who became his followers. 5He went
to his father's home in Ophrah and
on one stone murdered his seventy
9:5 ʷver 2; brothers,[w] the sons of Jerub-Baal. But
Jdg 8:30 Jotham, the youngest son of Jerub-
ˣ2Ki 11:2 Baal, escaped by hiding.[x] 6Then all the
citizens of Shechem and Beth Millo
gathered beside the great tree at the
pillar in Shechem to crown Abimelech
king.
7When Jotham was told about this,
he climbed up on the top of Mount
9:7 ʸDt 11:29; Gerizim[y] and shouted to them, "Listen
27:12; to me, citizens of Shechem, so that God
Jn 4:20 may listen to you. 8One day the trees
went out to anoint a king for themselves. They said to the olive tree, 'Be
our king.'
9"But the olive tree answered, 'Should
I give up my oil, by which both gods
and men are honored, to hold sway
over the trees?'
10"Next, the trees said to the fig tree,
'Come and be our king.'
11"But the fig tree replied, 'Should I
give up my fruit, so good and sweet, to
hold sway over the trees?'
12"Then the trees said to the vine,
'Come and be our king.'
13"But the vine answered, 'Should I
give up my wine,[z] which cheers both 9:13 ᶻEcc 2:3
gods and men, to hold sway over the
trees?'
14"Finally all the trees said to the
thornbush, 'Come and be our king.'
15"The thornbush said to the trees,
'If you really want to anoint me king
over you, come and take refuge in my
shade;[a] but if not, then let fire come 9:15 ᵃIsa 30:2
out[b] of the thornbush and consume the ᵇver 20
cedars of Lebanon!'[c] ᶜIsa 2:13
16"Now if you have acted honorably
and in good faith when you made
Abimelech king, and if you have been
fair to Jerub-Baal and his family, and if
you have treated him as he deserves—
17and to think that my father fought for
you, risked his life to rescue you from
the hand of Midian 18(but today you
have revolted against my father's family,
murdered his seventy sons[d] on a single 9:18 ᵈver 5-6;
stone, and made Abimelech, the son of Jdg 8:30
his slave girl, king over the citizens of
Shechem because he is your brother)—
19if then you have acted honorably and
in good faith toward Jerub-Baal and his
family today, may Abimelech be your
joy, and may you be his, too! 20But if
you have not, let fire come out[e] from 9:20 ᵉver 15
Abimelech and consume you, citizens
of Shechem and Beth Millo, and let
fire come out from you, citizens of Shechem and Beth Millo, and consume
Abimelech!"
21Then Jotham fled, escaping to Beer,
and he lived there because he was afraid
of his brother Abimelech.
22After Abimelech had governed Is-
rael three years, 23God sent an evil 9:23 ᶠ1Sa 16:14,23;
spirit[f] between Abimelech and the cit- 18:10;
izens of Shechem, who acted treach- 1Ki 22:22; Isa 19:14;
erously against Abimelech. 24God did 33:1

a4 That is, about 1 3/4 pounds (about 0.8 kilogram)

this in order that the crime against Jerub-Baal's seventy sons, the shedding[g] of their blood, might be avenged[h] on their brother Abimelech and on the citizens of Shechem, who had helped him[i] murder his brothers. 25 In opposition to him these citizens of Shechem set men on the hilltops to ambush and rob everyone who passed by, and this was reported to Abimelech.

26 Now Gaal son of Ebed moved with his brothers into Shechem, and its citizens put their confidence in him. 27 After they had gone out into the fields and gathered the grapes and trodden[j] them, they held a festival in the temple of their god.[k] While they were eating and drinking, they cursed Abimelech. 28 Then Gaal son of Ebed said, "Who[l] is Abimelech, and who is Shechem, that we should be subject to him? Isn't he Jerub-Baal's son, and isn't Zebul his deputy? Serve the men of Hamor,[m] Shechem's father! Why should we serve Abimelech? 29 If only this people were under my command![n] Then I would get rid of him. I would say to Abimelech, 'Call out your whole army!' "[a]

30 When Zebul the governor of the city heard what Gaal son of Ebed said, he was very angry. 31 Under cover he sent messengers to Abimelech, saying, "Gaal son of Ebed and his brothers have come to Shechem and are stirring up the city against you. 32 Now then, during the night you and your men should come and lie in wait[o] in the fields. 33 In the morning at sunrise, advance against the city. When Gaal and his men come out against you, do whatever your hand finds to do.[p]"

34 So Abimelech and all his troops set out by night and took up concealed positions near Shechem in four companies. 35 Now Gaal son of Ebed had gone out and was standing at the entrance to the city gate just as Abimelech and his soldiers came out from their hiding place.[q]

36 When Gaal saw them, he said to Zebul, "Look, people are coming down from the tops of the mountains!"

Zebul replied, "You mistake the shadows of the mountains for men."

37 But Gaal spoke up again: "Look, people are coming down from the center of the land, and a company is coming from the direction of the soothsayers' tree."

38 Then Zebul said to him, "Where is your big talk now, you who said, 'Who is Abimelech that we should be subject to him?' Aren't these the men you ridiculed?[r] Go out and fight them!"

39 So Gaal led out[b] the citizens of Shechem and fought Abimelech. 40 Abimelech chased him, and many fell wounded in the flight—all the way to the entrance to the gate. 41 Abimelech stayed in Arumah, and Zebul drove Gaal and his brothers out of Shechem.

42 The next day the people of Shechem went out to the fields, and this was reported to Abimelech. 43 So he took his men, divided them into three companies[s] and set an ambush in the fields. When he saw the people coming out of the city, he rose to attack them. 44 Abimelech and the companies with him rushed forward to a position at the entrance to the city gate. Then two companies rushed upon those in the fields and struck them down. 45 All that day Abimelech pressed his attack against the city until he had captured it and killed its people. Then he destroyed the city[t] and scattered salt[u] over it.

46 On hearing this, the citizens in the tower of Shechem went into the stronghold of the temple[v] of El-Berith. 47 When Abimelech heard that they had assembled there, 48 he and all his men went up Mount Zalmon.[w] He took an ax and cut off some branches, which he lifted to his shoulders. He ordered the men with him, "Quick! Do what you have seen me do!" 49 So all the men cut branches and followed Abimelech. They piled them against the stronghold and set it on fire over the people inside. So all the people in the tower of Shechem, about a thousand men and women, also died.

50 Next Abimelech went to Thebez[x] and besieged it and captured it. 51 Inside the city, however, was a strong tower, to which all the men and women—all the people of the city—fled. They locked themselves in and climbed up on the tower roof. 52 Abimelech went to the tower and stormed it. But as he ap-

9:24 [g]Nu 35:33; 1Ki 2:32 [h]ver 56-57 [i]Dt 27:25
9:27 [j]Am 9:13 [k]Jdg 8:33
9:28 [l]1Sa 25:10; 1Ki 12:16 [m]Ge 34:2,6
9:29 [n]2Sa 15:4
9:32 [o]Jos 8:2
9:33 [p]1Sa 10:7
9:35 [q]Ps 32:7; Jer 49:10
9:38 [r]ver 28-29
9:43 [s]Jdg 7:16
9:45 [t]ver 20; 2Ki 3:25 [u]Dt 29:23
9:46 [v]Jdg 8:33
9:48 [w]Ps 68:14
9:50 [x]2Sa 11:21

[a] *29* Septuagint; Hebrew *him." Then he said to Abimelech, "Call out your whole army!"* [b] *39* Or *Gaal went out in the sight of*

proached the entrance to the tower to
set it on fire, 53a woman dropped an upper millstone on his head and cracked
9:53 his skull.[y]
[y]2Sa 11:21 54Hurriedly he called to his armor-
9:54 [z]1Sa 31:4; bearer, "Draw your sword and kill me,[z]
2Sa 1:9 so that they can't say, 'A woman killed
him.'" So his servant ran him through,
and he died. 55When the Israelites saw
that Abimelech was dead, they went
home.

56Thus God repaid the wickedness
that Abimelech had done to his father by
murdering his seventy brothers. 57God
also made the men of Shechem pay for
9:57 [a]ver 20 all their wickedness.[a] The curse of Jotham son of Jerub-Baal came on them.

Tola

10 After the time of Abimelech a
10:1 [b]Ge 30:18 man of Issachar,[b] Tola son of
[c]Ge 46:13 Puah,[c] the son of Dodo, rose to save[d]
[d]Jdg 2:16; 6:14 Israel. He lived in Shamir, in the hill
country of Ephraim. 2He led[a] Israel
twenty-three years; then he died, and
was buried in Shamir.

Jair

3He was followed by Jair of Gilead,
who led Israel twenty-two years. 4He
had thirty sons, who rode thirty donkeys. They controlled thirty towns in
Gilead, which to this day are called
10:4 Havvoth Jair.[b][e] 5When Jair died, he was
[e]Nu 32:41 buried in Kamon.

GOODNESS

SPOILED MORALITY

Judges 10:6–7

Goodness gone soft thinks sin is unimportant. Morality then dies. God is ignored until some saint, completely ignorant of his or her importance, stands up and cries, "Repent!" Virtue then lives again.

Jephthah

6Again the Israelites did evil in the
10:6 [f]Jdg 2:11 eyes of the LORD.[f] They served the Ba-
[g]Jdg 2:13 als and the Ashtoreths,[g] and the gods of
[h]Jdg 2:12 Aram, the gods of Sidon, the gods of
[i]Dt 32:15 Moab, the gods of the Ammonites and
the gods of the Philistines.[h] And be-
10:7 [j]Dt 31:17 cause the Israelites forsook the LORD[i]
[k]Dt 32:30; Jdg 2:14; and no longer served him, 7he became
1Sa 12:9 angry[j] with them. He sold them[k] into
the hands of the Philistines and the
Ammonites, 8who that year shattered
and crushed them. For eighteen years
they oppressed all the Israelites on the
east side of the Jordan in Gilead, the
land of the Amorites. 9The Ammonites also crossed the Jordan to fight
against Judah, Benjamin and the house
of Ephraim; and Israel was in great distress. 10Then the Israelites cried out to
the LORD, "We have sinned against
you, forsaking our God and serving the
Baals."[l] 10:10 [l]1Sa 12:10

11The LORD replied, "When the
Egyptians,[m] the Amorites, the Ammon- 10:11 [m]Ex 14:30
ites,[n] the Philistines,[o] 12the Sidonians, [n]Nu 21:21; Jdg 3:13
the Amalekites and the Maonites[c] op- [o]Jdg 3:31
pressed you[p] and you cried to me for
help, did I not save you from their 10:12 [p]Ps 106:42
hands? 13But you have forsaken me and
served other gods, so I will no longer
save you. 14Go and cry out to the gods
you have chosen. Let them save you
when you are in trouble![q]"

15But the Israelites said to the LORD, 10:14 [q]Dt 32:37
"We have sinned. Do with us whatever
you think best,[r] but please rescue us 10:15 [r]1Sa 3:18;
now." 16Then they got rid of the for- 2Sa 15:26
eign gods among them and served the
LORD.[s] And he could bear Israel's mis- 10:16 [s]Jos 24:23; Jer 18:8
ery[t] no longer.[u] [t]Isa 63:9

17When the Ammonites were called [u]Dt 32:36; Ps 106:44-45
to arms and camped in Gilead, the
Israelites assembled and camped at 10:17 [v]Ge 31:49; Jdg 11:29
Mizpah.[v] 18The leaders of the people
of Gilead said to each other, "Whoever
will launch the attack against the Am-
monites will be the head[w] of all those 10:18 [w]Jdg 11:8,9
living in Gilead."

11 Jephthah[x] the Gileadite was a 11:1 [x]Heb 11:32
mighty warrior.[y] His father was [y]Jdg 6:12
Gilead; his mother was a prostitute.
2Gilead's wife also bore him sons, and
when they were grown up, they drove
Jephthah away. "You are not going to
get any inheritance in our family," they
said, "because you are the son of another woman." 3So Jephthah fled from his
brothers and settled in the land of Tob,[z] 11:3 [z]2Sa 10:6,8
where a group of adventurers[a] gathered [a]Jdg 9:4
around him and followed him.

4Some time later, when the Ammon-
ites[b] made war on Israel, 5the elders of 11:4 [b]Jdg 10:9
Gilead went to get Jephthah from the

[a]2 Traditionally *judged;* also in verse 3 [b]4 Or *called the settlements of Jair* [c]12 Hebrew; some Septuagint manuscripts *Midianites*

land of Tob. 6“Come,” they said, “be
our commander, so we can fight the
Ammonites.”
7Jephthah said to them, “Didn’t you
hate me and drive me from my father’s
11:7 house?[c] Why do you come to me now,
cGe 26:27 when you’re in trouble?”
8The elders of Gilead said to him,
“Nevertheless, we are turning to you
now; come with us to fight the Am-
11:8 monites, and you will be our head[d] over
dJdg 10:18 all who live in Gilead.”
9Jephthah answered, “Suppose you
take me back to fight the Ammonites
and the LORD gives them to me—will
I really be your head?”
10The elders of Gilead replied, “The
11:10 LORD is our witness;[e] we will certainly
eGe 31:50; do as you say.” 11So Jephthah went with
Jer 42:5 the elders of Gilead, and the people
made him head and commander over
them. And he repeated all his words be-
11:11 fore the LORD in Mizpah.[f]
fJos 11:3; Jdg 10:17; 12Then Jephthah sent messengers to
20:1; the Ammonite king with the question:
1Sa 10:17 “What do you have against us that you
have attacked our country?”
13The king of the Ammonites answered Jephthah’s messengers, “When
Israel came up out of Egypt, they took
away my land from the Arnon to the
11:13 Jabbok,[g] all the way to the Jordan. Now
gGe 32:22; Nu 21:24 give it back peaceably.”
14Jephthah sent back messengers to
the Ammonite king, 15saying:

“This is what Jephthah says: Israel
11:15 hDt 2:9 did not take the land of Moab[h] or
iDt 2:19 the land of the Ammonites.[i] 16But
when they came up out of Egypt,
Israel went through the desert to
11:16 the Red Sea[a][j] and on to Kadesh.[k]
jNu 14:25; Dt 1:40 17Then Israel sent messengers[l] to
kNu 20:1 the king of Edom, saying, ‘Give
11:17 us permission to go through your
lNu 20:14 country,’[m] but the king of Edom
mNu 20:18,21 would not listen. They sent also to
nJos 24:9 the king of Moab, and he refused.[n]
So Israel stayed at Kadesh.
18“Next they traveled through
the desert, skirted the lands of
11:18 Edom[o] and Moab, passed along
oNu 21:4 the eastern side[p] of the country of
pDt 2:8 qNu 21:13 Moab, and camped on the other
side of the Arnon.[q] They did not
enter the territory of Moab, for the
Arnon was its border.
19“Then Israel sent messengers
to Sihon king of the Amorites, who
ruled in Heshbon, and said to him,
‘Let us pass through your country
to our own place.’[r] 20Sihon, how- 11:19 rNu 21:21-22;
ever, did not trust Israel[b] to pass Dt 2:26-27
through his territory. He mustered
all his men and encamped at Jahaz 11:20
and fought with Israel.[s] sNu 21:23;
21“Then the LORD, the God of Dt 2:32
Israel, gave Sihon and all his men
into Israel’s hands, and they defeated them. Israel took over all the
land of the Amorites who lived in
that country, 22capturing all of it
from the Arnon to the Jabbok and
from the desert to the Jordan.[t] 11:22 tDt 2:36
23“Now since the LORD, the
God of Israel, has driven the Amorites out before his people Israel,
what right have you to take it
over? 24Will you not take what
your god Chemosh[u] gives you? 11:24 uNu 21:29;
Likewise, whatever the LORD our Jos 3:10;
God has given us, we will possess. 1Ki 11:7
25Are you better than Balak son
of Zippor,[v] king of Moab? Did he 11:25 vNu 22:2
ever quarrel with Israel or fight wJos 24:9
with them?[w] 26For three hundred
years Israel occupied[x] Heshbon, 11:26 xNu 21:25
Aroer, the surrounding settlements
and all the towns along the Arnon. Why didn’t you retake them
during that time? 27I have not
wronged you, but you are doing
me wrong by waging war against
me. Let the LORD, the Judge,[c][y] 11:27 yGe 18:25
decide[z] the dispute this day be- zGe 16:5;
tween the Israelites and the Am- 31:53; 1Sa 24:12,15
monites.”

28The king of Ammon, however, paid
no attention to the message Jephthah
sent him.
29Then the Spirit[a] of the LORD came 11:29 aNu 11:25;
upon Jephthah. He crossed Gilead and Jdg 3:10;
Manasseh, passed through Mizpah of 6:34; 14:6,19; 15:14;
Gilead, and from there he advanced 1Sa 11:6; 16:13;
against the Ammonites. 30And Jeph- Isa 11:2
thah made a vow[b] to the LORD: “If you 11:30
give the Ammonites into my hands, bGe 28:20
31whatever comes out of the door of my
house to meet me when I return in triumph from the Ammonites will be the
LORD’s, and I will sacrifice it as a burnt
offering.”

a16 Hebrew *Yam Suph*; that is, Sea of Reeds
b20 Or *however, would not make an agreement for Israel* c27 Or *Ruler*

32Then Jephthah went over to fight
the Ammonites, and the LORD gave
them into his hands. 33He devastated
twenty towns from Aroer to the vicinity
11:33 of Minnith,[c] as far as Abel Keramim.
[c]Eze 27:17 Thus Israel subdued Ammon.
34When Jephthah returned to his
home in Mizpah, who should come out
to meet him but his daughter, dancing
11:34 to the sound of tambourines![d] She was
[d]Ex 15:20; Jer 31:4 an only child. Except for her he had
neither son nor daughter. 35When he
saw her, he tore his clothes and cried,
"Oh! My daughter! You have made me
miserable and wretched, because I have
made a vow to the LORD that I cannot
11:35 break.[e]"
[e]Nu 30:2; Ecc 5:2,4,5 36"My father," she replied, "you have
given your word to the LORD. Do to
11:36 me just as you promised,[f] now that the
[f]Lk 1:38 [g]2Sa 18:19 LORD has avenged you of your enemies,[g] the Ammonites. 37But grant me
this one request," she said. "Give me
two months to roam the hills and weep
with my friends, because I will never
marry."
38"You may go," he said. And he let
her go for two months. She and the
girls went into the hills and wept because she would never marry. 39After
the two months, she returned to her father and he did to her as he had vowed.
And she was a virgin.
From this comes the Israelite custom 40that each year the young women
of Israel go out for four days to commemorate the daughter of Jephthah the
Gileadite.

Jephthah and Ephraim

12 The men of Ephraim called out
their forces, crossed over to Zaphon and said to Jephthah, "Why did
you go to fight the Ammonites with-
12:1 out calling us to go with you?[h] We're
[h]Jdg 8:1 going to burn down your house over
your head."
2Jephthah answered, "I and my people were engaged in a great struggle
with the Ammonites, and although I
called, you didn't save me out of their
hands. 3When I saw that you wouldn't
12:3 help, I took my life in my hands[i] and
[i]1Sa 19:5; 28:21; crossed over to fight the Ammonites,
Job 13:14 and the LORD gave me the victory over
them. Now why have you come up to-
day to fight me?"
4Jephthah then called together the
men of Gilead and fought against
Ephraim. The Gileadites struck them
down because the Ephraimites had said,
"You Gileadites are renegades from
Ephraim and Manasseh." 5The Gileadites captured the fords of the Jordan[j] 12:5
leading to Ephraim, and whenever a [j]Jos 22:11;
survivor of Ephraim said, "Let me cross Jdg 3:28
over," the men of Gilead asked him,
"Are you an Ephraimite?" If he replied,
"No," 6they said, "All right, say 'Shibboleth.'" If he said, "Sibboleth," because he could not pronounce the word
correctly, they seized him and killed
him at the fords of the Jordan. Forty-
two thousand Ephraimites were killed
at that time.
7Jephthah led[a] Israel six years. Then
Jephthah the Gileadite died, and was
buried in a town in Gilead.

Ibzan, Elon and Abdon

8After him, Ibzan of Bethlehem led
Israel. 9He had thirty sons and thirty
daughters. He gave his daughters away
in marriage to those outside his clan,
and for his sons he brought in thirty
young women as wives from outside
his clan. Ibzan led Israel seven years.
10Then Ibzan died, and was buried in
Bethlehem.
11After him, Elon the Zebulunite led
Israel ten years. 12Then Elon died, and
was buried in Aijalon in the land of
Zebulun.
13After him, Abdon son of Hillel,
from Pirathon, led Israel. 14He had forty sons and thirty grandsons,[k] who rode 12:14
on seventy donkeys.[l] He led Israel eight [k]Jdg 10:4 [l]Jdg 5:10
years. 15Then Abdon son of Hillel died,
and was buried at Pirathon in Ephraim,
in the hill country of the Amalekites.[m] 12:15 [m]Jdg 5:14

The Birth of Samson

13 Again the Israelites did evil in
the eyes of the LORD, so the
LORD delivered them into the hands of
the Philistines[n] for forty years. 13:1
2A certain man of Zorah,[o] named [n]Jdg 2:11; 1Sa 12:9
Manoah, from the clan of the Danites,
had a wife who was sterile and remained 13:2
childless. 3The angel of the LORD[p] ap- [o]Jos 15:33; 19:41
peared to her[q] and said, "You are ster- 13:3
ile and childless, but you are going to [p]ver 6,8; Jdg 6:12
conceive and have a son.[r] 4Now see [q]ver 10
to it that you drink no wine or other [r]Lk 1:13

[a]7 Traditionally *judged*; also in verses 8-14

fermented drink and that you do not eat anything unclean,[s] 5 because you will conceive and give birth to a son. No razor[t] may be used on his head, because the boy is to be a Nazirite,[u] set apart to God from birth, and he will begin[v] the deliverance of Israel from the hands of the Philistines."

6 Then the woman went to her husband and told him, "A man of God[w] came to me. He looked like an angel of God,[x] very awesome. I didn't ask him where he came from, and he didn't tell me his name. 7 But he said to me, 'You will conceive and give birth to a son. Now then, drink no wine or other fermented drink and do not eat anything unclean, because the boy will be a Nazirite of God from birth until the day of his death.'"

8 Then Manoah prayed to the LORD: "O Lord, I beg you, let the man of God you sent to us come again to teach us how to bring up the boy who is to be born."

9 God heard Manoah, and the angel of God came again to the woman while she was out in the field; but her husband Manoah was not with her. 10 The woman hurried to tell her husband, "He's here! The man who appeared to me the other day!"

11 Manoah got up and followed his wife. When he came to the man, he said, "Are you the one who talked to my wife?"

"I am," he said.

12 So Manoah asked him, "When your words are fulfilled, what is to be the rule for the boy's life and work?"

13 The angel of the LORD answered, "Your wife must do all that I have told her. 14 She must not eat anything that comes from the grapevine, nor drink any wine or other fermented drink[y] nor eat anything unclean.[z] She must do everything I have commanded her."

15 Manoah said to the angel of the LORD, "We would like you to stay until we prepare a young goat[a] for you."

16 The angel of the LORD replied, "Even though you detain me, I will not eat any of your food. But if you prepare a burnt offering,[b] offer it to the LORD." (Manoah did not realize that it was the angel of the LORD.)

17 Then Manoah inquired of the angel of the LORD, "What is your name,[c] so that we may honor you when your word comes true?"

18 He replied, "Why do you ask my name?[d] It is beyond understanding.[a]" 19 Then Manoah took a young goat, together with the grain offering, and sacrificed it on a rock[e] to the LORD. And the LORD did an amazing thing while Manoah and his wife watched: 20 As the flame[f] blazed up from the altar toward heaven, the angel of the LORD ascended in the flame. Seeing this, Manoah and his wife fell with their faces to the ground.[g] 21 When the angel of the LORD did not show himself again to Manoah and his wife, Manoah realized[h] that it was the angel of the LORD.

22 "We are doomed[i] to die!" he said to his wife. "We have seen[j] God!"

23 But his wife answered, "If the LORD had meant to kill us, he would not have accepted a burnt offering and grain offering from our hands, nor shown us all these things or now told us this."[k]

24 The woman gave birth to a boy and named him Samson.[l] He grew[m] and the LORD blessed him,[n] 25 and the Spirit of the LORD began to stir[o] him while he was in Mahaneh Dan,[p] between Zorah and Eshtaol.

Samson's Marriage

14 Samson went down to Timnah[q] and saw there a young Philistine woman. 2 When he returned, he said to his father and mother, "I have seen a Philistine woman in Timnah; now get her for me as my wife."[r]

3 His father and mother replied, "Isn't there an acceptable woman among your relatives or among all our people?[s] Must you go to the uncircumcised[t] Philistines to get a wife?[u]"

But Samson said to his father, "Get her for me. She's the right one for me." 4 (His parents did not know that this was from the LORD, who was seeking an occasion to confront the Philistines;[v] for at that time they were ruling over Israel.)[w] 5 Samson went down to Timnah together with his father and mother. As they approached the vineyards of Timnah, suddenly a young lion came roaring toward him. 6 The Spirit of the LORD came upon him in power[x] so that he tore the lion apart with his bare

[a] 18 Or *is wonderful*

13:4 [s] ver 14; Nu 6:2-4; Lk 1:15
13:5 [t] Nu 6:5; 1Sa 1:11 [u] Nu 6:2,13 [v] 1Sa 7:13
13:6 [w] ver 8; 1Sa 2:27; 9:6 [x] ver 17-18; Mt 28:3
13:14 [y] Nu 6:4 [z] ver 4
13:15 [a] ver 3; Jdg 6:19
13:16 [b] Jdg 6:20
13:17 [c] Ge 32:29
13:18 [d] Isa 9:6
13:19 [e] Jdg 6:20
13:20 [f] Lev 9:24 [g] 1Ch 21:16; Eze 1:28; Mt 17:6
13:21 [h] ver 16; Jdg 6:22
13:22 [i] Dt 5:26 [j] Ge 32:30; Jdg 6:22
13:23 [k] Ps 25:14
13:24 [l] Heb 11:32 [m] 1Sa 3:19 [n] Lk 1:80
13:25 [o] Jdg 3:10 [p] Jdg 18:12
14:1 [q] Ge 38:12
14:2 [r] Ge 21:21; 34:4
14:3 [s] Ge 24:4 [t] Dt 7:3 [u] Ex 34:16
14:4 [v] Jos 11:20 [w] Jdg 13:1
14:6 [x] Jdg 3:10; 13:25

hands as he might have torn a young
goat. But he told neither his father nor
his mother what he had done. 7Then he
went down and talked with the woman, and he liked her.

8Some time later, when he went back
to marry her, he turned aside to look
at the lion's carcass. In it was a swarm
of bees and some honey, 9which he
scooped out with his hands and ate as
he went along. When he rejoined his
parents, he gave them some, and they
too ate it. But he did not tell them that
he had taken the honey from the lion's
carcass.

10Now his father went down to see
the woman. And Samson made a feast
there, as was customary for bride-
grooms. 11When he appeared, he was
given thirty companions.

12"Let me tell you a riddle,[y]" Sam-
14:12 [y]1Ki 10:1; Eze 17:2 [z]Ge 29:27 [a]Ge 45:22; 2Ki 5:5 son said to them. "If you can give me
the answer within the seven days of the
feast,[z] I will give you thirty linen garments and thirty sets of clothes.[a] 13If
you can't tell me the answer, you must
give me thirty linen garments and thirty sets of clothes."

"Tell us your riddle," they said. "Let's
hear it."

14He replied,

"Out of the eater, something to eat;
out of the strong, something
sweet."

For three days they could not give the
answer.

15On the fourth[a] day, they said to
14:15 [b]Jdg 16:5; Ecc 7:26 [c]Jdg 15:6 Samson's wife, "Coax[b] your husband
into explaining the riddle for us, or we
will burn you and your father's household to death.[c] Did you invite us here
to rob us?"

16Then Samson's wife threw herself
on him, sobbing, "You hate me! You
14:16 [d]Jdg 16:15 don't really love me.[d] You've given my
people a riddle, but you haven't told me
the answer."

"I haven't even explained it to my father or mother," he replied, "so why
should I explain it to you?" 17She cried
14:17 [e]Est 1:5 the whole seven days[e] of the feast. So
on the seventh day he finally told her,
because she continued to press him.
She in turn explained the riddle to her
people.

18Before sunset on the seventh day
the men of the town said to him,

"What is sweeter than honey?
What is stronger than a lion?"[f] 14:18 [f]ver 14

Samson said to them,

"If you had not plowed with my
heifer,
you would not have solved my
riddle."

19Then the Spirit of the LORD came
upon him in power.[g] He went down to 14:19 [g]Nu 11:25; Jdg 3:10; 6:34; 11:29; 13:25; 15:14; 1Sa 11:6; 16:13; 1Ki 18:46; 2Ch 24:20; Isa 11:2 [h]1Sa 11:6
Ashkelon, struck down thirty of their
men, stripped them of their belongings and gave their clothes to those who
had explained the riddle. Burning with
anger,[h] he went up to his father's house.
20And Samson's wife was given to the
friend[i] who had attended him at his 14:20 [i]Jdg 15:2,6; Jn 3:29
wedding.

Samson's Vengeance on the Philistines

15 Later on, at the time of wheat
harvest, Samson took a young
goat[j] and went to visit his wife. He said, 15:1 [j]Ge 38:17
"I'm going to my wife's room." But her
father would not let him go in.

2"I was so sure you thoroughly hated
her," he said, "that I gave her to your
friend.[k] Isn't her younger sister more at- 15:2 [k]Jdg 14:20
tractive? Take her instead."

3Samson said to them, "This time I
have a right to get even with the Philistines; I will really harm them." 4So
he went out and caught three hundred
foxes and tied them tail to tail in pairs.
He then fastened a torch to every pair
of tails, 5lit the torches and let the foxes
loose in the standing grain of the Philistines. He burned up the shocks and
standing grain, together with the vineyards and olive groves.

6When the Philistines asked, "Who
did this?" they were told, "Samson, the
Timnite's son-in-law, because his wife
was given to his friend."

So the Philistines went up and burned
her and her father to death.[l] 7Samson 15:6 [l]Jdg 14:15
said to them, "Since you've acted like
this, I won't stop until I get my revenge
on you." 8He attacked them viciously
and slaughtered many of them. Then
he went down and stayed in a cave in
the rock of Etam.

9The Philistines went up and camped

[a]15 Some Septuagint manuscripts and Syriac; Hebrew *seventh*

15:9 [m]ver 14,17,19

in Judah, spreading out near Lehi.[m] 10The men of Judah asked, "Why have you come to fight us?"

"We have come to take Samson prisoner," they answered, "to do to him as he did to us."

11Then three thousand men from Judah went down to the cave in the rock of Etam and said to Samson, "Don't you realize that the Philistines are rulers over us?[n] What have you done to us?"

15:11 [n]Jdg 13:1; 14:4; Ps 106:40-42

He answered, "I merely did to them what they did to me."

12They said to him, "We've come to tie you up and hand you over to the Philistines."

Samson said, "Swear to me that you won't kill me yourselves."

13"Agreed," they answered. "We will only tie you up and hand you over to them. We will not kill you." So they bound him with two new ropes and led him up from the rock. 14As he approached Lehi, the Philistines came toward him shouting. The Spirit of the LORD came upon him in power.[o] The ropes on his arms became like charred flax, and the bindings dropped from his hands. 15Finding a fresh jawbone of a donkey, he grabbed it and struck down a thousand men.[p]

15:14 [o]Jdg 3:10; 14:19; 1Sa 11:6

15:15 [p]Lev 26:8; Jos 23:10; Jdg 3:31

16Then Samson said,

"With a donkey's jawbone
I have made donkeys of them.[a]
With a donkey's jawbone
I have killed a thousand men."

JOY

SAMSON'S SONG

Judges 15:16

Samson wrote only four lines as far as we know. His song seems a weak one. It mentions neither God's love nor his power. Yet everyone should sing some song.

We can't all be poets and composers, but when the downbeat comes, we must stand and sing something or the world will think we have no God.

17When he finished speaking, he threw away the jawbone; and the place was called Ramath Lehi.[b]

18Because he was very thirsty, he cried out to the LORD,[q] "You have given your servant this great victory. Must I now die of thirst and fall into the hands of the uncircumcised?" 19Then God opened up the hollow place in Lehi, and water came out of it. When Samson drank, his strength returned and he revived.[r] So the spring was called En Hakkore,[c] and it is still there in Lehi.

15:18 [q]Jdg 16:28

15:19 [r]Ge 45:27; Isa 40:29

20Samson led[d] Israel for twenty years[s] in the days of the Philistines.

15:20 [s]Jdg 13:1; 16:31; Heb 11:32

Samson and Delilah

16 One day Samson went to Gaza, where he saw a prostitute. He went in to spend the night with her. 2The people of Gaza were told, "Samson is here!" So they surrounded the place and lay in wait for him all night at the city gate.[t] They made no move during the night, saying, "At dawn we'll kill him."

16:2 [t]1Sa 23:26; Ps 118:10-12; Ac 9:24

3But Samson lay there only until the middle of the night. Then he got up and took hold of the doors of the city gate, together with the two posts, and tore them loose, bar and all. He lifted them to his shoulders and carried them to the top of the hill that faces Hebron.[u]

16:3 [u]Jos 10:36

4Some time later, he fell in love[v] with a woman in the Valley of Sorek whose name was Delilah. 5The rulers of the Philistines[w] went to her and said, "See if you can lure[x] him into showing you the secret of his great strength and how we can overpower him so we may tie him up and subdue him. Each one of us will give you eleven hundred shekels[e] of silver."[y]

16:4 [v]Ge 24:67

16:5 [w]Jos 13:3 [x]Ex 10:7; Jdg 14:15 [y]ver 18

6So Delilah said to Samson, "Tell me the secret of your great strength and how you can be tied up and subdued."

7Samson answered her, "If anyone ties me with seven fresh thongs[f] that have not been dried, I'll become as weak as any other man."

8Then the rulers of the Philistines brought her seven fresh thongs that had not been dried, and she tied him with them. 9With men hidden in the room,[z] she called to him, "Samson, the Philistines are upon you!" But he snapped the thongs as easily as a piece of string

16:9 [z]ver 12

[a]*16* Or *made a heap or two*; the Hebrew for *donkey* sounds like the Hebrew for *heap.* [b]*17 Ramath Lehi* means *jawbone hill.* [c]*19 En Hakkore* means *caller's spring.* [d]*20* Traditionally *judged* [e]*5* That is, about 28 pounds (about 13 kilograms) [f]*7* Or *bowstrings*; also in verses 8 and 9

snaps when it comes close to a flame.
So the secret of his strength was not discovered.
10 Then Delilah said to Samson, "You
16:10 [a]ver 13 have made a fool of me;[a] you lied to
me. Come now, tell me how you can be
tied."
11 He said, "If anyone ties me securely
16:11 with new ropes[b] that have never been
[b]Jdg 15:13 used, I'll become as weak as any other
man."
12 So Delilah took new ropes and tied
him with them. Then, with men hidden in the room, she called to him,
"Samson, the Philistines are upon you!"
But he snapped the ropes off his arms
as if they were threads.
13 Delilah then said to Samson, "Until now, you have been making a fool of
me and lying to me. Tell me how you
can be tied."
He replied, "If you weave the seven
braids of my head into the fabric ⌊on
the loom⌋ and tighten it with the pin,
I'll become as weak as any other man."
So while he was sleeping, Delilah took
the seven braids of his head, wove them
into the fabric 14 and[a] tightened it with
the pin.
Again she called to him, "Samson, the
16:14 Philistines are upon you!"[c] He awoke
[c]ver 9,20 from his sleep and pulled up the pin
and the loom, with the fabric.
15 Then she said to him, "How can
16:15 you say, 'I love you,'[d] when you won't
[d]Jdg 14:16 [e]Nu 24:10 confide in me? This is the third time[e]
[f]ver 5 you have made a fool of me and haven't
told me the secret of your great
strength.[f]" 16 With such nagging she
prodded him day after day until he was
tired to death.
16:17 [g]Mic 7:5 17 So he told her everything.[g] "No ra-
[h]Nu 6:2,5; Jdg 13:5 zor has ever been used on my head," he
said, "because I have been a Nazirite[h]
set apart to God since birth. If my head
were shaved, my strength would leave
me, and I would become as weak as any
other man."
18 When Delilah saw that he had told
16:18 [i]Jos 13:3; 1Sa 5:8 her everything, she sent word to the
rulers of the Philistines[i], "Come back
once more; he has told me everything."
So the rulers of the Philistines returned
with the silver in their hands. 19 Having
put him to sleep on her lap, she called a
man to shave off the seven braids of his
16:19 hair, and so began to subdue him.[b] And
[j]Pr 7:26-27 his strength left him.[j]

20 Then she called, "Samson, the Philistines are upon you!"
He awoke from his sleep and thought,
"I'll go out as before and shake myself
free." But he did not know that the
LORD had left him.[k] 16:20 [k]Nu 14:42; Jos 7:12; 1Sa 16:14; 18:12; 28:15
21 Then the Philistines[l] seized him,
gouged out his eyes[m] and took him
down to Gaza. Binding him with bronze
shackles, they set him to grinding[n] in 16:21 [l]Jer 47:1 [m]Nu 16:14 [n]Job 31:10; Isa 47:2
the prison. 22 But the hair on his head
began to grow again after it had been
shaved.

The Death of Samson

23 Now the rulers of the Philistines
assembled to offer a great sacrifice to
Dagon[o] their god and to celebrate, say- 16:23 [o]1Sa 5:2; 1Ch 10:10
ing, "Our god has delivered Samson,
our enemy, into our hands."
24 When the people saw him, they
praised their god,[p] saying, 16:24 [p]Da 5:4 [q]1Sa 31:9; 1Ch 10:9

"Our god has delivered our enemy
into our hands,[q]
the one who laid waste our land
and multiplied our slain."

25 While they were in high spirits,[r] 16:25 [r]Jdg 9:27; Ru 3:7; Est 1:10
they shouted, "Bring out Samson to en-
tertain us." So they called Samson out
of the prison, and he performed for
them.
When they stood him among the pillars, 26 Samson said to the servant who
held his hand, "Put me where I can feel
the pillars that support the temple, so
that I may lean against them." 27 Now
the temple was crowded with men and
women; all the rulers of the Philistines
were there, and on the roof[s] were about 16:27 [s]Dt 22:8; Jos 2:8
three thousand men and women watch-
ing Samson perform. 28 Then Samson
prayed to the LORD,[t] "O Sovereign 16:28 [t]Jdg 15:18 [u]Jer 15:15
LORD, remember me. O God, please
strengthen me just once more, and let
me with one blow get revenge[u] on the
Philistines for my two eyes." 29 Then
Samson reached toward the two central pillars on which the temple stood.
Bracing himself against them, his right
hand on the one and his left hand on
the other, 30 Samson said, "Let me die
with the Philistines!" Then he pushed

[a] *13,14* Some Septuagint manuscripts; Hebrew *"⌊I can⌋ if you weave the seven braids of my head into the fabric ⌊on the loom⌋." 14So she* [b] *19* Hebrew; some Septuagint manuscripts *and he began to weaken*

with all his might, and down came the
temple on the rulers and all the people
in it. Thus he killed many more when
he died than while he lived.
31Then his brothers and his father's
whole family went down to get him.
They brought him back and buried him
between Zorah and Eshtaol in the tomb
16:31 [v]Jdg 13:2 [w]Ru 1:1; 1Sa 4:18 [x]Jdg 15:20
of Manoah[v] his father. He had led[a][w] Israel twenty years.[x]

Micah's Idols

17:1 [y]Jdg 18:2,13
17 Now a man named Micah[y] from
the hill country of Ephraim
2said to his mother, "The eleven hundred shekels[b] of silver that were taken
from you and about which I heard you
utter a curse—I have that silver with
me; I took it."
Then his mother said, "The LORD
17:2 [z]Ru 2:20; 1Sa 15:13; 2Sa 2:5
bless you,[z] my son!"
3When he returned the eleven hundred shekels of silver to his mother, she
said, "I solemnly consecrate my silver
to the LORD for my son to make a
17:3 [a]Ex 20:4,23; 34:17; Lev 19:4
carved image and a cast idol.[a] I will give
it back to you."
4So he returned the silver to his mother, and she took two hundred shekels[c]
of silver and gave them to a silversmith,
who made them into the image and
17:4 [b]Ex 32:4; Isa 17:8
the idol.[b] And they were put in Micah's
house.
17:5 [c]Isa 44:13; Eze 8:10 [d]Jdg 8:27 [e]Ge 31:19; Jdg 18:14 [f]Nu 16:10 [g]Ex 29:9; Jdg 18:24
5Now this man Micah had a shrine,[c]
and he made an ephod[d] and some idols[e]
and installed[f] one of his sons as his
priest.[g] 6In those days Israel had no
king;[h] everyone did as he saw fit.[i]
7A young Levite from Bethlehem in
17:6 [h]Jdg 18:1; 19:1; 21:25 [i]Dt 12:8
Judah,[j] who had been living within the
clan of Judah, 8left that town in search
of some other place to stay. On his
17:7 [j]Jdg 19:1; Ru 1:1-2; Mic 5:2; Mt 2:1
way[d] he came to Micah's house in the
hill country of Ephraim.
9Micah asked him, "Where are you
from?"
"I'm a Levite from Bethlehem in Judah," he said, "and I'm looking for a
place to stay."
10Then Micah said to him, "Live
17:10 [k]Jdg 18:19
with me and be my father and priest,[k]
and I'll give you ten shekels[e] of silver a
year, your clothes and your food." 11So
the Levite agreed to live with him, and
the young man was to him like one of
17:12 [l]Nu 16:10
his sons. 12Then Micah installed[l] the
Levite, and the young man became his
priest and lived in his house. 13And Micah said, "Now I know that the LORD
will be good to me, since this Levite has
become my priest."

Danites Settle in Laish

18 In those days Israel had no
king.[m] 18:1 [m]Jdg 17:6; 19:1
And in those days the tribe of the [n]Jos 19:47
Danites was seeking a place of their
own where they might settle, because
they had not yet come into an inheritance among the tribes of Israel.[n] 2So
the Danites[o] sent five warriors from Zo- 18:2 [o]Jdg 13:25
rah and Eshtaol to spy out the land and [p]Jos 2:1 [q]Jdg 17:1
explore it. These men represented all
their clans. They told them, "Go, explore the land."[p]
The men entered the hill country
of Ephraim and came to the house of
Micah,[q] where they spent the night.
3When they were near Micah's house,
they recognized the voice of the young
Levite; so they turned in there and
asked him, "Who brought you here?
What are you doing in this place? Why
are you here?"
4He told them what Micah had done
for him, and said, "He has hired me
and I am his priest.[r]" 18:4 [r]Jdg 17:12
5Then they said to him, "Please inquire of God[s] to learn whether our jour- 18:5
ney will be successful." [s]1Ki 22:5
6The priest answered them, "Go in
peace[t]. Your journey has the LORD's ap- 18:6 [t]1Ki 22:6
proval."
7So the five men left and came to 18:7
Laish,[u] where they saw that the people [u]Jos 19:47 [v]ver 28
were living in safety, like the Sidoni-
ans, unsuspecting and secure. And since
their land lacked nothing, they were
prosperous.[f] Also, they lived a long way
from the Sidonians[v] and had no relationship with anyone else.[g]
8When they returned to Zorah and
Eshtaol, their brothers asked them,
"How did you find things?"
9They answered, "Come on, let's attack them! We have seen that the land
is very good. Aren't you going to do 18:9
something?[w] Don't hesitate to go there [w]Nu 13:30; 1Ki 22:3
and take it over. 10When you get there,

[a] *31* Traditionally *judged* [b] *2* That is, about 28 pounds (about 13 kilograms) [c] *4* That is, about 5 pounds (about 2.3 kilograms) [d] *8* Or *To carry on his profession* [e] *10* That is, about 4 ounces (about 110 grams) [f] *7* The meaning of the Hebrew for this clause is uncertain. [g] *7* Hebrew; some Septuagint manuscripts *with the Arameans*

you will find an unsuspecting people and a spacious land that God has put into your hands, a land that lacks nothing[x] whatever.[y]"

11Then six hundred men[z] from the clan of the Danites,[a] armed for battle, set out from Zorah and Eshtaol. 12On their way they set up camp near Kiriath Jearim in Judah. This is why the place west of Kiriath Jearim is called Mahaneh Dan[a][b] to this day. 13From there they went on to the hill country of Ephraim and came to Micah's house.

14Then the five men who had spied out the land of Laish said to their brothers, "Do you know that one of these houses has an ephod, other household gods, a carved image and a cast idol?[c] Now you know what to do." 15So they turned in there and went to the house of the young Levite at Micah's place and greeted him. 16The six hundred Danites,[d] armed for battle, stood at the entrance to the gate. 17The five men who had spied out the land went inside and took the carved image, the ephod, the other household gods[e] and the cast idol while the priest and the six hundred armed men stood at the entrance to the gate.

18When these men went into Micah's house and took[f] the carved image, the ephod, the other household gods and the cast idol, the priest said to them, "What are you doing?"

19They answered him, "Be quiet![g] Don't say a word. Come with us, and be our father and priest.[h] Isn't it better that you serve a tribe and clan in Israel as priest rather than just one man's household?" 20Then the priest was glad. He took the ephod, the other household gods and the carved image and went along with the people. 21Putting their little children, their livestock and their possessions in front of them, they turned away and left.

22When they had gone some distance from Micah's house, the men who lived near Micah were called together and overtook the Danites. 23As they shouted after them, the Danites turned and said to Micah, "What's the matter with you that you called out your men to fight?"

24He replied, "You took the gods I made, and my priest, and went away. What else do I have? How can you ask, 'What's the matter with you?' "

18:10 [x]ver 7,27; Dt 8:9 [y]1Ch 4:40
18:11 [z]ver 16,17 [a]Jdg 13:2
18:12 [b]Jdg 13:25
18:14 [c]Ge 31:19; Jdg 17:5
18:16 [d]ver 11
18:17 [e]Ge 31:19; Mic 5:13
18:18 [f]Isa 46:2; Jer 43:11; Hos 10:5
18:19 [g]Job 21:5; 29:9; 40:4; Mic 7:16 [h]Jdg 17:10

25The Danites answered, "Don't argue with us, or some hot-tempered men will attack you, and you and your family will lose your lives." 26So the Danites went their way, and Micah, seeing that they were too strong for him,[i] turned around and went back home.

27Then they took what Micah had made, and his priest, and went on to Laish, against a peaceful and unsuspecting people.[j] They attacked them with the sword and burned down their city.[k] 28There was no one to rescue them because they lived a long way from Sidon[l] and had no relationship with anyone else. The city was in a valley near Beth Rehob.[m]

The Danites rebuilt the city and settled there. 29They named it Dan[n] after their forefather Dan, who was born to Israel—though the city used to be called Laish.[o] 30There the Danites set up for themselves the idols, and Jonathan son of Gershom,[p] the son of Moses,[b] and his sons were priests for the tribe of Dan until the time of the captivity of the land. 31They continued to use the idols Micah had made, all the time the house of God[q] was in Shiloh.[r]

A Levite and His Concubine

19 In those days Israel had no king.

Now a Levite who lived in a remote area in the hill country of Ephraim[s] took a concubine from Bethlehem in Judah.[t] 2But she was unfaithful to him. She left him and went back to her father's house in Bethlehem, Judah. After she had been there four months, 3her husband went to her to persuade her to return. He had with him his servant and two donkeys. She took him into her father's house, and when her father saw him, he gladly welcomed him. 4His father-in-law, the girl's father, prevailed upon him to stay; so he remained with him three days, eating and drinking,[u] and sleeping there.

5On the fourth day they got up early and he prepared to leave, but the girl's father said to his son-in-law, "Refresh yourself[v] with something to eat; then you can go." 6So the two of them sat

[a]*12 Mahaneh Dan* means *Dan's camp.* [b]*30* An ancient Hebrew scribal tradition, some Septuagint manuscripts and Vulgate; Masoretic Text *Manasseh*

18:26 [i]Ps 18:17; 35:10
18:27 [j]ver 7,10 [k]Ge 49:17; Jos 19:47
18:28 [l]ver 7 [m]Nu 13:21; 2Sa 10:6
18:29 [n]Ge 14:14 [o]Jos 19:47; 1Ki 15:20
18:30 [p]Ex 2:22; Jdg 17:3,5
18:31 [q]Jdg 19:18 [r]Jos 18:1; Jer 7:14
19:1 [s]Jdg 18:1 [t]Ru 1:1
19:4 [u]Ex 32:6
19:5 [v]ver 8; Ge 18:5

down to eat and drink together. Afterward the girl's father said, "Please stay
19:6 [w]ver 9,22; Jdg 16:25 tonight and enjoy yourself.[w]" 7And
when the man got up to go, his fa-
ther-in-law persuaded him, so he stayed
there that night. 8On the morning of
the fifth day, when he rose to go, the
girl's father said, "Refresh yourself. Wait
till afternoon!" So the two of them ate
together.
9Then when the man, with his concubine and his servant, got up to leave,
his father-in-law, the girl's father, said,
"Now look, it's almost evening. Spend
the night here; the day is nearly over.
Stay and enjoy yourself. Early tomorrow morning you can get up and be
on your way home." 10But, unwilling
to stay another night, the man left and
19:10 [x]Ge 10:16; Jos 15:8; 1Ch 11:4-5 went toward Jebus[x] (that is, Jerusalem),
with his two saddled donkeys and his
concubine.
11When they were near Jebus and the
day was almost gone, the servant said to
his master, "Come, let's stop at this city
19:11 [y]Jos 3:10 of the Jebusites[y] and spend the night."
12His master replied, "No. We won't
go into an alien city, whose people are
not Israelites. We will go on to Gibeah."
13He added, "Come, let's try to reach
Gibeah or Ramah[z] and spend the night
19:13 [z]Jos 18:25 in one of those places." 14So they went
on, and the sun set as they neared Gib-
19:14 [a]1Sa 10:26; Isa 10:29 eah in Benjamin.[a] 15There they stopped
to spend the night. They went and sat
in the city square,[b] but no one took
19:15 [b]Ge 19:2 them into his home for the night.
19:16 [c]Ps 104:23 [d]ver 1 16That evening[c] an old man from the
hill country of Ephraim,[d] who was liv-
ing in Gibeah (the men of the place
were Benjamites), came in from his
work in the fields. 17When he looked
and saw the traveler in the city square,
the old man asked, "Where are you go-
19:17 [e]Ge 29:4 ing? Where did you come from?"[e]
18He answered, "We are on our way
from Bethlehem in Judah to a remote
area in the hill country of Ephraim
where I live. I have been to Bethlehem
in Judah and now I am going to the
19:18 [f]Jdg 18:31 house of the LORD.[f] No one has taken
me into his house. 19We have both
19:19 [g]Ge 24:25 [h]Ge 14:18 straw and fodder[g] for our donkeys and
bread and wine[h] for ourselves your ser-
vants—me, your maidservant, and the
young man with us. We don't need anything."
20"You are welcome at my house,"
the old man said. "Let me supply whatever you need. Only don't spend the
night in the square." 21So he took him
into his house and fed his donkeys. After they had washed their feet, they had
something to eat and drink.[i] 19:21 [i]Ge 24:32-33; Lk 7:44
22While they were enjoying them-
selves,[j] some of the wicked men[k] of the 19:22 [j]Jdg 16:25 [k]Dt 13:13 [l]Ge 19:4-5; Jdg 20:5; Ro 1:26-27
city surrounded the house. Pounding
on the door, they shouted to the old
man who owned the house, "Bring out
the man who came to your house so we
can have sex with him.[l]"
23The owner of the house went out-
side[m] and said to them, "No, my friends, 19:23 [m]Ge 19:6 [n]Ge 34:7; Lev 19:29; Dt 22:21; Jdg 20:6; 2Sa 13:12; Ro 1:27
don't be so vile. Since this man is my
guest, don't do this disgraceful thing.[n]
24Look, here is my virgin daughter,[o]
and his concubine. I will bring them
out to you now, and you can use them
and do to them whatever you wish. But 19:24 [o]Ge 19:8; Dt 21:14
to this man, don't do such a disgraceful
thing."
25But the men would not listen to
him. So the man took his concubine
and sent her outside to them, and they
raped her and abused her[p] throughout 19:25 [p]1Sa 31:4
the night, and at dawn they let her go.
26At daybreak the woman went back to
the house where her master was staying,
fell down at the door and lay there until
daylight.
27When her master got up in the
morning and opened the door of the
house and stepped out to continue on
his way, there lay his concubine, fallen
in the doorway of the house, with her
hands on the threshold. 28He said to
her, "Get up; let's go." But there was no
answer. Then the man put her on his
donkey and set out for home.
29When he reached home, he took a
knife[q] and cut up his concubine, limb 19:29 [q]Ge 22:6 [r]Jdg 20:6; 1Sa 11:7
by limb, into twelve parts and sent them
into all the areas of Israel.[r] 30Everyone
who saw it said, "Such a thing has never
been seen or done, not since the day
the Israelites came up out of Egypt.[s] 19:30 [s]Hos 9:9 [t]Jdg 20:7; Pr 13:10
Think about it! Consider it! Tell us
what to do![t]"

Israelites Fight the Benjamites

20 Then all the Israelites[u] from 20:1 [u]Jdg 21:5 [v]1Sa 3:20; 2Sa 3:10; 1Ki 4:25 [w]1Sa 11:7 [x]1Sa 7:5
Dan to Beersheba[v] and from the
land of Gilead came out as one man[w]
and assembled[x] before the LORD in
Mizpah. 2The leaders of all the people
of the tribes of Israel took their places

in the assembly of the people of God,
20:2 four hundred thousand soldiers[y] armed
[y]Jdg 8:10 with swords. 3(The Benjamites heard
that the Israelites had gone up to Mizpah.) Then the Israelites said, "Tell us
how this awful thing happened."
4So the Levite, the husband of the
murdered woman, said, "I and my con-
20:4 cubine came to Gibeah[z] in Benjamin
[z]Jos 15:57 [a]Jdg 19:15 to spend the night.[a] 5During the night
the men of Gibeah came after me and
surrounded the house, intending to kill
20:5 me.[b] They raped my concubine, and
[b]Jdg 19:22 [c]Jdg 19:25-26 she died.[c] 6I took my concubine, cut
her into pieces and sent one piece to
20:6 [d]Jdg 19:29 each region of Israel's inheritance,[d] be-
[e]Jos 7:15; Jdg 19:23 cause they committed this lewd and
disgraceful act[e] in Israel. 7Now, all you
Israelites, speak up and give your ver-
20:7 dict.[f]"
[f]Jdg 19:30 8All the people rose as one man, saying, "None of us will go home. No, not
one of us will return to his house. 9But
now this is what we'll do to Gibeah:
20:9 We'll go up against it as the lot directs.[g]
[g]Lev 16:8 10We'll take ten men out of every hundred from all the tribes of Israel, and a
hundred from a thousand, and a thousand from ten thousand, to get provisions for the army. Then, when the
army arrives at Gibeah[a] in Benjamin, it
can give them what they deserve for all
this vileness done in Israel." 11So all the
men of Israel got together and united as
20:11 one man[h] against the city.
[h]ver 1 12The tribes of Israel sent men
throughout the tribe of Benjamin, saying, "What about this awful crime that
was committed among you? 13Now sur-
20:13 render those wicked men[i] of Gibeah so
[i]Dt 13:13; Jdg 19:22 that we may put them to death and
[j]Dt 17:12 purge the evil from Israel.[j]"
But the Benjamites would not listen
to their fellow Israelites. 14From their
towns they came together at Gibeah to
fight against the Israelites. 15At once
the Benjamites mobilized twenty-six
thousand swordsmen from their towns,
in addition to seven hundred chosen
men from those living in Gibeah.
16Among all these soldiers there were
seven hundred chosen men who were
20:16 left-handed,[k] each of whom could sling
[k]Jdg 3:15; 1Ch 12:2 a stone at a hair and not miss.
17Israel, apart from Benjamin, mus-
tered four hundred thousand swordsmen, all of them fighting men.
18The Israelites went up to Bethel[b]

and inquired of God.[l] They said, "Who 20:18 [l]ver 26-27; Nu 27:21
of us shall go first to fight[m] against the [m]ver 23,28
Benjamites?"
The LORD replied, "Judah shall go
first."
19The next morning the Israelites
got up and pitched camp near Gibeah.
20The men of Israel went out to fight
the Benjamites and took up battle positions against them at Gibeah. 21The
Benjamites came out of Gibeah and cut
down twenty-two thousand Israelites[n] 20:21
on the battlefield that day. 22But the [n]ver 25
men of Israel encouraged one another
and again took up their positions where
they had stationed themselves the first
day. 23The Israelites went up and wept
before the LORD until evening,[o] and 20:23 [o]Jos 7:6
they inquired of the LORD. They said, [p]ver 18
"Shall we go up again to battle[p] against
the Benjamites, our brothers?"
The LORD answered, "Go up against
them."
24Then the Israelites drew near to
Benjamin the second day. 25This time,
when the Benjamites came out from
Gibeah to oppose them, they cut down
another eighteen thousand Israelites,[q] 20:25 [q]ver 21
all of them armed with swords.
26Then the Israelites, all the people,
went up to Bethel, and there they sat 20:26
weeping before the LORD.[r] They fast- [r]ver 23
ed that day until evening and presented [s]Jdg 21:4
burnt offerings and fellowship offer-
ings[c] to the LORD.[s] 27And the Israelites
inquired of the LORD. (In those days
the ark of the covenant of God[t] was 20:27 [t]Jos 18:1
there, 28with Phinehas son of Eleazar,[u] 20:28
the son of Aaron, ministering before [u]Jos 24:33 [v]Dt 18:5
it.)[v] They asked, "Shall we go up again [w]Jdg 7:9
to battle with Benjamin our brother, or
not?"
The LORD responded, "Go, for tomorrow I will give them into your
hands.[w]"
29Then Israel set an ambush[x] around 20:29 [x]Jos 8:2,4
Gibeah. 30They went up against the
Benjamites on the third day and took
up positions against Gibeah as they had
done before. 31The Benjamites came out
to meet them and were drawn away[y] 20:31 [y]Jos 8:16
from the city. They began to inflict casualties on the Israelites as before, so
that about thirty men fell in the open

[a]*10* One Hebrew manuscript; most Hebrew manuscripts *Geba,* a variant of *Gibeah*
[b]*18* Or *to the house of God*; also in verse 26
[c]*26* Traditionally *peace offerings*

field and on the roads—the one leading
to Bethel and the other to Gibeah.
32While the Benjamites were saying,
20:32 [z]ver 39 “We are defeating them as before,”[z] the
Israelites were saying, “Let’s retreat and
draw them away from the city to the
roads.”
33All the men of Israel moved from
their places and took up positions at
Baal Tamar, and the Israelite ambush
20:33 [a]Jos 8:19 charged out of its place[a] on the west[a]
of Gibeah.[b] 34Then ten thousand of Is-
rael’s finest men made a frontal attack
on Gibeah. The fighting was so heavy
20:34 [b]Jos 8:14 [c]Isa 47:11 that the Benjamites did not realize[b] how
near disaster was.[c] 35The LORD defeat-
ed Benjamin[d] before Israel, and on that
20:35 [d]1Sa 9:21 day the Israelites struck down 25,100
Benjamites, all armed with swords.
36Then the Benjamites saw that they
were beaten.
Now the men of Israel had given
20:36 [e]Jos 8:15 way[e] before Benjamin, because they relied on the ambush they had set near
Gibeah. 37The men who had been in
ambush made a sudden dash into Gibeah, spread out and put the whole city
20:37 [f]Jos 8:19 to the sword.[f] 38The men of Israel had
arranged with the ambush that they
20:38 [g]Jos 8:20 should send up a great cloud of smoke[g]
from the city, 39and then the men of Is-
rael would turn in the battle.
The Benjamites had begun to inflict
casualties on the men of Israel (about
thirty), and they said, “We are defeat-
20:39 [h]ver 32 ing them as in the first battle.”[h] 40But
when the column of smoke began to
rise from the city, the Benjamites turned
and saw the smoke of the whole city go-
20:40 [i]Jos 8:20 ing up into the sky.[i] 41Then the men
of Israel turned on them, and the men
of Benjamin were terrified, because they
realized that disaster had come upon
them. 42So they fled before the Israelites in the direction of the desert, but
they could not escape the battle. And
the men of Israel who came out of the
towns cut them down there. 43They surrounded the Benjamites, chased them
and easily[c] overran them in the vicinity
of Gibeah on the east. 44Eighteen thousand Benjamites fell, all of them valiant
20:44 [j]Ps 76:5 fighters.[j] 45As they turned and fled to-
20:45 [k]Jos 15:32; Jdg 21:13 ward the desert to the rock of Rimmon,[k]
the Israelites cut down five thousand
men along the roads. They kept pressing after the Benjamites as far as Gidom
and struck down two thousand more.

46On that day twenty-five thousand
Benjamite swordsmen fell, all of them
valiant fighters. 47But six hundred men
turned and fled into the desert to the
rock of Rimmon, where they stayed
four months. 48The men of Israel went
back to Benjamin and put all the towns
to the sword, including the animals
and everything else they found. All the
towns they came across they set on
fire.[l] 20:48 [l]Jdg 21:23

Wives for the Benjamites

21 The men of Israel had taken an
oath[m] at Mizpah:[n] “Not one of 21:1 [m]Jos 9:18 [n]Jdg 20:1 [o]ver 7,18
us will give[o] his daughter in marriage to
a Benjamite.”
2The people went to Bethel,[d] where
they sat before God until evening, raising their voices and weeping bitterly.
3“O LORD, the God of Israel,” they
cried, “why has this happened to Israel?
Why should one tribe be missing from
Israel today?”
4Early the next day the people built
an altar and presented burnt offerings
and fellowship offerings.[e][p] 21:4 [p]Jdg 20:26; 2Sa 24:25
5Then the Israelites asked, “Who
from all the tribes of Israel[q] has failed to 21:5 [q]Jdg 5:23; 20:1
assemble before the LORD?” For they
had taken a solemn oath that anyone
who failed to assemble before the LORD
at Mizpah should certainly be put to
death.
6Now the Israelites grieved for their
brothers, the Benjamites. “Today one
tribe is cut off from Israel,” they said.
7“How can we provide wives for those
who are left, since we have taken an
oath[r] by the LORD not to give them any 21:7 [r]ver 1
of our daughters in marriage?” 8Then
they asked, “Which one of the tribes
of Israel failed to assemble before the
LORD at Mizpah?” They discovered
that no one from Jabesh Gilead[s] had 21:8 [s]1Sa 11:1; 31:11
come to the camp for the assembly. 9For
when they counted the people, they
found that none of the people of Jabesh
Gilead were there.
10So the assembly sent twelve thousand fighting men with instructions to
go to Jabesh Gilead and put to the

[a]*33* Some Septuagint manuscripts and Vulgate; the meaning of the Hebrew for this word is uncertain. [b]*33* Hebrew *Geba,* a variant of *Gibeah*
[c]*43* The meaning of the Hebrew for this word is uncertain. [d]*2* Or *to the house of God*
[e]*4* Traditionally *peace offerings*

sword those living there, including the
women and children. 11“This is what
you are to do,” they said. “Kill every
male and every woman who is not a
21:11 [t]Nu 31:17-18 virgin.[t]” 12They found among the people living in Jabesh Gilead four hun-
dred young women who had never slept
with a man, and they took them to the
21:12 [u]Jos 18:1 camp at Shiloh[u] in Canaan.
13Then the whole assembly sent an
21:13 [v]Dt 20:10 [w]Jdg 20:47 offer of peace[v] to the Benjamites at the
rock of Rimmon.[w] 14So the Benjamites
returned at that time and were given
the women of Jabesh Gilead who had
been spared. But there were not enough
for all of them.
21:15 [x]ver 6 15The people grieved for Benjamin,[x]
because the LORD had made a gap in
the tribes of Israel. 16And the elders of
the assembly said, “With the women of
Benjamin destroyed, how shall we provide wives for the men who are left?
17The Benjamite survivors must have
heirs,” they said, “so that a tribe of Israel will not be wiped out. 18We can't give
them our daughters as wives, since we
Israelites have taken this oath: ‘Cursed
21:18 [y]ver 1 be anyone who gives[y] a wife to a Benjamite.’ 19But look, there is the annual
festival of the LORD in Shiloh,[z] to the 21:19 [z]Jos 18:1; Jdg 18:31; 1Sa 1:3
north of Bethel, and east of the road
that goes from Bethel to Shechem, and
to the south of Lebonah.”
20So they instructed the Benjamites,
saying, “Go and hide in the vineyards
21and watch. When the girls of Shiloh
come out to join in the dancing,[a] then 21:21 [a]Ex 15:20; Jdg 11:34
rush from the vineyards and each of
you seize a wife from the girls of Shiloh and go to the land of Benjamin.
22When their fathers or brothers complain to us, we will say to them, ‘Do
us a kindness by helping them, because
we did not get wives for them during
the war, and you are innocent, since
you did not give[b] your daughters to 21:22 [b]ver 1,18
them.’”
23So that is what the Benjamites did.
While the girls were dancing, each man
caught one and carried her off to be his
wife. Then they returned to their inheritance and rebuilt the towns and settled
in them.[c] 21:23 [c]Jdg 20:48
24At that time the Israelites left that
place and went home to their tribes and
clans, each to his own inheritance. 21:25 [d]Dt 12:8; Jdg 17:6; 18:1; 19:1
25In those days Israel had no king;
everyone did as he saw fit.[d]

RUTH

AUTHORSHIP AND DATE

The author is unknown.

Probably written after 1000 B.C., since David is referred to

KEY THEMES

The book of Ruth holds a vital place among the small but important books of the Bible. It fills in the genealogy of David (see 4:16–22), but it is so much more than a genealogical hyphen in the Old Testament. It is a story of kindness and faithfulness, a tale of integrity and hardship and blessing. It is an oasis of tenderness and kindness placed between the harsh exploits of the judges and the fierce military struggles of the new monarchy. The book of Ruth is a tender account of a Gentile woman from Moab and her friendship with a Hebrew woman from Bethlehem named Naomi. A parallel story is the developing romance between Ruth and a relative of Naomi's. This seemingly unimportant couple wrote themselves into the lineage of kings.

FRUIT OF THE SPIRIT IN RUTH

Goodness: The fruit of goodness is only slightly easier to see than are the fruits of love, gentleness or faithfulness. But *goodness* is the word that stands out when defining this book filled with heroes. Examine the quality of goodness exhibited by the three main characters that occupy the stage of this book.

Naomi: Having lost her husband and sons, she nonetheless was willing to take her daughter-in-law, Ruth, back to Bethlehem with her. Naomi insisted on being called Mara ("bitter") because she felt the Lord had dealt bitterly with her. Her broken heart left her open to the companionship of her virtuous daughter-in-law.

Ruth: Her goodness was manifested in many ways: She didn't want to abandon her grieving mother-in-law (see 1:16). In order to feed them both, she agreed to glean in the fields, gathering what meager food she could find (see 2:2). She was not contentious with her mother-in-law's advice, but she readily agreed to honor the older woman's counsel, saying, "I will do whatever you say" (3:5). And she did "everything her mother-in-law told her to do" (v. 6).

Boaz: He encouraged Ruth not to glean in any other field but his (see 2:8). He also told her that when she was thirsty, she could drink from the water jars used by the men on his farm. And Boaz guaranteed her security by instructing the men not to hurt her (see 2:9).

The result of so much goodness: Ruth and Boaz married and are a part of the line of Christ.

Naomi and Ruth

1:1 1 In the days when the judges ruled,[1][a]
[a]Jdg 2:16-18 [b]Ge 12:10; there was a famine in the land,[b]
Ps 105:16 [c]Jdg 3:30 and a man from Bethlehem in Judah,
together with his wife and two sons,
went to live for a while in the country
of Moab.[c] 2The man's name was Elimelech, his wife's name Naomi, and the
names of his two sons were Mahlon
1:2 and Kilion. They were Ephrathites from
[d]Ge 35:19 Bethlehem,[d] Judah. And they went to
Moab and lived there.
3Now Elimelech, Naomi's husband,
died, and she was left with her two
sons. 4They married Moabite women,
1:4 one named Orpah and the other Ruth.[e]
[e]Mt 1:5 After they had lived there about ten
years, 5both Mahlon and Kilion also
died, and Naomi was left without her
two sons and her husband.
6When she heard in Moab that the
LORD had come to the aid of his peo-
1:6 [f]Ex 4:31; ple[f] by providing food[g] for them, Na-
Jer 29:10; omi and her daughters-in-law prepared
Zep 2:7 [g]Ps 132:15; to return home from there. 7With her
Mt 6:11 two daughters-in-law she left the place
where she had been living and set out
on the road that would take them back
to the land of Judah.
8Then Naomi said to her two daughters-in-law, "Go back, each of you, to
1:8 your mother's home. May the LORD
[h]Ru 2:20; 2Ti 1:16 show kindness[h] to you, as you have
[i]ver 5 shown to your dead[i] and to me. 9May
the LORD grant that each of you will
1:9 [j]Ru 3:1 find rest[j] in the home of another husband."
Then she kissed them and they wept
aloud 10and said to her, "We will go
back with you to your people."
11But Naomi said, "Return home, my
daughters. Why would you come with
1:11 me? Am I going to have any more sons,
[k]Ge 38:11; Dt 25:5 who could become your husbands?[k]
12Return home, my daughters; I am too
old to have another husband. Even if
I thought there was still hope for me—
even if I had a husband tonight and
then gave birth to sons— 13would you
wait until they grew up? Would you
1:13 remain unmarried for them? No, my
[l]Jdg 2:15; daughters. It is more bitter for me than
Job 4:5; 19:21; for you, because the LORD's hand has
Ps 32:4 gone out against me![l]"
1:14 14At this they wept again. Then Or-
[m]Ru 2:11 [n]Pr 17:17; pah kissed her mother-in-law[m] good-
18:24 by, but Ruth clung to her.[n]

15"Look," said Naomi, "your sister-
in-law is going back to her people and
her gods.[o] Go back with her." 1:15 [o]Jos 24:14;
16But Ruth replied, "Don't urge me Jdg 11:24

[a]*1* Traditionally *judged*

DAY 5 FIVE

▸ GENTLENESS AND ITS PLACE IN MY PERSONAL WORSHIP

Ruth 1:16–17

To think of gentleness is to think of Ruth. This book is a beautiful little stopover of grace sandwiched between the frequently gruesome sagas of the judges and the checkered histories of the kings. Ruth isn't a book you study—it's a new pair of shoes that you wear and find that your heels are winged with all that is most noble in the human spirit.

"Don't urge me to leave you," Ruth begs with dignity. Her eloquence is steeped in tenderness—yes, in gentleness. She has lost her husband; she is unsupported and alone, yet her concern is for Naomi. She desires to be with Naomi through the coming trials and struggles. Are you not struck by the gentle form this strong commitment takes? Robert Harling's play *Steel Magnolias* is a story about five women whose gentle spirits could, when necessary, exhibit steel commitment. How blessed are all those who make gentle commitments of steel.

Now when Ruth and Naomi arrive in Bethlehem, bereaved and penniless, what does gentleness win them—a moment of grand worship in a splendid tabernacle? No, but it teaches them that life itself can become a worship experience. God is a balm for the pain of the gentle. His touch in a life can inspire worship through the difficult experience.

If you would know gentleness as a way of winning others and thrilling in personal worship, then observe a hopeless old woman become an ancestor of the Son of God. And see Ruth, a Gentile woman, contributing her bit of DNA to the makeup of Mary's baby a thousand years before his time. Gentleness is a part of the life of Ruth, and worship is the life lived for God.

To begin a study on the topic of Gentleness, a Way of Winning Others to Christ, turn to the home page on page 1303.

1:16 [p]2Ki 2:2 to leave you[p] or to turn back from you.
[q]Ru 2:11,12 Where you go I will go, and where
you stay I will stay. Your people will
be my people and your God my God.[q]
17Where you die I will die, and there
I will be buried. May the LORD deal
1:17 [r]1Sa 3:17; with me, be it ever so severely,[r] if any-
25:22; thing but death separates you and me."
2Sa 19:13; 18When Naomi realized that Ruth was
2Ki 6:31 determined to go with her, she stopped
1:18 urging her.[s]
[s]Ac 21:14 19So the two women went on until
they came to Bethlehem. When they arrived in Bethlehem, the whole town was
stirred[t] because of them, and the wom- 1:19 [t]Mt 21:10
en exclaimed, "Can this be Naomi?"
20"Don't call me Naomi,[a]" she told
them. "Call me Mara,[b] because the Al-
mighty[c] [u] has made my life very bitter.[v] 1:20 [u]Ex 6:3
21I went away full, but the LORD has [v]ver 13; Job 6:4
brought me back empty.[w] Why call me
Naomi? The LORD has afflicted[d] me; 1:21 [w]Job 1:21
the Almighty has brought misfortune
upon me."

[a]20 *Naomi* means *pleasant*; also in verse 21.
[b]20 *Mara* means *bitter.* [c]20 Hebrew *Shaddai*; also in verse 21 [d]21 Or *has testified against*

RUTH

Love Through the Tears (1:1-22)

There is no relationship stronger than the fellowship of suffering. Ruth and Naomi had gone through the pain of widowhood together and had clung to each other when all light seemed to have been shut out by the black mantle of death. Their tears watered their common trust, and it grew. Their love flourished in their brokenness, proving that we can never really know someone until we've wept with them.

Although Naomi left Bethlehem due to a famine, she was likely optimistic that this was but a temporary setback in life. Now, years later, she returned as an exile bludgeoned by life's brutality. Ruth became an alien, a Moabitess in a Jewish culture, a Gentile with nothing to commend her. Suffering had made these women partners in their sorrow, but the greatest bond between them was their trust.

The trust between Naomi and Ruth is revealed at the very beginning of their journey together. Naomi had two daughters-in-law, Ruth and Orpah. Both women set out with Naomi on the journey back to Bethlehem. But when Naomi told them both to return to their homes, only Orpah agreed to do so. Although Naomi was insistent, Ruth remained loyal to the path she had chosen. Ruth clung to Naomi in love. Even though Naomi set her free to return to her family in Moab, Ruth begged Naomi: "Don't urge me to leave you or to turn back from you" (Ruth 1:16). Thus began a love whose endurance would be marked through the centuries by its inclusion in the lineage of Christ.

Love as strong as Ruth's is a rare thing, for this kind of love always results in service. It has often been said that we can serve without loving, but we cannot love without serving. Ruth's love ordered her into the fields to serve in the backbreaking work of gleaning. She spent her days picking up grains of wheat that the harvesters had missed. It was wretched work. But when her service was over, Ruth's love yielded a harvest of grace and placed her name in the ancestry of Jesus.

Love as strong as Ruth's results in trust. When Naomi instructed Ruth to approach Boaz on the threshing floor and ask for his protection, Ruth obeyed without question. Such love brings rewards: "So Boaz took Ruth and she became his wife" (4:13). Love produced a harvest of blessing for both Ruth and Naomi. Naomi finally received her hope for the future; it came in the form of the child that lay in her lap (see v. 16). That child, the son of Ruth and Boaz, became the grandfather of King David.

Love is strong as steel—the manganese of rugged endurance. It is the platinum heart of all treasure.

Love binds those who must live beneath the stress of grief and separation, and it says to them, "Weep until you are malleable—God shapes best clay made soft by tears."

GENTLENESS

WHITE BANDAGES FROM OLD BITTERNESS

Ruth 1:20

Naomi's lessons are ours also. There is a Savior who catches all our tears in golden censers so the angels may esteem our pain. He waits for us in a land where bitterness has never entered. He, who at least four times wept himself, shall someday wipe away all tears.

22So Naomi returned from Moab accompanied by Ruth the Moabitess, her
daughter-in-law, arriving in Bethlehem
1:22 [x]Ex 9:31; Ru 2:23 [y]2Sa 21:9 as the barley harvest[x] was beginning.[y]

Ruth Meets Boaz

2:1 [z]Ru 3:2,12 [a]Ru 1:2 [b]Ru 4:21 2 Now Naomi had a relative[z] on her
husband's side, from the clan of
Elimelech,[a] a man of standing, whose
name was Boaz.[b]
2And Ruth the Moabitess said to Naomi, "Let me go to the fields and pick
up the leftover grain[c] behind anyone in
2:2 [c]ver 7; Lev 19:9; 23:22; Dt 24:19 whose eyes I find favor."
Naomi said to her, "Go ahead, my
daughter." 3So she went out and began
to glean in the fields behind the harvesters. As it turned out, she found herself
working in a field belonging to Boaz,
who was from the clan of Elimelech.
4Just then Boaz arrived from Bethle-
2:4 [d]Jdg 6:12; Lk 1:28; 2Th 3:16 [e]Ps 129:7-8 hem and greeted the harvesters, "The
LORD be with you!"[d]
"The LORD bless you![e]" they called
back.
5Boaz asked the foreman of his
harvesters, "Whose young woman is
that?"
6The foreman replied, "She is the
2:6 [f]Ru 1:22 Moabitess[f] who came back from Moab
with Naomi. 7She said, 'Please let me
glean and gather among the sheaves
behind the harvesters.' She went into
the field and has worked steadily from
morning till now, except for a short rest
in the shelter."
8So Boaz said to Ruth, "My daughter, listen to me. Don't go and glean in
another field and don't go away from
here. Stay here with my servant girls.
9Watch the field where the men are harvesting, and follow along after the girls.
I have told the men not to touch you.
And whenever you are thirsty, go and
get a drink from the water jars the men
have filled."
10At this, she bowed down with her
face to the ground.[g] She exclaimed, 2:10 [g]1Sa 25:23 [h]Ps 41:1 [i]Dt 15:3
"Why have I found such favor in your
eyes that you notice me[h]—a foreigner?[i]"
11Boaz replied, "I've been told all
about what you have done for your
mother-in-law[j] since the death of your 2:11 [j]Ru 1:14 [k]Ru 1:16-17
husband—how you left your father and
mother and your homeland and came
to live with a people you did not know
before.[k] 12May the LORD repay you for 2:12 [l]1Sa 24:19 [m]Ps 17:8; 36:7; 57:1; 61:4; 63:7; 91:4 [n]Ru 1:16
what you have done. May you be rich-
ly rewarded by the LORD,[l] the God of
Israel, under whose wings[m] you have
come to take refuge.[n]"

SELF-CONTROL

SELF-CONTROL: A METHODOLOGY FOR BUILDING REPUTATION

Ruth 2:11–12

When you speak the word *Christ* to someone in despair, you build a pedestal for discipline.
Discipline produces character.
That character entices all the world to think of God
and wish itself more moral.

13"May I continue to find favor in
your eyes, my lord," she said. "You
have given me comfort and have spoken kindly to your servant—though I
do not have the standing of one of your
servant girls."
14At mealtime Boaz said to her,
"Come over here. Have some bread and
dip it in the wine vinegar."
When she sat down with the harvesters, he offered her some roasted grain.
She ate all she wanted and had some
left over.[o] 15As she got up to glean, 2:14 [o]ver 18
Boaz gave orders to his men, "Even if
she gathers among the sheaves, don't
embarrass her. 16Rather, pull out some
stalks for her from the bundles and
leave them for her to pick up, and don't
rebuke her."
17So Ruth gleaned in the field until
evening. Then she threshed the barley
she had gathered, and it amounted to
about an ephah.[a] 18She carried it back

[a] *17* That is, probably about 3/5 bushel (about 22 liters)

to town, and her mother-in-law saw
how much she had gathered. Ruth also
brought out and gave her what she had
2:18 [p]ver 14 left over[p] after she had eaten enough.
19Her mother-in-law asked her,
"Where did you glean today? Where
did you work? Blessed be the man who
2:19 [q]ver 10; Ps 41:1 took notice of you![q]"
Then Ruth told her mother-in-law
about the one at whose place she had
been working. "The name of the man I
worked with today is Boaz," she said.

LOVE

THE KINSMAN-REDEEMER

Ruth 2:20

What a lovely word: *kinsman-redeemer*. It says we have a rich relative—a person whose affluence and power are known in heaven. He is on our side. His grace will stamp "Paid in Full" across our bankrupt lives.

20"The LORD bless him!" Naomi said
to her daughter-in-law. "He has not
2:20 [r]Ru 3:10; 2Sa 2:5; Pr 17:17 stopped showing his kindness[r] to the
living and the dead." She added, "That
[s]Ru 3:9,12; 4:1,14 man is our close relative; he is one of
our kinsman-redeemers.[s]"
21Then Ruth the Moabitess said, "He
even said to me, 'Stay with my workers until they finish harvesting all my
grain.' "
22Naomi said to Ruth her daughter-
in-law, "It will be good for you, my
daughter, to go with his girls, because
in someone else's field you might be
harmed."
23So Ruth stayed close to the servant
girls of Boaz to glean until the barley
2:23 [t]Dt 16:9 and wheat harvests[t] were finished. And
she lived with her mother-in-law.

Ruth and Boaz at the Threshing Floor

3 One day Naomi her mother-in-law
said to her, "My daughter, should I
3:1 [u]Ru 1:9 not try to find a home[a] [u] for you, where
you will be well provided for? 2Is not
3:2 [v]Dt 25:5-10; Ru 2:1 Boaz, with whose servant girls you have
been, a kinsman[v] of ours? Tonight he
will be winnowing barley on the thresh-
3:3 [w]2Sa 14:2 ing floor. 3Wash and perfume yourself,[w]
and put on your best clothes. Then go
down to the threshing floor, but don't
let him know you are there until he has
finished eating and drinking. 4When he
lies down, note the place where he is
lying. Then go and uncover his feet
and lie down. He will tell you what
to do."
5"I will do whatever you say,"[x] Ruth 3:5 [x]Eph 6:1; Col 3:20
answered. 6So she went down to the
threshing floor and did everything her
mother-in-law told her to do.
7When Boaz had finished eating and
drinking and was in good spirits,[y] he 3:7 [y]Jdg 19:6, 9,22; 2Sa 13:28; 1Ki 21:7; Est 1:10
went over to lie down at the far end of
the grain pile. Ruth approached quietly,
uncovered his feet and lay down. 8In
the middle of the night something startled the man, and he turned and discovered a woman lying at his feet.
9"Who are you?" he asked.
"I am your servant Ruth," she said.
"Spread the corner of your garment[z] 3:9 [z]Eze 16:8
over me, since you are a kinsman-re- [a]ver 12; Ru 2:20
deemer.[a]"
10"The LORD bless you, my daughter," he replied. "This kindness is greater than that which you showed earlier:
You have not run after the younger
men, whether rich or poor. 11And now,
my daughter, don't be afraid. I will do
for you all you ask. All my fellow townsmen know that you are a woman of no-
ble character.[b] 12Although it is true that 3:11 [b]Pr 12:4; 31:10
I am near of kin, there is a kinsman-
redeemer[c] nearer than[d] I. 13Stay here 3:12 [c]ver 9 [d]Ru 4:1
for the night, and in the morning if
he wants to redeem,[e] good; let him re- 3:13 [e]Dt 25:5; Ru 4:5; Mt 22:24
deem. But if he is not willing, as surely
as the LORD lives[f] I will do it. Lie here [f]Jdg 8:19; Jer 4:2
until morning."
14So she lay at his feet until morning, but got up before anyone could be
recognized; and he said, "Don't let it
be known that a woman came to the
threshing floor."[g] 3:14 [g]Ro 14:16; 2Co 8:21
15He also said, "Bring me the shawl
you are wearing and hold it out." When
she did so, he poured into it six measures of barley and put it on her. Then
he[b] went back to town.
16When Ruth came to her mother-
in-law, Naomi asked, "How did it go,
my daughter?"
Then she told her everything Boaz
had done for her 17and added, "He gave
me these six measures of barley, saying,

[a] *1* Hebrew *find rest* (see Ruth 1:9) [b] *15* Most Hebrew manuscripts; many Hebrew manuscripts, Vulgate and Syriac *she*

WEEK 8

GENTLENESS

DAY ONE

GENTLENESS, THE APPROACHABLE LIFE

Read Ruth 2:19–22

Naomi lived a life of sorrow and tragedy. She lost her husband while living in a strange land. Then both of her sons died. In chapter one of Ruth, Naomi begs her friends to call her Mara, or "Miss Bitter," for life's circumstances had made Naomi feel empty, sad and bitter.

Cynicism and gentleness are opposite responses to the same hardships. Some sufferings and trials break and wound, and those who are broken and wounded are made malleable—soft putty in the hands of God. These broken souls are gentle in every way. They become—because of all they have suffered—the best counselors of God.

But others are made cynical and hard. They become characterized by bitterness and brooding, unkind and harsh in their treatment of others. Naomi confesses to such bitterness.

But Naomi is home again in Bethlehem. Everything looks better when you're at home. Although she claims to be bitter, Naomi is gentle with Ruth. She advises Ruth to glean in Boaz's fields "because in someone else's field you might be harmed."

And Boaz, too, is gentle and kind. He tells Ruth, "Don't go and glean in another field" (Ruth 2:8). All in all, the book of Ruth may be the apex of our study on the fruit of the Spirit, and particularly the fruit of gentleness. Each aspect of the story sees gentleness as the approachable life—treating others with kindness so that all may approach and not be afraid.

DAY TWO

GENTLENESS AND THE PURPOSE OF GOD IN MY LIFE

"Hatred stirs up dissension," and dissension separates us into small, walled provinces of ego-defensiveness. Hatred is non-inviting. It crushes us into small cells of fear that cause us to shrink back into the center of our souls. That "I'd like to cross over to the other side of the road" feeling comes when people are in the presence of such hatred. But gentleness makes others feel comfortable at our approach. *Turn to Proverbs 10:12, page 743, for today's study.*

MEMORIZE THIS WEEK

MATTHEW 11:29

Take my yoke upon you and learn from me, for I am gentle and humble in heart, and you will find rest for your souls.

DAY THREE

GENTLENESS AND MY RELATIONSHIP WITH CHRIST

Here is the picture that well earns Jesus the title, "Gentle Jesus, Meek and Mild." It is not the Jesus who rebukes Pharisees who brings comfort to our souls. It is the Christ who blesses children. Childlikeness is the heart of gentleness. Children do not make us afraid. Rather, they invite us to love them and to summon up all the gentleness we can, so we will not make them afraid of us. *Turn to Mark 10:13–16, page 1183, for today's study.*

DAY FOUR

GENTLENESS AND MY SERVICE TO OTHERS

We're all in this together. When we serve others, we can look into the faces of those in need of our healing touch and know that we are a breath away from their situation. When we serve others, when we share gentle words and deeds, may we remember that God's grace allows us to be able to give. *Turn to Hebrews 5:1–3, page 1465, for today's study.*

DAY FIVE

GENTLENESS AND ITS PLACE IN MY PERSONAL WORSHIP

Jesus' ultimate gentleness is captured in this Messianic picture of a great king riding on a donkey. Isn't this the noblest challenge to our own hard-hearted lifestyles? We prefer the image of power and control—a white steed and the appropriate banner—just so we can feel good about ourselves. Surely when we feel like we ought to be treated royally, we will remember Zechariah's picture of the Servant-Messiah and worship God in a spirit of gentleness. *Turn to Zechariah 9:9, page 1105, for today's study.*

Week 9, Self-Control, the Path of Coming to Maturity, begins on page 364, 2 Samuel 11:1–5.
To begin a topical study on the Fruit of the Spirit, Gentleness, turn to the Topical Index, page 1548.

'Don't go back to your mother-in-law empty-handed.' "
18Then Naomi said, "Wait, my daughter, until you find out what happens. For the man will not rest until the matter is settled today."[b]

3:18 [b]Ps 37:3-5

Boaz Marries Ruth

4 Meanwhile Boaz went up to the town gate and sat there. When the kinsman-redeemer he had mentioned[i] came along, Boaz said, "Come over here, my friend, and sit down." So he went over and sat down.

4:1 [i]Ru 3:12

2Boaz took ten of the elders[j] of the
town and said, "Sit here," and they
did so. 3Then he said to the kinsman-
redeemer, "Naomi, who has come back
from Moab, is selling the piece of land
that belonged to our brother Elimelech.
4I thought I should bring the matter to
your attention and suggest that you buy
it in the presence of these seated here
and in the presence of the elders of my

4:2 [j]1Ki 21:8; Pr 31:23

BOAZ

Kindness, the Ensign of Romance (4:1–22)

In this beautiful tale of romance, we read of the first meeting between Ruth and Boaz, which appeared to be love at first sight for Boaz. When Ruth first arrived in Bethlehem from her homeland of Moab, she found work picking up leftover grain in barley fields. She and her mother-in-law, Naomi, were both widows and helplessly poor. But Boaz noticed Ruth in his field right away, and he questioned his foreman, "Whose young woman is that?" (Ruth 2:5). When he discovered who she was, his interest in her only seemed to increase. He approached her and over the next few weeks showed her nine specific kindnesses:

First, he told Ruth to stay under his protection: "Don't go and glean in another field" (v. 8).

Second, he ordered the field hands not to take any sexual liberties with her, since she was a foreign woman living in a strange land with no protector (v. 9).

Third, he told Ruth that whenever she was thirsty she could drink from the water jars that he kept for his own field hands (v. 9).

Fourth, he complimented her on the excellent kindness she had shown to her mother-in-law, Naomi (v. 11).

Fifth, he allowed Ruth to share in the noon meal with those he had hired (v. 14).

Sixth—and now we know this affair is getting serious—he ordered the harvesters to purposely leave some grain so Ruth would be able to glean a good amount (v. 16).

Seventh, he protected her reputation after she came to him on the threshing floor and asked that he be her kinsman-redeemer (3:14).

Eighth, he gave her six measures of barley as a gift, a very valuable present in Ruth and Naomi's time of hardship (v. 15).

Finally, he bought her hand in marriage by agreeing to become her kinsman-redeemer in the place of the nearer relative who had declined the role (4:1–10).

So the love affair that began with kindness was consummated in romance, and the child that was born to them was an ancestor of our Lord. One hears Boaz's sonnet forming as the events, and his heart, unfold:

There in the gold she stands, empress of grain,
The harvest just ahead of her. I see,
And in this glance I know why lovers die
For love. I own these fields, this realm she reigns.
She stops. Those almond eyes of Araby
Survey her new-found home. O God, she's come—
Beguiling immigrant of mystery,
And Isaac stares at Ishmael as dumb.
Bethlehem is charged. The desert's green.
Such fields as these might angels know in time.
Such beauty might conceive a royal king.
Such regal bearing tempts the light to shine.
May Moab mother infant princes here
And love be mine while ages stand and cheer.

people. If you will redeem it, do so. But
if you[a] will not, tell me, so I will know.
For no one has the right to do it except
4:4 [k]Lev 25:25; Jer 32:7-8 you,[k] and I am next in line."
"I will redeem it," he said.
5Then Boaz said, "On the day you
buy the land from Naomi and from
Ruth the Moabitess, you acquire[b] the
dead man's widow, in order to maintain
the name of the dead with his
4:5 [l]Ge 38:8; Dt 25:5-6; Ru 3:13; Mt 22:24 property."[l]
6At this, the kinsman-redeemer said,
"Then I cannot redeem[m] it because I
4:6 [m]Lev 25:25; Ru 3:13 might endanger my own estate. You redeem
deem it yourself. I cannot do it."
7(Now in earlier times in Israel, for
the redemption and transfer of property
to become final, one party took off
his sandal and gave it to the other. This
was the method of legalizing transactions
4:7 [n]Dt 25:7-9 tions in Israel.)[n]
8So the kinsman-redeemer said to
Boaz, "Buy it yourself." And he removed
moved his sandal.
9Then Boaz announced to the elders
and all the people, "Today you are witnesses
that I have bought from Naomi
all the property of Elimelech, Kilion
and Mahlon. 10I have also acquired
Ruth the Moabitess, Mahlon's widow,
as my wife, in order to maintain the
name of the dead with his property, so
that his name will not disappear from
4:10 [o]Dt 25:6 among his family or from the town
records.[o] Today you are witnesses!"
11Then the elders and all those at the
4:11 [p]Dt 25:9 [q]Ps 127:3; 128:3 [r]Ge 35:16 gate said, "We are witnesses.[p] May the
LORD make the woman who is coming
into your home like Rachel and Leah,[q]
who together built up the house of Israel.
May you have standing in Ephrathah[r]
and be famous in Bethlehem.
12Through the offspring the LORD gives
you by this young woman, may your
4:12 [s]ver 18; Ge 38:29 family be like that of Perez,[s] whom Tamar
bore to Judah."

The Genealogy of David

13So Boaz took Ruth and she became
his wife. Then he went to her, and the
4:13 [t]Ge 29:31; 33:5; Ru 3:11 LORD enabled her to conceive,[t] and she
gave birth to a son. 14The women[u] said
to Naomi: "Praise be to the LORD, who
4:14 [u]Lk 1:58 this day has not left you without a kinsman-redeemer.
May he become famous
throughout Israel! 15He will renew your
life and sustain you in your old age. For
your daughter-in-law, who loves you 4:15 [v]Ru 1:16-17; 2:11-12; 1Sa 1:8
and who is better to you than seven
sons,[v] has given him birth."

▸ JOY

THE JOY COMPULSION

Ruth 4:14

Joy is a boisterous compulsion. None can keep it quiet.

16Then Naomi took the child, laid
him in her lap and cared for him. 17The
women living there said, "Naomi has a
son." And they named him Obed. He
was the father of Jesse,[w] the father of 4:17 [w]ver 22; 1Sa 16:1,18; 1Ch 2:12,13
David.
18This, then, is the family line of Perez[x]: 4:18 [x]Mt 1:3-6

Perez was the father of Hezron,
19 Hezron the father of Ram,
Ram the father of Amminadab,[y] 4:19 [y]Ex 6:23
20 Amminadab the father of Nahshon,
Nahshon the father of Salmon,[c]
21 Salmon the father of Boaz,[z] 4:21 [z]Ru 2:1
Boaz the father of Obed,
22 Obed the father of Jesse,
and Jesse the father of David.

▸ PATIENCE

JESUS' GRANDMA AND GRANDPA

Ruth 4:22

God chose a bloodline in which to declare himself a Savior. He, by the very nature of his redeeming love, would rather make history than watch it. But the mills of God grind slowly. He took his own sweet eons to redeem us. He saved the world by making sure the Savior had a long succession of grandparents, stretching all the way back to a Bethlehem farmer.

[a]*4* Many Hebrew manuscripts, Septuagint, Vulgate and Syriac; most Hebrew manuscripts *he* [b]*5* Hebrew; Vulgate and Syriac *Naomi, you acquire Ruth the Moabitess,* [c]*20* A few Hebrew manuscripts, some Septuagint manuscripts and Vulgate (see also verse 21 and Septuagint of 1 Chron. 2:11); most Hebrew manuscripts *Salma*

1 SAMUEL

AUTHORSHIP AND DATE

The books of 1 and 2 Samuel were originally one book. The author is unknown; Samuel likely contributed to parts of 1 Samuel.

The date is uncertain, but probably soon after the division of the kingdom in 950 B.C.

KEY THEMES

Though the books of 1 and 2 Samuel span a period of many years, 1 Samuel is primarily a tale of how the kingdom of Israel became a monarchy. First Samuel begins during the last years of the era of the judges. The prophet Samuel is the last judge, and he remains the dominant religious figure throughout the book; however, the book deals mostly with Israel's first two kings: Saul and David. The most common themes of the book include the nature of the monarchy, the control of God, issues of leadership and God's requirements of Israel's leaders.

FRUIT OF THE SPIRIT IN 1 SAMUEL

Love: First Samuel pays great tribute to human friendship and love. Jonathan and David were friends: "After David had finished talking with Saul, Jonathan became one in spirit with David, and he loved him as himself" (18:1). This loving friendship endured through the greatest difficulties. David's worst enemy was Saul, his best friend's father; yet David and Jonathan's love endured.

Joy: Hannah, a matriarch and a mentor of all women of God, kept her word. God had given her a son, and she gave him back—as she had vowed—to the Lord. Hannah's prayer was a timeless prayer of great joy: "My heart rejoices in the LORD; in the LORD my horn is lifted high. My mouth boasts over my enemies, for I delight in your deliverance" (2:1).

Patience: Hannah had prayed for years for a child. Eli, seeing one of her desperate, unspoken prayers and believing her to be drunk, asked her, "How long will you keep on getting drunk? Get rid of your wine" (1:14). But Hannah's patience and persistence in prayer was heard in heaven, and patience always has its own reward.

Goodness: Samuel publicly agreed to keep praying that the Israelites would learn to do what was good and right (see 12:23).

Faithfulness: God let Eli know that his faithless, sacrilegious sons would never become high priest. The prophecy was given to inform Eli that God would raise up a high priest who would be faithful (see 2:35).

Gentleness: David and Jonathan, both capable of being fierce warriors, laid aside their armor and embraced in their willingness to honor their covenant of friendship (see ch. 20). This man-to-man picture of tender warriors is both gentle and infrequent in the annals of human relationships.

Self-Control: First Samuel 24:6 records David's chance to kill Saul. Most of Israel would have considered this an act of justifiable homicide, for Saul had tried to kill David many times. But David steeled himself against such an act of murder. He exercised self-control and told all those who might have agreed with Saul's assassination that he would not lift his hand against the God-anointed king. Self-control never forgets the debt it owes to God.

The Birth of Samuel

1 There was a certain man from Ramathaim, a Zuphite[a] from the hill
1:1 country[a] of Ephraim, whose name was
[a]Jos 17:17-18 [b]1Ch 6:27,34 Elkanah[b] son of Jeroham, the son of Elihu, the son of Tohu, the son of Zuph,
1:2 [c]Dt 21:15-17; Lk 2:36 an Ephraimite. 2He had two wives;[c] one
was called Hannah and the other Penin-
nah. Peninnah had children, but Hannah had none.
1:3 [d]ver 21; Ex 23:14; 34:23; Lk 2:41 3Year after year[d] this man went up
from his town to worship[e] and sacri-
fice to the LORD Almighty at Shiloh,[f]
[e]Dt 12:5-7 where Hophni and Phinehas, the two
[f]Jos 18:1 sons of Eli, were priests of the LORD.
4Whenever the day came for Elkanah
1:4 to sacrifice,[g] he would give portions of
[g]Dt 12:17-18 the meat to his wife Peninnah and to all
her sons and daughters. 5But to Han-
nah he gave a double portion because
he loved her, and the LORD had closed
1:5 her womb.[h] 6And because the LORD
[h]Ge 16:1; 30:2 had closed her womb, her rival kept
1:6 provoking her in order to irritate her.[i]
[i]Job 24:21 7This went on year after year. Whenever
Hannah went up to the house of the
LORD, her rival provoked her till she
wept and would not eat. 8Elkanah her
husband would say to her, "Hannah,
why are you weeping? Why don't you
1:8 eat? Why are you downhearted? Don't I
[j]Ru 4:15 mean more to you than ten sons?[j]"

▸ FAITHFULNESS

THE STERILE LIFE AND THE GODLY HEART

1 Samuel 1:5

Hannah found that, for those who please him, God brings forth life from barrenness. The heart that chooses to be fruitful can circumvent the unproductive life.

9Once when they had finished eating and drinking in Shiloh, Hannah
stood up. Now Eli the priest was sitting on a chair by the doorpost of the
1:9 [k]1Sa 3:3 LORD's temple.[b] [k] 10In bitterness of soul[l]
Hannah wept much and prayed to the
1:10 [l]Job 7:11 LORD. 11And she made a vow, saying,
"O LORD Almighty, if you will only
look upon your servant's misery and re-
1:11 [m]Ge 8:1; 28:20; 29:32 member[m] me, and not forget your servant but give her a son, then I will give
[n]Nu 6:1-21; Jdg 13:5 him to the LORD for all the days of his
life, and no razor[n] will ever be used on
his head."

DAY 5 FIVE

▸ PATIENCE AND ITS PLACE IN MY PERSONAL WORSHIP

1 Samuel 1:9–28

Prayers are voiced from the perspective of our timeframe, but they are all answered from God's timetable. So perhaps the least reasonable of all intercessions is "Give me *now*!" Yet often this is how we pray. We don't just ask God for what we want, but we tell him when we want it.

Patience in our petitioning covers the stretch between God's answering schedule and our asking schedule. Hannah knew this great truth of prayer: Praying is attuning ourselves to the timetable of God. We cannot speed his answers by trying to push God into action. "God, answer me now" is not prayer, but a case of spiritual nerves. Instead, we must always pray, "God, answer me when you will, how you will. I set my watch even now by heaven's clock."

The length of time between our asking and God's supply is patience. Hannah received exactly what she had asked for. But the key to her blessing lay in her steadfastness. She is not only to be commended for being patient with God; she is also to be commended for praying and worshiping without fail.

At long last, Hannah's prayers are answered. She has a child. And her response is to return gifts to the Giver. She dedicates her only child to God. Hannah's patience results in God's blessing. But in Hannah's response, we see her heart. Her love for God and thankfulness to him manifested themselves in great worship, leading to a cycle of ever-greater blessings.

To begin a study on the topic of Patience Brings the Blessing of God, turn to the home page on page 1476.

12As she kept on praying to the
LORD, Eli observed her mouth. 13Han-
nah was praying in her heart, and her
lips were moving but her voice was not
heard. Eli thought she was drunk 14and
said to her, "How long will you keep on
getting drunk? Get rid of your wine."
15"Not so, my lord," Hannah replied,
"I am a woman who is deeply troubled.
I have not been drinking wine or beer; I

[a]*1* Or *from Ramathaim Zuphim* [b]*9* That is, tabernacle

1:15 [o]Ps 42:4; 62:8; La 2:19

was pouring[o] out my soul to the LORD.
16Do not take your servant for a wicked
woman; I have been praying here out of
my great anguish and grief."

1:17 [p]Jdg 18:6; 1Sa 25:35; 2Ki 5:19; Mk 5:34 [q]Ps 20:3-5

17Eli answered, "Go in peace,[p] and
may the God of Israel grant you what
you have asked of him.[q]"
18She said, "May your servant find
favor in your eyes.[r]" Then she went her
way and ate something, and her face
was no longer downcast.[s]

1:18 [r]Ru 2:13 [s]Ecc 9:7; Ro 15:13

19Early the next morning they arose
and worshiped before the LORD and
then went back to their home at Ramah. Elkanah lay with Hannah his wife,
and the LORD remembered[t] her. 20So
in the course of time Hannah conceived
and gave birth to a son. She named[u]
him Samuel,[a] saying, "Because I asked
the LORD for him."

1:19 [t]Ge 4:1; 30:22

1:20 [u]Ge 41:51-52; Ex 2:10,22; Mt 1:21

Hannah Dedicates Samuel

21When the man Elkanah went up
with all his family to offer the annual[v]
sacrifice to the LORD and to fulfill his
vow,[w] 22Hannah did not go. She said to
her husband, "After the boy is weaned, I
will take him and present[x] him before the
LORD, and he will live there always."

1:21 [v]ver 3 [w]Dt 12:11

1:22 [x]ver 11,28; Lk 2:22

23"Do what seems best to you," Elkanah her husband told her. "Stay here
until you have weaned him; only may
the LORD make good[y] his[b] word." So
the woman stayed at home and nursed
her son until she had weaned him.

1:23 [y]ver 17; Nu 30:7

24After he was weaned, she took the
boy with her, young as he was, along
with a three-year-old bull,[c][z] an ephah[d]
of flour and a skin of wine, and brought
him to the house of the LORD at Shiloh. 25When they had slaughtered the
bull, they brought the boy to Eli, 26and
she said to him, "As surely as you live,
my lord, I am the woman who stood
here beside you praying to the LORD.
27I prayed[a] for this child, and the LORD
has granted me what I asked of him.
28So now I give him to the LORD. For
his whole life[b] he will be given over
to the LORD." And he worshiped the
LORD there.

1:24 [z]Nu 15:8-10; Dt 12:5; Jos 18:1

1:27 [a]ver 11-13; Ps 66:19-20

1:28 [b]ver 11,22; Ge 24:26,52

Hannah's Prayer

2 Then Hannah prayed and said:[c]

"My heart rejoices[d] in the LORD;
in the LORD my horn[e][e] is lifted
high.
My mouth boasts over my enemies,
for I delight in your deliverance.

2:1 [c]Lk 1:46-55 [d]Ps 9:14; 13:5 [e]Ps 89:17,24; 92:10; Isa 12:2-3

2"There is no one holy[f][f] like the
LORD;
there is no one besides you;
there is no Rock[g] like our God.

2:2 [f]Ex 15:11; Lev 19:2 [g]Dt 32:30-31; 2Sa 22:2,32

3"Do not keep talking so proudly
or let your mouth speak such
arrogance,[h]
for the LORD is a God who knows,
and by him deeds[i] are weighed.[j]

2:3 [h]Pr 8:13 [i]1Sa 16:7; 1Ki 8:39 [j]Pr 16:2; 24:11-12

4"The bows of the warriors are
broken,[k]
but those who stumbled are armed
with strength.
5Those who were full hire themselves
out for food,
but those who were hungry
hunger no more.
She who was barren[l] has borne seven
children,
but she who has had many sons
pines away.

2:4 [k]Ps 37:15

2:5 [l]Ps 113:9; Jer 15:9

6"The LORD brings death and makes
alive;[m]
he brings down to the grave[g] and
raises up.[n]

2:6 [m]Dt 32:39 [n]Isa 26:19

PEACE

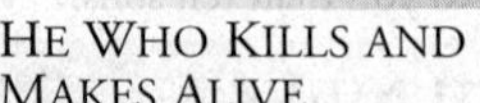

HE WHO KILLS AND MAKES ALIVE

1 Samuel 2:6

He who kills and makes alive was able to make the world alive precisely because he was killed.

God is not capricious in choosing whom he slays or lets live.

He has called the world to peace.
No price—even the life of his only Son—
Was considered too dear to purchase it.

7The LORD sends poverty and
wealth;[o]
he humbles and he exalts.[p]
8He raises[q] the poor from the dust
and lifts the needy from the ash
heap;

2:7 [o]Dt 8:18 [p]Job 5:11; Ps 75:7

2:8 [q]Ps 113:7-8

[a]20 *Samuel* sounds like the Hebrew for *heard of God.* [b]23 Masoretic Text; Dead Sea Scrolls, Septuagint and Syriac *your* [c]24 Dead Sea Scrolls, Septuagint and Syriac; Masoretic Text *with three bulls* [d]24 That is, probably about 3/5 bushel (about 22 liters) [e]1 *Horn* here symbolizes strength; also in verse 10. [f]2 Or *no Holy One* [g]6 Hebrew *Sheol*

he seats them with princes
and has them inherit a throne of
honor.[r]

2:8 [r]Job 36:7; [s]Job 38:4

"For the foundations[s] of the earth
are the LORD's;
upon them he has set the world.

2:9 [t]Ps 91:12; [u]Mt 8:12; [v]Ps 33:16-17

9 He will guard the feet[t] of his saints,
but the wicked will be silenced in
darkness.[u]

"It is not by strength[v] that one
prevails;
10 those who oppose the LORD will
be shattered.[w]

2:10 [w]Ps 2:9; [x]Ps 18:13; [y]Ps 96:13; [z]Ps 21:1; [a]Ps 89:24

He will thunder[x] against them from
heaven;
the LORD will judge[y] the ends of
the earth.

"He will give strength[z] to his king
and exalt the horn[a] of his
anointed."

11 Then Elkanah went home to Ramah, but the boy ministered[b] before the LORD under Eli the priest.

2:11 [b]ver 18; 1Sa 3:1

Eli's Wicked Sons

12 Eli's sons were wicked men; they had no regard[c] for the LORD. 13 Now it was the practice of the priests with the people that whenever anyone offered a sacrifice and while the meat[d] was being boiled, the servant of the priest would come with a three-pronged fork in his hand. 14 He would plunge it into the pan or kettle or caldron or pot, and the priest would take for himself whatever the fork brought up. This is how they treated all the Israelites who came to Shiloh. 15 But even before the fat was burned, the servant of the priest would come and say to the man who was sacrificing, "Give the priest some meat to roast; he won't accept boiled meat from you, but only raw."

2:12 [c]Jer 2:8; 9:6

2:13 [d]Lev 7:29-34

16 If the man said to him, "Let the fat be burned up first, and then take whatever you want," the servant would then answer, "No, hand it over now; if you don't, I'll take it by force."

17 This sin of the young men was very great in the LORD's sight, for they[a] were treating the LORD's offering with contempt.[e]

2:17 [e]Mal 2:7-9

18 But Samuel was ministering[f] before the LORD—a boy wearing a linen ephod.[g] 19 Each year his mother made him a little robe and took it to him when she went up with her husband to offer the annual[h] sacrifice. 20 Eli would bless Elkanah and his wife, saying, "May the LORD give you children by this woman to take the place of the one she prayed[i] for and gave to the LORD." Then they would go home. 21 And the LORD was gracious to Hannah;[j] she conceived and gave birth to three sons and two daughters. Meanwhile, the boy Samuel grew[k] up in the presence of the LORD.

2:18 [f]ver 11; 1Sa 3:1; [g]ver 28

2:19 [h]1Sa 1:3

2:20 [i]1Sa 1:11, 27-28; Lk 2:34

2:21 [j]Ge 21:1; [k]ver 26; Jdg 13:24; 1Sa 3:19; Lk 2:40

22 Now Eli, who was very old, heard about everything his sons were doing to all Israel and how they slept with the women[l] who served at the entrance to the Tent of Meeting. 23 So he said to them, "Why do you do such things? I hear from all the people about these wicked deeds of yours. 24 No, my sons; it is not a good report that I hear spreading among the LORD's people. 25 If a man sins against another man, God[b] may mediate for him; but if a man sins against the LORD, who will[m] intercede[n] for him?" His sons, however, did not listen to their father's rebuke, for it was the LORD's will to put them to death.

2:22 [l]Ex 38:8

2:25 [m]Nu 15:30; Jos 11:20; [n]Dt 1:17; 1Sa 3:14; Heb 10:26

26 And the boy Samuel continued to grow[o] in stature and in favor with the LORD and with men.

2:26 [o]ver 21; Lk 2:52

Prophecy Against the House of Eli

27 Now a man of God[p] came to Eli and said to him, "This is what the LORD says: 'Did I not clearly reveal myself to your father's house when they were in Egypt under Pharaoh? 28 I chose[q] your father out of all the tribes of Israel to be my priest, to go up to my altar, to burn incense, and to wear an ephod[r] in my presence. I also gave your father's house all the offerings made with fire by the Israelites. 29 Why do you[c] scorn my sacrifice and offering[s] that I prescribed for my dwelling?[t] Why do you honor your sons more than me by fattening yourselves on the choice parts of every offering made by my people Israel?'

2:27 [p]Ex 4:14-16; 1Ki 13:1

2:28 [q]Ex 28:1; [r]Lev 8:7-8

2:29 [s]ver 12-17; [t]Dt 12:5; Mt 10:37

30 "Therefore the LORD, the God of Israel, declares: 'I promised that your house and your father's house would minister before me forever.[u]' But now the LORD declares: 'Far be it from me!

2:30 [u]Ex 29:9

[a] *17* Or *men* [b] *25* Or *the judges* [c] *29* The Hebrew is plural.

2:30 [v]Ps 50:23; 91:15 [w]Mal 2:9
Those who honor me I will honor,[v]
but those who despise[w] me will be disdained. 31The time is coming when I
will cut short your strength and the
strength of your father's house, so that
there will not be an old man in your
2:31 [x]1Sa 4:11-18; 22:16-20
family line[x] 32and you will see distress
in my dwelling. Although good will be
done to Israel, in your family line there
2:32 [y]1Ki 2:26-27; Zec 8:4
will never be an old man.[y] 33Every one
of you that I do not cut off from my
altar will be spared only to blind your
eyes with tears and to grieve your heart,
and all your descendants will die in the
prime of life.

34" 'And what happens to your two
sons, Hophni and Phinehas, will be a
2:34 [z]1Sa 4:11 [a]1Ki 13:3
sign to you—they will both die[z] on the
same day.[a] 35I will raise up for myself a
2:35 [b]1Sa 12:3; 1Ki 2:35 [c]1Sa 16:13; 2Sa 7:11,27; 1Ki 11:38
faithful priest,[b] who will do according
to what is in my heart and mind. I will
firmly establish his house, and he will
minister before my anointed[c] one always. 36Then everyone left in your family line will come and bow down before
him for a piece of silver and a crust of
bread and plead, "Appoint me to some
priestly office so I can have food to
2:36 [d]1Ki 2:27
eat.[d]" ' "

The LORD Calls Samuel

3:1 [e]1Sa 2:11 [f]Ps 74:9 [g]Am 8:11
3 The boy Samuel ministered[e] before
the LORD under Eli. In those days
the word of the LORD was rare;[f] there
were not many visions.[g]

3:2 [h]1Sa 4:15
2One night Eli, whose eyes[h] were becoming so weak that he could barely
see, was lying down in his usual place.
3:3 [i]Lev 24:1-4
3The lamp[i] of God had not yet gone
out, and Samuel was lying down in the
temple[a] of the LORD, where the ark of
God was. 4Then the LORD called Samuel.

3:4 [j]Isa 6:8
Samuel answered, "Here I am.[j]" 5And
he ran to Eli and said, "Here I am; you
called me."

But Eli said, "I did not call; go back
and lie down." So he went and lay
down.

6Again the LORD called, "Samuel!"
And Samuel got up and went to Eli and
said, "Here I am; you called me."

"My son," Eli said, "I did not call; go
back and lie down."

7Now Samuel did not yet know the
LORD: The word of the LORD had not
3:7 [k]Ac 19:12
yet been revealed[k] to him.

8The LORD called Samuel a third
time, and Samuel got up and went to Eli
and said, "Here I am; you called me."

Then Eli realized that the LORD was
calling the boy. 9So Eli told Samuel,
"Go and lie down, and if he calls you,
say, 'Speak, LORD, for your servant is
listening.' " So Samuel went and lay
down in his place.

GENTLENESS

THE CHATTY DEAF

1 Samuel 3:9

Zealots have a major weakness: an inability to speak softly. Mouthy disciples talk themselves through life, never hearing the still, small voice that summons their allegiance. To know the will of God is to be skilled at the art of listening.

10The LORD came and stood there,
calling as at the other times, "Samuel!
Samuel!"

Then Samuel said, "Speak, for your
servant is listening."

11And the LORD said to Samuel:
"See, I am about to do something in Israel that will make the ears of everyone
who hears of it tingle.[l] 12At that time I 3:11 [l]2Ki 21:12; Jer 19:3
will carry out against Eli everything[m] I
spoke against his family—from begin- 3:12 [m]1Sa 2:27-36
ning to end. 13For I told him that I
would judge his family forever because
of the sin he knew about; his sons made
themselves contemptible,[b] and he failed
to restrain[n] them. 14Therefore, I swore 3:13 [n]1Sa 2:12, 17,22,29-31
to the house of Eli, 'The guilt of Eli's
house will never be atoned[o] for by sac- 3:14 [o]Lev 15:30-31; 1Sa 2:25; Isa 22:14
rifice or offering.' "

15Samuel lay down until morning
and then opened the doors of the house
of the LORD. He was afraid to tell Eli
the vision, 16but Eli called him and said,
"Samuel, my son."

Samuel answered, "Here I am."

17"What was it he said to you?" Eli
asked. "Do not hide it from me. May
God deal with you, be it ever so severe-
ly,[p] if you hide from me anything he 3:17 [p]Ru 1:17; 2Sa 3:35
told you." 18So Samuel told him every-
thing, hiding nothing from him. Then
Eli said, "He is the LORD; let him do 3:18 [q]Job 2:10; Isa 39:8
what is good in his eyes."[q]

[a]*3* That is, tabernacle [b]*13* Masoretic Text; an ancient Hebrew scribal tradition and Septuagint *sons blasphemed God*

GENTLENESS

WEEK 35

DAY ONE

1 GENTLENESS, CHILDLIKE GODLINESS

Read 1 Samuel 3:1–10

After hearing his name called three times, Samuel is instructed by the old priest Eli, "If he calls you, say, 'Speak, LORD, for your servant is listening.' " Consider the tenderness in this gentle story. The God who thundered on Sinai calls Samuel so quietly, so tenderly, that the old priest isn't sure at first that Samuel has heard from God at all.

God approaches us gently when he speaks to us, so that we won't be frightened. The Scriptures contain many examples of his gentle approaches. He whispered to Elijah, answered Gideon with a fleece instead of words, and came to Moses in a burning bush.

"Speak, for your servant is listening," said the boy Samuel, and God's gentleness began in the boy's life a long, vital ride of obedience and blessing. Gentle the entrance of God, but dynamic in the national life was Samuel's calling. Samuel led the nation from the era of the judges to the era of the monarchy. He anointed the first two kings of Israel—one of them would be the greatest king Israel would ever have. He blessed battles and condemned sin.

When Samuel began his role as national prophet, Israel was a loose confederacy of clans and tribes. By the end of Samuel's life, Israel was a nation on its way to walled cities, levied armies and world-class status. Yet throughout Samuel's life, God spoke gently to this prophet and used David, whom Samuel anointed as king, to sing his gentle praises to the nation.

MEMORIZE THIS WEEK

LUKE 10:21

At that time Jesus, full of joy through the Holy Spirit, said, "I praise you, Father, Lord of heaven and earth, because you have hidden these things from the wise and learned, and revealed them to little children. Yes, Father, for this was your good pleasure."

DAY TWO

2 GENTLENESS AND THE PURPOSE OF GOD IN MY LIFE

God's tenderness toward Israel models the sort of gentleness he would love to see in his followers. "Can a mother forget the baby at her breast?" asks the prophet. "Though she may forget," says Isaiah's God, "I will not forget you." God sees Israel as his child, and he is the gentle, loving Father. *Turn to Isaiah 49:15, page 848, for today's study.*

DAY THREE

3 GENTLENESS AND MY RELATIONSHIP WITH CHRIST

Who was Andrew? Some scholars have remarked that every time we see Andrew in Scripture, he is bringing someone to Jesus. This passage describes a little boy that Andrew introduces to Jesus. I like to believe that Andrew made friends with this wonderful, warm, little boy. I also like to believe the boy had a dog and that Andrew really liked dogs. All of this may be hypothetical, but we do know that Andrew's young friend had a lunch. And Andrew's gentleness, his childlike gentleness, won the day. *Turn to John 6:1–11, page 1256, for today's study.*

DAY FOUR

4 GENTLENESS AND MY SERVICE TO OTHERS

Heavenly wisdom is imbued with a gentleness that can only be called childlike godliness. Consider the adjectives that James used to describe godly wisdom: "pure; then peace-loving, considerate, submissive, full of mercy and good fruit, impartial and sincere." God is gentle, and his gentle wisdom should be our desire. His gentleness is exactly what we need as we minister to others. *Turn to James 3:13–18, page 1485, for today's study.*

DAY FIVE

5 GENTLENESS AND ITS PLACE IN MY PERSONAL WORSHIP

The children are the last to be silenced on Palm Sunday. They keep shouting, "Hosanna to the Son of David." The implication of Jesus' Messiahship was heretical to the chief priests and teachers of the law. If the heretics were adults, they could be stoned or burned, but what are you to do with a child heretic? The great thing about Christian truth is its simplicity. Children can celebrate its gentle doctrines as readily as those who are older and sometimes more grudging. *Turn to Matthew 21:14–17, page 1150, for today's study.*

Week 36, Self-Control, Managing My Moods, begins on page 179, Numbers 20:6–13.
To begin a topical study on the Fruit of the Spirit, Gentleness, turn to the Topical Index, page 1548.

19The LORD was with[r] Samuel as he
3:19 [r]Ge 21:22; grew[s] up, and he let none[t] of his words
39:2 fall to the ground. 20And all Israel
[s]1Sa 2:21 from Dan to Beersheba[u] recognized
[t]1Sa 9:6 that Samuel was attested as a prophet
3:20 of the LORD. 21The LORD continued
[u]Jdg 20:1 to appear at Shiloh, and there he re-
3:21 vealed[v] himself to Samuel through his
[v]ver 10 word.

4 And Samuel's word came to all Israel.

The Philistines Capture the Ark

Now the Israelites went out to fight
against the Philistines. The Israelites
4:1 camped at Ebenezer,[w] and the Philis-
[w]1Sa 7:12 tines at Aphek.[x] 2The Philistines de-
[x]Jos 12:18; 1Sa 29:1 ployed their forces to meet Israel, and
as the battle spread, Israel was defeat-
ed by the Philistines, who killed about
four thousand of them on the battlefield. 3When the soldiers returned to
4:3 camp, the elders of Israel asked, "Why[y]
[y]Jos 7:7 did the LORD bring defeat upon us
[z]Nu 10:35; Jos 6:7 today before the Philistines? Let us
bring the ark[z] of the LORD's covenant
from Shiloh, so that it[a] may go with
us and save us from the hand of our
enemies."

4So the people sent men to Shiloh,
and they brought back the ark of the
covenant of the LORD Almighty, who
4:4 is enthroned between the cherubim.[a]
[a]Ex 25:22; 2Sa 6:2 And Eli's two sons, Hophni and Phinehas, were there with the ark of the cov-
enant of God.

5When the ark of the LORD's covenant came into the camp, all Israel
4:5 raised such a great shout[b] that the
[b]Jos 6:5,10 ground shook. 6Hearing the uproar, the
Philistines asked, "What's all this shouting in the Hebrew camp?"

When they learned that the ark of
the LORD had come into the camp,
4:7 [c]Ex 15:14 7the Philistines were afraid.[c] "A god has
come into the camp," they said. "We're
in trouble! Nothing like this has happened before. 8Woe to us! Who will deliver us from the hand of these mighty
gods? They are the gods who struck the
Egyptians with all kinds of plagues in
the desert. 9Be strong, Philistines! Be
4:9 [d]Jdg 13:1; men, or you will be subject to the He-
1Co 16:13 brews, as they[d] have been to you. Be
4:10 men, and fight!"

[e]ver 2; 10So the Philistines fought, and the
Dt 28:25; 2Sa 18:17; Israelites were defeated[e] and every man
2Ki 14:12 fled to his tent. The slaughter was very
great; Israel lost thirty thousand foot
soldiers. 11The ark of God was captured, and Eli's two sons, Hophni and
Phinehas, died.[f] 4:11 [f]1Sa 2:34; Ps 78:61,64

Death of Eli

12That same day a Benjamite ran
from the battle line and went to Shiloh,
his clothes torn and dust[g] on his head. 4:12 [g]Jos 7:6;
13When he arrived, there was Eli[h] sit- 2Sa 1:2;
ting on his chair by the side of the road, 15:32; Ne 9:1;
watching, because his heart feared for Job 2:12
the ark of God. When the man entered 4:13
the town and told what had happened, [h]ver 18; 1Sa 1:9
the whole town sent up a cry.

14Eli heard the outcry and asked,
"What is the meaning of this uproar?"

The man hurried over to Eli, 15who
was ninety-eight years old and whose
eyes[i] were set so that he could not see. 4:15 [i]1Sa 3:2
16He told Eli, "I have just come from
the battle line; I fled from it this very
day."

Eli asked, "What happened, my
son?"

17The man who brought the news replied, "Israel fled before the Philistines,
and the army has suffered heavy losses.
Also your two sons, Hophni and Phinehas, are dead, and the ark of God has
been captured."

18When he mentioned the ark of
God, Eli fell backward off his chair by
the side of the gate. His neck was broken and he died, for he was an old man
and heavy. He had led[b][j] Israel forty 4:18 [j]ver 13
years.

19His daughter-in-law, the wife of
Phinehas, was pregnant and near the
time of delivery. When she heard the
news that the ark of God had been captured and that her father-in-law and her
husband were dead, she went into labor and gave birth, but was overcome
by her labor pains. 20As she was dying,
the women attending her said, "Don't
despair; you have given birth to a son."
But she did not respond or pay any attention.

21She named the boy Ichabod,[c][k] say- 4:21 [k]Ge 35:18
ing, "The glory[l] has departed from [l]Ps 26:8;
Israel"—because of the capture of the Jer 2:11
ark of God and the deaths of her father-
in-law and her husband. 22She said,

[a]3 Or *he* [b]18 Traditionally *judged* [c]21 *Ichabod* means *no glory.*

“The glory has departed from Israel, for
the ark of God has been captured.”

The Ark in Ashdod and Ekron

5 After the Philistines had captured
the ark of God, they took it from
5:1 Ebenezer[m] to Ashdod.[n] 2Then they car-
[m]1Sa 4:1; 7:12 [n]Jos 13:3 ried the ark into Dagon’s temple and
5:2 set it beside Dagon.[o] 3When the peo-
[o]Jdg 16:23 ple of Ashdod rose early the next day,
5:3 there was Dagon, fallen[p] on his face on
[p]Isa 19:1; 46:7 the ground before the ark of the LORD!
They took Dagon and put him back in
his place. 4But the following morning
when they rose, there was Dagon, fallen
on his face on the ground before the
ark of the LORD! His head and hands
5:4 [q]Eze 6:6; had been broken[q] off and were lying on
Mic 1:7 the threshold; only his body remained.
5That is why to this day neither the
priests of Dagon nor any others who
enter Dagon’s temple at Ashdod step on
5:5 [r]Zep 1:9 the threshold.[r]
6The LORD’s hand[s] was heavy upon
5:6 [s]ver 7; Ex 9:3; the people of Ashdod and its vicinity;
Ps 32:4; Ac 13:11 he brought devastation[t] upon them and
[t]ver 11; Ps 78:66 afflicted them with tumors.[a] [u] 7When
[u]Dt 28:27; 1Sa 6:5 the men of Ashdod saw what was happening, they said, “The ark of the god
of Israel must not stay here with us, because his hand is heavy upon us and
upon Dagon our god.” 8So they called
together all the rulers of the Philistines
and asked them, “What shall we do
with the ark of the god of Israel?”
They answered, “Have the ark of the
5:8 god of Israel moved to Gath.[v]” So they
[v]ver 11 moved the ark of the God of Israel.
9But after they had moved it, the
LORD’s hand was against that city,
5:9 [w]ver 6,11; throwing it into a great panic.[w] He af-
Dt 2:15; 1Sa 7:13; flicted the people of the city, both young
Ps 78:66 and old, with an outbreak of tumors.[b]
10So they sent the ark of God to Ekron.
As the ark of God was entering Ekron, the people of Ekron cried out,
“They have brought the ark of the god
of Israel around to us to kill us and our
people.” 11So they called together all
5:11 the rulers[x] of the Philistines and said,
[x]ver 6,8-9 “Send the ark of the god of Israel away;
let it go back to its own place, or it[c] will
kill us and our people.” For death had
filled the city with panic; God’s hand
was very heavy upon it. 12Those who
did not die were afflicted with tumors,
and the outcry of the city went up to
heaven.

The Ark Returned to Israel

6 When the ark of the LORD had been
in Philistine territory seven months,
2the Philistines called for the priests and
the diviners[y] and said, “What shall we do 6:2
with the ark of the LORD? Tell us how [y]Ge 41:8; Ex 7:11;
we should send it back to its place.” Isa 2:6
3They answered, “If you return the
ark of the god of Israel, do not send it
away empty,[z] but by all means send a 6:3 [z]Ex 23:15;
guilt offering[a] to him. Then you will Dt 16:16
be healed, and you will know why his [a]Lev 5:15 [b]ver 9
hand[b] has not been lifted from you.”
4The Philistines asked, “What guilt
offering should we send to him?”
They replied, “Five gold tumors and
five gold rats, according to the number[c] 6:4
of the Philistine rulers, because the same [c]ver 17-18; Jos 13:3;
plague has struck both you and your rul- Jdg 3:3
ers. 5Make models of the tumors[d] and 6:5
of the rats that are destroying the coun- [d]1Sa 5:6-11 [e]Jos 7:19;
try, and pay honor[e] to Israel’s god. Per- Isa 42:12; Jn 9:24;
haps he will lift his hand from you and Rev 14:7
your gods and your land. 6Why do you 6:6
harden[f] your hearts as the Egyptians and [f]Ex 7:13;
Pharaoh did? When he[d] treated them 8:15; 9:34;
harshly, did they[g] not send the Israelites 14:17 [g]Ex 12:31,33
out so they could go on their way?
7“Now then, get a new cart[h] ready, 6:7 [h]2Sa 6:3
with two cows that have calved and [i]Nu 19:2
have never been yoked.[i] Hitch the cows
to the cart, but take their calves away
and pen them up. 8Take the ark of the
LORD and put it on the cart, and in
a chest beside it put the gold objects
you are sending back to him as a guilt
offering. Send it on its way, 9but keep
watching it. If it goes up to its own 6:9
territory, toward Beth Shemesh,[j] then [j]ver 3;
the LORD has brought this great disas- Jos 15:10; 21:16
ter on us. But if it does not, then we
will know that it was not his hand that
struck us and that it happened to us by
chance.”
10So they did this. They took two
such cows and hitched them to the
cart and penned up their calves. 11They
placed the ark of the LORD on the cart
and along with it the chest containing
the gold rats and the models of the tumors. 12Then the cows went straight up
toward Beth Shemesh, keeping on the

[a]6 Hebrew; Septuagint and Vulgate *tumors. And rats appeared in their land, and death and destruction were throughout the city* [b]9 Or *with tumors in the groin* (see Septuagint) [c]11 Or *he*
[d]6 That is, God

road and lowing all the way; they did
not turn to the right or to the left. The
rulers of the Philistines followed them
as far as the border of Beth Shemesh.
13 Now the people of Beth Shemesh
were harvesting their wheat in the valley, and when they looked up and saw
the ark, they rejoiced at the sight. 14 The
cart came to the field of Joshua of Beth
Shemesh, and there it stopped beside
a large rock. The people chopped up
the wood of the cart and sacrificed the
6:14 cows as a burnt offering[k] to the LORD.
[k]2Sa 24:22; 1Ki 19:21 15 The Levites[l] took down the ark of
6:15 the LORD, together with the chest con-
[l]Jos 3:3 taining the gold objects, and placed
them on the large rock. On that day
the people of Beth Shemesh offered
burnt offerings and made sacrifices to
the LORD. 16 The five rulers of the Philistines saw all this and then returned
that same day to Ekron.
17 These are the gold tumors the Philistines sent as a guilt offering to the
6:17 LORD—one each[m] for Ashdod, Gaza,
[m]ver 4 Ashkelon, Gath and Ekron. 18 And the
number of the gold rats was according
to the number of Philistine towns belonging to the five rulers—the fortified
towns with their country villages. The
large rock, on which[a] they set the ark of
the LORD, is a witness to this day in the
field of Joshua of Beth Shemesh.
6:19 19 But God struck down[n] some of the
[n]2Sa 6:7 men of Beth Shemesh, putting seven-
[o]Ex 19:21; Nu 4:5,15,20 ty[b] of them to death because they had
looked[o] into the ark of the LORD. The
people mourned because of the heavy
blow the LORD had dealt them, 20 and
the men of Beth Shemesh asked, "Who
6:20 can stand[p] in the presence of the LORD,
[p]2Sa 6:9; Mal 3:2; Rev 6:17 this holy[q] God? To whom will the ark
[q]Lev 11:45 go up from here?"
6:21 21 Then they sent messengers to the
[r]Jos 9:17; 15:9,60; 1Ch 13:5-6 people of Kiriath Jearim,[r] saying, "The
Philistines have returned the ark of the
LORD. Come down and take it up to
7 your place." 1 So the men of Kiriath
Jearim came and took up the ark of
7:1 the LORD. They took it to Abinadab's[s]
[s]2Sa 6:3 house on the hill and consecrated Eleazar his son to guard the ark of the
LORD.

Samuel Subdues the Philistines at Mizpah

2 It was a long time, twenty years in
all, that the ark remained at Kiriath
Jearim, and all the people of Israel
mourned and sought after the LORD.
3 And Samuel said to the whole house
of Israel, "If you are returning[t] to the 7:3 [t]Dt 30:10; Isa 55:7; Hos 6:1
LORD with all your hearts, then rid[u]
yourselves of the foreign gods and the [u]Ge 35:2; Jos 24:14
Ashtoreths[v] and commit[w] yourselves to [v]Jdg 2:12-13; 1Sa 31:10
the LORD and serve him only,[x] and he [w]Joel 2:12
will deliver you out of the hand of the [x]Dt 6:13; Mt 4:10; Lk 4:8
Philistines." 4 So the Israelites put away
their Baals and Ashtoreths, and served
the LORD only.
5 Then Samuel said, "Assemble all Is-
rael at Mizpah[y] and I will intercede 7:5 [y]Jdg 20:1
with the LORD for you." 6 When they
had assembled at Mizpah, they drew
water and poured[z] it out before the 7:6 [z]Ps 62:8; La 2:19
LORD. On that day they fasted and
there they confessed, "We have sinned [a]Jdg 10:10; Ne 9:1; Ps 106:6
against the LORD." And Samuel was
leader[c][a] of Israel at Mizpah.
7 When the Philistines heard that Israel had assembled at Mizpah, the rulers of the Philistines came up to attack
them. And when the Israelites heard of
it, they were afraid[b] because of the Phi- 7:7 [b]1Sa 17:11
listines. 8 They said to Samuel, "Do not
stop crying[c] out to the LORD our God 7:8 [c]1Sa 12:19,23; Isa 37:4; Jer 15:1
for us, that he may rescue us from the
hand of the Philistines." 9 Then Sam-
uel[d] took a suckling lamb and offered 7:9 [d]Ps 99:6
it up as a whole burnt offering to the [e]Jer 15:1
LORD. He cried out to the LORD on
Israel's behalf, and the LORD answered
him.[e]
10 While Samuel was sacrificing the
burnt offering, the Philistines drew near
to engage Israel in battle. But that day
the LORD thundered[f] with loud thun- 7:10 [f]1Sa 2:10; 2Sa 22:14-15
der against the Philistines and threw
them into such a panic[g] that they were [g]Jos 10:10
routed before the Israelites. 11 The men
of Israel rushed out of Mizpah and pursued the Philistines, slaughtering them
along the way to a point below Beth
Car.
12 Then Samuel took a stone[h] and set 7:12 [h]Ge 35:14; Jos 4:9
it up between Mizpah and Shen. He
named it Ebenezer,[d] saying, "Thus far
has the LORD helped us." 13 So the Phi-
listines were subdued[i] and did not in- 7:13 [i]Jdg 13:1,5; 1Sa 13:5
vade Israelite territory again.

[a] *18* A few Hebrew manuscripts (see also Septuagint); most Hebrew manuscripts *villages as far as Greater Abel, where* [b] *19* A few Hebrew manuscripts; most Hebrew manuscripts and Septuagint *50,070* [c] *6* Traditionally *judge* [d] *12 Ebenezer* means *stone of help.*

Throughout Samuel's lifetime, the
hand of the LORD was against the Philistines. 14The towns from Ekron to
Gath that the Philistines had captured
from Israel were restored to her, and Israel delivered the neighboring territory
from the power of the Philistines. And
there was peace between Israel and the
Amorites.
7:15 [j]ver 6; 1Sa 12:11 15Samuel[j] continued as judge over Israel all the days of his life. 16From year
to year he went on a circuit from Bethel
to Gilgal to Mizpah, judging Israel in
all those places. 17But he always went
7:17 [k]1Sa 1:19; 8:4 [l]Jdg 21:4 back to Ramah,[k] where his home was,
and there he also judged Israel. And he
built an altar[l] there to the LORD.

Israel Asks for a King

8 When Samuel grew old, he ap-
pointed[m] his sons as judges for Isra- 8:1 [m]Dt 16:18-19
el. 2The name of his firstborn was Joel
and the name of his second was Abi-
jah, and they served at Beersheba.[n] 3But 8:2 [n]Ge 22:19; 1Ki 19:3; Am 5:4-5
his sons did not walk in his ways. They
turned aside after dishonest gain and
accepted bribes[o] and perverted justice. 8:3 [o]Ex 23:8; Dt 16:19; Ps 15:5
4So all the elders of Israel gathered to-
gether and came to Samuel at Ramah.[p] 8:4 [p]1Sa 7:17
5They said to him, "You are old, and
your sons do not walk in your ways;
now appoint a king[q] to lead[a] us, such 8:5 [q]Dt 17:14-20
as all the other nations have."

[a]5 Traditionally *judge*; also in verses 6 and 20

SAMUEL

Peace, the Resolution of Conflict (7:2–17)

Samuel was a prophet whose life was scarred by conflicts. First, his family life was filled with sorrow. He had two sons, Joel and Abijah, whom he appointed as judges in Israel. Alas, his sons did not "walk in his ways" (1 Samuel 8:3). They accepted bribes and were continually involved in dishonest dealings.

Second, Samuel was at an impasse with the people of Israel as to what kind of government Israel should have. The Israelites wanted Samuel to end the four-century era of the judges because they wanted a king. Samuel reminded the people of God's words: A king would levy a military draft, take common citizens as servants and institute a taxation system. Life would become unbearable under a monarchy. But the people did not listen to Samuel and continued to clamor for a king.

Samuel understood the frustration of conflict. He understood disappointment and broken dreams. But Samuel was a friend of God and turned to him when he needed answers to life's questions: "But when they said, 'Give us a king to lead us,' this displeased Samuel; so he prayed to the LORD" (v. 6). Instead of arguing that his sons would be fine leaders . . . instead of asking the people to see things his way . . . instead of getting into a shouting match . . . instead of letting conflict run his life, Samuel ran to God.

God resolved the conflicts in Samuel's life with his wisdom. Although Samuel may not have agreed with God's answers, there was a direction; there was a resolve, and Samuel could rest in the knowledge that God had directed the outcome. Following the decision came peace. Peace always follows the resolution of conflict. Our struggles are resolved when we acknowledge that God has spoken and we determine that we will obey his voice. Samuel may not have totally agreed with God's methodology, but he did obey. Obedience results in peace.

It is in the context of national direction that Samuel learned the beauty of conflict resolution. Peace, however, is always more than just the cessation of a quarrel. Peace is a single focus. Try to look at two different things at the same time, and your eyes will cross and your mind lose concentration. Look at one thing only, and that single focus will bring greater concentration and attention. A single focus brings peace to the mind. Samuel had learned that inner serenity Isaiah would later write about:

You will keep in perfect peace
him whose mind is steadfast,
because he trusts in you.
(Isaiah 26:3)

6But when they said, "Give us a king
8:6 [r]1Sa 15:11 to lead us," this displeased[r] Samuel;
so he prayed to the LORD. 7And the
LORD told him: "Listen to all that the
people are saying to you; it is not you
they have rejected, but they have re-
8:7 [s]Ex 16:8; 1Sa 10:19 jected me as their king.[s] 8As they have
done from the day I brought them up
out of Egypt until this day, forsaking
me and serving other gods, so they are
doing to you. 9Now listen to them;
8:9 [t]ver 11-18; 1Sa 10:25 but warn them solemnly and let them
know[t] what the king who will reign
over them will do."

GOODNESS

CELEBRATING DIFFERENCES

1 Samuel 8:20

The prayer cry that matters is "Lord, make me so different that my uniqueness will proclaim your glory. Help me to remember that the turnpike to hell is paved with carbon paper."

10Samuel told all the words of the
LORD to the people who were asking
him for a king. 11He said, "This is
what the king who will reign over you
8:11 [u]1Sa 10:25; 14:52 will do: He will take[u] your sons and
make them serve with his chariots and
[v]Dt 17:16; 2Sa 15:1 horses, and they will run in front of
his chariots.[v] 12Some he will assign to
be commanders of thousands and com-
8:12 [w]1Sa 22:7 manders[w] of fifties, and others to plow
his ground and reap his harvest, and
still others to make weapons of war and
equipment for his chariots. 13He will
take your daughters to be perfumers
and cooks and bakers. 14He will take
8:14 [x]Eze 46:18 the best of your fields[x] and vineyards[y]
[y]1Ki 21:7,15 and olive groves and give them to his
attendants. 15He will take a tenth of
your grain and of your vintage and give
it to his officials and attendants. 16Your
menservants and maidservants and the
best of your cattle[a] and donkeys he will
take for his own use. 17He will take
a tenth of your flocks, and you yourselves will become his slaves. 18When
that day comes, you will cry out for re-
8:18 [z]Pr 1:28; Isa 1:15; Mic 3:4 lief from the king you have chosen, and
the LORD will not answer[z] you in that
day."
8:19 [a]Isa 66:4; Jer 44:16 19But the people refused[a] to listen to
Samuel. "No!" they said. "We want a
king over us. 20Then we will be like all
8:20 [b]ver 5 the other nations,[b] with a king to lead
us and to go out before us and fight our
battles."
21When Samuel heard all that the
people said, he repeated[c] it before the 8:21 [c]Jdg 11:11
LORD. 22The LORD answered, "Listen[d]
to them and give them a king." 8:22 [d]ver 7
Then Samuel said to the men of Israel, "Everyone go back to his town."

Samuel Anoints Saul

9 There was a Benjamite, a man of
standing, whose name was Kish[e] 9:1 [e]1Sa 14:51; 1Ch 8:33; 9:39
son of Abiel, the son of Zeror, the son
of Becorath, the son of Aphiah of Benjamin. 2He had a son named Saul, an
impressive young man without equal[f] 9:2 [f]1Sa 10:24
among the Israelites—a head taller[g] [g]1Sa 10:23
than any of the others.
3Now the donkeys belonging to Saul's
father Kish were lost, and Kish said to
his son Saul, "Take one of the servants
with you and go and look for the don-
keys." 4So he passed through the hill[h] 9:4 [h]Jos 24:33
country of Ephraim and through the [i]2Ki 4:42
area around Shalisha,[i] but they did not
find them. They went on into the district of Shaalim, but the donkeys were
not there. Then he passed through the
territory of Benjamin, but they did not
find them.
5When they reached the district of
Zuph,[j] Saul said to the servant who was 9:5 [j]1Sa 1:1
with him, "Come, let's go back, or my [k]1Sa 10:2
father will stop thinking about the donkeys and start worrying[k] about us."
6But the servant replied, "Look, in
this town there is a man of God;[l] he 9:6 [l]Dt 33:1;
is highly respected, and everything[m] he 1Ki 13:1
says comes true. Let's go there now. Per- [m]1Sa 3:19
haps he will tell us what way to take." 9:7
7Saul said to his servant, "If we go, [n]1Ki 14:3; 2Ki 5:5,15;
what can we give the man? The food in 8:8
our sacks is gone. We have no gift[n] to
take to the man of God. What do we
have?"
8The servant answered him again.
"Look," he said, "I have a quarter of a
shekel[b] of silver. I will give it to the man
of God so that he will tell us what way
to take." 9(Formerly in Israel, if a man 9:9
went to inquire of God, he would say, [o]2Sa 24:11;
"Come, let us go to the seer," because 2Ki 17:13; 1Ch 9:22;
the prophet of today used to be called 26:28; 29:29;
a seer.)[o] Isa 30:10; Am 7:12
10"Good," Saul said to his servant,

[a]16 Septuagint; Hebrew *young men* [b]8 That is, about 1/10 ounce (about 3 grams)

"Come, let's go." So they set out for the
town where the man of God was.
11As they were going up the hill to
the town, they met some girls coming
9:11 [p]Ge 24:11,13 out to draw[p] water, and they asked
them, "Is the seer here?"
12"He is," they answered. "He's ahead
of you. Hurry now; he has just come to
our town today, for the people have a
9:12 sacrifice[q] at the high place.[r] 13As soon
[q]Nu 28:11-15; 1Sa 7:17 as you enter the town, you will find
[r]Ge 31:54; 1Sa 10:5; him before he goes up to the high place
1Ki 3:2 to eat. The people will not begin eating
until he comes, because he must bless
the sacrifice; afterward, those who are
invited will eat. Go up now; you should
find him about this time."
14They went up to the town, and as
they were entering it, there was Samuel,
coming toward them on his way up to
the high place.
15Now the day before Saul came,
the LORD had revealed this to Samuel:
16"About this time tomorrow I will
send you a man from the land of Benja-
9:16 min. Anoint[s] him leader over my peo-
[s]1Sa 10:1 [t]Ex 3:7-9 ple Israel; he will deliver[t] my people
from the hand of the Philistines. I have
looked upon my people, for their cry
has reached me."
17When Samuel caught sight of Saul,
9:17 [u]1Sa 16:12 the LORD said to him, "This[u] is the
man I spoke to you about; he will gov-
ern my people."
18Saul approached Samuel in the
gateway and asked, "Would you please
tell me where the seer's house is?"
19"I am the seer," Samuel replied.
"Go up ahead of me to the high place,
for today you are to eat with me, and in
the morning I will let you go and will
tell you all that is in your heart. 20As for
9:20 the donkeys[v] you lost three days ago, do
[v]ver 3 [w]1Sa 8:5; not worry about them; they have been
12:13 found. And to whom is all the desire[w]
of Israel turned, if not to you and all
your father's family?"
21Saul answered, "But am I not a
9:21 Benjamite, from the smallest tribe[x] of
[x]1Sa 15:17 [y]Jdg 20:35,46 Israel, and is not my clan the least
of all the clans of the tribe of Benja-
min?[y] Why do you say such a thing
to me?"
22Then Samuel brought Saul and his
servant into the hall and seated them at
the head of those who were invited—
about thirty in number. 23Samuel said
to the cook, "Bring the piece of meat
I gave you, the one I told you to lay
aside."
24So the cook took up the leg[z] with 9:24 [z]Lev 7:32-34; Nu 18:18
what was on it and set it in front of
Saul. Samuel said, "Here is what has
been kept for you. Eat, because it was
set aside for you for this occasion, from
the time I said, 'I have invited guests.' "
And Saul dined with Samuel that day.
25After they came down from the
high place to the town, Samuel talked
with Saul on the roof[a] of his house. 9:25 [a]Dt 22:8; Ac 10:9
26They rose about daybreak and Sam-
uel called to Saul on the roof, "Get
ready, and I will send you on your way."
When Saul got ready, he and Samuel
went outside together. 27As they were
going down to the edge of the town,
Samuel said to Saul, "Tell the servant
to go on ahead of us"—and the servant did so—"but you stay here awhile,
so that I may give you a message from
God."
10 Then Samuel took a flask[b] of 10:1 [b]1Sa 16:13; 2Ki 9:1,3,6
oil and poured it on Saul's head [c]Ps 2:12
and kissed him, saying, "Has not the [d]Dt 32:9;
LORD anointed[c] you leader over his Ps 78:62,71
inheritance?[a] [d] 2When you leave me today, you will meet two men near Ra- 10:2 [e]Ge 35:20
chel's tomb,[e] at Zelzah on the border [f]1Sa 9:4
of Benjamin. They will say to you, [g]1Sa 9:5
'The donkeys[f] you set out to look for
have been found. And now your father
has stopped thinking about them and
is worried[g] about you. He is asking,
"What shall I do about my son?"'
3"Then you will go on from there
until you reach the great tree of Tabor.
Three men going up to God at Bethel[h] 10:3 [h]Ge 28:22; 35:7-8
will meet you there. One will be car-
rying three young goats, another three
loaves of bread, and another a skin of
wine. 4They will greet you and offer
you two loaves of bread, which you will
accept from them.
5"After that you will go to Gibeah
of God, where there is a Philistine out- 10:5 [i]1Sa 13:3
post.[i] As you approach the town, you [j]1Sa 9:12
will meet a procession of prophets com- [k]2Ki 3:15
ing down from the high place[j] with [l]1Sa 19:20; 1Co 14:1
lyres, tambourines, flutes and harps[k] be- 10:6 [m]ver 10;
ing played before them, and they will Nu 11:25;
be prophesying.[l] 6The Spirit[m] of the 1Sa 19:23-24

[a] *1* Hebrew; Septuagint and Vulgate *over his people Israel? You will reign over the LORD's people and save them from the power of their enemies round about. And this will be a sign to you that the LORD has anointed you leader over his inheritance:*

LORD will come upon you in power,
and you will prophesy with them; and
you will be changed into a different
person. 7Once these signs are fulfilled,
10:7 [n]Ecc 9:10 [o]Jos 1:5; Jdg 6:12; Heb 13:5
do whatever[n] your hand finds to do, for
God is with[o] you.
8"Go down ahead of me to Gilgal.[p]
I will surely come down to you to
10:8 [p]1Sa 11:14-15
sacrifice burnt offerings and fellowship
offerings,[a] but you must wait seven days
until I come to you and tell you what
you are to do."

Saul Made King

9As Saul turned to leave Samuel, God
10:9 [q]ver 6
changed[q] Saul's heart, and all these signs
were fulfilled that day. 10When they arrived at Gibeah, a procession of prophets met him; the Spirit of God came
10:10 [r]ver 5-6; 1Sa 19:20
upon him in power, and he joined in
their prophesying.[r] 11When all those
who had formerly known him saw him
prophesying with the prophets, they
10:11 [s]Mt 13:54; Jn 7:15 [t]1Sa 19:24
asked each other, "What is this[s] that has
happened to the son of Kish? Is Saul
also among the prophets?"[t]
12A man who lived there answered,
"And who is their father?" So it became a saying: "Is Saul also among the
prophets?" 13After Saul stopped prophesying, he went to the high place.
10:14 [u]1Sa 14:50
14Now Saul's uncle[u] asked him and
his servant, "Where have you been?"
"Looking for the donkeys," he said.
"But when we saw they were not to be
found, we went to Samuel."
15Saul's uncle said, "Tell me what
Samuel said to you."
16Saul replied, "He assured us that
10:16 [v]1Sa 9:20
the donkeys[v] had been found." But he
did not tell his uncle what Samuel had
said about the kingship.
17Samuel summoned the people of
Israel to the LORD at Mizpah[w] 18and
10:17 [w]Jdg 20:1; 1Sa 7:5
said to them, "This is what the LORD,
the God of Israel, says: 'I brought Israel
up out of Egypt, and I delivered you
from the power of Egypt and all the
10:18 [x]Jdg 6:8-9
kingdoms that oppressed[x] you.' 19But
you have now rejected your God, who
saves you out of all your calamities and
distresses. And you have said, 'No, set
10:19 [y]1Sa 8:5-7; 12:12 [z]Jos 7:14; 24:1
a king[y] over us.' So now present[z] yourselves before the LORD by your tribes
and clans."
20When Samuel brought all the tribes
of Israel near, the tribe of Benjamin
was chosen. 21Then he brought forward
the tribe of Benjamin, clan by clan,
and Matri's clan was chosen. Finally
Saul son of Kish was chosen. But when
they looked for him, he was not to be
10:22 [a]1Sa 23:2,4, 9-11
found. 22So they inquired[a] further of
the LORD, "Has the man come here
yet?"
And the LORD said, "Yes, he has hidden himself among the baggage."
23They ran and brought him out,
and as he stood among the people he
10:23 [b]1Sa 9:2
was a head taller[b] than any of the others. 24Samuel said to all the people, "Do
10:24 [c]Dt 17:15; 2Sa 21:6 [d]1Ki 1:25, 34,39
you see the man the LORD has chosen?[c]
There is no one like him among all the
people."
Then the people shouted, "Long live[d]
the king!"
25Samuel explained to the people the
10:25 [e]Dt 17:14-20; 1Sa 8:11-18
regulations[e] of the kingship. He wrote
them down on a scroll and deposited
it before the LORD. Then Samuel dismissed the people, each to his own
home.
26Saul also went to his home in Gibe-
10:26 [f]1Sa 11:4
ah,[f] accompanied by valiant men whose
hearts God had touched. 27But some
10:27 [g]Dt 13:13 [h]1Ki 10:25; 2Ch 17:5
troublemakers[g] said, "How can this fellow save us?" They despised him and
brought him no gifts.[h] But Saul kept silent.

Saul Rescues the City of Jabesh

11:1 [i]1Sa 12:12 [j]Jdg 21:8 [k]1Ki 20:34; Eze 17:13
11 Nahash[i] the Ammonite went
up and besieged Jabesh Gilead.[j]
And all the men of Jabesh said to him,
"Make a treaty[k] with us, and we will be
subject to you."
2But Nahash the Ammonite replied,
"I will make a treaty with you only
11:2 [l]Nu 16:14 [m]1Sa 17:26
on the condition that I gouge[l] out the
right eye of every one of you and so
bring disgrace[m] on all Israel."
3The elders of Jabesh said to him,
"Give us seven days so we can send
messengers throughout Israel; if no one
comes to rescue us, we will surrender to
you."
4When the messengers came to Gib-
11:4 [n]1Sa 10:5,26; 15:34 [o]Jdg 2:4; 1Sa 30:4
eah[n] of Saul and reported these terms to
the people, they all wept[o] aloud. 5Just
then Saul was returning from the fields,
behind his oxen, and he asked, "What
is wrong with the people? Why are they
weeping?" Then they repeated to him
what the men of Jabesh had said.

[a]8 Traditionally *peace offerings*

6When Saul heard their words, the
11:6 [p]Jdg 3:10; Spirit[p] of God came upon him in pow-
6:34; 13:25; er, and he burned with anger. 7He took
14:6; 1Sa 10:10; a pair of oxen, cut them into pieces, and
16:13 sent the pieces by messengers through-
11:7 out Israel,[q] proclaiming, "This is what
[q]Jdg 19:29 [r]Jdg 21:5 will be done to the oxen of anyone[r]
who does not follow Saul and Sam-
uel." Then the terror of the LORD fell
on the people, and they turned out as
11:8 one man. 8When Saul mustered[s] them
[s]Jdg 20:2 at Bezek,[t] the men of Israel numbered
[t]Jdg 1:4 three hundred thousand and the men
of Judah thirty thousand.
9They told the messengers who had
come, "Say to the men of Jabesh Gilead, 'By the time the sun is hot tomorrow, you will be delivered.'" When the
messengers went and reported this to
the men of Jabesh, they were elated.
10They said to the Ammonites, "To-
11:10 [u]ver 3 morrow we will surrender[u] to you, and
you can do to us whatever seems good
to you."
11The next day Saul separated his
11:11 [v]Jdg 7:16 men into three divisions;[v] during the
last watch of the night they broke into
the camp of the Ammonites and slaughtered them until the heat of the day.
Those who survived were scattered, so
that no two of them were left together.

Saul Confirmed as King

11:12 12The people then said to Samuel,
[w]1Sa 10:27; Lk 19:27 "Who[w] was it that asked, 'Shall Saul
reign over us?' Bring these men to us
and we will put them to death."
13But Saul said, "No one shall be put
11:13 [x]2Sa 19:22 to death today,[x] for this day the LORD
[y]Ex 14:13; 1Sa 19:5 has rescued[y] Israel."
14Then Samuel said to the people,
11:14 [z]1Sa 10:8 "Come, let us go to Gilgal[z] and there re-
[a]1Sa 10:25 affirm the kingship.[a]" 15So all the peo-
11:15 ple went to Gilgal[b] and confirmed Saul
[b]1Sa 10:8,17 as king in the presence of the LORD.
There they sacrificed fellowship offerings[a] before the LORD, and Saul and all
the Israelites held a great celebration.

Samuel's Farewell Speech

12 Samuel said to all Israel, "I have
12:1 [c]1Sa 8:7 listened[c] to everything you said
[d]1Sa 10:24; 11:15 to me and have set a king[d] over you.
2Now you have a king as your leader.[e]
12:2 [e]1Sa 8:5 As for me, I am old and gray, and my
sons are here with you. I have been your
leader from my youth until this day.
3Here I stand. Testify against me in the
presence of the LORD and his anoint- 12:3
ed.[f] Whose ox have I taken? Whose [f]1Sa 10:1; 24:6;
donkey[g] have I taken? Whom have I 2Sa 1:14 [g]Nu 16:15
cheated? Whom have I oppressed? From [h]Dt 16:19
whose hand have I accepted a bribe[h] to [i]Ac 20:33
make me shut my eyes? If I have done[i]
any of these, I will make it right."
4"You have not cheated or oppressed
us," they replied. "You have not taken
anything[j] from anyone's hand.[k]" 12:5 [j]Ac 23:9;
5Samuel said to them, "The LORD is 24:20 [k]Ex 22:4
witness against you, and also his anointed is witness this day, that you have not
found anything in my hand."
"He is witness," they said.
6Then Samuel said to the people, "It
is the LORD who appointed Moses and
Aaron and brought[l] your forefathers up 12:6
out of Egypt. 7Now then, stand here, [l]Ex 6:26; Mic 6:4
because I am going to confront[m] you
with evidence before the LORD as to 12:7 [m]Isa 1:18;
all the righteous acts performed by the Mic 6:1-5
LORD for you and your fathers.
8"After Jacob entered Egypt, they
cried[n] to the LORD for help, and the 12:8 [n]Ex 2:23
LORD sent[o] Moses and Aaron, who [o]Ex 3:10; 4:16
brought your forefathers out of Egypt
and settled them in this place.
9"But they forgot[p] the LORD their 12:9
God; so he sold them into the hand of [p]Jdg 3:7 [q]Jdg 4:2
Sisera,[q] the commander of the army of [r]Jdg 10:7; 13:1
Hazor, and into the hands of the Phi- [s]Jdg 3:12
listines[r] and the king of Moab,[s] who
fought against them. 10They cried out
to the LORD and said, 'We have sinned;
we have forsaken[t] the LORD and served 12:10
the Baals and the Ashtoreths.[u] But now [t]Jdg 10:10,15 [u]Jdg 2:13
deliver us from the hands of our en-
emies, and we will serve you.' 11Then
the LORD sent Jerub-Baal,[b] [v] Barak,[c] [w] 12:11
Jephthah[x] and Samuel,[d] and he deliv- [v]Jdg 6:14,32 [w]Jdg 4:6
ered you from the hands of your en- [x]Jdg 11:1
emies on every side, so that you lived
securely.
12"But when you saw that Nahash[y] 12:12
king[z] of the Ammonites was moving [y]1Sa 11:1 [z]1Sa 8:5
against you, you said to me, 'No, we [a]Jdg 8:23; 1Sa 8:6,19
want a king to rule[a] over us'—even
though the LORD your God was your
king. 13Now here is the king[b] you have 12:13 [b]1Sa 8:5;
chosen, the one you asked[c] for; see, Hos 13:11
the LORD has set a king over you. [c]1Sa 10:24
14If you fear[d] the LORD and serve and 12:14 [d]Jos 24:14
obey him and do not rebel against his

[a] *15* Traditionally *peace offerings* [b] *11* Also called *Gideon* [c] *11* Some Septuagint manuscripts and Syriac; Hebrew *Bedan* [d] *11* Hebrew; some Septuagint manuscripts and Syriac *Samson*

commands, and if both you and the
king who reigns over you follow the
LORD your God—good! 15But if you
do not obey the LORD, and if you rebel
12:15 [e]ver 9; Jos 24:20; Isa 1:20 against[e] his commands, his hand will be
against you, as it was against your fa-
thers.
12:16 [f]Ex 14:13 16"Now then, stand still and see[f] this
great thing the LORD is about to do
before your eyes! 17Is it not wheat har-
12:17 [g]1Sa 7:9-10 [h]Jas 5:18 [i]Pr 26:1 [j]1Sa 8:6-7 vest[g] now? I will call[h] upon the LORD
to send thunder and rain.[i] And you will
realize what an evil[j] thing you did in
the eyes of the LORD when you asked
for a king."
18Then Samuel called upon the
LORD, and that same day the LORD
sent thunder and rain. So all the people
12:18 [k]Ex 14:31 stood in awe[k] of the LORD and of Samuel.
12:19 [l]ver 23; Ex 9:28; Jas 5:18; 1Jn 5:16 19The people all said to Samuel,
"Pray[l] to the LORD your God for your
servants so that we will not die, for we
have added to all our other sins the evil
of asking for a king."
20"Do not be afraid," Samuel replied.
"You have done all this evil; yet do not
turn away from the LORD, but serve
the LORD with all your heart. 21Do not
12:21 [m]Isa 41:24,29; Jer 16:19; Hab 2:18 [n]Dt 11:16 turn away after useless[m] idols.[n] They
can do you no good, nor can they res-
cue you, because they are useless. 22For
the sake[o] of his great name[p] the LORD
12:22 [o]Ps 106:8 [p]Jos 7:9 [q]1Ki 6:13 [r]Dt 7:7; 1Pe 2:9 will not reject[q] his people, because the
LORD was pleased to make[r] you his
own. 23As for me, far be it from me that
I should sin against the LORD by failing
12:23 [s]Ro 1:9-10; Col 1:9; 2Ti 1:3 [t]1Ki 8:36; Ps 34:11; Pr 4:11 to pray[s] for you. And I will teach[t] you
the way that is good and right. 24But
be sure to fear[u] the LORD and serve
him faithfully with all your heart; consider[v] what great[w] things he has done
12:24 [u]Ecc 12:13 [v]Isa 5:12 [w]Dt 10:21 for you. 25Yet if you persist[x] in doing
evil, both you and your king will be
12:25 [x]1Sa 31:1-5 [y]Jos 24:20 swept[y] away."

Samuel Rebukes Saul

13 Saul was ⌞thirty⌟[a] years old when
he became king, and he reigned
over Israel ⌞forty-⌟[b] two years.
2Saul[c] chose three thousand men
from Israel; two thousand were with
him at Micmash and in the hill country of Bethel, and a thousand were with
13:2 [z]1Sa 10:26 Jonathan at Gibeah[z] in Benjamin. The
rest of the men he sent back to their
homes.
3Jonathan attacked the Philistine out-
post[a] at Geba, and the Philistines heard 13:3 [a]1Sa 10:5
about it. Then Saul had the trumpet
blown throughout the land and said,
"Let the Hebrews hear!" 4So all Israel
heard the news: "Saul has attacked the
Philistine outpost, and now Israel has
become a stench[b] to the Philistines." 13:4 [b]Ge 34:30
And the people were summoned to join
Saul at Gilgal.
5The Philistines assembled to fight
Israel, with three thousand[d] chariots,
six thousand charioteers, and soldiers
as numerous as the sand[c] on the sea- 13:5 [c]Jos 11:4
shore. They went up and camped at
Micmash, east of Beth Aven. 6When
the men of Israel saw that their situation was critical and that their army
was hard pressed, they hid in caves
and thickets, among the rocks, and in
pits and cisterns.[d] 7Some Hebrews even 13:6 [d]Jdg 6:2
crossed the Jordan to the land of Gad[e]
and Gilead. 13:7 [e]Nu 32:33
Saul remained at Gilgal, and all the
troops with him were quaking with fear.
8He waited seven[f] days, the time set by 13:8 [f]1Sa 10:8
Samuel; but Samuel did not come to
Gilgal, and Saul's men began to scat- 13:9 [g]2Sa 24:25; 1Ki 3:4
ter. 9So he said, "Bring me the burnt
offering and the fellowship offerings.[e]"
And Saul offered[g] up the burnt offering. 10Just as he finished making the of-
fering, Samuel[h] arrived, and Saul went 13:10 [h]1Sa 15:13
out to greet him.
11"What have you done?" asked Samuel.
Saul replied, "When I saw that the
men were scattering, and that you did
not come at the set time, and that
the Philistines were assembling at Mic-
mash,[i] 12I thought, 'Now the Philistines 13:11 [i]ver 2,5,16,23
will come down against me at Gilgal,
and I have not sought the LORD's fa-
vor.[j]' So I felt compelled to offer the 13:12 [j]Jer 26:19
burnt offering."
13"You acted foolishly,[k]" Samuel said. 13:13 [k]2Ch 16:9 [l]1Sa 15:23,24
"You have not kept[l] the command the
LORD your God gave you; if you had,
he would have established your kingdom over Israel for all time. 14But now
your kingdom[m] will not endure; the 13:14 [m]1Sa 15:28 [n]Ac 7:46; 13:22 [o]2Sa 6:21
LORD has sought out a man after his
own heart[n] and appointed[o] him leader

[a]*1* A few late manuscripts of the Septuagint; Hebrew does not have *thirty.* [b]*1* See the round number in Acts 13:21; Hebrew does not have *forty-.* [c]*1,2* Or *and when he had reigned over Israel two years, 2he* [d]5 Some Septuagint manuscripts and Syriac; Hebrew *thirty thousand* [e]9 Traditionally *peace offerings*

KINDNESS

OBEY GOD AND EXTEND YOUR INFLUENCE

1 Samuel 13:13

Jesus said, "Whoever has my commands and obeys them, he is the one who loves me" (John 14:21). But it is best not to be flamboyant when you take a stand for humility. Those who want to claim a city should ride into it upon a borrowed donkey.

of his people, because you have not
kept the LORD's command."
15Then Samuel left Gilgal[a] and went
13:15 [p]1Sa 14:2 up to Gibeah[p] in Benjamin, and Saul
counted the men who were with him.
They numbered about six hundred.

Israel Without Weapons

16Saul and his son Jonathan and the
men with them were staying in Gibeah[b] in Benjamin, while the Philistines
camped at Micmash. 17Raiding par-
13:17 [q]1Sa 14:15 [r]Jos 18:23 ties[q] went out from the Philistine camp
in three detachments. One turned to-
ward Ophrah[r] in the vicinity of Shual,
13:18 [s]Jos 18:13-14 [t]Ne 11:34 18another toward Beth Horon,[s] and the
third toward the borderland overlook-
ing the Valley of Zeboim[t] facing the
desert.
13:19 [u]2Ki 24:14; Jer 24:1 19Not a blacksmith[u] could be found
in the whole land of Israel, because the
Philistines had said, "Otherwise the Hebrews will make swords or spears!" 20So
all Israel went down to the Philistines
to have their plowshares, mattocks, axes
and sickles[c] sharpened. 21The price was
two thirds of a shekel[d] for sharpening
plowshares and mattocks, and a third of
a shekel[e] for sharpening forks and axes
and for repointing goads.
22So on the day of the battle not a
13:22 [v]1Ch 9:39 [w]Jdg 5:8 soldier with Saul and Jonathan[v] had a
sword or spear[w] in his hand; only Saul
and his son Jonathan had them.

Jonathan Attacks the Philistines

23Now a detachment of Philistines
13:23 [x]1Sa 14:4 had gone out to the pass[x] at Micmash.

14 1One day Jonathan son of Saul
said to the young man bearing
his armor, "Come, let's go over to the
Philistine outpost on the other side."
But he did not tell his father.
2Saul was staying on the outskirts of
Gibeah[y] under a pomegranate tree in 14:2 [y]1Sa 13:15
Migron.[z] With him were about six hun- [z]Isa 10:28
dred men, 3among whom was Ahijah,
who was wearing an ephod. He was a
son of Ichabod's[a] brother Ahitub[b] son 14:3 [a]1Sa 4:21
of Phinehas, the son of Eli,[c] the LORD's [b]1Sa 22:11,20 [c]1Sa 2:28
priest in Shiloh. No one was aware that
Jonathan had left.
4On each side of the pass[d] that Jona- 14:4 [d]1Sa 13:23
than intended to cross to reach the Philistine outpost was a cliff; one was called
Bozez, and the other Seneh. 5One cliff
stood to the north toward Micmash,
the other to the south toward Geba.
6Jonathan said to his young armor-
bearer, "Come, let's go over to the out-
post of those uncircumcised[e] fellows. 14:6 [e]1Sa 17:26,36; Jer 9:26
Perhaps the LORD will act in our be- [f]Heb 11:34
half. Nothing[f] can hinder the LORD [g]Jdg 7:4
from saving, whether by many[g] or by [h]1Sa 17:46-47
few."[h]
7"Do all that you have in mind,"
his armor-bearer said. "Go ahead; I am
with you heart and soul."
8Jonathan said, "Come, then; we will
cross over toward the men and let them
see us. 9If they say to us, 'Wait there until we come to you,' we will stay where
we are and not go up to them. 10But
if they say, 'Come up to us,' we will
climb up, because that will be our sign[i] 14:10 [i]Ge 24:14;
that the LORD has given them into our Jdg 6:36-37
hands."
11So both of them showed themselves to the Philistine outpost. "Look!"
said the Philistines. "The Hebrews are
crawling out of the holes they were
hiding[j] in." 12The men of the outpost 14:11 [j]1Sa 13:6
shouted to Jonathan and his armor-
bearer, "Come up to us and we'll teach
you a lesson.[k]" 14:12 [k]1Sa 17:43-44
So Jonathan said to his armor-bearer, [l]2Sa 5:24
"Climb up after me; the LORD has giv-
en them into the hand[l] of Israel."
13Jonathan climbed up, using his
hands and feet, with his armor-bearer
right behind him. The Philistines fell
before Jonathan, and his armor-bearer
followed and killed behind him. 14In
that first attack Jonathan and his ar-

[a]*15* Hebrew; Septuagint *Gilgal and went his way; the rest of the people went after Saul to meet the army, and they went out of Gilgal* [b]*16* Two Hebrew manuscripts; most Hebrew manuscripts *Geba,* a variant of *Gibeah* [c]*20* Septuagint; Hebrew *plowshares* [d]*21* Hebrew *pim;* that is, about 1/4 ounce (about 8 grams) [e]*21* That is, about 1/8 ounce (about 4 grams)

mor-bearer killed some twenty men in
an area of about half an acre.[a]

Israel Routs the Philistines

14:15 [m]Ge 35:5; 15Then panic[m] struck the whole
2Ki 7:5-7 army—those in the camp and field, and
[n]1Sa 13:17 those in the outposts and raiding[n] parties—and the ground shook. It was a
panic sent by God.[b]
14:16 16Saul's lookouts[o] at Gibeah in Ben-
[o]2Sa 18:24 jamin saw the army melting away in all
directions. 17Then Saul said to the men
who were with him, "Muster the forces
and see who has left us." When they did,
it was Jonathan and his armor-bearer
who were not there.
18Saul said to Ahijah, "Bring[p] the
14:18 [p]1Sa 30:7 ark of God." (At that time it was with
the Israelites.)[c] 19While Saul was talk-
ing to the priest, the tumult in the Philistine camp increased more and more.
14:19 [q]Nu 27:21 So Saul said to the priest,[q] "Withdraw
your hand."
20Then Saul and all his men assembled and went to the battle. They
found the Philistines in total confusion,
14:20 [r]Jdg 7:22; striking[r] each other with their swords.
2Ch 20:23 21Those Hebrews who had previously
been with the Philistines and had gone
14:21 [s]1Sa 29:4 up with them to their camp went[s] over
to the Israelites who were with Saul
and Jonathan. 22When all the Israelites
14:22 [t]1Sa 13:6 who had hidden[t] in the hill country of
Ephraim heard that the Philistines were
on the run, they joined the battle in hot
14:23 [u]Ex 14:30; pursuit. 23So the LORD rescued[u] Israel
Ps 44:6-7 that day, and the battle moved on be-
[v]1Sa 13:5 yond Beth Aven.[v]

Jonathan Eats Honey

24Now the men of Israel were in distress that day, because Saul had bound
14:24 [w]Jos 6:26 the people under an oath,[w] saying,
"Cursed be any man who eats food
before evening comes, before I have
avenged myself on my enemies!" So
none of the troops tasted food.
25The entire army[d] entered the
woods, and there was honey on the
ground. 26When they went into the
woods, they saw the honey oozing out,
yet no one put his hand to his mouth,
because they feared the oath. 27But Jonathan had not heard that his father had
bound the people with the oath, so he
reached out the end of the staff that
14:27 [x]ver 43; was in his hand and dipped it into
1Sa 30:12 the honeycomb.[x] He raised his hand to
his mouth, and his eyes brightened.[e]
28Then one of the soldiers told him,
"Your father bound the army under a
strict oath, saying, 'Cursed be any man
who eats food today!' That is why the
men are faint."
29Jonathan said, "My father has made
trouble[y] for the country. See how my
eyes brightened[f] when I tasted a little 14:29 [y]Jos 7:25;
of this honey. 30How much better it 1Ki 18:18
would have been if the men had eaten
today some of the plunder they took
from their enemies. Would not the
slaughter of the Philistines have been
even greater?"
31That day, after the Israelites had
struck down the Philistines from Mic-
mash to Aijalon,[z] they were exhausted. 14:31 [z]Jos 10:12
32They pounced on the plunder[a] and,
taking sheep, cattle and calves, they 14:32 [a]1Sa 15:19
butchered them on the ground and ate [b]Ge 9:4;
them, together with the blood.[b] 33Then Lev 3:17;
someone said to Saul, "Look, the men 7:26; 17:10-14; 19:26;
are sinning against the LORD by eating Dt 12:16, 23-24
meat that has blood in it."
"You have broken faith," he said.
"Roll a large stone over here at once."
34Then he said, "Go out among the
men and tell them, 'Each of you bring
me your cattle and sheep, and slaughter them here and eat them. Do not sin
against the LORD by eating meat with
blood still in it.'"
So everyone brought his ox that night
and slaughtered it there. 35Then Saul
built an altar[c] to the LORD; it was the 14:35 [c]1Sa 7:17
first time he had done this.
36Saul said, "Let us go down after the
Philistines by night and plunder them
till dawn, and let us not leave one of
them alive."
"Do whatever seems best to you,"
they replied.
But the priest said, "Let us inquire of
God here."
37So Saul asked God, "Shall I go
down after the Philistines? Will you
give them into Israel's hand?" But God
did not answer[d] him that day. 14:37 [d]1Sa 10:22;
38Saul therefore said, "Come here, all 28:6,15
you who are leaders of the army, and

[a]*14* Hebrew *half a yoke*; a "yoke" was the land plowed by a yoke of oxen in one day. [b]*15* Or *a terrible panic* [c]*18* Hebrew; Septuagint *"Bring the ephod." (At that time he wore the ephod before the Israelites.)* [d]*25* Or *Now all the people of the land* [e]*27* Or *his strength was renewed* [f]*29* Or *my strength was renewed*

JESUS SPEAKS OUT *on the Fruit of the Spirit:* JOY

Luke 15:10
I tell you, there is rejoicing in the presence of the angels of God over one sinner who repents.

John 15:11
I have told you this so that my joy may be in you and that your joy may be complete.

John 16:20
I tell you the truth, you will weep and mourn while the world rejoices. You will grieve, but your grief will turn to joy.

John 16:22
Now is your time of grief, but I will see you again and you will rejoice, and no one will take away your joy.

John 16:24
Until now you have not asked for anything in my name. Ask and you will receive, and your joy will be complete.

John 17:13
I am coming to you now, but I say these things while I am still in the world, so that they may have the full measure of my joy within them.

▸ THE LOST SHEEP

The tax collectors and "sinners" were all gathering around to hear [Jesus]. But the Pharisees and the teachers of the law muttered, "This man welcomes sinners and eats with them."

Then Jesus told them this parable: "Suppose one of you has a hundred sheep and loses one of them. Does he not leave the ninety-nine in the open country and go after the lost sheep until he finds it? And when he finds it, he joyfully puts it on his shoulders and goes home. Then he calls his friends and neighbors together and says, 'Rejoice with me; I have found my lost sheep.' I tell you that in the same way there will be more rejoicing in heaven over one sinner who repents than over ninety-nine righteous persons who do not need to repent."

Luke 15:1–7

Paul Speaks Out *on the Fruit of the Spirit:* Joy

Galatians 5:22
The fruit of the Spirit is love, joy, peace, patience, kindness, goodness, faithfulness, gentleness and self-control.

Romans 14:17
The kingdom of God is not a matter of eating and drinking, but of righteousness, peace and joy in the Holy Spirit.

Romans 15:13
May the God of hope fill you with all joy and peace as you trust in him, so that you may overflow with hope by the power of the Holy Spirit.

Philippians 4:4
Rejoice in the Lord always. I will say it again: Rejoice!

1 Thessalonians 1:6
You became imitators of us and of the Lord; in spite of severe suffering, you welcomed the message with the joy given by the Holy Spirit.

1 Thessalonians 5:16
Be joyful always.

Joy in Believing

Once when we were going to the place of prayer, we were met by a slave girl who had a spirit by which she predicted the future. She earned a great deal of money for her owners by fortune-telling. This girl followed Paul and the rest of us, shouting, "These men are servants of the Most High God, who are telling you the way to be saved." She kept this up for many days. Finally Paul became so troubled that he turned around and said to the spirit, "In the name of Jesus Christ I command you to come out of her!" At that moment the spirit left her.

When the owners of the slave girl realized that their hope of making money was gone, they seized Paul and Silas and dragged them into the marketplace to face the authorities. They brought them before the magistrates and said, "These men are Jews, and are throwing our city into an uproar by advocating customs unlawful for us Romans to accept or practice."

The crowd joined in the attack against Paul and Silas, and the magistrates ordered them to be stripped and beaten. After they had been severely flogged, they were thrown into prison, and the jailer was commanded to guard them carefully. Upon receiving such orders, he put them in the inner cell and fastened their feet in the stocks.

About midnight Paul and Silas were praying and singing hymns to God, and the other prisoners were listening to them. Suddenly there was such a violent earthquake that the foundations of the prison were shaken. At once all the prison doors flew open, and everybody's chains came loose. The jailer woke up, and when he saw the prison doors open, he drew his sword and was about to kill himself because he thought the prisoners had escaped. But Paul shouted, "Don't harm yourself! We are all here!"

The jailer called for lights, rushed in and fell trembling before Paul and Silas. He then brought them out and asked, "Sirs, what must I do to be saved?"

They replied, "Believe in the Lord Jesus, and you will be saved—you and your household." Then they spoke the word of the Lord to him and to all the others in his house. At that hour of the night the jailer took them and washed their wounds; then immediately he and all his family were baptized. The jailer brought them into his house and set a meal before them; he was filled with joy because he had come to believe in God—he and his whole family.

Acts 16:16–34

let us find out what sin has been com-
14:38 [e]Jos 7:11; 1Sa 10:19 mitted[e] today. 39As surely as the LORD
who rescues Israel lives,[f] even if it lies
14:39 [f]2Sa 12:5 with my son Jonathan, he must die."
But not one of the men said a word.
40Saul then said to all the Israelites,
"You stand over there; I and Jonathan
my son will stand over here."
"Do what seems best to you," the
men replied.
41Then Saul prayed to the LORD,
14:41 [g]Ac 1:24 [h]Pr 16:33 the God of Israel, "Give[g] me the right[h]
answer."[a] And Jonathan and Saul were
taken by lot, and the men were cleared.
42Saul said, "Cast the lot between me
and Jonathan my son." And Jonathan
was taken.
43Then Saul said to Jonathan, "Tell
14:43 [i]Jos 7:19 [j]ver 27 me what you have done."[i]
So Jonathan told him, "I merely tast-
ed a little honey[j] with the end of my
staff. And now must I die?"
44Saul said, "May God deal with me,
14:44 [k]Ru 1:17 [l]ver 39 be it ever so severely,[k] if you do not die,
Jonathan.[l]"
45But the men said to Saul, "Should
Jonathan die—he who has brought
about this great deliverance in Israel?
Never! As surely as the LORD lives,
14:45 [m]1Ki 1:52; Lk 21:18; Ac 27:34 [n]2Sa 14:11 not a hair[m] of his head will fall to
the ground, for he did this today with
God's help." So the men rescued[n] Jonathan, and he was not put to death.
46Then Saul stopped pursuing the
Philistines, and they withdrew to their
own land.
47After Saul had assumed rule over
Israel, he fought against their enemies
14:47 [o]1Sa 11:1-13 [p]ver 52; 2Sa 10:6 on every side: Moab, the Ammonites,[o]
Edom, the kings[b] of Zobah,[p] and the
Philistines. Wherever he turned, he
inflicted punishment on them.[c] 48He
fought valiantly and defeated the
14:48 [q]1Sa 15:2,7 Amalekites,[q] delivering Israel from the
hands of those who had plundered
them.

Saul's Family

49Saul's sons were Jonathan, Ishvi and
14:49 [r]1Sa 31:2; 1Ch 8:33 [s]1Sa 18:17-20 Malki-Shua.[r] The name of his older
daughter was Merab, and that of the
younger was Michal.[s] 50His wife's name
was Ahinoam daughter of Ahimaaz.
The name of the commander of Saul's
army was Abner son of Ner, and Ner
14:51 [t]1Sa 9:1 was Saul's uncle. 51Saul's father Kish[t]
and Abner's father Ner were sons of
Abiel.

52All the days of Saul there was bitter war with the Philistines, and whenever Saul saw a mighty or brave man,
he took[u] him into his service. 14:52 [u]1Sa 8:11

The LORD Rejects Saul as King

15 Samuel said to Saul, "I am the
one the LORD sent to anoint[v] 15:1 [v]1Sa 9:16
you king over his people Israel; so listen
now to the message from the LORD.
2This is what the LORD Almighty says:
'I will punish the Amalekites[w] for what 15:2 [w]Ex 17:8-14; Nu 24:20; Dt 25:17-19
they did to Israel when they waylaid
them as they came up from Egypt.
3Now go, attack the Amalekites and to- 15:3 [x]Nu 24:20; Dt 20:16-18; Jos 6:17; 1Sa 22:19
tally[x] destroy[d] everything that belongs
to them. Do not spare them; put to
death men and women, children and
infants, cattle and sheep, camels and
donkeys.'"
4So Saul summoned the men and
mustered them at Telaim—two hundred thousand foot soldiers and ten
thousand men from Judah. 5Saul went
to the city of Amalek and set an ambush in the ravine. 6Then he said to the
Kenites,[y] "Go away, leave the Amalek- 15:6 [y]Ex 18:10,19; Nu 10:29-32; 24:22; Jdg 1:16; 4:1
ites so that I do not destroy you along
with them; for you showed kindness to
all the Israelites when they came up out
of Egypt." So the Kenites moved away
from the Amalekites.
7Then Saul attacked the Amalekites[z] 15:7 [z]1Sa 14:48 [a]Ge 16:7; 25:17-18; Ex 15:22
all the way from Havilah to Shur,[a] to
the east of Egypt. 8He took Agag king
of the Amalekites alive,[b] and all his peo- 15:8 [b]1Sa 30:1
ple he totally destroyed with the sword.
9But Saul and the army spared[c] Agag
and the best of the sheep and cattle, the 15:9 [c]ver 3,15
fat calves[e] and lambs—everything that
was good. These they were unwilling to
destroy completely, but everything that
was despised and weak they totally destroyed.
10Then the word of the LORD came 15:11 [d]Ge 6:6; 2Sa 24:16 [e]Jos 22:16
to Samuel: 11"I am grieved[d] that I have
made Saul king, because he has turned[e]
away from me and has not carried out

[a]*41* Hebrew; Septuagint *"Why have you not answered your servant today? If the fault is in me or my son Jonathan, respond with Urim, but if the men of Israel are at fault, respond with Thummim."*
[b]*47* Masoretic Text; Dead Sea Scrolls and Septuagint *king* [c]*47* Hebrew; Septuagint *he was victorious*
[d]*3* The Hebrew term refers to the irrevocable giving over of things or persons to the LORD, often by totally destroying them; also in verses 8, 9, 15, 18, 20 and 21. [e]*9* Or *the grown bulls*; the meaning of the Hebrew for this phrase is uncertain.

15:11 [f]1Sa 13:13; 1Ki 9:6-7 [g]ver 35

my instructions."[f] Samuel was troubled,[g] and he cried out to the LORD all
that night.
12Early in the morning Samuel got
up and went to meet Saul, but he was

15:12 [h]Jos 15:55

told, "Saul has gone to Carmel.[h] There
he has set up a monument in his own
honor and has turned and gone on
down to Gilgal."
13When Samuel reached him, Saul
said, "The LORD bless you! I have carried out the LORD's instructions."
14But Samuel said, "What then is this
bleating of sheep in my ears? What is
this lowing of cattle that I hear?"
15Saul answered, "The soldiers
brought them from the Amalekites; they
spared the best of the sheep and cattle
to sacrifice to the LORD your God, but
we totally destroyed the rest."
16"Stop!" Samuel said to Saul. "Let
me tell you what the LORD said to me
last night."
"Tell me," Saul replied.
17Samuel said, "Although you were

15:17 [i]1Sa 9:21

once small[i] in your own eyes, did you
not become the head of the tribes of
Israel? The LORD anointed you king
over Israel. 18And he sent you on a mission, saying, 'Go and completely destroy
those wicked people, the Amalekites;
make war on them until you have wiped
them out.' 19Why did you not obey
the LORD? Why did you pounce on the

15:19 [j]1Sa 14:32

plunder[j] and do evil in the eyes of the
LORD?"

15:20 [k]ver 13

20"But I did obey[k] the LORD," Saul
said. "I went on the mission the LORD
assigned me. I completely destroyed the
Amalekites and brought back Agag their
king. 21The soldiers took sheep and cattle from the plunder, the best of what
was devoted to God, in order to sacrifice them to the LORD your God at
Gilgal."
22But Samuel replied:

"Does the LORD delight in burnt
offerings and sacrifices
as much as in obeying the voice of
the LORD?
To obey is better than sacrifice,[l]
and to heed is better than the fat
of rams.
23For rebellion is like the sin of
divination,[m]
and arrogance like the evil of
idolatry.

15:22 [l]Ps 40:6-8; 51:16; Isa 1:11-15; Jer 7:22; Hos 6:6; Mic 6:6-8; Mt 12:7; Mk 12:33; Heb 10:6-9

15:23 [m]Dt 18:10

Because you have rejected[n] the word
of the LORD,
he has rejected you as king."

15:23 [n]1Sa 13:13

24Then Saul said to Samuel, "I have
sinned.[o] I violated the LORD's command and your instructions. I was
afraid[p] of the people and so I gave in to
them. 25Now I beg you, forgive[q] my sin
and come back with me, so that I may
worship the LORD."

15:24 [o]2Sa 12:13 [p]Pr 29:25; Isa 51:12-13

15:25 [q]Ex 10:17

26But Samuel said to him, "I will not
go back with you. You have rejected[r]
the word of the LORD, and the LORD
has rejected you as king over Israel!"

15:26 [r]1Sa 13:14

27As Samuel turned to leave, Saul
caught hold of the hem of his robe,
and it tore.[s] 28Samuel said to him, "The
LORD has torn[t] the kingdom of Israel
from you today and has given it to one
of your neighbors—to one better than
you. 29He who is the Glory of Israel
does not lie[u] or change[v] his mind; for
he is not a man, that he should change
his mind."

15:27 [s]1Ki 11:11,31

15:28 [t]1Sa 28:17; 1Ki 11:31

15:29 [u]1Ch 29:11; Tit 1:2 [v]Nu 23:19; Eze 24:14

30Saul replied, "I have sinned. But
please honor[w] me before the elders of
my people and before Israel; come back
with me, so that I may worship the
LORD your God." 31So Samuel went
back with Saul, and Saul worshiped the
LORD.

15:30 [w]Isa 29:13; Jn 5:44; 12:43

32Then Samuel said, "Bring me Agag
king of the Amalekites."
Agag came to him confidently,[a] thinking, "Surely the bitterness of death is
past."
33But Samuel said,

"As your sword has made women
childless,
so will your mother be childless
among women."[x]

15:33 [x]Ge 9:6; Jdg 1:7

And Samuel put Agag to death before
the LORD at Gilgal.
34Then Samuel left for Ramah,[y] but
Saul went up to his home in Gibeah[z]
of Saul. 35Until the day Samuel[a] died,
he did not go to see Saul again, though
Samuel mourned[b] for him. And the
LORD was grieved that he had made
Saul king over Israel.

15:34 [y]1Sa 7:17 [z]1Sa 11:4

15:35 [a]1Sa 19:24 [b]1Sa 16:1

Samuel Anoints David

16 The LORD said to Samuel,
"How long will you mourn[c] for

16:1 [c]1Sa 15:35

[a]32 Or *him trembling, yet*

16:1 [d]1Sa 15:23 [e]2Ki 9:1 [f]Ru 4:17; 1Sa 9:16 [g]Ps 78:70; Ac 13:22

Saul, since I have rejected[d] him as king over Israel? Fill your horn with oil[e] and be on your way; I am sending you to Jesse[f] of Bethlehem. I have chosen[g] one of his sons to be king."

[2]But Samuel said, "How can I go? Saul will hear about it and kill me."

16:3 [h]Ex 4:15 [i]Dt 17:15; 1Sa 9:16

The LORD said, "Take a heifer with you and say, 'I have come to sacrifice to the LORD.' [3]Invite Jesse to the sacrifice, and I will show[h] you what to do. You are to anoint[i] for me the one I indicate."

16:4 [j]Ge 48:7; Lk 2:4 [k]1Ki 2:13; 2Ki 9:17

[4]Samuel did what the LORD said. When he arrived at Bethlehem,[j] the elders of the town trembled when they met him. They asked, "Do you come in peace?"[k]

16:5 [l]Ex 19:10,22

[5]Samuel replied, "Yes, in peace; I have come to sacrifice to the LORD. Consecrate[l] yourselves and come to the sacrifice with me." Then he consecrated Jesse and his sons and invited them to the sacrifice.

16:6 [m]1Sa 17:13

[6]When they arrived, Samuel saw Eliab[m] and thought, "Surely the LORD's anointed stands here before the LORD."

GENTLENESS

GENTLENESS HAS NOTHING TO DO WITH PHYSICAL STRENGTH

1 Samuel 16:7

Tall people come in all sizes; the heart alone determines the believer's stature.

16:7 [n]Ps 147:10 [o]1Ki 8:39; 1Ch 28:9; Isa 55:8

[7]But the LORD said to Samuel, "Do not consider his appearance or his height, for I have rejected him. The LORD does not look at the things man looks at. Man looks at the outward appearance,[n] but the LORD looks at the heart."[o]

16:8 [p]1Sa 17:13

[8]Then Jesse called Abinadab[p] and had him pass in front of Samuel. But Samuel said, "The LORD has not chosen this one either." [9]Jesse then had Shammah pass by, but Samuel said, "Nor has the LORD chosen this one." [10]Jesse had seven of his sons pass before Samuel, but Samuel said to him, "The LORD has not chosen these." [11]So he asked Jesse, "Are these all[q] the sons you have?"

16:11 [q]1Sa 17:12

"There is still the youngest," Jesse answered, "but he is tending the sheep." Samuel said, "Send for him; we will not sit down[a] until he arrives."

16:12 [r]1Sa 9:17 [s]Ge 39:6; 1Sa 17:42

[12]So he[r] sent and had him brought in. He was ruddy, with a fine appearance and handsome[s] features.

Then the LORD said, "Rise and anoint him; he is the one."

16:13 [t]Nu 27:18; Jdg 11:29 [u]1Sa 10:1,6, 9-10; 11:6

[13]So Samuel took the horn of oil and anointed him in the presence of his brothers, and from that day on the Spirit of the LORD[t] came upon David in power.[u] Samuel then went to Ramah.

David in Saul's Service

16:14 [v]Jdg 16:20 [w]Jdg 9:23; 1Sa 18:10

[14]Now the Spirit of the LORD had departed[v] from Saul, and an evil[b] spirit[w] from the LORD tormented him.

[15]Saul's attendants said to him, "See, an evil spirit from God is tormenting you. [16]Let our lord command his servants here to search for someone who can play the harp.[x] He will play when the evil spirit from God comes upon you, and you will feel better."

16:16 [x]ver 23; 1Sa 18:10; 19:9; 2Ki 3:15

[17]So Saul said to his attendants, "Find someone who plays well and bring him to me."

[18]One of the servants answered, "I have seen a son of Jesse of Bethlehem who knows how to play the harp. He is a brave man and a warrior. He speaks well and is a fine-looking man. And the LORD is with[y] him."

16:18 [y]1Sa 3:19; 17:32-37

[19]Then Saul sent messengers to Jesse and said, "Send me your son David, who is with the sheep." [20]So Jesse took a donkey loaded with bread,[z] a skin of wine and a young goat and sent them with his son David to Saul.

16:20 [z]1Sa 10:27; Pr 18:16

[21]David came to Saul and entered his service.[a] Saul liked him very much, and David became one of his armor-bearers. [22]Then Saul sent word to Jesse, saying, "Allow David to remain in my service, for I am pleased with him."

16:21 [a]Ge 41:46; Pr 22:29

[23]Whenever the spirit from God came upon Saul, David would take his harp and play. Then relief would come to Saul; he would feel better, and the evil spirit[b] would leave him.

16:23 [b]ver 14-16

David and Goliath

17:1 [c]1Sa 13:5

17 Now the Philistines gathered their forces for war and assembled[c] at Socoh in Judah. They pitched

[a]*11* Some Septuagint manuscripts; Hebrew *not gather around* [b]*14* Or *injurious*; also in verses 15, 16 and 23

camp at Ephes Dammim, between Socoh[d] and Azekah. 2Saul and the Israelites assembled and camped in the Valley of Elah[e] and drew up their battle line to meet the Philistines. 3The Philistines occupied one hill and the Israelites another, with the valley between them.

4A champion named Goliath,[f] who was from Gath, came out of the Philistine camp. He was over nine feet[a] tall. 5He had a bronze helmet on his head and wore a coat of scale armor of bronze weighing five thousand shekels[b]; 6on his legs he wore bronze greaves, and a bronze javelin[g] was slung on his back. 7His spear shaft was like a weaver's rod,[h] and its iron point weighed six hundred shekels.[c] His shield bearer[i] went ahead of him.

8Goliath stood and shouted to the ranks of Israel, "Why do you come out and line up for battle? Am I not a Philistine, and are you not the servants of Saul? Choose[j] a man and have him come down to me. 9If he is able to fight and kill me, we will become your subjects; but if I overcome him and kill him, you will become our subjects and serve us." 10Then the Philistine said, "This day I defy[k] the ranks of Israel! Give me a man and let us fight each other." 11On hearing the Philistine's words, Saul and all the Israelites were dismayed and terrified.

12Now David was the son of an Ephrathite named Jesse,[l] who was from Bethlehem[m] in Judah. Jesse had eight[n] sons, and in Saul's time he was old and well advanced in years. 13Jesse's three oldest sons had followed Saul to the war: The firstborn was Eliab;[o] the second, Abinadab; and the third, Shammah.[p] 14David was the youngest. The three oldest followed Saul, 15but David went back and forth from Saul to tend his father's sheep[q] at Bethlehem.

16For forty days the Philistine came forward every morning and evening and took his stand.

17Now Jesse said to his son David, "Take this ephah[d] of roasted grain[r] and these ten loaves of bread for your brothers and hurry to their camp. 18Take along these ten cheeses to the commander of their unit.[e] See how your brothers[s] are and bring back some assurance[f] from them. 19They are with Saul and all the men of Israel in the Valley of Elah, fighting against the Philistines."

20Early in the morning David left the flock with a shepherd, loaded up and set out, as Jesse had directed. He reached the camp as the army was going out to its battle positions, shouting the war cry. 21Israel and the Philistines were drawing up their lines facing each other. 22David left his things with the keeper of supplies, ran to the battle lines and greeted his brothers. 23As he was talking with them, Goliath, the Philistine champion from Gath, stepped out from his lines and shouted his usual[t] defiance, and David heard it. 24When the Israelites saw the man, they all ran from him in great fear.

25Now the Israelites had been saying, "Do you see how this man keeps coming out? He comes out to defy Israel. The king will give great wealth to the man who kills him. He will also give him his daughter[u] in marriage and will exempt his father's family from taxes in Israel."

26David asked the men standing near him, "What will be done for the man who kills this Philistine and removes this disgrace[v] from Israel? Who is this uncircumcised[w] Philistine that he should defy[x] the armies of the living[y] God?"

27They repeated to him what they had been saying and told him, "This is what will be done for the man who kills him."

28When Eliab, David's oldest brother, heard him speaking with the men, he burned with anger[z] at him and asked, "Why have you come down here? And with whom did you leave those few sheep in the desert? I know how conceited you are and how wicked your heart is; you came down only to watch the battle."

29"Now what have I done?" said David. "Can't I even speak?" 30He then turned away to someone else and brought up the same matter, and the men answered him as before. 31What David said was overheard and reported to Saul, and Saul sent for him.

17:1 [d]Jos 15:35; 2Ch 28:18
17:2 [e]1Sa 21:9
17:4 [f]Jos 11:21-22; 2Sa 21:19
17:6 [g]ver 45
17:7 [h]2Sa 21:19 [i]ver 41
17:8 [j]1Sa 8:17
17:10 [k]ver 26,45; 2Sa 21:21
17:12 [l]Ru 4:17; 1Ch 2:13-15 [m]Ge 35:19 [n]1Sa 16:11
17:13 [o]1Sa 16:6 [p]1Sa 16:9
17:15 [q]1Sa 16:19
17:17 [r]1Sa 25:18
17:18 [s]Ge 37:14
17:23 [t]ver 8-10
17:25 [u]Jos 15:16; 1Sa 18:17
17:26 [v]1Sa 11:2 [w]1Sa 14:6 [x]ver 10 [y]Dt 5:26
17:28 [z]Ge 37:4,8, 11; Pr 18:19; Mt 10:36

[a]*4* Hebrew *was six cubits and a span* (about 3 meters)
[b]*5* That is, about 125 pounds (about 57 kilograms)
[c]*7* That is, about 15 pounds (about 7 kilograms)
[d]*17* That is, probably about 3/5 bushel (about 22 liters)
[e]*18* Hebrew *thousand*
[f]*18* Or *some token;* or *some pledge of spoils*

[32]David said to Saul, "Let no one lose heart[a] on account of this Philistine; your servant will go and fight him."

[33]Saul replied,[b] "You are not able to go out against this Philistine and fight him; you are only a boy, and he has been a fighting man from his youth."

[34]But David said to Saul, "Your servant has been keeping his father's sheep. When a lion[c] or a bear came and carried off a sheep from the flock, [35]I went after it, struck it and rescued the sheep from its mouth. When it turned on me, I seized it by its hair, struck it and killed it. [36]Your servant has killed both the lion and the bear; this uncircumcised Philistine will be like one of them, because he has defied the armies of the living God. [37]The LORD who delivered[d] me from the paw of the lion[e] and the paw of the bear will deliver me from the hand of this Philistine."

Saul said to David, "Go, and the LORD be with[f] you."

[38]Then Saul dressed David in his own tunic. He put a coat of armor on him and a bronze helmet on his head. [39]David fastened on his sword over the tunic and tried walking around, because he was not used to them.

"I cannot go in these," he said to Saul, "because I am not used to them." So he took them off. [40]Then he took his staff in his hand, chose five smooth stones from the stream, put them in the pouch of his shepherd's bag and, with his sling in his hand, approached the Philistine.

[41]Meanwhile, the Philistine, with his shield bearer in front of him, kept coming closer to David. [42]He looked David over and saw that he was only a boy, ruddy and handsome,[g] and he despised[h] him. [43]He said to David, "Am I a dog,[i] that you come at me with sticks?" And the Philistine cursed David by his gods. [44]"Come here," he said, "and I'll give your flesh to the birds of the air and the beasts of the field![j]"

[45]David said to the Philistine, "You come against me with sword and spear and javelin, but I come against you in the name[k] of the LORD Almighty, the God of the armies of Israel, whom you have defied.[l] [46]This day the LORD will hand you over to me, and I'll strike you down and cut off your head. Today I will give the carcasses[m] of the Philistine army to the birds of the air and the beasts of the earth, and the whole world[n] will know that there is a God in Israel.[o] [47]All those gathered here will know that it is not by sword[p] or spear that the LORD saves;[q] for the battle[r] is the LORD's, and he will give all of you into our hands."

[48]As the Philistine moved closer to attack him, David ran quickly toward the battle line to meet him. [49]Reaching into his bag and taking out a stone, he slung it and struck the Philistine on the forehead. The stone sank into his forehead, and he fell facedown on the ground.

PATIENCE

CONQUERING LIFE

1 Samuel 17:47

Conquering life is not a matter of being an overcomer. It's a matter of worship.
Great worship creates overcomers.
It trains the heart to see outside.
It looks up over ego
To behold a better guide.

[50]So David triumphed over the Philistine with a sling[s] and a stone; without a sword in his hand he struck down the Philistine and killed him.

[51]David ran and stood over him. He took hold of the Philistine's sword and drew it from the scabbard. After he killed him, he cut[t] off his head with the sword.[u]

When the Philistines saw that their hero was dead, they turned and ran. [52]Then the men of Israel and Judah surged forward with a shout and pursued the Philistines to the entrance of Gath[a] and to the gates of Ekron.[v] Their dead were strewn along the Shaaraim[w] road to Gath and Ekron. [53]When the Israelites returned from chasing the Philistines, they plundered their camp. [54]David took the Philistine's head and brought it to Jerusalem, and he put the Philistine's weapons in his own tent.

[55]As Saul watched David[x] going out to meet the Philistine, he said to Abner, commander of the army, "Abner, whose son is that young man?"

[a]*52* Some Septuagint manuscripts; Hebrew *a valley*

17:32 [a]Dt 20:3; 1Sa 16:18
17:33 [b]Nu 13:31
17:34 [c]Jer 49:19; Am 3:12
17:37 [d]2Co 1:10 [e]2Ti 4:17 [f]1Sa 20:13; 1Ch 22:11,16
17:42 [g]1Sa 16:12 [h]Ps 123:3-4; Pr 16:18
17:43 [i]1Sa 24:14; 2Sa 3:8; 9:8; 2Ki 8:13
17:44 [j]1Ki 20:10-11
17:45 [k]2Sa 22:33, 35; 2Ch 32:8; Ps 124:8; Heb 11:32-34 [l]ver 10
17:46 [m]Dt 28:26
17:46 [n]Jos 4:24; 1Ki 8:43; Isa 52:10 [o]1Ki 18:36; 2Ki 19:19; Isa 37:20
17:47 [p]Hos 1:7; Zec 4:6 [q]1Sa 14:6; 2Ch 14:11 [r]2Ch 20:15; Ps 44:6-7
17:50 [s]2Sa 23:21
17:51 [t]Heb 11:34 [u]1Sa 21:9
17:52 [v]Jos 15:11 [w]Jos 15:36
17:55 [x]1Sa 16:21

Abner replied, "As surely as you live, O king, I don't know."

56 The king said, "Find out whose son this young man is."

57 As soon as David returned from killing the Philistine, Abner took him and brought him before Saul, with David still holding the Philistine's head.

58 "Whose son are you, young man?" Saul asked him.

David said, "I am the son of your servant Jesse[y] of Bethlehem."

Saul's Jealousy of David

18 After David had finished talking with Saul, Jonathan became one in spirit with David, and he loved[z] him as himself.[a] 2 From that day Saul kept David with him and did not let him return to his father's house. 3 And Jonathan made a covenant[b] with David because he loved him as himself. 4 Jonathan took off the robe[c] he was wearing and gave it to David, along with his tunic, and even his sword, his bow and his belt.

5 Whatever Saul sent him to do, David did it so successfully[a] that Saul gave him a high rank in the army. This pleased all the people, and Saul's officers as well.

6 When the men were returning home after David had killed the Philistine, the women came out from all the towns of Israel to meet King Saul with singing and dancing,[d] with joyful songs and with tambourines[e] and lutes. 7 As they danced, they sang:[f]

"Saul has slain his thousands,
and David his tens[g] of thousands."

8 Saul was very angry; this refrain galled him. "They have credited David with tens of thousands," he thought, "but me with only thousands. What more can he get but the kingdom?[h]" 9 And from that time on Saul kept a jealous eye on David.

10 The next day an evil[b] spirit[i] from God came forcefully upon Saul. He was prophesying in his house, while David was playing the harp, as he usually[j] did. Saul had a spear in his hand 11 and he hurled it, saying to himself,[k] "I'll pin David to the wall." But David eluded[l] him twice.

12 Saul was afraid[m] of David, because the LORD[n] was with[o] David but had left Saul. 13 So he sent David away from him and gave him command over a thousand men, and David led[p] the troops in their campaigns.[q] 14 In everything he did he had great success,[c][r] because the LORD was with[s] him. 15 When Saul saw how successful[d] he was, he was afraid of him. 16 But all Israel and Judah loved David, because he led them in their campaigns.[t]

17 Saul said to David, "Here is my older daughter[u] Merab. I will give her to you in marriage; only serve me bravely and fight the battles[v] of the LORD." For Saul said to himself,[w] "I will not raise a hand against him. Let the Philistines do that!"

18 But David said to Saul, "Who am I,[x] and what is my family or my father's clan in Israel, that I should become the king's son-in-law?[y]" 19 So[e] when the time came for Merab,[z] Saul's daughter, to be given to David, she was given in marriage to Adriel of Meholah.[a]

20 Now Saul's daughter Michal[b] was in love with David, and when they told Saul about it, he was pleased. 21 "I will give her to him," he thought, "so that she may be a snare[c] to him and so that the hand of the Philistines may be against him." So Saul said to David, "Now you have a second opportunity to become my son-in-law."

22 Then Saul ordered his attendants: "Speak to David privately and say, 'Look, the king is pleased with you, and his attendants all like you; now become his son-in-law.'"

23 They repeated these words to David. But David said, "Do you think it is a small matter to become the king's son-in-law? I'm only a poor man and little known."

24 When Saul's servants told him what David had said, 25 Saul replied, "Say to David, 'The king wants no other price[d] for the bride than a hundred Philistine foreskins, to take revenge on his enemies.'" Saul's plan[e] was to have David fall by the hands of the Philistines.

26 When the attendants told David these things, he was pleased to become the king's son-in-law. So before the allotted time elapsed, 27 David and his men went out and killed two hundred

17:58 *y* ver 12
18:1 *z* 2Sa 1:26 *a* Ge 44:30
18:3 *b* 1Sa 20:8,16,17,42
18:4 *c* Ge 41:42
18:6 *d* Ex 15:20 *e* Jdg 11:34; Ps 68:25
18:7 *f* Ex 15:21 *g* 1Sa 21:11; 29:5
18:8 *h* 1Sa 15:8
18:10 *i* 1Sa 16:14 *j* 1Sa 19:7
18:11 *k* 1Sa 20:7,33 *l* 1Sa 19:10
18:12 *m* ver 15,29 *n* 1Sa 16:13 *o* 1Sa 28:15
18:13 *p* ver 16; Nu 27:17 *q* 2Sa 5:2
18:14 *r* Ge 39:3 *s* Ge 39:2,23; Jos 6:27; 1Sa 16:18
18:16 *t* ver 5
18:17 *u* 1Sa 17:25 *v* Nu 21:14; 1Sa 25:28 *w* ver 25
18:18 *x* 1Sa 9:21; 2Sa 7:18 *y* ver 23
18:19 *z* 2Sa 21:8 *a* Jdg 7:22
18:20 *b* ver 28
18:21 *c* ver 17,26
18:25 *d* Ge 34:12; Ex 22:17; 1Sa 14:24 *e* ver 17

[a] *5* Or *wisely* [b] *10* Or *injurious* [c] *14* Or *he was very wise* [d] *15* Or *wise* [e] *19* Or *However,*

DAY 2 TWO

▸ SELF-CONTROL AND THE PURPOSE OF GOD IN MY LIFE

1 Samuel 19:8–17

An evil spirit resided in Saul. When that spirit took over Saul's life, all that he did was devious. Saul was clearly out of control.

The Apostle Paul subjected each temptation to indulgence to three tests (1 Corinthians 10:23,31): First, is it beneficial? Second, is it constructive? Third, does it glorify God? Do we, like King Saul, surrender to evil so readily that we fail to face our temptations with these three questions?

The Greek word for having self-control, *egkrateuomai*, has to do with disciplining the self. Paul used the word in 1 Corinthians 7:9 when speaking of the Christian's mastery of sexual impulses, and again in 9:25 to speak of an athlete's disciplining of his or her body. It is a word that speaks of a realistic view of self. The word does not encourage us to hate ourselves, as expressed in this poem:

I hate my ego-evil-I.
I think I'll eat a worm and die.

Nor does the word encourage us to love ourselves in a narcissistic fashion:

I love me-self; I love me-self.
I pick me up and hug me-self.

Rather, the word encourages us to take a long, hard look at who we are. We are to be moderate as we understand and relate to our world—as expressed in the famous epitaph on an old tombstone:

Here lies Martin Elginbrod.
Have mercy on my soul, O God.
As I would have if I were God
And you were Martin Elginbrod.

As Martin Luther wrote, "We are at once saint and sinner." Self-control means that we make a conscious effort to make our saintliness more saintly and our sinfulness less sinful. King Saul lost that battle; the evil he wouldn't control, he at last couldn't control.

To begin a study on the topic of Self-Control, Managing My Moods, turn to the home page on page 179

Philistines. He brought their foreskins
and presented the full number to the
king so that he might become the king's
son-in-law. Then Saul gave him his
daughter Michal[f] in marriage.
28When Saul realized that the LORD
was with David and that his daughter
Michal loved David, 29Saul became still
more afraid of him, and he remained
his enemy the rest of his days.
30The Philistine commanders continued to go out to battle, and as often
as they did, David met with more success[a][g] than the rest of Saul's officers,
and his name became well known.

Saul Tries to Kill David

19 Saul told his son Jonathan[h] and
all the attendants to kill[i] David.
But Jonathan was very fond of David
2and warned him, "My father Saul is
looking for a chance to kill you. Be on
your guard tomorrow morning; go into
hiding and stay there. 3I will go out and
stand with my father in the field where
you are. I'll speak[j] to him about you
and will tell you what I find out."
4Jonathan spoke[k] well of David to
Saul his father and said to him, "Let not
the king do wrong[l] to his servant David; he has not wronged you, and what
he has done has benefited you greatly.
5He took his life in his hands when he
killed the Philistine. The LORD won a
great victory[m] for all Israel, and you saw
it and were glad. Why then would you
do wrong to an innocent[n] man like David by killing him for no reason?"
6Saul listened to Jonathan and took
this oath: "As surely as the LORD lives,
David will not be put to death."
7So Jonathan called David and told
him the whole conversation. He
brought him to Saul, and David was
with Saul as before.[o]
8Once more war broke out, and David went out and fought the Philistines.
He struck them with such force that
they fled before him.
9But an evil[b] spirit[p] from the LORD
came upon Saul as he was sitting in his
house with his spear in his hand. While
David was playing the harp, 10Saul tried
to pin him to the wall with his spear,
but David eluded[q] him as Saul drove

[a]30 Or *David acted more wisely* [b]9 Or *injurious*

18:27 [f]ver 13; 2Sa 3:14
18:30 [g]ver 5; 2Sa 11:1
19:1 [h]1Sa 18:1 [i]1Sa 18:9
19:3 [j]1Sa 20:12
19:4 [k]1Sa 20:32; Pr 31:8,9; Jer 18:20 [l]Ge 42:22; Pr 17:13
19:5 [m]1Sa 11:13; 17:49-50; 1Ch 11:14 [n]Dt 19:10-13; 1Sa 20:32; Mt 27:4
19:7 [o]1Sa 16:21; 18:2,13
19:9 [p]1Sa 16:14; 18:10-11
19:10 [q]1Sa 18:11

the spear into the wall. That night David made good his escape.
[11]Saul sent men to David's house to
19:11 watch[r] it and to kill him in the morning.
[r]Ps 59 Title But Michal, David's wife, warned him,
"If you don't run for your life tonight,
19:12 tomorrow you'll be killed." [12]So Michal
[s]Jos 2:15; let David down through a window,[s] and
Ac 9:25 he fled and escaped. [13]Then Michal
took an idol[a] and laid it on the bed,
covering it with a garment and putting
some goats' hair at the head.
[14]When Saul sent the men to capture
19:14 [t]Jos 2:4 David, Michal said,[t] "He is ill."
[15]Then Saul sent the men back to see
David and told them, "Bring him up to
me in his bed so that I may kill him."
[16]But when the men entered, there was
the idol in the bed, and at the head was
some goats' hair.
[17]Saul said to Michal, "Why did you
deceive me like this and send my enemy away so that he escaped?"
Michal told him, "He said to me, 'Let
me get away. Why should I kill you?'"
19:18 [18]When David had fled and made his
[u]1Sa 7:17 escape, he went to Samuel at Ramah[u]
and told him all that Saul had done
to him. Then he and Samuel went to
Naioth and stayed there. [19]Word came
to Saul: "David is in Naioth at Ramah"; [20]so he sent men to capture him.
But when they saw a group of proph-
19:20 ets[v] prophesying, with Samuel standing
[v]ver 11,14; Jn 7:32,45 there as their leader, the Spirit of God
[w]Nu 11:25 came upon[w] Saul's men and they also
[x]1Sa 10:5; Joel 2:28 prophesied.[x] [21]Saul was told about it,
and he sent more men, and they proph-
esied too. Saul sent men a third time,
and they also prophesied. [22]Finally, he
himself left for Ramah and went to the
great cistern at Secu. And he asked,
"Where are Samuel and David?"
"Over in Naioth at Ramah," they
said.
[23]So Saul went to Naioth at Ramah.
But the Spirit of God came even upon
19:23 him, and he walked along prophesying[y]
[y]1Sa 10:13 until he came to Naioth. [24]He stripped[z]
19:24 off his robes and also prophesied in
[z]2Sa 6:20; Isa 20:2; Samuel's presence. He lay that way
Mic 1:8 all that day and night. This is why
[a]1Sa 10:11 people say, "Is Saul also among the
prophets?"[a]

David and Jonathan

20 Then David fled from Naioth
at Ramah and went to Jonathan
and asked, "What have I done? What
is my crime? How have I wronged[b] 20:1 [b]1Sa 24:9
your father, that he is trying to take my
life?"
[2]"Never!" Jonathan replied. "You are
not going to die! Look, my father doesn't
do anything, great or small, without
confiding in me. Why would he hide
this from me? It's not so!"
[3]But David took an oath[c] and said, 20:3 [c]Dt 6:13
"Your father knows very well that I
have found favor in your eyes, and he
has said to himself, 'Jonathan must not
know this or he will be grieved.' Yet as
surely as the LORD lives and as you live,
there is only a step between me and
death."
[4]Jonathan said to David, "Whatever
you want me to do, I'll do for you."
[5]So David said, "Look, tomorrow is
the New Moon festival,[d] and I am sup- 20:5 [d]Nu 10:10; 28:11
posed to dine with the king; but let me [e]1Sa 19:2
go and hide[e] in the field until the evening of the day after tomorrow. [6]If your
father misses me at all, tell him, 'David
earnestly asked my permission to hurry
to Bethlehem,[f] his hometown, because 20:6 [f]1Sa 17:58
an annual[g] sacrifice is being made there [g]Dt 12:5
for his whole clan.' [7]If he says, 'Very
well,' then your servant is safe. But if
he loses his temper,[h] you can be sure 20:7 [h]1Sa 25:17
that he is determined to harm me. [8]As
for you, show kindness to your servant,
for you have brought him into a cov-
enant[i] with you before the LORD. If I 20:8 [i]1Sa 18:3;
am guilty, then kill[j] me yourself! Why 23:18
hand me over to your father?" [j]2Sa 14:32
[9]"Never!" Jonathan said. "If I had
the least inkling that my father was determined to harm you, wouldn't I tell
you?"
[10]David asked, "Who will tell me if
your father answers you harshly?"
[11]"Come," Jonathan said, "let's go
out into the field." So they went there
together.
[12]Then Jonathan said to David: "By
the LORD, the God of Israel, I will
surely sound out my father by this time
the day after tomorrow! If he is favorably disposed toward you, will I not
send you word and let you know? [13]But
if my father is inclined to harm you, 20:13 [k]Ru 1:17;
may the LORD deal with me, be it ever 1Sa 3:17
so severely,[k] if I do not let you know and
send you away safely. May the LORD

[a]*13* Hebrew *teraphim*; also in verse 16

20:13 [l]Jos 1:5; 1Sa 17:37; 18:12; 1Ch 22:11,16 be with[l] you as he has been with my
father. 14But show me unfailing kind-
ness like that of the LORD as long as I
live, so that I may not be killed, 15and
do not ever cut off your kindness from
20:15 [m]2Sa 9:7 my family[m]—not even when the LORD
has cut off every one of David's enemies
from the face of the earth."
20:16 [n]1Sa 25:22 16So Jonathan made a covenant[n] with
the house of David, saying, "May the
LORD call David's enemies to account."
17And Jonathan had David reaffirm his
20:17 [o]1Sa 18:3 oath[o] out of love for him, because he
loved him as he loved himself.
18Then Jonathan said to David: "Tomorrow is the New Moon festival. You
will be missed, because your seat will
20:18 [p]ver 5,25 be empty.[p] 19The day after tomorrow,
toward evening, go to the place where
20:19 [q]1Sa 19:2 you hid[q] when this trouble began, and
wait by the stone Ezel. 20I will shoot
three arrows to the side of it, as though
I were shooting at a target. 21Then I
will send a boy and say, 'Go, find the
arrows.' If I say to him, 'Look, the arrows are on this side of you; bring them
here,' then come, because, as surely as
the LORD lives, you are safe; there is no
danger. 22But if I say to the boy, 'Look,
20:22 [r]ver 37 the arrows are beyond[r] you,' then you
must go, because the LORD has sent you
away. 23And about the matter you and I
discussed—remember, the LORD is wit-
20:23 [s]ver 14-15; Ge 31:50 ness[s] between you and me forever."
24So David hid in the field, and
when the New Moon festival came, the
king sat down to eat. 25He sat in his
customary place by the wall, opposite
Jonathan,[a] and Abner sat next to Saul,
20:25 [t]ver 18 but David's place was empty.[t] 26Saul
said nothing that day, for he thought,
"Something must have happened to
David to make him ceremonially un-
20:26 [u]Lev 7:20-21; 15:5; 1Sa 16:5 clean—surely he is unclean.[u]" 27But the
next day, the second day of the month,
David's place was empty again. Then
Saul said to his son Jonathan, "Why
hasn't the son of Jesse come to the meal,
either yesterday or today?"
28Jonathan answered, "David earnest-
20:28 [v]ver 6 ly asked me for permission[v] to go to
Bethlehem. 29He said, 'Let me go, be-
cause our family is observing a sacrifice
in the town and my brother has ordered
me to be there. If I have found favor
in your eyes, let me get away to see my
brothers.' That is why he has not come
to the king's table."

30Saul's anger flared up at Jonathan
and he said to him, "You son of a perverse and rebellious woman! Don't I
know that you have sided with the son
of Jesse to your own shame and to the
shame of the mother who bore you?
31As long as the son of Jesse lives on this
earth, neither you nor your kingdom
will be established. Now send and bring
him to me, for he must die!"
32"Why[w] should he be put to death? 20:32 [w]1Sa 19:4; Mt 27:23 [x]Ge 31:36; Lk 23:22
What[x] has he done?" Jonathan asked
his father. 33But Saul hurled his spear at
him to kill him. Then Jonathan knew
that his father intended[y] to kill David. 20:33 [y]ver 7; 1Sa 18:11,17
34Jonathan got up from the table in
fierce anger; on that second day of the
month he did not eat, because he was
grieved at his father's shameful treatment of David.
35In the morning Jonathan went out
to the field for his meeting with David.
He had a small boy with him, 36and he
said to the boy, "Run and find the arrows I shoot." As the boy ran, he shot
an arrow beyond him. 37When the boy
came to the place where Jonathan's arrow had fallen, Jonathan called out
after him, "Isn't the arrow beyond[z] 20:37 [z]ver 22
you?" 38Then he shouted, "Hurry! Go
quickly! Don't stop!" The boy picked
up the arrow and returned to his master. 39(The boy knew nothing of all
this; only Jonathan and David knew.)
40Then Jonathan gave his weapons to
the boy and said, "Go, carry them
back to town."
41After the boy had gone, David got
up from the south side ⌊of the stone⌋
and bowed down before Jonathan three
times, with his face to the ground. Then
they kissed each other and wept together—but David wept the most.
42Jonathan said to David, "Go in
peace,[a] for we have sworn friendship[b] 20:42 [a]ver 22; 1Sa 1:17 [b]2Sa 1:26; Pr 18:24
with each other in the name of the
LORD, saying, 'The LORD is witness
between you and me, and between your
descendants and my descendants forever.' " Then David left, and Jonathan
went back to the town.

David at Nob

21 David went to Nob,[c] to Ahime- 21:1 [c]1Sa 14:3; 22:9,19; Ne 11:32; Isa 10:32 [d]1Sa 16:4
lech the priest. Ahimelech trem-
bled[d] when he met him, and asked,

[a]*25* Septuagint; Hebrew *wall. Jonathan arose*

"Why are you alone? Why is no one
with you?"
2David answered Ahimelech the
priest, "The king charged me with a
certain matter and said to me, 'No one
is to know anything about your mission
and your instructions.' As for my men,
I have told them to meet me at a certain
place. 3Now then, what do you have on
hand? Give me five loaves of bread, or
whatever you can find."
4But the priest answered David, "I

21:4 [e]Lev 24:8-9 [f]Ex 25:30; Mt 12:4 [g]Ex 19:15

don't have any ordinary bread[e] on hand;
however, there is some consecrated[f]
bread here—provided the men have
kept[g] themselves from women."
5David replied, "Indeed women have
been kept from us, as usual whenever[a]

21:5 [h]1Th 4:4

I set out. The men's things[b] are holy[h]
even on missions that are not holy. How
much more so today!" 6So the priest

21:6 [i]Lev 24:8-9; Mt 12:3-4; Mk 2:25-28; Lk 6:1-5

gave him the consecrated bread,[i] since
there was no bread there except the
bread of the Presence that had been removed from before the LORD and replaced by hot bread on the day it was
taken away.
7Now one of Saul's servants was there
that day, detained before the LORD; he

21:7 [j]1Sa 22:9,22 [k]1Sa 14:47; Ps 52 Title

was Doeg[j] the Edomite,[k] Saul's head
shepherd.
8David asked Ahimelech, "Don't you
have a spear or a sword here? I haven't
brought my sword or any other weapon, because the king's business was urgent."

21:9 [l]1Sa 17:51 [m]1Sa 17:2

9The priest replied, "The sword[l] of
Goliath the Philistine, whom you killed
in the Valley of Elah,[m] is here; it is
wrapped in a cloth behind the ephod.
If you want it, take it; there is no sword
here but that one."
David said, "There is none like it;
give it to me."

David at Gath

10That day David fled from Saul and

21:10 [n]1Sa 27:2

went[n] to Achish king of Gath. 11But the
servants of Achish said to him, "Isn't
this David, the king of the land? Isn't
he the one they sing about in their
dances:

"'Saul has slain his thousands,
and David his tens of
thousands'?"[o]

21:11 [o]1Sa 18:7; 29:5; Ps 56 Title

12David took these words to heart
and was very much afraid of Achish
king of Gath. 13So he pretended to be

21:13 [p]Ps 34 Title

insane[p] in their presence; and while he
was in their hands he acted like a madman, making marks on the doors of
the gate and letting saliva run down his
beard.

JOY

GOD IS THE ONLY SOURCE OF WORTHY REPUTATION

1 Samuel 21:11

Saul had slain his thousands, David his tens of thousands. It was a litany of numbers, the Dow-Jones of giant killing. It might have left David an ugly achiever had he not understood that God alone must be the source of our reputations.

14Achish said to his servants, "Look
at the man! He is insane! Why bring
him to me? 15Am I so short of madmen that you have to bring this fellow
here to carry on like this in front of me?
Must this man come into my house?"

David at Adullam and Mizpah

22 David left Gath and escaped to
the cave[q] of Adullam. When

22:1 [q]2Sa 23:13; Ps 57 Title; 142 Title

his brothers and his father's household
heard about it, they went down to
him there. 2All those who were in distress or in debt or discontented gath-

22:2 [r]1Sa 23:13; 25:13; 2Sa 15:20

ered[r] around him, and he became their
leader. About four hundred men were
with him.
3From there David went to Mizpah
in Moab and said to the king of Moab,
"Would you let my father and mother
come and stay with you until I learn
what God will do for me?" 4So he left
them with the king of Moab, and they
stayed with him as long as David was in
the stronghold.

22:5 [s]2Sa 24:11; 1Ch 21:9; 29:29; 2Ch 29:25

5But the prophet Gad[s] said to David,
"Do not stay in the stronghold. Go into
the land of Judah." So David left and
went to the forest of Hereth.

Saul Kills the Priests of Nob

6Now Saul heard that David and his
men had been discovered. And Saul,

22:6 [t]Jdg 4:5 [u]Ge 21:33

spear in hand, was seated[t] under the
tamarisk[u] tree on the hill at Gibeah,
with all his officials standing around

[a]5 Or *from us in the past few days since* [b]5 Or *bodies*

him. 7Saul said to them, "Listen, men
of Benjamin! Will the son of Jesse give
all of you fields and vineyards? Will he
22:7 make all of you commanders[v] of thou-
[v]1Sa 8:14 sands and commanders of hundreds? 8Is
that why you have all conspired against
me? No one tells me when my son
22:8 makes a covenant[w] with the son of Jes-
[w]1Sa 18:3; se. None of you is concerned[x] about me
20:16 [x]1Sa 23:21 or tells me that my son has incited my
servant to lie in wait for me, as he does
22:9 today."
[y]1Sa 21:7; 9But Doeg[y] the Edomite, who was
Ps 52 Title standing with Saul's officials, said, "I
[z]1Sa 21:1 saw the son of Jesse come to Ahimelech
22:10 son of Ahitub at Nob.[z] 10Ahimelech in-
[a]Nu 27:21; quired[a] of the LORD for him; he also
1Sa 10:22 [b]1Sa 21:6 gave him provisions[b] and the sword of
Goliath the Philistine."
11Then the king sent for the priest
Ahimelech son of Ahitub and his father's whole family, who were the priests
at Nob, and they all came to the king.
12Saul said, "Listen now, son of Ahitub."
"Yes, my lord," he answered.
13Saul said to him, "Why have you
22:13 conspired[c] against me, you and the son
[c]ver 8 of Jesse, giving him bread and a sword
and inquiring of God for him, so that
he has rebelled against me and lies in
wait for me, as he does today?"
14Ahimelech answered the king,
22:14 "Who[d] of all your servants is as loyal
[d]1Sa 19:4 as David, the king's son-in-law, captain
of your bodyguard and highly respected
in your household? 15Was that day the
first time I inquired of God for him?
Of course not! Let not the king accuse
your servant or any of his father's family, for your servant knows nothing at
all about this whole affair."
16But the king said, "You will surely
die, Ahimelech, you and your father's
whole family."
17Then the king ordered the guards
at his side: "Turn and kill the priests of
the LORD, because they too have sided
with David. They knew he was fleeing,
yet they did not tell me."
But the king's officials were not will-
22:17 ing[e] to raise a hand to strike the priests
[e]Ex 1:17 of the LORD.
18The king then ordered Doeg, "You
turn and strike down the priests." So
Doeg the Edomite turned and struck
22:18 them down. That day he killed eighty-
[f]1Sa 2:18,31 five men who wore the linen ephod.[f]

19He also put to the sword[g] Nob, the 22:19
town of the priests, with its men and [g]1Sa 15:3
women, its children and infants, and its 22:20
cattle, donkeys and sheep. [h]1Sa 23:6,9; 30:7;
20But Abiathar,[h] a son of Ahimelech 1Ki 2:22, 26,27
son of Ahitub, escaped and fled to join [i]1Sa 2:32
David.[i] 21He told David that Saul had
killed the priests of the LORD. 22Then
David said to Abiathar: "That day, when
Doeg[j] the Edomite was there, I knew 22:22
he would be sure to tell Saul. I am re- [j]1Sa 21:7
sponsible for the death of your father's
whole family. 23Stay with me; don't be
afraid; the man who is seeking your 22:23
life[k] is seeking mine also. You will be [k]1Ki 2:26
safe with me."

David Saves Keilah

23 When David was told, "Look,
the Philistines are fighting 23:1
against Keilah[l] and are looting the [l]Jos 15:44
threshing floors," 2he inquired[m] of the 23:2
LORD, saying, "Shall I go and attack [m]ver 4,12; 1Sa 30:8;
these Philistines?" 2Sa 5:19,23
The LORD answered him, "Go, attack the Philistines and save Keilah."
3But David's men said to him, "Here
in Judah we are afraid. How much
more, then, if we go to Keilah against
the Philistine forces!"
4Once again David inquired of the
LORD, and the LORD answered him,
"Go down to Keilah, for I am going to
give the Philistines into your hand.[n]" 23:4
5So David and his men went to Kei- [n]Jos 8:7; Jdg 7:7
lah, fought the Philistines and carried
off their livestock. He inflicted heavy
losses on the Philistines and saved the
people of Keilah. 6(Now Abiathar[o] son 23:6
of Ahimelech had brought the ephod [o]1Sa 22:20
down with him when he fled to David
at Keilah.)

Saul Pursues David

7Saul was told that David had gone to
Keilah, and he said, "God has handed
him over to me, for David has imprisoned himself by entering a town with
gates and bars." 8And Saul called up
all his forces for battle, to go down to
Keilah to besiege David and his men.
9When David learned that Saul was
plotting against him, he said to Abi- 23:9
athar[p] the priest, "Bring the ephod." [p]ver 6; 1Sa 22:20;
10David said, "O LORD, God of Israel, 30:7
your servant has heard definitely that
Saul plans to come to Keilah and destroy the town on account of me. 11Will

the citizens of Keilah surrender me to him? Will Saul come down, as your servant has heard? O LORD, God of Israel, tell your servant."

And the LORD said, "He will."

12 Again David asked, "Will the citizens of Keilah surrender[q] me and my men to Saul?"

And the LORD said, "They will."

13 So David and his men,[r] about six hundred in number, left Keilah and kept moving from place to place. When Saul was told that David had escaped from Keilah, he did not go there.

14 David stayed in the desert strongholds and in the hills of the Desert of Ziph.[s] Day after day Saul searched[t] for him, but God did not[u] give David into his hands.

15 While David was at Horesh in the Desert of Ziph, he learned that Saul had come out to take his life. 16 And Saul's son Jonathan went to David at Horesh and helped him find strength[v] in God. 17 "Don't be afraid," he said. "My father Saul will not lay a hand on you. You will be king[w] over Israel, and I will be second to you. Even my father Saul knows this." 18 The two of them made a covenant[x] before the LORD. Then Jonathan went home, but David remained at Horesh.

19 The Ziphites[y] went up to Saul at Gibeah and said, "Is not David hiding among us[z] in the strongholds at Horesh, on the hill of Hakilah,[a] south of Jeshimon? 20 Now, O king, come down whenever it pleases you to do so, and we will be responsible for handing[b] him over to the king."

21 Saul replied, "The LORD bless you for your concern[c] for me. 22 Go and make further preparation. Find out where David usually goes and who has seen him there. They tell me he is very crafty. 23 Find out about all the hiding places he uses and come back to me with definite information.[a] Then I will go with you; if he is in the area, I will track him down among all the clans of Judah."

24 So they set out and went to Ziph ahead of Saul. Now David and his men were in the Desert of Maon,[d] in the Arabah south of Jeshimon. 25 Saul and his men began the search, and when David was told about it, he went down to the rock and stayed in the Desert of Maon. When Saul heard this, he went into the Desert of Maon in pursuit of David.

26 Saul[e] was going along one side of the mountain, and David and his men were on the other side, hurrying to get away from Saul. As Saul and his forces were closing in on David and his men to capture them, 27 a messenger came to Saul, saying, "Come quickly! The Philistines are raiding the land." 28 Then Saul broke off his pursuit of David and went to meet the Philistines. That is why they call this place Sela Hammahlekoth.[b] 29 And David went up from there and lived in the strongholds of En Gedi.[f]

23:12 [q]ver 20
23:13 [r]1Sa 22:2; 25:13
23:14 [s]Jos 15:24,55 [t]Ps 54:3-4 [u]Ps 32:7
23:16 [v]1Sa 30:6
23:17 [w]1Sa 20:31; 24:20
23:18 [x]1Sa 18:3; 20:16,42; 2Sa 9:1; 21:7
23:19 [y]1Sa 26:1 [z]Ps 54 Title [a]1Sa 26:3
23:20 [b]ver 12
23:21 [c]1Sa 22:8
23:24 [d]Jos 15:55; 1Sa 25:2
23:26 [e]Ps 17:9
23:29 [f]2Ch 20:2

David Spares Saul's Life

24 After Saul returned from pursuing the Philistines, he was told, "David is in the Desert of En Gedi.[g]" 2 So Saul took three thousand chosen men from all Israel and set out to look[h] for David and his men near the Crags of the Wild Goats.

3 He came to the sheep pens along the way; a cave[i] was there, and Saul went in to relieve[j] himself. David and his men were far back in the cave. 4 The men said, "This is the day the LORD spoke[k] of when he said[c] to you, 'I will give your enemy into your hands for you to deal with as you wish.'"[l] Then David crept up unnoticed and cut off a corner of Saul's robe.

PEACE

THE LAURELS OF THE PEACEMAKER

1 Samuel 24:6

There would be no civil war. While David had the popularity to win, he knew that making peace is a greater triumph than merely winning wars.

5 Afterward, David was conscience-stricken[m] for having cut off a corner of his robe. 6 He said to his men, "The LORD forbid that I should do such a thing to my master, the LORD's anointed,[n] or lift my hand against him; for he is the anointed of the LORD." 7 With these words David rebuked his

24:1 [g]1Sa 23:28-29
24:2 [h]1Sa 26:2
24:3 [i]Ps 57 Title; 142 Title [j]Jdg 3:24
24:4 [k]1Sa 25:28-30 [l]1Sa 23:17; 26:8
24:5 [m]2Sa 24:10
24:6 [n]1Sa 26:11

[a]23 Or *me at Nacon* [b]28 *Sela Hammahlekoth* means *rock of parting.* [c]4 Or *"Today the LORD is saying*

men and did not allow them to attack
Saul. And Saul left the cave and went
his way.
8Then David went out of the cave
and called out to Saul, "My lord the
king!" When Saul looked behind him,
David bowed down and prostrated himself with his face to the ground.[o] 9He
said to Saul, "Why do you listen when
men say, 'David is bent on harming
you'? 10This day you have seen with
your own eyes how the LORD delivered
you into my hands in the cave. Some
urged me to kill you, but I spared you;
I said, 'I will not lift my hand against
my master, because he is the LORD's
anointed.' 11See, my father, look at this
piece of your robe in my hand! I cut
off the corner of your robe but did not
kill you. Now understand and recognize
that I am not guilty[p] of wrongdoing
or rebellion. I have not wronged you,
but you are hunting[q] me down to take
my life. 12May the LORD judge[r] between you and me. And may the LORD
avenge[s] the wrongs you have done to
me, but my hand will not touch you.
13As the old saying goes, 'From evildoers come evil deeds,[t]' so my hand will
not touch you.
14"Against whom has the king of Israel come out? Whom are you pursuing? A dead dog?[u] A flea?[v] 15May the
LORD be our judge[w] and decide between us. May he consider my cause
and uphold[x] it; may he vindicate[y] me
by delivering[z] me from your hand."
16When David finished saying this,
Saul asked, "Is that your voice,[a] David
my son?" And he wept aloud. 17"You
are more righteous than I,"[b] he said.
"You have treated me well,[c] but I have
treated you badly. 18You have just now
told me of the good you did to me; the
LORD delivered[d] me into your hands,
but you did not kill me. 19When a man
finds his enemy, does he let him get
away unharmed? May the LORD reward you well for the way you treated
me today. 20I know that you will surely
be king[e] and that the kingdom[f] of Israel will be established in your hands.
21Now swear[g] to me by the LORD that
you will not cut off my descendants
or wipe out my name from my father's
family.[h]"
22So David gave his oath to Saul.
Then Saul returned home, but David

24:8 [o]1Sa 25:23-24
24:11 [p]Ps 7:3 [q]1Sa 23:14, 23; 1Sa 26:20
24:12 [r]Ge 16:5; 31:53; Job 5:8 [s]Jdg 11:27; 1Sa 26:10
24:13 [t]Mt 7:20
24:14 [u]1Sa 17:43; 2Sa 9:8 [v]1Sa 26:20
24:15 [w]ver 12 [x]Ps 35:1,23; Mic 7:9 [y]Ps 43:1 [z]Ps 119:134, 154
24:16 [a]1Sa 26:17
24:17 [b]Ge 38:26; 1Sa 26:21 [c]Mt 5:44
24:18 [d]1Sa 26:23
24:20 [e]1Sa 23:17 [f]1Sa 13:14
24:21 [g]Ge 21:23; 2Sa 21:1-9 [h]1Sa 20:14-15

and his men went up to the stronghold.[i]

David, Nabal and Abigail

25 Now Samuel died,[j] and all Israel assembled and mourned[k] for
him; and they buried him at his home
in Ramah.[l]
Then David moved down into the
Desert of Maon.[a] 2A certain man in
Maon,[m] who had property there at Carmel, was very wealthy. He had a thousand goats and three thousand sheep,
which he was shearing in Carmel. 3His
name was Nabal and his wife's name
was Abigail.[n] She was an intelligent and
beautiful woman, but her husband, a
Calebite,[o] was surly and mean in his
dealings.
4While David was in the desert, he
heard that Nabal was shearing sheep.
5So he sent ten young men and said to
them, "Go up to Nabal at Carmel and
greet him in my name. 6Say to him:
'Long life to you! Good health[p] to you
and your household! And good health
to all that is yours![q]
7" 'Now I hear that it is sheep-shearing
time. When your shepherds were with
us, we did not mistreat[r] them, and the
whole time they were at Carmel nothing of theirs was missing. 8Ask your own
servants and they will tell you. Therefore be favorable toward my young men,
since we come at a festive time. Please
give your servants and your son David
whatever[s] you can find for them.' "
9When David's men arrived, they
gave Nabal this message in David's
name. Then they waited.
10Nabal answered David's servants,
"Who[t] is this David? Who is this son of
Jesse? Many servants are breaking away
from their masters these days. 11Why
should I take my bread[u] and water,
and the meat I have slaughtered for my
shearers, and give it to men coming
from who knows where?"
12David's men turned around and
went back. When they arrived, they reported every word. 13David said to his
men, "Put on your swords!" So they
put on their swords, and David put on
his. About four hundred men went[v] up
with David, while two hundred stayed
with the supplies.[w]

[a]*1* Some Septuagint manuscripts; Hebrew *Paran*

24:22 [i]1Sa 23:29
25:1 [j]1Sa 28:3 [k]Nu 20:29; Dt 34:8 [l]Ge 21:21; 2Ch 33:20
25:2 [m]Jos 15:55; 1Sa 23:24
25:3 [n]Pr 31:10 [o]Jos 15:13
25:6 [p]Ps 122:7; Lk 10:5 [q]1Ch 12:18
25:7 [r]ver 15
25:8 [s]Ne 8:10
25:10 [t]Jdg 9:28
25:11 [u]Jdg 8:6
25:13 [v]1Sa 23:13 [w]1Sa 30:24

14One of the servants told Nabal's
wife Abigail: "David sent messengers
from the desert to give our master
25:14 [x]1Sa 13:10 his greetings,[x] but he hurled insults
at them. 15Yet these men were very
25:15 [y]ver 7 [z]ver 21 good to us. They did not mistreat[y]
us, and the whole time we were out
in the fields near them nothing was
missing.[z] 16Night and day they were a
25:16 [a]Ex 14:22; Job 1:10 wall[a] around us all the time we were
herding our sheep near them. 17Now
think it over and see what you can
do, because disaster is hanging over our
master and his whole household. He is
25:17 [b]1Sa 20:7 such a wicked[b] man that no one can
talk to him."
18Abigail lost no time. She took two
hundred loaves of bread, two skins of
wine, five dressed sheep, five seahs[a] of
roasted grain, a hundred cakes of rai-
25:18 [c]1Ch 12:40 [d]2Sa 16:1 sins[c] and two hundred cakes of pressed
figs, and loaded them on donkeys.[d]
19Then she told her servants, "Go on
25:19 [e]Ge 32:20 ahead;[e] I'll follow you." But she did not
tell her husband Nabal.
20As she came riding her donkey into
a mountain ravine, there were David
and his men descending toward her,
and she met them. 21David had just
said, "It's been useless—all my watching
over this fellow's property in the desert
so that nothing of his was missing. He
25:21 [f]Ps 109:5 has paid[f] me back evil for good. 22May
God deal with David,[b] be it ever so se-
25:22 [g]1Sa 3:17; 20:13 [h]1Ki 14:10; 21:21; 2Ki 9:8 verely,[g] if by morning I leave alive one
male[h] of all who belong to him!"
23When Abigail saw David, she
quickly got off her donkey and bowed
down before David with her face to
25:23 [i]1Sa 20:41 the ground.[i] 24She fell at his feet and
said: "My lord, let the blame be on
me alone. Please let your servant speak
to you; hear what your servant has to
say. 25May my lord pay no attention to
that wicked man Nabal. He is just like
25:25 [j]Pr 14:16 his name—his name is Fool,[j] and folly
goes with him. But as for me, your ser-
vant, I did not see the men my master
sent.
26"Now since the LORD has kept
25:26 [k]ver 33 [l]Heb 10:30 [m]2Sa 18:32 you, my master, from bloodshed[k] and
from avenging[l] yourself with your own
hands, as surely as the LORD lives and
as you live, may your enemies and all
who intend to harm my master be
like Nabal.[m] 27And let this gift,[n] which
25:27 [n]Ge 33:11; 1Sa 30:26 your servant has brought to my master,
be given to the men who follow you.
28Please forgive[o] your servant's offense, 25:28 [o]ver 24 [p]2Sa 7:11,26 [q]1Sa 18:17 [r]1Sa 24:11
for the LORD will certainly make a last-
ing[p] dynasty for my master, because
he fights the LORD's battles.[q] Let no
wrongdoing[r] be found in you as long
as you live. 29Even though someone is
pursuing you to take your life, the life
of my master will be bound securely in
the bundle of the living by the LORD
your God. But the lives of your enemies
he will hurl[s] away as from the pocket of 25:29 [s]Jer 10:18
a sling. 30When the LORD has done for
my master every good thing he promised concerning him and has appointed
him leader[t] over Israel, 31my master will 25:30 [t]1Sa 13:14
not have on his conscience the stagger-
ing burden of needless bloodshed or of
having avenged himself. And when the
LORD has brought my master success,
remember[u] your servant." 25:31 [u]Ge 40:14
32David said to Abigail, "Praise[v] be 25:32 [v]Ge 24:27; Ex 18:10; Lk 1:68
to the LORD, the God of Israel, who
has sent you today to meet me. 33May
you be blessed for your good judgment
and for keeping me from bloodshed[w] 25:33 [w]ver 26
this day and from avenging myself with
my own hands. 34Otherwise, as surely
as the LORD, the God of Israel, lives,
who has kept me from harming you, if
you had not come quickly to meet me,
not one male belonging to Nabal would
have been left alive by daybreak."
35Then David accepted from her
hand what she had brought him and
said, "Go home in peace. I have heard
your words and granted[x] your re- 25:35 [x]Ge 19:21; 1Sa 20:42; 2Ki 5:19
quest."
36When Abigail went to Nabal, he
was in the house holding a banquet
like that of a king. He was in high[y] 25:36 [y]2Sa 13:23 [z]Pr 20:1; Isa 5:11,22; Hos 4:11 [a]ver 19
spirits and very drunk.[z] So she told[a]
him nothing until daybreak. 37Then in
the morning, when Nabal was sober, his
wife told him all these things, and his
heart failed him and he became like a
stone. 38About ten days later, the LORD
struck[b] Nabal and he died. 25:38 [b]1Sa 26:10; 2Sa 6:7
39When David heard that Nabal was
dead, he said, "Praise be to the LORD,
who has upheld my cause against Nabal
for treating me with contempt. He has
kept his servant from doing wrong and
has brought Nabal's wrongdoing down
on his own head."

[a] *18* That is, probably about a bushel (about 37 liters)
[b] *22* Some Septuagint manuscripts; Hebrew *with David's enemies*

KINDNESS

WEEK 41

DAY ONE

1 KINDNESS, THE APPROACH TO GRACE

Read 1 Samuel 25:32–34

David blesses Abigail for her good judgment and for keeping him from bloodshed when he was in a mood for self-willed vengeance. Kindness is a virtue that sometimes arrives only after we have enjoyed being as mad as we really wanted to be for as long as we wanted to be.

Abigail reminded David that vengefully killing our enemies is not a measure of the kindness of God. Martin Luther wrote that Jesus' kindness is but God's approach to grace and that we would do well to emulate Jesus' kindness.

> Christ gives you faith with all its benefits, and you are to give your neighbor love with all its benefits. You may ask then what are the good works that you should do for your neighbor. They have no name. Just as the good works which Christ has done for you have no name…they have no name for this reason, lest they be divided and this done and that left undone. Rather you must give yourself to your neighbor utterly, just as Christ did not confine himself to prayer and fasting for you…So this is not your good work, that you should give alms or pray, but rather that you should give yourself entirely to your neighbor, as he needs and as you can, with alms, prayer, fasting, counsel, comfort, teaching, appeal, reproof, pardon, clothes, food, and also suffering and death on his behalf. But tell me, where in all Christendom are such works?

Luther was asking where kindness exists in our world. It is noticeably infrequent. Where are the "Abigails" who stay our hands and tempers and beg us to be kind to our enemies? Wouldn't such kindness make a place for God's grace in a world that is looking to be loved and finding very few lovers?

MEMORIZE THIS WEEK

EPHESIANS 4:32

Be kind and compassionate to one another, forgiving each other, just as in Christ God forgave you.

DAY TWO

2 KINDNESS AND THE PURPOSE OF GOD IN MY LIFE

The Hebrew midwives feared God, and that reverence led to their kind acts to others. However, their kindness caused them to risk their lives by defying a royal decree. To cover their acts, they told a little white lie to the king of Egypt—that Hebrew women are vigorous and have short labor time, so their babies are born before a midwife is needed. God blessed the midwives for their lifesaving acts and showed kindness to them for their kindnesses. *Turn to Exodus 1:15–21, page 68, for today's study.*

DAY THREE

3 KINDNESS AND MY RELATIONSHIP WITH CHRIST

Josiah was spared. When he wept before God and confessed his sins, God granted him a reprieve from punishment. Josiah knew God's kindness. When you consider God's redeeming love in your own life, you are able to separate the smaller, everyday kindnesses of God from the truly great kindness of being spared from punishment for your sins. That is the grace of God and the kindness of Christ. Kindness and grace are sisters, if not identical twins. *Turn to 2 Chronicles 34:19–28, page 534, for today's study.*

DAY FOUR

4 KINDNESS AND MY SERVICE TO OTHERS

Kind women and kind men make a kind world. This is the approach of these two proverbs. They teach us that kindness is the demonstration that we are truly human beings. Isn't it nice that this one virtue, kindness, can make us appear to be human beings and at the same time open our world to be evangelized? *Turn to Proverbs 11:16–17, page 744, for today's study.*

DAY FIVE

5 KINDNESS AND ITS PLACE IN MY PERSONAL WORSHIP

Here is yet another passage linking kindness and grace and showing how both of them relate to faith in Christ. When we first saw grace, it was such an obvious blessing that we knew we dared not pass it by—for it was heaven that was being offered to us. Naturally, in the overwhelming presence of such grace, we must fall down in worship. Who could see grace in all of its beauty and not want to worship? *Turn to Ephesians 2:6–10, page 1405, for today's study.*

Week 42, Goodness, the Virtue of the Written Word of God, begins on page 918, Jeremiah 36:1–7,20–24. To begin a topical study on the Fruit of the Spirit, Kindness, turn to the Topical Index, page 1548.

Then David sent word to Abigail,
asking her to become his wife. 40His
servants went to Carmel and said to
Abigail, "David has sent us to you to
take you to become his wife."
41She bowed down with her face to
the ground and said, "Here is your
maidservant, ready to serve you and
wash the feet of my master's servants."
25:42 [c]Ge 24:61-67 42Abigail[c] quickly got on a donkey and,
attended by her five maids, went with
David's messengers and became his wife.
25:43 [d]Jos 15:56 [e]1Sa 27:3; 30:5 43David had also married Ahinoam[d] of
Jezreel, and they both were his wives.[e]
44But Saul had given his daughter Mi-
25:44 [f]2Sa 3:15 [g]Isa 10:30 chal, David's wife, to Paltiel[a][f] son of
Laish, who was from Gallim.[g]

David Again Spares Saul's Life

26:1 [h]1Sa 23:19 [i]Ps 54 Title 26 The Ziphites[h] went to Saul at
Gibeah and said, "Is not David
hiding[i] on the hill of Hakilah, which
faces Jeshimon?"
2So Saul went down to the Desert
of Ziph, with his three thousand cho-
26:2 [j]1Sa 13:2; 24:2 sen men of Israel, to search[j] there for
David. 3Saul made his camp beside
the road on the hill of Hakilah facing
Jeshimon, but David stayed in the
desert. When he saw that Saul had followed him there, 4he sent out scouts
and learned that Saul had definitely
arrived.[b]
5Then David set out and went to
the place where Saul had camped. He
26:5 [k]1Sa 14:50; 17:55 saw where Saul and Abner[k] son of Ner,
the commander of the army, had lain
down. Saul was lying inside the camp,
with the army encamped around him.
6David then asked Ahimelech the
26:6 [l]Jdg 7:10-11; 1Ch 2:16 Hittite and Abishai son of Zeruiah,[l]
Joab's brother, "Who will go down into
the camp with me to Saul?"
"I'll go with you," said Abishai.
7So David and Abishai went to the
army by night, and there was Saul, lying
asleep inside the camp with his spear
stuck in the ground near his head. Abner and the soldiers were lying around
him.
8Abishai said to David, "Today God
has delivered your enemy into your
hands. Now let me pin him to the
ground with one thrust of my spear; I
won't strike him twice."
9But David said to Abishai, "Don't
26:9 [m]2Sa 1:14 [n]1Sa 24:5 destroy him! Who can lay a hand on
the LORD's anointed[m] and be guiltless?[n]
10As surely as the LORD lives," he said, 26:10 [o]1Sa 25:38; Ro 12:19 [p]Ge 47:29; Dt 31:14; Ps 37:13 [q]1Sa 31:6; 2Sa 1:1
"the LORD himself will strike[o] him; ei-
ther his time[p] will come and he will
die,[q] or he will go into battle and perish.
11But the LORD forbid that I should lay
a hand on the LORD's anointed. Now
get the spear and water jug that are near
his head, and let's go."
12So David took the spear and water
jug near Saul's head, and they left. No
one saw or knew about it, nor did anyone wake up. They were all sleeping,
because the LORD had put them into a
deep sleep.[r] 26:12 [r]Ge 2:21; 15:12
13Then David crossed over to the
other side and stood on top of the hill
some distance away; there was a wide
space between them. 14He called out
to the army and to Abner son of Ner,
"Aren't you going to answer me, Abner?"
Abner replied, "Who are you who
calls to the king?"
15David said, "You're a man, aren't
you? And who is like you in Israel?
Why didn't you guard your lord the
king? Someone came to destroy your
lord the king. 16What you have done
is not good. As surely as the LORD
lives, you and your men deserve to die,
because you did not guard your master, the LORD's anointed. Look around
you. Where are the king's spear and water jug that were near his head?"
17Saul recognized David's voice and
said, "Is that your voice,[s] David my 26:17 [s]1Sa 24:16
son?"
David replied, "Yes it is, my lord the
king." 18And he added, "Why is my
lord pursuing his servant? What have
I done, and what wrong[t] am I guilty 26:18 [t]1Sa 24:9, 11-14
of? 19Now let my lord the king listen
to his servant's words. If the LORD has
incited you against me, then may he ac-
cept an offering.[u] If, however, men have 26:19 [u]2Sa 16:11 [v]2Sa 14:16
done it, may they be cursed before the
LORD! They have now driven me from
my share in the LORD's inheritance[v]
and have said, 'Go, serve other gods.'
20Now do not let my blood fall to the
ground far from the presence of the
LORD. The king of Israel has come out
to look for a flea[w]—as one hunts a par- 26:20 [w]1Sa 24:14
tridge in the mountains."
21Then Saul said, "I have sinned.[x] 26:21 [x]Ex 9:27; 1Sa 15:24

[a]44 Hebrew *Palti,* a variant of *Paltiel* [b]4 Or *had come to Nacon*

Come back, David my son. Because
26:21 you considered my life precious[y] today,
[y]1Sa 24:17 I will not try to harm you again. Surely
I have acted like a fool and have erred
greatly."
22"Here is the king's spear," David
answered. "Let one of your young men
come over and get it. 23The LORD re-
26:23 [z]Ps 62:12 wards[z] every man for his righteousness[a]
[a]Ps 7:8; and faithfulness. The LORD delivered
18:20,24 you into my hands today, but I would
not lay a hand on the LORD's anointed.
24As surely as I valued your life today,
so may the LORD value my life and de-
26:24 liver[b] me from all trouble."
[b]Ps 54:7 25Then Saul said to David, "May you
be blessed, my son David; you will do
great things and surely triumph."
So David went on his way, and Saul
returned home.

David Among the Philistines

27 But David thought to himself,
"One of these days I will be destroyed by the hand of Saul. The best
thing I can do is to escape to the land
of the Philistines. Then Saul will give
up searching for me anywhere in Israel,
and I will slip out of his hand."
27:2 2So David and the six hundred men[c]
[c]1Sa 25:13 [d]1Sa 21:10 with him left and went[d] over to
[e]1Ki 2:39 Achish[e] son of Maoch king of Gath.
3David and his men settled in Gath with
Achish. Each man had his family with
27:3 him, and David had his two wives:[f]
[f]1Sa 25:43; Ahinoam of Jezreel and Abigail of Car-
30:3 mel, the widow of Nabal. 4When Saul
was told that David had fled to Gath,
he no longer searched for him.
5Then David said to Achish, "If I
have found favor in your eyes, let a
place be assigned to me in one of the
country towns, that I may live there.
Why should your servant live in the
royal city with you?"
6So on that day Achish gave him
27:6 Ziklag,[g] and it has belonged to the
[g]Jos 15:31; kings of Judah ever since. 7David lived[h]
19:5; Ne 11:28 in Philistine territory a year and four
27:7 months.
[h]1Sa 29:3 8Now David and his men went up
27:8 and raided the Geshurites,[i] the Gir-
[i]Jos 13:2,13 [j]Ex 17:8; zites and the Amalekites.[j] (From an-
1Sa 15:7-8 cient times these peoples had lived in
[k]Ex 15:22 the land extending to Shur[k] and Egypt.)
27:9 9Whenever David attacked an area, he
[l]1Sa 15:3 did not leave a man or woman alive,[l]
but took sheep and cattle, donkeys and

camels, and clothes. Then he returned
to Achish.
10When Achish asked, "Where did
you go raiding today?" David would
say, "Against the Negev of Judah" or
"Against the Negev of Jerahmeel[m]" or 27:10
"Against the Negev of the Kenites.[n]" [m]1Sa 30:29; 1Ch 2:9,25
11He did not leave a man or woman [n]Jdg 1:16
alive to be brought to Gath, for he
thought, "They might inform on us
and say, 'This is what David did.'" And
such was his practice as long as he lived
in Philistine territory. 12Achish trusted
David and said to himself, "He has
become so odious to his people, the
Israelites, that he will be my servant
forever."

Saul and the Witch of Endor

28 In those days the Philistines
gathered[o] their forces to fight 28:1
against Israel. Achish said to David, [o]1Sa 29:1
"You must understand that you and
your men will accompany me in the
army."
2David said, "Then you will see for
yourself what your servant can do."
Achish replied, "Very well, I will
make you my bodyguard for life."
3Now Samuel was dead,[p] and all Is- 28:3 [p]1Sa 25:1
rael had mourned for him and buried [q]1Sa 7:17
him in his own town of Ramah.[q] Saul [r]Ex 22:18; Lev 19:31;
had expelled the mediums and spirit- 20:27; Dt 18:10-11;
ists[r] from the land. 1Sa 15:23

PATIENCE

IMPATIENCE LEADS TO WITCHES

1 Samuel 28:7

It is better to trust God than to take counsel with witches. Does God seem slow to answer? Take care. Look not for easier, swifter answers. At the end of all impatience are the witches of our doubt.

4The Philistines assembled and came
and set up camp at Shunem,[s] while 28:4
Saul gathered all the Israelites and set [s]Jos 19:18; 2Ki 4:8
up camp at Gilboa.[t] 5When Saul saw [t]1Sa 31:1,3
the Philistine army, he was afraid; ter- 28:6
ror filled his heart. 6He inquired[u] of the [u]1Sa 14:37; 1Ch 10:13-
LORD, but the LORD did not answer 14; Pr 1:28
him by dreams[v] or Urim[w] or prophets. [v]Nu 12:6
7Saul then said to his attendants, "Find [w]Ex 28:30; Nu 27:21
me a woman who is a medium,[x] so I 28:7
may go and inquire of her." [x]Ac 16:16
"There is one in Endor,[y]" they said. [y]Jos 17:11

28:8 [z]2Ch 18:29; 35:22 [a]Dt 18:10-11; 1Ch 10:13; Isa 8:19

8So Saul disguised[z] himself, putting
on other clothes, and at night he and
two men went to the woman. "Consult[a] a spirit for me," he said, "and
bring up for me the one I name."
9But the woman said to him, "Surely you know what Saul has done. He
has cut off[b] the mediums and spiritists
from the land. Why have you set a trap
for my life to bring about my death?"
10Saul swore to her by the LORD, "As
surely as the LORD lives, you will not
be punished for this."
11Then the woman asked, "Whom
shall I bring up for you?"
"Bring up Samuel," he said.
12When the woman saw Samuel, she
cried out at the top of her voice and
said to Saul, "Why have you deceived
me? You are Saul!"
13The king said to her, "Don't be
afraid. What do you see?"
The woman said, "I see a spirit[a] coming up out of the ground."
14"What does he look like?" he
asked.
"An old man wearing a robe[c] is coming up," she said.
Then Saul knew it was Samuel, and
he bowed down and prostrated himself
with his face to the ground.
15Samuel said to Saul, "Why have
you disturbed me by bringing me up?"
"I am in great distress," Saul said.
"The Philistines are fighting against me,
and God has turned[d] away from me.
He no longer answers me, either by
prophets or by dreams. So I have called
on you to tell me what to do."
16Samuel said, "Why do you consult
me, now that the LORD has turned
away from you and become your enemy? 17The LORD has done what he
predicted through me. The LORD has
torn[e] the kingdom out of your hands
and given it to one of your neighbors—
to David. 18Because you did not obey[f]
the LORD or carry out his fierce wrath[g]
against the Amalekites, the LORD has
done this to you today. 19The LORD
will hand over both Israel and you to
the Philistines, and tomorrow you and
your sons[h] will be with me. The LORD
will also hand over the army of Israel to
the Philistines."
20Immediately Saul fell full length on
the ground, filled with fear because of
Samuel's words. His strength was gone,
for he had eaten nothing all that day
and night.
21When the woman came to Saul and
saw that he was greatly shaken, she said,
"Look, your maidservant has obeyed
you. I took my life[i] in my hands and
did what you told me to do. 22Now
please listen to your servant and let me
give you some food so you may eat and
have the strength to go on your way."
23He refused[j] and said, "I will not
eat."
But his men joined the woman in
urging him, and he listened to them.
He got up from the ground and sat on
the couch.
24The woman had a fattened calf at
the house, which she butchered at once.
She took some flour, kneaded it and
baked bread without yeast. 25Then she
set it before Saul and his men, and they
ate. That same night they got up and
left.

28:9 [b]ver 3
28:14 [c]1Sa 15:27; 24:8
28:15 [d]ver 6; 1Sa 18:12
28:17 [e]1Sa 15:28
28:18 [f]1Sa 15:20 [g]1Ki 20:42
28:19 [h]1Sa 31:2
28:21 [i]Jdg 12:3; 1Sa 19:5; Job 13:14
28:23 [j]2Ki 5:13

Achish Sends David Back to Ziklag

29 The Philistines gathered[k] all
their forces at Aphek,[l] and Israel
camped by the spring in Jezreel.[m] 2As
the Philistine rulers marched with their
units of hundreds and thousands, David and his men were marching at the
rear[n] with Achish. 3The commanders
of the Philistines asked, "What about
these Hebrews?"
Achish replied, "Is this not David,
who was an officer of Saul king of Israel? He has already been with me for
over a year,[o] and from the day he left
Saul until now, I have found no fault in
him."
4But the Philistine commanders were
angry with him and said, "Send[p] the
man back, that he may return to the
place you assigned him. He must not
go with us into battle, or he will turn[q]
against us during the fighting. How
better could he regain his master's favor
than by taking the heads of our own
men? 5Isn't this the David they sang
about in their dances:

" 'Saul has slain his thousands,
and David his tens of
thousands'?"[r]

6So Achish called David and said
to him, "As surely as the LORD lives,

29:1 [k]1Sa 28:1 [l]Jos 12:18; 1Sa 4:1 [m]2Ki 9:30
29:2 [n]1Sa 28:2
29:3 [o]1Sa 27:7; Da 6:5
29:4 [p]1Ch 12:19 [q]1Sa 14:21
29:5 [r]1Sa 18:7; 21:11

[a]13 Or *see spirits*; or *see gods*

you have been reliable, and I would be
pleased to have you serve with me in the
29:6 [s]1Sa 27:8-12 [t]ver 3 army. From the day[s] you came to me
until now, I have found no fault in you,
but the rulers[t] don't approve of you.
7Turn back and go in peace; do nothing
to displease the Philistine rulers."
8"But what have I done?" asked David. "What have you found against your
servant from the day I came to you until
now? Why can't I go and fight against
the enemies of my lord the king?"
9Achish answered, "I know that you
have been as pleasing in my eyes as an
29:9 [u]2Sa 14:17, 20; 19:27 [v]ver 4 angel[u] of God; nevertheless, the Philistine commanders[v] have said, 'He must
not go up with us into battle.' 10Now
get up early, along with your master's
servants who have come with you, and
29:10 [w]1Ch 12:19 leave[w] in the morning as soon as it is
light."
11So David and his men got up early
in the morning to go back to the land
of the Philistines, and the Philistines
went up to Jezreel.

David Destroys the Amalekites

30 David and his men reached
30:1 [x]1Sa 29:4,11 [y]1Sa 15:7; 27:8 Ziklag[x] on the third day. Now
the Amalekites[y] had raided the Negev
and Ziklag. They had attacked Ziklag
and burned it, 2and had taken captive
the women and all who were in it, both
young and old. They killed none of
them, but carried them off as they went
on their way.
3When David and his men came to
Ziklag, they found it destroyed by fire
and their wives and sons and daughters
taken captive. 4So David and his men
wept aloud until they had no strength
30:5 [z]1Sa 25:43; 2Sa 2:2 left to weep. 5David's two wives[z] had
been captured—Ahinoam of Jezreel and
Abigail, the widow of Nabal of Carmel.
6David was greatly distressed because
30:6 [a]Ex 17:4; Jn 8:59 [b]Ps 27:14; 56:3-4,11; Ro 4:20 the men were talking of stoning[a] him;
each one was bitter in spirit because
of his sons and daughters. But David
found strength[b] in the LORD his God.
7Then David said to Abiathar[c] the
30:7 [c]1Sa 22:20 [d]1Sa 23:9 priest, the son of Ahimelech, "Bring
me the ephod.[d]" Abiathar brought it
to him, 8and David inquired[e] of the
30:8 [e]1Sa 23:2 [f]ver 18 LORD, "Shall I pursue this raiding party? Will I overtake them?"
"Pursue them," he answered. "You
will certainly overtake them and succeed[f] in the rescue."
9David and the six hundred men[g] 30:9 [g]1Sa 27:2
with him came to the Besor Ravine,
where some stayed behind, 10for two
hundred men were too exhausted[h] to 30:10 [h]ver 9,21
cross the ravine. But David and four
hundred men continued the pursuit.
11They found an Egyptian in a field
and brought him to David. They gave
him water to drink and food to eat—
12part of a cake of pressed figs and
two cakes of raisins. He ate and was
revived,[i] for he had not eaten any food 30:12 [i]Jdg 15:19
or drunk any water for three days and
three nights.
13David asked him, "To whom do
you belong, and where do you come
from?"
He said, "I am an Egyptian, the slave
of an Amalekite. My master abandoned
me when I became ill three days ago.
14We raided the Negev of the Kereth-
ites[j] and the territory belonging to Ju- 30:14 [j]2Sa 8:18; 1Ki 1:38,44; Eze 25:16; Zep 2:5 [k]ver 16; Jos 14:13; 15:13 [l]ver 1
dah and the Negev of Caleb.[k] And we
burned[l] Ziklag."
15David asked him, "Can you lead
me down to this raiding party?"
He answered, "Swear to me before
God that you will not kill me or hand
me over to my master, and I will take
you down to them."
16He led David down, and there they
were, scattered over the countryside, 30:16 [m]Lk 12:19 [n]ver 14
eating, drinking and reveling[m] because
of the great amount of plunder[n] they
had taken from the land of the Philis- 30:17 [o]1Sa 11:11 [p]1Sa 15:3
tines and from Judah. 17David fought[o]
them from dusk until the evening of
the next day, and none of them got
away, except four hundred young men
who rode off on camels and fled.[p] 18Da- 30:18 [q]Ge 14:16
vid recovered[q] everything the Amalek-
ites had taken, including his two wives.
19Nothing was missing: young or old,
boy or girl, plunder or anything else
they had taken. David brought everything back. 20He took all the flocks and
herds, and his men drove them ahead
of the other livestock, saying, "This is
David's plunder."
21Then David came to the two hundred men who had been too exhaust-
ed[r] to follow him and who were left 30:21 [r]ver 10
behind at the Besor Ravine. They came
out to meet David and the people with
him. As David and his men approached,
he greeted them. 22But all the evil
men and troublemakers among David's
followers said, "Because they did not

go out with us, we will not share with
them the plunder we recovered. However, each man may take his wife and
children and go."
23David replied, "No, my brothers,
you must not do that with what the
LORD has given us. He has protected
us and handed over to us the forces that
came against us. 24Who will listen to
what you say? The share of the man
who stayed with the supplies is to be the
same as that of him who went down to
30:24 [s]Nu 31:27; Jos 22:8 the battle. All will share alike.[s]" 25Da-
vid made this a statute and ordinance
for Israel from that day to this.
26When David arrived in Ziklag, he
sent some of the plunder to the elders
of Judah, who were his friends, saying,
30:27 [t]Jos 7:2 [u]Jos 19:8 [v]Jos 15:48 "Here is a present for you from the
plunder of the LORD's enemies."
27He sent it to those who were in
30:28 [w]Jos 13:16 [x]Jos 15:50 Bethel,[t] Ramoth[u] Negev and Jattir;[v]
28to those in Aroer,[w] Siphmoth, Eshte-
30:29 [y]1Sa 27:10 [z]Jdg 1:16; 1Sa 15:6 moa[x] 29and Racal; to those in the towns
of the Jerahmeelites[y] and the Kenites;[z]
30to those in Hormah,[a] Bor Ashan,[b]
30:30 [a]Nu 14:45; Jdg 1:17 [b]Jos 15:42 Athach 31and Hebron;[c] and to those in
all the other places where David and his
men had roamed.

30:31 [c]Jos 14:13; 2Sa 2:1,4

Saul Takes His Life

31 Now the Philistines fought
against Israel; the Israelites fled
before them, and many fell slain on
31:1 [d]1Sa 28:4; 1Ch 10:1-12 Mount Gilboa.[d] 2The Philistines pressed
hard after Saul and his sons, and they
killed his sons Jonathan, Abinadab and
Malki-Shua. 3The fighting grew fierce
around Saul, and when the archers over-
31:3 [e]2Sa 1:6 took him, they wounded[e] him critically.

4Saul said to his armor-bearer, "Draw
your sword and run me through,[f] or 31:4 [f]Jdg 9:54; 2Sa 1:6,10
these uncircumcised[g] fellows will come [g]1Sa 14:6
and run me through and abuse me."
But his armor-bearer was terrified
and would not do it; so Saul took his
own sword and fell on it. 5When the
armor-bearer saw that Saul was dead,
he too fell on his sword and died with
him. 6So Saul and his three sons and
his armor-bearer and all his men died
together that same day.
7When the Israelites along the valley
and those across the Jordan saw that the
Israelite army had fled and that Saul
and his sons had died, they abandoned
their towns and fled. And the Philistines came and occupied them.
8The next day, when the Philistines
came to strip the dead, they found Saul
and his three sons fallen on Mount Gilboa. 9They cut off his head and stripped
off his armor, and they sent messengers
throughout the land of the Philistines
to proclaim the news[h] in the temple 31:9 [h]2Sa 1:20
of their idols and among their people.[i] [i]Jdg 16:24
10They put his armor in the temple of
the Ashtoreths[j] and fastened his body 31:10 [j]Jdg 2:12-13; 1Sa 7:3
to the wall of Beth Shan.[k] [k]Jos 17:11; 2Sa 21:12
11When the people of Jabesh Gilead[l]
heard of what the Philistines had done
to Saul, 12all their valiant men jour- 31:11 [l]1Sa 11:1
neyed through the night to Beth Shan.
They took down the bodies of Saul
and his sons from the wall of Beth 31:12 [m]2Sa 2:4-7; 2Ch 16:14; Am 6:10
Shan and went to Jabesh, where they
burned[m] them. 13Then they took their
bones[n] and buried them under a tama- 31:13 [n]2Sa 21:12-14
risk[o] tree at Jabesh, and they fasted[p] [o]1Sa 22:6 [p]2Sa 1:12
seven days.[q] [q]Ge 50:10

2 SAMUEL

AUTHORSHIP AND DATE

The books of 1 and 2 Samuel were originally one book. The author is unknown; Samuel likely contributed to parts of 1 Samuel.

The date is uncertain, but probably soon after the division of the kingdom in 950 B.C.

KEY THEMES

David was a man after God's own heart (see 1 Samuel 13:14). Of all the heroes in the Old Testament, David stands front and center as the hero of Old Testament Israel. Under David's lengthy reign, the kingdom Samuel had wished to prevent—and the kingdom Saul had only dreamed of—actually came into being. David subdued the land, unified all Israel's quarreling and disorganized tribes, levied an army, captured the citadel of Jerusalem, brought the ark into the city and, in short, created a nation. But adultery and murder scandalized his reign (see 11–13). Following that time, his own family eventually divided the entire nation in civil war. But for all its dark side, Israel would never produce another king like David. David's kingdom, at its peak, stretched undisputed from Syria to Egypt. This book deals with nationalization, civic morality, God's judgment and his blessing.

FRUIT OF THE SPIRIT IN 2 SAMUEL

Love: David celebrated his friendship with Jonathan in a requiem after Jonathan's death in the battle at Mount Gilboa: "I grieve for you, Jonathan my brother; you were very dear to me. Your love for me was wonderful, more wonderful than that of women" (1:26).

Joy: As the ark was brought into the royal city, David danced in joy before the Lord with all his might (see 6:14).

Peace: God became angry over David's census of his fighting men and gave David a choice between three punishment alternatives—three years of famine, three months of fleeing from his enemies, or three days of plague. David cried out to God, whose avenging angel was striking down people, "I am the one who has sinned and done wrong. These are but sheep. What have they done? Let your hand fall upon me and my family" (24:17). David, in a sense, bought peace with God by offering himself as a supreme sacrifice for his wrong.

Kindness: Kindness is that quality that never forgets its humanity when it comes face to face with divinity. Kindness rehearses the Golden Rule until it really believes it and acts accordingly. In the presence of God, David was reminded of God's greatness, and his own resulting attitude was one of humility: "Who am I, O Sovereign LORD, and what is my family, that you have brought me this far?" (7:18).

Goodness: David asked, "Is there anyone still left of the house of Saul to whom I can show kindness for Jonathan's sake?" (9:1). Jonathan's crippled son Mephibosheth was found, and David brought him to the palace. David exercised goodness for the sake of an old friend.

Faithfulness: David's song of joy included this line: "To the faithful you show yourself faithful" (22:26). God's faithfulness causes us to respond by giving our own faithfulness to him.

David Hears of Saul's Death

1:1 [a]1Sa 31:6 [b]1Sa 30:17
1 After the death[a] of Saul, David returned from defeating[b] the Amalekites and stayed in Ziklag two days.
1:2 [c]2Sa 4:10 [d]1Sa 4:12
2On the third day a man[c] arrived from Saul's camp, with his clothes torn and with dust on his head.[d] When he came to David, he fell to the ground to pay him honor.

3"Where have you come from?" David asked him.

He answered, "I have escaped from the Israelite camp."

4"What happened?" David asked. "Tell me."

He said, "The men fled from the battle. Many of them fell and died. And Saul and his son Jonathan are dead."

5Then David said to the young man who brought him the report, "How do you know that Saul and his son Jonathan are dead?"

6"I happened to be on Mount Gilboa,[e]" the young man said, "and there was Saul, leaning on his spear, with the chariots and riders almost upon him. 1:6 [e]1Sa 28:4; 31:2-4
7When he turned around and saw me, he called out to me, and I said, 'What can I do?'

8"He asked me, 'Who are you?'

JONATHAN

Love, the Strength of Best Friends (1:1–27)

The love between David and Jonathan was a love that ranks among the greatest in history. There are several such examples of great friendships in world literature. The Gilgamesh Epic, one of the first sagas ever written, is the story of two famous friends, Gilgamesh and Enkidu. Their journeys and struggles with life and death are legendary. But the Biblical tale of David and Jonathan surpasses all the other accounts of famous best friends.

The story of their love is all the more remarkable because David and Jonathan's friendship existed under the pall of King Saul's erratic temper and furious jealousy. Saul, Jonathan's father, suffered from periods of psychotic rage. During those times of rage, he often tried to kill David.

Consider the burden life's circumstances had placed on this love: David's worst enemy was his best friend's father. The strongest testament of the strength of David and Jonathan's love was exhibited after Jonathan and his father were killed in the battle of Mount Gilboa. When David heard of his friend's death, in his sorrow he composed and sang a song of tribute to Jonathan:

I grieve for you, Jonathan my brother;
you were very dear to me.
Your love for me was wonderful,
more wonderful than that of women.
(1:26)

Today, with society's muddled definitions of love and friendship, love between two men or two women is often viewed through a homoerotic lens. But David and Jonathan had the value of a relationship grounded in long-term loyalty and friendship. On many occasions Jonathan supported David and saved him from Saul's vendettas. And Jonathan, too, experienced the strength and support that comes from the unfailing love of a best friend. David and Jonathan could have understood the wisdom of the proverb, "As iron sharpens iron, so one man sharpens another" (Proverbs 27:17).

After the deaths of Jonathan and Saul, David's love and respect for them overflowed in sorrow. Even though Saul had pursued David and had wished his death, David sang to both Saul and Jonathan:

Saul and Jonathan—
in life they were loved and gracious,
and in death they were not parted.
They were swifter than eagles,
they were stronger than lions.
(1:23)

Poor are those who must define love in terms of romance alone. Rich indeed are those who can say, "I have a friend—we love each other." In this friend's confident love every sunrise is welcomed, every crisis is easier, every pain has counsel and every midnight is safer.

1:8 [f]1Sa 15:2; 30:13,17 “‘An Amalekite,[f]’ I answered.
9“Then he said to me, ‘Stand over
me and kill me! I am in the throes of
death, but I’m still alive.’
10“So I stood over him and killed
him, because I knew that after he had
fallen he could not survive. And I took
1:10 [g]Jdg 9:54; 2Ki 11:12 the crown[g] that was on his head and
the band on his arm and have brought
them here to my lord.”
11Then David and all the men with
him took hold of their clothes and
1:11 [h]Ge 37:29; 2Sa 3:31; 13:31 tore[h] them. 12They mourned and wept
and fasted till evening for Saul and his
son Jonathan, and for the army of the
LORD and the house of Israel, because
they had fallen by the sword.
13David said to the young man who
brought him the report, “Where are
you from?”
“I am the son of an alien, an Amalek-
1:13 [i]ver 8 ite,[i]” he answered.
14David asked him, “Why were you
not afraid to lift your hand to destroy
1:14 [j]1Sa 24:6; 26:9 the LORD’s anointed?[j]”
15Then David called one of his men
1:15 [k]2Sa 4:12 [l]2Sa 4:10 and said, “Go, strike him down!”[k] So he
struck him down, and he died.[l] 16For
David had said to him, “Your blood be
1:16 [m]Lev 20:9; 2Sa 3:28-29; 1Ki 2:32; Mt 27:24-25; Ac 18:6 on your own head.[m] Your own mouth
testified against you when you said, ‘I
killed the LORD’s anointed.’”

David’s Lament for Saul and Jonathan

17David took up this lament[n] con-
1:17 [n]2Ch 35:25 cerning Saul and his son Jonathan,
18and ordered that the men of Judah
1:18 [o]Jos 10:13; 1Sa 31:3 be taught this lament of the bow (it is
written in the Book of Jashar):[o]

19“Your glory, O Israel, lies slain on
your heights.
1:19 [p]ver 27 How the mighty have fallen![p]

1:20 [q]Mic 1:10 [r]1Sa 31:8 [s]Ex 15:20; 1Sa 18:6 20“Tell it not in Gath,[q]
proclaim it not in the streets of
Ashkelon,
lest the daughters of the Philistines[r]
be glad,
lest the daughters of the
uncircumcised rejoice.[s]

1:21 [t]ver 6; 1Sa 31:1 [u]Eze 31:15 21“O mountains of Gilboa,[t]
may you have neither dew nor rain,
nor fields that yield offerings[u] ⌞of
grain⌟.
For there the shield of the mighty
was defiled,
the shield of Saul—no longer
rubbed with oil.[v] 1:21 [v]Isa 21:5
22From the blood[w] of the slain,
from the flesh of the mighty, 1:22 [w]Isa 34:3,7 [x]Dt 32:42; 1Sa 18:4
the bow[x] of Jonathan did not turn
back,
the sword of Saul did not return
unsatisfied.
23“Saul and Jonathan—
in life they were loved and
gracious,
and in death they were not parted. 1:23 [y]Dt 28:49; Jer 4:13 [z]Jdg 14:18
They were swifter than eagles,[y]
they were stronger than lions.[z]

24“O daughters of Israel,
weep for Saul,
who clothed you in scarlet and
finery,
who adorned your garments with
ornaments of gold.

25“How the mighty have fallen in
battle!
Jonathan lies slain on your heights.
26I grieve for you, Jonathan my 1:26 [a]1Sa 20:42 [b]1Sa 18:1
brother;[a]
you were very dear to me.
Your love for me was wonderful,[b]
more wonderful than that of
women.

27“How the mighty have fallen!
The weapons of war have 1:27 [c]ver 19,25; 1Sa 2:4
perished!”[c]

LOVE

HOLY LOVE

2 Samuel 1:26

There is a love that is given for its own sake. It is chaste. It is holy. It is present where two souls drop the gaudy robes of ego, choosing burlap instead for their garments.

David Anointed King Over Judah

2 In the course of time, David in- 2:1 [d]1Sa 23:2,11-12 [e]Ge 13:18; 1Sa 30:31
quired[d] of the LORD. “Shall I go
up to one of the towns of Judah?” he
asked.
The LORD said, “Go up.”
David asked, “Where shall I go?”
“To Hebron,”[e] the LORD answered.
2So David went up there with his
two wives,[f] Ahinoam of Jezreel and Ab- 2:2 [f]1Sa 25:43; 30:5 [g]1Sa 25:42
igail,[g] the widow of Nabal of Carmel.
3David also took the men who were

with him,[h] each with his family, and they settled in Hebron[i] and its towns. 4Then the men of Judah came to Hebron and there they anointed[j] David king over the house of Judah.

When David was told that it was the men of Jabesh Gilead[k] who had buried Saul, 5he sent messengers to the men of Jabesh Gilead to say to them, "The LORD bless[l] you for showing this kindness to Saul your master by burying him. 6May the LORD now show you kindness and faithfulness,[m] and I too will show you the same favor because you have done this. 7Now then, be strong and brave, for Saul your master is dead, and the house of Judah has anointed me king over them."

War Between the Houses of David and Saul

8Meanwhile, Abner[n] son of Ner, the commander of Saul's army, had taken Ish-Bosheth son of Saul and brought him over to Mahanaim.[o] 9He made him king over Gilead,[p] Ashuri[a][q] and Jezreel, and also over Ephraim, Benjamin and all Israel.[r]

10Ish-Bosheth son of Saul was forty years old when he became king over Israel, and he reigned two years. The house of Judah, however, followed David. 11The length of time David was king in Hebron over the house of Judah was seven years and six months.[s]

12Abner son of Ner, together with the men of Ish-Bosheth son of Saul, left Mahanaim and went to Gibeon.[t] 13Joab[u] son of Zeruiah and David's men went out and met them at the pool of Gibeon. One group sat down on one side of the pool and one group on the other side.

14Then Abner said to Joab, "Let's have some of the young men get up and fight hand to hand in front of us."

"All right, let them do it," Joab said.

15So they stood up and were counted off—twelve men for Benjamin and Ish-Bosheth son of Saul, and twelve for David. 16Then each man grabbed his opponent by the head and thrust his dagger into his opponent's side, and they fell down together. So that place in Gibeon was called Helkath Hazzurim.[b]

17The battle that day was very fierce, and Abner and the men of Israel were defeated[v] by David's men.

2:3 [h]1Sa 27:2; 30:9 [i]1Sa 30:31
2:4 [j]1Sa 2:35; 2Sa 5:3-5 [k]1Sa 31:11-13
2:5 [l]1Sa 23:21
2:6 [m]Ex 34:6; 1Ti 1:16
2:8 [n]1Sa 14:50 [o]Ge 32:2
2:9 [p]Nu 32:26 [q]Jdg 1:32 [r]1Ch 12:29
2:11 [s]2Sa 5:5
2:12 [t]Jos 18:25
2:13 [u]2Sa 8:16; 1Ch 2:16; 11:6
2:17 [v]2Sa 3:1

18The three sons of Zeruiah[w] were there: Joab,[x] Abishai[y] and Asahel.[z] Now Asahel was as fleet-footed as a wild gazelle.[a] 19He chased Abner, turning neither to the right nor to the left as he pursued him. 20Abner looked behind him and asked, "Is that you, Asahel?"

"It is," he answered.

21Then Abner said to him, "Turn aside to the right or to the left; take on one of the young men and strip him of his weapons." But Asahel would not stop chasing him.

22Again Abner warned Asahel, "Stop chasing me! Why should I strike you down? How could I look your brother Joab in the face?"[b]

23But Asahel refused to give up the pursuit; so Abner thrust the butt of his spear into Asahel's stomach,[c] and the spear came out through his back. He fell there and died on the spot. And every man stopped when he came to the place where Asahel had fallen and died.[d]

24But Joab and Abishai pursued Abner, and as the sun was setting, they came to the hill of Ammah, near Giah on the way to the wasteland of Gibeon. 25Then the men of Benjamin rallied behind Abner. They formed themselves into a group and took their stand on top of a hill.

26Abner called out to Joab, "Must the sword devour[e] forever? Don't you realize that this will end in bitterness? How long before you order your men to stop pursuing their brothers?"

27Joab answered, "As surely as God lives, if you had not spoken, the men would have continued the pursuit of their brothers until morning.[c]"

28So Joab[f] blew the trumpet,[g] and all the men came to a halt; they no longer pursued Israel, nor did they fight anymore.

29All that night Abner and his men marched through the Arabah. They crossed the Jordan, continued through the whole Bithron[d] and came to Mahanaim.[h]

[a]9 Or *Asher* [b]16 *Helkath Hazzurim* means *field of daggers* or *field of hostilities.* [c]27 Or *spoken this morning, the men would not have taken up the pursuit of their brothers;* or *spoken, the men would have given up the pursuit of their brothers by morning* [d]29 Or *morning;* or *ravine;* the meaning of the Hebrew for this word is uncertain.

2:18 [w]2Sa 3:39 [x]2Sa 3:30 [y]1Sa 26:6 [z]1Ch 2:16 [a]1Ch 12:8
2:22 [b]2Sa 3:27
2:23 [c]2Sa 3:27; 4:6 [d]2Sa 20:12
2:26 [e]Dt 32:42; Jer 46:10,14
2:28 [f]2Sa 18:16 [g]Jdg 3:27
2:29 [h]ver 8

30Then Joab returned from pursuing
Abner and assembled all his men.
Besides Asahel, nineteen of David's
men were found missing. 31But David's
men had killed three hundred and sixty Benjamites who were with Abner.
32They took Asahel and buried him in
2:32 [i]Ge 49:29 his father's tomb[i] at Bethlehem. Then
Joab and his men marched all night and
arrived at Hebron by daybreak.

3 The war between the house of Saul
and the house of David lasted a
3:1 [j]1Ki 14:30 long time.[j] David grew stronger and
[k]2Sa 5:10 stronger,[k] while the house of Saul grew
[l]2Sa 2:17 weaker and weaker.[l]
2Sons were born to David in Hebron:
3:2 [m]1Sa 25:43; His firstborn was Amnon the
1Ch 3:1-3 son of Ahinoam[m] of Jezreel;
3his second, Kileab the son of
3:3 [n]1Sa 25:42 Abigail[n] the widow of Nabal of
[o]2Sa 13:1,28 Carmel;
[p]1Sa 27:8; 2Sa 13:37; 14:32; the third, Absalom[o] the son of
15:8 Maacah daughter of Talmai king
3:4 [q]1Ki 1:5,11 of Geshur;[p]
4the fourth, Adonijah[q] the son of
Haggith;
the fifth, Shephatiah the son of
Abital;
5and the sixth, Ithream the son
of David's wife Eglah.
These were born to David in
Hebron.

Abner Goes Over to David

6During the war between the house
of Saul and the house of David, Abner
had been strengthening his own posi-
3:7 tion in the house of Saul. 7Now Saul
[r]2Sa 16:21-22 had had a concubine[r] named Rizpah[s]
[s]2Sa 21:8-11 daughter of Aiah. And Ish-Bosheth said
to Abner, "Why did you sleep with my
father's concubine?"
8Abner was very angry because of
3:8 what Ish-Bosheth said and he answered,
[t]1Sa 24:14; "Am I a dog's head[t]—on Judah's side?
2Sa 9:8; 16:9 This very day I am loyal to the house of
your father Saul and to his family and
friends. I haven't handed you over to
David. Yet now you accuse me of an offense involving this woman! 9May God
deal with Abner, be it ever so severely, if
I do not do for David what the LORD
3:9 [u]1Sa 15:28; promised[u] him on oath 10and transfer
1Ki 19:2 the kingdom from the house of Saul
3:10 and establish David's throne over Israel
[v]Jdg 20:1; and Judah from Dan to Beersheba."[v]
1Sa 3:20 11Ish-Bosheth did not dare to say another word to Abner, because he was
afraid of him.
12Then Abner sent messengers on his
behalf to say to David, "Whose land is
it? Make an agreement with me, and
I will help you bring all Israel over to
you."
13"Good," said David. "I will make
an agreement with you. But I demand
one thing of you: Do not come into
my presence unless you bring Michal
daughter of Saul when you come to see
me."[w] 14Then David sent messengers 3:13 [w]Ge 43:5;
to Ish-Bosheth son of Saul, demanding, 1Sa 18:20
"Give me my wife Michal,[x] whom I be- 3:14
trothed to myself for the price of a hun- [x]1Sa 18:27
dred Philistine foreskins."
15So Ish-Bosheth gave orders and had 3:15
her taken away from her husband[y] Pal- [y]Dt 24:1-4
tiel[z] son of Laish. 16Her husband, how- [z]1Sa 25:44
ever, went with her, weeping behind her 3:16
all the way to Bahurim.[a] Then Abner [a]2Sa 16:5;
said to him, "Go back home!" So he 19:16
went back.
17Abner conferred with the elders[b] 3:17 [b]Jdg 11:11
of Israel and said, "For some time you
have wanted to make David your king.
18Now do it! For the LORD promised
David, 'By my servant David I will rescue my people Israel from the hand of
the Philistines[c] and from the hand of 3:18
all their enemies.[d]'" [c]1Sa 9:16
19Abner also spoke to the Benjamites [d]1Sa 15:28; 2Sa 8:6
in person. Then he went to Hebron
to tell David everything that Israel and
the whole house of Benjamin[e] wanted 3:19
to do. 20When Abner, who had twenty [e]1Sa
men with him, came to David at He- 10:20-21; 1Ch 12:2,
bron, David prepared a feast for him 16,29
and his men. 21Then Abner said to David, "Let me go at once and assemble
all Israel for my lord the king, so that
they may make a compact[f] with you, 3:21 [f]ver 10,12
and that you may rule over all that your [g]1Ki 11:37
heart desires."[g] So David sent Abner
away, and he went in peace.

Joab Murders Abner

22Just then David's men and Joab returned from a raid and brought with
them a great deal of plunder. But Abner
was no longer with David in Hebron,
because David had sent him away, and
he had gone in peace. 23When Joab and
all the soldiers with him arrived, he was
told that Abner son of Ner had come to
the king and that the king had sent him
away and that he had gone in peace.

GOODNESS

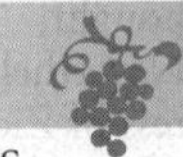

THE ART OF BLESSING ENEMIES

2 Samuel 3:22

Goodness never pursues power for the joy of ruling others. Goodness blesses enemies, lays down its sword, bares its neck upon the block and prays that God will give its executioner a sunny day.

24So Joab went to the king and said,
"What have you done? Look, Abner
came to you. Why did you let him go?
Now he is gone! 25You know Abner son
of Ner; he came to deceive you and observe your movements and find out everything you are doing."
26Joab then left David and sent messengers after Abner, and they brought
him back from the well of Sirah. But
David did not know it. 27Now when
3:27 Abner[h] returned to Hebron, Joab took
h2Sa 2:8 him aside into the gateway, as though
i2Sa 2:22; 20:9-10; to speak with him privately. And there,
1Ki 2:5 to avenge the blood of his brother Asahel, Joab stabbed him in the stomach,
and he died.[i]
28Later, when David heard about this,
he said, "I and my kingdom are forever
3:28 innocent[j] before the LORD concerning
jver 37; Dt 21:9 the blood of Abner son of Ner. 29May
3:29 his blood[k] fall upon the head of Joab
kLev 20:9 and upon all his father's house![l] May
l1Ki 2:31-33 Joab's house never be without someone
mLev 15:2 who has a running sore[m] or leprosy[a] or
who leans on a crutch or who falls by
the sword or who lacks food."
30(Joab and his brother Abishai murdered Abner because he had killed their
brother Asahel in the battle at Gibeon.)
31Then David said to Joab and all the
3:31 people with him, "Tear your clothes and
n2Sa 1:2,11; Ps 30:11; put on sackcloth[n] and walk in mourn-
Isa 20:2 ing[o] in front of Abner." King David
oGe 37:34 himself walked behind the bier. 32They
3:32 buried Abner in Hebron, and the king
pNu 14:1; Pr 24:17 wept[p] aloud at Abner's tomb. All the
people wept also.
3:33 33The king sang this lament[q] for Ab-
q2Sa 1:17 ner:

"Should Abner have died as the
lawless die?
34 Your hands were not bound,
your feet were not fettered.
You fell as one falls before wicked
men."

And all the people wept over him
again.
35Then they all came and urged David to eat something while it was still
day; but David took an oath, saying,
"May God deal with me, be it ever so
severely,[r] if I taste bread[s] or anything 3:35 rRu 1:17; 1Sa 3:17
else before the sun sets!" s1Sa 31:13; 2Sa 1:12; 12:17; Jer 16:7
36All the people took note and were
pleased; indeed, everything the king did
pleased them. 37So on that day all the
people and all Israel knew that the king
had no part[t] in the murder of Abner 3:37 tver 28
son of Ner.
38Then the king said to his men, "Do
you not realize that a prince and a great
man has fallen[u] in Israel this day? 39And 3:38 u2Sa 1:19
today, though I am the anointed king,
I am weak, and these sons of Zeruiah[v] 3:39 v2Sa 2:18
are too strong for me.[w] May the LORD w2Sa 19:5-7
repay[x] the evildoer according to his evil x1Ki 2:5-6, 33-34; Ps 41:10; 101:8
deeds!"

Ish-Bosheth Murdered

4 When Ish-Bosheth son of Saul
heard that Abner[y] had died in He- 4:1 y2Sa 3:27; Ezr 4:4
bron, he lost courage, and all Israel
became alarmed. 2Now Saul's son had
two men who were leaders of raiding
bands. One was named Baanah and the
other Recab; they were sons of Rimmon the Beerothite from the tribe of
Benjamin—Beeroth[z] is considered part 4:2 zJos 9:17; 18:25
of Benjamin, 3because the people of Be-
eroth fled to Gittaim[a] and have lived 4:3 aNe 11:33
there as aliens to this day.
4(Jonathan[b] son of Saul had a son 4:4 b1Sa 18:1
who was lame in both feet. He was c1Sa 31:1-4
five years old when the news[c] about dLev 21:18
Saul and Jonathan came from Jezreel. e2Sa 9:3,6; 1Ch 8:34; 9:40
His nurse picked him up and fled,
but as she hurried to leave, he fell
and became crippled.[d] His name was
Mephibosheth.)[e]
5Now Recab and Baanah, the sons
of Rimmon the Beerothite, set out for 4:5
the house of Ish-Bosheth,[f] and they ar- f2Sa 2:8
rived there in the heat of the day while
he was taking his noonday rest. 6They
went into the inner part of the house as 4:6
if to get some wheat, and they stabbed[g] g2Sa 2:23
him in the stomach. Then Recab and
his brother Baanah slipped away.
7They had gone into the house while
he was lying on the bed in his bedroom.

[a] *29* The Hebrew word was used for various diseases affecting the skin—not necessarily leprosy.

After they stabbed and killed him, they
cut off his head. Taking it with them,
they traveled all night by way of the Arabah. 8They brought the head of Ish-
Bosheth to David at Hebron and said
4:8 to the king, “Here is the head of Ish-
[b]1Sa 24:4; Bosheth son of Saul,[b] your enemy, who
25:29 tried to take your life. This day the
LORD has avenged my lord the king
against Saul and his offspring.”
9David answered Recab and his
brother Baanah, the sons of Rimmon
the Beerothite, “As surely as the LORD
4:9 lives, who has delivered[i] me out of all
[i]Ge 48:16; 1Ki 1:29 trouble, 10when a man told me, ‘Saul
is dead,’ and thought he was bringing
good news, I seized him and put him to
4:10 [j]2Sa 1:2-16 death in Ziklag.[j] That was the reward
I gave him for his news! 11How much
more—when wicked men have killed
an innocent man in his own house and
4:11 on his own bed—should I not now de-
[k]Ge 9:5; Ps 9:12 mand his blood[k] from your hand and
rid the earth of you!”
12So David gave an order to his men,
4:12 [l]2Sa 1:15 and they killed them.[l] They cut off their
hands and feet and hung the bodies by
the pool in Hebron. But they took the
head of Ish-Bosheth and buried it in
Abner's tomb at Hebron.

David Becomes King Over Israel

5:1 [m]2Sa 19:43 5 All the tribes of Israel[m] came to Da-
[n]1Ch 11:1 vid at Hebron and said, “We are
your own flesh and blood.[n] 2In the past,
while Saul was king over us, you were
the one who led Israel on their military
5:2 [o]1Sa 18:5, campaigns.[o] And the LORD said to you,
13,16 ‘You will shepherd[p] my people Israel,
[p]1Sa 16:1; 2Sa 7:7 and you will become their ruler.[q]’”
[q]1Sa 25:30 3When all the elders of Israel had
come to King David at Hebron, the
5:3 [r]2Sa 3:21 king made a compact[r] with them at
[s]2Sa 2:4 Hebron before the LORD, and they
anointed[s] David king over Israel.
5:4 [t]Lk 3:23 4David was thirty years old[t] when
[u]1Ki 2:11; 1Ch 3:4 he became king, and he reigned[u] forty[v]
[v]1Ch 26:31; 29:27 years. 5In Hebron he reigned over Ju-
5:5 dah seven years and six months,[w] and
[w]2Sa 2:11; 1Ch 3:4 in Jerusalem he reigned over all Israel
and Judah thirty-three years.

David Conquers Jerusalem

6The king and his men marched to
5:6 [x]Jdg 1:8 Jerusalem[x] to attack the Jebusites,[y] who
[y]Jos 15:8 lived there. The Jebusites said to David,
“You will not get in here; even the blind
and the lame can ward you off.” They
thought, “David cannot get in here.”
7Nevertheless, David captured the for- 5:7
tress of Zion, the City of David.[z] [z]2Sa 6:12,16; 1Ki 2:10
8On that day, David said, “Anyone
who conquers the Jebusites will have to
use the water shaft[a] to reach those ‘lame
and blind’ who are David's enemies.[b]”
That is why they say, “The ‘blind and
lame’ will not enter the palace.”
9David then took up residence in the
fortress and called it the City of David.
He built up the area around it, from 5:9
the supporting terraces[c] [a] inward. 10And [a]ver 7; 1Ki 9:15,24
he became more and more powerful,[b] 5:10
because the LORD God Almighty was [b]2Sa 3:1
with him.

FAITHFULNESS

THE PRESENCE OF GOD AND WIDENING INFLUENCE

2 Samuel 5:10

Lord, only you are great.

“No man is big who thinks he is big.
When we're uppity-up, we're only a clod.
We ought to remember we're made out of sod.”

Both servants and kings are people of God.

11Now Hiram[c] king of Tyre sent mes-
sengers to David, along with cedar logs 5:11 [c]1Ki 5:1,18; 1Ch 14:1
and carpenters and stonemasons, and
they built a palace for David. 12And
David knew that the LORD had established him as king over Israel and had
exalted his kingdom for the sake of his
people Israel.
13After he left Hebron, David took
more concubines and wives[d] in Jerusa- 5:13 [d]Dt 17:17;
lem, and more sons and daughters were 1Ch 3:9
born to him. 14These are the names of the
children born to him there:[e] Shammua, 5:14 [e]1Ch 3:5
Shobab, Nathan, Solomon, 15Ibhar, El-
ishua, Nepheg, Japhia, 16Elishama, Eliada and Eliphelet.

David Defeats the Philistines

17When the Philistines heard that
David had been anointed king over Israel, they went up in full force to search
for him, but David heard about it and 5:17 [f]2Sa 23:14;
went down to the stronghold.[f] 18Now 1Ch 11:16
the Philistines had come and spread out 5:18
in the Valley of Rephaim;[g] 19so David [g]Jos 15:8; 17:15; 18:16

[a]8 Or *use scaling hooks* [b]8 Or *are hated by David*
[c]9 Or *the Millo*

5:19 inquired[h] of the LORD, "Shall I go and
[h]1Sa 23:2; attack the Philistines? Will you hand
2Sa 2:1 them over to me?"
The LORD answered him, "Go, for I
will surely hand the Philistines over to
you."
20 So David went to Baal Perazim, and
there he defeated them. He said, "As
waters break out, the LORD has broken out against my enemies before me."
5:20 So that place was called Baal Perazim.[a][i]
[i]Isa 28:21 21 The Philistines abandoned their idols
5:21 there, and David and his men carried
[j]Dt 7:5; them off.[j]
1Ch 14:12; 22 Once more the Philistines came up
Isa 46:2 and spread out in the Valley of Rephaim; 23 so David inquired of the LORD,
and he answered, "Do not go straight
up, but circle around behind them and
attack them in front of the balsam trees.
5:24 24 As soon as you hear the sound[k] of
[k]2Ki 7:6 marching in the tops of the balsam
[l]Jdg 4:14 trees, move quickly, because that will
mean the LORD has gone out in front[l]
of you to strike the Philistine army."
25 So David did as the LORD commanded him, and he struck down the Phi-
5:25 listines all the way from Gibeon[b][m] to
[m]Isa 28:21 Gezer.[n]
[n]1Ch 14:16

The Ark Brought to Jerusalem

6 David again brought together out
of Israel chosen men, thirty thou-
6:2 sand in all. 2 He and all his men set
[o]Jos 15:9 out from Baalah[o] of Judah[c] to bring up
[p]1Sa 4:4; 7:1 from there the ark[p] of God, which is
[q]Lev 24:16; called by the Name,[d][q] the name of the
Isa 63:14 LORD Almighty, who is enthroned[r] be-
[r]Ps 99:1 tween the cherubim[s] that are on the
[s]Ex 25:22; 1Ch 13:5-6
6:3 ark. 3 They set the ark of God on a new
[t]Nu 7:4-9; cart[t] and brought it from the house of
1Sa 6:7 Abinadab, which was on the hill. Uzzah
and Ahio, sons of Abinadab, were guiding the new cart 4 with the ark of God
on it,[e] and Ahio was walking in front of
it. 5 David and the whole house of Israel were celebrating with all their might
before the LORD, with songs[f] and with
6:5 harps, lyres, tambourines, sistrums and
[u]1Sa 18:6-7; cymbals.[u]
Ezr 3:10; Ps 150:56: 6 When they came to the threshing
6:6 floor of Nacon, Uzzah reached out and
[v]Nu 4:15, took hold of[v] the ark of God, because
19-20; 1Ch 13:9 the oxen stumbled. 7 The LORD's anger
6:7 burned against Uzzah because of his ir-
[w]1Ch 15:13-15 reverent act;[w] therefore God struck him
[x]Ex 19:22; down[x] and he died there beside the ark
1Sa 6:19 of God.

8 Then David was angry because the
LORD's wrath[y] had broken out against 6:8
Uzzah, and to this day that place is [y]Ps 7:11 [z]Ge 38:29
called Perez Uzzah.[g][z]
9 David was afraid of the LORD that
day and said, "How[a] can the ark of the 6:9 [a]Ps 119:120
LORD ever come to me?" 10 He was not
willing to take the ark of the LORD
to be with him in the City of David.
Instead, he took it aside to the house 6:10
of Obed-Edom[b] the Gittite. 11 The ark [b]1Ch 13:13; 26:4-5
of the LORD remained in the house
of Obed-Edom the Gittite for three
months, and the LORD blessed him and 6:11 [c]Ge 30:27; 39:5
his entire household.[c]
12 Now King David[d] was told, "The 6:12
LORD has blessed the household of [d]1Ki 8:1; 1Ch 15:25
Obed-Edom and everything he has, be-
cause of the ark of God." So David went
down and brought up the ark of God
from the house of Obed-Edom to the
City of David with rejoicing. 13 When
those who were carrying the ark of the
LORD had taken six steps, he sacri-
ficed[e] a bull and a fattened calf. 14 Da- 6:13 [e]1Ki 8:5,62
vid, wearing a linen ephod,[f] danced[g] 6:14
before the LORD with all his might, [f]Ex 19:6; 1Sa 2:18
15 while he and the entire house of Israel [g]Ex 15:20
brought up the ark of the LORD with
shouts and the sound of trumpets.[h] 6:15 [h]Ps 47:5; 98:6
16 As the ark of the LORD was enter-
ing the City of David,[i] Michal daughter 6:16 [i]2Sa 5:7
of Saul watched from a window. And
when she saw King David leaping and
dancing before the LORD, she despised
him in her heart.
17 They brought the ark of the LORD
and set it in its place inside the tent that
David had pitched for it,[j] and David 6:17 [j]1Ch 15:1;
sacrificed burnt offerings[k] and fellow- 2Ch 1:4
ship offerings[h] before the LORD. 18 Af- [k]Lev 1:1-17; 1Ki 8:62-64
ter he had finished sacrificing[l] the burnt 6:18
offerings and fellowship offerings, he [l]1Ki 8:22
blessed the people in the name of the 6:19
LORD Almighty. 19 Then he gave a [m]Hos 3:1
loaf of bread, a cake of dates and a
cake of raisins[m] to each person in the

[a]20 *Baal Perazim* means *the lord who breaks out.*
[b]25 Septuagint (see also 1 Chron. 14:16); Hebrew *Geba* [c]2 That is, Kiriath Jearim; Hebrew *Baale Judah,* a variant of *Baalah of Judah* [d]2 Hebrew; Septuagint and Vulgate do not have *the Name.*
[e]3,4 Dead Sea Scrolls and some Septuagint manuscripts; Masoretic Text *cart* [4]*and they brought it with the ark of God from the house of Abinadab, which was on the hill* [f]5 See Dead Sea Scrolls, Septuagint and 1 Chronicles 13:8; Masoretic Text *celebrating before the LORD with all kinds of instruments made of pine.* [g]8 *Perez Uzzah* means *outbreak against Uzzah.*
[h]17 Traditionally *peace offerings*; also in verse 18

WEEK 11

JOY

1
DAY ONE
▸ JOY, A POSITIVE ATTITUDE

Read 2 Samuel 6:14–15

In this passage, David brings the ark of the covenant into Jerusalem. It is his desire that this chief artifact of Israel's sojourn in Sinai should be in his royal city. Why? Because the Jews believed that God himself dwelt on the *kapporeth* or the lid of the ark. Where the ark was, that was the dwelling place of God. David was bringing the ark into his new capital because he wanted God near him as he directed the nation. Further, if God were near him, then his praise would center on the nearness of God, and his joy would be continual and vibrant.

But David was not always joyful about moving the ark. Earlier in the chapter, David reacts with fear and anger when his first attempt to move the ark ends in disaster. Instead of following the law of God and having the Levites carry the ark with poles inserted through rings on its sides, David allows the ark to be placed on a cart (2 Samuel 6:3). When one of the oxen pulling the cart stumbles, Uzzah reaches out to steady the ark and is instantly killed by God.

After the tragic death of Uzzah, David's worship ceases, as does his fellowship with God. There is a barrier between David and his Lord. Disobedience and wrong attitudes impede his joy. But David's attitude changes when he begins to follow the laws of God and later moves the ark in the proper manner. His celebration is this time without disturbance or distraction. When his fellowship with God is restored, once more he can worship with joy.

2
DAY TWO
▸ JOY AND THE PURPOSE OF GOD IN MY LIFE

Although Ecclesiastes is a sometimes pessimistic study of the futility of positivism and happiness, there exists in this verse a brief salutation of joy. There is nothing better, says the writer of Ecclesiastes, "than to eat and drink and be glad." The existence of a day-to-day positive attitude will produce joy. This joy will accompany a person wherever he or she goes in life, on whatever mission God gives that person to achieve. *Turn to Ecclesiastes 8:14–15, page 776, for today's study.*

3
DAY THREE
▸ JOY AND MY RELATIONSHIP WITH CHRIST

We are able to sing to the Lord because we have experienced his saving grace. We are heirs with Christ, members of the family of God. Our joy is uncontainable when we think about the great gifts of God in Christ. *Turn to Psalm 30:4, page 649, for today's study.*

4
DAY FOUR
▸ JOY AND MY SERVICE TO OTHERS

Many churches are obsessed with getting bigger. "User-friendly" is a methodology or a series of methodologies that churches use to accomplish growth. But the book of Isaiah suggests that drawing large numbers to God may depend on nothing more than the church's developing a sense of authentic praise. When God is praised, the world will rush to our songs to see whether our joy can be appropriated into their own dull lives. *Turn to Isaiah 42:1,10–13, page 838, for today's study.*

5
DAY FIVE
▸ JOY AND ITS PLACE IN MY PERSONAL WORSHIP

Joy, like relationships themselves, binds whole nations together. In this passage of Scripture, Israel sees the manifestations of fire, and as God consumes their sin sacrifices, the whole nation falls facedown and praises God, who has personally received their offerings. In some ways this resembles the fire of the coming of the Holy Spirit that set the early church rejoicing on the day of Pentecost. When we behold the supernatural power of God, we are at first hushed and then set afire with outbursts of praise. *Turn to Leviticus 9:22–24, page 125, for today's study.*

MEMORIZE THIS WEEK

PHILIPPIANS 4:4

Rejoice in the Lord always. I will say it again: Rejoice!

Week 12, Peace and the Prince of Peace, begins on page 19, Genesis 14:17–20.
To begin a topical study on the Fruit of the Spirit, Joy, turn to the Topical Index, page 1548.

whole crowd of Israelites, both men and
6:19 [n]Ne 8:10 women.[n] And all the people went to
their homes.
[20]When David returned home to
bless his household, Michal daughter
of Saul came out to meet him and
said, "How the king of Israel has dis-
6:20 [o]ver 14,16 tinguished himself today, disrobing[o] in
the sight of the slave girls of his servants
as any vulgar fellow would!"
[21]David said to Michal, "It was before the LORD, who chose me rather
than your father or anyone from his
6:21 [p]1Sa 13:14; 15:28 house when he appointed[p] me ruler
over the LORD's people Israel—I will
celebrate before the LORD. [22]I will become even more undignified than this,
and I will be humiliated in my own
eyes. But by these slave girls you spoke
of, I will be held in honor."
[23]And Michal daughter of Saul had
no children to the day of her death.

God's Promise to David

7:1 [q]1Ch 17:1 7 After the king was settled in his palace[q] and the LORD had given him
rest from all his enemies around him,
7:2 [r]2Sa 5:11 [s]Ex 26:1; Ac 7:45-46 [2]he said to Nathan the prophet, "Here
I am, living in a palace[r] of cedar, while
the ark of God remains in a tent."[s]
[3]Nathan replied to the king, "Whatever you have in mind, go ahead and do
it, for the LORD is with you."
[4]That night the word of the LORD
came to Nathan, saying:
[5]"Go and tell my servant David,
7:5 [t]1Ki 8:19; 1Ch 22:8 [u]1Ki 5:3-5 'This is what the LORD says: Are
you[t] the one to build me a house
to dwell in?[u] [6]I have not dwelt in
a house from the day I brought
the Israelites up out of Egypt to
this day. I have been moving from
7:6 [v]Ex 40:18,34 [w]1Ki 8:16 place to place with a tent[v] as my
dwelling.[w] [7]Wherever I have moved
7:7 [x]Dt 23:14 [y]2Sa 5:2 [z]Lev 26:11-12 with all the Israelites,[x] did I ever
say to any of their rulers whom I
commanded to shepherd[y] my people Israel, "Why have you not built
me a house of cedar?[z]"'
[8]"Now then, tell my servant David, 'This is what the LORD Almighty says: I took you from the
7:8 [a]1Sa 16:11 [b]2Sa 6:21 [c]Ps 78:70-72; 2Co 6:18* pasture and from following the
flock[a] to be ruler[b] over my people
Israel.[c] [9]I have been with you wherever you have gone,[d] and I have
7:9 [d]2Sa 5:10 cut off all your enemies from before you.[e] Now I will make your 7:9 [e]Ps 18:37-42
name great, like the names of the
greatest men of the earth. [10]And I
will provide a place for my people
Israel and will plant[f] them so that 7:10 [f]Ex 15:17; Isa 5:1-7 [g]Ps 89:22-23 [h]Isa 60:18
they can have a home of their own
and no longer be disturbed. Wicked[g] people will not oppress them
anymore,[h] as they did at the begin-
ning [11]and have done ever since 7:11 [i]Jdg 2:16; 1Sa 12:9-11 [j]ver 1 [k]1Sa 25:28 [l]ver 27
the time I appointed leaders[a] [i] over
my people Israel. I will also give
you rest from all your enemies.[j]
" 'The LORD declares to you
that the LORD himself will estab-
lish[k] a house[l] for you: [12]When 7:12 [m]1Ki 2:1 [n]Ps 132:11-12
your days are over and you rest[m]
with your fathers, I will raise up
your offspring to succeed you, who
will come from your own body,[n]
and I will establish his kingdom.
[13]He is the one who will build a
house for my Name,[o] and I will es- 7:13 [o]1Ki 5:5; 8:19,29 [p]Isa 9:7
tablish the throne of his kingdom
forever.[p] [14]I will be his father, and
he will be my son.[q] When he does 7:14 [q]Ps 89:26; Heb 1:5* [r]Ps 89:30-33
wrong, I will punish him with the
rod[r] of men, with floggings inflicted by men. [15]But my love will never
be taken away from him, as I took it
away from Saul,[s] whom I removed 7:15 [s]1Sa 15:23,28
from before you. [16]Your house and
your kingdom will endure forever
before me[b]; your throne[t] will be 7:16 [t]Ps 89:36-37 [u]ver 13
established forever.[u]' "

PATIENCE

THE PROMISE OF THOSE WHO FOLLOW

2 Samuel 7:13

David's son Solomon would build the temple. David's ever-so-great grandson Jesus would make a temple of every human heart.

[17]Nathan reported to David all the
words of this entire revelation.

David's Prayer

[18]Then King David went in and sat
before the LORD, and he said:

"Who am I,[v] O Sovereign 7:18 [v]Ex 3:11; 1Sa 18:18
LORD, and what is my family, that

[a] *11* Traditionally *judges* [b] *16* Some Hebrew manuscripts and Septuagint; most Hebrew manuscripts *you*

you have brought me this far?
19And as if this were not enough
in your sight, O Sovereign LORD,
you have also spoken about the
future of the house of your ser-
7:19 vant. Is this your usual way of
[w]Isa 55:8-9 dealing with man,[w] O Sovereign
LORD?
20"What more can David say to
7:20 [x]Jn 21:17 you? For you know[x] your servant,[y]
[y]1Sa 16:7 O Sovereign LORD. 21For the sake
of your word and according to
your will, you have done this great
thing and made it known to your
servant.
7:22 [z]Ps 48:1; 22"How great[z] you are,[a] O Sover-
86:10; eign LORD! There is no one like
Jer 10:6 [a]Dt 3:24 you, and there is no God[b] but
[b]Ex 15:11 you, as we have heard with our
[c]Ex 10:2; Ps 44:1 own ears.[c] 23And who is like your
people Israel[d]—the one nation on
7:23 [d]Dt 4:32-38 earth that God went out to re-
[e]Dt 10:21 deem as a people for himself, and
[f]Dt 9:26; 15:15 to make a name for himself, and to
perform great and awesome won-
ders[e] by driving out nations and
their gods from before your people, whom you redeemed[f] from
Egypt?[a] 24You have established
7:24 your people Israel as your very
[g]Dt 26:18 [h]Ex 6:6-7; own[g] forever, and you, O LORD,
Ps 48:14 have become their God.[h]
25"And now, LORD God, keep
forever the promise you have made
concerning your servant and his
house. Do as you promised, 26so
that your name will be great forever. Then men will say, 'The
LORD Almighty is God over Israel!' And the house of your servant
David will be established before
you.
27"O LORD Almighty, God of
Israel, you have revealed this to
your servant, saying, 'I will build
a house for you.' So your servant
has found courage to offer you
this prayer. 28O Sovereign LORD,
7:28 you are God! Your words are
[i]Ex 34:6; Jn 17:17 trustworthy,[i] and you have promised these good things to your ser-
vant. 29Now be pleased to bless
the house of your servant, that it
may continue forever in your sight;
for you, O Sovereign LORD, have
7:29 spoken, and with your blessing[j]
[j]Nu 6:23-27 the house of your servant will be
blessed forever."

David's Victories

8 In the course of time, David defeated the Philistines and subdued
them, and he took Metheg Ammah
from the control of the Philistines.
2David also defeated the Moabites.[k] 8:2 [k]Ge 19:37;
He made them lie down on the ground Nu 24:17
and measured them off with a length of
cord. Every two lengths of them were
put to death, and the third length was
allowed to live. So the Moabites became
subject to David and brought tribute.
3Moreover, David fought Hadadezer[l] 8:3 [l]2Sa 10:16,19
son of Rehob, king of Zobah,[m] when [m]1Sa 14:47
he went to restore his control along
the Euphrates River. 4David captured
a thousand of his chariots, seven thousand charioteers[b] and twenty thousand
foot soldiers. He hamstrung[n] all but a 8:4
hundred of the chariot horses. [n]Jos 11:9
5When the Arameans of Damascus[o] 8:5 [o]1Ki 11:24
came to help Hadadezer king of Zobah,
David struck down twenty-two thousand of them. 6He put garrisons in the
Aramean kingdom of Damascus, and
the Arameans became subject to him
and brought tribute. The LORD gave 8:6 [p]ver 14;
David victory wherever he went.[p] 2Sa 3:18; 7:9
7David took the gold shields[q] that
belonged to the officers of Hadadezer 8:7 [q]1Ki 10:16
and brought them to Jerusalem. 8From
Tebah[c] and Berothai,[r] towns that be- 8:8 [r]Eze 47:16
longed to Hadadezer, King David took
a great quantity of bronze.
9When Tou[d] king of Hamath[s] heard 8:9 [s]1Ki 8:65;
that David had defeated the entire army 2Ch 8:4
of Hadadezer, 10he sent his son Joram[e]
to King David to greet him and congratulate him on his victory in battle
over Hadadezer, who had been at war
with Tou. Joram brought with him articles of silver and gold and bronze.
11King David dedicated[t] these articles 8:11 [t]1Ki 7:51;
to the LORD, as he had done with the 1Ch 26:26
silver and gold from all the nations he
had subdued: 12Edom[f] and Moab,[u] the 8:12 [u]ver 2
Ammonites[v] and the Philistines,[w] and [v]2Sa 10:14 [w]2Sa 5:25
Amalek.[x] He also dedicated the plunder [x]1Sa 27:8

[a]*23* See Septuagint and 1 Chron. 17:21; Hebrew *wonders for your land and before your people, whom you redeemed from Egypt, from the nations and their gods.* [b]*4* Septuagint (see also Dead Sea Scrolls and 1 Chron. 18:4); Masoretic Text *captured seventeen hundred of his charioteers* [c]*8* See some Septuagint manuscripts (see also 1 Chron. 18:8); Hebrew *Betah.* [d]*9* Hebrew *Toi,* a variant of *Tou;* also in verse 10 [e]*10* A variant of *Hadoram* [f]*12* Some Hebrew manuscripts, Septuagint and Syriac (see also 1 Chron. 18:11); most Hebrew manuscripts *Aram*

DAY 4 FOUR

▸ KINDNESS AND MY SERVICE TO OTHERS

2 Samuel 9:1–13

In spite of the abuse David received from King Saul, when David became king of Israel, he asked, "Is there anyone still left of the house of Saul to whom I can show kindness for Jonathan's sake?" Yes, there is always somebody to whom we can show kindness. Here, it is Mephibosheth, the disabled son of Jonathan. Jonathan was David's best friend, and David had not forgotten the promise he had made to care for Jonathan's family (1 Samuel 20:14–15).

David's desire that his own family would be the line of kings had left the house of Saul unwelcome in Israel. Jonathan's son was living in the land of Lo Debar. The name means "no pasture," indicating that Mephibosheth was living in extremity and need.

But David welcomes Mephibosheth to the palace. The outcast meets grace. Now he who was handicapped and without human support lives and dines at the king's table.

Kindness is the great virtue of the Christian life. Kindness is usually so automatic, so basic to our nature as Christians, that those who are kindest among us do not suspect themselves as kind. Watch those who regularly open doors for the elderly—they smile once the act is completed and hurry about their business never having seen the glory of their simple deed. Kindness is so Christ-like that it never stops to celebrate itself.

Bellhops, flight attendants and others represent the sort of kindness which is paid for and professional. But all of us like those people best who, having not been paid for behaving like a human being, behave like human beings just for the joy of it. That sort of kindness is Christ-like. It changes the world. It melts the hearts of gladiators. It lifts the orphans toward the Fatherhood of God. It smiles in frowning assemblies. It says, "what can I do to help you?" and actually hopes it will be given an assignment. Kindness wears the sandals of servants—it has since the first century.

To begin a study on the topic of Kindness As a Worldview, turn to the home page on page 1058.

taken from Hadadezer son of Rehob,
king of Zobah.
13And David became famous[y] after
he returned from striking down eighteen thousand Edomites[a] in the Valley
of Salt.[z]
14He put garrisons throughout Edom,
and all the Edomites[a] became subject
to David.[b] The LORD gave David victory wherever he went.[c]

David's Officials

15David reigned over all Israel, doing
what was just and right for all his people. 16Joab[d] son of Zeruiah was over the
army; Jehoshaphat[e] son of Ahilud was
recorder; 17Zadok[f] son of Ahitub and
Ahimelech son of Abiathar were priests;
Seraiah was secretary;[g] 18Benaiah[h] son
of Jehoiada was over the Kerethites[i] and
Pelethites; and David's sons were royal
advisers.[b]

David and Mephibosheth

9 David asked, "Is there anyone still
left of the house of Saul to whom
I can show kindness for Jonathan's
sake?"[j]
2Now there was a servant of Saul's
household named Ziba.[k] They called
him to appear before David, and the
king said to him, "Are you Ziba?"
"Your servant," he replied.
3The king asked, "Is there no one
still left of the house of Saul to whom I
can show God's kindness?"
Ziba answered the king, "There is
still a son of Jonathan;[l] he is crippled[m]
in both feet."
4"Where is he?" the king asked.
Ziba answered, "He is at the house of
Makir[n] son of Ammiel in Lo Debar."
5So King David had him brought
from Lo Debar, from the house of Makir son of Ammiel.
6When Mephibosheth son of Jonathan, the son of Saul, came to David,
he bowed down to pay him honor.[o]
David said, "Mephibosheth!"
"Your servant," he replied.
7"Don't be afraid," David said to him,
"for I will surely show you kindness for
the sake of your father Jonathan. I will
restore to you all the land that belonged

8:13 [y]2Sa 7:9 [z]2Ki 14:7; 1Ch 18:12
8:14 [a]Nu 24:17-18 [b]Ge 27:29, 37-40 [c]ver 6
8:16 [d]2Sa 19:13; 1Ch 11:6 [e]2Sa 20:24; 1Ki 4:3
8:17 [f]2Sa 15:24,29; 1Ch 16:39; 24:3 [g]1Ki 4:3; 2Ki 12:10
8:18 [h]2Sa 20:23; 1Ki 1:8,38; 1Ch 18:17 [i]1Sa 30:14
9:1 [j]1Sa 20:14-17,42
9:2 [k]2Sa 16:1-4; 19:17,26,29
9:3 [l]1Sa 20:14 [m]2Sa 4:4
9:4 [n]2Sa 17:27-29
9:6 [o]2Sa 16:4; 19:24-30

[a]*13* A few Hebrew manuscripts, Septuagint and Syriac (see also 1 Chron. 18:12); most Hebrew manuscripts *Aram* (that is, Arameans) [b]*18* Or *were priests*

to your grandfather Saul, and you will
9:7 [p]ver 1,3; 2Sa 12:8; 19:28; 1Ki 2:7; 2Ki 25:29 always eat at my table.[p]"
8 Mephibosheth bowed down and
said, "What is your servant, that you
should notice a dead dog[q] like me?"
9:8 [q]2Sa 16:9 9 Then the king summoned Ziba,
Saul's servant, and said to him, "I have
given your master's grandson everything
that belonged to Saul and his family.
10 You and your sons and your servants
are to farm the land for him and bring
9:10 [r]ver 7,11,13; 2Sa 19:28 in the crops, so that your master's grandson[r] may be provided for. And Mephib-
osheth, grandson of your master, will
always eat at my table." (Now Ziba had
fifteen sons and twenty servants.)
11 Then Ziba said to the king, "Your
servant will do whatever my lord the
king commands his servant to do." So
9:11 [s]Job 36:7; Ps 113:8 Mephibosheth ate at David's[a] table like
one of the king's sons.[s]
12 Mephibosheth had a young son
named Mica, and all the members
of Ziba's household were servants of
9:12 [t]1Ch 8:34 Mephibosheth.[t] 13 And Mephibosheth
lived in Jerusalem, because he always
ate at the king's table, and he was crippled in both feet.

GOODNESS

THE FEAST OF OUR FOREVERNESS

2 Samuel 9:13

Grace means that the disabled may sit at a king's table.

Are we ourselves not like Mephibosheth?
Maimed by sin we came
And feasted at the banquet grand—
A crippled horde, devouring grace
At the supper of the Lamb.

David Defeats the Ammonites

10 In the course of time, the king
of the Ammonites died, and his
son Hanun succeeded him as king. 2 Da-
10:2 [u]1Sa 11:1 vid thought, "I will show kindness to
Hanun son of Nahash,[u] just as his fa-
ther showed kindness to me." So David
sent a delegation to express his sympathy to Hanun concerning his father.
When David's men came to the land
of the Ammonites, 3 the Ammonite nobles said to Hanun their lord, "Do you
think David is honoring your father
by sending men to you to express
sympathy? Hasn't David sent them to
you to explore the city and spy it out
and overthrow it?" 4 So Hanun seized
David's men, shaved off half of each
man's beard,[v] cut off their garments in 10:4 [v]Lev 19:27; Isa 15:2; Jer 48:37 [w]Isa 20:4
the middle at the buttocks,[w] and sent
them away.
5 When David was told about this, he
sent messengers to meet the men, for
they were greatly humiliated. The king
said, "Stay at Jericho till your beards
have grown, and then come back."
6 When the Ammonites realized that
they had become a stench[x] in David's 10:6 [x]Ge 34:30 [y]2Sa 8:5 [z]Jdg 18:28 [a]Dt 3:14
nostrils, they hired twenty thousand Ar-
amean[y] foot soldiers from Beth Rehob[z]
and Zobah, as well as the king of Maacah[a] with a thousand men, and also
twelve thousand men from Tob.
7 On hearing this, David sent Joab
out with the entire army of fighting
men. 8 The Ammonites came out and
drew up in battle formation at the entrance to their city gate, while the Arameans of Zobah and Rehob and the
men of Tob and Maacah were by themselves in the open country.
9 Joab saw that there were battle lines
in front of him and behind him; so he
selected some of the best troops in Israel
and deployed them against the Arameans. 10 He put the rest of the men under
the command of Abishai his brother
and deployed them against the Ammonites. 11 Joab said, "If the Arameans
are too strong for me, then you are to
come to my rescue; but if the Ammonites are too strong for you, then I will
come to rescue you. 12 Be strong[b] and 10:12 [b]Dt 31:6; 1Co 16:13; Eph 6:10 [c]Jdg 10:15; 1Sa 3:18; Ne 4:14
let us fight bravely for our people and
the cities of our God. The LORD will
do what is good in his sight."[c]
13 Then Joab and the troops with him
advanced to fight the Arameans, and
they fled before him. 14 When the Ammonites saw that the Arameans were
fleeing, they fled before Abishai and
went inside the city. So Joab returned
from fighting the Ammonites and came
to Jerusalem.
15 After the Arameans saw that they
had been routed by Israel, they re-
grouped. 16 Hadadezer had Arameans
brought from beyond the River[b]; they
went to Helam, with Shobach the com-

[a] *11* Septuagint; Hebrew *my* [b] *16* That is, the Euphrates

mander of Hadadezer's army leading
them.
17When David was told of this, he
gathered all Israel, crossed the Jordan
and went to Helam. The Arameans
formed their battle lines to meet David and fought against him. 18But they
fled before Israel, and David killed sev-
en hundred of their charioteers and forty thousand of their foot soldiers.[a] He
also struck down Shobach the commander of their army, and he died there.
19When all the kings who were vassals
of Hadadezer saw that they had been
defeated by Israel, they made peace with
10:19 the Israelites and became subject[d] to
[d]2Sa 8:6 [e]1Ki 11:25; them.
2Ki 5:1 So the Arameans[e] were afraid to help
the Ammonites anymore.

David and Bathsheba

11:1 **11** In the spring,[f] at the time when
[f]1Ki 20:22,26 [g]2Sa 2:18 kings go off to war, David sent
[h]1Ch 20:1 [i]2Sa 12:26-28 Joab[g] out with the king's men and the
whole Israelite army.[h] They destroyed
the Ammonites and besieged Rabbah.[i]
But David remained in Jerusalem.

SELF-CONTROL

When Kings Presume

2 Samuel 11:1

A king must not forget the obligation of his office. At a time when "kings go off to war," David didn't. A true king does not despise the discipline of kings. His crown is forbearance; his scepter, self-control.

2One evening David got up from his
11:2 bed and walked around on the roof[j]
[j]Dt 22:8; Jos 2:8 of the palace. From the roof he saw[k] a
[k]Mt 5:28 woman bathing. The woman was very
beautiful, 3and David sent someone to
11:3 find out about her. The man said, "Isn't
[l]1Ch 3:5 [m]2Sa 23:34 this Bathsheba,[l] the daughter of Eliam[m]
[n]2Sa 23:39 and the wife of Uriah[n] the Hittite?"
11:4 4Then David sent messengers to get
[o]Lev 20:10; Ps 51 Title; her.[o] She came to him, and he slept[p]
Jas 1:14-15 [p]Dt 22:22 with her. (She had purified herself from
[q]Lev 15:25-30; 18:19 her uncleanness.)[q] Then[b] she went back
home. 5The woman conceived and sent
word to David, saying, "I am pregnant."
6So David sent this word to Joab:
11:6 [r]1Ch 11:41 "Send me Uriah[r] the Hittite." And Joab
sent him to David. 7When Uriah came
to him, David asked him how Joab was,
how the soldiers were and how the war
was going. 8Then David said to Uriah,
"Go down to your house and wash your
feet."[s] So Uriah left the palace, and a 11:8 [s]Ge 18:4;
gift from the king was sent after him. 43:24;
9But Uriah slept at the entrance to the Lk 7:44
palace with all his master's servants and
did not go down to his house.
10When David was told, "Uriah did
not go home," he asked him, "Haven't
you just come from a distance? Why
didn't you go home?"
11Uriah said to David, "The ark[t] and 11:11 [t]2Sa 7:2
Israel and Judah are staying in tents,
and my master Joab and my lord's men
are camped in the open fields. How
could I go to my house to eat and drink
and lie with my wife? As surely as you
live, I will not do such a thing!"
12Then David said to him, "Stay here
one more day, and tomorrow I will send
you back." So Uriah remained in Jerusalem that day and the next. 13At David's invitation, he ate and drank with
him, and David made him drunk. But
in the evening Uriah went out to sleep
on his mat among his master's servants;
he did not go home.
14In the morning David wrote a let- 11:14
ter[u] to Joab and sent it with Uriah. 15In [u]1Ki 21:8
it he wrote, "Put Uriah in the front
line where the fighting is fiercest. Then
withdraw from him so he will be struck 11:15
down[v] and die.[w]" [v]2Sa 12:9 [w]2Sa 12:12
16So while Joab had the city under
siege, he put Uriah at a place where
he knew the strongest defenders were.
17When the men of the city came out
and fought against Joab, some of the
men in David's army fell; moreover,
Uriah the Hittite died.
18Joab sent David a full account of
the battle. 19He instructed the messenger: "When you have finished giving
the king this account of the battle, 20the
king's anger may flare up, and he may
ask you, 'Why did you get so close
to the city to fight? Didn't you know
they would shoot arrows from the wall? 11:21
21Who killed Abimelech[x] son of Jerub- [x]Jdg 8:31
Besheth[c]? Didn't a woman throw an up- [y]Jdg 9:50-54
per millstone on him from the wall,[y] so
that he died in Thebez? Why did you
get so close to the wall?' If he asks you

[a]*18* Some Septuagint manuscripts (see also 1 Chron. 19:18); Hebrew *horsemen* [b]*4* Or *with her. When she purified herself from her uncleanness,* [c]*21* Also known as *Jerub-Baal* (that is, Gideon)

WEEK 9 SELF-CONTROL

1 DAY ONE
SELF-CONTROL, THE PATH OF COMING TO MATURITY

Read 2 Samuel 11:1–5

"In the spring, at the time when kings go off to war" is the sinister "once-upon-a-time" with which the author begins his tale of King David's affair with Bathsheba. Why are the words "at the time when kings go off to war" so significant? We may infer that this was probably the first time in his reign when David—unlike other kings—did not go to war.

From this short phrase, we understand that David sent his army into the field without him. He opted to forgo the rigors of field bivouac in favor of a life of ease. While his soldiers were suffering through the trauma of war, David wasn't suffering at all. In other words, David, who had always before chosen a life of self-denial, was now determining to live a life of self-indulgence.

"Taking a load off" is how our comfort-loving society phrases it. But taking a load off leads to secondary indulgences that the king allows himself while enjoying the castle comforts instead of living in the open field. At ease morally, he watches one of his soldier's wives take a bath. And watching Bathsheba begets lusting, and lusting begets adultery, which results in a pregnancy, a murder and a huge cover-up operation that the king institutes to hide his sin and protect his reputation. When indulgence comes into our lives, self-control leaves by the back door. In David's case, a great writer of many psalms and praises to God is debased to an indulgent adulterer.

Once we permit ourselves one sin and squelch our inner remorse, that remorse loses its voice. We commit other sins, leading to a spiral of despair. The only hope we have is to make self-control the keeper of our inner lives. Our path to maturity in Christ is paved by self-control. It is God's instrument, given by him, to lead us to victory.

2 DAY TWO
SELF-CONTROL AND THE PURPOSE OF GOD IN MY LIFE

The purposes of God are for each of us to live consistently in love with him. Loving God will result in sexual purity. And sexual purity makes us the kind of vessel God can use. In a day and age when sexual purity has been redefined as "loving consent" between two adults—any two adults—do we dare ask what the Bible has to say? Christians can ill-afford to live any other way. *Turn to Proverbs 5:15–20, page 738, for today's study.*

3 DAY THREE
SELF-CONTROL AND MY RELATIONSHIP WITH CHRIST

The refining work of God is like a metallurgist using a forge and foundry to work on us until all our impurities are gone and we approach the holiness that is so like God. When we have passed through the refiner's fire, and the dross and slag have been burned from our lives—only then will we know the importance of the refinery. Only then will we come forth as gold. *Turn to Job 23:10, page 608, for today's study.*

4 DAY FOUR
SELF-CONTROL AND MY SERVICE TO OTHERS

To achieve the extraordinary in discipleship, our self-control must also be extraordinary. We can only have victory over Satan when we have triumphed over spiritual laziness in our lives. Jesus remarks that only those who resolve to keep their relationship with God strong can ever wage war effectively against Satan. *Turn to Mark 9:14–18,29, page 1181, for today's study.*

5 DAY FIVE
SELF-CONTROL AND ITS PLACE IN MY PERSONAL WORSHIP

Nothing is sweeter than worship when we meet God having been cleansed of all sin and when our desire for secret sins has been cleansed as well. Being forgiven brings open fellowship with God. This psalm is perhaps David's greatest. More than any other, it deals with unconfessed sin and the cost such sin engenders in broken fellowship with God. *Turn to Psalm 51:1–12, page 666, for today's study.*

MEMORIZE THIS WEEK

PHILIPPIANS 2:12-13

Therefore, my dear friends, as you have always obeyed—not only in my presence, but now much more in my absence—continue to work out your salvation with fear and trembling, for it is God who works in you to will and to act according to his good purpose.

Week 10, Love Forgives, begins on page 1227, Luke 15:11–24.
To begin a topical study on the Fruit of the Spirit, Self-Control, turn to the Topical Index, page 1548.

this, then say to him, 'Also, your servant Uriah the Hittite is dead.'"
22The messenger set out, and when
he arrived he told David everything
Joab had sent him to say. 23The messenger said to David, "The men overpowered us and came out against us in
the open, but we drove them back to
the entrance to the city gate. 24Then
the archers shot arrows at your servants
from the wall, and some of the king's
men died. Moreover, your servant Uriah the Hittite is dead."
25David told the messenger, "Say this
to Joab: 'Don't let this upset you; the
sword devours one as well as another.
Press the attack against the city and destroy it.' Say this to encourage Joab."
26When Uriah's wife heard that her
husband was dead, she mourned for
him. 27After the time of mourning was
over, David had her brought to his
house, and she became his wife and
11:27 bore him a son. But the thing David
[z]2Sa 12:9; had done displeased[z] the LORD.
Ps 51:4-5

Nathan Rebukes David

12:1 **12** The LORD sent Nathan[a] to
[a]2Sa 7:2; David.[b] When he came to him,[c]
1Ki 20:35-41 [b]Ps 51 Title he said, "There were two men in a cer-
[c]2Sa 14:4 tain town, one rich and the other poor.
2The rich man had a very large number
of sheep and cattle, 3but the poor man
had nothing except one little ewe lamb
he had bought. He raised it, and it grew
up with him and his children. It shared
his food, drank from his cup and even
slept in his arms. It was like a daughter
to him.
4"Now a traveler came to the rich
man, but the rich man refrained from
taking one of his own sheep or cattle to
prepare a meal for the traveler who had
come to him. Instead, he took the ewe
lamb that belonged to the poor man
and prepared it for the one who had
come to him."
12:5 5David[d] burned with anger against
[d]1Ki 20:40 the man and said to Nathan, "As surely
as the LORD lives, the man who did
this deserves to die! 6He must pay for
12:6 that lamb four times over,[e] because he
[e]Ex 22:1; did such a thing and had no pity."
Lk 19:8
7Then Nathan said to David, "You
are the man! This is what the LORD,
12:7 the God of Israel, says: 'I anointed[f]
[f]1Sa 16:13 you[g] king over Israel, and I delivered
[g]1Ki 20:42 you from the hand of Saul. 8I gave your

master's house to you,[h] and your mas- 12:8
ter's wives into your arms. I gave you [h]2Sa 9:7
the house of Israel and Judah. And if all
this had been too little, I would have
given you even more. 9Why did you
despise[i] the word of the LORD by do- 12:9
ing what is evil in his eyes? You struck [i]Nu 15:31;
down[j] Uriah the Hittite with the sword 1Sa 15:19 [j]2Sa 11:15
and took his wife to be your own. You
killed him with the sword of the Am- 12:10
monites. 10Now, therefore, the sword[k] [k]2Sa 13:28;
will never depart from your house, be- 18:14-15;
cause you despised me and took the 1Ki 2:25
wife of Uriah the Hittite to be your
own.'
11"This is what the LORD says: 'Out
of your own household I am going to
bring calamity upon you. Before your
very eyes I will take your wives and give 12:11
them to one who is close to you,[l] and [l]Dt 28:30;
he will lie with your wives in broad 2Sa 16:21-22
daylight. 12You did it in secret,[m] but I 12:12
will do this thing in broad daylight[n] be- [m]2Sa 11:4-15
fore all Israel.'" [n]2Sa 16:22
13Then David said to Nathan, "I have 12:13
sinned[o] against the LORD." [o]Ge 13:13;
Nathan replied, "The LORD has tak- Nu 22:34; 1Sa 15:24; 2Sa 24:10
en away[p] your sin.[q] You are not going [p]Ps 32:1-5; 51:1,9;
to die.[r] 14But because by doing this you 103:12;
have made the enemies of the LORD Zec 3:4,9 [q]Pr 28:13;
show utter contempt,[a][s] the son born to Mic 7:18-19 [r]Lev 20:10;
you will die." 24:17
15After Nathan had gone home, the
LORD struck[t] the child that Uriah's 12:14
wife had borne to David, and he be- [s]Isa 52:5; Ro 2:24
came ill. 16David pleaded with God for 12:15
the child. He fasted and went into his [t]1Sa 25:38
house and spent the nights lying[u] on 12:16
the ground. 17The elders of his house- [u]2Sa 13:31; Ps 5:7
hold stood beside him to get him up
from the ground, but he refused, and 12:17
he would not eat any food with them.[v] [v]2Sa 3:35
18On the seventh day the child died.
David's servants were afraid to tell
him that the child was dead, for they
thought, "While the child was still living, we spoke to David but he would
not listen to us. How can we tell him
the child is dead? He may do something desperate."
19David noticed that his servants were
whispering among themselves and he
realized the child was dead. "Is the child
dead?" he asked.

[a]*14* Masoretic Text; an ancient Hebrew scribal tradition *this you have shown utter contempt for the LORD*

"Yes," they replied, "he is dead."
[20]Then David got up from the
12:20 [w]Mt 6:17 ground. After he had washed,[w] put on
[x]Job 1:20 lotions and changed his clothes,[x] he
went into the house of the LORD and
worshiped. Then he went to his own
house, and at his request they served
him food, and he ate.
[21]His servants asked him, "Why are
you acting this way? While the child
12:21 [y]Jdg 20:26 was alive, you fasted and wept,[y] but
now that the child is dead, you get up
and eat!"
[22]He answered, "While the child was
12:22 still alive, I fasted and wept. I thought,
[z]Jnh 3:9 'Who knows?[z] The LORD may be gra-
[a]Isa 38:1-5 cious to me and let the child live.'[a]
12:23 [b]Ge 37:35 [23]But now that he is dead, why should
[c]1Sa 31:13; 2Sa 13:39; I fast? Can I bring him back again? I
Job 7:10; 10:21 will go to him,[b] but he will not return
to me."[c]

JOY

FAMILY REUNION

2 Samuel 12:23

Heaven is a place of families in reunion. It is a place where grieving fathers may reclaim their lost children. Christ preceded us there and dries away all tears. We will discover that the joy of being with our loved ones is eclipsed only by the joy of being with him.

12:24 [24]Then David comforted his wife
[d]1Ki 1:11 Bathsheba,[d] and he went to her and
[e]1Ki 1:10; lay with her. She gave birth to a son,
1Ch 22:9; 28:5; and they named him Solomon.[e] The
Mt 1:6 LORD loved him; [25]and because the
LORD loved him, he sent word through
12:25 Nathan the prophet to name him
[f]Ne 13:26 Jedidiah.[a][f]
12:26 [26]Meanwhile Joab fought against
[g]Dt 3:11; Rabbah[g] of the Ammonites and cap-
1Ch 20:1-3 tured the royal citadel. [27]Joab then sent
messengers to David, saying, "I have
fought against Rabbah and taken its
water supply. [28]Now muster the rest of
the troops and besiege the city and capture it. Otherwise I will take the city,
and it will be named after me."
[29]So David mustered the entire army
12:30 [h]1Ch 20:2; and went to Rabbah, and attacked and
Est 8:15; captured it. [30]He took the crown[h] from
Ps 21:3; the head of their king[b]—its weight was
132:18 a talent[c] of gold, and it was set with
precious stones—and it was placed on
David's head. He took a great quantity
of plunder from the city [31]and brought
out the people who were there, consign-
ing them to labor with saws and with
iron picks and axes, and he made them
work at brickmaking.[d] He did this to
all the Ammonite[i] towns. Then David 12:31 [i]1Sa 14:47
and his entire army returned to Jeru-
salem.

Amnon and Tamar

13 In the course of time, Amnon[j] 13:1 [j]2Sa 3:2
son of David fell in love with [k]2Sa 14:27; 1Ch 3:9
Tamar,[k] the beautiful sister of Absalom[l] [l]2Sa 3:3
son of David.
[2]Amnon became frustrated to the
point of illness on account of his sister
Tamar, for she was a virgin, and it
seemed impossible for him to do anything to her.
[3]Now Amnon had a friend named 13:3
Jonadab son of Shimeah,[m] David's [m]1Sa 16:9
brother. Jonadab was a very shrewd
man. [4]He asked Amnon, "Why do you,
the king's son, look so haggard morning
after morning? Won't you tell me?"
Amnon said to him, "I'm in love with
Tamar, my brother Absalom's sister."
[5]"Go to bed and pretend to be ill,"
Jonadab said. "When your father comes
to see you, say to him, 'I would like
my sister Tamar to come and give me
something to eat. Let her prepare the
food in my sight so I may watch her
and then eat it from her hand.' "
[6]So Amnon lay down and pretended
to be ill. When the king came to see
him, Amnon said to him, "I would
like my sister Tamar to come and make
some special bread in my sight, so I
may eat from her hand."
[7]David sent word to Tamar at the
palace: "Go to the house of your brother Amnon and prepare some food for
him." [8]So Tamar went to the house
of her brother Amnon, who was lying
down. She took some dough, kneaded
it, made the bread in his sight and
baked it. [9]Then she took the pan and
served him the bread, but he refused
to eat.
"Send everyone out of here,"[n] Am- 13:9 [n]Ge 45:1
non said. So everyone left him. [10]Then
Amnon said to Tamar, "Bring the food
here into my bedroom so I may eat

[a]*25 Jedidiah* means *loved by the LORD.* [b]*30* Or *of Milcom* (that is, Molech) [c]*30* That is, about 75 pounds (about 34 kilograms) [d]*31* The meaning of the Hebrew for this clause is uncertain.

from your hand." And Tamar took the
bread she had prepared and brought it
to her brother Amnon in his bedroom.
11But when she took it to him to eat, he
13:11 [o]Ge 39:12 grabbed[o] her and said, "Come to bed
[p]Ge 38:16 with me, my sister."[p]
12"Don't, my brother!" she said to
him. "Don't force me. Such a thing
13:12 [q]Lev 20:17; should not be done in Israel![q] Don't do
Jdg 20:6 [r]Ge 34:7; this wicked thing.[r] 13What about me?[s]
Jdg 19:23 Where could I get rid of my disgrace?
13:13 And what about you? You would be like
[s]Ge 20:12; one of the wicked fools in Israel. Please
Lev 18:9; Dt 22:21, speak to the king; he will not keep me
23-24 from being married to you." 14But he
13:14 refused to listen to her, and since he
[t]Ge 34:2; Dt 22:25; was stronger than she, he raped her.[t]
Eze 22:11 15Then Amnon hated her with in-
tense hatred. In fact, he hated her more
than he had loved her. Amnon said to
her, "Get up and get out!"
16"No!" she said to him. "Sending
me away would be a greater wrong than
what you have already done to me."
But he refused to listen to her. 17He
called his personal servant and said,
"Get this woman out of here and bolt
the door after her." 18So his servant put
her out and bolted the door after her.
13:18 She was wearing a richly ornamented[a]
[u]Ge 37:23; robe,[u] for this was the kind of garment
Jdg 5:30 the virgin daughters of the king wore.
13:19 [v]Jos 7:6; 19Tamar put ashes[v] on her head and tore
1Sa 4:12; the ornamented[b] robe she was wearing.
2Sa 1:2; Est 4:1; She put her hand on her head and went
Da 9:3 away, weeping aloud as she went.
20Her brother Absalom said to her,
"Has that Amnon, your brother, been
with you? Be quiet now, my sister; he
is your brother. Don't take this thing to
heart." And Tamar lived in her brother
Absalom's house, a desolate woman.
13:21 21When King David heard all this,
[w]Ge 34:7 he was furious.[w] 22Absalom never said
13:22 [x]Ge 31:24 a word to Amnon, either good or bad;[x]
[y]Lev 19:17- he hated[y] Amnon because he had dis-
18; 1Jn 2:9-11 graced his sister Tamar.

Absalom Kills Amnon

23Two years later, when Absalom's
13:23 [z]1Sa 25:7 sheepshearers[z] were at Baal Hazor near
the border of Ephraim, he invited all
the king's sons to come there. 24Absa-
lom went to the king and said, "Your
servant has had shearers come. Will the
king and his officials please join me?"
25"No, my son," the king replied. "All
of us should not go; we would only be
a burden to you." Although Absalom
urged him, he still refused to go, but
gave him his blessing.
26Then Absalom said, "If not, please
let my brother Amnon come with us."
The king asked him, "Why should
he go with you?" 27But Absalom urged
him, so he sent with him Amnon and
the rest of the king's sons.
28Absalom[a] ordered his men, "Lis- 13:28 [a]2Sa 3:3
ten! When Amnon is in high[b] spirits [b]Jdg 19:6, 9,22;
from drinking wine and I say to you, Ru 3:7;
'Strike Amnon down,' then kill him. 1Sa 25:36 [c]2Sa 12:10
Don't be afraid. Have not I given you
this order? Be strong and brave.[c]" 29So
Absalom's men did to Amnon what Absalom had ordered. Then all the king's
sons got up, mounted their mules and
fled.
30While they were on their way, the
report came to David: "Absalom has
struck down all the king's sons; not one of
them is left." 31The king stood up, tore[d] 13:31 [d]Nu 14:6;
his clothes and lay down on the ground; 2Sa 1:11;
and all his servants stood by with their 12:16
clothes torn.
32But Jonadab son of Shimeah, David's brother, said, "My lord should not
think that they killed all the princes;
only Amnon is dead. This has been Absalom's expressed intention ever since
the day Amnon raped his sister Tamar.
33My lord the king should not be concerned about the report that all the
king's sons are dead. Only Amnon is
dead."
34Meanwhile, Absalom had fled.
Now the man standing watch looked
up and saw many people on the road
west of him, coming down the side of
the hill. The watchman went and told
the king, "I see men in the direction of
Horonaim, on the side of the hill."[c]
35Jonadab said to the king, "See, the
king's sons are here; it has happened
just as your servant said."
36As he finished speaking, the king's
sons came in, wailing loudly. The king,
too, and all his servants wept very bitterly.
37Absalom fled and went to Talmai[e] 13:37 [e]ver 34;
son of Ammihud, the king of Geshur. 2Sa 3:3;
But King David mourned for his son 14:23,32
every day.

[a] *18* The meaning of the Hebrew for this phrase is uncertain. [b] *19* The meaning of the Hebrew for this word is uncertain. [c] *34* Septuagint; Hebrew does not have this sentence.

38After Absalom fled and went to Geshur, he stayed there three years. 39And
13:39 the spirit of the king[a] longed to go to
f2Sa 14:13 Absalom,[f] for he was consoled[g] con-
g2Sa 12:19-23 cerning Amnon's death.

Absalom Returns to Jerusalem

14:1 14 Joab[b] son of Zeruiah knew that
b2Sa 2:18 the king's heart longed for Ab-
14:2 salom. 2So Joab sent someone to Tekoa[i]
i2Ch 11:6; and had a wise woman[j] brought from
Ne 3:5; Jer 6:1; there. He said to her, "Pretend you
Am 1:1 j2Sa 20:16 are in mourning. Dress in mourning
kRu 3:3; clothes, and don't use any cosmetic
2Sa 12:20; Isa 1:6 lotions.[k] Act like a woman who has
spent many days grieving for the dead.
3Then go to the king and speak these
14:3 words to him." And Joab[l] put the words
lver 19 in her mouth.
4When the woman from Tekoa went[b]
to the king, she fell with her face to the
ground to pay him honor, and she said,
"Help me, O king!"
5The king asked her, "What is troubling you?"
She said, "I am indeed a widow; my
husband is dead. 6I your servant had
two sons. They got into a fight with
each other in the field, and no one
was there to separate them. One struck
the other and killed him. 7Now the
whole clan has risen up against your
servant; they say, 'Hand over the one
14:7 who struck his brother down, so that
mNu 35:19 nMt 21:38 we may put him to death[m] for the life
oDt 19:10-13 of his brother whom he killed; then we
will get rid of the heir[n] as well.' They
would put out the only burning coal I
have left,[o] leaving my husband neither
name nor descendant on the face of the
earth."
14:8 8The king said to the woman, "Go
p1Sa 25:35 home,[p] and I will issue an order in your
behalf."
14:9 9But the woman from Tekoa said to
q1Sa 25:24 rMt 27:25 him, "My lord the king, let the blame[q]
s1Sa 25:28; rest on me and on my father's family,[r]
1Ki 2:33 and let the king and his throne be without guilt."[s]
10The king replied, "If anyone says
anything to you, bring him to me, and
he will not bother you again."
11She said, "Then let the king in-
14:11 voke the LORD his God to prevent the
tNu 35:12,21 avenger[t] of blood from adding to the
destruction, so that my son will not be
destroyed."
"As surely as the LORD lives," he
said, "not one hair[u] of your son's head 14:11 uMt 10:30
will fall to the ground.[v]" v1Sa 14:45
12Then the woman said, "Let your
servant speak a word to my lord the
king."
"Speak," he replied.
13The woman said, "Why then have
you devised a thing like this against
the people of God? When the king says 14:13
this, does he not convict himself,[w] for w2Sa 12:7;
the king has not brought back his ban- 1Ki 20:40; 1Sa 14:45; Mt 10:30
ished son?[x] 14Like water[y] spilled on the x2Sa 13:38-39
ground, which cannot be recovered, so 14:14
we must die.[z] But God does not take yJob 14:11;
away life; instead, he devises ways so Ps 58:7;
that a banished person[a] may not remain Isa 19:5 zJob 10:8;
estranged from him. 17:13; 30:23; Ps 22:15;
15"And now I have come to say this to Heb 9:27 aNu 35:15,
my lord the king because the people have 25-28;
made me afraid. Your servant thought, Job 34:15
'I will speak to the king; perhaps he
will do what his servant asks. 16Perhaps
the king will agree to deliver his servant
from the hand of the man who is trying
to cut off both me and my son from the 14:16
inheritance[b] God gave us.' bEx 34:9; 1Sa 26:19
17"And now your servant says, 'May
the word of my lord the king bring me
rest, for my lord the king is like an an-
gel[c] of God in discerning[d] good and 14:17 cver 20;
evil. May the LORD your God be with 1Sa 29:9; 2Sa 19:27
you.'" d1Ki 3:9; Da 2:21
18Then the king said to the woman,
"Do not keep from me the answer to
what I am going to ask you."
"Let my lord the king speak," the
woman said.
19The king asked, "Isn't the hand of 14:19
Joab[e] with you in all this?" ever 3
The woman answered, "As surely as
you live, my lord the king, no one can
turn to the right or to the left from
anything my lord the king says. Yes, it
was your servant Joab who instructed
me to do this and who put all these
words into the mouth of your servant.
20Your servant Joab did this to change
the present situation. My lord has wis- 14:20
dom[f] like that of an angel of God—he f1Ki 3:12,28;
knows everything that happens in the Isa 28:6 gver 17;
land.[g]" 2Sa 18:13; 19:27
21The king said to Joab, "Very well,
I will do it. Go, bring back the young
man Absalom."

[a]*39* Dead Sea Scrolls and some Septuagint manuscripts; Masoretic Text *But ⌊the spirit of⌋ David the king* [b]*4* Many Hebrew manuscripts, Septuagint, Vulgate and Syriac; most Hebrew manuscripts *spoke*

22Joab fell with his face to the ground
to pay him honor, and he blessed the
14:22 [h]Ge 47:7 king.[h] Joab said, "Today your servant
knows that he has found favor in your
eyes, my lord the king, because the king
has granted his servant's request."
23Then Joab went to Geshur and
brought Absalom back to Jerusalem.
24But the king said, "He must go to his
own house; he must not see my face."
So Absalom went to his own house and
did not see the face of the king.
25In all Israel there was not a man
so highly praised for his handsome appearance as Absalom. From the top of
his head to the sole of his foot there was
14:26 no blemish in him. 26Whenever he cut
[i]2Sa 18:9; Eze 44:20 the hair of his head[i]—he used to cut his
hair from time to time when it became
too heavy for him—he would weigh it,
and its weight was two hundred shekels[a] by the royal standard.
14:27 [j]2Sa 18:18 27Three sons[j] and a daughter were
[k]2Sa 13:1 born to Absalom. The daughter's name
was Tamar,[k] and she became a beautiful
woman.
28Absalom lived two years in Jerusalem without seeing the king's face.
29Then Absalom sent for Joab in order
to send him to the king, but Joab refused to come to him. So he sent a
second time, but he refused to come.
30Then he said to his servants, "Look,
Joab's field is next to mine, and he has
14:30 [l]Ex 9:31 barley[l] there. Go and set it on fire." So
Absalom's servants set the field on fire.
31Then Joab did go to Absalom's
14:31 house and he said to him, "Why have
[m]Jdg 15:5 your servants set my field on fire?"[m]
32Absalom said to Joab, "Look, I sent
word to you and said, 'Come here so I
14:32 can send you to the king to ask, "Why
[n]2Sa 3:3 [o]1Sa 20:8 have I come from Geshur?[n] It would
be better for me if I were still there!"'
Now then, I want to see the king's face,
and if I am guilty of anything, let him
put me to death."[o]
33So Joab went to the king and told
him this. Then the king summoned
Absalom, and he came in and bowed
down with his face to the ground be-
14:33 [p]Ge 33:4; Lk 15:20 fore the king. And the king kissed[p] Absalom.

Absalom's Conspiracy

15:1 15 In the course of time,[q] Absalom
[q]2Sa 12:11 [r]1Sa 8:11; 1Ki 1:5 provided himself with a chariot[r]
and horses and with fifty men to run
ahead of him. 2He would get up early
and stand by the side of the road leading to the city gate.[s] Whenever anyone 15:2
came with a complaint to be placed [s]Ge 23:10; 2Sa 19:8
before the king for a decision, Absalom
would call out to him, "What town are
you from?" He would answer, "Your
servant is from one of the tribes of
Israel." 3Then Absalom would say to
him, "Look, your claims are valid and
proper, but there is no representative of
the king to hear you."[t] 4And Absalom 15:3 [t]Pr 12:2
would add, "If only I were appointed 15:4
judge in the land![u] Then everyone who [u]Jdg 9:29
has a complaint or case could come to
me and I would see that he gets justice."
5Also, whenever anyone approached
him to bow down before him, Absalom
would reach out his hand, take hold of
him and kiss him. 6Absalom behaved in
this way toward all the Israelites who
came to the king asking for justice, and
so he stole the hearts[v] of the men of 15:6
Israel. [v]Ro 16:18

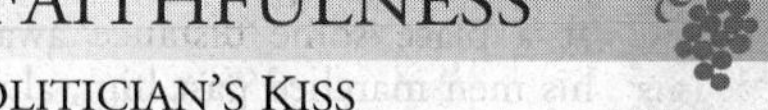

FAITHFULNESS

A Politician's Kiss

2 Samuel 15:5

Absalom kissed all his father's enemies with a politician's kiss. A politician's kiss is faithless. It is but ego kissing its own future. It is ballot-box affection, lasting only till the polls close.

7At the end of four[b] years, Absalom
said to the king, "Let me go to Hebron
and fulfill a vow I made to the LORD.
8While your servant was living at Ge- 15:8
shur[w] in Aram, I made this vow:[x] 'If [w]2Sa 3:3; 13:37-38
the LORD takes me back to Jerusalem, I [x]Ge 28:20
will worship the LORD in Hebron.[c]'"
9The king said to him, "Go in peace."
So he went to Hebron.
10Then Absalom sent secret messengers throughout the tribes of Israel to
say, "As soon as you hear the sound 15:10
of the trumpets,[y] then say, 'Absalom is [y]1Ki 1:34,39; 2Ki 9:13
king in Hebron.'" 11Two hundred men
from Jerusalem had accompanied Absalom. They had been invited as guests
and went quite innocently, knowing

[a]*26* That is, about 5 pounds (about 2.3 kilograms)
[b]*7* Some Septuagint manuscripts, Syriac and Josephus; Hebrew *forty* [c]*8* Some Septuagint manuscripts; Hebrew does not have *in Hebron.*

nothing about the matter. 12While Absalom was offering sacrifices, he also sent for Ahithophel[z] the Gilonite, David's counselor,[a] to come from Giloh,[b] his hometown. And so the conspiracy gained strength, and Absalom's following kept on increasing.[c]

David Flees

13A messenger came and told David, "The hearts of the men of Israel are with Absalom."

14Then David said to all his officials who were with him in Jerusalem, "Come! We must flee,[d] or none of us will escape from Absalom.[e] We must leave immediately, or he will move quickly to overtake us and bring ruin upon us and put the city to the sword."

15The king's officials answered him, "Your servants are ready to do whatever our lord the king chooses."

16The king set out, with his entire household following him; but he left ten concubines[f] to take care of the palace. 17So the king set out, with all the people following him, and they halted at a place some distance away. 18All his men marched past him, along with all the Kerethites[g] and Pelethites; and all the six hundred Gittites who had accompanied him from Gath marched before the king.

19The king said to Ittai[h] the Gittite, "Why should you come along with us? Go back and stay with King Absalom. You are a foreigner,[i] an exile from your homeland. 20You came only yesterday. And today shall I make you wander[j] about with us, when I do not know where I am going? Go back, and take your countrymen. May kindness and faithfulness[k] be with you."

21But Ittai replied to the king, "As surely as the LORD lives, and as my lord the king lives, wherever my lord the king may be, whether it means life or death, there will your servant be."[l]

22David said to Ittai, "Go ahead, march on." So Ittai the Gittite marched on with all his men and the families that were with him.

23The whole countryside wept aloud as all the people passed by. The king also crossed the Kidron Valley,[m] and all the people moved on toward the desert.

24Zadok[n] was there, too, and all the Levites who were with him were carrying the ark[o] of the covenant of God. They set down the ark of God, and Abiathar[p] offered sacrifices[a] until all the people had finished leaving the city.

25Then the king said to Zadok, "Take the ark of God back into the city. If I find favor in the LORD's eyes, he will bring me back and let me see it and his dwelling place[q] again. 26But if he says, 'I am not pleased with you,' then I am ready; let him do to me whatever seems good to him.[r]"

27The king also said to Zadok the priest, "Aren't you a seer?[s] Go back to the city in peace, with your son Ahimaaz and Jonathan[t] son of Abiathar. You and Abiathar take your two sons with you. 28I will wait at the fords[u] in the desert until word comes from you to inform me." 29So Zadok and Abiathar took the ark of God back to Jerusalem and stayed there.

30But David continued up the Mount of Olives, weeping[v] as he went; his head[w] was covered and he was barefoot. All the people with him covered their heads too and were weeping as they went up. 31Now David had been told, "Ahithophel[x] is among the conspirators with Absalom." So David prayed, "O LORD, turn Ahithophel's counsel into foolishness."

32When David arrived at the summit, where people used to worship God, Hushai the Arkite[y] was there to meet him, his robe torn and dust[z] on his head. 33David said to him, "If you go with me, you will be a burden[a] to me. 34But if you return to the city and say to Absalom, 'I will be your servant, O king; I was your father's servant in the past, but now I will be your servant,'[b] then you can help me by frustrating Ahithophel's advice. 35Won't the priests Zadok and Abiathar be there with you? Tell them anything you hear in the king's palace.[c] 36Their two sons, Ahimaaz son of Zadok and Jonathan[d] son of Abiathar, are there with them. Send them to me with anything you hear."

37So David's friend Hushai[e] arrived at Jerusalem as Absalom[f] was entering the city.

[a]24 Or *Abiathar went up*

15:12 [z]ver 31,34; 2Sa 16:15,23; 1Ch 27:33 [a]Job 19:14; Ps 41:9; 55:13; Jer 9:4 [b]Jos 15:51 [c]Ps 3:1
15:14 [d]2Sa 12:11; 1Ki 2:26; Ps 132:1; Ps 3 Title [e]2Sa 19:9
15:16 [f]2Sa 16:21-22; 20:3
15:18 [g]1Sa 30:14; 2Sa 8:18; 20:7,23; 1Ki 1:38,44; 1Ch 18:17
15:19 [h]2Sa 18:2 [i]Ge 31:15
15:20 [j]1Sa 23:13 [k]2Sa 2:6
15:21 [l]Ru 1:16-17; Pr 17:17
15:23 [m]2Ch 29:16
15:24 [n]2Sa 8:17
15:24 [o]Nu 4:15 [p]1Sa 22:20
15:25 [q]Ex 15:13; Ps 43:3; Jer 25:30
15:26 [r]1Sa 3:18; 2Sa 22:20; 1Ki 10:9
15:27 [s]1Sa 9:9 [t]2Sa 17:17
15:28 [u]2Sa 17:16
15:30 [v]2Sa 19:4; Ps 126:6 [w]Est 6:12; Isa 20:2-4
15:31 [x]ver 12; 2Sa 16:23; 17:14,23
15:32 [y]Jos 16:2 [z]2Sa 1:2
15:33 [a]2Sa 19:35
15:34 [b]2Sa 16:19
15:35 [c]2Sa 17:15-16
15:36 [d]ver 27; 2Sa 17:17
15:37 [e]2Sa 16:16-17; 1Ch 27:33 [f]2Sa 16:15

David and Ziba

16 When David had gone a short distance beyond the summit, there was Ziba,[g] the steward of Mephibosheth, waiting to meet him. He had a string of donkeys saddled and loaded with two hundred loaves of bread, a hundred cakes of raisins, a hundred cakes of figs and a skin of wine.[h]

2 The king asked Ziba, "Why have you brought these?"

Ziba answered, "The donkeys are for the king's household to ride on, the bread and fruit are for the men to eat, and the wine is to refresh[i] those who become exhausted in the desert."

3 The king then asked, "Where is your master's grandson?"[j]

Ziba said to him, "He is staying in Jerusalem, because he thinks, 'Today the house of Israel will give me back my grandfather's kingdom.' "

4 Then the king said to Ziba, "All that belonged to Mephibosheth is now yours."

"I humbly bow," Ziba said. "May I find favor in your eyes, my lord the king."

Shimei Curses David

5 As King David approached Bahurim,[k] a man from the same clan as Saul's family came out from there. His name was Shimei[l] son of Gera, and he cursed[m] as he came out. 6 He pelted David and all the king's officials with stones, though all the troops and the special guard were on David's right and left. 7 As he cursed, Shimei said, "Get out, get out, you man of blood, you scoundrel! 8 The LORD has repaid you for all the blood you shed in the household of Saul, in whose place you have reigned.[n] The LORD has handed the kingdom over to your son Absalom. You have come to ruin because you are a man of blood!"

9 Then Abishai[o] son of Zeruiah said to the king, "Why should this dead dog curse my lord the king? Let me go over and cut off his head."[p]

10 But the king said, "What do you and I have in common, you sons of Zeruiah?[q] If he is cursing because the LORD said to him, 'Curse David,' who can ask, 'Why do you do this?' "[r]

11 David then said to Abishai and all his officials, "My son,[s] who is of my own flesh, is trying to take my life. How much more, then, this Benjamite! Leave him alone; let him curse, for the LORD has told him to.[t] 12 It may be that the LORD will see my distress[u] and repay me with good[v] for the cursing I am receiving today.[w]"

13 So David and his men continued along the road while Shimei was going along the hillside opposite him, cursing as he went and throwing stones at him and showering him with dirt. 14 The king and all the people with him arrived at their destination exhausted.[x] And there he refreshed himself.

The Advice of Hushai and Ahithophel

15 Meanwhile, Absalom[y] and all the men of Israel came to Jerusalem, and Ahithophel[z] was with him. 16 Then Hushai[a] the Arkite, David's friend, went to Absalom and said to him, "Long live the king! Long live the king!"

17 Absalom asked Hushai, "Is this the love you show your friend? Why didn't you go with your friend?"[b]

18 Hushai said to Absalom, "No, the one chosen by the LORD, by these people, and by all the men of Israel—his I will be, and I will remain with him. 19 Furthermore, whom should I serve? Should I not serve the son? Just as I served your father, so I will serve you."[c]

20 Absalom said to Ahithophel, "Give us your advice. What should we do?"

21 Ahithophel answered, "Lie with your father's concubines whom he left to take care of the palace. Then all Israel will hear that you have made yourself a stench in your father's nostrils, and the hands of everyone with you will be strengthened." 22 So they pitched a tent for Absalom on the roof, and he lay with his father's concubines in the sight of all Israel.[d]

23 Now in those days the advice[e] Ahithophel gave was like that of one who inquires of God. That was how both David[f] and Absalom regarded all of Ahithophel's advice.

17 Ahithophel said to Absalom, "I would[a] choose twelve thousand men and set out tonight in pursuit of

[a] *1* Or *Let me*

16:1 [g] 2Sa 9:1-13 [h] 1Sa 25:18
16:2 [i] 2Sa 17:27-29
16:3 [j] 2Sa 9:9-10; 19:26-27
16:5 [k] 2Sa 3:16 [l] 2Sa 19:16-23; 1Ki 2:8-9, 36,44 [m] Ex 22:28
16:8 [n] 2Sa 21:9
16:9 [o] 2Sa 9:8 [p] Ex 22:28; Lk 9:54
16:10 [q] 2Sa 19:22 [r] Ro 9:20
16:11 [s] 2Sa 12:11 [t] Ge 45:5
16:12 [u] Ps 4:1; 25:18 [v] Dt 23:5; Ro 8:28 [w] Ps 109:28
16:14 [x] 2Sa 17:2
16:15 [y] 2Sa 15:37 [z] 2Sa 15:12
16:16 [a] 2Sa 15:37
16:17 [b] 2Sa 19:25
16:19 [c] 2Sa 15:34
16:22 [d] 2Sa 12:11-12; 15:16
16:23 [e] 2Sa 17:14,23 [f] 2Sa 15:12

David. 2 I would[a] attack him while he is weary and weak.[g] I would[a] strike him with terror, and then all the people with him will flee. I would[a] strike down only the king[h] 3 and bring all the people back to you. The death of the man you seek will mean the return of all; all the people will be unharmed." 4 This plan seemed good to Absalom and to all the elders of Israel.

5 But Absalom said, "Summon also Hushai[i] the Arkite, so we can hear what he has to say." 6 When Hushai came to him, Absalom said, "Ahithophel has given this advice. Should we do what he says? If not, give us your opinion."

7 Hushai replied to Absalom, "The advice Ahithophel has given is not good this time. 8 You know your father and his men; they are fighters, and as fierce as a wild bear robbed of her cubs.[j] Besides, your father is an experienced fighter;[k] he will not spend the night with the troops. 9 Even now, he is hidden in a cave or some other place.[l] If he should attack your troops first,[b] whoever hears about it will say, 'There has been a slaughter among the troops who follow Absalom.' 10 Then even the bravest soldier, whose heart is like the heart of a lion,[m] will melt[n] with fear, for all Israel knows that your father is a fighter and that those with him are brave.[o]

11 "So I advise you: Let all Israel, from Dan to Beersheba[p]—as numerous as the sand[q] on the seashore—be gathered to you, with you yourself leading them into battle. 12 Then we will attack him wherever he may be found, and we will fall on him as dew settles on the ground. Neither he nor any of his men will be left alive. 13 If he withdraws into a city, then all Israel will bring ropes to that city, and we will drag it down to the valley[r] until not even a piece of it can be found."

14 Absalom and all the men of Israel said, "The advice[s] of Hushai the Arkite is better than that of Ahithophel."[t] For the LORD had determined to frustrate[u] the good advice of Ahithophel in order to bring disaster[v] on Absalom.[w]

15 Hushai told Zadok and Abiathar, the priests, "Ahithophel has advised Absalom and the elders of Israel to do such and such, but I have advised them to do so and so. 16 Now send a message immediately and tell David, 'Do not spend the night at the fords in the desert;[x] cross over without fail, or the king and all the people with him will be swallowed up.[y]' "

17 Jonathan[z] and Ahimaaz were staying at En Rogel.[a] A servant girl was to go and inform them, and they were to go and tell King David, for they could not risk being seen entering the city. 18 But a young man saw them and told Absalom. So the two of them left quickly and went to the house of a man in Bahurim.[b] He had a well in his courtyard, and they climbed down into it. 19 His wife took a covering and spread it out over the opening of the well and scattered grain over it. No one knew anything about it.[c]

20 When Absalom's men came to the woman[d] at the house, they asked, "Where are Ahimaaz and Jonathan?"

The woman answered them, "They crossed over the brook."[c] The men searched but found no one, so they returned to Jerusalem.

21 After the men had gone, the two climbed out of the well and went to inform King David. They said to him, "Set out and cross the river at once; Ahithophel has advised such and such against you." 22 So David and all the people with him set out and crossed the Jordan. By daybreak, no one was left who had not crossed the Jordan.

23 When Ahithophel saw that his advice[e] had not been followed, he saddled his donkey and set out for his house in his hometown. He put his house in order[f] and then hanged himself. So he died and was buried in his father's tomb.

24 David went to Mahanaim,[g] and Absalom crossed the Jordan with all the men of Israel. 25 Absalom had appointed Amasa[h] over the army in place of Joab. Amasa was the son of a man named Jether,[d][i] an Israelite[e] who had married Abigail,[f] the daughter of Nahash and sister of Zeruiah the mother of Joab. 26 The Israelites and Absalom camped in the land of Gilead.

17:2 [g]2Sa 16:14 [h]1Ki 22:31; Zec 13:7
17:5 [i]2Sa 15:32
17:8 [j]Hos 13:8 [k]1Sa 16:18
17:9 [l]Jer 41:9
17:10 [m]1Ch 12:8 [n]Jos 2:9,11; Eze 21:15 [o]2Sa 23:8; 1Ch 11:11
17:11 [p]Jdg 20:1 [q]Ge 12:2; 22:17; Jos 11:4
17:13 [r]Mic 1:6
17:14 [s]2Sa 16:23 [t]2Sa 15:12 [u]2Sa 15:34; Ne 4:15 [v]Ps 9:16 [w]2Ch 10:8
17:16 [x]2Sa 15:28 [y]2Sa 15:35
17:17 [z]2Sa 15:27,36 [a]Jos 15:7; 18:16
17:18 [b]2Sa 3:16; 16:5
17:19 [c]Jos 2:6
17:20 [d]Ex 1:19; Jos 2:3-5; 1Sa 19:12-17
17:23 [e]2Sa 15:12; 16:23 [f]2Ki 20:1; Mt 27:5
17:24 [g]Ge 32:2; 2Sa 2:8
17:25 [h]2Sa 19:13; 20:4,9-12; 1Ki 2:5,32; 1Ch 12:18 [i]1Ch 2:13-17

[a]*2* Or *will* [b]*9* Or *When some of the men fall at the first attack* [c]*20* Or *"They passed by the sheep pen toward the water."* [d]*25* Hebrew *Ithra,* a variant of *Jether* [e]*25* Hebrew and some Septuagint manuscripts; other Septuagint manuscripts (see also 1 Chron. 2:17) *Ishmaelite* or *Jezreelite* [f]*25* Hebrew *Abigal,* a variant of *Abigail*

27When David came to Mahanaim,
17:27 [j]1Sa 11:1 [k]Dt 3:11; 2Sa 10:1-2; 12:26,29 [l]2Sa 9:4 [m]2Sa 19:31-39; 1Ki 2:7 [n]2Sa 19:31; Ezr 2:61
Shobi son of Nahash[j] from Rabbah[k]
of the Ammonites, and Makir[l] son of
Ammiel from Lo Debar, and Barzillai[m]
the Gileadite[n] from Rogelim 28brought
bedding and bowls and articles of pottery. They also brought wheat and barley, flour and roasted grain, beans and
lentils,[a] 29honey and curds, sheep, and
cheese from cows' milk for David and
17:29 [o]1Ch 12:40 [p]2Sa 16:2; Ro 12:13
his people to eat.[o] For they said, "The
people have become hungry and tired
and thirsty in the desert.[p]"

Absalom's Death

18 David mustered the men who were with him and appointed over them commanders of thousands
18:2 [q]Jdg 7:16; 1Sa 11:11 [r]1Sa 26:6 [s]2Sa 15:19
and commanders of hundreds. 2David
sent the troops out[q]—a third under the
command of Joab, a third under Joab's
brother Abishai[r] son of Zeruiah, and a
third under Ittai[s] the Gittite. The king
told the troops, "I myself will surely
march out with you."

3But the men said, "You must not go
out; if we are forced to flee, they won't
care about us. Even if half of us die, they
18:3 [t]1Sa 18:7 [u]2Sa 21:17
won't care; but you are worth ten[t] thousand of us.[b] It would be better now for
you to give us support from the city."[u]

4The king answered, "I will do whatever seems best to you."

So the king stood beside the gate while all the men marched out in units of hundreds and of thousands. 5The king commanded Joab, Abishai and Ittai, "Be gentle with the young man Absalom for my sake." And all the troops heard the king giving orders concerning Absalom to each of the commanders.

6The army marched into the field to
fight Israel, and the battle took place
18:6 [v]Jos 17:18
in the forest[v] of Ephraim. 7There the
army of Israel was defeated by David's
men, and the casualties that day were
great—twenty thousand men. 8The battle spread out over the whole countryside, and the forest claimed more lives that day than the sword.

9Now Absalom happened to meet
David's men. He was riding his mule,
and as the mule went under the thick
18:9 [w]2Sa 14:26
branches of a large oak, Absalom's head[w]
got caught in the tree. He was left hanging in midair, while the mule he was riding kept on going.

10When one of the men saw this, he

DAY 4 FOUR

▸ GENTLENESS AND MY SERVICE TO OTHERS

2 Samuel 18:1–5

David in this passage feels the lingering effects of old sins. His long-ago affair with Bathsheba demonstrated that he was capable of using power to get what he wanted in life. Now when he sees the same tendency in the life of his son, Absalom, he must be cut to the heart. For Absalom, like his father before him, is resorting to abusive power to get what he wants in life.

Power. What is this swaggering force that makes us puff ourselves up with grandiose self-congratulation? What is there in power that is drawn to brutal politics and cruel force to take what we want in life no matter the cost to others? The world has been a vast weeping planet for scores of centuries because of the lust for power.

But do not think that power is only the province of swaggering warlords like Absalom. Hardly. Power causes people in contemporary corporations to squelch their competition and hurt employees in lesser positions. Power causes ordinarily decent men and women to "do unto others before others do unto them." Power sponsors a new definition of the Golden Rule, "He who has the gold rules." So we come to a day when the powerful can buy the law they need in order to purchase the souls of the weak.

But nowhere is the abuse of power uglier than in the church. When competition, greed and ego displace gentle concern for others, we find the church a center of turmoil instead of a haven of rest. How we need to displace our egos with gentleness, to abandon control and let our spirits minister to others in the house of God! That is our call. That is our responsibility to our fellow human beings.

To begin a study on the topic of Gentleness, the Art of Ego Displacement, turn to the home page on page 1387.

[a]*28* Most Septuagint manuscripts and Syriac; Hebrew *lentils, and roasted grain* [b]*3* Two Hebrew manuscripts, some Septuagint manuscripts and Vulgate; most Hebrew manuscripts *care; for now there are ten thousand like us*

told Joab, "I just saw Absalom hanging in an oak tree."

11Joab said to the man who had told him this, "What! You saw him? Why didn't you strike[x] him to the ground right there? Then I would have had to give you ten shekels[a] of silver and a warrior's belt.[y]"

12But the man replied, "Even if a thousand shekels[b] were weighed out into my hands, I would not lift my hand against the king's son. In our hearing the king commanded you and Abishai and Ittai, 'Protect the young man Absalom for my sake.[c]' 13And if I had put my life in jeopardy[d]—and nothing is hidden from the king[z]—you would have kept your distance from me."

14Joab[a] said, "I'm not going to wait like this for you." So he took three javelins in his hand and plunged them into Absalom's heart while Absalom was still alive in the oak tree. 15And ten of Joab's armor-bearers surrounded Absalom, struck him and killed him.[b]

16Then Joab[c] sounded the trumpet, and the troops stopped pursuing Israel, for Joab halted them. 17They took Absalom, threw him into a big pit in the forest and piled up[d] a large heap of rocks[e] over him. Meanwhile, all the Israelites fled to their homes.

18During his lifetime Absalom had taken a pillar and erected it in the King's Valley[f] as a monument[g] to himself, for he thought, "I have no son[h] to carry on the memory of my name." He named the pillar after himself, and it is called Absalom's Monument to this day.

18:11 [x]2Sa 3:39 [y]1Sa 18:4
18:13 [z]2Sa 14:19-20
18:14 [a]2Sa 2:18; 14:30
18:15 [b]2Sa 12:10
18:16 [c]2Sa 2:28; 20:22
18:17 [d]Jos 7:26 [e]Jos 8:29
18:18 [f]Ge 14:17 [g]Ge 50:5; Nu 32:42; 1Sa 15:12 [h]2Sa 14:27

David Mourns

19Now Ahimaaz[i] son of Zadok said, "Let me run and take the news to the king that the LORD has delivered him from the hand of his enemies.[j]"

20"You are not the one to take the news today," Joab told him. "You may take the news another time, but you must not do so today, because the king's son is dead."

21Then Joab said to a Cushite, "Go, tell the king what you have seen." The Cushite bowed down before Joab and ran off.

22Ahimaaz son of Zadok again said to Joab, "Come what may, please let me run behind the Cushite."

But Joab replied, "My son, why do you want to go? You don't have any news that will bring you a reward."

23He said, "Come what may, I want to run."

So Joab said, "Run!" Then Ahimaaz ran by way of the plain[e] and outran the Cushite.

18:19 [i]2Sa 15:36 [j]ver 31; Jdg 11:36

24While David was sitting between the inner and outer gates, the watchman[k] went up to the roof of the gateway by the wall. As he looked out, he saw a man running alone. 25The watchman called out to the king and reported it.

The king said, "If he is alone, he must have good news." And the man came closer and closer.

26Then the watchman saw another man running, and he called down to the gatekeeper, "Look, another man running alone!"

The king said, "He must be bringing good news,[l] too."

27The watchman said, "It seems to me that the first one runs like[m] Ahimaaz son of Zadok."

"He's a good man," the king said. "He comes with good news."

28Then Ahimaaz called out to the king, "All is well!" He bowed down before the king with his face to the ground and said, "Praise be to the LORD your God! He has delivered up the men who lifted their hands against my lord the king."

29The king asked, "Is the young man Absalom safe?"

Ahimaaz answered, "I saw great confusion just as Joab was about to send the king's servant and me, your servant, but I don't know what it was."

30The king said, "Stand aside and wait here." So he stepped aside and stood there.

31Then the Cushite arrived and said, "My lord the king, hear the good news! The LORD has delivered you today from all who rose up against you."

32The king asked the Cushite, "Is the young man Absalom safe?"

The Cushite replied, "May the enemies of my lord the king and all who

18:24 [k]1Sa 14:16; 2Sa 19:8; 2Ki 9:17; Jer 51:12
18:26 [l]1Ki 1:42; Isa 52:7; 61:1
18:27 [m]2Ki 9:20

[a]*11* That is, about 4 ounces (about 115 grams)
[b]*12* That is, about 25 pounds (about 11 kilograms)
[c]*12* A few Hebrew manuscripts, Septuagint, Vulgate and Syriac; most Hebrew manuscripts may be translated *Absalom, whoever you may be.* [d]*13* Or *Otherwise, if I had acted treacherously toward him*
[e]*23* That is, the plain of the Jordan

LOVE

HOW KINGS LOVE SONS

2 Samuel 18:33

When a child is lost, the broken parents grieve. The Father of Jesus wept in the agony of loss, "My son, my son, my son!" The sobbing around the cross was surpassed only by the sobbing above it.

rise up to harm you be like that young
18:32 [n]Jdg 5:31; 1Sa 25:26 man."[n]
33The king was shaken. He went up
to the room over the gateway and wept.
As he went, he said: "O my son Absalom! My son, my son Absalom! If only I
18:33 [o]Ex 32:32 had died[o] instead of you—O Absalom,
[p]Ge 43:14; 2Sa 19:4; Ro 9:3 my son, my son!"[p]

19 Joab was told, "The king is
weeping and mourning for Absalom." 2And for the whole army the
victory that day was turned into mourning, because on that day the troops
heard it said, "The king is grieving
for his son." 3The men stole into the
city that day as men steal in who are
ashamed when they flee from battle.
4The king covered his face and cried
aloud, "O my son Absalom! O Absalom, my son, my son!"
5Then Joab went into the house to
the king and said, "Today you have humiliated all your men, who have just
saved your life and the lives of your
sons and daughters and the lives of your
wives and concubines. 6You love those
who hate you and hate those who love
you. You have made it clear today that
the commanders and their men mean
nothing to you. I see that you would
be pleased if Absalom were alive today
and all of us were dead. 7Now go out
and encourage your men. I swear by
the LORD that if you don't go out, not
a man will be left with you by nightfall. This will be worse for you than all
19:7 the calamities that have come upon you
[q]Pr 14:28 from your youth till now."[q]
8So the king got up and took his
seat in the gateway. When the men
were told, "The king is sitting in the
19:8 [r]2Sa 15:2 gateway,[r]" they all came before him.

David Returns to Jerusalem

Meanwhile, the Israelites had fled to
their homes. 9Throughout the tribes of
Israel, the people were all arguing with
each other, saying, "The king delivered
us from the hand of our enemies; he
is the one who rescued us from the
hand of the Philistines.[s] But now he has 19:9 [s]2Sa 8:1-14
fled the country because of Absalom;[t] [t]2Sa 15:14
10and Absalom, whom we anointed to
rule over us, has died in battle. So why
do you say nothing about bringing the
king back?"
11King David sent this message to 19:11
Zadok[u] and Abiathar, the priests: "Ask [u]2Sa 15:24
the elders of Judah, 'Why should you
be the last to bring the king back to his
palace, since what is being said throughout Israel has reached the king at his
quarters? 12You are my brothers, my
own flesh and blood. So why should
you be the last to bring back the king?'
13And say to Amasa,[v] 'Are you not my 19:13 [v]2Sa 17:25
own flesh and blood?[w] May God deal [w]Ge 29:14
with me, be it ever so severely,[x] if from [x]Ru 1:17; 1Ki 19:2;
now on you are not the commander of 8:16
my army in place of Joab.[y]'" [y]2Sa 2:13
14He won over the hearts of all the
men of Judah as though they were one
man. They sent word to the king, "Return, you and all your men." 15Then
the king returned and went as far as the
Jordan.
Now the men of Judah had come to 19:15
Gilgal[z] to go out and meet the king and [z]Jos 5:9; 1Sa 11:15
bring him across the Jordan. 16Shimei[a]
son of Gera, the Benjamite from Bahu- 19:16 [a]2Sa 16:5-13;
rim, hurried down with the men of Ju- 1Ki 2:8
dah to meet King David. 17With him
were a thousand Benjamites, along with 19:17
Ziba,[b] the steward of Saul's household,[c] [b]2Sa 9:2; 16:1-2
and his fifteen sons and twenty servants. [c]Ge 43:16
They rushed to the Jordan, where the
king was. 18They crossed at the ford to
take the king's household over and to
do whatever he wished.
When Shimei son of Gera crossed
the Jordan, he fell prostrate before the
king 19and said to him, "May my lord
not hold me guilty. Do not remember
how your servant did wrong on the day 19:19
my lord the king left Jerusalem.[d] May [d]1Sa 22:15; 2Sa 16:6-8
the king put it out of his mind. 20For I
your servant know that I have sinned,
but today I have come here as the first
of the whole house of Joseph to come
down and meet my lord the king."
21Then Abishai[e] son of Zeruiah said, 19:21 [e]1Sa 26:6
"Shouldn't Shimei be put to death [f]Ex 22:28 19:21
for this? He cursed[f] the LORD's [g]1Sa 12:3; 26:9;
anointed."[g] 2Sa 16:7-8

22David replied, "What do you and I have in common, you sons of Zeruiah?[h] This day you have become my adversaries! Should anyone be put to death in Israel today?[i] Do I not know that today I am king over Israel?" 23So the king said to Shimei, "You shall not die." And the king promised him on oath.[j]

24Mephibosheth,[k] Saul's grandson, also went down to meet the king. He had not taken care of his feet or trimmed his mustache or washed his clothes from the day the king left until the day he returned safely. 25When he came from Jerusalem to meet the king, the king asked him, "Why didn't you go with me,[l] Mephibosheth?"

26He said, "My lord the king, since I your servant am lame,[m] I said, 'I will have my donkey saddled and will ride on it, so I can go with the king.' But Ziba[n] my servant betrayed me. 27And he has slandered your servant to my lord the king. My lord the king is like an angel[o] of God; so do whatever pleases you. 28All my grandfather's descendants deserved nothing but death[p] from my lord the king, but you gave your servant a place among those who eat at your table.[q] So what right do I have to make any more appeals to the king?"

29The king said to him, "Why say more? I order you and Ziba to divide the fields."

30Mephibosheth said to the king, "Let him take everything, now that my lord the king has arrived home safely."

31Barzillai[r] the Gileadite also came down from Rogelim to cross the Jordan with the king and to send him on his way from there. 32Now Barzillai was a very old man, eighty years of age. He had provided for the king during his stay in Mahanaim, for he was a very wealthy[s] man. 33The king said to Barzillai, "Cross over with me and stay with me in Jerusalem, and I will provide for you."

34But Barzillai answered the king, "How many more years will I live, that I should go up to Jerusalem with the king? 35I am now eighty[t] years old. Can I tell the difference between what is good and what is not? Can your servant taste what he eats and drinks? Can I still hear the voices of men and women singers?[u] Why should your servant be an added[v] burden to my lord the king? 36Your servant will cross over the Jordan with the king for a short distance, but why should the king reward me in this way? 37Let your servant return, that I may die in my own town near the tomb of my father[w] and mother. But here is your servant Kimham.[x] Let him cross over with my lord the king. Do for him whatever pleases you."

38The king said, "Kimham shall cross over with me, and I will do for him whatever pleases you. And anything you desire from me I will do for you."

39So all the people crossed the Jordan, and then the king crossed over. The king kissed Barzillai and gave him his blessing,[y] and Barzillai returned to his home.

40When the king crossed over to Gilgal, Kimham crossed with him. All the troops of Judah and half the troops of Israel had taken the king over.

41Soon all the men of Israel were coming to the king and saying to him, "Why did our brothers, the men of Judah, steal the king away and bring him and his household across the Jordan, together with all his men?"[z]

42All the men of Judah answered the men of Israel, "We did this because the king is closely related to us. Why are you angry about it? Have we eaten any of the king's provisions? Have we taken anything for ourselves?"

43Then the men of Israel[a] answered the men of Judah, "We have ten shares in the king; and besides, we have a greater claim on David than you have. So why do you treat us with contempt? Were we not the first to speak of bringing back our king?"

But the men of Judah responded even more harshly than the men of Israel.

Sheba Rebels Against David

20 Now a troublemaker named Sheba son of Bicri, a Benjamite, happened to be there. He sounded the trumpet and shouted,

"We have no share[b] in David,[c]
no part in Jesse's son![d]
Every man to his tent, O Israel!"

2So all the men of Israel deserted David to follow Sheba son of Bicri. But the men of Judah stayed by their king all the way from the Jordan to Jerusalem.

19:22 [h]2Sa 2:18; 16:10 [i]1Sa 11:13
19:23 [j]1Ki 2:8,42
19:24 [k]2Sa 4:4; 9:6-10
19:25 [l]2Sa 16:17
19:26 [m]Lev 21:18 [n]2Sa 9:2
19:27 [o]1Sa 29:9; 2Sa 14:17,20
19:28 [p]2Sa 16:8; 21:6-9 [q]2Sa 9:7,13
19:31 [r]2Sa 17:27-29,27; 1Ki 2:7
19:32 [s]1Sa 25:2; 2Sa 17:27
19:35 [t]Ps 90:10 [u]2Ch 35:25; Ezr 2:65; Ecc 2:8; 12:1; Isa 5:11-12 [v]2Sa 15:33
19:37 [w]Ge 49:29; 1Ki 2:7 [x]ver 40; Jer 41:17
19:39 [y]Ge 31:55; Ge 47:7
19:41 [z]Jdg 8:1; 12:1
19:43 [a]2Sa 5:1
20:1 [b]Ge 31:14 [c]Ge 29:14; 1Ki 12:16 [d]1Sa 22:7-8; 2Ch 10:16

3 When David returned to his palace
in Jerusalem, he took the ten concu-
20:3 [e]2Sa 15:16; 16:21-22
bines[e] he had left to take care of the
palace and put them in a house under
guard. He provided for them, but did
not lie with them. They were kept in
confinement till the day of their death,
living as widows.

20:4 [f]2Sa 17:25; 19:13
4 Then the king said to Amasa,[f] "Summon the men of Judah to come to me
within three days, and be here yourself." 5 But when Amasa went to summon Judah, he took longer than the
time the king had set for him.

20:6 [g]2Sa 21:17
6 David said to Abishai,[g] "Now Sheba son of Bicri will do us more harm
than Absalom did. Take your master's
men and pursue him, or he will find
fortified cities and escape from us." 7 So
20:7 [h]1Sa 30:14; 2Sa 8:18; 15:18; 1Ki 1:38
Joab's men and the Kerethites[h] and Pelethites and all the mighty warriors went
out under the command of Abishai.
They marched out from Jerusalem to
pursue Sheba son of Bicri.

8 While they were at the great rock
20:8 [i]Jos 9:3 [j]2Sa 2:18
in Gibeon,[i] Amasa came to meet them.
Joab[j] was wearing his military tunic,
and strapped over it at his waist was a
belt with a dagger in its sheath. As he
stepped forward, it dropped out of its
sheath.

9 Joab said to Amasa, "How are you,
my brother?" Then Joab took Amasa
by the beard with his right hand to
20:10 [k]Jdg 3:21; 2Sa 2:23; 3:27 [l]1Ki 2:5
kiss him. 10 Amasa was not on his guard
against the dagger[k] in Joab's[l] hand, and
Joab plunged it into his belly, and his
intestines spilled out on the ground.
Without being stabbed again, Amasa
died. Then Joab and his brother Abishai pursued Sheba son of Bicri.

11 One of Joab's men stood beside
Amasa and said, "Whoever favors Joab,
and whoever is for David, let him follow Joab!" 12 Amasa lay wallowing in his
blood in the middle of the road, and
the man saw that all the troops came to
20:12 [m]2Sa 2:23
a halt[m] there. When he realized that everyone who came up to Amasa stopped,
he dragged him from the road into a
field and threw a garment over him.
13 After Amasa had been removed from
the road, all the men went on with Joab
to pursue Sheba son of Bicri.

14 Sheba passed through all the tribes
of Israel to Abel Beth Maacah[a] and
20:14 [n]Nu 21:16
through the entire region of the Berites,[n]
who gathered together and followed
him. 15 All the troops with Joab came
and besieged Sheba in Abel Beth
Maacah.[o] They built a siege ramp[p] up
20:15 [o]1Ki 15:20; 2Ki 15:29 [p]2Ki 19:32; Isa 37:33; Jer 6:6; 32:24
to the city, and it stood against the out-
er fortifications. While they were battering the wall to bring it down, 16 a
20:16 [q]2Sa 14:2
wise woman[q] called from the city, "Listen! Listen! Tell Joab to come here so I
can speak to him." 17 He went toward
her, and she asked, "Are you Joab?"

"I am," he answered.

She said, "Listen to what your servant has to say."

"I'm listening," he said.

18 She continued, "Long ago they used
to say, 'Get your answer at Abel,' and
20:19 [r]Dt 2:26 [s]1Sa 26:19; 2Sa 21:3
that settled it. 19 We are the peaceful[r]
and faithful in Israel. You are trying to
destroy a city that is a mother in Israel.
Why do you want to swallow up the
LORD's inheritance?"[s]

20 "Far be it from me!" Joab replied,
"Far be it from me to swallow up or
destroy! 21 That is not the case. A man
named Sheba son of Bicri, from the hill
country of Ephraim, has lifted up his
hand against the king, against David.
Hand over this one man, and I'll withdraw from the city."

20:21 [t]2Sa 4:8
The woman said to Joab, "His head[t]
will be thrown to you from the wall."

20:22 [u]Ecc 9:13
22 Then the woman went to all the
people with her wise advice,[u] and they
cut off the head of Sheba son of Bicri
and threw it to Joab. So he sounded the
trumpet, and his men dispersed from
the city, each returning to his home.
And Joab went back to the king in Jerusalem.

20:23 [v]2Sa 2:28; 8:16-18; 24:2
23 Joab[v] was over Israel's entire army;
Benaiah son of Jehoiada was over the
Kerethites and Pelethites; 24 Adoniram[b] [w]
20:24 [w]1Ki 4:6; 5:14; 12:18; 2Ch 10:18 [x]2Sa 8:16; 1Ki 4:3
was in charge of forced labor; Je-
hoshaphat[x] son of Ahilud was recorder;
25 Sheva was secretary; Zadok[y] and Abi-
20:25 [y]1Sa 2:35; 2Sa 8:17
athar were priests; 26 and Ira the Jairite
was David's priest.

The Gibeonites Avenged

21:1 [z]Ge 12:10; Dt 32:24 [a]Ex 32:11
21 During the reign of David, there
was a famine[z] for three successive years; so David sought[a] the face of
the LORD. The LORD said, "It is on
account of Saul and his blood-stained

[a] *14* Or *Abel, even Beth Maacah*; also in verse 15
[b] *24* Some Septuagint manuscripts (see also 1 Kings 4:6 and 5:14); Hebrew *Adoram*

house; it is because he put the Gibeonites to death."
[2]The king summoned the Gibeon-
21:2 [b]Jos 9:15 ites[b] and spoke to them. (Now the Gibeonites were not a part of Israel but
were survivors of the Amorites; the Israelites had sworn to ⌞spare⌟ them, but
Saul in his zeal for Israel and Judah
had tried to annihilate them.) [3]David
asked the Gibeonites, "What shall I do
for you? How shall I make amends so
21:3 that you will bless the LORD's inheri-
[c]1Sa 26:19; 2Sa 20:19 tance?"[c]
[4]The Gibeonites answered him, "We
have no right to demand silver or gold
from Saul or his family, nor do we have
21:4 the right to put anyone in Israel to
[d]Nu 35:33-34 death."[d]
"What do you want me to do for
you?" David asked.
[5]They answered the king, "As for
the man who destroyed us and plotted
against us so that we have been deci-
mated and have no place anywhere in
Israel, [6]let seven of his male descendants
21:6 be given to us to be killed and exposed[e]
[e]Nu 25:4 before the LORD at Gibeah of Saul—
[f]1Sa 10:24 the LORD's chosen[f] one."
So the king said, "I will give them to
you."
21:7 [7]The king spared Mephibosheth[g] son
[g]2Sa 4:4 of Jonathan, the son of Saul, because
[h]1Sa 18:3; 20:8,15; of the oath[h] before the LORD between
2Sa 9:7 David and Jonathan son of Saul. [8]But
the king took Armoni and Mephibo-
21:8 sheth, the two sons of Aiah's daughter
[i]2Sa 3:7 Rizpah,[i] whom she had borne to Saul,
[j]1Sa 18:19 together with the five sons of Saul's
daughter Merab,[a] whom she had borne
to Adriel son of Barzillai the Mehola-
thite.[j] [9]He handed them over to the
Gibeonites, who killed and exposed
them on a hill before the LORD. All
21:9 seven of them fell together; they were
[k]2Sa 16:8 put to death[k] during the first days of
[l]Ru 1:22 the harvest, just as the barley harvest
was beginning.[l]
[10]Rizpah daughter of Aiah took sackcloth and spread it out for herself on
a rock. From the beginning of the harvest till the rain poured down from the
heavens on the bodies, she did not let
the birds of the air touch them by day
21:10 [m]ver 8; or the wild animals by night.[m] [11]When
Dt 21:23; David was told what Aiah's daughter
1Sa 17:44 Rizpah, Saul's concubine, had done,
21:12 [12]he went and took the bones of Saul[n]
[n]1Sa 31:11-13 and his son Jonathan from the citizens
of Jabesh Gilead. (They had taken them
secretly from the public square at Beth
Shan,[o] where the Philistines had hung[p] 21:12 [o]Jos 17:11
them after they struck Saul down on [p]1Sa 31:10
Gilboa.) [13]David brought the bones of
Saul and his son Jonathan from there,
and the bones of those who had been
killed and exposed were gathered up.
[14]They buried the bones of Saul and
his son Jonathan in the tomb of Saul's
father Kish, at Zela[q] in Benjamin, and 21:14
did everything the king commanded. [q]Jos 18:28 [r]Jos 7:26
After that,[r] God answered prayer[s] in be- [s]2Sa 24:25
half of the land.

Wars Against the Philistines

[15]Once again there was a battle be- 21:15
tween the Philistines[t] and Israel. David [t]2Sa 5:25
went down with his men to fight against
the Philistines, and he became exhausted. [16]And Ishbi-Benob, one of the
descendants of Rapha, whose bronze
spearhead weighed three hundred shekels[b] and who was armed with a new
⌞sword⌟, said he would kill David. [17]But 21:17
Abishai[u] son of Zeruiah came to Da- [u]2Sa 20:6
vid's rescue; he struck the Philistine [v]1Ki 11:36 [w]2Sa 18:3
down and killed him. Then David's
men swore to him, saying, "Never again
will you go out with us to battle, so
that the lamp[v] of Israel will not be
extinguished.[w]"
[18]In the course of time, there was
another battle with the Philistines, at
Gob. At that time Sibbecai[x] the Hu- 21:18 [x]1Ch 11:29;
shathite killed Saph, one of the descen- 20:4; 27:11
dants of Rapha.
[19]In another battle with the Philistines at Gob, Elhanan son of Jaare-
Oregim[c] the Bethlehemite killed Goliath[d] the Gittite, who had a spear with a
shaft like a weaver's rod.[y] 21:19 [y]1Sa 17:7
[20]In still another battle, which took
place at Gath, there was a huge man
with six fingers on each hand and six
toes on each foot—twenty-four in all.
He also was descended from Rapha.
[21]When he taunted Israel, Jonathan son 21:21
of Shimeah,[z] David's brother, killed [z]1Sa 16:9
him.
[22]These four were descendants of Ra-

[a] *8* Two Hebrew manuscripts, some Septuagint manuscripts and Syriac (see also 1 Samuel 18:19); most Hebrew and Septuagint manuscripts *Michal*
[b] *16* That is, about 7 1/2 pounds (about 3.5 kilograms) [c] *19* Or *son of Jair the weaver*
[d] *19* Hebrew and Septuagint; 1 Chron. 20:5 *son of Jair killed Lahmi the brother of Goliath*

pha in Gath, and they fell at the hands of David and his men.

David's Song of Praise

22:1 [a]Ex 15:1; Jdg 5:1; Ps 18:2-50

22 David sang[a] to the LORD the
words of this song when the
LORD delivered him from the hand of
all his enemies and from the hand of
Saul. 2He said:

22:2 [b]Dt 32:4; Ps 71:3 [c]Ps 31:3; 91:2 [d]Ps 144:2

"The LORD is my rock,[b] my fortress[c]
and my deliverer;[d]

PEACE

THE STRONGHOLD

2 Samuel 22:2

"Would you escape the moral storms?"
All agonies decry.
Hide within the cliffs of God
Until those storms pass by.

22:3 [e]Dt 32:37; Jer 16:19 [f]Ge 15:1 [g]Lk 1:69 [h]Ps 9:9

3 my God is my rock, in whom I
take refuge,[e]
my shield[f] and the horn[a][g] of my
salvation.
He is my stronghold,[h] my refuge and
my savior—
from violent men you save me.

22:4 [i]Ps 48:1; 96:4

4I call to the LORD, who is worthy[i]
of praise,
and I am saved from my enemies.

22:5 [j]Ps 69:14-15; 93:4; Jnh 2:3

5"The waves[j] of death swirled about
me;
the torrents of destruction
overwhelmed me.

22:6 [k]Ps 116:3

6The cords of the grave[b][k] coiled around
me;
the snares of death confronted me.

22:7 [l]Ps 120:1 [m]Ps 34:6,15; 116:4

7In my distress[l] I called[m] to the
LORD;
I called out to my God.
From his temple he heard my voice;
my cry came to his ears.

22:8 [n]Jdg 5:4; Ps 97:4 [o]Ps 77:18 [p]Job 26:11

8"The earth[n] trembled and quaked,[o]
the foundations[p] of the heavens[c]
shook;
they trembled because he was
angry.

22:9 [q]Ps 97:3; Heb 12:29

9Smoke rose from his nostrils;
consuming fire[q] came from his
mouth,
burning coals blazed out of it.

22:10 [r]1Ki 8:12; Na 1:3

10He parted the heavens and came
down;
dark clouds[r] were under his feet.

22:11 [s]Ps 104:3

11He mounted the cherubim and flew;
he soared[d] on the wings of the
wind.[s]
12He made darkness his canopy
around him—
the dark[e] rain clouds of the sky.

22:13 [t]ver 9

13Out of the brightness of his presence
bolts of lightning[t] blazed forth.

22:14 [u]1Sa 2:10

14The LORD thundered[u] from heaven;
the voice of the Most High
resounded.

22:15 [v]Dt 32:23

15He shot arrows[v] and scattered ⌊the
enemies⌋,
bolts of lightning and routed them.

22:16 [w]Na 1:4

16The valleys of the sea were exposed
and the foundations of the earth
laid bare
at the rebuke[w] of the LORD,
at the blast of breath from his
nostrils.

22:17 [x]Ps 144:7 [y]Ex 2:10

17"He reached down from on high[x]
and took hold of me;
he drew[y] me out of deep waters.
18He rescued me from my powerful
enemy,
from my foes, who were too
strong for me.

22:19 [z]Ps 23:4

19They confronted me in the day of
my disaster,
but the LORD was my support.[z]

22:20 [a]Ps 31:8 [b]Ps 118:5 [c]Ps 22:8 [d]2Sa 15:26

20He brought me out into a spacious[a]
place;
he rescued[b] me because he
delighted[c] in me.[d]

22:21 [e]1Sa 26:23 [f]Ps 24:4

21"The LORD has dealt with me
according to my
righteousness;[e]
according to the cleanness of my
hands[f] he has rewarded me.

22:22 [g]Ge 18:19; Ps 128:1; Pr 8:32

22For I have kept[g] the ways of the
LORD;
I have not done evil by turning
from my God.

22:23 [h]Dt 6:4-9; Ps 119:30-32 [i]Ps 119:102

23All his laws are before me;[h]
I have not turned[i] away from his
decrees.

22:24 [j]Ge 6:9; Eph 1:4

24I have been blameless[j] before him
and have kept myself from sin.

22:25 [k]ver 21

25The Lord has rewarded me
according to my
righteousness,[k]

[a]*3 Horn* here symbolizes strength. [b]*6* Hebrew *Sheol* [c]*8* Hebrew; Vulgate and Syriac (see also Psalm 18:7) *mountains* [d]*11* Many Hebrew manuscripts (see also Psalm 18:10); most Hebrew manuscripts *appeared* [e]*12* Septuagint and Vulgate (see also Psalm 18:11); Hebrew *massed*

according to my cleanness[a] in his
sight.
26 "To the faithful you show yourself
faithful,
to the blameless you show yourself
blameless,
27 to the pure[l] you show yourself pure,
but to the crooked you show
yourself shrewd.[m]
28 You save the humble,[n]
but your eyes are on the haughty
to bring them low.[o]
29 You are my lamp,[p] O LORD;
the LORD turns my darkness into
light.
30 With your help I can advance
against a troop[b];
with my God I can scale a wall.

31 "As for God, his way is perfect;[q]
the word of the LORD is
flawless.[r]
He is a shield
for all who take refuge in him.
32 For who is God besides the LORD?
And who is the Rock[s] except our
God?
33 It is God who arms me with
strength[c]
and makes my way perfect.
34 He makes my feet like the feet of a
deer;[t]
he enables me to stand on the
heights.[u]
35 He trains my hands[v] for battle;
my arms can bend a bow of
bronze.
36 You give me your shield[w] of victory;
you stoop down to make me great.
37 You broaden the path[x] beneath me,
so that my ankles do not turn.

38 "I pursued my enemies and crushed
them;
I did not turn back till they were
destroyed.
39 I crushed[y] them completely, and
they could not rise;
they fell beneath my feet.
40 You armed me with strength for
battle;
you made my adversaries bow at
my feet.[z]
41 You made my enemies turn their
backs[a] in flight,
and I destroyed my foes.
42 They cried for help,[b] but there was
no one to save them—[c]

22:27 [l]Mt 5:8 [m]Lev 26:23-24
22:28 [n]Ex 3:8; Ps 72:12-13 [o]Isa 2:12,17; 5:15
22:29 [p]Ps 27:1
22:31 [q]Dt 32:4; Mt 5:48 [r]Ps 12:6; 119:140; Pr 30:5-6
22:32 [s]1Sa 2:2
22:34 [t]Hab 3:19 [u]Dt 32:13
22:35 [v]Ps 144:1
22:36 [w]Eph 6:16
22:37 [x]Pr 4:11
22:39 [y]Mal 4:3
22:40 [z]Ps 44:5
22:41 [a]Ex 23:27
22:42 [b]Isa 1:15 [c]Ps 50:22

to the LORD, but he did not
answer.
43 I beat them as fine as the dust of the
earth;
I pounded and trampled[d] them
like mud[e] in the streets.
44 "You have delivered[f] me from the
attacks of my people;
you have preserved[g] me as the
head of nations.
People[h] I did not know are subject
to me,
45 and foreigners come cringing[i] to
me;
as soon as they hear me, they obey
me.
46 They all lose heart;
they come trembling[d][j] from their
strongholds.

47 "The LORD lives! Praise be to my
Rock!
Exalted be God, the Rock, my
Savior![k]
48 He is the God who avenges me,[l]
who puts the nations under me,
49 who sets me free from my
enemies.[m]
You exalted me above my foes;
from violent men you rescued
me.
50 Therefore I will praise you,
O LORD, among the
nations;
I will sing praises to your name.[n]
51 He gives his king great victories;[o]
he shows unfailing kindness to his
anointed,[p]
to David[q] and his descendants
forever."[r]

22:43 [d]Mic 7:10 [e]Isa 10:6; Mic 7:10
22:44 [f]2Sa 3:1 [g]Dt 28:13 [h]2Sa 8:1-14; Isa 55:3-5
22:45 [i]Ps 66:3; 81:15
22:46 [j]Mic 7:17
22:47 [k]Ps 89:26
22:48 [l]Ps 94:1; 144:2; 1Sa 25:39
22:49 [m]Ps 140:1,4
22:50 [n]Ro 15:9*
22:51 [o]Ps 144:9-10 [p]Ps 89:20 [q]2Sa 7:13 [r]Ps 89:24,29

The Last Words of David

23 These are the last words of David:

"The oracle of David son of Jesse,
the oracle of the man exalted[s] by
the Most High,
the man anointed[t] by the God of
Jacob,
Israel's singer of songs[e]:

23:1 [s]2Sa 7:8-9; Ps 78:70-71; 89:27 [t]1Sa 16:12-13; Ps 89:20

[a]*25* Hebrew; Septuagint and Vulgate (see also Psalm 18:24) *to the cleanness of my hands* [b]*30* Or *can run through a barricade* [c]*33* Dead Sea Scrolls, some Septuagint manuscripts, Vulgate and Syriac (see also Psalm 18:32); Masoretic Text *who is my strong refuge* [d]*46* Some Septuagint manuscripts and Vulgate (see also Psalm 18:45); Masoretic Text *they arm themselves.* [e]*1* Or *Israel's beloved singer*

23:2 [u]Mt 22:43; 2Pe 1:21

2 “The Spirit[u] of the LORD spoke
through me;
his word was on my tongue.
3 The God of Israel spoke,
the Rock[v] of Israel said to me:
‘When one rules over men in
righteousness,[w]
when he rules in the fear of God,[x]
4 he is like the light of morning at
sunrise[y]
on a cloudless morning,
like the brightness after rain
that brings the grass from the
earth.’

23:3 [v]Dt 32:4; 2Sa 22:2,32 [w]Ps 72:3 [x]2Ch 19:7,9; Isa 11:1-5

23:4 [y]Jdg 5:31; Ps 89:36

5 “Is not my house right with God?
Has he not made with me an
everlasting covenant,[z]
arranged and secured in every
part?
Will he not bring to fruition my
salvation
and grant me my every desire?
6 But evil men are all to be cast aside
like thorns,[a]
which are not gathered with the
hand.
7 Whoever touches thorns
uses a tool of iron or the shaft of
a spear;
they are burned up where they
lie.”

23:5 [z]Ps 89:29; Isa 55:3

23:6 [a]Mt 13:40-41

David's Mighty Men

8 These are the names of David's
mighty men:
Josheb-Basshebeth,[a] a Tahkemonite,[b]
was chief of the Three; he raised his
spear against eight hundred men, whom
he killed[c] in one encounter.

GENTLENESS

THE HIGH, THE PROUD, THE GENTLE

2 Samuel 23:8–11

These mighty men were great heroes, chosen in a season of gentleness. It is doubtful that they appeared either great or gentle to themselves. Duty was the virtue that awarded them both attributes.

23:9 [b]1Ch 27:4 [c]1Ch 8:4

9 Next to him was Eleazar son of Dodai[b] the Ahohite.[c] As one of the three
mighty men, he was with David when
they taunted the Philistines gathered
⌊at Pas Dammim⌋[d] for battle. Then the
men of Israel retreated, 10 but he stood
his ground and struck down the Philistines till his hand grew tired and froze
to the sword. The LORD brought about
a great victory that day. The troops returned to Eleazar, but only to strip the
dead.
11 Next to him was Shammah son of
Agee the Hararite. When the Philistines
banded together at a place where there
was a field full of lentils, Israel's troops
fled from them. 12 But Shammah took
his stand in the middle of the field. He
defended it and struck the Philistines
down, and the LORD brought about a
great victory.
13 During harvest time, three of the
thirty chief men came down to David
at the cave of Adullam,[d] while a band
of Philistines was encamped in the Valley of Rephaim.[e] 14 At that time David
was in the stronghold,[f] and the Philistine garrison was at Bethlehem.[g] 15 David longed for water and said, “Oh, that
someone would get me a drink of water
from the well near the gate of Bethlehem!” 16 So the three mighty men broke
through the Philistine lines, drew water from the well near the gate of Bethlehem and carried it back to David.
But he refused to drink it; instead, he
poured[h] it out before the LORD. 17 “Far
be it from me, O LORD, to do this!” he
said. “Is it not the blood[i] of men who
went at the risk of their lives?” And David would not drink it.
Such were the exploits of the three
mighty men.
18 Abishai[j] the brother of Joab son
of Zeruiah was chief of the Three.[e] He
raised his spear against three hundred
men, whom he killed, and so he became as famous as the Three. 19 Was
he not held in greater honor than the
Three? He became their commander,
even though he was not included among
them.
20 Benaiah[k] son of Jehoiada was a valiant fighter from Kabzeel,[l] who per-

23:13 [d]1Sa 22:1 [e]2Sa 5:18

23:14 [f]1Sa 22:4-5 [g]Ru 1:19

23:16 [h]Ge 35:14

23:17 [i]Lev 17:10-12

23:18 [j]2Sa 10:10,14; 1Ch 11:20

23:20 [k]2Sa 8:18; 20:23 [l]Jos 15:21

[a]8 Hebrew; some Septuagint manuscripts suggest *Ish-Bosheth,* that is, *Esh-Baal* (see also 1 Chron. 11:11 *Jashobeam*). [b]8 Probably a variant of *Hacmonite* (see 1 Chron. 11:11) [c]8 Some Septuagint manuscripts (see also 1 Chron. 11:11); Hebrew and other Septuagint manuscripts *Three; it was Adino the Eznite who killed eight hundred men* [d]9 See 1 Chron. 11:13; Hebrew *gathered there.* [e]18 Most Hebrew manuscripts (see also 1 Chron. 11:20); two Hebrew manuscripts and Syriac *Thirty*

formed great exploits. He struck down two of Moab's best men. He also went down into a pit on a snowy day and killed a lion. 21And he struck down a huge Egyptian. Although the Egyptian had a spear in his hand, Benaiah went against him with a club. He snatched the spear from the Egyptian's hand and killed him with his own spear. 22Such were the exploits of Benaiah son of Jehoiada; he too was as famous as the three mighty men. 23He was held in greater honor than any of the Thirty, but he was not included among the Three. And David put him in charge of his bodyguard.

24Among the Thirty were:

23:24 [m]2Sa 2:18
Asahel[m] the brother of Joab,
Elhanan son of Dodo from Bethlehem,
25Shammah the Harodite,
23:25 [n]Jdg 7:1; 1Ch 11:27
Elika the Harodite,[n]
26Helez[o] the Paltite,
23:26 [o]1Ch 27:10
Ira son of Ikkesh from Tekoa,
27Abiezer from Anathoth,[p]
23:27 [p]Jos 21:18
Mebunnai[a] the Hushathite,
28Zalmon the Ahohite,
23:28 [q]1Ch 27:13 [r]2Ki 25:23; Ne 7:26
Maharai[q] the Netophathite,[r]
29Heled[b] son of Baanah the Netophathite,
23:29 [s]Jos 15:57
Ithai son of Ribai from Gibeah[s] in Benjamin,
23:30 [t]Jdg 12:13 [u]Jos 24:30
30Benaiah the Pirathonite,[t]
Hiddai[c] from the ravines of Gaash,[u]
31Abi-Albon the Arbathite,
23:31 [v]2Sa 3:16
Azmaveth the Barhumite,[v]
32Eliahba the Shaalbonite,
the sons of Jashen,
Jonathan 33son of[d] Shammah the Hararite,
Ahiam son of Sharar[e] the Hararite,
34Eliphelet son of Ahasbai the Maacathite,
23:34 [w]2Sa 11:3 [x]2Sa 15:12
Eliam[w] son of Ahithophel[x] the Gilonite,
23:35 [y]Jos 12:22
35Hezro the Carmelite,[y]
Paarai the Arbite,
23:36 [z]1Sa 14:47
36Igal son of Nathan from Zobah,[z]
the son of Hagri,[f]
37Zelek the Ammonite,
Naharai the Beerothite, the armor-bearer of Joab son of Zeruiah,
23:38 [a]2Sa 20:26; 1Ch 2:53
38Ira the Ithrite,[a]
Gareb the Ithrite
23:39 [b]2Sa 11:3
39and Uriah[b] the Hittite.
There were thirty-seven in all.

David Counts the Fighting Men

24:1 [c]Jos 9:15 [d]1Ch 27:23

24 Again[c] the anger of the LORD burned against Israel, and he incited David against them, saying, "Go and take a census of[d] Israel and Judah."

24:2 [e]2Sa 20:23 [f]Jdg 20:1; 2Sa 3:10

2So the king said to Joab[e] and the army commanders[g] with him, "Go throughout the tribes of Israel from Dan to Beersheba[f] and enroll the fighting men, so that I may know how many there are."

24:3 [g]Dt 1:11

3But Joab replied to the king, "May the LORD your God multiply the troops a hundred times over,[g] and may the eyes of my lord the king see it. But why does my lord the king want to do such a thing?"

4The king's word, however, overruled Joab and the army commanders; so they left the presence of the king to enroll the fighting men of Israel.

24:5 [h]Dt 2:36; Jos 13:9 [i]Nu 21:32

24:6 [j]Ge 10:19; Jos 19:28; Jdg 1:31

24:7 [k]Jos 19:29 [l]Ge 21:22-33 [m]Dt 1:7; Jos 11:3

5After crossing the Jordan, they camped near Aroer,[h] south of the town in the gorge, and then went through Gad and on to Jazer.[i] 6They went to Gilead and the region of Tahtim Hodshi, and on to Dan Jaan and around toward Sidon.[j] 7Then they went toward the fortress of Tyre[k] and all the towns of the Hivites and Canaanites. Finally, they went on to Beersheba[l] in the Negev[m] of Judah.

8After they had gone through the entire land, they came back to Jerusalem at the end of nine months and twenty days.

24:9 [n]Nu 1:44-46; 1Ch 21:5

9Joab reported the number of the fighting men to the king: In Israel there were eight hundred thousand able-bodied men who could handle a sword, and in Judah five hundred thousand.[n]

[a]*27* Hebrew; some Septuagint manuscripts (see also 1 Chron. 11:29) *Sibbecai* [b]*29* Some Hebrew manuscripts and Vulgate (see also 1 Chron. 11:30); most Hebrew manuscripts *Heleb* [c]*30* Hebrew; some Septuagint manuscripts (see also 1 Chron. 11:32) *Hurai* [d]*33* Some Septuagint manuscripts (see also 1 Chron. 11:34); Hebrew does not have *son of.* [e]*33* Hebrew; some Septuagint manuscripts (see also 1 Chron. 11:35) *Sacar* [f]*36* Some Septuagint manuscripts (see also 1 Chron. 11:38); Hebrew *Haggadi* [g]*2* Septuagint (see also verse 4 and 1 Chron. 21:2); Hebrew *Joab the army commander*

24:10 [o]1Sa 24:5 [p]2Sa 12:13 [q]Nu 12:11; 1Sa 13:13
10David was conscience-stricken[o] af-
ter he had counted the fighting men,
and he said to the LORD, "I have
sinned[p] greatly in what I have done.
Now, O LORD, I beg you, take away
the guilt of your servant. I have done a
very foolish thing.[q]"
11Before David got up the next morning, the word of the LORD had come to
24:11 [r]1Sa 22:5 [s]1Sa 9:9; 1Ch 29:29
Gad[r] the prophet, David's seer:[s] 12"Go
and tell David, 'This is what the LORD
says: I am giving you three options.
Choose one of them for me to carry out
against you.' "
13So Gad went to David and said to
him, "Shall there come upon you three[a]
24:13 [t]Dt 28:38-42, 48; Eze 14:21 [u]Lev 26:25
years of famine[t] in your land? Or three
months of fleeing from your enemies
while they pursue you? Or three days of
plague[u] in your land? Now then, think
it over and decide how I should answer
the one who sent me."
14David said to Gad, "I am in deep
distress. Let us fall into the hands of
24:14 [v]Ne 9:28; Ps 51:1; 103:8,13; 130:4
the LORD, for his mercy[v] is great; but
do not let me fall into the hands of
men."
15So the LORD sent a plague on Israel from that morning until the end of
the time designated, and seventy thousand of the people from Dan to Beer-
24:15 [w]1Ch 27:24
sheba died.[w] 16When the angel stretched
24:16 [x]Ge 6:6; 1Sa 15:11 [y]Ex 12:23; Ac 12:23
out his hand to destroy Jerusalem, the
LORD was grieved[x] because of the calamity and said to the angel who was af-
flicting the people, "Enough! Withdraw
your hand." The angel of the LORD[y]
was then at the threshing floor of Araunah the Jebusite.
17When David saw the angel who
was striking down the people, he said
to the LORD, "I am the one who has
sinned and done wrong. These are but
24:17 [z]Ps 74:1 [a]Jnh 1:12
sheep.[z] What have they done? Let your
hand fall upon me and my family."[a]

David Builds an Altar

18On that day Gad went to David
and said to him, "Go up and build an
altar to the LORD on the threshing floor
of Araunah the Jebusite." 19So David
went up, as the LORD had commanded
through Gad. 20When Araunah looked
and saw the king and his men coming
toward him, he went out and bowed
down before the king with his face to
the ground.
21Araunah said, "Why has my lord
the king come to his servant?"
"To buy your threshing floor," David
answered, "so I can build an altar to the
24:21 [b]Nu 16:44-50
LORD, that the plague on the people
may be stopped."[b]
22Araunah said to David, "Let my
24:22 [c]1Sa 6:14; 1Ki 19:21
lord the king take whatever pleases him
and offer it up. Here are oxen[c] for the
burnt offering, and here are threshing
24:23 [d]Eze 20:40-41
sledges and ox yokes for the wood.
23O king, Araunah gives[d] all this to the
king." Araunah also said to him, "May
the LORD your God accept you."
24But the king replied to Araunah,
"No, I insist on paying you for it. I
will not sacrifice to the LORD my God
24:24 [e]Mal 1:13-14
burnt offerings that cost me nothing."[e]
So David bought the threshing floor
and the oxen and paid fifty shekels[b] of
24:25 [f]1Sa 7:17 [g]2Sa 21:14
silver for them. 25David built an altar[f] to
the LORD there and sacrificed burnt offerings and fellowship offerings.[c] Then
the LORD answered prayer[g] in behalf
of the land, and the plague on Israel
was stopped.

[a]*13* Septuagint (see also 1 Chron. 21:12); Hebrew *seven* [b]*24* That is, about 1 1/4 pounds (about 0.6 kilogram) [c]*25* Traditionally *peace offerings*

1 KINGS

AUTHORSHIP AND DATE

Unknown

KEY THEMES

The first half of 1 Kings describes David's relinquishment of his kingdom to his son Solomon, who was the last of the great kings and the last king to govern the entire nation. At the beginning of his reign, Solomon asked God for wisdom, and God granted it. Solomon later proved himself unwise by collecting a harem of foreign wives, who ultimately became his undoing. The idolatries of his foreign wives became the downfall of the entire nation in the years following Solomon's reign. Unfortunately, upon Solomon's death, his son Rehoboam made no commitments to wisdom and, by listening to the foolish advice of his counselors, made decisions that resulted in the kingdom splitting into two smaller nations. From that point on, the greatness of both kingdoms diminished. While the southern kingdom endured the longest and generally had the best-behaved kings, both nations were beset with idolatry and foreign oppression, which ultimately destroyed them both. The themes of this book: abuses of power, duplicity, sin and repentance.

FRUIT OF THE SPIRIT IN 1 KINGS

Joy: Joy is an effervescent mood that celebrates great leadership. When Solomon was crowned king, public joy was the natural response: "Zadok the priest took the horn of oil from the sacred tent and anointed Solomon. Then they sounded the trumpet and all the people shouted, 'Long live King Solomon!' And all the people went up after him, playing flutes and rejoicing greatly, so that the ground shook with the sound" (1:39–40).

Peace: Elijah was in retreat from the fury of Jezebel. He was afraid for his life, and his inner turmoil was at least equal to his outer despair. Longing for peace in the midst of his troubles, he learned to listen for God in a new way. God sent wind, earthquake and fire to remind Elijah of his power. But when he actually spoke to Elijah, he did so in a "gentle whisper"

(19:12). God's peace is often less showy and far quieter than we might anticipate.

Patience: Elijah prophesied a drought of some years (see 17:1). The wheels of God do sometimes grind exceedingly slow. Prophecies we wish could be fulfilled within weeks often require years. But in the waiting we are conformed to a better image through obedience and repentance. Thus the fruit of our patience is a closer relationship with God.

Kindness: Solomon did not ask for vast power or great wealth; instead he pleaded for wisdom (see ch. 3). His kindness summoned forth the vast treasuries of God's supply, fulfilling all that Solomon asked for. Kindness never craves poor material gifts; it always seeks that which will magnify God rather than self (see 3:10). It cares for others and treats the needy with wisdom that craves the chance to do something loving.

Faithfulness: Solomon went to Gibeon to offer sacrifices. During the night, God appeared to him in a dream. God asked Solomon to name anything he would like to have. Solomon replied, "You have shown great kindness to your servant, my father David, because he was faithful to you... So give your servant a discerning heart" (3:6,9). God was pleased that Solomon cited David's faithfulness and that he asked for wisdom. Wisdom was granted and Solomon proved himself faithful.

Gentleness: Gentleness has a dreadful antonym—harshness. Choose gentleness and the world comes together unafraid. Choose harshness and the universe is split down the middle. Rehoboam chose to be harsh and his father's kingdom split. He threatened his people even before his coronation: "My little finger is thicker than my father's waist... My father scourged you with whips; I will scourge you with scorpions" (12:10–11).

Self-Control: God told Solomon that self-control would always be the key to blessing. Solomon had but to practice self-control and obey God's laws, and his self-control would provide him with all things (see 6:11–13).

Adonijah Sets Himself Up as King

1 When King David was old and well
advanced in years, he could not
keep warm even when they put covers
over him. 2So his servants said to him,
"Let us look for a young virgin to attend the king and take care of him. She
can lie beside him so that our lord the
king may keep warm."
3Then they searched throughout Israel for a beautiful girl and found Ab-
1:3 ishag, a Shunammite,[a] and brought her
aJos 19:18 to the king. 4The girl was very beautiful; she took care of the king and waited
on him, but the king had no intimate
relations with her.
1:5 5Now Adonijah,[b] whose mother was
b2Sa 3:4 c2Sa 15:1 Haggith, put himself forward and said,
"I will be king." So he got chariots[c]
and horses[a] ready, with fifty men to run
ahead of him. 6(His father had never
1:6 interfered[d] with him by asking, "Why
d2Sa 3:3-4 do you behave as you do?" He was also
very handsome and was born next after
Absalom.)
1:7 7Adonijah conferred with Joab[e] son of
e1Ki 2:22,28; 1Ch 11:6 Zeruiah and with Abiathar[f] the priest,
f1Sa 22:20; 2Sa 20:25 and they gave him their support. 8But
Zadok[g] the priest, Benaiah[h] son of Je-
1:8 hoiada, Nathan[i] the prophet, Shimei[j]
g2Sa 20:25 h2Sa 8:18 and Rei[b] and David's special guard[k] did
i2Sa 12:1 j1Ki 4:18 not join Adonijah.
k2Sa 23:8 9Adonijah then sacrificed sheep, cattle and fattened calves at the Stone of
1:9 l2Sa 17:17 Zoheleth near En Rogel.[l] He invited
all his brothers, the king's sons, and all
the men of Judah who were royal officials, 10but he did not invite Nathan
1:10 the prophet or Benaiah or the special
m2Sa 12:24 guard or his brother Solomon.[m]
1:11 11Then Nathan asked Bathsheba,[n]
n2Sa 12:24 o2Sa 3:4 Solomon's mother, "Have you not heard
that Adonijah,[o] the son of Haggith, has
become king without our lord David's
1:12 knowing it? 12Now then, let me advise[p]
pPr 15:22 you how you can save your own life and
the life of your son Solomon. 13Go in
to King David and say to him, 'My lord
1:13 the king, did you not swear[q] to me your
qver 30; 1Ch 22:9-13 servant: "Surely Solomon your son shall
be king after me, and he will sit on my
throne"? Why then has Adonijah become king?' 14While you are still there
talking to the king, I will come in and
confirm what you have said."
1:15 15So Bathsheba went to see the aged
rver 1 king in his room, where Abishag[r] the
Shunammite was attending him. 16Bath-
sheba bowed low and knelt before the
king.
"What is it you want?" the king
asked.
17She said to him, "My lord, you
yourself swore[s] to me your servant by 1:17
the LORD your God: 'Solomon your sver 13,30
son shall be king after me, and he will
sit on my throne.' 18But now Adonijah
has become king, and you, my lord the
king, do not know about it. 19He has
sacrificed[t] great numbers of cattle, fat- 1:19 tver 9
tened calves, and sheep, and has invited
all the king's sons, Abiathar the priest
and Joab the commander of the army,
but he has not invited Solomon your
servant. 20My lord the king, the eyes
of all Israel are on you, to learn from
you who will sit on the throne of my
lord the king after him. 21Otherwise, as
soon as my lord the king is laid to rest[u] 1:21 uDt 31:16;
with his fathers, I and my son Solomon 1Ki 2:10
will be treated as criminals."
22While she was still speaking with
the king, Nathan the prophet arrived.
23And they told the king, "Nathan the
prophet is here." So he went before the
king and bowed with his face to the
ground.
24Nathan said, "Have you, my lord
the king, declared that Adonijah shall
be king after you, and that he will sit on
your throne? 25Today he has gone down
and sacrificed great numbers of cattle,
fattened calves, and sheep. He has invited all the king's sons, the commanders of the army and Abiathar the priest.
Right now they are eating and drinking
with him and saying, 'Long live King
Adonijah!' 26But me your servant, and
Zadok the priest, and Benaiah son of
Jehoiada, and your servant Solomon he
did not invite.[v] 27Is this something my 1:26
lord the king has done without letting vver 8,10
his servants know who should sit on the
throne of my lord the king after him?"

David Makes Solomon King

28Then King David said, "Call in
Bathsheba." So she came into the king's
presence and stood before him.
29The king then took an oath: "As 1:29
surely as the LORD lives, who has deliv- w2Sa 4:9
ered me out of every trouble,[w] 30I will 1:30
surely carry out today what I swore[x] to xver 13,17

[a]5 Or *charioteers* [b]8 Or *and his friends*

you by the LORD, the God of Israel:
Solomon your son shall be king after
me, and he will sit on my throne in my
place."
31Then Bathsheba bowed low with
her face to the ground and, kneeling
before the king, said, "May my lord
King David live forever!"
32King David said, "Call in Zadok
the priest, Nathan the prophet and
Benaiah son of Jehoiada." When they
came before the king, 33he said to them:
"Take your lord's servants with you and
set Solomon my son on my own mule[y]
and take him down to Gihon.[z] 34There
have Zadok the priest and Nathan the
prophet anoint[a] him king over Israel.
Blow the trumpet[b] and shout, 'Long
live King Solomon!' 35Then you are to
go up with him, and he is to come and
sit on my throne and reign in my place.
I have appointed him ruler over Israel
and Judah."
36Benaiah son of Jehoiada answered
the king, "Amen! May the LORD, the
God of my lord the king, so declare it.
37As the LORD was with my lord the
king, so may he be with[c] Solomon to
make his throne even greater[d] than the
throne of my lord King David!"
38So Zadok[e] the priest, Nathan the
prophet, Benaiah son of Jehoiada, the
Kerethites[f] and the Pelethites went
down and put Solomon on King David's mule and escorted him to Gihon.[g]
39Zadok the priest took the horn of oil[h]
from the sacred tent and anointed Solomon. Then they sounded the trumpet and all the people shouted,[i] "Long
live King Solomon!" 40And all the people went up after him, playing flutes
and rejoicing greatly, so that the ground
shook with the sound.
41Adonijah and all the guests who
were with him heard it as they were finishing their feast. On hearing the sound
of the trumpet, Joab asked, "What's the
meaning of all the noise in the city?"
42Even as he was speaking, Jonathan[j]
son of Abiathar the priest arrived. Adonijah said, "Come in. A worthy man like
you must be bringing good news."[k]
43"Not at all!" Jonathan answered.
"Our lord King David has made Solomon king. 44The king has sent with him
Zadok the priest, Nathan the prophet,
Benaiah son of Jehoiada, the Kerethites and the Pelethites, and they have
put him on the king's mule, 45and Zadok the priest and Nathan the prophet
have anointed him king at Gihon. From
there they have gone up cheering, and
the city resounds[l] with it. That's the
noise you hear. 46Moreover, Solomon
has taken his seat on the royal throne.
47Also, the royal officials have come to
congratulate our lord King David, saying, 'May your God make Solomon's
name more famous than yours and his
throne greater[m] than yours!' And the
king bowed in worship on his bed 48and
said, 'Praise be to the LORD, the God
of Israel, who has allowed my eyes to
see a successor[n] on my throne today.'"
49At this, all Adonijah's guests rose
in alarm and dispersed. 50But Adonijah, in fear of Solomon, went and took
hold of the horns of the altar. 51Then
Solomon was told, "Adonijah is afraid
of King Solomon and is clinging to the
horns[o] of the altar. He says, 'Let King
Solomon swear to me today that he will
not put his servant to death with the
sword.'"
52Solomon replied, "If he shows himself to be a worthy man, not a hair[p]
of his head will fall to the ground; but
if evil is found in him, he will die."
53Then King Solomon sent men, and
they brought him down from the altar.
And Adonijah came and bowed down
to King Solomon, and Solomon said,
"Go to your home."

David's Charge to Solomon

2 When the time drew near for David to die,[q] he gave a charge to Solomon his son.
2"I am about to go the way of all the
earth,"[r] he said. "So be strong,[s] show
yourself a man, 3and observe[t] what the
LORD your God requires: Walk in his
ways, and keep his decrees and commands, his laws and requirements, as

1:33 [y]2Sa 20:6-7 [z]2Ch 32:30; 33:14
1:34 [a]1Sa 10:1; 16:3,12; 1Ki 19:16; 2Ki 9:3,13 [b]ver 25; 2Sa 5:3; 15:10
1:37 [c]Jos 1:5,17; 1Sa 20:13 [d]ver 47
1:38 [e]ver 8 [f]2Sa 8:18 [g]ver 33
1:39 [h]Ex 30:23-32; Ps 89:20 [i]ver 34; 1Sa 10:24
1:42 [j]2Sa 15:27,36 [k]2Sa 18:26
1:45 [l]ver 40
1:47 [m]ver 37; Ge 47:31
1:48 [n]2Sa 7:12; 1Ki 3:6
1:50 [o]1Ki 2:28
1:52 [p]1Sa 14:45; 2Sa 14:11
2:1 [q]Ge 47:29; Dt 31:14
2:2 [r]Jos 23:14 [s]Dt 31:7,23; Jos 1:6
2:3 [t]Dt 17:14-20; Jos 1:7

PEACE

DEATH BE NOT PROUD

1 Kings 2:1–2

Dying was once thought to be the end of everything. But that was before Jesus died. Now dying is the beginning of all things, the porch of a great house. That house is far larger than those outside imagine it to be.

written in the Law of Moses, so that
2:3 you may prosper[u] in all you do and
u1Ch 22:13 wherever you go, 4and that the LORD
2:4 may keep his promise[v] to me: 'If your
v2Sa 7:13,25; descendants watch how they live, and if
1Ki 8:25 w2Ki 20:3; they walk faithfully[w] before me with all
Ps 132:12 their heart and soul, you will never fail
to have a man on the throne of Israel.'
2:5 5"Now you yourself know what Joab[x]
x2Sa 2:18; 18:5,12,14 son of Zeruiah did to me—what he did
y2Sa 3:27 z2Sa 20:10 to the two commanders of Israel's armies,
mies, Abner[y] son of Ner and Amasa[z]
son of Jether. He killed them, shedding
their blood in peacetime as if in battle,
and with that blood stained the belt
around his waist and the sandals on his
feet. 6Deal with him according to your
2:6 wisdom,[a] but do not let his gray head
aver 9 go down to the grave[a] in peace.
7"But show kindness to the sons of
2:7 b2Sa 17:27; Barzillai[b] of Gilead and let them be
19:31-39 c2Sa 9:7 among those who eat at your table.[c]
They stood by me when I fled from
your brother Absalom.
8"And remember, you have with you
2:8 d2Sa 16:5-13 Shimei[d] son of Gera, the Benjamite
e2Sa 19:18-23 from Bahurim, who called down bitter
curses on me the day I went to Ma-
hanaim. When he came down to meet
me at the Jordan, I swore[e] to him by
the LORD: 'I will not put you to death
by the sword.' 9But now, do not consider him innocent. You are a man of
2:9 fver 6 wisdom;[f] you will know what to do to
him. Bring his gray head down to the
grave in blood."
10Then David rested with his fathers
2:10 gAc 2:29; and was buried[g] in the City of David.[h]
13:36 h2Sa 5:7 11He had reigned[i] forty years over Israel—seven years in Hebron and thirty-
2:11 i2Sa 5:4,5 three in Jerusalem. 12So Solomon sat on
the throne[j] of his father David, and his
2:12 rule was firmly established.[k]

j1Ch 29:23 k2Ch 1:1

Solomon's Throne Established

2:13 l1Sa 16:4 13Now Adonijah, the son of Haggith,
went to Bathsheba, Solomon's mother.
Bathsheba asked him, "Do you come
peacefully?"[l]
He answered, "Yes, peacefully."
14Then he added, "I have something to
say to you."
"You may say it," she replied.
15"As you know," he said, "the kingdom was mine. All Israel looked to me
as their king. But things changed, and
the kingdom has gone to my brother;
for it has come to him from the LORD.
16Now I have one request to make of
you. Do not refuse me."
"You may make it," she said.
17So he continued, "Please ask King
Solomon—he will not refuse you—to
give me Abishag[m] the Shunammite as 2:17 m1Ki 1:3
my wife."
18"Very well," Bathsheba replied, "I
will speak to the king for you."
19When Bathsheba went to King Solomon to speak to him for Adonijah, the
king stood up to meet her, bowed down
to her and sat down on his throne.
He had a throne brought for the king's 2:19
mother,[n] and she sat down at his right n1Ki 15:13
hand.[o] oPs 45:9
20"I have one small request to make
of you," she said. "Do not refuse me."
The king replied, "Make it, my mother; I will not refuse you."
21So she said, "Let Abishag[p] the Shu- 2:21 p1Ki 1:3
nammite be given in marriage to your
brother Adonijah."
22King Solomon answered his moth-
er, "Why do you request Abishag[q] the 2:22 q2Sa 12:8;
Shunammite for Adonijah? You might 1Ki 1:3 r1Ch 3:2
as well request the kingdom for him—
after all, he is my older brother[r]—yes,
for him and for Abiathar the priest and
Joab son of Zeruiah!"
23Then King Solomon swore by the
LORD: "May God deal with me, be it
ever so severely,[s] if Adonijah does not 2:23 sRu 1:17
pay with his life for this request! 24And
now, as surely as the LORD lives—he
who has established me securely on the
throne of my father David and has
founded a dynasty for me as he prom-
ised[t]—Adonijah shall be put to death 2:24 t2Sa 7:11;
today!" 25So King Solomon gave orders 1Ch 22:10
to Benaiah[u] son of Jehoiada, and he 2:25
struck down Adonijah and he died. u2Sa 8:18
26To Abiathar[v] the priest the king 2:26
said, "Go back to your fields in Ana- v1Sa 22:20
thoth.[w] You deserve to die, but I will wJos 21:18 x2Sa 15:24
not put you to death now, because you y1Sa 23:6
carried the ark[x] of the Sovereign LORD
before my father David and shared all
my father's hardships."[y] 27So Solomon
removed Abiathar from the priesthood
of the LORD, fulfilling[z] the word the 2:27 z1Sa 2:27-36
LORD had spoken at Shiloh about the
house of Eli.
28When the news reached Joab, who
had conspired with Adonijah though
not with Absalom, he fled to the tent of

[a]6 Hebrew *Sheol*; also in verse 9

2:28 [a]1Ki 1:7,50 the LORD and took hold of the horns[a]
of the altar. 29King Solomon was told
that Joab had fled to the tent of the
LORD and was beside the altar. Then
2:29 [b]ver 25 Solomon ordered Benaiah[b] son of Jehoiada, "Go, strike him down!"
30So Benaiah entered the tent of the
LORD and said to Joab, "The king says,
2:30 [c]Ex 21:14 'Come out![c]'"
But he answered, "No, I will die
here."
Benaiah reported to the king, "This
is how Joab answered me."
31Then the king commanded Benaiah, "Do as he says. Strike him down
and bury him, and so clear me and
my father's house of the guilt of the
2:31 [d]Nu 35:33; Dt 19:13; 21:8-9 innocent blood[d] that Joab shed. 32The
LORD will repay[e] him for the blood he
shed,[f] because without the knowledge
2:32 [e]Jdg 9:57; Ps 7:16 [f]Jdg 9:24 [g]2Sa 3:27; 20:10 [h]2Ch 21:13 of my father David he attacked two
men and killed them with the sword.
Both of them—Abner son of Ner, commander of Israel's army, and Amasa[g]
son of Jether, commander of Judah's
army—were better[h] men and more upright than he. 33May the guilt of their
blood rest on the head of Joab and
his descendants forever. But on David
and his descendants, his house and his
throne, may there be the LORD's peace
forever."
34So Benaiah son of Jehoiada went
up and struck down Joab and killed
him, and he was buried on his own
land[a] in the desert. 35The king put Be-
2:35 [i]1Ki 4:4 [j]ver 27; 1Ch 29:22 naiah[i] son of Jehoiada over the army
in Joab's position and replaced Abiathar
with Zadok[j] the priest.
2:36 [k]ver 8; 2Sa 16:5 36Then the king sent for Shimei[k] and
said to him, "Build yourself a house in
Jerusalem and live there, but do not
go anywhere else. 37The day you leave
2:37 [l]2Sa 15:23 [m]Lev 20:9; Jos 2:19; 2Sa 1:16 and cross the Kidron Valley,[l] you can be
sure you will die; your blood will be on
your own head."[m]
38Shimei answered the king, "What
you say is good. Your servant will do as
my lord the king has said." And Shimei
stayed in Jerusalem for a long time.
39But three years later, two of Shim-
2:39 [n]1Sa 27:2 ei's slaves ran off to Achish[n] son of Maacah, king of Gath, and Shimei was told,
"Your slaves are in Gath." 40At this, he
saddled his donkey and went to Achish
at Gath in search of his slaves. So Shimei went away and brought the slaves
back from Gath.

41When Solomon was told that Shimei had gone from Jerusalem to Gath and
had returned, 42the king summoned
Shimei and said to him, "Did I not
make you swear by the LORD and warn
you, 'On the day you leave to go anywhere else, you can be sure you will
die'? At that time you said to me, 'What
you say is good. I will obey.' 43Why
then did you not keep your oath to the
LORD and obey the command I gave
you?"
44The king also said to Shimei, "You
know in your heart all the wrong[o] you 2:44 [o]1Sa 25:39; 2Sa 16:5-13; Eze 17:19
did to my father David. Now the LORD
will repay you for your wrongdoing.
45But King Solomon will be blessed,
and David's throne will remain secure[p] 2:45 [p]2Sa 7:13; Pr 25:5
before the LORD forever."
46Then the king gave the order to
Benaiah son of Jehoiada, and he went
out and struck Shimei down and killed
him.
The kingdom was now firmly estab-
lished[q] in Solomon's hands. 2:46 [q]ver 12; 2Ch 1:1

Solomon Asks for Wisdom

3 Solomon made an alliance with
Pharaoh king of Egypt and mar-
ried[r] his daughter.[s] He brought her to 3:1 [r]1Ki 7:8 [s]1Ki 9:24 [t]2Sa 5:7 [u]1Ki 7:1; 9:15,19
the City of David[t] until he finished
building his palace[u] and the temple of
the LORD, and the wall around Jerusalem. 2The people, however, were still
sacrificing at the high places,[v] because 3:2 [v]Lev 17:3-5; Dt 12:2,4-5; 1Ki 22:43
a temple had not yet been built for the
Name of the LORD. 3Solomon showed
his love[w] for the LORD by walking ac- 3:3 [w]Dt 6:5; Ps 31:23; 1Co 8:3 [x]1Ki 2:3; 9:4; 11:4,6,38
cording to the statutes[x] of his father
David, except that he offered sacrifices
and burned incense on the high places.
4The king went to Gibeon[y] to offer 3:4 [y]1Ch 16:39
sacrifices, for that was the most important high place, and Solomon offered
a thousand burnt offerings on that al-
tar. 5At Gibeon the LORD appeared[z] to 3:5 [z]1Ki 9:2 [a]Nu 12:6; Mt 1:20
Solomon during the night in a dream,[a]
and God said, "Ask for whatever you
want me to give you."
6Solomon answered, "You have
shown great kindness to your servant,
my father David, because he was faith-
ful[b] to you and righteous and upright 3:6 [b]1Ki 2:4; 9:4 [c]1Ki 1:48
in heart. You have continued this great
kindness to him and have given him a
son[c] to sit on his throne this very day.

[a]34 Or *buried in his tomb*

7“Now, O LORD my God, you have made your servant king in place of my father David. But I am only a little child[d] and do not know how to carry out my duties. 8Your servant is here among the people you have chosen,[e] a great people, too numerous to count or number.[f] 9So give your servant a discerning[g] heart to govern your people and to distinguish[h] between right and wrong. For who is able[i] to govern this great people of yours?”

10The Lord was pleased that Solomon had asked for this. 11So God said to him, “Since you have asked[j] for this and not for long life or wealth for yourself, nor have asked for the death of your enemies but for discernment in administering justice, 12I will do what you have asked.[k] I will give you a wise[l] and discerning heart, so that there will never have been anyone like you, nor will there ever be. 13Moreover, I will give you what you have not[m] asked for—both riches and honor[n]—so that in your lifetime you will have no equal[o] among kings. 14And if you walk[p] in my ways and obey my statutes and commands as David your father did, I will give you a long life.”[q] 15Then Solomon awoke[r]—and he realized it had been a dream.

He returned to Jerusalem, stood before the ark of the Lord’s covenant and sacrificed burnt offerings[s] and fellowship offerings.[a][t] Then he gave a feast[u] for all his court.

3:7 [d]Nu 27:17; 1Ch 29:1
3:8 [e]Dt 7:6 [f]Ge 15:5
3:9 [g]2Sa 14:17; Jas 1:5 [h]Pr 2:3-9; Heb 5:14 [i]Ps 72:1-2
3:11 [j]Jas 4:3
3:12 [k]1Jn 5:14-15 [l]1Ki 4:29, 30,31; 5:12; 10:23; Ecc 1:16
3:13 [m]Mt 6:33; Eph 3:20 [n]1Ki 4:21-24; Pr 3:1-2,16 [o]1Ki 10:23
3:14 [p]ver 6; Pr 3:1-2,16 [q]Ps 61:6; 91:16
3:15 [r]Ge 41:7 [s]1Ki 8:65 [t]Mk 6:21 [u]Est 1:3,9; Da 5:1

A Wise Ruling

16Now two prostitutes came to the king and stood before him. 17One of them said, “My lord, this woman and I live in the same house. I had a baby while she was there with me. 18The third day after my child was born, this woman also had a baby. We were alone; there was no one in the house but the two of us.

19“During the night this woman’s son died because she lay on him. 20So she got up in the middle of the night and took my son from my side while I your servant was asleep. She put him by her breast and put her dead son by my breast. 21The next morning, I got up to nurse my son—and he was dead! But when I looked at him closely in the morning light, I saw that it wasn’t the son I had borne.”

22The other woman said, “No! The living one is my son; the dead one is yours.”

But the first one insisted, “No! The dead one is yours; the living one is mine.” And so they argued before the king.

23The king said, “This one says, ‘My son is alive and your son is dead,’ while that one says, ‘No! Your son is dead and mine is alive.’ ”

24Then the king said, “Bring me a sword.” So they brought a sword for the king. 25He then gave an order: “Cut the living child in two and give half to one and half to the other.”

26The woman whose son was alive was filled with compassion[v] for her son and said to the king, “Please, my lord, give her the living baby! Don’t kill him!”

But the other said, “Neither I nor you shall have him. Cut him in two!”

27Then the king gave his ruling: “Give the living baby to the first woman. Do not kill him; she is his mother.”

28When all Israel heard the verdict the king had given, they held the king in awe, because they saw that he had wisdom[w] from God to administer justice.

3:26 [v]Ge 43:30; Isa 49:15; Jer 31:20; Hos 11:8
3:28 [w]ver 9,11-12; Col 2:3

Solomon’s Officials and Governors

4 So King Solomon ruled over all Israel. 2And these were his chief officials:

Azariah[x] son of Zadok—the priest;
3Elihoreph and Ahijah, sons of Shisha—secretaries;
Jehoshaphat[y] son of Ahilud—recorder;
4Benaiah[z] son of Jehoiada—commander in chief;
Zadok[a] and Abiathar—priests;
5Azariah son of Nathan—in charge of the district officers;
Zabud son of Nathan—a priest and personal adviser to the king;
6Ahishar—in charge of the palace;
Adoniram son of Abda—in charge of forced labor.

4:2 [x]1Ch 6:10
4:3 [y]2Sa 8:16
4:4 [z]1Ki 2:35 [a]1Ki 2:27

[a] *15* Traditionally *peace offerings*

7 Solomon also had twelve district governors over all Israel, who supplied provisions for the king and the royal household. Each one had to provide supplies for one month in the year. 8 These are their names:

Ben-Hur—in the hill country[b] of Ephraim;

9 Ben-Deker—in Makaz, Shaalbim,[c] Beth Shemesh[d] and Elon Bethhanan;

10 Ben-Hesed—in Arubboth (Socoh[e] and all the land of Hepher[f] were his);

11 Ben-Abinadab—in Naphoth Dor[a][g] (he was married to Taphath daughter of Solomon);

12 Baana son of Ahilud—in Taanach and Megiddo, and in all of Beth Shan[h] next to Zarethan[i] below Jezreel, from Beth Shan to Abel Meholah[j] across to Jokmeam;[k]

13 Ben-Geber—in Ramoth Gilead (the settlements of Jair[l] son of Manasseh in Gilead were his, as well as the district of Argob in Bashan and its sixty large walled cities[m] with bronze gate bars);

14 Ahinadab son of Iddo—in Mahanaim;[n]

15 Ahimaaz[o]—in Naphtali (he had married Basemath daughter of Solomon);

16 Baana son of Hushai[p]—in Asher and in Aloth;

17 Jehoshaphat son of Paruah—in Issachar;

18 Shimei[q] son of Ela—in Benjamin;

19 Geber son of Uri—in Gilead (the country of Sihon king of the Amorites and the country of Og[r] king of Bashan). He was the only governor over the district.

4:8 [b]Jos 24:33
4:9 [c]Jdg 1:35 [d]Jos 21:16
4:10 [e]Jos 15:35 [f]Jos 12:17
4:11 [g]Jos 11:2
4:12 [h]Jos 17:11; Jdg 5:19 [i]Jos 3:16 [j]1Ki 19:16 [k]1Ch 6:68
4:13 [l]Nu 32:41 [m]Dt 3:4
4:14 [n]Jos 13:26
4:15 [o]2Sa 15:27
4:16 [p]2Sa 15:32
4:18 [q]1Ki 1:8
4:19 [r]Dt 3:8-10

Solomon's Daily Provisions

20 The people of Judah and Israel were as numerous as the sand[s] on the seashore; they ate, they drank and they were happy. 21 And Solomon ruled[t] over all the kingdoms from the River[b][u] to the land of the Philistines, as far as the border of Egypt.[v] These countries brought tribute[w] and were Solomon's subjects all his life.

22 Solomon's daily provisions were thirty cors[c] of fine flour and sixty cors[d] of meal, 23 ten head of stall-fed cattle, twenty of pasture-fed cattle and a hundred sheep and goats, as well as deer, gazelles, roebucks and choice fowl. 24 For he ruled over all the kingdoms west of the River, from Tiphsah[x] to Gaza, and had peace[y] on all sides. 25 During Solomon's lifetime Judah and Israel, from Dan to Beersheba,[z] lived in safety,[a] each man under his own vine and fig tree.[b]

26 Solomon had four[e] thousand stalls for chariot horses,[c] and twelve thousand horses.[f]

27 The district officers,[d] each in his month, supplied provisions for King Solomon and all who came to the king's table. They saw to it that nothing was lacking. 28 They also brought to the proper place their quotas of barley and straw for the chariot horses and the other horses.

4:20 [s]Ge 22:17; 32:12; 1Ki 3:8
4:21 [t]2Ch 9:26; Ps 72:11 [u]Jos 1:4; Ps 72:8 [v]Ge 15:18 [w]Ps 68:29
4:24 [x]Ps 72:11 [y]1Ch 22:9
4:25 [z]Jdg 20:1 [a]Jer 23:6 [b]Mic 4:4; Zec 3:10
4:26 [c]1Ki 10:26; 2Ch 1:14
4:27 [d]ver 7

Solomon's Wisdom

29 God gave Solomon wisdom[e] and very great insight, and a breadth of understanding as measureless as the sand on the seashore. 30 Solomon's wisdom was greater than the wisdom of all the men of the East,[f] and greater than all the wisdom of Egypt.[g] 31 He was wiser[h] than any other man, including Ethan the Ezrahite—wiser than Heman, Calcol and Darda, the sons of Mahol. And his fame spread to all the surrounding nations. 32 He spoke three thousand proverbs[i] and his songs[j] numbered a thousand and five. 33 He described plant life, from the cedar of Lebanon to the hyssop that grows out of walls. He also taught about animals and birds, reptiles and fish. 34 Men of all nations came to listen to Solomon's wisdom, sent by all the kings[k] of the world, who had heard of his wisdom.

4:29 [e]1Ki 3:12
4:30 [f]Ge 25:6 [g]Ac 7:22
4:31 [h]1Ki 3:12; 1Ch 2:6; 6:33; 15:19; Ps 89 Title
4:32 [i]Pr 1:1; Ecc 12:9 [j]SS 1:1
4:34 [k]1Ki 10:1; 2Ch 9:23

Preparations for Building the Temple

5 When Hiram[l] king of Tyre heard that Solomon had been anointed king to succeed his father David, he sent his envoys to Solomon, because he

5:1 [l]ver 10,18; 2Sa 5:11; 1Ch 14:1

[a] *11* Or *in the heights of Dor* [b] *21* That is, the Euphrates; also in verse 24 [c] *22* That is, probably about 185 bushels (about 6.6 kiloliters) [d] *22* That is, probably about 375 bushels (about 13.2 kiloliters) [e] *26* Some Septuagint manuscripts (see also 2 Chron. 9:25); Hebrew *forty* [f] *26* Or *charioteers*

had always been on friendly terms with
David. 2Solomon sent back this message to Hiram:

3"You know that because of the
5:3 wars[m] waged against my father Da-
[m]1Ch 22:8; vid from all sides, he could not
28:3 build a temple for the Name of the
LORD his God until the LORD put
his enemies under his feet. 4But
5:4 now the LORD my God has given
[n]1Ki 4:24; me rest[n] on every side, and there is
1Ch 22:9 no adversary or disaster. 5I intend,
5:5 therefore, to build a temple[o] for
[o]1Ch 17:12 the Name of the LORD my God,
[p]2Sa 7:13; 1Ch 22:10 as the LORD told my father David, when he said, 'Your son whom
I will put on the throne in your
place will build the temple for my
Name.'[p]

6"So give orders that cedars of
Lebanon be cut for me. My men
will work with yours, and I will
pay you for your men whatever
wages you set. You know that we
have no one so skilled in felling
timber as the Sidonians."

GOODNESS

CHILDREN AND PROMISES

1 Kings 5:5

David's boy lived to honor all his father's dreams. In honoring our parents' dreams, the work of God continues on across the years. We ourselves continue building Christ's kingdom on the dreams of simple fishermen, shepherds and potters.

"You're dying, old man,
With your dreams left undone."
"Yes!
But I've placed all my dreams
In the hands of my son."

7When Hiram heard Solomon's message, he was greatly pleased and said,
"Praise be to the LORD today, for he
has given David a wise son to rule over
this great nation."
8So Hiram sent word to Solomon:

"I have received the message you
sent me and will do all you want in
providing the cedar and pine logs.
9My men will haul them down
5:9 from Lebanon to the sea, and I
[q]Ezr 3:7 will float them in rafts by sea[q] to
the place you specify. There I will
separate them and you can take
them away. And you are to grant
my wish by providing food[r] for my 5:9 [r]Eze 27:17;
royal household." Ac 12:20

10In this way Hiram kept Solomon
supplied with all the cedar and pine
logs he wanted, 11and Solomon gave
Hiram twenty thousand cors[a] of wheat
as food for his household, in addition
to twenty thousand baths[b,c] of pressed
olive oil. Solomon continued to do this
for Hiram year after year. 12The LORD
gave Solomon wisdom,[s] just as he had 5:12
promised him. There were peaceful re- [s]1Ki 3:12 [t]Am 1:9
lations between Hiram and Solomon,
and the two of them made a treaty.[t]
13King Solomon conscripted laborers[u] from all Israel—thirty thousand 5:13
men. 14He sent them off to Lebanon [u]1Ki 9:15
in shifts of ten thousand a month, so
that they spent one month in Lebanon
and two months at home. Adoniram[v] 5:14 [v]1Ki 4:6;
was in charge of the forced labor. 15Sol- 2Ch 10:18
omon had seventy thousand carriers
and eighty thousand stonecutters in the
hills, 16as well as thirty-three hundred[d]
foremen[w] who supervised the project 5:16
and directed the workmen. 17At the [w]1Ki 9:23
king's command they removed from the
quarry[x] large blocks of quality stone[y] to 5:17
provide a foundation of dressed stone [x]1Ki 6:7
for the temple. 18The craftsmen of Sol- [y]1Ch 22:2
omon and Hiram and the men of Ge-
bal[e][z] cut and prepared the timber and 5:18
stone for the building of the temple. [z]Jos 13:5

Solomon Builds the Temple

6 In the four hundred and eightieth[f]
year after the Israelites had come
out of Egypt, in the fourth year of Solomon's reign over Israel, in the month
of Ziv, the second month, he began to
build the temple of the LORD.[a] 6:1 [a]Ac 7:47
2The temple[b] that King Solomon
built for the LORD was sixty cubits 6:2
long, twenty wide and thirty high.[g] [b]Eze 41:1
3The portico at the front of the main

[a]*11* That is, probably about 125,000 bushels (about 4,400 kiloliters) [b]*11* Septuagint (see also 2 Chron. 2:10); Hebrew *twenty cors* [c]*11* That is, about 115,000 gallons (about 440 kiloliters) [d]*16* Hebrew; some Septuagint manuscripts (see also 2 Chron. 2:2, 18) *thirty-six hundred* [e]*18* That is, Byblos [f]*1* Hebrew; Septuagint *four hundred and fortieth* [g]*2* That is, about 90 feet (about 27 meters) long and 30 feet (about 9 meters) wide and 45 feet (about 13.5 meters) high

hall of the temple extended the width
of the temple, that is twenty cubits,[a]
and projected ten cubits[b] from the front
of the temple. 4He made narrow clere-
6:4 story windows[c] in the temple. 5Against
cEze 40:16; the walls of the main hall and inner
41:16 sanctuary he built a structure around
the building, in which there were side
6:5 rooms.[d] 6The lowest floor was five cu-
dver 16,19-21; bits[c] wide, the middle floor six cubits[d]
Eze 41:5-6 and the third floor seven.[e] He made
offset ledges around the outside of the
temple so that nothing would be inserted into the temple walls.
7In building the temple, only blocks
6:7 dressed[e] at the quarry were used, and
eEx 20:25 no hammer, chisel or any other iron
fDt 27:5 tool[f] was heard at the temple site while
it was being built.
8The entrance to the lowest[f] floor
was on the south side of the temple; a
stairway led up to the middle level and
from there to the third. 9So he built
the temple and completed it, roofing it
6:9 with beams and cedar[g] planks. 10And
gver 14,38 he built the side rooms all along the
temple. The height of each was five cubits, and they were attached to the temple by beams of cedar.
11The word of the LORD came to
Solomon: 12"As for this temple you are
building, if you follow my decrees, carry out my regulations and keep all my
commands and obey them, I will fulfill
6:12 through you the promise[h] I gave to Da-
h2Sa 7:12-16; vid your father. 13And I will live among
1Ki 2:4; 9:5 the Israelites and will not abandon[i] my
6:13 people Israel."
iEx 25:8; 14So Solomon built the temple and
Lev 26:11; Dt 31:6; completed[j] it. 15He lined its interior
Heb 13:5 walls with cedar boards, paneling them
6:14 from the floor of the temple to the
jver 9,38 ceiling,[k] and covered the floor of the
6:15 temple with planks of pine. 16He par-
k1Ki 7:7 titioned off twenty cubits[a] at the rear
of the temple with cedar boards from
floor to ceiling to form within the temple an inner sanctuary, the Most Holy
6:16 Place.[l] 17The main hall in front of this
lEx 26:33; room was forty cubits[g] long. 18The in-
Lev 16:2; 1Ki 8:6 side of the temple was cedar,[m] carved
6:18 with gourds and open flowers. Every-
m1Ki 7:24; thing was cedar; no stone was to be
Ps 74:6 seen.
6:19 19He prepared the inner sanctuary[n]
n1Ki 8:6 within the temple to set the ark of the
o1Sa 3:3 covenant[o] of the LORD there. 20The in-
6:20 ner sanctuary[p] was twenty cubits long,
pEze 41:3-4 twenty wide and twenty high.[h] He overlaid the inside with pure gold, and he
also overlaid the altar of cedar. 21Solo-
mon covered the inside of the temple
with pure gold, and he extended gold
chains across the front of the inner sanctuary, which was overlaid with gold.
22So he overlaid the whole interior with
gold. He also overlaid with gold the
altar that belonged to the inner sanctuary.
23In the inner sanctuary he made a
pair of cherubim[q] of olive wood, each 6:23
ten cubits[b] high. 24One wing of the qEx 37:1-9
first cherub was five cubits long, and
the other wing five cubits—ten cubits
from wing tip to wing tip. 25The second cherub also measured ten cubits,
for the two cherubim were identical in
size and shape. 26The height of each
cherub was ten cubits. 27He placed the
cherubim[r] inside the innermost room 6:27
of the temple, with their wings spread rEx 25:20; 37:9;
out. The wing of one cherub touched 1Ki 8:7;
one wall, while the wing of the other 2Ch 5:8
touched the other wall, and their wings
touched each other in the middle of the
room. 28He overlaid the cherubim with
gold.
29On the walls all around the temple,
in both the inner and outer rooms, he
carved cherubim,[s] palm trees and open 6:29
flowers. 30He also covered the floors of sver 32,35
both the inner and outer rooms of the
temple with gold.
31For the entrance of the inner sanctuary he made doors of olive wood with
five-sided jambs. 32And on the two olive wood doors he carved cherubim,
palm trees and open flowers, and overlaid the cherubim and palm trees with
beaten gold. 33In the same way he made
four-sided jambs of olive wood for the
entrance to the main hall. 34He also
made two pine doors, each having two
leaves that turned in sockets. 35He
carved cherubim, palm trees and open
flowers on them and overlaid them with
gold hammered evenly over the carv-
ings.

[a] *3,16* That is, about 30 feet (about 9 meters) [b] *3,23* That is, about 15 feet (about 4.5 meters) [c] *6* That is, about 7 1/2 feet (about 2.3 meters); also in verses 10 and 24 [d] *6* That is, about 9 feet (about 2.7 meters) [e] *6* That is, about 10 1/2 feet (about 3.1 meters) [f] *8* Septuagint; Hebrew *middle* [g] *17* That is, about 60 feet (about 18 meters) [h] *20* That is, about 30 feet (about 9 meters) long, wide and high

36 And he built the inner courtyard of
6:36 [t]1Ki 7:12; Ezr 6:4 three courses[t] of dressed stone and one
course of trimmed cedar beams.
37 The foundation of the temple of
the LORD was laid in the fourth year, in
the month of Ziv. 38 In the eleventh year
in the month of Bul, the eighth month,
the temple was finished in all its details
6:38 according to its specifications.[u] He had
[u]Heb 8:5 spent seven years building it.

Solomon Builds His Palace

7 It took Solomon thirteen years,
7:1 [v]1Ki 9:10; 2Ch 8:1 however, to complete the construction of his palace.[v] 2 He built the Palace[w]
of the Forest of Lebanon[x] a hundred
7:2 [w]2Sa 7:2; [x]1Ki 10:17; 2Ch 9:16 cubits long, fifty wide and thirty high,[a]
with four rows of cedar columns sup-
porting trimmed cedar beams. 3 It was
roofed with cedar above the beams
that rested on the columns—forty-five
beams, fifteen to a row. 4 Its windows
were placed high in sets of three, facing
each other. 5 All the doorways had rect-
angular frames; they were in the front
part in sets of three, facing each other.[b]
6 He made a colonnade fifty cubits
long and thirty wide.[c] In front of it was
a portico, and in front of that were pillars and an overhanging roof.
7:7 [y]Ps 122:5; Pr 20:8 [z]1Ki 6:15 7 He built the throne hall, the Hall
of Justice, where he was to judge,[y] and
he covered it with cedar from floor to
ceiling.[d][z] 8 And the palace in which he
was to live, set farther back, was similar in design. Solomon also made a palace like this hall for Pharaoh's daughter,
7:8 [a]1Ki 3:1; 2Ch 8:11 whom he had married.[a]
9 All these structures, from the outside
to the great courtyard and from foundation to eaves, were made of blocks
of high-grade stone cut to size and
trimmed with a saw on their inner and
outer faces. 10 The foundations were laid
with large stones of good quality, some
measuring ten cubits[e] and some eight.[f]
11 Above were high-grade stones, cut
to size, and cedar beams. 12 The great
7:12 [b]1Ki 6:36 courtyard was surrounded by a wall of
three courses[b] of dressed stone and one
course of trimmed cedar beams, as was
the inner courtyard of the temple of the
LORD with its portico.

The Temple's Furnishings

13 King Solomon sent to Tyre and
7:13 [c]2Ch 2:13 brought Huram,[g][c] 14 whose mother was
a widow from the tribe of Naphtali and
whose father was a man of Tyre and a
craftsman in bronze. Huram was highly
skilled[d] and experienced in all kinds of 7:14 [d]Ex 31:2-5; 35:31; 36:1; 2Ch 2:14 [e]2Ch 4:11,16
bronze work. He came to King Solo-
mon and did all[e] the work assigned to
him. 7:15 [f]2Ki 25:17; 2Ch 3:15; 4:12; 52:17,21
15 He cast two bronze pillars,[f] each
eighteen cubits high and twelve cubits
around,[h] by line. 16 He also made two
capitals[g] of cast bronze to set on the 7:16 [g]2Ki 25:17
tops of the pillars; each capital was five
cubits[i] high. 17 A network of interwoven
chains festooned the capitals on top of
the pillars, seven for each capital. 18 He
made pomegranates in two rows[j] encircling each network to decorate the capitals on top of the pillars.[k] He did the
same for each capital. 19 The capitals on
top of the pillars in the portico were
in the shape of lilies, four cubits[l] high.
20 On the capitals of both pillars, above
the bowl-shaped part next to the network, were the two hundred pomegran-
ates[h] in rows all around. 21 He erected 7:20 [h]2Ch 3:16; 4:13; Jer 52:23
the pillars at the portico of the temple.
The pillar to the south he named Jakin[m]
and the one to the north Boaz.[n][i] 22 The 7:21 [i]1Ki 6:3; 2Ch 3:17
capitals on top were in the shape of lil-
ies. And so the work on the pillars was
completed.
23 He made the Sea[j] of cast metal, cir- 7:23 [j]2Ki 25:13; 1Ch 18:8; Jer 52:17
cular in shape, measuring ten cubits[e]
from rim to rim and five cubits high.
It took a line of thirty cubits[o] to measure around it. 24 Below the rim, gourds
encircled it—ten to a cubit. The gourds
were cast in two rows in one piece with
the Sea. 7:25 [k]2Ch 4:4-5; Jer 52:20
25 The Sea stood on twelve bulls,[k]

[a] *2* That is, about 150 feet (about 46 meters) long, 75 feet (about 23 meters) wide and 45 feet (about 13.5 meters) high [b] *5* The meaning of the Hebrew for this verse is uncertain. [c] *6* That is, about 75 feet (about 23 meters) long and 45 feet (about 13.5 meters) wide [d] *7* Vulgate and Syriac; Hebrew *floor* [e] *10,23* That is, about 15 feet (about 4.5 meters) [f] *10* That is, about 12 feet (about 3.6 meters) [g] *13* Hebrew *Hiram,* a variant of *Huram;* also in verses 40 and 45 [h] *15* That is, about 27 feet (about 8.1 meters) high and 18 feet (about 5.4 meters) around [i] *16* That is, about 7 1/2 feet (about 2.3 meters); also in verse 23 [j] *18* Two Hebrew manuscripts and Septuagint; most Hebrew manuscripts *made the pillars, and there were two rows* [k] *18* Many Hebrew manuscripts and Syriac; most Hebrew manuscripts *pomegranates* [l] *19* That is, about 6 feet (about 1.8 meters); also in verse 38 [m] *21 Jakin* probably means *he establishes.* [n] *21 Boaz* probably means *in him is strength.* [o] *23* That is, about 45 feet (about 13.5 meters)

three facing north, three facing west,
three facing south and three facing east.
The Sea rested on top of them, and
their hindquarters were toward the center. 26It was a handbreadth[a] in thickness, and its rim was like the rim of
a cup, like a lily blossom. It held two
thousand baths.[b]
7:27 [l]ver 38; 2Ch 4:14 27He also made ten movable stands[l]
of bronze; each was four cubits long,
four wide and three high.[c] 28This is how
the stands were made: They had side
panels attached to uprights. 29On the
panels between the uprights were lions,
bulls and cherubim—and on the uprights as well. Above and below the lions
and bulls were wreaths of hammered
7:30 [m]2Ki 16:17 work. 30Each stand[m] had four bronze
wheels with bronze axles, and each had a
basin resting on four supports, cast with
wreaths on each side. 31On the inside of
the stand there was an opening that had
a circular frame one cubit[d] deep. This
opening was round, and with its base-
work it measured a cubit and a half.[e]
Around its opening there was engraving.
The panels of the stands were square,
not round. 32The four wheels were under the panels, and the axles of the
wheels were attached to the stand. The
diameter of each wheel was a cubit and a
half. 33The wheels were made like chariot wheels; the axles, rims, spokes and
hubs were all of cast metal.

34Each stand had four handles, one
on each corner, projecting from the
stand. 35At the top of the stand there
was a circular band half a cubit[f] deep.
The supports and panels were attached
to the top of the stand. 36He engraved
cherubim, lions and palm trees on the
surfaces of the supports and on the
panels, in every available space, with
wreaths all around. 37This is the way he
made the ten stands. They were all cast
in the same molds and were identical in
size and shape.

7:38 [n]Ex 30:18; 2Ch 4:6 38He then made ten bronze basins,[n]
each holding forty baths[g] and measur-
ing four cubits across, one basin to go
on each of the ten stands. 39He placed
five of the stands on the south side of
the temple and five on the north. He
placed the Sea on the south side, at the
southeast corner of the temple. 40He
also made the basins and shovels and
sprinkling bowls.

So Huram finished all the work he
had undertaken for King Solomon in
the temple of the LORD:

41 the two pillars;
the two bowl-shaped capitals on top of the pillars;
the two sets of network decorating the two bowl-shaped capitals on top of the pillars;
42 the four hundred pomegranates for the two sets of network (two rows of pomegranates for each network, decorating the bowl-
shaped capitals[o] on top of the pillars); 7:42 [o]ver 20
43 the ten stands with their ten basins;
44 the Sea and the twelve bulls under it;
45 the pots, shovels and sprinkling
bowls.[p] 7:45 [p]Ex 27:3

All these objects that Huram made
for King Solomon for the temple of the
LORD were of burnished bronze. 46The
king had them cast in clay molds in the
plain[q] of the Jordan between Succoth[r] 7:46 [q]2Ch 4:17 [r]Ge 33:17; Jos 13:27
and Zarethan.[s] 47Solomon left all these [s]Jos 3:16
things unweighed,[t] because there were 7:47 [t]1Ch 22:3
so many; the weight of the bronze was
not determined.

48Solomon also made all the furnishings that were in the LORD's temple:

the golden altar;
the golden table[u] on which was the
bread of the Presence;[v] 7:48 [u]Ex 37:10 [v]Ex 25:30
49 the lampstands[w] of pure gold (five
on the right and five on the left, 7:49 [w]Ex 25:31-38
in front of the inner sanctuary);
the gold floral work and lamps and tongs;
50 the pure gold basins, wick trimmers, sprinkling bowls, dishes
and censers;[x] 7:50 [x]2Ki 25:13
and the gold sockets for the doors of the innermost room, the Most Holy Place, and also for the doors of the main hall of the temple.

[a]*26* That is, about 3 inches (about 8 centimeters)
[b]*26* That is, probably about 11,500 gallons (about 44 kiloliters); the Septuagint does not have this sentence.
[c]*27* That is, about 6 feet (about 1.8 meters) long and wide and about 4 1/2 feet (about 1.3 meters) high
[d]*31* That is, about 1 1/2 feet (about 0.5 meter)
[e]*31* That is, about 2 1/4 feet (about 0.7 meter); also in verse 32
[f]*35* That is, about 3/4 foot (about 0.2 meter)
[g]*38* That is, about 230 gallons (about 880 liters)

51When all the work King Solomon
had done for the temple of the LORD
was finished, he brought in the things
7:51 his father David had dedicated[y]—the
[y]2Sa 8:11 silver and gold and the furnishings—
and he placed them in the treasuries of
the LORD's temple.

The Ark Brought to the Temple

8 Then King Solomon summoned
into his presence at Jerusalem the
elders of Israel, all the heads of the tribes
8:1 [z]Nu 7:2 and the chiefs[z] of the Israelite families,
[a]2Sa 6:17 to bring up the ark[a] of the LORD's cov-
[b]2Sa 5:7 enant from Zion, the City of David.[b]
2All the men of Israel came together to
King Solomon at the time of the festi-
8:2 val[c] in the month of Ethanim, the sev-
[c]2Ch 7:8 enth month.[d]
[d]Lev 23:34 3When all the elders of Israel had ar-
8:3 [e]Nu 7:9; rived, the priests[e] took up the ark, 4and
Jos 3:3 they brought up the ark of the LORD
8:4 and the Tent of Meeting[f] and all the sa-
[f]1Ki 3:4; cred furnishings in it. The priests and
2Ch 1:3 Levites carried them up, 5and King Solomon and the entire assembly of Israel
that had gathered about him were be-
8:5 fore the ark, sacrificing[g] so many sheep
[g]2Sa 6:13 and cattle that they could not be recorded or counted.
6The priests then brought the ark of
8:6 the LORD's covenant[h] to its place in
[h]2Sa 6:17 the inner sanctuary of the temple, the
[i]1Ki 6:19,27 Most Holy Place, and put it beneath
the wings of the cherubim.[i] 7The cherubim spread their wings over the place of
the ark and overshadowed the ark and
its carrying poles. 8These poles were
so long that their ends could be seen
from the Holy Place in front of the inner sanctuary, but not from outside the
8:8 Holy Place; and they are still there to-
[j]Ex 25:13-15 day.[j] 9There was nothing in the ark ex-
8:9 cept the two stone tablets[k] that Moses
[k]Ex 24:7-8; had placed in it at Horeb, where the
25:21; 40:20; LORD made a covenant with the Israel-
Dt 10:2-5; Heb 9:4 ites after they came out of Egypt.
10When the priests withdrew from
8:10 the Holy Place, the cloud[l] filled the
[l]Ex 40:34-35; 2Ch 7:1-2 temple of the LORD. 11And the priests
could not perform their service because
of the cloud, for the glory of the LORD
filled his temple.
8:12 12Then Solomon said, "The LORD
[m]Ps 18:11; 97:2 has said that he would dwell in a dark
8:13 cloud;[m] 13I have indeed built a magnifi-
[n]Ex 15:17; 2Sa 7:13; cent temple for you, a place for you to
Ps 132:13 dwell[n] forever."

14While the whole assembly of Israel
was standing there, the king turned
around and blessed[o] them. 15Then he 8:14
said: [o]2Sa 6:18

"Praise be to the LORD,[p] the 8:15
God of Israel, who with his own [p]2Sa 7:12-13; 1Ch 29:10,
hand has fulfilled what he prom- 20; Ne 9:5;
ised with his own mouth to my fa- Lk 1:68
ther David. For he said, 16'Since
the day I brought my people Israel
out of Egypt, I have not chosen a
city in any tribe of Israel to have a
temple built for my Name[q] to be 8:16 [q]Dt 12:5
there, but I have chosen[r] David[s] to [r]1Sa 16:1
rule my people Israel.' [s]2Sa 7:4-6,8
17"My father David had it in his
heart to build a temple[t] for the 8:17 [t]2Sa 7:2;
Name of the LORD, the God of Is- 1Ch 17:1
rael. 18But the LORD said to my
father David, 'Because it was in
your heart to build a temple for
my Name, you did well to have
this in your heart. 19Nevertheless,
you[u] are not the one to build the 8:19 [u]2Sa 7:5
temple, but your son, who is your [v]2Sa 7:13;
own flesh and blood—he is the 1Ki 5:3,5
one who will build the temple for
my Name.'[v]
20"The LORD has kept the
promise he made: I have succeeded David my father and now I sit
on the throne of Israel, just as the
LORD promised, and I have built[w] 8:20
the temple for the Name of the [w]1Ch 28:6
LORD, the God of Israel. 21I have
provided a place there for the ark,
in which is the covenant of the
LORD that he made with our fathers when he brought them out
of Egypt."

Solomon's Prayer of Dedication

22Then Solomon stood before the altar of the LORD in front of the whole
assembly of Israel, spread out his hands[x] 8:22 [x]Ex 9:29;
toward heaven 23and said: Ezr 9:5

"O LORD, God of Israel, there is
no God like[y] you in heaven above 8:23
or on earth below—you who keep [y]1Sa 2:2; 2Sa 7:22
your covenant of love[z] with your [z]Dt 7:9,12;
servants who continue wholeheart- Ne 1:5; 9:32; Da 9:4
edly in your way. 24You have kept
your promise to your servant David my father; with your mouth
you have promised and with your
hand you have fulfilled it—as it is
today.

GOODNESS

THE GOD WHO HONORS GOODNESS

1 Kings 8:23

There is no God like him who is the Father of our Savior. No God loves like he does! No God saves like he does! No other God could touch the earth, bleed for it and leave it ever after a colony of heaven.

25"Now LORD, God of Israel,
keep for your servant David my
8:25 [a]1Ki 2:4 father the promises[a] you made to
him when you said, 'You shall
never fail to have a man to sit before me on the throne of Israel,
if only your sons are careful in all
they do to walk before me as you
have done.' 26And now, O God
of Israel, let your word that you
8:26 [b]2Sa 7:25 promised[b] your servant David my
father come true.
8:27 27"But will God really dwell[c] on
[c]Ac 7:48 earth? The heavens, even the high-
[d]2Ch 2:6; Ps 139:7-16; est heaven, cannot contain[d] you.
Isa 66:1; How much less this temple I have
Jer 23:24 built! 28Yet give attention to your
servant's prayer and his plea for
mercy, O LORD my God. Hear
the cry and the prayer that your
servant is praying in your presence
8:29 this day. 29May your eyes be open[e]
[e]2Ch 7:15; Ne 1:6 toward[f] this temple night and day,
[f]Da 6:10 this place of which you said, 'My
[g]Dt 12:11 Name[g] shall be there,' so that you
will hear the prayer your servant
prays toward this place. 30Hear the
supplication of your servant and of
your people Israel when they pray
toward this place. Hear from heav-
en, your dwelling place, and when
8:30 [h]Ps 85:2 you hear, forgive.[h]
31"When a man wrongs his
neighbor and is required to take
an oath and he comes and swears
8:31 [i]Ex 22:11 the oath[i] before your altar in this
temple, 32then hear from heaven
and act. Judge between your servants, condemning the guilty and
bringing down on his own head
what he has done. Declare the in-
8:32 [j]Dt 25:1 nocent not guilty, and so establish
his innocence.[j]
8:33 [k]Lev 26:17; 33"When your people Israel have
Dt 28:25 been defeated[k] by an enemy because they have sinned[l] against 8:33 [l]Lev 26:39
you, and when they turn back to
you and confess your name, praying and making supplication to
you in this temple, 34then hear
from heaven and forgive the sin of
your people Israel and bring them
back to the land you gave to their
fathers.
35"When the heavens are shut
up and there is no rain[m] because 8:35 [m]Lev 26:19;
your people have sinned against Dt 28:24
you, and when they pray toward
this place and confess your name
and turn from their sin because
you have afflicted them, 36then
hear from heaven and forgive the
sin of your servants, your people
Israel. Teach[n] them the right way[o] 8:36 [n]1Sa 12:23;
to live, and send rain on the land Ps 25:4; 94:12
you gave your people for an inher- [o]Ps 5:8; 27:11;
itance. Jer 6:16
37"When famine[p] or plague 8:37 [p]Lev 26:26
comes to the land, or blight[q] or [q]Dt 28:22
mildew, locusts or grasshoppers, or
when an enemy besieges them in
any of their cities, whatever disaster or disease may come, 38and
when a prayer or plea is made by
any of your people Israel—each
one aware of the afflictions of his
own heart, and spreading out his
hands toward this temple— 39then
hear from heaven, your dwelling
place. Forgive and act; deal with
each man according to all he does,
since you know his heart (for you
alone know[r] the hearts of all men), 8:39 [r]1Sa 16:7;
40so that they will fear[s] you all the 1Ch 28:9;
time they live in the land you gave Ps 11:4;
our fathers. Jer 17:10; Jn 2:24;
41"As for the foreigner who does Ac 1:24
not belong to your people Israel 8:40 [s]Ps 130:4
but has come from a distant land
because of your name— 42for men
will hear of your great name and 8:42
your mighty hand[t] and your out- [t]Dt 3:24
stretched arm—when he comes
and prays toward this temple,
43then hear from heaven, your
dwelling place, and do whatever
the foreigner asks of you, so that
all the peoples of the earth may
know[u] your name and fear[v] you, 8:43 [u]1Sa 17:46;
as do your own people Israel, and 2Ki 19:19
may know that this house I have [v]Ps 102:15
built bears your Name.
44"When your people go to war

WEEK 34 FAITHFULNESS

DAY ONE

FAITHFULNESS, A STUBBORN COMMITMENT TO THE RIGHT

Read 1 Kings 8:54–61

Solomon's blessing on the newly finished temple includes a blessing on the people of Israel. Solomon dedicates the temple by thanking God for the ways God had expressed his faithfulness in the past and by asking God to perform five wonderful things in Israel's future.

Solomon's thanksgiving for God's past faithfulness includes these celebration points:

- God had given rest to his people. War is over. Peace has come.
- God never fell short in a single one of his promises.
- God kept his word to his people.
- God was with Israel's ancestors from Abraham to the present moment.

Solomon's thanksgiving gives us a reason to believe God will also be faithful in the future. Here are the five invocations of the king:

- He prays that God will turn the hearts of the relatively new nation toward himself.
- He prays that God will enable Israel to keep all God's commandments and live in purity.
- He invokes God's promise for the future.
- He petitions God to be as faithful in his future providence as he has been in the past.
- Solomon's fifth and final entreaty is that God will use Israel's future faithfulness to prove to the entire world that Israel's God is the only God.

These blessings and invocations of Solomon remind us of God's faithfulness and encourage our own.

DAY TWO

FAITHFULNESS AND THE PURPOSE OF GOD IN MY LIFE

Diógenes of Sinope once took a lantern and thrust it into every nook and cranny of Athens in broad daylight, seeking for truth. The same imagery is used in Jeremiah, referring to Jeremiah's decadent hometown. It was as though Jeremiah took a lantern and ran up and down through the streets of Jerusalem crying, "I seek an honest person!" But how did Jeremiah live in this corrupt city? First, he was faithful to God. Second, he had a stubborn commitment to what was right. *Turn to Jeremiah 5:1–2, page 878, for today's study.*

DAY THREE

FAITHFULNESS AND MY RELATIONSHIP WITH CHRIST

The Jewish officials were attempting to get this man who had been born blind to condemn Jesus as a sinner or as a religious charlatan. But a healed blind man, who has lived his life in darkness, may not be the best person to pressure into giving a condemnation of his healer. Jesus had riled official institutionalism to the point that the leaders wanted to discredit and destroy him. But in this man whom Jesus had healed they found only stubborn commitment to the Son of God. *Turn to John 9:24–34, page 1263, for today's study.*

DAY FOUR

FAITHFULNESS AND MY SERVICE TO OTHERS

Surely those of us who love God recognize our special obligation to honor those who love God. How do we serve others? The Jews who were doing better financially after repatriation were taking advantage of those who were not faring as well. We can apply the principle to our own day: The church that reaches out is always under obligation to care for those it has. *Turn to Nehemiah 5:6–11, page 558, for today's study.*

DAY FIVE

FAITHFULNESS AND ITS PLACE IN MY PERSONAL WORSHIP

Never did a martyr die without scanning the sky, hoping for Jesus to return before the fires of the stake destroyed his or her life. While most martyrs pray to be delivered, many pray more fervently that they will be found faithful. Daniel faced his own martyrdom by remaining faithful to his worship of God, no matter what the cost. *Turn to Daniel 6:11–22, page 1020, for today's study.*

MEMORIZE THIS WEEK

LUKE 9:62

Jesus replied, "No one who puts his hand to the plow and looks back is fit for service in the kingdom of God."

Week 35, Gentleness, Childlike Godliness, begins on page 315, 1 Samuel 3:1–10.
To begin a topical study on the Fruit of the Spirit, Faithfulness, turn to the Topical Index, page 1548.

against their enemies, wherever you
send them, and when they pray
to the LORD toward the city you
have chosen and the temple I have
built for your Name, 45then hear
from heaven their prayer and their
plea, and uphold their cause.
46"When they sin against you—
for there is no one who does not
sin[w]—and you become angry with
them and give them over to the enemy, who takes them captive to his
own land, far away or near; 47and if
they have a change of heart in the
land where they are held captive,[x]
and repent and plead[y] with you in
the land of their conquerors and
say, 'We have sinned, we have done
wrong, we have acted wickedly';[z]
48and if they turn back to you with
all their heart[a] and soul in the land
of their enemies who took them
captive, and pray[b] to you toward
the land you gave their fathers, toward the city you have chosen and
the temple[c] I have built for your
Name; 49then from heaven, your
dwelling place, hear their prayer
and their plea, and uphold their
cause. 50And forgive your people,
who have sinned against you; forgive all the offenses they have committed against you, and cause their
conquerors to show them mercy;[d]
51for they are your people and your
inheritance,[e] whom you brought
out of Egypt, out of that iron-
smelting furnace.[f]
52"May your eyes be open to
your servant's plea and to the plea
of your people Israel, and may you
listen to them whenever they cry
out to you. 53For you singled them
out from all the nations of the
world to be your own inheritance,[g]
just as you declared through your
servant Moses when you, O Sovereign LORD, brought our fathers
out of Egypt."

54When Solomon had finished all
these prayers and supplications to the
LORD, he rose from before the altar of
the LORD, where he had been kneeling with his hands spread out toward
heaven. 55He stood[h] and blessed the
whole assembly of Israel in a loud voice,
saying:

8:46 [w]Pr 20:9; Ecc 7:20; Ro 3:9; 1Jn 1:8-10 [x]Lev 26:33-39; Dt 28:64
8:47 [y]Lev 26:40; Ne 1:6 [z]Ps 106:6; Da 9:5
8:48 [a]Dt 4:29; Jer 29:12-14 [b]Da 6:10 [c]Jnh 2:4
8:50 [d]2Ch 30:9; Ps 106:46
8:51 [e]Dt 4:20; 9:29; Ne 1:10 [f]Jer 11:4
8:53 [g]Ex 19:5; Dt 9:26-29
8:55 [h]ver 14; 2Sa 6:18

56"Praise be to the LORD, who
has given rest[i] to his people Israel
just as he promised. Not one word
has failed of all the good promises[j]
he gave through his servant Moses.
57May the LORD our God be with
us as he was with our fathers; may
he never leave us nor forsake[k] us.
58May he turn our hearts[l] to him,
to walk in all his ways and to keep
the commands, decrees and regulations he gave our fathers. 59And
may these words of mine, which I
have prayed before the LORD, be
near to the LORD our God day
and night, that he may uphold
the cause of his servant and the
cause of his people Israel according to each day's need, 60so that
all the peoples[m] of the earth may
know that the LORD is God and
that there is no other.[n] 61But your
hearts must be fully committed[o] to
the LORD our God, to live by his
decrees and obey his commands,
as at this time."

The Dedication of the Temple

62Then the king and all Israel with
him offered sacrifices before the LORD.
63Solomon offered a sacrifice of fellowship offerings[a] to the LORD: twenty-
two thousand cattle and a hundred and
twenty thousand sheep and goats. So
the king and all the Israelites dedicated
the temple of the LORD.
64On that same day the king consecrated the middle part of the courtyard
in front of the temple of the LORD,
and there he offered burnt offerings,
grain offerings and the fat of the fellowship offerings, because the bronze altar[p]
before the LORD was too small to hold
the burnt offerings, the grain offerings
and the fat of the fellowship offerings.
65So Solomon observed the festival[q]
at that time, and all Israel with him—a
vast assembly, people from Lebo[b] Hamath[r] to the Wadi of Egypt.[s] They celebrated it before the LORD our God for
seven days and seven days more, fourteen days in all. 66On the following day
he sent the people away. They blessed
the king and then went home, joyful

[a]*63* Traditionally *peace offerings*; also in verse 64
[b]*65* Or *from the entrance to*

8:56 [i]Dt 12:10 [j]Jos 21:45; 23:15
8:57 [k]Dt 31:6; Jos 1:5; Heb 13:5
8:58 [l]Ps 119:36
8:60 [m]Jos 4:24; 1Sa 17:46 [n]Dt 4:35; 1Ki 18:39; Jer 10:10-12
8:61 [o]1Ki 11:4; 15:3,14; 2Ki 20:3
8:64 [p]2Ch 4:1
8:65 [q]ver 2; Lev 23:34 [r]Nu 34:8; Jos 13:5; Jdg 3:3; 2Ki 14:25 [s]Ge 15:18

and glad in heart for all the good things
the LORD had done for his servant David and his people Israel.

The LORD Appears to Solomon

9:1 [t]1Ki 7:1; 2Ch 8:6

9 When Solomon had finished[t] building the temple of the LORD and
the royal palace, and had achieved all
he had desired to do, 2the LORD appeared[u] to him a second time, as he
had appeared to him at Gibeon. 3The
LORD said to him:

9:2 [u]1Ki 3:5

"I have heard[v] the prayer and
plea you have made before me;
I have consecrated this temple,
which you have built, by putting
my Name there forever. My eyes[w]
and my heart will always be there.
4"As for you, if you walk before
me in integrity of heart[x] and uprightness, as David[y] your father
did, and do all I command and observe my decrees and laws, 5I will
establish[z] your royal throne over
Israel forever, as I promised David
your father when I said, 'You shall
never fail[a] to have a man on the
throne of Israel.'

9:3 [v]2Ki 20:5; Ps 10:17 [w]Dt 11:12; 1Ki 8:29

9:4 [x]Ge 17:1 [y]1Ki 15:5

9:5 [z]1Ch 22:10 [a]2Sa 7:15; 1Ki 2:4

KINDNESS

A LINE OF KINGS

1 Kings 9:5

The Lord promised David a throne forever. Jesus was the last king in David's dynasty. He made royalty of us all.

Cain begat and that was that—
A thousand sons of dynasty.
But God begat an entire race,
A kingdom born at Calvary.

6"But if you[a] or your sons turn
away[b] from me and do not observe
the commands and decrees I have
given you[a] and go off to serve other gods and worship them, 7then I
will cut off Israel from the land[c] I
have given them and will reject this
temple I have consecrated for my
Name.[d] Israel will then become a
byword[e] and an object of ridicule[f]
among all peoples. 8And though
this temple is now imposing, all
who pass by will be appalled and
will scoff and say, 'Why has the
LORD done such a thing to this
land and to this temple?'[g] 9People
will answer, 'Because they have forsaken the LORD their God, who
brought their fathers out of Egypt,
and have embraced other gods,
worshiping and serving them—
that is why the LORD brought all
this disaster on them.'"

9:6 [b]2Sa 7:14

9:7 [c]2Ki 17:23; 25:21 [d]Jer 7:14 [e]Ps 44:14 [f]Dt 28:37

9:8 [g]Dt 29:24; Jer 22:8-9

Solomon's Other Activities

10At the end of twenty years, during
which Solomon built these two buildings—the temple of the LORD and the
royal palace— 11King Solomon gave
twenty towns in Galilee to Hiram king
of Tyre, because Hiram had supplied
him with all the cedar and pine and
gold[h] he wanted. 12But when Hiram
went from Tyre to see the towns that
Solomon had given him, he was not
pleased with them. 13"What kind of
towns are these you have given me, my
brother?" he asked. And he called them
the Land of Cabul,[b][i] a name they have
to this day. 14Now Hiram had sent to
the king 120 talents[c] of gold.

9:11 [h]2Ch 8:2

9:13 [i]Jos 19:27

15Here is the account of the forced
labor King Solomon conscripted[j] to
build the LORD's temple, his own palace, the supporting terraces,[d][k] the wall
of Jerusalem, and Hazor,[l] Megiddo and
Gezer.[m] 16(Pharaoh king of Egypt had
attacked and captured Gezer. He had
set it on fire. He killed its Canaanite inhabitants and then gave it as a wedding
gift to his daughter, Solomon's wife.
17And Solomon rebuilt Gezer.) He built
up Lower Beth Horon,[n] 18Baalath,[o] and
Tadmor[e] in the desert, within his land,
19as well as all his store cities[p] and
the towns for his chariots[q] and for his
horses[f]—whatever he desired to build
in Jerusalem, in Lebanon and throughout all the territory he ruled.

9:15 [j]Jos 16:10; 1Ki 5:13 [k]ver 24; 2Sa 5:9 [l]Jos 19:36 [m]Jos 17:11

9:17 [n]Jos 16:3; 2Ch 8:5

9:18 [o]Jos 19:44

9:19 [p]ver 1 [q]1Ki 4:26

20All the people left from the Amorites, Hittites, Perizzites, Hivites and
Jebusites (these peoples were not Israelites), 21that is, their descendants[r]
remaining in the land, whom the Israelites could not exterminate[g][s]—these

9:21 [r]Ge 9:25-26 [s]Jos 15:63; 17:12; Jdg 1:21, 27,29

[a]*6* The Hebrew is plural. [b]*13 Cabul* sounds like the Hebrew for *good-for-nothing.* [c]*14* That is, about 4 1/2 tons (about 4 metric tons) [d]*15* Or *the Millo*; also in verse 24 [e]*18* The Hebrew may also be read *Tamar.* [f]*19* Or *charioteers* [g]*21* The Hebrew term refers to the irrevocable giving over of things or persons to the LORD, often by totally destroying them.

Solomon conscripted for his slave labor
9:21 [t]Ezr 2:55,58 force,[t] as it is to this day. [22]But Solo-
9:22 mon did not make slaves[u] of any of the
[u]Lev 25:39 Israelites; they were his fighting men,
his government officials, his officers, his
captains, and the commanders of his
chariots and charioteers. [23]They were
9:23 [v]1Ki 5:16 also the chief officials[v] in charge of Solomon's projects—550 officials supervis-
ing the men who did the work.
9:24 [w]1Ki 3:1; 7:8 [24]After Pharaoh's daughter[w] had come
[x]2Sa 5:9; 1Ki 11:27; up from the City of David to the pal-
2Ch 32:5 ace Solomon had built for her, he con-
9:25 structed the supporting terraces.[x]
[y]Ex 23:14; 2Ch 8:12-13, 16 [25]Three[y] times a year Solomon sacrificed burnt offerings and fellowship of-
ferings[a] on the altar he had built for
the LORD, burning incense before the
LORD along with them, and so fulfilled
the temple obligations.
9:26 [z]1Ki 22:48 [26]King Solomon also built ships[z] at
[a]Nu 33:35; Dt 2:8 Ezion Geber,[a] which is near Elath in
Edom, on the shore of the Red Sea.[b]
9:27 [b]1Ki 10:11; [27]And Hiram sent his men—sailors[b]
Eze 27:8 who knew the sea—to serve in the fleet
with Solomon's men. [28]They sailed to
9:28 [c]1Ch 29:4 Ophir[c] and brought back 420 talents[c]
of gold, which they delivered to King
Solomon.

The Queen of Sheba Visits Solomon

10:1 [d]Ge 10:7,28; **10** When the queen of Sheba[d]
Mt 12:42; heard about the fame of Solo-
Lk 11:31 mon and his relation to the name of
[e]Jdg 14:12 the LORD, she came to test him with
hard questions.[e] [2]Arriving at Jerusalem
with a very great caravan—with camels carrying spices, large quantities of
gold, and precious stones—she came to
Solomon and talked with him about all
that she had on her mind. [3]Solomon
answered all her questions; nothing was
too hard for the king to explain to her.
[4]When the queen of Sheba saw all the
wisdom of Solomon and the palace he
10:5 [f]1Ch 26:16 had built, [5]the food on his table,[f] the
seating of his officials, the attending
servants in their robes, his cupbearers,
and the burnt offerings he made at[d]
the temple of the LORD, she was overwhelmed.
[6]She said to the king, "The report I
heard in my own country about your
achievements and your wisdom is true.
[7]But I did not believe these things until I came and saw with my own eyes.
Indeed, not even half was told me; in
wisdom and wealth[g] you have far ex- 10:7 [g]1Ch 29:25
ceeded the report I heard. [8]How happy
your men must be! How happy your
officials, who continually stand before
you and hear[h] your wisdom! [9]Praise[i] be 10:8 [h]Pr 8:34
to the LORD your God, who has de-
lighted in you and placed you on the 10:9 [i]1Ki 5:7
throne of Israel. Because of the LORD's [j]2Sa 8:15; Ps 33:5; 72:2
eternal love for Israel, he has made
you king, to maintain justice[j] and righteousness."
[10]And she gave the king 120 talents[e]
of gold,[k] large quantities of spices, and 10:10 [k]ver 2
precious stones. Never again were so
many spices brought in as those the
queen of Sheba gave to King Solomon.
[11](Hiram's ships brought gold from
Ophir;[l] and from there they brought 10:11 [l]Ge 10:29;
great cargoes of almugwood[f] and pre- 1Ki 9:27-28
cious stones. [12]The king used the almugwood to make supports for the
temple of the LORD and for the royal
palace, and to make harps and lyres
for the musicians. So much almugwood
has never been imported or seen since
that day.)
[13]King Solomon gave the queen of
Sheba all she desired and asked for,
besides what he had given her out of
his royal bounty. Then she left and returned with her retinue to her own
country.

Solomon's Splendor

[14]The weight of the gold[m] that Solo- 10:14 [m]1Ki 9:28
mon received yearly was 666 talents,[g]
[15]not including the revenues from merchants and traders and from all the Ara-
bian kings and the governors of the
land.
[16]King Solomon made two hundred
large shields[n] of hammered gold; six
hundred bekas[h] of gold went into each 10:16 [n]1Ki 14:26-28
shield. [17]He also made three hundred
small shields of hammered gold, with
three minas[i] of gold in each shield. The
king put them in the Palace of the Forest of Lebanon.[o] 10:17 [o]1Ki 7:2
[18]Then the king made a great throne

[a]*25* Traditionally *peace offerings* [b]*26* Hebrew *Yam Suph*; that is, Sea of Reeds [c]*28* That is, about 16 tons (about 14.5 metric tons) [d]*5* Or *the ascent by which he went up to* [e]*10* That is, about 4 1/2 tons (about 4 metric tons) [f]*11* Probably a variant of *algumwood*; also in verse 12 [g]*14* That is, about 25 tons (about 23 metric tons) [h]*16* That is, about 7 1/2 pounds (about 3.5 kilograms) [i]*17* That is, about 3 3/4 pounds (about 1.7 kilograms)

inlaid with ivory and overlaid with fine
gold. [19]The throne had six steps, and its
back had a rounded top. On both sides
of the seat were armrests, with a lion
standing beside each of them. [20]Twelve
lions stood on the six steps, one at either end of each step. Nothing like it
had ever been made for any other kingdom. [21]All King Solomon's goblets were
gold, and all the household articles in
the Palace of the Forest of Lebanon
were pure gold. Nothing was made of
silver, because silver was considered of
little value in Solomon's days. [22]The
10:22 king had a fleet of trading ships[a][p] at sea
[p]1Ki 9:26 along with the ships of Hiram. Once
every three years it returned, carrying
gold, silver and ivory, and apes and baboons.
10:23 [23]King Solomon was greater in riches[q]
[q]1Ki 3:13 and wisdom[r] than all the other kings
[r]1Ki 4:30 of the earth. [24]The whole world sought
audience with Solomon to hear the wis-
10:24 dom[s] God had put in his heart. [25]Year
[s]1Ki 3:9,12,28 after year, everyone who came brought
a gift—articles of silver and gold, robes,
weapons and spices, and horses and
mules.
[26]Solomon accumulated chariots and
10:26 horses;[t] he had fourteen hundred chari-
[t]Dt 17:16; 1Ki 4:26; ots and twelve thousand horses,[b] which
9:19; he kept in the chariot cities and also with
2Ch 1:14; 9:25 him in Jerusalem. [27]The king made silver as common[u] in Jerusalem as stones,
10:27 [u]Dt 17:17 and cedar as plentiful as sycamore-fig
trees in the foothills. [28]Solomon's horses
were imported from Egypt[c] and from
Kue[d]—the royal merchants purchased
them from Kue. [29]They imported a
chariot from Egypt for six hundred
shekels[e] of silver, and a horse for a hundred and fifty.[f] They also exported them
10:29 to all the kings of the Hittites[v] and of
[v]2Ki 7:6-7 the Arameans.

Solomon's Wives

11 King Solomon, however, loved
many foreign women[w] besides
11:1 [w]Dt 17:17; Pharaoh's daughter—Moabites, Am-
Ne 13:26 monites, Edomites, Sidonians and Hittites. [2]They were from nations about
which the LORD had told the Israel-
11:2 ites, "You must not intermarry[x] with
[x]Ex 34:16; them, because they will surely turn your
Dt 7:3-4 hearts after their gods." Nevertheless,
Solomon held fast to them in love. [3]He
had seven hundred wives of royal birth
and three hundred concubines, and his
wives led him astray. [4]As Solomon grew
old, his wives turned his heart after other gods, and his heart was not fully de-
voted[y] to the LORD his God, as the 11:4 [y]1Ki 8:61; 9:4
heart of David his father had been. [5]He
followed Ashtoreth[z] the goddess of the 11:5 [z]ver 33;
Sidonians, and Molech[g][a] the detestable Jdg 2:13;
god of the Ammonites. [6]So Solomon 2Ki 23:13 [a]ver 7
did evil in the eyes of the LORD; he
did not follow the LORD completely, as
David his father had done.
[7]On a hill[b] east of Jerusalem, Solo- 11:7
mon built a high place for Chemosh[c] [b]2Ki 23:13 [c]Nu 21:29;
the detestable god of Moab, and for Jdg 11:24
Molech[d] the detestable god of the Am- [d]Lev 20:2-5; Ac 7:43
monites. [8]He did the same for all his
foreign wives, who burned incense and
offered sacrifices to their gods.

▸ SELF-CONTROL

UNTHINKABLE IDOLATRY

1 Kings 11:9

Idols recruit their worshipers with cheap enticements. Judas did not reject Christ outright. He only made Christ equal with his love of silver.

[9]The LORD became angry with Solomon because his heart had turned
away from the LORD, the God of Is-
rael, who had appeared[e] to him twice. 11:9 [e]ver 2-3;
[10]Although he had forbidden Solomon 1Ki 3:5; 9:2
to follow other gods,[f] Solomon did not 11:10
keep the LORD's command.[g] [11]So the [f]1Ki 9:6 [g]1Ki 6:12
LORD said to Solomon, "Since this is
your attitude and you have not kept
my covenant and my decrees, which
I commanded you, I will most certainly tear[h] the kingdom away from you 11:11
and give it to one of your subordinates. [h]ver 31; 1Ki 12:15-16;
[12]Nevertheless, for the sake of David 2Ki 17:21
your father, I will not do it during your
lifetime. I will tear it out of the hand of
your son. [13]Yet I will not tear the whole
kingdom from him, but will give him
one tribe[i] for the sake[j] of David my 11:13
servant and for the sake of Jerusalem, [i]1Ki 12:20 [j]2Sa 7:15
which I have chosen."[k] [k]Dt 12:11

[a]22 Hebrew *of ships of Tarshish* [b]26 Or *charioteers* [c]28 Or possibly *Muzur,* a region in Cilicia; also in verse 29 [d]28 Probably *Cilicia* [e]29 That is, about 15 pounds (about 7 kilograms) [f]29 That is, about 3 3/4 pounds (about 1.7 kilograms) [g]5 Hebrew *Milcom;* also in verse 33

Solomon's Adversaries

14Then the LORD raised up against
Solomon an adversary, Hadad the
Edomite, from the royal line of Edom.
15Earlier when David was fighting with
Edom, Joab the commander of the
army, who had gone up to bury the
dead, had struck down all the men
11:15 [l]Dt 20:13; 2Sa 8:14; 1Ch 18:12 in Edom.[l] 16Joab and all the Israelites
stayed there for six months, until they
had destroyed all the men in Edom.
17But Hadad, still only a boy, fled
to Egypt with some Edomite officials
who had served his father. 18They set
11:18 [m]Nu 10:12 out from Midian and went to Paran.[m]
Then taking men from Paran with
them, they went to Egypt, to Pharaoh
king of Egypt, who gave Hadad a
house and land and provided him with
food.

19Pharaoh was so pleased with Hadad that he gave him a sister of his
own wife, Queen Tahpenes, in marriage. 20The sister of Tahpenes bore him
a son named Genubath, whom Tahpenes brought up in the royal palace.
There Genubath lived with Pharaoh's
own children.

21While he was in Egypt, Hadad
heard that David rested with his fathers
and that Joab the commander of the
army was also dead. Then Hadad said
to Pharaoh, "Let me go, that I may return to my own country."

22"What have you lacked here that
you want to go back to your own country?" Pharaoh asked.

"Nothing," Hadad replied, "but do
let me go!"

23And God raised up against Solo-
11:23 [n]ver 14 [o]2Sa 8:3 mon another adversary,[n] Rezon son of
Eliada, who had fled from his master,
Hadadezer[o] king of Zobah. 24He gathered men around him and became the
leader of a band of rebels when David
destroyed the forces[a] ⌞of Zobah⌟; the
11:24 [p]2Sa 8:5; 10:8,18 rebels went to Damascus,[p] where they
settled and took control. 25Rezon was
Israel's adversary as long as Solomon
lived, adding to the trouble caused by
11:25 [q]2Sa 10:19 Hadad. So Rezon ruled in Aram[q] and
was hostile toward Israel.

Jeroboam Rebels Against Solomon

11:26 [r]2Sa 20:21; 1Ki 12:2; 2Ch 13:6 26Also, Jeroboam son of Nebat rebelled[r] against the king. He was one of
Solomon's officials, an Ephraimite from
Zeredah, and his mother was a widow
named Zeruah.

27Here is the account of how he rebelled against the king: Solomon had
built the supporting terraces[b][s] and had 11:27 [s]1Ki 9:24
filled in the gap in the wall of the city
of David his father. 28Now Jeroboam
was a man of standing,[t] and when Solo- 11:28 [t]Ru 2:1 [u]Pr 22:29
mon saw how well[u] the young man did
his work, he put him in charge of the
whole labor force of the house of Joseph.

29About that time Jeroboam was go-
ing out of Jerusalem, and Ahijah[v] the 11:29 [v]1Ki 12:15; 14:2; 2Ch 9:29
prophet of Shiloh met him on the way,
wearing a new cloak. The two of them
were alone out in the country, 30and
Ahijah took hold of the new cloak he
was wearing and tore[w] it into twelve 11:30 [w]1Sa 15:27
pieces. 31Then he said to Jeroboam,
"Take ten pieces for yourself, for this is
what the LORD, the God of Israel, says:
'See, I am going to tear[x] the kingdom 11:31 [x]ver 11
out of Solomon's hand and give you ten
tribes. 32But for the sake of my servant
David and the city of Jerusalem, which
I have chosen out of all the tribes of
Israel, he will have one tribe. 33I will
do this because they have[c] forsaken me
and worshiped[y] Ashtoreth the goddess 11:33 [y]ver 5-7 [z]1Ki 3:3
of the Sidonians, Chemosh the god of
the Moabites, and Molech the god of
the Ammonites, and have not walked
in my ways, nor done what is right in
my eyes, nor kept my statutes[z] and laws
as David, Solomon's father, did.

34" 'But I will not take the whole
kingdom out of Solomon's hand; I have
made him ruler all the days of his life
for the sake of David my servant, whom
I chose and who observed my commands and statutes. 35I will take the
kingdom from his son's hands and give
you ten tribes. 36I will give one tribe[a] to 11:36 [a]ver 13; 1Ki 12:17 [b]1Ki 15:4; 2Ki 8:19
his son so that David my servant may
always have a lamp[b] before me in Jerusalem, the city where I chose to put
my Name. 37However, as for you, I will
take you, and you will rule over all that
your heart desires;[c] you will be king 11:37 [c]2Sa 3:21
over Israel. 38If you do whatever I com-
mand you and walk in my ways and
do what is right in my eyes by keeping
my statutes[d] and commands, as David 11:38 [d]Dt 17:19

[a]*24* Hebrew *destroyed them* [b]*27* Or *the Millo*
[c]*33* Hebrew; Septuagint, Vulgate and Syriac *because he has*

my servant did, I will be with you. I will build you a dynasty[e] as enduring as the one I built for David and will give Israel to you. [39]I will humble David's descendants because of this, but not forever.' "

[40]Solomon tried to kill Jeroboam, but Jeroboam fled to Egypt, to Shishak[f] the king, and stayed there until Solomon's death.

Solomon's Death

[41]As for the other events of Solomon's reign—all he did and the wisdom he displayed—are they not written in the book of the annals of Solomon? [42]Solomon reigned in Jerusalem over all Israel forty years. [43]Then he rested with his fathers and was buried in the city of David his father. And Rehoboam[g] his son succeeded him as king.

Israel Rebels Against Rehoboam

12 Rehoboam went to Shechem, for all the Israelites had gone there to make him king. [2]When Jeroboam son of Nebat heard this (he was still in Egypt, where he had fled[h] from King Solomon), he returned from[a] Egypt. [3]So they sent for Jeroboam, and he and the whole assembly of Israel went to Rehoboam and said to him: [4]"Your father put a heavy yoke[i] on us, but now lighten the harsh labor and the heavy yoke he put on us, and we will serve you."

[5]Rehoboam answered, "Go away for three days and then come back to me." So the people went away.

[6]Then King Rehoboam consulted the elders[j] who had served his father Solomon during his lifetime. "How would you advise me to answer these people?" he asked.

[7]They replied, "If today you will be a servant to these people and serve them and give them a favorable answer,[k] they will always be your servants."

[8]But Rehoboam rejected the advice the elders gave him and consulted the young men who had grown up with him and were serving him. [9]He asked them, "What is your advice? How should we answer these people who say to me, 'Lighten the yoke your father put on us'?"

[10]The young men who had grown up with him replied, "Tell these people who have said to you, 'Your father put a heavy yoke on us, but make our yoke lighter'—tell them, 'My little finger is thicker than my father's waist. [11]My father laid on you a heavy yoke; I will make it even heavier. My father scourged you with whips; I will scourge you with scorpions.' "

[12]Three days later Jeroboam and all the people returned to Rehoboam, as the king had said, "Come back to me in three days." [13]The king answered the people harshly. Rejecting the advice given him by the elders, [14]he followed the advice of the young men and said, "My father made your yoke heavy; I will make it even heavier. My father scourged[l] you with whips; I will scourge you with scorpions." [15]So the king did not listen to the people, for this turn of events was from the LORD,[m] to fulfill the word the LORD had spoken to Jeroboam son of Nebat through Ahijah[n] the Shilonite.

[16]When all Israel saw that the king refused to listen to them, they answered the king:

"What share do we have in David,
what part in Jesse's son?
To your tents, O Israel![o]
Look after your own house,
O David!"

So the Israelites went home. [17]But as for the Israelites who were living in the towns of Judah,[p] Rehoboam still ruled over them.

[18]King Rehoboam sent out Adoniram,[b][q] who was in charge of forced labor, but all Israel stoned him to death. King Rehoboam, however, managed to get into his chariot and escape to Jerusalem. [19]So Israel has been in rebellion against the house of David[r] to this day.

[20]When all the Israelites heard that Jeroboam had returned, they sent and called him to the assembly and made him king over all Israel. Only the tribe of Judah remained loyal to the house of David.[s]

[21]When Rehoboam arrived in Jerusalem, he mustered the whole house of Judah and the tribe of Benjamin—a hundred and eighty thousand fighting

11:38 [e]Jos 1:5; 2Sa 7:11,27
11:40 [f]2Ch 12:2
11:43 [g]1Ki 14:21; Mt 1:7
12:2 [h]1Ki 11:40
12:4 [i]1Sa 8:11-18; 1Ki 4:20-28
12:6 [j]1Ki 4:2
12:7 [k]Pr 15:1
12:14 [l]Ex 1:14; 5:5-9,16-18
12:15 [m]ver 24; Dt 2:30; Jdg 14:4; 2Ch 22:7; 25:20 [n]1Ki 11:29
12:16 [o]2Sa 20:1
12:17 [p]1Ki 11:13,36
12:18 [q]2Sa 20:24; 1Ki 4:6; 5:14
12:19 [r]2Ki 17:21
12:20 [s]1Ki 11:13,32

[a]*2* Or *he remained in* [b]*18* Some Septuagint manuscripts and Syriac (see also 1 Kings 4:6 and 5:14); Hebrew *Adoram*

12:21 [t]2Ch 11:1 men—to make war[t] against the house
of Israel and to regain the kingdom for
Rehoboam son of Solomon.
22But this word of God came to She-
12:22 [u]2Ch 12:5-7 maiah[u] the man of God: 23"Say to Rehoboam son of Solomon king of Judah,
to the whole house of Judah and Benjamin, and to the rest of the people,
24'This is what the LORD says: Do not
go up to fight against your brothers, the
Israelites. Go home, every one of you,
for this is my doing.'" So they obeyed
the word of the LORD and went home
again, as the LORD had ordered.

Golden Calves at Bethel and Dan

12:25 [v]Jdg 9:45 [w]Jdg 8:8,17 25Then Jeroboam fortified Shechem[v]
in the hill country of Ephraim and lived
there. From there he went out and built
up Peniel.[a][w]
26Jeroboam thought to himself, "The
kingdom will now likely revert to the
house of David. 27If these people go
up to offer sacrifices at the temple of
12:27 [x]Dt 12:5-6 the LORD in Jerusalem,[x] they will again
give their allegiance to their lord, Reho-
boam king of Judah. They will kill me
and return to King Rehoboam."
28After seeking advice, the king made
12:28 [y]Ex 32:4; 2Ki 10:29; 17:16 [z]Ex 32:8 two golden calves.[y] He said to the people, "It is too much for you to go up to
Jerusalem. Here are your gods, O Israel, who brought you up out of Egypt."[z]
12:29 [a]Ge 28:19 [b]Jdg 18:27-31 29One he set up in Bethel,[a] and the
other in Dan.[b] 30And this thing became
12:30 [c]1Ki 13:34; 2Ki 17:21 a sin;[c] the people went even as far as
Dan to worship the one there.
12:31 [d]1Ki 13:32 [e]Nu 3:10; 1Ki 13:33; 2Ki 17:32; 2Ch 11:14-15; 13:9 31Jeroboam built shrines[d] on high
places and appointed priests[e] from all
sorts of people, even though they were
not Levites. 32He instituted a festival on
the fifteenth day of the eighth[f] month,
like the festival held in Judah, and of-
12:32 [f]Lev 23:33-34; Nu 29:12 fered sacrifices on the altar. This he
did in Bethel, sacrificing to the calves
he had made. And at Bethel he also
installed priests at the high places he
had made. 33On the fifteenth day of
the eighth month, a month of his own
choosing, he offered sacrifices on the al-
12:33 [g]Nu 15:39; 1Ki 13:1; Am 7:13 tar he had built at Bethel.[g] So he instituted the festival for the Israelites and
went up to the altar to make offerings.

The Man of God From Judah

13:1 [h]2Ki 23:17 [i]1Ki 12:32-33 **13** By the word of the LORD a man
of God[h] came from Judah to
Bethel,[i] as Jeroboam was standing by
the altar to make an offering. 2He cried
out against the altar by the word of the
LORD: "O altar, altar! This is what the
LORD says: 'A son named Josiah[j] will 13:2 [j]2Ki 23:15-16,20
be born to the house of David. On you
he will sacrifice the priests of the high
places who now make offerings here,
and human bones will be burned on
you.'" 3That same day the man of God
gave a sign:[k] "This is the sign the LORD 13:3 [k]Jdg 6:17; Isa 7:14; Jn 2:11; 1Co 1:22
has declared: The altar will be split apart
and the ashes on it will be poured out."
4When King Jeroboam heard what
the man of God cried out against the
altar at Bethel, he stretched out his
hand from the altar and said, "Seize
him!" But the hand he stretched out toward the man shriveled up, so that he
could not pull it back. 5Also, the altar
was split apart and its ashes poured out
according to the sign given by the man
of God by the word of the LORD.
6Then the king said to the man of
God, "Intercede[l] with the LORD your 13:6 [l]Ex 8:8; 9:28; 10:17; Lk 6:27-28; Ac 8:24; Jas 5:16
God and pray for me that my hand may
be restored." So the man of God interceded with the LORD, and the king's
hand was restored and became as it was
before.
7The king said to the man of God,
"Come home with me and have something to eat, and I will give you a
gift."[m] 13:7 [m]1Sa 9:7; 2Ki 5:15
8But the man of God answered the
king, "Even if you were to give me half
your possessions,[n] I would not go with 13:8 [n]Nu 22:18; 24:13 [o]ver 16
you, nor would I eat bread[o] or drink
water here. 9For I was commanded by
the word of the LORD: 'You must not
eat bread or drink water or return by
the way you came.'" 10So he took another road and did not return by the
way he had come to Bethel.
11Now there was a certain old prophet living in Bethel, whose sons came and
told him all that the man of God had
done there that day. They also told their
father what he had said to the king.
12Their father asked them, "Which way
did he go?" And his sons showed him
which road the man of God from Judah had taken. 13So he said to his sons,
"Saddle the donkey for me." And when
they had saddled the donkey for him,
he mounted it 14and rode after the man
of God. He found him sitting under an

[a] *25* Hebrew *Penuel,* a variant of *Peniel*

oak tree and asked, "Are you the man of
God who came from Judah?"
"I am," he replied.
15So the prophet said to him, "Come
home with me and eat."
16The man of God said, "I cannot
turn back and go with you, nor can I
13:16 [p]ver 8 eat bread[p] or drink water with you in
this place. 17I have been told by the
word of the LORD: 'You must not eat
bread or drink water there or return by
the way you came.'"
18The old prophet answered, "I too
am a prophet, as you are. And an angel
said to me by the word of the LORD:
'Bring him back with you to your house
so that he may eat bread and drink wa-
13:18 [q]Dt 13:3 ter.'" (But he was lying[q] to him.) 19So
the man of God returned with him and
ate and drank in his house.
20While they were sitting at the table,
the word of the LORD came to the old
prophet who had brought him back.
21He cried out to the man of God who
had come from Judah, "This is what
13:21 [r]ver 26 the LORD says: 'You have defied[r] the
word of the LORD and have not kept
the command the LORD your God gave
you. 22You came back and ate bread
and drank water in the place where he
told you not to eat or drink. Therefore
your body will not be buried in the
tomb of your fathers.'"
23When the man of God had finished eating and drinking, the prophet
who had brought him back saddled his
donkey for him. 24As he went on his
13:24 [s]1Ki 20:36 way, a lion[s] met him on the road and
killed him, and his body was thrown
down on the road, with both the donkey and the lion standing beside it.
25Some people who passed by saw the
body thrown down there, with the lion
standing beside the body, and they went
and reported it in the city where the old
prophet lived.
26When the prophet who had
brought him back from his journey
heard of it, he said, "It is the man of
God who defied the word of the LORD.
The LORD has given him over to the
lion, which has mauled him and killed
him, as the word of the LORD had
warned him."
27The prophet said to his sons, "Saddle the donkey for me," and they did
so. 28Then he went out and found the
body thrown down on the road, with
the donkey and the lion standing beside
it. The lion had neither eaten the body
nor mauled the donkey. 29So the prophet picked up the body of the man of
God, laid it on the donkey, and brought
it back to his own city to mourn for him
and bury him. 30Then he laid the body
in his own tomb, and they mourned
over him and said, "Oh, my brother!"[t] 13:30 [t]Jer 22:18
31After burying him, he said to his
sons, "When I die, bury me in the grave
where the man of God is buried; lay
my bones beside his bones.[u] 32For the 13:31 [u]2Ki 23:18
message he declared by the word of
the LORD against the altar in Bethel 13:32 [v]ver 2;
and against all the shrines on the high Lev 26:30
places[v] in the towns of Samaria[w] will [w]1Ki 16:24,28
certainly come true."[x] [x]2Ki 23:16

▸ SELF-CONTROL

GOOD-TIME PRIESTS

1 Kings 13:33

Jeroboam didn't want godly priests. He chose priests who picnicked in Gethsemane. If the priests are unclean, where will the soiled go for cleansing? If the gold rusts, what will the iron do?

33Even after this, Jeroboam did not
change his evil ways, but once more appointed priests for the high places from
all sorts[y] of people. Anyone who want- 13:33 [y]1Ki 12:31;
ed to become a priest he consecrated 2Ch 11:15;
for the high places. 34This was the sin[z] 13:9
of the house of Jeroboam that led to its 13:34 [z]1Ki 12:30
downfall and to its destruction[a] from [a]1Ki 14:10
the face of the earth.

Ahijah's Prophecy Against Jeroboam

14 At that time Abijah son of Jeroboam became ill, 2and Jeroboam said to his wife, "Go, disguise
yourself, so you won't be recognized as
the wife of Jeroboam. Then go to Shi-
loh. Ahijah[b] the prophet is there—the 14:2 [b]1Sa 28:8;
one who told me I would be king over 2Sa 14:2;
this people. 3Take ten loaves of bread[c] 1Ki 11:29
with you, some cakes and a jar of hon- 14:3 [c]1Sa 9:7
ey, and go to him. He will tell you what
will happen to the boy." 4So Jeroboam's
wife did what he said and went to Ahijah's house in Shiloh.
Now Ahijah could not see; his sight
was gone because of his age. 5But the
LORD had told Ahijah, "Jeroboam's

wife is coming to ask you about her son, for he is ill, and you are to give her such and such an answer. When she arrives, she will pretend to be someone else."

6 So when Ahijah heard the sound of her footsteps at the door, he said, "Come in, wife of Jeroboam. Why this pretense? I have been sent to you with bad news. 7 Go, tell Jeroboam that this is what the LORD, the God of Israel, says: 'I raised you up from among the people and made you a leader[d] over my people Israel. 8 I tore[e] the kingdom away from the house of David and gave it to you, but you have not been like my servant David, who kept my commands and followed me with all his heart, doing only what was right[f] in my eyes. 9 You have done more evil than all who lived before you. You have made for yourself other gods, idols[g] made of metal; you have provoked me to anger and thrust me behind your back.[h]

10 " 'Because of this, I am going to bring disaster on the house of Jeroboam. I will cut off from Jeroboam every last male in Israel—slave or free.[i] I will burn up the house of Jeroboam as one burns dung, until it is all gone.[j] 11 Dogs[k] will eat those belonging to Jeroboam who die in the city, and the birds of the air will feed on those who die in the country. The LORD has spoken!'

12 "As for you, go back home. When you set foot in your city, the boy will die. 13 All Israel will mourn for him and bury him. He is the only one belonging to Jeroboam who will be buried, because he is the only one in the house of Jeroboam in whom the LORD, the God of Israel, has found anything good.[l]

14 "The LORD will raise up for himself a king over Israel who will cut off the family of Jeroboam. This is the day! What? Yes, even now.[a] 15 And the LORD will strike Israel, so that it will be like a reed swaying in the water. He will uproot[m] Israel from this good land that he gave to their forefathers and scatter them beyond the River,[b] because they provoked[n] the LORD to anger by making Asherah[o] poles.[c] 16 And he will give Israel up because of the sins[p] Jeroboam has committed and has caused Israel to commit."

17 Then Jeroboam's wife got up and left and went to Tirzah.[q] As soon as she stepped over the threshold of the house, the boy died. 18 They buried him, and all Israel mourned for him, as the LORD had said through his servant the prophet Ahijah.

19 The other events of Jeroboam's reign, his wars and how he ruled, are written in the book of the annals of the kings of Israel. 20 He reigned for twenty-two years and then rested with his fathers. And Nadab his son succeeded him as king.

Rehoboam King of Judah

21 Rehoboam son of Solomon was king in Judah. He was forty-one years old when he became king, and he reigned seventeen years in Jerusalem, the city the LORD had chosen out of all the tribes of Israel in which to put his Name. His mother's name was Naamah; she was an Ammonite.[r]

22 Judah[s] did evil in the eyes of the LORD. By the sins they committed they stirred up his jealous anger[t] more than their fathers had done. 23 They also set up for themselves high places, sacred stones[u] and Asherah poles on every high hill and under every spreading tree.[v] 24 There were even male shrine prostitutes[w] in the land; the people engaged in all the detestable practices of the nations the LORD had driven out before the Israelites.

25 In the fifth year of King Rehoboam, Shishak king of Egypt attacked[x] Jerusalem. 26 He carried off the treasures of the temple[y] of the LORD and the treasures of the royal palace. He took everything, including all the gold shields[z] Solomon had made. 27 So King Rehoboam made bronze shields to replace them and assigned these to the commanders of the guard on duty at the entrance to the royal palace. 28 Whenever the king went to the LORD's temple, the guards bore the shields, and afterward they returned them to the guardroom.

29 As for the other events of Rehoboam's reign, and all he did, are they not written in the book of the annals of the kings of Judah? 30 There was continual warfare[a] between Rehoboam and Jeroboam. 31 And Rehoboam rested with his

14:7 [d]2Sa 12:7-8; 1Ki 16:2
14:8 [e]1Ki 11:31, 33,38 [f]1Ki 15:5
14:9 [g]Ex 34:17; 1Ki 12:28; 2Ch 11:15 [h]Ne 9:26; Ps 50:17; Eze 23:35
14:10 [i]Dt 32:36; 1Ki 21:21; 2Ki 9:8-9; 14:26 [j]1Ki 15:29
14:11 [k]1Ki 16:4; 21:24
14:13 [l]2Ch 12:12; 19:3
14:15 [m]Dt 29:28; 2Ki 15:29; 17:6; Ps 52:5 [n]Jos 23:15-16 [o]Ex 34:13; Dt 12:3
14:16 [p]1Ki 12:30; 13:34; 15:30,34; 16:2
14:17 [q]ver 12; 1Ki 15:33; 16:6-9
14:21 [r]ver 31; 1Ki 11:1; 2Ch 12:13
14:22 [s]2Ch 12:1 [t]Dt 32:21; Ps 78:58; 1Co 10:22
14:23 [u]Dt 16:22; 2Ki 17:9-10; Eze 16:24-25 [v]Dt 12:2; Isa 57:5
14:24 [w]Dt 23:17; 1Ki 15:12; 2Ki 23:7
14:25 [x]1Ki 11:40; 2Ch 12:2
14:26 [y]1Ki 15:15,18 [z]1Ki 10:17
14:30 [a]1Ki 12:21; 15:6

[a] *14* The meaning of the Hebrew for this sentence is uncertain. [b] *15* That is, the Euphrates [c] *15* That is, symbols of the goddess Asherah; here and elsewhere in 1 Kings

fathers and was buried with them in
the City of David. His mother's name
was Naamah; she was an Ammonite.[b]
And Abijah[a] his son succeeded him as
king.

Abijah King of Judah

15 In the eighteenth year of the
reign of Jeroboam son of Nebat,
Abijah[b] became king of Judah, 2and he
reigned in Jerusalem three years. His
mother's name was Maacah[c] daughter
of Abishalom.[c]

3He committed all the sins his father
had done before him; his heart was not
fully devoted[d] to the LORD his God,
as the heart of David his forefather had
been. 4Nevertheless, for David's sake
the LORD his God gave him a lamp[e] in
Jerusalem by raising up a son to succeed
him and by making Jerusalem strong.
5For David had done what was right
in the eyes of the LORD and had not
failed to keep[f] any of the LORD's commands all the days of his life—except in
the case of Uriah[g] the Hittite.

6There was war[h] between Rehoboam[d]
and Jeroboam throughout ⌊Abijah's⌋ lifetime. 7As for the other events of Abijah's reign, and all he did, are they not
written in the book of the annals of the
kings of Judah? There was war between
Abijah and Jeroboam. 8And Abijah rested with his fathers and was buried in
the City of David. And Asa his son succeeded him as king.

Asa King of Judah

9In the twentieth year of Jeroboam
king of Israel, Asa became king of Judah,
10and he reigned in Jerusalem forty-
one years. His grandmother's name was
Maacah[i] daughter of Abishalom.

11Asa did what was right in the eyes
of the LORD, as his father David had
done. 12He expelled the male shrine
prostitutes[j] from the land and got rid of
all the idols his fathers had made. 13He
even deposed his grandmother Maacah
from her position as queen mother, because she had made a repulsive Asherah pole. Asa cut the pole down[k] and
burned it in the Kidron Valley. 14Al-
though he did not remove the high
places, Asa's heart was fully committed[l]
to the LORD all his life. 15He brought
into the temple of the LORD the silver

14:31 [b]ver 21; 2Ch 12:16
15:2 [c]2Ch 11:20; 13:2
15:3 [d]1Ki 11:4; Ps 119:80
15:4 [e]2Sa 21:17; 1Ki 11:36; 2Ch 21:7
15:5 [f]1Ki 9:4; 14:8 [g]2Sa 11:2-27; 12:9
15:6 [h]1Ki 14:30
15:10 [i]ver 2
15:12 [j]1Ki 14:24; 22:46
15:13 [k]Ex 32:20
15:14 [l]ver 3; 1Ki 8:61; 22:43

and gold and the articles that he and his
father had dedicated.[m]

16There was war[n] between Asa and
Baasha king of Israel throughout their
reigns. 17Baasha king of Israel went up
against Judah and fortified Ramah[o] to
prevent anyone from leaving or entering the territory of Asa king of Judah.

18Asa then took all the silver and
gold that was left in the treasuries of
the LORD's temple[p] and of his own palace. He entrusted it to his officials and
sent[q] them to Ben-Hadad[r] son of Tab-
rimmon, the son of Hezion, the king
of Aram, who was ruling in Damascus.
19"Let there be a treaty between me and
you," he said, "as there was between my
father and your father. See, I am sending you a gift of silver and gold. Now
break your treaty with Baasha king of
Israel so he will withdraw from me."

20Ben-Hadad agreed with King Asa
and sent the commanders of his forces
against the towns of Israel. He conquered[s] Ijon, Dan, Abel Beth Maacah
and all Kinnereth in addition to Naphtali. 21When Baasha heard this, he
stopped building Ramah and withdrew
to Tirzah. 22Then King Asa issued an
order to all Judah—no one was exempt—and they carried away from Ramah the stones and timber Baasha had
been using there. With them King Asa
built up Geba[t] in Benjamin, and also
Mizpah.

23As for all the other events of Asa's
reign, all his achievements, all he did
and the cities he built, are they not
written in the book of the annals of the
kings of Judah? In his old age, however, his feet became diseased. 24Then
Asa rested with his fathers and was buried with them in the city of his father
David. And Jehoshaphat[u] his son succeeded him as king.

Nadab King of Israel

25Nadab son of Jeroboam became
king of Israel in the second year of Asa
king of Judah, and he reigned over Is-

[a] *31* Some Hebrew manuscripts and Septuagint (see also 2 Chron. 12:16); most Hebrew manuscripts *Abijam* [b] *1* Some Hebrew manuscripts and Septuagint (see also 2 Chron. 12:16); most Hebrew manuscripts *Abijam*; also in verses 7 and 8
[c] *2* A variant of *Absalom*; also in verse 10 [d] *6* Most Hebrew manuscripts; some Hebrew manuscripts and Syriac *Abijam* (that is, Abijah)

15:15 [m]1Ki 7:51
15:16 [n]ver 32
15:17 [o]Jos 18:25; 1Ki 12:27
15:18 [p]ver 15; 1Ki 14:26 [q]2Ki 12:18 [r]1Ki 11:23-24
15:20 [s]Jdg 18:29; 2Sa 20:14; 2Ki 15:29
15:22 [t]Jos 18:24; 21:17
15:24 [u]Mt 1:8

rael two years. 26He did evil in the eyes of the LORD, walking in the ways of his father[v] and in his sin, which he had caused Israel to commit.

27Baasha son of Ahijah of the house of Issachar plotted against him, and he struck him down[w] at Gibbethon,[x] a Philistine town, while Nadab and all Israel were besieging it. 28Baasha killed Nadab in the third year of Asa king of Judah and succeeded him as king.

29As soon as he began to reign, he killed Jeroboam's whole family.[y] He did not leave Jeroboam anyone that breathed, but destroyed them all, according to the word of the LORD given through his servant Ahijah the Shilonite— 30because of the sins[z] Jeroboam had committed and had caused Israel to commit, and because he provoked the LORD, the God of Israel, to anger.

31As for the other events of Nadab's reign, and all he did, are they not written in the book of the annals of the kings of Israel? 32There was war[a] between Asa and Baasha king of Israel throughout their reigns.

Baasha King of Israel

33In the third year of Asa king of Judah, Baasha son of Ahijah became king of all Israel in Tirzah, and he reigned twenty-four years. 34He did evil[b] in the eyes of the LORD, walking in the ways of Jeroboam and in his sin, which he had caused Israel to commit.

16 Then the word of the LORD came to Jehu[c] son of Hanani[d] against Baasha: 2"I lifted you up from the dust[e] and made you leader[f] of my people Israel, but you walked in the ways of Jeroboam and caused[g] my people Israel to sin and to provoke me to anger by their sins. 3So I am about to consume Baasha and his house, and I will make your house[h] like that of Jeroboam son of Nebat. 4Dogs[i] will eat those belonging to Baasha who die in the city, and the birds of the air will feed on those who die in the country."

5As for the other events of Baasha's reign, what he did and his achievements, are they not written in the book of the annals[j] of the kings of Israel? 6Baasha rested with his fathers and was buried in Tirzah.[k] And Elah his son succeeded him as king.

7Moreover, the word of the LORD came[l] through the prophet Jehu[m] son of Hanani to Baasha and his house, because of all the evil he had done in the eyes of the LORD, provoking him to anger by the things he did, and becoming like the house of Jeroboam—and also because he destroyed it.

Elah King of Israel

8In the twenty-sixth year of Asa king of Judah, Elah son of Baasha became king of Israel, and he reigned in Tirzah two years.

9Zimri, one of his officials, who had command of half his chariots, plotted against him. Elah was in Tirzah at the time, getting drunk[n] in the home of Arza, the man in charge[o] of the palace at Tirzah. 10Zimri came in, struck him down and killed him in the twenty-seventh year of Asa king of Judah. Then he succeeded him as king.

11As soon as he began to reign and was seated on the throne, he killed off Baasha's whole family.[p] He did not spare a single male, whether relative or friend. 12So Zimri destroyed the whole family of Baasha, in accordance with the word of the LORD spoken against Baasha through the prophet Jehu— 13because of all the sins Baasha and his son Elah had committed and had caused Israel to commit, so that they provoked the LORD, the God of Israel, to anger by their worthless idols.[q]

14As for the other events of Elah's reign, and all he did, are they not written in the book of the annals of the kings of Israel?

Zimri King of Israel

15In the twenty-seventh year of Asa king of Judah, Zimri reigned in Tirzah seven days. The army was encamped near Gibbethon,[r] a Philistine town. 16When the Israelites in the camp heard that Zimri had plotted against the king and murdered him, they proclaimed Omri, the commander of the army, king over Israel that very day there in the camp. 17Then Omri and all the Israelites with him withdrew from Gibbethon and laid siege to Tirzah. 18When Zimri saw that the city was taken, he went into the citadel of the royal palace and set the palace on fire around him. So he died, 19because of the sins he had committed, doing evil in the eyes of the

15:26 [v]1Ki 12:30; 14:16
15:27 [w]1Ki 14:14 [x]Jos 19:44; 21:23
15:29 [y]1Ki 14:10,14
15:30 [z]1Ki 14:9,16
15:32 [a]ver 16
15:34 [b]ver 26; 1Ki 12:28-29; 13:33; 14:16
16:1 [c]ver 7; 2Ch 19:2; 20:34 [d]2Ch 16:7
16:2 [e]1Sa 2:8 [f]1Ki 14:7-9 [g]1Ki 15:34
16:3 [h]ver 11; 1Ki 14:10; 15:29; 21:22
16:4 [i]1Ki 14:11
16:5 [j]1Ki 14:19; 15:31
16:6 [k]1Ki 14:17; 15:33
16:7 [l]1Ki 15:27,29 [m]ver 1
16:9 [n]2Ki 9:30-33 [o]1Ki 18:3
16:11 [p]ver 3
16:13 [q]Dt 32:21; 1Sa 12:21; Isa 41:29
16:15 [r]Jos 19:44; 1Ki 15:27

LORD and walking in the ways of Jeroboam and in the sin he had committed and had caused Israel to commit.

20As for the other events of Zimri's reign, and the rebellion he carried out, are they not written in the book of the annals of the kings of Israel?

Omri King of Israel

21Then the people of Israel were split into two factions; half supported Tibni son of Ginath for king, and the other half supported Omri. 22But Omri's followers proved stronger than those of Tibni son of Ginath. So Tibni died and Omri became king.

23In the thirty-first year of Asa king of Judah, Omri became king of Israel, and he reigned twelve years, six of them in Tirzah.[s] 24He bought the hill of Samaria from Shemer for two talents[a] of silver and built a city on the hill, calling it Samaria,[t] after Shemer, the name of the former owner of the hill.

25But Omri did evil[u] in the eyes of the LORD and sinned more than all those before him. 26He walked in all the ways of Jeroboam son of Nebat and in his sin, which he had caused[v] Israel to commit, so that they provoked the LORD, the God of Israel, to anger by their worthless idols.[w]

27As for the other events of Omri's reign, what he did and the things he achieved, are they not written in the book of the annals of the kings of Israel? 28Omri rested with his fathers and was buried in Samaria. And Ahab his son succeeded him as king.

Ahab Becomes King of Israel

29In the thirty-eighth year of Asa king of Judah, Ahab son of Omri became king of Israel, and he reigned in Samaria over Israel twenty-two years. 30Ahab son of Omri did more[x] evil in the eyes of the LORD than any of those before him. 31He not only considered it trivial to commit the sins of Jeroboam son of Nebat, but he also married[y] Jezebel daughter[z] of Ethbaal king of the Sidonians, and began to serve Baal[a] and worship him. 32He set up an altar for Baal in the temple[b] of Baal that he built in Samaria. 33Ahab also made an Asherah pole[c] and did more[d] to provoke the LORD, the God of Israel, to anger

16:23 [s]1Ki 15:21
16:24 [t]1Ki 13:32; Jn 4:4
16:25 [u]Dt 4:25; Mic 6:16
16:26 [v]ver 19 [w]Dt 32:21
16:30 [x]ver 25; 1Ki 14:9
16:31 [y]Dt 7:3; 1Ki 11:2 [z]Jdg 18:7; 2Ki 9:34 [a]2Ki 10:18; 17:16
16:32 [b]2Ki 10:21, 27; 11:18
16:33 [c]2Ki 13:6 [d]ver 29,30; 1Ki 14:9; 21:25

than did all the kings of Israel before him.

34In Ahab's time, Hiel of Bethel rebuilt Jericho. He laid its foundations at the cost of his firstborn son Abiram, and he set up its gates at the cost of his youngest son Segub, in accordance with the word of the LORD spoken by Joshua son of Nun.[e]

Elijah Fed by Ravens

17 Now Elijah[f] the Tishbite, from Tishbe[b] in Gilead,[g] said to Ahab, "As the LORD, the God of Israel, lives, whom I serve, there will be neither dew nor rain[h] in the next few years except at my word."

2Then the word of the LORD came to Elijah: 3"Leave here, turn eastward and hide in the Kerith Ravine, east of the Jordan. 4You will drink from the brook, and I have ordered the ravens[i] to feed you there."

5So he did what the LORD had told him. He went to the Kerith Ravine, east of the Jordan, and stayed there. 6The ravens brought him bread and meat in the morning[j] and bread and meat in the evening, and he drank from the brook.

The Widow at Zarephath

7Some time later the brook dried up because there had been no rain in the land. 8Then the word of the LORD came to him: 9"Go at once to Zarephath[k] of Sidon and stay there. I have commanded a widow in that place to supply you with food." 10So he went to Zarephath. When he came to the town gate, a widow[l] was there gathering sticks. He called to her and asked, "Would you bring me a little water in a jar so I may have a drink?"[m] 11As she was going to get it, he called, "And bring me, please, a piece of bread."

12"As surely as the LORD your God lives," she replied, "I don't have any bread—only a handful of flour in a jar and a little oil[n] in a jug. I am gathering a few sticks to take home and make a meal for myself and my son, that we may eat it—and die."

13Elijah said to her, "Don't be afraid. Go home and do as you have said. But

16:34 [e]Jos 6:26
17:1 [f]Mal 4:5; Jas 5:17 [g]Jdg 12:4 [h]Dt 10:8; 1Ki 18:1; 2Ki 3:14; Lk 4:25
17:4 [i]Ge 8:7
17:6 [j]Ex 16:8
17:9 [k]Ob 1:20 [l]Lk 4:26
17:10 [m]Ge 24:17; Jn 4:7
17:12 [n]ver 1; 2Ki 4:2

[a]*24* That is, about 150 pounds (about 70 kilograms)
[b]*1* Or *Tishbite, of the settlers*

first make a small cake of bread for me from what you have and bring it to me, and then make something for yourself and your son. 14For this is what the LORD, the God of Israel, says: 'The jar of flour will not be used up and the jug of oil will not run dry until the day the LORD gives rain on the land.'"

15She went away and did as Elijah

DAY 4 FOUR

▸ GENTLENESS AND MY SERVICE TO OTHERS

1 Kings 17:17–24

"O LORD my God, let this boy's life return to him!" (1 Kings 17:21). With this gentle cry, the prophet's God restores a dead boy to life. This touch is always to be ours. Not so dramatically, of course. Still, we who follow Christ exist to make dead things live. The key is never in us. We have no power in ourselves, but as we touch lifeless things, they can live because the Christ who lives in us gives life through us and then beyond us.

We touch dead worship and, if we are in touch with Christ the living center, the whole church comes alive.

We touch dead hope, and those who had given up on life see that the church exists to make alive a world in need of hope.

We touch a child with affirmation and that child—who may be dying for a compliment—is suddenly alive.

We touch an old woman in a nursing home—a woman who has been waiting in vain for anyone to call—and suddenly Jesus is all around us, using our touch to make dead eyes sparkle and a dead heart beat again in fountains of refreshing waters.

Gentleness is our calling. We are to go where people are afraid and leave them without fear. We are to go where there is no food, and feed; where there is nakedness, and clothe. But above all, we are to do all gently, not roaring about our own goodness or swaggering over our Bible knowledge. We are the gentle "touchers." We know the touch, for it changed us. Now we pass it on to all those yet unhealed.

To begin a study on the topic of Gentleness, the Healing Touch of God, turn to the home page on page 1175.

had told her. So there was food every
day for Elijah and for the woman and
her family. 16For the jar of flour was not
used up and the jug of oil did not run
dry, in keeping with the word of the
LORD spoken by Elijah.
17Some time later the son of the
woman who owned the house became
ill. He grew worse and worse, and finally stopped breathing. 18She said to
Elijah, "What do you have against me,
man of God? Did you come to remind
me of my sin[o] and kill my son?"
19"Give me your son," Elijah replied.
He took him from her arms, carried
him to the upper room where he was
staying, and laid him on his bed. 20Then
he cried out to the LORD, "O LORD
my God, have you brought tragedy also
upon this widow I am staying with,
by causing her son to die?" 21Then he
stretched[p] himself out on the boy three
times and cried to the LORD, "O LORD
my God, let this boy's life return to
him!"
22The LORD heard Elijah's cry, and
the boy's life returned to him, and he
lived. 23Elijah picked up the child and
carried him down from the room into
the house. He gave him to his mother
and said, "Look, your son is alive!"
24Then the woman said to Elijah,
"Now I know[q] that you are a man of
God and that the word of the LORD
from your mouth is the truth."[r]

17:18 [o]2Ki 3:13; Lk 5:8
17:21 [p]2Ki 4:34; Ac 20:10
17:24 [q]Jn 3:2; 16:30 [r]Ps 119:43; Jn 17:17

Elijah and Obadiah

18 After a long time, in the third[s]
year, the word of the LORD
came to Elijah: "Go and present yourself to Ahab, and I will send rain[t] on the
land." 2So Elijah went to present himself to Ahab.
Now the famine was severe in Samaria, 3and Ahab had summoned Obadiah, who was in charge[u] of his palace.
(Obadiah was a devout believer[v] in
the LORD. 4While Jezebel[w] was killing
off the LORD's prophets, Obadiah had
taken a hundred prophets and hidden[x]
them in two caves, fifty in each, and
had supplied them with food and water.) 5Ahab had said to Obadiah, "Go
through the land to all the springs and
valleys. Maybe we can find some grass
to keep the horses and mules alive so
we will not have to kill any of our animals." 6So they divided the land they

18:1 [s]1Ki 17:1; Lk 4:25; Jas 5:17 [t]Dt 28:12
18:3 [u]1Ki 16:9 [v]Ne 7:2
18:4 [w]2Ki 9:7 [x]ver 13; Isa 16:3

were to cover, Ahab going in one direction and Obadiah in another.
7As Obadiah was walking along, Eli-
18:7 jah met him. Obadiah recognized[y] him,
[y]2Ki 1:8 bowed down to the ground, and said,
"Is it really you, my lord Elijah?"
8"Yes," he replied. "Go tell your master, 'Elijah is here.' "
9"What have I done wrong," asked
Obadiah, "that you are handing your
servant over to Ahab to be put to death?
10As surely as the LORD your God lives,
there is not a nation or kingdom where
my master has not sent someone to
18:10 look[z] for you. And whenever a nation
[z]1Ki 17:3 or kingdom claimed you were not there,
he made them swear they could not
find you. 11But now you tell me to go
18:12 to my master and say, 'Elijah is here.'
[a]2Ki 2:16; 12I don't know where the Spirit[a] of the
Eze 3:14; LORD may carry you when I leave you.
Ac 8:39 If I go and tell Ahab and he doesn't find
you, he will kill me. Yet I your servant
have worshiped the LORD since my
youth. 13Haven't you heard, my lord,
what I did while Jezebel was killing the
prophets of the LORD? I hid a hundred
of the LORD's prophets in two caves,
fifty in each, and supplied them with
food and water. 14And now you tell me
to go to my master and say, 'Elijah is
here.' He will kill me!"
15Elijah said, "As the LORD Almighty
18:15 lives, whom I serve, I will surely pre-
[b]1Ki 17:1 sent[b] myself to Ahab today."

Elijah on Mount Carmel

16So Obadiah went to meet Ahab
and told him, and Ahab went to meet
Elijah. 17When he saw Elijah, he said
18:17 to him, "Is that you, you troubler[c] of
[c]Jos 7:25; 1Ki 21:20; Israel?"
Ac 16:20 18"I have not made trouble for Isra-
18:18 el," Elijah replied. "But you[d] and your
[d]1Ki 16:31, 33; 21:25 father's family have. You have aban-
[e]2Ch 15:2 doned[e] the LORD's commands and have
followed the Baals. 19Now summon the
people from all over Israel to meet me

on Mount Carmel.[f] And bring the four 18:19
hundred and fifty prophets of Baal and [f]Jos 19:26
the four hundred prophets of Asherah,
who eat at Jezebel's table."
20So Ahab sent word throughout all
Israel and assembled the prophets on
Mount Carmel. 21Elijah went before
the people and said, "How long will
you waver[g] between two opinions? If 18:21
the LORD is God, follow him; but if [g]Jos 24:15; 2Ki 17:41;
Baal is God, follow him." Mt 6:24
But the people said nothing.
22Then Elijah said to them, "I am
the only one of the LORD's prophets 18:22
left,[h] but Baal has four hundred and fif- [h]1Ki 19:10
ty prophets.[i] 23Get two bulls for us. Let [i]ver 19
them choose one for themselves, and let
them cut it into pieces and put it on
the wood but not set fire to it. I will
prepare the other bull and put it on the
wood but not set fire to it. 24Then you
call on the name of your god, and I will
call on the name of the LORD. The god 18:24
who answers by fire[j]—he is God." [j]ver 38; 1Ch 21:26
Then all the people said, "What you
say is good."
25Elijah said to the prophets of Baal,
"Choose one of the bulls and prepare
it first, since there are so many of you.
Call on the name of your god, but do
not light the fire." 26So they took the
bull given them and prepared it.
Then they called on the name of Baal
from morning till noon. "O Baal, answer us!" they shouted. But there was
no response;[k] no one answered. And
they danced around the altar they had 18:26 [k]Ps 115:4-5;
made. Jer 10:5; 1Co 8:4; 12:2
27At noon Elijah began to taunt them.
"Shout louder!" he said. "Surely he is
a god! Perhaps he is deep in thought,
or busy, or traveling. Maybe he is sleep-
ing and must be awakened."[l] 28So they 18:27 [l]Hab 2:19
shouted louder and slashed[m] themselves 18:28
with swords and spears, as was their cus- [m]Lev 19:28;
tom, until their blood flowed. 29Mid- Dt 14:1
day passed, and they continued their
frantic prophesying until the time for
the evening sacrifice.[n] But there was no 18:29 [n]Ex 29:41
response, no one answered, no one paid [o]ver 26
attention.[o]
30Then Elijah said to all the people,
"Come here to me." They came to him,
and he repaired the altar[p] of the LORD, 18:30
which was in ruins. 31Elijah took twelve [p]1Ki 19:10
stones, one for each of the tribes descended from Jacob, to whom the word
of the LORD had come, saying, "Your

PEACE

WANTING ONLY ONE THING AT A TIME

1 Kings 18:21

The troubled always want two or more things at once, while peace serves a single hunger.

JOY

WEEK 38

DAY ONE

1 ▸ JOY, FOCUSING ON A HIGHER REALITY

Read 1 Kings 18:20–21,38–39

There is nothing that brings joy to the human heart like actually beholding the power of God in action. On Mount Carmel Elijah sets up the arena for just such a display in 1 Kings 18:20–21. He throws out a challenge: "How long will you waver between two opinions? If the LORD is God, follow him; but if Baal is God, follow him." In this dramatic contest between the living God and a false god, the fire of God falls and the people, in high elation, shout, "The LORD—he is God! The LORD—he is God!" (v. 39).

Joy is the spontaneous result of seeing God in action, of focusing on a higher reality. We forget this great truth in so many contemporary churches. We somehow feel that joy is our responsibility. We plan productively and coordinate creatively. We think that if we can really get the people singing, joy will come. Thus is often born a kind of "Hallelujah hype." Hype and joy can almost pass for the same thing, but the heart that is hungry for the visitation of God's power will always know the difference. When the power comes near, the joy proclaims itself. It's like the electrical phenomenon of felt and silk. When they pass close to each other, the static fire can actually be seen.

When Evan Roberts arrived back in Laughor, Wales, at the turn of the last century, the demeanor of prayer, which at first occupied his family and later his entire hometown, made it clear that the fire of God was on the way. While the Welsh Revival was igniting the souls of the United Kingdom, it was very clear that when Pentecost is poured out, so is joy. The people began to focus on the transforming reality of God. Joy was the result. It always has been and always will be.

DAY TWO

2 ▸ JOY AND THE PURPOSE OF GOD IN MY LIFE

Ezekiel's experience of God has alternately been deemed unusual and unearthly. Yet this vision, as all of his visions, is a wild revelation of God's psychedelic ability to work with all different sorts of prophets. One thing is certain: the color, the fire, the form, the images and the far-out conceptions say that joy—wild and sometimes indefinable—marked Ezekiel's life. They may seem hard to understand. But who would want a God of only-vanilla sensibilities? In the book of Ezekiel, the joy of the Lord gets gaudy and electric—but mostly, it is undeniable. *Turn to Ezekiel 1:4–28, page 953, for today's study.*

DAY THREE

3 ▸ JOY AND MY RELATIONSHIP WITH CHRIST

At the time of the writing of this passage, the apostle John has not seen Jesus since his post-resurrection appearances years before. But the Christ he now sees is the Christ who rules over the Apocalypse. John is so overwhelmed by Christ's glory that he can only fall at his feet as though dead. Joy inevitably causes us to deepen our adoration as we worship Christ. *Turn to Revelation 1:12–16, page 1522, for today's study.*

DAY FOUR

4 ▸ JOY AND MY SERVICE TO OTHERS

The dedication of the temple had the same effect among the Jews as Evan Roberts's revival had among the Welsh. Joy broke out among the people as they began to witness what God was doing among them. Joy begets joy, and the result was that they were soon serving others even greater helpings of the grace of God. *Turn to Ezra 6:16, page 545, for today's study.*

DAY FIVE

5 ▸ JOY AND ITS PLACE IN MY PERSONAL WORSHIP

Paul confessed elation that makes communicating our best experiences with God nearly impossible. Paul's joy flung him, it would seem, at the very feet of God. He was lost in wonder, love and praise. But Paul confesses to a pain, "a thorn in [his] flesh," which God allowed to be visited upon him "to keep [him] from becoming conceited because of these surpassingly great revelations." Joy and pain are both elements of focus in our worship. Pain creates a need for God, and joy is the footprint of his presence in our lives. *Turn to 2 Corinthians 12:1–10, page 1390, for today's study.*

MEMORIZE THIS WEEK

PSALM 32:11

Rejoice in the LORD and be glad,
you righteous;
sing, all you who are upright in heart!

Week 39, Peace, the Companionship of Christ, begins on page 1243, Luke 24:13–16,30–35.
To begin a topical study on the Fruit of the Spirit, Joy, turn to the Topical Index, page 1548.

18:31 [q]Ge 32:28; name shall be Israel."[q] 32With the stones
35:10; he built an altar in the name[r] of the
2Ki 17:34 LORD, and he dug a trench around it
18:32 [r]Col 3:17 large enough to hold two seahs[a] of seed.
33He arranged[s] the wood, cut the bull
18:33 [s]Ge 22:9; into pieces and laid it on the wood.
Lev 1:6-8 Then he said to them, "Fill four large
jars with water and pour it on the offering and on the wood."
34"Do it again," he said, and they did
it again.
"Do it a third time," he ordered, and
they did it the third time. 35The water
ran down around the altar and even
filled the trench.
36At the time of sacrifice, the prophet Elijah stepped forward and prayed:
18:36 [t]Ex 3:6; "O LORD, God of Abraham,[t] Isaac
Mt 22:32 and Israel, let it be known[u] today that
[u]1Ki 8:43; 2Ki 19:19 you are God in Israel and that I am
[v]Nu 16:28 your servant and have done all these
things at your command.[v] 37Answer me,
O LORD, answer me, so these people
will know that you, O LORD, are God,
and that you are turning their hearts
back again."
18:38 38Then the fire[w] of the LORD fell
[w]Lev 9:24; Jdg 6:21; and burned up the sacrifice, the wood,
1Ch 21:26; 2Ch 7:1; the stones and the soil, and also licked
Job 1:16 up the water in the trench.
39When all the people saw this, they
fell prostrate and cried, "The LORD—
18:39 [x]ver 24 he is God! The LORD—he is God!"[x]
40Then Elijah commanded them,
"Seize the prophets of Baal. Don't let
anyone get away!" They seized them,
and Elijah had them brought down
18:40 [y]Jdg 4:7 to the Kishon Valley[y] and slaughtered[z]
[z]Dt 13:5; 18:20; there.
2Ki 10:24-25 41And Elijah said to Ahab, "Go, eat
and drink, for there is the sound of
a heavy rain." 42So Ahab went off
to eat and drink, but Elijah climbed
to the top of Carmel, bent down to the
ground and put his face between his
18:42 [a]ver 19-20; knees.[a]
Jas 5:18 43"Go and look toward the sea," he
told his servant. And he went up and
looked.
"There is nothing there," he said.
Seven times Elijah said, "Go back."
44The seventh time the servant re-
18:44 [b]Lk 12:54 ported, "A cloud[b] as small as a man's
hand is rising from the sea."
So Elijah said, "Go and tell Ahab,
'Hitch up your chariot and go down
before the rain stops you.'"
45Meanwhile, the sky grew black with
clouds, the wind rose, a heavy rain came
on and Ahab rode off to Jezreel. 46The
power[c] of the LORD came upon Elijah 18:46 [c]2Ki 3:15
and, tucking his cloak into his belt,[d] [d]2Ki 4:29; 9:1
he ran ahead of Ahab all the way to
Jezreel.

Elijah Flees to Horeb

19 Now Ahab told Jezebel everything Elijah had done and how 19:1
he had killed[e] all the prophets with the [e]1Ki 18:40
sword. 2So Jezebel sent a messenger to
Elijah to say, "May the gods deal with 19:2
me, be it ever so severely,[f] if by this [f]1Ki 20:10;
time tomorrow I do not make your life 2Ki 6:31; Ru 1:17
like that of one of them."
3Elijah was afraid[b] and ran[g] for his 19:3 [g]Ge 31:21
life. When he came to Beersheba in Ju-
dah, he left his servant there, 4while
he himself went a day's journey into
the desert. He came to a broom tree,
sat down under it and prayed that he
might die. "I have had enough, LORD,"
he said. "Take my life;[h] I am no better 19:4 [h]Nu 11:15;
than my ancestors." 5Then he lay down Jer 20:18; Jnh 4:8
under the tree and fell asleep.[i]
All at once an angel touched him 19:5 [i]Ge 28:11
and said, "Get up and eat." 6He looked
around, and there by his head was a
cake of bread baked over hot coals, and
a jar of water. He ate and drank and
then lay down again.
7The angel of the LORD came back a
second time and touched him and said,
"Get up and eat, for the journey is too
much for you." 8So he got up and ate
and drank. Strengthened by that food,
he traveled forty days and forty[j] nights 19:8 [j]Ex 24:18;
until he reached Horeb,[k] the mountain 34:28;
of God. 9There he went into a cave[l] and Dt 9:9-11,18; Mt 4:2
spent the night. [k]Ex 3:1

The LORD Appears to Elijah 19:9 [l]Ex 33:22

And the word of the LORD came to
him: "What are you doing here, Elijah?"
10He replied, "I have been very zeal-
ous[m] for the LORD God Almighty. The 19:10 [m]Nu 25:13
Israelites have rejected your covenant, [n]1Ki 18:4,22;
broken down your altars, and put your Ro 11:3*
prophets to death with the sword. I am
the only one left,[n] and now they are
trying to kill me too."
11The LORD said, "Go out and stand

[a]*32* That is, probably about 13 quarts (about 15 liters) [b]*3* Or *Elijah saw*

19:11 [o]Ex 24:12 on the mountain[o] in the presence of
[p]Eze 1:4; 37:7 the LORD, for the LORD is about to
pass by."
Then a great and powerful wind[p] tore
the mountains apart and shattered the
rocks before the LORD, but the LORD
was not in the wind. After the wind
there was an earthquake, but the LORD
was not in the earthquake. 12After the
earthquake came a fire, but the LORD
19:12 [q]Job 4:16; was not in the fire. And after the fire
Zec 4:6 came a gentle whisper.[q] 13When Elijah
19:13 heard it, he pulled his cloak over his
[r]ver 9; face[r] and went out and stood at the
Ex 3:6 mouth of the cave.

DAY 2 TWO

GENTLENESS AND THE PURPOSE OF GOD IN MY LIFE

1 Kings 19:11–14

In the turbulent life of Elijah, God spoke in a gentle whisper.

Elijah had been threatened with death. Queen Jezebel was seeking his life, and he was afraid. He who had only recently called down fire from heaven on Mount Carmel had run for his life and lost himself in the pits of personal depression.

Perhaps under the broom tree (1 Kings 19:4), he had become so depressed that he forgot who he was and who he worked for. He may even have forgotten what God's purpose for his life was. But enter the whispering God—the God who wants no one to live ill-informed about his purpose for life.

But see how hard it is to hear and know. First comes a great and powerful wind. The wind is so powerful that the rocks are shattered. But the Lord is not in the wind. Then comes an earthquake, but the Lord is not in the earthquake. Next, the fire roars, but God is not in the fire. And after the fire comes a gentle whisper, so soft that the prophet has to strain his ears to hear it. Suddenly, the Lord is there.

God's whisper defines both our calling and our own gentle manner of living it out. When we quiet ourselves to hear God's whispers, we find that our purpose in life becomes clearer.

To begin a study on the topic of Gentleness, a Way of Winning Others to Christ, turn to the home page on page 1303.

GENTLENESS

GENTLE WHISPERS

1 Kings 19:12

Look not for Jesus in rock-splitting displays and lightning-shattered skies. Sit still in a quiet place. He will come to you in whispers, which the loud display of your affairs has camouflaged.

Then a voice said to him, "What are
you doing here, Elijah?"
14He replied, "I have been very zealous for the LORD God Almighty. The
Israelites have rejected your covenant,
broken down your altars, and put your
prophets to death with the sword. I am
the only one left,[s] and now they are try- 19:14 [s]ver 10
ing to kill me too."
15The LORD said to him, "Go back
the way you came, and go to the Desert
of Damascus. When you get there,
anoint Hazael[t] king over Aram. 16Also, 19:15 [t]2Ki 8:7-15
anoint[u] Jehu son of Nimshi king over
Israel, and anoint Elisha[v] son of Sha- 19:16 [u]2Ki 9:1-3,6
phat from Abel Meholah to succeed you [v]ver 21;
as prophet. 17Jehu will put to death any 2Ki 2:9,15
who escape the sword of Hazael,[w] and 19:17 [w]2Ki 8:12,29;
Elisha will put to death any who escape 9:14;
the sword of Jehu. 18Yet I reserve[x] seven 13:3,7,22
thousand in Israel—all whose knees 19:18 [x]Ro 11:4*
have not bowed down to Baal and all [y]Hos 13:2
whose mouths have not kissed[y] him."

The Call of Elisha

19So Elijah went from there and
found Elisha son of Shaphat. He was
plowing with twelve yoke of oxen, and
he himself was driving the twelfth pair.
Elijah went up to him and threw his
cloak[z] around him. 20Elisha then left his 19:19 [z]2Ki 2:8,14
oxen and ran after Elijah. "Let me kiss
my father and mother good-by,"[a] he 19:20 [a]Mt 8:21-22;
said, "and then I will come with you." Lk 9:61

JOY

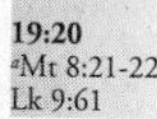

BURNING PLOWS

1 Kings 19:21

He who puts his hand to the plow and looks back is not fit for the kingdom.

When the call comes, burn your plow,
Roast your oxen, leave the sod.
See what glory follows farming
When you tend the fields of God.

"Go back," Elijah replied. "What have I done to you?"

21So Elisha left him and went back. He took his yoke of oxen[b] and slaughtered them. He burned the plowing equipment to cook the meat and gave it to the people, and they ate. Then he set out to follow Elijah and became his attendant.[c]

19:21 [b]2Sa 24:22 [c]ver 16

Ben-Hadad Attacks Samaria

20 Now Ben-Hadad[d] king of Aram mustered his entire army. Accompanied by thirty-two kings with their horses and chariots, he went up and besieged Samaria and attacked it. 2He sent messengers into the city to Ahab king of Israel, saying, "This is what Ben-Hadad says: 3'Your silver and gold are mine, and the best of your wives and children are mine.'"

20:1 [d]1Ki 15:18; 22:31; 2Ki 6:24

4The king of Israel answered, "Just as you say, my lord the king. I and all I have are yours."

5The messengers came again and said, "This is what Ben-Hadad says: 'I sent to demand your silver and gold, your wives and your children. 6But about this time tomorrow I am going to send my officials to search your palace and the houses of your officials. They will seize everything you value and carry it away.'"

7The king of Israel summoned all the elders of the land and said to them, "See how this man is looking for trouble![e] When he sent for my wives and my children, my silver and my gold, I did not refuse him."

20:7 [e]2Ki 5:7

8The elders and the people all answered, "Don't listen to him or agree to his demands."

9So he replied to Ben-Hadad's messengers, "Tell my lord the king, 'Your servant will do all you demanded the first time, but this demand I cannot meet.'" They left and took the answer back to Ben-Hadad.

10Then Ben-Hadad sent another message to Ahab: "May the gods deal with me, be it ever so severely, if enough dust[f] remains in Samaria to give each of my men a handful."

20:10 [f]2Sa 22:43; 1Ki 19:2

11The king of Israel answered, "Tell him: 'One who puts on his armor should not boast[g] like one who takes it off.'"

20:11 [g]Pr 27:1; Jer 9:23

12Ben-Hadad heard this message while he and the kings were drinking[h] in their tents,[a] and he ordered his men: "Prepare to attack." So they prepared to attack the city.

20:12 [h]ver 16; 1Ki 16:9

Ahab Defeats Ben-Hadad

13Meanwhile a prophet came to Ahab king of Israel and announced, "This is what the LORD says: 'Do you see this vast army? I will give it into your hand today, and then you will know[i] that I am the LORD.'"

20:13 [i]ver 28; Ex 6:7

14"But who will do this?" asked Ahab.

The prophet replied, "This is what the LORD says: 'The young officers of the provincial commanders will do it.'"

"And who will start[j] the battle?" he asked.

20:14 [j]Jdg 1:1

The prophet answered, "You will."

15So Ahab summoned the young officers of the provincial commanders, 232 men. Then he assembled the rest of the Israelites, 7,000 in all. 16They set out at noon while Ben-Hadad and the 32 kings allied with him were in their tents getting drunk.[k] 17The young officers of the provincial commanders went out first.

20:16 [k]ver 12; 1Ki 16:9

Now Ben-Hadad had dispatched scouts, who reported, "Men are advancing from Samaria."

18He said, "If they have come out for peace, take them alive; if they have come out for war, take them alive."

19The young officers of the provincial commanders marched out of the city with the army behind them 20and each one struck down his opponent. At that, the Arameans fled, with the Israelites in pursuit. But Ben-Hadad king of Aram escaped on horseback with some of his horsemen. 21The king of Israel advanced and overpowered the horses and chariots and inflicted heavy losses on the Arameans.

22Afterward, the prophet[l] came to the king of Israel and said, "Strengthen your position and see what must be done, because next spring[m] the king of Aram will attack you again."

20:22 [l]ver 13 [m]ver 26; 2Sa 11:1

23Meanwhile, the officials of the king of Aram advised him, "Their gods are gods[n] of the hills. That is why they were too strong for us. But if we fight them

20:23 [n]1Ki 14:23; Ro 1:21-23

[a]*12* Or *in Succoth*; also in verse 16

on the plains, surely we will be stronger than they. 24Do this: Remove all
the kings from their commands and replace them with other officers. 25You
must also raise an army like the one you
lost—horse for horse and chariot for
chariot—so we can fight Israel on the
plains. Then surely we will be stronger
than they." He agreed with them and
acted accordingly.
20:26 [o]ver 22 [p]2Ki 13:17
26The next spring[o] Ben-Hadad mustered the Arameans and went up to
Aphek[p] to fight against Israel. 27When
the Israelites were also mustered and
given provisions, they marched out to
meet them. The Israelites camped opposite them like two small flocks of
goats, while the Arameans covered the
20:27 [q]Jdg 6:6; 1Sa 13:6
countryside.[q]
28The man of God came up and
told the king of Israel, "This is what
the LORD says: 'Because the Arameans
20:28 [r]ver 23 [s]ver 13
think the LORD is a god[r] of the hills
and not a god of the valleys, I will deliver this vast army into your hands, and
you will know[s] that I am the LORD.' "
29For seven days they camped opposite each other, and on the seventh day
the battle was joined. The Israelites inflicted a hundred thousand casualties on
the Aramean foot soldiers in one day.
30The rest of them escaped to the city
20:30 [t]ver 26 [u]1Ki 22:25; 2Ch 18:24
of Aphek,[t] where the wall collapsed on
twenty-seven thousand of them. And
Ben-Hadad fled to the city and hid[u] in
an inner room.
31His officials said to him, "Look, we
have heard that the kings of the house
of Israel are merciful. Let us go to the
20:31 [v]Ge 37:34
king of Israel with sackcloth[v] around
our waists and ropes around our heads.
Perhaps he will spare your life."
32Wearing sackcloth around their
waists and ropes around their heads,
they went to the king of Israel and said,
"Your servant Ben-Hadad says: 'Please
let me live.' "
The king answered, "Is he still alive?
He is my brother."
33The men took this as a good sign
and were quick to pick up his word.
"Yes, your brother Ben-Hadad!" they
said.
"Go and get him," the king said.
When Ben-Hadad came out, Ahab had
him come up into his chariot.
20:34 [w]1Ki 15:20
34"I will return the cities[w] my father
took from your father," Ben-Hadad offered. "You may set up your own market areas in Damascus,[x] as my father
did in Samaria."
20:34 [x]Jer 49:23-27 [y]Ex 23:32
⌞Ahab said,⌟ "On the basis of a treaty[y] I will set you free." So he made a
treaty with him, and let him go.

A Prophet Condemns Ahab

35By the word of the LORD one of
the sons of the prophets said to his companion, "Strike me with your weapon,"
20:35 [z]1Ki 13:21; 2Ki 2:3-7
but the man refused.[z]
36So the prophet said, "Because you
have not obeyed the LORD, as soon as
20:36 [a]1Ki 13:24
you leave me a lion[a] will kill you." And
after the man went away, a lion found
him and killed him.
37The prophet found another man
and said, "Strike me, please." So the
man struck him and wounded him.
38Then the prophet went and stood by
the road waiting for the king. He disguised himself with his headband down
over his eyes. 39As the king passed by,
the prophet called out to him, "Your
servant went into the thick of the battle, and someone came to me with a
captive and said, 'Guard this man. If he
is missing, it will be your life for his
20:39 [b]2Ki 10:24
life,[b] or you must pay a talent[a] of silver.'
40While your servant was busy here and
there, the man disappeared."
"That is your sentence," the king of
Israel said. "You have pronounced it
yourself."
41Then the prophet quickly removed
the headband from his eyes, and the
king of Israel recognized him as one
of the prophets. 42He said to the king,
"This is what the LORD says: 'You have
set free a man I had determined should
20:42 [c]Jer 48:10 [d]ver 39; Jos 2:14; 1Ki 22:31-37
die.[b][c] Therefore it is your life[d] for his
life, your people for his people.' " 43Sul-
20:43 [e]1Ki 21:4
len and angry,[e] the king of Israel went
to his palace in Samaria.

Naboth's Vineyard

21 Some time later there was an incident involving a vineyard be-
21:1 [f]2Ki 9:21 [g]1Ki 18:45-46
longing to Naboth[f] the Jezreelite. The
vineyard was in Jezreel,[g] close to the
palace of Ahab king of Samaria. 2Ahab
said to Naboth, "Let me have your vineyard to use for a vegetable garden, since

[a]*39* That is, about 75 pounds (about 34 kilograms) [b]*42* The Hebrew term refers to the irrevocable giving over of things or persons to the LORD, often by totally destroying them.

it is close to my palace. In exchange
I will give you a better vineyard or, if
you prefer, I will pay you whatever it is
worth."
[3]But Naboth replied, "The LORD
forbid that I should give you the inheri-
21:3 tance[h] of my fathers."
[h]Lev 25:23; Nu 36:7; [4]So Ahab went home, sullen and an-
Eze 46:18 gry[i] because Naboth the Jezreelite had
21:4 said, "I will not give you the inheri-
[i]1Ki 20:43 tance of my fathers." He lay on his bed
sulking and refused to eat.
[5]His wife Jezebel came in and asked
him, "Why are you so sullen? Why
won't you eat?"
[6]He answered her, "Because I said
to Naboth the Jezreelite, 'Sell me your
vineyard; or if you prefer, I will give
you another vineyard in its place.' But
he said, 'I will not give you my vineyard.' "
[7]Jezebel his wife said, "Is this how
you act as king over Israel? Get up and
eat! Cheer up. I'll get you the vineyard[j]
21:7 [j]1Sa 8:14 of Naboth the Jezreelite."
[8]So she wrote letters in Ahab's name,
21:8 placed his seal[k] on them, and sent them
[k]Ge 38:18; Est 3:12; to the elders and nobles who lived in
8:8,10 Naboth's city with him. [9]In those letters
she wrote:

"Proclaim a day of fasting and
seat Naboth in a prominent place
among the people. [10]But seat two
21:10 scoundrels[l] opposite him and have
[l]Ac 6:11 [m]Ex 22:28; them testify that he has cursed[m]
Lev 24:15-16 both God and the king. Then take
him out and stone him to death."

[11]So the elders and nobles who lived
in Naboth's city did as Jezebel directed
in the letters she had written to them.
21:12 [12]They proclaimed a fast[n] and seated
[n]Isa 58:4 Naboth in a prominent place among the
people. [13]Then two scoundrels came and
sat opposite him and brought charges
against Naboth before the people, saying, "Naboth has cursed both God and
the king." So they took him outside the
21:13 city and stoned him to death.[o] [14]Then
[o]2Ki 9:26 they sent word to Jezebel: "Naboth has
been stoned and is dead."
[15]As soon as Jezebel heard that Naboth had been stoned to death, she said
to Ahab, "Get up and take possession
21:15 of the vineyard[p] of Naboth the Jezree-
[p]1Sa 8:14 lite that he refused to sell you. He is no
longer alive, but dead." [16]When Ahab
heard that Naboth was dead, he got up

and went down to take possession of
Naboth's vineyard.
[17]Then the word of the LORD came
to Elijah the Tishbite: [18]"Go down to
meet Ahab king of Israel, who rules in
Samaria. He is now in Naboth's vineyard, where he has gone to take possession of it. [19]Say to him, 'This is what
the LORD says: Have you not murdered
a man and seized his property?' Then
say to him, 'This is what the LORD
says: In the place where dogs licked up
Naboth's blood,[q] dogs[r] will lick up your 21:19 [q]2Ki 9:26;
blood—yes, yours!' " Ps 9:12;
[20]Ahab said to Elijah, "So you have Isa 14:20
found me, my enemy!"[s] [r]1Ki 22:38
"I have found you," he answered, 21:20 [s]1Ki 18:17
"because you have sold[t] yourself to do [t]ver 25;
evil in the eyes of the LORD. [21]'I am 2Ki 17:17; Ro 7:14
going to bring disaster on you. I will
consume your descendants and cut off
from Ahab every last male[u] in Israel— 21:21
slave or free. [22]I will make your house[v] [u]1Ki 14:10; 2Ki 9:8
like that of Jeroboam son of Nebat and
that of Baasha son of Ahijah, because 21:22
you have provoked me to anger and [v]1Ki 15:29; 16:3
have caused Israel to sin.'[w] [w]1Ki 12:30
[23]"And also concerning Jezebel the
LORD says: 'Dogs[x] will devour Jezebel 21:23 [x]2Ki 9:10,
by the wall of[a] Jezreel.' 34-36
[24]"Dogs[y] will eat those belonging to 21:24
Ahab who die in the city, and the birds [y]1Ki 14:11;
of the air will feed on those who die in 16:4
the country."
[25](There was never[z] a man like Ahab, 21:25
who sold himself to do evil in the eyes [z]ver 20; 1Ki 16:33
of the LORD, urged on by Jezebel his
wife. [26]He behaved in the vilest manner 21:26 [a]Ge 15:16;
by going after idols, like the Amorites[a] Lev 18:25-30;
the LORD drove out before Israel.) 2Ki 21:11
[27]When Ahab heard these words, he
tore his clothes, put on sackcloth[b] and 21:27 [b]Ge 37:34;
fasted. He lay in sackcloth and went 2Sa 3:31;
around meekly. 2Ki 6:30
[28]Then the word of the LORD came
to Elijah the Tishbite: [29]"Have you noticed how Ahab has humbled himself
before me? Because he has humbled
himself, I will not bring this disaster in
his day, but I will bring it on his house
in the days of his son."[c] 21:29 [c]2Ki 9:26

Micaiah Prophesies Against Ahab

22 For three years there was no war
between Aram and Israel. [2]But

[a]*23* Most Hebrew manuscripts; a few Hebrew manuscripts, Vulgate and Syriac (see also 2 Kings 9:26) *the plot of ground at*

in the third year Jehoshaphat king of
Judah went down to see the king of
Israel. 3The king of Israel had said to
his officials, "Don't you know that Ra-
22:3 [d]Dt 4:43; moth Gilead[d] belongs to us and yet we
Jos 21:38 are doing nothing to retake it from the
king of Aram?"
4So he asked Jehoshaphat, "Will you
22:4 [e]2Ki 3:7 go with me to fight[e] against Ramoth
Gilead?"
Jehoshaphat replied to the king of Israel, "I am as you are, my people as
your people, my horses as your horses."
5But Jehoshaphat also said to the king
22:5 [f]Ex 33:7; of Israel, "First seek the counsel[f] of the
2Ki 3:11 LORD."
6So the king of Israel brought together the prophets—about four hundred
men—and asked them, "Shall I go to
war against Ramoth Gilead, or shall I
refrain?"
22:6 [g]1Ki 18:19 "Go,"[g] they answered, "for the Lord
will give it into the king's hand."
7But Jehoshaphat asked, "Is there not
22:7 [h]2Ki 3:11 a prophet[h] of the LORD here whom we
can inquire of?"
8The king of Israel answered Jehoshaphat, "There is still one man
through whom we can inquire of the
22:8 [i]Am 5:10 LORD, but I hate[i] him because he never
[j]Isa 5:20 prophesies anything good[j] about me,
but always bad. He is Micaiah son of
Imlah."
"The king should not say that," Jehoshaphat replied.
9So the king of Israel called one of
his officials and said, "Bring Micaiah
son of Imlah at once."
10Dressed in their royal robes, the
king of Israel and Jehoshaphat king of
Judah were sitting on their thrones at
22:10 [k]ver 6 the threshing floor[k] by the entrance of
the gate of Samaria, with all the proph-
ets prophesying before them. 11Now
Zedekiah son of Kenaanah had made
22:11 [l]Dt 33:17; iron horns[l] and he declared, "This is
Zec 1:18-21 what the LORD says: 'With these you
will gore the Arameans until they are
destroyed.'"
12All the other prophets were prophesying the same thing. "Attack Ramoth
Gilead and be victorious," they said,
"for the LORD will give it into the king's
hand."
13The messenger who had gone to
summon Micaiah said to him, "Look,
as one man the other prophets are pre-
dicting success for the king. Let your
word agree with theirs, and speak favorably."
14But Micaiah said, "As surely as the
LORD lives, I can tell him only what
the LORD tells me."[m] 22:14 [m]Nu 22:18; 24:13; 1Ki 18:10,15
15When he arrived, the king asked
him, "Micaiah, shall we go to war
against Ramoth Gilead, or shall I refrain?"
"Attack and be victorious," he answered, "for the LORD will give it into
the king's hand."
16The king said to him, "How many
times must I make you swear to tell me
nothing but the truth in the name of
the LORD?"
17Then Micaiah answered, "I saw all
Israel scattered on the hills like sheep
without a shepherd,[n] and the LORD 22:17 [n]ver 34-36; Nu 27:17; Mt 9:36
said, 'These people have no master. Let
each one go home in peace.'"
18The king of Israel said to Jehoshaphat, "Didn't I tell you that he
never prophesies anything good about
me, but only bad?"
19Micaiah continued, "Therefore hear
the word of the LORD: I saw the LORD
sitting on his throne[o] with all the host[p] 22:19 [o]Isa 6:1; Eze 1:26; Da 7:9 [p]Job 1:6; 2:1; Ps 103:20-21; Mt 18:10; Heb 1:7,14
of heaven standing around him on his
right and on his left. 20And the LORD
said, 'Who will entice Ahab into attacking Ramoth Gilead and going to his
death there?'
"One suggested this, and another
that. 21Finally, a spirit came forward,
stood before the LORD and said, 'I will
entice him.'
22"'By what means?' the LORD
asked.
"'I will go out and be a lying[q] spirit 22:22 [q]Jdg 9:23; 1Sa 16:14; 18:10; 19:9; Eze 14:9; 2Th 2:11
in the mouths of all his prophets,' he
said.
"'You will succeed in enticing him,'
said the LORD. 'Go and do it.'
23"So now the LORD has put a lying
spirit in the mouths of all these prophets[r] of yours. The LORD has decreed disaster for you." 22:23 [r]Eze 14:9
24Then Zedekiah[s] son of Kenaanah 22:24 [s]ver 11
went up and slapped[t] Micaiah in the [t]Ac 23:2
face. "Which way did the spirit from[a]
the LORD go when he went from me to
speak to you?" he asked.
25Micaiah replied, "You will find out
on the day you go to hide[u] in an inner 22:25 [u]1Ki 20:30
room."

[a]24 Or *Spirit of*

26 The king of Israel then ordered,
"Take Micaiah and send him back to
Amon the ruler of the city and to Joash
the king's son 27 and say, 'This is what
22:27 the king says: Put this fellow in prison[v]
[v] 2Ch 16:10 and give him nothing but bread and
water until I return safely.'"
28 Micaiah declared, "If you ever re-
22:28 turn safely, the LORD has not spoken[w]
[w] Dt 18:22 through me." Then he added, "Mark
my words, all you people!"

Ahab Killed at Ramoth Gilead

29 So the king of Israel and Jehoshaphat king of Judah went up to Ramoth Gilead. 30 The king of Israel said
to Jehoshaphat, "I will enter the battle
22:30 in disguise,[x] but you wear your royal
[x] 2Ch 35:32 robes." So the king of Israel disguised
himself and went into battle.
31 Now the king of Aram had ordered his thirty-two chariot commanders, "Do not fight with anyone, small
22:31 or great, except the king[y] of Israel."
[y] 2Sa 17:2 32 When the chariot commanders saw
Jehoshaphat, they thought, "Surely this
is the king of Israel." So they turned
to attack him, but when Jehoshaphat
cried out, 33 the chariot commanders
saw that he was not the king of Israel
22:34 and stopped pursuing him.
[z] 2Ch 35:23 34 But someone drew his bow[z] at random and hit the king of Israel between
the sections of his armor. The king told
his chariot driver, "Wheel around and
get me out of the fighting. I've been
wounded." 35 All day long the battle
raged, and the king was propped up in
his chariot facing the Arameans. The
blood from his wound ran onto the
floor of the chariot, and that evening
he died. 36 As the sun was setting, a cry
22:36 spread through the army: "Every man
[a] 2Ki 14:12 to his town; everyone to his land!"[a]
37 So the king died and was brought
to Samaria, and they buried him there.
38 They washed the chariot at a pool in
Samaria (where the prostitutes bathed),[a]
22:38 and the dogs[b] licked up his blood, as
[b] 1Ki 21:19 the word of the LORD had declared.
39 As for the other events of Ahab's
reign, including all he did, the palace
22:39 he built and inlaid with ivory,[c] and the
[c] 2Ch 9:17; cities he fortified, are they not written
Am 3:15 in the book of the annals of the kings
of Israel? 40 Ahab rested with his fathers.
And Ahaziah his son succeeded him as
king.

Jehoshaphat King of Judah

41 Jehoshaphat son of Asa became
king of Judah in the fourth year of Ahab
king of Israel. 42 Jehoshaphat was thirty-
five years old when he became king,
and he reigned in Jerusalem twenty-five
years. His mother's name was Azubah
daughter of Shilhi. 43 In everything he
walked in the ways of his father Asa[d] 22:43 [d] 2Ch 17:3
and did not stray from them; he did [e] 1Ki 3:2; 15:14;
what was right in the eyes of the LORD. 2Ki 12:3
The high places,[e] however, were not removed, and the people continued to
offer sacrifices and burn incense there.
44 Jehoshaphat was also at peace with
the king of Israel.
45 As for the other events of Jehoshaphat's reign, the things he achieved
and his military exploits, are they not
written in the book of the annals of the
kings of Judah? 46 He rid the land of
the rest of the male shrine prostitutes[f] 22:46
who remained there even after the reign [f] Dt 23:17; 1Ki 14:24;
of his father Asa. 47 There was then no 15:12
king[g] in Edom; a deputy ruled. 22:47
48 Now Jehoshaphat built a fleet of [g] 2Sa 8:14;
trading ships[b][h] to go to Ophir for gold, 2Ki 3:9; 8:20
but they never set sail—they were 22:48 [h] 1Ki 9:26;
wrecked at Ezion Geber. 49 At that time 10:22
Ahaziah son of Ahab said to Jehoshaphat, "Let my men sail with your men,"
but Jehoshaphat refused.
50 Then Jehoshaphat rested with his
fathers and was buried with them in the
city of David his father. And Jehoram
his son succeeded him.

Ahaziah King of Israel

51 Ahaziah son of Ahab became king
of Israel in Samaria in the seventeenth
year of Jehoshaphat king of Judah, and
he reigned over Israel two years. 52 He
did evil[i] in the eyes of the LORD, be- 22:52
cause he walked in the ways of his fa- [i] 1Ki 15:26; 21:25
ther and mother and in the ways of
Jeroboam son of Nebat, who caused Israel to sin. 53 He served and worshiped
Baal[j] and provoked the LORD, the God 22:53
of Israel, to anger, just as his father[k] had [j] Jdg 2:11 [k] 1Ki 16:30-32
done.

[a] 38 Or *Samaria and cleaned the weapons*
[b] 48 Hebrew *of ships of Tarshish*

2 Kings

Authorship and Date

Unknown

Key Themes

The book of 2 Kings falls into two broad divisions. The first section deals with events taking place in both the northern and the southern kingdoms of Israel and Judah. The exploits of the kings of each kingdom are explained in terms of what was going on during the reign of the king in the other monarchy. This system of coordinating the tales of each kingdom can, in some ways, be confusing to one unschooled in the history of Israel. It is best to keep a chart of the history of Israel at hand to mark the separate dynasties and deeds of Judah and Israel.

The second part of the book is the history of the decline and fall of Judah after Israel, the northern kingdom, was destroyed. More detailed attention is given to the fall of Judah than Israel, suggesting that the writer of the book was himself from the southern kingdom and therefore more partial to the telling of its story. There are many themes that occur in the book. As in 1 Kings, we see abuses of power and the exasperation of God's patience. The book also deals with national idolatry and God's judgment on wickedness. As Elijah provided a colorful figure in 1 Kings, Elisha performs the same function in 2 Kings. These glorious loners—these non-writing prophets—portray the heart of all that's best and noble in the godly spirit.

Fruit of the Spirit in 2 Kings

Love: Love is the strongest of passions when it sets its heart on pleasing God. Josiah, in his newfound love for God, broke down the idols and shrines and called the nation back to the adoration of the God his own soul adored (see 23:8). When people come back to the adoration of the only God, their idols must soon melt in the sheer heat of their revitalized worship.

Joy: Joy results when we get anywhere near the grace of God. Naaman the leper, warrior of Syria, was healed of his leprosy. His gratitude could not help but erupt in joy as he exclaimed:

"Now I know that there is no God in all the world except in Israel" (5:15).

Peace: Elisha sent Naaman the leper home clean and whole. Naaman came to Israel diseased and in turmoil, but he left in peace and health. The difference between turmoil and peace lies in our willingness to come close to the source of all peace, Almighty God (see 5:19).

Kindness: Kindness results when great kings trust in the Lord rather than in their own understanding. So it was with Hezekiah (see 18:5). Hezekiah was kind in a day when cruelty was the custom. Perhaps this was the reason that God agreed to answer his dying prayer, adding 15 years to his life (see 20:6).

Goodness: Manasseh is remembered as a man void of goodness. By his evil, he condemned himself as well as an entire nation (see 21:10–12). Goodness is not a yoke that God lays on our heads to make us miserable. Goodness is the red carpet that ends at the throne; God summons us to walk upon that carpet, drawing us toward himself and making us his friends.

Faithfulness: Faithfulness enlarges the celebration of our hearts beyond our own egos. The lepers in chapter 7 had undoubtedly been shunned and mistreated all their lives. But suddenly they came upon a cache of material glory. Having discovered a vast treasure, they at first planned to keep it for themselves. But their lack of faithfulness settled on their consciences, and they agreed among themselves, "We're not doing right. This is a day of good news and we are keeping it to ourselves" (7:9). They went into town and reported the truth that the Arameans had fled and the nation was delivered. Faithfulness always serves God and others even when it must be done at some expense to ourselves. There is, perhaps, no one healthier than a leper who understands the obligation of faithfulness.

The LORD's Judgment on Ahaziah

1:1 [a]Ge 19:37; 2Sa 8:2; 2Ki 3:5
1 After Ahab's death, Moab[a] rebelled
against Israel. 2Now Ahaziah had
fallen through the lattice of his upper
room in Samaria and injured himself.
1:2 [b]ver 16 [c]Mk 3:22 [d]1Sa 6:2; Isa 2:6; 14:29; Mt 10:25 [e]Jdg 18:5; 2Ki 8:7-10
So he sent messengers,[b] saying to them,
"Go and consult Baal-Zebub,[c] the god
of Ekron,[d] to see if I will recover[e] from
this injury."
3But the angel[f] of the LORD said to
1:3 [f]ver 15; Ge 16:7 [g]1Ki 17:1 [h]1Sa 28:8
Elijah[g] the Tishbite, "Go up and meet
the messengers of the king of Samaria
and ask them, 'Is it because there is no
God in Israel[h] that you are going off to
consult Baal-Zebub, the god of Ekron?'
4Therefore this is what the LORD says:
1:4 [i]ver 6,16; Ps 41:8
'You will not leave[i] the bed you are lying on. You will certainly die!' " So Elijah went.
5When the messengers returned to
the king, he asked them, "Why have
you come back?"
6"A man came to meet us," they replied. "And he said to us, 'Go back to
the king who sent you and tell him,
"This is what the LORD says: Is it because there is no God in Israel that you
are sending men to consult Baal-Zebub,
the god of Ekron? Therefore you will
not leave the bed you are lying on. You
will certainly die!" ' "
7The king asked them, "What kind
of man was it who came to meet you
and told you this?"
8They replied, "He was a man with a
1:8 [j]1Ki 18:7; Zec 13:4; Mt 3:4; Mk 1:6
garment of hair[j] and with a leather belt
around his waist."
The king said, "That was Elijah the
Tishbite."
1:9 [k]2Ki 6:14 [l]Ex 18:25; Isa 3:3
9Then he sent[k] to Elijah a captain[l]
with his company of fifty men. The
captain went up to Elijah, who was
sitting on the top of a hill, and said
to him, "Man of God, the king says,
'Come down!' "
10Elijah answered the captain, "If I
am a man of God, may fire come down
from heaven and consume you and
1:10 [m]1Ki 18:38; Lk 9:54; Rev 11:5; 13:13
your fifty men!" Then fire[m] fell from
heaven and consumed the captain and
his men.
11At this the king sent to Elijah another captain with his fifty men. The
captain said to him, "Man of God, this
is what the king says, 'Come down at
once!' "
12"If I am a man of God," Elijah replied, "may fire come down from heaven
and consume you and your fifty men!"
Then the fire of God fell from heaven
and consumed him and his fifty men.
13So the king sent a third captain
with his fifty men. This third captain
went up and fell on his knees before Elijah. "Man of God," he begged, "please
have respect for my life[n] and the lives of 1:13 [n]1Sa 26:21; Ps 72:14
these fifty men, your servants! 14See, fire
has fallen from heaven and consumed
the first two captains and all their men.
But now have respect for my life!"
15The angel[o] of the LORD said to Eli- 1:15 [o]ver 3 [p]Isa 51:12; 57:11; Jer 1:17; Eze 2:6
jah, "Go down with him; do not be
afraid[p] of him." So Elijah got up and
went down with him to the king.
16He told the king, "This is what the
LORD says: Is it because there is no God
in Israel for you to consult that you
have sent messengers[q] to consult Baal- 1:16 [q]ver 2 [r]ver 4
Zebub, the god of Ekron? Because you
have done this, you will never leave[r]
the bed you are lying on. You will cer-
tainly die!" 17So he died,[s] according to 1:17 [s]2Ki 8:15; Jer 20:6; 28:17 [t]2Ki 3:1; 8:16
the word of the LORD that Elijah had
spoken.
Because Ahaziah had no son, Joram[a t]
succeeded him as king in the second
year of Jehoram son of Jehoshaphat
king of Judah. 18As for all the other
events of Ahaziah's reign, and what he
did, are they not written in the book of
the annals of the kings of Israel?

Elijah Taken Up to Heaven

2 When the LORD was about to take[u] 2:1 [u]Ge 5:24; Heb 11:5 [v]ver 11; 1Ki 19:11; Isa 5:28; 66:15; Jer 4:13; Na 1:3 [w]1Ki 19:16,21 [x]Dt 11:30; 2Ki 4:38
Elijah up to heaven in a whirlwind,[v]
Elijah and Elisha[w] were on their way
from Gilgal.[x] 2Elijah said to Elisha,
"Stay here;[y] the LORD has sent me to
Bethel."
But Elisha said, "As surely as the
LORD lives and as you live, I will not
leave you."[z] So they went down to 2:2 [y]ver 6 [z]Ru 1:16; 1Sa 1:26; 2Ki 4:30
Bethel.
3The company[a] of the prophets at
Bethel came out to Elisha and asked,
"Do you know that the LORD is going 2:3 [a]1Sa 10:5; 2Ki 4:1,38
to take your master from you today?"
"Yes, I know," Elisha replied, "but do
not speak of it."
4Then Elijah said to him, "Stay here,
Elisha; the LORD has sent me to Jeri- 2:4 [b]Jos 3:16; 6:26
cho.[b]"
And he replied, "As surely as the

[a] *17* Hebrew *Jehoram,* a variant of *Joram*

LORD lives and as you live, I will not
leave you." So they went to Jericho.
2:5 5The company[c] of the prophets at
[c]ver 3 Jericho went up to Elisha and asked
him, "Do you know that the LORD
is going to take your master from you
today?"
"Yes, I know," he replied, "but do
not speak of it."
2:6 6Then Elijah said to him, "Stay here;[d]
[d]ver 2 [e]Jos 3:15 the LORD has sent me to the Jordan."[e]
[f]Ru 1:16 And he replied, "As surely as the
LORD lives and as you live, I will
not leave you."[f] So the two of them
walked on.
7Fifty men of the company of the
prophets went and stood at a distance,
facing the place where Elijah and Elisha had stopped at the Jordan. 8Elijah
took his cloak,[g] rolled it up and struck[h] 2:8
the water with it. The water divided[i] to [g]1Ki 19:19 [h]ver 14
the right and to the left, and the two of [i]Ex 14:21
them crossed over on dry[j] ground. [j]Ex 14:22,29
9When they had crossed, Elijah said
to Elisha, "Tell me, what can I do for
you before I am taken from you?"
"Let me inherit a double[k] portion of 2:9 [k]Dt 21:17
your spirit,"[l] Elisha replied. [l]Nu 11:17
10"You have asked a difficult thing,"
Elijah said, "yet if you see me when I
am taken from you, it will be yours—
otherwise not."
11As they were walking along and
talking together, suddenly a chariot of
fire[m] and horses of fire appeared and 2:11 [m]2Ki 6:17; Ps 68:17; 104:3,4; Isa 66:15; Hab 3:8; Zec 6:1
separated the two of them, and Elijah
went up to heaven[n] in a whirlwind.[o] [n]Ge 5:24
12Elisha saw this and cried out, "My [o]ver 1
father! My father! The chariots[p] and
horsemen of Israel!" And Elisha saw
him no more. Then he took hold of his 2:12 [p]2Ki 6:17; 13:14
own clothes and tore[q] them apart. [q]Ge 37:29
13He picked up the cloak that had
fallen from Elijah and went back and
stood on the bank of the Jordan. 14Then
he took the cloak[r] that had fallen from 2:14 [r]1Ki 19:19
him and struck[s] the water with it. [s]ver 8
"Where now is the LORD, the God of
Elijah?" he asked. When he struck the
water, it divided to the right and to the
left, and he crossed over.

DAY 4 FOUR

Goodness and My Service to Others

2 Kings 2:6–15

Elisha wanted to be like Elijah. Elisha had, no doubt, studied the older prophet and imitated his devotion. Elisha followed Elijah on the very last day of Elijah's life. When Elijah told Elisha not to accompany him to the end, Elisha refused to leave his teacher and mentor. Later, Elisha received what he asked for—"a double portion" of Elijah's spirit. There is no teacher like a good mentor, and there is no better way to learn a lifestyle than to imitate it.

Elisha looked around and noted the person that he most wanted to emulate. He saw Elijah's power and goodness, his desire to help others and his impact on their lives. Then Elisha set about trying to bring his own life into accord with the one he wished to imitate.

Who is the person you are trying to become? Who is the person you would most like to be like? Could it be Jesus? Imitating Christ will produce a life of goodness. Study him. Learn how he lived. Learn how he ministered to others. Learn how he died and why he died.

Then as you study Christ, imitate him. Be prepared for a life of goodness and usefulness to others.

To begin a study on the topic of Goodness, the Result of Imitating Christ, turn to the home page on page 1409.

Gentleness

The Cloak of Power

2 Kings 2:14

The mantle of the Spirit fell, and people were amazed by what God accomplished through everyday heroes. At Pentecost the splendor of God's flame was given to insignificant people who had done nothing more than call Jesus "Lord."

15The company[t] of the prophets from 2:15 [t]ver 7;
Jericho, who were watching, said, "The 1Sa 10:5
spirit[u] of Elijah is resting on Elisha." [u]Nu 11:17
And they went to meet him and bowed
to the ground before him. 16"Look,"
they said, "we your servants have fifty
able men. Let them go and look for
your master. Perhaps the Spirit[v] of the 2:16
LORD has picked him up[w] and set him [v]1Ki 18:12 [w]Ac 8:39
down on some mountain or in some
valley."

"No," Elisha replied, "do not send
them."
[17]But they persisted until he was too
2:17 [x]2Ki 8:11 ashamed[x] to refuse. So he said, "Send
them." And they sent fifty men, who
searched for three days but did not find
him. [18]When they returned to Elisha,
who was staying in Jericho, he said to
them, "Didn't I tell you not to go?"

Healing of the Water

[19]The men of the city said to Elisha,
"Look, our lord, this town is well situated,
as you can see, but the water is
bad and the land is unproductive."
[20]"Bring me a new bowl," he said,
"and put salt in it." So they brought it
to him.
2:21 [y]Ex 15:25; 2Ki 4:41; 6:6 [21]Then he went out to the spring and
threw[y] the salt into it, saying, "This is
what the LORD says: 'I have healed this
water. Never again will it cause death or
make the land unproductive.'" [22]And
the water has remained wholesome[z] to 2:22 [z]Ex 15:25
this day, according to the word Elisha
had spoken.

GOODNESS

MOCKING HOLINESS

2 Kings 2:23

God will have honor. When children mock prophets, the culture must grieve.

Elisha Is Jeered

[23]From there Elisha went up to Bethel.
As he was walking along the road,
some youths came out of the town

ELISHA

Patience, the Secret of Active Waiting (2:1–25)

Patience is not passivity. Patience is informed waiting—waiting with the understanding that God has an answer and that we can be at peace, though not completely fulfilled, until that answer comes. Elisha knew what he wanted, and he actively waited for the gifts he sought by charging the gates of God.

Elijah didn't want any company on his last day on earth. Elijah knew (as did most everyone he saw that day) that God was going to take him to heaven. He continually asked Elisha to stay at various stopping points along their journey. Elijah said to Elisha, "Stay here; the LORD has sent me to Bethel" (2 Kings 2:2). But Elisha insisted on accompanying Elijah, saying, "As surely as the LORD lives and as you live, I will not leave you" (v. 2). The two of them had this same conversation at Jericho and again at the Jordan (vv. 4,6).

Elisha's goal was to be with Elijah that day. His final request was dependent upon his presence with Elijah: "Let me inherit a double portion of your spirit" (v. 9). Elijah informed Elisha that his request would only be granted if Elisha were present at the time Elijah was taken. Elisha's patience remained, and when the chariot and horses separated them and Elijah was whisked away, not only did Elisha see it happen, but Elijah's cloak fell off and landed at the young prophet's feet. When Elisha picked up the cloak and walked back to the Jordan, he approached the river and perhaps wondered, *Can I do what Elijah did?* He struck the river with Elijah's cloak and cried, "Where now is the LORD, the God of Elijah?" (v. 14). The river parted just as it had done for Elijah, and Elisha knew the reward for his patience.

Patience achieves the hunger of our heart without hurriedness. In Elisha's case, the hunger was for a life calling, to inherit a double portion of Elijah's spirit—an expression of Elisha's desire to continue Elijah's ministry. Elisha got what he waited for, but his wait was not a yawning, sleepy rest during which God dumped his life's goal on him while he slept. His waiting was an active patience. It knew how to wait with ardent hoping. Such waiting blesses those who honor it with the best gifts of God, the final product of all patience.

Elisha demonstrated that patience requires pacing. Patience is never a sprint and rarely a jog. It is a steady walk. Patience will not let anxiety hurry it, lest it run after God and pass him by.

2:23 [a]Ex 22:28; 2Ch 36:16; Job 19:18; Ps 31:18
and jeered[a] at him. "Go on up, you
baldhead!" they said. "Go on up, you
baldhead!" 24He turned around, looked
at them and called down a curse[b] on
2:24 [b]Ge 4:11; Ne 13:25-27 [c]Dt 18:19
them in the name[c] of the LORD. Then
two bears came out of the woods and
mauled forty-two of the youths. 25And
2:25 [d]1Ki 18:20; 2Ki 4:25
he went on to Mount Carmel[d] and
from there returned to Samaria.

Moab Revolts

3:1 [e]2Ki 1:17
3 Joram[a][e] son of Ahab became king
of Israel in Samaria in the eighteenth year of Jehoshaphat king of Judah, and he reigned twelve years. 2He
3:2 [f]1Ki 15:26 [g]1Ki 16:30-32 [h]Ex 23:24; 2Ki 10:18, 26-28
did evil[f] in the eyes of the LORD, but
not as his father[g] and mother had done.
He got rid of the sacred stone[h] of Baal
that his father had made. 3Nevertheless
3:3 [i]1Ki 12:28-32; 14:9,16
he clung to the sins[i] of Jeroboam son
of Nebat, which he had caused Israel
to commit; he did not turn away from
them.
4Now Mesha king of Moab[j] raised
3:4 [j]Ge 19:37; 2Ki 1:1 [k]Ezr 7:17; Isa 16:1
sheep, and he had to supply the king of
Israel with a hundred thousand lambs[k]
and with the wool of a hundred thousand rams. 5But after Ahab died, the
3:5 [l]2Ki 1:1
king of Moab[l] rebelled against the king
of Israel. 6So at that time King Joram
set out from Samaria and mobilized all
Israel. 7He also sent this message to Jehoshaphat king of Judah: "The king of
Moab has rebelled against me. Will you
3:7 [m]1Ki 22:4
go with me to fight[m] against Moab?"
"I will go with you," he replied. "I
am as you are, my people as your people, my horses as your horses."
8"By what route shall we attack?" he
asked.
"Through the Desert of Edom," he
answered.
9So the king of Israel set out with the
3:9 [n]1Ki 22:47
king of Judah and the king of Edom.[n]
After a roundabout march of seven days,
the army had no more water for themselves or for the animals with them.
10"What!" exclaimed the king of Israel. "Has the LORD called us three
kings together only to hand us over to
Moab?"
11But Jehoshaphat asked, "Is there no
prophet of the LORD here, that we may
3:11 [o]Ge 25:22; 1Ki 22:7 [p]Ge 20:7 [q]1Ki 19:16
inquire[o] of the LORD through him?"
An officer of the king of Israel answered, "Elisha[p] son of Shaphat is here.
He used to pour water on the hands of
Elijah.[b][q]"

12Jehoshaphat said, "The word[r] of 3:12 [r]Nu 11:17
the LORD is with him." So the king
of Israel and Jehoshaphat and the king
of Edom went down to him.
13Elisha said to the king of Israel,
"What do we have to do with each other? Go to the prophets of your father
and the prophets of your mother."
"No," the king of Israel answered,
"because it was the LORD who called us
three kings together to hand us over to
Moab."
14Elisha said, "As surely as the LORD
Almighty lives, whom I serve, if I did
not have respect for the presence of Jehoshaphat king of Judah, I would not
look at you or even notice you. 15But
now bring me a harpist."[s] 3:15 [s]1Sa 16:23 [t]Jer 15:17; Eze 1:3
While the harpist was playing, the
hand[t] of the LORD came upon Elisha
16and he said, "This is what the LORD
says: Make this valley full of ditches.
17For this is what the LORD says: You
will see neither wind nor rain, yet this
valley will be filled with water,[u] and 3:17 [u]Ps 107:35; Isa 32:2; 35:6; 41:18
you, your cattle and your other animals
will drink. 18This is an easy[v] thing in
the eyes of the LORD; he will also hand 3:18 [v]Ge 18:14; 2Ki 20:10; Isa 49:6; Jer 32:17,27; Mk 10:27
Moab over to you. 19You will over-
throw every fortified city and every major town. You will cut down every good
tree, stop up all the springs, and ruin
every good field with stones."
20The next morning, about the time[w] 3:20 [w]Ex 29:39-40 [x]Ex 17:6
for offering the sacrifice, there it was—
water flowing from the direction of
Edom! And the land was filled with
water.[x]
21Now all the Moabites had heard
that the kings had come to fight against
them; so every man, young and old,
who could bear arms was called up and
stationed on the border. 22When they
got up early in the morning, the sun was
shining on the water. To the Moabites
across the way, the water looked red—
like blood. 23"That's blood!" they said.
"Those kings must have fought and
slaughtered each other. Now to the
plunder, Moab!"
24But when the Moabites came to the
camp of Israel, the Israelites rose up and
fought them until they fled. And the
Israelites invaded the land and slaugh-

[a]*1* Hebrew *Jehoram,* a variant of *Joram;* also in verse 6 [b]*11* That is, he was Elijah's personal servant.

tered the Moabites. 25They destroyed the towns, and each man threw a stone on every good field until it was covered. They stopped up all the springs and cut down every good tree. Only Kir Hareseth[y] was left with its stones in place, but men armed with slings surrounded it and attacked it as well.

3:25 [y]ver 19; Isa 15:1; 16:7; Jer 48:31,36

26When the king of Moab saw that the battle had gone against him, he took with him seven hundred swordsmen to break through to the king of Edom, but they failed. 27Then he took his firstborn[z] son, who was to succeed him as king, and offered him as a sacrifice on the city wall. The fury against Israel was great; they withdrew and returned to their own land.

3:27 [z]Dt 12:31; 2Ki 16:3; 21:6; 2Ch 28:3; Ps 106:38; Jer 19:4-5; Am 2:1; Mic 6:7

The Widow's Oil

4 The wife of a man from the company[a] of the prophets cried out to Elisha, "Your servant my husband is dead, and you know that he revered the LORD. But now his creditor[b] is coming to take my two boys as his slaves."

4:1 [a]1Sa 10:5; 2Ki 2:3 [b]Ex 22:26; Lev 25:39-43; Ne 5:3-5; Job 22:6; 24:9

2Elisha replied to her, "How can I help you? Tell me, what do you have in your house?"

"Your servant has nothing there at all," she said, "except a little oil."[c]

4:2 [c]1Ki 17:12

3Elisha said, "Go around and ask all your neighbors for empty jars. Don't ask for just a few. 4Then go inside and shut the door behind you and your sons. Pour oil into all the jars, and as each is filled, put it to one side."

5She left him and afterward shut the door behind her and her sons. They brought the jars to her and she kept pouring. 6When all the jars were full, she said to her son, "Bring me another one."

But he replied, "There is not a jar left." Then the oil stopped flowing.

7She went and told the man of God,[d] and he said, "Go, sell the oil and pay your debts. You and your sons can live on what is left."

4:7 [d]1Ki 12:22

The Shunammite's Son Restored to Life

8One day Elisha went to Shunem.[e] And a well-to-do woman was there, who urged him to stay for a meal. So whenever he came by, he stopped there to eat. 9She said to her husband, "I know that this man who often comes our way is a holy man of God. 10Let's make a small room on the roof and put in it a bed and a table, a chair and a lamp for him. Then he can stay[f] there whenever he comes to us."

4:8 [e]Jos 19:18

4:10 [f]Mt 10:41; Ro 12:13

11One day when Elisha came, he went up to his room and lay down there. 12He said to his servant Gehazi, "Call the Shunammite."[g] So he called her, and she stood before him. 13Elisha said to him, "Tell her, 'You have gone to all this trouble for us. Now what can be done for you? Can we speak on your behalf to the king or the commander of the army?' "

4:12 [g]2Ki 8:1

She replied, "I have a home among my own people."

14"What can be done for her?" Elisha asked.

Gehazi said, "Well, she has no son and her husband is old."

15Then Elisha said, "Call her." So he called her, and she stood in the doorway. 16"About this time[h] next year," Elisha said, "you will hold a son in your arms."

4:16 [h]Ge 18:10

"No, my lord," she objected. "Don't mislead your servant, O man of God!"

17But the woman became pregnant, and the next year about that same time she gave birth to a son, just as Elisha had told her.

18The child grew, and one day he went out to his father, who was with the reapers.[i] 19"My head! My head!" he said to his father.

4:18 [i]Ru 2:3

His father told a servant, "Carry him to his mother." 20After the servant had lifted him up and carried him to his mother, the boy sat on her lap until noon, and then he died. 21She went up and laid him on the bed[j] of the man of God, then shut the door and went out.

4:21 [j]ver 32

22She called her husband and said, "Please send me one of the servants and a donkey so I can go to the man of God quickly and return."

23"Why go to him today?" he asked. "It's not the New Moon[k] or the Sabbath."

4:23 [k]Nu 10:10; 1Ch 23:31; Ps 81:3

"It's all right," she said.

24She saddled the donkey and said to her servant, "Lead on; don't slow down for me unless I tell you." 25So she set out and came to the man of God at Mount Carmel.[l]

4:25 [l]1Ki 18:20; 2Ki 2:25

When he saw her in the distance, the man of God said to his servant Gehazi,

"Look! There's the Shunammite! 26Run
to meet her and ask her, 'Are you all
right? Is your husband all right? Is your
child all right?' "

"Everything is all right," she said.

27When she reached the man of God
at the mountain, she took hold of his
feet. Gehazi came over to push her
away, but the man of God said, "Leave
4:27 her alone! She is in bitter distress,[m] but
[m]1Sa 1:15 the LORD has hidden it from me and
has not told me why."

28"Did I ask you for a son, my lord?"
she said. "Didn't I tell you, 'Don't raise
my hopes'?"

29Elisha said to Gehazi, "Tuck your
4:29 cloak into your belt,[n] take my staff[o] in
[n]1Ki 18:46; 2Ki 2:8,14; 9:1 your hand and run. If you meet any-
[o]Ex 4:2; 7:19; 14:16 one, do not greet him, and if anyone
greets you, do not answer. Lay my staff
on the boy's face."

30But the child's mother said, "As
surely as the LORD lives and as you live,
I will not leave you." So he got up and
followed her.

31Gehazi went on ahead and laid the
staff on the boy's face, but there was
no sound or response. So Gehazi went
back to meet Elisha and told him, "The
boy has not awakened."

32When Elisha reached the house,
there was the boy lying dead on his
4:32 couch.[p] 33He went in, shut the door
[p]ver 21 on the two of them and prayed[q] to the
4:33 LORD. 34Then he got on the bed and
[q]1Ki 17:20; Mt 6:6 lay upon the boy, mouth to mouth, eyes
4:34 to eyes, hands to hands. As he stretched[r]
[r]1Ki 17:21; Ac 20:10 himself out upon him, the boy's body
grew warm. 35Elisha turned away and
walked back and forth in the room and
then got on the bed and stretched out
upon him once more. The boy sneezed
4:35 seven times[s] and opened his eyes.[t]
[s]Jos 6:15 [t]2Ki 8:5 36Elisha summoned Gehazi and said,
"Call the Shunammite." And he did.
When she came, he said, "Take your
4:36 son."[u] 37She came in, fell at his feet and
[u]Heb 11:35 bowed to the ground. Then she took
her son and went out.

Death in the Pot

4:38 38Elisha returned to Gilgal[v] and there
[v]2Ki 2:1 [w]Lev 26:26; 2Ki 8:1 was a famine[w] in that region. While the
company of the prophets was meeting
with him, he said to his servant, "Put
on the large pot and cook some stew for
these men."

39One of them went out into the
fields to gather herbs and found a wild
vine. He gathered some of its gourds
and filled the fold of his cloak. When
he returned, he cut them up into the
pot of stew, though no one knew what
they were. 40The stew was poured out
for the men, but as they began to eat it,
they cried out, "O man of God, there is
death in the pot!" And they could not
eat it.

41Elisha said, "Get some flour." He
put it into the pot and said, "Serve it to
the people to eat." And there was noth-
ing harmful in the pot.[x] 4:41 [x]Ex 15:25; 2Ki 2:21

Feeding of a Hundred

42A man came from Baal Shalishah,[y] 4:42 [y]1Sa 9:4
bringing the man of God twenty loaves[z] [z]Mt 14:17; 15:36
of barley bread[a] baked from the first [a]1Sa 9:7
ripe grain, along with some heads of
new grain. "Give it to the people to
eat," Elisha said.

43"How can I set this before a hundred men?" his servant asked.

But Elisha answered, "Give it to the
people to eat.[b] For this is what the 4:43 [b]Lk 9:13
LORD says: 'They will eat and have [c]Mt 14:20; Jn 6:12
some left over.[c]' " 44Then he set it before them, and they ate and had some
left over, according to the word of the
LORD.

Naaman Healed of Leprosy

5 Now Naaman was commander of
the army of the king of Aram.[d] 5:1 [d]Ge 10:22; 2Sa 10:19
He was a great man in the sight of [e]Ex 4:6;
his master and highly regarded, because Nu 12:10; Lk 4:27
through him the LORD had given vic-
tory to Aram. He was a valiant soldier,
but he had leprosy.[a][e]

2Now bands[f] from Aram had gone 5:2 [f]2Ki 6:23; 13:20; 24:2
out and had taken captive a young girl
from Israel, and she served Naaman's
wife. 3She said to her mistress, "If only
my master would see the prophet[g] who 5:3 [g]Ge 20:7
is in Samaria! He would cure him of his
leprosy."

4Naaman went to his master and
told him what the girl from Israel had
said. 5"By all means, go," the king of
Aram replied. "I will send a letter to
the king of Israel." So Naaman left, taking with him ten talents[b] of silver, six

[a] *1* The Hebrew word was used for various diseases affecting the skin—not necessarily leprosy; also in verses 3, 6, 7, 11 and 27. [b] *5* That is, about 750 pounds (about 340 kilograms)

thousand shekels[a] of gold and ten sets
5:5 [h]ver 22; of clothing.[h] 6The letter that he took to
Ge 24:53; the king of Israel read: "With this let-
Jdg 14:12; ter I am sending my servant Naaman
1Sa 9:7 to you so that you may cure him of his
leprosy."
5:7 7As soon as the king of Israel read the
[i]2Ki 19:14 letter,[i] he tore his robes and said, "Am I
[j]Ge 30:2 God?[j] Can I kill and bring back to
[k]Dt 32:39; 1Sa 2:6 life?[k] Why does this fellow send some-

DAY 2 TWO

▸ KINDNESS AND THE PURPOSE OF GOD IN MY LIFE

2 Kings 5:1,8–15

Naaman receives the prescription for his healing and at first rejects it. The prophet's command for him to dip himself in the Jordan was not to his liking. He wanted to be free of his leprosy—but by some form of healing that would both cure him and allow him to retain his dignity.

One would think a leper would have so little dignity that any requirement for healing would be acceptable. But this particular leper, eroded and disfigured, rails at the requirements of God. This story presents a puzzling contradiction: To be cured in any way would seem to be an act of grace, yet Naaman's ego refuses to yield, still in the way of God's cleansing. The metaphor fits all of us. Which of us, drowning in our sin and much in need of God, will not live to the very last making demands rather than yielding to God?

Finally, because lepers have very few options, Naaman obeys. At that point his stormy anger is made calm by his obedience. He is washed by grace. And once he is clean, he becomes kind. "Please accept this gift from me," he begs the prophet. His hostility has completely dissipated.

There is a domesticating force in the heart of grace. Once we obey God, our wild ego struggles are given peace. We find our anger has been given a new, tolerant heart. Then we can—like Naaman—fulfill God's desire for our lives and minister to those we once considered enemies.

To begin a study on the topic of Kindness, Anger Washed by Grace, turn to the home page on page 751.

one to me to be cured of his leprosy?
See how he is trying to pick a quarrel[l] 5:7 [l]1Ki 20:7
with me!"
8When Elisha the man of God heard
that the king of Israel had torn his
robes, he sent him this message: "Why
have you torn your robes? Have the
man come to me and he will know that
there is a prophet[m] in Israel." 9So Na- 5:8 [m]1Ki 22:7
aman went with his horses and chari-
ots and stopped at the door of Elisha's
house. 10Elisha sent a messenger to
say to him, "Go, wash[n] yourself seven 5:10 [n]Jn 9:7
times[o] in the Jordan, and your flesh will [o]Ge 33:3;
be restored and you will be cleansed." Lev 14:7
11But Naaman went away angry and
said, "I thought that he would surely
come out to me and stand and call on
the name of the LORD his God, wave
his hand[p] over the spot and cure me of 5:11 [p]Ex 7:19
my leprosy. 12Are not Abana and Phar-
par, the rivers of Damascus, better than
any of the waters[q] of Israel? Couldn't I 5:12 [q]Isa 8:6
wash in them and be cleansed?" So he [r]Pr 14:17,29;
turned and went off in a rage.[r] 19:11; 29:11

▸ PATIENCE

SCRUBBING LEPERS

2 Kings 5:12

Waiting to get well is a recipe for health. Leprosy was not as terminal as the ancients thought it was. It was just that the prescription that could heal leprosy was kept in the pharmacy of the living God. Most cures come in the waiting. Perhaps that is why we call the suffering "patients."

13Naaman's servants went to him and
said, "My father,[s] if the prophet had 5:13 [s]2Ki 6:21;
told you to do some great thing, would 13:14
you not have done it? How much more,
then, when he tells you, 'Wash and
be cleansed'!" 14So he went down and
dipped himself in the Jordan seven
times,[t] as the man of God had told him, 5:14 [t]Ge 33:3;
and his flesh was restored[u] and became Lev 14:7; Jos 6:15 [u]Ex 4:7
clean like that of a young boy.[v] [v]Job 33:25; Lk 4:27
15Then Naaman and all his atten-
dants went back to the man of God.[w]
He stood before him and said, "Now 5:15 [w]Jos 2:11
I know[x] that there is no God in all [x]Jos 4:24;
the world except in Israel. Please accept 1Sa 17:46; Da 2:47
now a gift[y] from your servant." [y]1Sa 9:7; 25:27

[a]5 That is, about 150 pounds (about 70 kilograms)

16The prophet answered, "As surely
as the LORD lives, whom I serve, I will
not accept a thing." And even though
5:16 [z]ver 20,26; Ge 14:23; Da 5:17 Naaman urged him, he refused.[z]
17"If you will not," said Naaman,
"please let me, your servant, be given
5:17 [a]Ex 20:24 as much earth[a] as a pair of mules can
carry, for your servant will never again
make burnt offerings and sacrifices to
any other god but the LORD. 18But
may the LORD forgive your servant for
this one thing: When my master enters
the temple of Rimmon to bow down
5:18 [b]2Ki 7:2 and he is leaning[b] on my arm and I bow
there also—when I bow down in the
temple of Rimmon, may the LORD forgive your servant for this."
5:19 [c]1Sa 1:17; Ac 15:33 19"Go in peace,"[c] Elisha said.
After Naaman had traveled some dis-
tance, 20Gehazi, the servant of Elisha the
man of God, said to himself, "My master was too easy on Naaman, this Aramean, by not accepting from him what
5:20 [d]Ex 20:7 he brought. As surely as the LORD[d]
lives, I will run after him and get something from him."
21So Gehazi hurried after Naaman.
When Naaman saw him running toward him, he got down from the chariot
to meet him. "Is everything all right?"
he asked.
22"Everything is all right," Gehazi
answered. "My master sent me to say,
'Two young men from the company of
the prophets have just come to me from
the hill country of Ephraim. Please give
them a talent[a] of silver and two sets of
5:22 [e]ver 5; Ge 45:22 clothing.' "[e]
23"By all means, take two talents,"
said Naaman. He urged Gehazi to accept them, and then tied up the two
talents of silver in two bags, with two
sets of clothing. He gave them to two of
his servants, and they carried them
ahead of Gehazi. 24When Gehazi came
to the hill, he took the things from the
servants and put them away in the
house. He sent the men away and they
left. 25Then he went in and stood before his master Elisha.
"Where have you been, Gehazi?" Elisha asked.
"Your servant didn't go anywhere,"
Gehazi answered.
26But Elisha said to him, "Was not
my spirit with you when the man got
down from his chariot to meet you?
5:26 [f]ver 16 Is this the time[f] to take money, or
to accept clothes, olive groves, vineyards, flocks, herds, or menservants and
maidservants?[g] 27Naaman's leprosy[h] will 5:26 [g]Jer 45:5
cling to you and to your descendants
forever." Then Gehazi[i] went from Eli- 5:27 [h]Nu 12:10; 2Ki 15:5 [i]Col 3:5 [j]Ex 4:6
sha's presence and he was leprous, as
white as snow.[j]

An Axhead Floats

6 The company[k] of the prophets said 6:1 [k]1Sa 10:5; 2Ki 4:38
to Elisha, "Look, the place where
we meet with you is too small for us.
2Let us go to the Jordan, where each
of us can get a pole; and let us build a
place there for us to live."
And he said, "Go."
3Then one of them said, "Won't you
please come with your servants?"
"I will," Elisha replied. 4And he went
with them.
They went to the Jordan and began
to cut down trees. 5As one of them was
cutting down a tree, the iron axhead fell
into the water. "Oh, my lord," he cried
out, "it was borrowed!"
6The man of God asked, "Where did
it fall?" When he showed him the place,
Elisha cut a stick and threw[l] it there, 6:6 [l]Ex 15:25; 2Ki 2:21
and made the iron float. 7"Lift it out,"
he said. Then the man reached out his
hand and took it.

Elisha Traps Blinded Arameans

8Now the king of Aram was at war
with Israel. After conferring with his officers, he said, "I will set up my camp
in such and such a place."
9The man of God sent word to the
king[m] of Israel: "Beware of passing that 6:9 [m]ver 12
place, because the Arameans are going
down there." 10So the king of Israel
checked on the place indicated by the
man of God. Time and again Elisha
warned[n] the king, so that he was on his 6:10 [n]Jer 11:18
guard in such places.
11This enraged the king of Aram. He
summoned his officers and demanded
of them, "Will you not tell me which of
us is on the side of the king of Israel?"
12"None of us, my lord the king,"[o] 6:12 [o]ver 9
said one of his officers, "but Elisha, the
prophet who is in Israel, tells the king
of Israel the very words you speak in
your bedroom."
13"Go, find out where he is," the king
ordered, "so I can send men and cap-

[a]22 That is, about 75 pounds (about 34 kilograms)

ture him." The report came back: "He
6:13 is in Dothan."[p] 14Then he sent[q] horses
[p]Ge 37:17 and chariots and a strong force there.
6:14 They went by night and surrounded
[q]2Ki 1:9 the city.
15When the servant of the man of
God got up and went out early the
next morning, an army with horses and
chariots had surrounded the city. "Oh,
my lord, what shall we do?" the servant
asked.
6:16 16"Don't be afraid,"[r] the prophet an-
[r]Ge 15:1 swered. "Those who are with us are
[s]2Ch 32:7; more[s] than those who are with them."
Ps 55:18; 17And Elisha prayed, "O LORD, open
Ro 8:31; his eyes so he may see." Then the LORD
1Jn 4:4 opened the servant's eyes, and he looked
and saw the hills full of horses and char-
6:17 iots[t] of fire all around Elisha.
[t]2Ki 2:11,12; 18As the enemy came down toward
Ps 68:17; him, Elisha prayed to the LORD, "Strike
Zec 6:1-7 these people with blindness."[u] So he
6:18 struck them with blindness, as Elisha
[u]Ge 19:11; had asked.
Ac 13:11 19Elisha told them, "This is not the
road and this is not the city. Follow me,
and I will lead you to the man you are
looking for." And he led them to Samaria.
20After they entered the city, Elisha
said, "LORD, open the eyes of these
men so they can see." Then the LORD
opened their eyes and they looked, and
there they were, inside Samaria.
21When the king of Israel saw them,
he asked Elisha, "Shall I kill them, my
6:21 father?[v] Shall I kill them?"
[v]2Ki 5:13 22"Do not kill them," he answered.
"Would you kill men you have cap-
6:22 tured[w] with your own sword or bow?
[w]Dt 20:11; Set food and water before them so that
2Ch 28:8-15; they may eat and drink and then go
Ro 12:20 back to their master." 23So he prepared
a great feast for them, and after they
had finished eating and drinking, he
sent them away, and they returned to
6:23 their master. So the bands[x] from Aram
[x]2Ki 5:2 stopped raiding Israel's territory.

Famine in Besieged Samaria

6:24 24Some time later, Ben-Hadad[y] king
[y]1Ki 15:18; of Aram mobilized his entire army and
20:1; marched up and laid siege[z] to Samaria.
2Ki 8:7 25There was a great famine[a] in the city;
[z]Dt 28:52 the siege lasted so long that a donkey's
6:25 head sold for eighty shekels[a] of silver,
[a]Lev 26:26; and a quarter of a cab[b] of seed pods[c][b]
Ru 1:1 for five shekels.[d]
[b]Isa 36:12

26As the king of Israel was passing
by on the wall, a woman cried to him,
"Help me, my lord the king!"
27The king replied, "If the LORD
does not help you, where can I get
help for you? From the threshing floor?
From the winepress?" 28Then he asked
her, "What's the matter?"
She answered, "This woman said to
me, 'Give up your son so we may eat
him today, and tomorrow we'll eat my
son.' 29So we cooked my son and ate[c] 6:29
him. The next day I said to her, 'Give [c]Lev 26:29;
up your son so we may eat him,' but Dt 28:53-55
she had hidden him."
30When the king heard the woman's
words, he tore[d] his robes. As he went 6:30
along the wall, the people looked, and [d]2Ki 18:37;
there, underneath, he had sackcloth[e] on Isa 22:15
his body. 31He said, "May God deal [e]Ge 37:34;
with me, be it ever so severely, if the 1Ki 21:27
head of Elisha son of Shaphat remains
on his shoulders today!"
32Now Elisha was sitting in his house,
and the elders[f] were sitting with him. 6:32
The king sent a messenger ahead, but [f]Eze 8:1; 14:1;
before he arrived, Elisha said to the el- 20:1
ders, "Don't you see how this murderer[g] [g]1Ki 18:4
is sending someone to cut off my head?[h] [h]ver 31
Look, when the messenger comes, shut
the door and hold it shut against him.
Is not the sound of his master's footsteps behind him?"
33While he was still talking to them,
the messenger came down to him. And
⌞the king⌟ said, "This disaster is from
the LORD. Why should I wait[i] for the 6:33
LORD any longer?" [i]Lev 24:11;
Job 2:9;
7 Elisha said, "Hear the word of the 14:14;
LORD. This is what the LORD says: Isa 40:31
About this time tomorrow, a seah[e] of
flour will sell for a shekel[f] and two
seahs[g] of barley for a shekel[j] at the gate 7:1
of Samaria." [j]ver 16
2The officer on whose arm the king 7:2
was leaning[k] said to the man of God, [k]2Ki 5:18
"Look, even if the LORD should open [l]ver 19;
the floodgates[l] of the heavens, could Ge 7:11;
this happen?" Ps 78:23;
Mal 3:10

[a]*25* That is, about 2 pounds (about 1 kilogram)
[b]*25* That is, probably about 1/2 pint (about 0.3 liter)
[c]*25* Or *of dove's dung*
[d]*25* That is, about 2 ounces (about 55 grams)
[e]*1* That is, probably about 7 quarts (about 7.3 liters); also in verses 16 and 18
[f]*1* That is, about 2/5 ounce (about 11 grams); also in verses 16 and 18
[g]*1* That is, probably about 13 quarts (about 15 liters); also in verses 16 and 18

"You will see it with your own eyes,"
7:2 answered Elisha, "but you will not eat[m]
any of it!"

The Siege Lifted

[3]Now there were four men with lep-
7:3 rosy[a][n] at the entrance of the city gate.
They said to each other, "Why stay here
until we die? [4]If we say, 'We'll go into
the city'—the famine is there, and we
will die. And if we stay here, we will die.
So let's go over to the camp of the Arameans and surrender. If they spare us,
we live; if they kill us, then we die."
[5]At dusk they got up and went to
the camp of the Arameans. When they
reached the edge of the camp, not a
man was there, [6]for the Lord had caused
the Arameans to hear the sound[o] of
chariots and horses and a great army, so
that they said to one another, "Look,
the king of Israel has hired[p] the Hittite[q]
and Egyptian kings to attack us!" [7]So
they got up and fled[r] in the dusk and
abandoned their tents and their horses
and donkeys. They left the camp as it
was and ran for their lives.
[8]The men who had leprosy[s] reached
the edge of the camp and entered one
of the tents. They ate and drank, and
carried away silver, gold and clothes,
and went off and hid them. They returned and entered another tent and
took some things from it and hid them
also.
[9]Then they said to each other, "We're
not doing right. This is a day of good
news and we are keeping it to ourselves.
If we wait until daylight, punishment
will overtake us. Let's go at once and
report this to the royal palace."
[10]So they went and called out to the
city gatekeepers and told them, "We
went into the Aramean camp and not
a man was there—not a sound of anyone—only tethered horses and donkeys,
and the tents left just as they were."
[11]The gatekeepers shouted the news,
and it was reported within the palace.
[12]The king got up in the night and
said to his officers, "I will tell you what
the Arameans have done to us. They
know we are starving; so they have left
the camp to hide[t] in the countryside,
thinking, 'They will surely come out,
and then we will take them alive and
get into the city.'"
[13]One of his officers answered, "Have

7:2 [m]ver 17
7:3 [n]Lev 13:45-46; Nu 5:1-4
7:6 [o]Ex 14:24; 2Sa 5:24; Eze 1:24 [p]2Sa 10:6; Jer 46:21 [q]Nu 13:29
7:7 [r]Jdg 7:21; Ps 48:4-6; Pr 28:1; Isa 30:17
7:8 [s]Isa 33:23; 35:6
7:12 [t]Jos 8:4; 2Ki 6:25-29

[a]3 The Hebrew word is used for various diseases affecting the skin—not necessarily leprosy; also in verse 8.

DAY 4 FOUR

Kindness and My Service to Others

2 Kings 7:3–11

The lepers described in this passage undoubtedly wanted a life without leprosy—they wanted to be free of every threat to their existence. Their disease probably affected their entire outlook on life and most likely consumed their consciousness. Therefore, it is remarkable that these lepers would be diseased and yet concerned about a world that had forced upon them an unclean, outcast status. Yet grace makes its requirements even on lepers.

The four lepers, in their helplessness and hopelessness, stumble upon the camp of the Arameans, who had put the city to siege. In the dead of night, God had defeated the camp of soldiers and sent them fleeing into the darkness. Now the lepers, once without hope and willing to surrender to their enemies, find a camp full of riches. In obedience to God, they inform the people of the city this wonderful news. Their unselfish actions brought blessings on others.

But these lepers are not healed. They do not serve God in order to get well. They remain lepers. And even though they are diseased, they become agents of healing in the life of Israel. The most beautiful people are not necessarily those who serve God after they are healed, but those who serve God from the center of their afflictions. These are the glorious lepers of grace.

To begin a study on the topic of Kindness, Anger Washed by Grace, turn to the home page on page 751.

Goodness

Lepers of Conscience

2 Kings 7:9

"Abashed the Devil stood, / And felt how awful goodness is," said John Milton. Having been excluded from the world, these noble lepers did not keep grace for themselves.

everything all right? Why did this madman[v] come to you?"

"You know the man and the sort of things he says," Jehu replied.

[12]"That's not true!" they said. "Tell us."

Jehu said, "Here is what he told me: 'This is what the LORD says: I anoint you king over Israel.'"

[13]They hurried and took their cloaks and spread[w] them under him on the bare steps. Then they blew the trumpet[x] and shouted, "Jehu is king!"

Jehu Kills Joram and Ahaziah

[14]So Jehu son of Jehoshaphat, the son of Nimshi, conspired against Joram. (Now Joram and all Israel had been defending Ramoth Gilead[y] against Hazael king of Aram, [15]but King Joram[a] had returned to Jezreel to recover[z] from the wounds the Arameans had inflicted on him in the battle with Hazael king of Aram.) Jehu said, "If this is the way you feel, don't let anyone slip out of the city to go and tell the news in Jezreel." [16]Then he got into his chariot and rode to Jezreel, because Joram was resting there and Ahaziah[a] king of Judah had gone down to see him.

[17]When the lookout[b] standing on the tower in Jezreel saw Jehu's troops approaching, he called out, "I see some troops coming."

"Get a horseman," Joram ordered. "Send him to meet them and ask, 'Do you come in peace?[c]'"

[18]The horseman rode off to meet Jehu and said, "This is what the king says: 'Do you come in peace?'"

"What do you have to do with peace?" Jehu replied. "Fall in behind me."

The lookout reported, "The messenger has reached them, but he isn't coming back."

[19]So the king sent out a second horseman. When he came to them he said, "This is what the king says: 'Do you come in peace?'"

Jehu replied, "What do you have to do with peace? Fall in behind me."

[20]The lookout reported, "He has reached them, but he isn't coming back either. The driving is like[d] that of Jehu son of Nimshi—he drives like a madman."

[21]"Hitch up my chariot," Joram ordered. And when it was hitched up, Joram king of Israel and Ahaziah king of Judah rode out, each in his own chariot, to meet Jehu. They met him at the plot of ground that had belonged to Naboth[e] the Jezreelite. [22]When Joram saw Jehu he asked, "Have you come in peace, Jehu?"

"How can there be peace," Jehu replied, "as long as all the idolatry and witchcraft of your mother Jezebel[f] abound?"

[23]Joram turned about and fled, calling out to Ahaziah, "Treachery,[g] Ahaziah!"

[24]Then Jehu drew his bow[h] and shot Joram between the shoulders. The arrow pierced his heart and he slumped down in his chariot. [25]Jehu said to Bidkar, his chariot officer, "Pick him up and throw him on the field that belonged to Naboth the Jezreelite. Remember how you and I were riding together in chariots behind Ahab his father when the LORD made this prophecy[i] about him: [26]'Yesterday I saw the blood of Naboth[j] and the blood of his sons, declares the LORD, and I will surely make you pay for it on this plot of ground, declares the LORD.'[b] Now then, pick him up and throw him on that plot, in accordance with the word of the LORD."[k]

[27]When Ahaziah king of Judah saw what had happened, he fled up the road to Beth Haggan.[c] Jehu chased him, shouting, "Kill him too!" They wounded him in his chariot on the way up to Gur near Ibleam,[l] but he escaped to Megiddo[m] and died there. [28]His servants took him by chariot[n] to Jerusalem and buried him with his fathers in his tomb in the City of David. [29](In the eleventh[o] year of Joram son of Ahab, Ahaziah had become king of Judah.)

Jezebel Killed

[30]Then Jehu went to Jezreel. When Jezebel heard about it, she painted[p] her eyes, arranged her hair and looked out of a window. [31]As Jehu entered the gate, she asked, "Have you come in peace, Zimri,[q] you murderer of your master?"[d]

[a]*15* Hebrew *Jehoram,* a variant of *Joram;* also in verses 17 and 21-24 [b]*26* See 1 Kings 21:19. [c]*27* Or *fled by way of the garden house* [d]*31* Or *"Did Zimri have peace, who murdered his master?"*

9:11 [v]Jer 29:26; Jn 10:20; Ac 26:24
9:13 [w]Mt 21:8; Lk 19:36 [x]2Sa 15:10; 1Ki 1:34,39
9:14 [y]Dt 4:43; 2Ki 8:28
9:15 [z]2Ki 8:29
9:16 [a]2Ch 22:7
9:17 [b]Isa 21:6 [c]1Sa 16:4
9:20 [d]2Sa 18:27; 1Sa 16:4
9:21 [e]ver 26; 1Ki 21:1-7, 15-19
9:22 [f]1Ki 16:30-33; 18:19; 2Ch 21:13; Rev 2:20
9:23 [g]2Ki 11:14
9:24 [h]1Ki 22:34
9:25 [i]1Ki 21:19-22,24-29
9:26 [j]1Ki 21:19 [k]1Ki 21:29
9:27 [l]Jdg 1:27 [m]2Ki 23:29
9:28 [n]2Ki 14:20; 23:30
9:29 [o]2Ki 8:25
9:30 [p]Jer 4:30; Eze 23:40
9:31 [q]1Ki 16:9-10

32 He looked up at the window and called out, "Who is on my side? Who?" Two or three eunuchs looked down at him. 33 "Throw her down!" Jehu said. So they threw her down, and some of her blood spattered the wall and the horses as they trampled her underfoot.[r]

34 Jehu went in and ate and drank. "Take care of that cursed woman," he said, "and bury her, for she was a king's daughter."[s] 35 But when they went out to bury her, they found nothing except her skull, her feet and her hands. 36 They went back and told Jehu, who said, "This is the word of the LORD that he spoke through his servant Elijah the Tishbite: On the plot of ground at Jezreel dogs[t] will devour Jezebel's flesh.[a][u] 37 Jezebel's body will be like refuse[v] on the ground in the plot at Jezreel, so that no one will be able to say, 'This is Jezebel.' "

9:33 [r]Ps 7:5
9:34 [s]1Ki 16:31; 21:25
9:36 [t]Ps 68:23; Jer 15:3 [u]1Ki 21:23
9:37 [v]Ps 83:10; Isa 5:25; Jer 8:2; 9:22; 16:4; 25:33; Zep 1:17

Ahab's Family Killed

10 Now there were in Samaria[w] seventy sons[x] of the house of Ahab. So Jehu wrote letters and sent them to Samaria: to the officials of Jezreel,[b][y] to the elders and to the guardians[z] of Ahab's children. He said, 2 "As soon as this letter reaches you, since your master's sons are with you and you have chariots and horses, a fortified city and weapons, 3 choose the best and most worthy of your master's sons and set him on his father's throne. Then fight for your master's house."

4 But they were terrified and said, "If two kings could not resist him, how can we?"

5 So the palace administrator, the city governor, the elders and the guardians sent this message to Jehu: "We are your servants[a] and we will do anything you say. We will not appoint anyone as king; you do whatever you think best."

6 Then Jehu wrote them a second letter, saying, "If you are on my side and will obey me, take the heads of your master's sons and come to me in Jezreel by this time tomorrow."

Now the royal princes, seventy of them, were with the leading men of the city, who were rearing them. 7 When the letter arrived, these men took the princes and slaughtered all seventy[b] of them. They put their heads[c] in baskets and sent them to Jehu in Jezreel. 8 When the messenger arrived, he told Jehu, "They have brought the heads of the princes."

Then Jehu ordered, "Put them in two piles at the entrance of the city gate until morning."

9 The next morning Jehu went out. He stood before all the people and said, "You are innocent. It was I who conspired against my master and killed him, but who killed all these? 10 Know then, that not a word the LORD has spoken against the house of Ahab will fail. The LORD has done what he promised[d] through his servant Elijah."[e] 11 So Jehu[f] killed everyone in Jezreel who remained of the house of Ahab, as well as all his chief men, his close friends and his priests, leaving him no survivor.[g]

12 Jehu then set out and went toward Samaria. At Beth Eked of the Shepherds, 13 he met some relatives of Ahaziah king of Judah and asked, "Who are you?"

They said, "We are relatives of Ahaziah,[h] and we have come down to greet the families of the king and of the queen mother.[i]"

14 "Take them alive!" he ordered. So they took them alive and slaughtered them by the well of Beth Eked—forty-two men. He left no survivor.

15 After he left there, he came upon Jehonadab[j] son of Recab,[k] who was on his way to meet him. Jehu greeted him and said, "Are you in accord with me, as I am with you?"

"I am," Jehonadab answered.

"If so," said Jehu, "give me your hand."[l] So he did, and Jehu helped him up into the chariot. 16 Jehu said, "Come with me and see my zeal[m] for the LORD." Then he had him ride along in his chariot.

17 When Jehu came to Samaria, he killed all who were left there of Ahab's family;[n] he destroyed them, according to the word of the LORD spoken to Elijah.

Ministers of Baal Killed

18 Then Jehu brought all the people together and said to them, "Ahab served Baal a little; Jehu will serve[o] him much.

10:1 [w]1Ki 13:32 [x]Jdg 8:30 [y]1Ki 21:1 [z]ver 5
10:5 [a]Jos 9:8; 1Ki 20:4,32
10:7 [b]1Ki 21:21 [c]2Sa 4:8
10:10 [d]2Ki 9:7-10 [e]1Ki 21:29
10:11 [f]Hos 1:4 [g]ver 14; Job 18:19
10:13 [h]2Ki 8:24,29; 2Ch 22:8 [i]1Ki 2:19
10:15 [j]Jer 35:6, 14-19 [k]1Ch 2:55; Jer 35:2 [l]Ezr 10:19; Eze 17:18
10:16 [m]Nu 25:13; 1Ki 19:10
10:17 [n]2Ki 9:8
10:18 [o]Jdg 2:11; 1Ki 16:31-32

[a] *36* See 1 Kings 21:23. [b] *1* Hebrew; some Septuagint manuscripts and Vulgate *of the city*

19Now summon[p] all the prophets of
Baal, all his ministers and all his priests.
See that no one is missing, because I
am going to hold a great sacrifice for
Baal. Anyone who fails to come will no
longer live." But Jehu was acting decep-
tively in order to destroy the ministers
of Baal.
20Jehu said, "Call an assembly[q] in
honor of Baal." So they proclaimed it.
21Then he sent word throughout Israel,
and all the ministers of Baal came; not
one stayed away. They crowded into the
temple of Baal until it was full from
one end to the other. 22And Jehu said
to the keeper of the wardrobe, "Bring
robes for all the ministers of Baal." So
he brought out robes for them.
23Then Jehu and Jehonadab son of
Recab went into the temple of Baal.
Jehu said to the ministers of Baal, "Look
around and see that no servants of the
LORD are here with you—only ministers of Baal." 24So they went in to make
sacrifices and burnt offerings. Now Jehu
had posted eighty men outside with this
warning: "If one of you lets any of the
men I am placing in your hands escape,
it will be your life for his life."[r]
25As soon as Jehu had finished making the burnt offering, he ordered the
guards and officers: "Go in and kill[s]
them; let no one escape."[t] So they cut
them down with the sword. The guards
and officers threw the bodies out and
then entered the inner shrine of the
temple of Baal. 26They brought the sacred stone[u] out of the temple of Baal
and burned it. 27They demolished the
sacred stone of Baal and tore down the
temple[v] of Baal, and people have used
it for a latrine to this day.
28So Jehu[w] destroyed Baal worship in
Israel. 29However, he did not turn away
from the sins[x] of Jeroboam son of Nebat, which he had caused Israel to commit—the worship of the golden calves[y]
at Bethel[z] and Dan.
30The LORD said to Jehu, "Because
you have done well in accomplishing
what is right in my eyes and have done
to the house of Ahab all I had in
mind to do, your descendants will sit
on the throne of Israel to the fourth
generation."[a] 31Yet Jehu was not careful[b] to keep the law of the LORD, the
God of Israel, with all his heart. He did
not turn away from the sins[c] of Jeroboam, which he had caused Israel to commit.
32In those days the LORD began to
reduce[d] the size of Israel. Hazael[e] overpowered the Israelites throughout their
territory 33east of the Jordan in all the
land of Gilead (the region of Gad, Reuben and Manasseh), from Aroer[f] by the
Arnon Gorge through Gilead to Bashan.
34As for the other events of Jehu's
reign, all he did, and all his achievements, are they not written in the book
of the annals[g] of the kings of Israel?
35Jehu rested with his fathers and was
buried in Samaria. And Jehoahaz his
son succeeded him as king. 36The time
that Jehu reigned over Israel in Samaria
was twenty-eight years.

Athaliah and Joash

11 When Athaliah[h] the mother of
Ahaziah saw that her son was
dead, she proceeded to destroy the
whole royal family. 2But Jehosheba, the
daughter of King Jehoram[a] and sister
of Ahaziah, took Joash[i] son of Ahaziah
and stole him away from among the
royal princes, who were about to be
murdered. She put him and his nurse
in a bedroom to hide him from Athaliah; so he was not killed.[j] 3He remained
hidden with his nurse at the temple of
the LORD for six years while Athaliah
ruled the land.
4In the seventh year Jehoiada sent
for the commanders of units of a hundred, the Carites[k] and the guards and
had them brought to him at the temple
of the LORD. He made a covenant with
them and put them under oath at the
temple of the LORD. Then he showed
them the king's son. 5He commanded
them, saying, "This is what you are to
do: You who are in the three companies that are going on duty on the Sabbath[l]—a third of you guarding the royal
palace,[m] 6a third at the Sur Gate, and
a third at the gate behind the guard,
who take turns guarding the temple—
7and you who are in the other two
companies that normally go off Sabbath duty are all to guard the temple
for the king. 8Station yourselves around
the king, each man with his weapon in
his hand. Anyone who approaches your

[a]2 Hebrew *Joram,* a variant of *Jehoram*

10:19 [p]1Ki 18:19; 22:6
10:20 [q]Ex 32:5; Joel 1:14
10:24 [r]1Ki 20:39
10:25 [s]Ex 22:20; 2Ki 11:18 [t]1Ki 18:40
10:26 [u]1Ki 14:23
10:27 [v]1Ki 16:32
10:28 [w]1Ki 19:17
10:29 [x]1Ki 12:30 [y]1Ki 12:28-29 [z]1Ki 12:32
10:30 [a]ver 35; 2Ki 15:12
10:31 [b]Pr 4:23 [c]1Ki 12:30
10:32 [d]2Ki 13:25 [e]1Ki 19:17; 2Ki 8:12
10:33 [f]Nu 32:34; Dt 2:36; Jdg 11:26; Isa 17:2
10:34 [g]1Ki 15:31
11:1 [h]2Ki 8:18
11:2 [i]ver 21; 2Ki 12:1 [j]Jdg 9:5
11:4 [k]ver 19
11:5 [l]1Ch 9:25 [m]1Ki 14:27

ranks[a] must be put to death. Stay close
to the king wherever he goes."
9 The commanders of units of a hundred did just as Jehoiada the priest ordered. Each one took his men—those
who were going on duty on the Sabbath and those who were going off
duty—and came to Jehoiada the priest.
10 Then he gave the commanders the
11:10 [n]2Sa 8:7; 1Ch 18:7 spears and shields[n] that had belonged to
King David and that were in the tem-
ple of the LORD. 11 The guards, each
with his weapon in his hand, stationed
themselves around the king—near the
altar and the temple, from the south
side to the north side of the temple.
12 Jehoiada brought out the king's son
and put the crown on him; he presented him with a copy of the cov-
11:12 [o]Ex 25:16; 2Ki 23:3 [p]1Sa 9:16; 1Ki 1:39 [q]Ps 47:1; 98:8; Isa 55:12 [r]1Sa 10:24 enant[o] and proclaimed him king. They
anointed[p] him, and the people clapped
their hands[q] and shouted, "Long live
the king!"[r]
13 When Athaliah heard the noise
made by the guards and the people, she
went to the people at the temple of the
11:14 [s]1Ki 7:15; 2Ki 23:3; 2Ch 34:31 [t]1Ki 1:39 [u]Ge 37:29 [v]2Ki 9:23 LORD. 14 She looked and there was the
king, standing by the pillar,[s] as the cus-
tom was. The officers and the trumpeters were beside the king, and all the
people of the land were rejoicing and
blowing trumpets.[t] Then Athaliah tore[u]
her robes and called out, "Treason! Treason!"[v]
15 Jehoiada the priest ordered the commanders of units of a hundred, who
were in charge of the troops: "Bring her
out between the ranks[b] and put to the
sword anyone who follows her." For the
priest had said, "She must not be put
11:15 [w]1Ki 2:30 to death in the temple[w] of the LORD."
11:16 [x]Ne 3:28; Jer 31:40 [y]Ge 4:14 16 So they seized her as she reached the
place where the horses enter[x] the pal-
ace grounds, and there she was put to
death.[y]
11:17 [z]Ex 24:8; 2Sa 5:3; 2Ch 15:12; 23:3; 29:10; 34:31; Ezr 10:3 [a]2Ki 23:3; Jer 34:8 17 Jehoiada then made a covenant[z]
between the LORD and the king and
people that they would be the LORD's
people. He also made a covenant between the king and the people.[a] 18 All
the people of the land went to the tem-
11:18 [b]1Ki 16:32 [c]Dt 12:3 [d]1Ki 18:40; 2Ki 10:25; 23:20 ple[b] of Baal and tore it down. They
smashed[c] the altars and idols to pieces
and killed Mattan the priest[d] of Baal in
front of the altars.
Then Jehoiada the priest posted
guards at the temple of the LORD.
19 He took with him the commanders
of hundreds, the Carites,[e] the guards 11:19 [e]ver 4
and all the people of the land, and
together they brought the king down
from the temple of the LORD and went
into the palace, entering by way of the
gate of the guards. The king then took
his place on the royal throne, 20 and all
the people of the land rejoiced.[f] And 11:20 [f]Pr 11:10; 28:12; 29:2
the city was quiet, because Athaliah
had been slain with the sword at the
palace.
21 Joash[c] was seven years old when he
began to reign.

Joash Repairs the Temple

12 In the seventh year of Jehu,
Joash[d][g] became king, and he 12:1 [g]2Ki 11:2
reigned in Jerusalem forty years. His
mother's name was Zibiah; she was
from Beersheba. 2 Joash did what was
right in the eyes of the LORD all the
years Jehoiada the priest instructed him.
3 The high places,[h] however, were not 12:3 [h]1Ki 3:3; 2Ki 14:4; 15:35; 18:4
removed; the people continued to offer
sacrifices and burn incense there.
4 Joash said to the priests, "Collect[i] all 12:4 [i]2Ki 22:4 [j]Ex 35:5 [k]Ex 30:12 [l]Ex 35:29; 1Ch 29:3-9
the money that is brought as sacred of-
ferings[j] to the temple of the LORD—
the money collected in the census,[k] the
money received from personal vows and
the money brought voluntarily[l] to the
temple. 5 Let every priest receive the
money from one of the treasurers, and
let it be used to repair whatever damage
is found in the temple."
6 But by the twenty-third year of King
Joash the priests still had not repaired
the temple. 7 Therefore King Joash summoned Jehoiada the priest and the other priests and asked them, "Why aren't
you repairing the damage done to the
temple? Take no more money from your
treasurers, but hand it over for repairing
the temple." 8 The priests agreed that
they would not collect any more money
from the people and that they would
not repair the temple themselves.
9 Jehoiada the priest took a chest and
bored a hole in its lid. He placed it beside the altar, on the right side as one
enters the temple of the LORD. The 12:9 [m]Jer 35:4
priests who guarded the entrance[m] put

[a]8 Or *approaches the precincts* [b]15 Or *out from the precincts* [c]21 Hebrew *Jehoash,* a variant of *Joash* [d]1 Hebrew *Jehoash,* a variant of *Joash;* also in verses 2, 4, 6, 7 and 18

12:9 [n]2Ch 24:8; into the chest all the money[n] that was
Mk 12:41; brought to the temple of the LORD.
Lk 21:1 10Whenever they saw that there was a
large amount of money in the chest,
12:10 the royal secretary[o] and the high priest
[o]2Sa 8:17 came, counted the money that had
been brought into the temple of the
LORD and put it into bags. 11When
the amount had been determined, they
gave the money to the men appointed
to supervise the work on the temple.
With it they paid those who worked
on the temple of the LORD—the carpenters and builders, 12the masons and
12:12 stonecutters.[p] They purchased timber
[p]2Ki 22:5-6 and dressed stone for the repair of
the temple of the LORD, and met
all the other expenses of restoring the
temple.
13The money brought into the temple was not spent for making silver ba-
12:13 sins, wick trimmers, sprinkling bowls,
[q]1Ki 7:48-51; trumpets or any other articles of gold[q]
2Ch 24:14 or silver for the temple of the LORD;
14it was paid to the workmen, who used
it to repair the temple. 15They did not
require an accounting from those to
whom they gave the money to pay the
workers, because they acted with com-
12:15 [r]2Ki 22:7; plete honesty.[r] 16The money from the
1Co 4:2 guilt offerings[s] and sin offerings[t] was
12:16 not brought into the temple of the
[s]Lev 5:14-19; Nu 18:9 LORD; it belonged[u] to the priests.
[t]Lev 4:1-35 17About this time Hazael[v] king of
[u]Lev 7:7 Aram went up and attacked Gath and
12:17 captured it. Then he turned to attack
[v]2Ki 8:12 Jerusalem. 18But Joash king of Judah
took all the sacred objects dedicated by
his fathers—Jehoshaphat, Jehoram and
Ahaziah, the kings of Judah—and the
gifts he himself had dedicated and all
the gold found in the treasuries of the
temple of the LORD and of the royal
12:18 [w]1Ki 15:18; palace, and he sent[w] them to Hazael
2Ch 21:16-17 king of Aram, who then withdrew[x] from
[x]1Ki 15:21 Jerusalem.
19As for the other events of the reign
of Joash, and all he did, are they not
written in the book of the annals of
12:20 the kings of Judah? 20His officials[y] con-
[y]2Ki 14:5 [z]2Ch 24:25 spired against him and assassinated[z] him
[a]Jdg 9:6 at Beth Millo,[a] on the road down to
Silla. 21The officials who murdered him
were Jozabad son of Shimeath and Jehozabad son of Shomer. He died and
was buried with his fathers in the City
of David. And Amaziah his son succeeded him as king.

Jehoahaz King of Israel

13 In the twenty-third year of Joash son of Ahaziah king of Judah, Jehoahaz son of Jehu became king
of Israel in Samaria, and he reigned sev-
enteen years. 2He did evil[b] in the eyes 13:2 [b]1Ki 12:26-33
of the LORD by following the sins of
Jeroboam son of Nebat, which he had
caused Israel to commit, and he did not
turn away from them. 3So the LORD's
anger[c] burned against Israel, and for 13:3 [c]Dt 31:17;
a long time he kept them under the Jdg 2:14
power[d] of Hazael king of Aram and [d]1Ki 8:12; 12:17; 19:17
Ben-Hadad[e] his son. [e]ver 24
4Then Jehoahaz sought[f] the LORD's 13:4 [f]Dt 4:29;
favor, and the LORD listened to him, for Ps 78:34
he saw[g] how severely the king of Aram [g]Ex 3:7; Dt 26:7
was oppressing[h] Israel. 5The LORD pro- [h]2Ki 14:26
vided a deliverer[i] for Israel, and they escaped from the power of Aram. So the 13:5 [i]ver 25;
Israelites lived in their own homes as 2Ki 14:25,27
they had before. 6But they did not turn
away from the sins[j] of the house of Jer- 13:6 [j]1Ki 12:30
oboam, which he had caused Israel to [k]1Ki 16:33
commit; they continued in them. Also,
the Asherah pole[a] [k] remained standing
in Samaria.
7Nothing had been left[l] of the army 13:7 [l]2Ki 10:32-33
of Jehoahaz except fifty horsemen, ten [m]2Sa 22:43
chariots and ten thousand foot soldiers,
for the king of Aram had destroyed the
rest and made them like the dust[m] at
threshing time.
8As for the other events of the reign
of Jehoahaz, all he did and his achievements, are they not written in the book
of the annals of the kings of Israel? 9Je-
hoahaz rested with his fathers and was
buried in Samaria. And Jehoash[b] his
son succeeded him as king.

Jehoash King of Israel

10In the thirty-seventh year of Joash
king of Judah, Jehoash son of Jehoahaz
became king of Israel in Samaria, and
he reigned sixteen years. 11He did evil
in the eyes of the LORD and did not
turn away from any of the sins of Jeroboam son of Nebat, which he had
caused Israel to commit; he continued
in them.
12As for the other events of the
reign of Jehoash, all he did and his
achievements, including his war against

[a]6 That is, a symbol of the goddess Asherah; here and elsewhere in 2 Kings [b]9 Hebrew *Joash,* a variant of *Jehoash*; also in verses 12-14 and 25

13:12 ⁿ2Ki 14:15 Amaziah[n] king of Judah, are they not
ᵒ1Ki 15:31 written in the book of the annals[o] of
the kings of Israel? 13Jehoash rested
13:13 with his fathers, and Jeroboam[p] suc-
ᵖ2Ki 14:23; Hos 1:1 ceeded him on the throne. Jehoash was
buried in Samaria with the kings of
Israel.
14Now Elisha was suffering from the
illness from which he died. Jehoash king
of Israel went down to see him and
wept over him. "My father! My father!"
13:14 he cried. "The chariots[q] and horsemen
ᑫ2Ki 2:12 of Israel!"
15Elisha said, "Get a bow and some
13:15 arrows,"[r] and he did so. 16"Take the
ʳ1Sa 20:20 bow in your hands," he said to the king
of Israel. When he had taken it, Elisha
put his hands on the king's hands.
17"Open the east window," he said,
13:17 and he opened it. "Shoot!"[s] Elisha said,
ˢJos 8:18 and he shot. "The LORD's arrow of vic-
ᵗ1Ki 20:26 tory, the arrow of victory over Aram!"
Elisha declared. "You will completely
destroy the Arameans at Aphek."[t]
18Then he said, "Take the arrows,"
and the king took them. Elisha told
him, "Strike the ground." He struck it
three times and stopped. 19The man of
God was angry with him and said, "You
should have struck the ground five or
six times; then you would have defeated Aram and completely destroyed it.
But now you will defeat it only three
13:19 ᵘver 25 times."[u]
20Elisha died and was buried.
13:20 ᵛ2Ki 3:7; 24:2 Now Moabite raiders[v] used to enter
the country every spring. 21Once while
some Israelites were burying a man,
suddenly they saw a band of raiders; so
they threw the man's body into Elisha's
tomb. When the body touched Elisha's
13:21 ʷMt 27:52 bones, the man came to life[w] and stood
up on his feet.
13:22 ˣ1Ki 19:17; 2Ki 8:12 22Hazael king of Aram oppressed[x] Israel throughout the reign of Jehoahaz.
23But the LORD was gracious to them
and had compassion and showed con-
13:23 ʸGe 13:16-17; cern for them because of his covenant[y]
Ex 2:24 with Abraham, Isaac and Jacob. To this
ᶻDt 29:20 day he has been unwilling to destroy[z]
ᵃEx 33:15; 2Ki 14:27; 17:18; 24:3,20 them or banish them from his presence.[a]
24Hazael king of Aram died, and Ben-
13:24 ᵇver 3 Hadad[b] his son succeeded him as king.
25Then Jehoash son of Jehoahaz recap-
tured from Ben-Hadad son of Hazael
the towns he had taken in battle from
13:25 ᶜver 18,19 his father Jehoahaz. Three times[c] Jehoash defeated him, and so he recovered[d]
the Israelite towns. 13:25 ᵈ2Ki 10:32

Amaziah King of Judah

14 In the second year of Jehoash[a]
son of Jehoahaz king of Israel,
Amaziah son of Joash king of Judah
began to reign. 2He was twenty-five
years old when he became king, and he
reigned in Jerusalem twenty-nine years.
His mother's name was Jehoaddin; she
was from Jerusalem. 3He did what was
right in the eyes of the LORD, but not
as his father David had done. In everything he followed the example of his father Joash. 4The high places,[e] however, 14:4
were not removed; the people contin- ᵉ2Ki 12:3; 16:4
ued to offer sacrifices and burn incense
there.
5After the kingdom was firmly in his
grasp, he executed[f] the officials[g] who 14:5
had murdered his father the king. 6Yet ᶠ2Ki 21:24 ᵍ2Ki 12:20
he did not put the sons of the assassins
to death, in accordance with what is
written in the Book of the Law[h] of Mo- 14:6
ses where the LORD commanded: "Fa- ʰDt 28:61 ⁱNu 26:11;
thers shall not be put to death for their Job 21:20;
children, nor children put to death for Jer 31:30; 44:3;
their fathers; each is to die for his own Eze 18:4,20
sins."[b][i]
7He was the one who defeated ten
thousand Edomites in the Valley of Salt[j] 14:7
and captured Sela[k] in battle, calling it ʲ2Sa 8:13; 2Ch 25:11
Joktheel, the name it has to this day. ᵏJdg 1:36
8Then Amaziah sent messengers to
Jehoash son of Jehoahaz, the son of
Jehu, king of Israel, with the challenge:
"Come, meet me face to face."
9But Jehoash king of Israel replied to
Amaziah king of Judah: "A thistle[l] in 14:9
Lebanon sent a message to a cedar in ˡJdg 9:8-15
Lebanon, 'Give your daughter to my
son in marriage.' Then a wild beast
in Lebanon came along and trampled
the thistle underfoot. 10You have indeed defeated Edom and now you are
arrogant.[m] Glory in your victory, but 14:10
stay at home! Why ask for trouble and ᵐDt 8:14; 2Ch 26:16;
cause your own downfall and that of 32:25
Judah also?"
11Amaziah, however, would not listen, so Jehoash king of Israel attacked.
He and Amaziah king of Judah faced
each other at Beth Shemesh[n] in Judah. 14:11
12Judah was routed by Israel, and every ⁿJos 15:10

[a] *1* Hebrew *Joash,* a variant of *Jehoash;* also in verses 13, 23 and 27 [b] *6* Deut. 24:16

14:12 [o]2Sa 18:17 man fled to his home.[o] 13Jehoash king
of Israel captured Amaziah king of Ju-
dah, the son of Joash, the son of Ahaziah, at Beth Shemesh. Then Jehoash
went to Jerusalem and broke down the
14:13 [p]1Ki 3:1; 2Ch 33:14; 36:19; Jer 39:2 [q]Ne 8:16; 12:39 [r]2Ch 25:23; Jer 31:38; Zec 14:10 wall[p] of Jerusalem from the Ephraim
Gate[q] to the Corner Gate[r]—a section
about six hundred feet long.[a] 14He took
all the gold and silver and all the articles
found in the temple of the LORD and
in the treasuries of the royal palace. He
also took hostages and returned to Samaria.

15As for the other events of the reign
of Jehoash, what he did and his achieve-
14:15 [s]2Ki 13:12 ments, including his war[s] against Amaziah king of Judah, are they not written
in the book of the annals of the kings
of Israel? 16Jehoash rested with his fathers and was buried in Samaria with
the kings of Israel. And Jeroboam his
son succeeded him as king.

17Amaziah son of Joash king of Judah
lived for fifteen years after the death of
Jehoash son of Jehoahaz king of Israel.
18As for the other events of Amaziah's
reign, are they not written in the book
of the annals of the kings of Judah?
14:19 [t]2Ki 12:20 [u]Jos 10:3; 2Ki 18:14,17 19They conspired[t] against him in Jerusalem, and he fled to Lachish,[u] but
they sent men after him to Lachish and
killed him there. 20He was brought back
14:20 [v]2Ki 9:28 by horse[v] and was buried in Jerusalem
with his fathers, in the City of David.

21Then all the people of Judah took
14:21 [w]2Ki 15:1; 2Ch 26:23 Azariah,[b][w] who was sixteen years old,
and made him king in place of his fa-
ther Amaziah. 22He was the one who
14:22 [x]1Ki 9:26; 2Ki 16:6 rebuilt Elath[x] and restored it to Judah
after Amaziah rested with his fathers.

Jeroboam II King of Israel

23In the fifteenth year of Amaziah
14:23 [y]2Ki 13:13 son of Joash king of Judah, Jeroboam[y]
son of Jehoash king of Israel became
king in Samaria, and he reigned forty-
one years. 24He did evil in the eyes
of the LORD and did not turn away
from any of the sins of Jeroboam son
of Nebat, which he had caused Israel to
14:24 [z]1Ki 15:30 commit.[z] 25He was the one who restored
the boundaries of Israel from Lebo[c] Ha-
14:25 [a]Nu 13:21; 1Ki 8:65 [b]Dt 3:17 [c]Jnh 1:1; Mt 12:39 math[a] to the Sea of the Arabah,[d][b] in accordance with the word of the LORD,
the God of Israel, spoken through his
servant Jonah[c] son of Amittai, the
prophet from Gath Hepher.

26The LORD had seen how bitterly
everyone in Israel, whether slave or
free,[d] was suffering;[e] there was no one 14:26 [d]Dt 32:36 [e]2Ki 13:4 [f]Ps 18:41; 22:11; 72:12; 107:12; Isa 63:5; La 1:7
to help them.[f] 27And since the LORD
had not said he would blot out[g] the
name of Israel from under heaven, he
saved[h] them by the hand of Jeroboam
son of Jehoash. 14:27 [g]2Ki 13:23 [h]Jdg 6:14

28As for the other events of Jeroboam's reign, all he did, and his military
achievements, including how he recov-
ered for Israel both Damascus[i] and Ha- 14:28 [i]2Sa 8:5; 1Ki 11:24 [j]2Ch 8:3 [k]1Ki 15:31
math,[j] which had belonged to Yaudi,[e]
are they not written in the book of the
annals[k] of the kings of Israel? 29Jerobo-
am rested with his fathers, the kings of
Israel. And Zechariah his son succeeded
him as king.

Azariah King of Judah

15 In the twenty-seventh year of
Jeroboam king of Israel, Azari-
ah[l] son of Amaziah king of Judah be- 15:1 [l]ver 32; 2Ki 14:21
gan to reign. 2He was sixteen years old
when he became king, and he reigned
in Jerusalem fifty-two years. His mother's name was Jecoliah; she was from
Jerusalem. 3He did what was right in
the eyes of the LORD, just as his father
Amaziah had done. 4The high places,
however, were not removed; the people
continued to offer sacrifices and burn
incense there.

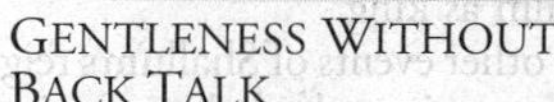

GENTLENESS

GENTLENESS WITHOUT BACK TALK

2 Kings 15:3

Azariah was gentle. Gentleness is ever appealing to God. "What God desires," said Francois Fenelon, "is pure intention, true identity and sincere self-renunciation."

5The LORD afflicted[m] the king with
leprosy[f] until the day he died, and he 15:5 [m]Ge 12:17 [n]Lev 13:46 [o]2Ch 27:1 [p]Ge 41:40
lived in a separate house.[g][n] Jotham[o] the
king's son had charge of the palace[p] and
governed the people of the land.

6As for the other events of Azariah's
reign, and all he did, are they not written

[a] *13* Hebrew *four hundred cubits* (about 180 meters)
[b] *21* Also called *Uzziah* [c] *25* Or *from the entrance to* [d] *25* That is, the Dead Sea [e] *28* Or *Judah* [f] *5* The Hebrew word was used for various diseases affecting the skin—not necessarily leprosy.
[g] *5* Or *in a house where he was relieved of responsibility*

in the book of the annals of the kings of
15:7 qIsa 6:1; 14:28 Judah? 7Azariah rested[q] with his fathers
rver 5 and was buried near them in the City of
David. And Jotham[r] his son succeeded
him as king.

Zechariah King of Israel

8In the thirty-eighth year of Azariah
king of Judah, Zechariah son of Jeroboam became king of Israel in Samaria, and he reigned six months. 9He did
15:9 s1Ki 15:26 evil[s] in the eyes of the LORD, as his fathers had done. He did not turn away
from the sins of Jeroboam son of Nebat, which he had caused Israel to commit.

10Shallum son of Jabesh conspired
against Zechariah. He attacked him in
15:10 front of the people,[a] assassinated[t] him
t2Ki 12:20 and succeeded him as king. 11The other
events of Zechariah's reign are written
15:11 in the book of the annals[u] of the kings
u1Ki 15:31 of Israel. 12So the word of the LORD
15:12 spoken to Jehu was fulfilled:[v] "Your de-
v2Ki 10:30 scendants will sit on the throne of Israel
to the fourth generation."[b]

Shallum King of Israel

13Shallum son of Jabesh became king
in the thirty-ninth year of Uzziah king
15:13 of Judah, and he reigned in Samaria[w]
wver 1,8 one month. 14Then Menahem son of
15:14 Gadi went from Tirzah[x] up to Samar-
x1Ki 14:17 ia. He attacked Shallum son of Jabesh
y2Ki 12:20 in Samaria, assassinated[y] him and succeeded him as king.

15The other events of Shallum's reign,
and the conspiracy he led, are written
15:15 in the book of the annals[z] of the kings
z1Ki 15:31 of Israel.

16At that time Menahem, starting
15:16 a1Ki 4:24 out from Tirzah, attacked Tiphsah[a] and
b2Ki 8:12; everyone in the city and its vicinity, be-
Hos 13:16 cause they refused to open[b] their gates.
He sacked Tiphsah and ripped open all
the pregnant women.

Menahem King of Israel

17In the thirty-ninth year of Azariah
king of Judah, Menahem son of Gadi
became king of Israel, and he reigned
in Samaria ten years. 18He did evil in
the eyes of the LORD. During his entire reign he did not turn away from the
sins of Jeroboam son of Nebat, which
15:19 he had caused Israel to commit.
c1Ch 5:6,26 19Then Pul[c][c] king of Assyria invaded the land, and Menahem gave him a
thousand talents[d] of silver to gain his
support and strengthen his own hold
on the kingdom. 20Menahem exacted
this money from Israel. Every wealthy
man had to contribute fifty shekels[e] of
silver to be given to the king of Assyria.
So the king of Assyria withdrew[d] and 15:20
stayed in the land no longer. d2Ki 12:18

21As for the other events of Menahem's reign, and all he did, are they
not written in the book of the annals of
the kings of Israel? 22Menahem rested
with his fathers. And Pekahiah his son
succeeded him as king.

Pekahiah King of Israel

23In the fiftieth year of Azariah king
of Judah, Pekahiah son of Menahem
became king of Israel in Samaria, and
he reigned two years. 24Pekahiah did
evil in the eyes of the LORD. He did
not turn away from the sins of Jeroboam son of Nebat, which he had caused
Israel to commit. 25One of his chief
officers, Pekah[e] son of Remaliah, con- 15:25 e2Ch 28:6;
spired against him. Taking fifty men of Isa 7:1
Gilead with him, he assassinated[f] Pek- f2Ki 12:20
ahiah, along with Argob and Arieh, in
the citadel of the royal palace at Samaria. So Pekah killed Pekahiah and succeeded him as king.

26The other events of Pekahiah's reign,
and all he did, are written in the book
of the annals of the kings of Israel.

Pekah King of Israel

27In the fifty-second year of Azariah
king of Judah, Pekah[g] son of Remaliah[h] 15:27 g2Ch 28:6;
became king of Israel in Samaria, and Isa 7:1
he reigned twenty years. 28He did evil hIsa 7:4
in the eyes of the LORD. He did not
turn away from the sins of Jeroboam 15:29 i2Ki 16:7;
son of Nebat, which he had caused Is- 17:6; 1Ch 5:26;
rael to commit. 2Ch 28:20;

29In the time of Pekah king of Israel, Jer 50:17 j1Ki 15:20
Tiglath-Pileser[i] king of Assyria came k2Ki 16:9;
and took Ijon,[j] Abel Beth Maacah, 17:24; 2Ch 16:4;
Janoah, Kedesh and Hazor. He took Isa 9:1
Gilead and Galilee, including all the l2Ki 24:14-16; 1Ch 5:22;
land of Naphtali,[k] and deported[l] the Isa 14:6,17;
people to Assyria. 30Then Hoshea[m] son 36:17; 45:13
of Elah conspired against Pekah son of 15:30 m2Ki 17:1
Remaliah. He attacked and assassinated[n] n2Ki 12:20

[a] *10* Hebrew; some Septuagint manuscripts *in Ibleam*
[b] *12* 2 Kings 10:30 [c] *19* Also called *Tiglath-Pileser*
[d] *19* That is, about 37 tons (about 34 metric tons)
[e] *20* That is, about 1 1/4 pounds (about 0.6 kilogram)

him, and then succeeded him as king in the twentieth year of Jotham son of Uzziah.

31As for the other events of Pekah's reign, and all he did, are they not written in the book of the annals of the kings of Israel?

Jotham King of Judah

32In the second year of Pekah son of Remaliah king of Israel, Jotham[o] son of Uzziah king of Judah began to reign. 33He was twenty-five years old when he became king, and he reigned in Jerusalem sixteen years. His mother's name was Jerusha daughter of Zadok. 34He did what was right[p] in the eyes of the LORD, just as his father Uzziah had done. 35The high places,[q] however, were not removed; the people continued to offer sacrifices and burn incense there. Jotham rebuilt the Upper Gate[r] of the temple of the LORD.

36As for the other events of Jotham's reign, and what he did, are they not written in the book of the annals of the kings of Judah? 37(In those days the LORD began to send Rezin[s] king of Aram and Pekah son of Remaliah against Judah.) 38Jotham rested with his fathers and was buried with them in the City of David, the city of his father. And Ahaz his son succeeded him as king.

15:32 [o]1Ch 5:17
15:34 [p]ver 3; 1Ki 14:8; 2Ch 26:4-5
15:35 [q]2Ki 12:3 [r]2Ch 23:20
15:37 [s]2Ki 16:5; Isa 7:1

Ahaz King of Judah

16 In the seventeenth year of Pekah son of Remaliah, Ahaz[t] son of Jotham king of Judah began to reign. 2Ahaz was twenty years old when he became king, and he reigned in Jerusalem sixteen years. Unlike David his father, he did not do what was right[u] in the eyes of the LORD his God. 3He walked in the ways of the kings of Israel and even sacrificed his son[v] in[a] the fire, following the detestable[w] ways of the nations the LORD had driven out before the Israelites. 4He offered sacrifices and burned incense at the high places, on the hilltops and under every spreading tree.[x]

5Then Rezin[y] king of Aram and Pekah son of Remaliah king of Israel marched up to fight against Jerusalem and besieged Ahaz, but they could not overpower him. 6At that time, Rezin[z] king of Aram recovered Elath[a] for Aram by driving out the men of Judah. Edomites then moved into Elath and have lived there to this day.

16:1 [t]Isa 1:1; 14:28
16:2 [u]1Ki 14:8
16:3 [v]Lev 18:21; 2Ki 21:6 [w]Lev 18:3; Dt 9:4; 12:31
16:4 [x]Dt 12:2; Eze 6:13
16:5 [y]2Ki 15:37; Isa 7:1,4
16:6 [z]Isa 9:12 [a]2Ki 14:22; 2Ch 26:2

7Ahaz sent messengers to say to Tiglath-Pileser[b] king of Assyria, "I am your servant and vassal. Come up and save[c] me out of the hand of the king of Aram and of the king of Israel, who are attacking me." 8And Ahaz took the silver and gold found in the temple of the LORD and in the treasuries of the royal palace and sent it as a gift[d] to the king of Assyria. 9The king of Assyria complied by attacking Damascus[e] and capturing it. He deported its inhabitants to Kir[f] and put Rezin to death.

10Then King Ahaz went to Damascus to meet Tiglath-Pileser king of Assyria. He saw an altar in Damascus and sent to Uriah[g] the priest a sketch of the altar, with detailed plans for its construction. 11So Uriah the priest built an altar in accordance with all the plans that King Ahaz had sent from Damascus and finished it before King Ahaz returned. 12When the king came back from Damascus and saw the altar, he approached it and presented offerings[b][h] on it. 13He offered up his burnt offering[i] and grain offering, poured out his drink offering, and sprinkled the blood of his fellowship offerings[c][j] on the altar. 14The bronze altar[k] that stood before the LORD he brought from the front of the temple—from between the new altar and the temple of the LORD—and put it on the north side of the new altar.

15King Ahaz then gave these orders to Uriah the priest: "On the large new altar, offer the morning[l] burnt offering and the evening grain offering, the king's burnt offering and his grain offering, and the burnt offering of all the people of the land, and their grain offering and their drink offering. Sprinkle on the altar all the blood of the burnt offerings and sacrifices. But I will use the bronze altar for seeking guidance."[m] 16And Uriah the priest did just as King Ahaz had ordered.

17King Ahaz took away the side panels and removed the basins from the movable stands. He removed the Sea from the bronze bulls that supported

16:7 [b]2Ki 15:29 [c]Isa 2:6; Jer 2:18; Eze 16:28; Hos 10:6
16:8 [d]2Ki 12:18
16:9 [e]2Ki 15:29 [f]Isa 22:6; Am 1:5; 9:7
16:10 [g]Isa 8:2
16:12 [h]2Ch 26:16
16:13 [i]Lev 6:8-13 [j]Lev 7:11-21
16:14 [k]2Ch 4:1
16:15 [l]Ex 29:38-41 [m]1Sa 9:9

[a]3 Or *even made his son pass through* [b]12 Or *and went up* [c]13 Traditionally *peace offerings*

16:17 it and set it on a stone base.[n] [18]He
[n]1Ki 7:27 took away the Sabbath canopy[a] that
had been built at the temple and removed the royal entryway outside the
temple of the LORD, in deference to
16:18 the king of Assyria.[o]
[o]Eze 16:28 [19]As for the other events of the reign
of Ahaz, and what he did, are they not
written in the book of the annals of the
kings of Judah? [20]Ahaz rested with his
fathers and was buried with them in the
City of David. And Hezekiah his son
succeeded him as king.

Hoshea Last King of Israel

17 In the twelfth year of Ahaz king
of Judah, Hoshea[p] son of Elah
17:1 [p]2Ki 15:30 became king of Israel in Samaria, and
he reigned nine years. [2]He did evil in
the eyes of the LORD, but not like the
kings of Israel who preceded him.
17:3 [3]Shalmaneser[q] king of Assyria came
[q]2Ki 18:9-12; up to attack Hoshea, who had been
Hos 10:14 Shalmaneser's vassal and had paid him
tribute. [4]But the king of Assyria discovered that Hoshea was a traitor, for he
had sent envoys to So[b] king of Egypt,
and he no longer paid tribute to the
king of Assyria, as he had done year by
year. Therefore Shalmaneser seized him
and put him in prison. [5]The king of Assyria invaded the entire land, marched
17:5 against Samaria and laid siege[r] to it for
[r]Hos 13:16 three years. [6]In the ninth year of Hoshea, the king of Assyria captured Sa-
17:6 [s]Hos 13:16 maria[s] and deported[t] the Israelites to
[t]Dt 28:36,64; Assyria. He settled them in Halah, in
2Ki 18:10-11 [u]1Ch 5:26 Gozan[u] on the Habor River and in the
towns of the Medes.

Israel Exiled Because of Sin

[7]All this took place because the Is-
17:7 raelites had sinned[v] against the LORD
[v]Jos 23:16; their God, who had brought them up
Jdg 6:10 [w]Ex 14:15-31 out of Egypt[w] from under the power
of Pharaoh king of Egypt. They wor-
shiped other gods [8]and followed the
17:8 [x]Lev 18:3; practices of the nations[x] the LORD had
Dt 18:9; driven out before them, as well as the
2Ki 16:3 practices that the kings of Israel had
introduced. [9]The Israelites secretly did
things against the LORD their God that
were not right. From watchtower to for-
17:9 tified city[y] they built themselves high
[y]2Ki 18:8 places in all their towns. [10]They set
17:10 up sacred stones and Asherah poles[z] on
[z]Ex 34:13; Mic 5:14 every high hill and under every spread-
[a]1Ki 14:23 ing tree.[a] [11]At every high place they
burned incense, as the nations whom
the LORD had driven out before them
had done. They did wicked things that
provoked the LORD to anger. [12]They
worshiped idols,[b] though the LORD had 17:12
said, "You shall not do this."[c] [13]The [b]Ex 20:4
LORD warned Israel and Judah through
all his prophets and seers:[c] "Turn from 17:13
your evil ways.[d] Observe my commands [c]1Sa 9:9 [d]Jer 18:11;
and decrees, in accordance with the en- 25:5; 35:15
tire Law that I commanded your fa-
thers to obey and that I delivered to you
through my servants the prophets."
[14]But they would not listen and were
as stiff-necked[e] as their fathers, who 17:14
did not trust in the LORD their God. [e]Ex 32:9; Dt 31:27;
[15]They rejected his decrees and the Ac 7:51
covenant[f] he had made with their fa- 17:15
thers and the warnings he had given [f]Dt 29:25 [g]Dt 32:21;
them. They followed worthless idols[g] Ro 1:21-23 [h]Dt 12:30-31
and themselves became worthless. They
imitated the nations[h] around them although the LORD had ordered them,
"Do not do as they do," and they did
the things the LORD had forbidden
them to do.
[16]They forsook all the commands of
the LORD their God and made for
themselves two idols cast in the shape
of calves,[i] and an Asherah[j] pole. They 17:16
bowed down to all the starry hosts,[k] [i]1Ki 12:28 [j]1Ki 14:15,23
and they worshiped Baal.[l] [17]They sacri- [k]2Ki 21:3 [l]1Ki 16:31
ficed[m] their sons and daughters in[d] the
fire. They practiced divination and sor- 17:17 [m]Dt 18:10-
cery[n] and sold[o] themselves to do evil in 12; 2Ki 16:3
the eyes of the LORD, provoking him [n]Lev 19:26
to anger. [o]1Ki 21:20
[18]So the LORD was very angry with
Israel and removed them from his presence. Only the tribe of Judah was left,
[19]and even Judah did not keep the commands of the LORD their God. They
followed the practices Israel had introduced.[p] [20]Therefore the LORD reject- 17:19 [p]1Ki
ed all the people of Israel; he afflicted 14:22-23; 2Ki 16:3
them and gave them into the hands of
plunderers,[q] until he thrust them from 17:20 [q]2Ki 15:29
his presence.
[21]When he tore[r] Israel away from the 17:21
house of David, they made Jeroboam [r]1Ki 11:11 [s]1Ki 12:20
son of Nebat their king.[s] Jeroboam en-
ticed Israel away from following the
LORD and caused them to commit a

[a]*18* Or *the dais of his throne* (see Septuagint) [b]*4* Or *to Sais, to the*; *So* is possibly an abbreviation for *Osorkon.* [c]*12* Exodus 20:4, 5 [d]*17* Or *They made their sons and daughters pass through*

great sin. 22The Israelites persisted in all
the sins of Jeroboam and did not turn
away from them 23until the LORD removed them from his presence, as he
had warned through all his servants the
prophets. So the people of Israel were
taken from their homeland into exile in
Assyria, and they are still there.

Samaria Resettled

17:24 [t]Ezr 4:2,10 24The king of Assyria[t] brought people
[u]2Ki 18:34 from Babylon, Cuthah, Avva, Hamath
and Sepharvaim[u] and settled them in
the towns of Samaria to replace the Israelites. They took over Samaria and
lived in its towns. 25When they first
lived there, they did not worship the
17:25 [v]Ge 37:20 LORD; so he sent lions[v] among them
and they killed some of the people. 26It
was reported to the king of Assyria:
"The people you deported and resettled
in the towns of Samaria do not know
what the god of that country requires.
He has sent lions among them, which
are killing them off, because the people
do not know what he requires."
27Then the king of Assyria gave this
order: "Have one of the priests you took
captive from Samaria go back to live
there and teach the people what the god
of the land requires." 28So one of the
priests who had been exiled from Samaria came to live in Bethel and taught
them how to worship the LORD.
29Nevertheless, each national group
17:29 made its own gods in the several towns[w]
[w]Jer 2:28 where they settled, and set them up
[x]1Ki 12:31 [y]Mic 4:5 in the shrines[x] the people of Samaria
had made at the high places.[y] 30The
men from Babylon made Succoth Be-
noth, the men from Cuthah made Ner-
gal, and the men from Hamath made
Ashima; 31the Avvites made Nibhaz
and Tartak, and the Sepharvites burned
their children in the fire as sacrifices to
17:31 [z]2Ki 19:37 Adrammelech[z] and Anammelech, the
[a]ver 24 gods of Sepharvaim.[a] 32They worshiped
the LORD, but they also appointed all
17:32 [b]1Ki 12:31 sorts[b] of their own people to officiate
for them as priests in the shrines at
the high places. 33They worshiped the
LORD, but they also served their own
gods in accordance with the customs of
the nations from which they had been
brought.
34To this day they persist in their former practices. They neither worship the
LORD nor adhere to the decrees and ordinances, the laws and commands that
the LORD gave the descendants of Ja- 17:34
cob, whom he named Israel.[c] 35When [c]Ge 32:28;
the LORD made a covenant with the 35:10;
Israelites, he commanded them: "Do 1Ki 18:31
not worship[d] any other gods or bow 17:35 [d]Ex 20:5;
down to them, serve them or sacrifice Jdg 6:10
to them. 36But the LORD, who brought
you up out of Egypt with mighty power and outstretched arm,[e] is the one 17:36
you must worship. To him you shall [e]Ex 3:20; 6:6;
bow down and to him offer sacrifices. Ps 136:12
37You must always be careful[f] to keep 17:37 [f]Dt 5:32
the decrees and ordinances, the laws
and commands he wrote for you. Do
not worship other gods. 38Do not forget[g] the covenant I have made with 17:38
you, and do not worship other gods. [g]Dt 4:23; 6:12
39Rather, worship the LORD your God;
it is he who will deliver you from the
hand of all your enemies."
40They would not listen, however,
but persisted in their former practices.
41Even while these people were worshiping the LORD,[h] they were serving 17:41
their idols. To this day their children [h]ver 32-33;
and grandchildren continue to do as 1Ki 18:21;
their fathers did. Mt 6:24

Hezekiah King of Judah

18 In the third year of Hoshea son
of Elah king of Israel, Hezeki-
ah[i] son of Ahaz king of Judah began 18:1 [i]Isa 1:1;
to reign. 2He was twenty-five years old 2Ch 28:27
when he became king, and he reigned
in Jerusalem twenty-nine years.[j] His 18:2
mother's name was Abijah[a] daughter of [j]Isa 38:5
Zechariah. 3He did what was right in 18:3
the eyes of the LORD, just as his father [k]Isa 38:5
David[k] had done. 4He removed[l] the 18:4
high places, smashed the sacred stones[m] [l]2Ch 31:1
and cut down the Asherah poles. He [m]Ex 23:24

[a]2 Hebrew *Abi*, a variant of *Abijah*

▸ FAITHFULNESS

NEHUSHTAN: THE SIN OF WORSHIPING A SNAKE

2 Kings 18:4

Never worship brazen snakes. Worship the God who called you to "Look at it and live" (Numbers 21:8). If you want to be saved, crave God and not salvation. Those who long for Jesus own redemption, never having hungered for it.

18:4 [n]Nu 21:9 broke into pieces the bronze snake[n]
Moses had made, for up to that time
the Israelites had been burning incense
to it. (It was called[a] Nehushtan.[b])
18:5 [o]2Ki 19:10; 23:25 5Hezekiah trusted[o] in the LORD, the
God of Israel. There was no one like
him among all the kings of Judah, either before him or after him. 6He held
18:6 [p]Dt 10:20; Jos 23:8 fast[p] to the LORD and did not cease
to follow him; he kept the commands
the LORD had given Moses. 7And the
18:7 [q]Ge 39:3; 1Sa 18:14 [r]2Ki 16:7 LORD was with him; he was successful[q]
in whatever he undertook. He rebelled[r]
against the king of Assyria and did not
serve him. 8From watchtower to forti-
18:8 [s]2Ki 17:9; Isa 14:29 fied city,[s] he defeated the Philistines, as
far as Gaza and its territory.
18:9 [t]Isa 1:1 9In King Hezekiah's fourth year,[t]
which was the seventh year of Hoshea
son of Elah king of Israel, Shalmaneser
king of Assyria marched against Samaria and laid siege to it. 10At the end
of three years the Assyrians took it.
So Samaria was captured in Hezekiah's
18:11 [u]Isa 37:12 sixth year, which was the ninth year of
Hoshea king of Israel. 11The king[u] of
Assyria deported Israel to Assyria and
settled them in Halah, in Gozan on the
Habor River and in towns of the Medes.
12This happened because they had not
obeyed the LORD their God, but had
violated his covenant[v]—all that Moses 18:12 [v]2Ki 17:15
the servant of the LORD commanded.[w] [w]Da 9:6,10
They neither listened to the commands[x] [x]1Ki 9:6
nor carried them out.
13In the fourteenth year of King Hezekiah's reign, Sennacherib king of Assyria attacked all the fortified cities of
Judah[y] and captured them. 14So Hez- 18:13 [y]2Ch 32:1; Isa 1:7; Mic 1:9
ekiah king of Judah sent this message
to the king of Assyria at Lachish: "I
have done wrong.[z] Withdraw from me, 18:14 [z]Isa 24:5
and I will pay whatever you demand of
me." The king of Assyria exacted from
Hezekiah king of Judah three hundred
talents[c] of silver and thirty talents[d] of 18:15 [a]1Ki 15:18; 2Ki 16:8
gold. 15So Hezekiah gave[a] him all the

[a]*4* Or *He called it* [b]*4 Nehushtan* sounds like the Hebrew for *bronze* and *snake* and *unclean thing.*
[c]*14* That is, about 11 tons (about 10 metric tons)
[d]*14* That is, about 1 ton (about 1 metric ton)

HEZEKIAH

Peace, Walking With God Through Trials (18:1–37)

Hezekiah came to the throne of Judah when he was twenty-five years old. He lived and reigned in troubled times. Great empires feuded and powerful armies marched all around his kingdom. In the fourteenth year of Hezekiah's reign, Sennacherib of Assyria marched against all the fortified cities of Hezekiah's kingdom, capturing all of them except Jerusalem. When Jerusalem was threatened, Hezekiah went to the Lord for help, and God heard his prayer. God's words of comfort came to Hezekiah through the prophet Isaiah, and the Scriptures record what God did: "That night the angel of the LORD went out and put to death a hundred and eighty-five thousand men in the Assyrian camp . . . So Sennacherib king of Assyria broke camp and withdrew" (2 Kings 19:35–36).

Hezekiah was a great leader who looked to God for guidance, and in spite of a reign dominated by foreign wars, he walked with God. Under his leadership Jerusalem itself avoided siege and knew peace. Hezekiah's own peace was the result of a life committed to God. "He did what was right in the eyes of the LORD, just as his father David had done" (18:3).

Peace results when we focus completely on God. Hezekiah destroyed idol worship in the nation of Judah. When there were no longer false gods to worship, the people gave their adoration to the Lord alone. This single focus of our adoration still results in peace. Have you ever been torn between loving God and loving your idols? In pursuing secondary affections, you can lose both your single focus on worship and your peace. Anything more important than God to you, is god to you. Do you object to the idea of idolatry in your life? Idols take many forms in the lives of Christians, but they always demand the honor and affection that should be given to God alone. Tear down those high places, and the God of Hezekiah will walk in peace through your life.

silver that was found in the temple of
the LORD and in the treasuries of the
royal palace.
16At this time Hezekiah king of Judah stripped off the gold with which he
had covered the doors and doorposts of
the temple of the LORD, and gave it to
the king of Assyria.

Sennacherib Threatens Jerusalem

17The king of Assyria sent his su-
18:17 [b]Isa 20:1 [c]2Ki 20:20; 2Ch 32:4,30; Isa 7:3 preme commander,[b] his chief officer
and his field commander with a large
army, from Lachish to King Hezekiah
at Jerusalem. They came up to Jerusalem and stopped at the aqueduct of
the Upper Pool,[c] on the road to the
Washerman's Field. 18They called for
18:18 [d]2Ki 19:2; Isa 22:20 [e]Isa 22:15 the king; and Eliakim[d] son of Hilkiah
the palace administrator, Shebna[e] the
secretary, and Joah son of Asaph the recorder went out to them.
19The field commander said to them,
"Tell Hezekiah:

" 'This is what the great king,
the king of Assyria, says: On what
are you basing this confidence of
yours? 20You say you have strategy and military strength—but
you speak only empty words. On
whom are you depending, that
you rebel against me? 21Look now,
18:21 [f]Isa 20:5; Eze 29:6 [g]Isa 30:5,7 you are depending on Egypt,[f] that
splintered reed of a staff,[g] which
pierces a man's hand and wounds
him if he leans on it! Such is Pharaoh king of Egypt to all who depend on him. 22And if you say
to me, "We are depending on
the LORD our God"—isn't he the
one whose high places and altars
Hezekiah removed, saying to Judah and Jerusalem, "You must
worship before this altar in Jerusalem"?
23" 'Come now, make a bargain
with my master, the king of Assyria: I will give you two thousand
horses—if you can put riders on
them! 24How can you repulse one
18:24 [h]Isa 10:8 officer[h] of the least of my master's
officials, even though you are de-
pending on Egypt for chariots and
horsemen[a]? 25Furthermore, have I
come to attack and destroy this
place without word from the
18:25 [i]2Ki 19:6,22 LORD?[i] The LORD himself told
me to march against this country
and destroy it.' "
26Then Eliakim son of Hilkiah, and
Shebna and Joah said to the field commander, "Please speak to your servants
in Aramaic,[j] since we understand it. 18:26 [j]Ezr 4:7
Don't speak to us in Hebrew in the
hearing of the people on the wall."
27But the commander replied, "Was
it only to your master and you that my
master sent me to say these things, and
not to the men sitting on the wall—
who, like you, will have to eat their
own filth and drink their own urine?"
28Then the commander stood and
called out in Hebrew: "Hear the word
of the great king, the king of Assyria!
29This is what the king says: Do not let
Hezekiah deceive[k] you. He cannot de- 18:29 [k]2Ki 19:10
liver you from my hand. 30Do not let
Hezekiah persuade you to trust in the
LORD when he says, 'The LORD will
surely deliver us; this city will not be
given into the hand of the king of Assyria.'
31"Do not listen to Hezekiah. This
is what the king of Assyria says: Make
peace with me and come out to me.
Then every one of you will eat from his
own vine and fig tree[l] and drink water 18:31 [l]Nu 13:23; 1Ki 4:25 [m]Jer 14:3; La 4:4
from his own cistern,[m] 32until I come
and take you to a land like your own,
a land of grain and new wine, a land
of bread and vineyards, a land of olive
trees and honey. Choose life[n] and not 18:32 [n]Dt 8:7-9; 30:19
death!
"Do not listen to Hezekiah, for he
is misleading you when he says, 'The 18:33 [o]2Ki 19:12; Isa 10:10-11
LORD will deliver us.' 33Has the god[o]
of any nation ever delivered his land
from the hand of the king of Assyria?
34Where are the gods of Hamath[p] and 18:34 [p]2Ki 17:24; 19:13 [q]Isa 10:9
Arpad?[q] Where are the gods of Sephar-
vaim, Hena and Ivvah? Have they rescued Samaria from my hand? 35Who of
all the gods of these countries has been
able to save his land from me? How
then can the LORD deliver Jerusalem
from my hand?"[r] 18:35 [r]Ps 2:1-2
36But the people remained silent and
said nothing in reply, because the king
had commanded, "Do not answer
him."
37Then Eliakim son of Hilkiah the palace administrator, Shebna the secretary

[a]24 Or *charioteers*

and Joah son of Asaph the recorder went
18:37 to Hezekiah, with their clothes torn,[s]
s2Ki 6:30 and told him what the field commander
had said.

Jerusalem's Deliverance Foretold

19 When King Hezekiah heard
19:1 this, he tore[t] his clothes and put
tGe 37:34; on sackcloth and went into the temple
1Ki 21:27; 2Ch 32:20-22 of the LORD. 2He sent Eliakim the
palace administrator, Shebna the secre-
tary and the leading priests, all wearing
19:2 sackcloth, to the prophet Isaiah[u] son of
uIsa 1:1 Amoz. 3They told him, "This is what
Hezekiah says: This day is a day of distress and rebuke and disgrace, as when
children come to the point of birth and
there is no strength to deliver them.
4It may be that the LORD your God
will hear all the words of the field commander, whom his master, the king of
19:4 Assyria, has sent to ridicule[v] the living
v2Ki 18:35 w2Sa 16:12 God, and that he will rebuke[w] him for
the words the LORD your God has
heard. Therefore pray for the remnant
that still survives."
5When King Hezekiah's officials came
to Isaiah, 6Isaiah said to them, "Tell
your master, 'This is what the LORD
says: Do not be afraid of what you have
heard—those words with which the un-
19:6 derlings of the king of Assyria have blas-
x2Ki 18:25 phemed[x] me. 7Listen! I am going to put
such a spirit in him that when he hears
a certain report, he will return to his
19:7 own country, and there I will have him
yver 37 cut down with the sword.[y]' "
8When the field commander heard
that the king of Assyria had left
19:8 Lachish,[z] he withdrew and found the
z2Ki 18:14 king fighting against Libnah.
9Now Sennacherib received a report
that Tirhakah, the Cushite[a] king ⌞of
Egypt⌟, was marching out to fight
against him. So he again sent messengers to Hezekiah with this word: 10"Say
to Hezekiah king of Judah: Do not let
19:10 the god you depend[a] on deceive[b] you
a2Ki 18:5 b2Ki 18:29 when he says, 'Jerusalem will not be
handed over to the king of Assyria.'
11Surely you have heard what the kings
of Assyria have done to all the countries, destroying them completely. And
will you be delivered? 12Did the gods of
the nations that were destroyed by my
19:12 forefathers deliver[c] them: the gods of
c2Ki 18:33 d2Ki 17:6 Gozan,[d] Haran,[e] Rezeph and the people
eGe 11:31 of Eden who were in Tel Assar? 13Where

is the king of Hamath, the king of Arpad, the king of the city of Sepharvaim,
or of Hena or Ivvah?"[f] 19:13 f2Ki 18:34

Hezekiah's Prayer

14Hezekiah received the letter from the
messengers and read it. Then he went up
to the temple of the LORD and spread
it out before the LORD. 15And Hezekiah
prayed to the LORD: "O LORD, God of
Israel, enthroned between the cherubim,[g] 19:15
you alone are God over all the kingdoms gEx 25:22
of the earth. You have made heaven and
earth. 16Give ear,[h] O LORD, and hear;[i] 19:16
open your eyes,[j] O LORD, and see; lis- hPs 31:2
ten to the words Sennacherib has sent to i1Ki 8:29
insult the living God. jver 4; 2Ch 6:40
17"It is true, O LORD, that the Assyrian kings have laid waste these nations
and their lands. 18They have thrown
their gods into the fire and destroyed
them, for they were not gods[k] but only 19:18
wood and stone, fashioned by men's kIsa 44:9-11;
hands.[l] 19Now, O LORD our God, de- Jer 10:3-10
liver us from his hand, so that all king- lPs 115:4; Ac 17:29
doms[m] on earth may know[n] that you 19:19 m1Ki 8:43
alone, O LORD, are God." nPs 83:18

Isaiah Prophesies Sennacherib's Fall

20Then Isaiah son of Amoz sent a
message to Hezekiah: "This is what
the LORD, the God of Israel, says:
I have heard[o] your prayer concerning 19:20
Sennacherib king of Assyria. 21This is o2Ki 20:5
the word that the LORD has spoken
against him:

" 'The Virgin Daughter[p] of Zion 19:21
despises you and mocks[q] you. pJer 14:17; La 2:13
The Daughter of Jerusalem qPs 22:7-8
tosses her head[r] as you flee. rJob 16:4; Ps 109:25
22Who is it you have insulted and
blasphemed?
Against whom have you raised
your voice
and lifted your eyes in pride?
Against the Holy One[s] of Israel! 19:22
23By your messengers sPs 71:22; Isa 5:24
you have heaped insults on the
Lord.
And you have said,[t] 19:23
"With my many chariots[u] tIsa 10:18
I have ascended the heights of the uPs 20:7
mountains,
the utmost heights of Lebanon.
I have cut down its tallest cedars,

a9 That is, from the upper Nile region

the choicest of its pines.
I have reached its remotest parts,
the finest of its forests.
24 I have dug wells in foreign lands
and drunk the water there.
With the soles of my feet
I have dried up all the streams of
Egypt."

19:25 [v]Isa 40:21,28 [w]Isa 10:5; 45:7 [x]Mic 1:6
25 " 'Have you not heard?[v]
Long ago I ordained it.
In days of old I planned[w] it;
now I have brought it to pass,
that you have turned fortified cities
into piles of stone.[x]
19:26 [y]Ps 6:10 [z]Isa 4:2 [a]Ps 129:6
26 Their people, drained of power,
are dismayed[y] and put to
shame.
They are like plants in the field,
like tender green shoots,[z]
like grass sprouting on the roof,
scorched[a] before it grows up.
19:27 [b]Ps 139:1-4
27 " 'But I know[b] where you stay
and when you come and go
and how you rage against me.
28 Because you rage against me
and your insolence has reached
my ears,
19:28 [c]Eze 19:9; 29:4 [d]Isa 30:28 [e]ver 33
I will put my hook[c] in your nose
and my bit[d] in your mouth,
and I will make you return[e]
by the way you came.'

19:29 [f]2Ki 20:8-9; Lk 2:12 [g]Lev 25:5 [h]Ps 107:37
29 "This will be the sign[f] for you,
O Hezekiah:

"This year you will eat what grows
by itself,[g]
and the second year what springs
from that.
But in the third year sow and reap,
plant vineyards[h] and eat their
fruit.
30 Once more a remnant of the house
of Judah
19:30 [i]2Ch 32:22-23
will take root[i] below and bear fruit
above.
31 For out of Jerusalem will come a
remnant,
and out of Mount Zion a band of
survivors.
19:31 [j]Isa 9:7
The zeal[j] of the LORD Almighty will
accomplish this.

32 "Therefore this is what the LORD
says concerning the king of Assyria:

"He will not enter this city
or shoot an arrow here.
He will not come before it with
shield
or build a siege ramp against it.
19:33 [k]ver 28
33 By the way that he came he will
return;[k]
he will not enter this city,
declares the LORD.
19:34 [l]2Ki 20:6 [m]1Ki 11:12-13
34 I will defend[l] this city and save it,
for my sake and for the sake of
David[m] my servant."

19:35 [n]Ex 12:23 [o]Job 24:24
35 That night the angel of the LORD[n]
went out and put to death a hundred
and eighty-five thousand men in the
Assyrian camp. When the people got up
the next morning—there were all the
dead bodies![o] 36 So Sennacherib king of
19:36 [p]Ge 10:11; Jnh 1:2
Assyria broke camp and withdrew. He
returned to Nineveh[p] and stayed there.

JOY

THE MIRACLE ARMY

2 Kings 19:35

Joy only seems far away when we focus on our fears. Do your circumstances gang up on you like the armies of hell? Remember Sennacherib. He thought he could overwhelm the people of God. He lost his army on the very night the Israelites learned that their enemies were irrelevant if God was their friend.

37 One day, while he was worshiping
in the temple of his god Nisroch, his
sons Adrammelech and Sharezer cut
19:37 [q]ver 7 [r]Ge 8:4 [s]Ezr 4:2
him down with the sword,[q] and they
escaped to the land of Ararat.[r] And
Esarhaddon[s] his son succeeded him as
king.

Hezekiah's Illness

20 In those days Hezekiah became
ill and was at the point of death.
The prophet Isaiah son of Amoz went
to him and said, "This is what the
LORD says: Put your house in order,
because you are going to die; you will
not recover."

2 Hezekiah turned his face to the wall
20:3 [t]Ne 13:22 [u]2Ki 18:3-6
and prayed to the LORD, 3 "Remember,[t]
O LORD, how I have walked before
you faithfully[u] and with wholehearted
devotion and have done what is good
in your eyes." And Hezekiah wept bitterly.

4 Before Isaiah had left the middle
court, the word of the LORD came to

him: 5"Go back and tell Hezekiah, the
leader of my people, 'This is what the
LORD, the God of your father David,
20:5 says: I have heard[v] your prayer and seen
[v]1Sa 9:16; 1Ki 9:3; 2Ki 19:20 your tears;[w] I will heal you. On the
[w]Ps 39:12; 56:8 third day from now you will go up to
the temple of the LORD. 6I will add fif-
teen years to your life. And I will deliver you and this city from the hand of
the king of Assyria. I will defend[x] this 20:6 [x]2Ki 19:34
city for my sake and for the sake of my
servant David.' "

KINDNESS

PRAYING FOR TIME

2 Kings 20:6

God is kind. On his deathbed, Hezekiah asked God to spare his life, and God gave him 15 more years. Come to Christ, beg life and see how Hezekiah's gift is diminished when compared with the eternity God offers you.

7Then Isaiah said, "Prepare a poultice of figs." They did so and applied it
to the boil,[y] and he recovered. 20:7 [y]Isa 38:21
8Hezekiah had asked Isaiah, "What
will be the sign that the LORD will heal
me and that I will go up to the temple
of the LORD on the third day from
now?"
9Isaiah answered, "This is the LORD's
sign[z] to you that the LORD will do 20:9 [z]Dt 13:2; Jer 44:29
what he has promised: Shall the shadow
go forward ten steps, or shall it go back
ten steps?"
10"It is a simple matter for the shadow to go forward ten steps," said Hezekiah. "Rather, have it go back ten
steps."
11Then the prophet Isaiah called upon
the LORD, and the LORD made the
shadow go back[a] the ten steps it had 20:11 [a]Jos 10:13
gone down on the stairway of Ahaz.

Envoys From Babylon

12At that time Merodach-Baladan son
of Baladan king of Babylon sent Hezekiah letters and a gift, because he had
heard of Hezekiah's illness. 13Hezekiah
received the messengers and showed
them all that was in his storehouses—
the silver, the gold, the spices and the
fine oil—his armory and everything
found among his treasures. There was
nothing in his palace or in all his
kingdom that Hezekiah did not show
them.
14Then Isaiah the prophet went to
King Hezekiah and asked, "What did
those men say, and where did they come
from?"
"From a distant land," Hezekiah replied. "They came from Babylon."
15The prophet asked, "What did they
see in your palace?"

DAY 2 TWO

PATIENCE AND THE PURPOSE OF GOD IN MY LIFE

2 Kings 20:1–7

"I'll die when my number's up" is an adage used by those who have forgotten the hold that the world has on us. Hezekiah was a king whose number was up, and he turned his face to the wall and begged God for an extension. God answered and extended his life fifteen more years.

Hezekiah did not want to die. Perhaps this is the ironic element of the story. Most of us Christians are confident about eternity. We all are confident of heaven when we die. But no one wants to go on the next load. In spite of the fact that we are counting on heaven being better than this world, we cling to this world as tightly as we can for as long as we can.

Hezekiah, at the hour of death, begs for more life. After all, when has any life been long enough? One can only imagine Methuselah at the gates of death asking God for another nine hundred years. Still, Hebrews reminds us that each of us is destined to die. Since the last heartbeat is an approaching reality, maybe patience would teach us that the heartbeats along the way are our means of coming to terms with our mortality. Our purpose from God is to use wisely the minutes we have allotted to us.

Hezekiah's life was extended. Have you ever wondered how he used his final fifteen years? Perhaps he lived the paced life. He looked at sundials and was determined that they would not master him, but instead they would inform him. They would not make him hurry life, but they would make him use life—all of it for God's purposes.

To begin a study on the topic of Patience, Living by God's Timetable, turn to the home page on page 593.

"They saw everything in my palace," Hezekiah said. "There is nothing among my treasures that I did not show them."

16Then Isaiah said to Hezekiah, "Hear the word of the LORD: 17The time will surely come when everything in your palace, and all that your fathers have stored up until this day, will be carried off to Babylon.[b] Nothing will be left, says the LORD. 18And some of your descendants,[c] your own flesh and blood, that will be born to you, will be taken away, and they will become eunuchs in the palace of the king of Babylon."

19"The word of the LORD you have spoken is good," Hezekiah replied. For he thought, "Will there not be peace and security in my lifetime?"

20As for the other events of Hezekiah's reign, all his achievements and how he made the pool[d] and the tunnel by which he brought water into the city, are they not written in the book of the annals of the kings of Judah? 21Hezekiah rested with his fathers. And Manasseh his son succeeded him as king.

Manasseh King of Judah

21 Manasseh was twelve years old when he became king, and he reigned in Jerusalem fifty-five years. His mother's name was Hephzibah.[e] 2He did evil[f] in the eyes of the LORD, following the detestable practices[g] of the nations the LORD had driven out before the Israelites. 3He rebuilt the high places[h] his father Hezekiah had destroyed; he also erected altars to Baal[i] and made an Asherah pole, as Ahab king of Israel had done. He bowed down to all the starry hosts[j] and worshiped them. 4He built altars[k] in the temple of the LORD, of which the LORD had said, "In Jerusalem I will put my Name."[l] 5In both courts[m] of the temple of the LORD, he built altars to all the starry hosts. 6He sacrificed his own son[n] in[a] the fire, practiced sorcery and divination, and consulted mediums and spiritists.[o] He did much evil in the eyes of the LORD, provoking him to anger.

7He took the carved Asherah pole[p] he had made and put it in the temple, of which the LORD had said to David and to his son Solomon, "In this temple and in Jerusalem, which I have chosen out of all the tribes of Israel, I will put my Name[q] forever. 8I will not again[r] make the feet of the Israelites wander from the land I gave their forefathers, if only they will be careful to do everything I commanded them and will keep the whole Law that my servant Moses[s] gave them." 9But the people did not listen. Manasseh led them astray, so that they did more evil[t] than the nations[u] the LORD had destroyed before the Israelites.

10The LORD said through his servants the prophets: 11"Manasseh king of Judah has committed these detestable sins. He has done more evil[v] than the Amorites[w] who preceded him and has led Judah into sin with his idols. 12Therefore this is what the LORD, the God of Israel, says: I am going to bring such disaster[x] on Jerusalem and Judah that the ears of everyone who hears of it will tingle.[y] 13I will stretch out over Jerusalem the measuring line used against Samaria and the plumb line[z] used against the house of Ahab. I will wipe[a] out Jerusalem as one wipes a dish, wiping it and turning it upside down. 14I will forsake[b] the remnant[c] of my inheritance and hand them over to their enemies. They will be looted and plundered by all their foes, 15because they have done evil[d] in my eyes and have provoked[e] me to anger from the day their forefathers came out of Egypt until this day."

16Moreover, Manasseh also shed so much innocent blood[f] that he filled Jerusalem from end to end—besides the sin that he had caused Judah to commit, so that they did evil in the eyes of the LORD.

17As for the other events of Manasseh's reign, and all he did, including the sin he committed, are they not written in the book of the annals of the kings of Judah? 18Manasseh rested with his fathers and was buried in his palace garden,[g] the garden of Uzza. And Amon his son succeeded him as king.

Amon King of Judah

19Amon was twenty-two years old when he became king, and he reigned in Jerusalem two years. His mother's name was Meshullemeth daughter of

20:17 [b]2Ki 24:13; 25:13; 2Ch 36:10; Jer 27:22; 52:17-23
20:18 [c]2Ki 24:15; 2Ch 33:11; Da 1:3
20:20 [d]Ne 3:16
21:1 [e]Isa 62:4
21:2 [f]Jer 15:4 [g]2Ki 16:3
21:3 [h]2Ki 18:4 [i]Jdg 6:28; 1Ki 16:32 [j]Dt 17:3; 2Ki 17:16
21:4 [k]Jer 32:34 [l]2Sa 7:13; 1Ki 8:29
21:5 [m]1Ki 7:12; 2Ki 23:12
21:6 [n]Lev 18:21; Dt 18:10; 2Ki 16:3; 17:17 [o]Lev 19:31
21:7 [p]Dt 16:21; 2Ki 23:4
21:7 [q]2Sa 7:13; 1Ki 8:29; 9:3; 2Ki 23:27; Jer 32:34
21:8 [r]2Sa 7:10 [s]2Ki 18:12
21:9 [t]Pr 29:12 [u]Dt 9:4
21:11 [v]2Ki 24:3-4 [w]Ge 15:16; 1Ki 21:26
21:12 [x]2Ki 23:26; 24:3; Jer 15:4 [y]1Sa 3:11; Jer 19:3
21:13 [z]Isa 34:11; La 2:8; Am 7:7-9 [a]2Ki 23:27
21:14 [b]Ps 78:58-60 [c]2Ki 19:4; Mic 2:12
21:15 [d]Ex 32:22 [e]Jer 25:7
21:16 [f]2Ki 24:4
21:18 [g]ver 26

[a]6 Or *He made his own son pass through*

WEEK 52 SELF-CONTROL

DAY ONE
SELF-CONTROL, FREEDOM FROM PERMISSIVENESS

Read 2 Kings 21:1–9

There is one name that stands out as the arch-villain in the lineage of the kings of Judah. That name is Manasseh. Consider all the evil things he did:

> He built altars to Baal and made an Asherah pole (2 Kings 21:3).
> He worshiped astral deities (v. 3).
> He built altars to false gods in the very temple of God (vv. 4–5).
> He sacrificed his own son in the fire of pagan ritual (v. 6).
> He practiced witchcraft and sorcery (v. 6).

In short, he lived a more wicked life than did the Amorites, whom Israel had conquered to establish the holiness of God in the land (see v. 11).

Indulgence is a comfort-loving attitude that constantly makes a wider bed for itself. Indulgence and self-control are alike in one way: They are both addictive. For instance, a person who is sexually promiscuous will continue to push this latitude into wider and wider areas of permissiveness. Indulgence in one area, like sexual libertinism, is also easily extended to another area, such as alcoholism or gluttony.

Across the gamut from indulgence lies self-control. When we deny any appetite, it is easier to extend that denial into other areas. The person who remains temperate in one area will likely be temperate in other areas.

What made Manasseh Judah's most evil king? He likely lacked the ability to say no to himself. He skirted self-denial, opting for the "if-it-feels-good-do-it" philosophy. He likely thought he was living free, but he was enslaved by the ugliest of monsters—his own permissiveness.

MEMORIZE THIS WEEK

TITUS 2:11-12

For the grace of God that brings salvation has appeared to all men. It teaches us to say "No" to ungodliness and worldly passions, and to live self-controlled, upright and godly lives in this present age.

DAY TWO
SELF-CONTROL AND THE PURPOSE OF GOD IN MY LIFE

The work of rebuilding the temple had begun in 538 B.C. upon Israel's return from exile in Babylon. But the work was interrupted for a period of years and not taken up again until 520 B.C. Haggai preached this sermon to remind Israel that the work had been halted because the people had become more interested in their own personal agendas than in being obedient to God. *Turn to Haggai 1:5–6, page 1094, for today's study.*

DAY THREE
SELF-CONTROL AND MY RELATIONSHIP WITH CHRIST

Now that we have been set free from libertinism, says the apostle, we have elected a wonderful, new, voluntary slavery. We have been set free from a reckless, old, irresponsible freedom and have elected voluntarily to be slaves to God. Slavery is bad when the slave's master is evil. But we serve a good Master, who loves us to the point of dying for us. So we are truly free, free not to have our own way, but free to have a meaningful life in our world. *Turn to Romans 6:19–23, page 1340, for today's study.*

DAY FOUR
SELF-CONTROL AND MY SERVICE TO OTHERS

The prophet Joel noticed the similarity between individual license and national hedonism. He cried out for a new craving for self-control. The nations were casting lots for human beings, trading in prostitution, selling children to finance their debauchery (3:3). Such nations cannot be practicing self-control. A nation only arrives at virtue when the individual citizens practice it. *Turn to Joel 3:1–3, page 1049, for today's study.*

DAY FIVE
SELF-CONTROL AND ITS PLACE IN MY PERSONAL WORSHIP

Spiritual self-control is lost when we give to God only what is second best. Those who went to the temple were sacrificing only blemished animals, keeping the best for themselves. When God is given only our hand-me-downs, we are clothing ourselves in ego. When God gets our best and we give it freely, we have set ourselves free from the libertine life. *Turn to Malachi 3:8–10, page 1112, for today's study.*

Week 1, The Evidence of Love Is Giving, begins on page 5, Genesis 1:29.
To begin a topical study on the Fruit of the Spirit, Self-Control, turn to the Topical Index, page 1548.

Haruz; she was from Jotbah. 20He did
21:20 [h]ver 2-6 evil[h] in the eyes of the LORD, as his father Manasseh had done. 21He walked
in all the ways of his father; he worshiped the idols his father had worshiped, and bowed down to them. 22He
forsook the LORD, the God of his fa-
21:22 [i]1Ki 11:33 thers, and did not walk[i] in the way of
the LORD.

23Amon's officials conspired against
21:23 [j]2Ki 12:20; 2Ch 33:24-25 him and assassinated[j] the king in his
palace. 24Then the people of the land
21:24 [k]2Ki 14:5 killed[k] all who had plotted against King
Amon, and they made Josiah his son
king in his place.

25As for the other events of Amon's
reign, and what he did, are they not
written in the book of the annals of the
kings of Judah? 26He was buried in his
21:26 [l]ver 18 grave in the garden[l] of Uzza. And Josiah
his son succeeded him as king.

The Book of the Law Found

22 Josiah was eight years old when
he became king, and he reigned
in Jerusalem thirty-one years. His mother's name was Jedidah daughter of Ada-
22:1 [m]Jos 15:39 iah; she was from Bozkath.[m] 2He did
22:2 [n]Dt 17:19 what was right[n] in the eyes of the LORD
and walked in all the ways of his father
[o]Dt 5:32 David, not turning aside to the right[o]
or to the left.

3In the eighteenth year of his reign,
22:3 [p]2Ch 34:20; Jer 39:14 King Josiah sent the secretary, Shaphan[p]
son of Azaliah, the son of Meshullam,
to the temple of the LORD. He said:
4"Go up to Hilkiah the high priest and
have him get ready the money that has
been brought into the temple of the
LORD, which the doorkeepers have col-
22:4 [q]2Ki 12:4-5 lected[q] from the people. 5Have them
entrust it to the men appointed to su-
pervise the work on the temple. And
have these men pay the workers who
22:5 [r]2Ki 12:5, 11-14 repair[r] the temple of the LORD— 6the
carpenters, the builders and the masons.
Also have them purchase timber and
22:6 [s]2Ki 12:11-12 dressed stone to repair the temple.[s] 7But
they need not account for the money
entrusted to them, because they are act-
22:7 [t]2Ki 12:15 ing faithfully."[t]

8Hilkiah the high priest said to Shaphan the secretary, "I have found the
22:8 [u]Dt 31:24 Book of the Law[u] in the temple of the
LORD." He gave it to Shaphan, who
read it. 9Then Shaphan the secretary
went to the king and reported to him:
"Your officials have paid out the money
that was in the temple of the LORD and
have entrusted it to the workers and supervisors at the temple." 10Then Shaphan the secretary informed the king,
"Hilkiah the priest has given me a
book." And Shaphan read from it in
the presence of the king.[v] 22:10 [v]Jer 36:21

11When the king heard the words of
the Book of the Law, he tore his robes.
12He gave these orders to Hilkiah the
priest, Ahikam[w] son of Shaphan, Acbor 22:12 [w]2Ki 25:22; Jer 26:24
son of Micaiah, Shaphan the secretary
and Asaiah the king's attendant: 13"Go
and inquire of the LORD for me and
for the people and for all Judah about
what is written in this book that has
been found. Great is the LORD's an-
ger[x] that burns against us because our 22:13 [x]Dt 29:24-28; 31:17
fathers have not obeyed the words of
this book; they have not acted in accordance with all that is written there concerning us."

LOVE

WHEN KINGS REPENT

2 Kings 22:11

When kings repent, the world is safe. When kings repent, God steps to the edge of heaven, looks over the ramparts and smiles. When kings repent, God remembers the sixth day of creation and says again, "That's good!"

14Hilkiah the priest, Ahikam, Acbor,
Shaphan and Asaiah went to speak to
the prophetess Huldah, who was the
wife of Shallum son of Tikvah, the son
of Harhas, keeper of the wardrobe. She
lived in Jerusalem, in the Second District.

15She said to them, "This is what
the LORD, the God of Israel, says: Tell
the man who sent you to me, 16'This
is what the LORD says: I am going to
bring disaster[y] on this place and its peo- 22:16 [y]Dt 31:29; Jos 23:15
ple, according to everything written in
the book[z] the king of Judah has read. [z]Dt 29:27; Da 9:11
17Because they have forsaken[a] me and 22:17 [a]Dt 29:25-27
burned incense to other gods and pro-
voked me to anger by all the idols their
hands have made,[a] my anger will burn
against this place and will not be
quenched.' 18Tell the king of Judah,
who sent you to inquire[b] of the LORD, 22:18 [b]2Ch 34:26; Jer 21:2

[a]17 Or *by everything they have done*

'This is what the LORD, the God of Israel, says concerning the words you heard: 19 Because your heart was responsive and you humbled[c] yourself before the LORD when you heard what I have spoken against this place and its people, that they would become accursed[d] and laid waste,[e] and because you tore your robes and wept in my presence, I have heard you, declares the LORD. 20 Therefore I will gather you to your fathers, and you will be buried in peace.[f] Your eyes will not see all the disaster I am going to bring on this place.' "

So they took her answer back to the king.

Josiah Renews the Covenant

23 Then the king called together all the elders of Judah and Jerusalem. 2 He went up to the temple of the LORD with the men of Judah, the people of Jerusalem, the priests and the prophets—all the people from the least to the greatest. He read[g] in their hearing all the words of the Book of the Covenant, which had been found in the temple of the LORD. 3 The king stood by the pillar and renewed the covenant[h] in the presence of the LORD—to follow[i] the LORD and keep his commands, regulations and decrees with all his heart and all his soul, thus confirming the words of the covenant written in this book. Then all the people pledged themselves to the covenant.

4 The king ordered Hilkiah the high priest, the priests next in rank and the doorkeepers[j] to remove[k] from the temple of the LORD all the articles made for Baal and Asherah and all the starry hosts. He burned them outside Jerusalem in the fields of the Kidron Valley and took the ashes to Bethel. 5 He did away with the pagan priests appointed by the kings of Judah to burn incense on the high places of the towns of Judah and on those around Jerusalem—those who burned incense to Baal, to the sun and moon, to the constellations and to all the starry hosts.[l] 6 He took the Asherah pole from the temple of the LORD to the Kidron Valley outside Jerusalem and burned it there. He ground it to powder and scattered the dust over the graves of the common people.[m] 7 He also tore down the quarters of the male shrine prostitutes,[n] which were in the temple of the LORD and where women did weaving for Asherah.

8 Josiah brought all the priests from the towns of Judah and desecrated the high places, from Geba[o] to Beersheba, where the priests had burned incense. He broke down the shrines[a] at the gates—at the entrance to the Gate of Joshua, the city governor, which is on the left of the city gate. 9 Although the priests of the high places did not serve[p] at the altar of the LORD in Jerusalem, they ate unleavened bread with their fellow priests.

10 He desecrated Topheth,[q] which was in the Valley of Ben Hinnom,[r] so no one could use it to sacrifice his son[s] or daughter in[b] the fire to Molech. 11 He removed from the entrance to the temple of the LORD the horses that the kings of Judah had dedicated to the sun. They were in the court near the room of an official named Nathan-Melech. Josiah then burned the chariots dedicated to the sun.[t]

12 He pulled down the altars the kings of Judah had erected on the roof[u] near the upper room of Ahaz, and the altars Manasseh had built in the two courts[v] of the temple of the LORD. He removed them from there, smashed them to pieces and threw the rubble into the Kidron Valley. 13 The king also desecrated the high places that were east of Jerusalem on the south of the Hill of Corruption—the ones Solomon[w] king of Israel had built for Ashtoreth the vile goddess of the Sidonians, for Chemosh the vile god of Moab, and for Molech[c] the detestable god of the people of Ammon. 14 Josiah smashed[x] the sacred stones and cut down the Asherah poles and covered the sites with human bones.

15 Even the altar[y] at Bethel, the high place made by Jeroboam[z] son of Nebat, who had caused Israel to sin—even that altar and high place he demolished. He burned the high place and ground it to powder, and burned the Asherah pole also. 16 Then Josiah[a] looked around, and when he saw the tombs that were there on the hillside, he had the bones removed from them and burned on the altar to defile it, in accordance with the

22:19 [c]Ex 10:3; 1Ki 21:29; Ps 51:17; Isa 57:15; Mic 6:8 [d]Jer 26:6 [e]Lev 26:31
22:20 [f]Isa 57:1
23:2 [g]Dt 31:11; 2Ki 22:8
23:3 [h]2Ki 11:14,17 [i]Dt 13:4
23:4 [j]2Ki 25:18 [k]2Ki 21:7
23:5 [l]2Ki 21:3; Jer 8:2
23:6 [m]Jer 26:23
23:7 [n]1Ki 14:24; 15:12; Eze 16:16
23:8 [o]1Ki 15:22
23:9 [p]Eze 44:10-14
23:10 [q]Isa 30:33; Jer 7:31,32; 19:6 [r]Jos 15:8 [s]Lev 18:21; Dt 18:10
23:11 [t]Dt 4:19
23:12 [u]Jer 19:13; Zep 1:5 [v]2Ki 21:5
23:13 [w]1Ki 11:7
23:14 [x]Ex 23:24; Dt 7:5,25
23:15 [y]1Ki 13:1-3 [z]1Ki 12:33
23:16 [a]1Ki 13:2

[a]8 Or *high places* [b]10 Or *to make his son or daughter pass through* [c]13 Hebrew *Milcom*

word of the LORD proclaimed by the
man of God who foretold these things.
17The king asked, "What is that
tombstone I see?"
The men of the city said, "It marks
the tomb of the man of God who came
from Judah and pronounced against the
altar of Bethel the very things you have
done to it."
18"Leave it alone," he said. "Don't
23:18 let anyone disturb his bones.[b]" So they
[b]1Ki 13:31 spared his bones and those of the prophet who had come from Samaria.
19Just as he had done at Bethel, Josiah removed and defiled all the shrines
at the high places that the kings of Israel
had built in the towns of Samaria that
had provoked the LORD to anger. 20Jo-
23:20 siah slaughtered[c] all the priests of those
[c]Ex 22:20; high places on the altars and burned
2Ki 10:25; human bones[d] on them. Then he went
11:18 [d]1Ki 13:2 back to Jerusalem.
21The king gave this order to all the
23:21 people: "Celebrate the Passover[e] to the
[e]Ex 12:11; LORD your God, as it is written in this
Nu 9:2; Dt 16:1-8 Book of the Covenant." 22Not since the
days of the judges who led Israel, nor
throughout the days of the kings of Israel and the kings of Judah, had any
such Passover been observed. 23But in
the eighteenth year of King Josiah, this
Passover was celebrated to the LORD in
Jerusalem.
24Furthermore, Josiah got rid of the
23:24 mediums and spiritists,[f] the household
[f]Lev 19:31; gods,[g] the idols and all the other de-
Dt 18:11; 2Ki 21:6 testable things seen in Judah and Je-
[g]Ge 31:19 rusalem. This he did to fulfill the
requirements of the law written in the
book that Hilkiah the priest had discovered in the temple of the LORD. 25Nei-
ther before nor after Josiah was there a
23:25 king like him who turned[h] to the LORD
[h]2Ki 18:5 as he did—with all his heart and with
all his soul and with all his strength, in
accordance with all the Law of Moses.
26Nevertheless, the LORD did not
turn away from the heat of his fierce
anger, which burned against Judah be-
23:26 cause of all that Manasseh[i] had done to
[i]2Ki 21:12; provoke him to anger. 27So the LORD
Jer 15:4 said, "I will remove[j] Judah also from
23:27 my presence[k] as I removed Israel, and
[j]2Ki 21:13 [k]2Ki 18:11 I will reject Jerusalem, the city I chose,
and this temple, about which I said,
'There shall my Name be.'[a]"
28As for the other events of Josiah's
reign, and all he did, are they not written in the book of the annals of the
kings of Judah?
29While Josiah was king, Pharaoh
Neco[l] king of Egypt went up to the Eu- 23:29 [l]Jer 46:2
phrates River to help the king of As- [m]Zec 12:11
syria. King Josiah marched out to meet
him in battle, but Neco faced him and
killed him at Megiddo.[m] 30Josiah's servants brought his body in a chariot[n] 23:30 [n]2Ki 9:28
from Megiddo to Jerusalem and buried
him in his own tomb. And the people
of the land took Jehoahaz son of Josiah
and anointed him and made him king
in place of his father.

Jehoahaz King of Judah

31Jehoahaz[o] was twenty-three years 23:31
old when he became king, and he [o]1Ch 3:15;
reigned in Jerusalem three months. His Jer 22:11 [p]2Ki 24:18
mother's name was Hamutal[p] daugh-
ter of Jeremiah; she was from Libnah.
32He did evil in the eyes of the LORD,
just as his fathers had done. 33Pharaoh
Neco put him in chains at Riblah[q] in 23:33 [q]2Ki 25:6
the land of Hamath[b][r] so that he might [r]1Ki 8:65
not reign in Jerusalem, and he imposed
on Judah a levy of a hundred talents[c]
of silver and a talent[d] of gold. 34Phar-
aoh Neco made Eliakim[s] son of Josiah 23:34 [s]1Ch 3:15;
king in place of his father Josiah and 2Ch 36:5-8
changed Eliakim's name to Jehoiakim. [t]Jer 22:12; Eze 19:3-4
But he took Jehoahaz and carried him
off to Egypt, and there he died.[t] 35Je-
hoiakim paid Pharaoh Neco the silver
and gold he demanded. In order to do
so, he taxed the land and exacted the
silver and gold from the people of the
land according to their assessments.[u] 23:35 [u]ver 33

Jehoiakim King of Judah

36Jehoiakim[v] was twenty-five years 23:36
old when he became king, and he [v]Jer 26:1
reigned in Jerusalem eleven years. His
mother's name was Zebidah daughter of
Pedaiah; she was from Rumah. 37And
he did evil in the eyes of the LORD, just
as his fathers had done.

24 During Jehoiakim's reign, Nebuchadnezzar[w] king of Babylon 24:1 [w]Jer 25:1,9;
invaded the land, and Jehoiakim be- Da 1:1
came his vassal for three years. But
then he changed his mind and rebelled
against Nebuchadnezzar. 2The LORD

[a]*27* 1 Kings 8:29 [b]*33* Hebrew; Septuagint (see also 2 Chron. 36:3) *Neco at Riblah in Hamath removed him* [c]*33* That is, about 3 3/4 tons (about 3.4 metric tons) [d]*33* That is, about 75 pounds (about 34 kilograms)

sent Babylonian,[a] Aramean,[x] Moabite
and Ammonite raiders against him. He
sent them to destroy[y] Judah, in accordance with the word of the LORD proclaimed by his servants the prophets.
3Surely these things happened to Judah
according to the LORD's command,[z] in
order to remove them from his presence
because of the sins of Manasseh[a] and all
he had done, 4including the shedding
of innocent blood.[b] For he had filled Jerusalem with innocent blood, and the
LORD was not willing to forgive.

5As for the other events of Jehoiakim's reign, and all he did, are they not
written in the book of the annals of the
kings of Judah? 6Jehoiakim rested[c] with
his fathers. And Jehoiachin his son succeeded him as king.

7The king of Egypt[d] did not march
out from his own country again, because the king of Babylon[e] had taken all
his territory, from the Wadi of Egypt to
the Euphrates River.

Jehoiachin King of Judah

8Jehoiachin[f] was eighteen years old
when he became king, and he reigned
in Jerusalem three months. His mother's name was Nehushta daughter of Elnathan; she was from Jerusalem. 9He
did evil in the eyes of the LORD, just as
his father had done.

10At that time the officers of Nebuchadnezzar[g] king of Babylon advanced
on Jerusalem and laid siege to it, 11and
Nebuchadnezzar himself came up to
the city while his officers were besieging it. 12Jehoiachin king of Judah, his
mother, his attendants, his nobles and
his officials all surrendered[h] to him.

In the eighth year of the reign of
the king of Babylon, he took Jehoiachin
prisoner. 13As the LORD had declared,[i]
Nebuchadnezzar removed all the treasures[j] from the temple of the LORD
and from the royal palace, and took
away all the gold articles[k] that Solomon[l]
king of Israel had made for the temple
of the LORD. 14He carried into exile[m]
all Jerusalem: all the officers and fighting men, and all the craftsmen and artisans—a total of ten thousand. Only the
poorest[n] people of the land were left.

15Nebuchadnezzar took Jehoiachin
captive to Babylon. He also took from
Jerusalem to Babylon the king's mother,[o]
his wives, his officials and the leading
men[p] of the land. 16The king of Babylon also deported to Babylon the entire force of seven thousand fighting
men, strong and fit for war, and a
thousand craftsmen and artisans.[q] 17He
made Mattaniah, Jehoiachin's uncle,
king in his place and changed his name
to Zedekiah.[r]

Zedekiah King of Judah

18Zedekiah[s] was twenty-one years old
when he became king, and he reigned
in Jerusalem eleven years. His mother's
name was Hamutal[t] daughter of Jeremiah; she was from Libnah. 19He did
evil in the eyes of the LORD, just as Jehoiakim had done. 20It was because of
the LORD's anger that all this happened
to Jerusalem and Judah, and in the end
he thrust[u] them from his presence.

The Fall of Jerusalem

Now Zedekiah rebelled against the
king of Babylon.

25 So in the ninth year of Zedekiah's reign, on the tenth day of
the tenth month, Nebuchadnezzar[v] king
of Babylon marched against Jerusalem
with his whole army. He encamped outside the city and built siege works[w] all
around it. 2The city was kept under siege
until the eleventh year of King Zedekiah. 3By the ninth day of the ⌞fourth⌟[b]
month the famine[x] in the city had become so severe that there was no food
for the people to eat. 4Then the city wall
was broken through,[y] and the whole
army fled at night through the gate
between the two walls near the king's
garden, though the Babylonians[c] were
surrounding[z] the city. They fled toward
the Arabah,[d] 5but the Babylonian[e] army
pursued the king and overtook him in
the plains of Jericho. All his soldiers were
separated from him and scattered,[a] 6and
he was captured.[b] He was taken to the
king of Babylon at Riblah,[c] where sentence was pronounced on him. 7They
killed the sons of Zedekiah before his
eyes. Then they put out his eyes, bound
him with bronze shackles and took him
to Babylon.[d]

8On the seventh day of the fifth

[a]2 Or *Chaldean* [b]3 See Jer. 52:6. [c]4 Or *Chaldeans*; also in verses 13, 25 and 26 [d]4 Or *the Jordan Valley* [e]5 Or *Chaldean*; also in verses 10 and 24

24:2 [x]Jer 35:11 [y]Jer 25:9
24:3 [z]2Ki 18:25 [a]2Ki 21:12; 23:26
24:4 [b]2Ki 21:16
24:6 [c]Jer 22:19
24:7 [d]Ge 15:18 [e]Jer 37:5-7; 46:2
24:8 [f]1Ch 3:16
24:10 [g]Da 1:1
24:12 [h]2Ki 25:27; Jer 22:24-30; 24:1; 25:1; 29:2; 52:28
24:13 [i]2Ki 20:17 [j]2Ki 25:15; Isa 39:6 [k]2Ki 25:14; Jer 20:5 [l]1Ki 7:51
24:14 [m]Jer 24:1; 52:28 [n]2Ki 25:12; Jer 40:7; 52:16
24:15 [o]Jer 22:24-28
24:15 [p]Est 2:6; Eze 17:12-14
24:16 [q]Jer 52:28
24:17 [r]1Ch 3:15; 2Ch 36:11; Jer 37:1
24:18 [s]Jer 52:1 [t]2Ki 23:31
24:20 [u]Dt 4:26; 29:27
25:1 [v]Jer 34:1-7 [w]Eze 24:2
25:3 [x]Jer 14:18; La 4:9
25:4 [y]Eze 33:21 [z]Jer 4:17
25:5 [a]Eze 12:14
25:6 [b]Jer 34:21-22 [c]2Ki 23:33
25:7 [d]Jer 21:7; 32:4-5; Eze 12:11

month, in the nineteenth year of Nebuchadnezzar king of Babylon, Nebuzaradan commander of the imperial
guard, an official of the king of Bab-
25:9 [e]Isa 60:7; [f]Ps 74:3-8; Jer 2:15; Am 2:5; Mic 3:12
ylon, came to Jerusalem. 9He set fire[e]
to the temple of the LORD, the royal
palace and all the houses of Jerusalem.
Every important building he burned
down.[f] 10The whole Babylonian army,
under the commander of the imperial
25:10 [g]Ne 1:3
guard, broke down the walls[g] around
Jerusalem. 11Nebuzaradan the com-
25:11 [h]2Ki 24:14 [i]2Ki 24:1
mander of the guard carried into exile[h]
the people who remained in the city,
along with the rest of the populace and
those who had gone over to the king
25:12 [j]2Ki 24:14
of Babylon.[i] 12But the commander left
behind some of the poorest people[j]
of the land to work the vineyards and
fields.

13The Babylonians broke up the
bronze pillars, the movable stands and
the bronze Sea that were at the temple of
the LORD and they carried the bronze
to Babylon. 14They also took away the
pots, shovels, wick trimmers, dishes and
25:14 [k]Ex 27:3; 1Ki 7:47-50
all the bronze articles[k] used in the temple service. 15The commander of the
imperial guard took away the censers
and sprinkling bowls—all that were
made of pure gold or silver.

16The bronze from the two pillars,
the Sea and the movable stands, which
Solomon had made for the temple of
the LORD, was more than could be
25:17 [l]1Ki 7:15-22
weighed. 17Each pillar[l] was twenty-seven
feet[a] high. The bronze capital on top
of one pillar was four and a half feet[b]
high and was decorated with a network
and pomegranates of bronze all around.
The other pillar, with its network, was
similar.

18The commander of the guard took
25:18 [m]1Ch 6:14; Ezr 7:1; Ne 11:11 [n]Jer 21:1; 29:25
as prisoners Seraiah[m] the chief priest,
Zephaniah[n] the priest next in rank and
the three doorkeepers. 19Of those still
in the city, he took the officer in charge
of the fighting men and five royal advisers. He also took the secretary who was
chief officer in charge of conscripting
the people of the land and sixty of his
men who were found in the city. 20Neb-
uzaradan the commander took them all
and brought them to the king of Babylon at Riblah. 21There at Riblah, in
the land of Hamath, the king had them
executed.

So Judah went into captivity, away
from her land.[o]
25:21 [o]Ge 12:7; Dt 28:64; Jos 23:13; 2Ki 23:27

22Nebuchadnezzar king of Babylon
appointed Gedaliah[p] son of Ahikam,
the son of Shaphan, to be over the
people he had left behind in Judah.
25:22 [p]Jer 39:14; 40:5,7
23When all the army officers and their
men heard that the king of Babylon
had appointed Gedaliah as governor,
they came to Gedaliah at Mizpah—Ishmael son of Nethaniah, Johanan son of
Kareah, Seraiah son of Tanhumeth the
Netophathite, Jaazaniah the son of the
Maacathite, and their men. 24Gedaliah
took an oath to reassure them and their
men. "Do not be afraid of the Babylonian officials," he said. "Settle down in
the land and serve the king of Babylon,
and it will go well with you."

25In the seventh month, however,
Ishmael son of Nethaniah, the son of
Elishama, who was of royal blood, came
with ten men and assassinated Gedaliah
and also the men of Judah and the Babylonians who were with him at Mizpah.
26At this, all the people from the least
to the greatest, together with the army
officers, fled to Egypt[q] for fear of the
Babylonians.
25:26 [q]Isa 30:2; Jer 43:7

Jehoiachin Released

27In the thirty-seventh year of the
exile of Jehoiachin king of Judah, in
the year Evil-Merodach[c] became king of
Babylon, he released Jehoiachin[r] from
25:27 [r]2Ki 24:12; Jer 52:31-34
prison on the twenty-seventh day of the
twelfth month. 28He spoke kindly to
him and gave him a seat of honor[s] high-
25:28 [s]Ezr 5:5; Ne 2:1; Da 2:48
er than those of the other kings who
were with him in Babylon. 29So Jehoiachin put aside his prison clothes and
for the rest of his life ate regularly at
25:29 [t]2Sa 9:7
the king's table.[t] 30Day by day the king
25:30 [u]Est 2:9; Jer 28:4
gave Jehoiachin a regular allowance as
long as he lived.[u]

[a] *17* Hebrew *eighteen cubits* (about 8.1 meters)
[b] *17* Hebrew *three cubits* (about 1.3 meters)
[c] *27* Also called *Amel-Marduk*

1 CHRONICLES

▸ AUTHORSHIP AND DATE

Ezra, according to Jewish tradition

c. 430 B.C.

▸ KEY THEMES

Large parts of both 1 and 2 Chronicles are dedicated to the lineage and dynasty of the leadership of the nation of Israel. First Chronicles specifically concerns itself with David and his rise to power and the enlarging of the borders of the country. First and Second Chronicles were originally one book. Both books virtually ignore the split-off of the northern kingdom and focus almost entirely on Judah. They are more positive in tone than their sister volumes of 1 and 2 Kings. In Chronicles the darker sides of David and Solomon are played down, while the later kings of the northern kingdom are shown in the worst possible light. First and Second Chronicles were written from a priestly point of view after the exile. The tone of both books is brisk, formal and filled with genealogies and other incidentals that may distract the reader who lacks appreciation for history. These books attempt to preserve the highest and holiest part of Israel's identity and suffrage. They focus on the temple—its building, its service to the nation and its restoration after the exile (described in the very closing verses of 2 Chronicles). Keeping the temple central in Israel's history is what we would expect from a recounting of truth written by a priest and scribe like Ezra.

▸ FRUIT OF THE SPIRIT IN 1 CHRONICLES

Love: After David had the ark brought into the newly acquired capital of Jerusalem, there were celebrations of devotion and grace. David sang a long psalm of thanksgiving during this celebration. He recalled the love of God for his people, saying, "Give thanks to the LORD, for he is good; his love endures forever" (16:34).

Joy: In preparation for the return of the ark, David built a great tent to house it. In response to the return of the ark, David created a psalm of thanks for God's goodness. That song of thanksgiving presaged the glory of the temple, where the ark would remain at the center of Israel's worship. The praise and thanksgiving offered in David's psalm is best exemplified by the following: "Cry out, 'Save us, O God our Savior; gather us and deliver us from the nations, that we may give thanks to your holy name, that we may glory in your praise'" (16:35).

Patience: God asked David to remain patient, for the building of the temple was not his to supervise. Waiting on the Lord sometimes means that the great achievements we dream of are to be given to our children. God said to David, "Solomon your son is the one who will build my house and my courts, for I have chosen him to be my son" (28:6). God's timing sometimes demands our waiting.

Goodness: Goodness is a word that often describes David's reign, and the Chronicler made this observation: "David reigned over all Israel, doing what was just and right for all his people" (18:14).

Faithfulness: David's charge to Solomon to build the temple was a charge to faithfulness. Surely it is in the heart of every godly father that his child be faithful to God: "Now, my son, the LORD be with you, and may you have success and build the house of the LORD your God, as he said you would" (22:11). It is clear that not only is our worship related to faithfulness, but our success in every spiritual arena of our lives is also related to it.

Self-Control: After David told Solomon that he was to build the temple, God gave David a mandate to be disciplined. It would have been easy for David to be less than enthusiastic about the work that his son was to do. But David, strong in self-discipline, encouraged Solomon to be self-controlled in the building of the temple. David said, "Be strong and courageous, and do the work" (28:20).

1:1 [a]Ge 5:1-32; Lk 3:36-38
1:2 [b]Ge 5:9 [c]Ge 5:12 [d]Ge 5:15
1:3 [e]Ge 5:18; Jude 1:14 [f]Ge 5:21 [g]Ge 5:25 [h]Ge 5:29
1:4 [i]Ge 6:10; 10:1 [j]Ge 5:32

Historical Records From Adam to Abraham

To Noah's Sons

1 Adam,[a] Seth, Enosh, 2Kenan,[b] Mahalalel,[c] Jared,[d] 3Enoch,[e] Methuselah,[f] Lamech,[g] Noah.[h]

4The sons of Noah:[a] [i]
Shem, Ham and Japheth.[j]

LOVE

ONE MAN'S FAMILY

1 Chronicles 1:4

God redeemed the world through a chain of children. Never consider the genealogies of the Bible boring. When you come to the family lists, salute. God's tale of earth's salvation is the story of one Man's family.

The Japhethites

5The sons[b] of Japheth:
Gomer, Magog, Madai, Javan, Tubal, Meshech and Tiras.
6The sons of Gomer:
Ashkenaz, Riphath[c] and Togarmah.
7The sons of Javan:
Elishah, Tarshish, the Kittim and the Rodanim.

The Hamites

8The sons of Ham:
Cush, Mizraim,[d] Put and Canaan.
9The sons of Cush:
Seba, Havilah, Sabta, Raamah and Sabteca.
The sons of Raamah:
Sheba and Dedan.
10Cush was the father[e] of
Nimrod, who grew to be a mighty warrior on earth.
11Mizraim was the father of
the Ludites, Anamites, Lehabites, Naphtuhites, 12Pathrusites, Casluhites (from whom the Philistines came) and Caphtorites.
13Canaan was the father of
Sidon his firstborn,[f] and of the Hittites, 14Jebusites, Amorites, Girgashites, 15Hivites, Arkites, Sinites, 16Arvadites, Zemarites and Hamathites.

The Semites

17The sons of Shem:
Elam, Asshur, Arphaxad, Lud and Aram.
The sons of Aram[g]:
Uz, Hul, Gether and Meshech.
18Arphaxad was the father of Shelah,
and Shelah the father of Eber.
19Two sons were born to Eber:
One was named Peleg,[h] because in his time the earth was divided; his brother was named Joktan.
20Joktan was the father of
Almodad, Sheleph, Hazarmaveth, Jerah, 21Hadoram, Uzal, Diklah, 22Obal,[i] Abimael, Sheba, 23Ophir, Havilah and Jobab. All these were sons of Joktan.

24Shem,[k] Arphaxad,[j] Shelah, 1:24 [k]Ge 10:21-25; Lk 3:34-36
25Eber, Peleg, Reu,
26Serug, Nahor, Terah
27and Abram (that is, Abraham).

The Family of Abraham

28The sons of Abraham:
Isaac and Ishmael.

Descendants of Hagar

29These were their descendants:
Nebaioth the firstborn of Ishmael, Kedar, Adbeel, Mibsam, 30Mishma, Dumah, Massa, Hadad, Tema, 31Jetur, Naphish and Kedemah. These were the sons of Ishmael.

Descendants of Keturah

32The sons born to Keturah, Abraham's concubine:[l] 1:32 [l]Ge 22:24
Zimran, Jokshan, Medan, Midian, Ishbak and Shuah.

[a]*4* Septuagint; Hebrew does not have *The sons of Noah:* [b]*5 Sons* may mean *descendants* or *successors* or *nations*; also in verses 6-10, 17 and 20. [c]*6* Many Hebrew manuscripts and Vulgate (see also Septuagint and Gen. 10:3); most Hebrew manuscripts *Diphath* [d]*8* That is, Egypt; also in verse 11 [e]*10 Father* may mean *ancestor* or *predecessor* or *founder*; also in verses 11, 13, 18 and 20. [f]*13* Or *of the Sidonians, the foremost* [g]*17* One Hebrew manuscript and some Septuagint manuscripts (see also Gen. 10:23); most Hebrew manuscripts do not have this line. [h]*19 Peleg* means *division.* [i]*22* Some Hebrew manuscripts and Syriac (see also Gen. 10:28); most Hebrew manuscripts *Ebal* [j]*24* Hebrew; some Septuagint manuscripts *Arphaxad, Cainan* (see also note at Gen. 11:10)

The sons of Jokshan:
1:32 Sheba and Dedan.[m]
[m]Ge 10:7

33 The sons of Midian:
Ephah, Epher, Hanoch, Abida and Eldaah.
All these were descendants of Keturah.

Descendants of Sarah

1:34 34 Abraham[n] was the father of Isaac.[o]
The sons of Isaac:
Esau and Israel.[p]
[n]Lk 3:34 [o]Ge 21:2-3; Mt 1:2; Ac 7:8 [p]Ge 17:5; 25:25-26

Esau's Sons

1:35 35 The sons of Esau:[q]
Eliphaz, Reuel,[r] Jeush, Jalam and Korah.
[q]Ge 36:19 [r]Ge 36:4

36 The sons of Eliphaz:
Teman, Omar, Zepho,[a] Gatam and Kenaz;
1:36 by Timna: Amalek.[b s]
[s]Ex 17:14

1:37 37 The sons of Reuel:[t]
Nahath, Zerah, Shammah and Mizzah.
[t]Ge 36:17

The People of Seir in Edom

38 The sons of Seir:
Lotan, Shobal, Zibeon, Anah, Dishon, Ezer and Dishan.

39 The sons of Lotan:
Hori and Homam. Timna was Lotan's sister.

40 The sons of Shobal:
Alvan,[c] Manahath, Ebal, Shepho and Onam.
The sons of Zibeon:
1:40 Aiah and Anah.[u]
[u]Ge 36:2

41 The son of Anah:
Dishon.
The sons of Dishon:
Hemdan,[d] Eshban, Ithran and Keran.

42 The sons of Ezer:
Bilhan, Zaavan and Akan.[e]
The sons of Dishan[f]:
Uz and Aran.

The Rulers of Edom

43 These were the kings who reigned in Edom before any Israelite king reigned[g]:
Bela son of Beor, whose city was named Dinhabah.

44 When Bela died, Jobab son of Zerah from Bozrah succeeded him as king.

45 When Jobab died, Husham from
1:45 the land of the Temanites[v] succeeded him as king.
[v]Ge 36:11

46 When Husham died, Hadad son of Bedad, who defeated Midian in the country of Moab, succeeded him as king. His city was named Avith.

47 When Hadad died, Samlah from Masrekah succeeded him as king.

48 When Samlah died, Shaul from Rehoboth on the river[h] succeeded him as king.

49 When Shaul died, Baal-Hanan son of Acbor succeeded him as king.

50 When Baal-Hanan died, Hadad succeeded him as king. His city was named Pau,[i] and his wife's name was Mehetabel daughter of Matred, the daughter of Me-Zahab. 51 Hadad also died.

The chiefs of Edom were:
Timna, Alvah, Jetheth, 52 Oholibamah, Elah, Pinon, 53 Kenaz, Teman, Mibzar, 54 Magdiel and Iram. These were the chiefs of Edom.

Israel's Sons

2 These were the sons of Israel:
Reuben, Simeon, Levi, Judah, Issachar, Zebulun, 2 Dan, Joseph, Benjamin, Naphtali, Gad and Asher.

Judah

To Hezron's Sons

2:3 3 The sons of Judah:[w]
Er, Onan and Shelah.[x] These three were born to him by a Ca-
[w]Ge 29:35; 38:2-10 [x]Ge 38:5

[a] *36* Many Hebrew manuscripts, some Septuagint manuscripts and Syriac (see also Gen. 36:11); most Hebrew manuscripts *Zephi* [b] *36* Some Septuagint manuscripts (see also Gen. 36:12); Hebrew *Gatam, Kenaz, Timna and Amalek* [c] *40* Many Hebrew manuscripts and some Septuagint manuscripts (see also Gen. 36:23); most Hebrew manuscripts *Alian* [d] *41* Many Hebrew manuscripts and some Septuagint manuscripts (see also Gen. 36:26); most Hebrew manuscripts *Hamran* [e] *42* Many Hebrew and Septuagint manuscripts (see also Gen. 36:27); most Hebrew manuscripts *Zaavan, Jaakan* [f] *42* Hebrew *Dishon,* a variant of *Dishan* [g] *43* Or *before an Israelite king reigned over them* [h] *48* Possibly the Euphrates [i] *50* Many Hebrew manuscripts, some Septuagint manuscripts, Vulgate and Syriac (see also Gen. 36:39); most Hebrew manuscripts *Pai*

naanite woman, the daughter of
2:3 [y]Ge 38:2 [z]Nu 26:19 Shua.[y] Er, Judah's firstborn, was
wicked in the LORD's sight; so
the LORD put him to death.[z]
2:4 [a]Ge 38:11-30 [b]Ge 11:31 [c]Ge 38:29 4Tamar,[a] Judah's daughter-in-
law,[b] bore him Perez[c] and Zerah.
Judah had five sons in all.

2:5 [d]Ge 46:12 [e]Nu 26:21 5 The sons of Perez:[d]
Hezron[e] and Hamul.
6 The sons of Zerah:
Zimri, Ethan, Heman, Calcol
and Darda[a]—five in all.
7 The son of Carmi:
2:7 [f]Jos 7:1 [g]Jos 6:18 Achar,[b][f] who brought trouble
on Israel by violating the ban on
taking devoted things.[c][g]
8 The son of Ethan:
Azariah.
2:9 [h]Nu 26:21 9 The sons born to Hezron[h] were:
Jerahmeel, Ram and Caleb.[d]

From Ram Son of Hezron

2:10 [i]Lk 3:32-33 [j]Ex 6:23 [k]Nu 1:7 10 Ram[i] was the father of
Amminadab,[j] and Amminadab
the father of Nahshon,[k] the
leader of the people of Judah.
11Nahshon was the father of
Salmon,[e] Salmon the father of
2:12 [l]Ru 2:1 [m]Ru 4:17 Boaz, 12Boaz[l] the father of Obed
and Obed the father of Jesse.[m]
13 Jesse[n] was the father of
2:13 [n]Ru 4:17 [o]1Sa 16:6 Eliab[o] his firstborn; the second
son was Abinadab, the third
Shimea, 14the fourth Nethanel,
the fifth Raddai, 15the sixth
Ozem and the seventh David.
2:16 [p]1Sa 26:6 [q]2Sa 2:18 [r]2Sa 2:13 16Their sisters were Zeruiah[p] and
Abigail. Zeruiah's[q] three sons
were Abishai, Joab[r] and Asahel.
17Abigail was the mother of
2:17 [s]2Sa 17:25 Amasa,[s] whose father was Jether
the Ishmaelite.

Caleb Son of Hezron

18 Caleb son of Hezron had children
by his wife Azubah (and by Jeri-
oth). These were her sons: Jesher,
Shobab and Ardon. 19When
2:19 [t]ver 42,50 Azubah died, Caleb[t] married
Ephrath, who bore him Hur.
20Hur was the father of Uri, and
2:20 [u]Ex 31:2 Uri the father of Bezalel.[u]
21 Later, Hezron lay with the daughter of Makir the father of Gil-
2:21 [v]Nu 27:1 ead[v] (he had married her when
he was sixty years old), and she
bore him Segub. 22Segub was
the father of Jair, who controlled
twenty-three towns in Gilead.
23(But Geshur and Aram cap-
tured Havvoth Jair,[f][w] as well 2:23 [w]Nu 32:41; Dt 3:14; Jos 13:30
as Kenath[x] with its surround- [x]Nu 32:42
ing settlements—sixty towns.)
All these were descendants of
Makir the father of Gilead.

24 After Hezron died in Caleb Ephrathah, Abijah the wife of Hezron
bore him Ashhur[y] the father[g] of 2:24 [y]1Ch 4:5
Tekoa.

Jerahmeel Son of Hezron

25 The sons of Jerahmeel the first-
born of Hezron:
Ram his firstborn, Bunah, Oren,
Ozem and[h] Ahijah. 26Jerahmeel
had another wife, whose name
was Atarah; she was the mother
of Onam.
27 The sons of Ram the firstborn of
Jerahmeel:
Maaz, Jamin and Eker.
28 The sons of Onam:
Shammai and Jada.
The sons of Shammai:
Nadab and Abishur.
29 Abishur's wife was named Abihail,
who bore him Ahban and
Molid.
30 The sons of Nadab:
Seled and Appaim. Seled died
without children.
31 The son of Appaim:
Ishi, who was the father of
Sheshan.
Sheshan was the father of Ahlai.
32 The sons of Jada, Shammai's
brother:
Jether and Jonathan. Jether died
without children.
33 The sons of Jonathan:
Peleth and Zaza.
These were the descendants of
Jerahmeel.

[a]*6* Many Hebrew manuscripts, some Septuagint manuscripts and Syriac (see also 1 Kings 4:31); most Hebrew manuscripts *Dara* [b]*7 Achar* means *trouble*; *Achar* is called *Achan* in Joshua. [c]*7* The Hebrew term refers to the irrevocable giving over of things or persons to the LORD, often by totally destroying them. [d]*9* Hebrew *Kelubai,* a variant of *Caleb* [e]*11* Septuagint (see also Ruth 4:21); Hebrew *Salma* [f]*23* Or *captured the settlements of Jair* [g]*24 Father* may mean *civic leader* or *military leader*; also in verses 42, 45, 49-52 and possibly elsewhere. [h]*25* Or *Oren and Ozem, by*

34 Sheshan had no sons—only daughters.
He had an Egyptian servant named Jarha. 35 Sheshan gave his daughter in marriage to his servant Jarha, and she bore him Attai.
36 Attai was the father of Nathan,
Nathan the father of Zabad,[z]
37 Zabad the father of Ephlal,
Ephlal the father of Obed,
38 Obed the father of Jehu,
Jehu the father of Azariah,
39 Azariah the father of Helez,
Helez the father of Eleasah,
40 Eleasah the father of Sismai,
Sismai the father of Shallum,
41 Shallum the father of Jekamiah,
and Jekamiah the father of Elishama.

2:36 [z]1Ch 11:41

The Clans of Caleb

42 The sons of Caleb[a] the brother of Jerahmeel:
Mesha his firstborn, who was the father of Ziph, and his son Mareshah,[a] who was the father of Hebron.
43 The sons of Hebron:
Korah, Tappuah, Rekem and Shema. 44 Shema was the father of Raham, and Raham the father of Jorkeam. Rekem was the father of Shammai. 45 The son of Shammai was Maon,[b] and Maon was the father of Beth Zur.[c]
46 Caleb's concubine Ephah was the mother of Haran, Moza and Gazez. Haran was the father of Gazez.
47 The sons of Jahdai:
Regem, Jotham, Geshan, Pelet, Ephah and Shaaph.
48 Caleb's concubine Maacah was the mother of Sheber and Tirhanah. 49 She also gave birth to Shaaph the father of Madmannah[d] and to Sheva the father of Macbenah and Gibea. Caleb's daughter was Acsah.[e] 50 These were the descendants of Caleb.

2:42 [a]ver 19
2:45 [b]Jos 15:55 [c]Jos 15:58
2:49 [d]Jos 15:31 [e]Jos 15:16

The sons of Hur[f] the firstborn of Ephrathah:
Shobal the father of Kiriath Jearim,[g] 51 Salma the father of Bethlehem, and Hareph the father of Beth Gader.
52 The descendants of Shobal the father of Kiriath Jearim were:
Haroeh, half the Manahathites, 53 and the clans of Kiriath Jearim: the Ithrites,[h] Puthites, Shumathites and Mishraites. From these descended the Zorathites and Eshtaolites.
54 The descendants of Salma:
Bethlehem, the Netophathites,[i] Atroth Beth Joab, half the Manahathites, the Zorites, 55 and the clans of scribes[b] who lived at Jabez: the Tirathites, Shimeathites and Sucathites. These are the Kenites[j] who came from Hammath,[k] the father of the house of Recab.[c l]

2:50 [f]1Ch 4:4 [g]ver 19
2:53 [h]2Sa 23:38
2:54 [i]Ezr 2:22; Ne 7:26; 12:28
2:55 [j]Ge 15:19; Jdg 1:16; Jdg 4:11 [k]Jos 19:35 [l]2Ki 10:15,23; Jer 35:2-19

The Sons of David

3 These were the sons of David[m] born to him in Hebron:
The firstborn was Amnon the son of Ahinoam of Jezreel;[n]
the second, Daniel the son of Abigail[o] of Carmel;
2 the third, Absalom the son of Maacah daughter of Talmai king of Geshur;
the fourth, Adonijah[p] the son of Haggith;
3 the fifth, Shephatiah the son of Abital;
and the sixth, Ithream, by his wife Eglah.
4 These six were born to David in Hebron,[q] where he reigned seven years and six months.[r]
David reigned in Jerusalem thirty-three years, 5 and these were the children born to him there:
Shammua,[d] Shobab, Nathan and Solomon. These four were by Bathsheba[e s] daughter of Ammiel. 6 There were also Ibhar, Elishua,[f] Eliphelet, 7 Nogah, Nepheg, Japhia, 8 Elishama, Eliada and Eliphelet—nine in all.

3:1 [m]1Ch 14:3; 28:5 [n]Jos 15:56 [o]1Sa 25:42
3:2 [p]1Ki 2:22
3:4 [q]2Sa 5:4; 1Ch 29:27 [r]2Sa 2:11; 5:5
3:5 [s]2Sa 11:3; 12:24

[a] *42* The meaning of the Hebrew for this phrase is uncertain. [b] *55* Or *of the Sopherites* [c] *55* Or *father of Beth Recab* [d] *5* Hebrew *Shimea,* a variant of *Shammua* [e] *5* One Hebrew manuscript and Vulgate (see also Septuagint and 2 Samuel 11:3); most Hebrew manuscripts *Bathshua* [f] *6* Two Hebrew manuscripts (see also 2 Samuel 5:15 and 1 Chron. 14:5); most Hebrew manuscripts *Elishama*

9 All these were the sons of David, besides his sons by his concubines. And Tamar[t] was their sister.[u]

The Kings of Judah

10 Solomon's son was Rehoboam,[v]
Abijah his son,
Asa his son,
Jehoshaphat[w] his son,
11 Jehoram[a x] his son,
Ahaziah[y] his son,
Joash[z] his son,
12 Amaziah[a] his son,
Azariah his son,
Jotham[b] his son,
13 Ahaz[c] his son,
Hezekiah[d] his son,
Manasseh[e] his son,
14 Amon[f] his son,
Josiah[g] his son.
15 The sons of Josiah:
Johanan the firstborn,
Jehoiakim[h] the second son,
Zedekiah[i] the third,
Shallum[j] the fourth.
16 The successors of Jehoiakim:
Jehoiachin[b k] his son,
and Zedekiah.[l]

The Royal Line After the Exile

17 The descendants of Jehoiachin the captive:
Shealtiel[m] his son, 18 Malkiram,
Pedaiah, Shenazzar,[n] Jekamiah,
Hoshama and Nedabiah.[o]
19 The sons of Pedaiah:
Zerubbabel[p] and Shimei.
The sons of Zerubbabel:
Meshullam and Hananiah.
Shelomith was their sister.
20 There were also five others:
Hashubah, Ohel, Berekiah, Hasadiah and Jushab-Hesed.
21 The descendants of Hananiah:
Pelatiah and Jeshaiah, and the sons of Rephaiah, of Arnan, of Obadiah and of Shecaniah.
22 The descendants of Shecaniah:
Shemaiah and his sons:
Hattush,[q] Igal, Bariah, Neariah and Shaphat—six in all.
23 The sons of Neariah:
Elioenai, Hizkiah and Azrikam—three in all.
24 The sons of Elioenai:
Hodaviah, Eliashib, Pelaiah, Akkub, Johanan, Delaiah and Anani—seven in all.

3:9 [t]2Sa 13:1 [u]1Ch 14:4
3:10 [v]1Ki 11:43; 14:21-31; 2Ch 12:16 [w]2Ch 17:1-21:3
3:11 [x]2Ki 8:16-24; 2Ch 21:1 [y]2Ch 22:1-10 [z]2Ki 11:1-12:21
3:12 [a]2Ki 14:1-22; 2Ch 25:1-28 [b]Isa 1:1; Hos 1:1; Mic 1:1
3:13 [c]2Ki 16:1-20; 2Ch 28:1; Isa 7:1 [d]2Ki 18:1-20:21; 2Ch 29:1; Jer 26:19 [e]2Ch 33:1
3:14 [f]2Ki 21:19-26; 2Ch 33:21; Zep 1:1 [g]2Ch 34:1; Jer 1:2; 3:6; 25:3
3:15 [h]2Ki 23:34 [i]Jer 37:1 [j]2Ki 23:31
3:16 [k]2Ki 24:6,8; Mt 1:11 [l]2Ki 24:18
3:17 [m]Ezr 3:2
3:18 [n]Ezr 1:8; 5:14 [o]Jer 22:30
3:19 [p]Ezr 2:2; 3:2; 5:2; Ne 7:7; 12:1; Hag 1:1; 2:2; Zec 4:6
3:22 [q]Ezr 8:2-3

Other Clans of Judah

4 The descendants of Judah:[r]
Perez, Hezron,[s] Carmi, Hur and Shobal.
2 Reaiah son of Shobal was the father of Jahath, and Jahath the father of Ahumai and Lahad. These were the clans of the Zorathites.
3 These were the sons[c] of Etam:
Jezreel, Ishma and Idbash. Their sister was named Hazzelelponi.
4 Penuel was the father of Gedor, and Ezer the father of Hushah.
These were the descendants of Hur,[t] the firstborn of Ephrathah and father[d] of Bethlehem.[u]
5 Ashhur[v] the father of Tekoa had two wives, Helah and Naarah.
6 Naarah bore him Ahuzzam, Hepher, Temeni and Haahashtari. These were the descendants of Naarah.
7 The sons of Helah:
Zereth, Zohar, Ethnan, 8 and Koz, who was the father of Anub and Hazzobebah and of the clans of Aharhel son of Harum.

9 Jabez was more honorable than his
brothers. His mother had named him
Jabez,[e] saying, "I gave birth to him in
pain." 10 Jabez cried out to the God of
Israel, "Oh, that you would bless me
and enlarge my territory! Let your hand
be with me, and keep me from harm so
that I will be free from pain." And God
granted his request.

11 Kelub, Shuhah's brother, was the father of Mehir, who was the father of Eshton. 12 Eshton was the father of Beth Rapha, Paseah and Tehinnah the father of Ir Nahash.[f] These were the men of Recah.

13 The sons of Kenaz:
Othniel[w] and Seraiah.

4:1 [r]Ge 29:35; 46:12; 1Ch 2:3 [s]Nu 26:21 [t]1Ch 2:50 [u]Ru 1:19
4:5 [v]1Ch 2:24
4:13 [w]Jos 15:17

[a] *11* Hebrew *Joram,* a variant of *Jehoram*
[b] *16* Hebrew *Jeconiah,* a variant of *Jehoiachin*; also in verse 17
[c] *3* Some Septuagint manuscripts (see also Vulgate); Hebrew *father*
[d] *4 Father* may mean *civic leader* or *military leader*; also in verses 12, 14, 17, 18 and possibly elsewhere.
[e] *9 Jabez* sounds like the Hebrew for *pain.*
[f] *12* Or *of the city of Nahash*

DAY 4 FOUR

▸ GOODNESS AND MY SERVICE TO OTHERS

1 Chronicles 4:9–10

"Reputation, reputation, reputation," mutters Shakespeare's Cassio. Certainly the importance of reputation is reflected in this short Scripture passage. Nearly hidden among the list of names is the name of one of God's followers—Jabez. He must have made quite an impact on those around him, for he is specifically mentioned by the Chronicler in this book.

In our day the church is ever counting on people of reputation to have an effective ministry. The goodness that is the basis of our reputation must come from the Bible. What does this ancient yet remarkably up-to-date book have to say about our behavior? One cannot read very far before one discovers that nearly every page is a manual of instruction dedicated to our behavior. From the Ten Commandments to the Sermon on the Mount to the hundreds of other verses instructing those who would become good, we find a guide for our behavior and examples for us to follow.

And, as we know, becoming good is the foreword to becoming holy. Our goodness will be a light to others and lead them closer to God. How do we become good? The Word will guide us.

I have hidden your word in my heart
that I might not sin against you.
(Psalm 119:11)

With my lips I recount
all the laws that come from your mouth.
I rejoice in following your statutes
as one rejoices in great riches.
(vv. 13–14)

Give me understanding, and I will keep
your law
and obey it with all my heart.
(v. 34)

This Word-saturated disciple is a person of reputation. This is the kind of person God seeks to be a servant to others.

To begin a study on the topic of Goodness, the Virtue of the Written Word of God, turn to the home page on page 918.

The sons of Othniel:
Hathath and Meonothai.[a] 14 Meonothai was the father of Ophrah.
Seraiah was the father of Joab,
the father of Ge Harashim.[b] It was called this because its people were craftsmen.
15 The sons of Caleb son of Jephunneh:
Iru, Elah and Naam.
The son of Elah:
Kenaz.
16 The sons of Jehallelel:
Ziph, Ziphah, Tiria and Asarel.
17 The sons of Ezrah:
Jether, Mered, Epher and Jalon.
One of Mered's wives gave birth
to Miriam,[x] Shammai and Ishbah the father of Eshtemoa. 4:17 [x]Ex 15:20
18 (His Judean wife gave birth to
Jered the father of Gedor, Heber
the father of Soco, and Jekuthiel the father of Zanoah.[y]) These 4:18 [y]Jos 15:34
were the children of Pharaoh's
daughter Bithiah, whom Mered
had married.
19 The sons of Hodiah's wife, the sister of Naham:
the father of Keilah[z] the Garmite, and Eshtemoa the Maacathite.[a] 4:19 [z]Jos 15:44 [a]Dt 3:14
20 The sons of Shimon:
Amnon, Rinnah, Ben-Hanan and Tilon.
The descendants of Ishi:
Zoheth and Ben-Zoheth.
21 The sons of Shelah[b] son of Judah: 4:21 [b]Ge 38:5
Er the father of Lecah, Laadah
the father of Mareshah and the
clans of the linen workers at
Beth Ashbea, 22 Jokim, the men
of Cozeba, and Joash and Saraph, who ruled in Moab and
Jashubi Lehem. (These records
are from ancient times.) 23 They
were the potters who lived at Netaim and Gederah; they stayed
there and worked for the king.

Simeon

24 The descendants of Simeon:[c] 4:24 [c]Ge 29:33 [d]Nu 26:12
Nemuel, Jamin, Jarib,[d] Zerah
and Shaul;

[a]*13* Some Septuagint manuscripts and Vulgate; Hebrew does not have *and Meonothai.*
[b]*14 Ge Harashim* means *valley of craftsmen.*

25 Shallum was Shaul's son, Mibsam
his son and Mishma his son.
26 The descendants of Mishma:
Hammuel his son, Zaccur his
son and Shimei his son.
27 Shimei had sixteen sons and six
daughters, but his brothers did not
have many children; so their entire
clan did not become as numerous as
4:28 the people of Judah. 28 They lived in
[e]Ge 21:14 Beersheba,[e] Moladah,[f] Hazar Shual,
[f]Jos 15:26 29 Bilhah, Ezem,[g] Tolad, 30 Bethuel,
4:29 Hormah,[h] Ziklag, 31 Beth Marcaboth,
[g]Jos 15:29 Hazar Susim, Beth Biri and Shaaraim.[i]
4:30 These were their towns until the reign
[h]Nu 14:45 of David. 32 Their surrounding villages
4:31 were Etam, Ain,[j] Rimmon, Token and
[i]Jos 15:36 Ashan[k]—five towns— 33 and all the
4:32 [j]Nu 34:11 villages around these towns as far as
[k]Jos 15:42 Baalath.[a] These were their settlements.
And they kept a genealogical record.

34 Meshobab, Jamlech, Joshah son
of Amaziah, 35 Joel, Jehu son of
Joshibiah, the son of Seraiah, the
son of Asiel, 36 also Elioenai, Jaa-
kobah, Jeshohaiah, Asaiah, Adiel,
Jesimiel, Benaiah, 37 and Ziza son
of Shiphi, the son of Allon, the
son of Jedaiah, the son of Shimri,
the son of Shemaiah.

38 The men listed above by name were
leaders of their clans. Their families
4:39 increased greatly, 39 and they went to
[l]Jos 15:58 the outskirts of Gedor[l] to the east of
the valley in search of pasture for their
flocks. 40 They found rich, good pasture,
4:40 and the land was spacious, peaceful and
[m]Jdg 18:7-10 quiet.[m] Some Hamites had lived there
formerly.
41 The men whose names were listed
came in the days of Hezekiah king of Judah. They attacked the Hamites in their
4:41 dwellings and also the Meunites[n] who
[n]2Ch 20:1; 26:7 were there and completely destroyed[b]
them, as is evident to this day. Then
they settled in their place, because there
was pasture for their flocks. 42 And five
hundred of these Simeonites, led by
Pelatiah, Neariah, Rephaiah and Uzziel,
4:42 the sons of Ishi, invaded the hill coun-
[o]Ge 14:6 try of Seir.[o] 43 They killed the remaining
4:43 Amalekites[p] who had escaped, and they
[p]1Sa 15:8; 30:17; 2Sa 8:12; Est 3:1; 9:16 have lived there to this day.

Reuben

5:1 [q]Ge 29:32 5 The sons of Reuben[q] the firstborn
of Israel (he was the firstborn, but
when he defiled his father's marriage
bed,[r] his rights as firstborn were given 5:1 [r]Ge 35:22; 49:4
to the sons of Joseph[s] son of Israel;[t] [s]Ge 48:16,22; 49:26
so he could not be listed in the gene-
alogical record in accordance with his [t]Ge 48:5 [u]1Ch 26:10
birthright,[u] 2 and though Judah[v] was the
strongest of his brothers and a ruler[w] 5:2 [v]Ge 49:10,12
came from him, the rights of the first- [w]1Sa 9:16; 12:12;
born[x] belonged to Joseph)— 3 the sons 2Sa 6:21;
of Reuben[y] the firstborn of Israel: 1Ch 11:2; 2Ch 7:18;
Hanoch, Pallu,[z] Hezron and Car- Ps 60:7;
mi. Mic 5:2; Mt 2:6
4 The descendants of Joel: [x]Ge 25:31
Shemaiah his son, Gog his son, 5:3
Shimei his son, 5 Micah his son, [y]Ge 29:32; 46:9; Ex 6:14;
Reaiah his son, Baal his son, Nu 26:5-11 [z]Nu 26:5
6 and Beerah his son, whom Tig-
lath-Pileser[c][a] king of Assyria 5:6 [a]ver 26; 2Ki
took into exile. Beerah was a 15:19; 16:10;
leader of the Reubenites. 2Ch 28:20
7 Their relatives by clans,[b] listed 5:7 [b]ver 17
according to their genealogical
records:
Jeiel the chief, Zechariah, 8 and
Bela son of Azaz, the son of
Shema, the son of Joel. They
settled in the area from Aroer[c] 5:8 [c]Nu 32:34
to Nebo and Baal Meon. 9 To
the east they occupied the land
up to the edge of the desert that
extends to the Euphrates River,
because their livestock had in- 5:9
creased in Gilead.[d] [d]Nu 32:26; Jos 22:9
10 During Saul's reign they waged
war against the Hagrites,[e] who were 5:10 [e]ver 18-21
defeated at their hands; they occu-
pied the dwellings of the Hagrites
throughout the entire region east
of Gilead.

Gad

11 The Gadites[f] lived next to them in 5:11 [f]Jos 13:24-28
Bashan, as far as Salecah:[g] [g]Dt 3:10; Jos 13:11
12 Joel was the chief, Shapham the
second, then Janai and Shaphat,
in Bashan.
13 Their relatives, by families, were:
Michael, Meshullam, Sheba, Jo-
rai, Jacan, Zia and Eber—seven
in all.
14 These were the sons of Abihail
son of Huri, the son of Jaroah,

[a]*33* Some Septuagint manuscripts (see also Joshua 19:8); Hebrew *Baal* [b]*41* The Hebrew term refers to the irrevocable giving over of things or persons to the LORD, often by totally destroying them.
[c]*6* Hebrew *Tilgath-Pilneser,* a variant of *Tiglath-Pileser*; also in verse 26

the son of Gilead, the son of Michael, the son of Jeshishai, the son of Jahdo, the son of Buz.
[15]Ahi son of Abdiel, the son of Guni, was head of their family.
[16]The Gadites lived in Gilead, in Bashan and its outlying villages, and on all the pasturelands of Sharon as far as they extended.

[17]All these were entered in the genealogical records during the reigns of Jotham[h] king of Judah and Jeroboam[i] king of Israel.

5:17 [h]2Ki 15:32 [i]2Ki 14:16,28

[18]The Reubenites, the Gadites and the half-tribe of Manasseh had 44,760 men ready for military service[j]—able-bodied men who could handle shield and sword, who could use a bow, and who were trained for battle. [19]They waged war against the Hagrites, Jetur,[k] Naphish and Nodab. [20]They were helped[l] in fighting them, and God handed the Hagrites and all their allies over to them, because they cried[m] out to him during the battle. He answered their prayers, because they trusted[n] in him. [21]They seized the livestock of the Hagrites—fifty thousand camels, two hundred fifty thousand sheep and two thousand donkeys. They also took one hundred thousand people captive, [22]and many others fell slain, because the battle[o] was God's. And they occupied the land until the exile.[p]

5:18 [j]Nu 1:3
5:19 [k]ver 10; Ge 25:15; 1Ch 1:31
5:20 [l]Ps 37:40 [m]1Ki 8:44; 2Ch 13:14; 14:11; Ps 20:7-9; 22:5 [n]Ps 26:1; Da 6:23
5:22 [o]2Ch 32:8 [p]2Ki 15:29; 17:6

The Half-Tribe of Manasseh

[23]The people of the half-tribe of Manasseh were numerous; they settled in the land from Bashan to Baal Hermon, that is, to Senir (Mount Hermon).[q]

[24]These were the heads of their families: Epher, Ishi, Eliel, Azriel, Jeremiah, Hodaviah and Jahdiel. They were brave warriors, famous men, and heads of their families. [25]But they were unfaithful[r] to the God of their fathers and prostituted[s] themselves to the gods of the peoples of the land, whom God had destroyed before them. [26]So the God of Israel stirred up the spirit of Pul[t] king of Assyria (that is, Tiglath-Pileser[u] king of Assyria), who took the Reubenites, the Gadites and the half-tribe of Manasseh into exile. He took them to Halah,[v] Habor, Hara and the river of Gozan, where they are to this day.

5:23 [q]Dt 3:8,9; SS 4:8
5:25 [r]Dt 32:15-18; 2Ki 17:7; 1Ch 9:1; 2Ch 26:16 [s]Ex 34:15
5:26 [t]2Ki 15:19 [u]2Ki 15:29 [v]2Ki 17:6; 18:11

Levi

6 The sons of Levi:[w]
Gershon, Kohath and Merari.
[2]The sons of Kohath:
Amram, Izhar, Hebron and Uzziel.
[3]The children of Amram:
Aaron, Moses and Miriam.
The sons of Aaron:
Nadab, Abihu,[x] Eleazar and Ithamar.
[4]Eleazar was the father of Phinehas,
Phinehas the father of Abishua,
[5]Abishua the father of Bukki,
Bukki the father of Uzzi,
[6]Uzzi the father of Zerahiah,
Zerahiah the father of Meraioth,
[7]Meraioth the father of Amariah,
Amariah the father of Ahitub,
[8]Ahitub the father of Zadok,[y]
Zadok the father of Ahimaaz,
[9]Ahimaaz the father of Azariah,
Azariah the father of Johanan,
[10]Johanan the father of Azariah[z] (it was he who served as priest in the temple Solomon built in Jerusalem),
[11]Azariah the father of Amariah,
Amariah the father of Ahitub,
[12]Ahitub the father of Zadok,
Zadok the father of Shallum,
[13]Shallum the father of Hilkiah,[a]
Hilkiah the father of Azariah,
[14]Azariah the father of Seraiah,[b]
and Seraiah the father of Jehozadak.

[15]Jehozadak[c] was deported when the LORD sent Judah and Jerusalem into exile by the hand of Nebuchadnezzar.

[16]The sons of Levi:[d]
Gershon,[a] Kohath and Merari.[e]
[17]These are the names of the sons of Gershon:
Libni and Shimei.
[18]The sons of Kohath:
Amram, Izhar, Hebron and Uzziel.
[19]The sons of Merari:[f]
Mahli and Mushi.
These are the clans of the Levites

6:1 [w]Ge 46:11; Ex 6:16; Nu 26:57; 1Ch 23:6
6:3 [x]Lev 10:1
6:8 [y]2Sa 8:17; 15:27; Ezr 7:2
6:10 [z]1Ki 4:2; 6:1; 2Ch 3:1; 26:17-18
6:13 [a]2Ki 22:1-20; 2Ch 34:9; 35:8
6:14 [b]2Ki 25:18; Ezr 2:2; Ne 11:11
6:15 [c]2Ki 25:18; Ne 12:1; Hag 1:1,14; 2:2,4; Zec 6:11
6:16 [d]Ge 29:34; Ex 6:16; Nu 3:17-20 [e]Nu 26:57
6:19 [f]Ge 46:11; 1Ch 23:21; 24:26

[a]*16* Hebrew *Gershom,* a variant of *Gershon;* also in verses 17, 20, 43, 62 and 71

listed according to their fathers:
20 Of Gershon:
Libni his son, Jehath his son,
Zimmah his son, 21 Joah his son,
Iddo his son, Zerah his son
and Jeatherai his son.
22 The descendants of Kohath:
6:22 [g]Ex 6:24
Amminadab his son, Korah[g] his son,
Assir his son, 23 Elkanah his son,
Ebiasaph his son, Assir his son,
6:24 [h]1Ch 15:5
24 Tahath his son, Uriel[h] his son,
Uzziah his son and Shaul his son.
25 The descendants of Elkanah:
Amasai, Ahimoth,
26 Elkanah his son,[a] Zophai his son,
Nahath his son, 27 Eliab his son,
Jeroham his son, Elkanah[i] his son
6:27 [i]1Sa 1:1 [j]1Sa 1:20
and Samuel[j] his son.[b]
28 The sons of Samuel:
6:28 [k]ver 33; 1Sa 8:2
Joel[c][k] the firstborn
and Abijah the second son.
29 The descendants of Merari:
Mahli, Libni his son,
Shimei his son, Uzzah his son,
30 Shimea his son, Haggiah his son
and Asaiah his son.

JOY

PRAISE IS THE ANTHEM OF PEACE

1 Chronicles 6:31–46

Our joy is in our music. Here are the names of the men David put in charge of praise. The nation that sings to God rarely does so while thinking about other gods.

The Temple Musicians

6:31 [l]1Ch 25:1; 2Ch 29:25-26; Ne 12:45 [m]1Ch 9:33; 15:19; Ezr 3:10; Ps 68:25

31 These are the men[l] David put in
charge of the music[m] in the house of the
LORD after the ark came to rest there.
32 They ministered with music before
the tabernacle, the Tent of Meeting,
until Solomon built the temple of the
LORD in Jerusalem. They performed
their duties according to the regulations
laid down for them.
33 Here are the men who served, together with their sons:

From the Kohathites:
6:33 [n]1Ki 4:31; 1Ch 15:17; 25:1 [o]ver 28
Heman,[n] the musician,
the son of Joel,[o] the son of Samuel,
6:34 [p]1Sa 1:1
34 the son of Elkanah,[p] the son of Jeroham,
the son of Eliel, the son of Toah,
35 the son of Zuph, the son of Elkanah,
the son of Mahath, the son of Amasai,
36 the son of Elkanah, the son of Joel,
the son of Azariah, the son of Zephaniah,
37 the son of Tahath, the son of Assir,
the son of Ebiasaph, the son of Korah,[q]
6:37 [q]Ex 6:24
38 the son of Izhar,[r] the son of Kohath,
6:38 [r]Ex 6:21
the son of Levi, the son of Israel;
39 and Heman's associate Asaph,[s] who served at his right hand:
6:39 [s]1Ch 25:1,9; 2Ch 29:13; Ne 11:17 [t]1Ch 15:17
Asaph son of Berekiah, the son of Shimea,[t]
40 the son of Michael, the son of Baaseiah,[d]
the son of Malkijah, 41 the son of Ethni,
the son of Zerah, the son of Adaiah,
42 the son of Ethan, the son of Zimmah,
the son of Shimei, 43 the son of Jahath,
the son of Gershon, the son of Levi;
44 and from their associates, the Merarites, at his left hand:
Ethan son of Kishi, the son of Abdi,
the son of Malluch, 45 the son of Hashabiah,
the son of Amaziah, the son of Hilkiah,

[a]*26* Some Hebrew manuscripts, Septuagint and Syriac; most Hebrew manuscripts *Ahimoth* [26]*and Elkanah. The sons of Elkanah:* [b]*27* Some Septuagint manuscripts (see also 1 Samuel 1:19,20 and 1 Chron. 6:33,34); Hebrew does not have *and Samuel his son.* [c]*28* Some Septuagint manuscripts and Syriac (see also 1 Samuel 8:2 and 1 Chron. 6:33); Hebrew does not have *Joel.* [d]*40* Most Hebrew manuscripts; some Hebrew manuscripts, one Septuagint manuscript and Syriac *Maaseiah*

46 the son of Amzi, the son of
Bani,
the son of Shemer, 47 the son of
Mahli,
the son of Mushi, the son of
Merari,
the son of Levi.

6:48 [u]1Ch 23:32

48 Their fellow Levites[u] were assigned
to all the other duties of the tabernacle, the house of God. 49 But Aaron and
his descendants were the ones who presented offerings on the altar[v] of burnt
offering and on the altar of incense[w]
in connection with all that was done
in the Most Holy Place, making atonement for Israel, in accordance with all
that Moses the servant of God had commanded.

6:49 [v]Ex 27:1-8 [w]Ex 30:1-7, 10; 2Ch 26:18

50 These were the descendants of
Aaron:
Eleazar his son, Phinehas his
son,
Abishua his son, 51 Bukki his
son,
Uzzi his son, Zerahiah his son,
52 Meraioth his son, Amariah his
son,
Ahitub his son, 53 Zadok[x] his son
and Ahimaaz his son.

6:53 [x]2Sa 8:17

54 These were the locations of their
settlements[y] allotted as their territory
(they were assigned to the descendants
of Aaron who were from the Kohathite clan, because the first lot was for
them):
55 They were given Hebron in
Judah with its surrounding pasturelands. 56 But the fields and villages around the city were given to
Caleb son of Jephunneh.[z]
57 So the descendants of Aaron
were given Hebron (a city of refuge), and Libnah,[a] [a] Jattir,[b] Eshtemoa, 58 Hilen, Debir,[c] 59 Ashan,[d]
Juttah[b] and Beth Shemesh, together with their pasturelands. 60 And
from the tribe of Benjamin they
were given Gibeon,[c] Geba, Alemeth and Anathoth,[e] together with
their pasturelands.
These towns, which were distributed among the Kohathite clans,
were thirteen in all.
61 The rest of Kohath's descendants
were allotted ten towns from the clans
of half the tribe of Manasseh.

6:54 [y]Nu 31:10
6:56 [z]Jos 14:13; 15:13
6:57 [a]Nu 33:20 [b]Jos 15:48
6:58 [c]Jos 10:3
6:59 [d]Jos 15:42
6:60 [e]Jer 1:1

62 The descendants of Gershon, clan
by clan, were allotted thirteen towns
from the tribes of Issachar, Asher and
Naphtali, and from the part of the tribe
of Manasseh that is in Bashan.
63 The descendants of Merari, clan by
clan, were allotted twelve towns from
the tribes of Reuben, Gad and Zebulun.
64 So the Israelites gave the Levites
these towns[f] and their pasturelands.
65 From the tribes of Judah, Simeon and
Benjamin they allotted the previously
named towns.
66 Some of the Kohathite clans were
given as their territory towns from the
tribe of Ephraim.
67 In the hill country of Ephraim
they were given Shechem (a city of
refuge), and Gezer,[d] [g] 68 Jokmeam,[h]
Beth Horon,[i] 69 Aijalon[j] and Gath
Rimmon,[k] together with their pasturelands.
70 And from half the tribe of
Manasseh the Israelites gave Aner
and Bileam, together with their
pasturelands, to the rest of the Kohathite clans.

6:64 [f]Nu 35:1-8; Jos 21:3, 41-42
6:67 [g]Jos 10:33
6:68 [h]1Ki 4:12 [i]Jos 10:10
6:69 [j]Jos 10:12 [k]Jos 19:45

71 The Gershonites[l] received the following:
From the clan of the half-tribe of
Manasseh
they received Golan in Bashan[m]
and also Ashtaroth, together
with their pasturelands;
72 from the tribe of Issachar
they received Kedesh, Daberath,[n] 73 Ramoth and Anem, together with their pasturelands;
74 from the tribe of Asher
they received Mashal, Abdon,[o]
75 Hukok[p] and Rehob,[q] together
with their pasturelands;
76 and from the tribe of Naphtali
they received Kedesh in Galilee, Hammon[r] and Kiriathaim,[s]
together with their pasturelands.

6:71 [l]1Ch 23:7 [m]Jos 20:8
6:72 [n]Jos 19:12
6:74 [o]Jos 19:28
6:75 [p]Jos 19:34 [q]Nu 13:21
6:76 [r]Jos 19:28 [s]Nu 32:37

77 The Merarites (the rest of the Levites) received the following:
From the tribe of Zebulun

[a]57 See Joshua 21:13; Hebrew *given the cities of refuge: Hebron, Libnah.* [b]59 Syriac (see also Septuagint and Joshua 21:16); Hebrew does not have *Juttah.* [c]60 See Joshua 21:17; Hebrew does not have *Gibeon.* [d]67 See Joshua 21:21; Hebrew *given the cities of refuge: Shechem, Gezer.*

they received Jokneam, Kartah,[a]
Rimmono and Tabor, together
with their pasturelands;
78 from the tribe of Reuben across
the Jordan east of Jericho
they received Bezer[t] in the desert, Jahzah, 79 Kedemoth[u] and
Mephaath, together with their
pasturelands;
80 and from the tribe of Gad
they received Ramoth in Gilead,[v] Mahanaim,[w] 81 Heshbon
and Jazer,[x] together with their
pasturelands.[y]

6:78 [t]Jos 20:8
6:79 [u]Dt 2:26
6:80 [v]Jos 20:8 [w]Ge 32:2
6:81 [x]Nu 21:32 [y]2Ch 11:14

Issachar

7 The sons of Issachar:[z]
Tola, Puah,[a] Jashub and Shimron—four in all.
2 The sons of Tola:
Uzzi, Rephaiah, Jeriel, Jahmai,
Ibsam and Samuel—heads of
their families. During the reign
of David, the descendants of
Tola listed as fighting men in their
genealogy numbered 22,600.
3 The son of Uzzi:
Izrahiah.
The sons of Izrahiah:
Michael, Obadiah, Joel and Isshiah. All five of them were
chiefs. 4 According to their family genealogy, they had 36,000
men ready for battle, for they
had many wives and children.
5 The relatives who were fighting
men belonging to all the clans
of Issachar, as listed in their genealogy, were 87,000 in all.

7:1 [z]Ge 30:18; Nu 26:23 [a]Ge 46:13

Benjamin

6 Three sons of Benjamin:[b]
Bela, Beker and Jediael.
7 The sons of Bela:
Ezbon, Uzzi, Uzziel, Jerimoth
and Iri, heads of families—five
in all. Their genealogical record
listed 22,034 fighting men.
8 The sons of Beker:
Zemirah, Joash, Eliezer, Elioenai, Omri, Jeremoth, Abijah,
Anathoth and Alemeth. All these
were the sons of Beker. 9 Their
genealogical record listed the
heads of families and 20,200
fighting men.
10 The son of Jediael:
Bilhan.

7:6 [b]Ge 46:21; Nu 26:38; 1Ch 8:1-40

The sons of Bilhan:
Jeush, Benjamin, Ehud, Ke-
naanah, Zethan, Tarshish and
Ahishahar. 11 All these sons of
Jediael were heads of families.
There were 17,200 fighting men
ready to go out to war.
12 The Shuppites and Huppites were
the descendants of Ir, and the
Hushites the descendants of
Aher.

Naphtali

13 The sons of Naphtali:[c]
Jahziel, Guni, Jezer and Shillem[b]—the descendants of Bilhah.

7:13 [c]Ge 30:8; 46:24

Manasseh

14 The descendants of Manasseh:[d]
Asriel was his descendant
through his Aramean concubine.
She gave birth to Makir the father
of Gilead.[e] 15 Makir took a wife
from among the Huppites and
Shuppites. His sister's name was
Maacah.
Another descendant was named
Zelophehad,[f] who had only daugh-
ters.
16 Makir's wife Maacah gave birth
to a son and named him Peresh.
His brother was named Sheresh,
and his sons were Ulam and
Rakem.
17 The son of Ulam:
Bedan.
These were the sons of Gilead[g] son
of Makir, the son of Manasseh.
18 His sister Hammoleketh gave
birth to Ishhod, Abiezer[h] and
Mahlah.
19 The sons of Shemida were:
Ahian, Shechem, Likhi and
Aniam.

7:14 [d]Ge 41:51; Jos 17:1; 1Ch 5:23 [e]Nu 26:30
7:15 [f]Nu 26:33; 36:1-12
7:17 [g]Nu 26:30; 1Sa 12:11
7:18 [h]Jos 17:2

Ephraim

20 The descendants of Ephraim:[i]
Shuthelah, Bered his son,
Tahath his son, Eleadah his
son,
Tahath his son, 21 Zabad his son
and Shuthelah his son.

7:20 [i]Ge 41:52; Nu 1:33; 26:35

[a]*77* See Septuagint and Joshua 21:34; Hebrew does not have *Jokneam, Kartah.* [b]*13* Some Hebrew and Septuagint manuscripts (see also Gen. 46:24 and Num. 26:49); most Hebrew manuscripts *Shallum*

Ezer and Elead were killed by the
native-born men of Gath, when
they went down to seize their
livestock. 22 Their father Ephraim
mourned for them many days, and
his relatives came to comfort him.
23 Then he lay with his wife again,
and she became pregnant and gave
birth to a son. He named him
Beriah,[a] because there had been
misfortune in his family. 24 His
daughter was Sheerah, who built
7:24 [j]Jos 10:10; 16:3,5 Lower and Upper Beth Horon[j] as
well as Uzzen Sheerah.
25 Rephah was his son, Resheph his
son,[b]
Telah his son, Tahan his son,
26 Ladan his son, Ammihud his
son,
Elishama his son, 27 Nun his
son
and Joshua his son.
28 Their lands and settlements included Bethel and its surrounding villages,
7:28 [k]Jos 10:33; 16:7 Naaran to the east, Gezer[k] and its villages to the west, and Shechem and its
villages all the way to Ayyah and its
villages. 29 Along the borders of Manas-
7:29 [l]Jos 17:11 seh were Beth Shan,[l] Taanach, Megiddo
[m]Jos 11:2 and Dor,[m] together with their villages.
The descendants of Joseph son of Israel
lived in these towns.

Asher

7:30 [n]Ge 46:17; Nu 1:40; 26:44 30 The sons of Asher:[n]
Imnah, Ishvah, Ishvi and Beri-
ah. Their sister was Serah.
31 The sons of Beriah:
Heber and Malkiel, who was the
father of Birzaith.
32 Heber was the father of Japhlet,
Shomer and Hotham and of
their sister Shua.
33 The sons of Japhlet:
Pasach, Bimhal and Ashvath.
These were Japhlet's sons.
34 The sons of Shomer:
Ahi, Rohgah,[c] Hubbah and
Aram.
35 The sons of his brother Helem:
Zophah, Imna, Shelesh and
Amal.
36 The sons of Zophah:
Suah, Harnepher, Shual, Beri,
Imrah, 37 Bezer, Hod, Shamma,
Shilshah, Ithran[d] and Beera.
38 The sons of Jether:
Jephunneh, Pispah and Ara.
39 The sons of Ulla:
Arah, Hanniel and Rizia.
40 All these were descendants of Asher—heads of families, choice men, brave
warriors and outstanding leaders. The
number of men ready for battle, as listed in their genealogy, was 26,000.

The Genealogy of Saul the Benjamite

8 Benjamin[o] was the father of Bela 8:1 [o]Ge 46:21; 1Ch 7:6
his firstborn,
Ashbel the second son, Aharah
the third,
2 Nohah the fourth and Rapha
the fifth.
3 The sons of Bela were:
Addar,[p] Gera, Abihud,[e] 4 Abish- 8:3 [p]Ge 46:21
ua, Naaman, Ahoah,[q] 5 Gera,
Shephuphan and Huram. 8:4 [q]2Sa 23:9
6 These were the descendants of
Ehud,[r] who were heads of fami- 8:6 [r]Jdg 3:12-30; 1Ch 2:52
lies of those living in Geba and
were deported to Manahath:
7 Naaman, Ahijah, and Gera, who
deported them and who was the
father of Uzza and Ahihud.
8 Sons were born to Shaharaim in
Moab after he had divorced his
wives Hushim and Baara. 9 By
his wife Hodesh he had Jobab,
Zibia, Mesha, Malcam, 10 Jeuz,
Sakia and Mirmah. These were
his sons, heads of families. 11 By
Hushim he had Abitub and Elpaal.
12 The sons of Elpaal:
Eber, Misham, Shemed (who
built Ono[s] and Lod with its sur- 8:12 [s]Ezr 2:33; Ne 6:2; 7:37; 11:35
rounding villages), 13 and Beri-
ah and Shema, who were heads
of families of those living in Ai-
jalon[t] and who drove out the in- 8:13 [t]Jos 10:12
habitants of Gath.[u] [u]Jos 11:22
14 Ahio, Shashak, Jeremoth, 15 Zebadiah, Arad, Eder, 16 Michael, Ish-
pah and Joha were the sons of
Beriah.
17 Zebadiah, Meshullam, Hizki, Heber, 18 Ishmerai, Izliah and Jobab
were the sons of Elpaal.
19 Jakim, Zicri, Zabdi, 20 Elienai, Zil-
lethai, Eliel, 21 Adaiah, Beraiah

[a] *23 Beriah* sounds like the Hebrew for *misfortune.* [b] *25* Some Septuagint manuscripts; Hebrew does not have *his son.* [c] *34* Or *of his brother Shomer: Rohgah* [d] *37* Possibly a variant of *Jether* [e] *3* Or *Gera the father of Ehud*

and Shimrath were the sons of
Shimei.
22 Ishpan, Eber, Eliel, 23 Abdon, Zicri,
Hanan, 24 Hananiah, Elam, Anthothijah, 25 Iphdeiah and Penuel were the sons of Shashak.
26 Shamsherai, Shehariah, Athaliah,
27 Jaareshiah, Elijah and Zicri were the sons of Jeroham.

28 All these were heads of families, chiefs as listed in their genealogy, and they lived in Jerusalem.

29 Jeiel[a] the father[b] of Gibeon lived
8:29 [v]Jos 9:3 in Gibeon.[v]
His wife's name was Maacah,
30 and his firstborn son was Abdon, followed by Zur, Kish, Baal, Ner,[c] Nadab, 31 Gedor, Ahio, Zeker 32 and Mikloth, who was the father of Shimeah. They too lived near their relatives in Jerusalem.
8:33 [w]1Sa 28:19 [x]1Sa 9:1 [y]1Sa 14:49 [z]2Sa 2:8
33 Ner[w] was the father of Kish,[x] Kish the father of Saul,[y] and Saul the father of Jonathan, Malki-Shua, Abinadab and Esh-Baal.[d z]
8:34 [a]2Sa 9:12 [b]2Sa 4:4
34 The son of Jonathan:[a]
Merib-Baal,[e b] who was the father of Micah.
35 The sons of Micah:
Pithon, Melech, Tarea and Ahaz.
36 Ahaz was the father of Jehoaddah, Jehoaddah was the father of Alemeth, Azmaveth and Zimri, and Zimri was the father of Moza. 37 Moza was the father of Binea; Raphah was his son, Eleasah his son and Azel his son.
38 Azel had six sons, and these were their names:
Azrikam, Bokeru, Ishmael, Sheariah, Obadiah and Hanan. All these were the sons of Azel.
39 The sons of his brother Eshek:
Ulam his firstborn, Jeush the second son and Eliphelet the third. 40 The sons of Ulam were brave warriors who could handle the bow. They had many sons and grandsons—150 in all.
All these were the descendants of
8:40 [c]Nu 26:38 Benjamin.[c]

9 All Israel was listed in the genealogies recorded in the book of the kings of Israel.

FAITHFULNESS

ONLY THE UNFAITHFUL ARE REALLY SLAVES

1 Chronicles 9:1

One cannot be a slave if one is a true believer. Slavery is only for those who forget that God holds the keys to the jail door.

The People in Jerusalem

The people of Judah were taken
captive to Babylon because of their
unfaithfulness.[d] 2 Now the first to reset- 9:1 [d]1Ch 5:25
tle on their own property in their own
towns[e] were some Israelites, priests, Le- 9:2 [e]Jos 9:27; Ezr 2:70 [f]Ezr 2:43,58; 8:20; Ne 7:60
vites and temple servants.[f]
3 Those from Judah, from Benjamin,
and from Ephraim and Manasseh who
lived in Jerusalem were:
4 Uthai son of Ammihud, the son of Omri, the son of Imri, the son of Bani, a descendant of Perez son of Judah.[g] 9:4 [g]Ge 38:29; 46:12
5 Of the Shilonites:
Asaiah the firstborn and his sons.
6 Of the Zerahites:
Jeuel.
The people from Judah numbered 690.
7 Of the Benjamites:
Sallu son of Meshullam, the son of Hodaviah, the son of Hassenuah;
8 Ibneiah son of Jeroham; Elah son of Uzzi, the son of Micri; and Meshullam son of Shephatiah, the son of Reuel, the son of Ibnijah.
9 The people from Benjamin, as listed in their genealogy, numbered 956. All these men were heads of their families.
10 Of the priests:
Jedaiah; Jehoiarib; Jakin;
11 Azariah son of Hilkiah, the son of Meshullam, the son of Zadok, the son of Meraioth, the son of Ahitub, the official in charge of the house of God;

[a]*29* Some Septuagint manuscripts (see also 1 Chron. 9:35); Hebrew does not have *Jeiel.* [b]*29 Father* may mean *civic leader* or *military leader.* [c]*30* Some Septuagint manuscripts (see also 1 Chron. 9:36); Hebrew does not have *Ner.* [d]*33* Also known as *Ish-Bosheth* [e]*34* Also known as *Mephibosheth*

12 Adaiah son of Jeroham, the son of Pashhur,[h] the son of Malkijah; and Maasai son of Adiel, the son of Jahzerah, the son of Meshullam, the son of Meshillemith, the son of Immer.

13 The priests, who were heads of families, numbered 1,760. They were able men, responsible for ministering in the house of God.

14 Of the Levites:

Shemaiah son of Hasshub, the son of Azrikam, the son of Hashabiah, a Merarite; 15 Bakbakkar, Heresh, Galal and Mattaniah[i] son of Mica, the son of Zicri, the son of Asaph; 16 Obadiah son of Shemaiah, the son of Galal, the son of Jeduthun; and Berekiah son of Asa, the son of Elkanah, who lived in the villages of the Netophathites.[j]

17 The gatekeepers:[k]

Shallum, Akkub, Talmon, Ahiman and their brothers, Shallum their chief 18 being stationed at the King's Gate[l] on the east, up to the present time. These were the gatekeepers belonging to the camp of the Levites. 19 Shallum[m] son of Kore, the son of Ebiasaph, the son of Korah, and his fellow gatekeepers from his family (the Korahites) were responsible for guarding the thresholds of the Tent[a] just as their fathers had been responsible for guarding the entrance to the dwelling of the LORD. 20 In earlier times Phinehas[n] son of Eleazar was in charge of the gatekeepers, and the LORD was with him. 21 Zechariah[o] son of Meshelemiah was the gatekeeper[p] at the entrance to the Tent of Meeting.

22 Altogether, those chosen to be gatekeepers at the thresholds numbered 212. They were registered by genealogy in their villages. The gatekeepers had been assigned to their positions of trust by David and Samuel the seer.[q] 23 They and their descendants were in charge of guarding the gates of the house of the LORD—the house called the Tent. 24 The gatekeepers were on the four sides: east, west, north and south. 25 Their brothers in their villages had to come from time to time and share their duties for seven-day[r] periods. 26 But the four principal gatekeepers, who were Levites, were entrusted with the responsibility for the rooms and treasuries[s] in the house of God. 27 They would spend the night stationed around the house of God,[t] because they had to guard it; and they had charge of the key[u] for opening it each morning.

28 Some of them were in charge of the articles used in the temple service; they counted them when they were brought in and when they were taken out. 29 Others were assigned to take care of the furnishings and all the other articles of the sanctuary,[v] as well as the flour and wine, and the oil, incense and spices. 30 But some[w] of the priests took care of mixing the spices. 31 A Levite named Mattithiah, the firstborn son of Shallum the Korahite, was entrusted with the responsibility for baking the offering bread. 32 Some of their Kohathite brothers were in charge of preparing for every Sabbath the bread set out on the table.[x]

33 Those who were musicians,[y] heads of Levite families, stayed in the rooms of the temple and were exempt from other duties because they were responsible for the work day and night.[z]

34 All these were heads of Levite families, chiefs as listed in their genealogy, and they lived in Jerusalem.

The Genealogy of Saul

35 Jeiel[a] the father[b] of Gibeon lived in Gibeon.

His wife's name was Maacah, 36 and his firstborn son was Abdon, followed by Zur, Kish, Baal, Ner, Nadab, 37 Gedor, Ahio, Zechariah and Mikloth. 38 Mikloth was the father of Shimeam. They too lived near their relatives in Jerusalem.

39 Ner[b] was the father of Kish,[c] Kish the father of Saul, and Saul the father of Jonathan,[d] Malki-Shua, Abinadab and Esh-Baal.[c][e]

40 The son of Jonathan:

Merib-Baal,[d][f] who was the father of Micah.

[a] *19* That is, the temple; also in verses 21 and 23
[b] *35* *Father* may mean *civic leader* or *military leader.*
[c] *39* Also known as *Ish-Bosheth* [d] *40* Also known as *Mephibosheth*

9:12 [h]Ezr 2:38; 10:22; Ne 10:3; Jer 21:1; 38:1
9:15 [i]2Ch 20:14; Ne 11:22
9:16 [j]Ne 12:28
9:17 [k]ver 22; 1Ch 26:1; 2Ch 8:14; 31:14; Ezr 2:42; Ne 7:45
9:18 [l]1Ch 26:14; Eze 43:1; 46:1
9:19 [m]Jer 35:4
9:20 [n]Nu 25:7-13
9:21 [o]1Ch 26:2,14
9:22 [p]ver 17; 1Ch 26:1-2; 2Ch 31:15,18 [q]1Sa 9:9
9:25 [r]2Ki 11:5; 2Ch 23:8
9:26 [s]1Ch 26:22
9:27 [t]Nu 3:38; 1Ch 23:30-32 [u]Isa 22:22
9:29 [v]Nu 3:28; 1Ch 23:29
9:30 [w]Ex 30:23-25
9:32 [x]Lev 24:5-8; 1Ch 23:29; 2Ch 13:11
9:33 [y]1Ch 6:31; 25:1-31 [z]Ps 134:1
9:35 [a]1Ch 8:29
9:39 [b]1Ch 8:33 [c]1Sa 9:1 [d]1Sa 13:22 [e]2Sa 2:8
9:40 [f]2Sa 4:4

41 The sons of Micah:
Pithon, Melech, Tahrea and Ahaz.[a]
42 Ahaz was the father of Jadah, Jadah[b] was the father of Alemeth, Azmaveth and Zimri, and Zimri was the father of Moza.
43 Moza was the father of Binea; Rephaiah was his son, Eleasah his son and Azel his son.
44 Azel had six sons, and these were their names:
Azrikam, Bokeru, Ishmael, Sheariah, Obadiah and Hanan. These were the sons of Azel.

Saul Takes His Life

10 Now the Philistines fought against Israel; the Israelites fled before them, and many fell slain on Mount Gilboa. 2The Philistines pressed hard after Saul and his sons, and they killed his sons Jonathan, Abinadab and Malki-Shua. 3The fighting grew fierce around Saul, and when the archers overtook him, they wounded him.

4Saul said to his armor-bearer, "Draw your sword and run me through, or these uncircumcised fellows will come and abuse me."

But his armor-bearer was terrified and would not do it; so Saul took his own sword and fell on it. 5When the armor-bearer saw that Saul was dead, he too fell on his sword and died. 6So Saul and his three sons died, and all his house died together.

7When all the Israelites in the valley saw that the army had fled and that Saul and his sons had died, they abandoned their towns and fled. And the Philistines came and occupied them.

8The next day, when the Philistines came to strip the dead, they found Saul and his sons fallen on Mount Gilboa. 9They stripped him and took his head and his armor, and sent messengers throughout the land of the Philistines to proclaim the news among their idols and their people. 10They put his armor in the temple of their gods and hung up
10:10 [g]Jdg 16:23
his head in the temple of Dagon.[g]
10:11 [h]Jdg 21:8
11When all the inhabitants of Jabesh Gilead[h] heard of everything the Philistines had done to Saul, 12all their valiant men went and took the bodies of Saul and his sons and brought them to Jabesh. Then they buried their bones under the great tree in Jabesh, and they fasted seven days.

13Saul died[i] because he was unfaithful[j] to the LORD; he did not keep[k] the word of the LORD and even consulted a medium[l] for guidance, 14and did not inquire of the LORD. So the LORD put him to death and turned[m] the kingdom[n] over to David son of Jesse.

10:13 [i]2Sa 1:1 [j]1Sa 15:23; 1Ch 5:25 [k]1Sa 13:13 [l]Lev 19:31; 20:6; Dt 18:9-14; 1Sa 28:7

10:14 [m]1Ch 12:23 [n]1Sa 13:14; 15:28

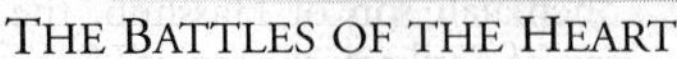

PEACE

THE BATTLES OF THE HEART

1 Chronicles 10:13

Saul died a troubled man. There was an absence of God in his life. He counseled with witches and lost the battle of Mount Gilboa. The outcomes of our inner wars determine the outcomes of our outer ones.

David Becomes King Over Israel

11 All Israel[o] came together to David at Hebron[p] and said, "We are your own flesh and blood. 2In the past, even while Saul was king, you were the one who led Israel on their military campaigns.[q] And the LORD your God said to you, 'You will shepherd[r] my people Israel, and you will become their ruler.[s]' "

11:1 [o]1Ch 9:1 [p]Ge 13:18; 23:19

11:2 [q]1Sa 18:5,16 [r]Ps 78:71; Mt 2:6 [s]1Ch 5:2

3When all the elders of Israel had come to King David at Hebron, he made a compact with them at Hebron before the LORD, and they anointed[t] David king over Israel, as the LORD had promised through Samuel.

11:3 [t]1Sa 16:1-13

David Conquers Jerusalem

4David and all the Israelites marched to Jerusalem (that is, Jebus). The Jebusites[u] who lived there 5said to David, "You will not get in here." Nevertheless, David captured the fortress of Zion, the City of David.

11:4 [u]Ge 10:16; 15:18-21; Jos 3:10; 15:8; Jdg 1:21; 19:10

6David had said, "Whoever leads the attack on the Jebusites will become commander-in-chief." Joab[v] son of Zeruiah went up first, and so he received the command.

11:6 [v]2Sa 2:13; 8:16

7David then took up residence in the fortress, and so it was called the City of

[a]*41* Vulgate and Syriac (see also Septuagint and 1 Chron. 8:35); Hebrew does not have *and Ahaz.*
[b]*42* Some Hebrew manuscripts and Septuagint (see also 1 Chron. 8:36); most Hebrew manuscripts *Jarah, Jarah*

David. [8]He built up the city around it,
11:8 [w]2Sa 5:9; from the supporting terraces[a][w] to the
2Ch 32:5 surrounding wall, while Joab restored
the rest of the city. [9]And David became
11:9 [x]2Sa 3:1; more and more powerful,[x] because the
Est 9:4 LORD Almighty was with him.

David's Mighty Men

[10]These were the chiefs of David's
mighty men—they, together with all Is-
11:10 [y]ver 1 rael,[y] gave his kingship strong support
[z]ver 3; to extend it over the whole land, as the
1Ch 12:23 LORD had promised[z]— [11]this is the list
11:11 [a]2Sa 17:10 of David's mighty men:[a]

Jashobeam,[b] a Hacmonite, was chief
of the officers[c]; he raised his spear
against three hundred men, whom he
killed in one encounter.

[12]Next to him was Eleazar son of Dodai the Ahohite, one of the three mighty
men. [13]He was with David at Pas Dammim when the Philistines gathered there
for battle. At a place where there was a
field full of barley, the troops fled from
the Philistines. [14]But they took their
stand in the middle of the field. They
defended it and struck the Philistines
down, and the LORD brought about a
11:14 [b]Ex 14:30; great victory.[b]
1Sa 11:13 [15]Three of the thirty chiefs came
down to David to the rock at the cave
of Adullam, while a band of Philistines
11:15 [c]1Ch 14:9; was encamped in the Valley[c] of Reph-
Isa 17:5 aim. [16]At that time David was in the
11:16 stronghold,[d] and the Philistine garri-
[d]2Sa 5:17 son was at Bethlehem. [17]David longed
for water and said, "Oh, that someone
would get me a drink of water from the
well near the gate of Bethlehem!" [18]So
the Three broke through the Philistine
lines, drew water from the well near the
gate of Bethlehem and carried it back
to David. But he refused to drink it;
11:18 [e]Dt 12:16 instead, he poured[e] it out before the
LORD. [19]"God forbid that I should do
this!" he said. "Should I drink the blood
of these men who went at the risk of
their lives?" Because they risked their
lives to bring it back, David would not
drink it.

Such were the exploits of the three
mighty men.
11:20 [f]1Sa 26:6 [20]Abishai[f] the brother of Joab was
chief of the Three. He raised his spear
against three hundred men, whom he
killed, and so he became as famous as
the Three. [21]He was doubly honored
above the Three and became their commander, even though he was not included among them.

[22]Benaiah son of Jehoiada was a valiant fighter from Kabzeel,[g] who per- 11:22
formed great exploits. He struck down [g]Jos 15:21 [h]1Sa 17:36
two of Moab's best men. He also went
down into a pit on a snowy day and
killed a lion.[h] [23]And he struck down
an Egyptian who was seven and a half
feet[d] tall. Although the Egyptian had a
spear like a weaver's rod[i] in his hand, 11:23 [i]1Sa 17:7
Benaiah went against him with a club.
He snatched the spear from the Egyptian's hand and killed him with his own
spear. [24]Such were the exploits of Benaiah son of Jehoiada; he too was as famous as the three mighty men. [25]He
was held in greater honor than any of
the Thirty, but he was not included
among the Three. And David put him
in charge of his bodyguard.

[26]The mighty men were:
Asahel[j] the brother of Joab, 11:26 [j]2Sa 2:18
Elhanan son of Dodo from
Bethlehem,
[27]Shammoth[k] the Harorite, 11:27 [k]1Ch 27:8
Helez the Pelonite,
[28]Ira son of Ikkesh from Tekoa,
Abiezer[l] from Anathoth, 11:28 [l]1Ch 27:12
[29]Sibbecai[m] the Hushathite, 11:29 [m]2Sa 21:18
Ilai the Ahohite,
[30]Maharai the Netophathite,
Heled son of Baanah the Netophathite,
[31]Ithai son of Ribai from Gibeah
in Benjamin,
Benaiah[n] the Pirathonite,[o] 11:31 [n]1Ch 27:14 [o]Jdg 12:13
[32]Hurai from the ravines of
Gaash,
Abiel the Arbathite,
[33]Azmaveth the Baharumite,
Eliahba the Shaalbonite,
[34]the sons of Hashem the Gi-
zonite,
Jonathan son of Shagee the Hararite,
[35]Ahiam son of Sacar the Hararite,
Eliphal son of Ur,
[36]Hepher the Mekerathite,
Ahijah the Pelonite,
[37]Hezro the Carmelite,
Naarai son of Ezbai,

[a]*8* Or *the Millo* [b]*11* Possibly a variant of *Jashob-Baal* [c]*11* Or *Thirty*; some Septuagint manuscripts *Three* (see also 2 Samuel 23:8) [d]*23* Hebrew *five cubits* (about 2.3 meters)

38 Joel the brother of Nathan,
Mibhar son of Hagri,
39 Zelek the Ammonite,
Naharai the Berothite, the armor-
bearer of Joab son of Zeruiah,
40 Ira the Ithrite,
Gareb the Ithrite,
11:41 [p]2Sa 11:6 41 Uriah[p] the Hittite,
[q]1Ch 2:36 Zabad[q] son of Ahlai,
42 Adina son of Shiza the Reubenite, who was chief of the
Reubenites, and the thirty with
him,
43 Hanan son of Maacah,
Joshaphat the Mithnite,
11:44 [r]Dt 1:4 44 Uzzia the Ashterathite,[r]
Shama and Jeiel the sons of Ho-
tham the Aroerite,
45 Jediael son of Shimri,
his brother Joha the Tizite,
46 Eliel the Mahavite,
Jeribai and Joshaviah the sons of
Elnaam,
Ithmah the Moabite,
47 Eliel, Obed and Jaasiel the Me-
zobaite.

Warriors Join David

12:1 [s]Jos 15:31; 1Sa 27:2-6 12 These were the men who came
to David at Ziklag,[s] while he
was banished from the presence of
Saul son of Kish (they were among
the warriors who helped him in battle;
2 they were armed with bows and were
able to shoot arrows or to sling stones
12:2 [t]Jdg 3:15; 20:16 right-handed or left-handed;[t] they were
[u]2Sa 3:19 kinsmen of Saul[u] from the tribe of Benjamin):

3 Ahiezer their chief and Joash the
sons of Shemaah the Gibeathite;
Jeziel and Pelet the sons of Azmaveth; Beracah, Jehu the Anathothite, 4 and Ishmaiah the Gibeonite,
a mighty man among the Thirty,
who was a leader of the Thirty;
12:4 [v]Jos 15:36 Jeremiah, Jahaziel, Johanan, Jozabad the Gederathite,[v] 5 Eluzai, Jerimoth, Bealiah, Shemariah and
Shephatiah the Haruphite; 6 Elka-
12:7 [w]Jos 15:58 nah, Isshiah, Azarel, Joezer and
Jashobeam the Korahites; 7 and Jo-
elah and Zebadiah the sons of Je-
12:8 [x]Ge 30:11 roham from Gedor.[w]

8 Some Gadites[x] defected to David at
his stronghold in the desert. They were
brave warriors, ready for battle and able
to handle the shield and spear. Their 12:8
faces were the faces of lions,[y] and they [y]2Sa 17:10
were as swift as gazelles[z] in the moun- [z]2Sa 2:18
tains.

9 Ezer was the chief,
Obadiah the second in command,
Eliab the third,
10 Mishmannah the fourth, Jeremiah
the fifth,
11 Attai the sixth, Eliel the seventh,
12 Johanan the eighth, Elzabad the
ninth,
13 Jeremiah the tenth and Macban-
nai the eleventh.

14 These Gadites were army com-
manders; the least was a match for 12:14 [a]Lev 26:8
a hundred,[a] and the greatest for a [b]Dt 32:30
thousand.[b] 15 It was they who crossed
the Jordan in the first month when it 12:15
was overflowing all its banks,[c] and they [c]Jos 3:15
put to flight everyone living in the valleys, to the east and to the west. 12:16
16 Other Benjamites[d] and some men [d]2Sa 3:19
from Judah also came to David in his
stronghold. 17 David went out to meet
them and said to them, "If you have
come to me in peace, to help me, I am
ready to have you unite with me. But
if you have come to betray me to my
enemies when my hands are free from
violence, may the God of our fathers
see it and judge you." 12:18
18 Then the Spirit[e] came upon Amas- [e]Jdg 3:10; 6:34;
ai,[f] chief of the Thirty, and he said: 1Ch 28:12; 2Ch 15:1; 20:14; 24:20

"We are yours, O David! [f]2Sa 17:25
We are with you, O son of Jesse! [g]1Sa 25:5-6
Success,[g] success to you,
and success to those who help
you,
for your God will help you."

So David received them and made
them leaders of his raiding bands.
19 Some of the men of Manasseh defected to David when he went with the
Philistines to fight against Saul. (He
and his men did not help the Philistines
because, after consultation, their rulers
sent him away. They said, "It will cost
us our heads if he deserts to his master 12:19
Saul.")[h] 20 When David went to Ziklag,[i] [h]1Sa 29:2-11
these were the men of Manasseh who 12:20
defected to him: Adnah, Jozabad, Jedi- [i]1Sa 27:6
ael, Michael, Jozabad, Elihu and Zille-
thai, leaders of units of a thousand in
Manasseh. 21 They helped David against
raiding bands, for all of them were brave

warriors, and they were commanders in his army. 22Day after day men came to help David, until he had a great army, like the army of God.[a]

Others Join David at Hebron

23These are the numbers of the men armed for battle who came to David at Hebron[j] to turn[k] Saul's kingdom over to him, as the LORD had said:[l]

12:23 [j]2Sa 2:3-4 [k]1Ch 10:14 [l]1Sa 16:1; 1Ch 11:10

24men of Judah, carrying shield and spear—6,800 armed for battle;
25men of Simeon, warriors ready for battle—7,100;
26men of Levi—4,600, 27including Jehoiada, leader of the family of Aaron, with 3,700 men, 28and Zadok,[m] a brave young warrior, with 22 officers from his family;

12:28 [m]2Sa 8:17; 1Ch 6:8; 15:11; 16:39; 27:17

29men of Benjamin,[n] Saul's kinsmen—3,000, most[o] of whom had remained loyal to Saul's house until then;

12:29 [n]2Sa 3:19 [o]2Sa 2:8-9

30men of Ephraim, brave warriors, famous in their own clans—20,800;
31men of half the tribe of Manasseh, designated by name to come and make David king—18,000;
32men of Issachar, who understood the times and knew what Israel should do[p]—200 chiefs, with all their relatives under their command;

12:32 [p]Est 1:13

33men of Zebulun, experienced soldiers prepared for battle with every type of weapon, to help David with undivided loyalty—50,000;
34men of Naphtali—1,000 officers, together with 37,000 men carrying shields and spears;
35men of Dan, ready for battle—28,600;
36men of Asher, experienced soldiers prepared for battle—40,000;
37and from east of the Jordan, men of Reuben, Gad and the half-tribe of Manasseh, armed with every type of weapon—120,000.

38All these were fighting men who volunteered to serve in the ranks. They came to Hebron fully determined to make David king over all Israel.[q] All the rest of the Israelites were also of one mind to make David king. 39The men spent three days there with David, eating and drinking,[r] for their families had supplied provisions for them. 40Also, their neighbors from as far away as Issachar, Zebulun and Naphtali came bringing food on donkeys, camels, mules and oxen. There were plentiful supplies[s] of flour, fig cakes, raisin[t] cakes, wine, oil, cattle and sheep, for there was joy[u] in Israel.

12:38 [q]2Sa 5:1-3; 1Ch 9:1

12:39 [r]2Sa 3:20; Isa 25:6-8

12:40 [s]2Sa 16:1; 17:29 [t]1Sa 25:18 [u]1Ch 29:22

Bringing Back the Ark

13 David conferred with each of his officers, the commanders of thousands and commanders of hundreds. 2He then said to the whole assembly of Israel, "If it seems good to you and if it is the will of the LORD our God, let us send word far and wide to the rest of our brothers throughout the territories of Israel, and also to the priests and Levites who are with them in their towns and pasturelands, to come and join us. 3Let us bring the ark of our God back to us,[v] for we did not inquire[w] of[b] it[c] during the reign of Saul." 4The whole assembly agreed to do this, because it seemed right to all the people.

13:3 [v]1Sa 7:1-2 [w]2Ch 1:5

5So David assembled all the Israelites,[x] from the Shihor River[y] in Egypt to Lebo[d] Hamath,[z] to bring the ark of God from Kiriath Jearim.[a] 6David and all the Israelites with him went to Baalah[b] of Judah (Kiriath Jearim) to bring up from there the ark of God the LORD, who is enthroned between the cherubim[c]—the ark that is called by the Name.

13:5 [x]1Ch 11:1; 15:3 [y]Jos 13:3 [z]Nu 13:21 [a]1Sa 6:21; 7:2

13:6 [b]Jos 15:9; 2Sa 6:2 [c]Ex 25:22; 2Ki 19:15

7They moved the ark of God from Abinadab's[d] house on a new cart, with Uzzah and Ahio guiding it. 8David and all the Israelites were celebrating with all their might before God, with songs and with harps, lyres, tambourines, cymbals and trumpets.[e]

13:7 [d]Nu 4:15; 1Sa 7:1

13:8 [e]2Sa 6:5; 1Ch 15:16,19,24; 2Ch 5:12; Ps 92:3

9When they came to the threshing floor of Kidon, Uzzah reached out his hand to steady the ark, because the oxen stumbled. 10The LORD's anger[f] burned against Uzzah, and he struck him down[g] because he had put his hand on the ark. So he died there before God.

13:10 [f]1Ch 15:13,15 [g]Lev 10:2

11Then David was angry because the LORD's wrath had broken out against

[a]22 Or *a great and mighty army* [b]3 Or *we neglected* [c]3 Or *him* [d]5 Or *to the entrance to*

PATIENCE

UZZAH WAS . . . GOD IS

1 Chronicles 13:10

Uzzah loved the ark and would not wait for God to save it in his own way. God dwelt upon the ark's gold lid, so it would never have fallen like some clumsy Cannanite idol. God never needed Uzzah to rescue him. Saving God is not our calling. It's the other way around.

Uzzah, and to this day that place is
13:11 [h]1Ch 15:13; Ps 7:11 called Perez Uzzah.[a][h]
12David was afraid of God that day
and asked, "How can I ever bring the
ark of God to me?" 13He did not take
the ark to be with him in the City
of David. Instead, he took it aside to
13:13 [i]1Ch 15:18, 24; 16:38; 26:4-5,15 the house of Obed-Edom[i] the Gittite.
14The ark of God remained with the
family of Obed-Edom in his house for
three months, and the LORD blessed
13:14 [j]2Sa 6:11; 1Ch 26:4-5 his household[j] and everything he had.

David's House and Family

14 Now Hiram king of Tyre sent
messengers to David, along with
14:1 [k]2Ch 2:3; Ezr 3:7 cedar logs,[k] stonemasons and carpenters to build a palace for him. 2And
David knew that the LORD had established him as king over Israel and that
14:2 [l]Nu 24:7; Dt 26:19 his kingdom had been highly exalted[l]
for the sake of his people Israel.
14:3 [m]1Ch 3:1 3In Jerusalem David took more wives
and became the father of more sons[m]
and daughters. 4These are the names of
14:4 [n]1Ch 3:9 the children born to him there:[n] Shammua, Shobab, Nathan, Solomon, 5Ib-
har, Elishua, Elpelet, 6Nogah, Nepheg,
Japhia, 7Elishama, Beeliada[b] and Eliphelet.

David Defeats the Philistines

8When the Philistines heard that David had been anointed king over all
14:8 [o]1Ch 11:1 Israel,[o] they went up in full force to
search for him, but David heard about
it and went out to meet them. 9Now
the Philistines had come and raided
14:9 [p]ver 13; Jos 15:8; 1Ch 11:15 the Valley[p] of Rephaim; 10so David inquired of God: "Shall I go and attack
the Philistines? Will you hand them
over to me?"
The LORD answered him, "Go, I will
hand them over to you."
11So David and his men went up to
Baal Perazim,[q] and there he defeated 14:11 [q]Isa 28:21
them. He said, "As waters break out,
God has broken out against my enemies by my hand." So that place was
called Baal Perazim.[c] 12The Philistines
had abandoned their gods there, and
David gave orders to burn[r] them in the 14:12 [r]Ex 32:20 [s]Jos 7:15
fire.[s]
13Once more the Philistines raided
the valley;[t] 14so David inquired of God 14:13 [t]ver 9
again, and God answered him, "Do not
go straight up, but circle around them
and attack them in front of the balsam
trees. 15As soon as you hear the sound
of marching in the tops of the balsam
trees, move out to battle, because that
will mean God has gone out in front
of you to strike the Philistine army."
16So David did as God commanded
him, and they struck down the Philis-
tine army, all the way from Gibeon[u] to 14:16 [u]Jos 9:3 [v]Jos 10:33
Gezer.[v]
17So David's fame[w] spread through- 14:17 [w]Jos 6:27; 2Ch 26:8 [x]Ex 15:14-16; Dt 2:25
out every land, and the LORD made all
the nations fear[x] him.

The Ark Brought to Jerusalem

15 After David had constructed
buildings for himself in the City
of David, he prepared[y] a place for the 15:1 [y]Ps 132:1-18 [z]1Ch 16:1; 17:1
ark of God and pitched[z] a tent for it.
2Then David said, "No one but the
Levites[a] may carry[b] the ark of God, be- 15:2 [a]Nu 4:15; Dt 10:8; 2Ch 5:5 [b]Dt 31:9 [c]1Ch 23:13
cause the LORD chose them to carry
the ark of the LORD and to minister[c]
before him forever."
3David assembled all Israel[d] in Jeru- 15:3 [d]1Ki 8:1; 1Ch 13:5
salem to bring up the ark of the LORD
to the place he had prepared for it. 4He
called together the descendants of Aaron and the Levites:

5From the descendants of Kohath,
Uriel the leader and 120 relatives;
6from the descendants of Merari,
Asaiah the leader and 220 relatives;
7from the descendants of Gershon,[d]
Joel the leader and 130 relatives;
8from the descendants of Elizaphan,[e] 15:8 [e]Ex 6:22

[a]11 *Perez Uzzah* means *outbreak against Uzzah.*
[b]7 A variant of *Eliada* [c]11 *Baal Perazim* means *the lord who breaks out.* [d]7 Hebrew *Gershom,* a variant of *Gershon*

Jesus Speaks Out *on the Fruit of the Spirit:* Peace

Matthew 5:9
Blessed are the peacemakers, for they will be called sons of God.

Matthew 11:28
Come to me, all you who are weary and burdened, and I will give you rest.

John 14:27
Peace I leave with you; my peace I give you. I do not give to you as the world gives. Do not let your hearts be troubled and do not be afraid.

John 16:33
I have told you these things, so that in me you may have peace. In this world you will have trouble. But take heart! I have overcome the world.

John 20:19
On the evening of that first day of the week, when the disciples were together, with the doors locked for fear of the Jews, Jesus came and stood among them and said, "Peace be with you!"

John 14:1
Do not let your hearts be troubled. Trust in God; trust also in me.

The Peace of God

Then Judas (not Judas Iscariot) said, "But, Lord, why do you intend to show yourself to us and not to the world?"

Jesus replied, "If anyone loves me, he will obey my teaching. My Father will love him, and we will come to him and make our home with him. He who does not love me will not obey my teaching. These words you hear are not my own; they belong to the Father who sent me.

"All this I have spoken while still with you. But the Counselor, the Holy Spirit, whom the Father will send in my name, will teach you all things and will remind you of everything I have said to you. Peace I leave with you; my peace I give you. I do not give to you as the world gives. Do not let your hearts be troubled and do not be afraid.

"You heard me say, 'I am going away and I am coming back to you.' If you loved me, you would be glad that I am going to the Father, for the Father is greater than I. I have told you now before it happens, so that when it does happen you will believe. I will not speak with you much longer, for the prince of this world is coming. He has no hold on me, but the world must learn that I love the Father and that I do exactly what my Father has commanded me.

"Come now; let us leave."

John 14:22–31

Paul Speaks Out
on the Fruit of the Spirit:
Peace

Romans 5:1

Since we have been justified through faith, we have peace with God through our Lord Jesus Christ.

Romans 8:6

The mind of sinful man is death, but the mind controlled by the Spirit is life and peace.

Romans 14:17

The kingdom of God is not a matter of eating and drinking, but of righteousness, peace and joy in the Holy Spirit.

Ephesians 2:14–18

He himself is our peace, who has made the two one and has destroyed the barrier, the dividing wall of hostility, by abolishing in his flesh the law with its commandments and regulations. His purpose was to create in himself one new man out of the two, thus making peace, and in this one body to reconcile both of them to God through the cross, by which he put to death their hostility. He came and preached peace to you who were far away and peace to those who were near. For through him we both have access to the Father by one Spirit.

Ephesians 4:3

Make every effort to keep the unity of the Spirit through the bond of peace.

Philippians 4:7

The peace of God, which transcends all understanding, will guard your hearts and your minds in Christ Jesus.

1 Thessalonians 5:13

Hold them in the highest regard in love because of their work. Live in peace with each other.

▸ Peace in the Storm

On the fourteenth night we were still being driven across the Adriatic Sea, when about midnight the sailors sensed they were approaching land. They took soundings and found that the water was a hundred and twenty feet deep. A short time later they took soundings again and found it was ninety feet deep. Fearing that we would be dashed against the rocks, they dropped four anchors from the stern and prayed for daylight. In an attempt to escape from the ship, the sailors let the lifeboat down into the sea, pretending they were going to lower some anchors from the bow. Then Paul said to the centurion and the soldiers, "Unless these men stay with the ship, you cannot be saved." So the soldiers cut the ropes that held the lifeboat and let it fall away.

Just before dawn Paul urged them all to eat. "For the last fourteen days," he said, "you have been in constant suspense and have gone without food—you haven't eaten anything. Now I urge you to take some food. You need it to survive. Not one of you will lose a single hair from his head." After he said this, he took some bread and gave thanks to God in front of them all. Then he broke it and began to eat. They were all encouraged and ate some food themselves. Altogether there were 276 of us on board.

The soldiers planned to kill the prisoners to prevent any of them from swimming away and escaping. But the centurion wanted to spare Paul's life and kept them from carrying out their plan. He ordered those who could swim to jump overboard first and get to land. The rest were to get there on planks or on pieces of the ship. In this way everyone reached land in safety.

Acts 27:27–37,42–44

Shemaiah the leader and 200
relatives;
15:9 [f]Ex 6:18 9 from the descendants of Hebron,[f]
Eliel the leader and 80 relatives;
10 from the descendants of Uzziel,
Amminadab the leader and 112
relatives.
15:11 [g]1Ch 12:28 11 Then David summoned Zadok[g]
[h]1Sa 22:20 and Abiathar[h] the priests, and Uriel,
Asaiah, Joel, Shemaiah, Eliel and Amminadab the Levites. 12 He said to them,
"You are the heads of the Levitical families; you and your fellow Levites are to
15:12 consecrate[i] yourselves and bring up the
[i]Ex 19:14-15; Lev 11:44; ark of the LORD, the God of Israel, to
2Ch 35:6 the place I have prepared for it. 13 It was
15:13 because you, the Levites,[j] did not bring
[j]1Ki 8:4 it up the first time that the LORD our
[k]2Sa 6:3; 1Ch 13:7-10 God broke out in anger against us.[k] We
did not inquire of him about how to
do it in the prescribed way." 14 So the
priests and Levites consecrated themselves in order to bring up the ark of
the LORD, the God of Israel. 15 And
the Levites carried the ark of God with
the poles on their shoulders, as Moses
15:15 had commanded[l] in accordance with
[l]Ex 25:14; Nu 4:5,15 the word of the LORD.
16 David told the leaders of the Le-
15:16 vites to appoint their brothers as sing-
[m]Ps 68:25 ers[m] to sing joyful songs, accompanied
[n]1Ch 13:8; 25:1; by musical instruments: lyres, harps and
Ne 12:27,36 cymbals.[n]
15:17 17 So the Levites appointed Heman[o]
[o]1Ch 6:33 [p]1Ch 6:39 son of Joel; from his brothers, Asaph[p]
[q]1Ch 6:44 son of Berekiah; and from their brothers the Merarites,[q] Ethan son of Ku-
shaiah; 18 and with them their brothers
next in rank: Zechariah,[a] Jaaziel, Shemiramoth, Jehiel, Unni, Eliab, Benaiah, Maaseiah, Mattithiah, Eliphelehu,
15:18 Mikneiah, Obed-Edom[r] and Jeiel,[b] the
[r]1Ch 26:4-5 gatekeepers.
15:19 19 The musicians Heman,[s] Asaph and
[s]1Ch 25:6 Ethan were to sound the bronze cymbals; 20 Zechariah, Aziel, Shemiramoth,
Jehiel, Unni, Eliab, Maaseiah and Benaiah were to play the lyres according
to *alamoth*,[c] 21 and Mattithiah, Eliphelehu, Mikneiah, Obed-Edom, Jeiel and
Azaziah were to play the harps, direct-
ing according to *sheminith*.[c] 22 Kenaniah the head Levite was in charge of the
singing; that was his responsibility because he was skillful at it.
23 Berekiah and Elkanah were to be
doorkeepers for the ark. 24 Shebaniah,
Joshaphat, Nethanel, Amasai, Zechariah, Benaiah and Eliezer the priests were
to blow trumpets[t] before the ark of 15:24
God. Obed-Edom and Jehiah were also [t]ver 28; 1Ch 16:6;
to be doorkeepers for the ark. 2Ch 7:6
25 So David and the elders of Israel
and the commanders of units of a
thousand went to bring up the ark[u] of 15:25
the covenant of the LORD from the [u]1Ch 13:13; 2Ch 1:4
house of Obed-Edom, with rejoicing.
26 Because God had helped the Levites
who were carrying the ark of the covenant of the LORD, seven bulls and 15:26
seven rams[v] were sacrificed. 27 Now Da- [v]Nu 23:1-4,29
vid was clothed in a robe of fine lin-
en, as were all the Levites who were
carrying the ark, and as were the singers, and Kenaniah, who was in charge
of the singing of the choirs. David
also wore a linen ephod. 28 So all Israel
brought up the ark of the covenant of
the LORD with shouts, with the sounding of rams' horns[w] and trumpets, and 15:28
of cymbals, and the playing of lyres [w]1Ch 13:8
and harps.
29 As the ark of the covenant of the
LORD was entering the City of David,
Michal daughter of Saul watched from
a window. And when she saw King David dancing and celebrating, she despised him in her heart.

16 They brought the ark of God
and set it inside the tent that
David had pitched[x] for it, and they 16:1
presented burnt offerings and fellow- [x]1Ch 15:1
ship offerings[d] before God. 2 After David had finished sacrificing the burnt
offerings and fellowship offerings, he 16:2
blessed[y] the people in the name of the [y]Ex 39:43
LORD. 3 Then he gave a loaf of bread,
a cake of dates and a cake of raisins to
each Israelite man and woman.
4 He appointed some of the Levites to
minister[z] before the ark of the LORD, 16:4
to make petition, to give thanks, and [z]1Ch 15:2
to praise the LORD, the God of Israel:
5 Asaph was the chief, Zechariah second,
then Jeiel, Shemiramoth, Jehiel, Mattithiah, Eliab, Benaiah, Obed-Edom
and Jeiel. They were to play the lyres
and harps, Asaph was to sound the
cymbals, 6 and Benaiah and Jahaziel

[a] *18* Three Hebrew manuscripts and most Septuagint manuscripts (see also verse 20 and 1 Chron. 16:5); most Hebrew manuscripts *Zechariah son and* or *Zechariah, Ben and* [b] *18* Hebrew; Septuagint (see also verse 21) *Jeiel and Azaziah* [c] *20,21* Probably a musical term [d] *1* Traditionally *peace offerings*; also in verse 2

the priests were to blow the trumpets regularly before the ark of the covenant of God.

DAY 2 TWO

▸ Gentleness and the Purpose of God in My Life

1 Chronicles 16:8,19–22

In this psalm David rejoices with the people of Israel over the gentle leadership of God. God had, after all, cared for them in the wilderness and gently led them to Canaan. The exodus might seem anything but gentle; nevertheless, that's what it was. When Hosea pictured it, he wrote:

When Israel was a child, I loved him,
and out of Egypt I called my son.
But the more I called Israel,
the further they went from me . . .
It was I who taught Ephraim to walk,
taking them by the arms;
but they did not realize
it was I who healed them.
I led them with cords of human kindness,
with ties of love;
I lifted the yoke from their neck
and bent down to feed them.
(Hosea 11:1–4)

This tender picture of the Father with his child is the same gentle genre David chooses in the writing of his great thanksgiving psalm:

Give thanks to the LORD, call on his name . . .
When they were but few in number,
few indeed, and strangers in it,
they wandered from nation to nation,
from one kingdom to another.
He allowed no man to oppress them;
for their sake he rebuked kings:
"Do not touch my anointed ones;
do my prophets no harm."
(1 Chronicles 16:8,19–22)

These gentle metaphors speak clearly of the tenderness of God and call us to approach our own wilderness experiences with the same gentleness toward our fellow travelers.

To begin a study on the topic of Gentleness, the Healing Touch of God, turn to the home page on page 1175.

David's Psalm of Thanks

7That day David first committed to Asaph and his associates this psalm[a] of thanks to the LORD: 16:7 [a]2Sa 23:1

8Give thanks[b] to the LORD, call on his name; 16:8 [b]ver 34; Ps 136:1 [c]2Ki 19:19
make known among the nations[c] what he has done.

▸ Kindness

The Face in the Mirror of God

1 Chronicles 16:8

David thanked God for his kindness—and so he should have. The poet's opinion:
"It is a heart born free and kind
That frames the love of God."

9Sing to him, sing praise[d] to him; 16:9 [d]Ex 15:1
tell of all his wonderful acts.
10Glory in his holy name;
let the hearts of those who seek the LORD rejoice.
11Look to the LORD and his strength;
seek[e] his face always. 16:11 [e]1Ch 28:9; 2Ch 7:14; Ps 24:6; 119:2,58
12Remember[f] the wonders he has done,
his miracles,[g] and the judgments he pronounced, 16:12 [f]Ps 77:11 [g]Ps 78:43
13O descendants of Israel his servant,
O sons of Jacob, his chosen ones.

14He is the LORD our God;
his judgments[h] are in all the earth. 16:14 [h]Isa 26:9
15He remembers[a] his covenant forever,
the word he commanded, for a thousand generations,
16the covenant[i] he made with Abraham, 16:16 [i]Ge 12:7; 15:18; 17:2; 22:16-18; 26:3; 28:13; 35:11
the oath he swore to Isaac.
17He confirmed it to Jacob[j] as a decree, 16:17 [j]Ge 35:9-12
to Israel as an everlasting covenant:
18"To you I will give the land of Canaan[k] 16:18 [k]Ge 13:14-17
as the portion you will inherit."

19When they were but few in number,[l] 16:19 [l]Ge 34:30; Dt 7:7
few indeed, and strangers in it,
20they[b] wandered from nation to nation,

[a]*15* Some Septuagint manuscripts (see also Psalm 105:8); Hebrew *Remember* [b]*18-20* One Hebrew manuscript, Septuagint and Vulgate (see also Psalm 105:12); most Hebrew manuscripts *inherit, / [19]though you are but few in number, / few indeed, and strangers in it." / [20]They*

from one kingdom to another.
21 He allowed no man to oppress them;
for their sake he rebuked kings:[m]
22 "Do not touch my anointed ones;
do my prophets[n] no harm."
23 Sing to the LORD, all the earth;
proclaim his salvation day after day.
24 Declare his glory among the nations,
his marvelous deeds among all peoples.
25 For great is the LORD and most worthy of praise;[o]
he is to be feared[p] above all gods.[q]
26 For all the gods of the nations are idols,
but the LORD made the heavens.[r]
27 Splendor and majesty are before him;
strength and joy in his dwelling place.
28 Ascribe to the LORD, O families of nations,
ascribe to the LORD glory and strength,[s]
29 ascribe to the LORD the glory due his name.
Bring an offering and come before him;
worship the LORD in the splendor of his[a] holiness.[t]
30 Tremble[u] before him, all the earth!
The world is firmly established; it cannot be moved.
31 Let the heavens rejoice, let the earth be glad;[v]
let them say among the nations,
"The LORD reigns![w]"
32 Let the sea resound, and all that is in it;[x]
let the fields be jubilant, and everything in them!
33 Then the trees[y] of the forest will sing,
they will sing for joy before the LORD,
for he comes to judge[z] the earth.
34 Give thanks[a] to the LORD, for he is good;[b]
his love endures forever.[c]
35 Cry out, "Save us, O God our Savior;[d]
gather us and deliver us from the nations,
that we may give thanks to your holy name,
that we may glory in your praise."

16:21 [m]Ge 12:17; 20:3; Ex 7:15-18
16:22 [n]Ge 20:7
16:25 [o]Ps 48:1 [p]Ps 76:7; 89:7 [q]Dt 32:39
16:26 [r]Lev 19:4; Ps 102:25
16:28 [s]Ps 29:1-2
16:29 [t]Ps 29:1-2
16:30 [u]Ps 114:7
16:31 [v]Isa 44:23; 49:13 [w]Ps 93:1
16:32 [x]Ps 98:7
16:33 [y]Isa 55:12 [z]Ps 96:10; 98:9
16:34 [a]ver 8 [b]Na 1:7 [c]2Ch 5:13; 7:3; Ezr 3:11; Ps 136:1-26; Jer 33:11
16:35 [d]Mic 7:7

36 Praise be to the LORD, the God of Israel,[e]
from everlasting to everlasting.

Then all the people said "Amen" and "Praise the LORD."

37 David left Asaph and his associates
before the ark of the covenant of the
LORD to minister there regularly, according to each day's requirements.[f]
38 He also left Obed-Edom[g] and his
sixty-eight associates to minister with
them. Obed-Edom son of Jeduthun,
and also Hosah,[h] were gatekeepers.
39 David left Zadok[i] the priest and
his fellow priests before the tabernacle
of the LORD at the high place in Gibeon[j] 40 to present burnt offerings to the
LORD on the altar of burnt offering
regularly, morning and evening, in accordance with everything written in the
Law[k] of the LORD, which he had giv-
en Israel. 41 With them were Heman[l]
and Jeduthun and the rest of those chosen and designated by name to give
thanks to the LORD, "for his love endures forever." 42 Heman and Jeduthun
were responsible for the sounding of
the trumpets and cymbals and for the
playing of the other instruments for sacred song.[m] The sons of Jeduthun were
stationed at the gate.
43 Then all the people left, each for his
own home, and David returned home
to bless his family.

God's Promise to David

17 After David was settled in his palace, he said to Nathan the prophet, "Here I am, living in a palace of cedar, while the ark of the covenant of the LORD is under a tent.[n]"

2 Nathan replied to David, "Whatever you have in mind,[o] do it, for God is with you."

3 That night the word of God came to Nathan, saying:

4 "Go and tell my servant David,
'This is what the LORD says: You[p]
are not the one to build me a house
to dwell in. 5 I have not dwelt in a
house from the day I brought Israel
up out of Egypt to this day. I have
moved from one tent site to another, from one dwelling place to

[a]29 Or *LORD with the splendor of*

16:36 [e]Dt 27:15; 1Ki 8:15; Ps 72:18-19
16:37 [f]2Ch 8:14
16:38 [g]1Ch 13:13 [h]1Ch 26:10
16:39 [i]2Sa 8:17; 1Ch 15:11 [j]1Ki 3:4; 2Ch 1:3
16:40 [k]Ex 29:38; Nu 28:1-8
16:41 [l]1Ch 6:33; 25:1-6; 2Ch 5:13
16:42 [m]2Ch 7:6
17:1 [n]1Ch 15:1
17:2 [o]2Ch 6:7
17:4 [p]1Ch 28:3

another. 6Wherever I have moved with all the Israelites, did I ever say to any of their leaders[a] whom I commanded to shepherd my people, "Why have you not built me a house of cedar?"'

7"Now then, tell my servant David, 'This is what the LORD Almighty says: I took you from the pasture and from following the flock, to be ruler[q] over my people Israel. 8I have been with you wherever you have gone, and I have cut off all your enemies from before you. Now I will make your name like the names of the greatest men of the earth. 9And I will provide a place for my people Israel and will plant them so that they can have a home of their own and no longer be disturbed. Wicked people will not oppress them anymore, as they did at the beginning 10and have done ever since the time I appointed leaders[r] over my people Israel. I will also subdue all your enemies.

"'I declare to you that the LORD will build a house for you: 11When your days are over and you go to be with your fathers, I will raise up your offspring to succeed you, one of your own sons, and I will establish his kingdom. 12He is the one who will build[s] a house for me, and I will establish his throne forever.[t] 13I will be his father,[u] and he will be my son.[v] I will never take my love away from him, as I took it away from your predecessor. 14I will set him over my house and my kingdom forever; his throne[w] will be established forever.[x]'"

15Nathan reported to David all the words of this entire revelation.

17:7 [q]2Sa 6:21
17:10 [r]Jdg 2:16
17:12 [s]1Ki 5:5 [t]2Ch 7:18
17:13 [u]2Co 6:18 [v]Lk 1:32; Heb 1:5*
17:14 [w]1Ki 2:12; 1Ch 28:5 [x]Ps 132:11; Jer 33:17

David's Prayer

16Then King David went in and sat before the LORD, and he said:

"Who am I, O LORD God, and what is my family, that you have brought me this far? 17And as if this were not enough in your sight, O God, you have spoken about the future of the house of your servant. You have looked on me as though I were the most exalted of men, O LORD God.

18"What more can David say to you for honoring your servant? For you know your servant, 19O LORD. For the sake[y] of your servant and according to your will, you have done this great thing and made known all these great promises.[z]

20"There is no one like you, O LORD, and there is no God but you,[a] as we have heard with our own ears. 21And who is like your people Israel—the one nation on earth whose God went out to redeem[b] a people for himself, and to make a name for yourself, and to perform great and awesome wonders by driving out nations from before your people, whom you redeemed from Egypt? 22You made your people Israel your very own forever,[c] and you, O LORD, have become their God.

23"And now, LORD, let the promise[d] you have made concerning your servant and his house be established forever. Do as you promised, 24so that it will be established and that your name will be great forever. Then men will say, 'The LORD Almighty, the God over Israel, is Israel's God!' And the house of your servant David will be established before you.

25"You, my God, have revealed to your servant that you will build a house for him. So your servant has found courage to pray to you. 26O LORD, you are God! You have promised these good things to your servant. 27Now you have been pleased to bless the house of your servant, that it may continue forever in your sight;[e] for you, O LORD, have blessed it, and it will be blessed forever."

David's Victories

18 In the course of time, David defeated the Philistines and subdued them, and he took Gath and its surrounding villages from the control of the Philistines.

2David also defeated the Moabites,[f] and they became subject to him and brought tribute.

17:19 [y]2Sa 7:16-17; 2Ki 20:6; Isa 9:7; 37:35; 55:3 [z]2Sa 7:25
17:20 [a]Ex 8:10; 9:14; 15:11; Isa 44:6; 46:9
17:21 [b]Ex 6:6
17:22 [c]Ex 19:5-6
17:23 [d]1Ki 8:25
17:27 [e]Ps 16:11; 21:6
18:2 [f]Nu 21:29

[a]6 Traditionally *judges*; also in verse 10

3Moreover, David fought Hadadezer king of Zobah,[g] as far as Hamath, when he went to establish his control along the Euphrates River.[h] 4David captured a thousand of his chariots, seven thousand charioteers and twenty thousand foot soldiers. He hamstrung[i] all but a hundred of the chariot horses.

5When the Arameans of Damascus[j] came to help Hadadezer king of Zobah, David struck down twenty-two thousand of them. 6He put garrisons in the Aramean kingdom of Damascus, and the Arameans became subject to him and brought tribute. The LORD gave David victory everywhere he went.

7David took the gold shields carried by the officers of Hadadezer and brought them to Jerusalem. 8From Tebah[a] and Cun, towns that belonged to Hadadezer, David took a great quantity of bronze, which Solomon used to make the bronze Sea,[k] the pillars and various bronze articles.

9When Tou king of Hamath heard that David had defeated the entire army of Hadadezer king of Zobah, 10he sent his son Hadoram to King David to greet him and congratulate him on his victory in battle over Hadadezer, who had been at war with Tou. Hadoram brought all kinds of articles of gold and silver and bronze.

11King David dedicated these articles to the LORD, as he had done with the silver and gold he had taken from all these nations: Edom[l] and Moab, the Ammonites and the Philistines, and Amalek.[m]

12Abishai son of Zeruiah struck down eighteen thousand Edomites[n] in the Valley of Salt. 13He put garrisons in Edom, and all the Edomites became subject to David. The LORD gave David victory everywhere he went.

David's Officials

14David reigned[o] over all Israel,[p] doing what was just and right for all his people. 15Joab[q] son of Zeruiah was over the army; Jehoshaphat son of Ahilud was recorder; 16Zadok[r] son of Ahitub and Ahimelech[b][s] son of Abiathar were priests; Shavsha was secretary; 17Benaiah son of Jehoiada was over the Kerethites and Pelethites;[t] and David's sons were chief officials at the king's side.

18:3 [g]1Ch 19:6 [h]Ge 2:14
18:4 [i]Ge 49:6
18:5 [j]2Ki 16:9; 1Ch 19:6
18:8 [k]1Ki 7:23; 2Ch 4:12, 15-16
18:11 [l]Nu 24:18 [m]Nu 24:20
18:12 [n]1Ki 11:15
18:14 [o]1Ch 29:26 [p]1Ch 11:1
18:15 [q]2Sa 5:6-8; 1Ch 11:6
18:16 [r]2Sa 8:17; 1Ch 6:8 [s]1Ch 24:6
18:17 [t]1Sa 30:14; 2Sa 8:18; 15:18

The Battle Against the Ammonites

19 In the course of time, Nahash king of the Ammonites[u] died, and his son succeeded him as king. 2David thought, "I will show kindness to Hanun son of Nahash, because his father showed kindness to me." So David sent a delegation to express his sympathy to Hanun concerning his father.

When David's men came to Hanun in the land of the Ammonites to express sympathy to him, 3the Ammonite nobles said to Hanun, "Do you think David is honoring your father by sending men to you to express sympathy? Haven't his men come to you to explore and spy out[v] the country and overthrow it?" 4So Hanun seized David's men, shaved them, cut off their garments in the middle at the buttocks, and sent them away.

5When someone came and told David about the men, he sent messengers to meet them, for they were greatly humiliated. The king said, "Stay at Jericho till your beards have grown, and then come back."

6When the Ammonites realized that they had become a stench[w] in David's nostrils, Hanun and the Ammonites sent a thousand talents[c] of silver to hire chariots and charioteers from Aram Naharaim,[d] Aram Maacah and Zobah.[x] 7They hired thirty-two thousand chariots and charioteers, as well as the king of Maacah with his troops, who came and camped near Medeba,[y] while the Ammonites were mustered from their towns and moved out for battle.

8On hearing this, David sent Joab out with the entire army of fighting men. 9The Ammonites came out and drew up in battle formation at the entrance to their city, while the kings who had come were by themselves in the open country.

10Joab saw that there were battle lines in front of him and behind him; so he selected some of the best troops in Israel and deployed them against the Arameans. 11He put the rest of the men under the command of Abishai[z] his brother,

[a]*8* Hebrew *Tibhath,* a variant of *Tebah* [b]*16* Some Hebrew manuscripts, Vulgate and Syriac (see also 2 Samuel 8:17); most Hebrew manuscripts *Abimelech* [c]*6* That is, about 37 tons (about 34 metric tons) [d]*6* That is, Northwest Mesopotamia

19:1 [u]Ge 19:38; Jdg 10:17-11:33; 2Ch 20:1-2; Zep 2:8-11
19:3 [v]Nu 21:32
19:6 [w]Ge 34:30 [x]1Ch 18:3,5,9
19:7 [y]Nu 21:30; Jos 13:9,16
19:11 [z]1Sa 26:6

and they were deployed against the Ammonites. 12Joab said, "If the Arameans
are too strong for me, then you are to
rescue me; but if the Ammonites are
too strong for you, then I will rescue
you. 13Be strong and let us fight bravely for our people and the cities of our
God. The LORD will do what is good
in his sight."
14Then Joab and the troops with him
advanced to fight the Arameans, and
they fled before him. 15When the Ammonites saw that the Arameans were
fleeing, they too fled before his brother Abishai and went inside the city. So
Joab went back to Jerusalem.
19:17 16After the Arameans saw that they
[a]1Ch 9:1 had been routed by Israel,[a] they sent
messengers and had Arameans brought
from beyond the River,[a] with Shophach
the commander of Hadadezer's army
leading them.
17When David was told of this, he
gathered all Israel and crossed the Jordan; he advanced against them and
formed his battle lines opposite them.
David formed his lines to meet the
Arameans in battle, and they fought
against him. 18But they fled before Israel, and David killed seven thousand of
their charioteers and forty thousand of
their foot soldiers. He also killed Shophach the commander of their army.
19When the vassals of Hadadezer saw
that they had been defeated by Israel,
they made peace with David and became subject to him.
So the Arameans were not willing to
help the Ammonites anymore.

The Capture of Rabbah

20 In the spring, at the time when
kings go off to war, Joab led
out the armed forces. He laid waste
the land of the Ammonites and went
to Rabbah and besieged it, but David
remained in Jerusalem. Joab attacked
20:1 [b]Dt 3:11; Rabbah[b] and left it in ruins.[c] 2David
2Sa 12:26 took the crown from the head of their
[c]Am 1:13-15 king[b]—its weight was found to be a
talent[c] of gold, and it was set with
precious stones—and it was placed on
David's head. He took a great quantity
of plunder from the city 3and brought
out the people who were there, con-
20:3 signing them to labor with saws and
[d]Dt 29:11 with iron picks and axes.[d] David did
this to all the Ammonite towns. Then
David and his entire army returned to
Jerusalem.

War With the Philistines

4In the course of time, war broke
out with the Philistines, at Gezer.[e] At 20:4
that time Sibbecai the Hushathite killed [e]Jos 10:33 [f]Ge 14:5
Sippai, one of the descendants of the
Rephaites,[f] and the Philistines were sub-
jugated.
5In another battle with the Philistines, Elhanan son of Jair killed Lahmi
the brother of Goliath the Gittite, who
had a spear with a shaft like a weaver's 20:5
rod.[g] [g]1Sa 17:7
6In still another battle, which took
place at Gath, there was a huge man
with six fingers on each hand and six
toes on each foot—twenty-four in all.
He also was descended from Rapha.
7When he taunted Israel, Jonathan son
of Shimea, David's brother, killed him.
8These were descendants of Rapha in
Gath, and they fell at the hands of David and his men.

David Numbers the Fighting Men

21:1
21 Satan[h] rose up against Israel and [h]2Ch 18:21;
incited David to take a census[i] Ps 109:6 [i]2Ch 14:8;
of Israel. 2So David said to Joab and the 25:5
commanders of the troops, "Go and 21:2
count[j] the Israelites from Beersheba to [j]1Ch 27:23-
Dan. Then report back to me so that I 24
may know how many there are."
3But Joab replied, "May the LORD
multiply his troops a hundred times 21:3
over.[k] My lord the king, are they not all [k]Dt 1:11
my lord's subjects? Why does my lord
want to do this? Why should he bring
guilt on Israel?"
4The king's word, however, overruled
Joab; so Joab left and went throughout
Israel and then came back to Jerusalem.
5Joab reported the number of the fight- 21:5
ing men to David: In all Israel[l] there [l]1Ch 9:1
were one million one hundred thousand
men who could handle a sword, including four hundred and seventy thousand
in Judah.
6But Joab did not include Levi and
Benjamin in the numbering, because
the king's command was repulsive to
him. 7This command was also evil in
the sight of God; so he punished Israel.

[a] *16* That is, the Euphrates [b] *2* Or *of Milcom,* that is, Molech [c] *2* That is, about 75 pounds (about 34 kilograms)

8Then David said to God, "I have
sinned greatly by doing this. Now, I beg
you, take away the guilt of your servant. I have done a very foolish thing."
9The LORD said to Gad,[m] David's
seer,[n] 10"Go and tell David, 'This is
what the LORD says: I am giving you
three options. Choose one of them for
me to carry out against you.'"
11So Gad went to David and said to
him, "This is what the LORD says: 'Take
your choice: 12three years of famine,[o]
three months of being swept away[a] before your enemies, with their swords
overtaking you, or three days of the
sword[p] of the LORD[q]—days of plague
in the land, with the angel of the LORD
ravaging every part of Israel.' Now then,
decide how I should answer the one
who sent me."
13David said to God, "I am in deep
distress. Let me fall into the hands of
the LORD, for his mercy[r] is very great;
but do not let me fall into the hands of
men."
14So the LORD sent a plague on Israel, and seventy thousand men of Israel fell dead.[s] 15And God sent an angel[t]
to destroy Jerusalem.[u] But as the angel
was doing so, the LORD saw it and was
grieved[v] because of the calamity and
said to the angel who was destroying[w]
the people, "Enough! Withdraw your
hand." The angel of the LORD was then
standing at the threshing floor of Araunah[b] the Jebusite.
16David looked up and saw the angel
of the LORD standing between heaven
and earth, with a drawn sword in his
hand extended over Jerusalem. Then
David and the elders, clothed in sackcloth, fell facedown.[x]
17David said to God, "Was it not I
who ordered the fighting men to be
counted? I am the one who has sinned
and done wrong. These are but sheep.[y]
What have they done? O LORD my
God, let your hand fall upon me and
my family,[z] but do not let this plague
remain on your people."
18Then the angel of the LORD ordered Gad to tell David to go up and
build an altar to the LORD on the
threshing floor[a] of Araunah the Jebusite. 19So David went up in obedience
to the word that Gad had spoken in the
name of the LORD.
20While Araunah was threshing
wheat,[b] he turned and saw the angel; his
four sons who were with him hid themselves. 21Then David approached, and
when Araunah looked and saw him,
he left the threshing floor and bowed
down before David with his face to the
ground.
22David said to him, "Let me have
the site of your threshing floor so I can
build an altar to the LORD, that the
plague on the people may be stopped.
Sell it to me at the full price."
23Araunah said to David, "Take it! Let
my lord the king do whatever pleases
him. Look, I will give the oxen for the
burnt offerings, the threshing sledges
for the wood, and the wheat for the
grain offering. I will give all this."
24But King David replied to Araunah, "No, I insist on paying the full
price. I will not take for the LORD what
is yours, or sacrifice a burnt offering
that costs me nothing."
25So David paid Araunah six hundred shekels[c] of gold for the site. 26Da-
vid built an altar to the LORD there and
sacrificed burnt offerings and fellowship offerings.[d] He called on the LORD,
and the LORD answered him with fire[c]
from heaven on the altar of burnt offering.
27Then the LORD spoke to the angel, and he put his sword back into its
sheath. 28At that time, when David saw
that the LORD had answered him on
the threshing floor of Araunah the Jebusite, he offered sacrifices there. 29The
tabernacle of the LORD, which Moses
had made in the desert, and the altar
of burnt offering were at that time on
the high place at Gibeon.[d] 30But David could not go before it to inquire
of God, because he was afraid of the
sword of the angel of the LORD.

22 Then David said, "The house
of the LORD God[e] is to be here,
and also the altar of burnt offering for
Israel."

Preparations for the Temple

2So David gave orders to assemble
the aliens[f] living in Israel, and from
among them he appointed stonecutters[g]

[a]*12* Hebrew; Septuagint and Vulgate (see also 2 Samuel 24:13) *of fleeing* [b]*15* Hebrew *Ornan,* a variant of *Araunah;* also in verses 18-28 [c]*25* That is, about 15 pounds (about 7 kilograms)
[d]*26* Traditionally *peace offerings*

21:9 [m]1Sa 22:5 [n]1Sa 9:9
21:12 [o]Dt 32:24 [p]Eze 30:25 [q]Ge 19:13
21:13 [r]Ps 6:4; 86:15; 130:4,7
21:14 [s]1Ch 27:24
21:15 [t]Ge 32:1 [u]Ps 125:2 [v]Ge 6:6; Ex 32:14 [w]Ge 19:13
21:16 [x]Nu 14:5; Jos 7:6
21:17 [y]2Sa 7:8; Ps 74:1 [z]Jnh 1:12
21:18 [a]2Ch 3:1
21:20 [b]Jdg 6:11
21:26 [c]Lev 9:24; Jdg 6:21
21:29 [d]1Ki 3:4; 1Ch 16:39
22:1 [e]Ge 28:17; 1Ch 21:18-29; 2Ch 3:1
22:2 [f]1Ki 9:21; Isa 56:6 [g]1Ki 5:17-18

to prepare dressed stone for building the house of God. 3 He provided a large amount of iron to make nails for the doors of the gateways and for the fittings, and more bronze than could be weighed.[h] 4 He also provided more cedar logs[i] than could be counted, for the Sidonians and Tyrians had brought large numbers of them to David.

5 David said, "My son Solomon is young[j] and inexperienced, and the house to be built for the LORD should be of great magnificence and fame and splendor in the sight of all the nations. Therefore I will make preparations for it." So David made extensive preparations before his death.

6 Then he called for his son Solomon and charged him to build[k] a house for the LORD, the God of Israel. 7 David said to Solomon: "My son, I had it in my heart[l] to build[m] a house for the Name[n] of the LORD my God. 8 But this word of the LORD came to me: 'You have shed much blood and have fought many wars.[o] You are not to build a house for my Name,[p] because you have shed much blood on the earth in my sight. 9 But you will have a son who will be a man of peace[q] and rest, and I will give him rest from all his enemies on every side. His name will be Solomon,[a][r] and I will grant Israel peace and quiet[s] during his reign. 10 He is the one who will build a house for my Name.[t] He will be my son,[u] and I will be his father. And I will establish the throne of his kingdom over Israel forever.'[v]

11 "Now, my son, the LORD be with[w] you, and may you have success and build the house of the LORD your God, as he said you would. 12 May the LORD give you discretion and understanding[x] when he puts you in command over Israel, so that you may keep the law of the LORD your God. 13 Then you will have success if you are careful to observe the decrees and laws[y] that the LORD gave Moses for Israel. Be strong and courageous.[z] Do not be afraid or discouraged.

14 "I have taken great pains to provide for the temple of the LORD a hundred thousand talents[b] of gold, a million talents[c] of silver, quantities of bronze and iron too great to be weighed, and wood and stone. And you may add to them.[a] 15 You have many workmen: stonecutters, masons and carpenters, as well as men skilled in every kind of work 16 in gold and silver, bronze and iron—craftsmen[b] beyond number. Now begin the work, and the LORD be with you."

17 Then David ordered[c] all the leaders of Israel to help his son Solomon. 18 He said to them, "Is not the LORD your God with you? And has he not granted you rest[d] on every side?[e] For he has handed the inhabitants of the land over to me, and the land is subject to the LORD and to his people. 19 Now devote your heart and soul to seeking the LORD your God.[f] Begin to build the sanctuary of the LORD God, so that you may bring the ark of the covenant of the LORD and the sacred articles belonging to God into the temple that will be built for the Name of the LORD."

22:3 [h]ver 14; 1Ki 7:47; 1Ch 29:2-5
22:4 [i]1Ki 5:6
22:5 [j]1Ki 3:7; 1Ch 29:1
22:6 [k]Ac 7:47
22:7 [l]1Ch 17:2 [m]2Sa 7:2; 1Ki 8:17 [n]Dt 12:5,11
22:8 [o]1Ki 5:3 [p]1Ch 28:3
22:9 [q]1Ki 5:4 [r]2Sa 12:24 [s]1Ki 4:20
22:10 [t]1Ch 17:12 [u]2Sa 7:13 [v]2Sa 7:14; 2Ch 6:15
22:11 [w]ver 16
22:12 [x]1Ki 3:9-12; 2Ch 1:10
22:13 [y]1Ch 28:7 [z]Dt 31:6; Jos 1:6-9; 1Ch 28:20
22:14 [a]ver 3; 1Ch 29:2-5, 19
22:16 [b]ver 11; 2Ch 2:7
22:17 [c]1Ch 28:1-6
22:18 [d]ver 9; 1Ch 23:25 [e]2Sa 7:1
22:19 [f]ver 7; 1Ki 8:6; 1Ch 28:9; 2Ch 5:7; 7:14

▸ GOODNESS

PITCH IN AND HELP

1 Chronicles 22:19

David challenged the people to help his son Solomon build the temple. David was too much a man of war to build it himself. "How is heaven opened?" asked Catherine of Siena. "With the key of his dear blood." Goodness spent on honoring God makes temples in its own time.

The Levites

23 When David was old and full of years, he made his son Solomon[g] king over Israel.[h]

2 He also gathered together all the leaders of Israel, as well as the priests and Levites. 3 The Levites thirty years old or more[i] were counted, and the total number of men was thirty-eight thousand.[j] 4 David said, "Of these, twenty-four thousand are to supervise[k] the work of the temple of the LORD and six thousand are to be officials and judges.[l] 5 Four thousand are to be gatekeepers and four thousand are to praise the LORD with the musical instruments[m] I have provided for that purpose."[n]

6 David divided[o] the Levites into

23:1 [g]1Ki 1:33-39; 1Ch 28:5 [h]1Ki 1:30; 1Ch 29:28
23:3 [i]ver 24; Nu 8:24 [j]Nu 4:3-49
23:4 [k]Ezr 3:8 [l]1Ch 26:29; 2Ch 19:8
23:5 [m]1Ch 15:16 [n]Ne 12:45
23:6 [o]2Ch 8:14; 29:25

[a]9 *Solomon* sounds like and may be derived from the Hebrew for *peace.* [b]14 That is, about 3,750 tons (about 3,450 metric tons) [c]14 That is, about 37,500 tons (about 34,500 metric tons)

groups corresponding to the sons of Levi: Gershon, Kohath and Merari.

Gershonites

7 Belonging to the Gershonites:
Ladan and Shimei.
8 The sons of Ladan:
Jehiel the first, Zetham and Joel—three in all.
9 The sons of Shimei:
Shelomoth, Haziel and Haran—three in all.
These were the heads of the families of Ladan.
10 And the sons of Shimei:
Jahath, Ziza,[a] Jeush and Beriah.
These were the sons of Shimei—four in all.
11 Jahath was the first and Ziza the second, but Jeush and Beriah did not have many sons; so they were counted as one family with one assignment.

Kohathites

23:12 12 The sons of Kohath:[p]
[p]Ex 6:18 Amram, Izhar, Hebron and Uzziel—four in all.
13 The sons of Amram:[q]
23:13 [q]Ex 6:20; 28:1 [r]Ex 30:7-10; Dt 21:5 [s]Nu 6:23
Aaron and Moses.
Aaron was set apart,[r] he and his descendants forever, to consecrate the most holy things, to offer sacrifices before the LORD, to minister before him and to pronounce blessings[s] in his name forever. 14 The sons of Moses the man of God were counted as part[t] of the tribe of
23:14 [t]Dt 33:1 Levi.
15 The sons of Moses:
23:15 [u]Ex 18:4 Gershom and Eliezer.[u]
16 The descendants of Gershom:[v]
23:16 [v]1Ch 26:24-28 Shubael was the first.
17 The descendants of Eliezer:
Rehabiah was the first.
Eliezer had no other sons, but the sons of Rehabiah were very numerous.
18 The sons of Izhar:
Shelomith was the first.
23:19 [w]1Ch 24:23 19 The sons of Hebron:[w]
Jeriah the first, Amariah the second, Jahaziel the third and Jekameam the fourth.
20 The sons of Uzziel:
Micah the first and Isshiah the second.

Merarites

21 The sons of Merari:[x] 23:21 [x]1Ch 24:26
Mahli and Mushi.
The sons of Mahli:
Eleazar and Kish.
22 Eleazar died without having sons: he had only daughters. Their cousins, the sons of Kish, married them.
23 The sons of Mushi:
Mahli, Eder and Jerimoth—three in all.

24 These were the descendants of Levi
by their families—the heads of families as they were registered under their
names and counted individually, that is,
the workers twenty years old or more[y] 23:24 [y]Nu 4:3; 10:17,21
who served in the temple of the LORD.
25 For David had said, "Since the LORD,
the God of Israel, has granted rest[z] 23:25 [z]1Ch 22:9
to his people and has come to dwell
in Jerusalem forever, 26 the Levites no
longer need to carry the tabernacle or
any of the articles used in its service."[a] 23:26 [a]Nu 4:5,15; 7:9; Dt 10:8
27 According to the last instructions of
David, the Levites were counted from
those twenty years old or more.
28 The duty of the Levites was to help
Aaron's descendants in the service of the
temple of the LORD: to be in charge
of the courtyards, the side rooms, the
purification[b] of all sacred things and 23:28 [b]2Ch 29:15; Ne 13:9; Mal 3:3
the performance of other duties at the
house of God. 29 They were in charge of
the bread set out on the table,[c] the flour 23:29 [c]Ex 25:30 [d]Lev 2:4-7; 6:20-23 [e]Lev 19:35-36; 1Ch 9:29,32
for the grain offerings,[d] the unleavened
wafers, the baking and the mixing, and
all measurements of quantity and size.[e]
30 They were also to stand every morning to thank and praise the LORD.
They were to do the same in the eve-
ning 31 and whenever burnt offerings[f] 23:30 [f]1Ch 9:33; Ps 134:1
were presented to the LORD on Sab-
baths and at New Moon[g] festivals and 23:31 [g]2Ki 4:23 [h]Lev 23:4; Nu 28:9-29:39; Isa 1:13-14; Col 2:16
at appointed feasts.[h] They were to serve
before the LORD regularly in the proper number and in the way prescribed
for them.
32 And so the Levites[i] carried out their 23:32 [i]Nu 1:53; 1Ch 6:48 [j]Nu 3:6-8,38 [k]2Ch 23:18; 31:2; Eze 44:14
responsibilities for the Tent of Meet-
ing,[j] for the Holy Place and, under
their brothers the descendants of Aaron, for the service of the temple of the
LORD.[k]

[a] *10* One Hebrew manuscript, Septuagint and Vulgate (see also verse 11); most Hebrew manuscripts *Zina*

The Divisions of Priests

24 These were the divisions[l] of the
sons of Aaron:[m]
The sons of Aaron were Nadab, Abihu, Eleazar and Ithamar.[n] 2But Nadab
and Abihu died before their father did,[o]
and they had no sons; so Eleazar and
Ithamar served as the priests. 3With
the help of Zadok[p] a descendant of
Eleazar and Ahimelech a descendant
of Ithamar, David separated them into
divisions for their appointed order of
ministering. 4A larger number of leaders were found among Eleazar's descendants than among Ithamar's, and
they were divided accordingly: sixteen
heads of families from Eleazar's descendants and eight heads of families from
Ithamar's descendants. 5They divided
them impartially by drawing lots,[q] for
there were officials of the sanctuary
and officials of God among the descendants of both Eleazar and Ithamar.
6The scribe Shemaiah son of Nethanel, a Levite, recorded their names in the
presence of the king and of the officials: Zadok the priest, Ahimelech[r] son
of Abiathar and the heads of families
of the priests and of the Levites—one
family being taken from Eleazar and
then one from Ithamar.

7The first lot fell to Jehoiarib,
the second to Jedaiah,[s]
8the third to Harim,[t]
the fourth to Seorim,
9the fifth to Malkijah,
the sixth to Mijamin,
10the seventh to Hakkoz,
the eighth to Abijah,[u]
11the ninth to Jeshua,
the tenth to Shecaniah,
12the eleventh to Eliashib,
the twelfth to Jakim,
13the thirteenth to Huppah,
the fourteenth to Jeshebeab,
14the fifteenth to Bilgah,
the sixteenth to Immer,[v]
15the seventeenth to Hezir,[w]
the eighteenth to Happizzez,
16the nineteenth to Pethahiah,
the twentieth to Jehezkel,
17the twenty-first to Jakin,
the twenty-second to Gamul,
18the twenty-third to Delaiah
and the twenty-fourth to Maaziah.

24:1 [l]1Ch 23:6; 28:13; 2Ch 5:11; 8:14; 23:8; 31:2; 35:4,5; Ezr 6:18 [m]Nu 3:2-4 [n]Ex 6:23
24:2 [o]Lev 10:1-2; Nu 3:4
24:3 [p]2Sa 8:17
24:5 [q]ver 31; 1Ch 25:8
24:6 [r]1Ch 18:16
24:7 [s]Ezr 2:36; Ne 12:6
24:8 [t]Ezr 2:39; Ne 10:5
24:10 [u]Ne 12:4,17; Lk 1:5
24:14 [v]Jer 20:1
24:15 [w]Ne 10:20

19This was their appointed order of
ministering when they entered the temple of the LORD, according to the regulations prescribed for them by their
forefather Aaron, as the LORD, the God
of Israel, had commanded him.

The Rest of the Levites

20As for the rest of the descendants of
Levi:[x]
from the sons of Amram: Shubael;
from the sons of Shubael: Jehdeiah.
21As for Rehabiah,[y] from his sons:
Isshiah was the first.
22From the Izharites: Shelomoth;
from the sons of Shelomoth: Jahath.
23The sons of Hebron:[z] Jeriah the
first,[a] Amariah the second, Jahaziel the third and Jekameam the
fourth.
24The son of Uzziel: Micah;
from the sons of Micah: Shamir.
25The brother of Micah: Isshiah;
from the sons of Isshiah: Zechariah.
26The sons of Merari:[a] Mahli and
Mushi.
The son of Jaaziah: Beno.
27The sons of Merari:
from Jaaziah: Beno, Shoham,
Zaccur and Ibri.
28From Mahli: Eleazar, who had no
sons.
29From Kish: the son of Kish:
Jerahmeel.
30And the sons of Mushi: Mahli,
Eder and Jerimoth.

These were the Levites, according to
their families. 31They also cast lots,[b]
just as their brothers the descendants of
Aaron did, in the presence of King David and of Zadok, Ahimelech, and the
heads of families of the priests and of
the Levites. The families of the oldest
brother were treated the same as those
of the youngest.

The Singers

25 David, together with the commanders of the army, set apart

24:20 [x]1Ch 23:6
24:21 [y]1Ch 23:17
24:23 [z]1Ch 23:19
24:26 [a]1Ch 6:19; 23:21
24:31 [b]ver 5

[a] *23* Two Hebrew manuscripts and some Septuagint manuscripts (see also 1 Chron. 23:19); most Hebrew manuscripts *The sons of Jeriah:*

25:1 [c]1Ch 6:39 [d]1Ch 6:33 [e]1Ch 16:41, 42; Ne 11:17 [f]1Sa 10:5; 2Ki 3:15 [g]1Ch 15:16 [h]1Ch 6:31 [i]2Ch 5:12; 8:14; 34:12; 35:15; Ezr 3:10

some of the sons of Asaph,[c] Heman[d] and
Jeduthun[e] for the ministry of prophesying,[f] accompanied by harps, lyres and
cymbals.[g] Here is the list of the men[h]
who performed this service:[i]

2 From the sons of Asaph:
Zaccur, Joseph, Nethaniah and Asarelah. The sons of Asaph were under the supervision of Asaph, who prophesied under the king's supervision.

25:3 [j]1Ch 16:41-42 [k]Ge 4:21; Ps 33:2

3 As for Jeduthun, from his sons:[j]
Gedaliah, Zeri, Jeshaiah, Shimei,[a] Hashabiah and Mattithiah, six in all, under the supervision of their father Jeduthun, who prophesied, using the harp[k] in thanking and praising the LORD.

4 As for Heman, from his sons:
Bukkiah, Mattaniah, Uzziel, Shubael and Jerimoth; Hananiah, Hanani, Eliathah, Giddalti and Romamti-Ezer; Joshbekashah, Mallothi, Hothir and Mahazioth. 5 All
these were sons of Heman the king's seer. They were given him through the promises of God to exalt him.[b] God gave Heman fourteen sons and three daughters.

25:6 [l]1Ch 15:16 [m]1Ch 15:19 [n]2Ch 23:18; 29:25

6 All these men were under the supervision of their fathers[l] for the music
of the temple of the LORD, with cymbals, lyres and harps, for the ministry at
the house of God. Asaph, Jeduthun and
Heman[m] were under the supervision of
the king.[n] 7 Along with their relatives—
all of them trained and skilled in music for the LORD—they numbered 288.
8 Young and old alike, teacher as well as
student, cast lots[o] for their duties.

25:8 [o]1Ch 26:13

25:9 [p]1Ch 6:39

9 The first lot, which was for
Asaph,[p] fell to Joseph,
his sons and relatives,[c] 12[d]
the second to Gedaliah,
he and his relatives and
sons, 12
10 the third to Zaccur,
his sons and relatives, 12
11 the fourth to Izri,[e]
his sons and relatives, 12
12 the fifth to Nethaniah,
his sons and relatives, 12
13 the sixth to Bukkiah,
his sons and relatives, 12
14 the seventh to Jesarelah,[f]
his sons and relatives, 12
15 the eighth to Jeshaiah,
his sons and relatives, 12
16 the ninth to Mattaniah,
his sons and relatives, 12
17 the tenth to Shimei,
his sons and relatives, 12
18 the eleventh to Azarel,[g]
his sons and relatives, 12
19 the twelfth to Hashabiah,
his sons and relatives, 12
20 the thirteenth to Shubael,
his sons and relatives, 12
21 the fourteenth to Mattithiah,
his sons and relatives, 12
22 the fifteenth to Jerimoth,
his sons and relatives, 12
23 the sixteenth to Hananiah,
his sons and relatives, 12
24 the seventeenth to
Joshbekashah,
his sons and relatives, 12
25 the eighteenth to Hanani,
his sons and relatives, 12
26 the nineteenth to Mallothi,
his sons and relatives, 12
27 the twentieth to Eliathah,
his sons and relatives, 12
28 the twenty-first to Hothir,
his sons and relatives, 12
29 the twenty-second to
Giddalti,
his sons and relatives, 12
30 the twenty-third to
Mahazioth,
his sons and relatives, 12
31 the twenty-fourth to
Romamti-Ezer,
his sons and relatives, 12[q]

25:31 [q]1Ch 9:33

The Gatekeepers

26:1 [r]1Ch 9:17

26 The divisions of the gatekeepers:[r]

From the Korahites: Meshelemiah son of Kore, one of the sons of Asaph.

26:2 [s]1Ch 9:21

2 Meshelemiah had sons:
Zechariah[s] the firstborn,
Jediael the second,
Zebadiah the third,
Jathniel the fourth,

[a] *3* One Hebrew manuscript and some Septuagint manuscripts (see also verse 17); most Hebrew manuscripts do not have *Shimei.* [b] *5* Hebrew *exalt the horn* [c] *9* See Septuagint; Hebrew does not have *his sons and relatives.* [d] *9* See the total in verse 7; Hebrew does not have *twelve.* [e] *11* A variant of *Zeri* [f] *14* A variant of *Asarelah* [g] *18* A variant of *Uzziel*

3Elam the fifth,
Jehohanan the sixth
and Eliehoenai the seventh.
4Obed-Edom also had sons:
Shemaiah the firstborn,
Jehozabad the second,
Joah the third,
Sacar the fourth,
Nethanel the fifth,
5Ammiel the sixth,
Issachar the seventh
and Peullethai the eighth.
(For God had blessed Obed-
26:5 [t]2Sa 6:10; 1Ch 13:13; 16:38 Edom.[t])
6His son Shemaiah also had sons,
who were leaders in their
father's family because they were
very capable men. 7The sons
of Shemaiah: Othni, Rephael,
Obed and Elzabad; his relatives
Elihu and Semakiah were also
able men. 8All these were descendants of Obed-Edom; they
and their sons and their relatives were capable men with the
strength to do the work—descendants of Obed-Edom, 62
in all.
9Meshelemiah had sons and relatives, who were able men—18
in all.
10Hosah the Merarite had sons:
Shimri the first (although he was
not the firstborn, his father had
26:10 [u]Dt 21:16; 1Ch 5:1 appointed him the first),[u] 11Hil-
kiah the second, Tabaliah the
third and Zechariah the fourth.
The sons and relatives of Hosah
were 13 in all.
12These divisions of the gatekeepers,
through their chief men, had duties for
26:12 [v]1Ch 9:22 ministering[v] in the temple of the LORD,
just as their relatives had. 13Lots[w] were
26:13 [w]1Ch 24:5, 31; 25:8 cast for each gate, according to their
families, young and old alike.
14The lot for the East Gate[x] fell to
26:14 [x]1Ch 9:18 [y]1Ch 9:21 Shelemiah.[a] Then lots were cast for his
son Zechariah,[y] a wise counselor, and
the lot for the North Gate fell to him.
15The lot for the South Gate fell to
26:15 [z]1Ch 13:13; 2Ch 25:24 Obed-Edom,[z] and the lot for the storehouse fell to his sons. 16The lots for
the West Gate and the Shalleketh Gate
on the upper road fell to Shuppim and
Hosah.
Guard was alongside of guard:
17There were six Levites a day on the
east, four a day on the north, four a
day on the south and two at a time at
the storehouse. 18As for the court to the
west, there were four at the road and
two at the court itself.
19These were the divisions of the 26:19 [a]2Ch 35:15; Ne 7:1; Eze 44:11
gatekeepers who were descendants of
Korah and Merari.[a]

▸ LOVE

GREASING THE GATES WITH GRACE

1 Chronicles 26:19

The gatekeepers did not bolt the gates to keep the needy out. The gates led into a holy presence. It was at the gates that the insecure studied their unworthiness and quailed before their entrance. Yet grace greased the gates.

The Treasurers and Other Officials

20Their fellow Levites[b] were[b] in 26:20 [b]2Ch 24:5 [c]1Ch 28:12
charge of the treasuries of the house of
God and the treasuries for the dedicated things.[c]
21The descendants of Ladan, who
were Gershonites[d] through Ladan and 26:21 [d]1Ch 23:7; 29:8
who were heads of families belonging
to Ladan the Gershonite, were Jehieli, 26:22 [e]1Ch 9:26
22the sons of Jehieli, Zetham and his
brother Joel. They were in charge of the
treasuries[e] of the temple of the LORD.
23From the Amramites, the Izharites,
the Hebronites and the Uzzielites:[f] 26:23 [f]Nu 3:27
24Shubael,[g] a descendant of Ger- 26:24 [g]1Ch 23:16
shom son of Moses, was the of-
ficer in charge of the treasuries.
25His relatives through Eliezer:
Rehabiah his son, Jeshaiah his
son, Joram his son, Zicri his son
and Shelomith[h] his son. 26She- 26:25 [h]1Ch 23:18
lomith and his relatives were in
charge of all the treasuries for
the things dedicated[i] by King 26:26 [i]2Sa 8:11
David, by the heads of families
who were the commanders of
thousands and commanders of
hundreds, and by the other army
commanders. 27Some of the
plunder taken in battle they
dedicated for the repair of the
temple of the LORD. 28And everything dedicated by Samuel
the seer [j]and by Saul son of 26:28 [j]1Sa 9:9

[a]14 A variant of *Meshelemiah* [b]20 Septuagint; Hebrew *As for the Levites, Ahijah was*

Kish, Abner son of Ner and Joab
son of Zeruiah, and all the other dedicated things were in the
care of Shelomith and his relatives.
29 From the Izharites: Kenaniah and
his sons were assigned duties
away from the temple, as offi-
26:29 [k]Dt 17:8-13; 1Ch 23:4; Ne 11:16
cials and judges[k] over Israel.
30 From the Hebronites: Hashabiah[l]
and his relatives—seventeen
26:30 [l]1Ch 27:17
hundred able men—were re-
sponsible in Israel west of the
Jordan for all the work of the
26:31 [m]1Ch 23:19 [n]2Sa 5:4
LORD and for the king's service.
31 As for the Hebronites,[m] Jeriah was their chief according to
the genealogical records of their
families. In the fortieth[n] year
of David's reign a search was
made in the records, and capable men among the Hebronites
were found at Jazer in Gilead.
32 Jeriah had twenty-seven hundred relatives, who were able
men and heads of families, and
King David put them in charge
of the Reubenites, the Gadites
and the half-tribe of Manasseh
for every matter pertaining to
God and for the affairs of the
king.

Army Divisions

27 This is the list of the Israelites—
heads of families, commanders
of thousands and commanders of hundreds, and their officers, who served the
king in all that concerned the army divisions that were on duty month by
month throughout the year. Each division consisted of 24,000 men.

2 In charge of the first division, for the
27:2 [o]2Sa 23:8; 1Ch 11:11
first month, was Jashobeam[o] son of
Zabdiel. There were 24,000 men
in his division. 3 He was a descendant of Perez and chief of all the
army officers for the first month.
27:4 [p]2Sa 23:9
4 In charge of the division for the second month was Dodai[p] the Ahohite; Mikloth was the leader of his
division. There were 24,000 men
in his division.
27:5 [q]2Sa 23:20
5 The third army commander, for the
third month, was Benaiah[q] son of
Jehoiada the priest. He was chief
and there were 24,000 men in his
division. 6 This was the Benaiah
who was a mighty man among the
Thirty and was over the Thirty.
His son Ammizabad was in charge
of his division.
7 The fourth, for the fourth month,
was Asahel[r] the brother of Joab; 27:7 [r]2Sa 2:18; 1Ch 11:26
his son Zebadiah was his succes-
sor. There were 24,000 men in his
division.
8 The fifth, for the fifth month, was
the commander Shamhuth[s] the Iz- 27:8 [s]1Ch 11:27
rahite. There were 24,000 men in
his division.
9 The sixth, for the sixth month, was
Ira[t] the son of Ikkesh the Tekoite. 27:9 [t]2Sa 23:26; 1Ch 11:28
There were 24,000 men in his
division.
10 The seventh, for the seventh month,
was Helez[u] the Pelonite, an Ephra- 27:10 [u]2Sa 23:26; 1Ch 11:27
imite. There were 24,000 men in
his division.
11 The eighth, for the eighth month, was
Sibbecai[v] the Hushathite, a Zera- 27:11 [v]2Sa 21:18
hite. There were 24,000 men in
his division.
12 The ninth, for the ninth month, was
Abiezer[w] the Anathothite, a Ben- 27:12 [w]2Sa 23:27; 1Ch 11:28
jamite. There were 24,000 men in
his division.
13 The tenth, for the tenth month, was
Maharai[x] the Netophathite, a Ze- 27:13 [x]2Sa 23:28; 1Ch 11:30
rahite. There were 24,000 men in
his division.
14 The eleventh, for the eleventh month,
was Benaiah[y] the Pirathonite, an 27:14 [y]1Ch 11:31
Ephraimite. There were 24,000
men in his division.
15 The twelfth, for the twelfth month,
was Heldai[z] the Netophathite, 27:15 [z]2Sa 23:29 [a]Jos 15:17
from the family of Othniel.[a] There
were 24,000 men in his division.

Officers of the Tribes

16 The officers over the tribes of Israel:
over the Reubenites: Eliezer son of
Zicri;
over the Simeonites: Shephatiah
son of Maacah; 27:17 [b]1Ch 26:30 [c]2Sa 8:17; 1Ch 12:28
17 over Levi: Hashabiah[b] son of Kem-
uel;
over Aaron: Zadok;[c]
18 over Judah: Elihu, a brother of David;
over Issachar: Omri son of Michael;

19 over Zebulun: Ishmaiah son of Obadiah;
over Naphtali: Jerimoth son of Azriel;
20 over the Ephraimites: Hoshea son of Azaziah;
over half the tribe of Manasseh: Joel son of Pedaiah;
21 over the half-tribe of Manasseh in Gilead: Iddo son of Zechariah;
over Benjamin: Jaasiel son of Abner;
22 over Dan: Azarel son of Jeroham.

These were the officers over the tribes of Israel.

23 David did not take the number
of the men twenty years old or less,[d]
because the LORD had promised to
make Israel as numerous as the stars[e]
in the sky. 24 Joab son of Zeruiah began to count the men but did not finish. Wrath came on Israel on account of this numbering,[f] and the number was not entered in the book[a] of the annals of King David.

27:23 [d]1Ch 21:2-5 [e]Ge 15:5

27:24 [f]2Sa 24:15; 1Ch 21:7

The King's Overseers

25 Azmaveth son of Adiel was in charge of the royal storehouses.

Jonathan son of Uzziah was in charge of the storehouses in the outlying districts, in the towns, the villages and the watchtowers.

26 Ezri son of Kelub was in charge of the field workers who farmed the land.

27 Shimei the Ramathite was in charge of the vineyards.

Zabdi the Shiphmite was in charge of the produce of the vineyards for the wine vats.

28 Baal-Hanan the Gederite was in charge of the olive and sycamore-fig[g] trees in the western foothills.

27:28 [g]1Ki 10:27; 2Ch 1:15

Joash was in charge of the supplies of olive oil.

29 Shitrai the Sharonite was in charge of the herds grazing in Sharon.

Shaphat son of Adlai was in charge of the herds in the valleys.

30 Obil the Ishmaelite was in charge of the camels.

Jehdeiah the Meronothite was in charge of the donkeys.

31 Jaziz the Hagrite[h] was in charge of the flocks.

27:31 [h]1Ch 5:10

All these were the officials in charge of King David's property.

32 Jonathan, David's uncle, was a counselor, a man of insight and a scribe. Jehiel son of Hacmoni took care of the king's sons.

33 Ahithophel[i] was the king's counselor.

Hushai[j] the Arkite was the king's friend. 34 Ahithophel was succeeded by Jehoiada son of Benaiah and by Abiathar.[k]

Joab[l] was the commander of the royal army.

27:33 [i]2Sa 15:12 [j]2Sa 15:37

27:34 [k]1Ki 1:7 [l]1Ch 11:6

David's Plans for the Temple

28 David summoned all the officials[m] of Israel to assemble at Jerusalem: the officers over the tribes, the commanders of the divisions in the service of the king, the commanders of thousands and commanders of hundreds, and the officials in charge of all the property and livestock belonging to the king and his sons, together with the palace officials, the mighty men and all the brave warriors.

28:1 [m]1Ch 11:10; 27:1-31

2 King David rose to his feet and said: "Listen to me, my brothers and my people. I had it in my heart[n] to build a house as a place of rest for the ark of the covenant of the LORD, for the footstool[o] of our God, and I made plans to
build it. 3 But God said to me,[p] 'You are not to build a house for my Name,[q] because you are a warrior and have shed blood.[r]

28:2 [n]1Ch 17:2 [o]Ps 99:5; 132:7

28:3 [p]2Sa 7:5 [q]1Ch 22:8 [r]1Ki 5:3; 1Ch 17:4

▸GENTLENESS

A TEMPLE FOR ALL SEASONS

1 Chronicles 28:3

The temple was to be raised by those who were gentle of spirit. Robert Whittington said of Thomas More: "He was a man of gentleness—a man for all seasons." Such people should build God's temple—a temple for all seasons.

4 "Yet the LORD, the God of Israel, chose me[s] from my whole family[t] to be king over Israel forever. He chose Judah[u] as leader, and from the house of Judah he chose my family, and from my father's sons he was pleased to make me king over all Israel. 5 Of all my sons—

28:4 [s]1Ch 17:23,27; 2Ch 6:6 [t]1Sa 16:1-13 [u]Ge 49:10; 1Ch 5:2

[a]*24* Septuagint; Hebrew *number*

and the LORD has given me many[v]—he has chosen my son Solomon[w] to sit on the throne of the kingdom of the LORD over Israel. 6He said to me: 'Solomon your son is the one who will build my house and my courts, for I have chosen him to be my son,[x] and I will be his father. 7I will establish his kingdom forever if he is unswerving in carrying out my commands and laws,[y] as is being done at this time.'

8"So now I charge you in the sight of all Israel and of the assembly of the LORD, and in the hearing of our God: Be careful to follow all the commands[z] of the LORD your God, that you may possess this good land and pass it on as an inheritance to your descendants forever.[a]

9"And you, my son Solomon, acknowledge the God of your father, and serve him with wholehearted devotion[b] and with a willing mind, for the LORD searches every heart[c] and understands every motive behind the thoughts. If you seek him,[d] he will be found by you; but if you forsake[e] him, he will reject[f] you forever. 10Consider now, for the LORD has chosen you to build a temple as a sanctuary. Be strong and do the work."

11Then David gave his son Solomon the plans[g] for the portico of the temple, its buildings, its storerooms, its upper parts, its inner rooms and the place of atonement. 12He gave him the plans of all that the Spirit[h] had put in his mind for the courts of the temple of the LORD and all the surrounding rooms, for the treasuries of the temple of God and for the treasuries for the dedicated things.[i] 13He gave him instructions for the divisions[j] of the priests and Levites, and for all the work of serving in the temple of the LORD, as well as for all the articles to be used in its service. 14He designated the weight of gold for all the gold articles to be used in various kinds of service, and the weight of silver for all the silver articles to be used in various kinds of service: 15the weight of gold for the gold lampstands[k] and their lamps, with the weight for each lampstand and its lamps; and the weight of silver for each silver lampstand and its lamps, according to the use of each lampstand; 16the weight of gold for each table[l] for consecrated bread; the weight of silver for the silver tables; 17the weight of pure gold for the forks, sprinkling bowls[m] and pitchers; the weight of gold for each gold dish; the weight of silver for each silver dish; 18and the weight of the refined gold for the altar of incense.[n] He also gave him the plan for the chariot,[o] that is, the cherubim of gold that spread their wings and shelter[p] the ark of the covenant of the LORD.

19"All this," David said, "I have in writing from the hand of the LORD upon me, and he gave me understanding in all the details[q] of the plan.[r]"

20David also said to Solomon his son, "Be strong and courageous,[s] and do the work. Do not be afraid or discouraged, for the LORD God, my God, is with you. He will not fail you or forsake[t] you until all the work for the service of the temple of the LORD is finished.[u] 21The divisions of the priests and Levites are ready for all the work on the temple of God, and every willing man skilled[v] in any craft will help you in all the work. The officials and all the people will obey your every command."

Gifts for Building the Temple

29 Then King David said to the whole assembly: "My son Solomon, the one whom God has chosen, is young and inexperienced.[w] The task is great, because this palatial structure is not for man but for the LORD God. 2With all my resources I have provided for the temple of my God—gold[x] for the gold work, silver for the silver, bronze for the bronze, iron for the iron and wood for the wood, as well as onyx for the settings, turquoise,[a][y] stones of various colors, and all kinds of fine stone and marble—all of these in large quantities.[z] 3Besides, in my devotion to the temple of my God I now give my personal treasures of gold and silver for the temple of my God, over and above everything I have provided[a] for this holy temple: 4three thousand talents[b] of gold (gold of Ophir)[b] and seven thousand talents[c] of refined silver,[c] for the overlaying of the walls of the buildings, 5for the gold work and the

[a]2 The meaning of the Hebrew for this word is uncertain. [b]4 That is, about 110 tons (about 100 metric tons) [c]4 That is, about 260 tons (about 240 metric tons)

28:5 [v]1Ch 3:1 [w]1Ch 22:9; 23:1
28:6 [x]2Sa 7:13; 1Ch 22:9-10
28:7 [y]1Ch 22:13
28:8 [z]Dt 6:1 [a]Dt 4:1
28:9 [b]1Ch 29:19 [c]1Sa 16:7; Ps 7:9 [d]Ps 40:16; Jer 29:13 [e]Jos 24:20; 2Ch 15:2 [f]Ps 44:23
28:11 [g]Ex 25:9
28:12 [h]1Ch 12:18 [i]1Ch 26:20
28:13 [j]1Ch 24:1
28:15 [k]Ex 25:31
28:16 [l]Ex 25:23
28:17 [m]Ex 27:3
28:18 [n]Ex 30:1-10 [o]Ex 25:18-22 [p]Ex 25:20
28:19 [q]1Ki 6:38 [r]Ex 25:9
28:20 [s]Dt 31:6; 1Ch 22:13; 2Ch 19:11; Hag 2:4 [t]Dt 4:31; Jos 24:20 [u]1Ki 6:14; 2Ch 7:11
28:21 [v]Ex 35:25-36:5
29:1 [w]1Ki 3:7; 1Ch 22:5; 2Ch 13:7
29:2 [x]ver 7,14,16; Ezr 1:4; 6:5; Hag 2:8 [y]Isa 54:11 [z]1Ch 22:2-5
29:3 [a]2Ch 24:10; 31:3; 35:8
29:4 [b]Ge 10:29 [c]1Ch 22:14

silver work, and for all the work to be done by the craftsmen. Now, who is willing to consecrate himself today to the LORD?"

6Then the leaders of families, the officers of the tribes of Israel, the commanders of thousands and commanders of hundreds, and the officials[d] in charge of the king's work gave willingly.[e] 7They[f] gave toward the work on the temple of God five thousand talents[a] and ten thousand darics[b] of gold, ten thousand talents[c] of silver, eighteen thousand talents[d] of bronze and a hundred thousand talents[e] of iron. 8Any who had precious stones[g] gave them to the treasury of the temple of the LORD in the custody of Jehiel the Gershonite.[h] 9The people rejoiced at the willing response of their leaders, for they had given freely and wholeheartedly[i] to the LORD. David the king also rejoiced greatly.

David's Prayer

10David praised the LORD in the presence of the whole assembly, saying,

"Praise be to you, O LORD,
God of our father Israel,
from everlasting to everlasting.
11Yours, O LORD, is the greatness and the power[j]
and the glory and the majesty and the splendor,
for everything in heaven and earth is yours.[k]
Yours, O LORD, is the kingdom;
you are exalted as head over all.[l]
12Wealth and honor[m] come from you;
you are the ruler[n] of all things.
In your hands are strength and power
to exalt and give strength to all.
13Now, our God, we give you thanks,
and praise your glorious name.

14"But who am I, and who are my people, that we should be able to give as generously as this? Everything comes from you, and we have given you only what comes from your hand. 15We are aliens and strangers[o] in your sight, as were all our forefathers. Our days on earth are like a shadow,[p] without hope. 16O LORD our God, as for all this abundance that we have provided for building you a temple for your Holy Name, it comes from your hand, and all of it belongs to you. 17I know, my God, that you test the heart[q] and are pleased with integrity. All these things have I given willingly and with honest intent. And now I have seen with joy how willingly your people who are here have given to you.[r] 18O LORD, God of our fathers Abraham, Isaac and Israel, keep this desire in the hearts of your people forever, and keep their hearts loyal to you. 19And give my son Solomon the wholehearted devotion[s] to keep your commands, requirements and decrees[t] and to do everything to build the palatial structure for which I have provided."[u]

20Then David said to the whole assembly, "Praise the LORD your God." So they all praised the LORD, the God of their fathers; they bowed low and fell prostrate before the LORD and the king.

Solomon Acknowledged as King

21The next day they made sacrifices to the LORD and presented burnt offerings to him:[v] a thousand bulls, a thousand rams and a thousand male lambs, together with their drink offerings, and other sacrifices in abundance for all Israel. 22They ate and drank with great joy[w] in the presence of the LORD that day.

Then they acknowledged Solomon son of David as king a second time, anointing him before the LORD to be ruler and Zadok[x] to be priest. 23So Solomon sat on the throne[y] of the LORD as king in place of his father David. He prospered and all Israel obeyed him. 24All the officers and mighty men, as well as all of King David's sons, pledged their submission to King Solomon.

25The LORD highly exalted Solomon in the sight of all Israel and bestowed on him royal splendor[z] such as no king over Israel ever had before.[a]

The Death of David

26David son of Jesse was king[b] over all Israel. 27He ruled over Israel forty years—seven in Hebron and thirty-three in Jerusalem.[c] 28He died[d] at a

a 7 That is, about 190 tons (about 170 metric tons)
b 7 That is, about 185 pounds (about 84 kilograms)
c 7 That is, about 375 tons (about 345 metric tons)
d 7 That is, about 675 tons (about 610 metric tons)
e 7 That is, about 3,750 tons (about 3,450 metric tons)

29:6 d1Ch 27:1; 28:1 ever 9; Ex 25:1-8; 35:20-29; 36:2; 2Ch 24:10; Ezr 7:15
29:7 fEx 25:2; Ne 7:70-71
29:8 gEx 35:27 h1Ch 26:21
29:9 i1Ki 8:61; 2Co 9:7
29:11 jPs 24:8; 59:17; 62:11 kPs 89:11 lRev 5:12-13
29:12 m2Ch 1:12 n2Ch 20:6; Ro 11:36
29:15 oPs 39:12; Heb 11:13 pJob 14:2
29:17 qPs 139:23; Pr 15:11; 17:3; Jer 11:20; 17:10 r1Ch 28:9; Ps 15:1-5
29:19 s1Ch 28:9 tPs 72:1 u1Ch 22:14
29:21 v1Ki 8:62
29:22 w1Ch 23:1 x1Ki 1:33-39
29:23 y1Ki 2:12
29:25 z2Ch 1:1,12 a1Ki 3:13; Ecc 2:9
29:26 b1Ch 18:14
29:27 c2Sa 5:4-5; 1Ki 2:11; 1Ch 3:4
29:28 dGe 15:15; Ac 13:36

good old age, having enjoyed long life,
wealth and honor. His son Solomon
succeeded him as king.[e]
29As for the events of King David's
reign, from beginning to end, they are
written in the records of Samuel the
seer,[f] the records of Nathan[g] the prophet and the records of Gad[h] the seer, 30to-
gether with the details of his reign and
power, and the circumstances that surrounded him and Israel and the kingdoms of all the other lands.

29:28
[e]1Ch 23:1

29:29
[f]1Sa 9:9
[g]2Sa 7:2
[h]1Sa 22:5

2 CHRONICLES

AUTHORSHIP AND DATE

Ezra, according to Jewish tradition

c. 430 B.C.

KEY THEMES

The book of 2 Chronicles deals with a diversity of themes chronicling the time period between the building of Solomon's temple and the siege of Jerusalem in 586 B.C. After Solomon's reign, the nation of Israel was divided into the northern and southern kingdoms. Both kingdoms had a few powerful kings and many bad, self-indulgent, evil kings. The bane of both kingdoms was idolatry, and the gradual descent of them both toward oblivion was the result of idol worship.

FRUIT OF THE SPIRIT IN 2 CHRONICLES

Love: It is difficult in this tale of kings and quarreling dynasties to find great moments when the love of God is triumphant. But at the dedication of the temple, a national euphoria settled over the still undivided kingdom. During the service of temple consecration, the people seemed to be very much in love with God. Amid the resounding of instruments, they played and sang, "[The LORD] is good; his love endures forever" (5:13).

Joy: The praising by the people at the dedication of Solomon's temple was prompted by Solomon's own joy as he exulted, "Praise be to the LORD, the God of Israel, who with his hands has fulfilled what he promised with his mouth to my father David" (6:4). This joy before the living God would shortly wane. At the forefront of Israel's decline into depravity was idolatry, which demonstrated that the nation had forgotten how and whom to worship.

Patience: Uzziah became king at the age of sixteen. "He did what was right in the eyes of the LORD" (26:4). He learned to wait on the Lord, and his patient and devotional spirit led him to achieve great things for Judah in the early part of his reign. But in the end, he abandoned his life of patient waiting on God. After a temper tantrum in the temple, he was smitten with leprosy (see 26:19–21), and he died a leper king in his own quarantined house, the antithesis of all he had been when first he loved the Lord and served in patience.

Faithfulness: Solomon confessed, "The LORD has kept the promise he made. I have succeeded David my father and now I sit on the throne of Israel, just as the LORD promised, and I have built the temple for the Name of the LORD, the God of Israel" (6:10). The faithfulness of God is meant to elicit the faithfulness of those who love him.

Gentleness: Josiah's gentle and dependent spirit was revealed when the Book of the Law was discovered in the temple. In gentleness, repentance and real humility, he tore his clothes because of his sin and cried out to those around him, "Go and inquire of the LORD for me…about what is written in this book that has been found" (34:21).

Solomon Asks for Wisdom

1 Solomon son of David established[a] himself firmly over his kingdom, for the LORD his God was with[b] him and made him exceedingly great.[c]

2 Then Solomon spoke to all Israel[d]—to the commanders of thousands and commanders of hundreds, to the judges and to all the leaders in Israel, the heads of families— 3 and Solomon and the whole assembly went to the high place at Gibeon, for God's Tent of Meeting[e] was there, which Moses[f] the LORD's servant had made in the desert. 4 Now David had brought up the ark[g] of God from Kiriath Jearim to the place he had prepared for it, because he had pitched a tent[h] for it in Jerusalem. 5 But the bronze altar[i] that Bezalel[j] son of Uri, the son of Hur, had made was in Gibeon in front of the tabernacle of the LORD; so Solomon and the assembly inquired[k] of him there. 6 Solomon went up to the bronze altar before the LORD in the Tent of Meeting and offered a thousand burnt offerings on it.

7 That night God appeared[l] to Solomon and said to him, "Ask for whatever you want me to give you."

8 Solomon answered God, "You have shown great kindness to David my father and have made me[m] king in his place. 9 Now, LORD God, let your promise[n] to my father David be confirmed, for you have made me king over a people who are as numerous as the dust of the earth.[o] 10 Give me wisdom and knowledge, that I may lead[p] this people, for who is able to govern this great people of yours?"

11 God said to Solomon, "Since this is your heart's desire and you have not asked for wealth,[q] riches or honor, nor for the death of your enemies, and since you have not asked for a long life but for wisdom and knowledge to govern my people over whom I have made you king, 12 therefore wisdom and knowledge will be given you. And I will also give you wealth, riches and honor,[r] such as no king who was before you ever had and none after you will have.[s]"

13 Then Solomon went to Jerusalem from the high place at Gibeon, from before the Tent of Meeting. And he reigned over Israel.

14 Solomon accumulated chariots[t] and horses; he had fourteen hundred chariots and twelve thousand horses,[a] which he kept in the chariot cities and also with him in Jerusalem. 15 The king made silver and gold[u] as common in Jerusalem as stones, and cedar as plentiful as sycamore-fig trees in the foothills. 16 Solomon's horses were imported from Egypt[b] and from Kue[c]—the royal merchants purchased them from Kue. 17 They imported a chariot[v] from Egypt for six hundred shekels[d] of silver, and a horse for a hundred and fifty.[e] They also exported them to all the kings of the Hittites and of the Arameans.

1:1 [a]1Ki 2:12,26; 2Ch 12:1 [b]Ge 21:22; 39:2; Nu 14:43 [c]1Ch 29:25
1:2 [d]1Ch 9:1; 28:1
1:3 [e]Ex 36:8 [f]Ex 40:18
1:4 [g]2Sa 6:2; 1Ch 15:25 [h]2Sa 6:17; 1Ch 15:1
1:5 [i]Ex 38:2 [j]Ex 31:2 [k]1Ch 13:3
1:7 [l]2Ch 7:12
1:8 [m]1Ch 23:1; 28:5
1:9 [n]2Sa 7:25; 1Ki 8:25 [o]Ge 12:2
1:10 [p]Nu 27:17; 2Sa 5:2; Pr 8:15-16
1:11 [q]Dt 17:17
1:12 [r]1Ch 29:12 [s]1Ch 29:25; 2Ch 9:22; Ne 13:26
1:14 [t]1Sa 8:11; 1Ki 4:26; 9:19
1:15 [u]1Ki 9:28; Isa 60:5
1:17 [v]SS 1:9

Preparations for Building the Temple

2 Solomon gave orders to build a temple[w] for the Name of the LORD and a royal palace for himself.[x] 2 He conscripted seventy thousand men as carriers and eighty thousand as stonecutters in the hills and thirty-six hundred as foremen over them.[y]

3 Solomon sent this message to Hiram[f][z] king of Tyre:

> "Send me cedar logs[a] as you did for my father David when you sent him cedar to build a palace to live in. 4 Now I am about to build a temple[b] for the Name of the LORD my God and to dedicate it to him for burning fragrant incense[c] before him, for setting out the consecrated bread[d] regularly, and for making burnt offerings[e] every morning and evening and on Sabbaths[f] and New Moons

2:1 [w]Dt 12:5 [x]Ecc 2:4
2:2 [y]ver 18; 2Ch 10:4
2:3 [z]2Sa 5:11 [a]1Ch 14:1
2:4 [b]ver 1; Dt 12:5 [c]Ex 30:7 [d]Ex 25:30 [e]Ex 29:42; 2Ch 13:11 [f]Nu 28:9-10

[a] *14* Or *charioteers* [b] *16* Or possibly *Muzur,* a region in Cilicia; also in verse 17 [c] *16* Probably Cilicia [d] *17* That is, about 15 pounds (about 7 kilograms) [e] *17* That is, about 3 3/4 pounds (about 1.7 kilograms) [f] *3* Hebrew *Huram,* a variant of *Hiram;* also in verses 11 and 12

PATIENCE

A STEADY WALK: A GRAND CONFORMITY

2 Chronicles 1:10

Solomon must have desired many material things, but when asked by God what he wanted most, he replied, "Wisdom." Wisdom is a gift we gain by pain. We receive it after we have known despair.

and at the appointed feasts of the
LORD our God. This is a lasting
ordinance for Israel.
5"The temple I am going to
build will be great,[g] because our
God is greater than all other gods.[h]
6But who is able to build a temple for him, since the heavens, even
the highest heavens, cannot contain
him?[i] Who then am I[j] to build a
temple for him, except as a place
to burn sacrifices before him?

2:5 [g]1Ch 22:5; Ps 135:5 [h]1Ch 16:25
2:6 [i]1Ki 8:27; 2Ch 6:18; Jer 23:24 [j]Ex 3:11

7"Send me, therefore, a man
skilled to work in gold and silver,
bronze and iron, and in purple,
crimson and blue yarn, and experienced in the art of engraving, to
work in Judah and Jerusalem with
my skilled craftsmen,[k] whom my
father David provided.

2:7 [k]ver 13-14; Ex 35:31; 1Ch 22:16

8"Send me also cedar, pine and
algum[a] logs from Lebanon, for I
know that your men are skilled in
cutting timber there. My men will
work with yours 9to provide me
with plenty of lumber, because the
temple I build must be large and
magnificent. 10I will give your servants, the woodsmen who cut the
timber, twenty thousand cors[b] of
ground wheat, twenty thousand
cors of barley, twenty thousand
baths[c] of wine and twenty thousand baths of olive oil.[l]"

2:10 [l]Ezr 3:7

11Hiram king of Tyre replied by letter to Solomon:

"Because the LORD loves[m] his
people, he has made you their
king."

2:11 [m]1Ki 10:9; 2Ch 9:8

12And Hiram added:

"Praise be to the LORD, the God
of Israel, who made heaven and
earth![n] He has given King David
a wise son, endowed with intelligence and discernment, who will
build a temple for the LORD and
a palace for himself.

2:12 [n]Ne 9:6; Ps 8:3; 33:6; 102:25

13"I am sending you Huram-
Abi,[o] a man of great skill, 14whose
mother was from Dan[p] and whose
father was from Tyre. He is trained[q]
to work in gold and silver, bronze
and iron, stone and wood, and
with purple and blue[r] and crimson yarn and fine linen. He is experienced in all kinds of engraving
and can execute any design given
to him. He will work with your
craftsmen and with those of my
lord, David your father.

2:13 [o]1Ki 7:13
2:14 [p]Ex 31:6 [q]Ex 35:31 [r]Ex 35:35

15"Now let my lord send his servants the wheat and barley and the
olive oil[s] and wine he promised,
16and we will cut all the logs from
Lebanon that you need and will
float them in rafts by sea down to
Joppa.[t] You can then take them up
to Jerusalem."

2:15 [s]ver 10; Ezr 3:7
2:16 [t]Jos 19:46; Jnh 1:3

17Solomon took a census of all the
aliens[u] who were in Israel, after the census[v] his father David had taken; and
they were found to be 153,600. 18He
assigned[w] 70,000 of them to be carriers and 80,000 to be stonecutters in the
hills, with 3,600 foremen over them to
keep the people working.

2:17 [u]1Ch 22:2 [v]2Sa 24:2
2:18 [w]ver 2; 1Ch 22:2; 2Ch 8:8

Solomon Builds the Temple

3 Then Solomon began to build[x] the
temple of the LORD[y] in Jerusalem
on Mount Moriah, where the LORD
had appeared to his father David. It was
on the threshing floor of Araunah[d][z] the
Jebusite, the place provided by David.
2He began building on the second day
of the second month in the fourth year
of his reign.[a]
3The foundation Solomon laid for
building the temple of God was sixty cubits long and twenty cubits wide[e][b] (using the cubit of the old standard). 4The
portico at the front of the temple was
twenty cubits[f] long across the width of
the building and twenty cubits[g] high.
He overlaid the inside with pure gold.
5He paneled the main hall with pine
and covered it with fine gold and decorated it with palm tree[c] and chain
designs. 6He adorned the temple with
precious stones. And the gold he used
was gold of Parvaim. 7He overlaid the
ceiling beams, doorframes, walls and
doors of the temple with gold, and he
carved cherubim[d] on the walls.

3:1 [x]Ac 7:47 [y]Ge 28:17 [z]2Sa 24:18; 1Ch 21:18
3:2 [a]Ezr 5:11
3:3 [b]Eze 41:2
3:5 [c]Eze 40:16
3:7 [d]Ge 3:24; 1Ki 6:29-35; Eze 41:18

[a]*8* Probably a variant of *almug*; possibly juniper
[b]*10* That is, probably about 125,000 bushels (about 4,400 kiloliters) [c]*10* That is, probably about 115,000 gallons (about 440 kiloliters) [d]*1* Hebrew *Ornan,* a variant of *Araunah* [e]*3* That is, about 90 feet (about 27 meters) long and 30 feet (about 9 meters) wide [f]*4* That is, about 30 feet (about 9 meters); also in verses 8, 11 and 13
[g]*4* Some Septuagint and Syriac manuscripts; Hebrew *and a hundred and twenty*

3:8 [e]Ex 26:33 8He built the Most Holy Place,[e] its
length corresponding to the width of
the temple—twenty cubits long and
twenty cubits wide. He overlaid the inside with six hundred talents[a] of fine
3:9 [f]Ex 26:32 gold. 9The gold nails[f] weighed fifty
shekels.[b] He also overlaid the upper
parts with gold.

10In the Most Holy Place he made a
3:10 [g]Ex 25:18 pair[g] of sculptured cherubim and overlaid them with gold. 11The total wing-
span of the cherubim was twenty cubits.
One wing of the first cherub was five
cubits[c] long and touched the temple
wall, while its other wing, also five
cubits long, touched the wing of the
other cherub. 12Similarly one wing of
the second cherub was five cubits long
and touched the other temple wall, and
its other wing, also five cubits long,
touched the wing of the first cherub.
3:13 [h]Ex 25:18 13The wings of these cherubim[h] extended twenty cubits. They stood on their
feet, facing the main hall.[d]

3:14 [i]Ex 26:31,33; Heb 9:3 [j]Ge 3:24 14He made the curtain[i] of blue, purple and crimson yarn and fine linen,
with cherubim[j] worked into it.

3:15 [k]1Ki 7:15; Rev 3:12 [l]1Ki 7:22 15In the front of the temple he made
two pillars,[k] which together were thirty-
five cubits[e] long, each with a capital[l] on
top measuring five cubits. 16He made
3:16 [m]1Ki 7:17 [n]1Ki 7:20 interwoven chains[f][m] and put them on
top of the pillars. He also made a hun-
dred pomegranates[n] and attached them
to the chains. 17He erected the pillars
in the front of the temple, one to the
south and one to the north. The one to
the south he named Jakin[g] and the one
to the north Boaz.[h]

The Temple's Furnishings

4:1 [o]Ex 20:24; 27:1-2; 40:6; 1Ki 8:64; 2Ki 16:14 4 He made a bronze altar[o] twenty cubits long, twenty cubits wide and
ten cubits high.[i] 2He made the Sea[p] of
4:2 [p]Rev 4:6; 15:2 cast metal, circular in shape, measuring
ten cubits from rim to rim and five cu-
bits[j] high. It took a line of thirty cubits[k] to measure around it. 3Below the
rim, figures of bulls encircled it—ten to
a cubit.[l] The bulls were cast in two rows
in one piece with the Sea.

4The Sea stood on twelve bulls, three
facing north, three facing west, three
4:4 [q]Nu 2:3-25; Eze 48:30-34; Rev 21:13 facing south and three facing east.[q] The
Sea rested on top of them, and their
hindquarters were toward the center.
5It was a handbreadth[m] in thickness,
and its rim was like the rim of a cup,
like a lily blossom. It held three thousand baths.[n]

6He then made ten basins[r] for wash- 4:6 [r]Ex 30:18 [s]Ne 13:5,9; Eze 40:38
ing and placed five on the south side
and five on the north. In them the
things to be used for the burnt offerings[s] were rinsed, but the Sea was to be
used by the priests for washing.

SELF-CONTROL

CLEANLINESS IS NEXT TO HOLINESS

2 Chronicles 4:6

Much space in Solomon's temple was given for the task of cleansing. Cleanliness is the preface to godliness. Holiness cannot be achieved by those who are comfortable with filth.

7He made ten gold lampstands[t] ac- 4:7 [t]Ex 25:31 [u]Ex 25:40
cording to the specifications[u] for them
and placed them in the temple, five on
the south side and five on the north.

8He made ten tables[v] and placed 4:8 [v]Ex 25:23 [w]Nu 4:14
them in the temple, five on the south
side and five on the north. He also made
a hundred gold sprinkling bowls.[w]

9He made the courtyard[x] of the 4:9 [x]1Ki 6:36; 2Ki 21:5; 2Ch 33:5
priests, and the large court and the
doors for the court, and overlaid the
doors with bronze. 10He placed the Sea
on the south side, at the southeast corner.

11He also made the pots and shovels
and sprinkling bowls.

So Huram finished[y] the work he had 4:11 [y]1Ki 7:14
undertaken for King Solomon in the
temple of God:

12the two pillars;
the two bowl-shaped capitals on
top of the pillars;
the two sets of network decorating

[a]*8* That is, about 23 tons (about 21 metric tons) [b]*9* That is, about 1 1/4 pounds (about 0.6 kilogram) [c]*11* That is, about 7 1/2 feet (about 2.3 meters); also in verse 15 [d]*13* Or *facing inward* [e]*15* That is, about 52 feet (about 16 meters) [f]*16* Or possibly *made chains in the inner sanctuary*; the meaning of the Hebrew for this phrase is uncertain. [g]*17 Jakin* probably means *he establishes.* [h]*17 Boaz* probably means *in him is strength.* [i]*1* That is, about 30 feet (about 9 meters) long and wide, and about 15 feet (about 4.5 meters) high [j]*2* That is, about 7 1/2 feet (about 2.3 meters) [k]*2* That is, about 45 feet (about 13.5 meters) [l]*3* That is, about 1 1/2 feet (about 0.5 meter) [m]*5* That is, about 3 inches (about 8 centimeters) [n]*5* That is, about 17,500 gallons (about 66 kiloliters)

the two bowl-shaped capitals on top of the pillars;
13 the four hundred pomegranates for the two sets of network (two rows of pomegranates for each network, decorating the bowl-shaped capitals on top of the pillars);
4:14 [z]1Ki 7:27-30
14 the stands[z] with their basins;
15 the Sea and the twelve bulls under it;
16 the pots, shovels, meat forks and all related articles.

4:16 [a]1Ki 7:13
4:17 [b]Ge 33:17
4:18 [c]1Ki 7:23

All the objects that Huram-Abi[a] made for King Solomon for the temple of the LORD were of polished bronze. 17 The king had them cast in clay molds in the plain of the Jordan between Succoth[b] and Zarethan.[a] 18 All these things that Solomon made amounted to so much that the weight of the bronze[c] was not determined.

19 Solomon also made all the furnishings that were in God's temple:

4:19 [d]Ex 25:23,30
4:20 [e]Ex 25:31
4:22 [f]Nu 7:14 [g]Lev 10:1

the golden altar;
the tables[d] on which was the bread of the Presence;
20 the lampstands[e] of pure gold with their lamps, to burn in front of the inner sanctuary as prescribed;
21 the gold floral work and lamps and tongs (they were solid gold);
22 the pure gold wick trimmers, sprinkling bowls, dishes[f] and censers;[g] and the gold doors of the temple: the inner doors to the Most Holy Place and the doors of the main hall.

5:1 [h]1Ki 6:14 [i]2Sa 8:11

5 When all the work Solomon had done for the temple of the LORD was finished,[h] he brought in the things his father David had dedicated[i]—the silver and gold and all the furnishings—and he placed them in the treasuries of God's temple.

The Ark Brought to the Temple

5:2 [j]Nu 3:31; 2Sa 6:12; 1Ch 15:25
5:3 [k]1Ch 9:1; 2Ch 7:8-10

2 Then Solomon summoned to Jerusalem the elders of Israel, all the heads of the tribes and the chiefs of the Israelite families, to bring up the ark[j] of the LORD's covenant from Zion, the City of David. 3 And all the men of Israel[k] came together to the king at the time of the festival in the seventh month.

5:5 [l]Nu 3:31; 1Ch 15:2

4 When all the elders of Israel had arrived, the Levites took up the ark, 5 and they brought up the ark and the Tent of Meeting and all the sacred furnishings in it. The priests, who were Levites,[l] carried them up; 6 and King Solomon and the entire assembly of Israel that had gathered about him were before the ark, sacrificing so many sheep and cattle that they could not be recorded or counted.

5:7 [m]Rev 11:19
5:8 [n]Ge 3:24
5:10 [o]Heb 9:4 [p]Ex 16:34; Dt 10:2

7 The priests then brought the ark[m] of the LORD's covenant to its place in the inner sanctuary of the temple, the Most Holy Place, and put it beneath the wings of the cherubim. 8 The cherubim[n] spread their wings over the place of the ark and covered the ark and its carrying poles. 9 These poles were so long that their ends, extending from the ark, could be seen from in front of the inner sanctuary, but not from outside the Holy Place; and they are still there today. 10 There was nothing in the ark except[o] the two tablets[p] that Moses had placed in it at Horeb, where the LORD made a covenant with the Israelites after they came out of Egypt.

5:11 [q]1Ch 24:1
5:12 [r]1Ki 10:12; 1Ch 25:1; Ps 68:25 [s]1Ch 13:8; 15:24
5:13 [t]1Ch 16:34,41; 2Ch 7:3; 20:21; Ezr 3:11; Ps 100:5; 136:1; Jer 33:11

11 The priests then withdrew from the Holy Place. All the priests who were there had consecrated themselves, regardless of their divisions.[q] 12 All the Levites who were musicians[r]—Asaph, Heman, Jeduthun and their sons and relatives—stood on the east side of the altar, dressed in fine linen and playing cymbals, harps and lyres. They were accompanied by 120 priests sounding trumpets.[s] 13 The trumpeters and singers joined in unison, as with one voice, to give praise and thanks to the LORD. Accompanied by trumpets, cymbals and other instruments, they raised their voices in praise to the LORD and sang:

"He is good;
his love endures forever."[t]

5:14 [u]Ex 40:35; Rev 15:8 [v]Ex 19:16 [w]Ex 29:43; 2Ch 7:2

Then the temple of the LORD was filled with a cloud, 14 and the priests could not perform[u] their service because of the cloud,[v] for the glory[w] of the LORD filled the temple of God.

6:1 [x]Ex 19:9; 1Ki 8:12-50

6 Then Solomon said, "The LORD has said that he would dwell in a dark cloud;[x] 2 I have built a magnificent

[a] *17* Hebrew *Zeredatha,* a variant of *Zarethan*

temple for you, a place for you to dwell forever.[y]"

3While the whole assembly of Israel was standing there, the king turned around and blessed them. 4Then he said:

"Praise be to the LORD, the God of Israel, who with his hands has fulfilled what he promised with his mouth to my father David. For he said, 5'Since the day I brought my people out of Egypt, I have not chosen a city in any tribe of Israel to have a temple built for my Name to be there, nor have I chosen anyone to be the leader over my people Israel. 6But now I have chosen Jerusalem[z] for my Name[a] to be there, and I have chosen David[b] to rule my people Israel.'

7"My father David had it in his heart[c] to build a temple for the Name of the LORD, the God of Israel. 8But the LORD said to my father David, 'Because it was in your heart to build a temple for my Name, you did well to have this in your heart. 9Nevertheless, you are not the one to build the temple, but your son, who is your own flesh and blood—he is the one who will build the temple for my Name.'

10"The LORD has kept the promise he made. I have succeeded David my father and now I sit on the throne of Israel, just as the LORD promised, and I have built the temple for the Name of the LORD, the God of Israel. 11There I have placed the ark, in which is the covenant[d] of the LORD that he made with the people of Israel."

Solomon's Prayer of Dedication

12Then Solomon stood before the altar of the LORD in front of the whole assembly of Israel and spread out his hands. 13Now he had made a bronze platform,[e] five cubits[a] long, five cubits wide and three cubits[b] high, and had placed it in the center of the outer court. He stood on the platform and then knelt down[f] before the whole assembly of Israel and spread out his hands toward heaven. 14He said:

"O LORD, God of Israel, there is no God like you[g] in heaven or on earth—you who keep your covenant of love[h] with your servants who continue wholeheartedly in your way. 15You have kept your promise to your servant David my father; with your mouth you have promised[i] and with your hand you have fulfilled it—as it is today.

16"Now LORD, God of Israel, keep for your servant David my father the promises you made to him when you said, 'You shall never fail[j] to have a man to sit before me on the throne of Israel, if only your sons are careful in all they do to walk before me according to my law,[k] as you have done.' 17And now, O LORD, God of Israel, let your word that you promised your servant David come true.

18"But will God really dwell[l] on earth with men? The heavens,[m] even the highest heavens, cannot contain you. How much less this temple I have built! 19Yet give attention to your servant's prayer and his plea for mercy, O LORD my God. Hear the cry and the prayer that your servant is praying in your presence. 20May your eyes[n] be open toward this temple day and night, this place of which you said you would put your Name[o] there. May you hear[p] the prayer your servant prays toward this place. 21Hear the supplications of your servant and of your people Israel when they pray toward this place. Hear from heaven, your dwelling place; and when you hear, forgive.[q]

22"When a man wrongs his neighbor and is required to take an oath[r] and he comes and swears the oath before your altar in this temple, 23then hear from heaven and act. Judge between your servants, repaying[s] the guilty by bringing down on his own head what he has done. Declare the innocent not guilty and so establish his innocence.

24"When your people Israel have been defeated[t] by an enemy because they have sinned against you

[a] *13* That is, about 7 1/2 feet (about 2.3 meters)
[b] *13* That is, about 4 1/2 feet (about 1.3 meters)

6:2 [y]Ezr 6:12; 7:15; Ps 135:21
6:6 [z]Dt 12:5; Isa 14:1 [a]Ex 20:24; 2Ch 12:13 [b]1Ch 28:4
6:7 [c]1Sa 10:7; 1Ch 17:2; 28:2; Ac 7:46
6:11 [d]Dt 10:2; 2Ch 5:10; Ps 25:10; 50:5
6:13 [e]Ne 8:4 [f]Ps 95:6
6:14 [g]Ex 8:10; 15:11
6:14 [h]Dt 7:9
6:15 [i]1Ch 22:10
6:16 [j]2Sa 7:13,15; 1Ki 2:4; 2Ch 7:18; 23:3 [k]Ps 132:12
6:18 [l]Rev 21:3 [m]2Ch 2:6; Ps 11:4; Isa 40:22; 66:1; Ac 7:49
6:20 [n]Ex 3:16; Ps 34:15 [o]Dt 12:11 [p]2Ch 7:14; 30:20
6:21 [q]Ps 51:1; Isa 33:24; 40:2; 43:25; 44:22; 55:7; Mic 7:18
6:22 [r]Ex 22:11
6:23 [s]Isa 3:11; 65:6; Mt 16:27
6:24 [t]Lev 26:17

and when they turn back and confess your name, praying and making supplication before you in this
temple, 25then hear from heaven
and forgive the sin of your people
Israel and bring them back to the
land you gave to them and their
fathers.
26"When the heavens are shut
up and there is no rain[u] because
your people have sinned against
you, and when they pray toward
this place and confess your name
and turn from their sin because
you have afflicted them, 27then
hear from heaven and forgive[v] the
sin of your servants, your people
Israel. Teach them the right way
to live, and send rain on the land
you gave your people for an inheritance.
28"When famine[w] or plague
comes to the land, or blight or
mildew, locusts or grasshoppers, or
when enemies besiege them in any
of their cities, whatever disaster
or disease may come, 29and when
a prayer or plea is made by any
of your people Israel—each one
aware of his afflictions and pains,
and spreading out his hands toward this temple— 30then hear
from heaven, your dwelling place.
Forgive,[x] and deal with each man
according to all he does, since you
know his heart (for you alone know
the hearts of men),[y] 31so that they
will fear you[z] and walk in your
ways all the time they live in the
land you gave our fathers.
32"As for the foreigner who does
not belong to your people Israel
but has come[a] from a distant land
because of your great name and
your mighty hand[b] and your outstretched arm—when he comes
and prays toward this temple,
33then hear from heaven, your
dwelling place, and do whatever
the foreigner[c] asks of you, so that
all the peoples of the earth may
know your name and fear you, as
do your own people Israel, and
may know that this house I have
built bears your Name.
34"When your people go to war
against their enemies,[d] wherever
you send them, and when they

6:26 [u]Lev 26:19; Dt 11:17; 28:24; 2Sa 1:21; 1Ki 17:1
6:27 [v]ver 30,39; 2Ch 7:14
6:28 [w]2Ch 20:9
6:30 [x]ver 27 [y]1Sa 16:7; 1Ch 28:9; Ps 7:9; 44:21; Pr 16:2; 17:3
6:31 [z]Ps 103:11,13; Pr 8:13
6:32 [a]2Ch 9:6; Jn 12:20; Ac 8:27 [b]Ex 3:19,20
6:33 [c]2Ch 7:14
6:34 [d]Dt 28:7

pray[e] to you toward this city you
have chosen and the temple I have
built for your Name, 35then hear
from heaven their prayer and their
plea, and uphold their cause.
36"When they sin against you—
for there is no one who does not
sin[f]—and you become angry with
them and give them over to the
enemy, who takes them captive[g] to
a land far away or near; 37and if
they have a change of heart[h] in the
land where they are held captive,
and repent and plead with you in
the land of their captivity and say,
'We have sinned, we have done
wrong and acted wickedly'; 38and
if they turn back to you with all
their heart and soul in the land
of their captivity where they were
taken, and pray toward the land
you gave their fathers, toward the
city you have chosen and toward
the temple I have built for your
Name; 39then from heaven, your
dwelling place, hear their prayer
and their pleas, and uphold their
cause. And forgive your people,
who have sinned against you.
40"Now, my God, may your eyes
be open and your ears attentive[i] to
the prayers offered in this place.

41"Now arise,[j] O LORD God,
and come to your
resting place,[k]
you and the ark of your
might.
May your priests,[l] O LORD
God, be clothed with
salvation,
may your saints rejoice in
your goodness.[m]
42O LORD God, do not reject
your anointed one.
Remember the great love[n]
promised to David your
servant."

The Dedication of the Temple

7 When Solomon finished praying,
fire[o] came down from heaven and
consumed the burnt offering and the
sacrifices, and the glory of the LORD
filled[p] the temple.[q] 2The priests could
not enter[r] the temple of the LORD because the glory[s] of the LORD filled it.
3When all the Israelites saw the fire

6:34 [e]1Ch 5:20
6:36 [f]Job 15:14; Ps 143:2; Ecc 7:20; Jer 17:9; Jas 3:1; 1Jn 1:8-10 [g]Lev 26:44
6:37 [h]2Ch 7:14; 33:12,19,23; Jer 29:13
6:40 [i]2Ch 7:15; Ne 1:6,11; Ps 17:1,6
6:41 [j]Isa 33:10 [k]1Ch 28:2 [l]Ps 132:16 [m]Ps 116:12
6:42 [n]Ps 89:24,28; Isa 55:3
7:1 [o]Lev 9:24; 1Ki 18:38 [p]Ex 16:10 [q]Ps 26:8
7:2 [r]1Ki 8:11 [s]Ex 29:43; 40:35; 2Ch 5:14

coming down and the glory of the
LORD above the temple, they knelt on
the pavement with their faces to the
ground, and they worshiped and gave
thanks to the LORD, saying,

"He is good;
his love endures forever."[t]

7:3 [t]1Ch 16:34; 2Ch 5:13; 20:21

4Then the king and all the people offered sacrifices before the LORD. 5And
King Solomon offered a sacrifice of
twenty-two thousand head of cattle and
a hundred and twenty thousand sheep
and goats. So the king and all the
people dedicated the temple of God.
6The priests took their positions, as did
the Levites[u] with the LORD's musical
instruments,[v] which King David had
made for praising the LORD and which
were used when he gave thanks, saying, "His love endures forever." Opposite the Levites, the priests blew their
trumpets, and all the Israelites were
standing.

7:6 [u]1Ch 15:16 [v]2Ch 5:12

7Solomon consecrated the middle
part of the courtyard in front of the
temple of the LORD, and there he offered burnt offerings and the fat of
the fellowship offerings,[a] because the
bronze altar he had made could not
hold the burnt offerings, the grain offerings and the fat portions.

8So Solomon observed the festival[w]
at that time for seven days, and all Israel
with him—a vast assembly, people from
Lebo[b] Hamath to the Wadi of Egypt.[x]
9On the eighth day they held an assembly, for they had celebrated the dedication of the altar for seven days and the
festival[y] for seven days more. 10On the
twenty-third day of the seventh month
he sent the people to their homes, joyful and glad in heart for the good things
the LORD had done for David and Solomon and for his people Israel.

7:8 [w]2Ch 30:26 [x]Ge 15:18

7:9 [y]Lev 23:36

The LORD Appears to Solomon

11When Solomon had finished the
temple of the LORD and the royal palace, and had succeeded in carrying out
all he had in mind to do in the temple
of the LORD and in his own palace,
12the LORD appeared to him at night
and said:

"I have heard your prayer and
have chosen this place for myself[z]
as a temple for sacrifices.

7:12 [z]Dt 12:5

13"When I shut up the heavens
so that there is no rain,[a] or command locusts to devour the land
or send a plague among my people, 14if my people, who are called
by my name, will humble[b] themselves and pray and seek my face[c]
and turn[d] from their wicked ways,
then will I hear from heaven and
will forgive[e] their sin and will heal[f]
their land. 15Now my eyes will
be open and my ears attentive to
the prayers offered in this place.[g]
16I have chosen[h] and consecrated
this temple so that my Name may
be there forever. My eyes and my
heart will always be there.

7:13 [a]2Ch 6:26-28; Am 4:7

7:14 [b]Lev 26:41; 2Ch 6:37; Jas 4:10 [c]1Ch 16:11 [d]Isa 55:7; Zec 1:4 [e]2Ch 6:27 [f]2Ch 30:20; Isa 30:26; 57:18

7:15 [g]2Ch 6:40

7:16 [h]ver 12; 2Ch 6:6

FAITHFULNESS

THE NAME, THE PRAYER, THE HEALING

2 Chronicles 7:14

This verse—as a philosophy of life—was condensed by the Christ, who said, "You may ask me for anything in my name, and I will do it" (John 14:14).

17"As for you, if you walk before me [i]as David your father did,
and do all I command, and observe my decrees and laws, 18I will
establish your royal throne, as I
covenanted with David your father
when I said, 'You shall never fail to
have a man[j] to rule over Israel.'[k]

19"But if you[c] turn away[l] and
forsake[m] the decrees and commands I have given you[c] and go off
to serve other gods and worship
them, 20then I will uproot[n] Israel
from my land,[o] which I have given
them, and will reject this temple I
have consecrated for my Name. I
will make it a byword and an object of ridicule[p] among all peoples.
21And though this temple is now
so imposing, all who pass by will
be appalled and say,[q] 'Why has the
LORD done such a thing to this
land and to this temple?' 22People
will answer, 'Because they have
forsaken the LORD, the God of
their fathers, who brought them

7:17 [i]1Ki 9:4

7:18 [j]2Ch 6:16 [k]2Sa 7:13; 2Ch 13:5

7:19 [l]Dt 28:15 [m]Lev 26:14,33

7:20 [n]Dt 29:28 [o]1Ki 14:15 [p]Dt 28:37

7:21 [q]Dt 29:24

[a]7 Traditionally *peace offerings* [b]8 Or *from the entrance to* [c]19 The Hebrew is plural.

out of Egypt, and have embraced
other gods, worshiping and serving them—that is why he brought
all this disaster on them.' "

Solomon's Other Activities

8 At the end of twenty years, during
which Solomon built the temple of
the LORD and his own palace, 2Solo-
mon rebuilt the villages that Hiram[a]
had given him, and settled Israelites in
them. 3Solomon then went to Hamath
Zobah and captured it. 4He also built
up Tadmor in the desert and all the
8:5 store cities he had built in Hamath.
[r]1Ch 7:24; 5He rebuilt Upper Beth Horon[r] and
2Ch 14:7 Lower Beth Horon as fortified cities,
with walls and with gates and bars, 6as
well as Baalath and all his store cities,
and all the cities for his chariots and
for his horses[b]—whatever he desired
to build in Jerusalem, in Lebanon and
throughout all the territory he ruled.
7All the people left from the Hittites,
Amorites, Perizzites, Hivites and Jebu-
8:7 sites[s] (these peoples were not Israelites),
[s]Ge 10:16 8that is, their descendants remaining in
8:8 the land, whom the Israelites had not
[t]1Ki 4:6; 9:21 destroyed—these Solomon conscripted[t]
for his slave labor force, as it is to this
day. 9But Solomon did not make slaves
of the Israelites for his work; they were
his fighting men, commanders of his
captains, and commanders of his chariots and charioteers. 10They were also
King Solomon's chief officials—two
hundred and fifty officials supervising
the men.
8:11 11Solomon brought Pharaoh's daugh-
[u]1Ki 3:1; 7:8 ter[u] up from the City of David to the
palace he had built for her, for he said,
"My wife must not live in the palace
of David king of Israel, because the
places the ark of the LORD has entered
8:12 are holy."
[v]1Ki 8:64; 12On the altar[v] of the LORD that
2Ch 4:1; 15:8 he had built in front of the portico,
Solomon sacrificed burnt offerings to
8:13 the LORD, 13according to the daily re-
[w]Ex 29:38; quirement[w] for offerings commanded by
Nu 28:3 Moses for Sabbaths,[x] New Moons and
[x]Nu 28:9 [y]Ex 23:14; the three[y] annual feasts—the Feast of
Dt 16:16 [z]Ex 23:16 Unleavened Bread, the Feast of Weeks[z]
and the Feast of Tabernacles. 14In keep-
ing with the ordinance of his father
8:14 [a]1Ch 24:1 David, he appointed the divisions[a] of
[b]1Ch 25:1 the priests for their duties, and the Levites[b] to lead the praise and to assist the
priests according to each day's requirement. He also appointed the gatekeep-
ers[c] by divisions for the various gates, 8:14 [c]1Ch 9:17;
because this was what David the man 26:1
of God[d] had ordered.[e] 15They did not [d]Ne 12:24,36 [e]1Ch 23:6;
deviate from the king's commands to Ne 12:45
the priests or to the Levites in any matter, including that of the treasuries.
16All Solomon's work was carried out,
from the day the foundation of the
temple of the LORD was laid until its
completion. So the temple of the LORD
was finished.
17Then Solomon went to Ezion Geber and Elath on the coast of Edom.
18And Hiram sent him ships commanded by his own officers, men who knew
the sea. These, with Solomon's men,
sailed to Ophir and brought back four 8:18
hundred and fifty talents[c] of gold,[f] [f]2Ch 9:9
which they delivered to King Solo-
mon.

The Queen of Sheba Visits Solomon

9 When the queen of Sheba[g] heard of 9:1
Solomon's fame, she came to Jeru- [g]Ge 10:7;
salem to test him with hard questions. Eze 23:42; Mt 12:42;
Arriving with a very great caravan— Lk 11:31
with camels carrying spices, large quantities of gold, and precious stones—she
came to Solomon and talked with him
about all she had on her mind. 2Solo-
mon answered all her questions; nothing was too hard for him to explain to
her. 3When the queen of Sheba saw the 9:3
wisdom of Solomon,[h] as well as the pal- [h]1Ki 5:12
ace he had built, 4the food on his table,
the seating of his officials, the attending
servants in their robes, the cupbearers
in their robes and the burnt offerings
he made at[d] the temple of the LORD,
she was overwhelmed.
5She said to the king, "The report I
heard in my own country about your
achievements and your wisdom is true.
6But I did not believe what they said 9:6
until I came[i] and saw with my own [i]2Ch 6:32
eyes. Indeed, not even half the greatness of your wisdom was told me; you
have far exceeded the report I heard.
7How happy your men must be! How
happy your officials, who continually
stand before you and hear your wisdom!

[a]*2* Hebrew *Huram,* a variant of *Hiram*; also in verse 18 [b]*6* Or *charioteers* [c]*18* That is, about 17 tons (about 16 metric tons) [d]*4* Or *the ascent by which he went up to*

GENTLENESS 

BLESSING BUTTERFLIES

2 Chronicles 9:6

Affirmation is a tender tool. The queen of Sheba was an observer of Solomon's kingdom. She praised Solomon with a gentle word, and her kindness earned her a place in Scripture. Gentleness makes the world better merely by walking through it.

8 Praise be to the LORD your God, who
has delighted in you and placed you
9:8 [j]1Ki 2:12; 1Ch 17:14; 28:5; 29:23; 2Ch 13:8 [k]2Ch 2:11 on his throne[j] as king to rule for the
LORD your God. Because of the love
of your God for Israel and his desire
to uphold them forever, he has made
you king[k] over them, to maintain justice and righteousness."
9 Then she gave the king 120 talents[a]
9:9 [l]2Ch 8:18 of gold,[l] large quantities of spices, and
precious stones. There had never been
such spices as those the queen of Sheba
gave to King Solomon.
10 (The men of Hiram and the men
9:10 [m]2Ch 8:18 of Solomon brought gold from Ophir;[m]
they also brought algumwood[b] and pre-
cious stones. 11 The king used the algumwood to make steps for the temple
of the LORD and for the royal palace,
and to make harps and lyres for the
musicians. Nothing like them had ever
been seen in Judah.)
12 King Solomon gave the queen of
Sheba all she desired and asked for; he
gave her more than she had brought to
him. Then she left and returned with
her retinue to her own country.

Solomon's Splendor

13 The weight of the gold that Solomon received yearly was 666 talents,[c]
14 not including the revenues brought in
9:14 [n]2Ch 17:11; Isa 21:13; Jer 25:24; Eze 27:21; 30:5 by merchants and traders. Also all the
kings of Arabia[n] and the governors of
the land brought gold and silver to Solomon.
15 King Solomon made two hundred
large shields of hammered gold; six
hundred bekas[d] of hammered gold went
into each shield. 16 He also made three
9:16 [o]2Ch 12:9 [p]1Ki 7:2 hundred small shields[o] of hammered
gold, with three hundred bekas[e] of gold
in each shield. The king put them in
the Palace of the Forest of Lebanon.[p]
17 Then the king made a great throne
inlaid with ivory[q] and overlaid with 9:17 [q]1Ki 22:39
pure gold. 18 The throne had six steps,
and a footstool of gold was attached to
it. On both sides of the seat were armrests, with a lion standing beside each
of them. 19 Twelve lions stood on the
six steps, one at either end of each step.
Nothing like it had ever been made
for any other kingdom. 20 All King Solomon's goblets were gold, and all the
household articles in the Palace of the
Forest of Lebanon were pure gold.
Nothing was made of silver, because
silver was considered of little value in
Solomon's day. 21 The king had a fleet
of trading ships[f] manned by Hiram's[g]
men. Once every three years it returned,
carrying gold, silver and ivory, and apes
and baboons.
22 King Solomon was greater in riches
and wisdom than all the other kings of
the earth.[r] 23 All the kings[s] of the earth 9:22 [r]1Ki 3:13; 2Ch 1:12
sought audience with Solomon to hear
the wisdom God had put in his heart. 9:23 [s]1Ki 4:34
24 Year after year, everyone who came
brought a gift[t]—articles of silver and 9:24 [t]2Ch 32:23; Ps 45:12; 68:29; 72:10; Isa 18:7
gold, and robes, weapons and spices,
and horses and mules.
25 Solomon had four thousand stalls
for horses and chariots,[u] and twelve 9:25 [u]1Sa 8:11; 1Ki 4:26
thousand horses,[h] which he kept in the
chariot cities and also with him in Je-
rusalem. 26 He ruled[v] over all the kings 9:26 [v]1Ki 4:21 [w]Ps 72:8-9 [x]Ge 15:18-21
from the River[i][w] to the land of the Phi-
listines, as far as the border of Egypt.[x]
27 The king made silver as common in
Jerusalem as stones, and cedar as plentiful as sycamore-fig trees in the foothills.
28 Solomon's horses were imported from
Egypt[j] and from all other countries.

Solomon's Death

29 As for the other events of Solomon's
reign, from beginning to end, are they
not written in the records of Nathan[y] 9:29 [y]2Sa 7:2; 1Ch 29:29 [z]1Ki 11:29 [a]2Ch 10:2
the prophet, in the prophecy of Ahijah[z]
the Shilonite and in the visions of Iddo
the seer concerning Jeroboam[a] son of
Nebat? 30 Solomon reigned in Jerusalem

[a]*9* That is, about 4 1/2 tons (about 4 metric tons) [b]*10* Probably a variant of *almugwood* [c]*13* That is, about 25 tons (about 23 metric tons) [d]*15* That is, about 7 1/2 pounds (about 3.5 kilograms) [e]*16* That is, about 3 3/4 pounds (about 1.7 kilograms) [f]*21* Hebrew *of ships that could go to Tarshish* [g]*21* Hebrew *Huram,* a variant of *Hiram* [h]*25* Or *charioteers* [i]*26* That is, the Euphrates [j]*28* Or possibly *Muzur,* a region in Cilicia

over all Israel forty years. 31Then he
9:31 [b]1Ki 2:10 rested with his fathers and was buried
in the city of David[b] his father. And
Rehoboam his son succeeded him as
king.

Israel Rebels Against Rehoboam

10 Rehoboam went to Shechem,
for all the Israelites had gone
10:2 [c]2Ch 9:29 there to make him king. 2When Jer-
[d]1Ki 11:40 oboam[c] son of Nebat heard this (he was
in Egypt, where he had fled[d] from King
Solomon), he returned from Egypt. 3So
10:3 they sent for Jeroboam, and he and all
[e]1Ch 9:1 Israel[e] went to Rehoboam and said to
10:4 him: 4"Your father put a heavy yoke on
[f]2Ch 2:2 us,[f] but now lighten the harsh labor
and the heavy yoke he put on us, and
we will serve you."
5Rehoboam answered, "Come back
to me in three days." So the people
went away.
10:6 6Then King Rehoboam consulted the
[g]Job 8:8-9; elders[g] who had served his father Solo-
12:12; 15:10; mon during his lifetime. "How would
32:7 you advise me to answer these people?"
he asked.
7They replied, "If you will be kind to
10:7 these people and please them and give
[h]Pr 15:1 them a favorable answer[h], they will al-
10:8 ways be your servants."
[i]2Sa 17:14 8But Rehoboam rejected[i] the advice
[j]Pr 13:20 the elders[j] gave him and consulted
the young men who had grown up
with him and were serving him. 9He
asked them, "What is your advice? How
should we answer these people who say
to me, 'Lighten the yoke your father
put on us'?"
10The young men who had grown
up with him replied, "Tell the people
who have said to you, 'Your father put
a heavy yoke on us, but make our
yoke lighter'—tell them, 'My little finger is thicker than my father's waist.
11My father laid on you a heavy yoke;
I will make it even heavier. My father
scourged you with whips; I will scourge
you with scorpions.'"
12Three days later Jeroboam and all
the people returned to Rehoboam, as
the king had said, "Come back to me in
three days." 13The king answered them
harshly. Rejecting the advice of the elders, 14he followed the advice of the
young men and said, "My father made
your yoke heavy; I will make it even
heavier. My father scourged you with
whips; I will scourge you with scorpions." 15So the king did not listen to the
people, for this turn of events was from
God,[k] to fulfill the word the LORD
had spoken to Jeroboam son of Nebat 10:15
through Ahijah the Shilonite.[l] [k]2Ch 11:4; 25:16-20
16When all Israel[m] saw that the king [l]1Ki 11:29
refused to listen to them, they answered 10:16 [m]1Ch 9:1
the king: [n]ver 19; 2Sa 20:1

"What share do we have in David,[n]
what part in Jesse's son?
To your tents, O Israel!
Look after your own house,
O David!"

So all the Israelites went home. 17But as
for the Israelites who were living in the
towns of Judah, Rehoboam still ruled
over them.
18King Rehoboam sent out Adoni-
ram,[a][o] who was in charge of forced la- 10:18
bor, but the Israelites stoned him to [o]1Ki 5:14
death. King Rehoboam, however, man-
aged to get into his chariot and escape
to Jerusalem. 19So Israel has been in rebellion against the house of David to
this day.

11 When Rehoboam arrived in Je-
rusalem,[p] he mustered the house 11:1 [p]1Ki 12:21
of Judah and Benjamin—a hundred
and eighty thousand fighting men—to
make war against Israel and to regain
the kingdom for Rehoboam.
2But this word of the LORD came to 11:2
Shemaiah[q] the man of God: 3"Say to [q]2Ch 12:5-7,
Rehoboam son of Solomon king of Ju- 15
dah and to all the Israelites in Judah
and Benjamin, 4'This is what the LORD
says: Do not go up to fight against your 11:4
brothers.[r] Go home, every one of you, [r]2Ch 28:8-11
for this is my doing.'" So they obeyed
the words of the LORD and turned back
from marching against Jeroboam.

[a]*18* Hebrew *Hadoram,* a variant of *Adoniram*

GENTLENESS

LIVE TO MAKE THE WORLD UNAFRAID

2 Chronicles 10:10

Rehoboam promised Israel only severity. Harsh words lose kingdoms. How wise he would have been to reply, "Mercy is not weakness; strength is unafraid of gentleness."

Rehoboam Fortifies Judah

5Rehoboam lived in Jerusalem and
built up towns for defense in Judah:
6Bethlehem, Etam, Tekoa, 7Beth Zur,
Soco, Adullam, 8Gath, Mareshah, Ziph,
9Adoraim, Lachish, Azekah, 10Zorah,
Aijalon and Hebron. These were fortified cities in Judah and Benjamin.
11He strengthened their defenses and
put commanders in them, with supplies
of food, olive oil and wine. 12He put
shields and spears in all the cities, and
made them very strong. So Judah and
Benjamin were his.
13The priests and Levites from all
their districts throughout Israel sided
11:14 [s]Nu 35:2-5 with him. 14The Levites[s] even aban-
[t]2Ch 13:9 doned their pasturelands and property,[t]
and came to Judah and Jerusalem be-
cause Jeroboam and his sons had rejected them as priests of the LORD. 15And
11:15 [u]1Ki 13:33 he appointed[u] his own priests[v] for the
[v]1Ki 12:31 high places and for the goat[w] and calf[x]
[w]Lev 17:7 [x]1Ki 12:28; idols he had made. 16Those from every
2Ch 13:8 tribe of Israel[y] who set their hearts on
11:16 [y]2Ch 15:9 seeking the LORD, the God of Israel,
followed the Levites to Jerusalem to of-
fer sacrifices to the LORD, the God of
11:17 [z]2Ch 12:1 their fathers. 17They strengthened[z] the
kingdom of Judah and supported Re-
hoboam son of Solomon three years,
walking in the ways of David and Solomon during this time.

Rehoboam's Family

18Rehoboam married Mahalath, who
was the daughter of David's son Jerimoth and of Abihail, the daughter of
Jesse's son Eliab. 19She bore him sons:
Jeush, Shemariah and Zaham. 20Then
11:20 [a]1Ki 15:2 he married Maacah[a] daughter of Absa-
[b]2Ch 13:2 lom, who bore him Abijah,[b] Attai, Ziza
and Shelomith. 21Rehoboam loved Ma-
11:21 acah daughter of Absalom more than
[c]Dt 17:17 any of his other wives[c] and concubines.
In all, he had eighteen wives and sixty
concubines, twenty-eight sons and sixty
daughters.
11:22 [d]Dt 21:15-17 22Rehoboam appointed Abijah[d] son
of Maacah to be the chief prince among
his brothers, in order to make him king.
23He acted wisely, dispersing some of
his sons throughout the districts of Judah and Benjamin, and to all the fortified cities. He gave them abundant
provisions and took many wives for
them.

Shishak Attacks Jerusalem

12 After Rehoboam's position as
king was established[e] and he had 12:1 [e]ver 13
become strong,[f] he and all Israel[a] with [f]2Ch 11:17
him abandoned the law of the LORD.
2Because they had been unfaithful[g] to 12:2 [g]1Ki 14:22-24
the LORD, Shishak[h] king of Egypt at- [h]1Ki 11:40
tacked Jerusalem in the fifth year of
King Rehoboam. 3With twelve hundred
chariots and sixty thousand horsemen
and the innumerable troops of Libyans,
Sukkites and Cushites[b] [i] that came with 12:3 [i]2Ch 16:8;
him from Egypt, 4he captured the forti- Na 3:9
fied cities[j] of Judah and came as far as 12:4 [j]2Ch 11:10
Jerusalem.
5Then the prophet Shemaiah[k] came 12:5 [k]2Ch 11:2
to Rehoboam and to the leaders of Ju- [l]Dt 28:15;
dah who had assembled in Jerusalem 2Ch 15:2
for fear of Shishak, and he said to them,
"This is what the LORD says, 'You have
abandoned me; therefore, I now abandon[l] you to Shishak.'"
6The leaders of Israel and the king
humbled themselves and said, "The 12:6 [m]Ex 9:27;
LORD is just."[m] Da 9:14
7When the LORD saw that they
humbled themselves, this word of the
LORD came to Shemaiah: "Since they
have humbled themselves, I will not
destroy them but will soon give them 12:7
deliverance.[n] My wrath will not be [n]1Ki 21:29; Ps 78:38
poured out on Jerusalem through Shi-
shak. 8They will, however, become sub- 12:8
ject[o] to him, so that they may learn the [o]Dt 28:48
difference between serving me and serv-
ing the kings of other lands."
9When Shishak king of Egypt attacked Jerusalem, he carried off the
treasures of the temple of the LORD
and the treasures of the royal palace.
He took everything, including the gold
shields[p] Solomon had made. 10So King 12:9 [p]2Ch 9:16
Rehoboam made bronze shields to re-
place them and assigned these to the
commanders of the guard on duty at the
entrance to the royal palace. 11When-
ever the king went to the LORD's temple, the guards went with him, bearing
the shields, and afterward they returned
them to the guardroom.
12Because Rehoboam humbled himself, the LORD's anger turned from him,
and he was not totally destroyed. In- 12:12
deed, there was some good[q] in Judah. [q]1Ki 14:13;
13King Rehoboam established him- 2Ch 19:3

[a]*1* That is, Judah, as frequently in 2 Chronicles
[b]*3* That is, people from the upper Nile region

self firmly in Jerusalem and continued as king. He was forty-one years old when he became king, and he reigned seventeen years in Jerusalem, the city the LORD had chosen out of all the tribes of Israel in which to put his Name.[r] His mother's name was Naamah; she was an Ammonite. 14He did evil because he had not set his heart on seeking the LORD.

15As for the events of Rehoboam's reign, from beginning to end, are they not written in the records of Shemaiah[s] the prophet and of Iddo the seer that deal with genealogies? There was continual warfare between Rehoboam and Jeroboam. 16Rehoboam rested with his fathers and was buried in the City of David. And Abijah[t] his son succeeded him as king.

Abijah King of Judah

13 In the eighteenth year of the reign of Jeroboam, Abijah became king of Judah, 2and he reigned in Jerusalem three years. His mother's name was Maacah,[a] a daughter[b] of Uriel of Gibeah.

There was war between Abijah[u] and Jeroboam.[v] 3Abijah went into battle with a force of four hundred thousand able fighting men, and Jeroboam drew up a battle line against him with eight hundred thousand able troops.

4Abijah stood on Mount Zemaraim,[w] in the hill country of Ephraim, and said, "Jeroboam and all Israel,[x] listen to me! 5Don't you know that the LORD, the God of Israel, has given the kingship of Israel to David and his descendants forever[y] by a covenant of salt?[z] 6Yet Jeroboam son of Nebat, an official of Solomon son of David, rebelled[a] against his master. 7Some worthless scoundrels[b] gathered around him and opposed Rehoboam son of Solomon when he was young and indecisive and not strong enough to resist them.

8"And now you plan to resist the kingdom of the LORD, which is in the hands of David's descendants. You are indeed a vast army and have with you the golden calves[c] that Jeroboam made to be your gods. 9But didn't you drive out the priests of the LORD,[d] the sons of Aaron, and the Levites, and make priests of your own as the peoples of other lands do? Whoever comes to consecrate himself with a young bull[e] and seven rams may become a priest of what are not gods.[f]

10"As for us, the LORD is our God, and we have not forsaken him. The priests who serve the LORD are sons of Aaron, and the Levites assist them. 11Every morning and evening[g] they present burnt offerings and fragrant incense to the LORD. They set out the bread on the ceremonially clean table[h] and light the lamps on the gold lampstand every evening. We are observing the requirements of the LORD our God. But you have forsaken him. 12God is with us; he is our leader. His priests with their trumpets will sound the battle cry against you.[i] Men of Israel, do not fight against the LORD,[j] the God of your fathers, for you will not succeed."

13Now Jeroboam had sent troops around to the rear, so that while he was in front of Judah the ambush[k] was behind them. 14Judah turned and saw that they were being attacked at both front and rear. Then they cried out[l] to the LORD. The priests blew their trumpets 15and the men of Judah raised the battle cry. At the sound of their battle cry, God routed Jeroboam and all Israel[m] before Abijah and Judah. 16The Israelites fled before Judah, and God delivered[n] them into their hands. 17Abijah and his men inflicted heavy losses on them, so that there were five hundred thousand casualties among Israel's able men. 18The men of Israel were subdued on that occasion, and the men of Judah were victorious because they relied[o] on the LORD, the God of their fathers.

19Abijah pursued Jeroboam and took from him the towns of Bethel, Jeshanah and Ephron, with their surrounding villages. 20Jeroboam did not regain power during the time of Abijah. And the LORD struck him down and he died.

21But Abijah grew in strength. He married fourteen wives and had twenty-two sons and sixteen daughters.

22The other events of Abijah's reign, what he did and what he said, are written in the annotations of the prophet Iddo.

[a]*2* Most Septuagint manuscripts and Syriac (see also 2 Chron. 11:20 and 1 Kings 15:2); Hebrew *Micaiah* [b]*2* Or *granddaughter*

12:13 [r]Dt 12:5; 2Ch 6:6
12:15 [s]2Ch 9:29; 11:2
12:16 [t]2Ch 11:20
13:2 [u]2Ch 11:20 [v]1Ki 15:6
13:4 [w]Jos 18:22 [x]1Ch 11:1
13:5 [y]2Sa 7:13 [z]Lev 2:13; Nu 18:19
13:6 [a]1Ki 11:26
13:7 [b]Jdg 9:4
13:8 [c]1Ki 12:28; 2Ch 11:15
13:9 [d]2Ch 11:14-15
13:9 [e]Ex 29:35-36 [f]Jer 2:11
13:11 [g]Ex 29:39; 2Ch 2:4 [h]Lev 24:5-9
13:12 [i]Nu 10:8-9 [j]Ac 5:39
13:13 [k]Jos 8:9
13:14 [l]2Ch 14:11
13:15 [m]2Ch 14:12
13:16 [n]2Ch 16:8
13:18 [o]1Ch 5:20; 2Ch 14:11; Ps 22:5

14 And Abijah rested with his fathers and was buried in the City
of David. Asa his son succeeded him as
king, and in his days the country was at
peace for ten years.

Asa King of Judah

2 Asa did what was good and right in
the eyes of the LORD his God. 3 He removed the foreign altars and the high
places, smashed the sacred stones and
cut down the Asherah poles.[a][p] 4 He
commanded Judah to seek the LORD,
the God of their fathers, and to obey
his laws and commands. 5 He removed
the high places and incense altars[q] in
every town in Judah, and the kingdom
was at peace under him. 6 He built up
the fortified cities of Judah, since the
land was at peace. No one was at war
with him during those years, for the
LORD gave him rest.[r]
7 "Let us build up these towns," he
said to Judah, "and put walls around
them, with towers, gates and bars. The
land is still ours, because we have sought
the LORD our God; we sought him and
he has given us rest on every side." So
they built and prospered.
8 Asa had an army of three hundred
thousand men from Judah, equipped
with large shields and with spears, and
two hundred and eighty thousand from
Benjamin, armed with small shields and
with bows. All these were brave fighting
men.
9 Zerah the Cushite[s] marched out
against them with a vast army[b] and three
hundred chariots, and came as far as
Mareshah.[t] 10 Asa went out to meet him,
and they took up battle positions in the
Valley of Zephathah near Mareshah.
11 Then Asa called[u] to the LORD his
God and said, "LORD, there is no one
like you to help the powerless against
the mighty. Help us, O LORD our God,
for we rely[v] on you, and in your name[w]
we have come against this vast army.
O LORD, you are our God; do not let
man prevail[x] against you."
12 The LORD struck down[y] the Cushites before Asa and Judah. The Cushites
fled, 13 and Asa and his army pursued
them as far as Gerar.[z] Such a great number of Cushites fell that they could not
recover; they were crushed before the
LORD and his forces. The men of Judah
carried off a large amount of plunder.

14:3 [p]Ex 34:13; Dt 7:5; 1Ki 15:12-14
14:5 [q]2Ch 34:4,7
14:6 [r]1Ch 22:9; 2Ch 15:15
14:9 [s]2Ch 12:3; 16:8 [t]2Ch 11:8
14:11 [u]2Ch 13:14 [v]2Ch 13:18 [w]1Sa 17:45 [x]1Sa 14:6; Ps 9:19
14:12 [y]2Ch 13:15
14:13 [z]Ge 10:19

14 They destroyed all the villages around
Gerar, for the terror[a] of the LORD had
fallen upon them. They plundered all
these villages, since there was much
booty there. 15 They also attacked the
camps of the herdsmen and carried off
droves of sheep and goats and camels.
Then they returned to Jerusalem.

Asa's Reform

15 The Spirit of God came upon[b]
Azariah son of Oded. 2 He went
out to meet Asa and said to him, "Listen to me, Asa and all Judah and Benjamin. The LORD is with you[c] when
you are with him.[d] If you seek[e] him, he
will be found by you, but if you forsake him, he will forsake you.[f] 3 For a
long time Israel was without the true
God, without a priest to teach[g] and
without the law.[h] 4 But in their distress
they turned to the LORD, the God of
Israel, and sought him,[i] and he was
found by them. 5 In those days it was
not safe to travel about,[j] for all the inhabitants of the lands were in great turmoil. 6 One nation was being crushed
by another and one city by another,[k]
because God was troubling them with
every kind of distress. 7 But as for you,
be strong[l] and do not give up, for your
work will be rewarded."[m]
8 When Asa heard these words and
the prophecy of Azariah son of[c] Oded
the prophet, he took courage. He removed the detestable idols from the
whole land of Judah and Benjamin and
from the towns he had captured[n] in the
hills of Ephraim. He repaired the altar[o]
of the LORD that was in front of the
portico of the LORD's temple.

14:14 [a]Ge 35:5; 2Ch 17:10
15:1 [b]Nu 11:25,26; 24:2; 2Ch 20:14; 24:20
15:2 [c]ver 4,15; 2Ch 20:17 [d]Jas 4:8 [e]Jer 29:13 [f]1Ch 28:9; 2Ch 24:20
15:3 [g]Lev 10:11 [h]2Ch 17:9; La 2:9
15:4 [i]Dt 4:29
15:5 [j]Jdg 5:6
15:6 [k]Mt 24:7
15:7 [l]Jos 1:7,9 [m]Ps 58:11
15:8 [n]2Ch 13:19 [o]2Ch 8:12

[a]3 That is, symbols of the goddess Asherah; here and elsewhere in 2 Chronicles [b]9 Hebrew *with an army of a thousand thousands* or *with an army of thousands upon thousands* [c]8 Vulgate and Syriac (see also Septuagint and verse 1); Hebrew does not have *Azariah son of.*

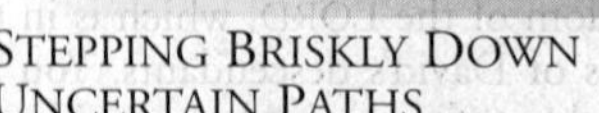

FAITHFULNESS

STEPPING BRISKLY DOWN UNCERTAIN PATHS

2 Chronicles 15:8

Faithfulness takes courage. Asa meddled with bogus gods and removed them at the risk of offending idolaters. To turn a nation unto God is fearsome work.

9 Then he assembled all Judah and Benjamin and the people from Ephraim, Manasseh and Simeon who had settled among them, for large numbers[p] had come over to him from Israel when they saw that the LORD his God was with him.

10 They assembled at Jerusalem in the third month of the fifteenth year of Asa's reign. 11 At that time they sacrificed to the LORD seven hundred head of cattle and seven thousand sheep and goats from the plunder[q] they had brought back. 12 They entered into a covenant[r] to seek the LORD,[s] the God of their fathers, with all their heart and soul. 13 All who would not seek the LORD, the God of Israel, were to be put to death,[t] whether small or great, man or woman. 14 They took an oath to the LORD with loud acclamation, with shouting and with trumpets and horns. 15 All Judah rejoiced about the oath because they had sworn it wholeheartedly. They sought God[u] eagerly, and he was found by them. So the LORD gave them rest[v] on every side.

16 King Asa also deposed his grandmother Maacah from her position as queen mother, because she had made a repulsive Asherah pole.[w] Asa cut the pole down, broke it up and burned it in the Kidron Valley. 17 Although he did not remove the high places from Israel, Asa's heart was fully committed ⌊to the LORD⌋ all his life. 18 He brought into the temple of God the silver and gold and the articles that he and his father had dedicated.

19 There was no more war until the thirty-fifth year of Asa's reign.

Asa's Last Years

16 In the thirty-sixth year of Asa's reign Baasha[x] king of Israel went up against Judah and fortified Ramah to prevent anyone from leaving or entering the territory of Asa king of Judah.

2 Asa then took the silver and gold out of the treasuries of the LORD's temple and of his own palace and sent it to Ben-Hadad king of Aram, who was ruling in Damascus. 3 "Let there be a treaty[y] between me and you," he said, "as there was between my father and your father. See, I am sending you silver and gold. Now break your treaty with Baasha king of Israel so he will withdraw from me."

4 Ben-Hadad agreed with King Asa and sent the commanders of his forces against the towns of Israel. They conquered Ijon, Dan, Abel Maim[a] and all the store cities of Naphtali. 5 When Baasha heard this, he stopped building Ramah and abandoned his work. 6 Then King Asa brought all the men of Judah, and they carried away from Ramah the stones and timber Baasha had been using. With them he built up Geba and Mizpah.

7 At that time Hanani[z] the seer came to Asa king of Judah and said to him: "Because you relied on the king of Aram and not on the LORD your God, the army of the king of Aram has escaped from your hand. 8 Were not the Cushites[b][a] and Libyans a mighty army with great numbers of chariots and horsemen[c]? Yet when you relied on the LORD, he delivered[b] them into your hand. 9 For the eyes[c] of the LORD range throughout the earth to strengthen those whose hearts are fully committed to him. You have done a foolish[d] thing, and from now on you will be at war."

10 Asa was angry with the seer because of this; he was so enraged that he put him in prison. At the same time Asa brutally oppressed some of the people.

11 The events of Asa's reign, from beginning to end, are written in the book of the kings of Judah and Israel. 12 In the thirty-ninth year of his reign Asa was afflicted with a disease in his feet. Though his disease was severe, even in his illness he did not seek help from the LORD,[e] but only from the physicians. 13 Then in the forty-first year of his reign Asa died and rested with his fathers. 14 They buried him in the tomb that he had cut out for himself in the City of David. They laid him on a bier covered with spices and various blended perfumes,[f] and they made a huge fire[g] in his honor.

Jehoshaphat King of Judah

17 Jehoshaphat his son succeeded him as king and strengthened himself against Israel. 2 He stationed

[a] 4 Also known as *Abel Beth Maacah* [b] 8 That is, people from the upper Nile region [c] 8 Or *charioteers*

15:9 [p] 2Ch 11:16-17
15:11 [q] 2Ch 14:13
15:12 [r] 2Ki 11:17; 2Ch 23:16; 34:31 [s] 1Ch 16:11
15:13 [t] Ex 22:20; Dt 13:9-16
15:15 [u] Dt 4:29 [v] 1Ch 22:9; 2Ch 14:7
15:16 [w] Ex 34:13; 2Ch 14:2-5
16:1 [x] Jer 41:9
16:3 [y] 2Ch 20:35
16:7 [z] 1Ki 16:1
16:8 [a] 2Ch 12:3; 14:9 [b] 2Ch 13:16
16:9 [c] Pr 15:3; Jer 16:17; Zec 4:10 [d] 1Sa 13:13
16:12 [e] Jer 17:5-6
16:14 [f] Ge 50:2; Jn 19:39-40 [g] 2Ch 21:19; Jer 34:5

troops in all the fortified cities of Judah
and put garrisons in Judah and in the
towns of Ephraim that his father Asa
17:2 [h]2Ch 15:8 had captured.[h]
3The LORD was with Jehoshaphat
because in his early years he walked
17:3 [i]1Ki 22:43 in the ways his father David[i] had followed. He did not consult the Baals
17:4 [j]1Ki 12:28; 2Ch 22:9 4but sought[j] the God of his father and
followed his commands rather than the
practices of Israel. 5The LORD established the kingdom under his control;
17:5 [k]1Sa 10:27 [l]2Ch 18:1 and all Judah brought gifts[k] to Jehoshaphat, so that he had great wealth and
17:6 [m]1Ki 8:61; 2Ch 15:17 [n]1Ki 15:14; 2Ch 19:3; 20:33 [o]Ex 34:13 [p]2Ch 21:12 honor.[l] 6His heart was devoted[m] to the
ways of the LORD; furthermore, he re-
moved the high places[n] and the Asherah poles[o] from Judah.[p]
7In the third year of his reign he
sent his officials Ben-Hail, Obadiah,
17:7 [q]Lev 10:11; Dt 6:4-9; 2Ch 15:3; 35:3 Zechariah, Nethanel and Micaiah to
teach[q] in the towns of Judah. 8With
them were certain Levites[r]—Shemaiah,
Nethaniah, Zebadiah, Asahel, Shemir-
17:8 [r]2Ch 19:8; Ne 8:7-8 amoth, Jehonathan, Adonijah, Tobijah
and Tob-Adonijah—and the priests
Elishama and Jehoram. 9They taught
throughout Judah, taking with them
17:9 [s]Dt 6:4-9; 28:61 the Book of the Law[s] of the LORD; they
went around to all the towns of Judah
and taught the people.
17:10 [t]Ge 35:5; Dt 2:25; 2Ch 14:14 10The fear[t] of the LORD fell on all
the kingdoms of the lands surround-
ing Judah, so that they did not make
war with Jehoshaphat. 11Some Philis-
17:11 [u]2Ch 9:14; 26:8 [v]2Ch 21:16 tines brought Jehoshaphat gifts and silver as tribute, and the Arabs[u] brought
him flocks:[v] seven thousand seven hundred rams and seven thousand seven
hundred goats.
12Jehoshaphat became more and
more powerful; he built forts and store
cities in Judah 13and had large supplies
in the towns of Judah. He also kept
experienced fighting men in Jerusalem.
17:14 [w]2Sa 24:2 14Their enrollment[w] by families was as
follows:

From Judah, commanders of units of 1,000:
Adnah the commander, with 300,000 fighting men;
15next, Jehohanan the command-
er, with 280,000;
16next, Amasiah son of Zicri, who
17:16 [x]Jdg 5:9; 1Ch 29:9 volunteered[x] himself for the
service of the LORD, with
200,000.
17From Benjamin:[y] 17:17 [y]Nu 1:36
Eliada, a valiant soldier, with 200,000 men armed with bows and shields;
18next, Jehozabad, with 180,000
men armed for battle.

19These were the men who served the
king, besides those he stationed in the
fortified cities[z] throughout Judah.[a] 17:19 [z]2Ch 11:10 [a]2Ch 25:5

Micaiah Prophesies Against Ahab

18 Now Jehoshaphat had great 18:1 [b]2Ch 17:5 [c]2Ch 19:1-3; 22:3 [d]2Ch 21:6
wealth and honor,[b] and he al-
lied[c] himself with Ahab[d] by marriage.
2Some years later he went down to visit Ahab in Samaria. Ahab slaughtered
many sheep and cattle for him and the
people with him and urged him to attack Ramoth Gilead. 3Ahab king of Israel asked Jehoshaphat king of Judah,
"Will you go with me against Ramoth
Gilead?"
Jehoshaphat replied, "I am as you are,
and my people as your people; we will
join you in the war." 4But Jehoshaphat
also said to the king of Israel, "First seek
the counsel of the LORD."
5So the king of Israel brought together the prophets—four hundred men—
and asked them, "Shall we go to war
against Ramoth Gilead, or shall I refrain?"
"Go," they answered, "for God will
give it into the king's hand."
6But Jehoshaphat asked, "Is there not
a prophet of the LORD here whom we
can inquire of?"
7The king of Israel answered Jehoshaphat, "There is still one man
through whom we can inquire of the
LORD, but I hate him because he never prophesies anything good about me,
but always bad. He is Micaiah son of
Imlah."
"The king should not say that," Jehoshaphat replied.
8So the king of Israel called one of
his officials and said, "Bring Micaiah
son of Imlah at once."
9Dressed in their royal robes, the king
of Israel and Jehoshaphat king of Judah were sitting on their thrones at the
threshing floor by the entrance to the
gate of Samaria, with all the prophets
prophesying before them. 10Now Zedekiah son of Kenaanah had made iron
horns, and he declared, "This is what

the LORD says: 'With these you will
gore the Arameans until they are destroyed.'"
11All the other prophets were prophesying the same thing. "Attack Ramoth
18:11 Gilead[e] and be victorious," they said,
e2Ch 22:5 "for the LORD will give it into the king's
hand."
12The messenger who had gone to
summon Micaiah said to him, "Look,
as one man the other prophets are pre-
dicting success for the king. Let your
word agree with theirs, and speak favorably."
13But Micaiah said, "As surely as the
LORD lives, I can tell him only what
18:13 my God says."[f]
fNu 22:18, 14When he arrived, the king asked
20,35 him, "Micaiah, shall we go to war
against Ramoth Gilead, or shall I refrain?"
"Attack and be victorious," he answered, "for they will be given into your
hand."
15The king said to him, "How many
times must I make you swear to tell me
nothing but the truth in the name of
the LORD?"
16Then Micaiah answered, "I saw all
18:16 gIsrael[g] scattered on the hills like sheep
g1Ch 9:1 hNu 27:17; without a shepherd,[h] and the LORD
Eze 34:5-8 said, 'These people have no master. Let
each one go home in peace.'"
17The king of Israel said to Jehoshaphat, "Didn't I tell you that he
never prophesies anything good about
me, but only bad?"
18Micaiah continued, "Therefore hear
the word of the LORD: I saw the LORD
18:18 iDa 7:9 sitting on his throne[i] with all the host
of heaven standing on his right and on
his left. 19And the LORD said, 'Who
will entice Ahab king of Israel into attacking Ramoth Gilead and going to
his death there?'
"One suggested this, and another
that. 20Finally, a spirit came forward,
stood before the LORD and said, 'I will
entice him.'
"'By what means?' the LORD asked.
18:21 21"'I will go and be a lying spirit[j] in
j1Ch 21:1; Job 1:6; the mouths of all his prophets,' he said.
Zec 3:1; Jn 8:44 "'You will succeed in enticing him,'
said the LORD. 'Go and do it.'
22"So now the LORD has put a lying
18:22 spirit in the mouths of these prophets
kJob 12:16; of yours.[k] The LORD has decreed disas-
Isa 19:14; Eze 14:9 ter for you."

23Then Zedekiah son of Kenaanah
went up and slapped[l] Micaiah in the 18:23
face. "Which way did the spirit from[a] lJer 20:2;
the LORD go when he went from me to Mk 14:65; Ac 23:2
speak to you?" he asked.
24Micaiah replied, "You will find out
on the day you go to hide in an inner
room."
25The king of Israel then ordered,
"Take Micaiah and send him back to
Amon the ruler of the city and to Joash
the king's son, 26and say, 'This is what 18:26
the king says: Put this fellow in prison[m] m2Ch 16:10;
and give him nothing but bread and Heb 11:36
water until I return safely.'"
27Micaiah declared, "If you ever return safely, the LORD has not spoken
through me." Then he added, "Mark
my words, all you people!"

Ahab Killed at Ramoth Gilead

28So the king of Israel and Jehoshaphat king of Judah went up to Ramoth Gilead. 29The king of Israel said
to Jehoshaphat, "I will enter the battle
in disguise, but you wear your royal
robes." So the king of Israel disguised[n] 18:29
himself and went into battle. n1Sa 28:8
30Now the king of Aram had ordered his chariot commanders, "Do not
fight with anyone, small or great, except the king of Israel." 31When the
chariot commanders saw Jehoshaphat,
they thought, "This is the king of Israel." So they turned to attack him, but 18:31
Jehoshaphat cried out,[o] and the LORD o2Ch 13:14
helped him. God drew them away from
him, 32for when the chariot commanders saw that he was not the king of Israel, they stopped pursuing him.
33But someone drew his bow at random and hit the king of Israel between
the sections of his armor. The king told
the chariot driver, "Wheel around and
get me out of the fighting. I've been
wounded." 34All day long the battle
raged, and the king of Israel propped
himself up in his chariot facing the Arameans until evening. Then at sunset he 18:34
died.[p] p2Ch 22:5

19 When Jehoshaphat king of Judah returned safely to his palace
in Jerusalem, 2Jehu[q] the seer, the son 19:2 q1Ki 16:1
of Hanani, went out to meet him and r2Ch 16:2-9
said to the king, "Should you help the
wicked[r] and love[b] those who hate the

[a]23 Or *Spirit of* [b]2 Or *and make alliances with*

LORD?[s] Because of this, the wrath[t] of the LORD is upon you. 3There is, however, some good[u] in you, for you have rid the land of the Asherah poles[v] and have set your heart on seeking God."[w]

Jehoshaphat Appoints Judges

4Jehoshaphat lived in Jerusalem, and he went out again among the people from Beersheba to the hill country of Ephraim and turned them back to the LORD, the God of their fathers. 5He appointed judges[x] in the land, in each of the fortified cities of Judah. 6He told them, "Consider carefully what you do,[y] because you are not judging for man[z] but for the LORD, who is with you whenever you give a verdict. 7Now let the fear of the LORD be upon you. Judge carefully, for with the LORD our God there is no injustice[a] or partiality[b] or bribery."

8In Jerusalem also, Jehoshaphat appointed some of the Levites, priests and heads of Israelite families to administer[c] the law of the LORD and to settle disputes. And they lived in Jerusalem. 9He gave them these orders: "You must serve faithfully and wholeheartedly in the fear of the LORD. 10In every case that comes before you from your fellow countrymen who live in the cities—whether bloodshed or other concerns of the law, commands, decrees or ordinances—you are to warn them not to sin against the LORD;[d] otherwise his wrath will come on you and your brothers. Do this, and you will not sin.

11"Amariah the chief priest will be over you in any matter concerning the LORD, and Zebadiah son of Ishmael, the leader of the tribe of Judah, will be over you in any matter concerning the king, and the Levites will serve as officials before you. Act with courage,[e] and may the LORD be with those who do well."

Jehoshaphat Defeats Moab and Ammon

20 After this, the Moabites and Ammonites with some of the Meunites[a][f] came to make war on Jehoshaphat.

2Some men came and told Jehoshaphat, "A vast army is coming against you from Edom,[b] from the other side of the Sea.[c] It is already in Hazazon Tamar"[g] (that is, En Gedi). 3Alarmed, Jehoshaphat resolved to inquire of the LORD, and he proclaimed a fast[h] for all Judah. 4The people of Judah came together to seek help from the LORD; indeed, they came from every town in Judah to seek him.

5Then Jehoshaphat stood up in the assembly of Judah and Jerusalem at the temple of the LORD in the front of the new courtyard 6and said:

"O LORD, God of our fathers,[i] are you not the God who is in heaven?[j] You rule over all the kingdoms[k] of the nations. Power and might are in your hand, and no one can withstand you. 7O our God, did you not drive out the inhabitants of this land before your people Israel and give it forever to the descendants of Abraham your friend?[l] 8They have lived in it and have built in it a sanctuary[m] for your Name, saying, 9'If calamity comes upon us, whether the sword of judgment, or plague or famine,[n] we will stand in your presence before this temple that bears your Name and will cry out to you in our distress, and you will hear us and save us.'

10"But now here are men from Ammon, Moab and Mount Seir, whose territory you would not allow Israel to invade when they came from Egypt;[o] so they turned away from them and did not destroy them. 11See how they are repaying us by coming to drive us out of the possession[p] you gave us as an inheritance. 12O our God, will you not judge them?[q] For we have no power to face this vast army that is attacking us. We do not know what to do, but our eyes are upon you."[r]

13All the men of Judah, with their wives and children and little ones, stood there before the LORD.

14Then the Spirit[s] of the LORD came upon Jahaziel son of Zechariah, the son

[a] *1* Some Septuagint manuscripts; Hebrew *Ammonites*
[b] *2* One Hebrew manuscript; most Hebrew manuscripts, Septuagint and Vulgate *Aram*
[c] *2* That is, the Dead Sea

19:2 [s]Ps 139:21-22 [t]2Ch 24:18; 32:25; Ps 7:11
19:3 [u]1Ki 14:13; 2Ch 12:12 [v]2Ch 17:6 [w]2Ch 18:1; 20:35; 25:7; Ezr 7:10
19:5 [x]Ge 47:6; Ex 18:26
19:6 [y]Lev 19:15 [z]Dt 1:17; 16:18-20; 17:8-13
19:7 [a]Ge 18:25; Dt 32:4 [b]Dt 10:17; Job 34:19; Ro 2:11; Col 3:25
19:8 [c]2Ch 17:8-9
19:10 [d]Dt 17:8-13
19:11 [e]1Ch 28:20
20:1 [f]1Ch 4:41
20:2 [g]Ge 14:7
20:3 [h]1Sa 7:6; 2Ch 19:3; Ezr 8:21; Jer 36:9; Jnh 3:5,7
20:6 [i]Mt 6:9 [j]Dt 4:39 [k]1Ch 29:11-12
20:7 [l]Isa 41:8; Jas 2:23
20:8 [m]2Ch 6:20
20:9 [n]2Ch 6:28
20:10 [o]Nu 20:14-21; Dt 2:4-6,9, 18-19
20:11 [p]Ps 83:1-12
20:12 [q]Jdg 11:27 [r]Ps 25:15; 121:1-2
20:14 [s]2Ch 15:1

of Benaiah, the son of Jeiel, the son of
Mattaniah, a Levite and descendant of
Asaph, as he stood in the assembly.
15He said: "Listen, King Jehoshaphat
and all who live in Judah and Jerusalem! This is what the LORD says to you:
20:15 [t]2Ch 32:7 [u]Ex 14:13-14; 1Sa 17:47 'Do not be afraid or discouraged[t] because of this vast army. For the battle[u]
is not yours, but God's. 16Tomorrow
march down against them. They will be
climbing up by the Pass of Ziz, and you
will find them at the end of the gorge in
the Desert of Jeruel. 17You will not have
to fight this battle. Take up your posi-
20:17 [v]Ex 14:13; 2Ch 15:2 tions; stand firm and see[v] the deliverance the LORD will give you, O Judah
and Jerusalem. Do not be afraid; do not
be discouraged. Go out to face them
tomorrow, and the LORD will be with
you.'"
18Jehoshaphat bowed[w] with his face 20:18 [w]Ex 4:31
to the ground, and all the people of Ju-
dah and Jerusalem fell down in worship before the LORD. 19Then some
Levites from the Kohathites and Korahites stood up and praised the LORD,
the God of Israel, with very loud voice.
20Early in the morning they left for
the Desert of Tekoa. As they set out,
Jehoshaphat stood and said, "Listen to
me, Judah and people of Jerusalem!
Have faith in the LORD your God and
you will be upheld; have faith[x] in his 20:20 [x]Isa 7:9 [y]Ge 39:3; Pr 16:3
prophets and you will be successful."[y]
21After consulting the people, Jehoshaphat appointed men to sing to the
LORD and to praise him for the splen-
dor of his[a] holiness[z] as they went out at 20:21 [z]1Ch 16:29; Ps 29:2 [a]2Ch 5:13; Ps 136:1
the head of the army, saying:

"Give thanks to the LORD,
for his love endures forever."[a]

DAY 2 TWO

FAITHFULNESS AND THE PURPOSE OF GOD IN MY LIFE

2 Chronicles 20:20–30

Stay faithful, and you will remain a conqueror. Victory is the end reward of faithfulness. King Jehoshaphat experienced this truth. He had been following the Lord for a long time. In fact, we read in 2 Chronicles 17:3 that "the LORD was with Jehoshaphat because in his early years he walked in the ways his father David had followed." Even as a young man, Jehoshaphat was faithful to God. In fact, his foundational beliefs set the stage for the later blessings from God. Jehosaphat's devotion to God began at an early age and the relationship lasted a lifetime.

Although Jehoshaphat wasn't perfect—he allied himself with evil King Ahab—he did tear down the high places of idol worship in his kingdom (17:6). And he was still consulting God later on in his life for direction—both for his own life as well as for governing the kingdom. God blessed Jehoshaphat's faithfulness by guiding him and giving him victory over his enemies. By relying on God, Jehoshaphat didn't even have to fight his enemies. When he and his army approached the plain of battle, he saw that the work had already been done (see 20:24). The enemy was defeated. God had given the victory to those he knew to be faithful.

To begin a study on the topic of Faithfulness, the Road That Ends in Victory, turn to the home page on page 1540.

JOY

SONGS FOR THE FRAY

2 Chronicles 20:21

Singing their way into the fray, Jehoshaphat's soldiers were victorious. So, too, will we be victors and joy will be our shield and buckler. We will be armored with the breastplate of St. Patrick:

"Christ with me, Christ before me, Christ behind me,
Christ in me, Christ beneath me, Christ above me."

22As they began to sing and praise,
the LORD set ambushes[b] against the 20:22 [b]Jdg 7:22; 2Ch 13:13
men of Ammon and Moab and Mount
Seir who were invading Judah, and they
were defeated. 23The men of Ammon[c] 20:23 [c]Ge 19:38 [d]2Ch 21:8 [e]Jdg 7:22; 1Sa 14:20; Eze 38:21
and Moab rose up against the men from
Mount Seir[d] to destroy and annihilate
them. After they finished slaughtering
the men from Seir, they helped to destroy one another.[e]
24When the men of Judah came to
the place that overlooks the desert and
looked toward the vast army, they saw
only dead bodies lying on the ground;
no one had escaped. 25So Jehoshaphat
and his men went to carry off their

[a]21 Or *him with the splendor of*

plunder, and they found among them a
great amount of equipment and clothing[a] and also articles of value—more
than they could take away. There was
so much plunder that it took three
days to collect it. 26On the fourth day
they assembled in the Valley of Beracah, where they praised the LORD. This
is why it is called the Valley of Beracah[b]
to this day.
27Then, led by Jehoshaphat, all the
men of Judah and Jerusalem returned
joyfully to Jerusalem, for the LORD had
given them cause to rejoice over their
enemies. 28They entered Jerusalem and
went to the temple of the LORD with
harps and lutes and trumpets.
20:29 29The fear[f] of God came upon all
[f]Ge 35:5; the kingdoms of the countries when
Dt 2:25; 2Ch 14:14; they heard how the LORD had fought[g]
17:10 [g]Ex 14:14 against the enemies of Israel. 30And the
kingdom of Jehoshaphat was at peace,
20:30 [h]1Ch 22:9; for his God had given him rest[h] on
2Ch 14:6-7; 15:15 every side.

The End of Jehoshaphat's Reign

31So Jehoshaphat reigned over Judah.
He was thirty-five years old when he
became king of Judah, and he reigned in
Jerusalem twenty-five years. His mother's name was Azubah daughter of Shilhi. 32He walked in the ways of his father
Asa and did not stray from them; he did
what was right in the eyes of the LORD.
20:33 [i]2Ch 17:6; 33The high places,[i] however, were not
19:3 removed, and the people still had not
set their hearts on the God of their fathers.
34The other events of Jehoshaphat's
reign, from beginning to end, are writ-
20:34 [j]1Ki 16:1 ten in the annals of Jehu[j] son of Hanani, which are recorded in the book of
the kings of Israel.
35Later, Jehoshaphat king of Judah
20:35 [k]2Ch 16:3 made an alliance[k] with Ahaziah king of
[l]2Ch 19:1-3 Israel, who was guilty of wickedness.[l]
36He agreed with him to construct
a fleet of trading ships.[c] After these
were built at Ezion Geber, 37Eliezer son
of Dodavahu of Mareshah prophesied
against Jehoshaphat, saying, "Because
you have made an alliance with Ahaziah, the LORD will destroy what you
20:37 have made." The ships[m] were wrecked
[m]1Ki 9:26; 2Ch 9:21 and were not able to set sail to trade.[d]

21 Then Jehoshaphat rested with
his fathers and was buried with
them in the City of David. And Je-
horam[n] his son succeeded him as king. 21:1 [n]1Ch 3:11
2Jehoram's brothers, the sons of Je-
hoshaphat, were Azariah, Jehiel, Zechariah, Azariahu, Michael and Shephatiah. All these were sons of Jehoshaphat
king of Israel.[e] 3Their father had given
them many gifts[o] of silver and gold and 21:3
articles of value, as well as fortified cit- [o]2Ch 11:23
ies[p] in Judah, but he had given the [p]2Ch 11:10
kingdom to Jehoram because he was
his firstborn son.

Jehoram King of Judah

4When Jehoram established[q] himself 21:4
firmly over his father's kingdom, he put [q]1Ki 2:12
all his brothers[r] to the sword along with [r]Jdg 9:5
some of the princes of Israel. 5Jehoram
was thirty-two years old when he became king, and he reigned in Jerusalem eight years. 6He walked in the ways
of the kings of Israel,[s] as the house of 21:6
Ahab had done, for he married a daugh- [s]1Ki 12:28-30
ter of Ahab.[t] He did evil in the eyes [t]2Ch 18:1; 22:3
of the LORD. 7Nevertheless, because of
the covenant the LORD had made with
David,[u] the LORD was not willing to 21:7
destroy the house of David.[v] He had [u]2Sa 7:13
promised to maintain a lamp[w] for him [v]2Sa 7:15; 2Ch 23:3
and his descendants forever. [w]2Sa 21:17; 1Ki 11:36
8In the time of Jehoram, Edom[x] re-
belled against Judah and set up its own 21:8 [x]2Ch 20:22-23
king. 9So Jehoram went there with his
officers and all his chariots. The Edomites surrounded him and his chariot
commanders, but he rose up and broke
through by night. 10To this day Edom
has been in rebellion against Judah.
Libnah[y] revolted at the same time, because Jehoram had forsaken the LORD, 21:10
the God of his fathers. 11He had also [y]Nu 33:20
built high places on the hills of Judah
and had caused the people of Jerusalem
to prostitute themselves and had led Judah astray.
12Jehoram received a letter from Elijah[z] the prophet, which said:

"This is what the LORD, the God 21:12
of your father[a] David, says: 'You [z]2Ki 1:16-17
have not walked in the ways of [a]2Ch 17:3-6
your father Jehoshaphat or of Asa[b] [b]2Ch 14:2
king of Judah. 13But you have
walked in the ways of the kings of

[a]*25* Some Hebrew manuscripts and Vulgate; most Hebrew manuscripts *corpses* [b]*26 Beracah* means *praise.* [c]*36* Hebrew *of ships that could go to Tarshish* [d]*37* Hebrew *sail for Tarshish* [e]*2* That is, Judah, as frequently in 2 Chronicles

Israel, and you have led Judah and
the people of Jerusalem to prostitute themselves, just as the house
of Ahab did.[c] You have also murdered your own brothers, members of your father's house, men
who were better[d] than you. 14So
now the LORD is about to strike
your people, your sons, your wives
and everything that is yours, with a
heavy blow. 15You yourself will be
very ill with a lingering disease[e] of
the bowels, until the disease causes
your bowels to come out.'"

16The LORD aroused against Jehoram the hostility of the Philistines and
of the Arabs[f] who lived near the Cushites. 17They attacked Judah, invaded it
and carried off all the goods found in
the king's palace, together with his sons
and wives. Not a son was left to him
except Ahaziah,[a] the youngest.[g]

18After all this, the LORD afflicted
Jehoram with an incurable disease of
the bowels. 19In the course of time, at
the end of the second year, his bowels
came out because of the disease, and he
died in great pain. His people made no
fire in his honor,[h] as they had for his
fathers.

20Jehoram was thirty-two years old
when he became king, and he reigned in
Jerusalem eight years. He passed away,
to no one's regret, and was buried[i] in
the City of David, but not in the tombs
of the kings.

21:13 [c]ver 6,11; 1Ki 16:29-33 [d]ver 4; 1Ki 2:32
21:15 [e]ver 18-19; Nu 12:10
21:16 [f]2Ch 17:10-11; 22:1; 26:7
21:17 [g]2Ki 12:18; 2Ch 22:1; 25:23; Joel 3:5
21:19 [h]2Ch 16:14
21:20 [i]2Ch 24:25; 28:27; 33:20; Jer 22:18,28

Ahaziah King of Judah

22 The people[j] of Jerusalem[k] made
Ahaziah, Jehoram's youngest
son, king in his place, since the raiders,[l]
who came with the Arabs into the camp,
had killed all the older sons. So Ahaziah
son of Jehoram king of Judah began to
reign.

2Ahaziah was twenty-two[b] years old
when he became king, and he reigned
in Jerusalem one year. His mother's
name was Athaliah, a granddaughter of
Omri.

3He too walked[m] in the ways of the
house of Ahab,[n] for his mother encouraged him in doing wrong. 4He did evil
in the eyes of the LORD, as the house
of Ahab had done, for after his father's
death they became his advisers, to his
undoing. 5He also followed their counsel when he went with Joram[c] son of
Ahab king of Israel to war against Hazael king of Aram at Ramoth Gilead.[o]
The Arameans wounded Joram; 6so he
returned to Jezreel to recover from the
wounds they had inflicted on him at
Ramoth[d] in his battle with Hazael[p] king
of Aram.

Then Ahaziah[e] son of Jehoram king
of Judah went down to Jezreel to see Joram son of Ahab because he had been
wounded.

7Through Ahaziah's[q] visit to Joram,
God brought about Ahaziah's downfall.
When Ahaziah arrived, he went out
with Joram to meet Jehu son of Nimshi, whom the LORD had anointed to
destroy the house of Ahab. 8While Jehu
was executing judgment on the house
of Ahab,[r] he found the princes of Judah and the sons of Ahaziah's relatives,
who had been attending Ahaziah, and
he killed them. 9He then went in search
of Ahaziah, and his men captured him
while he was hiding[s] in Samaria. He was
brought to Jehu and put to death. They
buried him, for they said, "He was a
son of Jehoshaphat, who sought[t] the
LORD with all his heart." So there was
no one in the house of Ahaziah powerful enough to retain the kingdom.

22:1 [j]2Ch 33:25; 36:1 [k]2Ch 23:20-21; 26:1 [l]2Ch 21:16-17
22:3 [m]2Ch 18:1 [n]2Ch 21:6
22:5 [o]2Ch 18:11,34
22:6 [p]1Ki 19:15; 2Ki 8:13-15; 9:15
22:7 [q]2Ki 9:16; 2Ch 10:15
22:8 [r]2Ki 10:13
22:9 [s]Jdg 9:5 [t]2Ch 17:4

Athaliah and Joash

10When Athaliah the mother of Ahaziah saw that her son was dead, she proceeded to destroy the whole royal family
of the house of Judah. 11But Jehosheba,[f]
the daughter of King Jehoram, took Joash son of Ahaziah and stole him away
from among the royal princes who were
about to be murdered and put him
and his nurse in a bedroom. Because
Jehosheba,[f] the daughter of King Jehoram and wife of the priest Jehoiada, was
Ahaziah's sister, she hid the child from
Athaliah so she could not kill him. 12He
remained hidden with them at the temple of God for six years while Athaliah
ruled the land.

[a] *17* Hebrew *Jehoahaz,* a variant of *Ahaziah*
[b] *2* Some Septuagint manuscripts and Syriac (see also 2 Kings 8:26); Hebrew *forty-two*
[c] *5* Hebrew *Jehoram,* a variant of *Joram*; also in verses 6 and 7
[d] *6* Hebrew *Ramah,* a variant of *Ramoth*
[e] *6* Some Hebrew manuscripts, Septuagint, Vulgate and Syriac (see also 2 Kings 8:29); most Hebrew manuscripts *Azariah*
[f] *11* Hebrew *Jehoshabeath,* a variant of *Jehosheba*

23 In the seventh year Jehoiada
showed his strength. He made a
covenant with the commanders of units
of a hundred: Azariah son of Jeroham,
Ishmael son of Jehohanan, Azariah son
of Obed, Maaseiah son of Adaiah, and
Elishaphat son of Zicri. [2]They went
throughout Judah and gathered the Le-
23:2 [u]Nu 35:2-5 vites[u] and the heads of Israelite families
from all the towns. When they came to
Jerusalem, [3]the whole assembly made a
23:3 [v]2Ki 11:17; [w]2Sa 7:12; 1Ki 2:4; 2Ch 6:16; 7:18; 21:7 covenant[v] with the king at the temple
of God.

Jehoiada said to them, "The king's
son shall reign, as the LORD promised
concerning the descendants of David.[w]
[4]Now this is what you are to do: A third
of you priests and Levites who are going on duty on the Sabbath are to keep
watch at the doors, [5]a third of you at
the royal palace and a third at the Foundation Gate, and all the other men are
to be in the courtyards of the temple of
the LORD. [6]No one is to enter the temple of the LORD except the priests and
Levites on duty; they may enter because
they are consecrated, but all the other
23:6 [x]1Ch 23:28-29; Zec 3:7 men are to guard[x] what the LORD has
assigned to them.[a] [7]The Levites are to
station themselves around the king,
each man with his weapons in his hand.
Anyone who enters the temple must
be put to death. Stay close to the king
wherever he goes."

[8]The Levites and all the men of Judah did just as Jehoiada the priest or-
23:8 [y]2Ki 11:9 [z]1Ch 24:1 dered.[y] Each one took his men—those
who were going on duty on the Sabbath
and those who were going off duty—
for Jehoiada the priest had not released
any of the divisions.[z] [9]Then he gave the
commanders of units of a hundred the
spears and the large and small shields
that had belonged to King David and
that were in the temple of God. [10]He
stationed all the men, each with his
weapon in his hand, around the king—
near the altar and the temple, from
the south side to the north side of the
temple.

[11]Jehoiada and his sons brought out
the king's son and put the crown on
23:11 [a]Ex 25:16; Dt 17:18; 1Sa 10:24 him; they presented him with a copy[a]
of the covenant and proclaimed him
king. They anointed him and shouted,
"Long live the king!"

[12]When Athaliah heard the noise of
the people running and cheering the
king, she went to them at the temple
of the LORD. [13]She looked, and there 23:13
was the king,[b] standing by his pillar[c] [b]1Ki 1:41 [c]1Ki 7:15
at the entrance. The officers and the
trumpeters were beside the king, and
all the people of the land were rejoicing
and blowing trumpets, and singers with
musical instruments were leading the
praises. Then Athaliah tore her robes
and shouted, "Treason! Treason!"

[14]Jehoiada the priest sent out the
commanders of units of a hundred, who
were in charge of the troops, and said
to them: "Bring her out between the
ranks[b] and put to the sword anyone
who follows her." For the priest had
said, "Do not put her to death at the
temple of the LORD." [15]So they seized
her as she reached the entrance of the
Horse Gate[d] on the palace grounds, 23:15 [d]Ne 3:28; Jer 31:40
and there they put her to death.

[16]Jehoiada then made a covenant[e] 23:16 [e]2Ch 29:10; 34:31; Ne 9:38
that he and the people and the king[c]
would be the LORD's people. [17]All the
people went to the temple of Baal and
tore it down. They smashed the altars
and idols and killed[f] Mattan the priest 23:17 [f]Dt 13:6-9
of Baal in front of the altars.

[18]Then Jehoiada placed the oversight
of the temple of the LORD in the hands
of the priests, who were Levites,[g] to 23:18 [g]1Ch 23:28-32; 2Ch 5:5 [h]1Ch 23:6; 25:6
whom David had made assignments in
the temple,[h] to present the burnt offerings of the LORD as written in the Law
of Moses, with rejoicing and singing, as
David had ordered. [19]He also stationed
doorkeepers[i] at the gates of the LORD's 23:19 [i]1Ch 9:22
temple so that no one who was in any
way unclean might enter.

[20]He took with him the commanders
of hundreds, the nobles, the rulers of
the people and all the people of the land
and brought the king down from the
temple of the LORD. They went into
the palace through the Upper Gate[j] 23:20 [j]2Ki 15:35
and seated the king on the royal throne,
[21]and all the people of the land rejoiced.
And the city was quiet, because Athali-
ah had been slain with the sword.[k] 23:21 [k]2Ch 22:1

Joash Repairs the Temple

24 Joash was seven years old when
he became king, and he reigned
in Jerusalem forty years. His mother's

[a]6 Or *to observe the LORD's command* ⌊*not to enter*⌋
[b]14 Or *out from the precincts* [c]16 Or *covenant between* ⌊*the LORD*⌋ *and the people and the king that they* (see 2 Kings 11:17)

name was Zibiah; she was from Beersheba. [2]Joash did what was right in the
eyes of the LORD[l] all the years of Jehoiada the priest. [3]Jehoiada chose two
wives for him, and he had sons and
daughters.

24:2 [l]2Ch 25:2; 26:5

[4]Some time later Joash decided to
restore the temple of the LORD. [5]He
called together the priests and Levites
and said to them, "Go to the towns
of Judah and collect the money[m] due
annually from all Israel,[n] to repair the
temple of your God. Do it now." But
the Levites[o] did not act at once.

24:5 [m]Ex 30:16; Ne 10:32-33; Mt 17:24 [n]1Ch 11:1 [o]1Ch 26:20

[6]Therefore the king summoned Jehoiada the chief priest and said to him,
"Why haven't you required the Levites
to bring in from Judah and Jerusalem
the tax imposed by Moses the servant
of the LORD and by the assembly of Israel for the Tent of the Testimony?"[p]

24:6 [p]Ex 30:12-16; Nu 1:50

[7]Now the sons of that wicked woman Athaliah had broken into the temple
of God and had used even its sacred objects for the Baals.

[8]At the king's command, a chest was
made and placed outside, at the gate of
the temple of the LORD. [9]A proclamation was then issued in Judah and Jerusalem that they should bring to the
LORD the tax that Moses the servant
of God had required of Israel in the
desert. [10]All the officials and all the
people brought their contributions
gladly,[q] dropping them into the chest
until it was full. [11]Whenever the chest
was brought in by the Levites to the
king's officials and they saw that there
was a large amount of money, the royal secretary and the officer of the chief
priest would come and empty the chest
and carry it back to its place. They
did this regularly and collected a great
amount of money. [12]The king and Jehoiada gave it to the men who carried
out the work required for the temple of
the LORD. They hired[r] masons and carpenters to restore the LORD's temple,
and also workers in iron and bronze to
repair the temple.

24:10 [q]Ex 25:2; 1Ch 29:3,6,9

24:12 [r]2Ch 34:11

[13]The men in charge of the work
were diligent, and the repairs progressed
under them. They rebuilt the temple
of God according to its original design
and reinforced it. [14]When they had finished, they brought the rest of the money to the king and Jehoiada, and with
it were made articles for the LORD's
temple: articles for the service and for
the burnt offerings, and also dishes and
other objects of gold and silver. As long
as Jehoiada lived, burnt offerings were
presented continually in the temple of
the LORD.

[15]Now Jehoiada was old and full of
years, and he died at the age of a hundred and thirty. [16]He was buried with
the kings in the City of David, because
of the good he had done in Israel for
God and his temple.

The Wickedness of Joash

[17]After the death of Jehoiada, the officials of Judah came and paid homage
to the king, and he listened to them.
[18]They abandoned[s] the temple of the
LORD, the God of their fathers, and
worshiped Asherah poles and idols.[t] Because of their guilt, God's anger[u] came
upon Judah and Jerusalem. [19]Although
the LORD sent prophets to the people
to bring them back to him, and though
they testified against them, they would
not listen.[v]

24:18 [s]ver 4; Jos 24:20; 2Ch 7:19 [t]Ex 34:13; 1Ki 14:23; 2Ch 33:3; Jer 17:2 [u]Jos 22:20; 2Ch 19:2

24:19 [v]Nu 11:29; Jer 7:25; Zec 1:4

[20]Then the Spirit[w] of God came upon
Zechariah[x] son of Jehoiada the priest.
He stood before the people and said,
"This is what God says: 'Why do you
disobey the LORD's commands? You
will not prosper.[y] Because you have
forsaken the LORD, he has forsaken[z]
you.' "

24:20 [w]Jdg 3:10; 1Ch 12:18; 2Ch 20:14 [x]Mt 23:35; Lk 11:51 [y]Nu 14:41 [z]Dt 31:17; 2Ch 15:2

[21]But they plotted against him, and
by order of the king they stoned[a] him to
death[b] in the courtyard of the LORD's
temple.[c] [22]King Joash did not remember
the kindness Zechariah's father Jehoiada
had shown him but killed his son, who
said as he lay dying, "May the LORD
see this and call you to account."[d]

24:21 [a]Jos 7:25; Ac 7:58-59 [b]Ne 9:26; Jer 26:21 [c]Jer 20:2; Mt 23:35

24:22 [d]Ge 9:5

[23]At the turn of the year,[a] the army
of Aram marched against Joash; it invaded Judah and Jerusalem and killed
all the leaders of the people.[e] They sent
all the plunder to their king in Damascus. [24]Although the Aramean army had
come with only a few men,[f] the LORD
delivered into their hands a much larger
army.[g] Because Judah had forsaken the
LORD, the God of their fathers, judgment was executed on Joash. [25]When
the Arameans withdrew, they left Joash
severely wounded. His officials conspired against him for murdering the

24:23 [e]2Ki 12:17-18

24:24 [f]2Ch 14:9; 16:8; 20:2,12 [g]Lev 26:23-25; Dt 28:25

[a]*23* Probably in the spring

son of Jehoiada the priest, and they
killed him in his bed. So he died and
24:25 was buried[b] in the City of David, but
[b]2Ch 21:20 not in the tombs of the kings.
26Those who conspired against him
were Zabad,[a] son of Shimeath an Ammonite woman, and Jehozabad, son of
24:26 [i]2Ki 12:21 Shimrith[b] [i] a Moabite woman.[j] 27The
[j]Ru 1:4 account of his sons, the many prophecies about him, and the record of the
restoration of the temple of God are
written in the annotations on the book
of the kings. And Amaziah his son succeeded him as king.

Amaziah King of Judah

25 Amaziah was twenty-five years
old when he became king, and
he reigned in Jerusalem twenty-nine
years. His mother's name was Jehoaddin[c]; she was from Jerusalem. 2He did
25:2 what was right in the eyes of the
[k]ver 14; LORD, but not wholeheartedly.[k] 3After
1Ki 8:61; the kingdom was firmly in his control,
2Ch 24:2 he executed the officials who had murdered his father the king. 4Yet he did
not put their sons to death, but acted in
accordance with what is written in the
25:4 Law, in the Book of Moses,[l] where the
[l]Dt 28:61 [m]Nu 26:11; LORD commanded: "Fathers shall not
Dt 24:16 be put to death for their children, nor
children put to death for their fathers;
each is to die for his own sins."[d] [m]

GOODNESS

UNCONTAMINATED

2 Chronicles 25:2

Amaziah did what was right, but not wholeheartedly. In other words, he was "sorta good." The problem with being "sorta good" is that the part that isn't good is "sorta bad." Holiness never comes in league with any contamination.

5Amaziah called the people of Judah
together and assigned them according to
their families to commanders of thousands and commanders of hundreds for
all Judah and Benjamin. He then mus-
25:5 [n]2Sa 24:2 tered[n] those twenty years old[o] or more
[o]Ex 30:14 and found that there were three hun-
[p]Nu 1:3; 1Ch 21:1; dred thousand men ready for military
2Ch 17:14-19 service,[p] able to handle the spear and
shield. 6He also hired a hundred thou-
sand fighting men from Israel for a
hundred talents[e] of silver.

7But a man of God came to him
and said, "O king, these troops from
Israel[q] must not march with you, for 25:7 [q]2Ch 16:2-9;
the LORD is not with Israel—not with 19:1-3
any of the people of Ephraim. 8Even if
you go and fight courageously in battle,
God will overthrow you before the enemy, for God has the power to help or
to overthrow."[r] 25:8 [r]2Ch 14:11;
9Amaziah asked the man of God, 20:6
"But what about the hundred talents I
paid for these Israelite troops?"
The man of God replied, "The LORD 25:9
can give you much more than that."[s] [s]Dt 8:18; Pr 10:22
10So Amaziah dismissed the troops
who had come to him from Ephraim
and sent them home. They were furious
with Judah and left for home in a great
rage.[t] 25:10
11Amaziah then marshaled his [t]ver 13
strength and led his army to the Valley
of Salt, where he killed ten thousand
men of Seir. 12The army of Judah also
captured ten thousand men alive, took
them to the top of a cliff and threw
them down so that all were dashed to 25:12
pieces.[u] [u]Ps 141:6;
13Meanwhile the troops that Amazi- Ob 1:3
ah had sent back and had not allowed
to take part in the war raided Judean
towns from Samaria to Beth Horon.
They killed three thousand people and
carried off great quantities of plunder.
14When Amaziah returned from
slaughtering the Edomites, he brought
back the gods of the people of Seir. He
set them up as his own gods,[v] bowed 25:14
down to them and burned sacrifices to [v]Ex 20:3; 2Ch 28:23;
them. 15The anger of the LORD burned Isa 44:15
against Amaziah, and he sent a prophet to him, who said, "Why do you
consult this people's gods, which could
not save[w] their own people from your 25:15 [w]Ps 96:5;
hand?" Isa 36:20
16While he was still speaking, the
king said to him, "Have we appointed
you an adviser to the king? Stop! Why
be struck down?"
So the prophet stopped but said, "I
know that God has determined to destroy you, because you have done this
and have not listened to my counsel."
17After Amaziah king of Judah con-

[a]*26* A variant of *Jozabad* [b]*26* A variant of *Shomer*
[c]*1* Hebrew *Jehoaddan,* a variant of *Jehoaddin*
[d]*4* Deut. 24:16 [e]*6* That is, about 3 3/4 tons (about 3.4 metric tons); also in verse 9

sulted his advisers, he sent this challenge to Jehoash[a] son of Jehoahaz, the
son of Jehu, king of Israel: "Come, meet
me face to face."
18But Jehoash king of Israel replied
25:18 to Amaziah king of Judah: "A thistle[x]
[x]Jdg 9:8-15 in Lebanon sent a message to a cedar
in Lebanon, 'Give your daughter to my
son in marriage.' Then a wild beast in
Lebanon came along and trampled the
thistle underfoot. 19You say to yourself
that you have defeated Edom, and now
you are arrogant and proud. But stay at
home! Why ask for trouble and cause
your own downfall and that of Judah
also?"
20Amaziah, however, would not listen, for God so worked that he might
hand them over to ⌞Jehoash⌟, because
25:20 [y]1Ki 12:15; they sought the gods of Edom.[y] 21So Je-
2Ch 10:15; hoash king of Israel attacked. He and
22:7 Amaziah king of Judah faced each other
at Beth Shemesh in Judah. 22Judah was
routed by Israel, and every man fled to
his home. 23Jehoash king of Israel captured Amaziah king of Judah, the son
of Joash, the son of Ahaziah,[b] at Beth
Shemesh. Then Jehoash brought him
to Jerusalem and broke down the wall
25:23 [z]2Ki 14:13; of Jerusalem from the Ephraim Gate[z]
Ne 8:16; 12:39 to the Corner Gate[a]—a section about
[a]2Ch 26:9; six hundred feet[c] long. 24He took all the
Jer 31:38 gold and silver and all the articles found
in the temple of God that had been in
25:24 [b]1Ch 26:15 the care of Obed-Edom,[b] together with
the palace treasures and the hostages,
and returned to Samaria.
25Amaziah son of Joash king of Judah
lived for fifteen years after the death of
Jehoash son of Jehoahaz king of Israel.
26As for the other events of Amaziah's
reign, from beginning to end, are they
not written in the book of the kings of
Judah and Israel? 27From the time that
Amaziah turned away from following
the LORD, they conspired against him
25:27 in Jerusalem and he fled to Lachish[c],
[c]Jos 10:3 but they sent men after him to Lachish
and killed him there. 28He was brought
back by horse and was buried with his
fathers in the City of Judah.

Uzziah King of Judah

26:1 [d]2Ch 22:1 26 Then all the people of Judah[d]
took Uzziah,[d] who was sixteen
years old, and made him king in place
of his father Amaziah. 2He was the one
who rebuilt Elath and restored it to Judah after Amaziah rested with his fathers.
3Uzziah was sixteen years old when
he became king, and he reigned in Jerusalem fifty-two years. His mother's
name was Jecoliah; she was from Jerusalem. 4He did what was right in the eyes
of the LORD, just as his father Amaziah had done. 5He sought God during
the days of Zechariah, who instructed
him in the fear[e] of God.[e] As long as he 26:5 [e]2Ch 15:2;
sought the LORD, God gave him suc- 24:2; Da 1:17
cess.[f] [f]2Ch 27:6
6He went to war against the Phi-
listines[g] and broke down the walls of 26:6 [g]Isa 2:6;
Gath, Jabneh and Ashdod.[h] He then re- 11:14; 14:29;
built towns near Ashdod and elsewhere Jer 25:20
among the Philistines. 7God helped [h]Am 1:8; 3:9
him against the Philistines and against
the Arabs[i] who lived in Gur Baal and 26:7 [i]2Ch 21:16
against the Meunites.[j] 8The Ammon- [j]2Ch 20:1
ites[k] brought tribute to Uzziah, and 26:8 [k]Ge 19:38;
his fame spread as far as the border 2Ch 17:11
of Egypt, because he had become very
powerful.
9Uzziah built towers in Jerusalem at
the Corner Gate,[l] at the Valley Gate[m] 26:9 [l]2Ki 14:13;
and at the angle of the wall, and he 2Ch 25:23
fortified them. 10He also built towers [m]Ne 2:13;
in the desert and dug many cisterns, 3:13
because he had much livestock in the
foothills and in the plain. He had people working his fields and vineyards in
the hills and in the fertile lands, for he
loved the soil.
11Uzziah had a well-trained army,
ready to go out by divisions according
to their numbers as mustered by Jeiel
the secretary and Maaseiah the officer
under the direction of Hananiah, one
of the royal officials. 12The total number of family leaders over the fighting
men was 2,600. 13Under their command was an army of 307,500 men
trained for war, a powerful force to support the king against his enemies. 14Uz-
ziah provided shields, spears, helmets,
coats of armor, bows and slingstones
for the entire army.[n] 15In Jerusalem he 26:14 [n]Jer 46:4
made machines designed by skillful men
for use on the towers and on the corner
defenses to shoot arrows and hurl large

[a] *17* Hebrew *Joash,* a variant of *Jehoash;* also in verses 18, 21, 23 and 25 [b] *23* Hebrew *Jehoahaz,* a variant of *Ahaziah* [c] *23* Hebrew *four hundred cubits* (about 180 meters) [d] *1* Also called *Azariah* [e] *5* Many Hebrew manuscripts, Septuagint and Syriac; other Hebrew manuscripts *vision*

stones. His fame spread far and wide,
for he was greatly helped until he became powerful.
16 But after Uzziah became powerful,
26:16 his pride[o] led to his downfall.[p] He was
[o]2Ki 14:10 [p]Dt 32:15; 2Ch 25:19 unfaithful[q] to the LORD his God, and
[q]1Ch 5:25 entered the temple of the LORD to burn
[r]2Ki 16:12 incense[r] on the altar of incense. 17 Aza-
26:17 riah[s] the priest with eighty other cou-
[s]1Ki 4:2; 1Ch 6:10 rageous priests of the LORD followed
him in. 18 They confronted him and
said, "It is not right for you, Uzziah, to
burn incense to the LORD. That is for
26:18 the priests,[t] the descendants[u] of Aaron,[v]
[t]Nu 16:39 who have been consecrated to burn
[u]Nu 18:1-7 [v]Ex 30:7 incense.[w] Leave the sanctuary, for you
[w]1Ch 6:49 have been unfaithful; and you will not
be honored by the LORD God."

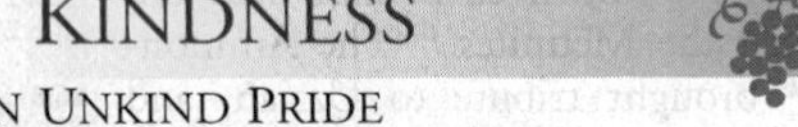

KINDNESS

AN UNKIND PRIDE

2 Chronicles 26:16

The proud are rarely kind. Thinking of their greatness requires all their time.

19 Uzziah, who had a censer in his
hand ready to burn incense, became angry. While he was raging at the priests
in their presence before the incense altar
26:19 in the LORD's temple, leprosy[a][x] broke
[x]Nu 12:10; 2Ki 5:25-27 out on his forehead. 20 When Azariah
the chief priest and all the other priests
looked at him, they saw that he had
leprosy on his forehead, so they hurried
him out. Indeed, he himself was eager
to leave, because the LORD had afflicted him.
21 King Uzziah had leprosy until the
day he died. He lived in a separate
26:21 house[b][y]—leprous, and excluded from
[y]Ex 4:6; Lev 13:46; 14:8; Nu 5:2; 19:12 the temple of the LORD. Jotham his
son had charge of the palace and gov-
erned the people of the land.
22 The other events of Uzziah's reign,
from beginning to end, are recorded by
26:22 the prophet Isaiah[z] son of Amoz. 23 Uz-
[z]2Ki 15:1; Isa 1:1; 6:1 ziah[a] rested with his fathers and was
26:23 buried near them in a field for burial
[a]Isa 1:1; 6:1 that belonged to the kings, for people
[b]2Ki 14:21; 15:7; Am 1:1 said, "He had leprosy." And Jotham his
son succeeded him as king.[b]

Jotham King of Judah

27:1 **27** Jotham[c] was twenty-five years
[c]2Ki 15:5,32; 1Ch 3:12 old when he became king, and
he reigned in Jerusalem sixteen years.
His mother's name was Jerusha daughter of Zadok. 2 He did what was right in
the eyes of the LORD, just as his father
Uzziah had done, but unlike him he

[a]*19* The Hebrew word was used for various diseases affecting the skin—not necessarily leprosy; also in verses 20, 21 and 23. [b]*21* Or *in a house where he was relieved of responsibilities*

DAY 2 TWO

FAITHFULNESS AND THE PURPOSE OF GOD IN MY LIFE

2 Chronicles 27:1–6

Jotham grew powerful because he walked with the Lord his God. He was steadfast and persistent, and his unswerving faithfulness brought powerful influence to the throne of Judah.

It is what we are not told about Jotham that most fascinates me. What had happened in Jotham's life to break his spirit and teach him his persistent dependency upon God? It can hardly be doubted that somewhere in the unrecorded tears of his life he had learned the lessons of brokenness, dependency and trust. The beauty of broken pride is that it is a gift we lay on the highest level of God's altars. The gift comes wrapped in our bandages and slings. It is saturated with a handkerchief once filled with our tears.

Gene Edwards writes so beautifully in *A Tale of Three Kings*:

> **God has a university. It's a small school. Few enroll, even fewer graduate. Very, very few indeed. God has this school because he does not have broken men. Instead he has several other types of men. He has men who claim to be God's authority...and aren't; men who claim to be broken and aren't...He has, regretfully, a spectroscopic mixture of everything in between. All of these he has in abundance; but broken men, hardly at all.**

There is more than a casual relationship between brokenness and persistence. Jotham found that balance and knew his purpose in the world. When we grow mature enough to applaud our brokenness, we will know our purpose in life.

To begin a study on the topic of Faithfulness, the High Art of Persistence, turn to the home page on page 635.

did not enter the temple of the LORD. The people, however, continued their corrupt practices. 3 Jotham rebuilt the Upper Gate of the temple of the LORD and did extensive work on the wall at the hill of Ophel.[d] 4 He built towns in the Judean hills and forts and towers in the wooded areas.

5 Jotham made war on the king of the Ammonites[e] and conquered them. That year the Ammonites paid him a hundred talents[a] of silver, ten thousand cors[b] of wheat and ten thousand cors of barley. The Ammonites brought him the same amount also in the second and third years.

6 Jotham grew powerful[f] because he walked steadfastly before the LORD his God.

7 The other events in Jotham's reign, including all his wars and the other things he did, are written in the book of the kings of Israel and Judah. 8 He was twenty-five years old when he became king, and he reigned in Jerusalem sixteen years. 9 Jotham rested with his fathers and was buried in the City of David. And Ahaz his son succeeded him as king.

Ahaz King of Judah

28 Ahaz[g] was twenty years old when he became king, and he reigned in Jerusalem sixteen years. Unlike David his father, he did not do what was right in the eyes of the LORD. 2 He walked in the ways of the kings of Israel and also made cast idols[h] for worshiping the Baals. 3 He burned sacrifices in the Valley of Ben Hinnom[i] and sacrificed his sons[j] in the fire, following the detestable[k] ways of the nations the LORD had driven out before the Israelites. 4 He offered sacrifices and burned incense at the high places, on the hilltops and under every spreading tree.

5 Therefore the LORD his God handed him over to the king of Aram.[l] The Arameans defeated him and took many of his people as prisoners and brought them to Damascus.

He was also given into the hands of the king of Israel, who inflicted heavy casualties on him. 6 In one day Pekah[m] son of Remaliah killed a hundred and twenty thousand soldiers in Judah[n]—because Judah had forsaken the LORD, the God of their fathers. 7 Zicri, an Ephraimite warrior, killed Maaseiah the king's son, Azrikam the officer in charge of the palace, and Elkanah, second to the king. 8 The Israelites took captive from their kinsmen[o] two hundred thousand wives, sons and daughters. They also took a great deal of plunder, which they carried back to Samaria.[p]

9 But a prophet of the LORD named Oded was there, and he went out to meet the army when it returned to Samaria. He said to them, "Because the LORD, the God of your fathers, was angry[q] with Judah, he gave them into your hand. But you have slaughtered them in a rage that reaches to heaven.[r] 10 And now you intend to make the men and women of Judah and Jerusalem your slaves.[s] But aren't you also guilty of sins against the LORD your God? 11 Now listen to me! Send back your fellow countrymen you have taken as prisoners, for the LORD's fierce anger rests on you.[t]"

12 Then some of the leaders in Ephraim—Azariah son of Jehohanan, Berekiah son of Meshillemoth, Jehizkiah son of Shallum, and Amasa son of Hadlai—confronted those who were arriving from the war. 13 "You must not bring those prisoners here," they said, "or we will be guilty before the LORD. Do you intend to add to our sin and guilt? For our guilt is already great, and his fierce anger rests on Israel."

14 So the soldiers gave up the prisoners and plunder in the presence of the officials and all the assembly. 15 The men designated by name took the prisoners, and from the plunder they clothed all who were naked. They provided them with clothes and sandals, food and drink,[u] and healing balm. All those who were weak they put on donkeys. So they took them back to their fellow countrymen at Jericho, the City of Palms,[v] and returned to Samaria.

16 At that time King Ahaz sent to the king[c] of Assyria[w] for help. 17 The Edomites[x] had again come and attacked Judah and carried away prisoners,[y] 18 while the Philistines[z] had raided towns in the foothills and in the Negev of Judah.

[a] 5 That is, about 3 3/4 tons (about 3.4 metric tons) [b] 5 That is, probably about 62,000 bushels (about 2,200 kiloliters) [c] *16* One Hebrew manuscript, Septuagint and Vulgate (see also 2 Kings 16:7); most Hebrew manuscripts *kings*

27:3 [d]2Ch 33:14; Ne 3:26
27:5 [e]Ge 19:38
27:6 [f]2Ch 26:5
28:1 [g]1Ch 3:13; Isa 1:1
28:2 [h]Ex 34:17; 2Ch 22:3
28:3 [i]Jos 15:8; 2Ki 23:10 [j]Lev 18:21; 2Ki 3:27; 2Ch 33:6; Eze 20:26 [k]Dt 18:9; 2Ch 33:2
28:5 [l]Isa 7:1
28:6 [m]2Ki 15:25, 27 [n]ver 8; Isa 9:21; 11:13
28:8 [o]Dt 28:25-41; 2Ch 11:4 [p]2Ch 29:9
28:9 [q]2Ch 25:15; Isa 10:6; 47:6; Zec 1:15 [r]Ezr 9:6; Rev 18:5
28:10 [s]Lev 25:39-46
28:11 [t]2Ch 11:4; Jas 2:13
28:15 [u]2Ki 6:22; Pr 25:21-22 [v]Dt 34:3; Jdg 1:16
28:16 [w]2Ki 16:7
28:17 [x]Ps 137:7; Isa 34:5 [y]2Ch 29:9
28:18 [z]Eze 16:27,57

They captured and occupied Beth She-
28:18 [a]Jos 10:12 mesh, Aijalon[a] and Gederoth, as well as
Soco, Timnah and Gimzo, with their
surrounding villages. 19The LORD had
humbled Judah because of Ahaz king of
Israel,[a] for he had promoted wickedness
28:19 [b]2Ch 21:2 in Judah and had been most unfaithful[b]
to the LORD. 20Tiglath-Pileser[b][c] king
28:20 [c]2Ki 15:29; 1Ch 5:6 [d]2Ki 16:7 of Assyria came to him, but he gave
him trouble instead of help.[d] 21Ahaz
took some of the things from the temple of the LORD and from the royal
palace and from the princes and presented them to the king of Assyria, but
that did not help him.
22In his time of trouble King Ahaz
28:22 [e]Jer 5:3 became even more unfaithful[e] to the
LORD. 23He offered sacrifices to the
28:23 [f]2Ch 25:14 [g]Jer 44:17-18 gods[f] of Damascus, who had defeated
him; for he thought, "Since the gods of
the kings of Aram have helped them, I
will sacrifice to them so they will help
me."[g] But they were his downfall and
the downfall of all Israel.
24Ahaz gathered together the furnishings from the temple of God[h] and took
28:24 [h]2Ki 16:18 [i]2Ch 29:7 [j]2Ch 30:14 them away.[c] He shut the doors[i] of the
LORD's temple and set up altars[j] at
every street corner in Jerusalem. 25In
every town in Judah he built high places
to burn sacrifices to other gods and
provoked the LORD, the God of his fathers, to anger.
26The other events of his reign and
all his ways, from beginning to end, are
written in the book of the kings of Ju-
28:27 [k]Isa 14:28-32 [l]2Ch 21:20; 24:25 dah and Israel. 27Ahaz rested[k] with his
fathers and was buried[l] in the city of Je-
rusalem, but he was not placed in the
tombs of the kings of Israel. And Hezekiah his son succeeded him as king.

Hezekiah Purifies the Temple

29:1 [m]1Ch 3:13 29 Hezekiah[m] was twenty-five years
old when he became king, and
he reigned in Jerusalem twenty-nine
years. His mother's name was Abijah
daughter of Zechariah. 2He did what
was right in the eyes of the LORD, just
29:2 [n]2Ch 28:1; 34:2 as his father David[n] had done.
3In the first month of the first year
of his reign, he opened the doors of
29:3 [o]2Ch 28:24 the temple of the LORD and repaired[o]
them. 4He brought in the priests and
the Levites, assembled them in the
square on the east side 5and said: "Lis-
29:5 [p]2Ch 35:6 ten to me, Levites! Consecrate[p] yourselves now and consecrate the temple
of the LORD, the God of your fathers.
Remove all defilement from the sanc-
tuary. 6Our fathers[q] were unfaithful;[r] 29:6 [q]Ps 106:6-47; Jer 2:27 [r]1Ch 5:25; Eze 8:16
they did evil in the eyes of the LORD
our God and forsook him. They turned
their faces away from the LORD's dwelling place and turned their backs on
him. 7They also shut the doors of the
portico and put out the lamps. They
did not burn incense or present any
burnt offerings at the sanctuary to the
God of Israel. 8Therefore, the anger of
the LORD has fallen on Judah and Jerusalem; he has made them an object
of dread and horror[s] and scorn,[t] as 29:8 [s]Dt 28:25; 2Ch 24:18 [t]Jer 18:16; 19:8; 25:9,18
you can see with your own eyes. 9This
is why our fathers have fallen by the
sword and why our sons and daughters
and our wives are in captivity.[u] 10Now 29:9 [u]2Ch 28:5-8, 17
I intend to make a covenant[v] with the
LORD, the God of Israel, so that his 29:10 [v]2Ch 15:12; 23:16
fierce anger will turn away from us.
11My sons, do not be negligent now, for 29:11 [w]Nu 3:6; 8:6,14 [x]1Ch 15:2
the LORD has chosen you to stand be-
fore him and serve him,[w] to minister[x]
before him and to burn incense."

PATIENCE

RENOVATING TEMPLES

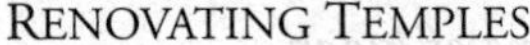

2 Chronicles 29:3

Reconstructing broken temples is a high calling from God. But hurry not the repair. And when rebuilding temples, restore the altar first. There meet with God to discuss how the renovation should be done.

12Then these Levites[y] set to work: 29:12 [y]Nu 3:17-20 [z]2Ch 31:15
from the Kohathites,
Mahath son of Amasai and Joel
son of Azariah;
from the Merarites,
Kish son of Abdi and Azariah
son of Jehallelel;
from the Gershonites,
Joah son of Zimmah and Eden[z]
son of Joah;
13from the descendants of Elizaphan,
Shimri and Jeiel;
from the descendants of Asaph,[a] 29:13 [a]1Ch 6:39
Zechariah and Mattaniah;
14from the descendants of Heman,
Jehiel and Shimei;

[a]*19* That is, Judah, as frequently in 2 Chronicles
[b]*20* Hebrew *Tilgath-Pilneser,* a variant of *Tiglath-Pileser* [c]*24* Or *and cut them up*

from the descendants of Jeduthun,
Shemaiah and Uzziel.

15When they had assembled their brothers and consecrated themselves, they went in to purify[b] the temple of the LORD, as the king had ordered, following the word of the LORD. 16The priests went into the sanctuary of the LORD to purify it. They brought out to the courtyard of the LORD's temple everything unclean that they found in the temple of the LORD. The Levites took it and carried it out to the Kidron Valley.[c] 17They began the consecration on the first day of the first month, and by the eighth day of the month they reached the portico of the LORD. For eight more days they consecrated the temple of the LORD itself, finishing on the sixteenth day of the first month.

18Then they went in to King Hezekiah and reported: "We have purified the entire temple of the LORD, the altar of burnt offering with all its utensils, and the table for setting out the consecrated bread, with all its articles. 19We have prepared and consecrated all the articles[d] that King Ahaz removed in his unfaithfulness while he was king. They are now in front of the LORD's altar."

20Early the next morning King Hezekiah gathered the city officials together and went up to the temple of the LORD. 21They brought seven bulls, seven rams, seven male lambs and seven male goats as a sin offering[e] for the kingdom, for the sanctuary and for Judah. The king commanded the priests, the descendants of Aaron, to offer these on the altar of the LORD. 22So they slaughtered the bulls, and the priests took the blood[f] and sprinkled it on the altar; next they slaughtered the rams and sprinkled their blood on the altar; then they slaughtered the lambs and sprinkled their blood on the altar. 23The goats for the sin offering were brought before the king and the assembly, and they laid their hands[g] on them. 24The priests then slaughtered the goats and presented their blood on the altar for a sin offering to atone[h] for all Israel, because the king had ordered the burnt offering and the sin offering for all Israel.

25He stationed the Levites in the temple of the LORD with cymbals, harps and lyres in the way prescribed by David[i] and Gad[j] the king's seer and Nathan the prophet; this was commanded by the LORD through his prophets. 26So the Levites stood ready with David's instruments,[k] and the priests with their trumpets.[l]

27Hezekiah gave the order to sacrifice the burnt offering on the altar. As the offering began, singing to the LORD began also, accompanied by trumpets and the instruments[m] of David king of Israel. 28The whole assembly bowed in worship, while the singers sang and the trumpeters played. All this continued until the sacrifice of the burnt offering was completed.

29When the offerings were finished, the king and everyone present with him knelt down and worshiped.[n] 30King Hezekiah and his officials ordered the Levites to praise the LORD with the words of David and of Asaph the seer. So they sang praises with gladness and bowed their heads and worshiped.

31Then Hezekiah said, "You have now dedicated yourselves to the LORD. Come and bring sacrifices[o] and thank offerings to the temple of the LORD." So the assembly brought sacrifices and thank offerings, and all whose hearts were willing[p] brought burnt offerings.

32The number of burnt offerings the assembly brought was seventy bulls, a hundred rams and two hundred male lambs—all of them for burnt offerings to the LORD. 33The animals consecrated as sacrifices amounted to six hundred bulls and three thousand sheep and goats. 34The priests, however, were too few to skin all the burnt offerings;[q] so their kinsmen the Levites helped them until the task was finished and until other priests had been consecrated,[r] for the Levites had been more conscientious in

29:15 [b]ver 5; 1Ch 23:28; 2Ch 30:12
29:16 [c]2Sa 15:23
29:19 [d]2Ch 28:24
29:21 [e]Lev 4:13-14
29:22 [f]Lev 4:18
29:23 [g]Lev 4:15
29:24 [h]Ex 29:36; Lev 4:26
29:25 [i]1Ch 25:6; 2Ch 8:14 [j]1Sa 22:5; 2Sa 24:11
29:26 [k]1Ch 15:16 [l]1Ch 15:24; 23:5; 2Ch 5:12
29:27 [m]2Ch 23:18
29:29 [n]2Ch 20:18
29:31 [o]Heb 13:15-16 [p]Ex 25:2; 35:22
29:34 [q]2Ch 35:11 [r]2Ch 30:3,15

JOY

A SACRIFICE OF PRAISE

2 Chronicles 30:21

Joy ought to be as regular as worship. "When he has broken my bands in sunder, I will offer to Thee the sacrifice of praise," wrote Augustine. The singing Levites were reminded that those who serve the altar best are souls filled with volatile joy.

consecrating themselves than the priests had been. 35There were burnt offerings in abundance, together with the fat[s] of the fellowship offerings[a][t] and the drink offerings[u] that accompanied the burnt offerings.

So the service of the temple of the LORD was reestablished. 36Hezekiah and all the people rejoiced at what God had brought about for his people, because it was done so quickly.

Hezekiah Celebrates the Passover

30 Hezekiah sent word to all Israel and Judah and also wrote letters to Ephraim and Manasseh,[v] inviting them to come to the temple of the LORD in Jerusalem and celebrate the Passover[w] to the LORD, the God of Israel. 2The king and his officials and the whole assembly in Jerusalem decided to celebrate[x] the Passover in the second month. 3They had not been able to celebrate it at the regular time because not enough priests had consecrated[y] themselves and the people had not assembled in Jerusalem. 4The plan seemed right both to the king and to the whole assembly. 5They decided to send a proclamation throughout Israel, from Beersheba to Dan,[z] calling the people to come to Jerusalem and celebrate the Passover to the LORD, the God of Israel. It had not been celebrated in large numbers according to what was written.

6At the king's command, couriers went throughout Israel and Judah with letters from the king and from his officials, which read:

"People of Israel, return to the LORD, the God of Abraham, Isaac and Israel, that he may return to you who are left, who have escaped from the hand of the kings of Assyria. 7Do not be like your fathers[a] and brothers, who were unfaithful to the LORD, the God of their fathers, so that he made them an object of horror,[b] as you see. 8Do not be stiff-necked,[c] as your fathers were; submit to the LORD. Come to the sanctuary, which he has consecrated forever. Serve the LORD your God, so that his fierce anger[d] will turn away from you. 9If you return[e] to the LORD, then your brothers and your children will be shown compassion[f] by their captors and will come back to this land, for the LORD your God is gracious and compassionate.[g] He will not turn his face from you if you return to him."

10The couriers went from town to town in Ephraim and Manasseh, as far as Zebulun, but the people scorned and ridiculed[h] them. 11Nevertheless, some men of Asher, Manasseh and Zebulun humbled themselves and went to Jerusalem.[i] 12Also in Judah the hand of God was on the people to give them unity[j] of mind to carry out what the king and his officials had ordered, following the word of the LORD.

13A very large crowd of people assembled in Jerusalem to celebrate the Feast of Unleavened Bread[k] in the second month. 14They removed the altars[l] in Jerusalem and cleared away the incense altars and threw them into the Kidron Valley.[m]

15They slaughtered the Passover lamb on the fourteenth day of the second month. The priests and the Levites were ashamed and consecrated[n] themselves and brought burnt offerings to the temple of the LORD. 16Then they took up their regular positions[o] as prescribed in the Law of Moses the man of God. The priests sprinkled the blood handed to them by the Levites. 17Since many in the crowd had not consecrated themselves, the Levites had to kill[p] the Passover lambs for all those who were not ceremonially clean and could not consecrate ⌞their lambs⌟ to the LORD. 18Although most of the many people who came from Ephraim, Manasseh, Issachar and Zebulun had not purified themselves,[q] yet they ate the Passover, contrary to what was written. But Hezekiah prayed for them, saying, "May the LORD, who is good, pardon everyone 19who sets his heart on seeking God—the LORD, the God of his fathers—even if he is not clean according to the rules of the sanctuary." 20And the LORD heard[r] Hezekiah and healed[s] the people.[t]

21The Israelites who were present in Jerusalem celebrated the Feast of Un-

29:35 [s]Ex 29:13; Lev 3:16 [t]Lev 7:11-21 [u]Nu 15:5-10
30:1 [v]Ge 41:52 [w]Ex 12:11; Nu 28:16
30:2 [x]Nu 9:10
30:3 [y]2Ch 29:34
30:5 [z]Jdg 20:1
30:7 [a]Ps 78:8,57; 106:6; Eze 20:18 [b]2Ch 29:8
30:8 [c]Ex 32:9 [d]Nu 25:4; 2Ch 29:10
30:9 [e]Dt 30:2-5; Isa 1:16; 55:7
30:9 [f]1Ki 8:50; Ps 106:46 [g]Ex 34:6-7; Dt 4:31; Mic 7:18
30:10 [h]2Ch 36:16
30:11 [i]ver 25
30:12 [j]Jer 32:39; Eze 11:19; Php 2:13
30:13 [k]Nu 28:16
30:14 [l]2Ch 28:24 [m]2Sa 15:23
30:15 [n]2Ch 29:34
30:16 [o]2Ch 35:10
30:17 [p]2Ch 29:34
30:18 [q]Ex 12:43-49; Nu 9:6-10
30:20 [r]2Ch 6:20 [s]2Ch 7:14; Mal 4:2 [t]Jas 5:16

[a]35 Traditionally *peace offerings*

leavened Bread[u] for seven days with
great rejoicing, while the Levites and
priests sang to the LORD every day, accompanied by the LORD's instruments
of praise.[a]
22 Hezekiah spoke encouragingly to
all the Levites, who showed good understanding of the service of the LORD.
For the seven days they ate their assigned portion and offered fellowship
offerings[b] and praised the LORD, the
God of their fathers.
23 The whole assembly then agreed to
celebrate[v] the festival seven more days;
so for another seven days they celebrated joyfully. 24 Hezekiah king of Judah
provided[w] a thousand bulls and seven
thousand sheep and goats for the assembly, and the officials provided them
with a thousand bulls and ten thousand sheep and goats. A great number
of priests consecrated themselves. 25 The
entire assembly of Judah rejoiced, along
with the priests and Levites and all who
had assembled from Israel,[x] including
the aliens who had come from Israel
and those who lived in Judah. 26 There
was great joy in Jerusalem, for since the
days of Solomon[y] son of David king of
Israel there had been nothing like this in
Jerusalem. 27 The priests and the Levites
stood to bless[z] the people, and God
heard them, for their prayer reached
heaven, his holy dwelling place.

31 When all this had ended, the
Israelites who were there went
out to the towns of Judah, smashed
the sacred stones and cut down[a] the
Asherah poles. They destroyed the high
places and the altars throughout Judah
and Benjamin and in Ephraim and
Manasseh. After they had destroyed all
of them, the Israelites returned to their
own towns and to their own property.

Contributions for Worship

2 Hezekiah[b] assigned the priests and
Levites to divisions[c]—each of them according to their duties as priests or
Levites—to offer burnt offerings and
fellowship offerings,[b] to minister,[d] to
give thanks and to sing praises[e] at the
gates of the LORD's dwelling.[f] 3 The
king contributed[g] from his own possessions for the morning and evening
burnt offerings and for the burnt offerings on the Sabbaths, New Moons and
appointed feasts as written in the Law
of the LORD.[h] 4 He ordered the people
living in Jerusalem to give the portion[i]
due the priests and Levites so they could
devote themselves to the Law of the
LORD. 5 As soon as the order went out,
the Israelites generously gave the firstfruits[j] of their grain, new wine,[k] oil and
honey and all that the fields produced.
They brought a great amount, a tithe
of everything. 6 The men of Israel and
Judah who lived in the towns of Judah
also brought a tithe[l] of their herds and
flocks and a tithe of the holy things
dedicated to the LORD their God, and
they piled them in heaps.[m] 7 They began doing this in the third month and
finished in the seventh month.[n] 8 When
Hezekiah and his officials came and saw
the heaps, they praised the LORD and
blessed[o] his people Israel.
9 Hezekiah asked the priests and Levites about the heaps; 10 and Azariah the
chief priest, from the family of Zadok,[p]
answered, "Since the people began to
bring their contributions to the temple
of the LORD, we have had enough to
eat and plenty to spare, because the
LORD has blessed his people, and this
great amount is left over."[q]
11 Hezekiah gave orders to prepare
storerooms in the temple of the LORD,
and this was done. 12 Then they faithfully brought in the contributions, tithes
and dedicated gifts. Conaniah,[r] a Levite, was in charge of these things,
and his brother Shimei was next in
rank. 13 Jehiel, Azaziah, Nahath, Asahel, Jerimoth, Jozabad,[s] Eliel, Ismakiah,
Mahath and Benaiah were supervisors
under Conaniah and Shimei his brother, by appointment of King Hezekiah
and Azariah the official in charge of the
temple of God.
14 Kore son of Imnah the Levite, keeper of the East Gate, was in charge of
the freewill offerings given to God, distributing the contributions made to the
LORD and also the consecrated gifts.
15 Eden,[t] Miniamin, Jeshua, Shemaiah,
Amariah and Shecaniah assisted him
faithfully in the towns[u] of the priests,
distributing to their fellow priests according to their divisions, old and young
alike.

[a] *21* Or *priests praised the LORD every day with resounding instruments belonging to the LORD*
[b] *22,2* Traditionally *peace offerings*

30:21 [u]Ex 12:15,17; 13:6
30:23 [v]1Ki 8:65; 2Ch 7:9
30:24 [w]1Ki 8:5; 2Ch 29:34; 35:7; Ezr 6:17; 8:35
30:25 [x]ver 11
30:26 [y]2Ch 7:8
30:27 [z]Ex 39:43; Nu 6:23; Dt 26:15; 2Ch 23:18; Ps 68:5
31:1 [a]2Ki 18:4; 2Ch 32:12; Isa 36:7
31:2 [b]2Ch 29:9 [c]1Ch 24:1 [d]1Ch 15:2 [e]Ps 7:17; 9:2; 47:6; 71:22 [f]1Ch 23:28-32
31:3 [g]1Ch 29:3; 2Ch 35:7; Eze 45:17
31:3 [h]Nu 28:1-29:40
31:4 [i]Nu 18:8; Dt 18:8; Ne 13:10; Mal 2:7
31:5 [j]Nu 18:12,24; Ne 13:12; Eze 44:30 [k]Dt 12:17
31:6 [l]Lev 27:30; Ne 13:10-12 [m]Dt 14:28; Ru 3:7
31:7 [n]Ex 23:16
31:8 [o]Ps 144:13-15
31:10 [p]2Sa 8:17 [q]Ex 36:5; Eze 44:30; Mal 3:10-12
31:12 [r]2Ch 35:9
31:13 [s]2Ch 35:9
31:15 [t]2Ch 29:12 [u]Jos 21:9-19

16In addition, they distributed to
the males three years old or more
whose names were in the genealogical
31:16 [v]1Ch 23:3; Ezr 3:4 records[v]—all who would enter the temple of the LORD to perform the daily
duties of their various tasks, according
to their responsibilities and their divisions. 17And they distributed to the
priests enrolled by their families in the
genealogical records and likewise to
the Levites twenty years old or more,
according to their responsibilities and
their divisions. 18They included all the
little ones, the wives, and the sons and
daughters of the whole community listed in these genealogical records. For
they were faithful in consecrating themselves.
19As for the priests, the descendants
of Aaron, who lived on the farm lands
around their towns or in any other
31:19 [w]ver 12-15; Lev 25:34; Nu 35:2-5 towns,[w] men were designated by name to
distribute portions to every male among
them and to all who were recorded in
the genealogies of the Levites.
20This is what Hezekiah did throughout Judah, doing what was good and
31:20 [x]2Ki 20:3; 22:2 right and faithful[x] before the LORD his
God. 21In everything that he under-
took in the service of God's temple and
in obedience to the law and the commands, he sought his God and worked
31:21 [y]Dt 29:9 wholeheartedly. And so he prospered.[y]

Sennacherib Threatens Jerusalem

32 After all that Hezekiah had so
32:1 [z]2Ki 18:13-19; Isa 36:1; 37:9,17,37 faithfully done, Sennacherib[z]
king of Assyria came and invaded Ju-
dah. He laid siege to the fortified cities,
thinking to conquer them for himself.
2When Hezekiah saw that Sennacherib
had come and that he intended to make
32:2 [a]Isa 22:7; Jer 1:15 war on Jerusalem,[a] 3he consulted with
his officials and military staff about
blocking off the water from the springs
outside the city, and they helped him.
4A large force of men assembled, and
32:4 [b]2Ki 18:17; 20:20; Isa 22:9,11; Na 3:14 they blocked all the springs[b] and the
stream that flowed through the land.
"Why should the kings[a] of Assyria come
and find plenty of water?" they said.
5Then he worked hard repairing all the
32:5 [c]2Ch 25:23; Isa 22:10 [d]1Ki 9:24; 1Ch 11:8 [e]Isa 22:8 broken sections of the wall[c] and building towers on it. He built another wall
outside that one and reinforced the supporting terraces[b][d] of the City of David.
He also made large numbers of weapons[e] and shields.

6He appointed military officers over
the people and assembled them before
him in the square at the city gate
and encouraged them with these words:
7"Be strong and courageous.[f] Do not 32:7 [f]Dt 31:6; 1Ch 22:13 [g]2Ch 20:15 [h]Nu 14:9; 2Ki 6:16
be afraid or discouraged[g] because of the
king of Assyria and the vast army with
him, for there is a greater power with us
than with him.[h] 8With him is only the
arm of flesh,[i] but with us[j] is the LORD 32:8 [i]Job 40:9; Isa 52:10; Jer 17:5; 32:21 [j]Dt 3:22; 1Sa 17:45; 2Ch 13:12 [k]1Ch 5:22; 2Ch 20:17; Ps 20:7; Isa 28:6
our God to help us and to fight our
battles."[k] And the people gained confidence from what Hezekiah the king of
Judah said.
9Later, when Sennacherib king of Assyria and all his forces were laying siege
to Lachish,[l] he sent his officers to Jerusalem with this message for Hezekiah 32:9 [l]Jos 10:3,31
king of Judah and for all the people of
Judah who were there:

10"This is what Sennacherib
king of Assyria says: On what are
you basing your confidence,[m] that 32:10 [m]Eze 29:16
you remain in Jerusalem under
siege? 11When Hezekiah says, 'The
LORD our God will save us from
the hand of the king of Assyria,'
he is misleading[n] you, to let you 32:11 [n]Isa 37:10
die of hunger and thirst. 12Did
not Hezekiah himself remove this
god's high places and altars, saying
to Judah and Jerusalem, 'You must
worship before one altar[o] and burn 32:12 [o]2Ch 31:1
sacrifices on it'?
13"Do you not know what I
and my fathers have done to all
the peoples of the other lands?
Were the gods of those nations
ever able to deliver their land from
my hand?[p] 14Who of all the gods 32:13 [p]ver 15
of these nations that my fathers
destroyed has been able to save
his people from me? How then
can your god deliver you from my
hand? 15Now do not let Hezekiah
deceive[q] you and mislead you like 32:15 [q]Isa 37:10 [r]Da 3:15 [s]Ex 5:2
this. Do not believe him, for no
god of any nation or kingdom has
been able to deliver[r] his people
from my hand or the hand of my
fathers.[s] How much less will your
god deliver you from my hand!"

16Sennacherib's officers spoke further
against the LORD God and against his

[a]4 Hebrew; Septuagint and Syriac *king* [b]5 Or *the Millo*

servant Hezekiah. 17The king also wrote letters[t] insulting[u] the LORD, the God of Israel, and saying this against him: "Just as the gods[v] of the peoples of the other lands did not rescue their people from my hand, so the god of Hezekiah will not rescue his people from my hand." 18Then they called out in Hebrew to the people of Jerusalem who were on the wall, to terrify them and make them afraid in order to capture the city. 19They spoke about the God of Jerusalem as they did about the gods of the other peoples of the world—the work of men's hands.[w]

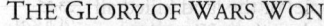

32:17 [t]Isa 37:14 [u]Ps 74:22; Isa 37:4,17 [v]2Ki 19:12

32:19 [w]2Ki 19:18; Ps 115:4,4-8; Isa 2:8; 17:8

20King Hezekiah and the prophet Isaiah son of Amoz cried out in prayer to heaven about this. 21And the LORD sent an angel,[x] who annihilated all the fighting men and the leaders and officers in the camp of the Assyrian king. So he withdrew to his own land in disgrace. And when he went into the temple of his god, some of his sons cut him down with the sword.[y]

32:21 [x]Ge 19:13 [y]2Ki 19:7

PEACE

THE GLORY OF WARS WON

2 Chronicles 32:20–21

There is no place where peace so abounds as the place where God fights for us. In such a place there is no doubt about who should have the glory for the victory.

22So the LORD saved Hezekiah and the people of Jerusalem from the hand of Sennacherib king of Assyria and from the hand of all others. He took care of them[a] on every side. 23Many brought offerings to Jerusalem for the LORD and valuable gifts[z] for Hezekiah king of Judah. From then on he was highly regarded by all the nations.

32:23 [z]2Ch 9:24; 17:5; Isa 45:14; Zec 14:16-17

Hezekiah's Pride, Success and Death

24In those days Hezekiah became ill and was at the point of death. He prayed to the LORD, who answered him and gave him a miraculous sign. 25But Hezekiah's heart was proud[a] and he did not respond to the kindness shown him; therefore the LORD's wrath[b] was on him and on Judah and Jerusalem. 26Then Hezekiah repented[c] of the pride of his heart, as did the people of Jerusalem; therefore the LORD's wrath did not come upon them during the days of Hezekiah.[d]

32:25 [a]2Ki 14:10; 2Ch 26:16 [b]2Ch 19:2; 24:18

32:26 [c]Jer 26:18-19

32:26 [d]2Ch 34:27, 28; Isa 39:8

27Hezekiah had very great riches and honor,[e] and he made treasuries for his silver and gold and for his precious stones, spices, shields and all kinds of valuables. 28He also made buildings to store the harvest of grain, new wine and oil; and he made stalls for various kinds of cattle, and pens for the flocks. 29He built villages and acquired great numbers of flocks and herds, for God had given him very great riches.[f]

32:27 [e]1Ch 29:12

32:29 [f]1Ch 29:12

30It was Hezekiah who blocked[g] the upper outlet of the Gihon[h] spring and channeled the water down to the west side of the City of David. He succeeded in everything he undertook. 31But when envoys were sent by the rulers of Babylon[i] to ask him about the miraculous sign[j] that had occurred in the land, God left him to test[k] him and to know everything that was in his heart.

32:30 [g]2Ki 18:17 [h]1Ki 1:33

32:31 [i]Isa 39:1 [j]ver 24; Isa 38:7 [k]Ge 22:1; Dt 8:16

32The other events of Hezekiah's reign and his acts of devotion are written in the vision of the prophet Isaiah son of Amoz in the book of the kings of Judah and Israel. 33Hezekiah rested with his fathers and was buried on the hill where the tombs of David's descendants are. All Judah and the people of Jerusalem honored him when he died. And Manasseh his son succeeded him as king.

Manasseh King of Judah

33 Manasseh[l] was twelve years old when he became king, and he reigned in Jerusalem fifty-five years. 2He did evil in the eyes of the LORD,[m] following the detestable[n] practices of the nations the LORD had driven out before the Israelites. 3He rebuilt the high places his father Hezekiah had demolished; he also erected altars to the Baals and made Asherah poles.[o] He bowed down[p] to all the starry hosts and worshiped them. 4He built altars in the temple of the LORD, of which the LORD had said, "My Name[q] will remain in Jerusalem forever." 5In both courts of the temple of the LORD,[r] he built altars to all the starry hosts. 6He sacrificed his sons[s] in[b] the fire in the Valley of Ben Hinnom, practiced

33:1 [l]1Ch 3:13

33:2 [m]Jer 15:4 [n]Dt 18:9; 2Ch 28:3

33:3 [o]Dt 16:21-22 [p]Dt 17:3; 2Ch 31:1

33:4 [q]2Ch 7:16

33:5 [r]2Ch 4:9

33:6 [s]Lev 18:21; Dt 18:10; 2Ch 28:3

[a]22 Hebrew; Septuagint and Vulgate *He gave them rest* [b]6 Or *He made his sons pass through*

sorcery, divination and witchcraft, and consulted mediums[t] and spiritists.[u] He did much evil in the eyes of the LORD, provoking him to anger.

7 He took the carved image he had made and put it in God's temple,[v] of which God had said to David and to his son Solomon, "In this temple and in Jerusalem, which I have chosen out of all the tribes of Israel, I will put my Name forever. 8 I will not again make the feet of the Israelites leave the land[w] I assigned to your forefathers, if only they will be careful to do everything I commanded them concerning all the laws, decrees and ordinances given through Moses." 9 But Manasseh led Judah and the people of Jerusalem astray, so that they did more evil than the nations the LORD had destroyed before the Israelites.[x]

10 The LORD spoke to Manasseh and his people, but they paid no attention. 11 So the LORD brought against them the army commanders of the king of Assyria, who took Manasseh prisoner,[y] put a hook in his nose, bound him with bronze shackles[z] and took him to Babylon. 12 In his distress he sought the favor of the LORD his God and humbled[a] himself greatly before the God of his fathers. 13 And when he prayed to him, the LORD was moved by his entreaty and listened to his plea; so he brought him back to Jerusalem and to his kingdom. Then Manasseh knew that the LORD is God.

14 Afterward he rebuilt the outer wall of the City of David, west of the Gihon[b] spring in the valley, as far as the entrance of the Fish Gate[c] and encircling the hill of Ophel;[d] he also made it much higher. He stationed military commanders in all the fortified cities in Judah.

15 He got rid of the foreign gods and removed[e] the image from the temple of the LORD, as well as all the altars he had built on the temple hill and in Jerusalem; and he threw them out of the city. 16 Then he restored the altar of the LORD and sacrificed fellowship offerings[a] and thank offerings on it,[f] and told Judah to serve the LORD, the God of Israel. 17 The people, however, continued to sacrifice at the high places, but only to the LORD their God.

18 The other events of Manasseh's reign, including his prayer to his God and the words the seers spoke to him in the name of the LORD, the God of Israel, are written in the annals of the kings of Israel.[b] 19 His prayer and how God was moved by his entreaty, as well as all his sins and unfaithfulness, and the sites where he built high places and set up Asherah poles and idols before he humbled[g] himself—all are written in the records of the seers.[c][h] 20 Manasseh rested with his fathers and was buried[i] in his palace. And Amon his son succeeded him as king.

Amon King of Judah

21 Amon[j] was twenty-two years old when he became king, and he reigned in Jerusalem two years. 22 He did evil in the eyes of the LORD, as his father Manasseh had done. Amon worshiped and offered sacrifices to all the idols Manasseh had made. 23 But unlike his father Manasseh, he did not humble[k] himself before the LORD; Amon increased his guilt.

24 Amon's officials conspired against him and assassinated him in his palace. 25 Then the people[l] of the land killed all who had plotted against King Amon, and they made Josiah his son king in his place.

Josiah's Reforms

34 Josiah[m] was eight years old when he became king,[n] and he reigned in Jerusalem thirty-one years. 2 He did what was right in the eyes of the LORD and walked in the ways of his father David,[o] not turning aside to the right or to the left.

3 In the eighth year of his reign, while he was still young, he began to seek the God[p] of his father David. In his twelfth year he began to purge Judah and Jerusalem of high places, Asherah poles, carved idols and cast images. 4 Under his direction the altars of the Baals were torn down; he cut to pieces the incense altars that were above them, and smashed the Asherah poles,[q] the idols and the images. These he broke to pieces and scattered over the graves of those who had sacrificed to them.[r] 5 He burned[s]

[a] *16* Traditionally *peace offerings* [b] *18* That is, Judah, as frequently in 2 Chronicles [c] *19* One Hebrew manuscript and Septuagint; most Hebrew manuscripts *of Hozai*

33:6 [t]Lev 19:31 [u]1Sa 28:13
33:7 [v]2Ch 7:16
33:8 [w]2Sa 7:10
33:9 [x]Jer 15:4
33:11 [y]Dt 28:36 [z]Ps 149:8
33:12 [a]2Ch 6:37; 32:26; 1Pe 5:6
33:14 [b]1Ki 1:33 [c]Ne 3:3; 12:39; Zep 1:10 [d]2Ch 27:3; Ne 3:26
33:15 [e]ver 3-7; 2Ki 23:12
33:16 [f]Lev 7:11-18
33:19 [g]2Ch 6:37 [h]2Ki 21:17
33:20 [i]2Ki 21:18; 2Ch 21:20
33:21 [j]1Ch 3:14
33:23 [k]ver 12; Ex 10:3; 2Ch 7:14; Ps 18:27; 147:6; Pr 3:34
33:25 [l]2Ch 22:1
34:1 [m]1Ch 3:14 [n]Zep 1:1
34:2 [o]2Ch 29:2
34:3 [p]1Ki 13:2; 1Ch 16:11; 2Ch 15:2; 33:17,22
34:4 [q]Ex 34:13 [r]Ex 32:20; Lev 26:30; 2Ki 23:11; Mic 1:5
34:5 [s]1Ki 13:2

the bones of the priests on their altars,
and so he purged Judah and Jerusalem.
6 In the towns of Manasseh, Ephraim
and Simeon, as far as Naphtali, and in
the ruins around them, 7 he tore down
the altars and the Asherah poles and
34:7 [t] Ex 32:20; 2Ch 31:1
crushed the idols to powder[t] and cut
to pieces all the incense altars throughout Israel. Then he went back to Jerusalem.
8 In the eighteenth year of Josiah's
reign, to purify the land and the temple, he sent Shaphan son of Azaliah and
Maaseiah the ruler of the city, with Joah
son of Joahaz, the recorder, to repair the
temple of the LORD his God.
34:9 [u] 1Ch 6:13; 2Ch 35:8
9 They went to Hilkiah[u] the high
priest and gave him the money that had
been brought into the temple of God,
which the Levites who were the doorkeepers had collected from the people
of Manasseh, Ephraim and the entire
remnant of Israel and from all the people of Judah and Benjamin and the
inhabitants of Jerusalem. 10 Then they
entrusted it to the men appointed to supervise the work on the LORD's temple.
These men paid the workers who repaired and restored the temple. 11 They
34:11 [v] 2Ch 24:12 [w] 2Ch 33:4-7
also gave money[v] to the carpenters and
builders to purchase dressed stone, and
timber for joists and beams for the
buildings that the kings of Judah had
allowed to fall into ruin.[w]
34:12 [x] 2Ki 12:15 [y] 1Ch 25:1
12 The men did the work faithfully.[x]
Over them to direct them were Jahath
and Obadiah, Levites descended from
Merari, and Zechariah and Meshullam, descended from Kohath. The Levites—all who were skilled in playing
musical instruments—[y] 13 had charge
34:13 [z] 1Ch 23:4
of the laborers[z] and supervised all the
workers from job to job. Some of the
Levites were secretaries, scribes and
doorkeepers.

The Book of the Law Found

14 While they were bringing out the
money that had been taken into the
temple of the LORD, Hilkiah the priest
34:15 [a] 2Ki 22:8; Ezr 7:6; Ne 8:1
found the Book of the Law of the LORD
that had been given through Moses.
15 Hilkiah said to Shaphan the secretary,
"I have found the Book of the Law[a] in
the temple of the LORD." He gave it to
Shaphan.
16 Then Shaphan took the book to
the king and reported to him: "Your
officials are doing everything that has
been committed to them. 17 They have
paid out the money that was in the
temple of the LORD and have entrusted it to the supervisors and workers."
18 Then Shaphan the secretary informed
the king, "Hilkiah the priest has given
me a book." And Shaphan read from it
in the presence of the king.
19 When the king heard the words
34:19 [b] Dt 28:3-68 [c] Jos 7:6; Isa 36:22; 37:1
of the Law,[b] he tore[c] his robes. 20 He
gave these orders to Hilkiah, Ahikam
son of Shaphan,[d] Abdon son of Micah,[a]
34:20 [d] 2Ki 22:3
Shaphan the secretary and Asaiah the
king's attendant: 21 "Go and inquire of
the LORD for me and for the remnant
in Israel and Judah about what is written in this book that has been found.
Great is the LORD's anger that is poured
34:21 [e] 2Ch 29:8; La 2:4; 4:11; Eze 36:18
out[e] on us because our fathers have not
kept the word of the LORD; they have
not acted in accordance with all that is
written in this book."
22 Hilkiah and those the king had
sent with him[b] went to speak to the
34:22 [f] Ex 15:20; Ne 6:14
prophetess[f] Huldah, who was the wife
of Shallum son of Tokhath,[c] the son of
34:24 [g] Pr 16:4; Isa 3:9; Jer 40:2; 42:10; 44:2,11 [h] 2Ch 36:14-20 [i] Dt 28:15-68
Hasrah,[d] keeper of the wardrobe. She
lived in Jerusalem, in the Second District.
23 She said to them, "This is what
the LORD, the God of Israel, says: Tell
the man who sent you to me, 24 'This
is what the LORD says: I am going to
bring disaster[g] on this place and its people[h]—all the curses[i] written in the book
that has been read in the presence of the
king of Judah. 25 Because they have for-
34:25 [j] 2Ch 33:3-6; Jer 22:9
saken me[j] and burned incense to other
gods and provoked me to anger by all
that their hands have made,[e] my anger
will be poured out on this place and
will not be quenched.' 26 Tell the king
of Judah, who sent you to inquire of
the LORD, 'This is what the LORD, the
God of Israel, says concerning the words
you heard: 27 Because your heart was re-
34:27 [k] 2Ch 12:7; 32:26 [l] Ex 10:3; 2Ch 6:37
sponsive[k] and you humbled[l] yourself
before God when you heard what he
spoke against this place and its people,
and because you humbled yourself before me and tore your robes and wept in
my presence, I have heard you, declares

[a] *20* Also called *Acbor son of Micaiah* [b] *22* One Hebrew manuscript, Vulgate and Syriac; most Hebrew manuscripts do not have *had sent with him.* [c] *22* Also called *Tikvah* [d] *22* Also called *Harhas* [e] *25* Or *by everything they have done*

DAY 3 THREE

▸ KINDNESS AND MY RELATIONSHIP WITH CHRIST

2 Chronicles 34:19–28

Josiah experienced the kindness of God firsthand. He understood God's kindness when he became the recipient of God's grace. Josiah knew his people and nation had sinned and forgotten God. Yet this king received incredible news from God: Josiah would be spared from disaster. His humility and contrition had led to forgiveness. God demonstrated grace to Josiah through these simple words, "I have heard you."

Grace saves us. But how different is grace from kindness? Distinguish them for me if you can. But after you have tried, I will still, like Josiah, often find them indistinguishable.

Here is my litany of grace, and as I speak it, I celebrate with every phrase my relationship with Christ, who showed ultimate grace by sacrificing himself for me:

Dear Christ,
With every slice of warm bread, I praise your name.
For rain on a warm evening and the smell of ground, I praise your name.
For a child's laughter and a woman's lullaby, I praise your name.
For the Word of God, the word of novelists, for my own words,
For the stars when I can see them and when I can't,
For the truth when I can figure it out and when I can't,
For a robed choir and one who can't afford robes,
For preachers who use pulpits and those who don't,
For barefoot on warm concrete and barefoot in the park,
For barefoot on carpet and barefoot in mountain brooks,
For barefoot before the fire and barefoot in the rain:
For all things, I measure your kindness, and I thank you.

To begin a study on the topic of Kindness, the Approach to Grace, turn to the home page on page 343.

the LORD. 28Now I will gather you to
your fathers,[m] and you will be buried in
peace. Your eyes will not see all the disaster I am going to bring on this place
and on those who live here.'"[n]
So they took her answer back to the
king.
29Then the king called together all
the elders of Judah and Jerusalem. 30He
went up to the temple of the LORD[o]
with the men of Judah, the people of
Jerusalem, the priests and the Levites—
all the people from the least to the
greatest. He read in their hearing all
the words of the Book of the Covenant,
which had been found in the temple of
the LORD. 31The king stood by his pillar[p] and renewed the covenant[q] in the
presence of the LORD—to follow[r] the
LORD and keep his commands, regulations and decrees with all his heart and
all his soul, and to obey the words of
the covenant written in this book.
32Then he had everyone in Jerusalem
and Benjamin pledge themselves to it;
the people of Jerusalem did this in accordance with the covenant of God, the
God of their fathers.
33Josiah removed all the detestable[s]
idols from all the territory belonging to
the Israelites, and he had all who were
present in Israel serve the LORD their
God. As long as he lived, they did not
fail to follow the LORD, the God of
their fathers.

Josiah Celebrates the Passover

35 Josiah celebrated the Passover[t]
to the LORD in Jerusalem, and
the Passover lamb was slaughtered on
the fourteenth day of the first month.
2He appointed the priests to their duties and encouraged them in the service of the LORD's temple. 3He said
to the Levites, who instructed[u] all Israel and who had been consecrated to
the LORD: "Put the sacred ark in the
temple that Solomon son of David king
of Israel built. It is not to be carried
about on your shoulders. Now serve the
LORD your God and his people Israel.
4Prepare yourselves by families in your
divisions,[v] according to the directions
written by David king of Israel and by
his son Solomon.
5"Stand in the holy place with a
group of Levites for each subdivision
of the families of your fellow coun-

34:28 [m]2Ch 35:20-25 [n]2Ch 32:26
34:30 [o]2Ki 23:2; Ne 8:1-3
34:31 [p]1Ki 7:15; 2Ki 11:14 [q]2Ki 11:17; 2Ch 23:16; 29:10 [r]Dt 13:4
34:33 [s]ver 3-7; Dt 18:9
35:1 [t]Ex 12:1-30; Nu 9:3; 28:16
35:3 [u]Dt 33:10; 1Ch 23:26; 2Ch 5:7; 17:7
35:4 [v]ver 10; 1Ch 9:10-13; 24:1; 2Ch 8:14; Ezr 6:18

trymen, the lay people. 6Slaughter the Passover lambs, consecrate yourselves[w] and prepare ⌊the lambs⌋ for your fellow countrymen, doing what the LORD commanded through Moses."

7Josiah provided for all the lay people who were there a total of thirty thousand sheep and goats for the Passover offerings,[x] and also three thousand cattle—all from the king's own possessions.[y]

8His officials also contributed[z] voluntarily to the people and the priests and Levites. Hilkiah,[a] Zechariah and Jehiel, the administrators of God's temple, gave the priests twenty-six hundred Passover offerings and three hundred cattle. 9Also Conaniah[b] along with Shemaiah and Nethanel, his brothers, and Hashabiah, Jeiel and Jozabad,[c] the leaders of the Levites, provided five thousand Passover offerings and five hundred head of cattle for the Levites.

10The service was arranged and the priests stood in their places with the Levites in their divisions[d] as the king had ordered.[e] 11The Passover lambs were slaughtered,[f] and the priests sprinkled the blood handed to them, while the Levites skinned the animals. 12They set aside the burnt offerings to give them to the subdivisions of the families of the people to offer to the LORD, as is written in the Book of Moses. They did the same with the cattle. 13They roasted the Passover animals over the fire as prescribed,[g] and boiled the holy offerings in pots, caldrons and pans and served them quickly to all the people. 14After this, they made preparations for themselves and for the priests, because the priests, the descendants of Aaron, were sacrificing the burnt offerings and the fat portions[h] until nightfall. So the Levites made preparations for themselves and for the Aaronic priests.

15The musicians,[i] the descendants of Asaph, were in the places prescribed by David, Asaph, Heman and Jeduthun the king's seer. The gatekeepers at each gate did not need to leave their posts, because their fellow Levites made the preparations for them.

16So at that time the entire service of the LORD was carried out for the celebration of the Passover and the offering of burnt offerings on the altar of the LORD, as King Josiah had ordered.

35:6 [w]Lev 11:44; 2Ch 29:5,15
35:7 [x]2Ch 30:24 [y]2Ch 31:3
35:8 [z]1Ch 29:3; 2Ch 29:31-36 [a]1Ch 6:13
35:9 [b]2Ch 31:12 [c]2Ch 31:13
35:10 [d]ver 4; Ezr 6:18 [e]2Ch 30:16
35:11 [f]2Ch 29:22, 34; 30:17
35:13 [g]Ex 12:2-11; Lev 6:25; 1Sa 2:13-15
35:14 [h]Ex 29:13
35:15 [i]1Ch 25:1; 26:12-19; 2Ch 29:30; Ne 12:46; Ps 68:25

17The Israelites who were present celebrated the Passover at that time and observed the Feast of Unleavened Bread for seven days. 18The Passover had not been observed like this in Israel since the days of the prophet Samuel; and none of the kings of Israel had ever celebrated such a Passover as did Josiah, with the priests, the Levites and all Judah and Israel who were there with the people of Jerusalem. 19This Passover was celebrated in the eighteenth year of Josiah's reign.

The Death of Josiah

20After all this, when Josiah had set the temple in order, Neco king of Egypt went up to fight at Carchemish[j] on the Euphrates,[k] and Josiah marched out to meet him in battle. 21But Neco sent messengers to him, saying, "What quarrel is there between you and me, O king of Judah? It is not you I am attacking at this time, but the house with which I am at war. God has told[l] me to hurry; so stop opposing God, who is with me, or he will destroy you."

22Josiah, however, would not turn away from him, but disguised[m] himself to engage him in battle. He would not listen to what Neco had said at God's command but went to fight him on the plain of Megiddo.

35:20 [j]Isa 10:9; Jer 46:2 [k]Ge 2:14
35:21 [l]1Ki 13:18; 2Ki 18:25
35:22 [m]Jdg 5:19; 1Sa 28:8; 2Ch 18:29

LOVE

WHAT WE ARE WILLING TO DIE FOR

2 Chronicles 35:22

Josiah was willing to die for God. Unfortunately, God would rather Josiah had lived for him.

23Archers[n] shot King Josiah, and he told his officers, "Take me away; I am badly wounded." 24So they took him out of his chariot, put him in the other chariot he had and brought him to Jerusalem, where he died. He was buried in the tombs of his fathers, and all Judah and Jerusalem mourned for him.

25Jeremiah composed laments for Josiah, and to this day all the men and women singers commemorate Josiah in the laments.[o] These became a tradition in Israel and are written in the Laments.

26The other events of Josiah's reign

35:23 [n]1Ki 22:34
35:25 [o]Jer 22:10, 15-16

and his acts of devotion, according
to what is written in the Law of the
LORD— [27]all the events, from beginning to end, are written in the
book of the kings of Israel and Judah.

36 [1]And the people of the land
took Jehoahaz son of Josiah and
made him king in Jerusalem in place of
his father.

Jehoahaz King of Judah

[2]Jehoahaz[a] was twenty-three years old
when he became king, and he reigned
in Jerusalem three months. [3]The king
of Egypt dethroned him in Jerusalem
and imposed on Judah a levy of a hundred talents[b] of silver and a talent[c] of
gold. [4]The king of Egypt made Eliakim,
a brother of Jehoahaz, king over Judah
and Jerusalem and changed Eliakim's
36:4 [p]Jer 22:10-12 name to Jehoiakim. But Neco[p] took
Eliakim's brother Jehoahaz and carried
him off to Egypt.

Jehoiakim King of Judah

36:5 [q]Jer 22:18; 26:1; 35:1 [5]Jehoiakim[q] was twenty-five years old
when he became king, and he reigned
in Jerusalem eleven years. He did evil in
the eyes of the LORD his God. [6]Nebu-
36:6 [r]Jer 25:9; 27:6; Eze 29:18 [s]2Ch 33:11; Eze 19:9; Da 1:1 chadnezzar[r] king of Babylon attacked
him and bound him with bronze shack-
les to take him to Babylon.[s] [7]Nebu-
chadnezzar also took to Babylon articles
from the temple of the LORD and put
36:7 [t]2Ki 24:13; Ezr 1:7; Da 1:2 them in his temple[d] there.[t]
[8]The other events of Jehoiakim's
reign, the detestable things he did and
all that was found against him, are written in the book of the kings of Israel
and Judah. And Jehoiachin his son succeeded him as king.

Jehoiachin King of Judah

36:9 [u]Jer 22:24-28; 52:31 [9]Jehoiachin[u] was eighteen[e] years old
when he became king, and he reigned
in Jerusalem three months and ten days.
He did evil in the eyes of the LORD. [10]In
the spring, King Nebuchadnezzar sent
36:10 [v]ver 18; 2Ki 20:17; Ezr 1:7; Jer 22:25; 24:1; 29:1; 37:1; Eze 17:12 for him and brought him to Babylon,[v]
together with articles of value from the
temple of the LORD, and he made Jehoiachin's uncle,[f] Zedekiah, king over
Judah and Jerusalem.

Zedekiah King of Judah

36:11 [w]2Ki 24:17; Jer 27:1; 28:1 [11]Zedekiah[w] was twenty-one years old
when he became king, and he reigned
in Jerusalem eleven years. [12]He did evil 36:12 [x]Jer 37:1-39:18 [y]Dt 8:3; 2Ch 7:14; 2Ch 33:23; Jer 21:3-7
in the eyes of the LORD[x] his God and
did not humble[y] himself before Jeremiah the prophet, who spoke the word of
the LORD. [13]He also rebelled against
King Nebuchadnezzar, who had made
him take an oath[z] in God's name. He 36:13 [z]Eze 17:13 [a]2Ki 17:14; 2Ch 30:8
became stiff-necked[a] and hardened his
heart and would not turn to the LORD,
the God of Israel. [14]Furthermore, all
the leaders of the priests and the people
became more and more unfaithful,[b] fol- 36:14 [b]1Ch 5:25
lowing all the detestable practices of the
nations and defiling the temple of the
LORD, which he had consecrated in Je- 36:15 [c]Isa 5:4; 44:26; Jer 7:25; Hag 1:13; Zec 1:4; Mal 2:7; 3:1 [d]Jer 7:13,25; 25:3-4; 35:14,15; 44:4-6
rusalem.

The Fall of Jerusalem

[15]The LORD, the God of their fathers, sent word to them through his
messengers[c] again and again,[d] because
he had pity on his people and on 36:16 [e]2Ki 2:23; Pr 1:25; Jer 5:13 [f]Ezr 5:12; Pr 1:30-31 [g]2Ch 30:10; Pr 29:1; Zec 1:2
his dwelling place. [16]But they mocked
God's messengers, despised his words
and scoffed[e] at his prophets until the
wrath[f] of the LORD was aroused against
his people and there was no remedy.[g]
[17]He brought up against them the king 36:17 [h]Jer 6:11 [i]Ezr 5:12; Jer 32:28
of the Babylonians,[g] who killed their
young men with the sword in the
sanctuary, and spared neither young 36:18 [j]ver 7,10
man nor young woman, old man[h] or
aged. God handed all of them over to 36:19 [k]Jer 11:16; 17:27; 21:10,14; 22:7; 32:29; 39:8; La 4:11; Eze 20:47; Am 2:5; Zec 11:1 [l]1Ki 9:8-9 [m]2Ki 14:13 [n]La 2:6 [o]Ps 79:1-3
Nebuchadnezzar.[i] [18]He carried to Bab-
ylon all the articles[j] from the temple
of God, both large and small, and the
treasures of the LORD's temple and the
treasures of the king and his officials.
[19]They set fire[k] to God's temple[l] and
broke down the wall[m] of Jerusalem; they
burned all the palaces and destroyed[n]
everything of value there.[o]
[20]He carried into exile[p] to Babylon 36:20 [p]Lev 26:44; 2Ki 24:14; Ezr 2:1; Ne 7:6 [q]Jer 27:7
the remnant, who escaped from the
sword, and they became servants[q] to
him and his sons until the kingdom of
Persia came to power. [21]The land en- 36:21 [r]Lev 25:4; 26:34 [s]1Ch 22:9
joyed its sabbath rests;[r] all the time of
its desolation it rested,[s] until the seven-

[a]*2* Hebrew *Joahaz,* a variant of *Jehoahaz;* also in verse 4 [b]*3* That is, about 3 3/4 tons (about 3.4 metric tons) [c]*3* That is, about 75 pounds (about 34 kilograms) [d]*7* Or *palace* [e]*9* One Hebrew manuscript, some Septuagint manuscripts and Syriac (see also 2 Kings 24:8); most Hebrew manuscripts *eight* [f]*10* Hebrew *brother,* that is, relative (see 2 Kings 24:17) [g]*17* Or *Chaldeans*

36:21 [t]Jer 1:1; 25:11; 27:22; 29:10; 40:1; Da 9:2; Zec 1:12; 7:5

36:22 [u]Isa 44:28; 45:1,13; Jer 25:12; 29:10; Da 1:21; 6:28; 10:1

ty years[t] were completed in fulfillment
of the word of the LORD spoken by Jeremiah.
22 In the first year of Cyrus[u] king
of Persia, in order to fulfill the word
of the LORD spoken by Jeremiah,
the LORD moved the heart of Cyrus
king of Persia to make a proclamation
throughout his realm and to put it in
writing:

23 "This is what Cyrus king of Persia
says:

"'The LORD, the God of heaven, has given me all the kingdoms of the earth and he has appointed[v] me to build a temple for him at Jerusalem in Judah. Anyone of his people among you—may the LORD his God be with him, and let him go up.'"

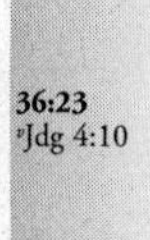

36:23 [v]Jdg 4:10

EZRA

AUTHORSHIP AND DATE

The author isn't specifically named, but credit for the work is often given to Ezra.

c. 450 B.C.

KEY THEMES

The name *Ezra* means "help." According to Jewish tradition, Ezra was one of the 120 men who helped designate and establish the canon of the Old Testament. There are, however, notable facts about Ezra that are more than tradition. We know he led the second migration of exiles from Babylon back to Jerusalem. This occurred 58 years after Zerubbabel led the first migration of 42,360 exiles. Because the closing of 2 Chronicles is so similar in style, tone and account to the opening of Ezra, many scholars believe that Ezra was responsible for writing the Chronicles as well as this book that bears his name. We also know that Ezra was—in addition to being a great leader—both a priest and a scribe. More than this, he was also a man of faith and a servant of God who desired obedience above all else. He was a priest who interceded on behalf of the people (see ch. 9), and his humble confession led to a national revival (see ch. 10).

FRUIT OF THE SPIRIT IN EZRA

Kindness: This fruit of the Spirit can be seen in any number of events and passages in the life of Ezra.

First, consider this testament to his devoted spirit: "Ezra had devoted himself to the study and observance of the Law of the LORD" (7:10).

Second, consider this statement: "There, by the Ahava Canal, I proclaimed a fast, so that we might humble ourselves before our God" (8:21). Whether he was in exile or whether he was free, Ezra considered the spiritual needs of others.

Third, Ezra's kindness was not a soft touch, as can be seen in his reaction to the intermarriage of Jews and Canaanites: "When I heard this, I tore my tunic and cloak, pulled hair from my head and beard and sat down appalled...And I sat there appalled until the evening sacrifice" (9:3–4).

Finally, Ezra's kindness was shown in his personal confession, which called the fledgling new Jerusalem back to obedience to God's law: "While Ezra was praying and confessing, weeping and throwing himself down before the house of God, a large crowd of Israelites—men, women and children—gathered around him. They too wept bitterly" (10:1). And out of this collective mourning a new zeal for God and obedience to the Lord was born. Kindness before the Lord always sparks the beginning of revival.

Cyrus Helps the Exiles to Return

1 In the first year of Cyrus king of
Persia, in order to fulfill the word
of the LORD spoken by Jeremiah,[a]
the LORD moved the heart[b] of Cyrus
king of Persia to make a proclamation
throughout his realm and to put it in
writing:

2“This is what Cyrus king of Persia
says:

“ ‘The LORD, the God of heav-
en, has given me all the kingdoms
of the earth and he has appointed[c]
me to build[d] a temple for him at
Jerusalem in Judah. 3Anyone of his
people among you—may his God
be with him, and let him go up to
Jerusalem in Judah and build the
temple of the LORD, the God of
Israel, the God who is in Jerusalem. 4And the people of any place
where survivors[e] may now be living are to provide him with silver
and gold, with goods and livestock,
and with freewill offerings[f] for the
temple of God in Jerusalem.’ ”[g]

5Then the family heads of Judah
and Benjamin,[h] and the priests and Levites—everyone whose heart God had
moved[i]—prepared to go up and build
the house[j] of the LORD in Jerusalem.
6All their neighbors assisted them with
articles of silver and gold, with goods
and livestock, and with valuable gifts,
in addition to all the freewill offerings.
7Moreover, King Cyrus brought out
the articles belonging to the temple of
the LORD, which Nebuchadnezzar had
carried away from Jerusalem and had
placed in the temple of his god.[a][k] 8Cy-
rus king of Persia had them brought by
Mithredath the treasurer, who counted
them out to Sheshbazzar[l] the prince of
Judah.

9This was the inventory:

gold dishes	30
silver dishes	1,000
silver pans[b]	29
10 gold bowls	30
matching silver bowls	410
other articles	1,000

11In all, there were 5,400 articles of
gold and of silver. Sheshbazzar brought
all these along when the exiles came up
from Babylon to Jerusalem.

1:1 [a]Jer 25:11-12; 29:10-14 [b]2Ch 36:22, 23
1:2 [c]Isa 44:28; 45:13 [d]Ezr 5:13
1:4 [e]Isa 10:20-22 [f]Nu 15:3; Ps 50:14; 54:6; 116:17 [g]Ezr 4:3; 5:13; 6:3,14
1:5 [h]Ezr 4:1; Ne 11:4 [i]ver 1; Ex 35:20-22; 2Ch 36:22; Hag 1:14; Php 2:13 [j]Ps 127:1
1:7 [k]2Ki 24:13; 2Ch 36:7,10; Ezr 5:14; 6:5
1:8 [l]Ezr 5:14

The List of the Exiles Who Returned

2 Now these are the people of the
province who came up from the
captivity of the exiles,[m] whom Nebuchadnezzar king of Babylon[n] had tak-
en captive to Babylon (they returned to
Jerusalem and Judah, each to his own
town,[o] 2in company with Zerubbabel,[p]
Jeshua,[q] Nehemiah, Seraiah,[r] Reelaiah,
Mordecai, Bilshan, Mispar, Bigvai, Rehum and Baanah):

The list of the men of the people of Israel:

3 the descendants of Parosh[s]	2,172
4 of Shephatiah	372
5 of Arah	775
6 of Pahath-Moab (through the line of Jeshua and Joab)	2,812
7 of Elam	1,254
8 of Zattu	945
9 of Zaccai	760
10 of Bani	642
11 of Bebai	623
12 of Azgad	1,222
13 of Adonikam[t]	666
14 of Bigvai	2,056
15 of Adin	454
16 of Ater (through Hezekiah)	98
17 of Bezai	323
18 of Jorah	112
19 of Hashum	223
20 of Gibbar	95
21 the men of Bethlehem[u]	123
22 of Netophah	56
23 of Anathoth	128
24 of Azmaveth	42
25 of Kiriath Jearim,[c] Kephirah and Beeroth	743
26 of Ramah[v] and Geba	621
27 of Micmash	122
28 of Bethel and Ai[w]	223
29 of Nebo	52
30 of Magbish	156
31 of the other Elam	1,254
32 of Harim	320
33 of Lod, Hadid and Ono	725
34 of Jericho[x]	345
35 of Senaah	3,630

2:1 [m]2Ch 36:20; Ne 7:6 [n]2Ki 24:16; 25:12 [o]Ne 7:73
2:2 [p]1Ch 3:19 [q]Ezr 3:2 [r]Ne 10:2
2:3 [s]Ezr 8:3
2:13 [t]Ezr 8:13
2:21 [u]Mic 5:2
2:26 [v]Jos 18:25
2:28 [w]Ge 12:8
2:34 [x]1Ki 16:34; 2Ch 28:15

[a]7 Or *gods* [b]9 The meaning of the Hebrew for this word is uncertain. [c]25 See Septuagint (see also Neh. 7:29); Hebrew *Kiriath Arim.*

36 The priests:

the descendants of Jedaiah[y]
(through the family
of Jeshua) 973
37 of Immer[z] 1,052
38 of Pashhur[a] 1,247
39 of Harim[b] 1,017

40 The Levites:[c]

the descendants of Jeshua[d]
and Kadmiel (through
the line of Hodaviah) 74

41 The singers:[e]

the descendants of Asaph 128

42 The gatekeepers[f] of the temple:

the descendants of
Shallum, Ater, Talmon,
Akkub, Hatita and
Shobai 139

43 The temple servants:[g]

the descendants of
Ziha, Hasupha, Tabbaoth,
44 Keros, Siaha, Padon,
45 Lebanah, Hagabah, Akkub,
46 Hagab, Shalmai, Hanan,
47 Giddel, Gahar, Reaiah,
48 Rezin, Nekoda, Gazzam,
49 Uzza, Paseah, Besai,
50 Asnah, Meunim, Nephussim,
51 Bakbuk, Hakupha, Harhur,
52 Bazluth, Mehida, Harsha,
53 Barkos, Sisera, Temah,
54 Neziah and Hatipha

55 The descendants of the servants
of Solomon:

the descendants of
Sotai, Hassophereth, Peruda,
56 Jaala, Darkon, Giddel,
57 Shephatiah, Hattil,
Pokereth-Hazzebaim and Ami

58 The temple servants[h] and the
descendants of the
servants of Solomon 392

59 The following came up from
the towns of Tel Melah, Tel Harsha, Kerub, Addon and Immer, but
they could not show that their families were descended[i] from Israel:

60 The descendants of
Delaiah, Tobiah and
Nekoda 652

2:36 [y]1Ch 24:7
2:37 [z]1Ch 24:14
2:38 [a]1Ch 9:12
2:39 [b]1Ch 24:8
2:40 [c]Ge 29:34; Nu 3:9; Dt 18:6-7; 1Ch 16:4; Ezr 7:7; 8:15; Ne 12:24 [d]Ezr 3:9
2:41 [e]1Ch 15:16
2:42 [f]1Sa 3:15; 1Ch 9:17
2:43 [g]1Ch 9:2; Ne 11:21
2:58 [h]1Ki 9:21; 1Ch 9:2
2:59 [i]Nu 1:18

61 And from among the priests:

The descendants of
Hobaiah, Hakkoz and
Barzillai (a man who had
married a daughter of
Barzillai the Gileadite[j] and
was called by that name).

62 These searched for their family records, but they could not find
them and so were excluded from
the priesthood[k] as unclean. 63 The
governor ordered them not to eat
any of the most sacred food[l] until
there was a priest ministering with
the Urim and Thummim.[m]

64 The whole company numbered 42,360, 65 besides their 7,337
menservants and maidservants; and
they also had 200 men and women
singers.[n] 66 They had 736 horses,[o]
245 mules, 67 435 camels and 6,720
donkeys.

68 When they arrived at the house of
the LORD in Jerusalem, some of the
heads of the families[p] gave freewill offerings toward the rebuilding of the
house of God on its site. 69 According
to their ability they gave to the treasury
for this work 61,000 drachmas[a] of gold,
5,000 minas[b] of silver and 100 priestly
garments.

70 The priests, the Levites, the singers,
the gatekeepers and the temple servants
settled in their own towns, along with
some of the other people, and the rest
of the Israelites settled in their towns.[q]

Rebuilding the Altar

3 When the seventh month came and
the Israelites had settled in their
towns,[r] the people assembled[s] as one
man in Jerusalem. 2 Then Jeshua[t] son
of Jozadak[u] and his fellow priests and
Zerubbabel son of Shealtiel[v] and his associates began to build the altar of the
God of Israel to sacrifice burnt offerings on it, in accordance with what is
written in the Law of Moses[w] the man
of God. 3 Despite their fear[x] of the peoples around them, they built the altar
on its foundation and sacrificed burnt
offerings on it to the LORD, both the
morning and evening sacrifices.[y] 4 Then

[a] *69* That is, about 1,100 pounds (about 500 kilograms) [b] *69* That is, about 3 tons (about 2.9 metric tons)

2:61 [j]2Sa 17:27
2:62 [k]Nu 3:10; 16:39-40
2:63 [l]Lev 2:3,10 [m]Ex 28:30; Nu 27:21
2:65 [n]2Sa 19:35
2:66 [o]Isa 66:20
2:68 [p]Ex 25:2
2:70 [q]ver 1; 1Ch 9:2; Ne 11:3-4
3:1 [r]Ne 7:73; 8:1 [s]Lev 23:24
3:2 [t]Ezr 2:2; Ne 12:1,8; Hag 2:2 [u]Hag 1:1; Zec 6:11 [v]1Ch 3:17 [w]Ex 20:24; Dt 12:5-6
3:3 [x]Ezr 4:4; Da 9:25 [y]Ex 29:39; Nu 28:1-8

LOVE

AN IMPULSE UPWARD

Ezra 3:3

The grand motivator in the face of terror is love. Jewish mothers in the trench executions of Babi Yar, a ravine near Kiev, doubled their bodies around their little ones, trying to protect them from the bullets of the Nazi firing squads. Love raises altars in the presence of its enemies. Heaven opens to those who climb toward it on the stairs of their fears.

3:4 [z]Ex 23:16; Nu 29:12-38; Ne 8:14-18; Zec 14:16-19 in accordance with what is written, they
celebrated the Feast of Tabernacles[z] with
the required number of burnt offerings
prescribed for each day. 5After that, they
presented the regular burnt offerings,
3:5 [a]Nu 28:3, 11,14; Col 2:16 [b]Lev 23:1-44; Nu 29:39 the New Moon[a] sacrifices and the sacrifices for all the appointed sacred feasts
of the LORD,[b] as well as those brought
as freewill offerings to the LORD. 6On
the first day of the seventh month they
began to offer burnt offerings to the
LORD, though the foundation of the
LORD's temple had not yet been laid.

Rebuilding the Temple

7Then they gave money to the masons and carpenters, and gave food and
drink and oil to the people of Sidon and
Tyre, so that they would bring cedar
3:7 [c]1Ch 14:1 [d]Isa 35:2 [e]Ezr 1:2-4; 6:3 logs[c] by sea from Lebanon[d] to Joppa, as
authorized by Cyrus[e] king of Persia.
8In the second month of the second
3:8 [f]Zec 4:9 [g]1Ch 23:24 year after their arrival at the house of
God in Jerusalem, Zerubbabel[f] son of
Shealtiel, Jeshua son of Jozadak and the
rest of their brothers (the priests and
the Levites and all who had returned
from the captivity to Jerusalem) began
the work, appointing Levites twenty[g]
years of age and older to supervise the
building of the house of the LORD.
3:9 [h]Ezr 2:40 9Jeshua[h] and his sons and brothers
and Kadmiel and his sons (descendants
of Hodaviah[a]) and the sons of Henadad and their sons and brothers—all
Levites—joined together in supervising
those working on the house of God.
10When the builders laid[i] the foundation of the temple of the LORD,
the priests in their vestments and with
3:10 [i]Ezr 5:16 [j]Nu 10:2; 1Ch 16:6 [k]1Ch 25:1 trumpets,[j] and the Levites (the sons of
Asaph) with cymbals, took their places
to praise[k] the LORD, as prescribed by
David[l] king of Israel.[m] 11With praise and 3:10 [l]1Ch 6:31 [m]Zec 6:12
thanksgiving they sang to the LORD:

"He is good; 3:11 [n]1Ch 16:34,41; 2Ch 7:3; Ps 107:1; 118:1 [o]Ne 12:24
his love to Israel endures forever."[n]

And all the people gave a great shout[o] of
praise to the LORD, because the foundation of the house of the LORD was
laid. 12But many of the older priests
and Levites and family heads, who had
seen the former temple,[p] wept aloud 3:12 [p]Hag 2:3,9
when they saw the foundation of this
temple being laid, while many others
shouted for joy. 13No one could distin-
guish the sound of the shouts of joy[q] 3:13 [q]Job 8:21; Ps 27:6; Isa 16:9
from the sound of weeping, because the
people made so much noise. And the
sound was heard far away.

Opposition to the Rebuilding

4 When the enemies of Judah and
Benjamin heard that the exiles were
building a temple for the LORD, the
God of Israel, 2they came to Zerubbabel and to the heads of the families and
said, "Let us help you build because,
like you, we seek your God and have
been sacrificing to him since the time
of Esarhaddon[r] king of Assyria, who 4:2 [r]2Ki 17:24; 19:37 [s]2Ki 17:41
brought us here."[s]
3But Zerubbabel, Jeshua and the rest
of the heads of the families of Israel
answered, "You have no part with us
in building a temple to our God. We
alone will build it for the LORD, the
God of Israel, as King Cyrus, the king
of Persia, commanded us."[t] 4:3 [t]Ezr 1:1-4; Ne 2:20
4Then the peoples around them set
out to discourage the people of Judah
and make them afraid to go on
building.[b][u] 5They hired counselors to 4:4 [u]Ezr 3:3
work against them and frustrate their
plans during the entire reign of Cyrus
king of Persia and down to the reign of
Darius king of Persia.

Later Opposition Under Xerxes and Artaxerxes

6At the beginning of the reign of
Xerxes,[c][v] they lodged an accusation 4:6 [v]Est 1:1; Da 9:1 [w]Est 3:13; 9:5
against the people of Judah and Jeru-
salem.[w]
7And in the days of Artaxerxes[x] king 4:7 [x]Ezr 7:1; Ne 2:1
of Persia, Bishlam, Mithredath, Tabeel
and the rest of his associates wrote a let-

[a]9 Hebrew *Yehudah,* probably a variant of *Hodaviah*
[b]4 Or *and troubled them as they built*
[c]6 Hebrew *Ahasuerus,* a variant of Xerxes' Persian name

4:7 [y]2Ki 18:26; Isa 36:11; Da 2:4

ter to Artaxerxes. The letter was written
in Aramaic script and in the Aramaic[y]
language.[a,b]
8Rehum the commanding officer and
Shimshai the secretary wrote a letter
against Jerusalem to Artaxerxes the king
as follows:

9Rehum the commanding officer
and Shimshai the secretary, together with the rest of their as-

4:9 [z]Ezr 5:6; 6:6,13

sociates[z]—the judges and officials
over the men from Tripolis, Persia,[c]
Erech and Babylon, the Elamites of
Susa, 10and the other people whom
the great and honorable Ashurbanipal[d] deported and settled in the
city of Samaria and elsewhere in
Trans-Euphrates.[a]

4:10 [a]ver 17; Ne 4:2

11(This is a copy of the letter they
sent him.)

To King Artaxerxes,

From your servants, the men of
Trans-Euphrates:

12The king should know that the
Jews who came up to us from you
have gone to Jerusalem and are rebuilding that rebellious and wicked city. They are restoring the walls
and repairing the foundations.[b]

4:12 [b]Ezr 5:3,9

13Furthermore, the king should
know that if this city is built and
its walls are restored, no more
taxes, tribute or duty[c] will be paid,
and the royal revenues will suffer.

4:13 [c]Ezr 7:24; Ne 5:4

14Now since we are under obligation to the palace and it is not
proper for us to see the king dishonored, we are sending this message to inform the king, 15so that
a search may be made in the archives[d] of your predecessors. In
these records you will find that
this city is a rebellious city, troublesome to kings and provinces,
a place of rebellion from ancient
times. That is why this city was
destroyed.[e] 16We inform the king
that if this city is built and its walls
are restored, you will be left with
nothing in Trans-Euphrates.[f]

4:15 [d]Ezr 5:17; 6:1 [e]Est 3:8

4:17 [f]ver 10

17The king sent this reply:

To Rehum the commanding officer, Shimshai the secretary and
the rest of their associates living
in Samaria and elsewhere in Trans-Euphrates:

Greetings.

18The letter you sent us has been
read and translated in my presence. 19I issued an order and a
search was made, and it was found
that this city has a long history
of revolt[g] against kings and has
been a place of rebellion and sedition. 20Jerusalem has had powerful kings ruling over the whole of
Trans-Euphrates,[h] and taxes, tribute and duty were paid to them.
21Now issue an order to these men
to stop work, so that this city will
not be rebuilt until I so order. 22Be
careful not to neglect this matter.
Why let this threat grow, to the
detriment of the royal interests?[i]

4:19 [g]2Ki 18:7

4:20 [h]Ge 15:18-21; Ex 23:31; Jos 1:4; 1Ki 4:21; 1Ch 18:3; Ps 72:8-11

4:22 [i]Da 6:2

23As soon as the copy of the letter
of King Artaxerxes was read to Rehum
and Shimshai the secretary and their associates,[j] they went immediately to the
Jews in Jerusalem and compelled them
by force to stop.

4:23 [j]ver 9

24Thus the work on the house of
God in Jerusalem came to a standstill
until the second year of the reign of
Darius[k] king of Persia.

4:24 [k]Ne 2:1-8; Da 9:25; Hag 1:1,15; Zec 1:1

Tattenai's Letter to Darius

5 Now Haggai[l] the prophet and Zechariah[m] the prophet, a descendant of
Iddo, prophesied[n] to the Jews in Judah
and Jerusalem in the name of the God
of Israel, who was over them. 2Then
Zerubbabel[o] son of Shealtiel and Jeshua[p] son of Jozadak set to work[q] to rebuild the house of God in Jerusalem.
And the prophets of God were with
them, helping them.
3At that time Tattenai,[r] governor of
Trans-Euphrates, and Shethar-Bozenai[s]
and their associates went to them and
asked, "Who authorized you to rebuild
this temple and restore this structure?"[t]
4They also asked, "What are the names
of the men constructing this building?"[e]

5:1 [l]Ezr 6:14; Hag 1:1,3,12; 2:1,10,20 [m]Zec 1:1; 7:1 [n]Hag 1:14-2:9; Zec 4:9-10; 8:9

5:2 [o]1Ch 3:19; Hag 1:14; 2:21; Zec 4:6-10 [p]Ezr 2:2; 3:2 [q]ver 8; Hag 2:2-5

5:3 [r]Ezr 6:6 [s]Ezr 6:6 [t]ver 9; Ezr 1:3; 4:12

[a]7 Or *written in Aramaic and translated* [b]7 The text of Ezra 4:8—6:18 is in Aramaic. [c]9 Or *officials, magistrates and governors over the men from* [d]10 Aramaic *Osnappar,* a variant of *Ashurbanipal* [e]4 See Septuagint; Aramaic [4]*We told them the names of the men constructing this building.*

5:5 [u]2Ki 25:28; Ezr 7:6,9,28; 8:18,22,31; Ne 2:8,18; Ps 33:18; Isa 66:14

5But the eye of their God[u] was watching over the elders of the Jews, and they were not stopped until a report could go to Darius and his written reply be received.

6This is a copy of the letter that Tattenai, governor of Trans-Euphrates, and Shethar-Bozenai and their associates, the officials of Trans-Euphrates, sent to King Darius. 7The report they sent him read as follows:

To King Darius:

Cordial greetings.

8The king should know that we went to the district of Judah, to the temple of the great God. The people are building it with large stones and placing the timbers in the

5:8 [v]ver 2

walls. The work[v] is being carried on with diligence and is making rapid progress under their direction.

9We questioned the elders and asked them, "Who authorized you to rebuild this temple and restore

5:9 [w]Ezr 4:12

this structure?"[w] 10We also asked them their names, so that we could write down the names of their leaders for your information.

11This is the answer they gave us:

"We are the servants of the God of heaven and earth, and we are

5:11 [x]1Ki 6:1; 2Ch 3:1-2

rebuilding the temple[x] that was built many years ago, one that a great king of Israel built and finished. 12But because our fathers

5:12 [y]2Ch 36:16 [z]Dt 21:10; 28:36; 2Ki 24:1; 25:8,9,11; Jer 1:3

angered[y] the God of heaven, he handed them over to Nebuchadnezzar the Chaldean, king of Babylon, who destroyed this temple and deported the people to Babylon.[z]

13"However, in the first year of Cyrus king of Babylon, King Cyrus issued a decree[a] to rebuild this house of God. 14He even removed from the temple[a] of Babylon the gold and silver articles of the house of God, which Nebuchadnezzar had taken from the temple in Jerusalem and brought to the temple[a] in Babylon.[b]

5:13 [a]Ezr 1:1

5:14 [b]Ezr 1:7; 6:5; Da 5:2 [c]1Ch 3:18

"Then King Cyrus gave them to a man named Sheshbazzar,[c] whom he had appointed governor, 15and he told him, 'Take these articles and go and deposit them in the temple in Jerusalem. And rebuild the house of God[d] on its site.' 16So this Sheshbazzar came and laid the foundations of the house of God in Jerusalem. From that day to the present it has been under construction but is not yet finished."

5:16 [d]Ezr 3:10; 6:15

17Now if it pleases the king, let a search be made in the royal archives[e] of Babylon to see if King Cyrus did in fact issue a decree to rebuild this house of God in Jerusalem. Then let the king send us his decision in this matter.

5:17 [e]Ezr 4:15; 6:1,2

The Decree of Darius

6 King Darius then issued an order, and they searched in the archives[f] stored in the treasury at Babylon. 2A scroll was found in the citadel of Ecbatana in the province of Media, and this was written on it:

6:1 [f]Ezr 4:15; 5:17

Memorandum:

3In the first year of King Cyrus, the king issued a decree concerning the temple of God in Jerusalem:

Let the temple be rebuilt as a place to present sacrifices, and let its foundations be laid.[g] It is to be ninety feet[b] high and ninety feet wide, 4with three courses[h] of large stones and one of timbers. The costs are to be paid by the royal treasury.[i] 5Also, the gold[j] and silver articles of the house of God, which Nebuchadnezzar took from the temple in Jerusalem and brought to Babylon, are to be returned to their places in the temple in Jerusalem; they are to be deposited in the house of God.[k]

6:3 [g]Ezr 3:10; Hag 2:3

6:4 [h]1Ki 6:36 [i]ver 8; Ezr 7:20

6:5 [j]1Ch 29:2 [k]Ezr 1:7; 5:14

6Now then, Tattenai,[l] governor of Trans-Euphrates, and Shethar-Bozenai[m] and you, their fellow officials of that province, stay away from there. 7Do not interfere with the work on this temple of God. Let the governor of the Jews and

6:6 [l]Ezr 5:3 [m]Ezr 5:3

[a]*14* Or *palace* [b]*3* Aramaic *sixty cubits* (about 27 meters)

the Jewish elders rebuild this house
of God on its site.
8 Moreover, I hereby decree what
you are to do for these elders of
the Jews in the construction of this
house of God:
The expenses of these men are
to be fully paid out of the royal
treasury,[n] from the revenues[o] of
Trans-Euphrates, so that the work
will not stop. 9 Whatever is need-

6:8 [n]ver 4 [o]1Sa 9:20

DAY 4 FOUR

▸ JOY AND MY SERVICE TO OTHERS

Ezra 6:16

The people, former exiles, celebrated the dedication of the temple with joy. They had reason to be joyful. They had witnessed the miraculous workings of God to bring them back to their land and restore to them their house of worship. They joyfully celebrated God's power in a simple recipe that woke the world around them to joy. These are the kinds of things that can happen when God's people begin to witness God working in the world around them. And joy is always noticed by the world.

This higher reality that brings such joy often hides in simple things near at hand. Martin Luther believed this higher reality lived in much lower verities.

> **If we had eyes and ears, we would be able to see and hear what the wheat says to us: "Rejoice in God, eat and drink, use me and serve your neighbors. Soon I will fill the barns." If I were not deaf, I would hear the cows say: "Be glad, we bring you butter and cheese. Eat and drink and give to others." So the hens say, "We lay eggs for you." And the birds, "Be joyful, we are hatching chicks" . . . So speak all the animals to us, and everyone should say, "I will use what God has given, and I will give to others."**

Joy is easy to come by. We have but to open our eyes and ears, and it will overwhelm us. But it will never be more authentic than after we have served someone else and given all the credit to Christ.

To begin a study on the topic of Joy, Focusing on a Higher Reality, turn to the home page on page 413.

ed—young bulls, rams, male lambs
for burnt offerings[p] to the God of
heaven, and wheat, salt, wine and
oil, as requested by the priests in Jerusalem—must be given them daily without fail, 10 so that they may
offer sacrifices pleasing to the God
of heaven and pray for the well-
being of the king and his sons.[q]
11 Furthermore, I decree that if
anyone changes this edict, a beam
is to be pulled from his house and
he is to be lifted up and impaled[r]
on it. And for this crime his house
is to be made a pile of rubble.[s]
12 May God, who has caused his
Name to dwell there,[t] overthrow
any king or people who lifts a hand
to change this decree or to destroy
this temple in Jerusalem.
I Darius[u] have decreed it. Let it
be carried out with diligence.

Completion and Dedication of the Temple

13 Then, because of the decree King
Darius had sent, Tattenai, governor of
Trans-Euphrates, and Shethar-Bozenai
and their associates[v] carried it out with
diligence. 14 So the elders of the Jews
continued to build and prosper under
the preaching[w] of Haggai the prophet
and Zechariah, a descendant of Iddo.
They finished building the temple according to the command of the God
of Israel and the decrees of Cyrus,[x] Darius[y] and Artaxerxes,[z] kings of Persia.
15 The temple was completed on the
third day of the month Adar, in the
sixth year of the reign of King Darius.[a]
16 Then the people of Israel—the
priests, the Levites and the rest of the
exiles—celebrated the dedication[b] of
the house of God with joy. 17 For the
dedication of this house of God they
offered[c] a hundred bulls, two hundred
rams, four hundred male lambs and, as
a sin offering for all Israel, twelve male
goats, one for each of the tribes of Israel. 18 And they installed the priests in
their divisions[d] and the Levites in their
groups[e] for the service of God at Jerusalem, according to what is written in
the Book of Moses.[f]

The Passover

19 On the fourteenth day of the first
month, the exiles celebrated the Passover.[g]

6:9 [p]Lev 1:3,10
6:10 [q]Ezr 7:23; 1Ti 2:1-2
6:11 [r]Dt 21:22-23; Est 2:23; 5:14; 9:14 [s]Ezr 7:26; Da 2:5; 3:29
6:12 [t]Ex 20:24; Dt 12:5; 1Ki 9:3; 2Ch 6:2 [u]ver 14
6:13 [v]Ezr 4:9
6:14 [w]Ezr 5:1 [x]Ezr 1:1-4 [y]ver 12 [z]Ezr 7:1; Ne 2:1
6:15 [a]Zec 1:1; 4:9
6:16 [b]1Ki 8:63; 2Ch 7:5
6:17 [c]2Sa 6:13; 2Ch 29:21; 30:24; Ezr 8:35
6:18 [d]1Ch 23:6; 2Ch 35:4; Lk 1:5 [e]1Ch 24:1 [f]Nu 3:6-9; 8:9-11; 18:1-32
6:19 [g]Ex 12:11; Nu 28:16

20 The priests and Levites had purified
themselves and were all ceremonially
6:20 [h]2Ch 30:15, 17; 35:11
clean. The Levites slaughtered[h] the Passover lamb for all the exiles, for their
brothers the priests and for themselves.
21 So the Israelites who had returned
from the exile ate it, together with all
6:21 [i]Ezr 9:1; Ne 9:2 [j]Dt 18:9; Ezr 9:11; Eze 36:25 [k]1Ch 22:19; Ps 14:2
who had separated themselves[i] from
the unclean practices[j] of their Gentile
neighbors in order to seek the LORD,[k]
the God of Israel. 22 For seven days they
celebrated with joy the Feast of Un-
6:22 [l]Ex 12:17 [m]Ezr 1:1
leavened Bread,[l] because the LORD had
filled them with joy by changing the attitude[m] of the king of Assyria, so that
he assisted them in the work on the
house of God, the God of Israel.

Ezra Comes to Jerusalem

7 After these things, during the reign
7:1 [n]Ezr 4:7; 6:14; Ne 2:1 [o]2Ki 22:4
of Artaxerxes[n] king of Persia, Ezra
son of Seraiah, the son of Azariah, the
son of Hilkiah,[o] 2 the son of Shallum,
7:2 [p]1Ki 1:8; 1Ch 6:8 [q]Ne 11:11
the son of Zadok,[p] the son of Ahitub,[q]
3 the son of Amariah, the son of Azariah, the son of Meraioth, 4 the son of
Zerahiah, the son of Uzzi, the son of
Bukki, 5 the son of Abishua, the son
of Phinehas, the son of Eleazar, the son
of Aaron the chief priest— 6 this Ezra[r]
7:6 [r]Ne 12:36 [s]Ezr 5:5; Isa 41:20
came up from Babylon. He was a teacher well versed in the Law of Moses,
which the LORD, the God of Israel,
had given. The king had granted him
everything he asked, for the hand of
the LORD his God was on him.[s] 7 Some
of the Israelites, including priests, Levites, singers, gatekeepers and temple
servants, also came up to Jerusalem in
7:7 [t]Ezr 8:1
the seventh year of King Artaxerxes.[t]
8 Ezra arrived in Jerusalem in the fifth
month of the seventh year of the king.
9 He had begun his journey from Babylon on the first day of the first month,
and he arrived in Jerusalem on the first
day of the fifth month, for the gra-
7:9 [u]ver 6
cious hand of his God was on him.[u]
10 For Ezra had devoted himself to the
study and observance of the Law of the
7:10 [v]ver 25; Dt 33:10; Ne 8:1-8
LORD, and to teaching[v] its decrees and
laws in Israel.

King Artaxerxes' Letter to Ezra

11 This is a copy of the letter King
Artaxerxes had given to Ezra the priest
and teacher, a man learned in matters
concerning the commands and decrees
of the LORD for Israel:

12[a] Artaxerxes, king of kings,[w] 7:12 [w]Eze 26:7; Da 2:37

To Ezra the priest, a teacher of the
Law of the God of heaven:

Greetings.

13 Now I decree that any of the
Israelites in my kingdom, including priests and Levites, who wish
to go to Jerusalem with you, may
go. 14 You are sent by the king and
his seven advisers[x] to inquire about 7:14 [x]Est 1:14
Judah and Jerusalem with regard
to the Law of your God, which
is in your hand. 15 Moreover, you
are to take with you the silver and
gold that the king and his advisers
have freely given[y] to the God of 7:15 [y]1Ch 29:6
Israel, whose dwelling[z] is in Jeru- [z]1Ch 29:6,9; 2Ch 6:2
salem, 16 together with all the silver
and gold[a] you may obtain from 7:16 [a]Ezr 8:25
the province of Babylon, as well [b]Zec 6:10
as the freewill offerings of the people and priests for the temple of
their God in Jerusalem.[b] 17 With
this money be sure to buy bulls,
rams and male lambs,[c] together 7:17 [c]2Ki 3:4
with their grain offerings and drink [d]Nu 15:5-12
offerings,[d] and sacrifice[e] them on [e]Dt 12:5-11
the altar of the temple of your God
in Jerusalem.

LOVE

A PAGAN BLESSING

Ezra 7:13

In loving what God loves, pagans soon
love God.
In loving God himself,
They offer benedictions to those
They once thought were their foes.

18 You and your brother Jews
may then do whatever seems best
with the rest of the silver and gold,
in accordance with the will of your
God. 19 Deliver[f] to the God of Je- 7:19 [f]Ezr 5:14; Jer 27:22
rusalem all the articles entrusted
to you for worship in the temple
of your God. 20 And anything else
needed for the temple of your God
that you may have occasion to supply, you may provide from the royal treasury.[g] 7:20 [g]Ezr 6:4
21 Now I, King Artaxerxes, order all the treasurers of Trans-

[a]*12* The text of Ezra 7:12-26 is in Aramaic.

Euphrates to provide with diligence
whatever Ezra the priest, a teacher
of the Law of the God of heaven,
may ask of you— 22 up to a hundred talents[a] of silver, a hundred
cors[b] of wheat, a hundred baths[c] of
wine, a hundred baths[c] of olive oil,
and salt without limit. 23 Whatever
the God of heaven has prescribed,
let it be done with diligence for
the temple of the God of heaven.
Why should there be wrath against
the realm of the king and of his
7:23 [h]Ezr 6:10 sons?[h] 24 You are also to know that
you have no authority to impose
taxes, tribute or duty[i] on any of
the priests, Levites, singers, gatekeepers, temple servants or other
7:24 [i]Ezr 4:13 workers at this house of God.[j]
[j]Ezr 8:36 25 And you, Ezra, in accordance
with the wisdom of your God,
7:25 [k]Ex 18:21,26; which you possess, appoint[k] mag-
Dt 16:18 istrates and judges to administer
[l]ver 10; justice to all the people of Trans-
Lev 10:11 Euphrates—all who know the laws
of your God. And you are to
teach[l] any who do not know them.
26 Whoever does not obey the law
of your God and the law of the
king must surely be punished by
death, banishment, confiscation of
7:26 [m]Ezr 6:11 property, or imprisonment.[m]

27 Praise be to the LORD, the God
of our fathers, who has put it into the
7:27 [n]Ezr 1:1; 6:22 king's heart[n] to bring honor[o] to the
[o]1Ch 29:12 house of the LORD in Jerusalem in this
way 28 and who has extended his good
7:28 [p]2Ki 25:28 favor[p] to me before the king and his
[q]Ezr 5:5; 9:9 advisers and all the king's powerful officials. Because the hand of the LORD
my God was on me,[q] I took courage
and gathered leading men from Israel
to go up with me.

List of the Family Heads Returning With Ezra

8 These are the family heads and
those registered with them who
came up with me from Babylon during
8:1 [r]Ezr 7:7 the reign of King Artaxerxes:[r]

2 of the descendants of Phinehas,
Gershom;
of the descendants of Ithamar,
Daniel;
of the descendants of David, Hat-
8:3 [s]1Ch 3:22 tush 3 of the descendants of Shecaniah;[s]
of the descendants of Parosh,[t] 8:3 [t]Ezr 2:3
Zechariah, and with him were
registered 150 men;
4 of the descendants of Pahath-
Moab,[u] Eliehoenai son of Zera- 8:4 [u]Ezr 2:6
hiah, and with him 200 men;
5 of the descendants of Zattu,[d] Shecaniah son of Jahaziel, and with
him 300 men;
6 of the descendants of Adin,[v] Ebed 8:6 [v]Ezr 2:15;
son of Jonathan, and with him Ne 7:20;
50 men; 10:16
7 of the descendants of Elam, Jeshaiah son of Athaliah, and with
him 70 men;
8 of the descendants of Shephatiah,
Zebadiah son of Michael, and
with him 80 men;
9 of the descendants of Joab, Obadiah son of Jehiel, and with him
218 men;
10 of the descendants of Bani,[e] Shelomith son of Josiphiah, and with
him 160 men;
11 of the descendants of Bebai, Zechariah son of Bebai, and with
him 28 men;
12 of the descendants of Azgad, Johanan son of Hakkatan, and with
him 110 men;
13 of the descendants of Adonikam,[w] 8:13 [w]Ezr 2:13
the last ones, whose names were
Eliphelet, Jeuel and Shemaiah,
and with them 60 men;
14 of the descendants of Bigvai, Uthai
and Zaccur, and with them 70
men.

The Return to Jerusalem

15 I assembled them at the canal that
flows toward Ahava,[x] and we camped 8:15 [x]ver 21,31
there three days. When I checked among [y]Ezr 2:40; 7:7
the people and the priests, I found no
Levites[y] there. 16 So I summoned Eliezer, Ariel, Shemaiah, Elnathan, Jarib,
Elnathan, Nathan, Zechariah and Meshullam, who were leaders, and Joiarib
and Elnathan, who were men of learning, 17 and I sent them to Iddo, the leader in Casiphia. I told them what to say
to Iddo and his kinsmen, the temple

[a] *22* That is, about 3 3/4 tons (about 3.4 metric tons) [b] *22* That is, probably about 600 bushels (about 22 kiloliters) [c] *22* That is, probably about 600 gallons (about 2.2 kiloliters) [d] *5* Some Septuagint manuscripts (also 1 Esdras 8:32); Hebrew does not have *Zattu.* [e] *10* Some Septuagint manuscripts (also 1 Esdras 8:36); Hebrew does not have *Bani.*

8:17 servants[z] in Casiphia, so that they might
[z]Ezr 2:43 bring attendants to us[a] for the house of
8:18 our God. 18Because the gracious hand
[a]Ezr 5:5 of our God was on us, they brought
us Sherebiah, a capable man, from the
descendants of Mahli son of Levi, the
son of Israel, and Sherebiah's sons and
brothers, 18 men; 19and Hashabiah, together with Jeshaiah from the descendants of Merari, and his brothers and
nephews, 20 men. 20They also brought
8:20 220 of the temple servants[b]—a body
[b]1Ch 9:2; that David and the officials had estab-
Ezr 2:43 lished to assist the Levites. All were registered by name.
8:21 [c]ver 15; 21There, by the Ahava Canal,[c] I pro-
2Ch 20:3 claimed a fast, so that we might humble
[d]Ps 5:8; 107:7 ourselves before our God and ask him
for a safe journey[d] for us and our chil-
8:22 dren, with all our possessions. 22I was
[e]Ne 2:9; ashamed to ask the king for soldiers[e]
Ezr 7:6,9,28 [f]Ezr 5:5 and horsemen to protect us from en-
[g]Dt 31:17; emies on the road, because we had told
2Ch 15:2 the king, "The gracious hand of our
God is on everyone[f] who looks to him,
but his great anger is against all who
8:23 forsake him.[g]" 23So we fasted[h] and pe-
[h]2Ch 20:3; titioned our God about this, and he an-
33:13 swered our prayer.
24Then I set apart twelve of the lead-
8:24 ing priests, together with Sherebiah,[i]
[i]ver 18 Hashabiah and ten of their brothers,
8:25 [j]ver 33; 25and I weighed out[j] to them the offer-
Ezr 7:15,16 ing of silver and gold and the articles
that the king, his advisers, his officials
and all Israel present there had donated
for the house of our God. 26I weighed
out to them 650 talents[a] of silver, silver
articles weighing 100 talents,[b] 100 talents[b] of gold, 27 20 bowls of gold valued
at 1,000 darics,[c] and two fine articles of
polished bronze, as precious as gold.
28I said to them, "You as well as these
8:28 articles are consecrated to the LORD.[k]
[k]Lev 21:6; The silver and gold are a freewill offer-
22:2-3 ing to the LORD, the God of your fathers. 29Guard them carefully until you
weigh them out in the chambers of the
house of the LORD in Jerusalem before
the leading priests and the Levites and
the family heads of Israel." 30Then the
priests and Levites received the silver
and gold and sacred articles that had
been weighed out to be taken to the
house of our God in Jerusalem.
31On the twelfth day of the first
8:31 month we set out from the Ahava Ca-
[l]ver 15 nal[l] to go to Jerusalem. The hand of

our God was on us, and he protected
us from enemies and bandits along the
way. 32So we arrived in Jerusalem, where 8:32
we rested three days.[m] [m]Ge 40:13;
33On the fourth day, in the house Ne 2:11
of our God, we weighed out the silver
and gold and the sacred articles into
the hands of Meremoth[n] son of Uriah, 8:33 [n]Ne 3:4,21
the priest. Eleazar son of Phinehas was [o]Ne 3:24
with him, and so were the Levites Jozabad son of Jeshua and Noadiah son
of Binnui.[o] 34Everything was accounted
for by number and weight, and the entire weight was recorded at that time.
35Then the exiles who had returned
from captivity sacrificed burnt offerings to the God of Israel: twelve bulls
for all Israel, ninety-six rams, seventy-
seven male lambs and, as a sin offer-
ing, twelve male goats.[p] All this was 8:35 [p]2Ch 29:21;
a burnt offering to the LORD. 36They Ezr 6:17
also delivered the king's orders[q] to the 8:36
royal satraps and to the governors of [q]Ezr 7:21-24
Trans-Euphrates, who then gave assis- [r]Est 9:3
tance to the people and to the house
of God.[r]

JOY

CHRIST: A SINGER'S MELODY

Ezra 8:35

The exiles had come home. Their years of pain were over. They sacrificed in joy. They had found the ecstasy of Matthew Simpson: "Rejoice in God! Dry up those tears! Cast away that downcast look! Child of Christ, you are an heir to Glory!"

Ezra's Prayer About Intermarriage

9 After these things had been done, the
leaders came to me and said, "The
people of Israel, including the priests
and the Levites, have not kept themselves separate[s] from the neighboring 9:1
peoples with their detestable practices, [s]Ezr 6:21; Ne 9:2
like those of the Canaanites, Hittites, [t]Ge 19:38
Perizzites, Jebusites, Ammonites,[t] Mo- [u]Ex 13:5
abites, Egyptians and Amorites.[u] 2They
have taken some of their daughters[v] as
wives for themselves and their sons, and 9:2 [v]Ex 34:16
have mingled the holy race[w] with the [w]Ex 22:31

[a]26 That is, about 25 tons (about 22 metric tons)
[b]26 That is, about 3 3/4 tons (about 3.4 metric tons) [c]27 That is, about 19 pounds (about 8.5 kilograms)

peoples around them. And the leaders
and officials have led the way in this
9:2 [x]Ezr 10:2 unfaithfulness."[x]
3When I heard this, I tore my tunic
and cloak, pulled hair from my head
and beard and sat down appalled. 4Then
9:4 [y]Ezr 10:3 everyone who trembled[y] at the words of
the God of Israel gathered around me
because of this unfaithfulness of the exiles. And I sat there appalled until the
evening sacrifice.
9:5 [z]Ex 29:41 5Then, at the evening sacrifice,[z] I rose
from my self-abasement, with my tunic
and cloak torn, and fell on my knees
with my hands spread out to the LORD
my God 6and prayed:

"O my God, I am too ashamed
and disgraced to lift up my face to
you, my God, because our sins are
higher than our heads and our guilt
9:6 [a]2Ch 28:9; Job 42:6; Ps 38:4; Rev 18:5 has reached to the heavens.[a] 7From
the days of our forefathers[b] until
now, our guilt has been great. Because of our sins, we and our kings
9:7 [b]2Ch 29:6 [c]Eze 21:1-32 [d]Dt 28:64 [e]Dt 28:37 and our priests have been subjected
to the sword[c] and captivity,[d] to pil-
lage and humiliation[e] at the hand
of foreign kings, as it is today.
8"But now, for a brief moment,
the LORD our God has been gra-
9:8 [f]Ps 25:16; Isa 33:2 [g]Ge 45:7 [h]Ecc 12:11; Isa 22:23 [i]Ps 13:3 cious[f] in leaving us a remnant[g] and
giving us a firm place[h] in his sanc-
tuary, and so our God gives light
to our eyes[i] and a little relief in our
bondage. 9Though we are slaves,[j]
9:9 [j]Ex 1:14; Ne 9:36 [k]Ezr 7:28 [l]Ps 69:35; Isa 43:1; Jer 32:44 our God has not deserted us in our
bondage. He has shown us kind-
ness[k] in the sight of the kings of
Persia: He has granted us new life to
rebuild the house of our God and
repair its ruins,[l] and he has given us
a wall of protection in Judah and
Jerusalem.
10"But now, O our God, what
can we say after this? For we have
9:10 [m]Dt 11:8; Isa 1:19-20 disregarded the commands[m] 11you
gave through your servants the
prophets when you said: 'The land
you are entering to possess is a land
9:11 [n]Lev 18:25-28 [o]Dt 9:4 polluted[n] by the corruption of its
peoples. By their detestable prac-
tices[o] they have filled it with their
impurity from one end to the other. 12Therefore, do not give your
daughters in marriage to their sons
or take their daughters for your
sons. Do not seek a treaty of friend-
ship with them[p] at any time, that 9:12 [p]Ex 34:15; Dt 7:3; 23:6
you may be strong and eat the
good things of the land and leave
it to your children as an everlasting inheritance.'
13"What has happened to us is
a result of our evil deeds and our
great guilt, and yet, our God, you
have punished us less than our
sins have deserved[q] and have given 9:13 [q]Job 11:6; Ps 103:10
us a remnant like this. 14Shall we
again break your commands and
intermarry[r] with the peoples who 9:14 [r]Ne 13:27 [s]Dt 9:8 [t]Dt 9:14
commit such detestable practices?
Would you not be angry enough
with us to destroy us,[s] leaving us no
remnant[t] or survivor? 15O LORD, 9:15 [u]Ge 18:25; Ps 51:4; Jer 12:1; Da 9:7 [v]Ne 9:33; Ps 130:3; Mal 3:2 [w]1Ki 8:47
God of Israel, you are righteous![u]
We are left this day as a remnant.
Here we are before you in our guilt,
though because of it not one of us
can stand[v] in your presence.[w]"

PEACE

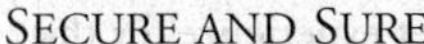

SECURE AND SURE

Ezra 10:1

Peace does not only result from people offering us encouragement. Peace results from people being willing to weep with us. Empathy is the music of the church—the confirmation that we are not alone in the dark passages of life.

The People's Confession of Sin

10 While Ezra was praying and 10:1 [x]2Ch 20:9; Da 9:20
confessing,[x] weeping and
throwing himself down before the
house of God, a large crowd of Israelites—men, women and children—
gathered around him. They too wept
bitterly. 2Then Shecaniah son of Jehiel,
one of the descendants of Elam, said to
Ezra, "We have been unfaithful[y] to our 10:2 [y]Ezr 9:2; Ne 13:27 [z]Dt 30:8-10
God by marrying foreign women from
the peoples around us. But in spite of
this, there is still hope for Israel.[z] 3Now 10:3 [a]2Ch 34:31 [b]Ex 34:16; Dt 7:2-3; Ezr 9:4
let us make a covenant[a] before our God
to send away[b] all these women and
their children, in accordance with the
counsel of my lord and of those who
fear the commands of our God. Let it
be done according to the Law. 4Rise
up; this matter is in your hands. We
will support you, so take courage and
do it."
5So Ezra rose up and put the leading

priests and Levites and all Israel under
10:5 [c]Ne 5:12; 13:25 oath[c] to do what had been suggested.
And they took the oath. [6]Then Ezra
withdrew from before the house of God
and went to the room of Jehohanan son
of Eliashib. While he was there, he ate
10:6 [d]Ex 34:28; Dt 9:18 no food and drank no water,[d] because
he continued to mourn over the unfaithfulness of the exiles.

[7]A proclamation was then issued
throughout Judah and Jerusalem for
all the exiles to assemble in Jerusalem.
[8]Anyone who failed to appear within
three days would forfeit all his property,
in accordance with the decision of the
officials and elders, and would himself
be expelled from the assembly of the
exiles.

[9]Within the three days, all the men
of Judah and Benjamin[e] had gathered 10:9 [e]Ezr 1:5
in Jerusalem. And on the twentieth day

EZRA

Goodness, the Product of the Confessional (9:5–15)

After the fall of Babylon to Persia in 539 B.C., the Jewish exiles who had been captives in Babylon were allowed to return to their land. Zerubbabel had led the first wave of exiles, and he led the effort to rebuild the temple in Jerusalem. Restoring the ruins of Solomon's temple was a bittersweet experience for the people. "Many of the older priests and Levites and family heads, who had seen the former temple, wept aloud when they saw the foundation of this temple being laid, while many others shouted for joy" (Ezra 3:12).

Eighty years after the beginning of the building of Zerubbabel's temple, Ezra also returned to his homeland to begin a program of religious education. But as Ezra began teaching the people the laws of the Lord, he saw the fragmentation of the nation due to various kinds of sins and indulgences. Notably, many of the men, including some of the priests and Levites, had married foreign women, who were leading their families away from the true faith. Israel's earlier acceptance of interfaith marriages had continually led the nation into the worship of foreign gods. For example, King Solomon and King Ahab had corrupted their reputations with idolatrous queens who had led their nations into impure worship.

Ezra believed that only repentance could return the nation to a state of godly morality, the only kind of goodness he could accept. Struck by the national immorality, he stood at the time of evening sacrifice and cried:

> **O my God, I am too ashamed and disgraced to lift up my face to you, my God, because our sins are higher than our heads and our guilt has reached to the heavens. From the days of our forefathers until now, our guilt has been great. Because of our sins, we and our kings and our priests have been subjected to the sword and captivity, to pillage and humiliation at the hand of foreign kings, as it is today . . . But now, O our God, what can we say after this? For we have disregarded the commands you gave through your servants the prophets . . . O LORD, God of Israel, you are righteous! We are left this day as a remnant. Here we are before you in our guilt, though because of it not one of us can stand in your presence. (9:6–7,10–11,15)**

This plea for renewal, for a return to goodness, was sponsored by a truly good man and resulted in a good outcome. "While Ezra was praying and confessing, weeping and throwing himself down before the house of God, a large crowd of Israelites—men, women and children—gathered around him. They too wept bitterly" (10:1).

When good people cry out to be better, goodness is established and the kingdom of God is ushered in. Goodness springs from a longing in the soul to bring pleasure to God by our behavior. Goodness allows people to look each other directly in the eye when doing business. Goodness is the highest definition of righteousness. Goodness is the porch of holiness.

of the ninth month, all the people were
sitting in the square before the house
of God, greatly distressed by the occasion and because of the rain. 10Then
Ezra the priest stood up and said to
them, "You have been unfaithful; you
have married foreign women, adding to
Israel's guilt. 11Now make confession to
the LORD, the God of your fathers, and
do his will. Separate yourselves from
the peoples around you and from your
10:11 [f]ver 3; Dt 24:1; Ne 9:2; Mal 2:10-16 foreign wives."[f]
12The whole assembly responded
with a loud voice:[g] "You are right! We
must do as you say. 13But there are
10:12 [g]Jos 6:5 many people here and it is the rainy
season; so we cannot stand outside. Besides, this matter cannot be taken care
of in a day or two, because we have
sinned greatly in this thing. 14Let our
officials act for the whole assembly.
Then let everyone in our towns who has
married a foreign woman come at a set
10:14 [h]Dt 16:18 [i]Nu 25:4; 2Ch 29:10; 30:8 time, along with the elders and judges[h]
of each town, until the fierce anger[i] of
our God in this matter is turned away
from us." 15Only Jonathan son of Asahel and Jahzeiah son of Tikvah, sup-
10:15 [j]Ne 11:16 ported by Meshullam and Shabbethai[j]
the Levite, opposed this.
16So the exiles did as was proposed.
Ezra the priest selected men who were
family heads, one from each family division, and all of them designated by
name. On the first day of the tenth
month they sat down to investigate the
cases, 17and by the first day of the first
month they finished dealing with all the
men who had married foreign women.

Those Guilty of Intermarriage

18Among the descendants of the
priests, the following had mar-
10:18 [k]Jdg 3:6 [l]Ezr 2:2 ried foreign women:[k]

From the descendants of Jeshua[l]
son of Jozadak, and his brothers: Maaseiah, Eliezer, Jarib and
Gedaliah. 19(They all gave their
10:19 [m]2Ki 10:15 [n]Lev 5:15; 6:6 hands[m] in pledge to put away
their wives, and for their guilt
they each presented a ram from
10:20 [o]1Ch 24:14 the flock as a guilt offering.)[n]
20From the descendants of Immer:[o]
Hanani and Zebadiah.
10:21 [p]1Ch 24:8 21From the descendants of Harim:[p]
Maaseiah, Elijah, Shemaiah, Je-
hiel and Uzziah.

22From the descendants of Pashhur:[q] 10:22 [q]1Ch 9:12
Elioenai, Maaseiah, Ishmael, Nethanel, Jozabad and Elasah.

23Among the Levites:[r] 10:23 [r]Ne 8:7; 9:4

Jozabad, Shimei, Kelaiah (that
is, Kelita), Pethahiah, Judah and
Eliezer.
24From the singers:
Eliashib.[s] 10:24 [s]Ne 3:1; 12:10; 13:7,28
From the gatekeepers:
Shallum, Telem and Uri.

25And among the other Israelites:

From the descendants of Parosh:[t] 10:25 [t]Ezr 2:3
Ramiah, Izziah, Malkijah, Mija-
min, Eleazar, Malkijah and Be-
naiah.
26From the descendants of Elam:[u] 10:26 [u]ver 2
Mattaniah, Zechariah, Jehiel,
Abdi, Jeremoth and Elijah.
27From the descendants of Zattu:
Elioenai, Eliashib, Mattaniah,
Jeremoth, Zabad and Aziza.
28From the descendants of Bebai:
Jehohanan, Hananiah, Zabbai
and Athlai.
29From the descendants of Bani:
Meshullam, Malluch, Adaiah,
Jashub, Sheal and Jeremoth.
30From the descendants of Pahath-
Moab:
Adna, Kelal, Benaiah, Maaseiah,
Mattaniah, Bezalel, Binnui and
Manasseh.
31From the descendants of Harim:
Eliezer, Ishijah, Malkijah, She-
maiah, Shimeon, 32Benjamin,
Malluch and Shemariah.
33From the descendants of Ha-
shum:
Mattenai, Mattattah, Zabad,
Eliphelet, Jeremai, Manasseh
and Shimei.
34From the descendants of Bani:
Maadai, Amram, Uel, 35Bena-
iah, Bedeiah, Keluhi, 36Vaniah,
Meremoth, Eliashib, 37Mattani-
ah, Mattenai and Jaasu.
38From the descendants of Binnui:[a]
Shimei, 39Shelemiah, Nathan,
Adaiah, 40Macnadebai, Shashai,
Sharai, 41Azarel, Shelemiah, Shem-

[a] *37,38* See Septuagint (also 1 Esdras 9:34); Hebrew *Jaasu 38and Bani and Binnui,*

ariah, [42]Shallum, Amariah and Joseph.

[43]From the descendants of Nebo:
Jeiel, Mattithiah, Zabad, Zebina, Jaddai, Joel and Benaiah.

[44]All these had married foreign women, and some of them had children by these wives.[a]

[a]44 Or *and they sent them away with their children*

NEHEMIAH

AUTHORSHIP AND DATE

Nehemiah probably wrote the book that bears his name, but many suggest that Ezra may have written part of it and edited most of it.

Between 445 B.C. and 430 B.C.

KEY THEMES

The Jewish exiles first began to return to Jerusalem to rebuild the city-state in 538 B.C. This first return was led by Zerubbabel. A second wave of exiles returned under Ezra's leadership in 458 B.C. Nehemiah led the third group in 445 B.C. The book of Nehemiah is easily divided into two sections. The first section (1:1—7:73) deals with the rebuilding of the wall. The second section (8:1—13:31) deals with reforming the people and getting the theology of post-exilic Judaism back into concert with the general theology of the nation. Nehemiah was a great person of motivation and leadership; therefore, the themes that dominate the book are leadership, vision, prayer and a spirit of revival.

FRUIT OF THE SPIRIT IN NEHEMIAH

Faithfulness: The book opens with Nehemiah in deep meditation concerning the exiles who had previously returned to Jerusalem. The wall was broken and unrepaired. The mood was dour. Nehemiah confessed for the nation and apologized to God for the national state of disobedience. God then called Nehemiah, who was the royal cupbearer to Artaxerxes, to return to Jerusalem and rebuild the wall. Nehemiah responded.

Nehemiah's life is not just a study in faithfulness; it is also a study in leadership. When Tobiah the Ammonite criticized Nehemiah's attempt to rebuild the wall by saying that if a fox jumped upon it, the wall would fall to pieces (see 4:3), Nehemiah continued to be faithful to God, inspiring the workers to carry on. Ultimately, Nehemiah's call to faithfulness brought about national repentance and revival. Nehemiah confessed, perhaps as a tribute to his own faithfulness, "We will not neglect the house of our God" (10:39). His faithfulness stood at the center of his desire to be of use to God.

Nehemiah's Prayer

1 The words of Nehemiah son of Hacaliah:

1:1 In the month of Kislev[a] in the twen-
[a]Ne 10:1; tieth year, while I was in the citadel
Zec 7:1 of Susa, 2Hanani,[b] one of my brothers,
1:2 [b]Ne 7:2 came from Judah with some other men,
[c]Jer 52:28 and I questioned them about the Jewish
remnant[c] that survived the exile, and
also about Jerusalem.
3They said to me, "Those who survived the exile and are back in the province are in great trouble and disgrace.
The wall of Jerusalem is broken down,
and its gates have been burned with
1:3 fire."[d]
[d]2Ki 25:10; Ne 2:3,13,17 4When I heard these things, I sat
down and wept.[e] For some days I
1:4 [e]Ps 137:1 mourned and fasted[f] and prayed before
[f]Ezr 9:4 the God of heaven. 5Then I said:

"O LORD, God of heaven, the
1:5 great and awesome God,[g] who
[g]Dt 7:21; keeps his covenant of love[h] with
Ne 4:14 [h]Ex 20:6; those who love him and obey his
Da 9:4 commands, 6let your ear be attentive and your eyes open to hear[i]
1:6 [i]1Ki 8:29 the prayer[j] your servant is praying
[j]Da 9:17 before you day and night for your
servants, the people of Israel. I confess the sins we Israelites, including myself and my father's house,
have committed against you. 7We
1:7 have acted very wickedly[k] toward
[k]Dt 28:14-15; Ps 106:6 you. We have not obeyed the commands, decrees and laws you gave
your servant Moses.
1:8 8"Remember[l] the instruction
[l]2Ki 20:3 [m]Lev 26:33 you gave your servant Moses, saying, 'If you are unfaithful, I will
scatter[m] you among the nations,
9but if you return to me and obey
my commands, then even if your
exiled people are at the farthest
1:9 horizon, I will gather them[n] from
[n]Dt 30:4 [o]1Ki 8:48; there and bring them to the place
Jer 29:14 I have chosen as a dwelling for my
Name.'[o]
10"They are your servants and
your people, whom you redeemed
by your great strength and your
1:10 mighty hand.[p] 11O Lord, let your
[p]Ex 32:11; Dt 9:29 ear be attentive[q] to the prayer of
1:11 this your servant and to the prayer
[q]ver 6 of your servants who delight in
revering your name. Give your
servant success today by granting
him favor in the presence of this
man."
I was cupbearer[r] to the king. 1:11 [r]Ge 40:1

Artaxerxes Sends Nehemiah to Jerusalem

2 In the month of Nisan in the
twentieth year of King Artaxerxes,[s] 2:1
when wine was brought for him, I took [s]Ezr 7:1
the wine and gave it to the king. I had
not been sad in his presence before; 2so
the king asked me, "Why does your face
look so sad when you are not ill? This
can be nothing but sadness of heart."
I was very much afraid, 3but I said
to the king, "May the king live forever![t] 2:3 [t]1Ki 1:31;
Why should my face not look sad when Da 2:4; 5:10; 6:6,21
the city[u] where my fathers are buried [u]Ps 137:6
lies in ruins, and its gates have been de- [v]Ne 1:3
stroyed by fire?[v]"
4The king said to me, "What is it
you want?"
Then I prayed to the God of heaven,
5and I answered the king, "If it pleases
the king and if your servant has found
favor in his sight, let him send me to
the city in Judah where my fathers are
buried so that I can rebuild it."

▸ PATIENCE

THE BROKEN QUEEN

Nehemiah 2:5

Jerusalem once lay broken in the ashes of rebellion. But God is the God of the second chance. He restored the fallen queen. The city rose again and in five hundred years hosted Jesus' life and teachings. But Jerusalem shall soon descend once more, gilded with apocalypse and a new, urban holiness—a throne incomparable for a reign everlasting.

6Then the king,[w] with the queen sit- 2:6
ting beside him, asked me, "How long [w]Ne 5:14; 13:6
will your journey take, and when will
you get back?" It pleased the king to
send me; so I set a time.
7I also said to him, "If it pleases the
king, may I have letters to the gover- 2:7
nors of Trans-Euphrates,[x] so that they [x]Ezr 8:36
will provide me safe-conduct until I arrive in Judah? 8And may I have a letter
to Asaph, keeper of the king's forest, so
he will give me timber to make beams 2:8
for the gates of the citadel[y] by the tem- [y]Ne 7:2
ple and for the city wall and for the

residence I will occupy?" And because
the gracious hand of my God was upon
2:8 [z]ver 18; Ezr 5:5; 7:6 me,[z] the king granted my requests.
9 So I went to the governors of Trans-
Euphrates and gave them the king's
letters. The king had also sent army of-
2:9 [a]Ezr 8:22 ficers and cavalry[a] with me.
10 When Sanballat[b] the Horonite and
2:10 [b]ver 19; Ne 4:1,7 [c]Ne 4:3; 13:4-7 [d]Est 10:3 Tobiah[c] the Ammonite official heard
about this, they were very much dis-
turbed that someone had come to promote the welfare of the Israelites.[d]

Nehemiah Inspects Jerusalem's Walls

11 I went to Jerusalem, and after stay-
2:11 [e]Ge 40:13 ing there three days[e] 12 I set out during
the night with a few men. I had not
told anyone what my God had put in
my heart to do for Jerusalem. There
were no mounts with me except the
one I was riding on.
13 By night I went out through the
2:13 [f]2Ch 26:9 [g]Ne 3:13 [h]Ne 1:3 Valley Gate[f] toward the Jackal[a] Well
and the Dung Gate,[g] examining the
walls[h] of Jerusalem, which had been
broken down, and its gates, which had
been destroyed by fire. 14 Then I moved
2:14 [i]Ne 3:15 [j]2Ki 18:17 on toward the Fountain Gate[i] and the
King's Pool,[j] but there was not enough
room for my mount to get through;
15 so I went up the valley by night, examining the wall. Finally, I turned back
and reentered through the Valley Gate.
16 The officials did not know where I
had gone or what I was doing, because
as yet I had said nothing to the Jews or
the priests or nobles or officials or any
others who would be doing the work.
17 Then I said to them, "You see the
trouble we are in: Jerusalem lies in ruins, and its gates have been burned with
2:17 [k]Ne 1:3 [l]Ps 102:16; Isa 30:13; 58:12 [m]Eze 5:14 fire.[k] Come, let us rebuild the wall[l] of
Jerusalem, and we will no longer be in
disgrace."[m] 18 I also told them about the
gracious hand of my God upon me[n]
2:18 [n]2Sa 2:7 and what the king had said to me.
They replied, "Let us start rebuild-
ing." So they began this good work.
19 But when Sanballat the Horonite,
Tobiah the Ammonite official and Ge-
2:19 [o]Ne 6:1,2,6 [p]Ps 44:13-16 shem[o] the Arab heard about it, they
mocked and ridiculed us.[p] "What is
this you are doing?" they asked. "Are
you rebelling against the king?"
20 I answered them by saying, "The
God of heaven will give us success. We
his servants will start rebuilding, but
as for you, you have no share[q] in Je- 2:20 [q]Ezr 4:3
rusalem or any claim or historic right
to it."

Builders of the Wall

3 Eliashib[r] the high priest and his fel- 3:1 [r]Ezr 10:24 [s]Isa 58:12 [t]ver 32; Ne 12:39 [u]Ne 12:39; Jer 31:38; Zec 14:10
low priests went to work and re-
built[s] the Sheep Gate.[t] They dedicated
it and set its doors in place, building as
far as the Tower of the Hundred, which
they dedicated, and as far as the Tower
of Hananel.[u] 2 The men of Jericho[v] built 3:2 [v]Ne 7:36
the adjoining section, and Zaccur son
of Imri built next to them.

3 The Fish Gate[w] was rebuilt by the 3:3 [w]2Ch 33:14; Ne 12:39
sons of Hassenaah. They laid its beams
and put its doors and bolts and bars in
place. 4 Meremoth son of Uriah, the son
of Hakkoz, repaired the next section.
Next to him Meshullam son of Berekiah, the son of Meshezabel, made repairs,
and next to him Zadok son of Baana
also made repairs. 5 The next section was
repaired by the men of Tekoa,[x] but their 3:5 [x]2Sa 14:2
nobles would not put their shoulders to
the work under their supervisors.[b]

6 The Jeshanah[c] Gate[y] was repaired 3:6 [y]Ne 12:39
by Joiada son of Paseah and Meshullam
son of Besodeiah. They laid its beams 3:7 [z]Jos 9:3; Ne 2:7
and put its doors and bolts and bars in
place. 7 Next to them, repairs were made
by men from Gibeon[z] and Mizpah—
Melatiah of Gibeon and Jadon of Me-
ronoth—places under the authority of
the governor of Trans-Euphrates. 8 Uzziel son of Harhaiah, one of the goldsmiths, repaired the next section; and
Hananiah, one of the perfume-makers,
made repairs next to that. They restored[d] Jerusalem as far as the Broad
Wall.[a] 9 Rephaiah son of Hur, ruler of 3:8 [a]Ne 12:38
a half-district of Jerusalem, repaired the
next section. 10 Adjoining this, Jedaiah
son of Harumaph made repairs opposite
his house, and Hattush son of Hashab-
neiah made repairs next to him. 11 Malkijah son of Harim and Hasshub son of
Pahath-Moab repaired another section
and the Tower of the Ovens.[b] 12 Shal- 3:11 [b]Ne 12:38
lum son of Hallohesh, ruler of a half-
district of Jerusalem, repaired the next
section with the help of his daughters.

[a] *13* Or *Serpent* or *Fig* [b] *5* Or *their Lord* or *the governor* [c] *6* Or *Old* [d] *8* Or *They left out part of*

3:13 [c]2Ch 26:9 13The Valley Gate[c] was repaired by
[d]Jos 15:34 Hanun and the residents of Zanoah.[d]
[e]Ne 2:13 They rebuilt it and put its doors and
bolts and bars in place. They also repaired five hundred yards[a] of the wall as
far as the Dung Gate.[e]

14The Dung Gate was repaired by
Malkijah son of Recab, ruler of the dis-
3:14 trict of Beth Hakkerem.[f] He rebuilt it
[f]Jer 6:1 and put its doors and bolts and bars in
place.

15The Fountain Gate was repaired by
Shallun son of Col-Hozeh, ruler of the
district of Mizpah. He rebuilt it, roofing it over and putting its doors and
bolts and bars in place. He also repaired
3:15 [g]Isa 8:6; the wall of the Pool of Siloam,[b][g] by the
Jn 9:7 King's Garden, as far as the steps going
down from the City of David. 16Be-
yond him, Nehemiah son of Azbuk,
3:16 ruler of a half-district of Beth Zur,[h]
[h]Jos 15:58 made repairs up to a point opposite the
[i]Ac 2:29 tombs[c][i] of David, as far as the artificial
pool and the House of the Heroes.

17Next to him, the repairs were made
by the Levites under Rehum son of
Bani. Beside him, Hashabiah, ruler of
3:17 half the district of Keilah,[j] carried out
[j]Jos 15:44 repairs for his district. 18Next to him,
the repairs were made by their coun-
trymen under Binnui[d] son of Henadad,
ruler of the other half-district of Keilah. 19Next to him, Ezer son of Jeshua,
ruler of Mizpah, repaired another section, from a point facing the ascent to
the armory as far as the angle. 20Next to
him, Baruch son of Zabbai zealously repaired another section, from the angle
to the entrance of the house of Eliashib
the high priest. 21Next to him, Mere-
3:21 moth[k] son of Uriah, the son of Hak-
[k]Ezr 8:33 koz, repaired another section, from the
entrance of Eliashib's house to the end
of it.

22The repairs next to him were made
by the priests from the surrounding region. 23Beyond them, Benjamin and
Hasshub made repairs in front of their
house; and next to them, Azariah son
of Maaseiah, the son of Ananiah, made
repairs beside his house. 24Next to him,
3:24 Binnui[l] son of Henadad repaired an-
[l]Ezr 8:33 other section, from Azariah's house to
the angle and the corner, 25and Palal
son of Uzai worked opposite the angle
3:25 [m]Jer 32:2; and the tower projecting from the up-
37:21; 39:14 per palace near the court of the guard.[m]
Next to him, Pedaiah son of Parosh[n] 3:25 [n]Ezr 2:3
26and the temple servants[o] living on
the hill of Ophel[p] made repairs up 3:26 [o]Ne 7:46;
to a point opposite the Water Gate[q] 11:21
toward the east and the projecting tow- [p]2Ch 33:14 [q]Ne 8:1,3,16;
er. 27Next to them, the men of Tekoa[r] 12:37
repaired another section, from the 3:27
great projecting tower[s] to the wall of [r]ver 5 [s]Ps 48:12
Ophel.

28Above the Horse Gate,[t] the priests 3:28 [t]2Ki 11:16;
made repairs, each in front of his own 2Ch 23:15; Jer 31:40
house. 29Next to them, Zadok son of
Immer made repairs opposite his house.
Next to him, Shemaiah son of Shecaniah, the guard at the East Gate, made repairs. 30Next to him, Hananiah son of
Shelemiah, and Hanun, the sixth son of
Zalaph, repaired another section. Next
to them, Meshullam son of Berekiah
made repairs opposite his living quarters. 31Next to him, Malkijah, one of
the goldsmiths, made repairs as far
as the house of the temple servants and
the merchants, opposite the Inspection
Gate, and as far as the room above
the corner; 32and between the room
above the corner and the Sheep Gate[u] 3:32 [u]ver 1;
the goldsmiths and merchants made re- Jn 5:2
pairs.

Opposition to the Rebuilding

4 When Sanballat[v] heard that we were 4:1
rebuilding the wall, he became an- [v]Ne 2:10
gry and was greatly incensed. He ridiculed the Jews, 2and in the presence of 4:2
his associates[w] and the army of Samaria, [w]Ezr 4:9-10
he said, "What are those feeble Jews do- [x]Ps 79:1;
ing? Will they restore their wall? Will Jer 26:18
they offer sacrifices? Will they finish in
a day? Can they bring the stones back 4:3
to life from those heaps of rubble[x]— [y]Ne 2:10
burned as they are?" [z]Job 13:12; 15:3

3Tobiah[y] the Ammonite, who was at
his side, said, "What they are building—
if even a fox climbed up on it, he would
break down their wall of stones!"[z]

4Hear us, O our God, for we are de- 4:4 [a]Ps 44:13; 79:12;
spised.[a] Turn their insults back on their 123:3-4;
own heads. Give them over as plunder Jer 33:24
in a land of captivity. 5Do not cover up 4:5 [b]Isa 2:9;
their guilt[b] or blot out their sins from La 1:22

[a]*13* Hebrew *a thousand cubits* (about 450 meters)
[b]*15* Hebrew *Shelah,* a variant of *Shiloah,* that is, Siloam
[c]*16* Hebrew; Septuagint, some Vulgate manuscripts and Syriac *tomb*
[d]*18* Two Hebrew manuscripts and Syriac (see also Septuagint and verse 24); most Hebrew manuscripts *Bavvai*

4:5 c 2Ki 14:27; Ps 51:1; 69:27-28; 109:14; Jer 18:23 your sight,[c] for they have thrown insults in the face of[a] the builders.
6 So we rebuilt the wall till all of it
reached half its height, for the people
worked with all their heart.
4:7 d Ne 2:10 7 But when Sanballat, Tobiah,[d] the
Arabs, the Ammonites and the men of
Ashdod heard that the repairs to Jerusalem's walls had gone ahead and that
the gaps were being closed, they were
4:8 e Ps 2:2; 83:1-18 very angry. 8 They all plotted together[e]
to come and fight against Jerusalem
and stir up trouble against it. 9 But we
prayed to our God and posted a guard
day and night to meet this threat.
10 Meanwhile, the people in Judah
4:10 f 1Ch 23:4 said, "The strength of the laborers[f] is
giving out, and there is so much rubble
that we cannot rebuild the wall."
11 Also our enemies said, "Before they
know it or see us, we will be right there
among them and will kill them and put
an end to the work."
12 Then the Jews who lived near them
came and told us ten times over, "Wherever you turn, they will attack us."
13 Therefore I stationed some of the
people behind the lowest points of the
wall at the exposed places, posting them
by families, with their swords, spears
and bows. 14 After I looked things over, I
stood up and said to the nobles, the officials and the rest of the people, "Don't
4:14 g Ge 28:15; Nu 14:9; Dt 1:29 h Ne 1:8 i Ne 1:5 j 2Sa 10:12 be afraid[g] of them. Remember[h] the
Lord, who is great and awesome,[i] and
fight[j] for your brothers, your sons and
your daughters, your wives and your
homes."
15 When our enemies heard that we
were aware of their plot and that God
4:15 k 2Sa 17:14; Job 5:12 had frustrated it,[k] we all returned to the
wall, each to his own work.
16 From that day on, half of my men
did the work, while the other half were
equipped with spears, shields, bows and
armor. The officers posted themselves
behind all the people of Judah 17 who
were building the wall. Those who carried materials did their work with one
hand and held a weapon[l] in the other,
4:17 l Ps 149:6 18 and each of the builders wore his
sword at his side as he worked. But the
4:18 m Nu 10:2 man who sounded the trumpet[m] stayed
with me.
19 Then I said to the nobles, the officials and the rest of the people, "The
work is extensive and spread out, and

PEACE

BUILDING IN TIMES OF DURESS

Nehemiah 4:17

Amid powerful enemies, Nehemiah linked hands with the everlasting God and rebuilt the holy city.

But consider what Christ did. He came to a world in turbulence and, while all the enemies of God stared him in the face, he built a kingdom whose founder and maker is God.

we are widely separated from each other
along the wall. 20 Wherever you hear the
sound of the trumpet,[n] join us there. 4:20 n Eze 33:3
Our God will fight[o] for us!" o Ex 14:14; Dt 1:30; 20:4; Jos 10:14
21 So we continued the work with half
the men holding spears, from the first
light of dawn till the stars came out.
22 At that time I also said to the people,
"Have every man and his helper stay
inside Jerusalem at night, so they can
serve us as guards by night and workmen by day." 23 Neither I nor my brothers nor my men nor the guards with
me took off our clothes; each had his
weapon, even when he went for water.[b]

Nehemiah Helps the Poor

5 Now the men and their wives raised
a great outcry against their Jewish
brothers. 2 Some were saying, "We and
our sons and daughters are numerous;
in order for us to eat and stay alive, we
must get grain."
3 Others were saying, "We are mort-
gaging our fields,[p] our vineyards and 5:3 p Ps 109:11
our homes to get grain during the q Ge 47:23
famine."[q]
4 Still others were saying, "We have
had to borrow money to pay the king's
tax[r] on our fields and vineyards. 5 Al- 5:4 r Ezr 4:13
though we are of the same flesh and
blood[s] as our countrymen and though 5:5 s Ge 29:14
our sons are as good as theirs, yet we t Lev
have to subject our sons and daughters 25:39-43,47;
to slavery.[t] Some of our daughters have 2Ki 4:1;
already been enslaved, but we are pow- Isa 50:1
erless, because our fields and our vine- u Dt 15:7-11; 2Ki 4:1
yards belong to others."[u]
6 When I heard their outcry and these
charges, I was very angry. 7 I pondered
them in my mind and then accused

[a] 5 Or *have provoked you to anger before* [b] 23 The meaning of the Hebrew for this clause is uncertain.

the nobles and officials. I told them,
"You are exacting usury[v] from your
own countrymen!" So I called together
a large meeting to deal with them
8and said: "As far as possible, we have
bought[w] back our Jewish brothers who
were sold to the Gentiles. Now you
are selling your brothers, only for them
to be sold back to us!" They kept quiet, because they could find nothing to
say.[x]

5:7 [v]Ex 22:25-27; Lev 25:35-37; Dt 23:19-20; 24:10-13
5:8 [w]Lev 25:47 [x]Jer 34:8

DAY 4 FOUR

▸ FAITHFULNESS AND MY SERVICE TO OTHERS

Nehemiah 5:6–11

How do the redeemed treat the redeemed? Faithfulness includes a commitment to right behavior toward all our brothers and sisters in Christ.

One famous non-Christian said he would be a Christian if it weren't for Christians. I wonder whether he had witnessed those who claim the name of Christ mistreating one another.

There is a story that circulated among one of the high Reformed churches of South Africa during the terrible apartheid days of racial segregation. In those days (as in America during the civil rights struggle), blacks were not permitted to worship or pray in white churches. Blacks who tried to crash through these "color lines" were thrown out of the church by the angry whites who worshiped there.

On one occasion a wealthy white woman entered her church and, as she knelt and prayed on the kneeler of her pew, she noticed a black woman down on her knees just ahead of her. "What are you doing in this church?" shouted the angry white woman.

"Nothing, ma'am, just scrubbing the floor. I'm the new janitor. The church hired me just this morning."

"Oh, all right," said the white woman, softening her insulting tone. "But God help you if I catch you praying."

When Christians mistreat each other, God bleeds yet again. Nehemiah would castigate all believers who hold to hate or profit from prejudice while they make pretenses of devotion.

To begin a study on the topic of Faithfulness, a Stubborn Commitment to the Right, turn to the home page on page 398.

9So I continued, "What you are doing is not right. Shouldn't you walk in
the fear of our God to avoid the reproach[y] of our Gentile enemies? 10I and
my brothers and my men are also lending the people money and grain. But let
the exacting of usury stop![z] 11Give back
to them immediately their fields, vineyards, olive groves and houses, and also
the usury[a] you are charging them—the
hundredth part of the money, grain,
new wine and oil."

12"We will give it back," they said.
"And we will not demand anything
more from them. We will do as you
say."

Then I summoned the priests and
made the nobles and officials take an
oath[b] to do what they had promised.
13I also shook[c] out the folds of my robe
and said, "In this way may God shake
out of his house and possessions every
man who does not keep this promise.
So may such a man be shaken out and
emptied!"

At this the whole assembly said,
"Amen,"[d] and praised the LORD. And
the people did as they had promised.

14Moreover, from the twentieth year
of King Artaxerxes,[e] when I was appointed to be their governor[f] in the
land of Judah, until his thirty-second
year—twelve years—neither I nor my
brothers ate the food allotted to the
governor. 15But the earlier governors—
those preceding me—placed a heavy
burden on the people and took forty
shekels[a] of silver from them in addition
to food and wine. Their assistants also
lorded it over the people. But out of
reverence for God[g] I did not act like
that. 16Instead,[h] I devoted myself to the
work on this wall. All my men were assembled there for the work; we[b] did not
acquire any land.

17Furthermore, a hundred and fifty
Jews and officials ate at my table, as well
as those who came to us from the surrounding nations. 18Each day one ox,
six choice sheep and some poultry[i] were
prepared for me, and every ten days an
abundant supply of wine of all kinds.
In spite of all this, I never demanded
the food allotted to the governor, be-

5:9 [y]Isa 52:5
5:10 [z]Ex 22:25
5:11 [a]Isa 58:6
5:12 [b]Ezr 10:5
5:13 [c]Mt 10:14; Ac 18:6 [d]Dt 27:15-26
5:14 [e]Ne 2:6; 13:6 [f]Ge 42:6; Ezr 6:7; Jer 40:7; Hag 1:1
5:15 [g]Ge 20:11
5:16 [h]2Th 3:7-10
5:18 [i]1Ki 4:23

[a]*15* That is, about 1 pound (about 0.5 kilogram)
[b]*16* Most Hebrew manuscripts; some Hebrew manuscripts, Septuagint, Vulgate and Syriac *I*

cause the demands were heavy on these people.

[19]Remember[j] me with favor, O my God, for all I have done for these people.

5:19 [j]Ge 8:1; 2Ki 20:3; Ne 1:8; 13:14,22,31

Further Opposition to the Rebuilding

6 When word came to Sanballat, Tobiah,[k] Geshem[l] the Arab and the rest of our enemies that I had rebuilt the wall and not a gap was left in it—though up to that time I had not set the doors in the gates—[2]Sanballat and Geshem sent me this message: "Come, let us meet together in one of the villages[a] on the plain of Ono.[m]"

6:1 [k]Ne 2:10 [l]Ne 2:19

6:2 [m]1Ch 8:12

But they were scheming to harm me; [3]so I sent messengers to them with this reply: "I am carrying on a great project and cannot go down. Why should the work stop while I leave it and go down to you?" [4]Four times they sent me the same message, and each time I gave them the same answer.

[5]Then, the fifth time, Sanballat[n] sent his aide to me with the same message, and in his hand was an unsealed letter [6]in which was written:

6:5 [n]Ne 2:10

> "It is reported among the nations—and Geshem[b][o] says it is true—that you and the Jews are plotting to revolt, and therefore you are building the wall. Moreover, according to these reports you are about to become their king [7]and have even appointed prophets to make this proclamation about you in Jerusalem: 'There is a king in Judah!' Now this report will get back to the king; so come, let us confer together."

6:6 [o]Ne 2:19

[8]I sent him this reply: "Nothing like what you are saying is happening; you are just making it up out of your head."

[9]They were all trying to frighten us, thinking, "Their hands will get too weak for the work, and it will not be completed."

⌞But I prayed,⌟ "Now strengthen my hands."

[10]One day I went to the house of Shemaiah son of Delaiah, the son of Mehetabel, who was shut in at his home. He said, "Let us meet in the house of God, inside the temple, and let us close the temple[p] doors, because men are coming to kill you—by night they are coming to kill you."

6:10 [p]Nu 18:7

[11]But I said, "Should a man like me run away? Or should one like me go into the temple to save his life? I will not go!" [12]I realized that God had not sent him, but that he had prophesied against me[q] because Tobiah and Sanballat[r] had hired him. [13]He had been hired to intimidate me so that I would commit a sin by doing this, and then they would give me a bad name to discredit me.[s]

6:12 [q]Eze 13:22-23 [r]Ne 2:10

6:13 [s]Jer 20:10

[14]Remember[t] Tobiah and Sanballat,[u] O my God, because of what they have done; remember also the prophetess[v] Noadiah and the rest of the prophets[w] who have been trying to intimidate me.

6:14 [t]Ne 1:8 [u]Ne 2:10 [v]Ex 15:20; Eze 13:17-23; Ac 21:9; Rev 2:20 [w]Ne 13:29; Jer 23:9-40; Zec 13:2-3

The Completion of the Wall

[15]So the wall was completed on the twenty-fifth of Elul, in fifty-two days. [16]When all our enemies heard about this, all the surrounding nations were afraid and lost their self-confidence, because they realized that this work had been done with the help of our God.

[17]Also, in those days the nobles of Judah were sending many letters to Tobiah, and replies from Tobiah kept coming to them. [18]For many in Judah were under oath to him, since he was son-in-law to Shecaniah son of Arah, and his son Jehohanan had married the daughter of Meshullam son of Berekiah. [19]Moreover, they kept reporting to me his good deeds and then telling him what I said. And Tobiah sent letters to intimidate me.

7 After the wall had been rebuilt and I had set the doors in place, the gatekeepers[x] and the singers[y] and the Levites[z] were appointed. [2]I put in charge of Jerusalem my brother Hanani,[a] along with[c] Hananiah[b] the commander of the citadel,[c] because he was a man of integrity and feared[d] God more than most men do. [3]I said to them, "The gates of Jerusalem are not to be opened until the sun is hot. While the gatekeepers are still on duty, have them shut the doors and bar them. Also appoint residents of Jerusalem as guards, some

7:1 [x]1Ch 9:27; 26:12-19; Ne 6:1,15 [y]Ps 68:25 [z]Ne 8:9

7:2 [a]Ne 1:2 [b]Ne 10:23 [c]Ne 2:8 [d]1Ki 18:3

[a]2 Or *in Kephirim* [b]6 Hebrew *Gashmu,* a variant of *Geshem* [c]2 Or *Hanani, that is,*

at their posts and some near their own
houses."

The List of the Exiles Who Returned

[4]Now the city was large and spacious,
7:4 [e]Ne 11:1 but there were few people in it,[e] and the
houses had not yet been rebuilt. [5]So my
God put it into my heart to assemble
the nobles, the officials and the common people for registration by families.
I found the genealogical record of those
who had been the first to return. This
is what I found written there:

[6]These are the people of the
province who came up from the
7:6 [f]2Ch 36:20; Ezr 2:1-70; Ne 1:2 captivity of the exiles[f] whom
Nebuchadnezzar king of Babylon
had taken captive (they returned
to Jerusalem and Judah, each to
his own town, [7]in company with
7:7 [g]1Ch 3:19; Ezr 2:2 Zerubbabel,[g] Jeshua, Nehemiah,
Azariah, Raamiah, Nahamani,
Mordecai, Bilshan, Mispereth, Bigvai, Nehum and Baanah):

The list of the men of Israel:

[8]the descendants of Parosh	2,172
[9]of Shephatiah	372
[10]of Arah	652
[11]of Pahath-Moab (through the line of Jeshua and Joab)	2,818
[12]of Elam	1,254
[13]of Zattu	845
[14]of Zaccai	760
[15]of Binnui	648
[16]of Bebai	628
[17]of Azgad	2,322
[18]of Adonikam	667
[19]of Bigvai	2,067
7:20 [h]Ezr 8:6 [20]of Adin[h]	655
[21]of Ater (through Hezekiah)	98
[22]of Hashum	328
[23]of Bezai	324
[24]of Hariph	112
[25]of Gibeon	95
7:26 [i]2Sa 23:28; 1Ch 2:54 [26]the men of Bethlehem and Netophah[i]	188
7:27 [j]Jos 21:18 [27]of Anathoth[j]	128
[28]of Beth Azmaveth	42
7:29 [k]Jos 18:26 [l]Jos 18:25 [29]of Kiriath Jearim, Kephirah[k] and Beeroth[l]	743
[30]of Ramah and Geba	621
[31]of Micmash	122
[32]of Bethel and Ai[m]	123 7:32 [m]Ge 12:8
[33]of the other Nebo	52
[34]of the other Elam	1,254
[35]of Harim	320
[36]of Jericho[n]	345 7:36 [n]Ne 3:2
[37]of Lod, Hadid and Ono[o]	721 7:37 [o]1Ch 8:12
[38]of Senaah	3,930

[39]The priests:

the descendants of Jedaiah (through the family of Jeshua)	973
[40]of Immer	1,052
[41]of Pashhur	1,247
[42]of Harim	1,017

[43]The Levites:

the descendants of Jeshua (through Kadmiel through the line of Hodaviah)	74

[44]The singers:[p] 7:44 [p]Ne 11:23

the descendants of Asaph	148

[45]The gatekeepers:[q] 7:45 [q]1Ch 9:17

the descendants of Shallum, Ater, Talmon, Akkub, Hatita and Shobai	138

[46]The temple servants:[r] 7:46 [r]Ne 3:26

the descendants of
Ziha, Hasupha, Tabbaoth,
[47]Keros, Sia, Padon,
[48]Lebana, Hagaba, Shalmai,
[49]Hanan, Giddel, Gahar,
[50]Reaiah, Rezin, Nekoda,
[51]Gazzam, Uzza, Paseah,
[52]Besai, Meunim, Nephussim,
[53]Bakbuk, Hakupha, Harhur,
[54]Bazluth, Mehida, Harsha,
[55]Barkos, Sisera, Temah,
[56]Neziah and Hatipha

[57]The descendants of the servants of Solomon:

the descendants of
Sotai, Sophereth, Perida,
[58]Jaala, Darkon, Giddel,
[59]Shephatiah, Hattil,
Pokereth-Hazzebaim and
Amon

[60]The temple servants and the descendants of the servants of Solomon[s]	392 7:60 [s]1Ch 9:2

[61]The following came up from the
towns of Tel Melah, Tel Harsha, Kerub,
Addon and Immer, but they could not

show that their families were descended
from Israel:
62 the descendants of
Delaiah, Tobiah and
Nekoda 642
63And from among the priests:
the descendants of
Hobaiah, Hakkoz and Barzillai
(a man who had married a
daughter of Barzillai the
Gileadite and was called by
that name).
64These searched for their family records, but they could not
find them and so were excluded
from the priesthood as unclean.
65The governor, therefore, ordered
them not to eat any of the most
sacred food until there should be
a priest ministering with the Urim
and Thummim.[t]

7:65 [t]Ex 28:30; Ne 8:9

66The whole company num-
bered 42,360, 67besides their 7,337
menservants and maidservants; and
they also had 245 men and women
singers. 68There were 736 horses,
245 mules,[a] 69435 camels and
6,720 donkeys.
70Some of the heads of the families contributed to the work. The
governor gave to the treasury 1,000
drachmas[b] of gold, 50 bowls and
530 garments for priests. 71Some
of the heads of the families[u] gave
to the treasury for the work 20,000
drachmas[c] of gold and 2,200
minas[d] of silver. 72The total given
by the rest of the people was
20,000 drachmas of gold, 2,000
minas[e] of silver and 67 garments
for priests.[v]
73The priests, the Levites, the
gatekeepers, the singers and the
temple servants,[w] along with certain of the people and the rest of
the Israelites, settled in their own
towns.[x]

7:71 [u]1Ch 29:7

7:72 [v]Ex 25:2

7:73 [w]Ne 1:10; Ps 34:22; 103:21; 113:1; 135:1 [x]Ezr 3:1; Ne 11:1 [y]Ezr 3:1

Ezra Reads the Law

When the seventh month came and
the Israelites had settled in their towns,[y]
8 1all the people assembled as one
man in the square before the Water
Gate.[z] They told Ezra the scribe to bring
out the Book of the Law of Moses,[a]
which the LORD had commanded for
Israel.
2So on the first day of the seventh
month[b] Ezra the priest brought the
Law[c] before the assembly, which was
made up of men and women and all
who were able to understand. 3He read
it aloud from daybreak till noon as he
faced the square before the Water Gate[d]
in the presence of the men, women and
others who could understand. And all
the people listened attentively to the
Book of the Law.

8:1 [z]Ne 3:26

8:1 [a]Dt 28:61; 2Ch 34:15; Ezr 7:6

8:2 [b]Lev 23:23-25; Nu 29:1-6 [c]Dt 31:11

8:3 [d]Ne 3:26

GOODNESS

THE READING OF THE WORD

Nehemiah 8:3

In the mere reading of the Word, there is a cry to be better than we are, a longing for a holiness we wish we owned. It is amazing that mere verbs and nouns can stir such hunger in our souls.

4Ezra the scribe stood on a high
wooden platform[e] built for the occasion.
Beside him on his right stood Mattithiah, Shema, Anaiah, Uriah, Hilkiah and
Maaseiah; and on his left were Pedaiah,
Mishael, Malkijah, Hashum, Hashbad-
danah, Zechariah and Meshullam.
5Ezra opened the book. All the people could see him because he was standing[f] above them; and as he opened it,
the people all stood up. 6Ezra praised
the LORD, the great God; and all the
people lifted their hands[g] and responded, "Amen! Amen!" Then they bowed
down and worshiped the LORD with
their faces to the ground.
7The Levites[h]—Jeshua, Bani, Sherebiah, Jamin, Akkub, Shabbethai, Hodiah, Maaseiah, Kelita, Azariah, Jozabad,
Hanan and Pelaiah—instructed[i] the
people in the Law while the people
were standing there. 8They read from
the Book of the Law of God, making
it clear[f] and giving the meaning so that

8:4 [e]2Ch 6:13

8:5 [f]Jdg 3:20

8:6 [g]Ex 4:31; Ezr 9:5; 1Ti 2:8

8:7 [h]Ezr 10:23 [i]Lev 10:11; 2Ch 17:7

[a]*68* Some Hebrew manuscripts (see also Ezra 2:66); most Hebrew manuscripts do not have this verse. [b]*70* That is, about 19 pounds (about 8.5 kilograms) [c]*71* That is, about 375 pounds (about 170 kilograms); also in verse 72 [d]*71* That is, about 1 1/3 tons (about 1.2 metric tons) [e]*72* That is, about 1 1/4 tons (about 1.1 metric tons) [f]*8* Or *God, translating it*

the people could understand what was
being read.
9 Then Nehemiah the governor, Ezra
the priest and scribe, and the Levites[j]
who were instructing the people said
to them all, "This day is sacred to the

8:9 [j]Ne 7:1,65,70

DAY 5 FIVE

▸ PATIENCE AND ITS PLACE IN MY PERSONAL WORSHIP

Nehemiah 8:3–10

Let us approach worship in an unhurried fashion. Notice in this passage that Ezra the priest and scribe read the Bible from daybreak till noon (Nehemiah 8:3), and as far as we can tell from the Hebrew text, no one complained, "How can we ever beat everyone else to the local diner if our worship services keep going on so long?"

Worship takes time. And apparently the Israelites realized that they had the time. No one was hurried, and they took all the time they needed for praising God. Their worship mainly was given to the reading of the Word of God, although "all the people lifted their hands and responded, 'Amen! Amen!'" They also "bowed down and worshiped the LORD with their faces to the ground" (v. 6).

What was the overall response to this long, "your-roast-back-home-is-probably-burning" service? The people began to weep at the privilege, the responsibility and the burden of hearing the Word of God spoken directly to them.

It was at this time that Nehemiah reminded them that the Word is sometimes meant to bring us to tears and conviction, but that on this particular occasion, God's Word was to be their source of joy. They had time; the unhurried virtue of patience was on their side. Nehemiah called out to all the people: "Do not mourn or weep... Go and enjoy choice food and sweet drinks... Do not grieve, for the joy of the LORD is your strength" (vv. 9–10).

God desires to invade our unhurried worship, and we are to take all the time we need to make patience during our worship the unhurried heart of our praise.

To begin a study on the topic of Patience, the Unhurried Virtue, turn to the home page on page 1146.

LORD your God. Do not mourn or
weep."[k] For all the people had been
weeping as they listened to the words of
the Law.
10 Nehemiah said, "Go and enjoy
choice food and sweet drinks, and send
some to those who have nothing[l] prepared.
This day is sacred to our Lord.
Do not grieve, for the joy[m] of the LORD
is your strength."
11 The Levites calmed all the people,
saying, "Be still, for this is a sacred day.
Do not grieve."
12 Then all the people went away to
eat and drink, to send portions of food
and to celebrate with great joy,[n] because
they now understood the words that
had been made known to them.
13 On the second day of the month,
the heads of all the families, along with
the priests and the Levites, gathered
around Ezra the scribe to give attention
to the words of the Law. 14 They
found written in the Law, which the
LORD had commanded through Moses,
that the Israelites were to live in
booths during the feast of the seventh
month 15 and that they should proclaim
this word and spread it throughout their
towns and in Jerusalem: "Go out into
the hill country and bring back branches
from olive and wild olive trees, and
from myrtles, palms and shade trees, to
make booths"—as it is written.[a]
16 So the people went out and brought
back branches and built themselves
booths on their own roofs, in their
courtyards, in the courts of the house
of God and in the square by the Water
Gate and the one by the Gate of
Ephraim.[o] 17 The whole company that
had returned from exile built booths
and lived in them. From the days of
Joshua son of Nun until that day, the
Israelites had not celebrated[p] it like this.
And their joy was very great.
18 Day after day, from the first day to
the last, Ezra read[q] from the Book of
the Law of God. They celebrated the
feast for seven days, and on the eighth
day, in accordance with the regulation,[r]
there was an assembly.

8:9 [k]Dt 12:7,12; 16:14-15
8:10 [l]1Sa 25:8; Lk 14:12-14 [m]Lev 23:40; Dt 12:18; 16:11,14-15
8:12 [n]Est 9:22
8:16 [o]2Ki 14:13; Ne 12:39
8:17 [p]2Ch 7:8; 8:13; 30:21
8:18 [q]Dt 31:11 [r]Lev 23:36,40; Nu 29:35

The Israelites Confess Their Sins

9 On the twenty-fourth day of the
same month, the Israelites gathered

[a]*15* See Lev. 23:37-40.

together, fasting and wearing sackcloth
and having dust on their heads.[s] 2Those
of Israelite descent had separated themselves from all foreigners.[t] They stood
in their places and confessed their sins
and the wickedness of their fathers.[u]
3They stood where they were and read
from the Book of the Law of the LORD
their God for a quarter of the day,
and spent another quarter in confession and in worshiping the LORD their
God. 4Standing on the stairs were the
Levites[v]—Jeshua, Bani, Kadmiel, Shebaniah, Bunni, Sherebiah, Bani and Ke-
nani—who called with loud voices to
the LORD their God. 5And the Levites—Jeshua, Kadmiel, Bani, Hashab-
neiah, Sherebiah, Hodiah, Shebaniah
and Pethahiah—said: "Stand up and
praise the LORD your God,[w] who is
from everlasting to everlasting.[a]"

"Blessed be your glorious name,
and may it be exalted above all
blessing and praise. 6You alone are
the LORD.[x] You made the heavens,
even the highest heavens,[y] and all
their starry host, the earth[z] and all
that is on it, the seas[a] and all that
is in them.[b] You give life to everything, and the multitudes of heav-
en worship you.

7"You are the LORD God, who
chose Abram and brought him out
of Ur of the Chaldeans[c] and named
him Abraham.[d] 8You found his
heart faithful to you, and you made
a covenant with him to give to his
descendants the land of the Canaanites, Hittites, Amorites, Perizzites, Jebusites and Girgashites.[e]
You have kept your promise[f] because you are righteous.[g]

9"You saw the suffering of our
forefathers in Egypt;[h] you heard
their cry at the Red Sea.[b][i] 10You
sent miraculous signs[j] and wonders against Pharaoh, against all his
officials and all the people of his
land, for you knew how arrogantly the Egyptians treated them. You
made a name[k] for yourself, which
remains to this day. 11You divided
the sea before them,[l] so that they
passed through it on dry ground,
but you hurled their pursuers into
the depths, like a stone into mighty
waters.[m] 12By day you led[n] them
with a pillar of cloud,[o] and by
night with a pillar of fire to give
them light on the way they were to
take.

13"You came down on Mount
Sinai;[p] you spoke[q] to them from
heaven. You gave them regulations
and laws that are just[r] and right,
and decrees and commands that
are good.[s] 14You made known to
them your holy Sabbath[t] and gave
them commands, decrees and laws
through your servant Moses. 15In
their hunger you gave them bread
from heaven[u] and in their thirst
you brought them water from the
rock;[v] you told them to go in and
take possession of the land you had
sworn with uplifted hand to give
them.[w]

16"But they, our forefathers, became arrogant and stiff-necked,
and did not obey your commands.[x]
17They refused to listen and failed
to remember[y] the miracles you
performed among them. They became stiff-necked and in their rebellion appointed a leader in order
to return to their slavery.[z] But you
are a forgiving God, gracious and
compassionate, slow to anger[a] and
abounding in love.[b] Therefore you
did not desert them,[c] 18even when
they cast for themselves an image
of a calf[d] and said, 'This is your
god, who brought you up out of
Egypt,' or when they committed
awful blasphemies.

19"Because of your great compassion you did not abandon them
in the desert. By day the pillar of
cloud did not cease to guide them
on their path, nor the pillar of fire
by night to shine on the way they
were to take. 20You gave your good
Spirit[e] to instruct them. You did
not withhold your manna[f] from
their mouths, and you gave them
water[g] for their thirst. 21For forty
years you sustained them in the
desert; they lacked nothing,[h] their
clothes did not wear out nor did
their feet become swollen.[i]

22"You gave them kingdoms and
nations, allotting to them even the

[a]5 Or *God for ever and ever* [b]9 Hebrew *Yam Suph;* that is, Sea of Reeds

9:1 [s]Jos 7:6; 1Sa 4:12
9:2 [t]Ne 13:3,30 [u]Ezr 10:11; Ps 106:6
9:4 [v]Ezr 10:23
9:5 [w]Ps 78:4
9:6 [x]Dt 6:4 [y]2Ki 19:15 [z]Ge 1:1; Isa 37:16 [a]Ps 95:5 [b]Dt 10:14
9:7 [c]Ge 11:31 [d]Ge 17:5
9:8 [e]Ge 15:18-21 [f]Jos 21:45 [g]Ge 15:6; Ezr 9:15
9:9 [h]Ex 3:7 [i]Ex 14:10-30
9:10 [j]Ex 10:1 [k]Jer 32:20; Da 9:15
9:11 [l]Ex 14:21; Ps 78:13 [m]Ex 15:4-5, 10; Heb 11:29
9:12 [n]Ex 15:13
9:12 [o]Ex 13:21
9:13 [p]Ex 19:11 [q]Ex 19:19 [r]Ps 119:137 [s]Ex 20:1
9:14 [t]Ge 2:3; Ex 20:8-11
9:15 [u]Ex 16:4; Jn 6:31 [v]Ex 17:6; Nu 20:7-13 [w]Dt 1:8,21
9:16 [x]Dt 1:26-33; 31:29
9:17 [y]Ps 78:42 [z]Nu 14:1-4 [a]Ex 34:6 [b]Nu 14:17-19 [c]Ps 78:11
9:18 [d]Ex 32:4
9:20 [e]Nu 11:17; Isa 63:11,14 [f]Ex 16:15 [g]Ex 17:6
9:21 [h]Dt 2:7 [i]Dt 8:4

remotest frontiers. They took over
9:22 [j]Nu 21:21 [k]Nu 21:33 the country of Sihon[a][j] king of
Heshbon and the country of Og
king of Bashan.[k] 23You made their
sons as numerous as the stars in the
sky, and you brought them into
the land that you told their fathers
to enter and possess. 24Their sons
went in and took possession of the
9:24 [l]Jos 11:23 land.[l] You subdued before them
the Canaanites, who lived in the
land; you handed the Canaanites
over to them, along with their
kings and the peoples of the land,
to deal with them as they pleased.
25They captured fortified cities and
fertile land; they took possession
of houses filled with all kinds of
good things, wells already dug,
vineyards, olive groves and fruit
trees in abundance. They ate to the
9:25 [m]Dt 6:10-12 [n]Nu 13:27; Dt 32:12-15 full and were well-nourished;[m] they
reveled in your great goodness.[n]
26"But they were disobedient
and rebelled against you; they put
9:26 [o]1Ki 14:9 [p]Mt 21:35-36 [q]Jdg 2:12-13 your law behind their backs.[o] They
killed your prophets,[p] who had ad-
monished them in order to turn
them back to you; they committed
awful blasphemies.[q] 27So you hand-
9:27 [r]Jdg 2:14 [s]Ps 106:45 ed them over to their enemies,[r]
who oppressed them. But when
they were oppressed they cried out
to you. From heaven you heard
them, and in your great compassion[s] you gave them deliverers,
who rescued them from the hand
of their enemies.
28"But as soon as they were at
rest, they again did what was evil in
your sight. Then you abandoned
them to the hand of their enemies so that they ruled over them.
And when they cried out to you
again, you heard from heaven, and
in your compassion you delivered
9:28 [t]Ps 106:43 them[t] time after time.
29"You warned them to return
to your law, but they became ar-
9:29 [u]Ps 5:5; Isa 2:11; Jer 43:2 [v]Dt 30:16 [w]Zec 7:11-12 rogant[u] and disobeyed your commands. They sinned against your
ordinances, by which a man will
live if he obeys them.[v] Stubbornly
they turned their backs on you,
became stiff-necked and refused to
listen.[w] 30For many years you were
patient with them. By your Spirit
you admonished them through
your prophets.[x] Yet they paid no 9:30 [x]2Ki 17:13-18; 2Ch 36:16
attention, so you handed them
over to the neighboring peoples.
31But in your great mercy you did 9:31 [y]Isa 48:9; Jer 4:27
not put an end[y] to them or aban-
don them, for you are a gracious
and merciful God.
32"Now therefore, O our God,
the great, mighty[z] and awesome 9:32 [z]Ps 24:8 [a]Dt 7:9
God, who keeps his covenant of
love,[a] do not let all this hardship
seem trifling in your eyes—the
hardship that has come upon us,
upon our kings and leaders, upon
our priests and prophets, upon our
fathers and all your people, from
the days of the kings of Assyria until today. 33In all that has happened
to us, you have been just;[b] you 9:33 [b]Ge 18:25 [c]Jer 44:3; Da 9:7-8,14 [d]2Ki 23:11 [e]Jer 44:17
have acted faithfully, while we did
wrong.[c] 34Our kings,[d] our leaders,
our priests and our fathers[e] did not
follow your law; they did not pay
attention to your commands or the
warnings you gave them. 35Even
while they were in their kingdom, 9:35 [f]Isa 63:7 [g]Dt 28:45-48
enjoying your great goodness[f] to
them in the spacious and fertile
land you gave them, they did not
serve you[g] or turn from their evil
ways.
36"But see, we are slaves[h] today, 9:36 [h]Dt 28:48; Ezr 9:9
slaves in the land you gave our
forefathers so they could eat its
fruit and the other good things it
produces. 37Because of our sins, its
abundant harvest goes to the kings
you have placed over us. They
rule over our bodies and our cat-
tle as they please. We are in great 9:37 [i]Dt 28:33; La 5:5
distress.[i]

The Agreement of the People

38"In view of all this, we are making
a binding agreement,[j] putting it in 9:38 [j]2Ch 23:16 [k]Isa 44:5
writing,[k] and our leaders, our Levites
and our priests are affixing their seals
to it."

10

Those who sealed it were:

Nehemiah the governor, the son of
Hacaliah.

Zedekiah, 2Seraiah,[l] Azariah, Jere- 10:2 [l]Ezr 2:2
miah,

[a]*22* One Hebrew manuscript and Septuagint; most
Hebrew manuscripts *Sihon, that is, the country of the*

WEEK 40

PATIENCE

1 DAY ONE

PATIENCE, THE SLOWLY ACQUIRED VIRTUE

Read Nehemiah 9:29–31

Nehemiah 9:30 says that God's historical motif is his patience. He was patient with the Israelites when:

> they became arrogant;
> they disobeyed the commandments of God;
> they sinned against God's ordinances;
> they turned their backs on God's desires for them;
> they became stiff-necked and refused to listen (v. 29).

All of these transgressions brought the judgment of God, who used other nations to admonish Israel. Yet God's people would not listen. Through all of their disobedience, the patience of God waited on Israel to return his love and behave like his children.

The spirit of this Nehemiah passage is echoed in 2 Peter 3:8–9: "But do not forget this one thing, dear friends: With the Lord a day is like a thousand years, and a thousand years are like a day. The Lord is not slow in keeping his promise, as some understand slowness. He is patient with you, not wanting anyone to perish, but everyone to come to repentance."

To our frenzied, earthbound view, God may appear slow in keeping his second-coming promises. Yet it is not so, said Peter. God is not slow; he just works from a different timetable than we do. He is deliberate in extending the day when Jesus comes again so that as many people as possible may be saved.

Patience is not a flaw in God; it is the glory of God. If God can extend his all-important, worldwide agenda by pacing himself so as to save all, perhaps the practice of patience would do us all good.

2 DAY TWO

PATIENCE AND THE PURPOSE OF GOD IN MY LIFE

God, in his unhurried way, causes us to remember that he is never through with us. Elizabeth and Zechariah were elderly, yet they had no idea of the grandeur that awaited them in their future. Nor could they begin to understand that they were about to play a role that would impact world history. A pregnant elderly woman is evidence that the divine providence for any of our lives must necessarily be glorious—though hard to explain. God must smile a lot! *Turn to Luke 1:5–7,13, page 1196, for today's study.*

3 DAY THREE

PATIENCE AND MY RELATIONSHIP WITH CHRIST

"Here is a trustworthy saying," says the apostle, "that deserves full acceptance: Christ Jesus came into the world to save sinners—of whom I am the worst." Paul probably wasn't the worst of sinners; after all, he lived about the time of Nero. Nonetheless, the glorious thing about drawing close to Christ is that the closer we draw to perfection, the more our imperfections become apparent to us. So it must have been with the apostle Paul. He stood so near the light of God that his own shadow fell dark around him. *Turn to 1 Timothy 1:15–16, page 1438, for today's study.*

4 DAY FOUR

PATIENCE AND MY SERVICE TO OTHERS

The singing of songs is a sign that we are pacing our lives. Deborah and Barak sing a duet, and they do not resent the fact that they have to take the time to sing it. It is a rare person who discovers the purpose of God for his or her life and knows exactly why he or she is in the world. But Deborah and Barak knew. Their purpose was to inspire Israel in matters of freedom; it was to incite the people to unify behind the national cause. *Turn to Judges 5:1–2, page 279, for today's study.*

5 DAY FIVE

PATIENCE AND ITS PLACE IN MY PERSONAL WORSHIP

Paul had learned patience through hardship. But the pain of the present moment is never significant in light of all the time we have. The creation itself has learned to wait in eager expectation for its post-second-coming renovation. In light of that, we must wait to see how we shall look in God's ultimate plan for our lives. *Turn to Romans 8:18–25, page 1343, for today's study.*

MEMORIZE THIS WEEK

PSALM 37:7

Be still before the LORD and wait patiently for him;
do not fret when men succeed in their ways,
when they carry out their wicked schemes.

Week 41, Kindness, the Approach to Grace, begins on page 343, 1 Samuel 25:32–34.
To begin a topical study on the Fruit of the Spirit, Patience, turn to the Topical Index, page 1548.

10:3 [m]1Ch 9:12
3 Pashhur,[m] Amariah, Malkijah,
4 Hattush, Shebaniah, Malluch,
10:5 [n]1Ch 24:8
5 Harim,[n] Meremoth, Obadiah,
6 Daniel, Ginnethon, Baruch,
7 Meshullam, Abijah, Mijamin,
8 Maaziah, Bilgai and Shemaiah.
These were the priests.

10:9 [o]Ne 12:1
9 The Levites:[o]

Jeshua son of Azaniah, Binnui of
the sons of Henadad, Kadmiel,
10 and their associates: Shebaniah,
Hodiah, Kelita, Pelaiah, Hanan,
11 Mica, Rehob, Hashabiah,
12 Zaccur, Sherebiah, Shebaniah,
13 Hodiah, Bani and Beninu.

14 The leaders of the people:

Parosh, Pahath-Moab, Elam, Zattu, Bani,
15 Bunni, Azgad, Bebai,
10:16 [p]Ezr 8:6
16 Adonijah, Bigvai, Adin,[p]
17 Ater, Hezekiah, Azzur,
18 Hodiah, Hashum, Bezai,
19 Hariph, Anathoth, Nebai,
20 Magpiash, Meshullam, Hezir,[q]
10:20 [q]1Ch 24:15
21 Meshezabel, Zadok, Jaddua,
22 Pelatiah, Hanan, Anaiah,
23 Hoshea, Hananiah,[r] Hasshub,
10:23 [r]Ne 7:2
24 Hallohesh, Pilha, Shobek,
25 Rehum, Hashabnah, Maaseiah,
26 Ahiah, Hanan, Anan,
27 Malluch, Harim and Baanah.

28 "The rest of the people—
priests, Levites, gatekeepers, singers, temple servants[s] and all who
10:28 [s]Ps 135:1 [t]2Ch 6:26; Ne 9:2
separated themselves from the
neighboring peoples[t] for the sake
of the Law of God, together with
their wives and all their sons and
daughters who are able to understand— 29 all these now join
their brothers the nobles, and bind
themselves with a curse and an
10:29 [u]Nu 5:21; Ps 119:106
oath[u] to follow the Law of God
given through Moses the servant
of God and to obey carefully all
the commands, regulations and decrees of the LORD our Lord.

30 "We promise not to give our
daughters in marriage to the peo-
10:30 [v]Ex 34:16; Dt 7:3; Ne 13:23
ples around us or take their daughters for our sons.[v]

31 "When the neighboring peo-
10:31 [w]Ne 13:16,18; Jer 17:27; Eze 23:38; Am 8:5
ples bring merchandise or grain to
sell on the Sabbath, we will not
buy from them on the Sabbath[w]
or on any holy day. Every seventh
year we will forgo working the
land[x] and will cancel all debts.[y]
10:31 [x]Ex 23:11; Lev 25:1-7 [y]Dt 15:1

32 "We assume the responsibility
for carrying out the commands to
give a third of a shekel[a] each year
for the service of the house of our
God: 33 for the bread set out on the
table;[z] for the regular grain offer-
10:33 [z]Lev 24:6 [a]Nu 10:10; Ps 81:3; Isa 1:14 [b]2Ch 24:5
ings and burnt offerings; for the
offerings on the Sabbaths, New
Moon[a] festivals and appointed
feasts; for the holy offerings; for
sin offerings to make atonement
for Israel; and for all the duties of
the house of our God.[b]

34 "We—the priests, the Levites
and the people—have cast lots[c] to
10:34 [c]Lev 16:8 [d]Ne 13:31
determine when each of our families is to bring to the house of our
God at set times each year a contribution of wood[d] to burn on the
altar of the LORD our God, as it is
written in the Law.

35 "We also assume responsibility for bringing to the house of the
LORD each year the firstfruits[e] of
10:35 [e]Ex 22:29; 23:19; Nu 18:12 [f]Dt 26:1-11
our crops and of every fruit tree.[f]

36 "As it is also written in the
Law, we will bring the firstborn[g]
10:36 [g]Ex 13:2; Nu 18:14-16 [h]Ne 13:31
of our sons and of our cattle, of
our herds and of our flocks to the
house of our God, to the priests
ministering there.[h]

37 "Moreover, we will bring to
the storerooms of the house of our
God, to the priests, the first of our
ground meal, of our ⌞grain⌟ offerings, of the fruit of all our trees
and of our new wine and oil.[i] And
10:37 [i]Lev 23:17; Nu 18:12 [j]Lev 27:30; Nu 18:21 [k]Dt 14:22-29 [l]Eze 44:30
we will bring a tithe[j] of our crops
to the Levites,[k] for it is the Levites
who collect the tithes in all the
towns where we work.[l] 38 A priest
descended from Aaron is to accompany the Levites when they receive the tithes, and the Levites are
10:38 [m]Nu 18:26
to bring a tenth of the tithes[m] up
to the house of our God, to the
storerooms of the treasury. 39 The
people of Israel, including the Levites, are to bring their contributions of grain, new wine and oil
to the storerooms where the articles for the sanctuary are kept
and where the ministering priests,

[a]32 That is, about 1/8 ounce (about 4 grams)

the gatekeepers and the singers
stay.
"We will not neglect the house
10:39 [n]Dt 12:6; Ne 13:11,12 of our God."[n]

The New Residents of Jerusalem

11 Now the leaders of the people
settled in Jerusalem, and the rest
of the people cast lots to bring one out
11:1 [o]Ne 7:4 [p]ver 18; Isa 48:2; 52:1; 64:10; Zec 14:20-21 [q]Ne 7:73 of every ten to live in Jerusalem,[o] the
holy city,[p] while the remaining nine
were to stay in their own towns.[q] 2The
people commended all the men who
volunteered to live in Jerusalem.
3These are the provincial leaders who
settled in Jerusalem (now some Israelites, priests, Levites, temple servants
and descendants of Solomon's servants
lived in the towns of Judah, each on
11:3 [r]1Ch 9:2-3; Ezr 2:1 his own property in the various towns,[r]
4while other people from both Judah
and Benjamin[s] lived in Jerusalem):[t]
11:4 [s]Ezr 1:5 [t]Ezr 2:70

From the descendants of Judah:

Athaiah son of Uzziah, the son of
Zechariah, the son of Amariah, the
son of Shephatiah, the son of Mahalalel, a descendant of Perez; 5and
Maaseiah son of Baruch, the son
of Col-Hozeh, the son of Hazaiah,
the son of Adaiah, the son of Joiarib, the son of Zechariah, a descendant of Shelah. 6The descendants
of Perez who lived in Jerusalem totaled 468 able men.

7From the descendants of Benjamin:

Sallu son of Meshullam, the son
of Joed, the son of Pedaiah, the
son of Kolaiah, the son of Maaseiah, the son of Ithiel, the son of Jeshaiah, 8and his followers, Gabbai
and Sallai—928 men. 9Joel son of
Zicri was their chief officer, and
Judah son of Hassenuah was over
the Second District of the city.

10From the priests:

Jedaiah; the son of Joiarib; Jakin;
11:11 [u]2Ki 25:18; Ezr 2:2 [v]Ezr 7:2 11Seraiah[u] son of Hilkiah, the son
of Meshullam, the son of Zadok,
the son of Meraioth, the son of
Ahitub,[v] supervisor in the house of
God, 12and their associates, who
carried on work for the temple—822 men; Adaiah son of Jeroham, the son of Pelaliah, the
son of Amzi, the son of Zechariah, the son of Pashhur, the son
of Malkijah, 13and his associates,
who were heads of families—242
men; Amashsai son of Azarel, the
son of Ahzai, the son of Meshillemoth, the son of Immer, 14and
his[a] associates, who were able
men—128. Their chief officer was
Zabdiel son of Haggedolim.

15From the Levites:

Shemaiah son of Hasshub, the son
of Azrikam, the son of Hashabiah,
the son of Bunni; 16Shabbethai[w] 11:16 [w]Ezr 10:15 [x]Ezr 8:33
and Jozabad,[x] two of the heads of
the Levites, who had charge of the
outside work of the house of God;
17Mattaniah[y] son of Mica, the son 11:17 [y]1Ch 9:15; Ne 12:8 [z]2Ch 5:12 [a]1Ch 25:1
of Zabdi, the son of Asaph,[z] the di-
rector who led in thanksgiving and
prayer; Bakbukiah, second among
his associates; and Abda son of
Shammua, the son of Galal, the
son of Jeduthun.[a] 18The Levites in
the holy city[b] totaled 284. 11:18 [b]Rev 21:2

19The gatekeepers:

Akkub, Talmon and their associates, who kept watch at the
gates—172 men.

20The rest of the Israelites, with the
priests and Levites, were in all the towns
of Judah, each on his ancestral property.
21The temple servants[c] lived on the 11:21 [c]Ezr 2:43; Ne 3:26
hill of Ophel, and Ziha and Gishpa
were in charge of them.
22The chief officer of the Levites in
Jerusalem was Uzzi son of Bani, the son
of Hashabiah, the son of Mattaniah,[d] 11:22 [d]1Ch 9:15
the son of Mica. Uzzi was one of Asaph's
descendants, who were the singers responsible for the service of the house
of God. 23The singers[e] were under the 11:23 [e]Ne 7:44
king's orders, which regulated their dai-
ly activity.
24Pethahiah son of Meshezabel, one
of the descendants of Zerah[f] son of Ju- 11:24 [f]Ge 38:30
dah, was the king's agent in all affairs
relating to the people.
25As for the villages with their fields,
some of the people of Judah lived
in Kiriath Arba[g] and its surrounding 11:25 [g]Ge 35:27; Jos 14:15 [h]Nu 21:30
settlements, in Dibon[h] and its settle-
ments, in Jekabzeel and its villages, 26in

[a]*14* Most Septuagint manuscripts; Hebrew *their*

11:26 [i]Jos 15:27 Jeshua, in Moladah, in Beth Pelet,[i] 27in
Hazar Shual, in Beersheba[j] and its set-
11:27 [j]Ge 21:14 tlements, 28in Ziklag,[k] in Meconah and
11:28 its settlements, 29in En Rimmon, in
[k]1Sa 27:6 Zorah,[l] in Jarmuth,[m] 30Zanoah, Adul-
11:29 lam[n] and their villages, in Lachish[o] and
[l]Jos 15:33 its fields, and in Azekah[p] and its settle-
[m]Jos 10:3 ments. So they were living all the way
11:30 from Beersheba[q] to the Valley of Hin-
[n]Jos 15:35 [o]Jos 10:3 nom.
[p]Jos 10:10 [q]Jos 15:28 31The descendants of the Benjamites
from Geba[r] lived in Micmash,[s] Aija,
11:31 [r]Jos 21:17; Bethel and its settlements, 32in Ana-
Isa 10:29 thoth,[t] Nob[u] and Ananiah, 33in Hazor,[v]
[s]1Sa 13:2 Ramah and Gittaim,[w] 34in Hadid, Ze-
11:32 [t]Jos 21:18; boim[x] and Neballat, 35in Lod and Ono,[y]
Isa 10:30 [u]1Sa 21:1 and in the Valley of the Craftsmen.
36Some of the divisions of the Levites
11:33 [v]Jos 11:1 [w]2Sa 4:3 of Judah settled in Benjamin.

11:34 [x]1Sa 13:18

Priests and Levites

11:35 [y]1Ch 8:12 12 These were the priests[z] and Levites who returned with Zerubba-
12:1 [z]Ne 10:1-8 bel[a] son of Shealtiel and with Jeshua:[b]
[a]1Ch 3:19 Seraiah,[c] Jeremiah, Ezra,
[b]Ezr 2:2 2Amariah, Malluch, Hattush,
[c]Ezr 2:2 3Shecaniah, Rehum, Meremoth,
12:4 [d]Zec 1:1 4Iddo,[d] Ginnethon,[a] Abijah,[e]
[e]Lk 1:5 5Mijamin,[b] Moadiah, Bilgah,
12:6 6Shemaiah, Joiarib, Jedaiah,[f]
[f]1Ch 24:7 7Sallu, Amok, Hilkiah and Jedaiah.
These were the leaders of the priests
and their associates in the days of Jeshua.
8The Levites were Jeshua, Binnui,
Kadmiel, Sherebiah, Judah, and also
12:8 [g]Ne 11:17 Mattaniah,[g] who, together with his associates, was in charge of the songs
of thanksgiving. 9Bakbukiah and Unni,
their associates, stood opposite them in
the services.
10Jeshua was the father of Joiakim,
12:10 [h]Ezr 10:24 Joiakim the father of Eliashib,[h] Eliashib
the father of Joiada, 11Joiada the father
of Jonathan, and Jonathan the father of
Jaddua.
12In the days of Joiakim, these were
the heads of the priestly families:
of Seraiah's family, Meraiah;
of Jeremiah's, Hananiah;
13of Ezra's, Meshullam;
of Amariah's, Jehohanan;
14of Malluch's, Jonathan;
of Shecaniah's,[c] Joseph;
15of Harim's, Adna;
12:16 of Meremoth's,[d] Helkai;
[i]ver 4 16of Iddo's,[i] Zechariah;
of Ginnethon's, Meshullam;
17of Abijah's, Zicri;
of Miniamin's and of Moadiah's,
Piltai;
18of Bilgah's, Shammua;
of Shemaiah's, Jehonathan;
19of Joiarib's, Mattenai;
of Jedaiah's, Uzzi;
20of Sallu's, Kallai;
of Amok's, Eber;
21of Hilkiah's, Hashabiah;
of Jedaiah's, Nethanel.
22The family heads of the Levites
in the days of Eliashib, Joiada, Johanan and Jaddua, as well as those of the
priests, were recorded in the reign of
Darius the Persian. 23The family heads
among the descendants of Levi up to
the time of Johanan son of Eliashib
were recorded in the book of the an-
nals. 24And the leaders of the Levites[j] 12:24 [j]Ezr 2:40
were Hashabiah, Sherebiah, Jeshua son
of Kadmiel, and their associates, who
stood opposite them to give praise and
thanksgiving, one section responding to
the other, as prescribed by David the
man of God.
25Mattaniah, Bakbukiah, Obadiah,
Meshullam, Talmon and Akkub were
gatekeepers who guarded the storerooms
at the gates. 26They served in the days
of Joiakim son of Jeshua, the son of
Jozadak, and in the days of Nehemiah
the governor and of Ezra the priest and
scribe.

Dedication of the Wall of Jerusalem

27At the dedication[k] of the wall of 12:27 [k]Dt 20:5
Jerusalem, the Levites were sought out [l]2Sa 6:5 [m]1Ch 15:16,
from where they lived and were brought 28; 25:6;
to Jerusalem to celebrate joyfully the Ps 92:3
dedication with songs of thanksgiving
and with the music of cymbals,[l] harps
and lyres.[m] 28The singers also were
brought together from the region
around Jerusalem—from the villages of
the Netophathites,[n] 29from Beth Gil- 12:28 [n]1Ch 2:54;
gal, and from the area of Geba and 9:16
Azmaveth, for the singers had built villages for themselves around Jerusalem.

[a]*4* Many Hebrew manuscripts and Vulgate (see also Neh. 12:16); most Hebrew manuscripts *Ginnethoi* [b]*5* A variant of *Miniamin* [c]*14* Very many Hebrew manuscripts, some Septuagint manuscripts and Syriac (see also Neh. 12:3); most Hebrew manuscripts *Shebaniah's* [d]*15* Some Septuagint manuscripts (see also Neh. 12:3); Hebrew *Meraioth's*

[30]When the priests and Levites had purified themselves ceremonially, they purified the people,[o] the gates and the wall.

12:30 [o]Ex 19:10; Job 1:5

JOY

WHERE GLOOM KNOWS NO FEAR

Nehemiah 12:27

The broken citadel was resurrected! Singing was the order of the day. The joy of the Lord was a joy that leveled humankind to one age. The old, through joy, became instantly childlike. Children washed by it became instantly mature.

[31]I had the leaders of Judah go up on top[a] of the wall. I also assigned two large choirs to give thanks. One was to proceed on top[b] of the wall to the right, toward the Dung Gate.[p] [32]Hoshaiah and half the leaders of Judah followed them, [33]along with Azariah, Ezra, Meshullam, [34]Judah, Benjamin,[q] Shemaiah, Jeremiah, [35]as well as some priests with trumpets,[r] and also Zechariah son of Jonathan, the son of Shemaiah, the son of Mattaniah, the son of Micaiah, the son of Zaccur, the son of Asaph, [36]and his associates—Shemaiah, Azarel, Milalai, Gilalai, Maai, Nethanel, Judah and Hanani—with musical instruments[s] ⌞prescribed by⌟ David the man of God.[t] Ezra[u] the scribe led the procession. [37]At the Fountain Gate[v] they continued directly up the steps of the City of David on the ascent to the wall and passed above the house of David to the Water Gate[w] on the east.

[38]The second choir proceeded in the opposite direction. I followed them on top[c] of the wall, together with half the people—past the Tower of the Ovens[x] to the Broad Wall,[y] [39]over the Gate of Ephraim,[z] the Jeshanah[d] Gate,[a] the Fish Gate,[b] the Tower of Hananel[c] and the Tower of the Hundred,[d] as far as the Sheep Gate.[e] At the Gate of the Guard they stopped.

[40]The two choirs that gave thanks then took their places in the house of God; so did I, together with half the officials, [41]as well as the priests—Eliakim, Maaseiah, Miniamin, Micaiah, Elioenai, Zechariah and Hananiah with their trumpets— [42]and also Maaseiah, Shemaiah, Eleazar, Uzzi, Jehohanan, Malkijah, Elam and Ezer. The choirs sang under the direction of Jezrahiah. [43]And on that day they offered great sacrifices, rejoicing because God had given them great joy. The women and children also rejoiced. The sound of rejoicing in Jerusalem could be heard far away.

12:31 [p]Ne 2:13
12:34 [q]Ezr 1:5
12:35 [r]Ezr 3:10
12:36 [s]1Ch 15:16 [t]2Ch 8:14 [u]Ezr 7:6
12:37 [v]Ne 2:14; 3:15 [w]Ne 3:26
12:38 [x]Ne 3:11 [y]Ne 3:8
12:39 [z]2Ki 14:13; Ne 8:16 [a]Ne 3:6 [b]2Ch 33:14; Ne 3:3 [c]Ne 3:1 [d]Ne 3:1 [e]Ne 3:1

[44]At that time men were appointed to be in charge of the storerooms[f] for the contributions, firstfruits and tithes.[g] From the fields around the towns they were to bring into the storerooms the portions required by the Law for the priests and the Levites, for Judah was pleased with the ministering priests and Levites.[h] [45]They performed the service of their God and the service of purification, as did also the singers and gatekeepers, according to the commands of David[i] and his son Solomon.[j] [46]For long ago, in the days of David and Asaph,[k] there had been directors for the singers and for the songs of praise[l] and thanksgiving to God. [47]So in the days of Zerubbabel and of Nehemiah, all Israel contributed the daily portions for the singers and gatekeepers. They also set aside the portion for the other Levites, and the Levites set aside the portion for the descendants of Aaron.[m]

Nehemiah's Final Reforms

13 On that day the Book of Moses was read aloud in the hearing of the people and there it was found written that no Ammonite or Moabite should ever be admitted into the assembly of God,[n] [2]because they had not met the Israelites with food and water but had hired Balaam[o] to call a curse down on them.[p] (Our God, however, turned the curse into a blessing.)[q] [3]When the people heard this law, they excluded from Israel all who were of foreign descent.[r]

[4]Before this, Eliashib the priest had been put in charge of the storerooms[s] of the house of our God. He was closely associated with Tobiah,[t] [5]and he had provided him with a large room formerly used to store the grain offerings and incense and temple articles, and also the tithes[u] of grain, new wine and oil prescribed for the Levites, singers

12:44 [f]Ne 13:4,13 [g]Lev 27:30 [h]Dt 18:8
12:45 [i]1Ch 25:1; 2Ch 8:14 [j]1Ch 6:31; 23:5
12:46 [k]2Ch 35:15 [l]2Ch 29:27; Ps 137:4
12:47 [m]Nu 18:21; Dt 18:8
13:1 [n]ver 23; Dt 23:3
13:2 [o]Nu 22:3-11 [p]Nu 23:7; Dt 23:3 [q]Nu 23:11; Dt 23:4-5
13:3 [r]ver 23; Ne 9:2
13:4 [s]Ne 12:44 [t]Ne 2:10
13:5 [u]Lev 27:30; Nu 18:21

[a]31 Or *go alongside* [b]31 Or *proceed alongside*
[c]38 Or *them alongside* [d]39 Or *Old*

and gatekeepers, as well as the contributions for the priests.
6 But while all this was going on, I
was not in Jerusalem, for in the thirty-
13:6 second year of Artaxerxes[v] king of Bab-
vNe 2:6; 5:14 ylon I had returned to the king. Some
time later I asked his permission 7 and
came back to Jerusalem. Here I learned
13:7 about the evil thing Eliashib[w] had done
wEzr 10:24 in providing Tobiah a room in the
courts of the house of God. 8 I was
greatly displeased and threw all Tobiah's
13:8 household goods out of the room.[x] 9 I
xMt 21:12-13; gave orders to purify the rooms,[y] and
Jn 2:13-16 then I put back into them the equip-
13:9 y1Ch 23:28; ment of the house of God, with the
2Ch 29:5 grain offerings and the incense.
10 I also learned that the portions assigned to the Levites had not been given
13:10 to them,[z] and that all the Levites and
zDt 12:19 singers responsible for the service had
gone back to their own fields. 11 So I
rebuked the officials and asked them,
13:11 aNe 10:37-39; "Why is the house of God neglected?"[a]
Hag 1:1-9 Then I called them together and stationed them at their posts.
13:12 b2Ch 31:6 12 All Judah brought the tithes[b] of
c1Ki 7:51; grain, new wine and oil into the store-
Ne 10:37-39; Mal 3:10 rooms.[c] 13 I put Shelemiah the priest,
Zadok the scribe, and a Levite named
Pedaiah in charge of the storerooms and
made Hanan son of Zaccur, the son of
Mattaniah, their assistant, because these
men were considered trustworthy. They
13:13 were made responsible for distributing
dNe 12:44; Ac 6:1-5 the supplies to their brothers.[d]
14 Remember[e] me for this, O my God,
13:14 and do not blot out what I have so
eGe 8:1 faithfully done for the house of my God
and its services.
15 In those days I saw men in Judah
treading winepresses on the Sabbath and
bringing in grain and loading it on donkeys, together with wine, grapes, figs
and all other kinds of loads. And they
were bringing all this into Jerusalem on
13:15 the Sabbath.[f] Therefore I warned them
fEx 20:8-11; 34:21; against selling food on that day. 16 Men
Dt 5:12-15; from Tyre who lived in Jerusalem were
Ne 10:31 bringing in fish and all kinds of merchandise and selling them in Jerusalem
13:16 on the Sabbath[g] to the people of Ju-
gNe 10:31 dah. 17 I rebuked the nobles of Judah
and said to them, "What is this wicked
thing you are doing—desecrating the
Sabbath day? 18 Didn't your forefathers
do the same things, so that our God
brought all this calamity upon us and
upon this city? Now you are stirring up
more wrath against Israel by desecrating the Sabbath."[h] 13:18 hNe 10:31;
19 When evening shadows fell on the Jer 17:21-23
gates of Jerusalem before the Sabbath,[i] 13:19
I ordered the doors to be shut and not iLev 23:32
opened until the Sabbath was over. I
stationed some of my own men at the
gates so that no load could be brought
in on the Sabbath day. 20 Once or twice
the merchants and sellers of all kinds
of goods spent the night outside Jerusalem. 21 But I warned them and said,
"Why do you spend the night by the
wall? If you do this again, I will lay
hands on you." From that time on
they no longer came on the Sabbath.
22 Then I commanded the Levites to
purify themselves and go and guard the
gates in order to keep the Sabbath day
holy.

Remember[j] me for this also, O my 13:22
God, and show mercy to me according jGe 8:1; Ne 12:30
to your great love.

23 Moreover, in those days I saw men
of Judah who had married[k] women from 13:23 kEzr 9:1-2;
Ashdod, Ammon and Moab.[l] 24 Half of Mal 2:11
their children spoke the language of lver 1; Ne 10:30
Ashdod or the language of one of the
other peoples, and did not know how
to speak the language of Judah. 25 I rebuked them and called curses down
on them. I beat some of the men and
pulled out their hair. I made them take
an oath[m] in God's name and said: "You 13:25 mEzr 10:5
are not to give your daughters in mar-
riage to their sons, nor are you to take
their daughters in marriage for your
sons or for yourselves. 26 Was it not because of marriages like these that Solomon king of Israel sinned? Among the
many nations there was no king like 13:26
him.[n] He was loved by his God,[o] and n1Ki 3:13;
God made him king over all Israel, but 2Ch 1:12
even he was led into sin by foreign o2Sa 12:25
women.[p] 27 Must we hear now that you p1Ki 11:3
too are doing all this terrible wickedness and are being unfaithful to our
God by marrying[q] foreign women?" 13:27
28 One of the sons of Joiada son of qEzr 9:14; 10:2
Eliashib[r] the high priest was son-in-law 13:28
to Sanballat[s] the Horonite. And I drove rEzr 10:24
him away from me. sNe 2:10

29 Remember[t] them, O my God, be- 13:29 tNe 6:14
cause they defiled the priestly office and

the covenant of the priesthood and of
the Levites.

30So I purified the priests and the
13:30 [u]Ne 10:30 Levites of everything foreign,[u] and assigned them duties, each to his own
task. 31I also made provision for contributions of wood[v] at designated times,
and for the firstfruits.

Remember[w] me with favor, O my
God.

13:31 [v]Ne 10:34 [w]ver 14,22; Ge 8:1

ESTHER

AUTHORSHIP AND DATE

The author is unknown.

c. 470 B.C. since Esther became queen in 479 B.C.

KEY THEMES

The book of Esther portrays the sovereignty of God over Israel in exile. God was not only sovereign over the Jews in captivity; he was also sovereign over all those nations with which the Israelites interacted.

Esther sought to save her people from annihilation. She was a beautiful woman who became queen in Persia. She then used her power and her goodness to great advantage. In February or March, on the fourteenth day of the Hebrew month of Adar, all of Judaism still celebrates the Feast of Purim, or the Feast of the "Lots." The lots were those cast by Haman to determine the date for the extermination of the Jews. Purim is a significant day dating back to the courage and goodness of Queen Esther, who saved Israel from extinction.

FRUIT OF THE SPIRIT IN ESTHER

Goodness: The courage of Esther came directly from her goodness. Esther never forgot who she was—a Jew who could not live as queen while her people suffered or were martyred in misery. This goodness can be seen throughout the book and witnessed primarily in the following verses: "Then Esther sent this reply to Mordecai: 'Go, gather together all the Jews who are in Susa, and fast for me. Do not eat or drink for three days, night or day. I and my maids will fast as you do. When this is done, I will go to the king, even though it is against the law. And if I perish, I perish' " (4:15–16). "Then Queen Esther answered,... 'Spare my people—this is my request. For I and my people have been sold for destruction and slaughter and annihilation' " (7:3–4).

Esther's goodness stood for all that was right and good, but it was also steeled in courage and diplomacy. Goodness that has learned all the skills of successful negotiation is goodness indeed. The summation of the book and its dependency on Esther's goodness is found in this key verse—a charge given to Esther by her cousin Mordecai: "For if you remain silent at this time, relief and deliverance for the Jews will arise from another place, but you and your father's family will perish. And who knows but that you have come to royal position for such a time as this?" (4:14). Esther's goodness was not only measured by doing the right thing, it was also measured by doing things right.

Queen Vashti Deposed

1 This is what happened during the
time of Xerxes,[a][a] the Xerxes who
ruled over 127 provinces[b] stretching
from India to Cush[b]:[c] 2At that time
King Xerxes reigned from his royal
throne in the citadel of Susa,[d] 3and in
the third year of his reign he gave a
banquet[e] for all his nobles and officials.
The military leaders of Persia and Media, the princes, and the nobles of the
provinces were present.
4For a full 180 days he displayed
the vast wealth of his kingdom and
the splendor and glory of his majesty.
5When these days were over, the king
gave a banquet, lasting seven days,[f] in
the enclosed garden[g] of the king's palace, for all the people from the least
to the greatest, who were in the citadel
of Susa. 6The garden had hangings of
white and blue linen, fastened with
cords of white linen and purple material
to silver rings on marble pillars. There
were couches[h] of gold and silver on a
mosaic pavement of porphyry, marble,
mother-of-pearl and other costly stones.
7Wine was served in goblets of gold,
each one different from the other, and
the royal wine was abundant, in keeping with the king's liberality.[i] 8By the
king's command each guest was allowed
to drink in his own way, for the king
instructed all the wine stewards to serve
each man what he wished.
9Queen Vashti also gave a banquet[j]
for the women in the royal palace of
King Xerxes.
10On the seventh day, when King
Xerxes was in high spirits[k] from wine,[l]
he commanded the seven eunuchs who
served him—Mehuman, Biztha, Harbona,[m] Bigtha, Abagtha, Zethar and
Carcas— 11to bring[n] before him Queen
Vashti, wearing her royal crown, in order to display her beauty[o] to the people
and nobles, for she was lovely to look
at. 12But when the attendants delivered
the king's command, Queen Vashti refused to come. Then the king became
furious and burned with anger.[p]
13Since it was customary for the king
to consult experts in matters of law and
justice, he spoke with the wise men who
understood the times[q] 14and were closest to the king—Carshena, Shethar, Ad-
matha, Tarshish, Meres, Marsena and
Memucan, the seven nobles[r] of Persia
and Media who had special access to the
king and were highest in the kingdom.
15"According to law, what must be
done to Queen Vashti?" he asked. "She
has not obeyed the command of King
Xerxes that the eunuchs have taken to
her."
16Then Memucan replied in the presence of the king and the nobles, "Queen
Vashti has done wrong, not only against
the king but also against all the nobles
and the peoples of all the provinces
of King Xerxes. 17For the queen's conduct will become known to all the
women, and so they will despise their
husbands and say, 'King Xerxes commanded Queen Vashti to be brought
before him, but she would not come.'
18This very day the Persian and Median
women of the nobility who have heard
about the queen's conduct will respond
to all the king's nobles in the same way.
There will be no end of disrespect and
discord.[s]
19"Therefore, if it pleases the king,[t]
let him issue a royal decree and let it be
written in the laws of Persia and Media,
which cannot be repealed,[u] that Vashti
is never again to enter the presence of
King Xerxes. Also let the king give her
royal position to someone else who is
better than she. 20Then when the king's
edict is proclaimed throughout all his
vast realm, all the women will respect
their husbands, from the least to the
greatest."
21The king and his nobles were
pleased with this advice, so the king did
as Memucan proposed. 22He sent dispatches to all parts of the kingdom, to
each province in its own script and to
each people in its own language,[v] proclaiming in each people's tongue that
every man should be ruler over his own
household.

Esther Made Queen

2 Later when the anger of King Xerxes had subsided,[w] he remembered
Vashti and what she had done and
what he had decreed about her. 2Then
the king's personal attendants proposed,
"Let a search be made for beautiful

1:1 [a]Ezr 4:6; Da 9:1 [b]Est 9:30; Da 3:2; 6:1 [c]Est 8:9
1:2 [d]Ezr 4:9; Ne 1:1; Est 2:8
1:3 [e]1Ki 3:15; Est 2:18
1:5 [f]Jdg 14:17 [g]2Ki 21:18; Est 7:7-8
1:6 [h]Est 7:8; Eze 23:41; Am 3:12; 6:4
1:7 [i]Est 2:18; Da 5:2
1:9 [j]1Ki 3:15
1:10 [k]Jdg 16:25; Ru 3:7 [l]Ge 14:18; Est 3:15; 5:6; 7:2; Pr 31:4-7; Da 5:1-4 [m]Est 7:9
1:11 [n]SS 2:4 [o]Ps 45:11; Eze 16:14
1:12 [p]Ge 39:19; Est 2:21; 7:7; Pr 19:12
1:13 [q]1Ch 12:32; Jer 10:7; Da 2:12
1:14 [r]2Ki 25:19; Ezr 7:14
1:18 [s]Pr 19:13; 27:15
1:19 [t]Ecc 8:4 [u]Est 8:8; Da 6:8,12
1:22 [v]Ne 13:24; Est 8:9; Eph 5:22-24; 1Ti 2:12
2:1 [w]Est 1:19-20; 7:10

[a] *1* Hebrew *Ahasuerus,* a variant of Xerxes' Persian name; here and throughout Esther [b] *1* That is, the upper Nile region

young virgins for the king. [3]Let the king appoint commissioners in every province of his realm to bring all these beautiful girls into the harem at the citadel of Susa. Let them be placed under the care of Hegai, the king's eunuch, who is in charge of the women; and let beauty treatments be given to them. [4]Then let the girl who pleases the king be queen instead of Vashti." This advice appealed to the king, and he followed it.

[5]Now there was in the citadel of Susa a Jew of the tribe of Benjamin, named Mordecai son of Jair, the son of Shimei, the son of Kish,[x] [6]who had been carried into exile from Jerusalem by Nebuchadnezzar king of Babylon, among those taken captive with Jehoiachin[a][y] king of Judah.[z] [7]Mordecai had a cousin named Hadassah, whom he had brought up because she had neither father nor mother. This girl, who was also known as Esther,[a] was lovely[b] in form and features, and Mordecai had taken her as his own daughter when her father and mother died.

[8]When the king's order and edict had been proclaimed, many girls were brought to the citadel of Susa[c] and put under the care of Hegai. Esther also was taken to the king's palace and entrusted to Hegai, who had charge of the harem. [9]The girl pleased him and won his favor.[d] Immediately he provided her with her beauty treatments and special food.[e] He assigned to her seven maids selected from the king's palace and moved her and her maids into the best place in the harem.

[10]Esther had not revealed her nationality and family background, because Mordecai had forbidden her to do so.[f] [11]Every day he walked back and forth near the courtyard of the harem to find out how Esther was and what was happening to her.

[12]Before a girl's turn came to go in to King Xerxes, she had to complete twelve months of beauty treatments prescribed for the women, six months with oil of myrrh and six with perfumes[g] and cosmetics. [13]And this is how she would go to the king: Anything she wanted was given her to take with her from the harem to the king's palace. [14]In the evening she would go there and in the morning return to another part of the harem to the care of Shaashgaz, the king's eunuch who was in charge of the concubines.[h] She would not return to the king unless he was pleased with her and summoned her by name.[i]

[15]When the turn came for Esther (the girl Mordecai had adopted, the daughter of his uncle Abihail[j]) to go to the king,[k] she asked for nothing other than what Hegai, the king's eunuch who was in charge of the harem, suggested. And Esther won the favor[l] of everyone who saw her. [16]She was taken to King Xerxes in the royal residence in the tenth month, the month of Tebeth, in the seventh year of his reign.

[17]Now the king was attracted to Esther more than to any of the other women, and she won his favor and approval more than any of the other virgins. So he set a royal crown on her head and made her queen[m] instead of Vashti. [18]And the king gave a great banquet,[n] Esther's banquet, for all his nobles and officials.[o] He proclaimed a holiday throughout the provinces and distributed gifts with royal liberality.[p]

Mordecai Uncovers a Conspiracy

[19]When the virgins were assembled a second time, Mordecai was sitting at the king's gate.[q] [20]But Esther had kept secret her family background and nationality just as Mordecai had told her to do, for she continued to follow Mordecai's instructions as she had done when he was bringing her up.[r]

[21]During the time Mordecai was sitting at the king's gate, Bigthana[b] and Teresh, two of the king's officers[s] who guarded the doorway, became angry[t] and conspired to assassinate King Xerxes. [22]But Mordecai found out about the plot and told Queen Esther, who in turn reported it to the king, giving credit to Mordecai. [23]And when the report was investigated and found to be true, the two officials were hanged[u] on a gallows.[c] All this was recorded in the book of the annals[v] in the presence of the king.

Haman's Plot to Destroy the Jews

3 After these events, King Xerxes honored Haman son of Hamme-

[a]*6* Hebrew *Jeconiah,* a variant of *Jehoiachin*
[b]*21* Hebrew *Bigthan,* a variant of *Bigthana* [c]*23* Or *were hung* (or *impaled*) *on poles*; similarly elsewhere in Esther

2:5 [x]1Sa 9:1; Est 3:2
2:6 [y]2Ki 24:6,15; 2Ch 36:10,20 [z]Da 1:1-5; 5:13
2:7 [a]Ge 41:45 [b]Ge 39:6
2:8 [c]ver 3,15; Ne 1:1; Est 1:2; Da 8:2
2:9 [d]Ge 39:21 [e]ver 3,12; Ge 37:3; 1Sa 9:22-24; 2Ki 25:30; Eze 16:9-13; Da 1:5
2:10 [f]ver 20
2:12 [g]Pr 27:9; SS 1:3; Isa 3:24
2:14 [h]1Ki 11:3; SS 6:8; Da 5:2 [i]Est 4:11
2:15 [j]Est 9:29 [k]Ps 45:14 [l]Ge 18:3; 30:27; Est 5:8
2:17 [m]Est 1:11; Eze 16:9-13
2:18 [n]1Ki 3:15; Est 1:3 [o]Ge 40:20 [p]Est 1:7
2:19 [q]ver 21; Est 3:2; 4:2; 5:13
2:20 [r]ver 10
2:21 [s]Ge 40:2; Est 6:2 [t]Est 1:12; 3:5; 5:9; 7:7
2:23 [u]Ge 40:19; Ps 7:14-16; Pr 26:27 [v]Est 6:1; 10:2

datha, the Agagite,[w] elevating him and
giving him a seat of honor higher than
that of all the other nobles. 2All the royal officials at the king's gate knelt down
and paid honor to Haman, for the king
had commanded this concerning him.
But Mordecai would not kneel down or
pay him honor.
3Then the royal officials at the king's
gate asked Mordecai, "Why do you disobey the king's command?"[x] 4Day after
day they spoke to him but he refused
to comply.[y] Therefore they told Haman
about it to see whether Mordecai's behavior would be tolerated, for he had
told them he was a Jew.
5When Haman saw that Mordecai
would not kneel down or pay him
honor, he was enraged.[z] 6Yet having
learned who Mordecai's people were, he
scorned the idea of killing only Mordecai. Instead Haman looked for a way[a]
to destroy[b] all Mordecai's people, the
Jews,[c] throughout the whole kingdom of
Xerxes.
7In the twelfth year of King Xerxes,
in the first month, the month of Ni-
san, they cast the *pur*[d] (that is, the lot[e])
in the presence of Haman to select a
day and month. And the lot fell on[a] the
twelfth month, the month of Adar.[f]
8Then Haman said to King Xerxes,
"There is a certain people dispersed and
scattered among the peoples in all the
provinces of your kingdom whose customs[g] are different from those of all
other people and who do not obey[h] the
king's laws; it is not in the king's best interest to tolerate them.[i] 9If it pleases the
king, let a decree be issued to destroy
them, and I will put ten thousand talents[b] of silver into the royal treasury for
the men who carry out this business."[j]
10So the king took his signet ring[k]
from his finger and gave it to Haman
son of Hammedatha, the Agagite, the
enemy of the Jews. 11"Keep the money," the king said to Haman, "and do
with the people as you please."
12Then on the thirteenth day of the
first month the royal secretaries were
summoned. They wrote out in the script
of each province and in the language[l]
of each people all Haman's orders to
the king's satraps, the governors of the
various provinces and the nobles of the
various peoples. These were written in
the name of King Xerxes himself and
sealed[m] with his own ring. 13Dispatches
were sent by couriers to all the king's
provinces with the order to destroy,
kill and annihilate all the Jews[n]—young
and old, women and little children—
on a single day, the thirteenth day of
the twelfth month, the month of Adar,[o]
and to plunder[p] their goods. 14A copy
of the text of the edict was to be issued as law in every province and made
known to the people of every nationality so they would be ready for that
day.[q]
15Spurred on by the king's command,
the couriers went out, and the edict was
issued in the citadel of Susa.[r] The king
and Haman sat down to drink,[s] but the
city of Susa was bewildered.[t]

Mordecai Persuades Esther to Help

4 When Mordecai learned of all that
had been done, he tore his clothes,[u]
put on sackcloth and ashes,[v] and went
out into the city, wailing[w] loudly and
bitterly. 2But he went only as far as the
king's gate,[x] because no one clothed in
sackcloth was allowed to enter it. 3In
every province to which the edict and
order of the king came, there was great
mourning among the Jews, with fasting, weeping and wailing. Many lay in
sackcloth and ashes.
4When Esther's maids and eunuchs
came and told her about Mordecai, she
was in great distress. She sent clothes
for him to put on instead of his sackcloth, but he would not accept them.
5Then Esther summoned Hathach, one
of the king's eunuchs assigned to attend
her, and ordered him to find out what
was troubling Mordecai and why.
6So Hathach went out to Mordecai
in the open square of the city in front
of the king's gate. 7Mordecai told him
everything that had happened to him,
including the exact amount of money
Haman had promised to pay into the
royal treasury for the destruction of the
Jews.[y] 8He also gave him a copy of the
text of the edict for their annihilation,
which had been published in Susa, to
show to Esther and explain it to her,
and he told him to urge her to go into
the king's presence to beg for mercy and
plead with him for her people.

[a]7 Septuagint; Hebrew does not have *And the lot fell on.* [b]9 That is, about 375 tons (about 345 metric tons)

3:1 [w]ver 10; Ex 17:8-16; Nu 24:7; Dt 25:17-19; 1Sa 14:48; Est 5:11
3:3 [x]Est 5:9; Da 3:12
3:4 [y]Ge 39:10
3:5 [z]Est 2:21; 5:9
3:6 [a]Pr 16:25 [b]Ps 74:8; 83:4 [c]Est 9:24
3:7 [d]Est 9:24,26 [e]Lev 16:8; 1Sa 10:21 [f]ver 13; Ezr 6:15; Est 9:19
3:8 [g]Ac 16:20-21 [h]Jer 29:7; Da 6:13 [i]Ezr 4:15
3:9 [j]Est 7:4
3:10 [k]Ge 41:42; Est 7:6; 8:2
3:12 [l]Ne 13:24
3:12 [m]Ge 38:18; 1Ki 21:8; Est 8:8-10
3:13 [n]1Sa 15:3; Ezr 4:6; Est 8:10-14 [o]ver 7 [p]Est 8:11; 9:10
3:14 [q]Est 8:8; 9:1
3:15 [r]Est 8:14 [s]Est 1:10 [t]Est 8:15
4:1 [u]Nu 14:6 [v]2Sa 13:19; Eze 27:30-31; Jnh 3:5-6 [w]Ex 11:6; Ps 30:11
4:2 [x]Est 2:19
4:7 [y]Est 3:9; 7:4

[9]Hathach went back and reported to
Esther what Mordecai had said. [10]Then
she instructed him to say to Mordecai,
[11]"All the king's officials and the people of the royal provinces know that
for any man or woman who approaches
the king in the inner court without being summoned[z] the king has but one
law:[a] that he be put to death. The only
exception to this is for the king to extend the gold scepter[b] to him and spare
his life. But thirty days have passed
since I was called to go to the king."

4:11 [z]Est 2:14 [a]Da 2:9 [b]Est 5:1,2; 8:4

[12]When Esther's words were reported to Mordecai, [13]he sent back this answer: "Do not think that because you
are in the king's house you alone of all
the Jews will escape. [14]For if you remain silent[c] at this time, relief[d] and deliverance[e] for the Jews will arise from
another place, but you and your father's
family will perish. And who knows but
that you have come to royal position
for such a time as this?"[f]
[15]Then Esther sent this reply to Mordecai: [16]"Go, gather together all the

4:14 [c]Ecc 3:7; Isa 62:1; Am 5:13 [d]Est 9:16,22 [e]Ge 45:7; Dt 28:29 [f]Ge 50:20

ESTHER

Kindness, the Soft Underbelly of Courage (4:15)

Esther, a Jew, found herself in the high position of queen in the court of King Xerxes of Persia. Her unique position allowed her to be a central player in disclosing a horrifying plot to exterminate all the Jews living in the vast kingdom of Persia. Esther was able to use her position and influence to prevent the planned genocide and bring justice to those involved in the scheme. This tale of courage shows us that underneath courage lies a heart of kindness.

It has been said that courage is fear that has said its prayers. Esther, fearing for her life, asked her people to pray before she approached King Xerxes (see Esther 4:16). Each time she approached the king, she began her pleas by using the tenuous word *if.*

Esther 5:4: "If it pleases the king . . . let the king, together with Haman, come today to a banquet I have prepared for him."

Esther 5:8: "If the king regards me with favor . . ." Esther said cautiously and kindly as she appealed to Xerxes to attend a second banquet.

Esther 7:3: "If I have found favor with you, O king . . ." pleaded the queen as she was about to make her great move of courage, denouncing Haman, the one who had plotted the destruction of an entire race of people.

Esther 8:5: "If it pleases the king . . ."

Each of these beginnings reveals Esther using courage that had practiced kindness. Courage without thought or regard for others may offend or accomplish little, but kindly courage achieves its goals.

Esther is remembered for having said, "I will go to the king, even though it is against the law. And if I perish, I perish" (4:16). But what she really meant was, "I will go to the king and kindly but courageously make my case. Then if I perish, so be it."

Consider Esther's acrostic:

E . . . Everyone is ushered into the heart of God and left unafraid of the usher.

S . . . Smiling is the way kindness says, "Be not afraid."

T . . . Thanksgiving is the heart of kindness.

H . . . Hope is the sermon kindness preaches.

E . . . Eager is the adjective of the kindhearted.

R . . . Reassurance is the gift kindness gives to those who would be afraid.

Kindness and courage add up to charisma. The winning person with whom everyone desires friendship may be afraid, but he or she has the inner strength to stand up to fear. Kindness is the simple act of putting others before self. Such kindness is what the Jews called *chesed.* This word is a synonym for grace. The New Testament word for grace is *charis,* which means "gift." Giving is putting others ahead of yourself. Kindness is all of these things taken together and acted upon with courage.

4:16 [g]2Ch 20:3; Est 9:31 [h]Ge 43:14

Jews who are in Susa, and fast[g] for me.
Do not eat or drink for three days,
night or day. I and my maids will fast as
you do. When this is done, I will go to
the king, even though it is against the
law. And if I perish, I perish."[h]
17So Mordecai went away and carried out all of Esther's instructions.

SELF-CONTROL

IF I PERISH, I PERISH

Esther 4:16

There are stands that must be taken if the faith is to endure. We cannot know at the outset of our daring whether we shall live after we have told the truth.

Some would advise us, "Compromise!
After all, we must go on living."
But those who bear the cross reply,
"Must we?"

Esther's Request to the King

5:1 [i]Est 4:16; Eze 16:13 [j]Est 6:4; Pr 21:1

5 On the third day Esther put on
her royal robes[i] and stood in the
inner court of the palace, in front of
the king's[j] hall. The king was sitting on
his royal throne in the hall, facing the
entrance. 2When he saw Queen Esther
standing in the court, he was pleased
with her and held out to her the gold
scepter that was in his hand. So Esther
approached and touched the tip of the
scepter.[k]

5:2 [k]Est 4:11; 8:4; Pr 21:1

3Then the king asked, "What is it,
Queen Esther? What is your request?
Even up to half the kingdom,[l] it will be
given you."

5:3 [l]Est 7:2; Da 5:16; Mk 6:23

4"If it pleases the king," replied Esther, "let the king, together with Haman, come today to a banquet I have
prepared for him."
5"Bring Haman at once," the king
said, "so that we may do what Esther
asks."
So the king and Haman went to the
banquet Esther had prepared. 6As they
were drinking wine,[m] the king again
asked Esther, "Now what is your petition? It will be given you. And what
is your request? Even up to half the
kingdom,[n] it will be granted."[o]
7Esther replied, "My petition and my
request is this: 8If the king regards me
with favor[p] and if it pleases the king
to grant my petition and fulfill my request, let the king and Haman come
tomorrow to the banquet[q] I will prepare for them. Then I will answer the
king's question."

5:6 [m]Est 1:10 [n]Mk 6:23 [o]Est 7:2; 9:12

5:8 [p]Est 2:15; 7:3; 8:5

5:8 [q]1Ki 3:15; Est 6:14

Haman's Rage Against Mordecai

9Haman went out that day happy
and in high spirits. But when he saw
Mordecai at the king's gate and observed that he neither rose nor showed
fear in his presence, he was filled with
rage[r] against Mordecai.[s] 10Nevertheless,
Haman restrained himself and went
home.
Calling together his friends and
Zeresh,[t] his wife, 11Haman boasted[u] to
them about his vast wealth, his many
sons,[v] and all the ways the king had
honored him and how he had elevated
him above the other nobles and officials. 12"And that's not all," Haman
added. "I'm the only person[w] Queen
Esther invited to accompany the king
to the banquet she gave. And she has
invited me along with the king tomorrow. 13But all this gives me no satisfaction as long as I see that Jew Mordecai
sitting at the king's gate.[x]"
14His wife Zeresh and all his friends
said to him, "Have a gallows built, seventy-five feet[a] high,[y] and ask the king in
the morning to have Mordecai hanged[z]
on it. Then go with the king to the dinner and be happy." This suggestion delighted Haman, and he had the gallows
built.

5:9 [r]Est 2:21; Pr 14:17 [s]Est 3:3,5

5:10 [t]Est 6:13

5:11 [u]Pr 13:16 [v]Est 9:7-10,13

5:12 [w]Job 22:29; Pr 16:18; 29:23

5:13 [x]Est 2:19

5:14 [y]Est 7:9 [z]Ezr 6:11; Est 6:4

Mordecai Honored

6 That night the king could not
sleep;[a] so he ordered the book of
the chronicles,[b] the record of his reign,
to be brought in and read to him. 2It
was found recorded there that Mordecai had exposed Bigthana and Teresh,
two of the king's officers who guarded
the doorway, who had conspired to assassinate King Xerxes.
3"What honor and recognition has
Mordecai received for this?" the king
asked.
"Nothing has been done for him,"[c]
his attendants answered.
4The king said, "Who is in the court?"
Now Haman had just entered the outer
court of the palace to speak to the king

6:1 [a]Da 2:1; 6:18 [b]Est 2:23; 10:2

6:3 [c]Ecc 9:13-16

[a]14 Hebrew *fifty cubits* (about 23 meters)

about hanging Mordecai on the gallows
he had erected for him.
5His attendants answered, "Haman
is standing in the court."
"Bring him in," the king ordered.
6When Haman entered, the king
asked him, "What should be done for
the man the king delights to honor?"
Now Haman thought to himself,
"Who is there that the king would rather honor than me?" 7So he answered
the king, "For the man the king delights to honor, 8have them bring a roy-
6:8 [d]Ge 41:42; Isa 52:1 [e]1Ki 1:33 al robe[d] the king has worn and a horse[e]
the king has ridden, one with a royal
crest placed on its head. 9Then let the
robe and horse be entrusted to one of
the king's most noble princes. Let them
robe the man the king delights to hon-
or, and lead him on the horse through
the city streets, proclaiming before him,
'This is what is done for the man the
6:9 [f]Ge 41:43 king delights to honor![f]' "
10"Go at once," the king command-
ed Haman. "Get the robe and the horse
and do just as you have suggested for
Mordecai the Jew, who sits at the king's
gate. Do not neglect anything you have
recommended."
6:11 [g]Ge 41:42 11So Haman got[g] the robe and the
horse. He robed Mordecai, and led him
on horseback through the city streets,
proclaiming before him, "This is what
is done for the man the king delights to
honor!"
12Afterward Mordecai returned to
the king's gate. But Haman rushed
6:12 [h]2Sa 15:30; Jer 14:3,4; Mic 3:7 home, with his head covered[h] in grief,
13and told Zeresh[i] his wife and all his
friends everything that had happened
6:13 [i]Est 5:10 [j]Ps 57:6; Pr 26:27; 28:18 to him.
His advisers and his wife Zeresh said
to him, "Since Mordecai, before whom
your downfall[j] has started, is of Jewish
origin, you cannot stand against him—
you will surely come to ruin!" 14While
they were still talking with him, the
king's eunuchs arrived and hurried Ha-
6:14 [k]1Ki 3:15; Est 5:8 man away to the banquet[k] Esther had
prepared.

Haman Hanged

7 So the king and Haman went to
7:1 [l]Ge 40:20-22; Mt 22:1-14 dine[l] with Queen Esther, 2and as
they were drinking wine[m] on that sec-
7:2 [m]Est 1:10 ond day, the king again asked, "Queen
Esther, what is your petition? It will
be given you. What is your request?
Even up to half the kingdom,[n] it will be 7:2 [n]Est 5:3 [o]Est 9:12
granted.[o]"
3Then Queen Esther answered, "If I
have found favor[p] with you, O king, 7:3 [p]Est 2:15
and if it pleases your majesty, grant
me my life—this is my petition. And
spare my people—this is my request.
4For I and my people have been sold
for destruction and slaughter and
annihilation.[q] If we had merely been 7:4 [q]Est 3:9
sold as male and female slaves, I would
have kept quiet, because no such distress
would justify disturbing the king.[a]"
5King Xerxes asked Queen Esther,
"Who is he? Where is the man who has
dared to do such a thing?"
6Esther said, "The adversary and enemy is this vile Haman."
Then Haman was terrified before the
king and queen. 7The king got up in a
rage,[r] left his wine and went out into 7:7 [r]Ge 34:7; Est 1:12; Pr 19:12; 20:1-2 [s]2Ki 21:18 [t]Est 6:13
the palace garden.[s] But Haman, realiz-
ing that the king had already decided
his fate,[t] stayed behind to beg Queen
Esther for his life.
8Just as the king returned from the
palace garden to the banquet hall, Ha-
man was falling on the couch[u] where 7:8 [u]Est 1:6 [v]Ge 39:14 [w]Ge 34:7 [x]Est 6:12
Esther was reclining.[v]
The king exclaimed, "Will he even
molest the queen while she is with me
in the house?"[w]
As soon as the word left the king's
mouth, they covered Haman's face.[x]
9Then Harbona,[y] one of the eunuchs 7:9 [y]Est 1:10 [z]Est 5:14 [a]Ps 7:14-16; 9:16; Pr 11:5-6; 26:27; Mt 7:2
attending the king, said, "A gallows
seventy-five feet[b] high[z] stands by Haman's house. He had it made for Mordecai, who spoke up to help the king."
The king said, "Hang him on it!"[a]
10So they hanged Haman[b] on the gal- 7:10 [b]Pr 10:28 [c]Est 9:25 [d]Da 6:24 [e]Est 2:1
lows[c] he had prepared for Mordecai.[d]
Then the king's fury subsided.[e]

The King's Edict in Behalf of the Jews

8 That same day King Xerxes gave
Queen Esther the estate of Ha-
man,[f] the enemy of the Jews. And Mor- 8:1 [f]Est 2:7; 7:6; Pr 22:22-23
decai came into the presence of the
king, for Esther had told how he was
related to her. 2The king took off his
signet ring,[g] which he had reclaimed 8:2 [g]Ge 41:42; Est 3:10
from Haman, and presented it to Mor-

[a]4 Or *quiet, but the compensation our adversary offers cannot be compared with the loss the king would suffer* [b]9 Hebrew *fifty cubits* (about 23 meters)

decai. And Esther appointed him over
Haman's estate.[h]
3Esther again pleaded with the king,
falling at his feet and weeping. She
begged him to put an end to the evil
plan of Haman the Agagite, which he
had devised against the Jews. 4Then the
king extended the gold scepter[i] to Esther and she arose and stood before
him.
5"If it pleases the king," she said,
"and if he regards me with favor and
thinks it the right thing to do, and if he
is pleased with me, let an order be written overruling the dispatches that Haman son of Hammedatha, the Agagite,
devised and wrote to destroy the Jews
in all the king's provinces. 6For how can
I bear to see disaster fall on my people?
How can I bear to see the destruction
of my family?"[j]
7King Xerxes replied to Queen Esther
and to Mordecai the Jew, "Because Haman attacked the Jews, I have given his
estate to Esther, and they have hanged
him on the gallows. 8Now write another decree[k] in the king's name in behalf of the Jews as seems best to you,
and seal it with the king's signet ring[l]—
for no document written in the king's
name and sealed with his ring can be
revoked."[m]
9At once the royal secretaries were
summoned—on the twenty-third day
of the third month, the month of Si-
van. They wrote out all Mordecai's orders to the Jews, and to the satraps,
governors and nobles of the 127 provinces stretching from India to Cush.[a][n]
These orders were written in the script
of each province and the language of
each people and also to the Jews in
their own script and language.[o] 10Mor-
decai wrote in the name of King Xerxes, sealed the dispatches with the king's
signet ring, and sent them by mounted
couriers, who rode fast horses especially
bred for the king.
11The king's edict granted the Jews
in every city the right to assemble and
protect themselves; to destroy, kill and
annihilate any armed force of any nationality or province that might attack
them and their women and children;
and to plunder[p] the property of their
enemies. 12The day appointed for the
Jews to do this in all the provinces of
King Xerxes was the thirteenth day of
the twelfth month, the month of Adar.[q]
13A copy of the text of the edict was
to be issued as law in every province
and made known to the people of every
nationality so that the Jews would be
ready on that day[r] to avenge themselves
on their enemies.
14The couriers, riding the royal
horses, raced out, spurred on by the
king's command. And the edict was also
issued in the citadel of Susa.
15Mordecai[s] left the king's presence
wearing royal garments of blue and
white, a large crown of gold and a purple robe of fine linen.[t] And the city of
Susa held a joyous celebration.[u] 16For
the Jews it was a time of happiness
and joy,[v] gladness and honor.[w] 17In every province and in every city, wherever
the edict of the king went, there was
joy[x] and gladness among the Jews, with
feasting and celebrating. And many people of other nationalities became Jews
because fear[y] of the Jews had seized
them.[z]

Triumph of the Jews

9 On the thirteenth day of the twelfth
month, the month of Adar,[a] the
edict commanded by the king was to be
carried out. On this day the enemies of
the Jews had hoped to overpower them,
but now the tables were turned and the
Jews got the upper hand[b] over those
who hated them.[c] 2The Jews assembled
in their cities[d] in all the provinces of
King Xerxes to attack those seeking
their destruction. No one could stand
against them,[e] because the people of all
the other nationalities were afraid of
them. 3And all the nobles of the provinces, the satraps, the governors and the
king's administrators helped the Jews,[f]
because fear of Mordecai had seized
them. 4Mordecai was prominent[g] in the
palace; his reputation spread throughout the provinces, and he became more
and more powerful.[h]
5The Jews struck down all their enemies with the sword, killing and destroying them, and they did what they
pleased to those who hated them.[i] 6In
the citadel of Susa, the Jews killed and
destroyed five hundred men. 7They also
killed Parshandatha, Dalphon, Aspatha,

8:2 [h]Pr 13:22; Da 2:48
8:4 [i]Est 4:11; 5:2
8:6 [j]Est 7:4; 9:1
8:8 [k]Est 3:12-14 [l]Ge 41:42 [m]Est 1:19; Da 6:15
8:9 [n]Est 1:1 [o]Est 1:22
8:11 [p]Est 9:10, 15,16
8:12 [q]Est 3:13; 9:1
8:13 [r]Est 3:14
8:15 [s]Est 9:4 [t]Ge 41:42 [u]Est 3:15
8:16 [v]Ps 97:10-12 [w]Ps 112:4
8:17 [x]Est 9:19,27; Ps 35:27; Pr 11:10 [y]Ex 15:14,16; Dt 11:25 [z]Est 9:3
9:1 [a]Est 8:12 [b]Jer 29:4-7 [c]Est 3:12-14; Pr 22:22-23
9:2 [d]ver 15-18 [e]Est 8:11,17; Ps 71:13,24
9:3 [f]Ezr 8:36
9:4 [g]Ex 11:3 [h]2Sa 3:1; 1Ch 11:9
9:5 [i]Ezr 4:6

[a]9 That is, the upper Nile region

WEEK 29

JOY

1 DAY ONE

▸ JOY, THE REWARD OF ENDURANCE

Read Esther 8:15–17

The great celebration of Esther 8 follows on the heels of Esther's courage. In Esther 4:16, Esther sends word to her cousin Mordecai, and says, "I will go to the king, even though it is against the law. And if I perish, I perish."

Courage often precedes joy. Esther's courage not only saved the Jewish people but also led to the institution of the Feast of Purim, a Jewish holiday. Esther acted in a spirit of courage because she knew that what she was about to do was right. The cost to her personally was not as great a concern to her as her obedience to principle. Esther is on the list of Old Testament heroes for one simple reason: She was not for sale. Her life was subject to negotiation, but not her beliefs.

Esther was a woman who dared to stand up for truth in a world dominated by men. To lobby for truth against power structures is to face power with integrity. I wrote the following quatrain in one of my novels years ago:

The original sin is ultimate sin—
Claim thrones or be gods as you may!
And the last pair alive, like the first pair alive,
Would rather have power than obey.

I have long admired the martyrs and those who say, "I believe what I believe. I preach Christ because Christ is all that matters. My life and the truth it contains are not for sale." Esther is a model for all those who cherish truth. "I will go to the king, which is not according to custom, and if I perish, I perish." Compromise is out of the question.

What is the result of such determination? For Esther, it was the celebration of the Feast of Purim. For us, it is the inner joy that wells up when we know we have chosen to live for Christ.

2 DAY TWO

▸ JOY AND THE PURPOSE OF GOD IN MY LIFE

Joy marks the lives of Paul and Silas as they sing in a jail cell in the dead of night. Too bad there were no cassette recorders in those days. The song has been lost to us. Was its tonal quality good? Its vibrato? What would they have said at The Julliard School? It doesn't matter. The song was grand—a duet sung by two who had been beaten and jailed for Jesus. Their lives existed for Jesus, and their song was music to his ears. *Turn to Acts 16:22–26, page 1314, for today's study.*

3 DAY THREE

▸ JOY AND MY RELATIONSHIP WITH CHRIST

One of the elders asks John, "These in white robes—who are they, and where did they come from?" John answers, "Sir, you know." The elder replies, "These are they who have come out of the great tribulation; they have washed their robes and made them white in the blood of the Lamb." The white-robed ones love Jesus to the point of death, if necessary, yet their legacy is a song of joy. *Turn to Revelation 7:13–17, page 1530, for today's study.*

4 DAY FOUR

▸ JOY AND MY SERVICE TO OTHERS

It is a common expression among us: Life is the pits. Have you prayed from a pit? God loiters around the pits and listens intently. Pit prayers tend to be more intense than those uttered places of our lives. Jeremiah was in a literal pit because of his crusade for truth in a day when virtually all souls praised folly. God listened to Jeremiah as he called out from the depths of the pit. You may be sure God hears our pit prayers, too. *Turn to Lamentations 3:55–57, page 948, for today's study.*

5 DAY FIVE

▸ JOY AND ITS PLACE IN MY PERSONAL WORSHIP

Job's life caused him much pain, but he endured faithfully and was confident that God, who had called him, would not abandon him. Job worshiped his Redeemer through all his trials. Worship was not a take-it-or-leave-it luxury for Job. He reveled in every moment of praise. When he worshiped, he could stand anything. *Turn to Job 19:23–27, page 604, for today's study.*

MEMORIZE THIS WEEK

PSALM 126:5-6

Those who sow in tears
will reap with songs of joy.
He who goes out weeping,
carrying seed to sow,
will return with songs of joy,
carrying sheaves with him.

Week 30, Peace, Accepting a Higher Will, begins on page 1282, John 21:15–19.
To begin a topical study on the Fruit of the Spirit, Joy, turn to the Topical Index, page 1548.

8Poratha, Adalia, Aridatha, 9Parmashta,
Arisai, Aridai and Vaizatha, 10the ten
9:10 sons[j] of Haman son of Hammedatha,
[j]Est 5:11 [k]Ge 14:23; the enemy of the Jews. But they did not
1Sa 14:32; lay their hands on the plunder.[k]
Est 3:13; 8:11 11The number of those slain in the
citadel of Susa was reported to the
king that same day. 12The king said to
Queen Esther, "The Jews have killed
and destroyed five hundred men and
the ten sons of Haman in the citadel
of Susa. What have they done in the
rest of the king's provinces? Now what
is your petition? It will be given you.
What is your request? It will also be
9:12 granted."[l]
[l]Est 5:6; 7:2 13"If it pleases the king," Esther answered, "give the Jews in Susa per-
mission to carry out this day's edict
tomorrow also, and let Haman's ten
9:13 sons[m] be hanged[n] on gallows."
[m]Est 5:11 14So the king commanded that this
[n]Dt 21:22-23 be done. An edict was issued in Susa,
9:14 and they hanged[o] the ten sons of Ha-
[o]Ezr 6:11 man. 15The Jews in Susa came together on the fourteenth day of the month
of Adar, and they put to death in Susa
three hundred men, but they did not
9:15 lay their hands on the plunder.[p]
[p]Ge 14:23; Est 8:11 16Meanwhile, the remainder of the
Jews who were in the king's provinces
also assembled to protect themselves
9:16 and get relief[q] from their enemies.[r]
[q]Est 4:14 They killed seventy-five thousand of
[r]Dt 25:19 [s]1Ch 4:43 them[s] but did not lay their hands on
the plunder. 17This happened on the
thirteenth day of the month of Adar,
and on the fourteenth they rested and
9:17 made it a day of feasting[t] and joy.
[t]1Ki 3:15

Purim Celebrated

18The Jews in Susa, however, had assembled on the thirteenth and fourteenth, and then on the fifteenth they
rested and made it a day of feasting and
joy.
19That is why rural Jews—those living in villages—observe the fourteenth
9:19 of the month of Adar[u] as a day of joy
[u]Est 3:7 [v]ver 22; and feasting, a day for giving presents
Dt 16:11,14; Ne 8:10,12; to each other.[v]
Est 2:9; Rev 11:10 20Mordecai recorded these events, and
he sent letters to all the Jews through-
out the provinces of King Xerxes, near
and far, 21to have them celebrate annually the fourteenth and fifteenth days of
the month of Adar 22as the time when
9:22 [w]Est 4:14 the Jews got relief[w] from their enemies,

JOY

OUT OF THE PRISON, FORTH FROM THE PORTAL

Esther 9:19

Out of Esther's courage the Feast of Purim was born. Out of Jesus' obedience the festival of Easter life was born. Goethe reminds us that joy is the response after courage has done its difficult work:

"Christ is arisen, Joy to Thee mortal!
Out of his Prison, forth from its portal."

and as the month when their sorrow
was turned into joy and their mourning into a day of celebration.[x] He wrote 9:22
them to observe the days as days of [x]Ne 8:12; Ps 30:11-12
feasting and joy and giving presents of [y]2Ki 25:30
food[y] to one another and gifts to the
poor.
23So the Jews agreed to continue
the celebration they had begun, doing
what Mordecai had written to them.
24For Haman son of Hammedatha, the
Agagite,[z] the enemy of all the Jews, 9:24 [z]Ex 17:8-16
had plotted against the Jews to destroy [a]Est 3:7
them and had cast the *pur*[a] (that is, [b]Lev 16:8
the lot[b]) for their ruin and destruction. 25But when the plot came to the
king's attention,[a] he issued written orders that the evil scheme Haman had
devised against the Jews should come
back onto his own head,[c] and that he 9:25 [c]Ps 7:16
and his sons should be hanged[d] on the [d]Dt 21:22-23
gallows.[e] 26(Therefore these days were [e]Est 7:10
called Purim, from the word *pur*.[f]) Be- 9:26 [f]ver 20;
cause of everything written in this letter Est 3:7
and because of what they had seen and
what had happened to them, 27the Jews
took it upon themselves to establish the
custom that they and their descendants
and all who join them should without
fail observe these two days every year,
in the way prescribed and at the time
appointed. 28These days should be remembered and observed in every generation by every family, and in every
province and in every city. And these
days of Purim should never cease to be
celebrated by the Jews, nor should the
memory of them die out among their
descendants.
29So Queen Esther, daughter of Ab- 9:29
ihail,[g] along with Mordecai the Jew, [g]Est 2:15

[a]25 Or *when Esther came before the king*

wrote with full authority to confirm
this second letter concerning Purim.
30And Mordecai sent letters to all the
9:30 [h]Est 1:1 Jews in the 127 provinces[h] of the kingdom of Xerxes—words of goodwill and
assurance— 31to establish these days
of Purim at their designated times, as
Mordecai the Jew and Queen Esther
had decreed for them, and as they had
established for themselves and their descendants in regard to their times of
9:31 [i]Est 4:16 fasting[i] and lamentation.[j] 32Esther's de-
[j]Est 4:1-3 cree confirmed these regulations about
Purim, and it was written down in the
records.

The Greatness of Mordecai

10 King Xerxes imposed tribute
throughout the empire, to its 10:1 [k]Ps 72:10; 97:1; Isa 24:15
distant shores.[k] 2And all his acts of pow-
er and might, together with a full ac-
count of the greatness of Mordecai[l] to 10:2 [l]Est 8:15; 9:4
which the king had raised him,[m] are [m]Ge 41:44
they not written in the book of the an- [n]Est 2:23
nals[n] of the kings of Media and Persia?
3Mordecai the Jew was second[o] in rank[p] 10:3 [o]Da 5:7
to King Xerxes,[q] preeminent among the [p]Ge 41:43 [q]Ge 41:40
Jews, and held in high esteem by his [r]Ne 2:10; Jer 29:4-7; Da 6:3
many fellow Jews, because he worked
for the good of his people and spoke up
for the welfare of all the Jews.[r]

JOB

AUTHORSHIP AND DATE

The author is unknown.

The book seems to chronicle events that happened in the age of the patriarchs (c. 2000 B.C. to c. 1800 B.C.).

KEY THEMES

The book of Job was written in a dramatic style that examines the problem of why the righteous suffer. The book deals with such subjects as the nature of evil and why Satan attacks us. It also looks at pride, patience, love and self-examination. It considers issues of faith, confession, trust, God's goodness and God's inscrutability. It considers the philosophical, the banal and the grand. It is a book of introspection in which Job is constantly asking "Why?" and "Why me?" Job is portrayed as an upright man who in no way deserved all the evil things that befell him.

In the opening chapters, Satan and God examine Job's life and make him the subject of their power and their philosophical debate. God was confident that Job's love and trust were unimpeachable. Satan was convinced that Job, when confronted with the direst circumstances, would eventually turn from true faith. God ultimately rewarded Job's faithfulness by giving him twice as much as he had lost. The book unfolds into an unparalleled piece of literature that examines the nature of trial and faith.

FRUIT OF THE SPIRIT IN JOB

Patience: Job's patience is noteworthy. Job's godly life is summarized by these words: "In all this, Job did not sin in what he said" (2:10). Job's patience allowed him always to remain true—although he confessed that he was often bewildered as he went through incredible personal pain. He testified, "I have no peace, no quietness; I have no rest, but only turmoil" (3:26). Job's patience bore an impatience at times, especially when he was undergoing extreme testing: "If only my anguish could be weighed and all my misery be placed on the scales! It would surely outweigh the sand of the seas—no wonder my words have been impetuous" (6:2–3).

Job was forced to confess that life is harsh: "Does not

man have hard service on earth? Are not his days like those of a hired man?" (7:1). The hard days make one ponder the very point of life. Time on the way to the grave flies: "My days are swifter than a runner; they fly away without a glimpse of joy. They skim past like boats of papyrus, like eagles swooping down on their prey" (9:25–26).

In the final chapters of Job, the drama ends with God reminding Job of God's immensity—his visible as well as invisible workings, his earthly as well as cosmic majesty. The patience of Job was, in the end, rewarded as Job's wealth and family were restored to him. Job demonstrated great endurance in the midst of severe trials, and hence the world has applied to him, more than any other single virtue, the virtue of patience.

Prologue

1:1 [a]Jer 25:20 [b]Eze 14:14,20; Jas 5:11 [c]Ge 6:9; 17:1 [d]Ge 22:12; Ex 18:21
1 In the land of Uz[a] there lived a
man whose name was Job.[b] This
man was blameless[c] and upright; he
feared God[d] and shunned evil. 2He had
seven sons and three daughters,[e] 3and
1:2 [e]Job 42:13
he owned seven thousand sheep, three
thousand camels, five hundred yoke of
oxen and five hundred donkeys, and
had a large number of servants. He was
1:3 [f]Job 29:25
the greatest man[f] among all the people
of the East.
4His sons used to take turns holding
feasts in their homes, and they would
invite their three sisters to eat and drink
with them. 5When a period of feasting
had run its course, Job would send and
have them purified. Early in the morn-
ing he would sacrifice a burnt offering[g] 1:5 [g]Ge 8:20; Job 42:8 [h]Job 8:4 [i]1Ki 21:10,13
for each of them, thinking, "Perhaps
my children have sinned[h] and cursed
God[i] in their hearts." This was Job's
regular custom.

Job's First Test

6One day the angels[a][j] came to pre- 1:6 [j]Job 38:7 [k]Job 2:1
sent themselves before the LORD, and
Satan[b] also came with them.[k] 7The
LORD said to Satan, "Where have you
come from?"
Satan answered the LORD, "From
roaming through the earth and going
back and forth in it."[l] 1:7 [l]1Pe 5:8
8Then the LORD said to Satan, "Have

[a]6 Hebrew *the sons of God* [b]6 *Satan* means *accuser.*

JOB

Patience, the Endurance of Meaningful Suffering (1:1–5)

Patience is how the godly mind occupies itself when it can't get a clear answer to the question "Why do the righteous suffer?" Patience is the art of suffering without sinning against God. Patience loves God even when he is silent. Patience credits God with knowing what's best even when troubles overwhelm and cloud the horizon of hope.

In the book of Job, we read about a godly man who was blameless and upright, feared God and turned away from evil. He cared for others and prayed for his family. Everyone assumed that God had honored Job's righteousness by giving him extreme wealth (Job 1:3). Then, within a short period of time, his children and their families were killed, and most of his possessions were destroyed. However, we read that "in all this, Job did not sin by charging God with wrongdoing" (v. 22).

Although Job never cursed God in his suffering, he did have various reactions to his situation. He complained about his suffering (6:2–3; 10:1). He philosophized over his lot in life (7:1; 14:1). He even wished he had never come to exist (3:3; 10:19).

But a lesson we can learn from the tragedy in Job's life is that suffering is never meaningless. None of it is pointless! Job stands as a reference point in the midst of our own collapsing private worlds. How many times have we picked up Job's book to find out how he handled something? Job may have felt he wasn't handling life at all, but his reactions to his struggles teach us the value of our own patient suffering. When we don't fully understand the reason we're on the planet, it is a great comfort to read about Job's patience and trust in a time of great sorrow. Reading of his patience, we know we can hold on yet a while longer:

Naked I came from my mother's womb,
and naked I will depart.
The Lord gave and the Lord has taken away;
may the name of the Lord be praised.

(1:21)

Sometimes suffering hurts so badly that the only healing balm is praise. It is those who cry who also sing to God the sweetest songs. Such songs are never hurried. They are born in patience and sung in soft acceptance.

you considered my servant Job?[m] There is no one on earth like him; he is blameless and upright, a man who fears God and shuns evil."[n]

9"Does Job fear God for nothing?"[o] Satan replied. 10"Have you not put a hedge around him and his household and everything he has?[p] You have blessed the work of his hands, so that his flocks and herds are spread throughout the land.[q] 11But stretch out your hand and strike everything he has,[r] and he will surely curse you to your face."[s]

12The LORD said to Satan, "Very well, then, everything he has is in your hands, but on the man himself do not lay a finger."

Then Satan went out from the presence of the LORD.

13One day when Job's sons and daughters were feasting and drinking wine at the oldest brother's house, 14a messenger came to Job and said, "The oxen were plowing and the donkeys were grazing nearby, 15and the Sabeans[t] attacked and carried them off. They put the servants to the sword, and I am the only one who has escaped to tell you!"

16While he was still speaking, another messenger came and said, "The fire of God fell from the sky[u] and burned up the sheep and the servants,[v] and I am the only one who has escaped to tell you!"

17While he was still speaking, another messenger came and said, "The Chaldeans[w] formed three raiding parties and swept down on your camels and carried them off. They put the servants to the sword, and I am the only one who has escaped to tell you!"

18While he was still speaking, yet another messenger came and said, "Your sons and daughters were feasting and drinking wine at the oldest brother's house, 19when suddenly a mighty wind[x] swept in from the desert and struck the four corners of the house. It collapsed on them and they are dead, and I am the only one who has escaped to tell you!"

20At this, Job got up and tore his robe[y] and shaved his head. Then he fell to the ground in worship[z] 21and said:

"Naked I came from my mother's
womb,
and naked I will depart.[a] [a]
The LORD gave and the LORD has
taken away;[b]
may the name of the LORD be
praised."[c]

22In all this, Job did not sin by charging God with wrongdoing.[d]

1:8 [m]Jos 1:7; Job 42:7-8 [n]ver 1
1:9 [o]1Ti 6:5
1:10 [p]Ps 34:7 [q]ver 3; Job 29:6; 31:25; Ps 128:1-2
1:11 [r]Job 19:21 [s]Job 2:5
1:15 [t]Ge 10:7; Job 6:19
1:16 [u]Ge 19:24 [v]Lev 10:2; Nu 11:1-3
1:17 [w]Ge 11:28,31
1:19 [x]Jer 4:11; 13:24
1:20 [y]Ge 37:29 [z]1Pe 5:6
1:21 [a]Ecc 5:15; 1Ti 6:7
1:21 [b]1Sa 2:7 [c]Job 2:10; Eph 5:20; 1Th 5:18
1:22 [d]Job 2:10

FAITHFULNESS

NAKED INTEGRITY

Job 1:21

Bless Christ when all life's circumstances are in your favor.
Bless Christ when you do not own a single triumph.
Bless Christ for his cross even when it is your own to carry.
Bless Christ till every day is Easter and every tomb is empty.

Job's Second Test

2 On another day the angels[b] came to present themselves before the LORD, and Satan also came with them[e] to present himself before him. 2And the LORD said to Satan, "Where have you come from?"

Satan answered the LORD, "From roaming through the earth and going back and forth in it."

3Then the LORD said to Satan, "Have you considered my servant Job? There is no one on earth like him; he is blameless and upright, a man who fears God and shuns evil.[f] And he still maintains his integrity,[g] though you incited me against him to ruin him without any reason."[h]

4"Skin for skin!" Satan replied. "A man will give all he has for his own life. 5But stretch out your hand and strike his flesh and bones,[i] and he will surely curse you to your face."[j]

6The LORD said to Satan, "Very well, then, he is in your hands; but you must spare his life."[k]

7So Satan went out from the presence of the LORD and afflicted Job with painful sores from the soles of his feet to the top of his head.[l] 8Then Job took a piece of broken pottery and scraped himself with it as he sat among the ashes.[m]

9His wife said to him, "Are you still

[a]21 Or *will return there* [b]1 Hebrew *the sons of God*

2:1 [e]Job 1:6
2:3 [f]Job 1:1,8 [g]Job 27:6 [h]Job 9:17
2:5 [i]Job 19:20 [j]Job 1:11
2:6 [k]Job 1:12
2:7 [l]Dt 28:35; Job 7:5
2:8 [m]Job 42:6; Jer 6:26; Eze 27:30; Mt 11:21

holding on to your integrity? Curse
God and die!"

10 He replied, "You are talking like a
foolish[a] woman. Shall we accept good
from God, and not trouble?"[n]
In all this, Job did not sin in what he
said.[o]

2:10 [n]Job 1:21 [o]Job 1:22; Ps 39:1; Jas 1:12; 5:11

Job's Three Friends

11 When Job's three friends, Eliphaz
the Temanite,[p] Bildad the Shuhite[q] and
Zophar the Naamathite, heard about all
the troubles that had come upon him,
they set out from their homes and met
together by agreement to go and sympathize with him and comfort him.[r]
12 When they saw him from a distance,
they could hardly recognize him; they
began to weep aloud, and they tore
their robes and sprinkled dust on their
heads.[s] 13 Then they sat on the ground
with him for seven days and seven
nights.[t] No one said a word to him,
because they saw how great his suffering was.

2:11 [p]Ge 36:11; Jer 49:7 [q]Ge 25:2 [r]Job 42:11; Ro 12:15
2:12 [s]Jos 7:6; Ne 9:1; La 2:10; Eze 27:30
2:13 [t]Ge 50:10; Eze 3:15

Job Speaks

3 After this, Job opened his mouth
and cursed the day of his birth. 2 He
said:

3 "May the day of my birth perish,
and the night it was said, 'A boy
is born!'[u]
4 That day—may it turn to darkness;
may God above not care about it;
may no light shine upon it.
5 May darkness and deep shadow[b][v]
claim it once more;
may a cloud settle over it;
may blackness overwhelm its
light.
6 That night—may thick darkness[w]
seize it;
may it not be included among the
days of the year
nor be entered in any of the
months.
7 May that night be barren;
may no shout of joy be heard in
it.
8 May those who curse days[c] curse
that day,
those who are ready to rouse
Leviathan.[x]
9 May its morning stars become dark;
may it wait for daylight in vain
and not see the first rays of dawn,[y]
10 for it did not shut the doors of the
womb on me
to hide trouble from my eyes.

11 "Why did I not perish at birth,
and die as I came from the
womb?[z]
12 Why were there knees to receive me[a]
and breasts that I might be
nursed?
13 For now I would be lying down[b] in
peace;
I would be asleep and at rest[c]
14 with kings and counselors of the
earth,[d]
who built for themselves places
now lying in ruins,[e]
15 with rulers[f] who had gold,
who filled their houses with silver.[g]
16 Or why was I not hidden in
the ground like a stillborn
child,[h]
like an infant who never saw the
light of day?
17 There the wicked cease from
turmoil,
and there the weary are at rest.[i]
18 Captives also enjoy their ease;
they no longer hear the slave
driver's shout.[j]
19 The small and the great are there,
and the slave is freed from his
master.

20 "Why is light given to those in
misery,
and life to the bitter of soul,[k]
21 to those who long for death that
does not come,[l]
who search for it more than for
hidden treasure,[m]
22 who are filled with gladness
and rejoice when they reach the
grave?
23 Why is life given to a man
whose way is hidden,
whom God has hedged in?[n]
24 For sighing comes to me instead of
food;[o]
my groans pour out like water.[p]
25 What I feared has come upon me;
what I dreaded[q] has happened to
me.
26 I have no peace, no quietness;
I have no rest,[r] but only turmoil."

3:1 [u]Job 10:18-19; Jer 20:14-18
3:5 [v]Job 10:21, 22; Ps 23:4; Jer 2:6; 13:16
3:6 [w]Job 23:17
3:8 [x]Job 41:1,8, 10,25
3:9 [y]Job 41:18
3:11 [z]Job 10:18
3:12 [a]Ge 30:3; Isa 66:12
3:13 [b]Job 17:13 [c]Job 7:8-10, 21; 10:22; 14:10-12; 19:27; 21:13,23
3:14 [d]Job 12:17 [e]Job 15:28
3:15 [f]Job 12:21 [g]Job 27:17
3:16 [h]Ps 58:8; Ecc 6:3
3:17 [i]Job 17:16
3:18 [j]Job 39:7
3:20 [k]1Sa 1:10; Jer 20:18; Eze 27:30-31
3:21 [l]Rev 9:6 [m]Pr 2:4
3:23 [n]Job 19:6,8,12; Ps 88:8; La 3:7
3:24 [o]Job 6:7; 33:20 [p]Ps 42:3,4
3:25 [q]Job 30:15
3:26 [r]Job 7:4,14

[a] *10* The Hebrew word rendered *foolish* denotes moral deficiency. [b] *5* Or *and the shadow of death* [c] *8* Or *the sea*

Eliphaz

4 Then Eliphaz the Temanite replied:

2 "If someone ventures a word with you, will you be impatient?
But who can keep from speaking?[s]
3 Think how you have instructed many,
how you have strengthened feeble hands.[t]

4:2 [s]Job 32:20
4:3 [t]Isa 35:3; Heb 12:12

DAY 2 TWO

▸ PEACE AND THE PURPOSE OF GOD IN MY LIFE

Job 4:1–6

If there is hypocrisy in our Christian practice of discipleship, it may well lie in the area of personal peace. Like Job, it may be that we talk about peace better than we live it out. One of the greatest secular philosophers of our time refused to become a Christian because he thought there was something "warlike" in the way Christians went about preaching peace. Christians are always making new converts with the appeal, "Come to Christ and find peace." The truth, according to this philosopher, is that Christians are fierce—even peaceless—in maintaining their individual viewpoints.

The continuing proliferation of denominations is evidence that peace is not easy to attain. Christians have been known to resort to "holy wars" over the minutest nuances of Scriptural interpretation. Families have become divided over doctrinal quarrels. Surely it is important to fight for those cardinal doctrines that define us, but what about those highly individual viewpoints that isolate Christians into camps over less significant doctrinal differences? Should we abandon our peace over every divergence?

Eliphaz reminds Job that Job has long taught that the path of peace is dependent on our ability to trust God in the hard times. Now, he says it is time for Job to practice all that he preaches. It is time for him to demonstrate the life of confident peace he has insisted that others display. God is honored by the obedience of his servants. We, like Job, spread peace to others by allowing it to reign in our own lives.

To begin a study on the topic of Peace, the Evidence of Confidence, turn to the home page on page 1173.

4 Your words have supported those who stumbled;
you have strengthened faltering knees.[u]
5 But now trouble comes to you, and you are discouraged;
it strikes[v] you, and you are dismayed.[w]
6 Should not your piety be your confidence[x]
and your blameless[y] ways your hope?

7 "Consider now: Who, being innocent, has ever perished?[z]
Where were the upright ever destroyed?[a]
8 As I have observed, those who plow evil[b]
and those who sow trouble reap it.[c]
9 At the breath of God[d] they are destroyed;
at the blast of his anger they perish.[e]
10 The lions may roar and growl,
yet the teeth of the great lions are broken.[f]
11 The lion perishes for lack of prey,[g]
and the cubs of the lioness are scattered.

12 "A word was secretly brought to me,
my ears caught a whisper[h] of it.[i]
13 Amid disquieting dreams in the night,
when deep sleep falls on men,[j]
14 fear and trembling seized me
and made all my bones shake.[k]
15 A spirit glided past my face,
and the hair on my body stood on end.
16 It stopped,
but I could not tell what it was.
A form stood before my eyes,
and I heard a hushed voice:
17 'Can a mortal be more righteous than God?[l]
Can a man be more pure than his Maker?[m]
18 If God places no trust in his servants,
if he charges his angels with error,[n]
19 how much more those who live in houses of clay,[o]
whose foundations[p] are in the dust,[q]
who are crushed more readily than a moth!

4:4 [u]Isa 35:3; Heb 12:12
4:5 [v]Job 19:21 [w]Job 6:14
4:6 [x]Pr 3:26 [y]Job 1:1
4:7 [z]Job 36:7 [a]Job 8:20; Ps 37:25
4:8 [b]Job 15:35 [c]Pr 22:8; Hos 10:13; Gal 6:7-8
4:9 [d]Job 15:30; Isa 30:33; 2Th 2:8 [e]Job 40:13
4:10 [f]Job 5:15; Ps 58:6
4:11 [g]Job 27:14; Ps 34:10
4:12 [h]Job 26:14 [i]Job 33:14
4:13 [j]Job 33:15
4:14 [k]Jer 23:9; Hab 3:16
4:17 [l]Job 9:2 [m]Job 35:10
4:18 [n]Job 15:15
4:19 [o]Job 10:9 [p]Job 22:16 [q]Ge 2:7

20 Between dawn and dusk they are
broken to pieces;
unnoticed, they perish forever.[r]
21 Are not the cords of their tent pulled
up,[s]
so that they die without
wisdom?'[a][t]

5 "Call if you will, but who will
answer you?
To which of the holy ones[u] will
you turn?
2 Resentment kills a fool,
and envy slays the simple.[v]
3 I myself have seen a fool taking
root,[w]
but suddenly his house was
cursed.[x]
4 His children are far from safety,[y]
crushed in court[z] without a
defender.
5 The hungry consume his harvest,[a]
taking it even from among thorns,
and the thirsty pant after his
wealth.
6 For hardship does not spring from
the soil,
nor does trouble sprout from the
ground.
7 Yet man is born to trouble[b]
as surely as sparks fly upward.

8 "But if it were I, I would appeal to
God;
I would lay my cause before him.[c]
9 He performs wonders that cannot be
fathomed,[d]
miracles that cannot be counted.
10 He bestows rain on the earth;
he sends water upon the
countryside.[e]
11 The lowly he sets on high,[f]
and those who mourn are lifted to
safety.
12 He thwarts the plans[g] of the crafty,
so that their hands achieve no
success.
13 He catches the wise in their
craftiness,[h]
and the schemes of the wily are
swept away.
14 Darkness[i] comes upon them in the
daytime;
at noon they grope as in the
night.[j]
15 He saves the needy[k] from the sword
in their mouth;
he saves them from the clutches of
the powerful.[l]
16 So the poor have hope,
and injustice shuts its mouth.[m]
17 "Blessed is the man whom God
corrects;[n]
so do not despise the discipline[o] of
the Almighty.[b][p]

4:20 [r]Job 14:2,20; 20:7; Ps 90:5-6
4:21 [s]Job 8:22 [t]Job 18:21; 36:12
5:1 [u]Job 15:15
5:2 [v]Pr 12:16
5:3 [w]Ps 37:35; Jer 12:2 [x]Job 24:18
5:4 [y]Job 4:11 [z]Am 5:12
5:5 [a]Job 18:8-10
5:7 [b]Job 14:1
5:8 [c]Ps 35:23; 50:15
5:9 [d]Job 42:3; Ps 40:5
5:10 [e]Job 36:28
5:11 [f]Ps 113:7-8
5:12 [g]Ne 4:15; Ps 33:10
5:13 [h]1Co 3:19*
5:14 [i]Job 12:25 [j]Dt 28:29
5:15 [k]Ps 35:10 [l]Job 4:10
5:16 [m]Ps 107:42
5:17 [n]Jas 1:12 [o]Ps 94:12; Pr 3:11 [p]Heb 12:5-11

JOY
HURT AND HONOR

Job 5:17

Does life hurt? Job found that the mere act of getting out of bed can overwhelm us with unseen grief. Pain can come so fast. It sears the heart with lost fortunes and swift obituaries. But like an injured child, Job clung to his Father, and in the pain he found a hidden hallelujah.

So love Jesus and linger at the cross. There you will see what it means to honor God, and the world will be astonished that in your hurting you have found the voice of praise.

18 For he wounds, but he also binds
up;[q]
he injures, but his hands also
heal.[r]
19 From six calamities he will rescue
you;
in seven no harm will befall you.[s]
20 In famine[t] he will ransom you from
death,
and in battle from the stroke of
the sword.[u]
21 You will be protected from the lash
of the tongue,[v]
and need not fear[w] when
destruction comes.
22 You will laugh at destruction and
famine,
and need not fear the beasts of the
earth.[x]
23 For you will have a covenant with
the stones[y] of the field,
and the wild animals will be at
peace with you.[z]
24 You will know that your tent is
secure;
you will take stock of your
property and find nothing
missing.[a]
25 You will know that your children
will be many,[b]

5:18 [q]Isa 30:26 [r]1Sa 2:6
5:19 [s]Ps 34:19; 91:10
5:20 [t]Ps 33:19 [u]Ps 144:10
5:21 [v]Ps 31:20 [w]Ps 91:5
5:22 [x]Ps 91:13; Eze 34:25
5:23 [y]Ps 91:12 [z]Isa 11:6-9
5:24 [a]Job 8:6
5:25 [b]Ps 112:2

[a]*21* Some interpreters end the quotation after verse 17. [b]*17* Hebrew *Shaddai*; here and throughout Job

and your descendants like the
grass of the earth.[c]
5:25 [c]Ps 72:16; Isa 44:3-4
26 You will come to the grave in full
vigor,[d]
5:26 [d]Ge 15:15
like sheaves gathered in season.

27 "We have examined this, and it is
true.
So hear it and apply it to
yourself."

Job

6 Then Job replied:

2 "If only my anguish could be
weighed
and all my misery be placed on
6:2 [e]Job 31:6
the scales![e]
3 It would surely outweigh the sand[f]
6:3 [f]Pr 27:3 [g]Job 23:2
of the seas—
no wonder my words have been
impetuous.[g]
6:4 [h]Ps 38:2 [i]Job 16:12,13 [j]Job 21:20 [k]Job 30:15 [l]Ps 88:15-18
4 The arrows[h] of the Almighty are in
me,[i]
my spirit drinks[j] in their poison;
God's terrors[k] are marshaled
against me.[l]
5 Does a wild donkey bray when it has
grass,
or an ox bellow when it has
fodder?
6 Is tasteless food eaten without salt,
or is there flavor in the white of
an egg[a]?
7 I refuse to touch it;
6:7 [m]Job 3:24
such food makes me ill.[m]
6:8 [n]Job 14:13
8 "Oh, that I might have my request,
that God would grant what I hope
for,[n]
9 that God would be willing to crush
me,
6:9 [o]Nu 11:15; 1Ki 19:4
to let loose his hand and cut me
off![o]
10 Then I would still have this
consolation—
6:10 [p]Job 22:22; 23:12 [q]Lev 19:2; Isa 57:15
my joy in unrelenting pain—
that I had not denied the words[p]
of the Holy One.[q]

11 "What strength do I have, that I
should still hope?
6:11 [r]Job 21:4
What prospects, that I should be
patient?[r]
12 Do I have the strength of stone?
Is my flesh bronze?
6:13 [s]Job 26:2
13 Do I have any power to help myself,[s]
now that success has been driven
from me?

6:14 [t]Job 4:5 [u]Job 15:4
14 "A despairing man[t] should have the
devotion[u] of his friends,
even though he forsakes the fear of
the Almighty.
6:15 [v]Ps 38:11; Jer 15:18
15 But my brothers are as undependable
as intermittent streams,[v]
as the streams that overflow
16 when darkened by thawing ice
and swollen with melting snow,
17 but that cease to flow in the dry
season,
6:17 [w]Job 24:19
and in the heat[w] vanish from their
channels.
18 Caravans turn aside from their
routes;
they go up into the wasteland and
perish.
6:19 [x]Ge 25:15; Isa 21:14
19 The caravans of Tema[x] look for
water,
the traveling merchants of Sheba
look in hope.
20 They are distressed, because they had
been confident;
they arrive there, only to be
6:20 [y]Jer 14:3
disappointed.[y]
21 Now you too have proved to be of
no help;
you see something dreadful and
6:21 [z]Ps 38:11
are afraid.[z]
22 Have I ever said, 'Give something on
my behalf,
pay a ransom for me from your
wealth,
23 deliver me from the hand of the
enemy,
ransom me from the clutches of
the ruthless'?

6:24 [a]Ps 39:1
24 "Teach me, and I will be quiet;[a]
show me where I have been
wrong.
6:25 [b]Ecc 12:11
25 How painful are honest words![b]
But what do your arguments
prove?
26 Do you mean to correct what I say,
6:26 [c]Job 8:2; 15:3
and treat the words of a despairing
man as wind?[c]
6:27 [d]Joel 3:3; Na 3:10; 2Pe 2:3
27 You would even cast lots[d] for the
fatherless
and barter away your friend.

6:28 [e]Job 27:4; 33:1,3; 36:3,4
28 "But now be so kind as to look at me.
Would I lie to your face?[e]
29 Relent, do not be unjust;
6:29 [f]Job 23:7,10; 34:5,36; 42:6
reconsider, for my integrity is at
stake.[b][f]

[a]*6* The meaning of the Hebrew for this phrase is uncertain. [b]*29* Or *my righteousness still stands*

6:30 [g]Job 27:4 [h]Job 12:11

30 Is there any wickedness on my lips?[g]
Can my mouth not discern[h]
malice?

7:1 [i]Job 14:14; Isa 40:2 [j]Job 5:7 [k]Job 14:6

7 "Does not man have hard service[i]
on earth?[j]
Are not his days like those of a
hired man?[k]
2 Like a slave longing for the evening
shadows,
or a hired man waiting eagerly for
his wages,[l]

7:2 [l]Lev 19:13

3 so I have been allotted months of
futility,
and nights of misery have been
assigned to me.[m]

7:3 [m]Job 16:7; Ps 6:6

4 When I lie down I think, 'How long
before I get up?'[n]
The night drags on, and I toss till
dawn.

7:4 [n]Dt 28:67

5 My body is clothed with worms[o] and
scabs,
my skin is broken and festering.

7:5 [o]Job 17:14; Isa 14:11

6 "My days are swifter than a weaver's
shuttle,[p]
and they come to an end without
hope.[q]

7:6 [p]Job 9:25 [q]Job 13:15; 17:11,15

LOVE

LOVE AT THE ABYSS

Job 7:6

Does life hurry toward the wide abyss of death? Do not despair. God himself plays along the precipice, keeping his children safe.

7 Remember, O God, that my life is
but a breath;[r]
my eyes will never see happiness
again.[s]
8 The eye that now sees me will see me
no longer;
you will look for me, but I will be
no more.[t]

7:7 [r]Ps 78:39; Jas 4:14 [s]Job 9:25

7:8 [t]Job 20:7,9,21

9 As a cloud vanishes and is gone,
so he who goes down to the
grave[a][u] does not return.[v]

7:9 [u]Job 11:8 [v]2Sa 12:23; Job 30:15

10 He will never come to his house
again;
his place[w] will know him no
more.[x]

7:10 [w]Job 27:21,23 [x]Job 8:18

11 "Therefore I will not keep silent;[y]
I will speak out in the anguish of
my spirit,
I will complain in the bitterness of
my soul.[z]

7:11 [y]Ps 40:9 [z]1Sa 1:10

12 Am I the sea, or the monster of the
deep,[a]
that you put me under guard?

7:12 [a]Eze 32:2-3

13 When I think my bed will comfort
me
and my couch will ease my
complaint,[b]

7:13 [b]Job 9:27

14 even then you frighten me with
dreams
and terrify[c] me with visions,

7:14 [c]Job 9:34

15 so that I prefer strangling and
death,[d]
rather than this body of mine.

7:15 [d]1Ki 19:4

16 I despise my life;[e] I would not live
forever.
Let me alone; my days have no
meaning.

7:16 [e]Job 9:21; 10:1

17 "What is man that you make so
much of him,
that you give him so much
attention,[f]

7:17 [f]Ps 8:4; 144:3; Heb 2:6

18 that you examine him every morning
and test him every moment?[g]

7:18 [g]Job 14:3

19 Will you never look away from me,
or let me alone even for an
instant?[h]

7:19 [h]Job 9:18

20 If I have sinned, what have I done
to you,[i]
O watcher of men?
Why have you made me your target?[j]
Have I become a burden to you?[b]

7:20 [i]Job 35:6 [j]Job 16:12

21 Why do you not pardon my offenses
and forgive my sins?[k]
For I will soon lie down in the dust;[l]
you will search for me, but I will
be no more."

7:21 [k]Job 10:14 [l]Job 10:9; Ps 104:29

Bildad

8 Then Bildad the Shuhite replied:

2 "How long will you say such things?
Your words are a blustering
wind.[m]

8:2 [m]Job 6:26

3 Does God pervert justice?[n]
Does the Almighty pervert what is
right?[o]

8:3 [n]Dt 32:4; 2Ch 19:7; Ro 3:5 [o]Ge 18:25

4 When your children sinned against
him,
he gave them over to the penalty
of their sin.[p]

8:4 [p]Job 1:19

5 But if you will look to God
and plead[q] with the Almighty,
6 if you are pure and upright,

8:5 [q]Job 11:13

[a]9 Hebrew *Sheol* [b]20 A few manuscripts of the Masoretic Text, an ancient Hebrew scribal tradition and Septuagint; most manuscripts of the Masoretic Text *I have become a burden to myself.*

WEEK 22

PATIENCE

1 DAY ONE

PATIENCE, LIVING BY GOD'S TIMETABLE

Read Job 7:6

In this passage, Job laments that his days are "swifter than a weaver's shuttle." They are not only brief; they're pointless. Routine is at once our killer and our savior. To get up and do the same thing every day gives us a way to live and a reason to get up every morning. But Job's reaction is one often made by people whose routines do not furnish them with meaning. Job had to cry out in his despair that all the requirements of his life weren't providing him with much hope.

Still, the crisis itself may speak to that which is noblest. Since we cannot outrun a weaver's shuttle, maybe we ought to focus on those values that the passing of time cannot steal.

What values are timeless? What makes values valuable? Only one thing—values assigned by God never fade. The sense of the hurriedness of life belongs to us all—those who use their time well and those who don't. But those who give their days and years to God do triumph over time. Those who focus on cultivating the values of God find that life is meaningful even in the rush of life.

Job, like all of us, must still get up, even on those hopeless days, and determine to pace his living. He must determine that the larger goals are to cultivate a heart for God, no matter what the day may bring. The habit of patience is reflective. It thinks about God and his purposes in our lives.

Patience—the pacing of our affairs—says to the hurried, frantic clocks that surround us: "You can speed my day toward the grave, but I alone determine the quality of meaning those days will hold."

MEMORIZE THIS WEEK

PSALM 90:12

Teach us to number our days aright,
that we may gain a heart of wisdom.

2 DAY TWO

PATIENCE AND THE PURPOSE OF GOD IN MY LIFE

Who wants to die? Not many of us. But don't we long for God's presence? Don't we want to be with God? As our minutes on this earth slip away, we are faced with the recognition that all people must die. So our challenge becomes how to live for God before we die and spend the rest of our existence with God. *Turn to 2 Kings 20:1–7, page 450, for today's study.*

3 DAY THREE

PATIENCE AND MY RELATIONSHIP WITH CHRIST

Who can change time by hurrying through life? Patience is that virtue that stares down the clock, and says, "I live life by an inner rhythm, borne in me by a perfect will. Your spastic hands will not force me to run at a pace that has forgotten to trust." This passage in Ecclesiastes says that there is a time for everything. But how do we fit everything into our time here on earth? Let's look to Jesus as our role model. *Turn to Ecclesiastes 3:1–8, page 771, for today's study.*

4 DAY FOUR

PATIENCE AND MY SERVICE TO OTHERS

This "rich fool" is both wealthy and stupid. He raced the clocks with bank accounts. There exists all about us a foolish notion that, if we can make enough money, we will succeed in our race against time. Here dies a man who could buy almost anything but was poor spiritually. He did not defeat the calendar and the clock. They triumphed over him. *Turn to Luke 12:16–21, page 1221, for today's study.*

5 DAY FIVE

PATIENCE AND ITS PLACE IN MY PERSONAL WORSHIP

When Daniel's life is under threat for his allegiance to God, he goes to his room where the windows open toward Jerusalem, and prays—"just as he had done before." It is this phrase that speaks of faith as a lifestyle. Patience is in part a spiritual habit that keeps us paced, even when the threats of life would make us anxious. *Turn to Daniel 6:6–10, page 1018, for today's study.*

Week 23, Kindness, Anger Washed by Grace, begins on page 751, Proverbs 16:32.
To begin a topical study on the Fruit of the Spirit, Patience, turn to the Topical Index, page 1548.

even now he will rouse himself on
your behalf[r]
and restore you to your rightful
place.[s]
7 Your beginnings will seem humble,
so prosperous[t] will your future be.
8 "Ask the former generations[u]
and find out what their fathers
learned,
9 for we were born only yesterday and
know nothing,[v]
and our days on earth are but a
shadow.[w]
10 Will they not instruct you and tell
you?
Will they not bring forth words
from their understanding?
11 Can papyrus grow tall where there is
no marsh?
Can reeds thrive without water?
12 While still growing and uncut,
they wither more quickly than
grass.[x]
13 Such is the destiny of all who forget
God;[y]
so perishes the hope of the
godless.[z]
14 What he trusts in is fragile[a];
what he relies on is a spider's
web.[a]
15 He leans on his web,[b] but it gives
way;
he clings to it, but it does not
hold.[c]
16 He is like a well-watered plant in the
sunshine,
spreading its shoots[d] over the
garden;[e]
17 it entwines its roots around a pile of
rocks
and looks for a place among the
stones.
18 But when it is torn from its spot,
that place disowns it and says,
'I never saw you.'[f]
19 Surely its life withers[g] away,
and[b] from the soil other plants
grow.[h]
20 "Surely God does not reject a
blameless[i] man
or strengthen the hands of
evildoers.[j]
21 He will yet fill your mouth with
laughter[k]
and your lips with shouts of joy.[l]
22 Your enemies will be clothed in
shame,[m]
and the tents of the wicked will be
no more."[n]

8:6 [r]Ps 7:6 [s]Job 5:24 **8:7** [t]Job 42:12 **8:8** [u]Dt 4:32; 32:7; Job 15:18 **8:9** [v]Ge 47:9 [w]1Ch 29:15; Job 7:6 **8:12** [x]Ps 129:6; Jer 17:6 **8:13** [y]Ps 9:17 [z]Job 11:20; 13:16; 15:34; Pr 10:28 **8:14** [a]Isa 59:5 **8:15** [b]Job 27:18 [c]Ps 49:11 **8:16** [d]Ps 80:11 [e]Ps 37:35; Jer 11:16 **8:18** [f]Job 7:8; Ps 37:36 **8:19** [g]Job 20:5 [h]Ecc 1:4 **8:20** [i]Job 1:1 [j]Job 21:30 **8:21** [k]Job 5:22 [l]Ps 126:2; 132:16 **8:22** [m]Ps 35:26; 109:29; 132:18 [n]Job 18:6,14,21

Job

9 Then Job replied:

2 "Indeed, I know that this is true.
But how can a mortal be righteous
before God?[o]
3 Though one wished to dispute with
him,
he could not answer him one time
out of a thousand.[p]
4 His wisdom[q] is profound, his power
is vast.[r]
Who has resisted him and come
out unscathed?[s]
5 He moves mountains without their
knowing it
and overturns them in his anger.[t]
6 He shakes the earth[u] from its place
and makes its pillars tremble.[v]
7 He speaks to the sun and it does not
shine;
he seals off the light of the stars.[w]
8 He alone stretches out the heavens[x]
and treads on the waves of the
sea.[y]
9 He is the Maker of the Bear and
Orion,
the Pleiades and the constellations
of the south.[z]

PEACE

RECKONING WITH GALAXIES

Job 9:9

The heavens hush even infidels
with crushing, fiery lights.
So before you claim there is no God,
or deny he has a Son named Jesus,
take up your argument with the stars.
Then, at the very place you stood
to rail against the God of galaxies,
you shall be enveloped in such silence
you will know all argument is over.

10 He performs wonders[a] that cannot
be fathomed,
miracles that cannot be counted.[b]
11 When he passes me, I cannot see
him;
when he goes by, I cannot perceive
him.[c]

9:2 [o]Job 4:17; Ps 143:2; Ro 3:20 **9:3** [p]Job 10:2; 40:2 **9:4** [q]Job 11:6 [r]Job 36:5 [s]2Ch 13:12 **9:5** [t]Mic 1:4 **9:6** [u]Isa 2:21; Hag 2:6; Heb 12:26 [v]Job 26:11 **9:7** [w]Isa 13:10; Eze 32:8 **9:8** [x]Ge 1:6; Ps 104:2-3 [y]Job 38:16; Ps 77:19 **9:9** [z]Ge 1:16; Job 38:31; Am 5:8 **9:10** [a]Ps 71:15 [b]Job 5:9 **9:11** [c]Job 23:8-9; 35:14

[a] *14* The meaning of the Hebrew for this word is uncertain. [b] *19* Or *Surely all the joy it has / is that*

12 If he snatches away, who can stop
him?[d]
Who can say to him, 'What are
you doing?'[e]
13 God does not restrain his anger;
even the cohorts of Rahab[f]
cowered at his feet.

14 "How then can I dispute with him?
How can I find words to argue
with him?
15 Though I were innocent, I could not
answer him;[g]
I could only plead[h] with my Judge
for mercy.
16 Even if I summoned him and he
responded,
I do not believe he would give me
a hearing.
17 He would crush me[i] with a storm[j]
and multiply[k] my wounds for no
reason.[l]
18 He would not let me regain my
breath
but would overwhelm me with
misery.[m]
19 If it is a matter of strength, he is
mighty!
And if it is a matter of justice,
who will summon him[a]?
20 Even if I were innocent, my mouth
would condemn me;
if I were blameless, it would
pronounce me guilty.

21 "Although I am blameless,[n]
I have no concern for myself;
I despise my own life.[o]
22 It is all the same; that is why I say,
'He destroys both the blameless
and the wicked.'[p]
23 When a scourge[q] brings sudden
death,
he mocks the despair of the
innocent.[r]
24 When a land falls into the hands of
the wicked,[s]
he blindfolds its judges.[t]
If it is not he, then who is it?

25 "My days are swifter than a runner;[u]
they fly away without a glimpse of
joy.
26 They skim past like boats of
papyrus,[v]
like eagles swooping down on
their prey.[w]
27 If I say, 'I will forget my
complaint,[x]

9:12 [d]Job 11:10 [e]Isa 45:9; Ro 9:20
9:13 [f]Job 26:12; Ps 89:10; Isa 30:7; 51:9
9:15 [g]Job 10:15 [h]Job 8:5
9:17 [i]Job 16:12 [j]Job 30:22 [k]Job 16:14 [l]Job 2:3
9:18 [m]Job 7:19; 27:2
9:21 [n]Job 1:1 [o]Job 7:16
9:22 [p]Job 10:8; Ecc 9:2,3; Eze 21:3
9:23 [q]Heb 11:36 [r]Job 24:1,12
9:24 [s]Job 10:3; 16:11 [t]Job 12:6
9:25 [u]Job 7:6
9:26 [v]Isa 18:2 [w]Hab 1:8
9:27 [x]Job 7:11

I will change my expression, and
smile,'
28 I still dread[y] all my sufferings,
for I know you will not hold me
innocent.[z]
29 Since I am already found guilty,
why should I struggle in vain?[a]
30 Even if I washed myself with soap[b]
and my hands[b] with washing
soda,[c]
31 you would plunge me into a slime
pit
so that even my clothes would
detest me.

32 "He is not a man like me that I
might answer him,[d]
that we might confront each other
in court.[e]
33 If only there were someone to
arbitrate between us,[f]
to lay his hand upon us both,
34 someone to remove God's rod from
me,[g]
so that his terror would frighten
me no more.
35 Then I would speak up without fear
of him,
but as it now stands with me, I
cannot.[h]

10

1 "I loathe my very life;[i]
therefore I will give free rein to
my complaint
and speak out in the bitterness of
my soul.[j]
2 I will say to God: Do not condemn
me,
but tell me what charges[k] you have
against me.
3 Does it please you to oppress me,[l]
to spurn the work of your hands,[m]
while you smile on the schemes of
the wicked?[n]
4 Do you have eyes of flesh?
Do you see as a mortal sees?[o]
5 Are your days like those of a mortal
or your years like those of a
man,[p]
6 that you must search out my faults
and probe after my sin[q]—
7 though you know that I am not
guilty
and that no one can rescue me
from your hand?

8 "Your hands shaped[r] me and made
me.

9:28 [y]Job 3:25; Ps 119:120 [z]Job 7:21
9:29 [a]Ps 37:33
9:30 [b]Job 31:7 [c]Jer 2:22
9:32 [d]Ro 9:20 [e]Ps 143:2; Ecc 6:10
9:33 [f]1Sa 2:25
9:34 [g]Job 13:21; Ps 39:10
9:35 [h]Job 13:21
10:1 [i]1Ki 19:4 [j]Job 7:11
10:2 [k]Job 9:29
10:3 [l]Job 9:22 [m]Job 14:15; Ps 138:8; Isa 64:8 [n]Job 21:16; 22:18
10:4 [o]1Sa 16:7
10:5 [p]Ps 90:2,4; 2Pe 3:8
10:6 [q]Job 14:16
10:8 [r]Ps 119:73

[a] *19* See Septuagint; Hebrew *me.* [b] *30* Or *snow*

Will you now turn and destroy
me?
9 Remember that you molded me like
clay.[s]
Will you now turn me to dust
again?[t]
10 Did you not pour me out like milk
and curdle me like cheese,
11 clothe me with skin and flesh
and knit me together[u] with bones
and sinews?
12 You gave me life[v] and showed me
kindness,
and in your providence watched
over my spirit.

10:9 [s]Isa 64:8 [t]Ge 2:7
10:11 [u]Ps 139:13,15
10:12 [v]Job 33:4

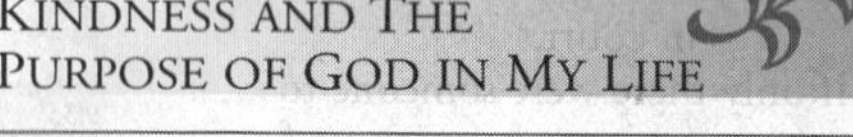

DAY 2 TWO

Kindness and The Purpose of God in My Life

Job 10:8–12

The kindness of God endears us to him. His kindness is made obvious through his providence, says Job. God does provide. Our daily bread would not exist to be buttered without his providence. Job, who it would seem has of late received only tough times from God, speaks of the amazing and wonderful ways that God created him: "Did you not pour me out like milk and curdle me like cheese, clothe me with skin and flesh and knit me together with bones and sinews?" (Job 10:10–11).

Lost in the wonders of God's creativity, Job must reckon with all the difficult things that have happened to him. There is a kind of harmony suggested here. Would a God who shaped him and carefully created him, turn on him to destroy him? Job cannot really think so. And Job's conclusion helps us to see that God's kindness allows us to fulfill his purposes for us.

God is consistently love, so we must not be quick to indict him as responsible for our misfortunes. Let us rather see if we can read into our circumstances a bit of his larger purpose. When the pain overwhelms us, we may have to struggle harder to see his deeper purpose, but it must be our goal. In all things we must strive to see the kindness of God, and then we can look past our present struggles to see his purposes in our lives.

To begin a study on the topic of Kindness in the Time of Need, turn to the home page on page 246.

13 "But this is what you concealed in
your heart,
and I know that this was in your
mind:[w]
14 If I sinned, you would be watching
me
and would not let my offense go
unpunished.[x]
15 If I am guilty—woe to me![y]
Even if I am innocent, I cannot
lift my head,[z]
for I am full of shame
and drowned in[a] my affliction.
16 If I hold my head high, you stalk me
like a lion[a]
and again display your awesome
power against me.[b]
17 You bring new witnesses against me[c]
and increase your anger toward
me;[d]
your forces come against me wave
upon wave.
18 "Why then did you bring me out of
the womb?[e]
I wish I had died before any eye
saw me.
19 If only I had never come into
being,
or had been carried straight from
the womb to the grave!
20 Are not my few days[f] almost over?[g]
Turn away from me[h] so I can have
a moment's joy
21 before I go to the place of no return,[i]
to the land of gloom and deep
shadow,[b][j]
22 to the land of deepest night,
of deep shadow and disorder,
where even the light is like
darkness."

Zophar

11 Then Zophar the Naamathite
replied:
2 "Are all these words to go
unanswered?[k]
Is this talker to be vindicated?
3 Will your idle talk reduce men to
silence?
Will no one rebuke you when you
mock?[l]
4 You say to God, 'My beliefs are
flawless[m]
and I am pure[n] in your sight.'

[a]*15* Or *and aware of* [b]*21* Or *and the shadow of death*; also in verse 22

10:13 [w]Job 23:13
10:14 [x]Job 7:21
10:15 [y]Job 9:13; Isa 3:11 [z]Job 9:15
10:16 [a]Isa 38:13; La 3:10 [b]Job 5:9
10:17 [c]Job 16:8 [d]Ru 1:21
10:18 [e]Job 3:11
10:20 [f]Job 14:1 [g]Job 7:19 [h]Job 7:16
10:21 [i]2Sa 12:23; Job 3:13; 16:22 [j]Ps 23:4; 88:12
11:2 [k]Job 8:2
11:3 [l]Job 17:2; 21:3
11:4 [m]Job 6:10 [n]Job 10:7

[5]Oh, how I wish that God would
speak,
that he would open his lips against
you
[6]and disclose to you the secrets of
wisdom,[o]
for true wisdom has two sides.
Know this: God has even
forgotten some of your sin.[p]

[7]"Can you fathom[q] the mysteries of
God?
Can you probe the limits of the
Almighty?
[8]They are higher than the heavens[r]—
what can you do?
They are deeper than the depths
of the grave[a]—what can you
know?
[9]Their measure is longer than the
earth
and wider than the sea.
[10]"If he comes along and confines you
in prison
and convenes a court, who can
oppose him?[s]
[11]Surely he recognizes deceitful men;
and when he sees evil, does he not
take note?[t]
[12]But a witless man can no more
become wise
than a wild donkey's colt can be
born a man.[b]

[13]"Yet if you devote your heart[u] to him
and stretch out your hands to
him,[v]
[14]if you put away the sin that is in
your hand
and allow no evil[w] to dwell in
your tent,[x]
[15]then you will lift up your face[y]
without shame;
you will stand firm and without
fear.
[16]You will surely forget your trouble,[z]
recalling it only as waters gone
by.[a]
[17]Life will be brighter than noonday,[b]
and darkness will become like
morning.
[18]You will be secure, because there is
hope;
you will look about you and take
your rest[c] in safety.[d]
[19]You will lie down, with no one to
make you afraid,[e]
and many will court your favor.[f]
[20]But the eyes of the wicked will
fail,[g]
and escape will elude them;[h]
their hope will become a dying
gasp."[i]

Job

12 Then Job replied:

[2]"Doubtless you are the people,
and wisdom will die with you![j]
[3]But I have a mind as well as you;
I am not inferior to you.
Who does not know all these
things?[k]

[4]"I have become a laughingstock[l] to
my friends,
though I called upon God and he
answered[m]—
a mere laughingstock, though
righteous and blameless![n]
[5]Men at ease have contempt for
misfortune
as the fate of those whose feet are
slipping.
[6]The tents of marauders are
undisturbed,[o]
and those who provoke God are
secure[p]—
those who carry their god in their
hands.[c]

[7]"But ask the animals, and they will
teach you,
or the birds of the air, and they
will tell you;
[8]or speak to the earth, and it will
teach you,
or let the fish of the sea inform
you.
[9]Which of all these does not know
that the hand of the LORD has
done this?[q]
[10]In his hand is the life of every
creature
and the breath of all mankind.[r]
[11]Does not the ear test words
as the tongue tastes food?[s]
[12]Is not wisdom found among the
aged?[t]
Does not long life bring
understanding?[u]

[13]"To God belong wisdom[v] and
power;[w]

[a]8 Hebrew *than Sheol* [b]12 Or *wild donkey can be born tame* [c]6 Or *secure / in what God's hand brings them*

11:6 [o]Job 9:4 [p]Ezr 9:13; Job 15:5
11:7 [q]Ecc 3:11; Ro 11:33
11:8 [r]Job 22:12
11:10 [s]Job 9:12; Rev 3:7
11:11 [t]Job 34:21-25; Ps 10:14
11:13 [u]1Sa 7:3; Ps 78:8 [v]Ps 88:9
11:14 [w]Ps 101:4 [x]Job 22:23
11:15 [y]Job 22:26; 1Jn 3:21
11:16 [z]Isa 65:16 [a]Job 22:11
11:17 [b]Job 22:28; Ps 37:6; Isa 58:8,10
11:18 [c]Ps 3:5 [d]Lev 26:6; Pr 3:24
11:19 [e]Lev 26:6 [f]Isa 45:14
11:20 [g]Dt 28:65; Job 17:5 [h]Job 27:22; 34:22 [i]Job 8:13
12:2 [j]Job 17:10
12:3 [k]Job 13:2
12:4 [l]Job 21:3 [m]Ps 91:15 [n]Job 6:29
12:6 [o]Job 22:18 [p]Job 9:24; 21:9
12:9 [q]Isa 41:20
12:10 [r]Job 27:3; 33:4; Ac 17:28
12:11 [s]Job 34:3
12:12 [t]Job 15:10 [u]Job 32:7,9
12:13 [v]Job 11:6 [w]Job 9:4

counsel and understanding are
his.[x]
14 What he tears down[y] cannot be
rebuilt;[z]
the man he imprisons cannot be
released.
15 If he holds back the waters,[a] there is
drought;[b]
if he lets them loose, they
devastate the land.[c]
16 To him belong strength and victory;
both deceived and deceiver are
his.[d]
17 He leads counselors away stripped[e]
and makes fools of judges.[f]
18 He takes off the shackles[g] put on by
kings
and ties a loincloth[a] around their
waist.
19 He leads priests away stripped
and overthrows men long
established.[h]
20 He silences the lips of trusted
advisers
and takes away the discernment of
elders.[i]
21 He pours contempt on nobles
and disarms the mighty.
22 He reveals the deep things of
darkness[j]
and brings deep shadows[k] into the
light.[l]
23 He makes nations great, and destroys
them;[m]
he enlarges nations,[n] and disperses
them.
24 He deprives the leaders of the earth
of their reason;
he sends them wandering through
a trackless waste.[o]
25 They grope in darkness with no
light;[p]
he makes them stagger like
drunkards.[q]

12:13 [x]Job 32:8; 38:36
12:14 [y]Job 19:10 [z]Job 37:7; Isa 25:2
12:15 [a]1Ki 8:35 [b]1Ki 17:1 [c]Ge 7:11
12:16 [d]Job 13:7,9
12:17 [e]Job 19:9 [f]Job 3:14
12:18 [g]Ps 116:16
12:19 [h]Job 24:12,22; 34:20,28; 35:9
12:20 [i]Job 32:9
12:22 [j]1Co 4:5 [k]Job 3:5 [l]Da 2:22
12:23 [m]Jer 25:9 [n]Ps 107:38; Isa 9:3; 26:15
12:24 [o]Ps 107:40
12:25 [p]Job 5:14 [q]Ps 107:27; Isa 24:20

13

"My eyes have seen all this,
my ears have heard and
understood it.
2 What you know, I also know;
I am not inferior to you.[r]
3 But I desire to speak to the Almighty
and to argue my case with God.[s]
4 You, however, smear me with lies;[t]
you are worthless physicians, all of
you!
5 If only you would be altogether
silent!
For you, that would be wisdom.[u]
6 Hear now my argument;
listen to the plea of my lips.
7 Will you speak wickedly on God's
behalf?
Will you speak deceitfully for
him?[v]
8 Will you show him partiality?[w]
Will you argue the case for God?
9 Would it turn out well if he
examined you?
Could you deceive him as you
might deceive men?[x]
10 He would surely rebuke you
if you secretly showed partiality.
11 Would not his splendor[y] terrify you?
Would not the dread of him fall
on you?
12 Your maxims are proverbs of ashes;
your defenses are defenses of clay.
13 "Keep silent and let me speak;
then let come to me what may.
14 Why do I put myself in jeopardy
and take my life in my hands?
15 Though he slay me, yet will I hope[z]
in him;[a]
I will surely[b] defend my ways to
his face.[b]

13:2 [r]Job 12:3
13:3 [s]Job 23:3-4
13:4 [t]Ps 119:69; Jer 23:32
13:5 [u]Pr 17:28
13:7 [v]Job 36:4
13:8 [w]Lev 19:15
13:9 [x]Job 12:16; Gal 6:7
13:11 [y]Job 31:23
13:15 [z]Job 7:6 [a]Ps 23:4; Pr 14:32 [b]Job 27:5

FAITHFULNESS

KISS THE HAND THAT HOLDS THE BLADE

Job 13:15

When you cannot manage the theology to explain your predicament…trust.

When none will stand beside you to bless your dreams…trust.

When all condemn you and the blade is at your throat…trust.

Jesus did.

16 Indeed, this will turn out for my
deliverance,[c]
for no godless man would dare
come before him!
17 Listen carefully to my words;[d]
let your ears take in what I say.
18 Now that I have prepared my case,[e]
I know I will be vindicated.
19 Can anyone bring charges against
me?[f]
If so, I will be silent and die.[g]
20 "Only grant me these two things,
O God,

13:16 [c]Isa 12:1
13:17 [d]Job 21:2
13:18 [e]Job 23:4
13:19 [f]Job 40:4; Isa 50:8 [g]Job 10:8

[a]18 Or *shackles of kings / and ties a belt* [b]15 Or *He will surely slay me; I have no hope — / yet I will*

and then I will not hide from you:
21 Withdraw your hand[h] far from me,
and stop frightening me with your
terrors.
22 Then summon me and I will
answer,[i]
or let me speak, and you reply.[j]
23 How many wrongs and sins have I
committed?[k]

13:21 [h]Ps 39:10
13:22 [i]Job 14:15 [j]Job 9:16
13:23 [k]1Sa 26:18

DAY 3 THREE

Faithfulness and My Relationship With Christ

Job 13:15

"Though he slay me, yet will I hope in him." Job had made a decision to stick with God. Although bad things had happened in Job's life, he was not about to give up his relationship with God.

Why was Job so dogmatic about his faithfulness? Could it be that our own faithfulness is a response to the faithfulness of God? Consider the words of this well-known passage:

**Because of the LORD's great love we are
not consumed,
for his compassions never fail.
They are new every morning;
great is your faithfulness.**

Lamentations 3:22–23

If our persistence needs a role model, God's own persistent faithfulness will certainly supply it. Job understood this. When we think about the compassion of God in offering his own Son as a sacrifice for our sin, we better understand true faithfulness. Christ suffered for us. How could we ever question God's steadfast love when our circumstances look grim?

Faithfulness involves developing the habit of hanging around God, not so that we'll have less suffering, but so that in the clear light of our nearness to God, we will better see what our suffering means and what our faithfulness should produce.

God has been faithful. He will be faithful. Jesus his Son was faithful to the point of death, and our relationship with God is guaranteed by Christ's constancy.

To begin a study on the topic of Faithfulness, the High Art of Persistence, turn to the home page on page 635.

Show me my offense and my sin.
24 Why do you hide your face[l]
and consider me your enemy?[m]
25 Will you torment a windblown leaf?[n]
Will you chase after dry chaff?[o]
26 For you write down bitter things
against me
and make me inherit the sins of
my youth.[p]
27 You fasten my feet in shackles;[q]
you keep close watch on all my
paths
by putting marks on the soles of
my feet.

28 "So man wastes away like something
rotten,
like a garment eaten by moths.[r]

14 "Man born of woman
is of few days and full of
trouble.[s]
2 He springs up like a flower[t] and
withers away;[u]
like a fleeting shadow,[v] he does
not endure.
3 Do you fix your eye on such a one?[w]
Will you bring him[a] before you
for judgment?[x]
4 Who can bring what is pure[y] from
the impure?[z]
No one![a]
5 Man's days are determined;
you have decreed the number of
his months[b]
and have set limits he cannot
exceed.
6 So look away from him and let him
alone,[c]
till he has put in his time like a
hired man.[d]

7 "At least there is hope for a tree:
If it is cut down, it will sprout
again,
and its new shoots will not fail.
8 Its roots may grow old in the ground
and its stump die in the soil,
9 yet at the scent of water it will bud
and put forth shoots like a plant.
10 But man dies and is laid low;
he breathes his last and is no
more.[e]
11 As water disappears from the sea
or a riverbed becomes parched and
dry,[f]
12 so man lies down and does not rise;

[a]3 Septuagint, Vulgate and Syriac; Hebrew *me*

13:24 [l]Dt 32:20; Ps 13:1; Isa 8:17 [m]Job 19:11; La 2:5
13:25 [n]Lev 26:36 [o]Job 21:18; Isa 42:3
13:26 [p]Ps 25:7
13:27 [q]Job 33:11
13:28 [r]Isa 50:9; Jas 5:2
14:1 [s]Job 5:7; Ecc 2:23
14:2 [t]Jas 1:10 [u]Ps 90:5-6 [v]Job 8:9
14:3 [w]Ps 8:4; 144:3 [x]Ps 143:2
14:4 [y]Ps 51:10 [z]Eph 2:1-3 [a]Jn 3:6; Ro 5:12
14:5 [b]Job 21:21
14:6 [c]Job 7:19 [d]Job 7:1,2; Ps 39:13
14:10 [e]Job 13:19
14:11 [f]Isa 19:5

till the heavens are no more,[g] men will not awake
or be roused from their sleep.[h]
13 "If only you would hide me in the grave[a]
and conceal me till your anger has passed![i]
If only you would set me a time
and then remember me!
14 If a man dies, will he live again?
All the days of my hard service
I will wait for my renewal[b] to come.

14:12 [g]Rev 20:11; 21:1 [h]Ac 3:21
14:13 [i]Isa 26:20

FAITHFULNESS

If a Man Dies, Will He Live Again?

Job 14:14

Job raised the question. Christ resolved it.
An odd, round stone once rolled away
From a dark and cold and "empty" cave.
"He is risen!" was the cry of all his miracle-stunned followers.
Pilgrims through the ages have believed—
Made treks to that odd cave
Where a dead man, bored with death, got up.

15 You will call and I will answer you;[j]
you will long for the creature your hands have made.
16 Surely then you will count my steps[k]
but not keep track of my sin.[l]
17 My offenses will be sealed up in a bag;[m]
you will cover over my sin.[n]
18 "But as a mountain erodes and crumbles
and as a rock is moved from its place,
19 as water wears away stones
and torrents wash away the soil,
so you destroy man's hope.[o]
20 You overpower him once for all, and he is gone;
you change his countenance and send him away.
21 If his sons are honored, he does not know it;
if they are brought low, he does not see it.[p]
22 He feels but the pain of his own body
and mourns only for himself."

14:15 [j]Job 13:22
14:16 [k]Ps 139:1-3; Pr 5:21; Jer 32:19 [l]Job 10:6
14:17 [m]Dt 32:34 [n]Hos 13:12
14:19 [o]Job 7:6
14:21 [p]Ecc 9:5; Isa 63:16

Eliphaz

15 Then Eliphaz the Temanite replied:

2 "Would a wise man answer with empty notions
or fill his belly with the hot east wind?[q]
3 Would he argue with useless words,
with speeches that have no value?
4 But you even undermine piety
and hinder devotion to God.
5 Your sin prompts your mouth;
you adopt the tongue of the crafty.[r]
6 Your own mouth condemns you, not mine;
your own lips testify against you.[s]
7 "Are you the first man ever born?[t]
Were you brought forth before the hills?[u]
8 Do you listen in on God's council?[v]
Do you limit wisdom to yourself?
9 What do you know that we do not know?
What insights do you have that we do not have?[w]
10 The gray-haired and the aged[x] are on our side,
men even older than your father.
11 Are God's consolations[y] not enough for you,
words[z] spoken gently to you?[a]
12 Why has your heart[b] carried you away,
and why do your eyes flash,
13 so that you vent your rage against God
and pour out such words from your mouth?
14 "What is man, that he could be pure,
or one born of woman,[c] that he could be righteous?[d]
15 If God places no trust in his holy ones,
if even the heavens are not pure in his eyes,[e]
16 how much less man, who is vile and corrupt,[f]
who drinks up evil like water![g]
17 "Listen to me and I will explain to you;
let me tell you what I have seen,
18 what wise men have declared,

15:2 [q]Job 6:26
15:5 [r]Job 5:13
15:6 [s]Lk 19:22
15:7 [t]Job 38:21 [u]Ps 90:2; Pr 8:25
15:8 [v]Ro 11:34; 1Co 2:11
15:9 [w]Job 13:2
15:10 [x]Job 32:6-7
15:11 [y]2Co 1:3-4 [z]Zec 1:13 [a]Job 36:16
15:12 [b]Job 11:13
15:14 [c]Job 14:4; 25:4 [d]Pr 20:9; Ecc 7:20
15:15 [e]Job 4:18; 25:5
15:16 [f]Ps 14:1 [g]Job 34:7; Pr 19:28

[a]13 Hebrew *Sheol* [b]14 Or *release*

hiding nothing received from their fathers[b]
19(to whom alone the land was given
when no alien passed among them):
20All his days the wicked man suffers torment,
the ruthless through all the years stored up for him.[i]
21Terrifying sounds fill his ears;[j]
when all seems well, marauders attack him.[k]
22He despairs of escaping the darkness;
he is marked for the sword.[l]
23He wanders about[m]—food for vultures[a];
he knows the day of darkness is at hand.[n]
24Distress and anguish fill him with terror;
they overwhelm him, like a king poised to attack,
25because he shakes his fist at God
and vaunts himself against the Almighty,[o]
26defiantly charging against him
with a thick, strong shield.

27"Though his face is covered with fat
and his waist bulges with flesh,[p]
28he will inhabit ruined towns
and houses where no one lives,[q]
houses crumbling to rubble.[r]
29He will no longer be rich and his wealth will not endure,[s]
nor will his possessions spread over the land.
30He will not escape the darkness;[t]
a flame[u] will wither his shoots,
and the breath of God's mouth[v] will carry him away.
31Let him not deceive himself by trusting what is worthless,[w]
for he will get nothing in return.
32Before his time[x] he will be paid in full,[y]
and his branches will not flourish.[z]
33He will be like a vine stripped of its unripe grapes,[a]
like an olive tree shedding its blossoms.
34For the company of the godless will be barren,
and fire will consume the tents of those who love bribes.[b]
35They conceive trouble and give birth to evil;[c]
their womb fashions deceit."

15:18 [h]Job 8:8
15:20 [i]Job 24:1; 27:13-23
15:21 [j]Job 18:11; 20:25 [k]Job 27:20; 1Th 5:3
15:22 [l]Job 19:29; 27:14
15:23 [m]Ps 59:15; 109:10 [n]Job 18:12
15:25 [o]Job 36:9
15:27 [p]Ps 17:10
15:28 [q]Isa 5:9 [r]Job 3:14
15:29 [s]Job 27:16-17
15:30 [t]Job 5:14 [u]Job 22:20 [v]Job 4:9
15:31 [w]Isa 59:4
15:32 [x]Ecc 7:17 [y]Job 22:16; Ps 55:23 [z]Job 18:16
15:33 [a]Hab 3:17
15:34 [b]Job 8:22
15:35 [c]Ps 7:14; Isa 59:4; Hos 10:13

Job

16

Then Job replied:
2"I have heard many things like these;
miserable comforters are you all![d]

KINDNESS

MISERABLE COMFORTERS

Job 16:2

Job needed counselors who could bring him soft-souled hope. Alas, he met only arrogant philosophers who offered nothing but cold pride.

Love the brokenhearted if you would be like God. Let kindness coat your abrasive arrogance with tolerance.

Offer hope.
Disperse no faulty counsel.
Summon the meek to instruct you,
And be meek when you pass their instruction on.

3Will your long-winded speeches never end?
What ails you that you keep on arguing?[e]
4I also could speak like you,
if you were in my place;
I could make fine speeches against you
and shake my head[f] at you.
5But my mouth would encourage you;
comfort from my lips would bring you relief.

6"Yet if I speak, my pain is not relieved;
and if I refrain, it does not go away.
7Surely, O God, you have worn me out;[g]
you have devastated my entire household.
8You have bound me—and it has become a witness;
my gauntness[h] rises up and testifies against me.[i]
9God assails me and tears[j] me in his anger
and gnashes his teeth at me;[k]
my opponent fastens on me his piercing eyes.[l]

[a]23 Or *about, looking for food*

16:2 [d]Job 13:4
16:3 [e]Job 6:26
16:4 [f]Ps 22:7; 109:25; La 2:15; Zep 2:15; Mt 27:39
16:7 [g]Job 7:3
16:8 [h]Job 19:20 [i]Job 10:17
16:9 [j]Hos 6:1 [k]Ps 35:16; La 2:16; Ac 7:54 [l]Job 13:24

[10]Men open their mouths[m] to jeer at
me;
they strike my cheek[n] in scorn
and unite together against me.[o]
[11]God has turned me over to evil men
and thrown me into the clutches
of the wicked.[p]
[12]All was well with me, but he
shattered me;
he seized me by the neck and
crushed me.[q]
He has made me his target;[r]
[13] his archers surround me.
Without pity, he pierces[s] my kidneys
and spills my gall on the ground.
[14]Again and again[t] he bursts upon me;
he rushes at me like a warrior.[u]

[15]"I have sewed sackcloth[v] over my
skin
and buried my brow in the dust.
[16]My face is red with weeping,
deep shadows ring my eyes;
[17]yet my hands have been free of
violence[w]
and my prayer is pure.

[18]"O earth, do not cover my blood;[x]
may my cry never be laid to rest![y]
[19]Even now my witness[z] is in heaven;
my advocate is on high.
[20]My intercessor is my friend[a]
as my eyes pour out[a] tears to God;
[21]on behalf of a man he pleads[b] with
God
as a man pleads for his friend.

[22]"Only a few years will pass
before I go on the journey of no
return.[c]

17 [1]My spirit is broken,
my days are cut short,
the grave awaits me.[d]
[2]Surely mockers[e] surround me;
my eyes must dwell on their
hostility.

[3]"Give me, O God, the pledge you
demand.[f]
Who else will put up security[g] for
me?[h]
[4]You have closed their minds to
understanding;
therefore you will not let them
triumph.
[5]If a man denounces his friends for
reward,
the eyes of his children will fail.[i]

16:10 [m]Ps 22:13 [n]Isa 50:6; La 3:30; Mic 5:1; Ac 23:2 [o]Ps 35:15
16:11 [p]Job 1:15,17
16:12 [q]Job 9:17 [r]La 3:12
16:13 [s]Job 20:24
16:14 [t]Job 9:17 [u]Joel 2:7
16:15 [v]Ge 37:34
16:17 [w]Isa 59:6; Jnh 3:8
16:18 [x]Isa 26:21 [y]Ps 66:18-19
16:19 [z]Ge 31:50; Ro 1:9; 1Th 2:5
16:20 [a]La 2:19
16:21 [b]Ps 9:4
16:22 [c]Ecc 12:5
17:1 [d]Ps 88:3-4
17:2 [e]1Sa 1:6-7
17:3 [f]Ps 119:122 [g]Pr 6:1 [h]Isa 38:14
17:5 [i]Job 11:20

[6]"God has made me a byword[j] to
everyone,
a man in whose face people spit.
[7]My eyes have grown dim with grief;[k]
my whole frame is but a shadow.
[8]Upright men are appalled at this;
the innocent are aroused[l] against
the ungodly.
[9]Nevertheless, the righteous[m] will
hold to their ways,
and those with clean hands[n] will
grow stronger.

[10]"But come on, all of you, try again!
I will not find a wise man among
you.[o]
[11]My days have passed, my plans are
shattered,
and so are the desires of my
heart.[p]
[12]These men turn night into day;
in the face of darkness they say,
'Light is near.'
[13]If the only home I hope for is the
grave,[b][q]
if I spread out my bed in darkness,
[14]if I say to corruption,[r] 'You are my
father,'
and to the worm,[s] 'My mother' or
'My sister,'
[15]where then is my hope?[t]
Who can see any hope for me?
[16]Will it go down to the gates of
death[b]?[u]
Will we descend together into the
dust?"

Bildad

18 Then Bildad the Shuhite replied:

[2]"When will you end these speeches?
Be sensible, and then we can talk.
[3]Why are we regarded as cattle
and considered stupid in your
sight?[v]
[4]You who tear yourself[w] to pieces in
your anger,
is the earth to be abandoned for
your sake?
Or must the rocks be moved from
their place?

[5]"The lamp of the wicked is snuffed
out;[x]
the flame of his fire stops burning.

[a]*20* Or *My friends treat me with scorn*
[b]*13,16* Hebrew *Sheol*

17:6 [j]Job 30:9
17:7 [k]Job 16:8
17:8 [l]Job 22:19
17:9 [m]Pr 4:18 [n]Job 22:30
17:10 [o]Job 12:2
17:11 [p]Job 7:6
17:13 [q]Job 3:13
17:14 [r]Job 13:28; 30:28,30; Ps 16:10 [s]Job 21:26
17:15 [t]Job 7:6
17:16 [u]Job 3:17-19; Jnh 2:6
18:3 [v]Ps 73:22
18:4 [w]Job 13:14
18:5 [x]Job 21:17; Pr 13:9; 20:20; 24:20

[6]The light in his tent becomes dark;
the lamp beside him goes out.
[7]The vigor of his step is weakened;[y]
his own schemes[z] throw him
down.[a]
[8]His feet thrust him into a net[b]
and he wanders into its mesh.
[9]A trap seizes him by the heel;
a snare holds him fast.
[10]A noose is hidden for him on the
ground;
a trap lies in his path.
[11]Terrors startle him on every side[c]
and dog[d] his every step.
[12]Calamity is hungry[e] for him;
disaster is ready for him when he
falls.
[13]It eats away parts of his skin;
death's firstborn devours his
limbs.[f]
[14]He is torn from the security of his
tent[g]
and marched off to the king of
terrors.
[15]Fire resides[a] in his tent;
burning sulfur[h] is scattered over
his dwelling.
[16]His roots dry up below[i]
and his branches wither above.[j]
[17]The memory of him perishes from
the earth;
he has no name in the land.[k]
[18]He is driven from light into
darkness[l]
and is banished from the world.
[19]He has no offspring[m] or
descendants[n] among his
people,
no survivor where once he
lived.[o]
[20]Men of the west are appalled at his
fate;[p]
men of the east are seized with
horror.
[21]Surely such is the dwelling[q] of an
evil man;
such is the place of one who
knows not God."[r]

18:7 [y]Pr 4:12 [z]Job 5:13 [a]Job 15:6
18:8 [b]Job 22:10; Ps 9:15; 35:7
18:11 [c]Job 15:21; Jer 6:25; 20:3 [d]Job 20:8
18:12 [e]Isa 8:21
18:13 [f]Zec 14:12
18:14 [g]Job 8:22
18:15 [h]Ps 11:6
18:16 [i]Isa 5:24; Hos 9:1-16; Am 2:9 [j]Job 15:30; Mal 4:1
18:17 [k]Ps 34:16; Pr 2:22; 10:7
18:18 [l]Job 5:14
18:19 [m]Jer 22:30 [n]Isa 14:22 [o]Job 27:14-15
18:20 [p]Ps 37:13; Jer 50:27,31
18:21 [q]Job 21:28 [r]Jer 9:3; 1Th 4:5

Job

19 Then Job replied:

[2]"How long will you torment me
and crush me with words?
[3]Ten times now you have reproached
me;
shamelessly you attack me.
[4]If it is true that I have gone astray,
my error[s] remains my concern
alone.
[5]If indeed you would exalt yourselves
above me[t]
and use my humiliation against
me,
[6]then know that God has wronged
me[u]
and drawn his net[v] around me.
[7]"Though I cry, 'I've been wronged!' I
get no response;[w]
though I call for help, there is no
justice.[x]
[8]He has blocked my way so I cannot
pass;[y]
he has shrouded my paths in
darkness.[z]
[9]He has stripped[a] me of my honor
and removed the crown from my
head.[b]
[10]He tears me down[c] on every side till
I am gone;
he uproots my hope[d] like a tree.[e]
[11]His anger[f] burns against me;
he counts me among his
enemies.[g]
[12]His troops advance in force;[h]
they build a siege ramp[i] against
me
and encamp around my tent.
[13]"He has alienated my brothers[j] from
me;
my acquaintances are completely
estranged from me.[k]
[14]My kinsmen have gone away;
my friends have forgotten me.
[15]My guests and my maidservants
count me a stranger;
they look upon me as an alien.
[16]I summon my servant, but he does
not answer,
though I beg him with my own
mouth.
[17]My breath is offensive to my wife;
I am loathsome to my own
brothers.
[18]Even the little boys[l] scorn me;
when I appear, they ridicule me.
[19]All my intimate friends[m] detest me;[n]
those I love have turned against
me.
[20]I am nothing but skin and bones;[o]
I have escaped with only the skin
of my teeth.[b]

19:4 [s]Job 6:24
19:5 [t]Ps 35:26; 38:16; 55:12
19:6 [u]Job 27:2 [v]Job 18:8
19:7 [w]Job 30:20 [x]Job 9:24; Hab 1:2-4
19:8 [y]Job 3:23; La 3:7 [z]Job 30:26
19:9 [a]Job 12:17 [b]Ps 89:39,44; La 5:16
19:10 [c]Job 12:14 [d]Job 7:6 [e]Job 24:20
19:11 [f]Job 16:9 [g]Job 13:24
19:12 [h]Job 16:13 [i]Job 30:12
19:13 [j]Ps 69:8 [k]Job 16:7; Ps 88:8
19:18 [l]2Ki 2:23
19:19 [m]Ps 55:12-13 [n]Ps 38:11
19:20 [o]Job 33:21; Ps 102:5

[a]*15* Or *Nothing he had remains* [b]*20* Or *only my gums*

21 "Have pity on me, my friends, have pity,
for the hand of God has struck me.
22 Why do you pursue[p] me as God does?
Will you never get enough of my flesh?[q]

23 "Oh, that my words were recorded,
that they were written on a scroll,[r]
24 that they were inscribed with an iron tool on[a] lead,

19:22 [p]Job 13:25; 16:11 [q]Ps 69:26
19:23 [r]Isa 30:8

DAY 5 FIVE

▸ JOY AND ITS PLACE IN MY PERSONAL WORSHIP

Job 19:23–27

It is, perhaps, not possible to understand these verses without empathizing with Job's frustration in his attempt to break through the silence of God. Job felt that God was not hearing him. Job thought that he was enduring his hardships alone and that God didn't care much.

Job cries out in 19:7–10:

Though I cry, "I've been wronged!" I get no response;
though I call for help, there is no justice.
He has blocked my way so I cannot pass;
he has shrouded my paths in darkness.
He has stripped me of my honor
and removed the crown from my head.
He tears me down on every side till I am gone;
he uproots my hope like a tree.

Job felt that people should not have to meet the silence of God—particularly when they are so needy—and have their despair go unnoticed. Surely no one should have to die with his or her suffering unrecorded. "Hurt this bad," reasons Job, "should be noticed somewhere in the universe."

Still, following this deep pain, hope finds enough joy to sing. After the despair there is a kind of instantaneous spark of joy when Job realizes that his Redeemer lives. Our worship is strengthened when we too realize the truth that Job found through his sorrows—that someday we will see God.

To begin a study on the topic of Joy, the Reward of Endurance, turn to the home page on page 581.

or engraved in rock forever!
25 I know that my Redeemer[b][s] lives,[t]
and that in the end he will stand upon the earth.[c]
26 And after my skin has been destroyed,
yet[d] in[e] my flesh I will see God;[u]
27 I myself will see him
with my own eyes—I, and not another.
How my heart yearns[v] within me!

28 "If you say, 'How we will hound him,
since the root of the trouble lies in him,[f]'
29 you should fear the sword yourselves;
for wrath will bring punishment by the sword,[w]
and then you will know that there is judgment.[g]"[x]

19:25 [s]Ps 78:35; Pr 23:11; Isa 43:14; Jer 50:34 [t]Job 16:19
19:26 [u]Ps 17:15; Mt 5:8; 1Co 13:12; 1Jn 3:2
19:27 [v]Ps 73:26
19:29 [w]Job 15:22 [x]Job 22:4; Ps 1:5; 9:7

▸ FAITHFULNESS

PURSUE THE ELUSIVE: HE LIVES

Job 19:25

He lives? He is elusive in his glory! But does he not live? Have you not seen him here and there—yet not quite with a clear eye? Then look again. There he is! Or is it only his indistinct self? Look for him. Search him out. He lives! Chase him. Pursue him. Find again his stopping place. Cling to his reality. Hang around the place you saw him last.

Zophar

20 Then Zophar the Naamathite replied:

2 "My troubled thoughts prompt me to answer
because I am greatly disturbed.
3 I hear a rebuke[y] that dishonors me,
and my understanding inspires me to reply.

4 "Surely you know how it has been from of old,
ever since man[h] was placed on the earth,
5 that the mirth of the wicked is brief,

20:3 [y]Job 19:3

[a]24 Or *and* [b]25 Or *defender* [c]25 Or *upon my grave* [d]26 Or *And after I awake, / though this ⌊body⌋ has been destroyed, / then* [e]26 Or */ apart from* [f]28 Many Hebrew manuscripts, Septuagint and Vulgate; most Hebrew manuscripts *me* [g]29 Or */ that you may come to know the Almighty* [h]4 Or *Adam*

the joy of the godless lasts but a
moment.[z]
6 Though his pride reaches to the
heavens
and his head touches the clouds,[a]
7 he will perish forever,[b] like his own
dung;
those who have seen him will say,
'Where is he?'[c]
8 Like a dream[d] he flies away,[e] no
more to be found,
banished[f] like a vision of the
night.[g]
9 The eye that saw him will not see
him again;
his place will look on him no
more.[h]
10 His children[i] must make amends to
the poor;
his own hands must give back his
wealth.[j]
11 The youthful vigor[k] that fills his
bones
will lie with him in the dust.[l]

12 "Though evil is sweet in his mouth
and he hides it under his tongue,
13 though he cannot bear to let it go
and keeps it in his mouth,[m]
14 yet his food will turn sour in his
stomach;
it will become the venom of
serpents within him.
15 He will spit out the riches he
swallowed;
God will make his stomach vomit
them up.
16 He will suck the poison[n] of serpents;
the fangs of an adder will kill
him.[o]
17 He will not enjoy the streams,
the rivers flowing with honey[p] and
cream.[q]
18 What he toiled for he must give back
uneaten;
he will not enjoy the profit from
his trading.
19 For he has oppressed the poor and
left them destitute;[r]
he has seized houses he did not
build.

20 "Surely he will have no respite from
his craving;[s]
he cannot save himself by his
treasure.
21 Nothing is left for him to devour;
his prosperity will not endure.[t]
22 In the midst of his plenty, distress
will overtake him;
the full force of misery will come
upon him.
23 When he has filled his belly,
God will vent his burning anger
against him
and rain down his blows upon
him.[u]
24 Though he flees[v] from an iron
weapon,
a bronze-tipped arrow pierces him.
25 He pulls it out of his back,
the gleaming point out of his
liver.
Terrors[w] will come over him;[x]
26 total darkness[y] lies in wait for his
treasures.
A fire unfanned will consume him[z]
and devour what is left in his tent.
27 The heavens will expose his guilt;
the earth will rise up against him.[a]
28 A flood will carry off his house,[b]
rushing waters[a] on the day of
God's wrath.[c]
29 Such is the fate God allots the
wicked,
the heritage appointed for them
by God."[d]

Job

21

Then Job replied:

2 "Listen carefully to my words;
let this be the consolation you give
me.
3 Bear with me while I speak,
and after I have spoken, mock on.[e]

4 "Is my complaint directed to man?
Why should I not be impatient?[f]
5 Look at me and be astonished;
clap your hand over your mouth.[g]
6 When I think about this, I am
terrified;
trembling seizes my body.
7 Why do the wicked live on,
growing old and increasing in
power?[h]
8 They see their children established
around them,
their offspring before their eyes.[i]
9 Their homes are safe and free from
fear;[j]
the rod of God is not upon them.
10 Their bulls never fail to breed;

[a]28 Or *The possessions in his house will be carried off, / washed away*

20:5 [z]Job 8:12; Ps 37:35-36; 73:19
20:6 [a]Isa 14:13-14; Ob 1:3-4
20:7 [b]Job 4:20 [c]Job 7:10; 8:18
20:8 [d]Ps 73:20 [e]Job 27:21-23 [f]Job 18:18 [g]Ps 90:5
20:9 [h]Job 7:8
20:10 [i]Job 5:4 [j]Job 27:16-17
20:11 [k]Job 13:26 [l]Job 21:26
20:13 [m]Nu 11:18-20
20:16 [n]Dt 32:32 [o]Dt 32:24
20:17 [p]Dt 32:13 [q]Job 29:6
20:19 [r]Job 24:4,14; 35:9
20:20 [s]Ecc 5:12-14
20:21 [t]Job 15:29
20:23 [u]Ps 78:30-31
20:24 [v]Isa 24:18; Am 5:19
20:25 [w]Job 18:11 [x]Job 16:13
20:26 [y]Job 18:18 [z]Ps 21:9
20:27 [a]Dt 31:28
20:28 [b]Dt 28:31 [c]Job 21:17, 20,30
20:29 [d]Job 27:13
21:3 [e]Job 16:10
21:4 [f]Job 6:11
21:5 [g]Jdg 18:19; Job 29:9; 40:4
21:7 [h]Job 12:6; Ps 73:3; Jer 12:1; Hab 1:13
21:8 [i]Ps 17:14
21:9 [j]Ps 73:5

their cows calve and do not
miscarry.[k]
11 They send forth their children as a
flock;
their little ones dance about.
12 They sing to the music of
tambourine and harp;
they make merry to the sound of
the flute.[l]
13 They spend their years in
prosperity[m]
and go down to the grave[a] in
peace.[b]
14 Yet they say to God, 'Leave us
alone![n]
We have no desire to know your
ways.[o]
15 Who is the Almighty, that we should
serve him?[p]
What would we gain by praying
to him?'
16 But their prosperity is not in their
own hands,
so I stand aloof from the counsel
of the wicked.

17 "Yet how often is the lamp of the
wicked snuffed out?[q]
How often does calamity come
upon them,
the fate God allots in his anger?
18 How often are they like straw before
the wind,
like chaff[r] swept away by a gale?
19 ⌊It is said,⌋ 'God stores up a man's
punishment for his sons.'[s]
Let him repay the man himself, so
that he will know it!
20 Let his own eyes see his destruction;
let him drink[t] of the wrath of the
Almighty.[c][u]
21 For what does he care about the
family he leaves behind
when his allotted months[v] come
to an end?

22 "Can anyone teach knowledge to
God,[w]
since he judges even the highest?[x]
23 One man dies in full vigor,
completely secure and at ease,
24 his body[d] well nourished,
his bones rich with marrow.[y]
25 Another man dies in bitterness of
soul,
never having enjoyed anything
good.
26 Side by side they lie in the dust,
and worms cover them both.[z]

27 "I know full well what you are
thinking,
the schemes by which you would
wrong me.
28 You say, 'Where now is the great
man's[a] house,
the tents where wicked men
lived?'[b]
29 Have you never questioned those
who travel?
Have you paid no regard to their
accounts—
30 that the evil man is spared from the
day of calamity,[c]
that he is delivered from[e] the day
of wrath?[d]
31 Who denounces his conduct to his
face?
Who repays him for what he has
done?
32 He is carried to the grave,
and watch is kept over his tomb.
33 The soil in the valley is sweet to him;
all men follow after him,[e]
and a countless throng goes[f]
before him.[f]

34 "So how can you console me[g] with
your nonsense?
Nothing is left of your answers
but falsehood!"

Eliphaz

22 Then Eliphaz the Temanite replied:

2 "Can a man be of benefit to God?[h]
Can even a wise man benefit him?
3 What pleasure would it give the
Almighty if you were
righteous?
What would he gain if your ways
were blameless?

4 "Is it for your piety that he rebukes
you
and brings charges against you?[i]
5 Is not your wickedness great?
Are not your sins[j] endless?
6 You demanded security[k] from your
brothers for no reason;
you stripped men of their clothing,
leaving them naked.

[a]*13* Hebrew *Sheol* [b]*13* Or *in an instant*
[c]*17-20* Verses 17 and 18 may be taken as exclamations and 19 and 20 as declarations.
[d]*24* The meaning of the Hebrew for this word is uncertain. [e]*30* Or *man is reserved for the day of calamity, / that he is brought forth to*
[f]*33* Or / *as a countless throng went*

21:10 [k]Ex 23:26
21:12 [l]Ps 81:2
21:13 [m]Job 36:11
21:14 [n]Job 22:17 [o]Pr 1:29
21:15 [p]Ex 5:2; Job 34:9; Mal 3:14
21:17 [q]Job 18:5
21:18 [r]Job 13:25; Ps 1:4
21:19 [s]Ex 20:5; Jer 31:29; Eze 18:2
21:20 [t]Ps 75:8; Isa 51:17 [u]Jer 25:15; Rev 14:10
21:21 [v]Job 14:5
21:22 [w]Job 35:11; 36:22; Isa 40:13-14; Ro 11:34 [x]Ps 82:1
21:24 [y]Pr 3:8
21:26 [z]Job 24:20; Ecc 9:2-3; Isa 14:11
21:28 [a]Job 1:3; 12:21; 31:37 [b]Job 8:22
21:30 [c]Pr 16:4 [d]Job 20:22,28; 2Pe 2:9
21:33 [e]Job 3:22; 17:16; 24:24 [f]Job 3:19
21:34 [g]Job 16:2
22:2 [h]Lk 17:10
22:4 [i]Job 14:3; 19:29; Ps 143:2
22:5 [j]Job 11:6; 15:5
22:6 [k]Ex 22:26; Dt 24:6,17; Eze 18:12,16

[7] You gave no water to the weary
and you withheld food from the hungry,[l]
[8] though you were a powerful man, owning land—
an honored man,[m] living on it.
[9] And you sent widows away empty-handed[n]
and broke the strength of the fatherless.
[10] That is why snares are all around you,
why sudden peril terrifies you,
[11] why it is so dark[o] you cannot see,
and why a flood of water covers you.[p]

[12] "Is not God in the heights of heaven?[q]
And see how lofty are the highest stars!
[13] Yet you say, 'What does God know?[r]
Does he judge through such darkness?[s]
[14] Thick clouds[t] veil him, so he does not see us
as he goes about in the vaulted heavens.'
[15] Will you keep to the old path
that evil men have trod?
[16] They were carried off before their time,[u]
their foundations washed away by a flood.[v]
[17] They said to God, 'Leave us alone!
What can the Almighty do to us?'[w]
[18] Yet it was he who filled their houses with good things,[x]
so I stand aloof from the counsel of the wicked.[y]

[19] "The righteous see their ruin and rejoice;[z]
the innocent mock[a] them, saying,
[20] 'Surely our foes are destroyed,
and fire[b] devours their wealth.'
[21] "Submit to God and be at peace with him;
in this way prosperity will come to you.[c]
[22] Accept instruction from his mouth
and lay up his words in your heart.
[23] If you return[d] to the Almighty, you will be restored:[e]
If you remove wickedness far from your tent[f]
[24] and assign your nuggets to the dust,
your gold of Ophir to the rocks in the ravines,[g]
[25] then the Almighty will be your gold,
the choicest silver for you.[h]
[26] Surely then you will find delight in the Almighty[i]
and will lift up your face to God.
[27] You will pray to him,[j] and he will hear you,
and you will fulfill your vows.
[28] What you decide on will be done,
and light will shine on your ways.
[29] When men are brought low and you say, 'Lift them up!'
then he will save the downcast.[k]
[30] He will deliver even one who is not innocent,
who will be delivered through the cleanness of your hands."[l]

22:7 [l]Job 31:17,21,31
22:8 [m]Isa 3:3; 9:15
22:9 [n]Job 24:3,21
22:11 [o]Job 5:14 [p]Ps 69:1-2; 124:4-5; La 3:54
22:12 [q]Job 11:8
22:13 [r]Ps 10:11; Isa 29:15 [s]Eze 8:12
22:14 [t]Job 26:9
22:16 [u]Job 15:32 [v]Job 14:19; Mt 7:26-27
22:17 [w]Job 21:15
22:18 [x]Job 12:6 [y]Job 21:16
22:19 [z]Ps 58:10; 107:42 [a]Ps 52:6
22:20 [b]Job 15:30
22:21 [c]Ps 34:8-10
22:23 [d]Job 8:5; Isa 31:6; Zec 1:3 [e]Isa 19:22; Ac 20:32 [f]Job 11:14
22:24 [g]Job 31:25
22:25 [h]Isa 33:6
22:26 [i]Job 27:10; Isa 58:14
22:27 [j]Job 33:26; 34:28; Isa 58:9
22:29 [k]Mt 23:12; 1Pe 5:5
22:30 [l]Job 42:7-8

Job

23

Then Job replied:

[2] "Even today my complaint[m] is bitter;[n]
his hand[a] is heavy in spite of[b] my groaning.
[3] If only I knew where to find him;
if only I could go to his dwelling!

▸ PEACE

IF ONLY I KNEW WHERE TO FIND HIM

Job 23:3

Our search for God is the light at the center of our faith. Like Mary Magdalene, we will one day think we're talking to the gardener, only to find that it is Jesus. When it's still dark at early twilight, how can we know the difference? We'll know! Peace will find its Prince. Mere gardeners will not supply our hearts for long. We must have Jesus.

[4] I would state my case[o] before him
and fill my mouth with arguments.
[5] I would find out what he would answer me,
and consider what he would say.
[6] Would he oppose me with great power?[p]

23:2 [m]Job 7:11 [n]Job 6:3
23:4 [o]Job 13:18
23:6 [p]Job 9:4

[a]2 Septuagint and Syriac; Hebrew / *the hand on me*
[b]2 Or *heavy on me in*

No, he would not press charges
against me.
7 There an upright man could present
his case before him,[q]
and I would be delivered forever
from my judge.

8 "But if I go to the east, he is not
there;
if I go to the west, I do not find
him.
9 When he is at work in the north, I
do not see him;
when he turns to the south, I
catch no glimpse of him.[r]
10 But he knows the way that I take;
when he has tested me,[s] I will
come forth as gold.[t]
11 My feet have closely followed his
steps;[u]
I have kept to his way without
turning aside.[v]
12 I have not departed from the
commands of his lips;[w]
I have treasured the words of his
mouth more than my daily
bread.[x]

13 "But he stands alone, and who can
oppose him?
He does whatever he pleases.[y]
14 He carries out his decree against me,
and many such plans he still has
in store.[z]
15 That is why I am terrified before
him;
when I think of all this, I fear
him.
16 God has made my heart faint;[a]
the Almighty[b] has terrified me.
17 Yet I am not silenced by the
darkness,[c]
by the thick darkness that covers
my face.

24 "Why does the Almighty not set
times for judgment?[d]
Why must those who know him
look in vain for such days?[e]
2 Men move boundary stones;[f]
they pasture flocks they have
stolen.
3 They drive away the orphan's donkey
and take the widow's ox in
pledge.[g]
4 They thrust the needy from the path
and force all the poor[h] of the land
into hiding.[i]
5 Like wild donkeys in the desert,
the poor go about their labor[j] of
foraging food;
the wasteland provides food for
their children.
6 They gather fodder in the fields
and glean in the vineyards of the
wicked.
7 Lacking clothes, they spend the
night naked;

23:7 [q]Job 13:3
23:9 [r]Job 9:11
23:10 [s]Ps 66:10; 139:1-3 [t]1Pe 1:7
23:11 [u]Ps 17:5 [v]Ps 44:18
23:12 [w]Job 6:10 [x]Jn 4:32,34
23:13 [y]Ps 115:3
23:14 [z]1Th 3:3
23:16 [a]Dt 20:3; Ps 22:14; Jer 51:46 [b]Job 27:2
23:17 [c]Job 19:8
24:1 [d]Jer 46:10 [e]Ac 1:7
24:2 [f]Dt 19:14; 27:17; Pr 23:10
24:3 [g]Dt 24:6,10, 12,17; Job 22:6
24:4 [h]Job 29:12; 30:25; Ps 41:1 [i]Pr 28:28
24:5 [j]Ps 104:23

DAY 3 THREE

Self-Control and My Relationship With Christ

Job 23:10

Holiness is the only soil in which a relationship with Christ can be rooted. But how do we strive for holiness? Do we simply decide to be holy and then try to be good enough to be welcomed into God's circle of friends?

Job says that God has "tested" us so that we can "come forth as gold." Trials do indeed refine us as if in a fire. One can imagine a clump of gold ore protesting in the foundry. The metallurgist would seem cruel as he heated the gold almost beyond endurance. But as the gold is smelted in the heat and the flame, it is purified into real, true metal without any flaws.

Yet who is so mature that he or she welcomes the refining fire? Almost no one. The discipline of God hurts. Hebrews reminds us that God's discipline is on our behalf. "God disciplines us for our good, that we may share in his holiness. No discipline seems pleasant at the time, but painful. Later on, however, it produces a harvest of righteousness and peace for those who have been trained by it" (Hebrews 12:10–11).

Almost every time we meet a great believer whose life has been schooled in holiness, that believer has passed through the furnaces of God. Those souls have wept, and their tears have purified their world views, their value systems and their hearts. Then, tried and cleansed, they have moved freely into a relationship with Christ that is more powerful than it was before their trials. They are at home in the presence and fellowship of God, for they are heirs with Christ, more like him than they could ever have dreamed possible.

To begin a study on the topic of Self-Control, the Path of Coming to Maturity, turn to the home page on page 364.

they have nothing to cover
themselves in the cold.[k]

24:7 kEx 22:27; Job 22:6

8 They are drenched by mountain
rains
and hug[l] the rocks for lack of
shelter.

24:8 lLa 4:5

9 The fatherless[m] child is snatched
from the breast;
the infant of the poor is seized for
a debt.

24:9 mDt 24:17

10 Lacking clothes, they go about
naked;
they carry the sheaves, but still go
hungry.
11 They crush olives among the
terraces[a];
they tread the winepresses, yet
suffer thirst.
12 The groans of the dying rise from
the city,
and the souls of the wounded cry
out for help.[n]
But God charges no one with
wrongdoing.[o]

24:12 nEze 26:15 oJob 9:23

13 "There are those who rebel against
the light,[p]
who do not know its ways
or stay in its paths.[q]

24:13 pJn 3:19-20 qIsa 5:20

14 When daylight is gone, the murderer
rises up
and kills the poor and needy;
in the night he steals forth like a
thief.[r]

24:14 rPs 10:9

15 The eye of the adulterer watches for
dusk;[s]
he thinks, 'No eye will see me,'[t]
and he keeps his face concealed.

24:15 sPr 7:8-9 tPs 10:11

16 In the dark, men break into houses,[u]
but by day they shut themselves
in;
they want nothing to do with the
light.[v]

24:16 uEx 22:2; Mt 6:19 vJn 3:20

17 For all of them, deep darkness is
their morning[b];
they make friends with the terrors
of darkness.[c]
18 "Yet they are foam[w] on the surface of
the water;[x]
their portion of the land is cursed,
so that no one goes to the
vineyards.

24:18 wJob 9:26 xJob 22:16

19 As heat and drought snatch away the
melted snow,[y]
so the grave[d][z] snatches away those
who have sinned.

24:19 yJob 6:17 zJob 21:13

20 The womb forgets them,
the worm feasts on them;
evil men are no longer remembered[a]
but are broken like a tree.[b]

24:20 aJob 18:17; Pr 10:7 bPs 31:12; Da 4:14

21 They prey on the barren and
childless woman,
and to the widow show no
kindness.[c]

24:21 cJob 22:9

22 But God drags away the mighty by
his power;
though they become established,
they have no assurance of
life.[d]

24:22 dDt 28:66

23 He may let them rest in a feeling of
security,[e]
but his eyes are on their ways.[f]

24:23 eJob 12:6 fJob 11:11

24 For a little while they are exalted,
and then they are gone;[g]
they are brought low and gathered
up like all others;
they are cut off like heads of
grain.[h]

24:24 gJob 14:21; Ps 37:10 hIsa 17:5

25 "If this is not so, who can prove me
false
and reduce my words to
nothing?"[i]

24:25 iJob 6:28; 27:4

Bildad

25 Then Bildad the Shuhite replied:

2 "Dominion and awe belong to God;[j]
he establishes order in the heights
of heaven.

25:2 jJob 9:4; Rev 1:6

3 Can his forces be numbered?
Upon whom does his light not
rise?[k]

25:3 kJas 1:17

4 How then can a man be righteous
before God?
How can one born of woman be
pure?[l]

25:4 lJob 4:17; 14:4

5 If even the moon[m] is not bright
and the stars are not pure in his
eyes,[n]

25:5 mJob 31:26 nJob 15:15

6 how much less man,[o] who is but a
maggot—
a son of man, who is only a
worm!"[p]

25:6 oJob 7:17 pPs 22:6

Job

26 Then Job replied:

2 "How you have helped the
powerless![q]

26:2 qJob 6:12

[a]11 Or *olives between the millstones*; the meaning of the Hebrew for this word is uncertain.
[b]17 Or *them, their morning is like the shadow of death*
[c]17 Or *of the shadow of death*
[d]19 Hebrew *Sheol*

26:2 [r]Ps 71:9
How you have saved the arm that
is feeble![r]
3 What advice you have offered to one
without wisdom!
And what great insight you have
displayed!
4 Who has helped you utter these
words?
And whose spirit spoke from your
mouth?

26:5 [s]Ps 88:10
5 "The dead are in deep anguish,[s]
those beneath the waters and all
that live in them.
26:6 [t]Ps 139:8 [u]Job 41:11; Pr 15:11; Heb 4:13
6 Death[a] [t] is naked before God;
Destruction[b] lies uncovered.[u]
26:7 [v]Job 9:8
7 He spreads out the northern ⌊skies⌋[v]
over empty space;
he suspends the earth over
nothing.
26:8 [w]Pr 30:4 [x]Job 37:11
8 He wraps up the waters[w] in his
clouds,[x]
yet the clouds do not burst under
their weight.
26:9 [y]Job 22:14; Ps 97:2
9 He covers the face of the full moon,
spreading his clouds[y] over it.
26:10 [z]Pr 8:27,29 [a]Job 38:8-11
10 He marks out the horizon on the
face of the waters[z]
for a boundary between light and
darkness.[a]
11 The pillars of the heavens quake,
aghast at his rebuke.
26:12 [b]Ex 14:21; Isa 51:15; Jer 31:35 [c]Job 12:13
12 By his power he churned up the sea;[b]
by his wisdom[c] he cut Rahab to
pieces.
26:13 [d]Isa 27:1
13 By his breath the skies became fair;
his hand pierced the gliding
serpent.[d]
14 And these are but the outer fringe of
his works;
how faint the whisper we hear of
him!
26:14 [e]Job 36:29
Who then can understand the
thunder of his power?"[e]

27:1 [f]Job 29:1
27 And Job continued his discourse:[f]

27:2 [g]Job 34:5 [h]Job 9:18
2 "As surely as God lives, who has
denied me justice,[g]
the Almighty, who has made me
taste bitterness of soul,[h]
27:3 [i]Job 32:8; 33:4
3 as long as I have life within me,
the breath of God[i] in my nostrils,
27:4 [j]Job 6:28
4 my lips will not speak wickedness,
and my tongue will utter no
deceit.[j]
5 I will never admit you are in the
right;

PATIENCE

THE SCIENCE OF SILENCE

Job 27:3-4

Evil words are born of impatience. Those who will not wait on God usually talk too much. Walk, don't talk. Keep company with God, and let his holy patience purify your speech. "When anything disagreeable happens to you, remember Christ crucified and keep silent," said Thomas à Kempis. Words are cheap; silence, quite expensive.

till I die, I will not deny my
integrity.[k] 27:5 [k]Job 2:9; 13:15
6 I will maintain my righteousness and
never let go of it;
my conscience will not reproach
me as long as I live.[l] 27:6 [l]Job 2:3

7 "May my enemies be like the
wicked,
my adversaries like the unjust!
8 For what hope has the godless[m] 27:8 [m]Job 8:13 [n]Job 11:20; Lk 12:20
when he is cut off,
when God takes away his life?[n]
9 Does God listen to his cry 27:9 [o]Job 35:12; Pr 1:28; Isa 1:15; Jer 14:12; Mic 3:4
when distress comes upon him?[o]
10 Will he find delight in the
Almighty?[p]
Will he call upon God at all 27:10 [p]Job 22:26
times?

11 "I will teach you about the power of
God;
the ways of the Almighty I will
not conceal.
12 You have all seen this yourselves.
Why then this meaningless talk?

13 "Here is the fate God allots to the
wicked,
the heritage a ruthless man
receives from the Almighty:[q] 27:13 [q]Job 15:20; 20:29
14 However many his children, their
fate is the sword;[r] 27:14 [r]Dt 28:41; Job 15:22; Hos 9:13 [s]Job 20:10
his offspring will never have
enough to eat.[s]
15 The plague will bury those who
survive him,
and their widows will not weep 27:15 [t]Ps 78:64
for them.[t]
16 Though he heaps up silver like dust 27:16 [u]Zec 9:3
and clothes like piles of clay,[u]
17 what he lays up the righteous will 27:17 [v]Pr 28:8; Ecc 2:26
wear,[v]

[a]6 Hebrew *Sheol* [b]6 Hebrew *Abaddon*

and the innocent will divide his
silver.
18 The house he builds is like a moth's
cocoon,[w]
like a hut[x] made by a watchman.
19 He lies down wealthy, but will do so
no more;[y]
when he opens his eyes, all is gone.
20 Terrors overtake him like a flood;[z]
a tempest snatches him away in
the night.[a]
21 The east wind carries him off, and
he is gone;
it sweeps him out of his place.[b]
22 It hurls itself against him without
mercy[c]
as he flees headlong from its
power.[d]
23 It claps its hands in derision
and hisses him out of his place.[e]

27:18 [w]Job 8:14 [x]Isa 1:8
27:19 [y]Job 7:8
27:20 [z]Job 15:21 [a]Job 20:8
27:21 [b]Job 7:10; 21:18
27:22 [c]Jer 13:14; Eze 5:11; 24:14 [d]Job 11:20
27:23 [e]Job 18:18

28

"There is a mine for silver
and a place where gold is
refined.
2 Iron is taken from the earth,
and copper is smelted from ore.[f]
3 Man puts an end to the darkness;[g]
he searches the farthest recesses
for ore in the blackest darkness.
4 Far from where people dwell he cuts
a shaft,
in places forgotten by the foot of
man;
far from men he dangles and
sways.
5 The earth, from which food comes,[h]
is transformed below as by fire;
6 sapphires[a] come from its rocks,
and its dust contains nuggets of
gold.
7 No bird of prey knows that hidden
path,
no falcon's eye has seen it.
8 Proud beasts do not set foot on it,
and no lion prowls there.
9 Man's hand assaults the flinty rock
and lays bare the roots of the
mountains.
10 He tunnels through the rock;
his eyes see all its treasures.
11 He searches[b] the sources of the rivers
and brings hidden things to light.
12 "But where can wisdom be found?[i]
Where does understanding dwell?
13 Man does not comprehend its
worth;[j]
it cannot be found in the land of
the living.

28:2 [f]Dt 8:9
28:3 [g]Ecc 1:13
28:5 [h]Ps 104:14
28:12 [i]Ecc 7:24
28:13 [j]Pr 3:15; Mt 13:44-46

14 The deep says, 'It is not in me';
the sea says, 'It is not with me.'
15 It cannot be bought with the finest
gold,
nor can its price be weighed in
silver.[k]
16 It cannot be bought with the gold of
Ophir,
with precious onyx or sapphires.
17 Neither gold nor crystal can compare
with it,
nor can it be had for jewels of
gold.[l]
18 Coral and jasper are not worthy of
mention;
the price of wisdom is beyond
rubies.[m]
19 The topaz of Cush cannot compare
with it;
it cannot be bought with pure
gold.[n]
20 "Where then does wisdom come
from?
Where does understanding dwell?[o]
21 It is hidden from the eyes of every
living thing,
concealed even from the birds of
the air.
22 Destruction[c][p] and Death say,
'Only a rumor of it has reached
our ears.'
23 God understands the way to it
and he alone knows where it
dwells,[q]
24 for he views the ends of the earth[r]
and sees everything under the
heavens.[s]
25 When he established the force of the
wind
and measured out the waters,[t]
26 when he made a decree for the rain
and a path for the thunderstorm,[u]
27 then he looked at wisdom and
appraised it;
he confirmed it and tested it.
28 And he said to man,
'The fear of the Lord—that is
wisdom,
and to shun evil is
understanding.[v]' "

29

Job continued his discourse:[w]
2 "How I long for the months gone
by,

[a]6 Or *lapis lazuli*; also in verse 16 [b]11 Septuagint, Aquila and Vulgate; Hebrew *He dams up* [c]22 Hebrew *Abaddon*

28:15 [k]Pr 3:13-14; 8:10-11; 16:16
28:17 [l]Pr 16:16
28:18 [m]Pr 3:15
28:19 [n]Pr 8:19
28:20 [o]ver 23,28
28:22 [p]Job 26:6
28:23 [q]Pr 8:22-31
28:24 [r]Ps 33:13-14 [s]Pr 15:3
28:25 [t]Job 12:15; Ps 135:7
28:26 [u]Job 37:3,8,11; 38:25,27
28:28 [v]Dt 4:6; Ps 111:10; Pr 1:7; 9:10
29:1 [w]Job 13:12; 27:1

for the days when God watched over me,[x]
[3]when his lamp shone upon my head
and by his light I walked through darkness![y]
[4]Oh, for the days when I was in my prime,
when God's intimate friendship blessed my house,[z]
[5]when the Almighty was still with me
and my children were around me,
[6]when my path was drenched with cream[a]
and the rock[b] poured out for me streams of olive oil.[c]

[7]"When I went to the gate[d] of the city
and took my seat in the public square,
[8]the young men saw me and stepped aside
and the old men rose to their feet;
[9]the chief men refrained from speaking
and covered their mouths with their hands;[e]
[10]the voices of the nobles were hushed,
and their tongues stuck to the roof of their mouths.[f]
[11]Whoever heard me spoke well of me,
and those who saw me commended me,
[12]because I rescued the poor[g] who cried for help,
and the fatherless[h] who had none to assist him.[i]
[13]The man who was dying blessed me;[j]
I made the widow's[k] heart sing.
[14]I put on righteousness[l] as my clothing;
justice was my robe and my turban.
[15]I was eyes[m] to the blind
and feet to the lame.
[16]I was a father to the needy;[n]
I took up the case of the stranger.
[17]I broke the fangs of the wicked
and snatched the victims from their teeth.[o]

[18]"I thought, 'I will die in my own house,
my days as numerous as the grains of sand.[p]
[19]My roots will reach to the water,[q]
and the dew will lie all night on my branches.
[20]My glory will remain fresh in me,
the bow[r] ever new in my hand.'[s]

[21]"Men listened to me expectantly,
waiting in silence for my counsel.
[22]After I had spoken, they spoke no more;
my words fell gently on their ears.[t]
[23]They waited for me as for showers
and drank in my words as the spring rain.
[24]When I smiled at them, they scarcely believed it;
the light of my face was precious to them.[a]
[25]I chose the way for them and sat as their chief;
I dwelt as a king[u] among his troops;
I was like one who comforts mourners.[v]

30

"But now they mock me,[w]
men younger than I,
whose fathers I would have disdained
to put with my sheep dogs.
[2]Of what use was the strength of their hands to me,
since their vigor had gone from them?
[3]Haggard from want and hunger,
they roamed[b] the parched land
in desolate wastelands at night.
[4]In the brush they gathered salt herbs,
and their food[c] was the root of the broom tree.
[5]They were banished from their fellow men,
shouted at as if they were thieves.
[6]They were forced to live in the dry stream beds,
among the rocks and in holes in the ground.
[7]They brayed among the bushes
and huddled in the undergrowth.
[8]A base and nameless brood,
they were driven out of the land.

[9]"And now their sons mock me[x] in song;[y]
I have become a byword[z] among them.
[10]They detest me and keep their distance;
they do not hesitate to spit in my face.[a]

[a]*24* The meaning of the Hebrew for this clause is uncertain. [b]*3* Or *gnawed* [c]*4* Or *fuel*

29:2 [x]Jer 31:28
29:3 [y]Job 11:17
29:4 [z]Ps 25:14; Pr 3:32
29:6 [a]Job 20:17 [b]Ps 81:16 [c]Dt 32:13
29:7 [d]Job 31:21
29:9 [e]Job 21:5
29:10 [f]Ps 137:6
29:12 [g]Job 24:4 [h]Job 31:17,21 [i]Ps 72:12; Pr 21:13
29:13 [j]Job 31:20 [k]Job 22:9
29:14 [l]Job 27:6; Ps 132:9; Isa 59:17; 61:10; Eph 6:14
29:15 [m]Nu 10:31
29:16 [n]Job 24:4; Pr 29:7
29:17 [o]Ps 3:7
29:18 [p]Ps 30:6
29:19 [q]Job 18:16; Jer 17:8
29:20 [r]Ps 18:34 [s]Ge 49:24
29:22 [t]Dt 32:2
29:25 [u]Job 1:3; 31:37 [v]Job 4:4
30:1 [w]Job 12:4
30:9 [x]Ps 69:11 [y]Job 12:4; La 3:14,63 [z]Job 17:6
30:10 [a]Nu 12:14; Dt 25:9; Isa 50:6; Mt 26:67

11 Now that God has unstrung my bow
and afflicted me,[b]
they throw off restraint[c] in my
presence.
12 On my right the tribe[a] attacks;
they lay snares for my feet,[d]
they build their siege ramps
against me.[e]
13 They break up my road;[f]
they succeed in destroying me—
without anyone's helping them.[b]
14 They advance as through a gaping
breach;
amid the ruins they come rolling
in.
15 Terrors overwhelm me;[g]
my dignity is driven away as by
the wind,
my safety vanishes like a cloud.[h]
16 "And now my life ebbs away;[i]
days of suffering grip me.
17 Night pierces my bones;
my gnawing pains never rest.
18 In his great power ⌊God⌋ becomes like
clothing to me[c];
he binds me like the neck of my
garment.
19 He throws me into the mud,[j]
and I am reduced to dust and
ashes.

20 "I cry out to you, O God, but you
do not answer;[k]
I stand up, but you merely look
at me.
21 You turn on me ruthlessly;[l]
with the might of your hand[m] you
attack me.[n]
22 You snatch me up and drive me
before the wind;[o]
you toss me about in the storm.[p]
23 I know you will bring me down to
death,[q]
to the place appointed for all the
living.[r]

24 "Surely no one lays a hand on a
broken man
when he cries for help in his
distress.[s]
25 Have I not wept for those in trouble?
Has not my soul grieved for the
poor?[t]
26 Yet when I hoped for good, evil
came;
when I looked for light, then
came darkness.[u]
27 The churning inside me never stops;[v]
days of suffering confront me.
28 I go about blackened,[w] but not by
the sun;
I stand up in the assembly and cry
for help.[x]
29 I have become a brother of jackals,[y]
a companion of owls.[z]
30 My skin grows black and peels;[a]
my body burns with fever.[b]
31 My harp is tuned to mourning,[c]
and my flute to the sound of
wailing.

31 "I made a covenant with my
eyes
not to look lustfully at a girl.[d]
2 For what is man's lot from God
above,
his heritage from the Almighty on
high?[e]
3 Is it not ruin[f] for the wicked,
disaster for those who do wrong?[g]
4 Does he not see my ways[h]
and count my every step?[i]

5 "If I have walked in falsehood
or my foot has hurried after
deceit[j]—
6 let God weigh me in honest scales[k]
and he will know that I am
blameless—
7 if my steps have turned from the
path,[l]
if my heart has been led by my
eyes,
or if my hands[m] have been
defiled,
8 then may others eat what I have
sown,[n]
and may my crops be uprooted.[o]

9 "If my heart has been enticed[p] by a
woman,
or if I have lurked at my
neighbor's door,
10 then may my wife grind another
man's grain,
and may other men sleep with
her.[q]
11 For that would have been shameful,
a sin to be judged.[r]
12 It is a fire[s] that burns to
Destruction[d];[t]
it would have uprooted my
harvest.[u]

[a] *12* The meaning of the Hebrew for this word is uncertain. [b] *13* Or *me. / 'No one can help him,' ⌊they say⌋.* [c] *18* Hebrew; Septuagint ⌊*God*⌋ *grasps my clothing* [d] *12* Hebrew *Abaddon*

30:11 [b]Ru 1:21 [c]Ps 32:9
30:12 [d]Ps 140:4-5 [e]Job 19:12
30:13 [f]Isa 3:12
30:15 [g]Job 31:23; Ps 55:4-5 [h]Job 3:25; Hos 13:3
30:16 [i]Job 3:24; Ps 22:14; 42:4
30:19 [j]Ps 69:2,14
30:20 [k]Job 19:7
30:21 [l]Job 19:6,22 [m]Job 16:9,14 [n]Job 10:3
30:22 [o]Job 27:21 [p]Job 9:17
30:23 [q]Job 9:22; 10:8 [r]Job 3:19
30:24 [s]Job 19:7
30:25 [t]Job 24:4; Ps 35:13-14; Ro 12:15
30:26 [u]Job 3:25-26; 19:8; Jer 8:15
30:27 [v]La 2:11
30:28 [w]Ps 38:6; 42:9; 43:2 [x]Job 19:7
30:29 [y]Ps 44:19 [z]Ps 102:6; Mic 1:8
30:30 [a]La 4:8 [b]Ps 102:3
30:31 [c]Isa 24:8
31:1 [d]Mt 5:28
31:2 [e]Job 20:29
31:3 [f]Job 21:30 [g]Job 34:22
31:4 [h]2Ch 16:9 [i]Pr 5:21
31:5 [j]Mic 2:11
31:6 [k]Job 6:2; 27:5-6
31:7 [l]Job 23:11 [m]Job 9:30
31:8 [n]Lev 26:16; Job 20:18 [o]Mic 6:15
31:9 [p]Job 24:15
31:10 [q]Dt 28:30; Jer 8:10
31:11 [r]Ge 38:24; Lev 20:10; Dt 22:22-24
31:12 [s]Job 15:30 [t]Job 26:6 [u]Job 20:28

13 “If I have denied justice to my
menservants and
maidservants
when they had a grievance against
me,[v]
31:13 [v]Dt 24:14-15
14 what will I do when God confronts
me?
What will I answer when called to
account?
15 Did not he who made me in the
womb make them?
Did not the same one form us
both within our mothers?[w]
31:15 [w]Job 10:3

16 “If I have denied the desires of the
poor[x]
or let the eyes of the widow[y] grow
weary,
31:16 [x]Job 5:16; 20:19 [y]Job 22:9
17 if I have kept my bread to myself,
not sharing it with the
fatherless[z]—
31:17 [z]Job 22:7; 29:12
18 but from my youth I reared him as
would a father,
and from my birth I guided the
widow—
19 if I have seen anyone perishing for
lack of clothing,[a]
or a needy[b] man without a
garment,
31:19 [a]Job 22:6 [b]Job 24:4
20 and his heart did not bless me
for warming him with the fleece
from my sheep,
21 if I have raised my hand against the
fatherless,[c]
knowing that I had influence in
court,
31:21 [c]Job 22:9
22 then let my arm fall from the
shoulder,
let it be broken off at the joint.[d]
31:22 [d]Job 38:15
23 For I dreaded destruction from God,
and for fear of his splendor[e] I
could not do such things.
31:23 [e]Job 13:11

24 “If I have put my trust in gold[f]
or said to pure gold, ‘You are my
security,’[g]
31:24 [f]Job 22:25 [g]Mt 6:24; Mk 10:24
25 if I have rejoiced over my great
wealth,[h]
the fortune my hands had gained,
31:25 [h]Ps 62:10
26 if I have regarded the sun[i] in its
radiance
or the moon moving in splendor,
31:26 [i]Eze 8:16
27 so that my heart was secretly enticed
and my hand offered them a kiss
of homage,
28 then these also would be sins to be
judged,[j]
for I would have been unfaithful
to God on high.
31:28 [j]Dt 17:2-7

29 “If I have rejoiced at my enemy’s
misfortune[k]
or gloated over the trouble that
came to him[l]—
31:29 [k]Ob 1:12 [l]Pr 17:5; 24:17-18
30 I have not allowed my mouth to sin
by invoking a curse against his
life—
31 if the men of my household have
never said,
‘Who has not had his fill of Job’s
meat?’[m]—
31:31 [m]Job 22:7
32 but no stranger had to spend the
night in the street,
for my door was always open to
the traveler[n]—
31:32 [n]Ge 19:2-3; Ro 12:13
33 if I have concealed[o] my sin as men
do,[a]
by hiding[p] my guilt in my heart
31:33 [o]Pr 28:13 [p]Ge 3:8
34 because I so feared the crowd[q]
and so dreaded the contempt of
the clans
that I kept silent and would not
go outside
31:34 [q]Ex 23:2
35 (“Oh, that I had someone to hear
me!
I sign now my defense—let the
Almighty answer me;[r]
let my accuser[s] put his indictment
in writing.
31:35 [r]Job 19:7; 30:28 [s]Job 27:7; 35:14
36 Surely I would wear it on my
shoulder,
I would put it on like a crown.
37 I would give him an account of my
every step;
like a prince[t] I would approach
him.)—
31:37 [t]Job 1:3; 29:25
38 “if my land cries out against me[u]
and all its furrows are wet with
tears,
31:38 [u]Ge 4:10
39 if I have devoured its yield without
payment[v]
or broken the spirit of its tenants,[w]
31:39 [v]1Ki 21:19 [w]Lev 19:13; Jas 5:4
40 then let briers[x] come up instead of
wheat
and weeds instead of barley.”
31:40 [x]Ge 3:18

The words of Job are ended.

Elihu

32 So these three men stopped answering Job, because he was
righteous in his own eyes.[y] 2 But Elihu
son of Barakel the Buzite,[z] of the family of Ram, became very angry with
Job for justifying himself rather than
God.[a] 3 He was also angry with the three

32:1 [y]Job 10:7; 33:9
32:2 [z]Ge 22:21 [a]Job 27:5; 30:21

[a]33 Or *as Adam did*

friends, because they had found no way
to refute Job, and yet had condemned
him.[a] 4Now Elihu had waited before
speaking to Job because they were older than he. 5But when he saw that the
three men had nothing more to say, his
anger was aroused.

6So Elihu son of Barakel the Buzite
said:

"I am young in years,
and you are old;[b]
that is why I was fearful,
not daring to tell you what I
know.
7I thought, 'Age should speak;
advanced years should teach
wisdom.'
8But it is the spirit[b] in a man,
the breath of the Almighty,[c] that
gives him understanding.[d]
9It is not only the old[c] who are wise,[e]
not only the aged who understand
what is right.

10"Therefore I say: Listen to me;
I too will tell you what I know.
11I waited while you spoke,
I listened to your reasoning;
while you were searching for words,
12 I gave you my full attention.
But not one of you has proved Job
wrong;
none of you has answered his
arguments.
13Do not say, 'We have found
wisdom;[f]
let God refute him, not man.'
14But Job has not marshaled his words
against me,
and I will not answer him with
your arguments.

15"They are dismayed and have no
more to say;
words have failed them.
16Must I wait, now that they are silent,
now that they stand there with no
reply?
17I too will have my say;
I too will tell what I know.
18For I am full of words,
and the spirit within me compels
me;
19inside I am like bottled-up wine,
like new wineskins ready to burst.
20I must speak and find relief;
I must open my lips and reply.
21I will show partiality[g] to no one,[h]
nor will I flatter any man;
22for if I were skilled in flattery,
my Maker would soon take me
away.

33

"But now, Job, listen to my
words;
pay attention to everything I say.[i]
2I am about to open my mouth;
my words are on the tip of my
tongue.
3My words come from an upright
heart;
my lips sincerely speak what I
know.[j]
4The Spirit of God has made me;[k]
the breath of the Almighty[l] gives
me life.
5Answer me[m] then, if you can;
prepare[n] yourself and confront
me.
6I am just like you before God;
I too have been taken from clay.[o]
7No fear of me should alarm you,
nor should my hand be heavy
upon you.[p]

8"But you have said in my hearing—
I heard the very words—
9'I am pure[q] and without sin;[r]
I am clean and free from guilt.
10Yet God has found fault with me;
he considers me his enemy.[s]
11He fastens my feet in shackles;[t]
he keeps close watch on all my
paths.'[u]

12"But I tell you, in this you are not
right,
for God is greater than man.[v]
13Why do you complain to him[w]
that he answers none of man's
words[d]?
14For God does speak[x]—now one way,
now another—
though man may not perceive it.
15In a dream,[y] in a vision of the
night,
when deep sleep falls on men
as they slumber in their beds,
16he may speak[z] in their ears
and terrify them with warnings,
17to turn man from wrongdoing
and keep him from pride,

[a]3 Masoretic Text; an ancient Hebrew scribal tradition *Job, and so had condemned God* [b]8 Or *Spirit*; also in verse 18 [c]9 Or *many*; or *great* [d]13 Or *that he does not answer for any of his actions*

32:6 [b]Job 15:10
32:8 [c]Job 27:3; 33:4 [d]Pr 2:6
32:9 [e]1Co 1:26
32:13 [f]Jer 9:23
32:21 [g]Lev 19:15; Job 13:10 [h]Mt 22:16
33:1 [i]Job 13:6
33:3 [j]Job 6:28; 27:4; 36:4
33:4 [k]Ge 2:7; Job 10:3 [l]Job 27:3
33:5 [m]ver 32 [n]Job 13:18
33:6 [o]Job 4:19
33:7 [p]Job 9:34; 13:21; 2Co 2:4
33:9 [q]Job 10:7 [r]Job 13:23; 16:17
33:10 [s]Job 13:24
33:11 [t]Job 13:27 [u]Job 14:16
33:12 [v]Ecc 7:20
33:13 [w]Job 40:2; Isa 45:9
33:14 [x]Ps 62:11
33:15 [y]Job 4:13
33:16 [z]Job 36:10,15

33:18 [a]ver 22,24, 28,30 [b]Job 15:22
[18]to preserve his soul from the pit,[a][a]
his life from perishing by the sword.[b][b]
[19]Or a man may be chastened on a bed of pain
33:19 [c]Job 30:17
with constant distress in his bones,[c]
33:20 [d]Ps 107:18 [e]Job 3:24; 6:6
[20]so that his very being finds food[d] repulsive
and his soul loathes the choicest meal.[e]
33:21 [f]Job 16:8; 19:20
[21]His flesh wastes away to nothing,
and his bones, once hidden, now stick out.[f]
33:22 [g]Ps 88:3
[22]His soul draws near to the pit,[c]
and his life to the messengers of death.[d][g]
[23]"Yet if there is an angel on his side
as a mediator, one out of a thousand,
33:23 [h]Mic 6:8
to tell a man what is right for him,[h]
[24]to be gracious to him and say,
'Spare him from going down to the pit[e];[i]
33:24 [i]Isa 38:17
I have found a ransom for him'—
[25]then his flesh is renewed like a child's;
it is restored as in the days of his youth.[j]
33:25 [j]2Ki 5:14
33:26 [k]Job 34:28 [l]Job 22:26 [m]Ps 50:15; 51:12
[26]He prays to God and finds favor with him,[k]
he sees God's face and shouts for joy;[l]
he is restored by God to his righteous state.[m]
33:27 [n]2Sa 12:13 [o]Lk 15:21 [p]Ro 6:21
[27]Then he comes to men and says,
'I sinned,[n] and perverted what was right,[o]
but I did not get what I deserved.[p]
[28]He redeemed my soul from going down to the pit,[f]
33:28 [q]Job 22:28
and I will live to enjoy the light.'[q]
33:29 [r]1Co 12:6; Eph 1:11; Php 2:13
[29]"God does all these things to a man[r]—
twice, even three times—
33:30 [s]Ps 56:13
[30]to turn back his soul from the pit,[g]
that the light of life[s] may shine on him.

[31]"Pay attention, Job, and listen to me;
be silent, and I will speak.
[32]If you have anything to say, answer me;
speak up, for I want you to be cleared.
[33]But if not, then listen to me;
be silent, and I will teach you wisdom."[t]
33:33 [t]Ps 34:11

34

Then Elihu said:

[2]"Hear my words, you wise men;
listen to me, you men of learning.
[3]For the ear tests words
as the tongue tastes food.[u]
34:3 [u]Job 12:11
[4]Let us discern for ourselves what is right;
let us learn together what is good.[v]
34:4 [v]1Th 5:21
[5]"Job says, 'I am innocent,[w]
34:5 [w]Job 33:9 [x]Job 27:2
but God denies me justice.[x]
[6]Although I am right,
I am considered a liar;
although I am guiltless,
his arrow inflicts an incurable wound.'[y]
34:6 [y]Job 6:4
[7]What man is like Job,
34:7 [z]Job 15:16
who drinks scorn like water?[z]
[8]He keeps company with evildoers;
34:8 [a]Job 22:15; Ps 50:18
he associates with wicked men.[a]
[9]For he says, 'It profits a man nothing
34:9 [b]Job 21:15; 35:3
when he tries to please God.'[b]
[10]"So listen to me, you men of understanding.
34:10 [c]Ge 18:25 [d]Dt 32:4; Job 8:3; Ro 9:14
Far be it from God to do evil,[c]
from the Almighty to do wrong.[d]
[11]He repays a man for what he has done;[e]
34:11 [e]Ps 62:12; Mt 16:27; Ro 2:6; 2Co 5:10 [f]Jer 32:19; Eze 33:20
he brings upon him what his conduct deserves.[f]
[12]It is unthinkable that God would do wrong,
that the Almighty would pervert justice.[g]
34:12 [g]Job 8:3
[13]Who appointed him over the earth?
Who put him in charge of the whole world?[h]
34:13 [h]Job 38:4,6
[14]If it were his intention
and he withdrew his spirit[h] and breath,[i]
34:14 [i]Ps 104:29
[15]all mankind would perish together
and man would return to the dust.[j]
34:15 [j]Ge 3:19; Job 9:22

[16]"If you have understanding, hear this;
listen to what I say.
[17]Can he who hates justice govern?[k]
34:17 [k]2Sa 23:3-4 [l]Job 40:8
Will you condemn the just and mighty One?[l]

[a]18 Or *preserve him from the grave* [b]18 Or *from crossing the River* [c]22 Or *He draws near to the grave* [d]22 Or *to the dead* [e]24 Or *grave* [f]28 Or *redeemed me from going down to the grave* [g]30 Or *turn him back from the grave* [h]14 Or *Spirit*

18 Is he not the One who says to kings,
'You are worthless,'
and to nobles, 'You are wicked,'[m]
19 who shows no partiality[n] to princes
and does not favor the rich over
the poor,[o]
for they are all the work of his
hands?[p]
20 They die in an instant, in the middle
of the night;[q]
the people are shaken and they
pass away;
the mighty are removed without
human hand.[r]

21 "His eyes are on the ways of men;
he sees their every step.[s]
22 There is no dark place,[t] no deep
shadow,[u]
where evildoers can hide.
23 God has no need to examine men
further,
that they should come before him
for judgment.[v]
24 Without inquiry he shatters the
mighty[w]
and sets up others in their place.[x]
25 Because he takes note of their deeds,
he overthrows them in the night
and they are crushed.
26 He punishes them for their
wickedness
where everyone can see them,
27 because they turned from following
him[y]
and had no regard for any of his
ways.[z]
28 They caused the cry of the poor to
come before him,
so that he heard the cry of the
needy.[a]
29 But if he remains silent, who can
condemn him?
If he hides his face, who can see
him?
Yet he is over man and nation alike,
30 to keep a godless man from
ruling,
from laying snares for the people.[b]

31 "Suppose a man says to God,
'I am guilty but will offend no
more.
32 Teach me what I cannot see;[c]
if I have done wrong, I will not do
so again.'[d]
33 Should God then reward you on
your terms,
when you refuse to repent?[e]
You must decide, not I;
so tell me what you know.

34 "Men of understanding declare,
wise men who hear me say to me,
35 'Job speaks without knowledge;[f]
his words lack insight.'
36 Oh, that Job might be tested to the
utmost
for answering like a wicked man![g]
37 To his sin he adds rebellion;
scornfully he claps his hands[h]
among us
and multiplies his words against
God."[i]

35

Then Elihu said:

2 "Do you think this is just?
You say, 'I will be cleared by
God.[a]'
3 Yet you ask him, 'What profit is it
to me,[b]
and what do I gain by not
sinning?'[j]

4 "I would like to reply to you
and to your friends with you.
5 Look up at the heavens[k] and see;
gaze at the clouds so high above
you.[l]
6 If you sin, how does that affect
him?[m]
If your sins are many, what does
that do to him?
7 If you are righteous, what do you
give to him,[n]
or what does he receive[o] from
your hand?[p]
8 Your wickedness affects only a man
like yourself,
and your righteousness only the
sons of men.

9 "Men cry out[q] under a load of
oppression;
they plead for relief from the arm
of the powerful.[r]
10 But no one says, 'Where is God my
Maker,[s]
who gives songs in the night,[t]
11 who teaches[u] more to us than to[c] the
beasts of the earth
and makes us wiser than[d] the birds
of the air?'
12 He does not answer[v] when men cry
out

[a]2 Or *My righteousness is more than God's* [b]3 Or *you* [c]11 Or *teaches us by* [d]11 Or *us wise by*

34:18 [m]Ex 22:28
34:19 [n]Dt 10:17; Ac 10:34 [o]Lev 19:15 [p]Job 10:3
34:20 [q]Ex 12:29 [r]Job 12:19
34:21 [s]Job 31:4; Pr 15:3
34:22 [t]Ps 139:12 [u]Am 9:2-3
34:23 [v]Job 11:11
34:24 [w]Job 12:19 [x]Da 2:21
34:27 [y]Ps 28:5; Isa 5:12 [z]1Sa 15:11
34:28 [a]Ex 22:23; Job 35:9; Jas 5:4
34:30 [b]Pr 29:2-12
34:32 [c]Job 35:11; Ps 25:4 [d]Job 33:27
34:33 [e]Job 41:11
34:35 [f]Job 35:16; 38:2
34:36 [g]Job 22:15
34:37 [h]Job 27:23 [i]Job 23:2
35:3 [j]Job 9:29-31; 34:9
35:5 [k]Ge 15:5 [l]Job 22:12
35:6 [m]Pr 8:36
35:7 [n]Ro 11:35 [o]Pr 9:12 [p]Job 22:2-3; Lk 17:10
35:9 [q]Ex 2:23 [r]Job 12:19
35:10 [s]Job 27:10; Isa 51:13 [t]Ps 42:8; 149:5; Ac 16:25
35:11 [u]Ps 94:12
35:12 [v]Pr 1:28

because of the arrogance of the wicked.
[13]Indeed, God does not listen to their empty plea;
the Almighty pays no attention to it.[w]
[14]How much less, then, will he listen
when you say that you do not see him,[x]
that your case[y] is before him
and you must wait for him,
[15]and further, that his anger never punishes
and he does not take the least notice of wickedness.[a]
[16]So Job opens his mouth with empty talk;
without knowledge he multiplies words."[z]

35:13 [w]Job 27:9; Pr 15:29; Isa 1:15; Jer 11:11
35:14 [x]Job 9:11 [y]Ps 37:6
35:16 [z]Job 34:35,37

36

Elihu continued:

[2]"Bear with me a little longer and I will show you
that there is more to be said in God's behalf.
[3]I get my knowledge from afar;
I will ascribe justice to my Maker.[a]
[4]Be assured that my words are not false;[b]
one perfect in knowledge[c] is with you.
[5]"God is mighty, but does not despise men;[d]
he is mighty, and firm in his purpose.[e]
[6]He does not keep the wicked alive[f]
but gives the afflicted their rights.[g]
[7]He does not take his eyes off the righteous;[h]
he enthrones them with kings[i]
and exalts them forever.
[8]But if men are bound in chains,[j]
held fast by cords of affliction,
[9]he tells them what they have done—
that they have sinned arrogantly.[k]
[10]He makes them listen[l] to correction
and commands them to repent of their evil.[m]
[11]If they obey and serve him,[n]
they will spend the rest of their days in prosperity
and their years in contentment.
[12]But if they do not listen,
they will perish by the sword[b] [o]
and die without knowledge.[p]

36:3 [a]Job 8:3; 37:23
36:4 [b]Job 33:3 [c]Job 37:5, 16,23
36:5 [d]Ps 22:24 [e]Job 12:13
36:6 [f]Job 8:22 [g]Job 5:15
36:7 [h]Ps 33:18 [i]Ps 113:8
36:8 [j]Ps 107:10,14
36:9 [k]Job 15:25
36:10 [l]Job 33:16 [m]2Ki 17:13
36:11 [n]Isa 1:19
36:12 [o]Job 15:22 [p]Job 4:21

[13]"The godless in heart[q] harbor resentment;
even when he fetters them, they do not cry for help.
[14]They die in their youth,
among male prostitutes of the shrines.[r]
[15]But those who suffer he delivers in their suffering;
he speaks to them in their affliction.
[16]"He is wooing[s] you from the jaws of distress
to a spacious place free from restriction,
to the comfort of your table[t]
laden with choice food.
[17]But now you are laden with the judgment due the wicked;
judgment and justice have taken hold of you.[u]
[18]Be careful that no one entices you by riches;
do not let a large bribe turn you aside.[v]
[19]Would your wealth
or even all your mighty efforts
sustain you so you would not be in distress?
[20]Do not long for the night,[w]
to drag people away from their homes.[c]
[21]Beware of turning to evil,[x]
which you seem to prefer to affliction.[y]
[22]"God is exalted in his power.
Who is a teacher like him?[z]
[23]Who has prescribed his ways for him,[a]
or said to him, 'You have done wrong'?[b]
[24]Remember to extol his work,[c]
which men have praised in song.[d]
[25]All mankind has seen it;
men gaze on it from afar.
[26]How great is God—beyond our understanding![e]
The number of his years is past finding out.[f]
[27]"He draws up the drops of water,
which distill as rain to the streams[d];[g]

[a]*15* Symmachus, Theodotion and Vulgate; the meaning of the Hebrew for this word is uncertain. [b]*12* Or *will cross the River* [c]*20* The meaning of the Hebrew for verses 18-20 is uncertain. [d]*27* Or *distill from the mist as rain*

36:13 [q]Ro 2:5
36:14 [r]Dt 23:17
36:16 [s]Hos 2:14 [t]Ps 23:5
36:17 [u]Job 22:11
36:18 [v]Job 34:33
36:20 [w]Job 34:20,25
36:21 [x]Ps 66:18 [y]Heb 11:25
36:22 [z]Isa 40:13; 1Co 2:16
36:23 [a]Job 34:13 [b]Job 8:3
36:24 [c]Ps 92:5; 138:5 [d]Ps 59:16; Rev 15:3
36:26 [e]1Co 13: 12 [f]Job 10:5; Ps 90:2; 102:24; Heb 1:12
36:27 [g]Job 38:28; Ps 147:8

28 the clouds pour down their moisture
and abundant showers fall on
mankind.[h]
29 Who can understand how he spreads
out the clouds,
how he thunders from his
pavilion?[i]
30 See how he scatters his lightning
about him,
bathing the depths of the sea.
31 This is the way he governs[a] the
nations[j]
and provides food in abundance.[k]
32 He fills his hands with lightning
and commands it to strike its
mark.[l]
33 His thunder announces the coming
storm;
even the cattle make known its
approach.[b]

36:28 [h]Job 5:10
36:29 [i]Job 26:14; 37:16
36:31 [j]Job 37:13 [k]Ps 136:25; Ac 14:17
36:32 [l]Job 37:12,15

37

"At this my heart pounds
and leaps from its place.
2 Listen! Listen to the roar of his
voice,
to the rumbling that comes from
his mouth.[m]
3 He unleashes his lightning beneath
the whole heaven
and sends it to the ends of the
earth.
4 After that comes the sound of his
roar;
he thunders with his majestic
voice.
When his voice resounds,
he holds nothing back.
5 God's voice thunders in marvelous
ways;
he does great things beyond our
understanding.[n]
6 He says to the snow,[o] 'Fall on the
earth,'
and to the rain shower, 'Be a
mighty downpour.'[p]
7 So that all men he has made may
know his work,
he stops every man from his
labor.[c][q]
8 The animals take cover;
they remain in their dens.[r]
9 The tempest comes out from its
chamber,
the cold from the driving winds.
10 The breath of God produces ice,
and the broad waters become
frozen.[s]
11 He loads the clouds with moisture;
he scatters his lightning through
them.[t]
12 At his direction they swirl around
over the face of the whole earth
to do whatever he commands
them.[u]
13 He brings the clouds to punish men,[v]
or to water his earth[d] and show
his love.[w]

14 "Listen to this, Job;
stop and consider God's wonders.
15 Do you know how God controls the
clouds
and makes his lightning flash?
16 Do you know how the clouds hang
poised,
those wonders of him who is
perfect in knowledge?[x]
17 You who swelter in your clothes
when the land lies hushed under
the south wind,
18 can you join him in spreading out
the skies,[y]
hard as a mirror of cast bronze?

19 "Tell us what we should say to him;
we cannot draw up our case
because of our darkness.
20 Should he be told that I want to
speak?
Would any man ask to be
swallowed up?
21 Now no one can look at the sun,
bright as it is in the skies
after the wind has swept them
clean.
22 Out of the north he comes in golden
splendor;
God comes in awesome majesty.
23 The Almighty is beyond our reach
and exalted in power;[z]
in his justice[a] and great
righteousness, he does not
oppress.[b]
24 Therefore, men revere him,[c]
for does he not have regard for all
the wise[d] in heart?[e]"

37:2 [m]Ps 29:3-9
37:5 [n]Job 5:9
37:6 [o]Job 38:22 [p]Job 36:27
37:7 [q]Job 12:14
37:8 [r]Job 38:40; Ps 104:22
37:10 [s]Job 38:29-30; Ps 147:17
37:11 [t]Job 36:27,29
37:12 [u]Ps 148:8
37:13 [v]1Sa 12:17 [w]Ex 9:18; 1Ki 18:45; Job 38:27
37:16 [x]Job 36:4
37:18 [y]Job 9:8; Ps 104:2; Isa 44:24
37:23 [z]Job 9:4; 36:4; 1Ti 6:16 [a]Job 8:3 [b]Isa 63:9; Eze 18:23,32
37:24 [c]Mt 10:28 [d]Mt 11:25

The LORD Speaks

38

Then the LORD answered Job
out of the storm.[e] He said:

2 "Who is this that darkens my
counsel

38:1 [e]Job 40:6

[a] *31* Or *nourishes* [b] *33* Or *announces his coming— / the One zealous against evil* [c] *7* Or */ he fills all men with fear by his power* [d] *13* Or *to favor them* [e] *24* Or *for he does not have regard for any who think they are wise.*

DAY 2 TWO

▸ JOY AND THE PURPOSE OF GOD IN MY LIFE

Job 38:1–7

Come, rejoice, and offer God this prayer:

God,

When I contemplate creation, I know you are God. When I face your power, I remember where I am in the world. It is your creative power that puts me in my place. I must face the same questions you asked Job: Where was I when you laid the foundations of the world? Where was I when you stretched out the heavens like a canvas? Where was I when all the morning stars sang together?

I ask these questions before the immensity of your creation. I am hushed by its beauty. I am stopped by its size. Before your majesty, I remember that I am small, atom-like and of little consequence in the scheme of things universal. Yet you saw me, and even as you did with Job, you began a conversation with me. And as we talked, I saw you in the natural world, and I sang anthems to your great creativity.

Then when I had praised you for your creative works, I knew that whatever purpose you had for my life should be my reason to live. For you made me just as you made my world. And joy is my response of gratitude for your including me in your grand design.

God, I know your purposes in my life are most important. And when I see the works of your hands, I know that you want my hands to create also. I'm here to use my body—fearfully and wonderfully made—to create works to honor you. So give me the gift of facing the sin and heartache all around me and doing my part to create the kingdom of God. I want to touch hate and rename it love. I want to touch vengeance and rename it mercy. I want to touch resentment and rename it understanding. I want to touch defiance and rename it submission. Create in me a servant who worships you and cherishes the kingdom Jesus died to establish.

Amen.

To begin a study on the topic of The Joy of Creativity, turn to the home page on page 639.

with words without knowledge?[f]
3 Brace yourself like a man;
I will question you,
and you shall answer me.[g]
4 "Where were you when I laid the earth's foundation?[h]
Tell me, if you understand.

▸ KINDNESS

MERCY'S BADGE

Job 38:4

It is the kindness of God that reminds us of his power. For all his strength, he does not crush us in our weakness. "Sweet mercy is nobility's true badge," said Shakespeare. Who would not love a God whose power flies at us with mercy?

5 Who marked off its dimensions?[i]
Surely you know!
Who stretched a measuring line across it?
6 On what were its footings set,
or who laid its cornerstone[j]—
7 while the morning stars sang together
and all the angels[a] shouted for joy?
8 "Who shut up the sea behind doors[k]
when it burst forth from the womb,[l]
9 when I made the clouds its garment
and wrapped it in thick darkness,
10 when I fixed limits for it[m]
and set its doors and bars in place,[n]
11 when I said, 'This far you may come and no farther;
here is where your proud waves halt'?[o]
12 "Have you ever given orders to the morning,
or shown the dawn its place,
13 that it might take the earth by the edges
and shake the wicked[p] out of it?
14 The earth takes shape like clay under a seal;
its features stand out like those of a garment.
15 The wicked are denied their light,[q]
and their upraised arm is broken.[r]

[a]7 Hebrew *the sons of God*

38:2 [f]Job 35:16; 42:3; 1Ti 1:7
38:3 [g]Job 40:7
38:4 [h]Ps 104:5; Pr 8:29
38:5 [i]Pr 8:29; Isa 40:12
38:6 [j]Job 26:7
38:8 [k]Jer 5:22 [l]Ge 1:9-10
38:10 [m]Ps 33:7; 104:9 [n]Job 26:10
38:11 [o]Ps 89:9
38:13 [p]Ps 104:35
38:15 [q]Job 18:5 [r]Ps 10:15

16 "Have you journeyed to the springs of the sea
or walked in the recesses of the deep?[s]
17 Have the gates of death[t] been shown to you?
Have you seen the gates of the shadow of death[a]?
18 Have you comprehended the vast expanses of the earth?[u]
Tell me, if you know all this.

19 "What is the way to the abode of light?
And where does darkness reside?
20 Can you take them to their places?
Do you know the paths[v] to their dwellings?
21 Surely you know, for you were already born![w]
You have lived so many years!

22 "Have you entered the storehouses of the snow[x]
or seen the storehouses of the hail,
23 which I reserve for times of trouble,[y]
for days of war and battle?[z]
24 What is the way to the place where the lightning is dispersed,
or the place where the east winds are scattered over the earth?
25 Who cuts a channel for the torrents of rain,
and a path for the thunderstorm,[a]
26 to water[b] a land where no man lives,
a desert with no one in it,
27 to satisfy a desolate wasteland
and make it sprout with grass?[c]
28 Does the rain have a father?[d]
Who fathers the drops of dew?
29 From whose womb comes the ice?
Who gives birth to the frost from the heavens[e]
30 when the waters become hard as stone,
when the surface of the deep is frozen?[f]

31 "Can you bind the beautiful[b] Pleiades?
Can you loose the cords of Orion?[g]
32 Can you bring forth the constellations in their seasons[c]
or lead out the Bear[d] with its cubs?
33 Do you know the laws[h] of the heavens?

38:16 [s]Ps 77:19
38:17 [t]Ps 9:13
38:18 [u]Job 28:24
38:20 [v]Job 26:10
38:21 [w]Job 15:7
38:22 [x]Job 37:6
38:23 [y]Isa 30:30; Eze 13:11 [z]Ex 9:18; Jos 10:11; Rev 16:21
38:25 [a]Job 28:26
38:26 [b]Job 36:27
38:27 [c]Ps 104:14; 107:35
38:28 [d]Ps 147:8; Jer 14:22
38:29 [e]Ps 147:16-17
38:30 [f]Job 37:10
38:31 [g]Job 9:9; Am 5:8
38:33 [h]Ps 148:6; Jer 31:36

Can you set up ⌞God's[e]⌟ dominion over the earth?

34 "Can you raise your voice to the clouds
and cover yourself with a flood of water?[i]
35 Do you send the lightning bolts on their way?[j]
Do they report to you, 'Here we are'?
36 Who endowed the heart[f] with wisdom[k]
or gave understanding[l] to the mind[f]?
37 Who has the wisdom to count the clouds?
Who can tip over the water jars of the heavens
38 when the dust becomes hard
and the clods of earth stick together?

39 "Do you hunt the prey for the lioness
and satisfy the hunger of the lions[m]
40 when they crouch in their dens[n]
or lie in wait in a thicket?
41 Who provides food for the raven[o]
when its young cry out to God
and wander about for lack of food?[p]

39 "Do you know when the mountain goats[q] give birth?
Do you watch when the doe bears her fawn?
2 Do you count the months till they bear?
Do you know the time they give birth?
3 They crouch down and bring forth their young;
their labor pains are ended.
4 Their young thrive and grow strong in the wilds;
they leave and do not return.

5 "Who let the wild donkey[r] go free?
Who untied his ropes?
6 I gave him the wasteland[s] as his home,
the salt flats as his habitat.[t]

[a]*17* Or *gates of deep shadows* [b]*31* Or *the twinkling;* or *the chains of the* [c]*32* Or *the morning star in its season* [d]*32* Or *out Leo* [e]*33* Or *his;* or *their* [f]*36* The meaning of the Hebrew for this word is uncertain.

38:34 [i]Job 22:11; 36:27-28
38:35 [j]Job 36:32; 37:3
38:36 [k]Job 9:4 [l]Job 32:8; Ps 51:6; Ecc 2:26
38:39 [m]Ps 104:21
38:40 [n]Job 37:8
38:41 [o]Lk 12:24 [p]Ps 147:9; Mt 6:26
39:1 [q]Dt 14:5
39:5 [r]Job 6:5; 11:12; 24:5
39:6 [s]Job 24:5; Ps 107:34; Jer 2:24 [t]Hos 8:9

[7]He laughs at the commotion in the
town;
39:7 [u]Job 3:18
he does not hear a driver's shout.[u]
[8]He ranges the hills for his pasture
and searches for any green thing.
39:9 [v]Nu 23:22; Dt 33:17
[9]"Will the wild ox[v] consent to serve
you?
Will he stay by your manger at
night?
[10]Can you hold him to the furrow
with a harness?
Will he till the valleys behind you?
[11]Will you rely on him for his great
strength?
Will you leave your heavy work to
him?
[12]Can you trust him to bring in your
grain
and gather it to your threshing
floor?

[13]"The wings of the ostrich flap
joyfully,
but they cannot compare with the
pinions and feathers of the
stork.
[14]She lays her eggs on the ground
and lets them warm in the sand,
[15]unmindful that a foot may crush
them,
that some wild animal may
trample them.
39:16 [w]La 4:3
[16]She treats her young harshly,[w] as if
they were not hers;
she cares not that her labor was in
vain,
[17]for God did not endow her with
wisdom
or give her a share of good sense.[x]
39:17 [x]Job 35:11
[18]Yet when she spreads her feathers to
run,
she laughs at horse and rider.

[19]"Do you give the horse his strength
or clothe his neck with a flowing
mane?
39:20 [y]Joel 2:4-5 [z]Jer 8:16
[20]Do you make him leap like a locust,[y]
striking terror with his proud
snorting?[z]
[21]He paws fiercely, rejoicing in his
strength,
39:21 [a]Jer 8:6
and charges into the fray.[a]
[22]He laughs at fear, afraid of nothing;
he does not shy away from the
sword.
[23]The quiver rattles against his side,
along with the flashing spear and
lance.
[24]In frenzied excitement he eats up the
ground;
he cannot stand still when the
trumpet sounds.[b] 39:24 [b]Jer 4:5,19; Eze 7:14; Am 3:6
[25]At the blast of the trumpet[c] he
snorts, 'Aha!' 39:25 [c]Jos 6:5 [d]Am 1:14; 2:2
He catches the scent of battle
from afar,
the shout of commanders and the
battle cry.[d]

[26]"Does the hawk take flight by your
wisdom
and spread his wings toward the
south?
[27]Does the eagle soar at your
command
and build his nest on high?[e] 39:27 [e]Jer 49:16; Ob 1:4
[28]He dwells on a cliff and stays there
at night;
a rocky crag is his stronghold.
[29]From there he seeks out his food;[f] 39:29 [f]Job 9:26
his eyes detect it from afar.
[30]His young ones feast on blood, 39:30 [g]Mt 24:28; Lk 17:37
and where the slain are, there is
he."[g]

40

The LORD said to Job:[h] 40:1 [h]Job 10:2; 13:3; 23:4; 31:35; 33:13

[2]"Will the one who contends with the
Almighty correct him?
Let him who accuses God answer
him!"

[3]Then Job answered the LORD:

[4]"I am unworthy[i]—how can I reply 40:4 [i]Job 42:6 [j]Job 29:9
to you?
I put my hand over my mouth.[j]
[5]I spoke once, but I have no
answer[k]— 40:5 [k]Job 9:3 [l]Job 9:15
twice, but I will say no more."[l]

[6]Then the LORD spoke to Job out of
the storm:[m] 40:6 [m]Job 38:1

[7]"Brace yourself like a man;
I will question you,
and you shall answer me.[n] 40:7 [n]Job 38:3; 42:4

[8]"Would you discredit my justice?[o]
Would you condemn me to justify 40:8 [o]Job 27:2; Ro 3:3
yourself?
[9]Do you have an arm like God's,[p] 40:9 [p]2Ch 32:8 [q]Job 37:5; Ps 29:3-4
and can your voice thunder like
his?[q]
[10]Then adorn yourself with glory and 40:10 [r]Ps 93:1; 104:1
splendor,
and clothe yourself in honor and
majesty.[r] 40:11 [s]Isa 42:25; Na 1:6
[11]Unleash the fury of your wrath,[s]

look at every proud man and
bring him low,[t]
12 look at every proud man and
humble him,[u]
crush[v] the wicked where they
stand.
13 Bury them all in the dust together;
shroud their faces in the grave.
14 Then I myself will admit to you
that your own right hand can save
you.[w]
15 "Look at the behemoth,[a]
which I made along with you
and which feeds on grass like an
ox.
16 What strength he has in his loins,
what power in the muscles of his
belly!
17 His tail[b] sways like a cedar;
the sinews of his thighs are
close-knit.
18 His bones are tubes of bronze,
his limbs like rods of iron.
19 He ranks first among the works of
God,[x]
yet his Maker can approach him
with his sword.
20 The hills bring him their produce,[y]
and all the wild animals play[z]
nearby.
21 Under the lotus plants he lies,
hidden among the reeds in the
marsh.
22 The lotuses conceal him in their
shadow;
the poplars by the stream[a]
surround him.
23 When the river rages, he is not
alarmed;
he is secure, though the Jordan
should surge against his
mouth.
24 Can anyone capture him by the
eyes,[c]
or trap him and pierce his nose?[b]

41 "Can you pull in the leviathan[d][c]
with a fishhook
or tie down his tongue with a
rope?
2 Can you put a cord through his nose
or pierce his jaw with a hook?[d]
3 Will he keep begging you for mercy?
Will he speak to you with gentle
words?
4 Will he make an agreement with you
for you to take him as your slave
for life?[e]

40:11 [t]Isa 2:11,12,17; Da 4:37
40:12 [u]1Sa 2:7 [v]Isa 13:11; 63:2-3,6
40:14 [w]Ps 20:6; 60:5; 108:6
40:19 [x]Job 41:33
40:20 [y]Ps 104:14 [z]Ps 104:26
40:22 [a]Isa 44:4
40:24 [b]Job 41:2,7,26
41:1 [c]Job 3:8; Ps 104:26; Isa 27:1
41:2 [d]Isa 37:29
41:4 [e]Ex 21:6

GOODNESS

THE TERROR OF LEVIATHAN

Job 41:1

There is a dragon that devours our courage and stops our ministry with fear. Leviathan is his name. He is not a sportsman's trophy. He is the terror that would send us, paralyzed, to hell were it not for the goodness of God. But God rebukes the monster, touches our paralysis and gives us legs of faith on which to stand.

5 Can you make a pet of him like a
bird
or put him on a leash for your
girls?
6 Will traders barter for him?
Will they divide him up among
the merchants?
7 Can you fill his hide with harpoons
or his head with fishing spears?
8 If you lay a hand on him,
you will remember the struggle
and never do it again!
9 Any hope of subduing him is false;
the mere sight of him is
overpowering.
10 No one is fierce enough to rouse
him.[f]
Who then is able to stand against
me?[g]
11 Who has a claim against me that I
must pay?[h]
Everything under heaven belongs
to me.[i]
12 "I will not fail to speak of his limbs,
his strength and his graceful form.
13 Who can strip off his outer coat?
Who would approach him with a
bridle?
14 Who dares open the doors of his
mouth,
ringed about with his fearsome
teeth?
15 His back has[e] rows of shields
tightly sealed together;
16 each is so close to the next
that no air can pass between.
17 They are joined fast to one another;
they cling together and cannot be
parted.
18 His snorting throws out flashes of
light;

41:10 [f]Job 3:8 [g]Jer 50:44
41:11 [h]Ro 11:35 [i]Ex 19:5; Dt 10:14; Ps 24:1; 50:12; 1Co 10:26

[a] *15* Possibly the hippopotamus or the elephant
[b] *17* Possibly trunk [c] *24* Or *by a water hole*
[d] *1* Possibly the crocodile [e] *15* Or *His pride is his*

41:18 [j]Job 3:9

his eyes are like the rays of dawn.[j]
19 Firebrands stream from his mouth;
sparks of fire shoot out.
20 Smoke pours from his nostrils
as from a boiling pot over a fire of reeds.

41:21 [k]Isa 40:7 [l]Ps 18:8

21 His breath[k] sets coals ablaze,
and flames dart from his mouth.[l]
22 Strength resides in his neck;
dismay goes before him.
23 The folds of his flesh are tightly joined;
they are firm and immovable.
24 His chest is hard as rock,
hard as a lower millstone.
25 When he rises up, the mighty are terrified;
they retreat before his thrashing.
26 The sword that reaches him has no effect,
nor does the spear or the dart or the javelin.
27 Iron he treats like straw
and bronze like rotten wood.
28 Arrows do not make him flee;
slingstones are like chaff to him.
29 A club seems to him but a piece of straw;
he laughs at the rattling of the lance.

41:30 [m]Isa 41:15

30 His undersides are jagged potsherds,
leaving a trail in the mud like a threshing sledge.[m]
31 He makes the depths churn like a boiling caldron
and stirs up the sea like a pot of ointment.
32 Behind him he leaves a glistening wake;
one would think the deep had white hair.

41:33 [n]Job 40:19

33 Nothing on earth is his equal[n]—
a creature without fear.
34 He looks down on all that are haughty;
he is king over all that are proud."[o]

41:34 [o]Job 28:8

Job

42 Then Job replied to the LORD:

42:2 [p]Ge 18:14; Mt 19:26 [q]2Ch 20:6

2 "I know that you can do all things;[p]
no plan of yours can be thwarted.[q]
3 ⌊You asked,⌋ 'Who is this that obscures my counsel without knowledge?'[r]

42:3 [r]Job 38:2

Surely I spoke of things I did not understand,

LOVE

ALL THINGS

Job 42:2

In your brokenness rehearse this truth alone:
"I know, dear Jesus, you can do all things.
Enable me to love my enemies
And baby-sit the children of my would-be assassins.
Let me teach the raucous world a hymn of love."

things too wonderful for me to know.[s]

42:3 [s]Ps 40:5; 131:1; 139:6

4 "⌊You said,⌋ 'Listen now, and I will speak;
I will question you,
and you shall answer me.'[t]

42:4 [t]Job 38:3; 40:7

5 My ears had heard of you[u]
but now my eyes have seen you.[v]

42:5 [u]Job 26:14; Ro 10:17 [v]Jdg 13:22; Isa 6:5; Eph 1:17-18

6 Therefore I despise myself[w]
and repent in dust and ashes."[x]

42:6 [w]Job 40:4 [x]Ezr 9:6

Epilogue

7 After the LORD had said these things
to Job, he said to Eliphaz the Temanite, "I am angry with you and your
two friends,[y] because you have not spoken of me what is right, as my servant
Job has. 8 So now take seven bulls and
seven rams[z] and go to my servant Job
and sacrifice a burnt offering[a] for yourselves. My servant Job will pray for you,
and I will accept his prayer[b] and not
deal with you according to your folly.[c]
You have not spoken of me what is
right, as my servant Job has." 9 So Eliphaz the Temanite, Bildad the Shuhite
and Zophar the Naamathite did what
the LORD told them; and the LORD
accepted Job's prayer.

42:7 [y]Job 32:3

42:8 [z]Nu 23:1,29 [a]Job 1:5 [b]Ge 20:17; Jas 5:15-16; 1Jn 5:16 [c]Job 22:30

10 After Job had prayed for his friends,
the LORD made him prosperous again[d]
and gave him twice as much as he had
before.[e] 11 All his brothers and sisters
and everyone who had known him before[f] came and ate with him in his
house. They comforted and consoled
him over all the trouble the LORD had
brought upon him, and each one gave
him a piece of silver[a] and a gold ring.
12 The LORD blessed the latter part

42:10 [d]Dt 30:3; Ps 14:7 [e]Job 1:3; Ps 85:1-3; 126:5-6

42:11 [f]Job 19:13

[a] *11* Hebrew *him a kesitah*; a kesitah was a unit of money of unknown weight and value.

of Job's life more than the first. He had
fourteen thousand sheep, six thousand
camels, a thousand yoke of oxen and a
thousand donkeys. 13And he also had
seven sons and three daughters. 14The
first daughter he named Jemimah, the
second Keziah and the third Keren-
Happuch. 15Nowhere in all the land
were there found women as beautiful as
Job's daughters, and their father granted them an inheritance along with their
brothers.

16After this, Job lived a hundred and
forty years; he saw his children and their
children to the fourth generation. 17And
so he died, old and full of years.[g]

42:17 [g]Ge 15:15; 25:8

Psalms

Authorship and Date

The psalms were written by many different authors. The most famous composer of psalms was King David.

Some of the psalms date to the time of David in the tenth century B.C. Most of them were compiled across the centuries that comprise the history of Old Testament Israel.

Key Themes

The traditional Hebrew title is *tehillim*, meaning *praises*. Psalms is a collection of hymns, prayers and poems to be used in worship. The Psalter, as it came to exist in its final form, was divided into five Books (1–41, 42–72, 73–89, 90–106, and 107–150). Of the entire collection of 150 psalms, only 34 lack some kind of superscription. These superscriptions, which have differing functions, denote authorship, musical direction, dedication of the psalm, and so forth. The dominant themes deal with praise.

Fruit of the Spirit in Psalms

Joy: Joy is the mood of all great praise. The words *joy* and *praise* are so closely related that there can rarely be praise that is not joyous or joy that does not praise. Nonetheless, the Psalter finds variant moods of joy and various focuses for praise. It would be impossible in such a small space to denote the wide focuses of the Psalms, but a sampling of them fall into the following categories:

Psalm 1—The joy of being righteous

Psalm 3—The joy of being delivered from evil

Psalm 7—The joy of personal, spiritual or physical security

Psalm 15—The joy of going to the sanctuary of God and the privilege of worship

Psalm 19—The joy that comes as a response to nature

Psalm 23—The joy that responds to God's protection, care and providence

Psalm 37—The joy of contentment

Psalm 51—The joy of having our sins forgiven and the blessing of confession

Psalm 91—The joy of God's protection when our lives are in danger

Psalm 119—The joy of the Word of God and all that it does to stabilize, counsel and instruct us

Psalm 139—The joy of serving the everywhere-present God

Praise (Psalm 150) and thanksgiving (Psalm 100) are the dominant themes of the book, leading to joy, which is both the manner and product of our praise.

BOOK I

Psalms 1–41

Psalm 1

1 Blessed is the man
1:1 [a]Pr 4:14 [b]Ps 26:4; Jer 15:17
who does not walk[a] in the counsel
of the wicked
or stand in the way of sinners
or sit[b] in the seat of mockers.
1:2 [c]Ps 119:16,35 [d]Ps 119:1 [e]Jos 1:8
2 But his delight[c] is in the law of the
LORD,[d]
and on his law he meditates[e] day
and night.
1:3 [f]Ps 128:3 [g]Jer 17:8 [h]Eze 47:12 [i]Ge 39:3
3 He is like a tree[f] planted by streams
of water,[g]
which yields its fruit[h] in season
and whose leaf does not wither.
Whatever he does prospers.[i]

4 Not so the wicked!
1:4 [j]Job 21:18; Isa 17:13
They are like chaff[j]
that the wind blows away.
1:5 [k]Ps 5:5 [l]Ps 9:7-8,16
5 Therefore the wicked will not stand[k]
in the judgment,[l]
nor sinners in the assembly of the
righteous.

1:6 [m]Ps 37:18; 2Ti 2:19 [n]Ps 9:6
6 For the LORD watches over[m] the way
of the righteous,
but the way of the wicked will
perish.[n]

Psalm 2

1 Why do the nations conspire[a]
2:1 [o]Ps 21:11
and the peoples plot[o] in vain?
2 The kings[p] of the earth take their
2:2 [p]Ps 48:4 [q]Jn 1:41 [r]Ps 74:18,23; Ac 4:25-26*
stand
and the rulers gather together
against the LORD
and against his Anointed[q] One.[b] [r]
3 "Let us break their chains," they say,
2:3 [s]Jer 5:5
"and throw off their fetters."[s]

2:4 [t]Ps 37:13; 59:8; Pr 1:26
4 The One enthroned in heaven
laughs;[t]
the Lord scoffs at them.
2:5 [u]Ps 21:9; 78:49-50
5 Then he rebukes them in his anger
and terrifies them in his wrath,[u]
saying,
6 "I have installed my King[c]
on Zion, my holy hill."

7 I will proclaim the decree of the LORD:

2:7 [v]Ac 13:33*; Heb 1:5*
He said to me, "You are my Son[d];
today I have become your
Father.[e] [v]

LOVE

LIKE FATHER, LIKE SON

Psalm 2:7

**Does not the power of heaven's intimacy
hang about the words *Father* and *Son*?
Does not the Son glory in the word *Father*?
Does not the Father celebrate the word
Son?
Does God not say in every worship service
where Christ is preached,
"This is my Son, whom I love; with him I
am well pleased"?
Does not the Son say in the splendor of
every sunrise,
"How great is the love the Father has
lavished on us, that we should be called
children of God"?**

8 Ask of me,
and I will make the nations your
inheritance,
the ends of the earth[w] your 2:8 [w]Ps 22:27
possession.
9 You will rule them with an iron
scepter[f]; [x] 2:9 [x]Rev 12:5 [y]Ps 89:23 [z]Rev 2:27*
you will dash them to pieces[y] like
pottery.[z]"

10 Therefore, you kings, be wise;
be warned, you rulers of the earth.
11 Serve the LORD with fear 2:11 [a]Heb 12:28 [b]Ps 119:119-120
and rejoice[a] with trembling.[b]
12 Kiss the Son,[c] lest he be angry
and you be destroyed in your way, 2:12 [c]Jn 5:23 [d]Rev 6:16 [e]Ps 34:8; Ro 9:33
for his wrath[d] can flare up in a
moment.
Blessed are all who take refuge[e] in
him.

Psalm 3

A psalm of David. When he fled
from his son Absalom.[f] 3:1 [f]2Sa 15:14

1 O LORD, how many are my foes!
How many rise up against me!
2 Many are saying of me, 3:2 [g]Ps 71:11
"God will not deliver him.[g]" *Selah*[g]

3 But you are a shield[h] around me, 3:3 [h]Ge 15:1; Ps 28:7
O LORD;

[a] *1* Hebrew; Septuagint *rage* [b] *2* Or *anointed one* [c] *6* Or *king* [d] *7* Or *son*; also in verse 12 [e] *7* Or *have begotten you* [f] *9* Or *will break them with a rod of iron* [g] *2* A word of uncertain meaning, occurring frequently in the Psalms; possibly a musical term

3:3 [i]Ps 27:6

you bestow glory on me and lift[a]
up my head.[i]

3:4 [j]Ps 2:6

4 To the LORD I cry aloud,
and he answers me from his holy
hill.[j] *Selah*

3:5 [k]Lev 26:6; Pr 3:24

5 I lie down and sleep;[k]
I wake again, because the LORD
sustains me.

3:6 [l]Ps 27:3

6 I will not fear[l] the tens of thousands
drawn up against me on every
side.

3:7 [m]Ps 7:6 [n]Ps 6:4 [o]Job 16:10 [p]Ps 58:6

7 Arise,[m] O LORD!
Deliver me,[n] O my God!
Strike[o] all my enemies on the jaw;
break the teeth[p] of the wicked.

3:8 [q]Isa 43:3,11

8 From the LORD comes deliverance.[q]
May your blessing be on your
people. *Selah*

JOY

DELIVERANCE

Psalm 3:8

Deliverance never mires us down in heavy praise. It flows about us like a river of joy.

Psalm 4

For the director of music. With stringed
instruments. A psalm of David.

1 Answer me when I call to you,
O my righteous God.
Give me relief from my distress;

4:1 [r]Ps 25:16 [s]Ps 17:6

be merciful[r] to me and hear my
prayer.[s]
2 How long, O men, will you turn my
glory into shame[b]?
How long will you love delusions

4:2 [t]Ps 31:6

and seek false gods[c]?[t] *Selah*

4:3 [u]Ps 31:23 [v]Ps 6:8

3 Know that the LORD has set apart
the godly[u] for himself;
the LORD will hear[v] when I call
to him.

4:4 [w]Eph 4:26* [x]Ps 77:6

4 In your anger do not sin;[w]
when you are on your beds,[x]
search your hearts and be silent.
Selah

4:5 [y]Dt 33:19; Ps 37:3

5 Offer right sacrifices
and trust in the LORD.[y]
6 Many are asking, "Who can show us
any good?"

4:6 [z]Nu 6:25

Let the light of your face shine
upon us,[z] O LORD.

4:7 [a]Ac 14:17 [b]Isa 9:3

7 You have filled my heart[a] with
greater joy[b]
than when their grain and new
wine abound.

4:8 [c]Ps 3:5 [d]Lev 25:18

8 I will lie down and sleep[c] in peace,
for you alone, O LORD,
make me dwell in safety.[d]

Psalm 5

For the director of music. For flutes.
A psalm of David.

1 Give ear to my words, O LORD,
consider my sighing.

5:2 [e]Ps 3:4 [f]Ps 84:3

2 Listen to my cry for help,[e]
my King and my God,[f]
for to you I pray.

5:3 [g]Ps 88:13

3 In the morning,[g] O LORD, you hear
my voice;
in the morning I lay my requests
before you
and wait in expectation.
4 You are not a God who takes
pleasure in evil;

5:4 [h]Ps 11:5; 92:15

with you the wicked[h] cannot
dwell.

5:5 [i]Ps 73:3 [j]Ps 1:5 [k]Ps 11:5

5 The arrogant[i] cannot stand[j] in your
presence;
you hate[k] all who do wrong.

5:6 [l]Ps 55:23; Rev 21:8

6 You destroy those who tell lies;[l]
bloodthirsty and deceitful men
the LORD abhors.
7 But I, by your great mercy,
will come into your house;

5:7 [m]Ps 138:2

in reverence will I bow down[m]
toward your holy temple.

5:8 [n]Ps 31:1 [o]Ps 27:11

8 Lead me, O LORD, in your
righteousness[n]
because of my enemies—
make straight your way[o] before
me.
9 Not a word from their mouth can be
trusted;
their heart is filled with
destruction.

5:9 [p]Lk 11:44 [q]Ro 3:13*

Their throat is an open grave;[p]
with their tongue they speak
deceit.[q]
10 Declare them guilty, O God!
Let their intrigues be their
downfall.

5:10 [r]Ps 9:16 [s]Ps 107:11

Banish them for their many sins,[r]
for they have rebelled[s] against you.

[a]3 Or *LORD, / my Glorious One, who lifts* [b]2 Or *you dishonor my Glorious One* [c]2 Or *seek lies*

11 But let all who take refuge in you
be glad;
let them ever sing for joy.[t]
Spread your protection over them,
that those who love your name[u]
may rejoice in you.[v]
12 For surely, O LORD, you bless the
righteous;
you surround them[w] with your
favor as with a shield.

5:11 [t]Ps 2:12 [u]Ps 69:36 [v]Isa 65:13
5:12 [w]Ps 32:7

Psalm 6

For the director of music. With stringed instruments. According to *sheminith.*[a] A psalm of David.

1 O LORD, do not rebuke me in your
anger[x]
or discipline me in your wrath.
2 Be merciful to me, LORD, for I am
faint;
O LORD, heal me,[y] for my bones
are in agony.[z]
3 My soul is in anguish.[a]
How long,[b] O LORD, how long?
4 Turn, O LORD, and deliver me;
save me because of your unfailing
love.[c]

6:1 [x]Ps 38:1
6:2 [y]Hos 6:1 [z]Ps 22:14; 31:10
6:3 [a]Jn 12:27 [b]Ps 90:13
6:4 [c]Ps 17:13

PEACE

UNFAILING LOVE

Psalm 6:4

The product of God's love is peace. There is a subtle force at work in the world: "Love unfailing" is its name. Salvation is its dream. Like sunlight, it is constant. Like an untiring parent, it swims the tides of desperation, seeking every lost and frightened child.

5 No one remembers you when he is
dead.
Who praises you from the grave[b]?[d]
6 I am worn out[e] from groaning;
all night long I flood my bed with
weeping
and drench my couch with tears.[f]
7 My eyes grow weak[g] with sorrow;
they fail because of all my foes.
8 Away from me,[h] all you who do evil,[i]
for the LORD has heard my
weeping.
9 The LORD has heard my cry for
mercy;[j]
the LORD accepts my prayer.
10 All my enemies will be ashamed and
dismayed;
they will turn back in sudden
disgrace.[k]

6:5 [d]Ps 30:9; 88:10-12; Ecc 9:10; Isa 38:18
6:6 [e]Ps 69:3 [f]Ps 42:3
6:7 [g]Ps 31:9
6:8 [h]Ps 119:115 [i]Mt 7:23; Lk 13:27
6:9 [j]Ps 116:1
6:10 [k]Ps 71:24; 73:19

Psalm 7

A *shiggaion*[c] of David, which he sang to the LORD concerning Cush, a Benjamite.

1 O LORD my God, I take refuge in
you;
save and deliver me from all who
pursue me,[l]
2 or they will tear me like a lion[m]
and rip me to pieces with no one
to rescue[n] me.

3 O LORD my God, if I have done
this
and there is guilt on my hands[o]—
4 if I have done evil to him who is at
peace with me
or without cause have robbed my
foe—
5 then let my enemy pursue and
overtake me;
let him trample my life to the
ground
and make me sleep in the dust.
Selah

6 Arise,[p] O LORD, in your anger;
rise up against the rage of my
enemies.[q]
Awake,[r] my God; decree justice.
7 Let the assembled peoples gather
around you.
Rule over them from on high;
8 let the LORD judge the peoples.
Judge me, O LORD, according to
my righteousness,[s]
according to my integrity, O Most
High.
9 O righteous God,[t]
who searches minds and hearts,[u]
bring to an end the violence of the
wicked
and make the righteous secure.[v]

10 My shield[d] is God Most High,
who saves the upright in heart.[w]
11 God is a righteous judge,[x]
a God who expresses his wrath
every day.
12 If he does not relent,

7:1 [l]Ps 31:15
7:2 [m]Isa 38:13 [n]Ps 50:22
7:3 [o]1Sa 24:11; Isa 59:3
7:6 [p]Ps 94:2 [q]Ps 138:7 [r]Ps 44:23
7:8 [s]Ps 18:20; 96:13
7:9 [t]Jer 11:20 [u]1Ch 28:9; Ps 26:2; Rev 2:23 [v]Ps 37:23
7:10 [w]Ps 125:4
7:11 [x]Ps 50:6

[a]Title: Probably a musical term [b]5 Hebrew *Sheol*
[c]Title: Probably a literary or musical term [d]10 Or *sovereign*

7:12 [y]Dt 32:41 he[a] will sharpen his sword;[y]
he will bend and string his bow.
[13]He has prepared his deadly weapons;
he makes ready his flaming
arrows.

[14]He who is pregnant with evil
7:14 [z]Job 15:35; Isa 59:4; Jas 1:15 and conceives trouble gives birth[z]
to disillusionment.
[15]He who digs a hole and scoops it out
7:15 [a]Job 4:8 falls into the pit he has made.[a]
[16]The trouble he causes recoils on
himself;
his violence comes down on his
own head.

7:17 [b]Ps 71:15-16 [c]Ps 9:2 [17]I will give thanks to the LORD
because of his righteousness[b]
and will sing praise[c] to the name
of the LORD Most High.

Psalm 8

For the director of music. According
to *gittith.*[b] A psalm of David.

[1]O LORD, our Lord,
how majestic is your name in all
the earth!

You have set your glory
8:1 [d]Ps 57:5; 113:4; 148:13 above the heavens.[d]
[2]From the lips of children and infants
8:2 [e]Mt 21:16* [f]Ps 44:16; 1Co 1:27 you have ordained praise[c][e]
because of your enemies,
to silence the foe[f] and the
avenger.

8:3 [g]Ps 89:11 [h]Ps 136:9 [3]When I consider your heavens,[g]
the work of your fingers,
the moon and the stars,[h]
which you have set in place,
[4]what is man that you are mindful of
8:4 [i]Job 7:17; Ps 144:3; Heb 2:6 him,
the son of man that you care for
him?[i]

PATIENCE

LOVED WITHOUT A REASON

Psalm 8:4

"God, shall I tell you why I love you? Here is my reason: Secure in the heavenlies with no real need of me, you still loved me to the point of incarnation. What am I, God, that you should desire me? What good was in me to lure your patient grace? It is both unreasonable and glorious that I belong to you—and it was all your doing."

[5]You made him a little lower than the
heavenly beings[d]
and crowned him with glory and
honor.[j] 8:5 [j]Ps 21:5; 103:4
[6]You made him ruler[k] over the works
of your hands; 8:6 [k]Ge 1:28 [l]Heb 2:6-8* [m]1Co 15:25, 27*; Eph 1:22
you put everything under his
feet:[l][m]
[7]all flocks and herds,
and the beasts of the field,
[8]the birds of the air,
and the fish of the sea,
all that swim the paths of the seas.

[9]O LORD, our Lord,
how majestic is your name in all 8:9 [n]ver 1
the earth![n]

Psalm 9[e]

For the director of music. To ⌊the tune
of⌋ "The Death of the Son."
A psalm of David.

[1]I will praise you, O LORD, with all 9:1 [o]Ps 86:12 [p]Ps 26:7
my heart;[o]
I will tell of all your wonders.[p]
[2]I will be glad and rejoice[q] in you; 9:2 [q]Ps 5:11 [r]Ps 92:1; 83:18
I will sing praise to your name,[r]
O Most High.

[3]My enemies turn back;
they stumble and perish before
you.
[4]For you have upheld my right and
my cause;[s] 9:4 [s]Ps 140:12 [t]1Pe 2:23
you have sat on your throne,
judging righteously.[t]
[5]You have rebuked the nations and
destroyed the wicked;
you have blotted out their name[u] 9:5 [u]Pr 10:7
for ever and ever.
[6]Endless ruin has overtaken the
enemy,
you have uprooted their cities;
even the memory of them[v] has 9:6 [v]Ps 34:16
perished.

[7]The LORD reigns forever;
he has established his throne[w] for 9:7 [w]Ps 89:14
judgment.
[8]He will judge the world in
righteousness;[x] 9:8 [x]Ps 96:13

[a]*12* Or *If a man does not repent, / God* [b]Title: Probably a musical term [c]*2* Or *strength* [d]*5* Or *than God* [e]Psalms 9 and 10 may have been originally a single acrostic poem, the stanzas of which begin with the successive letters of the Hebrew alphabet. In the Septuagint they constitute one psalm.

he will govern the peoples with
justice.

9:9 [y]Ps 32:7

9 The LORD is a refuge for the
oppressed,
a stronghold in times of trouble.[y]

9:10 [z]Ps 91:14 [a]Ps 37:28

10 Those who know your name[z] will
trust in you,
for you, LORD, have never
forsaken[a] those who seek
you.

9:11 [b]Ps 76:2 [c]Ps 107:22 [d]Ps 105:1

11 Sing praises to the LORD, enthroned
in Zion;[b]
proclaim among the nations[c] what
he has done.[d]

9:12 [e]Ge 9:5

12 For he who avenges blood[e]
remembers;
he does not ignore the cry of the
afflicted.

9:13 [f]Ps 38:19

13 O LORD, see how my enemies[f]
persecute me!
Have mercy and lift me up from
the gates of death,

9:14 [g]Ps 106:2 [h]Ps 13:5; 51:12

14 that I may declare your praises[g]
in the gates of the Daughter of
Zion
and there rejoice in your
salvation.[h]

9:15 [i]Ps 7:15-16 [j]Ps 35:8; 57:6

15 The nations have fallen into the pit
they have dug;[i]
their feet are caught in the net
they have hidden.[j]

16 The LORD is known by his justice;
the wicked are ensnared by the
work of their hands.
Higgaion.[a] *Selah*

9:17 [k]Ps 49:14 [l]Job 8:13; Ps 50:22

17 The wicked return to the grave,[b][k]
all the nations that forget God.[l]

9:18 [m]Ps 71:5; Pr 23:18 [n]Ps 12:5

18 But the needy will not always be
forgotten,
nor the hope[m] of the afflicted[n]
ever perish.

19 Arise, O LORD, let not man
triumph;
let the nations be judged in your
presence.

9:20 [o]Ps 62:9; Isa 31:3

20 Strike them with terror, O LORD;
let the nations know they are but
men.[o] *Selah*

Psalm 10[c]

10:1 [p]Ps 22:1,11 [q]Ps 13:1

1 Why, O LORD, do you stand far off?[p]
Why do you hide yourself[q] in
times of trouble?

2 In his arrogance the wicked man
hunts down the weak,
who are caught in the schemes he
devises.

10:3 [r]Ps 94:4

3 He boasts[r] of the cravings of his
heart;
he blesses the greedy and reviles
the LORD.

10:4 [s]Ps 14:1; 36:1

4 In his pride the wicked does not seek
him;
in all his thoughts there is no
room for God.[s]

5 His ways are always prosperous;
he is haughty and your laws are far
from him;
he sneers at all his enemies.

10:6 [t]Rev 18:7

6 He says to himself, "Nothing will
shake me;
I'll always be happy[t] and never
have trouble."

10:7 [u]Ro 3:14* [v]Ps 73:8 [w]Ps 140:3

7 His mouth is full of curses[u] and lies
and threats;[v]
trouble and evil are under his
tongue.[w]

10:8 [x]Ps 94:6

8 He lies in wait near the villages;
from ambush he murders the
innocent,[x]
watching in secret for his victims.

10:9 [y]Ps 17:12; 59:3; 140:5

9 He lies in wait like a lion in cover;
he lies in wait to catch the
helpless;[y]
he catches the helpless and drags
them off in his net.

10 His victims are crushed, they
collapse;
they fall under his strength.

10:11 [z]Job 22:13

11 He says to himself, "God has
forgotten;[z]
he covers his face and never sees."

10:12 [a]Ps 17:7; Mic 5:9 [b]Ps 9:12

12 Arise, LORD! Lift up your hand,[a]
O God.
Do not forget the helpless.[b]

13 Why does the wicked man revile
God?
Why does he say to himself,
"He won't call me to account"?

10:14 [c]Ps 22:11 [d]Ps 37:5 [e]Ps 68:5

14 But you, O God, do see trouble[c] and
grief;
you consider it to take it in hand.
The victim commits himself to
you;[d]
you are the helper[e] of the
fatherless.

[a]*16* Or *Meditation*; possibly a musical notation
[b]*17* Hebrew *Sheol* [c]Psalms 9 and 10 may have been originally a single acrostic poem, the stanzas of which begin with the successive letters of the Hebrew alphabet. In the Septuagint they constitute one psalm.

15 Break the arm of the wicked and evil
man;[f]
call him to account for his
wickedness
that would not be found out.
16 The LORD is King for ever and
ever;[g]
the nations[h] will perish from his
land.
17 You hear, O LORD, the desire of the
afflicted;[i]
you encourage them, and you
listen to their cry,
18 defending the fatherless[j] and the
oppressed,[k]
in order that man, who is of the
earth, may terrify no more.

10:15 [f]Ps 37:17
10:16 [g]Ps 29:10 [h]Dt 8:20
10:17 [i]1Ch 29:18; Ps 34:15
10:18 [j]Ps 82:3 [k]Ps 9:9

Psalm 11

For the director of music. Of David.

1 In the LORD I take refuge.[l]
How then can you say to me:
"Flee like a bird to your
mountain.
2 For look, the wicked bend their
bows;
they set their arrows[m] against the
strings
to shoot from the shadows
at the upright in heart.[n]
3 When the foundations[o] are being
destroyed,
what can the righteous do[a]?"
4 The LORD is in his holy temple;[p]
the LORD is on his heavenly
throne.[q]
He observes the sons of men;[r]
his eyes examine[s] them.
5 The LORD examines the righteous,[t]
but the wicked[b] and those who
love violence
his soul hates.[u]
6 On the wicked he will rain
fiery coals and burning sulfur;[v]
a scorching wind[w] will be their lot.
7 For the LORD is righteous,[x]
he loves justice;[y]
upright men will see his face.[z]

11:1 [l]Ps 56:11
11:2 [m]Ps 7:13 [n]Ps 64:3-4
11:3 [o]Ps 82:5
11:4 [p]Ps 18:6 [q]Ps 103:19 [r]Ps 33:13 [s]Ps 34:15-16
11:5 [t]Ge 22:1; Jas 1:12 [u]Ps 5:5
11:6 [v]Eze 38:22 [w]Jer 4:11-12
11:7 [x]Ps 7:9,11; 45:7 [y]Ps 33:5 [z]Ps 17:15

Psalm 12

For the director of music. According to *sheminith*.[c] A psalm of David.

1 Help, LORD, for the godly are no
more;[a]
the faithful have vanished from
among men.
2 Everyone lies to his neighbor;
their flattering lips speak with
deception.[b]
3 May the LORD cut off all flattering
lips
and every boastful tongue[c]
4 that says, "We will triumph with our
tongues;
we own our lips[d]—who is our
master?"
5 "Because of the oppression of the
weak
and the groaning of the needy,
I will now arise," says the LORD.
"I will protect them[d] from those
who malign them."
6 And the words of the LORD are
flawless,[e]
like silver refined in a furnace of
clay,
purified seven times.
7 O LORD, you will keep us safe
and protect us from such people
forever.[f]
8 The wicked freely strut[g] about
when what is vile is honored
among men.

12:1 [a]Isa 57:1
12:2 [b]Ps 10:7; 41:6; 55:21; Ro 16:18
12:3 [c]Da 7:8; Rev 13:5
12:5 [d]Ps 10:18; 34:6
12:6 [e]2Sa 22:31; Ps 18:30; Pr 30:5
12:7 [f]Ps 37:28
12:8 [g]Ps 55:10-11

Psalm 13

For the director of music.
A psalm of David.

1 How long, O LORD? Will you forget
me forever?
How long will you hide your face[h]
from me?
2 How long must I wrestle with my
thoughts[i]
and every day have sorrow in my
heart?
How long will my enemy triumph
over me?[j]
3 Look on me and answer,[k] O LORD
my God.
Give light to my eyes,[l] or I will
sleep in death;[m]
4 my enemy will say, "I have overcome
him,[n]"
and my foes will rejoice when I
fall.

13:1 [h]Job 13:24; Ps 44:24
13:2 [i]Ps 42:4 [j]Ps 42:9
13:3 [k]Ps 5:1 [l]Ezr 9:8 [m]Jer 51:39
13:4 [n]Ps 25:2

[a]3 Or *what is the Righteous One doing* [b]5 Or *The LORD, the Righteous One, examines the wicked, /* [c]Title: Probably a musical term [d]4 Or */ our lips are our plowshares*

13:5 [o]Ps 52:8 [p]Ps 9:14

[5] But I trust in your unfailing love;[o]
my heart rejoices in your salvation.[p]

13:6 [q]Ps 116:7

[6] I will sing[q] to the LORD,
for he has been good to me.

Psalm 14

For the director of music. Of David.

14:1 [r]Ps 10:4

[1] The fool[a] says in his heart,
"There is no God."[r]
They are corrupt, their deeds are vile;
there is no one who does good.

KINDNESS

THE HOUND OF HEAVEN

Psalm 14:1

Who says, "There is a God"? The wise believer. The one who says otherwise is a fool. But fool or not, there is a grace that hounds all infidels. Heaven never ceases to love those who doubt it. Angels—invisible, on tiptoe—throng atheists, begging them to be wise.

14:2 [s]Ps 33:13 [t]Ps 92:6

[2] The LORD looks down from heaven[s]
on the sons of men
to see if there are any who understand,[t]
any who seek God.

14:3 [u]Ps 58:3 [v]Ps 143:2 [w]Ro 3:10-12*

[3] All have turned aside,
they have together become corrupt;[u]
there is no one who does good,[v]
not even one.[w]

14:4 [x]Ps 82:5 [y]Ps 27:2 [z]Ps 79:6; Isa 64:7

[4] Will evildoers never learn—[x]
those who devour my people[y] as men eat bread
and who do not call on the LORD?[z]
[5] There they are, overwhelmed with dread,
for God is present in the company of the righteous.

14:6 [a]Ps 9:9; 40:17

[6] You evildoers frustrate the plans of the poor,
but the LORD is their refuge.[a]

14:7 [b]Ps 53:6

[7] Oh, that salvation for Israel would come out of Zion!
When the LORD restores the fortunes[b] of his people,
let Jacob rejoice and Israel be glad!

Psalm 15

A psalm of David.

15:1 [c]Ps 27:5-6 [d]Ps 24:3-5

[1] LORD, who may dwell in your sanctuary?[c]
Who may live on your holy hill?[d]

15:2 [e]Ps 24:4; Zec 8:3,16; Eph 4:25

[2] He whose walk is blameless
and who does what is righteous,
who speaks the truth[e] from his heart

15:3 [f]Ex 23:1

[3] and has no slander[f] on his tongue,
who does his neighbor no wrong
and casts no slur on his fellowman,

15:4 [g]Ac 28:10 [h]Jdg 11:35

[4] who despises a vile man
but honors[g] those who fear the LORD,
who keeps his oath[h]
even when it hurts,

15:5 [i]Ex 22:25 [j]Ex 23:8; Dt 16:19 [k]2Pe 1:10

[5] who lends his money without usury[i]
and does not accept a bribe[j]
against the innocent.

He who does these things
will never be shaken.[k]

Psalm 16

A *miktam*[b] of David.

16:1 [l]Ps 17:8 [m]Ps 7:1

[1] Keep me safe,[l] O God,
for in you I take refuge.[m]

16:2 [n]Ps 73:25

[2] I said to the LORD, "You are my Lord;
apart from you I have no good thing."[n]

16:3 [o]Ps 101:6

[3] As for the saints who are in the land,[o]
they are the glorious ones in whom is all my delight.[c]

16:4 [p]Ps 32:10 [q]Ps 106:37-38 [r]Ex 23:13

[4] The sorrows[p] of those will increase
who run after other gods.[q]
I will not pour out their libations of blood
or take up their names[r] on my lips.

16:5 [s]Ps 73:26 [t]Ps 23:5

[5] LORD, you have assigned me my portion[s] and my cup;[t]
you have made my lot secure.

16:6 [u]Ps 78:55; Jer 3:19

[6] The boundary lines have fallen for me in pleasant places;
surely I have a delightful inheritance.[u]

[a]*1* The Hebrew words rendered *fool* in Psalms denote one who is morally deficient. [b]Title: Probably a literary or musical term [c]*3* Or *As for the pagan priests who are in the land / and the nobles in whom all delight, I said:*

WEEK 16 FAITHFULNESS

1 DAY ONE

FAITHFULNESS, THE HIGH ART OF PERSISTENCE

Read Psalm 15:1–5

"Who may dwell in your sanctuary?" asks the psalmist and then answers his own question by saying it is he "who keeps his oath even when it hurts." Faithfulness is one of the greatest of all virtues. For to believe much but not be faithful brings life at last to nothing. Further, faithfulness begets a hunger to have, not just the blessings of God, but God himself. Faithfulness will not be satisfied until it sees at close range the God it cannot quit dreaming about.

This is the grand distinction between true Christianity and any one of its many counterfeits. True Christians hunger, not for evidences of the presence, but for the presence itself. True Christianity hungers, not even for the blessings of God, but for God.

Thomas à Kempis perfectly expressed the heart of faithfulness when he wrote:

> Grant me, O most loving Lord, to rest in thee above all creatures, above all health and beauty, above all glory and honor, above all power and dignity, above all knowledge and subtility, above all riches and art, above all fame and praise, above all sweetness and comfort, above all hope and promise, above all gifts and favors that thou canst give and impart to us, and above all jubilee that the mind of man can receive and feel; finally above all angels and archangels, and above all heavenly hosts, and above all things visible and invisible, and above all that thou art not, O my God. It is too small and unsatisfying, whatever thou bestowest on me apart from thee, or revealed to me or promised, whilst thou are not seen, and not fully obtained. For surely my heart cannot truly rest or be entirely contented, unless it rest in thee.

Faithfulness is the unswerving pursuit of the presence of God.

MEMORIZE THIS WEEK

1 THESSALONIANS 5:16-18

Be joyful always; pray continually; give thanks in all circumstances, for this is God's will for you in Christ Jesus.

2 DAY TWO

FAITHFULNESS AND THE PURPOSE OF GOD IN MY LIFE

What if you were a king or queen of a country—how would you rule? Would you live a life of ease without a care for others? Or would you try to make your country better for all those living there? Jotham was a young king faced with this decision, and he chose to be faithful to God and base his rulings on what God would have him do. His faithfulness brought him God's blessings and showed him God's purpose for his life. *Turn to 2 Chronicles 27:1–6, page 524, for today's study.*

3 DAY THREE

FAITHFULNESS AND MY RELATIONSHIP WITH CHRIST

Job said, "Though he slay me, yet will I hope in him." Job made persistence such a high agenda that not even death would end his constant struggle to be with God. He would trust and live or trust and die. And even if God were to become homicidal and Job were his first victim, Job would never stop pursuing his Lover. So ought we to pursue our Christ until the union we seek from him is ours for eternity. *Turn to Job 13:15, page 599, for today's study.*

4 DAY FOUR

FAITHFULNESS AND MY SERVICE TO OTHERS

The man in this story is persistent on behalf of a friend who has stopped in to see him. When we bring the needs of others before God, our persistence takes on new meaning. Now, more is at stake than our own wants and desires—we are ministering to others through our prayers for them. Nothing is more beautiful than the prayer warrior who is persistent on behalf of someone else's need. *Turn to Luke 11:5–8, page 1218, for today's study.*

5 DAY FIVE

FAITHFULNESS AND ITS PLACE IN MY PERSONAL WORSHIP

Would you have persistent faithfulness defined? Ask and ask and ask and ask and ask; never stop asking until the answer is given, and then go back and ask for more. Seek God until you find him. Knock until he opens. Keep on keeping on until you reach the Keeper. Persist until you have said a thousand times, "God, here I am," and you hear all the angels say, "Not you again." *Turn to Luke 18:1–8, page 1231, for today's study.*

Week 17, Gentleness, a Way of Winning Others to Christ, begins on page 1303, Acts 9:36–42.
To begin a topical study on the Fruit of the Spirit, Faithfulness, turn to the Topical Index, page 1548.

16:7 [v]Ps 73:24 [w]Ps 77:6

[7]I will praise the LORD, who counsels
me;[v]
even at night[w] my heart instructs
me.
[8]I have set the LORD always before
me.
Because he is at my right hand,[x]
I will not be shaken.

16:8 [x]Ps 73:23

16:9 [y]Ps 4:7; 30:11 [z]Ps 4:8

[9]Therefore my heart is glad[y] and my
tongue rejoices;
my body also will rest secure,[z]
[10]because you will not abandon me to
the grave,[a]
nor will you let your Holy One[b]
see decay.[a]

16:10 [a]Ac 13:35*

16:11 [b]Mt 7:14 [c]Ac 2:25-28* [d]Ps 36:7-8

[11]You have made[c] known to me the
path of life;[b]
you will fill me with joy in your
presence,[c]
with eternal pleasures[d] at your
right hand.

GENTLENESS

THE PROMISE OF LIFE

Psalm 16:9–10

Jesus was so loved by Love himself that his body died but never decayed. His grieving Father ordered the earth to quake and shake open his grave. When we cry, "Hallelujah, he is risen!" we celebrate the central work of our Father. God is ever busy prying triumph from the tombs—his and ours.

Psalm 17

A prayer of David.

17:1 [e]Ps 61:1 [f]Isa 29:13

[1]Hear, O LORD, my righteous plea;
listen to my cry.[e]
Give ear to my prayer—
it does not rise from deceitful lips.[f]
[2]May my vindication come from you;
may your eyes see what is right.

17:3 [g]Ps 26:2; 66:10 [h]Job 23:10; Jer 50:20 [i]Ps 39:1

[3]Though you probe my heart and
examine me at night,
though you test me,[g] you will find
nothing;[h]
I have resolved that my mouth
will not sin.[i]
[4]As for the deeds of men—
by the word of your lips
I have kept myself
from the ways of the violent.

17:5 [j]Ps 44:18; 119:133 [k]Ps 18:36

[5]My steps have held to your paths;[j]
my feet have not slipped.[k]

17:6 [l]Ps 86:7 [m]Ps 116:2 [n]Ps 88:2

[6]I call on you, O God, for you will
answer me;[l]
give ear to me[m] and hear my
prayer.[n]

17:7 [o]Ps 31:21 [p]Ps 20:6

[7]Show the wonder of your great love,[o]
you who save by your right hand[p]
those who take refuge in you from
their foes.

17:8 [q]Dt 32:10

[8]Keep me as the apple of your eye;[q]
hide me in the shadow of your
wings
[9]from the wicked who assail me,
from my mortal enemies who
surround me.[r]

17:9 [r]Ps 31:20; 109:3

17:10 [s]Ps 73:7 [t]1Sa 2:3

[10]They close up their callous hearts,[s]
and their mouths speak with
arrogance.[t]
[11]They have tracked me down, they
now surround me,[u]
with eyes alert, to throw me to the
ground.

17:11 [u]Ps 37:14; 88:17

17:12 [v]Ps 7:2; 10:9

[12]They are like a lion[v] hungry for prey,
like a great lion crouching in
cover.

17:13 [w]Ps 7:12; 22:20; 73:18

[13]Rise up, O LORD, confront them,
bring them down;[w]
rescue me from the wicked by
your sword.
[14]O LORD, by your hand save me
from such men,
from men of this world[x] whose
reward is in this life.

17:14 [x]Lk 16:8 [y]Ps 73:3-7

You still the hunger of those you
cherish;
their sons have plenty,
and they store up wealth[y] for their
children.
[15]And I—in righteousness I will see
your face;
when I awake, I will be satisfied
with seeing your likeness.[z]

17:15 [z]Nu 12:8; Ps 4:6-7; 16:11; 1Jn 3:2

Psalm 18

For the director of music. Of David
the servant of the LORD. He sang
to the LORD the words of this song
when the LORD delivered him from
the hand of all his enemies and
from the hand of Saul. He said:

[1]I love you, O LORD, my strength.

18:2 [a]Ps 19:14

[2]The LORD is my rock,[a] my fortress
and my deliverer;

[a]10 Hebrew *Sheol* [b]10 Or *your faithful one*
[c]11 Or *You will make*

my God is my rock, in whom I
take refuge.
He is my shield[b] and the horn[a]
of my salvation,[c] my
stronghold.
3 I call to the LORD, who is worthy
of praise,[d]
and I am saved from my enemies.

4 The cords of death[e] entangled me;
the torrents[f] of destruction
overwhelmed me.
5 The cords of the grave[b] coiled
around me;
the snares of death[g] confronted
me.
6 In my distress I called to the LORD;
I cried to my God for help.
From his temple he heard my voice;[h]
my cry came before him, into his
ears.

7 The earth trembled and quaked,[i]
and the foundations of the
mountains shook;
they trembled because he was
angry.[j]
8 Smoke rose from his nostrils;
consuming fire[k] came from his
mouth,
burning coals blazed out of it.
9 He parted the heavens and came
down;[l]
dark clouds were under his feet.
10 He mounted the cherubim[m] and
flew;
he soared on the wings of the
wind.[n]
11 He made darkness his covering,[o] his
canopy around him—
the dark rain clouds of the sky.
12 Out of the brightness of his
presence[p] clouds advanced,
with hailstones and bolts of
lightning.[q]
13 The LORD thundered[r] from heaven;
the voice of the Most High
resounded.[c]
14 He shot his arrows and scattered ⌞the
enemies⌟,
great bolts of lightning and routed
them.[s]
15 The valleys of the sea were exposed
and the foundations of the earth
laid bare
at your rebuke,[t] O LORD,
at the blast of breath from your
nostrils.

18:2 [b]Ps 59:11 [c]Ps 75:10
18:3 [d]Ps 48:1
18:4 [e]Ps 116:3 [f]Ps 124:4
18:5 [g]Ps 116:3
18:6 [h]Ps 34:15
18:7 [i]Jdg 5:4 [j]Ps 68:7-8
18:8 [k]Ps 50:3
18:9 [l]Ps 144:5
18:10 [m]Ps 80:1 [n]Ps 104:3
18:11 [o]Dt 4:11; Ps 97:2
18:12 [p]Ps 104:2 [q]Ps 97:3
18:13 [r]Ps 29:3; 104:7
18:14 [s]Ps 144:6
18:15 [t]Ps 76:6; 106:9

16 He reached down from on high and
took hold of me;
he drew me out of deep waters.[u]
17 He rescued me from my powerful
enemy,
from my foes, who were too
strong for me.[v]
18 They confronted me in the day of
my disaster,
but the LORD was my support.[w]
19 He brought me out into a spacious
place;[x]
he rescued me because he
delighted in me.[y]

20 The LORD has dealt with me
according to my
righteousness;
according to the cleanness of my
hands[z] he has rewarded me.
21 For I have kept the ways of the
LORD;[a]
I have not done evil by turning[b]
from my God.
22 All his laws are before me;[c]
I have not turned away from his
decrees.
23 I have been blameless before him
and have kept myself from sin.
24 The LORD has rewarded me
according to my
righteousness,[d]
according to the cleanness of my
hands in his sight.

25 To the faithful[e] you show yourself
faithful,
to the blameless you show yourself
blameless,
26 to the pure you show yourself pure,
but to the crooked you show
yourself shrewd.[f]
27 You save the humble
but bring low those whose eyes are
haughty.[g]
28 You, O Lord, keep my lamp
burning;
my God turns my darkness into
light.[h]
29 With your help[i] I can advance
against a troop[d];
with my God I can scale a wall.

[a]*2 Horn* here symbolizes strength. [b]*5* Hebrew *Sheol*
[c]*13* Some Hebrew manuscripts and Septuagint (see also 2 Samuel 22:14); most Hebrew manuscripts *resounded, / amid hailstones and bolts of lightning*
[d]*29* Or *can run through a barricade*

18:16 [u]Ps 144:7
18:17 [v]Ps 35:10
18:18 [w]Ps 59:16
18:19 [x]Ps 31:8 [y]Ps 118:5
18:20 [z]Ps 24:4
18:21 [a]2Ch 34:33 [b]Ps 119:102
18:22 [c]Ps 119:30
18:24 [d]1Sa 26:23
18:25 [e]1Ki 8:32; Ps 62:12; Mt 5:7
18:26 [f]Pr 3:34
18:27 [g]Pr 6:17
18:28 [h]Job 18:6; 29:3
18:29 [i]Heb 11:34

30 As for God, his way is perfect;[j]
the word of the LORD is flawless.[k]
He is a shield
for all who take refuge[l] in him.
31 For who is God besides the LORD?[m]
And who is the Rock[n] except our God?
32 It is God who arms me with strength[o]
and makes my way perfect.
33 He makes my feet like the feet of a deer;[p]
he enables me to stand on the heights.[q]
34 He trains my hands for battle;[r]
my arms can bend a bow of bronze.
35 You give me your shield of victory,
and your right hand sustains[s] me;
you stoop down to make me great.
36 You broaden the path beneath me,
so that my ankles do not turn.

37 I pursued my enemies[t] and overtook them;
I did not turn back till they were destroyed.
38 I crushed them so that they could not rise;[u]
they fell beneath my feet.[v]
39 You armed me with strength for battle;
you made my adversaries bow at my feet.
40 You made my enemies turn their backs[w] in flight,
and I destroyed[x] my foes.
41 They cried for help, but there was no one to save them[y]—
to the LORD, but he did not answer.[z]
42 I beat them as fine as dust borne on the wind;
I poured them out like mud in the streets.

43 You have delivered me from the attacks of the people;
you have made me the head of nations;[a]
people I did not know[b] are subject to me.
44 As soon as they hear me, they obey me;
foreigners[c] cringe before me.
45 They all lose heart;
they come trembling from their strongholds.[d]

18:30 [j]Dt 32:4; Rev 15:3 [k]Ps 12:6 [l]Ps 17:7
18:31 [m]Dt 32:39; 86:8; Isa 45:5,6, 14,18,21 [n]Dt 32:31; 1Sa 2:2
18:32 [o]Isa 45:5
18:33 [p]Hab 3:19 [q]Dt 32:13
18:34 [r]Ps 144:1
18:35 [s]Ps 119:116
18:37 [t]Ps 37:20; 44:5
18:38 [u]Ps 36:12 [v]Ps 47:3
18:40 [w]Ps 21:12 [x]Ps 94:23
18:41 [y]Ps 50:22 [z]Job 27:9; Pr 1:28
18:43 [a]2Sa 8:1-14 [b]Isa 52:15; 55:5
18:44 [c]Ps 66:3
18:45 [d]Mic 7:17

46 The LORD lives! Praise be to my Rock!
Exalted be God my Savior![e]
47 He is the God who avenges me,
who subdues nations[f] under me,
48 who saves[g] me from my enemies.
You exalted me above my foes;
from violent men you rescued me.
49 Therefore I will praise you among the nations, O LORD;
I will sing[h] praises to your name.[i]
50 He gives his king great victories;
he shows unfailing kindness to his anointed,
to David[j] and his descendants forever.[k]

18:46 [e]Ps 51:14
18:47 [f]Ps 47:3
18:48 [g]Ps 59:1
18:49 [h]Ps 108:1 [i]Ro 15:9*
18:50 [j]Ps 144:10 [k]Ps 89:4

Psalm 19

For the director of music.
A psalm of David.

1 The heavens[l] declare[m] the glory of God;
the skies proclaim the work of his hands.
2 Day after day they pour forth speech;
night after night they display knowledge.[n]
3 There is no speech or language
where their voice is not heard.[a]
4 Their voice[b] goes out into all the earth,
their words to the ends of the world.[o]

In the heavens he has pitched a tent[p] for the sun,
5 which is like a bridegroom coming forth from his pavilion,
like a champion rejoicing to run his course.
6 It rises at one end of the heavens
and makes its circuit to the other;[q]
nothing is hidden from its heat.

7 The law of the LORD is perfect,
reviving the soul.[r]
The statutes of the LORD are trustworthy,[s]
making wise the simple.[t]
8 The precepts of the LORD are right,[u]
giving joy to the heart.

19:1 [l]Isa 40:22 [m]Ps 50:6; Ro 1:19
19:2 [n]Ps 74:16
19:4 [o]Ro 10:18* [p]Ps 104:2
19:6 [q]Ps 113:3; Ecc 1:5
19:7 [r]Ps 23:3 [s]Ps 93:5; 111:7 [t]Ps 119:98-100
19:8 [u]Ps 12:6; 119:128

[a]3 Or *They have no speech, there are no words; / no sound is heard from them* [b]4 Septuagint, Jerome and Syriac; Hebrew *line*

JOY

WEEK 2

DAY ONE
THE JOY OF CREATIVITY

Read Psalm 19:1–4

In this passage God's creativity is honored by David's flamboyant praise. David reminds us that God's glory can be seen in God's handiwork in our world.

If your joy grows weak, take your Bible to a lonely hillside, and there where the horizon is wide, the air is fragrant and the clouds tend toward silver, study the Scriptures and open your life to praise. In such a place it is impossible to keep your joy to yourself.

The ancient Egyptians and Greeks often looked to the skies and drew pictures of their gods and goddesses, their demons, dragons and heroes in the fiery distant stars. But the psalmist looked up into the stars and saw that beneath the entire canopy of space there was only one great constellation. This constellation, etched by all the stars at once, formed a picture of God.

The heavens declare the glory!

When God finished each and every day of creation, he remarked that it was good. We are like God when we stop and appreciate all that he has created. When we stop and survey his created order, we can only exalt in his work and cry, "It is good!"

So may it be with your soul. May the beautiful things of God never permit you a speechless moment. May you recognize God's creativity in all of your creativity.

When you see God's great works, may you fully appreciate the true concept of joy.

DAY TWO
JOY AND THE PURPOSE OF GOD IN MY LIFE

Our world brims with the creative touch of God. He created everything from nothing. He brought about the very foundations of the earth. In light of his grand design, our purpose is to do his work and our response is to live in joy. *Turn to Job 38:1–7, page 620, for today's study.*

DAY THREE
JOY AND MY RELATIONSHIP WITH CHRIST

Christ is your best friend, isn't he? He furnishes the deepest fabric of friendship that can be known. What he brings each time you meet in the closet of prayer is joy, isn't it? After all, when you are in his presence, isn't the burden you thought you couldn't carry lighter? *Turn to Matthew 6:28–30, page 1126, for today's study.*

DAY FOUR
JOY AND MY SERVICE TO OTHERS

A glass of cold water offered a dying man only adds pain to his dying when offered by a morose servant. The needy require our service, but they need it to be offered to them with a smile that comes from our inner soul. Unless we offer joy with every crust of bread, our offerings fall short. Joy takes away the hesitant edge of fear from those we want to help. *Turn to James 2:14–17, page 1483, for today's study.*

DAY FIVE
JOY AND ITS PLACE IN MY PERSONAL WORSHIP

When we pause and contemplate the creativity and blessings of God, we can't help but praise him. When we consider everyday events that we take for granted, like a sunrise or a rainstorm, we can see in God's divine creative plan the goodness that he means for us and for his own glory. And our response to his good gifts is praise. *Turn to Genesis 1:1–5, page 3, for today's study.*

MEMORIZE THIS WEEK

PSALM 19:1-2

The heavens declare the glory of God;
the skies proclaim the work of his hands.
Day after day they pour forth speech;
night after night they display knowledge.

Week 3, Peace, a Truce With God to End My Alienation From Him, begins on page 1353, Romans 16:20.
To begin a topical study on the Fruit of the Spirit, Joy, turn to the Topical Index, page 1548.

The commands of the LORD are radiant,
giving light to the eyes.
9 The fear of the LORD is pure,
enduring forever.
The ordinances of the LORD are sure
and altogether righteous.[v]
10 They are more precious than gold,[w]
than much pure gold;
they are sweeter than honey,
than honey from the comb.
11 By them is your servant warned;
in keeping them there is great reward.
12 Who can discern his errors?
Forgive my hidden faults.[x]
13 Keep your servant also from willful sins;
may they not rule over me.
Then will I be blameless,
innocent of great transgression.
14 May the words of my mouth and the meditation of my heart
be pleasing[y] in your sight,
O LORD, my Rock[z] and my Redeemer.[a]

19:9 [v]Ps 119:138, 142
19:10 [w]Pr 8:10
19:12 [x]Ps 51:2; 90:8; 139:6
19:14 [y]Ps 104:34 [z]Ps 18:2 [a]Isa 47:4

Psalm 20

For the director of music.
A psalm of David.

1 May the LORD answer you when you are in distress;
may the name of the God of Jacob[b] protect you.[c]
2 May he send you help from the sanctuary[d]
and grant you support from Zion.
3 May he remember[e] all your sacrifices
and accept your burnt offerings.[f]
Selah
4 May he give you the desire of your heart[g]
and make all your plans succeed.
5 We will shout for joy when you are victorious
and will lift up our banners[h] in the name of our God.
May the LORD grant all your requests.[i]

6 Now I know that the LORD saves his anointed;[j]
he answers him from his holy heaven
with the saving power of his right hand.
7 Some trust in chariots and some in horses,[k]
but we trust in the name of the LORD our God.[l]
8 They are brought to their knees and fall,
but we rise up[m] and stand firm.[n]

9 O LORD, save the king!
Answer[a] us[o] when we call!

20:1 [b]Ps 46:7,11 [c]Ps 91:14
20:2 [d]Ps 3:4
20:3 [e]Ac 10:4 [f]Ps 51:19
20:4 [g]Ps 21:2; 145:16,19
20:5 [h]Ps 9:14; 60:4 [i]1Sa 1:17
20:6 [j]Ps 28:8; 41:11; Isa 58:9
20:7 [k]Ps 33:17; Isa 31:1 [l]2Ch 32:8
20:8 [m]Mic 7:8 [n]Ps 37:23
20:9 [o]Ps 3:7; 17:6

Psalm 21

For the director of music.
A psalm of David.

1 O LORD, the king rejoices in your strength.
How great is his joy in the victories you give![p]
2 You have granted him the desire of his heart[q]
and have not withheld the request of his lips. *Selah*
3 You welcomed him with rich blessings
and placed a crown of pure gold[r] on his head.
4 He asked you for life, and you gave it to him—
length of days, for ever and ever.[s]
5 Through the victories[t] you gave, his glory is great;
you have bestowed on him splendor and majesty.
6 Surely you have granted him eternal blessings
and made him glad with the joy[u] of your presence.[v]
7 For the king trusts in the LORD;
through the unfailing love of the Most High
he will not be shaken.

8 Your hand will lay hold[w] on all your enemies;
your right hand will seize your foes.
9 At the time of your appearing
you will make them like a fiery furnace.
In his wrath the LORD will swallow them up,
and his fire will consume them.[x]
10 You will destroy their descendants from the earth,
their posterity from mankind.[y]
11 Though they plot evil[z] against you

21:1 [p]Ps 59:16-17
21:2 [q]Ps 37:4
21:3 [r]2Sa 12:30
21:4 [s]Ps 61:5-6; 91:16; 133:3
21:5 [t]Ps 18:50
21:6 [u]Ps 43:4 [v]1Ch 17:27
21:8 [w]Isa 10:10
21:9 [x]Ps 50:3; La 2:2; Mal 4:1
21:10 [y]Dt 28:18; Ps 37:28
21:11 [z]Ps 2:1

[a]9 Or *save! / O King, answer*

Jesus Speaks Out *on the Fruit of the Spirit:* Patience

Luke 8:15
The seed on good soil stands for those with a noble and good heart, who hear the word, retain it, and by persevering produce a crop.

Luke 21:19
By standing firm you will gain life.

Luke 6:21-23
"Blessed are you who hunger now,
for you will be satisfied.
Blessed are you who weep now,
for you will laugh.
Blessed are you when men hate you,
when they exclude you and insult you
and reject your name as evil,
because of the Son of Man.

Rejoice in that day and leap for joy, because great is your reward in heaven. For that is how their fathers treated the prophets."

Matthew 6:25
I tell you, do not worry about your life, what you will eat or drink; or about your body, what you will wear. Is not life more important than food, and the body more important than clothes?

Revelation 3:10
Since you have kept my command to endure patiently, I will also keep you from the hour of trial that is going to come upon the whole world to test those who live on the earth.

▸ The Unforgiving Steward

Therefore, the kingdom of heaven is like a king who wanted to settle accounts with his servants. As he began the settlement, a man who owed him ten thousand talents was brought to him. Since he was not able to pay, the master ordered that he and his wife and his children and all that he had be sold to repay the debt.

The servant fell on his knees before him. "Be patient with me," he begged, "and I will pay back everything." The servant's master took pity on him, canceled the debt and let him go.

But when that servant went out, he found one of his fellow servants who owed him a hundred denarii. He grabbed him and began to choke him. "Pay back what you owe me!" he demanded.

His fellow servant fell to his knees and begged him, "Be patient with me, and I will pay you back."

But he refused. Instead, he went off and had the man thrown into prison until he could pay the debt. When the other servants saw what had happened, they were greatly distressed and went and told their master everything that had happened.

Then the master called the servant in. "You wicked servant," he said, "I canceled all that debt of yours because you begged me to. Shouldn't you have had mercy on your fellow servant just as I had on you?" In anger his master turned him over to the jailers to be tortured, until he should pay back all he owed.

Matthew 18:23–35

Paul Speaks Out *on the Fruit of the Spirit:* Patience

Romans 9:22
What if God, choosing to show his wrath and make his power known, bore with great patience the objects of his wrath—prepared for destruction?

Romans 12:12
Be joyful in hope, patient in affliction, faithful in prayer.

Ephesians 4:2
Be completely humble and gentle; be patient, bearing with one another in love.

Colossians 1:11
[Be] strengthened with all power according to his glorious might so that you may have great endurance and patience.

Colossians 3:12
As God's chosen people, holy and dearly loved, clothe yourselves with compassion, kindness, humility, gentleness and patience.

1 Thessalonians 5:14
We urge you, brothers, warn those who are idle, encourage the timid, help the weak, be patient with everyone.

1 Timothy 1:16
But for that very reason I was shown mercy so that in me, the worst of sinners, Christ Jesus might display his unlimited patience as an example for those who would believe on him and receive eternal life.

Patience in All Things

I repeat: Let no one take me for a fool. But if you do, then receive me just as you would a fool, so that I may do a little boasting. In this self-confident boasting I am not talking as the Lord would, but as a fool. Since many are boasting in the way the world does, I too will boast. You gladly put up with fools since you are so wise! In fact, you even put up with anyone who enslaves you or exploits you or takes advantage of you or pushes himself forward or slaps you in the face. To my shame I admit that we were too weak for that!

What anyone else dares to boast about—I am speaking as a fool—I also dare to boast about. Are they Hebrews? So am I. Are they Israelites? So am I. Are they Abraham's descendants? So am I. Are they servants of Christ? (I am out of my mind to talk like this.) I am more. I have worked much harder, been in prison more frequently, been flogged more severely, and been exposed to death again and again. Five times I received from the Jews the forty lashes minus one. Three times I was beaten with rods, once I was stoned, three times I was shipwrecked, I spent a night and a day in the open sea, I have been constantly on the move. I have been in danger from rivers, in danger from bandits, in danger from my own countrymen, in danger from Gentiles; in danger in the city, in danger in the country, in danger at sea; and in danger from false brothers. I have labored and toiled and have often gone without sleep; I have known hunger and thirst and have often gone without food; I have been cold and naked. Besides everything else, I face daily the pressure of my concern for all the churches. Who is weak, and I do not feel weak? Who is led into sin, and I do not inwardly burn?

If I must boast, I will boast of the things that show my weakness. The God and Father of the Lord Jesus, who is to be praised forever, knows that I am not lying.

2 Corinthians 11:16–31

21:11 [a]Ps 10:2 and devise wicked schemes,[a] they
cannot succeed;
12 for you will make them turn their
21:12 [b]Ps 7:12-13; 18:40 backs[b]
when you aim at them with drawn
bow.
13 Be exalted, O LORD, in your
strength;
we will sing and praise your
might.

Psalm 22

For the director of music. To ⌞the tune
of⌟ "The Doe of the Morning."
A psalm of David.

22:1 [c]Mt 27:46*; Mk 15:34* [d]Ps 10:1 1 My God, my God, why have you
forsaken me?[c]
Why are you so far[d] from saving
me,
so far from the words of my
groaning?

KINDNESS

THE ABSENTEE LOVER

Psalm 22:1

Have you not known the pain of private crucifixion? Have you not sometime felt that God was absent at your point of need? Wait awhile. Lift your eyes. He is always there. Beyond the suffering, his promises still live.

2 O my God, I cry out by day, but you
do not answer,
22:2 [e]Ps 42:3 by night,[e] and am not silent.
3 Yet you are enthroned as the Holy
22:3 [f]Ps 99:9 One;[f]
[g]Dt 10:21 you are the praise[g] of Israel.[a]
4 In you our fathers put their trust;
they trusted and you delivered
them.
5 They cried to you and were saved;
22:5 in you they trusted and were not
[h]Isa 49:23 disappointed.[h]
6 But I am a worm[i] and not a man,
22:6 [i]Job 25:6; Isa 41:14 scorned by men[j] and despised[k] by
[j]Ps 31:11 the people.
[k]Isa 49:7; 53:3 7 All who see me mock me;
22:7 [l]Mt 27:39,44 they hurl insults,[l] shaking their
[m]Mk 15:29 heads:[m]
8 "He trusts in the LORD;
22:8 let the LORD rescue him.[n]
[n]Ps 91:14 Let him deliver him,
[o]Mt 27:43 since he delights[o] in him."

DAY THREE

LOVE AND MY RELATIONSHIP WITH CHRIST

Psalm 22:1–5

This is the psalm Christ quotes as one of the last words spoken on the cross. Theologians largely agree that Jesus cried the words, "My God, my God, why have you forsaken me?" (Matthew 27:46) because of a great divorce between God and his Son. God in his holiness could not bear to look on his Son who bore the hideous and grotesque sins of humankind. God is holy and cannot gaze upon the kind of universal sin Jesus had to carry to save us.

Jesus quoted this psalm, and sometimes when we are in despair, we paraphrase a different line, "I cry out... but you do not answer." Isn't this our frequent response in life when we face a crisis? We groan our pleas, and it sometimes seems as though our words slide into an abyss. And God—who, in our better times, we say is love—seems to ignore us.

I try to remember during these times when it seems God is silent, that the promise of Scripture is that the Holy Spirit is answering our groaning needs not from beyond us but from within us (see Romans 8:26). God is never really silent; he is in constant concourse with our pain. Our tears are so precious to him that he cries out from within us, constantly making intercession for our sin.

There may be moments when we feel an unresponsive silence from God. But we know that Jesus, who also lived as a human, experienced the same discouragement and sorrow. We know that he cried out to God, pleading for a response, just as we do. Isn't Jesus the ultimate picture of love? He came to earth to suffer for us. He came to earth to save us. The next time we feel abandoned by God, we can look to Jesus and know that he felt the same sorrows that we do. But we can also look to Jesus and know that God is love and will never leave us. God gave us his Son to seal that promise.

To begin a study on the topic of Love, the Definition of God, turn to the home page on page 1033.

[a]3 Or *Yet you are holy, / enthroned on the praises of Israel*

22:9 [p]Ps 71:6
9 Yet you brought me out of the womb;[p]
you made me trust in you
even at my mother's breast.
22:10 [q]Isa 46:3
10 From birth[q] I was cast upon you;
from my mother's womb you have been my God.
11 Do not be far from me,
22:11 [r]Ps 72:12
for trouble is near
and there is no one to help.[r]
22:12 [s]Ps 68:30 [t]Dt 32:14
12 Many bulls[s] surround me;
strong bulls of Bashan[t] encircle me.
22:13 [u]Ps 17:12 [v]Ps 35:21
13 Roaring lions[u] tearing their prey
open their mouths wide[v] against me.
14 I am poured out like water,
22:14 [w]Ps 31:10 [x]Job 30:16; Da 5:6
and all my bones are out of joint.[w]
My heart has turned to wax;
it has melted away[x] within me.
15 My strength is dried up like a potsherd,
22:15 [y]Ps 38:10; Jn 19:28 [z]Ps 104:29
and my tongue sticks to the roof of my mouth;[y]
you lay me[a] in the dust[z] of death.
22:16 [a]Ps 59:6 [b]Isa 53:5; Zec 12:10; Jn 19:34
16 Dogs[a] have surrounded me;
a band of evil men has encircled me,
they have pierced[b][b] my hands and my feet.
17 I can count all my bones;
22:17 [c]Lk 23:35 [d]Lk 23:27
people stare[c] and gloat over me.[d]
18 They divide my garments among them
22:18 [e]Mt 27:35*; Lk 23:34; Jn 19:24*
and cast lots[e] for my clothing.
19 But you, O LORD, be not far off;
22:19 [f]Ps 70:5
O my Strength, come quickly[f] to help me.
22:20 [g]Ps 35:17
20 Deliver my life[g] from the sword,
my precious life from the power of the dogs.
21 Rescue me from the mouth of the lions;
save[c] me from the horns of the wild oxen.

22 I will declare your name to my brothers;
in the congregation I will praise you.[h] 22:22 [h]Heb 2:12*
23 You who fear the LORD, praise him![i] 22:23 [i]Ps 86:12; 135:19 [j]Ps 33:8
All you descendants of Jacob, honor him!
Revere him,[j] all you descendants of Israel!
24 For he has not despised or disdained
the suffering of the afflicted one; 22:24 [k]Ps 69:17 [l]Heb 5:7
he has not hidden his face[k] from him
but has listened to his cry for help.[l]

25 From you comes the theme of my praise in the great assembly;[m] 22:25 [m]Ps 35:18 [n]Ecc 5:4
before those who fear you[d] will I fulfill my vows.[n]
26 The poor will eat[o] and be satisfied; 22:26 [o]Ps 107:9 [p]Ps 40:16
they who seek the LORD will praise him—[p]
may your hearts live forever!
27 All the ends of the earth[q] 22:27 [q]Ps 2:8 [r]Ps 86:9
will remember and turn to the LORD,
and all the families of the nations
will bow down before him,[r]
28 for dominion belongs to the LORD[s] 22:28 [s]Ps 47:7-8
and he rules over the nations.
29 All the rich[t] of the earth will feast and worship; 22:29 [t]Ps 45:12 [u]Isa 26:19
all who go down to the dust[u] will kneel before him—
those who cannot keep themselves alive.
30 Posterity[v] will serve him; 22:30 [v]Ps 102:28
future generations will be told about the Lord.
31 They will proclaim his righteousness 22:31 [w]Ps 78:6
to a people yet unborn[w]—
for he has done it.

Psalm 23

A psalm of David.

1 The LORD is my shepherd,[x] I shall not be in want.[y] 23:1 [x]Isa 40:11; Jn 10:11; 1Pe 2:25 [y]Php 4:19
2 He makes me lie down in green pastures, 23:2 [z]Eze 34:14; Rev 7:17
he leads me beside quiet waters,[z]

[a]*15* Or / *I am laid* [b]*16* Some Hebrew manuscripts, Septuagint and Syriac; most Hebrew manuscripts / *like the lion,* [c]*21* Or / *you have heard* [d]*25* Hebrew *him*

PEACE

GARMENT GAMBLING

Psalm 22:18

Jesus died above those gamers who, unwilling to split his seamless robe, diced for the prize. Yet even while they gambled, the issue of their salvation was settled on the wood above them. There are better garments than what they won. The God of grace will someday clothe us in the final uniform of Christ's apocalypse.

GOODNESS

THE GOOD SHEPHERD

Psalm 23:1

Jesus is the shepherd. It is his sheep who use the word *good* to describe their shepherd. Those who will not be his sheep squander the word by using it in lesser ways.

23:3 [a]Ps 19:7 [b]Ps 5:8; 85:13

3 he restores my soul.[a]
He guides me in paths of
righteousness[b]
for his name's sake.
4 Even though I walk
through the valley of the shadow
of death,[a c]
I will fear no evil,[d]
for you are with me;[e]
your rod and your staff,
they comfort me.

23:4 [c]Job 10:21-22 [d]Ps 3:6; 27:1 [e]Isa 43:2

5 You prepare a table before me
in the presence of my enemies.
You anoint my head with oil;[f]
my cup[g] overflows.
6 Surely goodness and love will follow
me
all the days of my life,
and I will dwell in the house of the
LORD
forever.

23:5 [f]Ps 92:10 [g]Ps 16:5

Psalm 24

Of David. A psalm.

1 The earth is the LORD's,[b] and
everything in it,

24:1 [b]Ex 9:29; Job 41:11; Ps 89:11

[a]4 Or *through the darkest valley*

DAVID

Joy, the Force in the Psalmist's Heart (23:1–6)

Whenever we think of David, we see in our minds a man as diverse as the world itself. He was a giant-killer, king, adulterer and warrior. He was capable of honor and capable of crime. He sang to God's glory and offended God's holiness. But David's highest office was an office of joy. He was a singer of songs, and we hold his songs, far more than his weaknesses, in our hearts. David sang with joy, praising God through all his psalms.

He sang to God when he needed provision and care: "The LORD is my shepherd" (Psalm 23:1).

He sang to God when he needed protection: "But you are a shield around me, O LORD" (3:3).

He sang to God when he saw God's brilliant display through all of nature: "The heavens declare the glory of God" (19:1).

He sang to God when he was insecure: "Trust in the LORD and do good" (37:3).

He sang to God when he was in trouble: "He lifted me out of the slimy pit, out of the mud and mire" (40:2).

He sang to God when he felt the Lord's rebuke for his own sin: "Have mercy on me, O God, according to your unfailing love; according to your great compassion blot out my transgressions" (51:1).

Ironically, he also sang to God when he was in need of joy: "Restore to me the joy of your salvation and grant me a willing spirit, to sustain me" (51:12).

David was a man of joy, and nothing else awakens liberty of the soul like praise. Joy is that rare force in the human heart that creates lightness of being. It places within us a wonderful spirit of triumph. It is the antidote to all despair. It causes us to abandon our questioning of the mysteries of God's power. Through joy we gain a nearness to God that makes life worthwhile. Those who cannot praise become so sullied by the grime of living that they cannot see God. David sang and was free. His joy brings liberation to our souls every time we pick up the Psalms.

The Psalms sing us into the conviction that we are, in fact, worthwhile. They lift our heavy souls, restore our amputated wings and allow us to fly. Soaring over our sin and trials, we can see all things in perspective, and we realize that the size of our troubles is not as large as we had supposed.

24:1 [i]1Co 10:26*
24:3 [j]Ps 2:6

the world, and all who live in it;[i]
2 for he founded it upon the seas
and established it upon the waters.
3 Who may ascend the hill[j] of the LORD?

DAY 5 FIVE

▸ GOODNESS AND ITS PLACE IN MY PERSONAL WORSHIP

Psalm 24:3–6

Who shall enter into the presence of the Lord? The psalmist suggests that it is time for worship-readiness inspection.

Look at your hands: Are they clean? Have you taken a bribe or struck out at a fellow human being in physical anger? Have your hands been mucking about in side deals that have profited you and hurt someone else? Have your hands touched things forbidden or shaken other hands in political side deals that hurt others but put you in office?

Look at your heart: Is it pure? Here in the center of your life where you have raised a throne to God is there some new motive that hides truth from your family, your church friends or the IRS? What devious morality or inner flirtations with Satan have you permitted to live in your heart—the very throne room of his lordship over your once holy life?

Look at your soul: Has it trafficked with idols? Has it admired the material world or set its heart on affections that God could not honor?

All in all, goodness is the inspector that examines our worship. When goodness approves of the state of our hands, heart and soul, we are ready to enter into worship. We should make sure of this. It is important to get ready to worship. In worship we enter into audience with a holy God. If we were to be invited to a private audience with a queen, would we not spend infinite time preparing ourselves to meet her?

By contrast how shoddily—how thoughtlessly—do we run into the presence of God. Let us slow down and prepare ourselves for worship. Are our hands clean? Are our hearts pure? Are our souls free of all idolatries?

To begin a study on the topic of Goodness and the Desire for Holiness, turn to the home page on page 790.

Who may stand in his holy place?[k]
4 He who has clean hands[l] and a pure heart,[m]
who does not lift up his soul to an idol
or swear by what is false.[a]
5 He will receive blessing from the LORD
and vindication from God his Savior.
6 Such is the generation of those who seek him,
who seek your face,[n] O God of Jacob.[b] *Selah*
7 Lift up your heads, O you gates;[o]
be lifted up, you ancient doors,
that the King of glory[p] may come in.
8 Who is this King of glory?
The LORD strong and mighty,
the LORD mighty in battle.[q]
9 Lift up your heads, O you gates;
lift them up, you ancient doors,
that the King of glory may come in.
10 Who is he, this King of glory?
The LORD Almighty—
he is the King of glory. *Selah*

24:3 [k]Ps 15:1; 65:4
24:4 [l]Job 17:9 [m]Mt 5:8
24:6 [n]Ps 27:8
24:7 [o]Isa 26:2 [p]Ps 97:6; 1Co 2:8
24:8 [q]Ps 76:3-6

Psalm 25[c]

Of David.

1 To you, O LORD, I lift up my soul;[r]
2 in you I trust,[s] O my God.
Do not let me be put to shame,
nor let my enemies triumph over me.
3 No one whose hope is in you
will ever be put to shame,[t]
but they will be put to shame
who are treacherous without excuse.

4 Show me your ways, O LORD,
teach me your paths;[u]
5 guide me in your truth and teach me,
for you are God my Savior,
and my hope is in you all day long.

25:1 [r]Ps 86:4
25:2 [s]Ps 41:11
25:3 [t]Isa 49:23
25:4 [u]Ex 33:13

[a]4 Or *swear falsely* [b]6 Two Hebrew manuscripts and Syriac (see also Septuagint); most Hebrew manuscripts *face, Jacob* [c]This psalm is an acrostic poem, the verses of which begin with the successive letters of the Hebrew alphabet.

25:6 [v]Ps 103:17; Isa 63:7,15

6 Remember, O LORD, your great mercy and love,[v]
for they are from of old.

25:7 [w]Job 13:26; Jer 3:25 [x]Ps 51:1

7 Remember not the sins of my youth[w]
and my rebellious ways;
according to your love[x] remember me,
for you are good, O LORD.

25:8 [y]Ps 92:15 [z]Ps 32:8

8 Good and upright[y] is the LORD;
therefore he instructs[z] sinners in his ways.

25:9 [a]Ps 23:3 [b]Ps 27:11

9 He guides[a] the humble in what is right
and teaches them[b] his way.

25:10 [c]Ps 40:11 [d]Ps 103:18

10 All the ways of the LORD are loving and faithful[c]
for those who keep the demands of his covenant.[d]

25:11 [e]Ps 31:3; 79:9

11 For the sake of your name,[e] O LORD,
forgive my iniquity, though it is great.

12 Who, then, is the man that fears the LORD?

25:12 [f]Ps 37:23

He will instruct him in the way[f] chosen for him.

25:13 [g]Pr 19:23 [h]Ps 37:11

13 He will spend his days in prosperity,[g]
and his descendants will inherit the land.[h]

25:14 [i]Pr 3:32 [j]Jn 7:17

14 The LORD confides[i] in those who fear him;
he makes his covenant known[j] to them.

25:15 [k]Ps 141:8

15 My eyes are ever on the LORD,[k]
for only he will release my feet from the snare.

25:16 [l]Ps 69:16

16 Turn to me[l] and be gracious to me,
for I am lonely and afflicted.
17 The troubles of my heart have multiplied;

25:17 [m]Ps 107:6

free me from my anguish.[m]

25:18 [n]2Sa 16:12

18 Look upon my affliction and my distress[n]
and take away all my sins.

25:19 [o]Ps 3:1

19 See how my enemies[o] have increased
and how fiercely they hate me!

25:20 [p]Ps 86:2

20 Guard my life[p] and rescue me;
let me not be put to shame,
for I take refuge in you.

25:21 [q]Ps 41:12

21 May integrity[q] and uprightness protect me,
because my hope is in you.

25:22 [r]Ps 130:8

22 Redeem Israel,[r] O God,
from all their troubles!

Psalm 26

Of David.

1 Vindicate me, O LORD,
for I have led a blameless life;[s]
I have trusted[t] in the LORD
without wavering.[u]
2 Test me,[v] O LORD, and try me,
examine my heart and my mind;[w]
3 for your love is ever before me,
and I walk continually[x] in your truth.
4 I do not sit[y] with deceitful men,
nor do I consort with hypocrites;
5 I abhor[z] the assembly of evildoers
and refuse to sit with the wicked.
6 I wash my hands in innocence,[a]
and go about your altar, O LORD,
7 proclaiming aloud your praise
and telling of all your wonderful deeds.[b]
8 I love[c] the house where you live, O LORD,
the place where your glory dwells.
9 Do not take away my soul along with sinners,
my life with bloodthirsty men,[d]
10 in whose hands are wicked schemes,
whose right hands are full of bribes.[e]
11 But I lead a blameless life;
redeem me[f] and be merciful to me.

12 My feet stand on level ground;[g]
in the great assembly[h] I will praise the LORD.

26:1 [s]Ps 7:8; Pr 20:7 [t]Ps 28:7 [u]2Ki 20:3; Heb 10:23
26:2 [v]Ps 17:3 [w]Ps 7:9
26:3 [x]2Ki 20:3
26:4 [y]Ps 1:1
26:5 [z]Ps 31:6; 139:21
26:6 [a]Ps 73:13
26:7 [b]Ps 9:1
26:8 [c]Ps 27:4
26:9 [d]Ps 28:3
26:10 [e]1Sa 8:3
26:11 [f]Ps 69:18
26:12 [g]Ps 27:11; 40:2 [h]Ps 22:22

LOVE

LEVEL GROUND

Psalm 26:12

Did Jesus die upon a hill? For those who understand the real topography of faith, where the cross stands, the ground is level. Here there are no Jews or Gentiles, no slaves or free, no ethnic specialties, no gender favorites. Here, on this level ground, there are only sinners who have seen their neediness in the light of the cross.

Psalm 27

Of David.

1 The LORD is my light[i] and my salvation[j]—

27:1 [i]Isa 60:19 [j]Ex 15:2

PEACE

LIGHT AND SALVATION

Psalm 27:1

The Lord is my light—a light bright enough to lead me through the darkest thickets of my sin. The Lord is my salvation—salvation thorough enough to save me beyond every possibility of being lost.

whom shall I fear?
The LORD is the stronghold of my life—
of whom shall I be afraid?[k]
2 When evil men advance against me
to devour my flesh,[a]
when my enemies and my foes
attack me,
they will stumble and fall.[l]
3 Though an army besiege me,
my heart will not fear;[m]
though war break out against me,
even then will I be confident.[n]
4 One thing[o] I ask of the LORD,
this is what I seek:
that I may dwell in the house of the LORD
all the days of my life,[p]
to gaze upon the beauty of the LORD
and to seek him in his temple.
5 For in the day of trouble
he will keep me safe in his dwelling;
he will hide me[q] in the shelter of his tabernacle
and set me high upon a rock.[r]
6 Then my head will be exalted[s]
above the enemies who surround me;
at his tabernacle will I sacrifice[t] with shouts of joy;
I will sing and make music to the LORD.
7 Hear my voice when I call, O LORD;
be merciful to me and answer me.[u]
8 My heart says of you, "Seek his[b] face!"
Your face, LORD, I will seek.
9 Do not hide your face[v] from me,
do not turn your servant away in anger;
you have been my helper.
Do not reject me or forsake me,
O God my Savior.
10 Though my father and mother forsake me,
the LORD will receive me.
11 Teach me your way, O LORD;
lead me in a straight path[w]
because of my oppressors.
12 Do not turn me over to the desire of my foes,
for false witnesses[x] rise up against me,
breathing out violence.
13 I am still confident of this:
I will see the goodness of the LORD[y]
in the land of the living.[z]
14 Wait[a] for the LORD;
be strong and take heart
and wait for the LORD.

27:1 [k]Ps 118:6
27:2 [l]Ps 9:3; 14:4
27:3 [m]Ps 3:6 [n]Job 4:6
27:4 [o]Ps 90:17 [p]Ps 23:6; 26:8
27:5 [q]Ps 17:8; 31:20 [r]Ps 40:2
27:6 [s]Ps 3:3 [t]Ps 107:22
27:7 [u]Ps 13:3
27:9 [v]Ps 69:17
27:11 [w]Ps 5:8; 25:4; 86:11
27:12 [x]Mt 26:60; Ac 9:1
27:13 [y]Ps 31:19 [z]Jer 11:19; Eze 26:20
27:14 [a]Ps 40:1

Psalm 28

Of David.

1 To you I call, O LORD my Rock;
do not turn a deaf ear to me.
For if you remain silent,[b]
I will be like those who have gone down to the pit.[c]
2 Hear my cry for mercy[d]
as I call to you for help,
as I lift up my hands
toward your Most Holy Place.[e]
3 Do not drag me away with the wicked,
with those who do evil,
who speak cordially with their neighbors
but harbor malice in their hearts.[f]
4 Repay them for their deeds
and for their evil work;
repay them for what their hands have done[g]
and bring back upon them what they deserve.[h]
5 Since they show no regard for the works of the LORD
and what his hands have done,[i]
he will tear them down
and never build them up again.
6 Praise be to the LORD,
for he has heard my cry for mercy.
7 The LORD is my strength[j] and my shield;

28:1 [b]Ps 83:1 [c]Ps 88:4
28:2 [d]Ps 138:2; 140:6 [e]Ps 5:7
28:3 [f]Ps 12:2; Ps 26:9; Jer 9:8
28:4 [g]2Ti 4:14; Rev 22:12 [h]Rev 18:6
28:5 [i]Isa 5:12
28:7 [j]Ps 18:1

[a]2 Or *to slander me* [b]8 Or *To you, O my heart, he has said, "Seek my*

28:7 [k]Ps 13:5 [l]Ps 40:3; 69:30

my heart trusts[k] in him, and I am helped.
My heart leaps for joy
and I will give thanks to him in song.[l]

28:8 [m]Ps 20:6

8 The LORD is the strength of his people,
a fortress of salvation for his anointed one.[m]

28:9 [n]Dt 9:29; Ezr 1:4 [o]Isa 40:11 [p]Dt 1:31; 32:11

9 Save your people and bless your inheritance;[n]
be their shepherd[o] and carry them[p] forever.

Psalm 29

A psalm of David.

29:1 [q]1Ch 16:28 [r]Ps 96:7-9

1 Ascribe to the LORD,[q] O mighty ones,
ascribe to the LORD glory[r] and strength.
2 Ascribe to the LORD the glory due his name;
worship the LORD in the splendor of his[a] holiness.[s]

29:2 [s]2Ch 20:21

29:3 [t]Job 37:5 [u]Ps 18:13

3 The voice[t] of the LORD is over the waters;
the God of glory thunders,[u]
the LORD thunders over the mighty waters.

29:4 [v]Ps 68:33

4 The voice of the LORD is powerful;[v]
the voice of the LORD is majestic.
5 The voice of the LORD breaks the cedars;
the LORD breaks in pieces the cedars of Lebanon.[w]

29:5 [w]Jdg 9:15

29:6 [x]Ps 114:4 [y]Dt 3:9

6 He makes Lebanon skip[x] like a calf,
Sirion[b][y] like a young wild ox.
7 The voice of the LORD strikes
with flashes of lightning.
8 The voice of the LORD shakes the desert;
the LORD shakes the Desert of Kadesh.[z]

29:8 [z]Nu 13:26

9 The voice of the LORD twists the oaks[c]
and strips the forests bare.
And in his temple all cry, "Glory!"[a]

29:9 [a]Ps 26:8

10 The LORD sits[d] enthroned over the flood;[b]
the LORD is enthroned as King forever.[c]

29:10 [b]Ge 6:17 [c]Ps 10:16

11 The LORD gives strength to his people;[d]
the LORD blesses his people with peace.[e]

29:11 [d]Ps 28:8 [e]Ps 37:11

DAY 3 THREE

▸ JOY AND MY RELATIONSHIP WITH CHRIST

Psalm 30:4

Perhaps the place to begin our Bible study is to ask this question: "When the word *Jesus* comes to your mind, does a smile dominate your consciousness?" Your relationship with Christ should be such a pleasant affair that merely to think of his name tends to kick your emotional outlook up a notch or two.

The psalmist tells us to "Sing to the LORD." When we think on the great gifts God has given us in Jesus, we should break out in songs and hymns. Jesus brings joy. Do we not affirm this each time we sing,

There is a Name I love to hear,
I love to sing its worth;
It sounds like music in my ear,
The sweetest Name on earth.

It is his name that stirs our best joy.

One day on an airplane, I watched a flight attendant as she served her none-too-gracious public. She never seemed to run into any emotional snags. She had a sparkle—so effervescent it was hard not to be impressed with her joy. Finally, I took a chance and said, "I'll bet you know Jesus, don't you?" At that, her already happy face broke into an uncontainably joyous smile.

"Is it that obvious?" she asked.

When I told her that it was, she seemed extraordinarily delighted.

To but think of Christ produces such joy in most of us, for his name suggests all the wonderful paths our common pilgrimage has traversed. To hear his name suggests all that he has meant to us. Jesus and a sour spirit rarely live long together in our lives. When either one is dominant, the other has no chance at dwelling in us.

To begin a study on the topic of Joy, a Positive Attitude, turn to the home page on page 358.

[a]2 Or *LORD with the splendor of* [b]6 That is, Mount Hermon [c]9 Or *LORD makes the deer give birth* [d]*10* Or *sat*

Psalm 30

A psalm. A song. For the dedication of the temple.[a] Of David.

1 I will exalt you, O LORD,
for you lifted me out of the depths
and did not let my enemies gloat
30:1 [f]Ps 25:2; 28:9 over me.[f]
30:2 [g]Ps 88:13 [h]Ps 6:2 2 O LORD my God, I called to you
for help[g]
and you healed me.[h]
3 O LORD, you brought me up from
the grave[b];
you spared me from going down
30:3 [i]Ps 28:1; 86:13 into the pit.[i]
4 Sing to the LORD, you saints[j] of his;
30:4 [j]Ps 149:1 [k]Ps 97:12 praise his holy name.[k]
5 For his anger[l] lasts only a moment,
30:5 [l]Ps 103:9 [m]2Co 4:17 but his favor lasts a lifetime;
weeping may remain for a night,
but rejoicing comes in the
morning.[m]
6 When I felt secure, I said,
"I will never be shaken."
7 O LORD, when you favored me,
you made my mountain[c] stand
firm;
30:7 [n]Dt 31:17; Ps 104:29 but when you hid your face,[n]
I was dismayed.
8 To you, O LORD, I called;
to the Lord I cried for mercy:
9 "What gain is there in my
destruction,[d]
in my going down into the pit?
Will the dust praise you?
Will it proclaim your
30:9 [o]Ps 6:5 faithfulness?[o]
10 Hear, O LORD, and be merciful to
me;
O LORD, be my help."
11 You turned my wailing into dancing;
you removed my sackcloth and
30:11 [p]Ps 4:7; Jer 31:4,13 clothed me with joy,[p]
12 that my heart may sing to you and
not be silent.
30:12 [q]Ps 16:9 [r]Ps 44:8 O LORD my God, I will give you
thanks[q] forever.[r]

Psalm 31

For the director of music.
A psalm of David.

1 In you, O LORD, I have taken
refuge;
let me never be put to shame;
deliver me in your righteousness.
2 Turn your ear to me,
come quickly to my rescue;
be my rock of refuge,[s] 31:2 [s]Ps 18:2
a strong fortress to save me.
3 Since you are my rock and my
fortress,[t] 31:3 [t]Ps 18:2 [u]Ps 23:3
for the sake of your name[u] lead
and guide me.
4 Free me from the trap that is set for
me,
for you are my refuge.[v] 31:4 [v]Ps 25:15
5 Into your hands I commit my
spirit;[w] 31:5 [w]Lk 23:46; Ac 7:59
redeem me, O LORD, the God of
truth.

6 I hate those who cling to worthless
idols;
I trust in the LORD.[x] 31:6 [x]Jnh 2:8
7 I will be glad and rejoice in your
love,
for you saw my affliction[y] 31:7 [y]Ps 90:14
and knew the anguish[z] of my soul. [z]Ps 10:14; Jn 10:27
8 You have not handed me over[a] to the
enemy 31:8 [a]Dt 32:30
but have set my feet in a spacious
place.
9 Be merciful to me, O LORD, for I
am in distress;
my eyes grow weak with sorrow,[b] 31:9 [b]Ps 6:7
my soul and my body with grief.
10 My life is consumed by anguish
and my years by groaning;[c] 31:10 [c]Ps 13:2 [d]Ps 38:3; 39:11
my strength fails because of my
affliction,[e]
and my bones grow weak.[d]
11 Because of all my enemies,
I am the utter contempt of my
neighbors;[e] 31:11 [e]Job 19:13; Ps 38:11; 64:8; Isa 53:4
I am a dread to my friends—
those who see me on the street flee
from me.
12 I am forgotten by them as though I
were dead;[f] 31:12 [f]Ps 88:4
I have become like broken pottery.
13 For I hear the slander of many;
there is terror on every side;[g] 31:13 [g]Jer 20:3,10; La 2:22 [h]Mt 27:1
they conspire against me
and plot to take my life.[h]

14 But I trust[i] in you, O LORD; 31:14 [i]Ps 140:6
I say, "You are my God."
15 My times[j] are in your hands; 31:15 [j]Job 24:1; Ps 143:9
deliver me from my enemies
and from those who pursue me.
16 Let your face shine[k] on your servant; 31:16 [k]Nu 6:25; Ps 4:6

[a] Title: Or *palace* [b] 3 Hebrew *Sheol* [c] 7 Or *hill country* [d] 9 Or *there if I am silenced* [e] 10 Or *guilt*

save me in your unfailing love.
31:17 [l]Ps 25:2-3 [m]Ps 115:17
17 Let me not be put to shame,[l]
O LORD,
for I have cried out to you;
but let the wicked be put to shame
31:18 [n]Ps 120:2 [o]Ps 94:4
and lie silent[m] in the grave.[a]
18 Let their lying lips[n] be silenced,
for with pride and contempt
they speak arrogantly[o] against the
righteous.

31:19 [p]Ro 11:22 [q]Isa 64:4
19 How great is your goodness,[p]
which you have stored up for
those who fear you,
which you bestow in the sight of
men[q]
on those who take refuge in you.
31:20 [r]Ps 27:5 [s]Job 5:21
20 In the shelter of your presence you
hide[r] them
from the intrigues of men;[s]
31:21 [t]Ps 17:7 [u]1Sa 23:7
in your dwelling you keep them safe
from accusing tongues.

21 Praise be to the LORD,
for he showed his wonderful love[t]
to me
when I was in a besieged city.[u]
31:22 [v]Ps 116:11 [w]La 3:54
22 In my alarm[v] I said,
"I am cut off from your sight!"
Yet you heard my cry[w] for mercy
when I called to you for help.

31:23 [x]Ps 34:9 [y]Ps 145:20 [z]Ps 94:2
23 Love the LORD, all his saints![x]
The LORD preserves the faithful,[y]
but the proud he pays back[z] in full.
31:24 [a]Ps 27:14
24 Be strong and take heart,[a]
all you who hope in the LORD.

Psalm 32

Of David. A *maskil*.[b]

1 Blessed is he
whose transgressions are forgiven,
32:1 [b]Ps 85:2
whose sins are covered.[b]
32:2 [c]Ro 4:7-8*; 2Co 5:19 [d]Jn 1:47
2 Blessed is the man
whose sin the LORD does not
count against him[c]
and in whose spirit is no deceit.[d]

[a]17 Hebrew *Sheol* [b]Title: Probably a literary or musical term

SELF-CONTROL

BLESSED IS THE FORGIVEN; BLESSED IS THE FORGIVER

Psalm 32:1

Are you free?
I am not.
What bonds have fettered you?
None but the ones I forged by tasting everything that pleased me.
Come then, discipline your appetites with self-control.
Touch Jesus and live free.

DAY 5 FIVE

LOVE AND ITS PLACE IN MY PERSONAL WORSHIP

Psalm 32:1–2

"Blessed is the man whose sin the LORD does not count against him," reckons the poet. How true! A forgiven soul may enter into the presence of God unobstructed. He may meet God, not just as forgiven, but as clean. *Clean* is a more human synonym for *holy*. God is holy and incapable of sin. He is not only incapable of sin; he is too holy even to look on it. But his instant forgiveness of our sins makes it possible for us to approach him freely in our worship. Thus God's forgiveness of us makes possible our fellowship with him, and this is worship: face-to-face fellowship with God.

Worship is loving God, but sin is an impediment to our loving. While we languish under what we will not confess, the only bridge between our Father and ourselves is barricaded. Sin stiff-arms our approach to God. We can never embrace God while we hold him at arms' length. God's forgiveness gives us elbows; our arms can bend. They can fold around our heavenly Father.

A child who has disobeyed her earthly father will be reluctant to come into his presence. She knows that she has wronged him, and while she wishes she might feel his embrace and sleep against his chest, she also knows that there is an estrangement between the two of them that cannot be bridged until she receives his forgiveness. Still, she must ask for it. There lies before such a child the sheepish work of approaching her father and confessing. But after the honesty comes the embrace. What power can work such transformation? Grace! All has been removed that was formerly in the way of honest fellowship and love.

To begin a study on the topic of Love Forgives, turn to the home page on page 1227.

[3]When I kept silent,
32:3 [e]Ps 31:10
my bones wasted away[e]
through my groaning all day long.
[4]For day and night
32:4 [f]Job 33:7
your hand was heavy[f] upon me;
my strength was sapped
as in the heat of summer. *Selah*
[5]Then I acknowledged my sin to you
and did not cover up my iniquity.
32:5 [g]Pr 28:13 [h]Ps 103:12 [i]Lev 26:40
I said, "I will confess[g]
my transgressions[h] to the
LORD"—
and you forgave
the guilt of my sin.[i] *Selah*

[6]Therefore let everyone who is godly
pray to you
32:6 [j]Ps 69:13; Isa 55:6 [k]Isa 43:2
while you may be found;[j]
surely when the mighty waters rise,
they will not reach him.[k]
[7]You are my hiding place;
you will protect me from trouble[l]
32:7 [l]Ps 9:9 [m]Ex 15:1
and surround me with songs of
deliverance.[m] *Selah*

32:8 [n]Ps 25:8 [o]Ps 33:18
[8]I will instruct[n] you and teach you in
the way you should go;
I will counsel you and watch over[o]
you.
[9]Do not be like the horse or the
mule,
which have no understanding
but must be controlled by bit and
32:9 [p]Pr 26:3
bridle[p]
or they will not come to you.
32:10 [q]Ro 2:9 [r]Pr 16:20
[10]Many are the woes of the wicked,[q]
but the LORD's unfailing love
surrounds the man who trusts[r] in
him.
32:11 [s]Ps 64:10
[11]Rejoice in the LORD[s] and be glad,
you righteous;
sing, all you who are upright in
heart!

Psalm 33

[1]Sing joyfully to the LORD, you
righteous;
33:1 [t]Ps 147:1 [u]Ps 32:11
it is fitting[t] for the upright[u] to
praise him.
[2]Praise the LORD with the harp;
make music to him on the
33:2 [v]Ps 92:3
ten-stringed lyre.[v]
33:3 [w]Ps 96:1
[3]Sing to him a new song;[w]
play skillfully, and shout for joy.

33:4 [x]Ps 19:8
[4]For the word of the LORD is right[x]
and true;
he is faithful in all he does.
[5]The LORD loves righteousness and
33:5 [y]Ps 11:7 [z]Ps 119:64
justice;[y]
the earth is full of his unfailing
love.[z]

33:6 [a]Heb 11:3
[6]By the word[a] of the LORD were the
heavens made,
their starry host by the breath of
his mouth.
[7]He gathers the waters of the sea into
jars[a];
he puts the deep into storehouses.
[8]Let all the earth fear the LORD;
33:8 [b]Ps 67:7; 96:9
let all the people of the world
revere him.[b]
33:9 [c]Ge 1:3; Ps 148:5
[9]For he spoke, and it came to be;
he commanded,[c] and it stood
firm.
33:10 [d]Isa 8:10
[10]The LORD foils the plans of the
nations;[d]
he thwarts the purposes of the
peoples.
[11]But the plans of the LORD stand
firm forever,
33:11 [e]Job 23:13
the purposes[e] of his heart through
all generations.
[12]Blessed is the nation whose God is
33:12 [f]Ps 144:15 [g]Ex 19:5; Dt 7:6
the LORD,[f]
the people he chose[g] for his
inheritance.
33:13 [h]Job 28:24; Ps 11:4
[13]From heaven the LORD looks down
and sees all mankind;[h]
[14]from his dwelling place[i] he watches
33:14 [i]1Ki 8:39
all who live on earth—
33:15 [j]Job 10:8 [k]Jer 32:19
[15]he who forms[j] the hearts of all,
who considers everything they
do.[k]
[16]No king is saved by the size of his
33:16 [l]Ps 44:6
army;[l]
no warrior escapes by his great
strength.
33:17 [m]Ps 20:7; Pr 21:31
[17]A horse[m] is a vain hope for
deliverance;
despite all its great strength it
cannot save.
33:18 [n]Job 36:7; Ps 34:15 [o]Ps 147:11
[18]But the eyes[n] of the LORD are on
those who fear him,
on those whose hope is in his
unfailing love,[o]
[19]to deliver them from death
33:19 [p]Job 5:20
and keep them alive in famine.[p]
33:20 [q]Ps 130:6
[20]We wait[q] in hope for the LORD;
he is our help and our shield.
33:21 [r]Zec 10:7; Jn 16:22
[21]In him our hearts rejoice,[r]
for we trust in his holy name.

[a]7 Or *sea as into a heap*

22 May your unfailing love rest upon
us, O LORD,
even as we put our hope in you.

Psalm 34[a]

Of David. When he pretended to be insane before Abimelech, who drove him away, and he left.

34:1 [s]Ps 71:6; Eph 5:20
34:2 [t]Jer 9:24; 1Co 1:31 [u]Ps 119:74
34:3 [v]Lk 1:46
34:4 [w]Mt 7:7
34:5 [x]Ps 36:9 [y]Ps 25:3
34:7 [z]2Ki 6:17; Da 6:22
34:8 [a]1Pe 2:3 [b]Ps 2:12
34:9 [c]Ps 23:1
34:10 [d]Ps 84:11
34:11 [e]Ps 32:8
34:12 [f]1Pe 3:10
34:13 [g]1Pe 2:22
34:14 [h]Ps 37:27 [i]Heb 12:14
34:15 [j]Ps 33:18 [k]Job 36:7
34:16 [l]Lev 17:10; Jer 44:11 [m]1Pe 3:10-12*

1 I will extol the LORD at all times;[s]
his praise will always be on my
lips.
2 My soul will boast[t] in the LORD;
let the afflicted hear and rejoice.[u]
3 Glorify the LORD with me;
let us exalt[v] his name together.
4 I sought the LORD,[w] and he
answered me;
he delivered me from all my fears.
5 Those who look to him are radiant;[x]
their faces are never covered with
shame.[y]
6 This poor man called, and the LORD
heard him;
he saved him out of all his
troubles.
7 The angel of the LORD encamps[z]
around those who fear him,
and he delivers them.

8 Taste and see that the LORD is
good;[a]
blessed is the man who takes
refuge[b] in him.
9 Fear the LORD, you his saints,
for those who fear him lack
nothing.[c]
10 The lions may grow weak and
hungry,
but those who seek the LORD lack
no good thing.[d]
11 Come, my children, listen to me;
I will teach you[e] the fear of the
LORD.
12 Whoever of you loves life[f]
and desires to see many good days,
13 keep your tongue from evil
and your lips from speaking lies.[g]
14 Turn from evil and do good;[h]
seek peace[i] and pursue it.
15 The eyes of the LORD[j] are on the
righteous[k]
and his ears are attentive to their
cry;
16 the face of the LORD is against[l]
those who do evil,[m]
to cut off the memory[n] of them
from the earth.
17 The righteous cry out, and the
LORD hears[o] them;
he delivers them from all their
troubles.
18 The LORD is close[p] to the
brokenhearted[q]
and saves those who are crushed in
spirit.
19 A righteous man may have many
troubles,[r]
but the LORD delivers him from
them all;[s]
20 he protects all his bones,
not one of them will be broken.[t]
21 Evil will slay the wicked;[u]
the foes of the righteous will be
condemned.
22 The LORD redeems[v] his servants;
no one will be condemned who
takes refuge in him.

34:16 [n]Pr 10:7
34:17 [o]Ps 145:19
34:18 [p]Ps 145:18 [q]Isa 57:15
34:19 [r]ver 17 [s]ver 4,6; Pr 24:16
34:20 [t]Jn 19:36*
34:21 [u]Ps 94:23
34:22 [v]1Ki 1:29; Ps 71:23

Psalm 35

Of David.

1 Contend, O LORD, with those who
contend with me;
fight[w] against those who fight
against me.
2 Take up shield and buckler;
arise[x] and come to my aid.
3 Brandish spear and javelin[b]
against those who pursue me.
Say to my soul,
"I am your salvation."

4 May those who seek my life
be disgraced[y] and put to shame;
may those who plot my ruin
be turned back in dismay.
5 May they be like chaff[z] before the
wind,
with the angel of the LORD
driving them away;
6 may their path be dark and
slippery,
with the angel of the LORD
pursuing them.
7 Since they hid their net for me
without cause
and without cause dug a pit for
me,

35:1 [w]Ps 43:1
35:2 [x]Ps 62:2
35:4 [y]Ps 70:2
35:5 [z]Job 21:18; Ps 1:4; Isa 29:5

[a]This psalm is an acrostic poem, the verses of which begin with the successive letters of the Hebrew alphabet. [b]3 Or *and block the way*

8 may ruin overtake them by
surprise—[a]
may the net they hid entangle
them,
may they fall into the pit,[b] to their
ruin.

35:8 [a]1Th 5:3 [b]Ps 9:15

9 Then my soul will rejoice[c] in the
LORD
and delight in his salvation.[d]

35:9 [c]Lk 1:47 [d]Isa 61:10

10 My whole being will exclaim,
"Who is like you,[e] O LORD?
You rescue the poor from those too
strong[f] for them,
the poor and needy[g] from those
who rob them."

35:10 [e]Ex 15:11 [f]Ps 18:17 [g]Ps 37:14

11 Ruthless witnesses[h] come forward;
they question me on things I
know nothing about.

35:11 [h]Ps 27:12

12 They repay me evil for good[i]
and leave my soul forlorn.

35:12 [i]Jn 10:32

13 Yet when they were ill, I put on
sackcloth
and humbled myself with fasting.[j]
When my prayers returned to me
unanswered,

35:13 [j]Job 30:25; Ps 69:10

14 I went about mourning
as though for my friend or
brother.
I bowed my head in grief
as though weeping for my mother.
15 But when I stumbled, they gathered
in glee;
attackers gathered against me
when I was unaware.
They slandered[k] me without
ceasing.

35:15 [k]Job 30:1,8

16 Like the ungodly they maliciously
mocked[a];
they gnashed their teeth[l] at me.

35:16 [l]Job 16:9; La 2:16

17 O Lord, how long[m] will you look
on?
Rescue my life from their ravages,
my precious life[n] from these lions.

35:17 [m]Hab 1:13 [n]Ps 22:20

18 I will give you thanks in the great
assembly;[o]
among throngs of people I will
praise you.[p]

35:18 [o]Ps 22:25 [p]Ps 22:22

19 Let not those gloat over me
who are my enemies without
cause;
let not those who hate me without
reason[q]
maliciously wink the eye.[r]

35:19 [q]Ps 38:19; 69:4; Jn 15:25* [r]Ps 13:4; Pr 6:13

20 They do not speak peaceably,
but devise false accusations
against those who live quietly in
the land.
21 They gape[s] at me and say, "Aha!
Aha![t]
With our own eyes we have seen
it."

35:21 [s]Ps 22:13 [t]Ps 40:15

22 O LORD, you have seen[u] this; be not
silent.
Do not be far[v] from me, O Lord.

35:22 [u]Ex 3:7 [v]Ps 10:1; 28:1

23 Awake,[w] and rise to my defense!
Contend for me, my God and
Lord.

35:23 [w]Ps 44:23

24 Vindicate me in your righteousness,
O LORD my God;
do not let them gloat over me.
25 Do not let them think, "Aha, just
what we wanted!"
or say, "We have swallowed him
up."[x]

35:25 [x]La 2:16

26 May all who gloat over my distress
be put to shame[y] and confusion;
may all who exalt themselves over
me[z]
be clothed with shame and
disgrace.

35:26 [y]Ps 40:14; 109:29 [z]Ps 38:16

27 May those who delight in my
vindication[a]
shout for joy[b] and gladness;
may they always say, "The LORD be
exalted,
who delights[c] in the well-being of
his servant."

35:27 [a]Ps 9:4 [b]Ps 32:11 [c]Ps 40:16; 147:11

28 My tongue will speak of your
righteousness[d]
and of your praises all day long.

35:28 [d]Ps 51:14

Psalm 36

For the director of music.
Of David the servant of the LORD.

1 An oracle is within my heart
concerning the sinfulness of the
wicked:[b]
There is no fear of God
before his eyes.[e]

36:1 [e]Ro 3:18*

2 For in his own eyes he flatters
himself
too much to detect or hate his sin.
3 The words of his mouth[f] are wicked
and deceitful;
he has ceased to be wise[g] and to
do good.[h]

36:3 [f]Ps 10:7 [g]Ps 94:8 [h]Jer 4:22

4 Even on his bed he plots evil;[i]
he commits himself to a sinful
course[j]

36:4 [i]Pr 4:16; Mic 2:1 [j]Isa 65:2

[a] *16* Septuagint; Hebrew may mean *ungodly circle of mockers.* [b] *1* Or *heart: / Sin proceeds from the wicked.*

and does not reject what is
wrong.[k]

36:4 [k]Ps 52:3; Ro 12:9

5 Your love, O LORD, reaches to the heavens,
your faithfulness to the skies.
6 Your righteousness is like the mighty mountains,
your justice like the great deep.[l]
O LORD, you preserve both man and beast.

36:6 [l]Job 11:8; Ps 77:19; Ro 11:33

7 How priceless is your unfailing love!
Both high and low among men
find[a] refuge in the shadow of your wings.[m]
8 They feast on the abundance of your house;[n]
you give them drink from your river[o] of delights.
9 For with you is the fountain of life;[p]
in your light[q] we see light.

36:7 [m]Ru 2:12; Ps 17:8

36:8 [n]Ps 65:4 [o]Job 20:17; Rev 22:1

36:9 [p]Jer 2:13 [q]1Pe 2:9

10 Continue your love to those who know you,
your righteousness to the upright in heart.
11 May the foot of the proud not come against me,
nor the hand of the wicked drive me away.
12 See how the evildoers lie fallen—
thrown down, not able to rise![r]

36:12 [r]Ps 140:10

Psalm 37[b]

Of David.

1 Do not fret because of evil men
or be envious[s] of those who do wrong;[t]
2 for like the grass they will soon wither,
like green plants they will soon die away.[u]

37:1 [s]Pr 23:17-18 [t]Ps 73:3

37:2 [u]Ps 90:6

3 Trust in the LORD and do good;
dwell in the land[v] and enjoy safe pasture.[w]
4 Delight[x] yourself in the LORD
and he will give you the desires of your heart.

37:3 [v]Dt 30:20 [w]Isa 40:11; Jn 10:9

37:4 [x]Isa 58:14

5 Commit your way to the LORD;
trust in him[y] and he will do this:
6 He will make your righteousness[z] shine like the dawn,[a]
the justice of your cause like the noonday sun.

37:5 [y]Ps 4:5; Ps 55:22; Pr 16:3; 1Pe 5:7

37:6 [z]Mic 7:9 [a]Job 11:17

7 Be still[b] before the LORD and wait patiently[c] for him;
do not fret when men succeed in their ways,
when they carry out their wicked schemes.

37:7 [b]Ps 62:5; La 3:26 [c]Ps 40:1

8 Refrain from anger[d] and turn from wrath;
do not fret—it leads only to evil.
9 For evil men will be cut off,
but those who hope in the LORD will inherit the land.[e]

37:8 [d]Eph 4:31; Col 3:8

37:9 [e]Isa 57:13; 60:21

10 A little while, and the wicked will be no more;[f]
though you look for them, they will not be found.
11 But the meek will inherit the land[g]
and enjoy great peace.

37:10 [f]Job 7:10; 24:24

37:11 [g]Mt 5:5

12 The wicked plot against the righteous
and gnash their teeth[h] at them;
13 but the Lord laughs at the wicked,
for he knows their day is coming.[i]

37:12 [h]Ps 35:16

37:13 [i]1Sa 26:10; Ps 2:4

14 The wicked draw the sword
and bend the bow[j]
to bring down the poor and needy,[k]
to slay those whose ways are upright.
15 But their swords will pierce their own hearts,[l]
and their bows will be broken.

37:14 [j]Ps 11:2 [k]Ps 35:10

37:15 [l]Ps 9:16

16 Better the little that the righteous have
than the wealth[m] of many wicked;
17 for the power of the wicked will be broken,[n]
but the LORD upholds the righteous.

37:16 [m]Pr 15:16

37:17 [n]Job 38:15; Ps 10:15

18 The days of the blameless are known to the LORD,[o]
and their inheritance will endure forever.

37:18 [o]Ps 1:6

GOODNESS

BELIEVE AND BEHAVE

Psalm 37:3

"Trust in the Lord and do good"—an entire recipe for life with only two ingredients.

[a]7 Or *love, O God! / Men find*; or *love! / Both heavenly beings and men / find* [b]This psalm is an acrostic poem, the stanzas of which begin with the successive letters of the Hebrew alphabet.

19 In times of disaster they will not
wither;
in days of famine they will enjoy
plenty.
20 But the wicked will perish:
The LORD's enemies will be like
the beauty of the fields,
they will vanish—vanish like
smoke.[p]
21 The wicked borrow and do not
repay,
but the righteous give generously;[q]
22 those the LORD blesses will inherit
the land,
but those he curses[r] will be cut off.
23 If the LORD delights[s] in a man's way,
he makes his steps firm;[t]
24 though he stumble, he will not fall,[u]
for the LORD upholds[v] him with
his hand.

25 I was young and now I am old,
yet I have never seen the righteous
forsaken[w]
or their children begging bread.
26 They are always generous and lend
freely;
their children will be blessed.[x]

27 Turn from evil and do good;[y]
then you will dwell in the land
forever.
28 For the LORD loves the just
and will not forsake his faithful
ones.

They will be protected forever,
but the offspring of the wicked
will be cut off;[z]
29 the righteous will inherit the land[a]
and dwell in it forever.

30 The mouth of the righteous man
utters wisdom,
and his tongue speaks what is just.
31 The law of his God is in his heart;[b]
his feet do not slip.[c]

32 The wicked lie in wait[d] for the
righteous,
seeking their very lives;
33 but the LORD will not leave them in
their power
or let them be condemned when
brought to trial.[e]

34 Wait for the LORD[f]
and keep his way.
He will exalt you to inherit the land;

37:20 [p]Ps 102:3
37:21 [q]Ps 112:5
37:22 [r]Job 5:3; Pr 3:33
37:23 [s]Ps 147:11 [t]1Sa 2:9
37:24 [u]Pr 24:16 [v]Ps 145:14; 147:6
37:25 [w]Heb 13:5
37:26 [x]Ps 147:13
37:27 [y]Ps 34:14
37:28 [z]Ps 21:10; Isa 14:20
37:29 [a]ver 9; Pr 2:21
37:31 [b]Dt 6:6; Ps 40:8; Isa 51:7 [c]ver 23
37:32 [d]Ps 10:8
37:33 [e]Ps 109:31; 2Pe 2:9
37:34 [f]Ps 27:14

when the wicked are cut off, you
will see[g] it.

35 I have seen a wicked and ruthless
man
flourishing[h] like a green tree in its
native soil,
36 but he soon passed away and was no
more;
though I looked for him, he could
not be found.[i]

37 Consider the blameless, observe the
upright;
there is a future[a] for the man of
peace.[j]
38 But all sinners will be destroyed;
the future[b] of the wicked will be
cut off.[k]

39 The salvation[l] of the righteous comes
from the LORD;
he is their stronghold in time of
trouble.[m]
40 The LORD helps[n] them and delivers[o]
them;
he delivers them from the wicked
and saves them,
because they take refuge in him.

Psalm 38

A psalm of David. A petition.

1 O LORD, do not rebuke me in your
anger
or discipline me in your wrath.[p]
2 For your arrows[q] have pierced me,
and your hand has come down
upon me.
3 Because of your wrath there is no
health in my body;
my bones[r] have no soundness
because of my sin.
4 My guilt has overwhelmed me
like a burden too heavy to bear.[s]

5 My wounds fester and are
loathsome
because of my sinful folly.[t]
6 I am bowed down and brought very
low;
all day long I go about
mourning.[u]
7 My back is filled with searing pain;[v]
there is no health in my body.
8 I am feeble and utterly crushed;
I groan[w] in anguish of heart.

37:34 [g]Ps 52:6
37:35 [h]Job 5:3
37:36 [i]Job 20:5
37:37 [j]Isa 57:1-2
37:38 [k]Ps 1:4
37:39 [l]Ps 3:8 [m]Ps 9:9
37:40 [n]1Ch 5:20 [o]Isa 31:5
38:1 [p]Ps 6:1
38:2 [q]Job 6:4; Ps 32:4
38:3 [r]Ps 6:2; Isa 1:6
38:4 [s]Ezr 9:6
38:5 [t]Ps 69:5
38:6 [u]Job 30:28; Ps 35:14; 42:9
38:7 [v]Ps 102:3
38:8 [w]Ps 22:1

[a]*37* Or *there will be posterity* [b]*38* Or *posterity*

[9]All my longings lie open before you,
O Lord;
38:9 [x]Job 3:24; Ps 6:6; 10:17 my sighing[x] is not hidden from
you.
38:10 [y]Ps 31:10 [z]Ps 6:7 [10]My heart pounds, my strength fails[y]
me;
even the light has gone from my
eyes.[z]
38:11 [a]Ps 31:11 [11]My friends and companions avoid
me because of my wounds;[a]
my neighbors stay far away.
38:12 [b]Ps 140:5 [c]Ps 35:4; 54:3 [d]Ps 35:20 [12]Those who seek my life set their
traps,[b]
those who would harm me talk of
my ruin;[c]
all day long they plot deception.[d]

[13]I am like a deaf man, who cannot
hear,
like a mute, who cannot open his
mouth;
[14]I have become like a man who does
not hear,
38:15 [e]Ps 39:7 [f]Ps 17:6 whose mouth can offer no reply.
[15]I wait[e] for you, O LORD;
you will answer,[f] O Lord my God.
38:16 [g]Ps 35:26 [h]Ps 13:4 [16]For I said, "Do not let them gloat[g]
or exalt themselves over me when
my foot slips."[h]

[17]For I am about to fall,
and my pain is ever with me.
38:18 [i]Ps 32:5 [18]I confess my iniquity;[i]
I am troubled by my sin.
[19]Many are those who are my vigorous
38:19 [j]Ps 18:17 [k]Ps 35:19 enemies;[j]
those who hate me without
reason[k] are numerous.
38:20 [l]Ps 35:12; 1Jn 3:12 [20]Those who repay my good with evil[l]
slander me when I pursue what is
good.

38:21 [m]Ps 35:22 [21]O LORD, do not forsake me;
be not far[m] from me, O my God.
38:22 [n]Ps 40:13 [o]Ps 27:1 [22]Come quickly to help me,[n]
O Lord my Savior.[o]

Psalm 39

For the director of music. For Jeduthun.
A psalm of David.

39:1 [p]1Ki 2:4 [q]Job 2:10; Jas 3:2 [1]I said, "I will watch my ways[p]
and keep my tongue from sin;[q]
I will put a muzzle on my mouth
as long as the wicked are in my
presence."
39:2 [r]Ps 38:13 [2]But when I was silent[r] and still,
not even saying anything good,
my anguish increased.

DAY 3 THREE

Patience and My Relationship With Christ

Psalm 39:1–5

How fast the days of our lives pass by. If ever we are to become good stewards, we must find a way to measure the years so they do not steal from us our sense of patience, but rather improve the stewardship of our lives. Long ago I learned this little scheme for reckoning life in the very way that the psalmist is speaking of it here.

If you lived to be 72 years of age and could reckon all the years of your life on one giant clock, you might sequence your life in this manner: Plot all 72 years of your anticipated life span on that 12-hour dial. Each hour on that dial would then represent six years of your life. Figuratively, you would then be born at 7 o'clock in the morning and would die at 7 o'clock in the evening.

When it was 8 o'clock on that great clock,
you would be 6 years old.
When it was 10 o'clock on that great clock,
you would be 18 years old.
When it was 12 o'clock on that great clock,
you would be 30 years old.
When it was 4 o'clock on that great clock,
you would be 54 years old.
When it was 6 o'clock on that great clock,
you would be 66 years old.

Indeed, the psalmist is right: "You have made my days a mere handbreadth; the span of my years is as nothing before you. Each man's life is but a breath" (Psalm 39:5). During these fast-tumbling years, let us practice a determined patience and decide that these years will all be used for Christ. If we focus on using our time to develop our relationship with him, we will never look at the time as wasted, for we will someday have eternity to reap the benefits of our time with him now. A great hymn sums up the attitude of a life filled with patience: "Only one life, 'twill soon be past; only what's done for Christ will last."

To begin a study on the topic of Patience, the Unhurried Virtue, turn to the home page on page 1146.

[3]My heart grew hot within me,
and as I meditated, the fire burned;
then I spoke with my tongue:

39:4 [s]Ps 90:12 [t]Ps 103:14
[4]"Show me, O LORD, my life's end
and the number of my days;[s]
let me know how fleeting is my life.[t]

39:5 [u]Ps 89:45 [v]Ps 62:9
[5]You have made my days[u] a mere handbreadth;
the span of my years is as nothing before you.
Each man's life is but a breath.[v]
Selah

39:6 [w]1Pe 1:24 [x]Ps 127:2 [y]Lk 12:20
[6]Man is a mere phantom[w] as he goes to and fro:
He bustles about, but only in vain;[x]
he heaps up wealth, not knowing who will get it.[y]

SELF-CONTROL

THE STRONGBOX

Psalm 39:6

There is a vault where all that's stored is God-locked and secure.

The combination to this lofty safe has but one set of numbers:

Jesus first, others second, things last.

Lose this combination and nothing that you own can be kept safe until eternity.

39:7 [z]Ps 38:15
[7]"But now, Lord, what do I look for?
My hope is in you.[z]

39:8 [a]Ps 51:9 [b]Ps 44:13
[8]Save me[a] from all my transgressions;[b]
do not make me the scorn of fools.

39:9 [c]Job 2:10
[9]I was silent; I would not open my mouth,[c]
for you are the one who has done this.

39:10 [d]Job 9:34; Ps 32:4
[10]Remove your scourge from me;
I am overcome by the blow of your hand.[d]

39:11 [e]2Pe 2:16 [f]Job 13:28
[11]You rebuke[e] and discipline men for their sin;
you consume their wealth like a moth[f]—
each man is but a breath. *Selah*

39:12 [g]1Pe 2:11 [h]Heb 11:13
[12]"Hear my prayer, O LORD,
listen to my cry for help;
be not deaf to my weeping.
For I dwell with you as an alien,[g]
a stranger,[h] as all my fathers were.

DAY 3 THREE

PATIENCE AND MY RELATIONSHIP WITH CHRIST

Psalm 40:1–3

Out of the pit, out of the mire—the biography of all believers. It is this pit that creates in us a yearning after freedom. We long for his joy and above all for his liberty. But the pit will not let us be free.

In John Bunyan's *The Pilgrim's Progress,* Christian goes through the "Slough of Despond." This despond is the milieu that causes us to acknowledge our need. We cry out for rescue simply because we know in ourselves that we are helpless. We can do nothing but wait for rescue. We wait and God acts. We have patience and the Savior comes. Floundering, entrapped, ensnared, dying, we wait; and our patience is rewarded by the coming of our rescuer. He lifts us from the pit, and we are in love with him because he has saved us and endowed us with great liberty. We believe in and celebrate the word *grace* because we know we did not—nor could not—extricate ourselves from the pit. Only Christ, who knows the depths of sorrow and the darkness of night, can bring us freedom and salvation.

The poet in this psalm feels trapped in the mire. Circumstances—like quicksand—have grasped him and are dragging him down. His greatest strength lies in his desire to be free.

To fall into quicksand and live through it demands that the victim cease struggle. Lay back gently, fin with your hands and let your calm be your strength. The same law will lift us from the Slough of Despond. The more we flail to achieve our own freedom, the more certain we are to sink deeper. But if we wait...if we trust and wait...rescue is certain.

Turn to Christ for rescue. He knows what it's like in the quicksand. He has been there before and has overcome it. He can help you if you will trust in him.

To begin a study on the topic of Patience, the Art of Waiting on God, turn to the home page on page 1500.

[13]Look away from me, that I may rejoice again
before I depart and am no more."[i]
39:13 [i]Job 10:21; 14:10

Psalm 40

For the director of music.
Of David. A psalm.

40:1 [j]Ps 27:14 [k]Ps 34:15

[1]I waited patiently[j] for the LORD;
he turned to me and heard my cry.[k]

40:2 [l]Ps 69:14 [m]Ps 27:5

[2]He lifted me out of the slimy pit,
out of the mud and mire;[l]
he set my feet on a rock[m]
and gave me a firm place to stand.

40:3 [n]Ps 33:3

[3]He put a new song[n] in my mouth,
a hymn of praise to our God.
Many will see and fear
and put their trust in the LORD.

40:4 [o]Ps 34:8 [p]Ps 84:12

[4]Blessed is the man[o]
who makes the LORD his trust,[p]
who does not look to the proud,
to those who turn aside to false gods.[a]

DAY 2 TWO

▸ PEACE AND THE PURPOSE OF GOD IN MY LIFE

Psalm 40:6–8

"I desire to do your will, O my God; your law is within my heart."

This desire to discover God's will in our lives is fundamental to all of God's children who seek peace. We come to receive our desire by doing these five things:

P . . . Pray and seek the Father's plan for life,
Abandoning all things that lead to strife.
E . . . Engaging hearts, in sweet relinquishments
Of all that selfishness alone invents.
A . . . Abandoning ambitions we have known
And clinging to God's purpose as our own.
C . . . Consecrating ourselves to walk in grace,
Accepting both his sovereign path and pace.
E . . . Endowing our mind with focus, then to fill
It up with his sweet, higher will.

This acrostic is a recipe for peace. Make it your own. Then you will find that not only will turmoil disappear, but new meaning will flood your life because you've replaced a selfish agenda with the noblest of desires.

To begin a study on the topic of Peace, Accepting a Higher Will, turn to the home page on page 1282.

40:5 [q]Ps 136:4 [r]Ps 139:18; Isa 55:8

[5]Many, O LORD my God,
are the wonders[q] you have done.
The things you planned for us
no one can recount[r] to you;
were I to speak and tell of them,
they would be too many to declare.

40:6 [s]1Sa 15:22; Am 5:22 [t]Isa 1:11

[6]Sacrifice and offering you did not desire,[s]
but my ears you have pierced[b,c];
burnt offerings[t] and sin offerings
you did not require.
[7]Then I said, "Here I am, I have come—
it is written about me in the scroll.[d]

40:8 [u]Jn 4:34 [v]Ps 37:31

[8]I desire to do your will,[u] O my God;
your law is within my heart."[v]

▸ PEACE

TO WANT ONE THING

Psalm 40:8

Jesus had but one ambition: to please his Father. Want this one thing and your eye will be single-focused, your body full of light.

40:9 [w]Ps 22:25 [x]Jos 22:22; Ps 119:13

[9]I proclaim righteousness in the great assembly;[w]
I do not seal my lips,
as you know,[x] O LORD.

40:10 [y]Ps 89:1 [z]Ac 20:20

[10]I do not hide your righteousness in my heart;
I speak of your faithfulness[y] and salvation.
I do not conceal your love and your truth
from the great assembly.[z]

40:11 [a]Pr 20:28 [b]Ps 43:3

[11]Do not withhold your mercy from me, O LORD;
may your love[a] and your truth[b]
always protect me.

40:12 [c]Ps 116:3 [d]Ps 38:4 [e]Ps 69:4 [f]Ps 73:26

[12]For troubles[c] without number
surround me;
my sins have overtaken me, and I cannot see.[d]
They are more than the hairs of my head,[e]
and my heart fails[f] within me.

[13]Be pleased, O LORD, to save me;

[a]4 Or *to falsehood* [b]6 Hebrew; Septuagint *but a body you have prepared for me* (see also Symmachus and Theodotion) [c]6 Or *opened* [d]7 Or *come / with the scroll written for me*

O LORD, come quickly to help
me.[g] 40:13 [g]Ps 70:1
[14]May all who seek to take my life
be put to shame and confusion; 40:14 [h]Ps 35:4
may all who desire my ruin[h]
be turned back in disgrace.
[15]May those who say to me, "Aha!
Aha!"
be appalled at their own shame.
[16]But may all who seek you
rejoice and be glad in you;
may those who love your salvation
always say,
"The LORD be exalted!"[i] 40:16 [i]Ps 35:27
[17]Yet I am poor and needy;
may the Lord think of me.
You are my help and my deliverer;
O my God, do not delay.[j] 40:17 [j]Ps 70:5

Psalm 41

For the director of music.
A psalm of David.

[1]Blessed is he who has regard for the
weak;[k] 41:1 [k]Ps 82:3-4; Pr 14:21
the LORD delivers him in times of
trouble.
[2]The LORD will protect him and
preserve his life;
he will bless him in the land[l] 41:2 [l]Ps 37:22 [m]Ps 27:12
and not surrender him to the
desire of his foes.[m]
[3]The LORD will sustain him on his
sickbed
and restore him from his bed of
illness.
[4]I said, "O LORD, have mercy[n] on 41:4 [n]Ps 6:2 [o]Ps 51:4
me;
heal me, for I have sinned[o] against
you."
[5]My enemies say of me in malice,
"When will he die and his name
perish?"[p] 41:5 [p]Ps 38:12
[6]Whenever one comes to see me,
he speaks falsely,[q] while his heart 41:6 [q]Ps 12:2 [r]Pr 26:24
gathers slander;[r]
then he goes out and spreads it
abroad.
[7]All my enemies whisper together[s] 41:7 [s]Ps 56:5; 71:10-11
against me;
they imagine the worst for me,
saying,
[8]"A vile disease has beset him;
he will never get up from the place
where he lies."
[9]Even my close friend,[t] whom I 41:9 [t]2Sa 15:12; Ps 55:12 [u]Job 19:19; Ps 55:20; Mt 26:23; Jn 13:18*
trusted,
he who shared my bread,
has lifted up his heel against me.[u]
[10]But you, O LORD, have mercy on
me;
raise me up,[v] that I may repay 41:10 [v]Ps 3:3
them.
[11]I know that you are pleased with
me,[w] 41:11 [w]Ps 147:11 [x]Ps 25:2
for my enemy does not triumph
over me.[x]
[12]In my integrity you uphold me[y] 41:12 [y]Ps 37:17 [z]Job 36:7
and set me in your presence
forever.[z]

[13]Praise be to the LORD, the God of 41:13 [a]Ps 72:18 [b]Ps 89:52; 106:48
Israel,[a]
from everlasting to everlasting.
Amen and Amen.[b]

BOOK II

Psalms 42–72

Psalm 42[a]

For the director of music.
A *maskil*[b] of the Sons of Korah.

[1]As the deer pants for streams of
water,
so my soul pants[c] for you, O God. 42:1 [c]Ps 119:131
[2]My soul thirsts[d] for God, for the
living God.[e] 42:2 [d]Ps 63:1 [e]Jer 10:10 [f]Ps 43:4
When can I go[f] and meet with
God?
[3]My tears[g] have been my food 42:3 [g]Ps 80:5 [h]Ps 79:10
day and night,
while men say to me all day long,
"Where is your God?"[h]

[a]In many Hebrew manuscripts Psalms 42 and 43 constitute one psalm. [b]Title: Probably a literary or musical term

LOVE

Treachery, the Offense of Love

Psalm 41:9

Who has not felt the betrayal of someone trusted? Judas's offense lay not in being an enemy of Christ, but in his sustained rehearsal of pretended friendship.

GOODNESS 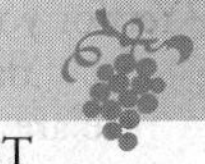

HUNGERING TO PLEASE CHRIST

Psalm 42:2

Teach your appetites to wait their turn to be satisfied. Allow none of them to feed until the heart has had its fill of intimacy with Christ. Then you won't have to try to be good. Goodness, like a storm of grace, will smother you with blessings.

4 These things I remember
as I pour out my soul:
how I used to go with the multitude,
leading the procession to the
house of God,[i]
with shouts of joy and thanksgiving[j]
among the festive throng.

42:4 [i]Isa 30:29 [j]Ps 100:4

5 Why are you downcast,[k] O my soul?
Why so disturbed within me?
Put your hope in God,[l]
for I will yet praise him,
my Savior[m] and 6 my God.

42:5 [k]Ps 38:6; 77:3 [l]La 3:24 [m]Ps 44:3

My[a] soul is downcast within me;
therefore I will remember you
from the land of the Jordan,
the heights of Hermon—from
Mount Mizar.

7 Deep calls to deep
in the roar of your waterfalls;
all your waves and breakers
have swept over me.[n]

42:7 [n]Ps 88:7; Jnh 2:3

8 By day the LORD directs his love,[o]
at night[p] his song[q] is with me—
a prayer to the God of my life.

42:8 [o]Ps 57:3 [p]Job 35:10 [q]Ps 63:6; 149:5

9 I say to God my Rock,
"Why have you forgotten me?
Why must I go about mourning,[r]
oppressed by the enemy?"

42:9 [r]Ps 38:6

10 My bones suffer mortal agony
as my foes taunt me,
saying to me all day long,
"Where is your God?"

11 Why are you downcast, O my soul?
Why so disturbed within me?
Put your hope in God,
for I will yet praise him,
my Savior and my God.[s]

42:11 [s]Ps 43:5

Psalm 43[b]

1 Vindicate me, O God,
and plead my cause[t] against an
ungodly nation;
rescue me from deceitful and
wicked men.[u]

43:1 [t]1Sa 24:15; Ps 26:1; 35:1 [u]Ps 5:6

2 You are God my stronghold.
Why have you rejected[v] me?
Why must I go about mourning,
oppressed by the enemy?[w]

43:2 [v]Ps 44:9 [w]Ps 42:9

3 Send forth your light[x] and your
truth,
let them guide me;
let them bring me to your holy
mountain,[y]
to the place where you dwell.[z]

43:3 [x]Ps 36:9 [y]Ps 42:4 [z]Ps 84:1

4 Then will I go to the altar[a] of God,
to God, my joy and my delight.
I will praise you with the harp,[b]
O God, my God.

43:4 [a]Ps 26:6 [b]Ps 33:2

5 Why are you downcast, O my soul?
Why so disturbed within me?
Put your hope in God,
for I will yet praise him,
my Savior and my God.[c]

43:5 [c]Ps 42:6

Psalm 44

For the director of music.
Of the Sons of Korah. A *maskil*.[c]

1 We have heard with our ears,
O God;
our fathers have told us[d]
what you did in their days,
in days long ago.

44:1 [d]Ex 12:26; Ps 78:3

2 With your hand you drove out[e] the
nations
and planted[f] our fathers;
you crushed the peoples
and made our fathers flourish.[g]

44:2 [e]Ps 78:55 [f]Ex 15:17 [g]Ps 80:9

3 It was not by their sword[h] that they
won the land,
nor did their arm bring them
victory;
it was your right hand, your arm,[i]
and the light of your face, for you
loved[j] them.

44:3 [h]Dt 8:17; Jos 24:12 [i]Ps 77:15 [j]Dt 4:37; 7:7-8

4 You are my King[k] and my God,
who decrees[d] victories for Jacob.

44:4 [k]Ps 74:12

5 Through you we push back our
enemies;
through your name we trample[l]
our foes.

44:5 [l]Ps 108:13

6 I do not trust in my bow,[m]

44:6 [m]Ps 33:16

[a]*5,6* A few Hebrew manuscripts, Septuagint and Syriac; most Hebrew manuscripts *praise him for his saving help. / 6O my God, my* [b]In many Hebrew manuscripts Psalms 42 and 43 constitute one psalm. [c]Title: Probably a literary or musical term
[d]*4* Septuagint, Aquila and Syriac; Hebrew *King, O God; / command*

my sword does not bring me victory;

44:7 [n]Ps 136:24 [o]Ps 53:5

[7] but you give us victory[n] over our enemies,
you put our adversaries to shame.[o]

44:8 [p]Ps 34:2 [q]Ps 30:12

[8] In God we make our boast[p] all day long,
and we will praise your name forever.[q] *Selah*

44:9 [r]Ps 74:1 [s]Ps 60:1,10

[9] But now you have rejected[r] and humbled us;
you no longer go out with our armies.[s]

44:10 [t]Lev 26:17; Jos 7:8; Ps 89:41

[10] You made us retreat[t] before the enemy,
and our adversaries have plundered us.

44:11 [u]Ro 8:36 [v]Dt 4:27; 28:64; Ps 10

[11] You gave us up to be devoured like sheep[u]
and have scattered us among the nations.[v]

44:12 [w]Isa 52:3; Jer 15:13; 52:3; Jer 15:13

[12] You sold your people for a pittance,[w]
gaining nothing from their sale.

44:13 [x]Ps 79:4; 80:6 [y]Dt 28:37

[13] You have made us a reproach to our neighbors,[x]
the scorn[y] and derision of those around us.

44:14 [z]Ps 109:25; Jer 24:9

[14] You have made us a byword among the nations;
the peoples shake their heads[z] at us.

[15] My disgrace is before me all day long,
and my face is covered with shame

44:16 [a]Ps 74:10

[16] at the taunts of those who reproach and revile[a] me,
because of the enemy, who is bent on revenge.

44:17 [b]Ps 78:7,57; Da 9:13

[17] All this happened to us,
though we had not forgotten[b] you
or been false to your covenant.

44:18 [c]Job 23:11

[18] Our hearts had not turned[c] back;
our feet had not strayed from your path.

44:19 [d]Ps 51:8 [e]Job 3:5

[19] But you crushed[d] us and made us a haunt for jackals
and covered us over with deep darkness.[e]

44:20 [f]Ps 78:11 [g]Dt 6:14; Ps 81:9

[20] If we had forgotten[f] the name of our God
or spread out our hands to a foreign god,[g]

44:21 [h]Ps 139:1-2; Jer 17:10

[21] would not God have discovered it,
since he knows the secrets of the heart?[h]

44:22 [i]Isa 53:7; Ro 8:36*

[22] Yet for your sake we face death all day long;
we are considered as sheep to be slaughtered.[i]

LOVE

THE MARTYRS' MASTER

Psalm 44:22

Facing death all day long for love? Yes. Each martyr's passion is unafraid of gallows. Two thousand years of hate have left every sunset a witness to some martyr's faith. Yet never has this daily dying left heaven unaffected. Christ weeps each time faith bleeds.

44:23 [j]Ps 7:6 [k]Ps 78:65 [l]Ps 77:7

[23] Awake,[j] O Lord! Why do you sleep?[k]
Rouse yourself! Do not reject us forever.[l]

44:24 [m]Job 13:24 [n]Ps 42:9

[24] Why do you hide your face[m]
and forget our misery and oppression?[n]

44:25 [o]Ps 119:25

[25] We are brought down to the dust;[o]
our bodies cling to the ground.

44:26 [p]Ps 35:2 [q]Ps 25:22

[26] Rise up[p] and help us;
redeem[q] us because of your unfailing love.

Psalm 45

For the director of music. To ⌊the tune of⌋ "Lilies." Of the Sons of Korah. A *maskil*.[a] A wedding song.

[1] My heart is stirred by a noble theme
as I recite my verses for the king;
my tongue is the pen of a skillful writer.

45:2 [r]Lk 4:22

[2] You are the most excellent of men
and your lips have been anointed with grace,[r]
since God has blessed you forever.

45:3 [s]Heb 4:12; Rev 1:16 [t]Isa 9:6

[3] Gird your sword[s] upon your side,
O mighty one;[t]
clothe yourself with splendor and majesty.

45:4 [u]Rev 6:2

[4] In your majesty ride forth victoriously[u]
in behalf of truth, humility and righteousness;
let your right hand display awesome deeds.

[5] Let your sharp arrows pierce the hearts of the king's enemies;

[a]Title: Probably a literary or musical term

let the nations fall beneath your
feet.
6 Your throne, O God, will last for
ever and ever;[v]
a scepter of justice will be the
scepter of your kingdom.
7 You love righteousness[w] and hate
wickedness;
therefore God, your God, has set
you above your companions
by anointing[x] you with the oil of
joy.[y]
8 All your robes are fragrant[z] with
myrrh and aloes and cassia;
from palaces adorned with ivory
the music of the strings makes you
glad.
9 Daughters of kings[a] are among your
honored women;
at your right hand[b] is the royal
bride in gold of Ophir.

10 Listen, O daughter, consider and
give ear:
Forget your people[c] and your
father's house.
11 The king is enthralled by your
beauty;
honor[d] him, for he is your lord.[e]
12 The Daughter of Tyre will come
with a gift,[a][f]
men of wealth will seek your favor.
13 All glorious[g] is the princess within
her chamber;
her gown is interwoven with gold.
14 In embroidered garments she is led
to the king;[h]
her virgin companions follow her
and are brought to you.
15 They are led in with joy and
gladness;
they enter the palace of the king.

16 Your sons will take the place of your
fathers;
you will make them princes
throughout the land.
17 I will perpetuate your memory
through all generations;[i]
therefore the nations will praise
you[j] for ever and ever.

Psalm 46

For the director of music. Of the Sons
of Korah. According to *alamoth*.[b] A song.

1 God is our refuge[k] and strength,
an ever-present[l] help in trouble.

45:6 [v]Ps 93:2; 98:9
45:7 [w]Ps 33:5 [x]Isa 61:1 [y]Ps 21:6; Heb 1:8-9*
45:8 [z]SS 1:3
45:9 [a]SS 6:8 [b]1Ki 2:19
45:10 [c]Dt 21:13
45:11 [d]Ps 95:6 [e]Isa 54:5
45:12 [f]Ps 22:29; Isa 49:23
45:13 [g]Isa 61:10
45:14 [h]SS 1:4
45:17 [i]Mal 1:11 [j]Ps 138:4
46:1 [k]Ps 9:9; 14:6 [l]Dt 4:7

2 Therefore we will not fear,[m] though
the earth give way[n]
and the mountains fall[o] into the
heart of the sea,
3 though its waters roar[p] and foam
and the mountains quake with
their surging. *Selah*

4 There is a river whose streams make
glad the city of God,[q]
the holy place where the Most
High dwells.
5 God is within her,[r] she will not fall;
God will help[s] her at break of day.
6 Nations[t] are in uproar, kingdoms[u]
fall;
he lifts his voice, the earth melts.[v]

7 The LORD Almighty is with us;[w]
the God of Jacob is our fortress.[x]
Selah

8 Come and see the works of the
LORD,[y]
the desolations[z] he has brought on
the earth.
9 He makes wars[a] cease to the ends of
the earth;
he breaks the bow[b] and shatters
the spear,
he burns the shields[c] with fire.[c]
10 "Be still, and know that I am God;[d]
I will be exalted[e] among the
nations,
I will be exalted in the earth."
11 The LORD Almighty is with us;
the God of Jacob is our fortress.
Selah

Psalm 47

For the director of music.
Of the Sons of Korah. A psalm.

1 Clap your hands,[f] all you nations;
shout to God with cries of joy.[g]
2 How awesome[h] is the LORD Most
High,
the great King[i] over all the earth!
3 He subdued[j] nations under us,
peoples under our feet.
4 He chose our inheritance[k] for us,
the pride of Jacob, whom he
loved.
Selah

5 God has ascended amid shouts of
joy,

46:2 [m]Ps 23:4 [n]Ps 82:5 [o]Ps 18:7
46:3 [p]Ps 93:3
46:4 [q]Ps 48:1,8; Isa 60:14
46:5 [r]Isa 12:6; Eze 43:7 [s]Ps 37:40
46:6 [t]Ps 2:1 [u]Ps 68:32 [v]Mic 1:4
46:7 [w]2Ch 13:12 [x]Ps 9:9
46:8 [y]Ps 66:5 [z]Isa 61:4
46:9 [a]Isa 2:4 [b]Ps 76:3 [c]Eze 39:9
46:10 [d]Ps 100:3 [e]Isa 2:11
47:1 [f]Ps 98:8; Isa 55:12 [g]Ps 106:47
47:2 [h]Dt 7:21 [i]Mal 1:14
47:3 [j]Ps 18:39,47
47:4 [k]1Pe 1:4

[a] *12* Or *A Tyrian robe is among the gifts* [b] Title: Probably a musical term [c] *9* Or *chariots*

47:5 [l]Ps 68:33; 98:6

the LORD amid the sounding of
trumpets.[l]

47:6 [m]Ps 68:4; 89:18

6 Sing praises[m] to God, sing praises;
sing praises to our King, sing
praises.

47:7 [n]Zec 14:9 [o]Col 3:16

7 For God is the King of all the earth;[n]
sing to him a psalm[a] [o] of praise.

47:8 [p]1Ch 16:31

8 God reigns[p] over the nations;
God is seated on his holy throne.
9 The nobles of the nations assemble
as the people of the God of
Abraham,

47:9 [q]Ps 72:11; 89:18 [r]Ps 97:9

for the kings[b] of the earth belong to
God;[q]
he is greatly exalted.[r]

Psalm 48

A song. A psalm of the Sons of Korah.

48:1 [s]Ps 96:4 [t]Ps 46:4 [u]Isa 2:2-3; Mic 4:1; Zec 8:3

1 Great is the LORD,[s] and most
worthy of praise,
in the city of our God,[t] his holy
mountain.[u]

48:2 [v]Ps 50:2; La 2:15 [w]Mt 5:35

2 It is beautiful[v] in its loftiness,
the joy of the whole earth.
Like the utmost heights of Zaphon[c]
is Mount Zion,
the[d] city of the Great King.[w]
3 God is in her citadels;
he has shown himself to be her
fortress.[x]

48:3 [x]Ps 46:7

48:4 [y]2Sa 10:1-19

4 When the kings joined forces,
when they advanced together,[y]
5 they saw ⌊her⌋ and were astounded;
they fled in terror.[z]

48:5 [z]Ex 15:16

6 Trembling seized them there,
pain like that of a woman in labor.
7 You destroyed them like ships of
Tarshish
shattered by an east wind.[a]

48:7 [a]Jer 18:17; Eze 27:26

8 As we have heard,
so have we seen
in the city of the LORD Almighty,
in the city of our God:
God makes her secure forever.[b]
Selah

48:8 [b]Ps 87:5

9 Within your temple, O God,
we meditate on your unfailing
love.[c]

48:9 [c]Ps 26:3

48:10 [d]Dt 28:58; Jos 7:9 [e]Isa 41:10

10 Like your name,[d] O God,
your praise reaches to the ends of
the earth;[e]
your right hand is filled with
righteousness.
11 Mount Zion rejoices,
the villages of Judah are glad
because of your judgments.[f]

48:11 [f]Ps 97:8

12 Walk about Zion, go around her,
count her towers,
13 consider well her ramparts,
view her citadels,[g]
that you may tell of them to the
next generation.[h]

48:13 [g]ver 3; Ps 122:7 [h]Ps 78:6

14 For this God is our God for ever and
ever;
he will be our guide[i] even to the
end.

48:14 [i]Ps 23:4

Psalm 49

For the director of music.
Of the Sons of Korah. A psalm.

49:1 [j]Ps 78:1 [k]Ps 33:8

1 Hear this, all you peoples;[j]
listen, all who live in this world,[k]
2 both low and high,
rich and poor alike:

49:3 [l]Ps 37:30 [m]Ps 119:130

3 My mouth will speak words of
wisdom;[l]
the utterance from my heart will
give understanding.[m]

49:4 [n]Ps 78:2

4 I will turn my ear to a proverb;[n]
with the harp I will expound my
riddle:[o]

49:4 [o]Nu 12:8

5 Why should I fear[p] when evil days
come,
when wicked deceivers surround
me—

49:5 [p]Ps 23:4

49:6 [q]Job 31:24

6 those who trust in their wealth[q]
and boast of their great riches?
7 No man can redeem the life of
another
or give to God a ransom for
him—
8 the ransom for a life is costly,
no payment is ever enough—[r]

49:8 [r]Mt 16:26

9 that he should live on[s] forever
and not see decay.

49:9 [s]Ps 22:29; 89:48

10 For all can see that wise men die;[t]
the foolish and the senseless alike
perish
and leave their wealth to others.[u]

49:10 [t]Ecc 2:16 [u]Ecc 2:18,21

11 Their tombs will remain their
houses[e] forever,
their dwellings for endless
generations,

[a]7 Or *a maskil* (probably a literary or musical term) [b]9 Or *shields* [c]2 *Zaphon* can refer to a sacred mountain or the direction north. [d]2 Or *earth, / Mount Zion, on the northern side / of the* [e]11 Septuagint and Syriac; Hebrew *In their thoughts their houses will remain*

though they had[a] named[v] lands
after themselves.
[12]But man, despite his riches, does not
endure;
he is[b] like the beasts that perish.
[13]This is the fate of those who trust in
themselves,[w]
and of their followers, who
approve their sayings. *Selah*
[14]Like sheep they are destined for the
grave,[c x]
and death will feed on them.
The upright will rule[y] over them in
the morning;
their forms will decay in the
grave,[c]
far from their princely mansions.
[15]But God will redeem my life[d] from
the grave;[z]
he will surely take me to himself.[a]
Selah
[16]Do not be overawed when a man
grows rich,
when the splendor of his house
increases;
[17]for he will take nothing with him
when he dies,
his splendor will not descend with
him.[b]
[18]Though while he lived he counted
himself blessed—[c]
and men praise you when you
prosper—
[19]he will join the generation of his
fathers,[d]
who will never see the light[e] ⌊of
life⌋.
[20]A man who has riches without
understanding
is like the beasts that perish.[f]

49:11 [v]Ge 4:17; Dt 3:14
49:13 [w]Lk 12:20
49:14 [x]Job 24:19; Ps 9:17 [y]Da 7:18; Mal 4:3; 1Co 6:2; Rev 2:26
49:15 [z]Ps 56:13; Hos 13:14 [a]Ps 73:24
49:17 [b]Ps 17:14; 1Ti 6:7
49:18 [c]Dt 29:19; Lk 12:19
49:19 [d]Ge 15:15 [e]Job 33:30
49:20 [f]Ecc 3:19

Psalm 50

A psalm of Asaph.

[1]The Mighty One, God, the LORD,[g]
speaks and summons the earth
from the rising of the sun to the
place where it sets.[h]
[2]From Zion, perfect in beauty,[i]
God shines forth.[j]
[3]Our God comes[k] and will not be
silent;
a fire devours before him,[l]
and around him a tempest rages.
[4]He summons the heavens above,
and the earth,[m] that he may judge
his people:
[5]"Gather to me my consecrated
ones,[n]
who made a covenant[o] with me by
sacrifice."
[6]And the heavens proclaim[p] his
righteousness,
for God himself is judge.[q] *Selah*
[7]"Hear, O my people, and I will
speak,
O Israel, and I will testify[r] against
you:
I am God, your God.[s]
[8]I do not rebuke you for your
sacrifices
or your burnt offerings,[t] which are
ever before me.
[9]I have no need of a bull[u] from your
stall
or of goats from your pens,
[10]for every animal of the forest is
mine,
and the cattle on a thousand hills.[v]
[11]I know every bird in the mountains,
and the creatures of the field are
mine.
[12]If I were hungry I would not tell
you,
for the world[w] is mine, and all
that is in it.
[13]Do I eat the flesh of bulls
or drink the blood of goats?
[14]Sacrifice thank offerings[x] to God,
fulfill your vows[y] to the Most
High,
[15]and call[z] upon me in the day of
trouble;
I will deliver you, and you will
honor[a] me."
[16]But to the wicked, God says:
"What right have you to recite my
laws
or take my covenant on your lips?[b]

50:1 [g]Jos 22:22 [h]Ps 113:3
50:2 [i]Ps 48:2 [j]Dt 33:2; Ps 80:1
50:3 [k]Ps 96:13 [l]Ps 97:3; Da 7:10
50:4 [m]Dt 4:26; Isa 1:2
50:5 [n]Ps 30:4 [o]Ex 24:7
50:6 [p]Ps 89:5 [q]Ps 75:7
50:7 [r]Ps 81:8 [s]Ex 20:2
50:8 [t]Ps 40:6; Hos 6:6
50:9 [u]Ps 69:31
50:10 [v]Ps 104:24
50:12 [w]Ex 19:5
50:14 [x]Heb 13:15 [y]Dt 23:21
50:15 [z]Ps 81:7 [a]Ps 22:23
50:16 [b]Isa 29:13

JOY
THE COSMIC CHRIST

Psalm 50:1

Jesus reigns over the entire world. Yet for all his cosmic sovereignty, he still meets all the needy, one lover at a time.

[a]*11* Or */ for they have* [b]*12* Hebrew; Septuagint and Syriac read verse 12 the same as verse 20.
[c]*14* Hebrew *Sheol*; also in verse 15 [d]*15* Or *soul*

50:17 [c]Ne 9:26; Ro 2:21-22
50:18 [d]Ro 1:32; 1Ti 5:22

[17]You hate my instruction
and cast my words behind[c] you.
[18]When you see a thief, you join[d] with him;
you throw in your lot with adulterers.
[19]You use your mouth for evil
and harness your tongue to deceit.[e]
[20]You speak continually against your brother[f]
and slander your own mother's son.
[21]These things you have done and I kept silent;[g]
you thought I was altogether[a] like you.
But I will rebuke you
and accuse[h] you to your face.

[22]"Consider this, you who forget God,[i]
or I will tear you to pieces, with none to rescue:[j]
[23]He who sacrifices thank offerings honors me,
and he prepares the way[k]
so that I may show him[b] the salvation of God.[l]"

50:19 [e]Ps 10:7; 52:2
50:20 [f]Mt 10:21
50:21 [g]Ecc 8:11; Isa 42:14 [h]Ps 90:8
50:22 [i]Job 8:13; Ps 9:17 [j]Ps 7:2
50:23 [k]Ps 85:13 [l]Ps 91:16

DAY FIVE

▸ SELF-CONTROL AND ITS PLACE IN MY PERSONAL WORSHIP

Psalm 51:1–12

This psalm is an exposé of the heart. It was written by a person who is not only desirous of forgiveness, but also hungry for a new lifestyle. Most people want to be forgiven, but many times their plea for forgiveness leaves them without the slightest desire to really become better people. Even as they seek cleansing, they fully expect to become dirty the next time.

The plea for forgiveness and the desire to live a cleansed life together amount to holiness. Holiness has about it a preemptive desire for sinlessness. It is that "second step" of self-control. After self-control alone has failed, the sinner seeks primarily to be forgiven for sin, but holiness only results when the person seeks to stop doing the sin altogether.

David in Psalm 51 realizes that his sin was never a private affair. "Against you, you only" are the four words of personal reformation that lead us into holy living. Personal reformation requires that we live in an attitude of open confession before God. God has a simple formula for forgiveness and cleansing. It is found in 1 John 1:9, "If we confess our sins, he is faithful and just and will forgive us our sins and purify us from all unrighteousness." If we do this, writes John, we will "walk in the light, as he is in the light." Then we will "have fellowship with one another" (v. 7). David had to learn, as do we, that we cannot sin without fracturing our whole world of relationships.

So our worship centers on our self-control. But then so does our entire world of relationships. Our self-control finds the energy to be consistent in its driving desire to bring pleasure to our Heavenly Father.

To begin a study on the topic of Self-Control, the Path of Coming to Maturity, turn to the home page on page 364.

Psalm 51

For the director of music. A psalm of David. When the prophet Nathan came to him after David had committed adultery with Bathsheba.

[1]Have mercy on me, O God,
according to your unfailing love;
according to your great compassion
blot out[m] my transgressions.[n]
[2]Wash away[o] all my iniquity
and cleanse[p] me from my sin.

[3]For I know my transgressions,
and my sin is always before me.[q]
[4]Against you, you only, have I sinned
and done what is evil in your sight,[r]
so that you are proved right when you speak
and justified when you judge.[s]
[5]Surely I was sinful[t] at birth,
sinful from the time my mother conceived me.
[6]Surely you desire truth in the inner parts[c];
you teach[d] me wisdom[u] in the inmost place.[v]

51:1 [m]Ac 3:19 [n]Isa 43:25; Col 2:14
51:2 [o]1Jn 1:9 [p]Heb 9:14
51:3 [q]Isa 59:12
51:4 [r]Ge 20:6; Lk 15:21 [s]Ro 3:4*
51:5 [t]Job 14:4
51:6 [u]Pr 2:6 [v]Ps 15:2

[a]21 Or *thought the 'I AM' was* [b]23 Or *and to him who considers his way*/ *I will show* [c]6 The meaning of the Hebrew for this phrase is uncertain. [d]6 Or *you desired . . . ; / you taught*

51:7 [w]Lev 14:4; Heb 9:19 [x]Isa 1:18

[7]Cleanse me with hyssop,[w] and I will be clean;
wash me, and I will be whiter than snow.[x]

51:8 [y]Isa 35:10

[8]Let me hear joy and gladness;[y]
let the bones you have crushed rejoice.

51:9 [z]Jer 16:17

[9]Hide your face from my sins[z]
and blot out all my iniquity.

51:10 [a]Ps 78:37; Ac 15:9 [b]Eze 18:31

[10]Create in me a pure heart,[a] O God,
and renew a steadfast spirit within me.[b]
[11]Do not cast me from your presence
or take your Holy Spirit[c] from me.

51:11 [c]Eph 4:30

[12]Restore to me the joy of your salvation[d]
and grant me a willing spirit, to sustain me.

51:12 [d]Ps 13:5

51:13 [e]Ac 9:21-22 [f]Ps 22:27

[13]Then I will teach transgressors your ways,[e]
and sinners will turn back to you.[f]

51:14 [g]2Sa 12:9 [h]Ps 25:5 [i]Ps 35:28

[14]Save me from bloodguilt,[g] O God,
the God who saves me,[h]
and my tongue will sing of your righteousness.[i]

51:15 [j]Ps 9:14

[15]O Lord, open my lips,[j]
and my mouth will declare your praise.

51:16 [k]1Sa 15:22; Ps 40:6

[16]You do not delight in sacrifice,[k] or I would bring it;
you do not take pleasure in burnt offerings.
[17]The sacrifices of God are[a] a broken spirit;
a broken and contrite heart,[l]
O God, you will not despise.

51:17 [l]Ps 34:18

GENTLENESS

THE SACRIFICES OF GOD

Psalm 51:17

It is a haughty heart that brags of its sufficiency. Broken hearts are through with boasting. Broken hearts love only God.

51:18 [m]Ps 102:16; Isa 51:3

[18]In your good pleasure make Zion[m] prosper;
build up the walls of Jerusalem.

51:19 [n]Ps 4:5 [o]Ps 66:13 [p]Ps 66:15

[19]Then there will be righteous sacrifices,[n]
whole burnt offerings[o] to delight you;
then bulls[p] will be offered on your altar.

Psalm 52

For the director of music. A *maskil*[b] of David. When Doeg the Edomite[q] had gone to Saul and told him: "David has gone to the house of Ahimelech."

52:1 [q]1Sa 22:9 [r]Ps 94:4

[1]Why do you boast of evil, you mighty man?
Why do you boast[r] all day long,
you who are a disgrace in the eyes of God?
[2]Your tongue plots destruction;
it is like a sharpened razor,[s]
you who practice deceit.[t]

52:2 [s]Ps 57:4 [t]Ps 50:19

[3]You love evil rather than good,
falsehood[u] rather than speaking the truth. *Selah*

52:3 [u]Jer 9:5

[4]You love every harmful word,
O you deceitful tongue![v]

52:4 [v]Ps 120:2,3

[5]Surely God will bring you down to everlasting ruin:
He will snatch you up and tear[w] you from your tent;
he will uproot[x] you from the land of the living.[y] *Selah*

52:5 [w]Isa 22:19 [x]Pr 2:22 [y]Ps 27:13

[6]The righteous will see and fear;
they will laugh[z] at him, saying,

52:6 [z]Job 22:19; Ps 37:34; 40:3

[7]"Here now is the man
who did not make God his stronghold
but trusted in his great wealth[a]
and grew strong by destroying others!"

52:7 [a]Ps 49:6

[8]But I am like an olive tree[b]
flourishing in the house of God;
I trust[c] in God's unfailing love
for ever and ever.

52:8 [b]Jer 11:16 [c]Ps 13:5

[9]I will praise you forever[d] for what you have done;
in your name I will hope, for your name is good.[e]
I will praise you in the presence of your saints.

52:9 [d]Ps 30:12 [e]Ps 54:6

Psalm 53

For the director of music. According to *mahalath.*[c] A *maskil*[b] of David.

53:1 [f]Ps 14:1-7; Ro 3:10 [g]Ps 10:4

[1]The fool[f] says in his heart,
"There is no God."[g]
They are corrupt, and their ways are vile;
there is no one who does good.

[a] *17* Or *My sacrifice, O God, is* [b] Title: Probably a literary or musical term [c] Title: Probably a musical term

53:2 [h]Ps 33:13 [i]2Ch 15:2

2 God looks down from heaven[h]
on the sons of men
to see if there are any who
understand,
any who seek God.[i]
3 Everyone has turned away,
they have together become
corrupt;
there is no one who does good,
not even one.[j]

53:3 [j]Ro 3:10-12*

PEACE

THE NECESSITY OF THE CROSS

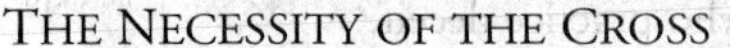

Psalm 53:3

Consider the following:

Major Premise: All are sinners.

Minor Premise: Sinners cannot dwell with God.

Conclusion: Therefore Jesus . . . therefore peace.

4 Will the evildoers never learn—
those who devour my people as
men eat bread
and who do not call on God?
5 There they were, overwhelmed with
dread,[k]
where there was nothing to dread.
God scattered the bones[l] of those
who attacked you;
you put them to shame, for God
despised them.
6 Oh, that salvation for Israel would
come out of Zion!
When God restores the fortunes
of his people,
let Jacob rejoice and Israel be glad!

53:5 [k]Lev 26:17 [l]Eze 6:5

Psalm 54

For the director of music. With stringed instruments. A *maskil*[a] of David. When the Ziphites had gone to Saul and said, "Is not David hiding among us?"

1 Save me, O God, by your name;[m]
vindicate me by your might.[n]
2 Hear my prayer, O God;[o]
listen to the words of my mouth.
3 Strangers are attacking me;[p]
ruthless men seek my life[q]—
men without regard for God.[r]
Selah
4 Surely God is my help;[s]
the Lord is the one who sustains
me.[t]
5 Let evil recoil[u] on those who slander
me;
in your faithfulness[v] destroy them.
6 I will sacrifice a freewill offering[w] to
you;
I will praise your name, O LORD,
for it is good.[x]
7 For he has delivered me[y] from all my
troubles,
and my eyes have looked in
triumph on my foes.[z]

54:1 [m]Ps 20:1 [n]2Ch 20:6
54:2 [o]Ps 5:1; 55:1
54:3 [p]Ps 86:14 [q]Ps 40:14 [r]Ps 36:1
54:4 [s]Ps 118:7
54:4 [t]Ps 41:12
54:5 [u]Ps 94:23 [v]Ps 89:49; 143:12
54:6 [w]Ps 50:14 [x]Ps 52:9
54:7 [y]Ps 34:6 [z]Ps 59:10

Psalm 55

For the director of music. With stringed instruments. A *maskil*[a] of David.

1 Listen to my prayer, O God,
do not ignore my plea;[a]
2 hear me and answer me.[b]
My thoughts trouble me and I am
distraught[c]
3 at the voice of the enemy,
at the stares of the wicked;
for they bring down suffering upon
me[d]
and revile me in their anger.[e]
4 My heart is in anguish within me;
the terrors[f] of death assail me.
5 Fear and trembling[g] have beset me;
horror has overwhelmed me.
6 I said, "Oh, that I had the wings of
a dove!
I would fly away and be at rest—
7 I would flee far away
and stay in the desert; *Selah*
8 I would hurry to my place of shelter,
far from the tempest and storm.[h]"
9 Confuse the wicked, O Lord,
confound their speech,
for I see violence and strife[i] in the
city.
10 Day and night they prowl about on
its walls;
malice and abuse are within it.
11 Destructive forces[j] are at work in the
city;
threats and lies[k] never leave its
streets.
12 If an enemy were insulting me,
I could endure it;
if a foe were raising himself against
me,

55:1 [a]Ps 27:9; 61:1
55:2 [b]Ps 66:19 [c]Ps 77:3; Isa 38:14
55:3 [d]2Sa 16:6-8; Ps 17:9 [e]Ps 71:11
55:4 [f]Ps 116:3
55:5 [g]Job 21:6; Ps 119:120
55:8 [h]Isa 4:6
55:9 [i]Jer 6:7
55:11 [j]Ps 5:9 [k]Ps 10:7

[a]Title: Probably a literary or musical term

KINDNESS
THE URBAN CHRIST

Psalm 55:11

Cities are places where sociology and sin team up to break a million hearts. Cities harbor weeping. No wonder Jesus left his small hometown and hung around the cities with their teeming, needy people. No wonder he wept above Jerusalem.

I could hide from him.
13 But it is you, a man like myself,
my companion, my close friend,[l]
14 with whom I once enjoyed sweet fellowship
as we walked with the throng at the house of God.[m]

15 Let death take my enemies by surprise;[n]
let them go down alive to the grave,[a] [o]
for evil finds lodging among them.

16 But I call to God,
and the LORD saves me.
17 Evening,[p] morning[q] and noon
I cry out in distress,
and he hears my voice.
18 He ransoms me unharmed
from the battle waged against me,
even though many oppose me.
19 God, who is enthroned forever,[r]
will hear[s] them and afflict them— *Selah*
men who never change their ways
and have no fear of God.

20 My companion attacks his friends;[t]
he violates his covenant.[u]
21 His speech is smooth as butter,
yet war is in his heart;
his words are more soothing than oil,[v]
yet they are drawn swords.[w]

22 Cast your cares on the LORD
and he will sustain you;[x]
he will never let the righteous fall.[y]
23 But you, O God, will bring down the wicked
into the pit[z] of corruption;
bloodthirsty and deceitful men[a]
will not live out half their days.[b]

But as for me, I trust in you.[c]

55:13 [l]2Sa 15:12; Ps 41:9
55:14 [m]Ps 42:4
55:15 [n]Ps 64:7 [o]Nu 16:30,33
55:17 [p]Ps 141:2; Ac 3:1 [q]Ps 5:3
55:19 [r]Dt 33:27 [s]Ps 78:59
55:20 [t]Ps 7:4 [u]Ps 89:34
55:21 [v]Pr 5:3 [w]Ps 28:3; Ps 57:4; 59:7
55:22 [x]Ps 37:5; Mt 6:25-34; 1Pe 5:7 [y]Ps 37:24
55:23 [z]Ps 73:18 [a]Ps 5:6 [b]Job 15:32; Pr 10:27 [c]Ps 25:2

Psalm 56

For the director of music. To ⌊the tune of⌋ "A Dove on Distant Oaks." Of David. A *miktam*.[b] When the Philistines had seized him in Gath.

1 Be merciful to me, O God, for men hotly pursue me;[d]
all day long they press their attack.
2 My slanderers pursue me all day long;[e]
many are attacking me in their pride.[f]

3 When I am afraid,[g]
I will trust in you.
4 In God, whose word I praise,
in God I trust; I will not be afraid.
What can mortal man do to me?[h]

5 All day long they twist my words;[i]
they are always plotting to harm me.
6 They conspire,[j] they lurk,
they watch my steps,
eager to take my life.[k]

7 On no account let them escape;
in your anger, O God, bring down the nations.[l]
8 Record my lament;
list my tears on your scroll[c]—
are they not in your record?[m]

9 Then my enemies will turn back[n]
when I call for help.[o]
By this I will know that God is for me.[p]

10 In God, whose word I praise,
in the LORD, whose word I praise—
11 in God I trust; I will not be afraid.
What can man do to me?

12 I am under vows[q] to you, O God;
I will present my thank offerings to you.
13 For you have delivered me[d] from death[r]
and my feet from stumbling,
that I may walk before God
in the light of life.[e] [s]

56:1 [d]Ps 57:1-3
56:2 [e]Ps 57:3 [f]Ps 35:1
56:3 [g]Ps 55:4-5
56:4 [h]Ps 118:6; Heb 13:6
56:5 [i]Ps 41:7
56:6 [j]Ps 59:3 [k]Ps 71:10
56:7 [l]Ps 36:12; 55:23
56:8 [m]Mal 3:16
56:9 [n]Ps 9:3 [o]Ps 102:2 [p]Ro 8:31
56:12 [q]Ps 50:14
56:13 [r]Ps 116:8 [s]Job 33:30

[a] *15* Hebrew *Sheol* [b] Title: Probably a literary or musical term [c] *8* Or / *put my tears in your wineskin* [d] *13* Or *my soul* [e] *13* Or *the land of the living*

Psalm 57

For the director of music. ⌞To the tune of⌟ "Do Not Destroy." Of David. A *miktam*.[a] When he had fled from Saul into the cave.

[1]Have mercy on me, O God, have
mercy on me,
for in you my soul takes refuge.[t]
I will take refuge in the shadow of
your wings[u]
until the disaster has passed.[v]

57:1 [t]Ps 2:12 [u]Ps 17:8 [v]Isa 26:20

[2]I cry out to God Most High,
to God, who fulfills ⌞his purpose⌟
for me.[w]

57:2 [w]Ps 138:8

[3]He sends from heaven and saves
me,[x]
rebuking those who hotly pursue
me;[y] *Selah*
God sends his love and his
faithfulness.[z]

57:3 [x]Ps 18:9,16 [y]Ps 56:1 [z]Ps 40:11

[4]I am in the midst of lions;[a]
I lie among ravenous beasts—
men whose teeth are spears and
arrows,
whose tongues are sharp swords.[b]

57:4 [a]Ps 35:17 [b]Ps 55:21; Pr 30:14

[5]Be exalted, O God, above the
heavens;
let your glory be over all the
earth.[c]

57:5 [c]Ps 108:5

[6]They spread a net for my feet—
I was bowed down[d] in distress.
They dug a pit[e] in my path—
but they have fallen into it
themselves.[f] *Selah*

57:6 [d]Ps 145:14 [e]Ps 35:7 [f]Ps 7:15; Pr 28:10

[7]My heart is steadfast, O God,
my heart is steadfast;[g]
I will sing and make music.

57:7 [g]Ps 108:1

[8]Awake, my soul!
Awake, harp and lyre![h]
I will awaken the dawn.

57:8 [h]Ps 16:9; 30:12; 150:3

[9]I will praise you, O Lord, among the
nations;
I will sing of you among the
peoples.
[10]For great is your love, reaching to
the heavens;
your faithfulness reaches to the
skies.[i]

57:10 [i]Ps 36:5; 103:11

[11]Be exalted, O God, above the
heavens;
let your glory be over all the
earth.[j]

57:11 [j]ver 5

Psalm 58

For the director of music. ⌞To the tune of⌟ "Do Not Destroy." Of David. A *miktam*.[a]

[1]Do you rulers indeed speak
justly?[k]
Do you judge uprightly among
men?

58:1 [k]Ps 82:2

[2]No, in your heart you devise
injustice,
and your hands mete out violence
on the earth.[l]

58:2 [l]Ps 94:20; Mal 3:15

[3]Even from birth the wicked go
astray;
from the womb they are wayward
and speak lies.
[4]Their venom is like the venom of a
snake,[m]
like that of a cobra that has
stopped its ears,
[5]that will not heed the tune of the
charmer,
however skillful the enchanter
may be.

58:4 [m]Ps 140:3; Ecc 10:11

[6]Break the teeth in their mouths,
O God;[n]
tear out, O LORD, the fangs of
the lions![o]

58:6 [n]Ps 3:7 [o]Job 4:10

[7]Let them vanish like water that flows
away;[p]
when they draw the bow, let their
arrows be blunted.[q]

58:7 [p]Jos 7:5; Ps 112:10 [q]Ps 64:3

[8]Like a slug melting away as it moves
along,
like a stillborn child,[r] may they
not see the sun.

58:8 [r]Job 3:16

[9]Before your pots can feel ⌞the heat of⌟
the thorns[s]—
whether they be green or dry—the
wicked will be swept
away.[b][t]

58:9 [s]Ps 118:12 [t]Pr 10:25

[10]The righteous will be glad when they
are avenged,[u]
when they bathe their feet in the
blood of the wicked.[v]

58:10 [u]Ps 64:10; 91:8 [v]Ps 68:23

[11]Then men will say,
"Surely the righteous still are
rewarded;
surely there is a God who judges
the earth."[w]

58:11 [w]Ps 9:8; 18:20

[a]Title: Probably a literary or musical term
[b]9 The meaning of the Hebrew for this verse is uncertain.

Psalm 59

For the director of music. ⌞To the tune of⌟ "Do Not Destroy." Of David. A *miktam*.[a] When Saul had sent men to watch David's house in order to kill him.

[1]Deliver me from my enemies,
59:1 [x]Ps 143:9 O God;[x]
protect me from those who rise up
against me.
[2]Deliver me from evildoers
59:2 [y]Ps 139:19 and save me from bloodthirsty
men.[y]

[3]See how they lie in wait for me!
59:3 [z]Ps 56:6 Fierce men conspire[z] against me
for no offense or sin of mine,
O LORD.
59:4 [a]Ps 35:19,23 [4]I have done no wrong, yet they are
ready to attack me.[a]
Arise to help me; look on my
plight!
[5]O LORD God Almighty, the God of
Israel,
rouse yourself to punish all the
nations;
59:5 [b]Jer 18:23 show no mercy to wicked
traitors.[b] *Selah*

59:6 [c]ver 14 [6]They return at evening,
snarling like dogs,[c]
and prowl about the city.
[7]See what they spew from their
mouths—
59:7 [d]Ps 57:4 [e]Ps 10:11 they spew out swords[d] from their
lips,
59:8 [f]Ps 37:13; Pr 1:26 [g]Ps 2:4 and they say, "Who can hear us?"[e]
[8]But you, O LORD, laugh at them;[f]
you scoff at all those nations.[g]
59:9 [h]Ps 9:9; 62:2 [9]O my Strength, I watch for you;
you, O God, are my fortress,[h]
[10]my loving God.

God will go before me
and will let me gloat over those
who slander me.
59:11 [i]Ps 84:9 [j]Dt 4:9 [k]Ps 106:27 [11]But do not kill them, O Lord our
shield,[b] [i]
or my people will forget.[j]
In your might make them wander
about,
59:12 [l]Ps 10:7 [m]Pr 12:13 [n]Zep 3:11 and bring them down.[k]
[12]For the sins of their mouths,[l]
for the words of their lips,[m]
let them be caught in their pride.[n]
For the curses and lies they utter,
[13] consume them in wrath,
59:13 [o]Ps 104:35 consume them till they are no
more.[o]
Then it will be known to the ends of
the earth
59:13 [p]Ps 83:18 that God rules over Jacob.[p] *Selah*

[14]They return at evening,
snarling like dogs,
and prowl about the city.
59:15 [q]Job 15:23 [15]They wander about for food[q]
and howl if not satisfied.
59:16 [r]Ps 21:13 [s]Ps 88:13 [t]Ps 101:1 [u]Ps 46:1 [16]But I will sing of your strength,[r]
in the morning[s] I will sing of your
love;[t]
for you are my fortress,
my refuge in times of trouble.[u]

[17]O my Strength, I sing praise to you;
you, O God, are my fortress, my
loving God.

Psalm 60

For the director of music. To ⌞the tune of⌟ "The Lily of the Covenant." A *miktam*[a] of David. For teaching. When he fought Aram Naharaim[c] and Aram Zobah,[d] and when Joab returned and struck down twelve thousand Edomites in the Valley of Salt.

60:1 [v]2Sa 5:20; Ps 44:9 [w]Ps 79:5 [x]Ps 80:3 [1]You have rejected us,[v] O God, and
burst forth upon us;
you have been angry[w]—now
restore us![x]
60:2 [y]Ps 18:7 [z]2Ch 7:14 [2]You have shaken the land[y] and torn
it open;
mend its fractures,[z] for it is
quaking.
60:3 [a]Ps 71:20 [b]Isa 51:17; Jer 25:16 [3]You have shown your people
desperate times;[a]
you have given us wine that makes
us stagger.[b]

[4]But for those who fear you, you have
raised a banner
to be unfurled against the bow.
Selah
60:5 [c]Ps 17:7; 108:6 [d]Ps 127:2 [5]Save us and help us with your right
hand,[c]
that those you love[d] may be
delivered.
60:6 [e]Ge 12:6 [6]God has spoken from his sanctuary:
"In triumph I will parcel out
Shechem[e]
and measure off the Valley of
Succoth.

[a]Title: Probably a literary or musical term [b]*11* Or *sovereign* [c]Title: That is, Arameans of Northwest Mesopotamia [d]Title: That is, Arameans of central Syria

7 Gilead[f] is mine, and Manasseh is mine;
Ephraim is my helmet,
Judah[g] my scepter.[h]
8 Moab is my washbasin,
upon Edom I toss my sandal;
over Philistia I shout in triumph.[i]"
9 Who will bring me to the fortified city?
Who will lead me to Edom?
10 Is it not you, O God, you who have rejected us
and no longer go out with our armies?[j]
11 Give us aid against the enemy,
for the help of man is worthless.[k]
12 With God we will gain the victory,
and he will trample down our enemies.[l]

Psalm 61

For the director of music. With stringed instruments. Of David.

1 Hear my cry, O God;[m]
listen to my prayer.[n]

2 From the ends of the earth I call to you,
I call as my heart grows faint;[o]
lead me to the rock[p] that is higher than I.
3 For you have been my refuge,[q]
a strong tower against the foe.[r]

4 I long to dwell[s] in your tent forever
and take refuge in the shelter of your wings.[t] *Selah*
5 For you have heard my vows,[u] O God;
you have given me the heritage of those who fear your name.[v]

6 Increase the days of the king's life,
his years for many generations.[w]
7 May he be enthroned in God's presence forever;[x]
appoint your love and faithfulness to protect him.[y]

8 Then will I ever sing praise to your name[z]
and fulfill my vows day after day.

Psalm 62

For the director of music. For Jeduthun. A psalm of David.

1 My soul finds rest[a] in God alone;
my salvation comes from him.
2 He alone is my rock[b] and my salvation;
he is my fortress, I will never be shaken.

3 How long will you assault a man?
Would all of you throw him down—
this leaning wall,[c] this tottering fence?
4 They fully intend to topple him
from his lofty place;
they take delight in lies.
With their mouths they bless,
but in their hearts they curse.[d] *Selah*

5 Find rest, O my soul, in God alone;
my hope comes from him.
6 He alone is my rock and my salvation;
he is my fortress, I will not be shaken.
7 My salvation and my honor depend on God[a];
he is my mighty rock, my refuge.[e]
8 Trust in him at all times, O people;
pour out your hearts to him,[f]
for God is our refuge. *Selah*

9 Lowborn men are but a breath,[g]
the highborn are but a lie;
if weighed on a balance,[h] they are nothing;
together they are only a breath.
10 Do not trust in extortion
or take pride in stolen goods;[i]
though your riches increase,
do not set your heart on them.[j]
11 One thing God has spoken,
two things have I heard:
that you, O God, are strong,
12 and that you, O Lord, are loving.
Surely you will reward each person
according to what he has done.[k]

Psalm 63

A psalm of David.
When he was in the Desert of Judah.

1 O God, you are my God,
earnestly I seek you;[l]
my soul thirsts for you,[l]
my body longs for you,
in a dry and weary land
where there is no water.

[a]7 Or / *God Most High is my salvation and my honor*

60:7 [f]Jos 13:31 [g]Dt 33:17 [h]Ge 49:10
60:8 [i]2Sa 8:1
60:10 [j]Jos 7:12; Ps 44:9; 108:11
60:11 [k]Ps 146:3
60:12 [l]Nu 24:18; Ps 44:5
61:1 [m]Ps 64:1 [n]Ps 86:6
61:2 [o]Ps 77:3 [p]Ps 18:2
61:3 [q]Ps 62:7 [r]Pr 18:10
61:4 [s]Ps 23:6 [t]Ps 91:4
61:5 [u]Ps 56:12 [v]Ps 86:11
61:6 [w]Ps 21:4
61:7 [x]Ps 41:12 [y]Ps 40:11
61:8 [z]Ps 65:1; 71:22
62:1 [a]Ps 33:20
62:2 [b]Ps 89:26
62:3 [c]Isa 30:13
62:4 [d]Ps 28:3
62:7 [e]Ps 46:1; 85:9; Jer 3:23
62:8 [f]1Sa 1:15; Ps 42:4; La 2:19
62:9 [g]Ps 39:5,11 [h]Isa 40:15
62:10 [i]Isa 61:8 [j]Job 31:25; 1Ti 6:6-10
62:12 [k]Job 34:11; Mt 16:27
63:1 [l]Ps 42:2; 84:2

63:2 [m]Ps 27:4
2 I have seen you in the sanctuary[m]
and beheld your power and your glory.
3 Because your love is better than
63:3 [n]Ps 69:16
life,[n]
my lips will glorify you.
63:4 [o]Ps 104:33 [p]Ps 28:2
4 I will praise you as long as I live,[o]
and in your name I will lift up my hands.[p]
63:5 [q]Ps 36:8
5 My soul will be satisfied as with the richest of foods;[q]
with singing lips my mouth will praise you.

6 On my bed I remember you;
I think of you through the
63:6 [r]Ps 42:8
watches of the night.[r]
7 Because you are my help,[s]
63:7 [s]Ps 27:9
I sing in the shadow of your wings.
63:8 [t]Ps 18:35
8 My soul clings to you;
your right hand upholds me.[t]

63:9 [u]Ps 40:14 [v]Ps 55:15
9 They who seek my life will be destroyed;[u]
they will go down to the depths of the earth.[v]
10 They will be given over to the sword
and become food for jackals.

11 But the king will rejoice in God;
63:11 [w]Dt 6:13; Ps 21:1; Isa 45:23
all who swear by God's name will praise him,[w]
while the mouths of liars will be silenced.

Psalm 64

For the director of music.
A psalm of David.

64:1 [x]Ps 55:2 [y]Ps 140:1
1 Hear me, O God, as I voice my complaint;[x]
protect my life from the threat of the enemy.[y]
2 Hide me from the conspiracy of the
64:2 [z]Ps 56:6; 59:2
wicked,[z]
from that noisy crowd of evildoers.

3 They sharpen their tongues like swords
64:3 [a]Ps 58:7
and aim their words like deadly arrows.[a]
4 They shoot from ambush at the
64:4 [b]Ps 11:2 [c]Ps 55:19
innocent man;[b]
they shoot at him suddenly, without fear.[c]

5 They encourage each other in evil plans,
they talk about hiding their snares;
64:5 [d]Ps 10:11
they say, "Who will see them[a]?"[d]
6 They plot injustice and say,
"We have devised a perfect plan!"
Surely the mind and heart of man are cunning.

7 But God will shoot them with arrows;
suddenly they will be struck down.
64:8 [e]Ps 9:3; Pr 18:7 [f]Ps 22:7
8 He will turn their own tongues against them[e]
and bring them to ruin;
all who see them will shake their heads[f] in scorn.
9 All mankind will fear;
they will proclaim the works of God
64:9 [g]Jer 51:10
and ponder what he has done.[g]
10 Let the righteous rejoice in the LORD
64:10 [h]Ps 25:20 [i]Ps 32:11
and take refuge in him;[h]
let all the upright in heart praise him![i]

Psalm 65

For the director of music.
A psalm of David. A song.

1 Praise awaits[b] you, O God, in Zion;
65:1 [j]Ps 116:18
to you our vows will be fulfilled.[j]
65:2 [k]Isa 66:23
2 O you who hear prayer,
to you all men will come.[k]
65:3 [l]Ps 38:4 [m]Heb 9:14
3 When we were overwhelmed by sins,[l]
you forgave[c] our transgressions.[m]
65:4 [n]Ps 4:3; 33:12 [o]Ps 36:8
4 Blessed are those you choose[n]
and bring near to live in your courts!
We are filled with the good things of your house,[o]
of your holy temple.

5 You answer us with awesome deeds of righteousness,
65:5 [p]Ps 85:4 [q]Ps 107:23
O God our Savior,[p]
the hope of all the ends of the earth
and of the farthest seas,[q]
6 who formed the mountains by your power,
65:6 [r]Ps 93:1
having armed yourself with strength,[r]
65:7 [s]Mt 8:26
7 who stilled the roaring of the seas,[s]

[a]5 Or *us* [b]*1* Or *befits*; the meaning of the Hebrew for this word is uncertain. [c]*3* Or *made atonement for*

65:7 [t]Isa 17:12-13

the roaring of their waves,
and the turmoil of the nations.[t]
8 Those living far away fear your wonders;
where morning dawns and evening fades
you call forth songs of joy.

65:9 [u]Ps 68:9-10 [v]Ps 46:4; 104:14

9 You care for the land and water it;[u]
you enrich it abundantly.
The streams of God are filled with water
to provide the people with grain,[v]
for so you have ordained it.[a]
10 You drench its furrows
and level its ridges;
you soften it with showers
and bless its crops.
11 You crown the year with your bounty,
and your carts overflow with abundance.

65:12 [w]Job 28:26

12 The grasslands of the desert overflow;[w]
the hills are clothed with gladness.

65:13 [x]Ps 144:13 [y]Ps 72:16 [z]Ps 98:8; Isa 55:12

13 The meadows are covered with flocks[x]
and the valleys are mantled with grain;[y]
they shout for joy and sing.[z]

Psalm 66

For the director of music.
A song. A psalm.

66:1 [a]Ps 100:1

1 Shout with joy to God, all the earth![a]

66:2 [b]Ps 79:9

2 Sing the glory of his name;[b]
make his praise glorious!

66:3 [c]Ps 65:5 [d]Ps 18:44

3 Say to God, "How awesome are your deeds![c]
So great is your power
that your enemies cringe[d] before you.

66:4 [e]Ps 22:27 [f]Ps 67:3

4 All the earth bows down[e] to you;
they sing praise[f] to you,
they sing praise to your name."
Selah

66:5 [g]Ps 106:22

5 Come and see what God has done,
how awesome his works[g] in man's behalf!

66:6 [h]Ex 14:22

6 He turned the sea into dry land,[h]
they passed through the waters on foot—
come, let us rejoice in him.

66:7 [i]Ps 145:13 [j]Ps 11:4 [k]Ps 140:8

7 He rules forever[i] by his power,
his eyes watch[j] the nations—
let not the rebellious[k] rise up against him.
Selah

66:8 [l]Ps 98:4

8 Praise[l] our God, O peoples,
let the sound of his praise be heard;

66:9 [m]Ps 121:3

9 he has preserved our lives
and kept our feet from slipping.[m]

66:10 [n]Ps 17:3; Isa 48:10; Zec 13:9; 1Pe 1:6-7

10 For you, O God, tested us;
you refined us like silver.[n]

66:11 [o]La 1:13

11 You brought us into prison
and laid burdens[o] on our backs.

66:12 [p]Isa 51:23 [q]Isa 43:2

12 You let men ride over our heads;[p]
we went through fire and water,
but you brought us to a place of abundance.[q]

66:13 [r]Ecc 5:4

13 I will come to your temple with burnt offerings
and fulfill my vows[r] to you—
14 vows my lips promised and my mouth spoke
when I was in trouble.

66:15 [s]Nu 6:14; Ps 51:19

15 I will sacrifice fat animals to you
and an offering of rams;
I will offer bulls and goats.[s] *Selah*

66:16 [t]Ps 34:11 [u]Ps 71:15,24

16 Come and listen,[t] all you who fear God;
let me tell[u] you what he has done for me.
17 I cried out to him with my mouth;
his praise was on my tongue.

66:18 [v]Job 36:21; Isa 1:15; Jas 4:3

18 If I had cherished sin in my heart,
the Lord would not have listened;[v]

66:19 [w]Ps 116:1-2

19 but God has surely listened
and heard my voice[w] in prayer.

66:20 [x]Ps 22:24; 68:35

20 Praise be to God,
who has not rejected[x] my prayer
or withheld his love from me!

Psalm 67

For the director of music. With stringed instruments. A psalm. A song.

67:1 [y]Nu 6:24-26; Ps 4:6

1 May God be gracious to us and bless us
and make his face shine upon us,[y]
Selah

67:2 [z]Isa 52:10 [a]Tit 2:11

2 that your ways may be known on earth,
your salvation[z] among all nations.[a]
3 May the peoples praise you, O God;
may all the peoples praise you.

67:4 [b]Ps 96:10-13

4 May the nations be glad and sing for joy,
for you rule the peoples justly[b]

[a]9 Or *for that is how you prepare the land*

and guide the nations of the earth. *Selah*

5 May the peoples praise you,
O God;
may all the peoples praise you.

6 Then the land will yield its harvest,[c]
and God, our God, will bless us.
7 God will bless us,
and all the ends of the earth will
fear him.[d]

67:6 [c]Lev 26:4; Ps 85:12; Eze 34:27
67:7 [d]Ps 33:8

Psalm 68

For the director of music. Of David.
A psalm. A song.

1 May God arise, may his enemies be
scattered;
may his foes flee[e] before him.
2 As smoke[f] is blown away by the
wind,
may you blow them away;
as wax melts[g] before the fire,
may the wicked perish before
God.
3 But may the righteous be glad
and rejoice[h] before God;
may they be happy and joyful.

4 Sing to God, sing praise to his
name,[i]
extol him who rides on the
clouds[a][j]—
his name is the LORD[k]—
and rejoice before him.
5 A father to the fatherless,[l] a defender
of widows,[m]
is God in his holy dwelling.[n]
6 God sets the lonely in families,[b][o]
he leads forth the prisoners[p] with
singing;
but the rebellious live in a
sun-scorched land.[q]

7 When you went out[r] before your
people, O God,
when you marched through the
wasteland, *Selah*
8 the earth shook,
the heavens poured down rain,[s]
before God, the One of Sinai,[t]
before God, the God of Israel.
9 You gave abundant showers,[u]
O God;
you refreshed your weary
inheritance.
10 Your people settled in it,
and from your bounty, O God,
you provided[v] for the poor.

68:1 [e]Nu 10:35; Isa 33:3
68:2 [f]Hos 13:3 [g]Isa 9:18; Mic 1:4
68:3 [h]Ps 32:11
68:4 [i]Ps 66:2 [j]Dt 33:26 [k]Ex 6:3; Ps 83:18
68:5 [l]Ps 10:14 [m]Dt 10:18 [n]Dt 26:15
68:6 [o]Ps 113:9 [p]Ac 12:6 [q]Ps 107:34
68:7 [r]Ex 13:21; Jdg 4:14
68:8 [s]Jdg 5:4 [t]Ex 19:16,18
68:9 [u]Dt 11:11
68:10 [v]Ps 74:19

11 The Lord announced the word,
and great was the company of
those who proclaimed it:
12 "Kings and armies flee[w] in haste;
in the camps men divide the
plunder.
13 Even while you sleep among the
campfires,[c][x]
the wings of ⌞my⌟ dove are sheathed
with silver,
its feathers with shining gold."
14 When the Almighty[d] scattered[y] the
kings in the land,
it was like snow fallen on Zalmon.

15 The mountains of Bashan are
majestic mountains;
rugged are the mountains of
Bashan.
16 Why gaze in envy, O rugged
mountains,
at the mountain where God
chooses[z] to reign,
where the LORD himself will
dwell forever?
17 The chariots of God are tens of
thousands
and thousands of thousands;[a]
the Lord ⌞has come⌟ from Sinai
into his sanctuary.
18 When you ascended on high,
you led captives[b] in your train;
you received gifts from men,[c]
even from[e] the rebellious—
that you,[f] O LORD God, might
dwell there.

68:12 [w]Jos 10:16
68:13 [x]Ge 49:14
68:14 [y]Jos 10:10
68:16 [z]Dt 12:5
68:17 [a]Dt 33:2; Da 7:10
68:18 [b]Jdg 5:12 [c]Eph 4:8*

FAITHFULNESS

CAPTURING CAPTIVITY

Psalm 68:18

Here we see the mighty processional of God. Like an ancient conqueror, he strode the earth incarnate as a carpenter and led captivity captive. How thorough was his work? Behind him in his victory retinue were such poor captives as we ourselves—cleansed and ready for the grand revue of heaven.

19 Praise be to the Lord, to God our
Savior,[d]
who daily bears our burdens.[e]
Selah

68:19 [d]Ps 65:5 [e]Ps 55:22

[a]4 Or / *prepare the way for him who rides through the deserts* [b]6 Or *the desolate in a homeland* [c]13 Or *saddlebags* [d]14 Hebrew *Shaddai* [e]18 Or *gifts for men, / even* [f]18 Or *they*

[20]Our God is a God who saves;
from the Sovereign LORD comes
escape from death.[f]

[21]Surely God will crush the heads[g] of
his enemies,
the hairy crowns of those who go
on in their sins.
[22]The Lord says, "I will bring them
from Bashan;
I will bring them from the depths
of the sea,[h]
[23]that you may plunge your feet in the
blood of your foes,[i]
while the tongues of your dogs[j]
have their share."

[24]Your procession has come into view,
O God,
the procession of my God and
King into the sanctuary.[k]
[25]In front are the singers, after them
the musicians;
with them are the maidens playing
tambourines.[l]
[26]Praise God in the great congregation;
praise the LORD in the assembly
of Israel.[m]
[27]There is the little tribe[n] of Benjamin,
leading them,
there the great throng of Judah's
princes,
and there the princes of Zebulun
and of Naphtali.

[28]Summon your power, O God[a];
show us your strength, O God, as
you have done before.
[29]Because of your temple at Jerusalem
kings will bring you gifts.[o]
[30]Rebuke the beast among the reeds,
the herd of bulls[p] among the
calves of the nations.
Humbled, may it bring bars of silver.
Scatter the nations[q] who delight in
war.
[31]Envoys will come from Egypt;[r]
Cush[b] will submit herself to God.

[32]Sing to God, O kingdoms of the
earth,
sing praise to the Lord, *Selah*
[33]to him who rides[s] the ancient skies
above,
who thunders with mighty voice.[t]
[34]Proclaim the power[u] of God,
whose majesty is over Israel,
whose power is in the skies.
[35]You are awesome, O God, in your
sanctuary;

68:20 [f]Ps 56:13
68:21 [g]Ps 110:5; Hab 3:13
68:22 [h]Nu 21:33
68:23 [i]Ps 58:10 [j]1Ki 21:19
68:24 [k]Ps 63:2
68:25 [l]Jdg 11:34; 1Ch 13:8
68:26 [m]Ps 26:12; Isa 48:1
68:27 [n]1Sa 9:21
68:29 [o]Ps 72:10
68:30 [p]Ps 22:12 [q]Ps 89:10
68:31 [r]Isa 19:19; 45:14
68:33 [s]Ps 18:10 [t]Ps 29:4
68:34 [u]Ps 29:1

the God of Israel gives power and
strength to his people.[v]

Praise be to God![w]

Psalm 69

For the director of music. To ⌞the tune of⌟ "Lilies." Of David.

[1]Save me, O God,
for the waters have come up to my
neck.[x]
[2]I sink in the miry depths,[y]
where there is no foothold.
I have come into the deep waters;
the floods engulf me.
[3]I am worn out calling for help;[z]
my throat is parched.
My eyes fail,[a]
looking for my God.
[4]Those who hate me without reason[b]
outnumber the hairs of my head;
many are my enemies without
cause,[c]
those who seek to destroy me.
I am forced to restore
what I did not steal.

[5]You know my folly,[d] O God;
my guilt is not hidden from you.[e]

[6]May those who hope in you
not be disgraced because of me,
O Lord, the LORD Almighty;
may those who seek you
not be put to shame because of
me,
O God of Israel.
[7]For I endure scorn for your sake,[f]
and shame covers my face.[g]
[8]I am a stranger to my brothers,
an alien to my own mother's
sons;[h]
[9]for zeal for your house consumes
me,[i]
and the insults of those who insult
you fall on me.[j]
[10]When I weep and fast,[k]
I must endure scorn;
[11]when I put on sackcloth,[l]
people make sport of me.
[12]Those who sit at the gate mock me,
and I am the song of the
drunkards.[m]

[a]*28* Many Hebrew manuscripts, Septuagint and Syriac; most Hebrew manuscripts *Your God has summoned power for you* [b]*31* That is, the upper Nile region

68:35 [v]Ps 29:11 [w]Ps 66:20
69:1 [x]Jnh 2:5
69:2 [y]Ps 40:2
69:3 [z]Ps 6:6 [a]Ps 119:82; Isa 38:14
69:4 [b]Jn 15:25* [c]Ps 35:19; 38:19
69:5 [d]Ps 38:5 [e]Ps 44:21
69:7 [f]Jer 15:15 [g]Ps 44:15
69:8 [h]Ps 31:11; Isa 53:3
69:9 [i]Jn 2:17* [j]Ps 89:50-51; Ro 15:3*
69:10 [k]Ps 35:13
69:11 [l]Ps 35:13
69:12 [m]Job 30:9

13 But I pray to you, O LORD,
in the time of your favor;[n]
in your great love,[o] O God,
answer me with your sure
salvation.
14 Rescue me from the mire,
do not let me sink;
deliver me from those who hate me,
from the deep waters.[p]
15 Do not let the floodwaters[q] engulf
me
or the depths swallow me up[r]
or the pit close its mouth over me.
16 Answer me, O LORD, out of the
goodness of your love;[s]
in your great mercy turn to me.
17 Do not hide your face[t] from your
servant;
answer me quickly, for I am in
trouble.[u]
18 Come near and rescue me;
redeem[v] me because of my foes.

19 You know how I am scorned,[w]
disgraced and shamed;
all my enemies are before you.
20 Scorn has broken my heart
and has left me helpless;
I looked for sympathy, but there was
none,
for comforters,[x] but I found
none.[y]
21 They put gall in my food
and gave me vinegar for my
thirst.[z]

22 May the table set before them
become a snare;
may it become retribution and[a] a
trap.
23 May their eyes be darkened so they
cannot see,
and their backs be bent forever.[a]
24 Pour out your wrath[b] on them;
let your fierce anger overtake
them.
25 May their place be deserted;[c]
let there be no one to dwell in
their tents.[d]
26 For they persecute those you wound
and talk about the pain of those
you hurt.[e]
27 Charge them with crime upon
crime;[f]
do not let them share in your
salvation.[g]
28 May they be blotted out of the book
of life[h]

69:13 [n]Isa 49:8; 2Co 6:2 [o]Ps 51:1
69:14 [p]ver 2; Ps 144:7
69:15 [q]Ps 124:4-5 [r]Nu 16:33
69:16 [s]Ps 63:3
69:17 [t]Ps 27:9 [u]Ps 66:14
69:18 [v]Ps 49:15
69:19 [w]Ps 22:6
69:20 [x]Job 16:2 [y]Isa 63:5
69:21 [z]Mt 27:34; Mk 15:23; Jn 19:28-30
69:23 [a]Isa 6:9-10; Ro 11:9-10*
69:24 [b]Ps 79:6
69:25 [c]Mt 23:38 [d]Ac 1:20*
69:26 [e]Isa 53:4; Zec 1:15
69:27 [f]Ne 4:5 [g]Ps 109:14; Isa 26:10
69:28 [h]Ex 32:32-33; Lk 10:20; Php 4:3

and not be listed with the
righteous.[i]
29 I am in pain and distress;
may your salvation, O God,
protect me.[j]

30 I will praise God's name in song[k]
and glorify him[l] with
thanksgiving.
31 This will please the LORD more than
an ox,
more than a bull with its horns
and hoofs.[m]
32 The poor will see and be glad[n]—
you who seek God, may your
hearts live![o]
33 The LORD hears the needy[p]
and does not despise his captive
people.

34 Let heaven and earth praise him,
the seas and all that move in
them,[q]
35 for God will save Zion[r]
and rebuild the cities of Judah.[s]
Then people will settle there and
possess it;
36 the children of his servants will
inherit it,
and those who love his name will
dwell there.[t]

Psalm 70

For the director of music.
Of David. A petition.

1 Hasten, O God, to save me;
O LORD, come quickly to help
me.[u]
2 May those who seek my life[v]
be put to shame and confusion;
may all who desire my ruin
be turned back in disgrace.[w]
3 May those who say to me, "Aha!
Aha!"
turn back because of their shame.
4 But may all who seek you
rejoice and be glad in you;
may those who love your salvation
always say,
"Let God be exalted!"

5 Yet I am poor and needy;[x]
come quickly to me,[y] O God.
You are my help and my deliverer;
O LORD, do not delay.

[a]22 Or *snare / and their fellowship become*

69:28 [i]Eze 13:9
69:29 [j]Ps 59:1; 70:5
69:30 [k]Ps 28:7 [l]Ps 34:3
69:31 [m]Ps 50:9-13
69:32 [n]Ps 34:2 [o]Ps 22:26
69:33 [p]Ps 12:5; 68:6
69:34 [q]Ps 96:11; 148:1; Isa 44:23; 49:13; 55:12
69:35 [r]Ob 1:17 [s]Ps 51:18; Isa 44:26
69:36 [t]Ps 37:29; 102:28
70:1 [u]Ps 40:13
70:2 [v]Ps 35:4 [w]Ps 35:26
70:5 [x]Ps 40:17 [y]Ps 141:1

Psalm 71

[1]In you, O LORD, I have taken
refuge;
let me never be put to shame.[z]
[2]Rescue me and deliver me in your
righteousness;
turn your ear[a] to me and save me.
[3]Be my rock of refuge,
to which I can always go;
give the command to save me,
for you are my rock and my
fortress.[b]
[4]Deliver me, O my God, from the
hand of the wicked,[c]
from the grasp of evil and cruel
men.
[5]For you have been my hope,
O Sovereign LORD,
my confidence[d] since my youth.

KINDNESS

THE CROSS-GENERATIONAL CHRIST

Psalm 71:5

Lord, when I was young, I learned to hope. Each day I age and cry to own hope still. I must have hope, or heaven is cursed and earth doesn't matter much.

[6]From birth[e] I have relied on you;
you brought me forth from my
mother's womb.[f]
I will ever praise[g] you.
[7]I have become like a portent[h] to
many,
but you are my strong refuge.[i]
[8]My mouth[j] is filled with your praise,
declaring your splendor[k] all day
long.
[9]Do not cast[l] me away when I am
old;[m]
do not forsake me when my
strength is gone.
[10]For my enemies speak against me;
those who wait to kill[n] me
conspire[o] together.
[11]They say, "God has forsaken him;
pursue him and seize him,
for no one will rescue[p] him."
[12]Be not far[q] from me, O God;
come quickly, O my God, to help[r]
me.
[13]May my accusers perish in shame;
may those who want to harm me
be covered with scorn and
disgrace.[s]
[14]But as for me, I will always have
hope;[t]
I will praise you more and more.
[15]My mouth will tell[u] of your
righteousness,
of your salvation all day long,
though I know not its measure.
[16]I will come and proclaim your
mighty acts,[v] O Sovereign
LORD;
I will proclaim your righteousness,
yours alone.
[17]Since my youth, O God, you have
taught[w] me,
and to this day I declare your
marvelous deeds.[x]
[18]Even when I am old and gray,[y]
do not forsake me, O God,
till I declare your power to the next
generation,
your might to all who are to come.[z]
[19]Your righteousness reaches to the
skies,[a] O God,
you who have done great things.[b]
Who, O God, is like you?[c]
[20]Though you have made me see
troubles,[d] many and bitter,
you will restore[e] my life again;
from the depths of the earth
you will again bring me up.
[21]You will increase my honor[f]
and comfort[g] me once again.
[22]I will praise you with the harp[h]
for your faithfulness, O my God;
I will sing praise to you with the
lyre,[i]
O Holy One of Israel.[j]
[23]My lips will shout for joy
when I sing praise to you—
I, whom you have redeemed.[k]
[24]My tongue will tell of your righteous
acts
all day long,[l]
for those who wanted to harm me[m]
have been put to shame and
confusion.

Psalm 72

Of Solomon.

[1]Endow the king with your justice,
O God,
the royal son with your
righteousness.

71:1 [z]Ps 25:2-3; 31:1
71:2 [a]Ps 17:6
71:3 [b]Ps 18:2; 31:2-3; 44:4
71:4 [c]Ps 140:4
71:5 [d]Job 4:6; Jer 17:7
71:6 [e]Ps 22:10 [f]Ps 22:9; Isa 46:3 [g]Ps 9:1; 34:1; 52:9; 119:164; 145:2
71:7 [h]Isa 8:18; 1Co 4:9 [i]2Sa 22:3; Ps 61:3
71:8 [j]Ps 51:15; 63:5 [k]Ps 35:28; 96:6; 104:1
71:9 [l]Ps 51:11 [m]ver 18; Ps 92:14; Isa 46:4
71:10 [n]Ps 10:8; 59:3; Pr 1:18 [o]Ps 31:13; 56:6; Mt 12:14
71:11 [p]Ps 7:2
71:12 [q]Ps 35:22; 38:21 [r]Ps 38:22; 70:1
71:13 [s]ver 24
71:14 [t]Ps 130:7
71:15 [u]Ps 35:28; 40:5
71:16 [v]Ps 106:2
71:17 [w]Dt 4:5 [x]Ps 26:7
71:18 [y]ver 9 [z]Ps 22:30,31; 78:4
71:19 [a]Ps 36:5; 57:10 [b]Ps 126:2; Lk 1:49 [c]Ps 35:10
71:20 [d]Ps 60:3 [e]Hos 6:2
71:21 [f]Ps 18:35 [g]Ps 23:4; 86:17; Isa 12:1; 49:13
71:22 [h]Ps 33:2 [i]Ps 92:3; 144:9 [j]2Ki 19:22
71:23 [k]Ps 103:4
71:24 [l]Ps 35:28 [m]ver 13

72:2 [n]Isa 9:7; 11:4-5; 32:1

2 He will[a] judge your people in
righteousness,[n]
your afflicted ones with justice.
3 The mountains will bring prosperity
to the people,
the hills the fruit of righteousness.
4 He will defend the afflicted among
the people
and save the children of the

72:4 [o]Isa 11:4

needy;[o]
he will crush the oppressor.

5 He will endure[b] as long as the sun,
as long as the moon, through all
generations.

72:6 [p]Dt 32:2; Hos 6:3

6 He will be like rain[p] falling on a
mown field,
like showers watering the earth.
7 In his days the righteous will

72:7 [q]Ps 92:12; Isa 2:4

flourish;[q]
prosperity will abound till the
moon is no more.

8 He will rule from sea to sea

72:8 [r]Ex 23:31 [s]Zec 9:10

and from the River[c][r] to the ends
of the earth.[d][s]
9 The desert tribes will bow before
him
and his enemies will lick the dust.
10 The kings of Tarshish and of distant
shores
will bring tribute to him;

72:10 [t]Ge 10:7 [u]2Ch 9:24

the kings of Sheba[t] and Seba
will present him gifts.[u]
11 All kings will bow down to him
and all nations will serve him.

12 For he will deliver the needy who cry
out,
the afflicted who have no one to
help.
13 He will take pity on the weak and
the needy
and save the needy from death.

72:14 [v]Ps 69:18 [w]1Sa 26:21; Ps 116:15

14 He will rescue[v] them from
oppression and violence,
for precious[w] is their blood in his
sight.

15 Long may he live!

72:15 [x]Isa 60:6

May gold from Sheba[x] be given
him.
May people ever pray for him
and bless him all day long.
16 Let grain abound throughout the
land;
on the tops of the hills may it
sway.
Let its fruit flourish like

72:16 [y]Ps 104:16

Lebanon;[y]
let it thrive like the grass of the
field.

72:17 [z]Ex 3:15 [a]Ps 89:36 [b]Ge 12:3; Lk 1:48

17 May his name endure forever;[z]
may it continue as long as the
sun.[a]

All nations will be blessed through
him,
and they will call him blessed.[b]

18 Praise be to the LORD God, the God

72:18 [c]1Ch 29:10; Ps 41:13; 106:48 [d]Job 5:9

of Israel,[c]
who alone does marvelous deeds.[d]
19 Praise be to his glorious name
forever;

72:19 [e]Nu 14:21; Ne 9:5 [f]Ps 41:13

may the whole earth be filled with
his glory.[e]
Amen and Amen.[f]

20 This concludes the prayers of David
son of Jesse.

BOOK III

Psalms 73–89

Psalm 73

A psalm of Asaph.

73:1 [g]Mt 5:8

1 Surely God is good to Israel,
to those who are pure in heart.[g]

2 But as for me, my feet had almost
slipped;
I had nearly lost my foothold.

73:3 [h]Ps 37:1; Pr 23:17 [i]Job 21:7; Jer 12:1

3 For I envied[h] the arrogant
when I saw the prosperity of the
wicked.[i]

4 They have no struggles;
their bodies are healthy and
strong.[e]

73:5 [j]Job 21:9

5 They are free[j] from the burdens
common to man;
they are not plagued by human
ills.

73:6 [k]Ge 41:42 [l]Ps 109:18

6 Therefore pride is their necklace;[k]
they clothe themselves with
violence.[l]

73:7 [m]Ps 17:10

7 From their callous hearts[m] comes
iniquity[f];
the evil conceits of their minds
know no limits.

[a]*2* Or *May he*; similarly in verses 3-11 and 17
[b]*5* Septuagint; Hebrew *You will be feared* [c]*8* That is, the Euphrates [d]*8* Or *the end of the land*
[e]*4* With a different word division of the Hebrew; Masoretic Text *struggles at their death; / their bodies are healthy* [f]*7* Syriac (see also Septuagint); Hebrew *Their eyes bulge with fat*

73:8 [n]Ps 17:10; Jude 16

8 They scoff, and speak with malice;
in their arrogance[n] they threaten
oppression.
9 Their mouths lay claim to heaven,
and their tongues take possession
of the earth.
10 Therefore their people turn to them
and drink up waters in
abundance.[a]
11 They say, "How can God know?
Does the Most High have
knowledge?"

73:12 [o]Ps 49:6

12 This is what the wicked are like—
always carefree, they increase in
wealth.[o]

73:13 [p]Job 21:15; 34:9 [q]Ps 26:6

13 Surely in vain[p] have I kept my heart
pure;
in vain have I washed my hands in
innocence.[q]
14 All day long I have been plagued;
I have been punished every
morning.

15 If I had said, "I will speak thus,"
I would have betrayed your
children.

73:16 [r]Ecc 8:17

16 When I tried to understand[r] all this,
it was oppressive to me

73:17 [s]Ps 77:13 [t]Ps 37:38

17 till I entered the sanctuary[s] of God;
then I understood their final
destiny.[t]

73:18 [u]Ps 35:6

18 Surely you place them on slippery
ground;[u]
you cast them down to ruin.

73:19 [v]Isa 47:11

19 How suddenly[v] are they destroyed,
completely swept away by
terrors!

73:20 [w]Job 20:8 [x]Ps 78:65

20 As a dream[w] when one awakes,[x]
so when you arise, O Lord,
you will despise them as
fantasies.

73:22 [y]Ps 49:10; 92:6 [z]Ecc 3:18

21 When my heart was grieved
and my spirit embittered,
22 I was senseless[y] and ignorant;
I was a brute beast[z] before you.

73:24 [a]Ps 48:14 [b]Ps 32:8

23 Yet I am always with you;
you hold me by my right hand.
24 You guide[a] me with your counsel,[b]
and afterward you will take me
into glory.

73:25 [c]Php 3:8

25 Whom have I in heaven but you?
And earth has nothing I desire
besides you.[c]

73:26 [d]Ps 84:2 [e]Ps 40:12

26 My flesh and my heart[d] may fail,[e]
but God is the strength of my
heart
and my portion forever.

73:27 [f]Ps 119:155

27 Those who are far from you will
perish;[f]
you destroy all who are unfaithful
to you.

73:28 [g]Heb 10:22; Jas 4:8 [h]Ps 40:5

28 But as for me, it is good to be near
God.[g]
I have made the Sovereign LORD
my refuge;
I will tell of all your deeds.[h]

Psalm 74

A *maskil*[b] of Asaph.

74:1 [i]Dt 29:20; Ps 44:23 [j]Ps 79:13; 95:7; 100:3

1 Why have you rejected us forever,[i]
O God?
Why does your anger smolder
against the sheep of your
pasture?[j]

74:2 [k]Ex 15:16 [l]Dt 32:7 [m]Ex 15:13 [n]Ps 68:16

2 Remember the people you
purchased[k] of old,[l]
the tribe of your inheritance,
whom you redeemed[m]—
Mount Zion, where you dwelt.[n]
3 Turn your steps toward these
everlasting ruins,
all this destruction the enemy has
brought on the sanctuary.

74:4 [o]La 2:7 [p]Nu 2:2

4 Your foes roared[o] in the place where
you met with us;
they set up their standards[p] as
signs.

74:5 [q]Jer 46:22

5 They behaved like men wielding axes
to cut through a thicket of trees.[q]

74:6 [r]1Ki 6:18

6 They smashed all the carved[r]
paneling
with their axes and hatchets.
7 They burned your sanctuary to the
ground;
they defiled the dwelling place of
your Name.

74:8 [s]Ps 83:4

8 They said in their hearts, "We will
crush[s] them completely!"
They burned every place where
God was worshiped in the
land.

74:9 [t]1Sa 3:1

9 We are given no miraculous signs;
no prophets[t] are left,
and none of us knows how long
this will be.

[a] *10* The meaning of the Hebrew for this verse is uncertain. [b] Title: Probably a literary or musical term

[10]How long will the enemy mock you,
O God?
Will the foe revile[u] your name
forever?
[11]Why do you hold back your hand,
your right hand?[v]
Take it from the folds of your
garment and destroy them!

[12]But you, O God, are my king[w] from
of old;
you bring salvation upon the
earth.
[13]It was you who split open the sea[x] by
your power;
you broke the heads of the
monster[y] in the waters.
[14]It was you who crushed the heads of
Leviathan
and gave him as food to the
creatures of the desert.
[15]It was you who opened up springs[z]
and streams;
you dried up[a] the ever flowing
rivers.
[16]The day is yours, and yours also the
night;
you established the sun and
moon.[b]
[17]It was you who set all the
boundaries[c] of the earth;
you made both summer and
winter.[d]

[18]Remember how the enemy has
mocked you, O LORD,
how foolish people[e] have reviled
your name.
[19]Do not hand over the life of your
dove to wild beasts;
do not forget the lives of your
afflicted[f] people forever.
[20]Have regard for your covenant,[g]
because haunts of violence fill the
dark places of the land.
[21]Do not let the oppressed[h] retreat in
disgrace;
may the poor and needy[i] praise
your name.

[22]Rise up, O God, and defend your
cause;
remember how fools[j] mock you
all day long.
[23]Do not ignore the clamor of your
adversaries,[k]
the uproar of your enemies, which
rises continually.

74:10 [u]Ps 44:16
74:11 [v]La 2:3
74:12 [w]Ps 44:4
74:13 [x]Ex 14:21 [y]Isa 51:9; Eze 29:3
74:15 [z]Ex 17:6; Nu 20:11 [a]Jos 2:10; 3:13
74:16 [b]Ge 1:16; Ps 136:7-9
74:17 [c]Dt 32:8; Ac 17:26 [d]Ge 8:22
74:18 [e]Dt 32:6; Ps 39:8
74:19 [f]Ps 9:18
74:20 [g]Ge 17:7; Ps 106:45
74:21 [h]Ps 103:6 [i]Ps 35:10
74:22 [j]Ps 53:1
74:23 [k]Ps 65:7

Psalm 75

For the director of music.
⌊To the tune of⌋ "Do Not Destroy."
A psalm of Asaph. A song.

[1]We give thanks to you, O God,
we give thanks, for your Name is
near;[l]
men tell of your wonderful
deeds.[m]

[2]You say, "I choose the appointed
time;
it is I who judge uprightly.
[3]When the earth and all its people
quake,[n]
it is I who hold its pillars[o] firm.
Selah
[4]To the arrogant I say, 'Boast no
more,'
and to the wicked, 'Do not lift up
your horns.[p]
[5]Do not lift your horns against
heaven;
do not speak with outstretched
neck.' "
[6]No one from the east or the west
or from the desert can exalt a
man.
[7]But it is God who judges:[q]
He brings one down, he exalts
another.[r]
[8]In the hand of the LORD is a cup
full of foaming wine mixed[s] with
spices;
he pours it out, and all the wicked
of the earth
drink it down to its very dregs.[t]

[9]As for me, I will declare[u] this forever;
I will sing praise to the God of
Jacob.
[10]I will cut off the horns of all the
wicked,
but the horns of the righteous will
be lifted up.[v]

Psalm 76

For the director of music. With
stringed instruments. A psalm
of Asaph. A song.

[1]In Judah God is known;
his name is great in Israel.
[2]His tent is in Salem,[w]
his dwelling place in Zion.
[3]There he broke the flashing arrows,
the shields and the swords, the
weapons of war.[x] *Selah*

75:1 [l]Ps 145:18 [m]Ps 44:1; 71:16
75:3 [n]Isa 24:19 [o]1Sa 2:8
75:4 [p]Zec 1:21
75:7 [q]Ps 50:6 [r]1Sa 2:7; Ps 147:6; Da 2:21
75:8 [s]Pr 23:30 [t]Job 21:20; Jer 25:15
75:9 [u]Ps 40:10
75:10 [v]Ps 89:17; 92:10; 148:14
76:2 [w]Ge 14:18
76:3 [x]Ps 46:9

4 You are resplendent with light,
more majestic than mountains
rich with game.
5 Valiant men lie plundered,
they sleep their last sleep;[y]
not one of the warriors
can lift his hands.
6 At your rebuke, O God of Jacob,
both horse and chariot[z] lie still.
7 You alone are to be feared.[a]
Who can stand[b] before you when
you are angry?[c]
8 From heaven you pronounced
judgment,
and the land feared[d] and was
quiet—
9 when you, O God, rose up to judge,[e]
to save all the afflicted of the land.
Selah
10 Surely your wrath against men
brings you praise,[f]
and the survivors of your wrath
are restrained.[a]
11 Make vows to the LORD your God
and fulfill them;[g]
let all the neighboring lands
bring gifts[h] to the One to be
feared.
12 He breaks the spirit of rulers;
he is feared by the kings of the
earth.

76:5 [y]Ps 13:3
76:6 [z]Ex 15:1
76:7 [a]1Ch 16:25 [b]Ezr 9:15; Rev 6:17 [c]Ps 2:5; Na 1:6
76:8 [d]1Ch 16:30; 2Ch 20:29-30
76:9 [e]Ps 9:8
76:10 [f]Ex 9:16; Ro 9:17
76:11 [g]Ps 50:14; Ecc 5:4-5 [h]2Ch 32:23; Ps 68:29

Psalm 77

For the director of music. For Jeduthun.
Of Asaph. A psalm.

1 I cried out to God[i] for help;
I cried out to God to hear me.
2 When I was in distress,[j] I sought the
Lord;
at night I stretched out untiring
hands[k]
and my soul refused to be
comforted.[l]

3 I remembered you, O God, and I
groaned;
I mused, and my spirit grew
faint.[m] *Selah*
4 You kept my eyes from closing;
I was too troubled to speak.
5 I thought about the former days,[n]
the years of long ago;
6 I remembered my songs in the night.
My heart mused and my spirit
inquired:

77:1 [i]Ps 3:4
77:2 [j]Ps 50:15; Isa 26:9,16 [k]Job 11:13 [l]Ge 37:35
77:3 [m]Ps 143:4
77:5 [n]Dt 32:7; Ps 44:1; 143:5; Isa 51:9

7 "Will the Lord reject forever?
Will he never show his favor[o]
again?
8 Has his unfailing love vanished
forever?
Has his promise[p] failed for all
time?
9 Has God forgotten to be merciful?[q]
Has he in anger withheld his
compassion?[r]" *Selah*

10 Then I thought, "To this I will
appeal:
the years of the right hand[s] of the
Most High."
11 I will remember the deeds of the
LORD;
yes, I will remember your
miracles[t] of long ago.
12 I will meditate on all your works
and consider all your mighty
deeds.

13 Your ways, O God, are holy.
What god is so great as our
God?[u]
14 You are the God who performs
miracles;
you display your power among the
peoples.
15 With your mighty arm you
redeemed your people,[v]
the descendants of Jacob and
Joseph. *Selah*

16 The waters[w] saw you, O God,
the waters saw you and writhed;[x]
the very depths were convulsed.
17 The clouds poured down water,[y]
the skies resounded with
thunder;
your arrows flashed back and
forth.
18 Your thunder was heard in the
whirlwind,
your lightning lit up the world;
the earth trembled and quaked.[z]
19 Your path led through the sea,[a]
your way through the mighty
waters,
though your footprints were not
seen.

20 You led your people[b] like a flock[c]
by the hand of Moses and Aaron.

77:7 [o]Ps 85:1
77:8 [p]2Pe 3:9
77:9 [q]Ps 25:6; 40:11; 51:1 [r]Isa 49:15
77:10 [s]Ps 31:22
77:11 [t]Ps 143:5
77:13 [u]Ex 15:11; Ps 71:19; 86:8
77:15 [v]Ex 6:6; Dt 9:29
77:16 [w]Ex 14:21,28; Hab 3:8 [x]Ps 114:4; Hab 3:10
77:17 [y]Jdg 5:4
77:18 [z]Jdg 5:4
77:19 [a]Hab 3:15
77:20 [b]Ex 13:21 [c]Ps 78:52; Isa 63:11

[a] *10* Or *Surely the wrath of men brings you praise, / and with the remainder of wrath you arm yourself*

Psalm 78

A *maskil*[a] of Asaph.

78:1 [d]Isa 51:4; 55:3
1 O my people, hear my teaching;[d]
listen to the words of my mouth.
78:2 [e]Ps 49:4; Mt 13:35*
2 I will open my mouth in parables,[e]
I will utter hidden things, things
from of old—

GENTLENESS

THE STORYTELLER

Psalm 78:2

Christ hid the riches of his kingdom in his stories—in fascinating forms of gentle truth. Jesus knew that to tell these truths without his stories might have left the Good News boring and the truth too plain to survive the centuries.

3 what we have heard and known,
78:3 [f]Ps 44:1
what our fathers have told us.[f]
4 We will not hide them from their
78:4 [g]Dt 11:19 [h]Ps 26:7; 71:17
children;[g]
we will tell the next generation
the praiseworthy deeds[h] of the
LORD,
his power, and the wonders he has
done.
78:5 [i]Ps 19:7; 81:5 [j]Ps 147:19
5 He decreed statutes[i] for Jacob[j]
and established the law in Israel,
which he commanded our
forefathers
to teach their children,
6 so the next generation would know
them,
78:6 [k]Ps 22:31; 102:18
even the children yet to be born,[k]
and they in turn would tell their
children.
7 Then they would put their trust in
God
78:7 [l]Dt 6:12 [m]Dt 5:29
and would not forget[l] his deeds
but would keep his commands.[m]
8 They would not be like their
78:8 [n]2Ch 30:7 [o]Ex 32:9 [p]ver 37; Isa 30:9
forefathers[n]—
a stubborn[o] and rebellious[p]
generation,
whose hearts were not loyal to God,
whose spirits were not faithful to
him.

78:9 [q]ver 57; 1Ch 12:2 [r]Jdg 20:39
9 The men of Ephraim, though armed
with bows,[q]
turned back on the day of battle;[r]
78:10 [s]2Ki 17:15
10 they did not keep God's covenant[s]
and refused to live by his law.
78:11 [t]Ps 106:13
11 They forgot what he had done,[t]
the wonders he had shown them.
12 He did miracles[u] in the sight of their
fathers
in the land of Egypt,[v] in the
region of Zoan.[w]
78:12 [u]Ps 106:22 [v]Ex 7-12 [w]Nu 13:22
13 He divided the sea[x] and led them
through;
he made the water stand firm like
a wall.[y]
78:13 [x]Ex 14:21; Ps 136:13 [y]Ex 15:8
14 He guided them with the cloud by
day
and with light from the fire all
night.[z]
78:14 [z]Ex 13:21; Ps 105:39
15 He split the rocks[a] in the desert
and gave them water as abundant
as the seas;
78:15 [a]Nu 20:11; 1Co 10:4
16 he brought streams out of a rocky
crag
and made water flow down like
rivers.

17 But they continued to sin[b] against
him,
rebelling in the desert against the
Most High.
78:17 [b]Dt 9:22; Isa 63:10; Heb 3:16
18 They willfully put God to the test[c]
by demanding the food they
craved.[d]
78:18 [c]1Co 10:9 [d]Ex 16:2; Nu 11:4
19 They spoke against God,[e] saying,
"Can God spread a table in the
desert?
78:19 [e]Nu 21:5
20 When he struck the rock, water
gushed out,[f]
and streams flowed abundantly.
But can he also give us food?
Can he supply meat[g] for his
people?"
78:20 [f]Nu 20:11 [g]Nu 11:18
21 When the LORD heard them, he was
very angry;
his fire broke out[h] against Jacob,
and his wrath rose against Israel,
78:21 [h]Nu 11:1
22 for they did not believe in God
or trust[i] in his deliverance.
78:22 [i]Dt 1:32; Heb 3:19
23 Yet he gave a command to the skies
above
and opened the doors of the
heavens;[j]
78:23 [j]Ge 7:11; Mal 3:10
24 he rained down manna[k] for the
people to eat,
he gave them the grain of heaven.
78:24 [k]Ex 16:4; Jn 6:31*
25 Men ate the bread of angels;
he sent them all the food they
could eat.
26 He let loose the east wind[l] from the
heavens
and led forth the south wind by
his power.
78:26 [l]Nu 11:31

[a]Title: Probably a literary or musical term

[27]He rained meat down on them like
dust,
flying birds like sand on the
seashore.
[28]He made them come down inside
their camp,
all around their tents.
[29]They ate till they had more than
enough,[m]
for he had given them what they
craved.
[30]But before they turned from the
food they craved,
even while it was still in their
mouths,[n]
[31]God's anger rose against them;
he put to death the sturdiest[o]
among them,
cutting down the young men of
Israel.

[32]In spite of all this, they kept on
sinning;
in spite of his wonders,[p] they did
not believe.[q]
[33]So he ended their days in futility[r]
and their years in terror.
[34]Whenever God slew them, they
would seek[s] him;
they eagerly turned to him again.
[35]They remembered that God was
their Rock,[t]
that God Most High was their
Redeemer.[u]
[36]But then they would flatter him with
their mouths,[v]
lying to him with their tongues;
[37]their hearts were not loyal[w] to him,
they were not faithful to his
covenant.
[38]Yet he was merciful;[x]
he forgave[y] their iniquities[z]
and did not destroy them.
Time after time he restrained his
anger
and did not stir up his full wrath.
[39]He remembered that they were but
flesh,[a]
a passing breeze[b] that does not
return.

[40]How often they rebelled[c] against him
in the desert[d]
and grieved him[e] in the wasteland!
[41]Again and again they put God to the
test;[f]
they vexed the Holy One of
Israel.[g]
[42]They did not remember his power—
the day he redeemed them from
the oppressor,
[43]the day he displayed his miraculous
signs in Egypt,
his wonders in the region of Zoan.
[44]He turned their rivers to blood;[h]
they could not drink from their
streams.
[45]He sent swarms of flies[i] that
devoured them,
and frogs[j] that devastated them.
[46]He gave their crops to the
grasshopper,
their produce to the locust.[k]
[47]He destroyed their vines with hail[l]
and their sycamore-figs with sleet.
[48]He gave over their cattle to the hail,
their livestock[m] to bolts of
lightning.
[49]He unleashed against them his hot
anger,[n]
his wrath, indignation and
hostility—
a band of destroying angels.
[50]He prepared a path for his anger;
he did not spare them from death
but gave them over to the plague.
[51]He struck down all the firstborn of
Egypt,[o]
the firstfruits of manhood in the
tents of Ham.[p]
[52]But he brought his people out like
a flock;[q]
he led them like sheep through
the desert.
[53]He guided them safely, so they were
unafraid;
but the sea engulfed[r] their
enemies.[s]
[54]Thus he brought them to the border
of his holy land,
to the hill country his right hand[t]
had taken.
[55]He drove out nations[u] before them
and allotted their lands to them as
an inheritance;[v]
he settled the tribes of Israel in
their homes.

[56]But they put God to the test
and rebelled against the Most
High;
they did not keep his statutes.
[57]Like their fathers[w] they were disloyal
and faithless,
as unreliable as a faulty bow.[x]
[58]They angered him[y] with their high
places;[z]

78:29 [m]Nu 11:20
78:30 [n]Nu 11:33
78:31 [o]Isa 10:16
78:32 [p]ver 11 [q]ver 22
78:33 [r]Nu 14:29,35
78:34 [s]Hos 5:15
78:35 [t]Dt 32:4 [u]Dt 9:26
78:36 [v]Eze 33:31
78:37 [w]ver 8; Ac 8:21
78:38 [x]Ex 34:6 [y]Isa 48:10 [z]Nu 14:18,20
78:39 [a]Ge 6:3; Ps 103:14 [b]Job 7:7; Jas 4:14
78:40 [c]Heb 3:16 [d]Ps 95:8; 106:14 [e]Eph 4:30
78:41 [f]Nu 14:22 [g]2Ki 19:22; Ps 89:18
78:44 [h]Ex 7:20-21; Ps 105:29
78:45 [i]Ex 8:24; Ps 105:31 [j]Ex 8:2,6
78:46 [k]Ex 10:13
78:47 [l]Ex 9:23; Ps 105:32
78:48 [m]Ex 9:25
78:49 [n]Ex 15:7
78:51 [o]Ex 12:29; Ps 135:8 [p]Ps 105:23; 106:22
78:52 [q]Ps 77:20
78:53 [r]Ex 14:28 [s]Ps 106:10
78:54 [t]Ex 15:17; Ps 44:3
78:55 [u]Ps 44:2 [v]Jos 13:7
78:57 [w]Eze 20:27 [x]Hos 7:16
78:58 [y]Jdg 2:12 [z]Lev 26:30

they aroused his jealousy with
their idols.[a]
59 When God heard them, he was very
angry;
he rejected Israel[b] completely.
60 He abandoned the tabernacle of
Shiloh,[c]
the tent he had set up among
men.
61 He sent ⌊the ark of⌋ his might[d] into
captivity,[e]
his splendor into the hands of the
enemy.
62 He gave his people over to the
sword;
he was very angry with his
inheritance.
63 Fire consumed[f] their young men,
and their maidens had no
wedding songs;[g]
64 their priests were put to the sword,[h]
and their widows could not weep.
65 Then the Lord awoke as from
sleep,[i]
as a man wakes from the stupor
of wine.
66 He beat back his enemies;
he put them to everlasting
shame.[j]
67 Then he rejected the tents of Joseph,
he did not choose the tribe of
Ephraim;
68 but he chose the tribe of Judah,
Mount Zion,[k] which he loved.
69 He built his sanctuary like the
heights,
like the earth that he established
forever.
70 He chose David[l] his servant
and took him from the sheep
pens;
71 from tending the sheep he brought
him
to be the shepherd[m] of his people
Jacob,
of Israel his inheritance.
72 And David shepherded them with
integrity of heart;[n]
with skillful hands he led them.

78:58 [a]Ex 20:4; Dt 32:21
78:59 [b]Dt 32:19
78:60 [c]Jos 18:1
78:61 [d]Ps 132:8 [e]1Sa 4:17
78:63 [f]Nu 11:1 [g]Jer 7:34; 16:9
78:64 [h]1Sa 4:17; 22:18
78:65 [i]Ps 44:23
78:66 [j]1Sa 5:6
78:68 [k]Ps 87:2
78:70 [l]1Sa 16:1
78:71 [m]2Sa 5:2; Ps 28:9
78:72 [n]1Ki 9:4

Psalm 79

A psalm of Asaph.

1 O God, the nations have invaded
your inheritance;[o]
they have defiled your holy
temple,
they have reduced Jerusalem to
rubble.[p]
2 They have given the dead bodies of
your servants
as food to the birds of the air,
the flesh of your saints to the
beasts of the earth.[q]
3 They have poured out blood like
water
all around Jerusalem,
and there is no one to bury the
dead.[r]
4 We are objects of reproach to our
neighbors,
of scorn and derision to those
around us.[s]

5 How long,[t] O LORD? Will you be
angry[u] forever?
How long will your jealousy burn
like fire?[v]
6 Pour out your wrath[w] on the
nations
that do not acknowledge[x] you,
on the kingdoms
that do not call on your name;[y]
7 for they have devoured Jacob
and destroyed his homeland.
8 Do not hold against us the sins of
the fathers;[z]
may your mercy come quickly to
meet us,
for we are in desperate need.[a]
9 Help us,[b] O God our Savior,
for the glory of your name;
deliver us and forgive our sins
for your name's sake.[c]
10 Why should the nations say,
"Where is their God?"[d]
Before our eyes, make known among
the nations
that you avenge[e] the outpoured
blood of your servants.
11 May the groans of the prisoners
come before you;
by the strength of your arm
preserve those condemned to
die.
12 Pay back into the laps[f] of our
neighbors seven times[g]
the reproach they have hurled at
you, O Lord.
13 Then we your people, the sheep of
your pasture,[h]
will praise you forever;[i]
from generation to generation
we will recount your praise.

79:1 [o]Ps 74:2
79:1 [p]2Ki 25:9
79:2 [q]Dt 28:26; Jer 7:33
79:3 [r]Jer 16:4
79:4 [s]Ps 44:13; 80:6
79:5 [t]Ps 74:10 [u]Ps 74:1; 85:5 [v]Dt 29:20; Ps 89:46; Zep 3:8
79:6 [w]Ps 69:24; Rev 16:1 [x]Jer 10:25; 2Th 1:8 [y]Ps 14:4
79:8 [z]Isa 64:9 [a]Ps 116:6; 142:6
79:9 [b]2Ch 14:11 [c]Ps 25:11; 31:3; Jer 14:7
79:10 [d]Ps 42:10 [e]Ps 94:1
79:12 [f]Isa 65:6; Jer 32:18 [g]Ge 4:15
79:13 [h]Ps 74:1; 95:7 [i]Ps 44:8

Psalm 80

For the director of music. To ⌞the tune of⌟ "The Lilies of the Covenant." Of Asaph. A psalm.

80:1 [j]Ps 77:20 [k]Ex 25:22

[1]Hear us, O Shepherd of Israel,
you who lead Joseph like a flock;[j]
you who sit enthroned between the cherubim,[k] shine forth

80:2 [l]Nu 2:18-24 [m]Ps 35:23

[2] before Ephraim, Benjamin and Manasseh.[l]
Awaken[m] your might;
come and save us.

80:3 [n]Ps 85:4; La 5:21 [o]Nu 6:25

[3]Restore[n] us,[o] O God;
make your face shine upon us,
that we may be saved.

[4]O LORD God Almighty,
how long will your anger smolder
against the prayers of your people?

80:5 [p]Ps 42:3; Isa 30:20

[5]You have fed them with the bread of tears;
you have made them drink tears by the bowlful.[p]

80:6 [q]Ps 79:4

[6]You have made us a source of contention to our neighbors,
and our enemies mock us.[q]

[7]Restore us, O God Almighty;
make your face shine upon us,
that we may be saved.

80:8 [r]Isa 5:1-2; Jer 2:21 [s]Jos 13:6; Ac 7:45

[8]You brought a vine[r] out of Egypt;
you drove out[s] the nations and planted it.
[9]You cleared the ground for it,
and it took root and filled the land.
[10]The mountains were covered with its shade,
the mighty cedars with its branches.

80:11 [t]Ps 72:8

[11]It sent out its boughs to the Sea,[a]
its shoots as far as the River.[b][t]

80:12 [u]Ps 89:40; Isa 5:5

[12]Why have you broken down its walls[u]
so that all who pass by pick its grapes?

80:13 [v]Jer 5:6

[13]Boars from the forest ravage[v] it
and the creatures of the field feed on it.

80:14 [w]Isa 63:15

[14]Return to us, O God Almighty!
Look down from heaven and see![w]
Watch over this vine,
[15] the root your right hand has planted,
the son[c] you have raised up for yourself.

80:16 [x]Ps 39:11; 76:6

[16]Your vine is cut down, it is burned with fire;
at your rebuke[x] your people perish.
[17]Let your hand rest on the man at your right hand,
the son of man you have raised up for yourself.
[18]Then we will not turn away from you;
revive us, and we will call on your name.

[19]Restore us, O LORD God Almighty;
make your face shine upon us,
that we may be saved.

Psalm 81

For the director of music. According to *gittith*.[d] Of Asaph.

81:1 [y]Ps 66:1

[1]Sing for joy to God our strength;
shout aloud to the God of Jacob![y]

81:2 [z]Ex 15:20 [a]Ps 92:3

[2]Begin the music, strike the tambourine,[z]
play the melodious harp[a] and lyre.

[3]Sound the ram's horn at the New Moon,
and when the moon is full, on the day of our Feast;
[4]this is a decree for Israel,
an ordinance of the God of Jacob.

81:5 [b]Ex 11:4 [c]Ps 114:1

[5]He established it as a statute for Joseph
when he went out against Egypt,[b]
where we heard a language we did not understand.[e][c]

81:6 [d]Isa 9:4

[6]He says, "I removed the burden from their shoulders;[d]
their hands were set free from the basket.

81:7 [e]Ex 2:23; Ps 50:15 [f]Ex 19:19 [g]Ex 17:7

[7]In your distress you called[e] and I rescued you,
I answered[f] you out of a thundercloud;
I tested you at the waters of Meribah.[g] *Selah*

81:8 [h]Ps 50:7

[8]"Hear, O my people,[h] and I will warn you—
if you would but listen to me, O Israel!

[a]*11* Probably the Mediterranean [b]*11* That is, the Euphrates [c]*15* Or *branch* [d]Title: Probably a musical term [e]*5* Or / *and we heard a voice we had not known*

81:9 [i]Ex 20:3; Dt 32:12; Isa 43:12

9 You shall have no foreign god[i]
among you;
you shall not bow down to an
alien god.
10 I am the LORD your God,
who brought you up out of
Egypt.[j]

81:10 [j]Ex 20:2 [k]Ps 107:9

Open wide your mouth and I will
fill[k] it.

11 "But my people would not listen to
me;
Israel would not submit to me.[l]

81:11 [l]Ex 32:1-6
81:12 [m]Ac 7:42; Ro 1:24

12 So I gave them over[m] to their
stubborn hearts
to follow their own devices.

81:13 [n]Dt 5:29; Isa 48:18

13 "If my people would but listen to
me,[n]
if Israel would follow my ways,

81:14 [o]Ps 47:3 [p]Am 1:8

14 how quickly would I subdue[o] their
enemies
and turn my hand against[p] their
foes!
15 Those who hate the LORD would
cringe before him,
and their punishment would last
forever.

81:16 [q]Dt 32:14

16 But you would be fed with the finest
of wheat;[q]
with honey from the rock I would
satisfy you."

Psalm 82

A psalm of Asaph.

82:1 [r]Ps 58:11; Isa 3:13

1 God presides in the great assembly;
he gives judgment[r] among the
"gods":

82:2 [s]Dt 1:17 [t]Ps 58:1-2; Pr 18:5

2 "How long will you[a] defend the
unjust
and show partiality[s] to the
wicked?[t] *Selah*

82:3 [u]Dt 24:17 [v]Jer 22:16

3 Defend the cause of the weak and
fatherless;[u]
maintain the rights of the poor[v]
and oppressed.
4 Rescue the weak and needy;
deliver them from the hand of the
wicked.

82:5 [w]Ps 14:4; Mic 3:1 [x]Isa 59:9 [y]Ps 11:3

5 "They know nothing, they
understand nothing.[w]
They walk about in darkness;[x]
all the foundations[y] of the earth
are shaken.

82:6 [z]Jn 10:34*

6 "I said, 'You are "gods";[z]
you are all sons of the Most High.'

82:7 [a]Ps 49:12; Eze 31:14

7 But you will die[a] like mere men;
you will fall like every other ruler."

82:8 [b]Ps 12:5 [c]Ps 2:8; Rev 11:15

8 Rise up,[b] O God, judge the earth,
for all the nations are your
inheritance.[c]

Psalm 83

A song. A psalm of Asaph.

83:1 [d]Ps 28:1; 35:22

1 O God, do not keep silent;[d]
be not quiet, O God, be not still.

83:2 [e]Ps 2:1; Isa 17:12 [f]Jdg 8:28; Ps 81:15

2 See how your enemies are astir,[e]
how your foes rear their heads.[f]

83:3 [g]Ps 31:13

3 With cunning they conspire[g] against
your people;
they plot against those you
cherish.

83:4 [h]Est 3:6 [i]Jer 11:19

4 "Come," they say, "let us destroy[h]
them as a nation,
that the name of Israel be
remembered[i] no more."

83:5 [j]Ps 2:2

5 With one mind they plot together;[j]
they form an alliance against
you—

83:6 [k]Ps 137:7 [l]2Ch 20:1 [m]Ge 25:16

6 the tents of Edom[k] and the
Ishmaelites,
of Moab[l] and the Hagrites,[m]

83:7 [n]Jos 13:5 [o]Eze 27:3

7 Gebal,[b][n] Ammon and Amalek,
Philistia, with the people of Tyre.[o]
8 Even Assyria has joined them
to lend strength to the

83:8 [p]Dt 2:9

descendants of Lot.[p] *Selah*

83:9 [q]Jdg 7:1-23 [r]Jdg 4:23-24

9 Do to them as you did to Midian,[q]
as you did to Sisera and Jabin at
the river Kishon,[r]

83:10 [s]Zep 1:17

10 who perished at Endor
and became like refuse[s] on the
ground.

83:11 [t]Jdg 7:25 [u]Jdg 8:12,21

11 Make their nobles like Oreb and
Zeeb,[t]
all their princes like Zebah and
Zalmunna,[u]

83:12 [v]2Ch 20:11

12 who said, "Let us take possession[v]
of the pasturelands of God."

83:13 [w]Ps 35:5; Isa 17:13

13 Make them like tumbleweed, O my
God,
like chaff[w] before the wind.

83:14 [x]Dt 32:22; Isa 9:18

14 As fire consumes the forest
or a flame sets the mountains
ablaze,[x]

83:15 [y]Job 9:17

15 so pursue them with your tempest
and terrify them with your
storm.[y]

83:16 [z]Ps 109:29; 132:18

16 Cover their faces with shame[z]

[a]*2* The Hebrew is plural. [b]*7* That is, Byblos

so that men will seek your name,
O LORD.

17 May they ever be ashamed and
dismayed;
83:17 [a]Ps 35:4 may they perish in disgrace.[a]
18 Let them know that you, whose
name is the LORD—
that you alone are the Most High
83:18 [b]Ps 59:13 over all the earth.[b]

Psalm 84

For the director of music. According to *gittith*.[a] Of the Sons of Korah. A psalm.

84:1 [c]Ps 27:4; 43:3; 132:5 1 How lovely is your dwelling place,[c]
O LORD Almighty!
84:2 [d]Ps 42:1-2 2 My soul yearns,[d] even faints,
for the courts of the LORD;
my heart and my flesh cry out
for the living God.

PATIENCE

FINAL THINGS

Psalm 84:1–2

Does the noisy city seem dull and pointless? Then close your eyes till in your heart of hearts you see a city built foursquare, coming down from God out of heaven. This city will someday replace the one where you now live.

3 Even the sparrow has found a home,
and the swallow a nest for herself,
84:3 [e]Ps 43:4 [f]Ps 5:2 where she may have her young—
a place near your altar,[e]
O LORD Almighty, my King and
my God.[f]
4 Blessed are those who dwell in your
house;
they are ever praising you. *Selah*
84:5 [g]Ps 81:1 [h]Jer 31:6 5 Blessed are those whose strength[g] is
in you,
who have set their hearts on
pilgrimage.[h]
6 As they pass through the Valley of
Baca,
they make it a place of springs;
84:6 [i]Joel 2:23 the autumn[i] rains also cover it
with pools.[b]
84:7 [j]Pr 4:18 [k]Dt 16:16 7 They go from strength to strength,[j]
till each appears[k] before God in
Zion.
8 Hear my prayer, O LORD God
Almighty;
listen to me, O God of Jacob.
Selah
9 Look upon our shield,[c][l] O God; 84:9 [l]Ps 59:11 [m]1Sa 16:6; Ps 2:2; 132:17
look with favor on your anointed
one.[m]
10 Better is one day in your courts
than a thousand elsewhere;
I would rather be a doorkeeper[n] in 84:10 [n]1Ch 23:5
the house of my God
than dwell in the tents of the
wicked.
11 For the LORD God is a sun[o] and 84:11 [o]Isa 60:19; Rev 21:23 [p]Ge 15:1 [q]Ps 34:10
shield;[p]
the LORD bestows favor and
honor;
no good thing does he withhold[q]
from those whose walk is
blameless.
12 O LORD Almighty,
blessed[r] is the man who trusts in 84:12 [r]Ps 2:12
you.

Psalm 85

For the director of music. Of the Sons of Korah. A psalm.

1 You showed favor to your land,
O LORD;
you restored the fortunes[s] of 85:1 [s]Ps 14:7; Jer 30:18; Eze 39:25
Jacob.
2 You forgave[t] the iniquity[u] of your
people 85:2 [t]Nu 14:19 [u]Ps 78:38
and covered all their sins. *Selah*
3 You set aside all your wrath[v] 85:3 [v]Ps 106:23 [w]Ex 32:12; Dt 13:17; Ps 78:38; Jnh 3:9
and turned from your fierce
anger.[w]
4 Restore[x] us again, O God our Savior,
and put away your displeasure 85:4 [x]Ps 80:3,7
toward us.
5 Will you be angry with us forever?[y] 85:5 [y]Ps 79:5
Will you prolong your anger
through all generations?
6 Will you not revive[z] us again, 85:6 [z]Ps 80:18; Hab 3:2
that your people may rejoice in
you?
7 Show us your unfailing love,
O LORD,
and grant us your salvation.
8 I will listen to what God the LORD
will say;
he promises peace[a] to his people, 85:8 [a]Zec 9:10
his saints—
but let them not return to folly.

[a]Title: Probably a musical term [b]6 Or *blessings* [c]9 Or *sovereign*

85:9 [b]Isa 46:13 [c]Zec 2:5

9 Surely his salvation[b] is near those
who fear him,
that his glory[c] may dwell in our
land.

85:10 [d]Ps 89:14; Pr 3:3 [e]Ps 72:2-3; Isa 32:17

10 Love and faithfulness[d] meet together;
righteousness[e] and peace kiss each
other.

85:11 [f]Isa 45:8

11 Faithfulness springs forth from the
earth,
and righteousness[f] looks down
from heaven.

85:12 [g]Ps 84:11; Jas 1:17 [h]Lev 26:4; Ps 67:6; Zec 8:12

12 The LORD will indeed give what is
good,[g]
and our land will yield[h] its
harvest.
13 Righteousness goes before him
and prepares the way for his steps.

Psalm 86

A prayer of David.

86:1 [i]Ps 17:6

1 Hear, O LORD, and answer[i] me,
for I am poor and needy.
2 Guard my life, for I am devoted to
you.

86:2 [j]Ps 25:2; 31:14

You are my God; save your servant
who trusts in you.[j]

86:3 [k]Ps 4:1; 57:1 [l]Ps 88:9

3 Have mercy[k] on me, O Lord,
for I call[l] to you all day long.

86:4 [m]Ps 25:1; 143:8

4 Bring joy to your servant,
for to you, O Lord,
I lift[m] up my soul.

86:5 [n]Ex 34:6; Ne 9:17; Ps 103:8; 145:8; Joel 2:13; Jnh 4:2

5 You are forgiving and good, O Lord,
abounding in love[n] to all who call
to you.
6 Hear my prayer, O LORD;
listen to my cry for mercy.

86:7 [o]Ps 50:15

7 In the day of my trouble[o] I will call
to you,
for you will answer me.

86:8 [p]Ex 15:11; Dt 3:24; Ps 89:6

8 Among the gods there is none like
you,[p] O Lord;
no deeds can compare with yours.

86:9 [q]Ps 66:4; Rev 15:4 [r]Isa 43:7

9 All the nations you have made
will come and worship[q] before
you, O Lord;
they will bring glory[r] to your
name.

86:10 [s]Ps 72:18 [t]Dt 6:4; Mk 12:29; 1Co 8:4

10 For you are great and do marvelous
deeds;[s]
you alone[t] are God.

86:11 [u]Ps 25:5 [v]Jer 32:39

11 Teach me your way,[u] O LORD,
and I will walk in your truth;
give me an undivided[v] heart,
that I may fear your name.
12 I will praise you, O Lord my God,
with all my heart;
I will glorify your name forever.
13 For great is your love toward me;
you have delivered me from the
depths of the grave.[a]

86:14 [w]Ps 54:3

14 The arrogant are attacking me,
O God;
a band of ruthless men seeks my
life—
men without regard for you.[w]

86:15 [x]Ps 103:8 [y]Ex 34:6; Ne 9:17; Joel 2:13

15 But you, O Lord, are a
compassionate and gracious[x]
God,
slow to anger, abounding in love
and faithfulness.[y]

86:16 [z]Ps 116:16

16 Turn to me and have mercy on me;
grant your strength to your
servant
and save the son of your
maidservant.[b][z]
17 Give me a sign of your goodness,
that my enemies may see it and be
put to shame,
for you, O LORD, have helped me
and comforted me.

Psalm 87

Of the Sons of Korah. A psalm. A song.

1 He has set his foundation on the
holy mountain;

87:2 [a]Ps 78:68

2 the LORD loves the gates of Zion[a]
more than all the dwellings of
Jacob.

87:3 [b]Ps 46:4; Isa 60:1

3 Glorious things are said of you,
O city of God:[b] *Selah*

87:4 [c]Job 9:13 [d]Ps 45:12 [e]Isa 19:25

4 "I will record Rahab[c][c] and Babylon
among those who acknowledge
me—
Philistia too, and Tyre,[d] along with
Cush[d]—
and will say, 'This[e] one was born
in Zion.[e]' "
5 Indeed, of Zion it will be said,
"This one and that one were born
in her,
and the Most High himself will
establish her."

87:6 [f]Ps 69:28; Isa 4:3; Eze 13:9

6 The LORD will write in the register[f]
of the peoples:

[a]13 Hebrew *Sheol* [b]16 Or *save your faithful son* [c]4 A poetic name for Egypt [d]4 That is, the upper Nile region [e]4 Or *"O Rahab and Babylon, / Philistia, Tyre and Cush, / I will record concerning those who acknowledge me: / 'This*

"This one was born in Zion." *Selah*
7 As they make music[g] they will sing,
"All my fountains[h] are in you."

87:7 [g]Ps 149:3 [h]Ps 36:9

Psalm 88

A song. A psalm of the Sons of Korah. For the director of music. According to *mahalath leannoth.*[a] A *maskil*[b] of Heman the Ezrahite.

1 O LORD, the God who saves me,[i]
day and night I cry out[j] before you.
2 May my prayer come before you;
turn your ear to my cry.
3 For my soul is full of trouble
and my life draws near the grave.[c][k]
4 I am counted among those who go down to the pit;[l]
I am like a man without strength.
5 I am set apart with the dead,
like the slain who lie in the grave,
whom you remember no more,
who are cut off[m] from your care.
6 You have put me in the lowest pit,
in the darkest depths.[n]
7 Your wrath lies heavily upon me;
you have overwhelmed me with all your waves.[o] *Selah*
8 You have taken from me my closest friends[p]
and have made me repulsive to them.
I am confined[q] and cannot escape;
9 my eyes[r] are dim with grief.
I call[s] to you, O LORD, every day;
I spread out my hands[t] to you.
10 Do you show your wonders to the dead?
Do those who are dead rise up and praise you?[u] *Selah*
11 Is your love declared in the grave,
your faithfulness[v] in Destruction[d]?
12 Are your wonders known in the place of darkness,
or your righteous deeds in the land of oblivion?
13 But I cry to you for help,[w] O LORD;
in the morning[x] my prayer comes before you.[y]
14 Why, O LORD, do you reject[z] me
and hide your face[a] from me?
15 From my youth I have been afflicted and close to death;
I have suffered your terrors[b] and am in despair.
16 Your wrath has swept over me;
your terrors have destroyed me.
17 All day long they surround me like a flood;[c]
they have completely engulfed me.
18 You have taken my companions[d] and loved ones from me;
the darkness is my closest friend.

88:1 [i]Ps 51:14 [j]Ps 22:2; 27:9; Lk 18:7
88:3 [k]Ps 107:18,26
88:4 [l]Ps 28:1
88:5 [m]Ps 31:22; Isa 53:8
88:6 [n]Ps 69:15; La 3:55
88:7 [o]Ps 42:7
88:8 [p]Job 19:13; Ps 31:11 [q]Jer 32:2
88:9 [r]Ps 38:10 [s]Ps 86:3 [t]Job 11:13; Ps 143:6
88:10 [u]Ps 6:5
88:11 [v]Ps 30:9
88:13 [w]Ps 30:2 [x]Ps 5:3 [y]Ps 119:147
88:14 [z]Ps 43:2 [a]Job 13:24; Ps 13:1
88:15 [b]Job 6:4
88:17 [c]Ps 22:16; 124:4
88:18 [d]ver 8; Job 19:13; Ps 38:11

Psalm 89

A *maskil*[b] of Ethan the Ezrahite.

1 I will sing[e] of the LORD's great love forever;
with my mouth I will make your faithfulness known[f] through all generations.
2 I will declare that your love stands firm forever,
that you established your faithfulness in heaven itself.[g]
3 You said, "I have made a covenant with my chosen one,
I have sworn to David my servant,
4 'I will establish your line forever
and make your throne firm through all generations.' "[h] *Selah*
5 The heavens[i] praise your wonders, O LORD,
your faithfulness too, in the assembly of the holy ones.
6 For who in the skies above can compare with the LORD?
Who is like the LORD among the heavenly beings?[j]
7 In the council of the holy ones God is greatly feared;
he is more awesome than all who surround him.[k]
8 O LORD God Almighty, who is like you?[l]
You are mighty, O LORD, and your faithfulness surrounds you.
9 You rule over the surging sea;
when its waves mount up, you still them.[m]
10 You crushed Rahab[n] like one of the slain;

89:1 [e]Ps 59:16; Ps 101:1 [f]Ps 36:5; 40:10
89:2 [g]Ps 36:5
89:4 [h]2Sa 7:12-16; 1Ki 8:16; Ps 132:11-12; Isa 9:7; Lk 1:33
89:5 [i]Ps 19:1
89:6 [j]Ps 113:5
89:7 [k]Ps 47:2
89:8 [l]Ps 71:19
89:9 [m]Ps 65:7
89:10 [n]Ps 87:4

[a]Title: Possibly a tune, "The Suffering of Affliction" [b]Title: Probably a literary or musical term [c]*3* Hebrew *Sheol* [d]*11* Hebrew *Abaddon*

with your strong arm you
scattered[o] your enemies.
11 The heavens are yours, and yours
also the earth;[p]
you founded the world and all
that is in it.[q]
12 You created the north and the south;
Tabor[r] and Hermon[s] sing for joy[t]
at your name.
13 Your arm is endued with power;
your hand is strong, your right
hand exalted.

14 Righteousness and justice are the
foundation of your throne;[u]
love and faithfulness go before
you.
15 Blessed are those who have learned
to acclaim you,
who walk in the light[v] of your
presence, O LORD.
16 They rejoice in your name[w] all day
long;
they exult in your righteousness.
17 For you are their glory and strength,
and by your favor you exalt our
horn.[a][x]
18 Indeed, our shield[b] belongs to the
LORD,
our king[y] to the Holy One of
Israel.
19 Once you spoke in a vision,
to your faithful people you said:
"I have bestowed strength on a
warrior;
I have exalted a young man from
among the people.
20 I have found David[z] my servant;[a]
with my sacred oil I have
anointed[b] him.
21 My hand will sustain him;
surely my arm will strengthen
him.[c]
22 No enemy will subject him to
tribute;
no wicked man will oppress[d] him.
23 I will crush his foes before him[e]
and strike down his adversaries.[f]
24 My faithful love will be with him,[g]
and through my name his horn[c]
will be exalted.
25 I will set his hand over the sea,
his right hand over the rivers.[h]
26 He will call out to me, 'You are my
Father,[i]
my God, the Rock my Savior.'[j]
27 I will also appoint him my
firstborn,[k]
the most exalted[l] of the kings[m] of
the earth.
28 I will maintain my love to him
forever,
and my covenant with him will
never fail.[n]
29 I will establish his line forever,
his throne as long as the heavens
endure.[o]

30 "If his sons forsake my law
and do not follow my statutes,
31 if they violate my decrees
and fail to keep my commands,
32 I will punish their sin with the rod,
their iniquity with flogging;[p]
33 but I will not take my love from
him,[q]
nor will I ever betray my
faithfulness.
34 I will not violate my covenant
or alter what my lips have
uttered.[r]
35 Once for all, I have sworn by my
holiness—
and I will not lie to David—
36 that his line will continue forever
and his throne endure before me
like the sun;
37 it will be established forever like the
moon,
the faithful witness in the sky."
Selah

38 But you have rejected,[s] you have
spurned,
you have been very angry with
your anointed one.
39 You have renounced the covenant
with your servant
and have defiled his crown in the
dust.[t]
40 You have broken through all his
walls[u]
and reduced his strongholds[v] to
ruins.
41 All who pass by have plundered
him;
he has become the scorn of his
neighbors.[w]
42 You have exalted the right hand of
his foes;
you have made all his enemies
rejoice.[x]
43 You have turned back the edge of his
sword

[a]*17 Horn* here symbolizes strong one. [b]*18* Or *sovereign* [c]*24 Horn* here symbolizes strength.

89:10 [o]Ps 68:1
89:11 [p]1Ch 29:11; Ps 24:1 [q]Ge 1:1
89:12 [r]Jos 19:22 [s]Dt 3:8; Jos 12:1 [t]Ps 98:8
89:14 [u]Ps 97:2
89:15 [v]Ps 44:3
89:16 [w]Ps 105:3
89:17 [x]Ps 75:10; 92:10; 148:14
89:18 [y]Ps 47:9
89:20 [z]Ac 13:22 [a]Ps 78:70 [b]1Sa 16:1,12
89:21 [c]Ps 18:35
89:22 [d]2Sa 7:10
89:23 [e]Ps 18:40 [f]2Sa 7:9
89:24 [g]2Sa 7:15
89:25 [h]Ps 72:8
89:26 [i]2Sa 7:14 [j]2Sa 22:47
89:27 [k]Col 1:18
89:27 [l]Nu 24:7 [m]Rev 1:5; 19:16
89:28 [n]ver 33-34; Isa 55:3
89:29 [o]ver 4,36; Dt 11:21; Jer 33:17
89:32 [p]2Sa 7:14
89:33 [q]2Sa 7:15
89:34 [r]Nu 23:19
89:38 [s]Dt 32:19; 1Ch 28:9; Ps 44:9
89:39 [t]La 5:16
89:40 [u]Ps 80:12 [v]La 2:2
89:41 [w]Ps 44:13
89:42 [x]Ps 13:2; 80:6

and have not supported him in
battle.[y]
89:43 [y]Ps 44:10
44 You have put an end to his splendor
and cast his throne to the ground.
45 You have cut short the days of his
youth;
you have covered him with a
mantle of shame.[z] *Selah*
89:45 [z]Ps 44:15; 109:29

46 How long, O LORD? Will you hide
yourself forever?
How long will your wrath burn
like fire?[a]
89:46 [a]Ps 79:5
47 Remember how fleeting is my life.[b]
89:47 [b]Job 7:7; Ps 39:5
For what futility you have created
all men!
48 What man can live and not see
death,
or save himself from the power of
the grave[a]?[c] *Selah*
89:48 [c]Ps 22:29; 49:9
49 O Lord, where is your former great
love,
which in your faithfulness you
swore to David?
50 Remember, Lord, how your servant
has[b] been mocked,[d]
89:50 [d]Ps 69:19
how I bear in my heart the taunts
of all the nations,
51 the taunts with which your enemies
have mocked, O LORD,
with which they have mocked
every step of your anointed
one.[e]
89:51 [e]Ps 74:10

52 Praise be to the LORD forever!
Amen and Amen.[f]
89:52 [f]Ps 41:13; 72:19

BOOK IV

Psalms 90–106

Psalm 90

A prayer of Moses the man of God.

1 Lord, you have been our dwelling
place[g]
90:1 [g]Dt 33:27; Eze 11:16
throughout all generations.
2 Before the mountains were born[h]
90:2 [h]Job 15:7; Pr 8:25 [i]Ps 102:24-27
or you brought forth the earth and
the world,
from everlasting to everlasting you
are God.[i]
3 You turn men back to dust,
saying, "Return to dust, O sons of
men."[j]
90:3 [j]Ge 3:19; Job 34:15
4 For a thousand years in your sight

PEACE

A NEW TIME ZONE

Psalm 90:4

Heaven Standard Time is on the way. When you hear the trumpet sound, be prepared to set your clocks a thousand years ahead. Welcome then the clockless age, when Eden shall be born again. Then peace will be our anthem, and we'll study war no more.

are like a day that has just gone
by,
or like a watch in the night.[k]
90:4 [k]2Pe 3:8
5 You sweep men away[l] in the sleep of
death;
90:5 [l]Ps 73:20; Isa 40:6
they are like the new grass of the
morning—
6 though in the morning it springs up
new,
by evening it is dry and
withered.[m]
90:6 [m]Mt 6:30; Jas 1:10

7 We are consumed by your anger
and terrified by your indignation.
8 You have set our iniquities before
you,
our secret sins[n] in the light of your
presence.
90:8 [n]Ps 19:12
9 All our days pass away under your
wrath;
we finish our years with a moan.[o]
90:9 [o]Ps 78:33
10 The length of our days is seventy
years—
or eighty, if we have the strength;
yet their span[c] is but trouble and
sorrow,
for they quickly pass, and we fly
away.[p]
90:10 [p]Job 20:8
11 Who knows the power of your
anger?
For your wrath is as great as the
fear that is due you.[q]
90:11 [q]Ps 76:7
12 Teach us to number our days[r]
aright,
90:12 [r]Ps 39:4 [s]Dt 32:29
that we may gain a heart of
wisdom.[s]
13 Relent, O LORD! How long[t] will it
be?
90:13 [t]Ps 6:3 [u]Dt 32:36; Ps 135:14
Have compassion on your
servants.[u]
14 Satisfy[v] us in the morning with your
unfailing love,
90:14 [v]Ps 103:5

[a] *48* Hebrew *Sheol* [b] *50* Or *your servants have*
[c] *10* Or *yet the best of them*

that we may sing for joy[w] and be
glad all our days.[x]
15 Make us glad for as many days as
you have afflicted us,
for as many years as we have seen
trouble.
16 May your deeds be shown to your
servants,
your splendor to their children.[y]
17 May the favor[a] of the Lord our God
rest upon us;
establish the work of our hands
for us—
yes, establish the work of our
hands.[z]

90:14 [w]Ps 85:6 [x]Ps 31:7
90:16 [y]Ps 44:1; Hab 3:2
90:17 [z]Isa 26:12

Psalm 91

1 He who dwells in the shelter[a] of the
Most High
will rest in the shadow[b] of the
Almighty.[b]
2 I will say[c] of the LORD, "He is my
refuge[c] and my fortress,
my God, in whom I trust."

3 Surely he will save you from the
fowler's snare[d]
and from the deadly pestilence.[e]
4 He will cover you with his feathers,
and under his wings you will find
refuge;[f]
his faithfulness will be your shield[g]
and rampart.
5 You will not fear[h] the terror of night,
nor the arrow that flies by day,
6 nor the pestilence that stalks in the
darkness,
nor the plague that destroys at
midday.
7 A thousand may fall at your side,
ten thousand at your right hand,
but it will not come near you.
8 You will only observe with your eyes
and see the punishment of the
wicked.[i]

9 If you make the Most High your
dwelling—
even the LORD, who is my
refuge—
10 then no harm[j] will befall you,
no disaster will come near your
tent.
11 For he will command his angels[k]
concerning you
to guard you in all your ways;[l]
12 they will lift you up in their hands,
so that you will not strike your
foot against a stone.[m]
13 You will tread upon the lion and the
cobra;
you will trample the great lion and
the serpent.[n]

91:1 [a]Ps 31:20 [b]Ps 17:8
91:2 [c]Ps 142:5
91:3 [d]Ps 124:7; Pr 6:5 [e]1Ki 8:37
91:4 [f]Ps 17:8 [g]Ps 35:2
91:5 [h]Job 5:21
91:8 [i]Ps 37:34; 58:10; Mal 1:5
91:10 [j]Pr 12:21
91:11 [k]Heb 1:14 [l]Ps 34:7
91:12 [m]Mt 4:6*; Lk 4:10-11*
91:13 [n]Da 6:22; Lk 10:19

SELF-CONTROL

TREADING ON COBRAS

Psalm 91:13

This authority is yours. The Christ who lives within you will empower you. Shod in boots of grace, you'll walk through serpents without fear. Your self-control will order lions.

14 "Because he loves me," says the
LORD, "I will rescue him;
I will protect him, for he
acknowledges my name.
15 He will call upon me, and I will
answer him;
I will be with him in trouble,
I will deliver him and honor him.[o]
16 With long life[p] will I satisfy him
and show him my salvation.[q]"

91:15 [o]1Sa 2:30; Ps 50:15; Jn 12:26
91:16 [p]Dt 6:2; Ps 21:4 [q]Ps 50:23

Psalm 92

A psalm. A song. For the Sabbath day.

1 It is good to praise the LORD
and make music to your name,[r]
O Most High,[s]
2 to proclaim your love in the
morning[t]
and your faithfulness at night,
3 to the music of the ten-stringed lyre
and the melody of the harp.[u]

4 For you make me glad by your
deeds, O LORD;
I sing for joy at the works of your
hands.[v]
5 How great are your works,[w]
O LORD,
how profound your thoughts![x]
6 The senseless man[y] does not know,
fools do not understand,
7 that though the wicked spring up
like grass
and all evildoers flourish,
they will be forever destroyed.

8 But you, O LORD, are exalted
forever.

92:1 [r]Ps 147:1 [s]Ps 135:3
92:2 [t]Ps 89:1
92:3 [u]1Sa 10:5; Ne 12:27; Ps 33:2
92:4 [v]Ps 8:6; 143:5
92:5 [w]Rev 15:3 [x]Ps 40:5; 139:17; Isa 28:29; Ro 11:33
92:6 [y]Ps 73:22

[a]*17* Or *beauty* [b]*1* Hebrew *Shaddai* [c]*2* Or *He says*

[9]For surely your enemies, O LORD,
surely your enemies will perish;
92:9 [z]Ps 68:1; 89:10
all evildoers will be scattered.[z]
[10]You have exalted my horn[a] [a] like that
92:10 [a]Ps 89:17 [b]Ps 23:5
of a wild ox;
fine oils[b] have been poured upon
me.
[11]My eyes have seen the defeat of my
adversaries;
92:11 [c]Ps 54:7; 91:8
my ears have heard the rout of my
wicked foes.[c]

[12]The righteous will flourish like a
palm tree,
92:12 [d]Ps 1:3; 52:8; Jer 17:8; Hos 14:6
they will grow like a cedar of
Lebanon;[d]
[13]planted in the house of the LORD,
92:13 [e]Ps 100:4
they will flourish in the courts of
our God.[e]
92:14 [f]Jn 15:2
[14]They will still bear fruit[f] in old age,
they will stay fresh and green,
[15]proclaiming, "The LORD is upright;
92:15 [g]Job 34:10
he is my Rock, and there is no
wickedness in him.[g]"

Psalm 93

93:1 [h]Ps 97:1 [i]Ps 104:1 [j]Ps 65:6 [k]Ps 96:10
[1]The LORD reigns,[h] he is robed in
majesty;[i]
the LORD is robed in majesty
and is armed with strength.[j]
The world is firmly established;
it cannot be moved.[k]
[2]Your throne was established long
ago;
93:2 [l]Ps 45:6
you are from all eternity.[l]
93:3 [m]Ps 96:11
[3]The seas[m] have lifted up, O LORD,
the seas have lifted up their voice;
the seas have lifted up their
pounding waves.
93:4 [n]Ps 65:7
[4]Mightier than the thunder[n] of the
great waters,
mightier than the breakers of the
sea—
the LORD on high is mighty.

93:5 [o]Ps 29:2
[5]Your statutes stand firm;
holiness[o] adorns your house
for endless days, O LORD.

Psalm 94

94:1 [p]Na 1:2; Ro 12:19 [q]Ps 80:1
[1]O LORD, the God who avenges,[p]
O God who avenges, shine forth.[q]
94:2 [r]Ge 18:25 [s]Ps 31:23
[2]Rise up, O Judge[r] of the earth;
pay back[s] to the proud what they
deserve.
[3]How long will the wicked, O LORD,
how long will the wicked be
jubilant?
94:4 [t]Ps 31:18 [u]Ps 52:1
[4]They pour out arrogant[t] words;
all the evildoers are full of
boasting.[u]
94:5 [v]Isa 3:15
[5]They crush your people,[v] O LORD;
they oppress your inheritance.
[6]They slay the widow and the alien;
they murder the fatherless.
94:7 [w]Job 22:14; Ps 10:11
[7]They say, "The LORD does not see;[w]
the God of Jacob pays no heed."
94:8 [x]Ps 92:6
[8]Take heed, you senseless ones[x]
among the people;
you fools, when will you become
wise?
[9]Does he who implanted the ear not
hear?
94:9 [y]Ex 4:11; Pr 20:12
Does he who formed the eye not
see?[y]
[10]Does he who disciplines nations not
punish?
94:10 [z]Job 35:11; Isa 28:26
Does he who teaches[z] man lack
knowledge?
[11]The LORD knows the thoughts of
man;
94:11 [a]1Co 3:20*
he knows that they are futile.[a]
94:12 [b]Job 5:17; Heb 12:5 [c]Dt 8:3
[12]Blessed is the man you discipline,[b]
O LORD,
the man you teach[c] from your law;
[13]you grant him relief from days of
trouble,
94:13 [d]Ps 55:23
till a pit[d] is dug for the wicked.
[14]For the LORD will not reject his
94:14 [e]1Sa 12:22; Ps 37:28; Ro 11:2
people;[e]
he will never forsake his
inheritance.
[15]Judgment will again be founded on
94:15 [f]Ps 97:2
righteousness,[f]
and all the upright in heart will
follow it.
94:16 [g]Nu 10:35; Ps 17:13 [h]Ps 59:2
[16]Who will rise up[g] for me against the
wicked?
Who will take a stand for me
against evildoers?[h]
94:17 [i]Ps 124:2
[17]Unless the LORD had given me
help,[i]
I would soon have dwelt in the
silence of death.
94:18 [j]Ps 38:16
[18]When I said, "My foot is slipping,[j]"
your love, O LORD, supported
me.
[19]When anxiety was great within me,
your consolation brought joy to
my soul.

[a] *10 Horn* here symbolizes strength.

20 Can a corrupt throne be allied with you—
one that brings on misery by its decrees?[k]
21 They band together[l] against the righteous
and condemn the innocent[m] to death.
22 But the LORD has become my fortress,
and my God the rock in whom I take refuge.[n]
23 He will repay[o] them for their sins
and destroy them for their wickedness;
the LORD our God will destroy them.

94:20 [k]Ps 58:2
94:21 [l]Ps 56:6 [m]Ps 106:38; Pr 17:15,26
94:22 [n]Ps 18:2; 59:9
94:23 [o]Ps 7:16

Psalm 95

1 Come, let us sing for joy to the LORD;
let us shout aloud[p] to the Rock[q] of our salvation.
2 Let us come before him[r] with thanksgiving
and extol him with music[s] and song.
3 For the LORD is the great God,[t]
the great King above all gods.[u]
4 In his hand are the depths of the earth,
and the mountain peaks belong to him.
5 The sea is his, for he made it,
and his hands formed the dry land.[v]

6 Come, let us bow down[w] in worship,
let us kneel[x] before the LORD our Maker;[y]
7 for he is our God
and we are the people of his pasture,[z]
the flock under his care.

Today, if you hear his voice,
8 do not harden your hearts as you did at Meribah,[a][a]
as you did that day at Massah[b] in the desert,
9 where your fathers tested[b] and tried me,
though they had seen what I did.
10 For forty years[c] I was angry with that generation;
I said, "They are a people whose hearts go astray,
and they have not known my ways."
11 So I declared on oath[d] in my anger,
"They shall never enter my rest."[e]

95:1 [p]Ps 81:1 [q]2Sa 22:47
95:2 [r]Mic 6:6 [s]Ps 81:2; Eph 5:19
95:3 [t]Ps 48:1; 145:3 [u]Ps 96:4; 97:9
95:5 [v]Ge 1:9; Ps 146:6
95:6 [w]Php 2:10 [x]2Ch 6:13 [y]Ps 100:3; 149:2; Isa 17:7; Da 6:10-11; Hos 8:14
95:7 [z]Ps 74:1; 79:13
95:8 [a]Ex 17:7
95:9 [b]Nu 14:22; Ps 78:18; 1Co 10:9
95:10 [c]Ac 7:36; Heb 3:17
95:11 [d]Nu 14:23 [e]Dt 1:35; Heb 4:3*

Psalm 96

1 Sing to the LORD[f] a new song;
sing to the LORD, all the earth.
2 Sing to the LORD, praise his name;
proclaim his salvation[g] day after day.
3 Declare his glory among the nations,
his marvelous deeds among all peoples.

4 For great is the LORD and most worthy of praise;[h]
he is to be feared[i] above all gods.[j]
5 For all the gods of the nations are idols,
but the LORD made the heavens.[k]
6 Splendor and majesty are before him;
strength and glory[l] are in his sanctuary.

7 Ascribe to the LORD,[m] O families of nations,[n]
ascribe to the LORD glory and strength.
8 Ascribe to the LORD the glory due his name;
bring an offering[o] and come into his courts.
9 Worship the LORD in the splendor of his[c] holiness;[p]
tremble[q] before him, all the earth.[r]
10 Say among the nations, "The LORD reigns.[s]"
The world is firmly established, it cannot be moved;[t]
he will judge the peoples with equity.[u]
11 Let the heavens rejoice, let the earth be glad;[v]
let the sea resound, and all that is in it;
12 let the fields be jubilant, and everything in them.
Then all the trees of the forest[w] will sing for joy;[x]
13 they will sing before the LORD,
for he comes,
he comes to judge[y] the earth.

[a]8 *Meribah* means *quarreling.* [b]8 *Massah* means *testing.* [c]9 Or *LORD with the splendor of*

96:1 [f]1Ch 16:23
96:2 [g]Ps 71:15
96:4 [h]Ps 18:3; 145:3 [i]Ps 89:7 [j]Ps 95:3
96:5 [k]Ps 115:15
96:6 [l]Ps 29:1
96:7 [m]Ps 29:1 [n]Ps 22:27
96:8 [o]Ps 45:12; 72:10
96:9 [p]Ps 29:2 [q]Ps 114:7 [r]Ps 33:8
96:10 [s]Ps 97:1 [t]Ps 93:1 [u]Ps 67:4
96:11 [v]Ps 97:1; 98:7; Isa 49:13
96:12 [w]Isa 44:23 [x]Ps 65:13
96:13 [y]Rev 19:11

He will judge the world in
righteousness
and the peoples in his truth.

Psalm 97

97:1 [z]Ps 96:10 [a]Ps 96:11

1 The LORD reigns,[z] let the earth be glad;[a]
let the distant shores rejoice.

97:2 [b]Ex 19:9; Ps 18:11 [c]Ps 89:14

2 Clouds and thick darkness[b] surround him;
righteousness and justice are the foundation of his throne.[c]

97:3 [d]Da 7:10 [e]Hab 3:5 [f]Ps 18:8

3 Fire[d] goes before[e] him
and consumes[f] his foes on every side.

97:4 [g]Ps 104:32

4 His lightning lights up the world;
the earth sees and trembles.[g]

97:5 [h]Ps 46:2,6; Mic 1:4 [i]Jos 3:11

5 The mountains melt[h] like wax before the LORD,
before the Lord of all the earth.[i]

97:6 [j]Ps 50:6 [k]Ps 19:1

6 The heavens proclaim his righteousness,[j]
and all the peoples see his glory.[k]

97:7 [l]Lev 26:1 [m]Jer 10:14 [n]Heb 1:6

7 All who worship images[l] are put to shame,[m]
those who boast in idols—
worship him,[n] all you gods!

97:8 [o]Ps 48:11

8 Zion hears and rejoices
and the villages of Judah are glad
because of your judgments,[o]
O LORD.

97:9 [p]Ps 83:18; 95:3 [q]Ex 18:11

9 For you, O LORD, are the Most High over all the earth;[p]
you are exalted[q] far above all gods.

97:10 [r]Ps 34:14; Am 5:15; Ro 12:9 [s]Pr 2:8 [t]Da 3:28 [u]Ps 37:40; Jer 15:21

10 Let those who love the LORD hate evil,[r]
for he guards the lives of his faithful ones[s]
and delivers[t] them from the hand of the wicked.[u]

97:11 [v]Job 22:28

11 Light is shed[v] upon the righteous
and joy on the upright in heart.

97:12 [w]Ps 30:4

12 Rejoice in the LORD, you who are righteous,
and praise his holy name.[w]

Psalm 98

A psalm.

98:1 [x]Ps 96:1 [y]Ps 96:3 [z]Ex 15:6 [a]Isa 52:10

1 Sing to the LORD a new song,[x]
for he has done marvelous things;[y]
his right hand[z] and his holy arm[a]
have worked salvation for him.

98:2 [b]Isa 52:10

2 The LORD has made his salvation known[b]
and revealed his righteousness to the nations.

98:3 [c]Lk 1:54

3 He has remembered[c] his love
and his faithfulness to the house of Israel;
all the ends of the earth have seen
the salvation of our God.

98:4 [d]Isa 44:23

4 Shout for joy[d] to the LORD, all the earth,
burst into jubilant song with music;

98:5 [e]Ps 92:3 [f]Isa 51:3

5 make music to the LORD with the harp,[e]
with the harp and the sound of singing,[f]

98:6 [g]Nu 10:10 [h]Ps 47:7

6 with trumpets[g] and the blast of the ram's horn—
shout for joy before the LORD, the King.[h]

98:7 [i]Ps 24:1

7 Let the sea resound, and everything in it,
the world, and all who live in it.[i]

98:8 [j]Isa 55:12

8 Let the rivers clap their hands,
let the mountains[j] sing together for joy;
9 let them sing before the LORD,
for he comes to judge the earth.
He will judge the world in righteousness
and the peoples with equity.[k]

98:9 [k]Ps 96:10

KINDNESS

A SCEPTER FOR THE SON

Psalm 99:1–2

Jesus holds a king's scepter. His domain is no tiny province. This world of ours—this third rock from the sun—is but the footstool of his Father. Yet for all his awesome power, he walks in the sandals of kindness, seeking those whom he may redeem.

Psalm 99

99:1 [l]Ps 97:1 [m]Ex 25:22

1 The LORD reigns,[l]
let the nations tremble;
he sits enthroned between the cherubim,[m]
let the earth shake.

99:2 [n]Ps 48:1 [o]Ps 97:9; 113:4

2 Great is the LORD[n] in Zion;
he is exalted[o] over all the nations.

99:3 [p]Ps 76:1

3 Let them praise your great and awesome name[p]—
he is holy.

[4]The King is mighty, he loves justice[q]—
you have established equity;[r]
in Jacob you have done
what is just and right.
[5]Exalt[s] the LORD our God
and worship at his footstool;
he is holy.

[6]Moses[t] and Aaron were among his priests,
Samuel[u] was among those who called on his name;
they called on the LORD
and he answered[v] them.
[7]He spoke to them from the pillar of cloud;[w]
they kept his statutes and the decrees he gave them.

[8]O LORD our God,
you answered them;
you were to Israel[a] a forgiving God,[x]
though you punished their misdeeds.[b]
[9]Exalt the LORD our God
and worship at his holy mountain,
for the LORD our God is holy.

99:4 [q]Ps 11:7 [r]Ps 98:9
99:5 [s]Ps 132:7
99:6 [t]Ex 24:6 [u]Jer 15:1 [v]1Sa 7:9
99:7 [w]Ex 33:9
99:8 [x]Nu 14:20

Psalm 100

A psalm. For giving thanks.

[1]Shout for joy[y] to the LORD, all the earth.
[2]Worship the LORD with gladness;
come before him[z] with joyful songs.
[3]Know that the LORD is God.[a]
It is he who made us,[b] and we are his[c];
we are his people, the sheep of his pasture.[c]

[4]Enter his gates with thanksgiving
and his courts with praise;
give thanks to him and praise his name.[d]
[5]For the LORD is good[e] and his love endures forever;[f]
his faithfulness[g] continues through all generations.

100:1 [y]Ps 98:4
100:2 [z]Ps 95:2
100:3 [a]Ps 46:10 [b]Job 10:3 [c]Ps 74:1; Eze 34:31
100:4 [d]Ps 116:17
100:5 [e]1Ch 16:34; Ps 25:8 [f]Ezr 3:11; Ps 106:1 [g]Ps 119:90

Psalm 101

Of David. A psalm.

[1]I will sing of your love[h] and justice;
to you, O LORD, I will sing praise.
[2]I will be careful to lead a blameless life—
when will you come to me?

I will walk in my house
with blameless heart.
[3]I will set before my eyes
no vile thing.[i]

The deeds of faithless men I hate;[j]
they will not cling to me.
[4]Men of perverse heart[k] shall be far from me;
I will have nothing to do with evil.

[5]Whoever slanders his neighbor[l] in secret,
him will I put to silence;
whoever has haughty eyes[m] and a proud heart,
him will I not endure.

[6]My eyes will be on the faithful in the land,
that they may dwell with me;
he whose walk is blameless[n]
will minister to me.
[7]No one who practices deceit
will dwell in my house;
no one who speaks falsely
will stand in my presence.
[8]Every morning[o] I will put to silence
all the wicked[p] in the land;
I will cut off every evildoer[q]
from the city of the LORD.[r]

101:1 [h]Ps 51:14; 89:1; 145:7
101:3 [i]Dt 15:9 [j]Ps 40:4
101:4 [k]Pr 11:20
101:5 [l]Ps 50:20 [m]Ps 10:5; Pr 6:17
101:6 [n]Ps 119:1
101:8 [o]Jer 21:12 [p]Ps 75:10 [q]Ps 118:10-12 [r]Ps 46:4

Psalm 102

A prayer of an afflicted man.
When he is faint and pours out
his lament before the LORD.

[1]Hear my prayer, O LORD;
let my cry for help[s] come to you.
[2]Do not hide your face[t] from me
when I am in distress.
Turn your ear to me;
when I call, answer me quickly.

[3]For my days vanish like smoke;[u]
my bones burn like glowing embers.
[4]My heart is blighted and withered like grass;[v]
I forget to eat my food.
[5]Because of my loud groaning
I am reduced to skin and bones.

102:1 [s]Ex 2:23
102:2 [t]Ps 69:17
102:3 [u]Jas 4:14
102:4 [v]Ps 37:2

[a]8 Hebrew *them* [b]8 Or *I an avenger of the wrongs done to them* [c]3 Or *and not we ourselves*

102:6 [w]Job 30:29; Isa 34:11
[6]I am like a desert owl,[w]
like an owl among the ruins.
102:7 [x]Ps 77:4 [y]Ps 38:11
[7]I lie awake;[x] I have become
like a bird alone[y] on a roof.
[8]All day long my enemies taunt me;
those who rail against me use my
name as a curse.
[9]For I eat ashes as my food
102:9 [z]Ps 42:3
and mingle my drink with tears[z]
[10]because of your great wrath,[a]
102:10 [a]Ps 38:3
for you have taken me up and
thrown me aside.
102:11 [b]Job 14:2
[11]My days are like the evening
shadow;[b]
I wither away like grass.
[12]But you, O LORD, sit enthroned
102:12 [c]Ps 9:7 [d]Ps 135:13
forever;[c]
your renown endures[d] through all
generations.
102:13 [e]Isa 60:10
[13]You will arise and have compassion[e]
on Zion,
for it is time to show favor to her;
the appointed time has come.
[14]For her stones are dear to your
servants;
102:15 [f]1Ki 8:43 [g]Ps 138:4
her very dust moves them to pity.
[15]The nations will fear[f] the name of
the LORD,
all the kings[g] of the earth will
revere your glory.
[16]For the LORD will rebuild Zion
102:16 [h]Isa 60:1-2
and appear in his glory.[h]
102:17 [i]Ne 1:6
[17]He will respond to the prayer[i] of the
destitute;
he will not despise their plea.
102:18 [j]Ro 15:4 [k]Ps 22:31
[18]Let this be written[j] for a future
generation,
that a people not yet created[k] may
praise the LORD:

JOY

A FUTURE SONG

Psalm 102:18

There are unborn continents of children who will, when they have come to be, bless the name of Jesus, for whose sake they will be given life.

[19]"The LORD looked down[l] from his
102:19 [l]Dt 26:15
sanctuary on high,
102:20 [m]Ps 79:11
from heaven he viewed the earth,
[20]to hear the groans of the prisoners[m]
and release those condemned to
death."

[21]So the name of the LORD will be
102:21 [n]Ps 22:22
declared[n] in Zion
and his praise in Jerusalem
[22]when the peoples and the kingdoms
assemble to worship the LORD.

[23]In the course of my life[a] he broke my
strength;
he cut short my days.
[24]So I said:
"Do not take me away, O my
God, in the midst of my
days;
102:24 [o]Ps 90:2; Isa 38:10
your years go on[o] through all
generations.
102:25 [p]Ge 1:1; Heb 1:10-12*
[25]In the beginning[p] you laid the
foundations of the earth,
and the heavens are the work of
your hands.
102:26 [q]Isa 34:4; Mt 24:35; 2Pe 3:7-10; Rev 20:11
[26]They will perish,[q] but you remain;
they will all wear out like a
garment.
Like clothing you will change them
and they will be discarded.
102:27 [r]Mal 3:6; Heb 13:8; Jas 1:17
[27]But you remain the same,[r]
and your years will never end.
102:28 [s]Ps 69:36 [t]Ps 89:4
[28]The children of your servants[s] will
live in your presence;
their descendants[t] will be
established before you."

Psalm 103

Of David.

103:1 [u]Ps 104:1
[1]Praise the LORD, O my soul;[u]
all my inmost being, praise his
holy name.
[2]Praise the LORD, O my soul,
and forget not all his benefits—
103:3 [v]Ps 130:8 [w]Ex 15:26
[3]who forgives all your sins[v]
and heals[w] all your diseases,
[4]who redeems your life from the pit
and crowns you with love and
compassion,
[5]who satisfies your desires with good
things
so that your youth is renewed like
103:5 [x]Isa 40:31
the eagle's.[x]

[6]The LORD works righteousness
103:7 [y]Ps 99:7; 147:19 [z]Ex 33:13 [a]Ps 106:22
and justice for all the oppressed.

[7]He made known[y] his ways[z] to
Moses,
103:8 [b]Ex 34:6; Ps 86:15; Jas 5:11
his deeds[a] to the people of Israel:
[8]The LORD is compassionate and
gracious,[b]

[a]23 Or *By his power*

slow to anger, abounding in love.
[9]He will not always accuse,
nor will he harbor his anger
forever;[c]
[10]he does not treat us as our sins
deserve[d]
or repay us according to our
iniquities.
[11]For as high as the heavens are above
the earth,
so great is his love[e] for those who
fear him;
[12]as far as the east is from the west,
so far has he removed our
transgressions[f] from us.
[13]As a father has compassion[g] on his
children,
so the LORD has compassion on
those who fear him;
[14]for he knows how we are formed,[h]
he remembers that we are dust.
[15]As for man, his days are like grass,[i]
he flourishes like a flower[j] of the
field;
[16]the wind blows[k] over it and it is
gone,
and its place[l] remembers it no
more.
[17]But from everlasting to everlasting
the LORD's love is with those who
fear him,
and his righteousness with their
children's children—
[18]with those who keep his covenant
and remember to obey his
precepts.[m]
[19]The LORD has established his throne
in heaven,
and his kingdom rules[n] over all.
[20]Praise the LORD, you his angels,[o]
you mighty ones[p] who do his
bidding,
who obey his word.
[21]Praise the LORD, all his heavenly
hosts,[q]
you his servants who do his will.
[22]Praise the LORD, all his works[r]
everywhere in his dominion.

Praise the LORD, O my soul.

103:9 [c]Ps 30:5; Isa 57:16; Jer 3:5,12; Mic 7:18
103:10 [d]Ezr 9:13
103:11 [e]Ps 57:10
103:12 [f]2Sa 12:13
103:13 [g]Mal 3:17
103:14 [h]Isa 29:16
103:15 [i]Ps 90:5 [j]Job 14:2; Jas 1:10; 1Pe 1:24
103:16 [k]Isa 40:7 [l]Job 7:10
103:18 [m]Dt 7:9
103:19 [n]Ps 47:2
103:20 [o]Ps 148:2; Heb 1:14 [p]Ps 29:1
103:21 [q]1Ki 22:19
103:22 [r]Ps 145:10

Psalm 104

[1]Praise the LORD, O my soul.[s]

O LORD my God, you are very
great;
you are clothed with splendor and
majesty.
[2]He wraps[t] himself in light as with a
garment;
he stretches out the heavens[u] like
a tent
[3] and lays the beams[v] of his upper
chambers on their waters.
He makes the clouds[w] his chariot
and rides on the wings of the
wind.[x]
[4]He makes winds his messengers,[a][y]
flames of fire[z] his servants.
[5]He set the earth[a] on its foundations;
it can never be moved.
[6]You covered it[b] with the deep[c] as
with a garment;
the waters stood above the
mountains.
[7]But at your rebuke[d] the waters fled,
at the sound of your thunder they
took to flight;
[8]they flowed over the mountains,
they went down into the valleys,
to the place you assigned[e] for
them.
[9]You set a boundary they cannot
cross;
never again will they cover the
earth.
[10]He makes springs[f] pour water into
the ravines;
it flows between the mountains.
[11]They give water to all the beasts of
the field;
the wild donkeys quench their
thirst.
[12]The birds of the air[g] nest by the
waters;
they sing among the branches.
[13]He waters the mountains[h] from his
upper chambers;
the earth is satisfied by the fruit of
his work.
[14]He makes grass grow[i] for the cattle,
and plants for man to
cultivate—
bringing forth food[j] from the
earth:
[15]wine[k] that gladdens the heart of
man,
oil[l] to make his face shine,
and bread that sustains his heart.
[16]The trees of the LORD are well
watered,

104:1 [s]Ps 103:22
104:2 [t]Da 7:9 [u]Isa 40:22
104:3 [v]Am 9:6 [w]Isa 19:1 [x]Ps 18:10
104:4 [y]Ps 148:8; Heb 1:7* [z]2Ki 2:11
104:5 [a]Job 26:7; Ps 24:1-2
104:6 [b]Ge 7:19 [c]Ge 1:2
104:7 [d]Ps 18:15
104:8 [e]Ps 33:7
104:10 [f]Ps 107:33; Isa 41:18
104:12 [g]Mt 8:20
104:13 [h]Ps 147:8; Jer 10:13
104:14 [i]Job 38:27; Ps 147:8 [j]Ge 1:30; Job 28:5
104:15 [k]Jdg 9:13 [l]Ps 23:5; 92:10; Lk 7:46

[a]4 Or *angels*

WEEK 47

JOY

1 DAY ONE

JOY, THE REVELING OF ANGELS

Read Psalm 103:20–22

"Praise the LORD, you his angels." This passage instructs angels to praise God, but aren't we his messengers of joy as well? In this gloomy world don't we need an occasional extra baptism of happiness? Don't we need to share that joy with others?

"You mighty ones who do his bidding." His bidding is not grievous. His task for us is the reason we exist. Therefore, whatever work he commands us is joy.

"Who obey his word." Obedience will make those who love God sing his praises. Obedience and music are both divine compositions. Those who obey have a reason to sing. Those who sing have a reason to obey.

"Praise the LORD, all his heavenly hosts." Notice, God said *all* the hosts. He will have no dour angels. Any who will not sing will find no happiness among the soaring voices of praise. Let there not be even one grumpy angel in the presence of God. In fact, Lucifer may have begun his fall by skipping his morning "Hallelujahs."

"You his servants who do his will." Joy is the business of angels. Joy is humanity's business too. The angels praise God when they see his mighty works and when they bask in the glory of his presence. That is our position as well: We look around our world and see God's hand in the scenic vistas and quiet streams. We come before God in prayer and feel his presence wash over us. We sing with the angels our praises to God.

2 DAY TWO

JOY AND THE PURPOSE OF GOD IN MY LIFE

When Jesus is victorious over the tempter in the wilderness, the angels come and minister to him. Joy is the automatic response of heaven every time we stand true in the midst of any trial. God is looking for those who can stand up in a moral onslaught and keep the faith. When we prove ourselves true, heaven takes an interest in our character. Listen carefully after you have stood for truth, and you will hear the fluttering of angel wings. Joy is heaven's response to godly courage. *Turn to Matthew 4:10–11, page 1122, for today's study.*

3 DAY THREE

JOY AND MY RELATIONSHIP WITH CHRIST

Gloria in excelsis deo is Latin. But whether the Bethlehem angels sang in Latin or Aramaic, the issue here is joy. Jesus has been born; the world has been blessed; salvation for humankind is on the way. What else would any good God-fearing angel do but sing? *Turn to Luke 2:13–14, page 1200, for today's study.*

4 DAY FOUR

JOY AND MY SERVICE TO OTHERS

Hospitality: Why is God so interested in it? Maybe because when we extend it, we are somehow forced to interrupt our own selfish agendas, take time, food, money or sleeping space and extend that to someone else. Guests are never just people we're nice to. Guests are souls who bring something unexpected to our lives. They contribute more to us than we do to them. They are angels, and they are never aware of it. Neither were we at the time; it was only later, when we were remaking the bed, that we found the feathers. *Turn to Hebrews 13:2, page 1477, for today's study.*

5 DAY FIVE

JOY AND ITS PLACE IN MY PERSONAL WORSHIP

We worship when we are reminded of God's goodness. The angels rejoice when a lost one is found. Shouldn't we also share their joy when we witness the miracle of a soul being introduced to eternal life? *Turn to Luke 15:1–7, page 1225, for today's study.*

MEMORIZE THIS WEEK

PSALM 148:1-2

Praise the LORD.

Praise the LORD from the heavens,
praise him in the heights above.
Praise him, all his angels,
praise him, all his heavenly hosts.

Week 48, Peace, the Reign of the Holy Spirit, begins on page 1429, 1 Thessalonians 1:4–10.
To begin a topical study on the Fruit of the Spirit, Joy, turn to the Topical Index, page 1548.

the cedars of Lebanon that he
planted.

104:17 [m]ver 12

17 There the birds[m] make their nests;
the stork has its home in the pine
trees.

18 The high mountains belong to the
wild goats;
the crags are a refuge for the
coneys.[a n]

104:18 [n]Pr 30:26

104:19 [o]Ge 1:14 [p]Ps 19:6

19 The moon marks off the seasons,[o]
and the sun[p] knows when to go
down.

104:20 [q]Isa 45:7 [r]Ps 74:16 [s]Ps 50:10

20 You bring darkness,[q] it becomes
night,[r]
and all the beasts of the forest[s]
prowl.

104:21 [t]Job 38:39; Ps 145:15; Joel 1:20

21 The lions roar for their prey
and seek their food from God.[t]

22 The sun rises, and they steal away;
they return and lie down in their
dens.[u]

104:22 [u]Job 37:8

104:23 [v]Ge 3:19

23 Then man goes out to his work,[v]
to his labor until evening.

104:24 [w]Ps 40:5 [x]Pr 3:19

24 How many are your works,[w]
O LORD!
In wisdom you made[x] them all;
the earth is full of your creatures.

104:25 [y]Ps 69:34

25 There is the sea,[y] vast and spacious,
teeming with creatures beyond
number—
living things both large and small.

104:26 [z]Ps 107:23; Eze 27:9 [a]Job 41:1

26 There the ships[z] go to and fro,
and the leviathan,[a] which you
formed to frolic there.

104:27 [b]Job 36:31; Ps 136:25; 145:15; 147:9

27 These all look to you
to give them their food[b] at the
proper time.

28 When you give it to them,
they gather it up;
when you open your hand,
they are satisfied[c] with good
things.

104:28 [c]Ps 145:16

104:29 [d]Dt 31:17 [e]Job 34:14; Ecc 12:7

29 When you hide your face,[d]
they are terrified;
when you take away their breath,
they die and return to the dust.[e]

30 When you send your Spirit,
they are created,
and you renew the face of the
earth.

31 May the glory of the LORD endure
forever;
may the LORD rejoice in his
works[f]—

104:31 [f]Ge 1:31

104:32 [g]Ps 97:4

32 he who looks at the earth, and it
trembles,[g]
who touches the mountains,[h] and
they smoke.[i]

104:32 [h]Ex 19:18 [i]Ps 144:5

104:33 [j]Ps 63:4

33 I will sing[j] to the LORD all my life;
I will sing praise to my God as
long as I live.

34 May my meditation be pleasing to
him,
as I rejoice[k] in the LORD.

104:34 [k]Ps 9:2

104:35 [l]Ps 37:38 [m]Ps 105:45; 106:48

35 But may sinners vanish[l] from the
earth
and the wicked be no more.

Praise the LORD, O my soul.

Praise the LORD.[b m]

Psalm 105

105:1 [n]1Ch 16:34 [o]Ps 99:6

1 Give thanks to the LORD,[n] call on
his name;[o]
make known among the nations
what he has done.

105:2 [p]Ps 96:1

2 Sing to him,[p] sing praise to him;
tell of all his wonderful acts.

FAITHFULNESS

A MAGNIFICENT OBSESSION

Psalm 105:1–2

***Silent witness* is an oxymoron. Witnesses, by definition, do two things: First they see and then they tell. No one can experience the fullness of Christ and remain silent. The glory of Christ's inner presence forbids all reticence. Witnessing is not an endeavor. It is a compulsion. It is a loud song, not a lullaby. It has something to say and has to say something.**

3 Glory in his holy name;
let the hearts of those who seek
the LORD rejoice.

4 Look to the LORD and his strength;
seek his face[q] always.

105:4 [q]Ps 27:8

105:5 [r]Ps 40:5 [s]Ps 77:11

5 Remember the wonders[r] he has
done,
his miracles, and the judgments he
pronounced,[s]

6 O descendants of Abraham his
servant,[t]
O sons of Jacob, his chosen[u] ones.

105:6 [t]ver 42 [u]Ps 106:5

7 He is the LORD our God;
his judgments are in all the earth.

[a] *18* That is, the hyrax or rock badger [b] *35* Hebrew *Hallelu Yah*; in the Septuagint this line stands at the beginning of Psalm 105.

8 He remembers his covenant[v] forever,
the word he commanded, for a
thousand generations,
9 the covenant he made with
Abraham,[w]
the oath he swore to Isaac.
10 He confirmed it[x] to Jacob as a
decree,
to Israel as an everlasting
covenant:
11 "To you I will give the land of
Canaan[y]
as the portion you will inherit."

12 When they were but few in number,[z]
few indeed, and strangers in it,[a]
13 they wandered from nation to
nation,
from one kingdom to another.
14 He allowed no one to oppress[b] them;
for their sake he rebuked kings:[c]
15 "Do not touch[d] my anointed ones;
do my prophets no harm."
16 He called down famine[e] on the land
and destroyed all their supplies of
food;
17 and he sent a man before them—
Joseph, sold as a slave.[f]
18 They bruised his feet with
shackles,[g]
his neck was put in irons,
19 till what he foretold[h] came to pass,
till the word of the LORD proved
him true.
20 The king sent and released him,
the ruler of peoples set him free.[i]
21 He made him master of his
household,
ruler over all he possessed,
22 to instruct his princes[j] as he pleased
and teach his elders wisdom.

23 Then Israel entered Egypt;[k]
Jacob lived as an alien in the land
of Ham.
24 The LORD made his people very
fruitful;
he made them too numerous[l] for
their foes,
25 whose hearts he turned[m] to hate his
people,
to conspire[n] against his servants.
26 He sent Moses[o] his servant,
and Aaron, whom he had
chosen.[p]
27 They performed[q] his miraculous
signs among them,
his wonders in the land of Ham.
28 He sent darkness[r] and made the land
dark—
for had they not rebelled against
his words?
29 He turned their waters into blood,[s]
causing their fish to die.[t]
30 Their land teemed with frogs,[u]
which went up into the bedrooms
of their rulers.
31 He spoke, and there came swarms of
flies,[v]
and gnats[w] throughout their
country.
32 He turned their rain into hail,[x]
with lightning throughout their
land;
33 he struck down their vines[y] and fig
trees
and shattered the trees of their
country.
34 He spoke, and the locusts came,[z]
grasshoppers without number;
35 they ate up every green thing in their
land,
ate up the produce of their soil.
36 Then he struck down all the
firstborn[a] in their land,
the firstfruits of all their
manhood.
37 He brought out Israel, laden with
silver and gold,[b]
and from among their tribes no
one faltered.
38 Egypt was glad when they left,
because dread of Israel[c] had fallen
on them.
39 He spread out a cloud[d] as a
covering,
and a fire to give light at night.[e]
40 They asked,[f] and he brought them
quail[g]
and satisfied them with the bread
of heaven.[h]
41 He opened the rock,[i] and water
gushed out;
like a river it flowed in the desert.

42 For he remembered his holy
promise[j]
given to his servant Abraham.
43 He brought out his people with
rejoicing,[k]
his chosen ones with shouts of
joy;
44 he gave them the lands of the
nations,[l]
and they fell heir to what others
had toiled for—

105:8 [v]Ps 106:45; Lk 1:72
105:9 [w]Ge 12:7; 17:2; 22:16-18; Gal 3:15-18
105:10 [x]Ge 28:13-15
105:11 [y]Ge 13:15; 15:18
105:12 [z]Ge 34:30; Dt 7:7 [a]Ge 23:4; Heb 11:9
105:14 [b]Ge 35:5 [c]Ge 12:17-20
105:15 [d]Ge 26:11
105:16 [e]Ge 41:54; Lev 26:26; Isa 3:1; Eze 4:16
105:17 [f]Ge 37:28; 45:5; Ac 7:9
105:18 [g]Ge 40:15
105:19 [h]Ge 40:20-22
105:20 [i]Ge 41:14
105:22 [j]Ge 41:43-44
105:23 [k]Ge 46:6; Ac 13:17
105:24 [l]Ex 1:7,9
105:25 [m]Ex 4:21 [n]Ex 1:6-10; Ac 7:19
105:26 [o]Ex 3:10 [p]Nu 16:5; 17:5-8
105:27 [q]Ex 7:8-12:51
105:28 [r]Ex 10:22
105:29 [s]Ps 78:44 [t]Ex 7:21
105:30 [u]Ex 8:2,6
105:31 [v]Ex 8:21-24 [w]Ex 8:16-18
105:32 [x]Ex 9:22-25
105:33 [y]Ps 78:47
105:34 [z]Ex 10:4, 12-15
105:36 [a]Ex 12:29
105:37 [b]Ex 12:35
105:38 [c]Ex 12:33; 15:16
105:39 [d]Ex 13:21 [e]Ne 9:12; Ps 78:14
105:40 [f]Ps 78:18,24 [g]Ex 16:13 [h]Jn 6:31
105:41 [i]Ex 17:6; Nu 20:11; Ps 78:15-16; 1Co 10:4
105:42 [j]Ge 15:13-16
105:43 [k]Ex 15:1-18; Ps 106:12
105:44 [l]Jos 13:6-7

105:45 [m]Dt 4:40; 6:21-24

45 that they might keep his precepts
and observe his laws.[m]

Praise the LORD.[a]

Psalm 106

1 Praise the LORD.[b]

106:1 [n]Ps 100:5; 105:1

Give thanks to the LORD, for he is good;[n]
his love endures forever.

106:2 [o]Ps 145:4,12

2 Who can proclaim the mighty acts[o] of the LORD
or fully declare his praise?
3 Blessed are they who maintain justice,
who constantly do what is right.[p]

106:3 [p]Ps 15:2

106:4 [q]Ps 119:132

4 Remember me,[q] O LORD, when you show favor to your people,
come to my aid when you save them,

106:5 [r]Ps 1:3 [s]Ps 118:15

5 that I may enjoy the prosperity[r] of your chosen ones,
that I may share in the joy[s] of your nation
and join your inheritance in giving praise.

106:6 [t]Da 9:5

6 We have sinned,[t] even as our fathers did;
we have done wrong and acted wickedly.
7 When our fathers were in Egypt,
they gave no thought to your miracles;

106:7 [u]Ps 78:11,42 [v]Ex 14:11-12

they did not remember[u] your many kindnesses,
and they rebelled by the sea,[v] the Red Sea.[c]

106:8 [w]Ex 9:16

8 Yet he saved them for his name's sake,[w]
to make his mighty power known.

106:9 [x]Ps 18:15 [y]Ex 14:21; Na 1:4 [z]Isa 63:11-14

9 He rebuked[x] the Red Sea, and it dried up;[y]
he led them through[z] the depths as through a desert.

106:10 [a]Ex 14:30 [b]Ps 107:2

10 He saved them[a] from the hand of the foe;
from the hand of the enemy he redeemed them.[b]

106:11 [c]Ex 14:28; 15:5

11 The waters covered[c] their adversaries;
not one of them survived.

106:12 [d]Ex 15:1-21

12 Then they believed his promises
and sang his praise.[d]

106:13 [e]Ex 15:24

13 But they soon forgot[e] what he had done
and did not wait for his counsel.

14 In the desert they gave in to their craving;
in the wasteland they put God to the test.[f]

106:14 [f]1Co 10:9

106:15 [g]Nu 11:31 [h]Isa 10:16

15 So he gave them[g] what they asked for,
but sent a wasting disease[h] upon them.

106:16 [i]Nu 16:1-3

16 In the camp they grew envious[i] of Moses
and of Aaron, who was consecrated to the LORD.

106:17 [j]Dt 11:6

17 The earth opened[j] up and swallowed Dathan;
it buried the company of Abiram.

106:18 [k]Nu 16:35

18 Fire blazed[k] among their followers;
a flame consumed the wicked.

106:19 [l]Ex 32:4

19 At Horeb they made a calf[l]
and worshiped an idol cast from metal.

106:20 [m]Jer 2:11; Ro 1:23

20 They exchanged their Glory[m]
for an image of a bull, which eats grass.

106:21 [n]Ps 78:11 [o]Dt 10:21

21 They forgot the God[n] who saved them,
who had done great things[o] in Egypt,

SELF-CONTROL

SING, EVEN WHEN THE HEART IS SOUR

Psalm 106:21

Israel forgot who saved her. Too bad, for praise is the goad of memory. If we forget our hallelujahs, we may soon forget our Savior.

106:22 [p]Ps 105:27

22 miracles in the land of Ham[p]
and awesome deeds by the Red Sea.

106:23 [q]Ex 32:10 [r]Ex 32:11-14

23 So he said he would destroy[q] them—
had not Moses, his chosen one,
stood in the breach[r] before him
to keep his wrath from destroying them.

106:24 [s]Dt 8:7; Eze 20:6 [t]Heb 3:18-19

24 Then they despised the pleasant land;[s]
they did not believe[t] his promise.

106:25 [u]Nu 14:2

25 They grumbled[u] in their tents
and did not obey the LORD.

106:26 [v]Eze 20:15; Heb 3:11

26 So he swore[v] to them with uplifted hand

[a] *45* Hebrew *Hallelu Yah* [b] *1* Hebrew *Hallelu Yah*; also in verse 48 [c] *7* Hebrew *Yam Suph*; that is, Sea of Reeds; also in verses 9 and 22

that he would make them fall in
the desert,[w]
27 make their descendants fall among
the nations
and scatter[x] them throughout the
lands.

28 They yoked themselves to the Baal
of Peor[y]
and ate sacrifices offered to lifeless
gods;
29 they provoked the LORD to anger by
their wicked deeds,
and a plague broke out among
them.
30 But Phinehas stood up and
intervened,
and the plague was checked.[z]
31 This was credited to him[a] as
righteousness
for endless generations to come.

32 By the waters of Meribah[b] they
angered the LORD,
and trouble came to Moses
because of them;
33 for they rebelled against the Spirit of
God,
and rash words came from Moses'
lips.[a c]

34 They did not destroy[d] the peoples
as the LORD had commanded[e]
them,
35 but they mingled[f] with the nations
and adopted their customs.
36 They worshiped their idols,[g]
which became a snare to them.
37 They sacrificed their sons[h]
and their daughters to demons.
38 They shed innocent blood,
the blood of their sons[i] and
daughters,
whom they sacrificed to the idols of
Canaan,
and the land was desecrated by
their blood.
39 They defiled themselves[j] by what
they did;
by their deeds they prostituted[k]
themselves.

40 Therefore the LORD was angry[l] with
his people
and abhorred his inheritance.[m]
41 He handed them over[n] to the
nations,
and their foes ruled over them.
42 Their enemies oppressed them
and subjected them to their
power.
43 Many times he delivered them,
but they were bent on rebellion[o]
and they wasted away in their sin.

44 But he took note of their distress
when he heard their cry;[p]
45 for their sake he remembered his
covenant[q]
and out of his great love[r] he
relented.
46 He caused them to be pitied[s]
by all who held them captive.

47 Save us, O LORD our God,
and gather us[t] from the nations,
that we may give thanks to your holy
name
and glory in your praise.

48 Praise be to the LORD, the God of
Israel,
from everlasting to everlasting.
Let all the people say, "Amen!"[u]

Praise the LORD.

106:26 [w]Nu 14:28-35
106:27 [x]Lev 26:33; Ps 44:11
106:28 [y]Nu 25:2-3; Hos 9:10
106:30 [z]Nu 25:8
106:31 [a]Nu 25:11-13
106:32 [b]Nu 20:2-13; Ps 81:7
106:33 [c]Nu 20:8-12
106:34 [d]Jdg 1:21 [e]Dt 7:16
106:35 [f]Jdg 3:5-6
106:36 [g]Jdg 2:12
106:37 [h]2Ki 16:3; 17:17
106:38 [i]Nu 35:33
106:39 [j]Eze 20:18 [k]Lev 17:7; Nu 15:39
106:40 [l]Jdg 2:14; Ps 78:59 [m]Dt 9:29
106:41 [n]Jdg 2:14; Ne 9:27
106:43 [o]Jdg 2:16-19
106:44 [p]Jdg 3:9; 10:10
106:45 [q]Lev 26:42; Ps 105:8 [r]Jdg 2:18
106:46 [s]Ezr 9:9; Jer 42:12
106:47 [t]Ps 147:2
106:48 [u]Ps 41:13

BOOK V

Psalms 107–150

Psalm 107

1 Give thanks to the LORD,[v] for he is
good;
his love endures forever.
2 Let the redeemed[w] of the LORD say
this—
those he redeemed from the hand
of the foe,
3 those he gathered[x] from the lands,

107:1 [v]Ps 106:1
107:2 [w]Ps 106:10
107:3 [x]Ps 106:47; Isa 43:5-6

[a]33 Or *against his spirit, / and rash words came from his lips*

GENTLENESS

GENTLE MUSIC

Psalm 107:2

Let the redeemed of the Lord say so . . . but let them say so gently. Let not their exuberance frighten the inquirers. Robert Whittington said of Thomas More that he was a man of angel's wit and gentleness. Such men never keep quiet about God, but they rarely speak loudly of him.

from east and west, from north
and south.[a]

107:4 [y]Nu 14:33; 32:13

4 Some wandered in desert[y]
wastelands,
finding no way to a city where
they could settle.
5 They were hungry and thirsty,
and their lives ebbed away.

107:6 [z]Ps 50:15

6 Then they cried out[z] to the LORD in
their trouble,
and he delivered them from their
distress.

107:7 [a]Ezr 8:21

7 He led them by a straight way[a]
to a city where they could settle.
8 Let them give thanks to the LORD
for his unfailing love
and his wonderful deeds for men,

107:9 [b]Ps 22:26; Lk 1:53 [c]Ps 34:10

9 for he satisfies[b] the thirsty
and fills the hungry with good
things.[c]

107:10 [d]Lk 1:79 [e]Job 36:8

10 Some sat in darkness[d] and the
deepest gloom,
prisoners suffering in iron chains,[e]

107:11 [f]Ps 106:7; La 3:42 [g]2Ch 36:16

11 for they had rebelled[f] against the
words of God
and despised the counsel[g] of the
Most High.
12 So he subjected them to bitter labor;
they stumbled, and there was no
one to help.[h]

107:12 [h]Ps 22:11

13 Then they cried to the LORD in
their trouble,
and he saved them from their
distress.
14 He brought them out of darkness
and the deepest gloom
and broke away their chains.[i]

107:14 [i]Ps 116:16; Lk 13:16; Ac 12:7

15 Let them give thanks to the LORD
for his unfailing love
and his wonderful deeds for men,
16 for he breaks down gates of bronze
and cuts through bars of iron.

17 Some became fools through their
rebellious ways
and suffered affliction[j] because of
their iniquities.

107:17 [j]Isa 65:6-7; La 3:39

18 They loathed all food[k]
and drew near the gates of
death.[l]

107:18 [k]Job 33:20 [l]Job 33:22; Ps 9:13; 88:3

19 Then they cried to the LORD in
their trouble,
and he saved them from their
distress.

107:20 [m]Mt 8:8 [n]Ps 103:3 [o]Job 33:28 [p]Ps 30:3; 49:15

20 He sent forth his word[m] and healed
them;[n]
he rescued[o] them from the grave.[p]

21 Let them give thanks to the LORD
for his unfailing love
and his wonderful deeds for men.

107:22 [q]Lev 7:12; Ps 50:14; 116:17 [r]Ps 9:11; 73:28; 118:17

22 Let them sacrifice thank offerings[q]
and tell of his works[r] with songs
of joy.

23 Others went out on the sea in ships;
they were merchants on the
mighty waters.
24 They saw the works of the LORD,
his wonderful deeds in the deep.

107:25 [s]Ps 105:31 [t]Jnh 1:4 [u]Ps 93:3

25 For he spoke[s] and stirred up a
tempest[t]
that lifted high the waves.[u]
26 They mounted up to the heavens
and went down to the
depths;
in their peril their courage melted[v]
away.

107:26 [v]Ps 22:14

27 They reeled and staggered like
drunken men;
they were at their wits' end.
28 Then they cried out to the LORD in
their trouble,
and he brought them out of their
distress.

107:29 [w]Mt 8:26 [x]Ps 89:9

29 He stilled the storm[w] to a whisper;
the waves[x] of the sea were hushed.
30 They were glad when it grew calm,
and he guided them to their
desired haven.
31 Let them give thanks to the LORD
for his unfailing love
and his wonderful deeds for men.

107:32 [y]Ps 22:22,25; 35:18

32 Let them exalt him in the assembly[y]
of the people
and praise him in the council of
the elders.

107:33 [z]1Ki 17:1; Ps 74:15

33 He turned rivers into a desert,[z]
flowing springs into thirsty
ground,

107:34 [a]Ge 13:10; 14:3; 19:25

34 and fruitful land into a salt waste,[a]
because of the wickedness of those
who lived there.

107:35 [b]Ps 114:8; Isa 41:18

35 He turned the desert into pools of
water[b]
and the parched ground into
flowing springs;
36 there he brought the hungry to live,
and they founded a city where
they could settle.

107:37 [c]Isa 65:21

37 They sowed fields and planted
vineyards[c]
that yielded a fruitful harvest;

[a]3 Hebrew *north and the sea*

38 he blessed them, and their numbers
greatly increased,[d]
and he did not let their herds
diminish.

107:38 [d]Ge 12:2; 17:16,20; Ex 1:7

39 Then their numbers decreased,[e] and
they were humbled
by oppression, calamity and
sorrow;

107:39 [e]2Ki 10:32; Eze 5:12

40 he who pours contempt on nobles[f]
made them wander in a trackless
waste.[g]

107:40 [f]Job 12:21 [g]Job 12:24

41 But he lifted the needy[h] out of their
affliction
and increased their families like
flocks.

107:41 [h]1Sa 2:8; Ps 113:7-9

42 The upright see and rejoice,[i]
but all the wicked shut their
mouths.[j]

107:42 [i]Job 22:19 [j]Job 5:16; Ps 63:11; Ro 3:19

43 Whoever is wise,[k] let him heed these
things
and consider the great love[l] of the
LORD.

107:43 [k]Jer 9:12; Hos 14:9 [l]Ps 64:9

Psalm 108

A song. A psalm of David.

1 My heart is steadfast, O God;
I will sing and make music with
all my soul.
2 Awake, harp and lyre!
I will awaken the dawn.
3 I will praise you, O LORD, among
the nations;
I will sing of you among the
peoples.
4 For great is your love, higher than
the heavens;
your faithfulness reaches to the
skies.
5 Be exalted, O God, above the
heavens,
and let your glory be over all the
earth.[m]

108:5 [m]Ps 57:5

6 Save us and help us with your right
hand,
that those you love may be
delivered.
7 God has spoken from his sanctuary:
"In triumph I will parcel out
Shechem
and measure off the Valley of
Succoth.
8 Gilead is mine, Manasseh is mine;
Ephraim is my helmet,
Judah[n] my scepter.

108:8 [n]Ge 49:10

9 Moab is my washbasin,
upon Edom I toss my sandal;
over Philistia I shout in triumph."
10 Who will bring me to the fortified
city?
Who will lead me to Edom?
11 Is it not you, O God, you who have
rejected us
and no longer go out with our
armies?[o]

108:11 [o]Ps 44:9

12 Give us aid against the enemy,
for the help of man is worthless.
13 With God we will gain the victory,
and he will trample down our
enemies.

Psalm 109

For the director of music.
Of David. A psalm.

1 O God, whom I praise,
do not remain silent,[p]

109:1 [p]Ps 83:1

2 for wicked and deceitful men
have opened their mouths against
me;
they have spoken against me with
lying tongues.[q]

109:2 [q]Ps 52:4; 120:2

3 With words of hatred[r] they surround
me;
they attack me without cause.[s]

109:3 [r]Ps 69:4 [s]Ps 35:7; Jn 15:25

4 In return for my friendship they
accuse me,
but I am a man of prayer.[t]

109:4 [t]Ps 69:13

5 They repay me evil for good,[u]
and hatred for my friendship.

109:5 [u]Ps 35:12; 38:20

6 Appoint[a] an evil man[b] to oppose
him;
let an accuser[c][v] stand at his right
hand.

109:6 [v]Zec 3:1

7 When he is tried, let him be found
guilty,
and may his prayers condemn[w]
him.

109:7 [w]Pr 28:9

8 May his days be few;
may another take his place[x] of
leadership.

109:8 [x]Ac 1:20*

9 May his children be fatherless
and his wife a widow.[y]

109:9 [y]Ex 22:24

10 May his children be wandering
beggars;
may they be driven[d] from their
ruined homes.
11 May a creditor seize all he has;

[a]*6* Or ⌊*They say:*⌋ "*Appoint* (with quotation marks at the end of verse 19) [b]*6* Or *the Evil One* [c]*6* Or *let Satan* [d]*10* Septuagint; Hebrew *sought*

109:11 [z]Job 5:5

may strangers plunder the fruits of
his labor.[z]

109:12 [a]Isa 9:17

12 May no one extend kindness to him
or take pity[a] on his fatherless
children.

109:13 [b]Job 18:19; Ps 37:28 [c]Pr 10:7

13 May his descendants be cut off,[b]
their names blotted out[c] from the
next generation.

109:14 [d]Ex 20:5; Ne 4:5; Jer 18:23

14 May the iniquity of his fathers[d]
be remembered before the
LORD;
may the sin of his mother never be
blotted out.
15 May their sins always remain before
the LORD,

109:15 [e]Job 18:17; Ps 34:16

that he may cut off the memory[e]
of them from the earth.

16 For he never thought of doing a
kindness,
but hounded to death the poor

109:16 [f]Ps 37:14,32 [g]Ps 34:18

and the needy[f] and the
brokenhearted.[g]

109:17 [h]Pr 14:14; Eze 35:6

17 He loved to pronounce a curse—
may it[a] come on him;[h]
he found no pleasure in blessing—
may it be[b] far from him.

109:18 [i]Ps 73:6 [j]Nu 5:22

18 He wore cursing[i] as his garment;
it entered into his body like
water,[j]
into his bones like oil.
19 May it be like a cloak wrapped about
him,
like a belt tied forever around
him.

109:20 [k]Ps 94:23; 2Ti 4:14 [l]Ps 71:10

20 May this be the LORD's payment[k] to
my accusers,
to those who speak evil[l] of me.

21 But you, O Sovereign LORD,

109:21 [m]Ps 79:9 [n]Ps 69:16

deal well with me for your name's
sake;[m]
out of the goodness of your love,[n]
deliver me.
22 For I am poor and needy,
and my heart is wounded within
me.

109:23 [o]Ps 102:11

23 I fade away like an evening shadow;[o]

109:24 [p]Heb 12:12

I am shaken off like a locust.
24 My knees give[p] way from fasting;

109:25 [q]Ps 22:6 [r]Mt 27:39; Mk 15:29

my body is thin and gaunt.
25 I am an object of scorn[q] to my
accusers;
when they see me, they shake their
heads.[r]

109:26 [s]Ps 119:86

26 Help me,[s] O LORD my God;
save me in accordance with your
love.

109:27 [t]Job 37:7

27 Let them know[t] that it is your hand,
that you, O LORD, have done it.

109:28 [u]2Sa 16:12 [v]Isa 65:14

28 They may curse,[u] but you will bless;
when they attack they will be put
to shame,
but your servant will rejoice.[v]
29 My accusers will be clothed with
disgrace

109:29 [w]Ps 35:26; 132:18

and wrapped in shame[w] as in a
cloak.

30 With my mouth I will greatly extol
the LORD;

109:30 [x]Ps 35:18; 111:1

in the great throng[x] I will praise
him.

109:31 [y]Ps 16:8; 73:23; 121:5

31 For he stands at the right hand[y] of
the needy one,
to save his life from those who
condemn him.

Psalm 110

Of David. A psalm.

110:1 [z]Mt 22:44*; Mk 12:36*; Lk 20:42*; Ac 2:34* [a]1Co 15:25

1 The LORD says[z] to my Lord:
"Sit at my right hand
until I make your enemies
a footstool for your feet."[a]
2 The LORD will extend your mighty

110:2 [b]Ps 45:6

scepter[b] from Zion;
you will rule in the midst of your
enemies.
3 Your troops will be willing

110:3 [c]Jdg 5:2; Ps 96:9

on your day of battle.
Arrayed in holy majesty,[c]
from the womb of the dawn
you will receive the dew of your
youth.[c]

110:4 [d]Nu 23:19 [e]Heb 5:6*; 7:21* [f]Heb 7:15-17*

4 The LORD has sworn
and will not change his mind:[d]
"You are a priest forever,[e]
in the order of Melchizedek.[f]"

110:5 [g]Ps 16:8 [h]Ps 2:12 [i]Ps 2:5; Ro 2:5

5 The Lord is at your right hand;[g]
he will crush kings[h] on the day of
his wrath.[i]

110:6 [j]Isa 2:4 [k]Isa 66:24 [l]Ps 68:21

6 He will judge the nations,[j] heaping
up the dead[k]
and crushing the rulers[l] of the
whole earth.
7 He will drink from a brook beside
the way[d];

110:7 [m]Ps 27:6

therefore he will lift up his head.[m]

[a] *17* Or *curse, / and it has* [b] *17* Or *blessing, / and it is*
[c] *3* Or */ your young men will come to you like the dew*
[d] *7* Or */ The One who grants succession will set him in authority*

Psalm 111[a]

[1] Praise the LORD.[b]

I will extol the LORD with all my
heart
in the council of the upright and
in the assembly.

[2] Great are the works[n] of the LORD;
they are pondered by all who
delight in them.

111:2 [n]Ps 92:5; 143:5

[3] Glorious and majestic are his deeds,
and his righteousness endures
forever.

[4] He has caused his wonders to be
remembered;
the LORD is gracious and
compassionate.[o]

111:4 [o]Ps 103:8

[5] He provides food[p] for those who fear
him;
he remembers his covenant
forever.

111:5 [p]Mt 6:26, 31-33

[6] He has shown his people the power
of his works,
giving them the lands of other
nations.

[7] The works of his hands are faithful
and just;
all his precepts are trustworthy.[q]

111:7 [q]Ps 19:7; Rev 15:3

[8] They are steadfast for ever[r] and ever,
done in faithfulness and
uprightness.

111:8 [r]Isa 40:8; Mt 5:18

[9] He provided redemption[s] for his
people;
he ordained his covenant
forever—
holy and awesome[t] is his name.

111:9 [s]Lk 1:68 [t]Ps 99:3; Lk 1:49

[10] The fear of the LORD is the
beginning of wisdom;[u]
all who follow his precepts have
good understanding.[v]
To him belongs eternal praise.[w]

111:10 [u]Pr 9:10 [v]Ecc 12:13 [w]Ps 145:2

Psalm 112[a]

[1] Praise the LORD.[b]

Blessed is the man who fears the
LORD,[x]
who finds great delight[y] in his
commands.

112:1 [x]Ps 128:1 [y]Ps 119:14, 16,47,92

[2] His children will be mighty in the
land;
the generation of the upright will
be blessed.

[3] Wealth and riches are in his house,
and his righteousness endures
forever.

[4] Even in darkness light dawns[z] for the
upright,
for the gracious and
compassionate and
righteous[a] man.[c]

112:4 [z]Job 11:17 [a]Ps 97:11

[5] Good will come to him who is
generous and lends freely,[b]
who conducts his affairs with
justice.

112:5 [b]Ps 37:21,26

[6] Surely he will never be shaken;
a righteous man will be
remembered[c] forever.

112:6 [c]Pr 10:7

[7] He will have no fear of bad news;
his heart is steadfast,[d] trusting in
the LORD.

112:7 [d]Ps 57:7; Pr 1:33

[8] His heart is secure, he will have no
fear;
in the end he will look in triumph
on his foes.[e]

112:8 [e]Ps 59:10

[9] He has scattered abroad his gifts to
the poor,[f]
his righteousness endures
forever;
his horn[d] will be lifted[g] high in
honor.

112:9 [f]2Co 9:9* [g]Ps 75:10

[10] The wicked man will see[h] and be
vexed,
he will gnash his teeth[i] and waste
away;[j]
the longings of the wicked will
come to nothing.[k]

112:10 [h]Ps 86:17 [i]Ps 37:12 [j]Ps 58:7-8 [k]Pr 11:7

Psalm 113

[1] Praise the LORD.[e]

Praise, O servants of the LORD,[l]
praise the name of the LORD.

113:1 [l]Ps 135:1

[2] Let the name of the LORD be
praised,
both now and forevermore.[m]

113:2 [m]Da 2:20

[3] From the rising of the sun[n] to the
place where it sets,
the name of the LORD is to be
praised.

113:3 [n]Isa 59:19; Mal 1:11

[4] The LORD is exalted[o] over all the
nations,
his glory above the heavens.[p]

113:4 [o]Ps 99:2 [p]Ps 8:1; 97:9

[5] Who is like the LORD our God,[q]
the One who sits enthroned[r] on
high,

113:5 [q]Ps 89:6 [r]Ps 103:19

[a]This psalm is an acrostic poem, the lines of which begin with the successive letters of the Hebrew alphabet. [b]*1* Hebrew *Hallelu Yah*
[c]*4* Or / *for ⌞the LORD⌟ is gracious and compassionate and righteous* [d]*9* *Horn* here symbolizes dignity.
[e]*1* Hebrew *Hallelu Yah*; also in verse 9

113:6 [s]Ps 11:4; 138:6; Isa 57:15

6 who stoops down to look[s]
on the heavens and the earth?

113:7 [t]1Sa 2:8 [u]Ps 107:41

7 He raises the poor[t] from the dust
and lifts the needy[u] from the ash heap;

113:8 [v]Job 36:7

8 he seats them[v] with princes,
with the princes of their people.

113:9 [w]1Sa 2:5; Ps 68:6; Isa 54:1

9 He settles the barren[w] woman in her home
as a happy mother of children.

Praise the LORD.

Psalm 114

114:1 [x]Ex 13:3

1 When Israel came out of Egypt,[x]
the house of Jacob from a people of foreign tongue,
2 Judah became God's sanctuary,
Israel his dominion.

114:3 [y]Ex 14:21; Ps 77:16 [z]Jos 3:16

3 The sea looked and fled,[y]
the Jordan turned back;[z]
4 the mountains skipped like rams,
the hills like lambs.

5 Why was it, O sea, that you fled,
O Jordan, that you turned back,
6 you mountains, that you skipped like rams,
you hills, like lambs?

114:7 [a]Ps 96:9

7 Tremble, O earth,[a] at the presence of the Lord,
at the presence of the God of Jacob,

114:8 [b]Ex 17:6; Nu 20:11; Ps 107:35

8 who turned the rock into a pool,
the hard rock into springs of water.[b]

Psalm 115

115:1 [c]Ps 96:8; Isa 48:11; Eze 36:32

1 Not to us, O LORD, not to us
but to your name be the glory,[c]
because of your love and faithfulness.

115:2 [d]Ps 42:3; 79:10

2 Why do the nations say,
"Where is their God?"[d]

115:3 [e]Ps 103:19 [f]Ps 135:6; Da 4:35

3 Our God is in heaven;[e]
he does whatever pleases him.[f]
4 But their idols are silver and gold,
made by the hands of men.[g]

115:4 [g]Dt 4:28; Jer 10:3-5

5 They have mouths, but cannot speak,[h]
eyes, but they cannot see;

115:5 [h]Jer 10:5

6 they have ears, but cannot hear,
noses, but they cannot smell;
7 they have hands, but cannot feel,
feet, but they cannot walk;
nor can they utter a sound with their throats.
8 Those who make them will be like them,
and so will all who trust in them.

9 O house of Israel, trust in the LORD—
he is their help and shield.

115:10 [i]Ps 118:3

10 O house of Aaron,[i] trust in the LORD—
he is their help and shield.
11 You who fear him, trust in the LORD—
he is their help and shield.

12 The LORD remembers us and will bless us:
He will bless the house of Israel,
he will bless the house of Aaron,

115:13 [j]Ps 128:1,4

13 he will bless those who fear[j] the LORD—
small and great alike.

115:14 [k]Dt 1:11

14 May the LORD make you increase,[k]
both you and your children.

115:15 [l]Ge 1:1; 14:19; Ps 96:5

15 May you be blessed by the LORD,
the Maker of heaven[l] and earth.

115:16 [m]Ps 89:11 [n]Ps 8:6-8

16 The highest heavens belong to the LORD,[m]
but the earth he has given[n] to man.

115:17 [o]Ps 6:5; 88:10-12; Isa 38:18

17 It is not the dead[o] who praise the LORD,
those who go down to silence;

115:18 [p]Ps 113:2; Da 2:20

18 it is we who extol the LORD,
both now and forevermore.[p]

Praise the LORD.[a]

Psalm 116

116:1 [q]Ps 18:1 [r]Ps 66:19

1 I love the LORD,[q] for he heard my voice;
he heard my cry[r] for mercy.

116:2 [s]Ps 40:1

2 Because he turned his ear[s] to me,
I will call on him as long as I live.

116:3 [t]Ps 18:4-5

3 The cords of death[t] entangled me,
the anguish of the grave[b] came upon me;
I was overcome by trouble and sorrow.

116:4 [u]Ps 118:5 [v]Ps 22:20

4 Then I called on the name[u] of the LORD:
"O LORD, save me![v]"

116:5 [w]Ezr 9:15; Ne 9:8; Ps 103:8; 145:17

5 The LORD is gracious and righteous;[w]

[a] *18* Hebrew *Hallelu Yah* [b] *3* Hebrew *Sheol*

our God is full of compassion.
[6]The LORD protects the simplehearted;
when I was in great need,[x] he saved me.

116:6 [x]Ps 19:7; 79:8

[7]Be at rest[y] once more, O my soul,
for the LORD has been good[z] to you.

116:7 [y]Jer 6:16; Mt 11:29 [z]Ps 13:6

[8]For you, O LORD, have delivered my soul[a] from death,
my eyes from tears,
my feet from stumbling,
[9]that I may walk before the LORD
in the land of the living.[b]
[10]I believed;[c] therefore[a] I said,
"I am greatly afflicted."
[11]And in my dismay I said,
"All men are liars."[d]

116:8 [a]Ps 56:13
116:9 [b]Ps 27:13
116:10 [c]2Co 4:13*
116:11 [d]Ro 3:4

[12]How can I repay the LORD
for all his goodness to me?
[13]I will lift up the cup of salvation
and call on the name[e] of the LORD.
[14]I will fulfill my vows[f] to the LORD
in the presence of all his people.

116:13 [e]Ps 16:5; 80:18
116:14 [f]Ps 22:25; Jnh 2:9

[15]Precious in the sight[g] of the LORD
is the death of his saints.
[16]O LORD, truly I am your servant;[h]
I am your servant, the son of your maidservant[b];[i]
you have freed me from my chains.

116:15 [g]Ps 72:14
116:16 [h]Ps 119:125; 143:12 [i]Ps 86:16

[17]I will sacrifice a thank offering[j] to you
and call on the name of the LORD.
[18]I will fulfill my vows to the LORD
in the presence of all his people,
[19]in the courts[k] of the house of the LORD—
in your midst, O Jerusalem.

116:17 [j]Lev 7:12; Ps 50:14
116:19 [k]Ps 96:8; 135:2

Praise the LORD.[c]

Psalm 117

[1]Praise the LORD, all you nations;[l]
extol him, all you peoples.
[2]For great is his love toward us,
and the faithfulness of the LORD[m] endures forever.

117:1 [l]Ro 15:11*
117:2 [m]Ps 100:5

Praise the LORD.[c]

Psalm 118

[1]Give thanks to the LORD,[n] for he is good;
his love endures forever.[o]

118:1 [n]1Ch 16:8 [o]Ps 106:1; 136:1

[2]Let Israel say:[p]
"His love endures forever."
[3]Let the house of Aaron say:
"His love endures forever."
[4]Let those who fear the LORD say:
"His love endures forever."

118:2 [p]Ps 115:9

[5]In my anguish[q] I cried to the LORD,
and he answered[r] by setting me free.
[6]The LORD is with me;[s] I will not be afraid.
What can man do to me?[t]
[7]The LORD is with me; he is my helper.[u]
I will look in triumph on my enemies.[v]

118:5 [q]Ps 120:1 [r]Ps 18:19
118:6 [s]Heb 13:6* [t]Ps 27:1; 56:4
118:7 [u]Ps 54:4 [v]Ps 59:10

[8]It is better to take refuge in the LORD[w]
than to trust in man.[x]
[9]It is better to take refuge in the LORD
than to trust in princes.[y]

118:8 [w]Ps 40:4 [x]Jer 17:5
118:9 [y]Ps 146:3

[10]All the nations surrounded me,
but in the name of the LORD I cut them off.[z]
[11]They surrounded me[a] on every side,[b]
but in the name of the LORD I cut them off.
[12]They swarmed around me like bees,[c]
but they died out as quickly as burning thorns;[d]
in the name of the LORD I cut them off.

118:10 [z]Ps 18:40
118:11 [a]Ps 88:17 [b]Ps 3:6
118:12 [c]Dt 1:44 [d]Ps 58:9

[13]I was pushed back and about to fall,
but the LORD helped me.[e]
[14]The LORD is my strength[f] and my song;
he has become my salvation.[g]
[15]Shouts of joy[h] and victory
resound in the tents of the righteous:
"The LORD's right hand[i] has done mighty things!
[16] The LORD's right hand is lifted high;
the LORD's right hand has done mighty things!"

118:13 [e]Ps 86:17; 140:4
118:14 [f]Ex 15:2 [g]Isa 12:2
118:15 [h]Ps 68:3 [i]Ps 89:13

[a]*10* Or *believed even when* [b]*16* Or *servant, your faithful son* [c]*19,2* Hebrew *Hallelu Yah*

118:17 [j]Ps 6:5; Hab 1:12 [k]Ex 15:6; Ps 73:28

17I will not die[j] but live,
and will proclaim[k] what the LORD
has done.
18The LORD has chastened me
severely,
but he has not given me over to
death.[l]

118:18 [l]2Co 6:9

118:19 [m]Isa 26:2

19Open for me the gates[m] of
righteousness;
I will enter and give thanks to the
LORD.
20This is the gate of the LORD
through which the righteous may
enter.[n]

118:20 [n]Ps 24:7; Isa 35:8; Rev 22:14

21I will give you thanks, for you
answered me;[o]
you have become my salvation.

118:21 [o]Ps 116:1

118:22 [p]Mt 21:42; Mk 12:10; Lk 20:17*; Ac 4:11*; 1Pe 2:7*

22The stone the builders rejected
has become the capstone;[p]
23the LORD has done this,
and it is marvelous in our eyes.
24This is the day the LORD has made;
let us rejoice and be glad in it.

25O LORD, save us;
O LORD, grant us success.
26Blessed is he who comes[q] in the
name of the LORD.
From the house of the LORD we
bless you.[a]

118:26 [q]Mt 21:9*; Mk 11:9*; Lk 13:35*; 19:38*; Jn 12:13*

27The LORD is God,
and he has made his light shine[r]
upon us.
With boughs in hand, join in the
festal procession
up[b] to the horns of the altar.

118:27 [r]1Pe 2:9

28You are my God, and I will give you
thanks;
you are my God,[s] and I will exalt[t]
you.

118:28 [s]Isa 25:1 [t]Ex 15:2

29Give thanks to the LORD, for he is
good;
his love endures forever.

Psalm 119[c]

א Aleph

1Blessed are they whose ways are
blameless,
who walk[u] according to the law of
the LORD.

119:1 [u]Ps 128:1

2Blessed are they who keep his
statutes
and seek him with all their heart.[v]

119:2 [v]Dt 6:5

3They do nothing wrong;[w]
they walk in his ways.

119:3 [w]1Jn 3:9; 5:18

4You have laid down precepts
that are to be fully obeyed.
5Oh, that my ways were steadfast
in obeying your decrees!
6Then I would not be put to shame
when I consider all your
commands.
7I will praise you with an upright
heart
as I learn your righteous laws.
8I will obey your decrees;
do not utterly forsake me.

ב Beth

9How can a young man keep his way
pure?
By living according to your word.[x]

119:9 [x]2Ch 6:16

10I seek you with all my heart;[y]
do not let me stray from your
commands.[z]

119:10 [y]2Ch 15:15 [z]ver 21,118

11I have hidden your word in my
heart[a]
that I might not sin against you.

119:11 [a]Ps 37:31; Lk 2:19,51

SELF-CONTROL

NO VACANCY

Psalm 119:11

Sinlessness issues from the force of God hidden in our hearts. Hide God's Word within you, and your heart will be so clean that sin will feel unwelcome, and it will not stay for long.

12Praise be to you, O LORD;
teach me your decrees.[b]

119:12 [b]ver 26

13With my lips I recount
all the laws that come from your
mouth.[c]

119:13 [c]Ps 40:9

14I rejoice in following your statutes
as one rejoices in great riches.
15I meditate on your precepts[d]
and consider your ways.

119:15 [d]Ps 1:2

16I delight[e] in your decrees;
I will not neglect your word.

119:16 [e]Ps 1:2

ג Gimel

17Do good to your servant,[f] and I will
live;
I will obey your word.

119:17 [f]Ps 13:6; 116:7

18Open my eyes that I may see
wonderful things in your law.
19I am a stranger on earth;[g]

119:19 [g]1Ch 29:15; Ps 39:12; 2Co 5:6; Heb 11:13

[a]*26* The Hebrew is plural. [b]*27* Or *Bind the festal sacrifice with ropes / and take it* [c]This psalm is an acrostic poem; the verses of each stanza begin with the same letter of the Hebrew alphabet.

do not hide your commands from
me.
119:20 [h]Ps 42:2; 84:2 [i]Ps 63:1
20 My soul is consumed[h] with longing
for your laws[i] at all times.
21 You rebuke the arrogant, who are
cursed
119:21 [j]ver 10
and who stray[j] from your
commands.
119:22 [k]Ps 39:8
22 Remove from me scorn[k] and
contempt,
for I keep your statutes.
23 Though rulers sit together and
slander me,
your servant will meditate on your
decrees.
24 Your statutes are my delight;
they are my counselors.

ד Daleth

119:25 [l]Ps 44:25 [m]Ps 143:11
25 I am laid low in the dust;[l]
preserve my life[m] according to
your word.
119:26 [n]Ps 25:4; 27:11; 86:11
26 I recounted my ways and you
answered me;
teach me your decrees.[n]
27 Let me understand the teaching of
your precepts;
then I will meditate on your
119:27 [o]Ps 145:5
wonders.[o]
119:28 [p]Ps 107:26 [q]Ps 20:2; 1Pe 5:10
28 My soul is weary with sorrow;[p]
strengthen me[q] according to your
word.
29 Keep me from deceitful ways;
be gracious to me through your
law.
30 I have chosen the way of truth;
I have set my heart on your laws.
119:31 [r]Dt 11:22
31 I hold fast[r] to your statutes,
O LORD;
do not let me be put to shame.
32 I run in the path of your commands,
for you have set my heart free.

ה He

119:33 [s]ver 12
33 Teach me,[s] O LORD, to follow your
decrees;
then I will keep them to the end.
34 Give me understanding, and I will
keep your law
and obey it with all my heart.
35 Direct me in the path of your
commands,
for there I find delight.
119:36 [t]1Ki 8:58 [u]Eze 33:31; Mk 7:21-22; Lk 12:15; Heb 13:5
36 Turn my heart[t] toward your statutes
and not toward selfish gain.[u]
37 Turn my eyes away from worthless
things;
preserve my life[v] according to your
word.[a]
119:37 [v]Ps 71:20; Isa 33:15
119:38 [w]2Sa 7:25
38 Fulfill your promise[w] to your
servant,
so that you may be feared.
39 Take away the disgrace I dread,
for your laws are good.
119:40 [x]ver 20
40 How I long[x] for your precepts!
Preserve my life in your
righteousness.

ו Waw

41 May your unfailing love come to me,
O LORD,
your salvation according to your
promise;
119:42 [y]Pr 27:11
42 then I will answer[y] the one who
taunts me,
for I trust in your word.
43 Do not snatch the word of truth
from my mouth,
for I have put my hope in your
laws.
44 I will always obey your law,
for ever and ever.
45 I will walk about in freedom,
for I have sought out your
precepts.
119:46 [z]Mt 10:18; Ac 26:1-2
46 I will speak of your statutes before
kings[z]
and will not be put to shame,
47 for I delight in your commands
because I love them.
48 I lift up my hands to[b] your
commands, which I love,
and I meditate on your decrees.

ז Zayin

49 Remember your word to your
servant,
for you have given me hope.
50 My comfort in my suffering is this:
119:50 [a]Ro 15:4
Your promise preserves my life.[a]
119:51 [b]Jer 20:7 [c]ver 157; Job 23:11; Ps 44:18
51 The arrogant mock me[b] without
restraint,
but I do not turn[c] from your law.
119:52 [d]Ps 103:18
52 I remember[d] your ancient laws,
O LORD,
and I find comfort in them.
119:53 [e]Ezr 9:3 [f]Ps 89:30
53 Indignation grips me[e] because of the
wicked,
who have forsaken your law.[f]
54 Your decrees are the theme of my
song

[a]*37* Two manuscripts of the Masoretic Text and Dead Sea Scrolls; most manuscripts of the Masoretic Text *life in your way* [b]*48* Or *for*

wherever I lodge.

119:55 [g]Ps 63:6

55 In the night I remember[g] your name, O LORD,
and I will keep your law.
56 This has been my practice:
I obey your precepts.

ח Heth

119:57 [h]Ps 16:5; La 3:24

57 You are my portion,[h] O LORD;
I have promised to obey your words.
58 I have sought your face with all my heart;
be gracious to me[i] according to your promise.[j]

119:58 [i]1Ki 13:6 [j]ver 41

119:59 [k]Lk 15:17-18

59 I have considered my ways[k]
and have turned my steps to your statutes.
60 I will hasten and not delay
to obey your commands.
61 Though the wicked bind me with ropes,
I will not forget[l] your law.

119:61 [l]Ps 140:5

62 At midnight[m] I rise to give you thanks
for your righteous laws.

119:62 [m]Ac 16:25

63 I am a friend to all who fear you,[n]
to all who follow your precepts.

119:63 [n]Ps 101:6-7

64 The earth is filled with your love,[o] O LORD;
teach me your decrees.

119:64 [o]Ps 33:5

ט Teth

65 Do good to your servant
according to your word, O LORD.
66 Teach me knowledge and good judgment,
for I believe in your commands.
67 Before I was afflicted I went astray,[p]
but now I obey your word.

119:67 [p]Jer 31:18-19; Heb 12:11

68 You are good,[q] and what you do is good;
teach me your decrees.[r]

119:68 [q]Ps 106:1; 107:1; Mt 19:17 [r]ver 12

69 Though the arrogant have smeared me with lies,[s]
I keep your precepts with all my heart.

119:69 [s]Job 13:4; Ps 109:2

70 Their hearts are callous[t] and unfeeling,
but I delight in your law.

119:70 [t]Ps 17:10; Isa 6:10; Ac 28:27

71 It was good for me to be afflicted
so that I might learn your decrees.
72 The law from your mouth is more precious to me
than thousands of pieces of silver and gold.[u]

119:72 [u]Ps 19:10; Pr 8:10-11,19

י Yodh

73 Your hands made me[v] and formed me;
give me understanding to learn your commands.

119:73 [v]Job 10:8; Ps 100:3; 138:8; 139:13-16

74 May those who fear you rejoice[w] when they see me,
for I have put my hope in your word.

119:74 [w]Ps 34:2

75 I know, O LORD, that your laws are righteous,

DAY 5 FIVE

▸ GOODNESS AND ITS PLACE IN MY PERSONAL WORSHIP

Psalm 119:65–68

"Teach me knowledge and good judgment, for I believe in your commands," cries the psalmist. Psalm 119 is dedicated to the Word of God. This theme pervades the entire psalm, for God desired that we never forget the importance of his Word to our lives. The word *bible* means "book." How essential "The Book" is to our worship. How essential is our worship to all we are.

The Book! The Book! . . .

Our God *can* write!
He lifts his starry quill,
And the ages beg for parchment.
A thousand pages of Adam's sad biography,
And on each one
The grace-drawn portrait of his Son.
His words, wide as Andromeda,
Stir the artist to create,
The compassionate to care,
The disconsolate to laughter,
The mute to oratorios,
The paralytics to fervent dancing . . .

His Book is ours—a light-year lithograph
Printed in a thousand etchings
Of the never-fading face of God—
Burning through our weak morality
Like a new-born sun ordered into sky—
Circling the earth
And orbiting our private world in light.

To begin a study on the topic of Goodness, the Virtue of the Written Word of God, turn to the home page on page 918.

119:75 [x]Heb 12:5-11 and in faithfulness[x] you have
afflicted me.
76 May your unfailing love be my
comfort,
according to your promise to your
servant.
119:77 [y]ver 41 77 Let your compassion[y] come to me
that I may live,
for your law is my delight.
119:78 [z]Jer 50:32 [a]ver 86,161 78 May the arrogant[z] be put to shame
for wronging me without
cause;[a]
but I will meditate on your
precepts.
79 May those who fear you turn to me,
those who understand your
statutes.
80 May my heart be blameless toward
your decrees,
that I may not be put to shame.

כ Kaph

119:81 [b]Ps 84:2 81 My soul faints[b] with longing for
your salvation,
but I have put my hope in your
word.
119:82 [c]Ps 69:3; La 2:11 82 My eyes fail,[c] looking for your
promise;
I say, "When will you comfort
me?"
83 Though I am like a wineskin in the
smoke,
I do not forget your decrees.
119:84 [d]Ps 39:4; Rev 6:10 84 How long[d] must your servant wait?
When will you punish my
persecutors?
119:85 [e]Ps 35:7; Jer 18:20,22 85 The arrogant dig pitfalls[e] for me,
contrary to your law.
119:86 [f]Ps 35:19 [g]Ps 109:26 [h]ver 78 86 All your commands are trustworthy;[f]
help me,[g] for men persecute me
without cause.[h]
87 They almost wiped me from the
earth,
119:87 [i]Isa 58:2 but I have not forsaken[i] your
precepts.
88 Preserve my life according to your
love,
and I will obey the statutes of
your mouth.

ל Lamedh

119:89 [j]Mt 24:34-35; 1Pe 1:25 89 Your word, O LORD, is eternal;[j]
it stands firm in the heavens.
119:90 [k]Ps 36:5 [l]Ps 148:6; Ecc 1:4 90 Your faithfulness[k] continues through
all generations;
you established the earth, and it
endures.[l]
119:91 [m]Jer 33:25 91 Your laws endure[m] to this day,
for all things serve you.
92 If your law had not been my delight,
I would have perished in my
affliction.
93 I will never forget your precepts,
for by them you have preserved
my life.
94 Save me, for I am yours;
I have sought out your precepts.
95 The wicked are waiting to destroy
me,
but I will ponder your statutes.
96 To all perfection I see a limit;
but your commands are
boundless.

מ Mem

97 Oh, how I love your law!
I meditate[n] on it all day long. 119:97 [n]Ps 1:2
98 Your commands make me wiser[o]
than my enemies, 119:98 [o]Dt 4:6
for they are ever with me.
99 I have more insight than all my
teachers,
for I meditate on your statutes.
100 I have more understanding than the
elders,
for I obey your precepts.[p] 119:100 [p]Job 32:7-9
101 I have kept my feet[q] from every evil 119:101 [q]Pr 1:15
path
so that I might obey your word.
102 I have not departed from your laws,
for you yourself have taught me.
103 How sweet are your words to my
taste,
sweeter than honey[r] to my 119:103 [r]Ps 19:10; Pr 8:11
mouth![s] [s]Pr 24:13-14
104 I gain understanding from your
precepts;
therefore I hate every wrong path.[t] 119:104 [t]ver 128

נ Nun

105 Your word is a lamp to my feet
and a light[u] for my path. 119:105 [u]Pr 6:23
106 I have taken an oath[v] and
confirmed it, 119:106 [v]Ne 10:29
that I will follow your righteous
laws.
107 I have suffered much;
preserve my life, O LORD,
according to your word.
108 Accept, O LORD, the willing praise 119:108 [w]Hos 14:2; Heb 13:15
of my mouth,[w]
and teach me your laws.
109 Though I constantly take my life in 119:109 [x]Jdg 12:3; Job 13:14
my hands,[x]
I will not forget your law. 119:110 [y]Ps 140:5; 141:9
110 The wicked have set a snare[y] for me,

119:110 [z]ver 10 but I have not strayed[z] from your
precepts.
111Your statutes are my heritage
forever;
they are the joy of my heart.
112My heart is set on keeping your
decrees
119:112 [a]ver 33 to the very end.[a]

ס Samekh

119:113 [b]Jas 1:8 113I hate double-minded men,[b]
but I love your law.
119:114 [c]Ps 32:7; 91:1 114You are my refuge and my shield;[c]
[d]ver 74 I have put my hope[d] in your
119:115 word.
[e]Ps 6:8; 139:19; Mt 7:23 115Away from me,[e] you evildoers,
that I may keep the commands of
my God!
119:116 [f]Ps 54:4 [g]Ps 25:2; Ro 5:5; 9:33 116Sustain me[f] according to your
promise, and I will live;
do not let my hopes be dashed.[g]
117Uphold me, and I will be delivered;
I will always have regard for your
decrees.
118You reject all who stray from your
decrees,
for their deceitfulness is in vain.
119All the wicked of the earth you
119:119 [h]Eze 22:18,19 discard like dross;[h]
therefore I love your statutes.
119:120 [i]Hab 3:16 120My flesh trembles[i] in fear of you;
I stand in awe of your laws.

ע Ayin

121I have done what is righteous and
just;
119:122 [j]Job 17:3 do not leave me to my oppressors.
122Ensure your servant's well-being;[j]
let not the arrogant oppress me.
123My eyes fail, looking for your
salvation,
119:123 [k]ver 82 looking for your righteous
promise.[k]
124Deal with your servant according to
your love
119:124 [l]ver 12 and teach me your decrees.[l]
125I am your servant;[m] give me
119:125 [m]Ps 116:16 discernment
that I may understand your
statutes.
126It is time for you to act, O LORD;
your law is being broken.
119:127 [n]Ps 19:10 127Because I love your commands
more than gold,[n] more than pure
gold,
128and because I consider all your
119:128 [o]ver 104,163 precepts right,
I hate every wrong path.[o]

פ Pe

129Your statutes are wonderful;
therefore I obey them.
130The unfolding of your words gives
light;[p] 119:130 [p]Pr 6:23 [q]Ps 19:7
it gives understanding to the
simple.[q]
131I open my mouth and pant,[r] 119:131 [r]Ps 42:1 [s]ver 20
longing for your commands.[s]
132Turn to me and have mercy[t] on me, 119:132 [t]Ps 25:16; 106:4
as you always do to those who
love your name.
133Direct my footsteps according to 119:133 [u]Ps 17:5 [v]Ps 19:13; Ro 6:12
your word;[u]
let no sin rule[v] over me.
134Redeem me from the oppression of
men,[w] 119:134 [w]Ps 142:6; Lk 1:74
that I may obey your precepts.
135Make your face shine[x] upon your 119:135 [x]Nu 6:25; Ps 4:6
servant
and teach me your decrees.
136Streams of tears[y] flow from my eyes, 119:136 [y]Jer 9:1,18 [z]Eze 9:4
for your law is not obeyed.[z]

צ Tsadhe

137Righteous are you,[a] O LORD, 119:137 [a]Ezr 9:15; Jer 12:1 [b]Ne 9:13
and your laws are right.[b]
138The statutes you have laid down are
righteous;[c] 119:138 [c]Ps 19:7
they are fully trustworthy.
139My zeal wears me out,[d] 119:139 [d]Ps 69:9; Jn 2:17
for my enemies ignore your words.
140Your promises have been thoroughly
tested,[e] 119:140 [e]Ps 12:6
and your servant loves them.
141Though I am lowly and despised,[f] 119:141 [f]Ps 22:6
I do not forget your precepts.
142Your righteousness is everlasting
and your law is true.[g] 119:142 [g]Ps 19:7
143Trouble and distress have come
upon me,
but your commands are my
delight.
144Your statutes are forever right; 119:144 [h]Ps 19:9
give me understanding[h] that I may
live.

ק Qoph

145I call with all my heart; answer me,
O LORD,
and I will obey your decrees.
146I call out to you; save me
and I will keep your statutes.
147I rise before dawn[i] and cry for help; 119:147 [i]Ps 5:3; 57:8; 108:2
I have put my hope in your word.
148My eyes stay open through the 119:148 [j]Ps 63:6
watches of the night,[j]

that I may meditate on your
promises.
149 Hear my voice in accordance with
your love;
preserve my life, O LORD,
according to your laws.
150 Those who devise wicked schemes
are near,
but they are far from your law.
151 Yet you are near,[k] O LORD,
and all your commands are true.[l]
152 Long ago I learned from your
statutes
that you established them to last
forever.[m]

ר Resh

153 Look upon my suffering[n] and
deliver me,
for I have not forgotten[o] your law.
154 Defend my cause[p] and redeem me;[q]
preserve my life according to your
promise.
155 Salvation is far from the wicked,
for they do not seek out[r] your
decrees.
156 Your compassion is great, O LORD;
preserve my life[s] according to your
laws.
157 Many are the foes who
persecute me,[t]
but I have not turned from your
statutes.
158 I look on the faithless with
loathing,[u]
for they do not obey your word.
159 See how I love your precepts;
preserve my life, O LORD,
according to your love.
160 All your words are true;
all your righteous laws are eternal.

שׁ Sin and Shin

161 Rulers persecute me[v] without cause,
but my heart trembles at your
word.
162 I rejoice in your promise
like one who finds great spoil.[w]
163 I hate and abhor falsehood
but I love your law.
164 Seven times a day I praise you
for your righteous laws.
165 Great peace[x] have they who love
your law,
and nothing can make them
stumble.

166 I wait for your salvation,[y] O LORD,
and I follow your commands.
167 I obey your statutes,
for I love them greatly.
168 I obey your precepts and your
statutes,
for all my ways are known[z] to you.

ת Taw

169 May my cry come[a] before you,
O LORD;
give me understanding according
to your word.
170 May my supplication come[b] before
you;
deliver me[c] according to your
promise.
171 May my lips overflow with praise,[d]
for you teach me[e] your decrees.
172 May my tongue sing of your word,
for all your commands are
righteous.
173 May your hand be ready to
help[f] me,
for I have chosen[g] your precepts.
174 I long for your salvation,[h] O LORD,
and your law is my delight.
175 Let me live[i] that I may praise you,
and may your laws sustain me.
176 I have strayed like a lost sheep.[j]
Seek your servant,
for I have not forgotten your
commands.

Psalm 120

A song of ascents.

1 I call on the LORD in my distress,[k]
and he answers me.
2 Save me, O LORD, from lying lips[l]
and from deceitful tongues.[m]

3 What will he do to you,
and what more besides,
O deceitful tongue?
4 He will punish you with a warrior's
sharp arrows,[n]
with burning coals of the broom
tree.

5 Woe to me that I dwell in Meshech,
that I live among the tents of
Kedar![o]
6 Too long have I lived
among those who hate peace.
7 I am a man of peace;
but when I speak, they are for war.

119:151 [k]Ps 34:18; 145:18 [l]ver 142
119:152 [m]Lk 21:33
119:153 [n]La 5:1 [o]Pr 3:1
119:154 [p]Mic 7:9 [q]1Sa 24:15
119:155 [r]Job 5:4
119:56 [s]2Sa 24:14
119:157 [t]Ps 7:1
119:158 [u]Ps 139:21
119:161 [v]1Sa 24:11
119:162 [w]1Sa 30:16
119:165 [x]Pr 3:2; Isa 26:3,12; 32:17
119:166 [y]Ge 49:18
119:168 [z]Pr 5:21
119:169 [a]Ps 18:6
119:170 [b]Ps 28:2 [c]Ps 31:2
119:171 [d]Ps 51:15 [e]Ps 94:12
119:173 [f]Ps 37:24 [g]Jos 24:22
119:174 [h]ver 166
119:175 [i]Isa 55:3
119:176 [j]Isa 53:6
120:1 [k]Ps 102:2; Jnh 2:2
120:2 [l]Pr 12:22 [m]Ps 52:4
120:4 [n]Ps 45:5
120:5 [o]Ge 25:13; Jer 49:28

Psalm 121

A song of ascents.

1 I lift up my eyes to the hills—
where does my help come from?
2 My help comes from the LORD,
the Maker of heaven and earth.[p]

121:2 [p]Ps 115:15; 124:8

3 He will not let your foot slip—
he who watches over you will not
slumber;
4 indeed, he who watches over Israel
will neither slumber nor sleep.

121:5 [q]Isa 25:4

5 The LORD watches over[q] you—
the LORD is your shade at your
right hand;

121:6 [r]Ps 91:5; Isa 49:10; Rev 7:16

6 the sun[r] will not harm you by day,
nor the moon by night.

121:7 [s]Ps 41:2; 91:10-12

7 The LORD will keep you from all
harm[s]—
he will watch over your life;
8 the LORD will watch over your
coming and going
both now and forevermore.[t]

121:8 [t]Dt 28:6

Psalm 122

A song of ascents. Of David.

1 I rejoiced with those who said to me,
"Let us go to the house of the
LORD."
2 Our feet are standing
in your gates, O Jerusalem.

3 Jerusalem is built like a city
that is closely compacted together.
4 That is where the tribes go up,
the tribes of the LORD,
to praise the name of the LORD
according to the statute given to
Israel.
5 There the thrones for judgment
stand,
the thrones of the house of David.

6 Pray for the peace of Jerusalem:
"May those who love[u] you be
secure.

122:6 [u]Ps 51:18

7 May there be peace within your walls
and security within your citadels."
8 For the sake of my brothers and
friends,
I will say, "Peace be within you."
9 For the sake of the house of the
LORD our God,
I will seek your prosperity.[v]

122:9 [v]Ne 2:10

Psalm 123

A song of ascents.

1 I lift up my eyes to you,
to you whose throne[w] is in heaven.

123:1 [w]Ps 11:4; 121:1; 141:8

2 As the eyes of slaves look to the hand
of their master,
as the eyes of a maid look to the
hand of her mistress,
so our eyes look to the LORD[x] our
God,
till he shows us his mercy.

123:2 [x]Ps 25:15

3 Have mercy on us, O LORD, have
mercy on us,
for we have endured much
contempt.
4 We have endured much ridicule
from the proud,
much contempt from the
arrogant.

Psalm 124

A song of ascents. Of David.

1 If the LORD had not been on our
side—
let Israel say[y]—

124:1 [y]Ps 129:1

2 if the LORD had not been on our
side
when men attacked us,
3 when their anger flared against us,
they would have swallowed us
alive;
4 the flood would have engulfed us,
the torrent would have swept over
us,
5 the raging waters
would have swept us away.
6 Praise be to the LORD,
who has not let us be torn by their
teeth.
7 We have escaped like a bird
out of the fowler's snare;[z]
the snare has been broken,
and we have escaped.

124:7 [z]Ps 91:3; Pr 6:5

8 Our help is in the name of the
LORD,
the Maker of heaven[a] and earth.

124:8 [a]Ge 1:1; Ps 121:2; 134:3

Psalm 125

A song of ascents.

1 Those who trust in the LORD are
like Mount Zion,
which cannot be shaken[b] but
endures forever.

125:1 [b]Ps 46:5

[2]As the mountains surround
Jerusalem,
so the LORD surrounds[c] his
people
both now and forevermore.
[3]The scepter of the wicked will not
remain[d]
over the land allotted to the
righteous,
for then the righteous might use
their hands to do evil.[e]
[4]Do good, O LORD,[f] to those who
are good,
to those who are upright in heart.[g]
[5]But those who turn[h] to crooked
ways[i]
the LORD will banish with the
evildoers.

Peace be upon Israel.[j]

125:2 [c]Ps 121:8; Zec 2:4-5
125:3 [d]Ps 89:22; Pr 22:8; Isa 14:5 [e]1Sa 24:10; Ps 55:20
125:4 [f]Ps 119:68 [g]Ps 7:10; 36:10; 94:15
125:5 [h]Job 23:11 [i]Pr 2:15; Isa 59:8 [j]Ps 128:6

Psalm 126

A song of ascents.

[1]When the LORD brought back[k] the
captives to[a] Zion,
we were like men who dreamed.[b]
[2]Our mouths were filled with
laughter,
our tongues with songs of joy.[l]
Then it was said among the nations,
"The LORD has done great
things[m] for them."
[3]The LORD has done great things for
us,
and we are filled with joy.[n]
[4]Restore our fortunes,[c] O LORD,
like streams in the Negev.[o]
[5]Those who sow in tears
will reap with songs of joy.[p]
[6]He who goes out weeping,
carrying seed to sow,
will return with songs of joy,
carrying sheaves with him.

126:1 [k]Ps 85:1; Hos 6:11
126:2 [l]Job 8:21; Ps 51:14 [m]Ps 71:19
126:3 [n]Isa 25:9
126:4 [o]Isa 35:6; 43:19
126:5 [p]Isa 35:10

Psalm 127

A song of ascents. Of Solomon.

[1]Unless the LORD builds[q] the house,
its builders labor in vain.
Unless the LORD watches[r] over the
city,
the watchmen stand guard in vain.
[2]In vain you rise early
and stay up late,
toiling for food[s] to eat—
for he grants sleep[t] to[d] those he
loves.
[3]Sons are a heritage from the LORD,
children a reward[u] from him.
[4]Like arrows in the hands of a warrior
are sons born in one's youth.
[5]Blessed is the man
whose quiver is full of them.
They will not be put to shame
when they contend with their
enemies[v] in the gate.

127:1 [q]Ps 78:69 [r]Ps 121:4
127:2 [s]Ge 3:17 [t]Job 11:18
127:3 [u]Ge 33:5
127:5 [v]Pr 27:11

Psalm 128

A song of ascents.

[1]Blessed are all who fear the LORD,[w]
who walk in his ways.[x]
[2]You will eat the fruit of your labor;[y]
blessings and prosperity[z] will be
yours.
[3]Your wife will be like a fruitful vine[a]
within your house;
your sons will be like olive shoots[b]
around your table.
[4]Thus is the man blessed
who fears the LORD.
[5]May the LORD bless you from Zion[c]
all the days of your life;
may you see the prosperity of
Jerusalem,
[6] and may you live to see your
children's children.[d]

Peace be upon Israel.[e]

128:1 [w]Ps 112:1 [x]Ps 119:1-3
128:2 [y]Isa 3:10 [z]Ecc 8:12
128:3 [a]Eze 19:10 [b]Ps 52:8; 144:12
128:5 [c]Ps 20:2; 134:3
128:6 [d]Ge 50:23; Job 42:16 [e]Ps 125:5

Psalm 129

A song of ascents.

[1]They have greatly oppressed me
from my youth[f]—
let Israel say[g]—
[2]they have greatly oppressed me from
my youth,
but they have not gained the
victory[h] over me.
[3]Plowmen have plowed my back
and made their furrows long.
[4]But the LORD is righteous;[i]
he has cut me free from the cords
of the wicked.
[5]May all who hate Zion[j]
be turned back in shame.[k]

129:1 [f]Ps 88:15; Hos 2:15 [g]Ps 124:1
129:2 [h]Mt 16:18
129:4 [i]Ps 119:137
129:5 [j]Mic 4:11 [k]Ps 71:13

[a]*1* Or *LORD restored the fortunes of* [b]*1* Or *men restored to health* [c]*4* Or *Bring back our captives* [d]*2* Or *eat— / for while they sleep he provides for*

[6]May they be like grass on the roof,
which withers[l] before it can grow;
[7]with it the reaper cannot fill his hands,
nor the one who gathers fill his arms.
[8]May those who pass by not say,
"The blessing of the LORD be upon you;
we bless you[m] in the name of the LORD."

129:6 [l]Ps 37:2
129:8 [m]Ru 2:4; Ps 118:26

Psalm 130

A song of ascents.

[1]Out of the depths[n] I cry to you, O LORD;
[2] O Lord, hear my voice.[o]
Let your ears be attentive[p]
to my cry for mercy.
[3]If you, O LORD, kept a record of sins,
O Lord, who could stand?[q]
[4]But with you there is forgiveness;[r]
therefore you are feared.[s]
[5]I wait for the LORD,[t] my soul waits,
and in his word[u] I put my hope.
[6]My soul waits for the Lord
more than watchmen[v] wait for the morning,
more than watchmen wait for the morning.[w]
[7]O Israel, put your hope[x] in the LORD,
for with the LORD is unfailing love
and with him is full redemption.
[8]He himself will redeem[y] Israel
from all their sins.

130:1 [n]Ps 42:7; 69:2; La 3:55
130:2 [o]Ps 28:2 [p]2Ch 6:40; Ps 64:1
130:3 [q]Ps 76:7; 143:2
130:4 [r]Ex 34:7; Isa 55:7; Jer 33:8 [s]1Ki 8:40
130:5 [t]Ps 27:14; 33:20; Isa 8:17 [u]Ps 119:81
130:6 [v]Ps 63:6 [w]Ps 119:147
130:7 [x]Ps 131:3
130:8 [y]Lk 1:68

Psalm 131

A song of ascents. Of David.

[1]My heart is not proud,[z] O LORD,
my eyes are not haughty;
I do not concern myself with great matters
or things too wonderful for me.
[2]But I have stilled and quieted my soul;
like a weaned child with its mother,
like a weaned child is my soul[a] within me.
[3]O Israel, put your hope[b] in the LORD
both now and forevermore.

131:1 [z]Ps 101:5; Ro 12:16
131:2 [a]Mt 18:3; 1Co 14:20
131:3 [b]Ps 130:7

DAY 2 TWO

LOVE AND THE PURPOSE OF GOD IN MY LIFE

Psalm 130:1–5

What part does God's forgiveness play in fulfilling his purposes for our lives? Just this: We cannot work to perform his will while we swelter under the necessity of carrying our own sins. We must be forgiven, for unforgiven sin dominates the focus of the needy soul. If we carry unforgiven sin, we cannot even think of what good, clear, positive focuses God would perform in our lives if we were free of our burden.

Guilt is the great debilitator. It puts a cramping paralysis on our desire to do good. It sits down, exhausted by the weight of all its grudges. It staggers under self-absorption because it no longer has the energy or inclination to care about others. It causes the best of Christians to avoid Christ and ignore their friends. It stalks the heart of all relationships, divine or human.

A husband may want to serve his family by contributing financially, caring for the needs of his children, and generally protecting and loving each member of the family. But if he and his wife have had even a small marital struggle that is largely his fault, he will likely not prove himself a good father until all has been forgiven. So, like the psalmist, such a tortured soul must ask for forgiveness and wait. When the sinner has been forgiven, he is possessed of a new lightness of soul that allows him to rise to his other family responsibilities and accomplish them speedily. The awesome difference between asking forgiveness from a fellow human and asking forgiveness from God is that God's great love for us allows instant reconciliation when we are humble and penitent before him.

So the moment we ask God's forgiveness, that very moment he forgives us; and then we are instantly free to focus on all that he wants to achieve next in our lives. His purposes are once again sweet and central to our worldview. Once we have God's forgiveness, no cloud of sin obscures what we are called to do.

To begin a study on the topic of Love Forgives, turn to the home page on page 1227.

DAY 5 FIVE

▸ PATIENCE AND ITS PLACE IN MY PERSONAL WORSHIP

Psalm 131:1–3

In this psalm David refutes those who find their egos demanding that God set aside his majesty and pay attention to them. In all ego there is a writhing impatience—impatience to have more glory, more recognition, greater fame. The self-centered believer is marked by an unholy impatience that keeps him or her from really seeing beyond self-importance to the full glory of God.

The ego ever clamors for increasing recognition. Is there an answer? How can we focus our worship on God when our tendency is to focus on self?

David says, "I have stilled and quieted my soul." How has he done this? Like a mother weans her child, breaking the child from an infant diet, so David has broken his ego from its diet of narcissism, the constant feeding on self-importance.

This is not as easy to do as one might think. The ego is like a sparrow chick. It keeps its overlarge beak turned up, crying "feed me."

"Feed you? With what?"

"Feed me with all I want; for I—your ego—cannot conceive of being happy with less than all I want. Oh, yes. And did I mention I want it now? Not just enough—more than enough. Don't feed me. Gorge me. Don't compliment me—flatter me. Don't give me a glass of wine—intoxicate me."

Ego keeps shouting at us for more. But when the Holy Spirit moves into our lives, teaching us the twin arts of temperance and patience, then ego at last is relegated to its place. Now it is finally quiet. Now we can praise God freely without the ugly impediment of self-will.

To begin a study on the topic of Patience, the Art of Waiting on God, turn to the home page on page 1500.

Psalm 132

A song of ascents.

1 O LORD, remember David
and all the hardships he endured.
2 He swore an oath to the LORD
and made a vow to the Mighty
One of Jacob:[c]
3 "I will not enter my house
or go to my bed—
4 I will allow no sleep to my eyes,
no slumber to my eyelids,
5 till I find a place[d] for the LORD,
a dwelling for the Mighty One of
Jacob."
6 We heard it in Ephrathah,[e]
we came upon it in the fields of
Jaar[a]:[b][f]
7 "Let us go to his dwelling place;[g]
let us worship at his footstool[h]—
8 arise, O LORD,[i] and come to your
resting place,
you and the ark of your might.
9 May your priests be clothed with
righteousness;[j]
may your saints sing for joy."
10 For the sake of David your servant,
do not reject your anointed one.
11 The LORD swore an oath to David,[k]
a sure oath that he will not revoke:
"One of your own descendants[l]
I will place on your throne—
12 if your sons keep my covenant
and the statutes I teach them,
then their sons will sit
on your throne[m] for ever and
ever."
13 For the LORD has chosen Zion,[n]
he has desired it for his dwelling:
14 "This is my resting place for ever
and ever;[o]
here I will sit enthroned, for I
have desired it—
15 I will bless her with abundant
provisions;
her poor will I satisfy with food.[p]
16 I will clothe her priests[q] with
salvation,
and her saints will ever sing for
joy.
17 "Here I will make a horn[c] grow[r] for
David
and set up a lamp[s] for my
anointed one.
18 I will clothe his enemies with shame,[t]
but the crown on his head will be
resplendent."

132:2 [c]Ge 49:24
132:5 [d]Ac 7:46
132:6 [e]1Sa 17:12 [f]1Sa 7:2
132:7 [g]Ps 5:7 [h]Ps 99:5
132:8 [i]Nu 10:35; Ps 78:61
132:9 [j]Job 29:14; Isa 61:3,10
132:11 [k]Ps 89:3-4,35 [l]2Sa 7:12
132:12 [m]Lk 1:32; Ac 2:30
132:13 [n]Ps 48:1-2
132:14 [o]Ps 68:16
132:15 [p]Ps 107:9; 147:14
132:16 [q]2Ch 6:41
132:17 [r]Eze 29:21; Lk 1:69 [s]1Ki 11:36; 2Ch 21:7
132:18 [t]Ps 35:26; 109:29

[a]6 That is, Kiriath Jearim [b]6 Or *heard of it in Ephrathah, / we found it in the fields of Jaar.* (And no quotes around verses 7-9) [c]17 *Horn* here symbolizes strong one, that is, king.

Psalm 133

A song of ascents. Of David.

[1] How good and pleasant it is
when brothers live together[u] in unity!

133:1 [u]Ge 13:8; Heb 13:1

GENTLENESS

A FERTILE LAND

Psalm 133:1

Love one another and your unity will mark out for itself a fertile zone for miracles. Hate one another and you will find only wide deserts of separation.

[2] It is like precious oil poured on the head,[v]
running down on the beard,
running down on Aaron's beard,
down upon the collar of his robes.
[3] It is as if the dew of Hermon[w]
were falling on Mount Zion.
For there the LORD bestows his blessing,[x]
even life forevermore.[y]

133:2 [v]Ex 30:25
133:3 [w]Dt 4:48 [x]Lev 25:21; Dt 28:8 [y]Ps 42:8

Psalm 134

A song of ascents.

[1] Praise the LORD, all you servants[z] of the LORD
who minister by night[a] in the house of the LORD.
[2] Lift up your hands[b] in the sanctuary
and praise the LORD.

[3] May the LORD, the Maker of heaven[c] and earth,
bless you from Zion.[d]

134:1 [z]Ps 135:1-2 [a]1Ch 9:33
134:2 [b]Ps 28:2; 1Ti 2:8
134:3 [c]Ps 124:8 [d]Ps 128:5

Psalm 135

[1] Praise the LORD.[a]

Praise the name of the LORD;
praise him, you servants[e] of the LORD,
[2] you who minister in the house[f] of the LORD,
in the courts[g] of the house of our God.

[3] Praise the LORD, for the LORD is good;[h]
sing praise to his name, for that is pleasant.[i]
[4] For the LORD has chosen Jacob[j] to be his own,
Israel to be his treasured possession.[k]

[5] I know that the LORD is great,[l]
that our Lord is greater than all gods.[m]
[6] The LORD does whatever pleases him,[n]
in the heavens and on the earth,
in the seas and all their depths.
[7] He makes clouds rise from the ends of the earth;
he sends lightning with the rain[o]
and brings out the wind[p] from his storehouses.[q]

[8] He struck down the firstborn[r] of Egypt,
the firstborn of men and animals.
[9] He sent his signs[s] and wonders into your midst, O Egypt,
against Pharaoh and all his servants.[t]
[10] He struck down many[u] nations
and killed mighty kings—
[11] Sihon[v] king of the Amorites,
Og king of Bashan
and all the kings of Canaan[w]—
[12] and he gave their land as an inheritance,[x]
an inheritance to his people Israel.

[13] Your name, O LORD, endures forever,[y]
your renown,[z] O LORD, through all generations.
[14] For the LORD will vindicate his people
and have compassion on his servants.[a]
[15] The idols of the nations are silver and gold,
made by the hands of men.
[16] They have mouths, but cannot speak,
eyes, but they cannot see;
[17] they have ears, but cannot hear,
nor is there breath in their mouths.
[18] Those who make them will be like them,
and so will all who trust in them.

[19] O house of Israel, praise the LORD;
O house of Aaron, praise the LORD;

[a]*1* Hebrew *Hallelu Yah*; also in verses 3 and 21

135:1 [e]Ps 113:1; 134:1
135:2 [f]Lk 2:37 [g]Ps 116:19
135:3 [h]Ps 119:68 [i]Ps 147:1
135:4 [j]Dt 10:15; 1Pe 2:9 [k]Ex 19:5; Dt 7:6
135:5 [l]Ps 48:1 [m]Ps 97:9
135:6 [n]Ps 115:3
135:7 [o]Jer 10:13; Zec 10:1 [p]Job 28:25 [q]Job 38:22
135:8 [r]Ex 12:12; Ps 78:51
135:9 [s]Dt 6:22 [t]Ps 136:10-15
135:10 [u]Nu 21:21-25; Ps 136:17-21
135:11 [v]Nu 21:21 [w]Jos 12:7-24
135:12 [x]Ps 78:55
135:13 [y]Ex 3:15 [z]Ps 102:12
135:14 [a]Dt 32:36

20 O house of Levi, praise the LORD;
you who fear him, praise the LORD.
21 Praise be to the LORD from Zion,[b]
to him who dwells in Jerusalem.

Praise the LORD.

135:21 [b]Ps 134:3

Psalm 136

1 Give thanks to the LORD, for he is good.[c]
His love endures forever.[d]
2 Give thanks to the God of gods.[e]
His love endures forever.
3 Give thanks to the Lord of lords:
His love endures forever.

4 to him who alone does great wonders,[f]
His love endures forever.
5 who by his understanding[g] made the heavens,[h]
His love endures forever.
6 who spread out the earth[i] upon the waters,[j]
His love endures forever.
7 who made the great lights[k]—
His love endures forever.
8 the sun to govern[l] the day,
His love endures forever.
9 the moon and stars to govern the night;
His love endures forever.

10 to him who struck down the firstborn[m] of Egypt
His love endures forever.
11 and brought Israel out[n] from among them
His love endures forever.
12 with a mighty hand and outstretched arm;[o]
His love endures forever.

13 to him who divided the Red Sea[a][p] asunder
His love endures forever.
14 and brought Israel through[q] the midst of it,
His love endures forever.
15 but swept Pharaoh and his army into the Red Sea;[r]
His love endures forever.

16 to him who led his people through the desert,[s]
His love endures forever.

17 who struck down great kings,[t]
His love endures forever.
18 and killed mighty kings[u]—
His love endures forever.
19 Sihon king of the Amorites[v]
His love endures forever.
20 and Og king of Bashan—
His love endures forever.
21 and gave their land[w] as an inheritance,
His love endures forever.
22 an inheritance to his servant Israel;
His love endures forever.

23 to the One who remembered us[x] in our low estate
His love endures forever.
24 and freed us from our enemies,[y]
His love endures forever.
25 and who gives food[z] to every creature.
His love endures forever.

26 Give thanks to the God of heaven.
His love endures forever.

136:1 [c]Ps 106:1 [d]1Ch 16:34; 2Ch 20:21
136:2 [e]Dt 10:17
136:4 [f]Ps 72:18
136:5 [g]Pr 3:19; Jer 51:15 [h]Ge 1:1
136:6 [i]Ge 1:9; Jer 10:12 [j]Ps 24:2
136:7 [k]Ge 1:14,16
136:8 [l]Ge 1:16
136:10 [m]Ex 12:29; Ps 135:8
136:11 [n]Ex 6:6; 12:51
136:12 [o]Dt 4:34; Ps 44:3
136:13 [p]Ex 14:21; Ps 78:13
136:14 [q]Ex 14:22
136:15 [r]Ex 14:27; Ps 135:9
136:16 [s]Ex 13:18
136:17 [t]Ps 135:9-12
136:18 [u]Dt 29:7
136:19 [v]Nu 21:21-25
136:21 [w]Jos 12:1
136:23 [x]Ps 113:7
136:24 [y]Ps 107:2
136:25 [z]Ps 104:27; 145:15

Psalm 137

1 By the rivers of Babylon[a] we sat and wept[b]
when we remembered Zion.
2 There on the poplars
we hung our harps,
3 for there our captors asked us for songs,
our tormentors demanded[c] songs of joy;
they said, "Sing us one of the songs of Zion!"

4 How can we sing the songs of the LORD
while in a foreign land?
5 If I forget you, O Jerusalem,
may my right hand forget ⌊its skill⌋.
6 May my tongue cling to the roof[d] of my mouth
if I do not remember you,
if I do not consider Jerusalem
my highest joy.

7 Remember, O LORD, what the Edomites[e] did
on the day Jerusalem fell.[f]
"Tear it down," they cried,
"tear it down to its foundations!"
8 O Daughter of Babylon, doomed to destruction,[g]

137:1 [a]Eze 1:1,3 [b]Ne 1:4
137:3 [c]Ps 80:6
137:6 [d]Eze 3:26
137:7 [e]Jer 49:7; La 4:21-22; Eze 25:12 [f]Ob 1:11
137:8 [g]Isa 13:1,19; Jer 25:12,26; Jer 50:15; Rev 18:6

[a]*13* Hebrew *Yam Suph*; that is, Sea of Reeds; also in verse 15

happy is he who repays you
for what you have done to us—
[9]he who seizes your infants
and dashes them[b] against the
rocks.

137:9 [b]2Ki 8:12; Isa 13:16

DAY 5 FIVE

▸ KINDNESS AND ITS PLACE IN MY PERSONAL WORSHIP

Psalm 137:1–9

Psalm 137 is a poem written by someone whose heart has been stirred by racial abuse. The people of Israel have been conquered and captured by the Babylonians, and the writer of this psalm cries out to God for justice.

But anger unextinguished by grace burns in the hearts of those who harbor grudges or hatred toward others. In the New Testament, Jesus gives us a perspective on our attitude toward our enemies. In Matthew 18:21–22, Jesus instructs Peter to forgive his enemies. How our unkind hearts are freed from prejudice when we quit making those we perceive as God's enemies our own enemies! Martin Niemoeller, imprisoned in a Nazi concentration camp said that each time the Nazi guards abused him—shoved him into the mud, slammed his head or body with a rifle butt—he practiced hating them. Niemoeller's resentment continued for a long time until he remembered that, while he considered the Nazis to be his enemies, it was not so with God. God hates no lost soul. This single insight transformed his life. He learned that kindness is merely anger washed by grace.

Ernest Gordon had a similar experience in the valley of the Kwai. He had to learn that his torturous Japanese overlords were all God's targets of grace. Gordon replaced all his resentment with love, and his attitude affected everyone in the concentration camp as a result.

Let us ever guard against prejudice. It is the result of trying to goad God into having our friends as his friends and our enemies as his enemies. There is a better way of seeing people. Seeing others God's way will free us up to worship a God who exists above our limited perspective.

To begin a study on the topic of Kindness, Anger Washed by Grace, turn to the home page on page 751.

Psalm 138

Of David.

[1]I will praise you, O LORD, with all
my heart;
before the "gods"[i] I will sing your
praise.
[2]I will bow down toward your holy
temple[j]
and will praise your name
for your love and your
faithfulness,
for you have exalted above all things
your name and your word.[k]
[3]When I called, you answered me;
you made me bold and
stouthearted.[l]

[4]May all the kings of the earth[m] praise
you, O LORD,
when they hear the words of your
mouth.
[5]May they sing of the ways of the
LORD,
for the glory of the LORD is great.

[6]Though the LORD is on high, he
looks upon the lowly,[n]
but the proud[o] he knows from
afar.
[7]Though I walk[p] in the midst of
trouble,
you preserve my life;
you stretch out your hand against
the anger of my foes,[q]
with your right hand[r] you save
me.[s]
[8]The LORD will fulfill ⌊his purpose⌋[t]
for me;
your love, O LORD, endures
forever—
do not abandon the works of your
hands.[u]

138:1 [i]Ps 95:3; 96:4
138:2 [j]1Ki 8:29; Ps 5:7; 28:2 [k]Isa 42:21
138:3 [l]Ps 28:7
138:4 [m]Ps 102:15
138:6 [n]Ps 113:6; Isa 57:15 [o]Pr 3:34; Jas 4:6
138:7 [p]Ps 23:4 [q]Jer 51:25 [r]Ps 20:6 [s]Ps 71:20
138:8 [t]Ps 57:2; Php 1:6 [u]Job 10:3,8; 14:15

Psalm 139

For the director of music.
Of David. A psalm.

[1]O LORD, you have searched me[v]
and you know[w] me.
[2]You know when I sit and when I
rise;[x]
you perceive my thoughts[y] from
afar.
[3]You discern my going out and my
lying down;
you are familiar with all my
ways.[z]
[4]Before a word is on my tongue

139:1 [v]Ps 17:3 [w]Jer 12:3
139:2 [x]2Ki 19:27 [y]Mt 9:4; Jn 2:24
139:3 [z]Job 31:4

139:4 [a]Heb 4:13
you know it completely,[a]
O LORD.

139:5 [b]Ps 34:7
5 You hem me in[b]—behind and before;
you have laid your hand upon me.
6 Such knowledge is too wonderful for me,
139:6 [c]Job 42:3; Ro 11:33
too lofty[c] for me to attain.

7 Where can I go from your Spirit?
139:7 [d]Jer 23:24; Jnh 1:3
Where can I flee[d] from your presence?

LOVE

THE GREAT PURSUIT

Psalm 139:7

God, our pursuing lover, spends his wide eternities in a chase of grace. He cannot quit loving us and therefore will not quit pursuing us. The great hound of heaven is on our heels, seeking, tracking, loving—until we decide to end the chase and open to his love.

8 If I go up to the heavens,[e] you are there;
139:8 [e]Am 9:2-3 [f]Pr 15:11
if I make my bed[f] in the depths,[a]
you are there.
9 If I rise on the wings of the dawn,
if I settle on the far side of the sea,
139:10 [g]Ps 23:3
10 even there your hand will guide me,[g]
your right hand will hold me fast.

11 If I say, "Surely the darkness will hide me
and the light become night around me,"
139:12 [h]Job 34:22; Da 2:22
12 even the darkness will not be dark[h] to you;
the night will shine like the day,
for darkness is as light to you.

139:13 [i]Ps 119:73 [j]Job 10:11
13 For you created my inmost being;[i]
you knit me together[j] in my mother's womb.
14 I praise you because I am fearfully and wonderfully made;
139:14 [k]Ps 40:5
your works are wonderful,[k]
I know that full well.
15 My frame was not hidden from you
when I was made in the secret place.
139:15 [l]Job 10:11 [m]Ps 63:9
When I was woven together[l] in the depths of the earth,[m]
16 your eyes saw my unformed body.
All the days ordained for me
were written in your book
before one of them came to be.
17 How precious to[b] me are your thoughts, O God![n]
139:17 [n]Ps 40:5
How vast is the sum of them!
18 Were I to count them,
they would outnumber the grains of sand.
When I awake,
I am still with you.

19 If only you would slay the wicked,[o] O God!
139:19 [o]Isa 11:4 [p]Ps 119:115
Away from me,[p] you bloodthirsty men!
20 They speak of you with evil intent;
your adversaries misuse your name.[q]
139:20 [q]Jude 15
21 Do not I hate those[r] who hate you, O LORD,
139:21 [r]2Ch 19:2; Ps 31:6; 119:113; Ps 119:158
and abhor those who rise up against you?
22 I have nothing but hatred for them;
I count them my enemies.
23 Search me,[s] O God, and know my heart;[t]
139:23 [s]Job 31:6; Ps 26:2 [t]Jer 11:20
test me and know my anxious thoughts.
24 See if there is any offensive way in me,
139:24 [u]Ps 5:8; 143:10; Pr 15:9
and lead me[u] in the way everlasting.

Psalm 140

For the director of music.
A psalm of David.

140:1 [v]Ps 17:13 [w]Ps 18:48
1 Rescue me,[v] O LORD, from evil men;
protect me from men of violence,[w]
140:2 [x]Ps 36:4; 56:6
2 who devise evil plans[x] in their hearts
and stir up war every day.
140:3 [y]Ps 57:4 [z]Ps 58:4; Jas 3:8
3 They make their tongues as sharp as[y] a serpent's;
the poison of vipers[z] is on their lips. *Selah*

140:4 [a]Ps 141:9 [b]Ps 71:4
4 Keep me,[a] O LORD, from the hands of the wicked;[b]
protect me from men of violence
who plan to trip my feet.
5 Proud men have hidden a snare for me;
they have spread out the cords of their net

[a]8 Hebrew *Sheol* [b]17 Or *concerning*

140:5 [c]Ps 31:4; 35:7 and have set traps[c] for me along
my path. *Selah*
140:6 [d]Ps 16:2 [e]Ps 116:1; 143:1 6 O LORD, I say to you, "You are my
God."[d]
Hear, O LORD, my cry for mercy.[e]
140:7 [f]Ps 28:8 7 O Sovereign LORD,[f] my strong
deliverer,
who shields my head in the day of
battle—
140:8 [g]Ps 10:2-3 8 do not grant the wicked[g] their
desires, O LORD;
do not let their plans succeed,
or they will become proud. *Selah*
9 Let the heads of those who surround
me
140:9 [h]Ps 7:16 be covered with the trouble their
lips have caused.[h]
140:10 [i]Ps 11:6; 21:9 10 Let burning coals fall upon them;
may they be thrown into the fire,[i]
into miry pits, never to rise.
11 Let slanderers not be established in
the land;
may disaster hunt down men of
140:11 [j]Ps 34:21 violence.[j]

12 I know that the LORD secures justice
for the poor
140:12 [k]Ps 9:4 [l]Ps 35:10 and upholds the cause[k] of the
needy.[l]
140:13 [m]Ps 97:12 [n]Ps 11:7 13 Surely the righteous will praise your
name[m]
and the upright will live[n] before
you.

Psalm 141

A psalm of David.

1 O LORD, I call to you; come
141:1 [o]Ps 22:19; 70:5 [p]Ps 143:1 quickly[o] to me.
Hear my voice[p] when I call to
you.
2 May my prayer be set before you like
141:2 [q]Rev 5:8; 8:3 [r]1Ti 2:8 [s]Ex 29:39,41 incense;[q]
may the lifting up of my hands[r] be
like the evening sacrifice.[s]
3 Set a guard over my mouth,
O LORD;
keep watch over the door of my
lips.
4 Let not my heart be drawn to what
is evil,
to take part in wicked deeds
with men who are evildoers;
141:4 [t]Pr 23:6 let me not eat of their delicacies.[t]
5 Let a righteous man[a] strike me—it is
a kindness;
let him rebuke me[u]—it is oil on 141:5 [u]Pr 9:8 [v]Ps 23:5
my head.[v]
My head will not refuse it.

Yet my prayer is ever against the
deeds of evildoers;
6 their rulers will be thrown down
from the cliffs,
and the wicked will learn that my
words were well spoken.
7 ⌞They will say,⌟ "As one plows and
breaks up the earth,
so our bones have been scattered
at the mouth[w] of the grave.[b]" 141:7 [w]Ps 53:5

8 But my eyes are fixed[x] on you, 141:8 [x]Ps 25:15 [y]Ps 2:12
O Sovereign LORD;
in you I take refuge[y]—do not give
me over to death.
9 Keep me[z] from the snares they have 141:9 [z]Ps 140:4 [a]Ps 38:12
laid for me,
from the traps set[a] by evildoers.
10 Let the wicked fall[b] into their own 141:10 [b]Ps 35:8
nets,
while I pass by in safety.

Psalm 142

A *maskil*[c] of David.
When he was in the cave. A prayer.

1 I cry aloud to the LORD;
I lift up my voice to the LORD for 142:1 [c]Ps 30:8
mercy.[c]
2 I pour out my complaint[d] before 142:2 [d]Isa 26:16
him;
before him I tell my trouble.

3 When my spirit grows faint[e] within 142:3 [e]Ps 140:5; 143:4,7
me,
it is you who know my way.
In the path where I walk
men have hidden a snare for me.
4 Look to my right and see;
no one is concerned for me.
I have no refuge;
no one cares[f] for my life. 142:4 [f]Ps 31:11; Jer 30:17

5 I cry to you, O LORD;
I say, "You are my refuge,[g] 142:5 [g]Ps 46:1 [h]Ps 16:5 [i]Ps 27:13
my portion[h] in the land of the
living."[i]
6 Listen to my cry,[j] 142:6 [j]Ps 17:1 [k]Ps 79:8; 116:6
for I am in desperate need;[k]
rescue me from those who pursue
me,
for they are too strong for me.
7 Set me free from my prison,[l] 142:7 [l]Ps 146:7

[a]5 Or *Let the Righteous One* [b]7 Hebrew *Sheol*
[c]Title: Probably a literary or musical term

that I may praise your name.
Then the righteous will gather about
me
because of your goodness to me.[m]

142:7 [m]Ps 13:6

Psalm 143

A psalm of David.

[1]O LORD, hear my prayer,
listen to my cry for mercy;[n]
in your faithfulness[o] and
righteousness[p]
come to my relief.

143:1 [n]Ps 140:6 [o]Ps 89:1-2 [p]Ps 71:2

[2]Do not bring your servant into
judgment,
for no one living is righteous[q]
before you.

143:2 [q]Ps 14:3; Ecc 7:20; Ro 3:20

[3]The enemy pursues me,
he crushes me to the ground;
he makes me dwell in darkness
like those long dead.
[4]So my spirit grows faint within me;
my heart within me is dismayed.[r]

143:4 [r]Ps 142:3

[5]I remember[s] the days of long ago;
I meditate on all your works
and consider what your hands
have done.

143:5 [s]Ps 77:6

[6]I spread out my hands[t] to you;
my soul thirsts for you like a
parched land. *Selah*

143:6 [t]Ps 63:1; 88:9

[7]Answer me quickly,[u] O LORD;
my spirit fails.
Do not hide your face[v] from me
or I will be like those who go
down to the pit.

143:7 [u]Ps 69:17 [v]Ps 27:9; 28:1

[8]Let the morning bring me word of
your unfailing love,[w]
for I have put my trust in you.
Show me the way[x] I should go,
for to you I lift up my soul.[y]

143:8 [w]Ps 46:5; 90:14 [x]Ps 27:11 [y]Ps 25:1-2

[9]Rescue me from my enemies,[z]
O LORD,
for I hide myself in you.

143:9 [z]Ps 31:15

[10]Teach me to do your will,
for you are my God;
may your good Spirit
lead[a] me on level ground.

143:10 [a]Ne 9:20; Ps 23:3; 25:4-5

[11]For your name's sake, O LORD,
preserve my life;[b]
in your righteousness,[c] bring me
out of trouble.

143:11 [b]Ps 119:25 [c]Ps 31:1

[12]In your unfailing love, silence my
enemies;
destroy all my foes,[d]
for I am your servant.[e]

143:12 [d]Ps 52:5; 54:5 [e]Ps 116:16

Psalm 144

Of David.

[1]Praise be to the LORD my Rock,[f]
who trains my hands for war,
my fingers for battle.

144:1 [f]Ps 18:2,34

[2]He is my loving God and my
fortress,[g]
my stronghold and my deliverer,
my shield,[h] in whom I take refuge,
who subdues peoples[a] under me.

144:2 [g]Ps 59:9; 91:2 [h]Ps 84:9

[3]O LORD, what is man[i] that you care
for him,
the son of man that you think of
him?

144:3 [i]Ps 8:4; Heb 2:6

[4]Man is like a breath;
his days are like a fleeting shadow.[j]

144:4 [j]Ps 39:11; 102:11

[5]Part your heavens,[k] O LORD, and
come down;
touch the mountains, so that they
smoke.[l]

144:5 [k]Ps 18:9; Isa 64:1 [l]Ps 104:32

[6]Send forth lightning and scatter ⌞the
enemies⌟;
shoot your arrows[m] and rout
them.

144:6 [m]Ps 7:12-13; 18:14

[7]Reach down your hand from on
high;
deliver me and rescue me
from the mighty waters,[n]
from the hands of foreigners[o]
[8]whose mouths are full of lies,[p]
whose right hands are deceitful.

144:7 [n]Ps 69:2 [o]Ps 18:44

144:8 [p]Ps 12:2

[9]I will sing a new song to you,
O God;
on the ten-stringed lyre[q] I will
make music to you,
[10]to the One who gives victory to
kings,
who delivers his servant David[r]
from the deadly sword.

144:9 [q]Ps 33:2-3

144:10 [r]Ps 18:50

[11]Deliver me and rescue me
from the hands of foreigners
whose mouths are full of lies,
whose right hands are deceitful.[s]

144:11 [s]Ps 12:2; Isa 44:20

[12]Then our sons in their youth
will be like well-nurtured plants,[t]
and our daughters will be like pillars
carved to adorn a palace.

144:12 [t]Ps 128:3

[13]Our barns will be filled
with every kind of provision.
Our sheep will increase by
thousands,

[a]*2* Many manuscripts of the Masoretic Text, Dead Sea Scrolls, Aquila, Jerome and Syriac; most manuscripts of the Masoretic Text *subdues my people*

by tens of thousands in our fields;
14 our oxen will draw heavy loads.[a]
There will be no breaching of walls,
no going into captivity,
no cry of distress in our streets.

144:15 [u]Ps 33:12

15 Blessed are the people[u] of whom this
is true;
blessed are the people whose God
is the LORD.

Psalm 145[b]

A psalm of praise. Of David.

145:1 [v]Ps 30:1; 34:1 [w]Ps 5:2
145:2 [x]Ps 71:6

1 I will exalt you,[v] my God the King;[w]
I will praise your name for ever
and ever.
2 Every day I will praise[x] you
and extol your name for ever and
ever.

145:3 [y]Job 5:9; Ps 147:5; Ro 11:33
145:4 [z]Isa 38:19

3 Great is the LORD and most worthy
of praise;
his greatness no one can
fathom.[y]
4 One generation[z] will commend your
works to another;
they will tell of your mighty acts.
5 They will speak of the glorious
splendor of your majesty,
and I will meditate on your
wonderful works.[c][a]

145:5 [a]Ps 119:27
145:6 [b]Ps 66:3 [c]Dt 32:3
145:7 [d]Isa 63:7 [e]Ps 51:14

6 They will tell of the power of your
awesome works,[b]
and I will proclaim[c] your great
deeds.
7 They will celebrate your abundant
goodness[d]
and joyfully sing of your
righteousness.[e]

145:8 [f]Ps 86:15 [g]Ex 34:6; Nu 14:18
145:9 [h]Ps 100:5
145:10 [i]Ps 19:1 [j]Ps 68:26

8 The LORD is gracious and
compassionate,[f]
slow to anger and rich in love.[g]
9 The LORD is good[h] to all;
he has compassion on all he has
made.
10 All you have made will praise you,[i]
O LORD;
your saints will extol you.[j]
11 They will tell of the glory of your
kingdom
and speak of your might,

145:12 [k]Ps 105:1
145:13 [l]1Ti 1:17; 2Pe 1:11

12 so that all men may know of your
mighty acts[k]
and the glorious splendor of your
kingdom.
13 Your kingdom is an everlasting
kingdom,[l]
and your dominion endures
through all generations.

The LORD is faithful to all his
promises
and loving toward all he has
made.[d]

145:14 [m]Ps 37:24 [n]Ps 146:8
145:15 [o]Ps 104:27; 136:25
145:16 [p]Ps 104:28

14 The LORD upholds[m] all those who
fall
and lifts up all[n] who are bowed
down.
15 The eyes of all look to you,
and you give them their food[o] at
the proper time.
16 You open your hand
and satisfy the desires[p] of every
living thing.

145:18 [q]Dt 4:7 [r]Jn 4:24
145:19 [s]Ps 37:4 [t]Pr 15:29
145:20 [u]Ps 31:23; 97:10 [v]Ps 9:5
145:21 [w]Ps 71:8 [x]Ps 65:2

17 The LORD is righteous in all his
ways
and loving toward all he has made.
18 The LORD is near[q] to all who call
on him,[r]
to all who call on him in truth.
19 He fulfills the desires[s] of those who
fear him;
he hears their cry[t] and saves them.
20 The LORD watches over all who love
him,[u]
but all the wicked he will destroy.[v]

21 My mouth will speak[w] in praise of
the LORD.
Let every creature[x] praise his holy
name
for ever and ever.

Psalm 146

146:1 [y]Ps 103:1
146:2 [z]Ps 104:33
146:3 [a]Ps 118:9 [b]Isa 2:22
146:4 [c]Ps 104:29; Ecc 12:7

1 Praise the LORD.[e]

Praise the LORD,[y] O my soul.
2 I will praise the LORD all my life;[z]
I will sing praise to my God as
long as I live.

3 Do not put your trust in princes,[a]
in mortal men,[b] who cannot save.
4 When their spirit departs, they
return to the ground;[c]

[a]*14* Or *our chieftains will be firmly established*
[b]This psalm is an acrostic poem, the verses of which (including verse 13b) begin with the successive letters of the Hebrew alphabet. [c]*5* Dead Sea Scrolls and Syriac (see also Septuagint); Masoretic Text *On the glorious splendor of your majesty / and on your wonderful works I will meditate* [d]*13* One manuscript of the Masoretic Text, Dead Sea Scrolls and Syriac (see also Septuagint); most manuscripts of the Masoretic Text do not have the last two lines of verse 13. [e]*1* Hebrew *Hallelu Yah*; also in verse 10

on that very day their plans come
to nothing.[d]
5 Blessed is he[e] whose help[f] is the God
of Jacob,
whose hope is in the LORD his
God,
6 the Maker of heaven[g] and earth,
the sea, and everything in them—
the LORD, who remains faithful[h]
forever.
7 He upholds the cause of the
oppressed[i]
and gives food to the hungry.[j]
The LORD sets prisoners free,[k]
8 the LORD gives sight to the blind,[l]
the LORD lifts up those who are
bowed down,
the LORD loves the righteous.
9 The LORD watches over the alien
and sustains the fatherless and the
widow,[m]
but he frustrates the ways of the
wicked.
10 The LORD reigns[n] forever,
your God, O Zion, for all
generations.

Praise the LORD.

Psalm 147

1 Praise the LORD.[a]

How good it is to sing praises to our
God,
how pleasant[o] and fitting to praise
him![p]
2 The LORD builds up Jerusalem;[q]
he gathers the exiles[r] of Israel.
3 He heals the brokenhearted
and binds up their wounds.
4 He determines the number of the
stars[s]
and calls them each by name.
5 Great is our Lord[t] and mighty in
power;
his understanding has no limit.[u]
6 The LORD sustains the humble[v]
but casts the wicked to the
ground.
7 Sing to the LORD[w] with
thanksgiving;
make music to our God on the
harp.
8 He covers the sky with clouds;
he supplies the earth with rain[x]

146:4 [d]Ps 33:10; 1Co 2:6
146:5 [e]Ps 144:15; Jer 17:7 [f]Ps 71:5
146:6 [g]Ps 115:15; Ac 14:15; Rev 14:7 [h]Ps 117:2
146:7 [i]Ps 103:6 [j]Ps 107:9 [k]Ps 68:6
146:8 [l]Mt 9:30
146:9 [m]Ex 22:22; Dt 10:18; Ps 68:5
146:10 [n]Ex 15:18; Ps 10:16
147:1 [o]Ps 135:3 [p]Ps 33:1
147:2 [q]Ps 102:16 [r]Dt 30:3
147:4 [s]Isa 40:26
147:5 [t]Ps 48:1 [u]Isa 40:28
147:6 [v]Ps 146:8-9
147:7 [w]Ps 33:3
147:8 [x]Job 38:26

and makes grass grow[y] on the
hills.
9 He provides food[z] for the cattle
and for the young ravens[a] when
they call.
10 His pleasure is not in the strength[b]
of the horse,[c]
nor his delight in the legs of a
man;
11 the LORD delights in those who fear
him,
who put their hope in his
unfailing love.

12 Extol the LORD, O Jerusalem;
praise your God, O Zion,
13 for he strengthens the bars of your
gates
and blesses your people within
you.
14 He grants peace[d] to your borders
and satisfies you[e] with the finest of
wheat.
15 He sends his command[f] to the
earth;
his word runs swiftly.
16 He spreads the snow[g] like wool
and scatters the frost[h] like ashes.
17 He hurls down his hail like pebbles.
Who can withstand his icy blast?
18 He sends his word[i] and melts them;
he stirs up his breezes, and the
waters flow.
19 He has revealed his word to Jacob,
his laws and decrees[j] to Israel.
20 He has done this for no other
nation;[k]
they do not know his laws.

Praise the LORD.

Psalm 148

1 Praise the LORD.[b]

Praise the LORD from the heavens,
praise him in the heights above.
2 Praise him, all his angels,[l]
praise him, all his heavenly hosts.
3 Praise him, sun and moon,
praise him, all you shining stars.
4 Praise him, you highest heavens
and you waters above the skies.[m]
5 Let them praise the name of the
LORD,

[a] *1* Hebrew *Hallelu Yah*; also in verse 20
[b] *1* Hebrew *Hallelu Yah*; also in verse 14

147:8 [y]Ps 104:14
147:9 [z]Ps 104:27-28; Mt 6:26 [a]Job 38:41
147:10 [b]1Sa 16:7 [c]Ps 33:16-17
147:14 [d]Isa 60:17-18 [e]Ps 132:15
147:15 [f]Job 37:12
147:16 [g]Job 37:6 [h]Job 38:29
147:18 [i]Ps 33:9
147:19 [j]Dt 33:4; Mal 4:4
147:20 [k]Dt 4:7-8, 32-34
148:2 [l]Ps 103:20
148:4 [m]Ge 1:7; 1Ki 8:27

148:5 [n]Ge 1:1,6; Ps 33:6,9
148:6 [o]Job 38:33; Ps 89:37; Jer 33:25
148:7 [p]Ps 74:13-14
148:8 [q]Ps 147:15-18
148:9 [r]Isa 44:23; 49:13; 55:12
148:13 [s]Isa 12:4 [t]Ps 8:1; 113:4
148:14 [u]Ps 75:10

for he commanded[n] and they were
created.
6 He set them in place for ever and
ever;
he gave a decree[o] that will never
pass away.
7 Praise the LORD from the earth,
you great sea creatures[p] and all
ocean depths,
8 lightning and hail, snow and clouds,
stormy winds that do his bidding,[q]
9 you mountains and all hills,[r]
fruit trees and all cedars,
10 wild animals and all cattle,
small creatures and flying birds,
11 kings of the earth and all nations,
you princes and all rulers on earth,
12 young men and maidens,
old men and children.

13 Let them praise the name of the
LORD,[s]
for his name alone is exalted;
his splendor is above the earth and
the heavens.[t]
14 He has raised up for his people a
horn,[a] [u]
the praise of all his saints,
of Israel, the people close to his
heart.

Praise the LORD.

Psalm 149

149:1 [v]Ps 33:2 [w]Ps 35:18

1 Praise the LORD.[b] [v]

Sing to the LORD a new song,
his praise in the assembly[w] of the
saints.

JOY

FRESH GRACE

Psalm 149:1

Grace is never stale. It is fresh every morning. It is the light in old men's eyes, the laughter in the aging heart. It is manna in Sinai. It is bread that endures to the end of life's journey.

149:2 [x]Ps 95:6 [y]Ps 47:6; Zec 9:9
149:3 [z]Ps 81:2; 150:4

2 Let Israel rejoice in their Maker;[x]
let the people of Zion be glad in
their King.[y]
3 Let them praise his name with
dancing
and make music to him with
tambourine and harp.[z]

DAY 5 FIVE

JOY AND ITS PLACE IN MY PERSONAL WORSHIP

Psalm 150:1–6

One cannot read this psalm without seeing that the joy of our personal worship must be guided by four powerful questions:

Where shall we praise God?
Why shall we praise God?
How shall we praise God?
Who is to praise God?

Where shall we praise God? The psalmist says we should praise both in the sanctuary and in the heavens. Christians gather in God's holy house, and from this local address we enter the heavens. Do not be too amazed at this requirement to praise God in the heavens. The heavens themselves represent the evidence of great adoration. When we praise, we are caught up in such lightness of being that we belong more to the heavens than to our dull and plodding earth.

Why shall we praise God? We see God in his works. We see the presence of God through the miracles that take place in our lives every day. He has done so much in our lives that we would sin in the very act of keeping such wonderful works to ourselves.

How shall we praise God? Let us praise God with all sorts of instruments. Let none object that accordions or tambourines or guitars lack dignity. God must be praised. Those who have no instruments must give themselves to singing or dancing—even in more traditional assemblies. Further, our praise should neither be quietly done nor hesitantly done. We should praise God with such force of soul that we are transformed by the force.

Who is to praise God? Anyone with a pulse is required to praise God. Anyone with a breath is living evidence of God's presence, and what better reason to praise than to see him living among us?

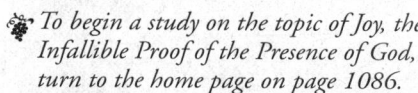

To begin a study on the topic of Joy, the Infallible Proof of the Presence of God, turn to the home page on page 1086.

[a] *14 Horn* here symbolizes strong one, that is, king.
[b] *1* Hebrew *Hallelu Yah*; also in verse 9

149:4 [a]Ps 35:27 [b]Ps 132:16
4 For the LORD takes delight[a] in his people;
he crowns the humble with salvation.[b]

149:5 [c]Ps 132:16 [d]Job 35:10
5 Let the saints rejoice[c] in this honor
and sing for joy on their beds.[d]

149:6 [e]Ps 66:17 [f]Heb 4:12; Rev 1:16
6 May the praise of God be in their mouths[e]
and a double-edged[f] sword in their hands,
7 to inflict vengeance on the nations
and punishment on the peoples,
8 to bind their kings with fetters,
their nobles with shackles of iron,

149:9 [g]Dt 7:1; Eze 28:26 [h]Ps 148:14
9 to carry out the sentence written against them.[g]
This is the glory of all his saints.[h]

Praise the LORD.

Psalm 150

150:1 [i]Ps 102:19 [j]Ps 19:1
1 Praise the LORD.[a]

Praise God in his sanctuary;[i]
praise him in his mighty heavens.[j]

150:2 [k]Dt 3:24 [l]Ps 145:5-6
2 Praise him for his acts of power;[k]
praise him for his surpassing greatness.[l]

150:3 [m]Ps 149:3
3 Praise him with the sounding of the trumpet,
praise him with the harp and lyre,[m]

150:4 [n]Ex 15:20 [o]Isa 38:20
4 praise him with tambourine and dancing,[n]
praise him with the strings[o] and flute,

150:5 [p]1Ch 13:8; 15:16
5 praise him with the clash of cymbals,[p]
praise him with resounding cymbals.

150:6 [q]Ps 145:21
6 Let everything[q] that has breath praise the LORD.

Praise the LORD.

[a]1 Hebrew *Hallelu Yah*; also in verse 6

PROVERBS

AUTHORSHIP AND DATE

Solomon compiled most of the book; other contributors may have been Lemuel and Agur, whose names appear later in the book.

The tenth century B.C. (if Solomon is credited as the author); however, there is internal evidence to suggest that the book grew over a period of three centuries, ending with the reign of Hezekiah about 700 B.C. (see 25:1).

KEY THEMES

The book was written "for giving prudence to the simple, [and] knowledge and discretion to the young" (1:4), as well as enabling the wise to gain further wisdom and increase their knowledge and discernment (see v. 5). In a general sense, the book seems to fall into three divisions:

1. Advice and counsel for the young (see 1:1—9:18)
2. Advice and counsel for people of all ages (see 10:1—24:34)
3. Adages and guidance for leaders (see 25:1—31:31)

FRUIT OF THE SPIRIT IN PROVERBS

Self-Control: The book of Proverbs is a set of admonitions to practice self-control. It also contains instructions and examples of guidance for building a disciplined life.

First, there are admonitions to learn self-control by emulating parents: "Listen, my son, to your father's instruction and do not forsake your mother's teaching" (1:8). "My son, if sinners entice you, do not give in to them" (v. 10).

Second, there are many admonitions not to fall into evil, but rather to stand up against evil with self-control: "Wisdom will save you from the ways of wicked men, from men whose words are perverse" (2:12).

Third, there are passages dealing with various topics related to self-control. For example, there are passages—both short (see 2:16) and long (see 5:15–20)—dealing with the trap of illicit sexuality. There are passages that encourage us to watch what we say (see 6:1–5), avoid folly (see 9:13–18), and avoid being lazy (see 10:4; 13:4; 24:33–34). There are many admonitions to love knowledge and industry and to avoid sloth.

Overall, the best and most disciplined persons become so because they love God, crave wisdom and treasure virtue. One passage that best expresses this idea is found in Proverbs 3:5–6: "Trust in the LORD with all your heart and lean not on your own understanding; in all your ways acknowledge him, and he will make your paths straight."

Prologue: Purpose and Theme

1:1 [a]1Ki 4:29-34 [b]Pr 10:1; 25:1; Ecc 1:1 **1** The proverbs of Solomon[a] son of
David, king of Israel:[b]

[2]for attaining wisdom and discipline;
for understanding words of
insight;
[3]for acquiring a disciplined and
prudent life,
doing what is right and just and
fair;
1:4 [c]Pr 8:5 [d]Pr 2:10-11; 8:12 [4]for giving prudence to the simple,[c]
knowledge and discretion[d] to the
young—
1:5 [e]Pr 9:9 [5]let the wise listen and add to their
learning,[e]
and let the discerning get
guidance—
1:6 [f]Ps 49:4; 78:2 [g]Nu 12:8 [6]for understanding proverbs and
parables,[f]
the sayings and riddles[g] of the
wise.

1:7 [h]Job 28:28; Ps 111:10; Pr 9:10; 15:33; Ecc 12:13 [7]The fear of the LORD[h] is the
beginning of knowledge,
but fools[a] despise wisdom and
discipline.

Exhortations to Embrace Wisdom

Warning Against Enticement

1:8 [i]Pr 4:1 [j]Pr 6:20 [8]Listen, my son,[i] to your father's
instruction
and do not forsake your mother's
teaching.[j]
[9]They will be a garland to grace your
head
1:9 [k]Pr 4:1-9 and a chain to adorn your neck.[k]

1:10 [l]Ge 39:7 [m]Dt 13:8 [n]Pr 16:29; Eph 5:11 [10]My son, if sinners entice[l] you,
do not give in[m] to them.[n]
[11]If they say, "Come along with us;
1:11 [o]Ps 10:8 let's lie in wait[o] for someone's
blood,
let's waylay some harmless soul;
[12]let's swallow them alive, like the
grave,[b]
1:12 [p]Ps 28:1 and whole, like those who go
down to the pit;[p]
[13]we will get all sorts of valuable things
and fill our houses with plunder;
[14]throw in your lot with us,
and we will share a common
purse"—

[a]*7* The Hebrew words rendered *fool* in Proverbs, and often elsewhere in the Old Testament, denote one who is morally deficient. [b]*12* Hebrew *Sheol*

DAY 2 TWO

▸ SELF-CONTROL AND THE PURPOSE OF GOD IN MY LIFE

Proverbs 1:1–6

Self-control is the opening theme of Proverbs. The writer implies that self-control will make those who honor it effective in four areas:

1. *Wisdom.* Wisdom is not intelligence. Wisdom is that God-given ability to use our intelligence to apply what we know to practical living.

2. *Discipline.* Discipline is the ability to do the things that are good for us, rather than opting for those things that are fun or easy for us. For example, Jesus' wilderness temptations involved Satan's allurements to make Jesus the Messiah without the ugly necessity of the cross. But Jesus was not bought off.

3. *Understanding.* Understanding is that gift of God that sits and waits, that sorts and sifts through all the information available before it makes a decision on anything.

4. *Doing what is right.* Many of us have no problem doing this once we have determined what it is. We ought always to pray as Abraham Lincoln did, "Lord, give me the power to do the right, as I can understand what it is."

Our ministry to others is always God's purpose in our life. Proverbs takes those four areas of effectiveness and applies them to our actions. These areas of self-control manifest themselves as we minister to others:

When we offer prudence to the simple—which means that we have a ministry of helping others think things through.

When we hold out discretion for the young. *Brash* is often a more realistic adjective for the young than *discreet.* Yet the young often need a little "cross-generational" insight to help them handle life.

When we give guidance to those who lack the insight and understanding of Proverbs.

Our enhanced understanding of interior truths can only be supplied by more of the grace of God to our lives. Then we can pass along our mature life-lessons to others.

To begin a study on the topic of Self-Control, the Disciplined Life, turn to the home page on page 1367.

15 my son, do not go along with them,
do not set foot[q] on their paths;[r]
16 for their feet rush into sin,
they are swift to shed blood.
17 How useless to spread a net
in full view of all the birds!
18 These men lie in wait for their own blood;[s]
they waylay only themselves!
19 Such is the end of all who go after ill-gotten gain;
it takes away the lives of those who get it.[t]

Warning Against Rejecting Wisdom

20 Wisdom calls aloud[u] in the street,
she raises her voice in the public squares;
21 at the head of the noisy streets[a] she cries out,
in the gateways of the city she makes her speech:
22 "How long will you simple ones[b][v]
love your simple ways?
How long will mockers delight in mockery
and fools hate knowledge?
23 If you had responded to my rebuke,
I would have poured out my heart to you
and made my thoughts known to you.
24 But since you rejected me when I called[w]
and no one gave heed when I stretched out my hand,
25 since you ignored all my advice
and would not accept my rebuke,
26 I in turn will laugh[x] at your disaster;
I will mock when calamity overtakes you[y]—
27 when calamity overtakes you like a storm,
when disaster sweeps over you like a whirlwind,
when distress and trouble overwhelm you.
28 "Then they will call to me but I will not answer;[z]
they will look for me but will not find me.[a]
29 Since they hated knowledge
and did not choose to fear the LORD,[b]
30 since they would not accept my advice
and spurned my rebuke,[c]

1:15 [q]Ps 119:101 [r]Ps 1:1; Pr 4:14
1:16 [s]Pr 6:18; Isa 59:7
1:19 [t]Pr 15:27
1:20 [u]Pr 8:1; 9:1-3,13-15
1:22 [v]Pr 8:5; 9:4,16
1:24 [w]Isa 65:12; 66:4; Jer 7:13; Zec 7:11
1:26 [x]Ps 2:4 [y]Pr 6:15; 10:24
1:28 [z]1Sa 8:18; Isa 1:15; Jer 11:11; Mic 3:4 [a]Job 27:9; Pr 8:17; Eze 8:18; Zec 7:13
1:29 [b]Job 21:14
1:30 [c]ver 25; Ps 81:11

31 they will eat the fruit of their ways
and be filled with the fruit of their schemes.[d]
32 For the waywardness of the simple will kill them,[e]
and the complacency of fools will destroy them;
33 but whoever listens to me will live in safety[f]
and be at ease, without fear of harm."[g]

Moral Benefits of Wisdom

2 My son, if you accept my words
and store up my commands within you,
2 turning your ear to wisdom
and applying your heart to understanding,[h]
3 and if you call out for insight
and cry aloud for understanding,
4 and if you look for it as for silver
and search for it as for hidden treasure,[i]
5 then you will understand the fear of the LORD
and find the knowledge of God.[j]
6 For the LORD gives wisdom,[k]
and from his mouth come knowledge and understanding.
7 He holds victory in store for the upright,
he is a shield[l] to those whose walk is blameless,[m]
8 for he guards the course of the just
and protects the way of his faithful ones.[n]
9 Then you will understand what is right and just
and fair—every good path.
10 For wisdom will enter your heart,[o]
and knowledge will be pleasant to your soul.
11 Discretion will protect you,
and understanding will guard you.[p]
12 Wisdom will save you from the ways of wicked men,
from men whose words are perverse,
13 who leave the straight paths
to walk in dark ways,[q]

1:31 [d]Job 4:8; Pr 14:14; Isa 3:11; Jer 6:19
1:32 [e]Jer 2:19
1:33 [f]Ps 25:12; Pr 3:23 [g]Ps 112:8
2:2 [h]Pr 22:17
2:4 [i]Job 3:21; Pr 3:14; Mt 13:44
2:5 [j]Pr 1:7
2:6 [k]1Ki 3:9,12; Jas 1:5
2:7 [l]Pr 30:5-6 [m]Ps 84:11
2:8 [n]1Sa 2:9; Ps 66:9
2:10 [o]Pr 14:33
2:11 [p]Pr 4:6; 6:22
2:13 [q]Pr 4:19; Jn 3:19

[a]*21* Hebrew; Septuagint / *on the tops of the walls*
[b]*22* The Hebrew word rendered *simple* in Proverbs generally denotes one without moral direction and inclined to evil.

[14]who delight in doing wrong
and rejoice in the perverseness of evil,[r]
[15]whose paths are crooked[s]
and who are devious in their ways.[t]

[16]It will save you also from the adulteress,[u]
from the wayward wife with her seductive words,
[17]who has left the partner of her youth
and ignored the covenant she made before God.[a][v]
[18]For her house leads down to death
and her paths to the spirits of the dead.[w]
[19]None who go to her return
or attain the paths of life.[x]

[20]Thus you will walk in the ways of good men
and keep to the paths of the righteous.
[21]For the upright will live in the land,[y]
and the blameless will remain in it;
[22]but the wicked will be cut off from the land,[z]
and the unfaithful will be torn from it.[a]

Further Benefits of Wisdom

3 My son, do not forget my teaching,[b]
but keep my commands in your heart,
[2]for they will prolong your life many years[c]
and bring you prosperity.

[3]Let love and faithfulness never leave you;
bind them around your neck,
write them on the tablet of your heart.[d]
[4]Then you will win favor and a good name
in the sight of God and man.[e]

[5]Trust in the LORD[f] with all your heart
and lean not on your own understanding;
[6]in all your ways acknowledge him,
and he will make your paths[g] straight.[b][h]

[7]Do not be wise in your own eyes;[i]
fear the LORD and shun evil.[j]
[8]This will bring health to your body[k]
and nourishment to your bones.[l]

[9]Honor the LORD with your wealth,
with the firstfruits[m] of all your crops;
[10]then your barns will be filled[n] to overflowing,
and your vats will brim over with new wine.[o]

[11]My son, do not despise the LORD's discipline[p]
and do not resent his rebuke,
[12]because the LORD disciplines those he loves,[q]
as a father[c] the son he delights in.[r]

[13]Blessed is the man who finds wisdom,
the man who gains understanding,
[14]for she is more profitable than silver
and yields better returns than gold.[s]
[15]She is more precious than rubies;[t]
nothing you desire can compare with her.[u]
[16]Long life is in her right hand;
in her left hand are riches and honor.[v]
[17]Her ways are pleasant ways,
and all her paths are peace.[w]
[18]She is a tree of life[x] to those who embrace her;
those who lay hold of her will be blessed.

[19]By wisdom the LORD laid the earth's foundations,[y]
by understanding he set the heavens[z] in place;
[20]by his knowledge the deeps were divided,
and the clouds let drop the dew.

[21]My son, preserve sound judgment and discernment,
do not let them out of your sight;[a]
[22]they will be life for you,
an ornament to grace your neck.[b]
[23]Then you will go on your way in safety,
and your foot will not stumble;[c]
[24]when you lie down,[d] you will not be afraid;
when you lie down, your sleep[e] will be sweet.
[25]Have no fear of sudden disaster

[a]*17* Or *covenant of her God* [b]*6* Or *will direct your paths* [c]*12* Hebrew; Septuagint / *and he punishes*

2:14 [r]Pr 10:23; Jer 11:15
2:15 [s]Ps 125:5 [t]Pr 21:8
2:16 [u]Pr 5:1-6; 6:20-29; 7:5-27
2:17 [v]Mal 2:14
2:18 [w]Pr 7:27
2:19 [x]Ecc 7:26
2:21 [y]Ps 37:29
2:22 [z]Job 18:17; Ps 37:38 [a]Dt 28:63; Pr 10:30
3:1 [b]Pr 4:5
3:2 [c]Pr 4:10
3:3 [d]Ex 13:9; Pr 6:21; 7:3; 2Co 3:3
3:4 [e]1Sa 2:26; Lk 2:52
3:5 [f]Ps 37:3,5
3:6 [g]1Ch 28:9 [h]Pr 16:3; Isa 45:13
3:7 [i]Ro 12:16 [j]Job 1:1; Pr 16:6
3:8 [k]Pr 4:22 [l]Job 21:24
3:9 [m]Ex 22:29; 23:19; Dt 26:1-15
3:10 [n]Dt 28:8 [o]Joel 2:24
3:11 [p]Job 5:17
3:12 [q]Pr 13:24; Rev 3:19 [r]Dt 8:5; Heb 12:5-6*
3:14 [s]Job 28:15; Pr 8:19; 16:16
3:15 [t]Job 28:18 [u]Pr 8:11
3:16 [v]Pr 8:18
3:17 [w]Pr 16:7; Mt 11:28-30
3:18 [x]Ge 2:9; Pr 11:30; Rev 2:7
3:19 [y]Ps 104:24 [z]Pr 8:27-29
3:21 [a]Pr 4:20-22
3:22 [b]Pr 1:8-9
3:23 [c]Ps 37:24; Pr 4:12
3:24 [d]Lev 26:6; Ps 3:5 [e]Job 11:18

or of the ruin that overtakes the
wicked,
26 for the LORD will be your
confidence
3:26 [f]1Sa 2:9
and will keep your foot[f] from
being snared.
27 Do not withhold good from those
who deserve it,
when it is in your power to act.
28 Do not say to your neighbor,
"Come back later; I'll give it
tomorrow"—
3:28 [g]Lev 19:13; Dt 24:15
when you now have it with you.[g]
29 Do not plot harm against your
neighbor,
who lives trustfully near you.
30 Do not accuse a man for no
reason—
when he has done you no harm.
3:31 [h]Ps 37:1; Pr 24:1-2
31 Do not envy[h] a violent man
or choose any of his ways,
3:32 [i]Pr 11:20 [j]Job 29:4; Ps 25:14
32 for the LORD detests a perverse man[i]
but takes the upright into his
confidence.[j]
3:33 [k]Dt 11:28; Mal 2:2 [l]Zec 5:4 [m]Ps 1:3
33 The LORD's curse[k] is on the house
of the wicked,[l]
but he blesses the home of the
righteous.[m]
3:34 [n]Jas 4:6*; 1Pe 5:5*
34 He mocks proud mockers
but gives grace to the humble.[n]
35 The wise inherit honor,
but fools he holds up to shame.

Wisdom Is Supreme

4:1 [o]Pr 1:8
4 Listen, my sons,[o] to a father's
instruction;
pay attention and gain
understanding.
2 I give you sound learning,
so do not forsake my teaching.
3 When I was a boy in my father's
house,
still tender, and an only child of
my mother,
4 he taught me and said,
"Lay hold of my words with all
your heart;
keep my commands and you will
live.[p]
4:4 [p]Pr 7:2
4:5 [q]Pr 16:16
5 Get wisdom,[q] get understanding;
do not forget my words or swerve
from them.
4:6 [r]2Th 2:10
6 Do not forsake wisdom, and she will
protect you;[r]
love her, and she will watch over
you.

DAY 2 TWO

GOODNESS AND THE PURPOSE OF GOD IN MY LIFE

Proverbs 4:3–4

"Keep my commands and you will live" is counsel that can add years, as well as quality, to our lives. This can be demonstrated with a very practical illustration: American tobacco companies have been sued within a few trillion dollars of their existence. Most of the lawsuits have been brought against the tobacco companies by smokers who have contracted some smoke-related disease such as lung cancer. I would be squarely in favor of the diseased suers except that these sick and dying people invited their diseases by pulling their cigarettes out of a pack one at a time. Each time they drew out a cigarette, they were greeted with a stern warning printed on the package: "Cigarette smoking can be hazardous to your health" or "Cigarette smoking can cause cancer." There it was, the incontrovertible law: Smoke and die! But they smoked and became ill and sued.

God has his own labels and warnings. They appear in Exodus 20. Proverbs 4 says that if you keep his laws, you will live. Otherwise, well . . . This study is to challenge you to get comfortable with God's laws. Indeed, you should love God's laws. God's laws were given because God loves you. He did not snuggle Exodus 20 between Exodus 19 and Exodus 21 to make you miserable. No, he gave his law to give you life upon the earth.

To begin a study on the topic of Goodness, a Contentment With the Commandments, turn to the home page on page 1233.

7 Wisdom is supreme; therefore get
wisdom.
Though it cost all[s] you have,[a] get
understanding.[t]
4:7 [s]Mt 13:44-46 [t]Pr 23:23
8 Esteem her, and she will exalt you;
embrace her, and she will honor
you.[u]
4:8 [u]1Sa 2:30; Pr 3:18
9 She will set a garland of grace on
your head
and present you with a crown of
splendor.[v]"
4:9 [v]Pr 1:8-9

[a]7 Or *Whatever else you get*

PEACE

GOODNESS REHEARSAL

Proverbs 4:6

Rehearse education, and you will only be smart. Rehearse what it takes to understand the heart of God, and you will be wise. Knowledge is bought and sold in marketplaces. Wisdom is purchased by desolation and anguish.

10 Listen, my son, accept what I say,
and the years of your life will be
many.[w]
11 I guide[x] you in the way of wisdom
and lead you along straight paths.
12 When you walk, your steps will not
be hampered;
when you run, you will not
stumble.[y]
13 Hold on to instruction, do not let
it go;
guard it well, for it is your life.[z]
14 Do not set foot on the path of the
wicked
or walk in the way of evil men.[a]
15 Avoid it, do not travel on it;
turn from it and go on your way.
16 For they cannot sleep till they do
evil;[b]
they are robbed of slumber till
they make someone fall.
17 They eat the bread of wickedness
and drink the wine of violence.
18 The path of the righteous[c] is like the
first gleam of dawn,
shining ever brighter till the full
light of day.[d]
19 But the way of the wicked is like
deep darkness;[e]
they do not know what makes
them stumble.

20 My son, pay attention to what I say;
listen closely to my words.[f]
21 Do not let them out of your sight,[g]
keep them within your heart;
22 for they are life to those who find
them
and health to a man's whole body.[h]
23 Above all else, guard your heart,
for it is the wellspring of life.[i]
24 Put away perversity from your
mouth;
keep corrupt talk far from your
lips.
25 Let your eyes look straight ahead,
fix your gaze directly before you.
26 Make level[a] paths for your feet[j]
and take only ways that are firm.
27 Do not swerve to the right or the
left;[k]
keep your foot from evil.

4:10 [w]Pr 3:2
4:11 [x]1Sa 12:23
4:12 [y]Job 18:7; Pr 3:23
4:13 [z]Pr 3:22
4:14 [a]Ps 1:1; Pr 1:15
4:16 [b]Ps 36:4; Mic 2:1
4:18 [c]Isa 26:7 [d]2Sa 23:4; Da 12:3; Mt 5:14; Php 2:15
4:19 [e]Job 18:5; Pr 2:13; Isa 59:9-10; Jn 12:35
4:20 [f]Pr 5:1
4:21 [g]Pr 3:21; 7:1-2
4:22 [h]Pr 3:8; 12:18
4:23 [i]Mt 12:34; Lk 6:45
4:26 [j]Heb 12:13*
4:27 [k]Dt 5:32; 28:14

Warning Against Adultery

5 My son, pay attention to my
wisdom,
listen well to my words[l] of insight,
2 that you may maintain discretion
and your lips may preserve
knowledge.
3 For the lips of an adulteress drip
honey,
and her speech is smoother than
oil;[m]
4 but in the end she is bitter as gall,[n]
sharp as a double-edged sword.
5 Her feet go down to death;
her steps lead straight to the
grave.[b][o]
6 She gives no thought to the way of
life;
her paths are crooked, but she
knows it not.[p]

7 Now then, my sons, listen[q] to me;
do not turn aside from what I say.
8 Keep to a path far from her,[r]
do not go near the door of her
house,
9 lest you give your best strength to
others
and your years to one who is cruel,
10 lest strangers feast on your wealth
and your toil enrich another man's
house.
11 At the end of your life you will
groan,
when your flesh and body are
spent.
12 You will say, "How I hated
discipline!
How my heart spurned
correction![s]
13 I would not obey my teachers
or listen to my instructors.
14 I have come to the brink of utter
ruin
in the midst of the whole
assembly."

15 Drink water from your own cistern,
running water from your own
well.

5:1 [l]Pr 4:20; 22:17
5:3 [m]Ps 55:21; Pr 2:16; 7:5
5:4 [n]Ecc 7:26
5:5 [o]Pr 7:26-27
5:6 [p]Pr 30:20
5:7 [q]Pr 7:24
5:8 [r]Pr 7:1-27
5:12 [s]Pr 1:29; 12:1

[a]*26* Or *Consider the* [b]5 Hebrew *Sheol*

[16]Should your springs overflow in the streets,
your streams of water in the public squares?
[17]Let them be yours alone,
never to be shared with strangers.
[18]May your fountain[t] be blessed,
and may you rejoice in the wife of your youth.[u]
[19]A loving doe, a graceful deer[v]—
may her breasts satisfy you always,
may you ever be captivated by her love.

5:18 [t]SS 4:12-15 [u]Ecc 9:9; Mal 2:14
5:19 [v]SS ; 2:9; 4:5

DAY 2 TWO

Self-Control and the Purpose of God in My Life

Proverbs 5:15–20

This metaphor on fidelity in marriage is one of the most powerful in Scripture. It reminds us that in every marriage sexual fidelity is the hallmark of God's blessing. To drink water from our own cistern means that we have agreed with God that we are willing to practice sexual self-control and that any suggestion of sexual infidelity injures not just our relationship with God but also with our fellow human beings as well. Yet in every age the temptation to be unfaithful endures.

In a recent survey, twelve percent of ministers admitted to having committed sexual indiscretions for which they "had never been caught." While they had apparently gotten away with their sin, none of them felt that their outward purity had enabled them to serve God effectively and whole-heartedly. While it is important to maintain a positive reputation, looking good on the outside is only part of the purpose of God in our lives. God requires pure hearts, willing to serve him. Only self-control provides hearts that are prepared for God's service.

Indeed, we cannot live out God's purpose for our lives while we indulge in immorality. God requires a clean vessel into which he can pour his purposes. Self-control allows us to hear God's voice. Without this voice, we are depraved and incapable of holiness.

To begin a study on the topic of Self-Control, the Path of Coming to Maturity, turn to the home page on page 364.

[20]Why be captivated, my son, by an adulteress?
Why embrace the bosom of another man's wife?
[21]For a man's ways are in full view[w] of the LORD,
and he examines all his paths.[x]
[22]The evil deeds of a wicked man ensnare him;[y]
the cords of his sin hold him fast.[z]
[23]He will die for lack of discipline,[a]
led astray by his own great folly.

5:21 [w]Ps 119:168; Hos 7:2 [x]Job 14:16; Job 31:4; 34:21; Pr 15:3; Jer 16:17; 32:19; Heb 4:13
5:22 [y]Ps 9:16 [z]Nu 32:23; Ps 7:15-16; Pr 1:31-32
5:23 [a]Job 4:21; 36:12

Warnings Against Folly

6 My son, if you have put up security for your neighbor,[b]
if you have struck hands in pledge[c] for another,
[2]if you have been trapped by what you said,
ensnared by the words of your mouth,
[3]then do this, my son, to free yourself,
since you have fallen into your neighbor's hands:
Go and humble yourself;
press your plea with your neighbor!
[4]Allow no sleep to your eyes,
no slumber to your eyelids.[d]
[5]Free yourself, like a gazelle from the hand of the hunter,
like a bird from the snare of the fowler.[e]
[6]Go to the ant, you sluggard;[f]
consider its ways and be wise!

6:1 [b]Pr 17:18 [c]Pr 11:15; 22:26-27
6:4 [d]Ps 132:4
6:5 [e]Ps 91:3
6:6 [f]Pr 20:4

Faithfulness

Insects That Praise

Proverbs 6:6

The ant has been given an agenda by a God it cannot name. Still, God is praised by insects that glorify their Maker, and they show that glory by keeping to his agenda.

[7]It has no commander,
no overseer or ruler,
[8]yet it stores its provisions in summer
and gathers its food at harvest.[g]
[9]How long will you lie there, you sluggard?[h]
When will you get up from your sleep?

6:8 [g]Pr 10:4
6:9 [h]Pr 24:30-34

10 A little sleep, a little slumber,
a little folding of the hands to rest[i]—
11 and poverty[j] will come on you like a bandit
and scarcity like an armed man.[a]

12 A scoundrel and villain,
who goes about with a corrupt mouth,
13 who winks with his eye,[k]
signals with his feet
and motions with his fingers,
14 who plots evil[l] with deceit in his heart—
he always stirs up dissension.[m]
15 Therefore disaster will overtake him in an instant;
he will suddenly be destroyed—without remedy.[n]

16 There are six things the LORD hates,
seven that are detestable to him:
17 haughty eyes,
a lying tongue,[o]
hands that shed innocent blood,[p]
18 a heart that devises wicked schemes,
feet that are quick to rush into evil,[q]
19 a false witness[r] who pours out lies
and a man who stirs up dissension among brothers.[s]

Warning Against Adultery

20 My son, keep your father's commands
and do not forsake your mother's teaching.[t]
21 Bind them upon your heart forever;
fasten them around your neck.[u]
22 When you walk, they will guide you;
when you sleep, they will watch over you;
when you awake, they will speak to you.
23 For these commands are a lamp,
this teaching is a light,[v]
and the corrections of discipline
are the way to life,
24 keeping you from the immoral woman,
from the smooth tongue of the wayward wife.[w]
25 Do not lust in your heart after her beauty
or let her captivate you with her eyes,
26 for the prostitute reduces you to a loaf of bread,
and the adulteress preys upon your very life.[x]
27 Can a man scoop fire into his lap
without his clothes being burned?
28 Can a man walk on hot coals
without his feet being scorched?
29 So is he who sleeps[y] with another man's wife;[z]
no one who touches her will go unpunished.

30 Men do not despise a thief if he steals
to satisfy his hunger when he is starving.
31 Yet if he is caught, he must pay sevenfold,[a]
though it costs him all the wealth of his house.
32 But a man who commits adultery[b] lacks judgment;[c]
whoever does so destroys himself.
33 Blows and disgrace are his lot,
and his shame will never[d] be wiped away;
34 for jealousy[e] arouses a husband's fury,[f]
and he will show no mercy when he takes revenge.
35 He will not accept any compensation;
he will refuse the bribe, however great it is.[g]

Warning Against the Adulteress

7 My son,[h] keep my words
and store up my commands within you.
2 Keep my commands and you will live;[i]
guard my teachings as the apple of your eye.
3 Bind them on your fingers;
write them on the tablet of your heart.[j]
4 Say to wisdom, "You are my sister,"
and call understanding your kinsman;
5 they will keep you from the adulteress,
from the wayward wife with her seductive words.[k]

[a] *11* Or *like a vagrant / and scarcity like a beggar*

6:10 [i]Pr 24:33
6:11 [j]Pr 24:30-34
6:13 [k]Ps 35:19
6:14 [l]Mic 2:1 [m]ver 16-19
6:15 [n]2Ch 36:16
6:17 [o]Ps 120:2; Pr 12:22 [p]Dt 19:10; Isa 1:15; 59:7
6:18 [q]Ge 6:5
6:19 [r]Ps 27:12 [s]ver 12-15
6:20 [t]Pr 1:8
6:21 [u]Pr 3:3; 7:1-3
6:23 [v]Ps 19:8; 119:105
6:24 [w]Pr 2:16; 7:5
6:26 [x]Pr 7:22-23; 29:3
6:29 [y]Ex 20:14 [z]Pr 2:16-19; 5:8
6:31 [a]Ex 22:1-14
6:32 [b]Ex 20:14 [c]Pr 7:7; 9:4,16
6:33 [d]Pr 5:9-14
6:34 [e]Nu 5:14 [f]Ge 34:7
6:35 [g]Job 31:9-11; SS 8:7
7:1 [h]Pr 1:8; 2:1
7:2 [i]Pr 4:4
7:3 [j]Dt 6:8; Pr 3:3
7:5 [k]ver 21; Job 31:9; Pr 2:16; 6:24

6 At the window of my house
I looked out through the lattice.
7 I saw among the simple,
I noticed among the young men,
a youth who lacked judgment.[l]
8 He was going down the street near her corner,
walking along in the direction of her house
9 at twilight,[m] as the day was fading,
as the dark of night set in.

10 Then out came a woman to meet him,
dressed like a prostitute and with crafty intent.
11 (She is loud[n] and defiant,
her feet never stay at home;
12 now in the street, now in the squares,
at every corner she lurks.)[o]
13 She took hold of him[p] and kissed him
and with a brazen face she said:[q]

14 "I have fellowship offerings[a] [r] at home;
today I fulfilled my vows.
15 So I came out to meet you;
I looked for you and have found you!
16 I have covered my bed
with colored linens from Egypt.
17 I have perfumed my bed[s]
with myrrh,[t] aloes and cinnamon.
18 Come, let's drink deep of love till morning;
let's enjoy ourselves with love![u]
19 My husband is not at home;
he has gone on a long journey.
20 He took his purse filled with money
and will not be home till full moon."

21 With persuasive words she led him astray;
she seduced him with her smooth talk.[v]
22 All at once he followed her
like an ox going to the slaughter,
like a deer[b] stepping into a noose[c] [w]
23 till an arrow pierces[x] his liver,
like a bird darting into a snare,
little knowing it will cost him his life.[y]

24 Now then, my sons, listen[z] to me;
pay attention to what I say.
25 Do not let your heart turn to her ways

7:7 [l]Pr 1:22; 6:32
7:9 [m]Job 24:15
7:11 [n]Pr 9:13; 1Ti 5:13
7:12 [o]Pr 8:1-36; 23:26-28
7:13 [p]Ge 39:12 [q]Pr 1:20
7:14 [r]Lev 7:11-18
7:17 [s]Est 1:6; Isa 57:7; Eze 23:41; Am 6:4 [t]Ge 37:25
7:18 [u]Ge 39:7
7:21 [v]Pr 5:3
7:22 [w]Job 18:10
7:23 [x]Job 15:22; 16:13 [y]Pr 6:26; Ecc 7:26; 9:12
7:24 [z]Pr 1:8-9; 5:7; 8:32

or stray into her paths.[a]
26 Many are the victims she has brought down;
her slain are a mighty throng.
27 Her house is a highway to the grave,[d]
leading down to the chambers of death.[b]

Wisdom's Call

8 Does not wisdom call out?[c]
Does not understanding raise her voice?
2 On the heights along the way,
where the paths meet, she takes her stand;
3 beside the gates leading into the city,
at the entrances, she cries aloud:[d]
4 "To you, O men, I call out;
I raise my voice to all mankind.
5 You who are simple,[e] gain prudence;[f]
you who are foolish, gain understanding.
6 Listen, for I have worthy things to say;
I open my lips to speak what is right.
7 My mouth speaks what is true,[g]
for my lips detest wickedness.
8 All the words of my mouth are just;
none of them is crooked or perverse.
9 To the discerning all of them are right;
they are faultless to those who have knowledge.
10 Choose my instruction instead of silver,
knowledge rather than choice gold,[h]
11 for wisdom is more precious[i] than rubies,
and nothing you desire can compare with her.[j]

12 "I, wisdom, dwell together with prudence;
I possess knowledge and discretion.[k]
13 To fear the LORD is to hate evil;[l]
I hate[m] pride and arrogance,
evil behavior and perverse speech.
14 Counsel and sound judgment are mine;
I have understanding and power.[n]

7:25 [a]Pr 5:7-8
7:27 [b]Pr 2:18; 5:5; 9:18; Rev 22:15
8:1 [c]Pr 1:20; 9:3
8:3 [d]Job 29:7
8:5 [e]Pr 1:22 [f]Pr 1:4
8:7 [g]Ps 37:30; Jn 8:14
8:10 [h]Pr 3:14-15
8:11 [i]Job 28:17-19 [j]Pr 3:13-15
8:12 [k]Pr 1:4
8:13 [l]Pr 16:6 [m]Jer 44:4
8:14 [n]Pr 21:22; Ecc 7:19

[a] *14* Traditionally *peace offerings* [b] *22* Syriac (see also Septuagint); Hebrew *fool* [c] *22* The meaning of the Hebrew for this line is uncertain. [d] *27* Hebrew *Sheol*

[15]By me kings reign
and rulers[o] make laws that are just;
[16]by me princes govern,
and all nobles who rule on earth.[a]
[17]I love those who love me,[p]
and those who seek me find me.[q]
[18]With me are riches and honor,[r]
enduring wealth and prosperity.[s]
[19]My fruit is better than fine gold;
what I yield surpasses choice silver.[t]
[20]I walk in the way of righteousness,
along the paths of justice,
[21]bestowing wealth on those who love me
and making their treasuries full.[u]

[22]"The LORD brought me forth as the first of his works,[b,c]
before his deeds of old;
[23]I was appointed[d] from eternity,
from the beginning, before the world began.
[24]When there were no oceans, I was given birth,
when there were no springs abounding with water;[v]
[25]before the mountains were settled in place,
before the hills, I was given birth,[w]
[26]before he made the earth or its fields
or any of the dust of the world.[x]
[27]I was there when he set the heavens in place,[y]
when he marked out the horizon on the face of the deep,
[28]when he established the clouds above
and fixed securely the fountains of the deep,
[29]when he gave the sea its boundary[z]
so the waters would not overstep his command,[a]
and when he marked out the foundations of the earth.[b]
[30]Then I was the craftsman at his side.[c]
I was filled with delight day after day,
rejoicing always in his presence,
[31]rejoicing in his whole world
and delighting in mankind.[d]

[32]"Now then, my sons, listen to me;
blessed are[e] those who keep my ways.[f]
[33]Listen to my instruction and be wise;
do not ignore it.
[34]Blessed is the man who listens[g] to me,
watching daily at my doors,
waiting at my doorway.
[35]For whoever finds me[h] finds life
and receives favor from the LORD.[i]
[36]But whoever fails to find me harms himself;[j]
all who hate me love death."

Invitations of Wisdom and of Folly

9 Wisdom has built[k] her house;
she has hewn out its seven pillars.
[2]She has prepared her meat and mixed her wine;
she has also set her table.[l]
[3]She has sent out her maids, and she calls[m]
from the highest point of the city.[n]
[4]"Let all who are simple come in here!"
she says to those who lack judgment.[o]
[5]"Come, eat my food
and drink the wine I have mixed.[p]
[6]Leave your simple ways and you will live;[q]
walk in the way of understanding.

[7]"Whoever corrects a mocker invites insult;
whoever rebukes a wicked man incurs abuse.[r]
[8]Do not rebuke a mocker[s] or he will hate you;[t]
rebuke a wise man and he will love you.
[9]Instruct a wise man and he will be wiser still;
teach a righteous man and he will add to his learning.[u]

[10]"The fear of the LORD[v] is the beginning of wisdom,
and knowledge of the Holy One is understanding.
[11]For through me your days will be many,
and years will be added to your life.[w]
[12]If you are wise, your wisdom will reward you;

[a]*16* Many Hebrew manuscripts and Septuagint; most Hebrew manuscripts *and nobles—all righteous rulers* [b]*22* Or *way*; or *dominion* [c]*22* Or *The LORD possessed me at the beginning of his work*; or *The LORD brought me forth at the beginning of his work* [d]*23* Or *fashioned*

8:15 [o]Da 2:21; Ro 13:1
8:17 [p]1Sa 2:30; Ps 91:14; Jn 14:21-24 [q]Pr 1:28; Jas 1:5
8:18 [r]Pr 3:16 [s]Dt 8:18; Mt 6:33
8:19 [t]Pr 3:13-14; 10:20
8:21 [u]Pr 24:4
8:24 [v]Ge 7:11
8:25 [w]Job 15:7
8:26 [x]Ps 90:2
8:27 [y]Pr 3:19
8:29 [z]Ge 1:9; Job 38:10; Ps 16:6 [a]Ps 104:9 [b]Job 38:5
8:30 [c]Jn 1:1-3
8:31 [d]Ps 16:3; 104:1-30
8:32 [e]Lk 11:28 [f]Ps 119:1-2
8:34 [g]Pr 3:13,18
8:35 [h]Pr 3:13-18 [i]Pr 12:2
8:36 [j]Pr 15:32
9:1 [k]Eph 2:20-22; 1Pe 2:5
9:2 [l]Lk 14:16-23
9:3 [m]Pr 8:1-3 [n]ver 14
9:4 [o]Pr 6:32
9:5 [p]Isa 55:1
9:6 [q]Pr 8:35
9:7 [r]Pr 23:9
9:8 [s]Pr 15:12 [t]Ps 141:5
9:9 [u]Pr 1:5,7
9:10 [v]Job 28:28; Pr 1:7
9:11 [w]Pr 3:16; 10:27

if you are a mocker, you alone will
suffer."

[9:13 [x]Pr 7:11 [y]Pr 5:6]

13 The woman Folly is loud;[x]
she is undisciplined and without
knowledge.[y]
14 She sits at the door of her house,
on a seat at the highest point of
the city,[z]

[9:14 [z]ver 3]

15 calling out to those who pass by,
who go straight on their way.
16 "Let all who are simple come in
here!"
she says to those who lack
judgment.
17 "Stolen water is sweet;
food eaten in secret is delicious!"[a]

[9:17 [a]Pr 20:17]

18 But little do they know that the dead
are there,
that her guests are in the depths of
the grave.[a] [b]

[9:18 [b]Pr 2:18; 7:26-27]

Proverbs of Solomon

[10:1 [c]Pr 1:1 [d]Pr 15:20; 29:3]

10 The proverbs of Solomon:[c]

A wise son brings joy to his father,[d]
but a foolish son grief to his
mother.

[10:2 [e]Pr 21:6 [f]Pr 11:4,19]

2 Ill-gotten treasures are of no value,[e]
but righteousness delivers from
death.[f]

3 The LORD does not let the righteous
go hungry[g]
but he thwarts the craving of the
wicked.

[10:3 [g]Mt 6:25-34]

4 Lazy hands make a man poor,[h]
but diligent hands bring wealth.[i]

[10:4 [h]Pr 19:15 [i]Pr 12:24; 13:4; 21:5]

5 He who gathers crops in summer is
a wise son,
but he who sleeps during harvest
is a disgraceful son.

6 Blessings crown the head of the
righteous,
but violence overwhelms the
mouth of the wicked.[b] [j]

[10:6 [j]ver 8,11,14]

7 The memory of the righteous[k] will
be a blessing,
but the name of the wicked[l] will
rot.[m]

[10:7 [k]Ps 112:6 [l]Ps 109:13 [m]Ps 9:6]

8 The wise in heart accept commands,
but a chattering fool comes to
ruin.[n]

[10:8 [n]Mt 7:24-27]

9 The man of integrity[o] walks
securely,[p]
but he who takes crooked paths
will be found out.[q]

[10:9 [o]Isa 33:15 [p]Ps 23:4 [q]Pr 28:18]

10 He who winks maliciously[r] causes
grief,
and a chattering fool comes to
ruin.

[10:10 [r]Ps 35:19]

11 The mouth of the righteous is a
fountain of life,[s]
but violence overwhelms the
mouth of the wicked.[t]

[10:11 [s]Ps 37:30; Pr 13:12, 14,19 [t]ver 6]

12 Hatred stirs up dissension,
but love covers over all wrongs.[u]

[10:12 [u]Pr 17:9; 1Co 13:4-7; 1Pe 4:8]

LOVE

"LOVE GOD AND DO WHAT YOU WILL"

Proverbs 10:12

"He values not Christ at all who does not value Christ above all," said Augustine. When our love is steadfast in its ardor, our sin will hold no power to damn us nor even cripple us with guilt. So "love God and do what you will."

13 Wisdom is found on the lips of the
discerning,[v]
but a rod is for the back of him
who lacks judgment.[w]

[10:13 [v]ver 31 [w]Pr 26:3]

14 Wise men store up knowledge,
but the mouth of a fool invites
ruin.[x]

[10:14 [x]Pr 18:6,7]

15 The wealth of the rich is their
fortified city,[y]
but poverty is the ruin of the
poor.[z]

[10:15 [y]Pr 18:11 [z]Pr 19:7]

16 The wages of the righteous bring
them life,
but the income of the wicked
brings them punishment.[a]

[10:16 [a]Pr 11:18-19]

17 He who heeds discipline shows the
way to life,[b]
but whoever ignores correction
leads others astray.

[10:17 [b]Pr 6:23]

18 He who conceals his hatred has lying
lips,
and whoever spreads slander is a
fool.

19 When words are many, sin is not
absent,

[a]*18* Hebrew *Sheol* [b]*6* Or *but the mouth of the wicked conceals violence*; also in verse 11

but he who holds his tongue is wise.[c]

10:19 [c]Pr 17:28; Ecc 5:3; Jas 1:19; 3:2-12

20 The tongue of the righteous is choice silver,
but the heart of the wicked is of little value.

21 The lips of the righteous nourish many,
but fools die for lack of judgment.[d]

10:21 [d]Pr 5:22-23; Hos 4:1,6,14

22 The blessing of the LORD brings wealth,[e]
and he adds no trouble to it.

10:22 [e]Ge 24:35; Ps 37:22

DAY 2 TWO

Gentleness and the Purpose of God in My Life

Proverbs 10:12

Hate does indeed stir dissension—but gentleness brings camaraderie and openness. When we are filled with gentleness, we are able to live out the purposes of God in our lives. For only when we are gentle, will people see us as approachable. Only then will they trust us. Only then will we be able to minister to them.

Ministry is the purpose of God in our lives. Therefore, it is mandatory that we embrace gentleness. The writer of Proverbs says we must always be aware that to harbor any hatred or to permit ourselves any grudge will keep us in such a state of dissension that a gentle spirit will elude us.

"Hatred stirs . . . but love covers," in Proverbs 10:12 really means: Hate agitates . . . love pacifies; hate boils in the soul . . . love sails on a placid sea of forgiveness; hate spreads its cancerous tentacles . . . love removes the ugly tissue of resentment and replaces it with the clean, healed tissue of health.

Watch a person who is filled with hatred. That person will vent, spew and be unable to talk without a vitriolic spirit owning his or her speech.

Conversely, watch a person who is under the compulsion of love. That person will serve Christ, and the manner of service will be gentleness.

To begin a study on the topic of Gentleness, the Approachable Life, turn to the home page on page 306.

23 A fool finds pleasure in evil conduct,[f]
but a man of understanding delights in wisdom.

10:23 [f]Pr 2:14; 15:21

24 What the wicked dreads[g] will overtake him;
what the righteous desire will be granted.[h]

10:24 [g]Isa 66:4 [h]Ps 145:17-19; Mt 5:6; 1Jn 5:14-15

25 When the storm has swept by, the wicked are gone,
but the righteous stand firm[i] forever.[j]

10:25 [i]Ps 15:5 [j]Pr 12:3,7; Mt 7:24-27

26 As vinegar to the teeth and smoke to the eyes,
so is a sluggard to those who send him.[k]

10:26 [k]Pr 26:6

27 The fear of the LORD adds length to life,[l]
but the years of the wicked are cut short.[m]

10:27 [l]Pr 9:10-11 [m]Job 15:32

28 The prospect of the righteous is joy,
but the hopes of the wicked come to nothing.[n]

10:28 [n]Job 8:13; Pr 11:7

29 The way of the LORD is a refuge for the righteous,
but it is the ruin of those who do evil.[o]

10:29 [o]Pr 21:15

30 The righteous will never be uprooted,
but the wicked will not remain in the land.[p]

10:30 [p]Ps 37:9,28-29; Pr 2:20-22

31 The mouth of the righteous brings forth wisdom,[q]
but a perverse tongue will be cut out.

10:31 [q]Ps 37:30

32 The lips of the righteous know what is fitting,[r]
but the mouth of the wicked only what is perverse.

10:32 [r]Ecc 10:12

11 The LORD abhors dishonest scales,[s]
but accurate weights are his delight.[t]

11:1 [s]Lev 19:36; Dt 25:13-16; Pr 20:10,23 [t]Pr 16:11

2 When pride comes, then comes disgrace,[u]
but with humility comes wisdom.[v]

11:2 [u]Pr 16:18 [v]Pr 18:12; 29:23

3 The integrity of the upright guides them,
but the unfaithful are destroyed by their duplicity.[w]

11:3 [w]Pr 13:6

11:4 [x]Eze 7:19; Zep 1:18 [y]Ge 7:1; Pr 10:2

[4]Wealth is worthless in the day of
wrath,[x]
but righteousness delivers from
death.[y]

11:5 [z]Pr 5:21-23

[5]The righteousness of the blameless
makes a straight way for
them,
but the wicked are brought down
by their own wickedness.[z]

[6]The righteousness of the upright
delivers them,
but the unfaithful are trapped by
evil desires.

DAY FOUR

▸ KINDNESS AND MY SERVICE TO OTHERS

Proverbs 11:16–17

This passage uses the word *ruthless*, and *ruthless* is a word that not only isn't kind, but is actually cruel. Kind people care when those around them hurt. Ruthless people do not. There is a little rhyme that goes:

I rode on my motor bike. Ruth rode in
back of me.
Suddenly I hit a bump and rode on
Ruth-lessly.

This is a fair illustration of the uncaring nature of the ruthless.

Kindness is quite the opposite as it paves the way to grace and to the service of others. Evangeline Booth, it is said, one day rescued a homeless person from the sidewalks. She took the woman into one of the Salvation Army hostels and began to care for her. The woman she rescued was unconscious and did not revive for a few hours. But just as Evangeline Booth leaned over and kissed her, the woman regained consciousness. The woman responded, "Thank you for doing that. Ain't nobody done that since my mama died."

Grace that saves sometimes waits for kindness to pave the way. If you want to win people to Christ, steep yourself in kindness. Spend no more time memorizing Scripture than you spend kissing the unconscious awake.

To begin a study on the topic of Kindness, the Approach to Grace, turn to the home page on page 343.

[7]When a wicked man dies, his hope
perishes;
all he expected from his power
comes to nothing.[a] 11:7 [a]Pr 10:28

[8]The righteous man is rescued from
trouble,
and it comes on the wicked
instead.[b] 11:8 [b]Pr 21:18

[9]With his mouth the godless destroys
his neighbor,
but through knowledge the
righteous escape.

[10]When the righteous prosper, the city
rejoices;[c] 11:10 [c]Pr 28:12
when the wicked perish, there are
shouts of joy.

[11]Through the blessing of the upright
a city is exalted,
but by the mouth of the wicked it
is destroyed.[d] 11:11 [d]Pr 29:8

[12]A man who lacks judgment derides
his neighbor,[e] 11:12 [e]Pr 14:21
but a man of understanding holds
his tongue.

[13]A gossip betrays a confidence,[f] 11:13 [f]Lev 19:16; Pr 20:19; 1Ti 5:13
but a trustworthy man keeps a
secret.

[14]For lack of guidance a nation falls,[g] 11:14 [g]Pr 20:18 [h]Pr 15:22; 24:6
but many advisers make victory
sure.[h]

[15]He who puts up security[i] for another 11:15 [i]Pr 6:1
will surely suffer,
but whoever refuses to strike
hands in pledge is safe.

[16]A kindhearted woman gains
respect,[j] 11:16 [j]Pr 31:31
but ruthless men gain only wealth.

[17]A kind man benefits himself,
but a cruel man brings trouble on
himself.

[18]The wicked man earns deceptive
wages,
but he who sows righteousness
reaps a sure reward.[k] 11:18 [k]Hos 10:12-13

[19]The truly righteous man attains life,
but he who pursues evil goes to
his death.

[20]The LORD detests men of perverse
heart 11:20 [l]1Ch 29:17; Ps 119:1; Pr 12:2,22
but he delights in those whose
ways are blameless.[l]

21 Be sure of this: The wicked will not
go unpunished,
but those who are righteous will
go free.[m]

11:21 [m]Pr 16:5

22 Like a gold ring in a pig's snout
is a beautiful woman who shows
no discretion.

23 The desire of the righteous ends only
in good,
but the hope of the wicked only
in wrath.

24 One man gives freely, yet gains even
more;
another withholds unduly, but
comes to poverty.

25 A generous man will prosper;
he who refreshes others will
himself be refreshed.[n]

11:25 [n]Mt 5:7; 2Co 9:6-9

26 People curse the man who hoards
grain,
but blessing crowns him who is
willing to sell.

27 He who seeks good finds goodwill,
but evil comes to him who
searches for it.[o]

11:27 [o]Est 7:10; Ps 7:15-16

28 Whoever trusts in his riches will fall,[p]
but the righteous will thrive like a
green leaf.[q]

11:28 [p]Job 31:24-28; Ps 49:6; 52:7; Mk 10:25; 1Ti 6:17 [q]Ps 1:3; 92:12-14; Jer 17:8

29 He who brings trouble on his family
will inherit only wind,
and the fool will be servant to the
wise.[r]

11:29 [r]Pr 14:19

30 The fruit of the righteous is a tree
of life,[s]
and he who wins souls is wise.

11:30 [s]Jas 5:20

31 If the righteous receive their due[t] on
earth,
how much more the ungodly and
the sinner!

11:31 [t]Pr 13:21; Jer 25:29; 1Pe 4:18

12 Whoever loves discipline loves
knowledge,
but he who hates correction is
stupid.[u]

12:1 [u]Pr 9:7-9; 15:5,10,12,32

2 A good man obtains favor from the
LORD,
but the LORD condemns a crafty
man.

3 A man cannot be established
through wickedness,
but the righteous cannot be
uprooted.[v]

12:3 [v]Pr 10:25

4 A wife of noble character is her
husband's crown,
but a disgraceful wife is like decay
in his bones.[w]

12:4 [w]Pr 14:30

5 The plans of the righteous are just,
but the advice of the wicked is
deceitful.

6 The words of the wicked lie in wait
for blood,
but the speech of the upright
rescues them.[x]

12:6 [x]Pr 14:3

7 Wicked men are overthrown and are
no more,[y]
but the house of the righteous
stands firm.[z]

12:7 [y]Ps 37:36 [z]Pr 10:25

8 A man is praised according to his
wisdom,
but men with warped minds are
despised.

9 Better to be a nobody and yet have
a servant
than pretend to be somebody and
have no food.

10 A righteous man cares for the needs
of his animal,
but the kindest acts of the wicked
are cruel.

11 He who works his land will have
abundant food,
but he who chases fantasies lacks
judgment.[a]

12:11 [a]Pr 28:19

12 The wicked desire the plunder of evil
men,
but the root of the righteous
flourishes.

13 An evil man is trapped by his sinful
talk,[b]
but a righteous man escapes
trouble.[c]

12:13 [b]Pr 18:7 [c]Pr 21:23; 2Pe 2:9

14 From the fruit of his lips a man is
filled with good things[d]
as surely as the work of his hands
rewards him.[e]

12:14 [d]Pr 13:2; 15:23; 18:20 [e]Isa 3:10-11

15 The way of a fool seems right to
him,[f]
but a wise man listens to advice.

12:15 [f]Pr 14:12; 16:2,25; Lk 18:11

16 A fool shows his annoyance at once,
but a prudent man overlooks an
insult.[g]

12:16 [g]Pr 29:11

17 A truthful witness gives honest testimony,
but a false witness tells lies.[h]
18 Reckless words pierce like a sword,[i]
but the tongue of the wise brings healing.[j]
19 Truthful lips endure forever,
but a lying tongue lasts only a moment.

12:17 [h]Pr 14:5,25
12:18 [i]Ps 57:4 [j]Pr 15:4

DAY 5 FIVE

▸ PEACE AND ITS PLACE IN MY PERSONAL WORSHIP

Proverbs 12:20

There is indeed "deceit in the hearts of those who plot evil." But there is also joy in the hearts of "those who promote peace." Peace brings joy. Once again the angels at the nativity remind us of this relationship. Joy is the watchword of the Christmas season, but then so is peace.

In the spring of 1945, Mrs. Pace called us into the tiny auditorium of Woodrow Wilson Grade School and told us that the war with Germany was over. The European Theater was at last silent. In response, we celebrated. From inside the school, I could hear the firecrackers going off in the town. This little scene occurred in Enid, Oklahoma, where I grew up. I could not even imagine how far Berlin was from our hometown center of life in Garfield County, but the announcement of peace was indeed a pronouncement of worldwide joy. Even there in Enid, this announcement of peace brought dancing in the streets.

Peace brings joy!

That very year was the year that I came to faith in Christ. I learned—even as a nine-year-old child—that peace quieted the human heart on quite another level. The final year of the war had been a terrible ordeal for me. I had suffered much that year as I watched my mother agonizing over the news from all the U.S. fronts. My older sisters were all married to servicemen. So when Jesus entered my life, peace calmed my childish heart, and joy—a welcome reprieve after so many joyless years—was mine and has remained mine to this day.

To begin a study on the topic of Peace and the Prince of Peace, turn to the home page on page 19.

20 There is deceit in the hearts of those who plot evil,
but joy for those who promote peace.
21 No harm befalls the righteous,[k]
but the wicked have their fill of trouble.
22 The LORD detests lying lips,[l]
but he delights in men who are truthful.[m]
23 A prudent man keeps his knowledge to himself,[n]
but the heart of fools blurts out folly.
24 Diligent hands will rule,
but laziness ends in slave labor.[o]
25 An anxious heart weighs a man down,[p]
but a kind word cheers him up.
26 A righteous man is cautious in friendship,[a]
but the way of the wicked leads them astray.
27 The lazy man does not roast[b] his game,
but the diligent man prizes his possessions.
28 In the way of righteousness there is life;[q]
along that path is immortality.

13

A wise son heeds his father's instruction,
but a mocker does not listen to rebuke.[r]
2 From the fruit of his lips a man enjoys good things,[s]
but the unfaithful have a craving for violence.
3 He who guards his lips[t] guards his life,[u]
but he who speaks rashly will come to ruin.[v]
4 The sluggard craves and gets nothing,
but the desires of the diligent are fully satisfied.
5 The righteous hate what is false,
but the wicked bring shame and disgrace.

12:21 [k]Ps 91:10
12:22 [l]Pr 6:17; Rev 22:15 [m]Pr 11:20
12:23 [n]Pr 10:14; 13:16
12:24 [o]Pr 10:4
12:25 [p]Pr 15:13; Isa 50:4
12:28 [q]Dt 30:15
13:1 [r]Pr 10:1
13:2 [s]Pr 12:14
13:3 [t]Jas 3:2 [u]Pr 21:23 [v]Pr 18:7, 20-21

[a]*26* Or *man is a guide to his neighbor* [b]*27* The meaning of the Hebrew for this word is uncertain.

6 Righteousness guards the man of integrity,
but wickedness overthrows the sinner.[w]

7 One man pretends to be rich, yet has nothing;
another pretends to be poor, yet has great wealth.[x]

8 A man's riches may ransom his life,
but a poor man hears no threat.

9 The light of the righteous shines brightly,
but the lamp of the wicked is snuffed out.[y]

10 Pride only breeds quarrels,
but wisdom is found in those who take advice.

11 Dishonest money dwindles away,[z]
but he who gathers money little by little makes it grow.

12 Hope deferred makes the heart sick,
but a longing fulfilled is a tree of life.

13 He who scorns instruction will pay for it,[a]
but he who respects a command is rewarded.

14 The teaching of the wise is a fountain of life,[b]
turning a man from the snares of death.[c]

15 Good understanding wins favor,
but the way of the unfaithful is hard.[a]

16 Every prudent man acts out of knowledge,
but a fool exposes his folly.[d]

17 A wicked messenger falls into trouble,
but a trustworthy envoy brings healing.[e]

18 He who ignores discipline comes to poverty and shame,
but whoever heeds correction is honored.[f]

19 A longing fulfilled is sweet to the soul,
but fools detest turning from evil.

20 He who walks with the wise grows wise,
but a companion of fools suffers harm.[g]

21 Misfortune pursues the sinner,
but prosperity is the reward of the righteous.[h]

22 A good man leaves an inheritance for his children's children,
but a sinner's wealth is stored up for the righteous.[i]

23 A poor man's field may produce abundant food,
but injustice sweeps it away.

24 He who spares the rod hates his son,
but he who loves him is careful to discipline him.[j]

25 The righteous eat to their hearts' content,
but the stomach of the wicked goes hungry.[k]

14 The wise woman builds her house,[l]
but with her own hands the foolish one tears hers down.

2 He whose walk is upright fears the LORD,
but he whose ways are devious despises him.

3 A fool's talk brings a rod to his back,
but the lips of the wise protect them.[m]

4 Where there are no oxen, the manger is empty,
but from the strength of an ox comes an abundant harvest.

5 A truthful witness does not deceive,
but a false witness pours out lies.[n]

6 The mocker seeks wisdom and finds none,
but knowledge comes easily to the discerning.

7 Stay away from a foolish man,
for you will not find knowledge on his lips.

8 The wisdom of the prudent is to give thought to their ways,
but the folly of fools is deception.[o]

9 Fools mock at making amends for sin,

[a] *15* Or *unfaithful does not endure*

13:6 [w]Pr 11:3,5
13:7 [x]2Co 6:10
13:9 [y]Job 18:5; Pr 4:18-19; 24:20
13:11 [z]Pr 10:2
13:13 [a]Nu 15:31; 2Ch 36:16
13:14 [b]Pr 10:11 [c]Pr 14:27
13:16 [d]Pr 12:23
13:17 [e]Pr 25:13
13:18 [f]Pr 15:5,31-32
13:20 [g]Pr 15:31
13:21 [h]Ps 32:10
13:22 [i]Job 27:17; Ecc 2:26
13:24 [j]Pr 19:18; 22:15; 23:13-14; 29:15,17; Heb 12:7
13:25 [k]Ps 34:10; Pr 10:3
14:1 [l]Pr 24:3
14:3 [m]Pr 12:6
14:5 [n]Pr 6:19; 12:17
14:8 [o]ver 24

but goodwill is found among the
upright.

10 Each heart knows its own bitterness,
and no one else can share its joy.

11 The house of the wicked will be
destroyed,
but the tent of the upright will
14:11 [p]Pr 3:33; 12:7
flourish.[p]

14:12 [q]Pr 12:15 [r]Pr 16:25
12 There is a way that seems right to a
man,[q]
but in the end it leads to death.[r]

GOODNESS

ONE WAY STREET

Proverbs 14:12

There is but one way to God, though there seem to be many. Why do you waver between opinions? Call out to any god the world will name. Then let the true God buy you with his blood. You will see. There is but one way.

14:13 [s]Ecc 2:2
13 Even in laughter[s] the heart may ache,
and joy may end in grief.

14:14 [t]Pr 1:31 [u]Pr 12:14
14 The faithless will be fully repaid for
their ways,[t]
and the good man rewarded for
his.[u]

15 A simple man believes anything,
but a prudent man gives thought
to his steps.

14:16 [v]Pr 22:3
16 A wise man fears the LORD and
shuns evil,[v]
but a fool is hotheaded and
reckless.

14:17 [w]ver 29
17 A quick-tempered man does foolish
things,[w]
and a crafty man is hated.

18 The simple inherit folly,
but the prudent are crowned with
knowledge.

19 Evil men will bow down in the
presence of the good,
and the wicked at the gates of the
14:19 [x]Pr 11:29
righteous.[x]

20 The poor are shunned even by their
neighbors,
14:20 [y]Pr 19:4,7
but the rich have many friends.[y]

14:21 [z]Pr 11:12 [a]Ps 41:1; Pr 19:17
21 He who despises his neighbor sins,[z]
but blessed is he who is kind to
the needy.[a]

22 Do not those who plot evil go
astray?
But those who plan what is good
find[a] love and faithfulness.

23 All hard work brings a profit,
but mere talk leads only to
poverty.

24 The wealth of the wise is their
crown,
but the folly of fools yields folly.

25 A truthful witness saves lives,
but a false witness is deceitful.[b] 14:25 [b]ver 5

26 He who fears the LORD has a secure
fortress,[c] 14:26 [c]Pr 18:10; 19:23; Isa 33:6
and for his children it will be a
refuge.

27 The fear of the LORD is a fountain
of life,
turning a man from the snares of 14:27 [d]Pr 13:14
death.[d]

28 A large population is a king's glory,
but without subjects a prince is
ruined.

29 A patient man has great
understanding,
but a quick-tempered man 14:29 [e]Ecc 7:8-9; Jas 1:19
displays folly.[e]

30 A heart at peace gives life to the
body,
but envy rots the bones.[f] 14:30 [f]Pr 12:4

31 He who oppresses the poor shows 14:31 [g]Pr 17:5
contempt for their Maker,[g]
but whoever is kind to the needy
honors God.

32 When calamity comes, the wicked 14:32 [h]Pr 6:15 [i]Job 13:15; 2Ti 4:18
are brought down,[h]
but even in death the righteous
have a refuge.[i]

33 Wisdom reposes in the heart of the 14:33 [j]Pr 2:6-10
discerning[j]
and even among fools she lets
herself be known.[b]

34 Righteousness exalts a nation,[k] 14:34 [k]Pr 11:11
but sin is a disgrace to any people.

35 A king delights in a wise servant,
but a shameful servant incurs his 14:35 [l]Mt 24:45-51; 25:14-30
wrath.[l]

[a]*22 Or show* [b]*33* Hebrew; Septuagint and Syriac / *but in the heart of fools she is not known*

15

15:1 [m]Pr 25:15

A gentle answer turns away wrath,[m]
but a harsh word stirs up anger.

[2]The tongue of the wise commends knowledge,
but the mouth of the fool gushes folly.[n]

15:2 [n]Pr 12:23

15:3 [o]2Ch 16:9 [p]Job 31:4; Heb 4:13 [q]Job 34:21; Jer 16:17

[3]The eyes[o] of the LORD are everywhere,[p]
keeping watch on the wicked and the good.[q]

[4]The tongue that brings healing is a tree of life,
but a deceitful tongue crushes the spirit.

[5]A fool spurns his father's discipline,
but whoever heeds correction shows prudence.[r]

15:5 [r]Pr 13:1

[6]The house of the righteous contains great treasure,[s]
but the income of the wicked brings them trouble.

15:6 [s]Pr 8:21

[7]The lips of the wise spread knowledge;
not so the hearts of fools.

[8]The LORD detests the sacrifice of the wicked,[t]
but the prayer of the upright pleases him.[u]

15:8 [t]Pr 21:27; Isa 1:11; Jer 6:20 [u]ver 29

[9]The LORD detests the way of the wicked
but he loves those who pursue righteousness.[v]

15:9 [v]Pr 21:21; 1Ti 6:11

[10]Stern discipline awaits him who leaves the path;
he who hates correction will die.[w]

15:10 [w]Pr 1:31-32; 5:12

[11]Death and Destruction[a] lie open before the LORD[x]—
how much more the hearts of men![y]

15:11 [x]Job 26:6; Ps 139:8 [y]2Ch 6:30; Ps 44:21

[12]A mocker resents correction;[z]
he will not consult the wise.

15:12 [z]Am 5:10

[13]A happy heart makes the face cheerful,
but heartache crushes the spirit.[a]

15:13 [a]Pr 12:25; 17:22; 18:14

[14]The discerning heart seeks knowledge,[b]
but the mouth of a fool feeds on folly.

15:14 [b]Pr 18:15

[15]All the days of the oppressed are wretched,
but the cheerful heart has a continual feast.[c]

15:15 [c]ver 13

[a]11 Hebrew *Sheol and Abaddon*

DAY 4 FOUR

▸ PATIENCE AND MY SERVICE TO OTHERS

Proverbs 15:18

We all want to serve others, but we have noticed that there is some truth in the philosopher Jean Paul Sartre's sour adage that "hell is other people." It is so hard to be patient when the kingdom of God seems to be filled with those who have been saved but have done so little growing in the image of Christ. But we must be honest here. It is sometimes easier to overlook our own immaturity when we see the same quality in someone else. O that we might be so generous to excuse the same faults in others that we see in ourselves!

We sing so many songs like, "*When we all get to heaven, what a day of rejoicing that will be.*" But the truth is that we are going to be with a lot of people up there who didn't necessarily bring us much joy down here. There is an old rhyme that expresses the very difficult task of living with God's people and liking it:

To live above with saints we love, oh that will be the glory, but
To live below with saints we know, well that's a different story.

It is hard to be patient with those we know. One Sunday after a particularly hard and ugly business conference, where members of the congregation were praying through clenched teeth, my son remarked to me on the way home from church, "Dad, will all these people be in heaven?"

"Most of them, Son," I allowed.

"Well," he said, "When I get to heaven, I'm going to ask to live by some new people that I don't know so well."

No wonder the book of Proverbs blesses the men and women who pour the oil of peace and patience on human squabbles. Surely such patience invites the blessings of God.

To begin a study on the topic of Patience Brings the Blessing of God, turn to the home page on page 1476.

16 Better a little with the fear of the LORD
than great wealth with turmoil.[d]

17 Better a meal of vegetables where there is love
than a fattened calf with hatred.[e]

18 A hot-tempered man stirs up dissension,[f]
but a patient man calms a quarrel.[g]

19 The way of the sluggard is blocked with thorns,[h]
but the path of the upright is a highway.

20 A wise son brings joy to his father,[i]
but a foolish man despises his mother.

21 Folly delights a man who lacks judgment,[j]
but a man of understanding keeps a straight course.

22 Plans fail for lack of counsel,
but with many advisers they succeed.[k]

23 A man finds joy in giving an apt reply[l]—
and how good is a timely word![m]

24 The path of life leads upward for the wise
to keep him from going down to the grave.[a]

25 The LORD tears down the proud man's house[n]
but he keeps the widow's boundaries intact.[o]

26 The LORD detests the thoughts of the wicked,[p]
but those of the pure are pleasing to him.

27 A greedy man brings trouble to his family,
but he who hates bribes will live.[q]

28 The heart of the righteous weighs its answers,[r]
but the mouth of the wicked gushes evil.

29 The LORD is far from the wicked
but he hears the prayer of the righteous.[s]

30 A cheerful look brings joy to the heart,
and good news gives health to the bones.

31 He who listens to a life-giving rebuke
will be at home among the wise.[t]

32 He who ignores discipline despises himself,[u]
but whoever heeds correction gains understanding.

33 The fear of the LORD[v] teaches a man wisdom,[b]
and humility comes before honor.[w]

16

1 To man belong the plans of the heart,
but from the LORD comes the reply of the tongue.[x]

2 All a man's ways seem innocent to him,
but motives are weighed by the LORD.[y]

3 Commit to the LORD whatever you do,
and your plans will succeed.[z]

4 The LORD works out everything for his own ends[a]—
even the wicked for a day of disaster.[b]

5 The LORD detests all the proud of heart.[c]
Be sure of this: They will not go unpunished.[d]

6 Through love and faithfulness sin is atoned for;
through the fear of the LORD a man avoids evil.[e]

7 When a man's ways are pleasing to the LORD,
he makes even his enemies live at peace with him.

8 Better a little with righteousness
than much gain[f] with injustice.

9 In his heart a man plans his course,
but the LORD determines his steps.[g]

10 The lips of a king speak as an oracle,
and his mouth should not betray justice.

15:16 [d]Ps 37:16-17; Pr 16:8; 1Ti 6:6
15:17 [e]Pr 17:1
15:18 [f]Pr 26:21 [g]Ge 13:8
15:19 [h]Pr 22:5
15:20 [i]Pr 10:1
15:21 [j]Pr 10:23
15:22 [k]Pr 11:14
15:23 [l]Pr 12:14 [m]Pr 25:11
15:25 [n]Pr 12:7 [o]Dt 19:14; Ps 68:5-6; Pr 23:10-11
15:26 [p]Pr 6:16
15:27 [q]Ex 23:8; Isa 33:15
15:28 [r]1Pe 3:15
15:29 [s]Ps 145:18-19
15:31 [t]ver 5
15:32 [u]Pr 1:7
15:33 [v]Pr 1:7 [w]Pr 18:12
16:1 [x]Pr 19:21
16:2 [y]Pr 21:2
16:3 [z]Ps 37:5-6; Pr 3:5-6
16:4 [a]Isa 43:7 [b]Ro 9:22
16:5 [c]Pr 6:16 [d]Pr 11:20-21
16:6 [e]Pr 14:16
16:8 [f]Ps 37:16
16:9 [g]Jer 10:23

[a]24 Hebrew *Sheol* [b]33 Or *Wisdom teaches the fear of the LORD*

WEEK 23 KINDNESS

DAY ONE
1 KINDNESS, ANGER WASHED BY GRACE

Read Proverbs 16:32

This proverb seems to be preaching patience more than kindness, but consider its instruction in a deeper way. Examine the proverbs on either side of this one. Proverbs 16:31 says, "Gray hair is a crown of splendor; it is attained by a righteous life." Proverbs 16:33 says, "The lot is cast into the lap, but its every decision is from the LORD." These three proverbs taken together seem to speak of a lifestyle controlled by God.

Kindness is the hallmark of God's control of our lives. People who have submitted themselves to God's control exhibit this grace. What is the evidence of kindness in life? Kind people are interruptible. They can stop what they are doing and care for others. Jesus' biography appears sometimes a haphazard hodgepodge of good deeds. Why is this so when he came to establish the kingdom of God? Because Jesus' compassion allowed him to be interrupted by the needs of others; his great heart of kindness could not pass by anyone's call for help. So he established the kingdom, but never by being unkind to the needy who thronged about him throughout his ministry.

When Jesus was on his way to heal the daughter of a very important religious official, a woman touched him in order to be healed (see Luke 8:40–48). Did Jesus rebuke the woman for her audacity? Did Jesus become angry that his schedule had been interrupted? Not at all—Jesus said to the woman, "Daughter, your faith has healed you. Go in peace." Kindness is controlling our emotions and allowing the needs of others to interrupt our scheduled lives.

The world is looking for kindness. When people see our lives of openness and accessibility, then God opens a door for us to minister to them. In fact, kindness paves the way for our service. Kindness brings God close to those who need him.

DAY TWO
2 KINDNESS AND THE PURPOSE OF GOD IN MY LIFE

"Better a patient man than a warrior, a man who controls his temper than one who takes a city" (Proverbs 16:32). Angry people do not serve the world well. In fact, anger distorts our vision. Angry people have murdered when they didn't want to, brutalized their loving supporters or lashed out in verbal abuse—all because the person got so angry he or she was no longer in control. Yet when people who struggle with anger allow God to scrub up their tempers, they are capable of great kindness. *Turn to 2 Kings 5:1,8–15, page 429, for today's study.*

DAY THREE
3 KINDNESS AND MY RELATIONSHIP WITH CHRIST

Peter was probably more of a fisherman than a warrior. A better soldier would have disemboweled the arresting troops as they came for Jesus. Peter became a mad hacker, chopping ears in a foolish attempt to defend his Lord. Jesus told him to put up his sword. Ear-chopping was a pitiful and small response in light of all Christ had come to achieve by establishing his kingdom. *Turn to John 18:10–11, page 1276, for today's study.*

DAY FOUR
4 KINDNESS AND MY SERVICE TO OTHERS

Here are lepers, who, given the years of contempt from the healthy, might have enjoyed the bounty of their discovery without a thought for others. What is it that makes a grudging leper kind? Well, oddly, there are lepers who are others-motivated. Sometimes the most diseased of souls may become kind when grudges are washed by the grace of God. Such outcasts then become lepers to be celebrated. *Turn to 2 Kings 7:3–11, page 432, for today's study.*

DAY FIVE
5 KINDNESS AND ITS PLACE IN MY PERSONAL WORSHIP

"I will praise you, O LORD, with all my heart," says Psalm 138:1. How washed by grace is this verse when compared with Psalm 137:8–9! Psalm 137 is filled with violations and violence. But Jesus admonishes his followers to forgive and be free of hate. If we clean away hate, love will fit perfectly in the space it leaves, and we will worship God with all of our hearts. *Turn to Psalm 137, page 723, for today's study.*

MEMORIZE THIS WEEK

EPHESIANS 4:26-27

"In your anger do not sin": Do not let the sun go down while you are still angry, and do not give the devil a foothold.

Week 24, Goodness Implanted Into Our Lives Through Christ, begins on page 1484, James 2:20–24. To begin a topical study on the Fruit of the Spirit, Kindness, turn to the Topical Index, page 1548.

[11]Honest scales and balances are from the LORD;
all the weights in the bag are of his making.[h]
16:11 [h]Pr 11:1

[12]Kings detest wrongdoing,
for a throne is established through righteousness.[i]
16:12 [i]Pr 25:5

[13]Kings take pleasure in honest lips;
they value a man who speaks the truth.[j]
16:13 [j]Pr 14:35

[14]A king's wrath is a messenger of death,[k]
but a wise man will appease it.
16:14 [k]Pr 19:12

[15]When a king's face brightens, it means life;[l]
his favor is like a rain cloud in spring.
16:15 [l]Job 29:24

[16]How much better to get wisdom than gold,
to choose understanding rather than silver![m]
16:16 [m]Pr 8:10,19

[17]The highway of the upright avoids evil;
he who guards his way guards his life.

[18]Pride goes before destruction,
a haughty spirit before a fall.[n]
16:18 [n]Pr 11:2; 18:12

[19]Better to be lowly in spirit and among the oppressed
than to share plunder with the proud.

[20]Whoever gives heed to instruction prospers,
and blessed is he who trusts in the LORD.[o]
16:20 [o]Ps 2:12; 34:8; Pr 19:8; Jer 17:7

[21]The wise in heart are called discerning,
and pleasant words promote instruction.[a][p]
16:21 [p]ver 23

[22]Understanding is a fountain of life to those who have it,[q]
but folly brings punishment to fools.
16:22 [q]Pr 13:14

[23]A wise man's heart guides his mouth,
and his lips promote instruction.[b]

[24]Pleasant words are a honeycomb,
sweet to the soul and healing to the bones.[r]
16:24 [r]Pr 24:13-14

[25]There is a way that seems right to a man,[s]
but in the end it leads to death.[t]
16:25 [s]Pr 12:15 [t]Pr 14:12

[26]The laborer's appetite works for him;
his hunger drives him on.

[27]A scoundrel plots evil,
and his speech is like a scorching fire.[u]
16:27 [u]Jas 3:6

[28]A perverse man stirs up dissension,[v]
and a gossip separates close friends.[w]
16:28 [v]Pr 15:18 [w]Pr 17:9

[29]A violent man entices his neighbor
and leads him down a path that is not good.[x]
16:29 [x]Pr 1:10; 12:26

[30]He who winks with his eye is plotting perversity;
he who purses his lips is bent on evil.

[31]Gray hair is a crown of splendor;[y]
it is attained by a righteous life.
16:31 [y]Pr 20:29

[32]Better a patient man than a warrior,
a man who controls his temper than one who takes a city.

[33]The lot is cast into the lap,
but its every decision is from the LORD.[z]
16:33 [z]Pr 18:18; 29:26

17 Better a dry crust with peace and quiet
than a house full of feasting,[c] with strife.[a]
17:1 [a]Pr 15:16,17

[2]A wise servant will rule over a disgraceful son,
and will share the inheritance as one of the brothers.

[3]The crucible for silver and the furnace for gold,[b]
but the LORD tests the heart.[c]
17:3 [b]Pr 27:21 [c]1Ch 29:17; Ps 26:2; Jer 17:10

[4]A wicked man listens to evil lips;
a liar pays attention to a malicious tongue.

[5]He who mocks the poor shows contempt for their Maker;[d]
whoever gloats over disaster[e] will not go unpunished.[f]
17:5 [d]Pr 14:31 [e]Job 31:29 [f]Ob 1:12

[6]Children's children[g] are a crown to the aged,
and parents are the pride of their children.
17:6 [g]Pr 13:22

[7]Arrogant[d] lips are unsuited to a fool—

[a]*21* Or *words make a man persuasive* [b]*23* Or *mouth / and makes his lips persuasive* [c]*1* Hebrew *sacrifices* [d]*7* Or *Eloquent*

how much worse lying lips to a
ruler!

8 A bribe is a charm to the one who
gives it;
wherever he turns, he succeeds.

9 He who covers over an offense
promotes love,[h]
but whoever repeats the matter
separates close friends.[i]

17:9 [h]Pr 10:12 [i]Pr 16:28

10 A rebuke impresses a man of
discernment
more than a hundred lashes a fool.

11 An evil man is bent only on
rebellion;
a merciless official will be sent
against him.

12 Better to meet a bear robbed of her
cubs
than a fool in his folly.

13 If a man pays back evil[j] for good,
evil will never leave his house.

17:13 [j]Ps 109:4-5; Jer 18:20

14 Starting a quarrel is like breaching a
dam;
so drop the matter before a
dispute breaks out.[k]

17:14 [k]Pr 20:3

15 Acquitting the guilty and
condemning the innocent[l]—
the LORD detests them both.[m]

17:15 [l]Pr 18:5 [m]Ex 23:6-7; Isa 5:23

16 Of what use is money in the hand
of a fool,
since he has no desire to get
wisdom?[n]

17:16 [n]Pr 23:23

17 A friend loves at all times,
and a brother is born for
adversity.

18 A man lacking in judgment strikes
hands in pledge
and puts up security for his
neighbor.[o]

17:18 [o]Pr 6:1-5; 11:15; 22:26-27

19 He who loves a quarrel loves sin;
he who builds a high gate invites
destruction.

20 A man of perverse heart does not
prosper;
he whose tongue is deceitful falls
into trouble.

21 To have a fool for a son brings grief;
there is no joy for the father of a
fool.[p]

17:21 [p]Pr 10:1

22 A cheerful heart is good medicine,
but a crushed spirit dries up the
bones.[q]

17:22 [q]Ps 22:15; Pr 15:13

23 A wicked man accepts a bribe[r] in
secret
to pervert the course of justice.

17:23 [r]Ex 23:8

24 A discerning man keeps wisdom in
view,
but a fool's eyes[s] wander to the
ends of the earth.

17:24 [s]Ecc 2:14

25 A foolish son brings grief to his
father
and bitterness to the one who bore
him.[t]

17:25 [t]Pr 10:1

26 It is not good to punish an innocent
man,[u]
or to flog officials for their
integrity.

17:26 [u]Pr 18:5

27 A man of knowledge uses words with
restraint,
and a man of understanding is
even-tempered.[v]

17:27 [v]Pr 14:29; Jas 1:19

28 Even a fool is thought wise if he
keeps silent,
and discerning if he holds his
tongue.[w]

17:28 [w]Job 13:5

18 An unfriendly man pursues
selfish ends;
he defies all sound judgment.

2 A fool finds no pleasure in
understanding
but delights in airing his own
opinions.[x]

18:2 [x]Pr 12:23

3 When wickedness comes, so does
contempt,
and with shame comes disgrace.

4 The words of a man's mouth are
deep waters,
but the fountain of wisdom is a
bubbling brook.

5 It is not good to be partial to the
wicked[y]
or to deprive the innocent of
justice.[z]

18:5 [y]Lev 19:15; Pr 24:23-25; 28:21 [z]Ps 82:2; Pr 17:15

6 A fool's lips bring him strife,
and his mouth invites a beating.

7 A fool's mouth is his undoing,
and his lips are a snare[a] to his
soul.[b]

18:7 [a]Ps 140:9 [b]Ps 64:8; Pr 10:14; 12:13; 13:3; Ecc 10:12

8 The words of a gossip are like choice
morsels;

they go down to a man's inmost
parts.[c]

18:8 [c]Pr 26:22

9 One who is slack in his work
is brother to one who destroys.[d]

18:9 [d]Pr 28:24

10 The name of the LORD is a strong
tower;[e]
the righteous run to it and are
safe.

18:10 [e]2Sa 22:3; Ps 61:3

11 The wealth of the rich is their
fortified city;[f]
they imagine it an unscalable wall.

18:11 [f]Pr 10:15

12 Before his downfall a man's heart is
proud,
but humility comes before honor.[g]

18:12 [g]Pr 11:2; 15:33; 16:18

13 He who answers before listening—
that is his folly and his shame.[h]

18:13 [h]Pr 20:25; Jn 7:51

14 A man's spirit sustains him in
sickness,
but a crushed spirit who can bear?[i]

18:14 [i]Pr 15:13; 17:22

15 The heart of the discerning acquires
knowledge;[j]
the ears of the wise seek it out.

18:15 [j]Pr 15:14

16 A gift[k] opens the way for the giver
and ushers him into the presence
of the great.

18:16 [k]Ge 32:20

17 The first to present his case seems
right,
till another comes forward and
questions him.

18 Casting the lot settles disputes[l]
and keeps strong opponents apart.

18:18 [l]Pr 16:33

19 An offended brother is more
unyielding than a fortified
city,
and disputes are like the barred
gates of a citadel.

20 From the fruit of his mouth a man's
stomach is filled;
with the harvest from his lips he is
satisfied.[m]

18:20 [m]Pr 12:14

21 The tongue has the power of life and
death,
and those who love it will eat its
fruit.[n]

18:21 [n]Pr 13:2-3; Mt 12:37

22 He who finds a wife finds what is
good[o]
and receives favor from the
LORD.[p]

18:22 [o]Pr 12:4 [p]Pr 19:14; 31:10

23 A poor man pleads for mercy,
but a rich man answers harshly.

24 A man of many companions may
come to ruin,
but there is a friend who sticks
closer than a brother.[q]

18:24 [q]Pr 17:17; Jn 15:13-15

19

1 Better a poor man whose walk
is blameless
than a fool whose lips are
perverse.[r]

19:1 [r]Pr 28:6

2 It is not good to have zeal without
knowledge,
nor to be hasty and miss the way.[s]

19:2 [s]Pr 29:20

3 A man's own folly ruins his life,
yet his heart rages against the
LORD.

4 Wealth brings many friends,
but a poor man's friend deserts
him.[t]

19:4 [t]Pr 14:20

5 A false witness[u] will not go
unpunished,
and he who pours out lies will not
go free.[v]

19:5 [u]Ex 23:1 [v]Dt 19:19; Pr 21:28

6 Many curry favor with a ruler,[w]
and everyone is the friend of a
man who gives gifts.[x]

19:6 [w]Pr 29:26 [x]Pr 17:8; 18:16

7 A poor man is shunned by all his
relatives—
how much more do his friends
avoid him!
Though he pursues them with
pleading,
they are nowhere to be found.[a][y]

19:7 [y]ver 4; Ps 38:11

8 He who gets wisdom loves his own
soul;
he who cherishes understanding
prospers.[z]

19:8 [z]Pr 16:20

9 A false witness will not go
unpunished,
and he who pours out lies will
perish.[a]

19:9 [a]ver 5

10 It is not fitting for a fool[b] to live in
luxury—
how much worse for a slave to
rule over princes![c]

19:10 [b]Pr 26:1 [c]Pr 30:21-23; Ecc 10:5-7

11 A man's wisdom gives him patience;[d]
it is to his glory to overlook an
offense.

19:11 [d]Pr 16:32

12 A king's rage is like the roar of a lion,
but his favor is like dew[e] on the
grass.[f]

19:12 [e]Ps 133:3 [f]Pr 16:14-15

[a] 7 The meaning of the Hebrew for this sentence is uncertain.

13 A foolish son is his father's ruin,[g]
and a quarrelsome wife is like a constant dripping.[h]

14 Houses and wealth are inherited from parents,[i]
but a prudent wife is from the LORD.[j]

15 Laziness brings on deep sleep,
and the shiftless man goes hungry.[k]

16 He who obeys instructions guards his life,
but he who is contemptuous of his ways will die.[l]

17 He who is kind to the poor lends to the LORD,
and he will reward him for what he has done.[m]

18 Discipline your son, for in that there is hope;
do not be a willing party to his death.[n]

19 A hot-tempered man must pay the penalty;
if you rescue him, you will have to do it again.

20 Listen to advice and accept instruction,[o]
and in the end you will be wise.[p]

21 Many are the plans in a man's heart,
but it is the LORD's purpose that prevails.[q]

22 What a man desires is unfailing love[a];
better to be poor than a liar.

23 The fear of the LORD leads to life:
Then one rests content, untouched by trouble.[r]

24 The sluggard buries his hand in the dish;
he will not even bring it back to his mouth![s]

25 Flog a mocker, and the simple will learn prudence;
rebuke a discerning man, and he will gain knowledge.[t]

26 He who robs his father and drives out his mother[u]
is a son who brings shame and disgrace.

27 Stop listening to instruction, my son,
and you will stray from the words of knowledge.

28 A corrupt witness mocks at justice,
and the mouth of the wicked gulps down evil.[v]

29 Penalties are prepared for mockers,
and beatings for the backs of fools.[w]

20 Wine is a mocker and beer a brawler;
whoever is led astray by them is not wise.[x]

2 A king's wrath is like the roar of a lion;[y]
he who angers him forfeits his life.[z]

3 It is to a man's honor to avoid strife,
but every fool is quick to quarrel.[a]

4 A sluggard does not plow in season;
so at harvest time he looks but finds nothing.

5 The purposes of a man's heart are deep waters,
but a man of understanding draws them out.

6 Many a man claims to have unfailing love,
but a faithful man who can find?[b]

7 The righteous man leads a blameless life;
blessed are his children after him.[c]

8 When a king sits on his throne to judge,
he winnows out all evil with his eyes.[d]

9 Who can say, "I have kept my heart pure;
I am clean and without sin"?[e]

10 Differing weights and differing measures—
the LORD detests them both.[f]

11 Even a child is known by his actions,
by whether his conduct is pure[g] and right.

12 Ears that hear and eyes that see—
the LORD has made them both.[h]

13 Do not love sleep or you will grow poor;[i]

[a]22 Or *A man's greed is his shame*

19:13 [g]Pr 10:1 [h]Pr 21:9
19:14 [i]2Co 12:14 [j]Pr 18:22
19:15 [k]Pr 6:9; 10:4
19:16 [l]Pr 16:17; Lk 10:28
19:17 [m]Mt 10:42; 2Co 9:6-8
19:18 [n]Pr 13:24; 23:13-14
19:20 [o]Pr 4:1 [p]Pr 12:15
19:21 [q]Ps 33:11; Pr 16:9; Isa 14:24,27
19:23 [r]Ps 25:13; Pr 12:21; 1Ti 4:8
19:24 [s]Pr 26:15
19:25 [t]Pr 9:9; 21:11
19:26 [u]Pr 28:24
19:28 [v]Job 15:16
19:29 [w]Pr 26:3
20:1 [x]Pr 31:4
20:2 [y]Pr 19:12 [z]Pr 8:36
20:3 [a]Pr 17:14
20:6 [b]Ps 12:1
20:7 [c]Ps 37:25-26; 112:2
20:8 [d]ver 26; Pr 25:4-5
20:9 [e]1Ki 8:46; Ecc 7:20; 1Jn 1:8
20:10 [f]ver 23; Pr 11:1
20:11 [g]Mt 7:16
20:12 [h]Ps 94:9
20:13 [i]Pr 6:11; 19:15

stay awake and you will have food
to spare.

14 “It’s no good, it’s no good!” says the
buyer;
then off he goes and boasts about
his purchase.

15 Gold there is, and rubies in
abundance,
but lips that speak knowledge are
a rare jewel.

16 Take the garment of one who puts
up security for a stranger;
hold it in pledge[j] if he does it for
a wayward woman.[k]

20:16 [j]Ex 22:26 [k]Pr 27:13

17 Food gained by fraud tastes sweet to
a man,[l]
but he ends up with a mouth full
of gravel.

20:17 [l]Pr 9:17

18 Make plans by seeking advice;
if you wage war, obtain guidance.[m]

20:18 [m]Pr 11:14; 24:6

19 A gossip betrays a confidence;[n]
so avoid a man who talks too
much.

20:19 [n]Pr 11:13

20 If a man curses his father or mother,[o]
his lamp will be snuffed out in
pitch darkness.[p]

20:20 [o]Pr 30:11 [p]Ex 21:17; Job 18:5

21 An inheritance quickly gained at the
beginning
will not be blessed at the end.

22 Do not say, “I’ll pay you back for
this wrong!”[q]
Wait for the LORD, and he will
deliver you.[r]

20:22 [q]Pr 24:29 [r]Ro 12:19

23 The LORD detests differing weights,
and dishonest scales do not please
him.[s]

20:23 [s]ver 10

24 A man’s steps are directed by the
LORD.
How then can anyone understand
his own way?[t]

20:24 [t]Jer 10:23

25 It is a trap for a man to dedicate
something rashly
and only later to consider his
vows.[u]

20:25 [u]Ecc 5:2,4-5

26 A wise king winnows out the
wicked;
he drives the threshing wheel over
them.[v]

20:26 [v]ver 8

27 The lamp of the LORD searches the
spirit of a man[a];
it searches out his inmost being.

28 Love and faithfulness keep a king
safe;
through love his throne is made
secure.[w]

20:28 [w]Pr 29:14

29 The glory of young men is their
strength,
gray hair the splendor of the old.[x]

20:29 [x]Pr 16:31

30 Blows and wounds cleanse[y] away
evil,
and beatings purge the inmost
being.

20:30 [y]Pr 22:15

21

1 The king’s heart is in the hand
of the LORD;
he directs it like a watercourse
wherever he pleases.

2 All a man’s ways seem right to him,
but the LORD weighs the heart.[z]

21:2 [z]Pr 16:2; 24:12; Lk 16:15

3 To do what is right and just
is more acceptable to the LORD
than sacrifice.[a]

21:3 [a]1Sa 15:22; Pr 15:8; Isa 1:11; Hos 6:6; Mic 6:6-8

4 Haughty eyes[b] and a proud heart,
the lamp of the wicked, are sin!

21:4 [b]Pr 6:17

5 The plans of the diligent lead to
profit[c]
as surely as haste leads to poverty.

21:5 [c]Pr 10:4; 28:22

6 A fortune made by a lying tongue
is a fleeting vapor and a deadly
snare.[b] [d]

21:6 [d]2Pe 2:3

7 The violence of the wicked will drag
them away,
for they refuse to do what is right.

8 The way of the guilty is devious,[e]
but the conduct of the innocent is
upright.

21:8 [e]Pr 2:15

9 Better to live on a corner of the roof
than share a house with a
quarrelsome wife.[f]

21:9 [f]Pr 25:24

10 The wicked man craves evil;
his neighbor gets no mercy from
him.

11 When a mocker is punished, the
simple gain wisdom;
when a wise man is instructed, he
gets knowledge.[g]

21:11 [g]Pr 19:25

12 The Righteous One[c] takes note of
the house of the wicked
and brings the wicked to ruin.[h]

21:12 [h]Pr 14:11

[a] 27 Or *The spirit of man is the LORD’s lamp*
[b] 6 Some Hebrew manuscripts, Septuagint and Vulgate; most Hebrew manuscripts *vapor for those who seek death*
[c] 12 Or *The righteous man*

[13]If a man shuts his ears to the cry of the poor,
he too will cry out and not be answered.[i]

[14]A gift given in secret soothes anger,
and a bribe concealed in the cloak pacifies great wrath.[j]

[15]When justice is done, it brings joy to the righteous
but terror to evildoers.[k]

[16]A man who strays from the path of understanding
comes to rest in the company of the dead.[l]

[17]He who loves pleasure will become poor;
whoever loves wine and oil will never be rich.[m]

[18]The wicked become a ransom[n] for the righteous,
and the unfaithful for the upright.

[19]Better to live in a desert
than with a quarrelsome and ill-tempered wife.[o]

[20]In the house of the wise are stores of choice food and oil,
but a foolish man devours all he has.

[21]He who pursues righteousness and love
finds life, prosperity[a] and honor.[p]

[22]A wise man attacks the city of the mighty[q]
and pulls down the stronghold in which they trust.

[23]He who guards his mouth[r] and his tongue
keeps himself from calamity.[s]

[24]The proud and arrogant[t] man—
"Mocker" is his name;
he behaves with overweening pride.

[25]The sluggard's craving will be the death of him,[u]
because his hands refuse to work.

[26]All day long he craves for more,
but the righteous give without sparing.[v]

[27]The sacrifice of the wicked is detestable[w]—
how much more so when brought with evil intent![x]

21:13 [i]Mt 18:30-34; Jas 2:13
21:14 [j]Pr 18:16; 19:6
21:15 [k]Pr 10:29
21:16 [l]Ps 49:14
21:17 [m]Pr 23:20-21, 29-35
21:18 [n]Pr 11:8; Isa 43:3
21:19 [o]ver 9
21:21 [p]Mt 5:6
21:22 [q]Ecc 9:15-16
21:23 [r]Jas 3:2 [s]Pr 12:13; 13:3
21:24 [t]Ps 1:1; Pr 1:22; Isa 16:6; Jer 48:29
21:25 [u]Pr 13:4
21:26 [v]Ps 37:26; Mt 5:42; Eph 4:28
21:27 [w]Isa 66:3; Jer 6:20; Am 5:22 [x]Pr 15:8

[28]A false witness will perish,[y]
and whoever listens to him will be destroyed forever.[b]

[29]A wicked man puts up a bold front,
but an upright man gives thought to his ways.

[30]There is no wisdom,[z] no insight, no plan
that can succeed against the LORD.[a]

[31]The horse is made ready for the day of battle,
but victory rests with the LORD.[b]

22

A good name is more desirable than great riches;
to be esteemed is better than silver or gold.[c]

[2]Rich and poor have this in common:
The LORD is the Maker of them all.[d]

[3]A prudent man sees danger and takes refuge,[e]
but the simple keep going and suffer for it.[f]

[4]Humility and the fear of the LORD
bring wealth and honor and life.

[5]In the paths of the wicked lie thorns and snares,[g]
but he who guards his soul stays far from them.

[6]Train[c] a child in the way he should go,[h]
and when he is old he will not turn from it.

KINDNESS

A MENTOR FOR OUR CHILDREN

Proverbs 22:6

Train a child to be like God by being so like God yourself that your life becomes the lesson.

[7]The rich rule over the poor,
and the borrower is servant to the lender.

[8]He who sows wickedness reaps trouble,[i]

21:28 [y]Pr 19:5
21:30 [z]Jer 9:23 [a]Isa 8:10; Ac 5:39
21:31 [b]Ps 3:8; 33:12-19; Isa 31:1
22:1 [c]Ecc 7:1
22:2 [d]Job 31:15
22:3 [e]Pr 14:16 [f]Pr 27:12
22:5 [g]Pr 15:19
22:6 [h]Eph 6:4
22:8 [i]Job 4:8

[a]*21 Or righteousness* [b]*28 Or / but the words of an obedient man will live on* [c]*6 Or Start*

and the rod of his fury will be
destroyed.[j]

22:8 [j]Ps 125:3

9 A generous man will himself be
blessed,[k]
for he shares his food with the
poor.[l]

22:9 [k]2Co 9:6 [l]Pr 19:17

10 Drive out the mocker, and out goes
strife;
quarrels and insults are ended.[m]

22:10 [m]Pr 18:6; 26:20

11 He who loves a pure heart and
whose speech is gracious
will have the king for his friend.[n]

22:11 [n]Pr 16:13; Mt 5:8

12 The eyes of the LORD keep watch
over knowledge,
but he frustrates the words of the
unfaithful.

13 The sluggard says, "There is a lion
outside!"[o]
or, "I will be murdered in the
streets!"

22:13 [o]Pr 26:13

14 The mouth of an adulteress is a deep
pit;[p]
he who is under the LORD's wrath
will fall into it.[q]

22:14 [p]Pr 2:16; 5:3-5; 7:5; 23:27 [q]Ecc 7:26

15 Folly is bound up in the heart of a
child,
but the rod of discipline will drive
it far from him.[r]

22:15 [r]Pr 13:24; 23:14

16 He who oppresses the poor to
increase his wealth
and he who gives gifts to the
rich—both come to poverty.

Sayings of the Wise

17 Pay attention and listen to the
sayings of the wise;[s]
apply your heart to what I teach,
18 for it is pleasing when you keep
them in your heart
and have all of them ready on
your lips.
19 So that your trust may be in the
LORD,
I teach you today, even you.
20 Have I not written thirty[a] sayings for
you,
sayings of counsel and knowledge,
21 teaching you true and reliable
words,[t]
so that you can give sound answers
to him who sent you?

22:17 [s]Pr 5:1

22:21 [t]Lk 1:3-4; 1Pe 3:15

22 Do not exploit the poor[u] because
they are poor
and do not crush the needy in
court,[v]
23 for the LORD will take up their case[w]
and will plunder those who
plunder them.[x]

22:22 [u]Zec 7:10 [v]Ex 23:6; Mal 3:5

22:23 [w]Ps 12:5 [x]1Sa 25:39; Pr 23:10-11

24 Do not make friends with a
hot-tempered man,
do not associate with one easily
angered,
25 or you may learn his ways
and get yourself ensnared.[y]

22:25 [y]1Co 15:33

26 Do not be a man who strikes hands
in pledge[z]
or puts up security for debts;
27 if you lack the means to pay,
your very bed will be snatched
from under you.[a]

22:26 [z]Pr 11:15

22:27 [a]Pr 17:18

28 Do not move an ancient boundary
stone[b]
set up by your forefathers.

22:28 [b]Dt 19:14; Pr 23:10

29 Do you see a man skilled in his
work?
He will serve[c] before kings;
he will not serve before obscure
men.

22:29 [c]Ge 41:46

23 When you sit to dine with a
ruler,
note well what[b] is before you,
2 and put a knife to your throat
if you are given to gluttony.
3 Do not crave his delicacies,[d]
for that food is deceptive.
4 Do not wear yourself out to get rich;
have the wisdom to show
restraint.
5 Cast but a glance at riches, and they
are gone,
for they will surely sprout wings
and fly off to the sky like an
eagle.[e]

23:3 [d]ver 6-8

23:5 [e]Pr 27:24

6 Do not eat the food of a stingy man,
do not crave his delicacies;[f]
7 for he is the kind of man
who is always thinking about the
cost.[c]
"Eat and drink," he says to you,
but his heart is not with you.
8 You will vomit up the little you have
eaten
and will have wasted your
compliments.

23:6 [f]Ps 141:4

[a]*20* Or *not formerly written*; or *not written excellent*
[b]*1* Or *who* [c]*7* Or *for as he thinks within himself, / so he is*; or *for as he puts on a feast, / so he is*

9 Do not speak to a fool,
for he will scorn the wisdom of your words.[g]
10 Do not move an ancient boundary stone[h]
or encroach on the fields of the fatherless,
11 for their Defender[i] is strong;
he will take up their case against you.[j]

12 Apply your heart to instruction
and your ears to words of knowledge.

13 Do not withhold discipline from a child;
if you punish him with the rod, he will not die.
14 Punish him with the rod
and save his soul from death.[a]

15 My son, if your heart is wise,
then my heart will be glad;
16 my inmost being will rejoice
when your lips speak what is right.[k]

17 Do not let your heart envy[l] sinners,
but always be zealous for the fear of the LORD.
18 There is surely a future hope for you,
and your hope will not be cut off.[m]

19 Listen, my son, and be wise,
and keep your heart on the right path.
20 Do not join those who drink too much wine[n]
or gorge themselves on meat,
21 for drunkards and gluttons become poor,[o]
and drowsiness clothes them in rags.

22 Listen to your father, who gave you life,
and do not despise your mother when she is old.[p]
23 Buy the truth and do not sell it;
get wisdom, discipline and understanding.[q]
24 The father of a righteous man has great joy;
he who has a wise son delights in him.[r]
25 May your father and mother be glad;
may she who gave you birth rejoice!

23:9 [g]Pr; 1:7; 9:7; Mt 7:6
23:10 [h]Dt 19:14; Pr 22:28
23:11 [i]Job 19:25 [j]Pr 22:22-23
23:16 [k]ver 24; Pr 27:11
23:17 [l]Ps 37:1; Pr 28:14
23:18 [m]Ps 9:18; Pr 24:14, 19-20
23:20 [n]Isa 5:11,22; Ro 13:13; Eph 5:18
23:21 [o]Pr 21:17
23:22 [p]Lev 19:32; Pr 1:8; 30:17; Eph 6:1-2
23:23 [q]Pr 4:7
23:24 [r]ver 15-16; Pr 10:1; 15:20

26 My son,[s] give me your heart
and let your eyes keep to my ways,[t]
27 for a prostitute is a deep pit[u]
and a wayward wife is a narrow well.
28 Like a bandit she lies in wait,[v]
and multiplies the unfaithful among men.

29 Who has woe? Who has sorrow?
Who has strife? Who has complaints?
Who has needless bruises? Who has bloodshot eyes?
30 Those who linger over wine,[w]
who go to sample bowls of mixed wine.
31 Do not gaze at wine when it is red,
when it sparkles in the cup,
when it goes down smoothly!
32 In the end it bites like a snake
and poisons like a viper.
33 Your eyes will see strange sights
and your mind imagine confusing things.
34 You will be like one sleeping on the high seas,
lying on top of the rigging.
35 "They hit me," you will say, "but I'm not hurt!
They beat me, but I don't feel it!
When will I wake up
so I can find another drink?"

24

Do not envy[x] wicked men,
do not desire their company;
2 for their hearts plot violence,
and their lips talk about making trouble.[y]

3 By wisdom a house is built,[z]
and through understanding it is established;
4 through knowledge its rooms are filled
with rare and beautiful treasures.[a]
5 A wise man has great power,
and a man of knowledge increases strength;
6 for waging war you need guidance,
and for victory many advisers.[b]

7 Wisdom is too high for a fool;
in the assembly at the gate he has nothing to say.

8 He who plots evil
will be known as a schemer.

[a] *14* Hebrew *Sheol*

23:26 [s]Pr 3:1; 5:1-6 [t]Ps 18:21; Pr 4:4
23:27 [u]Pr 22:14
23:28 [v]Pr 7:11-12; Ecc 7:26
23:30 [w]Ps 75:8; Isa 5:11; Eph 5:18
24:1 [x]Ps 37:1; 73:3; Pr 3:31-32; 23:17-18
24:2 [y]Ps 10:7
24:3 [z]Pr 14:1
24:4 [a]Pr 8:21
24:6 [b]Pr 11:14; 20:18; Lk 14:31

[9]The schemes of folly are sin,
and men detest a mocker.

[10]If you falter in times of trouble,
how small is your strength![c]

[11]Rescue those being led away to death;
hold back those staggering toward slaughter.[d]
[12]If you say, "But we knew nothing about this,"
does not he who weighs[e] the heart perceive it?
Does not he who guards your life know it?
Will he not repay each person according to what he has done?[f]

[13]Eat honey, my son, for it is good;
honey from the comb is sweet to your taste.
[14]Know also that wisdom is sweet to your soul;
if you find it, there is a future hope for you,
and your hope will not be cut off.[g h]

[15]Do not lie in wait like an outlaw against a righteous man's house,
do not raid his dwelling place;
[16]for though a righteous man falls seven times, he rises again,
but the wicked are brought down by calamity.[i]

[17]Do not gloat[j] when your enemy falls;
when he stumbles, do not let your heart rejoice,[k]
[18]or the LORD will see and disapprove
and turn his wrath away from him.

[19]Do not fret[l] because of evil men
or be envious of the wicked,
[20]for the evil man has no future hope,
and the lamp of the wicked will be snuffed out.[m]

[21]Fear the LORD and the king,[n] my son,
and do not join with the rebellious,
[22]for those two will send sudden destruction upon them,
and who knows what calamities they can bring?

24:10 [c]Job 4:5; Jer 51:46; Heb 12:3
24:11 [d]Ps 82:4; Isa 58:6-7
24:12 [e]Pr 21:2 [f]Job 34:11; Ps 62:12; Ro 2:6*
24:14 [g]Ps 119:103; Pr 16:24 [h]Pr 23:18
24:16 [i]Job 5:19; Ps 34:19; Mic 7:8
24:17 [j]Ob 1:12 [k]Job 31:29
24:19 [l]Ps 37:1
24:20 [m]Job 18:5; Pr 13:9; 23:17-18
24:21 [n]Ro 13:1-5; 1Pe 2:17

Further Sayings of the Wise

[23]These also are sayings of the wise:[o]

To show partiality[p] in judging is not good:[q]
[24]Whoever says to the guilty, "You are innocent"[r]—
peoples will curse him and nations denounce him.
[25]But it will go well with those who convict the guilty,
and rich blessing will come upon them.

[26]An honest answer
is like a kiss on the lips.

[27]Finish your outdoor work
and get your fields ready;
after that, build your house.

[28]Do not testify against your neighbor without cause,[s]
or use your lips to deceive.
[29]Do not say, "I'll do to him as he has done to me;
I'll pay that man back for what he did."[t]

[30]I went past the field of the sluggard,[u]
past the vineyard of the man who lacks judgment;
[31]thorns had come up everywhere,
the ground was covered with weeds,
and the stone wall was in ruins.
[32]I applied my heart to what I observed
and learned a lesson from what I saw:
[33]A little sleep, a little slumber,
a little folding of the hands to rest[v]—
[34]and poverty will come on you like a bandit
and scarcity like an armed man.[a w]

More Proverbs of Solomon

25 These are more proverbs[x] of Solomon, copied by the men of Hezekiah king of Judah:[y]

[2]It is the glory of God to conceal a matter;
to search out a matter is the glory of kings.[z]

[3]As the heavens are high and the earth is deep,

[a]34 Or *like a vagrant / and scarcity like a beggar*

24:23 [o]Pr 1:6 [p]Lev 19:15 [q]Pr 28:21
24:24 [r]Pr 17:15
24:28 [s]Ps 7:4; Pr 25:18; Eph 4:25
24:29 [t]Pr 20:22; Mt 5:38-41; Ro 12:17
24:30 [u]Pr 6:6-11; 26:13-16
24:33 [v]Pr 6:10
24:34 [w]Pr 10:4; Ecc 10:18
25:1 [x]1Ki 4:32 [y]Pr 1:1
25:2 [z]Pr 16:10-15

so the hearts of kings are
unsearchable.

[4]Remove the dross from the silver,
and out comes material for[a] the
silversmith;

25:5 [a]Pr 20:8 [b]2Sa 7:13 [c]Pr 16:12; 29:14
[5]remove the wicked from the king's
presence,[a]
and his throne will be
established[b] through
righteousness.[c]

[6]Do not exalt yourself in the king's
presence,
and do not claim a place among
great men;

25:7 [d]Lk 14:7-10
[7]it is better for him to say to you,
"Come up here,"[d]
than for him to humiliate you
before a nobleman.

What you have seen with your eyes
[8] do not bring[b] hastily to court,
for what will you do in the end
if your neighbor puts you to
shame?[e]

25:8 [e]Mt 5:25-26

[9]If you argue your case with a
neighbor,
do not betray another man's
confidence,
[10]or he who hears it may shame you
and you will never lose your bad
reputation.

25:11 [f]ver 12; Pr 15:23
[11]A word aptly spoken
is like apples of gold in settings of
silver.[f]

25:12 [g]ver 11; Ps 141:5; Pr 13:18; 15:31
[12]Like an earring of gold or an
ornament of fine gold
is a wise man's rebuke to a
listening ear.[g]

25:13 [h]Pr 10:26; 13:17
[13]Like the coolness of snow at harvest
time
is a trustworthy messenger to
those who send him;
he refreshes the spirit of his
masters.[h]

[14]Like clouds and wind without rain
is a man who boasts of gifts he
does not give.

25:15 [i]Ecc 10:4 [j]Pr 15:1
[15]Through patience a ruler can be
persuaded,[i]
and a gentle tongue can break a
bone.[j]

25:16 [k]ver 27
[16]If you find honey, eat just enough—
too much of it, and you will
vomit.[k]

[17]Seldom set foot in your neighbor's
house—
too much of you, and he will hate
you.

25:18 [l]Ps 57:4; Pr 12:18
[18]Like a club or a sword or a sharp
arrow
is the man who gives false
testimony against his
neighbor.[l]

[19]Like a bad tooth or a lame foot
is reliance on the unfaithful in
times of trouble.

[20]Like one who takes away a garment
on a cold day,
or like vinegar poured on soda,
is one who sings songs to a heavy
heart.

[21]If your enemy is hungry, give him
food to eat;
if he is thirsty, give him water to
drink.

▸ PEACE

THE UPSIDE DOWN KINGDOM

Proverbs 25:21
When we fully understand the love of Christ, we become more interested in feeding our enemies than in eating with our friends.

25:22 [m]Ps 18:8 [n]2Sa 16:12; 2Ch 28:15; Mt 5:44; Ro 12:20*
[22]In doing this, you will heap burning
coals[m] on his head,
and the LORD will reward you.[n]

[23]As a north wind brings rain,
so a sly tongue brings angry looks.

25:24 [o]Pr 21:9
[24]Better to live on a corner of the roof
than share a house with a
quarrelsome wife.[o]

25:25 [p]Pr 15:30
[25]Like cold water to a weary soul
is good news from a distant
land.[p]

[26]Like a muddied spring or a polluted
well
is a righteous man who gives way
to the wicked.

25:27 [q]ver 16 [r]Pr 27:2; Mt 23:12
[27]It is not good to eat too much
honey,[q]
nor is it honorable to seek one's
own honor.[r]

[a]4 Or *comes a vessel from* [b]7,8 Or *nobleman / on whom you had set your eyes. / [8]Do not go*

28 Like a city whose walls are broken
down
is a man who lacks self-control.

26

1 Like snow in summer or rain[s] in harvest,
honor is not fitting for a fool.[t]

26:1 [s]1Sa 12:17 [t]ver 8; Pr 19:10

2 Like a fluttering sparrow or a darting
swallow,
an undeserved curse does not
come to rest.[u]

26:2 [u]Nu 23:8; Dt 23:5

3 A whip for the horse, a halter for the
donkey,[v]
and a rod for the backs of fools![w]

26:3 [v]Ps 32:9 [w]Pr 10:13

4 Do not answer a fool according to
his folly,
or you will be like him yourself.[x]

26:4 [x]ver 5; Isa 36:21

5 Answer a fool according to his folly,
or he will be wise in his own
eyes.[y]

26:5 [y]ver 4; Pr 3:7

6 Like cutting off one's feet or
drinking violence
is the sending of a message by the
hand of a fool.[z]

26:6 [z]Pr 10:26

7 Like a lame man's legs that hang
limp
is a proverb in the mouth of a
fool.[a]

26:7 [a]ver 9

8 Like tying a stone in a sling
is the giving of honor to a fool.[b]

26:8 [b]ver 1

9 Like a thornbush in a drunkard's
hand
is a proverb in the mouth of a
fool.[c]

26:9 [c]ver 7

10 Like an archer who wounds at
random
is he who hires a fool or any
passer-by.

11 As a dog returns to its vomit,[d]
so a fool repeats his folly.[e]

26:11 [d]2Pe 2:22* [e]Ex 8:15; Ps 85:8

12 Do you see a man wise in his own
eyes?[f]
There is more hope for a fool than
for him.[g]

26:12 [f]Pr 3:7 [g]Pr 29:20

13 The sluggard says,[h] "There is a lion
in the road,
a fierce lion roaming the streets!"[i]

26:13 [h]Pr 6:6-11; 24:30-34 [i]Pr 22:13

14 As a door turns on its hinges,
so a sluggard turns on his bed.[j]

26:14 [j]Pr 6:9

15 The sluggard buries his hand in the
dish;
he is too lazy to bring it back to
his mouth.[k]

26:15 [k]Pr 19:24

16 The sluggard is wiser in his own eyes
than seven men who answer
discreetly.

17 Like one who seizes a dog by the ears
is a passer-by who meddles in a
quarrel not his own.

18 Like a madman shooting
firebrands or deadly arrows
19 is a man who deceives his neighbor
and says, "I was only joking!"

20 Without wood a fire goes out;
without gossip a quarrel dies
down.[l]

26:20 [l]Pr 22:10

21 As charcoal to embers and as wood
to fire,
so is a quarrelsome man for
kindling strife.[m]

26:21 [m]Pr 14:17; 15:18

22 The words of a gossip are like choice
morsels;
they go down to a man's inmost
parts.[n]

26:22 [n]Pr 18:8

23 Like a coating of glaze[a] over
earthenware
are fervent lips with an evil heart.

24 A malicious man disguises himself
with his lips,[o]
but in his heart he harbors deceit.[p]
25 Though his speech is charming,[q] do
not believe him,
for seven abominations fill his
heart.[r]

26:24 [o]Ps 31:18 [p]Ps 41:6; Pr 10:18; 12:20

26:25 [q]Ps 28:3 [r]Jer 9:4-8

26 His malice may be concealed by
deception,
but his wickedness will be exposed
in the assembly.

27 If a man digs a pit,[s] he will fall into
it;[t]
if a man rolls a stone, it will roll
back on him.[u]

26:27 [s]Ps 7:15 [t]Est 6:13 [u]Est 2:23; 7:9; Ps 35:8; 141:10; Pr 28:10; 29:6; Isa 50:11

28 A lying tongue hates those it hurts,
and a flattering mouth[v] works
ruin.

26:28 [v]Ps 12:3; Pr 29:5

27

1 Do not boast[w] about
tomorrow,
for you do not know what a day
may bring forth.[x]

27:1 [w]1Ki 20:11 [x]Mt 6:34; Lk 12:19-20; Jas 4:13-16

2 Let another praise you, and not your
own mouth;

[a]*23* With a different word division of the Hebrew; Masoretic Text *of silver dross*

someone else, and not your own
lips.[y]

[3]Stone is heavy and sand[z] a burden,
but provocation by a fool is
heavier than both.

[4]Anger is cruel and fury
overwhelming,
but who can stand before
jealousy?[a]

[5]Better is open rebuke
than hidden love.

[6]Wounds from a friend can be
trusted,
but an enemy multiplies kisses.[b]

[7]He who is full loathes honey,
but to the hungry even what is
bitter tastes sweet.

[8]Like a bird that strays from its nest[c]
is a man who strays from his
home.

[9]Perfume[d] and incense bring joy to
the heart,
and the pleasantness of one's
friend springs from his
earnest counsel.

[10]Do not forsake your friend and the
friend of your father,
and do not go to your brother's
house when disaster[e] strikes
you—
better a neighbor nearby than a
brother far away.

[11]Be wise, my son, and bring joy to
my heart;[f]
then I can answer anyone who
treats me with contempt.[g]

[12]The prudent see danger and take
refuge,
but the simple keep going and
suffer for it.[h]

[13]Take the garment of one who puts
up security for a stranger;
hold it in pledge if he does it for a
wayward woman.[i]

[14]If a man loudly blesses his neighbor
early in the morning,
it will be taken as a curse.

[15]A quarrelsome wife is like
a constant dripping[j] on a rainy
day;

[16]restraining her is like restraining the
wind
or grasping oil with the hand.

[17]As iron sharpens iron,
so one man sharpens another.

[18]He who tends a fig tree will eat its
fruit,[k]
and he who looks after his master
will be honored.[l]

[19]As water reflects a face,
so a man's heart reflects the man.

[20]Death and Destruction[a] are never
satisfied,[m]
and neither are the eyes of man.[n]

[21]The crucible for silver and the
furnace for gold,[o]
but man is tested by the praise he
receives.

[22]Though you grind a fool in a
mortar,
grinding him like grain with a
pestle,
you will not remove his folly from
him.

[23]Be sure you know the condition of
your flocks,[p]
give careful attention to your
herds;
[24]for riches do not endure forever,[q]
and a crown is not secure for all
generations.
[25]When the hay is removed and new
growth appears
and the grass from the hills is
gathered in,
[26]the lambs will provide you with
clothing,
and the goats with the price of a
field.
[27]You will have plenty of goats' milk
to feed you and your family
and to nourish your servant girls.

28

The wicked man flees[r] though
no one pursues,[s]
but the righteous are as bold as a
lion.[t]

[2]When a country is rebellious, it has
many rulers,
but a man of understanding and
knowledge maintains order.

[3]A ruler[b] who oppresses the poor

[a]20 Hebrew *Sheol and Abaddon* [b]3 Or *A poor man*

27:2 [y]Pr 25:27
27:3 [z]Job 6:3
27:4 [a]Nu 5:14
27:6 [b]Ps 141:5; Pr 28:23
27:8 [c]Isa 16:2
27:9 [d]Est 2:12; Ps 45:8
27:10 [e]Pr 17:17; 18:24
27:11 [f]Pr 10:1; 23:15-16 [g]Ge 24:60
27:12 [h]Pr 22:3
27:13 [i]Pr 20:16
27:15 [j]Est 1:18; Pr 19:13
27:18 [k]1Co 9:7 [l]Lk 19:12-27
27:20 [m]Pr 30:15-16; Hab 2:5 [n]Ecc 1:8; 6:7
27:21 [o]Pr 17:3
27:23 [p]Pr 12:10
27:24 [q]Pr 23:5
28:1 [r]2Ki 7:7 [s]Lev 26:17; Ps 53:5 [t]Ps 138:3

is like a driving rain that leaves no crops.

[4] Those who forsake the law praise the wicked,
but those who keep the law resist them.

[5] Evil men do not understand justice,
but those who seek the LORD understand it fully.

[6] Better a poor man whose walk is blameless
than a rich man whose ways are perverse.[u]

[7] He who keeps the law is a discerning son,
but a companion of gluttons disgraces his father.[v]

[8] He who increases his wealth by exorbitant interest[w]
amasses it for another,[x] who will be kind to the poor.[y]

[9] If anyone turns a deaf ear to the law,
even his prayers are detestable.[z]

[10] He who leads the upright along an evil path
will fall into his own trap,[a]
but the blameless will receive a good inheritance.

[11] A rich man may be wise in his own eyes,
but a poor man who has discernment sees through him.

[12] When the righteous triumph, there is great elation;[b]
but when the wicked rise to power, men go into hiding.[c]

[13] He who conceals his sins[d] does not prosper,
but whoever confesses and renounces them finds mercy.[e]

[14] Blessed is the man who always fears the LORD,
but he who hardens his heart falls into trouble.

[15] Like a roaring lion or a charging bear
is a wicked man ruling over a helpless people.

[16] A tyrannical ruler lacks judgment,
but he who hates ill-gotten gain will enjoy a long life.

[17] A man tormented by the guilt of murder
will be a fugitive[f] till death;
let no one support him.

[18] He whose walk is blameless is kept safe,
but he whose ways are perverse will suddenly fall.[g]

[19] He who works his land will have abundant food,
but the one who chases fantasies will have his fill of poverty.[h]

[20] A faithful man will be richly blessed,
but one eager to get rich will not go unpunished.[i]

[21] To show partiality is not good[j]—
yet a man will do wrong for a piece of bread.[k]

[22] A stingy man is eager to get rich
and is unaware that poverty awaits him.[l]

[23] He who rebukes a man will in the end gain more favor
than he who has a flattering tongue.[m]

[24] He who robs his father or mother[n]
and says, "It's not wrong"—
he is partner to him who destroys.[o]

[25] A greedy man stirs up dissension,
but he who trusts in the LORD[p] will prosper.

[26] He who trusts in himself is a fool,[q]
but he who walks in wisdom is kept safe.

[27] He who gives to the poor will lack nothing,[r]
but he who closes his eyes to them receives many curses.

[28] When the wicked rise to power,
people go into hiding;[s]
but when the wicked perish, the righteous thrive.

29 A man who remains stiff-necked after many rebukes
will suddenly be destroyed—
without remedy.[t]

[2] When the righteous thrive, the people rejoice;[u]

28:6 [u]Pr 19:1
28:7 [v]Pr 23:19-21
28:8 [w]Ex 18:21 [x]Job 27:17; Pr 13:22 [y]Ps 112:9; Pr 14:31; Lk 14:12-14
28:9 [z]Ps 66:18; 109:7; Pr 15:8; Isa 1:13
28:10 [a]Pr 26:27
28:12 [b]2Ki 11:20 [c]Pr 11:10; 29:2
28:13 [d]Job 31:33 [e]Ps 32:1-5; 1Jn 1:9
28:17 [f]Ge 9:6
28:18 [g]Pr 10:9
28:19 [h]Pr 12:11
28:20 [i]ver 22; Pr 10:6; 1Ti 6:9
28:21 [j]Pr 18:5 [k]Eze 13:19
28:22 [l]ver 20; Pr 23:6
28:23 [m]Pr 27:5-6
28:24 [n]Pr 19:26 [o]Pr 18:9
28:25 [p]Pr 29:25
28:26 [q]Ps 4:5; Pr 3:5
28:27 [r]Dt 15:7; 24:19; Pr 19:17; 22:9
28:28 [s]ver 12
29:1 [t]2Ch 36:16; Pr 6:15
29:2 [u]Est 8:15

when the wicked rule, the people
groan.[v]
3 A man who loves wisdom brings joy
to his father,[w]
but a companion of prostitutes
squanders his wealth.[x]
4 By justice a king gives a country
stability,[y]
but one who is greedy for bribes
tears it down.
5 Whoever flatters his neighbor
is spreading a net for his feet.
6 An evil man is snared by his own sin,[z]
but a righteous one can sing and
be glad.
7 The righteous care about justice for
the poor,[a]
but the wicked have no such
concern.
8 Mockers stir up a city,
but wise men turn away anger.[b]
9 If a wise man goes to court with a
fool,
the fool rages and scoffs, and there
is no peace.
10 Bloodthirsty men hate a man of
integrity
and seek to kill the upright.[c]
11 A fool gives full vent to his anger,
but a wise man keeps himself
under control.[d]
12 If a ruler listens to lies,
all his officials become wicked.
13 The poor man and the oppressor
have this in common:
The LORD gives sight to the eyes
of both.[e]
14 If a king judges the poor with
fairness,
his throne will always be secure.[f]
15 The rod of correction imparts
wisdom,
but a child left to himself disgraces
his mother.[g]
16 When the wicked thrive, so does sin,
but the righteous will see their
downfall.[h]
17 Discipline your son, and he will give
you peace;
he will bring delight to your soul.[i]

29:2 [v]Pr 28:12
29:3 [w]Pr 10:1 [x]Pr 5:8-10; Lk 15:11-32
29:4 [y]Pr 8:15-16
29:6 [z]Ecc 9:12
29:7 [a]Job 29:16; Ps 41:1; Pr 31:8-9
29:8 [b]Pr 11:11; 16:14
29:10 [c]1Jn 3:12
29:11 [d]Pr 12:16; 19:11
29:13 [e]Pr 22:2; Mt 5:45
29:14 [f]Ps 72:1-5; Pr 16:12
29:15 [g]Pr 10:1; 13:24; 17:21,25
29:16 [h]Ps 37:35-36; 58:10; 91:8; 92:11
29:17 [i]ver 15; Pr 10:1

18 Where there is no revelation, the
people cast off restraint;
but blessed is he who keeps the
law.[j]
19 A servant cannot be corrected by
mere words;
though he understands, he will
not respond.
20 Do you see a man who speaks in
haste?
There is more hope for a fool than
for him.[k]
21 If a man pampers his servant from
youth,
he will bring grief[a] in the end.
22 An angry man stirs up dissension,
and a hot-tempered one commits
many sins.[l]
23 A man's pride brings him low,
but a man of lowly spirit gains
honor.[m]
24 The accomplice of a thief is his own
enemy;
he is put under oath and dare not
testify.[n]
25 Fear of man will prove to be a snare,
but whoever trusts in the LORD[o]
is kept safe.
26 Many seek an audience with a ruler,[p]
but it is from the LORD that man
gets justice.
27 The righteous detest the dishonest;
the wicked detest the upright.[q]

Sayings of Agur

30 The sayings of Agur son of
Jakeh—an oracle[b]:

This man declared to Ithiel,
to Ithiel and to Ucal:[c]

2 "I am the most ignorant of men;
I do not have a man's
understanding.
3 I have not learned wisdom,
nor have I knowledge of the Holy
One.[r]
4 Who has gone up[s] to heaven and
come down?

[a]*21* The meaning of the Hebrew for this word is uncertain. [b]*1* Or *Jakeh of Massa* [c]*1* Masoretic Text; with a different word division of the Hebrew *declared, "I am weary, O God; / I am weary, O God, and faint.*

29:18 [j]Ps 1:1-2; 119:1-2; Jn 13:17
29:20 [k]Pr 26:12; Jas 1:19
29:22 [l]Pr 14:17; 15:18; 26:21
29:23 [m]Pr 11:2; 15:33; 16:18; Isa 66:2; Mt 23:12
29:24 [n]Lev 5:1
29:25 [o]Pr 28:25
29:26 [p]Pr 19:6
29:27 [q]ver 10
30:3 [r]Pr 9:10
30:4 [s]Ps 24:1-2; Jn 3:13; Eph 4:7-10

Who has gathered up the wind in
the hollow[t] of his hands?
Who has wrapped up the waters[u] in
his cloak?[v]
Who has established all the ends
of the earth?
What is his name,[w] and the name of
his son?
Tell me if you know!

5 "Every word of God is flawless;[x]
he is a shield[y] to those who take
refuge in him.
6 Do not add[z] to his words,
or he will rebuke you and prove
you a liar.

7 "Two things I ask of you, O LORD;
do not refuse me before I die:
8 Keep falsehood and lies far from me;
give me neither poverty nor riches,
but give me only my daily bread.[a]
9 Otherwise, I may have too much
and disown[b] you
and say, 'Who is the LORD?'[c]
Or I may become poor and steal,
and so dishonor the name of my
God.[d]

10 "Do not slander a servant to his
master,
or he will curse you, and you will
pay for it.

11 "There are those who curse their
fathers
and do not bless their mothers;[e]
12 those who are pure in their own eyes[f]
and yet are not cleansed of their
filth;[g]
13 those whose eyes are ever so
haughty,[h]
whose glances are so disdainful;
14 those whose teeth[i] are swords
and whose jaws are set with
knives[j]
to devour[k] the poor[l] from the earth,
the needy from among mankind.[m]

15 "The leech has two daughters.
'Give! Give!' they cry.

"There are three things that are
never satisfied,[n]
four that never say, 'Enough!':
16 the grave,[a][o] the barren womb,
land, which is never satisfied with
water,
and fire, which never says,
'Enough!'

30:4 [t]Ps 104:3; Isa 40:12 [u]Job 26:8; 38:8-9 [v]Ge 1:2 [w]Rev 19:12
30:5 [x]Ps 12:6; 18:30 [y]Ge 15:1; Ps 84:11
30:6 [z]Dt 4:2; 12:32; Rev 22:18
30:8 [a]Mt 6:11
30:9 [b]Jos 24:27; Isa 1:4; 59:13 [c]Dt 6:12; 8:10-14; Hos 13:6 [d]Dt 8:12
30:11 [e]Pr 20:20
30:12 [f]Pr 16:2; Lk 18:11 [g]Jer 2:23,35
30:13 [h]2Sa 22:28; Job 41:34; Ps 131:1; Pr 6:17
30:14 [i]Job 4:11; 29:17; Ps 3:7 [j]Ps 57:4 [k]Job 24:9; Ps 14:4 [l]Am 8:4; Mic 2:2 [m]Job 19:22
30:15 [n]Pr 27:20
30:16 [o]Pr 27:20; Isa 5:14; 14:9,11; Hab 2:5

17 "The eye that mocks[p] a father,
that scorns obedience to a mother,
will be pecked out by the ravens of
the valley,
will be eaten by the vultures.[q]

18 "There are three things that are too
amazing for me,
four that I do not understand:
19 the way of an eagle in the sky,
the way of a snake on a rock,
the way of a ship on the high seas,
and the way of a man with a
maiden.

20 "This is the way of an adulteress:
She eats and wipes her mouth
and says, 'I've done nothing
wrong.'[r]

21 "Under three things the earth
trembles,
under four it cannot bear up:
22 a servant who becomes king,[s]
a fool who is full of food,
23 an unloved woman who is married,
and a maidservant who displaces
her mistress.

24 "Four things on earth are small,
yet they are extremely wise:
25 Ants are creatures of little strength,
yet they store up their food in the
summer;[t]
26 coneys[b][u] are creatures of little power,
yet they make their home in the
crags;
27 locusts[v] have no king,
yet they advance together in ranks;
28 a lizard can be caught with the hand,
yet it is found in kings' palaces.

29 "There are three things that are
stately in their stride,
four that move with stately
bearing:
30 a lion, mighty among beasts,
who retreats before nothing;
31 a strutting rooster, a he-goat,
and a king with his army around
him.[c]

32 "If you have played the fool and
exalted yourself,
or if you have planned evil,
clap your hand over your mouth![w]
33 For as churning the milk produces
butter,

30:17 [p]Dt 21:18-21; Pr 23:22
30:17 [q]Job 15:23
30:20 [r]Pr 5:6
30:22 [s]Pr 19:10; 29:2
30:25 [t]Pr 6:6-8
30:26 [u]Ps 104:18
30:27 [v]Ex 10:4
30:32 [w]Job 21:5; 29:9

[a] *16* Hebrew *Sheol* [b] *26* That is, the hyrax or rock badger [c] *31* Or *king secure against revolt*

and as twisting the nose produces blood,
so stirring up anger produces strife."

Sayings of King Lemuel

31 The sayings[x] of King Lemuel—an oracle[a] his mother taught him:

2 "O my son, O son of my womb,
O son of my vows,[b][y]
3 do not spend your strength on women,
your vigor on those who ruin kings.[z]

4 "It is not for kings, O Lemuel—
not for kings to drink wine,[a]
not for rulers to crave beer,
5 lest they drink[b] and forget what the law decrees,[c]
and deprive all the oppressed of their rights.
6 Give beer to those who are perishing,
wine[d] to those who are in anguish;
7 let them drink[e] and forget their poverty
and remember their misery no more.

8 "Speak[f] up for those who cannot speak for themselves,
for the rights of all who are destitute.
9 Speak up and judge fairly;
defend the rights of the poor and needy."[g]

Epilogue: The Wife of Noble Character

10 [c]A wife of noble character[h] who can find?[i]
She is worth far more than rubies.
11 Her husband[j] has full confidence in her
and lacks nothing of value.[k]
12 She brings him good, not harm,
all the days of her life.
13 She selects wool and flax
and works with eager hands.[l]
14 She is like the merchant ships,
bringing her food from afar.
15 She gets up while it is still dark;
she provides food for her family
and portions for her servant girls.
16 She considers a field and buys it;
out of her earnings she plants a vineyard.
17 She sets about her work vigorously;
her arms are strong for her tasks.
18 She sees that her trading is profitable,
and her lamp does not go out at night.
19 In her hand she holds the distaff
and grasps the spindle with her fingers.
20 She opens her arms to the poor
and extends her hands to the needy.[m]
21 When it snows, she has no fear for her household;
for all of them are clothed in scarlet.
22 She makes coverings for her bed;
she is clothed in fine linen and purple.
23 Her husband is respected at the city gate,
where he takes his seat among the elders[n] of the land.
24 She makes linen garments and sells them,
and supplies the merchants with sashes.
25 She is clothed with strength and dignity;
she can laugh at the days to come.
26 She speaks with wisdom,
and faithful instruction is on her tongue.[o]
27 She watches over the affairs of her household
and does not eat the bread of idleness.
28 Her children arise and call her blessed;
her husband also, and he praises her:
29 "Many women do noble things,
but you surpass them all."
30 Charm is deceptive, and beauty is fleeting;
but a woman who fears the LORD is to be praised.
31 Give her the reward she has earned,
and let her works bring her praise[p]
at the city gate.

[a] *1* Or *of Lemuel king of Massa, which* [b] *2* Or / *the answer to my prayers* [c] *10* Verses 10-31 are an acrostic, each verse beginning with a successive letter of the Hebrew alphabet.

31:1 [x]Pr 22:17
31:2 [y]Jdg 11:30; Isa 49:15
31:3 [z]Dt 17:17; 1Ki 11:3; Ne 13:26; Pr 5:1-14
31:4 [a]Pr 20:1; Ecc 10:16-17; Isa 5:22
31:5 [b]1Ki 16:9 [c]Pr 16:12; Hos 4:11
31:6 [d]Ge 14:18
31:7 [e]Est 1:10
31:8 [f]1Sa 19:4; Job 29:12-17
31:9 [g]Lev 19:15; Dt 1:16; Pr 24:23; 29:7; Isa 1:17; Jer 22:16
31:10 [h]Ru 3:11; Pr 12:4; 18:22 [i]Pr 8:35; 19:14
31:11 [j]Ge 2:18 [k]Pr 12:4
31:13 [l]1Ti 2:9-10
31:20 [m]Dt 15:11; Eph 4:28; Heb 13:16
31:23 [n]Ex 3:16; Ru 4:1,11; Pr 12:4
31:26 [o]Pr 10:31
31:31 [p]Pr 11:16

ECCLESIASTES

AUTHORSHIP AND DATE

Evidence points to Solomon as the author.

c. 935 B.C.

KEY THEMES

The central focus of Ecclesiastes is the peacelessness that is produced by a meaningless life.

FRUIT OF THE SPIRIT IN ECCLESIASTES

Peace: A peaceless person's struggle to find meaning in life is exemplified in the negative tone of this book. An unhappy person looking for personal peace finds that, however ardently she or he seeks it, peace cannot be found. The mood of the book reveals the hollowness, emptiness and futility of life. Consider the verses that indicate the emptiness of this writer's search for meaning:

"Meaningless! Meaningless! . . . Utterly meaningless! Everything is meaningless" (1:2).

"All things are wearisome, more than one can say" (1:8).

"For the wise man, like the fool, will not be long remembered; in days to come both will be forgotten" (2:16).

"And I declared that the dead, who had already died, are happier than the living, who are still alive" (4:2).

"Naked a man comes from his mother's womb, and as he comes, so he departs" (5:15).

"Light is sweet, and it pleases the eyes to see the sun. However many years a man may live, let him enjoy them all. But let him remember the days of darkness, for they will be many. Everything to come is meaninglessness" (11:7–8).

The book of Ecclesiastes does, however, have a very positive ending. Peace can be ours if we "fear God and keep his commandments" (12:13).

Everything Is Meaningless

1 The words of the Teacher,[a][a] son of
David, king in Jerusalem:[b]

2 "Meaningless! Meaningless!"
says the Teacher.
"Utterly meaningless!
Everything is meaningless."[c]

3 What does man gain from all his
labor
at which he toils under the sun?[d]

4 Generations come and generations
go,
but the earth remains forever.[e]

5 The sun rises and the sun sets,
and hurries back to where it rises.[f]

6 The wind blows to the south
and turns to the north;
round and round it goes,
ever returning on its course.

7 All streams flow into the sea,
yet the sea is never full.
To the place the streams come from,
there they return again.[g]

8 All things are wearisome,
more than one can say.
The eye never has enough of seeing,[h]
nor the ear its fill of hearing.

9 What has been will be again,
what has been done will be done
again;[i]
there is nothing new under the
sun.

10 Is there anything of which one can
say,
"Look! This is something new"?
It was here already, long ago;
it was here before our time.

11 There is no remembrance of men of
old,
and even those who are yet to
come
will not be remembered
by those who follow.[j]

Wisdom Is Meaningless

12 I, the Teacher,[k] was king over Israel in Jerusalem. 13 I devoted myself to
study and to explore by wisdom all that
is done under heaven. What a heavy
burden God has laid on men![l] 14 I have
seen all the things that are done under
the sun; all of them are meaningless, a
chasing after the wind.[m]

15 What is twisted cannot be
straightened;[n]
what is lacking cannot be counted.

1:1 [a]ver 12; Ecc 7:27; 12:10 [b]Pr 1:1
1:2 [c]Ps 39:5-6; 62:9; 144:4; Ecc 12:8; Ro 8:20-21
1:3 [d]Ecc 2:11,22; 3:9; 5:15-16
1:4 [e]Ps 104:5; 119:90
1:5 [f]Ps 19:5-6
1:7 [g]Job 36:28
1:8 [h]Pr 27:20
1:9 [i]Ecc 2:12; 3:15
1:11 [j]Ecc 2:16
1:12 [k]ver 1
1:13 [l]Ge 3:17; Ecc 3:10
1:14 [m]Ecc 2:11,17
1:15 [n]Ecc 7:13

16 I thought to myself, "Look, I have
grown and increased in wisdom more
than anyone who has ruled over Jerusalem before me;[o] I have experienced
much of wisdom and knowledge."
17 Then I applied myself to the understanding of wisdom,[p] and also of madness and folly,[q] but I learned that this,
too, is a chasing after the wind.

18 For with much wisdom comes much
sorrow;
the more knowledge, the more
grief.[r]

Pleasures Are Meaningless

2 I thought in my heart, "Come now,
I will test you with pleasure[s] to find
out what is good." But that also proved
to be meaningless. 2 "Laughter,"[t] I said,
"is foolish. And what does pleasure accomplish?" 3 I tried cheering myself with
wine,[u] and embracing folly[v]—my mind
still guiding me with wisdom. I wanted
to see what was worthwhile for men to
do under heaven during the few days of
their lives.

4 I undertook great projects: I built
houses for myself[w] and planted vineyards.[x] 5 I made gardens and parks and
planted all kinds of fruit trees in them.
6 I made reservoirs to water groves of
flourishing trees. 7 I bought male and
female slaves and had other slaves who
were born in my house. I also owned
more herds and flocks than anyone in
Jerusalem before me. 8 I amassed silver
and gold[y] for myself, and the treasure
of kings and provinces. I acquired men
and women singers,[z] and a harem[b] as
well—the delights of the heart of man.
9 I became greater by far than anyone
in Jerusalem before me.[a] In all this my
wisdom stayed with me.

10 I denied myself nothing my eyes
desired;
I refused my heart no pleasure.
My heart took delight in all my
work,
and this was the reward for all my
labor.

11 Yet when I surveyed all that my
hands had done
and what I had toiled to achieve,

[a] *1* Or *leader of the assembly;* also in verses 2 and 12
[b] *8* The meaning of the Hebrew for this phrase is uncertain.

1:16 [o]1Ki 3:12; 4:30; Ecc 2:9
1:17 [p]Ecc 7:23 [q]Ecc 2:3,12; 7:25
1:18 [r]Ecc 2:23; 12:12
2:1 [s]Ecc 7:4; 8:15; Lk 12:19
2:2 [t]Pr 14:13; Ecc 7:6
2:3 [u]ver 24-25; Ecc 3:12-13 [v]Ecc 1:17
2:4 [w]1Ki 7:1-12 [x]SS 8:11
2:8 [y]1Ki 9:28; 10:10,14,21 [z]2Sa 19:35
2:9 [a]1Ch 29:25; Ecc 1:16

everything was meaningless, a
chasing after the wind;[b]
nothing was gained under the
sun.[c]

2:11 [b]Ecc 1:14 [c]Ecc 1:3

Wisdom and Folly Are Meaningless

12Then I turned my thoughts to
consider wisdom,
and also madness and folly.[d]
What more can the king's successor
do
than what has already been done?[e]

2:12 [d]Ecc 1:17 [e]Ecc 1:9; 7:25

13I saw that wisdom[f] is better than
folly,[g]
just as light is better than
darkness.

2:13 [f]Ecc 7:19; 9:18 [g]Ecc 7:11-12

14The wise man has eyes in his head,
while the fool walks in the
darkness;
but I came to realize
that the same fate overtakes them
both.[h]

2:14 [h]Ps 49:10; Pr 17:24; Ecc 3:19; 6:6; 7:2; 9:3,11-12

15Then I thought in my heart,
"The fate of the fool will overtake
me also.
What then do I gain by being
wise?"[i]
I said in my heart,
"This too is meaningless."

2:15 [i]Ecc 6:8

16For the wise man, like the fool, will
not be long remembered;
in days to come both will be
forgotten.[j]
Like the fool, the wise man too must
die!

2:16 [j]Ecc 1:11; 9:5

Toil Is Meaningless

17So I hated life, because the work
that is done under the sun was grievous
to me. All of it is meaningless, a chasing
after the wind.[k] 18I hated all the things
I had toiled for under the sun, because I
must leave them to the one who comes
after me.[l] 19And who knows whether
he will be a wise man or a fool? Yet
he will have control over all the work
into which I have poured my effort and
skill under the sun. This too is meaningless. 20So my heart began to despair
over all my toilsome labor under the
sun. 21For a man may do his work with
wisdom, knowledge and skill, and then
he must leave all he owns to someone
who has not worked for it. This too
is meaningless and a great misfortune.
22What does a man get for all the toil
and anxious striving with which he labors under the sun?[m] 23All his days his
work is pain and grief;[n] even at night
his mind does not rest. This too is
meaningless.
24A man can do nothing better than
to eat and drink[o] and find satisfaction
in his work.[p] This too, I see, is from
the hand of God,[q] 25for without him,
who can eat or find enjoyment? 26To
the man who pleases him, God gives
wisdom, knowledge and happiness, but
to the sinner he gives the task of gathering and storing up wealth[r] to hand it
over to the one who pleases God.[s] This
too is meaningless, a chasing after the
wind.

2:17 [k]Ecc 4:2
2:18 [l]Ps 39:6; 49:10
2:22 [m]Ecc 1:3; 3:9
2:23 [n]Job 5:7; 14:1; Ecc 1:18
2:24 [o]Ecc 8:15; 1Co 15:32 [p]Ecc 3:22 [q]Ecc 3:12-13; 5:17-19; 9:7-10
2:26 [r]Job 27:17 [s]Pr 13:22

A Time for Everything

3 There is a time[t] for everything,
and a season for every activity
under heaven:

3:1 [t]ver 11,17; Ecc 8:6

2 a time to be born and a time to
die,
a time to plant and a time to
uproot,
3 a time to kill and a time to heal,
a time to tear down and a time to
build,
4 a time to weep and a time to
laugh,
a time to mourn and a time to
dance,
5 a time to scatter stones and a time
to gather them,
a time to embrace and a time to
refrain,
6 a time to search and a time to give
up,
a time to keep and a time to
throw away,
7 a time to tear and a time to mend,
a time to be silent[u] and a time to
speak,
8 a time to love and a time to hate,
a time for war and a time for
peace.

3:7 [u]Am 5:13

LOVE

THE NOBLE ESSENCE

Ecclesiastes 2:17

Love is the only antidote to meaningless living. Loving is more important than being loved. Those who require love sometimes doubt; those who give love, never.

DAY 3 THREE

▸ PATIENCE AND MY RELATIONSHIP WITH CHRIST

Ecclesiastes 3:1–8

The playwright Henrik Ibsen said that mental illness is always an extreme case of self-absorption. The word *always* may be too strong, but self-absorption is indeed a real killer of the soul. It causes us to hurry ever faster to avoid the imagined disasters that loom in our minds. Impatience may in some cases be our attempt at self-preservation. If we hurry, we feel we may avoid some dire circumstances. Impatience in itself, therefore, becomes a kind of self-absorption. Impatience can be viewed as an indication that we are serious about life, while patience can be a sign that we are blasé about success. Those who will not hurry seem to us to be lazy. They seem to be in grave danger of becoming irrelevant, for surely they will never amount to anything in this world.

But if there is truly a time for everything in this world, surely we should be able in some way to find a balance between getting the things done that we can accomplish and having patience for the rest.

Jesus is a wonderful model for patience. He had only a few years to minister on this earth, yet he never worried that he would not have time to accomplish all that God had planned for him. He trusted God's perfect timetable.

Jesus said that mental frenzy is to no avail. Jesus suggested we take a cue from nature. The birds do not worry, yet they are cared for (Matthew 6:25–27). Since inner turmoil is pointless, why not give ourselves instead to patience? Patience walks slowly and shouts to the self-absorption that would cause us to hurry, "To succeed is not to hurry toward success. It is to trust God, to walk slowly, to live long, and to see the world we once hurried through."

Let's take our cue from Jesus and dismiss any worry from our lives. We were allotted enough time to do exactly what God has created us to do. Jesus spent 33 years on this earth. Only three of those years he devoted to ministry. If Jesus felt no hurry, neither should we.

To begin a study on the topic of Patience, Living by God's Timetable, turn to the home page on page 593.

9What does the worker gain from his
toil?[v] 10I have seen the burden God has
laid on men.[w] 11He has made everything beautiful in its time.[x] He has
also set eternity in the hearts of men;
yet they cannot fathom[y] what God has
done from beginning to end.[z] 12I know
that there is nothing better for men
than to be happy and do good while
they live. 13That everyone may eat and
drink,[a] and find satisfaction[b] in all his
toil—this is the gift of God.[c] 14I know
that everything God does will endure
forever; nothing can be added to it and
nothing taken from it. God does it so
that men will revere him.[d]

15Whatever is has already been,[e]
and what will be has been before;[f]
and God will call the past to
account.[a]

16And I saw something else under the
sun:

In the place of judgment—
wickedness was there,
in the place of justice—
wickedness was there.

17I thought in my heart,

"God will bring to judgment[g]
both the righteous and the
wicked,
for there will be a time for every
activity,
a time for every deed."[h]

18I also thought, "As for men, God
tests them so that they may see that
they are like the animals.[i] 19Man's fate[j]
is like that of the animals; the same fate
awaits them both: As one dies, so dies
the other. All have the same breath[b];
man has no advantage over the animal.
Everything is meaningless. 20All go to
the same place; all come from dust, and
to dust all return.[k] 21Who knows if the
spirit of man rises upward[l] and if the
spirit of the animal[c] goes down into the
earth?"

22So I saw that there is nothing better
for a man than to enjoy his work,[m] because that is his lot.[n] For who can bring
him to see what will happen after him?

[a]15 Or *God calls back the past* [b]19 Or *spirit*
[c]21 Or *Who knows the spirit of man, which rises upward, or the spirit of the animal, which*

3:9 [v]Ecc 1:3
3:10 [w]Ecc 1:13
3:11 [x]ver 1 [y]Job 11:7; Ecc 8:17 [z]Job 28:23; Ro 11:33
3:13 [a]Ecc 2:3 [b]Ps 34:12 [c]Dt 12:7,18; Ecc 2:24; 5:19
3:14 [d]Job 23:15; Ecc 5:7; 7:18; 8:12-13; Jas 1:17
3:15 [e]Ecc 6:10 [f]Ecc 1:9
3:17 [g]Job 19:29; Ecc 11:9; Mt 16:27; Ro 2:6-8; 2Th 1:6-7 [h]ver 1
3:18 [i]Ps 73:22
3:19 [j]Ecc 2:14
3:20 [k]Ge 2:7; 3:19; Job 34:15
3:21 [l]Ecc 12:7
3:22 [m]Ecc 2:24; 5:18 [n]Job 31:2

Oppression, Toil, Friendlessness

4:1 [o]Ps 12:5; Ecc 3:16 [p]La 1:16

4 Again I looked and saw all the oppression[o] that was taking place under the sun:

I saw the tears of the oppressed—
and they have no comforter;
power was on the side of their
oppressors—
and they have no comforter.[p]

4:2 [q]Jer 20:17-18; 22:10 [r]Job 3:17; 10:18

2 And I declared that the dead,[q]
who had already died,
are happier than the living,
who are still alive.[r]

4:3 [s]Job 3:16; Ecc 6:3 [t]Job 3:22

3 But better than both
is he who has not yet been,[s]
who has not seen the evil
that is done under the sun.[t]

4:4 [u]Ecc 1:14

4 And I saw that all labor and all achievement spring from man's envy of his neighbor. This too is meaningless, a chasing after the wind.[u]

PEACE

THE BLISS OF DEATH

Ecclesiastes 4:2

Peace is evidence of a life that cannot die. The dead are happier than the living—if the dead have died in Christ. But then, the dead in Christ are more alive than those who can only offer their breath and pulse to prove themselves alive.

4:5 [v]Pr 6:10

5 The fool folds his hands[v]
and ruins himself.

4:6 [w]Pr 15:16-17; 16:8

6 Better one handful with tranquillity
than two handfuls with toil[w]
and chasing after the wind.

7 Again I saw something meaningless under the sun:

4:8 [x]Pr 27:20

8 There was a man all alone;
he had neither son nor brother.
There was no end to his toil,
yet his eyes were not content[x] with
his wealth.
"For whom am I toiling," he asked,
"and why am I depriving myself of
enjoyment?"
This too is meaningless—
a miserable business!

9 Two are better than one,
because they have a good return
for their work:
10 If one falls down,
his friend can help him up.
But pity the man who falls
and has no one to help him up!
11 Also, if two lie down together, they
will keep warm.
But how can one keep warm
alone?
12 Though one may be overpowered,
two can defend themselves.
A cord of three strands is not quickly
broken.

Advancement Is Meaningless

13 Better a poor but wise youth than
an old but foolish king who no longer
knows how to take warning. 14 The
youth may have come from prison to
the kingship, or he may have been born
in poverty within his kingdom. 15 I saw
that all who lived and walked under
the sun followed the youth, the king's
successor. 16 There was no end to all
the people who were before them. But
those who came later were not pleased
with the successor. This too is meaningless, a chasing after the wind.

Stand in Awe of God

5 Guard your steps when you go to the house of God. Go near to listen rather than to offer the sacrifice of fools, who do not know that they do wrong.

5:2 [y]Jdg 11:35; Job 6:24; Pr 10:19; 20:25

2 Do not be quick with your mouth,
do not be hasty in your heart
to utter anything before God.[y]
God is in heaven
and you are on earth,
so let your words be few.[z]

5:3 [a]Job 20:8 [b]Ecc 10:14

3 As a dream[a] comes when there are
many cares,
so the speech of a fool when there
are many words.[b]

5:4 [c]Dt 23:21; Jdg 11:35; Ps 119:60 [d]Nu 30:2; Ps 66:13-14; 76:11

5:5 [e]Nu 30:2-4; Pr 20:25; Jnh 2:9; Ac 5:4

5:7 [f]Ecc 3:14; 12:13

4 When you make a vow to God, do
not delay in fulfilling it.[c] He has no
pleasure in fools; fulfill your vow.[d] 5 It
is better not to vow than to make a
vow and not fulfill it.[e] 6 Do not let your
mouth lead you into sin. And do not
protest to the ⌊temple⌋ messenger, "My
vow was a mistake." Why should God
be angry at what you say and destroy
the work of your hands? 7 Much dreaming and many words are meaningless.
Therefore stand in awe of God.[f]

Riches Are Meaningless

5:8 [g]Ps 12:5; Ecc 4:1

8If you see the poor oppressed[g] in a
district, and justice and rights denied,
do not be surprised at such things; for
one official is eyed by a higher one, and
over them both are others higher still.
9The increase from the land is taken by
all; the king himself profits from the
fields.

10Whoever loves money never has
money enough;
whoever loves wealth is never
satisfied with his income.
This too is meaningless.

11As goods increase,
so do those who consume them.
And what benefit are they to the
owner
except to feast his eyes on them?

12The sleep of a laborer is sweet,
whether he eats little or much,
but the abundance of a rich man
permits him no sleep.[h]

5:12 [h]Job 20:20

13I have seen a grievous evil under
the sun:[i]

5:13 [i]Ecc 6:1-2

wealth hoarded to the harm of its
owner,
14 or wealth lost through some
misfortune,
so that when he has a son
there is nothing left for him.
15Naked a man comes from his
mother's womb,
and as he comes, so he departs.[j]
He takes nothing from his labor[k]
that he can carry in his hand.[l]

5:15 [j]Job 1:21 [k]Ps 49:17; 1Ti 6:7 [l]Ecc 1:3

16This too is a grievous evil:

As a man comes, so he departs,
and what does he gain,
since he toils for the wind?[m]
17All his days he eats in darkness,
with great frustration, affliction
and anger.

5:16 [m]Pr 11:29; Ecc 1:3

18Then I realized that it is good and
proper for a man to eat and drink,[n] and
to find satisfaction in his toilsome labor[o] under the sun during the few days
of life God has given him—for this is
his lot. 19Moreover, when God gives
any man wealth and possessions,[p] and
enables him to enjoy them,[q] to accept
his lot[r] and be happy in his work—this
is a gift of God.[s] 20He seldom reflects
on the days of his life, because God
keeps him occupied with gladness of
heart.[t]

5:18 [n]Ecc 2:3 [o]Ecc 2:10,24

5:19 [p]1Ch 29:12; 2Ch 1:12 [q]Ecc 6:2 [r]Job 31:2 [s]Ecc 2:24; 3:13

5:20 [t]Dt 12:7,18

6 I have seen another evil under the
sun, and it weighs heavily on men:
2God gives a man wealth, possessions
and honor, so that he lacks nothing his
heart desires, but God does not enable
him to enjoy them,[u] and a stranger enjoys them instead. This is meaningless,
a grievous evil.[v]

6:2 [u]Ps 17:14; Ecc 5:19 [v]Ecc 5:13

3A man may have a hundred children and live many years; yet no matter
how long he lives, if he cannot enjoy his
prosperity and does not receive proper
burial, I say that a stillborn[w] child is
better off than he.[x] 4It comes without
meaning, it departs in darkness, and in
darkness its name is shrouded. 5Though
it never saw the sun or knew anything,
it has more rest than does that man—
6even if he lives a thousand years twice
over but fails to enjoy his prosperity.
Do not all go to the same place?

6:3 [w]Job 3:16; Ecc 4:3 [x]Job 3:3

7All man's efforts are for his mouth,
yet his appetite is never satisfied.[y]
8What advantage has a wise man
over a fool?[z]
What does a poor man gain
by knowing how to conduct
himself before others?
9Better what the eye sees
than the roving of the appetite.
This too is meaningless,
a chasing after the wind.[a]

6:7 [y]Pr 16:26; 27:20

6:8 [z]Ecc 2:15

6:9 [a]Ecc 1:14

10Whatever exists has already been
named,
and what man is has been known;
no man can contend
with one who is stronger than he.
11The more the words,
the less the meaning,
and how does that profit anyone?

12For who knows what is good for a
man in life, during the few and meaningless days[b] he passes through like a
shadow?[c] Who can tell him what will
happen under the sun after he is gone?

6:12 [b]Job 10:20 [c]Job 14:2; Ps 39:6; Jas 4:14

Wisdom

7 A good name is better than fine
perfume,[d]
and the day of death better than
the day of birth.
2It is better to go to a house of
mourning

7:1 [d]Pr 22:1; SS 1:3

than to go to a house of feasting,
for death[e] is the destiny[f] of every
man;
the living should take this to
heart.
[3]Sorrow is better than laughter,[g]
because a sad face is good for the
heart.
[4]The heart of the wise is in the house
of mourning,
but the heart of fools is in the
house of pleasure.[h]
[5]It is better to heed a wise man's
rebuke[i]
than to listen to the song of fools.
[6]Like the crackling of thorns[j] under
the pot,
so is the laughter[k] of fools.
This too is meaningless.

[7]Extortion turns a wise man into a
fool,
and a bribe[l] corrupts the heart.
[8]The end of a matter is better than its
beginning,
and patience[m] is better than pride.
[9]Do not be quickly provoked[n] in your
spirit,
for anger resides in the lap of
fools.

[10]Do not say, "Why were the old days
better than these?"
For it is not wise to ask such
questions.

[11]Wisdom, like an inheritance, is a
good thing[o]
and benefits those who see the
sun.[p]
[12]Wisdom is a shelter
as money is a shelter,
but the advantage of knowledge is
this:
that wisdom preserves the life of
its possessor.

[13]Consider what God has done:[q]

Who can straighten
what he has made crooked?[r]
[14]When times are good, be happy;
but when times are bad, consider:
God has made the one
as well as the other.
Therefore, a man cannot discover
anything about his future.

[15]In this meaningless life[s] of mine I
have seen both of these:

7:2 [e]Pr 11:19 [f]Ps 90:12
7:3 [g]Pr 14:13
7:4 [h]Ecc 2:1; Jer 16:8
7:5 [i]Ps 141:5; Pr 13:18; 15:31-32
7:6 [j]Ps 58:9; 118:12 [k]Ecc 2:2
7:7 [l]Ex 18:21; 23:8; Dt 16:19
7:8 [m]Pr 14:29; Gal 5:22; Eph 4:2
7:9 [n]Mt 5:22; Pr 14:17; Jas 1:19
7:11 [o]Pr 8:10-11; Ecc 2:13 [p]Ecc 11:7
7:13 [q]Ecc 2:24 [r]Ecc 1:15
7:15 [s]Job 7:7

a righteous man perishing in his
righteousness,
and a wicked man living long in
his wickedness.[t]
[16]Do not be overrighteous,
neither be overwise—
why destroy yourself?
[17]Do not be overwicked,
and do not be a fool—
why die before your time?[u]
[18]It is good to grasp the one
and not let go of the other.
The man who fears God[v] will
avoid all ⌊extremes⌋.[a]

[19]Wisdom[w] makes one wise man more
powerful[x]
than ten rulers in a city.

[20]There is not a righteous man[y] on
earth
who does what is right and never
sins.[z]

[21]Do not pay attention to every word
people say,
or you[a] may hear your servant
cursing you—
[22]for you know in your heart
that many times you yourself have
cursed others.

[23]All this I tested by wisdom and I
said,

"I am determined to be wise"[b]—
but this was beyond me.
[24]Whatever wisdom may be,
it is far off and most profound—
who can discover it?[c]
[25]So I turned my mind to understand,
to investigate and to search out
wisdom and the scheme of
things[d]
and to understand the stupidity of
wickedness
and the madness of folly.[e]

[26]I find more bitter than death
the woman who is a snare,[f]
whose heart is a trap
and whose hands are chains.
The man who pleases God will
escape her,
but the sinner she will ensnare.[g]

[27]"Look," says the Teacher,[b][h] "this is
what I have discovered:

[a]*18* Or *will follow them both* [b]*27* Or *leader of the assembly*

7:15 [t]Ecc 8:12-14; Jer 12:1
7:17 [u]Job 15:32; Ps 55:23
7:18 [v]Ecc 3:14
7:19 [w]Ecc 2:13 [x]Ecc 9:13-18
7:20 [y]Ps 14:3 [z]1Ki 8:46; 2Ch 6:36; Pr 20:9; Ro 3:23
7:21 [a]Pr 30:10
7:23 [b]Ecc 1:17; Ro 1:22
7:24 [c]Job 28:12
7:25 [d]Job 28:3 [e]Ecc 1:17
7:26 [f]Ex 10:7; Jdg 14:15 [g]Pr 2:16-19; 5:3-5; 7:23; 22:14
7:27 [h]Ecc 1:1

"Adding one thing to another to
discover the scheme of
things—
28 while I was still searching
but not finding—
I found one ⌊upright⌋ man among a
thousand,
but not one ⌊upright⌋ woman[i] 7:28 [i]1Ki 11:3
among them all.
29 This only have I found:
God made mankind upright,
but men have gone in search of
many schemes."

8 Who is like the wise man?
Who knows the explanation of
things?
Wisdom brightens a man's face
and changes its hard appearance.

Obey the King

2 Obey the king's command, I say, because you took an oath before God.
3 Do not be in a hurry to leave the
king's presence.[j] Do not stand up for a 8:3 [j]Ecc 10:4
bad cause, for he will do whatever he
pleases. 4 Since a king's word is supreme,
who can say to him, "What are you 8:4 [k]Job 9:12; Est 1:19; Da 4:35
doing?"[k]

5 Whoever obeys his command will
come to no harm,
and the wise heart will know the
proper time and procedure.
6 For there is a proper time and
procedure for every matter,[l] 8:6 [l]Ecc 3:1
though a man's misery weighs
heavily upon him.

7 Since no man knows the future,
who can tell him what is to come?
8 No man has power over the wind to
contain it[a];
so no one has power over the day
of his death.
As no one is discharged in time of
war,
so wickedness will not release
those who practice it.

9 All this I saw, as I applied my mind
to everything done under the sun. There
is a time when a man lords it over others to his own[b] hurt. 10 Then too, I saw
the wicked buried[m]—those who used 8:10 [m]Ecc 1:11
to come and go from the holy place and
receive praise[c] in the city where they
did this. This too is meaningless.
11 When the sentence for a crime is
not quickly carried out, the hearts of
the people are filled with schemes to do
wrong. 12 Although a wicked man commits a hundred crimes and still lives a
long time, I know that it will go better[n] 8:12 [n]Dt 12:28; Ps 37:11, 18-19; Pr 1:32-33; Isa 3:10-11 [o]Ex 1:20 [p]Ecc 3:14
with God-fearing men,[o] who are rev-
erent before God.[p] 13 Yet because the
wicked do not fear God,[q] it will not go
well with them, and their days[r] will not 8:13 [q]Ecc 3:14; Isa 3:11 [r]Dt 4:40; Job 5:26; Ps 34:12; Isa 65:20
lengthen like a shadow.
14 There is something else meaningless that occurs on earth: righteous men
who get what the wicked deserve, and
wicked men who get what the righteous
deserve.[s] This too, I say, is meaningless.[t] 8:14 [s]Job 21:7; Ps 73:14; Mal 3:15 [t]Ecc 7:15
15 So I commend the enjoyment of life,[u]
because nothing is better for a man under the sun than to eat and drink[v] and
be glad.[w] Then joy will accompany him 8:15 [u]Ps 42:8 [v]Ex 32:6; Ecc 2:3 [w]Ecc 2:24; 3:12-13; 5:18; 9:7
in his work all the days of the life God
has given him under the sun.
16 When I applied my mind to know
wisdom[x] and to observe man's labor on
earth[y]—his eyes not seeing sleep day 8:16 [x]Ecc 1:17 [y]Ecc 1:13
or night— 17 then I saw all that God
has done.[z] No one can comprehend
what goes on under the sun. Despite 8:17 [z]Job 28:3 [a]Job 5:9; 28:23; Ecc 3:11; Ro 11:33
all his efforts to search it out, man can-
not discover its meaning. Even if a wise
man claims he knows, he cannot really
comprehend it.[a]

A Common Destiny for All

9 So I reflected on all this and concluded that the righteous and the
wise and what they do are in God's
hands, but no man knows whether love
or hate awaits him.[b] 2 All share a com- 9:1 [b]Dt 33:3; Job 12:10; Ecc 10:14
mon destiny—the righteous and the
wicked, the good and the bad,[d] the
clean and the unclean, those who offer
sacrifices and those who do not.

As it is with the good man,
so with the sinner;
as it is with those who take oaths,
so with those who are afraid to
take them.[c] 9:2 [c]Job 9:22; Ecc 2:14; 6:6; 7:2

3 This is the evil in everything that
happens under the sun: The same des-
tiny overtakes all.[d] The hearts of men, 9:3 [d]Job 9:22; Ecc 2:14 [e]Jer 11:8; 13:10; 16:12; 17:9 [f]Job 21:26
moreover, are full of evil and there
is madness in their hearts while they
live,[e] and afterward they join the dead.[f]

[a]8 Or *over his spirit to retain it* [b]9 Or *to their*
[c]10 Some Hebrew manuscripts and Septuagint (Aquila); most Hebrew manuscripts *and are forgotten*
[d]2 Septuagint (Aquila), Vulgate and Syriac; Hebrew does not have *and the bad.*

[4]Anyone who is among the living has hope[a]—even a live dog is better off than a dead lion!

DAY 2 TWO

▸ JOY AND THE PURPOSE OF GOD IN MY LIFE

Ecclesiastes 8:14–15

The writer of Ecclesiastes is convinced that the best short-term solution for unhappiness in life is to get up every morning, put on a happy face and decide we're going to enjoy life. A certain Christian writer speaks of approaching life with a "Be Happy Attitude." If this seems too intentional, let the writer of Ecclesiastes convince us that the best way to be happy in life is to be intentional about it.

This passage seems to suggest that moods do not track us down and force themselves upon us. They should not be the master of our circumstances. We should be master of both our circumstances and our moods.

Happiness is a choice, and misery is an option. When we agree with God that we are going to be joyous by intention, we are pretty much saying that our happiness will not be left to circumstances or to other people. Generally, when our joy is missing, we tend to blame one or the other. But for any set of circumstances or any people to make us unhappy, we do in a sense have to agree to it. God wants us consistently to choose the joy-option as our way of life.

"But," some might object, "isn't joy a by-product of our relationship with God? Shouldn't we rather try to get our relationship right, and the joy will come automatically?" There can be no question that this is one way to achieve joy, but a corollary truth is that we should be able to simply obey this simple directive from Ecclesiastes—whether we feel like it or not. Whatever our mood, we should assume an attitude of joy. If we deliberately choose this as our way of life, the mood with which we approach our days will manifest inner contentment. So Ecclesiastes reinforces our purpose of a positive life by simply commanding us to take charge of our moods and choose joy.

To begin a study on the topic of Joy, a Positive Attitude, turn to the home page on page 358.

[5]For the living know that they will
die,
but the dead know nothing;[g]
they have no further reward,
and even the memory of them[h] is
forgotten.[i]
[6]Their love, their hate
and their jealousy have long since
vanished;
never again will they have a part
in anything that happens under
the sun.[j]

9:5 [g]Job 14:21 [h]Ps 9:6 [i]Ecc 1:11; 2:16; Isa 26:14
9:6 [j]Job 21:21

[7]Go, eat your food with gladness, and
drink your wine[k] with a joyful heart,[l]
for it is now that God favors what you
do. [8]Always be clothed in white,[m] and
always anoint your head with oil. [9]En-
joy life with your wife,[n] whom you love,
all the days of this meaningless life that
God has given you under the sun— all
your meaningless days. For this is your
lot[o] in life and in your toilsome labor
under the sun. [10]Whatever[p] your hand
finds to do, do it with all your might,[q]
for in the grave,[b][r] where you are going,
there is neither working nor planning
nor knowledge nor wisdom.[s]

9:7 [k]Nu 6:20 [l]Ecc 2:24; 8:15
9:8 [m]Ps 23:5; Rev 3:4
9:9 [n]Pr 5:18 [o]Job 31:2
9:10 [p]1Sa 10:7 [q]Ecc 11:6; Ro 12:11; Col 3:23 [r]Nu 16:33 [s]Ecc 2:24

[11]I have seen something else under
the sun:

The race is not to the swift
or the battle to the strong,[t]
nor does food come to the wise[u]
or wealth to the brilliant
or favor to the learned;
but time and chance[v] happen to
them all.[w]

9:11 [t]Am 2:14-15 [u]Job 32:13; Isa 47:10; Jer 9:23 [v]Ecc 2:14 [w]Dt 8:18

[12]Moreover, no man knows when his
hour will come:

As fish are caught in a cruel net,
or birds are taken in a snare,
so men are trapped by evil times[x]
that fall unexpectedly upon them.[y]

9:12 [x]Pr 29:6 [y]Ps 73:22; Ecc 2:14; 8:7

Wisdom Better Than Folly

[13]I also saw under the sun this example of wisdom[z] that greatly impressed
me: [14]There was once a small city with
only a few people in it. And a powerful king came against it, surrounded it
and built huge siegeworks against it.
[15]Now there lived in that city a man

9:13 [z]2Sa 20:22

[a]4 Or *What then is to be chosen? With all who live, there is hope* [b]10 Hebrew *Sheol*

poor but wise, and he saved the city by
his wisdom. But nobody remembered
that poor man.[a] 16 So I said, "Wisdom
is better than strength." But the poor
man's wisdom is despised, and his words
are no longer heeded.[b]

17 The quiet words of the wise are more
to be heeded
than the shouts of a ruler of fools.
18 Wisdom[c] is better than weapons of
war,
but one sinner destroys much
good.

10

As dead flies give perfume a
bad smell,
so a little folly[d] outweighs wisdom
and honor.
2 The heart of the wise inclines to the
right,
but the heart of the fool to the left.
3 Even as he walks along the road,
the fool lacks sense
and shows everyone[e] how stupid
he is.
4 If a ruler's anger rises against you,
do not leave your post;[f]
calmness can lay great errors to
rest.[g]

5 There is an evil I have seen under
the sun,
the sort of error that arises from
a ruler:
6 Fools are put in many high
positions,[h]
while the rich occupy the low
ones.
7 I have seen slaves on horseback,
while princes go on foot like
slaves.[i]

8 Whoever digs a pit may fall into it;[j]
whoever breaks through a wall
may be bitten by a snake.[k]
9 Whoever quarries stones may be
injured by them;
whoever splits logs may be
endangered by them.[l]

10 If the ax is dull
and its edge unsharpened,
more strength is needed
but skill will bring success.

11 If a snake bites before it is charmed,
there is no profit for the charmer.[m]

12 Words from a wise man's mouth are
gracious,[n]
but a fool is consumed by his own
lips.[o]
13 At the beginning his words are folly;
at the end they are wicked
madness—
14 and the fool multiplies words.[p]

No one knows what is coming—
who can tell him what will happen
after him?[q]

15 A fool's work wearies him;
he does not know the way to
town.

16 Woe to you, O land whose king was
a servant[a][r]
and whose princes feast in the
morning.
17 Blessed are you, O land whose king
is of noble birth
and whose princes eat at a proper
time—
for strength and not for
drunkenness.[s]

18 If a man is lazy, the rafters sag;
if his hands are idle, the house
leaks.[t]

19 A feast is made for laughter,
and wine[u] makes life merry,
but money is the answer for
everything.

20 Do not revile the king[v] even in your
thoughts,
or curse the rich in your bedroom,
because a bird of the air may carry
your words,
and a bird on the wing may report
what you say.

Bread Upon the Waters

11

Cast[w] your bread upon the
waters,
for after many days you will find
it again.[x]
2 Give portions to seven, yes to eight,
for you do not know what disaster
may come upon the land.

3 If clouds are full of water,
they pour rain upon the earth.
Whether a tree falls to the south or
to the north,
in the place where it falls, there
will it lie.
4 Whoever watches the wind will not
plant;

[a] 16 Or *king is a child*

9:15 [a]Ge 40:14; Ecc 1:11; 2:16; 4:13
9:16 [b]Pr 21:22; Ecc 7:19
9:18 [c]ver 16
10:1 [d]Pr 13:16; 18:2
10:3 [e]Pr 13:16; 18:2
10:4 [f]Ecc 8:3 [g]Pr 16:14; 25:15
10:6 [h]Pr 29:2
10:7 [i]Pr 19:10
10:8 [j]Ps 7:15; 57:6; Pr 26:27 [k]Est 2:23; Ps 9:16; Am 5:19
10:9 [l]Pr 26:27
10:11 [m]Ps 58:5; Isa 3:3
10:12 [n]Pr 10:32
10:12 [o]Pr 10:14; 14:3; 15:2; 18:7
10:14 [p]Pr 15:2; Ecc 5:3; 6:12; 8:7 [q]Ecc 9:1
10:16 [r]Isa 3:4-5,12
10:17 [s]Dt 14:26; 1Sa 25:36; Pr 31:4
10:18 [t]Pr 20:4; 24:30-34
10:19 [u]Ge 14:18; Jdg 9:13
10:20 [v]Ex 22:28
11:1 [w]ver 6; Isa 32:20; Hos 10:12 [x]Dt 24:19; Pr 19:17; Mt 10:42

whoever looks at the clouds will
not reap.
[5]As you do not know the path of the
wind,[y]
or how the body is formed[a] in a
mother's womb,[z]
so you cannot understand the work
of God,
the Maker of all things.

[6]Sow your seed in the morning,
and at evening let not your hands
be idle,[a]
for you do not know which will
succeed,
whether this or that,
or whether both will do equally
well.

Remember Your Creator While Young

[7]Light is sweet,
and it pleases the eyes to see the
sun.[b]
[8]However many years a man may live,
let him enjoy them all.
But let him remember[c] the days of
darkness,
for they will be many.
Everything to come is meaningless.

[9]Be happy, young man, while you are
young,
and let your heart give you joy in
the days of your youth.
Follow the ways of your heart
and whatever your eyes see,
but know that for all these things
God will bring you to judgment.[d]
[10]So then, banish anxiety[e] from your
heart
and cast off the troubles of your
body,
for youth and vigor are
meaningless.[f]

12 Remember[g] your Creator
in the days of your youth,
before the days of trouble[h] come
and the years approach when you
will say,
"I find no pleasure in them"—
[2]before the sun and the light
and the moon and the stars grow
dark,
and the clouds return after the
rain;
[3]when the keepers of the house
tremble,
and the strong men stoop,
when the grinders cease because they
are few,
and those looking through the
windows grow dim;
[4]when the doors to the street are
closed
and the sound of grinding fades;
when men rise up at the sound of
birds,
but all their songs grow faint;[i]
[5]when men are afraid of heights
and of dangers in the streets;
when the almond tree blossoms
and the grasshopper drags himself
along
and desire no longer is stirred.
Then man goes to his eternal home[j]
and mourners[k] go about the
streets.

[6]Remember him—before the silver
cord is severed,
or the golden bowl is broken;
before the pitcher is shattered at the
spring,
or the wheel broken at the well,
[7]and the dust returns[l] to the ground
it came from,
and the spirit returns to God[m]
who gave it.[n]

[8]"Meaningless! Meaningless!" says the
Teacher.[b]
"Everything is meaningless!"[o]

The Conclusion of the Matter

[9]Not only was the Teacher wise, but
also he imparted knowledge to the
people. He pondered and searched out
and set in order many proverbs.[p] [10]The
Teacher searched to find just the right
words, and what he wrote was upright
and true.[q]

[11]The words of the wise are like
goads, their collected sayings like firmly
embedded nails[r]—given by one Shepherd. [12]Be warned, my son, of anything
in addition to them.

Of making many books there is
no end, and much study wearies the
body.[s]

[13]Now all has been heard;
here is the conclusion of the
matter:

[a]5 Or *know how life* (or *the spirit*) / *enters the body being formed* [b]8 Or *the leader of the assembly*; also in verses 9 and 10

11:5 [y]Jn 3:8-10 [z]Ps 139:14-16
11:6 [a]Ecc 9:10
11:7 [b]Ecc 7:11
11:8 [c]Ecc 12:1
11:9 [d]Job 19:29; Ecc 2:24; 3:17; 12:14; Ro 14:10
11:10 [e]Ps 94:19 [f]Ecc 2:24
12:1 [g]Ecc 11:8 [h]2Sa 19:35
12:4 [i]Jer 25:10
12:5 [j]Job 17:13; 10:21 [k]Jer 9:17; Am 5:16
12:7 [l]Ge 3:19; Job 34:15; Ps 146:4 [m]Ecc 3:21 [n]Job 20:8; Zec 12:1
12:8 [o]Ecc 1:2
12:9 [p]1Ki 4:32
12:10 [q]Pr 22:20-21
12:11 [r]Ezr 9:8
12:12 [s]Ecc 1:18

FAITHFULNESS

REGULARITY OF FAITH

Ecclesiastes 12:13

Be content to keep the law of God faithfully, for you shall never keep it perfectly.

Fear God and keep his
commandments,[t]
for this is the whole ⌞duty⌟ of
man.[u]
14For God will bring every deed into
judgment,[v]
including every hidden thing,[w]
whether it is good or evil.

12:13 [t]Dt 4:2; 10:12 [u]Mic 6:8

12:14 [v]Ecc 3:17 [w]Mt 10:26; 1Co 4:5

SONG OF SONGS 

AUTHORSHIP AND DATE

Solomon may have been the author.

Date uncertain; probably written during Solomon's reign, 970–930 B.C.

KEY THEMES

This brief book contains the story of love between a man and a woman. The pastoral tale deals with the ideal of marital love.

FRUIT OF THE SPIRIT IN SONG OF SONGS

Love: In the various exchanges between a new bride and groom, a dialogue of marital love unfolds. The following excerpts are examples of this grand love:

Beloved: Let him kiss me with the kisses of his mouth—
for your love is more delightful than wine.
(1:2)

Lover: How beautiful you are, my darling!
Oh, how beautiful!
Your eyes are doves.
(1:15)

Beloved: Listen! My lover!
Look! Here he comes,
leaping across the mountains,
bounding over the hills.
(2:8)

Beloved: My lover is mine and I am his.
(2:16)

So runs the dialogue in a beautiful and affirming picture of a bride and groom. The picture celebrates the physical and spiritual dimensions of love. The most defining theme verse points out God's intention in the enduring nature of marital love:

"Many waters cannot quench love; rivers cannot wash it away" (8:7).

1:1 [a]1Ki 4:32

1 Solomon's Song of Songs.[a]

Beloved[a]

2 Let him kiss me with the kisses of his
mouth—
for your love[b] is more delightful
than wine.

1:2 [b]SS 4:10

3 Pleasing is the fragrance of your
perfumes;[c]
your name[d] is like perfume
poured out.
No wonder the maidens[e] love you!

1:3 [c]SS 4:10 [d]Ecc 7:1 [e]Ps 45:14

4 Take me away with you—let us
hurry!
Let the king bring me into his
chambers.[f]

1:4 [f]Ps 45:15

Friends

We rejoice and delight in you[b];
we will praise your love more than
wine.

Beloved

How right they are to adore you!

5 Dark am I, yet lovely,[g]
O daughters of Jerusalem,[h]
dark like the tents of Kedar,
like the tent curtains of Solomon.[c]

1:5 [g]SS 2:14; 4:3 [h]SS 2:7; 5:8; 5:16

6 Do not stare at me because I am
dark,
because I am darkened by the sun.
My mother's sons were angry with me
and made me take care of the
vineyards;[i]
my own vineyard I have neglected.

1:6 [i]Ps 69:8; SS 8:12

7 Tell me, you whom I love, where
you graze your flock
and where you rest your sheep[j] at
midday.
Why should I be like a veiled
woman
beside the flocks of your friends?

1:7 [j]SS 3:1-4; Isa 13:20

Friends

8 If you do not know, most beautiful
of women,[k]
follow the tracks of the sheep
and graze your young goats
by the tents of the shepherds.

1:8 [k]SS 5:9; 6:1

Lover

9 I liken you, my darling, to a mare
harnessed to one of the chariots[l] of
Pharaoh.

1:9 [l]2Ch 1:17

10 Your cheeks[m] are beautiful with
earrings,
your neck with strings of jewels.[n]

1:10 [m]SS 5:13 [n]Isa 61:10

11 We will make you earrings of gold,
studded with silver.

Beloved

12 While the king was at his table,
my perfume spread its fragrance.[o]

1:12 [o]SS 4:11-14

13 My lover is to me a sachet of myrrh
resting between my breasts.
14 My lover is to me a cluster of henna[p]
blossoms
from the vineyards of En Gedi.[q]

1:14 [p]SS 4:13 [q]1Sa 23:29

Lover

15 How beautiful[r] you are, my darling!
Oh, how beautiful!
Your eyes are doves.[s]

1:15 [r]SS 4:7 [s]SS ; 2:14; 4:1; 5:2,12; 6:9

Beloved

16 How handsome you are, my lover!
Oh, how charming!
And our bed is verdant.

Lover

17 The beams of our house are cedars;[t]
our rafters are firs.

1:17 [t]1Ki 6:9

Beloved[d]

2 I am a rose[e][u] of Sharon,[v]
a lily[w] of the valleys.

2:1 [u]Isa 35:1 [v]1Ch 27:29 [w]SS 5:13; Hos 14:5

Lover

2 Like a lily among thorns
is my darling among the maidens.

Beloved

3 Like an apple tree among the trees of
the forest
is my lover[x] among the young
men.
I delight[y] to sit in his shade,
and his fruit is sweet to my taste.[z]

2:3 [x]SS 1:14 [y]SS 1:4 [z]SS 4:16

4 He has taken me to the banquet
hall,[a]
and his banner[b] over me is love.

2:4 [a]Est 1:11 [b]Nu 1:52

5 Strengthen me with raisins,
refresh me with apples,[c]
for I am faint with love.[d]

2:5 [c]SS 7:8 [d]SS 5:8

6 His left arm is under my head,
and his right arm embraces me.[e]

2:6 [e]SS 8:3

[a]Primarily on the basis of the gender of the Hebrew pronouns used, male and female speakers are indicated in the margins by the captions *Lover* and *Beloved* respectively. The words of others are marked *Friends.* In some instances the divisions and their captions are debatable. [b]*4* The Hebrew is masculine singular. [c]*5* Or *Salma* [d]*1* Or *Lover* [e]*1* Possibly a member of the crocus family

2:7 [f]SS 5:8 [g]SS 3:5; 8:4

[7]Daughters of Jerusalem, I charge
you[f]
by the gazelles and by the does of
the field:
Do not arouse or awaken love
until it so desires.[g]

2:8 [h]ver 17; SS 8:14

[8]Listen! My lover!
Look! Here he comes,
leaping across the mountains,
bounding over the hills.[h]

2:9 [i]2Sa 2:18 [j]ver 17; SS 8:14

[9]My lover is like a gazelle[i] or a young
stag.[j]
Look! There he stands behind our
wall,
gazing through the windows,
peering through the lattice.
[10]My lover spoke and said to me,
"Arise, my darling,
my beautiful one, and come with
me.
[11]See! The winter is past;
the rains are over and gone.
[12]Flowers appear on the earth;
the season of singing has come,
the cooing of doves
is heard in our land.

2:13 [k]Isa 28:4; Jer 24:2; Hos 9:10; Mic 7:1; Na 3:12 [l]SS 7:12

[13]The fig tree forms its early fruit;[k]
the blossoming[l] vines spread their
fragrance.
Arise, come, my darling;
my beautiful one, come with me."

Lover

2:14 [m]Ge 8:8; SS 1:15 [n]SS 1:5; 8:13

[14]My dove[m] in the clefts of the rock,
in the hiding places on the
mountainside,
show me your face,
let me hear your voice;
for your voice is sweet,
and your face is lovely.[n]

2:15 [o]Jdg 15:4 [p]SS 1:6 [q]SS 7:12

[15]Catch for us the foxes,[o]
the little foxes
that ruin the vineyards,[p]
our vineyards that are in bloom.[q]

Beloved

2:16 [r]SS 7:10 [s]SS 4:5; 6:3

[16]My lover is mine and I am his;[r]
he browses among the lilies.[s]

2:17 [t]SS 4:6 [u]SS 1:14 [v]ver 9 [w]ver 8

[17]Until the day breaks
and the shadows flee,[t]
turn, my lover,[u]
and be like a gazelle
or like a young stag[v]
on the rugged hills.[a][w]

3:1 [x]SS 5:6; Isa 26:9

3 All night long on my bed
I looked[x] for the one my heart
loves;
I looked for him but did not find
him.
[2]I will get up now and go about the
city,
through its streets and squares;
I will search for the one my heart
loves.
So I looked for him but did not
find him.

3:1 [y]SS 5:7

[3]The watchmen found me
as they made their rounds in the
city.[y]
"Have you seen the one my heart
loves?"

3:4 [z]SS 8:2 [a]SS 6:9

[4]Scarcely had I passed them
when I found the one my heart
loves.
I held him and would not let him go
till I had brought him to my
mother's house,[z]
to the room of the one who
conceived me.[a]

3:5 [b]SS 2:7 [c]SS 8:4

[5]Daughters of Jerusalem, I charge
you[b]
by the gazelles and by the does of
the field:
Do not arouse or awaken love
until it so desires.[c]

3:6 [d]SS 8:5 [e]SS ; 1:13; 4:6,14 [f]Ex 30:34

[6]Who is this coming up from the
desert[d]
like a column of smoke,
perfumed with myrrh[e] and incense
made from all the spices[f] of the
merchant?

3:7 [g]1Sa 8:11

[7]Look! It is Solomon's carriage,
escorted by sixty warriors,[g]
the noblest of Israel,
[8]all of them wearing the sword,
all experienced in battle,
each with his sword at his side,
prepared for the terrors of the
night.[h]

3:8 [h]Job 15:22; Ps 91:5

[9]King Solomon made for himself the
carriage;
he made it of wood from
Lebanon.
[10]Its posts he made of silver,
its base of gold.
Its seat was upholstered with
purple,
its interior lovingly inlaid
by[b] the daughters of Jerusalem.

3:11 [i]Isa 4:4

[11]Come out, you daughters of Zion,[i]
and look at King Solomon
wearing the crown,

[a]17 Or *the hills of Bether* [b]10 Or *its inlaid interior a gift of love / from*

the crown with which his mother
crowned him
on the day of his wedding,
the day his heart rejoiced.[j]

Lover

4 How beautiful you are, my
darling!
Oh, how beautiful!
Your eyes behind your veil are
doves.[k]
Your hair is like a flock of goats
descending from Mount Gilead.[l]
2 Your teeth are like a flock of sheep
just shorn,
coming up from the washing.
Each has its twin;
not one of them is alone.[m]
3 Your lips are like a scarlet ribbon;
your mouth[n] is lovely.
Your temples behind your veil
are like the halves of a
pomegranate.[o]
4 Your neck is like the tower[p] of
David,
built with elegance[a];
on it hang a thousand shields,[q]
all of them shields of warriors.
5 Your two breasts[r] are like two fawns,
like twin fawns of a gazelle[s]
that browse among the lilies.[t]
6 Until the day breaks
and the shadows flee,[u]
I will go to the mountain of myrrh[v]
and to the hill of incense.
7 All beautiful[w] you are, my darling;
there is no flaw in you.

8 Come with me from Lebanon, my
bride,[x]
come with me from Lebanon.
Descend from the crest of Amana,
from the top of Senir,[y] the
summit of Hermon,[z]
from the lions' dens
and the mountain haunts of the
leopards.
9 You have stolen my heart, my sister,
my bride;
you have stolen my heart
with one glance of your eyes,
with one jewel of your necklace.[a]
10 How delightful[b] is your love,[c] my
sister, my bride!
How much more pleasing is your
love than wine,
and the fragrance of your perfume
than any spice!

3:11 [j]Isa 62:5
4:1 [k]SS 1:15; 5:12 [l]SS 6:5; Mic 7:14
4:2 [m]SS 6:6
4:3 [n]SS 5:16 [o]SS 6:7
4:4 [p]SS 7:4 [q]Eze 27:10
4:5 [r]SS 7:3 [s]Pr 5:19 [t]SS 2:16; 6:2-3
4:6 [u]SS 2:17 [v]ver 14
4:7 [w]SS 1:15
4:8 [x]SS 5:1 [y]Dt 3:9 [z]1Ch 5:23
4:9 [a]Ge 41:42
4:10 [b]SS 7:6 [c]SS 1:2

11 Your lips drop sweetness as the
honeycomb, my bride;
milk and honey are under your
tongue.[d]
The fragrance of your garments is
like that of Lebanon.[e]
12 You are a garden locked up, my
sister, my bride;
you are a spring enclosed, a sealed
fountain.[f]
13 Your plants are an orchard of
pomegranates[g]
with choice fruits,
with henna[h] and nard,
14 nard and saffron,
calamus and cinnamon,[i]
with every kind of incense tree,
with myrrh[j] and aloes
and all the finest spices.[k]
15 You are[b] a garden fountain,
a well of flowing water
streaming down from Lebanon.

Beloved

16 Awake, north wind,
and come, south wind!
Blow on my garden,
that its fragrance may spread
abroad.
Let my lover come into his garden
and taste its choice fruits.[l]

Lover

5 I have come into my garden, my
sister, my bride;[m]
I have gathered my myrrh with
my spice.
I have eaten my honeycomb and my
honey;
I have drunk my wine and my
milk.[n]

Friends

Eat, O friends, and drink;
drink your fill, O lovers.

Beloved

2 I slept but my heart was awake.
Listen! My lover is knocking:
"Open to me, my sister, my darling,
my dove, my flawless[o] one.[p]
My head is drenched with dew,
my hair with the dampness of the
night."
3 I have taken off my robe—

[a]4 The meaning of the Hebrew for this word is uncertain. [b]15 Or *I am* (spoken by the *Beloved*)

4:11 [d]Ps 19:10; SS 5:1 [e]Hos 14:6
4:12 [f]Pr 5:15-18
4:13 [g]SS ; 6:11; 7:12 [h]SS 1:14
4:14 [i]Ex 30:23 [j]SS 3:6 [k]SS 1:12
4:16 [l]SS ; 2:3; 5:1
5:1 [m]SS 4:8 [n]SS 4:11; Isa 55:1
5:2 [o]SS 4:7 [p]SS 6:9

must I put it on again?
I have washed my feet—
must I soil them again?
4 My lover thrust his hand through
the latch-opening;
my heart began to pound for him.
5 I arose to open for my lover,
and my hands dripped with
myrrh,
my fingers with flowing myrrh,[q]
on the handles of the lock.
6 I opened for my lover,[r]
but my lover had left; he was
gone.[s]
My heart sank at his departure.[a]
I looked[t] for him but did not find
him.
I called him but he did not
answer.
7 The watchmen found me
as they made their rounds in the
city.[u]
They beat me, they bruised me;
they took away my cloak,
those watchmen of the walls!
8 O daughters of Jerusalem, I charge
you[v]—
if you find my lover,
what will you tell him?
Tell him I am faint with love.[w]

Friends

9 How is your beloved better than
others,
most beautiful of women?[x]
How is your beloved better than
others,
that you charge us so?

Beloved

10 My lover is radiant and ruddy,
outstanding among ten
thousand.[y]
11 His head is purest gold;
his hair is wavy
and black as a raven.
12 His eyes are like doves[z]
by the water streams,
washed in milk,[a]
mounted like jewels.
13 His cheeks[b] are like beds of spice[c]
yielding perfume.
His lips are like lilies[d]
dripping with myrrh.
14 His arms are rods of gold
set with chrysolite.
His body is like polished ivory
decorated with sapphires.[b][e]

5:5 [q]ver 13
5:6 [r]SS 6:1 [s]SS 6:2 [t]SS 3:1
5:7 [u]SS 3:3
5:8 [v]SS 2:7; 3:5 [w]SS 2:5
5:9 [x]SS 1:8; 6:1
5:10 [y]Ps 45:2
5:12 [z]SS 1:15; 4:1 [a]Ge 49:12
5:13 [b]SS 1:10 [c]SS 6:2 [d]SS 2:1
5:14 [e]Job 28:6

15 His legs are pillars of marble
set on bases of pure gold.
His appearance is like Lebanon,[f]
choice as its cedars.
16 His mouth[g] is sweetness itself;
he is altogether lovely.
This is my lover,[h] this my friend,
O daughters of Jerusalem.[i]

5:15 [f]1Ki 4:33; SS 7:4
5:16 [g]SS 4:3 [h]SS 7:9 [i]SS 1:5

Friends

6 Where has your lover[j] gone,
most beautiful of women?[k]
Which way did your lover turn,
that we may look for him with
you?

Beloved

2 My lover has gone[l] down to his
garden,[m]
to the beds of spices,[n]
to browse in the gardens
and to gather lilies.
3 I am my lover's and my lover is
mine;[o]
he browses among the lilies.[p]

Lover

4 You are beautiful, my darling, as
Tirzah,[q]
lovely as Jerusalem,[r]
majestic as troops with banners.[s]
5 Turn your eyes from me;
they overwhelm me.
Your hair is like a flock of goats
descending from Gilead.[t]
6 Your teeth are like a flock of sheep
coming up from the washing.
Each has its twin,
not one of them is alone.[u]
7 Your temples behind your veil[v]
are like the halves of a
pomegranate.[w]
8 Sixty queens[x] there may be,
and eighty concubines,[y]
and virgins beyond number;
9 but my dove,[z] my perfect one,[a] is
unique,
the only daughter of her mother,
the favorite of the one who bore
her.[b]
The maidens saw her and called her
blessed;
the queens and concubines praised
her.

6:1 [j]SS 5:6 [k]SS 1:8
6:2 [l]SS 5:6 [m]SS 4:12 [n]SS 5:13
6:3 [o]SS 7:10 [p]SS 2:16
6:4 [q]Jos 12:24 [r]Ps 48:2; 50:2 [s]ver 10
6:5 [t]SS 4:1
6:6 [u]SS 4:2
6:7 [v]Ge 24:65 [w]SS 4:3
6:8 [x]Ps 45:9 [y]Ge 22:24
6:9 [z]SS 1:15 [a]SS 5:2 [b]SS 3:4

[a]6 Or *heart had gone out to him when he spoke*
[b]14 Or *lapis lazuli*

Friends

[10]Who is this that appears like the
dawn,
fair as the moon, bright as the
sun,
majestic as the stars in procession?

Lover

[11]I went down to the grove of nut
trees
to look at the new growth in the
valley,
to see if the vines had budded
or the pomegranates were in
bloom.[c]
6:11 [c]SS 7:12
[12]Before I realized it,
my desire set me among the royal
chariots of my people.[a]

Friends

[13]Come back, come back,
O Shulammite;
come back, come back, that we
may gaze on you!

Lover

Why would you gaze on the
Shulammite
6:13 [d]Ex 15:20
as on the dance[d] of Mahanaim?

7 How beautiful your sandaled feet,
7:1 [e]Ps 45:13
O prince's[e] daughter!
Your graceful legs are like jewels,
the work of a craftsman's hands.
[2]Your navel is a rounded goblet
that never lacks blended wine.
Your waist is a mound of wheat
encircled by lilies.
7:3 [f]SS 4:5
[3]Your breasts[f] are like two fawns,
twins of a gazelle.
7:4 [g]Ps 144:12; SS 4:4 [h]Nu 21:26 [i]SS 5:15
[4]Your neck is like an ivory tower.[g]
Your eyes are the pools of Heshbon[h]
by the gate of Bath Rabbim.
Your nose is like the tower of
Lebanon[i]
looking toward Damascus.
[5]Your head crowns you like Mount
7:5 [j]Isa 35:2
Carmel.[j]
Your hair is like royal tapestry;
the king is held captive by its
tresses.
7:6 [k]SS 1:15 [l]SS 4:10
[6]How beautiful[k] you are and how
pleasing,
O love, with your delights![l]
[7]Your stature is like that of the palm,
7:7 [m]SS 4:5
and your breasts[m] like clusters of
fruit.
[8]I said, "I will climb the palm tree;
I will take hold of its fruit."
May your breasts be like the clusters
of the vine,
the fragrance of your breath like
apples,[n]
7:8 [n]SS 2:5
[9] and your mouth like the best wine.

Beloved

May the wine go straight to my
lover,[o]
7:9 [o]SS 5:16
flowing gently over lips and teeth.[b]
[10]I belong to my lover,
7:10 [p]Ps 45:11 [q]SS 2:16; 6:3
and his desire[p] is for me.[q]
[11]Come, my lover, let us go to the
countryside,
let us spend the night in the
villages.[c]
7:12 [r]SS 1:6 [s]SS 2:15 [t]SS 2:13 [u]SS 4:13 [v]SS 6:11
[12]Let us go early to the vineyards[r]
to see if the vines have budded,[s]
if their blossoms[t] have opened,
and if the pomegranates[u] are in
bloom[v]—
there I will give you my love.
7:13 [w]Ge 30:14 [x]SS 4:16
[13]The mandrakes[w] send out their
fragrance,
and at our door is every delicacy,
both new and old,
that I have stored up for you, my
lover.[x]

8 If only you were to me like a
brother,
who was nursed at my mother's
breasts!
Then, if I found you outside,
I would kiss you,
and no one would despise me.
[2]I would lead you
and bring you to my mother's
house[y]—
8:2 [y]SS 3:4
she who has taught me.
I would give you spiced wine to
drink,
the nectar of my pomegranates.
[3]His left arm is under my head
8:3 [z]SS 2:6
and his right arm embraces me.[z]
[4]Daughters of Jerusalem, I charge you:
Do not arouse or awaken love
8:4 [a]SS 2:7; 3:5
until it so desires.[a]

Friends

[5]Who is this coming up from the
desert[b]
8:5 [b]SS 3:6
leaning on her lover?

[a]12 Or *among the chariots of Amminadab*; or *among the chariots of the people of the prince* [b]9 Septuagint, Aquila, Vulgate and Syriac; Hebrew *lips of sleepers* [c]11 Or *henna bushes*

Beloved

Under the apple tree I roused you;
there your mother conceived[e] you, 8:5 [e]SS 3:4
there she who was in labor gave you birth.

DAY 2 TWO

▸ LOVE AND THE PURPOSE OF GOD IN MY LIFE

Song of Songs 8:6–7

It is easy to understand why Saint John of the Cross wrote "The Divine Flame of Love." This passage says love "burns like blazing fire, like a mighty flame. Many waters cannot quench love; rivers cannot wash it away." There is great passion in God's saving love. It not only saves us, but it also daily reveals God's purpose in our lives. His love is the fuel and energy of our calling.

Paul celebrated this purpose-revealing, energy-driving love in what some have called the believer's victory hymn:

> **Who shall separate us from the love of Christ? Shall trouble or hardship or persecution or famine or nakedness or danger or sword? As it is written:**
>
> **"For your sake we face death all day long;**
> **we are considered as sheep to be slaughtered."**
>
> **No, in all these things we are more than conquerors through him who loved us. For I am convinced that neither death nor life, neither angels nor demons, neither the present nor the future, nor any powers, neither height nor depth, nor anything else in all creation, will be able to separate us from the love of God that is in Christ Jesus our Lord.**
> **(Romans 8:35–39)**

George Mattheson wrote, "Oh Love that will not let me Go, I rest my weary soul in thee. I give thee back the life I owe, that in the blessed crimson flow my life may richer, fuller be." So we are owned by, managed by, as well as indebted to the burning passion of God, a love unquenchable for the life everlasting.

To begin a study on the topic of Love, the Unconditional Longing of God, turn to the home page on page 89.

6 Place me like a seal over your heart,
like a seal on your arm;
for love[d] is as strong as death, 8:6 [d]SS 1:2
its jealousy[a][e] unyielding as the grave.[b] [e]Nu 5:14
It burns like blazing fire,
like a mighty flame.[c]
7 Many waters cannot quench love;
rivers cannot wash it away.
If one were to give
all the wealth of his house for love,
it[d] would be utterly scorned.[f] 8:7 [f]Pr 6:35

Friends

8 We have a young sister,
and her breasts are not yet grown.
What shall we do for our sister
for the day she is spoken for?
9 If she is a wall,
we will build towers of silver on her.
If she is a door,
we will enclose her with panels of cedar.

Beloved

10 I am a wall,
and my breasts are like towers.
Thus I have become in his eyes
like one bringing contentment.
11 Solomon had a vineyard[g] in Baal Hamon; 8:11 [g]Ecc 2:4
he let out his vineyard to tenants.
Each was to bring for its fruit
a thousand shekels[e][h] of silver. [h]Isa 7:23
12 But my own vineyard[i] is mine to give; 8:12 [i]SS 1:6
the thousand shekels are for you, O Solomon,
and two hundred[f] are for those who tend its fruit.

Lover

13 You who dwell in the gardens
with friends in attendance,
let me hear your voice!

Beloved

14 Come away, my lover,
and be like a gazelle[j] 8:14 [j]Pr 5:19
or like a young stag[k] [k]SS 2:9
on the spice-laden mountains.[l] [l]SS 2:8,17

[a]6 Or *ardor* [b]6 Hebrew *Sheol* [c]6 Or */ like the very flame of the LORD* [d]7 Or *he* [e]11 That is, about 25 pounds (about 11.5 kilograms); also in verse 12 [f]12 That is, about 5 pounds (about 2.3 kilograms)

ISAIAH

AUTHORSHIP AND DATE

Isaiah

Chapters 1–39 may have been written c. 700 B.C.; chapters 40–66 were probably written after 681 B.C.

KEY THEMES

Isaiah, like most of the prophets, preached a stern warning of God's coming judgment on Israel and the surrounding nations. Isaiah seems to have been more of a court prophet than some of the other prophets were, and the literary quality of his sermons and poems are of the finest quality. This high literary style points to Isaiah's fine education and aristocratic sensibilities.

Isaiah 1–39 contains denunciations and rebukes for the sins of the nations that surrounded Israel. But chapters 40–66 point to a time of God's ultimate redemption from exile and the coming of the Messiah. Holiness is one of the themes of the book of Isaiah, and that theme can be easily seen in the tone of Isaiah 6. Punishment and salvation are other themes of the book. But the most lucid and wonderful themes of the book deal with the coming Messiah. This suffering-servant Messiah is the theme of chapters 40–66. These chapters make it clear that the people of Israel must stop pinning all their hopes on the warrior-like Davidic Messiah and begin to exult the Messiah as a suffering servant.

FRUIT OF THE SPIRIT IN ISAIAH

Love: Isaiah gives us a "love-forecast" of the exiles returning to their homeland. God was in love with Israel and so he said, "Comfort, comfort my people . . . Speak tenderly to Jerusalem, and proclaim to her that her hard service has been completed, that her sin has been paid for, that she has received from the LORD's hand double for all her sins" (40:1–2). The people of Israel had sinned and would be taken captive. In exile, as they once were in Egypt, they would meet the love of God. And once again they were to be set free. God in his great grace was going to help them return home. He would make the way easy. His love would raise every valley, chop off every mountain and make every rugged place a level plain. God's chosen people were going home.

Joy: When the Israelites' long imprisonment was over, they would return once again to their God. In that day they would praise God, and they would cry in great joy: "Surely God is my salvation; I will trust and not be afraid. The LORD, the LORD, is my strength and my song; he has become my salvation... Give thanks to the LORD, call on his name... Sing to the LORD, for he has done glorious things" (12:2,4–5).

Peace: In the "peaceable kingdom," as it has been called, universal Eden will come again. The wolf will live with the lamb, the leopard with the goat, the calf with the lion. Then "the earth will be full of the knowledge of the LORD as the waters cover the sea" (11:9).

Patience: The famous sign to Ahaz ("The virgin will be with child...") gave the king God's assurance, but he still had to wait to see the prophecy come to pass. Before Ahaz could see his deliverance, he would have to wait until sometime before the promised child knew enough to choose between right and wrong (see 7:16). God usually gives us all the peace and security we ask for, but he often asks us to learn patience in the process.

Kindness: God's Messiah—his suffering servant—was one in whom God would delight. He would be gentle: "A bruised reed he will not break, and a smoldering wick he will not snuff out" (42:3). His kindness would be the mark of his gentle servanthood.

Goodness: "Water will gush forth in the wilderness and streams in the desert. The burning sand will become a pool, the thirsty ground bubbling springs. In the haunts where jackals once lay, grass and reeds and papyrus will grow. And a highway will be there; it will be called the Way of Holiness" (35:6–8). In the middle of this new utopia will be a highway called Holiness, and holiness is the final stage of goodness.

Gentleness: It is a gentle God who offers a drink of cold water to the thirsty. It is a gentle God who offers milk and wine without cost to the poor and hungry (see 55:1). God's gentleness is his robe of love, and his sandals are his grace.

1:1 [a]Nu 12:6 [b]Isa 40:9 [c]Isa 2:1 [d]2Ch 26:22 [e]2Ki 16:1

1 The vision[a] concerning Judah and Jerusalem[b] that Isaiah son of Amoz saw[c] during the reigns of Uzziah,[d] Jotham, Ahaz[e] and Hezekiah, kings of Judah.

A Rebellious Nation

1:2 [f]Mic 1:2 [g]Isa 30:1,9; 65:2

[2]Hear, O heavens! Listen, O earth!
For the LORD has spoken:[f]
"I reared children and brought them up,
but they have rebelled[g] against me.
[3]The ox knows his master,
the donkey his owner's manger,
but Israel does not know,[h]
my people do not understand."

1:3 [h]Jer 8:7; 9:3,6

[4]Ah, sinful nation,
a people loaded with guilt,
a brood of evildoers,[i]
children given to corruption!
They have forsaken the LORD;
they have spurned the Holy One[j] of Israel
and turned their backs on him.

1:4 [i]Isa 14:20 [j]Isa 5:19,24

[5]Why should you be beaten anymore?
Why do you persist in rebellion?[k]
Your whole head is injured,
your whole heart afflicted.[l]
[6]From the sole of your foot to the top of your head
there is no soundness[m]—
only wounds and welts
and open sores,
not cleansed or bandaged[n]
or soothed with oil.[o]

1:5 [k]Isa 31:6 [l]Isa 33:6,24

1:6 [m]Ps 38:3 [n]Isa 30:26; Jer 8:22 [o]Lk 10:34

[7]Your country is desolate,[p]
your cities burned with fire;
your fields are being stripped by foreigners
right before you,
laid waste as when overthrown by strangers.
[8]The Daughter of Zion is left
like a shelter in a vineyard,
like a hut[q] in a field of melons,
like a city under siege.
[9]Unless the LORD Almighty
had left us some survivors,[r]
we would have become like Sodom,
we would have been like Gomorrah.[s]

1:7 [p]Lev 26:34

1:8 [q]Job 27:18

1:9 [r]Isa 10:20-22; 37:4,31-32 [s]Ge 19:24; Ro 9:29*

[10]Hear the word of the LORD,[t]
you rulers of Sodom;[u]
listen to the law[v] of our God,
you people of Gomorrah!
[11]"The multitude of your sacrifices—
what are they to me?" says the LORD.
"I have more than enough of burnt offerings,
of rams and the fat of fattened animals;[w]
I have no pleasure
in the blood of bulls[x] and lambs and goats.[y]
[12]When you come to appear before me,
who has asked this of you,[z]
this trampling of my courts?
[13]Stop bringing meaningless offerings![a]
Your incense[b] is detestable to me.
New Moons, Sabbaths and convocations[c]—
I cannot bear your evil assemblies.
[14]Your New Moon festivals and your appointed feasts[d]
my soul hates.
They have become a burden to me;
I am weary[e] of bearing them.
[15]When you spread out your hands in prayer,
I will hide[f] my eyes from you;
even if you offer many prayers,
I will not listen.
Your hands are full of blood;[g]
[16]wash and make yourselves clean.
Take your evil deeds
out of my sight![h]
Stop doing wrong,[i]
[17]learn to do right!
Seek justice,[j]
encourage the oppressed.[a]
Defend the cause of the fatherless,[k]
plead the case of the widow.

1:10 [t]Isa 28:14 [u]Isa 3:9; Eze 16:49; Ro 9:29; Rev 11:8 [v]Isa 8:20

1:11 [w]Ps 50:8 [x]Jer 6:20 [y]1Sa 15:22; Mal 1:10

1:12 [z]Ex 23:17

1:13 [a]Isa 66:3 [b]Jer 7:9 [c]1Ch 23:31

1:14 [d]Lev 23:1-44; Nu 28:11-29:39; Isa 29:1 [e]Isa 7:13; 43:22,24

1:15 [f]Isa 8:17; 59:2; Mic 3:4 [g]Isa 59:3

1:16 [h]Isa 52:11 [i]Isa 55:7; Jer 25:5

1:17 [j]Zep 2:3 [k]Ps 82:3

GENTLENESS

THE SOCIOLOGY OF GOD

> *Isaiah 1:17*
> **Seek justice;**
> **Encourage the oppressed;**
> **Defend the cause of the fatherless;**
> **Plead the case of the widow.**
> **Be gentle if you would paint the best portrait of God.**

[18]"Come now, let us reason together,"[l]
says the LORD.
"Though your sins are like scarlet,
they shall be as white as snow;[m]
though they are red as crimson,

1:18 [l]Isa 41:1; 43:9,26 [m]Ps 51:7; Rev 7:14

[a]17 Or / *rebuke the oppressor*

WEEK 15 GOODNESS

1 DAY ONE

GOODNESS AND THE DESIRE FOR HOLINESS

Read Isaiah 1:1–6

God wants his children to be good. In this he is a most typical parent. How differently our children behave at their various phases of growth.

When they are very young, they pass through the "he hit me"—"I did not" phase of quarreling.
When they are older, it's "he's been in the bathroom two hours"—"I have not" phase of quarreling.
When they are teenagers, it's "she got to drive the car last week"—"I did not" phase of quarreling.

Whatever the phase, parents genuinely wish their children wouldn't argue. They want their children to behave, to be good. They want their children to love each other.

Isaiah says that the children of Israel were not good. They hadn't the slightest urge to be like their Father God—holy. "I reared children and brought them up, but they have rebelled against me," laments God (Isaiah 1:2). God had tried "spanking them" to bring them into line, but nothing was really working: "From the sole of your foot to the top of your head there is no soundness—only wounds and welts and open sores" (v. 6). God had spanked his children until they were covered with welts, but they were still disobedient.

The consequence of Israel's disobedience and later punishment was that God's people never saw the relationship between obedience and righteousness. Therefore, they lost that special relationship with God that they might have had if they had craved holiness and truth.

2 DAY TWO

GOODNESS AND THE PURPOSE OF GOD IN MY LIFE

Good seems so often an adjective too despised, for it passes awfully close to its ugly sister adjective, *goody.* In this passage Zechariah is opting for being good and not goody-goody. He says that true children of God will do the honest thing—the neighborly thing. They will be good people. *Turn to Zechariah 8:14–17, page 1103, for today's study.*

3 DAY THREE

GOODNESS AND MY RELATIONSHIP WITH CHRIST

This one-verse injunction on being holy follows hard upon the prior verse, which endorses the kosher system of eating. This pairing implies that obedience is a requirement of holiness. God gave good laws to keep his children from harm. When the Israelites respected those laws, they moved in the direction of God-likeness. They craved obedience and goodness, and in the process, they moved closer to the holiness of God. *Turn to Leviticus 20:26, page 139, for today's study.*

4 DAY FOUR

GOODNESS AND MY SERVICE TO OTHERS

Goodness involves a natural concern for the welfare of others. A good person does not want to hurt another for any reason. A good person remembers Shylock's defense of Judaism and Jews in Shakespeare's *Merchant of Venice* and says of Jews as of any other person, "If you prick us, do we not bleed?" We all have nervous systems. We all feel pain and elation. To forget that and to hurt someone is to bar the way to showing that person any kind of ministry. *Turn to 1 Corinthians 10:23—11:1, page 1368, for today's study.*

5 DAY FIVE

GOODNESS AND ITS PLACE IN MY PERSONAL WORSHIP

Worship is a kind of meal we share with the Almighty. If God were our dinner guest, we wouldn't consider serving him leftover devotion nor consider hurrying to the table, unwashed, unkempt and fouled by our own immorality. There must always come a time of preparation when we meet with God. Once we are clean, once we are morally pure, then we shall enter in and find our worship sweet. *Turn to Psalm 24:3–6, page 646, for today's study.*

MEMORIZE THIS WEEK

TITUS 1:8

Rather he must be hospitable, one who loves what is good, who is self-controlled, upright, holy and disciplined.

Week 16, Faithfulness, the High Art of Persistence, begins on page 635, Psalm 15:1–5.
To begin a topical study on the Fruit of the Spirit, Goodness, turn to the Topical Index, page 1548.

DAY 5 FIVE

▸ GOODNESS AND ITS PLACE IN MY PERSONAL WORSHIP

Isaiah 1:18

"Come now, let us reason together . . . Though your sins are like scarlet, they shall be as white as snow . . . They shall be like wool." In this passage wool and snow are held up as standards of the redeemed life. General William Booth of the Salvation Army longed to bring this white-as-snow, white-as-wool forgiveness to those outside of Christ.

Have you been to Jesus for the cleansing power?
Are you washed in the blood of the Lamb?
Are you fully trusting in His grace this hour?
Are you washed in the blood of the Lamb?

To those who needed Jesus, he offered sidewalk altars and Hyde Park pews. But the needy didn't require cathedrals. They just wanted that white-as-snow, white-as-wool cleansing, and so they welcomed the words:

Lay aside your garments that are stained with sin,
And be washed in the blood of the Lamb;
There's a fountain flowing for the soul unclean,
O be washed in the blood of the Lamb!

Self-righteous "religious" people may never have felt the real glory of this hymn. But when you know the joy of forgiveness, you may want to find a big tuba and try to harmonize with the others, singing:

When the Bridegroom cometh will your robes be white?
Are you washed in the blood of the Lamb?
Will your soul be ready for the mansions bright,
And be washed in the blood of the Lamb?"

Notice that the first and last verses of this hymn are a series of three questions. Your answers to these questions will tell you whose goodness you are counting on: his or yours.

To begin a study on the topic of Goodness, a Contentment With the Commandments, turn to the home page on page 1233.

they shall be like wool.
19 If you are willing and obedient,
you will eat the best from the land;[n]
20 but if you resist and rebel,
you will be devoured by the sword."[o]
For the mouth of the LORD has spoken.[p]

21 See how the faithful city has become a harlot![q]
She once was full of justice;
righteousness used to dwell in her—
but now murderers!
22 Your silver has become dross,
your choice wine is diluted with water.
23 Your rulers are rebels,
companions of thieves;
they all love bribes[r]
and chase after gifts.
They do not defend the cause of the fatherless;
the widow's case does not come before them.[s]
24 Therefore the Lord, the LORD Almighty,
the Mighty One of Israel, declares:
"Ah, I will get relief from my foes
and avenge[t] myself on my enemies.
25 I will turn my hand against you;
I will thoroughly purge away your dross
and remove all your impurities.[u]
26 I will restore your judges as in days of old,[v]
your counselors as at the beginning.
Afterward you will be called
the City of Righteousness,[w]
the Faithful City.[x]"

27 Zion will be redeemed with justice,
her penitent ones with righteousness.[y]
28 But rebels and sinners will both be broken,
and those who forsake the LORD will perish.[z]

29 "You will be ashamed because of the sacred oaks[a]
in which you have delighted;
you will be disgraced because of the gardens[b]
that you have chosen.

1:19 [n]Dt 30:15-16; Isa 55:2
1:20 [o]Isa 3:25; 65:12 [p]Isa 34:16; 40:5; 58:14; Mic 4:4
1:21 [q]Isa 57:3-9; Jer 2:20
1:23 [r]Ex 23:8 [s]Isa 10:2; Jer 5:28; Eze 22:6-7; Zec 7:10
1:24 [t]Isa 35:4; 59:17; 61:2; 63:4
1:25 [u]Eze 22:22; Mal 3:3
1:26 [v]Jer 33:7,11 [w]Isa 33:5; 62:1; Zec 8:3 [x]Isa 60:14; 62:2
1:27 [y]Isa 35:10; 62:12; 63:4
1:28 [z]Ps 9:5; Isa 24:20; 66:24; 2Th 1:8-9
1:29 [a]Isa 57:5 [b]Isa 65:3; 66:17

30 You will be like an oak with fading
leaves,
like a garden without water.
31 The mighty man will become
tinder
and his work a spark;
both will burn together,
with no one to quench the fire.[c]"

1:31 [c]Isa 5:24; 9:18-19; 26:11; 33:14; 66:15-16,24

The Mountain of the LORD

2 This is what Isaiah son of Amoz saw concerning Judah and Jerusalem:[d]

2:1 [d]Isa 1:1

2 In the last days

the mountain[e] of the LORD's temple
will be established
as chief among the mountains;
it will be raised above the hills,
and all nations will stream to it.

2:2 [e]Isa 27:13; 56:7; 66:20; Mic 4:7

3 Many peoples will come and say,

"Come, let us go up to the mountain
of the LORD,
to the house of the God of Jacob.
He will teach us his ways,
so that we may walk in his paths."
The law[f] will go out from Zion,
the word of the LORD from
Jerusalem.[g]

2:3 [f]Isa 51:4,7 [g]Lk 24:47

LOVE

WHOSOEVER WILL

Isaiah 2:3

Jesus died so that none would ever have to say, "God made me live outside of grace, for his kingdom was for others!"

4 He will judge between the nations
and will settle disputes for many
peoples.
They will beat their swords into
plowshares
and their spears into pruning
hooks.[h]
Nation will not take up sword
against nation,[i]
nor will they train for war
anymore.

2:4 [h]Joel 3:10 [i]Ps 46:9; Isa 9:5; 11:6-9; 32:18; Hos 2:18; Zec 9:10

5 Come, O house of Jacob,[j]
let us walk in the light[k] of the
LORD.

2:5 [j]Isa 58:1 [k]Isa 60:1, 19-20; 1Jn 1:5,7

The Day of the LORD

6 You have abandoned[l] your people,
the house of Jacob.

2:6 [l]Dt 31:17

They are full of superstitions from
the East;
they practice divination like the
Philistines[m]
and clasp hands[n] with pagans.[o]

2:6 [m]2Ki 1:2 [n]Pr 6:1 [o]2Ki 16:7

7 Their land is full of silver and gold;
there is no end to their treasures.
Their land is full of horses;[p]
there is no end to their chariots.[q]

2:7 [p]Dt 17:16 [q]Isa 31:1; Mic 5:10

8 Their land is full of idols;[r]
they bow down to the work of
their hands,
to what their fingers[s] have made.

2:8 [r]Isa 10:9-11 [s]Isa 17:8

9 So man will be brought low[t]
and mankind humbled[u]—
do not forgive them.[a][v]

2:9 [t]Ps 62:9 [u]Isa 5:15 [v]Ne 4:5

10 Go into the rocks,
hide in the ground
from dread of the LORD
and the splendor of his majesty![w]

2:10 [w]2Th 1:9; Rev 6:15-16

11 The eyes of the arrogant man will be
humbled
and the pride[x] of men brought
low;
the LORD alone will be exalted in
that day.

2:11 [x]Isa 5:15; 37:23

12 The LORD Almighty has a day in
store
for all the proud and lofty,
for all that is exalted[y]
(and they will be humbled),[z]
13 for all the cedars of Lebanon, tall
and lofty,
and all the oaks of Bashan,[a]
14 for all the towering mountains
and all the high hills,[b]
15 for every lofty tower
and every fortified wall,[c]
16 for every trading ship[b][d]
and every stately vessel.
17 The arrogance of man will be
brought low
and the pride of men humbled;
the LORD alone will be exalted in
that day,[e]
18 and the idols will totally
disappear.[f]

2:12 [y]Isa 24:4,21; Mal 4:1 [z]Job 40:11
2:13 [a]Zec 11:2
2:14 [b]Isa 30:25; 40:4
2:15 [c]Isa 25:2,12
2:16 [d]1Ki 10:22
2:17 [e]ver 11
2:18 [f]Isa 21:9

19 Men will flee to caves in the rocks
and to holes in the ground
from dread of the LORD
and the splendor of his majesty,
when he rises to shake the earth.[g]

2:19 [g]Heb 12:26

20 In that day men will throw away
to the rodents and bats[h]

2:20 [h]Lev 11:19

[a]9 Or *not raise them up* [b]16 Hebrew *every ship of Tarshish*

their idols of silver and idols of gold,
which they made to worship.
21 They will flee to caverns in the rocks
and to the overhanging crags
from dread of the LORD
and the splendor of his majesty,
when he rises to shake the earth.[i]

2:21 [i]ver 19

22 Stop trusting in man,[j]
who has but a breath in his
nostrils.
Of what account is he?[k]

2:22 [j]Ps 146:3; Jer 17:5 [k]Ps 8:4; 144:3; Isa 40:15; Jas 4:14

Judgment on Jerusalem and Judah

3 See now, the Lord,
the LORD Almighty,
is about to take from Jerusalem and
Judah
both supply and support:
all supplies of food[l] and all supplies
of water,[m]
2 the hero and warrior,[n]
the judge and prophet,
the soothsayer and elder,[o]
3 the captain of fifty and man of rank,
the counselor, skilled craftsman
and clever enchanter.

3:1 [l]Lev 26:26 [m]Isa 5:13; Eze 4:16
3:2 [n]Eze 17:13 [o]2Ki 24:14; Isa 9:14-15

4 I will make boys their officials;
mere children will govern them.[p]
5 People will oppress each other—
man against man, neighbor
against neighbor.[q]
The young will rise up against the
old,
the base against the honorable.

3:4 [p]Ecc 10:16 fn
3:5 [q]Isa 9:19; Jer 9:8; Mic 7:2,6

6 A man will seize one of his brothers
at his father's home, and say,
"You have a cloak, you be our leader;
take charge of this heap of ruins!"
7 But in that day he will cry out,
"I have no remedy.[r]
I have no food or clothing in my
house;
do not make me the leader of the
people."

3:7 [r]Eze 34:4; Hos 5:13

8 Jerusalem staggers,
Judah is falling;[s]
their words[t] and deeds are against
the LORD,
defying[u] his glorious presence.
9 The look on their faces testifies
against them;
they parade their sin like Sodom;[v]
they do not hide it.
Woe to them!
They have brought disaster[w] upon
themselves.

3:8 [s]Isa 1:7 [t]Isa 9:15,17 [u]Ps 73:9,11
3:9 [v]Ge 13:13 [w]Pr 8:36; Ro 6:23

10 Tell the righteous it will be well[x]
with them,
for they will enjoy the fruit of
their deeds.[y]
11 Woe to the wicked! Disaster[z] is upon
them!
They will be paid back for what their
hands have done.

3:10 [x]Dt 28:1-14 [y]Ps 128:2
3:11 [z]Dt 28:15-68

12 Youths[a] oppress my people,
women rule over them.
O my people, your guides lead you
astray;[b]
they turn you from the path.

3:12 [a]ver 4 [b]Isa 9:16

13 The LORD takes his place in court;
he rises to judge[c] the people.
14 The LORD enters into judgment[d]
against the elders and leaders of
his people:
"It is you who have ruined my
vineyard;
the plunder[e] from the poor is in
your houses.
15 What do you mean by crushing my
people[f]
and grinding the faces of the
poor?"
declares the Lord,
the LORD Almighty.

3:13 [c]Mic 6:2
3:14 [d]Job 22:4 [e]Job 24:9; Jas 2:6
3:15 [f]Ps 94:5

16 The LORD says,
"The women of Zion[g] are
haughty,
walking along with outstretched
necks,
flirting with their eyes,
tripping along with mincing steps,
with ornaments jingling on their
ankles.
17 Therefore the Lord will bring sores
on the heads of the women
of Zion;
the LORD will make their scalps
bald."

3:16 [g]SS 3:11

18 In that day the Lord will snatch
away their finery: the bangles and
headbands and crescent necklaces,[h] 19 the
earrings and bracelets and veils, 20 the
headdresses[i] and ankle chains and
sashes, the perfume bottles and charms,
21 the signet rings and nose rings, 22 the
fine robes and the capes and cloaks, the
purses 23 and mirrors, and the linen garments and tiaras and shawls.

3:18 [h]Jdg 8:21
3:20 [i]Ex 39:28

24 Instead of fragrance[j] there will be a
stench;

3:24 [j]Est 2:12

instead of a sash,[k] a rope;
instead of well-dressed hair,
baldness;[l]
instead of fine clothing,
sackcloth;[m]
instead of beauty,[n] branding.
25 Your men will fall by the sword,[o]
your warriors in battle.
26 The gates of Zion will lament and
mourn;[p]
destitute, she will sit on the
ground.[q]

4 In that day seven women
will take hold of one man[r]
and say, "We will eat our own food[s]
and provide our own clothes;
only let us be called by your name.
Take away our disgrace!"[t]

The Branch of the LORD

2 In that day the Branch of the LORD[u]
will be beautiful and glorious, and the
fruit[v] of the land will be the pride and
glory of the survivors in Israel. 3 Those
who are left in Zion, who remain[w] in
Jerusalem, will be called holy,[x] all who
are recorded[y] among the living in Jerusalem. 4 The Lord will wash away the
filth[z] of the women of Zion; he will
cleanse the bloodstains[a] from Jerusalem
by a spirit[a] of judgment[b] and a spirit[a] of
fire.[c] 5 Then the LORD will create over
all of Mount Zion and over those who
assemble there a cloud of smoke by day
and a glow of flaming fire by night;[d]
over all the glory[e] will be a canopy. 6 It
will be a shelter[f] and shade from the
heat of the day, and a refuge[g] and hiding place from the storm and rain.

The Song of the Vineyard

5 I will sing for the one I love
a song about his vineyard:[h]
My loved one had a vineyard
on a fertile hillside.
2 He dug it up and cleared it of stones
and planted it with the choicest
vines.[i]
He built a watchtower in it
and cut out a winepress as well.
Then he looked for a crop of good
grapes,
but it yielded only bad fruit.[j]

3 "Now you dwellers in Jerusalem and
men of Judah,
judge between me and my
vineyard.[k]

3:24 [k]Pr 31:24 [l]Isa 22:12 [m]La 2:10; Eze 27:30-31 [n]1Pe 3:3
3:25 [o]Isa 1:20
3:26 [p]Jer 14:2 [q]La 2:10
4:1 [r]Isa 13:12 [s]2Th 3:12 [t]Ge 30:23
4:2 [u]Isa 11:1-5; 53:2; Jer 23:5-6; Zec 3:8; 6:12 [v]Ps 72:16
4:3 [w]Ro 11:5 [x]Isa 52:1; 60:21 [y]Lk 10:20
4:4 [z]Isa 3:24 [a]Isa 1:15 [b]Isa 28:6 [c]Isa 1:31; Mt 3:11
4:5 [d]Ex 13:21 [e]Isa 60:1
4:6 [f]Ps 27:5 [g]Isa 25:4
5:1 [h]Ps 80:8-9
5:2 [i]Jer 2:21 [j]Mt 21:19; Mk 11:13; Lk 13:6
5:3 [k]Mt 21:40

4 What more could have been done
for my vineyard
than I have done for it?[l]
When I looked for good grapes,
why did it yield only bad?
5 Now I will tell you
what I am going to do to my
vineyard:
I will take away its hedge,
and it will be destroyed;
I will break down its wall,[m]
and it will be trampled.[n]
6 I will make it a wasteland,
neither pruned nor cultivated,
and briers and thorns[o] will grow
there.
I will command the clouds
not to rain on it."

7 The vineyard[p] of the LORD
Almighty
is the house of Israel,
and the men of Judah
are the garden of his delight.
And he looked for justice,[q] but saw
bloodshed;
for righteousness, but heard cries
of distress.

Woes and Judgments

8 Woe[r] to you who add house to
house
and join field to field[s]
till no space is left
and you live alone in the land.

9 The LORD Almighty has declared
in my hearing:[t]
"Surely the great houses will become
desolate,[u]
the fine mansions left without
occupants.
10 A ten-acre[b] vineyard will produce
only a bath[c] of wine,
a homer[d] of seed only an ephah[e]
of grain."[v]

11 Woe to those who rise early in the
morning
to run after their drinks,
who stay up late at night
till they are inflamed with wine.[w]

5:4 [l]2Ch 36:15; Jer 2:5-7; Mic 6:3-4; Mt 23:37
5:5 [m]Ps 80:12 [n]Isa 28:3,18; La 1:15; Lk 21:24
5:6 [o]Isa 7:23,24; Heb 6:8
5:7 [p]Ps 80:8 [q]Isa 59:15
5:8 [r]Jer 22:13 [s]Mic 2:2; Hab 2:9-12
5:9 [t]Isa 22:14 [u]Isa 6:11-12; Mt 23:38
5:10 [v]Lev 26:26
5:11 [w]Pr 23:29-30

[a]4 Or *the Spirit* [b]10 Hebrew *ten-yoke,* that is, the land plowed by 10 yoke of oxen in one day [c]10 That is, probably about 6 gallons (about 22 liters) [d]10 That is, probably about 6 bushels (about 220 liters) [e]10 That is, probably about 3/5 bushel (about 22 liters)

5:12
[x]Job 34:27
[y]Ps 28:5;
Am 6:5-6

12They have harps and lyres at their
banquets,
tambourines and flutes and wine,
but they have no regard[x] for the
deeds of the LORD,
no respect for the work of his
hands.[y]

5:13
[z]Hos 4:6
[a]Isa 1:3;
Hos 4:6

13Therefore my people will go into
exile[z]
for lack of understanding;[a]
their men of rank will die of hunger
and their masses will be parched
with thirst.

5:14
[b]Pr 30:16
[c]Nu 16:30

14Therefore the grave[a][b] enlarges its
appetite
and opens its mouth[c] without
limit;
into it will descend their nobles and
masses
with all their brawlers and
revelers.

5:15
[d]Isa 10:33
[e]Isa 2:9
[f]Isa 2:11

15So man will be brought low[d]
and mankind humbled,[e]
the eyes of the arrogant[f] humbled.

5:16
[g]Isa 28:17;
30:18; 33:5;
61:8
[h]Isa 29:23

16But the LORD Almighty will be
exalted by his justice,[g]
and the holy God will show
himself holy[h] by his
righteousness.

5:17
[i]Isa 7:25;
Zep 2:6,14

17Then sheep will graze as in their own
pasture;[i]
lambs will feed[b] among the ruins
of the rich.

5:18
[j]Isa 59:4-8;
Jer 23:14

18Woe to those who draw sin along
with cords of deceit,
and wickedness[j] as with cart
ropes,
19to those who say, "Let God hurry,
let him hasten his work
so we may see it.
Let it approach,
let the plan of the Holy One of
Israel come,
so we may know it."[k]

5:19
[k]Jer 17:15;
Eze 12:22;
2Pe 3:4

20Woe to those who call evil good
and good evil,
who put darkness for light
and light for darkness,[l]
who put bitter for sweet
and sweet for bitter.[m]

5:20
[l]Mt 6:22-23;
Lk 11:34-35
[m]Am 5:7

21Woe to those who are wise in their
own eyes[n]
and clever in their own sight.

5:21
[n]Pr 3:7;
Ro 12:16;
1Co 3:18-20

22Woe to those who are heroes at
drinking wine[o]
and champions at mixing drinks,

5:22
[o]Pr 23:20

23who acquit the guilty for a bribe,[p]
but deny justice[q] to the innocent.[r]

5:23
[p]Ex 23:8
[q]Isa 10:2
[r]Ps 94:21;
Jas 5:6

24Therefore, as tongues of fire lick up
straw
and as dry grass sinks down in the
flames,
so their roots will decay[s]
and their flowers blow away like
dust;
for they have rejected the law of the
LORD Almighty
and spurned the word[t] of the Holy
One of Israel.

5:24
[s]Job 18:16
[t]Isa 8:6;
30:9,12

25Therefore the LORD's anger[u] burns
against his people;
his hand is raised and he strikes
them down.
The mountains shake,
and the dead bodies are like
refuse[v] in the streets.

Yet for all this, his anger is not
turned away,[w]
his hand is still upraised.[x]

5:25
[u]2Ki 22:13
[v]2Ki 9:37
[w]Jer 4:8;
Da 9:16
[x]Isa 9:12,
17,21; 10:4

26He lifts up a banner for the distant
nations,
he whistles[y] for those at the ends
of the earth.[z]
Here they come,
swiftly and speedily!

5:26
[y]Isa 7:18;
Zec 10:8
[z]Dt 28:49;
Isa 13:5; 18:3

27Not one of them grows tired or
stumbles,
not one slumbers or sleeps;
not a belt is loosened at the waist,[a]
not a sandal thong is broken.[b]

5:27
[a]Job 12:18
[b]Joel 2:7-8

28Their arrows are sharp,[c]
all their bows[d] are strung;
their horses' hoofs seem like flint,
their chariot wheels like a
whirlwind.

5:28
[c]Ps 45:5
[d]Ps 7:12

29Their roar is like that of the lion,[e]
they roar like young lions;
they growl as they seize[f] their prey
and carry it off with no one to
rescue.[g]

5:29
[e]Jer 51:38;
Zep 3:3;
Zec 11:3
[f]Isa 10:6;
49:24-25
[g]Isa 42:22;
Mic 5:8

30In that day they will roar over it
like the roaring of the sea.[h]
And if one looks at the land,
he will see darkness and distress;[i]
even the light will be darkened[j] by
the clouds.

5:30
[h]Lk 21:25
[i]Isa 8:22; Jer
4:23-28
[j]Joel 2:10

Isaiah's Commission

6 In the year that King Uzziah[k] died,[l]
I saw the Lord[m] seated on a throne,[n]

6:1
[k]2Ch
26:22,23
[l]2Ki 15:7
[m]Jn 12:41
[n]Rev 4:2

[a]*14* Hebrew *Sheol* [b]*17* Septuagint; Hebrew / *strangers will eat*

high and exalted, and the train of his
6:2 robe filled the temple. [2]Above him were
[o]Rev 4:8 [p]Eze 1:11 seraphs,[o] each with six wings: With two
wings they covered their faces, with
two they covered their feet,[p] and with
two they were flying. [3]And they were
calling to one another:

"Holy, holy, holy is the LORD
Almighty;
6:3 [q]Ps 72:19; Rev 4:8 the whole earth is full of his
glory."[q]

[4]At the sound of their voices the doorposts and thresholds shook and the
temple was filled with smoke.
6:5 [r]Jer 9:3-8 [5]"Woe to me!" I cried. "I am ruined!
For I am a man of unclean lips, and
I live among a people of unclean lips,[r]
and my eyes have seen the King,[s] the 6:5 [s]Jer 51:57
LORD Almighty."
[6]Then one of the seraphs flew to me
with a live coal in his hand, which he
had taken with tongs from the altar.
[7]With it he touched my mouth and
said, "See, this has touched your lips;[t] 6:7 [t]Jer 1:9 [u]1Jn 1:7
your guilt is taken away and your sin
atoned for.[u]"
[8]Then I heard the voice[v] of the Lord 6:8 [v]Ac 9:4
saying, "Whom shall I send? And who
will go for us?"
And I said, "Here am I. Send me!"
[9]He said, "Go[w] and tell this peo- 6:9 [w]Eze 3:11
ple:

" 'Be ever hearing, but never
understanding;

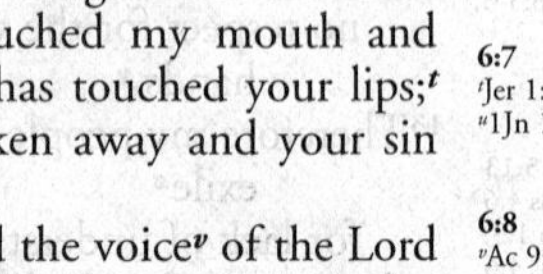
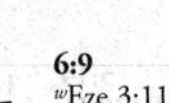
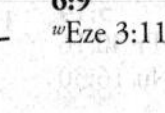

ISAIAH

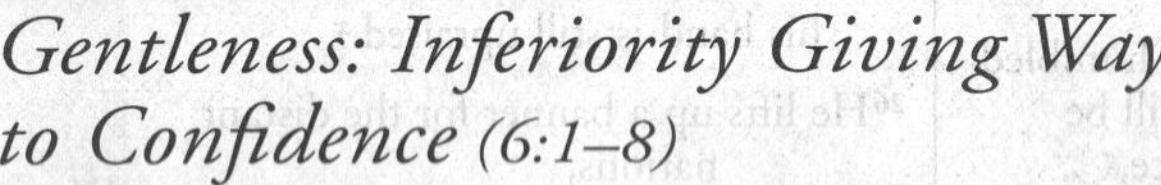

Gentleness: Inferiority Giving Way to Confidence (6:1–8)

Gentleness, in the best New Testament sense of the word, could be defined as "power under control." It is the image of a great stallion under the control of a small and lightweight jockey. The great horse can be controlled by the smallest tug of the reins. In the strictest sense of the word, *gentleness* does not mean inferiority. Yet all of us are plagued by feelings of inferiority from time to time. Frightened people are not gentle, yet they may seem so because of their timidity.

Isaiah protested his spiritual inferiority as the recipient of so noble a call: " 'Woe to me!' [he] cried, 'I am ruined! For I am a man of unclean lips, and I live among a people of unclean lips, and my eyes have seen the King, the LORD Almighty' " (Isaiah 6:5). But God has a way of dealing with our sense of inferiority—a way of applying healing salve to all our whipped feelings. As Isaiah told it: "Then one of the seraphs flew to me with a live coal in his hand, which he had taken with tongs from the altar. With it he touched my mouth and said, 'See, this has touched your lips; your guilt is taken away and your sin atoned for' " (vv. 6–7). With this searing, flaming image, Isaiah's inferiority complex was taken away, and he was ready to serve. Thus when God asked, "Whom shall I send? And who will go for us?" Isaiah was ready to answer: "Here am I. Send me!" (v. 8).

Isaiah in time became one of Israel's greatest poets. His sensitive poet's heart left him vulnerable to feelings of insecurity, but that very insecurity burst forth in a thousand poems that glorified God from the center of his gentle spirit. Gentleness and the heart of a poet are almost always companions. Isaiah's gentleness will continue to praise God forever, for out of such gentleness he praised the suffering and gentle servant, our Redeemer:

Here is my servant, whom I uphold,
my chosen one in whom I delight;
I will put my Spirit on him
and he will bring justice to the nations.
He will not shout or cry out,
or raise his voice in the streets.
A bruised reed he will not break,
and a smoldering wick he will not snuff out.
In faithfulness he will bring forth justice;
he will not falter or be discouraged
till he establishes justice on earth.
In his law the islands will put their hope.
(42:1–4)

6:9 [x]Mt 13:15*; Lk 8:10*
6:10 [y]Dt 32:15; Ps 119:70

be ever seeing, but never
perceiving.'[x]
10Make the heart of this people
calloused;[y]

DAY 4 FOUR

GOODNESS AND MY SERVICE TO OTHERS

Isaiah 6:1–7

Isaiah acknowledged his own moral shortcomings even as God was calling him to service. Isaiah focused on goodness before he accepted God's call. Goodness must be the bedrock character trait for all who take up the special mantle of service. We have had an overabundance of morally depraved servants in our time, and wherever these "men and women of God" have become corrupt, their work has been hampered or even nullified in the lives of those around them. Goodness is essential in performing our call to serve others.

Sadly, the word *good* has taken on bad connotations in our time. It smacks too much of *goody-goody.* It implies a kind of hypocrisy. To be a "goody-two-shoes" or to be "so heavenly minded we are of no earthly good" seems the ultimate slur, especially when it is laid at the feet of *churchy* people.

But genuinely good people have never been in great supply. Those who hunger to be of use to God have not set out to achieve some kind of moral reform and thus appear holy or godly. The truly good have been called by God, just as Isaiah was, to live in the world. They don't become good by grunting and sweating in their attempt to keep all the commandments. They love God. They want to please him. Soon, all God desires for them they desire for themselves. Ironically, when they have become good, they see themselves as Paul perceived: the worst of sinners. Such people readily concede that whatever good is in their lives has been placed in them from the perfect sacrifice of Christ and was nothing they achieved on their own. Then they live in the daily demonstration of the very goodness they deny. They serve others. They have no choice about it. It's what God expects of them, and his expectation is their delight.

To begin a study on the topic of Goodness, Caring How God Feels About My Morality, turn to the home page on page 51.

make their ears dull
and close their eyes.[a]
Otherwise they might see with their
eyes,
hear with their ears,[z]
understand with their hearts,
and turn and be healed."[a]

6:10 [z]Jer 5:21 [a]Mt 13:13-15; Mk 4:12*; Ac 28:26-27*

FAITHFULNESS

THE EXAMINER

Isaiah 6:10

Faith cannot be turned in the hands and examined like a potato. It may only be evaluated after it has been internalized. That is why even the wisest atheist can have no sound opinion on the subject of faith. This examination is held within the heart, and the examiner is God.

11Then I said, "For how long,
O Lord?"[b]
And he answered:

"Until the cities lie ruined[c]
and without inhabitant,
until the houses are left deserted
and the fields ruined and ravaged,
12until the LORD has sent everyone far
away[d]
and the land is utterly forsaken.[e]
13And though a tenth remains[f] in the
land,
it will again be laid waste.
But as the terebinth and oak
leave stumps when they are cut
down,
so the holy seed will be the stump
in the land."[g]

6:11 [b]Ps 79:5 [c]Lev 26:31
6:12 [d]Dt 28:64 [e]Jer 4:29
6:13 [f]Isa 1:9 [g]Job 14:7

The Sign of Immanuel

7 When Ahaz son of Jotham, the son
of Uzziah, was king of Judah, King
Rezin[h] of Aram[i] and Pekah[j] son of
Remaliah king of Israel marched up to
fight against Jerusalem, but they could
not overpower it.
2Now the house of David[k] was told,
"Aram has allied itself with[b] Ephraim[l]";
so the hearts of Ahaz and his people
were shaken, as the trees of the forest
are shaken by the wind.
3Then the LORD said to Isaiah, "Go

7:1 [h]2Ki 15:37 [i]2Ch 28:5 [j]2Ki 15:25
7:2 [k]ver 13; Isa 22:22 [l]Isa 9:9

[a]9,10 Hebrew; Septuagint *'You will be ever hearing, but never understanding; / you will be ever seeing, but never perceiving.' / 10This people's heart has become calloused; / they hardly hear with their ears, / and they have closed their eyes* [b]2 Or *has set up camp in*

out, you and your son Shear-Jashub,[a] to
meet Ahaz at the end of the aqueduct
of the Upper Pool, on the road to the
Washerman's Field.[m] 4Say to him, 'Be
careful, keep calm[n] and don't be afraid.[o]
Do not lose heart[p] because of these
two smoldering stubs[q] of firewood—
because of the fierce anger[r] of Rezin
and Aram and of the son of Remaliah.
5Aram, Ephraim and Remaliah's son
have plotted your ruin, saying, 6"Let us
invade Judah; let us tear it apart and divide it among ourselves, and make the
son of Tabeel king over it." 7Yet this is
what the Sovereign LORD says:

" 'It will not take place,
it will not happen,[s]
8for the head of Aram is Damascus,[t]
and the head of Damascus is only
Rezin.
Within sixty-five years
Ephraim will be too shattered[u] to
be a people.
9The head of Ephraim is Samaria,
and the head of Samaria is only
Remaliah's son.
If you do not stand firm in your
faith,[v]
you will not stand at all.' "[w]

10Again the LORD spoke to Ahaz,
11"Ask the LORD your God for a sign,
whether in the deepest depths or in the
highest heights."
12But Ahaz said, "I will not ask; I will
not put the LORD to the test."
13Then Isaiah said, "Hear now, you
house of David! Is it not enough to try
the patience of men? Will you try the
patience of my God[x] also? 14Therefore
the Lord himself will give you[b] a sign:
The virgin will be with child and will
give birth to a son,[y] and[c] will call him
Immanuel.[d z] 15He will eat curds and
honey[a] when he knows enough to reject the wrong and choose the right.
16But before the boy knows[b] enough to
reject the wrong and choose the right,
the land of the two kings you dread
will be laid waste.[c] 17The LORD will

7:3 [m]2Ki 18:17; Isa 36:2
7:4 [n]Isa 30:15 [o]Isa 35:4 [p]Dt 20:3 [q]Zec 3:2 [r]Isa 10:24
7:7 [s]Isa 8:10; Ac 4:25
7:8 [t]Ge 14:15 [u]Isa 17:1-3
7:9 [v]2Ch 20:20 [w]Isa 8:6-8; 30:12-14
7:13 [x]Isa 25:1
7:14 [y]Lk 1:31 [z]Isa 8:8,10; Mt 1:23*
7:15 [a]ver 22
7:16 [b]Isa 8:4 [c]Isa 17:3; Hos 5:9,13; Am 1:3-5

[a]*3 Shear-Jashub* means *a remnant will return.*
[b]*14* The Hebrew is plural. [c]*14* Masoretic Text; Dead Sea Scrolls *and he* or *and they* [d]*14 Immanuel* means *God with us.*

DAY 3 THREE

▸ PEACE AND MY RELATIONSHIP WITH CHRIST

Isaiah 7:10–17

"The Lord himself will give you a sign," said Isaiah. "The virgin will be with child and will give birth to a son, and will call him Immanuel." God's presence is the promise, for *Immanuel* means "God is with us." Peace is the promise, for God's presence is the end of turmoil. Immanuel is the grand promise. Peace is the grand by-product.

Years ago I wrote of this promise and its resultant peace in *A Symphony in Sand*:

Once in every universe
Some world is worry-torn
And hungry for a global lullaby.
O rest, poor race, and hurtle on through
space—
God has umbilicaled himself to straw,
Laid by his thunderbolts and learned to cry.

When God got serious about peace, he came as a baby—as the baby and Lord Jesus Christ. Babies are powerful forces for peace. They come to us in utter dependency. They are helpless, needy, nonthreatening, and they require love to exist. No wonder Isaiah's sign of peace was a baby.

But Immanuel doesn't just say, "God is with us." We must couple the word Immanuel with Golgotha. Then we understand the permanence of peace and the victory of peace. These two words—*Immanuel* and *Golgotha*—say not merely that God is with us but that God is with us *regardless.*

To begin a study on the topic of Peace, the Companionship of Christ, turn to the home page on page 1243.

▸ GENTLENESS

THE VIRGIN SIGN

Isaiah 7:14

How wonderful that the sign given to Ahaz should signify the symbol of Christ's coming. The Messiah would come softly—as a baby with no human father! The sign revealed that the gentle God was about to dress himself in flesh. Did life at any other time spring into being without the normal baggage of genetics? No. Only once did this occur, for that is the number of times God became a man.

JESUS SPEAKS OUT *on the Fruit of the Spirit:* KINDNESS

Matthew 5:43–44
You have heard that it was said, "Love your neighbor and hate your enemy." But I tell you: Love your enemies and pray for those who persecute you.

Luke 6:35–36
Love your enemies, do good to them, and lend to them without expecting to get anything back. Then your reward will be great, and you will be sons of the Most High, because he is kind to the ungrateful and wicked. Be merciful, just as your Father is merciful.

John 13:35
By this all men will know that you are my disciples, if you love one another.

Matthew 7:12
In everything, do to others what you would have them do to you, for this sums up the Law and the Prophets.

Matthew 5:7
Blessed are the merciful, for they will be shown mercy.

▸ THE STORY OF THE GOOD SAMARITAN

On one occasion an expert in the law stood up to test Jesus. "Teacher," he asked, "what must I do to inherit eternal life?"

"What is written in the Law?" he replied. "How do you read it?"

He answered: " 'Love the Lord your God with all your heart and with all your soul and with all your strength and with all your mind'; and, 'Love your neighbor as yourself.' "

"You have answered correctly," Jesus replied. "Do this and you will live."

But he wanted to justify himself, so he asked Jesus, "And who is my neighbor?"

In reply Jesus said: "A man was going down from Jerusalem to Jericho, when he fell into the hands of robbers. They stripped him of his clothes, beat him and went away, leaving him half dead. A priest happened to be going down the same road, and when he saw the man, he passed by on the other side. So too, a Levite, when he came to the place and saw him, passed by on the other side. But a Samaritan, as he traveled, came where the man was; and when he saw him, he took pity on him. He went to him and bandaged his wounds, pouring on oil and wine. Then he put the man on his own donkey, took him to an inn and took care of him. The next day he took out two silver coins and gave them to the innkeeper. 'Look after him,' he said, 'and when I return, I will reimburse you for any extra expense you may have.'

"Which of these three do you think was a neighbor to the man who fell into the hands of robbers?"

The expert in the law replied, "The one who had mercy on him."

Jesus told him, "Go and do likewise."

Luke 10:25–37

Paul Speaks Out *on the Fruit of the Spirit:* Kindness

Romans 2:4

Do you show contempt for the riches of his kindness, tolerance and patience, not realizing that God's kindness leads you toward repentance?

Romans 11:22

Consider therefore the kindness and sternness of God: sternness to those who fell, but kindness to you, provided that you continue in his kindness. Otherwise, you also will be cut off.

2 Corinthians 6:4,6

As servants of God we commend ourselves in every way: in great endurance; in troubles, hardships and distresses . . . in purity, understanding, patience and kindness; in the Holy Spirit and in sincere love.

Ephesians 2:6–7

God raised us up with Christ and seated us with him in the heavenly realms in Christ Jesus, in order that in the coming ages he might show the incomparable riches of his grace, expressed in his kindness to us in Christ Jesus.

Titus 3:4–5

When the kindness and love of God our Savior appeared, he saved us, not because of righteous things we had done, but because of his mercy. He saved us through the washing of rebirth and renewal by the Holy Spirit.

Philippians 1:3–9

I thank my God every time I remember you. In all my prayers for all of you, I always pray with joy because of your partnership in the gospel from the first day until now, being confident of this, that he who began a good work in you will carry it on to completion until the day of Christ Jesus.

It is right for me to feel this way about all of you, since I have you in my heart; for whether I am in chains or defending and confirming the gospel, all of you share in God's grace with me. God can testify how I long for all of you with the affection of Christ Jesus.

And this is my prayer: that your love may abound more and more in knowledge and depth of insight.

▸ Kindness Brings Comfort

I hope in the Lord Jesus to send Timothy to you soon, that I also may be cheered when I receive news about you. I have no one else like him, who takes a genuine interest in your welfare. For everyone looks out for his own interests, not those of Jesus Christ. But you know that Timothy has proved himself, because as a son with his father he has served with me in the work of the gospel. I hope, therefore, to send him as soon as I see how things go with me. And I am confident in the Lord that I myself will come soon.

But I think it is necessary to send back to you Epaphroditus, my brother, fellow worker and fellow soldier, who is also your messenger, whom you sent to take care of my needs. For he longs for all of you and is distressed because you heard he was ill. Indeed he was ill, and almost died. But God had mercy on him, and not on him only but also on me, to spare me sorrow upon sorrow. Therefore I am all the more eager to send him, so that when you see him again you may be glad and I may have less anxiety. Welcome him in the Lord with great joy, and honor men like him, because he almost died for the work of Christ, risking his life to make up for the help you could not give me.

Philippians 2:19–30

bring on you and on your people and
on the house of your father a time un-
7:17 [d]1Ki 12:16 [e]2Ch 28:20 like any since Ephraim broke away[d]
from Judah—he will bring the king of
Assyria.[e]”
7:18 [f]Isa 5:26 [g]Isa 13:5 18 In that day the LORD will whistle[f]
for flies from the distant streams of
Egypt and for bees from the land of
Assyria.[g] 19 They will all come and settle
in the steep ravines and in the crevices[h] 7:19 [h]Isa 2:19
in the rocks, on all the thornbushes
and at all the water holes. 20 In that day
the Lord will use[i] a razor hired from 7:20 [i]Isa 10:15 [j]Isa 8:7; 10:5
beyond the River[a]—the king of Assyr-
ia[j]—to shave your head and the hair of
your legs, and to take off your beards
also. 21 In that day, a man will keep
alive a young cow and two goats. 22 And
because of the abundance of the milk
they give, he will have curds to eat.
All who remain in the land will eat
curds and honey. 23 In that day, in every
place where there were a thousand vines
worth a thousand silver shekels,[b] there
will be only briers and thorns.[k] 24 Men 7:23 [k]Isa 5:6
will go there with bow and arrow, for
the land will be covered with briers and
thorns. 25 As for all the hills once cultivated by the hoe, you will no longer go
there for fear of the briers and thorns;
they will become places where cattle are
turned loose and where sheep run.[l] 7:25 [l]Isa 5:17

Assyria, the LORD's Instrument

8 The LORD said to me, “Take a
large scroll[m] and write on it with 8:1 [m]Isa 30:8; Hab 2:2 [n]ver 3; Hab 2:2
an ordinary pen: Maher-Shalal-Hash-
Baz.[c][n] 2 And I will call in Uriah[o] the
priest and Zechariah son of Jeberekiah 8:2 [o]2Ki 16:10
as reliable witnesses for me.”

3 Then I went to the prophetess, and
she conceived and gave birth to a son.
And the LORD said to me, “Name
him Maher-Shalal-Hash-Baz. 4 Before
the boy knows[p] how to say ‘My father’ 8:4 [p]Isa 7:16 [q]Isa 7:8
or ‘My mother,’ the wealth of Damas-
cus and the plunder of Samaria will be
carried off by the king of Assyria.[q]”

5 The LORD spoke to me again:

6 “Because this people has rejected[r] 8:6 [r]Isa 5:24 [s]Jn 9:7 [t]Isa 7:1
the gently flowing waters of
Shiloah[s]
and rejoices over Rezin
and the son of Remaliah,[t]
7 therefore the Lord is about to bring
against them
the mighty floodwaters[u] of the 8:7 [u]Isa 17:12-13 [v]Isa 7:20
River[a]—
the king of Assyria[v] with all his
pomp.
It will overflow all its channels,
run over all its banks

[a] *20,7* That is, the Euphrates [b] *23* That is, about 25 pounds (about 11.5 kilograms) [c] *1* *Maher-Shalal-Hash-Baz* means *quick to the plunder, swift to the spoil*; also in verse 3.

DAY 2 TWO

Gentleness and the Purpose of God in My Life

Isaiah 8:6–8

In this passage Isaiah contrasts two waters, the gentle waters of Shiloah and the floodwaters of a mighty river. Those who live near rivers understand the incredible force of a river at flood stage. When the waters rise and overspread their banks, nothing can hold back the flow. Everything in the path of the river is swept away and destroyed: vegetation, homes, belongings. A flood is terrible and awe-inspiring to behold.

But notice that Isaiah describes the gentle waters as God's blessing for the people who follow him. Although a river can be terrifying at flood stage, it can be life sustaining and beneficial when it is flowing gently. Water provides for the needs of those who live near it: irrigation for crops, a mode of transportation, a source of food for people and animals.

Isaiah tells the people that God will gently sustain them if they follow his purposes for their lives. And what does God want from his people? Acceptance. Love. Faithfulness. Humility. The people Isaiah addresses thought that they could arrogantly choose their own path. Their egos led them to think that they didn't need to follow God, that they could do as they pleased. But God has promised that consequences follow our choices. And in the case of the ego-infused, the floodwaters surge all around.

But when we follow the plans of God for our lives, we will find that our needs are met through his kindness and gentle sustenance. When we are following God, the waters of gentleness lap at our feet, and we are unafraid.

To begin a study on the topic of Gentleness, the Art of Ego Displacement, turn to the home page on page 1387.

[8]and sweep on into Judah, swirling
over it,
passing through it and reaching
up to the neck.
Its outspread wings will cover the
breadth of your land,
8:8 [w]Isa 7:14 O Immanuel[a]!"[w]

8:9 [x]Isa 17:12-13 [y]Joel 3:9 [9]Raise the war cry,[b][x] you nations, and
be shattered!
Listen, all you distant lands.
Prepare[y] for battle, and be shattered!
Prepare for battle, and be
shattered!
[10]Devise your strategy, but it will be
8:10 [z]Job 5:12 [a]Isa 7:7 [b]Isa 7:14; Ro 8:31 thwarted;[z]
propose your plan, but it will not
stand,[a]
for God is with us.[c][b]

Fear God

[11]The LORD spoke to me with his
8:11 [c]Eze 3:14 [d]Eze 2:8 strong hand upon me,[c] warning me not
to follow[d] the way of this people. He
said:

8:12 [e]Isa 7:2; 30:1 [f]1Pe 3:14* [12]"Do not call conspiracy[e]
everything that these people call
conspiracy[d];
do not fear what they fear,
and do not dread it.[f]
8:13 [g]Nu 20:12 [h]Isa 29:23 [13]The LORD Almighty is the one you
are to regard as holy,[g]
he is the one you are to fear,
he is the one you are to dread,[h]
8:14 [i]Isa 4:6; Eze 11:16 [j]Lk 2:34; Ro 9:33*; 1Pe 2:8* [k]Isa 24:17-18 [14]and he will be a sanctuary;[i]
but for both houses of Israel he
will be
a stone that causes men to stumble
and a rock that makes them fall.[j]
8:15 [l]Isa 28:13; 59:10; Lk 20:18; Ro 9:32 And for the people of Jerusalem he
will be
a trap and a snare.[k]
[15]Many of them will stumble;[l]
they will fall and be broken,
they will be snared and captured."
[16]Bind up the testimony
and seal[m] up the law among my 8:16 [m]Isa 29:11-12
disciples.
[17]I will wait[n] for the LORD, 8:17 [n]Hab 2:3 [o]Dt 31:17; Isa 54:8
who is hiding[o] his face from the
house of Jacob.
I will put my trust in him.

[18]Here am I, and the children the 8:18 [p]Heb 2:13* [q]Lk 2:34 [r]Ps 9:11
LORD has given me.[p] We are signs[q] and
symbols in Israel from the LORD Al-
mighty, who dwells on Mount Zion.[r] 8:19 [s]1Sa 28:8 [t]Isa 29:4
[19]When men tell you to consult[s] me-
diums and spiritists, who whisper and
mutter,[t] should not a people inquire of
their God? Why consult the dead on be- 8:20 [u]Isa 1:10; Lk 16:29 [v]Mic 3:6
half of the living? [20]To the law[u] and to
the testimony! If they do not speak according to this word, they have no light[v]
of dawn. [21]Distressed and hungry, they
will roam through the land; when they
are famished, they will become enraged 8:21 [w]Rev 16:11
and, looking upward, will curse[w] their
king and their God. [22]Then they will
look toward the earth and see only dis-
tress and darkness and fearful gloom, and 8:22 [x]ver 20; Isa 5:30
they will be thrust into utter darkness.[x]

To Us a Child Is Born

9 Nevertheless, there will be no more
gloom for those who were in dis-
tress. In the past he humbled the land 9:1 [y]2Ki 15:29
of Zebulun and the land of Naphtali,[y]
but in the future he will honor Galilee
of the Gentiles, by the way of the sea,
along the Jordan—
[2]The people walking in darkness 9:2 [z]Eph 5:8
have seen a great light;[z]

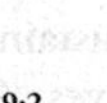

[a]8 *Immanuel* means *God with us.* [b]9 Or *Do your worst* [c]10 Hebrew *Immanuel* [d]12 Or *Do not call for a treaty / every time these people call for a treaty*

KINDNESS

THE STUMBLING STONE OF JUDGMENT

Isaiah 8:13–14

Jesus is a problem for those who don't believe, but a blessing to all who do. He is either a rock of glory or a stone of offense. He is either the Savior or the subject of debate. He is either the kind manifestation of God, gentle in all his ways, or the source of human judgment.

PEACE

THE LIGHT OF PEACE

Isaiah 9:2

Groping, stumbling, falling, dying—this is the utterly dark and senseless experience of all who long for peace.

Then suddenly Jesus!
Then light incomparable.
Then hope everlasting.
Then peace enduring.

on those living in the land of the shadow of death[a][a]
a light has dawned.[b]
3 You have enlarged the nation
and increased their joy;
they rejoice before you
as people rejoice at the harvest,
as men rejoice
when dividing the plunder.
4 For as in the day of Midian's defeat,[c]
you have shattered
the yoke[d] that burdens them,
the bar across their shoulders,[e]
the rod of their oppressor.[f]
5 Every warrior's boot used in battle
and every garment rolled in blood
will be destined for burning,[g]
will be fuel for the fire.
6 For to us a child is born,[h]
to us a son is given,[i]
and the government[j] will be on his shoulders.
And he will be called
Wonderful Counselor,[b][k] Mighty God,[l]
Everlasting Father, Prince of Peace.[m]

KINDNESS

THE KIND MESSIAH

Isaiah 9:6

Unto us a kind king!
Unto us a child!
Unto us a son!
Unto us a wonderful counselor!
Unto us a mighty God!
Unto us Jesus!
A baby God, who whimpered in his infancy,
Leaving none afraid to know him.

7 Of the increase of his government and peace
there will be no end.[n]
He will reign on David's throne
and over his kingdom,
establishing and upholding it
with justice[o] and righteousness
from that time on and forever.
The zeal[p] of the LORD Almighty
will accomplish this.

The LORD's Anger Against Israel

8 The Lord has sent a message against Jacob;
it will fall on Israel.
9 All the people will know it—
Ephraim and the inhabitants of Samaria[q]—
who say with pride
and arrogance[r] of heart,
10 "The bricks have fallen down,
but we will rebuild with dressed stone;
the fig trees have been felled,
but we will replace them with cedars."
11 But the LORD has strengthened
Rezin's[s] foes against them
and has spurred their enemies on.
12 Arameans[t] from the east and
Philistines[u] from the west
have devoured[v] Israel with open mouth.

Yet for all this, his anger is not turned away,
his hand is still upraised.[w]

13 But the people have not returned to
him who struck[x] them,
nor have they sought[y] the LORD Almighty.
14 So the LORD will cut off from Israel
both head and tail,
both palm branch and reed[z] in a single day;[a]
15 the elders[b] and prominent men are the head,
the prophets who teach lies are the tail.
16 Those who guide[c] this people
mislead them,
and those who are guided are led astray.[d]
17 Therefore the Lord will take no
pleasure in the young men,[e]
nor will he pity[f] the fatherless and widows,
for everyone is ungodly[g] and wicked,[h]
every mouth speaks vileness.[i]

Yet for all this, his anger is not turned away,
his hand is still upraised.[j]

18 Surely wickedness burns like a fire;[k]
it consumes briers and thorns,
it sets the forest thickets ablaze,[l]
so that it rolls upward in a column of smoke.

[a] 2 Or *land of darkness* [b] 6 Or *Wonderful, Counselor*

9:2 [a]Lk 1:79 [b]Mt 4:15-16*
9:4 [c]Jdg 7:25 [d]Isa 14:25 [e]Isa 10:27 [f]Isa 14:4; 49:26; 51:13; 54:14
9:5 [g]Isa 2:4
9:6 [h]Isa 53:2; Lk 2:11 [i]Jn 3:16 [j]Mt 28:18 [k]Isa 28:29 [l]Isa 10:21; 11:2 [m]Isa 26:3,12; 66:12
9:7 [n]Da 2:44; Lk 1:33 [o]Isa 11:4; 16:5; 32:1,16 [p]Isa 37:32; 59:17
9:9 [q]Isa 7:9 [r]Isa 46:12
9:11 [s]Isa 7:8
9:12 [t]2Ki 16:6 [u]2Ch 28:18 [v]Ps 79:7 [w]Isa 5:25
9:13 [x]Jer 5:3 [y]Isa 31:1; Hos 7:7,10
9:14 [z]Isa 19:15 [a]Rev 18:8
9:15 [b]Isa 3:2-3
9:16 [c]Mt 15:14; 23:16,24 [d]Isa 3:12
9:17 [e]Jer 18:21 [f]Isa 27:11 [g]Isa 10:6 [h]Isa 1:4 [i]Mt 12:34 [j]Isa 5:25
9:18 [k]Mal 4:1 [l]Ps 83:14

9:19 [m]Isa 13:9,13 [n]Isa 1:31 [o]Mic 7:2,6

[19]By the wrath[m] of the LORD Almighty
the land will be scorched
and the people will be fuel for the fire;[n]
no one will spare his brother.[o]
[20]On the right they will devour,
but still be hungry;[p]
on the left they will eat,[q]
but not be satisfied.
Each will feed on the flesh of his own offspring[a]:
[21] Manasseh will feed on Ephraim,
and Ephraim on Manasseh;
together they will turn against Judah.[r]

9:20 [p]Lev 26:26 [q]Isa 49:26

9:21 [r]2Ch 28:6 [s]Isa 5:25

Yet for all this, his anger is not turned away,
his hand is still upraised.[s]

10

Woe to those who make unjust laws,
to those who issue oppressive decrees,[t]
[2]to deprive[u] the poor of their rights
and withhold justice from the oppressed of my people,[v]
making widows their prey
and robbing the fatherless.
[3]What will you do on the day of reckoning,[w]
when disaster[x] comes from afar?
To whom will you run for help?[y]
Where will you leave your riches?
[4]Nothing will remain but to cringe among the captives[z]
or fall among the slain.[a]
Yet for all this, his anger is not turned away,[b]
his hand is still upraised.

10:1 [t]Ps 58:2

10:2 [u]Isa 3:14 [v]Isa 5:23

10:3 [w]Job 31:14; Hos 9:7 [x]Lk 19:44 [y]Isa 20:6

10:4 [z]Isa 24:22 [a]Isa 22:2; 34:3; 66:16 [b]Isa 5:25

God's Judgment on Assyria

[5]"Woe to the Assyrian,[c] the rod of my anger,
in whose hand is the club[d] of my wrath![e]
[6]I send him against a godless[f] nation,
I dispatch him against a people who anger me,[g]
to seize loot and snatch plunder,[h]
and to trample them down like mud in the streets.
[7]But this is not what he intends,[i]
this is not what he has in mind;
his purpose is to destroy,
to put an end to many nations.

10:5 [c]Isa 14:25; Zep 2:13 [d]Jer 51:20 [e]Isa 13:3,5,13; 30:30; 66:14

10:6 [f]Isa 9:17 [g]Isa 9:19 [h]Isa 5:29

10:7 [i]Ge 50:20; Ac 4:23-28

[8]'Are not my commanders[j] all kings?'
he says.
[9] 'Has not Calno[k] fared like Carchemish?[l]
Is not Hamath like Arpad,
and Samaria[m] like Damascus?[n]
[10]As my hand seized the kingdoms of the idols,[o]
kingdoms whose images excelled those of Jerusalem and Samaria—
[11]shall I not deal with Jerusalem and her images
as I dealt with Samaria and her idols?' "

10:8 [j]2Ki 18:24

10:9 [k]Ge 10:10 [l]2Ch 35:20 [m]2Ki 17:6 [n]2Ki 16:9

10:10 [o]2Ki 19:18

[12]When the Lord has finished all his
work[p] against Mount Zion[q] and Jerusalem, he will say, "I will punish the king
of Assyria[r] for the willful pride of his
heart and the haughty look in his eyes.
[13]For he says:

10:12 [p]Isa 28:21-22; 65:7 [q]2Ki 19:31 [r]Jer 50:18

" 'By the strength of my hand I have done this,[s]
and by my wisdom, because I have understanding.
I removed the boundaries of nations,
I plundered their treasures;[t]
like a mighty one I subdued[b] their kings.
[14]As one reaches into a nest,[u]
so my hand reached for the wealth[v] of the nations;
as men gather abandoned eggs,
so I gathered all the countries;
not one flapped a wing,
or opened its mouth to chirp.' "

10:13 [s]Isa 37:24; Da 4:30 [t]Eze 28:4

10:14 [u]Jer 49:16; Ob 1:4 [v]Job 31:25

[15]Does the ax raise itself above him who swings it,
or the saw boast against him who uses it?[w]
As if a rod were to wield him who lifts it up,
or a club[x] brandish him who is not wood!
[16]Therefore, the Lord, the LORD Almighty,
will send a wasting disease[y] upon his sturdy warriors;
under his pomp[z] a fire will be kindled
like a blazing flame.
[17]The Light of Israel will become a fire,[a]
their Holy One[b] a flame;
in a single day it will burn and consume

10:15 [w]Isa 45:9; Ro 9:20-21 [x]ver 5

10:16 [y]ver 18; Isa 17:4 [z]Isa 8:7

10:17 [a]Isa 31:9 [b]Isa 37:23

[a]*20* Or *arm* [b]*13* Or / *I subdued the mighty,*

10:17 [c]Nu 11:1-3 [d]Isa 9:18
his thorns[c] and his briers.[d]
[18]The splendor of his forests[e] and
fertile fields
10:18 [e]2Ki 19:23
it will completely destroy,
as when a sick man wastes away.
[19]And the remaining trees of his
10:19 [f]Isa 21:17
forests will be so few[f]
that a child could write them
down.

The Remnant of Israel

10:20 [g]Isa 11:10,11 [h]2Ki 16:7 [i]2Ch 28:20 [j]Isa 17:7
[20]In that day[g] the remnant of Israel,
the survivors of the house of
Jacob,
will no longer rely[h] on him
who struck them down[i]
but will truly rely[j] on the LORD,
the Holy One of Israel.
10:21 [k]Isa 6:13 [l]Isa 9:6
[21]A remnant[k] will return,[a] a remnant
of Jacob
will return to the Mighty God.[l]
[22]Though your people, O Israel, be
like the sand by the sea,
10:22 [m]Ro 9:27-28 [n]Isa 28:22; Da 9:27
only a remnant will return.[m]
Destruction has been decreed,[n]
overwhelming and righteous.
[23]The Lord, the LORD Almighty, will
carry out
the destruction decreed upon the
10:23 [o]Isa 28:22; Ro 9:27-28*
whole land.[o]

[24]Therefore, this is what the Lord,
the LORD Almighty, says:
10:24 [p]Ps 87:5-6 [q]Ex 5:14
"O my people who live in Zion,[p]
do not be afraid of the Assyrians,
who beat[q] you with a rod
and lift up a club against you, as
Egypt did.
10:25 [r]Isa 17:14 [s]ver 5; Da 11:36
[25]Very soon[r] my anger against you will
end
and my wrath[s] will be directed to
their destruction."
10:26 [t]Isa 37:36-38 [u]Isa 9:4 [v]Ex 14:16
[26]The LORD Almighty will lash[t] them
with a whip,
as when he struck down Midian[u]
at the rock of Oreb;
and he will raise his staff over the
waters,[v]
as he did in Egypt.
[27]In that day their burden will be
lifted from your shoulders,
10:27 [w]Isa 9:4 [x]Isa 14:25
their yoke[w] from your neck;[x]
the yoke will be broken
because you have grown so fat.[b]

[28]They enter Aiath;
10:28 [y]1Sa 14:2 [z]1Sa 13:2
they pass through Migron;[y]
they store supplies at Micmash.[z]
[29]They go over the pass, and say,
"We will camp overnight at Geba."
10:29 [a]Jos 18:25
Ramah[a] trembles;
Gibeah of Saul flees.
10:30 [b]1Sa 25:44 [c]Ne 11:32
[30]Cry out, O Daughter of Gallim![b]
Listen, O Laishah!
Poor Anathoth![c]
[31]Madmenah is in flight;
the people of Gebim take cover.
10:32 [d]1Sa 21:1 [e]Jer 6:23
[32]This day they will halt at Nob;[d]
they will shake their fist
at the mount of the Daughter of
Zion,[e]
at the hill of Jerusalem.
[33]See, the Lord, the LORD Almighty,
will lop off the boughs with great
power.
10:33 [f]Am 2:9
The lofty trees will be felled,
the tall[f] ones will be brought low.
[34]He will cut down the forest thickets
with an ax;
Lebanon will fall before the
Mighty One.

The Branch From Jesse

11:1 [g]ver 10; Isa 9:7; Rev 5:5 [h]Isa 4:2
11 A shoot will come up from the
stump of Jesse;[g]
from his roots a Branch[h] will bear
fruit.

GOODNESS

A ROOT OUT OF JESSE

Isaiah 11:1

Is humanity beyond saving? Is the tree dead? No, see here, at the base of the burned out trunk is a young, green sprout. The tree lives!

Is the grave forever? No, see here, at the base of humanity's headstone the grave is empty. We shall live!

11:2 [i]Isa 42:1; 48:16; 61:1; Mt 3:16; Jn 1:32-33 [j]Eph 1:17 [k]2Ti 1:7
[2]The Spirit[i] of the LORD will rest on
him—
the Spirit of wisdom[j] and of
understanding,
the Spirit of counsel and of
power,[k]
the Spirit of knowledge and of the
fear of the LORD—
[3]and he will delight in the fear of the
LORD.

11:3 [l]Jn 7:24
He will not judge by what he sees
with his eyes,[l]

[a]*21* Hebrew *shear-jashub*; also in verse 22
[b]*27* Hebrew; Septuagint *broken / from your shoulders*

11:3 [m]Jn 2:25
11:4 [n]Ps 72:2 [o]Isa 9:7 [p]Isa 3:14 [q]Mal 4:6 [r]Job 4:9; 2Th 2:8

or decide by what he hears with
his ears;[m]
4 but with righteousness[n] he will judge
the needy,
with justice[o] he will give decisions
for the poor[p] of the earth.
He will strike[q] the earth with the rod
of his mouth;
with the breath[r] of his lips he will
slay the wicked.
5 Righteousness will be his belt
and faithfulness[s] the sash around
his waist.[t]

11:5 [s]Isa 25:1 [t]Eph 6:14
11:6 [u]Isa 65:25

6 The wolf will live with the lamb,[u]
the leopard will lie down with the
goat,
the calf and the lion and the
yearling[a] together;
and a little child will lead them.
7 The cow will feed with the bear,
their young will lie down together,
and the lion will eat straw like the
ox.
8 The infant will play near the hole of
the cobra,
and the young child put his hand
into the viper's nest.
9 They will neither harm nor destroy[v]
on all my holy mountain,
for the earth[w] will be full of the
knowledge[x] of the LORD
as the waters cover the sea.

11:9 [v]Job 5:23 [w]Ps 98:2-3; Isa 52:10 [x]Isa 45:6,14; Hab 2:14

▸ PEACE

THE PEACEABLE KINGDOM

Isaiah 11:6–9

Nature, like all of humankind, will at last be redeemed. The era of tooth and claw is passing even now. Jesus comes. We've a cobra for our bracelet and a lion for our pet. The deer and leopard have signed a truce. Eden's gates are about to swing open! Look! The tree of life has sprouted once again.

11:10 [y]Jn 12:32 [z]Isa 49:23; Lk 2:32 [a]Ro 15:12* [b]Isa 14:3; 28:12; 32:17-18
11:11 [c]Isa 10:20 [d]Isa 19:24; Hos 11:11; Mic 7:12; Zec 10:10 [e]Ge 10:22 [f]Isa 42:4, 10,12; 66:19

10 In that day the Root of Jesse will
stand as a banner[y] for the peoples; the
nations[z] will rally to him,[a] and his place
of rest[b] will be glorious. 11 In that day[c]
the Lord will reach out his hand a second time to reclaim the remnant that
is left of his people from Assyria,[d] from
Lower Egypt, from Upper Egypt,[b] from
Cush,[c] from Elam,[e] from Babylonia,[d]
from Hamath and from the islands[f] of
the sea.

12 He will raise a banner for the nations
and gather the exiles of Israel;
he will assemble the scattered
peoples[g] of Judah
from the four quarters of the
earth.
13 Ephraim's jealousy will vanish,
and Judah's enemies[e] will be cut
off;
Ephraim will not be jealous of
Judah,
nor Judah hostile toward
Ephraim.[h]
14 They will swoop down on the slopes
of Philistia to the west;
together they will plunder the
people to the east.
They will lay hands on Edom[i] and
Moab,[j]
and the Ammonites will be subject
to them.
15 The LORD will dry up
the gulf of the Egyptian sea;
with a scorching wind he will sweep
his hand[k]
over the Euphrates River.[f][l]
He will break it up into seven
streams
so that men can cross over in
sandals.
16 There will be a highway[m] for the
remnant of his people
that is left from Assyria,
as there was for Israel
when they came up from Egypt.[n]

11:12 [g]Zep 3:10
11:13 [h]Jer 3:18; Eze 37:16-17,22; Hos 1:11
11:14 [i]Da 11:41; Joel 3:19 [j]Isa 16:14; 25:10
11:15 [k]Isa 19:16 [l]Isa 7:20
11:16 [m]Isa 19:23; 62:10 [n]Ex 14:26-31

Songs of Praise

12 In that day you will say:

"I will praise[o] you, O LORD.
Although you were angry with
me,
your anger has turned away
and you have comforted me.
2 Surely God is my salvation;
I will trust[p] and not be afraid.
The LORD, the LORD, is my
strength and my song;
he has become my salvation.[q]"
3 With joy you will draw water[r]
from the wells of salvation.

4 In that day you will say:

12:1 [o]Isa 25:1
12:2 [p]Isa 26:3 [q]Ex 15:2; Ps 118:14
12:3 [r]Jn 4:10,14

[a]6 Hebrew; Septuagint *lion will feed* [b]11 Hebrew *from Pathros* [c]11 That is, the upper Nile region [d]11 Hebrew *Shinar* [e]13 Or *hostility* [f]15 Hebrew *the River*

"Give thanks to the LORD, call on
his name;[s]
make known among the nations
what he has done,
and proclaim that his name is
exalted.
5 Sing[t] to the LORD, for he has done
glorious things;[u]
let this be known to all the world.
6 Shout aloud and sing for joy, people
of Zion,
for great is the Holy One of Israel[v]
among you."[w]

12:4 [s]Ps 105:1; Isa 24:15
12:5 [t]Ex 15:1 [u]Ps 98:1
12:6 [v]Isa 49:26 [w]Zep 3:14-17

A Prophecy Against Babylon

13 An oracle concerning Babylon
that Isaiah son of Amoz saw:

2 Raise a banner[x] on a bare hilltop,
shout to them;
beckon to them
to enter the gates of the nobles.
3 I have commanded my holy ones;
I have summoned my warriors[y] to
carry out my wrath—
those who rejoice[z] in my
triumph.
4 Listen, a noise on the mountains,
like that of a great multitude![a]
Listen, an uproar among the
kingdoms,
like nations massing together!
The LORD Almighty is mustering
an army for war.
5 They come from faraway lands,
from the ends of the heavens[b]—
the LORD and the weapons of his
wrath—
to destroy[c] the whole country.
6 Wail,[d] for the day[e] of the LORD is
near;
it will come like destruction from
the Almighty.[a]
7 Because of this, all hands will go
limp,
every man's heart will melt.[f]
8 Terror[g] will seize them,
pain and anguish will grip them;
they will writhe like a woman in
labor.
They will look aghast at each other,
their faces aflame.[h]
9 See, the day of the LORD is coming
—a cruel day, with wrath and
fierce anger—
to make the land desolate
and destroy the sinners within it.

13:2 [x]Jer 50:2; 51:27
13:3 [y]Joel 3:11 [z]Ps 149:2
13:4 [a]Joel 3:14
13:5 [b]Isa 5:26 [c]Isa 24:1
13:6 [d]Eze 30:2 [e]Isa 2:12; Joel 1:15
13:7 [f]Eze 21:7
13:8 [g]Isa 21:4 [h]Na 2:10

10 The stars of heaven and their
constellations
will not show their light.
The rising sun[i] will be darkened[j]
and the moon will not give its
light.[k]
11 I will punish[l] the world for its evil,
the wicked for their sins.
I will put an end to the arrogance of
the haughty
and will humble the pride of the
ruthless.
12 I will make man[m] scarcer than pure
gold,
more rare than the gold of Ophir.
13 Therefore I will make the heavens
tremble;[n]
and the earth will shake from its
place
at the wrath of the LORD Almighty,
in the day of his burning anger.
14 Like a hunted gazelle,
like sheep without a shepherd,[o]
each will return to his own people,
each will flee to his native land.[p]
15 Whoever is captured will be thrust
through;
all who are caught will fall[q] by the
sword.[r]
16 Their infants[s] will be dashed to
pieces before their eyes;
their houses will be looted and
their wives ravished.
17 See, I will stir up[t] against them the
Medes,
who do not care for silver
and have no delight in gold.[u]
18 Their bows will strike down the
young men;
they will have no mercy on infants
nor will they look with
compassion on children.
19 Babylon, the jewel of kingdoms,
the glory[v] of the Babylonians'[b]
pride,
will be overthrown[w] by God
like Sodom and Gomorrah.[x]
20 She will never be inhabited[y]
or lived in through all generations;
no Arab[z] will pitch his tent there,
no shepherd will rest his flocks
there.
21 But desert creatures[a] will lie there,
jackals will fill her houses;
there the owls will dwell,

[a] *6* Hebrew *Shaddai* [b] *19* Or *Chaldeans'*

13:10 [i]Isa 24:23 [j]Isa 5:30; Rev 8:12 [k]Eze 32:7; Mt 24:29*; Mk 13:24*
13:11 [l]Isa 3:11; 11:4; 26:21
13:12 [m]Isa 4:1
13:13 [n]Isa 34:4; 51:6; Hag 2:6
13:14 [o]1Ki 22:17 [p]Jer 50:16
13:15 [q]Jer 51:4 [r]Isa 14:19; Jer 50:25
13:16 [s]Ps 137:9
13:17 [t]Jer 51:1 [u]Pr 6:34-35
13:19 [v]Da 4:30 [w]Rev 14:8 [x]Ge 19:24
13:20 [y]Isa 14:23; 34:10-15 [z]2Ch 17:11
13:21 [a]Rev 18:2

and there the wild goats will leap
about.
22 Hyenas will howl in her
strongholds,[b]
jackals[c] in her luxurious palaces.
Her time is at hand,[d]
and her days will not be
prolonged.

13:22 [b]Isa 25:2 [c]Isa 34:13 [d]Jer 51:33

14

The LORD will have
compassion[e] on Jacob;
once again he will choose[f] Israel
and will settle them in their own
land.
Aliens[g] will join them
and unite with the house of Jacob.
2 Nations will take them
and bring[h] them to their own
place.
And the house of Israel will possess
the nations[i]
as menservants and maidservants
in the LORD's land.
They will make captives of their
captors
and rule over their oppressors.[j]

14:1 [e]Ps 102:13; Isa 49:10,13; 54:7-8,10 [f]Isa 41:8; 44:1; 49:7; Zec 1:17; 2:12 [g]Eph 2:12-19
14:2 [h]Isa 60:9 [i]Isa 49:7,23 [j]Isa 60:14; 61:5

3 On the day the LORD gives you relief[k] from suffering and turmoil and
cruel bondage, 4 you will take up this
taunt[l] against the king of Babylon:

How the oppressor[m] has come to an
end!
How his fury[a] has ended!
5 The LORD has broken the rod of the
wicked,[n]
the scepter of the rulers,
6 which in anger struck down peoples[o]
with unceasing blows,
and in fury subdued nations
with relentless aggression.[p]
7 All the lands are at rest and at peace;
they break into singing.[q]
8 Even the pine trees[r] and the cedars
of Lebanon
exult over you and say,
"Now that you have been laid low,
no woodsman comes to cut us
down."
9 The grave[b][s] below is all astir
to meet you at your coming;
it rouses the spirits of the departed
to greet you—
all those who were leaders in the
world;
it makes them rise from their
thrones—

14:3 [k]Isa 11:10
14:4 [l]Hab 2:6 [m]Isa 9:4
14:5 [n]Ps 125:3
14:6 [o]Isa 10:14 [p]Isa 47:6
14:7 [q]Ps 98:1; 126:1-3
14:8 [r]Eze 31:16
14:9 [s]Eze 32:21

all those who were kings over the
nations.
10 They will all respond,
they will say to you,
"You also have become weak, as we
are;
you have become like us."[t]
11 All your pomp has been brought
down to the grave,
along with the noise of your
harps;
maggots are spread out beneath you
and worms[u] cover you.
12 How you have fallen[v] from heaven,
O morning star,[w] son of the dawn!
You have been cast down to the
earth,
you who once laid low the
nations!

14:10 [t]Eze 32:21
14:11 [u]Isa 51:8
14:12 [v]Isa 34:4; Lk 10:18 [w]2Pe 1:19; Rev 2:28; 8:10; 9:1

▸ JOY

THE SIN OF SKIPPING HALLELUJAHS

Isaiah 14:12–13

Pride is turning from the adoration of the living God and falling, instead, on our knees before the icon of our own ego. Satan didn't begin his rebellion by destroying God's throne. He began his fall by skipping his morning hallelujahs. Once we quit praising God, defiance is not far behind.

13 You said in your heart,
"I will ascend[x] to heaven;
I will raise my throne[y]
above the stars of God;
I will sit enthroned on the mount of
assembly,
on the utmost heights of the
sacred mountain.[c]
14 I will ascend above the tops of the
clouds;
I will make myself like the Most
High."[z]
15 But you are brought down to the
grave,
to the depths[a] of the pit.
16 Those who see you stare at you,
they ponder your fate:[b]
"Is this the man who shook the earth
and made kingdoms tremble,

14:13 [x]Da 5:23; 8:10; Mt 11:23 [y]Eze 28:2; 2Th 2:4
14:14 [z]Isa 47:8; 2Th 2:4
14:15 [a]Mt 11:23; Lk 10:15
14:16 [b]Jer 50:23

[a]*4* Dead Sea Scrolls, Septuagint and Syriac; the meaning of the word in the Masoretic Text is uncertain. [b]*9* Hebrew *Sheol*; also in verses 11 and 15 [c]*13* Or *the north*; Hebrew *Zaphon*

17 the man who made the world a
desert,[c]
who overthrew its cities
and would not let his captives go
home?"

14:17 [c]Joel 2:3

18 All the kings of the nations lie in
state,
each in his own tomb.
19 But you are cast out[d] of your tomb
like a rejected branch;
you are covered with the slain,
with those pierced by the sword,
those who descend to the stones of
the pit.[e]
Like a corpse trampled underfoot,
20 you will not join them in burial,
for you have destroyed your land
and killed your people.

14:19 [d]Isa 22:16-18 [e]Jer 41:7-9

The offspring[f] of the wicked[g]
will never be mentioned[h] again.
21 Prepare a place to slaughter his sons
for the sins of their forefathers;[i]
they are not to rise to inherit the
land
and cover the earth with their
cities.

14:20 [f]Job 18:19 [g]Isa 1:4 [h]Ps 21:10
14:21 [i]Ex 20:5; Lev 26:39

22 "I will rise up against them,"
declares the LORD Almighty.
"I will cut off from Babylon her
name and survivors,
her offspring and descendants,[j]"
declares the LORD.
23 "I will turn her into a place for owls[k]
and into swampland;
I will sweep her with the broom of
destruction,"
declares the LORD Almighty.

14:22 [j]1Ki 14:10; Job 18:19
14:23 [k]Isa 34:11-15; Zep 2:14

A Prophecy Against Assyria

24 The LORD Almighty has sworn,[l]
"Surely, as I have planned, so it will
be,
and as I have purposed, so it will
stand.[m]
25 I will crush the Assyrian[n] in my land;
on my mountains I will trample
him down.
His yoke[o] will be taken from my
people,
and his burden removed from
their shoulders."[p]
26 This is the plan[q] determined for the
whole world;
this is the hand[r] stretched out over
all nations.

14:24 [l]Isa 45:23 [m]Ac 4:28
14:25 [n]Isa 10:5,12 [o]Isa 9:4 [p]Isa 10:27
14:26 [q]Isa 23:9 [r]Ex 15:12

27 For the LORD Almighty has
purposed, and who can
thwart him?
His hand is stretched out, and
who can turn it back?[s]

14:27 [s]2Ch 20:6; Isa 43:13; Da 4:35

A Prophecy Against the Philistines

28 This oracle[t] came in the year King
Ahaz[u] died:

14:28 [t]Isa 13:1 [u]2Ki 16:20

29 Do not rejoice, all you Philistines,[v]
that the rod that struck you is
broken;
from the root of that snake will
spring up a viper,[w]
its fruit will be a darting,
venomous serpent.
30 The poorest of the poor will find
pasture,
and the needy[x] will lie down in
safety.[y]
But your root I will destroy by
famine;[z]
it will slay[a] your survivors.

14:29 [v]2Ch 26:6 [w]Isa 11:8
14:30 [x]Isa 3:15 [y]Isa 7:21-22 [z]Isa 8:21; 9:20; 51:19 [a]Jer 25:16

31 Wail, O gate![b] Howl, O city!
Melt away, all you Philistines!
A cloud of smoke comes from the
north,[c]
and there is not a straggler in its
ranks.
32 What answer shall be given
to the envoys[d] of that nation?
"The LORD has established Zion,[e]
and in her his afflicted people will
find refuge.[f]"

14:31 [b]Isa 3:26 [c]Jer 1:14
14:32 [d]Isa 37:9 [e]Ps 87:2,5; Isa 44:28; 54:11 [f]Isa 4:6; Jas 2:5

A Prophecy Against Moab

15 An oracle concerning Moab:[g]

Ar in Moab is ruined,[h]
destroyed in a night!
Kir in Moab is ruined,
destroyed in a night!
2 Dibon goes up to its temple,
to its high places[i] to weep;
Moab wails over Nebo and
Medeba.
Every head is shaved[j]
and every beard cut off.
3 In the streets they wear sackcloth;
on the roofs and in the public
squares[k]
they all wail,
prostrate with weeping.[l]
4 Heshbon and Elealeh[m] cry out,
their voices are heard all the way
to Jahaz.

15:1 [g]Isa 11:14
15:2 [h]Jer 48:24,41 [i]Jer 48:35 [j]Lev 21:5
15:3 [k]Jer 48:38 [l]Isa 22:4
15:4 [m]Nu 32:3

Therefore the armed men of Moab
cry out,
and their hearts are faint.
5 My heart cries out over Moab;[n]
her fugitives flee as far as Zoar,
as far as Eglath Shelishiyah.
They go up the way to Luhith,
weeping as they go;
on the road to Horonaim[o]
they lament their destruction.[p]
6 The waters of Nimrim are dried up[q]
and the grass is withered;[r]
the vegetation is gone
and nothing green is left.
7 So the wealth they have acquired[s]
and stored up
they carry away over the Ravine of
the Poplars.
8 Their outcry echoes along the border
of Moab;
their wailing reaches as far as
Eglaim,
their lamentation as far as Beer
Elim.
9 Dimon's[a] waters are full of blood,
but I will bring still more upon
Dimon[a]—
a lion[t] upon the fugitives of Moab
and upon those who remain in the
land.

16 Send lambs[u] as tribute
to the ruler of the land,
from Sela,[v] across the desert,
to the mount of the Daughter of
Zion.[w]
2 Like fluttering birds
pushed from the nest,[x]
so are the women of Moab
at the fords of the Arnon.[y]

3 "Give us counsel,
render a decision.
Make your shadow like night—
at high noon.
Hide the fugitives,[z]
do not betray the refugees.
4 Let the Moabite fugitives stay with
you;
be their shelter from the
destroyer."
The oppressor[a] will come to an
end,
and destruction will cease;
the aggressor will vanish from the
land.
5 In love a throne[b] will be established;
in faithfulness a man will sit on
it—
one from the house[b] of David[c]—
one who in judging seeks justice[d]
and speeds the cause of
righteousness.

6 We have heard of Moab's[e] pride[f]—
her overweening pride and
conceit,
her pride and her insolence—
but her boasts are empty.
7 Therefore the Moabites wail,[g]
they wail together for Moab.
Lament and grieve
for the men[c][h] of Kir Hareseth.[i]
8 The fields of Heshbon wither,
the vines of Sibmah also.
The rulers of the nations
have trampled down the choicest
vines,
which once reached Jazer
and spread toward the desert.
Their shoots spread out
and went as far as the sea.
9 So I weep,[j] as Jazer weeps,
for the vines of Sibmah.
O Heshbon, O Elealeh,
I drench you with tears!
The shouts of joy over your ripened
fruit
and over your harvests[k] have been
stilled.
10 Joy and gladness are taken away
from the orchards;[l]
no one sings or shouts in the
vineyards;
no one treads[m] out wine at the
presses,[n]
for I have put an end to the
shouting.
11 My heart laments for Moab[o] like a
harp,
my inmost being[p] for Kir
Hareseth.
12 When Moab appears at her high
place,
she only wears herself out;
when she goes to her shrine[q] to pray,
it is to no avail.[r]

13 This is the word the LORD has already spoken concerning Moab. 14 But
now the LORD says: "Within three
years, as a servant bound by contract

15:5 [n]Jer 48:31 [o]Jer 48:3,34 [p]Jer 4:20; 48:5
15:6 [q]Isa 19:5-7; Jer 48:34 [r]Joel 1:12
15:7 [s]Isa 30:6; Jer 48:36
15:9 [t]2Ki 17:25
16:1 [u]2Ki 3:4 [v]2Ki 14:7 [w]Isa 10:32
16:2 [x]Pr 27:8 [y]Nu 21:13-14; Jer 48:20
16:3 [z]1Ki 18:4
16:4 [a]Isa 9:4
16:5 [b]Da 7:14; Mic 4:7 [c]Lk 1:32 [d]Isa 9:7
16:6 [e]Am 2:1; Zep 2:8 [f]Ob 1:3; Zep 2:10
16:7 [g]Jer 48:20 [h]1Ch 16:3 [i]2Ki 3:25
16:9 [j]Isa 15:3 [k]Jer 40:12
16:10 [l]Isa 24:7-8 [m]Jdg 9:27 [n]Job 24:11
16:11 [o]Isa 15:5 [p]Isa 63:15; Hos 11:8; Php 2:1
16:12 [q]Isa 15:2 [r]1Ki 18:29

[a] *9* Masoretic Text; Dead Sea Scrolls, some Septuagint manuscripts and Vulgate *Dibon* [b] *5* Hebrew *tent* [c] *7* Or "*raisin cakes,*" a wordplay

would count them, Moab's splendor and all her many people will be despised,[s] and her survivors will be very few and feeble."[t]

16:14 [s]Isa 25:10; Jer 48:42 [t]Isa 21:17

An Oracle Against Damascus

17 An oracle concerning Damascus:[u]

"See, Damascus will no longer be a city
but will become a heap of ruins.[v]
2 The cities of Aroer will be deserted
and left to flocks,[w] which will lie down,
with no one to make them afraid.[x]
3 The fortified city will disappear from Ephraim,
and royal power from Damascus;
the remnant of Aram will be
like the glory[y] of the Israelites,"[z]
declares the LORD Almighty.

17:1 [u]Ge 14:15; Jer 49:23; Ac 9:2 [v]Isa 25:2; Am 1:3; Zec 9:1
17:2 [w]Isa 7:21; Eze 25:5 [x]Jer 7:33; Mic 4:4
17:3 [y]ver 4; Hos 9:11 [z]Isa 7:8,16; 8:4

4 "In that day the glory of Jacob will fade;
the fat of his body will waste[a] away.
5 It will be as when a reaper gathers the standing grain
and harvests[b] the grain with his arm—
as when a man gleans heads of grain
in the Valley of Rephaim.
6 Yet some gleanings will remain,[c]
as when an olive tree is beaten,[d]
leaving two or three olives on the topmost branches,
four or five on the fruitful boughs,"
declares the LORD, the God of Israel.

17:4 [a]Isa 10:16
17:5 [b]ver 11; Jer 51:33; Joel 3:13; Mt 13:30
17:6 [c]Dt 4:27; Isa 24:13 [d]Isa 27:12

7 In that day men will look[e] to their Maker
and turn their eyes to the Holy One[f] of Israel.
8 They will not look to the altars,
the work of their hands,[g]
and they will have no regard for the Asherah poles[a]
and the incense altars their fingers have made.

17:7 [e]Isa 10:20 [f]Mic 7:7
17:8 [g]Isa 2:18,20; 30:22

9 In that day their strong cities, which they left because of the Israelites, will be like places abandoned to thickets and undergrowth. And all will be desolation.

10 You have forgotten[h] God your Savior;[i]
you have not remembered the Rock, your fortress.
Therefore, though you set out the finest plants
and plant imported vines,
11 though on the day you set them out,
you make them grow,
and on the morning[j] when you plant them, you bring them to bud,
yet the harvest will be as nothing[k]
in the day of disease and incurable pain.[l]

17:10 [h]Isa 51:13 [i]Ps 68:19; Isa 12:2
17:11 [j]Ps 90:6 [k]Hos 8:7 [l]Job 4:8

12 Oh, the raging of many nations—
they rage like the raging sea![m]
Oh, the uproar of the peoples—
they roar like the roaring of great waters!
13 Although the peoples roar like the roar of surging waters,
when he rebukes[n] them they flee[o] far away,
driven before the wind like chaff[p] on the hills,
like tumbleweed before a gale.[q]
14 In the evening, sudden terror!
Before the morning, they are gone![r]
This is the portion of those who loot us,
the lot of those who plunder us.

17:12 [m]Ps 18:4; Jer 6:23; Lk 21:25
17:13 [n]Ps 9:5 [o]Isa 13:14 [p]Isa 41:2,15-16 [q]Job 21:18
17:14 [r]2Ki 19:35

A Prophecy Against Cush

18 Woe to the land of whirring wings[b]
along the rivers of Cush,[c][s]
2 which sends envoys by sea
in papyrus[t] boats over the water.

Go, swift messengers,
to a people tall and smooth-skinned,
to a people feared far and wide,
an aggressive[u] nation of strange speech,
whose land is divided by rivers.[v]

3 All you people of the world,
you who live on the earth,
when a banner[w] is raised on the mountains,
you will see it,
and when a trumpet sounds,
you will hear it.
4 This is what the LORD says to me:

18:1 [s]Isa 20:3-5; Eze 30:4-5,9; Zep 2:12; 3:10
18:2 [t]Ex 2:3 [u]Ge 10:8-9; 2Ch 12:3 [v]ver 7
18:3 [w]Isa 5:26

[a]8 That is, symbols of the goddess Asherah
[b]1 Or *of locusts* [c]1 That is, the upper Nile region

"I will remain quiet and will look
on from my dwelling place,[x]
like shimmering heat in the
sunshine,
like a cloud of dew[y] in the heat of
harvest."
5 For, before the harvest, when the
blossom is gone
and the flower becomes a ripening
grape,
he will cut off the shoots with
pruning knives,
and cut down and take away the
spreading branches.[z]
6 They will all be left to the mountain
birds of prey
and to the wild animals;[a]
the birds will feed on them all
summer,
the wild animals all winter.

7 At that time gifts will be brought to
the LORD Almighty
from a people tall and
smooth-skinned,
from a people feared far and wide,
an aggressive nation of strange
speech,
whose land is divided by rivers—

the gifts will be brought to Mount Zion,
the place of the Name of the LORD
Almighty.[b]

18:4 [x]Isa 26:21; Hos 5:15 [y]Isa 26:19; Hos 14:5
18:5 [z]Isa 17:10-11; Eze 17:6
18:6 [a]Isa 56:9; Jer 7:33; Eze 32:4; 39:17
18:7 [b]Ps 68:31

A Prophecy About Egypt

19 An oracle[c] concerning Egypt:[d][e]

See, the LORD rides on a swift
cloud[f]
and is coming to Egypt.
The idols of Egypt tremble before
him,
and the hearts of the Egyptians
melt[g] within them.

2 "I will stir up Egyptian against
Egyptian—
brother will fight against brother,[h]
neighbor against neighbor,
city against city,
kingdom against kingdom.[i]
3 The Egyptians will lose heart,
and I will bring their plans to
nothing;
they will consult the idols and the
spirits of the dead,
the mediums and the spiritists.[j]
4 I will hand the Egyptians over
to the power of a cruel master,
and a fierce king[k] will rule over
them,"
declares the Lord, the LORD
Almighty.

5 The waters of the river will dry up,[l]
and the riverbed will be parched
and dry.
6 The canals will stink;[m]
the streams of Egypt will dwindle
and dry up.[n]
The reeds and rushes will wither,[o]
7 also the plants along the Nile,
at the mouth of the river.
Every sown field[p] along the Nile
will become parched, will blow
away and be no more.
8 The fishermen[q] will groan and
lament,
all who cast hooks[r] into the
Nile;
those who throw nets on the water
will pine away.
9 Those who work with combed flax
will despair,
the weavers of fine linen[s] will lose
hope.
10 The workers in cloth will be
dejected,
and all the wage earners will be
sick at heart.

11 The officials of Zoan[t] are nothing
but fools;
the wise counselors of Pharaoh
give senseless advice.
How can you say to Pharaoh,
"I am one of the wise men,[u]
a disciple of the ancient kings"?

12 Where are your wise men[v] now?
Let them show you and make
known
what the LORD Almighty
has planned[w] against Egypt.
13 The officials of Zoan have become
fools,
the leaders of Memphis[a][x] are
deceived;
the cornerstones of her peoples
have led Egypt astray.
14 The LORD has poured into them
a spirit of dizziness;[y]
they make Egypt stagger in all that
she does,
as a drunkard staggers around in
his vomit.

[a] *13* Hebrew *Noph*

19:1 [c]Isa 13:1; Jer 43:12 [d]Joel 3:19 [e]Ex 12:12 [f]Ps 18:10; 104:3; Rev 1:7 [g]Jos 2:11
19:2 [h]Jdg 7:22; Mt 10:21,36 [i]2Ch 20:23
19:3 [j]Isa 8:19; 47:13; Da 2:2,10
19:4 [k]Isa 20:4; Jer 46:26; Eze 29:19
19:5 [l]Jer 51:36
19:6 [m]Ex 7:18 [n]Isa 37:25; Eze 30:12 [o]Isa 15:6
19:7 [p]Isa 23:3
19:8 [q]Eze 47:10 [r]Hab 1:15
19:9 [s]Pr 7:16; Eze 27:7
19:11 [t]Nu 13:22 [u]1Ki 4:30; Ac 7:22
19:12 [v]1Co 1:20 [w]Isa 14:24; Ro 9:17
19:13 [x]Jer 2:16; Eze 30:13,16
19:14 [y]Mt 17:17

KINDNESS

REDEEMING LOVE

Isaiah 19:14

God was kind to afflict Egypt with vertigo. He wanted the people to turn from their dizziness and walk with clearer vision. So let it be for us.

[15]There is nothing Egypt can do—
19:15 [z]Isa 9:14
head or tail, palm branch or reed.[z]

[16]In that day the Egyptians will be
19:16 [a]51:30; Na 3:13 [b]Heb 10:31 [c]Isa 11:15
like women.[a] They will shudder with
fear[b] at the uplifted hand[c] that the
LORD Almighty raises against them.
[17]And the land of Judah will bring terror to the Egyptians; everyone to whom
Judah is mentioned will be terrified, because of what the LORD Almighty is
19:17 [d]Isa 14:24
planning[d] against them.
[18]In that day five cities in Egypt will
speak the language of Canaan and swear
19:18 [e]Zep 3:9
allegiance[e] to the LORD Almighty. One
of them will be called the City of Destruction.[a]
19:19 [f]Jos 22:10 [g]Ge 28:18
[19]In that day there will be an altar[f]
to the LORD in the heart of Egypt, and
a monument[g] to the LORD at its border. [20]It will be a sign and witness to the
LORD Almighty in the land of Egypt.
When they cry out to the LORD because of their oppressors, he will send
19:20 [h]Isa 49:24-26
them a savior and defender, and he will
rescue[h] them. [21]So the LORD will make
himself known to the Egyptians, and
19:21 [i]Isa 11:9 [j]Isa 56:7; Mal 1:11
in that day they will acknowledge[i] the
LORD. They will worship[j] with sacrifices and grain offerings; they will make
vows to the LORD and keep them.
19:22 [k]Heb 12:11 [l]Isa 45:14; Hos 14:1 [m]Dt 32:39
[22]The LORD will strike Egypt with a
plague; he will strike[k] them and heal
them. They will turn[l] to the LORD, and
he will respond to their pleas and heal[m]
them.
19:23 [n]Isa 11:16 [o]Isa 27:13
[23]In that day there will be a highway[n] from Egypt to Assyria. The Assyrians will go to Egypt and the Egyptians
to Assyria. The Egyptians and Assyrians
will worship[o] together. [24]In that day Israel will be the third, along with Egypt
19:25 [p]Ps 100:3 [q]Isa 29:23; 45:11; 60:21; 64:8; Eph 2:10 [r]Hos 2:23
and Assyria, a blessing on the earth.
[25]The LORD Almighty will bless them,
saying, "Blessed be Egypt my people,[p]
Assyria my handiwork,[q] and Israel my
inheritance.[r]"

A Prophecy Against Egypt and Cush

20:1 [s]2Ki 18:17
20 In the year that the supreme
commander,[s] sent by Sargon
king of Assyria, came to Ashdod and attacked and captured it— [2]at that time
the LORD spoke through Isaiah son of
20:2 [t]Isa 13:1 [u]Zec 13:4; Mt 3:4 [v]Eze 24:17,23 [w]1Sa 19:24 [x]Mic 1:8
Amoz.[t] He said to him, "Take off the
sackcloth[u] from your body and the sandals[v] from your feet." And he did so,
going around stripped[w] and barefoot.[x]
[3]Then the LORD said, "Just as my
servant Isaiah has gone stripped and
20:3 [y]Isa 8:18 [z]Isa 37:9; 43:3
barefoot for three years, as a sign[y] and
portent against Egypt and Cush,[b][z] [4]so
20:4 [a]Isa 19:4 [b]Isa 47:3; Jer 13:22,26
the king[a] of Assyria will lead away
stripped and barefoot the Egyptian captives and Cushite exiles, young and
old, with buttocks bared—to Egypt's
shame.[b] [5]Those who trusted in Cush
and boasted in Egypt[c] will be afraid and
20:5 [c]2Ki 18:21; Isa 30:5
put to shame. [6]In that day the people
who live on this coast will say, 'See what
20:6 [d]Isa 10:3 [e]Jer 30:15-17; Mt 23:33; 1Th 5:3; Heb 2:3
has happened to those we relied on,
those we fled to for help[d] and deliverance from the king of Assyria! How
then can we escape?[e]'"

A Prophecy Against Babylon

21:1 [f]Isa 13:21; Jer 51:43 [g]Zec 9:14
21 An oracle concerning the Desert[f] by the Sea:

Like whirlwinds sweeping through
the southland,[g]
an invader comes from the desert,
from a land of terror.

21:2 [h]Ps 60:3 [i]Isa 33:1 [j]Isa 22:6; Jer 49:34
[2]A dire[h] vision has been shown to
me:
The traitor betrays,[i] the looter
takes loot.
Elam,[j] attack! Media, lay siege!
I will bring to an end all the
groaning she caused.

[3]At this my body is racked with pain,
21:3 [k]Ps 48:6; Isa 26:17
pangs seize me, like those of a
woman in labor;[k]
I am staggered by what I hear,
I am bewildered by what I see.
[4]My heart falters,
fear makes me tremble;
the twilight I longed for
has become a horror to me.

[a]*18* Most manuscripts of the Masoretic Text; some manuscripts of the Masoretic Text, Dead Sea Scrolls and Vulgate *City of the Sun* (that is, Heliopolis)
[b]*3* That is, the upper Nile region; also in verse 5

21:5 [l]Jer 51:39,57; Da 5:2

5 They set the tables,
they spread the rugs,
they eat, they drink![l]
Get up, you officers,
oil the shields!

6 This is what the Lord says to me:

"Go, post a lookout
and have him report what he sees.

21:7 [m]ver 9

7 When he sees chariots[m]
with teams of horses,
riders on donkeys
or riders on camels,
let him be alert,
fully alert."

21:8 [n]Hab 2:1

8 And the lookout[a n] shouted,

"Day after day, my lord, I stand on
the watchtower;
every night I stay at my post.
9 Look, here comes a man in a chariot
with a team of horses.
And he gives back the answer:

21:9 [o]Rev 14:8 [p]Jer 51:8; Rev 18:2 [q]Isa 46:1; Jer 50:2; 51:44

'Babylon[o] has fallen[p], has fallen!
All the images of its gods[q]
lie shattered on the ground!'"

21:10 [r]Jer 51:33

10 O my people, crushed on the
threshing floor,[r]
I tell you what I have heard
from the LORD Almighty,
from the God of Israel.

A Prophecy Against Edom

21:11 [s]Ge 25:14 [t]Ge 32:3

11 An oracle concerning Dumah[b,s]:

Someone calls to me from Seir,[t]
"Watchman, what is left of the
night?
Watchman, what is left of the
night?"
12 The watchman replies,
"Morning is coming, but also the
night.
If you would ask, then ask;
and come back yet again."

A Prophecy Against Arabia

21:13 [u]Isa 13:1

13 An oracle[u] concerning Arabia:

You caravans of Dedanites,
who camp in the thickets of
Arabia,
14 bring water for the thirsty;

21:14 [v]Ge 25:15

you who live in Tema,[v]
bring food for the fugitives.

21:15 [w]Isa 13:14

15 They flee[w] from the sword,
from the drawn sword,
from the bent bow
and from the heat of battle.

16 This is what the Lord says to me: "Within one year, as a servant bound by contract[x] would count it, all the pomp[y] of Kedar[z] will come to an end. 17 The survivors of the bowmen, the warriors of Kedar, will be few.[a]" The LORD, the God of Israel, has spoken.

21:16 [x]Isa 16:14 [y]Isa 17:3 [z]Ps 120:5; Isa 60:7

21:17 [a]Isa 10:19

A Prophecy About Jerusalem

22:1 [b]Isa 13:1 [c]Ps 125:2; Jer 21:13; Joel 3:2,12,14

22 An oracle[b] concerning the Valley[c] of Vision:

What troubles you now,
that you have all gone up on the
roofs,
2 O town full of commotion,
O city of tumult and revelry?[d]

22:2 [d]Isa 32:13

Your slain were not killed by the
sword,
nor did they die in battle.
3 All your leaders have fled together;
they have been captured without
using the bow.
All you who were caught were taken
prisoner together,
having fled while the enemy was
still far away.
4 Therefore I said, "Turn away from
me;
let me weep[e] bitterly.
Do not try to console me
over the destruction of my
people."[f]

22:4 [e]Isa 15:3; Lk 19:41 [f]Jer 9:1

5 The Lord, the LORD Almighty, has
a day
of tumult and trampling and
terror[g]
in the Valley of Vision,
a day of battering down walls
and of crying out to the
mountains.

22:5 [g]La 1:5

6 Elam[h] takes up the quiver,[i]
with her charioteers and horses;
Kir[j] uncovers the shield.

22:6 [h]Isa 21:2 [i]Jer 49:35 [j]2Ki 16:9

7 Your choicest valleys are full of
chariots,
and horsemen are posted at the
city gates;[k]
8 the defenses of Judah are stripped
away.

22:7 [k]2Ch 32:1-2

[a]8 Dead Sea Scrolls and Syriac; Masoretic Text *A lion* [b]11 *Dumah* means *silence* or *stillness,* a wordplay on *Edom.*

22:8 [l]2Ch 32:5 [m]1Ki 7:2

And you looked in that day
to the weapons[l] in the Palace of the Forest;[m]
9 you saw that the City of David
had many breaches in its defenses;
you stored up water
in the Lower Pool.[n]

22:9 [n]2Ch 32:4

10 You counted the buildings in Jerusalem
and tore down houses to strengthen the wall.

22:11 [o]2Ki 25:4; Jer 39:4 [p]2Ch 32:4

11 You built a reservoir between the two walls[o]
for the water of the Old Pool,[p]
but you did not look to the One who made it,
or have regard for the One who planned it long ago.

22:12 [q]Joel 2:17 [r]Mic 1:16 [s]Joel 1:13

12 The Lord, the LORD Almighty,
called you on that day
to weep[q] and to wail,
to tear out your hair[r] and put on sackcloth.[s]

22:13 [t]Isa 5:22; 28:7-8; 56:12; Lk 17:26-29 [u]1Co 15:32*

13 But see, there is joy and revelry,
slaughtering of cattle and killing of sheep,
eating of meat and drinking of wine![t]
"Let us eat and drink," you say,
"for tomorrow we die!"[u]

22:14 [v]Isa 5:9 [w]Isa 13:11; 26:21; 30:13-14; Eze 24:13

14 The LORD Almighty has revealed
this in my hearing:[v] "Till your dying
day this sin will not be atoned[w] for,"
says the Lord, the LORD Almighty.

15 This is what the Lord, the LORD
Almighty, says:

22:15 [x]2Ki 18:18; Isa 36:3

"Go, say to this steward,
to Shebna,[x] who is in charge of the palace:
16 What are you doing here and who
gave you permission
to cut out a grave[y] for yourself here,
hewing your grave on the height
and chiseling your resting place in the rock?

22:16 [y]Mt 27:60

17 "Beware, the LORD is about to take
firm hold of you
and hurl you away, O you mighty man.
18 He will roll you up tightly like a ball
and throw[z] you into a large country.
There you will die

22:18 [z]Isa 17:13

and there your splendid chariots
will remain—
you disgrace to your master's house!
19 I will depose you from your office,
and you will be ousted from your position.

22:20 [a]2Ki 18:18; Isa 36:3

20 "In that day I will summon my servant, Eliakim[a] son of Hilkiah. 21 I will
clothe him with your robe and fasten
your sash around him and hand your
authority over to him. He will be a father to those who live in Jerusalem and
to the house of Judah. 22 I will place on
his shoulder the key[b] to the house of
David;[c] what he opens no one can shut,
and what he shuts no one can open.[d]
23 I will drive him like a peg[e] into a firm
place;[f] he will be a seat[a] of honor[g] for
the house of his father. 24 All the glory
of his family will hang on him: its offspring and offshoots—all its lesser vessels, from the bowls to all the jars.

22:22 [b]Rev 3:7 [c]Isa 7:2 [d]Job 12:14

22:23 [e]Zec 10:4 [f]Ezr 9:8 [g]1Sa 2:7-8; Job 36:7

25 "In that day," declares the LORD
Almighty, "the peg[h] driven into the firm
place will give way; it will be sheared
off and will fall, and the load hanging
on it will be cut down." The LORD has
spoken.[i]

22:25 [h]ver 23 [i]Isa 46:11; Mic 4:4

A Prophecy About Tyre

23:1 [j]Jos 19:29; 1Ki 5:1; Jer 47:4; Eze 26,27,28; Joel 3:4-8; Am 1:9-10; Zec 9:2-4 [k]1Ki 10:22 [l]Ge 10:4; Isa 2:16 fn

23 An oracle concerning Tyre:[j]

Wail, O ships[k] of Tarshish![l]
For Tyre is destroyed
and left without house or harbor.
From the land of Cyprus[b]
word has come to them.

2 Be silent, you people of the island
and you merchants of Sidon,
whom the seafarers have enriched.
3 On the great waters
came the grain of the Shihor;
the harvest of the Nile[c][m] was the revenue of Tyre,[n]
and she became the marketplace of the nations.

23:3 [m]Isa 19:7 [n]Eze 27:3

4 Be ashamed, O Sidon,[o] and you,
O fortress of the sea,
for the sea has spoken:

23:4 [o]Ge 10:15,19

[a]23 Or *throne* [b]1 Hebrew *Kittim*
[c]2,3 Masoretic Text; one Dead Sea Scroll *Sidon, / who cross over the sea; / your envoys* 3*are on the great waters. / The grain of the Shihor, / the harvest of the Nile,*

"I have neither been in labor nor
given birth;
I have neither reared sons nor
brought up daughters."
5 When word comes to Egypt,
they will be in anguish at the
report from Tyre.

6 Cross over to Tarshish;
wail, you people of the island.
7 Is this your city of revelry,[p]
the old, old city,
whose feet have taken her
to settle in far-off lands?
8 Who planned this against Tyre,
the bestower of crowns,
whose merchants are princes,
whose traders are renowned in the
earth?
9 The LORD Almighty planned it,
to bring low[q] the pride of all glory
and to humble[r] all who are
renowned[s] on the earth.

10 Till[a] your land as along the Nile,
O Daughter of Tarshish,
for you no longer have a harbor.
11 The LORD has stretched out his
hand[t] over the sea
and made its kingdoms tremble.
He has given an order concerning
Phoenicia[b]
that her fortresses be destroyed.[u]
12 He said, "No more of your reveling,[v]
O Virgin Daughter[w] of Sidon,
now crushed!

"Up, cross over to Cyprus[c];
even there you will find no rest."
13 Look at the land of the
Babylonians,[d]
this people that is now of no
account!
The Assyrians[x] have made it
a place for desert creatures;
they raised up their siege towers,
they stripped its fortresses bare
and turned it into a ruin.[y]

14 Wail, you ships of Tarshish;[z]
your fortress is destroyed!

15 At that time Tyre[a] will be forgotten
for seventy years, the span of a king's
life. But at the end of these seventy
years, it will happen to Tyre as in the
song of the prostitute:

16 "Take up a harp, walk through the
city,
O prostitute forgotten;
play the harp well, sing many a song,
so that you will be remembered."

17 At the end of seventy years, the
LORD will deal with Tyre. She will return to her hire as a prostitute[b] and will
ply her trade with all the kingdoms on
the face of the earth. 18 Yet her profit
and her earnings will be set apart for
the LORD;[c] they will not be stored up
or hoarded. Her profits will go to those
who live before the LORD,[d] for abundant food and fine clothes.

The LORD's Devastation of the Earth

24 See, the LORD is going to lay
waste the earth[e]
and devastate it;
he will ruin its face
and scatter its inhabitants—
2 it will be the same
for priest as for people,[f]
for master as for servant,
for mistress as for maid,
for seller as for buyer,[g]
for borrower as for lender,
for debtor as for creditor.[h]
3 The earth will be completely laid
waste
and totally plundered.[i]
The LORD has spoken
this word.

4 The earth dries up and withers,
the world languishes and withers,
the exalted[j] of the earth languish.
5 The earth is defiled[k] by its people;
they have disobeyed[l] the laws,
violated the statutes
and broken the everlasting
covenant.
6 Therefore a curse consumes the
earth;
its people must bear their guilt.
Therefore earth's inhabitants are
burned up,[m]
and very few are left.
7 The new wine dries up and the vine
withers;[n]
all the merrymakers groan.[o]
8 The gaiety of the tambourines[p] is
stilled,
the noise[q] of the revelers has
stopped,

[a] *10* Dead Sea Scrolls and some Septuagint manuscripts; Masoretic Text *Go through*
[b] *11* Hebrew *Canaan* [c] *12* Hebrew *Kittim*
[d] *13* Or *Chaldeans*

23:7 [p]Isa 22:2; 32:13
23:9 [q]Job 40:11 [r]Isa 13:11 [s]Isa 5:13; 9:15
23:11 [t]Ex 14:21 [u]Isa 25:2; Zec 9:3-4
23:12 [v]Rev 18:22 [w]Isa 47:1
23:13 [x]Isa 10:5 [y]Isa 10:7
23:14 [z]Isa 2:16 fn
23:15 [a]Jer 25:22
23:17 [b]Eze 16:26; Na 3:4; Rev 17:1
23:18 [c]Ex 28:36; Ps 72:10 [d]Isa 60:5-9; Mic 4:13
24:1 [e]ver 20; Isa 2:19-21; 33:9
24:2 [f]Hos 4:9 [g]Eze 7:12 [h]Lev 25:35-37; Dt 23:19-20
24:3 [i]Isa 6:11-12
24:4 [j]Isa 2:12
24:5 [k]Ge 3:17; Nu 35:33 [l]Isa 10:6; 59:12
24:6 [m]Isa 1:31
24:7 [n]Joel 1:10-12 [o]Isa 16:8-10
24:8 [p]Isa 5:12 [q]Jer 7:34; 16:9; 25:10; Hos 2:11

24:8 [r]Rev 18:22 [s]Eze 26:13

the joyful harp[r] is silent.[s]
9 No longer do they drink wine[t] with
a song;
the beer is bitter[u] to its drinkers.

24:9 [t]Isa 5:11,22 [u]Isa 5:20

10 The ruined city lies desolate;
the entrance to every house is
barred.
11 In the streets they cry out for wine;
all joy turns to gloom,[v]
all gaiety is banished from the
earth.

24:11 [v]Isa 16:10; 32:13; Jer 14:3

12 The city is left in ruins,
its gate is battered to pieces.
13 So will it be on the earth
and among the nations,
as when an olive tree is beaten,[w]
or as when gleanings are left after
the grape harvest.

24:13 [w]Isa 17:6

14 They raise their voices, they shout
for joy;[x]
from the west they acclaim the
LORD's majesty.

24:14 [x]Isa 12:6

15 Therefore in the east give glory[y] to
the LORD;
exalt[z] the name of the LORD, the
God of Israel,
in the islands of the sea.

24:15 [y]Isa 66:19 [z]Isa 25:3; Mal 1:11

16 From the ends of the earth we hear
singing:
"Glory[a] to the Righteous One."

But I said, "I waste away, I waste
away!
Woe to me!
The treacherous betray!
With treachery the treacherous
betray!"[b]

24:16 [a]Isa 28:5 [b]Isa 21:2; Jer 5:11

17 Terror and pit and snare[c] await you,
O people of the earth.
18 Whoever flees at the sound of terror
will fall into a pit;
whoever climbs out of the pit
will be caught in a snare.

24:17 [c]Jer 48:43

The floodgates of the heavens[d] are
opened,
the foundations of the earth
shake.[e]

24:18 [d]Ge 7:11 [e]Ps 18:7

19 The earth is broken up,
the earth is split asunder,[f]
the earth is thoroughly shaken.
20 The earth reels like a drunkard,[g]
it sways like a hut in the wind;
so heavy upon it is the guilt of its
rebellion[h]
that it falls—never to rise again.

24:19 [f]Dt 11:6

24:20 [g]Isa 19:14 [h]Isa 1:2,28; 43:27

21 In that day the LORD will punish[i]
the powers in the heavens above
and the kings on the earth below.

24:21 [i]Isa 10:12

22 They will be herded together
like prisoners[j] bound in a
dungeon;[k]
they will be shut up in prison
and be punished[a] after many days.[l]
23 The moon will be abashed, the sun[m]
ashamed;
for the LORD Almighty will reign[n]
on Mount Zion[o] and in Jerusalem,
and before its elders, gloriously.[p]

24:22 [j]Isa 10:4 [k]Isa 42:7,22 [l]Eze 38:8

24:23 [m]Isa 13:10 [n]Rev 22:5 [o]Heb 12:22 [p]Isa 60:19

Praise to the LORD

25 O LORD, you are my God;
I will exalt you and praise your
name,
for in perfect faithfulness
you have done marvelous things,[q]
things planned[r] long ago.

25:1 [q]Ps 98:1 [r]Nu 23:19

▸ JOY

A SONG FOR GOD'S SWEET BEING

Isaiah 25:1

Be not dour and petty-spirited. Exalt and praise our God! Sing to him whose presence is a song. Shout to him whose reality is triumph.

2 You have made the city a heap of
rubble,[s]
the fortified[t] town a ruin,
the foreigners' stronghold[u] a city no
more;
it will never be rebuilt.

25:2 [s]Isa 17:1 [t]Isa 17:3 [u]Isa 13:22

3 Therefore strong peoples will honor
you;
cities of ruthless[v] nations will
revere you.

25:3 [v]Isa 13:11

4 You have been a refuge[w] for the
poor,
a refuge for the needy in his
distress,
a shelter from the storm
and a shade from the heat.
For the breath of the ruthless[x]
is like a storm driving against a
wall
5 and like the heat of the desert.
You silence[y] the uproar of foreigners;
as heat is reduced by the shadow
of a cloud,
so the song of the ruthless is
stilled.

25:4 [w]Isa 4:6; 17:10; 27:5; 33:16 [x]Isa 29:5; 49:25

25:5 [y]Jer 51:55

[a]22 Or *released*

[6]On this mountain[z] the LORD
Almighty will prepare
a feast[a] of rich food for all peoples,
a banquet of aged wine—
the best of meats and the finest of
wines.[b]
[7]On this mountain he will destroy
the shroud[c] that enfolds all
peoples,
the sheet that covers all nations;
[8] he will swallow up death[d] forever.
The Sovereign LORD will wipe away
the tears[e]
from all faces;
he will remove the disgrace[f] of his
people
from all the earth.
The LORD has spoken.

[9]In that day they will say,

"Surely this is our God;[g]
we trusted in him, and he saved[h]
us.
This is the LORD, we trusted in him;
let us rejoice[i] and be glad in his
salvation."

[10]The hand of the LORD will rest on
this mountain;
but Moab[j] will be trampled under
him
as straw is trampled down in the
manure.
[11]They will spread out their hands in
it,
as a swimmer spreads out his
hands to swim.
God will bring down[k] their pride[l]
despite the cleverness[a] of their
hands.
[12]He will bring down your high
fortified walls
and lay them low;[m]
he will bring them down to the
ground,
to the very dust.

A Song of Praise

26 In that day this song will be
sung in the land of Judah:

We have a strong city;[n]
God makes salvation
its walls[o] and ramparts.
[2]Open the gates
that the righteous[p] nation may
enter,
the nation that keeps faith.
[3]You will keep in perfect peace
him whose mind is steadfast,
because he trusts in you.
[4]Trust[q] in the LORD forever,
for the LORD, the LORD, is the
Rock eternal.
[5]He humbles those who dwell on
high,
he lays the lofty city low;
he levels it to the ground[r]
and casts it down to the dust.
[6]Feet trample it down—
the feet of the oppressed,
the footsteps of the poor.[s]

[7]The path of the righteous is level;
O upright One, you make the way
of the righteous smooth.[t]
[8]Yes, LORD, walking in the way of
your laws,[b][u]
we wait for you;
your name[v] and renown
are the desire of our hearts.
[9]My soul yearns for you in the night;
in the morning my spirit longs[w]
for you.
When your judgments come upon
the earth,
the people of the world learn
righteousness.[x]
[10]Though grace is shown to the
wicked,
they do not learn righteousness;
even in a land of uprightness they go
on doing evil[y]
and regard[z] not the majesty of the
LORD.
[11]O LORD, your hand is lifted high,
but they do not see[a] it.
Let them see your zeal for your
people and be put to shame;
let the fire[b] reserved for your
enemies consume them.

[12]LORD, you establish peace for us;
all that we have accomplished you
have done for us.
[13]O LORD, our God, other lords[c]
besides you have ruled over
us,
but your name alone do we
honor.[d]
[14]They are now dead,[e] they live no
more;
those departed spirits do not rise.
You punished them and brought
them to ruin;[f]

[a]*11* The meaning of the Hebrew for this word is uncertain. [b]*8* Or *judgments*

25:6 [z]Isa 2:2 [a]Isa 1:19; Mt 8:11; 22:4 [b]Pr 9:2
25:7 [c]2Co 3:15-16; Eph 4:18
25:8 [d]Hos 13:14; 1Co 15:54-55* [e]Isa 30:19; 35:10; 51:11; 65:19; Rev 7:17; 21:4 [f]Mt 5:11; 1Pe 4:14
25:9 [g]Isa 40:9 [h]Ps 20:5; Isa 33:22; 35:4; 49:25-26; 60:16 [i]Isa 35:2,10
25:10 [j]Am 2:1-3
25:11 [k]Isa 5:25; 14:26; 16:14 [l]Job 40:12
25:12 [m]Isa 15:1
26:1 [n]Isa 14:32 [o]Isa 60:18
26:2 [p]Isa 54:14; 58:8; 62:2
26:4 [q]Isa 12:2; 50:10
26:5 [r]Isa 25:12
26:6 [s]Isa 3:15
26:7 [t]Isa 42:16
26:8 [u]Isa 56:1 [v]Isa 12:4
26:9 [w]Ps 63:1; 78:34; Isa 55:6 [x]Mt 6:33
26:10 [y]Isa 32:6 [z]Isa 22:12-13; Hos 11:7; Jn 5:37-38; Ro 2:4
26:11 [a]Isa 44:9,18 [b]Heb 10:27
26:13 [c]Isa 2:8; 10:5,11 [d]Isa 63:7
26:14 [e]Dt 4:28 [f]Isa 10:3

you wiped out all memory of
them.
[15]You have enlarged the nation,
O LORD;
you have enlarged the nation.
You have gained glory for yourself;
you have extended all the borders[g]
of the land.

26:15 [g]Isa 33:17

[16]LORD, they came to you in their
distress;[h]
when you disciplined them,
they could barely whisper a
prayer.[a]

26:16 [h]Hos 5:15

[17]As a woman with child and about to
give birth[i]
writhes and cries out in her pain,
so were we in your presence,
O LORD.

26:17 [i]Jn 16:21

[18]We were with child, we writhed in
pain,
but we gave birth[j] to wind.
We have not brought salvation[k] to
the earth;
we have not given birth to people
of the world.

26:18 [j]Isa 33:11; 59:4 [k]Ps 17:14

[19]But your dead[l] will live;
their bodies will rise.
You who dwell in the dust,
wake up and shout for joy.
Your dew is like the dew of the
morning;
the earth will give birth to her
dead.[m]

26:19 [l]Isa 25:8; Eph 5:14 [m]Eze 37:1-14; Da 12:2

[20]Go, my people, enter your rooms
and shut the doors[n] behind you;
hide[o] yourselves for a little while
until his wrath has passed by.[p]

26:20 [n]Ex 12:23 [o]Ps 91:1,4 [p]Ps 30:5; Isa 54:7-8

[21]See, the LORD is coming[q] out of his
dwelling[r]
to punish[s] the people of the earth
for their sins.
The earth will disclose the blood[t]
shed upon her;
she will conceal her slain no
longer.

26:21 [q]Jude 1:14 [r]Mic 1:3 [s]Isa 13:9,11; 30:12-14 [t]Job 16:18; Lk 11:50-51

Deliverance of Israel

27 In that day,

the LORD will punish with his
sword,[u]
his fierce, great and powerful
sword,
Leviathan[v] the gliding serpent,
Leviathan the coiling serpent;
he will slay the monster[w] of the sea.

27:1 [u]Isa 34:6; 66:16 [v]Job 3:8 [w]Ps 74:13

[2]In that day—

"Sing about a fruitful vineyard:[x]
[3] I, the LORD, watch over it;
I water[y] it continually.
I guard it day and night
so that no one may harm it.
[4] I am not angry.
If only there were briers and thorns
confronting me!
I would march against them in
battle;
I would set them all on fire.[z]
[5]Or else let them come to me for
refuge;[a]
let them make peace[b] with me,
yes, let them make peace with
me."

27:2 [x]Jer 2:21
27:3 [y]Isa 58:11
27:4 [z]Isa 10:17; Mt 3:12; Heb 6:8
27:5 [a]Isa 25:4 [b]Job 22:21; Ro 5:1; 2Co 5:20

[6]In days to come Jacob will take root,
Israel will bud and blossom[c]
and fill all the world with fruit.[d]

27:6 [c]Hos 14:5-6 [d]Isa 37:31

[7]Has ⌞the LORD⌟ struck her
as he struck[e] down those who
struck her?
Has she been killed
as those were killed who killed
her?

27:7 [e]Isa 37:36-38

[8]By warfare[b] and exile[f] you contend
with her—
with his fierce blast he drives her
out,
as on a day the east wind blows.

27:8 [f]Isa 50:1; 54:7

[9]By this, then, will Jacob's guilt be
atoned for,
and this will be the full fruitage of
the removal of his sin:[g]
When he makes all the altar stones
to be like chalk stones crushed to
pieces,
no Asherah poles[c][h] or incense altars
will be left standing.

27:9 [g]Ro 11:27* [h]Ex 34:13

[10]The fortified city stands desolate,[i]
an abandoned settlement, forsaken
like the desert;
there the calves graze,
there they lie down;[j]
they strip its branches bare.
[11]When its twigs are dry, they are
broken off
and women come and make fires
with them.
For this is a people without
understanding;[k]

27:10 [i]Isa 32:14; Jer 26:6 [j]Isa 17:2
27:11 [k]Dt 32:28; Isa 1:3; Jer 8:7

[a]*16* The meaning of the Hebrew for this clause is uncertain. [b]*8* See Septuagint; the meaning of the Hebrew for this word is uncertain. [c]*9* That is, symbols of the goddess Asherah

27:11 [l]Dt 32:18; Isa 43:1,7,15; 44:1-2,21,24 [m]Isa 9:17

so their Maker has no compassion
on them,
and their Creator[l] shows them no
favor.[m]

27:12 [n]Ge 15:18 [o]Dt 30:4; Isa 11:12; 17:6
27:13 [p]Lev 25:9; Mt 24:31 [q]Isa 19:21,25

12In that day the LORD will thresh
from the flowing Euphrates[a] to the
Wadi of Egypt,[n] and you, O Israelites,
will be gathered[o] up one by one. 13And
in that day a great trumpet[p] will sound.
Those who were perishing in Assyria
and those who were exiled in Egypt[q]
will come and worship the LORD on
the holy mountain in Jerusalem.

Woe to Ephraim

28:1 [r]ver 3; Isa 9:9 [s]ver 4 [t]Hos 7:5

28 Woe to that wreath, the pride of
Ephraim's[r] drunkards,
to the fading flower, his glorious
beauty,
set on the head of a fertile valley[s]—
to that city, the pride of those laid
low by wine![t]

28:2 [u]Isa 40:10 [v]Isa 30:30; Eze 13:11 [w]Isa 29:6 [x]Isa 8:7

2See, the Lord has one who is
powerful[u] and strong.
Like a hailstorm[v] and a destructive
wind,[w]
like a driving rain and a flooding[x]
downpour,
he will throw it forcefully to the
ground.

28:3 [y]ver 1

3That wreath, the pride of Ephraim's[y]
drunkards,
will be trampled underfoot.

28:4 [z]ver 1 [a]Hos 9:10; Na 3:12

4That fading flower, his glorious
beauty,
set on the head of a fertile valley,[z]
will be like a fig[a] ripe before
harvest—
as soon as someone sees it and
takes it in his hand,
he swallows it.

28:5 [b]Isa 62:3

5In that day the LORD Almighty
will be a glorious crown,[b]
a beautiful wreath
for the remnant of his people.

28:6 [c]Isa 11:2-4; 32:1,16 [d]Jn 5:30 [e]2Ch 32:8

6He will be a spirit of justice[c]
to him who sits in judgment,[d]
a source of strength
to those who turn back the battle[e]
at the gate.

28:7 [f]Isa 22:13 [g]Isa 56:10-12 [h]Isa 24:2 [i]Isa 9:15 [j]Isa 29:11; Hos 4:11

7And these also stagger from wine[f]
and reel[g] from beer:
Priests[h] and prophets[i] stagger from
beer
and are befuddled with wine;
they reel from beer,
they stagger when seeing visions,[j]
they stumble when rendering
decisions.

28:8 [k]Jer 48:26

8All the tables are covered with
vomit[k]
and there is not a spot without
filth.

28:9 [l]ver 26; Isa 30:20; 48:17; 50:4; 54:13 [m]Ps 131:2 [n]Heb 5:12-13

9"Who is it he is trying to teach?[l]
To whom is he explaining his
message?
To children weaned[m] from their
milk,[n]
to those just taken from the
breast?
10For it is:
Do and do, do and do,
rule on rule, rule on rule[b];
a little here, a little there."

28:11 [o]Isa 33:19 [p]1Co 14:21*

11Very well then, with foreign lips and
strange tongues[o]
God will speak to this people,[p]

28:12 [q]Isa 11:10; Mt 11:28-29

12to whom he said,
"This is the resting place, let the
weary rest";[q]
and, "This is the place of repose"—
but they would not listen.

28:13 [r]Mt 21:44 [s]Isa 8:15

13So then, the word of the LORD to
them will become:
Do and do, do and do,
rule on rule, rule on rule;
a little here, a little there—
so that they will go and fall
backward,
be injured[r] and snared and
captured.[s]

28:14 [t]Isa 1:10

14Therefore hear the word of the
LORD,[t] you scoffers
who rule this people in Jerusalem.
15You boast, "We have entered into a
covenant with death,

[a]*12* Hebrew *River* [b]*10* Hebrew / *sav lasav sav lasav / kav lakav kav lakav* (possibly meaningless sounds; perhaps a mimicking of the prophet's words); also in verse 13

FAITHFULNESS

CHRIST THE CORNERSTONE

Isaiah 28:16

Lay this stone first, and the kingdom it supports will make Rome's coliseum look makeshift and temporary. He who is faithful will finish the kingdom he founded on himself. His kingdom's architecture is of the heart. His citadel is an airy vault of spirit set in spires.

with the grave[a] we have made an
 agreement.
When an overwhelming scourge
 sweeps by,[u]
 it cannot touch us,
for we have made a lie[v] our refuge
 and falsehood[b] our hiding place.[w]"

28:15 [u]ver 2,18; Isa 8:7-8; 30:28; Da 11:22 [v]Isa 9:15 [w]Isa 29:15

16So this is what the Sovereign LORD says:

"See, I lay a stone in Zion,
 a tested stone,[x]
a precious cornerstone for a sure
 foundation;
 the one who trusts will never be
 dismayed.[y]
17I will make justice[z] the measuring
 line
 and righteousness the plumb line;[a]
hail will sweep away your refuge, the
 lie,
 and water will overflow your
 hiding place.
18Your covenant with death will be
 annulled;
 your agreement with the grave will
 not stand.[b]
When the overwhelming scourge
 sweeps by,[c]
 you will be beaten down[d] by it.
19As often as it comes it will carry you
 away;[e]
 morning after morning, by day
 and by night,
 it will sweep through."

28:16 [x]Ps 118:22; Isa 8:14-15; Mt 21:42; Ac 4:11; Eph 2:20 [y]Ro 9:33*; 10:11*; 1Pe 2:6*
28:17 [z]Isa 5:16 [a]2Ki 21:13
28:18 [b]Isa 7:7 [c]ver 15 [d]Da 8:13
28:19 [e]2Ki 24:2 [f]Job 18:11

The understanding of this message
 will bring sheer terror.[f]
20The bed is too short to stretch out
 on,
 the blanket too narrow to wrap
 around you.[g]
21The LORD will rise up as he did at
 Mount Perazim,[h]
 he will rouse himself as in the
 Valley of Gibeon[i]—
to do his work,[j] his strange work,
 and perform his task, his alien
 task.
22Now stop your mocking,
 or your chains will become
 heavier;
the Lord, the LORD Almighty, has
 told me
 of the destruction decreed[k] against
 the whole land.[l]

28:20 [g]Isa 59:6
28:21 [h]1Ch 14:11 [i]Jos 10:10,12; 1Ch 14:16 [j]Isa 10:12; Lk 19:41-44
28:22 [k]Isa 10:22 [l]Isa 10:23

23Listen and hear my voice;
 pay attention and hear what I say.
24When a farmer plows for planting,
 does he plow continually?
 Does he keep on breaking up and
 harrowing the soil?
25When he has leveled the surface,
 does he not sow caraway and
 scatter cummin?[m]
Does he not plant wheat in its
 place,[c]
 barley in its plot,[c]
 and spelt[n] in its field?
26His God instructs him
 and teaches him the right way.

28:25 [m]Mt 23:23 [n]Ex 9:32

27Caraway is not threshed with a
 sledge,
 nor is a cartwheel rolled over
 cummin;
caraway is beaten out with a rod,
 and cummin with a stick.
28Grain must be ground to make
 bread;
 so one does not go on threshing
 it forever.
Though he drives the wheels of his
 threshing cart over it,
 his horses do not grind it.
29All this also comes from the LORD
 Almighty,
 wonderful in counsel[o] and
 magnificent in wisdom.[p]

28:29 [o]Isa 9:6 [p]Ro 11:33

Woe to David's City

29 Woe[q] to you, Ariel, Ariel,[r]
 the city where David settled!
Add year to year
 and let your cycle of festivals[s] go
 on.
2Yet I will besiege Ariel;
 she will mourn and lament,[t]
 she will be to me like an altar
 hearth.[d]
3I will encamp against you all around;
 I will encircle[u] you with towers
 and set up my siege works against
 you.
4Brought low, you will speak from the
 ground;
 your speech will mumble[v] out of
 the dust.
Your voice will come ghostlike from
 the earth;
 out of the dust your speech will
 whisper.

29:1 [q]Isa 22:12-13 [r]2Sa 5:9 [s]Isa 1:14
29:2 [t]Isa 3:26; La 2:5
29:3 [u]Lk 19:43-44
29:4 [v]Isa 8:19

[a]*15* Hebrew *Sheol*; also in verse 18 [b]*15* Or *false gods* [c]*25* The meaning of the Hebrew for this word is uncertain. [d]*2* The Hebrew for *altar hearth* sounds like the Hebrew for *Ariel*.

5 But your many enemies will become
like fine dust,
the ruthless hordes like blown
chaff.[w]
Suddenly,[x] in an instant,
6 the LORD Almighty will come
with thunder and earthquake[y] and
great noise,
with windstorm and tempest and
flames of a devouring fire.

29:5 [w]Isa 17:13 [x]Isa 17:14; 1Th 5:3
29:6 [y]Mt 24:7; Mk 13:8; Lk 21:11; Rev 11:19

DAY 2 TWO

Love and the Purpose of God in My Life

Isaiah 29:16

Our love for God is displayed in a state of yielding that forbids all back talk. Our love for God says, "Yes, Lord" to whatever it is that God asks of us. Isaiah, in describing a "sassy pot," makes the point that it is the potter who forms, and it is the clay who yields. When the clay becomes resistant in the hands of the potter and refuses to be shaped according to the potter's desires, then the purposes of the potter are brought to a standstill. Similarly, in our relationship with God, when we resist God's will for us, we stand defiantly before God's all-shaping love and refuse to accept his divine purposes for our lives.

What then is the next step for such defiant clay? Brokenness. But brokenness is painful for both the potter and his recalcitrant clay. God is a loving parent who does not enjoy breaking his self-willed children. He would much rather they yield to him of their own accord. We must never suppose that the breaking process that God uses to change our lives ever brings him any delight. Indeed, he weeps for the process of forcing our stubbornness into usefulness.

This is God's love for us: that he cares for us enough to bring about his will in our lives. But we must mark this love as behind all of God's dealings with us. He celebrates our instant yielding as a triumph of his love. When he has to break our hard hearts, he celebrates that, too. He is willing—if we will have it no other way—to use a cross to fashion us in the image of his dear Son.

To begin a study on the topic of Love, the Definition of God, turn to the home page on page 1033.

7 Then the hordes of all the nations[z]
that fight against Ariel,
that attack her and her fortress
and besiege her,
will be as it is with a dream,[a]
with a vision in the night—
8 as when a hungry man dreams that
he is eating,
but he awakens, and his hunger
remains;
as when a thirsty man dreams that
he is drinking,
but he awakens[b] faint, with his
thirst unquenched.
So will it be with the hordes of all
the nations
that fight against Mount Zion.

29:7 [z]Mic 4:11-12; Zec 12:9 [a]Job 20:8
29:8 [b]Ps 73:20

9 Be stunned and amazed,
blind yourselves and be sightless;
be drunk,[c] but not from wine,[d]
stagger, but not from beer.
10 The LORD has brought over you a
deep sleep:
He has sealed your eyes[e] (the
prophets);[f]
he has covered your heads (the
seers).[g]

29:9 [c]Isa 51:17 [d]Isa 51:21-22
29:10 [e]Ps 69:23; Isa 6:9-10; Ro 11:8* [f]Mic 3:6 [g]1Sa 9:9

11 For you this whole vision is nothing but words sealed[h] in a scroll. And
if you give the scroll to someone who
can read, and say to him, "Read this,
please," he will answer, "I can't; it is
sealed." 12 Or if you give the scroll to
someone who cannot read, and say,
"Read this, please," he will answer, "I
don't know how to read."

29:11 [h]Isa 8:16; Mt 13:11; Rev 5:1-2

13 The Lord says:

"These people come near to me with
their mouth
and honor me with their lips,
but their hearts are far from me.
Their worship of me[i]
is made up only of rules taught by
men.[a][j]
14 Therefore once more I will astound
these people
with wonder upon wonder;[k]
the wisdom of the wise[l] will perish,
the intelligence of the intelligent
will vanish."[m]
15 Woe to those who go to great depths
to hide their plans from the LORD,
who do their work in darkness and
think,

29:13 [i]Eze 33:31 [j]Mt 15:8-9*; Mk 7:6-7*; Col 2:22
29:14 [k]Hab 1:5 [l]Jer 8:9; 49:7 [m]Isa 6:9-10; 1Co 1:19*

[a] *13* Hebrew; Septuagint *They worship me in vain; / their teachings are but rules taught by men*

29:15 [n]Ps 10:11-13; 94:7; Isa 57:12 [o]Job 22:13

"Who sees us?[n] Who will know?"[o]
16 You turn things upside down,
as if the potter were thought to be like the clay!
Shall what is formed say to him who formed it,
"He did not make me"?
Can the pot say of the potter,[p]
"He knows nothing"?

29:16 [p]Isa 45:9; 64:8; Ro 9:20-21*

17 In a very short time, will not
Lebanon be turned into a fertile field[q]
and the fertile field seem like a forest?[r]

29:17 [q]Ps 84:6 [r]Isa 32:15

18 In that day the deaf[s] will hear the words of the scroll,
and out of gloom and darkness
the eyes of the blind will see.[t]

29:18 [s]Mk 7:37 [t]Isa 32:3; 35:5; Mt 11:5

19 Once more the humble[u] will rejoice in the LORD;
the needy[v] will rejoice in the Holy One of Israel.

29:19 [u]Isa 61:1; Mt 5:5; 11:29 [v]Isa 14:30; Mt 11:5; Jas 1:9; 2:5

20 The ruthless will vanish,
the mockers[w] will disappear,
and all who have an eye for evil[x] will be cut down—

29:20 [w]Isa 28:22 [x]Isa 59:4; Mic 2:1

21 those who with a word make a man out to be guilty,
who ensnare the defender in court[y]
and with false testimony deprive the innocent of justice.[z]

29:21 [y]Am 5:10,15 [z]Isa 5:23; 32:7

22 Therefore this is what the LORD,
who redeemed Abraham,[a] says to the
house of Jacob:

29:22 [a]Isa 41:8; 63:16 [b]Isa 49:23

"No longer will Jacob be ashamed;[b]
no longer will their faces grow pale.
23 When they see among them their children,[c]
the work of my hands,[d]
they will keep my name holy;
they will acknowledge the holiness of the Holy One of Jacob,
and will stand in awe of the God of Israel.

29:23 [c]Isa 49:20-26 [d]Isa 19:25

24 Those who are wayward[e] in spirit
will gain understanding;[f]
those who complain will accept instruction."[g]

29:24 [e]Isa 28:7; Heb 5:2 [f]Isa 41:20; 60:16 [g]Isa 30:21

Woe to the Obstinate Nation

30:1 [h]Isa 29:15 [i]Isa 1:2

30 "Woe[h] to the obstinate children,"[i]
declares the LORD,
"to those who carry out plans that are not mine,
forming an alliance,[j] but not by my Spirit,
heaping sin upon sin;

30:1 [j]Isa 8:12

2 who go down to Egypt[k]
without consulting[l] me;
who look for help to Pharaoh's protection,[m]
to Egypt's shade for refuge.

30:2 [k]Isa 31:1 [l]Nu 27:21 [m]Isa 36:9

3 But Pharaoh's protection will be to your shame,
Egypt's shade will bring you disgrace.[n]

30:3 [n]Isa 20:4-5; 36:6

4 Though they have officials in Zoan[o]
and their envoys have arrived in Hanes,

30:4 [o]Isa 19:11

5 everyone will be put to shame
because of a people[p] useless to them,
who bring neither help nor advantage,
but only shame and disgrace."

30:5 [p]ver 7

6 An oracle concerning the animals of
the Negev:

Through a land of hardship and distress,[q]
of lions and lionesses,
of adders and darting snakes,[r]
the envoys carry their riches on donkeys' backs,
their treasures[s] on the humps of camels,
to that unprofitable nation,
7 to Egypt, whose help is utterly useless.
Therefore I call her
Rahab the Do-Nothing.

30:6 [q]Ex 5:10,21; Isa 8:22; Jer 11:4 [r]Dt 8:15 [s]Isa 15:7

8 Go now, write it on a tablet for them,
inscribe it on a scroll,[t]
that for the days to come
it may be an everlasting witness.

30:8 [t]Isa 8:1; Hab 2:2

9 These are rebellious people,
deceitful[u] children,
children unwilling to listen to the LORD's instruction.[v]

30:9 [u]Isa 28:15; 59:3-4 [v]Isa 1:10

10 They say to the seers,
"See no more visions[w]!"
and to the prophets,
"Give us no more visions of what is right!
Tell us pleasant things,[x]
prophesy illusions.[y]
11 Leave this way,
get off this path,

30:10 [w]Jer 11:21; Am 7:13 [x]1Ki 22:8 [y]Eze 13:7; Ro 16:18

and stop confronting[z] us
with the Holy One of Israel!"

12Therefore, this is what the Holy
One of Israel says:

"Because you have rejected this
message,[a]
relied on oppression[b]
and depended on deceit,
13this sin will become for you
like a high wall,[c] cracked and
bulging,
that collapses[d] suddenly,[e] in an
instant.
14It will break in pieces like pottery,[f]
shattered so mercilessly
that among its pieces not a fragment
will be found
for taking coals from a hearth
or scooping water out of a
cistern."

15This is what the Sovereign LORD,
the Holy One of Israel, says:

"In repentance and rest is your
salvation,
in quietness and trust[g] is your
strength,
but you would have none of it.
16You said, 'No, we will flee on
horses.'[h]
Therefore you will flee!
You said, 'We will ride off on swift
horses.'
Therefore your pursuers will be
swift!
17A thousand will flee
at the threat of one;
at the threat of five[i]
you will all flee[j] away,
till you are left
like a flagstaff on a mountaintop,
like a banner on a hill."

18Yet the LORD longs[k] to be gracious
to you;
he rises to show you compassion.
For the LORD is a God of justice.[l]
Blessed are all who wait for him![m]

19O people of Zion, who live in Jerusalem, you will weep no more.[n] How
gracious he will be when you cry for
help! As soon as he hears, he will answer[o] you. 20Although the Lord gives
you the bread[p] of adversity and the water of affliction, your teachers will be
hidden[q] no more; with your own eyes
you will see them. 21Whether you turn
to the right or to the left, your ears will
hear a voice[r] behind you, saying, "This
is the way; walk in it." 22Then you
will defile your idols[s] overlaid with silver and your images covered with gold;
you will throw them away like a men-
strual cloth and say to them, "Away
with you!"

23He will also send you rain[t] for the
seed you sow in the ground, and the
food that comes from the land will be
rich and plentiful. In that day your cattle will graze in broad meadows.[u] 24The
oxen and donkeys that work the soil will
eat fodder and mash, spread out with
fork[v] and shovel. 25In the day of great
slaughter, when the towers[w] fall, streams
of water will flow[x] on every high mountain and every lofty hill. 26The moon
will shine like the sun,[y] and the sunlight will be seven times brighter, like
the light of seven full days, when the
LORD binds up the bruises of his people
and heals[z] the wounds he inflicted.

27See, the Name[a] of the LORD comes
from afar,
with burning anger[b] and dense
clouds of smoke;
his lips are full of wrath,[c]
and his tongue is a consuming
fire.
28His breath[d] is like a rushing torrent,
rising up to the neck.[e]
He shakes the nations in the sieve[f] of
destruction;
he places in the jaws of the
peoples
a bit[g] that leads them astray.
29And you will sing
as on the night you celebrate a
holy festival;
your hearts will rejoice
as when people go up with flutes
to the mountain[h] of the LORD,
to the Rock of Israel.
30The LORD will cause men to hear
his majestic voice
and will make them see his arm
coming down
with raging anger and consuming
fire,
with cloudburst, thunderstorm
and hail.
31The voice of the LORD will shatter
Assyria;[i]
with his scepter he will strike[j]
them down.

30:11 [z]Job 21:14
30:12 [a]Isa 5:24 [b]Isa 5:7
30:13 [c]Ps 62:3 [d]1Ki 20:30 [e]Isa 29:5
30:14 [f]Ps 2:9; Jer 19:10-11
30:15 [g]Isa 32:17
30:16 [h]Isa 31:1,3
30:17 [i]Lev 26:8; Jos 23:10 [j]Lev 26:36; Dt 28:25
30:18 [k]Isa 42:14; 2Pe 3:9,15 [l]Isa 5:16 [m]Isa 25:9
30:19 [n]Isa 60:20; 61:3 [o]Ps 50:15; Isa 58:9; 65:24; Mt 7:7-11
30:20 [p]1Ki 22:27 [q]Ps 74:9; Am 8:11
30:21 [r]Isa 29:24
30:22 [s]Ex 32:4
30:23 [t]Isa 65:21-22 [u]Ps 65:13
30:24 [v]Mt 3:12; Lk 3:17
30:25 [w]Isa 2:15 [x]Isa 41:18
30:26 [y]Isa 24:23; 60:19-20; Rev 21:23; 22:5 [z]Dt 32:39; Isa 1:5
30:27 [a]Isa 59:19 [b]Isa 66:14 [c]Isa 10:5
30:28 [d]Isa 11:4 [e]Isa 8:8 [f]Am 9:9 [g]2Ki 19:28; Isa 37:29
30:29 [h]Ps 42:4
30:31 [i]Isa 10:5,12 [j]Isa 11:4

32 Every stroke the LORD lays on them
with his punishing rod
will be to the music of tambourines
and harps,
as he fights them in battle with
the blows of his arm.[k]
33 Topheth[l] has long been prepared;
it has been made ready for the
king.
Its fire pit has been made deep and
wide,
with an abundance of fire and
wood;
the breath of the LORD,
like a stream of burning sulfur,[m]
sets it ablaze.

30:32 [k]Isa 11:15; Eze 32:10
30:33 [l]2Ki 23:10 [m]Ge 19:24

Woe to Those Who Rely on Egypt

31 Woe to those who go down to
Egypt[n] for help,
who rely on horses,
who trust in the multitude of their
chariots[o]
and in the great strength of their
horsemen,
but do not look to the Holy One of
Israel,
or seek help from the LORD.[p]
2 Yet he too is wise[q] and can bring
disaster;[r]
he does not take back his words.[s]
He will rise up against the house of
the wicked,[t]
against those who help evildoers.
3 But the Egyptians[u] are men and not
God;[v]
their horses are flesh and not
spirit.
When the LORD stretches out his
hand,[w]
he who helps will stumble,
he who is helped[x] will fall;
both will perish together.

4 This is what the LORD says to me:

"As a lion[y] growls,
a great lion over his prey—
and though a whole band of
shepherds
is called together against him,
he is not frightened by their shouts
or disturbed by their clamor—
so the LORD Almighty will come
down[z]
to do battle on Mount Zion and
on its heights.
5 Like birds hovering overhead,
the LORD Almighty will shield[a]
Jerusalem;
he will shield it and deliver[b] it,
he will 'pass over' it and will
rescue it."

6 Return to him you have so greatly
revolted against, O Israelites. 7 For in
that day every one of you will reject
the idols of silver and gold[c] your sinful
hands have made.

8 "Assyria[d] will fall by a sword that is
not of man;
a sword, not of mortals, will
devour[e] them.
They will flee before the sword
and their young men will be put
to forced labor.[f]
9 Their stronghold[g] will fall because of
terror;
at sight of the battle standard their
commanders will panic,"
declares the LORD,
whose fire[h] is in Zion,
whose furnace is in Jerusalem.

31:1 [n]Dt 17:16; Isa 30:2,5 [o]Isa 2:7 [p]Ps 20:7; Da 9:13
31:2 [q]Ro 16:27 [r]Isa 45:7 [s]Nu 23:19 [t]Isa 32:6
31:3 [u]Isa 36:9 [v]Eze 28:9; 2Th 2:4 [w]Isa 9:17,21 [x]Isa 30:5-7
31:4 [y]Nu 24:9; Hos 11:10; Am 3:8 [z]Isa 42:13
31:5 [a]Ps 91:4 [b]Isa 37:35; 38:6
31:7 [c]Isa 2:20; 30:22
31:8 [d]Isa 10:12 [e]Isa 14:25; 37:7 [f]Ge 49:15
31:9 [g]Dt 32:31,37 [h]Isa 10:17

The Kingdom of Righteousness

32 See, a king[i] will reign in
righteousness
and rulers will rule with justice.[j]
2 Each man will be like a shelter[k] from
the wind
and a refuge from the storm,
like streams of water in the desert
and the shadow of a great rock in
a thirsty land.
3 Then the eyes of those who see will
no longer be closed,[l]
and the ears of those who hear will
listen.
4 The mind of the rash will know and
understand,[m]
and the stammering tongue will
be fluent and clear.
5 No longer will the fool[n] be called
noble
nor the scoundrel be highly
respected.
6 For the fool speaks folly,[o]
his mind is busy with evil:
He practices ungodliness[p]
and spreads error[q] concerning the
LORD;
the hungry he leaves empty[r]
and from the thirsty he withholds
water.
7 The scoundrel's methods are wicked,[s]

32:1 [i]Eze 37:24 [j]Ps 72:1-4; Isa 9:7
32:2 [k]Isa 4:6
32:3 [l]Isa 29:18
32:4 [m]Isa 29:24
32:5 [n]1Sa 25:25
32:6 [o]Pr 19:3 [p]Isa 9:17 [q]Isa 9:16 [r]Isa 3:15
32:7 [s]Jer 5:26-28

he makes up evil schemes[t]
to destroy the poor with lies,
even when the plea of the needy[u]
is just.
8 But the noble man makes noble
plans,
and by noble deeds[v] he stands.

The Women of Jerusalem

9 You women who are so complacent,
rise up and listen[w] to me;
you daughters who feel secure,[x]
hear what I have to say!
10 In little more than a year
you who feel secure will tremble;
the grape harvest will fail,[y]
and the harvest of fruit will not
come.
11 Tremble, you complacent women;
shudder, you daughters who feel
secure!
Strip off your clothes,[z]
put sackcloth around your waists.
12 Beat your breasts[a] for the pleasant
fields,
for the fruitful vines
13 and for the land of my people,
a land overgrown with thorns and
briers[b]—
yes, mourn for all houses of
merriment
and for this city of revelry.[c]
14 The fortress[d] will be abandoned,
the noisy city deserted;[e]
citadel and watchtower[f] will become
a wasteland forever,
the delight of donkeys,[g] a pasture
for flocks,
15 till the Spirit[h] is poured upon us
from on high,
and the desert becomes a fertile
field,[i]
and the fertile field seems like a
forest.[j]
16 Justice will dwell in the desert
and righteousness live in the fertile
field.
17 The fruit of righteousness will be
peace;[k]
the effect of righteousness will
be quietness and confidence[l]
forever.
18 My people will live in peaceful
dwelling places,
in secure homes,
in undisturbed places of rest.[m]
19 Though hail[n] flattens the forest[o]
and the city is leveled[p] completely,
20 how blessed you will be,
sowing[q] your seed by every stream,
and letting your cattle and
donkeys range free.[r]

Distress and Help

33 Woe to you, O destroyer,
you who have not been
destroyed!
Woe to you, O traitor,
you who have not been betrayed!
When you stop destroying,
you will be destroyed;[s]
when you stop betraying,
you will be betrayed.[t]

2 O LORD, be gracious to us;
we long for you.
Be our strength[u] every morning,
our salvation[v] in time of distress.
3 At the thunder of your voice, the
peoples flee;
when you rise up,[w] the nations
scatter.
4 Your plunder, O nations, is harvested
as by young locusts;
like a swarm of locusts men
pounce on it.
5 The LORD is exalted,[x] for he dwells
on high;
he will fill Zion with justice[y] and
righteousness.[z]
6 He will be the sure foundation for
your times,
a rich store of salvation[a] and
wisdom and knowledge;
the fear[b] of the LORD is the key to
this treasure.[a]
7 Look, their brave men cry aloud in
the streets;
the envoys[c] of peace weep bitterly.
8 The highways are deserted,
no travelers are on the roads.[d]
The treaty is broken,
its witnesses[b][e] are despised,
no one is respected.
9 The land mourns[c] and wastes away,
Lebanon[f] is ashamed and withers;[g]
Sharon is like the Arabah,
and Bashan and Carmel drop their
leaves.
10 "Now will I arise,[h]" says the LORD.
"Now will I be exalted;
now will I be lifted up.

32:7 [t]Mic 7:3 [u]Isa 61:1
32:8 [v]Pr 11:25
32:9 [w]Isa 28:23 [x]Isa 47:8; Am 6:1; Zep 2:15
32:10 [y]Isa 5:5-6; 24:7
32:11 [z]Isa 47:2
32:12 [a]Na 2:7
32:13 [b]Isa 5:6 [c]Isa 22:2
32:14 [d]Isa 13:22 [e]Isa 6:11; 27:10 [f]Isa 34:13 [g]Ps 104:11
32:15 [h]Isa 11:2; Joel 2:28 [i]Ps 107:35; Isa 35:1-2 [j]Isa 29:17
32:17 [k]Ps 119:165; Ro 14:17; Jas 3:18 [l]Isa 30:15
32:18 [m]Hos 2:18-23
32:19 [n]Isa 28:17; 30:30 [o]Isa 10:19; Zec 11:2 [p]Isa 24:10; 27:10
32:20 [q]Ecc 11:1 [r]Isa 30:24
33:1 [s]Hab 2:8; Mt 7:2 [t]Isa 21:2
33:2 [u]Isa 40:10; 51:9; 59:16 [v]Isa 25:9
33:3 [w]Isa 59:16-18
33:5 [x]Ps 97:9 [y]Isa 28:6 [z]Isa 1:26
33:6 [a]Isa 51:6 [b]Isa 11:2-3; Mt 6:33
33:7 [c]2Ki 18:37
33:8 [d]Jdg 5:6; Isa 35:8
33:9 [e]Isa 3:26 [f]Isa 2:13; 35:2 [g]Isa 24:4
33:10 [h]Ps 12:5; Isa 2:21

[a]6 Or *is a treasure from him* [b]8 Dead Sea Scrolls; Masoretic Text / *the cities* [c]9 Or *dries up*

DAY 2 TWO

Faithfulness and the Purpose of God in My Life

Isaiah 33:5–6

The best friend that our spiritual dependency can have is the fear of the Lord. What power there is in the reverence we give God! This awe releases in us the power to be more than we are. All fear is outlawed for the believer except the fear of the Lord. The only trembling permitted is the reverent awe we feel when standing face-to-face with utter holiness. Those who tremble before God are people who cannot forget the immensity of him to whom their lives are owed. Our calling is to fear not just his size and power, but to tremble lest we let go of the task he has put us in the world to accomplish.

Frederick Faber understood Isaiah and agreed with him!

Thy goodness to thy saints of old, An awful thing appeared;
For were thy majesty less good, much less would it be feared.

A special joy is in all love, for objects we revere;
Thus joy in God will always be proportioned to our fear.

When most I fear thee, Lord! Then most familiar I appear,
And I am in my soul most free, When I am most in fear.

They love thee little, if at all, Who do not fear thee much:
If love is thine attraction, Lord! Fear is thy very touch.

We fear because thou art so good, Also because we sin;
And when we make most show of love, We tremble most within.

It is when we tremble most within that we understand and rejoice in our own need. It is in this fear we find that our faithfulness is truly the habit of spiritual dependency, and only then are we able to fully live as God has purposed.

To begin a study on the topic of Faithfulness, the Habit of Spiritual Dependency, turn to the home page on page 260.

11 You conceive[i] chaff,
you give birth[j] to straw;
your breath is a fire[k] that consumes you.
12 The peoples will be burned as if to lime;
like cut thornbushes they will be set ablaze.[l]"

13 You who are far away,[m] hear[n] what I have done;
you who are near, acknowledge my power!
14 The sinners in Zion are terrified;
trembling[o] grips the godless:
"Who of us can dwell with the consuming fire?[p]
Who of us can dwell with everlasting burning?"
15 He who walks righteously[q]
and speaks what is right,[r]
who rejects gain from extortion
and keeps his hand from accepting bribes,
who stops his ears against plots of murder
and shuts his eyes[s] against contemplating evil—
16 this is the man who will dwell on the heights,
whose refuge[t] will be the mountain fortress.[u]
His bread will be supplied,
and water will not fail[v] him.

17 Your eyes will see the king[w] in his beauty
and view a land that stretches afar.[x]
18 In your thoughts you will ponder the former terror:[y]
"Where is that chief officer?
Where is the one who took the revenue?
Where is the officer in charge of the towers?"
19 You will see those arrogant people no more,
those people of an obscure speech,
with their strange, incomprehensible tongue.[z]

20 Look upon Zion, the city of our festivals;
your eyes will see Jerusalem,
a peaceful abode,[a] a tent that will not be moved;[b]
its stakes will never be pulled up,
nor any of its ropes broken.

33:11 [i]Ps 7:14; Isa 59:4; Jas 1:15 [j]Isa 26:18 [k]Isa 1:31
33:12 [l]Isa 10:17
33:13 [m]Ps 48:10; 49:1 [n]Isa 49:1
33:14 [o]Isa 32:11 [p]Isa 30:30; Heb 12:29
33:15 [q]Isa 58:8 [r]Ps 15:2; 24:4 [s]Ps 119:37
33:16 [t]Isa 25:4 [u]Isa 26:1 [v]Isa 49:10
33:17 [w]Isa 6:5 [x]Isa 26:15
33:18 [y]Isa 17:14
33:19 [z]Isa 28:11; Jer 5:15
33:20 [a]Isa 32:18 [b]Ps 46:5; 125:1-2

21 There the LORD will be our Mighty
One.
It will be like a place of broad
rivers and streams.[c]
No galley with oars will ride them,
no mighty ship will sail them.
22 For the LORD is our judge,[d]
the LORD is our lawgiver,[e]
the LORD is our king;[f]
it is he who will save[g] us.

23 Your rigging hangs loose:
The mast is not held secure,
the sail is not spread.
Then an abundance of spoils will be
divided
and even the lame[h] will carry off
plunder.[i]
24 No one living in Zion will say, "I am
ill";[j]
and the sins of those who dwell
there will be forgiven.[k]

Judgment Against the Nations

34 Come near, you nations, and
listen;
pay attention, you peoples![l]
Let the earth hear,[m] and all that is
in it,
the world, and all that comes out
of it![n]
2 The LORD is angry with all nations;
his wrath is upon all their armies.
He will totally destroy[a][o] them,
he will give them over to
slaughter.[p]
3 Their slain will be thrown out,
their dead bodies will send up a
stench;[q]
the mountains will be soaked with
their blood.[r]
4 All the stars of the heavens will be
dissolved[s]
and the sky rolled up[t] like a scroll;
all the starry host will fall[u]
like withered leaves from the vine,
like shriveled figs from the fig tree.

5 My sword[v] has drunk its fill in the
heavens;
see, it descends in judgment on
Edom,[w]
the people I have totally
destroyed.[x]
6 The sword of the LORD is bathed in
blood,
it is covered with fat—
the blood of lambs and goats,
fat from the kidneys of rams.

33:21 [c]Isa 41:18; 48:18; 66:12
33:22 [d]Isa 11:4 [e]Isa 2:3; Jas 4:12 [f]Ps 89:18 [g]Isa 25:9
33:23 [h]2Ki 7:8 [i]2Ki 7:16
33:24 [j]Isa 30:26 [k]Jer 50:20; 1Jn 1:7-9
34:1 [l]Isa 41:1; 43:9 [m]Ps 49:1 [n]Dt 32:1
34:2 [o]Isa 13:5 [p]Isa 30:25
34:3 [q]Joel 2:20; Am 4:10 [r]ver 7; Eze 14:19; 35:6; 38:22
34:4 [s]Isa 13:13; 2Pe 3:10 [t]Eze 32:7-8 [u]Joel 2:31; Mt 24:29*; Rev 6:13
34:5 [v]Dt 32:41-42; Jer 46:10; Eze 21:5 [w]Am 1:11-12 [x]Isa 24:6; Mal 1:4

For the LORD has a sacrifice in
Bozrah
and a great slaughter in Edom.
7 And the wild oxen will fall with
them,
the bull calves and the great bulls.[y]
Their land will be drenched with
blood,
and the dust will be soaked with
fat.

8 For the LORD has a day of
vengeance,[z]
a year of retribution, to uphold
Zion's cause.
9 Edom's streams will be turned into
pitch,
her dust into burning sulfur;
her land will become blazing
pitch!
10 It will not be quenched night and
day;
its smoke will rise forever.[a]
From generation to generation it will
lie desolate;[b]
no one will ever pass through it
again.
11 The desert owl[b][c] and screech owl[b]
will possess it;
the great owl[b] and the raven will
nest there.
God will stretch out over Edom
the measuring line of chaos
and the plumb line[d] of desolation.
12 Her nobles will have nothing there
to be called a kingdom,
all her princes[e] will vanish[f] away.
13 Thorns will overrun her citadels,
nettles and brambles her
strongholds.[g]
She will become a haunt for jackals,[h]
a home for owls.
14 Desert creatures will meet with
hyenas,[i]
and wild goats will bleat to each
other;
there the night creatures will also
repose
and find for themselves places of
rest.
15 The owl will nest there and lay eggs,
she will hatch them, and care for
her young under the shadow
of her wings;

34:7 [y]Ps 68:30
34:8 [z]Isa 63:4
34:10 [a]Rev 14:10-11; 19:3 [b]Isa 13:20; 24:1; Eze 29:12; Mal 1:3
34:11 [c]Zep 2:14; Rev 18:2 [d]2Ki 21:13; La 2:8
34:12 [e]Jer 27:20; 39:6 [f]Isa 41:11-12
34:13 [g]Isa 13:22; 32:13 [h]Ps 44:19; Jer 9:11; 10:22
34:14 [i]Isa 13:22

[a] *2* The Hebrew term refers to the irrevocable giving over of things or persons to the LORD, often by totally destroying them; also in verse 5. [b] *11* The precise identification of these birds is uncertain.

34:15 [j]Dt 14:13

there also the falcons[j] will gather,
each with its mate.

34:16 [k]Isa 30:8 [l]Isa 1:20; 58:14

16 Look in the scroll[k] of the LORD and read:

None of these will be missing,
not one will lack her mate.
For it is his mouth[l] that has given the order,
and his Spirit will gather them together.

34:17 [m]Isa 17:14; Jer 13:25 [n]ver 10

17 He allots their portions;[m]
his hand distributes them by measure.
They will possess it forever
and dwell there from generation to generation.[n]

Joy of the Redeemed

35:1 [o]Isa 27:10; 41:18-19 [p]Isa 51:3

35 The desert[o] and the parched land will be glad;
the wilderness will rejoice and blossom.[p]
Like the crocus, 2 it will burst into bloom;
it will rejoice greatly and shout for joy.[q]

35:2 [q]Isa 25:9; 55:12 [r]Isa 32:15 [s]SS 7:5 [t]Isa 25:9

The glory of Lebanon[r] will be given to it,
the splendor of Carmel[s] and Sharon;
they will see the glory of the LORD,
the splendor of our God.[t]

JOY

THE VOICE OF BELLS

Isaiah 35:1–2

Jesus comes and wintry hearts awake to springtime. Jesus comes and monstrous natures change. Taste the splendor of our Lord and tell me, who can withstand the storm of grace? Joy flies! Bells ring! We are loved!

35:3 [u]Job 4:4; Heb 12:12

3 Strengthen the feeble hands,
steady the knees[u] that give way;
4 say to those with fearful hearts,
"Be strong, do not fear;
your God will come,
he will come with vengeance;[v]
with divine retribution
he will come to save you."

35:4 [v]Isa 1:24; 34:8

35:5 [w]Mt 11:5; Jn 9:6-7 [x]Isa 29:18; 50:4

5 Then will the eyes of the blind be opened[w]
and the ears of the deaf[x] unstopped.

6 Then will the lame[y] leap like a deer,
and the mute tongue[z] shout for joy.
Water will gush forth in the wilderness
and streams[a] in the desert.

35:6 [y]Mt 15:30; Jn 5:8-9; Ac 3:8 [z]Isa 32:4; Mt 9:32-33; 12:22; Lk 11:14 [a]Isa 41:18; Jn 7:38

7 The burning sand will become a pool,
the thirsty ground bubbling springs.[b]
In the haunts where jackals[c] once lay,
grass and reeds and papyrus will grow.

35:7 [b]Isa 49:10 [c]Isa 13:22

8 And a highway[d] will be there;
it will be called the Way of Holiness.[e]
The unclean[f] will not journey on it;
it will be for those who walk in that Way;
wicked fools will not go about on it.[a]

35:8 [d]Isa 11:16; 33:8; Mt 7:13-14 [e]Isa 4:3; 1Pe 1:15 [f]Isa 52:1

9 No lion[g] will be there,
nor will any ferocious beast[h] get up on it;
they will not be found there.
But only the redeemed will walk there,
10 and the ransomed[i] of the LORD will return.
They will enter Zion with singing;
everlasting joy will crown their heads.
Gladness and joy[j] will overtake them,
and sorrow and sighing will flee away.[k]

35:9 [g]Isa 30:6 [h]Isa 34:14 [i]Isa 51:11; 62:12; 63:4

35:10 [j]Isa 25:9 [k]Isa 30:19; 51:11; Rev 7:17; 21:4

Sennacherib Threatens Jerusalem

36 In the fourteenth year of King
Hezekiah's reign, Sennacherib[l]
king of Assyria attacked all the fortified
cities of Judah and captured them. 2 Then
the king of Assyria sent his field commander with a large army from Lachish
to King Hezekiah at Jerusalem. When
the commander stopped at the aqueduct
of the Upper Pool, on the road to the
Washerman's Field,[m] 3 Eliakim[n] son of
Hilkiah the palace administrator, Shebna[o] the secretary, and Joah son of Asaph
the recorder went out to him.

36:1 [l]2Ch 32:1

36:2 [m]Isa 7:3

36:3 [n]Isa 22:20-21 [o]2Ki 18:18

4 The field commander said to them, "Tell Hezekiah,

" 'This is what the great king, the king of Assyria, says: On what are you basing this confidence

[a]8 Or / *the simple will not stray from it*

DAY 5 FIVE

▸ PEACE AND ITS PLACE IN MY PERSONAL WORSHIP

Isaiah 36:4–6

King Sennacherib's field commander—an Assyrian pagan—sends a message to Hezekiah, king of Judah, reminding him that he has falsely put his trust in military alliances when he should have put his trust in God. While King Hezekiah is still remembered as one of the best kings of Judah, this taunt from his godless enemy should have been a prompt for him to renew his trust in the true God of Israel. God is able to use pagans as well as fellow believers to remind us of the source of true peace.

Listen to the counsel of a hobo, particularly when it rebukes your weak righteousness. A beggar approached the front door of a house. He intended to ask for charity, but when he met the woman of the house, she rebuked him for his unkempt appearance, his lazy lifestyle and his poverty. She slammed the door in his face and left him dejected, still feeling the stabbing force of her sharp tongue.

The beggar then went around to the rear of her house and knocked on the back door. When the same woman opened the door, the poor beggar remarked, "Oh, please forgive me. I came to this door hoping that the angry woman I met at the front of the house might have a sister who would be kinder and more like our dear Lord Jesus at the back door."

The woman felt the surgical scalpel of his truth. Peacelessness often erupts in anger. If this is true in your life, claim your confidence in grace and let peace guide you into better worship.

When we embrace the peace that God has to offer, our outlook on life is changed. We rely on God for our confidence and find ourselves free to worship him. Let the events of your life today remind you of your reliance on God. Listen to those pagan and not-so-pagan voices, and find your worship for God once again.

To begin a study on the topic of Peace, the Evidence of Confidence, turn to the home page on page 1173.

of yours? 5You say you have strategy and military strength—but
you speak only empty words. On
whom are you depending, that 36:5
you rebel[p] against me? 6Look now, [p]2Ki 18:7
you are depending on Egypt,[q] that 36:6
splintered reed[r] of a staff, which [q]Isa 30:2,5
pierces a man's hand and wounds [r]Eze 29:6-7
him if he leans on it! Such is Pharaoh king of Egypt to all who depend on him. 7And if you say to
me, "We are depending on the
LORD our God"—isn't he the one
whose high places and altars Hezekiah removed,[s] saying to Judah 36:7
and Jerusalem, "You must worship [s]2Ki 18:4
before this altar"?[t] [t]Dt 12:2-5
8" 'Come now, make a bargain
with my master, the king of Assyria: I will give you two thousand horses—if you can put riders
on them! 9How then can you repulse one officer of the least of
my master's officials, even though
you are depending on Egypt[u] for 36:9
chariots and horsemen?[v] 10Further- [u]Isa 31:3
more, have I come to attack and de- [v]Isa 30:2-5
stroy this land without the LORD?
The LORD himself told[w] me to 36:10
march against this country and de- [w]1Ki 13:18
stroy it.' "

11Then Eliakim, Shebna and Joah
said to the field commander, "Please
speak to your servants in Aramaic,[x] 36:11
since we understand it. Don't speak to [x]Ezr 4:7
us in Hebrew in the hearing of the people on the wall."
12But the commander replied, "Was
it only to your master and you that my
master sent me to say these things, and
not to the men sitting on the wall—
who, like you, will have to eat their
own filth and drink their own urine?"
13Then the commander stood and
called out in Hebrew,[y] "Hear the words 36:13
of the great king, the king of Assyria! [y]2Ch 32:18
14This is what the king says: Do not let
Hezekiah deceive you. He cannot deliver you! 15Do not let Hezekiah persuade
you to trust in the LORD when he says,
'The LORD will surely deliver us; this
city will not be given into the hand of
the king of Assyria.'[z] 36:15
16"Do not listen to Hezekiah. This [z]Isa 37:10
is what the king of Assyria says: Make
peace with me and come out to me.
Then every one of you will eat from

his own vine and fig tree[a] and drink water from his own cistern,[b] 17until I come and take you to a land like your own—a land of grain and new wine, a land of bread and vineyards.

18"Do not let Hezekiah mislead you when he says, 'The LORD will deliver us.' Has the god of any nation ever delivered his land from the hand of the king of Assyria? 19Where are the gods of Hamath and Arpad? Where are the gods of Sepharvaim? Have they rescued Samaria from my hand? 20Who of all the gods[c] of these countries has been able to save his land from me? How then can the LORD deliver Jerusalem from my hand?"[d]

21But the people remained silent and said nothing in reply, because the king had commanded, "Do not answer him."

22Then Eliakim son of Hilkiah the palace administrator, Shebna the secretary, and Joah son of Asaph the recorder went to Hezekiah, with their clothes torn, and told him what the field commander had said.

Jerusalem's Deliverance Foretold

37 When King Hezekiah heard this, he tore his clothes and put on sackcloth and went into the temple of the LORD. 2He sent Eliakim the palace administrator, Shebna the secretary, and the leading priests, all wearing sackcloth, to the prophet Isaiah son of Amoz.[e] 3They told him, "This is what Hezekiah says: This day is a day of distress and rebuke and disgrace, as when children come to the point of birth[f] and there is no strength to deliver them. 4It may be that the LORD your God will hear the words of the field commander, whom his master, the king of Assyria, has sent to ridicule the living God, and that he will rebuke him for the words the LORD your God has heard.[g] Therefore pray for the remnant[h] that still survives."

5When King Hezekiah's officials came to Isaiah, 6Isaiah said to them, "Tell your master, 'This is what the LORD says: Do not be afraid[i] of what you have heard—those words with which the underlings of the king of Assyria have blasphemed me. 7Listen! I am going to put a spirit in him so that when he hears a certain report,[j] he will return to his own country, and there I will have him cut down with the sword.' "

8When the field commander heard that the king of Assyria had left Lachish, he withdrew and found the king fighting against Libnah.[k]

9Now Sennacherib received a report[l] that Tirhakah, the Cushite[a] king ⌞of Egypt⌟, was marching out to fight against him. When he heard it, he sent messengers to Hezekiah with this word: 10"Say to Hezekiah king of Judah: Do not let the god you depend on deceive you when he says, 'Jerusalem will not be handed over to the king of Assyria.'[m] 11Surely you have heard what the kings of Assyria have done to all the countries, destroying them completely. And will you be delivered?[n] 12Did the gods of the nations that were destroyed by my forefathers[o] deliver them—the gods of Gozan, Haran,[p] Rezeph and the people of Eden who were in Tel Assar? 13Where is the king of Hamath, the king of Arpad, the king of the city of Sepharvaim, or of Hena or Ivvah?"

Hezekiah's Prayer

14Hezekiah received the letter from the messengers and read it. Then he went up to the temple of the LORD and spread it out before the LORD. 15And Hezekiah prayed to the LORD: 16"O LORD Almighty, God of Israel, enthroned between the cherubim, you alone are God[q] over all the kingdoms of the earth. You have made heaven and earth. 17Give ear, O LORD, and hear;[r] open your eyes, O LORD, and see;[s] listen to all the words Sennacherib has sent to insult the living God.

18"It is true, O LORD, that the Assyrian kings have laid waste all these peoples and their lands.[t] 19They have thrown their gods into the fire and destroyed them,[u] for they were not gods[v] but only wood and stone, fashioned by human hands. 20Now, O LORD our God, deliver us from his hand, so that all kingdoms on earth may know that you alone, O LORD, are God.[b][w]"

Sennacherib's Fall

21Then Isaiah son of Amoz[x] sent a message to Hezekiah: "This is what the

[a] *9* That is, from the upper Nile region
[b] *20* Dead Sea Scrolls (see also 2 Kings 19:19); Masoretic Text *alone are the LORD*

36:16 [a]1Ki 4:25; Zec 3:10 [b]Pr 5:15
36:20 [c]1Ki 20:23
36:21 [d]Pr 9:7-8; 26:4
37:2 [e]Isa 1:1
37:3 [f]Isa 26:18; 66:9; Hos 13:13
37:4 [g]Isa 36:13, 18-20 [h]Isa 1:9
37:6 [i]Isa 7:4
37:7 [j]ver 9
37:8 [k]Nu 33:20
37:9 [l]ver 7
37:10 [m]Isa 36:15
37:11 [n]Isa 36:18-20
37:12 [o]2Ki 18:11 [p]Ge 11:31; 12:1-4; Ac 7:2
37:16 [q]Dt 10:17; Ps 86:10; 136:2-3
37:17 [r]2Ch 6:40 [s]Da 9:18
37:18 [t]2Ki 15:29; Na 2:11-12
37:19 [u]Isa 26:14 [v]Isa 41:24,29
37:20 [w]Ps 46:10
37:21 [x]ver 2

LORD, the God of Israel, says: Because
you have prayed to me concerning Sennacherib king of Assyria, 22 this is the
word the LORD has spoken against
him:

"The Virgin Daughter of Zion
despises and mocks you.
The Daughter of Jerusalem
tosses her head[y] as you flee.
23 Who is it you have insulted and
blasphemed?[z]
Against whom have you raised
your voice
and lifted your eyes in pride?[a]
Against the Holy One of Israel!
24 By your messengers
you have heaped insults on the
Lord.
And you have said,
'With my many chariots
I have ascended the heights of the
mountains,
the utmost heights of Lebanon.[b]
I have cut down its tallest cedars,
the choicest of its pines.
I have reached its remotest heights,
the finest of its forests.
25 I have dug wells in foreign lands[a]
and drunk the water there.
With the soles of my feet
I have dried up all the streams of
Egypt.'[c]
26 "Have you not heard?
Long ago I ordained[d] it.
In days of old I planned[e] it;
now I have brought it to pass,
that you have turned fortified cities
into piles of stone.[f]
27 Their people, drained of power,
are dismayed and put to shame.
They are like plants in the field,
like tender green shoots,
like grass sprouting on the roof,[g]
scorched[b] before it grows up.
28 "But I know where you stay
and when you come and go[h]
and how you rage[i] against me.
29 Because you rage against me
and because your insolence[j] has
reached my ears,
I will put my hook in your nose[k]
and my bit in your mouth,
and I will make you return
by the way you came.[l]

30 "This will be the sign for you,
O Hezekiah:

"This year you will eat what grows
by itself,
and the second year what springs
from that.
But in the third year sow and reap,
plant vineyards and eat their fruit.
31 Once more a remnant of the house
of Judah
will take root below and bear
fruit[m] above.
32 For out of Jerusalem will come a
remnant,
and out of Mount Zion a band of
survivors.
The zeal[n] of the LORD Almighty
will accomplish this.

33 "Therefore this is what the LORD
says concerning the king of Assyria:

"He will not enter this city
or shoot an arrow here.
He will not come before it with
shield
or build a siege ramp against it.
34 By the way that he came he will
return;[o]
he will not enter this city,"
declares the LORD.
35 "I will defend[p] this city and save it,
for my sake[q] and for the sake of
David[r] my servant!"

36 Then the angel of the LORD went
out and put to death a hundred and
eighty-five thousand men in the Assyrian[s] camp. When the people got up the
next morning—there were all the dead
bodies! 37 So Sennacherib king of Assyria broke camp and withdrew. He returned to Nineveh[t] and stayed there.
38 One day, while he was worshiping
in the temple of his god Nisroch, his
sons Adrammelech and Sharezer cut
him down with the sword, and they escaped to the land of Ararat.[u] And Esarhaddon his son succeeded him as king.

Hezekiah's Illness

38 In those days Hezekiah became
ill and was at the point of death.
The prophet Isaiah son of Amoz[v] went
to him and said, "This is what the

37:22 [y]Job 16:4
37:23 [z]ver 4 [a]Isa 2:11
37:24 [b]Isa 14:8
37:25 [c]Dt 11:10
37:26 [d]Ac 2:23; 4:27-28; 1Pe 2:8 [e]Isa 10:6; 25:1 [f]Isa 25:2
37:27 [g]Ps 129:6
37:28 [h]Ps 139:1-3 [i]Ps 2:1
37:29 [j]Isa 10:12 [k]Isa 30:28; Eze 38:4 [l]ver 34
37:31 [m]Isa 27:6
37:32 [n]Isa 9:7
37:34 [o]ver 29
37:35 [p]Isa 31:5; 38:6 [q]Isa 43:25; 48:9,11 [r]2Ki 20:6
37:36 [s]Isa 10:12
37:37 [t]Ge 10:11
37:38 [u]Ge 8:4; Jer 51:27
38:1 [v]Isa 37:2

[a]*25* Dead Sea Scrolls (see also 2 Kings 19:24); Masoretic Text does not have *in foreign lands.*
[b]*27* Some manuscripts of the Masoretic Text, Dead Sea Scrolls and some Septuagint manuscripts (see also 2 Kings 19:26); most manuscripts of the Masoretic Text *roof / and terraced fields*

38:1 [w]2Sa 17:23 LORD says: Put your house in order,[w]
because you are going to die; you will
not recover."
2Hezekiah turned his face to the wall
and prayed to the LORD, 3"Remember,
38:3 [x]Ne 13:14; Ps 26:3 O LORD, how I have walked[x] before
you faithfully and with wholehearted
[y]1Ch 29:19 [z]Dt 6:18 devotion[y] and have done what is good
[a]Ps 6:8 in your eyes.[z]" And Hezekiah wept[a] bitterly.
4Then the word of the LORD came
to Isaiah: 5"Go and tell Hezekiah, 'This
is what the LORD, the God of your
father David, says: I have heard your
38:5 prayer and seen your tears; I will add
[b]2Ki 18:2 fifteen years[b] to your life. 6And I will
38:6 deliver you and this city from the hand
[c]Isa 31:5; 37:35 of the king of Assyria. I will defend[c] this
city.

GOODNESS

UNTIRING OBEDIENCE

Isaiah 38:5

God extended Hezekiah's life by 15 years—but not until Hezekiah had cast himself upon the mercy of God.

No wonder George Herbert wrote:
"Let him be rich and weary, then at least,
If goodness had him not, yet weariness
May toss him to my breast."

38:7 [d]Isa 7:11,14 7" 'This is the LORD's sign[d] to you
that the LORD will do what he has
promised: 8I will make the shadow cast
by the sun go back the ten steps it has
gone down on the stairway of Ahaz.' "
So the sunlight went back the ten steps
38:8 [e]Jos 10:13 it had gone down.[e]

9A writing of Hezekiah king of Judah
after his illness and recovery:

38:10 [f]Ps 102:24 10I said, "In the prime of my life[f]
[g]Ps 107:18; 2Co 1:9 must I go through the gates of
[h]Job 17:11 death[a][g]
and be robbed of the rest of my
years?"[h]
11I said, "I will not again see the LORD,
the LORD, in the land of the
38:11 [i]Ps 27:13; 116:9 living;[i]
no longer will I look on mankind,
or be with those who now dwell in
this world.[b]
38:12 [j]2Co 5:1,4; 2Pe 1:13-14 12Like a shepherd's tent[j] my house
has been pulled down[k] and taken
[k]Job 4:21 from me.
Like a weaver I have rolled[l] up my 38:12 [l]Heb 1:12
life,
and he has cut me off from the [m]Job 7:6
loom;[m] [n]Ps 73:14
day and night[n] you made an end
of me.
13I waited patiently till dawn,
but like a lion he broke[o] all my 38:13 [o]Ps 51:8
bones;[p] [p]Job 10:16; Da 6:24
day and night you made an end
of me.
14I cried like a swift or thrush,
I moaned like a mourning dove.[q] 38:14 [q]Isa 59:11
My eyes grew weak as I looked to the [r]Job 17:3
heavens.
I am troubled; O Lord, come to
my aid!"[r]

15But what can I say?
He has spoken to me, and he
himself has done this.[s] 38:15 [s]Ps 39:9
I will walk humbly[t] all my years [t]1Ki 21:27
because of this anguish of my [u]Job 7:11
soul.[u]
16Lord, by such things men live;
and my spirit finds life in them
too.
You restored me to health
and let me live.[v] 38:16 [v]Ps 119:25
17Surely it was for my benefit
that I suffered such anguish.
In your love you kept me 38:17 [w]Ps 30:3
from the pit[w] of destruction; [x]Jer 31:34
you have put all my sins[x] [y]Isa 43:25;
behind your back.[y] Mic 19:19
18For the grave[a][z] cannot praise you, 38:18 [z]Ecc 9:10
death cannot sing your praise;[a] [a]Ps 6:5;
those who go down to the pit[b] 88:10-11;
cannot hope for your faithfulness. 115:17 [b]Ps 30:9
19The living, the living—they praise[c] 38:19 [c]Dt 6:7;
you, Ps 118:17;
as I am doing today; 119:175
fathers tell their children[d] [d]Dt 11:19
about your faithfulness.

20The LORD will save me,
and we will sing[e] with stringed 38:20 [e]Ps 68:25
instruments[f] [f]Ps 33:2
all the days of our lives[g] [g]Ps 116:2
in the temple[h] of the LORD. [h]Ps 116:17-19

21Isaiah had said, "Prepare a poultice
of figs and apply it to the boil, and he
will recover."
22Hezekiah had asked, "What will be

[a]*10,18* Hebrew *Sheol* [b]*11* A few Hebrew manuscripts; most Hebrew manuscripts *in the place of cessation*

the sign that I will go up to the temple
of the LORD?"

Envoys From Babylon

39 At that time Merodach-Baladan
39:1 [i]2Ch 32:31 son of Baladan king of Babylon[i]
sent Hezekiah letters and a gift, because
he had heard of his illness and recovery.
39:2 [j]2Ch 32:31 [2]Hezekiah received the envoys[j] gladly
[k]2Ki 18:15 and showed them what was in his storehouses—the silver, the gold,[k] the spices,
the fine oil, his entire armory and everything found among his treasures. There
was nothing in his palace or in all his
kingdom that Hezekiah did not show
them.

[3]Then Isaiah the prophet went to
King Hezekiah and asked, "What did
those men say, and where did they come
from?"

39:3 [l]Dt 28:49 "From a distant land,[l]" Hezekiah replied. "They came to me from Bab-
ylon."

[4]The prophet asked, "What did they
see in your palace?"

"They saw everything in my palace," Hezekiah said. "There is nothing
among my treasures that I did not show
them."

[5]Then Isaiah said to Hezekiah, "Hear
the word of the LORD Almighty: [6]The
time will surely come when everything
in your palace, and all that your fathers
have stored up until this day, will be
39:6 [m]2Ki 24:13; Jer 20:5 carried off to Babylon.[m] Nothing will
be left, says the LORD. [7]And some of
your descendants, your own flesh and
blood who will be born to you, will
be taken away, and they will become
eunuchs in the palace of the king of
39:7 [n]2Ki 24:15; Da 1:1-7 Babylon.[n]"

[8]"The word of the LORD you have
spoken is good," Hezekiah replied. For
he thought, "There will be peace and
39:8 [o]2Ch 32:26 security in my lifetime.[o]"

Comfort for God's People

40:1 [p]Isa 12:1; 49:13; 51:3,12; 52:9; 61:2; 66:13; Jer 31:13; Zep 3:14-17; 2Co 1:3

40 Comfort, comfort[p] my people,
says your God.

40:2 [q]Isa 35:4 [r]Isa 41:11-13; 49:25 [s]Isa 61:7; Jer 16:18; Zec 9:12; Rev 18:6

[2]Speak tenderly[q] to Jerusalem,
and proclaim to her
that her hard service has been
completed,[r]
that her sin has been paid for,
that she has received from the
LORD's hand
double[s] for all her sins.

[3]A voice of one calling:
"In the desert prepare
the way[t] for the LORD[a]; 40:3 [t]Mal 3:1 [u]Mt 3:3*; Mk 1:3*; Jn 1:23*
make straight in the wilderness
a highway for our God.[b][u]

GENTLENESS

THE DESERT VOICE:
GENTLENESS IN FIRE

Isaiah 40:3–4

Out where tumbleweeds rolled and jackals howled, God laid a causeway to the human heart. Every valley was raised. Every mountain was lowered. The exiles of Babylon came home—home, where the gentle God would one day live in sandals, unafraid of lepers; home, where every runaway could return and every orphan could know a Father.

[4]Every valley shall be raised up,
every mountain and hill made
low;
the rough ground shall become
level,[v] 40:4 [v]Isa 45:2,13
the rugged places a plain.
[5]And the glory of the LORD will be
revealed,
and all mankind together will see
it.[w] 40:5 [w]Isa 52:10; Lk 3:4-6* [x]Isa 1:20; 58:14
For the mouth of the
LORD has spoken."[x]

[6]A voice says, "Cry out."
And I said, "What shall I cry?"
"All men are like grass,[y] 40:6 [y]Job 14:2
and all their glory is like the
flowers of the field.
[7]The grass withers and the flowers
fall,
because the breath[z] of the LORD 40:7 [z]Job 41:21
blows on them.
Surely the people are grass.
[8]The grass withers and the flowers
fall, 40:8 [a]Isa 55:11; 59:21 [b]Mt 5:18; 1Pe 1:24-25*
but the word[a] of our God stands
forever."[b]

[9]You who bring good tidings[c] to Zion, 40:9 [c]Isa 52:7-10; 61:1; Ro 10:15
go up on a high mountain.
You who bring good tidings to
Jerusalem,[c]

[a]3 Or *A voice of one calling in the desert: / "Prepare the way for the LORD* [b]3 Hebrew; Septuagint *make straight the paths of our God* [c]9 Or *O Zion, bringer of good tidings, / go up on a high mountain. / O Jerusalem, bringer of good tidings*

lift up your voice with a shout,
lift it up, do not be afraid;
say to the towns of Judah,
"Here is your God!"[d]
10 See, the Sovereign LORD comes[e]
with power,
and his arm[f] rules[g] for him.
See, his reward[h] is with him,
and his recompense accompanies
him.
11 He tends his flock like a shepherd:[i]
He gathers the lambs in his arms
and carries them close to his heart;
he gently leads those that have
young.
12 Who has measured the waters[j] in the
hollow of his hand,[k]
or with the breadth of his hand
marked off the heavens?[l]
Who has held the dust of the earth
in a basket,
or weighed the mountains on the
scales
and the hills in a balance?
13 Who has understood the mind[a] of
the LORD,
or instructed him as his
counselor?[m]
14 Whom did the LORD consult to
enlighten him,
and who taught him the right
way?
Who was it that taught him
knowledge[n]
or showed him the path of
understanding?
15 Surely the nations are like a drop in
a bucket;
they are regarded as dust on the
scales;
he weighs the islands as though
they were fine dust.
16 Lebanon is not sufficient for altar
fires,
nor its animals[o] enough for burnt
offerings.
17 Before him all the nations[p] are as
nothing;[q]
they are regarded by him as
worthless
and less than nothing.[r]
18 To whom, then, will you compare
God?[s]
What image[t] will you compare
him to?
19 As for an idol,[u] a craftsman casts it,

40:9 [d]Isa 25:9
40:10 [e]Rev 22:7 [f]Isa 59:16 [g]Isa 9:6-7 [h]Isa 62:11; Rev 22:12
40:11 [i]Eze 34:23; Mic 5:4; Jn 10:11
40:12 [j]Job 38:10 [k]Pr 30:4 [l]Heb 1:10-12
40:13 [m]Ro 11:34*; 1Co 2:16*
40:14 [n]Job 21:22; Col 2:3
40:16 [o]Ps 50:9-11; Mic 6:7; Heb 10:5-9
40:17 [p]Isa 30:28 [q]Isa 29:7 [r]Da 4:35
40:18 [s]Ex 8:10; 1Sa 2:2; Isa 46:5 [t]Ac 17:29
40:19 [u]Ps 115:4

and a goldsmith[v] overlays it with
gold[w]
and fashions silver chains for it.
20 A man too poor to present such an
offering
selects wood that will not rot.
He looks for a skilled craftsman
to set up an idol that will not
topple.[x]
21 Do you not know?
Have you not heard?
Has it not been told[y] you from the
beginning?
Have you not understood[z] since
the earth was founded?[a]
22 He sits enthroned above the circle of
the earth,
and its people are like
grasshoppers.[b]
He stretches out the heavens like a
canopy,[c]
and spreads them out like a tent[d]
to live in.
23 He brings princes[e] to naught
and reduces the rulers of this
world to nothing.[f]
24 No sooner are they planted,
no sooner are they sown,
no sooner do they take root in the
ground,
than he blows[g] on them and they
wither,
and a whirlwind sweeps them
away like chaff.
25 "To whom will you compare me?[h]
Or who is my equal?" says the
Holy One.
26 Lift your eyes and look to the
heavens:[i]
Who created[j] all these?
He who brings out the starry host[k]
one by one,
and calls them each by name.
Because of his great power and
mighty strength,
not one of them is missing.[l]
27 Why do you say, O Jacob,
and complain, O Israel,
"My way is hidden from the LORD;
my cause is disregarded by my
God"?[m]
28 Do you not know?
Have you not heard?[n]
The LORD is the everlasting[o] God,

[a]*13* Or *Spirit*; or *spirit*

40:19 [v]Isa 41:7; Jer 10:3 [w]Isa 2:20
40:20 [x]1Sa 5:3
40:21 [y]Ps 19:1; 50:6; Ac 14:17 [z]Ro 1:19 [a]Isa 48:13; 51:13
40:22 [b]Nu 13:33; Ps 104:2; Isa 42:5 [c]Job 22:14 [d]Job 36:29
40:23 [e]Isa 34:12 [f]Job 12:21; Ps 107:40
40:24 [g]Isa 41:16
40:25 [h]ver 18
40:26 [i]Isa 51:6 [j]Ps 89:11-13; Isa 42:5 [k]Ps 147:4 [l]Isa 34:16
40:27 [m]Job 27:2; Lk 18:7-8
40:28 [n]ver 21 [o]Ps 90:2

DAY 2 TWO

▸ PATIENCE AND THE PURPOSE OF GOD IN MY LIFE

Isaiah 40:30–31

Those who hope in the Lord, demonstrate the power of true inner spirituality. Here then is the fourfold benefit of godly patience. They who hope in the Lord:

"Will renew their strength." Here is the physical testament of a spiritual truth. Paul spoke of our mortal bodies being given life through the Spirit (see Romans 8:11). Is it possible that God will, on the basis of our asking, renew our ebbing physical strength? It is indeed.

"They will soar on wings like eagles." Spiritual elation is the second result of the expectant hope in God. Have you not experienced the buoyancy at the end of a long period of spiritual waiting? We wait and pray and pray and wait, and then a wonderful breakthrough comes. Jesus invades our hearts and all things ponderous and plodding now grow wings. Suddenly, we soar in faith, and heaven is nearer than we supposed it might be.

"They will run and not grow weary." When we trust God, our lives are supplied energy far beyond what we knew to be possible. An older missionary doctor was finally forced to return home because of his frailty and uncertain health. When asked whether he was glad for the rest, he said yes. "But," he went on, "when my clinic was full, and people were walking for miles to stand in line for treatment—when I never got a day off, and I worked till midnight treating their bodies and winning their souls...Oh, those were the days!" There is a grand inebriation in serving God by doing something in which we really believe. We run and never grow weary.

"They will walk and not be faint." Running is not the way to demonstrate steadiness. All who run must, at times, stop to walk. But those who walk can walk forever—steadily and patiently—free in Christ.

To begin a study on the topic of Patience, the Wait for What God Promises, turn to the home page on page 1201.

the Creator of the ends of the
earth.
He will not grow tired or weary,
and his understanding no one can
fathom.[p]
29 He gives strength to the weary[q]
and increases the power of the
weak.
30 Even youths grow tired and weary,
and young men[r] stumble and fall;
31 but those who hope[s] in the LORD
will renew their strength.[t]
They will soar on wings like eagles;[u]
they will run and not grow weary,
they will walk and not be faint.[v]

The Helper of Israel

41 "Be silent[w] before me, you
islands![x]
Let the nations renew their
strength!
Let them come forward[y] and speak;
let us meet together[z] at the place
of judgment.

2 "Who has stirred[a] up one from the
east,[b]
calling him in righteousness to his
service[a]?
He hands nations over to him
and subdues kings before him.
He turns them to dust[c] with his
sword,
to windblown chaff[d] with his bow.
3 He pursues them and moves on
unscathed,
by a path his feet have not traveled
before.
4 Who has done this and carried it
through,
calling forth the generations from
the beginning?[e]
I, the LORD—with the first of them
and with the last[f]—I am he."

5 The islands[g] have seen it and fear;
the ends of the earth tremble.
They approach and come forward;
6 each helps the other
and says to his brother, "Be
strong!"
7 The craftsman encourages the
goldsmith,[h]
and he who smooths with the
hammer
spurs on him who strikes the
anvil.

[a]2 Or / *whom victory meets at every step*

40:28 [p]Ps 147:5; Ro 11:33
40:29 [q]Isa 50:4; Jer 31:25
40:30 [r]Isa 9:17; Jer 6:11; 9:21
40:31 [s]Lk 18:1 [t]2Co 4:16 [u]Ex 19:4; Ps 103:5 [v]2Co 4:1; Heb 12:1-3
41:1 [w]Hab 2:20; Zec 2:13 [x]Isa 11:11 [y]Isa 48:16 [z]Isa 1:18; 34:1; 50:8
41:2 [a]Ezr 1:2 [b]ver 25; Isa 45:1,13 [c]2Sa 22:43 [d]Isa 40:24
41:4 [e]ver 26; Isa 46:10 [f]Isa 44:6; 48:12; Rev 1:8,17; 22:13
41:5 [g]Eze 26:17-18
41:7 [h]Isa 40:19

He says of the welding, "It is good."
He nails down the idol so it will
not topple.

8 "But you, O Israel, my servant,
Jacob, whom I have chosen,
you descendants of Abraham[i] my
friend,[j]
9 I took you from the ends of the
earth,[k]
from its farthest corners I called
you.
I said, 'You are my servant';
I have chosen[l] you and have not
rejected you.
10 So do not fear, for I am with you;[m]
do not be dismayed, for I am your
God.
I will strengthen you and help[n] you;
I will uphold you with my
righteous right hand.

11 "All who rage[o] against you
will surely be ashamed and
disgraced;[p]
those who oppose[q] you
will be as nothing and perish.[r]
12 Though you search for your
enemies,
you will not find them.[s]
Those who wage war against you
will be as nothing[t] at all.
13 For I am the LORD, your God,
who takes hold of your right
hand[u]
and says to you, Do not fear;
I will help[v] you.
14 Do not be afraid, O worm Jacob,
O little Israel,
for I myself will help you," declares
the LORD,
your Redeemer, the Holy One of
Israel.
15 "See, I will make you into a
threshing sledge,[w]
new and sharp, with many teeth.
You will thresh the mountains and
crush them,
and reduce the hills to chaff.
16 You will winnow[x] them, the wind
will pick them up,
and a gale will blow them away.
But you will rejoice in the LORD
and glory[y] in the Holy One of
Israel.

17 "The poor and needy search for
water,[z]
but there is none;
their tongues are parched with
thirst.
But I the LORD will answer[a] them;
I, the God of Israel, will not
forsake them.
18 I will make rivers flow[b] on barren
heights,
and springs within the valleys.
I will turn the desert[c] into pools of
water,
and the parched ground into
springs.[d]
19 I will put in the desert
the cedar and the acacia, the
myrtle and the olive.
I will set pines in the wasteland,
the fir and the cypress together,[e]
20 so that people may see and know,
may consider and understand,
that the hand of the LORD has done
this,
that the Holy One of Israel has
created[f] it.

21 "Present your case," says the LORD.
"Set forth your arguments," says
Jacob's King.[g]
22 "Bring in ⌞your idols⌟ to tell us
what is going to happen.[h]
Tell us what the former things were,
so that we may consider them
and know their final outcome.
Or declare to us the things to come,[i]
23 tell us what the future holds,
so we may know[j] that you are
gods.
Do something, whether good or
bad,[k]
so that we will be dismayed and
filled with fear.
24 But you are less than nothing[l]
and your works are utterly
worthless;
he who chooses you is detestable.[m]

25 "I have stirred up one from the
north,[n] and he comes—
one from the rising sun who calls
on my name.
He treads[o] on rulers as if they were
mortar,
as if he were a potter treading the
clay.
26 Who told of this from the
beginning, so we could
know,
or beforehand, so we could say,
'He was right'?
No one told of this,

41:8 [i]Isa 29:22; 51:2; 63:16 [j]2Ch 20:7; Jas 2:23
41:9 [k]Isa 11:12 [l]Dt 7:6
41:10 [m]Jos 1:9; Isa 43:2,5; Ro 8:31 [n]ver 13-14; Isa 44:2; 49:8
41:11 [o]Isa 17:12 [p]Isa 45:24 [q]Ex 23:22 [r]Isa 29:8
41:12 [s]Ps 37:35-36 [t]Isa 17:14
41:13 [u]Isa 42:6; 45:1 [v]ver 10
41:15 [w]Mic 4:13
41:16 [x]Jer 51:2 [y]Isa 45:25
41:17 [z]Isa 43:20 [a]Isa 30:19
41:18 [b]Isa 30:25 [c]Isa 43:19 [d]Isa 35:7
41:19 [e]Isa 60:13
41:20 [f]Job 12:9
41:21 [g]Isa 43:15
41:22 [h]Isa 43:9; 45:21 [i]Isa 46:10
41:23 [j]Isa 42:9; 44:7-8; 45:3 [k]Jer 10:5
41:24 [l]Isa 37:19; 44:9; 1Co 8:4 [m]Ps 115:8
41:25 [n]ver 2 [o]2Sa 22:43

no one foretold it,
no one heard any words[p] from you.
27 I was the first to tell[q] Zion, 'Look, here they are!'
I gave to Jerusalem a messenger of good tidings.[r]
28 I look but there is no one[s]—
no one among them to give counsel,[t]
no one to give answer when I ask them.
29 See, they are all false!
Their deeds amount to nothing;[u]

41:26 [p]Hab 2:18-19
41:27 [q]Isa 48:3,16 [r]Isa 40:9
41:28 [s]Isa 50:2; 59:16; 63:5 [t]Isa 40:13-14
41:29 [u]ver 24

DAY 4 FOUR

Joy and My Service to Others

Isaiah 42:1,10–13

Some years ago Coca-Cola used the song "I'd Like to Teach the World to Sing" for its advertising campaign. The commercial centered on the wild international elation people felt from drinking this brand of soda pop. To be sure, it is a reach to think that all the people of the world would lay down their separate constitutions and ethnic biases and become one from drinking cola.

Nonetheless, I think this is exactly the picture that is so often portrayed in the book of Isaiah. Here in this passage, the entire world—mountains, deserts, islands and seas—is caught up in a great and overwhelming song of praise. What the cola manufacturers only dreamed of, a world of people praising God have actually experienced.

Some years ago I preached to a Hawaiian congregation and was amazed that there was no one dominant nationality. It was truly an international worship service. For one brief shining moment, I actually felt the Isaiah passage come to life. All nations, it seemed to me, had joined together in that wonderful oneness that only our praise can achieve. Jesus himself has taught the world to sing in perfect harmony. In a world torn by racial prejudice and civil injustice, this message of harmony is one that we can share with others through our praise and joy.

To begin a study on the topic of Joy, a Positive Attitude, turn to the home page on page 358.

their images are but wind[v] and confusion.

41:29 [v]Jer 5:13

The Servant of the LORD

42 "Here is my servant, whom I uphold,
my chosen one[w] in whom I delight;
I will put my Spirit[x] on him
and he will bring justice to the nations.
2 He will not shout or cry out,
or raise his voice in the streets.
3 A bruised reed he will not break,
and a smoldering wick he will not snuff out.
In faithfulness he will bring forth justice;[y]

42:1 [w]Isa 43:10; Lk 9:35; 1Pe 2:4,6 [x]Isa 11:2; Mt 3:16-17; Jn 3:34
42:3 [y]Ps 72:2

Gentleness

Gentle Justice

Isaiah 42:3

Watch Christ and what he did with power. Did he excoriate his accusers? Did he wallop his executioners? No. See, he was gentle. Although holding the destiny of all men, he would not bruise the grass on which he walked.

Was ever power so vast, yet smaller still than love?

4 he will not falter or be discouraged
till he establishes justice on earth.
In his law the islands will put their hope."[z]
5 This is what God the LORD says—
he who created the heavens and stretched them out,
who spread out the earth and all that comes out of it,[a]
who gives breath[b] to its people,
and life to those who walk on it:
6 "I, the LORD, have called[c] you in righteousness;[d]
I will take hold of your hand.
I will keep[e] you and will make you
to be a covenant[f] for the people
and a light for the Gentiles,[g]
7 to open eyes that are blind,[h]
to free[i] captives from prison[j]
and to release from the dungeon
those who sit in darkness.
8 "I am the LORD; that is my name![k]
I will not give my glory to another[l]

42:4 [z]Ge 49:10; Mt 12:18-21*
42:5 [a]Ps 24:2 [b]Ac 17:25
42:6 [c]Isa 43:1 [d]Jer 23:6 [e]Isa 26:3 [f]Isa 49:8 [g]Lk 2:32; Ac 13:47
42:7 [h]Isa 35:5 [i]Isa 49:9; 61:1 [j]Lk 4:19; 2Ti 2:26; Heb 2:14-15
42:8 [k]Ex 3:15 [l]Isa 48:11

or my praise to idols.
9 See, the former things have taken place,
and new things I declare;
before they spring into being
I announce them to you."

Song of Praise to the LORD

10 Sing to the LORD a new song,[m]
his praise from the ends of the earth,[n]
you who go down to the sea, and all that is in it,[o]
you islands, and all who live in them.
11 Let the desert[p] and its towns raise their voices;
let the settlements where Kedar[q] lives rejoice.
Let the people of Sela sing for joy;
let them shout from the mountaintops.[r]
12 Let them give glory[s] to the LORD
and proclaim his praise in the islands.
13 The LORD will march out like a mighty[t] man,
like a warrior he will stir up his zeal;[u]
with a shout[v] he will raise the battle cry
and will triumph over his enemies.[w]

14 "For a long time I have kept silent,
I have been quiet and held myself back.
But now, like a woman in childbirth,
I cry out, I gasp and pant.
15 I will lay waste[x] the mountains and hills
and dry up all their vegetation;
I will turn rivers into islands
and dry up[y] the pools.
16 I will lead[z] the blind[a] by ways they have not known,
along unfamiliar paths I will guide them;
I will turn the darkness into light before them
and make the rough places smooth.[b]
These are the things I will do;
I will not forsake[c] them.
17 But those who trust in idols,
who say to images, 'You are our gods,'
will be turned back in utter shame.[d]

Israel Blind and Deaf

18 "Hear, you deaf;[e]
look, you blind, and see!
19 Who is blind[f] but my servant,[g]
and deaf like the messenger[h] I send?
Who is blind like the one committed[i] to me,
blind like the servant of the LORD?
20 You have seen many things, but have paid no attention;
your ears are open, but you hear nothing."[j]
21 It pleased the LORD
for the sake of his righteousness
to make his law[k] great and glorious.
22 But this is a people plundered and looted,
all of them trapped in pits[l]
or hidden away in prisons.[m]
They have become plunder,
with no one to rescue them;
they have been made loot,
with no one to say, "Send them back."

23 Which of you will listen to this
or pay close attention[n] in time to come?
24 Who handed Jacob over to become loot,
and Israel to the plunderers?
Was it not the LORD,
against whom we have sinned?
For they would not follow[o] his ways;
they did not obey his law.
25 So he poured out on them his burning anger,
the violence of war.
It enveloped them in flames,[p] yet they did not understand;
it consumed them, but they did not take it to heart.[q]

Israel's Only Savior

43 But now, this is what the LORD says—
he who created you, O Jacob,
he who formed you,[r] O Israel:[s]
"Fear not, for I have redeemed[t] you;
I have summoned you by name;[u]
you are mine.
2 When you pass through the waters,[v]

42:10 [m]Ps 33:3; 40:3; 98:1 [n]Isa 49:6 [o]1Ch 16:32; Ps 96:11
42:11 [p]Isa 32:16 [q]Isa 60:7 [r]Isa 52:7; Na 1:15
42:12 [s]Isa 24:15
42:13 [t]Isa 9:6 [u]Isa 26:11 [v]Hos 11:10 [w]Isa 66:14
42:15 [x]Eze 38:20 [y]Isa 50:2; Na 1:4-6
42:16 [z]Lk 1:78-79 [a]Isa 32:3 [b]Lk 3:5 [c]Heb 13:5
42:17 [d]Ps 97:7; Isa 1:29; 44:11; 45:16
42:18 [e]Isa 35:5
42:19 [f]Isa 43:8; Eze 12:2 [g]Isa 41:8-9 [h]Isa 44:26 [i]Isa 26:3
42:20 [j]Jer 6:10
42:21 [k]ver 4
42:22 [l]Isa 24:18 [m]Isa 24:22
42:23 [n]Isa 48:18
42:24 [o]Isa 30:15
42:25 [p]2Ki 25:9 [q]Isa 29:13; 47:7; 57:1,11; Hos 7:9
43:1 [r]ver 7 [s]Ge 32:28; Isa 44:21 [t]Isa 44:2,6 [u]Isa 42:6; 45:3-4
43:2 [v]Isa 8:7

I will be with you;[w]
and when you pass through the rivers,
they will not sweep over you.
When you walk through the fire,[x]
you will not be burned;
the flames will not set you ablaze.[y]

43:2 [w]Dt 31:6,8 [x]Isa 29:6; 30:27 [y]Ps 66:12; Da 3:25-27

3 For I am the LORD, your God,[z]
the Holy One of Israel, your Savior;
I give Egypt for your ransom,
Cush[a][a] and Seba in your stead.[b]

43:3 [z]Ex 20:2 [a]Isa 20:3 [b]Pr 21:18

4 Since you are precious and honored in my sight,
and because I love[c] you,
I will give men in exchange for you,
and people in exchange for your life.

43:4 [c]Isa 63:9

5 Do not be afraid,[d] for I am with you;[e]
I will bring your children[f] from the east
and gather you from the west.

43:5 [d]Isa 44:2 [e]Jer 30:10-11 [f]Isa 41:8

6 I will say to the north, 'Give them up!'
and to the south,[g] 'Do not hold them back.'
Bring my sons from afar
and my daughters[h] from the ends of the earth—

43:6 [g]Ps 107:3 [h]2Co 6:18

7 everyone who is called by my name,[i]
whom I created for my glory,
whom I formed and made."[j]

43:7 [i]Isa 56:5; 63:19; Jas 2:7 [j]ver 1,21; Ps 100:3; Eph 2:10; Eph 2:10

8 Lead out those who have eyes but are blind,[k]
who have ears but are deaf.[l]

43:8 [k]Isa 6:9-10 [l]Isa 42:20; Eze 12:2

9 All the nations gather together[m]
and the peoples assemble.
Which of them foretold[n] this
and proclaimed to us the former things?
Let them bring in their witnesses to prove they were right,
so that others may hear and say, "It is true."

43:9 [m]Isa 41:1 [n]Isa 41:26

10 "You are my witnesses," declares the LORD,
"and my servant[o] whom I have chosen,
so that you may know and believe me
and understand that I am he.
Before me no god[p] was formed,
nor will there be one after me.

43:10 [o]Isa 41:8-9 [p]Isa 44:6,8

11 I, even I, am the LORD,
and apart from me there is no savior.[q]

43:11 [q]Isa 45:21

12 I have revealed and saved and proclaimed—
I, and not some foreign god[r] among you.
You are my witnesses,[s]" declares the LORD, "that I am God.

43:12 [r]Dt 32:12; Ps 81:9 [s]Isa 44:8

13 Yes, and from ancient days[t] I am he.
No one can deliver out of my hand.
When I act, who can reverse it?"[u]

43:13 [t]Ps 90:2 [u]Job 9:12; Isa 14:27

God's Mercy and Israel's Unfaithfulness

14 This is what the LORD says—
your Redeemer, the Holy One of Israel:
"For your sake I will send to Babylon
and bring down as fugitives[v] all the Babylonians,[b][w]
in the ships in which they took pride.

43:14 [v]Isa 13:14-15 [w]Isa 23:13

15 I am the LORD, your Holy One,
Israel's Creator, your King."

16 This is what the LORD says—
he who made a way through the sea,
a path through the mighty waters,[x]

43:16 [x]Ps 77:19; Isa 11:15; 51:10

17 who drew out[y] the chariots and horses,
the army and reinforcements together,[z]
and they lay there, never to rise again,
extinguished, snuffed out like a wick:

43:17 [y]Ps 118:12; Isa 1:31 [z]Ex 14:9

18 "Forget the former things;
do not dwell on the past.
19 See, I am doing a new thing![a]
Now it springs up; do you not perceive it?
I am making a way in the desert[b]
and streams in the wasteland.

43:19 [a]2Co 5:17; Rev 21:5 [b]Ex 17:6; Nu 20:11

20 The wild animals honor me,
the jackals[c] and the owls,
because I provide water[d] in the desert
and streams in the wasteland,
to give drink to my people, my chosen,

43:20 [c]Isa 13:22 [d]Isa 48:21

21 the people I formed for myself
that they may proclaim my praise.[e]

43:21 [e]Ps 102:18; 1Pe 2:9

22 "Yet you have not called upon me, O Jacob,

[a] *3* That is, the upper Nile region [b] *14* Or *Chaldeans*

you have not wearied yourselves
for me, O Israel.[f]
23 You have not brought me sheep for
burnt offerings,
nor honored[g] me with your
sacrifices.[h]
I have not burdened you with grain
offerings
nor wearied you with demands[i]
for incense.[j]
24 You have not bought any fragrant
calamus[k] for me,
or lavished on me the fat of your
sacrifices.
But you have burdened me with
your sins
and wearied[l] me with your
offenses.[m]

25 "I, even I, am he who blots out
your transgressions,[n] for my own
sake,[o]
and remembers your sins no
more.[p]
26 Review the past for me,
let us argue the matter together;[q]
state the case[r] for your innocence.
27 Your first father sinned;
your spokesmen[s] rebelled against
me.
28 So I will disgrace the dignitaries of
your temple,
and I will consign Jacob to
destruction[a]
and Israel to scorn.[t]

Israel the Chosen

44 "But now listen, O Jacob, my
servant,[u]
Israel, whom I have chosen.
2 This is what the LORD says—
he who made you, who formed
you in the womb,
and who will help[v] you:
Do not be afraid, O Jacob, my
servant,
Jeshurun,[w] whom I have chosen.
3 For I will pour water[x] on the thirsty
land,
and streams on the dry ground;
I will pour out my Spirit[y] on your
offspring,
and my blessing on your
descendants.[z]
4 They will spring up like grass in a
meadow,
like poplar trees[a] by flowing
streams.[b]

43:22 [f]Isa 30:11
43:23 [g]Zec 7:5-6; Mal 1:6-8 [h]Am 5:25 [i]Jer 7:22 [j]Ex 30:35; Lev 2:1
43:24 [k]Ex 30:23 [l]Isa 1:14; 7:13 [m]Mal 2:17
43:25 [n]Ac 3:19 [o]Isa 37:35; Eze 36:22 [p]Isa 38:17; Jer 31:34
43:26 [q]Isa 1:18 [r]Isa 41:1; 50:8
43:27 [s]Isa 9:15; 28:7; Jer 5:31
43:28 [t]Jer 24:9; Eze 5:15
44:1 [u]ver 21; Jer 30:10; 46:27-28
44:2 [v]Isa 41:10 [w]Dt 32:15
44:3 [x]Joel 3:18 [y]Joel 2:28; Ac 2:17 [z]Isa 61:9; 65:23
44:4 [a]Lev 23:40 [b]Job 40:22

5 One will say, 'I belong to the LORD';
another will call himself by the
name of Jacob;
still another will write on his hand,[c]
'The LORD's,'[d]
and will take the name Israel.

The LORD, Not Idols

6 "This is what the LORD says—
Israel's King[e] and Redeemer,[f] the
LORD Almighty:
I am the first and I am the last;[g]
apart from me there is no God.
7 Who then is like me? Let him
proclaim it.
Let him declare and lay out before
me
what has happened since I
established my ancient
people,
and what is yet to come—
yes, let him foretell[h] what will
come.
8 Do not tremble, do not be afraid.
Did I not proclaim this and
foretell it long ago?
You are my witnesses. Is there any
God[i] besides me?
No, there is no other Rock;[j] I
know not one."

9 All who make idols are nothing,
and the things they treasure are
worthless.[k]
Those who would speak up for them
are blind;
they are ignorant, to their own
shame.
10 Who shapes a god and casts an idol,
which can profit him nothing?[l]
11 He and his kind will be put to
shame;[m]
craftsmen are nothing but men.
Let them all come together and take
their stand;
they will be brought down to
terror and infamy.[n]

12 The blacksmith[o] takes a tool
and works with it in the coals;
he shapes an idol with hammers,
he forges it with the might of his
arm.[p]
He gets hungry and loses his
strength;

44:5 [c]Ex 13:9 [d]Zec 8:20-22
44:6 [e]Isa 41:21 [f]Isa 43:1 [g]Isa 41:4; Rev 1:8,17; 22:13
44:7 [h]Isa 41:22,26
44:8 [i]Isa 43:10 [j]Dt 4:35; 1Sa 2:2
44:9 [k]Isa 41:24
44:10 [l]Isa 41:29; Jer 10:5; Ac 19:26
44:11 [m]Isa 1:29 [n]Isa 42:17
44:12 [o]Isa 40:19; 41:6-7 [p]Jer 10:3-5; Ac 17:29

[a] *28* The Hebrew term refers to the irrevocable giving over of things or persons to the LORD, often by totally destroying them.

he drinks no water and grows
faint.
13The carpenter[q] measures with a line
and makes an outline with a
marker;
he roughs it out with chisels
and marks it with compasses.
He shapes it in the form of man,[r]
of man in all his glory,
that it may dwell in a shrine.[s]
14He cut down cedars,
or perhaps took a cypress or oak.
He let it grow among the trees of the
forest,
or planted a pine, and the rain
made it grow.
15It is man's fuel[t] for burning;
some of it he takes and warms
himself,
he kindles a fire and bakes bread.
But he also fashions a god and
worships it;
he makes an idol and bows[u] down
to it.
16Half of the wood he burns in the fire;
over it he prepares his meal,
he roasts his meat and eats his fill.
He also warms himself and says,
"Ah! I am warm; I see the fire."
17From the rest he makes a god, his
idol;
he bows down to it and worships.
He prays[v] to it and says,
"Save[w] me; you are my god."
18They know nothing, they
understand[x] nothing;
their eyes[y] are plastered over so
they cannot see,
and their minds closed so they
cannot understand.
19No one stops to think,
no one has the knowledge or
understanding[z] to say,
"Half of it I used for fuel;
I even baked bread over its coals,
I roasted meat and I ate.
Shall I make a detestable[a] thing from
what is left?
Shall I bow down to a block of
wood?"
20He feeds on ashes,[b] a deluded[c] heart
misleads him;
he cannot save himself, or say,
"Is not this thing in my right hand
a lie?"[d]
21"Remember[e] these things, O Jacob,
for you are my servant, O Israel.
I have made you, you are my
servant;[f]
O Israel, I will not forget you.[g]
22I have swept away[h] your offenses like
a cloud,
your sins like the morning mist.
Return[i] to me,
for I have redeemed[j] you."
23Sing for joy,[k] O heavens, for the
LORD has done this;
shout aloud, O earth[l] beneath.
Burst into song, you mountains,[m]
you forests and all your trees,
for the LORD has redeemed Jacob,
he displays his glory[n] in Israel.

Jerusalem to Be Inhabited

24"This is what the LORD says—
your Redeemer,[o] who formed you
in the womb:

I am the LORD,
who has made all things,
who alone stretched out the
heavens,[p]
who spread out the earth by myself,
25who foils[q] the signs of false prophets
and makes fools of diviners,[r]
who overthrows the learning of the
wise[s]
and turns it into nonsense,[t]
26who carries out the words[u] of his
servants
and fulfills[v] the predictions of his
messengers,

who says of Jerusalem, 'It shall be
inhabited,'
of the towns of Judah, 'They shall
be built,'
and of their ruins, 'I will restore
them,'[w]
27who says to the watery deep, 'Be dry,
and I will dry up your streams,'
28who says of Cyrus,[x] 'He is my
shepherd
and will accomplish all that I
please;
he will say of Jerusalem,[y] "Let it
be rebuilt,"
and of the temple,[z] "Let its
foundations be laid."'

45 "This is what the LORD says to
his anointed,
to Cyrus, whose right hand I take
hold[a] of
to subdue nations[b] before him

44:13 [q]Isa 41:7 [r]Ps 115:4-7 [s]Jdg 17:4-5
44:15 [t]ver 19 [u]2Ch 25:14
44:17 [v]1Ki 18:26 [w]Isa 45:20
44:18 [x]Isa 1:3 [y]Isa 6:9-10
44:19 [z]Isa 5:13; 27:11; 45:20 [a]Dt 27:15
44:20 [b]Ps 102:9 [c]Job 15:31; Ro 1:21-23, 28; 2Th 2:11; 2Ti 3:13 [d]Isa 59:3,4,13; Ro 1:25
44:21 [e]Isa 46:8; Zec 10:9 [f]ver 1-2 [g]Isa 49:15
44:22 [h]Isa 43:25; Ac 3:19 [i]Isa 55:7 [j]1Co 6:20
44:23 [k]Isa 42:10 [l]Ps 148:7 [m]Ps 98:8 [n]Isa 61:3
44:24 [o]Isa 43:14 [p]Isa 42:5
44:25 [q]Ps 33:10 [r]Isa 47:13 [s]1Co 1:27 [t]2Sa 15:31; 1Co 1:19-20
44:26 [u]Zec 1:6 [v]Isa 55:11; Mt 5:18 [w]Isa 49:8-21
44:28 [x]2Ch 36:22 [y]Isa 14:32 [z]Ezr 1:2-4
45:1 [a]Ps 73:23; Isa 41:13; 42:6 [b]Jer 50:35

and to strip kings of their armor,
to open doors before him
so that gates will not be shut:
2 I will go before you
and will level[c] the mountains[a];
I will break down gates of bronze
and cut through bars of iron.[d]
3 I will give you the treasures[e] of darkness,
riches stored in secret places,[f]
so that you may know[g] that I am the LORD,
the God of Israel, who summons you by name.[h]
4 For the sake of Jacob my servant,[i]
of Israel my chosen,
I summon you by name
and bestow on you a title of honor,
though you do not acknowledge[j] me.
5 I am the LORD, and there is no other;[k]
apart from me there is no God.[l]
I will strengthen you,[m]
though you have not acknowledged me,
6 so that from the rising of the sun
to the place of its setting[n]
men may know there is none besides me.[o]
I am the LORD, and there is no other.
7 I form the light and create darkness,
I bring prosperity and create disaster;[p]
I, the LORD, do all these things.

8 "You heavens above, rain[q] down righteousness;[r]
let the clouds shower it down.
Let the earth open wide,
let salvation[s] spring up,
let righteousness grow with it;
I, the LORD, have created it.

9 "Woe to him who quarrels[t] with his Maker,
to him who is but a potsherd
among the potsherds on the ground.
Does the clay say to the potter,[u]
'What are you making?'
Does your work say,
'He has no hands'?
10 Woe to him who says to his father,
'What have you begotten?'
or to his mother,
'What have you brought to birth?'

11 "This is what the LORD says—
the Holy One of Israel, and its Maker:
Concerning things to come,
do you question me about my children,
or give me orders about the work of my hands?[v]
12 It is I who made the earth
and created mankind upon it.
My own hands stretched out the heavens;[w]
I marshaled their starry hosts.[x]
13 I will raise up Cyrus[b][y] in my righteousness:
I will make all his ways straight.
He will rebuild my city
and set my exiles free,
but not for a price or reward,[z]
says the LORD Almighty."

14 This is what the LORD says:

"The products of Egypt and the merchandise of Cush,[c]
and those tall Sabeans—
they will come over to you
and will be yours;
they will trudge behind you,
coming over to you in chains.[a]
They will bow down before you
and plead[b] with you, saying,
'Surely God is with you,[c] and there is no other;
there is no other god.'"

15 Truly you are a God who hides[d] himself,
O God and Savior of Israel.
16 All the makers of idols will be put to shame and disgraced;[e]
they will go off into disgrace together.
17 But Israel will be saved[f] by the LORD
with an everlasting salvation;[g]
you will never be put to shame or disgraced,
to ages everlasting.

18 For this is what the LORD says—
he who created the heavens,
he is God;
he who fashioned and made the earth,
he founded it;
he did not create it to be empty,[h]

[a] *2* Dead Sea Scrolls and Septuagint; the meaning of the word in the Masoretic Text is uncertain.
[b] *13* Hebrew *him*
[c] *14* That is, the upper Nile region

45:2 [c]Isa 40:4 [d]Ps 107:16; Jer 51:30
45:3 [e]Jer 50:37 [f]Jer 41:8 [g]Isa 41:23 [h]Ex 33:12; Isa 43:1
45:4 [i]Isa 41:8-9 [j]Ac 17:23
45:5 [k]Isa 44:8 [l]Ps 18:31 [m]Ps 18:39
45:6 [n]Isa 43:5; Mal 1:11 [o]ver 5,18
45:7 [p]Isa 31:2; Am 3:6
45:8 [q]Ps 72:6; Joel 3:18 [r]Ps 85:11; Isa 60:21; 61:10,11; Hos 10:12 [s]Isa 12:3
45:9 [t]Job 15:25 [u]Isa 29:16; Ro 9:20-21*
45:11 [v]Isa 19:25
45:12 [w]Ge 2:1; Isa 42:5 [x]Ne 9:6
45:13 [y]2Ch 36:22; Isa 41:2 [z]Isa 52:3
45:14 [a]Isa 14:1-2 [b]Jer 16:19; Zec 8:20-23 [c]1Co 14:25
45:15 [d]Ps 44:24
45:16 [e]Isa 44:9,11
45:17 [f]Ro 11:26 [g]Isa 26:4
45:18 [h]Ge 1:2

but formed it to be inhabited[i]—
he says:
"I am the LORD,
and there is no other.[j]
19 I have not spoken in secret,[k]
from somewhere in a land of
darkness;
I have not said to Jacob's
descendants,[l]
'Seek me in vain.'
I, the LORD, speak the truth;
I declare what is right.[m]
20 "Gather together[n] and come;
assemble, you fugitives from the
nations.
Ignorant[o] are those who carry[p] about
idols of wood,
who pray to gods that cannot
save.[q]
21 Declare what is to be, present it—
let them take counsel together.
Who foretold[r] this long ago,
who declared it from the distant
past?
Was it not I, the LORD?
And there is no God apart from
me,[s]
a righteous God and a Savior;
there is none but me.
22 "Turn[t] to me and be saved,[u]
all you ends of the earth;[v]
for I am God, and there is no
other.
23 By myself I have sworn,[w]
my mouth has uttered in all
integrity[x]
a word that will not be revoked:[y]
Before me every knee will bow;
by me every tongue will swear.[z]
24 They will say of me, 'In the LORD
alone
are righteousness[a] and strength.'"
All who have raged against him
will come to him and be put to
shame.[b]
25 But in the LORD all the descendants
of Israel
will be found righteous and will
exult.[c]

Gods of Babylon

46 Bel[d] bows down, Nebo stoops
low;
their idols are borne by beasts of
burden.[a]
The images that are carried[e] about
are burdensome,
a burden for the weary.
2 They stoop and bow down together;
unable to rescue the burden,
they themselves go off into
captivity.[f]
3 "Listen[g] to me, O house of Jacob,
all you who remain of the house
of Israel,
you whom I have upheld since you
were conceived,
and have carried since your birth.
4 Even to your old age and gray hairs[h]
I am he,[i] I am he who will sustain
you.
I have made you and I will carry you;
I will sustain you and I will rescue
you.
5 "To whom will you compare me or
count me equal?
To whom will you liken me that
we may be compared?[j]
6 Some pour out gold from their bags
and weigh out silver on the scales;
they hire a goldsmith[k] to make it
into a god,
and they bow down and worship
it.[l]
7 They lift it to their shoulders and
carry[m] it;
they set it up in its place, and
there it stands.
From that spot it cannot move.
Though one cries out to it, it does
not answer;
it cannot save[n] him from his
troubles.
8 "Remember[o] this, fix it in mind,
take it to heart, you rebels.
9 Remember the former things, those
of long ago;[p]
I am God, and there is no other;
I am God, and there is none like
me.[q]
10 I make known the end from the
beginning,
from ancient times,[r] what is still
to come.
I say: My purpose will stand,[s]
and I will do all that I please.
11 From the east I summon a bird of
prey;
from a far-off land, a man to
fulfill my purpose.
What I have said, that will I bring
about;

[a] 1 Or *are but beasts and cattle*

45:18 [i]Ge 1:26; Isa 42:5 [j]ver 5
45:19 [k]Isa 48:16 [l]Isa 41:8 [m]Dt 30:11
45:20 [n]Isa 43:9 [o]Isa 44:19 [p]Isa 46:1; Jer 10:5 [q]Isa 44:17; 46:6-7
45:21 [r]Isa 41:22 [s]ver 5
45:22 [t]Zec 12:10 [u]Nu 21:8-9; 2Ch 20:12 [v]Isa 49:6,12
45:23 [w]Ge 22:16 [x]Heb 6:13 [y]Isa 55:11 [z]Ps 63:11; Isa 19:18; Ro 14:11*; Php 2:10-11
45:24 [a]Jer 33:16 [b]Isa 41:11
45:25 [c]Isa 41:16
46:1 [d]Isa 21:9; Jer 50:2; 51:44 [e]Isa 45:20
46:2 [f]Jdg 18:17-18; 2Sa 5:21
46:3 [g]ver 12
46:4 [h]Ps 71:18 [i]Isa 43:13
46:5 [j]Isa 40:18,25
46:6 [k]Isa 40:19 [l]Isa 44:17
46:7 [m]ver 1 [n]Isa 44:17; Isa 45:20
46:8 [o]Isa 44:21
46:9 [p]Dt 32:7 [q]Isa 45:5,21
46:10 [r]Isa 45:21 [s]Pr 19:21; Ac 5:39

what I have planned, that will I
do.
12 Listen[t] to me, you stubborn-hearted,
you who are far from
righteousness.[u]
13 I am bringing my righteousness near,
it is not far away;
and my salvation will not be
delayed.
I will grant salvation to Zion,
my splendor[v] to Israel.

46:12 [t]ver 3 [u]Ps 119:150; Isa 48:1; Jer 2:5
46:13 [v]Isa 44:23

The Fall of Babylon

47 "Go down, sit in the dust,
Virgin Daughter[w] of Babylon;
sit on the ground without a throne,
Daughter of the Babylonians.[a][x]
No more will you be called
tender or delicate.[y]
2 Take millstones[z] and grind[a] flour;
take off your veil.[b]
Lift up your skirts,[c] bare your legs,
and wade through the streams.
3 Your nakedness[d] will be exposed
and your shame[e] uncovered.
I will take vengeance;[f]
I will spare no one."

4 Our Redeemer—the LORD
Almighty is his name[g]—
is the Holy One of Israel.

5 "Sit in silence, go into darkness,[h]
Daughter of the Babylonians;
no more will you be called
queen of kingdoms.[i]
6 I was angry[j] with my people
and desecrated my inheritance;
I gave them into your hand,[k]
and you showed them no mercy.
Even on the aged
you laid a very heavy yoke.
7 You said, 'I will continue forever—
the eternal queen!'[l]
But you did not consider these
things
or reflect[m] on what might
happen.[n]

8 "Now then, listen, you wanton
creature,
lounging in your security[o]
and saying to yourself,
'I am, and there is none besides
me.[p]
I will never be a widow[q]
or suffer the loss of children.'
9 Both of these will overtake you
in a moment,[r] on a single day:
loss of children[s] and widowhood.
They will come upon you in full
measure,
in spite of your many sorceries[t]
and all your potent spells.[u]
10 You have trusted[v] in your wickedness
and have said, 'No one sees me.'[w]
Your wisdom[x] and knowledge
mislead[y] you
when you say to yourself,
'I am, and there is none besides
me.'
11 Disaster will come upon you,
and you will not know how to
conjure it away.
A calamity will fall upon you
that you cannot ward off with a
ransom;
a catastrophe you cannot foresee
will suddenly[z] come upon you.

12 "Keep on, then, with your magic
spells
and with your many sorceries,[a]
which you have labored at since
childhood.
Perhaps you will succeed,
perhaps you will cause terror.
13 All the counsel you have received has
only worn you out![b]
Let your astrologers[c] come
forward,
those stargazers who make
predictions month by
month,
let them save[d] you from what is
coming upon you.
14 Surely they are like stubble;[e]
the fire will burn them up.
They cannot even save themselves
from the power of the flame.[f]
Here are no coals to warm anyone;
here is no fire to sit by.
15 That is all they can do for you—
these you have labored with
and trafficked[g] with since
childhood.
Each of them goes on in his error;
there is not one that can save you.

47:1 [w]Isa 23:12 [x]Ps 137:8; Jer 50:42; 51:33; Zec 2:7 [y]Dt 28:56
47:2 [z]Ex 11:5; Mt 24:41 [a]Jdg 16:21 [b]Ge 24:65 [c]Isa 32:11
47:3 [d]Eze 16:37; Na 3:5 [e]Isa 20:4 [f]Isa 34:8
47:4 [g]Jer 50:34
47:5 [h]Isa 13:10 [i]Isa 13:19
47:6 [j]2Ch 28:9 [k]Isa 10:13
47:7 [l]ver 5; Rev 18:7 [m]Isa 42:23,25 [n]Dt 32:29
47:8 [o]Isa 32:9 [p]Isa 45:6; Zep 2:15 [q]Rev 18:7
47:9 [r]Ps 73:19; 1Th 5:3; Rev 18:8-10 [s]Isa 13:18 [t]Na 3:4 [u]Rev 18:23
47:10 [v]Ps 52:7; 62:10 [w]Isa 29:15 [x]Isa 5:21 [y]Isa 44:20
47:11 [z]1Th 5:3
47:12 [a]ver 9
47:13 [b]Isa 57:10; Jer 51:58 [c]Isa 44:25 [d]ver 15
47:14 [e]Isa 5:24; Na 1:10 [f]Isa 10:17; Jer 51:30,32,58
47:15 [g]Rev 18:11

Stubborn Israel

48 "Listen to this, O house of
Jacob,
you who are called by the name
of Israel

[a] *1* Or *Chaldeans*; also in verse 5

and come from the line of Judah,
you who take oaths in the name of the LORD
and invoke[h] the God of Israel—
but not in truth[i] or righteousness—
[2] you who call yourselves citizens of the holy city[j]
and rely[k] on the God of Israel—
the LORD Almighty is his name:
[3] I foretold the former things[l] long ago,
my mouth announced[m] them and I made them known;
then suddenly I acted, and they came to pass.
[4] For I knew how stubborn[n] you were;
the sinews of your neck[o] were iron,
your forehead[p] was bronze.
[5] Therefore I told you these things long ago;
before they happened I announced them to you
so that you could not say,
'My idols did them;[q]
my wooden image and metal god ordained them.'
[6] You have heard these things; look at them all.
Will you not admit them?

"From now on I will tell you of new things,
of hidden things unknown to you.
[7] They are created now, and not long ago;
you have not heard of them before today.
So you cannot say,
'Yes, I knew of them.'
[8] You have neither heard nor understood;
from of old your ear has not been open.
Well do I know how treacherous you are;
you were called a rebel[r] from birth.
[9] For my own name's sake I delay my wrath;[s]
for the sake of my praise I hold it back from you,
so as not to cut you off.[t]
[10] See, I have refined you, though not as silver;
I have tested you in the furnace[u] of affliction.
[11] For my own sake,[v] for my own sake, I do this.
How can I let myself be defamed?[w]
I will not yield my glory to another.[x]

Israel Freed

[12] "Listen[y] to me, O Jacob,
Israel, whom I have called:
I am he;
I am the first and I am the last.[z]
[13] My own hand laid the foundations of the earth,[a]
and my right hand spread out the heavens;[b]
when I summon them,
they all stand up together.[c]

[14] "Come together,[d] all of you, and listen:
Which of ⌊the idols⌋ has foretold these things?
The LORD's chosen ally
will carry out his purpose[e] against Babylon;
his arm will be against the Babylonians.[a]
[15] I, even I, have spoken;
yes, I have called[f] him.
I will bring him,
and he will succeed in his mission.

[16] "Come near[g] me and listen to this:

"From the first announcement I have not spoken in secret;[h]
at the time it happens, I am there."

And now the Sovereign LORD has sent[i] me,
with his Spirit.

[17] This is what the LORD says—
your Redeemer,[j] the Holy One[k] of Israel:
"I am the LORD your God,
who teaches you what is best for you,
who directs[l] you in the way[m] you should go.
[18] If only you had paid attention[n] to my commands,
your peace[o] would have been like a river,
your righteousness[p] like the waves of the sea.

[a] *14* Or *Chaldeans*; also in verse 20

48:1 [h]Isa 58:2 [i]Jer 4:2
48:2 [j]Isa 52:1 [k]Isa 10:20; Mic 3:11; Ro 2:17
48:3 [l]Isa 41:22 [m]Isa 45:21
48:4 [n]Dt 31:27 [o]Ex 32:9; Ac 7:51 [p]Eze 3:9
48:5 [q]Jer 44:15-18
48:8 [r]Dt 9:7,24; Ps 58:3
48:9 [s]Ps 78:38; Isa 30:18 [t]Ne 9:31
48:10 [u]1Ki 8:51
48:11 [v]1Sa 12:22; Isa 37:35 [w]Dt 32:27; Jer 14:7,21; Eze 20:9,14, 22,44 [x]Isa 42:8
48:12 [y]Isa 46:3 [z]Isa 41:4; Rev 1:17; 22:13
48:13 [a]Heb 1:10-12 [b]Ex 20:11 [c]Isa 40:26
48:14 [d]Isa 43:9 [e]Isa 46:10-11
48:15 [f]Isa 45:1
48:16 [g]Isa 41:1 [h]Isa 45:19 [i]Zec 2:9,11
48:17 [j]Isa 49:7 [k]Isa 43:14 [l]Isa 49:10 [m]Ps 32:8
48:18 [n]Dt 32:29 [o]Ps 119:165; Isa 66:12 [p]Isa 45:8

[19]Your descendants would have been
like the sand,
your children like its numberless
grains;[q]
their name would never be cut off[r]
nor destroyed from before me."

48:19 [q]Ge 22:17 [r]Isa 56:5; 66:22

[20]Leave Babylon,
flee[s] from the Babylonians!
Announce this with shouts of joy[t]
and proclaim it.
Send it out to the ends of the earth;
say, "The LORD has redeemed[u]
his servant Jacob."

48:20 [s]Jer 50:8; 51:6,45; Zec 2:6-7; Rev 18:4 [t]Isa 49:13 [u]Isa 52:9; 63:9

[21]They did not thirst[v] when he led
them through the deserts;
he made water flow[w] for them
from the rock;
he split the rock
and water gushed out.[x]

48:21 [v]Isa 41:17 [w]Isa 30:25 [x]Ex 17:6; Nu 20:11; Ps 105:41; Isa 35:6

[22]"There is no peace," says the LORD,
"for the wicked."[y]

48:22 [y]Isa 57:21

The Servant of the LORD

49 Listen to me, you islands;
hear this, you distant nations:
Before I was born[z] the LORD called[a]
me;
from my birth he has made
mention of my name.

49:1 [z]Isa 44:24; 46:3; Mt 1:20 [a]Isa 7:14; 9:6; 44:2; Jer 1:5; Gal 1:15

[2]He made my mouth like a sharpened
sword,[b]
in the shadow of his hand he hid
me;
he made me into a polished arrow
and concealed me in his quiver.

49:2 [b]Isa 11:4; Rev 1:16

[3]He said to me, "You are my
servant,[c]
Israel, in whom I will display my
splendor.[d]"

49:3 [c]Zec 3:8 [d]Isa 44:23

[4]But I said, "I have labored to no
purpose;
I have spent my strength in vain[e]
and for nothing.
Yet what is due me is in the LORD's
hand,
and my reward[f] is with my God."

49:4 [e]Isa 65:23 [f]Isa 35:4

[5]And now the LORD says—
he who formed me in the womb
to be his servant
to bring Jacob back to him
and gather Israel[g] to himself,
for I am honored[h] in the eyes of the
LORD
and my God has been my
strength—

49:5 [g]Isa 11:12 [h]Isa 43:4

[6]he says:
"It is too small a thing for you to be
my servant
to restore the tribes of Jacob
and bring back those of Israel I
have kept.
I will also make you a light for the
Gentiles,[i]
that you may bring my salvation
to the ends of the earth."[j]

49:6 [i]Lk 2:32 [j]Ac 13:47*

[7]This is what the LORD says—
the Redeemer and Holy One of
Israel[k]—
to him who was despised[l] and
abhorred by the nation,
to the servant of rulers:
"Kings[m] will see you and rise up,
princes will see and bow down,
because of the LORD, who is faithful,
the Holy One of Israel, who has
chosen you."

49:7 [k]Isa 48:17 [l]Ps 22:6; 69:7-9 [m]Isa 52:15

LOVE

THE UNIVERSALLY ADORED CHRIST

Isaiah 49:7

Despised in the era of the caesars, our Lord is now enthroned for every age. Let smaller kings remove their crowns and enter into the presence of the exalted Christ. Heaven knows but one crown. Only he who wore the crown of thorns is fit to wear the final corona of love.

Restoration of Israel

[8]This is what the LORD says:
"In the time of my favor[n] I will
answer you,
and in the day of salvation I will
help you;[o]
I will keep[p] you and will make you
to be a covenant for the people,[q]
to restore the land[r]
and to reassign its desolate
inheritances,

49:8 [n]Ps 69:13 [o]2Co 6:2* [p]Isa 26:3 [q]Isa 42:6 [r]Isa 44:26

[9]to say to the captives,[s] 'Come out,'
and to those in darkness, 'Be free!'
"They will feed beside the roads
and find pasture on every barren
hill.[t]

49:9 [s]Isa 42:7; 61:1; Lk 4:19 [t]Isa 41:18

[10]They will neither hunger nor thirst,[u]
nor will the desert heat or the sun
beat upon them.[v]
He who has compassion[w] on them
will guide them

49:10 [u]Isa 33:16 [v]Ps 121:6; Rev 7:16 [w]Isa 14:1

DAY 2 TWO

Gentleness and the Purpose of God in My Life

Isaiah 49:15

Gentleness is God's demeanor in all of the tender ways he relates to us. The prophet's metaphor here is that of a nursing mother. Can a mother forget her child? Never! But, says the prophet, even if she does forget, God will never forget us. God is tender—he is gentle in his relationships to all his children. It is God's purpose to counter the heinous crimes of tyrants with gentleness. The world is all too often a brutal and ugly place, but God steps into the world's terror and horror and gently reminds us of his purpose.

Between 1534 and 1584 a pageant was performed on the steps of the old Coventry Cathedral. A lullaby was written, and it was sung in the pageant every year. It was a haunting theme that clung to the souls of those who heard it, for it was a lullaby that singers representing bereaved Bethlehem mothers sang to their little ones who had been massacred in their cribs by the wicked Herod.

Lully, Lullay, Thou little tiny Child,
By, by, Lully, Lullay,
Lullay, thou little tiny Child
By, by, Lully, Lullay.

O sisters too, how may we do,
For to preserve this day
This poor Youngling for whom we do sing
By, by, Lully, Lullay?

Herod the king, in his raging,
Charged he hath this day
His men of might, in his own sight,
All children young to slay.

Then woe is me, poor Child for Thee,
And ever morn and day
For Thy parting nor say nor sing,
By, by, Lully, Lullay.

Oh, the gentle tenderness of a caring God! God will never forget his children. Gently he loves us. Gently he leads us to celebrate his purposes in our lives.

To begin a study on the topic of Gentleness, Childlike Godliness, turn to the home page on page 315.

and lead them beside springs[x] of
water.
11 I will turn all my mountains into
roads,
and my highways[y] will be raised
up.[z]
12 See, they will come from afar[a]—
some from the north, some from
the west,
some from the region of Aswan.[a]"
13 Shout for joy, O heavens;
rejoice, O earth;
burst into song, O mountains![b]
For the LORD comforts[c] his people
and will have compassion on his
afflicted ones.
14 But Zion said, "The LORD has
forsaken me,
the Lord has forgotten me."
15 "Can a mother forget the baby at her
breast
and have no compassion on the
child she has borne?
Though she may forget,
I will not forget you![d]
16 See, I have engraved[e] you on the
palms of my hands;
your walls[f] are ever before me.
17 Your sons hasten back,
and those who laid you waste[g]
depart from you.
18 Lift up your eyes and look around;
all your sons gather[h] and come to
you.
As surely as I live,[i]" declares the
LORD,
"you will wear[j] them all as
ornaments;
you will put them on, like a bride.
19 "Though you were ruined and made
desolate[k]
and your land laid waste,[l]
now you will be too small for your
people,[m]
and those who devoured you will
be far away.
20 The children born during your
bereavement
will yet say in your hearing,
'This place is too small for us;
give us more space to live in.'[n]
21 Then you will say in your heart,
'Who bore me these?
I was bereaved and barren;

[a]*12* Dead Sea Scrolls; Masoretic Text *Sinim*

49:10 [x]Isa 35:7
49:11 [y]Isa 11:16 [z]Isa 40:4
49:12 [a]Isa 43:5-6
49:13 [b]Isa 44:23 [c]Isa 40:1
49:15 [d]Isa 44:21
49:16 [e]SS 8:6 [f]Ps 48:12-13; Isa 62:6
49:17 [g]Isa 10:6
49:18 [h]Isa 43:5; 54:7; Isa 60:4 [i]Isa 45:23 [j]Isa 52:1
49:19 [k]Isa 54:1,3 [l]Isa 5:6 [m]Zec 10:10
49:20 [n]Isa 54:1-3

49:21 [o]Isa 5:13 [p]Isa 1:8

I was exiled and rejected.[o]
Who brought these up?
I was left[p] all alone,
but these—where have they come from?' "

49:22 [q]Isa 11:10 [r]Isa 60:4

22 This is what the Sovereign LORD says:

"See, I will beckon to the Gentiles,
I will lift up my banner[q] to the peoples;
they will bring your sons in their arms
and carry your daughters on their shoulders.[r]

49:23 [s]Isa 60:3, 10-11 [t]Isa 60:16 [u]Ps 72:9 [v]Mic 7:17

23 Kings[s] will be your foster fathers,
and their queens your nursing mothers.[t]
They will bow down before you with their faces to the ground;
they will lick the dust[u] at your feet.
Then you will know that I am the LORD;[v]
those who hope in me will not be disappointed."

49:24 [w]Mt 12:29; Lk 11:21

24 Can plunder be taken from warriors,[w]
or captives rescued from the fierce[a]?

49:25 [x]Isa 14:2 [y]Jer 50:33-34 [z]Isa 25:9; 35:4

25 But this is what the LORD says:

"Yes, captives[x] will be taken from warriors,[y]
and plunder retrieved from the fierce;
I will contend with those who contend with you,
and your children I will save.[z]

49:26 [a]Isa 9:4 [b]Isa 9:20 [c]Rev 16:6 [d]Eze 39:7

26 I will make your oppressors[a] eat[b] their own flesh;
they will be drunk on their own blood,[c] as with wine.
Then all mankind will know[d]
that I, the LORD, am your Savior,
your Redeemer, the Mighty One of Jacob."

Israel's Sin and the Servant's Obedience

50:1 [e]Dt 24:1; Jer 3:8; Hos 2:2 [f]Ne 5:5; Mt 18:25 [g]Dt 32:30; Isa 52:3

50 This is what the LORD says:

"Where is your mother's certificate of divorce[e]
with which I sent her away?
Or to which of my creditors
did I sell[f] you?
Because of your sins you were sold;[g]
because of your transgressions
your mother was sent away.

50:2 [h]Isa 41:28 [i]Nu 11:23; Isa 59:1 [j]Ge 18:14 [k]Ex 14:22; Jos 3:16

2 When I came, why was there no one?
When I called, why was there no one to answer?[h]
Was my arm too short[i] to ransom you?
Do I lack the strength[j] to rescue you?
By a mere rebuke I dry up the sea,[k]
I turn rivers into a desert;
their fish rot for lack of water
and die of thirst.

50:3 [l]Rev 6:12

3 I clothe the sky with darkness
and make sackcloth[l] its covering."

50:4 [m]Ex 4:12 [n]Mt 11:28 [o]Ps 5:3; 119:147; 143:8

4 The Sovereign LORD has given me an instructed tongue,[m]
to know the word that sustains the weary.[n]
He wakens me morning by morning,[o]
wakens my ear to listen like one being taught.

50:5 [p]Isa 35:5 [q]Mt 26:39; Jn 8:29; 14:31; 15:10; Ac 26:19; Heb 5:8

5 The Sovereign LORD has opened my ears,[p]
and I have not been rebellious;[q]
I have not drawn back.

50:6 [r]Isa 53:5; Mt 27:30; Mk 14:65; 15:19; Lk 22:63 [s]La 3:30; Mt 26:67

6 I offered my back to those who beat[r] me,
my cheeks to those who pulled out my beard;
I did not hide my face
from mocking and spitting.[s]

FAITHFULNESS

THE SERVANT'S OBEDIENCE

Isaiah 50:6

There is little good in reaching out to those who would amputate our hands, yet Christ reached out in exactly this way. He is faithful. See how he died, and tell me, "Do we not mean the world to God?"

50:7 [t]Isa 42:1 [u]Eze 3:8-9

7 Because the Sovereign LORD helps[t] me,
I will not be disgraced.
Therefore have I set my face like flint,[u]
and I know I will not be put to shame.
8 He who vindicates me is near.

[a] *24* Dead Sea Scrolls, Vulgate and Syriac (see also Septuagint and verse 25); Masoretic Text *righteous*

Who then will bring charges
against me?[v]
Let us face each other![w]
Who is my accuser?
Let him confront me!
9 It is the Sovereign LORD who helps[x]
me.
Who is he that will condemn me?
They will all wear out like a
garment;
the moths[y] will eat them up.

10 Who among you fears the LORD
and obeys the word of his
servant?[z]
Let him who walks in the dark,
who has no light,
trust[a] in the name of the LORD
and rely on his God.
11 But now, all you who light fires
and provide yourselves with
flaming torches,[b]
go, walk in the light of your fires[c]
and of the torches you have set
ablaze.
This is what you shall receive from
my hand:
You will lie down in torment.[d]

50:8 [v]Isa 43:26; Ro 8:32-34 [w]Isa 41:1
50:9 [x]Isa 41:10 [y]Job 13:28; Isa 51:8
50:10 [z]Isa 49:3 [a]Isa 26:4
50:11 [b]Pr 26:18 [c]Jas 3:6 [d]Isa 65:13-15

Everlasting Salvation for Zion

51 "Listen[e] to me, you who pursue
righteousness[f]
and who seek the LORD:
Look to the rock from which you
were cut
and to the quarry from which you
were hewn;
2 look to Abraham,[g] your father,
and to Sarah, who gave you
birth.
When I called him he was but one,
and I blessed him and made him
many.[h]
3 The LORD will surely comfort[i] Zion
and will look with compassion on
all her ruins;[j]
he will make her deserts like Eden,[k]
her wastelands like the garden of
the LORD.
Joy and gladness[l] will be found in
her,
thanksgiving and the sound of
singing.

4 "Listen to me, my people;[m]
hear me, my nation:
The law will go out from me;
my justice[n] will become a light to
the nations.[o]

51:1 [e]Isa 46:3 [f]ver 7; Ps 94:15; Ro 9:30-31
51:2 [g]Isa 29:22; Ro 4:16; Heb 11:11 [h]Ge 12:2
51:3 [i]Isa 40:1 [j]Isa 52:9 [k]Ge 2:8 [l]Isa 25:9; 66:10
51:4 [m]Ps 50:7 [n]Isa 2:4 [o]Isa 42:4,6

5 My righteousness draws near
speedily,
my salvation is on the way,[p]
and my arm[q] will bring justice to
the nations.
The islands will look to me
and wait in hope for my arm.
6 Lift up your eyes to the heavens,
look at the earth beneath;
the heavens will vanish like smoke,[r]
the earth will wear out like a
garment[s]
and its inhabitants die like flies.
But my salvation will last forever,
my righteousness will never fail.

7 "Hear me, you who know what is
right,[t]
you people who have my law in
your hearts:[u]
Do not fear the reproach of men
or be terrified by their insults.[v]
8 For the moth will eat them up like
a garment;[w]
the worm will devour them like
wool.
But my righteousness will last
forever,[x]
my salvation through all
generations."

9 Awake, awake! Clothe yourself with
strength,[y]
O arm of the LORD;
awake, as in days gone by,
as in generations of old.[z]
Was it not you who cut Rahab to
pieces,
who pierced that monster[a]
through?
10 Was it not you who dried up the
sea,[b]
the waters of the great deep,
who made a road in the depths of
the sea
so that the redeemed might cross
over?
11 The ransomed[c] of the LORD will
return.
They will enter Zion with singing;
everlasting joy will crown their
heads.
Gladness and joy[d] will overtake them,
and sorrow and sighing will flee
away.[e]

12 "I, even I, am he who comforts[f] you.
Who are you that you fear mortal
men,[g]

51:5 [p]Isa 46:13 [q]Isa 40:10; 63:1,5
51:6 [r]Mt 24:35; 2Pe 3:10 [s]Ps 102:25-26
51:7 [t]ver 1 [u]Ps 37:31 [v]Mt 5:11; Ac 5:41
51:8 [w]Isa 50:9 [x]ver 6
51:9 [y]Isa 52:1 [z]Dt 4:34 [a]Ps 74:13
51:10 [b]Ex 14:22
51:11 [c]Isa 35:9 [d]Jer 33:11 [e]Rev 7:17
51:12 [f]2Co 1:4 [g]Ps 118:6; Isa 2:22

the sons of men, who are but
grass,[b]
13 that you forget[i] the LORD your
Maker,[j]
who stretched out the heavens[k]
and laid the foundations of the
earth,
that you live in constant terror[l] every
day
because of the wrath of the
oppressor,
who is bent on destruction?
For where is the wrath of the
oppressor?
14 The cowering prisoners will soon
be set free;
they will not die in their dungeon,
nor will they lack bread.[m]
15 For I am the LORD your God,
who churns up the sea[n] so that its
waves roar—
the LORD Almighty is his name.
16 I have put my words in your mouth[o]
and covered you with the shadow
of my hand[p]—
I who set the heavens in place,
who laid the foundations of the
earth,
and who say to Zion, 'You are my
people.' "

The Cup of the LORD's Wrath

17 Awake, awake![q]
Rise up, O Jerusalem,
you who have drunk from the hand
of the LORD
the cup of his wrath,[r]
you who have drained to its dregs
the goblet that makes men
stagger.[s]
18 Of all the sons[t] she bore
there was none to guide her;[u]
of all the sons she reared
there was none to take her by the
hand.
19 These double calamities[v] have come
upon you—
who can comfort you?—
ruin and destruction, famine[w] and
sword—
who can[a] console you?
20 Your sons have fainted;
they lie at the head of every
street,[x]
like antelope caught in a net.
They are filled with the wrath of the
LORD
and the rebuke of your God.

51:12 [b]Isa 40:6-7; 1Pe 1:24
51:13 [i]Isa 17:10 [j]Isa 45:11 [k]Ps 104:2; Isa 48:13 [l]Isa 7:4
51:14 [m]Isa 49:10
51:15 [n]Jer 31:35
51:16 [o]Dt 18:18; Isa 59:21 [p]Ex 33:22
51:17 [q]Isa 52:1 [r]Job 21:20; Rev 14:10; 16:19 [s]Ps 60:3
51:18 [t]Ps 88:18 [u]Isa 49:21
51:19 [v]Isa 47:9 [w]Isa 14:30
51:20 [x]Isa 5:25; Jer 14:16

21 Therefore hear this, you afflicted
one,
made drunk,[y] but not with wine.
22 This is what your Sovereign LORD
says,
your God, who defends[z] his
people:
"See, I have taken out of your hand
the cup[a] that made you stagger;
from that cup, the goblet of my
wrath,
you will never drink again.
23 I will put it into the hands of your
tormentors,[b]
who said to you,
'Fall prostrate[c] that we may walk[d]
over you.'
And you made your back like the
ground,
like a street to be walked over."

52 Awake, awake,[e] O Zion,
clothe yourself with strength.[f]
Put on your garments of splendor,[g]
O Jerusalem, the holy city.[h]
The uncircumcised and defiled
will not enter you again.[i]
2 Shake off your dust;[j]
rise up, sit enthroned,
O Jerusalem.
Free yourself from the chains on
your neck,
O captive Daughter of Zion.

3 For this is what the LORD says:

"You were sold for nothing,[k]
and without money[l] you will be
redeemed."

4 For this is what the Sovereign LORD
says:

"At first my people went down to
Egypt[m] to live;
lately, Assyria has oppressed them.

5 "And now what do I have here?" declares the LORD.

"For my people have been taken
away for nothing,
and those who rule them mock,[b]"
declares the LORD.
"And all day long
my name is constantly
blasphemed.[n]

[a] *19* Dead Sea Scrolls, Septuagint, Vulgate and Syriac; Masoretic Text / *how can I* [b] *5* Dead Sea Scrolls and Vulgate; Masoretic Text *wail*

51:21 [y]ver 17; Isa 29:9
51:22 [z]Isa 49:25 [a]ver 17
51:23 [b]Isa 49:26; Jer 25:15-17,26,28; 49:12 [c]Zec 12:2 [d]Jos 10:24
52:1 [e]Isa 51:17 [f]Isa 51:9 [g]Ex 28:2,40; Ps 110:3; Zec 3:4 [h]Ne 11:1; Mt 4:5; Rev 21:2 [i]Na 1:15; Rev 21:27
52:2 [j]Isa 29:4
52:3 [k]Ps 44:12 [l]Isa 45:13
52:4 [m]Ge 46:6
52:5 [n]Eze 36:20; Ro 2:24*

52:6 [o]Isa 49:23

6 Therefore my people will know[o] my name;
therefore in that day they will know
that it is I who foretold it.
Yes, it is I."

DAY 4 FOUR

▸ Love and My Service to Others

Isaiah 52:7

Love motivates the feet of the messenger. The messenger's "going" is just as much a part of the victory of grace as his "telling." Going and telling are a part of the Great Commission of Jesus (see Matthew 28:18–20). Many scholars translate the subjunctive force of the Great Commission this way: "Since you are going into the world anyway, preach the gospel as you go." In other words, since all of us are called by God to tell the story, let us do it as a natural outgrowth of our everyday involvement. Telling and going are a single action.

There is a tale of a grateful convert who walked over 60 miles to bring the missionary who had led him to Christ a simple gift. The gift was not expensive, for the poor convert had little of the world's goods to give.

When the missionary saw the simple gift, she received it with joy, but she offered her convert a small rebuke, "You should not have walked so far to bring me this gift."

"Ah," said the convert, "the walk is part of the gift."

This is the spirit of Isaiah 52:7—the "going" is part of the "telling." Going is part of the spirit that permeates the Scriptures. Indeed, the feet are what bring us to the place where we can tell the old, old story.

Can you recall the one whom God sent to reveal to you the Good News that God in love sent his Son to reconcile us all to him? The story brought to you made you alive in Christ, but in truth the walk—the person coming to you—was a part of the gift. How beautiful the message that redeems us, but how lovely also the obedience of those who have felt compelled to tell us of his love.

To begin a study on the topic of Love, the Definition of God, turn to the home page on page 1033.

7 How beautiful on the mountains
are the feet of those who bring good news,[p]
who proclaim peace,[q]
who bring good tidings,
who proclaim salvation,
who say to Zion,
"Your God reigns!"[r]

52:7 [p]Isa 40:9; Ro 10:15* [q]Na 1:15; Eph 6:15 [r]Ps 93:1

8 Listen! Your watchmen[s] lift up their voices;
together they shout for joy.
When the LORD returns to Zion,
they will see it with their own eyes.

52:8 [s]Isa 62:6

9 Burst into songs of joy[t] together,
you ruins[u] of Jerusalem,
for the LORD has comforted his people,
he has redeemed Jerusalem.[v]

52:9 [t]Ps 98:4 [u]Isa 51:3 [v]Isa 48:20

10 The LORD will lay bare his holy arm
in the sight of all the nations,[w]
and all the ends of the earth will see
the salvation[x] of our God.

52:10 [w]Isa 66:18 [x]Ps 98:2-3; Lk 3:6

11 Depart,[y] depart, go out from there!
Touch no unclean thing![z]
Come out from it and be pure,[a]
you who carry the vessels of the LORD.

52:11 [y]Isa 48:20 [z]Isa 1:16; 2Co 6:17* [a]2Ti 2:19

12 But you will not leave in haste[b]
or go in flight;
for the LORD will go before you,[c]
the God of Israel will be your rear guard.[d]

52:12 [b]Ex 12:11 [c]Mic 2:13 [d]Ex 14:19

The Suffering and Glory of the Servant

13 See, my servant[e] will act wisely[a];
he will be raised and lifted up and highly exalted.[f]

52:13 [e]Isa 42:1 [f]Isa 57:15; Php 2:9

14 Just as there were many who were appalled at him[b]—
his appearance was so disfigured
beyond that of any man
and his form marred beyond
human likeness—
15 so will he sprinkle many nations,[c]
and kings will shut their mouths
because of him.
For what they were not told, they will see,
and what they have not heard,
they will understand.[g]

52:15 [g]Ro 15:21*; Eph 3:4-5

53 Who has believed our message[h]
and to whom has the arm of the LORD been revealed?[i]

53:1 [h]Ro 10:16*; [i]Jn 12:38*

[a]13 Or *will prosper* [b]14 Hebrew *you* [c]15 Hebrew; Septuagint *so will many nations marvel at him*

[2] He grew up before him like a tender shoot,
and like a root out of dry ground.
He had no beauty or majesty to attract us to him,
53:2 [j]Isa 52:14
nothing in his appearance[j] that we should desire him.
[3] He was despised and rejected by men,
53:3 [k]ver 4,10; Lk 18:31-33 [l]Ps 22:6; Jn 1:10-11
a man of sorrows, and familiar with suffering.[k]
Like one from whom men hide their faces
he was despised,[l] and we esteemed him not.
53:4 [m]Mt 8:17* [n]Jn 19:7
[4] Surely he took up our infirmities
and carried our sorrows,[m]
yet we considered him stricken by God,[n]
smitten by him, and afflicted.
53:5 [o]Ro 4:25; 1Co 15:3; Heb 9:28 [p]1Pe 2:24-25
[5] But he was pierced for our transgressions,[o]
he was crushed for our iniquities;
the punishment that brought us peace was upon him,
and by his wounds we are healed.[p]

LOVE

THE WOUNDED HEALER

Isaiah 53:5

Trust no unscarred healer with your own wounds. Healing lesions is the work of love. Only those who've bled know where to apply the tourniquets of grace.

[6] We all, like sheep, have gone astray,
each of us has turned to his own way;
and the LORD has laid on him
the iniquity of us all.
53:7 [q]Mk 14:61
[7] He was oppressed and afflicted,
yet he did not open his mouth;[q]
he was led like a lamb to the slaughter,
and as a sheep before her shearers is silent,
so he did not open his mouth.
[8] By oppression[a] and judgment he was taken away.
And who can speak of his descendants?
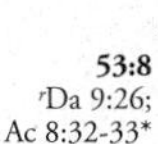
53:8 [r]Da 9:26; Ac 8:32-33*
For he was cut off from the land of the living;[r]
53:8 [s]ver 12
for the transgression[s] of my people
he was stricken.[b]
53:9 [t]Mt 27:57-60 [u]Isa 42:1-3 [v]1Pe 2:22*
[9] He was assigned a grave with the wicked,
and with the rich[t] in his death,
though he had done no violence,[u]
nor was any deceit in his mouth.[v]
53:10 [w]Isa 46:10 [x]ver 5 [y]ver 3 [z]Ps 22:30
[10] Yet it was the LORD's will[w] to crush[x] him and cause him to suffer,[y]
and though the LORD makes[c] his life a guilt offering,
he will see his offspring[z] and prolong his days,
and the will of the LORD will prosper in his hand.
53:11 [a]Jn 10:14-18 [b]Ro 5:18-19
[11] After the suffering[a] of his soul,
he will see the light ⌊of life⌋[d] and be satisfied[e];
by his knowledge[f] my righteous servant will justify[b] many,
and he will bear their iniquities.
53:12 [c]Php 2:9 [d]Mt 26:28, 38,39,42 [e]Mk 15:27*; Lk 22:37*; 23:32
[12] Therefore I will give him a portion among the great,[g][c]
and he will divide the spoils with the strong,[h]
because he poured out his life unto death,[d]
and was numbered with the transgressors.[e]
For he bore the sin of many,
and made intercession for the transgressors.

[a] 8 Or *From arrest* [b] 8 Or *away. / Yet who of his generation considered / that he was cut off from the land of the living / for the transgression of my people, / to whom the blow was due?* [c] 10 Hebrew *though you make* [d] 11 Dead Sea Scrolls (see also Septuagint); Masoretic Text does not have *the light ⌊of life⌋.* [e] 11 Or (with Masoretic Text) *[11] He will see the result of the suffering of his soul / and be satisfied* [f] 11 Or *by knowledge of him* [g] 12 Or *many* [h] 12 Or *numerous*

KINDNESS

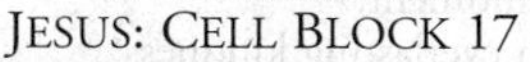

JESUS: CELL BLOCK 17

Isaiah 53:12

Be grateful that Christ died between two immoral and dishonest men, for in your heart you have been immoral—dishonest, too. Thank Christ that he was numbered with the transgressors, for you are a transgressor. It was the convict-Christ who took your sin to judgment.

The Future Glory of Zion

54 "Sing, O barren woman,
you who never bore a child;
burst into song, shout for joy,
you who were never in labor;
because more are the children[f] of the
desolate woman
than of her who has a husband,[g]"
says the LORD.

54:1 [f]Isa 49:20 [g]1Sa 2:5; Gal 4:27*
54:2 [h]Isa 49:19-20 [i]Ex 35:18; 39:40

2 "Enlarge the place of your tent,[h]
stretch your tent curtains wide,
do not hold back;
lengthen your cords,
strengthen your stakes.[i]
3 For you will spread out to the right
and to the left;
your descendants will dispossess
nations
and settle in their desolate[j] cities.

54:3 [j]Isa 49:19

4 "Do not be afraid; you will not
suffer shame.
Do not fear disgrace; you will not
be humiliated.
You will forget the shame of your
youth
and remember no more the
reproach[k] of your
widowhood.
5 For your Maker is your husband[l]—
the LORD Almighty is his name—
the Holy One of Israel is your
Redeemer;[m]
he is called the God of all the
earth.[n]
6 The LORD will call you back[o]
as if you were a wife deserted[p] and
distressed in spirit—
a wife who married young,
only to be rejected," says your
God.
7 "For a brief moment[q] I abandoned
you,
but with deep compassion I will
bring you back.[r]
8 In a surge of anger[s]
I hid my face from you for a
moment,
but with everlasting kindness[t]
I will have compassion on you,"
says the LORD your Redeemer.

9 "To me this is like the days of Noah,
when I swore that the waters
of Noah would never again
cover the earth.[u]
So now I have sworn not to be
angry[v] with you,
never to rebuke you again.
10 Though the mountains be shaken[w]
and the hills be removed,
yet my unfailing love for you will
not be shaken[x]
nor my covenant[y] of peace be
removed,"
says the LORD, who has
compassion[z] on you.

54:4 [k]Isa 51:7
54:5 [l]Jer 3:14 [m]Isa 48:17 [n]Isa 6:3
54:6 [o]Isa 49:14-21 [p]Isa 50:1-2; 62:4,12
54:7 [q]Isa 26:20 [r]Isa 49:18
54:8 [s]Isa 60:10 [t]ver 10
54:9 [u]Ge 8:21 [v]Isa 12:1
54:10 [w]Ps 46:2 [x]Isa 51:6 [y]Ps 89:34 [z]ver 8

11 "O afflicted[a] city, lashed by storms[b]
and not comforted,[c]
I will build you with stones of
turquoise,[a][d]
your foundations[e] with sapphires.[b]
12 I will make your battlements of
rubies,
your gates of sparkling jewels,
and all your walls of precious
stones.
13 All your sons will be taught by the
LORD,[f]
and great will be your children's
peace.[g]
14 In righteousness you will be
established:
Tyranny[h] will be far from you;
you will have nothing to fear.
Terror will be far removed;
it will not come near you.
15 If anyone does attack you, it will not
be my doing;
whoever attacks you will
surrender[i] to you.

16 "See, it is I who created the
blacksmith
who fans the coals into flame
and forges a weapon fit for its
work.
And it is I who have created the
destroyer to work havoc;
17 no weapon forged against you will
prevail,[j]
and you will refute[k] every tongue
that accuses you.
This is the heritage of the servants of
the LORD,
and this is their vindication from
me,"
declares the LORD.

54:11 [a]Isa 14:32 [b]Isa 28:2; 29:6 [c]Isa 51:19 [d]1Ch 29:2; Rev 21:18 [e]Isa 28:16; Rev 21:19-20
54:13 [f]Jn 6:45* [g]Isa 48:18
54:14 [h]Isa 9:4
54:15 [i]Isa 41:11-16
54:17 [j]Isa 29:8 [k]Isa 45:24-25

Invitation to the Thirsty

55 "Come, all you who are
thirsty,[l]
come to the waters;

55:1 [l]Jn 4:14; 7:37

[a] *11* The meaning of the Hebrew for this word is uncertain. [b] *11* Or *lapis lazuli*

and you who have no money,
come, buy[m] and eat!
Come, buy wine and milk[n]
without money and without cost.[o]
2 Why spend money on what is not bread,
and your labor on what does not satisfy?[p]
Listen, listen to me, and eat what is good,[q]
and your soul will delight in the richest of fare.
3 Give ear and come to me;
hear me, that your soul may live.[r]
I will make an everlasting covenant[s] with you,
my faithful love[t] promised to David.[u]
4 See, I have made him a witness to the peoples,
a leader and commander[v] of the peoples.
5 Surely you will summon nations[w] you know not,
and nations that do not know you will hasten to you,
because of the LORD your God,
the Holy One of Israel,
for he has endowed you with splendor."[x]

6 Seek the LORD while he may be found;[y]
call[z] on him while he is near.
7 Let the wicked forsake his way
and the evil man his thoughts.[a]
Let him turn[b] to the LORD, and he will have mercy[c] on him,
and to our God, for he will freely pardon.[d]

8 "For my thoughts are not your thoughts,
neither are your ways my ways,"[e]
declares the LORD.
9 "As the heavens are higher than the earth,[f]
so are my ways higher than your ways
and my thoughts than your thoughts.
10 As the rain[g] and the snow
come down from heaven,
and do not return to it
without watering the earth
and making it bud and flourish,
so that it yields seed for the sower
and bread for the eater,[h]
11 so is my word that goes out from my mouth:
It will not return to me empty,[i]
but will accomplish what I desire
and achieve the purpose[j] for which I sent it.
12 You will go out in joy
and be led forth in peace;[k]
the mountains and hills
will burst into song before you,
and all the trees[l] of the field
will clap their hands.[m]
13 Instead of the thornbush will grow the pine tree,
and instead of briers[n] the myrtle[o] will grow.
This will be for the LORD's renown,[p]
for an everlasting sign,
which will not be destroyed."

Salvation for Others

56 This is what the LORD says:

"Maintain justice[q]
and do what is right,
for my salvation[r] is close at hand
and my righteousness will soon be revealed.
2 Blessed[s] is the man who does this,
the man who holds it fast,
who keeps the Sabbath[t] without desecrating it,
and keeps his hand from doing any evil."

3 Let no foreigner who has bound himself to the LORD say,
"The LORD will surely exclude me from his people."
And let not any eunuch[u] complain,
"I am only a dry tree."

4 For this is what the LORD says:

"To the eunuchs who keep my Sabbaths,
who choose what pleases me
and hold fast to my covenant—
5 to them I will give within my temple and its walls[v]
a memorial and a name
better than sons and daughters;
I will give them an everlasting name
that will not be cut off.[w]
6 And foreigners who bind themselves to the LORD
to serve[x] him,
to love the name of the LORD,
and to worship him,

55:1 [m]La 5:4; Mt 13:44; Rev 3:18 [n]SS 5:1 [o]Hos 14:4; Mt 10:8; Rev 21:6
55:2 [p]Ps 22:26; Ecc 6:2; Hos 8:7 [q]Isa 1:19
55:3 [r]Lev 18:5; Ro 10:5 [s]Isa 61:8 [t]Isa 54:8 [u]Ac 13:34*
55:4 [v]Jer 30:9; Eze 34:23-24
55:5 [w]Isa 49:6 [x]Isa 60:9
55:6 [y]Ps 32:6; Isa 49:8; 2Co 6:1-2 [z]Isa 65:24
55:7 [a]Isa 32:7; 59:7 [b]Isa 44:22 [c]Isa 54:10 [d]Isa 1:18; 40:2
55:8 [e]Isa 53:6
55:9 [f]Ps 103:11
55:10 [g]Isa 30:23 [h]2Co 9:10
55:11 [i]Isa 45:23 [j]Isa 44:26
55:12 [k]Isa 54:10,13 [l]1Ch 16:33 [m]Ps 98:8
55:13 [n]Isa 5:6 [o]Isa 41:19 [p]Isa 63:12
56:1 [q]Isa 1:17 [r]Ps 85:9
56:2 [s]Ps 119:2 [t]Ex 20:8,10; Isa 58:13
56:3 [u]Jer 38:7 fn; Ac 8:27
56:5 [v]Isa 26:1; 60:18 [w]Isa 48:19; 55:13
56:6 [x]Isa 60:7,10; 61:5

all who keep the Sabbath[y] without
desecrating it
and who hold fast to my
covenant—
7 these I will bring to my holy
mountain[z]
and give them joy in my house of
prayer.
Their burnt offerings and sacrifices[a]
will be accepted on my altar;
for my house will be called
a house of prayer for all nations.[b]"[c]
8 The Sovereign LORD declares—
he who gathers the exiles of Israel:
"I will gather[d] still others to them
besides those already gathered."

God's Accusation Against the Wicked

9 Come, all you beasts of the field,[e]
come and devour, all you beasts of
the forest!
10 Israel's watchmen[f] are blind,
they all lack knowledge;
they are all mute dogs,
they cannot bark;
they lie around and dream,
they love to sleep.[g]
11 They are dogs with mighty appetites;
they never have enough.
They are shepherds[h] who lack
understanding;[i]
they all turn to their own way,
each seeks his own gain.[j]
12 "Come," each one cries, "let me get
wine!
Let us drink our fill of beer!
And tomorrow will be like today,
or even far better."[k]

57

The righteous perish,[l]
and no one ponders it in his
heart;[m]
devout men are taken away,
and no one understands
that the righteous are taken away
to be spared from evil.[n]
2 Those who walk uprightly[o]
enter into peace;
they find rest as they lie in death.
3 "But you—come here, you sons of a
sorceress,
you offspring of adulterers[p] and
prostitutes![q]
4 Whom are you mocking?
At whom do you sneer
and stick out your tongue?
Are you not a brood of rebels,
the offspring of liars?
5 You burn with lust among the oaks
and under every spreading tree;[r]
you sacrifice your children[s] in the
ravines
and under the overhanging crags.
6 ⌊The idols⌋[t] among the smooth
stones of the ravines are your
portion;
they, they are your lot.
Yes, to them you have poured out
drink offerings[u]
and offered grain offerings.
In the light of these things, should
I relent?[v]
7 You have made your bed on a high
and lofty hill;[w]
there you went up to offer your
sacrifices.
8 Behind your doors and your
doorposts
you have put your pagan symbols.
Forsaking me, you uncovered your
bed,
you climbed into it and opened it
wide;
you made a pact with those whose
beds you love,[x]
and you looked on their
nakedness.[y]
9 You went to Molech[a] with olive oil
and increased your perfumes.
You sent your ambassadors[b][z] far
away;
you descended to the grave[c] itself!
10 You were wearied by all your ways,
but you would not say, 'It is
hopeless.'[a]
You found renewal of your strength,
and so you did not faint.
11 "Whom have you so dreaded and
feared[b]
that you have been false to me,
and have neither remembered[c] me
nor pondered this in your hearts?
Is it not because I have long been
silent[d]
that you do not fear me?
12 I will expose your righteousness and
your works,[e]
and they will not benefit you.
13 When you cry out[f] for help,
let your collection ⌊of idols⌋ save
you!
The wind will carry all of them off,

[a]9 Or *to the king* [b]9 Or *idols* [c]9 Hebrew *Sheol*

56:6 [y]ver 2,4
56:7 [z]Isa 2:2 [a]Ro 12:1; Heb 13:15 [b]Mt 21:13*; Lk 19:46* [c]Mk 11:17*
56:8 [d]Isa 11:12; 60:3-11; Jn 10:16
56:9 [e]Isa 18:6; Jer 12:9
56:10 [f]Eze 3:17 [g]Na 3:18
56:11 [h]Eze 34:2 [i]Isa 1:3 [j]Isa 57:17; Eze 13:19; Mic 3:11
56:12 [k]Ps 10:6; Lk 12:18-19
57:1 [l]Ps 12:1 [m]Isa 42:25 [n]2Ki 22:20
57:2 [o]Isa 26:7
57:3 [p]Mt 16:4 [q]Isa 1:21
57:5 [r]2Ki 16:4 [s]Lev 18:21; Ps 106:37-38; Eze 16:20
57:6 [t]Jer 3:9 [u]Jer 7:18 [v]Jer 5:9,29; 9:9
57:7 [w]Jer 3:6; Eze 16:16
57:8 [x]Eze 16:26; 23:7 [y]Eze 23:18
57:9 [z]Eze 23:16,40
57:10 [a]Jer 2:25; 18:12
57:11 [b]Pr 29:25 [c]Jer 2:32; 3:21 [d]Ps 50:21
57:12 [e]Isa 29:15; Mic 3:2-4,8
57:13 [f]Jer 22:20; 30:15

a mere breath will blow them
away.
But the man who makes me his
refuge
will inherit the land[g]
and possess my holy mountain."[h]

57:13 [g]Ps 37:9 [h]Isa 65:9-11

Comfort for the Contrite

14 And it will be said:
"Build up, build up, prepare the
road!
Remove the obstacles out of the
way of my people."[i]
15 For this is what the high and lofty[j]
One says—
he who lives forever,[k] whose name
is holy:
"I live in a high and holy place,
but also with him who is contrite[l]
and lowly in spirit,[m]
to revive the spirit of the lowly
and to revive the heart of the
contrite.[n]
16 I will not accuse forever,
nor will I always be angry,[o]
for then the spirit of man would
grow faint before me—
the breath of man that I have
created.
17 I was enraged by his sinful greed;[p]
I punished him, and hid my face
in anger,
yet he kept on in his willful ways.[q]
18 I have seen his ways, but I will heal[r]
him;
I will guide him and restore
comfort[s] to him,
19 creating praise on the lips[t] of the
mourners in Israel.
Peace, peace,[u] to those far and
near,"[v]
says the LORD. "And I will heal
them."
20 But the wicked[w] are like the tossing
sea,
which cannot rest,
whose waves cast up mire and
mud.
21 "There is no peace,"[x] says my God,
"for the wicked."[y]

57:14 [i]Isa 62:10; Jer 18:15
57:15 [j]Isa 52:13 [k]Dt 33:27 [l]Ps 147:3 [m]Ps 34:18; 51:17; Isa 66:2 [n]Isa 61:1
57:16 [o]Ps 85:5; 103:9; Mic 7:18
57:17 [p]Isa 56:11 [q]Isa 1:4
57:18 [r]Isa 30:26 [s]Isa 61:1-3
57:19 [t]Isa 6:7; Heb 13:15 [u]Eph 2:17 [v]Ac 2:39
57:20 [w]Job 18:5-21
57:21 [x]Isa 59:8 [y]Isa 48:22

True Fasting

58 "Shout it aloud,[z] do not hold
back.
Raise your voice like a trumpet.
Declare to my people their
rebellion[a]
and to the house of Jacob their
sins.
2 For day after day they seek[b] me out;
they seem eager to know my ways,
as if they were a nation that does
what is right
and has not forsaken the
commands of its God.
They ask me for just decisions
and seem eager for God to come
near[c] them.
3 'Why have we fasted,'[d] they say,
'and you have not seen it?
Why have we humbled ourselves,
and you have not noticed?'[e]
"Yet on the day of your fasting, you
do as you please[f]
and exploit all your workers.
4 Your fasting ends in quarreling and
strife,[g]
and in striking each other with
wicked fists.
You cannot fast as you do today
and expect your voice to be heard[h]
on high.
5 Is this the kind of fast[i] I have
chosen,
only a day for a man to humble[j]
himself?
Is it only for bowing one's head like
a reed
and for lying on sackcloth and
ashes?[k]
Is that what you call a fast,
a day acceptable to the LORD?
6 "Is not this the kind of fasting I have
chosen:
to loose the chains of injustice[l]
and untie the cords of the yoke,
to set the oppressed[m] free
and break every yoke?
7 Is it not to share your food with the
hungry[n]
and to provide the poor wanderer
with shelter[o]—
when you see the naked, to clothe[p]
him,
and not to turn away from your
own flesh and blood?[q]
8 Then your light will break forth like
the dawn,[r]
and your healing[s] will quickly
appear;
then your righteousness[a] will go
before you,

58:1 [z]Isa 40:6 [a]Isa 48:8
58:2 [b]Isa 48:1; Tit 1:16; Jas 4:8 [c]Isa 29:13
58:3 [d]Lev 16:29 [e]Mal 3:14 [f]Isa 22:13; Zec 7:5-6
58:4 [g]1Ki 21:9-13; Isa 59:6 [h]Isa 59:2
58:5 [i]Zec 7:5 [j]1Ki 21:27 [k]Job 2:8
58:6 [l]Ne 5:10-11 [m]Jer 34:9
58:7 [n]Eze 18:16; Lk 3:11 [o]Isa 16:4; Heb 13:2 [p]Job 31:19-20; Mt 25:36 [q]Ge 29:14; Lk 10:31-32
58:8 [r]Job 11:17 [s]Isa 30:26

[a]8 Or *your righteous One*

and the glory of the LORD will be
your rear guard.[t]
9 Then you will call,[u] and the LORD
will answer;
you will cry for help, and he will
say: Here am I.

"If you do away with the yoke of
oppression,
with the pointing finger[v] and
malicious talk,[w]
10 and if you spend yourselves in behalf
of the hungry
and satisfy the needs of the
oppressed,[x]
then your light[y] will rise in the
darkness,
and your night will become like
the noonday.[z]
11 The LORD will guide you always;
he will satisfy your needs[a] in a
sun-scorched land
and will strengthen your frame.
You will be like a well-watered
garden,[b]
like a spring[c] whose waters never
fail.
12 Your people will rebuild the ancient
ruins[d]
and will raise up the age-old
foundations;[e]
you will be called Repairer of Broken
Walls,
Restorer of Streets with Dwellings.
13 "If you keep your feet from breaking
the Sabbath[f]
and from doing as you please on
my holy day,
if you call the Sabbath a delight[g]
and the LORD's holy day
honorable,
and if you honor it by not going
your own way
and not doing as you please or
speaking idle words,
14 then you will find your joy[h] in the
LORD,
and I will cause you to ride on the
heights[i] of the land
and to feast on the inheritance of
your father Jacob."
The mouth of the LORD
has spoken.[j]

Sin, Confession and Redemption

59 Surely the arm of the LORD is
not too short[k] to save,
nor his ear too dull to hear.[l]

58:8 [t]Ex 14:19
58:9 [u]Ps 50:15 [v]Pr 6:13 [w]Ps 12:2; Isa 59:13
58:10 [x]Dt 15:7-8 [y]Isa 42:16 [z]Job 11:17
58:11 [a]Ps 107:9 [b]SS 4:15 [c]Jn 4:14
58:12 [d]Isa 49:8 [e]Isa 44:28
58:13 [f]Isa 56:2 [g]Ps 84:2,10
58:14 [h]Job 22:26 [i]Dt 32:13 [j]Isa 1:20
59:1 [k]Nu 11:23; Isa 50:2 [l]Isa 58:9; 65:24

2 But your iniquities have separated
you from your God;
your sins have hidden his face from
you,
so that he will not hear.[m]
3 For your hands are stained with
blood,[n]
your fingers with guilt.
Your lips have spoken lies,
and your tongue mutters wicked
things.
4 No one calls for justice;
no one pleads his case with
integrity.
They rely on empty arguments and
speak lies;
they conceive trouble and give
birth to evil.[o]
5 They hatch the eggs of vipers
and spin a spider's web.[p]
Whoever eats their eggs will die,
and when one is broken, an adder
is hatched.
6 Their cobwebs are useless for
clothing;
they cannot cover themselves with
what they make.[q]
Their deeds are evil deeds,
and acts of violence[r] are in their
hands.
7 Their feet rush into sin;
they are swift to shed innocent
blood.[s]
Their thoughts are evil thoughts;[t]
ruin and destruction mark their
ways.[u]
8 The way of peace they do not know;
there is no justice in their paths.
They have turned them into crooked
roads;
no one who walks in them will
know peace.[v]

9 So justice is far from us,
and righteousness does not reach
us.
We look for light, but all is
darkness;[w]
for brightness, but we walk in
deep shadows.
10 Like the blind[x] we grope along the
wall,
feeling our way like men without
eyes.
At midday we stumble[y] as if it were
twilight;
among the strong, we are like the
dead.[z]

59:2 [m]Isa 1:15; 58:4
59:3 [n]Isa 1:15
59:4 [o]Job 15:35; Ps 7:14
59:5 [p]Job 8:14
59:6 [q]Isa 28:20 [r]Isa 58:4
59:7 [s]Pr 6:17 [t]Mk 7:21-22 [u]Ro 3:15-17*
59:8 [v]Isa 57:21; Lk 1:79
59:9 [w]Isa 5:30; 8:20
59:10 [x]Dt 28:29 [y]Isa 8:15 [z]La 3:6

[11]We all growl like bears;
we moan mournfully like doves.[a]
We look for justice, but find none;
for deliverance, but it is far away.
[12]For our offenses[b] are many in your sight,
and our sins testify[c] against us.
Our offenses are ever with us,
and we acknowledge our iniquities:
[13]rebellion and treachery against the LORD,
turning our backs[d] on our God,
fomenting oppression[e] and revolt,
uttering lies[f] our hearts have conceived.
[14]So justice is driven back,
and righteousness[g] stands at a distance;
truth[h] has stumbled in the streets,
honesty cannot enter.
[15]Truth is nowhere to be found,
and whoever shuns evil becomes a prey.

The LORD looked and was displeased
that there was no justice.
[16]He saw that there was no one,[i]
he was appalled that there was no one to intervene;
so his own arm worked salvation[j] for him,
and his own righteousness sustained him.
[17]He put on righteousness as his breastplate,[k]
and the helmet[l] of salvation on his head;
he put on the garments[m] of vengeance
and wrapped himself in zeal[n] as in a cloak.
[18]According to what they have done,
so will he repay
wrath to his enemies
and retribution to his foes;
he will repay the islands their due.
[19]From the west,[o] men will fear the name of the LORD,
and from the rising of the sun,[p]
they will revere his glory.
For he will come like a pent-up flood
that the breath of the LORD drives along.[a]

59:11 [a]Isa 38:14; Eze 7:16
59:12 [b]Ezr 9:6 [c]Isa 3:9
59:13 [d]Pr 30:9; Mt 10:33; Tit 1:16 [e]Isa 5:7 [f]Mk 7:21-22
59:14 [g]Isa 1:21 [h]Isa 48:1
59:16 [i]Isa 41:28 [j]Ps 98:1; Isa 63:5
59:17 [k]Eph 6:14 [l]Eph 6:17; 1Th 5:8 [m]Isa 63:3 [n]Isa 9:7
59:19 [o]Isa 49:12 [p]Ps 113:3

[20]"The Redeemer will come to Zion,
to those in Jacob who repent of their sins,"[q]
declares the LORD.

[21]"As for me, this is my covenant with
them," says the LORD. "My Spirit,[r]
who is on you, and my words that I
have put in your mouth will not depart
from your mouth, or from the mouths
of your children, or from the mouths
of their descendants from this time on
and forever," says the LORD.

The Glory of Zion

60 "Arise,[s] shine, for your light[t] has come,
and the glory of the LORD rises upon you.

JOY

THE GLORIOUS ANNOUNCEMENT

Isaiah 60:1

Arise! Shine! Jesus has conquered darkness. Find for me a single shadow in all of heaven, and the Scriptures may be proclaimed a lie.

[2]See, darkness covers the earth
and thick darkness[u] is over the peoples,
but the LORD rises upon you
and his glory appears over you.
[3]Nations[v] will come to your light,
and kings[w] to the brightness of your dawn.
[4]"Lift up your eyes and look about you:
All assemble[x] and come to you;
your sons come from afar,
and your daughters[y] are carried on the arm.[z]
[5]Then you will look and be radiant,
your heart will throb and swell with joy;
the wealth on the seas will be brought to you,
to you the riches of the nations will come.
[6]Herds of camels will cover your land,
young camels of Midian[a] and Ephah.[b]
And all from Sheba[c] will come,
bearing gold and incense[d]

[a]19 Or *When the enemy comes in like a flood, / the Spirit of the LORD will put him to flight*

59:20 [q]Ac 2:38-39; Ro 11:26-27*
59:21 [r]Isa 11:2; 44:3
60:1 [s]Isa 52:2 [t]Eph 5:14
60:2 [u]Jer 13:16; Col 1:13
60:3 [v]Isa 45:14; Rev 21:24 [w]Isa 49:23
60:4 [x]Isa 11:12 [y]Isa 43:6 [z]Isa 49:20-22
60:6 [a]Ge 25:2 [b]Ge 25:4 [c]Ps 72:10 [d]Isa 43:23; Mt 2:11

and proclaiming the praise[e] of the LORD.
7 All Kedar's[f] flocks will be gathered to you,
the rams of Nebaioth will serve you;
they will be accepted as offerings on my altar,
and I will adorn my glorious temple.[g]

8 "Who are these[h] that fly along like clouds,
like doves to their nests?
9 Surely the islands[i] look to me;
in the lead are the ships of Tarshish,[a][j]
bringing[k] your sons from afar,
with their silver and gold,
to the honor of the LORD your God,
the Holy One of Israel,
for he has endowed you with splendor.[l]

10 "Foreigners[m] will rebuild your walls,
and their kings[n] will serve you.
Though in anger I struck you,
in favor I will show you compassion.[o]
11 Your gates[p] will always stand open,
they will never be shut, day or night,
so that men may bring you the wealth of the nations[q]—
their kings[r] led in triumphal procession.
12 For the nation or kingdom that will not serve[s] you will perish;
it will be utterly ruined.

13 "The glory of Lebanon[t] will come to you,
the pine, the fir and the cypress together,[u]
to adorn the place of my sanctuary;
and I will glorify the place of my feet.[v]
14 The sons of your oppressors[w] will come bowing before you;
all who despise you will bow down[x] at your feet
and will call you the City of the LORD,
Zion[y] of the Holy One of Israel.

15 "Although you have been forsaken[z] and hated,
with no one traveling[a] through,
I will make you the everlasting pride[b]
and the joy[c] of all generations.
16 You will drink the milk of nations
and be nursed[d] at royal breasts.
Then you will know that I, the LORD, am your Savior,
your Redeemer,[e] the Mighty One of Jacob.
17 Instead of bronze I will bring you gold,
and silver in place of iron.
Instead of wood I will bring you bronze,
and iron in place of stones.
I will make peace your governor
and righteousness your ruler.
18 No longer will violence be heard in your land,
nor ruin or destruction within your borders,
but you will call your walls Salvation[f]
and your gates Praise.
19 The sun will no more be your light by day,
nor will the brightness of the moon shine on you,
for the LORD will be your everlasting light,[g]
and your God will be your glory.[h]
20 Your sun[i] will never set again,
and your moon will wane no more;
the LORD will be your everlasting light,
and your days of sorrow[j] will end.
21 Then will all your people be righteous[k]
and they will possess[l] the land forever.
They are the shoot I have planted,[m]
the work of my hands,[n]
for the display of my splendor.[o]
22 The least of you will become a thousand,
the smallest a mighty nation.
I am the LORD;
in its time I will do this swiftly."

The Year of the LORD's Favor

61 The Spirit[p] of the Sovereign LORD is on me,
because the LORD has anointed[q] me
to preach good news to the poor.[r]

[a]9 Or *the trading ships*

60:6 [e]Isa 42:10
60:7 [f]Ge 25:13 [g]ver 13; Hag 2:3,7,9
60:8 [h]Isa 49:21
60:9 [i]Isa 11:11 [j]Isa 2:16 fn [k]Isa 14:2; 43:6 [l]Isa 55:5
60:10 [m]Isa 14:1-2 [n]Isa 49:23; Rev 21:24 [o]Isa 54:8
60:11 [p]ver 18; Isa 62:10; Rev 21:25 [q]ver 5; Rev 21:26 [r]Ps 149:8
60:12 [s]Isa 14:2
60:13 [t]Isa 35:2 [u]Isa 41:19 [v]1Ch 28:2; Ps 132:7
60:14 [w]Isa 14:2 [x]Isa 49:23; Rev 3:9 [y]Heb 12:22
60:15 [z]Isa 1:7-9; 6:12 [a]Isa 33:8 [b]Isa 4:2 [c]Isa 65:18
60:16 [d]Isa 49:23; 66:11,12 [e]Isa 59:20
60:18 [f]Isa 26:1
60:19 [g]Rev 22:5 [h]Zec 2:5; Rev 21:23
60:20 [i]Isa 30:26 [j]Isa 35:10
60:21 [k]Rev 21:27 [l]Ps 37:11,22; Isa 57:13; 61:7 [m]Mt 15:13 [n]Isa 19:25; 29:23; Eph 2:10 [o]Isa 52:1
61:1 [p]Isa 11:2 [q]Ps 45:7 [r]Mt 11:5; Lk 7:22

61:1 [s]Isa 57:15 [t]Isa 42:7; 49:9

He has sent me to bind up[s] the
brokenhearted,
to proclaim freedom for the
captives[t]
and release from darkness for the
prisoners,[a]
2 to proclaim the year of the LORD's
favor[u]
and the day of vengeance[v] of our
God,
to comfort[w] all who mourn,

61:2 [u]Isa 49:8; Lk 4:18-19* [v]Isa 34:8 [w]Isa 57:18; Mt 5:4

DAY 4 FOUR

▸ LOVE AND MY SERVICE TO OTHERS

Isaiah 61:1–3

Is it not altogether wonderful that God, who is secure in the heavens, should care about things so remote and far away as earth? Is it not amazing that God, who transcends flesh and has no nervous system, should care about earthly preoccupations: pain, death and hunger? Isn't it wonderful that Jesus became a human being? He had a digestive system, a nervous system and a circulatory system. He was able to bleed and thereby redeem us. You can trust a God who willingly made it possible for himself to bleed, so that no one could accuse him of failing to understand human existence.

God's love is his passion for his world. He serves prisoners, the poor and the brokenhearted. God has made it possible for everyone to receive the Good News. Of course the truth is that we are the news-carriers; we must make sure that the Word gets out and that no one dies not having heard of God's love. This is how we serve the world he loves. We're the information people, the worldwide-webbers, the publishers of the worldwide hope.

We are the trustees of the most remarkable news: God, for no reason that profits himself, actually cares about us. This news is so good that, without it, the bad news would be very bad: The universe would be a madhouse without scheme or reason. Believe not only because there is nothing else worthy of trust. Believe it because it is not only true, but it is the most beautiful truth that can be imagined.

To begin a study on the topic of Love, God's Passion for His World, turn to the home page on page 1253.

3 and provide for those who grieve
in Zion—
to bestow on them a crown of
beauty
instead of ashes,
the oil of gladness
instead of mourning,
and a garment of praise
instead of a spirit of despair.
They will be called oaks of
righteousness,
a planting of the LORD
for the display of his splendor.[x]

61:3 [x]Isa 60:20-21

4 They will rebuild the ancient ruins[y]
and restore the places long
devastated;
they will renew the ruined cities
that have been devastated for
generations.

61:4 [y]Isa 49:8; Eze 36:33; Am 9:14

5 Aliens[z] will shepherd your flocks;
foreigners will work your fields
and vineyards.

61:5 [z]Isa 14:1-2

6 And you will be called priests[a] of the
LORD,
you will be named ministers of
our God.
You will feed on the wealth[b] of
nations,
and in their riches you will boast.

61:6 [a]Ex 19:6; 1Pe 2:5 [b]Isa 60:11

7 Instead of their shame
my people will receive a double[c]
portion,
and instead of disgrace
they will rejoice in their
inheritance;
and so they will inherit a double
portion in their land,
and everlasting joy will be theirs.

61:7 [c]Isa 40:2; Zec 9:12

8 "For I, the LORD, love justice;[d]
I hate robbery and iniquity.
In my faithfulness I will reward them
and make an everlasting covenant[e]
with them.
9 Their descendants will be known
among the nations
and their offspring among the
peoples.
All who see them will acknowledge
that they are a people the LORD
has blessed."

61:8 [d]Ps 11:7; Isa 5:16 [e]Isa 55:3

10 I delight greatly in the LORD;
my soul rejoices[f] in my God.
For he has clothed me with garments
of salvation

61:10 [f]Isa 25:9; Hab 3:18

[a]*1* Hebrew; Septuagint *the blind*

61:10 [g]Ps 132:9; Isa 52:1 [h]Isa 49:18; Rev 21:2

and arrayed me in a robe of
righteousness,[g]
as a bridegroom adorns his head like
a priest,
and as a bride[h] adorns herself with
her jewels.
11 For as the soil makes the sprout
come up
and a garden causes seeds to grow,
so the Sovereign LORD will make
righteousness[i] and praise
spring up before all nations.

61:11 [i]Ps 85:11

Zion's New Name

62 For Zion's sake I will not keep
silent,
for Jerusalem's sake I will not
remain quiet,
till her righteousness[j] shines out like
the dawn,
her salvation like a blazing torch.
2 The nations[k] will see your
righteousness,
and all kings your glory;
you will be called by a new name[l]
that the mouth of the LORD will
bestow.
3 You will be a crown[m] of splendor in
the LORD's hand,
a royal diadem in the hand of
your God.
4 No longer will they call you
Deserted,[n]
or name your land Desolate.
But you will be called Hephzibah,[a]
and your land Beulah[b];
for the LORD will take delight[o] in
you,
and your land will be married.[p]
5 As a young man marries a maiden,
so will your sons[c] marry you;
as a bridegroom rejoices over his
bride,
so will your God rejoice[q] over you.
6 I have posted watchmen[r] on your
walls, O Jerusalem;
they will never be silent day or
night.
You who call on the LORD,
give yourselves no rest,
7 and give him no rest[s] till he
establishes Jerusalem
and makes her the praise of the
earth.
8 The LORD has sworn by his right
hand
and by his mighty arm:

62:1 [j]Isa 1:26
62:2 [k]Isa 52:10; 60:3 [l]ver 4,12
62:3 [m]Isa 28:5; Zec 9:16; 1Th 2:19
62:4 [n]Isa 54:6 [o]Jer 32:41; Zep 3:17 [p]Jer 3:14; Hos 2:19
62:5 [q]Isa 65:19
62:6 [r]Isa 52:8; Eze 3:17
62:7 [s]Mt 15:21-28; Lk 18:1-8

"Never again will I give your grain[t]
as food for your enemies,
and never again will foreigners drink
the new wine
for which you have toiled;
9 but those who harvest it will eat it
and praise the LORD,
and those who gather the grapes will
drink it
in the courts of my sanctuary."
10 Pass through, pass through the
gates![u]
Prepare the way for the people.
Build up, build up the highway![v][w]
Remove the stones.
Raise a banner[x] for the nations.
11 The LORD has made proclamation
to the ends of the earth:
"Say to the Daughter of Zion,[y]
'See, your Savior comes![z]
See, his reward is with him,
and his recompense accompanies
him.'"[a]
12 They will be called[b] the Holy
People,[c]
the Redeemed[d] of the LORD;
and you will be called Sought After,
the City No Longer Deserted.[e]

62:8 [t]Dt 28:30-33; Isa 1:7; Jer 5:17
62:10 [u]Isa 60:11 [v]Isa 57:14 [w]Isa 11:16 [x]Isa 11:10
62:11 [y]Zec 9:9; Mt 21:5 [z]Rev 22:12 [a]Isa 40:10
62:12 [b]ver 4 [c]1Pe 2:9 [d]Isa 35:9 [e]Isa 42:16

God's Day of Vengeance and Redemption

63 Who is this coming from
Edom,
from Bozrah,[f] with his garments
stained crimson?
Who is this, robed in splendor,
striding forward in the greatness
of his strength?
"It is I, speaking in righteousness,
mighty to save."[g]
2 Why are your garments red,
like those of one treading the
winepress?
3 "I have trodden the winepress[h]
alone;
from the nations no one was with
me.
I trampled them in my anger
and trod them down in my wrath;[i]
their blood spattered my garments,[j]
and I stained all my clothing.
4 For the day of vengeance was in my
heart,

63:1 [f]Am 1:12 [g]Zep 3:17
63:3 [h]Rev 14:20; 19:15 [i]Isa 22:5 [j]Rev 19:13

[a]4 *Hephzibah* means *my delight is in her.* [b]4 *Beulah* means *married.* [c]5 Or *Builder*

and the year of my redemption
has come.
[63:5 k Isa 41:28]
5 I looked, but there was no one[k] to
help,
I was appalled that no one gave
support;
so my own arm[l] worked salvation for
me,
and my own wrath sustained me.[m]
[63:5 l Ps 44:3; 98:1 m Isa 59:16]
6 I trampled the nations in my anger;
in my wrath I made them drunk[n]
and poured their blood[o] on the
ground."
[63:6 n Isa 29:9 o Isa 34:3]

DAY 5 FIVE

Kindness and Its Place in My Personal Worship

Isaiah 63:7

Isaiah saw that we couldn't enter into a time of worship without the enduring presence of God's kindness beckoning us in. And sooner or later when we enter into our quiet adoration of Jesus on our own, we stop—one on one—at the cross. When we see his nail-scarred hands, the kindness that leads us to salvation now causes our quiet personal worship experience to soar.

Caught up in such quiet-time rapture, I wrote in my journal in 1986:

Hands. Broken, leathery, big and tough,
And weathered, hammer-gripping, sweating fists,
Quite used to driving nails into the rough
And bronze, blue-bruised where once the iron missed.
A hand's a thing of beauty, in the eye
Of those who, vision-trained, can pierce the skin
To see the steel of sturdy bones laid white,
And fragile tendons, filament and thin.

The riddle of the nails I understand—
How leathered calluses breed tougher skin,
Hiding tiny porcelain machines within
The flesh of your strong, injured, suff'ring hands.

Your hammer-wielding fists at last grew frail
And beckoned to each palm a killing nail.

It is altogether fitting that our quiet time should end here, at the cross. Now we experience for ourselves just how far the kindness of God goes. It sees our lostness, considers our unworthiness and dies for us anyway. Hallelujah!

To begin a study on the topic of Kindness in the Time of Need, turn to the home page on page 246.

Praise and Prayer

7 I will tell of the kindnesses[p] of the
LORD,
the deeds for which he is to be
praised,
according to all the LORD has
done for us—
yes, the many good things he has
done
for the house of Israel,
according to his compassion[q] and
many kindnesses.
[63:7 p Isa 54:8 q Ps 51:1; Eph 2:4]
8 He said, "Surely they are my people,[r]
sons who will not be false to me";
and so he became their Savior.
[63:8 r Isa 51:4]
9 In all their distress he too was
distressed,
and the angel of his presence[s]
saved them.
In his love and mercy he redeemed[t]
them;
he lifted them up and carried[u]
them
all the days of old.
[63:9 s Ex 33:14 t Dt 7:7-8 u Dt 1:31]
10 Yet they rebelled[v]
and grieved his Holy Spirit.[w]
So he turned and became their
enemy[x]
and he himself fought against
them.
[63:10 v Ps 78:40 w Ps 51:11; Ac 7:51; Eph 4:30 x Ps 106:40]

11 Then his people recalled[a] the days of
old,
the days of Moses and his
people—
where is he who brought them
through the sea,[y]
with the shepherd of his flock?
Where is he who set
his Holy Spirit[z] among them,
[63:11 y Ex 14:22,30 z Nu 11:17]
12 who sent his glorious arm of power
to be at Moses' right hand,
who divided the waters[a] before
them,
to gain for himself everlasting
renown,
[63:12 a Ex 14:21-22; Isa 11:15]
13 who led[b] them through the depths?
Like a horse in open country,
they did not stumble;[c]
[63:13 b Dt 32:12 c Jer 31:9]

[a] 11 Or *But may he recall*

[14]like cattle that go down to the plain,
they were given rest by the Spirit
of the LORD.
This is how you guided your people
to make for yourself a glorious
name.

DAY 3 THREE

▸ GOODNESS AND MY RELATIONSHIP WITH CHRIST

Isaiah 64:4–7

The reason for loving goodness and for championing the commandments should occur to us when reading Isaiah 64:6, "All our righteous acts are like filthy rags." Isaiah correctly pictures our culture, as well as his own, when he says, "No one calls on your name or strives to lay hold of you; for you have hidden your face from us and made us waste away because of our sins" (v. 7).

Our goodness must come from our contentment with the commandments. We must open our hearts to God when he says, "I am the LORD your God, who brought you out of Egypt, out of the land of slavery. You shall have no other gods before me" (Exodus 20:2–3). We are truly a nation in need of falling in love with God's commandments. We love fun. We love indulgence. We love comfort. We love marketing lies to pad our sales charts. We love fast foods, fast banks, fast drugs, the fast lane. But we do not love God's laws. And nations that do not love his laws will, in time, be consumed by lawlessness.

Isaiah saw the Israelites' hypocritical "righteous acts" as "filthy rags." Do we see sin in this vile way? It sometimes seems that we do not even believe in sin anymore. We believe in "live and let live." We believe in "safe sex" and "safe cars," and we see things that are unsafe as sin. We have lost our contempt for sin. We not only fail to honor the Ten Commandments, we don't even know what they are. We need to return to a goodness based on a love of God's law and close walk with Jesus Christ. If we follow Christ, if we make the choices he would make and choose the path he would follow, we will be drawn ever closer to the goodness of God.

To begin a study on the topic of Goodness, a Contentment With the Commandments, turn to the home page on page 1233.

[15]Look down from heaven[d] and see
from your lofty throne,[e] holy and
glorious.
Where are your zeal[f] and your
might?
Your tenderness and compassion[g]
are withheld from us.
[16]But you are our Father,
though Abraham does not know
us
or Israel acknowledge[h] us;
you, O LORD, are our Father,
our Redeemer[i] from of old is your
name.
[17]Why, O LORD, do you make us
wander from your ways
and harden our hearts so we do
not revere[j] you?
Return[k] for the sake of your servants,
the tribes that are your
inheritance.
[18]For a little while your people
possessed your holy place,
but now our enemies have
trampled down your
sanctuary.[l]
[19]We are yours from of old;
but you have not ruled over them,
they have not been called by your
name.[a]

64 Oh, that you would rend the
heavens[m] and come down,[n]
that the mountains[o] would
tremble before you!
[2]As when fire sets twigs ablaze
and causes water to boil,
come down to make your name
known to your enemies
and cause the nations to quake[p]
before you!
[3]For when you did awesome[q] things
that we did not expect,
you came down, and the
mountains trembled before
you.
[4]Since ancient times no one has
heard,
no ear has perceived,
no eye has seen any God besides
you,
who acts on behalf of those who
wait for him.[r]
[5]You come to the help of those who
gladly do right,[s]

63:15 [d]Dt 26:15; Ps 80:14 [e]Ps 123:1 [f]Isa 9:7; 26:11 [g]Jer 31:20; Hos 11:8
63:16 [h]Job 14:21 [i]Isa 41:14; 44:6
63:17 [j]Isa 29:13 [k]Nu 10:36
63:18 [l]Ps 74:3-8
64:1 [m]Ps 18:9; 144:5 [n]Mic 1:3 [o]Ex 19:18
64:2 [p]Ps 99:1; Jer 5:22; 33:9
64:3 [q]Ps 65:5
64:4 [r]Isa 30:18; 1Co 2:9*
64:5 [s]Isa 26:8

[a]19 Or *We are like those you have never ruled, / like those never called by your name*

who remember your ways.
But when we continued to sin
against them,
you were angry.
How then can we be saved?
6 All of us have become like one who
is unclean,
and all our righteous[t] acts are like
filthy rags;
we all shrivel up like a leaf,[u]
and like the wind our sins sweep
us away.
7 No one[v] calls on your name
or strives to lay hold of you;
for you have hidden[w] your face from
us
and made us waste away[x] because
of our sins.
8 Yet, O LORD, you are our Father.[y]
We are the clay, you are the
potter;[z]
we are all the work of your hand.
9 Do not be angry[a] beyond measure,
O LORD;
do not remember our sins[b]
forever.
Oh, look upon us, we pray,
for we are all your people.
10 Your sacred cities have become a
desert;
even Zion is a desert, Jerusalem a
desolation.
11 Our holy and glorious temple,[c]
where our fathers praised
you,
has been burned with fire,
and all that we treasured[d] lies in
ruins.
12 After all this, O LORD, will you hold
yourself back?[e]
Will you keep silent[f] and punish
us beyond measure?

Judgment and Salvation

65 "I revealed myself to those who
did not ask for me;
I was found by those who did not
seek me.[g]
To a nation[h] that did not call on my
name,
I said, 'Here am I, here am I.'
2 All day long I have held out my
hands
to an obstinate people,[i]
who walk in ways not good,
pursuing their own
imaginations[j]—
3 a people who continually provoke
me
to my very face,[k]
offering sacrifices in gardens[l]
and burning incense on altars of
brick;
4 who sit among the graves
and spend their nights keeping
secret vigil;
who eat the flesh of pigs,[m]
and whose pots hold broth of
unclean meat;
5 who say, 'Keep away; don't come
near me,
for I am too sacred[n] for you!'
Such people are smoke in my
nostrils,
a fire that keeps burning all day.
6 "See, it stands written before me:
I will not keep silent[o] but will pay
back[p] in full;
I will pay it back into their
laps[q]—
7 both your sins[r] and the sins of your
fathers,"[s]
says the LORD.
"Because they burned sacrifices on
the mountains
and defied me on the hills,[t]
I will measure into their laps
the full payment for their former
deeds."
8 This is what the LORD says:

"As when juice is still found in a
cluster of grapes
and men say, 'Don't destroy it,
there is yet some good in it,'
so will I do in behalf of my servants;
I will not destroy them all.
9 I will bring forth descendants[u] from
Jacob,
and from Judah those who will
possess[v] my mountains;
my chosen people will inherit them,
and there will my servants live.[w]
10 Sharon[x] will become a pasture for
flocks,
and the Valley of Achor[y] a resting
place for herds,
for my people who seek[z] me.
11 "But as for you who forsake[a] the
LORD
and forget my holy mountain,
who spread a table for Fortune
and fill bowls of mixed wine for
Destiny,

64:6 [t]Isa 46:12; 48:1 [u]Ps 90:5-6
64:7 [v]Isa 59:4 [w]Dt 31:18; Isa 1:15; 54:8 [x]Isa 9:18
64:8 [y]Isa 63:16 [z]Isa 29:16
64:9 [a]Isa 57:17; 60:10 [b]Isa 43:25
64:11 [c]Ps 74:3-7 [d]La 1:7,10
64:12 [e]Ps 74:10-11; Isa 42:14 [f]Ps 83:1
65:1 [g]Hos 1:10; Ro 9:24-26; 10:20* [h]Eph 2:12
65:2 [i]Isa 1:2,23; Ro 10:21* [j]Ps 81:11-12; Isa 66:18
65:3 [k]Job 1:11 [l]Isa 1:29
65:4 [m]Lev 11:7
65:5 [n]Mt 9:11; Lk 7:39; 18:9-12
65:6 [o]Ps 50:3 [p]Jer 16:18 [q]Ps 79:12
65:7 [r]Isa 22:14 [s]Ex 20:5 [t]Isa 57:7
65:9 [u]Isa 45:19 [v]Am 9:11-15 [w]Isa 32:18
65:10 [x]Isa 35:2 [y]Jos 7:26 [z]Isa 51:1
65:11 [a]Dt 29:24-25; Isa 1:28

12 I will destine you for the sword,[b]
and you will all bend down for the slaughter;
for I called but you did not answer,[c]
I spoke but you did not listen.[d]
You did evil in my sight
and chose what displeases me."

13 Therefore this is what the Sovereign LORD says:

"My servants will eat,[e]
but you will go hungry;
my servants will drink,
but you will go thirsty;[f]
my servants will rejoice,
but you will be put to shame.[g]
14 My servants will sing
out of the joy of their hearts,
but you will cry out[h]
from anguish of heart
and wail in brokenness of spirit.
15 You will leave your name
to my chosen ones as a curse;[i]
the Sovereign LORD will put you to death,
but to his servants he will give another name.
16 Whoever invokes a blessing in the land
will do so by the God of truth;[j]
he who takes an oath in the land
will swear[k] by the God of truth.
For the past troubles will be forgotten
and hidden from my eyes.

New Heavens and a New Earth

17 "Behold, I will create
new heavens and a new earth.[l]
The former things will not be remembered,[m]
nor will they come to mind.
18 But be glad and rejoice[n] forever
in what I will create,
for I will create Jerusalem to be a delight
and its people a joy.
19 I will rejoice[o] over Jerusalem
and take delight in my people;
the sound of weeping and of crying[p]
will be heard in it no more.

20 "Never again will there be in it
an infant who lives but a few days,
or an old man who does not live out his years;[q]
he who dies at a hundred
will be thought a mere youth;
he who fails to reach[a] a hundred
will be considered accursed.
21 They will build houses[r] and dwell in them;
they will plant vineyards and eat their fruit.[s]
22 No longer will they build houses and others live in them,
or plant and others eat.
For as the days of a tree,[t]
so will be the days[u] of my people;
my chosen ones will long enjoy
the works of their hands.
23 They will not toil in vain
or bear children doomed to misfortune;
for they will be a people blessed[v] by the LORD,
they and their descendants[w] with them.
24 Before they call[x] I will answer;
while they are still speaking[y] I will hear.
25 The wolf and the lamb[z] will feed together,
and the lion will eat straw like the ox,
but dust will be the serpent's[a] food.
They will neither harm nor destroy
on all my holy mountain,"
says the LORD.

Judgment and Hope

66 This is what the LORD says:

"Heaven is my throne,[b]
and the earth is my footstool.[c]
Where is the house[d] you will build for me?
Where will my resting place be?
2 Has not my hand made all these things,[e]
and so they came into being?"
declares the LORD.

"This is the one I esteem:
he who is humble and contrite in spirit,[f]
and trembles at my word.[g]
3 But whoever sacrifices a bull[h]
is like one who kills a man,
and whoever offers a lamb,
like one who breaks a dog's neck;
whoever makes a grain offering
is like one who presents pig's blood,

[a]20 Or / *the sinner who reaches*

65:12 [b]Isa 27:1 [c]Pr 1:24-25; Isa 41:28; 66:4 [d]2Ch 36:15-16; Jer 7:13
65:13 [e]Isa 1:19 [f]Isa 41:17 [g]Isa 44:9
65:14 [h]Mt 8:12; Lk 13:28
65:15 [i]Zec 8:13
65:16 [j]Ps 31:5 [k]Isa 19:18
65:17 [l]Isa 66:22; 2Pe 3:13 [m]Isa 43:18; Jer 3:16
65:18 [n]Ps 98:1-9; Isa 25:9
65:19 [o]Isa 35:10; 62:5 [p]Isa 25:8; Rev 7:17
65:20 [q]Ecc 8:13
65:21 [r]Isa 32:18 [s]Isa 37:30; Am 9:14
65:22 [t]Ps 92:12-14 [u]Ps 21:4; 91:16
65:23 [v]Dt 28:3-12; Isa 61:9 [w]Ac 2:39
65:24 [x]Isa 55:6 [y]Da 9:20-23; 10:12
65:25 [z]Isa 11:6 [a]Ge 3:14; Mic 7:17
66:1 [b]Mt 23:22 [c]1Ki 8:27; Mt 5:34-35 [d]2Sa 7:7; Jn 4:20-21; Ac 7:49*; 17:24
66:2 [e]Isa 40:26; Ac 7:50* [f]Isa 57:15; Mt 5:3-4; Lk 18:13-14 [g]Ezr 9:4
66:3 [h]Isa 1:11

and whoever burns memorial
incense,[i]
like one who worships an idol.
They have chosen their own ways,[j]
and their souls delight in their
abominations;
4 so I also will choose harsh treatment
for them
and will bring upon them what
they dread.[k]
For when I called, no one answered,[l]
when I spoke, no one listened.
They did evil[m] in my sight
and chose what displeases me."[n]

66:3 [i]Lev 2:2 [j]Isa 57:17
66:4 [k]Pr 10:24 [l]Pr 1:24; Jer 7:13 [m]2Ki 21:2,4,6 [n]Isa 65:12

5 Hear the word of the LORD,
you who tremble at his word:
"Your brothers who hate[o] you,
and exclude you because of my
name, have said,
'Let the LORD be glorified,
that we may see your joy!'
Yet they will be put to shame.[p]
6 Hear that uproar from the city,
hear that noise from the temple!
It is the sound of the LORD
repaying[q] his enemies all they
deserve.

66:5 [o]Ps 38:20; Isa 60:15 [p]Lk 13:17
66:6 [q]Isa 65:6; Joel 3:7

7 "Before she goes into labor,[r]
she gives birth;
before the pains come upon her,
she delivers a son.[s]
8 Who has ever heard of such a thing?
Who has ever seen[t] such things?
Can a country be born in a day
or a nation be brought forth in a
moment?
Yet no sooner is Zion in labor
than she gives birth to her
children.
9 Do I bring to the moment of birth[u]
and not give delivery?" says the
LORD.
"Do I close up the womb
when I bring to delivery?" says
your God.
10 "Rejoice[v] with Jerusalem and be glad
for her,
all you who love[w] her;
rejoice greatly with her,
all you who mourn over her.
11 For you will nurse[x] and be satisfied
at her comforting breasts;
you will drink deeply
and delight in her overflowing
abundance."

66:7 [r]Isa 54:1 [s]Rev 12:5
66:8 [t]Isa 64:4
66:9 [u]Isa 37:3
66:10 [v]Dt 32:43; Ro 15:10 [w]Ps 26:8
66:11 [x]Isa 60:16

12 For this is what the LORD says:

"I will extend peace to her like a
river,[y]
and the wealth[z] of nations like a
flooding stream;
you will nurse and be carried[a] on her
arm
and dandled on her knees.
13 As a mother comforts her child,
so will I comfort[b] you;
and you will be comforted over
Jerusalem."

66:12 [y]Isa 48:18 [z]Ps 72:3; Isa 60:5; 61:6 [a]Isa 60:4
66:13 [b]Isa 40:1; 2Co 1:4

14 When you see this, your heart will
rejoice
and you will flourish like grass;
the hand of the LORD will be made
known to his servants,
but his fury[c] will be shown to his
foes.
15 See, the LORD is coming with fire,
and his chariots[d] are like a
whirlwind;
he will bring down his anger with
fury,
and his rebuke[e] with flames of fire.
16 For with fire[f] and with his sword[g]
the LORD will execute judgment
upon all men,
and many will be those slain by
the LORD.

66:14 [c]Isa 10:5
66:15 [d]Ps 68:17 [e]Ps 9:5
66:16 [f]Isa 30:30 [g]Isa 27:1

17 "Those who consecrate and purify
themselves to go into the gardens,[h] following the one in the midst of[a] those
who eat the flesh of pigs[i] and rats
and other abominable things—they will
meet their end[j] together," declares the
LORD.
18 "And I, because of their actions and
their imaginations, am about to come[b]
and gather all nations and tongues, and
they will come and see my glory.
19 "I will set a sign[k] among them, and
I will send some of those who survive to
the nations—to Tarshish,[l] to the Libyans[c] and Lydians[m] (famous as archers),
to Tubal[n] and Greece, and to the distant
islands[o] that have not heard of my fame
or seen my glory.[p] They will proclaim
my glory among the nations. 20 And
they will bring all your brothers, from
all the nations, to my holy mountain in
Jerusalem as an offering to the LORD—
on horses, in chariots and wagons, and
on mules and camels," says the LORD.

66:17 [h]Isa 1:29 [i]Lev 11:7 [j]Ps 37:20; Isa 1:28
66:19 [k]Isa 11:10; 49:22 [l]Isa 2:16 [m]Eze 27:10 [n]Ge 10:2 [o]Isa 11:11 [p]1Ch 16:24; Isa 24:15

[a] *17* Or *gardens behind one of your temples, and*
[b] *18* The meaning of the Hebrew for this clause is uncertain.
[c] *19* Some Septuagint manuscripts *Put* (Libyans); Hebrew *Pul*

"They will bring them, as the Israelites
bring their grain offerings, to the temple of the LORD in ceremonially clean
vessels.[q] 21 And I will select some of
them also to be priests[r] and Levites,"
says the LORD.

22 "As the new heavens and the new
earth[s] that I make will endure before
me," declares the LORD, "so will your
name and descendants endure.[t] 23 From
one New Moon to another and from
one Sabbath[u] to another, all mankind
will come and bow down[v] before me,"
says the LORD. 24 "And they will go
out and look upon the dead bodies of
those who rebelled against me; their
worm[w] will not die, nor will their fire
be quenched,[x] and they will be loathsome to all mankind."

66:20 [q]Isa 52:11
66:21 [r]Ex 19:6; Isa 61:6; 1Pe 2:5,9
66:22 [s]Isa 65:17; Heb 12:26-27; 2Pe 3:13; Rev 21:1
66:22 [t]Jn 10:27-29; 1Pe 1:4-5
66:23 [u]Eze 46:1-3 [v]Isa 19:21
66:24 [w]Isa 14:11 [x]Isa 1:31; Mk 9:48*

JEREMIAH

AUTHORSHIP AND DATE

Jeremiah

Between 627 B.C. and 586 B.C.

KEY THEMES

Jeremiah is often called the "weeping prophet." He seemed a failure to most people. He was thrown into stocks, into dungeons, into cisterns and into pits. His preaching was very unpopular. He found few friends among either the royalty or the common people. Yet he went on preaching, never stopping in the face of pressure. Faithfulness best describes his entire life and ministry, for he continued to be faithful against impossible odds and outright opposition. He lived long enough to see many of his prophecies come true. The most notable of these was his prophecy of the siege and fall of Jerusalem. Other themes throughout his book include condemnation of sin, a heralding of judgment and a new revelation of covenants—the covenant of the heart (see 31:31–32).

FRUIT OF THE SPIRIT IN JEREMIAH

Love: Concerning Israel after the exodus: "I [the LORD] said, 'How gladly would I treat you like sons and give you a desirable land, the most beautiful inheritance of any nation.' I thought you would call me 'Father' and not turn away from following me" (3:19). God wanted Israel's response to his salvation to be love. But Israel turned from loving God to loving idols, and the nation's death brought tears to the Scriptures in the writings of Jeremiah.

Joy: We must anticipate the joy that will come with the fulfillment of God's plan. Jeremiah had been honest—and therefore negative—about the fate of the nation. But he promised that joy would return once more: "Yet in the towns of Judah and the streets of Jerusalem that are deserted, inhabited by neither men nor animals, there will be heard once more the sounds of joy and gladness, the voices of bride and bridegroom, and the voices of those who bring thank offerings to the house of the LORD saying, 'Give thanks to the LORD Almighty, for the LORD is good; his love endures forever'" (33:10–11).

Peace: Peace is the most decent word politicians ever speak; however, it is often only a sword of political promise. Those who promise peace sometimes are incapable of delivering it. "'Peace, peace,' they say, when there is no peace" (8:11). Still, every mother who has sent a son off to war has dreamed mostly of armistices: "We hoped for peace but no good has come, for a time of healing but there was only terror" (8:15). Wars and rumors of wars are our lot but not our dream. Our dream is always of peace.

Goodness: Jeremiah 5:1 was a plea for national integrity. Jeremiah set forth a standing offer from God: If anyone could run through the streets of Jerusalem and find a single honest person, God would pardon the city. There are times of decadence in the lives of nations—usually just before they fall, never to rise again—when goodness is at a premium. Yet our morality is the aspect of life which proves our devotion to God.

Self-Control: To provide an example and rebuke to the people of Judah, the Lord told Jeremiah to attempt to entice the Recabites to break their vow not to drink wine (see 35:4–11). But people with real self-control—those who honor God's convictions—can never be bought off. The Recabites stood likes stars of holiness in a corrupt culture.

1 The words of Jeremiah son of Hilkiah, one of the priests at Anathoth[a] in the territory of Benjamin.
2The word of the LORD came to him
in the thirteenth year of the reign of Josiah son of Amon king of Judah, 3and

1:1 [a]Jos 21:18; 1Ch 6:60; Jer 32:7-9

DAY 2 TWO

JOY AND THE PURPOSE OF GOD IN MY LIFE

Jeremiah 1:4–5

A sense of calling is the single greatest and most lasting impetus to seeing meaning in our lives. So often pastors hear their frustrated parishioners struggling to answer life's most basic questions: "What am I here for? Why am I in the world?" This sense of worthlessness can lead to depression or despair, and taken to an extreme, can result in the loss of the desire to live. Almost every suicide note centers around a perceived lack of significance and purpose.

Some years ago the body of a young girl was pulled out of the Missouri River only blocks from the small apartment where my wife and I lived. Pinned to her seedy, muddy blouse was a note in running, faded ink, "I haven't a friend in the world; nobody cares for me." How tragic that the girl didn't know that her perception was untrue. God not only cared for her; he had given his own Son for her and had a plan for her life.

When I was a parish pastor, I taught every believer to become familiar with the three major "gifts passages" (Romans 12, 1 Corinthians 12 and Ephesians 4). The members of the congregation were to read these passages until they understood God's specific gifts for them. I instructed people to find and claim their unique gifts because I did not want people to try to follow Christ with no explicit sense of purpose.

Salvation is a great gift. But our sense of spiritual security can be magnified into great joy when we see what Christ wants us to do with his marvelous gift of eternal life. For Jeremiah, the purposes of God for his life were rooted in the ages before he was born. He felt dwarfed by all that God had called him to do, but he never doubted why he was in the world.

To begin a study on the topic of Joy, the Infallible Proof of the Presence of God, turn to the home page on page 1086.

through the reign of Jehoiakim[b] son of
Josiah king of Judah, down to the fifth
month of the eleventh year of Zedekiah[c]
son of Josiah king of Judah, when the
people of Jerusalem went into exile.[d]

1:3 [b]2Ki 23:34 [c]2Ki 24:17; Jer 39:2 [d]Jer 52:15

The Call of Jeremiah

4The word of the LORD came to me,
saying,

5"Before I formed you in the womb I
knew[a][e] you,
before you were born[f] I set you
apart;
I appointed you as a prophet to
the nations."[g]

1:5 [e]Ps 139:16 [f]Isa 49:1 [g]ver 10; Jer 25:15-26

LOVE

CALLED FROM THE WOMB

Jeremiah 1:5

A God who loved us and called us to serve him while we were in the womb must surely be a God whose love will bear us up in the troubled world in which we must live.

6"Ah, Sovereign LORD," I said, "I do
not know how to speak;[h] I am only a
child."[i]
7But the LORD said to me, "Do not
say, 'I am only a child.' You must go to
everyone I send you to and say whatever I command you. 8Do not be afraid[j]
of them, for I am with you[k] and will
rescue you," declares the LORD.
9Then the LORD reached out his
hand and touched[l] my mouth and said
to me, "Now, I have put my words in
your mouth.[m] 10See, today I appoint
you over nations and kingdoms to uproot and tear down, to destroy and
overthrow, to build and to plant."[n]
11The word of the LORD came to
me: "What do you see, Jeremiah?"[o]
"I see the branch of an almond tree,"
I replied.
12The LORD said to me, "You have
seen correctly, for I am watching[b] to see
that my word is fulfilled."
13The word of the LORD came to me
again: "What do you see?"[p]
"I see a boiling pot, tilting away from
the north," I answered.
14The LORD said to me, "From the

1:6 [h]Ex 4:10; 6:12 [i]1Ki 3:7
1:8 [j]Eze 2:6 [k]Jos 1:5; Jer 15:20
1:9 [l]Isa 6:7 [m]Ex 4:12
1:10 [n]Jer 18:7-10; 24:6; 31:4,28
1:11 [o]Jer 24:3; Am 7:8
1:13 [p]Zec 4:2

[a]5 Or *chose* [b]*12* The Hebrew for *watching* sounds like the Hebrew for *almond tree.*

north disaster will be poured out on all
who live in the land. 15 I am about to
summon all the peoples of the northern
kingdoms," declares the LORD.

"Their kings will come and set up
their thrones
in the entrance of the gates of
Jerusalem;
they will come against all her
surrounding walls
and against all the towns of
Judah.[q]

1:15 [q]Jer 4:16; 9:11

16 I will pronounce my judgments on
my people
because of their wickedness[r] in
forsaking me,[s]
in burning incense to other gods[t]
and in worshiping what their
hands have made.

1:16 [r]Dt 28:20 [s]Jer 17:13 [t]Jer 7:9; 19:4

17 "Get yourself ready! Stand up and
say to them whatever I command you.
Do not be terrified[u] by them, or I will
terrify you before them. 18 Today I have
made you[v] a fortified city, an iron pillar
and a bronze wall to stand against the
whole land—against the kings of Judah, its officials, its priests and the people of the land. 19 They will fight against
you but will not overcome you, for I
am with you[w] and will rescue[x] you,"
declares the LORD.

1:17 [u]Eze 2:6
1:18 [v]Isa 50:7
1:19 [w]Jer 20:11 [x]ver 8

Israel Forsakes God

2 The word of the LORD came to
me: 2 "Go and proclaim in the hearing of Jerusalem:

"'I remember the devotion of your
youth,[y]
how as a bride you loved me
and followed me through the desert,[z]
through a land not sown.
3 Israel was holy[a] to the LORD,[b]
the firstfruits[c] of his harvest;
all who devoured[d] her were held
guilty,[e]
and disaster overtook them,'"
declares the LORD.

2:2 [y]Eze 16:8-14, 60; Hos 2:15 [z]Dt 2:7
2:3 [a]Dt 7:6 [b]Ex 19:6 [c]Jas 1:18; Rev 14:4 [d]Isa 41:11; Jer 30:16 [e]Jer 50:7

4 Hear the word of the LORD,
O house of Jacob,
all you clans of the house of Israel.

5 This is what the LORD says:

"What fault did your fathers find in
me,
that they strayed so far from me?
They followed worthless idols
and became worthless[f] themselves.
6 They did not ask, 'Where is the
LORD,
who brought us up out of Egypt[g]
and led us through the barren
wilderness,
through a land of deserts[h] and
rifts,[i]
a land of drought and darkness,[a]
a land where no one travels and
no one lives?'

2:5 [f]2Ki 17:15
2:6 [g]Hos 13:4 [h]Dt 8:15 [i]Dt 32:10

7 I brought you into a fertile land
to eat its fruit and rich produce.[j]
But you came and defiled my land
and made my inheritance
detestable.[k]
8 The priests did not ask,
'Where is the LORD?'
Those who deal with the law did not
know me;[l]
the leaders rebelled against me.
The prophets prophesied by Baal,[m]
following worthless idols.[n]

2:7 [j]Nu 13:27; Dt 8:7-9; 11:10-12 [k]Ps 106:34-39; Jer 16:18
2:8 [l]Jer 4:22 [m]Jer 23:13 [n]Jer 16:19

9 "Therefore I bring charges[o] against
you again,"
declares the LORD.
"And I will bring charges against
your children's children.
10 Cross over to the coasts of Kittim[b]
and look,
send to Kedar[c] and observe
closely;
see if there has ever been anything
like this:
11 Has a nation ever changed its gods?
(Yet they are not gods[p] at all.)
But my people have exchanged
their[d] Glory[q]
for worthless idols.
12 Be appalled at this, O heavens,
and shudder with great horror,"
declares the LORD.

2:9 [o]Eze 20:35-36; Mic 6:2
2:11 [p]Isa 37:19; Jer 16:20 [q]Ps 106:20; Ro 1:23

13 "My people have committed two
sins:
They have forsaken me,
the spring of living water,[r]
and have dug their own cisterns,
broken cisterns that cannot hold
water.
14 Is Israel a servant, a slave[s] by birth?
Why then has he become plunder?
15 Lions[t] have roared;
they have growled at him.

2:13 [r]Ps 36:9; Jn 4:14
2:14 [s]Ex 4:22
2:15 [t]Jer 4:7; 50:17

[a]*6* Or *and the shadow of death* [b]*10* That is, Cyprus and western coastlands [c]*10* The home of Bedouin tribes in the Syro-Arabian desert [d]*11* Masoretic Text; an ancient Hebrew scribal tradition *my*

SELF-CONTROL

BROKEN CISTERNS

Jeremiah 2:13

The Israelites had bypassed the sweet refreshment of God and had tried to quench their thirsty souls at broken cisterns. How foolish we are to cherish fetid water and bypass the grand cascades of his abundance.

They have laid waste[u] his land;
his towns are burned and deserted.
16Also, the men of Memphis[a][v] and
Tahpanhes[w]
have shaved the crown of your
head.[b]
17Have you not brought this on
yourselves[x]
by forsaking the LORD your God
when he led you in the way?
18Now why go to Egypt[y]
to drink water from the Shihor[c]?[z]
And why go to Assyria
to drink water from the River[d]?
19Your wickedness will punish you;
your backsliding[a] will rebuke[b] you.
Consider then and realize
how evil and bitter[c] it is for you
when you forsake the LORD your
God
and have no awe[d] of me,"
declares the Lord,
the LORD Almighty.

20"Long ago you broke off your yoke[e]
and tore off your bonds;
you said, 'I will not serve you!'
Indeed, on every high hill[f]
and under every spreading tree[g]
you lay down as a prostitute.
21I had planted[h] you like a choice vine[i]
of sound and reliable stock.
How then did you turn against me
into a corrupt,[j] wild vine?
22Although you wash yourself with
soda
and use an abundance of soap,
the stain of your guilt is still
before me,"
declares the Sovereign
LORD.
23"How can you say, 'I am not
defiled;[k]
I have not run after the Baals'?[l]
See how you behaved in the valley;[m]
consider what you have done.
You are a swift she-camel
running[n] here and there,
24a wild donkey[o] accustomed to the
desert,
sniffing the wind in her craving—
in her heat who can restrain her?
Any males that pursue her need not
tire themselves;
at mating time they will find her.
25Do not run until your feet are bare
and your throat is dry.
But you said, 'It's no use!
I love foreign gods,[p]
and I must go after them.'

26"As a thief is disgraced[q] when he is
caught,
so the house of Israel is
disgraced—
they, their kings and their officials,
their priests and their prophets.
27They say to wood, 'You are my
father,'
and to stone,[r] 'You gave me birth.'
They have turned their backs to me
and not their faces;[s]
yet when they are in trouble,[t] they
say,
'Come and save us!'
28Where then are the gods[u] you made
for yourselves?
Let them come if they can save
you
when you are in trouble![v]
For you have as many gods
as you have towns,[w] O Judah.

29"Why do you bring charges against
me?
You have all[x] rebelled against me,"
declares the LORD.
30"In vain I punished your people;
they did not respond to
correction.
Your sword has devoured your
prophets[y]
like a ravening lion.

31"You of this generation, consider
the word of the LORD:

"Have I been a desert to Israel
or a land of great darkness?[z]
Why do my people say, 'We are free
to roam;
we will come to you no more'?
32Does a maiden forget her jewelry,
a bride her wedding ornaments?

[a]*16* Hebrew *Noph* [b]*16* Or *have cracked your skull* [c]*18* That is, a branch of the Nile [d]*18* That is, the Euphrates

2:15 [u]Isa 1:7
2:16 [v]Isa 19:13 [w]Jer 43:7-9
2:17 [x]Jer 4:18
2:18 [y]Isa 30:2 [z]Jos 13:3
2:19 [a]Jer 3:11,22 [b]Isa 3:9; Hos 5:5 [c]Job 20:14; Am 8:10 [d]Ps 36:1
2:20 [e]Lev 26:13 [f]Isa 57:7; Jer 17:2 [g]Dt 12:2
2:21 [h]Ex 15:17 [i]Ps 80:8 [j]Isa 5:4
2:23 [k]Pr 30:12 [l]Jer 9:14 [m]Jer 7:31
2:23 [n]ver 33; Jer 31:22
2:24 [o]Jer 14:6
2:25 [p]Dt 32:16; Jer 3:13; 14:10
2:26 [q]Jer 48:27
2:27 [r]Jer 3:9 [s]Jer 18:17; 32:33 [t]Jdg 10:10; Isa 26:16
2:28 [u]Isa 45:20 [v]Dt 32:37 [w]2Ki 17:29; Jer 11:13
2:29 [x]Jer 5:1; 6:13; Da 9:11
2:30 [y]Ne 9:26; Ac 7:52; 1Th 2:15
2:31 [z]Isa 45:19

Yet my people have forgotten me,
days without number.
33 How skilled you are at pursuing love!
Even the worst of women can
learn from your ways.
34 On your clothes men find
the lifeblood[a] of the innocent
poor,
though you did not catch them
breaking in.[b]
Yet in spite of all this
35 you say, 'I am innocent;
he is not angry with me.'
But I will pass judgment[c] on you
because you say, 'I have not
sinned.'[d]
36 Why do you go about so much,
changing[e] your ways?
You will be disappointed by Egypt[f]
as you were by Assyria.
37 You will also leave that place
with your hands on your head,[g]
for the LORD has rejected those you
trust;
you will not be helped[h] by them.

2:34 [a]2Ki 21:16 [b]Ex 22:2
2:35 [c]Jer 25:31 [d]1Jn 1:8,10
2:36 [e]Jer 31:22 [f]Isa 30:2,3,7
2:37 [g]2Sa 13:19 [h]Jer 37:7

3 "If a man divorces[i] his wife
and she leaves him and marries
another man,
should he return to her again?
Would not the land be completely
defiled?
But you have lived as a prostitute
with many lovers[j]—
would you now return to me?"
declares the LORD.
2 "Look up to the barren heights and
see.
Is there any place where you have
not been ravished?
By the roadside[k] you sat waiting for
lovers,
sat like a nomad[a] in the desert.
You have defiled the land[l]
with your prostitution and
wickedness.
3 Therefore the showers have been
withheld,[m]
and no spring rains[n] have fallen.
Yet you have the brazen look of a
prostitute;
you refuse to blush with shame.[o]
4 Have you not just called to me:
'My Father,[p] my friend from my
youth,[q]
5 will you always be angry?[r]
Will your wrath continue
forever?'
This is how you talk,
but you do all the evil you can."

3:1 [i]Dt 24:1-4 [j]Jer 2:20,25; Eze 16:26,29
3:2 [k]Ge 38:14; Eze 16:25 [l]Jer 2:7
3:3 [m]Lev 26:19 [n]Jer 14:4 [o]Jer 6:15; 8:12; Zep 3:5
3:4 [p]ver 19 [q]Jer 2:2
3:5 [r]Ps 103:9; Isa 57:16

Unfaithful Israel

6 During the reign of King Josiah,
the LORD said to me, "Have you seen
what faithless Israel has done? She has
gone up on every high hill and under
every spreading tree[s] and has committed adultery[t] there. 7 I thought that after
she had done all this she would return
to me but she did not, and her unfaithful sister[u] Judah saw it. 8 I gave faithless
Israel her certificate of divorce and sent
her away because of all her adulteries.
Yet I saw that her unfaithful sister Judah had no fear;[v] she also went out
and committed adultery. 9 Because Israel's immorality mattered so little to her,
she defiled the land[w] and committed
adultery with stone[x] and wood.[y] 10 In
spite of all this, her unfaithful sister Judah did not return to me with all her
heart, but only in pretense,[z]" declares
the LORD.
11 The LORD said to me, "Faithless
Israel is more righteous[a] than unfaithful[b] Judah. 12 Go, proclaim this message
toward the north:[c]

" 'Return,[d] faithless Israel,' declares
the LORD,
'I will frown on you no longer,
for I am merciful,' declares the
LORD,
'I will not be angry[e] forever.
13 Only acknowledge[f] your guilt—
you have rebelled against the
LORD your God,
you have scattered your favors to
foreign gods[g]
under every spreading tree,[h]
and have not obeyed[i] me,' "
declares the LORD.

14 "Return,[j] faithless people," declares
the LORD, "for I am your husband.
I will choose you—one from a town
and two from a clan—and bring you
to Zion. 15 Then I will give you shepherds[k] after my own heart, who will
lead you with knowledge and understanding. 16 In those days, when your
numbers have increased greatly in the
land," declares the LORD, "men will no
longer say, 'The ark of the covenant
of the LORD.' It will never enter their

3:6 [s]Jer 17:2 [t]Jer 2:20
3:7 [u]Eze 16:46
3:8 [v]Eze 16:47; 23:11
3:9 [w]ver 2 [x]Isa 57:6 [y]Jer 2:27
3:10 [z]Jer 12:2
3:11 [a]Eze 16:52; 23:11 [b]ver 7
3:12 [c]2Ki 17:3-6 [d]ver 14; Jer 31:21,22; Eze 33:11 [e]Ps 86:15
3:13 [f]Dt 30:1-3; Jer 14:20; 1Jn 1:9 [g]Jer 2:25 [h]Dt 12:2 [i]ver 25
3:14 [j]Hos 2:19
3:15 [k]Ac 20:28

[a]2 Or *an Arab*

minds or be remembered;[l] it will not be
missed, nor will another one be made.
17 At that time they will call Jerusalem
The Throne[m] of the LORD, and all nations will gather in Jerusalem to honor[n]
the name of the LORD. No longer will
they follow the stubbornness of their
evil hearts.[o] 18 In those days the house of
Judah will join the house of Israel,[p] and
together[q] they will come from a northern[r] land to the land[s] I gave your forefathers as an inheritance.
19 "I myself said,

" 'How gladly would I treat you like
sons
and give you a desirable land,
the most beautiful inheritance of
any nation.'
I thought you would call me
'Father'[t]
and not turn away from following
me.
20 But like a woman unfaithful to her
husband,
so you have been unfaithful to me,
O house of Israel,"
declares the LORD.

21 A cry is heard on the barren
heights,[u]
the weeping and pleading of the
people of Israel,
because they have perverted their
ways
and have forgotten the LORD
their God.

22 "Return,[v] faithless people;
I will cure[w] you of backsliding."

"Yes, we will come to you,
for you are the LORD our God.
23 Surely the ⌊idolatrous⌋ commotion on
the hills
and mountains is a deception;
surely in the LORD our God
is the salvation[x] of Israel.
24 From our youth shameful[y] gods have
consumed
the fruits of our fathers' labor—
their flocks and herds,
their sons and daughters.
25 Let us lie down in our shame,[z]
and let our disgrace cover us.
We have sinned against the LORD
our God,
both we and our fathers;
from our youth[a] till this day

3:16 [l]Isa 65:17
3:17 [m]Jer 17:12; Eze 43:7 [n]Isa 60:9 [o]Jer 11:8
3:18 [p]Hos 1:11 [q]Isa 11:13; Jer 50:4 [r]Jer 16:15; 31:8 [s]Am 9:15
3:19 [t]ver 4; Isa 63:16
3:21 [u]ver 2
3:22 [v]Hos 14:4 [w]Jer 33:6; Hos 6:1
3:23 [x]Ps 3:8; Jer 17:14
3:24 [y]Hos 9:10
3:25 [z]Ezr 9:6 [a]Jer 22:21

we have not obeyed the LORD our
God."

4 "If you will return,[b] O Israel,
return to me,"
declares the LORD.
"If you put your detestable idols[c] out
of my sight
and no longer go astray,
2 and if in a truthful, just and
righteous way
you swear,[d] 'As surely as the LORD
lives,'[e]
then the nations will be blessed[f] by
him
and in him they will glory."

3 This is what the LORD says to the
men of Judah and to Jerusalem:

"Break up your unplowed ground[g]
and do not sow among thorns.[h]
4 Circumcise yourselves to the LORD,
circumcise your hearts,[i]
you men of Judah and people of
Jerusalem,
or my wrath[j] will break out and
burn like fire
because of the evil you have
done—
burn with no one to quench[k] it.

Disaster From the North

5 "Announce in Judah and proclaim in
Jerusalem and say:
'Sound the trumpet throughout
the land!'
Cry aloud and say:
'Gather together!
Let us flee to the fortified cities!'[l]
6 Raise the signal to go to Zion!
Flee for safety without delay!
For I am bringing disaster from the
north,[m]
even terrible destruction."

7 A lion[n] has come out of his lair;
a destroyer of nations has set out.
He has left his place
to lay waste[o] your land.
Your towns will lie in ruins[p]
without inhabitant.
8 So put on sackcloth,[q]
lament and wail,
for the fierce anger[r] of the LORD
has not turned away from us.

9 "In that day," declares the LORD,
"the king and the officials will lose
heart,

4:1 [b]Jer 3:1,22; Joel 2:12 [c]Jer 35:15
4:2 [d]Dt 10:20; Isa 65:16 [e]Jer 12:16 [f]Ge 22:18; Gal 3:8
4:3 [g]Hos 10:12 [h]Mk 4:18
4:4 [i]Dt 10:16; Jer 9:26; Ro 2:28-29 [j]Zep 2:2 [k]Am 5:6
4:5 [l]Jos 10:20; Jer 8:14
4:6 [m]Jer 1:13-15; 50:3
4:7 [n]2Ki 24:1; Jer 2:15 [o]Isa 1:7 [p]Jer 25:9
4:8 [q]Isa 22:12; Jer 6:26 [r]Jer 30:24

DAY 3 THREE

▸ GOODNESS AND MY RELATIONSHIP WITH CHRIST

Jeremiah 4:22

Those who are skilled at doing evil may not know how to do good. What else is characteristic of such people? They don't know God. It is impossible for anyone to truly comprehend God, but one person has made it possible to have a relationship with God and to enter God's presence without fear: Jesus Christ.

Romans 3:21–22 reminds us that we are good only through the work of Christ: "But now a righteousness from God, apart from law, has been made known, to which the Law and the Prophets testify. This righteousness from God comes through faith in Jesus Christ to all who believe. There is no difference." This "righteousness apart from law" is not a righteousness humans could have ever achieved on their own, for we were still in a sense accountable to the Ten Commandments and the Law. But Jesus did achieve this perfection. Now the righteousness he achieved can be ours as well.

Jesus was indeed the sinless Son of God. As the writer of Hebrews testifies, our Lord was tempted like we are, yet he was without sin. Because Christ never sinned, he could die as a perfect sacrifice and take away the sin of the world.

Our relationship with Christ does not demand that we be sinless. This of course we can never be. But every unconfessed sin becomes a kind of barrier to our communication. It is like a husband and wife who may be quarreling over some insignificant sin. Until one of them says "I'm sorry," there is little chance that love and harmony can flow once again in their home. Only when the root of their ill feelings is cleared out of the way by confession can their home be happy once again.

Our relationship with Christ is damaged when we cherish some evil that prevents our good will from being merged with his mercy. So when we know God, we know how to do good. Our relationship with the sinless Son of God means that we must understand that holiness and indecency can never keep company.

To begin a study on the topic of Goodness, Caring How God Feels About My Morality, turn to the home page on page 51.

the priests will be horrified,
and the prophets will be
appalled."[s]

10Then I said, "Ah, Sovereign LORD,
how completely you have deceived[t] this
people and Jerusalem by saying, 'You
will have peace,'[u] when the sword is at
our throats."
11At that time this people and Jerusalem will be told, "A scorching wind[v]
from the barren heights in the desert
blows toward my people, but not to
winnow or cleanse; 12a wind too strong
for that comes from me.[a] Now I pronounce my judgments[w] against them."

13Look! He advances like the clouds,[x]
his chariots[y] come like a
whirlwind,[z]
his horses are swifter than eagles.[a]
Woe to us! We are ruined!
14O Jerusalem, wash[b] the evil from
your heart and be saved.
How long will you harbor wicked
thoughts?
15A voice is announcing from Dan,[c]
proclaiming disaster from the hills
of Ephraim.
16"Tell this to the nations,
proclaim it to Jerusalem:
'A besieging army is coming from a
distant land,
raising a war cry[d] against the cities
of Judah.
17They surround[e] her like men
guarding a field,
because she has rebelled[f] against
me,' "
declares the LORD.
18"Your own conduct and actions[g]
have brought this upon you.[h]
This is your punishment.
How bitter[i] it is!
How it pierces to the heart!"

19Oh, my anguish, my anguish![j]
I writhe in pain.
Oh, the agony of my heart!
My heart pounds within me,
I cannot keep silent.[k]
For I have heard the sound of the
trumpet;
I have heard the battle cry.[l]
20Disaster follows disaster;[m]
the whole land lies in ruins.
In an instant my tents[n] are
destroyed,

[a]12 Or *comes at my command*

4:9 [s]Isa 29:9
4:10 [t]2Th 2:11 [u]Jer 14:13
4:11 [v]Eze 17:10; Hos 13:15
4:12 [w]Jer 1:16
4:13 [x]Isa 19:1 [y]Isa 66:15 [z]Isa 5:28 [a]Dt 28:49; Hab 1:8
4:14 [b]Jas 4:8
4:15 [c]Jer 8:16
4:16 [d]Eze 21:22
4:17 [e]2Ki 25:1,4 [f]Jer 5:23
4:18 [g]Ps 107:17; Isa 50:1 [h]Jer 2:17 [i]Jer 2:19
4:19 [j]Isa 16:11; 22:4; Jer 9:10 [k]Jer 20:9 [l]Nu 10:9
4:20 [m]Ps 42:7; Eze 7:26 [n]Jer 10:20

my shelter in a moment.
21 How long must I see the battle standard
and hear the sound of the trumpet?

4:22 [o]Jer 10:8 [p]Jer 2:8 [q]Jer 13:23; 1Co 14:20 [r]Ro 16:19

22 "My people are fools;[o]
they do not know me.[p]
They are senseless children;
they have no understanding.
They are skilled in doing evil;[q]
they know not how to do good."[r]

23 I looked at the earth,
4:23 [s]Ge 1:2
and it was formless and empty;[s]
and at the heavens,
and their light was gone.
24 I looked at the mountains,
4:24 [t]Isa 5:25; Eze 38:20
and they were quaking;[t]
all the hills were swaying.
25 I looked, and there were no people;
every bird in the sky had flown away.[u]
4:25 [u]Jer 9:10; 12:4; Zep 1:3
26 I looked, and the fruitful land was a desert;
all its towns lay in ruins
before the LORD, before his fierce anger.

27 This is what the LORD says:

4:27 [v]Jer 5:10,18; 12:12; 30:11; 46:28
"The whole land will be ruined,
though I will not destroy[v] it completely.
4:28 [w]Jer 12:4,11; 14:2; Hos 4:3 [x]Isa 5:30; 50:3 [y]Nu 23:19 [z]Jer 23:20; 30:24
28 Therefore the earth will mourn[w]
and the heavens above grow dark,[x]
because I have spoken and will not relent,[y]
I have decided and will not turn back."[z]

4:29 [a]Jer 6:23 [b]2Ki 25:4 [c]ver 7
29 At the sound of horsemen and archers[a]
every town takes to flight.[b]
Some go into the thickets;
some climb up among the rocks.
All the towns are deserted;[c]
no one lives in them.

4:30 [d]Isa 10:3-4 [e]Eze 23:40 [f]2Ki 9:30 [g]La 1:2; Eze 23:9,22
30 What are you doing,[d] O devastated one?
Why dress yourself in scarlet
and put on jewels[e] of gold?
Why shade your eyes with paint?[f]
You adorn yourself in vain.
Your lovers[g] despise you;
they seek your life.

4:31 [h]Jer 13:21 [i]Isa 42:14 [j]Isa 1:15; La 1:17
31 I hear a cry as of a woman in labor,[h]
a groan as of one bearing her first child—
the cry of the Daughter of Zion
gasping for breath,[i]
stretching out her hands[j] and saying,
"Alas! I am fainting;
my life is given over to murderers."

Not One Is Upright

5:1 [k]2Ch 16:9; Eze 22:30 [l]Ge 18:32 [m]Ge 18:24

5 "Go up and down[k] the streets of Jerusalem,
look around and consider,
search through her squares.
If you can find but one person[l]
who deals honestly and seeks the truth,
I will forgive[m] this city.

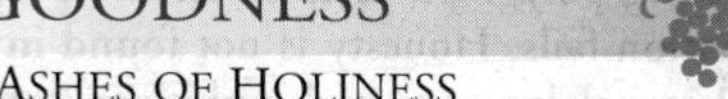

GOODNESS
THE ASHES OF HOLINESS

Jeremiah 5:1

Abraham once bartered with God to spare Sodom on behalf of ten righteous souls. In this passage Jeremiah notes that, in his time, one can rake the ashes of his evil culture in search of a single ember of truth and come away empty. If a few honest saints had been found in Jerusalem, God may well have driven Babylon from her gates.

5:2 [n]Jer 4:2
2 Although they say, 'As surely as the LORD lives,'[n]
still they are swearing falsely."
5:3 [o]2Ch 16:9 [p]Isa 9:13 [q]Jer 2:30; Zep 3:2 [r]Jer 7:26; 19:15; Eze 3:8-9
3 O LORD, do not your eyes[o] look for truth?
You struck[p] them, but they felt no pain;
you crushed them, but they refused correction.[q]
They made their faces harder than stone[r]
and refused to repent.
4 I thought, "These are only the poor;
they are foolish,
5:4 [s]Jer 8:7
for they do not know[s] the way of the LORD,
the requirements of their God.
5:5 [t]Mic 3:1,9 [u]Ps 2:3; Jer 2:20
5 So I will go to the leaders[t]
and speak to them;
surely they know the way of the LORD,
the requirements of their God."
But with one accord they too had broken off the yoke
and torn off the bonds.[u]

[6]Therefore a lion from the forest will
attack them,
a wolf from the desert will ravage
them,
a leopard[v] will lie in wait near their
towns
to tear to pieces any who venture
out,
for their rebellion is great
and their backslidings many.[w]
[7]"Why should I forgive you?
Your children have forsaken me
and sworn[x] by gods that are not
gods.[y]
I supplied all their needs,
yet they committed adultery[z]
and thronged to the houses of
prostitutes.
[8]They are well-fed, lusty stallions,
each neighing for another man's
wife.[a]
[9]Should I not punish them for this?"[b]
declares the LORD.
"Should I not avenge myself
on such a nation as this?

[10]"Go through her vineyards and
ravage them,
but do not destroy them
completely.[c]
Strip off her branches,
for these people do not belong to
the LORD.
[11]The house of Israel and the house of
Judah
have been utterly unfaithful[d] to
me,"
declares the LORD.
[12]They have lied about the LORD;
they said, "He will do nothing!
No harm will come to us;[e]
we will never see sword or
famine.[f]
[13]The prophets[g] are but wind
and the word is not in them;
so let what they say be done to
them."

[14]Therefore this is what the LORD
God Almighty says:

"Because the people have spoken
these words,
I will make my words in your
mouth[h] a fire[i]
and these people the wood it
consumes.
[15]O house of Israel," declares the
LORD,
"I am bringing a distant nation
against you—
an ancient and enduring nation,[j]
a people whose language[k] you do
not know,
whose speech you do not
understand.

5:6 [v]Hos 13:7 [w]Jer 30:14
5:7 [x]Jos 23:7; Zep 1:5 [y]Dt 32:21; Jer 2:11; Gal 4:8 [z]Nu 25:1
5:8 [a]Jer 29:23; Eze 22:11
5:9 [b]ver 29; Jer 9:9
5:10 [c]Jer 4:27
5:11 [d]Jer 3:20
5:12 [e]Jer 23:17 [f]2Ch 36:16; Jer 14:13
5:13 [g]Jer 14:15
5:14 [h]Jer 1:9; Hos 6:5 [i]Jer 23:29
5:15 [j]Dt 28:49; Isa 5:26; Jer 4:16 [k]Isa 28:11

DAY 2 TWO

FAITHFULNESS AND THE PURPOSE OF GOD IN MY LIFE

Jeremiah 5:1–2

Jeremiah's test of national morality is accomplished by his jogging through the capital and giving polygraph tests to all the people. The nation fails. Honesty is not found in the city. Personal interests and ambitious career goals have wiped out all social compassion.

We who have served Christ during the closing years of the twentieth century have witnessed the demise of personal character in many of our political figures. Two of the last five American presidents have faced impeachment trials. The sludge artists of election engineering have forced candidates to resign before and during public elections. Other lawmakers have been forced by public scandal to resign before their terms of office were completed. It is not surprising that Jeremiah's jog through Jerusalem found no men or women of character. The question that matters most to us is: "What would the prophet discover if he were to jog through our own cities with a polygraph machine?"

During a recent political scandal, lawmakers rated perjury—but not immorality—as an impeachable offense. In the search for national morality, the character of many other lawmakers was called into question as well. Integrity seemed in short supply.

We can understand Jeremiah's quest for an honest person, for we, too, live in dishonest times. But Jeremiah stayed true to God and committed to doing right. We can look to him for our own encouragement. We can be faithful to God's purposes for us even when others are doing evil.

To begin a study on the topic of Faithfulness, a Stubborn Commitment to the Right, turn to the home page on page 398.

16 Their quivers are like an open grave;
all of them are mighty warriors.
17 They will devour[l][m] your harvests
and food,
devour[n][o] your sons and daughters;
they will devour[p] your flocks and
herds,
devour your vines and fig trees.
With the sword they will destroy
the fortified cities in which you
trust.[q]

18 "Yet even in those days," declares
the LORD, "I will not destroy[r] you
completely. 19 And when the people ask,[s]
'Why has the LORD our God done all
this to us?' you will tell them, 'As you
have forsaken me and served foreign
gods[t] in your own land, so now you
will serve foreigners[u] in a land not your
own.'

20 "Announce this to the house of
Jacob
and proclaim it in Judah:
21 Hear this, you foolish and senseless
people,
who have eyes[v] but do not see,
who have ears but do not hear:[w]
22 Should you not fear[x] me?" declares
the LORD.
"Should you not tremble in my
presence?
I made the sand a boundary for the
sea,
an everlasting barrier it cannot
cross.
The waves may roll, but they cannot
prevail;
they may roar, but they cannot
cross it.
23 But these people have stubborn and
rebellious[y] hearts;
they have turned aside and gone
away.
24 They do not say to themselves,
'Let us fear the LORD our God,
who gives autumn and spring rains[z]
in season,
who assures us of the regular
weeks of harvest.'[a]
25 Your wrongdoings have kept these
away;
your sins have deprived you of
good.
26 "Among my people are wicked men
who lie in wait[b] like men who
snare birds

5:17 [l]Jer 8:16 [m]Lev 26:16 [n]Jer 50:7,17 [o]Dt 28:32 [p]Dt 28:31 [q]Dt 28:33
5:18 [r]Jer 4:27
5:19 [s]Dt 29:24-26; 1Ki 9:9 [t]Jer 16:13 [u]Dt 28:48
5:21 [v]Isa 6:10; Eze 12:2 [w]Mt 13:15; Mk 8:18
5:22 [x]Dt 28:58
5:23 [y]Dt 21:18
5:24 [z]Ps 147:8; Joel 2:23 [a]Ge 8:22; Ac 14:17
5:26 [b]Ps 10:8; Pr 1:11

and like those who set traps to
catch men.
27 Like cages full of birds,
their houses are full of deceit;[c]
they have become rich[d] and
powerful
28 and have grown fat[e] and sleek.
Their evil deeds have no limit;
they do not plead the case of the
fatherless[f] to win it,
they do not defend the rights of
the poor.[g]
29 Should I not punish them for this?"
declares the LORD.
"Should I not avenge myself
on such a nation as this?

30 "A horrible[h] and shocking thing
has happened in the land:
31 The prophets prophesy lies,[i]
the priests rule by their own
authority,
and my people love it this way.
But what will you do in the end?

Jerusalem Under Siege

6 "Flee for safety, people of
Benjamin!
Flee from Jerusalem!
Sound the trumpet in Tekoa![j]
Raise the signal over Beth
Hakkerem![k]
For disaster looms out of the north,[l]
even terrible destruction.
2 I will destroy the Daughter of Zion,
so beautiful and delicate.
3 Shepherds[m] with their flocks will
come against her;
they will pitch their tents around[n]
her,
each tending his own portion."

4 "Prepare for battle against her!
Arise, let us attack at noon![o]
But, alas, the daylight is fading,
and the shadows of evening grow
long.
5 So arise, let us attack at night
and destroy her fortresses!"

6 This is what the LORD Almighty
says:

"Cut down the trees[p]
and build siege ramps[q] against
Jerusalem.
This city must be punished;
it is filled with oppression.
7 As a well pours out its water,
so she pours out her wickedness.

5:27 [c]Jer 9:6 [d]Jer 12:1
5:28 [e]Dt 32:15 [f]Zec 7:10 [g]Isa 1:23; Jer 7:6
5:30 [h]Jer 23:14; Hos 6:10
5:31 [i]Eze 13:6; Mic 2:11
6:1 [j]2Ch 11:6 [k]Ne 3:14 [l]Jer 4:6
6:3 [m]Jer 12:10 [n]2Ki 25:4; Lk 19:43
6:4 [o]Jer 15:8
6:6 [p]Dt 20:19-20 [q]Jer 32:24

6:7 [r]Ps 55:9; Eze 7:11,23 [s]Jer 20:8

Violence[r] and destruction[s] resound
in her;
her sickness and wounds are ever
before me.
8 Take warning, O Jerusalem,
or I will turn away[t] from you
and make your land desolate
so no one can live in it."

6:8 [t]Eze 23:18; Hos 9:12

9 This is what the LORD Almighty
says:
"Let them glean the remnant of
Israel
as thoroughly as a vine;
pass your hand over the branches
again,
like one gathering grapes."
10 To whom can I speak and give
warning?
Who will listen to me?
Their ears are closed[a][u]
so they cannot hear.
The word[v] of the LORD is offensive
to them;
they find no pleasure in it.

6:10 [u]Ac 7:51 [v]Jer 20:8

11 But I am full of the wrath[w] of the
LORD,
and I cannot hold it in.[x]
"Pour it out on the children in the
street
and on the young men[y] gathered
together;
both husband and wife will be
caught in it,
and the old, those weighed down
with years.
12 Their houses will be turned over to
others,[z]
together with their fields and their
wives,[a]
when I stretch out my hand[b]
against those who live in the
land,"
declares the LORD.

6:11 [w]Jer 7:20 [x]Job 32:20; Jer 20:9 [y]Jer 9:21

6:12 [z]Dt 28:30 [a]Jer 8:10; 38:22 [b]Isa 5:25

13 "From the least to the greatest,
all are greedy for gain;[c]
prophets and priests alike,
all practice deceit.[d]
14 They dress the wound of my people
as though it were not serious.
'Peace, peace,' they say,
when there is no peace.[e]
15 Are they ashamed of their loathsome
conduct?
No, they have no shame at all;
they do not even know how to
blush.[f]

6:13 [c]Isa 56:11 [d]Jer 8:10

6:14 [e]Jer 4:10; 8:11; Eze 13:10

6:15 [f]Jer 3:3; 8:10-12

So they will fall among the fallen;
they will be brought down when I
punish them,"
says the LORD.

16 This is what the LORD says:
"Stand at the crossroads and look;
ask for the ancient paths,[g]
ask where the good way[h] is, and
walk in it,
and you will find rest[i] for your
souls.
But you said, 'We will not walk
in it.'
17 I appointed watchmen[j] over you and
said,
'Listen to the sound of the
trumpet!'
But you said, 'We will not listen.'[k]
18 Therefore hear, O nations;
observe, O witnesses,
what will happen to them.
19 Hear, O earth:[l]
I am bringing disaster on this
people,
the fruit of their schemes,[m]
because they have not listened to my
words
and have rejected my law.[n]
20 What do I care about incense from
Sheba
or sweet calamus[o] from a distant
land?
Your burnt offerings are not
acceptable;[p]
your sacrifices[q] do not please
me."[r]

6:16 [g]Jer 18:15 [h]Ps 119:3 [i]Mt 11:29

6:17 [j]Eze 3:17 [k]Jer 11:7-8; 25:4

6:19 [l]Isa 1:2; Jer 22:29 [m]Pr 1:31 [n]Jer 8:9

6:20 [o]Ex 30:23 [p]Am 5:22 [q]Ps 50:8-10; Jer 7:21; Mic 6:7-8 [r]Isa 1:11

21 Therefore this is what the LORD
says:
"I will put obstacles before this
people.
Fathers and sons alike will
stumble[s] over them;
neighbors and friends will perish."

6:21 [s]Isa 8:14

22 This is what the LORD says:
"Look, an army is coming
from the land of the north;[t]
a great nation is being stirred up
from the ends of the earth.
23 They are armed with bow and spear;
they are cruel and show no
mercy.[u]
They sound like the roaring sea
as they ride on their horses;[v]

6:22 [t]Jer 1:15; 10:22

6:23 [u]Isa 13:18 [v]Jer 4:29

[a]10 Hebrew *uncircumcised*

they come like men in battle
formation
to attack you, O Daughter of
Zion."
24We have heard reports about them,
and our hands hang limp.
6:24 [w]Jer 4:19; [x]Jer 4:31; 50:41-43
Anguish[w] has gripped us,
pain like that of a woman in
labor.[x]
25Do not go out to the fields
or walk on the roads,
6:25 [y]Jer 49:29
for the enemy has a sword,
and there is terror on every side.[y]
6:26 [z]Jer 4:8; [a]Jer 25:34; Mic 1:10; [b]Zec 12:10
26O my people, put on sackcloth[z]
and roll in ashes;[a]
mourn with bitter wailing
as for an only son,[b]
for suddenly the destroyer
will come upon us.
6:27 [c]Jer 9:7
27"I have made you a tester[c] of
metals
and my people the ore,
that you may observe
and test their ways.
6:28 [d]Jer 5:23; [e]Jer 9:4; [f]Eze 22:18
28They are all hardened rebels,[d]
going about to slander.[e]
They are bronze and iron;[f]
they all act corruptly.
29The bellows blow fiercely
to burn away the lead with fire,
but the refining goes on in vain;
the wicked are not purged out.
30They are called rejected silver,
6:30 [g]Ps 119:119; Jer 7:29; Hos 9:17
because the LORD has rejected
them."[g]

False Religion Worthless

7 This is the word that came to Jer-
7:2 [h]Jer 17:19
emiah from the LORD: 2"Stand[h] at
the gate of the LORD's house and there
proclaim this message:
" 'Hear the word of the LORD, all
you people of Judah who come through
these gates to worship the LORD. 3This
is what the LORD Almighty, the God
7:3 [i]Jer 18:11; 26:13
of Israel, says: Reform your ways[i] and
your actions, and I will let you live in
7:4 [j]Mic 3:11
this place. 4Do not trust in deceptive[j]
words and say, "This is the temple of
the LORD, the temple of the LORD,
the temple of the LORD!" 5If you really
change your ways and your actions and
7:5 [k]Jer 22:3
deal with each other justly,[k] 6if you do
not oppress the alien, the fatherless or
the widow and do not shed innocent
7:6 [l]Jer 2:34; 19:4; [m]Dt 8:19
blood[l] in this place, and if you do not
follow other gods[m] to your own harm,
7then I will let you live in this place,
in the land[n] I gave your forefathers for
7:7 [n]Dt 4:40
ever and ever. 8But look, you are trusting in deceptive words that are worthless.
9" 'Will you steal and murder, commit adultery and perjury,[a] burn in-
7:9 [o]Jer 11:13,17; [p]Ex 20:3
cense to Baal[o] and follow other gods[p]
you have not known, 10and then come
and stand before me in this house,[q]
7:10 [q]Jer 32:34; Eze 23:38-39
which bears my Name, and say, "We
are safe"—safe to do all these detestable
things? 11Has this house,[r] which bears
7:11 [r]Isa 56:7; [s]Mt 21:13*; Mk 11:17*; Lk 19:46*; [t]Jer 29:23
my Name, become a den of robbers[s]
to you? But I have been watching![t] declares the LORD.
12" 'Go now to the place in Shiloh[u]
7:12 [u]Jos 18:1; [v]1Sa 4:10-11,22; Ps 78:60-64
where I first made a dwelling for my
Name, and see what I did[v] to it because of the wickedness of my people
Israel. 13While you were doing all these
things, declares the LORD, I spoke to
7:13 [w]2Ch 36:15; [x]Isa 65:12; [y]Jer 35:17
you again and again,[w] but you did not
listen;[x] I called you, but you did not answer.[y] 14Therefore, what I did to Shiloh
I will now do to the house that bears
7:14 [z]1Ki 9:7
my Name,[z] the temple you trust in, the
place I gave to you and your fathers. 15I
will thrust you from my presence, just
as I did all your brothers, the people of
7:15 [a]Ps 78:67
Ephraim.'[a]
16"So do not pray for this people nor
7:16 [b]Ex 32:10; Dt 9:14; Jer 15:1
offer any plea[b] or petition for them;
do not plead with me, for I will not listen to you. 17Do you not see what they
are doing in the towns of Judah and
in the streets of Jerusalem? 18The children gather wood, the fathers light the
fire, and the women knead the dough
and make cakes of bread for the Queen
7:18 [c]Jer 44:17-19; [d]Jer 19:13; [e]1Ki 14:9
of Heaven.[c] They pour out drink offerings[d] to other gods to provoke[e] me to
anger. 19But am I the one they are pro-
7:19 [f]Jer 9:19
voking? declares the LORD. Are they
not rather harming themselves, to their
own shame?[f]
20" 'Therefore this is what the Sov-
7:20 [g]Jer 42:18; La 2:3-5
ereign LORD says: My anger[g] and my
wrath will be poured out on this place,
on man and beast, on the trees of the
field and on the fruit of the ground,
and it will burn and not be quenched.
21" 'This is what the LORD Almighty,
the God of Israel, says: Go ahead, add
7:21 [h]Isa 1:11; Am 5:21-22; [i]Hos 8:13
your burnt offerings to your other sacrifices[h] and eat[i] the meat yourselves!

[a]9 Or *and swear by false gods*

22For when I brought your forefathers out of Egypt and spoke to them, I did not just give them commands about burnt offerings and sacrifices,[j] 23but I gave them this command: Obey[k] me, and I will be your God and you will be my people.[l] Walk in all the ways I command you, that it may go well[m] with you. 24But they did not listen or pay attention;[n] instead, they followed the stubborn inclinations of their evil hearts. They went backward and not forward. 25From the time your forefathers left Egypt until now, day after day, again and again I sent you my servants the prophets.[o] 26But they did not listen to me or pay attention. They were stiff-necked and did more evil than their forefathers.'[p]

27"When you tell[q] them all this, they will not listen[r] to you; when you call to them, they will not answer. 28Therefore say to them, 'This is the nation that has not obeyed the LORD its God or responded to correction. Truth has perished; it has vanished from their lips. 29Cut off[s] your hair and throw it away; take up a lament on the barren heights, for the LORD has rejected and abandoned[t] this generation that is under his wrath.

The Valley of Slaughter

30" 'The people of Judah have done evil in my eyes, declares the LORD. They have set up their detestable idols[u] in the house that bears my Name and have defiled[v] it. 31They have built the high places of Topheth[w] in the Valley of Ben Hinnom to burn their sons and daughters[x] in the fire—something I did not command, nor did it enter my mind.[y] 32So beware, the days are coming, declares the LORD, when people will no longer call it Topheth or the Valley of Ben Hinnom, but the Valley of Slaughter,[z] for they will bury[a] the dead in Topheth until there is no more room. 33Then the carcasses of this people will become food[b] for the birds of the air and the beasts of the earth, and there will be no one to frighten them away. 34I will bring an end to the sounds[c] of joy and gladness and to the voices of bride and bridegroom[d] in the towns of Judah and the streets of Jerusalem, for the land will become desolate.[e]

7:22 [j]1Sa 15:22; Ps 51:16; Hos 6:6
7:23 [k]Ex 19:5 [l]Lev 26:12 [m]Ex 15:26
7:24 [n]Ps 81:11-12; Jer 11:8
7:25 [o]Jer 25:4
7:26 [p]Jer 16:12
7:27 [q]Eze 2:7 [r]Eze 3:7
7:29 [s]Job 1:20; Isa 15:2; Mic 1:16 [t]Jer 6:30
7:30 [u]Eze 7:20-22 [v]Jer 32:34
7:31 [w]2Ki 23:10 [x]Ps 106:38 [y]Jer 19:5
7:32 [z]Jer 19:6 [a]Jer 19:11
7:33 [b]Dt 28:26
7:34 [c]Isa 24:8; Eze 26:13 [d]Rev 18:23 [e]Lev 26:34

8 " 'At that time, declares the LORD, the bones of the kings and officials of Judah, the bones of the priests and prophets, and the bones of the people of Jerusalem will be removed from their graves. 2They will be exposed to the sun and the moon and all the stars of the heavens, which they have loved and served[f] and which they have followed and consulted and worshiped. They will not be gathered up or buried, but will be like refuse lying on the ground. 3Wherever I banish them, all the survivors of this evil nation will prefer death to life,[g] declares the LORD Almighty.'

Sin and Punishment

4"Say to them, 'This is what the LORD says:

" 'When men fall down, do they not
get up?[h]
When a man turns away, does he
not return?
5Why then have these people turned
away?
Why does Jerusalem always turn
away?
They cling to deceit;[i]
they refuse to return.[j]
6I have listened attentively,
but they do not say what is right.
No one repents[k] of his wickedness,
saying, "What have I done?"
Each pursues his own course[l]
like a horse charging into battle.
7Even the stork in the sky
knows her appointed seasons,
and the dove, the swift and the
thrush
observe the time of their
migration.
But my people do not know[m]
the requirements of the LORD.

8" 'How can you say, "We are wise,
for we have the law[n] of the
LORD,"
when actually the lying pen of the
scribes
has handled it falsely?
9The wise[o] will be put to shame;
they will be dismayed and
trapped.
Since they have rejected the word[p] of
the LORD,
what kind of wisdom do they
have?

8:2 [f]2Ki 23:5; Ac 7:42
8:3 [g]Job 3:22; Rev 9:6
8:4 [h]Pr 24:16
8:5 [i]Jer 5:27 [j]Jer 7:24; 9:6
8:6 [k]Rev 9:20 [l]Ps 14:1-3
8:7 [m]Isa 1:3; Jer 5:4-5
8:8 [n]Ro 2:17
8:9 [o]Jer 6:15 [p]Jer 6:19

10Therefore I will give their wives to
other men
and their fields to new owners.[q]
From the least to the greatest,
all are greedy for gain;[r]
prophets and priests alike,
all practice deceit.
11They dress the wound of my people
as though it were not serious.
"Peace, peace," they say,
when there is no peace.[s]
12Are they ashamed of their loathsome
conduct?
No, they have no shame[t] at all;
they do not even know how to
blush.
So they will fall among the fallen;
they will be brought down when
they are punished,[u]
says the LORD.[v]

13" 'I will take away their harvest,
declares the LORD.
There will be no grapes on the
vine.[w]
There will be no figs[x] on the tree,
and their leaves will wither.[y]
What I have given them
will be taken[z] from them.[a]' "

14"Why are we sitting here?
Gather together!
Let us flee to the fortified cities[a]
and perish there!
For the LORD our God has doomed
us to perish
and given us poisoned water[b] to
drink,
because we have sinned[c] against
him.
15We hoped for peace[d]
but no good has come,
for a time of healing
but there was only terror.[e]
16The snorting of the enemy's horses
is heard from Dan;[f]
at the neighing of their stallions
the whole land trembles.
They have come to devour
the land and everything in it,
the city and all who live there."

17"See, I will send venomous snakes[g]
among you,
vipers that cannot be charmed,[h]
and they will bite you,"
declares the LORD.

18O my Comforter[b] in sorrow,
my heart is faint[i] within me.
19Listen to the cry of my people
from a land far away:[j]
"Is the LORD not in Zion?
Is her King no longer there?"

"Why have they provoked me to
anger with their images,
with their worthless foreign
idols?"[k]

20"The harvest is past,
the summer has ended,
and we are not saved."

21Since my people are crushed, I am
crushed;
I mourn,[l] and horror grips me.
22Is there no balm in Gilead?[m]
Is there no physician there?
Why then is there no healing[n]
for the wound of my people?

9 1Oh, that my head were a spring
of water
and my eyes a fountain of tears!
I would weep[o] day and night
for the slain of my people.[p]
2Oh, that I had in the desert
a lodging place for travelers,
so that I might leave my people
and go away from them;
for they are all adulterers,[q]
a crowd of unfaithful people.

3"They make ready their tongue
like a bow, to shoot lies;[r]
it is not by truth
that they triumph[c] in the land.
They go from one sin to another;
they do not acknowledge me,"
declares the LORD.
4"Beware of your friends;
do not trust your brothers.[s]
For every brother is a deceiver,[d][t]
and every friend a slanderer.
5Friend deceives friend,
and no one speaks the truth.
They have taught their tongues to
lie;
they weary themselves with
sinning.
6You[e] live in the midst of deception;[u]
in their deceit they refuse to
acknowledge me,"
declares the LORD.

[a]*13* The meaning of the Hebrew for this sentence is uncertain. [b]*18* The meaning of the Hebrew for this word is uncertain. [c]*3* Or *lies; / they are not valiant for truth* [d]*4* Or *a deceiving Jacob* [e]*6* That is, Jeremiah (the Hebrew is singular)

8:10 [q]Jer 6:12 [r]Isa 56:11
8:11 [s]Jer 6:14
8:12 [t]Jer 3:3 [u]Ps 52:5-7; Isa 3:9 [v]Jer 6:15
8:13 [w]Joel 1:7 [x]Lk 13:6 [y]Mt 21:19 [z]Jer 5:17
8:14 [a]Jer 4:5; Jer 35:11 [b]Dt 29:18; Jer 9:15; 23:15 [c]Jer 14:7,20
8:15 [d]ver 11 [e]Jer 14:19
8:16 [f]Jer 4:15
8:17 [g]Nu 21:6; Dt 32:24 [h]Ps 58:5
8:18 [i]La 5:17
8:19 [j]Jer 9:16 [k]Dt 32:21
8:21 [l]Jer 14:17
8:22 [m]Ge 37:25 [n]Jer 30:12
9:1 [o]Jer 13:17; La 2:11,18 [p]Isa 22:4
9:2 [q]Jer 5:7-8; 23:10; Hos 4:2
9:3 [r]Ps 64:3
9:4 [s]Mic 7:5-6 [t]Ge 27:35
9:6 [u]Jer 5:27

7 Therefore this is what the LORD Almighty says:

"See, I will refine[v] and test[w] them,
for what else can I do
because of the sin of my people?
8 Their tongue[x] is a deadly arrow;
it speaks with deceit.
With his mouth each speaks
cordially to his neighbor,
but in his heart he sets a trap[y] for him.
9 Should I not punish them for this?"
declares the LORD.
"Should I not avenge[z] myself
on such a nation as this?"

10 I will weep and wail for the mountains
and take up a lament concerning the desert pastures.
They are desolate and untraveled,
and the lowing of cattle is not heard.
The birds of the air[a] have fled
and the animals are gone.

11 "I will make Jerusalem a heap of ruins,
a haunt of jackals;[b]
and I will lay waste the towns of Judah
so no one can live there."[c]

12 What man is wise[d] enough to understand this? Who has been instructed
by the LORD and can explain it? Why
has the land been ruined and laid waste
like a desert that no one can cross?
13 The LORD said, "It is because they
have forsaken my law, which I set before them; they have not obeyed me
or followed my law.[e] 14 Instead, they
have followed[f] the stubbornness of their
hearts;[g] they have followed the Baals, as
their fathers taught them." 15 Therefore,
this is what the LORD Almighty, the
God of Israel, says: "See, I will make
this people eat bitter food[h] and drink
poisoned water.[i] 16 I will scatter them
among nations[j] that neither they nor
their fathers have known,[k] and I will
pursue them with the sword[l] until I
have destroyed them."[m]

17 This is what the LORD Almighty
says:

"Consider now! Call for the wailing women[n] to come;
send for the most skillful of them.

9:7 [v]Isa 1:25 [w]Jer 6:27
9:8 [x]ver 3 [y]Jer 5:26
9:9 [z]Jer 5:9,29
9:10 [a]Jer 4:25; 12:4; Hos 4:3
9:11 [b]Isa 34:13 [c]Isa 25:2; Jer 26:9
9:12 [d]Ps 107:43; Hos 14:9
9:13 [e]2Ch 7:19; Ps 89:30-32
9:14 [f]Jer 2:8,23 [g]Jer 7:24
9:15 [h]La 3:15 [i]Jer 8:14
9:16 [j]Lev 26:33 [k]Dt 28:64 [l]Eze 5:2 [m]Jer 44:27; Eze 5:12
9:17 [n]2Ch 35:25; Ecc 12:5; Am 5:16

18 Let them come quickly
and wail over us
till our eyes overflow with tears
and water streams from our eyelids.[o]
19 The sound of wailing is heard from Zion:
'How ruined[p] we are!
How great is our shame!
We must leave our land
because our houses are in ruins.'"
20 Now, O women, hear the word of the LORD;
open your ears to the words of his mouth.
Teach your daughters how to wail;
teach one another a lament.[q]
21 Death has climbed in through our windows
and has entered our fortresses;
it has cut off the children from the streets
and the young men[r] from the public squares.

22 Say, "This is what the LORD declares:

"'The dead bodies of men will lie
like refuse[s] on the open field,
like cut grain behind the reaper,
with no one to gather them.'"

23 This is what the LORD says:

"Let not the wise man boast of his wisdom[t]
or the strong man boast of his strength[u]
or the rich man boast of his riches,[v]
24 but let him who boasts boast[w] about this:
that he understands and knows me,
that I am the LORD,[x] who exercises kindness,[y]
justice and righteousness[z] on earth,
for in these I delight,"
declares the LORD.

25 "The days are coming," declares
the LORD, "when I will punish all who
are circumcised only in the flesh[a]—
26 Egypt, Judah, Edom, Ammon, Moab
and all who live in the desert in distant places.[a][b] For all these nations are

[a]26 Or *desert and who clip the hair by their foreheads*

9:18 [o]Jer 14:17
9:19 [p]Jer 4:13
9:20 [q]Isa 32:9-13
9:21 [r]2Ch 36:17
9:22 [s]Jer 8:2
9:23 [t]Ecc 9:11 [u]1Ki 20:11 [v]Eze 28:4-5
9:24 [w]1Co 1:31*; Gal 6:14 [x]2Co 10:17* [y]Ps 51:1; Mic 7:18 [z]Ps 36:6
9:25 [a]Ro 2:8-9
9:26 [b]Jer 25:23

GOODNESS

A SERVANT FREE OF ARROGANCE

Jeremiah 9:25

How little good it does to brag of our morality or boast of those rituals by which we have become members of the church. Those whose hearts have felt the knife of circumcision have experienced the holiness of God, and they know their need for cleansing.

really uncircumcised, and even the
whole house of Israel is uncircumcised
9:26 [c]Lev 26:41; Ac 7:51; Ro 2:28 in heart.[c]"

God and Idols

10 Hear what the LORD says to
you, O house of Israel. 2 This is
what the LORD says:

"Do not learn the ways of the
nations[d]
10:2 [d]Lev 20:23
or be terrified by signs in the sky,
though the nations are terrified by
them.
3 For the customs of the peoples are
worthless;
they cut a tree out of the forest,
10:3 [e]Isa 40:19 and a craftsman[e] shapes it with his
chisel.
4 They adorn it with silver and gold;
they fasten it with hammer and
nails
10:4 [f]Isa 41:7 so it will not totter.[f]
5 Like a scarecrow in a melon patch,
10:5 [g]1Co 12:2 [h]Ps 115:5,7 [i]Isa 41:24; 46:7 their idols cannot speak;[g]
they must be carried
because they cannot walk.[h]
Do not fear them;
they can do no harm
nor can they do any good."[i]
6 No one is like you, O LORD;
10:6 [j]Ps 48:1 you are great,[j]
and your name is mighty in
power.
10:7 [k]Ps 22:28; Rev 15:4 7 Who should not revere you,
O King of the nations?[k]
This is your due.
Among all the wise men of the
nations
and in all their kingdoms,
there is no one like you.
10:8 [l]Isa 40:19; Jer 4:22 8 They are all senseless and foolish;[l]
they are taught by worthless
wooden idols.
9 Hammered silver is brought from
Tarshish
and gold from Uphaz.
What the craftsman and goldsmith
have made[m] 10:9 [m]Ps 115:4; Isa 40:19
is then dressed in blue and
purple—
all made by skilled workers.
10 But the LORD is the true God;
he is the living God, the eternal
King.
When he is angry, the earth
trembles;
the nations cannot endure his 10:10 [n]Ps 76:7
wrath.[n]

11 "Tell them this: 'These gods, who
did not make the heavens and the earth,
will perish[o] from the earth and from 10:11 [o]Ps 96:5; Isa 2:18
under the heavens.'"[a]

12 But God made the earth by his
power;
he founded the world by his
wisdom
and stretched out the heavens[p] by 10:12 [p]Ge 1:1,8; Job 9:8; Isa 40:22
his understanding.
13 When he thunders,[q] the waters in 10:13 [q]Job 36:29 [r]Ps 135:7
the heavens roar;
he makes clouds rise from the
ends of the earth.
He sends lightning with the rain[r]
and brings out the wind from his
storehouses.

14 Everyone is senseless and without
knowledge;
every goldsmith is shamed by his
idols.
His images are a fraud;
they have no breath in them.
15 They are worthless,[s] the objects of 10:15 [s]Isa 41:24; Jer 14:22
mockery;
when their judgment comes, they
will perish.
16 He who is the Portion[t] of Jacob is 10:16 [t]Dt 32:9; Ps 119:57 [u]ver 12 [v]Ps 74:2 [w]Jer 31:35; 32:18
not like these,
for he is the Maker of all things,[u]
including Israel, the tribe of his
inheritance[v]—
the LORD Almighty is his name.[w]

Coming Destruction

17 Gather up your belongings[x] to leave 10:17 [x]Eze 12:3-12
the land,
you who live under siege.
18 For this is what the LORD says: 10:18 [y]1Sa 25:29
"At this time I will hurl[y] out

[a] *11* The text of this verse is in Aramaic.

those who live in this land;
I will bring distress on them
so that they may be captured."
19Woe to me because of my injury!
My wound[z] is incurable!
Yet I said to myself,
"This is my sickness, and I must
endure[a] it."
20My tent[b] is destroyed;
all its ropes are snapped.
My sons are gone from me and are
no more;[c]
no one is left now to pitch my
tent
or to set up my shelter.
21The shepherds are senseless
and do not inquire of the LORD;
so they do not prosper
and all their flock is scattered.[d]
22Listen! The report is coming—
a great commotion from the land
of the north!
It will make the towns of Judah
desolate,
a haunt of jackals.[e]

Jeremiah's Prayer

23I know, O LORD, that a man's life is
not his own;
it is not for man to direct his
steps.[f]
24Correct me, LORD, but only with
justice—
not in your anger,[g]
lest you reduce me to nothing.[h]
25Pour out your wrath on the nations[i]
that do not acknowledge you,
on the peoples who do not call on
your name.[j]
For they have devoured[k] Jacob;
they have devoured him
completely
and destroyed his homeland.[l]

10:19 [z]Jer 14:17 [a]Mic 7:9
10:20 [b]Jer 4:20 [c]Jer 31:15; La 1:5
10:21 [d]Jer 23:2
10:22 [e]Jer 9:11
10:23 [f]Pr 20:24
10:24 [g]Ps 6:1; 38:1 [h]Jer 30:11
10:25 [i]Zep 3:8 [j]Job 18:21; Ps 14:4 [k]Ps 79:7; Jer 8:16 [l]Ps 79:6-7

The Covenant Is Broken

11 This is the word that came to
Jeremiah from the LORD: 2"Listen to the terms of this covenant and
tell them to the people of Judah and to
those who live in Jerusalem. 3Tell them
that this is what the LORD, the God of
Israel, says: 'Cursed[m] is the man who
does not obey the terms of this covenant— 4the terms I commanded your
forefathers when I brought them out
of Egypt, out of the iron-smelting
furnace.[n]' I said, 'Obey[o] me and do
everything I command you, and you
will be my people,[p] and I will be your
God. 5Then I will fulfill the oath I
swore[q] to your forefathers, to give them
a land flowing with milk and honey'—
the land you possess today."
I answered, "Amen, LORD."
6The LORD said to me, "Proclaim all
these words in the towns of Judah and
in the streets of Jerusalem: 'Listen to
the terms of this covenant and follow[r]
them. 7From the time I brought your
forefathers up from Egypt until today, I
warned them again and again,[s] saying,
"Obey me." 8But they did not listen
or pay attention;[t] instead, they followed
the stubbornness of their evil hearts. So
I brought on them all the curses[u] of
the covenant I had commanded them
to follow but that they did not keep.' "
9Then the LORD said to me, "There
is a conspiracy[v] among the people of
Judah and those who live in Jerusalem.
10They have returned to the sins of their
forefathers,[w] who refused to listen to
my words. They have followed other
gods[x] to serve them. Both the house
of Israel and the house of Judah have
broken the covenant I made with their
forefathers. 11Therefore this is what the
LORD says: 'I will bring on them a
disaster[y] they cannot escape. Although
they cry[z] out to me, I will not listen[a]
to them. 12The towns of Judah and
the people of Jerusalem will go and cry
out to the gods to whom they burn
incense,[b] but they will not help them at
all when disaster[c] strikes. 13You have as
many gods as you have towns, O Judah;
and the altars you have set up to burn
incense[d] to that shameful[e] god Baal are
as many as the streets of Jerusalem.'
14"Do not pray[f] for this people nor
offer any plea or petition for them, because I will not listen[g] when they call to
me in the time of their distress.

15"What is my beloved doing in my
temple
as she works out her evil schemes
with many?
Can consecrated meat avert ⌞your
punishment⌟?
When you engage in your
wickedness,
then you rejoice.[a]"

11:3 [m]Dt 27:26; Gal 3:10
11:4 [n]Dt 4:20; 1Ki 8:51 [o]Ex 24:8
11:4 [p]Jer 7:23; 31:33
11:5 [q]Ex 13:5; Dt 7:12; Ps 105:8-11
11:6 [r]Dt 15:5; Ro 2:13; Jas 1:22
11:7 [s]2Ch 36:15
11:8 [t]Jer 7:26 [u]Lev 26:14-43
11:9 [v]Eze 22:25
11:10 [w]Dt 9:7 [x]Jdg 2:12-13
11:11 [y]2Ki 22:16 [z]Jer 14:12; Eze 8:18 [a]ver 14; Pr 1:28; Isa 1:15; Zec 7:13
11:12 [b]Jer 44:17 [c]Dt 32:37
11:13 [d]Jer 7:9 [e]Jer 3:24
11:14 [f]Ex 32:10 [g]ver 11

[a]*15* Or *Could consecrated meat avert your punishment? / Then you would rejoice*

[16]The LORD called you a thriving
olive tree
with fruit beautiful in form.
But with the roar of a mighty storm
he will set it on fire,[h]
and its branches will be broken.[i]

[17]The LORD Almighty, who planted[j] you, has decreed disaster for you, because the house of Israel and the house of Judah have done evil and provoked me to anger by burning incense to Baal.[k]

11:16 [h]Jer 21:14 [i]Isa 27:11; Ro 11:17-24
11:17 [j]Isa 5:2; Jer 12:2 [k]Jer 7:9

Plot Against Jeremiah

[18]Because the LORD revealed their plot to me, I knew it, for at that time he showed me what they were doing.
[19]I had been like a gentle lamb led to the slaughter; I did not realize that they had plotted[l] against me, saying,

"Let us destroy the tree and its fruit;
let us cut him off from the land of the living,[m]
that his name be remembered[n] no more."

[20]But, O LORD Almighty, you who judge righteously
and test the heart and mind,[o]
let me see your vengeance upon them,
for to you I have committed my cause.

11:19 [l]Jer 18:18; 20:10 [m]Job 28:13; Isa 53:8 [n]Ps 83:4
11:20 [o]Ps 7:9

[21]"Therefore this is what the LORD says about the men of Anathoth who are seeking your life[p] and saying, 'Do not prophesy in the name of the LORD or you will die[q] by our hands'— [22]therefore this is what the LORD Almighty says: 'I will punish them. Their young men[r] will die by the sword, their sons and daughters by famine. [23]Not even a remnant[s] will be left to them, because I will bring disaster on the men of Anathoth in the year of their punishment.[t]' "

11:21 [p]Jer 12:6 [q]Jer 26:8,11; 38:4
11:22 [r]Jer 18:21
11:23 [s]Jer 6:9 [t]Jer 23:12

Jeremiah's Complaint

12 You are always righteous,[u] O LORD,
when I bring a case before you.
Yet I would speak with you about your justice:
Why does the way of the wicked prosper?[v]
Why do all the faithless live at ease?

12:1 [u]Ezr 9:15 [v]Jer 5:27-28

[2]You have planted[w] them, and they have taken root;
they grow and bear fruit.
You are always on their lips
but far from their hearts.[x]
[3]Yet you know me, O LORD;
you see me and test[y] my thoughts about you.
Drag them off like sheep to be butchered!
Set them apart for the day of slaughter![z]
[4]How long will the land lie parched[a][a]
and the grass in every field be withered?[b]
Because those who live in it are wicked,
the animals and birds have perished.[c]
Moreover, the people are saying,
"He will not see what happens to us."

12:2 [w]Jer 11:17 [x]Isa 29:13; Jer 3:10; Mt 15:8; Tit 1:16
12:3 [y]Ps 7:9; 11:5; 139:1-4; Jer 11:20 [z]Jer 17:18
12:4 [a]Jer 4:28 [b]Joel 1:10-12 [c]Jer 4:25; 9:10

God's Answer

[5]"If you have raced with men on foot
and they have worn you out,
how can you compete with horses?
If you stumble in safe country,[b]
how will you manage in the thickets[d] by[c] the Jordan?

12:5 [d]Jer 49:19; 50:44

PATIENCE

ENDURING TROUBLE

Jeremiah 12:5

Patience is a capacity for enduring trouble. People lacking endurance are soft because they have developed a lifestyle of avoiding hard times. But the judgment of God cannot be avoided, and best of all, his lessons sculpt the hardest granite into an enduring testimony.

[6]Your brothers, your own family—
even they have betrayed you;
they have raised a loud cry against you.[e]
Do not trust them,
though they speak well of you.[f]
[7]"I will forsake my house,
abandon[g] my inheritance;
I will give the one I love
into the hands of her enemies.
[8]My inheritance has become to me
like a lion in the forest.

12:6 [e]Pr 26:24-25; Jer 9:4 [f]Ps 12:2
12:7 [g]Jer 7:29

[a]4 Or *land mourn* [b]5 Or *If you put your trust in a land of safety* [c]5 Or *the flooding of*

She roars at me;
therefore I hate her.[b]
9 Has not my inheritance become to me
like a speckled bird of prey
that other birds of prey surround and attack?
Go and gather all the wild beasts;
bring them to devour.[i]
10 Many shepherds[j] will ruin my vineyard
and trample down my field;
they will turn my pleasant field
into a desolate wasteland.[k]
11 It will be made a wasteland,
parched and desolate before me;[l]
the whole land will be laid waste
because there is no one who cares.
12 Over all the barren heights in the desert
destroyers will swarm,
for the sword of the LORD[m] will devour
from one end of the land to the other;[n]
no one will be safe.
13 They will sow wheat but reap thorns;
they will wear themselves out but gain nothing.[o]
So bear the shame of your harvest
because of the LORD's fierce anger."[p]

14 This is what the LORD says: "As for all my wicked neighbors who seize the inheritance I gave my people Israel, I will uproot[q] them from their lands and I will uproot the house of Judah from among them. 15 But after I uproot them, I will again have compassion and will bring[r] each of them back to his own inheritance and his own country. 16 And if they learn well the ways of my people and swear by my name, saying, 'As surely as the LORD lives'[s]—even as they once taught my people to swear by Baal[t]—then they will be established among my people.[u] 17 But if any nation does not listen, I will completely uproot and destroy[v] it," declares the LORD.

A Linen Belt

13 This is what the LORD said to me: "Go and buy a linen belt and put it around your waist, but do not let it touch water." 2 So I bought a belt, as the LORD directed, and put it around my waist.

12:8 [h]Hos 9:15; Am 6:8
12:9 [i]Isa 56:9; Jer 15:3; Eze 23:25
12:10 [j]Jer 23:1 [k]Isa 5:1-7
12:11 [l]ver 4; Isa 42:25; Jer 23:10
12:12 [m]Jer 47:6 [n]Jer 3:2
12:13 [o]Lev 26:20; Dt 28:38; Mic 6:15; Hag 1:6 [p]Jer 4:26
12:14 [q]Zec 2:7-9
12:15 [r]Am 9:14-15
12:16 [s]Jer 4:2 [t]Jos 23:7 [u]Isa 49:6; Jer 3:17
12:17 [v]Isa 60:12

3 Then the word of the LORD came to me a second time: 4 "Take the belt you bought and are wearing around your waist, and go now to Perath[a] and hide it there in a crevice in the rocks." 5 So I went and hid it at Perath, as the LORD told me.[w]

6 Many days later the LORD said to me, "Go now to Perath and get the belt I told you to hide there." 7 So I went to Perath and dug up the belt and took it from the place where I had hidden it, but now it was ruined and completely useless.

8 Then the word of the LORD came to me: 9 "This is what the LORD says: 'In the same way I will ruin the pride[x] of Judah and the great pride of Jerusalem. 10 These wicked people, who refuse to listen to my words, who follow the stubbornness of their hearts[y] and go after other gods[z] to serve and worship them, will be like this belt—completely useless! 11 For as a belt is bound around a man's waist, so I bound the whole house of Israel and the whole house of Judah to me,' declares the LORD, 'to be my people for my renown[a] and praise and honor.[b] But they have not listened.'[c]

Wineskins

12 "Say to them: 'This is what the LORD, the God of Israel, says: Every wineskin should be filled with wine.' And if they say to you, 'Don't we know that every wineskin should be filled with wine?' 13 then tell them, 'This is what the LORD says: I am going to fill with drunkenness[d] all who live in this land, including the kings who sit on David's throne, the priests, the prophets and all those living in Jerusalem. 14 I will smash them one against the other, fathers and sons alike, declares the LORD. I will allow no pity or mercy or compassion[e] to keep me from destroying[f] them.'"

Threat of Captivity

15 Hear and pay attention,
do not be arrogant,
for the LORD has spoken.
16 Give glory[g] to the LORD your God
before he brings the darkness,
before your feet stumble[h]

13:5 [w]Ex 40:16
13:9 [x]Lev 26:19
13:10 [y]Jer 11:8; 16:12 [z]Jer 9:14
13:11 [a]Jer 32:20; 33:9 [b]Ex 19:5-6 [c]Jer 7:26
13:13 [d]Ps 60:3; 75:8; Isa 51:17; 63:6; Jer 51:57
13:14 [e]Jer 16:5 [f]Dt 29:20; Eze 5:10
13:16 [g]Jos 7:19 [h]Jer 23:12

[a]4 Or possibly *the Euphrates*; also in verses 5-7

on the darkening hills.
You hope for light,
but he will turn it to thick
darkness
and change it to deep gloom.[i]
[17]But if you do not listen,[j]
I will weep in secret
because of your pride;
my eyes will weep bitterly,
overflowing with tears,[k]
because the LORD's flock[l] will be
taken captive.[m]
[18]Say to the king and to the queen
mother,
"Come down from your thrones,
for your glorious crowns
will fall from your heads."
[19]The cities in the Negev will be shut
up,
and there will be no one to open
them.
All Judah[n] will be carried into exile,
carried completely away.

[20]Lift up your eyes and see
those who are coming from the
north.[o]
Where is the flock[p] that was
entrusted to you,
the sheep of which you boasted?
[21]What will you say when ⌊the LORD⌋
sets over you
those you cultivated as your
special allies?[q]
Will not pain grip you
like that of a woman in labor?[r]
[22]And if you ask yourself,
"Why has this happened to
me?"—
it is because of your many sins[s]
that your skirts have been torn off
and your body mistreated.[t]
[23]Can the Ethiopian[a] change his skin
or the leopard its spots?
Neither can you do good
who are accustomed to doing evil.

[24]"I will scatter you like chaff[u]
driven by the desert wind.[v]
[25]This is your lot,
the portion[w] I have decreed for
you,"
declares the LORD,
"because you have forgotten me
and trusted in false gods.
[26]I will pull up your skirts over your
face
that your shame may be seen[x]—
[27]your adulteries and lustful neighings,
your shameless prostitution![y]
I have seen your detestable acts
on the hills and in the fields.[z]
Woe to you, O Jerusalem!
How long will you be unclean?"[a]

Drought, Famine, Sword

14 This is the word of the LORD to Jeremiah concerning the drought:

[2]"Judah mourns,[b]
her cities languish;
they wail for the land,
and a cry goes up from Jerusalem.
[3]The nobles send their servants for
water;[c]
they go to the cisterns
but find no water.
They return with their jars unfilled;
dismayed and despairing,
they cover their heads.[d]
[4]The ground is cracked
because there is no rain in the
land;[e]
the farmers are dismayed
and cover their heads.
[5]Even the doe in the field
deserts her newborn fawn
because there is no grass.[f]
[6]Wild donkeys stand on the barren
heights[g]
and pant like jackals;
their eyesight fails
for lack of pasture."

[7]Although our sins testify[h] against us,
O LORD, do something for the
sake of your name.
For our backsliding[i] is great;
we have sinned[j] against you.
[8]O Hope[k] of Israel,
its Savior in times of distress,
why are you like a stranger in the
land,
like a traveler who stays only a
night?
[9]Why are you like a man taken by
surprise,
like a warrior powerless to save?[l]
You are among[m] us, O LORD,
and we bear your name;[n]
do not forsake us!

[10]This is what the LORD says about
this people:

[a]*23* Hebrew *Cushite* (probably a person from the upper Nile region)

13:16 [i]Isa 59:9
13:17 [j]Mal 2:2 [k]Jer 9:1 [l]Ps 80:1; Jer 23:1 [m]Jer 14:18
13:19 [n]Jer 20:4; 52:30
13:20 [o]Jer 6:22; Hab 1:6 [p]Jer 23:2
13:21 [q]Jer 38:22 [r]Jer 4:31
13:22 [s]Jer 9:2-6; 16:10-12 [t]Eze 16:37; Na 3:5-6
13:24 [u]Ps 1:4 [v]Lev 26:33
13:25 [w]Job 20:29; Mt 24:51
13:26 [x]La 1:8; Eze 16:37; Hos 2:10
13:27 [y]Jer 2:20 [z]Eze 6:13 [a]Hos 8:5
14:2 [b]Isa 3:26; Jer 8:21
14:3 [c]2Ki 18:31; Job 6:19-20 [d]2Sa 15:30
14:4 [e]Jer 3:3
14:5 [f]Isa 15:6
14:6 [g]Job 39:5-6; Jer 2:24
14:7 [h]Hos 5:5 [i]Jer 5:6 [j]Jer 8:14
14:8 [k]Jer 17:13
14:9 [l]Isa 50:2 [m]Jer 8:19 [n]Isa 63:19; Jer 15:16

"They greatly love to wander;
they do not restrain their feet.[o]
So the LORD does not accept[p] them;
he will now remember[q] their
wickedness
and punish them for their sins."[r]

11 Then the LORD said to me, "Do not pray[s] for the well-being of this people. 12 Although they fast, I will not listen to their cry;[t] though they offer burnt offerings[u] and grain offerings, I will not accept[v] them. Instead, I will destroy them with the sword, famine and plague."

13 But I said, "Ah, Sovereign LORD, the prophets keep telling them, 'You will not see the sword or suffer famine.[w] Indeed, I will give you lasting peace in this place.' "

14 Then the LORD said to me, "The prophets are prophesying lies[x] in my name. I have not sent[y] them or appointed them or spoken to them. They are prophesying to you false visions,[z] divinations,[a] idolatries[a] and the delusions of their own minds. 15 Therefore, this is what the LORD says about the prophets who are prophesying in my name: I did not send them, yet they are saying, 'No sword or famine will touch this land.' Those same prophets will perish[b] by sword and famine.[c] 16 And the people they are prophesying to will be thrown out into the streets of Jerusalem because of the famine and sword. There will be no one to bury[d] them or their wives, their sons or their daughters.[e] I will pour out on them the calamity they deserve.[f]

17 "Speak this word to them:

" 'Let my eyes overflow with tears[g]
night and day without ceasing;
for my virgin daughter—my
people—
has suffered a grievous wound,
a crushing blow.[h]
18 If I go into the country,
I see those slain by the sword;
if I go into the city,
I see the ravages of famine.[i]
Both prophet and priest
have gone to a land they know
not.' "

19 Have you rejected Judah
completely?[j]
Do you despise Zion?
Why have you afflicted us
so that we cannot be healed?[k]
We hoped for peace
but no good has come,
for a time of healing
but there is only terror.[l]
20 O LORD, we acknowledge our
wickedness
and the guilt of our fathers;
we have indeed sinned[m] against
you.
21 For the sake of your name[n] do not
despise us;
do not dishonor your glorious
throne.[o]
Remember your covenant with us
and do not break it.
22 Do any of the worthless idols of the
nations bring rain?[p]
Do the skies themselves send
down showers?
No, it is you, O LORD our God.
Therefore our hope is in you,
for you are the one who does all
this.

15

Then the LORD said to me: "Even if Moses[q] and Samuel[r] were to stand before me, my heart would not go out to this people.[s] Send them away from my presence![t] Let them go! 2 And if they ask you, 'Where shall we go?' tell them, 'This is what the LORD says:

" 'Those destined for death, to death;
those for the sword, to the sword;[u]
those for starvation, to starvation;[v]
those for captivity, to captivity.'[w]

3 "I will send four kinds of destroyers[x] against them," declares the LORD, "the sword to kill and the dogs to drag away and the birds[y] of the air and the beasts of the earth to devour and destroy.[z] 4 I will make them abhorrent[a] to all the kingdoms of the earth[b] because of what Manasseh[c] son of Hezekiah king of Judah did in Jerusalem.

5 "Who will have pity[d] on you,
O Jerusalem?
Who will mourn for you?
Who will stop to ask how you are?
6 You have rejected[e] me," declares the
LORD.
"You keep on backsliding.
So I will lay hands[f] on you and
destroy you;

[a] 14 Or *visions, worthless divinations*

14:10 [o]Ps 119:101; Jer 2:25 [p]Jer 6:20; Am 5:22 [q]Hos 9:9 [r]Jer 44:21-23; Hos 8:13
14:11 [s]Ex 32:10
14:12 [t]Isa 1:15; Jer 11:11 [u]Jer 7:21 [v]Jer 6:20
14:13 [w]Jer 5:12
14:14 [x]Jer 27:14 [y]Jer 23:21,32 [z]Jer 23:16 [a]Eze 12:24
14:15 [b]Eze 14:9 [c]Jer 5:12-13
14:16 [d]Ps 79:3 [e]Jer 7:33 [f]Pr 1:31
14:17 [g]Jer 9:1 [h]Jer 8:21
14:18 [i]Eze 7:15
14:19 [j]Jer 7:29
14:19 [k]Jer 30:12-13 [l]Jer 8:15
14:20 [m]Da 9:7-8
14:21 [n]ver 7 [o]Jer 3:17
14:22 [p]Ps 135:7
15:1 [q]Ex 32:11; Nu 14:13-20 [r]1Sa 7:9 [s]Jer 7:16; Eze 14:14,20 [t]2Ki 17:20
15:2 [u]Jer 43:11 [v]Jer 14:12 [w]Rev 13:10
15:3 [x]Lev 26:16 [y]Dt 28:26 [z]Lev 26:22; Eze 14:21
15:4 [a]Jer 24:9; 29:18 [b]Dt 28:25 [c]2Ki 21:2; 23:26-27
15:5 [d]Isa 51:19; Jer 13:14; 21:7; Na 3:7
15:6 [e]Jer 6:19; 7:24 [f]Zep 1:4

FAITHFULNESS

DRAWING NEAR

Jeremiah 15:6

Backsliding is a habit just as faithfulness is. Our lives are consumed by either moving toward God or moving away from him. Let us not delude ourselves by saying, "I'm semi-close to (or semi-far from) God, and I'm content." Move ever God-ward. Only then shall you live.

I can no longer show compassion.
[7]I will winnow them with a
winnowing fork
at the city gates of the land.
I will bring bereavement and
destruction on my people,[g]
for they have not changed their
ways.
[8]I will make their widows more
numerous
than the sand of the sea.
At midday I will bring a destroyer[h]
against the mothers of their young
men;
suddenly I will bring down on them
anguish and terror.
[9]The mother of seven will grow faint[i]
and breathe her last.
Her sun will set while it is still day;
she will be disgraced and
humiliated.
I will put the survivors to the sword[j]
before their enemies,"
declares the LORD.

[10]Alas, my mother, that you gave me
birth,[k]
a man with whom the whole land
strives and contends![l]
I have neither lent[m] nor borrowed,
yet everyone curses me.

[11]The LORD said,

"Surely I will deliver you[n] for a good
purpose;
surely I will make your enemies
plead[o] with you
in times of disaster and times of
distress.

[12]"Can a man break iron—
iron from the north[p]—or bronze?
[13]Your wealth and your treasures
I will give as plunder, without
charge,[q]

15:7 [g]Jer 18:21
15:8 [h]Jer 6:4
15:9 [i]1Sa 2:5 [j]Jer 21:7
15:10 [k]Job 3:1 [l]Jer 1:19 [m]Lev 25:36
15:11 [n]Jer 40:4 [o]Jer 21:1-2; 37:3; 42:1-3
15:12 [p]Jer 28:14
15:13 [q]Ps 44:12

because of all your sins
throughout your country.[r]
[14]I will enslave you to your enemies
in[a] a land you do not know,[s]
for my anger will kindle a fire[t]
that will burn against you."

[15]You understand, O LORD;
remember me and care for me.
Avenge me on my persecutors.[u]
You are long-suffering—do not take
me away;
think of how I suffer reproach for
your sake.[v]
[16]When your words came, I ate[w]
them;
they were my joy and my heart's
delight,[x]
for I bear your name,[y]
O LORD God Almighty.
[17]I never sat[z] in the company of
revelers,
never made merry with them;
I sat alone because your hand was
on me
and you had filled me with
indignation.
[18]Why is my pain unending
and my wound grievous and
incurable?[a]
Will you be to me like a deceptive
brook,
like a spring that fails?[b]

[19]Therefore this is what the LORD
says:

"If you repent, I will restore you
that you may serve[c] me;
if you utter worthy, not worthless,
words,
you will be my spokesman.
Let this people turn to you,
but you must not turn to them.
[20]I will make you a wall to this people,
a fortified wall of bronze;
they will fight against you
but will not overcome you,
for I am with you
to rescue and save you,"[d]
declares the LORD.
[21]"I will save you from the hands of
the wicked
and redeem[e] you from the grasp of
the cruel."[f]

[a]*14* Some Hebrew manuscripts, Septuagint and Syriac (see also Jer. 17:4); most Hebrew manuscripts *I will cause your enemies to bring you / into*

15:13 [r]Jer 17:3
15:14 [s]Dt 28:36; Jer 16:13 [t]Dt 32:22; Ps 21:9
15:5 [u]Jer 12:3 [v]Ps 69:7-9
15:16 [w]Eze 3:3; Rev 10:10 [x]Ps 119:72, 103 [y]Jer 14:9
15:17 [z]Ps 1:1; 26:4-5; Jer 16:8
15:18 [a]Jer 30:15; Mic 1:9 [b]Job 6:15
15:19 [c]Zec 3:7
15:20 [d]Jer 20:11; Eze 3:8
15:21 [e]Jer 50:34 [f]Ge 48:16

Day of Disaster

16 Then the word of the LORD came to me: 2"You must not marry[g] and have sons or daughters in this place." 3For this is what the LORD says about the sons and daughters born in this land and about the women who are their mothers and the men who are their fathers:[h] 4"They will die of deadly diseases. They will not be mourned or buried[i] but will be like refuse lying on the ground.[j] They will perish by sword and famine, and their dead bodies will become food for the birds of the air and the beasts of the earth."[k]

5For this is what the LORD says: "Do not enter a house where there is a funeral meal; do not go to mourn or show sympathy, because I have withdrawn my blessing, my love and my pity from this people," declares the LORD. 6"Both high and low will die in this land.[l] They will not be buried or mourned, and no one will cut[m] himself or shave[n] his head for them. 7No one will offer food to comfort those who mourn[o] for the dead—not even for a father or a mother—nor will anyone give them a drink to console them.

8"And do not enter a house where there is feasting and sit down to eat and drink.[p] 9For this is what the LORD Almighty, the God of Israel, says: Before your eyes and in your days I will bring an end to the sounds[q] of joy and gladness and to the voices of bride and bridegroom in this place.[r]

10"When you tell these people all this and they ask you, 'Why has the LORD decreed such a great disaster against us? What wrong have we done? What sin have we committed against the LORD our God?'[s] 11then say to them, 'It is because your fathers forsook me,' declares the LORD, 'and followed other gods and served and worshiped them. They forsook me and did not keep my law.[t] 12But you have behaved more wickedly than your fathers.[u] See how each of you is following the stubbornness of his evil heart[v] instead of obeying me. 13So I will throw you out of this land into a land neither you nor your fathers have known,[w] and there you will serve other gods[x] day and night, for I will show you no favor.'[y]

14"However, the days are coming," declares the LORD, "when men will no longer say, 'As surely as the LORD lives, who brought the Israelites up out of Egypt,'[z] 15but they will say, 'As surely as the LORD lives, who brought the Israelites up out of the land of the north and out of all the countries where he had banished them.'[a] For I will restore[b] them to the land I gave their forefathers.

16"But now I will send for many fishermen," declares the LORD, "and they will catch them.[c] After that I will send for many hunters, and they will hunt[d] them down on every mountain and hill and from the crevices of the rocks.[e] 17My eyes are on all their ways; they are not hidden[f] from me, nor is their sin concealed from my eyes.[g] 18I will repay them double[h] for their wickedness and their sin, because they have defiled my land[i] with the lifeless forms of their vile images and have filled my inheritance with their detestable idols."

19O LORD, my strength and my fortress,
  my refuge in time of distress,
to you the nations will come[j]
  from the ends of the earth and say,
"Our fathers possessed nothing but false gods,[k]
  worthless idols that did them no good.
20Do men make their own gods?
  Yes, but they are not gods!"[l]

21"Therefore I will teach them—
  this time I will teach them
  my power and might.
Then they will know
  that my name is the LORD.

17 "Judah's sin is engraved with an iron tool,[m]
  inscribed with a flint point,
on the tablets of their hearts[n]
  and on the horns of their altars.
2Even their children remember
  their altars and Asherah poles[a][o]
beside the spreading trees
  and on the high hills.[p]
3My mountain in the land
  and your[b] wealth and all your treasures
I will give away as plunder,[q]
  together with your high places,[r]

16:2 [g]1Co 7:26-27
16:3 [h]Jer 6:21
16:4 [i]Jer 25:33 [j]Ps 83:10; Jer 9:22 [k]Ps 79:1-3; Jer 15:3; 34:20
16:6 [l]Eze 9:5-6 [m]Lev 19:28 [n]Jer 41:5; 47:5
16:7 [o]Eze 24:17; Hos 9:4
16:8 [p]Ecc 7:2-4; Jer 15:17
16:9 [q]Isa 24:8; Eze 26:13; Hos 2:11 [r]Rev 18:23
16:10 [s]Dt 29:24; Jer 5:19
16:11 [t]Dt 29:25-26; 1Ki 9:9; Ps 106:35-43; Jer 22:9
16:12 [u]Jer 7:26 [v]Ecc 9:3; Jer 13:10
16:13 [w]Dt 28:36; Jer 5:19 [x]Dt 4:28 [y]Jer 15:5
16:14 [z]Dt 15:15; Jer 23:7-8
16:15 [a]Isa 11:11; Jer 23:8 [b]Jer 24:6
16:16 [c]Am 4:2; Hab 1:14-15 [d]Am 9:3; Mic 7:2 [e]1Sa 26:20
16:17 [f]1Co 4:5; Heb 4:13 [g]Pr 15:3
16:18 [h]Isa 40:2; Rev 18:6 [i]Nu 35:34; Jer 2:7
16:19 [j]Isa 2:2; Jer 3:17 [k]Ps 4:2
16:20 [l]Ps 115:4-7; Isa 37:19; Jer 2:11
17:1 [m]Job 19:24 [n]Pr 3:3; 2Co 3:3
17:2 [o]2Ch 24:18 [p]Jer 2:20
17:3 [q]2Ki 24:13 [r]Jer 26:18; Mic 3:12

[a]2 That is, symbols of the goddess Asherah
[b]2,3 Or *hills* / [3]*and the mountains of the land. / Your*

because of sin throughout your
country.[s]
[4]Through your own fault you will
lose
the inheritance[t] I gave you.
I will enslave you to your enemies[u]
in a land[v] you do not know,
for you have kindled my anger,
and it will burn[w] forever."

[5]This is what the LORD says:

"Cursed is the one who trusts in
man,[x]
who depends on flesh for his
strength
and whose heart turns away from
the LORD.
[6]He will be like a bush in the
wastelands;
he will not see prosperity when it
comes.
He will dwell in the parched places
of the desert,
in a salt[y] land where no one lives.
[7]"But blessed is the man who trusts[z]
in the LORD,
whose confidence is in him.
[8]He will be like a tree planted by the
water
that sends out its roots by the
stream.
It does not fear when heat comes;
its leaves are always green.
It has no worries in a year of
drought[a]
and never fails to bear fruit."[b]

[9]The heart[c] is deceitful above all things
and beyond cure.
Who can understand it?
[10]"I the LORD search the heart[d]
and examine the mind,[e]
to reward[f] a man according to his
conduct,
according to what his deeds
deserve."[g]

[11]Like a partridge that hatches eggs it
did not lay
is the man who gains riches by
unjust means.
When his life is half gone, they will
desert him,
and in the end he will prove to be
a fool.[h]

[12]A glorious throne,[i] exalted from the
beginning,
is the place of our sanctuary.
[13]O LORD, the hope[j] of Israel,
all who forsake[k] you will be put to
shame.
Those who turn away from you will
be written in the dust
because they have forsaken the
LORD,
the spring of living water.

[14]Heal me, O LORD, and I will be
healed;
save me and I will be saved,
for you are the one I praise.[l]
[15]They keep saying to me,
"Where is the word of the LORD?
Let it now be fulfilled!"[m]
[16]I have not run away from being your
shepherd;
you know I have not desired the
day of despair.
What passes my lips is open
before you.
[17]Do not be a terror[n] to me;
you are my refuge[o] in the day of
disaster.
[18]Let my persecutors be put to shame,
but keep me from shame;
let them be terrified,
but keep me from terror.
Bring on them the day of disaster;
destroy them with double
destruction.[p]

Keeping the Sabbath Holy

[19]This is what the LORD said to me:
"Go and stand at the gate of the people,
through which the kings of Judah go in
and out; stand also at all the other gates
of Jerusalem.[q] [20]Say to them, 'Hear the
word of the LORD, O kings of Judah
and all people of Judah and everyone
living in Jerusalem[r] who come through
these gates.[s] [21]This is what the LORD
says: Be careful not to carry a load on
the Sabbath[t] day or bring it through
the gates of Jerusalem. [22]Do not bring
a load out of your houses or do any
work on the Sabbath, but keep the Sabbath day holy, as I commanded your
forefathers.[u] [23]Yet they did not listen or
pay attention;[v] they were stiff-necked[w]
and would not listen or respond to
discipline.[x] [24]But if you are careful to
obey me, declares the LORD, and bring
no load through the gates of this city
on the Sabbath, but keep the Sabbath
day holy by not doing any work on it,

17:3 [s]Jer 15:13
17:4 [t]La 5:2 [u]Dt 28:48; Jer 12:7 [v]Jer 16:13 [w]Jer 7:20; 15:14
17:5 [x]Isa 2:22; 30:1-3
17:6 [y]Dt 29:23; Job 39:6
17:7 [z]Ps 34:8; 40:4; Pr 16:20
17:8 [a]Jer 14:1-6 [b]Ps 1:3; 92:12-14
17:9 [c]Ecc 9:3; Mt 13:15; Mk 7:21-22
17:10 [d]1Sa 16:7; Rev 2:23 [e]Ps 17:3; 139:23; Jer 11:20; 20:12; Ro 8:27 [f]Ps 62:12; Jer 32:19 [g]Ro 2:6
17:11 [h]Lk 12:20
17:12 [i]Jer 3:17
17:13 [j]Jer 14:8 [k]Isa 1:28; Jer 2:17
17:14 [l]Ps 109:1
17:15 [m]Isa 5:19; 2Pe 3:4
17:17 [n]Ps 88:15-16 [o]Jer 16:19; Na 1:7
17:18 [p]Ps 35:1-8
17:19 [q]Jer 7:2; 26:2
17:20 [r]Jer 19:3 [s]Jer 22:2
17:21 [t]Nu 15:32-36; Ne 13:15-21; Jn 5:10
17:22 [u]Ex 20:8; 31:13; Isa 56:2-6; Eze 20:12
17:23 [v]Jer 7:26 [w]Jer 19:15 [x]Jer 7:28

17:25 [y]2Sa 7:13; Isa 9:7; Jer 22:2,4; Lk 1:32 25then kings who sit on David's throne[y]
will come through the gates of this city
with their officials. They and their officials will come riding in chariots and
on horses, accompanied by the men of
Judah and those living in Jerusalem,
and this city will be inhabited forever.
26People will come from the towns of
Judah and the villages around Jerusalem, from the territory of Benjamin
and the western foothills, from the hill
17:26 [z]Jer 32:44; 33:13; Zec 7:7 country and the Negev,[z] bringing burnt
offerings and sacrifices, grain offerings,
incense and thank offerings to the house
17:27 [a]Jer 22:5 [b]Jer 7:20 [c]2Ki 25:9; Am 2:5 of the LORD. 27But if you do not obey[a]
me to keep the Sabbath day holy by not
carrying any load as you come through
the gates of Jerusalem on the Sabbath
day, then I will kindle an unquenchable
fire[b] in the gates of Jerusalem that will
consume her fortresses.'"[c]

At the Potter's House

18 This is the word that came to
Jeremiah from the LORD: 2"Go
down to the potter's house, and there
I will give you my message." 3So I
went down to the potter's house, and
I saw him working at the wheel. 4But
the pot he was shaping from the clay
was marred in his hands; so the potter
formed it into another pot, shaping it
as seemed best to him.

SELF-CONTROL

SHAPE UP!

Jeremiah 18:4

We are ultimately responsible for determining what shape our lives will take. The divine potter has a plan for us, but we must submit to and cooperate with that plan. The potter only dreams for us, leaving an openness to his design. If we would be what he would make of us, we must relax and bless his fingers—even as they shape us.

5Then the word of the LORD came
to me: 6"O house of Israel, can I not do
with you as this potter does?" declares
18:6 [d]Isa 45:9; Ro 9:20-21 the LORD. "Like clay[d] in the hand of
the potter, so are you in my hand, O
house of Israel. 7If at any time I an-
18:7 [e]Jer 1:10 nounce that a nation or kingdom is to
be uprooted,[e] torn down and destroyed,
18:8 [f]Jer 26:13; Jnh 3:8-10 8and if that nation I warned repents of
its evil, then I will relent[f] and not in-
flict on it the disaster[g] I had planned. 18:8 [g]Eze 18:21; Hos 11:8-9
9And if at another time I announce that
a nation or kingdom is to be built[h] up 18:9 [h]Jer 1:10; 31:28
and planted, 10and if it does evil[i] in my
sight and does not obey me, then I will
reconsider[j] the good I had intended to 18:10 [i]Eze 33:18 [j]1Sa 2:29-30
do for it.
11"Now therefore say to the people
of Judah and those living in Jerusalem,
'This is what the LORD says: Look! I 18:11 [k]Jer 4:6 [l]2Ki 17:13; Isa 1:16-19 [m]Jer 7:3
am preparing a disaster[k] for you and de-
vising a plan against you. So turn[l] from
your evil ways,[m] each one of you, and
reform your ways and your actions.' 18:12 [n]Isa 57:10; Jer 2:25
12But they will reply, 'It's no use.[n] We
will continue with our own plans; each
of us will follow the stubbornness of his
evil heart.'"

13Therefore this is what the LORD
says:

"Inquire among the nations:
Who has ever heard anything like 18:13 [o]Isa 66:8; Jer 2:10 [p]Jer 5:30
this?[o]
A most horrible[p] thing has been
done
by Virgin Israel.
14Does the snow of Lebanon
ever vanish from its rocky slopes?
Do its cool waters from distant
sources
ever cease to flow?[a]
15Yet my people have forgotten me;
they burn incense to worthless
idols,[q] 18:15 [q]Jer 10:15 [r]Jer 6:16 [s]Isa 57:14; 62:10
which made them stumble in their
ways
and in the ancient paths.[r]
They made them walk in bypaths
and on roads not built up.[s]
16Their land will be laid waste,[t] 18:16 [t]Jer 25:9 [u]Jer 19:8 [v]Ps 22:7
an object of lasting scorn;[u]
all who pass by will be appalled
and will shake their heads.[v]
17Like a wind[w] from the east, 18:17 [w]Jer 13:24 [x]Jer 2:27
I will scatter them before their
enemies;
I will show them my back and not
my face[x]
in the day of their disaster."

18They said, "Come, let's make plans[y] 18:18 [y]Jer 11:19 [z]Mal 2:7 [a]Jer 5:13
against Jeremiah; for the teaching of
the law by the priest[z] will not be lost,
nor will counsel from the wise, nor the
word from the prophets.[a] So come, let's

[a] *14* The meaning of the Hebrew for this sentence is uncertain.

18:18 [b]Ps 52:2 attack him with our tongues[b] and pay
no attention to anything he says."
19 Listen to me, O LORD;
hear what my accusers are saying!
18:20 20 Should good be repaid with evil?
[c]Ps 35:7; 57:6 [d]Ps 106:23 Yet they have dug a pit[c] for me.
Remember that I stood before you
and spoke in their behalf[d]
to turn your wrath away from
them.
18:21 21 So give their children over to famine;[e]
[e]Jer 11:22 [f]Ps 109:9 hand them over to the power of
the sword.
Let their wives be made childless and
widows;[f]
let their men be put to death,
their young men slain by the
sword in battle.
18:22 22 Let a cry[g] be heard from their houses
[g]Jer 6:26 [h]Ps 140:5 when you suddenly bring invaders
against them,
for they have dug a pit to capture me
and have hidden snares[h] for my
feet.
23 But you know, O LORD,
18:23 [i]Jer 11:21 all their plots to kill[i] me.
[j]Ps 109:14 Do not forgive[j] their crimes
or blot out their sins from your
sight.
Let them be overthrown before you;
deal with them in the time of your
anger.

19:1 **19** This is what the LORD says: "Go
[k]Jer 18:2 and buy a clay jar from a potter.[k]
[l]Nu 11:17 Take along some of the elders[l] of the
people and of the priests 2 and go out to
19:2 the Valley of Ben Hinnom,[m] near the
[m]Jos 15:8 entrance of the Potsherd Gate. There
19:3 proclaim the words I tell you, 3 and say,
[n]Jer 17:20 "Hear the word of the LORD, O kings[n]
[o]Jer 6:19 [p]1Sa 3:11 of Judah and people of Jerusalem. This
is what the LORD Almighty, the God of
Israel, says: Listen! I am going to bring
a disaster[o] on this place that will make
the ears of everyone who hears of it tin-
19:4 [q]Dt 28:20; gle.[p] 4 For they have forsaken[q] me and
Isa 65:11 [r]Lev 18:21 made this a place of foreign gods; they
[s]2Ki 21:16; have burned sacrifices[r] in it to gods that
Jer 2:34 neither they nor their fathers nor the
kings of Judah ever knew, and they have
filled this place with the blood of the
19:5 innocent.[s] 5 They have built the high
[t]Lev 18:21; Ps 106:37-38 places of Baal to burn their sons[t] in the
[u]Jer 7:31; 32:35 fire as offerings to Baal—something I
did not command or mention, nor did
it enter my mind.[u] 6 So beware, the days

are coming, declares the LORD, when
people will no longer call this place Topheth or the Valley of Ben Hinnom,[v] 19:6 [v]Jos 15:8
but the Valley of Slaughter.[w] [w]Jer 7:32
7 "'In this place I will ruin[a] the plans
of Judah and Jerusalem. I will make
them fall by the sword before their
enemies,[x] at the hands of those who 19:7 [x]Lev 26:17;
seek their lives, and I will give their car- Dt 28:25
casses[y] as food[z] to the birds of the air [y]Jer 16:4; 34:20
and the beasts of the earth. 8 I will dev- [z]Ps 79:2
astate this city and make it an object of
scorn;[a] all who pass by will be appalled 19:8 [a]Jer 18:16
and will scoff because of all its wounds.
9 I will make them eat[b] the flesh of their 19:9 [b]Lev 26:29;
sons and daughters, and they will eat Dt 28:49-57;
one another's flesh during the stress of La 4:10 [c]Isa 9:20
the siege imposed on them by the en-
emies[c] who seek their lives.'
10 "Then break the jar[d] while those 19:10 [d]ver 1
who go with you are watching, 11 and
say to them, 'This is what the LORD
Almighty says: I will smash[e] this na- 19:11 [e]Ps 2:9;
tion and this city just as this potter's Isa 30:14
jar is smashed and cannot be repaired. [f]Jer 7:32
They will bury[f] the dead in Topheth
until there is no more room. 12 This is
what I will do to this place and to those
who live here, declares the LORD. I
will make this city like Topheth. 13 The
houses[g] in Jerusalem and those of the 19:13 [g]Jer 32:29;
kings of Judah will be defiled like this 52:13
place, Topheth—all the houses where [h]Dt 4:19; Ac 7:42
they burned incense on the roofs to all [i]Jer 7:18;
the starry hosts[h] and poured out drink Eze 20:28
offerings[i] to other gods.'"
14 Jeremiah then returned from Topheth, where the LORD had sent him 19:14
to prophesy, and stood in the court[j] of [j]2Ch 20:5;
the LORD's temple and said to all the Jer 26:2
people, 15 "This is what the LORD Almighty, the God of Israel, says: 'Listen!
I am going to bring on this city and
the villages around it every disaster I
pronounced against them, because they 19:15
were stiff-necked[k] and would not listen [k]Ne 9:16; Jer 7:26;
to my words.'" 17:23

Jeremiah and Pashhur

20 When the priest Pashhur son 20:1
of Immer,[l] the chief officer[m] in [l]1Ch 24:14 [m]2Ki 25:18
the temple of the LORD, heard Jeremi-
ah prophesying these things, 2 he had
Jeremiah the prophet beaten[n] and put 20:2 [n]Jer 1:19
in the stocks[o] at the Upper Gate of [o]Job 13:27

[a]7 The Hebrew for *ruin* sounds like the Hebrew for *jar* (see verses 1 and 10).

20:2 [p]Jer 37:13; 38:7; Zec 14:10
Benjamin[p] at the LORD's temple. 3The
next day, when Pashhur released him
from the stocks, Jeremiah said to him,
20:3 [q]ver 10
"The LORD's name for you is not Pashhur, but Magor-Missabib.[a][q] 4For this
is what the LORD says: 'I will make
you a terror to yourself and to all your
20:4 [r]Jer 29:21 [s]Jer 21:10 [t]Jer 52:27
friends; with your own eyes[r] you will
see them fall by the sword of their enemies. I will hand[s] all Judah over to the
king of Babylon, who will carry[t] them
away to Babylon or put them to the
20:5 [u]Jer 17:3
sword. 5I will hand over to their enemies all the wealth[u] of this city—all
its products, all its valuables and all the
treasures of the kings of Judah. They
20:5 [v]2Ki 20:17
will take it away[v] as plunder and carry it
off to Babylon. 6And you, Pashhur, and
all who live in your house will go into
exile to Babylon. There you will die and
be buried, you and all your friends to
20:6 [w]Jer 14:15; La 2:14
whom you have prophesied[w] lies.'"

Jeremiah's Complaint

7O LORD, you deceived[b] me, and I
was deceived[b];

[a]3 *Magor-Missabib* means *terror on every side.*
[b]7 Or *persuaded*

JEREMIAH

Faithfulness: Standing When the Whole World Seems to Be in Disagreement (20:1–18)

Israel had two kinds of prophets: false and true. The false were always very popular, but the true always told the truth. Jeremiah found himself in utter pain because, like preachers in every age, he really wanted to have his sermons admired by those who heard them. But alas, his sermons were too truthful to be popular.

In Jeremiah 20, Pashhur, who was a priest with many friends, made it clear that Jeremiah must stop preaching negative sermons. To reinforce his request, he had Jeremiah beaten and put in the stocks at the temple's Gate of Benjamin. After Jeremiah was released the next day, he said to Pashhur, "The LORD's name for you is not Pashhur, but Magor-Missabib" (v. 3). *Pashhur* in Hebrew means "glad-free," and *Magor-Missabib* means "terror on every side." So Jeremiah was saying in essence, "Your name is no longer Rev. Glad Free (an indication that he was probably preaching the gospel of "Everything's Coming Up Roses") but is now Dr. Terror on Every Side (an indication that he would probably lose his pulpit when the Babylonians came charging through the walls—once the siege was over).

Faithfulness does not preach compromise, hoping the sermon might get printed in a theological journal. Rather, faithfulness preaches the truth when the truth is not popular. Jeremiah's sermon was preached to one man—Pashur: "I will make you a terror to yourself and to all your friends; with your own eyes you will see them fall by the sword of their enemies. I will hand all Judah over to the king of Babylon, who will carry them away to Babylon or put them to the sword. I will hand over to their enemies all the wealth of this city . . . And you, Pashhur, and all who live in your house will go into exile to Babylon. There you will die and be buried, you and all your friends to whom you have prophesied lies" (vv. 4–6).

This was not the kind of sermon that won friends and influenced people. Jeremiah's preaching did not suddenly become popular with this sermon. But God smiled down on a lone prophet's faithfulness, for God knew that, although Jeremiah would never be popular, the prophet would always remain faithful. Jeremiah knew his preaching wasn't winning him friends; he also knew that he would never cease to be faithful. His loyalty can be summed up by his own words: "But if I say, 'I will not mention [God] or speak any more in his name,' his word is in my heart like a fire, a fire shut up in my bones. I am weary of holding it in; indeed, I cannot" (v. 9).

Allegiance to faithful preaching is the burden of all pastors who will not trade truth for acceptance. Faithfulness is fire. It scorches the earth with God's requirements even as it consumes the committed.

you overpowered me and
prevailed.
I am ridiculed all day long;
everyone mocks me.
8 Whenever I speak, I cry out
proclaiming violence and
destruction.[x]
So the word of the LORD has
brought me
insult and reproach[y] all day long.
9 But if I say, "I will not mention him
or speak any more in his name,"
his word is in my heart like a fire,[z]
a fire shut up in my bones.
I am weary of holding it in;[a]
indeed, I cannot.
10 I hear many whispering,
"Terror[b] on every side!
Report[c] him! Let's report him!"
All my friends[d]
are waiting for me to slip,[e] saying,
"Perhaps he will be deceived;
then we will prevail[f] over him
and take our revenge on him."

20:8 [x]Jer 6:7 [y]2Ch 36:16; Jer 6:10
20:9 [z]Ps 39:3 [a]Job 32:18-20; Ac 4:20
20:10 [b]Ps 31:13; Jer 6:25 [c]Isa 29:21 [d]Ps 41:9 [e]Lk 11:53-54 [f]1Ki 19:2

FAITHFULNESS

A Flame Divine That Can't be Suppressed

Jeremiah 20:8–9

The fire in our bones should be the flame of divine obedience. The fire in Jeremiah's bones was the flame of God's message—a message that brought the prophet much suffering. In our own lives, we may deny its fire and seek to quench its force, but nothing will change. God put his flame within us, and it will either burn honoring his intentions or die out completely.

11 But the LORD[g] is with me like a
mighty warrior;
so my persecutors[h] will stumble
and not prevail.[i]
They will fail and be thoroughly
disgraced;[j]
their dishonor will never be
forgotten.
12 O LORD Almighty, you who
examine the righteous
and probe the heart and mind,[k]
let me see your vengeance[l] upon
them,
for to you I have committed[m] my
cause.

13 Sing to the LORD!
Give praise to the LORD!

20:11 [g]Jer 1:8; Ro 8:31 [h]Jer 17:18 [i]Jer 15:20 [j]Jer 23:40
20:12 [k]Jer 17:10 [l]Ps 54:7; 59:10 [m]Ps 62:8; Jer 11:20

He rescues[n] the life of the needy
from the hands of the wicked.

14 Cursed be the day I was born![o]
May the day my mother bore me
not be blessed!
15 Cursed be the man who brought my
father the news,
who made him very glad, saying,
"A child is born to you—a son!"
16 May that man be like the towns[p]
the LORD overthrew without pity.
May he hear wailing in the morning,
a battle cry at noon.
17 For he did not kill me in the womb,[q]
with my mother as my grave,
her womb enlarged forever.
18 Why did I ever come out of the
womb
to see trouble and sorrow
and to end my days in shame?[r]

20:13 [n]Ps 35:10
20:14 [o]Job 3:3; Jer 15:10
20:16 [p]Ge 19:25
20:17 [q]Job 10:18-19
20:18 [r]Ps 90:9

God Rejects Zedekiah's Request

21 The word came to Jeremiah
from the LORD when King Zed-
ekiah[s] sent to him Pashhur[t] son of Malkijah and the priest Zephaniah[u] son of
Maaseiah. They said: 2 "Inquire[v] now of
the LORD for us because Nebuchadnezzar[a][w] king of Babylon is attacking us.
Perhaps the LORD will perform wonders[x] for us as in times past so that he
will withdraw from us."
3 But Jeremiah answered them, "Tell
Zedekiah, 4 'This is what the LORD, the
God of Israel, says: I am about to turn[y]
against you the weapons of war that are
in your hands, which you are using to
fight the king of Babylon and the Babylonians[b] who are outside the wall besieging[z] you. And I will gather them
inside this city. 5 I myself will fight
against you with an outstretched hand[a]
and a mighty arm in anger and fury and
great wrath. 6 I will strike down those
who live in this city—both men and
animals—and they will die of a terrible
plague.[b] 7 After that, declares the LORD,
I will hand over Zedekiah[c] king of Judah, his officials and the people in
this city who survive the plague, sword
and famine, to Nebuchadnezzar king
of Babylon[d] and to their enemies who
seek their lives. He will put them to the

21:1 [s]2Ki 24:18; Jer 52:1 [t]Jer 38:1 [u]2Ki 25:18; Jer 29:25; 37:3
21:2 [v]Jer 37:3,7 [w]2Ki 25:1 [x]Ps 44:1-4; Jer 32:17
21:4 [y]Jer 32:5 [z]Jer 37:8-10
21:5 [a]Jer 6:12
21:6 [b]Jer 14:12
21:7 [c]2Ki 25:7; Jer 52:9 [d]Jer 37:17; 39:5

[a]2 Hebrew *Nebuchadrezzar,* of which *Nebuchadnezzar* is a variant; here and often in Jeremiah and Ezekiel [b]4 Or *Chaldeans*; also in verse 9

WEEK 43 FAITHFULNESS

1 DAY ONE
FAITHFULNESS: NO COMPROMISE

Read Jeremiah 20:1–2,7–10

Faithfulness is a fire in the bones. It may forswear its loyalty in moments of weak faith, but it will not stop burning. Faithfulness does not make compromises—as Esther said prior to approaching the king, "I will go to the king, even though it is against the law. And if I perish, I perish" (Esther 4:16).

The cross stands as the ultimate example of facing our extremities without any sense of compromise. Jesus was the no-quit Christ who demonstrated how to hold to principle—even to the point of death. Years ago I wrote in *Once Upon A Tree*:

> Joseph Wittig once said, "A man's biography ought really to begin not with his birth but with his death; it can be written only from the point of view of its end, because only from there can the whole of his life in its fulfillment be seen." So it is that when we tell anyone of Jesus we must begin with his death. One cannot even begin to understand the life of Christ without understanding his death. It is here at the cross that his biography begins.

Self-sacrifice is the fearsome way to say "self-denial." Jeremiah had denied himself in favor of what God wanted. Jeremiah understood that we must spend the small coins of self-denial in order to buy the great commitments of our lives. Anticipating our dying keeps us remembering that life is inherently serious. The apostle Paul said that he was "being poured out like a drink offering" (Philippians 2:17). Jeremiah's life was being poured out in utter faithfulness, with no hint of compromise.

MEMORIZE THIS WEEK

ESTHER 4:16

"Go, gather together all the Jews who are in Susa, and fast for me. Do not eat or drink for three days, night or day. I and my maids will fast as you do. When this is done, I will go to the king, even though it is against the law. And if I perish, I perish."

2 DAY TWO
FAITHFULNESS AND THE PURPOSE OF GOD IN MY LIFE

People did not leave following Stephen's sermon cooing, "Oh, Pastor, that was just the best sermon. Your preaching means so much to me." Stephen's sermon was a rare sermon, one after which the crowd picked up rocks. Stephen's death shows us that the purpose to which God calls us is not always easy to carry out. But Stephen well merits the epitaph: Faithful unto death. *Turn to Acts 7:52–60, page 1299, for today's study.*

3 DAY THREE
FAITHFULNESS AND MY RELATIONSHIP WITH CHRIST

We preach Christ crucified. How can the message of the Good News reach others? So many scoff or turn away. But as we are faithful, God supplies power to continue on, power to overcome. Our steadfast defense of God's kingdom will evoke his steadfast defense of our lives. *Turn to 1 Corinthians 1:20–25, page 1358, for today's study.*

4 DAY FOUR
FAITHFULNESS AND MY SERVICE TO OTHERS

This beautiful metaphor of our faithfulness and God's provision is made more picturesque by a challenge. God's protection is pictured as a soldier putting on armor. Each piece is described by the function it provides. But the main ideas of the metaphor occur in verses 10 and 14. Verse 10 says, "Be strong in the Lord and in his mighty power." And verse 14 says "Stand firm." *Turn to Ephesians 6:10–18, page 1410, for today's study.*

5 DAY FIVE
FAITHFULNESS AND ITS PLACE IN MY PERSONAL WORSHIP

Jeremiah's book of Lamentations reminds us that God's never-failing compassions are new every morning. Jeremiah exults in that wonderful assurance that so often marks our worship: Great is thy faithfulness! The faithfulness of God should be a constant impetus for us to be unyielding in our support of the truth. God loves us and has called us to produce for him exactly what he has promised us: no-compromise faithfulness. *Turn to Lamentations 3:22–24, page 947, for today's study.*

Week 44, Gentleness, the Healing Touch of God, begins on page 1175, Mark 5:24–34.
To begin a topical study on the Fruit of the Spirit, Faithfulness, turn to the Topical Index, page 1548.

sword; he will show them no mercy or
21:7 [e]2Ch 36:17; Eze 7:9; Hab 1:6 pity or compassion.’[e]
8“Furthermore, tell the people, ‘This
is what the LORD says: See, I am setting before you the way of life and the
way of death. 9Whoever stays in this
21:9 city will die by the sword, famine or
[f]Jer 14:12 plague.[f] But whoever goes out and sur-
[g]Jer 38:2,17; 39:18; 45:5 renders to the Babylonians who are besieging you will live; he will escape with
his life.[g] 10I have determined to do this
21:10 [h]Jer 44:11,27; Am 9:4 city harm[h] and not good, declares the
[i]Jer 32:28; 38:2-3 LORD. It will be given into the hands[i]
of the king of Babylon, and he will de-
[j]Jer 52:13 stroy it with fire.[j]
21:11 11“Moreover, say to the royal house[k]
[k]Jer 13:18 of Judah, ‘Hear the word of the LORD;
12O house of David, this is what the
LORD says:

21:12 [l]Jer 22:3 [m]Isa 1:31 “ ‘Administer justice[l] every morning;
rescue from the hand of his
oppressor
the one who has been robbed,
or my wrath will break out and burn
like fire
because of the evil you have
done—
burn with no one to quench[m] it.
21:13 [n]Eze 13:8 13I am against[n] you, ⌞Jerusalem,⌟
[o]Ps 125:2 you who live above this valley[o]
[p]Jer 49:4; Ob 1:3-4 on the rocky plateau,
declares the LORD—
you who say, “Who can come
against us?
Who can enter our refuge?”[p]
21:14 [q]Isa 3:10-11 14I will punish you as your deeds[q]
[r]2Ch 36:19; Jer 52:13 deserve,
[s]Eze 20:47 declares the LORD.
I will kindle a fire[r] in your forests[s]
that will consume everything
around you.’ ”

Judgment Against Evil Kings

22 This is what the LORD says:
“Go down to the palace of the
king of Judah and proclaim this message
there: 2‘Hear the word of the LORD, O
king of Judah, you who sit on David’s
22:2 [t]Jer 17:25; Lk 1:32 throne[t]—you, your officials and your
[u]Jer 17:20 people who come through these gates.[u]
3This is what the LORD says: Do what
22:3 [v]Mic 6:8; Zec 7:9 is just[v] and right. Rescue from the hand
[w]Ps 72:4; Jer 21:12 of his oppressor[w] the one who has been
robbed. Do no wrong or violence to
[x]Ex 22:22 the alien, the fatherless or the widow,[x]
and do not shed innocent blood in this
place. 4For if you are careful to carry
out these commands, then kings[y] who 22:4 [y]Jer 17:25
sit on David’s throne will come through
the gates of this palace, riding in chariots and on horses, accompanied by their
officials and their people. 5But if you
do not obey[z] these commands, declares 22:5 [z]Jer 17:27
the LORD, I swear[a] by myself that this [a]Heb 6:13
palace will become a ruin.’ ”
6For this is what the LORD says about
the palace of the king of Judah:

“Though you are like Gilead to me,
like the summit of Lebanon,
I will surely make you like a desert,[b] 22:6 [b]Mic 3:12
like towns not inhabited.
7I will send destroyers[c] against you, 22:7 [c]Jer 4:7
each man with his weapons, [d]Isa 10:34
and they will cut[d] up your fine cedar
beams
and throw them into the fire.

8“People from many nations will pass
by this city and will ask one another,
‘Why has the LORD done such a thing
to this great city?’[e] 9And the answer will 22:8 [e]Dt 29:25-26;
be: ‘Because they have forsaken the cov- 1Ki 9:8-9;
enant of the LORD their God and have Jer 16:10-11
worshiped and served other gods.[f]’ ” 22:9 [f]2Ki 22:17; 2Ch 34:25

10Do not weep for the dead[g] ⌞king⌟ or
mourn[h] his loss; 22:10 [g]Ecc 4:2
rather, weep bitterly for him who [h]ver 18
is exiled,
because he will never return
nor see his native land again.

11For this is what the LORD says about
Shallum[a][i] son of Josiah, who succeeded 22:11 [i]2Ki 23:31
his father as king of Judah but has gone
from this place: “He will never return.
12He will die[j] in the place where they 22:12 [j]2Ki 23:34
have led him captive; he will not see
this land again.”

13“Woe to him who builds[k] his palace 22:13 [k]Mic 3:10;
by unrighteousness, Hab 2:9
his upper rooms by injustice, [l]Lev 19:13;
making his countrymen work for Jas 5:4
nothing,
not paying[l] them for their labor.
14He says, ‘I will build myself a great
palace[m] 22:14 [m]Isa 5:8-9
with spacious upper rooms.’ [n]2Sa 7:2
So he makes large windows in it,
panels it with cedar[n]
and decorates it in red.

15“Does it make you a king
to have more and more cedar?

[a]*11* Also called *Jehoahaz*

Did not your father have food and
drink?
He did what was right and just,[o]
so all went well[p] with him.

22:15 [o]2Ki 23:25 [p]Ps 128:2; Isa 3:10

[16]He defended the cause of the poor
and needy,[q]
and so all went well.
Is that not what it means to know
me?"
declares the LORD.

22:16 [q]Ps 72:1-4, 12-13

[17]"But your eyes and your heart
are set only on dishonest gain,
on shedding innocent blood[r]
and on oppression and extortion."

22:17 [r]2Ki 24:4

[18]Therefore this is what the LORD says
about Jehoiakim son of Josiah king of
Judah:

"They will not mourn for him:
'Alas, my brother! Alas, my sister!'
They will not mourn for him:
'Alas, my master! Alas, his
splendor!'
[19]He will have the burial of a
donkey—
dragged away and thrown[s]
outside the gates of Jerusalem."

22:19 [s]Jer 36:30

[20]"Go up to Lebanon and cry out,
let your voice be heard in Bashan,
cry out from Abarim,[t]
for all your allies are crushed.

22:20 [t]Nu 27:12

[21]I warned you when you felt secure,
but you said, 'I will not listen!'
This has been your way from your
youth;[u]
you have not obeyed[v] me.

22:21 [u]Jer 3:25; 32:30 [v]Jer 7:23-28

[22]The wind will drive all your
shepherds away,
and your allies will go into exile.
Then you will be ashamed and
disgraced
because of all your wickedness.
[23]You who live in 'Lebanon,[a]'
who are nestled in cedar buildings,
how you will groan when pangs
come upon you,
pain[w] like that of a woman in
labor!

22:23 [w]Jer 4:31

[24]"As surely as I live," declares the
LORD, "even if you, Jehoiachin[b][x] son
of Jehoiakim king of Judah, were a signet ring on my right hand, I would still
pull you off. [25]I will hand you over[y]
to those who seek your life, those you
fear—to Nebuchadnezzar king of Babylon and to the Babylonians.[c] [26]I will
hurl[z] you and the mother who gave
you birth into another country, where
neither of you was born, and there
you both will die. [27]You will never
come back to the land you long to return to."

22:24 [x]2Ki 24:6,8; Jer 37:1

22:25 [y]2Ki 24:16; Jer 34:20

22:26 [z]2Ki 24:8; 2Ch 36:10

[28]Is this man Jehoiachin a despised,
broken pot,[a]
an object no one wants?
Why will he and his children be
hurled[b] out,
cast into a land[c] they do not
know?

22:28 [a]Ps 31:12; Jer 48:38; Hos 8:8 [b]Jer 15:1 [c]Jer 17:4

[29]O land,[d] land, land,
hear the word of the LORD!

22:29 [d]Jer 6:19; Mic 1:2

[30]This is what the LORD says:
"Record this man as if childless,[e]
a man who will not prosper[f] in his
lifetime,
for none of his offspring will prosper,
none will sit on the throne[g] of
David
or rule anymore in Judah."

22:30 [e]1Ch 3:18; Mt 1:12 [f]Jer 10:21 [g]Ps 94:20

The Righteous Branch

23 "Woe to the shepherds[h] who
are destroying and scattering[i]
the sheep of my pasture!"[j] declares
the LORD. [2]Therefore this is what the
LORD, the God of Israel, says to the
shepherds who tend my people: "Because you have scattered my flock and
driven them away and have not bestowed care on them, I will bestow punishment on you for the evil[k] you have
done," declares the LORD. [3]"I myself
will gather the remnant[l] of my flock out
of all the countries where I have driven
them and will bring them back to their
pasture, where they will be fruitful and
increase in number. [4]I will place shepherds[m] over them who will tend them,
and they will no longer be afraid[n] or
terrified, nor will any be missing,[o]" declares the LORD.

23:1 [h]Jer 10:21; Eze 34:1-10; Zec 11:15-17 [i]Isa 56:11 [j]Eze 34:31

23:2 [k]Jer 21:12

23:3 [l]Isa 11:10-12; Jer 32:37; Eze 34:11-16

23:4 [m]Jer 3:15; 31:10; Eze 34:23 [n]Jer 30:10; 46:27-28 [o]Jn 6:39

[5]"The days are coming," declares the
LORD,
"when I will raise up to David[d] a
righteous Branch,[p]
a King who will reign[q] wisely
and do what is just and right[r] in
the land.
[6]In his days Judah will be saved
and Israel will live in safety.

23:5 [p]Isa 4:2 [q]Isa 9:7 [r]Isa 11:1; Zec 6:12

[a]*23* That is, the palace in Jerusalem (see 1 Kings 7:2)
[b]*24* Hebrew *Coniah,* a variant of *Jehoiachin;* also in verse 28
[c]*25* Or *Chaldeans*
[d]*5* Or *up from David's line*

GOODNESS

THE LORD OUR RIGHTEOUSNESS

Jeremiah 23:6

The struggle to live in purity—free from sin—is a struggle that pleases God. Jesus came to earth and lived perfectly. All that he accomplished on the cross became a lavish cloak to drape across the shoulders of our imperfections.

23:6 [s]Jer 33:16; Mt 1:21-23 [t]Ro 3:21-22; 1Co 1:30

This is the name[s] by which he will
be called:
The LORD Our Righteousness.[t]

7"So then, the days are coming," declares the LORD, "when people will no
longer say, 'As surely as the LORD lives,
who brought the Israelites up out of
Egypt,'[u] 8but they will say, 'As surely as
the LORD lives, who brought the descendants of Israel up out of the land of
the north and out of all the countries
where he had banished them.' Then
they will live in their own land."[v]

23:7 [u]Jer 16:14

23:8 [v]Isa 43:5-6; Am 9:14-15

Lying Prophets

9Concerning the prophets:

My heart is broken within me;
all my bones tremble.
I am like a drunken man,
like a man overcome by wine,
because of the LORD
and his holy words.[w]
10The land is full of adulterers;[x]
because of the curse[a] the land lies
parched[b]
and the pastures[y] in the desert are
withered.[z]
The ⌊prophets⌋ follow an evil course
and use their power unjustly.

23:9 [w]Jer 20:8-9

23:10 [x]Jer 9:2 [y]Ps 107:34; Jer 9:10 [z]Hos 4:2-3

11"Both prophet and priest are
godless;[a]
even in my temple[b] I find their
wickedness,"
declares the LORD.
12"Therefore their path will become
slippery;[c]
they will be banished to darkness
and there they will fall.
I will bring disaster on them
in the year they are punished,[d]"
declares the LORD.

23:11 [a]Jer 6:13; 8:10; Zep 3:4 [b]Jer 7:10

23:12 [c]Ps 35:6; Jer 13:16 [d]Jer 11:23

13"Among the prophets of Samaria
I saw this repulsive thing:
They prophesied by Baal[e]
and led my people Israel astray.
14And among the prophets of
Jerusalem
I have seen something horrible:[f]
They commit adultery and live a
lie.[g]
They strengthen the hands of
evildoers,[h]
so that no one turns from his
wickedness.
They are all like Sodom[i] to me;
the people of Jerusalem are like
Gomorrah."[j]

23:13 [e]Jer 2:8

23:14 [f]Jer 5:30 [g]Jer 29:23 [h]Eze 13:22 [i]Ge 18:20 [j]Isa 1:9-10; Jer 20:16

15Therefore, this is what the LORD
Almighty says concerning the prophets:

"I will make them eat bitter food
and drink poisoned water,[k]
because from the prophets of
Jerusalem
ungodliness has spread throughout
the land."

23:15 [k]Jer 8:14; 9:15

16This is what the LORD Almighty
says:

"Do not listen[l] to what the prophets
are prophesying to you;
they fill you with false hopes.
They speak visions[m] from their own
minds,
not from the mouth[n] of the
LORD.
17They keep saying to those who
despise me,
'The LORD says: You will have
peace.'[o]
And to all who follow the
stubbornness[p] of their hearts
they say, 'No harm[q] will come to
you.'
18But which of them has stood in the
council of the LORD
to see or to hear his word?
Who has listened and heard his
word?
19See, the storm[r] of the LORD
will burst out in wrath,
a whirlwind swirling down
on the heads of the wicked.
20The anger[s] of the LORD will not
turn back[t]
until he fully accomplishes
the purposes of his heart.
In days to come

23:16 [l]Jer 27:9-10,14; Mt 7:15 [m]Jer 14:14 [n]Jer 9:20

23:17 [o]Jer 8:11 [p]Jer 13:10 [q]Jer 5:12; Am 9:10; Mic 3:11

23:19 [r]Jer 25:32; 30:23

23:20 [s]2Ki 23:26 [t]Jer 30:24

[a]10 Or *because of these things* [b]10 Or *land mourns*

you will understand it clearly.
23:21 [u]Jer 14:14; 27:15
21I did not send[u] these prophets,
yet they have run with their
message;
I did not speak to them,
yet they have prophesied.
22But if they had stood in my council,
they would have proclaimed my
words to my people
23:22 [v]Jer 25:5; Zec 1:4
and would have turned[v] them from
their evil ways
and from their evil deeds.
23:23 [w]Ps 139:1-10
23"Am I only a God nearby,[w]"
declares the LORD,
"and not a God far away?
23:24 [x]Job 22:12-14 [y]1Ki 8:27
24Can anyone hide[x] in secret places
so that I cannot see him?"
declares the LORD.
"Do not I fill heaven and earth?"[y]
declares the LORD.
25"I have heard what the prophets
23:25 [z]Jer 14:14 [a]ver 28,32; Jer 29:8
say who prophesy lies[z] in my name.
They say, 'I had a dream![a] I had a
dream!' 26How long will this continue
in the hearts of these lying prophets,
23:26 [b]1Ti 4:1-2
who prophesy the delusions[b] of their
own minds? 27They think the dreams
they tell one another will make my peo-
23:27 [c]Dt 13:1-3; Jer 29:8 [d]Jdg 3:7; 8:33-34
ple forget[c] my name, just as their fathers forgot[d] my name through Baal
worship. 28Let the prophet who has a
dream tell his dream, but let the one
who has my word speak it faithfully.
For what has straw to do with grain?"
declares the LORD. 29"Is not my word
23:29 [e]Jer 5:14
like fire,"[e] declares the LORD, "and like
a hammer that breaks a rock in pieces?
23:30 [f]Ps 34:16 [g]Dt 18:20; Jer 14:15
30"Therefore," declares the LORD, "I
am against[f] the prophets[g] who steal
from one another words supposedly
from me. 31Yes," declares the LORD,
"I am against the prophets who wag
23:31 [h]ver 17
their own tongues and yet declare, 'The
LORD declares.'[h] 32Indeed, I am against
23:32 [i]ver 25 [j]Jer 7:8; La 2:14
those who prophesy false dreams,[i]" declares the LORD. "They tell them and
lead my people astray with their reckless lies, yet I did not send or appoint
them. They do not benefit[j] these people in the least," declares the LORD.

False Oracles and False Prophets

33"When these people, or a prophet
or a priest, ask you, 'What is the ora-
23:33 [k]Mal 1:1 [l]ver 39
cle[a][k] of the LORD?' say to them, 'What
oracle?[b] I will forsake[l] you, declares the
LORD.' 34If a prophet or a priest or
anyone else claims, 'This is the oracle[m] 23:34 [m]La 2:14
of the LORD,' I will punish[n] that man [n]Zec 13:3
and his household. 35This is what each
of you keeps on saying to his friend or
relative: 'What is the LORD's answer?'[o] 23:35 [o]Jer 33:3; 42:4
or 'What has the LORD spoken?' 36But
you must not mention 'the oracle of the
LORD' again, because every man's own
word becomes his oracle and so you
distort[p] the words of the living God, 23:36 [p]Gal 1:7-8; 2Pe 3:16
the LORD Almighty, our God. 37This
is what you keep saying to a prophet:
'What is the LORD's answer to you?'
or 'What has the LORD spoken?' 38Al-
though you claim, 'This is the oracle of
the LORD,' this is what the LORD says:
You used the words, 'This is the oracle
of the LORD,' even though I told you
that you must not claim, 'This is the
oracle of the LORD.' 39Therefore, I will
surely forget you and cast[q] you out of 23:39 [q]Jer 7:15
my presence along with the city I gave
to you and your fathers. 40I will bring
upon you everlasting disgrace[r]—ever- 23:40 [r]Jer 20:11; Eze 5:14-15
lasting shame that will not be forgot-
ten."

Two Baskets of Figs

24 After Jehoiachin[c][s] son of Jehoi- 24:1 [s]2Ki 24:16; 2Ch 36:9; Jer 29:2
akim king of Judah and the of-
ficials, the craftsmen and the artisans of [t]Am 8:1-2
Judah were carried into exile from Jerusalem to Babylon by Nebuchadnezzar
king of Babylon, the LORD showed me
two baskets of figs[t] placed in front of
the temple of the LORD. 2One basket
had very good figs, like those that ripen 24:2 [u]Isa 5:4
early; the other basket had very poor[u]
figs, so bad they could not be eaten.
3Then the LORD asked me, "What
do you see,[v] Jeremiah?" 24:3 [v]Jer 1:11; Am 8:2
"Figs," I answered. "The good ones
are very good, but the poor ones are so
bad they cannot be eaten."
4Then the word of the LORD came
to me: 5"This is what the LORD, the
God of Israel, says: 'Like these good
figs, I regard as good the exiles from
Judah, whom I sent away from this
place to the land of the Babylonians.[d]
6My eyes will watch over them for their 24:6 [w]Jer 29:10; Eze 11:17
good, and I will bring them back[w] to [x]Jer 33:7; 42:10
this land. I will build[x] them up and not

[a]33 Or *burden* (see Septuagint and Vulgate)
[b]33 Hebrew; Septuagint and Vulgate *'You are the burden.* (The Hebrew for *oracle* and *burden* is the same.)
[c]1 Hebrew *Jeconiah,* a variant of *Jehoiachin*
[d]5 Or *Chaldeans*

tear them down; I will plant them and
not uproot them. [7]I will give them a
heart to know me, that I am the LORD.
24:7 [y]Isa 51:16; Jer 31:33; Heb 8:10 [z]Jer 32:40 [a]Eze 11:19
They will be my people,[y] and I will be
their God, for they will return[z] to me
with all their heart.[a]
[8]"'But like the poor[b] figs, which are
24:8 [b]Jer 29:17 [c]Jer 39:6 [d]Jer 39:9 [e]Jer 44:1,26
so bad they cannot be eaten,' says the
LORD, 'so will I deal with Zedekiah
king of Judah, his officials[c] and the survivors[d] from Jerusalem, whether they
24:9 [f]Jer 15:4; 34:17 [g]Dt 28:25; 1Ki 9:7 [h]Jer 29:18 [i]Dt 28:37
remain in this land or live in Egypt.[e] [9]I
will make them abhorrent[f] and an offense to all the kingdoms of the earth,
a reproach and a byword,[g] an object of
ridicule and cursing,[h] wherever I ban-
24:10 [j]Isa 51:19 [k]Jer 27:8
ish[i] them. [10]I will send the sword,[j] famine and plague[k] against them until they
are destroyed from the land I gave to
them and their fathers.'"

Seventy Years of Captivity

25 The word came to Jeremiah
concerning all the people of Ju-
25:1 [l]2Ki 24:2; Jer 36:1 [m]2Ki 24:1
dah in the fourth year of Jehoiakim[l] son
of Josiah king of Judah, which was the
first year of Nebuchadnezzar[m] king of
Babylon. [2]So Jeremiah the prophet said
25:2 [n]Jer 18:11
to all the people of Judah[n] and to all
those living in Jerusalem: [3]For twenty-
25:3 [o]Jer 1:2 [p]Jer 11:7; 26:5 [q]Jer 7:26
three years—from the thirteenth year
of Josiah[o] son of Amon king of Judah
until this very day—the word of the
LORD has come to me and I have spoken to you again and again,[p] but you
have not listened.[q]
[4]And though the LORD has sent all
25:4 [r]Jer 7:25
his servants the prophets[r] to you again
and again, you have not listened or paid
any attention. [5]They said, "Turn now,
each of you, from your evil ways and
your evil practices, and you can stay
in the land the LORD gave to you and
your fathers for ever and ever. [6]Do not
25:6 [s]Dt 8:19
follow other gods[s] to serve and worship
them; do not provoke me to anger with
what your hands have made. Then I
will not harm you."
[7]"But you did not listen to me," declares the LORD, "and you have provoked me with what your hands have
25:7 [t]Dt 32:21 [u]2Ki 21:15
made,[t] and you have brought harm[u] to
yourselves."
[8]Therefore the LORD Almighty says
this: "Because you have not listened
25:9 [v]Isa 13:3-5 [w]Jer 1:15 [x]Jer 27:6
to my words, [9]I will summon[v] all the
peoples of the north[w] and my servant[x]
Nebuchadnezzar king of Babylon," declares the LORD, "and I will bring them
against this land and its inhabitants
and against all the surrounding nations.
I will completely destroy[a] them and
make them an object of horror and
25:9 [y]Jer 18:16
scorn,[y] and an everlasting ruin. [10]I will
banish from them the sounds[z] of joy
25:10 [z]Isa 24:8; Eze 26:13 [a]Jer 7:34 [b]Ecc 12:3-4 [c]Rev 18:22-23
and gladness, the voices of bride and
bridegroom,[a] the sound of millstones[b]
and the light of the lamp.[c] [11]This
whole country will become a desolate
25:11 [d]Jer 4:26-27; 12:11-12 [e]2Ch 36:21
wasteland,[d] and these nations will serve
the king of Babylon seventy years.[e]
[12]"But when the seventy years[f] are
25:12 [f]Jer 29:10 [g]Isa 13:19-22; 14:22-23
fulfilled, I will punish the king of Babylon and his nation, the land of the
Babylonians,[b] for their guilt," declares
the LORD, "and will make it desolate[g]
forever. [13]I will bring upon that land all
the things I have spoken against it, all
that are written in this book and prophesied by Jeremiah against all the nations.
25:14 [h]Jer 27:7 [i]Jer 50:9; 51:27-28 [j]Jer 51:6
[14]They themselves will be enslaved[h] by
many nations[i] and great kings; I will repay[j] them according to their deeds and
the work of their hands."

The Cup of God's Wrath

[15]This is what the LORD, the God
of Israel, said to me: "Take from my
25:15 [k]Isa 51:17; Ps 75:8; Rev 14:10
hand this cup[k] filled with the wine of
my wrath and make all the nations to
whom I send you drink it. [16]When they
25:16 [l]Na 3:11 [m]Jer 51:7
drink it, they will stagger[l] and go mad[m]
because of the sword I will send among
them."
[17]So I took the cup from the LORD's
hand and made all the nations to whom
25:17 [n]Jer 1:10
he sent[n] me drink it: [18]Jerusalem and
the towns of Judah, its kings and offi-
25:18 [o]Jer 24:9 [p]Jer 44:22
cials, to make them a ruin and an object of horror and scorn and cursing,[o]
as they are today;[p] [19]Pharaoh king of
Egypt, his attendants, his officials and
all his people, [20]and all the foreign
25:20 [q]Job 1:1 [r]Jer 47:5
people there; all the kings of Uz;[q] all
the kings of the Philistines (those of
25:21 [s]Jer 49:1
Ashkelon,[r] Gaza, Ekron, and the people left at Ashdod); [21]Edom, Moab and
25:22 [t]Jer 47:4 [u]Jer 31:10
Ammon;[s] [22]all the kings of Tyre and
Sidon;[t] the kings of the coastlands[u]
across the sea; [23]Dedan, Tema, Buz and
25:23 [v]Jer 9:26; 49:32
all who are in distant places[c];[v] [24]all the

[a]9 The Hebrew term refers to the irrevocable giving over of things or persons to the LORD, often by totally destroying them. [b]*12* Or *Chaldeans* [c]*23* Or *who clip the hair by their foreheads*

25:24 kings of Arabia[w] and all the kings of the
[w]2Ch 9:14 foreign people who live in the desert;
25:25 [x]Ge 10:22 25all the kings of Zimri, Elam[x] and Media; 26and all the kings of the north,[y]
25:26 [y]Jer 50:3,9 near and far, one after the other—all the
[z]Jer 51:41 kingdoms on the face of the earth. And
after all of them, the king of Sheshach[a][z]
will drink it too.

27"Then tell them, 'This is what the
25:27 LORD Almighty, the God of Israel, says:
[a]ver 16,28; Hab 2:16 Drink, get drunk[a] and vomit, and fall
[b]Eze 21:4 to rise no more because of the sword[b]
I will send among you.' 28But if they
refuse to take the cup from your hand
and drink, tell them, 'This is what the
LORD Almighty says: You must drink
it! 29See, I am beginning to bring disas-
25:29 [c]Jer 13:12-14 ter[c] on the city that bears my Name,[d]
[d]1Pe 4:17 and will you indeed go unpunished?[e]
[e]Pr 11:31 You will not go unpunished, for I am
[f]ver 30-31 calling down a sword upon all[f] who
live on the earth, declares the LORD Almighty.'

30"Now prophesy all these words
against them and say to them:

25:30 [g]Isa 16:10; 42:13 " 'The LORD will roar[g] from on
high;
[h]Joel 3:16; Am 1:2 he will thunder[h] from his holy
dwelling
and roar mightily against his
land.
He will shout like those who tread
the grapes,
shout against all who live on the
earth.
31The tumult will resound to the ends
of the earth,
25:31 [i]Hos 4:1; Joel 3:2; Mic 6:2 for the LORD will bring charges[i]
against the nations;
he will bring judgment on all
mankind
and put the wicked to the
sword,' "
declares the LORD.

32This is what the LORD Almighty
says:

25:32 [j]Isa 34:2 "Look! Disaster is spreading
[k]Jer 23:19 from nation to nation;[j]
a mighty storm[k] is rising
from the ends of the earth."

25:33 33At that time those slain[l] by the LORD
[l]Isa 66:16; Eze 39:17-20 will be everywhere—from one end of
the earth to the other. They will not be
[m]Jer 16:4 [n]Ps 79:3 mourned or gathered[m] up or buried,[n]
but will be like refuse lying on the
ground.

34Weep and wail, you shepherds;
roll[o] in the dust, you leaders of the 25:34 [o]Jer 6:26
flock. [p]Isa 34:6; Jer 50:27
For your time to be slaughtered[p] has
come;
you will fall and be shattered like
fine pottery.
35The shepherds will have nowhere to
flee,
the leaders of the flock no place to 25:35
escape.[q] [q]Job 11:20
36Hear the cry of the shepherds,
the wailing of the leaders of the
flock,
for the LORD is destroying their
pasture.
37The peaceful meadows will be laid
waste
because of the fierce anger of the
LORD.
38Like a lion[r] he will leave his lair, 25:38 [r]Jer 4:7
and their land will become
desolate
because of the sword[b] of the
oppressor
and because of the LORD's fierce
anger.

Jeremiah Threatened With Death

26 Early in the reign of Jehoiakim[s] 26:1
son of Josiah king of Judah, [s]2Ki 23:36
this word came from the LORD: 2"This
is what the LORD says: Stand in the 26:2
courtyard[t] of the LORD's house and [t]Jer 19:14
speak to all the people of the towns [u]Jer 1:17;
of Judah who come to worship in the Mt 28:20;
house of the LORD. Tell[u] them every- Ac 20:27 [v]Dt 4:2
thing I command you; do not omit[v]
a word. 3Perhaps they will listen and
each will turn[w] from his evil way. Then 26:3 [w]Jer 36:7
I will relent[x] and not bring on them [x]Jer 18:8
the disaster I was planning because of
the evil they have done. 4Say to them,
'This is what the LORD says: If you 26:4
do not listen[y] to me and follow my [y]Lev 26:14
law,[z] which I have set before you, 5and [z]1Ki 9:6
if you do not listen to the words of
my servants the prophets, whom I have
sent to you again and again (though
you have not listened[a]), 6then I will 26:5 [a]Jer 25:4
make this house like Shiloh[b] and this
city an object of cursing[c] among all the 26:6 [b]Jos 18:1
nations of the earth.' " [c]2Ki 22:19

7The priests, the prophets and all

[a]*26 Sheshach* is a cryptogram for Babylon.
[b]*38* Some Hebrew manuscripts and Septuagint (see also Jer. 46:16 and 50:16); most Hebrew manuscripts *anger*

the people heard Jeremiah speak these
words in the house of the LORD. 8But
as soon as Jeremiah finished telling all
the people everything the LORD had
commanded him to say, the priests, the
prophets and all the people seized him
and said, "You must die! 9Why do you
prophesy in the LORD's name that this
house will be like Shiloh and this city
26:9 [d]Jer 9:11
will be desolate and deserted?"[d] And all
the people crowded around Jeremiah in
the house of the LORD.
10When the officials of Judah heard
about these things, they went up from
the royal palace to the house of the
LORD and took their places at the entrance
of the New Gate of the LORD's
house. 11Then the priests and the prophets
said to the officials and all the people,
"This man should be sentenced
26:11 [e]Dt 18:20; Jer 18:23; 38:4; Mt 26:66; Ac 6:11
to death[e] because he has prophesied
against this city. You have heard it with
your own ears!"
12Then Jeremiah said to all the officials[f]
26:12 [f]Jer 1:18 [g]Am 7:15; Ac 4:18-20; 5:29 [h]ver 2,15
and all the people: "The LORD
sent me to prophesy[g] against this house
and this city all the things you have
heard.[h] 13Now reform[i] your ways and
26:13 [i]Jer 7:5; Joel 2:12-14
your actions and obey the LORD your
God. Then the LORD will relent and not
bring the disaster he has pronounced
against you. 14As for me, I am in your
26:14 [j]Jer 38:5
hands;[j] do with me whatever you think
is good and right. 15Be assured, however,
that if you put me to death, you
will bring the guilt of innocent blood
on yourselves and on this city and on
those who live in it, for in truth the
LORD has sent me to you to speak all
these words in your hearing."
26:16 [k]Ac 23:9 [l]Ac 5:34-39; 23:29
16Then the officials[k] and all the people
said to the priests and the prophets,
"This man should not be sentenced to
death![l] He has spoken to us in the name
of the LORD our God."
17Some of the elders of the land
stepped forward and said to the entire
26:18 [m]Mic 1:1 [n]Isa 2:3 [o]Ne 4:2; Jer 9:11 [p]Mic 4:1; Zec 8:3 [q]Jer 17:3
assembly of people, 18"Micah[m] of Moresheth
prophesied in the days of Hezekiah
king of Judah. He told all the
people of Judah, 'This is what the LORD
Almighty says:

"'Zion[n] will be plowed like a field,
Jerusalem will become a heap of rubble,[o]
the temple hill[p] a mound
overgrown with thickets.'[a][q]

26:19 [r]2Ch 32:24-26; Isa 37:14-20 [s]Ex 32:14; 2Sa 24:16 [t]Jer 44:7 [u]Hab 2:10
19"Did Hezekiah king of Judah or anyone
else in Judah put him to death?
Did not Hezekiah[r] fear the LORD and
seek his favor? And did not the LORD
relent,[s] so that he did not bring the disaster[t]
he pronounced against them? We
are about to bring a terrible disaster[u] on
ourselves!"
20(Now Uriah son of Shemaiah from
26:20 [v]Jos 9:17
Kiriath Jearim[v] was another man who
prophesied in the name of the LORD;
he prophesied the same things against
this city and this land as Jeremiah did.
21When King Jehoiakim[w] and all his officers
26:21 [w]1Ki 19:2 [x]Mt 10:23
and officials heard his words, the
king sought to put him to death. But
Uriah heard of it and fled[x] in fear to
Egypt. 22King Jehoiakim, however, sent
26:22 [y]Jer 36:12,25
Elnathan[y] son of Acbor to Egypt, along
with some other men. 23They brought
Uriah out of Egypt and took him to
King Jehoiakim, who had him struck
down with a sword and his body thrown
into the burial place of the common
people.)
24Furthermore, Ahikam[z] son of Shaphan
26:24 [z]2Ki 22:12
supported Jeremiah, and so he
was not handed over to the people to be
put to death.

Judah to Serve Nebuchadnezzar

27:1 [a]2Ch 36:11
27 Early in the reign of Zedekiah[b][a]
son of Josiah king of Judah, this
word came to Jeremiah from the LORD:
2This is what the LORD said to me:
27:2 [b]Jer 28:10,13
"Make a yoke[b] out of straps and crossbars
and put it on your neck. 3Then
27:3 [c]Jer 25:21
send word to the kings of Edom, Moab,
Ammon,[c] Tyre and Sidon through the

[a] *18* Micah 3:12 [b] *1* A few Hebrew manuscripts and Syriac (see also Jer. 27:3, 12 and 28:1); most Hebrew manuscripts *Jehoiakim* (Most Septuagint manuscripts do not have this verse.)

GENTLENESS

Making Ourselves Soft for the Hard Work of Ministry

Jeremiah 27:2

God's manner is one of gentleness. He'll first give us what we must have in order to break our will. He may even wound us to let us know the joy of healing. But what he wants is to own our spirit. When we are broken, then we will have all we need to take up his yoke.

envoys who have come to Jerusalem to
Zedekiah king of Judah. 4Give them a
message for their masters and say, 'This
is what the LORD Almighty, the God of
Israel, says: "Tell this to your masters:
5With my great power and outstretched
27:5 [d]Dt 9:29 arm[d] I made the earth and its people
[e]Ps 115:16 and the animals that are on it, and I
give[e] it to anyone I please. 6Now I will
27:6 hand all your countries over to my ser-
[f]Jer 25:9 vant[f] Nebuchadnezzar[g] king of Bab-
[g]Jer 21:7; Eze 29:18-20 ylon; I will make even the wild animals
[h]Jer 28:14; Da 2:37-38 subject to him.[h] 7All nations will serve[i]
him and his son and his grandson un-
27:7 [i]2Ch 36:20 til the time[j] for his land comes; then
[j]Jer 25:12 many nations and great kings will sub-
[k]Jer 25:14; Da 5:28 jugate[k] him.
8" '"If, however, any nation or kingdom will not serve Nebuchadnezzar
king of Babylon or bow its neck under
his yoke, I will punish that nation with
the sword, famine and plague, declares
the LORD, until I destroy it by his
hand. 9So do not listen to your proph-
27:9 ets, your diviners, your interpreters of
[l]Dt 18:11 dreams, your mediums[l] or your sorcerers who tell you, 'You will not serve
the king of Babylon.' 10They prophesy
27:10 [m]Jer 23:25 lies[m] to you that will only serve to remove you far from your lands; I will
banish you and you will perish. 11But if
27:11 any nation will bow its neck under the
[n]Jer 21:9 yoke[n] of the king of Babylon and serve
him, I will let that nation remain in its
own land to till it and to live there, declares the LORD."' "
12I gave the same message to Zedekiah king of Judah. I said, "Bow your
neck under the yoke of the king of Babylon; serve him and his people, and
you will live. 13Why will you and your
27:13 [o]Eze 18:31 people die[o] by the sword, famine and
plague with which the LORD has threat-
ened any nation that will not serve the
king of Babylon? 14Do not listen to the
words of the prophets who say to you,
'You will not serve the king of Bab-
27:14 ylon,' for they are prophesying lies[p] to
[p]Jer 14:14 you. 15'I have not sent[q] them,' declares
27:15 [q]Jer 23:21 the LORD. 'They are prophesying lies
[r]Jer 29:9 in my name.[r] Therefore, I will banish
[s]Jer 6:15 you and you will perish,[s] both you and
the prophets who prophesy to you.' "
16Then I said to the priests and all
these people, "This is what the LORD
27:16 [t]2Ki 24:13; says: Do not listen to the prophets who
2Ch 36:7,10; say, 'Very soon now the articles[t] from
Jer 28:3; Da 1:2 the LORD's house will be brought back

from Babylon.' They are prophesying
lies to you. 17Do not listen to them.
Serve the king of Babylon, and you
will live. Why should this city become
a ruin? 18If they are prophets and have
the word of the LORD, let them plead[u] 27:18 [u]1Sa 7:8
with the LORD Almighty that the fur-
nishings remaining in the house of the
LORD and in the palace of the king
of Judah and in Jerusalem not be tak-
en to Babylon. 19For this is what the
LORD Almighty says about the pillars,
the Sea,[v] the movable stands and the 27:19 [v]2Ki 25:13
other furnishings[w] that are left in this [w]Jer 52:17-23
city, 20which Nebuchadnezzar king of
Babylon did not take away when he
carried[x] Jehoiachin[a y] son of Jehoiakim 27:20 [x]2Ch 36:10;
king of Judah into exile from Jerusa- Jer 24:1
lem to Babylon, along with all the no- [y]Jer 22:24
bles of Judah and Jerusalem— 21yes,
this is what the LORD Almighty, the
God of Israel, says about the things
that are left in the house of the LORD
and in the palace of the king of Judah
and in Jerusalem: 22'They will be tak-
en[z] to Babylon and there they will re- 27:22 [z]2Ki 25:13
main until the day[a] I come for them,' [a]2Ch 36:21
declares the LORD. 'Then I will bring[b] [b]Ezr 1:7; 7:19
them back and restore them to this
place.' "

The False Prophet Hananiah

28 In the fifth month of that same
year, the fourth year, early in the
reign of Zedekiah[c] king of Judah, the 28:1 [c]Jer 27:1,3
prophet Hananiah son of Azzur, who [d]Jos 9:3
was from Gibeon,[d] said to me in the
house of the LORD in the presence of
the priests and all the people: 2"This is
what the LORD Almighty, the God of
Israel, says: 'I will break the yoke[e] of the 28:2 [e]Jer 27:12
king of Babylon. 3Within two years I
will bring back to this place all the ar- 28:3
ticles[f] of the LORD's house that Neb- [f]2Ki 24:13
uchadnezzar king of Babylon removed
from here and took to Babylon. 4I will
also bring back to this place Jehoia-
chin[a g] son of Jehoiakim king of Judah 28:4 [g]Jer 22:24-27
and all the other exiles from Judah who
went to Babylon,' declares the LORD,
'for I will break the yoke of the king of
Babylon.' "
5Then the prophet Jeremiah replied
to the prophet Hananiah before the
priests and all the people who were
standing in the house of the LORD.

[a]20,4 Hebrew *Jeconiah,* a variant of *Jehoiachin*

6He said, "Amen! May the LORD do so! May the LORD fulfill the words you have prophesied by bringing the articles of the LORD's house and all the exiles back to this place from Babylon. 7Nevertheless, listen to what I have to say in your hearing and in the hearing of all the people: 8From early times the prophets who preceded you and me have prophesied war, disaster and plague[h] against many countries and great kingdoms. 9But the prophet who prophesies peace will be recognized as one truly sent by the LORD only if his prediction comes true.[i]"

10Then the prophet Hananiah took the yoke[j] off the neck of the prophet Jeremiah and broke it, 11and he said[k] before all the people, "This is what the LORD says: 'In the same way will I break the yoke of Nebuchadnezzar king of Babylon off the neck of all the nations within two years.'" At this, the prophet Jeremiah went on his way.

12Shortly after the prophet Hananiah had broken the yoke off the neck of the prophet Jeremiah, the word of the LORD came to Jeremiah: 13"Go and tell Hananiah, 'This is what the LORD says: You have broken a wooden yoke, but in its place you will get a yoke of iron. 14This is what the LORD Almighty, the God of Israel, says: I will put an iron yoke[l] on the necks of all these nations to make them serve Nebuchadnezzar king of Babylon, and they will serve[m] him. I will even give him control over the wild animals.[n]'"

15Then the prophet Jeremiah said to Hananiah the prophet, "Listen, Hananiah! The LORD has not sent[o] you, yet you have persuaded this nation to trust in lies.[p] 16Therefore, this is what the LORD says: 'I am about to remove you from the face of the earth.[q] This very year you are going to die, because you have preached rebellion[r] against the LORD.'"

17In the seventh month of that same year, Hananiah the prophet died.

28:8 [h]Lev 26:14-17; Isa 5:5-7
28:9 [i]Dt 18:22
28:10 [j]Jer 27:2
28:11 [k]Jer 14:14; 27:10
28:14 [l]Dt 28:48 [m]Jer 25:11 [n]Jer 27:6
28:15 [o]Jer 29:31 [p]Jer 20:6; 29:21; La 2:14; Eze 13:6
28:16 [q]Ge 7:4 [r]Dt 13:5; Jer 29:32

A Letter to the Exiles

29 This is the text of the letter that the prophet Jeremiah sent from Jerusalem to the surviving elders among the exiles and to the priests, the prophets and all the other people Nebuchadnezzar had carried into exile from Jerusalem to Babylon.[s] 2(This was after King Jehoiachin[a][t] and the queen mother, the court officials and the leaders of Judah and Jerusalem, the craftsmen and the artisans had gone into exile from Jerusalem.) 3He entrusted the letter to Elasah son of Shaphan and to Gemariah son of Hilkiah, whom Zedekiah king of Judah sent to King Nebuchadnezzar in Babylon. It said:

4This is what the LORD Almighty, the God of Israel, says to all those I carried[u] into exile from Jerusalem to Babylon: 5"Build[v] houses and settle down; plant gardens and eat what they produce. 6Marry and have sons and daughters; find wives for your sons and give your daughters in marriage, so that they too may have sons and daughters. Increase in number there; do not decrease. 7Also, seek the peace and prosperity of the city to which I have carried you into exile. Pray[w] to the LORD for it, because if it prospers, you too will prosper." 8Yes, this is what the LORD Almighty, the God of Israel, says: "Do not let the prophets and diviners among you deceive[x] you. Do not listen to the dreams you encourage them to have.[y] 9They are prophesying lies[z] to you in my name. I have not sent them," declares the LORD.

10This is what the LORD says: "When seventy years[a] are completed for Babylon, I will come to you and fulfill my gracious promise to bring you back[b] to this place. 11For I know the plans[c] I have for you," declares the LORD, "plans to prosper you and not to harm you, plans to give you hope and a future. 12Then you will call upon me and come and pray to me, and I will listen[d] to you. 13You will seek[e] me and find me when you seek me with all your heart.[f] 14I will be found by you," declares the LORD, "and will bring you back[g] from captivity.[b] I will gather you from all the nations and places where I have banished you," declares the LORD, "and will bring you back to

[a]2 Hebrew *Jeconiah,* a variant of *Jehoiachin*
[b]14 Or *will restore your fortunes*

29:1 [s]2Ch 36:10
29:2 [t]2Ki 24:12; Jer 22:24-28
29:4 [u]Jer 24:5
29:5 [v]ver 28
29:7 [w]Ezr 6:10; 1Ti 2:1-2
29:8 [x]Jer 37:9 [y]Jer 23:27
29:9 [z]Jer 14:14; 27:15
29:10 [a]2Ch 36:21; Jer 25:12; Da 9:2 [b]Jer 21:22
29:11 [c]Ps 40:5
29:12 [d]Ps 145:19
29:13 [e]Mt 7:7 [f]Dt 4:29; Jer 24:7
29:14 [g]Dt 30:3; Jer 30:3

the place from which I carried you into exile."[h]

15You may say, "The LORD has raised up prophets for us in Babylon," 16but this is what the LORD says about the king who sits on David's throne and all the people who remain in this city, your countrymen who did not go with you into exile— 17yes, this is what the LORD Almighty says: "I will send the sword, famine and plague[i] against them and I will make them like poor figs[j] that are so bad they cannot be eaten. 18I will pursue them with the sword, famine and plague and will make them abhorrent[k] to all the kingdoms of the earth and an object of cursing and horror,[l] of scorn and reproach, among all the nations where I drive them. 19For they have not listened to my words,"[m] declares the LORD, "words that I sent to them again and again by my servants the prophets.[n] And you exiles have not listened either," declares the LORD.

20Therefore, hear the word of the LORD, all you exiles whom I have sent[o] away from Jerusalem to Babylon. 21This is what the LORD Almighty, the God of Israel, says about Ahab son of Kolaiah and Zedekiah son of Maaseiah, who are prophesying lies[p] to you in my name: "I will hand them over to Nebuchadnezzar king of Babylon, and he will put them to death before your very eyes. 22Because of them, all the exiles from Judah who are in Babylon will use this curse: 'The LORD treat you like Zedekiah and Ahab, whom the king of Babylon burned[q] in the fire.' 23For they have done outrageous things in Israel; they have committed adultery[r] with their neighbors' wives and in my name have spoken lies, which I did not tell them to do. I know[s] it and am a witness to it," declares the LORD.

29:14 [h]Jer 23:3-4
29:17 [i]Jer 27:8 [j]Jer 24:8-10
29:18 [k]Jer 15:4 [l]Dt 28:25; Jer 42:18
29:19 [m]Jer 6:19 [n]Jer 25:4
29:20 [o]Jer 24:5
29:21 [p]ver 9; Jer 14:14
29:22 [q]Da 3:6
29:23 [r]Jer 23:14 [s]Heb 4:13

Message to Shemaiah

24Tell Shemaiah the Nehelamite, 25"This is what the LORD Almighty, the God of Israel, says: You sent letters in your own name to all the people in Jerusalem, to Zephaniah[t] son of Maaseiah the priest, and to all the other priests. You said to Zephaniah, 26'The LORD has appointed you priest in place of Jehoiada to be in charge of the house of the LORD; you should put any madman[u] who acts like a prophet into the stocks[v] and neck-irons. 27So why have you not reprimanded Jeremiah from Anathoth, who poses as a prophet among you? 28He has sent this message[w] to us in Babylon: It will be a long time.[x] Therefore build[y] houses and settle down; plant gardens and eat what they produce.' "

29Zephaniah the priest, however, read the letter to Jeremiah the prophet. 30Then the word of the LORD came to Jeremiah: 31"Send this message to all the exiles: 'This is what the LORD says about Shemaiah[z] the Nehelamite: Because Shemaiah has prophesied to you, even though I did not send[a] him, and has led you to believe a lie, 32this is what the LORD says: I will surely punish Shemaiah the Nehelamite and his descendants.[b] He will have no one left among this people, nor will he see the good[c] things I will do for my people, declares the LORD, because he has preached rebellion[d] against me.' "

Restoration of Israel

30 This is the word that came to Jeremiah from the LORD: 2"This is what the LORD, the God of Israel, says: 'Write[e] in a book all the words I have spoken to you. 3The days are coming,' declares the LORD, 'when I will bring[f] my people Israel and Judah back from captivity[a] and restore[g] them to the land I gave their forefathers to possess,' says the LORD."

4These are the words the LORD spoke concerning Israel and Judah: 5"This is what the LORD says:

" 'Cries of fear[h] are heard—
terror, not peace.
6Ask and see:
Can a man bear children?
Then why do I see every strong man
with his hands on his stomach like
a woman in labor,[i]
every face turned deathly pale?

29:25 [t]2Ki 25:18; Jer 21:1
29:26 [u]2Ki 9:11; Hos 9:7; Jn 10:20 [v]Jer 20:2
29:28 [w]ver 1 [x]ver 10 [y]ver 5
29:31 [z]ver 24 [a]Jer 14:14; 28:15
29:32 [b]1Sa 2:30-33 [c]ver 10 [d]Jer 28:16
30:2 [e]Isa 30:8
30:3 [f]Jer 29:14 [g]Jer 16:15
30:5 [h]Jer 6:25
30:6 [i]Jer 4:31

[a]3 Or *will restore the fortunes of my people Israel and Judah*

30:7 [j]Isa 2:12; Joel 2:11 [k]Zep 1:15 [l]ver 10

7 How awful that day[j] will be!
None will be like it.
It will be a time of trouble[k] for Jacob,
but he will be saved[l] out of it.

30:8 [m]Isa 9:4 [n]Eze 34:27

8 " 'In that day,' declares the LORD Almighty,
'I will break the yoke[m] off their necks
and will tear off their bonds;
no longer will foreigners enslave them.[n]
9 Instead, they will serve the LORD their God
and David[o] their king,[p]
whom I will raise up for them.

30:9 [o]Isa 55:3-4; Lk 1:69; Ac 2:30; 13:23 [p]Eze 34:23-24; 37:24; Hos 3:5

10 " 'So do not fear,[q] O Jacob my servant;[r]
do not be dismayed, O Israel,'
declares the LORD.
'I will surely save[s] you out of a distant place,
your descendants from the land of their exile.
Jacob will again have peace and security,[t]
and no one will make him afraid.

30:10 [q]Isa 43:5; Jer 46:27-28 [r]Isa 44:2 [s]Jer 29:14 [t]Isa 35:9

11 I am with you and will save you,'
declares the LORD.
'Though I completely destroy all the nations
among which I scatter you,
I will not completely destroy[u] you.
I will discipline[v] you but only with justice;
I will not let you go entirely unpunished.'[w]

30:11 [u]Jer 4:27; 46:28 [v]Jer 10:24 [w]Am 9:8

12 "This is what the LORD says:

" 'Your wound is incurable,
your injury beyond healing.[x]
13 There is no one to plead your cause,
no remedy for your sore,
no healing[y] for you.
14 All your allies[z] have forgotten you;
they care nothing for you.
I have struck you as an enemy[a] would
and punished you as would the cruel,[b]
because your guilt is so great
and your sins[c] so many.
15 Why do you cry out over your wound,
your pain that has no cure?
Because of your great guilt and many sins
I have done these things to you.

30:12 [x]Jer 15:18

30:13 [y]Jer 8:22; 14:19; 46:11

30:14 [z]Jer 22:20; La 1:2 [a]Job 13:24 [b]Job 30:21 [c]Jer 5:6

16 " 'But all who devour[d] you will be devoured;
all your enemies will go into exile.[e]
Those who plunder[f] you will be plundered;
all who make spoil of you I will despoil.
17 But I will restore you to health
and heal your wounds,'
declares the LORD,
'because you are called an outcast,[g]
Zion for whom no one cares.'

30:16 [d]Isa 33:1; Jer 2:3; 10:25 [e]Isa 14:2; Joel 3:4-8 [f]Jer 50:10

30:17 [g]Jer 33:24

18 "This is what the LORD says:

" 'I will restore the fortunes[h] of Jacob's tents
and have compassion[i] on his dwellings;
the city will be rebuilt[j] on her ruins,
and the palace will stand in its proper place.
19 From them will come songs[k] of thanksgiving[l]
and the sound of rejoicing.[m]
I will add to their numbers,[n]
and they will not be decreased;
I will bring them honor,[o]
and they will not be disdained.
20 Their children[p] will be as in days of old,
and their community will be established[q] before me;
I will punish all who oppress them.
21 Their leader[r] will be one of their own;
their ruler will arise from among them.
I will bring him near[s] and he will come close to me,
for who is he who will devote himself
to be close to me?'
declares the LORD.
22 " 'So you will be my people,
and I will be your God.' "

30:18 [h]ver 3; Jer 31:23 [i]Ps 102:13 [j]Jer 31:4, 24,38

30:19 [k]Isa 35:10; 51:11 [l]Isa 51:3 [m]Ps 126:1-2; Jer 31:4 [n]Jer 33:22 [o]Isa 60:9

30:20 [p]Isa 54:13; Jer 31:17 [q]Isa 54:14

30:21 [r]ver 9 [s]Nu 16:5

23 See, the storm[t] of the LORD
will burst out in wrath,
a driving wind swirling down
on the heads of the wicked.
24 The fierce anger[u] of the LORD will not turn back[v]
until he fully accomplishes
the purposes of his heart.
In days to come
you will understand[w] this.

30:23 [t]Jer 23:19

30:24 [u]Jer 4:8 [v]Jer 4:28 [w]Jer 23:19-20

31 "At that time," declares the LORD, "I will be the God[x] of all the clans of Israel, and they will be my people."

[2]This is what the LORD says:

"The people who survive the sword
will find favor[y] in the desert;
I will come to give rest[z] to Israel."

[3]The LORD appeared to us in the past,[a] saying:

"I have loved[a] you with an
everlasting love;
I have drawn[b] you with
loving-kindness.
[4]I will build you up again
and you will be rebuilt, O Virgin
Israel.
Again you will take up your
tambourines
and go out to dance with the
joyful.[c]
[5]Again you will plant vineyards
on the hills of Samaria;[d]
the farmers will plant them
and enjoy their fruit.[e]
[6]There will be a day when watchmen
cry out
on the hills of Ephraim,
'Come, let us go up to Zion,
to the LORD our God.'"[f]

[7]This is what the LORD says:

"Sing with joy for Jacob;
shout for the foremost[g] of the
nations.
Make your praises heard, and say,
'O LORD, save[h] your people,
the remnant[i] of Israel.'
[8]See, I will bring them from the land
of the north[j]
and gather[k] them from the ends of
the earth.
Among them will be the blind[l] and
the lame,[m]
expectant mothers and women in
labor;
a great throng will return.
[9]They will come with weeping;[n]
they will pray as I bring them
back.
I will lead[o] them beside streams of
water
on a level[p] path where they will
not stumble,
because I am Israel's father,[q]
and Ephraim is my firstborn son.

31:1 [x]Jer 30:22
31:2 [y]Nu 14:20 [z]Ex 33:14
31:3 [a]Dt 4:37 [b]Hos 11:4
31:4 [c]Jer 30:19
31:5 [d]Jer 50:19 [e]Isa 65:21; Am 9:14
31:6 [f]Isa 2:3; Jer 50:4-5; Mic 4:2
31:7 [g]Dt 28:13; Isa 61:9 [h]Ps 14:7; 28:9 [i]Isa 37:31
31:8 [j]Jer 3:18; 23:8 [k]Dt 30:4; Eze 34:12-14 [l]Isa 42:16 [m]Eze 34:16; Mic 4:6
31:9 [n]Ps 126:5 [o]Isa 63:13 [p]Isa 49:11 [q]Ex 4:22; Jer 3:4

[10]"Hear the word of the LORD,
O nations;
proclaim it in distant coastlands:[r]
'He who scattered Israel will gather[s]
them
and will watch over his flock like
a shepherd.'[t]
[11]For the LORD will ransom Jacob
and redeem[u] them from the hand
of those stronger[v] than they.
[12]They will come and shout for joy on
the heights[w] of Zion;
they will rejoice in the bounty[x] of
the LORD—
the grain, the new wine and the oil,[y]
the young of the flocks and
herds.
They will be like a well-watered
garden,[z]
and they will sorrow[a] no more.
[13]Then maidens will dance and be
glad,
young men and old as well.
I will turn their mourning[b] into
gladness;
I will give them comfort and joy[c]
instead of sorrow.
[14]I will satisfy[d] the priests with
abundance,
and my people will be filled with
my bounty,"
declares the LORD.

[15]This is what the LORD says:

"A voice is heard in Ramah,[e]
mourning and great weeping,
Rachel weeping for her children
and refusing to be comforted,[f]
because her children are no
more."[g]

[16]This is what the LORD says:

31:10 [r]Isa 66:19; Jer 25:22 [s]Jer 50:19 [t]Isa 40:11; Eze 34:12
31:11 [u]Isa 44:23; 48:20 [v]Ps 142:6
31:12 [w]Eze 17:23; Mic 4:1 [x]Joel 3:18 [y]Hos 2:21-22 [z]Isa 58:11 [a]Isa 65:19; Jn 16:22; Rev 7:17
31:13 [b]Isa 61:3 [c]Ps 30:11; Isa 51:11
31:14 [d]ver 25
31:15 [e]Jos 18:25 [f]Ge 37:35 [g]Jer 10:20; Mt 2:17-18*

[a]3 Or *LORD has appeared to us from afar*

JOY

WEEPING IN RAMAH

Jeremiah 31:15

Herod's blades, thrust into the cradles of Bethlehem, came out red. Mothers mourned. But the baby Herod sought to kill was already bound for Egypt the night that Rachel wept. When Jesus reached maturity, laughter marked Bethlehem as a town where tyranny at last had met its match. In every plan of God, weeping is at last resolved in joy.

"Restrain your voice from weeping
31:16 [b]Isa 25:8; 30:19 [i]Ru 2:12 [j]Jer 30:3; Eze 11:17 and your eyes from tears,[b]
for your work will be rewarded,[i]"
declares the LORD.
"They will return[j] from the land
of the enemy.
[17]So there is hope for your future,"
declares the LORD.
"Your children will return to their
own land.

[18]"I have surely heard Ephraim's
moaning:
31:18 [k]Job 5:17 [l]Hos 4:16 [m]Ps 80:3 'You disciplined[k] me like an
unruly calf,[l]
and I have been disciplined.
Restore[m] me, and I will return,
because you are the LORD my
God.
31:19 [n]Eze 36:31 [o]Eze 21:12; Lk 18:13 [19]After I strayed,[n]
I repented;
after I came to understand,
I beat[o] my breast.
I was ashamed and humiliated
because I bore the disgrace of my
youth.'
[20]Is not Ephraim my dear son,
the child in whom I delight?
Though I often speak against him,
31:20 [p]Hos 4:4; 11:8 [q]Isa 55:7; 63:15; Mic 7:18 I still remember[p] him.
Therefore my heart yearns for him;
I have great compassion[q] for him,"
declares the LORD.

[21]"Set up road signs;
put up guideposts.
31:21 [r]Jer 50:5 [s]Isa 52:11 [t]ver 4 Take note of the highway,[r]
the road that you take.
Return,[s] O Virgin[t] Israel,
return to your towns.
31:22 [u]Jer 2:23 [v]Jer 3:6 [22]How long will you wander,[u]
O unfaithful[v] daughter?
The LORD will create a new thing
on earth—
a woman will surround[a] a man."

[23]This is what the LORD Almighty,
the God of Israel, says: "When I bring
31:23 [w]Jer 30:18 [x]Isa 1:26 [y]Ps 48:1; Zec 8:3 them back from captivity,[b][w] the people
in the land of Judah and in its towns
will once again use these words: 'The
LORD bless you, O righteous dwelling,[x]
31:24 [z]Zec 8:4-8 O sacred mountain.'[y] [24]People will live[z]
together in Judah and all its towns—
farmers and those who move about with
31:25 [a]Jn 4:14 their flocks. [25]I will refresh the weary
and satisfy the faint."[a]
31:26 [b]Zec 4:1 [26]At this I awoke[b] and looked around.
My sleep had been pleasant to me.

[27]"The days are coming," declares the
LORD, "when I will plant[c] the house of 31:27 [c]Eze 36:9-11; Hos 2:23
Israel and the house of Judah with the
offspring of men and of animals. [28]Just
as I watched over them to uproot and
tear down, and to overthrow, destroy
and bring disaster,[d] so I will watch over 31:28 [d]Jer 18:8; 44:27 [e]Jer 1:10
them to build and to plant,"[e] declares
the LORD. [29]"In those days people will
no longer say,

'The fathers[f] have eaten sour grapes, 31:29 [f]La 5:7 [g]Eze 18:2
and the children's teeth are set on
edge.'[g]

[30]Instead, everyone will die for his own
sin;[h] whoever eats sour grapes—his own 31:30 [h]Isa 3:11; Gal 6:7
teeth will be set on edge.

[31]"The time is coming," declares the
LORD,
"when I will make a new
covenant[i] 31:31 [i]Jer 32:40; Eze 37:26; Lk 22:20; Heb 8:8-12*; 10:16-17
with the house of Israel
and with the house of Judah.
[32]It will not be like the covenant[j]
I made with their forefathers[k] 31:32 [j]Ex 24:8 [k]Dt 5:3
when I took them by the hand
to lead them out of Egypt,
because they broke my covenant,
though I was a husband to[c]
them,[d]"
declares the LORD.
[33]"This is the covenant I will make
with the house of Israel
after that time," declares the
LORD.
"I will put my law in their minds 31:33 [l]2Co 3:3 [m]Jer 24:7; Heb 10:16
and write it on their hearts.[l]
I will be their God,
and they will be my people.[m]

[a]22 Or *will go about* ⌊*seeking*⌋; or *will protect*
[b]23 Or *I restore their fortunes* [c]32 Hebrew; Septuagint and Syriac / *and I turned away from*
[d]32 Or *was their master*

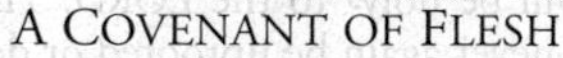

GENTLENESS

A COVENANT OF FLESH

Jeremiah 31:33

The Ten Commandments were written in stone.

Stone has its limitations.

The covenant of grace is written on the human heart.

God's gentleness in flesh outlasts earth's hardest granite.

31:34 [n]1Jn 2:27 [o]Jn 6:45 [p]Isa 54:13; Jer 33:8; 50:20 [q]Ro 11:27; Mic 7:19; Heb 10:17*

34 No longer will a man teach[n] his
neighbor,
or a man his brother, saying,
'Know the LORD,'
because they will all know[o] me,
from the least of them to the
greatest,"
declares the LORD.
"For I will forgive[p] their wickedness
and will remember their sins[q] no
more."

35 This is what the LORD says,

31:35 [r]Ps 136:7-9 [s]Ge 1:16 [t]Jer 10:16

he who appoints[r] the sun
to shine by day,
who decrees the moon and stars
to shine by night,[s]
who stirs up the sea
so that its waves roar—
the LORD Almighty is his name:[t]

31:36 [u]Isa 54:9-10; Jer 33:20-26 [v]Ps 89:36-37

36 "Only if these decrees[u] vanish from
my sight,"
declares the LORD,
"will the descendants[v] of Israel ever
cease
to be a nation before me."

37 This is what the LORD says:

"Only if the heavens above can be
measured[w]

31:37 [w]Jer 33:22 [x]Jer 33:24-26; Ro 11:1-5

and the foundations of the earth
below be searched out
will I reject[x] all the descendants of
Israel
because of all they have done,"
declares the LORD.

31:38 [y]Jer 30:18 [z]Ne 3:1 [a]2Ki 14:13; Zec 14:10

38 "The days are coming," declares the
LORD, "when this city will be rebuilt[y]
for me from the Tower of Hananel[z] to
the Corner Gate.[a] 39 The measuring line
will stretch from there straight to the
hill of Gareb and then turn to Goah.

31:40 [b]Jer 7:31-32 [c]Jer 8:2 [d]2Sa 15:23; Jn 18:1 [e]2Ki 11:16 [f]Joel 3:17; Zec 14:21

40 The whole valley[b] where dead bodies[c]
and ashes are thrown, and all the terraces out to the Kidron Valley[d] on the
east as far as the corner of the Horse
Gate,[e] will be holy[f] to the LORD. The
city will never again be uprooted or demolished."

Jeremiah Buys a Field

32:1 [g]2Ki 25:1 [h]Jer 25:1; 39:1

32 This is the word that came to
Jeremiah from the LORD in the
tenth[g] year of Zedekiah king of Judah,
which was the eighteenth[h] year of Nebuchadnezzar. 2 The army of the king of
Babylon was then besieging Jerusalem,
and Jeremiah the prophet was confined
in the courtyard of the guard[i] in the 32:2 [i]Ne 3:25; Jer 37:21
royal palace of Judah.
3 Now Zedekiah king of Judah had
imprisoned him there, saying, "Why do
you prophesy[j] as you do? You say, 'This 32:3 [j]Jer 26:8-9 [k]ver 28; Jer 34:2-3
is what the LORD says: I am about to
hand this city over to the king of Babylon, and he will capture[k] it. 4 Zedeki-
ah king of Judah will not escape[l] out of 32:4 [l]Jer 38:18,23; 39:5-7; 52:9
the hands of the Babylonians[a] but will
certainly be handed over to the king of
Babylon, and will speak with him face
to face and see him with his own eyes.
5 He will take[m] Zedekiah to Babylon, 32:5 [m]Jer 39:7; Eze 12:13 [n]Jer 21:4
where he will remain until I deal with
him, declares the LORD. If you fight
against the Babylonians, you will not
succeed.' "[n]
6 Jeremiah said, "The word of the
LORD came to me: 7 Hanamel son of
Shallum your uncle is going to come
to you and say, 'Buy my field at Anathoth, because as nearest relative it is
your right and duty[o] to buy it.' 32:7 [o]Lev 25:24-25; Ru 4:3-4; Mt 27:10*
8 "Then, just as the LORD had said,
my cousin Hanamel came to me in the
courtyard of the guard and said, 'Buy
my field at Anathoth in the territory of
Benjamin. Since it is your right to redeem it and possess it, buy it for yourself.'

JOY

BATTLEFIELD SONGS

Jeremiah 32:8

Joy can come even in a time of war. When the siege machines had surrounded the city and the conqueror was soon to own the country, Jeremiah bought a field for an inheritance. This unlikely transaction was like shopping for real estate in Berlin in 1944. It was a candle of joy, a statement of hope.

"I knew that this was the word of
the LORD; 9 so I bought the field at Anathoth from my cousin Hanamel and
weighed out for him seventeen shekels[b]
of silver.[p] 10 I signed and sealed the deed, 32:9 [p]Ge 23:16
had it witnessed,[q] and weighed out the 32:10 [q]Ru 4:9
silver on the scales. 11 I took the deed of
purchase—the sealed copy containing

[a]4 Or *Chaldeans*; also in verses 5, 24, 25, 28, 29 and 43 [b]9 That is, about 7 ounces (about 200 grams)

the terms and conditions, as well as the
32:12 [r]ver 16; Jer 36:4; 43:3,6; 45:1 [s]Jer 51:59
unsealed copy— 12and I gave this deed
to Baruch[r] son of Neriah,[s] the son of
Mahseiah, in the presence of my cousin
Hanamel and of the witnesses who had
signed the deed and of all the Jews sitting in the courtyard of the guard.
13"In their presence I gave Baruch
these instructions: 14'This is what the
LORD Almighty, the God of Israel, says:
Take these documents, both the sealed
and unsealed copies of the deed of purchase, and put them in a clay jar so they
will last a long time. 15For this is what
the LORD Almighty, the God of Israel,
32:15 [t]ver 43-44; Jer 30:18; Am 9:14-15
says: Houses, fields and vineyards will
again be bought in this land.'[t]
16"After I had given the deed of purchase to Baruch son of Neriah, I prayed
to the LORD:

32:17 [u]Jer 1:6 [v]2Ki 19:15; Ps 102:25 [w]Mt 19:26
17"Ah, Sovereign LORD,[u] you have
made the heavens and the earth by
your great power and outstretched
arm.[v] Nothing is too hard[w] for
32:18 [x]Dt 5:10 [y]Ex 20:5 [z]Jer 10:16
you. 18You show love[x] to thousands but bring the punishment
for the fathers' sins into the laps of
their children[y] after them. O great
and powerful God, whose name is
the LORD Almighty,[z] 19great are
your purposes and mighty are your
32:19 [a]Isa 28:29 [b]Pr 5:21; Jer 16:17 [c]Jer 17:10; Mt 16:27
deeds.[a] Your eyes are open to all
the ways of men;[b] you reward everyone according to his conduct
and as his deeds deserve.[c] 20You
performed miraculous signs and
32:20 [d]Ex 9:16
wonders in Egypt[d] and have continued them to this day, both in
Israel and among all mankind, and
have gained the renown that is still
yours. 21You brought your people
Israel out of Egypt with signs and
32:21 [e]Ex 6:6; 1Ch 17:21; Da 9:15 [f]Dt 26:8
wonders, by a mighty hand[e] and
an outstretched arm and with great
terror.[f] 22You gave them this land
you had sworn to give their forefathers, a land flowing with milk and
32:22 [g]Ex 3:8; Jer 11:5
honey.[g] 23They came in and took
possession[h] of it, but they did not
32:23 [h]Ps 44:2; 78:54-55 [i]Ne 9:26; Jer 11:8 [j]Da 9:14
obey you or follow your law;[i] they
did not do what you commanded
them to do. So you brought all
this disaster[j] upon them.
24"See how the siege ramps are
built up to take the city. Because
32:24 [k]Jer 14:12
of the sword, famine and plague,[k]
the city will be handed over to the
Babylonians who are attacking it. 32:24 [l]Dt 4:25-26; Jos 23:15-16
What you said[l] has happened, as
you now see. 25And though the city
will be handed over to the Babylonians, you, O Sovereign LORD,
say to me, 'Buy the field with silver and have the transaction witnessed.' "

26Then the word of the LORD came
to Jeremiah: 27"I am the LORD, the
God of all mankind.[m] Is anything too 32:27 [m]Nu 16:22
hard for me? 28Therefore, this is what
the LORD says: I am about to hand
this city over to the Babylonians and to
Nebuchadnezzar[n] king of Babylon, who 32:28 [n]2Ch 36:17 [o]ver 3
will capture it.[o] 29The Babylonians who
are attacking this city will come in and
set it on fire; they will burn it down,[p] 32:29 [p]2Ch 36:19; Jer 21:10; 37:8,10; 52:13 [q]Jer 19:13 [r]Jer 44:18
along with the houses[q] where the peo-
ple provoked me to anger by burning
incense on the roofs to Baal and by
pouring out drink offerings[r] to other
gods.
30"The people of Israel and Judah
have done nothing but evil in my sight
from their youth;[s] indeed, the people 32:30 [s]Jer 22:21 [t]Jer 8:19 [u]Jer 25:7
of Israel have done nothing but pro-
voke[t] me with what their hands have
made,[u] declares the LORD. 31From the
day it was built until now, this city has
so aroused my anger and wrath that I
must remove[v] it from my sight. 32The 32:31 [v]2Ki 23:27; 24:3
people of Israel and Judah have pro-
voked me by all the evil[w] they have 32:32 [w]Isa 1:4-6; Da 9:8
done—they, their kings and officials,
their priests and prophets, the men
of Judah and the people of Jerusalem.
33They turned their backs[x] to me and 32:33 [x]Jer 2:27; Eze 8:16 [y]Jer 7:13
not their faces; though I taught[y] them
again and again, they would not listen
or respond to discipline. 34They set up
their abominable idols in the house that
bears my Name and defiled[z] it. 35They 32:34 [z]Jer 7:30
built high places for Baal in the Valley
of Ben Hinnom to sacrifice their sons
and daughters[a] to Molech,[a] though I 32:35 [a]Lev 18:21 [b]Jer 7:31; 19:5
never commanded, nor did it enter my
mind,[b] that they should do such a detestable thing and so make Judah sin.
36"You are saying about this city, 'By
the sword, famine and plague[c] it will 32:36 [c]ver 24
be handed over to the king of Babylon';
but this is what the LORD, the God of
Israel, says: 37I will surely gather[d] them 32:37 [d]Jer 23:3,6
from all the lands where I banish them

[a]35 Or *to make their sons and daughters pass through* ⌊*the fire*⌋

in my furious anger and great wrath; I will bring them back to this place and let them live in safety.[e] 38They will be my people,[f] and I will be their God. 39I will give them singleness[g] of heart and action, so that they will always fear me for their own good and the good of their children after them. 40I will make an everlasting covenant[h] with them: I will never stop doing good to them, and I will inspire them to fear me, so that they will never turn away from me.[i] 41I will rejoice in doing them good[j] and will assuredly plant[k] them in this land with all my heart and soul.

42"This is what the LORD says: As I have brought all this great calamity on this people, so I will give them all the prosperity I have promised[l] them. 43Once more fields will be bought[m] in this land of which you say, 'It is a desolate waste, without men or animals, for it has been handed over to the Babylonians.' 44Fields will be bought for silver, and deeds[n] will be signed, sealed and witnessed in the territory of Benjamin, in the villages around Jerusalem, in the towns of Judah and in the towns of the hill country, of the western foothills and of the Negev,[o] because I will restore[p] their fortunes,[a] declares the LORD."

Promise of Restoration

33 While Jeremiah was still confined in the courtyard[q] of the guard, the word of the LORD came to him a second time: 2"This is what the LORD says, he who made the earth,[r] the LORD who formed it and established it—the LORD is his name:[s] 3'Call[t] to me and I will answer you and tell you great and unsearchable things you do not know.' 4For this is what the LORD, the God of Israel, says about the houses in this city and the royal palaces of Judah that have been torn down to be used against the siege[u] ramps[v] and the sword 5in the fight with the Babylonians[b]: 'They will be filled with the dead bodies of the men I will slay in my anger and wrath.[w] I will hide my face[x] from this city because of all its wickedness.

6" 'Nevertheless, I will bring health and healing to it; I will heal my people and will let them enjoy abundant peace and security. 7I will bring Judah[y] and Israel back from captivity[c][z] and will rebuild them as they were before.[a] 8I will cleanse[b] them from all the sin they have committed against me and will forgive[c] all their sins of rebellion against me. 9Then this city will bring me renown, joy, praise[d] and honor[e] before all nations on earth that hear of all the good things I do for it; and they will be in awe and will tremble at the abundant prosperity and peace I provide for it.'

10"This is what the LORD says: 'You say about this place, "It is a desolate waste, without men or animals."[f] Yet in the towns of Judah and the streets of Jerusalem that are deserted, inhabited by neither men nor animals, there will be heard once more 11the sounds of joy and gladness,[g] the voices of bride and bridegroom, and the voices of those who bring thank offerings[h] to the house of the LORD, saying,

"Give thanks to the LORD Almighty,
for the LORD is good;[i]
his love endures forever."[j]

For I will restore the fortunes of the land as they were before,' says the LORD.

12"This is what the LORD Almighty says: 'In this place, desolate[k] and without men or animals—in all its towns there will again be pastures for shepherds to rest their flocks.[l] 13In the towns of the hill country, of the western foothills and of the Negev,[m] in the territory of Benjamin, in the villages around Jerusalem and in the towns of Judah, flocks will again pass under the hand[n] of the one who counts them,' says the LORD.

14" 'The days are coming,' declares the LORD, 'when I will fulfill the gracious promise[o] I made to the house of Israel and to the house of Judah.

15" 'In those days and at that time
I will make a righteous[p] Branch[q]
sprout from David's line;
he will do what is just and right
in the land.
16In those days Judah will be saved[r]
and Jerusalem will live in safety.
This is the name by which it[d] will
be called:
The LORD Our Righteousness.'[s]

[a]44 Or *will bring them back from captivity*
[b]5 Or *Chaldeans* [c]7 Or *will restore the fortunes of Judah and Israel* [d]16 Or *he*

32:37 [e]Dt 30:3; Eze 34:28
32:38 [f]Jer 24:7; 2Co 6:16*
32:39 [g]Eze 11:19
32:40 [h]Isa 55:3 [i]Jer 24:7
32:41 [j]Dt 30:9 [k]Jer 24:6; 31:28; Am 9:15
32:42 [l]Jer 31:28
32:43 [m]ver 15
32:44 [n]ver 10 [o]Jer 17:26 [p]Jer 33:7, 11,26
33:1 [q]Jer 32:2-3; 37:21; 38:28
33:2 [r]Jer 10:16 [s]Ex 3:15; 15:3
33:3 [t]Isa 55:6; Jer 29:12
33:4 [u]Eze 4:2 [v]Jer 32:24; Hab 1:10
33:5 [w]Jer 21:4-7 [x]Isa 8:17
33:7 [y]Jer 32:44
33:7 [z]Jer 30:3; Am 9:14 [a]Isa 1:26
33:8 [b]Heb 9:13-14 [c]Jer 31:34; Mic 7:18; Zec 13:1
33:9 [d]Jer 13:11 [e]Isa 62:7; Jer 3:17
33:10 [f]Jer 32:43
33:11 [g]Isa 51:3 [h]Lev 7:12 [i]1Ch 16:8; Ps 136:1 [j]Ps 100:4-5
33:12 [k]Jer 32:43; 1Ch 16:34; 2Ch 5:13 [l]Isa 65:10; Eze 34:11-15
33:13 [m]Jer 17:26 [n]Lev 27:32
33:14 [o]Jer 29:10
33:15 [p]Ps 72:2 [q]Isa 4:2; 11:1; Jer 23:5
33:16 [r]Isa 45:17 [s]1Co 1:30

17For this is what the LORD says: 'David will never fail[t] to have a man to sit
on the throne of the house of Israel,
18nor will the priests, who are Levites,[u]
ever fail to have a man to stand before
me continually to offer burnt offerings,
to burn grain offerings and to present
sacrifices.[v]' "
19The word of the LORD came to Jeremiah: 20"This is what the LORD says:
'If you can break my covenant with the
day[w] and my covenant with the night,
so that day and night no longer come
at their appointed time, 21then my covenant[x] with David my servant—and
my covenant with the Levites who are
priests ministering before me—can be
broken and David will no longer have a
descendant to reign on his throne.[y] 22I
will make the descendants of David my
servant and the Levites who minister
before me as countless[z] as the stars of
the sky and as measureless as the sand
on the seashore.' "
23The word of the LORD came to
Jeremiah: 24"Have you not noticed that
these people are saying, 'The LORD has
rejected the two kingdoms[a][a] he chose'?
So they despise[b] my people and no longer regard them as a nation.[c] 25This is
what the LORD says: 'If I have not established my covenant with day and
night[d] and the fixed laws of heaven and
earth,[e] 26then I will reject[f] the descendants of Jacob[g] and David my servant
and will not choose one of his sons
to rule over the descendants of Abraham, Isaac and Jacob. For I will restore
their fortunes[b][h] and have compassion
on them.' "

33:17 [t]2Sa 7:13; 1Ki 2:4; Ps 89:29-37; Lk 1:33
33:18 [u]Dt 18:1 [v]Heb 13:15
33:20 [w]Ps 89:36
33:21 [x]Ps 89:34 [y]2Ch 7:18
33:22 [z]Ge 15:5
33:24 [a]Eze 37:22 [b]Ne 4:4 [c]Jer 30:17
33:25 [d]Jer 31:35-36 [e]Ps 74:16-17
33:26 [f]Jer 31:37 [g]Isa 14:1 [h]ver 7

Warning to Zedekiah

34 While Nebuchadnezzar king of
Babylon and all his army and all
the kingdoms and peoples[i] in the empire he ruled were fighting against Jerusalem[j] and all its surrounding towns,
this word came to Jeremiah from the
LORD: 2"This is what the LORD, the
God of Israel, says: Go to Zedekiah[k]
king of Judah and tell him, 'This is
what the LORD says: I am about to
hand this city over to the king of Babylon, and he will burn it down.[l] 3You
will not escape from his grasp but will
surely be captured and handed over[m] to
him. You will see the king of Babylon
with your own eyes, and he will speak
with you face to face. And you will go
to Babylon.
4" 'Yet hear the promise of the LORD,
O Zedekiah king of Judah. This is what
the LORD says concerning you: You
will not die by the sword; 5you will
die peacefully. As people made a funeral
fire[n] in honor of your fathers, the former kings who preceded you, so they
will make a fire in your honor and lament, "Alas,[o] O master!" I myself make
this promise, declares the LORD.' "
6Then Jeremiah the prophet told all
this to Zedekiah king of Judah, in Jerusalem, 7while the army of the king
of Babylon was fighting against Jerusalem and the other cities of Judah that
were still holding out—Lachish[p] and
Azekah.[q] These were the only fortified
cities left in Judah.

34:1 [i]Jer 27:7 [j]2Ki 25:1; Jer 39:1
34:2 [k]2Ch 36:11 [l]ver 22; Jer 32:29; 37:8
34:3 [m]2Ki 25:7; Jer 21:7; 32:4
34:5 [n]2Ch 16:14; 21:19 [o]Jer 22:18
34:7 [p]Jos 10:3 [q]Jos 10:10; 2Ch 11:9

Freedom for Slaves

8The word came to Jeremiah from
the LORD after King Zedekiah had
made a covenant with all the people[r] in
Jerusalem to proclaim freedom[s] for the
slaves. 9Everyone was to free his Hebrew
slaves, both male and female; no one
was to hold a fellow Jew in bondage.[t]
10So all the officials and people who entered into this covenant agreed that they
would free their male and female slaves
and no longer hold them in bondage.
They agreed, and set them free. 11But
afterward they changed their minds and
took back the slaves they had freed and
enslaved them again.
12Then the word of the LORD came
to Jeremiah: 13"This is what the LORD,
the God of Israel, says: I made a covenant with your forefathers[u] when I
brought them out of Egypt, out of the
land of slavery. I said, 14'Every seventh
year each of you must free any fellow
Hebrew who has sold himself to you.
After he has served you six years, you
must let him go free.'[c][v] Your fathers,
however, did not listen to me or pay attention[w] to me. 15Recently you repented and did what is right in my sight:
Each of you proclaimed freedom to his
countrymen.[x] You even made a covenant before me in the house that bears
my Name.[y] 16But now you have turned
around[z] and profaned[a] my name; each

34:8 [r]2Ki 11:17 [s]Ex 21:2; Lev 25:10, 39-41; Ne 5:5-8
34:9 [t]Lev 25:39-46
34:13 [u]Ex 24:8
34:14 [v]Ex 21:2 [w]Dt 15:12; 2Ki 17:14
34:15 [x]ver 8 [y]Jer 7:10-11; 32:34
34:16 [z]Eze 3:20; 18:24 [a]Ex 20:7; Lev 19:12

[a]*24* Or *families* [b]*26* Or *will bring them back from captivity* [c]*14* Deut. 15:12

of you has taken back the male and female slaves you had set free to go where they wished. You have forced them to become your slaves again.

17"Therefore, this is what the LORD says: You have not obeyed me; you have not proclaimed freedom for your fellow countrymen. So I now proclaim 'freedom' for you,[b] declares the LORD—'freedom' to fall by the sword, plague and famine. I will make you abhorrent to all the kingdoms of the earth.[c] 18The men who have violated my covenant and have not fulfilled the terms of the covenant they made before me, I will treat like the calf they cut in two and then walked between its pieces.[d] 19The leaders of Judah and Jerusalem, the court officials,[e] the priests and all the people of the land who walked between the pieces of the calf, 20I will hand over[f] to their enemies who seek their lives.[g] Their dead bodies will become food for the birds of the air and the beasts of the earth.[h]

21"I will hand Zedekiah[i] king of Judah and his officials[j] over to their enemies who seek their lives, to the army of the king of Babylon, which has withdrawn[k] from you. 22I am going to give the order, declares the LORD, and I will bring them back to this city. They will fight against it, take[l] it and burn[m] it down. And I will lay waste the towns of Judah so no one can live there."

The Recabites

35 This is the word that came to Jeremiah from the LORD during the reign of Jehoiakim[n] son of Josiah king of Judah: 2"Go to the Recabite[o] family and invite them to come to one of the side rooms[p] of the house of the LORD and give them wine to drink."

3So I went to get Jaazaniah son of Jeremiah, the son of Habazziniah, and his brothers and all his sons—the whole family of the Recabites. 4I brought them into the house of the LORD, into the room of the sons of Hanan son of Igdaliah the man of God.[q] It was next to the room of the officials, which was over that of Maaseiah son of Shallum[r] the doorkeeper.[s] 5Then I set bowls full of wine and some cups before the men of the Recabite family and said to them, "Drink some wine."

6But they replied, "We do not drink wine, because our forefather Jonadab[t] son of Recab gave us this command: 'Neither you nor your descendants must ever drink wine.[u] 7Also you must never build houses, sow seed or plant vineyards; you must never have any of these things, but must always live in tents.[v] Then you will live a long time in the land[w] where you are nomads.' 8We have obeyed everything our forefather[x] Jonadab son of Recab commanded us. Neither we nor our wives nor our sons and daughters have ever drunk wine 9or built houses to live in or had vineyards, fields or crops.[y] 10We have lived in tents and have fully obeyed everything our forefather Jonadab commanded us. 11But when Nebuchadnezzar king of Babylon invaded[z] this land, we said, 'Come, we must go to Jerusalem[a] to escape the Babylonian[a] and Aramean armies.' So we have remained in Jerusalem."

12Then the word of the LORD came to Jeremiah, saying: 13"This is what the LORD Almighty, the God of Israel, says: Go and tell the men of Judah and the people of Jerusalem, 'Will you not learn a lesson[b] and obey my words?' declares the LORD. 14'Jonadab son of Recab ordered his sons not to drink wine and this command has been kept. To this day they do not drink wine, because they obey their forefather's command. But I have spoken to you again and again,[c] yet you have not obeyed[d] me. 15Again and again I sent all my servants the prophets[e] to you. They said, "Each of you must turn[f] from your wicked ways and reform[g] your actions; do not follow other gods to serve them. Then you will live in the land[h] I have given to you and your fathers." But you have not paid attention or listened[i] to me. 16The descendants of Jonadab son of Recab have carried out the command their forefather[j] gave them, but these people have not obeyed me.'

17"Therefore, this is what the LORD God Almighty, the God of Israel, says: 'Listen! I am going to bring on Judah and on everyone living in Jerusalem every disaster[k] I pronounced against them. I spoke to them, but they did not listen;[l] I called to them, but they did not answer.' "[m]

[a]11 Or *Chaldean*

34:17 [b]Mt 7:2; Gal 6:7 [c]Dt 28:25,64; Jer 29:18
34:18 [d]Ge 15:10
34:19 [e]Zep 3:3-4
34:20 [f]Jer 21:7 [g]Jer 11:21 [h]Dt 28:26; Jer 7:33; 19:7
34:21 [i]Jer 32:4 [j]Jer 39:6; 52:24-27 [k]Jer 37:5
34:22 [l]Jer 39:1-2 [m]Jer 39:8
35:1 [n]2Ch 36:5
35:2 [o]2Ki 10:15; 1Ch 2:55 [p]1Ki 6:5
35:4 [q]Dt 33:1 [r]1Ch 9:19 [s]2Ki 12:9
35:6 [t]2Ki 10:15 [u]Lev 10:9; Nu 6:2-4; Lk 1:15
35:7 [v]Heb 11:9 [w]Ex 20:12; Eph 6:2-3
35:8 [x]Pr 1:8; Col 3:20
35:9 [y]1Ti 6:6
35:11 [z]2Ki 24:1 [a]Jer 8:14
35:13 [b]Jer 6:10; 32:33
35:14 [c]Jer 7:13; 25:3 [d]Isa 30:9
35:15 [e]Jer 7:25 [f]Jer 26:3 [g]Isa 1:16-17; Jer 4:1; 18:11; Eze 18:30 [h]Jer 25:5 [i]Jer 7:26
35:16 [j]Mal 1:6
35:17 [k]Jos 23:15; Jer 21:4-7 [l]Pr 1:24; Ro 10:21 [m]Isa 65:12; 66:4; Jer 7:13

18 Then Jeremiah said to the family of
the Recabites, "This is what the LORD
Almighty, the God of Israel, says: 'You
have obeyed the command of your forefather Jonadab and have followed all his
instructions and have done everything
he ordered.' 19 Therefore, this is what
the LORD Almighty, the God of Israel,
35:19 [n]Jer 33:17 [o]Jer 15:19 says: 'Jonadab son of Recab will never
fail[n] to have a man to serve[o] me.'"

Jehoiakim Burns Jeremiah's Scroll

36:1 [p]2Ch 36:5 **36** In the fourth year of Jehoiakim[p]
son of Josiah king of Judah, this
word came to Jeremiah from the LORD:
36:2 [q]Ex 17:14; Jer 30:2; Hab 2:2 [r]Jer 1:2; 25:3 2 "Take a scroll[q] and write on it all the
words I have spoken to you concerning
Israel, Judah and all the other nations
from the time I began speaking to you
in the reign of Josiah[r] till now. 3 Per-
36:3 [s]ver 7; Eze 12:3 [t]Mk 4:12 [u]Jer 26:3; Jnh 3:8; Ac 3:19 [v]Jer 18:8 haps[s] when the people of Judah hear[t]
about every disaster I plan to inflict on
them, each of them will turn[u] from his
wicked way; then I will forgive[v] their
wickedness and their sin."
36:4 [w]Jer 32:12 [x]ver 18 [y]Eze 2:9 4 So Jeremiah called Baruch[w] son of
Neriah, and while Jeremiah dictated[x]
all the words the LORD had spoken to
him, Baruch wrote them on the scroll.[y]
5 Then Jeremiah told Baruch, "I am restricted; I cannot go to the LORD's
temple. 6 So you go to the house of the
36:6 [z]ver 9 LORD on a day of fasting[z] and read to
the people from the scroll the words
of the LORD that you wrote as I dictated. Read them to all the people of
Judah who come in from their towns.
7 Perhaps they will bring their petition
36:7 [a]Jer 26:3 [b]Dt 31:17 before the LORD, and each will turn[a]
from his wicked ways, for the anger[b]
and wrath pronounced against this people by the LORD are great."
8 Baruch son of Neriah did everything
Jeremiah the prophet told him to do; at
the LORD's temple he read the words
of the LORD from the scroll. 9 In the
36:9 [c]ver 22 [d]2Ch 20:3 ninth month[c] of the fifth year of Jehoiakim son of Josiah king of Judah, a
time of fasting[d] before the LORD was
proclaimed for all the people in Jerusalem and those who had come from
the towns of Judah. 10 From the room of
36:10 [e]Jer 52:25 [f]Jer 26:10 Gemariah son of Shaphan the secretary,[e]
which was in the upper courtyard at the
entrance of the New Gate[f] of the temple, Baruch read to all the people at the
LORD's temple the words of Jeremiah
from the scroll.

11 When Micaiah son of Gemariah,
the son of Shaphan, heard all the words
of the LORD from the scroll, 12 he went
down to the secretary's room in the royal palace, where all the officials were
sitting: Elishama the secretary, Delaiah
son of Shemaiah, Elnathan[g] son of Ac- 36:12 [g]Jer 26:22
bor, Gemariah son of Shaphan, Zedeki-
ah son of Hananiah, and all the other
officials. 13 After Micaiah told them everything he had heard Baruch read to
the people from the scroll, 14 all the officials sent Jehudi[h] son of Nethaniah, 36:14 [h]ver 21
the son of Shelemiah, the son of Cu-
shi, to say to Baruch, "Bring the scroll
from which you have read to the people and come." So Baruch son of Neriah went to them with the scroll in his
hand. 15 They said to him, "Sit down,
please, and read it to us."
So Baruch read it to them. 16 When
they heard all these words, they looked
at each other in fear and said to Baruch,
"We must report all these words to the
king." 17 Then they asked Baruch, "Tell
us, how did you come to write all this?
Did Jeremiah dictate it?"
18 "Yes," Baruch replied, "he dictated[i] 36:18 [i]ver 4
all these words to me, and I wrote them
in ink on the scroll."
19 Then the officials said to Baruch,
"You and Jeremiah, go and hide.[j] Don't 36:19 [j]1Ki 17:3
let anyone know where you are."
20 After they put the scroll in the
room of Elishama the secretary, they
went to the king in the courtyard and
reported everything to him. 21 The king
sent Jehudi[k] to get the scroll, and Jehu- 36:21 [k]ver 14 [l]2Ki 22:10
di brought it from the room of Elisha-
ma the secretary and read it to the king[l]
and all the officials standing beside him.
22 It was the ninth month and the king
was sitting in the winter apartment,[m] 36:22 [m]Am 3:15
with a fire burning in the firepot in
front of him. 23 Whenever Jehudi had
read three or four columns of the scroll,
the king cut them off with a scribe's
knife and threw them into the firepot,
until the entire scroll was burned in the
fire.[n] 24 The king and all his attendants 36:23 [n]1Ki 22:8
who heard all these words showed no
fear,[o] nor did they tear their clothes.[p] 36:24 [o]Ps 36:1 [p]Ge 37:29; 2Ki 22:11; Isa 37:1
25 Even though Elnathan, Delaiah and
Gemariah urged the king not to burn
the scroll, he would not listen to them.
26 Instead, the king commanded Jerahmeel, a son of the king, Seraiah son of
Azriel and Shelemiah son of Abdeel to

WEEK 42

GOODNESS

DAY ONE

GOODNESS, THE VIRTUE OF THE WRITTEN WORD OF GOD

Read Jeremiah 36:1–7,20–24

We would not know who God is without the Word of God. The Word is God's revelation of himself to humankind. We would not know what righteousness is without the Word. The Word defines righteousness. We would not know the fullest definition of sin without the Word. We would know neither of our origin nor of our destiny without the Word. God's plan for the ages would never be ours without the Word of God.

In Jeremiah 36, Jeremiah receives instruction from the Lord that he is to write down a revelation of all that God plans to do with regard to Judah. The intention of God's revelation is not merely to inform the people of impending judgment. The real purpose is this: "Perhaps when the people of Judah hear about every disaster I plan to inflict on them, each of them will turn from his wicked way; then I will forgive their wickedness and their sin" (v. 3). God's Word is always meant to teach us God's requirements.

Because Jeremiah was restricted from going to the temple, probably because of his inflammatory messages, Baruch son of Neriah took the scroll to the temple. He went to the room of Gemariah, which was at the entrance of the New Gate of the temple. From this upper room he read aloud—out into the entrance of the courtyard of the temple—all the words of the scroll to the people. While some of the officials were concerned about the impending judgment, when the king heard the words, he threw the scroll into the fire. The king's disrespectful acts led to judgment from God.

The Word of God is alive and powerful, and it is set in our midst to inform us of what God wants with our lives. One of those things is the presence of genuine goodness. The Word of God exists not just to make us better than we might have been, but it exists to elevate us to the level of goodness that God requires of his children.

MEMORIZE THIS WEEK

PSALM 119:11

I have hidden your word in my heart that I might not sin against you.

DAY TWO

GOODNESS AND THE PURPOSE OF GOD IN MY LIFE

How is it that the Word of God creates goodness in our lives? It reckons life deep within us—down where the soul and spirit and the joints and marrow come together. It is at this deep level within us that it judges our thoughts and our intents. And down inside us, where none can see but God, it reprimands and congratulates, indicts and blesses, and we are re-created at the deepest possible level of who we are. *Turn to Hebrews 4:12, page 1464, for today's study.*

DAY THREE

GOODNESS AND MY RELATIONSHIP WITH CHRIST

Jesus taught with authority. When he spoke of goodness, where did this authority come from? Did it come from his long study on morality? Had he completed his Ph.D. in Ethics? No. His authority came from who he was and what he was, namely, the Son of God, sinless and holy. If you are going to speak with authority on goodness, you need to be pretty good. Jesus was perfect and perfectly qualified to speak on the subject. *Turn to Mark 1:21–22, page 1168, for today's study.*

DAY FOUR

GOODNESS AND MY SERVICE TO OTHERS

Jabez was an honorable man. He was singled out from a list of names to be remembered for his goodness. The church has always sought out good, moral examples. Goodness matters. Goodness is the seedbed of reputation. Reputation either draws all to Christ or causes would-be believers to back away from hypocrisies that proclaim more goodness than they possess. *Turn to 1 Chronicles 4:9–10, page 465, for today's study.*

DAY FIVE

GOODNESS AND ITS PLACE IN MY PERSONAL WORSHIP

In this psalm, the longest chapter in the Bible, is the psalmist's plea to God for goodness: "You are good, and what you do is good; teach me your decrees." We ought to pray to be good and learn goodness from its source—God. For when we are good, our personal worship will have its own altar of being—incised with holiness—and we will speak with God because we will be like him. *Turn to Psalm 119:65–68, page 713, for today's study.*

Week 43, Faithfulness: No Compromise, begins on page 898, Jeremiah 20:1–2,7–10.
To begin a topical study on the Fruit of the Spirit, Goodness, turn to the Topical Index, page 1548.

FAITHFULNESS

KEEPING TRUE

Jeremiah 36:24

When kings will not repent, God weeps. No nation can be saved without a weeping king.

36:26 [q]Mt 23:34 [r]Jer 15:21 arrest[q] Baruch the scribe and Jeremiah
the prophet. But the LORD had hid-
den[r] them.
27After the king burned the scroll
containing the words that Baruch had
36:27 [s]ver 4 written at Jeremiah's dictation,[s] the word
of the LORD came to Jeremiah: 28"Take
another scroll and write on it all the
words that were on the first scroll,
which Jehoiakim king of Judah burned
up. 29Also tell Jehoiakim king of Judah, 'This is what the LORD says: You
burned that scroll and said, "Why did
you write on it that the king of Babylon would certainly come and destroy
this land and cut off both men and ani-
36:29 [t]Isa 30:10 mals from it?"[t] 30Therefore, this is what
the LORD says about Jehoiakim king of
Judah: He will have no one to sit on
the throne of David; his body will be
36:30 [u]Jer 22:19 thrown out[u] and exposed to the heat by
day and the frost by night. 31I will pun-
ish him and his children and his attendants for their wickedness; I will bring
on them and those living in Jerusalem
36:31 [v]Pr 29:1 and the people of Judah every disaster[v] I
pronounced against them, because they
have not listened.'"
32So Jeremiah took another scroll and
gave it to the scribe Baruch son of Ne-
36:32 [w]ver 4 [x]Ex 34:1 [y]ver 23 riah, and as Jeremiah dictated,[w] Baruch wrote[x] on it all the words of the
scroll that Jehoiakim king of Judah had
burned[y] in the fire. And many similar
words were added to them.

Jeremiah in Prison

37:1 [z]2Ki 24:17 [a]Eze 17:13 [b]2Ki 24:8,12; 2Ch 36:10; Jer 22:24 37 Zedekiah[z] son of Josiah was
made king[a] of Judah by Nebu-
chadnezzar king of Babylon; he reigned
in place of Jehoiachin[a][b] son of Jehoiakim. 2Neither he nor his attendants nor
the people of the land paid any atten-
37:2 [c]2Ki 24:19; 2Ch 36:12,14 tion[c] to the words the LORD had spoken through Jeremiah the prophet.
3King Zedekiah, however, sent Jehucal son of Shelemiah with the priest
37:3 [d]Jer 29:25; 52:24 Zephaniah[d] son of Maaseiah to Jeremiah the prophet with this message:
"Please pray[e] to the LORD our God 37:3 [e]1Ki 13:6; Jer 21:1-2; 42:2
for us."
4Now Jeremiah was free to come and
go among the people, for he had not yet
been put in prison.[f] 5Pharaoh's army 37:4 [f]ver 15; Jer 32:2
had marched out of Egypt,[g] and when
the Babylonians[b] who were besieging 37:5 [g]Eze 17:15 [h]Jer 34:21 [i]2Ki 24:7
Jerusalem heard the report about them,
they withdrew[h] from Jerusalem.[i]
6Then the word of the LORD came
to Jeremiah the prophet: 7"This is what
the LORD, the God of Israel, says: Tell
the king of Judah, who sent you to in-
quire[j] of me, 'Pharaoh's army, which 37:7 [j]2Ki 22:18 [k]Jer 2:36; La 4:17
has marched out to support you, will go
back to its own land, to Egypt.[k] 8Then
the Babylonians will return and attack 37:8 [l]Jer 34:22; 39:8
this city; they will capture it and burn[l]
it down.'
9"This is what the LORD says: Do
not deceive[m] yourselves, thinking, 'The 37:9 [m]Jer 29:8
Babylonians will surely leave us.' They
will not! 10Even if you were to defeat the
entire Babylonian[c] army that is attacking you and only wounded men were
left in their tents, they would come out
and burn this city down."
11After the Babylonian army had
withdrawn[n] from Jerusalem because of 37:11 [n]ver 5
Pharaoh's army, 12Jeremiah started to
leave the city to go to the territory of
Benjamin to get his share of the prop-
erty[o] among the people there. 13But 37:12 [o]Jer 32:9
when he reached the Benjamin Gate,
the captain of the guard, whose name
was Irijah son of Shelemiah, the son of
Hananiah, arrested him and said, "You
are deserting to the Babylonians!"
14"That's not true!" Jeremiah said.
"I am not deserting to the Babylonians." But Irijah would not listen to
him; instead, he arrested[p] Jeremiah and 37:14 [p]Jer 40:4
brought him to the officials. 15They
were angry with Jeremiah and had him
beaten[q] and imprisoned in the house[r] 37:15 [q]Jer 20:2 [r]Jer 38:26
of Jonathan the secretary, which they
had made into a prison.
16Jeremiah was put into a vaulted cell
in a dungeon, where he remained a long
time. 17Then King Zedekiah sent for
him and had him brought to the pal-
ace, where he asked[s] him privately,[t] "Is 37:17 [s]Jer 15:11 [t]Jer 38:16
there any word from the LORD?"
"Yes," Jeremiah replied, "you will be

[a]*1* Hebrew *Coniah,* a variant of *Jehoiachin*
[b]*5* Or *Chaldeans;* also in verses 8, 9, 13 and 14
[c]*10* Or *Chaldean;* also in verse 11

37:17 [u]Jer 21:7 handed over[u] to the king of Babylon.”
18Then Jeremiah said to King Zede-
37:18 [v]1Sa 26:18; kiah, “What crime[v] have I committed
Jn 10:32; against you or your officials or this peo-
Ac 25:8 ple, that you have put me in prison?
19Where are your prophets who prophesied to you, ‘The king of Babylon will
not attack you or this land’? 20But now,
my lord the king, please listen. Let me
bring my petition before you: Do not
send me back to the house of Jonathan
the secretary, or I will die there.”
21King Zedekiah then gave orders for
Jeremiah to be placed in the courtyard
37:21 [w]Isa 33:16; of the guard and given bread[w] from the
Jer 38:9 street of the bakers each day until all
[x]2Ki 25:3; Jer 52:6 the bread in the city was gone.[x] So Jer-
[y]Jer 32:2; 38:6,13,28 emiah remained in the courtyard of the
guard.[y]

Jeremiah Thrown Into a Cistern

38 Shephatiah son of Mattan, Ged-
38:1 [z]Jer 37:3 aliah son of Pashhur, Jehucal[a][z]
son of Shelemiah, and Pashhur son of
Malkijah heard what Jeremiah was telling all the people when he said, 2“This
is what the LORD says: ‘Whoever stays
38:2 in this city will die by the sword, fam-
[a]Jer 34:17 ine or plague,[a] but whoever goes over
[b]Jer 21:9; 39:18; 45:5 to the Babylonians[b] will live. He will
escape with his life; he will live.’[b] 3And
this is what the LORD says: ‘This city
will certainly be handed over to the
army of the king of Babylon, who will
38:3 [c]Jer 21:4,10; capture it.’ ”[c]
32:3 4Then the officials[d] said to the king,
38:4 [d]Jer 36:12 “This man should be put to death.[e] He
[e]Jer 26:11 is discouraging the soldiers who are left
in this city, as well as the people, by
the things he is saying to them. This
man is not seeking the good of these
people but their ruin.”
5“He is in your hands,” King Zedekiah answered. “The king can do nothing to oppose you.”
6So they took Jeremiah and put him
into the cistern of Malkijah, the king’s
son, which was in the courtyard of the
38:6 guard.[f] They lowered Jeremiah by ropes
[f]Jer 37:21 into the cistern; it had no water in
it, only mud, and Jeremiah sank down
into the mud.
38:7 [g]Jer 39:16 7But Ebed-Melech,[g] a Cushite,[c][h] an
[h]Ac 8:27 official[d] in the royal palace, heard that
[i]Job 29:7 they had put Jeremiah into the cistern.
While the king was sitting in the Benjamin Gate,[i] 8Ebed-Melech went out of
the palace and said to him, 9“My lord
the king, these men have acted wickedly in all they have done to Jeremiah the
prophet. They have thrown him into a
cistern, where he will starve to death
when there is no longer any bread[j] in 38:9 [j]Jer 37:21
the city.”
10Then the king commanded Ebed-
Melech the Cushite, “Take thirty men
from here with you and lift Jeremiah
the prophet out of the cistern before he
dies.”
11So Ebed-Melech took the men with
him and went to a room under the treasury in the palace. He took some old
rags and worn-out clothes from there
and let them down with ropes to Jeremiah in the cistern. 12Ebed-Melech the
Cushite said to Jeremiah, “Put these old
rags and worn-out clothes under your
arms to pad the ropes.” Jeremiah did
so, 13and they pulled him up with the
ropes and lifted him out of the cistern.
And Jeremiah remained in the court- 38:13
yard of the guard.[k] [k]Jer 37:21

Zedekiah Questions Jeremiah Again

14Then King Zedekiah sent for Jeremiah the prophet and had him brought
to the third entrance to the temple of
the LORD. “I am going to ask you
something,” the king said to Jeremiah. 38:14
“Do not hide[l] anything from me.” [l]1Sa 3:17
15Jeremiah said to Zedekiah, “If I
give you an answer, will you not kill
me? Even if I did give you counsel, you
would not listen to me.”
16But King Zedekiah swore this oath 38:16
secretly[m] to Jeremiah: “As surely as the [m]Jer 37:17
LORD lives, who has given us breath,[n] I [n]Isa 42:5;
will neither kill you nor hand you over 57:16
to those who are seeking your life.”[o] [o]ver 4
17Then Jeremiah said to Zedekiah,
“This is what the LORD God Almighty,
the God of Israel, says: ‘If you surrender
to the officers of the king of Babylon,
your life will be spared and this city
will not be burned down; you and your 38:17
family will live.[p] 18But if you will not [p]2Ki 24:12;
surrender to the officers of the king of Jer 21:9
Babylon, this city will be handed over[q] 38:18 [q]ver 3;
to the Babylonians and they will burn[r] Jer 34:3
it down; you yourself will not escape[s] [r]Jer 37:8
from their hands.’ ” [s]Jer 24:8; 32:4

[a] *1* Hebrew *Jucal,* a variant of *Jehucal* [b] *2* Or *Chaldeans;* also in verses 18, 19 and 23
[c] *7* Probably from the upper Nile region [d] *7* Or *a eunuch*

38:19 [t]Isa 51:12; Jn 12:42 [u]Jer 39:9

[19]King Zedekiah said to Jeremiah, "I am afraid[t] of the Jews who have gone over[u] to the Babylonians, for the Babylonians may hand me over to them and they will mistreat me."

38:20 [v]Jer 11:4 [w]Isa 55:3

[20]"They will not hand you over," Jeremiah replied. "Obey[v] the LORD by doing what I tell you. Then it will go well with you, and your life[w] will be spared. [21]But if you refuse to surrender, this is what the LORD has revealed to me: [22]All the women[x] left in the palace of the king of Judah will be brought out to the officials of the king of Babylon. Those women will say to you:

38:22 [x]Jer 6:12

"'They misled you and overcame
you—
those trusted friends of yours.
Your feet are sunk in the mud;
your friends have deserted you.'

38:23 [y]2Ki 25:6 [z]Jer 41:10

[23]"All your wives and children[y] will be brought out to the Babylonians. You yourself will not escape from their hands but will be captured[z] by the king of Babylon; and this city will[a] be burned down."

[24]Then Zedekiah said to Jeremiah, "Do not let anyone know about this conversation, or you may die. [25]If the officials hear that I talked with you, and they come to you and say, 'Tell us what you said to the king and what the king said to you; do not hide it from us or we will kill you,' [26]then tell them, 'I was pleading with the king not to send me back to Jonathan's house[a] to die there.'"

38:26 [a]Jer 37:15

[27]All the officials did come to Jeremiah and question him, and he told them everything the king had ordered him to say. So they said no more to him, for no one had heard his conversation with the king.

38:28 [b]Jer 37:21; 39:14

[28]And Jeremiah remained in the courtyard of the guard[b] until the day Jerusalem was captured.

The Fall of Jerusalem

39:1 [c]2Ki 25:1; Jer 52:4; Eze 24:2

39 This is how Jerusalem was taken: [1]In the ninth year of Zedekiah king of Judah, in the tenth month, Nebuchadnezzar king of Babylon marched against Jerusalem with his whole army and laid siege[c] to it. [2]And on the ninth day of the fourth month of Zedekiah's eleventh year, the city wall was broken through. [3]Then all the officials[d] of the king of Babylon came and took seats in the Middle Gate: Nergal-Sharezer of Samgar, Nebo-Sarsekim[b] a chief officer, Nergal-Sharezer a high official and all the other officials of the king of Babylon. [4]When Zedekiah king of Judah and all the soldiers saw them, they fled; they left the city at night by way of the king's garden, through the gate between the two walls, and headed toward the Arabah.[c]

39:3 [d]Jer 21:4

39:5 [e]Jer 32:4 [f]2Ki 23:33

[5]But the Babylonian[d] army pursued them and overtook Zedekiah[e] in the plains of Jericho. They captured him and took him to Nebuchadnezzar king of Babylon at Riblah[f] in the land of Hamath, where he pronounced sentence on him. [6]There at Riblah the king of Babylon slaughtered the sons of Zedekiah before his eyes and also killed all the nobles of Judah. [7]Then he put out Zedekiah's eyes[g] and bound him with bronze shackles to take him to Babylon.[h]

39:7 [g]Eze 12:13 [h]Jer 32:5

39:8 [i]Jer 38:18 [j]Ne 1:3

[8]The Babylonians[e] set fire[i] to the royal palace and the houses of the people and broke down the walls[j] of Jerusalem. [9]Nebuzaradan commander of the imperial guard carried into exile to Babylon the people who remained in the city, along with those who had gone over to him, and the rest of the people.[k] [10]But Nebuzaradan the commander of the guard left behind in the land of Judah some of the poor people, who owned nothing; and at that time he gave them vineyards and fields.

39:9 [k]Jer 40:1

[11]Now Nebuchadnezzar king of Babylon had given these orders about Jeremiah through Nebuzaradan commander of the imperial guard: [12]"Take him and look after him; don't harm[l] him but do for him whatever he asks." [13]So Nebuzaradan the commander of the guard, Nebushazban a chief officer, Nergal-Sharezer a high official and all the other

39:12 [l]Pr 16:7; 1Pe 3:13

[a]23 Or *and you will cause this city to* [b]3 Or *Nergal-Sharezer, Samgar-Nebo, Sarsekim* [c]4 Or *the Jordan Valley* [d]5 Or *Chaldean* [e]8 Or *Chaldeans*

▸ LOVE

ADORING DESPERATION

Jeremiah 39:11–12

Grace adores desperation; it gives love opportunity to demonstrate its loving nature.

officers of the king of Babylon 14sent and had Jeremiah taken out of the courtyard of the guard.[m] They turned him over to Gedaliah son of Ahikam,[n] the son of Shaphan, to take him back to his home. So he remained among his own people.[o]

15While Jeremiah had been confined in the courtyard of the guard, the word of the LORD came to him: 16"Go and tell Ebed-Melech[p] the Cushite, 'This is what the LORD Almighty, the God of Israel, says: I am about to fulfill my words against this city through disaster,[q] not prosperity. At that time they will be fulfilled before your eyes. 17But I will rescue[r] you on that day, declares the LORD; you will not be handed over to those you fear. 18I will save you; you will not fall by the sword[s] but will escape with your life,[t] because you trust[u] in me, declares the LORD.' "

39:14 [m]Jer 38:28 [n]2Ki 22:12 [o]Jer 40:5
39:16 [p]Jer 38:7 [q]Jer 21:10; Da 9:12
39:17 [r]Ps 41:1-2
39:18 [s]Jer 45:5 [t]Jer 21:9; 38:2 [u]Jer 17:7

Jeremiah Freed

40 The word came to Jeremiah from the LORD after Nebuzaradan commander of the imperial guard had released him at Ramah. He had found Jeremiah bound in chains among all the captives from Jerusalem and Judah who were being carried into exile to Babylon. 2When the commander of the guard found Jeremiah, he said to him, "The LORD your God decreed this disaster for this place.[v] 3And now the LORD has brought it about; he has done just as he said he would. All this happened because you people sinned[w] against the LORD and did not obey[x] him. 4But today I am freeing you from the chains on your wrists. Come with me to Babylon, if you like, and I will look after you; but if you do not want to, then don't come. Look, the whole country lies before you; go wherever you please."[y] 5However, before Jeremiah turned to go,[a] Nebuzaradan added, "Go back to Gedaliah[z] son of Ahikam, the son of Shaphan, whom the king of Babylon has appointed over the towns of Judah, and live with him among the people, or go anywhere else you please."[a]

Then the commander gave him provisions and a present and let him go. 6So Jeremiah went to Gedaliah son of Ahikam at Mizpah[b] and stayed with him among the people who were left behind in the land.

40:2 [v]Jer 50:7
40:3 [w]Da 9:11 [x]Dt 29:24-28; Ro 2:5-9
40:4 [y]Ge 13:9; Jer 39:11-12
40:5 [z]2Ki 25:22 [a]Jer 39:14
40:6 [b]Jdg 20:1; 1Sa 7:5-17

Gedaliah Assassinated

7When all the army officers and their men who were still in the open country heard that the king of Babylon had appointed Gedaliah son of Ahikam as governor over the land and had put him in charge of the men, women and children who were the poorest[c] in the land and who had not been carried into exile to Babylon, 8they came to Gedaliah at Mizpah[d]—Ishmael[e] son of Nethaniah, Johanan and Jonathan the sons of Kareah, Seraiah son of Tanhumeth, the sons of Ephai the Netophathite,[f] and Jaazaniah[b] the son of the Maacathite,[g] and their men. 9Gedaliah son of Ahikam, the son of Shaphan, took an oath to reassure them and their men. "Do not be afraid to serve[h] the Babylonians,[c]" he said. "Settle down in the land and serve the king of Babylon, and it will go well with you.[i] 10I myself will stay at Mizpah[j] to represent you before the Babylonians who come to us, but you are to harvest the wine, summer fruit and oil, and put them in your storage jars, and live in the towns you have taken over."[k]

11When all the Jews in Moab,[l] Ammon, Edom and all the other countries heard that the king of Babylon had left a remnant in Judah and had appointed Gedaliah son of Ahikam, the son of Shaphan, as governor over them, 12they all came back to the land of Judah, to Gedaliah at Mizpah, from all the countries where they had been scattered.[m] And they harvested an abundance of wine and summer fruit.

13Johanan son of Kareah and all the army officers still in the open country came to Gedaliah at Mizpah[n] 14and said to him, "Don't you know that Baalis king of the Ammonites[o] has sent Ishmael son of Nethaniah to take your life?" But Gedaliah son of Ahikam did not believe them.

15Then Johanan son of Kareah said privately to Gedaliah in Mizpah, "Let me go and kill Ishmael son of Nethaniah, and no one will know it. Why should he take your life and cause all the Jews who are gathered around you to be scattered and the remnant of Judah to perish?"

40:7 [c]Jer 39:10
40:8 [d]ver 13 [e]ver 14; Jer 41:1,2 [f]2Sa 23:28 [g]Dt 3:14
40:9 [h]Jer 27:11 [i]Jer 38:20
40:10 [j]ver 6 [k]Dt 1:39
40:11 [l]Nu 25:1
40:12 [m]Jer 43:5
40:13 [n]ver 8
40:14 [o]2Sa 10:1-19; Jer 25:21; 41:10

[a]5 Or *Jeremiah answered* [b]8 Hebrew *Jezaniah*, a variant of *Jaazaniah* [c]9 Or *Chaldeans*; also in verse 10

16 But Gedaliah son of Ahikam said to Johanan son of Kareah, "Don't do such a thing! What you are saying about Ishmael is not true."

41 In the seventh month Ishmael[p] son of Nethaniah, the son of Elishama, who was of royal blood and had been one of the king's officers, came with ten men to Gedaliah son of Ahikam at Mizpah. While they were eating together there, 2 Ishmael[q] son of Nethaniah and the ten men who were with him got up and struck down Gedaliah son of Ahikam, the son of Shaphan, with the sword, killing the one whom the king of Babylon had appointed[r] as governor over the land.[s] 3 Ishmael also killed all the Jews who were with Gedaliah at Mizpah, as well as the Babylonian[a] soldiers who were there.

4 The day after Gedaliah's assassination, before anyone knew about it, 5 eighty men who had shaved off their beards,[t] torn their clothes and cut themselves came from Shechem,[u] Shiloh[v] and Samaria,[w] bringing grain offerings and incense with them to the house of the LORD.[x] 6 Ishmael son of Nethaniah went out from Mizpah to meet them, weeping[y] as he went. When he met them, he said, "Come to Gedaliah son of Ahikam." 7 When they went into the city, Ishmael son of Nethaniah and the men who were with him slaughtered them and threw them into a cistern. 8 But ten of them said to Ishmael, "Don't kill us! We have wheat and barley, oil and honey, hidden in a field."[z] So he let them alone and did not kill them with the others. 9 Now the cistern where he threw all the bodies of the men he had killed along with Gedaliah was the one King Asa[a] had made as part of his defense[b] against Baasha[c] king of Israel. Ishmael son of Nethaniah filled it with the dead.

10 Ishmael made captives of all the rest of the people[d] who were in Mizpah—the king's daughters along with all the others who were left there, over whom Nebuzaradan commander of the imperial guard had appointed Gedaliah son of Ahikam. Ishmael son of Nethaniah took them captive and set out to cross over to the Ammonites.[e]

11 When Johanan[f] son of Kareah and all the army officers who were with him heard about all the crimes Ishmael son of Nethaniah had committed, 12 they took all their men and went to fight Ishmael son of Nethaniah. They caught up with him near the great pool[g] in Gibeon. 13 When all the people[h] Ishmael had with him saw Johanan son of Kareah and the army officers who were with him, they were glad. 14 All the people Ishmael had taken captive at Mizpah turned and went over to Johanan son of Kareah. 15 But Ishmael son of Nethaniah and eight of his men escaped[i] from Johanan and fled to the Ammonites.

Flight to Egypt

16 Then Johanan son of Kareah and all the army officers who were with him led away all the survivors[j] from Mizpah whom he had recovered from Ishmael son of Nethaniah after he had assassinated Gedaliah son of Ahikam: the soldiers, women, children and court officials he had brought from Gibeon. 17 And they went on, stopping at Geruth Kimham[k] near Bethlehem on their way to Egypt[l] 18 to escape the Babylonians.[b] They were afraid[m] of them because Ishmael son of Nethaniah had killed Gedaliah[n] son of Ahikam, whom the king of Babylon had appointed as governor over the land.

42 Then all the army officers, including Johanan[o] son of Kareah and Jezaniah[c] son of Hoshaiah, and all the people from the least to the greatest[p] approached 2 Jeremiah the prophet and said to him, "Please hear our petition and pray[q] to the LORD your God for this entire remnant.[r] For as you now see, though we were once many, now only a few[s] are left. 3 Pray that the LORD your God will tell us where we should go and what we should do."[t]

4 "I have heard you," replied Jeremiah the prophet. "I will certainly pray[u] to the LORD your God as you have requested; I will tell you everything the LORD says and will keep nothing back from you."[v]

5 Then they said to Jeremiah, "May the LORD be a true and faithful witness[w] against us if we do not act in accordance with everything the LORD your God sends you to tell us. 6 Whether

[a] *3* Or *Chaldean* [b] *18* Or *Chaldeans* [c] *1* Hebrew; Septuagint (see also 43:2) *Azariah*

41:1 [p]Jer 40:8
41:2 [q]Ps 41:9; 109:5 [r]Jer 40:5 [s]2Sa 3:27; 20:9-10
41:5 [t]Lev 19:27 [u]Ge 33:18; Jdg 9:1-57; 1Ki 12:1 [v]Jos 18:1 [w]1Ki 16:24 [x]2Ki 25:9
41:6 [y]2Sa 3:16
41:8 [z]Isa 45:3
41:9 [a]1Ki 15:22; 2Ch 16:6 [b]Jdg 6:2 [c]2Ch 16:1
41:10 [d]Jer 40:7,12 [e]Jer 40:14
41:11 [f]Jer 40:8
41:12 [g]2Sa 2:13
41:13 [h]ver 10
41:15 [i]Job 21:30; Pr 28:17
41:16 [j]Jer 43:4
41:17 [k]2Sa 19:37 [l]Jer 42:14
41:18 [m]Isa 51:12; Jer 42:16; Lk 12:4-5 [n]Jer 40:5
42:1 [o]Jer 40:13; 41:11 [p]Jer 6:13; 44:12
42:2 [q]Jer 36:7; Ac 8:24; Jas 5:16 [r]Isa 1:9 [s]Lev 26:22; La 1:1
42:3 [t]Ps 86:11; Pr 3:6
42:4 [u]Ex 8:29; 1Sa 12:23 [v]1Ki 22:14; 1Sa 3:17
42:5 [w]Ge 31:50

it is favorable or unfavorable, we will
obey the LORD our God, to whom we
are sending you, so that it will go well[x]
with us, for we will obey[y] the LORD
our God."
7Ten days later the word of the LORD
came to Jeremiah. 8So he called together
Johanan son of Kareah and all the army
officers[z] who were with him and all the
people from the least to the greatest.
9He said to them, "This is what the
LORD, the God of Israel, to whom you
sent me to present your petition, says:[a]
10'If you stay in this land, I will build[b]
you up and not tear you down; I will
plant[c] you and not uproot you,[d] for
I am grieved over the disaster I have
inflicted on you.[e] 11Do not be afraid
of the king of Babylon,[f] whom you
now fear.[g] Do not be afraid of him, declares the LORD, for I am with you and
will save[h] you and deliver you from his
hands.[i] 12I will show you compassion
so that he will have compassion on you
and restore you to your land.'[j]
13"However, if you say, 'We will not
stay in this land,' and so disobey[k] the
LORD your God, 14and if you say, 'No,
we will go and live in Egypt,[l] where we
will not see war or hear the trumpet or
be hungry for bread,' 15then hear the
word of the LORD, O remnant of Judah. This is what the LORD Almighty,
the God of Israel, says: 'If you are determined to go to Egypt and you do go
to settle there, 16then the sword[m] you
fear will overtake you there, and the
famine you dread will follow you into
Egypt, and there you will die. 17Indeed,
all who are determined to go to Egypt
to settle there will die by the sword,
famine and plague;[n] not one of them
will survive or escape the disaster I
will bring on them.' 18This is what
the LORD Almighty, the God of Israel,
says: 'As my anger and wrath[o] have
been poured out on those who lived in
Jerusalem,[p] so will my wrath be poured
out on you when you go to Egypt. You
will be an object of cursing and horror,[q]
of condemnation and reproach; you will
never see this place again.'[r]
19"O remnant of Judah, the LORD
has told you, 'Do not go to Egypt.'[s] Be
sure of this: I warn you today 20that
you made a fatal mistake[a] when you
sent me to the LORD your God and
said, 'Pray to the LORD our God for us;

42:6 [x]Dt 5:29; 6:3; Jer 7:23 [y]Ex 24:7; Jos 24:24
42:8 [z]ver 1
42:9 [a]2Ki 22:15
42:10 [b]Jer 24:6 [c]Jer 31:28 [d]Eze 36:36 [e]Jer 18:8
42:11 [f]Jer 27:11 [g]Nu 14:9 [h]Isa 43:5 [i]Jer 1:8; Ro 8:31
42:12 [j]Ps 106:44-46
42:13 [k]Jer 44:16
42:14 [l]Nu 11:4-5
42:16 [m]Eze 11:8
42:17 [n]ver 22; Jer 44:13
42:18 [o]Dt 29:18-20; Jer 7:20 [p]2Ch 36:19; Jer 39:1-9 [q]Jer 29:18 [r]Jer 22:10
42:19 [s]Dt 17:16; Isa 30:7

tell us everything he says and we will
do it.'[t] 21I have told you today, but you
still have not obeyed the LORD your
God in all he sent me to tell you.[u] 22So
now, be sure of this: You will die by the
sword, famine and plague[v] in the place
where you want to go to settle."[w]

43

When Jeremiah finished telling
the people all the words of the
LORD their God—everything the
LORD had sent him to tell them[x]—
2Azariah son of Hoshaiah and Johanan[y]
son of Kareah and all the arrogant men
said to Jeremiah, "You are lying! The
LORD our God has not sent you to
say, 'You must not go to Egypt to settle
there.' 3But Baruch son of Neriah is inciting you against us to hand us over to
the Babylonians,[b] so they may kill us or
carry us into exile to Babylon."[z]
4So Johanan son of Kareah and all
the army officers and all the people disobeyed the LORD's command[a] to stay
in the land of Judah.[b] 5Instead, Johanan
son of Kareah and all the army officers
led away all the remnant of Judah who
had come back to live in the land of
Judah from all the nations where they
had been scattered.[c] 6They also led away
all the men, women and children and
the king's daughters whom Nebuzaradan commander of the imperial guard
had left with Gedaliah son of Ahikam,
the son of Shaphan, and Jeremiah the
prophet and Baruch son of Neriah.
7So they entered Egypt in disobedience to the LORD and went as far as
Tahpanhes.[d]
8In Tahpanhes[e] the word of the LORD
came to Jeremiah: 9"While the Jews
are watching, take some large stones
with you and bury them in clay in the
brick pavement at the entrance to Pharaoh's palace in Tahpanhes. 10Then say
to them, 'This is what the LORD Almighty, the God of Israel, says: I will
send for my servant[f] Nebuchadnezzar
king of Babylon, and I will set his
throne over these stones I have buried
here; he will spread his royal canopy
above them. 11He will come and attack
Egypt,[g] bringing death to those destined for death, captivity to those destined for captivity, and the sword[h] to
those destined for the sword. 12He[c] will

42:20 [t]ver 2
42:21 [u]Eze 2:7; Zec 7:11-12
42:22 [v]ver 17; Eze 6:11 [w]Hos 9:6
43:1 [x]Jer 26:8; 42:9-22
43:2 [y]Jer 42:1
43:3 [z]Jer 38:4
43:4 [a]Jer 42:5-6 [b]Jer 42:10
43:5 [c]Jer 40:12
43:7 [d]Jer 2:16; 44:1
43:8 [e]Jer 2:16
43:10 [f]Isa 44:28; Jer 25:9; 27:6
43:11 [g]Jer 46:13-26; Eze 29:19-20 [h]Jer 15:2; 44:13; Zec 11:9

[a]20 Or *you erred in your hearts* [b]3 Or *Chaldeans*
[c]12 Or *I*

set fire to the temples of the gods[i] of Egypt; he will burn their temples and take their gods captive. As a shepherd wraps[j] his garment around him, so will he wrap Egypt around himself and depart from there unscathed. 13There in the temple of the sun[a] in Egypt he will demolish the sacred pillars and will burn down the temples of the gods of Egypt.'"

Disaster Because of Idolatry

44 This word came to Jeremiah concerning all the Jews living in Lower Egypt—in Migdol,[k] Tahpanhes[l] and Memphis[b][m]—and in Upper Egypt[c]:[n] 2"This is what the LORD Almighty, the God of Israel, says: You saw the great disaster I brought on Jerusalem and on all the towns of Judah. Today they lie deserted and in ruins[o] 3because of the evil they have done. They provoked me to anger by burning incense and by worshiping other gods[p] that neither they nor you nor your fathers[q] ever knew. 4Again and again[r] I sent my servants the prophets,[s] who said, 'Do not do this detestable thing that I hate!' 5But they did not listen or pay attention; they did not turn from their wickedness or stop burning incense to other gods.[t] 6Therefore, my fierce anger was poured out; it raged against the towns of Judah and the streets of Jerusalem and made them the desolate ruins they are today.

7"Now this is what the LORD God Almighty, the God of Israel, says: Why bring such great disaster[u] on yourselves by cutting off from Judah the men and women,[v] the children and infants, and so leave yourselves without a remnant? 8Why provoke me to anger with what your hands have made,[w] burning incense to other gods in Egypt, where you have come to live?[x] You will destroy yourselves and make yourselves an object of cursing and reproach[y] among all the nations on earth. 9Have you forgotten the wickedness committed by your fathers and by the kings and queens of Judah and the wickedness committed by you and your wives in the land of Judah and the streets of Jerusalem?[z] 10To this day they have not humbled themselves or shown reverence, nor have they followed my law[a] and the decrees I set before you and your fathers.[b]

43:12 [i]Jer 46:25; Eze 30:13 [j]Ps 104:2; 109:18-19
44:1 [k]Ex 14:2 [l]Jer 43:7,8 [m]Isa 19:13 [n]Isa 11:11; Jer 46:14
44:2 [o]Isa 6:11; Jer 9:11; 34:22
44:3 [p]ver 8; Dt 13:6-11; 29:26 [q]Dt 32:17; Jer 19:4
44:4 [r]Jer 7:13 [s]Jer 7:25; 25:4; 26:5
44:5 [t]Jer 11:8-10
44:7 [u]Jer 26:19 [v]Jer 51:22
44:8 [w]Jer 25:6-7 [x]1Co 10:22 [y]Jer 42:18
44:9 [z]ver 17,21
44:10 [a]Jos 1:7 [b]1Ki 9:6-9

11"Therefore, this is what the LORD Almighty, the God of Israel, says: I am determined to bring disaster[c] on you and to destroy all Judah. 12I will take away the remnant[d] of Judah who were determined to go to Egypt to settle there. They will all perish in Egypt; they will fall by the sword or die from famine. From the least to the greatest, they will die by sword or famine.[e] They will become an object of cursing and horror, of condemnation and reproach.[f] 13I will punish those who live in Egypt with the sword, famine and plague,[g] as I punished Jerusalem. 14None of the remnant of Judah who have gone to live in Egypt will escape or survive to return to the land of Judah, to which they long to return and live; none will return except a few fugitives."[h]

15Then all the men who knew that their wives were burning incense to other gods, along with all the women who were present—a large assembly—and all the people living in Lower and Upper Egypt,[d] said to Jeremiah, 16"We will not listen[i] to the message you have spoken to us in the name of the LORD! 17We will certainly do everything we said we would:[j] We will burn incense to the Queen of Heaven[k] and will pour out drink offerings to her just as we and our fathers, our kings and our officials did in the towns of Judah and in the streets of Jerusalem. At that time we had plenty of food and were well off and suffered no harm.[l] 18But ever since we stopped burning incense to the Queen of Heaven and pouring out drink offerings to her, we have had nothing and have been perishing by sword and famine.[m]"

19The women added, "When we burned incense to the Queen of Heaven[n] and poured out drink offerings to her, did not our husbands know that we were making cakes like her image and pouring out drink offerings to her?"

20Then Jeremiah said to all the people, both men and women, who were answering him, 21"Did not the LORD remember[o] and think about the incense[p] burned in the towns of Judah and the streets of Jerusalem[q] by you and your fathers,[r] your kings and your offi-

[a]*13* Or *in Heliopolis* [b]*1* Hebrew *Noph* [c]*1* Hebrew *in Pathros* [d]*15* Hebrew *in Egypt and Pathros*

44:11 [c]Jer 21:10; Am 9:4
44:12 [d]ver 7 [e]Isa 1:28 [f]Jer 29:18; 42:15-18
44:13 [g]Jer 42:17
44:14 [h]ver 28; Jer 22:24-27; Ro 9:27
44:16 [i]Jer 11:8-10
44:17 [j]Dt 23:23 [k]ver 25; Jer 7:18 [l]Hos 2:5-13
44:18 [m]Mal 3:13-15
44:19 [n]Jer 7:18
44:21 [o]Isa 64:9; Jer 14:10 [p]Jer 11:13 [q]ver 9 [r]Ps 79:8

cials and the people of the land? 22When the LORD could no longer endure your wicked actions and the detestable things you did, your land became an object of cursing[s] and a desolate waste without inhabitants, as it is today.[t] 23Because you have burned incense and have sinned against the LORD and have not obeyed him or followed his law or his decrees or his stipulations, this disaster[u] has come upon you, as you now see."[v]

24Then Jeremiah said to all the people, including the women,[w] "Hear the word of the LORD, all you people of Judah in Egypt.[x] 25This is what the LORD Almighty, the God of Israel, says: You and your wives have shown by your actions what you promised when you said, 'We will certainly carry out the vows we made to burn incense and pour out drink offerings to the Queen of Heaven.'[y]

"Go ahead then, do what you promised! Keep your vows![z] 26But hear the word of the LORD, all Jews living in Egypt: 'I swear[a] by my great name,' says the LORD, 'that no one from Judah living anywhere in Egypt will ever again invoke my name or swear, "As surely as the Sovereign LORD lives."[b] 27For I am watching over them for harm,[c] not for good; the Jews in Egypt will perish by sword and famine until they are all destroyed. 28Those who escape the sword and return to the land of Judah from Egypt will be very few.[d] Then the whole remnant of Judah who came to live in Egypt will know whose word will stand—mine or theirs.[e]

29" 'This will be the sign to you that I will punish you in this place,' declares the LORD, 'so that you will know that my threats of harm against you will surely stand.'[f] 30This is what the LORD says: 'I am going to hand Pharaoh[g] Hophra king of Egypt over to his enemies who seek his life, just as I handed Zedekiah[h] king of Judah over to Nebuchadnezzar king of Babylon, the enemy who was seeking his life.' "[i]

A Message to Baruch

45 This is what Jeremiah the prophet told Baruch[j] son of Neriah in the fourth year of Jehoiakim[k] son of Josiah king of Judah, after Baruch had written on a scroll the words Jeremiah was then dictating: 2"This is what the LORD, the God of Israel, says to you, Baruch: 3You said, 'Woe to me! The LORD has added sorrow to my pain; I am worn out with groaning[l] and find no rest.' "

4⌊The LORD said,⌋ "Say this to him: 'This is what the LORD says: I will overthrow what I have built and uproot what I have planted,[m] throughout the land.[n] 5Should you then seek great things for yourself? Seek them not.[o] For I will bring disaster on all people, declares the LORD, but wherever you go I will let you escape with your life.' "[p]

44:22 [s]Jer 25:18 [t]Ge 19:13; Ps 107:33-34
44:23 [u]Jer 40:2 [v]1Ki 9:9; Jer 7:13-15; Da 9:11-12
44:24 [w]ver 15 [x]Jer 43:7
44:25 [y]ver 17 [z]Eze 20:39
44:26 [a]Ge 22:16; Isa 48:1; Heb 6:13-17 [b]Dt 32:40; Ps 50:16
44:27 [c]Jer 31:28
44:28 [d]ver 13-14; Isa 10:19 [e]ver 17,25-26
44:29 [f]Pr 19:21
44:30 [g]Jer 46:26; Eze 30:21 [h]2Ki 25:1-7 [i]Jer 39:5
45:1 [j]Jer 32:12; 36:4,18,32 [k]2Ch 36:5

A Message About Egypt

46 This is the word of the LORD that came to Jeremiah the prophet concerning the nations:[q]

2Concerning Egypt:

This is the message against the army of Pharaoh Neco[r] king of Egypt, which was defeated at Carchemish[s] on the Euphrates River by Nebuchadnezzar king of Babylon in the fourth year of Jehoiakim[t] son of Josiah king of Judah:

3"Prepare your shields,[u] both large
and small,
and march out for battle!
4Harness the horses,
mount the steeds!
Take your positions
with helmets on!
Polish[v] your spears,
put on your armor![w]
5What do I see?
They are terrified,
they are retreating,
their warriors are defeated.
They flee[x] in haste
without looking back,
and there is terror[y] on every side,"
declares the LORD.
6"The swift cannot flee[z]
nor the strong escape.
In the north by the River Euphrates
they stumble and fall.[a]

7"Who is this that rises like the Nile,
like rivers of surging waters?[b]
8Egypt rises like the Nile,
like rivers of surging waters.
She says, 'I will rise and cover the
earth;
I will destroy cities and their
people.'

45:3 [l]Ps 69:3
45:4 [m]Jer 11:17 [n]Isa 5:5-7; Jer 18:7-10
45:5 [o]Mt 6:25-27,33 [p]Jer 21:9; 38:2; 39:18
46:1 [q]Jer 1:10; 25:15-38
46:2 [r]2Ki 23:29 [s]2Ch 35:20 [t]Jer 45:1
46:3 [u]Isa 21:5; Jer 51:11-12
46:4 [v]Eze 21:9-11 [w]1Sa 17:5,38; 2Ch 26:14; Ne 4:16
46:5 [x]ver 21 [y]Jer 49:29
46:6 [z]Isa 30:16 [a]ver 12,16; Da 11:19
46:7 [b]Jer 47:2

46:9 [c]Jer 47:3 [d]Isa 66:19

9 Charge, O horses!
Drive furiously, O charioteers![c]
March on, O warriors—
men of Cush[a] and Put who carry shields,
men of Lydia[d] who draw the bow.

46:10 [e]Joel 1:15 [f]Dt 32:42 [g]Zep 1:7

10 But that day[e] belongs to the Lord,
the LORD Almighty—
a day of vengeance, for vengeance on his foes.
The sword will devour[f] till it is satisfied,
till it has quenched its thirst with blood.
For the Lord, the LORD Almighty,
will offer sacrifice[g]
in the land of the north by the River Euphrates.

PEACE

A COMPANION FOR HUMILITY

Jeremiah 46:8–10

Pride and peace do not keep company; humility and peace do.

46:11 [h]Jer 8:22 [i]Isa 47:1 [j]Jer 30:13; Mic 1:9

11 "Go up to Gilead and get balm,[h]
O Virgin[i] Daughter of Egypt.
But you multiply remedies in vain;
there is no healing[j] for you.
12 The nations will hear of your shame;
your cries will fill the earth.
One warrior will stumble over another;
both will fall[k] down together."

46:12 [k]Isa 19:4; Na 3:8-10

13 This is the message the LORD spoke
to Jeremiah the prophet about the coming of Nebuchadnezzar king of Babylon
to attack Egypt:[l]

46:13 [l]Isa 19:1

14 "Announce this in Egypt, and
proclaim it in Migdol;
proclaim it also in Memphis[b] and Tahpanhes:[m]
'Take your positions and get ready,
for the sword devours those around you.'

46:14 [m]Jer 43:8

15 Why will your warriors be laid low?
They cannot stand, for the LORD
will push them down.[n]

46:15 [n]Isa 66:15-16

16 They will stumble[o] repeatedly;
they will fall[p] over each other.
They will say, 'Get up, let us go back
to our own people and our native lands,
away from the sword of the oppressor.'
17 There they will exclaim,
'Pharaoh king of Egypt is only a loud noise;
he has missed his opportunity.[q]'

46:16 [o]Lev 26:37 [p]ver 6

46:17 [q]Isa 19:11-16

18 "As surely as I live," declares the King,[r]
whose name is the LORD Almighty,
"one will come who is like Tabor[s]
among the mountains,
like Carmel[t] by the sea.

46:18 [r]Jer 48:15 [s]Jos 19:22 [t]1Ki 18:42

19 Pack your belongings for exile,[u]
you who live in Egypt,
for Memphis will be laid waste
and lie in ruins without inhabitant.

46:19 [u]Isa 20:4

20 "Egypt is a beautiful heifer,
but a gadfly is coming
against her from the north.[v]

46:20 [v]ver 24; Jer 47:2

21 The mercenaries[w] in her ranks
are like fattened calves.
They too will turn and flee[x] together,
they will not stand their ground,
for the day[y] of disaster is coming upon them,
the time for them to be punished.

46:21 [w]2Ki 7:6 [x]ver 5 [y]Ps 37:13

22 Egypt will hiss like a fleeing serpent
as the enemy advances in force;
they will come against her with axes,
like men who cut down trees.
23 They will chop down her forest,"
declares the LORD,
"dense though it be.
They are more numerous than locusts,[z]
they cannot be counted.

46:23 [z]Jdg 7:12

24 The Daughter of Egypt will be put to shame,
handed over to the people of the north."[a]

46:24 [a]Jer 1:15

25 The LORD Almighty, the God of
Israel, says: "I am about to bring punishment on Amon god of Thebes,[c][b] on
Pharaoh, on Egypt and her gods[c] and
her kings, and on those who rely[d] on
Pharaoh. 26 I will hand them over[e] to
those who seek their lives, to Nebuchadnezzar king[f] of Babylon and his
officers. Later, however, Egypt will be
inhabited[g] as in times past," declares
the LORD.

46:25 [b]Eze 30:14; Na 3:8 [c]Jer 43:12 [d]Isa 20:6

46:26 [e]Jer 44:30 [f]Eze 32:11 [g]Eze 29:11-16

[a] *9* That is, the upper Nile region [b] *14* Hebrew *Noph*; also in verse 19 [c] *25* Hebrew *No*

46:27 [h]Isa 41:13; 43:5 [i]Isa 11:11; Jer 50:19

27 "Do not fear,[h] O Jacob my servant;
do not be dismayed, O Israel.
I will surely save you out of a distant place,
your descendants from the land of their exile.[i]
Jacob will again have peace and security,
and no one will make him afraid.

46:28 [j]Isa 8:9-10 [k]Jer 4:27

28 Do not fear, O Jacob my servant,
for I am with you,"[j] declares the LORD.
"Though I completely destroy[k] all the nations
among which I scatter you,
I will not completely destroy you.
I will discipline you but only with justice;
I will not let you go entirely unpunished."

A Message About the Philistines

47:1 [l]Ge 10:19; Am 1:6; Zec 9:5-7

47 This is the word of the LORD that came to Jeremiah the
prophet concerning the Philistines be-
fore Pharaoh attacked Gaza:[l]

2 This is what the LORD says:

47:2 [m]Isa 8:7; 14:31

"See how the waters are rising in the north;[m]
they will become an overflowing torrent.
They will overflow the land and everything in it,
the towns and those who live in them.
The people will cry out;
all who dwell in the land will wail
3 at the sound of the hoofs of galloping steeds,
at the noise of enemy chariots
and the rumble of their wheels.
Fathers will not turn to help their children;
their hands will hang limp.
4 For the day has come
to destroy all the Philistines
and to cut off all survivors

47:4 [n]Am 1:9-10; Zec 9:2-4 [o]Jer 25:22 [p]Ge 10:14; Joel 3:4 [q]Dt 2:23

who could help Tyre[n] and Sidon.[o]
The LORD is about to destroy the Philistines,[p]
the remnant from the coasts of Caphtor.[a][q]

47:5 [r]Jer 41:5; Mic 1:16 [s]Jer 25:20

5 Gaza will shave[r] her head in mourning;
Ashkelon[s] will be silenced.
O remnant on the plain,
how long will you cut yourselves?

47:6 [t]Jer 12:12

6 " 'Ah, sword[t] of the LORD,' ⌞you cry,⌟
'how long till you rest?
Return to your scabbard;
cease and be still.'
7 But how can it rest
when the LORD has commanded it,
when he has ordered it
to attack Ashkelon and the coast?"

A Message About Moab

48 Concerning Moab:

This is what the LORD Almighty, the
God of Israel, says:

48:1 [u]Nu 32:38 [v]Nu 32:37

"Woe to Nebo,[u] for it will be ruined.
Kiriathaim[v] will be disgraced and captured;
the stronghold[b] will be disgraced and shattered.

48:2 [w]Isa 16:14 [x]Nu 21:25

2 Moab will be praised[w] no more;
in Heshbon[c][x] men will plot her downfall:
'Come, let us put an end to that nation.'
You too, O Madmen,[d] will be silenced;
the sword will pursue you.

48:3 [y]Isa 15:5

3 Listen to the cries from Horonaim,[y]
cries of great havoc and destruction.
4 Moab will be broken;
her little ones will cry out.[e]

48:5 [z]Isa 15:5

5 They go up the way to Luhith,[z]
weeping bitterly as they go;
on the road down to Horonaim
anguished cries over the destruction are heard.

48:6 [a]Jer 17:6

6 Flee! Run for your lives;
become like a bush[f] in the desert.[a]
7 Since you trust in your deeds and riches,
you too will be taken captive,

48:7 [b]Nu 21:29 [c]Isa 46:1-2; Jer 49:3

and Chemosh[b] will go into exile,[c]
together with his priests and officials.
8 The destroyer will come against every town,
and not a town will escape.
The valley will be ruined
and the plateau destroyed,
because the LORD has spoken.

[a]4 That is, Crete [b]1 Or / *Misgab* [c]2 The Hebrew for *Heshbon* sounds like the Hebrew for *plot.* [d]2 The name of the Moabite town Madmen sounds like the Hebrew for *be silenced.* [e]4 Hebrew; Septuagint / *proclaim it to Zoar* [f]6 Or *like Aroer*

9 Put salt on Moab,
for she will be laid waste[a];
her towns will become desolate,
with no one to live in them.
10 "A curse on him who is lax in doing
the LORD's work!
A curse on him who keeps his
sword[d] from bloodshed![e]
11 "Moab has been at rest[f] from youth,
like wine left on its dregs,[g]
not poured from one jar to
another—
she has not gone into exile.
So she tastes as she did,
and her aroma is unchanged.
12 But days are coming,"
declares the LORD,
"when I will send men who pour
from jars,
and they will pour her out;
they will empty her jars
and smash her jugs.
13 Then Moab will be ashamed of
Chemosh,
as the house of Israel was
ashamed[h]
when they trusted in Bethel.
14 "How can you say, 'We are warriors,[i]
men valiant in battle'?
15 Moab will be destroyed and her
towns invaded;
her finest young men will go
down in the slaughter,[j]"
declares the King,[k] whose name is
the LORD Almighty.[l]
16 "The fall of Moab is at hand;[m]
her calamity will come quickly.
17 Mourn for her, all who live around
her,
all who know her fame;
say, 'How broken is the mighty
scepter,
how broken the glorious staff!'
18 "Come down from your glory
and sit on the parched ground,[n]
O inhabitants of the Daughter of
Dibon,[o]
for he who destroys Moab
will come up against you
and ruin your fortified cities.[p]
19 Stand by the road and watch,
you who live in Aroer.[q]
Ask the man fleeing and the woman
escaping,
ask them, 'What has happened?'
20 Moab is disgraced, for she is
shattered.
Wail[r] and cry out!
Announce by the Arnon[s]
that Moab is destroyed.
21 Judgment has come to the
plateau—
to Holon, Jahzah[t] and Mephaath,[u]
22 to Dibon,[v] Nebo and Beth
Diblathaim,
23 to Kiriathaim, Beth Gamul and
Beth Meon,[w]
24 to Kerioth[x] and Bozrah—
to all the towns of Moab, far and
near.
25 Moab's horn[b][y] is cut off;
her arm[z] is broken,"
declares the LORD.
26 "Make her drunk,[a]
for she has defied the LORD.
Let Moab wallow in her vomit;
let her be an object of ridicule.
27 Was not Israel the object of your
ridicule?[b]
Was she caught among thieves,
that you shake your head[c] in scorn[d]
whenever you speak of her?
28 Abandon your towns and dwell
among the rocks,
you who live in Moab.
Be like a dove[e] that makes its nest
at the mouth of a cave.[f]
29 "We have heard of Moab's pride[g]—
her overweening pride and
conceit,
her pride and arrogance
and the haughtiness of her heart.
30 I know her insolence but it is futile,"
declares the LORD,
"and her boasts accomplish
nothing.
31 Therefore I wail[h] over Moab,
for all Moab I cry out,
I moan for the men of Kir
Hareseth.[i]
32 I weep for you, as Jazer weeps,
O vines of Sibmah.[j]
Your branches spread as far as the
sea;
they reached as far as the sea of
Jazer.
The destroyer has fallen
on your ripened fruit and grapes.
33 Joy and gladness are gone

[a]9 Or *Give wings to Moab, / for she will fly away*
[b]25 *Horn* here symbolizes strength.

48:10 [d]Jer 47:6 [e]1Ki 20:42; 2Ki 13:15-19
48:11 [f]Zec 1:15 [g]Zep 1:12
48:13 [h]Hos 10:6
48:14 [i]Ps 33:16
48:15 [j]Jer 50:27 [k]Jer 46:18 [l]Jer 51:57
48:16 [m]Isa 13:22
48:18 [n]Isa 47:1 [o]Nu 21:30; Jos 13:9 [p]ver 8
48:19 [q]Dt 2:36
48:20 [r]Isa 16:7 [s]Nu 21:13
48:21 [t]Nu 21:23; Isa 15:4 [u]Jos 13:18
48:22 [v]Jos 13:9,17
48:23 [w]Jos 13:17
48:24 [x]Am 2:2
48:25 [y]Ps 75:10 [z]Ps 10:15; Eze 30:21
48:26 [a]Jer 25:16,27
48:27 [b]Jer 2:26 [c]Job 16:4; Jer 18:16 [d]Mic 7:8-10
48:28 [e]Ps 55:6-7 [f]Jdg 6:2
48:29 [g]Job 40:12; Isa 16:6
48:31 [h]Isa 15:5-8 [i]2Ki 3:25
48:32 [j]Isa 16:8-9

from the orchards and fields of
Moab.
I have stopped the flow of wine[k]
from the presses;
no one treads them with shouts of
joy.[l]
Although there are shouts,
they are not shouts of joy.
34 "The sound of their cry rises
from Heshbon to Elealeh[m] and
Jahaz,[n]
from Zoar[o] as far as Horonaim[p] and
Eglath Shelishiyah,
for even the waters of Nimrim are
dried up.[q]
35 In Moab I will put an end
to those who make offerings on
the high places[r]
and burn incense[s] to their gods,"
declares the LORD.
36 "So my heart laments[t] for Moab like
a flute;
it laments like a flute for the men
of Kir Hareseth.
The wealth they acquired[u] is gone.
37 Every head is shaved
and every beard cut off;
every hand is slashed[v]
and every waist is covered with
sackcloth.[w]
38 On all the roofs in Moab
and in the public squares
there is nothing but mourning,
for I have broken Moab
like a jar[x] that no one wants,"
declares the LORD.
39 "How shattered she is! How they
wail!
How Moab turns her back in
shame!
Moab has become an object of
ridicule,
an object of horror to all those
around her."

40 This is what the LORD says:

"Look! An eagle is swooping[y] down,
spreading its wings[z] over Moab.
41 Kerioth[a] will be captured
and the strongholds taken.
In that day the hearts of Moab's
warriors
will be like the heart of a woman
in labor.[a]
42 Moab will be destroyed[b] as a nation[c]
because she defied[d] the LORD.
43 Terror and pit and snare[e] await you,

48:33 [k]Isa 16:10 [l]Joel 1:12
48:34 [m]Nu 32:3 [n]Isa 15:4 [o]Ge 13:10 [p]Isa 15:5 [q]Isa 15:6
48:35 [r]Isa 15:2; 16:12 [s]Jer 11:13
48:36 [t]Isa 16:11 [u]Isa 15:7
48:37 [v]Isa 15:2; Jer 41:5 [w]Ge 37:34
48:38 [x]Jer 22:28
48:40 [y]Dt 28:49; Hab 1:8 [z]Isa 8:8
48:41 [a]Isa 21:3
48:42 [b]Ps 83:4; Isa 16:14 [c]ver 2 [d]ver 26
48:43 [e]Isa 24:17

O people of Moab,"
declares the LORD.
44 "Whoever flees[f] from the terror
will fall into a pit,
whoever climbs out of the pit
will be caught in a snare;
for I will bring upon Moab
the year[g] of her punishment,"
declares the LORD.

45 "In the shadow of Heshbon
the fugitives stand helpless,
for a fire has gone out from
Heshbon,
a blaze from the midst of Sihon;[h]
it burns the foreheads of Moab,
the skulls[i] of the noisy boasters.
46 Woe to you, O Moab![j]
The people of Chemosh are
destroyed;
your sons are taken into exile
and your daughters into captivity.

47 "Yet I will restore[k] the fortunes of
Moab
in days to come,"
declares the LORD.

Here ends the judgment on Moab.

A Message About Ammon

49 Concerning the Ammonites:[l]

This is what the LORD says:
"Has Israel no sons?
Has she no heirs?
Why then has Molech[b] taken
possession of Gad?
Why do his people live in its towns?
2 But the days are coming,"
declares the LORD,
"when I will sound the battle cry[m]
against Rabbah[n] of the
Ammonites;
it will become a mound of ruins,
and its surrounding villages will be
set on fire.
Then Israel will drive out
those who drove her out,[o]"
says the LORD.
3 "Wail, O Heshbon, for Ai[p] is
destroyed!
Cry out, O inhabitants of Rabbah!
Put on sackcloth and mourn;
rush here and there inside the
walls,

[a]41 Or *The cities* [b]1 Or *their king*; Hebrew *malcam*; also in verse 3

48:44 [f]1Ki 19:17; Isa 24:18 [g]Jer 11:23
48:45 [h]Nu 21:21,26-28 [i]Nu 24:17
48:46 [j]Nu 21:29
48:47 [k]Jer 12:15; 49:6,39
49:1 [l]Am 1:13; Zep 2:8-9
49:2 [m]Jer 4:19 [n]Dt 3:11 [o]Isa 14:2; Eze 21:28-32; 25:2-11
49:3 [p]Jos 8:28

49:3 [q]Jer 48:7
for Molech will go into exile,[q]
together with his priests and
officials.
[4]Why do you boast of your valleys,
boast of your valleys so fruitful?
O unfaithful daughter,
49:4 [r]Jer 9:23; 1Ti 6:17 [s]Jer 21:13
you trust in your riches[r] and say,
'Who will attack me?'[s]
[5]I will bring terror on you
from all those around you,"
declares the Lord,
the LORD Almighty.
"Every one of you will be driven
away,
and no one will gather the
fugitives.

49:6 [t]ver 39; Jer 48:47
[6]"Yet afterward, I will restore[t] the
fortunes of the Ammonites,"
declares the LORD.

A Message About Edom

49:7 [u]Ge 25:30; Eze 25:12 [v]Ge 36:11, 15,34
[7]Concerning Edom:[u]

This is what the LORD Almighty
says:

"Is there no longer wisdom in
Teman?[v]
Has counsel perished from the
prudent?
Has their wisdom decayed?
[8]Turn and flee, hide in deep caves,
49:8 [w]Jer 25:23
you who live in Dedan,[w]
for I will bring disaster on Esau
at the time I punish him.
[9]If grape pickers came to you,
would they not leave a few grapes?
If thieves came during the night,
would they not steal only as much
as they wanted?
[10]But I will strip Esau bare;
I will uncover his hiding places,
so that he cannot conceal himself.
His children, relatives and neighbors
49:10 [x]Mal 1:2-5
will perish,
and he will be no more.[x]
49:11 [y]Hos 14:3
[11]Leave your orphans;[y] I will protect
their lives.
Your widows too can trust in me."

[12]This is what the LORD says: "If
those who do not deserve to drink the
49:12 [z]Jer 25:15 [a]Jer 25:28-29
cup[z] must drink it, why should you go
unpunished?[a] You will not go unpun-
49:13 [b]Ge 22:16 [c]Ge 36:33; Isa 34:6
ished, but must drink it. [13]I swear[b] by
myself," declares the LORD, "that Bozrah[c] will become a ruin and an object of
horror, of reproach and of cursing; and
all its towns will be in ruins forever."

[14]I have heard a message from the
LORD:
An envoy was sent to the nations
to say,
"Assemble yourselves to attack it!
Rise up for battle!"

[15]"Now I will make you small among
the nations,
despised among men.
[16]The terror you inspire
and the pride of your heart have
deceived you,
you who live in the clefts of the
rocks,
who occupy the heights of the
hill.
Though you build your nest[d] as high 49:16 [d]Job 39:27; Am 9:2
as the eagle's,
from there I will bring you down,"
declares the LORD.
[17]"Edom will become an object of
horror;[e] 49:17 [e]ver 13 [f]Jer 50:13; Eze 35:7
all who pass by will be appalled
and will scoff
because of all its wounds.[f] 49:18 [g]Ge 19:24; Dt 29:23 [h]ver 33
[18]As Sodom and Gomorrah[g] were
overthrown,
along with their neighboring
towns,"
says the LORD,
"so no one will live there;
no man will dwell[h] in it.

[19]"Like a lion coming up from Jordan's
thickets[i] 49:19 [i]Jer 12:5 [j]Jer 50:44
to a rich pastureland,
I will chase Edom from its land in
an instant.
Who is the chosen one I will
appoint for this?
Who is like me and who can
challenge me?[j]
And what shepherd can stand
against me?"
[20]Therefore, hear what the LORD has
planned against Edom,
what he has purposed[k] against 49:20 [k]Isa 14:27 [l]Jer 50:45 [m]Mal 1:3-4
those who live in Teman:
The young of the flock[l] will be
dragged away;
he will completely destroy[m] their
pasture because of them.
[21]At the sound of their fall the earth
will tremble;[n] 49:21 [n]Eze 26:15 [o]Jer 50:46; Eze 26:18
their cry[o] will resound to the Red
Sea.[a]

[a]*21* Hebrew *Yam Suph*; that is, Sea of Reeds

49:22 [p]Hos 8:1 [q]Isa 13:8; Jer 48:40-41

22 Look! An eagle will soar and swoop[p]
down,
spreading its wings over Bozrah.
In that day the hearts of Edom's
warriors
will be like the heart of a woman
in labor.[q]

A Message About Damascus

49:23 [r]Ge 14:15; 2Ch 16:2; Ac 9:2 [s]Isa 10:9; Am 6:2; Zec 9:2 [t]2Ki 18:34 [u]Ge 49:4; Isa 57:20

23 Concerning Damascus:[r]

"Hamath[s] and Arpad[t] are dismayed,
for they have heard bad news.
They are disheartened,
troubled like[a] the restless sea.[u]
24 Damascus has become feeble,
she has turned to flee
and panic has gripped her;
anguish and pain have seized her,
pain like that of a woman in labor.
25 Why has the city of renown not
been abandoned,
the town in which I delight?
26 Surely, her young men will fall in the
streets;
all her soldiers will be silenced[v] in
that day,"
declares the LORD Almighty.
27 "I will set fire[w] to the walls of
Damascus;
it will consume the fortresses of
Ben-Hadad.[x]"

49:26 [v]Jer 50:30
49:27 [w]Jer 43:12; Am 1:4 [x]1Ki 15:18

A Message About Kedar and Hazor

49:28 [y]Ge 25:13 [z]Jdg 6:3

28 Concerning Kedar[y] and the kingdoms of Hazor, which Nebuchadnezzar
king of Babylon attacked:

This is what the LORD says:

"Arise, and attack Kedar
and destroy the people of the East.[z]
29 Their tents and their flocks will be
taken;
their shelters will be carried off
with all their goods and camels.
Men will shout to them,
'Terror[a] on every side!'

49:29 [a]Jer 6:25; 46:5

30 "Flee quickly away!
Stay in deep caves, you who live
in Hazor,"
declares the LORD.
"Nebuchadnezzar king of Babylon
has plotted against you;
he has devised a plan against you.
31 "Arise and attack a nation at ease,
which lives in confidence,"
declares the LORD,
"a nation that has neither gates nor
bars;[b]
its people live alone.
32 Their camels will become plunder,
and their large herds will be booty.
I will scatter to the winds those who
are in distant places[b][c]
and will bring disaster on them
from every side,"
declares the LORD.
33 "Hazor will become a haunt of
jackals,
a desolate[d] place forever.
No one will live there;
no man will dwell[e] in it."

49:31 [b]Eze 38:11
49:32 [c]Jer 9:26
49:33 [d]Jer 10:22 [e]ver 18; Jer 51:37

A Message About Elam

34 This is the word of the LORD that
came to Jeremiah the prophet concerning Elam,[f] early in the reign of Zedekiah[g] king of Judah:

49:34 [f]Ge 10:22 [g]2Ki 24:18

35 This is what the LORD Almighty
says:

"See, I will break the bow[h] of Elam,
the mainstay of their might.
36 I will bring against Elam the four
winds[i]
from the four quarters of the
heavens;
I will scatter them to the four winds,
and there will not be a nation
where Elam's exiles do not go.
37 I will shatter Elam before their foes,
before those who seek their lives;
I will bring disaster upon them,
even my fierce anger,"[j]
declares the LORD.
"I will pursue them with the sword[k]
until I have made an end of them.
38 I will set my throne in Elam
and destroy her king and
officials,"
declares the LORD.
39 "Yet I will restore[l] the fortunes of
Elam
in days to come,"
declares the LORD.

49:35 [h]Isa 22:6
49:36 [i]ver 32
49:37 [j]Jer 30:24 [k]Jer 9:16
49:39 [l]Jer 48:47

A Message About Babylon

50 This is the word the LORD
spoke through Jeremiah the
prophet concerning Babylon[m] and the
land of the Babylonians[c]:

50:1 [m]Ge 10:10; Isa 13:1

[a]23 Hebrew *on* or *by* [b]32 Or *who clip the hair by their foreheads* [c]1 Or *Chaldeans*; also in verses 8, 25, 35 and 45

50:2 [n]Jer 4:16 [o]Jer 51:31 [p]Isa 46:1 [q]Jer 51:47

2 "Announce and proclaim[n] among
the nations,
lift up a banner and proclaim it;
keep nothing back, but say,
'Babylon will be captured;[o]
Bel[p] will be put to shame,
Marduk[q] filled with terror.
Her images will be put to shame
and her idols filled with terror.'

PEACE

WHERE IDOLS DIE

Jeremiah 50:2

Marduk and Bel were Babylonian gods with widespread respect but no power. Our graven images may be our homes and cars and stock options. But, as was the case with the impotent lords of Babylon, we need to remember that peace cannot come till powerless idols die.

3 A nation from the north will attack
her
and lay waste her land.

50:3 [r]ver 13; Isa 14:22-23 [s]Zep 1:3

No one will live[r] in it;
both men and animals[s] will flee
away.
4 "In those days, at that time,"
declares the LORD,
"the people of Israel and the people
of Judah together[t]

50:4 [t]Jer 3:18; Hos 1:11 [u]Ezr 3:12; Jer 31:9 [v]Hos 3:5

will go in tears[u] to seek[v] the LORD
their God.
5 They will ask the way to Zion
and turn their faces toward it.

50:5 [w]Jer 33:7 [x]Isa 55:3; Jer 32:40; Heb 8:6-10

They will come[w] and bind
themselves to the LORD
in an everlasting covenant[x]
that will not be forgotten.

50:6 [y]Isa 53:6; Mt 9:36; 10:6 [z]Jer 3:6; Eze 34:6 [a]ver 19

6 "My people have been lost sheep;[y]
their shepherds have led them
astray
and caused them to roam on the
mountains.
They wandered over mountain and
hill[z]
and forgot their own resting
place.[a]
7 Whoever found them devoured
them;

50:7 [b]Jer 2:3 [c]Jer 14:8

their enemies said, 'We are not
guilty,[b]
for they sinned against the LORD,
their true pasture,
the LORD, the hope[c] of their
fathers.'

DAY 3 THREE

KINDNESS AND MY RELATIONSHIP WITH CHRIST

Jeremiah 50:6

The people were lost. They were called "lost sheep," meaning that they had no shepherd to guide them or protect them. What the people needed then was someone to save them. What people need now is someone to save them. The condition of people today is the same as it was when Jeremiah spoke God's words to lost Israel.

Jesus reminds us that we are to share what we have with the rest of the world. In Matthew 10:8 Jesus tells his disciples that they have received "freely." What was it they had received? They had received friendship with God's Son, so he was to be the grand offering to others. All missionaries have one message: "We have received the Son; now he is yours."

Freely Jesus came to us, but often we are not floodgates of grace but dams across the flow. Our cowardice or our separation from God stops the flow. Cowardice asks, "What right do I have to impose God's grace on others?" Separation from God leaves us too remote to remember that God wants to redeem all people. We pass in callous disregard those whom God longs to save. So Jesus is missed!

Consider the exotic glory that was yours when Jesus first came to you. He loved you as you were—a miracle in and of itself. He forgave your sins—a triumph, considering that he had carried his love for you to the hour of his death. He filled you with his Spirit—a welcome abundance, considering that your life had been so empty. He gave you a place in his community, a community filled with souls like yourself, who have wandered into wonder. The cost of all this? For you, nothing; for him, everything. There is a world of lost sheep waiting to hear from you. You have a Shepherd; now show him to others.

To begin a study on the topic of Kindness, Always Applying the Golden Rule, turn to the home page on page 1141.

8 "Flee[d] out of Babylon;
leave the land of the Babylonians,
and be like the goats that lead the
flock.

50:8 [d]Isa 48:20; Jer 51:6; Rev 18:4

[9]For I will stir up and bring against
Babylon
an alliance of great nations from
the land of the north.
They will take up their positions
against her,
and from the north she will be
captured.
Their arrows will be like skilled
warriors
who do not return empty-handed.
[10]So Babylonia[a] will be plundered;
all who plunder her will have their
fill,"
declares the LORD.

[11]"Because you rejoice and are glad,
you who pillage my inheritance,[e]
because you frolic like a heifer
threshing grain
and neigh like stallions,
[12]your mother will be greatly ashamed;
she who gave you birth will be
disgraced.
She will be the least of the nations—
a wilderness, a dry land, a desert.
[13]Because of the LORD's anger she will
not be inhabited
but will be completely desolate.
All who pass Babylon will be
horrified and scoff[f]
because of all her wounds.[g]

[14]"Take up your positions around
Babylon,
all you who draw the bow.[h]
Shoot at her! Spare no arrows,
for she has sinned against the
LORD.
[15]Shout[i] against her on every side!
She surrenders, her towers fall,
her walls[j] are torn down.
Since this is the vengeance[k] of the
LORD,
take vengeance on her;
do to her[l] as she has done to
others.
[16]Cut off from Babylon the sower,
and the reaper with his sickle at
harvest.
Because of the sword[m] of the
oppressor
let everyone return to his own
people,[n]
let everyone flee to his own land.[o]

[17]"Israel is a scattered flock
that lions[p] have chased away.
The first to devour him
was the king[q] of Assyria;
the last to crush his bones
was Nebuchadnezzar[r] king[s] of
Babylon."

[18]Therefore this is what the LORD
Almighty, the God of Israel, says:

"I will punish the king of Babylon
and his land
as I punished the king[t] of Assyria.[u]
[19]But I will bring[v] Israel back to his
own pasture
and he will graze on Carmel and
Bashan;
his appetite will be satisfied
on the hills[w] of Ephraim and
Gilead.
[20]In those days, at that time,"
declares the LORD,
"search will be made for Israel's guilt,
but there will be none,
and for the sins[x] of Judah,
but none will be found,
for I will forgive[y] the remnant[z] I
spare.

[21]"Attack the land of Merathaim
and those who live in Pekod.[a]
Pursue, kill and completely destroy[b]
them,"
declares the LORD.
"Do everything I have
commanded you.
[22]The noise[b] of battle is in the land,
the noise of great destruction!
[23]How broken and shattered
is the hammer of the whole earth!
How desolate[c] is Babylon
among the nations!
[24]I set a trap[d] for you, O Babylon,
and you were caught before you
knew it;
you were found and captured[e]
because you opposed[f] the LORD.
[25]The LORD has opened his arsenal
and brought out the weapons[g] of
his wrath,
for the Sovereign LORD Almighty
has work to do
in the land of the Babylonians.[h]
[26]Come against her from afar.
Break open her granaries;
pile her up like heaps of grain.
Completely destroy[i] her

50:11 [e]Isa 47:6
50:13 [f]Jer 18:16 [g]Jer 49:17
50:14 [h]ver 29,42
50:15 [i]Jer 51:14 [j]Jer 51:44,58 [k]Jer 51:6 [l]Ps 137:8; Rev 18:6
50:16 [m]Jer 25:38 [n]Isa 13:14 [o]Jer 51:9
50:17 [p]Jer 2:15
50:17 [q]2Ki 17:6 [r]2Ki 24:10,14 [s]2Ki 25:7
50:18 [t]Isa 10:12 [u]Eze 31:3
50:19 [v]Jer 31:10; Eze 34:13 [w]Jer 31:5; 33:12
50:20 [x]Mic 7:18,19 [y]Jer 31:34 [z]Isa 1:9
50:21 [a]Eze 23:23
50:22 [b]Jer 4:19-21; 51:54
50:23 [c]Isa 14:16
50:24 [d]Da 5:30-31 [e]Jer 51:31 [f]Job 9:4
50:25 [g]Isa 13:5 [h]Jer 51:25,55
50:26 [i]Isa 14:22-23

[a]*10* Or *Chaldea* [b]*21* The Hebrew term refers to the irrevocable giving over of things or persons to the LORD, often by totally destroying them; also in verse 26.

and leave her no remnant.
27 Kill all her young bulls;
let them go down to the slaughter!
Woe to them! For their day has come,
the time for them to be punished.
28 Listen to the fugitives and refugees from Babylon
declaring in Zion[j]
how the LORD our God has taken vengeance,[k]
vengeance for his temple.

29 "Summon archers against Babylon,
all those who draw the bow.[l]
Encamp all around her;
let no one escape.
Repay[m] her for her deeds;[n]
do to her as she has done.
For she has defied[o] the LORD,
the Holy One of Israel.
30 Therefore, her young men[p] will fall in the streets;
all her soldiers will be silenced in that day,"
declares the LORD.
31 "See, I am against[q] you, O arrogant one,"
declares the Lord, the LORD Almighty,
"for your day has come,
the time for you to be punished.
32 The arrogant one will stumble and fall
and no one will help her up;
I will kindle a fire[r] in her towns
that will consume all who are around her."

33 This is what the LORD Almighty says:

"The people of Israel are oppressed,[s]
and the people of Judah as well.
All their captors hold them fast,
refusing to let them go.[t]
34 Yet their Redeemer is strong;
the LORD Almighty[u] is his name.
He will vigorously defend their cause[v]
so that he may bring rest[w] to their land,
but unrest to those who live in Babylon.

35 "A sword[x] against the Babylonians!"
declares the LORD—
"against those who live in Babylon
and against her officials and wise[y] men!
36 A sword against her false prophets!
They will become fools.
A sword against her warriors![z]
They will be filled with terror.
37 A sword against her horses and chariots[a]
and all the foreigners in her ranks!
They will become women.[b]
A sword against her treasures!
They will be plundered.
38 A drought on[a] her waters!
They will dry[c] up.
For it is a land of idols,[d]
idols that will go mad with terror.

39 "So desert creatures and hyenas will live there,
and there the owl will dwell.
It will never again be inhabited
or lived in from generation to generation.[e]
40 As God overthrew Sodom and Gomorrah[f]
along with their neighboring towns,"
declares the LORD,
"so no one will live there;
no man will dwell in it.

41 "Look! An army is coming from the north;[g]
a great nation and many kings
are being stirred up from the ends of the earth.[h]
42 They are armed with bows[i] and spears;
they are cruel and without mercy.[j]
They sound like the roaring sea[k]
as they ride on their horses;
they come like men in battle formation
to attack you, O Daughter of Babylon.[l]
43 The king of Babylon has heard reports about them,
and his hands hang limp.
Anguish has gripped him,
pain like that of a woman in labor.
44 Like a lion coming up from Jordan's thickets
to a rich pastureland,
I will chase Babylon from its land in an instant.
Who is the chosen[m] one I will appoint for this?
Who is like me and who can challenge me?[n]

[a] 38 Or *A sword against*

50:28 [j] Isa 48:20; Jer 51:10 [k] ver 15
50:29 [l] ver 14 [m] Rev 18:6 [n] Jer 51:56 [o] Isa 47:10
50:30 [p] Isa 13:18; Jer 49:26
50:31 [q] Jer 21:13
50:32 [r] Jer 21:14; 49:27
50:33 [s] Isa 58:6 [t] Isa 14:17
50:34 [u] Jer 51:19 [v] Jer 15:21; 51:36 [w] Isa 14:7
50:35 [x] Jer 47:6 [y] Da 5:7
50:36 [z] Jer 49:22
50:37 [a] Jer 51:21 [b] Jer 51:30; Na 3:13
50:38 [c] Jer 51:36 [d] ver 2
50:39 [e] Isa 13:19-22; 34:13-15; Jer 51:37; Rev 18:2
50:40 [f] Ge 19:24
50:41 [g] Jer 6:22 [h] Isa 13:4; Jer 51:22-28
50:42 [i] ver 14 [j] Isa 13:18 [k] Isa 5:30 [l] Jer 6:23
50:44 [m] Nu 16:5 [n] Job 41:10; Isa 46:9; Jer 49:19

And what shepherd can stand
against me?"

50:45 [o]Ps 33:11; Isa 14:24; Jer 51:11

45 Therefore, hear what the LORD has
planned against Babylon,
what he has purposed[o] against the
land of the Babylonians:
The young of the flock will be
dragged away;
he will completely destroy their
pasture because of them.

50:46 [p]Rev 18:9-10

46 At the sound of Babylon's capture
the earth will tremble;
its cry[p] will resound among the
nations.

51

This is what the LORD says:
"See, I will stir up the spirit of a
destroyer
against Babylon and the people of
Leb Kamai.[a]

51:2 [q]Isa 41:16; Jer 15:7; Mt 3:12

2 I will send foreigners to Babylon
to winnow[q] her and to devastate
her land;
they will oppose her on every side
in the day of her disaster.

51:3 [r]Jer 50:29 [s]Jer 46:4

3 Let not the archer string his bow,[r]
nor let him put on his armor.[s]
Do not spare her young men;
completely destroy[b] her army.

51:4 [t]Isa 13:15 [u]Jer 49:26; 50:30

4 They will fall[t] down slain in
Babylon,[c]
fatally wounded in her streets.[u]

51:5 [v]Isa 54:6-8 [w]Hos 4:1

5 For Israel and Judah have not been
forsaken[v]
by their God, the LORD
Almighty,
though their land[d] is full of guilt[w]
before the Holy One of Israel.

51:6 [x]Jer 50:8 [y]Nu 16:26; Rev 18:4 [z]Jer 50:15 [a]Jer 25:14

6 "Flee[x] from Babylon!
Run for your lives!
Do not be destroyed because of
her sins.[y]
It is time for the LORD's vengeance;[z]
he will pay[a] her what she
deserves.

51:7 [b]Jer 25:15-16; Rev 14:8-10; 17:4

7 Babylon was a gold cup[b] in the
LORD's hand;
she made the whole earth drunk.
The nations drank her wine;
therefore they have now gone
mad.

51:8 [c]Isa 21:9; Rev 14:8 [d]Jer 46:11

8 Babylon will suddenly fall[c] and be
broken.
Wail over her!
Get balm[d] for her pain;
perhaps she can be healed.

51:9 [e]Isa 13:14; Jer 50:16 [f]Rev 18:4-5

9 " 'We would have healed Babylon,
but she cannot be healed;
let us leave[e] her and each go to his
own land,
for her judgment[f] reaches to the
skies,
it rises as high as the clouds.'

51:10 [g]Mic 7:9 [h]Jer 50:28

10 " 'The LORD has vindicated[g] us;
come, let us tell in Zion
what the LORD our God has
done.'[h]

51:11 [i]Jer 50:9 [j]Jer 46:4 [k]ver 28 [l]Jer 50:45 [m]Jer 50:28

11 "Sharpen the arrows,[i]
take up the shields![j]
The LORD has stirred up the kings
of the Medes,[k]
because his purpose[l] is to destroy
Babylon.
The LORD will take vengeance,
vengeance for his temple.[m]
12 Lift up a banner against the walls of
Babylon!
Reinforce the guard,
station the watchmen,
prepare an ambush!
The LORD will carry out his
purpose,
his decree against the people of
Babylon.

51:13 [n]Rev 17:1,15 [o]Isa 45:3; Hab 2:9

13 You who live by many waters[n]
and are rich in treasures,[o]
your end has come,
the time for you to be cut off.

51:14 [p]Am 6:8 [q]ver 27; Na 3:15 [r]Jer 50:15

14 The LORD Almighty has sworn by
himself:[p]
I will surely fill you with men, as
with a swarm of locusts,[q]
and they will shout[r] in triumph
over you.

51:15 [s]Ge 1:1; Job 9:8; Ps 104:2

15 "He made the earth by his power;
he founded the world by his
wisdom
and stretched[s] out the heavens by
his understanding.

51:16 [t]Ps 18:11-13 [u]Ps 135:7; Jnh 1:4

16 When he thunders,[t] the waters in the
heavens roar;
he makes clouds rise from the
ends of the earth.
He sends lightning with the rain
and brings out the wind from his
storehouses.[u]

[a]1 *Leb Kamai* is a cryptogram for Chaldea, that is, Babylonia. [b]3 The Hebrew term refers to the irrevocable giving over of things or persons to the LORD, often by totally destroying them. [c]4 Or *Chaldea* [d]5 Or / *and the land* ⌊*of the Babylonians*⌋

17"Every man is senseless and without
knowledge;
every goldsmith is shamed by his
idols.
His images are a fraud;[v]
they have no breath in them.
18They are worthless,[w] the objects of
mockery;
when their judgment comes, they
will perish.
19He who is the Portion of Jacob is not
like these,
for he is the Maker of all things,
including the tribe of his
inheritance—
the LORD Almighty is his name.

20"You are my war club,[x]
my weapon for battle—
with you I shatter[y] nations,
with you I destroy kingdoms,
21with you I shatter horse and rider,[z]
with you I shatter chariot and
driver,
22with you I shatter man and woman,
with you I shatter old man and
youth,
with you I shatter young man and
maiden,[a]
23with you I shatter shepherd and
flock,
with you I shatter farmer and
oxen,
with you I shatter governors and
officials.[b]

24"Before your eyes I will repay[c] Babylon and all who live in Babylonia[a] for
all the wrong they have done in Zion,"
declares the LORD.

25"I am against you, O destroying
mountain,
you who destroy the whole earth,"
declares the LORD.
"I will stretch out my hand against
you,
roll you off the cliffs,
and make you a burned-out
mountain.[d]
26No rock will be taken from you for a
cornerstone,
nor any stone for a foundation,
for you will be desolate[e] forever,"
declares the LORD.

27"Lift up a banner[f] in the land!
Blow the trumpet among the
nations!

51:17 [v]Isa 44:20; Hab 2:18-19
51:18 [w]Jer 18:15
51:20 [x]Isa 10:5 [y]Mic 4:13
51:21 [z]Ex 15:1
51:22 [a]2Ch 36:17; Isa 13:17-18
51:23 [b]ver 57
51:24 [c]Jer 50:15
51:25 [d]Zec 4:7
51:26 [e]ver 29; Isa 13:19-22; Jer 50:12
51:27 [f]Isa 13:2; Jer 50:2

Prepare the nations for battle against
her;
summon against her these
kingdoms:[g]
Ararat,[h] Minni and Ashkenaz.[i]
Appoint a commander against her;
send up horses like a swarm of
locusts.
28Prepare the nations for battle against
her—
the kings of the Medes,[j]
their governors and all their officials,
and all the countries they rule.
29The land trembles and writhes,
for the LORD's purposes against
Babylon stand—
to lay waste the land of Babylon
so that no one will live there.[k]
30Babylon's warriors[l] have stopped
fighting;
they remain in their strongholds.
Their strength is exhausted;
they have become like women.[m]
Her dwellings are set on fire;
the bars[n] of her gates are broken.
31One courier[o] follows another
and messenger follows messenger
to announce to the king of Babylon
that his entire city is captured,
32the river crossings seized,
the marshes set on fire,
and the soldiers terrified.[p]"

33This is what the LORD Almighty,
the God of Israel, says:

"The Daughter of Babylon is like a
threshing floor[q]
at the time it is trampled;
the time to harvest[r] her will soon
come."

34"Nebuchadnezzar[s] king of Babylon
has devoured us,
he has thrown us into confusion,
he has made us an empty jar.
Like a serpent he has swallowed us
and filled his stomach with our
delicacies,
and then has spewed us out.
35May the violence done to our flesh[b]
be upon Babylon,"
say the inhabitants of Zion.
"May our blood be on those who
live in Babylonia,"
says Jerusalem.[t]

[a]24 Or *Chaldea*; also in verse 35 [b]35 Or *done to us and to our children*

51:27 [g]Jer 25:14 [h]Ge 8:4 [i]Ge 10:3
51:28 [j]ver 11
51:29 [k]ver 43; Isa 13:20
51:30 [l]Jer 50:36 [m]Isa 19:16 [n]Isa 45:2; La 2:9; Na 3:13
51:31 [o]2Sa 18:19-31
51:32 [p]Jer 50:36
51:33 [q]Isa 21:10 [r]Isa 17:5; Hos 6:11
51:34 [s]Jer 50:17
51:35 [t]ver 24; Ps 137:8

36 Therefore, this is what the LORD says:

"See, I will defend your cause[u]
and avenge[v] you;
I will dry up[w] her sea
and make her springs dry.
37 Babylon will be a heap of ruins,
a haunt[x] of jackals,
an object of horror and scorn,
a place where no one lives.[y]
38 Her people all roar like young lions,
they growl like lion cubs.
39 But while they are aroused,
I will set out a feast for them
and make them drunk,
so that they shout with laughter—
then sleep forever and not awake,"
declares the LORD.[z]
40 "I will bring them down
like lambs to the slaughter,
like rams and goats.

41 "How Sheshach[a][a] will be captured,[b]
the boast of the whole earth seized!
What a horror Babylon will be
among the nations!
42 The sea will rise over Babylon;
its roaring waves[c] will cover her.
43 Her towns will be desolate,
a dry and desert land,
a land where no one lives,
through which no man travels.[d]
44 I will punish Bel[e] in Babylon
and make him spew out[f] what he
has swallowed.
The nations will no longer stream to
him.
And the wall[g] of Babylon will fall.

45 "Come out[h] of her, my people!
Run[i] for your lives!
Run from the fierce anger of the
LORD.
46 Do not lose heart or be afraid[j]
when rumors[k] are heard in the
land;
one rumor comes this year, another
the next,
rumors of violence in the land
and of ruler against ruler.
47 For the time will surely come
when I will punish the idols[l] of
Babylon;
her whole land will be disgraced[m]
and her slain will all lie fallen
within her.
48 Then heaven and earth and all that
is in them
will shout[n] for joy over Babylon,
for out of the north[o]
destroyers will attack her,"
declares the LORD.

49 "Babylon must fall because of Israel's
slain,
just as the slain in all the earth
have fallen because of Babylon.[p]
50 You who have escaped the sword,
leave[q] and do not linger!
Remember[r] the LORD in a distant
land,
and think on Jerusalem."

51 "We are disgraced,[s]
for we have been insulted
and shame covers our faces,
because foreigners have entered
the holy places of the LORD's
house."[t]

52 "But days are coming," declares the
LORD,
"when I will punish her idols,[u]
and throughout her land
the wounded will groan.
53 Even if Babylon reaches the sky[v]
and fortifies her lofty stronghold,
I will send destroyers[w] against her,"
declares the LORD.

54 "The sound of a cry comes from
Babylon,
the sound of great destruction[x]
from the land of the Babylonians.[b]
55 The LORD will destroy Babylon;
he will silence her noisy din.
Waves[y] of enemies will rage like
great waters;
the roar of their voices will
resound.
56 A destroyer[z] will come against
Babylon;
her warriors will be captured,
and their bows will be broken.[a]
For the LORD is a God of
retribution;
he will repay[b] in full.
57 I will make her officials and wise
men drunk,
her governors, officers and
warriors as well;
they will sleep[c] forever and not
awake,"
declares the King,[d] whose name is
the LORD Almighty.

[a] *41 Sheshach* is a cryptogram for Babylon.
[b] *54* Or *Chaldeans*

51:36 [u]Ps 140:12; Jer 50:34; La 3:58 [v]ver 6; Ro 12:19 [w]Jer 50:38
51:37 [x]Isa 13:22; Rev 18:2 [y]Jer 50:13,39
51:39 [z]ver 57
51:41 [a]Jer 25:26 [b]Isa 13:19
51:42 [c]Isa 8:7
51:43 [d]ver 29,62; Isa 13:20; Jer 2:6
51:44 [e]Isa 46:1 [f]ver 34 [g]ver 58; Jer 50:15
51:45 [h]Rev 18:4 [i]ver 6; Isa 48:20; Jer 50:8
51:46 [j]Jer 46:27 [k]2Ki 19:7
51:47 [l]ver 52; Isa 46:1-2; Jer 50:2 [m]Jer 50:12
51:48 [n]Isa 44:23; Rev 18:20 [o]ver 11
51:49 [p]Ps 137:8; Jer 50:29
51:50 [q]ver 45 [r]Ps 137:6
51:51 [s]Ps 44:13-16; 79:4 [t]La 1:10
51:52 [u]ver 47
51:53 [v]Ge 11:4; Isa 14:13-14 [w]Jer 49:16
51:54 [x]Jer 50:22
51:55 [y]Ps 18:4
51:56 [z]ver 48 [a]Ps 46:9 [b]ver 6; Ps 94:1-2; Hab 2:8
51:57 [c]Ps 76:5; Jer 25:27 [d]Jer 46:18; 48:15

58This is what the LORD Almighty
says:

51:58 [e]ver 44 “Babylon’s thick wall[e] will be leveled
[f]ver 64 [g]Hab 2:13 and her high gates set on fire;
the peoples[f] exhaust themselves for nothing,
the nations’ labor is only fuel for the flames.”[g]

59This is the message Jeremiah gave to
51:59 [h]Jer 36:4 the staff officer Seraiah son of Neriah,[h]
[i]Jer 52:1 the son of Mahseiah, when he went to
[j]Jer 28:1 Babylon with Zedekiah[i] king of Judah
51:60 in the fourth[j] year of his reign. 60Jer-
[k]Jer 30:2; 36:2 emiah had written on a scroll[k] about
all the disasters that would come upon
Babylon—all that had been recorded
concerning Babylon. 61He said to Seraiah, “When you get to Babylon, see that
you read all these words aloud. 62Then
say, ‘O LORD, you have said you will
destroy this place, so that neither man
nor animal will live in it; it will be deso-
51:62 [l]Isa 13:20; late[l] forever.’ 63When you finish read-
Jer 50:13,39 ing this scroll, tie a stone to it and
throw it into the Euphrates. 64Then say,
‘So will Babylon sink to rise no more
because of the disaster I will bring upon
51:64 [m]ver 58 her. And her people[m] will fall.’”
[n]Job 31:40 The words of Jeremiah end[n] here.

The Fall of Jerusalem

52:1 [o]2Ki 24:17 52 Zedekiah[o] was twenty-one years
[p]Jos 10:29; old when he became king, and
2Ki 8:22 he reigned in Jerusalem eleven years.
His mother’s name was Hamutal daughter of Jeremiah; she was from Libnah.[p]
2He did evil in the eyes of the LORD,
52:2 [q]Jer 36:30 just as Jehoiakim[q] had done. 3It was
52:3 because of the LORD’s anger that all
[r]Isa 3:1 this happened to Jerusalem and Judah,[r]
[s]Eze 17:12-16 and in the end he thrust them from his
presence.
Now Zedekiah rebelled[s] against the
king of Babylon.
4So in the ninth year of Zedekiah’s
52:4 reign, on the tenth[t] day of the tenth
[t]Zec 8:19 month, Nebuchadnezzar king of Bab-
[u]2Ki 25:1-7; Jer 39:1 ylon marched against Jerusalem[u] with
[v]Eze 24:1-2 his whole army. They camped outside
the city and built siege works all around
it.[v] 5The city was kept under siege until
the eleventh year of King Zedekiah.
6By the ninth day of the fourth
month the famine in the city had be-
52:6 come so severe that there was no food
[w]Isa 3:1 for the people to eat.[w] 7Then the city
wall was broken through, and the whole
army fled. They left the city at night
through the gate between the two walls
near the king’s garden, though the Babylonians[a] were surrounding the city.
They fled toward the Arabah,[b] 8but the
Babylonian[c] army pursued King Zedekiah and overtook him in the plains of
Jericho. All his soldiers were separated
from him and scattered, 9and he was
captured.[x] 52:9 [x]Jer 32:4
He was taken to the king of Bab- [y]Nu 34:11
ylon at Riblah[y] in the land of Hamath,[z] [z]Nu 13:21
where he pronounced sentence on him.
10There at Riblah the king of Babylon 52:10
slaughtered the sons[a] of Zedekiah before [a]Jer 22:30
his eyes; he also killed all the officials
of Judah. 11Then he put out Zedekiah’s
eyes, bound him with bronze shackles
and took him to Babylon, where he put 52:11
him in prison till the day of his death.[b] [b]Eze 12:13
12On the tenth day of the fifth[c] 52:12
month, in the nineteenth year of Neb- [c]Zec 7:5; 8:19
uchadnezzar king of Babylon, Nebu- [d]Jer 39:9
zaradan[d] commander of the imperial
guard, who served the king of Babylon,
came to Jerusalem. 13He set fire[e] to the 52:13 [e]2Ch 36:19;
temple[f] of the LORD, the royal palace Ps 74:8; La 2:6
and all the houses of Jerusalem. Every [f]Ps 79:1;
important building he burned down. Mic 3:12
14The whole Babylonian army under
the commander of the imperial guard
broke down all the walls[g] around Jeru- 52:14 [g]Ne 1:3
salem. 15Nebuzaradan the commander
of the guard carried into exile some of
the poorest people and those who remained in the city, along with the rest
of the craftsmen[d] and those who had
gone over to the king of Babylon. 16But
Nebuzaradan left behind[h] the rest of 52:16 [h]Jer 40:6
the poorest people of the land to work
the vineyards and fields.
17The Babylonians broke up the 52:17
bronze pillars,[i] the movable stands[j] and [i]1Ki 7:15 [j]1Ki 7:27-37
the bronze Sea[k] that were at the tem- [k]1Ki 7:23
ple of the LORD and they carried all [l]Jer 27:19-22
the bronze to Babylon.[l] 18They also
took away the pots, shovels, wick trimmers, sprinkling bowls, dishes and all
the bronze articles used in the temple 52:18
service.[m] 19The commander of the im- [m]Ex 27:3; 1Ki 7:45
perial guard took away the basins,
censers,[n] sprinkling bowls, pots, lamp- 52:19 [n]1Ki 7:50
stands, dishes and bowls used for drink

[a] *7* Or *Chaldeans;* also in verse 17 [b] *7* Or *the Jordan Valley* [c] *8* Or *Chaldean;* also in verse 14
[d] *15* Or *populace*

offerings—all that were made of pure
gold or silver.
20The bronze from the two pillars,
the Sea and the twelve bronze bulls under it, and the movable stands, which
King Solomon had made for the temple of the LORD, was more than could
52:20 be weighed.[o] 21Each of the pillars was
o1Ki 7:47 eighteen cubits high and twelve cubits
in circumference[a]; each was four fingers
52:21 thick, and hollow.[p] 22The bronze capi-
p1Ki 7:15 tal[q] on top of the one pillar was five
52:22 cubits[b] high and was decorated with a
q1Ki 7:16 network and pomegranates of bronze all
around. The other pillar, with its pomegranates, was similar. 23There were ninety-six pomegranates on the sides; the
52:23 total number of pomegranates[r] above
r1Ki 7:20 the surrounding network was a hundred.
24The commander of the guard took
52:24 s2Ki 25:18 as prisoners Seraiah[s] the chief priest,
tJer 21:1; 37:3 Zephaniah[t] the priest next in rank and
the three doorkeepers. 25Of those still
in the city, he took the officer in charge
of the fighting men, and seven royal advisers. He also took the secretary who
was chief officer in charge of conscripting the people of the land and sixty of
52:26 his men who were found in the city.
uver 12 26Nebuzaradan[u] the commander took
them all and brought them to the king
of Babylon at Riblah. 27There at Riblah, in the land of Hamath, the king
had them executed.

So Judah went into captivity, away[v] 52:27 vJer 20:4
from her land. 28This is the number
of the people Nebuchadnezzar carried
into exile:[w] 52:28 w2Ki 24:14-16; 2Ch 36:20

in the seventh year, 3,023 Jews;
29in Nebuchadnezzar's eighteenth year,
832 people from Jerusalem;
30in his twenty-third year,
745 Jews taken into exile by Nebuzaradan the commander of the imperial guard.
There were 4,600 people in all.

Jehoiachin Released

31In the thirty-seventh year of the
exile of Jehoiachin king of Judah, in
the year Evil-Merodach[c] became king
of Babylon, he released Jehoiachin king
of Judah and freed him from prison
on the twenty-fifth day of the twelfth
month. 32He spoke kindly to him and
gave him a seat of honor higher than
those of the other kings who were with
him in Babylon. 33So Jehoiachin put
aside his prison clothes and for the rest
of his life ate regularly at the king's
table.[x] 34Day by day the king of Bab- 52:33 x2Sa 9:7
ylon gave Jehoiachin a regular allow-
ance[y] as long as he lived, till the day of 52:34 y2Sa 9:10
his death.

[a]*21* That is, about 27 feet (about 8.1 meters) high and 18 feet (about 5.4 meters) in circumference
[b]*22* That is, about 7 1/2 feet (about 2.3 meters)
[c]*31* Also called *Amel-Marduk*

LAMENTATIONS

AUTHORSHIP AND DATE

Jeremiah, according to ancient Jewish and Christian tradition

After the fall of Jerusalem, which took place in 586 B.C.

KEY THEMES

Lamentations, which resonates with grief, deals with heavy subjects indeed. The fall of Jerusalem was an utter disaster that occasioned Jeremiah's tearful requiem. But his grief was not a grief without hope. In fact, hope is a key theme that appears throughout the book. While Jeremiah was careful to show the utter misery of the burned out city, he could not leave its one-time citizens to be hauled into slavery with no hope. God's great mercy would at last overcome the consequences of their sin. Still, the tearful absence of peace freezes the warmth of the human heart. The very first line of the book—"How deserted lies the city, once so full of people!"—sweeps the soul with melancholy. By the time Jeremiah's despair is discovered, our hearts are breaking with the sheer weight of his lamentation: "My eyes fail from weeping, I am in torment within, my heart is poured out on the ground because my people are destroyed, because children and infants faint in the streets of the city" (2:11).

FRUIT OF THE SPIRIT IN LAMENTATIONS

Joy: The laments of Jeremiah are so sorrowful that there seems to be no ray of light within them. But God is a God of hope, and Jeremiah, whose life was characterized by his "jeremiads" (complaints), wept his way through Lamentations to close with a benediction of great joy and ultimate hope: "Rejoice and be glad, O Daughter of Edom . . . O Daughter of Zion, your punishment will end; he will not prolong your exile" (4:21–22).

Patience: The hope in this book is dependent upon the Israelites patience, their ability to wait until God causes the sluggish hope to finally arrive. "You, O LORD, reign forever; your throne endures from generation to generation. Why do you always forget us? Why do you forsake us so long? Restore us to yourself, O LORD, that we may return; renew our days as of old" (5:19–21). The cry was for God to hasten the renewal. God's answer: Israel had to learn that patience is never empty.

Faithfulness: Perhaps the most famous promises in the book of Lamentations deal with God's faithfulness: "Because of the LORD's great love we are not consumed, for his compassions never fail. They are new every morning; great is your faithfulness" (3:22–23).

1:1 [a]Isa 47:8 [b]1Ki 4:21 [c]Isa 3:26; Jer 40:9

1[a] How deserted lies the city,
once so full of people!
How like a widow[a] is she,
who once was great[b] among the nations!
She who was queen among the provinces
has now become a slave.[c]

LOVE

A REQUIEM FOR JERUSALEM

Lamentations 1:1

Love writes requiems. Jerusalem the golden had become a dying pit of rubble. Like Dresden after the firestorms, her gallant citadels had been reduced to rotting lintels and crumbling stone. Yet ashes yield in time to younger masons. Love sees the domes and spires of God's dream rise again.

1:2 [d]Ps 6:6 [e]Jer 3:1 [f]Jer 4:30; Mic 7:5 [g]ver 16

2 Bitterly she weeps[d] at night,
tears are upon her cheeks.
Among all her lovers[e]
there is none to comfort her.
All her friends have betrayed[f] her;
they have become her enemies.[g]

1:3 [h]Jer 13:19 [i]Dt 28:65

3 After affliction and harsh labor,
Judah has gone into exile.[h]
She dwells among the nations;
she finds no resting place.[i]
All who pursue her have overtaken her
in the midst of her distress.

1:4 [j]Jer 9:11 [k]Joel 1:8-13

4 The roads to Zion mourn,
for no one comes to her appointed feasts.
All her gateways are desolate,[j]
her priests groan,
her maidens grieve,
and she is in bitter anguish.[k]

1:5 [l]Jer 30:15 [m]Jer 39:9; 52:28-30

5 Her foes have become her masters;
her enemies are at ease.
The LORD has brought her grief[l]
because of her many sins.
Her children have gone into exile,[m]
captive before the foe.

1:6 [n]Jer 13:18

6 All the splendor has departed
from the Daughter of Zion.[n]
Her princes are like deer
that find no pasture;
in weakness they have fled
before the pursuer.

1:7 [o]Jer 37:7; La 4:17

7 In the days of her affliction and wandering
Jerusalem remembers all the treasures
that were hers in days of old.
When her people fell into enemy hands,
there was no one to help her.[o]
Her enemies looked at her
and laughed at her destruction.

1:8 [p]ver 20; Isa 59:2-13 [q]Jer 13:22,26 [r]ver 21,22

8 Jerusalem has sinned[p] greatly
and so has become unclean.
All who honored her despise her,
for they have seen her nakedness;[q]
she herself groans[r]
and turns away.

1:9 [s]Dt 32:28-29; Isa 47:7; Eze 24:13 [t]Jer 13:18 [u]Ecc 4:1; Jer 16:7 [v]Ps 25:18

9 Her filthiness clung to her skirts;
she did not consider her future.[s]
Her fall[t] was astounding;
there was none to comfort[u] her.
"Look, O LORD, on my affliction,[v]
for the enemy has triumphed."

1:10 [w]Isa 64:11 [x]Ps 74:7-8; Jer 51:51 [y]Dt 23:3

10 The enemy laid hands
on all her treasures;[w]
she saw pagan nations
enter her sanctuary[x]—
those you had forbidden[y]
to enter your assembly.

1:11 [z]Ps 38:8 [a]Jer 52:6

11 All her people groan[z]
as they search for bread;[a]
they barter their treasures for food
to keep themselves alive.
"Look, O LORD, and consider,
for I am despised."

1:12 [b]Jer 18:16 [c]ver 18 [d]Isa 13:13; Jer 30:24

12 "Is it nothing to you, all you who pass by?[b]
Look around and see.
Is any suffering like my suffering[c]
that was inflicted on me,
that the LORD brought on me
in the day of his fierce anger?[d]

1:13 [e]Job 30:30 [f]Jer 44:6 [g]Hab 3:16

13 "From on high he sent fire,
sent it down into my bones.[e]
He spread a net for my feet
and turned me back.
He made me desolate,[f]
faint[g] all the day long.

1:14 [h]Dt 28:48; Isa 47:6

14 "My sins have been bound into a yoke[b];[h]
by his hands they were woven together.
They have come upon my neck

[a]This chapter is an acrostic poem, the verses of which begin with the successive letters of the Hebrew alphabet. [b]*14* Most Hebrew manuscripts; Septuagint *He kept watch over my sins*

and the Lord has sapped my
strength.
He has handed me over[i]
to those I cannot withstand.

15 "The Lord has rejected
all the warriors in my midst;[j]
he has summoned an army[k] against
me
to[a] crush my young men.[l]
In his winepress the Lord has
trampled
the Virgin Daughter of Judah.

16 "This is why I weep
and my eyes overflow with tears.[m]
No one is near to comfort[n] me,
no one to restore my spirit.
My children are destitute
because the enemy has prevailed."[o]

17 Zion stretches out her hands,[p]
but there is no one to comfort her.
The LORD has decreed for Jacob
that his neighbors become his
foes;
Jerusalem has become
an unclean thing among them.

18 "The LORD is righteous,
yet I rebelled[q] against his
command.
Listen, all you peoples;
look upon my suffering.[r]
My young men and maidens
have gone into exile.[s]

19 "I called to my allies
but they betrayed me.
My priests and my elders
perished[t] in the city
while they searched for food
to keep themselves alive.

20 "See, O LORD, how distressed[u] I am!
I am in torment[v] within,
and in my heart I am disturbed,
for I have been most rebellious.
Outside, the sword bereaves;
inside, there is only death.[w]

21 "People have heard my groaning,[x]
but there is no one to comfort
me.[y]
All my enemies have heard of my
distress;
they rejoice[z] at what you have
done.
May you bring the day[a] you have
announced
so they may become like me.

22 "Let all their wickedness come before
you;
deal with them
as you have dealt with me
because of all my sins.[b]
My groans are many
and my heart is faint."

2 [b]How the Lord has covered the
Daughter of Zion
with the cloud of his anger[c]![c]
He has hurled down the splendor of
Israel
from heaven to earth;
he has not remembered his
footstool[d]
in the day of his anger.

2 Without pity[e] the Lord has
swallowed[f] up
all the dwellings of Jacob;
in his wrath he has torn down
the strongholds[g] of the Daughter
of Judah.
He has brought her kingdom and its
princes
down to the ground[h] in dishonor.

3 In fierce anger he has cut off
every horn[d][i] of Israel.
He has withdrawn his right hand[j]
at the approach of the enemy.
He has burned in Jacob like a
flaming fire
that consumes everything around
it.[k]

4 Like an enemy he has strung his
bow;[l]
his right hand is ready.
Like a foe he has slain
all who were pleasing to the eye;[m]
he has poured out his wrath like fire[n]
on the tent of the Daughter of
Zion.

5 The Lord is like an enemy;[o]
he has swallowed up Israel.
He has swallowed up all her palaces
and destroyed her strongholds.[p]
He has multiplied mourning and
lamentation
for the Daughter of Judah.[q]

1:14 [i]Jer 32:5
1:15 [j]Jer 37:10 [k]Isa 41:2 [l]Isa 28:18; Jer 18:21
1:16 [m]La 2:11,18; 3:48-49 [n]Ps 69:20; Ecc 4:1 [o]ver 2; Jer 13:17; 14:17
1:17 [p]Jer 4:31
1:18 [q]1Sa 12:14 [r]ver 12 [s]Dt 28:32,41
1:19 [t]Jer 14:15; La 2:20
1:20 [u]Jer 4:19 [v]La 2:11 [w]Dt 32:25; Eze 7:15
1:21 [x]ver 8 [y]ver 4 [z]La 2:15 [a]Isa 47:11; Jer 30:16
1:22 [b]Ne 4:5
2:1 [c]La 3:44 [d]Ps 99:5; 132:7
2:2 [e]La 3:43 [f]Ps 21:9 [g]Ps 89:39-40; Mic 5:11 [h]Isa 25:12
2:3 [i]Ps 75:5,10 [j]Ps 74:11 [k]Isa 42:25; Jer 21:4-5,14
2:4 [l]Job 16:13; La 3:12-13 [m]Eze 24:16,25 [n]Isa 42:25; Jer 7:20
2:5 [o]Jer 30:14 [p]ver 2 [q]Jer 9:17-20

[a]*15* Or *has set a time for me / when he will*
[b]This chapter is an acrostic poem, the verses of which begin with the successive letters of the Hebrew alphabet. [c]*1* Or *How the Lord in his anger / has treated the Daughter of Zion with contempt* [d]*3* Or */ all the strength*; or *every king*; *horn* here symbolizes strength.

6 He has laid waste his dwelling like a
garden;
he has destroyed his place of
meeting.[r]
The LORD has made Zion forget
her appointed feasts and her
Sabbaths;[s]
in his fierce anger he has spurned
both king and priest.[t]

2:6 [r]Jer 52:13 [s]La 1:4; Zep 3:18 [t]La 4:16

7 The Lord has rejected his altar
and abandoned his sanctuary.
He has handed over to the enemy
the walls of her palaces;[u]
they have raised a shout in the house
of the LORD
as on the day of an appointed
feast.

2:7 [u]Ps 74:7-8; Isa 64:11; Jer 33:4-5

8 The LORD determined to tear down
the wall around the Daughter of
Zion.
He stretched out a measuring line[v]
and did not withhold his hand
from destroying.
He made ramparts and walls lament;
together they wasted away.[w]

2:8 [v]2Ki 21:13; Isa 34:11 [w]Isa 3:26

9 Her gates[x] have sunk into the
ground;
their bars he has broken and
destroyed.
Her king and her princes are exiled[y]
among the nations,
the law[z] is no more,
and her prophets no longer find
visions[a] from the LORD.

2:9 [x]Ne 1:3 [y]Dt 28:36; 2Ki 24:15 [z]2Ch 15:3 [a]Jer 14:14

10 The elders of the Daughter of Zion
sit on the ground in silence;
they have sprinkled dust on their
heads[b]
and put on sackcloth.[c]
The young women of Jerusalem
have bowed their heads to the
ground.[d]

2:10 [b]Job 2:12 [c]Isa 15:3 [d]Job 2:13; Isa 3:26

11 My eyes fail from weeping,[e]
I am in torment within,[f]
my heart is poured out[g] on the
ground
because my people are destroyed,
because children and infants faint[h]
in the streets of the city.

2:11 [e]La 1:16; 3:48-51 [f]La 1:20 [g]ver 19; Ps 22:14 [h]La 4:4

12 They say to their mothers,
"Where is bread and wine?"
as they faint like wounded men
in the streets of the city,
as their lives ebb away
in their mothers' arms.[i]

2:12 [i]La 4:4

13 What can I say for you?
With what can I compare you,
O Daughter of Jerusalem?
To what can I liken you,
that I may comfort you,
O Virgin Daughter of Zion?[j]
Your wound is as deep as the sea.[k]
Who can heal you?

2:13 [j]Isa 37:22 [k]Jer 14:17; La 1:12

14 The visions of your prophets
were false and worthless;
they did not expose your sin
to ward off your captivity.[l]
The oracles they gave you
were false and misleading.[m]

2:14 [l]Isa 58:1 [m]Jer 2:8; 23:25-32, 33-40; 29:9; Eze 13:3; 22:28

15 All who pass your way
clap their hands at you;[n]
they scoff[o] and shake their heads
at the Daughter of Jerusalem:
"Is this the city that was called
the perfection of beauty,[p]
the joy of the whole earth?"[q]

2:15 [n]Eze 25:6 [o]Jer 19:8 [p]Ps 50:2 [q]Ps 48:2

16 All your enemies open their mouths
wide against you;[r]
they scoff and gnash their teeth[s]
and say, "We have swallowed her
up.[t]
This is the day we have waited for;
we have lived to see it."

2:16 [r]Ps 56:2; La 3:46 [s]Job 16:9 [t]Ps 35:25

17 The LORD has done what he
planned;
he has fulfilled his word,
which he decreed long ago.[u]
He has overthrown you without
pity,[v]
he has let the enemy gloat over
you,
he has exalted the horn[a] of your
foes.[w]

2:17 [u]Dt 28:15-45 [v]ver 2; Eze 5:11 [w]Ps 89:42

18 The hearts of the people
cry out to the Lord.[x]
O wall of the Daughter of Zion,
let your tears[y] flow like a river
day and night;[z]
give yourself no relief,
your eyes no rest.[a]

2:18 [x]Ps 119:145 [y]La 1:16 [z]Jer 9:1 [a]La 3:49

19 Arise, cry out in the night,
as the watches of the night begin;
pour out your heart[b] like water
in the presence of the Lord.[c]
Lift up your hands to him
for the lives of your children,
who faint[d] from hunger
at the head of every street.

2:19 [b]1Sa 1:15; Ps 62:8 [c]Isa 26:9 [d]Isa 51:20

[a] *17 Horn* here symbolizes strength.

20 "Look, O LORD, and consider:
Whom have you ever treated like this?
Should women eat their offspring,[e]
the children they have cared for?[f]
Should priest and prophet be killed[g]
in the sanctuary of the Lord?

2:20
[e]Dt 28:53; Jer 19:9
[f]La 4:10
[g]Ps 78:64; Jer 14:15

21 "Young and old lie together
in the dust of the streets;
my young men and maidens
have fallen by the sword.[h]
You have slain them in the day of your anger;
you have slaughtered them without pity.[i]

2:21
[h]2Ch 36:17; Ps 78:62-63; Jer 6:11
[i]Jer 13:14; La 3:43; Zec 11:6

22 "As you summon to a feast day,
so you summoned against me terrors[j] on every side.
In the day of the LORD's anger
no one escaped or survived;
those I cared for and reared,[k]
my enemy has destroyed."

2:22
[j]Ps 31:13; Jer 6:25
[k]Hos 9:13

3 [a] I am the man who has seen affliction
by the rod of his wrath.[l]

3:1
[l]Job 19:21; Ps 88:7

2 He has driven me away and made me walk
in darkness[m] rather than light;

3:2
[m]Jer 4:23

3 indeed, he has turned his hand against me[n]
again and again, all day long.

3:3
[n]Isa 5:25

4 He has made my skin and my flesh grow old
and has broken my bones.[o]

3:4
[o]Ps 51:8; Isa 38:13; Jer 50:17

5 He has besieged me and surrounded me
with bitterness[p] and hardship.[q]

3:5
[p]ver 19
[q]Jer 23:15

6 He has made me dwell in darkness
like those long dead.[r]

3:6
[r]Ps 88:5-6

7 He has walled me in so I cannot escape;[s]
he has weighed me down with chains.[t]

3:7
[s]Job 3:23
[t]Jer 40:4

8 Even when I call out or cry for help,
he shuts out my prayer.[u]

3:8
[u]Job 30:20; Ps 22:2

9 He has barred my way with blocks of stone;
he has made my paths crooked.[v]

3:9
[v]Isa 63:17; Hos 2:6

10 Like a bear lying in wait,
like a lion in hiding,
11 he dragged me from the path and mangled[w] me
and left me without help.

3:11
[w]Hos 6:1

12 He drew his bow[x]
and made me the target[y] for his arrows.[z]

3:12
[x]La 2:4
[y]Job 7:20
[z]Ps 7:12-13; 38:2

13 He pierced my heart
with arrows from his quiver.[a]

3:13
[a]Job 6:4

14 I became the laughingstock[b] of all my people;
they mock me in song[c] all day long.

3:14
[b]Jer 20:7
[c]Job 30:9

15 He has filled me with bitter herbs
and sated me with gall.[d]

3:15
[d]Jer 9:15

16 He has broken my teeth with gravel;[e]
he has trampled me in the dust.

3:16
[e]Pr 20:17

17 I have been deprived of peace;
I have forgotten what prosperity is.
18 So I say, "My splendor is gone
and all that I had hoped from the LORD."[f]

3:18
[f]Job 17:15

19 I remember my affliction and my wandering,
the bitterness and the gall.
20 I well remember them,
and my soul is downcast[g] within me.[h]

3:20
[g]Ps 42:5
[h]Ps 42:11

21 Yet this I call to mind
and therefore I have hope:

22 Because of the LORD's great love we are not consumed,
for his compassions never fail.[i]

3:22
[i]Ps 78:38; Mal 3:6

23 They are new every morning;
great is your faithfulness.[j]

3:23
[j]Zep 3:5

FAITHFULNESS

THE VIRTUE OF PERSEVERANCE

Lamentations 3:23

"Great is your faithfulness" is the testimony of all who have borne the faith in pain and triumph. Need is the master of our music. Our faith is to be greater than our hurt.

24 I say to myself, "The LORD is my portion;[k]
therefore I will wait for him."

3:24
[k]Ps 16:5

25 The LORD is good to those whose hope is in him,
to the one who seeks him;[l]

3:25
[l]Isa 25:9; 30:18

26 it is good to wait quietly
for the salvation of the LORD.[m]

3:26
[m]Ps 37:7; 40:1

27 It is good for a man to bear the yoke
while he is young.

[a]This chapter is an acrostic poem; the verses of each stanza begin with the successive letters of the Hebrew alphabet, and the verses within each stanza begin with the same letter.

3:28 [n]Jer 15:17
28 Let him sit alone in silence,[n]
for the LORD has laid it on him.
29 Let him bury his face in the dust—
3:29 [o]Jer 31:17
there may yet be hope.[o]
30 Let him offer his cheek to one who
3:30 [p]Job 16:10; Isa 50:6
would strike him,[p]
and let him be filled with disgrace.

3:31 [q]Ps 94:14; Isa 54:7
31 For men are not cast off
by the Lord forever.[q]
32 Though he brings grief, he will show
compassion,
3:32 [r]Ps 78:38; Hos 11:8
so great is his unfailing love.[r]
33 For he does not willingly bring
affliction
3:33 [s]Eze 33:11
or grief to the children of men.[s]

34 To crush underfoot
all prisoners in the land,
35 to deny a man his rights
before the Most High,
36 to deprive a man of justice—
3:36 [t]Jer 22:3; Hab 1:13
would not the Lord see such
things?[t]

DAY 5 FIVE

▸ FAITHFULNESS AND ITS PLACE IN MY PERSONAL WORSHIP

Lamentations 3:22–24

This facet of our no-compromise faithfulness could hardly be said better than when it is said in Thomas Obediah Chisholm's great hymn that expresses God's faithfulness to us: "Great Is Thy Faithfulness."

Chisholm's inspired words are drawn directly from Scripture. This passage in Lamentations provides the thoughts that we now sing:

Because of the LORD's great love we are
not consumed,
for his compassions never fail.
They are new every morning;
great is your faithfulness.
(3:22–23)

Indeed, God is faithful. And when we have been faithful, he will constantly supply his protection and his blessing, and they will arrive regularly with each new sunrise.

To begin a study on the topic of Faithfulness: No Compromise, turn to the home page on page 898.

37 Who can speak and have it happen
3:37 [u]Ps 33:9-11
if the Lord has not decreed it?[u]
38 Is it not from the mouth of the Most
High
that both calamities and good
3:38 [v]Job 2:10; Isa 45:7; Jer 32:42
things come?[v]
39 Why should any living man
complain
3:39 [w]Jer 30:15; Mic 7:9
when punished for his sins?[w]
40 Let us examine our ways and test
3:40 [x]2Co 13:5 [y]Ps 119:59; 139:23-24
them,[x]
and let us return to the LORD.[y]
41 Let us lift up our hearts and our
hands
3:41 [z]Ps 25:1; 28:2
to God in heaven,[z] and say:
42 "We have sinned and rebelled[a]
3:42 [a]Da 9:5 [b]Jer 5:7-9
and you have not forgiven.[b]
43 "You have covered yourself with
anger and pursued us;
3:43 [c]La 2:2,17,21
you have slain without pity.[c]
44 You have covered yourself with a
3:44 [d]Ps 97:2 [e]ver 8
cloud[d]
so that no prayer[e] can get
through.
3:45 [f]1Co 4:13
45 You have made us scum[f] and refuse
among the nations.
46 "All our enemies have opened their
mouths
3:46 [g]La 2:16
wide against us.[g]
47 We have suffered terror and pitfalls,[h]
3:47 [h]Jer 48:43 [i]Isa 24:17-18; 51:19
ruin and destruction.[i]
48 Streams of tears flow from my eyes[j]
3:48 [j]La 1:16 [k]La 2:11
because my people are destroyed.[k]
49 My eyes will flow unceasingly,
without relief,[l]
3:49 [l]Jer 14:17
50 until the LORD looks down
3:50 [m]Isa 63:15
from heaven and sees.[m]
51 What I see brings grief to my soul
because of all the women of my
city.

52 Those who were my enemies
without cause
3:52 [n]Ps 35:7
hunted me like a bird.[n]
53 They tried to end my life in a pit[o]
3:53 [o]Jer 37:16
and threw stones at me;
54 the waters closed over my head,[p]
3:54 [p]Ps 69:2; Jnh 2:3-5
and I thought I was about to be
cut off.

55 I called on your name, O LORD,
3:55 [q]Ps 130:1; Jnh 2:2
from the depths of the pit.[q]
56 You heard my plea:[r] "Do not close
3:56 [r]Ps 55:1
your ears
to my cry for relief."
57 You came near when I called you,
3:57 [s]Isa 41:10
and you said, "Do not fear."[s]

3:58 [t]Jer 51:36 [u]Ps 34:22; Jer 50:34
3:59 [v]Jer 18:19-20

58 O Lord, you took up my case;[t]
you redeemed my life.[u]
59 You have seen, O LORD, the wrong
done to me.[v]
Uphold my cause!

DAY 4 FOUR

▸ Joy and My Service to Others

Lamentations 3:55–57

Let us examine, phrase by phrase, this brief excerpt from Jeremiah's weeping lamentation. From this passage, we see how our endurance may be resolved at last in joy, and we may better understand how to serve others in their times of despair.

"I called on your name, O LORD." This is the only wise thing to do in times of unbearable hurt. There is no other name that saves.

"From the depths of the pit." Despair is a megaphone in the hand of prayer. It amplifies all that we feel and makes it all the more audible in the courts of heaven. When we feel that we are in the pit or when we see others in that pit, our response should be prayer—earnest and heart-felt.

"You heard my plea." What the weeping heart whispers enters heaven as a shout.

"Do not close your ears to my cry for relief." God listens for the sobbing of his children. He hears their laughter, and he smiles. He hears their petitions, and he is thoughtful. But when he hears their sobbing, he orders the angels to be silent, so that all of heaven may listen and respond.

"You came near when I called you." One call to our heavenly Father and the gap is bridged. The pit is no longer so deep. Heaven gives up its cosmic address; the throne of God becomes an armchair of warm relief; and God—once starry galaxies away—now lives on our block.

"And you said, 'Do not fear.'" It is time for joy! God hears our calls.

These verses are wonderful to memorize so that when others need assurance or comfort, we are ready with an encouraging promise from God. Our own joy is magnified when we share that joy with others.

To begin a study on the topic of Joy, the Reward of Endurance, turn to the home page on page 581.

60 You have seen the depth of their
vengeance,
all their plots against me.[w] 3:60 [w]Jer 11:20; 18:18
61 O LORD, you have heard their
insults,
all their plots against me—
62 what my enemies whisper and
mutter
against me all day long.[x] 3:62 [x]Eze 36:3
63 Look at them! Sitting or standing,
they mock me in their songs.
64 Pay them back what they deserve,
O LORD,
for what their hands have done.[y] 3:64 [y]Ps 28:4
65 Put a veil over their hearts,[z]
and may your curse be on them! 3:65 [z]Isa 6:10
66 Pursue them in anger and destroy
them
from under the heavens of the
LORD.

4 [a] How the gold has lost its luster,
the fine gold become dull!
The sacred gems are scattered
at the head of every street.[a] 4:1 [a]Eze 7:19

2 How the precious sons of Zion,
once worth their weight in gold,
are now considered as pots of clay,
the work of a potter's hands!

3 Even jackals offer their breasts
to nurse their young,
but my people have become heartless 4:3 [b]Job 39:16
like ostriches in the desert.[b]
4 Because of thirst the infant's tongue 4:4 [c]Ps 22:15 [d]La 2:11,12
sticks to the roof of its mouth;[c]
the children beg for bread,
but no one gives it to them.[d]
5 Those who once ate delicacies
are destitute in the streets.
Those nurtured in purple[e] 4:5 [e]Jer 6:2 [f]Am 6:3-7
now lie on ash heaps.[f]
6 The punishment of my people
is greater than that of Sodom,[g] 4:6 [g]Ge 19:25
which was overthrown in a moment
without a hand turned to help her.
7 Their princes were brighter than
snow
and whiter than milk,
their bodies more ruddy than rubies,
their appearance like sapphires.[b]

[a]This chapter is an acrostic poem, the verses of which begin with the successive letters of the Hebrew alphabet. [b]7 Or *lapis lazuli*

[8]But now they are blacker[h] than soot;
they are not recognized in the streets.
Their skin has shriveled on their bones;[i]
it has become as dry as a stick.

[9]Those killed by the sword are better off
than those who die of famine;
racked with hunger, they waste away
for lack of food from the field.[j]

[10]With their own hands
compassionate women
have cooked their own children,[k]
who became their food
when my people were destroyed.

[11]The LORD has given full vent to his wrath;
he has poured out his fierce anger.
He kindled a fire[l] in Zion
that consumed her foundations.[m]

[12]The kings of the earth did not believe,
nor did any of the world's people,
that enemies and foes could enter
the gates of Jerusalem.[n]

[13]But it happened because of the sins of her prophets
and the iniquities of her priests,[o]
who shed within her
the blood of the righteous.

[14]Now they grope through the streets
like men who are blind.[p]
They are so defiled with blood[q]
that no one dares to touch their garments.

[15]"Go away! You are unclean!" men cry to them.
"Away! Away! Don't touch us!"
When they flee and wander about,
people among the nations say,
"They can stay here no longer."[r]

[16]The LORD himself has scattered them;
he no longer watches over them.[s]
The priests are shown no honor,
the elders[t] no favor.

[17]Moreover, our eyes failed,
looking in vain[u] for help;[v]
from our towers we watched
for a nation[w] that could not save us.

[18]Men stalked us at every step,
so we could not walk in our streets.
Our end was near, our days were numbered,
for our end had come.[x]

[19]Our pursuers were swifter
than eagles[y] in the sky;
they chased us[z] over the mountains
and lay in wait for us in the desert.

[20]The LORD's anointed,[a] our very life breath,
was caught in their traps.[b]
We thought that under his shadow
we would live among the nations.

[21]Rejoice and be glad, O Daughter of Edom,
you who live in the land of Uz.
But to you also the cup[c] will be passed;
you will be drunk and stripped naked.[d]

[22]O Daughter of Zion, your punishment will end;[e]
he will not prolong your exile.
But, O Daughter of Edom, he will punish your sin
and expose your wickedness.[f]

5 Remember, O LORD, what has happened to us;
look, and see our disgrace.[g]
[2]Our inheritance[h] has been turned over to aliens,
our homes[i] to foreigners.
[3]We have become orphans and fatherless,
our mothers like widows.[j]
[4]We must buy the water we drink;
our wood can be had only at a price.[k]
[5]Those who pursue us are at our heels;
we are weary[l] and find no rest.
[6]We submitted to Egypt and Assyria[m]
to get enough bread.
[7]Our fathers sinned and are no more,
and we bear their punishment.[n]
[8]Slaves[o] rule over us,
and there is none to free us from their hands.[p]
[9]We get our bread at the risk of our lives
because of the sword in the desert.
[10]Our skin is hot as an oven,

4:8 [h]Job 30:28 [i]Ps 102:3-5
4:9 [j]Jer 15:2; 16:4
4:10 [k]Lev 26:29; Dt 28:53-57; Jer 19:9; La 2:20; Eze 5:10
4:11 [l]Jer 17:27 [m]Dt 32:22; Jer 7:20; Eze 22:31
4:12 [n]1Ki 9:9; Jer 21:13
4:13 [o]Jer 5:31; 6:13; Eze 22:28; Mic 3:11
4:14 [p]Isa 59:10 [q]Jer 2:34; 19:4
4:15 [r]Lev 13:46
4:16 [s]Isa 9:14-16 [t]La 5:12
4:17 [u]Isa 20:5; Eze 29:16 [v]La 1:7 [w]Jer 37:7
4:18 [x]Eze 7:2-12; Am 8:2
4:19 [y]Dt 28:49 [z]Isa 5:26-28
4:20 [a]2Sa 19:21 [b]Jer 39:5; Eze 12:12-13; 19:4,8
4:21 [c]Jer 25:15 [d]Isa 34:6-10; Am 1:11-12; Ob 1:16
4:22 [e]Isa 40:2; Jer 33:8 [f]Ps 137:7; Mal 1:4
5:1 [g]Ps 44:13-16; 89:50
5:2 [h]Ps 79:1 [i]Zep 1:13
5:3 [j]Jer 15:8; 18:21
5:4 [k]Isa 3:1
5:5 [l]Ne 9:37
5:6 [m]Hos 9:3
5:7 [n]Jer 14:20; 16:12
5:8 [o]Ne 5:15 [p]Zec 11:6

5:10 [q]La 4:8-9
5:11 [r]Zec 14:2
5:12 [s]La 4:16

feverish from hunger.[q]
11 Women have been ravished[r] in Zion,
and virgins in the towns of Judah.
12 Princes have been hung up by their
hands;
elders are shown no respect.[s]
13 Young men toil at the millstones;
boys stagger under loads of wood.
14 The elders are gone from the city
gate;
the young men have stopped their
music.[t]
15 Joy is gone from our hearts;
our dancing has turned to
mourning.[u]
16 The crown[v] has fallen from our head.
Woe to us, for we have sinned![w]
17 Because of this our hearts[x] are faint,
because of these things our eyes[y]
grow dim
18 for Mount Zion, which lies
desolate,[z]
with jackals prowling over it.

19 You, O LORD, reign forever;
your throne endures[a] from
generation to generation.
20 Why do you always forget us?[b]
Why do you forsake us so long?
21 Restore[c] us to yourself, O LORD,
that we may return;
renew our days as of old
22 unless you have utterly rejected us
and are angry with us beyond
measure.[d]

5:14 [t]Isa 24:8; Jer 7:34
5:15 [u]Jer 25:10
5:16 [v]Ps 89:39 [w]Isa 3:11
5:17 [x]Isa 1:5 [y]Ps 6:7
5:18 [z]Mic 3:12
5:19 [a]Ps 45:6; 102:12,24-27
5:20 [b]Ps 13:1; 44:24
5:21 [c]Ps 80:3
5:22 [d]Isa 64:9

JOY

A Mourning Song Becomes a Morning Song

Lamentations 5:15

After the siege of Jerusalem, there was little joy to be found in the ashes of the once proud city. Only the psalmist can counsel such desolation: "Weeping may remain for a night, but rejoicing comes in the morning" (Psalm 30:5).

EZEKIEL

Authorship and Date

Ezekiel

571 B.C., the year of his last dated oracle, or shortly thereafter

Key Themes

The book of Ezekiel deals with sin, judgment and restoration. What was said of Jeremiah regarding faithfulness might also be said of Ezekiel. He was faithful, first as a priest in Jerusalem and later as a street preacher in Babylon. He was often called to prophesy through extreme illustrations (lying on his side for 430 days or showing no emotion when his wife died). Ezekiel faithfully preached hope—hope that would follow judgment. And his great message of God's ultimate deliverance haunts the words of Ezekiel 36:25–26: "I will cleanse you from all your impurities and from all your idols. I will give you a new heart and put a new spirit in you; I will remove from you your heart of stone and give you a heart of flesh."

Fruit of the Spirit in Ezekiel

Love: Ezekiel's best-known metaphor of love is his shepherd illustration. Condemning the false shepherds who had used the sheep by abusing them, he cried: "Woe to the shepherds of Israel who only take care of themselves! Should not shepherds take care of the flock?" (34:2). But God would demonstrate his love for the sheep, and his pure love would be the ensign of his care: "For this is what the Sovereign LORD says: I myself will search for my sheep and look after them" (v. 11). God is the Good Shepherd. His sheep know him, see his care for them and know he is love divine.

Goodness: We begin to lose our goodness when we willfully disobey the commandments. God pointed this out: "But the children rebelled against me: They did not follow my decrees, they were not careful to keep my laws—although the man who obeys them will live by them—and they desecrated my Sabbaths" (20:21). The loss of goodness inevitably results in depravity, and depravity results in judgment.

Self-Control: Israel was to practice self-control. God instructed Ezekiel to say to the Israelites: "This is what the Sovereign LORD says: Will you defile yourselves the way your fathers did and lust after their vile images?" (20:30). The point of the challenge is obvious. The more we allow unbridled lust in our lives, the more we become impervious to the purposes of God. Whether the lust is a sexual desire or a hankering after idols, we name our love for God as insignificant the moment we allow our lust to transcend our love. Self-control is the mandate of all those who would love rather than lust.

The Living Creatures and the Glory of the LORD

1 In the[a] thirtieth year, in the fourth
month on the fifth day, while I was
among the exiles[a] by the Kebar River,
the heavens were opened[b] and I saw visions[c] of God.
2On the fifth of the month—it was
the fifth year of the exile of King Je-

1:1 [a]Eze 11:24-25 [b]Mt 3:16; Ac 7:56 [c]Ex 24:10

DAY 2 TWO

JOY AND THE PURPOSE OF GOD IN MY LIFE

Ezekiel 1:4–28

Ezekiel saw a windstorm, a cloud flashing with lightning, the sky afire like glowing metal, and then four creatures, each with four faces and four wings (see 1:4–6). Ezekiel saw these four creatures flying in the midst of fire. The creatures sped back and forth like lightning in the sky and the fire moved back and forth between the creatures (see vv. 11–14).

Ezekiel saw a wheel a turning,
Way in the middle of the air,
A wheel within a wheel a-turning,
Way in the middle of the air,
And the little wheel turned by faith,
And the big wheel turned
By the grace of God.

This is the account of a Picasso-type religious experience. Ezekiel didn't see the kingdom of God like everyone else did. But when he did see it, it came to him in vivid impressions that told him that his Lord was no pastel God. This was not a Rembrandt-style God who liked umbers and ochers. This was a God who could combine stripes, prints, plaids and neon colors in such a way that he colored the earth with indescribable joy.

But best of all, when this God of the wild palette spoke, there was work to be done. Ezekiel received his purpose, wrote down his color-clashing visions and went off to do his work. Joy speaks to us in all kinds of ways—in ways as unique to each of us as his purposes are different for every believer.

To begin a study on the topic of Joy, Focusing on a Higher Reality, turn to the home page on page 413.

hoiachin[d]— 3the word of the LORD
came to Ezekiel the priest, the son of
Buzi,[b] by the Kebar River in the land of
the Babylonians.[c] There the hand of the
LORD was upon him.[e]
4I looked, and I saw a windstorm
coming out of the north[f]—an immense
cloud with flashing lightning and surrounded by brilliant light. The center of
the fire looked like glowing metal,[g] 5and
in the fire was what looked like four living creatures.[h] In appearance their form
was that of a man,[i] 6but each of them
had four faces[j] and four wings. 7Their
legs were straight; their feet were like
those of a calf and gleamed like burnished bronze.[k] 8Under their wings on
their four sides they had the hands of
a man.[l] All four of them had faces and
wings, 9and their wings touched one
another. Each one went straight ahead;
they did not turn as they moved.[m]
10Their faces looked like this: Each
of the four had the face of a man, and
on the right side each had the face of
a lion, and on the left the face of an
ox; each also had the face of an eagle.[n]
11Such were their faces. Their wings
were spread out upward; each had two
wings,[o] one touching the wing of another creature on either side, and two
wings covering its body. 12Each one
went straight ahead. Wherever the spirit would go, they would go, without
turning as they went. 13The appearance
of the living creatures was like burning
coals of fire or like torches. Fire moved
back and forth among the creatures; it
was bright, and lightning[p] flashed out
of it. 14The creatures sped back and
forth like flashes of lightning.[q]
15As I looked at the living creatures,
I saw a wheel on the ground beside
each creature with its four faces. 16This
was the appearance and structure of the
wheels: They sparkled like chrysolite,[r]
and all four looked alike. Each appeared
to be made like a wheel intersecting a
wheel. 17As they moved, they would go
in any one of the four directions the
creatures faced; the wheels did not turn[s]
about[d] as the creatures went. 18Their
rims were high and awesome, and all
four rims were full of eyes[t] all around.
19When the living creatures moved,

[a]*1* Or ⌞*my*⌟ [b]*3* Or *Ezekiel son of Buzi the priest* [c]*3* Or *Chaldeans* [d]*17* Or *aside*

1:2 [d]2Ki 24:15
1:3 [e]2Ki 3:15; Eze 3:14,22
1:4 [f]Jer 1:14 [g]Eze 8:2
1:5 [h]Rev 4:6 [i]ver 26
1:6 [j]Eze 10:14
1:7 [k]Da 10:6; Rev 1:15
1:8 [l]Eze 10:8
1:9 [m]Eze 10:22
1:10 [n]Eze 10:14; Rev 4:7
1:11 [o]Isa 6:2
1:13 [p]Rev 4:5
1:14 [q]Ps 29:7
1:16 [r]Eze 10:9-11; Da 10:6
1:17 [s]ver 9
1:18 [t]Eze 10:12; Rev 4:6

the wheels beside them moved; and
when the living creatures rose from the
ground, the wheels also rose. 20 Wherever the spirit would go, they would
1:20 [u]ver 12 go,[u] and the wheels would rise along
with them, because the spirit of the living creatures was in the wheels. 21 When
the creatures moved, they also moved;
when the creatures stood still, they also
stood still; and when the creatures rose
from the ground, the wheels rose along
with them, because the spirit of the liv-
1:21 [v]Eze 10:17 ing creatures was in the wheels.[v]
22 Spread out above the heads of the
1:22 [w]Eze 10:1 living creatures was what looked like an
expanse,[w] sparkling like ice, and awe-
some. 23 Under the expanse their wings
were stretched out one toward the other, and each had two wings covering its
body. 24 When the creatures moved, I
heard the sound of their wings, like the
1:24 [x]Eze 10:5; 43:2; Da 10:6; Rev 1:15; 19:6 [y]2Ki 7:6 roar of rushing waters, like the voice[x]
of the Almighty,[a] like the tumult of an
army.[y] When they stood still, they lowered their wings.
25 Then there came a voice from
above the expanse over their heads as
they stood with lowered wings. 26 Above
the expanse over their heads was what
1:26 [z]Ex 24:10; Eze 10:1 [a]Rev 1:13 looked like a throne of sapphire,[b] [z] and
high above on the throne was a figure
like that of a man.[a] 27 I saw that from
what appeared to be his waist up he
looked like glowing metal, as if full
of fire, and that from there down he
1:27 [b]Eze 8:2 looked like fire; and brilliant light surrounded him.[b] 28 Like the appearance of
a rainbow[c] in the clouds on a rainy day,
1:28 [c]Ge 9:13; Rev 10:1 [d]Rev 4:2 [e]Eze 8:4 [f]Eze 3:23; Da 8:17; Rev 1:17 so was the radiance around him.[d]
This was the appearance of the like-
ness of the glory[e] of the LORD. When I
saw it, I fell facedown,[f] and I heard the
voice of one speaking.

Ezekiel's Call

2:1 [g]Da 10:11 **2** He said to me, "Son of man, stand[g]
up on your feet and I will speak to
you." 2 As he spoke, the Spirit came into
2:2 [h]Eze 3:24; Da 8:18 me and raised me[h] to my feet, and I
heard him speaking to me.
3 He said: "Son of man, I am sending
you to the Israelites, to a rebellious nation that has rebelled against me; they
and their fathers have been in revolt
2:3 [i]Jer 3:25; Eze 20:8-24 against me to this very day.[i] 4 The people
to whom I am sending you are obsti-
nate and stubborn.[j] Say to them, 'This
2:4 [j]Eze 3:7 is what the Sovereign LORD says.' 5 And
whether they listen or fail to listen[k]—for 2:5 [k]Eze 3:11 [l]Eze 3:27 [m]Eze 33:33
they are a rebellious house[l]—they will
know that a prophet has been among
them.[m] 6 And you, son of man, do not
be afraid[n] of them or their words. Do 2:6 [n]Jer 1:8,17 [o]Isa 9:18; Mic 7:4 [p]Eze 3:9
not be afraid, though briers and thorns[o]
are all around you and you live among
scorpions. Do not be afraid of what they
say or terrified by them, though they
are a rebellious house.[p] 7 You must speak
my words to them, whether they listen
or fail to listen, for they are rebellious.[q] 2:7 [q]Jer 1:7; Eze 3:10-11
8 But you, son of man, listen to what I
say to you. Do not rebel like that rebel-
lious house;[r] open your mouth and eat[s] 2:8 [r]Isa 50:5 [s]Jer 15:16; Rev 10:9
what I give you."
9 Then I looked, and I saw a hand[t]
stretched out to me. In it was a scroll, 2:9 [t]Eze 8:3
10 which he unrolled before me. On
both sides of it were written words of 2:10 [u]Rev 8:13
lament and mourning and woe.[u]
3 And he said to me, "Son of man,
eat what is before you, eat this
scroll; then go and speak to the house
of Israel." 2 So I opened my mouth, and
he gave me the scroll to eat.

GOODNESS

THE LIFE OF THINGS GOD FAVORS

Ezekiel 3:1

When we internalize God's Word, we can speak it forthrightly. But more than that, we can see the world in all of its relationships.

3 Then he said to me, "Son of man,
eat this scroll I am giving you and fill
your stomach with it." So I ate[v] it, 3:3 [v]Jer 15:16 [w]Ps 19:10; Ps 119:103; Rev 10:9-10
and it tasted as sweet as honey[w] in my
mouth.
4 He then said to me: "Son of man,
go now to the house of Israel and speak
my words to them. 5 You are not being
sent to a people of obscure speech and
difficult language,[x] but to the house 3:5 [x]Isa 28:11; Jnh 1:2
of Israel— 6 not to many peoples of
obscure speech and difficult language,
whose words you cannot understand.
Surely if I had sent you to them, they
would have listened to you.[y] 7 But the 3:6 [y]Mt 11:21-23
house of Israel is not willing to listen to
you because they are not willing to listen to me, for the whole house of Israel
is hardened and obstinate.[z] 8 But I will 3:7 [z]Eze 2:4; Jn 15:20-23
make you as unyielding and hardened

[a]24 Hebrew *Shaddai* [b]26 Or *lapis lazuli*

as they are.[a] 9I will make your forehead like the hardest stone, harder than flint. Do not be afraid of them or terrified by them, though they are a rebellious house.[b]"

10And he said to me, "Son of man, listen carefully and take to heart all the words I speak to you. 11Go now to your countrymen in exile and speak to them. Say to them, 'This is what the Sovereign LORD says,' whether they listen or fail to listen.[c]"

12Then the Spirit lifted me up,[d] and I heard behind me a loud rumbling sound—May the glory of the LORD be praised in his dwelling place!— 13the sound of the wings of the living creatures brushing against each other and the sound of the wheels beside them, a loud rumbling sound.[e] 14The Spirit then lifted me up and took me away, and I went in bitterness and in the anger of my spirit, with the strong hand of the LORD upon me. 15I came to the exiles who lived at Tel Abib near the Kebar River.[f] And there, where they were living, I sat among them for seven days[g]—overwhelmed.

Warning to Israel

16At the end of seven days the word of the LORD came to me:[h] 17"Son of man, I have made you a watchman[i] for the house of Israel; so hear the word I speak and give them warning from me. 18When I say to a wicked man, 'You will surely die,' and you do not warn him or speak out to dissuade him from his evil ways in order to save his life, that wicked man will die for[a] his sin, and I will hold you accountable for his blood.[j] 19But if you do warn the wicked man and he does not turn from his wickedness or from his evil ways, he will die for his sin; but you will have saved yourself.[k]

20"Again, when a righteous man turns from his righteousness and does evil, and I put a stumbling block before him, he will die. Since you did not warn him, he will die for his sin. The righteous things he did will not be remembered, and I will hold you accountable for his blood.[l] 21But if you do warn the righteous man not to sin and he does not sin, he will surely live because he took warning, and you will have saved yourself."[m]

3:8 [a]Jer 1:18
3:9 [b]Isa 50:7; Eze 2:6; Mic 3:8
3:11 [c]Eze 2:4-5,7
3:12 [d]Eze 8:3; Ac 8:39
3:13 [e]Eze 1:24; 10:5,16-17
3:15 [f]Ps 137:1 [g]Job 2:13
3:16 [h]Jer 42:7
3:17 [i]Isa 52:8; Jer 6:17; Eze 33:7-9
3:18 [j]ver 20; Eze 33:6
3:19 [k]2Ki 17:13; Eze 14:14,20; Ac 18:6; 20:26; 1Ti 4:14-16
3:20 [l]Ps 125:5; Eze 18:24; 33:12,18
3:21 [m]Ac 20:31

22The hand of the LORD[n] was upon me there, and he said to me, "Get up and go[o] out to the plain,[p] and there I will speak to you." 23So I got up and went out to the plain. And the glory of the LORD was standing there, like the glory I had seen by the Kebar River,[q] and I fell facedown.[r]

24Then the Spirit came into me and raised me[s] to my feet. He spoke to me and said: "Go, shut yourself inside your house. 25And you, son of man, they will tie with ropes; you will be bound so that you cannot go out among the people.[t] 26I will make your tongue stick to the roof of your mouth so that you will be silent and unable to rebuke them, though they are a rebellious house.[u] 27But when I speak to you, I will open your mouth and you shall say to them, 'This is what the Sovereign LORD says.'[v] Whoever will listen let him listen, and whoever will refuse let him refuse; for they are a rebellious house.[w]

Siege of Jerusalem Symbolized

4 "Now, son of man, take a clay tablet, put it in front of you and draw the city of Jerusalem on it. 2Then lay siege to it: Erect siege works against it, build a ramp[x] up to it, set up camps against it and put battering rams around it.[y] 3Then take an iron pan, place it as an iron wall between you and the city and turn your face toward it. It will be under siege, and you shall besiege it. This will be a sign[z] to the house of Israel.[a]

4"Then lie on your left side and put the sin of the house of Israel upon yourself.[b] You are to bear their sin for the number of days you lie on your side. 5I have assigned you the same number of days as the years of their sin. So for 390 days you will bear the sin of the house of Israel.

6"After you have finished this, lie down again, this time on your right side, and bear the sin of the house of Judah. I have assigned you 40 days, a day for each year.[b] 7Turn your face toward the siege of Jerusalem and with bared arm prophesy against her. 8I will tie you up with ropes so that you cannot turn from one side to the other

[a]*18* Or *in;* also in verses 19 and 20 [b]*4* Or *your side*

3:22 [n]Eze 1:3 [o]Ac 9:6 [p]Eze 8:4
3:23 [q]Eze 1:1 [r]Eze 1:28
3:24 [s]Eze 2:2
3:25 [t]Eze 4:8
3:26 [u]Eze 2:5; 24:27; 33:22
3:27 [v]ver 11 [w]Eze 12:3; 24:27; 33:22
4:2 [x]Jer 6:6 [y]Eze 21:22
4:3 [z]Isa 8:18; 20:3; Eze 12:3-6; 24:24,27 [a]Jer 39:1
4:6 [b]Nu 14:34; Da 9:24-26; 12:11-12

until you have finished the days of your siege.[c]

9"Take wheat and barley, beans and lentils, millet and spelt;[d] put them in a storage jar and use them to make bread for yourself. You are to eat it during the 390 days you lie on your side. 10Weigh out twenty shekels[a] of food to eat each day and eat it at set times. 11Also measure out a sixth of a hin[b] of water and drink it at set times. 12Eat the food as you would a barley cake; bake it in the sight of the people, using human excrement[e] for fuel." 13The LORD said, "In this way the people of Israel will eat defiled food among the nations where I will drive them."[f]

14Then I said, "Not so, Sovereign LORD![g] I have never defiled myself. From my youth until now I have never eaten anything found dead[h] or torn by wild animals. No unclean meat has ever entered my mouth.[i]"

15"Very well," he said, "I will let you bake your bread over cow manure instead of human excrement."

16He then said to me: "Son of man, I will cut off[j] the supply of food in Jerusalem. The people will eat rationed food in anxiety and drink rationed water in despair,[k] 17for food and water will be scarce. They will be appalled at the sight of each other and will waste away because of[c] their sin.[l]

5 "Now, son of man, take a sharp sword and use it as a barber's razor[m] to shave[n] your head and your beard.[o] Then take a set of scales and divide up the hair. 2When the days of your siege come to an end, burn a third of the hair with fire inside the city. Take a third and strike it with the sword all around the city. And scatter a third to the wind. For I will pursue them with drawn sword.[p] 3But take a few strands of hair and tuck them away in the folds of your garment.[q] 4Again, take a few of these and throw them into the fire and burn them up. A fire will spread from there to the whole house of Israel.

5"This is what the Sovereign LORD says: This is Jerusalem, which I have set in the center of the nations, with countries all around her. 6Yet in her wickedness she has rebelled against my laws and decrees more than the nations and countries around her. She has rejected my laws and has not followed my decrees.[r]

4:8 [c]Eze 3:25
4:9 [d]Isa 28:25
4:12 [e]Isa 36:12
4:13 [f]Hos 9:3
4:14 [g]Jer 1:6; Eze 9:8; 20:49 [h]Lev 11:39 [i]Ex 22:31; Dt 14:3; Ac 10:14
4:16 [j]Ps 105:16; Eze 5:16 [k]ver 10-11; Lev 26:26; Isa 3:1; Eze 12:19
4:17 [l]Lev 26:39; Eze 24:23; 33:10
5:1 [m]Isa 7:20 [n]Eze 44:20 [o]Lev 21:5
5:2 [p]ver 12; Lev 26:33
5:3 [q]Jer 39:10

7"Therefore this is what the Sovereign LORD says: You have been more unruly than the nations around you and have not followed my decrees or kept my laws. You have not even[d] conformed to the standards of the nations around you.[s]

8"Therefore this is what the Sovereign LORD says: I myself am against you, Jerusalem, and I will inflict punishment on you in the sight of the nations.[t] 9Because of all your detestable idols, I will do to you what I have never done before and will never do again.[u] 10Therefore in your midst fathers will eat their children, and children will eat their fathers.[v] I will inflict punishment on you and will scatter all your survivors to the winds.[w] 11Therefore as surely as I live, declares the Sovereign LORD, because you have defiled my sanctuary with all your vile images[x] and detestable practices,[y] I myself will withdraw my favor; I will not look on you with pity or spare you.[z] 12A third of your people will die of the plague or perish by famine inside you; a third will fall by the sword outside your walls; and a third I will scatter to the winds and pursue with drawn sword.[a]

13"Then my anger will cease and my wrath[b] against them will subside, and I will be avenged.[c] And when I have spent my wrath upon them, they will know that I the LORD have spoken in my zeal.

14"I will make you a ruin and a reproach among the nations around you, in the sight of all who pass by.[d] 15You will be a reproach and a taunt, a warning and an object of horror to the nations around you when I inflict punishment on you in anger and in wrath and with stinging rebuke.[e] I the LORD have spoken.[f] 16When I shoot at you with my deadly and destructive arrows of famine, I will shoot to destroy you. I will bring more and more famine upon you and cut off your supply of food.[g] 17I will send famine and wild beasts against you, and they will leave you childless. Plague and bloodshed[h] will

[a]*10* That is, about 8 ounces (about 0.2 kilogram)
[b]*11* That is, about 2/3 quart (about 0.6 liter)
[c]*17* Or *away in* [d]*7* Most Hebrew manuscripts; some Hebrew manuscripts and Syriac *You have*

5:6 [r]Jer 11:10; Eze 16:47-51; Zec 7:11
5:7 [s]2Ch 33:9; Jer 2:10-11; Eze 16:47
5:8 [t]Eze 15:7
5:9 [u]Da 9:12; Mt 24:21
5:10 [v]Lev 26:29; La 2:20 [w]Lev 26:33; Ps 44:11; Eze 12:14; Zec 2:6
5:11 [x]Eze 7:20 [y]2Ch 36:14; Eze 8:6 [z]Eze 7:4,9
5:12 [a]ver 2,17; Jer 15:2; 21:9; Eze 6:11-12; 12:14
5:13 [b]Eze 21:17; 36:6 [c]Isa 1:24
5:14 [d]Lev 26:32; Ne 2:17; Ps 74:3-10; 79:1-4
5:15 [e]1Ki 9:7; Jer 22:8-9; 24:9 [f]Eze 25:17
5:16 [g]Dt 32:24
5:17 [h]Eze 38:22

sweep through you, and I will bring the sword against you. I the LORD have spoken.[i]"

5:17 [i]Eze 14:21

A Prophecy Against the Mountains of Israel

6 The word of the LORD came to me: 2"Son of man, set your face against the mountains[j] of Israel; prophesy against them 3and say: 'O mountains of Israel, hear the word of the Sovereign LORD. This is what the Sovereign LORD says to the mountains and hills, to the ravines and valleys:[k] I am about to bring a sword against you, and I will destroy your high places.[l] 4Your altars[m] will be demolished and your incense altars will be smashed; and I will slay your people in front of your idols. 5I will lay the dead bodies of the Israelites in front of their idols, and I will scatter your bones[n] around your altars. 6Wherever you live, the towns will be laid waste and the high places demolished, so that your altars will be laid waste and devastated, your idols[o] smashed and ruined, your incense altars[p] broken down, and what you have made wiped out.[q] 7Your people will fall slain among you, and you will know that I am the LORD.

8"'But I will spare some, for some of you will escape[r] the sword when you are scattered among the lands and nations.[s] 9Then in the nations where they have been carried captive, those who escape will remember me—how I have been grieved[t] by their adulterous hearts, which have turned away from me, and by their eyes, which have lusted after their idols.[u] They will loathe themselves for the evil they have done and for all their detestable practices.[v] 10And they will know that I am the LORD; I did not threaten in vain to bring this calamity on them.

11"'This is what the Sovereign LORD says: Strike your hands together and stamp your feet and cry out "Alas!" because of all the wicked and detestable practices of the house of Israel, for they will fall by the sword, famine and plague.[w] 12He that is far away will die of the plague, and he that is near will fall by the sword, and he that survives and is spared will die of famine. So will I spend my wrath upon them.[x] 13And they will know that I am the LORD, when their people lie slain among their idols around their altars, on every high hill and on all the mountaintops, under every spreading tree and every leafy oak[y]—places where they offered fragrant incense to all their idols.[z] 14And I will stretch out my hand[a] against them and make the land a desolate waste from the desert to Diblah[a]—wherever they live. Then they will know that I am the LORD.[b]'"

6:2 [j]Eze 36:1
6:3 [k]Eze 36:4 [l]Lev 26:30
6:4 [m]2Ch 14:5
6:5 [n]Jer 8:1-2
6:6 [o]Mic 1:7; Zec 13:2 [p]Lev 26:30 [q]Isa 6:11; Eze 5:14
6:8 [r]Jer 44:28 [s]Isa 6:13; Jer 44:14; Eze 12:16; 14:22
6:9 [t]Ps 78:40; Isa 7:13 [u]Eze 20:7,24 [v]Eze 20:43; 36:31
6:11 [w]Eze 5:12; 21:14,17; 25:6
6:12 [x]Eze 5:12
6:13 [y]Isa 57:5 [z]1Ki 14:23; Jer 2:20; Eze 20:28; Hos 4:13
6:14 [a]Isa 5:25 [b]Eze 14:13

The End Has Come

7 The word of the LORD came to me: 2"Son of man, this is what the Sovereign LORD says to the land of Israel: The end![c] The end has come upon the four corners[d] of the land. 3The end is now upon you and I will unleash my anger against you. I will judge you according to your conduct and repay you for all your detestable practices. 4I will not look on you with pity[e] or spare you; I will surely repay you for your conduct and the detestable practices among you. Then you will know that I am the LORD.

5"This is what the Sovereign LORD says: Disaster![f] An unheard-of[b] disaster is coming. 6The end has come! The end has come! It has roused itself against you. It has come! 7Doom has come upon you—you who dwell in the land. The time has come, the day is near;[g] there is panic, not joy, upon the mountains. 8I am about to pour out my wrath[h] on you and spend my anger against you; I will judge you according to your conduct and repay you for all your detestable practices.[i] 9I will not look on you with pity or spare you; I will repay you in accordance with your conduct and the detestable practices among you. Then you will know that it is I the LORD who strikes the blow.

10"The day is here! It has come! Doom has burst forth, the rod[j] has budded, arrogance has blossomed! 11Violence has grown into[c] a rod to punish wickedness; none of the people will be left, none of that crowd—no wealth, nothing of value.[k] 12The time has come, the day has arrived. Let not the buyer

7:2 [c]Am 8:2,10 [d]Rev 7:1; 20:8
7:4 [e]Eze 5:11
7:5 [f]2Ki 21:12
7:7 [g]Eze 12:23; Zep 1:14
7:8 [h]Isa 42:25; Eze 9:8; 14:19; Na 1:6 [i]Eze 20:8,21; 36:19
7:10 [j]Ps 89:32; Isa 10:5
7:11 [k]Jer 16:6; Zep 1:18

[a]14 Most Hebrew manuscripts; a few Hebrew manuscripts *Riblah* [b]5 Most Hebrew manuscripts; some Hebrew manuscripts and Syriac *Disaster after* [c]11 Or *The violent one has become*

rejoice nor the seller grieve, for wrath
is upon the whole crowd.[l] 13The seller
will not recover the land he has sold as
long as both of them live, for the vision concerning the whole crowd will
not be reversed. Because of their sins,
not one of them will preserve his life.[m]
14Though they blow the trumpet and
get everything ready, no one will go
into battle, for my wrath is upon the
whole crowd.
15"Outside is the sword, inside are
plague and famine; those in the country will die by the sword, and those in
the city will be devoured by famine and
plague.[n] 16All who survive and escape
will be in the mountains, moaning like
doves[o] of the valleys, each because of
his sins.[p] 17Every hand will go limp,[q]
and every knee will become as weak as
water. 18They will put on sackcloth and
be clothed with terror.[r] Their faces will
be covered with shame and their heads
will be shaved.[s] 19They will throw their
silver into the streets, and their gold
will be an unclean thing. Their silver
and gold will not be able to save them
in the day of the LORD's wrath.[t] They
will not satisfy their hunger or fill their
stomachs with it, for it has made them
stumble[u] into sin.[v] 20They were proud
of their beautiful jewelry and used it
to make their detestable idols and vile
images.[w] Therefore I will turn these
into an unclean thing for them. 21I will
hand it all over as plunder to foreigners
and as loot to the wicked of the earth,
and they will defile it.[x] 22I will turn my
face[y] away from them, and they will
desecrate my treasured place; robbers
will enter it and desecrate it.
23"Prepare chains, because the land is
full of bloodshed[z] and the city is full of
violence. 24I will bring the most wicked of the nations to take possession of

7:12 [l]ver 7; Isa 5:13-14; Eze 30:3
7:13 [m]Lev 25:24-28
7:15 [n]Dt 32:25; Jer 14:18; La 1:20; Eze 5:12
7:16 [o]Isa 59:11 [p]Ezr 9:15; Eze 6:8
7:17 [q]Isa 13:7; Eze 21:7; 22:14
7:18 [r]Ps 55:5 [s]Isa 15:2-3; Eze 27:31; Am 8:10
7:19 [t]Eze 13:5; Zep 1:7,18 [u]Eze 14:3 [v]Pr 11:4
7:20 [w]Jer 7:30
7:21 [x]2Ki 24:13
7:22 [y]Eze 39:23-24
7:23 [z]2Ki 21:16

FAITHFULNESS

THE TEMPLE SIN

Ezekiel 7:22

Jesus purged the temple not because he stood against the sacrificial system, but because God's altar had become just one more avenue of enterprise (see Luke 19:45–46).

But no vendor in the temple ever meant to make faith mercenary. It was just that profit gradually became more important than prayer.

their houses; I will put an end to the
pride of the mighty, and their sanctuaries[a] will be desecrated.[b] 25When terror
comes, they will seek peace, but there
will be none.[c] 26Calamity upon calamity[d] will come, and rumor upon rumor.
They will try to get a vision from the
prophet; the teaching of the law by the
priest will be lost, as will the counsel
of the elders.[e] 27The king will mourn,
the prince will be clothed with despair,[f]
and the hands of the people of the land
will tremble. I will deal with them according to their conduct,[g] and by their
own standards I will judge them. Then
they will know that I am the LORD.[h]"

Idolatry in the Temple

8 In the sixth year, in the sixth month
on the fifth day, while I was sitting
in my house and the elders[i] of Judah
were sitting before[j] me, the hand of the
Sovereign LORD came upon me there.[k]
2I looked, and I saw a figure like that of
a man.[a] From what appeared to be his
waist down he was like fire, and from
there up his appearance was as bright as
glowing metal.[l] 3He stretched out what
looked like a hand and took me by the
hair of my head. The Spirit lifted me
up[m] between earth and heaven and in
visions of God he took me to Jerusalem, to the entrance to the north gate
of the inner court, where the idol that
provokes to jealousy[n] stood. 4And there
before me was the glory[o] of the God of
Israel, as in the vision I had seen in the
plain.[p]
5Then he said to me, "Son of man,
look toward the north." So I looked,
and in the entrance north of the gate of
the altar I saw this idol[q] of jealousy.
6And he said to me, "Son of man, do
you see what they are doing—the utterly detestable[r] things the house of Israel
is doing here, things that will drive me
far from my sanctuary? But you will see
things that are even more detestable."
7Then he brought me to the entrance
to the court. I looked, and I saw a hole
in the wall. 8He said to me, "Son of
man, now dig into the wall." So I dug
into the wall and saw a doorway there.
9And he said to me, "Go in and see
the wicked and detestable things they
are doing here." 10So I went in and

7:24 [a]Eze 24:21 [b]2Ch 7:20; Eze 28:7
7:25 [c]Eze 13:10,16
7:26 [d]Jer 4:20 [e]Isa 47:11; Eze 20:1-3; Mic 3:6
7:27 [f]Ps 109:19; Eze 26:16 [g]Eze 18:20 [h]ver 4
8:1 [i]Eze 14:1 [j]Eze 33:31 [k]Eze 1:1-3
8:2 [l]Eze 1:4,26-27
8:3 [m]Eze 3:12; 11:1 [n]Ex 20:5; Dt 32:16
8:4 [o]Eze 1:28 [p]Eze 3:22
8:5 [q]Ps 78:58; Jer 32:34
8:6 [r]Eze 5:11

[a]2 Or *saw a fiery figure*

looked, and I saw portrayed all over the
walls all kinds of crawling things and
detestable animals and all the idols of
8:10 [s]Ex 20:4 — the house of Israel.[s] 11In front of them
stood seventy elders of the house of Is-
rael, and Jaazaniah son of Shaphan was
standing among them. Each had a cen-
8:11 [t]Nu 16:17 [u]Nu 16:35 — ser[t] in his hand, and a fragrant cloud of
incense[u] was rising.
12He said to me, "Son of man, have
you seen what the elders of the house
of Israel are doing in the darkness, each
at the shrine of his own idol? They
8:12 [v]Ps 10:11; Isa 29:15; Eze 9:9 — say, 'The LORD does not see[v] us; the
LORD has forsaken the land.'" 13Again,
he said, "You will see them doing things
that are even more detestable."
14Then he brought me to the entrance to the north gate of the house
of the LORD, and I saw women sitting
there, mourning for Tammuz. 15He said
to me, "Do you see this, son of man?
You will see things that are even more
detestable than this."
16He then brought me into the inner court of the house of the LORD,
and there at the entrance to the tem-
8:16 [w]Joel 2:17 [x]Dt 4:19; 17:3; Job 31:28; Jer 2:27; Eze 11:1,12 — ple, between the portico and the altar,[w]
were about twenty-five men. With their
backs toward the temple of the LORD
and their faces toward the east, they
were bowing down to the sun in the
east.[x]
17He said to me, "Have you seen this,
son of man? Is it a trivial matter for
the house of Judah to do the detestable things they are doing here? Must
8:17 [y]Eze 9:9 [z]Eze 16:26 — they also fill the land with violence[y]
and continually provoke me to anger?[z]
Look at them putting the branch to
their nose! 18Therefore I will deal with
them in anger; I will not look on them
8:18 [a]Eze 9:10; 24:14 [b]Isa 1:15; Jer 11:11; Mic 3:4; Zec 7:13 — with pity[a] or spare them. Although they
shout in my ears, I will not listen[b] to
them."

Idolaters Killed

9 Then I heard him call out in a loud
voice, "Bring the guards of the city
here, each with a weapon in his hand."
2And I saw six men coming from the
direction of the upper gate, which faces
north, each with a deadly weapon in his
hand. With them was a man clothed
9:2 [c]Lev 16:4; Eze 10:2; Rev 15:6 — in linen[c] who had a writing kit at his
side. They came in and stood beside the
bronze altar.
9:3 [d]Eze 10:4 — 3Now the glory[d] of the God of Israel went up from above the cherubim,[e] — 9:3 [e]Eze 11:22
where it had been, and moved to the
threshold of the temple. Then the LORD
called to the man clothed in linen who
had the writing kit at his side 4and said
to him, "Go throughout the city of Je-
rusalem and put a mark[f] on the fore- — 9:4 [f]Ex 12:7; 2Co 1:22; Rev 7:3; 9:4 [g]Ps 119:136; Jer 13:17; Eze 21:6 [h]Ps 119:53
heads of those who grieve and lament[g]
over all the detestable things that are
done in it.[h]"
5As I listened, he said to the others,
"Follow him through the city and kill,
without showing pity[i] or compassion. — 9:5 [i]Eze 5:11
6Slaughter old men, young men and
maidens, women and children, but do
not touch anyone who has the mark.
Begin at my sanctuary." So they began
with the elders[j] who were in front of — 9:6 [j]Eze 8:11-13,16 [k]2Ch 36:17; Jer 25:29; 1Pe 4:17
the temple.[k]
7Then he said to them, "Defile the
temple and fill the courts with the slain.
Go!" So they went out and began killing throughout the city. 8While they
were killing and I was left alone, I fell
facedown,[l] crying out, "Ah, Sovereign — 9:8 [l]Jos 7:6 [m]Eze 11:13; Am 7:1-6
LORD! Are you going to destroy the en-
tire remnant of Israel in this outpour-
ing of your wrath on Jerusalem?"[m]
9He answered me, "The sin of the
house of Israel and Judah is exceedingly great; the land is full of bloodshed
and the city is full of injustice.[n] They — 9:9 [n]Eze 22:29 [o]Job 22:13; Eze 8:12
say, 'The LORD has forsaken the land;
the LORD does not see.'[o] 10So I will
not look on them with pity[p] or spare — 9:10 [p]Eze 7:4; 8:18 [q]Isa 65:6; Eze 11:21
them, but I will bring down on their
own heads what they have done.[q]"
11Then the man in linen with the
writing kit at his side brought back
word, saying, "I have done as you commanded."

The Glory Departs From the Temple

10 I looked, and I saw the likeness — 10:1 [r]Rev 4:2 [s]Ex 24:10 [t]Eze 1:22
of a throne[r] of sapphire[a][s] above
the expanse[t] that was over the heads of
the cherubim. 2The LORD said to the
man clothed in linen,[u] "Go in among — 10:2 [u]Eze 9:2 [v]Eze 1:15 [w]Rev 8:5
the wheels[v] beneath the cherubim. Fill[w]
your hands with burning coals from
among the cherubim and scatter them
over the city." And as I watched, he
went in.
3Now the cherubim were standing
on the south side of the temple when

[a]1 Or *lapis lazuli*

the man went in, and a cloud filled
the inner court. 4Then the glory of the
10:4 [x]Eze 1:28; 9:3 LORD[x] rose from above the cherubim
and moved to the threshold of the tem-
ple. The cloud filled the temple, and
the court was full of the radiance of
the glory of the LORD. 5The sound of
the wings of the cherubim could be
heard as far away as the outer court, like
10:5 [y]Job 40:9; Eze 1:24 the voice[y] of God Almighty[a] when he
speaks.

6When the LORD commanded the
man in linen, "Take fire from among
the wheels, from among the cherubim," the man went in and stood beside
a wheel. 7Then one of the cherubim
reached out his hand to the fire that was
among them. He took up some of it
and put it into the hands of the man in
linen, who took it and went out. 8(Under the wings of the cherubim could be
seen what looked like the hands of a
10:8 [z]Eze 1:8 man.)[z]

9I looked, and I saw beside the cherubim four wheels, one beside each of
the cherubim; the wheels sparkled like
10:9 [a]Eze 1:15-16; Rev 21:20 chrysolite.[a] 10As for their appearance,
the four of them looked alike; each
was like a wheel intersecting a wheel.
11As they moved, they would go in any
one of the four directions the cherubim
faced; the wheels did not turn about[b]
as the cherubim went. The cherubim
went in whatever direction the head
faced, without turning as they went.
12Their entire bodies, including their
10:12 [b]Rev 4:6-8 [c]Eze 1:15-21 backs, their hands and their wings, were
completely full of eyes,[b] as were their
four wheels.[c] 13I heard the wheels being called "the whirling wheels." 14Each
10:14 [d]1Ki 7:36 [e]Eze 1:6 [f]Eze 1:10; Rev 4:7 of the cherubim[d] had four faces:[e] One
face was that of a cherub, the second
the face of a man, the third the face of
a lion, and the fourth the face of an
eagle.[f]

15Then the cherubim rose upward.
10:15 [g]Eze 1:3,5 These were the living creatures[g] I had
seen by the Kebar River. 16When the
cherubim moved, the wheels beside
them moved; and when the cherubim
spread their wings to rise from the
ground, the wheels did not leave their
side. 17When the cherubim stood still,
they also stood still; and when the cherubim rose, they rose with them, because
the spirit of the living creatures was in
10:17 [h]Eze 1:20-21 them.[h]

18Then the glory of the LORD departed from over the threshold of the tem-
ple and stopped above the cherubim.[i] 10:18 [i]Ps 18:10
19While I watched, the cherubim spread
their wings and rose from the ground,
and as they went, the wheels went with
them.[j] They stopped at the entrance to 10:19 [j]Eze 11:1,22
the east gate of the LORD's house, and
the glory of the God of Israel was above
them.

20These were the living creatures I
had seen beneath the God of Israel by 10:20 [k]Eze 1:1
the Kebar River,[k] and I realized that
they were cherubim. 21Each had four
faces[l] and four wings,[m] and under their 10:21 [l]Eze 41:18 [m]Eze 1:6
wings was what looked like the hands
of a man. 22Their faces had the same
appearance as those I had seen by the
Kebar River. Each one went straight
ahead.

Judgment on Israel's Leaders

11 Then the Spirit lifted me up
and brought me to the gate of
the house of the LORD that faces east.
There at the entrance to the gate were
twenty-five men, and I saw among them
Jaazaniah son of Azzur and Pelatiah son 11:1 [n]Eze 8:16; 10:19; 43:4-5
of Benaiah, leaders of the people.[n] 2The
LORD said to me, "Son of man, these
are the men who are plotting evil and
giving wicked advice in this city. 3They
say, 'Will it not soon be time to build
houses?[c] This city is a cooking pot,[o] and 11:3 [o]Jer 1:13; Eze 24:3 [p]ver 7,11
we are the meat.'[p] 4Therefore prophesy[q]
against them; prophesy, son of man."

5Then the Spirit of the LORD came 11:4 [q]Eze 3:4,17
upon me, and he told me to say: "This
is what the LORD says: That is what
you are saying, O house of Israel, but
I know what is going through your
mind.[r] 6You have killed many people in 11:5 [r]Jer 17:10
this city and filled its streets with the 11:6 [s]Eze 7:23; 22:6
dead.[s]

7"Therefore this is what the Sovereign LORD says: The bodies you have
thrown there are the meat and this city
is the pot, but I will drive you out of it.[t] 11:7 [t]Eze 24:3-13; Mic 3:2-3
8You fear the sword, and the sword is
what I will bring against you, declares
the Sovereign LORD.[u] 9I will drive you 11:8 [u]Pr 10:24
out of the city and hand you over[v] to
foreigners and inflict punishment on 11:9 [v]Ps 106:41 [w]Dt 28:36; Eze 5:8
you.[w] 10You will fall by the sword, and
I will execute judgment on you at the 11:10 [x]2Ki 14:25
borders of Israel.[x] Then you will know

[a]5 Hebrew *El-Shaddai* [b]11 Or *aside*
[c]3 Or *This is not the time to build houses.*

Jesus Speaks Out *on the Fruit of the Spirit:* Goodness

Matthew 5:6

Blessed are those who hunger and thirst for righteousness, for they will be filled.

Matthew 5:20

I tell you that unless your righteousness surpasses that of the Pharisees and the teachers of the law, you will certainly not enter the kingdom of heaven.

Matthew 6:33

Seek first his kingdom and his righteousness, and all these things will be given to you as well.

Matthew 12:35

The good man brings good things out of the good stored up in him, and the evil man brings evil things out of the evil stored up in him.

Luke 6:43–45

No good tree bears bad fruit, nor does a bad tree bear good fruit. Each tree is recognized by its own fruit. People do not pick figs from thornbushes, or grapes from briers. The good man brings good things out of the good stored up in his heart, and the evil man brings evil things out of the evil stored up in his heart. For out of the overflow of his heart his mouth speaks.

John 16:8–10

When [the Holy Spirit] comes, he will convict the world of guilt in regard to sin and righteousness and judgment: in regard to sin, because men do not believe in me; in regard to righteousness, because I am going to the Father, where you can see me no longer.

▸ The Salt of the Earth

You are the salt of the earth. But if the salt loses its saltiness, how can it be made salty again? It is no longer good for anything, except to be thrown out and trampled by men.

You are the light of the world. A city on a hill cannot be hidden. Neither do people light a lamp and put it under a bowl. Instead they put it on its stand, and it gives light to everyone in the house. In the same way, let your light shine before men, that they may see your good deeds and praise your Father in heaven.

Do not think that I have come to abolish the Law or the Prophets; I have not come to abolish them but to fulfill them. I tell you the truth, until heaven and earth disappear, not the smallest letter, not the least stroke of a pen, will by any means disappear from the Law until everything is accomplished. Anyone who breaks one of the least of these commandments and teaches others to do the same will be called least in the kingdom of heaven, but whoever practices and teaches these commands will be called great in the kingdom of heaven. For I tell you that unless your righteousness surpasses that of the Pharisees and the teachers of the law, you will certainly not enter the kingdom of heaven.

Matthew 5:13–20

Paul Speaks Out *on the Fruit of the Spirit:* Goodness

Romans 8:28

We know that in all things God works for the good of those who love him, who have been called according to his purpose.

Romans 15:14

I myself am convinced, my brothers, that you yourselves are full of goodness, complete in knowledge and competent to instruct one another.

Ephesians 5:8–9

You were once darkness, but now you are light in the Lord. Live as children of light (for the fruit of the light consists in all goodness, righteousness and truth).

Romans 7:18–21

I know that nothing good lives in me, that is, in my sinful nature. For I have the desire to do what is good, but I cannot carry it out. For what I do is not the good I want to do; no, the evil I do not want to do—this I keep on doing. Now if I do what I do not want to do, it is no longer I who do it, but it is sin living in me that does it.

So I find this law at work: When I want to do good, evil is right there with me.

2 Timothy 1:3–9

I thank God, whom I serve, as my forefathers did, with a clear conscience, as night and day I constantly remember you in my prayers. Recalling your tears, I long to see you, so that I may be filled with joy. I have been reminded of your sincere faith, which first lived in your grandmother Lois and in your mother Eunice and, I am persuaded, now lives in you also. For this reason I remind you to fan into flame the gift of God, which is in you through the laying on of my hands. For God did not give us a spirit of timidity, but a spirit of power, of love and of self-discipline.

So do not be ashamed to testify about our Lord, or ashamed of me his prisoner. But join with me in suffering for the gospel, by the power of God, who has saved us and called us to a holy life—not because of anything we have done but because of his own purpose and grace. This grace was given us in Christ Jesus before the beginning of time.

▸ Goodness Accomplishes God's Will

Keep reminding them of these things. Warn them before God against quarreling about words; it is of no value, and only ruins those who listen. Do your best to present yourself to God as one approved, a workman who does not need to be ashamed and who correctly handles the word of truth. Avoid godless chatter, because those who indulge in it will become more and more ungodly. Their teaching will spread like gangrene. Among them are Hymenaeus and Philetus, who have wandered away from the truth. They say that the resurrection has already taken place, and they destroy the faith of some. Nevertheless, God's solid foundation stands firm, sealed with this inscription: "The Lord knows those who are his," and, "Everyone who confesses the name of the Lord must turn away from wickedness."

In a large house there are articles not only of gold and silver, but also of wood and clay; some are for noble purposes and some for ignoble. If a man cleanses himself from the latter, he will be an instrument for noble purposes, made holy, useful to the Master and prepared to do any good work.

2 Timothy 2:14–21

that I am the LORD. 11 This city will
11:11 [y]ver 3 not be a pot[y] for you, nor will you be
the meat in it; I will execute judgment
on you at the borders of Israel. 12 And
you will know that I am the LORD,
11:12 [z]Lev 18:4; Eze 18:9 [a]Eze 8:10 for you have not followed my decrees[z]
or kept my laws but have conformed
to the standards of the nations around
you.[a]"
13 Now as I was prophesying, Pelati-
11:13 [b]ver 1 [c]Eze 9:8 ah[b] son of Benaiah died. Then I fell
facedown and cried out in a loud voice,
"Ah, Sovereign LORD! Will you completely destroy the remnant of Israel?[c]"
14 The word of the LORD came to
me: 15 "Son of man, your brothers—
your brothers who are your blood relatives[a] and the whole house of Israel—are
those of whom the people of Jerusalem
have said, 'They are[b] far away from the
LORD; this land was given to us as our
11:15 [d]Eze 33:24 possession.'[d]

Promised Return of Israel

16 "Therefore say: 'This is what the
Sovereign LORD says: Although I sent
them far away among the nations and
scattered them among the countries, yet
for a little while I have been a sanctu-
11:16 [e]Ps 90:1; 91:9; Isa 8:14 ary[e] for them in the countries where
they have gone.'
17 "Therefore say: 'This is what the
Sovereign LORD says: I will gather you
from the nations and bring you back
11:17 [f]Jer 3:18; 24:5-6; Eze 28:25; 34:13 from the countries where you have been
scattered, and I will give you back the
land of Israel again.'[f]

LOVE

MAKING ALL THINGS USABLE

Ezekiel 11:17
God loves repairing broken things.
He loves to make them new.
He loves collecting scattered things.
That's what a God should do.

18 "They will return to it and remove
11:18 [g]Eze 5:11 [h]Eze 37:23 all its vile images[g] and detestable idols.[h]
19 I will give them an undivided heart[i]
11:19 [i]Jer 32:39 [j]Zec 7:12 [k]Eze 18:31; 36:26; 2Co 3:3 and put a new spirit in them; I will remove from them their heart of stone[j]
and give them a heart of flesh.[k] 20 Then
they will follow my decrees and be care-
11:20 [l]Ps 105:45 [m]Eze 14:11; 36:26-28 ful to keep my laws.[l] They will be my
people, and I will be their God.[m] 21 But
as for those whose hearts are devoted
to their vile images and detestable idols,
I will bring down on their own heads
what they have done, declares the Sov- 11:21 [n]Eze 9:10; 16:43
ereign LORD.[n]"
22 Then the cherubim, with the wheels
beside them, spread their wings, and
the glory of the God of Israel was above 11:22 [o]Eze 10:19
them.[o] 23 The glory[p] of the LORD went
up from within the city and stopped 11:23 [p]Eze 8:4; 10:4 [q]Zec 14:4
above the mountain[q] east of it. 24 The
Spirit[r] lifted me up and brought me to
the exiles in Babylonia[c] in the vision[s] 11:24 [r]Eze 8:3 [s]2Co 12:2-4
given by the Spirit of God.
Then the vision I had seen went up
from me, 25 and I told the exiles everything the LORD had shown me.[t] 11:25 [t]Eze 3:4,11

The Exile Symbolized

12 The word of the LORD came
to me: 2 "Son of man, you are
living among a rebellious people. They
have eyes to see but do not see and ears
to hear but do not hear, for they are a 12:2 [u]Isa 6:10; Eze 2:6-8; Mt 13:15
rebellious people.[u]
3 "Therefore, son of man, pack your
belongings for exile and in the daytime, as they watch, set out and go
from where you are to another place. 12:3 [v]Jer 36:3 [w]Jer 26:3 [x]2Ti 2:25-26
Perhaps[v] they will understand,[w] though
they are a rebellious house.[x] 4 During
the daytime, while they watch, bring
out your belongings packed for exile.
Then in the evening, while they are
watching, go out like those who go into 12:4 [y]ver 12; Jer 39:4
exile.[y] 5 While they watch, dig through
the wall and take your belongings out
through it. 6 Put them on your shoulder as they are watching and carry them
out at dusk. Cover your face so that you
cannot see the land, for I have made
you a sign[z] to the house of Israel." 12:6 [z]ver 12; Isa 8:18; 20:3; Eze 4:3; 24:24
7 So I did as I was commanded.[a] Dur-
ing the day I brought out my things 12:7 [a]Eze 24:18; 37:10
packed for exile. Then in the evening I
dug through the wall with my hands. I
took my belongings out at dusk, carrying them on my shoulders while they
watched.
8 In the morning the word of the
LORD came to me: 9 "Son of man, did
not that rebellious house of Israel ask 12:9 [b]Eze 17:12; 20:49; 24:19
you, 'What are you doing?'[b]
10 "Say to them, 'This is what the
Sovereign LORD says: This oracle con-

[a] *15* Or *are in exile with you* (see Septuagint and Syriac) [b] *15* Or *those to whom the people of Jerusalem have said, 'Stay* [c] *24* Or *Chaldea*

cerns the prince in Jerusalem and the whole house of Israel who are there.' 11Say to them, 'I am a sign to you.'

"As I have done, so it will be done to them. They will go into exile as captives.[c]

12"The prince among them will put his things on his shoulder at dusk[d] and leave, and a hole will be dug in the wall for him to go through. He will cover his face so that he cannot see the land.[e] 13I will spread my net[f] for him, and he will be caught in my snare;[g] I will bring him to Babylonia, the land of the Chaldeans, but he will not see[h] it, and there he will die.[i] 14I will scatter to the winds all those around him—his staff and all his troops—and I will pursue them with drawn sword.[j]

15"They will know that I am the LORD, when I disperse them among the nations and scatter them through the countries. 16But I will spare a few of them from the sword, famine and plague, so that in the nations where they go they may acknowledge all their detestable practices. Then they will know that I am the LORD.[k]"

17The word of the LORD came to me: 18"Son of man, tremble as you eat your food,[l] and shudder in fear as you drink your water. 19Say to the people of the land: 'This is what the Sovereign LORD says about those living in Jerusalem and in the land of Israel: They will eat their food in anxiety and drink their water in despair, for their land will be stripped of everything[m] in it because of the violence of all who live there.[n] 20The inhabited towns will be laid waste and the land will be desolate. Then you will know that I am the LORD.[o]'"

21The word of the LORD came to me: 22"Son of man, what is this proverb you have in the land of Israel: 'The days go by and every vision comes to nothing'?[p] 23Say to them, 'This is what the Sovereign LORD says: I am going to put an end to this proverb, and they will no longer quote it in Israel.' Say to them, 'The days are near when every vision will be fulfilled.[q] 24For there will be no more false visions or flattering divinations[r] among the people of Israel. 25But I the LORD will speak what I will, and it shall be fulfilled without delay. For in your days, you rebellious house, I will fulfill whatever I say, declares the Sovereign LORD.[s]'"

26The word of the LORD came to me: 27"Son of man, the house of Israel is saying, 'The vision he sees is for many years from now, and he prophesies about the distant future.'[t]

28"Therefore say to them, 'This is what the Sovereign LORD says: None of my words will be delayed any longer; whatever I say will be fulfilled, declares the Sovereign LORD.'"

False Prophets Condemned

13 The word of the LORD came to me: 2"Son of man, prophesy against the prophets of Israel who are now prophesying. Say to those who prophesy out of their own imagination: 'Hear the word of the LORD![u] 3This is what the Sovereign LORD says: Woe to the foolish[a] prophets[v] who follow their own spirit and have seen nothing![w] 4Your prophets, O Israel, are like jackals among ruins. 5You have not gone up to the breaks in the wall to repair[x] it for the house of Israel so that it will stand firm in the battle on the day of the LORD.[y] 6Their visions are false and their divinations a lie. They say, "The LORD declares," when the LORD has not sent them; yet they expect their words to be fulfilled.[z] 7Have you not seen false visions and uttered lying divinations when you say, "The LORD declares," though I have not spoken?

8" 'Therefore this is what the Sovereign LORD says: Because of your false words and lying visions, I am against you, declares the Sovereign LORD. 9My hand will be against the prophets who see false visions and utter lying divinations. They will not belong to the council of my people or be listed in the records[a] of the house of Israel, nor will they enter the land of Israel. Then you will know that I am the Sovereign LORD.[b]

10" 'Because they lead my people astray,[c] saying, "Peace," when there is no peace, and because, when a flimsy wall is built, they cover it with whitewash,[d] 11therefore tell those who cover it with whitewash that it is going to fall. Rain will come in torrents, and I will send hailstones hurtling down, and violent

[a]3 Or *wicked*

12:11 [c]2Ki 25:7; Jer 15:2; 52:15
12:12 [d]Jer 39:4 [e]Jer 52:7
12:13 [f]Eze 17:20; 19:8; Hos 7:12 [g]Isa 24:17-18 [h]Jer 39:7 [i]Jer 52:11; Eze 17:16
12:14 [j]2Ki 25:5; Eze 5:10,12
12:16 [k]Jer 22:8-9; Eze 6:8-10; 14:22
12:18 [l]La 5:9; Eze 4:16
12:19 [m]Eze 6:6-14; Mic 7:13; Zec 7:14 [n]Eze 4:16; 23:33
12:20 [o]Isa 7:23-24; Jer 4:7
12:22 [p]Eze 11:3; Am 6:3; 2Pe 3:4
12:23 [q]Ps 37:13; Joel 2:1; Zep 1:14
12:24 [r]Jer 14:14; Eze 13:23; Zec 13:2-4
12:25 [s]Isa 14:24; Hab 1:5
12:27 [t]Da 10:14
13:2 [u]ver 17; Jer 23:16; 37:19
13:3 [v]La 2:14 [w]Jer 23:25-32
13:5 [x]Isa 58:12; Eze 22:30 [y]Eze 7:19
13:6 [z]Jer 28:15; Eze 22:28
13:9 [a]Jer 17:13 [b]Eze 20:38
13:10 [c]Jer 50:6 [d]Eze 7:25; 22:28

13:11 [e]Eze 38:22 winds will burst forth.[e] 12When the
wall collapses, will people not ask you,
"Where is the whitewash you covered it
with?"
13" 'Therefore this is what the Sovereign LORD says: In my wrath I will unleash a violent wind, and in my anger
13:13 [f]Rev 11:19; hailstones[f] and torrents of rain will fall
16:21 with destructive fury.[g] 14I will tear down
[g]Ex 9:25; the wall you have covered with white-
Isa 30:30 wash and will level it to the ground so
13:14 that its foundation[h] will be laid bare.
[h]Mic 1:6 When it[a] falls,[i] you will be destroyed
[i]Jer 6:15 in it; and you will know that I am
the LORD. 15So I will spend my wrath
against the wall and against those who
covered it with whitewash. I will say to
you, "The wall is gone and so are those
who whitewashed it, 16those prophets
of Israel who prophesied to Jerusalem
and saw visions of peace for her when
there was no peace, declares the Sover-
13:16 [j]Isa 57:21; eign LORD.[j]" '
Jer 6:14 17"Now, son of man, set your face
13:17 [k]Rev 2:20 against the daughters[k] of your people
[l]ver 2 who prophesy out of their own imagination. Prophesy against them[l] 18and
say, 'This is what the Sovereign LORD
says: Woe to the women who sew magic charms on all their wrists and make
veils of various lengths for their heads
in order to ensnare people. Will you en-
13:19 [m]Eze 20:39; snare the lives of my people but pre-
22:26 serve your own? 19You have profaned[m]
[n]Pr 28:21 me among my people for a few handfuls of barley and scraps of bread. By lying to my people, who listen to lies, you
have killed those who should not have
died and have spared those who should
not live.[n]
20" 'Therefore this is what the Sovereign LORD says: I am against your
magic charms with which you ensnare
people like birds and I will tear them
from your arms; I will set free the people that you ensnare like birds. 21I will
tear off your veils and save my people
from your hands, and they will no longer fall prey to your power. Then you
13:21 [o]Ps 91:3 will know that I am the LORD.[o] 22Be-
cause you disheartened the righteous
with your lies, when I had brought
13:22 them no grief, and because you en-
[p]Jer 23:14; couraged the wicked not to turn from
Eze 33:14-16 their evil ways and so save their lives,[p]
13:23 23therefore you will no longer see false
[q]ver 6; visions or practice divination.[q] I will
Eze 12:24 save my people from your hands. And

then you will know that I am the
LORD.[r]' " 13:23 [r]Mic 3:6

Idolaters Condemned

14 Some of the elders of Israel came
to me and sat down in front
of me.[s] 2Then the word of the LORD 14:1 [s]Eze 8:1; 20:1
came to me: 3"Son of man, these men
have set up idols in their hearts and put 14:3 [t]ver 7;
wicked stumbling blocks[t] before their Eze 7:19
faces. Should I let them inquire of me at [u]Isa 1:15;
all?[u] 4Therefore speak to them and tell Eze 20:31
them, 'This is what the Sovereign LORD
says: When any Israelite sets up idols in
his heart and puts a wicked stumbling
block before his face and then goes to
a prophet, I the LORD will answer him
myself in keeping with his great idolatry. 5I will do this to recapture the hearts
of the people of Israel, who have all de- 14:5 [v]Zec 11:8
serted[v] me for their idols.'[w] [w]Jer 2:11
6"Therefore say to the house of Israel, 'This is what the Sovereign LORD
says: Repent! Turn from your idols and 14:6
renounce all your detestable practices![x] [x]Isa 2:20; 30:22
7" 'When any Israelite or any alien[y]
living in Israel separates himself from 14:7 [y]Ex 12:48;
me and sets up idols in his heart and 20:10
puts a wicked stumbling block before
his face and then goes to a prophet to
inquire of me, I the LORD will answer 14:8
him myself. 8I will set my face against[z] [z]Eze 15:7
that man and make him an example [a]Eze 5:15
and a byword.[a] I will cut him off from
my people. Then you will know that I
am the LORD.
9" 'And if the prophet[b] is enticed[c] to 14:9 [b]Jer 14:15
utter a prophecy, I the LORD have en- [c]Jer 4:10
ticed that prophet, and I will stretch out [d]1Ki 22:23
my hand against him and destroy him
from among my people Israel.[d] 10They
will bear their guilt—the prophet will
be as guilty as the one who consults
him. 11Then the people of Israel will no 14:11
longer stray[e] from me, nor will they de- [e]Eze 48:11 [f]Eze 11:19-20;
file themselves anymore with all their 37:23
sins. They will be my people, and I
will be their God, declares the Sovereign LORD.[f]"

Judgment Inescapable

12The word of the LORD came to
me: 13"Son of man, if a country sins
against me by being unfaithful and I
stretch out my hand against it to cut 14:13
off its food supply[g] and send famine [g]Lev 26:26

[a]14 Or *the city*

upon it and kill its men and their
animals,[h] 14even if these three men—
Noah,[i] Daniel[a][j] and Job[k]—were in it,
they could save only themselves by their
righteousness,[l] declares the Sovereign
LORD.
15"Or if I send wild beasts[m] through
that country and they leave it childless
and it becomes desolate so that no
one can pass through it because of the
beasts,[n] 16as surely as I live, declares
the Sovereign LORD, even if these three
men were in it, they could not save
their own sons or daughters. They alone
would be saved, but the land would be
desolate.[o]
17"Or if I bring a sword[p] against that
country and say, 'Let the sword pass
throughout the land,' and I kill its men
and their animals,[q] 18as surely as I live,
declares the Sovereign LORD, even if
these three men were in it, they could
not save their own sons or daughters.
They alone would be saved.
19"Or if I send a plague into that
land and pour out my wrath[r] upon
it through bloodshed, killing its men
and their animals,[s] 20as surely as I live,
declares the Sovereign LORD, even if
Noah, Daniel and Job were in it, they
could save neither son nor daughter.
They would save only themselves by
their righteousness.[t]
21"For this is what the Sovereign
LORD says: How much worse will it
be when I send against Jerusalem my
four dreadful judgments—sword and
famine and wild beasts and plague—to
kill its men and their animals![u] 22Yet
there will be some survivors—sons and
daughters who will be brought out of
it.[v] They will come to you, and when
you see their conduct[w] and their actions, you will be consoled regarding
the disaster I have brought upon Jerusalem—every disaster I have brought
upon it. 23You will be consoled when
you see their conduct and their actions,
for you will know that I have done
nothing in it without cause, declares
the Sovereign LORD.[x]"

Jerusalem, A Useless Vine

15 The word of the LORD came to
me: 2"Son of man, how is the
wood of a vine[y] better than that of a
branch on any of the trees in the forest? 3Is wood ever taken from it to make
anything useful? Do they make pegs
from it to hang things on? 4And after
it is thrown on the fire as fuel and the
fire burns both ends and chars the middle, is it then useful for anything?[z] 5If it
was not useful for anything when it was
whole, how much less can it be made
into something useful when the fire has
burned it and it is charred?
6"Therefore this is what the Sovereign LORD says: As I have given the
wood of the vine among the trees of
the forest as fuel for the fire, so will
I treat the people living in Jerusalem.
7I will set my face against[a] them. Although they have come out of the fire,
the fire will yet consume them. And
when I set my face against them, you
will know that I am the LORD.[b] 8I will
make the land desolate[c] because they
have been unfaithful,[d] declares the Sovereign LORD."

An Allegory of Unfaithful Jerusalem

16 The word of the LORD came to
me: 2"Son of man, confront Jerusalem with her detestable practices[e]
3and say, 'This is what the Sovereign
LORD says to Jerusalem: Your ancestry[f]
and birth were in the land of the Canaanites; your father was an Amorite
and your mother a Hittite.[g] 4On the
day you were born[h] your cord was not
cut, nor were you washed with water to
make you clean, nor were you rubbed
with salt or wrapped in cloths. 5No one
looked on you with pity or had compassion enough to do any of these things
for you. Rather, you were thrown out
into the open field, for on the day you
were born you were despised.
6" 'Then I passed by and saw you
kicking about in your blood, and as
you lay there in your blood I said to
you, "Live!"[b][i] 7I made you grow[j] like
a plant of the field. You grew up and
developed and became the most beautiful of jewels.[c] Your breasts were formed
and your hair grew, you who were naked and bare.[k]
8" 'Later I passed by, and when I

14:13 [h]Eze 5:16; 6:14; 15:8
14:14 [i]Ge 6:8 [j]ver 20; Eze 28:3; Da 1:6; 6:13 [k]Job 1:1 [l]Job 42:9; Jer 15:1; Eze 18:20
14:15 [m]Eze 5:17 [n]Lev 26:22
14:16 [o]Eze 18:20
14:17 [p]Lev 26:25; Eze 5:12; 21:3-4 [q]Eze 25:13; Zep 1:3
14:19 [r]Eze 7:8 [s]Eze 38:22
14:20 [t]ver 14
14:21 [u]Jer 15:3; Eze 5:17; 33:27; Am 4:6-10; Rev 6:8
14:22 [v]Eze 12:16 [w]Eze 20:43
14:23 [x]Jer 22:8-9
15:2 [y]Isa 5:1-7; Jer 2:21; Hos 10:1
15:4 [z]Eze 19:14; Jn 15:6
15:7 [a]Ps 34:16; Eze 14:8 [b]Isa 24:18; Am 9:1-4
15:8 [c]Eze 14:13 [d]Eze 17:20
16:2 [e]Eze 20:4; 22:2
16:3 [f]Eze 21:30 [g]ver 45
16:4 [h]Hos 2:3
16:6 [i]Ex 19:4
16:7 [j]Dt 1:10 [k]Ex 1:7

[a]*14* Or *Danel*; the Hebrew spelling may suggest a person other than the prophet Daniel; also in verse 20. [b]*6* A few Hebrew manuscripts, Septuagint and Syriac; most Hebrew manuscripts *"Live!" And as you lay there in your blood I said to you, "Live!"*
[c]*7* Or *became mature*

looked at you and saw that you were old enough for love, I spread the corner of my garment[l] over you and covered your nakedness. I gave you my solemn oath and entered into a covenant with you, declares the Sovereign LORD, and you became mine.[m]

9 “ ‘I bathed[a] you with water and washed[n] the blood from you and put ointments on you. 10 I clothed you with an embroidered[o] dress and put leather sandals on you. I dressed you in fine linen[p] and covered you with costly garments.[q] 11 I adorned you with jewelry:[r] I put bracelets[s] on your arms and a necklace[t] around your neck, 12 and I put a ring on your nose,[u] earrings on your ears and a beautiful crown[v] on your head. 13 So you were adorned with gold and silver; your clothes were of fine linen and costly fabric and embroidered cloth. Your food was fine flour, honey and olive oil.[w] You became very beautiful and rose to be a queen.[x] 14 And your fame[y] spread among the nations on account of your beauty,[z] because the splendor I had given you made your beauty perfect, declares the Sovereign LORD.

15 “ ‘But you trusted in your beauty and used your fame to become a prostitute. You lavished your favors on anyone who passed by[a] and your beauty became his.[b][b] 16 You took some of your garments to make gaudy high places, where you carried on your prostitution.[c] Such things should not happen, nor should they ever occur. 17 You also took the fine jewelry I gave you, the jewelry made of my gold and silver, and you made for yourself male idols and engaged in prostitution with them.[d] 18 And you took your embroidered clothes to put on them, and you offered my oil and incense before them. 19 Also the food I provided for you—the fine flour, olive oil and honey I gave you to eat—you offered as fragrant incense before them. That is what happened, declares the Sovereign LORD.[e]

20 “ ‘And you took your sons and daughters[f] whom you bore to me[g] and sacrificed them as food to the idols. Was your prostitution not enough?[h] 21 You slaughtered my children and sacrificed them[c] to the idols.[i] 22 In all your detestable practices and your prostitution you did not remember the days of your youth,[j] when you were naked and bare, kicking about in your blood.[k]

23 “ ‘Woe! Woe to you, declares the Sovereign LORD. In addition to all your other wickedness, 24 you built a mound for yourself and made a lofty shrine[l] in every public square.[m] 25 At the head of every street you built your lofty shrines and degraded your beauty, offering your body with increasing promiscuity to anyone who passed by.[n] 26 You engaged in prostitution with the Egyptians, your lustful neighbors, and provoked[o] me to anger with your increasing promiscuity.[p] 27 So I stretched out my hand[q] against you and reduced your territory; I gave you over to the greed of your enemies, the daughters of the Philistines,[r] who were shocked by your lewd conduct. 28 You engaged in prostitution with the Assyrians[s] too, because you were insatiable; and even after that, you still were not satisfied. 29 Then you increased your promiscuity to include Babylonia,[d][t] a land of merchants, but even with this you were not satisfied.

30 “ ‘How weak-willed you are, declares the Sovereign LORD, when you do all these things, acting like a brazen prostitute![u] 31 When you built your mounds at the head of every street and made your lofty shrines[v] in every public square, you were unlike a prostitute, because you scorned payment.

32 “ ‘You adulterous wife! You prefer strangers to your own husband! 33 Every prostitute receives a fee, but you give gifts[w] to all your lovers, bribing them to come to you from everywhere for your illicit favors.[x] 34 So in your prostitution you are the opposite of others; no one runs after you for your favors. You are the very opposite, for you give payment and none is given to you.

35 “ ‘Therefore, you prostitute, hear the word of the LORD! 36 This is what the Sovereign LORD says: Because you poured out your wealth[e] and exposed your nakedness in your promiscuity with your lovers, and because of all your detestable idols, and because you gave them your children's blood,[y] 37 therefore I am going to gather all your lov-

16:8 [l]Ru 3:9 [m]Jer 2:2; Hos 2:7,19-20
16:9 [n]Ru 3:3
16:10 [o]Ex 26:36 [p]Eze 27:16 [q]ver 18
16:11 [r]Eze 23:40 [s]Isa 3:19; Eze 23:42 [t]Ge 41:42
16:12 [u]Isa 3:21 [v]Isa 28:5; Jer 13:18
16:13 [w]1Sa 10:1 [x]Dt 32:13-14; 1Ki 4:21
16:14 [y]1Ki 10:24 [z]La 2:15
16:15 [a]ver 25 [b]Isa 57:8; Jer 2:20; Eze 23:3; 27:3
16:16 [c]2Ki 23:7
16:17 [d]Eze 7:20
16:19 [e]Hos 2:8
16:20 [f]Jer 7:31 [g]Ex 13:2 [h]Ps 106:37-38; Isa 57:5; Eze 23:37
16:21 [i]2Ki 17:17; Jer 19:5
16:22 [j]Jer 2:2; Hos 11:1 [k]ver 6
16:24 [l]ver 31; Isa 57:7 [m]Ps 78:58; Jer 2:20; 3:2; Eze 20:28
16:25 [n]ver 15; Pr 9:14
16:26 [o]Eze 8:17 [p]Eze 20:8; 23:19-21
16:27 [q]Eze 20:33 [r]2Ch 28:18
16:28 [s]2Ki 16:7
16:29 [t]Eze 23:14-17
16:30 [u]Jer 3:3
16:31 [v]ver 24
16:33 [w]Isa 30:6; 57:9 [x]Hos 8:9-10
16:36 [y]Jer 19:5; Eze 23:10

[a]9 Or *I had bathed* [b]15 Most Hebrew manuscripts; one Hebrew manuscript (see some Septuagint manuscripts) *by. Such a thing should not happen* [c]21 Or *and made them pass through* ⌞*the fire*⌟ [d]29 Or *Chaldea* [e]36 Or *lust*

ers, with whom you found pleasure, those you loved as well as those you hated. I will gather them against you from all around and will strip you in front of them, and they will see all your nakedness.[z] 38I will sentence you to the punishment of women who commit adultery and who shed blood;[a] I will bring upon you the blood vengeance of my wrath and jealous anger.[b] 39Then I will hand you over to your lovers, and they will tear down your mounds and destroy your lofty shrines. They will strip you of your clothes and take your fine jewelry and leave you naked and bare.[c] 40They will bring a mob against you, who will stone[d] you and hack you to pieces with their swords. 41They will burn down[e] your houses and inflict punishment on you in the sight of many women.[f] I will put a stop[g] to your prostitution, and you will no longer pay your lovers. 42Then my wrath against you will subside and my jealous anger will turn away from you; I will be calm and no longer angry.[h]

43" 'Because you did not remember[i] the days of your youth but enraged me with all these things, I will surely bring down[j] on your head what you have done, declares the Sovereign LORD. Did you not add lewdness to all your other detestable practices?[k]

44" 'Everyone who quotes proverbs will quote this proverb about you: "Like mother, like daughter." 45You are a true daughter of your mother, who despised her husband and her children; and you are a true sister of your sisters, who despised their husbands and their children. Your mother was a Hittite and your father an Amorite.[l] 46Your older sister was Samaria, who lived to the north of you with her daughters; and your younger sister, who lived to the south of you with her daughters, was Sodom.[m] 47You not only walked in their ways and copied their detestable practices, but in all your ways you soon became more depraved than they.[n] 48As surely as I live, declares the Sovereign LORD, your sister Sodom and her daughters never did what you and your daughters have done.[o]

49" 'Now this was the sin of your sister Sodom:[p] She and her daughters were arrogant,[q] overfed and unconcerned; they did not help the poor and needy.[r] 50They were haughty and did detestable things before me. Therefore I did away with them as you have seen.[s] 51Samaria did not commit half the sins you did. You have done more detestable things than they, and have made your sisters seem righteous by all these things you have done.[t] 52Bear your disgrace, for you have furnished some justification for your sisters. Because your sins were more vile than theirs, they appear more righteous than you. So then, be ashamed and bear your disgrace, for you have made your sisters appear righteous.

53" 'However, I will restore[u] the fortunes of Sodom and her daughters and of Samaria and her daughters, and your fortunes along with them, 54so that you may bear your disgrace[v] and be ashamed of all you have done in giving them comfort. 55And your sisters, Sodom with her daughters and Samaria with her daughters, will return to what they were before; and you and your daughters will return to what you were before.[w] 56You would not even mention your sister Sodom in the day of your pride, 57before your wickedness was uncovered. Even so, you are now scorned by the daughters of Edom[a][x] and all her neighbors and the daughters of the Philistines—all those around you who despise you. 58You will bear the consequences of your lewdness and your detestable practices, declares the LORD.[y]

59" 'This is what the Sovereign LORD says: I will deal with you as you deserve, because you have despised my oath by breaking the covenant.[z] 60Yet I will remember the covenant I made with you in the days of your youth, and I will establish an everlasting covenant[a] with you. 61Then you will remember your ways and be ashamed[b] when you receive your sisters, both those who are older than you and those who are younger. I will give them to you as daughters, but not on the basis of my covenant with you. 62So I will establish my covenant with you, and you will know that I am the LORD.[c] 63Then, when I make atonement[d] for you for all you have done, you will remember and be ashamed and never again open your

[a]57 Many Hebrew manuscripts and Syriac; most Hebrew manuscripts, Septuagint and Vulgate *Aram*

16:37 [z]Jer 13:22
16:38 [a]Eze 23:45 [b]Lev 20:10; Eze 23:25
16:39 [c]Eze 23:26; Hos 2:3
16:40 [d]Jn 8:5,7
16:41 [e]Dt 13:16 [f]Eze 23:10 [g]Eze 23:27,48
16:42 [h]Isa 54:9; Eze 5:13; 39:29
16:43 [i]Ps 78:42 [j]Eze 22:31 [k]ver 22; Eze 11:21
16:45 [l]Eze 23:2
16:46 [m]Ge 13:10-13; Eze 23:4
16:47 [n]2Ki 21:9; Eze 5:7
16:48 [o]Mt 10:15; 11:23-24
16:49 [p]Ge 13:13 [q]Ps 138:6 [r]Eze 18:7,12,16; Lk 12:16-20
16:50 [s]Ge 18:20-21; 19:5
16:51 [t]Jer 3:8-11
16:53 [u]Isa 19:24-25
16:54 [v]Jer 2:26; Eze 14:22
16:55 [w]Mal 3:4
16:57 [x]2Ki 16:6
16:58 [y]Eze 23:49
16:59 [z]Eze 17:19
16:60 [a]Jer 32:40; Eze 37:26
16:61 [b]Eze 20:43
16:62 [c]Jer 24:7; Eze 20:37,43-44; Hos 2:19-20
16:63 [d]Ps 65:3; 79:9

mouth[e] because of your humiliation, declares the Sovereign LORD.[f]' "

Two Eagles and a Vine

17 The word of the LORD came to me: 2"Son of man, set forth an allegory and tell the house of Israel a parable.[g] 3Say to them, 'This is what the Sovereign LORD says: A great eagle[h] with powerful wings, long feathers and full plumage of varied colors came to Lebanon.[i] Taking hold of the top of a cedar, 4he broke off its topmost shoot and carried it away to a land of merchants, where he planted it in a city of traders.

5" 'He took some of the seed of your land and put it in fertile soil. He planted it like a willow by abundant water,[j] 6and it sprouted and became a low, spreading vine. Its branches turned toward him, but its roots remained under it. So it became a vine and produced branches and put out leafy boughs.

7" 'But there was another great eagle with powerful wings and full plumage. The vine now sent out its roots toward him from the plot where it was planted and stretched out its branches to him for water.[k] 8It had been planted in good soil by abundant water so that it would produce branches, bear fruit and become a splendid vine.'

9"Say to them, 'This is what the Sovereign LORD says: Will it thrive? Will it not be uprooted and stripped of its fruit so that it withers? All its new growth will wither. It will not take a strong arm or many people to pull it up by the roots. 10Even if it[l] is transplanted, will it thrive? Will it not wither completely when the east wind strikes it—wither away in the plot where it grew?' "

11Then the word of the LORD came to me: 12"Say to this rebellious house, 'Do you not know what these things mean?[m]' Say to them: 'The king of Babylon went to Jerusalem and carried off her king and her nobles,[n] bringing them back with him to Babylon.[o] 13Then he took a member of the royal family and made a treaty with him, putting him under oath.[p] He also carried away the leading men of the land, 14so that the kingdom would be brought low,[q] unable to rise again, surviving only by keeping his treaty. 15But the king rebelled[r] against him by sending his envoys to Egypt to get horses and a large army.[s] Will he succeed? Will he who does such things escape? Will he break the treaty and yet escape?[t]

16" 'As surely as I live, declares the Sovereign LORD, he shall die[u] in Babylon, in the land of the king who put him on the throne, whose oath he despised and whose treaty he broke.[v] 17Pharaoh[w] with his mighty army and great horde will be of no help to him in war, when ramps[x] are built and siege works erected to destroy many lives.[y] 18He despised the oath by breaking the covenant. Because he had given his hand in pledge[z] and yet did all these things, he shall not escape.

19" 'Therefore this is what the Sovereign LORD says: As surely as I live, I will bring down on his head my oath that he despised and my covenant that he broke.[a] 20I will spread my net[b] for him, and he will be caught in my snare. I will bring him to Babylon and execute judgment[c] upon him there because he was unfaithful to me. 21All his fleeing troops will fall by the sword,[d] and the survivors[e] will be scattered to the winds.[f] Then you will know that I the LORD have spoken.

22" 'This is what the Sovereign LORD says: I myself will take a shoot from the very top of a cedar and plant it; I will break off a tender sprig from its topmost shoots and plant it on a high and lofty mountain.[g] 23On the mountain heights of Israel I will plant it; it will produce branches and bear fruit and become a splendid cedar. Birds of every kind will nest in it; they will find shelter in the shade of its branches.[h] 24All the trees of the field[i] will know that I the LORD bring down the tall tree and make the low tree grow tall. I dry up the green tree and make the dry tree flourish.

" 'I the LORD have spoken, and I will do it.[j]' "

The Soul Who Sins Will Die

18 The word of the LORD came to me: 2"What do you people mean by quoting this proverb about the land of Israel:

" 'The fathers eat sour grapes,
and the children's teeth are set on edge'?[k]

16:63 [e]Ro 3:19 [f]Ps 39:9; Da 9:7-8
17:2 [g]Eze 20:49
17:3 [h]Hos 8:1 [i]Jer 22:23
17:5 [j]Dt 8:7-9; Isa 44:4
17:7 [k]Eze 31:4
17:10 [l]Hos 13:15
17:12 [m]Eze 12:9 [n]2Ki 24:15 [o]Eze 24:19
17:13 [p]2Ch 36:13
17:14 [q]Eze 29:14
17:15 [r]Jer 52:3
17:15 [s]Dt 17:16 [t]Jer 34:3; 38:18
17:16 [u]Jer 52:11; Eze 12:13 [v]2Ki 24:17
17:17 [w]Jer 37:7 [x]Eze 4:2 [y]Isa 36:6; Jer 37:5; Eze 29:6-7
17:18 [z]1Ch 29:24
17:19 [a]Eze 16:59
17:20 [b]Eze 12:13; 32:3 [c]Jer 2:35; Eze 20:36
17:21 [d]Eze 12:14 [e]2Ki 25:11 [f]2Ki 25:5
17:22 [g]Jer 23:5; Eze 20:40; 36:1,36; 37:22
17:23 [h]Ps 92:12; Isa 2:2; Eze 31:6; Da 4:12; Hos 14:5-7; Mt 13:32
17:24 [i]Ps 96:12 [j]Eze 19:12; 21:26; 22:14; Am 9:11
18:2 [k]Isa 3:15; Jer 31:29; La 5:7

SELF-CONTROL

LIVING FOR SELF, DYING ALONE

Ezekiel 18:4

The sinning soul dies in futility. It dies of thirst beside a reservoir from which it would not drink. It dies of hunger seated at the banquet table of forgiveness. It dies a leper on the banks of healing rivers in which it would not bathe. It decides to live for its appetites rather than live in glory forever.

3“As surely as I live, declares the Sovereign LORD, you will no longer quote
this proverb in Israel. 4For every living
soul belongs to me, the father as well as
the son—both alike belong to me. The
soul who sins is the one who will die.[l]

5“Suppose there is a righteous man
who does what is just and right.
6He does not eat at the mountain[m]
shrines
or look to the idols[n] of the house
of Israel.
He does not defile his neighbor’s
wife
or lie with a woman during her
period.
7He does not oppress[o] anyone,
but returns what he took in
pledge[p] for a loan.
He does not commit robbery
but gives his food to the hungry
and provides clothing for the
naked.[q]
8He does not lend at usury
or take excessive interest.[a][r]
He withholds his hand from doing
wrong
and judges fairly[s] between man
and man.
9He follows my decrees
and faithfully keeps my laws.
That man is righteous;[t]
he will surely live,[u]
declares the Sovereign
LORD.

10“Suppose he has a violent son, who
sheds blood[v] or does any of these other
things[b] 11(though the father has done
none of them):

“He eats at the mountain shrines.
He defiles his neighbor’s wife.
12He oppresses the poor[w] and needy.
He commits robbery.
He does not return what he took in
pledge.
He looks to the idols.
He does detestable things.[x]
13He lends at usury and takes excessive
interest.[y]

Will such a man live? He will not!
Because he has done all these detestable things, he will surely be put to
death and his blood will be on his own
head.[z]

14“But suppose this son has a son
who sees all the sins his father commits,
and though he sees them, he does not
do such things:[a]

15“He does not eat at the mountain
shrines
or look to the idols of the house
of Israel.
He does not defile his neighbor’s
wife.
16He does not oppress anyone
or require a pledge for a loan.
He does not commit robbery
but gives his food to the hungry
and provides clothing for the
naked.[b]
17He withholds his hand from sin[c]
and takes no usury or excessive
interest.
He keeps my laws and follows my
decrees.

He will not die for his father’s sin; he
will surely live. 18But his father will die
for his own sin, because he practiced
extortion, robbed his brother and did
what was wrong among his people.

19“Yet you ask, ‘Why does the son
not share the guilt of his father?’ Since
the son has done what is just and right
and has been careful to keep all my decrees, he will surely live.[c] 20The soul
who sins is the one who will die. The
son will not share the guilt of the father,
nor will the father share the guilt of
the son. The righteousness of the righteous man will be credited to him, and
the wickedness of the wicked will be
charged against him.[d]

21“But if a wicked man turns away
from all the sins he has committed and
keeps all my decrees and does what is
just and right, he will surely live; he will

[a]*8* Or *take interest*; similarly in verses 13 and 17
[b]*10* Or *things to a brother* [c]*17* Septuagint (see also verse 8); Hebrew *from the poor*

18:4 [l]ver 20; Isa 42:5; Ro 6:23
18:6 [m]Eze 22:9 [n]Dt 4:19; Eze 6:13; 20:24
18:7 [o]Ex 22:21 [p]Ex 22:26; Dt 24:12 [q]Dt 15:11; Mt 25:36
18:8 [r]Ex 22:25; Lev 25:35-37; Dt 23:19-20 [s]Zec 8:16
18:9 [t]Hab 2:4 [u]Lev 18:5; Eze 20:11; Am 5:4
18:10 [v]Ex 21:12
18:12 [w]Am 4:1
18:12 [x]2Ki 21:11; Isa 59:6-7; Jer 22:17; Eze 8:6,17
18:13 [y]Ex 22:25 [z]Eze 33:4-5
18:14 [a]2Ch 34:21; Pr 23:24
18:16 [b]Ps 41:1; Isa 58:10
18:19 [c]Ex 20:5; Dt 5:9; Jer 15:4; Zec 1:3-6
18:20 [d]Dt 24:16; 1Ki 8:32; 2Ki 14:6; Isa 3:11; Mt 16:27; Ro 2:9

not die.[e] 22None of the offenses he has
committed will be remembered against
him. Because of the righteous things
he has done, he will live.[f] 23Do I take
any pleasure in the death of the wicked?
declares the Sovereign LORD. Rather,
am I not pleased[g] when they turn from
their ways and live?[h]
24"But if a righteous man turns from
his righteousness and commits sin and
does the same detestable things the
wicked man does, will he live? None of
the righteous things he has done will be
remembered. Because of the unfaithfulness he is guilty of and because of the
sins he has committed, he will die.[i]
25"Yet you say, 'The way of the Lord
is not just.' Hear, O house of Israel:
Is my way unjust?[j] Is it not your ways
that are unjust? 26If a righteous man
turns from his righteousness and commits sin, he will die for it; because of
the sin he has committed he will die.
27But if a wicked man turns away from
the wickedness he has committed and
does what is just and right, he will save
his life.[k] 28Because he considers all the
offenses he has committed and turns
away from them, he will surely live; he
will not die. 29Yet the house of Israel
says, 'The way of the Lord is not just.'
Are my ways unjust, O house of Israel?
Is it not your ways that are unjust?
30"Therefore, O house of Israel, I
will judge you, each one according
to his ways, declares the Sovereign
LORD. Repent![l] Turn away from all
your offenses; then sin will not be your
downfall.[m] 31Rid yourselves of all the
offenses you have committed, and get a
new heart[n] and a new spirit. Why will
you die, O house of Israel?[o] 32For I take
no pleasure in the death of anyone, declares the Sovereign LORD. Repent and
live![p]

A Lament for Israel's Princes

19 "Take up a lament[q] concerning
the princes[r] of Israel 2and say:

"'What a lioness was your mother
among the lions!
She lay down among the young lions
and reared her cubs.
3She brought up one of her cubs,
and he became a strong lion.
He learned to tear the prey
and he devoured men.
4The nations heard about him,
and he was trapped in their pit.
They led him with hooks
to the land of Egypt.[s]

5"'When she saw her hope
unfulfilled,
her expectation gone,
she took another of her cubs
and made him a strong lion.[t]
6He prowled among the lions,
for he was now a strong lion.
He learned to tear the prey
and he devoured men.[u]

18:21 [e]Eze 33:12,19
18:22 [f]Ps 18:20-24; Isa 43:25; Mic 7:19
18:23 [g]Ps 147:11 [h]Eze 33:11; 1Ti 2:4
18:24 [i]1Sa 15:11; 2Ch 24:17-20; Eze 3:20; 20:27; 2Pe 2:20-22
18:25 [j]Ge 18:25; Jer 12:1; Eze 33:17; Zep 3:5; Mal 2:17; 3:13-15
18:27 [k]Isa 1:18
18:30 [l]Mt 3:2 [m]Eze 7:3; 33:20; Hos 12:6
18:31 [n]Ps 51:10 [o]Isa 1:16-17; Eze 11:19; 36:26
18:32 [p]Eze 33:11
19:1 [q]Eze 26:17; 27:2,32 [r]2Ki 24:6
19:4 [s]2Ki 23:33-34; 2Ch 36:4
19:5 [t]2Ki 23:34
19:6 [u]2Ki 24:9; 2Ch 36:9

DAY FOUR

▸ LOVE AND MY SERVICE TO OTHERS

Ezekiel 18:30–32

What is to be the heart of our service to others? To fall in love with love and to preach the unsearchable riches of Christ. Our service is to inform all people that God is after them and to beg them to quickly come to his love. Our service is to preach, "Rid yourselves of all the offenses you have committed, and get a new heart and a new spirit" (Ezekiel 18:31).

I have often wondered whether Ezekiel could have experienced the full light of the New Testament if he had been able to stand back and gaze at Calvary love. Seeing the cross high and lifted up makes visible the unconditional love of God. Jesus hung on Calvary to affirm Ezekiel 18:31, to speak it loudly: "Rid yourselves of all the offenses . . . and get a new heart and a new spirit."

Life's lessons come in wood and steel,
And hope is born where vengeance cries.
Forgiveness grows where God must feel
What tears the soul and crucifies.

Because of your deep guilt and sin
My life was counted loss;
I shuddered in the April wind,
I knew the chafing cross.

Earth's epoch hourglass spilling time
Has measured centuries since then;
You played your part in cosmic crime.
You need a cosmic friend.

To begin a study on the topic of Love, the Unconditional Longing of God, turn to the home page on page 89.

[7] He broke down[a] their strongholds
and devastated[v] their towns.
The land and all who were in it
were terrified by his roaring.
[8] Then the nations[w] came against him,
those from regions round about.
They spread their net for him,
and he was trapped in their pit.[x]
[9] With hooks they pulled him into a
cage
and brought him to the king of
Babylon.[y]
They put him in prison,
so his roar was heard no longer
on the mountains of Israel.[z]
[10] "'Your mother was like a vine in
your vineyard[b]
planted by the water;[a]
it was fruitful and full of branches
because of abundant water.
[11] Its branches were strong,
fit for a ruler's scepter.
It towered high
above the thick foliage,
conspicuous for its height
and for its many branches.[b]
[12] But it was uprooted[c] in fury
and thrown to the ground.
The east wind made it shrivel,[d]
it was stripped of its fruit;
its strong branches withered
and fire consumed them.[d]
[13] Now it is planted in the desert,[e]
in a dry and thirsty land.[f]
[14] Fire spread from one of its main[c]
branches
and consumed[g] its fruit.
No strong branch is left on it
fit for a ruler's scepter.'[h]

This is a lament and is to be used as a lament."

19:7 [v]Eze 30:12
19:8 [w]2Ki 24:2 [x]2Ki 24:11
19:9 [y]2Ch 36:6 [z]2Ki 24:15
19:10 [a]Ps 80:8-11
19:11 [b]Eze 31:3; Da 4:11
19:12 [c]Eze 17:10 [d]Isa 27:11; Eze 28:17; Hos 13:15
19:13 [e]Eze 20:35 [f]Hos 2:3
19:14 [g]Eze 20:47 [h]Eze 15:4

Rebellious Israel

20 In the seventh year, in the fifth
month on the tenth day, some
of the elders of Israel came to inquire of
the LORD, and they sat down in front
of me.[i]
[2] Then the word of the LORD came
to me: [3] "Son of man, speak to the elders of Israel and say to them, 'This is
what the Sovereign LORD says: Have
you come to inquire[j] of me? As surely
as I live, I will not let you inquire of
me, declares the Sovereign LORD.'[k]
[4] "Will you judge them? Will you
judge them, son of man? Then confront them with the detestable practices
of their fathers[l] [5] and say to them: 'This
is what the Sovereign LORD says: On
the day I chose[m] Israel, I swore with
uplifted hand to the descendants of the
house of Jacob and revealed myself to
them in Egypt. With uplifted hand I
said to them, "I am the LORD your
God.[n]" [6] On that day I swore to them
that I would bring them out of Egypt
into a land I had searched out for them,
a land flowing with milk and honey,[o]
the most beautiful of all lands.[p] [7] And I
said to them, "Each of you, get rid of
the vile images[q] you have set your eyes
on, and do not defile yourselves with
the idols of Egypt. I am the LORD your
God.[r]"
[8] "'But they rebelled against me and
would not listen to me; they did not
get rid of the vile images they had set
their eyes on, nor did they forsake the
idols of Egypt.[s] So I said I would pour
out my wrath on them and spend my
anger against them in Egypt.[t] [9] But for
the sake of my name I did what would
keep it from being profaned in the eyes
of the nations they lived among and
in whose sight I had revealed myself
to the Israelites by bringing them out
of Egypt.[u] [10] Therefore I led them out
of Egypt and brought them into the
desert.[v] [11] I gave them my decrees and
made known to them my laws, for
the man who obeys them will live by
them.[w] [12] Also I gave them my Sabbaths as a sign[x] between us, so they
would know that I the LORD made
them holy.
[13] "'Yet the people of Israel rebelled[y]
against me in the desert. They did
not follow my decrees but rejected my
laws—although the man who obeys
them will live by them—and they utterly desecrated my Sabbaths. So I said
I would pour out my wrath[z] on them
and destroy them in the desert.[a] [14] But
for the sake of my name I did what
would keep it from being profaned in
the eyes of the nations in whose sight I
had brought them out.[b] [15] Also with uplifted hand I swore to them in the desert that I would not bring them into the
land I had given them—a land flowing

20:1 [i]Eze 8:1
20:3 [j]Eze 14:3 [k]Mic 3:7
20:4 [l]Eze 16:2; 22:2; Mt 23:32
20:5 [m]Dt 7:6 [n]Ex 6:7
20:6 [o]Ex 3:8; Jer 32:22 [p]Dt 8:7; Ps 48:2; Da 8:9
20:7 [q]Ex 20:4 [r]Ex 20:2; Lev 18:3; Dt 29:18
20:8 [s]Eze 7:8 [t]Isa 63:10
20:9 [u]Eze 36:22; 39:7
20:10 [v]Ex 13:18
20:11 [w]Lev 18:5; Dt 4:7-8; Ro 10:5
20:12 [x]Ex 31:13
20:13 [y]Ps 78:40 [z]Dt 9:8 [a]Nu 14:29; Ps 95:8-10; Isa 56:6
20:14 [b]Eze 36:23

[a] *7* Targum (see Septuagint); Hebrew *He knew*
[b] *10* Two Hebrew manuscripts; most Hebrew manuscripts *your blood*
[c] *14* Or *from under its*

with milk and honey, most beautiful
20:15 [e]Ps 95:11; 106:26 of all lands[e]— 16because they rejected
my laws and did not follow my decrees
20:16 [d]Nu 15:39 [e]Am 5:26 and desecrated my Sabbaths. For their
hearts[d] were devoted to their idols.[e]
17Yet I looked on them with pity and
did not destroy them or put an end
to them in the desert. 18I said to their
20:18 [f]Zec 1:4 children in the desert, "Do not follow
the statutes of your fathers[f] or keep
20:19 [g]Ex 20:2 [h]Dt 5:32-33; 6:1-2; 8:1; 11:1; 12:1 their laws or defile yourselves with their
idols. 19I am the LORD your God;[g] fol-
low my decrees and be careful to keep
my laws.[h] 20Keep my Sabbaths holy,
that they may be a sign between us.
20:20 [i]Jer 17:22 Then you will know that I am the
LORD your God.[i]"
21" 'But the children rebelled against
me: They did not follow my decrees,
they were not careful to keep my laws—
although the man who obeys them will
live by them—and they desecrated my
Sabbaths. So I said I would pour out
my wrath on them and spend my an-
20:22 [j]Ps 78:38 ger against them in the desert. 22But I
withheld[j] my hand, and for the sake
of my name I did what would keep it
from being profaned in the eyes of the
nations in whose sight I had brought
them out. 23Also with uplifted hand
I swore to them in the desert that I
would disperse them among the nations
20:23 [k]Lev 26:33; Dt 28:64 and scatter[k] them through the countries, 24because they had not obeyed my
20:24 [l]ver 13 [m]Eze 6:9 [n]ver 16 laws but had rejected my decrees and
desecrated my Sabbaths,[l] and their eyes
⌞lusted⌟ after[m] their fathers' idols.[n] 25I
20:25 [o]Ps 81:12 [p]2Th 2:11 also gave them over[o] to statutes that
were not good and laws they could not
live by;[p] 26I let them become defiled
through their gifts—the sacrifice of every firstborn[a]—that I might fill them
20:26 [q]2Ki 17:17 with horror so they would know that I
am the LORD.[q]'
27"Therefore, son of man, speak to
the people of Israel and say to them,
'This is what the Sovereign LORD says:
20:27 [r]Ro 2:24 [s]Eze 18:24 In this also your fathers blasphemed[r]
me by forsaking me:[s] 28When I brought
20:28 [t]Ps 78:55,58 [u]Eze 6:13 them into the land[t] I had sworn to give
them and they saw any high hill or
any leafy tree, there they offered their
sacrifices, made offerings that provoked
me to anger, presented their fragrant
incense and poured out their drink
offerings.[u] 29Then I said to them: What
is this high place you go to?' " (It is
called Bamah[b] to this day.)

Judgment and Restoration

30"Therefore say to the house of Israel: 'This is what the Sovereign LORD
says: Will you defile yourselves[v] the way 20:30 [v]ver 43 [w]Jer 16:12
your fathers did and lust after their vile
images?[w] 31When you offer your gifts—
the sacrifice of your sons[x] in[c] the fire— 20:31 [x]Eze 16:20 [y]Ps 106:37-39; Jer 7:31
you continue to defile yourselves with all
your idols to this day. Am I to let you inquire of me, O house of Israel? As surely
as I live, declares the Sovereign LORD, I
will not let you inquire of me.[y]
32" 'You say, "We want to be like the
nations, like the peoples of the world,
who serve wood and stone." But what
you have in mind will never happen.
33As surely as I live, declares the Sovereign LORD, I will rule over you with a
mighty hand and an outstretched arm
and with outpoured wrath.[z] 34I will 20:33 [z]Jer 21:5
bring you from the nations[a] and gather
you from the countries where you have 20:34 [a]2Co 6:17* [b]Isa 27:12-13; Jer 44:6; La 2:4
been scattered—with a mighty hand and
an outstretched arm and with outpoured
wrath.[b] 35I will bring you into the desert
of the nations and there, face to face, I
will execute judgment[c] upon you. 36As I 20:35 [c]Jer 2:35
judged your fathers in the desert of the
land of Egypt, so I will judge you, de- 20:36 [d]Nu 11:1-35; 1Co 10:5-10
clares the Sovereign LORD.[d] 37I will take
note of you as you pass under my rod,[e]
and I will bring you into the bond of the 20:37 [e]Lev 27:32; Jer 33:13 [f]Eze 16:62
covenant.[f] 38I will purge[g] you of those
who revolt and rebel against me. Al-
though I will bring them out of the land 20:38 [g]Eze 34:17-22; Am 9:9-10 [h]Ps 95:11; Jer 44:14; Eze 13:9; Mal 3:3; Heb 4:3
where they are living, yet they will not
enter the land of Israel. Then you will
know that I am the LORD.[h]
39" 'As for you, O house of Israel,
this is what the Sovereign LORD says:
Go and serve your idols,[i] every one of 20:39 [i]Jer 44:25 [j]Isa 1:13; Eze 43:7; Am 4:4
you! But afterward you will surely lis-
ten to me and no longer profane my
holy name with your gifts and idols.[j]
40For on my holy mountain, the high
mountain of Israel, declares the Sovereign LORD, there in the land the entire
house of Israel will serve me, and there
I will accept them. There I will require
your offerings[k] and your choice gifts,[d] 20:40 [k]Isa 60:7 [l]Isa 56:7; Mal 3:4
along with all your holy sacrifices.[l] 41I
will accept you as fragrant incense when
I bring you out from the nations and

[a]26 Or *—making every firstborn pass through ⌞the fire⌟* [b]29 *Bamah* means *high place.* [c]31 Or *—making your sons pass through* [d]40 Or *and the gifts of your firstfruits*

gather you from the countries where you have been scattered, and I will show myself holy[m] among you in the sight of the nations.[n] 42 Then you will know that I am the LORD,[o] when I bring you into the land of Israel,[p] the land I had sworn with uplifted hand to give to your fathers. 43 There you will remember your conduct and all the actions by which you have defiled yourselves, and you will loathe yourselves for all the evil you have done.[q] 44 You will know that I am the LORD, when I deal with you for my name's sake[r] and not according to your evil ways and your corrupt practices, O house of Israel, declares the Sovereign LORD.[s]' "

Prophecy Against the South

45 The word of the LORD came to me: 46 "Son of man, set your face toward the south; preach against the south and prophesy against[t] the forest of the southland.[u] 47 Say to the southern forest: 'Hear the word of the LORD. This is what the Sovereign LORD says: I am about to set fire to you, and it will consume all your trees, both green and dry. The blazing flame will not be quenched, and every face from south to north will be scorched by it.[v] 48 Everyone will see that I the LORD have kindled it; it will not be quenched.[w]' "

49 Then I said, "Ah, Sovereign LORD! They are saying of me, 'Isn't he just telling parables?[x]' "

Babylon, God's Sword of Judgment

21 The word of the LORD came to me: 2 "Son of man, set your face against Jerusalem and preach against[y] the sanctuary. Prophesy against the land of Israel 3 and say to her: 'This is what the LORD says: I am against you.[z] I will draw my sword from its scabbard and cut off from you both the righteous and the wicked.[a] 4 Because I am going to cut off the righteous and the wicked, my sword will be unsheathed against everyone from south to north.[b] 5 Then all people will know that I the LORD have drawn my sword from its scabbard; it will not return[c] again.'[d]

6 "Therefore groan, son of man! Groan before them with broken heart and bitter grief.[e] 7 And when they ask you, 'Why are you groaning?' you shall say, 'Because of the news that is coming. Every heart will melt and every hand go limp;[f] every spirit will become faint and every knee become as weak as water.' It is coming! It will surely take place, declares the Sovereign LORD."

8 The word of the LORD came to me: 9 "Son of man, prophesy and say, 'This is what the Lord says:

" 'A sword, a sword,
sharpened and polished—
10 sharpened for the slaughter,[g]
polished to flash like lightning!

" 'Shall we rejoice in the scepter of my son ⌊Judah⌋? The sword despises every such stick.

11 " 'The sword is appointed to be polished,[h]
to be grasped with the hand;
it is sharpened and polished,
made ready for the hand of the slayer.
12 Cry out and wail, son of man,
for it is against my people;
it is against all the princes of Israel.
They are thrown to the sword
along with my people.
Therefore beat your breast.[i]

13 " 'Testing will surely come. And what if the scepter ⌊of Judah⌋, which the sword despises, does not continue? declares the Sovereign LORD.'

14 "So then, son of man, prophesy
and strike your hands[j] together.
Let the sword strike twice,
even three times.
It is a sword for slaughter—
a sword for great slaughter,
closing in on them from every side.[k]
15 So that hearts may melt[l]
and the fallen be many,
I have stationed the sword for slaughter[a]
at all their gates.
Oh! It is made to flash like lightning,
it is grasped for slaughter.[m]
16 O sword, slash to the right,
then to the left,
wherever your blade is turned.
17 I too will strike my hands[n] together,
and my wrath[o] will subside.
I the LORD have spoken."

[a] *15* Septuagint; the meaning of the Hebrew for this word is uncertain.

20:41 [m]Eze 28:25; 36:23 [n]Eze 11:17
20:42 [o]Eze 38:23 [p]Eze 34:13; 36:24
20:43 [q]Eze 6:9; 16:61; Hos 5:15
20:44 [r]Eze 36:22 [s]Eze 24:24
20:46 [t]Eze 21:2; Am 7:16 [u]Isa 30:6; Jer 13:19
20:47 [v]Isa 9:18-19; 13:8; Jer 21:14
20:48 [w]Jer 7:20
20:49 [x]Mt 13:13; Jn 16:25
21:2 [y]Eze 20:46
21:3 [z]Jer 21:13 [a]ver 9-11; Job 9:22
21:4 [b]Eze 20:47
21:5 [c]ver 30 [d]Na 1:9
21:6 [e]Isa 22:4
21:7 [f]Eze 22:14; 7:17
21:10 [g]Ps 110:5-6; Isa 34:5-6
21:11 [h]Jer 46:4
21:12 [i]Jer 31:19
21:14 [j]Nu 24:10 [k]Eze 6:11; 30:24
21:15 [l]2Sa 17:10 [m]Ps 22:14
21:17 [n]ver 14; Eze 22:13 [o]Eze 5:13

GOODNESS

AN INFINITY OF HURT

Ezekiel 21:17

God waits to extend his cup of mercy. The healing lies in the asking. Dante was right, "Infinite goodness has such wide arms that it takes in whatever turns to it."

18 The word of the LORD came to
me: 19 "Son of man, mark out two roads
for the sword of the king of Babylon to
take, both starting from the same country. Make a signpost where the road
branches off to the city. 20 Mark out
one road for the sword to come against
21:20 [p]Dt 3:11; Jer 49:2; Am 1:14 Rabbah of the Ammonites[p] and another against Judah and fortified Jerusa-
lem. 21 For the king of Babylon will stop
at the fork in the road, at the junction
of the two roads, to seek an omen: He
21:21 [q]Pr 16:33 [r]Nu 22:7; 23:23 will cast lots[q] with arrows, he will consult his idols, he will examine the liver.[r]
22 Into his right hand will come the lot
for Jerusalem, where he is to set up battering rams, to give the command to
slaughter, to sound the battle cry, to
set battering rams against the gates, to
21:22 [s]Eze 4:2; 26:9 build a ramp and to erect siege works.[s]
23 It will seem like a false omen to those
who have sworn allegiance to him, but
21:23 [t]Nu 5:15 he will remind[t] them of their guilt and
take them captive.
24 "Therefore this is what the Sovereign LORD says: 'Because you people
have brought to mind your guilt by
your open rebellion, revealing your sins
in all that you do—because you have
done this, you will be taken captive.
25 " 'O profane and wicked prince of
Israel, whose day has come, whose time
21:25 [u]Eze 35:5 of punishment has reached its climax,[u]
26 this is what the Sovereign LORD says:
21:26 [v]Jer 13:18 [w]Ps 75:7; Eze 17:24 Take off the turban, remove the crown.[v]
It will not be as it was: The lowly will be
exalted and the exalted will be brought
low.[w] 27 A ruin! A ruin! I will make it
a ruin! It will not be restored until he
comes to whom it rightfully belongs; to
21:27 [x]Ps 2:6; Jer 23:5-6; Eze 37:24; Hag 2:21-22 him I will give it.'[x]
28 "And you, son of man, prophesy
and say, 'This is what the Sovereign
21:28 [y]Zep 2:8 [z]Jer 12:12 LORD says about the Ammonites[y] and
their insults:

" 'A sword,[z] a sword,
drawn for the slaughter,
polished to consume
and to flash like lightning!
29 Despite false visions concerning you
and lying divinations about you,
it will be laid on the necks
of the wicked who are to be slain,
whose day has come,
whose time of punishment has
reached its climax.[a] 21:29 [a]ver 25; Eze 22:28; 35:5
30 Return the sword to its scabbard.[b]
In the place where you were
created,
in the land of your ancestry,[c] 21:30 [b]Jer 47:6 [c]Eze 16:3
I will judge you.
31 I will pour out my wrath upon you
and breathe out my fiery anger[d] 21:31 [d]Eze 22:20-21 [e]Jer 51:20-23
against you;
I will hand you over to brutal men,
men skilled in destruction.[e]
32 You will be fuel for the fire,[f] 21:32 [f]Mal 4:1 [g]Eze 25:10
your blood will be shed in your
land,
you will be remembered[g] no more;
for I the LORD have spoken.' "

Jerusalem's Sins

22 The word of the LORD came
to me: 2 "Son of man, will you
judge her? Will you judge this city of
bloodshed?[h] Then confront her with all 22:2 [h]Eze 24:6,9; Na 3:1 [i]Eze 16:2
her detestable practices[i] 3 and say: 'This
is what the Sovereign LORD says: O city
that brings on herself doom by shed-
ding blood[j] in her midst and defiles 22:3 [j]ver 6,13,27; Eze 23:37,45
herself by making idols, 4 you have be-
come guilty because of the blood you
have shed[k] and have become defiled 22:4 [k]2Ki 21:16 [l]Eze 21:25 [m]Eze 5:14
by the idols you have made. You have
brought your days to a close, and the
end of your years has come.[l] Therefore I
will make you an object of scorn to the
nations and a laughingstock to all the
countries.[m] 5 Those who are near and
those who are far away will mock you,
O infamous city, full of turmoil.
6 " 'See how each of the princes of Israel who are in you uses his power to
shed blood.[n] 7 In you they have treated 22:6 [n]Isa 1:23
father and mother with contempt;[o] in 22:7 [o]Dt 5:16; 27:16 [p]Ex 22:21-22
you they have oppressed the alien and
mistreated the fatherless and the wid-
ow.[p] 8 You have despised my holy things 22:8 [q]Eze 23:38-39
and desecrated my Sabbaths.[q] 9 In you
are slanderous men[r] bent on shedding 22:9 [r]Lev 19:16 [s]Eze 18:11 [t]Hos 4:10,14
blood; in you are those who eat at the
mountain shrines[s] and commit lewd
acts.[t] 10 In you are those who dishonor
their fathers' bed; in you are those

who violate women during their period,
when they are ceremonially unclean.[u]
11 In you one man commits a detestable
offense with his neighbor's wife, another shamefully defiles his daughter-in-
law,[v] and another violates his sister,[w] his
own father's daughter. 12 In you men
accept bribes[x] to shed blood; you take
usury and excessive interest[a] and make
unjust gain from your neighbors[y] by
extortion. And you have forgotten me,
declares the Sovereign LORD.
13 " 'I will surely strike my hands[z] together at the unjust gain[a] you have
made and at the blood[b] you have shed
in your midst. 14 Will your courage endure or your hands be strong in the
day I deal with you? I the LORD have
spoken,[c] and I will do it.[d] 15 I will disperse you among the nations and scatter[e] you through the countries; and I
will put an end to your uncleanness.[f]
16 When you have been defiled[b] in the
eyes of the nations, you will know that
I am the LORD.' "
17 Then the word of the LORD came
to me: 18 "Son of man, the house of Israel has become dross[g] to me; all of
them are the copper, tin, iron and lead
left inside a furnace. They are but the
dross of silver.[h] 19 Therefore this is what
the Sovereign LORD says: 'Because you
have all become dross, I will gather you
into Jerusalem. 20 As men gather silver,
copper, iron, lead and tin into a furnace
to melt it with a fiery blast, so will I
gather you in my anger and my wrath
and put you inside the city and melt
you.[i] 21 I will gather you and I will blow
on you with my fiery wrath, and you
will be melted[j] inside her. 22 As silver
is melted in a furnace, so you will be
melted inside her, and you will know
that I the LORD have poured out my
wrath upon you.' "[k]
23 Again the word of the LORD came
to me: 24 "Son of man, say to the land,
'You are a land that has had no rain or
showers[c] in the day of wrath.'[l] 25 There
is a conspiracy[m] of her princes[d] within
her like a roaring lion tearing its prey;
they devour people,[n] take treasures and
precious things and make many widows[o] within her. 26 Her priests do violence to my law[p] and profane my holy
things; they do not distinguish between
the holy and the common;[q] they teach
that there is no difference between the

22:10 [u]Lev 18:8,19
22:11 [v]Lev 18:15 [w]Lev 18:9; 2Sa 13:14
22:12 [x]Dt 27:25; Mic 7:3 [y]Lev 19:13
22:13 [z]Eze 21:17 [a]Isa 33:15 [b]ver 3
22:14 [c]Eze 24:14 [d]Eze 17:24; 21:7
22:15 [e]Dt 4:27; Zec 7:14 [f]Eze 23:27
22:18 [g]Ps 119:119; Isa 1:22 [h]Jer 6:28-30
22:20 [i]Mal 3:2
22:22 [j]Isa 1:25 [k]Eze 20:8,33
22:24 [l]Eze 24:13
22:25 [m]Jer 11:9 [n]Hos 6:9 [o]Jer 15:8
22:26 [p]Mal 2:7-8 [q]Eze 44:23

unclean and the clean;[r] and they shut
their eyes to the keeping of my Sabbaths, so that I am profaned among
them.[s] 27 Her officials within her are
like wolves tearing their prey; they shed
blood and kill people to make unjust
gain.[t] 28 Her prophets whitewash[u] these
deeds for them by false visions and lying divinations. They say, 'This is what
the Sovereign LORD says'—when the
LORD has not spoken.[v] 29 The people
of the land practice extortion and commit robbery; they oppress the poor and
needy and mistreat the alien,[w] denying
them justice.[x]
30 "I looked for a man among them
who would build up the wall[y] and stand
before me in the gap on behalf of the
land so I would not have to destroy it,
but I found none.[z] 31 So I will pour out
my wrath on them and consume them
with my fiery anger, bringing down[a] on
their own heads all they have done, declares the Sovereign LORD.[b]"

Two Adulterous Sisters

23 The word of the LORD came to
me: 2 "Son of man, there were
two women, daughters of the same
mother.[c] 3 They became prostitutes in
Egypt,[d] engaging in prostitution[e] from
their youth. In that land their breasts
were fondled and their virgin bosoms
caressed. 4 The older was named Oholah,
and her sister was Oholibah. They were
mine and gave birth to sons and daughters. Oholah is Samaria, and Oholibah
is Jerusalem.
5 "Oholah engaged in prostitution
while she was still mine; and she lusted
after her lovers, the Assyrians[f]—warriors[g] 6 clothed in blue, governors and
commanders, all of them handsome
young men, and mounted horsemen.
7 She gave herself as a prostitute to all
the elite of the Assyrians and defiled
herself with all the idols of everyone she
lusted after.[h] 8 She did not give up the
prostitution she began in Egypt,[i] when
during her youth men slept with her,
caressed her virgin bosom and poured
out their lust upon her.[j]
9 "Therefore I handed her over[k] to
her lovers, the Assyrians, for whom she

22:26 [r]Lev 10:10 [s]1Sa 2:12-17; Jer 2:8,26; Hag 2:11-14
22:27 [t]Isa 1:23
22:28 [u]Eze 13:10 [v]Eze 13:2,6-7
22:29 [w]Ex 22:21; 23:9 [x]Isa 5:7
22:30 [y]Eze 13:5 [z]Ps 106:23; Jer 5:1
22:31 [a]Eze 16:43 [b]Eze 7:8-9; 9:10; Ro 2:8
23:2 [c]Jer 3:7; Eze 16:45
23:3 [d]Jos 24:14 [e]Lev 17:7
23:5 [f]2Ki 16:7; Hos 5:13 [g]Hos 8:9
23:7 [h]Hos 5:3; 6:10
23:8 [i]Ex 32:4 [j]Eze 16:15
23:9 [k]2Ki 18:11

[a]*12* Or *usury and interest* [b]*16* Or *When I have allotted you your inheritance* [c]*24* Septuagint; Hebrew *has not been cleansed or rained on* [d]*25* Septuagint; Hebrew *prophets*

lusted.[l] 10They stripped[m] her naked, took away her sons and daughters and killed her with the sword. She became a byword among women,[n] and punishment was inflicted on her.[o]

11"Her sister Oholibah saw this, yet in her lust and prostitution she was more depraved than her sister.[p] 12She too lusted after the Assyrians—governors and commanders, warriors in full dress, mounted horsemen, all handsome young men.[q] 13I saw that she too defiled herself; both of them went the same way.

14"But she carried her prostitution still further. She saw men portrayed on a wall,[r] figures of Chaldeans[a] portrayed in red,[s] 15with belts around their waists and flowing turbans on their heads; all of them looked like Babylonian chariot officers, natives of Chaldea.[b] 16As soon as she saw them, she lusted after them and sent messengers to them in Chaldea. 17Then the Babylonians came to her, to the bed of love, and in their lust they defiled her. After she had been defiled by them, she turned away from them in disgust. 18When she carried on her prostitution openly and exposed her nakedness, I turned away[t] from her in disgust, just as I had turned away from her sister.[u] 19Yet she became more and more promiscuous as she recalled the days of her youth, when she was a prostitute in Egypt. 20There she lusted after her lovers, whose genitals were like those of donkeys and whose emission was like that of horses. 21So you longed for the lewdness of your youth, when in Egypt your bosom was caressed and your young breasts fondled.[c][v]

22"Therefore, Oholibah, this is what the Sovereign LORD says: I will stir up your lovers against you, those you turned away from in disgust, and I will bring them against you from every side[w]— 23the Babylonians[x] and all the Chaldeans, the men of Pekod[y] and Shoa and Koa, and all the Assyrians with them, handsome young men, all of them governors and commanders, chariot officers and men of high rank, all mounted on horses.[z] 24They will come against you with weapons,[d] chariots and wagons[a] and with a throng of people; they will take up positions against you on every side with large and small shields and with helmets. I will turn

23:9 [l]Hos 11:5
23:10 [m]Hos 2:10 [n]Eze 16:41 [o]Eze 16:36
23:11 [p]Jer 3:8-11; Eze 16:51
23:12 [q]2Ki 16:7-15; 2Ch 28:16
23:14 [r]Eze 8:10 [s]Jer 22:14
23:18 [t]Ps 78:59; 106:40; Jer 6:8 [u]Jer 12:8; Am 5:21
23:21 [v]Eze 16:26
23:22 [w]Eze 16:37
23:23 [x]2Ki 20:14-18 [y]Jer 50:21 [z]2Ki 24:2
23:24 [a]Jer 47:3; Eze 26:7,10; Na 2:4

you over to them for punishment[b], and they will punish you according to their standards. 25I will direct my jealous anger against you, and they will deal with you in fury. They will cut off your noses and your ears, and those of you who are left will fall by the sword. They will take away your sons and daughters,[c] and those of you who are left will be consumed by fire.[d] 26They will also strip[e] you of your clothes and take your fine jewelry.[f] 27So I will put a stop[g] to the lewdness and prostitution you began in Egypt. You will not look on these things with longing or remember Egypt anymore.

28"For this is what the Sovereign LORD says: I am about to hand you over[h] to those you hate, to those you turned away from in disgust. 29They will deal with you in hatred and take away everything you have worked for. They will leave you naked and bare, and the shame of your prostitution will be exposed. Your lewdness and promiscuity[i] 30have brought this upon you, because you lusted after the nations and defiled yourself with their idols.[j] 31You have gone the way of your sister; so I will put her cup[k] into your hand.[l]

32"This is what the Sovereign LORD says:

"You will drink your sister's cup,
a cup large and deep;
it will bring scorn and derision,
for it holds so much.[m]
33You will be filled with drunkenness
and sorrow,
the cup of ruin and desolation,
the cup of your sister Samaria.[n]
34You will drink it[o] and drain it dry;
you will dash it to pieces
and tear your breasts.

I have spoken, declares the Sovereign LORD.

35"Therefore this is what the Sovereign LORD says: Since you have forgotten[p] me and thrust me behind your back,[q] you must bear the consequences of your lewdness and prostitution."

36The LORD said to me: "Son of man, will you judge Oholah and Ohol-

[a]*14* Or *Babylonians* [b]*15* Or *Babylonia*; also in verse 16 [c]*21* Syriac (see also verse 3); Hebrew *caressed because of your young breasts* [d]*24* The meaning of the Hebrew for this word is uncertain.

23:24 [b]Jer 39:5-6
23:25 [c]ver 47 [d]Eze 20:47-48
23:26 [e]Jer 13:22 [f]Isa 3:18-23; Eze 16:39
23:27 [g]Eze 16:41
23:28 [h]Jer 34:20
23:29 [i]Dt 28:48
23:30 [j]Eze 6:9
23:31 [k]Jer 25:15 [l]2Ki 21:13
23:32 [m]Ps 60:3; Isa 51:17; Jer 25:15
23:33 [n]Jer 25:15-16
23:34 [o]Ps 75:8; Isa 51:17
23:35 [p]Isa 17:10; Jer 3:21 [q]1Ki 14:9

ibah? Then confront[r] them with their
detestable practices,[s] 37for they have
committed adultery and blood is on
their hands. They committed adultery
with their idols; they even sacrificed
their children, whom they bore to me,[a]
as food for them.[t] 38They have also
done this to me: At that same time they
defiled my sanctuary and desecrated my
Sabbaths. 39On the very day they sacrificed their children to their idols, they
entered my sanctuary and desecrated[u]
it. That is what they did in my house.[v]
40"They even sent messengers for
men who came from far away,[w] and
when they arrived you bathed yourself
for them, painted your eyes[x] and put
on your jewelry.[y] 41You sat on an elegant couch,[z] with a table[a] spread before
it on which you had placed the incense
and oil that belonged to me.
42"The noise of a carefree crowd
was around her; Sabeans[b] were brought
from the desert along with men from
the rabble, and they put bracelets[b] on
the arms of the woman and her sister
and beautiful crowns on their heads.[c]
43Then I said about the one worn out
by adultery, 'Now let them use her as a
prostitute,[d] for that is all she is.' 44And
they slept with her. As men sleep with a
prostitute, so they slept with those lewd
women, Oholah and Oholibah. 45But
righteous men will sentence them to
the punishment of women who commit adultery and shed blood, because
they are adulterous and blood is on
their hands.[e]
46"This is what the Sovereign LORD
says: Bring a mob[f] against them and
give them over to terror and plunder.
47The mob will stone them and cut
them down with their swords; they will
kill their sons and daughters and burn[g]
down their houses.[h]
48"So I will put an end to lewdness
in the land, that all women may take
warning and not imitate you.[i] 49You
will suffer the penalty for your lewdness
and bear the consequences of your sins
of idolatry. Then you will know that I
am the Sovereign LORD.[j]"

The Cooking Pot

24 In the ninth year, in the tenth
month on the tenth day, the
word of the LORD came to me:[k] 2"Son
of man, record this date, this very date,
because the king of Babylon has laid
siege to Jerusalem this very day.[l] 3Tell
this rebellious house[m] a parable[n] and
say to them: 'This is what the Sovereign
LORD says:

" 'Put on the cooking pot;[o] put it on
and pour water into it.
4Put into it the pieces of meat,
all the choice pieces—the leg and
the shoulder.
Fill it with the best of these bones;
5take the pick of the flock.[p]
Pile wood beneath it for the bones;
bring it to a boil
and cook the bones in it.[q]

6" 'For this is what the Sovereign LORD
says:

" 'Woe to the city of bloodshed,[r]
to the pot now encrusted,
whose deposit will not go away!
Empty it piece by piece
without casting lots[s] for them.
7" 'For the blood she shed is in her
midst:
She poured it on the bare rock;
she did not pour it on the ground,
where the dust would cover it.[t]
8To stir up wrath and take revenge
I put her blood on the bare rock,
so that it would not be covered.

9" 'Therefore this is what the Sovereign
LORD says:

" 'Woe to the city of bloodshed!
I, too, will pile the wood high.
10So heap on the wood
and kindle the fire.
Cook the meat well,
mixing in the spices;
and let the bones be charred.
11Then set the empty pot on the
coals
till it becomes hot and its copper
glows
so its impurities may be melted
and its deposit burned away.[u]
12It has frustrated all efforts;
its heavy deposit has not been
removed,
not even by fire.

13" 'Now your impurity is lewdness.
Because I tried to cleanse you but you
would not be cleansed from your impu-

23:36 [r]Eze 16:2 [s]Isa 58:1; Eze 22:2; Mic 3:8
23:37 [t]Eze 16:36
23:39 [u]2Ki 21:4 [v]Jer 7:10
23:40 [w]Isa 57:9 [x]2Ki 9:30 [y]Jer 4:30; Eze 16:13-19
23:41 [z]Est 1:6; Pr 7:17; Am 6:4 [a]Isa 65:11; Eze 44:16
23:42 [b]Ge 24:30 [c]Eze 16:11-12
23:43 [d]ver 3
23:45 [e]Lev 20:10; Eze 16:38; Hos 6:5
23:46 [f]Eze 16:40
23:47 [g]2Ch 36:19 [h]2Ch 36:17; Eze 16:40-41
23:48 [i]2Pe 2:6
23:49 [j]Eze 7:4; 9:10; 20:38
24:1 [k]Eze 8:1
24:2 [l]2Ki 25:1; Jer 39:1; 52:4
24:3 [m]Isa 1:2; Eze 2:3,6 [n]Eze 17:2; 20:49 [o]Jer 1:13; Eze 11:3
24:5 [p]Jer 52:10 [q]Jer 52:24-27
24:6 [r]Eze 22:2 [s]Ob 1:11; Na 3:10
24:7 [t]Lev 17:13
24:11 [u]Jer 21:10; Eze 22:15

[a]37 Or *even made the children they bore to me pass through ⌊the fire⌋* [b]42 Or *drunkards*

rity, you will not be clean again until my wrath against you has subsided.[v]

14"'I the LORD have spoken. The time has come for me to act. I will not hold back; I will not have pity, nor will I relent. You will be judged according to your conduct and your actions,[w] declares the Sovereign LORD.[x]'"

Ezekiel's Wife Dies

15The word of the LORD came to me: 16"Son of man, with one blow I am about to take away from you the delight of your eyes. Yet do not lament or weep or shed any tears.[y] 17Groan quietly; do not mourn for the dead. Keep your turban fastened and your sandals on your feet; do not cover the lower part of your face or eat the customary food ⌞of mourners⌟.[z]"

18So I spoke to the people in the morning, and in the evening my wife died. The next morning I did as I had been commanded.

19Then the people asked me, "Won't you tell us what these things have to do with us?[a]"

20So I said to them, "The word of the LORD came to me: 21Say to the house of Israel, 'This is what the Sovereign LORD says: I am about to desecrate my sanctuary—the stronghold in which you take pride, the delight of your eyes,[b] the object of your affection. The sons and daughters[c] you left behind will fall by the sword.[d] 22And you will do as I have done. You will not cover the lower part of your face or eat the customary food ⌞of mourners⌟.[e] 23You will keep your turbans on your heads and your sandals on your feet. You will not mourn[f] or weep but will waste away because of[a] your sins and groan among yourselves.[g] 24Ezekiel will be a sign[h] to you; you will do just as he has done. When this happens, you will know that I am the Sovereign LORD.'

25"And you, son of man, on the day I take away their stronghold, their joy and glory, the delight of their eyes, their heart's desire, and their sons and daughters[i] as well— 26on that day a fugitive will come to tell you[j] the news. 27At that time your mouth will be opened; you will speak with him and will no longer be silent. So you will be a sign to them, and they will know that I am the LORD.[k]"

A Prophecy Against Ammon

25 The word of the LORD came to me: 2"Son of man, set your face against the Ammonites[l] and prophesy against them.[m] 3Say to them, 'Hear the word of the Sovereign LORD. This is what the Sovereign LORD says: Because you said "Aha![n]" over my sanctuary when it was desecrated and over the land of Israel when it was laid waste and over the people of Judah when they went into exile,[o] 4therefore I am going to give you to the people of the East[p] as a possession. They will set up their camps and pitch their tents among you; they will eat your fruit and drink your milk.[q] 5I will turn Rabbah[r] into a pasture for camels and Ammon into a resting place for sheep.[s] Then you will know that I am the LORD. 6For this is what the Sovereign LORD says: Because you have clapped your hands and stamped your feet, rejoicing with all the malice of your heart against the land of Israel,[t] 7therefore I will stretch out my hand[u] against you and give you as plunder to the nations. I will cut you off from the nations and exterminate you from the countries. I will destroy[v] you, and you will know that I am the LORD.[w]'"

A Prophecy Against Moab

8"This is what the Sovereign LORD says: 'Because Moab[x] and Seir said, "Look, the house of Judah has become like all the other nations," 9therefore I will expose the flank of Moab, beginning at its frontier towns—Beth Jeshimoth,[y] Baal Meon[z] and Kiriathaim[a]—the glory of that land. 10I will give Moab along with the Ammonites to the people of the East as a possession, so that the Ammonites will not be remembered[b] among the nations; 11and I will inflict punishment on Moab. Then they will know that I am the LORD.'"

A Prophecy Against Edom

12"This is what the Sovereign LORD says: 'Because Edom[c] took revenge on the house of Judah and became very guilty by doing so, 13therefore this is

[a]23 Or *away in*

24:13 [v]Jer 6:28-30; Eze 16:42; 22:24
24:14 [w]Eze 36:19 [x]Eze 18:30
24:16 [y]Jer 13:17; 16:5; 22:10
24:17 [z]Jer 16:7
24:19 [a]Eze 12:9; 37:18
24:21 [b]Ps 27:4 [c]Eze 23:25 [d]Jer 7:14,15; Eze 23:47
24:22 [e]Jer 16:7
24:23 [f]Job 27:15 [g]Ps 78:64
24:24 [h]Isa 20:3; Eze 4:3; 12:11
24:25 [i]Jer 11:22
24:26 [j]1Sa 4:12; Job 1:15-19
24:27 [k]Eze 3:26; 33:22
25:2 [l]Eze 21:28; Zep 2:8-9 [m]Jer 49:1-6
25:3 [n]Eze 26:2; 36:2 [o]Pr 17:5
25:4 [p]Jdg 6:3 [q]Dt 28:33,51; Jdg 6:33
25:5 [r]Dt 3:11; Eze 21:20 [s]Isa 17:2
25:6 [t]Ob 1:12; Zep 2:8
25:7 [u]Zep 1:4 [v]Eze 21:31 [w]Am 1:14-15
25:8 [x]Jer 48:1; Am 2:1
25:9 [y]Nu 33:49 [z]Nu 32:3; Jos 13:17 [a]Nu 32:37; Jos 13:19
25:10 [b]Eze 21:32
25:12 [c]2Ch 28:17

what the Sovereign LORD says: I will
stretch out my hand against Edom and
25:13 [d]Eze 29:8 kill its men and their animals.[d] I will
[e]Jer 25:23 lay it waste, and from Teman to Dedan[e] they will fall by the sword. 14I
will take vengeance on Edom by the
hand of my people Israel, and they will
deal with Edom in accordance with my
25:14 [f]Eze 35:11 anger[f] and my wrath; they will know
my vengeance, declares the Sovereign
LORD.'"

A Prophecy Against Philistia

15"This is what the Sovereign LORD
25:15 [g]2Ch 28:18 says: 'Because the Philistines[g] acted in
vengeance and took revenge with malice
in their hearts, and with ancient hostility sought to destroy Judah, 16therefore
this is what the Sovereign LORD says:
25:16 I am about to stretch out my hand
[h]Jer 47:1-7 against the Philistines,[h] and I will cut
[i]1Sa 30:14; Zep 2:4-5 off the Kerethites[i] and destroy those remaining along the coast. 17I will carry
out great vengeance on them and punish them in my wrath. Then they will
know that I am the LORD, when I take
vengeance on them.'"

A Prophecy Against Tyre

26 In the eleventh year, on the first
day of the month, the word of
26:2 the LORD came to me: 2"Son of man,
[j]2Sa 5:11; Isa 23 because Tyre[j] has said of Jerusalem,
[k]Eze 25:3 'Aha![k] The gate to the nations is broken,
and its doors have swung open to me;
now that she lies in ruins I will prosper,' 3therefore this is what the Sovereign
LORD says: I am against you, O Tyre,
26:3 and I will bring many nations against
[l]Isa 5:30; Jer 50:42; you, like the sea[l] casting up its waves.
51:42 4They will destroy[m] the walls of Tyre[n]
26:4 and pull down her towers; I will scrape
[m]Isa 23:1,11 away her rubble and make her a bare
[n]Am 1:10 rock. 5Out in the sea[o] she will become
26:5 a place to spread fishnets, for I have spo-
[o]Eze 27:32 [p]Eze 29:19 ken, declares the Sovereign LORD. She
will become plunder[p] for the nations,
6and her settlements on the mainland
will be ravaged by the sword. Then they
will know that I am the LORD.
7"For this is what the Sovereign LORD
says: From the north I am going to
26:7 [q]Jer 27:6 bring against Tyre Nebuchadnezzar[a][q]
[r]Ezr 7:12; Da 2:37 king of Babylon, king of kings,[r] with
[s]Eze 23:24; horses and chariots,[s] with horsemen and
Na 2:3-4 a great army. 8He will ravage your settle-
26:8 ments on the mainland with the sword;
[t]Jer 6:6 he will set up siege works[t] against you,
build a ramp[u] up to your walls and 26:8 [u]Eze 21:22
raise his shields against you. 9He will
direct the blows of his battering rams
against your walls and demolish your
towers with his weapons. 10His horses
will be so many that they will cover
you with dust. Your walls will tremble
at the noise of the war horses, wagons 26:10
and chariots[v] when he enters your gates [v]Jer 4:13
as men enter a city whose walls have 26:11
been broken through. 11The hoofs[w] of [w]Isa 5:28
his horses will trample all your streets; [x]Jer 43:13 [y]Isa 26:5
he will kill your people with the sword,
and your strong pillars[x] will fall to
the ground.[y] 12They will plunder your
wealth and loot your merchandise; they
will break down your walls and demolish your fine houses and throw your 26:12
stones, timber and rubble into the sea.[z] [z]Isa 23:8;
13I will put an end[a] to your noisy songs, Eze 27:3-27; 28:8
and the music of your harps[b] will be 26:13
heard no more.[c] 14I will make you a [a]Jer 7:34
bare rock, and you will become a place [b]Isa 14:11 [c]Jer 25:10;
to spread fishnets. You will never be Rev 18:22
rebuilt,[d] for I the LORD have spoken, 26:14
declares the Sovereign LORD. [d]Job 12:14; Mal 1:4
15"This is what the Sovereign LORD
says to Tyre: Will not the coastlands[e] 26:15
tremble[f] at the sound of your fall, when [e]Eze 27:35 [f]Jer 49:21
the wounded groan and the slaughter
takes place in you? 16Then all the princes
of the coast will step down from their
thrones and lay aside their robes and
take off their embroidered garments.
Clothed[g] with terror, they will sit on 26:16
the ground, trembling[h] every moment, [g]Job 8:22 [h]Hos 11:10
appalled[i] at you. 17Then they will take [i]Eze 32:10
up a lament[j] concerning you and say to 26:17
you: [j]Eze 19:1; 27:32

"'How you are destroyed, O city of [k]Isa 14:12
renown,
peopled by men of the sea!
You were a power on the seas,
you and your citizens;
you put your terror
on all who lived there.[k]
18Now the coastlands tremble
on the day of your fall;
the islands in the sea 26:18
are terrified at your collapse.'[l] [l]Isa 23:5; 41:5; Eze 27:35

19"This is what the Sovereign LORD
says: When I make you a desolate city,
like cities no longer inhabited, and
when I bring the ocean depths over you

[a]7 Hebrew *Nebuchadrezzar,* of which *Nebuchadnezzar* is a variant; here and often in Ezekiel and Jeremiah

26:19 [m]Isa 8:7-8
and its vast waters cover you,[m] 20 then
I will bring you down with those who
26:20 [n]Eze 32:18; Am 9:2; Jnh 2:2,6 [o]Eze 32:24,30
go down to the pit,[n] to the people of
long ago. I will make you dwell in the
earth below, as in ancient ruins, with
those who go down to the pit, and you
will not return or take your place[a] in
the land of the living.[o] 21 I will bring
you to a horrible end and you will be
no more. You will be sought, but you
will never again be found, declares the
26:21 [p]Eze 27:36; 28:19; Rev 18:21
Sovereign LORD."[p]

A Lament for Tyre

27 The word of the LORD came
to me: 2 "Son of man, take up a
lament concerning Tyre. 3 Say to Tyre,
27:3 [q]ver 33 [r]Eze 28:2
situated at the gateway to the sea,[q] merchant of peoples on many coasts, 'This
is what the Sovereign LORD says:

" 'You say, O Tyre,
"I am perfect in beauty.[r]"
4 Your domain was on the high seas;
your builders brought your beauty
to perfection.
5 They made all your timbers
27:5 [s]Dt 3:9
of pine trees from Senir[b];[s]
they took a cedar from Lebanon
to make a mast for you.
27:6 [t]Nu 21:33; Jer 22:20; Zec 11:2 [u]Ge 10:4; Isa 23:12
6 Of oaks[t] from Bashan
they made your oars;
of cypress wood[c] from the coasts of
Cyprus[d][u]
they made your deck, inlaid with
ivory.
7 Fine embroidered linen from Egypt
was your sail
and served as your banner;
your awnings were of blue and
27:7 [v]Ex 25:4; Jer 10:9
purple[v]
from the coasts of Elishah.
27:8 [w]Ge 10:18 [x]1Ki 9:27
8 Men of Sidon and Arvad[w] were your
oarsmen;
your skilled men, O Tyre, were
aboard as your seamen.[x]
27:9 [y]Jos 13:5; 1Ki 5:18
9 Veteran craftsmen of Gebal[e][y] were
on board
as shipwrights to caulk your seams.
All the ships of the sea and their
sailors
came alongside to trade for your
wares.

27:10 [z]Eze 38:5 [a]Eze 30:5
10 " 'Men of Persia,[z] Lydia and Put[a]
served as soldiers in your army.
They hung their shields and helmets
on your walls,
bringing you splendor.
11 Men of Arvad and Helech
manned your walls on every side;
men of Gammad
were in your towers.
They hung their shields around your
walls;
they brought your beauty to
perfection.

27:12 [b]Ge 10:4 [c]ver 18,33
12 " 'Tarshish[b] did business with you
because of your great wealth of goods;[c]
they exchanged silver, iron, tin and lead
for your merchandise.
27:13 [d]Ge 10:2; Isa 66:19; Eze 38:2 [e]Rev 18:13
13 " 'Greece, Tubal and Meshech[d] traded with you; they exchanged slaves[e] and
articles of bronze for your wares.
27:14 [f]Ge 10:3; Eze 38:6
14 " 'Men of Beth Togarmah[f] exchanged work horses, war horses and
mules for your merchandise.
27:15 [g]Ge 10:7 [h]Jer 25:22 [i]1Ki 10:22; Rev 18:12
15 " 'The men of Rhodes[f][g] traded with
you, and many coastlands[h] were your
customers; they paid you with ivory[i]
tusks and ebony.
27:16 [j]Jdg 10:6; Isa 7:1-8 [k]Eze 28:13
16 " 'Aram[g][j] did business with you
because of your many products; they
exchanged turquoise,[k] purple fabric,
embroidered work, fine linen, coral and
rubies for your merchandise.
27:17 [l]Jdg 11:33
17 " 'Judah and Israel traded with you;
they exchanged wheat from Minnith[l]
and confections,[h] honey, oil and balm
for your wares.
27:18 [m]Ge 14:15; Eze 47:16-18
18 " 'Damascus,[m] because of your
many products and great wealth of
goods, did business with you in wine
from Helbon and wool from Zahar.
19 " 'Danites and Greeks from Uzal
bought your merchandise; they exchanged wrought iron, cassia and calamus for your wares.
20 " 'Dedan traded in saddle blankets
with you.
27:21 [n]Ge 25:13; Isa 60:7
21 " 'Arabia and all the princes of Kedar[n] were your customers; they did
business with you in lambs, rams and
goats.
27:22 [o]Ge 10:7,28; 1Ki 10:1-2; Isa 60:6 [p]Ge 43:11
22 " 'The merchants of Sheba[o] and Ra-
amah traded with you; for your merchandise they exchanged the finest of
all kinds of spices[p] and precious stones,
and gold.

[a] *20* Septuagint; Hebrew *return, and I will give glory*
[b] *5* That is, Hermon [c] *6* Targum; the Masoretic Text has a different division of the consonants.
[d] *6* Hebrew *Kittim* [e] *9* That is, Byblos
[f] *15* Septuagint; Hebrew *Dedan* [g] *16* Most Hebrew manuscripts; some Hebrew manuscripts and Syriac *Edom* [h] *17* The meaning of the Hebrew for this word is uncertain.

[23]“ ‘Haran,[q] Canneh and Eden[r] and merchants of Sheba, Asshur and Kilmad traded with you. [24]In your marketplace they traded with you beautiful garments, blue fabric, embroidered work and multicolored rugs with cords twisted and tightly knotted.

[25]“ ‘The ships of Tarshish[s] serve
as carriers for your wares.
You are filled with heavy cargo
in the heart of the sea.
[26]Your oarsmen take you
out to the high seas.
But the east wind[t] will break you to pieces
in the heart of the sea.
[27]Your wealth,[u] merchandise and wares,
your mariners, seamen and shipwrights,
your merchants and all your soldiers,
and everyone else on board
will sink into the heart of the sea
on the day of your shipwreck.
[28]The shorelands will quake[v]
when your seamen cry out.
[29]All who handle the oars
will abandon their ships;
the mariners and all the seamen
will stand on the shore.
[30]They will raise their voice
and cry bitterly over you;
they will sprinkle dust[w] on their heads
and roll[x] in ashes.[y]
[31]They will shave their heads because of you
and will put on sackcloth.
They will weep[z] over you with anguish of soul
and with bitter mourning.[a]
[32]As they wail and mourn over you,
they will take up a lament[b] concerning you:
“Who was ever silenced like Tyre,
surrounded by the sea?”
[33]When your merchandise went out on the seas,
you satisfied many nations;
with your great wealth[c] and your wares
you enriched the kings of the earth.
[34]Now you are shattered by the sea
in the depths of the waters;
your wares and all your company
have gone down with you.[d]
[35]All who live in the coastlands[e]
are appalled at you;
their kings shudder with horror
and their faces are distorted with fear.
[36]The merchants among the nations
hiss at you;[f]
you have come to a horrible end
and will be no more.[g]’ ”

27:23 [q]2Ki 19:12 [r]Isa 37:12
27:25 [s]Isa 2:16 fn
27:26 [t]Ps 48:7; Jer 18:17
27:27 [u]Pr 11:4
27:28 [v]Eze 26:15
27:30 [w]2Sa 1:2 [x]Jer 6:26 [y]Rev 18:18-19
27:31 [z]Isa 16:9 [a]Isa 22:12; Eze 7:18
27:32 [b]Eze 26:17
27:33 [c]ver 12; Eze 28:4-5
27:34 [d]Zec 9:4
27:35 [e]Eze 26:15
27:36 [f]Jer 18:16; 19:8; 49:17; 50:13; Zep 2:15 [g]Ps 37:10,36; Eze 26:21

A Prophecy Against the King of Tyre

28 The word of the LORD came to me: [2]“Son of man, say to the ruler of Tyre, ‘This is what the Sovereign LORD says:

“ ‘In the pride of your heart
you say, “I am a god;
I sit on the throne[h] of a god
in the heart of the seas.”
But you are a man and not a god,
though you think you are as wise as a god.[i]

SELF-CONTROL

IN CHARGE OF EXCESSES

Ezekiel 28:2

Idols are a breeze to please since they are but extensions of ourselves. Idols have our appetites; in fact, idols *are* our appetites. It is not surprising that idolatry is both easy and common. The true God requires our sacrifice, demands our adoration and asks for the spending of our souls.

[3]Are you wiser than Daniel[a]?[j]
Is no secret hidden from you?
[4]By your wisdom and understanding
you have gained wealth for yourself
and amassed gold and silver
in your treasuries.[k]
[5]By your great skill in trading
you have increased your wealth,
and because of your wealth
your heart has grown proud.[l]

[6]“ ‘Therefore this is what the Sovereign LORD says:

“ ‘Because you think you are wise,
as wise as a god,
[7]I am going to bring foreigners
against you,

28:2 [h]Isa 14:13 [i]Ps 9:20; 82:6-7; Isa 31:3; 2Th 2:4
28:3 [j]Da 1:20; 5:11-12
28:4 [k]Zec 9:3
28:5 [l]Job 31:25; Ps 52:7; 62:10; Hos 12:8; 13:6

[a]3 Or *Danel*; the Hebrew spelling may suggest a person other than the prophet Daniel.

28:7 [m]Eze 30:11; 31:12; 32:12; Hab 1:6

the most ruthless of nations;[m]
they will draw their swords against
your beauty and wisdom
and pierce your shining splendor.

28:8 [n]Eze 32:30 [o]Eze 27:27

8 They will bring you down to the
pit,[n]
and you will die a violent death
in the heart of the seas.[o]
9 Will you then say, "I am a god,"
in the presence of those who kill
you?
You will be but a man, not a god,
in the hands of those who slay
you.

28:10 [p]Eze 31:18; 32:19,24

10 You will die the death of the
uncircumcised[p]
at the hands of foreigners.

I have spoken, declares the Sovereign
LORD.'"

28:12 [q]Eze 19:1 [r]Eze 27:2-4

11 The word of the LORD came to
me: 12 "Son of man, take up a lament[q]
concerning the king of Tyre and say to
him: 'This is what the Sovereign LORD
says:

"'You were the model of perfection,
full of wisdom and perfect in
beauty.[r]

28:13 [s]Ge 2:8 [t]Eze 31:8-9 [u]Eze 27:16

13 You were in Eden,[s]
the garden of God;[t]
every precious stone adorned you:
ruby, topaz and emerald,
chrysolite, onyx and jasper,
sapphire,[a] turquoise[u] and beryl.[b]
Your settings and mountings[c] were
made of gold;
on the day you were created they
were prepared.

28:14 [v]Ex 30:26; 40:9 [w]Ex 25:17-20

14 You were anointed[v] as a guardian
cherub,[w]
for so I ordained you.
You were on the holy mount of God;
you walked among the fiery
stones.
15 You were blameless in your ways
from the day you were created
till wickedness was found in you.

28:16 [x]Hab 2:17 [y]Ge 3:24

16 Through your widespread trade
you were filled with violence,[x]
and you sinned.
So I drove you in disgrace from the
mount of God,
and I expelled you, O guardian
cherub,[y]
from among the fiery stones.

28:17 [z]Eze 31:10

17 Your heart became proud[z]
on account of your beauty,
and you corrupted your wisdom
because of your splendor.
So I threw you to the earth;
I made a spectacle of you before
kings.
18 By your many sins and dishonest
trade
you have desecrated your
sanctuaries.
So I made a fire come out from you,
and it consumed you,

28:18 [a]Mal 4:3

and I reduced you to ashes[a] on the
ground
in the sight of all who were
watching.
19 All the nations who knew you
are appalled at you;

28:19 [b]Jer 51:64; Eze 26:21; 27:36

you have come to a horrible end
and will be no more.[b]'"

A Prophecy Against Sidon

20 The word of the LORD came to me:

28:21 [c]Eze 6:2 [d]Ge 10:15; Jer 25:22

21 "Son of man, set your face against[c]
Sidon;[d] prophesy against her 22 and
say: 'This is what the Sovereign LORD
says:

28:22 [e]Eze 39:13 [f]Eze 30:19

"'I am against you, O Sidon,
and I will gain glory[e] within you.
They will know that I am the LORD,
when I inflict punishment[f] on her
and show myself holy within her.
23 I will send a plague upon her
and make blood flow in her
streets.
The slain will fall within her,
with the sword against her on
every side.
Then they will know that I am the
LORD.[g]

28:23 [g]Eze 38:22

24 "'No longer will the people of Is-

28:24 [h]Nu 33:55; Jos 23:13; Eze 2:6

rael have malicious neighbors who are
painful briers and sharp thorns.[h] Then
they will know that I am the Sovereign
LORD.
25 "'This is what the Sovereign LORD

28:25 [i]Ps 106:47; Jer 32:37 [j]Isa 11:12 [k]Eze 20:41 [l]Jer 23:8; Eze 11:17; 34:27; 37:25

says: When I gather[i] the people of Israel from the nations where they have
been scattered,[j] I will show myself holy[k]
among them in the sight of the nations. Then they will live in their own
land, which I gave to my servant Jacob.[l]

28:26 [m]Jer 23:6

26 They will live there in safety[m] and will
build houses and plant vineyards; they

[a] *13* Or *lapis lazuli* [b] *13* The precise identification of some of these precious stones is uncertain.
[c] *13* The meaning of the Hebrew for this phrase is uncertain.

will live in safety when I inflict punishment on all their neighbors who maligned them. Then they will know that
I am the LORD their God.[n]' "

A Prophecy Against Egypt

29 In the tenth year, in the tenth
month on the twelfth day, the
word of the LORD came to me:[o] 2"Son
of man, set your face against Pharaoh
king of Egypt[p] and prophesy against
him and against all Egypt.[q] 3Speak to
him and say: 'This is what the Sovereign LORD says:

" 'I am against you, Pharaoh[r] king of
Egypt,
you great monster[s] lying among
your streams.
You say, "The Nile is mine;
I made it for myself."
4But I will put hooks[t] in your jaws
and make the fish of your streams
stick to your scales.
I will pull you out from among your
streams,
with all the fish sticking to your
scales.[u]
5I will leave you in the desert,
you and all the fish of your
streams.
You will fall on the open field
and not be gathered or picked up.
I will give you as food
to the beasts of the earth and the
birds of the air.[v]

6Then all who live in Egypt will know
that I am the LORD.

" 'You have been a staff of reed[w] for
the house of Israel. 7When they grasped
you with their hands, you splintered[x]
and you tore open their shoulders; when
they leaned on you, you broke and their
backs were wrenched.[a][y]
8" 'Therefore this is what the Sovereign LORD says: I will bring a sword
against you and kill your men and their
animals.[z] 9Egypt will become a desolate
wasteland. Then they will know that I
am the LORD.
" 'Because you said, "The Nile is
mine; I made it,[a]" 10therefore I am
against you and against your streams,
and I will make the land of Egypt a ruin
and a desolate waste from Migdol to
Aswan,[b] as far as the border of Cush.[b]
11No foot of man or animal will pass
through it; no one will live there for
forty years.[c] 12I will make the land of
Egypt desolate among devastated lands,
and her cities will lie desolate forty years
among ruined cities. And I will disperse
the Egyptians among the nations and
scatter them through the countries.[d]
13" 'Yet this is what the Sovereign
LORD says: At the end of forty years I
will gather the Egyptians from the nations where they were scattered. 14I will
bring them back from captivity and return them to Upper Egypt,[c][e] the land
of their ancestry. There they will be a
lowly[f] kingdom. 15It will be the lowliest of kingdoms and will never again
exalt itself above the other nations.[g] I
will make it so weak that it will never
again rule over the nations. 16Egypt will
no longer be a source of confidence[h]
for the people of Israel but will be a reminder of their sin in turning to her for
help. Then they will know that I am the
Sovereign LORD.[i]' "
17In the twenty-seventh year, in the
first month on the first day, the word of
the LORD came to me:[j] 18"Son of man,
Nebuchadnezzar[k] king of Babylon drove
his army in a hard campaign against
Tyre; every head was rubbed bare[l] and
every shoulder made raw. Yet he and his
army got no reward from the campaign
he led against Tyre. 19Therefore this is
what the Sovereign LORD says: I am going to give Egypt to Nebuchadnezzar
king of Babylon, and he will carry off
its wealth. He will loot and plunder the
land as pay for his army.[m] 20I have given
him Egypt as a reward for his efforts because he and his army did it for me, declares the Sovereign LORD.[n]
21"On that day I will make a horn[d][o]
grow for the house of Israel, and I will
open your mouth[p] among them. Then
they will know that I am the LORD.[q]"

A Lament for Egypt

30 The word of the LORD came
to me: 2"Son of man, prophesy
and say: 'This is what the Sovereign
LORD says:

" 'Wail[r] and say,
"Alas for that day!"

[a]*7* Syriac (see also Septuagint and Vulgate); Hebrew *and you caused their backs to stand* [b]*10* That is, the upper Nile region [c]*14* Hebrew *to Pathros* [d]*21 Horn* here symbolizes strength.

28:26 [n]Isa 65:21; Jer 32:15; Eze 38:8; Am 9:14-15
29:1 [o]ver 17; Eze 26:1
29:2 [p]Jer 25:19 [q]Isa 19:1-17; Jer 46:2; Eze 30:1-26; 31:1-18; 32:1-32
29:3 [r]Jer 44:30 [s]Ps 74:13; Isa 27:1; Eze 32:2
29:4 [t]2Ki 19:28 [u]Eze 38:4
29:5 [v]Jer 7:33; 34:20; Eze 32:4-6; 39:4
29:6 [w]2Ki 18:21; Isa 36:6
29:7 [x]Isa 36:6 [y]Eze 17:15-17
29:8 [z]Eze 14:17; 32:11-13
29:9 [a]Eze 30:7-8, 13-19
29:10 [b]Eze 30:6
29:11 [c]Eze 32:13
29:12 [d]Jer 46:19; Eze 30:7, 23,26
29:14 [e]Eze 30:14 [f]Eze 17:14
29:15 [g]Zec 10:11
29:16 [h]Isa 36:4,6 [i]Isa 30:2; Hos 8:13
29:17 [j]Eze 24:1
29:18 [k]Jer 27:6; Eze 26:7-8 [l]Jer 48:37
29:19 [m]Jer 43:10-13; Eze 30:4,10, 24-25
29:20 [n]Isa 10:6-7; 45:1; Jer 25:9
29:21 [o]Ps 132:17 [p]Eze 33:22 [q]Eze 24:27
30:2 [r]Isa 13:6

30:3 [s]Eze 7:7; Joel 2:1,11; Ob 1:15 [t]ver 18; Eze 7:12,19

[3] For the day is near,[s]
the day of the LORD[t] is near—
a day of clouds,
a time of doom for the nations.
[4] A sword will come against Egypt,
and anguish will come upon
Cush.[a]
When the slain fall in Egypt,
her wealth will be carried away
and her foundations torn down.[u]

30:4 [u]Eze 29:19

30:5 [v]Eze 27:10 [w]Jer 25:20

[5] Cush and Put,[v] Lydia and all Arabia,
Libya[b] and the people[w] of the covenant
land will fall by the sword along with
Egypt.

[6] " 'This is what the LORD says:

" 'The allies of Egypt will fall
and her proud strength will fail.
From Migdol to Aswan[x]
they will fall by the sword within
her,
declares the Sovereign
LORD.

30:6 [x]Eze 29:10

[7] " 'They will be desolate
among desolate lands,
and their cities will lie
among ruined cities.[y]

30:7 [y]Eze 29:12

[8] Then they will know that I am the
LORD,
when I set fire to Egypt
and all her helpers are crushed.

30:9 [z]Isa 18:1-2 [a]Isa 23:5 [b]Eze 32:9-10

[9] " 'On that day messengers will go
out from me in ships to frighten Cush[z]
out of her complacency. Anguish[a] will
take hold of them on the day of Egypt's
doom, for it is sure to come.[b]

[10] " 'This is what the Sovereign LORD
says:

" 'I will put an end to the hordes of
Egypt
by the hand of Nebuchadnezzar
king of Babylon.[c]

30:10 [c]Eze 29:19
30:11 [d]Eze 28:7

[11] He and his army—the most ruthless
of nations[d]—
will be brought in to destroy the
land.
They will draw their swords against
Egypt
and fill the land with the slain.

30:12 [e]Isa 19:6 [f]Eze 29:9

[12] I will dry up[e] the streams of the Nile[f]
and sell the land to evil men;
by the hand of foreigners
I will lay waste the land and
everything in it.

I the LORD have spoken.

[13] " 'This is what the Sovereign LORD
says:

" 'I will destroy the idols[g]
and put an end to the images in
Memphis.[c][h]
No longer will there be a prince in
Egypt,[i]
and I will spread fear throughout
the land.

30:13 [g]Jer 43:12 [h]Isa 19:13 [i]Zec 10:11

[14] I will lay[j] waste Upper Egypt,[d]
set fire to Zoan[k]
and inflict punishment on
Thebes.[e][l]

30:14 [j]Eze 29:14 [k]Ps 78:12,43 [l]Jer 46:25

[15] I will pour out my wrath on
Pelusium,[f]
the stronghold of Egypt,
and cut off the hordes of Thebes.
[16] I will set fire to Egypt;
Pelusium will writhe in agony.
Thebes will be taken by storm;
Memphis will be in constant
distress.
[17] The young men of Heliopolis[g][m] and
Bubastis[h]
will fall by the sword,
and the cities themselves will go
into captivity.

30:17 [m]Ge 41:45

[18] Dark will be the day at Tahpanhes
when I break the yoke of Egypt;[n]
there her proud strength will come
to an end.
She will be covered with clouds,
and her villages will go into
captivity.[o]

30:18 [n]Lev 26:13 [o]ver 3

[19] So I will inflict punishment on
Egypt,
and they will know that I am the
LORD.' "

[20] In the eleventh year, in the first
month on the seventh day, the word of
the LORD came to me:[p] [21] "Son of man,
I have broken the arm[q] of Pharaoh king
of Egypt. It has not been bound up for
healing[r] or put in a splint so as to become strong enough to hold a sword.
[22] Therefore this is what the Sovereign
LORD says: I am against Pharaoh king
of Egypt.[s] I will break both his arms,
the good arm as well as the broken one,
and make the sword fall from his hand.[t]
[23] I will disperse the Egyptians among

30:20 [p]Eze 26:1; 29:17; 31:1
30:21 [q]Jer 48:25 [r]Jer 30:13; 46:11
30:22 [s]Jer 46:25 [t]Ps 37:17

[a] *4* That is, the upper Nile region; also in verses 5 and 9 [b] *5* Hebrew *Cub* [c] *13* Hebrew *Noph*; also in verse 16 [d] *14* Hebrew *waste Pathros* [e] *14* Hebrew *No*; also in verses 15 and 16 [f] *15* Hebrew *Sin*; also in verse 16 [g] *17* Hebrew *Awen* (or *On*) [h] *17* Hebrew *Pi Beseth*

the nations and scatter them through
30:23 [u]Eze 29:12 the countries.[u] 24I will strengthen[v] the
arms of the king of Babylon and put my
30:24 [v]Zec 10:6,12 [w]Eze 21:14; Zep 2:12 sword[w] in his hand, but I will break the
arms of Pharaoh, and he will groan be-
fore him like a mortally wounded man.
25I will strengthen the arms of the king
of Babylon, but the arms of Pharaoh
will fall limp. Then they will know that
I am the LORD, when I put my sword
into the hand of the king of Babylon
and he brandishes it against Egypt. 26I
will disperse the Egyptians among the
nations and scatter them through the
countries. Then they will know that I
30:26 [x]Eze 29:12 am the LORD.[x]"

A Cedar in Lebanon

31:1 [y]Jer 52:5 [z]Eze 30:20 31 In the eleventh year,[y] in the
third month on the first day, the
word of the LORD came to me:[z] 2"Son
of man, say to Pharaoh king of Egypt
and to his hordes:

"'Who can be compared with you in majesty?
3Consider Assyria, once a cedar in Lebanon,
with beautiful branches overshadowing the forest;
it towered on high,
31:3 [a]Isa 10:34 its top above the thick foliage.[a]
4The waters nourished it,
deep springs made it grow tall;
their streams flowed
all around its base
and sent their channels
to all the trees of the field.
5So it towered higher
than all the trees of the field;
its boughs increased
and its branches grew long,
31:5 [b]Eze 17:5 spreading because of abundant waters.[b]
6All the birds of the air
nested in its boughs,
all the beasts of the field
gave birth under its branches;
all the great nations
31:6 [c]Eze 17:23; Mt 13:32 lived in its shade.[c]
7It was majestic in beauty,
with its spreading boughs,
for its roots went down
to abundant waters.
31:8 [d]Ps 80:10 8The cedars[d] in the garden of God
could not rival it,
nor could the pine trees
equal its boughs,
nor could the plane trees
compare with its branches—
no tree in the garden of God
could match its beauty.[e] 31:8 [e]Ge 2:8-9
9I made it beautiful
with abundant branches,
the envy of all the trees of Eden[f] 31:9 [f]Ge 2:8 [g]Ge 13:10; Eze 28:13
in the garden of God.[g]

10"'Therefore this is what the Sovereign LORD says: Because it towered
on high, lifting its top above the thick 31:10 [h]Isa 14:13-14; Eze 28:17
foliage, and because it was proud[h] of
its height, 11I handed it over to the ruler of the nations, for him to deal with
according to its wickedness. I cast it 31:11 [i]Da 5:20
aside,[i] 12and the most ruthless of for-
eign nations[j] cut it down and left it. Its 31:12 [j]Eze 28:7 [k]Eze 32:5; 35:8 [l]Eze 32:11-12; Da 4:14
boughs fell on the mountains and in all
the valleys;[k] its branches lay broken in
all the ravines of the land. All the nations of the earth came out from under
its shade and left it.[l] 13All the birds of
the air settled on the fallen tree, and all
the beasts of the field were among its 31:13 [m]Isa 18:6; Eze 29:5; 32:4
branches.[m] 14Therefore no other trees
by the waters are ever to tower proudly
on high, lifting their tops above the
thick foliage. No other trees so well-wa-
tered are ever to reach such a height; 31:14 [n]Ps 82:7 [o]Ps 63:9; Eze 26:20; 32:24
they are all destined for death,[n] for the
earth below, among mortal men, with
those who go down to the pit.[o]
15"'This is what the Sovereign LORD
says: On the day it was brought down
to the grave[a] I covered the deep springs
with mourning for it; I held back its
streams, and its abundant waters were
restrained. Because of it I clothed Lebanon with gloom, and all the trees of
the field withered away. 16I made the 31:16 [p]Eze 26:15 [q]Isa 14:8 [r]Eze 14:22; 32:31 [s]Isa 14:15; Eze 32:18
nations tremble[p] at the sound of its fall
when I brought it down to the grave
with those who go down to the pit.
Then all the trees[q] of Eden, the choicest and best of Lebanon, all the trees
that were well-watered, were consoled[r]
in the earth below.[s] 17Those who lived
in its shade, its allies among the nations, had also gone down to the grave
with it, joining those killed by the 31:17 [t]Ps 9:17
sword.[t]
18"'Which of the trees of Eden can
be compared with you in splendor and
majesty? Yet you, too, will be brought
down with the trees of Eden to the
earth below; you will lie among the

[a]*15* Hebrew *Sheol*; also in verses 16 and 17

31:18 [u]Jer 9:26; Eze 32:19,21 uncircumcised,[u] with those killed by the sword.
" 'This is Pharaoh and all his hordes, declares the Sovereign LORD.' "

A Lament for Pharaoh

32 In the twelfth year, in the twelfth month on the first day, the word
32:1 [v]Eze 31:1; 33:21 of the LORD came to me:[v] 2 "Son of
man, take up a lament[w] concerning
32:2 [w]Eze 19:1; 27:2 [x]Eze 19:3,6; Na 2:11-13 [y]Eze 29:3; 34:18 Pharaoh king of Egypt and say to him:

" 'You are like a lion[x] among the nations;
you are like a monster in the seas
thrashing about in your streams,
churning the water with your feet
and muddying the streams.[y]

3 " 'This is what the Sovereign LORD says:

" 'With a great throng of people
I will cast my net over you,
and they will haul you up in my
32:3 [z]Eze 12:13 net.[z]
4 I will throw you on the land
and hurl you on the open field.
I will let all the birds of the air settle
32:4 [a]Isa 18:6; Eze 31:12-13 on you[a]
and all the beasts of the earth
gorge themselves on you.
5 I will spread your flesh on the mountains
32:5 [b]Eze 31:12 and fill the valleys[b] with your remains.
32:6 [c]Isa 34:3 6 I will drench the land with your flowing blood[c]
all the way to the mountains,
and the ravines will be filled with your flesh.
7 When I snuff you out, I will cover the heavens
and darken their stars;
I will cover the sun with a cloud,
32:7 [d]Isa 13:10; 34:4; Eze 30:3; Joel 2:2,31; 3:15; Mt 24:29; Rev 8:12 and the moon will not give its light.[d]
8 All the shining lights in the heavens
I will darken over you;
I will bring darkness over your land,
declares the Sovereign LORD.
9 I will trouble the hearts of many peoples
when I bring about your destruction among the nations,
among[a] lands you have not known.
10 I will cause many peoples to be appalled at you,
and their kings will shudder with horror because of you
when I brandish my sword before them.
32:10 [e]Jer 46:10 [f]Eze 26:16; 27:35 On the day[e] of your downfall
each of them will tremble
every moment for his life.[f]

11 " 'For this is what the Sovereign LORD says:

32:11 [g]Jer 46:26 " 'The sword of the king of Babylon[g]
will come against you.
12 I will cause your hordes to fall
32:12 [h]Eze 28:7 [i]Eze 31:11-12 by the swords of mighty men—
the most ruthless of all nations.[h]
They will shatter the pride of Egypt,
and all her hordes will be overthrown.[i]
13 I will destroy all her cattle
from beside abundant waters
no longer to be stirred by the foot of man
or muddied by the hoofs of
32:13 [j]Eze 29:8,11 cattle.[j]
14 Then I will let her waters settle
and make her streams flow like oil,
declares the Sovereign LORD.
15 When I make Egypt desolate
and strip the land of everything in it,
when I strike down all who live there,
32:15 [k]Ex 7:5; 14:4,18; Ps 107:33-34; Eze 6:7 then they will know that I am the LORD.[k]'

16 "This is the lament[l] they will chant
32:16 [l]2Sa 1:17; 2Ch 35:25; Eze 26:17 for her. The daughters of the nations
will chant it; for Egypt and all her
hordes they will chant it, declares the
Sovereign LORD."

17 In the twelfth year, on the fifteenth
day of the month, the word of the
32:17 [m]ver 1 LORD came to me:[m] 18 "Son of man,
32:18 [n]Jer 1:10 [o]Eze 31:14,16; Mic 1:8 wail for the hordes of Egypt and consign[n] to the earth below both her and
the daughters of mighty nations, with
those who go down to the pit.[o] 19 Say to
them, 'Are you more favored than oth-
32:19 [p]ver 29-30; Eze 28:10; 31:18 ers? Go down and be laid among the
uncircumcised.'[p] 20 They will fall among
those killed by the sword. The sword is
32:20 [q]Ps 28:3 drawn; let her be dragged[q] off with all

[a]9 Hebrew; Septuagint *bring you into captivity among the nations, / to*

32:21 [r]Isa 14:9
her hordes. 21From within the grave[a][r]
the mighty leaders will say of Egypt and
her allies, 'They have come down and
they lie with the uncircumcised, with
those killed by the sword.'
22"Assyria is there with her whole
army; she is surrounded by the graves of
all her slain, all who have fallen by the
sword. 23Their graves are in the depths
32:23 [s]Isa 14:15
of the pit[s] and her army lies around her
grave. All who had spread terror in the
land of the living are slain, fallen by the
sword.
32:24 [t]Ge 10:22 [u]Jer 49:37 [v]Job 28:13 [w]Eze 26:20
24"Elam[t] is there, with all her hordes
around her grave. All of them are slain,
fallen by the sword.[u] All who had spread
terror in the land of the living[v] went
down uncircumcised to the earth below.
They bear their shame with those who
go down to the pit.[w] 25A bed is made
for her among the slain, with all her
hordes around her grave. All of them
are uncircumcised, killed by the sword.
Because their terror had spread in the
land of the living, they bear their shame
with those who go down to the pit;
32:26 [x]Ge 10:2; Eze 27:13
they are laid among the slain.
26"Meshech and Tubal[x] are there, with
all their hordes around their graves. All
of them are uncircumcised, killed by the
sword because they spread their terror
in the land of the living. 27Do they not
lie with the other uncircumcised warriors who have fallen, who went down
to the grave with their weapons of war,
whose swords were placed under their
heads? The punishment for their sins
rested on their bones, though the terror
of these warriors had stalked through
the land of the living.
28"You too, O Pharaoh, will be broken and will lie among the uncircumcised, with those killed by the sword.
32:29 [y]Isa 34:5-15; Jer 49:7; Eze 35:15; Ob 1:1 [z]Eze 25:12-14
29"Edom[y] is there, her kings and all
her princes; despite their power, they
are laid with those killed by the sword.
They lie with the uncircumcised, with
those who go down to the pit.[z]
32:30 [a]Jer 25:26; Eze 38:6; 39:2 [b]Jer 25:22; Eze 28:21
30"All the princes of the north[a] and
all the Sidonians[b] are there; they went
down with the slain in disgrace despite
the terror caused by their power. They
lie uncircumcised with those killed by
the sword and bear their shame with
those who go down to the pit.
31"Pharaoh—he and all his army—
32:31 [c]Eze 14:22; 31:16
will see them and he will be consoled[c]
for all his hordes that were killed by the
sword, declares the Sovereign LORD.
32Although I had him spread terror in
the land of the living, Pharaoh and all
his hordes will be laid among the uncircumcised, with those killed by the
sword, declares the Sovereign LORD."

Ezekiel a Watchman

33 The word of the LORD came to
me: 2"Son of man, speak to your
countrymen and say to them: 'When I
bring the sword[d] against a land, and the
33:2 [d]Jer 12:12 [e]Eze 3:11
people of the land choose one of their
men and make him their watchman,[e]
3and he sees the sword coming against
33:3 [f]Hos 8:1
the land and blows the trumpet[f] to
warn the people, 4then if anyone hears
33:4 [g]2Ch 25:16 [h]Jer 6:17; Eze 18:13; Zec 1:4; Ac 18:6
the trumpet but does not take warning[g]
and the sword comes and takes his life,
his blood will be on his own head.[h]
5Since he heard the sound of the trumpet but did not take warning, his blood
will be on his own head. If he had taken
warning, he would have saved himself.
6But if the watchman sees the sword
coming and does not blow the trumpet to warn the people and the sword
comes and takes the life of one of them,
that man will be taken away because of
his sin, but I will hold the watchman
33:6 [i]Eze 3:18
accountable for his blood.'[i]
7"Son of man, I have made you a
watchman for the house of Israel; so
33:7 [j]Jer 26:2; Eze 3:17
hear the word I speak and give them
warning from me.[j] 8When I say to the
wicked, 'O wicked man, you will surely
33:8 [k]ver 14 [l]Eze 18:4
die,[k]' and you do not speak out to dissuade him from his ways, that wicked
man will die for[b] his sin, and I will hold
you accountable for his blood.[l] 9But if
you do warn the wicked man to turn
from his ways and he does not do so,
he will die for his sin, but you will have
33:9 [m]Eze 3:17-19
saved yourself.[m]
10"Son of man, say to the house of
Israel, 'This is what you are saying:
"Our offenses and sins weigh us down,
33:10 [n]Eze 24:23 [o]Lev 26:39; Eze 4:17
and we are wasting away[n] because of[c]
them. How then can we live?[o]"' 11Say
to them, 'As surely as I live, declares the
Sovereign LORD, I take no pleasure in
the death of the wicked, but rather that
33:11 [p]Eze 18:32; 2Pe 3:9 [q]Eze 18:23
they turn from their ways and live.[p]
Turn! Turn from your evil ways! Why
will you die, O house of Israel?'[q]

[a] *21* Hebrew *Sheol*; also in verse 27 [b] *8* Or *in*; also in verse 9 [c] *10* Or *away in*

12“Therefore, son of man, say to your
countrymen, ‘The righteousness of the
righteous man will not save him when
he disobeys, and the wickedness of the
wicked man will not cause him to fall
when he turns from it. The righteous
man, if he sins, will not be allowed to
live because of his former righteousness.’[r] 13If I tell the righteous man that
he will surely live, but then he trusts in
his righteousness and does evil, none of
the righteous things he has done will be
remembered; he will die for the evil he
has done.[s] 14And if I say to the wicked
man, ‘You will surely die,’ but he then
turns away from his sin and does what
is just[t] and right— 15if he gives back
what he took in pledge for a loan, returns what he has stolen,[u] follows the
decrees that give life, and does no evil,
he will surely live; he will not die.[v]
16None of the sins he has committed
will be remembered against him. He
has done what is just and right; he will
surely live.[w]

17“Yet your countrymen say, ‘The
way of the Lord is not just.’ But it is
their way that is not just. 18If a righteous man turns from his righteousness
and does evil, he will die for it.[x] 19And
if a wicked man turns away from his
wickedness and does what is just and
right, he will live by doing so. 20Yet,
O house of Israel, you say, ‘The way
of the Lord is not just.’ But I will
judge each of you according to his own
ways.”

Jerusalem’s Fall Explained

21In the twelfth year of our exile, in
the tenth month on the fifth day, a man
who had escaped[y] from Jerusalem came
to me and said, “The city has fallen![z]”
22Now the evening before the man arrived, the hand of the LORD was upon
me,[a] and he opened my mouth[b] before
the man came to me in the morning.
So my mouth was opened and I was no
longer silent.[c]

23Then the word of the LORD came
to me: 24“Son of man, the people living
in those ruins[d] in the land of Israel are
saying, ‘Abraham was only one man,
yet he possessed the land. But we are
many; surely the land has been given to
us as our possession.’[e] 25Therefore say
to them, ‘This is what the Sovereign
LORD says: Since you eat meat with
the blood[f] still in it and look to your
idols and shed blood, should you then
possess the land?[g] 26You rely on your
sword, you do detestable things, and
each of you defiles his neighbor’s wife.[h]
Should you then possess the land?’

27“Say this to them: ‘This is what the
Sovereign LORD says: As surely as I live,
those who are left in the ruins will fall
by the sword, those out in the country
I will give to the wild animals to be devoured, and those in strongholds and
caves will die of a plague.[i] 28I will make
the land a desolate waste, and her proud
strength will come to an end, and the
mountains of Israel will become desolate so that no one will cross them.
29Then they will know that I am the
LORD, when I have made the land a
desolate waste because of all the detestable things they have done.’

30“As for you, son of man, your countrymen are talking together about you
by the walls and at the doors of the
houses, saying to each other, ‘Come and
hear the message that has come from
the LORD.’ 31My people come to you,
as they usually do, and sit before[j] you
to listen to your words, but they do
not put them into practice. With their
mouths they express devotion, but their
hearts are greedy for unjust gain.[k] 32In-
deed, to them you are nothing more
than one who sings love songs with a
beautiful voice and plays an instrument
well, for they hear your words but do
not put them into practice.[l]

33“When all this comes true—and it
surely will—then they will know that a
prophet has been among them.[m]”

Shepherds and Sheep

34 The word of the LORD came
to me: 2“Son of man, prophesy
against the shepherds of Israel; prophesy and say to them: ‘This is what the
Sovereign LORD says: Woe to the shepherds of Israel who only take care of
themselves! Should not shepherds take
care of the flock?[n] 3You eat the curds,
clothe yourselves with the wool and
slaughter the choice animals, but you
do not take care of the flock.[o] 4You have
not strengthened the weak or healed the
sick or bound up the injured. You have
not brought back the strays or searched
for the lost. You have ruled them harshly and brutally.[p] 5So they were scat-

33:12 [r]2Ch 7:14; Eze 3:20
33:13 [s]Eze 18:24; Heb 10:38; 2Pe 2:20-21
33:14 [t]Eze 18:27
33:15 [u]Ex 22:1-4; Lev 6:2-5 [v]Eze 20:11; Lk 19:8
33:16 [w]Isa 43:25; Eze 18:22
33:18 [x]Eze 3:20; Eze 18:26
33:21 [y]Eze 24:26 [z]2Ki 25:4,10; Jer 39:1-2; Eze 32:1
33:22 [a]Eze 1:3 [b]Lk 1:64 [c]Eze 3:26-27; 24:27
33:24 [d]Eze 36:4 [e]Isa 51:2; Jer 40:7; Eze 11:15; Ac 7:5
33:25 [f]Ge 9:4; Dt 12:16 [g]Jer 7:9-10; Eze 22:6,27
33:26 [h]Eze 22:11
33:27 [i]1Sa 13:6; Isa 2:19; Jer 42:22; Eze 39:4
33:31 [j]Eze 8:1 [k]Ps 78:36-37; Isa 29:13; Eze 22:27; Mt 13:22; 1Jn 3:18
33:32 [l]Mk 6:20
33:33 [m]1Sa 3:20; Jer 28:9; Eze 2:5
34:2 [n]Ps 78:70-72; Isa 40:11; Jer 3:15; 23:1; Mic 3:11; Jn 10:11; 21:15-17
34:3 [o]Isa 56:11; Eze 22:27; Zec 11:16
34:4 [p]Zec 11:15-17

34:5 [q]Nu 27:17 tered because there was no shepherd,[q]
[r]ver 28; and when they were scattered they be-
Isa 56:9 came food for all the wild animals.[r] 6My
sheep wandered over all the mountains
34:6 and on every high hill. They were scat-
[s]Ps 142:4; tered over the whole earth, and no one
1Pe 2:25 searched or looked for them.[s]

KINDNESS 

A SHEPHERD'S SOUL

Ezekiel 34:6

Shepherds who love their sheep are ever in short supply. Sheep sometimes die waiting for someone to care.

7"'Therefore, you shepherds, hear the
word of the LORD: 8As surely as I live,
declares the Sovereign LORD, because
my flock lacks a shepherd and so has
been plundered and has become food
for all the wild animals, and because my
shepherds did not search for my flock
but cared for themselves rather than for
my flock, 9therefore, O shepherds, hear
the word of the LORD: 10This is what
34:10 [t]Jer 21:13 the Sovereign LORD says: I am against[t]
[u]Ps 72:14 the shepherds and will hold them ac-
[v]1Sa 2:29-30; countable for my flock. I will remove
Zec 10:3 them from tending the flock so that
the shepherds can no longer feed themselves. I will rescue[u] my flock from their
mouths, and it will no longer be food
for them.[v]
11"'For this is what the Sovereign
LORD says: I myself will search for
my sheep and look after them. 12As a
34:12 [w]Isa 40:11; shepherd[w] looks after his scattered flock
Jer 31:10; when he is with them, so will I look af-
Lk 19:10 ter my sheep. I will rescue them from
[x]Eze 30:3 all the places where they were scattered
on a day of clouds and darkness.[x] 13I
will bring them out from the nations
and gather them from the countries,
and I will bring them into their own
land. I will pasture them on the mountains of Israel, in the ravines and in
34:13 all the settlements in the land.[y] 14I will
[y]Jer 23:3 tend them in a good pasture, and the
34:14 mountain heights of Israel[z] will be their
[z]Eze 20:40 grazing land. There they will lie down
[a]Ps 23:2 [b]Eze 36:29-30 in good grazing land, and there they will
feed in a rich pasture[a] on the moun-
tains of Israel.[b] 15I myself will tend my
sheep and have them lie down, declares
34:15 the Sovereign LORD.[c] 16I will search for
[c]Ps 23:1-2 the lost and bring back the strays. I will
bind up the injured and strengthen the
weak,[d] but the sleek and the strong I 34:16 [d]Mic 4:6
will destroy. I will shepherd the flock [e]Isa 10:16;
with justice.[e] Lk 5:32
17"'As for you, my flock, this is what
the Sovereign LORD says: I will judge
between one sheep and another, and 34:17
between rams and goats.[f] 18Is it not [f]Mt 25:32-33
enough for you to feed on the good
pasture? Must you also trample the rest
of your pasture with your feet? Is it not
enough for you to drink clear water?
Must you also muddy the rest with your
feet? 19Must my flock feed on what you
have trampled and drink what you have
muddied with your feet?
20"'Therefore this is what the Sovereign LORD says to them: See, I myself will judge between the fat sheep
and the lean sheep. 21Because you shove
with flank and shoulder, butting all the 34:21
weak sheep with your horns[g] until you [g]Dt 33:17
have driven them away, 22I will save my
flock, and they will no longer be plundered. I will judge between one sheep 34:22
and another.[h] 23I will place over them [h]Ps 72:12-14;
one shepherd, my servant David, and Jer 23:2-3
he will tend[i] them; he will tend them 34:23
and be their shepherd. 24I the LORD [i]Isa 40:11
will be their God,[j] and my servant Da- 34:24
vid will be prince among them. I the [j]Eze 36:28
LORD have spoken.[k] [k]Jer 30:9
25"'I will make a covenant of peace
with them and rid the land of wild
beasts[l] so that they may live in the des- 34:25 [l]Lev 26:6
ert and sleep in the forests in safety.[m] [m]Isa 11:6-9;
26I will bless[n] them and the places sur- Hos 2:18
rounding my hill.[a] I will send down 34:26
showers in season;[o] there will be show- [n]Ge 12:2 [o]Ps 68:9
ers of blessing.[p] 27The trees of the field [p]Dt 11:13-15;
will yield their fruit and the ground will Isa 44:3
yield its crops; the people will be secure in their land. They will know that
I am the LORD, when I break the bars 34:27
of their yoke[q] and rescue them from [q]Lev 26:13
the hands of those who enslaved them.[r] [r]Jer 30:8
28They will no longer be plundered by
the nations, nor will wild animals devour them. They will live in safety, and 34:28
no one will make them afraid.[s] 29I will [s]Jer 30:10;
provide for them a land renowned[t] for Eze 39:26
its crops, and they will no longer be 34:29 [t]Isa 4:2
victims of famine[u] in the land or bear [u]Eze 36:29
the scorn[v] of the nations.[w] 30Then they [v]Eze 36:6
will know that I, the LORD their God, [w]Eze 36:15

[a]26 Or *I will make them and the places surrounding my hill a blessing*

am with them and that they, the house
of Israel, are my people, declares the
Sovereign LORD.[x] 31You my sheep, the
sheep of my pasture,[y] are people, and
I am your God, declares the Sovereign
LORD.' "

A Prophecy Against Edom

35 The word of the LORD came to
me: 2"Son of man, set your face
against Mount Seir; prophesy against it
3and say: 'This is what the Sovereign
LORD says: I am against you, Mount
Seir, and I will stretch out my hand[z]
against you and make you a desolate
waste.[a] 4I will turn your towns into ruins and you will be desolate. Then you
will know that I am the LORD.[b]

5" 'Because you harbored an ancient
hostility and delivered the Israelites over
to the sword at the time of their calamity, the time their punishment reached
its climax,[c] 6therefore as surely as I live,
declares the Sovereign LORD, I will give
you over to bloodshed and it will pursue you.[d] Since you did not hate bloodshed, bloodshed will pursue you. 7I will
make Mount Seir a desolate waste and
cut off from it all who come and go. 8I
will fill your mountains with the slain;
those killed by the sword will fall on
your hills and in your valleys and in all
your ravines.[e] 9I will make you desolate
forever; your towns will not be inhabited. Then you will know that I am the
LORD.[f]

10" 'Because you have said, "These
two nations and countries will be ours
and we will take possession[g] of them,"
even though I the LORD was there,
11therefore as surely as I live, declares
the Sovereign LORD, I will treat you in
accordance with the anger[h] and jealousy you showed in your hatred of them
and I will make myself known among
them when I judge you.[i] 12Then you
will know that I the LORD have heard
all the contemptible things you have
said against the mountains of Israel.
You said, "They have been laid waste
and have been given over to us to devour.[j]" 13You boasted against me and
spoke against me without restraint, and
I heard it.[k] 14This is what the Sovereign LORD says: While the whole
earth rejoices, I will make you desolate.[l]
15Because you rejoiced[m] when the inheritance of the house of Israel became

34:30 [x]Eze 14:11; 37:27
34:31 [y]Ps 100:3; Jer 23:1
35:3 [z]Jer 6:12 [a]Eze 25:12-14
35:4 [b]ver 9
35:5 [c]Ps 137:7; Eze 21:29
35:6 [d]Isa 63:2-6
35:8 [e]Eze 31:12
35:9 [f]Jer 49:13
35:10 [g]Ps 83:12; Eze 36:2,5
35:11 [h]Eze 25:14 [i]Ps 9:16; Mt 7:2
35:12 [j]Jer 50:7
35:13 [k]Da 11:36
35:14 [l]Jer 51:48
35:15 [m]Ob 1:12

desolate, that is how I will treat you.
You will be desolate, O Mount Seir,[n]
you and all of Edom.[o] Then they will
know that I am the LORD.' "

A Prophecy to the Mountains of Israel

36 "Son of man, prophesy to the
mountains of Israel and say,
'O mountains of Israel, hear the word
of the LORD. 2This is what the Sovereign LORD says: The enemy said of
you, "Aha![p] The ancient heights[q] have
become our possession.[r]" ' 3Therefore
prophesy and say, 'This is what the Sovereign LORD says: Because they ravaged and hounded you from every side
so that you became the possession of
the rest of the nations and the object
of people's malicious talk and slander,[s]
4therefore, O mountains of Israel, hear
the word of the Sovereign LORD: This
is what the Sovereign LORD says to the
mountains and hills, to the ravines and
valleys,[t] to the desolate ruins and the
deserted towns that have been plundered and ridiculed by the rest of the
nations around you[u]— 5this is what
the Sovereign LORD says: In my burning zeal I have spoken against the rest
of the nations, and against all Edom,
for with glee and with malice in their
hearts they made my land their own
possession so that they might plunder
its pastureland.'[v] 6Therefore prophesy
concerning the land of Israel and say to
the mountains and hills, to the ravines
and valleys: 'This is what the Sovereign
LORD says: I speak in my jealous wrath
because you have suffered the scorn of
the nations.[w] 7Therefore this is what
the Sovereign LORD says: I swear with
uplifted hand that the nations around
you will also suffer scorn.

8" 'But you, O mountains of Israel,
will produce branches and fruit[x] for my
people Israel, for they will soon come
home. 9I am concerned for you and will
look on you with favor; you will be
plowed and sown, 10and I will multiply
the number of people upon you, even
the whole house of Israel. The towns
will be inhabited and the ruins rebuilt.[y]
11I will increase the number of men
and animals upon you, and they will be
fruitful and become numerous. I will
settle people on you as in the past[z]
and will make you prosper more than

35:15 [n]ver 3 [o]Isa 34:5-6, 11; Jer 50:11-13; La 4:21
36:2 [p]Eze 25:3 [q]Dt 32:13 [r]Eze 35:10
36:3 [s]Ps 44:13-14
36:4 [t]Eze 6:3 [u]Dt 11:11; Ps 79:4; Eze 34:28
36:5 [v]Jer 50:11; Eze 25:12-14; 35:10,15
36:6 [w]Ps 123:3-4; Eze 34:29
36:8 [x]Isa 27:6
36:10 [y]ver 33; Isa 49:17-23
36:11 [z]Mic 7:14

36:11 [a]Jer 31:28; Eze 16:55
before.[a] Then you will know that I am
the LORD. 12I will cause people, my
people Israel, to walk upon you. They

DAY 5 FIVE

▸ PEACE AND ITS PLACE IN MY PERSONAL WORSHIP

Ezekiel 36:24–28

When we accept God's renovation of our lives, we are ready to worship for the first time. God's five-fold promise equips us to become his ambassadors of peace. Peace produces an inward calm, and we are truly ready to adore him.

"I will cleanse you from all your impurities and from all your idols." How blessed is this promise, for, whether or not we like to admit it, coming to Christ is not the first time that we have worshiped. It is merely the first time we have worshiped the right thing. Before that time we had given our attention to idols. Idols? Yes, for anything that is more important than God in our lives is the god of our lives. Each of us had plenty of these idols before Jesus came into our lives.

"I will give you a new heart." By this God is saying, "I am going to transplant your value system and give you a new worldview." With that transplant we are given a God's-eye-view of our world.

"I will . . . put a new spirit in you." We will have a new energy for desiring righteousness in our lives. We will no longer be left to manage life with a set of inferior appetites. The Spirit will alter our desires until they are all *God's* desires.

"I will remove from you your heart of stone and give you a heart of flesh." A soft, teachable spirit is the automatic by-product of our heart transplant. God causes us to forsake callous rebellion in favor of tenderness toward him, as well as toward the people around us.

"I will . . . move you to follow my decrees." With the renovation of one's heart comes the desire for a relationship with God that has obedience as a main ingredient.

In short, with this great renovation, not only will the peace of God occupy our lives, but we will be made ready to worship our Lord.

To begin a study on the topic of Peace, the Reign of the Holy Spirit, turn to the home page on page 1429.

will possess you, and you will be their
inheritance;[b] you will never again de- 36:12 [b]Eze 47:14,22
prive them of their children.
13" 'This is what the Sovereign LORD
says: Because people say to you, "You
devour men[c] and deprive your nation 36:13 [c]Nu 13:32
of its children," 14therefore you will no
longer devour men or make your nation
childless, declares the Sovereign LORD.
15No longer will I make you hear the
taunts of the nations, and no longer
will you suffer the scorn of the peoples
or cause your nation to fall, declares the 36:15 [d]Ps 89:50-51;
Sovereign LORD.[d]' " Eze 34:29
16Again the word of the LORD came
to me: 17"Son of man, when the people of Israel were living in their own
land, they defiled it by their conduct
and their actions. Their conduct was
like a woman's monthly uncleanness in
my sight.[e] 18So I poured out[f] my wrath 36:17 [e]Jer 2:7
on them because they had shed blood
in the land and because they had de- 36:18 [f]2Ch 34:21
filed it with their idols. 19I dispersed
them among the nations, and they
were scattered[g] through the countries; 36:19 [g]Dt 28:64
I judged them according to their con- [h]Eze 39:24
duct and their actions.[h] 20And wherever
they went among the nations they pro-
faned[i] my holy name, for it was said 36:20 [i]Ro 2:24
of them, 'These are the LORD's people, [j]Isa 52:5;
and yet they had to leave his land.'[j] 21I Jer 33:24;
had concern for my holy name, which Eze 12:16
the house of Israel profaned among the
nations where they had gone.[k] 36:21 [k]Ps 74:18;
22"Therefore say to the house of Is- Isa 48:9
rael, 'This is what the Sovereign LORD
says: It is not for your sake, O house
of Israel, that I am going to do these
things, but for the sake of my holy
name, which you have profaned[l] among 36:22 [l]Ro 2:24*
the nations where you have gone.[m] 23I [m]Ps 106:8
will show the holiness of my great name,
which has been profaned among the
nations, the name you have profaned
among them. Then the nations will
know that I am the LORD, declares the 36:23 [n]Eze 20:41
Sovereign LORD, when I show myself [o]Ps 126:2;
holy[n] through you before their eyes.[o] Isa 5:16
24" 'For I will take you out of the
nations; I will gather you from all the 36:24 [p]Eze 34:13;
countries and bring you back into your 37:21
own land.[p] 25I will sprinkle[q] clean wa- 36:25 [q]Heb 9:13;
ter on you, and you will be clean; I will 10:22
cleanse[r] you from all your impurities [r]Ps 51:2,7
and from all your idols.[s] 26I will give [s]Zec 13:2
you a new heart[t] and put a new spirit in 36:26 [t]Jer 24:7
you; I will remove from you your heart

36:26 [u]Ps 51:10; Eze 11:19 of stone and give you a heart of flesh.[u]
[27]And I will put my Spirit[v] in you and
36:27 [v]Eze 37:14 move you to follow my decrees and be
careful to keep my laws. [28]You will live
36:28 [w]Jer 30:22 [x]Eze 14:11; 37:14,27 in the land I gave your forefathers; you
will be my people,[w] and I will be your
God.[x] [29]I will save you from all your
uncleanness. I will call for the grain
and make it plentiful and will not bring
36:29 [y]Eze 34:29 famine[y] upon you. [30]I will increase
the fruit of the trees and the crops of
the field, so that you will no longer suffer disgrace among the nations because
36:30 [z]Lev 26:4-5; Eze 34:27; Hos 2:21-22 of famine.[z] [31]Then you will remember
your evil ways and wicked deeds, and
you will loathe yourselves for your sins
36:31 [a]Eze 6:9; 20:43 and detestable practices.[a] [32]I want you
to know that I am not doing this for
your sake, declares the Sovereign LORD.
Be ashamed and disgraced for your con-
36:32 [b]Dt 9:5 duct, O house of Israel![b]
[33]"'This is what the Sovereign LORD
says: On the day I cleanse you from all
your sins, I will resettle your towns, and
the ruins will be rebuilt. [34]The desolate land will be cultivated instead of lying desolate in the sight of all who pass
through it. [35]They will say, "This land
that was laid waste has become like the
36:35 [c]Joel 2:3 [d]Isa 51:3 garden of Eden;[c] the cities that were lying in ruins, desolate and destroyed, are
now fortified and inhabited.[d]" [36]Then
the nations around you that remain
will know that I the LORD have rebuilt
what was destroyed and have replanted
36:36 [e]Eze 17:22; 22:14; 37:14; 39:27-28 what was desolate. I the LORD have
spoken, and I will do it.'[e]
[37]"This is what the Sovereign LORD
says: Once again I will yield to the plea
of the house of Israel and do this for
them: I will make their people as nu-
36:38 [f]1Ki 8:63; 2Ch 35:7-9 merous as sheep, [38]as numerous as the
flocks for offerings[f] at Jerusalem during
her appointed feasts. So will the ruined
cities be filled with flocks of people.
Then they will know that I am the
LORD."

The Valley of Dry Bones

37:1 [g]Eze 1:3; 8:3 [h]Eze 11:24; Lk 4:1; Ac 8:39 [i]Jer 7:32 [j]Jer 8:2; Eze 40:1 **37** The hand of the LORD was
upon me,[g] and he brought me
out by the Spirit[h] of the LORD and set
me in the middle of a valley;[i] it was full
of bones.[j] [2]He led me back and forth
among them, and I saw a great many
bones on the floor of the valley, bones
that were very dry. [3]He asked me, "Son
of man, can these bones live?"

I said, "O Sovereign LORD, you alone 37:3 [k]Dt 32:39; 1Sa 2:6; Isa 26:19
know.[k]"
[4]Then he said to me, "Prophesy to
these bones and say to them, 'Dry
bones, hear the word of the LORD![l] 37:4 [l]Jer 22:29
[5]This is what the Sovereign LORD says
to these bones: I will make breath[a] en-
ter you, and you will come to life.[m] [6]I 37:5 [m]Ge 2:7; Ps 104:29-30
will attach tendons to you and make
flesh come upon you and cover you
with skin; I will put breath in you, and
you will come to life. Then you will
know that I am the LORD.[n]'" 37:6 [n]Eze 38:23; Joel 2:27; 3:17
[7]So I prophesied as I was command-
ed. And as I was prophesying, there
was a noise, a rattling sound, and the
bones came together, bone to bone. [8]I
looked, and tendons and flesh appeared
on them and skin covered them, but
there was no breath in them.
[9]Then he said to me, "Prophesy to 37:9 [o]Ps 104:30
the breath;[o] prophesy, son of man, and
say to it, 'This is what the Sovereign
LORD says: Come from the four winds,
O breath, and breathe into these slain,
that they may live.'" [10]So I prophesied
as he commanded me, and breath en-
tered them; they came to life and stood 37:10 [p]Rev 11:11
up on their feet—a vast army.[p]
[11]Then he said to me: "Son of man,
these bones are the whole house of Israel. They say, 'Our bones are dried up
and our hope is gone; we are cut off.'[q] 37:11 [q]La 3:54
[12]Therefore prophesy and say to them:
'This is what the Sovereign LORD says:
O my people, I am going to open your
graves and bring you up from them;
I will bring you back to the land of 37:12 [r]Dt 32:39; 1Sa 2:6; Isa 26:19; Hos 13:14; Am 9:14-15
Israel.[r] [13]Then you, my people, will
know that I am the LORD, when I open
your graves and bring you up from
them. [14]I will put my Spirit[s] in you and
you will live, and I will settle you in 37:14 [s]Joel 2:28-29

[a]5 The Hebrew for this word can also mean *wind* or *spirit* (see verses 6-14).

▸ PATIENCE

CAN THESE BONES LIVE?

Ezekiel 37:11

"The foot bone connected to the anklebone; the anklebone connected to the leg bone . . . the knee bone . . . the hipbone." Can these bones live? It all depends on whether or not they are all connected to God. And connecting to God is a process that takes time.

your own land. Then you will know that I the LORD have spoken, and I have done it, declares the LORD.[t]' "

One Nation Under One King

15 The word of the LORD came to me: 16 "Son of man, take a stick of wood and write on it, 'Belonging to Judah and the Israelites[u] associated with him.[v]' Then take another stick of wood, and write on it, 'Ephraim's stick, belonging to Joseph and all the house of Israel associated with him.' 17 Join them together into one stick so that they will become one in your hand.[w]

18 "When your countrymen ask you, 'Won't you tell us what you mean by this?'[x] 19 say to them, 'This is what the Sovereign LORD says: I am going to take the stick of Joseph—which is in Ephraim's hand—and of the Israelite tribes associated with him, and join it to Judah's stick, making them a single stick of wood, and they will become one in my hand.'[y] 20 Hold before their eyes the sticks you have written on 21 and say to them, 'This is what the Sovereign LORD says: I will take the Israelites out of the nations where they have gone. I will gather them from all around and bring them back into their own land.[z] 22 I will make them one nation in the land, on the mountains of Israel. There will be one king over all of them and they will never again be two nations or be divided into two kingdoms.[a] 23 They will no longer defile[b] themselves with their idols and vile images or with any of their offenses, for I will save them from all their sinful backsliding,[a] and I will cleanse them. They will be my people, and I will be their God.[c]

24 " 'My servant David[d] will be king over them, and they will all have one shepherd.[e] They will follow my laws and be careful to keep my decrees.[f] 25 They will live in the land I gave to my servant Jacob, the land where your fathers lived.[g] They and their children and their children's children will live there forever,[h] and David my servant will be their prince forever.[i] 26 I will make a covenant of peace[j] with them; it will be an everlasting covenant. I will establish them and increase their numbers,[k] and I will put my sanctuary among them forever.[l] 27 My dwelling place[m] will be with them; I will be their God, and they will be my people.[n] 28 Then the nations will know that I the LORD make Israel holy,[o] when my sanctuary is among them forever.' "

A Prophecy Against Gog

38 The word of the LORD came to me: 2 "Son of man, set your face against Gog, of the land of Magog,[p] the chief prince of[b] Meshech and Tubal;[q] prophesy against him 3 and say: 'This is what the Sovereign LORD says: I am against you, O Gog, chief prince of[c] Meshech and Tubal.[r] 4 I will turn you around, put hooks[s] in your jaws and bring you out with your whole army—your horses, your horsemen fully armed, and a great horde with large and small shields, all of them brandishing their swords.[t] 5 Persia, Cush[d][u] and Put[v] will be with them, all with shields and helmets, 6 also Gomer[w] with all its troops, and Beth Togarmah[x] from the far north with all its troops—the many nations with you.

7 " 'Get ready; be prepared,[y] you and all the hordes gathered about you, and take command of them. 8 After many days[z] you will be called to arms. In future years you will invade a land that has recovered from war, whose people were gathered from many nations[a] to the mountains of Israel, which had long been desolate. They had been brought out from the nations, and now all of them live in safety.[b] 9 You and all your troops and the many nations with you will go up, advancing like a storm;[c] you will be like a cloud[d] covering the land.

10 " 'This is what the Sovereign LORD says: On that day thoughts will come into your mind and you will devise an evil scheme.[e] 11 You will say, "I will invade a land of unwalled villages; I will attack a peaceful and unsuspecting people—all of them living without walls and without gates and bars.[f] 12 I will plunder and loot and turn my hand against the resettled ruins and the people gathered from the nations, rich in livestock and goods, living at the center of the land." 13 Sheba[g] and Dedan

37:14 [t]Eze 36:27-28, 36
37:16 [u]1Ki 12:20; 2Ch 10:17-19 [v]Nu 17:2-3; 2Ch 15:9
37:17 [w]ver 24; Isa 11:13; Jer 50:4; Hos 1:11
37:18 [x]Eze 24:19
37:19 [y]Zec 10:6
37:21 [z]Isa 43:5-6; Eze 36:24; 39:27
37:22 [a]Isa 11:13; Jer 3:18; Hos 1:11
37:23 [b]Eze 36:25; 43:7 [c]Eze 11:18; 36:28
37:24 [d]Hos 3:5 [e]Isa 40:11; Eze 34:23 [f]Ps 78:70-71
37:25 [g]Eze 28:25 [h]Am 9:15 [i]Isa 11:1
37:26 [j]Isa 55:3 [k]Jer 30:19 [l]Eze 16:62
37:27 [m]Lev 26:11; Jn 1:14 [n]2Co 6:16*
37:28 [o]Ex 31:13; Eze 20:12
38:2 [p]Ge 10:2 [q]Rev 20:8
38:3 [r]Eze 39:1
38:4 [s]2Ki 19:28 [t]Eze 29:4; Da 11:40
38:5 [u]Ge 10:6 [v]Eze 27:10
38:6 [w]Ge 10:2 [x]Eze 27:14
38:7 [y]Isa 8:9
38:8 [z]Isa 24:22 [a]Isa 11:11 [b]Jer 23:6
38:9 [c]Isa 28:2 [d]Jer 4:13; Joel 2:2
38:10 [e]Ps 36:4; Mic 2:1
38:11 [f]Jer 49:31; Zec 2:4
38:13 [g]Eze 27:22

[a]*23* Many Hebrew manuscripts (see also Septuagint); most Hebrew manuscripts *all their dwelling places where they sinned* [b]*2* Or *the prince of Rosh,* [c]*3* Or *Gog, prince of Rosh,* [d]*5* That is, the upper Nile region

and the merchants of Tarshish and all
her villages[a] will say to you, “Have you
come to plunder? Have you gathered
your hordes to loot, to carry off silver
and gold, to take away livestock and
38:13 [h]Isa 10:6; Jer 15:13 goods and to seize much plunder?[h]” ’
14“Therefore, son of man, prophesy
and say to Gog: ‘This is what the Sovereign LORD says: In that day, when my
38:14 [i]ver 8; Zec 2:5 people Israel are living in safety,[i] will
you not take notice of it? 15You will
come from your place in the far north,
you and many nations with you, all of
them riding on horses, a great horde,
38:15 [j]Eze 39:2 a mighty army.[j] 16You will advance
against my people Israel like a cloud[k]
38:16 [k]ver 9 [l]Isa 29:23; Eze 39:21 that covers the land. In days to come,
O Gog, I will bring you against my
land, so that the nations may know me
when I show myself holy through you
before their eyes.[l]
17“ ‘This is what the Sovereign LORD
says: Are you not the one I spoke of in
former days by my servants the prophets of Israel? At that time they prophesied for years that I would bring you
against them. 18This is what will happen in that day: When Gog attacks the
land of Israel, my hot anger will be
aroused, declares the Sovereign LORD.
19In my zeal and fiery wrath I declare
that at that time there shall be a great
38:19 [m]Ps 18:7; Eze 5:13; Hag 2:6,21 earthquake in the land of Israel.[m] 20The
fish of the sea, the birds of the air, the
beasts of the field, every creature that
moves along the ground, and all the
people on the face of the earth will
tremble at my presence. The mountains will be overturned, the cliffs will
crumble and every wall will fall to the
38:20 [n]Hos 4:3; Na 1:5 ground.[n] 21I will summon a sword[o]
against Gog on all my mountains, de-
38:21 [o]Eze 14:17 [p]1Sa 14:20; 2Ch 20:23; Hag 2:22 clares the Sovereign LORD. Every man’s
sword will be against his brother.[p] 22I
will execute judgment[q] upon him with
plague and bloodshed; I will pour down
38:22 [q]Isa 66:16; Jer 25:31 [r]Ps 18:12; Rev 16:21 torrents of rain, hailstones[r] and burning sulfur on him and on his troops and
on the many nations with him. 23And
so I will show my greatness and my holiness, and I will make myself known in
the sight of many nations. Then they
38:23 [s]Eze 36:23 will know that I am the LORD.[s]’

39 “Son of man, prophesy against
Gog and say: ‘This is what the
Sovereign LORD says: I am against you,
39:1 [t]Eze 38:2,3 O Gog, chief prince of[b] Meshech and
Tubal.[t] 2I will turn you around and
drag you along. I will bring you from
the far north and send you against the
mountains of Israel. 3Then I will strike
your bow[u] from your left hand and 39:3 [u]Hos 1:5 [v]Ps 76:3
make your arrows[v] drop from your right
hand. 4On the mountains of Israel you
will fall, you and all your troops and
the nations with you. I will give you as
food to all kinds of carrion birds and
to the wild animals.[w] 5You will fall in 39:4 [w]ver 17-20; Eze 29:5; 33:27
the open field, for I have spoken, de-
clares the Sovereign LORD. 6I will send
fire[x] on Magog and on those who live 39:6 [x]Eze 30:8; Am 1:4 [y]Jer 25:22
in safety in the coastlands,[y] and they
will know that I am the LORD.

▸ PATIENCE

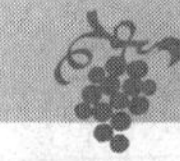

A Place to Start Our Worship

Ezekiel 39:6

Magog will answer for its belligerence toward God. When? When clocks run down and time has passed the point of starting over. At that time all things that have opposed God will at last confess his justice.

7“ ‘I will make known my holy name
among my people Israel. I will no lon-
ger let my holy name be profaned,[z] and 39:7 [z]Ex 20:7 [a]Isa 12:6; Eze 36:16,23
the nations will know that I the LORD
am the Holy One in Israel.[a] 8It is coming! It will surely take place, declares
the Sovereign LORD. This is the day I
have spoken of.
9“ ‘Then those who live in the towns
of Israel will go out and use the weapons for fuel and burn them up—the
small and large shields, the bows and
arrows, the war clubs and spears. For 39:9 [b]Ps 46:9
seven years they will use them for fuel.[b]
10They will not need to gather wood
from the fields or cut it from the forests, because they will use the weapons
for fuel. And they will plunder those
who plundered them and loot those
who looted them, declares the Sover- 39:10 [c]Isa 14:2; 33:1; Hab 2:8
eign LORD.[c]
11“ ‘On that day I will give Gog a
burial place in Israel, in the valley of
those who travel east toward[c] the Sea.[d]
It will block the way of travelers, because Gog and all his hordes will be

[a]*13* Or *her strong lions* [b]*1* Or *Gog, prince of Rosh,* [c]*11* Or *of* [d]*11* That is, the Dead Sea

buried there. So it will be called the Valley of Hamon Gog.[a][d]

12 "'For seven months the house of Israel will be burying them in order to cleanse the land.[e] 13 All the people of the land will bury them, and the day I am glorified[f] will be a memorable day for them, declares the Sovereign LORD.

14 "'Men will be regularly employed to cleanse the land. Some will go throughout the land and, in addition to them, others will bury those that remain on the ground. At the end of the seven months they will begin their search. 15 As they go through the land and one of them sees a human bone, he will set up a marker beside it until the gravediggers have buried it in the Valley of Hamon Gog. 16 (Also a town called Hamonah[b] will be there.) And so they will cleanse the land.'

17 "Son of man, this is what the Sovereign LORD says: Call out to every kind of bird[g] and all the wild animals: 'Assemble and come together from all around to the sacrifice I am preparing for you, the great sacrifice on the mountains of Israel. There you will eat flesh and drink blood. 18 You will eat the flesh of mighty men and drink the blood of the princes of the earth as if they were rams and lambs, goats and bulls—all of them fattened animals from Bashan.[h] 19 At the sacrifice I am preparing for you, you will eat fat till you are glutted and drink blood till you are drunk. 20 At my table you will eat your fill of horses and riders, mighty men and soldiers of every kind,' declares the Sovereign LORD.[i]

21 "I will display my glory among the nations, and all the nations will see the punishment I inflict and the hand I lay upon them.[j] 22 From that day forward the house of Israel will know that I am the LORD their God. 23 And the nations will know that the people of Israel went into exile for their sin, because they were unfaithful to me. So I hid my face from them and handed them over to their enemies, and they all fell by the sword.[k] 24 I dealt with them according to their uncleanness and their offenses, and I hid my face from them.[l]

25 "Therefore this is what the Sovereign LORD says: I will now bring Jacob back from captivity[c][m] and will have compassion[n] on all the people of Israel, and I will be zealous for my holy name.[o] 26 They will forget their shame and all the unfaithfulness they showed toward me when they lived in safety[p] in their land with no one to make them afraid.[q] 27 When I have brought them back from the nations and have gathered them from the countries of their enemies, I will show myself holy through them in the sight of many nations.[r] 28 Then they will know that I am the LORD their God, for though I sent them into exile among the nations, I will gather them to their own land, not leaving any behind. 29 I will no longer hide my face from them, for I will pour out my Spirit[s] on the house of Israel, declares the Sovereign LORD."

The New Temple Area

40 In the twenty-fifth year of our exile, at the beginning of the year, on the tenth of the month, in the fourteenth year after the fall of the city[t]—on that very day the hand of the LORD was upon me[u] and he took me there. 2 In visions[v] of God he took me to the land of Israel and set me on a very high mountain,[w] on whose south side were some buildings that looked like a city. 3 He took me there, and I saw a man whose appearance was like bronze;[x] he was standing in the gateway with a linen cord and a measuring rod[y] in his hand. 4 The man said to me, "Son of man, look with your eyes and hear with your ears and pay attention to everything I am going to show you, for that is why you have been brought here. Tell[z] the house of Israel everything you see.[a]"

The East Gate to the Outer Court

5 I saw a wall completely surrounding the temple area. The length of the measuring rod in the man's hand was six long cubits, each of which was a cubit[d] and a handbreadth.[e] He measured[b] the wall; it was one measuring rod thick and one rod high.

6 Then he went to the gate facing east.[c] He climbed its steps and measured the threshold of the gate; it was

39:11 [d]Eze 38:2
39:12 [e]Dt 21:23
39:13 [f]Eze 28:22
39:17 [g]Rev 19:17
39:18 [h]Ps 22:12; Jer 51:40
39:20 [i]Rev 19:17-18
39:21 [j]Ex 9:16; Isa 37:20; Eze 38:16
39:23 [k]Isa 1:15; 59:2; Jer 22:8-9; 44:23
39:24 [l]Jer 2:17,19; 4:18; Eze 36:19
39:25 [m]Jer 33:7; Eze 34:13 [n]Jer 30:18

39:25 [o]Isa 27:12-13
39:26 [p]1Ki 4:25 [q]Isa 17:2; Eze 34:28; Mic 4:4
39:27 [r]Eze 36:23-24; 37:21; 38:16
39:29 [s]Joel 2:28; Ac 2:17
40:1 [t]2Ki 25:7; Jer 39:1-10; 52:4-11; Eze 33:21 [u]Eze 1:3
40:2 [v]Da 7:1,7 [w]Eze 17:22; Rev 21:10
40:3 [x]Eze 1:7; Da 10:6; Rev 1:15 [y]Eze 47:3; Zec 2:1-2; Rev 11:1; 21:15
40:4 [z]Jer 26:2 [a]Eze 44:5
40:5 [b]Eze 42:20
40:6 [c]Eze 8:16

[a] *11 Hamon Gog* means *hordes of Gog.* [b] *16 Hamonah* means *horde.* [c] *25* Or *now restore the fortunes of Jacob* [d] 5 The common cubit was about 1 1/2 feet (about 0.5 meter). [e] 5 That is, about 3 inches (about 8 centimeters)

40:7 [d]ver 36

one rod deep.[a] 7The alcoves[d] for the guards were one rod long and one rod wide, and the projecting walls between the alcoves were five cubits thick. And the threshold of the gate next to the portico facing the temple was one rod deep.

8Then he measured the portico of the gateway; 9it[b] was eight cubits deep and its jambs were two cubits thick. The portico of the gateway faced the temple.

40:14 [e]Ex 27:9

40:16 [f]ver 21-22; 2Ch 3:5; Eze 41:26

10Inside the east gate were three alcoves on each side; the three had the same measurements, and the faces of the projecting walls on each side had the same measurements. 11Then he measured the width of the entrance to the gateway; it was ten cubits and its length was thirteen cubits. 12In front of each alcove was a wall one cubit high, and the alcoves were six cubits square. 13Then he measured the gateway from the top of the rear wall of one alcove to the top of the opposite one; the distance was twenty-five cubits from one parapet opening to the opposite one. 14He measured along the faces of the projecting walls all around the inside of the gateway—sixty cubits. The measurement was up to the portico[c] facing the courtyard.[d][e] 15The distance from the entrance of the gateway to the far end of its portico was fifty cubits. 16The alcoves and the projecting walls inside the gateway were surmounted by narrow parapet openings all around, as was the portico; the openings all around faced inward. The faces of the projecting walls were decorated with palm trees.[f]

The Outer Court

40:17 [g]Rev 11:2 [h]Eze 41:6 [i]Eze 42:1

40:19 [j]Eze 46:1 [k]ver 23,27

17Then he brought me into the outer court.[g] There I saw some rooms and a pavement that had been constructed all around the court; there were thirty rooms[h] along the pavement.[i] 18It abutted the sides of the gateways and was as wide as they were long; this was the lower pavement. 19Then he measured the distance from the inside of the lower gateway to the outside of the inner court;[j] it was a hundred cubits[k] on the east side as well as on the north.

The North Gate

40:21 [l]ver 7

40:22 [m]ver 49

40:23 [n]ver 19

20Then he measured the length and width of the gate facing north, leading into the outer court. 21Its alcoves[l]—three on each side—its projecting walls and its portico had the same measurements as those of the first gateway. It was fifty cubits long and twenty-five cubits wide. 22Its openings, its portico[m] and its palm tree decorations had the same measurements as those of the gate facing east. Seven steps led up to it, with its portico opposite them. 23There was a gate to the inner court facing the north gate, just as there was on the east. He measured from one gate to the opposite one; it was a hundred cubits.[n]

The South Gate

40:25 [o]ver 33

40:26 [p]ver 22

40:27 [q]ver 32

24Then he led me to the south side and I saw a gate facing south. He measured its jambs and its portico, and they had the same measurements as the others. 25The gateway and its portico had narrow openings all around, like the openings of the others. It was fifty cubits long and twenty-five cubits wide.[o] 26Seven steps led up to it, with its portico opposite them; it had palm tree decorations on the faces of the projecting walls on each side.[p] 27The inner court[q] also had a gate facing south, and he measured from this gate to the outer gate on the south side; it was a hundred cubits.

Gates to the Inner Court

40:28 [r]ver 35

40:30 [s]ver 21

40:31 [t]ver 22

28Then he brought me into the inner court through the south gate, and he measured the south gate; it had the same measurements[r] as the others. 29Its alcoves, its projecting walls and its portico had the same measurements as the others. The gateway and its portico had openings all around. It was fifty cubits long and twenty-five cubits wide. 30(The porticoes[s] of the gateways around the inner court were twenty-five cubits wide and five cubits deep.) 31Its portico[t] faced the outer court; palm trees decorated its jambs, and eight steps led up to it.

32Then he brought me to the inner court on the east side, and he measured

[a]*6* Septuagint; Hebrew *deep, the first threshold, one rod deep* [b]*8,9* Many Hebrew manuscripts, Septuagint, Vulgate and Syriac; most Hebrew manuscripts *gateway facing the temple; it was one rod deep. 9Then he measured the portico of the gateway; it* [c]*14* Septuagint; Hebrew *projecting wall* [d]*14* The meaning of the Hebrew for this verse is uncertain.

the gateway; it had the same measurements as the others. [33]Its alcoves, its
projecting walls and its portico had the
same measurements as the others. The
gateway and its portico had openings
all around. It was fifty cubits long and
40:34 [u]ver 22 twenty-five cubits wide. [34]Its portico[u]
faced the outer court; palm trees dec-
orated the jambs on either side, and
eight steps led up to it.
[35]Then he brought me to the north
40:35 [v]Eze 44:4; gate[v] and measured it. It had the same
47:2 measurements as the others, [36]as did
40:36 its alcoves,[w] its projecting walls and its
[w]ver 7 portico, and it had openings all around.
It was fifty cubits long and twenty-five
cubits wide. [37]Its portico[a] faced the outer court; palm trees decorated the jambs
on either side, and eight steps led up
to it.

The Rooms for Preparing Sacrifices

[38]A room with a doorway was by
40:38 the portico in each of the inner gate-
[x]2Ch 4:6; Eze 42:13 ways, where the burnt offerings[x] were
washed. [39]In the portico of the gateway
40:39 were two tables on each side, on which
[y]Eze 46:2 the burnt offerings,[y] sin offerings[z] and
[z]Lev 4:3,28 [a]Lev 7:1 guilt offerings[a] were slaughtered. [40]By
the outside wall of the portico of the
gateway, near the steps at the entrance
to the north gateway were two tables,
and on the other side of the steps were
two tables. [41]So there were four tables
on one side of the gateway and four
on the other—eight tables in all—on
which the sacrifices were slaughtered.
[42]There were also four tables of dressed
40:42 [b]Ex 20:25 stone[b] for the burnt offerings, each a
[c]ver 39 cubit and a half long, a cubit and a half
wide and a cubit high. On them were
placed the utensils for slaughtering the
burnt offerings and the other sacrifices.[c]
[43]And double-pronged hooks, each a
handbreadth long, were attached to the
wall all around. The tables were for the
flesh of the offerings.

Rooms for the Priests

[44]Outside the inner gate, within the
inner court, were two rooms, one[b] at
the side of the north gate and facing
south, and another at the side of the
40:45 south[c] gate and facing north. [45]He said
[d]1Ch 9:23 to me, "The room facing south is for the
priests who have charge of the temple,[d]
40:46 [46]and the room facing north[e] is for the
[e]Eze 42:13 [f]Nu 18:5 priests who have charge of the altar.[f]
These are the sons of Zadok,[g] who are 40:46 [g]1Ki 2:35
the only Levites who may draw near to [h]Nu 16:5;
the LORD to minister before him.[h]" Eze 43:19;
[47]Then he measured the court: It was 44:15; 45:4; 48:11
square—a hundred cubits long and a
hundred cubits wide. And the altar was
in front of the temple.

The Temple

[48]He brought me to the portico of 40:48
the temple[i] and measured the jambs of [i]1Ki 6:2
the portico; they were five cubits wide
on either side. The width of the entrance was fourteen cubits and its projecting walls were[d] three cubits wide on 40:49
either side. [49]The portico[j] was twenty [j]ver 22; 1Ki 6:3
cubits wide, and twelve[e] cubits from [k]1Ki 7:15
front to back. It was reached by a flight
of stairs,[f] and there were pillars[k] on each
side of the jambs.

41

Then the man brought me to
the outer sanctuary[l] and mea- 41:1 [l]ver 23
sured the jambs; the width of the jambs
was six cubits[g] on each side.[h] [2]The entrance was ten cubits wide, and the projecting walls on each side of it were five
cubits wide. He also measured the outer sanctuary; it was forty cubits long 41:2
and twenty cubits wide.[m] [m]2Ch 3:3
[3]Then he went into the inner sanctuary and measured the jambs of the entrance; each was two cubits wide. The
entrance was six cubits wide, and the
projecting walls on each side of it were
seven cubits wide. [4]And he measured
the length of the inner sanctuary; it was
twenty cubits, and its width was twenty cubits across the end of the outer
sanctuary.[n] He said to me, "This is the 41:4
Most Holy Place.[o]" [n]1Ki 6:20 [o]Ex 26:33;
[5]Then he measured the wall of the Heb 9:3-8
temple; it was six cubits thick, and each
side room around the temple was four
cubits wide. [6]The side rooms were on
three levels, one above another, thirty[p] 41:6 [p]Eze 40:17
on each level. There were ledges all [q]1Ki 6:5
around the wall of the temple to serve
as supports for the side rooms, so that
the supports were not inserted into the
wall of the temple.[q] [7]The side rooms all

[a]*37* Septuagint (see also verses 31 and 34); Hebrew *jambs* [b]*44* Septuagint; Hebrew *were rooms for singers, which were* [c]*44* Septuagint; Hebrew *east* [d]*48* Septuagint; Hebrew *entrance was* [e]*49* Septuagint; Hebrew *eleven* [f]*49* Hebrew; Septuagint *Ten steps led up to it* [g]*1* The common cubit was about 1 1/2 feet (about 0.5 meter). [h]*1* One Hebrew manuscript and Septuagint; most Hebrew manuscripts *side, the width of the tent*

around the temple were wider at each
successive level. The structure surrounding the temple was built in ascending
stages, so that the rooms widened as
41:7 one went upward. A stairway[r] went up
[r]1Ki 6:8 from the lowest floor to the top floor
through the middle floor.
8I saw that the temple had a raised
base all around it, forming the foundation of the side rooms. It was the
length of the rod, six long cubits. 9The
outer wall of the side rooms was five
cubits thick. The open area between
the side rooms of the temple 10and the
⌞priests'⌟ rooms was twenty cubits wide
all around the temple. 11There were
entrances to the side rooms from the
open area, one on the north and another on the south; and the base adjoining
the open area was five cubits wide all
around.
12The building facing the temple
courtyard on the west side was seventy
cubits wide. The wall of the building
was five cubits thick all around, and its
length was ninety cubits.
13Then he measured the temple; it
was a hundred cubits long, and the temple courtyard and the building with its
walls were also a hundred cubits long.
14The width of the temple courtyard on
the east, including the front of the tem-
41:14 ple, was a hundred cubits.[s]
[s]Eze 40:47 15Then he measured the length of
the building facing the courtyard at the
rear of the temple, including its galler-
41:15 ies[t] on each side; it was a hundred cu-
[t]Eze 42:3 bits.
The outer sanctuary, the inner sanctuary and the portico facing the court,
16as well as the thresholds and the nar-
41:16 [u]1Ki 6:4 row windows[u] and galleries around the
[v]ver 25-26; three of them—everything beyond and
1Ki 6:15; including the threshold was covered
Eze 42:3 with wood. The floor, the wall up to
the windows, and the windows were
41:18 covered.[v] 17In the space above the out-
[w]1Ki 6:18 side of the entrance to the inner sanctu-
[x]Ex 37:7; 2Ch 3:7 ary and on the walls at regular intervals
[y]1Ki 6:29; 7:36 all around the inner and outer sanctu-
[z]Eze 10:21 ary 18were carved[w] cherubim[x] and palm
trees.[y] Palm trees alternated with cherubim. Each cherub had two faces:[z] 19the
face of a man toward the palm tree on
one side and the face of a lion toward
the palm tree on the other. They were
41:19 carved all around the whole temple.[a]
[a]Eze 10:14 20From the floor to the area above the

entrance, cherubim and palm trees were
carved on the wall of the outer sanctuary.
21The outer sanctuary[b] had a rect- 41:21
angular doorframe, and the one at the [b]ver 1
front of the Most Holy Place was simi-
lar. 22There was a wooden altar[c] three 41:22 [c]Ex 30:1
cubits high and two cubits square[a]; its [d]Ex 25:23;
corners, its base[b] and its sides were of Eze 23:41; 44:16;
wood. The man said to me, "This is the Mal 1:7,12
table[d] that is before the LORD." 23Both
the outer sanctuary[e] and the Most Holy 41:23 [e]ver 1
Place had double doors.[f] 24Each door [f]1Ki 6:32
had two leaves—two hinged leaves[g] for 41:24
each door. 25And on the doors of the [g]1Ki 6:34
outer sanctuary were carved cherubim
and palm trees like those carved on the
walls, and there was a wooden over-
hang on the front of the portico. 26On
the sidewalls of the portico were narrow windows with palm trees carved on
each side. The side rooms of the temple 41:26
also had overhangs.[h] [h]ver 15-16; Eze 40:16

Rooms for the Priests

42 Then the man led me north-
ward into the outer court and 42:1
brought me to the rooms[i] opposite the [i]ver 13
temple courtyard[j] and opposite the out- [j]Eze 41:12-14
er wall on the north side.[k] 2The building [k]Eze 40:17
whose door faced north was a hundred
cubits[c] long and fifty cubits wide. 3Both
in the section twenty cubits from the
inner court and in the section opposite
the pavement of the outer court, gal- 42:3
lery[l] faced gallery at the three levels.[m] [l]Eze 41:15
4In front of the rooms was an inner [m]Eze 41:16
passageway ten cubits wide and a hundred cubits[d] long. Their doors were on
the north.[n] 5Now the upper rooms were 42:4 [n]Eze 46:19
narrower, for the galleries took more
space from them than from the rooms
on the lower and middle floors of the
building. 6The rooms on the third floor
had no pillars, as the courts had; so
they were smaller in floor space than
those on the lower and middle floors.
7There was an outer wall parallel to the
rooms and the outer court; it extended
in front of the rooms for fifty cubits.
8While the row of rooms on the side
next to the outer court was fifty cubits
long, the row on the side nearest the
sanctuary was a hundred cubits long.

[a]*22* Septuagint; Hebrew *long* [b]*22* Septuagint; Hebrew *length* [c]*2* The common cubit was about 1 1/2 feet (about 0.5 meter). [d]*4* Septuagint and Syriac; Hebrew *and one cubit*

42:9 9The lower rooms had an entrance[o] on
[o]Eze 44:5; the east side as one enters them from
46:19 the outer court.
10On the south side[a] along the length
of the wall of the outer court, adjoining
the temple courtyard and opposite the
42:10 outer wall, were rooms[p] 11with a pas-
[p]ver 1 sageway in front of them. These were
like the rooms on the north; they had
the same length and width, with similar exits and dimensions. Similar to the
doorways on the north 12were the doorways of the rooms on the south. There
was a doorway at the beginning of the
passageway that was parallel to the corresponding wall extending eastward, by
which one enters the rooms.
42:13 [q]Eze 40:46 13Then he said to me, "The north[q]
[r]Lev 10:17; and south rooms facing the temple
6:25 [s]Lev 14:13 courtyard are the priests' rooms, where
[t]Ex 29:31; the priests who approach the LORD
Lev 6:29; 7:6; 10:12-13; will eat the most holy offerings. There
Nu 18:9-10 they will put the most holy offerings—
the grain offerings, the sin offerings[r]
and the guilt offerings[s]—for the place is
holy.[t] 14Once the priests enter the holy
precincts, they are not to go into the
42:14 outer court until they leave behind the
[u]Eze 44:19 garments[u] in which they minister, for
[v]Ex 29:9; Lev 8:7-9 these are holy. They are to put on other
clothes before they go near the places
that are for the people.[v]"
15When he had finished measuring
what was inside the temple area, he led
42:15 [w]Eze 43:1 me out by the east gate[w] and measured
the area all around: 16He measured the
east side with the measuring rod; it was
five hundred cubits.[b] 17He measured
the north side; it was five hundred cubits[c] by the measuring rod. 18He measured the south side; it was five hundred
cubits by the measuring rod. 19Then he
turned to the west side and measured; it
was five hundred cubits by the measur-
42:20 [x]Eze 40:5 ing rod. 20So he measured[x] the area on
[y]Zec 2:5 all four sides. It had a wall around it,[y]
[z]Eze 45:2; Rev 21:16 five hundred cubits long and five hun-
[a]Eze 22:26 dred cubits wide,[z] to separate the holy
from the common.[a]

The Glory Returns to the Temple

43:1 [b]Eze 10:19; 43 Then the man brought me to
42:15; 44:1; the gate facing east,[b] 2and I saw
46:1 the glory of the God of Israel coming
43:2 from the east. His voice was like the
[c]Rev 1:15 [d]Isa 6:3; roar of rushing waters,[c] and the land
Eze 11:23; was radiant with his glory.[d] 3The vi-
Rev 18:1 sion I saw was like the vision I had
seen when he[d] came to destroy the city
and like the visions I had seen by the
Kebar River, and I fell facedown. 4The
glory[e] of the LORD entered the temple 43:4
through the gate facing east.[f] 5Then the [e]Eze 1:28
Spirit[g] lifted me up[h] and brought me [f]Eze 10:19
into the inner court, and the glory of 43:5
the LORD filled the temple. [g]Eze 11:24 [h]Eze 3:12; 8:3
6While the man was standing beside
me, I heard someone speaking to me
from inside the temple. 7He said: "Son
of man, this is the place of my throne
and the place for the soles of my feet.
This is where I will live among the
Israelites forever. The house of Israel
will never again defile my holy name—
neither they nor their kings—by their
prostitution[e] and the lifeless idols[f] of 43:7
their kings at their high places.[i] 8When [i]Lev 26:30
they placed their threshold next to my
threshold and their doorposts beside my
doorposts, with only a wall between me
and them, they defiled my holy name
by their detestable practices. So I destroyed them in my anger. 9Now let
them put away from me their prostitution and the lifeless idols of their kings, 43:9
and I will live among them forever.[j] [j]Eze 37:26-28
10"Son of man, describe the temple
to the people of Israel, that they may be 43:10
ashamed[k] of their sins. Let them con- [k]Eze 16:61
sider the plan, 11and if they are ashamed
of all they have done, make known to
them the design of the temple—its ar-
rangement, its exits and entrances—its
whole design and all its regulations[g] and
laws. Write these down before them so
that they may be faithful to its design 43:11
and follow all its regulations.[l] [l]Eze 44:5
12"This is the law of the temple: All
the surrounding area[m] on top of the 43:12 [m]Eze 40:2
mountain will be most holy. Such is the
law of the temple.

The Altar

13"These are the measurements of the 43:13
altar[n] in long cubits, that cubit being a [n]2Ch 4:1
cubit[h] and a handbreadth[i]: Its gutter is

[a] *10* Septuagint; Hebrew *Eastward* [b] *16* See Septuagint of verse 17; Hebrew *rods*; also in verses 18 and 19. [c] *17* Septuagint; Hebrew *rods*
[d] *3* Some Hebrew manuscripts and Vulgate; most Hebrew manuscripts *I* [e] *7* Or *their spiritual adultery*; also in verse 9 [f] *7* Or *the corpses*; also in verse 9 [g] *11* Some Hebrew manuscripts and Septuagint; most Hebrew manuscripts *regulations and its whole design* [h] *13* The common cubit was about 1 1/2 feet (about 0.5 meter). [i] *13* That is, about 3 inches (about 8 centimeters)

a cubit deep and a cubit wide, with a rim of one span[a] around the edge. And this is the height of the altar: **14**From the gutter on the ground up to the lower ledge it is two cubits high and a cubit wide, and from the smaller ledge up to the larger ledge it is four cubits high and a cubit wide. **15**The altar hearth is four cubits high, and four horns[o] project upward from the hearth. **16**The altar hearth is square, twelve cubits long and twelve cubits wide. **17**The upper ledge also is square, fourteen cubits long and fourteen cubits wide, with a rim of half a cubit and a gutter of a cubit all around. The steps[p] of the altar face east."

43:15 [o]Ex 27:2

43:17 [p]Ex 20:26

18Then he said to me, "Son of man, this is what the Sovereign LORD says: These will be the regulations for sacrificing burnt offerings[q] and sprinkling blood[r] upon the altar when it is built: **19**You are to give a young bull[s] as a sin offering to the priests, who are Levites, of the family of Zadok,[t] who come near[u] to minister before me, declares the Sovereign LORD. **20**You are to take some of its blood and put it on the four horns of the altar and on the four corners of the upper ledge[v] and all around the rim, and so purify the altar[w] and make atonement for it. **21**You are to take the bull for the sin offering and burn it in the designated part of the temple area outside the sanctuary.[x]

43:18 [q]Ex 40:29 [r]Lev 1:5,11; Heb 9:21-22

43:19 [s]Lev 4:3; Eze 45:18-19 [t]Eze 44:15 [u]Nu 16:40; Eze 40:46

43:20 [v]ver 17 [w]Lev 16:19

43:21 [x]Ex 29:14; Heb 13:11

22"On the second day you are to offer a male goat without defect for a sin offering, and the altar is to be purified as it was purified with the bull. **23**When you have finished purifying it, you are to offer a young bull and a ram from the flock, both without defect.[y] **24**You are to offer them before the LORD, and the priests are to sprinkle salt[z] on them and sacrifice them as a burnt offering to the LORD.

43:23 [y]Ex 29:1

43:24 [z]Lev 2:13; Mk 9:49-50

25"For seven days[a] you are to provide a male goat daily for a sin offering; you are also to provide a young bull and a ram from the flock, both without defect.[b] **26**For seven days they are to make atonement for the altar and cleanse it; thus they will dedicate it. **27**At the end of these days, from the eighth day[c] on, the priests are to present your burnt offerings and fellowship offerings[b][d] on the altar. Then I will accept you, declares the Sovereign LORD."

43:25 [a]Lev 8:33 [b]Ex 29:37

43:27 [c]Lev 9:1 [d]Lev 17:5

The Prince, the Levites, the Priests

44 Then the man brought me back to the outer gate of the sanctuary, the one facing east,[e] and it was shut. **2**The LORD said to me, "This gate is to remain shut. It must not be opened; no one may enter through it.[f] It is to remain shut because the LORD, the God of Israel, has entered through it. **3**The prince himself is the only one who may sit inside the gateway to eat in the presence[g] of the LORD. He is to enter by way of the portico of the gateway and go out the same way.[h]"

44:1 [e]Eze 43:1

44:2 [f]Eze 43:4-5

44:3 [g]Ex 24:9-11 [h]Eze 46:2,8

4Then the man brought me by way of the north gate to the front of the temple. I looked and saw the glory of the LORD filling the temple[i] of the LORD, and I fell facedown.[j]

44:4 [i]Isa 6:4; Rev 15:8 [j]Eze 1:28; 3:23

5The LORD said to me, "Son of man, look carefully, listen closely and give attention to everything I tell you concerning all the regulations regarding the temple of the LORD. Give attention to the entrance of the temple and all the exits of the sanctuary.[k] **6**Say to the rebellious house[l] of Israel, 'This is what the Sovereign LORD says: Enough of your detestable practices, O house of Israel! **7**In addition to all your other detestable practices, you brought foreigners uncircumcised in heart[m] and flesh into my sanctuary, desecrating my temple while you offered me food, fat and blood, and you broke my covenant.[n] **8**Instead of carrying out your duty in regard to my holy things, you put others in charge of my sanctuary.[o] **9**This is what the Sovereign LORD says: No foreigner uncircumcised in heart and flesh is to enter my sanctuary, not even the foreigners who live among the Israelites.[p]

44:5 [k]Eze 40:4; 43:10-11

44:6 [l]Eze 3:9

44:7 [m]Lev 26:41 [n]Ge 17:14; Ex 12:48; Lev 22:25

44:8 [o]Lev 22:2; Nu 18:7

44:9 [p]Joel 3:17; Zec 14:21

10" 'The Levites who went far from me when Israel went astray[q] and who wandered from me after their idols must bear the consequences of their sin.[r] **11**They may serve in my sanctuary, having charge of the gates of the temple and serving in it; they may slaughter the burnt offerings[s] and sacrifices for the people and stand before the people and serve them.[t] **12**But because they served them in the presence of their idols and made the house of Israel fall into sin, therefore I have sworn with uplifted

44:10 [q]2Ki 23:8 [r]Nu 18:23

44:11 [s]2Ch 29:34 [t]Nu 3:5-37; 16:9; 1Ch 26:12-19

[a]*13* That is, about 9 inches (about 22 centimeters)
[b]*27* Traditionally *peace offerings*

hand[u] that they must bear the consequences of their sin, declares the Sovereign LORD.[v] 13They are not to come near to serve me as priests or come near any of my holy things or my most holy offerings; they must bear the shame[w] of their detestable practices.[x] 14Yet I will put them in charge of the duties of the temple and all the work that is to be done in it.[y]

15" 'But the priests, who are Levites and descendants of Zadok and who faithfully carried out the duties of my sanctuary when the Israelites went astray from me, are to come near to minister before me; they are to stand before me to offer sacrifices of fat and blood, declares the Sovereign LORD.[z] 16They alone are to enter my sanctuary; they alone are to come near my table[a] to minister before me and perform my service.[b]

17" 'When they enter the gates of the inner court, they are to wear linen clothes;[c] they must not wear any woolen garment while ministering at the gates of the inner court or inside the temple. 18They are to wear linen turbans[d] on their heads and linen undergarments[e] around their waists. They must not wear anything that makes them perspire.[f] 19When they go out into the outer court where the people are, they are to take off the clothes they have been ministering in and are to leave them in the sacred rooms, and put on other clothes, so that they do not consecrate[g] the people by means of their garments.[h]

20" 'They must not shave their heads or let their hair grow long, but they are to keep the hair of their heads trimmed.[i] 21No priest is to drink wine when he enters the inner court.[j] 22They must not marry widows or divorced women; they may marry only virgins of Israelite descent or widows of priests.[k] 23They are to teach my people the difference between the holy and the common[l] and show them how to distinguish between the unclean and the clean.[m]

24" 'In any dispute, the priests are to serve as judges[n] and decide it according to my ordinances. They are to keep my laws and my decrees for all my appointed feasts, and they are to keep my Sabbaths holy.[o]

25" 'A priest must not defile himself by going near a dead person; however, if the dead person was his father or mother, son or daughter, brother or unmarried sister, then he may defile himself.[p] 26After he is cleansed, he must wait seven days.[q] 27On the day he goes into the inner court of the sanctuary to minister in the sanctuary, he is to offer a sin offering for himself, declares the Sovereign LORD.

28" 'I am to be the only inheritance[r] the priests have. You are to give them no possession in Israel; I will be their possession. 29They will eat the grain offerings, the sin offerings and the guilt offerings; and everything in Israel devoted[a] to the LORD[s] will belong to them.[t] 30The best of all the firstfruits[u] and of all your special gifts will belong to the priests. You are to give them the first portion of your ground meal[v] so that a blessing[w] may rest on your household.[x] 31The priests must not eat anything, bird or animal, found dead or torn by wild animals.[y]

Division of the Land

45 " 'When you allot the land as an inheritance,[z] you are to present to the LORD a portion of the land as a sacred district, 25,000 cubits long and 20,000[b] cubits wide; the entire area will be holy.[a] 2Of this, a section 500 cubits square[b] is to be for the sanctuary, with 50 cubits around it for open land. 3In the sacred district, measure off a section 25,000 cubits[c] long and 10,000 cubits[d] wide. In it will be the sanctuary, the Most Holy Place. 4It will be the sacred portion of the land for the priests,[c] who minister in the sanctuary and who draw near to minister before the LORD. It will be a place for their houses as well as a holy place for the sanctuary.[d] 5An area 25,000 cubits long and 10,000 cubits wide will belong to the Levites, who serve in the temple, as their possession for towns to live in.[e][e]

6" 'You are to give the city as its property an area 5,000 cubits wide and 25,000 cubits long, adjoining the sa-

44:12 [u]Ps 106:26 [v]2Ki 16:10-16
44:13 [w]Eze 16:61 [x]Nu 18:3
44:14 [y]Nu 18:4; 1Ch 23:28-32
44:15 [z]Jer 33:18; Eze 40:46; Zec 3:7
44:16 [a]Eze 41:22 [b]Nu 18:5
44:17 [c]Ex 39:27-28; Rev 19:8
44:18 [d]Ex 28:39; Isa 3:20 [e]Ex 28:42 [f]Lev 16:4
44:19 [g]Lev 6:27; Eze 46:20 [h]Lev 6:10-11; Eze 42:14
44:20 [i]Lev 21:5; Nu 6:5
44:21 [j]Lev 10:9
44:22 [k]Lev 21:7
44:23 [l]Eze 22:26 [m]Mal 2:7
44:24 [n]Dt 17:8-9; 1Ch 23:4 [o]2Ch 19:8
44:25 [p]Lev 21:1-4
44:26 [q]Nu 19:14
44:28 [r]Nu 18:20; Dt 10:9; 18:1-2; Jos 13:33
44:29 [s]Lev 27:21 [t]Nu 18:9,14
44:30 [u]Nu 18:12-13 [v]Nu 15:18-21 [w]Mal 3:10 [x]Ne 10:35-37
44:31 [y]Ex 22:31; Lev 22:8
45:1 [z]Eze 47:21-22 [a]Eze 48:8-9,29
45:2 [b]Eze 42:20
45:4 [c]Eze 40:46 [d]Eze 48:10-11
45:5 [e]Eze 48:13

[a]*29* The Hebrew term refers to the irrevocable giving over of things or persons to the LORD.
[b]*1* Septuagint (see also verses 3 and 5 and 48:9); Hebrew *10,000* [c]*3* That is, about 7 miles (about 12 kilometers) [d]*3* That is, about 3 miles (about 5 kilometers) [e]*5* Septuagint; Hebrew *temple; they will have as their possession 20 rooms*

cred portion; it will belong to the whole
45:6 [f]Eze 48:15-18 house of Israel.[f]
7“ ‘The prince will have the land bordering each side of the area formed by
the sacred district and the property of
the city. It will extend westward from
the west side and eastward from the
east side, running lengthwise from the
western to the eastern border parallel to
45:7 [g]Eze 48:21 one of the tribal portions.[g] 8This land
will be his possession in Israel. And my
princes will no longer oppress my people but will allow the house of Israel
to possess the land according to their
45:8 [h]Nu 26:53; Eze 46:18 tribes.[h]
9“ ‘This is what the Sovereign LORD
says: You have gone far enough,
O princes of Israel! Give up your violence and oppression and do what is
45:9 [i]Jer 22:3; Zec 7:9-10; 8:16 just and right.[i] Stop dispossessing my
people, declares the Sovereign LORD.
10You are to use accurate scales,[j] an ac-
45:10 [j]Dt 25:15; Pr 11:1; Am 8:4-6; Mic 6:10-11 [k]Lev 19:36 curate ephah[a][k] and an accurate bath.[b]
11The ephah[l] and the bath are to be the
same size, the bath containing a tenth
of a homer[c] and the ephah a tenth of a
45:11 [l]Isa 5:10 homer; the homer is to be the standard
measure for both. 12The shekel[d] is to
45:12 [m]Ex 30:13; Lev 27:25; Nu 3:47 consist of twenty gerahs.[m] Twenty shekels plus twenty-five shekels plus fifteen
shekels equal one mina.[e]

GENTLENESS

RAIN FROM HEAVEN

Ezekiel 45:9

God speaks to all brash tyrants who would inflict weaker souls with pain. God sees what the evil do. He will defend his people.

Offerings and Holy Days

13“ ‘This is the special gift you are to
offer: a sixth of an ephah from each homer of wheat and a sixth of an ephah
from each homer of barley. 14The prescribed portion of oil, measured by the
bath, is a tenth of a bath from each cor
(which consists of ten baths or one homer, for ten baths are equivalent to a
homer). 15Also one sheep is to be tak-
en from every flock of two hundred
from the well-watered pastures of Israel. These will be used for the grain of-
45:15 [n]Lev 1:4 [o]Lev 6:30 ferings, burnt offerings[n] and fellowship
offerings[f] to make atonement[o] for the
people, declares the Sovereign LORD.
16All the people of the land will participate in this special gift for the use of the
prince in Israel. 17It will be the duty of
the prince to provide the burnt offerings, grain offerings and drink offerings
at the festivals, the New Moons and the
Sabbaths[p]—at all the appointed feasts of 45:17 [p]Lev 23:38; Isa 66:23 [q]1Ki 8:62; 2Ch 31:3; Eze 46:4-12
the house of Israel. He will provide the
sin offerings, grain offerings, burnt offerings and fellowship offerings to make
atonement for the house of Israel.[q]
18“ ‘This is what the Sovereign LORD
says: In the first month[r] on the first day 45:18 [r]Ex 12:2 [s]Lev 22:20; Heb 9:14 [t]Lev 16:16,33
you are to take a young bull without
defect[s] and purify the sanctuary.[t] 19The
priest is to take some of the blood of
the sin offering and put it on the doorposts of the temple, on the four cor-
ners of the upper ledge[u] of the altar[v] 45:19 [u]Eze 43:17 [v]Lev 16:18-19; Eze 43:20
and on the gateposts of the inner court.
20You are to do the same on the seventh
day of the month for anyone who sins
unintentionally[w] or through ignorance; 45:20 [w]Lev 4:27
so you are to make atonement for the
temple.
21“ ‘In the first month on the fourteenth day you are to observe the
Passover,[x] a feast lasting seven days, dur- 45:21 [x]Ex 12:11; Lev 23:5-6
ing which you shall eat bread made
without yeast. 22On that day the prince
is to provide a bull as a sin offering
for himself and for all the people of
the land.[y] 23Every day during the seven 45:22 [y]Lev 4:14
days of the Feast he is to provide seven
bulls and seven rams[z] without defect as 45:23 [z]Job 42:8 [a]Nu 28:16-25
a burnt offering to the LORD, and a
male goat for a sin offering.[a] 24He is to
provide as a grain offering[b] an ephah 45:24 [b]Nu 28:12-13 [c]Eze 46:5-7
for each bull and an ephah for each
ram, along with a hin[g] of oil for each
ephah.[c]
25“ ‘During the seven days of the
Feast,[d] which begins in the seventh 45:25 [d]Dt 16:13 [e]Lev 23:34-43; Nu 29:12-38
month on the fifteenth day, he is to
make the same provision for sin offerings, burnt offerings, grain offerings
and oil.[e]

46 “ ‘This is what the Sovereign
LORD says: The gate of the inner
court[f] facing east[g] is to be shut on the 46:1 [f]Eze 40:19 [g]1Ch 9:18
six working days, but on the Sabbath

[a]*10* An ephah was a dry measure. [b]*10* A bath was a liquid measure. [c]*11* A homer was a dry measure. [d]*12* A shekel weighed about 2/5 ounce (about 11.5 grams). [e]*12* That is, 60 shekels; the common mina was 50 shekels. [f]*15* Traditionally *peace offerings*; also in verse 17 [g]*24* That is, probably about 4 quarts (about 4 liters)

day and on the day of the New Moon[h] it
is to be opened. 2The prince is to enter
from the outside through the portico[i] of
the gateway and stand by the gatepost.
The priests are to sacrifice his burnt offering and his fellowship offerings.[a] He
is to worship at the threshold of the
gateway and then go out, but the gate
will not be shut until evening.[j] 3On the
Sabbaths and New Moons the people
of the land are to worship in the presence of the LORD at the entrance to
that gateway.[k] 4The burnt offering the
prince brings to the LORD on the Sabbath day is to be six male lambs and a
ram, all without defect. 5The grain offering given with the ram is to be an
ephah,[b] and the grain offering with the
lambs is to be as much as he pleases,
along with a hin[c] of oil for each ephah.[l]
6On the day of the New Moon[m] he is
to offer a young bull, six lambs and a
ram, all without defect. 7He is to provide as a grain offering one ephah with
the bull, one ephah with the ram, and
with the lambs as much as he wants to
give, along with a hin of oil with each
ephah.[n] 8When the prince enters, he is
to go in through the portico[o] of the
gateway, and he is to come out the same
way.[p]
9" 'When the people of the land
come before the LORD at the appointed feasts,[q] whoever enters by the north
gate to worship is to go out the south
gate; and whoever enters by the south
gate is to go out the north gate. No one
is to return through the gate by which
he entered, but each is to go out the opposite gate. 10The prince is to be among
them, going in when they go in and going out when they go out.[r]
11" 'At the festivals and the appointed feasts, the grain offering is to be an
ephah with a bull, an ephah with a ram,
and with the lambs as much as one
pleases, along with a hin of oil for each
ephah.[s] 12When the prince provides[t] a
freewill offering[u] to the LORD—whether a burnt offering or fellowship offerings—the gate facing east is to be
opened for him. He shall offer his burnt
offering or his fellowship offerings as he
does on the Sabbath day. Then he shall
go out, and after he has gone out, the
gate will be shut.[v]
13" 'Every day you are to provide
a year-old lamb without defect for a
burnt offering to the LORD; morning
by morning you shall provide it.[w] 14You
are also to provide with it morning by
morning a grain offering, consisting of
a sixth of an ephah with a third of a hin
of oil to moisten the flour. The presenting of this grain offering to the LORD
is a lasting ordinance.[x] 15So the lamb
and the grain offering and the oil shall
be provided morning by morning for a
regular[y] burnt offering.[z]
16" 'This is what the Sovereign LORD
says: If the prince makes a gift from
his inheritance to one of his sons, it
will also belong to his descendants; it
is to be their property by inheritance.[a]
17If, however, he makes a gift from
his inheritance to one of his servants,
the servant may keep it until the year
of freedom;[b] then it will revert to the
prince. His inheritance belongs to his
sons only; it is theirs. 18The prince must
not take any of the inheritance[c] of the
people, driving them off their property.
He is to give his sons their inheritance
out of his own property, so that none
of my people will be separated from his
property.' "
19Then the man brought me through
the entrance[d] at the side of the gate to
the sacred rooms facing north, which
belonged to the priests, and showed
me a place at the western end. 20He
said to me, "This is the place where
the priests will cook the guilt offering
and the sin offering and bake the grain
offering, to avoid bringing them into
the outer court and consecrating[e] the
people."[f]
21He then brought me to the outer
court and led me around to its four corners, and I saw in each corner another
court. 22In the four corners of the outer
court were enclosed[d] courts, forty cubits long and thirty cubits wide; each of
the courts in the four corners was the
same size. 23Around the inside of each
of the four courts was a ledge of stone,
with places for fire built all around under the ledge. 24He said to me, "These
are the kitchens where those who minister at the temple will cook the sacrifices of the people."

[a]*2* Traditionally *peace offerings*; also in verse 12
[b]*5* That is, probably about 3/5 bushel (about 22 liters)
[c]*5* That is, probably about 4 quarts (about 4 liters)
[d]*22* The meaning of the Hebrew for this word is uncertain.

46:1 [h]ver 6; Isa 66:23
46:2 [i]ver 8 [j]ver 12; Eze 44:3
46:3 [k]Lk 1:10
46:5 [l]ver 11; Eze 45:24
46:6 [m]ver 1; Nu 10:10
46:7 [n]Eze 45:24
46:8 [o]ver 2 [p]Eze 44:3
46:9 [q]Ex 23:14; 34:20
46:10 [r]2Sa 6:14-15; Ps 42:4
46:11 [s]ver 5
46:12 [t]Eze 45:17 [u]Lev 7:16 [v]ver 2
46:13 [w]Ex 29:38; Nu 28:3
46:14 [x]Da 8:11
46:15 [y]Ex 29:42 [z]Ex 29:38; Nu 28:5-6
46:16 [a]2Ch 21:3
46:17 [b]Lev 25:10
46:18 [c]Lev 25:23; Eze 45:8; Mic 2:1-2
46:19 [d]Eze 42:9
46:20 [e]Lev 6:27 [f]Zec 14:20

The River From the Temple

47 The man brought me back to the entrance of the temple, and I saw water[g] coming out from under the threshold of the temple toward the east (for the temple faced east). The water was coming down from under the south side of the temple, south of the altar.[h] 2 He then brought me out through the north gate and led me around the outside to the outer gate facing east, and the water was flowing from the south side.

47:1 [g]Isa 55:1 [h]Ps 46:4; Joel 3:18; Rev 22:1

3 As the man went eastward with a measuring line[i] in his hand, he measured off a thousand cubits[a] and then led me through water that was ankle-deep. 4 He measured off another thousand cubits and led me through water that was knee-deep. He measured off another thousand and led me through water that was up to the waist. 5 He measured off another thousand, but now it was a river that I could not cross, because the water had risen and was deep enough to swim in—a river that no one could cross.[j] 6 He asked me, "Son of man, do you see this?"

47:3 [i]Eze 40:3

47:5 [j]Isa 11:9; Hab 2:14

Then he led me back to the bank of the river. 7 When I arrived there, I saw a great number of trees on each side of the river.[k] 8 He said to me, "This water flows toward the eastern region and goes down into the Arabah,[b][l] where it enters the Sea.[c] When it empties into the Sea,[c] the water there becomes fresh.[m] 9 Swarms of living creatures will live wherever the river flows. There will be large numbers of fish, because this water flows there and makes the salt water fresh; so where the river flows everything will live.[n] 10 Fishermen[o] will stand along the shore; from En Gedi[p] to En Eglaim there will be places for spreading nets.[q] The fish will be of many kinds[r]—like the fish of the Great Sea.[d][s] 11 But the swamps and marshes will not become fresh; they will be left for salt.[t] 12 Fruit trees of all kinds will grow on both banks of the river.[u] Their leaves will not wither, nor will their fruit[v] fail. Every month they will bear, because the water from the sanctuary flows to them. Their fruit will serve for food and their leaves for healing.[w]"

47:7 [k]ver 12; Rev 22:2

47:8 [l]Dt 3:17; Jos 3:16 [m]Isa 41:18

47:9 [n]Isa 12:3; 55:1; Jn 4:14; 7:37-38

47:10 [o]Mt 4:19 [p]Jos 15:62 [q]Eze 26:5 [r]Ps 104:25; Mt 13:47 [s]Nu 34:6

47:11 [t]Dt 29:23

47:12 [u]ver 7; Rev 22:2 [v]Ps 1:3 [w]Ge 2:9; Jer 17:8

The Boundaries of the Land

13 This is what the Sovereign LORD says: "These are the boundaries[x] by which you are to divide the land for an inheritance among the twelve tribes of Israel, with two portions for Joseph.[y] 14 You are to divide it equally among them. Because I swore with uplifted hand to give it to your forefathers, this land will become your inheritance.[z]

47:13 [x]Nu 34:2-12 [y]Ge 48:5

47:14 [z]Ge 12:7; Dt 1:8; Eze 20:5-6

15 "This is to be the boundary of the land:

"On the north side it will run from the Great Sea by the Hethlon road[a] past Lebo[e] Hamath to Zedad, 16 Berothah[f][b] and Sibraim (which lies on the border between Damascus and Hamath),[c] as far as Hazer Hatticon, which is on the border of Hauran. 17 The boundary will extend from the sea to Hazar Enan,[g] along the northern border of Damascus, with the border of Hamath to the north. This will be the north boundary.[d]

47:15 [a]Eze 48:1

47:16 [b]2Sa 8:8 [c]Nu 13:21; Eze 48:1

47:17 [d]Eze 48:1

18 "On the east side the boundary will run between Hauran and Damascus, along the Jordan between Gilead and the land of Israel, to the eastern sea and as far as Tamar.[h] This will be the east boundary.

19 "On the south side it will run from Tamar as far as the waters of Meribah Kadesh,[e] then along the Wadi of Egypt[f] to the Great Sea.[g] This will be the south boundary.

47:19 [e]Dt 32:51 [f]Isa 27:12 [g]Eze 48:28

20 "On the west side, the Great Sea will be the boundary to a point opposite Lebo[i] Hamath.[h] This will be the west boundary.[i]

47:20 [h]Eze 48:1 [i]Nu 34:6

21 "You are to distribute this land among yourselves according to the tribes of Israel. 22 You are to allot it as an inheritance for yourselves and for the aliens[j] who have settled among you and who have children. You are to consider them as native-born Israelites; along with you they are to be allotted an inheritance

47:22 [j]Isa 14:1

[a] *3* That is, about 1,500 feet (about 450 meters)
[b] *8* Or *the Jordan Valley*
[c] *8* That is, the Dead Sea
[d] *10* That is, the Mediterranean; also in verses 15, 19 and 20
[e] *15* Or *past the entrance to*
[f] *15,16* See Septuagint and Ezekiel 48:1; Hebrew *road to go into Zedad, 16Hamath, Berothah*
[g] *17* Hebrew *Enon,* a variant of *Enan*
[h] *18* Septuagint and Syriac; Hebrew *Israel. You will measure to the eastern sea*
[i] *20* Or *opposite the entrance to*

47:22 [k]Nu 26:55-56; Isa 56:6-7; Ro 10:12; Eph 2:12-16; 3:6; Col 3:11

among the tribes of Israel.[k] 23 In whatever tribe the alien settles, there you are
to give him his inheritance," declares
the Sovereign LORD.

The Division of the Land

48:1 [l]Ge 30:6 [m]Eze 47:15-17 [n]Eze 47:20

48 "These are the tribes, listed by
name: At the northern frontier,
Dan[l] will have one portion; it will follow
the Hethlon road[m] to Lebo[a] Hamath;[n]
Hazar Enan and the northern border of
Damascus next to Hamath will be part
of its border from the east side to the
west side.

48:2 [o]Jos 19:24-31

2 "Asher[o] will have one portion; it will
border the territory of Dan from east to
west.

48:3 [p]Jos 19:32-39

3 "Naphtali[p] will have one portion; it
will border the territory of Asher from
east to west.

48:4 [q]Jos 17:1-11

4 "Manasseh[q] will have one portion;
it will border the territory of Naphtali
from east to west.

48:5 [r]Jos 16:5-9 [s]Jos 17:7-10 [t]Jos 17:17

5 "Ephraim[r] will have one portion; it
will border the territory of Manasseh[s]
from east to west.[t]

48:6 [u]Jos 13:15-21

6 "Reuben[u] will have one portion; it
will border the territory of Ephraim
from east to west.

48:7 [v]Jos 15:1-63

7 "Judah[v] will have one portion; it will
border the territory of Reuben from
east to west.
8 "Bordering the territory of Judah
from east to west will be the portion
you are to present as a special gift. It
will be 25,000 cubits[b] wide, and its
length from east to west will equal one
of the tribal portions; the sanctuary will
be in the center of it.[w]

48:8 [w]ver 21

9 "The special portion you are to offer
to the LORD will be 25,000 cubits long
and 10,000 cubits[c] wide.[x] 10 This will
be the sacred portion for the priests. It
will be 25,000 cubits long on the north
side, 10,000 cubits wide on the west
side, 10,000 cubits wide on the east side
and 25,000 cubits long on the south
side. In the center of it will be the sanctuary of the LORD.[y] 11 This will be for
the consecrated priests, the Zadokites,[z]
who were faithful in serving me[a] and
did not go astray as the Levites did
when the Israelites went astray.[b] 12 It will
be a special gift to them from the sacred
portion of the land, a most holy portion, bordering the territory of the Levites.
13 "Alongside the territory of the

48:9 [x]Eze 45:1

48:10 [y]ver 21; Eze 45:3-4

48:11 [z]2Sa 8:17 [a]Lev 8:35 [b]Eze 14:11; 44:15

priests, the Levites will have an allotment 25,000 cubits long and 10,000 cubits wide. Its total length will be 25,000
cubits and its width 10,000 cubits.[c]
14 They must not sell or exchange any of
it. This is the best of the land and must
not pass into other hands, because it is
holy to the LORD.[d]
15 "The remaining area, 5,000 cubits
wide and 25,000 cubits long, will be for
the common use of the city, for houses
and for pastureland. The city will be in
the center of it 16 and will have these
measurements: the north side 4,500 cubits, the south side 4,500 cubits, the
east side 4,500 cubits, and the west side
4,500 cubits.[e] 17 The pastureland for the
city will be 250 cubits on the north,
250 cubits on the south, 250 cubits on
the east, and 250 cubits on the west.
18 What remains of the area, bordering
on the sacred portion and running the
length of it, will be 10,000 cubits on
the east side and 10,000 cubits on the
west side. Its produce will supply food
for the workers of the city.[f] 19 The workers from the city who farm it will come
from all the tribes of Israel. 20 The entire
portion will be a square, 25,000 cubits
on each side. As a special gift you will
set aside the sacred portion, along with
the property of the city.
21 "What remains on both sides of
the area formed by the sacred portion
and the city property will belong to the
prince. It will extend eastward from the
25,000 cubits of the sacred portion to
the eastern border, and westward from
the 25,000 cubits to the western border. Both these areas running the length
of the tribal portions will belong to the
prince, and the sacred portion with the
temple sanctuary will be in the center
of them.[g] 22 So the property of the Levites and the property of the city will
lie in the center of the area that belongs
to the prince. The area belonging to the
prince will lie between the border of Judah and the border of Benjamin.
23 "As for the rest of the tribes: Benjamin[h] will have one portion; it will
extend from the east side to the west
side.
24 "Simeon[i] will have one portion; it

48:13 [c]Eze 45:5

48:14 [d]Lev 25:34; 27:10,28

48:16 [e]Rev 21:16

48:18 [f]Eze 45:6

48:21 [g]ver 8,10; Eze 45:7

48:23 [h]Jos 18:11-28

48:24 [i]Ge 29:33; Jos 19:1-9

[a]*1* Or *to the entrance to* [b]*8* That is, about 7 miles (about 12 kilometers) [c]*9* That is, about 3 miles (about 5 kilometers)

will border the territory of Benjamin
from east to west.
48:25 [j]Jos 19:17-23 25“Issachar[j] will have one portion; it
will border the territory of Simeon from
east to west.
48:26 [k]Jos 19:10-16 26“Zebulun[k] will have one portion;
it will border the territory of Issachar
from east to west.
48:27 [l]Jos 13:24-28 27“Gad[l] will have one portion; it will
border the territory of Zebulun from
east to west.
28“The southern boundary of Gad
48:28 [m]Ge 14:7 will run south from Tamar[m] to the wa-
[n]Eze 47:19 ters of Meribah Kadesh, then along the
Wadi ⌊of Egypt⌋ to the Great Sea.[a][n]
29“This is the land you are to allot
as an inheritance to the tribes of Israel,
and these will be their portions,” declares the Sovereign LORD.

The Gates of the City

30“These will be the exits of the city:
Beginning on the north side, which is
4,500 cubits long, 31the gates of the city
will be named after the tribes of Israel.
The three gates on the north side will
be the gate of Reuben, the gate of Judah
and the gate of Levi.
32“On the east side, which is 4,500
cubits long, will be three gates: the gate
of Joseph, the gate of Benjamin and the
gate of Dan.
33“On the south side, which measures 4,500 cubits, will be three gates:
the gate of Simeon, the gate of Issachar
and the gate of Zebulun.
34“On the west side, which is 4,500
cubits long, will be three gates: the gate
of Gad, the gate of Asher and the gate
of Naphtali.
35“The distance all around will be
18,000 cubits.
“And the name of the city from that
time on will be: 48:35 [o]Isa 12:6; 24:23; Jer 3:17; 14:9; Jer 33:16; Joel 3:21; Zec 2:10; Rev 21:3

THE LORD IS THERE.[o]”

[a]*28* That is, the Mediterranean

DANIEL

AUTHORSHIP AND DATE

Daniel

c. 535 B.C.

KEY THEMES

The book of Daniel falls into two nearly equal divisions. The first half of the book (chs. 1–6) deals with events drawn from Daniel's life; the second half deals with Daniel's visions (chs. 7–12). There are two key themes that compose the content of the first half of the book. One of those themes is self-control. If self-control is defined as "spiritual and moral discipline," then indeed this is the theme of the entire book. But there is also the supporting theme of faithfulness. Daniel and his friends remain true to God even when their lives are at stake.

FRUIT OF THE SPIRIT IN DANIEL

Joy: There are three noteworthy passages of joy in the early chapters of Daniel. One passage is Daniel 2:20–23, which begins: "Praise be to the name of God for ever and ever; wisdom and power are his." When the renegade Nebuchadnezzar, filled with the joy of the true God, could hold his praise no longer, he broke into anthems of praise: "At the end of that time, I, Nebuchadnezzar, raised my eyes toward heaven, and my sanity was restored. Then I praised the Most High; I honored and glorified him who lives forever" (4:34). And Darius, after God delivered Daniel from the lions' den, offered the third thanksgiving praise: "For he is the living God and he endures forever; his kingdom will not be destroyed, his dominion will never end" (6:26).

Faithfulness: There are at least five clear statements regarding the faithfulness of Daniel and his friends:

First, Daniel was faithful to interpret Nebuchadnezzar's dream, even though there was some risk involved should the king decide the interpretation was wrong. Nebuchadnezzar's first dream held nothing inherently gloomy; still, Daniel was living pretty close to royalty, and honesty in close quarters can sometimes be dangerous (see 2:36–48).

Second, Shadrach, Meshach and Abednego refused to worship the king's statue but chose to remain faithful to the one true God. Their decision brought about the king's anger and the prospect of death by fire. Yet they were steadfast (see 3:16–18). Faithfulness does not depend upon God's rescue; it depends upon standing strong, even when facing annihilation.

Third, Daniel told Nebuchadnezzar the interpretation of a dream that could not have been good news to the king. Yet he was faithful despite the dour prophecy involved (see 4:19–27).

Fourth, Daniel interpreted the handwriting on the wall at Belshazzar's banquet. Despite great personal risk to himself, Daniel told the truth about what God said to Belshazzar (see 5:22–30). Babylon was overthrown on the very night of Daniel's interpretation.

Fifth, despite a royal edict outlawing prayers to God, Daniel's faithful life of prayer continued on exactly as it always had. Such faithfulness won the approval of God, and Daniel's future was far better than the futures of Darius' pagan counselors who had published the edict (see 6:24).

Self-Control: Neither Daniel nor his friends would sell out to live impure and undisciplined lives. In chapter 1, Daniel and his three friends, Hananiah, Mishael and Azariah (the Hebrew names of Shadrach, Meshach and Abednego), refuse to eat the king's rich food or wine. Self-control has its rewards. Daniel and his friends were healthier than their Babylonian counterparts as a result of their choices (see v. 15).

Daniel's Training in Babylon

1 In the third year of the reign of Jehoiakim king of Judah, Nebuchadnezzar[a] king of Babylon came to Jerusalem and besieged it.[b] 2And the Lord delivered Jehoiakim king of Judah into his hand, along with some of the articles from the temple of God. These he carried off to the temple of his god in Babylonia[a] and put in the treasure house of his god.[c]

3Then the king ordered Ashpenaz, chief of his court officials, to bring in some of the Israelites from the royal family and the nobility[d]— 4young men without any physical defect, handsome, showing aptitude for every kind of learning, well informed, quick to understand, and qualified to serve in the king's palace. He was to teach them the language and literature of the Babylonians.[b] 5The king assigned them a daily amount of food and wine[e] from the king's table. They were to be trained for three years, and after that they were to enter the king's service.[f]

6Among these were some from Judah: Daniel,[g] Hananiah, Mishael and Azariah. 7The chief official gave them new names: to Daniel, the name Belteshazzar;[h] to Hananiah, Shadrach; to Mishael, Meshach; and to Azariah, Abednego.[i]

1:1 [a]2Ki 24:1 [b]2Ch 36:6
1:2 [c]2Ch 36:7; Jer 27:19-20; Zec 5:5-11
1:3 [d]2Ki 20:18; 24:15; Isa 39:7
1:5 [e]ver 8,10 [f]ver 19
1:6 [g]Eze 14:14
1:7 [h]Da 4:8; 5:12 [i]Da 2:49; 3:12

SELF-CONTROL

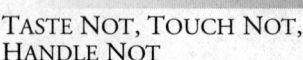

TASTE NOT, TOUCH NOT, HANDLE NOT

Daniel 1:8

Daniel resolved not to defile himself. He had learned the self-denial of the cross a half millennium before it rose above Golgotha. Daniel had learned the difficult art of saying no to himself.

8But Daniel resolved not to defile[j] himself with the royal food and wine, and he asked the chief official for permission not to defile himself this way. 9Now God had caused the official to show favor[k] and sympathy[l] to Daniel, 10but the official told Daniel, "I am afraid of my lord the king, who has assigned your[c] food and drink. Why should he see you looking worse than the other young men your age? The king would then have my head because of you."

11Daniel then said to the guard whom the chief official had appointed over Daniel, Hananiah, Mishael and Azariah, 12"Please test your servants for ten days: Give us nothing but vegetables to eat and water to drink. 13Then compare our appearance with that of the young men who eat the royal food, and treat your servants in accordance with what you see." 14So he agreed to this and tested them for ten days.

15At the end of the ten days they looked healthier and better nourished than any of the young men who ate the royal food.[m] 16So the guard took away their choice food and the wine they were to drink and gave them vegetables instead.[n]

17To these four young men God gave knowledge and understanding[o] of all kinds of literature and learning.[p] And Daniel could understand visions and dreams of all kinds.[q]

18At the end of the time[r] set by the king to bring them in, the chief official presented them to Nebuchadnezzar. 19The king talked with them, and he found none equal to Daniel, Hananiah, Mishael and Azariah; so they entered the king's service.[s] 20In every matter of wisdom and understanding about which the king questioned them, he found them ten times better than all the magicians and enchanters in his whole kingdom.[t]

21And Daniel remained there until the first year of King Cyrus.[u]

1:8 [j]Eze 4:13-14
1:9 [k]Ge 39:21; Pr 16:7 [l]1Ki 8:50; Ps 106:46
1:15 [m]Ex 23:25
1:16 [n]ver 12-13
1:17 [o]1Ki 3:12 [p]Da 2:23; Jas 1:5 [q]Da 2:19,30; 7:1; 8:1
1:18 [r]ver 5
1:19 [s]Ge 41:46
1:20 [t]1Ki 4:30; Da 2:13,28
1:21 [u]Da 6:28; 10:1

Nebuchadnezzar's Dream

2 In the second year of his reign, Nebuchadnezzar had dreams;[v] his mind was troubled[w] and he could not sleep.[x] 2So the king summoned the magicians,[y] enchanters, sorcerers[z] and astrologers[d][a] to tell him what he had dreamed.[b] When they came in and stood before the king, 3he said to them, "I have had a dream that troubles[c] me and I want to know what it means.[e]"

4Then the astrologers answered the king in Aramaic,[f][d] "O king, live forever![e]

2:1 [v]Job 33:15,18; Da 4:5
2:2 [w]Ge 41:8 [x]Est 6:1; Da 6:18 [y]Ge 41:8 [z]Ex 7:11 [a]ver 10; Da 5:7 [b]Da 4:6
2:3 [c]Da 4:5
2:4 [d]Ezr 4:7 [e]Da 3:9; 5:10

[a]*2* Hebrew *Shinar* [b]*4* Or *Chaldeans* [c]*10* The Hebrew for *your* and *you* in this verse is plural. [d]*2* Or *Chaldeans*; also in verses 4, 5 and 10 [e]*3* Or *was* [f]*4* The text from here through chapter 7 is in Aramaic.

WEEK 18

SELF-CONTROL

1 DAY ONE

SELF-CONTROL, THE MARK OF OBEDIENCE

Read Daniel 1:8–17

Most evangelicals I know wouldn't drink even a little wine and confess to it. They feel that while it might have been all right for Paul and Timothy, it would weaken their reputation in the church. Many sermons focus on the dangers of indulging in drinking alcohol. Gluttony, however, is a rare subject in sermons. It is the evangelical sin kept on reserve—a certified evangelical indulgence. If you need a certificate of moral permission for a real whopper of an iniquity, the church will sign off on gluttony.

I have ever been struck by the odd inconsistency of obese evangelists preaching against alcohol abuse. How wicked we become in excusing our own indulgences while excoriating others for theirs. Self-rationalization nearly always acquits the preacher but calls the audience to task. Nowhere is this truer than how Christians handle gluttony.

This permissive stance on overeating is an odd forgiveness since the Bible condemns it so often. Further, the Scriptures define fasting as a manner of self-control that enhances the prayer life and deepens the life in Christ. This passage in Daniel speaks to the spoiling of life and health by over-indulgence. Daniel survives very well on vegetables and water. But surviving was not Daniel's goal. He wanted to thrive spiritually. He wanted to be sure that permissive gluttony did not leave him a poor lover of God. It's a legitimate concern for us as well.

MEMORIZE THIS WEEK

2 PETER 1:5-7

For this very reason, make every effort to add to your faith goodness; and to goodness, knowledge; and to knowledge, self-control; and to self-control, perseverance; and to perseverance, godliness; and to godliness, brotherly kindness; and to brotherly kindness, love.

2 DAY TWO

SELF-CONTROL AND THE PURPOSE OF GOD IN MY LIFE

What is the purpose of God in your life? Just this: that whatever you do should exalt him. If you have any current activity or avocation that would detract from his immense love, then stop it. Resolve that you will accept his purpose for your life and live in such a way that when you walk into a room people will long to get to know the God you serve. *Turn to 1 Corinthians 10:31, page 1369, for today's study.*

3 DAY THREE

SELF-CONTROL AND MY RELATIONSHIP WITH CHRIST

Self-control is three things, says Moses. It is loving God, walking in his ways and keeping his laws. Here is the recipe for self-control with only three ingredients. And when the loaf is baked, the recipe proves so complete that we sit with Christ, feeling our relationship with him grow deeper as we eat of this simple recipe. *Turn to Deuteronomy 30:15–16, page 234, for today's study.*

4 DAY FOUR

SELF-CONTROL AND MY SERVICE TO OTHERS

One cannot escape the feeling in reading the New Testament that the closer one walks with Jesus Christ, the less self-control is an issue. One gets the feeling that the apostle Paul never woke on a single morning and said, "Hmm, let's see what I must avoid doing today to keep God happy." Rather, I think he woke up every morning saying, "Jesus I love, show me the worlds we shall conquer on this wonderful new day together." Self-control is the happy achievement of those truly enraptured with Christ. *Turn to 1 Corinthians 8:9–13, page 1364, for today's study.*

5 DAY FIVE

SELF-CONTROL AND ITS PLACE IN MY PERSONAL WORSHIP

Decide what to do for Christ and do it. Be conformed to the image of Christ. Live as one long W.W.J.D. bracelet. Only, the best servants don't wear it as jewelry but enshrine it in their hearts. When we are conformed to his image, we love his Father just like he did, and our quality of worship soars to new heights. *Turn to Romans 12:1–2, page 1348, for today's study.*

Week 19, Love, the Definition of God, begins on page 1033, Hosea 3:1–3.
To begin a topical study on the Fruit of the Spirit, Self-Control, turn to the Topical Index, page 1548.

Tell your servants the dream, and we
will interpret it."
5The king replied to the astrologers,
"This is what I have firmly decided:
If you do not tell me what my dream
was and interpret it, I will have you
2:5 [f]ver 12 cut into pieces[f] and your houses turned
[g]Ezr 6:11; Da 3:29 into piles of rubble.[g] 6But if you tell
me the dream and explain it, you will
2:6 receive from me gifts and rewards and
[h]ver 48; Da 5:7,16 great honor.[h] So tell me the dream and
interpret it for me."
7Once more they replied, "Let the
king tell his servants the dream, and we
will interpret it."
8Then the king answered, "I am certain that you are trying to gain time,
because you realize that this is what I
2:9 have firmly decided: 9If you do not tell
[i]Est 4:11 me the dream, there is just one penalty[i]
[j]Isa 41:22-24 for you. You have conspired to tell me
misleading and wicked things, hoping
the situation will change. So then, tell
me the dream, and I will know that you
can interpret it for me."[j]
10The astrologers answered the king,
"There is not a man on earth who can
do what the king asks! No king, however great and mighty, has ever asked such
2:10 a thing of any magician or enchanter
[k]ver 27 or astrologer.[k] 11What the king asks is
2:11 too difficult. No one can reveal it to the
[l]Da 5:11 king except the gods,[l] and they do not
live among men."
2:12 12This made the king so angry and
[m]Da 3:13,19 furious[m] that he ordered the execution[n]
[n]ver 5 of all the wise men of Babylon. 13So the
decree was issued to put the wise men
to death, and men were sent to look for
2:13 Daniel and his friends to put them to
[o]Da 1:20 death.[o]
14When Arioch, the commander of
the king's guard, had gone out to put to
death the wise men of Babylon, Daniel spoke to him with wisdom and tact.
15He asked the king's officer, "Why did
the king issue such a harsh decree?" Arioch then explained the matter to Daniel. 16At this, Daniel went in to the king
and asked for time, so that he might interpret the dream for him.
17Then Daniel returned to his house
and explained the matter to his friends
2:17 Hananiah, Mishael and Azariah.[p] 18He
[p]Da 1:6 urged them to plead for mercy[q] from
2:18 the God of heaven concerning this
[q]Isa 37:4 [r]Jer 33:3 mystery,[r] so that he and his friends
might not be executed with the rest of
the wise men of Babylon. 19During the
night the mystery[s] was revealed to Dan- 2:19 [s]ver 28
iel in a vision.[t] Then Daniel praised the [t]Job 33:15; Da 1:17
God of heaven 20and said:

"Praise be to the name of God for
ever and ever;[u] 2:20 [u]Ps 113:2; 145:1-2
wisdom and power[v] are his. [v]Jer 32:19
21He changes times and seasons;[w] 2:21 [w]Da 7:25
he sets up kings and deposes[x] [x]Job 12:19; Ps 75:6-7
them.
He gives wisdom[y] to the wise [y]Jas 1:5
and knowledge to the discerning.
22He reveals deep and hidden
things;[z] 2:22 [z]Job 12:22; Ps 25:14; Da 5:11
he knows what lies in darkness,[a] [a]Ps 139:11-12; Jer 23:24; Heb 4:13
and light[b] dwells with him. [b]Isa 45:7; Jas 1:17
23I thank and praise you, O God of
my fathers:[c]
You have given me wisdom[d] and
power,
you have made known to me what 2:23 [c]Ex 3:15 [d]Da 1:17
we asked of you,
you have made known to us the
dream of the king."

Daniel Interprets the Dream

24Then Daniel went to Arioch,[e] 2:24 [e]ver 14
whom the king had appointed to execute the wise men of Babylon, and said
to him, "Do not execute the wise men
of Babylon. Take me to the king, and I
will interpret his dream for him."
25Arioch took Daniel to the king at
once and said, "I have found a man
among the exiles from Judah[f] who can 2:25 [f]Da 1:6; 5:13; 6:13
tell the king what his dream means."
26The king asked Daniel (also called
Belteshazzar),[g] "Are you able to tell 2:26 [g]Da 1:7
me what I saw in my dream and inter-
pret it?"
27Daniel replied, "No wise man, enchanter, magician or diviner can explain
to the king the mystery he has asked
about,[h] 28but there is a God in heaven 2:27 [h]ver 10
who reveals mysteries.[i] He has shown 2:28 [i]Ge 40:8; Am 4:13
King Nebuchadnezzar what will happen
in days to come.[j] Your dream and the [j]Ge 49:1; Da 10:14
visions that passed through your mind[k] [k]Da 4:5
as you lay on your bed are these:
29"As you were lying there, O king,
your mind turned to things to come,
and the revealer of mysteries showed
you what is going to happen. 30As for 2:30
me, this mystery has been revealed[l] to [l]Isa 45:3; Da 1:17; Am 4:13
me, not because I have greater wisdom
than other living men, but so that you,
O king, may know the interpretation

and that you may understand what went through your mind.

31"You looked, O king, and there before you stood a large statue—an enormous, dazzling statue,[m] awesome in appearance. 32The head of the statue was made of pure gold, its chest and arms of silver, its belly and thighs of bronze, 33its legs of iron, its feet partly of iron and partly of baked clay. 34While you were watching, a rock was cut out, but not by human hands.[n] It struck the statue on its feet of iron and clay and smashed them.[o] 35Then the iron, the clay, the bronze, the silver and the gold were broken to pieces at the same time and became like chaff on a threshing floor in the summer. The wind swept them away[p] without leaving a trace. But the rock that struck the statue became a huge mountain[q] and filled the whole earth.

36"This was the dream, and now we will interpret it to the king. 37You, O king, are the king of kings.[r] The God of heaven has given you dominion[s] and power and might and glory; 38in your hands he has placed mankind and the beasts of the field and the birds of the air. Wherever they live, he has made you ruler over them all.[t] You are that head of gold.

39"After you, another kingdom will rise, inferior to yours. Next, a third kingdom, one of bronze, will rule over the whole earth. 40Finally, there will be a fourth kingdom, strong as iron—for iron breaks and smashes everything—and as iron breaks things to pieces, so it will crush and break all the others.[u] 41Just as you saw that the feet and toes were partly of baked clay and partly of iron, so this will be a divided kingdom; yet it will have some of the strength of iron in it, even as you saw iron mixed with clay. 42As the toes were partly iron and partly clay, so this kingdom will be partly strong and partly brittle. 43And just as you saw the iron mixed with baked clay, so the people will be a mixture and will not remain united, any more than iron mixes with clay.

44"In the time of those kings, the God of heaven will set up a kingdom that will never be destroyed, nor will it be left to another people. It will crush[v] all those kingdoms[w] and bring them to an end, but it will itself endure forever.[x] 45This is the meaning of the vision of the rock[y] cut out of a mountain, but not by human hands[z]—a rock that broke the iron, the bronze, the clay, the silver and the gold to pieces.

"The great God has shown the king what will take place in the future. The dream is true and the interpretation is trustworthy."

46Then King Nebuchadnezzar fell prostrate[a] before Daniel and paid him honor and ordered that an offering[b] and incense be presented to him. 47The king said to Daniel, "Surely your God is the God of gods[c] and the Lord of kings[d] and a revealer of mysteries,[e] for you were able to reveal this mystery."

48Then the king placed Daniel in a high position and lavished many gifts on him. He made him ruler over the entire province of Babylon and placed him in charge of all its wise men.[f] 49Moreover, at Daniel's request the king appointed Shadrach, Meshach and Abednego administrators over the province of Babylon,[g] while Daniel himself remained at the royal court.

The Image of Gold and the Fiery Furnace

3 King Nebuchadnezzar made an image[h] of gold, ninety feet high and nine feet[a] wide, and set it up on the plain of Dura in the province of Babylon. 2He then summoned the satraps, prefects, governors, advisers, treasurers, judges, magistrates and all the other provincial officials[i] to come to the dedication of the image he had set up. 3So the satraps, prefects, governors, advisers, treasurers, judges, magistrates and all the other provincial officials assembled for the dedication of the image that King Nebuchadnezzar had set up, and they stood before it.

4Then the herald loudly proclaimed, "This is what you are commanded to do, O peoples, nations and men of every language:[j] 5As soon as you hear the sound of the horn, flute, zither, lyre, harp, pipes and all kinds of music, you must fall down and worship the image of gold that King Nebuchadnezzar has set up.[k] 6Whoever does not fall

[a]*1* Aramaic *sixty cubits high and six cubits wide* (about 27 meters high and 2.7 meters wide)

2:31 [m]Hab 1:7
2:34 [n]Zec 4:6 [o]ver 44-45; Ps 2:9; Isa 60:12; Da 8:25
2:35 [p]Ps 1:4; 37:10; Isa 17:13 [q]Isa 2:3; Mic 4:1
2:37 [r]Eze 26:7 [s]Jer 27:7
2:38 [t]Jer 27:6; Da 4:21-22
2:40 [u]Da 7:7,23
2:44 [v]Ps 2:9; 1Co 15:24 [w]Isa 60:12 [x]Ps 145:13; Isa 9:7; Da 4:34; 6:26; 7:14,27; Mic 4:7,13; Lk 1:33
2:45 [y]Isa 28:16 [z]Da 8:25
2:46 [a]Da 8:17; Ac 10:25 [b]Ac 14:13
2:47 [c]Da 11:36 [d]Da 4:25 [e]ver 22,28
2:48 [f]ver 6; Da 4:9; 5:11
2:49 [g]Da 1:7
3:1 [h]Isa 46:6; Jer 16:20; Hab 2:19
3:2 [i]ver 27; Da 6:7
3:4 [j]Da 4:1; 6:25
3:5 [k]ver 10,15

down and worship will immediately be thrown into a blazing furnace."[l]

7Therefore, as soon as they heard the sound of the horn, flute, zither, lyre, harp and all kinds of music, all the peoples, nations and men of every language fell down and worshiped the image of gold that King Nebuchadnezzar had set up.[m]

8At this time some astrologers[a][n] came forward and denounced the Jews. 9They said to King Nebuchadnezzar, "O king, live forever![o] 10You have issued a decree,[p] O king, that everyone who hears the sound of the horn, flute, zither, lyre, harp, pipes and all kinds of music must fall down and worship the image of gold,[q] 11and that whoever does not fall down and worship will be thrown into a blazing furnace. 12But there are some Jews whom you have set over the affairs of the province of Babylon—Shadrach, Meshach and Abednego[r]—who pay no attention[s] to you, O king. They neither serve your gods nor worship the image of gold you have set up."[t]

13Furious[u] with rage, Nebuchadnezzar summoned Shadrach, Meshach and Abednego. So these men were brought before the king, 14and Nebuchadnezzar said to them, "Is it true, Shadrach, Meshach and Abednego, that you do not serve my gods[v] or worship the image[w] of gold I have set up? 15Now when you hear the sound of the horn, flute, zither, lyre, harp, pipes and all kinds of music, if you are ready to fall down and worship the image I made, very good. But if you do not worship it, you will be thrown immediately into a blazing furnace. Then what god[x] will be able to rescue[y] you from my hand?"

16Shadrach, Meshach and Abednego[z] replied to the king, "O Nebuchadnezzar, we do not need to defend ourselves

3:6 [l]ver 11,15,21; Jer 29:22; Da 6:7; Mt 13:42,50; Rev 13:15
3:7 [m]ver 5
3:8 [n]Da 2:10
3:9 [o]Ne 2:3; Da 5:10; 6:6
3:10 [p]Da 6:12 [q]ver 4-6
3:12 [r]Da 2:49 [s]Da 6:13 [t]Est 3:3
3:13 [u]Da 2:12
3:14 [v]Isa 46:1; Jer 50:2 [w]ver 1
3:15 [x]Isa 36:18-20 [y]Ex 5:2; 2Ch 32:15
3:16 [z]Da 1:7

FAITHFULNESS

Pray On, Stand Up!

Daniel 3:18

Whether or not God appears to answer us, we must pray on. Whether or not we can see him, we must stand. When God seems not to notice our conviction, we must still be faithful. Though he slay us, yet we must trust him.

before you in this matter. 17If we are thrown into the blazing furnace, the God we serve is able to save[a] us from it, and he will rescue[b] us from your hand, O king. 18But even if he does not, we want you to know, O king, that we will not serve your gods or worship the image of gold you have set up.[c]"

19Then Nebuchadnezzar was furious with Shadrach, Meshach and Abednego, and his attitude toward them changed. He ordered the furnace heated seven[d] times hotter than usual 20and commanded some of the strongest soldiers in his army to tie up Shadrach, Meshach and Abednego and throw them into the blazing furnace. 21So these men, wearing their robes, trousers, turbans and other clothes, were bound and thrown into the blazing furnace. 22The king's command was so urgent and the furnace so hot that the flames of the fire killed the soldiers who took up Shadrach, Meshach and Abednego,[e] 23and these three men, firmly tied, fell into the blazing furnace.

24Then King Nebuchadnezzar leaped to his feet in amazement and asked his advisers, "Weren't there three men that we tied up and threw into the fire?"

They replied, "Certainly, O king."

25He said, "Look! I see four men walking around in the fire, unbound and unharmed, and the fourth looks like a son of the gods."

26Nebuchadnezzar then approached the opening of the blazing furnace and shouted, "Shadrach, Meshach and Abednego, servants of the Most High God,[f] come out! Come here!"

So Shadrach, Meshach and Abednego came out of the fire, 27and the satraps, prefects, governors and royal advisers[g] crowded around them.[h] They saw that the fire[i] had not harmed their bodies, nor was a hair of their heads singed; their robes were not scorched, and there was no smell of fire on them.

28Then Nebuchadnezzar said, "Praise be to the God of Shadrach, Meshach and Abednego, who has sent his angel[j] and rescued his servants! They trusted[k] in him and defied the king's command and were willing to give up their lives rather than serve or worship any god except their own God.[l] 29Therefore I

[a]8 Or *Chaldeans*

3:17 [a]Ps 27:1-2 [b]Job 5:19; Jer 1:8
3:18 [c]ver 28; Jos 24:15
3:19 [d]Lev 26:18-28
3:22 [e]Da 1:7
3:26 [f]Da 4:2,34
3:27 [g]ver 2 [h]Isa 43:2; Heb 11:32-34 [i]Da 6:23
3:28 [j]Ps 34:7; Da 6:22; Ac 5:19 [k]Job 13:15; Ps 26:1; 84:12; Jer 17:7 [l]ver 18

decree[m] that the people of any nation or language who say anything against the God of Shadrach, Meshach and Abednego be cut into pieces and their houses be turned into piles of rubble,[n] for no other god can save[o] in this way."

30 Then the king promoted Shadrach, Meshach and Abednego in the province of Babylon.[p]

Nebuchadnezzar's Dream of a Tree

4 King Nebuchadnezzar,

To the peoples, nations and men of every language,[q] who live in all the world:

May you prosper greatly![r]

2 It is my pleasure to tell you about the miraculous signs[s] and wonders that the Most High God[t] has performed for me.

3 How great are his signs,
how mighty his wonders![u]
His kingdom is an eternal kingdom;
his dominion endures[v] from generation to generation.

4 I, Nebuchadnezzar, was at home in my palace, contented[w] and prosperous. 5 I had a dream[x] that made me afraid. As I was lying in my bed, the images and visions that passed through my mind[y] terrified me. 6 So I commanded that all the wise men of Babylon be brought before me to interpret[z] the dream for me. 7 When the magicians,[a] enchanters, astrologers[a] and diviners[b] came, I told them the dream, but they could not interpret it for me.[c] 8 Finally, Daniel came into my presence and I told him the dream. (He is called Belteshazzar,[d] after the name of my god, and the spirit of the holy gods[e] is in him.)

9 I said, "Belteshazzar, chief[f] of the magicians, I know that the spirit of the holy gods[g] is in you, and no mystery is too difficult for you. Here is my dream; interpret it for me. 10 These are the visions I saw while lying in my bed:[h] I looked, and there before me stood a tree in the middle of the land. Its height was enormous.[i] 11 The tree grew large and strong and its top touched the sky; it was visible to the ends of the earth. 12 Its leaves were beautiful, its fruit abundant, and on it was food for all. Under it the beasts of the field found shelter, and the birds of the air lived in its branches;[j] from it every creature was fed.

13 "In the visions I saw while lying in my bed,[k] I looked, and there before me was a messenger,[b] a holy one,[l] coming down from heaven. 14 He called in a loud voice: 'Cut down the tree and trim off its branches; strip off its leaves and scatter its fruit. Let the animals flee from under it and the birds from its branches.[m] 15 But let the stump and its roots, bound with iron and bronze, remain in the ground, in the grass of the field.

" 'Let him be drenched with the dew of heaven, and let him live with the animals among the plants of the earth. 16 Let his mind be changed from that of a man and let him be given the mind of an animal, till seven times[c] pass by for him.[n]

17 " 'The decision is announced by messengers, the holy ones declare the verdict, so that the living may know that the Most High[o] is sovereign[p] over the kingdoms of men and gives them to anyone he wishes and sets over them the lowliest[q] of men.'

18 "This is the dream that I, King Nebuchadnezzar, had. Now, Belteshazzar, tell me what it means, for none of the wise men in my kingdom can interpret it for me.[r] But you can,[s] because the spirit of the holy gods is in you."[t]

Daniel Interprets the Dream

19 Then Daniel (also called Belteshazzar) was greatly perplexed for a time, and his thoughts terrified[u] him. So the king said, "Belteshazzar, do not let the dream or its meaning alarm you."

[a] *7* Or *Chaldeans* [b] *13* Or *watchman*; also in verses 17 and 23 [c] *16* Or *years*; also in verses 23, 25 and 32

3:29 [m]Da 6:26 [n]Ezr 6:11 [o]Da 6:27
3:30 [p]Da 2:49
4:1 [q]Da 3:4 [r]Da 6:25
4:2 [s]Ps 74:9 [t]Da 3:26
4:3 [u]Ps 105:27; Da 6:27 [v]Da 2:44
4:4 [w]Ps 30:6
4:5 [x]Da 2:1 [y]Da 2:28
4:6 [z]Da 2:2
4:7 [a]Ge 41:8 [b]Isa 44:25; Da 2:2 [c]Da 2:10
4:8 [d]Da 1:7 [e]Da 5:11,14
4:9 [f]Da 2:48 [g]Da 5:11-12
4:10 [h]ver 5
4:10 [i]Eze 31:3-4
4:12 [j]Eze 17:23; Mt 13:32
4:13 [k]Da 7:1 [l]ver 23; Dt 33:2; Da 8:13
4:14 [m]Eze 31:12; Mt 3:10
4:16 [n]ver 23,32
4:17 [o]ver 2,25; Ps 83:18 [p]Jer 27:5-7; Da 2:21; 5:18-21 [q]Da 11:21
4:18 [r]Ge 41:8; Da 5:8,15 [s]Ge 41:15 [t]ver 7-9
4:19 [u]Da 7:15,28; 8:27; 10:16-17

Belteshazzar answered, "My lord, if only the dream applied to your enemies and its meaning to your adversaries! 20The tree you saw, which grew large and strong, with its top touching the sky, visible to the whole earth, 21with beautiful leaves and abundant fruit, providing food for all, giving shelter to the beasts of the field, and having nesting places in its branches for the birds of the air— 22you, O king, are that tree![v] You have become great and strong; your greatness has grown until it reaches the sky, and your dominion extends to distant parts of the earth.[w]

23"You, O king, saw a messenger, a holy one,[x] coming down from heaven and saying, 'Cut down the tree and destroy it, but leave the stump, bound with iron and bronze, in the grass of the field, while its roots remain in the ground. Let him be drenched with the dew of heaven; let him live like the wild animals, until seven times pass by for him.'[y]

24"This is the interpretation, O king, and this is the decree[z] the Most High has issued against my lord the king: 25You will be driven away from people and will live with the wild animals; you will eat grass like cattle and be drenched with the dew of heaven. Seven times will pass by for you until you acknowledge that the Most High[a] is sovereign over the kingdoms of men and gives them to anyone he wishes.[b] 26The command to leave the stump of the tree with its roots[c] means that your kingdom will be restored to you when you acknowledge that Heaven rules.[d] 27Therefore, O king, be pleased to accept my advice: Renounce your sins by doing what is right, and your wickedness by being kind to the oppressed.[e] It may be that then your prosperity will continue.[f]"

4:22 [v]2Sa 12:7 [w]Jer 27:7; Da 2:37-38; 5:18-19
4:23 [x]ver 13 [y]Da 5:21
4:24 [z]Job 40:12; Ps 107:40
4:25 [a]ver 17; Ps 83:18 [b]Jer 27:5; Da 5:21
4:26 [c]ver 15 [d]Da 2:37
4:27 [e]Isa 55:6-7 [f]1Ki 21:29; Ps 41:3; Eze 18:22

The Dream Is Fulfilled

28All this happened[g] to King Nebuchadnezzar. 29Twelve months later, as the king was walking on the roof of the royal palace of Babylon, 30he said, "Is not this the great Babylon I have built as the royal residence, by my mighty power and for the glory of my majesty?"[h]

31The words were still on his lips when a voice came from heaven, "This is what is decreed for you, King Nebuchadnezzar: Your royal authority has been taken from you. 32You will be driven away from people and will live with the wild animals; you will eat grass like cattle. Seven times will pass by for you until you acknowledge that the Most High is sovereign over the kingdoms of men and gives them to anyone he wishes."

33Immediately what had been said about Nebuchadnezzar was fulfilled. He was driven away from people and ate grass like cattle. His body was drenched with the dew of heaven until his hair grew like the feathers of an eagle and his nails like the claws of a bird.[i]

34At the end of that time, I, Nebuchadnezzar, raised my eyes toward heaven, and my sanity was restored. Then I praised the Most High; I honored and glorified him who lives forever.[j]

His dominion is an eternal
  dominion;
 his kingdom endures from
  generation to generation.[k]
35All the peoples of the earth
  are regarded as nothing.[l]
He does as he pleases[m]
  with the powers of heaven
  and the peoples of the earth.
No one can hold back his hand
  or say to him: "What have you
  done?"[n]

36At the same time that my sanity was restored, my honor and splendor were returned to me for the glory of my kingdom.[o] My advisers and nobles sought me out, and I was restored to my throne and became even greater than before. 37Now I, Nebuchadnezzar, praise and exalt and glorify the King of heaven, because everything he does is right and all his ways are just.[p] And those who walk in pride he is able to humble.[q]

4:28 [g]Nu 23:19
4:30 [h]Isa 37:24-25; Da 5:20; Hab 2:4
4:33 [i]Da 5:20-21
4:34 [j]Da 12:7; Rev 4:10 [k]Ps 145:13; Da 2:44; 5:21; 6:26; Lk 1:33
4:35 [l]Isa 40:17 [m]Ps 115:3; 135:6 [n]Isa 45:9; Ro 9:20
4:36 [o]Pr 22:4
4:37 [p]Dt 32:4; Ps 33:4-5 [q]Ex 18:11; Job 40:11-12; Da 5:20,23

The Writing on the Wall

5 King Belshazzar gave a great ban-
5:1 [r]Est 1:3 quet[r] for a thousand of his nobles
and drank wine with them. 2While
Belshazzar was drinking his wine, he
gave orders to bring in the gold and
5:2 silver goblets[s] that Nebuchadnezzar his
[s]2Ki 24:13; Jer 52:19 father[a] had taken from the temple in Je-
[t]Est 1:7; Da 1:2 rusalem, so that the king and his nobles,
his wives and his concubines might
drink from them.[t] 3So they brought in
the gold goblets that had been taken
from the temple of God in Jerusalem,
and the king and his nobles, his wives
and his concubines drank from them.
4As they drank the wine, they praised
5:4 the gods of gold and silver, of bronze,
[u]Ps 135:15-18; Hab 2:19; Rev 9:20 iron, wood and stone.[u]
5Suddenly the fingers of a human
hand appeared and wrote on the plaster of the wall, near the lampstand
in the royal palace. The king watched
the hand as it wrote. 6His face turned
5:6 [v]Da 4:5 pale and he was so frightened[v] that his
[w]Eze 7:17 knees knocked together and his legs
gave way.[w]
7The king called out for the enchant-
5:7 [x]Isa 44:25 ers, astrologers[b] and diviners[x] to be
[y]Da 4:6-7 brought and said to these wise[y] men
[z]Ge 41:42 [a]Da 2:5-6,48; of Babylon, "Whoever reads this writ-
6:2-3 ing and tells me what it means will be
clothed in purple and have a gold chain
placed around his neck,[z] and he will
be made the third highest ruler in the
kingdom."[a]
8Then all the king's wise men came
5:8 in, but they could not read the writing
[b]Da 2:10,27 or tell the king what it meant.[b] 9So
5:9 King Belshazzar became even more ter-
[c]Isa 21:4 rified[c] and his face grew more pale. His
nobles were baffled.
10The queen,[c] hearing the voices of
5:10 the king and his nobles, came into the
[d]Da 3:9 banquet hall. "O king, live forever!"[d]
she said. "Don't be alarmed! Don't look
so pale! 11There is a man in your kingdom who has the spirit of the holy
5:11 [e]Da 4:8-9,19 gods[e] in him. In the time of your fa-
[f]ver 14; Da 1:17 ther he was found to have insight and
[g]Da 2:47-48 intelligence and wisdom[f] like that of
the gods. King Nebuchadnezzar your
father—your father the king, I say—
appointed him chief of the magicians,
enchanters, astrologers and diviners.[g]
12This man Daniel, whom the king
5:12 [h]Da 1:7 called Belteshazzar,[h] was found to have
a keen mind and knowledge and un-

derstanding, and also the ability to
interpret dreams, explain riddles and
solve difficult problems.[i] Call for Dan- 5:12 [i]ver 14-16;
iel, and he will tell you what the writing Da 6:3
means."
13So Daniel was brought before the
king, and the king said to him, "Are
you Daniel, one of the exiles my father 5:13
the king brought from Judah?[j] 14I have [j]Da 6:13
heard that the spirit of the gods is in
you and that you have insight, intelligence and outstanding wisdom. 15The
wise men and enchanters were brought
before me to read this writing and tell
me what it means, but they could not
explain it. 16Now I have heard that you
are able to give interpretations and to
solve difficult problems. If you can read
this writing and tell me what it means,
you will be clothed in purple and have
a gold chain placed around your neck,
and you will be made the third highest
ruler in the kingdom."
17Then Daniel answered the king,
"You may keep your gifts for yourself 5:17
and give your rewards to someone else.[k] [k]2Ki 5:16
Nevertheless, I will read the writing for
the king and tell him what it means.
18"O king, the Most High God gave
your father Nebuchadnezzar sovereignty 5:18
and greatness and glory and splendor.[l] [l]Jer 27:7; Da 2:37-38
19Because of the high position he gave
him, all the peoples and nations and
men of every language dreaded and
feared him. Those the king wanted to 5:19
put to death,[m] he put to death; those [m]Da 2:12-13; 3:6
he wanted to spare, he spared; those he
wanted to promote, he promoted; and
those he wanted to humble, he humbled. 20But when his heart became ar-
rogant and hardened with pride,[n] he 5:20 [n]Da 4:30
was deposed from his royal throne and [o]Jer 13:18
stripped[o] of his glory.[p] 21He was driven [p]Job 40:12; Isa 14:13-15
away from people and given the mind
of an animal; he lived with the wild
donkeys and ate grass like cattle; and
his body was drenched with the dew of
heaven, until he acknowledged that the
Most High God is sovereign[q] over the 5:21
kingdoms of men and sets over them [q]Eze 17:24 [r]Da
anyone he wishes.[r] 4:16-17,35
22"But you his son,[d] O Belshazzar,
have not humbled[s] yourself, though you 5:22 [s]Ex 10:3;
knew all this. 23Instead, you have set 2Ch 33:23

[a]*2* Or *ancestor*; or *predecessor*; also in verses 11, 13 and 18 [b]*7* Or *Chaldeans*; also in verse 11 [c]*10* Or *queen mother* [d]*22* Or *descendant*; or *successor*

5:23 [t]Jer 50:29 yourself up against[t] the Lord of heav-
[u]Ps 115:4-8; en. You had the goblets from his tem-
Hab 2:19 ple brought to you, and you and your
[v]Job 12:10 nobles, your wives and your concubines
[w]Job 31:4; drank wine from them. You praised
Jer 10:23 the gods of silver and gold, of bronze,
iron, wood and stone, which cannot see
or hear or understand.[u] But you did not
honor the God who holds in his hand
your life[v] and all your ways.[w] 24Therefore he sent the hand that wrote the inscription.
25"This is the inscription that was written:

MENE, MENE, TEKEL, PARSIN[a]

26"This is what these words mean:

Mene[b]: God has numbered the
5:26 [x]Jer 27:7 days[x] of your reign and
[y]Isa 13:6 brought it to an end.[y]
27 *Tekel*[c]: You have been weighed on the scales and found
5:27 [z]Ps 62:9 wanting.[z]
28 *Peres*[d]: Your kingdom is divided
5:28 [a]Isa 13:17 and given to the Medes[a] and
[b]Da 6:28 Persians."[b]

GENTLENESS

THE BALANCES OF LIFE

Daniel 5:25

Mene, Mene, Tekel, Parsin **means the era of grace is over. The time of God's gentleness is past. God is at the gates with balances, and he will weigh our deeds.**

29Then at Belshazzar's command,
Daniel was clothed in purple, a gold
chain was placed around his neck, and
he was proclaimed the third highest ruler in the kingdom.
5:30 [c]ver 1 30That very night Belshazzar,[c] king
[d]Isa 21:9; of the Babylonians,[e] was slain,[d] 31and
Jer 51:31 Darius[e] the Mede took over the king-
5:31 [e]Da 6:1; 9:1 dom, at the age of sixty-two.

Daniel in the Den of Lions

6:1 [f]Da 5:31 6 It pleased Darius[f] to appoint 120
[g]Est 1:1 satraps[g] to rule throughout the kingdom, 2with three administrators over
6:2 [h]Da 2:48-49 them, one of whom was Daniel.[h] The
[i]Ezr 4:22 satraps were made accountable[i] to them
so that the king might not suffer loss.
3Now Daniel so distinguished himself
among the administrators and the satraps by his exceptional qualities that the

DAY FIVE

PATIENCE AND ITS PLACE IN MY PERSONAL WORSHIP

Daniel 6:6–10

Daniel prayed in this crisis, "just as he had done before." It is safe to say that Daniel was pacing his life with prayer. Those who believe in the importance of prayer do a rather remarkable thing in this hurried, over-scheduled world of ours. They simply stop running and take perfectly good time that they could use for success and achievement to pray. Why? Because to pray is to succeed. To arrive at any plateau of personal advancement having not prayed is to have gotten there the wrong way.

Prayer changes things, but the most important thing it changes is us. This is perhaps the first thing we should see about prayer and the last thing we usually do see. So many intercessors expend their spiritual energy asking God for changes they want to see in the world, and while they may see some changes, they fail to see that the major change is within themselves.

Prayer keeps us flexible and keeps us willing to modify or delete those personal parts of our ambitions that make us most neurotic. Those who, like Daniel, let prayer interrupt and slow their pace are able to focus on their relationship with God and to communicate with him.

Notice the methodology of Daniel's prayer routine in Daniel 6:10: First, he leaves what he has been doing. Second, he goes where he can be alone with God. Third, he prays and offers thanks to God. Notice that he does this three times a day. Daniel makes time for a relationship with God.

It is easy to see that Daniel had a prayer routine that broke into the demands of all his other routines. His devotion to his worship of God is evidenced in his willingness to make prayer a priority. Even during his hassled political struggles, Daniel leaned on God and made time for worship.

To begin a study on the topic of Patience, Living by God's Timetable, turn to the home page on page 593.

[a]25 Aramaic *UPARSIN* (that is, *AND PARSIN*)
[b]26 *Mene* can mean *numbered* or *mina* (a unit of money). [c]27 *Tekel* can mean *weighed* or *shekel.*
[d]28 *Peres* (the singular of *Parsin*) can mean *divided* or *Persia* or *a half mina* or *a half shekel.* [e]30 Or *Chaldeans*

king planned to set him over the whole
6:3 [j]Ge 41:41; Est 10:3; Da 5:12-14 kingdom.[j] 4At this, the administrators
and the satraps tried to find grounds for
charges against Daniel in his conduct
of government affairs, but they were
unable to do so. They could find no
corruption in him, because he was trustworthy and neither corrupt nor negligent. 5Finally these men said, "We will
never find any basis for charges against
this man Daniel unless it has something
6:5 [k]Ac 24:13-16 to do with the law of his God."[k]
6So the administrators and the sa-
traps went as a group to the king and
said: "O King Darius, live forever![l] 7The 6:6 [l]Ne 2:3; Da 2:4
royal administrators, prefects, satraps,
advisers and governors[m] have all agreed 6:7 [m]Da 3:2 [n]Ps 59:3; 64:2-6; Da 3:6
that the king should issue an edict and
enforce the decree that anyone who
prays to any god or man during the
next thirty days, except to you, O king,
shall be thrown into the lions' den.[n]
8Now, O king, issue the decree and put
it in writing so that it cannot be al-
tered—in accordance with the laws of
the Medes and Persians, which cannot
be repealed."[o] 9So King Darius put the 6:8 [o]Est 1:19
decree in writing.

DANIEL

Goodness, the Fruit of Our Convictions (6:1–28)

Our convictions define who we are. Convictions are the building blocks of character, the seeds of a growing morality, the sunlight that frowns on shady compromise. People without convictions neither know who they are nor are ever sure of their worship, for convictions are conceived only when we discover who God is.

Daniel was a person of no compromise. When a law was passed proclaiming that no one could pray to any god except the king (who had modestly agreed to his own legalized divinity), Daniel became a civil nuisance. The administrators and satraps had long been trying to find some reason to have Daniel removed from his position in government. They knew that deifying the king would be the perfect way to trap Daniel, for Daniel was so committed to the adoration of God alone that he would never agree to the worship of human royalty. So these conspirators said to the king, "O King Darius, live forever! The royal administrators, prefects, satraps, advisers and governors have all agreed that the king should issue an edict and enforce the decree that anyone who prays to any god or man during the next thirty days, except to you, O king, shall be thrown into the lions' den" (6:6–7).

People of conviction don't alter their worship merely because some king supposedly arrives at a state of divinity, even when his "deification" proceeds from an act of state. So "when Daniel learned that the decree had been published, he went home to his upstairs room where the windows opened toward Jerusalem. Three times a day he got down on his knees and prayed, giving thanks to his God, just as he had done before" (v. 10). Of course, Daniel was apprehended and thrown into the lions' den for his blatant disobedience.

The king, concerned for Daniel, "spent the night without eating and without any entertainment being brought to him. And he could not sleep" (v. 18). After his long night of insomnia, at the first light of morning, the king ran to the lions' den and called out in anguish, "Daniel, servant of the living God, has your God, whom you serve continually, been able to rescue you from the lions?" (v. 20). Daniel answered, "O king, live forever!" (v. 21).

These were welcome words to Darius, for he was a friend of Daniel's and knew that, in spite of the recent national legislation, he was just not good at being a god. There was only one thing left to do: He threw the legislators into the lions' den. The lions licked their chops, and civil government was much improved. This ended the recent volley of bad legislation, and things were soon back to normal. And what was normal? Normalcy, according to Daniel, prevails only when God is in heaven and the goodness of virtuous individuals goes on uninterrupted.

[10]Now when Daniel learned that the
decree had been published, he went
home to his upstairs room where the 6:10 [p]1Ki 8:48-49
windows opened toward[p] Jerusalem.
Three times a day he got down on his
knees[q] and prayed, giving thanks to 6:10 [q]Ps 95:6
his God, just as he had done before.[r] [r]Ac 5:29
[11]Then these men went as a group and
found Daniel praying and asking God
for help. [12]So they went to the king
and spoke to him about his royal decree: "Did you not publish a decree that
during the next thirty days anyone who
prays to any god or man except to you,
O king, would be thrown into the lions' den?"
The king answered, "The decree
stands—in accordance with the laws of
the Medes and Persians, which cannot
be repealed."[s] 6:12 [s]Est 1:19; Da 3:8-12
[13]Then they said to the king, "Dan-
iel, who is one of the exiles from Judah,[t] 6:13
pays no attention[u] to you, O king, or [t]Da 2:25; 5:13
to the decree you put in writing. He [u]Est 3:8; Da 3:12
still prays three times a day." [14]When
the king heard this, he was greatly
distressed;[v] he was determined to rescue 6:14
Daniel and made every effort until sun- [v]Mk 6:26
down to save him.
[15]Then the men went as a group to
the king and said to him, "Remember,
O king, that according to the law of the
Medes and Persians no decree or edict
that the king issues can be changed."[w] 6:15
[16]So the king gave the order, and they [w]Est 8:8
brought Daniel and threw him into the
lions' den.[x] The king said to Daniel, 6:16
"May your God, whom you serve con- [x]ver 7
tinually, rescue[y] you!" [y]Job 5:19; Ps 37:39-40
[17]A stone was brought and placed
over the mouth of the den, and the
king sealed[z] it with his own signet ring 6:17
and with the rings of his nobles, so [z]Mt 27:66
that Daniel's situation might not be
changed. [18]Then the king returned to
his palace and spent the night without
eating[a] and without any entertainment
being brought to him. And he could 6:18
not sleep.[b] [a]2Sa 12:17 [b]Est 6:1; Da 2:1
[19]At the first light of dawn, the king
got up and hurried to the lions' den.
[20]When he came near the den, he called
to Daniel in an anguished voice, "Daniel, servant of the living God, has your
God, whom you serve continually, been 6:20
able to rescue you from the lions?"[c] [c]Da 3:17
[21]Daniel answered, "O king, live 6:21
forever![d] [22]My God sent his angel,[e] and [d]Da 2:4
he shut the mouths of the lions.[f] They 6:22 [e]Da 3:28
have not hurt me, because I was found [f]Ps 91:11-13; Heb 11:33
innocent in his sight.[g] Nor have I ever [g]Ac 12:11; 2Ti 4:17
done any wrong before you, O king."

DAY 5 FIVE

▸ Faithfulness and Its Place in My Personal Worship

Daniel 6:11–22

God can deliver us from every trial—yet he doesn't always do so. As he faced an unfair decree that required him to cease worshiping God, Daniel must have realized that he was among the few fortunate Jews who had survived the rigors of the Babylonian siege and the horrors of Persian exile and imprisonment. He knew many who had died; he had heard the elder ones tell of the three-year siege during which the starving Jews had resorted to cannibalism. The horror of the living conditions had brought about epidemics of diseases. Typhus, in those days, claimed as many lives as the siege.

Why, then, would Daniel believe that God was more inclined to rescue him than the thousands who had paid in blood before Nebuchadnezzar had burned and leveled the city? The truth is, he didn't know. God would be able to deliver him from the lions' den if that were his will. In fact, God is so powerful that he could crush Daniel's enemies like flies on a tile wall. But even if God did not save Daniel—as he had not done for the thousands before Daniel—one thing was certain: Daniel was determined to worship the true God, even in the midst of a pagan culture.

Daniel might have to die, but he didn't have to be unfaithful.

God would be God, celebrated by Daniel's life or by Daniel's death.

So fill the lions' den, starve the lions, and throw commitment to the beasts. There will be no compromise. It is as easy for the committed to worship in the company of beasts as it is to worship in the temple.

To begin a study on the topic of Faithfulness, a Stubborn Commitment to the Right, turn to the home page on page 398.

23The king was overjoyed and gave
orders to lift Daniel out of the den.
And when Daniel was lifted from the
6:23 [b]Da 3:27 den, no wound[b] was found on him, be-
[i]1Ch 5:20 cause he had trusted[i] in his God.
24At the king's command, the men
who had falsely accused Daniel were
brought in and thrown into the lions'
6:24 [j]Dt 19:18-19; den,[j] along with their wives and
Est 7:9-10; children.[k] And before they reached the
Ps 54:5 [k]Dt 24:16; floor of the den, the lions overpowered
2Ki 14:6 [l]Isa 38:13 them and crushed all their bones.[l]
25Then King Darius wrote to all the
peoples, nations and men of every language throughout the land:

6:25 [m]Da 4:1 "May you prosper greatly![m]

26"I issue a decree that in every
part of my kingdom people must
fear and reverence the God of
6:26 [n]Ps 99:1-3; Da 3:29 Daniel.[n]

[o]Da 2:44; 4:34 "For he is the living God
and he endures forever;
his kingdom will not be destroyed,
his dominion will never end.[o]
6:27 [p]Da 4:3 [q]ver 22 27He rescues and he saves;
he performs signs and wonders[p]
in the heavens and on the earth.
He has rescued Daniel
from the power of the lions."[q]

28So Daniel prospered during the
6:28 [r]2Ch 36:22; reign of Darius and the reign of Cyrus[a][r]
Da 1:21 the Persian.

Daniel's Dream of Four Beasts

7:1 [s]Da 5:1 7 In the first year of Belshazzar's[s] king
[t]Da 1:17 of Babylon, Daniel had a dream,
[u]Jer 36:4 and visions passed through his mind[t]
as he was lying on his bed. He wrote[u]
down the substance of his dream.
2Daniel said: "In my vision at night
7:2 [v]Rev 7:1 I looked, and there before me were the
four winds of heaven[v] churning up the
7:3 [w]Rev 13:1 great sea. 3Four great beasts,[w] each different from the others, came up out of
the sea.
7:4 [x]Jer 4:7 4"The first was like a lion,[x] and it
[y]Eze 17:3 had the wings of an eagle.[y] I watched
until its wings were torn off and it was
lifted from the ground so that it stood
on two feet like a man, and the heart of
a man was given to it.
5"And there before me was a second
beast, which looked like a bear. It was
raised up on one of its sides, and it
had three ribs in its mouth between its
teeth. It was told, 'Get up and eat your
fill of flesh!'[z] 7:5 [z]Da 2:39
6"After that, I looked, and there before me was another beast, one that
looked like a leopard.[a] And on its back 7:6 [a]Rev 13:2
it had four wings like those of a bird.
This beast had four heads, and it was
given authority to rule.
7"After that, in my vision at night
I looked, and there before me was a
fourth beast—terrifying and frighten- 7:7
ing and very powerful. It had large iron[b] [b]Da 2:40 [c]Rev 12:3
teeth; it crushed and devoured its vic-
tims and trampled underfoot whatever
was left. It was different from all the
former beasts, and it had ten horns.[c]
8"While I was thinking about the
horns, there before me was another
horn, a little[d] one, which came up 7:8 [d]Da 8:9
among them; and three of the first [e]Rev 9:7 [f]Ps 12:3;
horns were uprooted before it. This Rev 13:5-6
horn had eyes like the eyes of a man[e]
and a mouth that spoke boastfully.[f]
9"As I looked,

"thrones were set in place,
and the Ancient of Days took his
seat.
His clothing was as white as snow;
the hair of his head was white like
wool.[g] 7:9 [g]Rev 1:14 [h]Eze 1:15;
His throne was flaming with fire, 10:6
and its wheels[h] were all ablaze.
10A river of fire[i] was flowing, 7:10 [i]Ps 50:3; 97:3;
coming out from before him.[j] Isa 30:27 [j]Dt 33:2;
Thousands upon thousands attended Ps 68:17;
him; Rev 5:11
ten thousand times ten thousand [k]Rev 20:11-15
stood before him.
The court was seated,
and the books[k] were opened.

11"Then I continued to watch because of the boastful words the horn
was speaking. I kept looking until the
beast was slain and its body destroyed 7:11
and thrown into the blazing fire.[l] 12(The [l]Rev 19:20
other beasts had been stripped of their
authority, but were allowed to live for a
period of time.)
13"In my vision at night I looked,
and there before me was one like a son
of man,[m] coming with the clouds of 7:13 [m]Mt 8:20*;
heaven.[n] He approached the Ancient Rev 1:13* [n]Mt 24:30;
of Days and was led into his presence. Rev 1:7
14He was given authority,[o] glory and 7:14
sovereign power; all peoples, nations [o]Mt 28:18

[a]28 Or *Darius, that is, the reign of Cyrus*

JOY

The Christ of Final Joy

Daniel 7:13

There is a double-exposure photograph in the heart of every believer. One image is of the dying Christ, a seeming captive to human laws and small decrees, crying, "It is finished." The other image is of the Christ of the Apocalypse, bursting through the skies, clothed in lightning, crying, "Ladies and gentlemen, it's closing time!"

7:14 pPs 72:11; 102:22; 1Co 15:27; Eph 1:22 qDa 2:44; Heb 12:28; Rev 11:15 and men of every language worshiped
him.[p] His dominion is an everlasting
dominion that will not pass away, and
his kingdom is one that will never be
destroyed.[q]

The Interpretation of the Dream

15"I, Daniel, was troubled in spirit,
and the visions that passed through my
7:15 rDa 4:19 mind disturbed me.[r] 16I approached
one of those standing there and asked
him the true meaning of all this.
"So he told me and gave me the in-
7:16 sDa 8:16; 9:22; Zec 1:9 terpretation[s] of these things: 17'The four
great beasts are four kingdoms that will
rise from the earth. 18But the saints of
the Most High will receive the kingdom and will possess it forever—yes,
7:18 tIsa 60:12-14; Rev 2:26; 20:4 for ever and ever.'[t]
19"Then I wanted to know the true
meaning of the fourth beast, which was
different from all the others and most
terrifying, with its iron teeth and bronze
claws—the beast that crushed and devoured its victims and trampled underfoot whatever was left. 20I also wanted
to know about the ten horns on its
head and about the other horn that
came up, before which three of them
fell—the horn that looked more imposing than the others and that had eyes
and a mouth that spoke boastfully. 21As
I watched, this horn was waging war
7:21 uRev 13:7 against the saints and defeating them,[u]
22until the Ancient of Days came and
pronounced judgment in favor of the
saints of the Most High, and the time
came when they possessed the kingdom.
23"He gave me this explanation: 'The
fourth beast is a fourth kingdom that
will appear on earth. It will be different from all the other kingdoms and
will devour the whole earth, trampling
it down and crushing it.[v] 24The ten 7:23 vDa 2:40
horns[w] are ten kings who will come
from this kingdom. After them another 7:24 wRev 17:12
king will arise, different from the earlier
ones; he will subdue three kings. 25He 7:25 xIsa 37:23; Da 11:36 yDa 2:21 zDa 8:24; 12:7; Rev 12:14
will speak against the Most High[x] and
oppress his saints and try to change the
set times[y] and the laws. The saints will
be handed over to him for a time, times
and half a time.[a z]
26" 'But the court will sit, and his
power will be taken away and completely destroyed forever. 27Then the
sovereignty, power and greatness of the
kingdoms under the whole heaven will
be handed over to the saints, the people
of the Most High. His kingdom will be
an everlasting[a] kingdom, and all rulers 7:27 aDa 2:44; 4:34; Lk 1:33; Rev 11:15; 22:5 bPs 22:27; 72:11; 86:9
will worship[b] and obey him.'
28"This is the end of the matter. I,
Daniel, was deeply troubled[c] by my
thoughts, and my face turned pale, but
I kept the matter to myself." 7:28 cDa 4:19

Daniel's Vision of a Ram and a Goat

8 In the third year of King Belshazzar's reign, I, Daniel, had a vision,
after the one that had already appeared
to me. 2In my vision I saw myself in
the citadel of Susa[d] in the province of 8:2 dEst 1:2 eGe 10:22
Elam;[e] in the vision I was beside the
Ulai Canal. 3I looked up,[f] and there 8:3 fDa 10:5
before me was a ram with two horns,
standing beside the canal, and the horns
were long. One of the horns was longer than the other but grew up later.
4I watched the ram as he charged toward the west and the north and the
south. No animal could stand against
him, and none could rescue from his
power. He did as he pleased[g] and be- 8:4 gDa 11:3,16
came great.
5As I was thinking about this, suddenly a goat with a prominent horn
between his eyes came from the west,
crossing the whole earth without touching the ground. 6He came toward the
two-horned ram I had seen standing
beside the canal and charged at him in
great rage. 7I saw him attack the ram
furiously, striking the ram and shatter-
ing his two horns. The ram was powerless to stand against him; the goat
knocked him to the ground and tram-

a25 Or *for a year, two years and half a year*

pled on him,[h] and none could rescue the ram from his power. 8 The goat became very great, but at the height of his power his large horn was broken off,[i] and in its place four prominent horns grew up toward the four winds of heaven.[j]

9 Out of one of them came another horn, which started small but grew in power to the south and to the east and toward the Beautiful Land.[k] 10 It grew until it reached[l] the host of the heavens, and it threw some of the starry host down to the earth[m] and trampled[n] on them. 11 It set itself up to be as great as the Prince of the host;[o] it took away the daily sacrifice[p] from him, and the place of his sanctuary was brought low.[q] 12 Because of rebellion, the host ⌞of the saints⌟[a] and the daily sacrifice were given over to it. It prospered in everything it did, and truth was thrown to the ground.

13 Then I heard a holy one[r] speaking, and another holy one said to him, "How long will it take for the vision to be fulfilled[s]—the vision concerning the daily sacrifice, the rebellion that causes desolation, and the surrender of the sanctuary and of the host that will be trampled[t] underfoot?"

14 He said to me, "It will take 2,300 evenings and mornings; then the sanctuary will be reconsecrated."[u]

The Interpretation of the Vision

15 While I, Daniel, was watching the vision[v] and trying to understand it, there before me stood one who looked like a man.[w] 16 And I heard a man's voice from the Ulai calling, "Gabriel,[x] tell this man the meaning of the vision."

17 As he came near the place where I was standing, I was terrified and fell prostrate.[y] "Son of man," he said to me, "understand that the vision concerns the time of the end."[z]

18 While he was speaking to me, I was in a deep sleep, with my face to the ground.[a] Then he touched me and raised me to my feet.[b]

19 He said: "I am going to tell you what will happen later in the time of wrath, because the vision concerns the appointed time of the end.[b][c] 20 The two-horned ram that you saw represents the kings of Media and Persia. 21 The shaggy goat is the king of Greece,[d] and the large horn between his eyes is the first king.[e] 22 The four horns that replaced the one that was broken off represent four kingdoms that will emerge from his nation but will not have the same power.

23 "In the latter part of their reign, when rebels have become completely wicked, a stern-faced king, a master of intrigue, will arise. 24 He will become very strong, but not by his own power. He will cause astounding devastation and will succeed in whatever he does. He will destroy the mighty men and the holy people.[f] 25 He will cause deceit to prosper, and he will consider himself superior. When they feel secure, he will destroy many and take his stand against the Prince of princes.[g] Yet he will be destroyed, but not by human power.[h]

26 "The vision of the evenings and mornings that has been given you is true,[i] but seal[j] up the vision, for it concerns the distant future."[k]

27 I, Daniel, was exhausted and lay ill for several days. Then I got up and went about the king's business.[l] I was appalled[m] by the vision; it was beyond understanding.

Daniel's Prayer

9 In the first year of Darius[n] son of Xerxes[c] (a Mede by descent), who was made ruler over the Babylonian[d] kingdom— 2 in the first year of his reign, I, Daniel, understood from the Scriptures, according to the word of the LORD given to Jeremiah the prophet, that the desolation of Jerusalem would last seventy[o] years. 3 So I turned to the Lord God and pleaded with him in prayer and petition, in fasting, and in sackcloth and ashes.[p]

4 I prayed to the LORD my God and confessed:

"O Lord, the great and awesome God,[q] who keeps his covenant of love[r] with all who love him and obey his commands, 5 we have sinned and done wrong.[s] We have been wicked and have rebelled; we have turned away[t] from your commands and laws.[u] 6 We have not listened to your servants the

[a]12 Or *rebellion, the armies* [b]19 Or *because the end will be at the appointed time* [c]1 Hebrew *Ahasuerus* [d]1 Or *Chaldean*

8:7 [h]Da 7:7
8:8 [i]2Ch 26:16-21; Da 5:20 [j]Da 7:2; Rev 7:1
8:9 [k]Da 11:16
8:10 [l]Isa 14:13 [m]Rev 12:4 [n]Da 7:7
8:11 [o]Da 11:36-37 [p]Eze 46:13-14 [q]Da 11:31; 12:11
8:13 [r]Da 4:23 [s]Da 12:6 [t]Lk 21:24; Rev 11:2
8:14 [u]Da 12:11-12
8:15 [v]ver 1 [w]Da 10:16-18
8:16 [x]Da 9:21; Lk 1:19
8:17 [y]Eze 1:28; Da 2:46; Rev 1:17 [z]Hab 2:3
8:18 [a]Da 10:9 [b]Eze 2:2; Da 10:16-18
8:19 [c]Hab 2:3
8:21 [d]Da 10:20
8:21 [e]Da 11:3
8:24 [f]Da 7:25; 11:36
8:25 [g]Da 11:36 [h]Da 2:34; 11:21
8:26 [i]Da 10:1 [j]Rev 22:10 [k]Da 10:14
8:27 [l]Da 2:48 [m]Da 7:28
9:1 [n]Da 5:31
9:2 [o]2Ch 36:21; Jer 29:10; Zec 7:5
9:3 [p]Ne 1:4; Jer 29:12
9:4 [q]Dt 7:21 [r]Dt 7:9
9:5 [s]Ps 106:6 [t]Isa 53:6 [u]ver 11; La 1:20

[9:6 v2Ch 36:16; Jer 44:5] prophets,[v] who spoke in your name
to our kings, our princes and our
fathers, and to all the people of the
land.
7“Lord, you are righteous, but
this day we are covered with
[9:7 wPs 44:15 xDt 4:27; Am 9:9 yJer 3:25] shame[w]—the men of Judah and
people of Jerusalem and all Israel,
both near and far, in all the countries where you have scattered[x] us
because of our unfaithfulness to
you.[y] 8O LORD, we and our kings,
our princes and our fathers are covered with shame because we have
sinned against you. 9The Lord our
[9:9 zPs 130:4 aNe 9:17; Jer 14:7] God is merciful and forgiving,[z]
even though we have rebelled
against him;[a] 10we have not obeyed
the LORD our God or kept the
[9:10 b2Ki 17:13-15; 18:12] laws he gave us through his servants the prophets.[b] 11All Israel has
transgressed your law and turned
away, refusing to obey you.
“Therefore the curses and sworn
judgments written in the Law of
Moses, the servant of God, have
been poured out on us, because
[9:11 cIsa 1:4-6; Jer 8:5-10] we have sinned[c] against you. 12You
have fulfilled[d] the words spoken
[9:12 dIsa 44:26; Zec 1:6 eJer 44:2-6; Eze 5:9] against us and against our rulers
by bringing upon us great disaster.
Under the whole heaven nothing
has ever been done like what has
been done to Jerusalem.[e] 13Just as
it is written in the Law of Moses,
all this disaster has come upon us,
yet we have not sought the favor
of the LORD our God by turning
from our sins and giving attention
[9:13 fIsa 9:13; Jer 2:30] to your truth.[f] 14The LORD did
not hesitate to bring the disaster[g]
[9:14 gJer 44:27 hNe 9:33] upon us, for the LORD our God
is righteous in everything he does;
yet we have not obeyed him.[h]
15“Now, O Lord our God, who
brought your people out of Egypt
[9:15 iJer 32:21 jNe 9:10] with a mighty hand[i] and who
made for yourself a name[j] that en-
dures to this day, we have sinned,
we have done wrong. 16O Lord,
in keeping with all your righteous
[9:16 kPs 31:1 lJer 32:32 mZec 8:3 nEze 5:14] acts,[k] turn away your anger and
your wrath from Jerusalem,[l] your
city, your holy hill.[m] Our sins and
the iniquities of our fathers have
made Jerusalem and your people
an object of scorn[n] to all those
around us.

17“Now, our God, hear the
prayers and petitions of your servant. For your sake, O Lord, look
with favor[o] on your desolate sanc- [9:17 oNu 6:24-26; Ps 80:19]
tuary. 18Give ear, O God, and hear;
open your eyes and see[p] the deso-
lation of the city that bears your [9:18 pPs 80:14 qIsa 37:17; Jer 7:10-12; 25:29]
Name.[q] We do not make requests
of you because we are righteous,
but because of your great mercy.
19O Lord, listen! O Lord, forgive![r] [9:19 rPs 44:23]
O Lord, hear and act! For your
sake, O my God, do not delay, because your city and your people
bear your Name.”

The Seventy “Sevens”

20While I was speaking and praying,
confessing my sin and the sin of my
people Israel and making my request to [9:20 sver 3; Ps 145:18; Isa 58:9]
the LORD my God for his holy hill[s]—
21while I was still in prayer, Gabriel,[t]
the man I had seen in the earlier vision, [9:21 tDa 8:16; Lk 1:19 uEx 29:39]
came to me in swift flight about the
time of the evening sacrifice.[u] 22He instructed me and said to me, “Daniel, I
have now come to give you insight and
understanding. 23As soon as you began
to pray, an answer was given, which I
have come to tell you, for you are high- [9:23 vDa 10:19; Lk 1:28 wDa 10:11-12; Mt 24:15]
ly esteemed.[v] Therefore, consider the
message and understand the vision:[w]
24“Seventy ‘sevens’[a] are decreed for
your people and your holy city to finish[b] transgression, to put an end to sin,
to atone[x] for wickedness, to bring in [9:24 xIsa 53:10 yIsa 56:1]
everlasting righteousness,[y] to seal up vi-
sion and prophecy and to anoint the
most holy.[c]
25“Know and understand this: From
the issuing of the decree[d] to restore and
rebuild[z] Jerusalem until the Anointed [9:25 zEzr 4:24 aJn 4:25]
One,[e][a] the ruler, comes, there will be
seven ‘sevens,’ and sixty-two ‘sevens.’ It
will be rebuilt with streets and a trench,
but in times of trouble. 26After the sixty-two ‘sevens,’ the Anointed One will
be cut off[b] and will have nothing.[f] The [9:26 bIsa 53:8 cNa 1:8]
people of the ruler who will come will
destroy the city and the sanctuary. The
end will come like a flood:[c] War will
continue until the end, and desolations
have been decreed. 27He will confirm a

[a]*24* Or *'weeks'*; also in verses 25 and 26 [b]*24* Or *restrain* [c]*24* Or *Most Holy Place*; or *most holy One* [d]*25* Or *word* [e]*25* Or *an anointed one*; also in verse 26 [f]*26* Or *off and will have no one*; or *off, but not for himself*

covenant with many for one 'seven.'[a] In the middle of the 'seven'[a] he will put an end to sacrifice and offering. And on a wing ⌊of the temple⌋ he will set up an abomination that causes desolation, until the end that is decreed[d] is poured out on him.[b]"[c]

Daniel's Vision of a Man

10 In the third year of Cyrus[e] king of Persia, a revelation was given to Daniel (who was called Belteshazzar).[f] Its message was true[g] and it concerned a great war.[d] The understanding of the message came to him in a vision.

2 At that time I, Daniel, mourned[h] for three weeks. 3 I ate no choice food; no meat or wine touched my lips; and I used no lotions at all until the three weeks were over.

4 On the twenty-fourth day of the first month, as I was standing on the bank of the great river, the Tigris,[i] 5 I looked up and there before me was a man dressed in linen,[j] with a belt of the finest gold[k] around his waist. 6 His body was like chrysolite, his face like lightning,[l] his eyes like flaming torches,[m] his arms and legs like the gleam of burnished bronze,[n] and his voice like the sound of a multitude.

7 I, Daniel, was the only one who saw the vision; the men with me did not see it,[o] but such terror overwhelmed them that they fled and hid themselves. 8 So I was left alone,[p] gazing at this great vision; I had no strength left,[q] my face turned deathly pale and I was helpless.[r] 9 Then I heard him speaking, and as I listened to him, I fell into a deep sleep, my face to the ground.[s]

10 A hand touched me[t] and set me trembling on my hands and knees.[u] 11 He said, "Daniel, you who are highly esteemed,[v] consider carefully the words I am about to speak to you, and stand up,[w] for I have now been sent to you." And when he said this to me, I stood up trembling.

12 Then he continued, "Do not be afraid, Daniel. Since the first day that you set your mind to gain understanding and to humble[x] yourself before your God, your words were heard, and I have come in response to them.[y] 13 But the prince of the Persian kingdom resisted me twenty-one days. Then Michael,[z] one of the chief princes, came to help me, because I was detained there with the king of Persia. 14 Now I have come to explain[a] to you what will happen to your people in the future, for the vision concerns a time yet to come.[b]"

15 While he was saying this to me, I bowed with my face toward the ground and was speechless.[c] 16 Then one who looked like a man[e] touched my lips, and I opened my mouth and began to speak.[d] I said to the one standing before me, "I am overcome with anguish[e] because of the vision, my lord, and I am helpless. 17 How can I, your servant, talk with you, my lord? My strength is gone and I can hardly breathe."[f]

18 Again the one who looked like a man touched[g] me and gave me strength. 19 "Do not be afraid, O man highly esteemed," he said. "Peace![h] Be strong now; be strong."[i]

When he spoke to me, I was strengthened and said, "Speak, my lord, since you have given me strength."[j]

20 So he said, "Do you know why I have come to you? Soon I will return to fight against the prince of Persia, and when I go, the prince of Greece[k] will come; 21 but first I will tell you what is written in the Book of Truth.[l] (No one supports me against them except

11 Michael,[m] your prince. 1 And in the first year of Darius[n] the Mede, I took my stand to support and protect him.)

The Kings of the South and the North

2 "Now then, I tell you the truth:[o] Three more kings will appear in Persia, and then a fourth, who will be far richer than all the others. When he has gained power by his wealth, he will stir up everyone against the kingdom of Greece.[p] 3 Then a mighty king will appear, who will rule with great power and do as he pleases.[q] 4 After he has appeared, his empire will be broken up and parceled out toward the four winds of heaven.[r] It

[a]*27* Or *'week'* [b]*27* Or *it* [c]*27* Or *And one who causes desolation will come upon the pinnacle of the abominable ⌊temple⌋, until the end that is decreed is poured out on the desolated ⌊city⌋* [d]*1* Or *true and burdensome* [e]*16* Most manuscripts of the Masoretic Text; one manuscript of the Masoretic Text, Dead Sea Scrolls and Septuagint *Then something that looked like a man's hand*

9:27 [d]Isa 10:22
10:1 [e]Da 1:21 [f]Da 1:7 [g]Da 8:26
10:2 [h]Ezr 9:4
10:4 [i]Ge 2:14
10:5 [j]Eze 9:2; Rev 15:6 [k]Jer 10:9
10:6 [l]Mt 17:2 [m]Rev 19:12 [n]Rev 1:15
10:7 [o]2Ki 6:17-20; Ac 9:7
10:8 [p]Ge 32:24 [q]Da 8:27 [r]Hab 3:16
10:9 [s]Da 8:18
10:10 [t]Jer 1:9 [u]Rev 1:17
10:11 [v]Da 9:23 [w]Eze 2:1
10:12 [x]Da 9:3 [y]Da 9:20
10:13 [z]ver 21; Da 12:1; Jude 1:9
10:14 [a]Da 9:22 [b]Da 2:28; 8:26; Hab 2:3
10:15 [c]Eze 24:27; Lk 1:20
10:16 [d]Isa 6:7; Jer 1:9; Da 8:15-18 [e]Isa 21:3
10:17 [f]Da 4:19
10:18 [g]ver 16
10:19 [h]Jdg 6:23; Isa 35:4 [i]Jos 1:9 [j]Isa 6:1-8
10:20 [k]Da 8:21; 11:2
10:21 [l]Da 11:2 [m]ver 13; Jude 1:9
11:1 [n]Da 5:31
11:2 [o]Da 10:21 [p]Da 10:20
11:3 [q]Da 8:4,21
11:4 [r]Da 7:2; 8:22

will not go to his descendants, nor will it have the power he exercised, because his empire will be uprooted and given to others.

5"The king of the South will become strong, but one of his commanders will become even stronger than he and will rule his own kingdom with great power. 6After some years, they will become allies. The daughter of the king of the South will go to the king of the North to make an alliance, but she will not retain her power, and he and his power[a] will not last. In those days she will be handed over, together with her royal escort and her father[b] and the one who supported her.

7"One from her family line will arise to take her place. He will attack the forces of the king of the North[s] and enter his fortress; he will fight against them and be victorious. 8He will also seize their gods,[t] their metal images and their valuable articles of silver and gold and carry them off to Egypt.[u] For some years he will leave the king of the North alone. 9Then the king of the North will invade the realm of the king of the South but will retreat to his own country. 10His sons will prepare for war and assemble a great army, which will sweep on like an irresistible flood[v] and carry the battle as far as his fortress.

11"Then the king of the South will march out in a rage and fight against the king of the North, who will raise a large army, but it will be defeated.[w] 12When the army is carried off, the king of the South will be filled with pride and will slaughter many thousands, yet he will not remain triumphant. 13For the king of the North will muster another army, larger than the first; and after several years, he will advance with a huge army fully equipped.

14"In those times many will rise against the king of the South. The violent men among your own people will rebel in fulfillment of the vision, but without success. 15Then the king of the North will come and build up siege ramps[x] and will capture a fortified city. The forces of the South will be powerless to resist; even their best troops will not have the strength to stand. 16The invader will do as he pleases;[y] no one will be able to stand against him.[z] He will establish himself in the Beautiful Land and will have the power to destroy it.[a] 17He will determine to come with the might of his entire kingdom and will make an alliance with the king of the South. And he will give him a daughter in marriage in order to overthrow the kingdom, but his plans[c] will not succeed[b] or help him. 18Then he will turn his attention to the coastlands[c] and will take many of them, but a commander will put an end to his insolence and will turn his insolence back upon him.[d] 19After this, he will turn back toward the fortresses of his own country but will stumble and fall,[e] to be seen no more.[f]

20"His successor will send out a tax collector to maintain the royal splendor.[g] In a few years, however, he will be destroyed, yet not in anger or in battle.

21"He will be succeeded by a contemptible[h] person who has not been given the honor of royalty.[i] He will invade the kingdom when its people feel secure, and he will seize it through intrigue. 22Then an overwhelming army will be swept away before him; both it and a prince of the covenant will be destroyed.[j] 23After coming to an agreement with him, he will act deceitfully,[k] and with only a few people he will rise to power. 24When the richest provinces feel secure, he will invade them and will achieve what neither his fathers nor his forefathers did. He will distribute plunder, loot and wealth among his followers.[l] He will plot the overthrow of fortresses—but only for a time.

25"With a large army he will stir up his strength and courage against the king of the South. The king of the South will wage war with a large and very powerful army, but he will not be able to stand because of the plots devised against him. 26Those who eat from the king's provisions will try to destroy him; his army will be swept away, and many will fall in battle. 27The two kings, with their hearts bent on evil,[m] will sit at the same table and lie[n] to each other, but to no avail, because an end will still come at the appointed time.[o] 28The king of the North will return to his own country with great wealth, but his heart will be set against the holy

11:7 [s]ver 6
11:8 [t]Isa 37:19; 46:1-2 [u]Jer 43:12
11:10 [v]Isa 8:8; Jer 46:8; Da 9:26
11:11 [w]Da 8:7-8
11:15 [x]Eze 4:2
11:16 [y]Da 8:4 [z]Jos 1:5; Da 8:7
11:16 [a]Da 8:9
11:17 [b]Ps 20:4
11:18 [c]Isa 66:19; Jer 25:22 [d]Hos 12:14
11:19 [e]Ps 27:2 [f]Ps 37:36; Eze 26:21
11:20 [g]Isa 60:17
11:21 [h]Da 4:17 [i]Da 8:25
11:22 [j]Da 8:10-11
11:23 [k]Da 8:25
11:24 [l]Ne 9:25
11:27 [m]Ps 64:6 [n]Ps 12:2; Jer 9:5 [o]Hab 2:3

[a]6 Or *offspring* [b]6 Or *child* (see Vulgate and Syriac) [c]17 Or *but she*

covenant. He will take action against it
and then return to his own country.
29"At the appointed time he will invade the South again, but this time the
outcome will be different from what
it was before. 30Ships of the western
coastlands[a][p] will oppose him, and he
will lose heart. Then he will turn back
and vent his fury against the holy covenant. He will return and show favor to
those who forsake the holy covenant.
31"His armed forces will rise up to
desecrate the temple fortress and will
abolish the daily sacrifice. Then they
will set up the abomination that causes
desolation.[q] 32With flattery he will corrupt those who have violated the covenant, but the people who know their
God will firmly resist[r] him.
33"Those who are wise will instruct[s]
many, though for a time they will fall by
the sword or be burned or captured or
plundered.[t] 34When they fall, they will
receive a little help, and many who are
not sincere[u] will join them. 35Some of
the wise will stumble, so that they may
be refined,[v] purified and made spotless
until the time of the end, for it will still
come at the appointed time.

11:30 [p]Ge 10:4
11:31 [q]Da 8:11-13; 9:27; Mt 24:15*; Mk 13:14*
11:32 [r]Mic 5:7-9
11:33 [s]Mal 2:7 [t]Mt 24:9; Jn 16:2; Heb 11:32-38
11:34 [u]Mt 7:15; Ro 16:18
11:35 [v]Ps 78:38; Da 12:10; Zec 13:9; Jn 15:2

The King Who Exalts Himself

36"The king will do as he pleases. He
will exalt and magnify himself above
every god and will say unheard-of
things[w] against the God of gods.[x] He
will be successful until the time of
wrath[y] is completed, for what has been
determined must take place. 37He will
show no regard for the gods of his fathers or for the one desired by women,
nor will he regard any god, but will exalt himself above them all. 38Instead of
them, he will honor a god of fortresses;
a god unknown to his fathers he will
honor with gold and silver, with precious stones and costly gifts. 39He will
attack the mightiest fortresses with the
help of a foreign god and will greatly
honor those who acknowledge him. He
will make them rulers over many people and will distribute the land at a
price.[b]
40"At the time of the end the king
of the South[z] will engage him in battle,
and the king of the North will storm[a]
out against him with chariots and cavalry and a great fleet of ships. He will invade many countries and sweep through
them like a flood.[b] 41He will also invade the Beautiful Land. Many countries will fall, but Edom,[c] Moab[d] and
the leaders of Ammon will be delivered from his hand. 42He will extend
his power over many countries; Egypt
will not escape. 43He will gain control
of the treasures of gold and silver and
all the riches of Egypt,[e] with the Libyans[f] and Nubians in submission. 44But
reports from the east and the north will
alarm him, and he will set out in a great
rage to destroy and annihilate many.
45He will pitch his royal tents between
the seas at[c] the beautiful holy mountain. Yet he will come to his end, and
no one will help him.

11:36 [w]Rev 13:5-6 [x]Dt 10:17; Isa 14:13-14; Da 7:25; 8:11-12,25; 2Th 2:4 [y]Isa 10:25; 26:20
11:40 [z]Isa 21:1 [a]Isa 5:28 [b]Eze 38:4
11:41 [c]Isa 11:14 [d]Jer 48:47
11:43 [e]Eze 30:4 [f]2Ch 12:3; Na 3:9

PATIENCE

THE WINDING DOWN OF TIME

Daniel 11:40

The end is on its way. Time is winding down. God holds the key that winds the universal clock. He is shaking his head from side to side. He will not wind the clock again.

The End Times

12 "At that time Michael,[g] the great
prince who protects your peo-
ple, will arise. There will be a time of
distress[h] such as has not happened from
the beginning of nations until then.
But at that time your people—everyone whose name is found written in
the book[i]—will be delivered.[j] 2Multi-
tudes who sleep in the dust of the earth
will awake: some to everlasting life, others to shame and everlasting contempt.[k]
3Those who are wise[d][l] will shine[m] like
the brightness of the heavens, and those
who lead many to righteousness, like
the stars for ever and ever.[n] 4But you,
Daniel, close up and seal[o] the words of
the scroll until the time of the end.[p]
Many will go here and there to increase
knowledge."

5Then I, Daniel, looked, and there
before me stood two others, one on this
bank of the river and one on the opposite bank.[q] 6One of them said to the
man clothed in linen,[r] who was above
the waters of the river, "How long will

12:1 [g]Da 10:13 [h]Da 9:12; Mt 24:21; Mk 13:19; Rev 16:18 [i]Ex 32:32; Ps 56:8 [j]Jer 30:7
12:2 [k]Isa 26:19; Mt 25:46; Jn 5:28-29
12:3 [l]Da 11:33 [m]Mt 13:43; Jn 5:35 [n]1Co 15:42
12:4 [o]Isa 8:16 [p]ver 9,13; Rev 22:10
12:5 [q]Da 10:4
12:6 [r]Eze 9:2

[a]30 Hebrew *of Kittim* [b]39 Or *land for a reward*
[c]45 Or *the sea and* [d]3 Or *who impart wisdom*

it be before these astonishing things are
fulfilled?"[s]
7The man clothed in linen, who was
above the waters of the river, lifted his
right hand and his left hand toward
heaven, and I heard him swear by him
who lives forever,[t] saying, "It will be for
a time, times and half a time.[a][u] When
the power of the holy people[v] has been
finally broken, all these things will be
completed.[w]"
8I heard, but I did not understand.
So I asked, "My lord, what will the outcome of all this be?"
9He replied, "Go your way, Daniel,
because the words are closed up and
sealed until the time of the end.[x] 10Many
will be purified, made spotless and refined,[y] but the wicked will continue to
be wicked.[z] None of the wicked will
understand, but those who are wise will
understand.[a]
11"From the time that the daily sacrifice is abolished and the abomination
that causes desolation[b] is set up, there
will be 1,290 days. 12Blessed is the one
who waits[c] for and reaches the end of
the 1,335 days.[d]
13"As for you, go your way till the
end. You will rest,[e] and then at the end
of the days you will rise to receive your
allotted inheritance.[f]"

[a]7 Or *a year, two years and half a year*

12:6 [s]Da 8:13
12:7 [t]Rev 10:5-6 [u]Da 7:25 [v]Da 8:24 [w]Lk 21:24; Rev 10:7
12:9 [x]ver 4
12:10 [y]Da 11:35 [z]Isa 32:7; Rev 22:11 [a]Hos 14:9
12:11 [b]Da 8:11; 9:27; Mt 24:15*; Mk 13:14*
12:12 [c]Isa 30:18 [d]Da 8:14
12:13 [e]Isa 57:2 [f]Ps 16:5; Rev 14:13

HOSEA

AUTHORSHIP AND DATE

Hosea

c. 715 B.C.

KEY THEMES

Hosea's preaching was addressed to the nation's need for repentance and its need to return to God's love. The book is divided into two unequal parts. The first three chapters address the immorality of Hosea's wife and her need for forgiveness. The remainder of the book reveals Israel's immorality and impending judgment. In this book, God's forgiveness of Israel's idolatry is likened to Hosea's forgiveness of his unfaithful wife. Hosea had been faithful to his wife as God had been faithful to Israel. But both trusts had been violated. And, while God would always love Israel, unfortunately judgment was on the way.

FRUIT OF THE SPIRIT IN HOSEA

Love: There are at least six aspects of love pictured in Hosea:

The book opens with a strong statement of family love. The prophet married Gomer, and they had three children (see 1:2–9). This family became the center of Hosea's earthly love and a metaphor of God's love affair with Israel.

God's love for Israel is demonstrated as he turned prophecies represented by the names of Hosea's children *(Jezreel* means "God scatters," *Lo-Ruhamah* means "not loved," and *Lo-Ammi* means "not my people"*)* into blessings. God would have mercy on the nation of Israel, and they would again be his people (see 2:23).

Hosea's love for his wife, rather than his more general love for his family, is the central story, and that love was at the heart of the prophet's woes and needs. His wife was unfaithful, and Hosea lost track of her for a period of time. But Hosea found her and bought her back, for she had evidently become a slave (see 3:1–3).

The fourth aspect of love pictured in the book is God's healing love. God never tired of the dream that the people would turn from their idolatry and return to his love.

"Come, let us return to the LORD. He has torn us to pieces but he will heal us; he has injured us but he will bind up our wounds" (6:1).

The fifth aspect of love pictured in Hosea is God's love for the child Israel. God never stopped regarding Israel as his child. The same is true of all parents: Their children always remain, even when grown up, their children. So God laments, "When Israel was a child, I loved him, and out of Egypt I called my son" (11:1).

The final aspect of God's love pictured in Hosea is triumphant love. At the end of all things is hope. After judgment comes restoration. Thus God cried out through the prophet, "Return, O Israel, to the LORD your God" (14:1).

1

The word of the LORD that came
to Hosea son of Beeri during the
reigns of Uzziah, Jotham, Ahaz and
1:1 [a]Isa 1:1; Mic 1:1 [b]2Ki 13:13 [c]Am 1:1
Hezekiah, kings of Judah,[a] and during
the reign of Jeroboam[b] son of Jehoash[a]
king of Israel:[c]

Hosea's Wife and Children

[2]When the LORD began to speak
1:2 [d]Jer 3:1; Hos 2:2,5; 3:1 [e]Dt 31:16; Jer 3:14; Eze 23:3-21; Hos 5:3
through Hosea, the LORD said to him,
"Go, take to yourself an adulterous[d]
wife and children of unfaithfulness, because the land is guilty of the vilest
adultery[e] in departing from the LORD."
[3]So he married Gomer daughter of Dib-
laim, and she conceived and bore him
a son.

LOVE

LOVE GOD FIRST, THEN LESSER THINGS

Hosea 1:2

Hosea loved a woman unworthy of his love, and he made his crumbling home life a metaphor of grace. To despise love must be the chief of sins. Those who spend their love in lesser ways will never love Christ.

1:4 [f]2Ki 10:1-14; Hos 2:22
[4]Then the LORD said to Hosea, "Call
him Jezreel,[f] because I will soon punish the house of Jehu for the massacre
at Jezreel, and I will put an end to
the kingdom of Israel. [5]In that day I
will break Israel's bow in the Valley of
1:5 [g]2Ki 15:29
Jezreel."[g]
[6]Gomer[h] conceived again and gave
1:6 [h]ver 3 [i]Hos 2:4
birth to a daughter. Then the LORD
said to Hosea, "Call her Lo-Ruhamah,[b]
for I will no longer show love to the
house of Israel,[i] that I should at all forgive them. [7]Yet I will show love to the
house of Judah; and I will save them—
1:7 [j]Ps 44:6 [k]Zec 4:6
not by bow,[j] sword or battle, or by
horses and horsemen, but by the LORD
their God."[k]
[8]After she had weaned Lo-Ruhamah,
Gomer had another son. [9]Then the
LORD said, "Call him Lo-Ammi,[c] for
you are not my people, and I am not
your God.
[10]"Yet the Israelites will be like the
sand on the seashore, which cannot
1:10 [l]Ge 22:17; Jer 33:22 [m]ver 9; Ro 9:26*
be measured or counted.[l] In the place
where it was said to them, 'You are not
my people,' they will be called 'sons
of the living God.'[m] [11]The people of
1:11 [n]Isa 11:12,13 [o]Jer 23:5-8 [p]Eze 37:15-28
Judah and the people of Israel will be
reunited,[n] and they will appoint one
leader[o] and will come up out of the
land,[p] for great will be the day of Jezreel.

2

2:1 [q]ver 23
"Say of your brothers, 'My people,' and of your sisters, 'My loved
one.'[q]

Israel Punished and Restored

2:2 [r]ver 5; Isa 50:1; Hos 1:2 [s]Eze 23:45
[2]"Rebuke your mother,[r] rebuke her,
for she is not my wife,
and I am not her husband.
Let her remove the adulterous[s] look
from her face
and the unfaithfulness from
between her breasts.
[3]Otherwise I will strip her naked
and make her as bare as on the
day she was born;[t]
2:3 [t]Eze 16:4,22 [u]Isa 32:13-14
I will make her like a desert,[u]
turn her into a parched land,
and slay her with thirst.
[4]I will not show my love to her
2:4 [v]Eze 8:18
children,[v]
because they are the children of
adultery.
[5]Their mother has been unfaithful
and has conceived them in
disgrace.
2:5 [w]Jer 3:6 [x]Jer 44:17-18
She said, 'I will go after my lovers,[w]
who give me my food and my
water,
my wool and my linen, my oil and
my drink.'[x]
[6]Therefore I will block her path with
thornbushes;
I will wall her in so that she
2:6 [y]Job 3:23; 19:8; La 3:9
cannot find her way.[y]
[7]She will chase after her lovers but
not catch them;
she will look for them but not
2:7 [z]Hos 5:13 [a]Jer 2:2; 3:1 [b]Eze 16:8
find them.[z]
Then she will say,
'I will go back to my husband as
at first,[a]
for then I was better off[b] than
now.'
2:8 [c]Isa 1:3 [d]Eze 16:15-19; Hos 8:4
[8]She has not acknowledged[c] that I
was the one
who gave her the grain, the new
wine and oil,
who lavished on her the silver and
gold—
which they used for Baal.[d]

[a]*1* Hebrew *Joash*, a variant of *Jehoash*
[b]*6 Lo-Ruhamah* means *not loved.* [c]*9 Lo-Ammi* means *not my people.*

2:9 [e]Hos 8:7 [f]Hos 9:2

9 "Therefore I will take away my
grain[e] when it ripens,
and my new wine[f] when it is
ready.
I will take back my wool and my
linen,
intended to cover her nakedness.
10 So now I will expose her lewdness
before the eyes of her lovers;
no one will take her out of my
hands.[g]

2:10 [g]Eze 16:37

11 I will stop[h] all her celebrations:
her yearly festivals, her New
Moons,
her Sabbath days—all her
appointed feasts.[i]

2:11 [h]Jer 7:34 [i]Isa 1:14; Jer 16:9; Hos 3:4; Am 8:10

12 I will ruin her vines[j] and her fig
trees,
which she said were her pay from
her lovers;
I will make them a thicket,[k]
and wild animals will devour
them.[l]

2:12 [j]Isa 7:23; Jer 8:13 [k]Isa 5:6 [l]Hos 13:8

13 I will punish her for the days
she burned incense to the Baals;[m]
she decked herself with rings and
jewelry,[n]
and went after her lovers,[o]
but me she forgot,"[p]
declares the LORD.

2:13 [m]Hos 11:2 [n]Eze 16:17 [o]Hos 4:13 [p]Hos 4:6; 8:14; 13:6

14 "Therefore I am now going to allure
her;
I will lead her into the desert
and speak tenderly to her.
15 There I will give her back her
vineyards,
and will make the Valley of
Achor[a][q] a door of hope.
There she will sing[b][r] as in the days
of her youth,[s]
as in the day she came up out of
Egypt.[t]

2:15 [q]Jos 7:24,26 [r]Ex 15:1-18 [s]Jer 2:2 [t]Hos 12:9

16 "In that day," declares the LORD,
"you will call me 'my husband';
you will no longer call me 'my
master.[c]
17 I will remove the names of the Baals
from her lips;[u]
no longer will their names be
invoked.[v]

2:17 [u]Ex 23:13; Ps 16:4 [v]Jos 23:7

18 In that day I will make a covenant
for them
with the beasts of the field and the
birds of the air
and the creatures that move along
the ground.[w]
Bow and sword and battle

2:18 [w]Job 5:22

I will abolish[x] from the land,
so that all may lie down in safety.[y]
19 I will betroth you to me forever;
I will betroth[z] you in[d]
righteousness and justice,[a]
in[e] love and compassion.
20 I will betroth you in faithfulness,
and you will acknowledge[b] the
LORD.

2:18 [x]Isa 2:4 [y]Jer 23:6; Eze 34:25
2:19 [z]Isa 62:4 [a]Isa 1:27
2:20 [b]Jer 31:34; Hos 6:6; 13:4

21 "In that day I will respond,"
declares the LORD—
"I will respond[c] to the skies,
and they will respond to the earth;
22 and the earth will respond to the
grain,
the new wine and oil,[d]
and they will respond to Jezreel.[f]
23 I will plant[e] her for myself in the
land;
I will show my love to the one I
called 'Not my loved one.[g][f]'
I will say to those called 'Not
my people,[h]' 'You are my
people';[g]
and they will say, 'You are my
God.[h]'"

2:21 [c]Isa 55:10; Zec 8:12
2:22 [d]Jer 31:12; Joel 2:19
2:23 [e]Jer 31:27 [f]Hos 1:6 [g]Hos 1:10 [h]Ro 9:25*; 1Pe 2:10

Hosea's Reconciliation With His Wife

3 The LORD said to me, "Go, show
your love to your wife again, though
she is loved by another and is an
adulteress.[i] Love her as the LORD loves
the Israelites, though they turn to other
gods and love the sacred raisin cakes.[j]"

3:1 [i]Hos 1:2 [j]2Sa 6:19

KINDNESS

EITHER BE KIND OR BE UNLIKE GOD

Hosea 3:1

We must love things unworthy of our love. We must do this or never be like God.

2 So I bought her for fifteen shekels[i] of
silver and about a homer and a lethek[j]
of barley. 3 Then I told her, "You are to
live with[k] me many days; you must not
be a prostitute or be intimate with any
man, and I will live with[k] you."

[a] 15 *Achor* means *trouble.* [b] 15 Or *respond*
[c] 16 Hebrew *baal* [d] 19 Or *with*; also in verse 20
[e] 19 Or *with* [f] 22 *Jezreel* means *God plants.*
[g] 23 Hebrew *Lo-Ruhamah* [h] 23 Hebrew *Lo-Ammi*
[i] 2 That is, about 6 ounces (about 170 grams)
[j] 2 That is, probably about 10 bushels (about 330 liters) [k] 3 Or *wait for*

WEEK 19

LOVE

1 DAY ONE

LOVE, THE DEFINITION OF GOD

Read Hosea 3:1–3

The very definition of God is love. If 1 John 4:7–8 states this definition, Hosea 3:1–3 demonstrates it. The prophet Hosea is commanded by God to buy his wife, Gomer, back from a slavery auction block. Gomer has been unfaithful to him, having lived as a prostitute. But Hosea's love for his unfaithful wife is a sign of God's love for the unfaithful nation of Israel.

The parallels between adultery and idolatry cannot be denied. Just as Gomer has been unfaithful in marriage, so has Israel been unfaithful in its covenant relationship with God. As Gomer has given herself to other lovers, so Israel has pursued idols, having abandoned the loving God.

But neither Gomer nor Israel feels chastisement from their true loves. In spite of her infidelity, Gomer is yet loved by her husband. Israel, in spite of its idolatries with foreign gods, is yet pursued by the unforsaking love of God.

Through this account of forgiveness and love between a husband and wife, we see that God is in love with his people, and his love is totally undeserved. His love has nothing to do with good things we have done, nor the time we have given him in prayer and adoration. God is God! God is love! Jesus saves . . . period!

How does all of this love story from the past apply to us today?

Grace was how God received us, giving us the forgiveness we never deserved and eternal life we could never have earned by our own moral struggle. We are accepted, not because we deserve God's love, but merely because it is God's nature to love. This is ours—this grace—this life—is ours while the ages steal.

MEMORIZE THIS WEEK

1 JOHN 4:7-8

Dear friends, let us love one another, for love comes from God. Everyone who loves has been born of God and knows God. Whoever does not love does not know God, because God is love.

2 DAY TWO

LOVE AND THE PURPOSE OF GOD IN MY LIFE

Clay is a medium of an artist. In this case, the artist is God, and he looks down on the clay of our lives with longing. He desires to give us a form that causes all who see us to think of his Son. With such a noble dream for us, dare we as clay defy the Potter and spoil his dream for our lives? *Turn to Isaiah 29:16, page 822, for today's study.*

3 DAY THREE

LOVE AND MY RELATIONSHIP WITH CHRIST

It seems at times that God is silent. At such times we stare into the gales of those storms that threaten us and beg the God of storms to cry, "Quiet! Be still!" But in spite of our desparate cries, the quiet does not come. The thunder rolls. The earth quakes beneath us. However, we must not suppose at such a moment that God laughs as our tears flow. It is not so. *Turn to Psalm 22:1–5, page 643, for today's study.*

4 DAY FOUR

LOVE AND MY SERVICE TO OTHERS

How beautiful are those who publish love in a world of hate. How lovely those who offer hope in a world of cynics. How graceful are the feet of those who travel to the ghettos of human despair and cry, "Rejoice! He lives!" This is the preaching that matters. *Turn to Isaiah 52:7, page 852, for today's study.*

5 DAY FIVE

LOVE AND ITS PLACE IN MY PERSONAL WORSHIP

In this passage, Moses is an old man. The Bible says he was 120 years old and in full health and strength. What do old men who have spent 120 years measuring the faithfulness of God do? They sing! Do not argue that these aged, faithful watchers of grace can't sing. They sing incontrovertible melodies, and the world is hushed by their praise. *Turn to Deuteronomy 32:1–4,9–12, page 236, for today's study.*

Week 20, Joy, the Infallible Proof of the Presence of God, begins on page 1086, Habakkuk 3:17–18. To begin a topical study on the Fruit of the Spirit, Love, turn to the Topical Index, page 1548.

4For the Israelites will live many days
without king or prince,[k] without sacrifice[l] or sacred stones, without ephod
or idol.[m] 5Afterward the Israelites will
return and seek the LORD their God
and David their king.[n] They will come
trembling to the LORD and to his blessings in the last days.[o]

3:4 [k]Hos 13:11 [l]Da 11:31; Hos 2:11 [m]Jdg 17:5-6; Zec 10:2
3:5 [n]Eze 34:23-24 [o]Jer 50:4-5

The Charge Against Israel

4 Hear the word of the LORD, you
Israelites,
because the LORD has a charge to
bring
against you who live in the land:
"There is no faithfulness, no love,
no acknowledgment[p] of God in
the land.
2There is only cursing,[a] lying[q] and
murder,[r]
stealing[s] and adultery;
they break all bounds,
and bloodshed follows
bloodshed.
3Because of this the land mourns,[b][t]
and all who live in it waste away;[u]
the beasts of the field and the birds
of the air
and the fish of the sea are dying.[v]

4"But let no man bring a charge,
let no man accuse another,
for your people are like those
who bring charges against a
priest.[w]
5You stumble day and night,
and the prophets stumble[x] with
you.
So I will destroy your mother[y]—
6 my people are destroyed from lack
of knowledge.[z]

"Because you have rejected
knowledge,
I also reject you as my priests;
because you have ignored the law[a] of
your God,
I also will ignore your children.
7The more the priests increased,
the more they sinned against me;
they exchanged[c] their[d] Glory[b] for
something disgraceful.[c]
8They feed on the sins of my people
and relish their wickedness.[d]
9And it will be: Like people, like
priests.[e]
I will punish both of them for
their ways
and repay them for their deeds.[f]

4:1 [p]Jer 7:28
4:2 [q]Hos 7:3; 10:4 [r]Hos 6:9 [s]Hos 7:1
4:3 [t]Jer 4:28 [u]Isa 33:9 [v]Jer 4:25; Zep 1:3
4:4 [w]Dt 17:12; Eze 3:26
4:5 [x]Eze 14:7 [y]Hos 2:2
4:6 [z]Hos 2:13; Mal 2:7-8 [a]Hos 8:1,12
4:7 [b]Hab 2:16 [c]Hos 10:1,6; 13:6
4:8 [d]Isa 56:11; Mic 3:11
4:9 [e]Isa 24:2 [f]Jer 5:31; Hos 8:13; 9:9,15

10"They will eat but not have enough;[g]
they will engage in prostitution
but not increase,
because they have deserted[h] the
LORD
to give themselves 11to
prostitution,[i]
to old wine and new,
which take away the
understanding[j] 12of my
people.
They consult a wooden idol[k]
and are answered by a stick of
wood.[l]
A spirit of prostitution leads them
astray;[m]
they are unfaithful to their God.
13They sacrifice on the mountaintops
and burn offerings on the hills,
under oak,[n] poplar and terebinth,
where the shade is pleasant.[o]
Therefore your daughters turn to
prostitution[p]
and your daughters-in-law to
adultery.[q]

14"I will not punish your daughters
when they turn to prostitution,
nor your daughters-in-law
when they commit adultery,
because the men themselves consort
with harlots[r]
and sacrifice with shrine
prostitutes—
a people without understanding
will come to ruin!

15"Though you commit adultery,
O Israel,
let not Judah become guilty.

"Do not go to Gilgal;[s]
do not go up to Beth Aven.[e]
And do not swear, 'As surely as the
LORD lives!'
16The Israelites are stubborn,
like a stubborn heifer.
How then can the LORD pasture
them
like lambs[t] in a meadow?
17Ephraim is joined to idols;
leave him alone!
18Even when their drinks are gone,

4:10 [g]Lev 26:26; Mic 6:14 [h]Hos 7:14; 9:17
4:11 [i]Hos 5:4 [j]Pr 20:1
4:12 [k]Jer 2:27 [l]Hab 2:19 [m]Isa 44:20
4:13 [n]Isa 1:29 [o]Jer 3:6; Hos 11:2 [p]Jer 2:20; Am 7:17 [q]Hos 2:13
4:14 [r]ver 11
4:15 [s]Hos 9:15; 12:11; Am 4:4
4:16 [t]Isa 5:17; 7:25

[a]*2* That is, to pronounce a curse upon [b]*3* Or *dries up* [c]*7* Syriac and an ancient Hebrew scribal tradition; Masoretic Text *I will exchange* [d]*7* Masoretic Text; an ancient Hebrew scribal tradition *my* [e]*15 Beth Aven* means *house of wickedness* (a name for Bethel, which means *house of God*).

they continue their prostitution;
their rulers dearly love shameful ways.
19 A whirlwind[u] will sweep them away,
and their sacrifices will bring them shame.[v]

Judgment Against Israel

5 "Hear this, you priests!
Pay attention, you Israelites!
Listen, O royal house!
This judgment is against you:
You have been a snare[w] at Mizpah,
a net spread out on Tabor.
2 The rebels are deep in slaughter.[x]
I will discipline all of them.[y]
3 I know all about Ephraim;
Israel is not hidden from me.
Ephraim, you have now turned to prostitution;
Israel is corrupt.[z]
4 "Their deeds do not permit them
to return to their God.
A spirit of prostitution[a] is in their heart;
they do not acknowledge[b] the LORD.
5 Israel's arrogance testifies[c] against them;
the Israelites, even Ephraim,
stumble in their sin;
Judah also stumbles with them.
6 When they go with their flocks and herds
to seek the LORD,[d]
they will not find him;
he has withdrawn[e] himself from them.
7 They are unfaithful[f] to the LORD;
they give birth to illegitimate[g] children.
Now their New Moon festivals
will devour[h] them and their fields.
8 "Sound the trumpet in Gibeah,[i]
the horn in Ramah.[j]
Raise the battle cry in Beth Aven[a];[k]
lead on, O Benjamin.
9 Ephraim will be laid waste
on the day of reckoning.[l]
Among the tribes of Israel
I proclaim what is certain.[m]
10 Judah's leaders are like those
who move boundary stones.[n]
I will pour out my wrath[o] on them
like a flood of water.
11 Ephraim is oppressed,
trampled in judgment,
intent on pursuing idols.[b][p]
12 I am like a moth[q] to Ephraim,
like rot to the people of Judah.
13 "When Ephraim saw his sickness,
and Judah his sores,
then Ephraim turned to Assyria,[r]
and sent to the great king for help.[s]
But he is not able to cure[t] you,
not able to heal your sores.[u]
14 For I will be like a lion[v] to Ephraim,
like a great lion to Judah.
I will tear them to pieces and go away;
I will carry them off, with no one to rescue them.[w]
15 Then I will go back to my place
until they admit their guilt.
And they will seek my face;[x]
in their misery[y] they will earnestly seek me.[z]"

Israel Unrepentant

6 "Come, let us return to the LORD.
He has torn us to pieces[a]
but he will heal us;
he has injured us
but he will bind up our wounds.[b]

PATIENCE

HEALED BY DEGREES

Hosea 6:1

God is a plastic surgeon of the spirit. He repairs all damaged souls with such beautifully crafted sutures that they leave no scars. Have patience, you hurting souls, for the cure for your deepest pain will come slowly. Shakespeare said, "What wound did ever heal but by degrees?"

2 After two days he will revive us;[c]
on the third day he will restore us,
that we may live in his presence.
3 Let us acknowledge the LORD;
let us press on to acknowledge him.
As surely as the sun rises,
he will appear;
he will come to us like the winter rains,[d]
like the spring rains that water the earth."[e]

[a]8 *Beth Aven* means *house of wickedness* (a name for Bethel, which means *house of God*). [b]11 The meaning of the Hebrew for this word is uncertain.

4:19 [u]Hos 12:1; 13:15 [v]Isa 1:29
5:1 [w]Hos 6:9; 9:8
5:2 [x]Hos 4:2 [y]Hos 9:15
5:3 [z]Hos 6:10
5:4 [a]Hos 4:11 [b]Hos 4:6
5:5 [c]Hos 7:10
5:6 [d]Mic 6:6-7 [e]Pr 1:28; Isa 1:15; Eze 8:6
5:7 [f]Hos 6:7 [g]Hos 2:4 [h]Hos 2:11-12
5:8 [i]Hos 9:9; 10:9 [j]Isa 10:29 [k]Hos 4:15
5:9 [l]Isa 37:3; Hos 9:11-17 [m]Isa 46:10; Zec 1:6
5:10 [n]Dt 19:14 [o]Eze 7:8
5:11 [p]Hos 9:16; Mic 6:16
5:12 [q]Isa 51:8
5:13 [r]Hos 7:11; 8:9 [s]Hos 10:6 [t]Hos 14:3 [u]Jer 30:12
5:14 [v]Am 3:4 [w]Mic 5:8
5:15 [x]Hos 3:5 [y]Jer 2:27 [z]Isa 64:9
6:1 [a]Hos 5:14 [b]Dt 32:39; Jer 30:17; Hos 14:4
6:2 [c]Ps 30:5
6:3 [d]Joel 2:23 [e]Ps 72:6

4 “What can I do with you, Ephraim?[f]
What can I do with you, Judah?
Your love is like the morning mist,
like the early dew that disappears.[g]
5 Therefore I cut you in pieces with
my prophets,
I killed you with the words of my
mouth;[h]
my judgments flashed like
lightning upon you.[i]
6 For I desire mercy, not sacrifice,[j]
and acknowledgment[k] of God
rather than burnt offerings.
7 Like Adam,[a] they have broken the
covenant[l]—
they were unfaithful[m] to me there.
8 Gilead is a city of wicked men,
stained with footprints of blood.
9 As marauders lie in ambush for a
man,
so do bands of priests;
they murder on the road to
Shechem,
committing shameful crimes.[n]
10 I have seen a horrible[o] thing
in the house of Israel.
There Ephraim is given to
prostitution
and Israel is defiled.[p]

11 “Also for you, Judah,
a harvest[q] is appointed.

“Whenever I would restore the
fortunes of my people,
7 1 whenever I would heal Israel,
the sins of Ephraim are exposed
and the crimes of Samaria
revealed.[r]
They practice deceit,[s]
thieves break into houses,[t]
bandits rob in the streets;
2 but they do not realize
that I remember[u] all their evil
deeds.
Their sins engulf them;[v]
they are always before me.

3 “They delight the king with their
wickedness,
the princes with their lies.[w]
4 They are all adulterers,[x]
burning like an oven
whose fire the baker need not stir
from the kneading of the dough
till it rises.
5 On the day of the festival of our king
the princes become inflamed with
wine,[y]
and he joins hands with the
mockers.
6 Their hearts are like an oven;[z]
they approach him with intrigue.
Their passion smolders all night;
in the morning it blazes like a
flaming fire.
7 All of them are hot as an oven;
they devour their rulers.
All their kings fall,
and none of them calls[a] on me.

8 “Ephraim mixes[b] with the nations;
Ephraim is a flat cake not turned
over.
9 Foreigners sap his strength,[c]
but he does not realize it.
His hair is sprinkled with gray,
but he does not notice.
10 Israel’s arrogance testifies against
him,[d]
but despite all this
he does not return to the LORD his
God
or search[e] for him.

11 “Ephraim is like a dove,[f]
easily deceived and senseless—
now calling to Egypt,
now turning to Assyria.[g]
12 When they go, I will throw my net[h]
over them;
I will pull them down like birds of
the air.
When I hear them flocking together,
I will catch them.
13 Woe[i] to them,
because they have strayed[j] from
me!
Destruction to them,
because they have rebelled against
me!
I long to redeem them
but they speak lies against me.[k]
14 They do not cry out to me from
their hearts[l]
but wail upon their beds.
They gather together[b] for grain and
new wine[m]
but turn away from me.[n]
15 I trained them and strengthened
them,
but they plot evil[o] against me.
16 They do not turn to the Most High;
they are like a faulty bow.[p]

[a]7 Or *As at Adam*; or *Like men* [b]14 Most Hebrew manuscripts; some Hebrew manuscripts and Septuagint *They slash themselves*

6:4 [f]Hos 11:8 [g]Hos 7:1; 13:3
6:5 [h]Jer 1:9-10; 23:29 [i]Heb 4:12
6:6 [j]Isa 1:11; Mt 9:13*; 12:7* [k]Hos 2:20
6:7 [l]Hos 8:1 [m]Hos 5:7
6:9 [n]Jer 7:9-10; Eze 22:9; Hos 7:1
6:10 [o]Jer 5:30 [p]Hos 5:3
6:11 [q]Jer 51:33; Joel 3:13
7:1 [r]Hos 6:4 [s]ver 13 [t]Hos 4:2
7:2 [u]Jer 14:10; Hos 8:13 [v]Jer 2:19
7:3 [w]Hos 4:2; Mic 7:3
7:4 [x]Jer 9:2
7:5 [y]Isa 28:1,7
7:6 [z]Ps 21:9
7:7 [a]ver 16
7:8 [b]ver 11; Ps 106:35; Hos 5:13
7:9 [c]Isa 1:7; Hos 8:7
7:10 [d]Hos 5:5 [e]Isa 9:13
7:11 [f]Hos 11:11 [g]Hos 5:13; 12:1
7:12 [h]Eze 12:13
7:13 [i]Hos 9:12 [j]Jer 14:10; Eze 34:4-6; Hos 9:17 [k]ver 1; Mt 23:37
7:14 [l]Jer 3:10 [m]Am 2:8 [n]Hos 13:16
7:15 [o]Na 1:9,11
7:16 [p]Ps 78:9,57

Their leaders will fall by the sword
because of their insolent words.
For this they will be ridiculed[q]
in the land of Egypt.[r]

Israel to Reap the Whirlwind

8 "Put the trumpet to your lips!
An eagle[s] is over the house of the LORD
because the people have broken my covenant
and rebelled against my law.[t]
2 Israel cries out to me,
'O our God, we acknowledge you!'
3 But Israel has rejected what is good;
an enemy will pursue him.
4 They set up kings without my consent;
they choose princes without my approval.[u]
With their silver and gold
they make idols[v] for themselves
to their own destruction.
5 Throw out your calf-idol,
O Samaria![w]
My anger burns against them.
How long will they be incapable of purity?[x]
6 They are from Israel!
This calf—a craftsman has made it;
it is not God.
It will be broken in pieces,
that calf of Samaria.
7 "They sow the wind
and reap the whirlwind.[y]
The stalk has no head;
it will produce no flour.
Were it to yield grain,
foreigners would swallow it up.[z]
8 Israel is swallowed up;[a]
now she is among the nations
like a worthless[b] thing.
9 For they have gone up to Assyria
like a wild donkey wandering alone.
Ephraim has sold herself to lovers.
10 Although they have sold themselves
among the nations,
I will now gather them together.[c]
They will begin to waste away[d]
under the oppression of the mighty king.
11 "Though Ephraim built many altars
for sin offerings,
these have become altars for sinning.[e]

7:16 [q]Eze 23:32 [r]Hos 9:3
8:1 [s]Dt 28:49; Jer 4:13 [t]Hos 4:6; 6:7
8:4 [u]Hos 13:10 [v]Hos 2:8
8:5 [w]Hos 10:5 [x]Jer 13:27
8:7 [y]Pr 22:8; Isa 66:15; Hos 10:12-13; Na 1:3 [z]Hos 2:9
8:8 [a]Jer 51:34 [b]Jer 22:28
8:10 [c]Eze 16:37; 22:20 [d]Jer 42:2
8:11 [e]Hos 10:1; 12:11

12 I wrote for them the many things of my law,
but they regarded them as something alien.
13 They offer sacrifices given to me
and they eat[f] the meat,
but the LORD is not pleased with them.
Now he will remember[g] their wickedness
and punish their sins:[h]
They will return to Egypt.[i]
14 Israel has forgotten[j] his Maker
and built palaces;
Judah has fortified many towns.
But I will send fire upon their cities
that will consume their fortresses."[k]

Punishment for Israel

9 Do not rejoice, O Israel;
do not be jubilant[l] like the other nations.
For you have been unfaithful[m] to your God;
you love the wages of a prostitute
at every threshing floor.
2 Threshing floors and winepresses
will not feed the people;
the new wine[n] will fail them.
3 They will not remain[o] in the LORD's land;
Ephraim will return to Egypt[p]
and eat unclean[a] food in Assyria.[q]
4 They will not pour out wine
offerings to the LORD,
nor will their sacrifices please[r] him.
Such sacrifices will be to them like
the bread of mourners;
all who eat them will be unclean.[s]
This food will be for themselves;
it will not come into the temple of the LORD.
5 What will you do[t] on the day of
your appointed feasts,[u]
on the festival days of the LORD?
6 Even if they escape from destruction,
Egypt will gather them,
and Memphis[v] will bury them.
Their treasures of silver will be taken over by briers,
and thorns[w] will overrun their tents.
7 The days of punishment[x] are coming,

[a] 3 That is, ceremonially unclean

8:13 [f]Jer 7:21 [g]Hos 7:2 [h]Hos 4:9 [i]Hos 9:3,6
8:14 [j]Dt 32:18; Hos 2:13 [k]Jer 17:27
9:1 [l]Isa 22:12-13 [m]Hos 10:5
9:2 [n]Hos 2:9
9:3 [o]Lev 25:23 [p]Hos 8:13 [q]Eze 4:13; Hos 7:11
9:4 [r]Jer 6:20; Hos 8:13 [s]Hag 2:13-14
9:5 [t]Isa 10:3; Jer 5:31 [u]Hos 2:11
9:6 [v]Isa 19:13 [w]Isa 5:6; Hos 10:8
9:7 [x]Isa 34:8; Jer 10:15; Mic 7:4

the days of reckoning are at hand.
Let Israel know this.
Because your sins[y] are so many
and your hostility so great,
the prophet is considered a fool,[z]
the inspired man a maniac.
8 The prophet, along with my God,
is the watchman over Ephraim,[a]
yet snares[a] await him on all his
paths,
and hostility in the house of his
God.
9 They have sunk deep into
corruption,
as in the days of Gibeah.[b]
God will remember[c] their
wickedness
and punish them for their sins.

10 "When I found Israel,
it was like finding grapes in the
desert;
when I saw your fathers,
it was like seeing the early fruit on
the fig tree.
But when they came to Baal Peor,[d]
they consecrated themselves to
that shameful idol[e]
and became as vile as the thing
they loved.
11 Ephraim's glory will fly away like a
bird[f]—
no birth, no pregnancy, no
conception.[g]
12 Even if they rear children,
I will bereave them of every one.
Woe[h] to them
when I turn away from them![i]
13 I have seen Ephraim, like Tyre,
planted in a pleasant place.[j]
But Ephraim will bring out
their children to the slayer."

14 Give them, O LORD—
what will you give them?
Give them wombs that miscarry
and breasts that are dry.[k]

15 "Because of all their wickedness in
Gilgal,[l]
I hated them there.
Because of their sinful deeds,[m]
I will drive them out of my house.
I will no longer love them;
all their leaders are rebellious.[n]
16 Ephraim[o] is blighted,
their root is withered,
they yield no fruit.[p]
Even if they bear children,

9:7 [y]Jer 16:18 [z]Isa 44:25; La 2:14; Eze 14:9-10
9:8 [a]Hos 5:1
9:9 [b]Jdg 19:16-30; Hos 5:8; 10:9 [c]Hos 8:13
9:10 [d]Nu 25:1-5; Ps 106:28-29 [e]Jer 11:13; Hos 4:14
9:11 [f]Hos 4:7; 10:5 [g]ver 14
9:12 [h]Hos 7:13 [i]Dt 31:17
9:13 [j]Eze 27:3
9:14 [k]ver 11; Lk 23:29
9:15 [l]Hos 4:15 [m]Hos 7:2 [n]Isa 1:23; Hos 4:9; 5:2
9:16 [o]Hos 5:11 [p]Hos 8:7

I will slay[q] their cherished
offspring."

17 My God will reject them
because they have not obeyed[r]
him;
they will be wanderers among the
nations.[s]

10 Israel was a spreading vine;[t]
he brought forth fruit for
himself.
As his fruit increased,
he built more altars;[u]
as his land prospered,
he adorned his sacred stones.[v]
2 Their heart is deceitful,[w]
and now they must bear their
guilt.[x]
The LORD will demolish their
altars[y]
and destroy their sacred stones.[z]
3 Then they will say, "We have no
king
because we did not revere the
LORD.
But even if we had a king,
what could he do for us?"
4 They make many promises,
take false oaths[a]
and make agreements;[b]
therefore lawsuits spring up
like poisonous weeds in a plowed
field.
5 The people who live in Samaria fear
for the calf-idol of Beth Aven.[b][c]
Its people will mourn over it,
and so will its idolatrous priests,[d]
those who had rejoiced over its
splendor,
because it is taken from them into
exile.[e]
6 It will be carried to Assyria[f]
as tribute for the great king.[g]
Ephraim will be disgraced;[h]
Israel will be ashamed of its
wooden idols.[c]
7 Samaria and its king will float away[i]
like a twig on the surface of the
waters.
8 The high places of wickedness[d][j] will
be destroyed—
it is the sin of Israel.

9:16 [q]ver 12
9:17 [r]Hos 4:10 [s]Dt 28:65; Hos 7:13
10:1 [t]Eze 15:2 [u]1Ki 14:23 [v]Hos 8:11; 12:11
10:2 [w]1Ki 18:21 [x]Hos 13:16 [y]ver 8 [z]Mic 5:13
10:4 [a]Hos 4:2 [b]Eze 17:19; Am 5:7
10:5 [c]Hos 5:8 [d]2Ki 23:5 [e]Hos 8:5; 9:1,3,11
10:6 [f]Hos 11:5 [g]Hos 5:13 [h]Isa 30:3; Hos 4:7
10:7 [i]Hos 13:11
10:8 [j]1Ki 12:28-30; Hos 4:13

[a]8 Or *The prophet is the watchman over Ephraim, / the people of my God* [b]5 *Beth Aven* means *house of wickedness* (a name for Bethel, which means *house of God*). [c]6 Or *its counsel* [d]8 Hebrew *aven,* a reference to Beth Aven (a derogatory name for Bethel)

10:8 [k]Hos 9:6 [l]ver 2; Isa 32:13 [m]Lk 23:30*; Rev 6:16

Thorns[k] and thistles will grow up
and cover their altars.[l]
Then they will say to the mountains,
"Cover us!"
and to the hills, "Fall on us!"[m]

DAY 5 FIVE

LOVE AND ITS PLACE IN MY PERSONAL WORSHIP

Hosea 11:1–9

This magnificent passage extolling love is—as much of the books of prophecy—written in exquisite poetry. Let us examine each of these rich phrases:

"When Israel was a child, I loved him"—Here God likens his giving love to that of a parent in love with a baby. Israel was God's child, and like all little children, Israel could not exist without a parent's loving care.

"It was I who taught Ephraim to walk"—Here is pictured a parent's joy at a baby's first steps. God gave Israel—here called Ephraim—the gift of maturing and protective love.

"I...bent down to feed them"—Here God says that his giving love nurtured Israel in the tender way a mother spoon-feeds or breast-feeds her infant.

In this passage God describes his great love for the people he calls his own. But in spite of God's giving love, Israel became a disobedient, delinquent child. So in verse 8 God laments, "How can I give you up, Ephraim?" God's giving love is a no-quitting love. How can we respond to such a love? We can exalt him in worship.

The beginning of all worship is love. Can those who do not have an intimate relationship with Christ praise him? Can they worship him if they have not experienced his gift of grace? If those who do not know God's love could but for one moment stand at the cross and gaze into the face of Christ, they would know how every value they esteem is trivial compared to what they behold in that one brief, thorn-crowned smile of grace.

What's left for us to do but to exalt him? What's left for us to sing, except "O, come let us adore him"?

To begin a study on the topic of The Evidence of Love Is Giving, turn to the home page on page 5.

9 "Since the days of Gibeah,[n] you have
sinned, O Israel,
and there you have remained.[a]
Did not war overtake
the evildoers in Gibeah?
10 When I please, I will punish[o] them;
nations will be gathered against
them
to put them in bonds for their
double sin.
11 Ephraim is a trained heifer
that loves to thresh;
so I will put a yoke
on her fair neck.
I will drive Ephraim,
Judah must plow,
and Jacob must break up the
ground.
12 Sow for yourselves righteousness,[p]
reap the fruit of unfailing love,
and break up your unplowed
ground;[q]
for it is time to seek[r] the LORD,
until he comes
and showers righteousness[s] on
you.
13 But you have planted wickedness,
you have reaped evil,[t]
you have eaten the fruit of
deception.
Because you have depended on your
own strength
and on your many warriors,[u]
14 the roar of battle will rise against
your people,
so that all your fortresses will be
devastated[v]—
as Shalman devastated Beth Arbel on
the day of battle,
when mothers were dashed to the
ground with their children.[w]
15 Thus will it happen to you,
O Bethel,
because your wickedness is great.
When that day dawns,
the king of Israel will be
completely destroyed.[x]

God's Love for Israel

11 "When Israel was a child, I loved
him,
and out of Egypt I called my son.[y]
2 But the more I[b] called Israel,
the further they went from me.[c]

10:9 [n]Hos 5:8
10:10 [o]Eze 5:13; Hos 4:9
10:12 [p]Pr 11:18 [q]Jer 4:3 [r]Hos 12:6 [s]Isa 45:8
10:13 [t]Job 4:8; Hos 7:3; 11:12; Gal 6:7-8 [u]Ps 33:16
10:14 [v]Isa 17:3 [w]Hos 13:16
10:15 [x]ver 7
11:1 [y]Ex 4:22; Hos 12:9,13; 13:4; Mt 2:15*

[a]9 Or *there a stand was taken* [b]2 Some Septuagint manuscripts; Hebrew *they* [c]2 Septuagint; Hebrew *them*

LOVE

THE HURT THAT HEALS

Hosea 11:1

His love should overflow our hearts. Such love did God spend on the infant Israel, the child he loved in Egypt. Yet when the child became a man, the man despised his childhood and his God.

They sacrificed to the Baals[z]
  and they burned incense to
    images.[a]
3 It was I who taught Ephraim to
    walk,
  taking them by the arms;[b]
but they did not realize
  it was I who healed[c] them.
4 I led them with cords of human
    kindness,
  with ties of love;[d]
I lifted the yoke[e] from their neck
  and bent down to feed[f] them.
5 "Will they not return to Egypt[g]
  and will not Assyria[h] rule over
    them
  because they refuse to repent?
6 Swords[i] will flash in their cities,
  will destroy the bars of their
    gates
  and put an end to their plans.
7 My people are determined to turn
    from me.[j]

11:2 [z]Hos 2:13 [a]2Ki 17:15; Isa 65:7; Jer 18:15
11:3 [b]Dt 1:31; Hos 7:15 [c]Jer 30:17
11:4 [d]Jer 31:2-3 [e]Lev 26:13 [f]Ex 16:32; Ps 78:25
11:5 [g]Hos 7:16 [h]Hos 10:6
11:6 [i]Hos 13:16
11:7 [j]Jer 3:6-7; 8:5

HOSEA

Love, the Unrelenting Pursuit of God (11:1–12)

God has been called the hound of heaven. He pursues us into the grand circle of his love. God said to Hosea, "Go, take to yourself an adulterous wife and children of unfaithfulness, because the land is guilty of the vilest adultery in departing from the LORD" (Hosea 1:2). This command initiated one of the most unusual relationships recorded in the Bible. Hosea married a woman whose adultery was met by his overcoming love for her. He loved Gomer and the children of their marriage, not all of whom may have been his (see v. 2). But his love was not enough to call Gomer back from her adultery. Even after Gomer left Hosea, God commanded him to find her and show her his love yet again.

The book of Hosea focuses on Hosea's undying love for his wife, but the real story is God's love for a faithless nation. God loved Israel to what would seem the very limits of his tolerance. But Israel continually turned away from God in a foolish love affair with idolatry and indulgence. In spite of Israel's unfaithfulness, God was unwilling to give up on his people. With a broken heart, he cried out:

When Israel was a child, I loved him,
** and out of Egypt I called my son.**
But the more I called Israel,
** the further they went from me.**
They sacrificed to the Baals
** and they burned incense to images.**
(11:1–2)

God pursued Israel, but the people were indifferent to his love. Perhaps there is no greater sin against the heart of a father than to spurn the majesty of his love. This rejection by Israel seems all the more tragic when we sense the brokenness that is revealed as God lovingly reached out and Israel continually rebelled: "How can I give you up, Ephraim?" (v. 8). This heart cry reveals a holy God in agony over human indifference to his love.

"How can I give you up?" This is a question born of weeping love. God still weeps each time we insist on having our way and, in the process, leave him in our indifference. Yet nothing will ever stop God's all-pursuing love. God's love is revealed in the near-silent tread of his footfalls when we think we're all alone. We are pursued by the power of God's immense affection. He is in love with us. We feel him all around us—even when the world tells us there's no one there. Ever onward he pursues us, chasing us at last into the very bosom of his divine embrace. We are surrounded by grace, irresistible and eternal. We are ensnared, and the entrapment is our glory.

Even if they call to the Most
High,
he will by no means exalt them.

11:8 [k]Hos 6:4 [l]Ge 14:8

[8]"How can I give you up, Ephraim?[k]
How can I hand you over, Israel?
How can I treat you like Admah?
How can I make you like
Zeboiim?[l]
My heart is changed within me;
all my compassion is aroused.

11:9 [m]Dt 13:17; Jer 30:11 [n]Mal 3:6 [o]Nu 23:19

[9]I will not carry out my fierce anger,[m]
nor will I turn and devastate[n]
Ephraim.
For I am God, and not man[o]—
the Holy One among you.
I will not come in wrath.[a]
[10]They will follow the LORD;
he will roar like a lion.
When he roars,
his children will come trembling
from the west.[p]

11:10 [p]Hos 6:1-3

[11]They will come trembling
like birds from Egypt,
like doves from Assyria.[q]
I will settle them in their homes,"[r]
declares the LORD.

11:11 [q]Isa 11:11 [r]Eze 28:26

Israel's Sin

11:12 [s]Hos 4:2

[12]Ephraim has surrounded me with
lies,[s]
the house of Israel with deceit.
And Judah is unruly against God,
even against the faithful Holy
One.

12:1 [t]Eze 17:10 [u]2Ki 17:4

12 [1]Ephraim feeds on the wind;[t]
he pursues the east wind all day
and multiplies lies and violence.
He makes a treaty with Assyria
and sends olive oil to Egypt.[u]

12:2 [v]Mic 6:2 [w]Hos 4:9

[2]The LORD has a charge[v] to bring
against Judah;
he will punish Jacob[b] according to
his ways
and repay him according to his
deeds.[w]

12:3 [x]Ge 25:26 [y]Ge 32:24-29

[3]In the womb he grasped his brother's
heel;[x]
as a man he struggled[y] with God.
[4]He struggled with the angel and
overcame him;
he wept and begged for his favor.

12:4 [z]Ge 28:12-15; 35:15

He found him at Bethel[z]
and talked with him there—
[5]the LORD God Almighty,

12:5 [a]Ex 3:15

the LORD is his name[a] of
renown!
[6]But you must return to your God;
maintain love and justice,[b]
and wait for your God always.[c]

12:6 [b]Mic 6:8 [c]Hos 6:1-3; 10:12; Mic 7:7

[7]The merchant uses dishonest scales;[d]
he loves to defraud.

12:7 [d]Am 8:5

[8]Ephraim boasts,
"I am very rich; I have become
wealthy.[e]
With all my wealth they will not
find in me
any iniquity or sin."

12:8 [e]Ps 62:10; Rev 3:17

[9]"I am the LORD your God,
⌊who brought you⌋ out of[c] Egypt;[f]
I will make you live in tents[g] again,
as in the days of your appointed
feasts.

12:9 [f]Lev 23:43; Hos 11:1 [g]Ne 8:17

[10]I spoke to the prophets,
gave them many visions
and told parables[h] through them."[i]

12:10 [h]Eze 20:49 [i]2Ki 17:13; Jer 7:25

[11]Is Gilead wicked?[j]
Its people are worthless!
Do they sacrifice bulls in Gilgal?[k]
Their altars will be like piles of
stones
on a plowed field.[l]

12:11 [j]Hos 6:8 [k]Hos 4:15 [l]Hos 8:11

[12]Jacob fled to the country of Aram[d];[m]
Israel served to get a wife,
and to pay for her he tended
sheep.[n]

12:12 [m]Ge 28:5 [n]Ge 29:18

[13]The LORD used a prophet to bring
Israel up from Egypt,
by a prophet he cared for him.[o]

12:13 [o]Ex 13:3; Isa 63:11-14

[14]But Ephraim has bitterly provoked
him to anger;
his Lord will leave upon him the
guilt of his bloodshed[p]
and will repay him for his
contempt.[q]

12:14 [p]Eze 18:13 [q]Da 11:18

The LORD's Anger Against Israel

13:1 [r]Jdg 12:1 [s]Jdg 8:1

13 When Ephraim spoke, men
trembled;[r]
he was exalted[s] in Israel.

[a]9 Or *come against any city* [b]2 *Jacob* means *he grasps the heel* (figuratively, *he deceives*). [c]9 Or *God / ever since you were in* [d]12 That is, Northwest Mesopotamia

SELF-CONTROL

IDOLATRY ABANDONED

Hosea 13:2

Kissing idols squanders godly worship. How odd that Israel was saved by El-Shaddai (God Almighty) yet gave drooling affection to cold, metallic calves.

But he became guilty of Baal
worship[t] and died.
2 Now they sin more and more;
they make idols for themselves
from their silver,[u]
cleverly fashioned images,
all of them the work of craftsmen.
It is said of these people,
"They offer human sacrifice
and kiss[a] the calf-idols.[v]"
3 Therefore they will be like the
morning mist,
like the early dew that
disappears,[w]
like chaff[x] swirling from a
threshing floor,[y]
like smoke[z] escaping through a
window.

4 "But I am the LORD your God,
⌊who brought you⌋ out of[b] Egypt.[a]
You shall acknowledge no God but
me,[b]
no Savior[c] except me.
5 I cared for you in the desert,
in the land of burning heat.
6 When I fed them, they were
satisfied;
when they were satisfied, they
became proud;
then they forgot me.[d]
7 So I will come upon them like a
lion,
like a leopard I will lurk by the
path.
8 Like a bear robbed of her cubs,[e]
I will attack them and rip them
open.
Like a lion I will devour them;
a wild animal will tear them
apart.[f]

9 "You are destroyed, O Israel,
because you are against me,[g]
against your helper.[h]
10 Where is your king,[i] that he may
save you?
Where are your rulers in all your
towns,
of whom you said,
'Give me a king and princes'?[j]
11 So in my anger I gave you a king,
and in my wrath I took him
away.[k]
12 The guilt of Ephraim is stored up,
his sins are kept on record.[l]
13 Pains as of a woman in childbirth[m]
come to him,
but he is a child without wisdom;

13:1 [t]Hos 11:2
13:2 [u]Isa 46:6; Jer 10:4 [v]Isa 44:17-20
13:3 [w]Hos 6:4 [x]Isa 17:13 [y]Da 2:35 [z]Ps 68:2
13:4 [a]Hos 12:9 [b]Ex 20:3 [c]Isa 43:11; 45:21-22
13:6 [d]Dt 32:12-15; Hos 2:13
13:8 [e]2Sa 17:8 [f]Ps 50:22
13:9 [g]Jer 2:17-19 [h]Dt 33:29
13:10 [i]2Ki 17:4 [j]1Sa 8:6; Hos 8:4
13:11 [k]1Ki 14:10; Hos 10:7
13:12 [l]Dt 32:34
13:13 [m]Isa 13:8; Mic 4:9-10

when the time arrives,
he does not come to the opening
of the womb.[n]

14 "I will ransom them from the power
of the grave[c];[o]
I will redeem them from death.
Where, O death, are your plagues?
Where, O grave,[c] is your
destruction?[p]

"I will have no compassion,
15 even though he thrives[q] among his
brothers.
An east wind[r] from the LORD will
come,
blowing in from the desert;
his spring will fail
and his well dry up.[s]
His storehouse will be plundered[t]
of all its treasures.
16 The people of Samaria must bear
their guilt,[u]
because they have rebelled[v] against
their God.
They will fall by the sword;[w]
their little ones will be dashed[x] to
the ground,
their pregnant women[y] ripped
open."

Repentance to Bring Blessing

14 Return, O Israel, to the LORD
your God.
Your sins have been your
downfall![z]
2 Take words with you
and return to the LORD.
Say to him:
"Forgive all our sins
and receive us graciously,[a]
that we may offer the fruit of our
lips.[d][b]
3 Assyria cannot save us;
we will not mount war-horses.[c]
We will never again say 'Our gods'[d]
to what our own hands have
made,
for in you the fatherless[e] find
compassion."

4 "I will heal[f] their waywardness
and love them freely,[g]
for my anger has turned away
from them.
5 I will be like the dew to Israel;

13:13 [n]Isa 66:9
13:14 [o]Ps 49:15; Eze 37:12-13 [p]1Co 15:55*
13:15 [q]Hos 10:1 [r]Eze 19:12 [s]Jer 51:36 [t]Jer 20:5
13:16 [u]Hos 10:2 [v]Hos 7:14 [w]Hos 11:6 [x]2Ki 8:12; Hos 10:14 [y]2Ki 15:16; Isa 13:16
14:1 [z]Hos 5:5
14:2 [a]Mic 7:18-19 [b]Heb 13:15
14:3 [c]Ps 33:17; Isa 31:1 [d]Hos 8:6 [e]Ps 10:14; 68:5
14:4 [f]Hos 6:1 [g]Zep 3:17

[a]2 Or *"Men who sacrifice / kiss* [b]4 Or *God / ever since you were in* [c]14 Hebrew *Sheol* [d]2 Or *offer our lips as sacrifices of bulls*

he will blossom like a lily.[h]
Like a cedar of Lebanon[i]
he will send down his roots;[j]
6 his young shoots will grow.
His splendor will be like an olive
tree,[k]
his fragrance like a cedar of
Lebanon.[l]
7 Men will dwell again in his shade.[m]
He will flourish like the grain.
He will blossom like a vine,
and his fame will be like the wine[n]
from Lebanon.[o]
8 O Ephraim, what more have I[a] to do
with idols?[p]
I will answer him and care for
him.
I am like a green pine tree;
your fruitfulness comes from me."

9 Who is wise?[q] He will realize these
things.
Who is discerning? He will
understand them.[r]
The ways of the LORD are right;[s]
the righteous walk[t] in them,
but the rebellious stumble in
them.

[a]8 Or *What more has Ephraim*

14:5 [h]SS 2:1 [i]Isa 35:2 [j]Job 29:19
14:6 [k]Ps 52:8; Jer 11:16 [l]SS 4:11
14:7 [m]Ps 91:1-4 [n]Hos 2:22 [o]Eze 17:23
14:8 [p]ver 3
14:9 [q]Ps 107:43 [r]Pr 10:29; Isa 1:28 [s]Ps 111:7-8; Zep 3:5; Ac 13:10 [t]Isa 26:7

JOEL

AUTHORSHIP AND DATE

Joel

Most likely sometime in the ninth century B.C.

KEY THEMES

While we know very little about Joel, we do know that he preached during a time of great prosperity. It was also a time of pagan worship. Joel warned Israel that idolatry would be the nation's undoing and that they should return to the Lord their God. He advised them to show a spirit of true repentance. To do this, they would have to rend their hearts and not just their garments (see 2:12–13). Joel's major reproof was in regard to the day of the Lord. That day of calamity and judgment would sweep down upon the people. They could not avoid the inescapable judgment of God.

FRUIT OF THE SPIRIT IN JOEL

Self-Control: There is a fourfold call in the book of Joel to embrace the life of self-denial and begin to love God. Self-control was to produce the following four virtues in the lives of the people:

Self-control is the way to repentance. Almost everything of value in the believer's life happens on the back side of saying "I'm sorry" to God. The prophet had a severe way of looking at repentance: Repentance was to be demonstrated by self-diminishing—by the taking off of fine clothes and the putting on of sackcloth. The dumping of old ashes on the head and face also symbolized how unlovely the sinner had become to God. "Put on sackcloth, O priests, and mourn" (1:13).

Self-control is the way to return to the love of God. If the people's repentance was sincere, it would enable them to return to the love of God; but it would require self-denial and spiritual discipline. "Rend your heart and not your garments" (2:13).

Self-control is a rehearsal for the coming of the kingdom. "And afterward, I will pour out my Spirit on all people. Your sons and daughters will prophesy, your old men will dream dreams, your young men will see visions. Even on my servants, both men and women, I will pour out my Spirit in those days" (2:28–29). When the kingdom came, God's Spirit would fall fully on the people. This would be a sign that the new age had come and Jesus lived in the hearts of his disciples. This was literally fulfilled on the day of Pentecost (see Acts 2).

The loss of self-control indicates depravity and solicits the judgment of God. Here was the apocalyptic picture of how the indulgent must ultimately face God: "Swing the sickle, for the harvest is ripe. Come, trample the grapes, for the winepress is full and the vats overflow—so great is their wickedness!" (Joel 3:13).

1 The word of the LORD that came[a] to Joel[b] son of Pethuel.

An Invasion of Locusts

2 Hear this,[c] you elders;
listen, all who live in the land.[d]
Has anything like this ever happened in your days
or in the days of your forefathers?[e]
3 Tell it to your children,[f]
and let your children tell it to their children,
and their children to the next generation.
4 What the locust swarm has left
the great locusts have eaten;
what the great locusts have left
the young locusts have eaten;
what the young locusts have left
other locusts[a] have eaten.[g]

5 Wake up, you drunkards, and weep!
Wail, all you drinkers of wine;[h]
wail because of the new wine,
for it has been snatched from your lips.
6 A nation has invaded my land,
powerful and without number;[i]
it has the teeth[j] of a lion,
the fangs of a lioness.
7 It has laid waste[k] my vines
and ruined my fig trees.[l]
It has stripped off their bark
and thrown it away,
leaving their branches white.

8 Mourn like a virgin[b] in sackcloth[m]
grieving for the husband[c] of her youth.
9 Grain offerings and drink offerings[n]
are cut off from the house of the LORD.
The priests are in mourning,
those who minister before the LORD.
10 The fields are ruined,
the ground is dried up[d];[o]
the grain is destroyed,
the new wine[p] is dried up,
the oil fails.
11 Despair, you farmers,[q]
wail, you vine growers;
grieve for the wheat and the barley,
because the harvest of the field is destroyed.[r]
12 The vine is dried up
and the fig tree is withered;
the pomegranate, the palm and the apple tree—
all the trees of the field—are dried up.[s]
Surely the joy of mankind
is withered away.

A Call to Repentance

13 Put on sackcloth,[t] O priests, and mourn;
wail, you who minister[u] before the altar.
Come, spend the night in sackcloth,
you who minister before my God;
for the grain offerings and drink offerings[v]
are withheld from the house of your God.
14 Declare a holy fast;[w]
call a sacred assembly.
Summon the elders
and all who live in the land
to the house of the LORD your God,
and cry out[x] to the LORD.

15 Alas for that[y] day!
For the day of the LORD[z] is near;
it will come like destruction from the Almighty.[e]

16 Has not the food been cut off[a]
before our very eyes—
joy and gladness
from the house of our God?[b]
17 The seeds are shriveled
beneath the clods.[f][c]
The storehouses are in ruins,
the granaries have been broken down,
for the grain has dried up.
18 How the cattle moan!
The herds mill about
because they have no pasture;
even the flocks of sheep are suffering.

19 To you, O LORD, I call,[d]
for fire[e] has devoured the open pastures[f]
and flames have burned up all the trees of the field.
20 Even the wild animals pant for you;[g]
the streams of water have dried up[h]
and fire has devoured the open pastures.

[a]4 The precise meaning of the four Hebrew words used here for locusts is uncertain. [b]8 Or *young woman* [c]8 Or *betrothed* [d]10 Or *ground mourns* [e]15 Hebrew *Shaddai* [f]17 The meaning of the Hebrew for this word is uncertain.

1:1 [a]Jer 1:2 [b]Ac 2:16
1:2 [c]Hos 5:1 [d]Hos 4:1 [e]Joel 2:2
1:3 [f]Ex 10:2; Ps 78:4
1:4 [g]Dt 28:39; Na 3:15
1:5 [h]Joel 3:3
1:6 [i]Joel 2:2,11,25 [j]Rev 9:8
1:7 [k]Isa 5:6 [l]Am 4:9
1:8 [m]ver 13; Isa 22:12; Am 8:10
1:9 [n]Hos 9:4; Joel 2:14,17
1:10 [o]Isa 24:4 [p]Hos 9:2
1:11 [q]Jer 14:3-4; Am 5:16 [r]Isa 17:11
1:12 [s]Hag 2:19
1:13 [t]Jer 4:8 [u]Joel 2:17 [v]ver 9
1:14 [w]2Ch 20:3 [x]Jnh 3:8
1:15 [y]Jer 30:7 [z]Isa 13:6,9; Joel 2:1,11,31
1:16 [a]Isa 3:7 [b]Dt 12:7
1:17 [c]Isa 17:10-11
1:19 [d]Ps 50:15 [e]Am 7:4 [f]Jer 9:10
1:20 [g]Ps 104:21 [h]1Ki 17:7

An Army of Locusts

2:1 [i]Jer 4:5 [j]ver 15

2 Blow the trumpet[i] in Zion;[j]
sound the alarm on my holy hill.
Let all who live in the land tremble,

DAY 5 FIVE

LOVE AND ITS PLACE IN MY PERSONAL WORSHIP

Joel 2:12–13

Ritual has a way of supplanting the truth it was formed to develop. Liturgies are written largely by poets to celebrate, in beautiful words, the unfailing love of God. So we repeat them, and we repeat them, and we repeat them. But before long their beauty becomes tarnished by coarse familiarity. At that point we are merely repeating dead words and cannot feel the love and life that captivated us when we were younger and when those words were newer.

The Israelites had a penchant for outward rituals; but, alas, they only mouthed old words that they never meant. God had been reduced to a topic of theological discussion in Israel. His people could talk about him for hours and never feel a thing for him. So the prophet encouraged them, "Rend your heart and not your garments"—let God into your life; quit meeting him for church while you refuse to speak to him on the streets. God says, in effect, "Don't talk about me anymore unless you're actually thinking about me and worshiping me. My love is too almighty, too gracious and too compassionate to be a mere subject of theology. I have loved you unconditionally. Love me the same way in return. Never stop celebrating our love in your personal worship."

Listen to the poet call you to God's unchanging heart of love:

Could we with ink, the oceans fill, and were
the skies of parchment made,
Were every stalk on earth a quill, and every
man a scribe by trade,
To write the love of God above, would
drain those oceans dry.
Nor would the scroll, contain the whole,
though stretched from sky to sky.

To begin a study on the topic of Love, the Unconditional Longing of God, turn to the home page on page 89.

for the day of the LORD[k] is
coming.
It is close at hand[l]—
2 a day of darkness[m] and gloom,[n]
a day of clouds and blackness.
Like dawn spreading across the
mountains
a large and mighty army[o] comes,
such as never was of old[p]
nor ever will be in ages to come.

3 Before them fire devours,
behind them a flame blazes.
Before them the land is like the
garden of Eden,[q]
behind them, a desert waste[r]—
nothing escapes them.
4 They have the appearance of horses;[s]
they gallop along like cavalry.
5 With a noise like that of chariots[t]
they leap over the mountaintops,
like a crackling fire[u] consuming
stubble,
like a mighty army drawn up for
battle.

6 At the sight of them, nations are in
anguish;[v]
every face turns pale.[w]
7 They charge like warriors;
they scale walls like soldiers.
They all march in line,
not swerving[x] from their course.
8 They do not jostle each other;
each marches straight ahead.
They plunge through defenses
without breaking ranks.
9 They rush upon the city;
they run along the wall.
They climb into the houses;
like thieves they enter through the
windows.[y]
10 Before them the earth shakes,[z]
the sky trembles,
the sun and moon are darkened,[a]
and the stars no longer shine.[b]
11 The LORD[c] thunders
at the head of his army;
his forces are beyond number,
and mighty are those who obey
his command.
The day of the LORD is great;[d]
it is dreadful.
Who can endure it?[e]

Rend Your Heart

12 "Even now," declares the LORD,
"return[f] to me with all your heart,

2:1 [k]Joel 1:15; Zep 1:14-16 [l]Ob 1:15
2:2 [m]Am 5:18 [n]Da 9:12 [o]Joel 1:6 [p]Joel 1:2
2:3 [q]Ge 2:8 [r]Ps 105:34-35
2:4 [s]Rev 9:7
2:5 [t]Rev 9:9 [u]Isa 5:24; 30:30
2:6 [v]Isa 13:8 [w]Na 2:10
2:7 [x]Isa 5:27
2:9 [y]Jer 9:21
2:10 [z]Ps 18:7 [a]Mt 24:29 [b]Isa 13:10; Eze 32:8
2:11 [c]Joel 1:15 [d]Zep 1:14; Rev 18:8 [e]Eze 22:14
2:12 [f]Jer 4:1; Hos 12:6

with fasting and weeping and
mourning."

2:13 [g]Ps 34:18; Isa 57:15 [h]Job 1:20 [i]Ex 34:6 [j]Jer 18:8

13 Rend your heart[g]
and not your garments.[h]
Return to the LORD your God,
for he is gracious and
compassionate,
slow to anger and abounding in
love,[i]
and he relents from sending
calamity.[j]

2:14 [k]Jer 26:3 [l]Hag 2:19 [m]Joel 1:13

14 Who knows? He may turn[k] and have
pity
and leave behind a blessing[l]—
grain offerings and drink offerings[m]
for the LORD your God.

2:15 [n]Nu 10:2 [o]Jer 36:9 [p]Joel 1:14

15 Blow the trumpet[n] in Zion,
declare a holy fast,[o]
call a sacred assembly.[p]
16 Gather the people,
consecrate[q] the assembly;
bring together the elders,
gather the children,
those nursing at the breast.
Let the bridegroom[r] leave his room
and the bride her chamber.

2:16 [q]Ex 19:10,22 [r]Ps 19:5

17 Let the priests, who minister before
the LORD,
weep between the temple porch
and the altar.[s]
Let them say, "Spare your people,
O LORD.
Do not make your inheritance an
object of scorn,[t]
a byword among the nations.
Why should they say among the
peoples,
'Where is their God?[u]' "

2:17 [s]Eze 8:16; Mt 23:35 [t]Dt 9:26-29; Ps 44:13 [u]Ps 42:3

The LORD's Answer

2:18 [v]Zec 1:14

18 Then the LORD will be jealous[v] for
his land
and take pity on his people.
19 The LORD will reply[a] to them:

"I am sending you grain, new wine
and oil,[w]
enough to satisfy you fully;
never again will I make you
an object of scorn[x] to the nations.

2:19 [w]Jer 31:12 [x]Eze 34:29

20 "I will drive the northern army[y] far
from you,
pushing it into a parched and
barren land,
with its front columns going into the
eastern[z] sea[b]
and those in the rear into the
western sea.[c]
And its stench[a] will go up;
its smell will rise."

2:20 [y]Jer 1:14-15 [z]Zec 14:8 [a]Isa 34:3

Surely he has done great things.[d]
21 Be not afraid,[b] O land;
be glad and rejoice.
Surely the LORD has done great
things.[c]

2:21 [b]Isa 54:4; Zep 3:16-17 [c]Ps 126:3

22 Be not afraid, O wild animals,
for the open pastures are
becoming green.[d]
The trees are bearing their fruit;
the fig tree and the vine yield their
riches.[e]

2:22 [d]Ps 65:12 [e]Joel 1:18-20

23 Be glad, O people of Zion,
rejoice[f] in the LORD your God,
for he has given you
the autumn rains in
righteousness.[e]
He sends you abundant showers,
both autumn and spring rains,[g] as
before.

2:23 [f]Ps 149:2; Isa 12:6; 41:16; Hab 3:18; Zec 10:7 [g]Lev 26:4

24 The threshing floors will be filled
with grain;
the vats will overflow[h] with new
wine[i] and oil.

2:24 [h]Lev 26:10; Mal 3:10 [i]Am 9:13

25 "I will repay you for the years the
locusts have eaten—
the great locust and the young
locust,
the other locusts and the locust
swarm[f]—
my great army that I sent among
you.
26 You will have plenty to eat, until you
are full,[j]
and you will praise[k] the name of
the LORD your God,
who has worked wonders[l] for
you;
never again will my people be
shamed.

2:26 [j]Lev 26:5 [k]Isa 62:9 [l]Ps 126:3; Isa 25:1

27 Then you will know that I am in
Israel,
that I am the LORD[m] your God,
and that there is no other;
never again will my people be
shamed.

2:27 [m]Joel 3:17

[a]*18,19* Or *LORD was jealous . . . / and took pity . . . / 19The LORD replied* [b]*20* That is, the Dead Sea [c]*20* That is, the Mediterranean [d]*20* Or *rise. / Surely it has done great things."* [e]*23* Or / *the teacher for righteousness:* [f]*25* The precise meaning of the four Hebrew words used here for locusts is uncertain.

The Day of the LORD

28 "And afterward,
I will pour out my Spirit[n] on all people.
Your sons and daughters will prophesy,
your old men will dream dreams,
your young men will see visions.

2:28
[n]Eze 39:29

▸ **JOY**

THE SPIRIT AGE

Joel 2:28

The dreamless dream. The youth are alive with zeal. The Spirit comes! Visions fall upon the aged, who thought they had no reason left to live.

Pentecost is glory!

The wind blew. The fire burned. The wind still blows. The fire still burns. The Spirit still roars over us in flame—unstoppable, redeeming.

29 Even on my servants,[o] both men and women,
I will pour out my Spirit in those days.
30 I will show wonders in the heavens[p]
and on the earth,[q]
blood and fire and billows of smoke.
31 The sun will be turned to darkness[r]
and the moon to blood
before the coming of the great and dreadful day of the LORD.[s]
32 And everyone who calls
on the name of the LORD will be saved;[t]
for on Mount Zion[u] and in Jerusalem
there will be deliverance,[v]
as the LORD has said,
among the survivors[w]
whom the LORD calls.

2:29
[o]1Co 12:13; Gal 3:28
2:30
[p]Lk 21:11
[q]Mk 13:24-25
2:31
[r]Mt 24:29
[s]Isa 13:9-10; Mal 4:1,5
2:32
[t]Ac 2:17-21*; Ro 10:13*
[u]Isa 46:13
[v]Ob 1:17
[w]Isa 11:11; Mic 4:7; Ro 9:27

The Nations Judged

3 "In those days and at that time,
when I restore the fortunes[x] of Judah and Jerusalem,
2 I will gather all nations
and bring them down to the Valley of Jehoshaphat.[a]
There I will enter into judgment[y]
against them
concerning my inheritance, my people Israel,

3:1
[x]Jer 16:15
3:2
[y]Eze 36:5

DAY 4 FOUR

▸ SELF-CONTROL AND MY SERVICE TO OTHERS

Joel 3:1–3

Nations generally move between a moral, values-driven culture and a culture of indulgence and moral decay. Joel says God wants to dialogue with the nations over the degeneration of their morality. God states, in effect, "I am going to judge them for institutionalizing sin." The sin life of a nation develops from individual indulgences to the decay of national character.

How can we live a life of self-control in a culture where indulgence is the rule? It is hard for Christian parents to say to their children, "You can't go," only to hear their children say, "But Mary's parents let her go." How do we instill values that derive from our self-control when all around us is a "let's-do-it" culture?

If we are going to minister to others, our lifestyles must reflect our relationship with Christ. When we minister to others, they will try to say to us, "I could never be a Christian because Christians don't . . ." The reason Christians don't do it—whatever "it" is—is that "it" is not good for the person individually or the culture as a whole. Sin hardly ever engages us head-on with "Decide here and now" or "Is this right or wrong?" Sin evolves gradually from wholehearted condemnation to wholesale acceptance. We are at first horrified by sin. Then we are merely shocked. Then we only argue about it. Then we're conversational about it. In time we become congenial about it. Finally, at last, we are indulgent.

My ministry to others means that I must serve others with a full understanding of the tendency we all have—to take life easy and to fail to practice self-control.

To begin a study on the topic of Self-Control, Freedom From Permissiveness, turn to the home page on page 452.

for they scattered my people among the nations
and divided up my land.
3 They cast lots for my people
and traded boys for prostitutes;

[a]*2 Jehoshaphat* means *the LORD judges*; also in verse 12.

3:3 [z]Am 2:6 they sold girls for wine[z]
that they might drink.

4“Now what have you against me,
3:4 [a]Mt 11:21 O Tyre and Sidon[a] and all you regions
[b]Isa 34:8 of Philistia? Are you repaying me for
something I have done? If you are paying me back, I will swiftly and speedily
return on your own heads what you
have done.[b] 5For you took my silver
and my gold and carried off my finest
3:5 [c]2Ch 21:16-17 treasures to your temples.[c] 6You sold the
people of Judah and Jerusalem to the
Greeks, that you might send them far
from their homeland.
7“See, I am going to rouse them out
3:7 [d]Isa 43:5-6; Jer 23:8 of the places to which you sold them,[d]
and I will return on your own heads
what you have done. 8I will sell your
3:8 [e]Isa 60:14 sons[e] and daughters to the people of Ju-
[f]Isa 14:2 dah,[f] and they will sell them to the Sabeans, a nation far away.” The LORD
has spoken.

9 Proclaim this among the nations:
3:9 [g]Isa 8:9 Prepare for war![g]
[h]Jer 46:4 Rouse the warriors![h]
Let all the fighting men draw near
and attack.
3:10 [i]Isa 2:4; Mic 4:3 10Beat your plowshares into swords
and your pruning hooks[i] into
[j]Zec 12:8 spears.
Let the weakling[j] say,
“I am strong!”
11Come quickly, all you nations from
every side,
3:11 [k]Eze 38:15-16; Zep 3:8 and assemble[k] there.
[l]Isa 13:3

Bring down your warriors,[l]
O LORD!

12“Let the nations be roused;
let them advance into the Valley of
Jehoshaphat,
for there I will sit
3:12 [m]Isa 2:4 to judge[m] all the nations on every
side.
3:13 [n]Hos 6:11; Mt 13:39; Rev 14:15-19 13Swing the sickle,
for the harvest[n] is ripe.
Come, trample the grapes,
[o]Rev 14:20 for the winepress[o] is full
and the vats overflow—
so great is their wickedness!”

14Multitudes, multitudes
in the valley of decision!
For the day of the LORD[p] is near 3:14 [p]Isa 34:2-8; Joel 1:15
in the valley of decision.
15The sun and moon will be darkened,
and the stars no longer shine.
16The LORD will roar from Zion 3:16
and thunder from Jerusalem;[q] [q]Am 1:2
the earth and the sky will [r]Eze 38:19
tremble.[r] [s]Jer 16:19
But the LORD will be a refuge for
his people,
a stronghold[s] for the people of
Israel.

Blessings for God’s People

17“Then you will know that I, the
LORD your God,[t] 3:17 [t]Joel 2:27
dwell in Zion,[u] my holy hill. [u]Isa 4:3
Jerusalem will be holy;
never again will foreigners invade
her.

18“In that day the mountains will drip
new wine,
and the hills will flow with milk;[v] 3:18 [v]Ex 3:8
all the ravines of Judah will run [w]Isa 30:25; 35:6
with water.[w] [x]Rev 22:1-2
A fountain will flow out of the [y]Eze 47:1; Am 9:13
LORD’s house[x]
and will water the valley of
acacias.[a][y]
19But Egypt will be desolate,
Edom a desert waste,
because of violence[z] done to the 3:19 [z]Ob 1:10
people of Judah,
in whose land they shed innocent
blood.
20Judah will be inhabited forever[a] 3:20 [a]Am 9:15
and Jerusalem through all
generations.
21Their bloodguilt, which I have not
pardoned,
I will pardon.”[b] 3:21 [b]Eze 36:25

The LORD dwells in Zion!

[a]18 Or *Valley of Shittim*

AMOS

AUTHORSHIP AND DATE

Amos

c. 750 B.C.

KEY THEMES

The book of Amos is a cry for justice: "Let justice roll on like a river, righteousness like a never-failing stream!" (5:24). This great cry came from a God-sensitive prophet to an insensitive people. Amos preached to a wealthy, self-satisfied nation. It was a nation divided into classes. The poor suffered at the hands of the rich and were sometimes sold into slavery for failure to repay a debt so small that a pair of sandals was the pledge (see 8:6). Amos cried out in judgment against this injustice. This book resounds with human rights, and Amos was among the first to preach that when any class of people hurt, all people should be concerned.

FRUIT OF THE SPIRIT IN AMOS

Kindness: The people of Israel had become so proud that they had lost every hint of godly humility. Scattered throughout the book are seven calls for Israel to return to humility and recover their lost sense of kindness.

Israel should have been kind because they had special status as the chosen people of God and knew God's requirements of them. "You only have I chosen of all the families of the earth; therefore I will punish you for all your sins" (3:2).

Israel should have developed men and women of moral propriety. But drunkenness and arrogance keep company (see 4:1); therefore, Amos tells the people to leave their drunkenness and return to humility, sobriety and, above all, kindness.

The Israelites should not have bragged about how much they were giving to God. Kind people don't boast about how much they give to God (see 4:5). They serve the poor and needy.

Kind people remember that they must ultimately reckon with God. Humility is born when we remember we are not sovereign over the living of our lives. "Therefore this is what

I will do to you, Israel, and because I will do this to you, prepare to meet your God, O Israel" (4:12).

The kind do not gain wealth at the expense of the poor. No one has the right to persecute others because of some self-adopted caste system. "You trample on the poor and force him to give you grain. Therefore, though you have built stone mansions, you will not live in them; though you have planted lush vineyards, you will not drink their wine" (5:11).

The kind do not cling to inordinate pride. "Woe to you who are complacent in Zion, and to you who feel secure on Mount Samaria, you notable men of the foremost nation, to whom the people of Israel come!" (6:1).

The kind treasure the words of God. Amos pictured a day when the harsh, who never seemed to need God's words, would suddenly find those words unobtainable. " 'The days are coming,' declares the Sovereign LORD, 'when I will send a famine through the land—not a famine of food or a thirst for water, but a famine of hearing the words of the LORD' " (8:11).

1 The words of Amos, one of the shepherds of Tekoa[a]—what he saw concerning Israel two years before the earthquake,[b] when Uzziah[c] was king of Judah and Jeroboam[d] son of Jehoash[a] was king of Israel.[e]

2 He said:

"The LORD roars[f] from Zion
and thunders from Jerusalem;[g]
the pastures of the shepherds dry up,[b]
and the top of Carmel[h] withers."[i]

1:1 [a]2Sa 14:2 [b]Zec 14:5 [c]2Ch 26:23 [d]2Ki 14:23 [e]Hos 1:1
1:2 [f]Isa 42:13 [g]Joel 3:16 [h]Am 9:3 [i]Jer 12:4

Judgment on Israel's Neighbors

3 This is what the LORD says:

"For three sins of Damascus,[j]
even for four, I will not turn back
⌊my wrath⌋.[k]
Because she threshed Gilead
with sledges having iron teeth,
4 I will send fire[l] upon the house of
Hazael
that will consume the fortresses[m]
of Ben-Hadad.[n]
5 I will break down the gate[o] of
Damascus;
I will destroy the king who is in[c]
the Valley of Aven[d]
and the one who holds the scepter in
Beth Eden.
The people of Aram will go into
exile to Kir,[p]"
says the LORD.

1:3 [j]Isa 8:4; 17:1-3 [k]Am 2:6
1:4 [l]Jer 49:27 [m]Jer 17:27 [n]1Ki 20:1; 2Ki 6:24
1:5 [o]Jer 51:30 [p]2Ki 16:9

6 This is what the LORD says:

"For three sins of Gaza,[q]
even for four, I will not turn back
⌊my wrath⌋.
Because she took captive whole
communities
and sold them to Edom,[r]
7 I will send fire upon the walls of
Gaza
that will consume her fortresses.
8 I will destroy the king[e] of Ashdod[s]
and the one who holds the scepter
in Ashkelon.
I will turn my hand[t] against Ekron,
till the last of the Philistines[u] is
dead,"
says the Sovereign LORD.[v]

1:6 [q]1Sa 6:17; Zep 2:4 [r]Ob 1:11
1:8 [s]2Ch 26:6 [t]Ps 81:14 [u]Eze 25:16 [v]Isa 14:28-32; Zep 2:4-7

9 This is what the LORD says:

"For three sins of Tyre,[w]
even for four, I will not turn back
⌊my wrath⌋.
Because she sold whole communities
of captives to Edom,
disregarding a treaty of
brotherhood,
10 I will send fire upon the walls of
Tyre
that will consume her fortresses."[x]

1:9 [w]1Ki 5:1; 9:11-14; Isa 23:1-18; Jer 25:22; Joel 3:4; Mt 11:21
1:10 [x]Zec 9:1-4

11 This is what the LORD says:

"For three sins of Edom,[y]
even for four, I will not turn back
⌊my wrath⌋.
Because he pursued his brother with
a sword,
stifling all compassion,[f]
because his anger raged continually
and his fury flamed unchecked,[z]
12 I will send fire upon Teman[a]
that will consume the fortresses of
Bozrah."

1:11 [y]Nu 20:14-21; 2Ch 28:17; Jer 49:7-22 [z]Eze 25:12-14
1:12 [a]Ob 1:9-10

13 This is what the LORD says:

"For three sins of Ammon,[b]
even for four, I will not turn back
⌊my wrath⌋.
Because he ripped open the pregnant
women[c] of Gilead
in order to extend his borders,
14 I will set fire to the walls of Rabbah[d]
that will consume her fortresses
amid war cries[e] on the day of battle,
amid violent winds on a stormy
day.
15 Her king[g] will go into exile,
he and his officials together,"
says the LORD.

1:13 [b]Jer 49:1-6; Eze 21:28; 25:2-7 [c]Hos 13:16
1:14 [d]Dt 3:11 [e]Am 2:2

2 This is what the LORD says:

"For three sins of Moab,
even for four, I will not turn back
⌊my wrath⌋.
Because he burned, as if to lime,
the bones of Edom's king,
2 I will send fire upon Moab
that will consume the fortresses of
Kerioth.[h]
Moab will go down in great tumult
amid war cries and the blast of the
trumpet.
3 I will destroy her ruler[f]
and kill all her officials with
him,"[g]
says the LORD.

2:3 [f]Ps 2:10 [g]Isa 40:23

[a] *1* Hebrew *Joash,* a variant of *Jehoash* [b] *2* Or *shepherds mourn* [c] *5* Or *the inhabitants of* [d] *5* *Aven* means *wickedness.* [e] *8* Or *inhabitants* [f] *11* Or *sword / and destroyed his allies* [g] *15* Or / *Molech;* Hebrew *malcam* [h] *2* Or *of her cities*

4 This is what the LORD says:

"For three sins of Judah,[h]
even for four, I will not turn back
my wrath⌋.
Because they have rejected the law[i]
of the LORD
and have not kept his decrees,[j]
because they have been led astray[k] by
false gods,[a][l]
the gods[b] their ancestors
followed,[m]
5 I will send fire upon Judah
that will consume the fortresses of
Jerusalem."[n]

2:4 [h]2Ki 17:19; Hos 12:2 [i]Jer 6:19 [j]Eze 20:24 [k]Isa 9:16 [l]Isa 28:15 [m]2Ki 22:13; Jer 16:12

2:5 [n]Jer 17:27; Hos 8:14

Judgment on Israel

6 This is what the LORD says:

"For three sins of Israel,
even for four, I will not turn back
my wrath⌋.
They sell the righteous for silver,
and the needy for a pair of
sandals.[o]
7 They trample on the heads of the
poor
as upon the dust of the ground
and deny justice to the oppressed.
Father and son use the same girl
and so profane my holy name.[p]
8 They lie down beside every altar
on garments taken in pledge.[q]
In the house of their god
they drink wine[r] taken as fines.

2:6 [o]Joel 3:3; Am 8:6

2:7 [p]Am 5:11-12; 8:4

2:8 [q]Ex 22:26 [r]Am 4:1; 6:6

9 "I destroyed the Amorite[s] before
them,
though he was tall as the cedars
and strong as the oaks.
I destroyed his fruit above
and his roots[t] below.

2:9 [s]Nu 21:23-26; Jos 10:12 [t]Eze 17:9; Mal 4:1

10 "I brought you up out of Egypt,[u]
and I led you forty years in the
desert[v]
to give you the land of the
Amorites.[w]
11 I also raised up prophets[x] from
among your sons
and Nazirites[y] from among your
young men.
Is this not true, people of Israel?"
declares the LORD.
12 "But you made the Nazirites drink
wine
and commanded the prophets not
to prophesy.[z]
13 "Now then, I will crush you
as a cart crushes when loaded with
grain.
14 The swift will not escape,
the strong[a] will not muster their
strength,
and the warrior will not save his
life.[b]
15 The archer[c] will not stand his
ground,
the fleet-footed soldier will not get
away,
and the horseman will not save his
life.
16 Even the bravest warriors[d]
will flee naked on that day,"
declares the LORD.

2:10 [u]Ex 20:2; Am 3:1 [v]Dt 2:7 [w]Ex 3:8; Am 9:7

2:11 [x]Dt 18:18; Jer 7:25 [y]Nu 6:2-3; Jdg 13:5

2:12 [z]Isa 30:10; Jer 11:21; Am 7:12-13; Mic 2:6

2:14 [a]Jer 9:23 [b]Ps 33:16; Isa 30:16-17

2:15 [c]Eze 39:3

2:16 [d]Jer 48:41

Witnesses Summoned Against Israel

3 Hear this word the LORD has spoken against you, O people of Israel—against the whole family I brought
up out of Egypt:[e]

2 "You only have I chosen[f]
of all the families of the earth;
therefore I will punish you
for all your sins."[g]

3:1 [e]Am 2:10

3:2 [f]Dt 7:6; Lk 12:47 [g]Jer 14:10

GOODNESS

AWE AND REVERENCE

Amos 3:2

God loves us. Let us all behave. We have a Father rich in grace. Let us not desecrate our wealth like urchins still in poverty.

3 Do two walk together
unless they have agreed to do so?
4 Does a lion roar in the thicket
when he has no prey?[h]
Does he growl in his den
when he has caught nothing?
5 Does a bird fall into a trap on the
ground
where no snare has been set?
Does a trap spring up from the earth
when there is nothing to catch?
6 When a trumpet sounds in a city,
do not the people tremble?
When disaster comes to a city,
has not the LORD caused it?[i]
7 Surely the Sovereign LORD does
nothing
without revealing his plan[j]
to his servants the prophets.[k]

3:4 [h]Ps 104:21; Hos 5:14

3:6 [i]Isa 14:24-27; 45:7

3:7 [j]Ge 18:17; Da 9:22; Jn 15:15; Rev 10:7 [k]Jer 23:22

[a]4 Or *by lies* [b]4 Or *lies*

3:8 [l]Jer 20:9; Jnh 1:1-3; 3:1-3; Ac 4:20

8 The lion has roared—
who will not fear?
The Sovereign LORD has spoken—
who can but prophesy?[l]

DAY 2 TWO

▸ SELF-CONTROL AND THE PURPOSE OF GOD IN MY LIFE

Amos 4:1–2

God has always been the champion of the poor. The poor are not closer to God because of their poverty, but their poverty creates a need for God. Amos prophesied against the uncaring attitudes of the rich women ("cows of Bashan"). The problem with their affluence was that it blinded them to the pain and suffering of the poor. The women of Israel were partygoers, eating and drinking in complete oblivion in a country where the poor were being sold into slavery for the price of a pair of shoes (Amos 2:6). Amos castigates these indulgent people on several other counts:

They denied justice to the oppressed (2:7).
They hoarded plunder and loot in their fortresses (3:10).
They crushed the needy and oppressed the poor (4:1).
They promoted a culture of drunkenness (4:1).
They gave little but bragged about their temple offerings (4:5).
They forced the poor into sharecrop status (5:11).
They accepted bribes in the courts (5:12).
They worshiped false gods (5:26).
They were gluttons (6:4).

All of these indulgences and cruelties were clearly the telltale signs of a culture in the last throes of moral collapse. Can we see parallels in our own times?

The number one question for us is: How can we learn self-control in the indulgent culture that we have become? Yet we must accomplish that goal. For if we will not say no to our own desires, our time in history will be futile, and God's purpose in our lives will come to no avail.

To begin a study on the topic of Self-Control, Saying No to Our Appetites, turn to the home page on page 105.

9 Proclaim to the fortresses of Ashdod
and to the fortresses of Egypt:
"Assemble yourselves on the
mountains of Samaria;[m]
see the great unrest within her
and the oppression among her
people."

10 "They do not know how to do
right,"[n] declares the LORD,
"who hoard plunder[o] and loot in
their fortresses."[p]

11 Therefore this is what the Sovereign LORD says:

"An enemy will overrun the land;
he will pull down your
strongholds
and plunder your fortresses.[q]"

12 This is what the LORD says:

"As a shepherd saves from the lion's[r]
mouth
only two leg bones or a piece of
an ear,
so will the Israelites be saved,
those who sit in Samaria
on the edge of their beds
and in Damascus on their
couches.[a][s]"

13 "Hear this and testify[t] against the
house of Jacob," declares the Lord, the
LORD God Almighty.

14 "On the day I punish Israel for her
sins,
I will destroy the altars of Bethel;[u]
the horns of the altar will be cut off
and fall to the ground.
15 I will tear down the winter house[v]
along with the summer house;[w]
the houses adorned with ivory[x] will
be destroyed
and the mansions will be
demolished,"
declares the LORD.

Israel Has Not Returned to God

4 Hear this word, you cows of
Bashan[y] on Mount Samaria,[z]
you women who oppress the poor
and crush the needy
and say to your husbands, "Bring
us some drinks!"[a]
2 The Sovereign LORD has sworn by
his holiness:

[a]*12* The meaning of the Hebrew for this line is uncertain.

3:9 [m]Am 4:1; 6:1
3:10 [n]Jer 4:22; Am 5:7; 6:12 [o]Hab 2:8 [p]Zep 1:9
3:11 [q]Am 2:5; 6:14
3:12 [r]1Sa 17:34 [s]Am 6:4
3:13 [t]Eze 2:7
3:14 [u]Am 5:5-6
3:15 [v]Jer 36:22 [w]Jdg 3:20 [x]1Ki 22:39
4:1 [y]Ps 22:12; Eze 39:18 [z]Am 3:9 [a]Am 2:8; 5:11; 8:6

"The time will surely come
4:2 [b]Am 6:8
when you will be taken away[b] with hooks,
the last of you with fishhooks.
3 You will each go straight out
4:3 [c]Eze 12:5
through breaks in the wall,[c]
and you will be cast out toward Harmon,[a]"
declares the LORD.
4 "Go to Bethel and sin;
4:4 [d]Hos 4:15 [e]Nu 28:3 [f]Dt 14:28 [g]Eze 20:39; Am 5:21-22
go to Gilgal[d] and sin yet more.
Bring your sacrifices every morning,[e]
your tithes[f] every three years.[b][g]
5 Burn leavened bread[h] as a thank offering
4:5 [h]Lev 7:13 [i]Lev 22:18-21
and brag about your freewill offerings[i]—
boast about them, you Israelites,
for this is what you love to do,"
declares the Sovereign LORD.

6 "I gave you empty stomachs[c] in every city
and lack of bread in every town,
4:6 [j]Isa 3:1; Jer 5:3; Hag 2:17
yet you have not returned to me,"
declares the LORD.[j]

7 "I also withheld rain from you
when the harvest was still three months away.
I sent rain on one town,
4:7 [k]Ex 9:4,26; Dt 11:17; 2Ch 7:13
but withheld it from another.[k]
One field had rain;
another had none and dried up.
8 People staggered from town to town
4:8 [l]Eze 4:16-17 [m]Jer 3:7 [n]Jer 14:4
for water[l]
but did not get enough to drink,
yet you have not returned[m] to me,"
declares the LORD.[n]

9 "Many times I struck your gardens and vineyards,
I struck them with blight and mildew.[o]
4:9 [o]Dt 28:22 [p]Joel 1:7 [q]Jer 3:10; Hag 2:17
Locusts devoured your fig and olive trees,[p]
yet you have not returned[q] to me,"
declares the LORD.

10 "I sent plagues[r] among you
4:10 [r]Ex 9:3; Dt 28:27 [s]Isa 9:13
as I did to Egypt.
I killed your young men with the sword,
along with your captured horses.
I filled your nostrils with the stench of your camps,
yet you have not returned to me,"
declares the LORD.[s]

11 "I overthrew some of you
as I[d] overthrew Sodom and Gomorrah.[t]
4:11 [t]Ge 19:24; Jer 23:14
You were like a burning stick
snatched from the fire,
yet you have not returned to me,"
declares the LORD.

12 "Therefore this is what I will do to you, Israel,
and because I will do this to you,
prepare to meet your God,
O Israel."

13 He who forms the mountains,[u]
4:13 [u]Ps 65:6 [v]Da 2:28 [w]Mic 1:3 [x]Isa 47:4; Am 5:8,27; 9:6
creates the wind,
and reveals his thoughts[v] to man,
he who turns dawn to darkness,
and treads the high places of the earth[w]—
the LORD God Almighty is his name.[x]

A Lament and Call to Repentance

5 Hear this word, O house of Israel,
5:1 [y]Eze 19:1
this lament[y] I take up concerning
you:

2 "Fallen is Virgin[z] Israel,
5:2 [z]Jer 14:17 [a]Jer 50:32; Am 8:14
never to rise again,
deserted in her own land,
with no one to lift her up.[a]"

3 This is what the Sovereign LORD
says:

"The city that marches out a thousand strong for Israel
will have only a hundred left;
the town that marches out a hundred strong
will have only ten left.[b]"
5:3 [b]Isa 6:13; Am 6:9

4 This is what the LORD says to the
house of Israel:

"Seek me and live;[c]
5:4 [c]Isa 55:3; Jer 29:13
5 do not seek Bethel,
do not go to Gilgal,[d]
5:5 [d]1Sa 11:14; Am 4:4 [e]Am 8:14 [f]1Sa 7:16
do not journey to Beersheba.[e]
For Gilgal will surely go into exile,
and Bethel will be reduced to nothing.[e][f]"
6 Seek[g] the LORD and live,[h]
5:6 [g]Isa 55:6 [h]ver 14 [i]Dt 4:24
or he will sweep through the
house of Joseph like a fire;[i]

[a]3 Masoretic Text; with a different word division of the Hebrew (see Septuagint) *out, O mountain of oppression* [b]4 Or *tithes on the third day* [c]6 Hebrew *you cleanness of teeth* [d]11 Hebrew *God* [e]5 Or *grief,* or *wickedness;* Hebrew *aven,* a reference to Beth Aven (a derogatory name for Bethel)

it will devour,
5:6 [j]Am 3:14
and Bethel[j] will have no one to quench it.

5:7 [k]Am 6:12
7 You who turn justice into bitterness[k]
and cast righteousness to the ground
8 (he who made the Pleiades and Orion,[l]
5:8 [l]Job 9:9 [m]Isa 42:16 [n]Ps 104:20; Am 8:9 [o]Ps 104:6-9; Am 4:13
who turns blackness into dawn[m]
and darkens day into night,[n]
who calls for the waters of the sea
and pours them out over the face of the land—
the LORD is his name[o]—

GENTLENESS

THE UNSELFISH SPIRIT

Amos 5:8

Consider the One who made the stars, and fear God. Fear is wise. It remembers that all flesh lives only because the God of wealth spent heaven's fortune on a hill called Calvary.

9 he flashes destruction on the stronghold
and brings the fortified city to ruin),[p]
5:9 [p]Mic 5:11
10 you hate the one who reproves in court[q]
5:10 [q]Isa 29:21 [r]1Ki 22:8
and despise him who tells the truth.[r]

5:11 [s]Am 8:6 [t]Am 3:15 [u]Mic 6:15
11 You trample on the poor[s]
and force him to give you grain.
Therefore, though you have built stone mansions,[t]
you will not live in them;
though you have planted lush vineyards,
you will not drink their wine.[u]
12 For I know how many are your offenses
and how great your sins.

You oppress the righteous and take bribes
and you deprive the poor of justice in the courts.[v]
5:12 [v]Isa 5:23; Am 2:6-7
13 Therefore the prudent man keeps quiet in such times,
for the times are evil.

14 Seek good, not evil,
that you may live.
Then the LORD God Almighty will be with you,
just as you say he is.

5:15 [w]Ps 97:10; Ro 12:9 [x]Joel 2:14 [y]Mic 5:7,8
15 Hate evil,[w] love good;
maintain justice in the courts.
Perhaps the LORD God Almighty will have mercy[x]
on the remnant[y] of Joseph.

16 Therefore this is what the Lord, the LORD God Almighty, says:

"There will be wailing[z] in all the streets
5:16 [z]Jer 9:17 [a]Joel 1:11
and cries of anguish in every public square.
The farmers[a] will be summoned to weep
and the mourners to wail.
17 There will be wailing in all the vineyards,
5:17 [b]Ex 12:12 [c]Isa 16:10; Jer 48:33
for I will pass through[b] your midst,"
says the LORD.[c]

The Day of the LORD

18 Woe to you who long
for the day of the LORD![d]
5:18 [d]Joel 1:15 [e]Joel 2:2 [f]Isa 5:19,30; Jer 30:7
Why do you long for the day of the LORD?
That day will be darkness,[e] not light.[f]
19 It will be as though a man fled from a lion
only to meet a bear,
as though he entered his house
and rested his hand on the wall
only to have a snake bite him.[g]
5:19 [g]Job 20:24; Isa 24:17-18; Jer 15:2-3; 48:44
20 Will not the day of the LORD be darkness, not light—
pitch-dark, without a ray of brightness?[h]
5:20 [h]Isa 13:10; Zep 1:15

21 "I hate, I despise your religious feasts;[i]
5:21 [i]Lev 26:31 [j]Isa 1:11-16
I cannot stand your assemblies.[j]
22 Even though you bring me burnt offerings and grain offerings,
I will not accept them.
Though you bring choice fellowship offerings,[a]
5:22 [k]Am 4:4; Mic 6:6-7 [l]Isa 66:3
I will have no regard for them.[k l]
23 Away with the noise of your songs!
I will not listen to the music of your harps.[m]
5:23 [m]Am 6:5
24 But let justice[n] roll on like a river,
5:24 [n]Jer 22:3 [o]Mic 6:8
righteousness like a never-failing stream![o]

25 "Did you bring me sacrifices[p] and offerings
5:25 [p]Isa 43:23

[a]22 Traditionally *peace offerings*

WEEK 5 — KINDNESS

DAY ONE
▸ KINDNESS AS A WORLDVIEW
Read Amos 5:11–13

Amos tells us the story of kindness by showing us what unkindness is. Listen to the brutality of the unkind. The unkind in Amos's day built stone mansions, elaborately landscaped with lush vineyards. Yet, they continued to take from the poor. The problem with wealth is that sometimes the wealthy suppose that everyone else's lifestyles are just like theirs. Nothing keeps people from feeling the hurt of the hurting like the magnification of their own comfort.

Marie Antoinette's detractors circulated this popular story about her, which makes the case for the insensitivity of the rich. The story goes that when Antoinette was told that her starving people had no bread, she replied, "Let them eat cake." Such a statement presupposes life in a French palace where, if the larders were low on one food, one might merely select another menu item. It is not believed that Marie Antoinette actually said this, but the story could easily be attributed to the attitudes of the wealthy people of Israel. Blinded by their own indulgent lifestyles, they could not see that the vast majority of their people had neither bread nor cake.

Amos points to the unkind and calls them to repentance. He promises that judgment will come upon those who continually disregard the needs of others.

Despite our own comfortable existence, we can become overwhelmed with the needs of the world. We wonder how one person can make any difference. We find we have little time to spare for the poor on the other side of the world, let alone those on the street corners of our cities. Kindness is our willingness to care about others who may not have our standard of living and may even live one comfortable ocean-moat away from our luxurious lifestyles. But the bottom line is that God expects our compassion. God desires our kindness to spread his healing to others.

MEMORIZE THIS WEEK

COLOSSIANS 3:12

Therefore, as God's chosen people, holy and dearly loved, clothe yourselves with compassion, kindness, humility, gentleness and patience.

DAY TWO
▸ KINDNESS AND THE PURPOSE OF GOD IN MY LIFE

The purpose of God in our lives, all lives, is to make us citizens of the kingdom of God. How do all such citizens appear? For one thing they radiate a kind of energy that leaves others unafraid of them, so they can offer help without impediment. Citizens of God's kingdom model the attributes of God and help others. Citizens of the kingdom bring in new citizens through their kind acts. *Turn to Deuteronomy 10:17–19, page 213, for today's study.*

DAY THREE
▸ KINDNESS AND MY RELATIONSHIP WITH CHRIST

Jesus weeps over Jerusalem with a gentle heart. And what do his tears prompt? They lead to an entry into Jerusalem the following day with Jesus' heart set on saving all who would call on him. Surely kindness and empathy will heighten our own relationship with Christ. It could be that kind people cry more easily than the unconcerned. Jesus weeps not because he feels sorry for the people of Jerusalem but because he sympathizes with their empty humanity. *Turn to Luke 19:41–42, page 1235, for today's study.*

DAY FOUR
▸ KINDNESS AND MY SERVICE TO OTHERS

When we are blessed by God and experience his mercies, we want to share his kindness with others. David wanted to show God's kindness to another. He had been the recipient of God's kindness himself, and so he shared that mercy with one seemingly cursed by God. As we show kindness to others, we share God with them and take away their sorrows. *Turn to 2 Samuel 9:1–13, page 361, for today's study.*

DAY FIVE
▸ KINDNESS AND ITS PLACE IN MY PERSONAL WORSHIP

Worship is only valuable when it comes from real, warm human beings. Harsh worshipers never really see God, for they have never seen their partnership in the human race. Jesus here teaches that it is a flawed idea that we can love God and remain indifferent to others. *Turn to Matthew 5:23–24, page 1124, for today's study.*

Week 6, Goodness, Caring How God Feels About My Morality, begins on page 51, Genesis 39:1–10. To begin a topical study on the Fruit of the Spirit, Kindness, turn to the Topical Index, page 1548.

forty years[q] in the desert, O house
of Israel?
26You have lifted up the shrine of your
king,
the pedestal of your idols,
the star of your god[a]—
which you made for yourselves.
27Therefore I will send you into exile
beyond Damascus,"
says the LORD, whose name is
God Almighty.[r]

Woe to the Complacent

6 Woe to you[s] who are complacent in
Zion,
and to you who feel secure on
Mount Samaria,
you notable men of the foremost
nation,
to whom the people of Israel
come![t]
2Go to Calneh[u] and look at it;
go from there to great Hamath,[v]
and then go down to Gath[w] in
Philistia.
Are they better off than[x] your two
kingdoms?
Is their land larger than yours?
3You put off the evil day
and bring near a reign of
terror.[y]
4You lie on beds inlaid with ivory
and lounge on your couches.
You dine on choice lambs
and fattened calves.[z]
5You strum away on your harps[a] like
David
and improvise on musical
instruments.[b]
6You drink wine[c] by the bowlful
and use the finest lotions,
but you do not grieve[d] over the
ruin of Joseph.
7Therefore you will be among the
first to go into exile;
your feasting and lounging will
end.

The LORD Abhors the Pride of Israel

8The Sovereign LORD has sworn by
himself[e]—the LORD God Almighty declares:

"I abhor[f] the pride of Jacob[g]
and detest his fortresses;
I will deliver up[h] the city
and everything in it.[i]"

5:25 [q]Dt 32:17
5:27 [r]Am 4:13; Ac 7:42-43*
6:1 [s]Lk 6:24 [t]Isa 32:9-11
6:2 [u]Ge 10:10 [v]2Ki 18:34 [w]2Ch 26:6 [x]Na 3:8
6:3 [y]Isa 56:12; Am 9:10
6:4 [z]Eze 34:2-3; Am 3:12
6:5 [a]Isa 5:12; Am 5:23 [b]1Ch 15:16
6:6 [c]Am 2:8 [d]Eze 9:4
6:8 [e]Ge 22:16; Heb 6:13 [f]Lev 26:30 [g]Ps 47:4 [h]Am 4:2 [i]Dt 32:19

9If ten[j] men are left in one house,
they too will die. 10And if a relative who
is to burn the bodies[k] comes to carry
them out of the house and asks anyone still hiding there, "Is anyone with
you?" and he says, "No," then he will
say, "Hush![l] We must not mention the
name of the LORD."

11For the LORD has given the
command,
and he will smash the great
house[m] into pieces
and the small house into bits.[n]

12Do horses run on the rocky crags?
Does one plow there with oxen?
But you have turned justice into
poison[o]
and the fruit of righteousness into
bitterness[p]—
13you who rejoice in the conquest of
Lo Debar[b]
and say, "Did we not take
Karnaim[c] by our own
strength?"[q]

14For the LORD God Almighty
declares,
"I will stir up a nation[r] against
you, O house of Israel,
that will oppress you all the way
from Lebo[d] Hamath[s] to the valley
of the Arabah.[t]"

Locusts, Fire and a Plumb Line

7 This is what the Sovereign LORD
showed me:[u] He was preparing
swarms of locusts[v] after the king's share
had been harvested and just as the second crop was coming up. 2When they
had stripped the land clean,[w] I cried
out, "Sovereign LORD, forgive! How
can Jacob survive?[x] He is so small![y]"
3So the LORD relented.[z]
"This will not happen," the LORD
said.[a]
4This is what the Sovereign LORD
showed me: The Sovereign LORD was
calling for judgment by fire;[b] it dried up
the great deep and devoured[c] the land.
5Then I cried out, "Sovereign LORD, I
beg you, stop! How can Jacob survive?
He is so small![d]"

6:9 [j]Am 5:3
6:10 [k]1Sa 31:12 [l]Am 8:3
6:11 [m]Am 3:15 [n]Isa 55:11
6:12 [o]Hos 10:4 [p]Am 5:7
6:13 [q]Job 8:15; Isa 28:14-15
6:14 [r]Jer 5:15 [s]1Ki 8:65 [t]Am 3:11
7:1 [u]Am 8:1 [v]Joel 1:4
7:2 [w]Ex 10:15 [x]Isa 37:4 [y]Eze 11:13
7:3 [z]Dt 32:36; Jer 26:19; Jnh 3:10 [a]Hos 11:8
7:4 [b]Isa 66:16 [c]Dt 32:22
7:5 [d]ver 1-2; Joel 2:17

[a]26 Or *lifted up Sakkuth your king / and Kaiwan your idols, / your star-gods;* Septuagint *lifted up the shrine of Molech / and the star of your god Rephan, / their idols* [b]13 *Lo Debar* means *nothing.* [c]13 *Karnaim* means *horns; horn* here symbolizes strength. [d]14 Or *from the entrance to*

7:6 [e]Jnh 3:10

[6]So the LORD relented.[e]
"This will not happen either," the
Sovereign LORD said.

[7]This is what he showed me: The
Lord was standing by a wall that had
been built true to plumb, with a plumb
line in his hand. [8]And the LORD asked
me, "What do you see,[f] Amos?[g]"

"A plumb line,[h]" I replied.

Then the Lord said, "Look, I am setting a plumb line among my people Israel; I will spare them no longer.[i]

7:8 [f]Jer 1:11,13 [g]Isa 28:17; La 2:8; Am 8:2 [h]2Ki 21:13 [i]Jer 15:6; Eze 7:2-9

FAITHFULNESS

A PLUMB LINE

Amos 7:8

God's plumb line measures faithfulness. Rectitude holds a straight course. Virtue must not lean toward chummy wickedness. For cultures die as they condone their tilting codes of ethics.

[9]"The high places of Isaac will be
destroyed
and the sanctuaries[j] of Israel will
be ruined;
with my sword I will rise against
the house of Jeroboam.[k]"

7:9 [j]Lev 26:31 [k]2Ki 15:9; Isa 63:18; Hos 10:8

Amos and Amaziah

[10]Then Amaziah the priest of Bethel[l]
sent a message to Jeroboam[m] king of
Israel: "Amos is raising a conspiracy[n]
against you in the very heart of Israel.
The land cannot bear all his words.[o]
[11]For this is what Amos is saying:

7:10 [l]1Ki 12:32 [m]2Ki 14:23 [n]Jer 38:4 [o]Jer 26:8-11

" 'Jeroboam will die by the sword,
and Israel will surely go into exile,
away from their native land.' "

[12]Then Amaziah said to Amos, "Get
out, you seer! Go back to the land of Judah. Earn your bread there and do your
prophesying there.[p] [13]Don't prophesy
anymore at Bethel, because this is the
king's sanctuary and the temple of the
kingdom.[q]"

7:12 [p]Mt 8:34

7:13 [q]Am 2:12; Ac 4:18

[14]Amos answered Amaziah, "I was
neither a prophet[r] nor a prophet's son,
but I was a shepherd, and I also took
care of sycamore-fig trees. [15]But the
LORD took me from tending the flock[s]
and said to me, 'Go, prophesy to my
people Israel.'[t] [16]Now then, hear the
word of the LORD. You say,

7:14 [r]2Ki 2:5; 4:38

7:15 [s]2Sa 7:8 [t]Jer 7:1-2; Eze 2:3-4

" 'Do not prophesy against[u] Israel,
and stop preaching against the
house of Isaac.'

7:16 [u]Eze 20:46; Mic 2:6

[17]"Therefore this is what the LORD
says:

" 'Your wife will become a prostitute[v]
in the city,
and your sons and daughters will
fall by the sword.
Your land will be measured and
divided up,
and you yourself will die in a
pagan[a] country.
And Israel will certainly go into
exile,
away from their native land.[w]' "

7:17 [v]Hos 4:13 [w]2Ki 17:6; Eze 4:13; Hos 9:3

A Basket of Ripe Fruit

8 This is what the Sovereign LORD
showed me: a basket of ripe fruit.
[2]"What do you see,[x] Amos?[y]" he asked.

"A basket of ripe fruit," I answered.

Then the LORD said to me, "The
time is ripe for my people Israel; I will
spare them no longer.[z]

8:2 [x]Jer 24:3 [y]Am 7:8 [z]Eze 7:2-9

[3]"In that day," declares the Sovereign
LORD, "the songs in the temple will
turn to wailing.[b] [a] Many, many bodies—
flung everywhere! Silence![b]"

8:3 [a]Am 5:16 [b]Am 5:23; 6:10

[4]Hear this, you who trample the
needy
and do away with the poor[c] of the
land,[d]

8:4 [c]Pr 30:14 [d]Ps 14:4; Am 2:7

[5]saying,

"When will the New Moon be over
that we may sell grain,
and the Sabbath be ended
that we may market wheat?"—
skimping the measure,
boosting the price
and cheating with dishonest
scales,[e]
[6]buying the poor with silver
and the needy for a pair of
sandals,
selling even the sweepings with
the wheat.[f]

8:5 [e]2Ki 4:23; Ne 13:15-16; Hos 12:7; Mic 6:10-11

8:6 [f]Am 2:6

[7]The LORD has sworn by the Pride
of Jacob:[g] "I will never forget[h] anything
they have done.

8:7 [g]Am 6:8 [h]Hos 8:13

[8]"Will not the land tremble[i] for this,
and all who live in it mourn?

8:8 [i]Hos 4:3

[a]17 Hebrew *an unclean* [b]3 Or *"the temple singers will wail*

The whole land will rise like the
Nile;
it will be stirred up and then sink
8:8 [j]Ps 18:7; Jer 46:8; Am 9:5 like the river of Egypt.[j]

9"In that day," declares the Sovereign
LORD,

8:9 [k]Job 5:14; Isa 59:9-10; Jer 15:9; Am 5:8; Mic 3:6 "I will make the sun go down at
noon
and darken the earth in broad
daylight.[k]

PATIENCE

THE DAY OF DARKNESS

Amos 8:9

The sun and stars are God's witnesses that all things will continue. But one day the sun will abandon its pilgrimage and the stars will shrink away. God's rule will overcome. Until then we wait in faith.

10I will turn your religious feasts into
mourning
8:10 [l]Jer 48:37 [m]Jer 6:26; Zec 12:10 [n]Eze 7:18 and all your singing into weeping.
I will make all of you wear sackcloth[l]
and shave your heads.
I will make that time like mourning
for an only son[m]
and the end of it like a bitter
day.[n]

11"The days are coming," declares the
Sovereign LORD,
"when I will send a famine
through the land—
not a famine of food or a thirst for
water,
but a famine of hearing the words
8:11 [o]1Sa 3:1; 2Ch 15:3; Eze 7:26 of the LORD.[o]
12Men will stagger from sea to sea
and wander from north to east,
8:12 [p]Eze 20:3,31 searching for the word of the LORD,
but they will not find it.[p]

13"In that day

"the lovely young women and strong
young men
8:13 [q]Isa 41:17; Hos 2:3 will faint because of thirst.[q]
14They who swear by the shame[a] of
Samaria,
or say, 'As surely as your god lives,
8:14 [r]1Ki 12:29 [s]Am 5:5 [t]Am 5:2 O Dan,'[r]
or, 'As surely as the god[b] of
Beersheba[s] lives'—
they will fall,
never to rise again.[t]"

Israel to Be Destroyed

9 I saw the Lord standing by the altar, and he said:

"Strike the tops of the pillars
so that the thresholds shake.
Bring them down on the heads[u] of 9:1 [u]Ps 68:21
all the people;
those who are left I will kill with
the sword.
Not one will get away,
none will escape.
2Though they dig down to the depths
of the grave,[c][v] 9:2 [v]Ps 139:8 [w]Jer 51:53 [x]Ob 1:4
from there my hand will take
them.
Though they climb up to the
heavens,[w]
from there I will bring them
down.[x]
3Though they hide themselves on the
top of Carmel,[y] 9:3 [y]Am 1:2 [z]Ps 139:8-10 [a]Jer 16:16-17
there I will hunt them down and
seize them.[z]
Though they hide from me at the
bottom of the sea,
there I will command the serpent
to bite them.[a]
4Though they are driven into exile by
their enemies,
there I will command the sword[b] 9:4 [b]Lev 26:33; Eze 5:12 [c]Jer 21:10 [d]Jer 39:16 [e]Jer 44:11
to slay them.
I will fix my eyes upon them
for evil[c] and not for good.[d]"[e]

5The Lord, the LORD Almighty,
he who touches the earth and it 9:5 [f]Ps 46:2; Mic 1:4 [g]Am 8:8
melts,[f]
and all who live in it mourn—
the whole land rises like the Nile,
then sinks like the river of
Egypt[g]—
6he who builds his lofty palace[d] in the
heavens
and sets its foundation[e] on the
earth,
who calls for the waters of the sea
and pours them out over the face
of the land— 9:6 [h]Ps 104:1-3,5-6,13; Am 5:8
the LORD is his name.[h]

7"Are not you Israelites
the same to me as the Cushites[f]?"[i] 9:7 [i]Isa 20:4; 43:3
declares the LORD.

[a]*14* Or *by Ashima*; or *by the idol* [b]*14* Or *power*
[c]*2* Hebrew *to Sheol* [d]*6* The meaning of the Hebrew for this phrase is uncertain. [e]*6* The meaning of the Hebrew for this word is uncertain. [f]*7* That is, people from the upper Nile region

"Did I not bring Israel up from
Egypt,
the Philistines from Caphtor[a][j]
and the Arameans from Kir?[k]

8 "Surely the eyes of the Sovereign
LORD
are on the sinful kingdom.
I will destroy it
from the face of the earth—
yet I will not totally destroy
the house of Jacob,"
declares the LORD.[l]

9 "For I will give the command,
and I will shake the house of Israel
among all the nations
as grain[m] is shaken in a sieve,[n]
and not a pebble will reach the
ground.

10 All the sinners among my people
will die by the sword,
all those who say,
'Disaster will not overtake or meet
us.'[o]

Israel's Restoration

11 "In that day I will restore
David's fallen tent.
I will repair its broken places,
restore its ruins,
and build it as it used to be,[p]

12 so that they may possess the remnant
of Edom[q]
and all the nations that bear my
name,[b][r]"
declares the LORD,
who will do these things.[s]

13 "The days are coming," declares the
LORD,

"when the reaper will be overtaken
by the plowman[t]
and the planter by the one
treading grapes.
New wine will drip from the
mountains
and flow from all the hills.[u]

14 I will bring back my exiled[c] people
Israel;
they will rebuild the ruined cities[v]
and live in them.
They will plant vineyards and drink
their wine;
they will make gardens and eat
their fruit.[w]

15 I will plant[x] Israel in their own land,
never again to be uprooted
from the land I have given them,"

says the LORD your God.[y]

9:7 [j]Dt 2:23; Jer 47:4 [k]2Ki 16:9; Isa 22:6; Am 1:5; 2:10
9:8 [l]Jer 44:27
9:9 [m]Lk 22:31 [n]Isa 30:28
9:10 [o]Am 6:3
9:11 [p]Ps 80:12
9:12 [q]Nu 24:18
9:12 [r]Isa 43:7 [s]Ac 15:16-17*
9:13 [t]Lev 26:5 [u]Joel 3:18
9:14 [v]Isa 61:4 [w]Jer 30:18; 31:28; Eze 28:25-26
9:15 [x]Isa 60:21 [y]Jer 24:6; Eze 34:25-28; 37:12,25

[a] *7* That is, Crete [b] *12* Hebrew; Septuagint *so that the remnant of men / and all the nations that bear my name may seek* ⌊*the Lord*⌋ [c] *14* Or *will restore the fortunes of my*

OBADIAH

▸ AUTHORSHIP AND DATE

Obadiah

Date uncertain.

▸ KEY THEMES

The Edomites lived in their high-cliff capital. Because of the precipitous heights on which their capital existed, Edom felt smug and secure. They had helped Israel's enemies loot and plunder Jerusalem in the time of siege. They were like scavengers, for they took advantage of Israel after others had broken down the walls and plundered the city. Edom's participation in Israel's devastation brought God's wrath, which was prophesied by the prophet Obadiah. The name *Obadiah* means "servant of the Lord."

▸ FRUIT OF THE SPIRIT IN OBADIAH

Gentleness: The book of Obadiah is a rebuke to the fierceness of a proud nation. Edom should have been gentle in Israel's time of need, but they were cruel and unkind. Notice these verses that speak of forfeited gentleness:

Verse 5: "If grape pickers came to you, would they not leave a few grapes?" The implication is that these harsh scavengers had left nothing.

Verse 10: "Because of the violence against your brother Jacob [the Edomites were the descendant of Jacob's twin brother Esau], you will be covered with shame; you will be destroyed forever." Violence earns judgment, and gentleness earns love.

Verse 14: "You should not wait at the crossroads to cut down their fugitives, nor hand over their survivors in the day of their trouble." The Edomites had helped the conquerors round up those Israelites who were trying to escape. Instead of helping Israel, Edom had helped Israel's conquerors. Grace and gentleness should have replaced their viciousness of spirit.

[1]The vision of Obadiah.

This is what the Sovereign LORD says about Edom[a]—

We have heard a message from the LORD:
An envoy[b] was sent to the nations to say,
"Rise, and let us go against her for battle"[c]—
[2]"See, I will make you small among the nations;
you will be utterly despised.
[3]The pride[d] of your heart has deceived you,
you who live in the clefts of the rocks[a]
and make your home on the heights,
you who say to yourself,
'Who can bring me down to the ground?'[e]
[4]Though you soar like the eagle
and make your nest[f] among the stars,
from there I will bring you down,"[g]
declares the LORD.[h]

1:1 [a]Isa 63:1-6; Jer 49:7-22; Eze 25:12-14; Am 1:11-12 [b]Isa 18:2 [c]Jer 6:4-5
1:3 [d]Isa 16:6 [e]Isa 14:13-15; Rev 18:7
1:4 [f]Hab 2:9 [g]Isa 14:13 [h]Job 20:6

DAY 5 FIVE

▸ Self-Control and Its Place in My Personal Worship

Obadiah 1–4

Self-control is less prone to be a factor in a culture that feels safe and impregnable. So it was with Edom. Edom, a nation south of the Dead Sea, was the desert's only superpower. Who could possibly bring it down? But Edom was brought down, never to rise again.

Foolish pride so often precedes a fall! Think of all the indulgent boasts that came to nothing: The Spanish Armada was supposed to be unbeatable. The Maginot Line could not be crossed. The Berlin Wall would stand forever. The Hindenburg was the safest way to cross the ocean. Hitler's bunker was impregnable. The Titanic was unsinkable. Communism would dominate the 20th century. Germany would never rise from the ashes of World War I. The Vietnam conflict would be resolved in six months with U.S. involvement. Consider the foolishness of *ne plus ultra*, the idea that nothing existed beyond the Pillars of Hercules.

Pride! Pride! Pride! How it always lures us into certain defeat. Arnold Toynbee notes that, of the 28 civilizations that have occupied the center stage of world history, not one of them was crushed from the outside before it had decayed and rotted from the inside.

Self-control is rarely the virtue of the proud. Security breeds indulgence and death—both personal and national death. Still, believers are called to live lives of self-denial in times of cultural decadence. Only then can we triumph over that pitiable pride that defeated Edom and live to praise God in any nation or circumstance.

To begin a study on the topic of Self-Control, Managing My Moods, turn to the home page on page 179.

▸ Goodness

Obey or Die

Obadiah 4

No one is exempt from God's requirement. Conceit was Edom's bread; in eating it, the Edomites thought themselves so high that they need not answer to any god. Yet God soon met them at the edge of hell and required a new humility.

[5]"If thieves came to you,
if robbers in the night—
Oh, what a disaster awaits you—
would they not steal only as much as they wanted?
If grape pickers came to you,
would they not leave a few grapes?[i]
[6]But how Esau will be ransacked,
his hidden treasures pillaged!
[7]All your allies[j] will force you to the border;
your friends will deceive and overpower you;
those who eat your bread[k] will set a trap for you,[b]
but you will not detect it.
[8]"In that day," declares the LORD,
"will I not destroy[l] the wise men of Edom,

1:5 [i]Dt 24:21
1:7 [j]Jer 30:14 [k]Ps 41:9
1:8 [l]Job 5:12; Isa 29:14

[a]3 Or *of Sela* [b]7 The meaning of the Hebrew for this clause is uncertain.

men of understanding in the
mountains of Esau?
1:9 [m]Ge 36:11,34 9 Your warriors, O Teman,[m] will be
terrified,
and everyone in Esau's mountains
will be cut down in the slaughter.
1:10 [n]Joel 3:19 [o]Ps 137:7; Am 1:11-12 [p]Eze 35:9 10 Because of the violence[n] against your
brother Jacob,[o]
you will be covered with shame;
you will be destroyed forever.[p]
11 On the day you stood aloof
while strangers carried off his
wealth
and foreigners entered his gates
1:11 [q]Na 3:10 and cast lots[q] for Jerusalem,
you were like one of them.
12 You should not look down on your
brother
in the day of his misfortune,
1:12 [r]Eze 35:15 [s]Pr 17:5 [t]Mic 4:11 nor rejoice[r] over the people of Judah
in the day of their destruction,[s]
nor boast so much
in the day of their trouble.[t]
13 You should not march through the
gates of my people
in the day of their disaster,
nor look down on them in their
1:13 [u]Eze 35:5 calamity[u]
in the day of their disaster,
nor seize their wealth
in the day of their disaster.
14 You should not wait at the crossroads
to cut down their fugitives,
nor hand over their survivors
in the day of their trouble.

1:15 [v]Eze 30:3 [w]Jer 50:29; Hab 2:8 15 "The day of the LORD is near[v]
for all nations.
As you have done, it will be done
to you;
your deeds[w] will return upon your
own head.
16 Just as you drank on my holy hill,
so all the nations will drink[x] 1:16 [x]Jer 25:15; 49:12
continually;
they will drink and drink
and be as if they had never been.
17 But on Mount Zion will be
deliverance;[y] 1:17 [y]Am 9:11-15 [z]Isa 4:3
it will be holy,[z]
and the house of Jacob
will possess its inheritance.
18 The house of Jacob will be a fire
and the house of Joseph a flame;
the house of Esau will be stubble,
and they will set it on fire and
consume[a] it. 1:18 [a]Zec 12:6
There will be no survivors
from the house of Esau."
The LORD has spoken.

19 People from the Negev will occupy
the mountains of Esau,
and people from the foothills will
possess
the land of the Philistines.[b] 1:19 [b]Isa 11:14 [c]Jer 31:5
They will occupy the fields of
Ephraim and Samaria,[c]
and Benjamin will possess Gilead.
20 This company of Israelite exiles who
are in Canaan
will possess ⌞the land⌟ as far as
Zarephath;[d] 1:20 [d]1Ki 17:9-10 [e]Jer 33:13
the exiles from Jerusalem who are in
Sepharad
will possess the towns of the
Negev.[e]
21 Deliverers will go up on[a] Mount
Zion
to govern the mountains of Esau. 1:21 [f]Ps 22:28; Zec 14:9,16; Rev 11:15
And the kingdom will be the
LORD's.[f]

[a] 21 Or *from*

JONAH

AUTHORSHIP AND DATE

Jonah

Sometime around 760 B.C.

KEY THEMES

Assyria was Israel's great enemy at the time of the writing of this book. So Jonah's assignment was similar to God calling an American evangelist to go to Berlin to bring revival to Germany in 1942. In some ways, it is easy to understand Jonah's prejudice. But God is in love with the world. Jonah was not at liberty to cling to his prejudices. God told Jonah that, spiritually speaking, Nineveh had more than 120,000 people who could not tell their right hand from their left (see 4:11). They needed a revival to call them to God. Once Jonah decided he didn't want to be that evangelist, peace was no longer his.

FRUIT OF THE SPIRIT IN JONAH

Peace: The only thing that will bring peace is obedience. There are three things that yield no peace.

The first thing that cannot yield peace is running away from the direct command of God (see 1:1–3). God gave Jonah the assignment to go to Nineveh (in the proximity of present-day Baghdad); he headed for Tarshish (probably in present-day Spain) instead.

The second thing that cannot yield peace is prejudice. Jonah's preaching was effective, and Nineveh repented. But Jonah's extreme prejudice led to his anger over their repentance. He didn't want God to spare Nineveh. "He prayed to the LORD, 'O LORD, is this not what I said when I was still at home? That is why I was so quick to flee to Tarshish. I knew that you are a gracious and compassionate God, slow to anger and abounding in love, a God who relents from sending calamity' " (4:2).

The third thing that cannot yield peace is being angry with God. "But the LORD replied, 'Have you any right to be angry?' " (4:4).

Jonah Flees From the LORD

1:1 [a]Mt 12:39-41 [b]2Ki 14:25
1:2 [c]Ge 10:11

1 The word of the LORD came to
Jonah[a] son of Amittai:[b] 2"Go to
the great city of Nineveh[c] and preach

DAY 2 TWO

▸ LOVE AND THE PURPOSE OF GOD IN MY LIFE

Jonah 1:1–17

Jonah had a deep-sea experience because he refused to love those whom God loved. How insanely proud are our prejudices. Jane Austen's novel *Pride and Prejudice* is the title borne by most of us. We are too self-involved to really respect others and too prejudiced to offer grace to those we don't care for. We assume both that God is like us and that God likes us. We also assume that God is unlike our enemies and that he doesn't particularly like them either.

In this way we keep God local—walled within our private worldview. He is the biggest thing in our province and prefers our town to every other town in the world. We think that God, if asked, would say he likes our denomination best and that he would prefer that other denominations change their foolish dogmas to more closely match our own glorious doctrines.

Jonah didn't like the Ninevites, and he was quite surprised to discover that God didn't feel the same way he did. In fact, God wanted the Ninevites to repent. Jonah could clearly see that the Ninevites had a lot of repenting to do, but he didn't want to head up the revival. Jonah didn't want to see the Ninevites get right with God. Rather, he wanted God to fry them for their wickedness.

But, from within the belly of the fish, Jonah discovered a great truth: His enemies were not God's enemies. God loves everyone. Jonah learned that God loved the Ninevites as much as the Jews. After being vomited up by a fish, Jonah went to help some of God's friends—people whom he had never much cared for. They would now have a chance for a relationship with God because Jonah learned a lesson on love.

To begin a study on the topic of Love, God's Passion for His World, turn to the home page on page 1253.

against it, because its wickedness has
come up before me."
3But Jonah ran[d] away from the LORD
and headed for Tarshish. He went down 1:3 [d]Ps 139:7
to Joppa,[e] where he found a ship bound [e]Jos 19:46; Ac 9:36,43
for that port. After paying the fare, he
went aboard and sailed for Tarshish to
flee from the LORD.
4Then the LORD sent a great wind
on the sea, and such a violent storm
arose that the ship threatened to break
up.[f] 5All the sailors were afraid and each 1:4 [f]Ps 107:23-26
cried out to his own god. And they
threw the cargo into the sea to lighten
the ship.[g] 1:5 [g]Ac 27:18-19
But Jonah had gone below deck,
where he lay down and fell into a
deep sleep. 6The captain went to him
and said, "How can you sleep? Get
up and call[h] on your god! Maybe he 1:6 [h]Jnh 3:8
will take notice of us, and we will not [i]Ps 107:28
perish."[i]
7Then the sailors said to each other,
"Come, let us cast lots to find out who
is responsible for this calamity."[j] They 1:7 [j]Jos 7:10-18; 1Sa 14:42
cast lots and the lot fell on Jonah.
8So they asked him, "Tell us, who
is responsible for making all this trouble
for us? What do you do? Where do
you come from? What is your country?
From what people are you?"
9He answered, "I am a Hebrew and I
worship the LORD, the God of heaven,[k] 1:9 [k]Ac 17:24
who made the sea and the land."[l] [l]Ps 146:6
10This terrified them and they asked,
"What have you done?" (They knew he
was running away from the LORD, because
he had already told them so.)
11The sea was getting rougher and
rougher. So they asked him, "What
should we do to you to make the sea
calm down for us?"
12"Pick me up and throw me into
the sea," he replied, "and it will become
calm. I know that it is my fault that this
great storm has come upon you."[m] 1:12 [m]2Sa 24:17; 1Ch 21:17
13Instead, the men did their best
to row back to land. But they could
not, for the sea grew even wilder than
before.[n] 14Then they cried to the LORD, 1:13 [n]Pr 21:30
"O LORD, please do not let us die
for taking this man's life. Do not hold
us accountable for killing an innocent 1:14 [o]Dt 21:8
man,[o] for you, O LORD, have done as [p]Ps 115:3
you pleased."[p] 15Then they took Jonah 1:15 [q]Ps 107:29; Lk 8:24
and threw him overboard, and the raging
sea grew calm.[q] 16At this the men 1:16 [r]Mk 4:41
greatly feared[r] the LORD, and they of-

fered a sacrifice to the LORD and made
vows to him.
[17]But the LORD provided a great fish
1:17 [s]Mt 12:40; 16:4; Lk 11:30 to swallow Jonah,[s] and Jonah was inside
the fish three days and three nights.

Jonah's Prayer

2 From inside the fish Jonah prayed
to the LORD his God. [2]He said:

"In my distress I called to the
2:1 [t]Ps 18:6; 120:1 LORD,[t]
and he answered me.
From the depths of the grave[a] I
called for help,
and you listened to my cry.

KINDNESS

TWENTY THOUSAND LEAGUES UNDER THE SEA

Jonah 2:2

Praying from inside a fish is real prayer. Twenty thousand leagues under the sea is a reasonable place to get serious about God. Condemning a prophet to living under water may seem severe, but kindness was God's purpose.

2:3 [u]Ps 88:6 [v]Ps 42:7 [3]You hurled me into the deep,[u]
into the very heart of the seas,
and the currents swirled about me;
all your waves and breakers
swept over me.[v]
[4]I said, 'I have been banished
2:4 [w]Ps 31:22 from your sight;[w]
yet I will look again
toward your holy temple.'
[5]The engulfing waters threatened
me,[b]
the deep surrounded me;
seaweed was wrapped around my
2:5 [x]Ps 69:1-2 head.[x]
[6]To the roots of the mountains I sank
down;
the earth beneath barred me in
forever.
But you brought my life up from the
pit,
O LORD my God.

[7]"When my life was ebbing away,
2:7 [y]Ps 77:11-12 [z]2Ch 30:27 [a]Ps 11:4; 18:6 I remembered[y] you, LORD,
and my prayer[z] rose to you,
to your holy temple.[a]

2:8 [b]2Ki 17:15; Jer 10:8 [8]"Those who cling to worthless idols[b]
forfeit the grace that could be
theirs.
[9]But I, with a song of thanksgiving,
will sacrifice[c] to you. 2:9 [c]Ps 50:14,23; Hos 14:2
What I have vowed[d] I will make [d]Ecc 5:4-5
good. [e]Ps 3:8
Salvation[e] comes from the LORD."

[10]And the LORD commanded the
fish, and it vomited Jonah onto dry
land.

Jonah Goes to Nineveh

3 Then the word of the LORD came
to Jonah[f] a second time: [2]"Go to 3:1 [f]Jnh 1:1
the great city of Nineveh and proclaim
to it the message I give you."
[3]Jonah obeyed the word of the LORD
and went to Nineveh. Now Nineveh
was a very important city—a visit required three days. [4]On the first day,
Jonah started into the city. He proclaimed: "Forty more days and Nineveh
will be overturned." [5]The Ninevites believed God. They declared a fast, and
all of them, from the greatest to the 3:5
least, put on sackcloth.[g] [g]Da 9:3; Lk 11:32
[6]When the news reached the king
of Nineveh, he rose from his throne,
took off his royal robes, covered himself with sackcloth and sat down in the
dust.[h] [7]Then he issued a proclamation 3:6 [h]Job 2:8,13;
in Nineveh: Eze 27:30-31

"By the decree of the king and his
nobles:

Do not let any man or beast,
herd or flock, taste anything; do
not let them eat or drink.[i] [8]But 3:7 [i]2Ch 20:3
let man and beast be covered with
sackcloth. Let everyone call[j] ur- 3:8 [j]Ps 130:1;
gently on God. Let them give up Jnh 1:6
their evil ways and their violence.
[9]Who knows?[k] God may yet relent 3:9 [k]2Sa 12:22
and with compassion turn[l] from [l]Joel 2:14
his fierce anger so that we will not
perish."

[10]When God saw what they did and
how they turned from their evil ways,
he had compassion[m] and did not bring 3:10
upon them the destruction[n] he had [m]Am 7:6 [n]Jer 18:8
threatened.[o] [o]Ex 32:14

Jonah's Anger at the LORD's Compassion

4 But Jonah was greatly displeased
and became angry.[p] [2]He prayed to 4:1 [p]ver 4;
the LORD, "O LORD, is this not what Lk 15:28

[a]2 Hebrew *Sheol* [b]5 Or *waters were at my throat*

I said when I was still at home? That
is why I was so quick to flee to Tarshish. I knew[q] that you are a gracious
and compassionate God, slow to anger
and abounding in love,[r] a God who
relents from sending calamity.[s] 3Now,
O LORD, take away my life,[t] for it is
better for me to die[u] than to live."
4But the LORD replied, "Have you
any right to be angry?"[v]
5Jonah went out and sat down at a
place east of the city. There he made
himself a shelter, sat in its shade and
waited to see what would happen to
the city. 6Then the LORD God provided a vine and made it grow up over Jonah to give shade for his head to ease
his discomfort, and Jonah was very
happy about the vine. 7But at dawn the
next day God provided a worm, which
chewed the vine so that it withered.[w]
8When the sun rose, God provided
a scorching east wind, and the sun
blazed on Jonah's head so that he grew
faint. He wanted to die, and said, "It
would be better for me to die than to
live."
9But God said to Jonah, "Do you
have a right to be angry about the
vine?"
"I do," he said. "I am angry enough
to die."
10But the LORD said, "You have been
concerned about this vine, though you
did not tend it or make it grow. It
sprang up overnight and died overnight.
11But Nineveh[x] has more than a hundred and twenty thousand people who
cannot tell their right hand from their
left, and many cattle as well. Should
I not be concerned[y] about that great
city?"

4:2 [q]Jer 20:7-8 [r]Ex 34:6; Ps 86:5,15 [s]Joel 2:13
4:3 [t]1Ki 19:4 [u]Job 7:15
4:4 [v]Mt 20:11-15
4:7 [w]Joel 1:12
4:11 [x]Jnh 1:2; 3:2 [y]Jnh 3:10

MICAH

AUTHORSHIP AND DATE

Micah

Probably written during the reigns of Ahaz and Hezekiah, c. 735 B.C. to c. 687 B.C.

KEY THEMES

The book of Micah, like most of the Minor Prophets, has a strong emphasis on sin and judgment. Probably one of the most memorized verses in the Old Testament is Micah 6:8: "He has showed you, O man, what is good. And what does the LORD require of you? To act justly and to love mercy and to walk humbly with your God."

The prophet Micah attacked all types of unrighteousness: greed, oppression, injustice, extortion and political abuse. See, for example, 2:1; 3:1–2; 6:9–12. Still, there runs throughout his book tender themes of a loving Redeemer.

FRUIT OF THE SPIRIT IN MICAH

Love: In his preaching Micah named four great qualities of the love of God.

The love of God never breaks its ancient commitments. God had promised Abraham that he would make a great nation of his descendants. In his great love, he also promised to rescue Israel from exile. "I will surely gather all of you, O Jacob; I will surely bring together the remnant of Israel. I will bring them together like sheep in a pen, like a flock in its pasture; the place will throng with people" (2:12).

God's love always rescues the disabled and the bereaved, who fall into special categories of his care. " 'In that day,' declares the LORD, 'I will gather the lame; I will assemble the exiles and those I have brought to grief' " (4:6).

God's love never sees anyone or any place as too small to experience his exaltation. Bethlehem was not a large place, but it was just the right size to introduce Jesus to the world. "But you, Bethlehem Ephrathah, though you are small among the clans of Judah, out of you will come for me one who will be ruler over Israel, whose origins are from of old, from ancient times" (5:2).

God's love constantly seeks to forgive. His anger will not exist forever, only his love will continue. "Who is a God like you, who pardons sin and forgives the transgression of the remnant of his inheritance? You do not stay angry forever but delight to show mercy" (7:18).

1 The word of the LORD that came to Micah of Moresheth[a] during the reigns of Jotham,[b] Ahaz[c] and Hezekiah, kings of Judah[d]—the vision[e] he saw concerning Samaria and Jerusalem.

1:1 [a]Jer 26:18 [b]1Ch 3:12 [c]1Ch 3:13 [d]Hos 1:1 [e]Isa 1:1

[2]Hear, O peoples, all of you,[f]
listen, O earth[g] and all who are in it,
that the Sovereign LORD may witness[h] against you,
the Lord from his holy temple.[i]

1:2 [f]Ps 50:7 [g]Jer 6:19 [h]Ge 31:50; Dt 4:26; Isa 1:2 [i]Ps 11:4

Judgment Against Samaria and Jerusalem

[3]Look! The LORD is coming from his dwelling[j] place;
he comes down and treads the high places of the earth.[k]
[4]The mountains melt[l] beneath him
and the valleys split apart,[m]
like wax before the fire,
like water rushing down a slope.
[5]All this is because of Jacob's transgression,
because of the sins of the house of Israel.
What is Jacob's transgression?
Is it not Samaria?[n]
What is Judah's high place?
Is it not Jerusalem?

1:3 [j]Isa 18:4 [k]Am 4:13
1:4 [l]Ps 46:2,6 [m]Nu 16:31; Na 1:5
1:5 [n]Am 8:14

[6]"Therefore I will make Samaria a heap of rubble,
a place for planting vineyards.
I will pour her stones[o] into the valley
and lay bare her foundations.[p]
[7]All her idols[q] will be broken to pieces;
all her temple gifts will be burned with fire;
I will destroy all her images.[r]
Since she gathered her gifts from the wages of prostitutes,[s]
as the wages of prostitutes they will again be used."

1:6 [o]Am 5:11 [p]Eze 13:14
1:7 [q]Eze 6:6 [r]Dt 9:21 [s]Dt 23:17-18

Weeping and Mourning

[8]Because of this I will weep[t] and wail;
I will go about barefoot and naked.
I will howl like a jackal
and moan like an owl.
[9]For her wound is incurable;[u]
it has come to Judah.[v]
It[a] has reached the very gate[w] of my people,
even to Jerusalem itself.
[10]Tell it not in Gath[b];
weep not at all.[c]
In Beth Ophrah[d]
roll in the dust.
[11]Pass on in nakedness[x] and shame,
you who live in Shaphir.[e]
Those who live in Zaanan[f]
will not come out.
Beth Ezel is in mourning;
its protection is taken from you.
[12]Those who live in Maroth[g] writhe in pain,
waiting for relief,[y]
because disaster has come from the LORD,
even to the gate of Jerusalem.
[13]You who live in Lachish,[h][z]
harness the team to the chariot.
You were the beginning of sin
to the Daughter of Zion,
for the transgressions of Israel
were found in you.
[14]Therefore you will give parting gifts[a]
to Moresheth Gath.
The town of Aczib[i][b] will prove deceptive[c]
to the kings of Israel.
[15]I will bring a conqueror against you
who live in Mareshah.[j][d]
He who is the glory of Israel
will come to Adullam.[e]
[16]Shave[f] your heads in mourning
for the children in whom you delight;
make yourselves as bald as the vulture,
for they will go from you into exile.

1:8 [t]Isa 15:3
1:9 [u]Jer 46:11 [v]2Ki 18:13 [w]Isa 3:26
1:11 [x]Eze 23:29
1:12 [y]Jer 14:19
1:13 [z]Jos 10:3
1:14 [a]2Ki 16:8 [b]Jos 15:44 [c]Jer 15:18
1:15 [d]Jos 15:44 [e]Jos 12:15
1:16 [f]Job 1:20

Man's Plans and God's

2 Woe to those who plan iniquity,
to those who plot evil on their beds![g]
At morning's light they carry it out
because it is in their power to do it.
[2]They covet fields[h] and seize them,
and houses, and take them.
They defraud[i] a man of his home,
a fellowman of his inheritance.

2:1 [g]Ps 36:4
2:2 [h]Isa 5:8 [i]Jer 22:17

[a]*9* Or *He* [b]*10 Gath* sounds like the Hebrew for *tell.* [c]*10* Hebrew; Septuagint may suggest *not in Acco.* The Hebrew for *in Acco* sounds like the Hebrew for *weep.* [d]*10 Beth Ophrah* means *house of dust.* [e]*11 Shaphir* means *pleasant.* [f]*11 Zaanan* sounds like the Hebrew for *come out.* [g]*12 Maroth* sounds like the Hebrew for *bitter.* [h]*13 Lachish* sounds like the Hebrew for *team.* [i]*14 Aczib* means *deception.* [j]*15 Mareshah* sounds like the Hebrew for *conqueror.*

3 Therefore, the LORD says:

2:3 [j]Jer 18:11; Am 3:1-2 [k]Isa 2:12

"I am planning disaster[j] against this
people,
from which you cannot save
yourselves.
You will no longer walk proudly,[k]
for it will be a time of calamity.
4 In that day men will ridicule you;
they will taunt you with this
mournful song:

2:4 [l]Jer 4:13

'We are utterly ruined;[l]
my people's possession is divided
up.
He takes it from me!
He assigns our fields to traitors.'"

5 Therefore you will have no one in
the assembly of the LORD
to divide the land[m] by lot.

2:5 [m]Jos 18:4

False Prophets

6 "Do not prophesy," their prophets
say.
"Do not prophesy about these
things;
disgrace[n] will not overtake us.[o]"

2:6 [n]Mic 6:16 [o]Am 2:12

7 Should it be said, O house of Jacob:
"Is the Spirit of the LORD angry?
Does he do such things?"

"Do not my words do good[p]
to him whose ways are upright?[q]

2:7 [p]Ps 119:65 [q]Ps 15:2; 84:11

8 Lately my people have risen up
like an enemy.
You strip off the rich robe
from those who pass by without a
care,
like men returning from battle.
9 You drive the women of my people
from their pleasant homes.[r]

2:9 [r]Jer 10:20

You take away my blessing
from their children forever.
10 Get up, go away!
For this is not your resting place,[s]
because it is defiled,[t]
it is ruined, beyond all remedy.

2:10 [s]Dt 12:9 [t]Lev 18:25-29; Ps 106:38-39

11 If a liar and deceiver[u] comes and
says,

2:11 [u]Jer 5:31 [v]Isa 30:10

'I will prophesy for you plenty of
wine and beer,'
he would be just the prophet for
this people![v]

Deliverance Promised

12 "I will surely gather all of you,
O Jacob;
I will surely bring together the
remnant[w] of Israel.

2:12 [w]Mic 4:7; 5:7; 7:18

I will bring them together like sheep
in a pen,
like a flock in its pasture;
the place will throng with people.
13 One who breaks open the way will
go up before[x] them;

2:13 [x]Isa 52:12

they will break through the gate
and go out.
Their king will pass through before
them,
the LORD at their head."

Leaders and Prophets Rebuked

3 Then I said,

"Listen, you leaders[y] of Jacob,
you rulers of the house of Israel.

3:1 [y]Jer 5:5

Should you not know justice,
2 you who hate good and love evil;
who tear the skin from my people
and the flesh from their bones;[z]

3:2 [z]Ps 53:4; Eze 22:27

3 who eat my people's flesh,[a]
strip off their skin
and break their bones in pieces;[b]
who chop them up like meat for the
pan,
like flesh for the pot?"[c]

3:3 [a]Ps 14:4 [b]Zep 3:3 [c]Eze 11:7

4 Then they will cry out to the LORD,
but he will not answer them.[d]
At that time he will hide his face[e]
from them
because of the evil they have done.

3:4 [d]Ps 18:41; Isa 1:15 [e]Dt 31:17

5 This is what the LORD says:

"As for the prophets
who lead my people astray,[f]

3:5 [f]Isa 3:12; 9:16

if one feeds them,
they proclaim 'peace';
if he does not,
they prepare to wage war against
him.
6 Therefore night will come over you,
without visions,
and darkness, without divination.[g]
The sun will set for the prophets,[h]
and the day will go dark for them.

3:6 [g]Isa 8:19-22 [h]Isa 29:10

7 The seers will be ashamed[i]
and the diviners disgraced.[j]

3:7 [i]Mic 7:16 [j]Isa 44:25

They will all cover their faces
because there is no answer from
God."

8 But as for me, I am filled with
power,
with the Spirit of the LORD,
and with justice and might,
to declare to Jacob his transgression,
to Israel his sin.[k]

3:8 [k]Isa 58:1

[9]Hear this, you leaders of the house
of Jacob,
you rulers of the house of Israel,
who despise justice
and distort all that is right;[l]
[10]who build[m] Zion with bloodshed,[n]
and Jerusalem with wickedness.[o]
[11]Her leaders judge for a bribe,
her priests teach for a price,
and her prophets tell fortunes for
money.[p]
Yet they lean upon the LORD and
say,
"Is not the LORD among us?
No disaster will come upon us."[q]
[12]Therefore because of you,
Zion will be plowed like a field,
Jerusalem will become a heap of
rubble,[r]
the temple hill a mound
overgrown with thickets.

3:9 [l]Ps 58:1-2; Isa 1:23
3:10 [m]Jer 22:13 [n]Hab 2:12 [o]Eze 22:27
3:11 [p]Isa 1:23; Jer 6:13; Hos 4:8,18 [q]Jer 7:4
3:12 [r]Jer 26:18

The Mountain of the LORD

4 In the last days
the mountain[s] of the LORD's temple
will be established
as chief among the mountains;
it will be raised above the hills,[t]
and peoples will stream to it.[u]

[2]Many nations will come and say,
"Come, let us go up to the mountain
of the LORD,[v]
to the house of the God of Jacob.[w]
He will teach us his ways,[x]
so that we may walk in his paths."
The law will go out from Zion,
the word of the LORD from
Jerusalem.
[3]He will judge between many peoples
and will settle disputes for strong
nations far and wide.[y]
They will beat their swords into
plowshares
and their spears into pruning
hooks.[z]
Nation will not take up sword
against nation,
nor will they train for war
anymore.[a]
[4]Every man will sit under his own
vine
and under his own fig tree,[b]
and no one will make them afraid,[c]
for the LORD Almighty has
spoken.[d]
[5]All the nations may walk
in the name of their gods;[e]
we will walk in the name of the
LORD
our God for ever and ever.[f]

4:1 [s]Zec 8:3 [t]Eze 17:22 [u]Ps 22:27; 86:9; Jer 3:17
4:2 [v]Jer 31:6 [w]Zec 2:11; 14:16 [x]Ps 25:8-9; Isa 54:13
4:3 [y]Isa 11:4
4:3 [z]Joel 3:10 [a]Isa 2:4
4:4 [b]1Ki 4:25 [c]Lev 26:6 [d]Isa 1:20; Zec 3:10
4:5 [e]2Ki 17:29 [f]Jos 24:14-15; Isa 26:8; Zec 10:12

The LORD's Plan

[6]"In that day," declares the LORD,

"I will gather the lame;
I will assemble the exiles[g]
and those I have brought to grief.[h]
[7]I will make the lame a remnant,[i]
those driven away a strong nation.
The LORD will rule over them in
Mount Zion
from that day and forever.[j]
[8]As for you, O watchtower of the
flock,
O stronghold[a] of the Daughter of
Zion,
the former dominion will be
restored[k] to you;
kingship will come to the
Daughter of Jerusalem."

[9]Why do you now cry aloud—
have you no king?[l]
Has your counselor perished,
that pain seizes you like that of a
woman in labor?[m]
[10]Writhe in agony, O Daughter of
Zion,
like a woman in labor,
for now you must leave the city
to camp in the open field.
You will go to Babylon;[n]
there you will be rescued.
There the LORD will redeem[o] you
out of the hand of your enemies.

[11]But now many nations
are gathered against you.
They say, "Let her be defiled,
let our eyes gloat[p] over Zion!"
[12]But they do not know

4:6 [g]Ps 147:2 [h]Eze 34:13, 16; 37:21; Zep 3:19
4:7 [i]Mic 2:12 [j]Da 7:14; Lk 1:33; Rev 11:15
4:8 [k]Isa 1:26
4:9 [l]Jer 8:19 [m]Jer 30:6
4:10 [n]2Ki 20:18; Isa 43:14 [o]Isa 48:20
4:11 [p]La 2:16; Ob 1:12

[a]8 Or *hill*

PEACE

SWORDS TO PLOWSHARES

Micah 4:3

Is Jesus truly the Prince of Peace? When God finally has his way, humankind will study war no more. Peace will come in smelting swords into plowshares. There will be food for all, for every unemployed soldier will take up farming.

the thoughts of the LORD;
they do not understand his plan,[q]
he who gathers them like sheaves
to the threshing floor.

[4:12 qIsa 55:8; Ro 11:33-34]

13 "Rise and thresh, O Daughter of
Zion,
for I will give you horns of iron;
I will give you hoofs of bronze
and you will break to pieces many
nations."[r]
You will devote their ill-gotten gains
to the LORD,
their wealth to the Lord of all the
earth.

[4:13 rDa 2:44]

DAY 4 FOUR

▸ PEACE AND MY SERVICE TO OTHERS

Micah 5:4–5

Micah's prophecy that Christ will be our peace suggests five truths. In fact Micah names five virtues that accompany Christ's peace: the shepherding of Christ, the strength of the Lord, the majesty of the Name, secure living, and a ministry that extends to the ends of the earth (see Micah 5:4–5).

It is Christ our shepherd who leads us.

It is Christ our strength who empowers us.

It is Christ the Name in whom we find our identities and our reasons for being in the world.

It is Christ our security by whose protective providence we bless each coming day and live unafraid.

It is Christ our ministry to the ends of the earth in whom the church finds its one supreme purpose in the world.

What a gift is this! When any church recognizes that this is its reason for its existence, then that church is indeed a place of unity and joy. But when any church forgets this, it is destined to live out an uneasy and quarrelsome life.

Christ has called us to be redemptive. Redemption saves the lost and prevents them from living all eternity without Christ. But it also saves each individual believer from a meaningless life.

To begin a study on the topic of Peace, the Companionship of Christ, turn to the home page on page 1243.

A Promised Ruler From Bethlehem

5 Marshal your troops, O city of
troops,[a]
for a siege is laid against us.
They will strike Israel's ruler
on the cheek[s] with a rod.

[5:1 sLa 3:30]

2 "But you, Bethlehem[t] Ephrathah,[u]
though you are small among the
clans[b] of Judah,
out of you will come for me
one who will be ruler over Israel,
whose origins[c] are from of old,[v]
from ancient times.[d]"[w]

[5:2 tJn 7:42 uGe 48:7 vPs 102:25 wMt 2:6*]

▸ PEACE

THE HEART AS GOD'S CRADLE

Micah 5:2

Bethlehem would be for all time a rural citadel of peace. John Banister Tabb counseled us to consider Micah's words and be pleased with peace:

"Let my heart thy cradle be,
of thy bleak nativity.
Then as grows the outer din,
greater peace shall reign within."

3 Therefore Israel will be abandoned
until the time when she who is in
labor gives birth
and the rest of his brothers return
to join the Israelites.

4 He will stand and shepherd his
flock[x]
in the strength of the LORD,
in the majesty of the name of the
LORD his God.
And they will live securely, for then
his greatness[y]
will reach to the ends of the earth.
5 And he will be their peace.[z]

[5:4 xIsa 40:11; 49:9; Eze 34:11-15,23; Mic 7:14 yIsa 52:13; Lk 1:32]

Deliverance and Destruction

When the Assyrian invades[a] our land
and marches through our
fortresses,
we will raise against him seven
shepherds,
even eight leaders of men.[b]
6 They will rule[e] the land of Assyria
with the sword,

[5:5 zIsa 9:6; Lk 2:14; Col 1:19-20 aIsa 8:7 bIsa 10:24-27]

[a] *1* Or *Strengthen your walls, O walled city* [b] *2* Or *rulers* [c] *2* Hebrew *goings out* [d] *2* Or *from days of eternity* [e] *6* Or *crush*

5:6 [c]Ge 10:8 [d]Zep 2:13 [e]Na 2:11-13 the land of Nimrod[c] with drawn
sword.[a][d]
He will deliver us from the Assyrian
when he invades our land
and marches into our borders.[e]

5:7 [f]Mic 2:12 [g]Isa 44:4 [7]The remnant[f] of Jacob will be
in the midst of many peoples
like dew from the LORD,
like showers on the grass,[g]
which do not wait for man
or linger for mankind.
[8]The remnant of Jacob will be among
the nations,
in the midst of many peoples,
like a lion among the beasts of the
5:8 [h]Ge 49:9 [i]Mic 4:13; Zec 10:5 [j]Ps 50:22; Hos 5:14 forest,[h]
like a young lion among flocks of
sheep,
which mauls and mangles[i] as it goes,
and no one can rescue.[j]
5:9 [k]Ps 10:12 [9]Your hand will be lifted up[k] in
triumph over your enemies,
and all your foes will be destroyed.

[10]"In that day," declares the LORD,

"I will destroy your horses from
among you
5:10 [l]Hos 14:3; Zec 9:10 and demolish your chariots.[l]
[11]I will destroy the cities[m] of your land
5:11 [m]Isa 6:11 [n]Hos 10:14; Am 5:9 and tear down all your
strongholds.[n]
[12]I will destroy your witchcraft
and you will no longer cast spells.[o]
5:12 [o]Dt 18:10-12; Isa 2:6; 8:19 [13]I will destroy your carved images
and your sacred stones from
among you;
you will no longer bow down
to the work of your hands.[p]
5:13 [p]Eze 6:9; Zec 13:2 [14]I will uproot from among you your
Asherah poles[b][q]
5:14 [q]Ex 34:13 and demolish your cities.
[15]I will take vengeance[r] in anger and
5:15 [r]Isa 65:12 wrath
upon the nations that have not
obeyed me."

The LORD's Case Against Israel

6 Listen to what the LORD says:

"Stand up, plead your case before the
6:1 [s]Ps 50:1; Eze 6:2 mountains;[s]
let the hills hear what you have to
say.
6:2 [t]Dt 32:1 [u]Hos 12:2 [2]Hear,[t] O mountains, the LORD's
accusation;[u]
listen, you everlasting foundations
of the earth.
For the LORD has a case against his
people;
he is lodging a charge[v] against 6:2 [v]Ps 50:7
Israel.

[3]"My people, what have I done to
you?
How have I burdened[w] you? 6:3 [w]Jer 2:5
Answer me.
[4]I brought you up out of Egypt
and redeemed you from the land
of slavery.[x] 6:4 [x]Dt 7:8
I sent Moses[y] to lead you, [y]Ex 4:16 [z]Ps 77:20
also Aaron[z] and Miriam.[a] [a]Ex 15:20
[5]My people, remember
what Balak[b] king of Moab 6:5
counseled [b]Nu 22:5-6 [c]Nu 25:1
and what Balaam son of Beor [d]Jos 5:9-10 [e]Jdg 5:11;
answered. 1Sa 12:7
Remember ⌞your journey⌟ from
Shittim[c] to Gilgal,[d]
that you may know the righteous
acts[e] of the LORD."

[6]With what shall I come before the
LORD
and bow down before the exalted
God?
Shall I come before him with burnt
offerings,
with calves a year old?[f] 6:6 [f]Ps 40:6-8; 51:16-17
[7]Will the LORD be pleased with
thousands of rams,[g] 6:7
with ten thousand rivers of oil?[h] [g]Isa 40:16 [h]Ps 50:8-10
Shall I offer my firstborn[i] for my [i]Lev 18:21
transgression, [j]2Ki 16:3
the fruit of my body for the sin of
my soul?[j]
[8]He has showed you, O man, what
is good.
And what does the LORD require
of you?
To act justly[k] and to love mercy 6:8 [k]Isa 1:17; Jer 22:3
and to walk humbly[l] with your [l]Isa 57:15
God.[m] [m]Dt 10:12-13; 1Sa 15:22; Hos 6:6

Israel's Guilt and Punishment

[9]Listen! The LORD is calling to the
city—
and to fear your name is
wisdom—
"Heed the rod and the One who
appointed it.[c]
[10]Am I still to forget, O wicked house,
your ill-gotten treasures

[a]6 Or *Nimrod in its gates* [b]14 That is, symbols of the goddess Asherah [c]9 The meaning of the Hebrew for this line is uncertain.

and the short ephah,[a] which is
accursed?[n]
6:10 [n]Eze 45:9-10; Am 3:10; 8:4-6
11 Shall I acquit a man with dishonest
scales,[o]
with a bag of false weights?
6:11 [o]Lev 19:36; Hos 12:7
12 Her rich men are violent;[p]
her people are liars[q]
and their tongues speak
deceitfully.[r]
6:12 [p]Isa 1:23 [q]Isa 3:8 [r]Jer 9:3
13 Therefore, I have begun to destroy[s]
you,
to ruin you because of your sins.
6:13 [s]Isa 1:7; 6:11
14 You will eat but not be satisfied;[t]
your stomach will still be empty.[b]
You will store up but save nothing,[u]
because what you save I will give
to the sword.
6:14 [t]Isa 9:20 [u]Isa 30:6
15 You will plant but not harvest;[v]
you will press olives but not use
the oil on yourselves,
you will crush grapes but not
drink the wine.[w]
6:15 [v]Dt 28:38; Jer 12:13 [w]Am 5:11; Zep 1:13
16 You have observed the statutes of
Omri[x]
and all the practices of Ahab's[y]
house,
and you have followed their
traditions.[z]
Therefore I will give you over to
ruin[a]
and your people to derision;
you will bear the scorn[b] of the
nations.[c]"
6:16 [x]1Ki 16:25 [y]1Ki 16:29-33 [z]Jer 7:24 [a]Jer 25:9 [b]Jer 51:51

Israel's Misery

7 What misery is mine!
I am like one who gathers summer
fruit
at the gleaning of the vineyard;
there is no cluster of grapes to eat,
none of the early figs that I crave.
2 The godly have been swept from the
land;[c]
not one upright man remains.
All men lie in wait to shed blood;[d]
each hunts his brother with a net.[e]
7:2 [c]Ps 12:1 [d]Mic 3:10 [e]Jer 5:26
3 Both hands are skilled in doing evil;[f]
the ruler demands gifts,
the judge accepts bribes,
the powerful dictate what they
desire—
they all conspire together.
7:3 [f]Pr 4:16
4 The best of them is like a brier,[g]
the most upright worse than a
thorn hedge.
The day of your watchmen has
come,
the day God visits you.
Now is the time of their
confusion.[h]
7:4 [g]Eze 2:6 [h]Isa 22:5; Hos 9:7
5 Do not trust a neighbor;
put no confidence in a friend.[i]
Even with her who lies in your
embrace
be careful of your words.
7:5 [i]Jer 9:4
6 For a son dishonors his father,
a daughter rises up against her
mother,[j]
a daughter-in-law against her mother-
in-law—
a man's enemies are the members
of his own household.[k]
7:6 [j]Eze 22:7 [k]Mt 10:35-36*
7 But as for me, I watch in hope[l] for
the LORD,
I wait for God my Savior;
my God will hear[m] me.
7:7 [l]Ps 130:5; Isa 25:9 [m]Ps 4:3

Israel Will Rise

8 Do not gloat over[n] me, my enemy!
Though I have fallen, I will rise.[o]
Though I sit in darkness,
the LORD will be my light.[p]
7:8 [n]Pr 24:17 [o]Ps 37:24; Am 9:11 [p]Isa 9:2
9 Because I have sinned against him,
I will bear the LORD's wrath,[q]
until he pleads my case
and establishes my right.
He will bring me out into the light;
I will see his righteousness.[r]
7:9 [q]La 3:39-40 [r]Isa 46:13
10 Then my enemy will see it
and will be covered with shame,[s]
she who said to me,
"Where is the LORD your God?"
My eyes will see her downfall;[t]
even now she will be trampled[u]
underfoot
like mire in the streets.
7:10 [s]Ps 35:26 [t]Isa 51:23 [u]Zec 10:5

11 The day for building your walls[v] will
come,
the day for extending your
boundaries.
7:11 [v]Isa 54:11
12 In that day people will come to you
from Assyria and the cities of
Egypt,
even from Egypt to the Euphrates
and from sea to sea
and from mountain to
mountain.[w]
7:12 [w]Isa 19:23-25
13 The earth will become desolate
because of its inhabitants,
as the result of their deeds.[x]
7:13 [x]Isa 3:10-11

[a] *10* An ephah was a dry measure. [b] *14* The meaning of the Hebrew for this word is uncertain. [c] *16* Septuagint; Hebrew *scorn due my people*

Prayer and Praise

14Shepherd[y] your people with your
staff,[z]
the flock of your inheritance,
which lives by itself in a forest,
in fertile pasturelands.[a]
Let them feed in Bashan and Gilead[a]
as in days long ago.
15"As in the days when you came out
of Egypt,
I will show them my wonders."[b]
16Nations will see and be ashamed,[c]
deprived of all their power.
They will lay their hands on their
mouths
and their ears will become deaf.
17They will lick dust like a snake,
like creatures that crawl on the
ground.
They will come trembling out of
their dens;
they will turn in fear[d] to the
LORD our God
and will be afraid of you.
18Who is a God like you,
who pardons sin[e] and forgives[f] the
transgression
of the remnant[g] of his
inheritance?[h]
You do not stay angry[i] forever
but delight to show mercy.[j]
19You will again have compassion on
us;
you will tread our sins underfoot
and hurl all our iniquities[k] into
the depths of the sea.[l]
20You will be true to Jacob,
and show mercy to Abraham,
as you pledged on oath to our
fathers[m]
in days long ago.

[a]14 Or *in the middle of Carmel*

7:14 [y]Mic 5:4 [z]Ps 23:4 [a]Jer 50:19
7:15 [b]Ex 3:20; Ps 78:12
7:16 [c]Isa 26:11
7:17 [d]Isa 25:3; 49:23; 59:19
7:18 [e]Isa 43:25; Jer 50:20 [f]Ps 103:8-13 [g]Mic 2:12 [h]Ex 34:9 [i]Ps 103:9 [j]Jer 32:41
7:19 [k]Isa 43:25 [l]Jer 31:34
7:20 [m]Dt 7:8; Lk 1:72

NAHUM

AUTHORSHIP AND DATE

Nahum

Between 663 B.C. and 612 B.C.

KEY THEMES

The nation of Assyria was a cruel oppressor. Their savage sieges and battles poured forth blood and pillage. Here is the picture of their cruelty: "The lion killed enough for his cubs and strangled the prey for his mate, filling his lairs with the kill and his dens with the prey" (2:12). Assyria was so vicious in battle that Nahum could only proclaim, "Woe to the city of blood, full of lies, full of plunder, never without victims! ... Many casualties, piles of dead, bodies without number, people stumbling over the corpses" (3:1,3).

FRUIT OF THE SPIRIT IN NAHUM

Goodness: The prophet Nahum sets the evil empire of Assyria in sharp contrast against the goodness of God. The goodness of God is seen in three ways.

First, the Lord's goodness comes to us in times of storm and crisis, when we need protection: "The LORD is good, a refuge in times of trouble. He cares for those who trust in him" (1:7).

Second, the Lord's goodness comes to us in the good news that the God of goodness is coming to deliver us: "Look, there on the mountains, the feet of one who brings good news, who proclaims peace!" (1:15).

Third, it is the God of goodness who restores us to that glory we abandoned when we turned from his faithful covenants to live lives of self-will: "The LORD will restore the splendor of Jacob like the splendor of Israel" (2:2).

1:1 [a]Isa 13:1; 19:1; Jer 23:33-34 [b]Jnh 1:2; Na 2:8; Zep 2:13

1 An oracle[a] concerning Nineveh.[b] The book of the vision of Nahum the Elkoshite.

The LORD's Anger Against Nineveh

1:2 [c]Ex 20:5 [d]Dt 32:41; Ps 94:1

2 The LORD is a jealous[c] and avenging God;
the LORD takes vengeance[d] and is filled with wrath.
The LORD takes vengeance on his foes
and maintains his wrath against his enemies.

1:3 [e]Ne 9:17 [f]Ex 34:7 [g]Ps 104:3

3 The LORD is slow to anger[e] and great in power;
the LORD will not leave the guilty unpunished.[f]
His way is in the whirlwind and the storm,
and clouds[g] are the dust of his feet.
4 He rebukes the sea and dries it up;
he makes all the rivers run dry.

1:4 [h]Isa 33:9

Bashan and Carmel[h] wither
and the blossoms of Lebanon fade.

1:5 [i]Ex 19:18 [j]Mic 1:4

5 The mountains quake[i] before him
and the hills melt away.[j]
The earth trembles at his presence,
the world and all who live in it.
6 Who can withstand his indignation?

1:6 [k]Mal 3:2 [l]Jer 10:10 [m]1Ki 19:11

Who can endure[k] his fierce anger?
His wrath is poured out like fire;[l]
the rocks are shattered[m] before him.

1:7 [n]Jer 33:11 [o]Ps 1:6

7 The LORD is good,[n]
a refuge in times of trouble.
He cares for[o] those who trust in him,
8 but with an overwhelming flood
he will make an end of ⌊Nineveh⌋;
he will pursue his foes into darkness.
9 Whatever they plot against the LORD
he[a] will bring to an end;
trouble will not come a second time.
10 They will be entangled among thorns[p]

1:10 [p]2Sa 23:6 [q]Isa 5:24; Mal 4:1

and drunk from their wine;
they will be consumed like dry stubble.[b][q]
11 From you, ⌊O Nineveh,⌋ has one come forth

[a]9 Or *What do you foes plot against the LORD? / He*
[b]10 The meaning of the Hebrew for this verse is uncertain.

DAY 5 FIVE

Kindness and Its Place in My Personal Worship

Nahum 1:3

Worship is a place of relationships, a place where we bring our cleansed hearts to put them in concord with the immaculate holiness of God. And so we approach him, having set our thirst for holiness and right relationships clearly out front for all to consider. But what if we detect a blemish on our deportment, the smudge of some intentional fault or grudging attitude? What then do we do?

God is slow to anger. We are to look to him for guidance regarding how we should live. We should observe God's kindness and love toward those who do wrong, and we should determine to mirror that patience, kindness and love. But God is also just. We can trust that he will judge those who sin against us. We can leave vengeance in his hands.

When we have been wronged, when we have been sinned against, we must leave our gift unoffered and go out into the world. We must find those with whom we have grievances and straighten out our relationships. When we have done our best to mend our broken world, we may return to the altar and offer praise. God loves the whole world, and when we allow ourselves the luxury of nursing a grudge toward any of his children, we cannot meet with God in open communion. God wants no subterfuge going on within his family. Peace in the family is what every loving father wants.

A certain man of my acquaintance was about to have all of his children together for a Christmas reunion. Before they came, he distinctly told them that he wanted only one gift that Christmas: He wanted his children to love each other throughout the entire Christmas season. Every public worship service is a meeting of the family of God. It is God's desire, as head of the family, that we give him one present above all—a universal love for the entire family he loves.

To begin a study on the topic of Kindness, Always Applying the Golden Rule, turn to the home page on page 1141.

who plots evil against the LORD
and counsels wickedness.

12 This is what the LORD says:

"Although they have allies and are
numerous,
they will be cut off[r] and pass
away.
Although I have afflicted you,
O Judah,
I will afflict you no more.[s]
13 Now I will break their yoke[t] from
your neck
and tear your shackles away."
14 The LORD has given a command
concerning you, ⌞Nineveh⌟:
"You will have no descendants to
bear your name.[u]
I will destroy the carved images[v] and
cast idols
that are in the temple of your
gods.
I will prepare your grave,[w]
for you are vile."

1:12 [r]Isa 10:34 [s]Isa 54:6-8; La 3:31-32
1:13 [t]Isa 9:4
1:14 [u]Isa 14:22 [v]Mic 5:13 [w]Eze 32:22-23

GENTLENESS

GENTLE FEET

Nahum 1:15

The messenger comes.
The herald proclaims.
The news is welcome!
None need ever die again.

15 Look, there on the mountains,
the feet of one who brings good
news,[x]
who proclaims peace![y]
Celebrate your festivals,[z] O Judah,
and fulfill your vows.
No more will the wicked invade
you;[a]
they will be completely
destroyed.

1:15 [x]Isa 40:9; Ro 10:15 [y]Isa 52:7 [z]Lev 23:2-4 [a]Isa 52:1

Nineveh to Fall

2 An attacker[b] advances against you,
⌞Nineveh⌟.
Guard the fortress,
watch the road,
brace yourselves,
marshal all your strength!

2 The LORD will restore[c] the splendor
of Jacob
like the splendor[d] of Israel,
though destroyers have laid them
waste
and have ruined their vines.

2:1 [b]Jer 51:20
2:2 [c]Eze 37:23 [d]Isa 60:15

3 The shields of his soldiers are red;
the warriors are clad in scarlet.[e]
The metal on the chariots flashes
on the day they are made ready;
the spears of pine are brandished.[a]
4 The chariots[f] storm through the
streets,
rushing back and forth through
the squares.
They look like flaming torches;
they dart about like lightning.

5 He summons his picked troops,
yet they stumble[g] on their way.
They dash to the city wall;
the protective shield is put in
place.
6 The river gates[h] are thrown open
and the palace collapses.
7 It is decreed[b] that ⌞the city⌟
be exiled and carried away.
Its slave girls moan[i] like doves
and beat upon their breasts.[j]
8 Nineveh is like a pool,
and its water is draining away.
"Stop! Stop!" they cry,
but no one turns back.
9 Plunder the silver!
Plunder the gold!
The supply is endless,
the wealth from all its treasures!
10 She is pillaged, plundered, stripped!
Hearts melt, knees give way,
bodies tremble, every face grows
pale.[k]
11 Where now is the lions' den,[l]
the place where they fed their
young,
where the lion and lioness went,
and the cubs, with nothing to fear?
12 The lion killed[m] enough for his cubs
and strangled the prey for his
mate,
filling his lairs with the kill
and his dens with the prey.

13 "I am against[n] you,"
declares the LORD Almighty.
"I will burn up your chariots in
smoke,[o]
and the sword will devour your
young lions.

2:3 [e]Eze 23:14-15
2:4 [f]Jer 4:13
2:5 [g]Jer 46:12
2:6 [h]Na 3:13
2:7 [i]Isa 59:11 [j]Isa 32:12
2:10 [k]Isa 29:22
2:11 [l]Isa 5:29
2:12 [m]Jer 51:34
2:13 [n]Jer 21:13; Na 3:5 [o]Ps 46:9

[a]3 Hebrew; Septuagint and Syriac / *the horsemen rush to and fro* [b]7 The meaning of the Hebrew for this word is uncertain.

I will leave you no prey on the
earth.
The voices of your messengers
will no longer be heard."

Woe to Nineveh

3:1 [p]Eze 22:2; Mic 3:10

3 Woe to the city of blood,[p]
full of lies,
full of plunder,
never without victims!
2 The crack of whips,
the clatter of wheels,
galloping horses
and jolting chariots!
3 Charging cavalry,
flashing swords
and glittering spears!
Many casualties,
piles of dead,
bodies without number,
people stumbling over the
corpses[q]—

3:3 [q]2Ki 19:35; Isa 34:3

4 all because of the wanton lust of a
harlot,
alluring, the mistress of sorceries,[r]
who enslaved nations by her
prostitution[s]
and peoples by her witchcraft.

3:4 [r]Isa 47:9 [s]Isa 23:17; Eze 16:25-29

5 "I am against[t] you," declares the
LORD Almighty.
"I will lift your skirts[u] over your
face.
I will show the nations your
nakedness[v]
and the kingdoms your shame.

3:5 [t]Na 2:13 [u]Jer 13:22 [v]Isa 47:3

6 I will pelt you with filth,[w]
I will treat you with contempt[x]
and make you a spectacle.[y]

3:6 [w]Job 9:31 [x]1Sa 2:30; Jer 51:37 [y]Isa 14:16

7 All who see you will flee from you
and say,
'Nineveh[z] is in ruins—who will
mourn for her?'[a]
Where can I find anyone to
comfort[b] you?"

3:7 [z]Na 1:1 [a]Jer 15:5 [b]Isa 51:19

8 Are you better than[c] Thebes,[a][d]
situated on the Nile,[e]
with water around her?
The river was her defense,
the waters her wall.

3:8 [c]Am 6:2 [d]Jer 46:25 [e]Isa 19:6-9

9 Cush[b][f] and Egypt were her
boundless strength;
Put[g] and Libya[h] were among her
allies.

3:9 [f]2Ch 12:3 [g]Eze 27:10 [h]Eze 30:5

10 Yet she was taken captive[i]
and went into exile.
Her infants were dashed[j] to pieces
at the head of every street.
Lots were cast for her nobles,
and all her great men were put in
chains.

3:10 [i]Isa 20:4 [j]Isa 13:16; Hos 13:16

11 You too will become drunk;[k]
you will go into hiding[l]
and seek refuge from the enemy.

3:11 [k]Isa 49:26 [l]Isa 2:10

12 All your fortresses are like fig trees
with their first ripe fruit;
when they are shaken,
the figs[m] fall into the mouth of the
eater.

3:12 [m]Isa 28:4

13 Look at your troops—
they are all women![n]
The gates[o] of your land
are wide open to your enemies;
fire has consumed their bars.[p]

3:13 [n]Isa 19:16; Jer 50:37 [o]Na 2:6 [p]Isa 45:2

14 Draw water for the siege,[q]
strengthen your defenses![r]
Work the clay,
tread the mortar,
repair the brickwork!

3:14 [q]2Ch 32:4 [r]Na 2:1

15 There the fire will devour you;
the sword will cut you down
and, like grasshoppers, consume
you.
Multiply like grasshoppers,
multiply like locusts![s]

3:15 [s]Joel 1:4

16 You have increased the number of
your merchants
till they are more than the stars of
the sky,
but like locusts they strip the land
and then fly away.
17 Your guards are like locusts,[t]
your officials like swarms of
locusts
that settle in the walls on a cold
day—
but when the sun appears they fly
away,
and no one knows where.

3:17 [t]Jer 51:27

18 O king of Assyria, your shepherds[c]
slumber;[u]
your nobles lie down to rest.[v]
Your people are scattered[w] on the
mountains
with no one to gather them.

3:18 [u]Ps 76:5-6 [v]Isa 56:10 [w]1Ki 22:17

19 Nothing can heal your wound;[x]
your injury is fatal.
Everyone who hears the news about
you
claps his hands[y] at your fall,
for who has not felt
your endless cruelty?

3:19 [x]Jer 30:13; Mic 1:9 [y]Job 27:23; La 2:15; Zep 2:15

[a]*8* Hebrew *No Amon* [b]*9* That is, the upper Nile region [c]*18* Or *rulers*

HABAKKUK

AUTHORSHIP AND DATE

Habakkuk

Around 600 B.C.

KEY THEMES

The book of Habakkuk deals with hard times and God's care for us during those times. While Habakkuk couldn't understand why God would use a pagan nation to chastise Israel, he nonetheless wrote a document of hope while he wrestled with the question. He brought his complaints and questions to the Lord, but finally he emerged with a spirit of joy. He did not have the overwhelming kind of joy that one finds in a giddy song; rather, he had the deep kind of joy that can use the dark threads of pain to ornament a tapestry of light.

FRUIT OF THE SPIRIT IN HABAKKUK

Joy: Joy may come packaged in pain, and the book of Habakkuk gives us four insights on joy and how to spot joy when it comes in its disguise of reflection and profundity.

First, joy is the passion of worship that swells and swells until it fills the empty places of all God's creation, including the empty places of our lives. "For the earth will be filled with the knowledge of the glory of the LORD, as the waters cover the sea" (2:14).

Second, joy is the splendor of God in his advance into our dry and barren world. If we are perceptive, it is easy to see that as he fills the world, he fills our days and barren lives as well. "God came from Teman, the Holy One from Mount Paran. His glory covered the heavens and his praise filled the earth" (3:3).

Third, joy sings its song all through the bad times—when there is too little to eat and too little to spend. "Though the fig tree does not bud and there are no grapes on the vines, though the olive crop fails and the fields produce no food, though there are no sheep in the pen and no cattle in the stalls, yet I will rejoice in the LORD, I will be joyful in God my Savior" (3:17–18).

Fourth, joy is the great enabler that sticks with us through all the difficult passages of our lives. "The Sovereign LORD is my strength; he makes my feet like the feet of a deer, he enables me to go on the heights" (3:19).

1:1 [a]Na 1:1

1 The oracle[a] that Habakkuk the prophet received.

Habakkuk's Complaint

1:2 [b]Ps 13:1-2; 22:1-2 [c]Jer 14:9

[2]How long, O LORD, must I call for help,
but you do not listen?[b]
Or cry out to you, "Violence!"
but you do not save?[c]
[3]Why do you make me look at injustice?

1:3 [d]ver 13 [e]Jer 20:8 [f]Ps 55:9

Why do you tolerate[d] wrong?
Destruction and violence[e] are before me;
there is strife,[f] and conflict abounds.

1:4 [g]Ps 119:126 [h]Job 19:7; Isa 1:23; 5:20; Eze 9:9

[4]Therefore the law[g] is paralyzed,
and justice never prevails.
The wicked hem in the righteous,
so that justice is perverted.[h]

The LORD's Answer

1:5 [i]Isa 29:9 [j]Ac 13:41*

[5]"Look at the nations and watch—
and be utterly amazed.[i]
For I am going to do something in your days
that you would not believe,
even if you were told.[j]

1:6 [k]2Ki 24:2 [l]Jer 13:20

[6]I am raising up the Babylonians,[a][k]
that ruthless and impetuous people,
who sweep across the whole earth
to seize dwelling places not their own.[l]

1:7 [m]Isa 18:7; Jer 39:5-9

[7]They are a feared and dreaded people;[m]
they are a law to themselves
and promote their own honor.

1:8 [n]Jer 4:13

[8]Their horses are swifter[n] than leopards,
fiercer than wolves at dusk.
Their cavalry gallops headlong;
their horsemen come from afar.
They fly like a vulture swooping to devour;
[9] they all come bent on violence.
Their hordes[b] advance like a desert wind

1:9 [o]Hab 2:5

and gather prisoners[o] like sand.

1:10 [p]2Ch 36:6

[10]They deride kings
and scoff at rulers.[p]
They laugh at all fortified cities;
they build earthen ramps and capture them.

1:11 [q]Jer 4:11-12 [r]Da 4:30

[11]Then they sweep past like the wind[q]
and go on—
guilty men, whose own strength is their god."[r]

Habakkuk's Second Complaint

1:12 [s]Isa 31:1 [t]Isa 10:6

[12]O LORD, are you not from everlasting?
My God, my Holy One,[s] we will not die.
O LORD, you have appointed[t] them
to execute judgment;
O Rock, you have ordained them
to punish.

1:13 [u]La 3:34-36

[13]Your eyes are too pure to look on evil;
you cannot tolerate wrong.[u]
Why then do you tolerate the treacherous?
Why are you silent while the wicked
swallow up those more righteous than themselves?
[14]You have made men like fish in the sea,
like sea creatures that have no ruler.

1:15 [v]Isa 19:8 [w]Jer 16:16

[15]The wicked foe pulls all of them up with hooks,[v]
he catches them in his net,[w]
he gathers them up in his dragnet;
and so he rejoices and is glad.

1:16 [x]Jer 44:8

[16]Therefore he sacrifices to his net
and burns incense[x] to his dragnet,
for by his net he lives in luxury
and enjoys the choicest food.

1:17 [y]Isa 14:6; 19:8

[17]Is he to keep on emptying his net,
destroying nations without mercy?[y]

2:1 [z]Isa 21:8 [a]Ps 48:13 [b]Ps 85:8 [c]Ps 5:3

2 I will stand at my watch[z]
and station myself on the ramparts;[a]
I will look to see what he will say[b] to me,
and what answer I am to give to this complaint.[c][c]

The LORD's Answer

2:2 [d]Rev 1:19

[2]Then the LORD replied:

"Write[d] down the revelation
and make it plain on tablets
so that a herald[d] may run with it.

2:3 [e]Da 8:17; 10:14 [f]Ps 27:14

[3]For the revelation awaits an appointed time;
it speaks of the end[e]
and will not prove false.
Though it linger, wait[f] for it;

[a]6 Or *Chaldeans* [b]9 The meaning of the Hebrew for this word is uncertain. [c]1 Or *and what to answer when I am rebuked* [d]2 Or *so that whoever reads it*

it[a] will certainly come and will not
delay.[g]

2:3 [g]Eze 12:25; Heb 10:37-38

4 "See, he is puffed up;
his desires are not upright—
but the righteous will live by his
faith[b][h]—

2:4 [h]Ro 1:17*; Gal 3:11*; Heb 10:37-38*

5 indeed, wine[i] betrays him;
he is arrogant and never at rest.
Because he is as greedy as the grave[c]
and like death is never satisfied,[j]
he gathers to himself all the nations
and takes captive all the peoples.

2:5 [i]Pr 20:1 [j]Pr 27:20; 30:15-16

6 "Will not all of them taunt[k] him
with ridicule and scorn, saying,

2:6 [k]Isa 14:4 [l]Am 2:8

" 'Woe to him who piles up stolen
goods
and makes himself wealthy by
extortion![l]
How long must this go on?'
7 Will not your debtors[d] suddenly arise?
Will they not wake up and make
you tremble?
Then you will become their
victim.[m]

2:7 [m]Pr 29:1

8 Because you have plundered many
nations,
the peoples who are left will
plunder you.[n]
For you have shed man's blood;[o]
you have destroyed lands and
cities and everyone in them.

2:8 [n]Isa 33:1; Zec 2:8-9 [o]ver 17

9 "Woe to him who builds[p] his realm
by unjust gain
to set his nest on high,
to escape the clutches of ruin!

2:9 [p]Jer 22:13

10 You have plotted the ruin[q] of many
peoples,
shaming[r] your own house and
forfeiting your life.

2:10 [q]Jer 26:19 [r]ver 16

11 The stones[s] of the wall will cry out,
and the beams of the woodwork
will echo it.

2:11 [s]Jos 24:27; Lk 19:40

12 "Woe to him who builds a city with
bloodshed[t]
and establishes a town by crime!

2:12 [t]Mic 3:10

13 Has not the LORD Almighty
determined
that the people's labor is only fuel
for the fire,[u]
that the nations exhaust
themselves for nothing?[v]

2:13 [u]Isa 50:11 [v]Isa 47:13

14 For the earth will be filled with the
knowledge of the glory[w] of
the LORD,
as the waters cover the sea.[x]

2:14 [w]Nu 14:21 [x]Isa 11:9

JOY

THE UNIVERSAL GLORY

Habakkuk 2:14

Jesus is the first word of every worthy anthem. It is the knowledge of his glory that not only fills the earth, but also keeps it from being an uninhabitable wasteland.

15 "Woe to him who gives drink to his
neighbors,
pouring it from the wineskin till
they are drunk,
so that he can gaze on their naked
bodies.
16 You will be filled with shame[y]
instead of glory.
Now it is your turn! Drink and be
exposed[e]![z]
The cup[a] from the LORD's right
hand is coming around to
you,
and disgrace will cover your glory.

2:16 [y]ver 10 [z]La 4:21 [a]Isa 51:22

17 The violence[b] you have done to
Lebanon will overwhelm
you,
and your destruction of animals
will terrify[c] you.
For you have shed man's blood;[d]
you have destroyed lands and
cities and everyone in them.

2:17 [b]Jer 51:35 [c]Jer 50:15 [d]ver 8

18 "Of what value is an idol,[e] since a
man has carved it?
Or an image that teaches lies?
For he who makes it trusts in his
own creation;
he makes idols that cannot speak.[f]

2:18 [e]Jer 5:21 [f]Ps 115:4-5; Jer 10:14

19 Woe to him who says to wood,
'Come to life!'
Or to lifeless stone, 'Wake up!'[g]
Can it give guidance?
It is covered with gold and silver;[h]
there is no breath in it.

2:19 [g]1Ki 18:27 [h]Jer 10:4

20 But the LORD is in his holy temple;[i]
let all the earth be silent[j] before
him."

2:20 [i]Ps 11:4 [j]Isa 41:1

Habakkuk's Prayer

3 A prayer of Habakkuk the prophet.
On *shigionoth*.[f]

[a]*3* Or *Though he linger, wait for him; / he* [b]*4* Or *faithfulness* [c]*5* Hebrew *Sheol* [d]*7* Or *creditors*
[e]*16* Masoretic Text; Dead Sea Scrolls, Aquila, Vulgate and Syriac (see also Septuagint) *and stagger*
[f]*1* Probably a literary or musical term

WEEK 20

DAY ONE
1 ▸ JOY, THE INFALLIBLE PROOF OF THE PRESENCE OF GOD

Read Habakkuk 3:17–18

Hard times come. But these are the times that really instruct. Hard times are the classrooms of the school of life. Don't show us a congregation of rich Christians yawning their way through hymns if you want us to believe. Show us, rather, poor Christians who never seem to notice their poverty since a holy God has made them rich in spiritual blessings.

Look at what our joy teaches others when God is our sole sufficiency. Those who have little are really those who have much.

They praise God when the fig tree does not bud.
They praise God when there are no grapes on the vines.
They praise God when the olive crop fails.
They praise God when the fields produce no food.
They praise God when there are no sheep in the pen.
They praise God when there are no cattle in the stalls.

How ironic in our culture that most parents seem to want to show their children how to succeed—how to get ahead in the world. What children need their parents to show them is how to fail. We have so few lessons on that. And if possible, good Christian parents need to show their children how to sing in times of failure. We have almost no one giving lessons on that.

Joy is not dependent on the sumptuousness of our circumstances but on the richness of him who orders all our lives. When God is present in our lives, we show our joy to others, no matter what our situation in life.

MEMORIZE THIS WEEK

ZEPHANIAH 3:17

"The LORD your God is with you,
he is mighty to save.
He will take great delight in you,
he will quiet you with his love,
he will rejoice over you with singing."

DAY TWO
2 ▸ JOY AND THE PURPOSE OF GOD IN MY LIFE

Erase from your thinking the notion that you met God by accident and that he casually revealed to you some happenstance program for your life. Jeremiah counsels you to remember that before you were born, the plan for your life already existed. Long before you were *in utero* God already ordained you for a calling so magnificent, so grand, that the scope of God's confidence in you should thrill you. *Turn to Jeremiah 1:4–5, page 871, for today's study.*

DAY THREE
3 ▸ JOY AND MY RELATIONSHIP WITH CHRIST

God wants you to see that you are chosen, regal, holy, and best of all, that you belong to him. Now try if you will to belittle yourself in front of a God who sees only excellence of purpose when he beholds your life. And what is that purpose? You are to declare your joy—your praises for him who saved you and called you into service. Salvation is your pedigree, joy your vocation. *Turn to 1 Peter 2:9, page 1491, for today's study.*

DAY FOUR
4 ▸ JOY AND MY SERVICE TO OTHERS

Joy is not just something we give to God to keep him happy with our positive attitude. Joy is the way we minister to others. When we are face-to-face with the presence of God, with God's work in our lives, we respond with joy. And in the process, we lead others to joy in God as well. *Turn to Exodus 15:19–21, page 83, for today's study.*

DAY FIVE
5 ▸ JOY AND ITS PLACE IN MY PERSONAL WORSHIP

Here is God in the orchestra pit. But there are no union musicians playing their instruments by contract. These are symphonies of spontaneity by those who praise God by ear and not by practice or rehearsal. Strings, percussion, brass: none can begin to tell the world how the orchestra really feels about worshiping the King of the universe. *Turn to Psalm 150:1–6, page 729, for today's study.*

Week 21, Peace, the Evidence of Confidence, begins on page 1173, Mark 4:35–41.
To begin a topical study on the Fruit of the Spirit, Joy, turn to the Topical Index, page 1548.

3:2 [k]Ps 44:1 [l]Ps 119:120 [m]Ps 85:6 [n]Isa 54:8 2 LORD, I have heard[k] of your fame;
I stand in awe[l] of your deeds,
O LORD.
Renew[m] them in our day,
in our time make them known;
in wrath remember mercy.[n]

3 God came from Teman,
the Holy One from Mount Paran.
Selah[a]
His glory covered the heavens
3:3 [o]Ps 48:10 and his praise filled the earth.[o]
4 His splendor was like the sunrise;
rays flashed from his hand,
where his power was hidden.
5 Plague went before him;
pestilence followed his steps.
6 He stood, and shook the earth;
he looked, and made the nations
tremble.
The ancient mountains crumbled
3:6 [p]Ps 114:1-6 and the age-old hills collapsed.[p]
His ways are eternal.
7 I saw the tents of Cushan in distress,
3:7 [q]Jdg 7:24-25 [r]Ex 15:14 the dwellings of Midian[q] in
anguish.[r]
3:8 [s]Ex 7:20 [t]Ps 68:17 8 Were you angry with the rivers,[s]
O LORD?
Was your wrath against the
streams?
Did you rage against the sea
when you rode with your horses
and your victorious chariots?[t]
9 You uncovered your bow,
3:9 [u]Ps 7:12-13 you called for many arrows.[u] *Selah*
You split the earth with rivers;
10 the mountains saw you and
writhed.
Torrents of water swept by;
3:10 [v]Ps 98:7 [w]Ps 93:3 the deep roared[v]
and lifted its waves[w] on high.

3:11 [x]Jos 10:13 [y]Ps 18:14 11 Sun and moon stood still[x] in the
heavens
at the glint of your flying arrows,[y]
at the lightning of your flashing
spear.
12 In wrath you strode through the
earth
3:12 [z]Isa 41:15 and in anger you threshed[z] the
nations.
3:13 [a]Ps 20:6; 28:8 13 You came out to deliver[a] your
people,
to save your anointed one.
3:13 [b]Ps 68:21; 110:6 You crushed[b] the leader of the land
of wickedness,
you stripped him from head to
foot. *Selah*
14 With his own spear you pierced his
head
when his warriors stormed out to
3:14 [c]Jdg 7:22 [d]Ps 64:2-5 scatter us,[c]
gloating as though about to devour
the wretched[d] who were in hiding.
15 You trampled the sea with your
3:15 [e]Ex 15:8; Ps 77:19 horses,
churning the great waters.[e]

16 I heard and my heart pounded,
my lips quivered at the sound;
decay crept into my bones,
and my legs trembled.
Yet I will wait patiently for the day
of calamity
to come on the nation invading
us.
17 Though the fig tree does not bud
and there are no grapes on the
vines,
3:17 [f]Joel 1:10-12,18 [g]Jer 5:17 though the olive crop fails
and the fields produce no food,[f]
though there are no sheep in the pen
3:18 [h]Isa 61:10; Php 4:4 and no cattle in the stalls,[g]
18 yet I will rejoice in the LORD,[h]
I will be joyful in God my Savior.

3:19 [i]Dt 33:29; Ps 46:1-5 [j]Dt 32:13; 2Sa 22:34; Ps 18:33 19 The Sovereign LORD is my
strength;[i]
he makes my feet like the feet of
a deer,
he enables me to go on the
heights.[j]

For the director of music. On my
stringed instruments.

[a] *3* A word of uncertain meaning; possibly a musical term; also in verses 9 and 13

JOY

IN THE HARD TIMES

Habakkuk 3:17–18

Providence is the evidence of God's abundance. But God is still there even when his abundance is not evident. When there is no food, and manna does not fall, it is still a good time to praise the Lord.

ZEPHANIAH

AUTHORSHIP AND DATE

Zephaniah

Probably between 640 B.C. and 627 B.C.

KEY THEMES

The key theme of this book is judgment. The day of the Lord was on the way; it was "near and coming quickly" (1:14). Still, it was a day that would require the patient waiting of the people of God. In this sense, it was not unlike the emphasis we put on the second coming of Christ. While the day of the Lord represents an aspect of judgment, it also holds out an aspect of hope. Christians who await "the day of the Lord" are like children trying to hurry Christmas. We are to anticipate the day with singing (see 3:14). We are to be glad with hope and sing in our hearts. We, like those in Israel, can say, "The LORD has taken away [our] punishment . . . The LORD . . . is mighty to save" (3:15,17).

FRUIT OF THE SPIRIT IN ZEPHANIAH

Patience: In a sense, Israel was not—as Christians are not—to have a dull patience lacking fire. We are to have an *impatient* patience. Our patience anticipates the appearance of our divine lover. Our patience will end in union with the coming Christ. God has promised:

The sorrows for the appointed feasts
I will remove from you;
they are a burden and a reproach to you.
At that time I will deal
with all who oppressed you;
I will rescue the lame
and gather those who have been scattered.
I will give them praise and honor
in every land where they were put to shame.
At that time I will gather you;
at that time I will bring you home.
I will give you honor and praise
among all the peoples of the earth
when I restore your fortunes
before your very eyes.

(3:18–20)

1 The word of the LORD that came
to Zephaniah son of Cushi, the son
of Gedaliah, the son of Amariah, the
son of Hezekiah, during the reign of Josiah[a] son of Amon king of Judah:

Warning of Coming Destruction

2 "I will sweep away everything
from the face of the earth,"[b]
declares the LORD.
3 "I will sweep away both men and
animals;
I will sweep away the birds of the
air[c]
and the fish of the sea.
The wicked will have only heaps of
rubble[a]
when I cut off man from the face
of the earth,"[d]
declares the LORD.

Against Judah

4 "I will stretch out my hand[e] against
Judah
and against all who live in
Jerusalem.
I will cut off from this place every
remnant of Baal,[f]
the names of the pagan and the
idolatrous priests[g]—
5 those who bow down on the roofs
to worship the starry host,
those who bow down and swear by
the LORD
and who also swear by Molech,[b][h]
6 those who turn back from following[i]
the LORD
and neither seek[j] the LORD nor
inquire[k] of him.
7 Be silent[l] before the Sovereign
LORD,
for the day of the LORD[m] is near.
The LORD has prepared a sacrifice;[n]
he has consecrated those he has
invited.
8 On the day of the LORD's sacrifice
I will punish[o] the princes
and the king's sons[p]
and all those clad
in foreign clothes.
9 On that day I will punish
all who avoid stepping on the
threshold,[c]
who fill the temple of their gods
with violence and deceit.[q]

10 "On that day," declares the LORD,
"a cry will go up from the Fish
Gate,[r]
wailing from the New Quarter,
and a loud crash from the hills.
11 Wail,[s] you who live in the market
district[d];
all your merchants will be wiped
out,
all who trade with[e] silver will be
ruined.[t]
12 At that time I will search Jerusalem
with lamps
and punish those who are
complacent,[u]
who are like wine left on its dregs,[v]
who think, 'The LORD will do
nothing,[w]
either good or bad.'
13 Their wealth will be plundered,[x]
their houses demolished.
They will build houses
but not live in them;
they will plant vineyards
but not drink the wine.[y]

The Great Day of the LORD

14 "The great day of the LORD[z] is
near[a]—
near and coming quickly.
Listen! The cry on the day of the
LORD will be bitter,
the shouting of the warrior there.
15 That day will be a day of wrath,
a day of distress and anguish,
a day of trouble and ruin,
a day of darkness and gloom,
a day of clouds and blackness,[b]
16 a day of trumpet and battle cry[c]
against the fortified cities
and against the corner towers.[d]
17 I will bring distress on the people
and they will walk like blind[e]
men,
because they have sinned against
the LORD.

1:1 [a]2Ki 22:1; 2Ch 34:1-35:25
1:2 [b]Ge 6:7
1:3 [c]Jer 4:25 [d]Hos 4:3
1:4 [e]Jer 6:12 [f]Mic 5:13 [g]Hos 10:5
1:5 [h]Jer 5:7
1:6 [i]Isa 1:4; Jer 2:13 [j]Isa 9:13 [k]Hos 7:7
1:7 [l]Hab 2:20; Zec 2:13 [m]ver 14; Isa 13:6 [n]Isa 34:6; Jer 46:10
1:8 [o]Isa 24:21 [p]Jer 39:6
1:9 [q]Am 3:10
1:10 [r]2Ch 33:14
1:11 [s]Jas 5:1 [t]Hos 9:6
1:12 [u]Am 6:1 [v]Jer 48:11 [w]Eze 8:12
1:13 [x]Jer 15:13 [y]Dt 28:30,39; Am 5:11; Mic 6:15
1:14 [z]ver 7; Joel 1:15 [a]Eze 7:7
1:15 [b]Isa 22:5; Joel 2:2
1:16 [c]Jer 4:19 [d]Isa 2:15
1:17 [e]Isa 59:10

[a]*3* The meaning of the Hebrew for this line is uncertain. [b]*5* Hebrew *Malcam,* that is, Milcom
[c]*9* See 1 Samuel 5:5. [d]*11* Or *the Mortar*
[e]*11* Or *in*

JOY

THE SILENCE BEFORE
THE MUSIC

Zephaniah 1:7

Joy knows how to keep silent and wait its turn to sing.

1:17 [f]Ps 79:3 [g]Jer 9:22

Their blood will be poured out[f] like
dust
and their entrails like filth.[g]
18 Neither their silver nor their gold
will be able to save them
on the day of the LORD's wrath.[h]

1:18 [h]Eze 7:19 [i]ver 2-3; Zep 3:8 [j]Ge 6:7

In the fire of his jealousy
the whole world will be
consumed,[i]
for he will make a sudden end
of all who live in the earth.[j]"

2:1 [k]2Ch 20:4; Joel 1:14 [l]Jer 3:3; 6:15

2

Gather together,[k] gather together,
O shameful[l] nation,
2 before the appointed time arrives
and that day sweeps on like
chaff,[m]

2:2 [m]Isa 17:13; Hos 13:3 [n]La 4:11

before the fierce anger[n] of the LORD
comes upon you,
before the day of the LORD's
wrath comes upon you.
3 Seek[o] the LORD, all you humble of
the land,

2:3 [o]Am 5:6 [p]Ps 45:4; Am 5:14-15 [q]Ps 57:1

you who do what he commands.
Seek righteousness, seek humility;[p]
perhaps you will be sheltered[q]
on the day of the LORD's anger.

Against Philistia

4 Gaza[r] will be abandoned
and Ashkelon left in ruins.

2:4 [r]Am 1:6,7-8; Zec 9:5-7

At midday Ashdod will be emptied
and Ekron uprooted.
5 Woe to you who live by the sea,
O Kerethite[s] people;

2:5 [s]Eze 25:16 [t]Am 3:1 [u]Isa 14:30

the word of the LORD is against
you,[t]
O Canaan, land of the Philistines.

"I will destroy you,
and none will be left."[u]

6 The land by the sea, where the
Kerethites[a] dwell,
will be a place for shepherds and
sheep pens.[v]

2:6 [v]Isa 5:17

7 It will belong to the remnant of the
house of Judah;
there they will find pasture.
In the evening they will lie down
in the houses of Ashkelon.
The LORD their God will care for
them;
he will restore their fortunes.[b][w]

2:7 [w]Ps 126:4; Jer 32:44

Against Moab and Ammon

8 "I have heard the insults[x] of Moab
and the taunts of the Ammonites,
who insulted[y] my people

2:8 [x]Jer 48:27 [y]Eze 25:3

and made threats against their
land.
9 Therefore, as surely as I live,"
declares the LORD Almighty, the
God of Israel,
"surely Moab[z] will become like
Sodom,[a]
the Ammonites[b] like Gomorrah—
a place of weeds and salt pits,
a wasteland forever.
The remnant of my people will
plunder[c] them;
the survivors of my nation will
inherit their land.[d]"

2:9 [z]Isa 15:1-16:14; Jer 48:1-47 [a]Dt 29:23 [b]Jer 49:1-6; Eze 25:1-7 [c]Isa 11:14 [d]Am 2:1-3

10 This is what they will get in return
for their pride,[e]
for insulting[f] and mocking the
people of the LORD
Almighty.

2:10 [e]Isa 16:6 [f]Jer 48:27

11 The LORD will be awesome[g] to them
when he destroys all the gods[h] of
the land.
The nations on every shore will
worship him,[i]
every one in its own land.

2:11 [g]Joel 2:11 [h]Zep 1:4 [i]Zep 3:9

Against Cush

12 "You too, O Cushites,[c][j]
will be slain by my sword.[k]"

2:12 [j]Isa 18:1; 20:4 [k]Jer 46:10

Against Assyria

13 He will stretch out his hand against
the north
and destroy Assyria,
leaving Nineveh[l] utterly desolate
and dry as the desert.[m]

2:13 [l]Na 1:1 [m]Mic 5:6

14 Flocks and herds will lie down there,
creatures of every kind.
The desert owl[n] and the screech owl
will roost on her columns.

2:14 [n]Isa 14:23

Their calls will echo through the
windows,
rubble will be in the doorways,
the beams of cedar will be
exposed.
15 This is the carefree[o] city
that lived in safety.[p]
She said to herself,
"I am, and there is none besides
me."[q]
What a ruin she has become,
a lair for wild beasts!
All who pass by her scoff[r]
and shake their fists.

2:15 [o]Isa 32:9 [p]Isa 47:8 [q]Eze 28:2 [r]Na 3:19

[a]*6* The meaning of the Hebrew for this word is uncertain. [b]*7* Or *will bring back their captives* [c]*12* That is, people from the upper Nile region

The Future of Jerusalem

3 Woe to the city of oppressors,[s]
rebellious and defiled![t]
2 She obeys[u] no one,
she accepts no correction.[v]
She does not trust in the LORD,
she does not draw near[w] to her God.
3 Her officials are roaring lions,
her rulers are evening wolves,[x]
who leave nothing for the morning.
4 Her prophets are arrogant;
they are treacherous[y] men.
Her priests profane the sanctuary
and do violence to the law.[z]
5 The LORD within her is righteous;
he does no wrong.[a]
Morning by morning he dispenses his justice,
and every new day he does not fail,
yet the unrighteous know no shame.

6 "I have cut off nations;
their strongholds are demolished.
I have left their streets deserted,
with no one passing through.
Their cities are destroyed;[b]
no one will be left—no one at all.
7 I said to the city,
'Surely you will fear me
and accept correction!'
Then her dwelling would not be cut off,
nor all my punishments come upon her.
But they were still eager
to act corruptly[c] in all they did.
8 Therefore wait[d] for me," declares the LORD,
"for the day I will stand up to testify.[a]
I have decided to assemble the nations,[e]
to gather the kingdoms
and to pour out my wrath on them—
all my fierce anger.
The whole world will be consumed[f]
by the fire of my jealous anger.

9 "Then will I purify the lips of the peoples,
that all of them may call[g] on the name of the LORD
and serve[h] him shoulder to shoulder.

3:1 [s]Jer 6:6 [t]Eze 23:30
3:2 [u]Jer 22:21 [v]Jer 7:28 [w]Ps 73:28; Jer 5:3
3:3 [x]Eze 22:27
3:4 [y]Jer 9:4 [z]Eze 22:26
3:5 [a]Dt 32:4
3:6 [b]Lev 26:31
3:7 [c]Hos 9:9
3:8 [d]Ps 27:14 [e]Joel 3:2 [f]Zep 1:18
3:9 [g]Zep 2:11 [h]Isa 19:18

10 From beyond the rivers of Cush[b][i]
my worshipers, my scattered people,
will bring me offerings.[j]
11 On that day you will not be put to shame[k]
for all the wrongs you have done to me,
because I will remove from this city
those who rejoice in their pride.
Never again will you be haughty
on my holy hill.
12 But I will leave within you
the meek[l] and humble,
who trust[m] in the name of the LORD.
13 The remnant[n] of Israel will do no wrong;[o]
they will speak no lies,[p]
nor will deceit be found in their mouths.
They will eat and lie down[q]
and no one will make them afraid.[r]"

14 Sing, O Daughter of Zion;[s]
shout aloud,[t] O Israel!
Be glad and rejoice with all your heart,
O Daughter of Jerusalem!
15 The LORD has taken away your punishment,
he has turned back your enemy.
The LORD, the King of Israel, is with you;[u]
never again will you fear[v] any harm.
16 On that day they will say to Jerusalem,
"Do not fear, O Zion;
do not let your hands hang limp.[w]
17 The LORD your God is with you,
he is mighty to save.[x]
He will take great delight[y] in you,
he will quiet you with his love,
he will rejoice over you with singing."

18 "The sorrows for the appointed feasts
I will remove from you;
they are a burden and a reproach to you.[c]
19 At that time I will deal

[a]*8* Septuagint and Syriac; Hebrew *will rise up to plunder* [b]*10* That is, the upper Nile region
[c]*18* Or *"I will gather you who mourn for the appointed feasts; / your reproach is a burden to you*

3:10 [i]Ps 68:31 [j]Isa 60:7
3:11 [k]Joel 2:26-27
3:12 [l]Isa 14:32 [m]Na 1:7
3:13 [n]Isa 10:21; Mic 4:7 [o]Ps 119:3 [p]Rev 14:5 [q]Eze 34:15; Zep 2:7 [r]Eze 34:25-28
3:14 [s]Zec 2:10 [t]Isa 12:6
3:15 [u]Eze 37:26-28 [v]Isa 54:14
3:16 [w]Job 4:3; Isa 35:3-4; Heb 12:12
3:17 [x]Isa 63:1 [y]Isa 62:4

with all who oppressed you;
I will rescue the lame
and gather those who have been scattered.[z]
I will give them praise[a] and honor
in every land where they were put to shame.
20At that time I will gather you;
at that time I will bring[b] you home.
I will give you honor[c] and praise
among all the peoples of the earth
when I restore your fortunes[a][d]
before your very eyes,"
says the LORD.

[a]20 Or *I bring back your captives*

3:19 [z]Eze 34:16; Mic 4:6 [a]Isa 60:18

3:20 [b]Jer 29:14; Eze 37:12 [c]Isa 56:5; 66:22 [d]Joel 3:1

HAGGAI

AUTHORSHIP AND DATE

Haggai

c. 520 B.C.

KEY THEMES

The Jews were imprisoned in Babylon after the fall of Jerusalem in 586 B.C. But Babylon soon fell to the Persians. Cyrus, the Persian king, permitted the first wave of Jewish refugees to return to their homeland in 538 B.C. Ezra motivated their restoration of the temple for a period of time, but soon the work—which was all but overwhelming for the remnant who had returned—stopped. It then fell to Haggai to motivate them to begin the work again. His stirring calls to faithfulness comprise what is written in his very short book.

FRUIT OF THE SPIRIT IN HAGGAI

Faithfulness: Israel's season of empty, hard days was soon to end. The people had been through very difficult days, but Haggai spoke out in favor of a new era of faithfulness. At the end of this new era of faithfulness, God would bless the people forever. Haggai used an interesting term for the days ahead: "From this day on…" (2:15,18). Through Haggai, God made this promise: "From this day on, from this twenty-fourth day of the ninth month, give careful thought to the day when the foundation of the LORD's temple was laid. Give careful thought: Is there yet any seed left in the barn? Until now, the vine and the fig tree…have not borne fruit. From this day on I will bless you." (2:18–19). What Haggai was saying was: "Cheer up! The hard times are over! Today really is the first day of the rest of your lives."

A Call to Build the House of the LORD

1:1 [a]Ezr 4:24 [b]Ezr 5:1 [c]Mt 1:12-13 [d]Ezr 5:3 [e]Ezr 2:2 [f]1Ch 6:15; Ezr 3:2
1 In the second year of King Darius,[a]
on the first day of the sixth month,
the word of the LORD came through
the prophet Haggai[b] to Zerubbabel[c] son
of Shealtiel, governor[d] of Judah, and
to Joshua[a][e] son of Jehozadak,[f] the high
priest:
2This is what the LORD Almighty
says: "These people say, 'The time has
not yet come for the LORD's house to
be built.' "
3Then the word of the LORD came
1:3 [g]Ezr 5:1 through the prophet Haggai:[g] 4"Is it a
1:4 time for you yourselves to be living in
[h]2Sa 7:2 your paneled houses,[h] while this house
[i]ver 9; Jer 33:12 remains a ruin?[i]"

▸ LOVE

LOVE JESUS FOR HIMSELF

Haggai 1:4

God's house is sometimes left unfinished while we build smaller empires of our own. It is not surprising that Thomas à Kempis said, "Love all for Jesus, but Jesus for himself."

5Now this is what the LORD Al-
1:5 [j]La 3:40 mighty says: "Give careful thought[j] to
your ways. 6You have planted much, but
1:6 [k]Dt 28:38 have harvested little.[k] You eat, but never
[l]Hag 2:16; Zec 8:10 have enough. You drink, but never have
your fill. You put on clothes, but are
not warm. You earn wages,[l] only to put
them in a purse with holes in it."
7This is what the LORD Almighty
says: "Give careful thought to your
ways. 8Go up into the mountains and
bring down timber and build the house,
1:8 [m]Ps 132:13-14 so that I may take pleasure[m] in it and
be honored," says the LORD. 9"You ex-
pected much, but see, it turned out to
be little. What you brought home, I
blew away. Why?" declares the LORD
Almighty. "Because of my house, which
1:9 [n]ver 4 remains a ruin,[n] while each of you is
busy with his own house. 10Therefore,
because of you the heavens have with-
1:10 [o]Lev 26:19; Dt 28:23 held their dew and the earth its crops.[o]
11I called for a drought[p] on the fields
1:11 [p]Dt 28:22; 1Ki 17:1 [q]Hag 2:17 and the mountains, on the grain, the
new wine, the oil and whatever the
ground produces, on men and cattle,
and on the labor of your hands."[q]

DAY 2 TWO

▸ SELF-CONTROL AND THE PURPOSE OF GOD IN MY LIFE

Haggai 1:5–6

Haggai wanted to set people free from their own permissiveness. He reminded them that the temptation to "do it if it feels good" is an open-ended proposition. To attempt to be happy by having more while giving God less is like a bucket with holes in it.

"You have planted much, but have harvested little. You eat, but never have enough . . . You put on clothes, but are not warm. You earn wages, only to put them in a purse with holes in it."

Self-gratification is the key to happiness, or so we are told. The pitch of nearly all advertising is: "Go ahead and indulge." "Let yourself go," entices one fast food restaurant. "Pamper yourself," says another firm.

Not many national advertising firms say, "Hey! Deny yourself! You must stop letting yourself go! You've pampered yourself far too long. You don't deserve a break."

Haggai reminds us that all the fun we think we're having by letting ourselves go has gotten out of hand. It's time to set ourselves free from these "freedoms" that kill and destroy our lives by spoonfuls.

I had a friend who said he had conquered fundamentalist legalisms and was free to take a drink whenever he wanted to; he died an alcoholic. I had a friend who said he was sexually faithful—generally—but he liked to window shop; he eventually left his wife for another woman. His children have never recovered. I had a friend who felt confident that he could get around some tax laws; he's now spent four years in prison.

Haggai said we can develop a close relationship with God only when we quit serving ourselves. Only then can we really convince ourselves that we are not gods, a realization that will allow us to truly know God's purposes for our lives.

To begin a study on the topic of Self-Control, Freedom From Permissiveness, turn to the home page on page 452.

[a]*1* A variant of *Jeshua*; here and elsewhere in Haggai

1:12 12Then Zerubbabel[r] son of Shealtiel,
[r]ver 1; [s]ver 14; Joshua son of Jehozadak, the high priest,
Isa 1:9; and the whole remnant[s] of the people
Hag 2:2; [t]Isa 50:10 obeyed[t] the voice of the LORD their
[u]Dt 31:12 God and the message of the prophet
Haggai, because the LORD their God
had sent him. And the people feared[u]
the LORD.
13Then Haggai, the LORD's messen-
1:13 ger, gave this message of the LORD to
[v]Mt 28:20; the people: "I am with[v] you," declares
Ro 8:31 the LORD. 14So the LORD stirred up
1:14 the spirit of Zerubbabel[w] son of Sheal-
[w]Ezr 5:2; [x]ver 12 tiel, governor of Judah, and the spirit
of Joshua son of Jehozadak, the high
priest, and the spirit of the whole remnant[x] of the people. They came and began to work on the house of the LORD
1:15 Almighty, their God, 15on the twenty-
[y]ver 1 fourth day of the sixth month[y] in the
second year of King Darius.

The Promised Glory of the New House

2 On the twenty-first day of the
seventh month, the word of the
LORD came through the prophet Haggai: 2"Speak to Zerubbabel son of Shealtiel, governor of Judah, to Joshua son
of Jehozadak, the high priest, and to
the remnant of the people. Ask them,
2:3 3'Who of you is left who saw this house[z]
[z]Ezr 3:12 in its former glory? How does it look
[a]Zec 4:10 to you now? Does it not seem to you
2:4 like nothing?[a] 4But now be strong,[b]
[b]1Ch 28:20; O Zerubbabel,' declares the Lord. 'Be
Zec 8:9; Eph 6:10 strong, O Joshua son of Jehozadak, the
[c]2Sa 5:10; high priest. Be strong, all you people of
Ac 7:9 the land,' declares the Lord, 'and work.
For I am with[c] you,' declares the Lord
Almighty. 5'This is what I covenanted
2:5 with you when you came out of Egypt.[d]
[d]Ex 29:46; [e]Ne 9:20; And my Spirit[e] remains among you.
Isa 63:11 Do not fear.'
6"This is what the LORD Almighty
2:6 [f]Isa 10:25 says: 'In a little while[f] I will once more
[g]Heb 12:26* shake the heavens and the earth,[g] the sea
and the dry land. 7I will shake all na-
tions, and the desired of all nations will
2:7 come, and I will fill this house[h] with
[h]Isa 60:7 glory,' says the LORD Almighty. 8'The
silver is mine and the gold is mine,' de-
2:9 [i]Ps 85:9 clares the LORD Almighty. 9'The glory[i]
of this present house will be greater
than the glory of the former house,'
says the LORD Almighty. 'And in this
place I will grant peace,' declares the
LORD Almighty."

DAY 5 FIVE

PEACE AND ITS PLACE IN MY PERSONAL WORSHIP

Haggai 2:1–9

Our individual worship is greater than the house of God. Yet how often do we go to church to feel its all-pervasive influence in our spiritual development?

When I was nine years old, I discovered the joy of corporate worship in a Pentecostal tent revival.

There was little use in asking Pentecostals where they got their tents. It was like asking Ringling Brothers where they got their tents. The Pentecostals had tents; that was all. And they came to our town. Their big-top tabernacle rose above a swampy, snaky tent site and as the wind billowed the canvas, the happy accordion sounds filled the cloth cathedral with melodies. The tent looked like a huge orange jack-o'-lantern, lit by dangling light bulbs, around which swarmed the candle-flies of August... I listened as a red-eyed, buck-skinned prophet told us of the Great Whore of Babylon who would be consort to the Anti-Christ until blood flowed to the horses' bridles.

I knew from my very first encounter with worship that I belonged in a world where people took God so seriously that they sang louder than necessary, preached longer than necessary and held public invitations that were probably more emotional than necessary. But one thing that was clearly necessary to them was God, and God happened to me in that church—every time I went. I worshiped and, even as a child, was reminded that the best realities were intangible and more cosmic than Oklahoma.

Ever since that time, I have agreed with Haggai: The best house of God is the one I'm in at whatever moment I happen to be in it. Any structure is significant where two or three are gathered together. There, peace is the offering, and peace is the concord of our union with Christ.

To begin a study on the topic of Peace, the Companionship of Christ, turn to the home page on page 1243.

Blessings for a Defiled People

10 On the twenty-fourth day of the ninth month,[j] in the second year of Darius, the word of the LORD came to the prophet Haggai: 11 "This is what the LORD Almighty says: 'Ask the priests[k] what the law says: 12 If a person carries consecrated meat in the fold of his garment, and that fold touches some bread or stew, some wine, oil or other food, does it become consecrated?[l]'"

The priests answered, "No."

13 Then Haggai said, "If a person defiled by contact with a dead body touches one of these things, does it become defiled?[m]"

"Yes," the priests replied, "it becomes defiled."

14 Then Haggai said, "'So it is with this people and this nation in my sight,' declares the LORD. 'Whatever they do and whatever they offer[n] there is defiled.

15 "'Now give careful thought[o] to this from this day on[a]—consider how things were before one stone was laid[p] on another in the LORD's temple.[q] 16 When anyone came to a heap of twenty measures, there were only ten. When anyone went to a wine vat to draw fifty measures, there were only twenty.[r] 17 I struck all the work of your hands[s] with blight,[t] mildew and hail, yet you did not turn to me,' declares the LORD.[u] 18 'From this day on, from this twenty-fourth day of the ninth month, give careful thought to the day when the foundation[v] of the LORD's temple was laid. Give careful thought: 19 Is there yet any seed left in the barn? Until now, the vine and the fig tree, the pomegranate and the olive tree have not borne fruit.

"'From this day on I will bless you.'"

Zerubbabel the LORD's Signet Ring

20 The word of the LORD came to Haggai a second time on the twenty-fourth day of the month: 21 "Tell Zerubbabel[w] governor of Judah that I will shake the heavens and the earth. 22 I will overturn royal thrones and shatter the power of the foreign kingdoms.[x] I will overthrow chariots[y] and their drivers; horses and their riders will fall, each by the sword of his brother.[z]

23 "'On that day,' declares the LORD Almighty, 'I will take you, my servant[a] Zerubbabel son of Shealtiel,' declares the LORD, 'and I will make you like my signet ring, for I have chosen you,' declares the LORD Almighty."

2:10 [j]ver 1
2:11 [k]Lev 10:10-11; Dt 17:8-11; Mal 2:7
2:12 [l]Lev 6:27; Mt 23:19
2:13 [m]Lev 22:4-6
2:14 [n]Isa 1:13
2:15 [o]Hag 1:5 [p]Ezr 3:10 [q]Ezr 4:24
2:16 [r]Hag 1:6
2:17 [s]Hag 1:11 [t]Dt 28:22; 1Ki 8:37; Am 4:9
2:17 [u]Am 4:6
2:18 [v]Zec 8:9
2:21 [w]Ezr 5:2
2:22 [x]Da 2:44 [y]Mic 5:10 [z]Jdg 7:22
2:23 [a]Isa 43:10

[a]15 Or *to the days past*

ZECHARIAH

AUTHORSHIP AND DATE

Zechariah

c. 520 B.C. to c. 480 B.C.

KEY THEMES

Zechariah ministered to the Jews returning from exile. He gave counsel and instruction, particularly to those who had come back to rebuild the temple. The book falls into two distinct divisions. Chapters 1–8 were probably sermons preached during the time the temple was being rebuilt. Chapters 9–14 were probably sermons preached after the temple project was completed. Hope runs like a scarlet ribbon through this book. It appears that—in Zechariah's mind—once the temple was rebuilt, the world would be ready for the coming of the Messiah.

FRUIT OF THE SPIRIT IN ZECHARIAH

Gentleness: Seven lessons of God's gentleness are nestled in this longest book of the Minor Prophets. Each of these lessons is pristine. Each one exemplifies values born in the human race before the fall in Eden.

First, God would come to live among the people as a gentle sojourner. Indeed his coming, when it did happen, attracted so little attention that many did not recognize that the Messiah had come. " 'Shout and be glad, O Daughter of Zion. For I am coming, and I will live among you,' declares the LORD" (2:10).

Second, when the Messiah's kingdom was complete, it would be a gentle society of the faithful. " 'In that day each of you will invite his neighbor to sit under his vine and fig tree,' declares the LORD Almighty" (3:10).

Third, Zechariah called for Israel to build a gentle nation. Surely these people, who had known the horrors of exile, could learn to be civil toward each other. "This is what the LORD Almighty says: 'Administer true justice; show mercy and compassion to one another. Do not oppress the widow or the fatherless, the alien or the poor. In your hearts do not think evil of each other' " (7:9–10).

Fourth, it is difficult to tell if Zechariah was only

speaking of how life ought to be in the rebuilt Jerusalem or if he was speaking of how life will be when the Messiah takes up his eternal residence in the city. "Once again men and women of ripe old age will sit in the streets of Jerusalem, each with cane in hand because of his age. The city streets will be filled with boys and girls playing there" (8:4–5).

Fifth, the gentle kingdom would have a gentle king. "Rejoice greatly, O Daughter of Zion! Shout, Daughter of Jerusalem! See, your king comes to you, righteous and having salvation, gentle and riding on a donkey, on a colt, the foal of a donkey" (9:9).

Sixth, the purified Israelites would know a loving and gentle covenant. "They will call on my name and I will answer them; I will say, 'They are my people,' and they will say, 'The LORD is our God' " (13:9).

Seventh, in its final state, this gentle kingdom will be so universally holy that temple vessels and housewares will hold the same sanctity. "On that day HOLY TO THE LORD will be inscribed on the bells of the horses, and the cooking pots in the LORD's house will be like the sacred bowls in front of the altar. Every pot in Jerusalem and Judah will be holy to the LORD Almighty, and all who come to sacrifice will take some of the pots and cook in them. And on that day there will no longer be a Canaanite in the house of the LORD Almighty" (14:20–21).

A Call to Return to the LORD

1 In the eighth month of the second year of Darius,[a] the word of the LORD came to the prophet Zechariah[b] son of Berekiah,[c] the son of Iddo:[d]

2“The LORD was very angry[e] with your forefathers. 3Therefore tell the people: This is what the LORD Almighty says: ‘Return to me,’ declares the LORD Almighty, ‘and I will return to you,’[f] says the LORD Almighty. 4Do not be like your forefathers,[g] to whom the earlier prophets proclaimed: This is what the LORD Almighty says: ‘Turn from your evil ways[h] and your evil practices.’ But they would not listen or pay attention to me,[i] declares the LORD. 5Where are your forefathers now? And the prophets, do they live forever? 6But did not my words and my decrees, which I commanded my servants the prophets, overtake your forefathers?

“Then they repented and said, ‘The LORD Almighty has done to us what our ways and practices deserve,[j] just as he determined to do.’ ”

The Man Among the Myrtle Trees

7On the twenty-fourth day of the eleventh month, the month of Shebat, in the second year of Darius, the word of the LORD came to the prophet Zechariah son of Berekiah, the son of Iddo.

8During the night I had a vision—and there before me was a man riding a red[k] horse! He was standing among the myrtle trees in a ravine. Behind him were red, brown and white horses.[l]

9I asked, “What are these, my lord?”

The angel[m] who was talking with me answered, “I will show you what they are.”

10Then the man standing among the myrtle trees explained, “They are the ones the LORD has sent to go throughout the earth.”[n]

11And they reported to the angel of the LORD, who was standing among the myrtle trees, “We have gone throughout the earth and found the whole world at rest and in peace.”[o]

12Then the angel of the LORD said, “LORD Almighty, how long will you withhold mercy from Jerusalem and from the towns of Judah, which you have been angry with these seventy[p] years?” 13So the LORD spoke kind and comforting words to the angel who talked with me.[q]

14Then the angel who was speaking to me said, “Proclaim this word: This is what the LORD Almighty says: ‘I am very jealous[r] for Jerusalem and Zion, 15but I am very angry with the nations that feel secure.[s] I was only a little angry, but they added to the calamity.’[t]

16“Therefore, this is what the LORD says: ‘I will return[u] to Jerusalem with mercy, and there my house will be rebuilt. And the measuring line[v] will be stretched out over Jerusalem,’ declares the LORD Almighty.

17“Proclaim further: This is what the LORD Almighty says: ‘My towns will again overflow with prosperity, and the LORD will again comfort[w] Zion and choose[x] Jerusalem.’ ”[y]

Four Horns and Four Craftsmen

18Then I looked up—and there before me were four horns! 19I asked the angel who was speaking to me, “What are these?”

He answered me, “These are the horns[z] that scattered Judah, Israel and Jerusalem.”

20Then the LORD showed me four craftsmen. 21I asked, “What are these coming to do?”

He answered, “These are the horns that scattered Judah so that no one could raise his head, but the craftsmen have come to terrify them and throw down these horns of the nations who lifted up their horns[a] against the land of Judah to scatter its people.”[b]

A Man With a Measuring Line

2 Then I looked up—and there before me was a man with a measuring line in his hand! 2I asked, “Where are you going?”

He answered me, “To measure Jerusalem, to find out how wide and how long it is.”[c]

3Then the angel who was speaking to me left, and another angel came to meet him 4and said to him: “Run, tell that young man, ‘Jerusalem will be a city without walls[d] because of the great number[e] of men and livestock in it. 5And I myself will be a wall[f] of fire around it,’ declares the LORD, ‘and I will be its glory[g] within.’

6“Come! Come! Flee from the land

1:1 [a]Ezr 4:24; 6:15 [b]Ezr 5:1 [c]Mt 23:35; Lk 11:51 [d]ver 7; Ne 12:4
1:2 [e]2Ch 36:16
1:3 [f]Mal 3:7; Jas 4:8
1:4 [g]2Ch 36:15 [h]Ps 106:6 [i]2Ch 24:19; Ps 78:8; Jer 6:17
1:6 [j]Jer 12:14-17; La 2:17
1:8 [k]Rev 6:4 [l]Zec 6:2-7
1:9 [m]Zec 4:1,4-5
1:10 [n]Zec 6:5-8
1:11 [o]Isa 14:7
1:12 [p]Da 9:2
1:13 [q]Zec 4:1
1:14 [r]Joel 2:18; Zec 8:2
1:15 [s]Jer 48:11 [t]Ps 123:3-4; Am 1:11
1:16 [u]Zec 8:3 [v]Zec 2:1-2
1:17 [w]Isa 51:3 [x]Isa 14:1 [y]Zec 2:12
1:19 [z]Am 6:13
1:21 [a]Ps 75:4 [b]Ps 75:10
2:2 [c]Eze 40:3; Rev 21:15
2:4 [d]Eze 38:11 [e]Isa 49:20; Jer 30:19; 33:22
2:5 [f]Isa 26:1 [g]Rev 21:23

of the north," declares the LORD, "for I
have scattered you to the four winds of
2:6 [h]Eze 17:21 heaven,"[h] declares the LORD.
7"Come, O Zion! Escape, you who
2:7 [i]Isa 48:20 live in the Daughter of Babylon!"[i] 8For
this is what the LORD Almighty says:
"After he has honored me and has sent
me against the nations that have plundered you—for whoever touches you
2:8 [j]Dt 32:10 touches the apple of his eye[j]— 9I will
surely raise my hand against them so
2:9 [k]Isa 14:2 [l]Zec 4:9 that their slaves will plunder them.[a][k]
Then you will know that the LORD Al-
mighty has sent me.[l]
10"Shout and be glad, O Daughter of
2:10 [m]Zep 3:14 [n]Zec 9:9 [o]Lev 26:12; Zec 8:3 Zion.[m] For I am coming,[n] and I will
live among you,"[o] declares the LORD.
11"Many nations will be joined with the
LORD in that day and will become my
people. I will live among you and you
will know that the LORD Almighty has
2:12 [p]Dt 32:9; Ps 33:12; Jer 10:16 [q]Zec 1:17 sent me to you. 12The LORD will inherit[p] Judah as his portion in the holy land
and will again choose[q] Jerusalem. 13Be
still[r] before the LORD, all mankind, be-
2:13 [r]Hab 2:20 cause he has roused himself from his
holy dwelling."

LOVE

I WILL LIVE AMONG YOU

Zechariah 2:10

Humankind has but one single boast that it may offer up in every age of history. The boast is this: We are loved by God. See, he lives among us in our same shabby circumstances. Why would a wealthy God choose to live in poverty? His palaces of light were too far away from the world he loved.

Clean Garments for the High Priest

3:1 [s]Hag 1:1; Zec 6:11 [t]Ps 109:6 3 Then he showed me Joshua[b][s] the
high priest standing before the an-
gel of the LORD, and Satan[c][t] standing at
his right side to accuse him. 2The LORD
3:2 [u]Jude 1:9 [v]Isa 14:1 [w]Am 4:11; Jude 1:23 said to Satan, "The LORD rebuke you,[u]
Satan! The LORD, who has chosen[v] Je-
rusalem, rebuke you! Is not this man a
burning stick snatched from the fire?"[w]
3Now Joshua was dressed in filthy
clothes as he stood before the angel.
4The angel said to those who were
standing before him, "Take off his filthy
clothes."
Then he said to Joshua, "See, I have
taken away your sin,[x] and I will put rich 3:4 [x]Eze 36:25; Mic 7:18 [y]Isa 52:1; Rev 19:8
garments[y] on you."
5Then I said, "Put a clean turban[z] on
his head." So they put a clean turban 3:5 [z]Ex 29:6
on his head and clothed him, while the
angel of the LORD stood by.
6The angel of the LORD gave this
charge to Joshua: 7"This is what the
LORD Almighty says: 'If you will walk
in my ways and keep my requirements,
then you will govern my house[a] and 3:7 [a]Dt 17:8-11; Eze 44:15-16
have charge of my courts, and I will
give you a place among these standing
here.
8" 'Listen, O high priest Joshua and
your associates seated before you, who
are men symbolic[b] of things to come: 3:8 [b]Eze 12:11 [c]Isa 4:2
I am going to bring my servant, the
Branch.[c] 9See, the stone I have set in
front of Joshua! There are seven eyes[d]
on that one stone,[d] and I will engrave 3:9 [d]Isa 28:16 [e]Jer 50:20
an inscription on it,' says the LORD Al-
mighty, 'and I will remove the sin[e] of
this land in a single day.
10" 'In that day each of you will invite his neighbor to sit under his vine
and fig tree,[f]' declares the LORD Al- 3:10 [f]1Ki 4:25; Mic 4:4
mighty."

The Gold Lampstand and the Two Olive Trees

4 Then the angel who talked with
me returned and wakened[g] me, as 4:1 [g]Da 8:18 [h]Jer 31:26
a man is wakened from his sleep.[h] 2He
asked me, "What do you see?"[i]
I answered, "I see a solid gold lamp- 4:2 [i]Jer 1:13 [j]Ex 25:31; Rev 1:12 [k]Rev 4:5
stand[j] with a bowl at the top and seven
lights[k] on it, with seven channels to the
lights. 3Also there are two olive trees[l] by 4:3 [l]ver 11; Rev 11:4
it, one on the right of the bowl and the
other on its left."
4I asked the angel who talked with
me, "What are these, my lord?"
5He answered, "Do you not know
what these are?"
"No, my lord," I replied.[m] 4:5 [m]Zec 1:9
6So he said to me, "This is the word
of the LORD to Zerubbabel:[n] 'Not by 4:6 [n]Ezr 5:2 [o]Isa 11:2-4; Hos 1:7
might nor by power, but by my Spirit,'[o]
says the LORD Almighty.
7"What[e] are you, O mighty mountain? Before Zerubbabel you will be-
come level ground.[p] Then he will bring 4:7 [p]Jer 51:25

[a] 8,9 Or *says after . . . eye:* 9"*I . . . plunder them.*"
[b] 1 A variant of *Jeshua;* here and elsewhere in Zechariah [c] 1 *Satan* means *accuser.* [d] 9 Or *facets*
[e] 7 Or *Who*

4:7 [q]Ps 118:22
out the capstone[q] to shouts of 'God
bless it! God bless it!' "
8Then the word of the LORD came
to me: 9"The hands of Zerubbabel have
4:9 [r]Ezr 3:11 [s]Ezr 3:8; 6:15; Zec 6:12 [t]Zec 2:9
laid the foundation[r] of this temple; his
hands will also complete it.[s] Then you
will know that the LORD Almighty has
sent me[t] to you.
10"Who despises the day of small
4:10 [u]Hag 2:3 [v]Zec 3:9; Rev 5:6
things?[u] Men will rejoice when they see
the plumb line in the hand of Zerubbabel.
"(These seven are the eyes[v] of the
LORD, which range throughout the
earth.)"
11Then I asked the angel, "What are
4:11 [w]ver 3; Rev 11:4
these two olive trees[w] on the right and
the left of the lampstand?"
12Again I asked him, "What are these
two olive branches beside the two gold
pipes that pour out golden oil?"
13He replied, "Do you not know
what these are?"
"No, my lord," I said.
14So he said, "These are the two who
4:14 [x]Ex 29:7; 40:15; Da 9:24-26; Zec 3:1-7
are anointed[x] to[a] serve the Lord of all
the earth."

The Flying Scroll

5 I looked again—and there before
5:1 [y]Eze 2:9; Rev 5:1
me was a flying scroll![y]
2He asked me, "What do you see?"
I answered, "I see a flying scroll,
thirty feet long and fifteen feet wide.[b]"
3And he said to me, "This is the
5:3 [z]Isa 24:6; 43:28; Mal 3:9; 4:6 [a]Ex 20:15; Mal 3:8 [b]Isa 48:1
curse[z] that is going out over the whole
land; for according to what it says on
one side, every thief[a] will be banished,
and according to what it says on the
other, everyone who swears falsely[b] will
be banished. 4The LORD Almighty declares, 'I will send it out, and it will enter the house of the thief and the house
of him who swears falsely by my name.
It will remain in his house and destroy
5:4 [c]Lev 14:34-45; Hab 2:9-11; Mal 3:5
it, both its timbers and its stones.' "[c]

The Woman in a Basket

5Then the angel who was speaking
to me came forward and said to me,
"Look up and see what this is that is appearing."
6I asked, "What is it?"
He replied, "It is a measuring basket.[c]" And he added, "This is the
iniquity[d] of the people throughout the
land."
7Then the cover of lead was raised,
and there in the basket sat a woman!
8He said, "This is wickedness," and he
pushed her back into the basket and
pushed the lead cover down over its
5:8 [d]Mic 6:11
mouth.[d]
9Then I looked up—and there before
me were two women, with the wind in
their wings! They had wings like those
5:9 [e]Lev 11:19
of a stork,[e] and they lifted up the basket
between heaven and earth.
10"Where are they taking the basket?" I asked the angel who was speaking to me.
11He replied, "To the country of Bab-
5:11 [f]Ge 10:10 [g]Jer 29:5,28 [h]Da 1:2
ylonia[e][f] to build a house[g] for it. When
it is ready, the basket will be set there in
its place."[h]

Four Chariots

6 I looked up again—and there before me were four chariots[i] coming
6:1 [i]ver 5
out from between two mountains—
mountains of bronze! 2The first chariot
6:2 [j]Rev 6:5
had red horses, the second black,[j] 3the
third white,[k] and the fourth dappled—
6:3 [k]Rev 6:2
all of them powerful. 4I asked the angel who was speaking to me, "What are
these, my lord?"
5The angel answered me, "These are
6:5 [l]Eze 37:9; Mt 24:31; Rev 7:1
the four spirits[f][l] of heaven, going out
from standing in the presence of the
Lord of the whole world. 6The one
with the black horses is going toward
the north country, the one with the
white horses toward the west,[g] and
the one with the dappled horses toward
the south."
7When the powerful horses went out,
they were straining to go throughout
6:7 [m]Zec 1:10
the earth.[m] And he said, "Go throughout the earth!" So they went throughout the earth.
8Then he called to me, "Look, those
going toward the north country have
6:8 [n]Eze 5:13; 24:13
given my Spirit[h] rest[n] in the land of the
north."

A Crown for Joshua

9The word of the LORD came to me:
10"Take ⌞silver and gold⌟ from the exiles
Heldai, Tobijah and Jedaiah, who have
6:10 [o]Ezr 7:14-16; Jer 28:6
arrived from Babylon.[o] Go the same day
to the house of Josiah son of Zephaniah.

[a]*14* Or *two who bring oil and* [b]*2* Hebrew *twenty cubits long and ten cubits wide* (about 9 meters long and 4.5 meters wide) [c]*6* Hebrew *an ephah;* also in verses 7-11 [d]*6* Or *appearance* [e]*11* Hebrew *Shinar* [f]*5* Or *winds* [g]*6* Or *horses after them* [h]*8* Or *spirit*

11Take the silver and gold and make a
crown,[p] and set it on the head of the
high priest, Joshua[q] son of Jehozadak.[r]
12Tell him this is what the LORD Almighty says: 'Here is the man whose
name is the Branch,[s] and he will branch
out from his place and build the temple of the LORD.[t] 13It is he who will
build the temple of the LORD, and he
will be clothed with majesty and will sit
and rule on his throne. And he will be
a priest[u] on his throne. And there will
be harmony between the two.' 14The
crown will be given to Heldai,[a] Tobijah, Jedaiah and Hen[b] son of Zephaniah as a memorial in the temple of the
LORD. 15Those who are far away will
come and help to build the temple of
the LORD,[v] and you will know that the
LORD Almighty has sent me to you.[w]
This will happen if you diligently obey[x]
the LORD your God."

Justice and Mercy, Not Fasting

7 In the fourth year of King Darius,
the word of the LORD came to
Zechariah on the fourth day of the
ninth month, the month of Kislev.[y]
2The people of Bethel had sent Sharezer
and Regem-Melech, together with their
men, to entreat[z] the LORD 3by asking
the priests of the house of the LORD
Almighty and the prophets, "Should I
mourn[a] and fast in the fifth[b] month, as
I have done for so many years?"
4Then the word of the LORD Almighty came to me: 5"Ask all the people of the land and the priests, 'When
you fasted[c] and mourned in the fifth
and seventh months for the past seventy
years, was it really for me that you fasted? 6And when you were eating and
drinking, were you not just feasting for
yourselves? 7Are these not the words the
LORD proclaimed through the earlier
prophets[d] when Jerusalem and its surrounding towns were at rest[e] and prosperous, and the Negev and the western
foothills[f] were settled?'"
8And the word of the LORD came
again to Zechariah: 9"This is what the
LORD Almighty says: 'Administer true
justice;[g] show mercy and compassion to
one another. 10Do not oppress the widow or the fatherless, the alien[h] or the
poor. In your hearts do not think evil of
each other.'[i]
11"But they refused to pay attention;

6:11 [p]Ps 21:3 [q]Zec 3:1 [r]Ezr 3:2
6:12 [s]Isa 4:2; Zec 3:8 [t]Ezr 3:8-10; Zec 4:6-9
6:13 [u]Ps 110:4
6:15 [v]Isa 60:10 [w]Zec 2:9-11 [x]Isa 58:12; Jer 7:23; Zec 3:7
7:1 [y]Ne 1:1
7:2 [z]Jer 26:19; Zec 8:21
7:3 [a]Zec 12:12-14 [b]Jer 52:12-14; Zec 8:19
7:5 [c]Isa 58:5
7:7 [d]Zec 1:4 [e]Jer 22:21 [f]Jer 17:26
7:9 [g]Zec 8:16
7:10 [h]Ex 22:21 [i]Ex 22:22; Isa 1:17

stubbornly they turned their backs
and stopped up their ears.[j] 12They
made their hearts as hard as flint[k] and
would not listen to the law or to the
words that the LORD Almighty had
sent by his Spirit through the earlier
prophets.[l] So the LORD Almighty was
very angry.[m]
13" 'When I called, they did not
listen;[n] so when they called, I would
not listen,'[o] says the LORD Almighty.[p]
14'I scattered[q] them with a whirlwind[r]
among all the nations, where they were
strangers. The land was left so desolate
behind them that no one could come
or go. This is how they made the pleasant land desolate.[s]' "

The LORD Promises to Bless Jerusalem

8 Again the word of the LORD Almighty came to me. 2This is what
the LORD Almighty says: "I am very
jealous for Zion; I am burning with
jealousy for her."
3This is what the LORD says: "I will
return[t] to Zion and dwell in Jerusalem.[u]
Then Jerusalem will be called the City
of Truth, and the mountain of the
LORD Almighty will be called the Holy
Mountain."
4This is what the LORD Almighty
says: "Once again men and women of
ripe old age will sit in the streets of
Jerusalem,[v] each with cane in hand because of his age. 5The city streets will
be filled with boys and girls playing
there."[w]
6This is what the LORD Almighty
says: "It may seem marvelous to the
remnant of this people at that time,[x]
but will it seem marvelous to me?[y]" declares the LORD Almighty.
7This is what the LORD Almighty
says: "I will save my people from the
countries of the east and the west.[z] 8I
will bring them back[a] to live in Jerusalem; they will be my people,[b] and I
will be faithful and righteous to them
as their God."
9This is what the LORD Almighty
says: "You who now hear these words
spoken by the prophets[c] who were there
when the foundation was laid for the

[a]14 Syriac; Hebrew *Helem* [b]14 Or *and the gracious one, the*

7:11 [j]Jer 8:5; 11:10; 17:23
7:12 [k]Jer 17:1; Eze 11:19 [l]Ne 9:29 [m]Da 9:12
7:13 [n]Pr 1:24 [o]Isa 1:15; Jer 11:11; 14:12; Mic 3:4 [p]Pr 1:28
7:14 [q]Dt 4:27; 28:64-67 [r]Jer 23:19 [s]Jer 44:6
8:3 [t]Zec 1:16 [u]Zec 2:10
8:4 [v]Isa 65:20
8:5 [w]Jer 30:20; 31:13
8:6 [x]Ps 118:23; 126:1-3 [y]Jer 32:17,27
8:7 [z]Ps 107:3; Isa 11:11; 43:5
8:8 [a]Zec 10:10 [b]Eze 11:19-20; 36:28; Zec 2:11
8:9 [c]Ezr 5:1

DAY 2 TWO

▸ GOODNESS AND THE PURPOSE OF GOD IN MY LIFE

Zechariah 8:14–17

This passage tells us that God will do good to Israel, but this goodness asks that those receiving it do some good of their own. From the passage, we can infer that the people were not doing good to others. God has to remind them to be truthful in their dealings and kind in their actions. God's not asking for a fake kind of illusion of goodness from his people. God wants the real thing.

To be good or goody-goody: how shall we ever determine the difference? Are we trying to build ourselves up so that we can feel good about how good we are or trying to build godly obedience and moral fiber into our lives? Here are four questions you may ask yourself to determine whether you're aiming at holiness or just a good reputation.

First, are you more prone to do good if someone sees it or recognizes it? It is a simple question but very defining. When we behave well under scrutiny, we may only be craving reputation. When we behave well when only God is looking, we are probably seeking holiness.

Second, do you want to be thought of as a person who does the proper thing or a person who can be counted on to die for the right cause? The martyrs hardly ever read Miss Manners, but they did devote a lot of time to seeking the heart of God.

Third, do you feel bad when someone else in your church is acknowledged for doing some ministry while something you did was entirely overlooked? This is a common fault. We really don't mind someone else getting the "Good Samaritan Award" as long as we're first runner-up. But true ministers of Christ turn from the accolades of peers in favor of the accolades of God.

Fourth, and this is the hardest question of all, are you prone to giving things anonymously so that no recognition could ever come back to you? You will know you are truly good when you reach this level of integrity.

To begin a study on the topic of Goodness and the Desire for Holiness, turn to the home page on page 790.

house of the LORD Almighty, let your
hands be strong[d] so that the temple
may be built. 10Before that time there
were no wages[e] for man or beast. No
one could go about his business safely
because of his enemy, for I had turned
every man against his neighbor. 11But
now I will not deal with the remnant
of this people as I did in the past,"[f] declares the LORD Almighty.

12"The seed will grow well, the vine
will yield its fruit,[g] the ground will produce its crops,[h] and the heavens will
drop their dew.[i] I will give all these
things as an inheritance[j] to the remnant of this people. 13As you have been
an object of cursing[k] among the nations, O Judah and Israel, so will I save
you, and you will be a blessing.[l] Do
not be afraid, but let your hands be
strong."

14This is what the LORD Almighty
says: "Just as I had determined to bring
disaster[m] upon you and showed no pity
when your fathers angered me," says
the LORD Almighty, 15"so now I have
determined to do good[n] again to Jerusalem and Judah. Do not be afraid.
16These are the things you are to do:
Speak the truth[o] to each other, and render true and sound judgment in your
courts;[p] 17do not plot evil[q] against your
neighbor, and do not love to swear
falsely.[r] I hate all this," declares the
LORD.

18Again the word of the LORD Almighty came to me. 19This is what
the LORD Almighty says: "The fasts of
the fourth,[s] fifth,[t] seventh[u] and tenth[v]
months will become joyful[w] and glad
occasions and happy festivals for Judah.
Therefore love truth[x] and peace."

20This is what the LORD Almighty
says: "Many peoples and the inhabitants of many cities will yet come, 21and
the inhabitants of one city will go to
another and say, 'Let us go at once to
entreat[y] the LORD and seek the LORD
Almighty. I myself am going.' 22And
many peoples and powerful nations will
come to Jerusalem to seek the LORD
Almighty and to entreat him."[z]

23This is what the LORD Almighty
says: "In those days ten men from all
languages and nations will take firm
hold of one Jew by the hem of his robe
and say, 'Let us go with you, because we
have heard that God is with you.' "[a]

8:9 [d]Hag 2:4
8:10 [e]Hag 1:6
8:11 [f]Isa 12:1
8:12 [g]Joel 2:22 [h]Ps 67:6 [i]Ge 27:28 [j]Ob 1:17
8:13 [k]Jer 42:18 [l]Ge 12:2
8:14 [m]Jer 31:28; Eze 24:14
8:15 [n]ver 13; Jer 29:11; Mic 7:18-20
8:16 [o]Ps 15:2; Eph 4:25 [p]Zec 7:9
8:17 [q]Pr 3:29 [r]Pr 6:16-19
8:19 [s]Jer 39:2 [t]Jer 52:12 [u]2Ki 25:25 [v]Jer 52:4 [w]Ps 30:11 [x]ver 16
8:21 [y]Zec 7:2
8:22 [z]Ps 117:1; Isa 60:3; Zec 2:11
8:23 [a]Isa 45:14; 1Co 14:25

Judgment on Israel's Enemies

An Oracle

9 The word of the LORD is against
the land of Hadrach
9:1 [b]Isa 17:1 and will rest upon Damascus[b]—
for the eyes of men and all the tribes
of Israel
are on the LORD—[a]
9:2 [c]Jer 49:23 [d]Eze 28:1-19 2 and upon Hamath[c] too, which
borders on it,
and upon Tyre[d] and Sidon,
though they are very skillful.
3 Tyre has built herself a stronghold;
she has heaped up silver like dust,
and gold like the dirt of the
9:3 [e]Job 27:16; Eze 28:4 streets.[e]
4 But the Lord will take away her
possessions
and destroy her power on the
sea,
and she will be consumed by
9:4 [f]Isa 23:1; Eze 26:3-5; 28:18 fire.[f]
5 Ashkelon will see it and fear;
Gaza will writhe in agony,
and Ekron too, for her hope will
wither.
Gaza will lose her king
and Ashkelon will be deserted.
6 Foreigners will occupy Ashdod,
and I will cut off the pride of the
Philistines.
7 I will take the blood from their
mouths,
the forbidden food from between
their teeth.
Those who are left will belong to our
God
and become leaders in Judah,
and Ekron will be like the
Jebusites.
8 But I will defend my house
against marauding forces.
Never again will an oppressor
overrun my people,
for now I am keeping watch.[g] 9:8 [g]Isa 52:1; 54:14

The Coming of Zion's King

9 Rejoice greatly, O Daughter of Zion!
Shout, Daughter of Jerusalem!
See, your king[b] comes to you,
righteous and having salvation,[h] 9:9 [h]Isa 9:6-7; 43:3-11; Jer 23:5-6; Zep 3:14-15; Zec 2:10 [i]Mt 21:5*; Jn 12:15*
gentle and riding on a donkey,
on a colt, the foal of a donkey.[i]
10 I will take away the chariots from
Ephraim
and the war-horses from
Jerusalem,
and the battle bow will be broken.[j] 9:10 [j]Hos 1:7; 2:18; Mic 4:3; 5:10; Zec 10:4 [k]Ps 72:8
He will proclaim peace to the
nations.
His rule will extend from sea to
sea
and from the River[c] to the ends of
the earth.[d][k]
11 As for you, because of the blood of
my covenant[l] with you,
I will free your prisoners[m] from 9:11 [l]Ex 24:8 [m]Isa 42:7
the waterless pit.
12 Return to your fortress,[n] O prisoners 9:12 [n]Joel 3:16
of hope;
even now I announce that I will
restore twice as much to you.
13 I will bend Judah as I bend my bow
and fill it with Ephraim.[o] 9:13 [o]Isa 49:2 [p]Joel 3:6 [q]Jer 51:20
I will rouse your sons, O Zion,
against your sons, O Greece,[p]
and make you like a warrior's
sword.[q]

The LORD Will Appear

14 Then the LORD will appear over
them;[r]
his arrow will flash like lightning.[s] 9:14 [r]Isa 31:5 [s]Ps 18:14; Hab 3:11 [t]Isa 21:1; 66:15
The Sovereign LORD will sound the
trumpet;
he will march in the storms[t] of the
south,
15 and the LORD Almighty will
shield[u] them. 9:15 [u]Isa 37:35; Zec 12:8 [v]Ex 27:2
They will destroy
and overcome with slingstones.
They will drink and roar as with
wine;
they will be full like a bowl
used for sprinkling[e] the corners[v]
of the altar.

JOY

THE COMING OF THE KING

Zechariah 9:9

**Bring round a steed; God's Son must ride
to coronation.
Oh, never mind;
This king prefers a lesser circumstance.
Bring him a donkey's colt.
The lower mount will let him ride a good
deal closer
To the people that he longs to save.**

[a] *1* Or *Damascus. / For the eye of the LORD is on all mankind, / as well as on the tribes of Israel,*
[b] *9* Or *King* [c] *10* That is, the Euphrates [d] *10* Or *the end of the land* [e] *15* Or *bowl, / like*

16 The LORD their God will save them
on that day
as the flock of his people.
They will sparkle in his land
like jewels in a crown.[w]
17 How attractive and beautiful they
will be!
Grain will make the young men
thrive,
and new wine the young women.

9:16 [w]Isa 62:3; Jer 31:11

DAY 5 FIVE

Gentleness and Its Place in My Personal Worship

Zechariah 9:9

Jesus rode into Jerusalem on a colt, the foal of a donkey. As he arrived, the mood was a wild celebration of his Messiahship. We cannot really imagine how Palm Sunday would have been pulled off if Jesus had ridden into town on a great white steed. Would the celebration have been as wonderful if the people had been in awe of Jesus' might and power? All that can be said is that our worship transcends glory when God—Jesus—is approachable. We offer our freest praise when we are unafraid.

Isn't God holy? Aren't we to live in sobriety and the fear of God? Surely the fear of God is the beginning of wisdom (see Psalm 111:10). But the whole point of God becoming a man in Christ is to take the severity out of our relationship with God. Christ called the majestic God "Abba" or "Daddy."

Now in Christ is God made gentle. He comes to us on a donkey, but with his power he will conquer death and hell. There will be no question that he is a great conqueror, but he chooses to present himself with humility and peace. Jesus here is consciously opting for the servant mentality and image. His gentle entrance to his final week of life could have left no one in doubt of that.

He is gentle. God who creates the cosmos and orders the tides is ours in Christ, and we cry in utter praise, "Hosanna! Blessed is the gentle one who comes in the name of the Lord!"

Our wildest praise is born in the wake of his gentle love.

To begin a study on the topic of Gentleness, the Approachable Life, turn to the home page on page 306.

The LORD Will Care for Judah

10 Ask the LORD for rain in the
springtime;
it is the LORD who makes the
storm clouds.
He gives showers of rain to men,
and plants of the field to everyone.
2 The idols[x] speak deceit,
diviners see visions that lie;
they tell dreams that are false,
they give comfort in vain.
Therefore the people wander like
sheep
oppressed for lack of a shepherd.[y]
3 "My anger burns against the
shepherds,
and I will punish the leaders;[z]
for the LORD Almighty will care
for his flock, the house of Judah,
and make them like a proud horse
in battle.
4 From Judah will come the
cornerstone,
from him the tent peg,[a]
from him the battle bow,[b]
from him every ruler.
5 Together they[a] will be like mighty
men
trampling the muddy streets in
battle.[c]
Because the LORD is with them,
they will fight and overthrow the
horsemen.[d]
6 "I will strengthen the house of Judah
and save the house of Joseph.
I will restore them
because I have compassion on
them.[e]
They will be as though
I had not rejected them,
for I am the LORD their God
and I will answer[f] them.
7 The Ephraimites will become like
mighty men,
and their hearts will be glad as
with wine.[g]
Their children will see it and be
joyful;
their hearts will rejoice in the
LORD.
8 I will signal[h] for them
and gather them in.
Surely I will redeem them;
they will be as numerous[i] as
before.

[a]4,5 Or *ruler, all of them together.* / [5]They

10:2 [x]Eze 21:21 [y]Eze 34:5; Hos 3:4; Mt 9:36
10:3 [z]Jer 25:34
10:4 [a]Isa 22:23 [b]Zec 9:10
10:5 [c]2Sa 22:43 [d]Am 2:15; Hag 2:22
10:6 [e]Zec 8:7-8 [f]Zec 13:9
10:7 [g]Zec 9:15
10:8 [h]Isa 5:26 [i]Jer 33:22; Eze 36:11

9 Though I scatter them among the
peoples,
yet in distant lands they will
10:9 [j]Eze 6:9 remember me.[j]
They and their children will survive,
and they will return.
10 I will bring them back from Egypt
10:10 [k]Isa 11:11 and gather them from Assyria.[k]
[l]Jer 50:19 I will bring them to Gilead[l] and
[m]Isa 49:19 Lebanon,
and there will not be room[m]
enough for them.
11 They will pass through the sea of
trouble;
the surging sea will be subdued
10:11 and all the depths of the Nile will
[n]Isa 19:5-7; dry up.[n]
51:10 Assyria's pride[o] will be brought down
[o]Zep 2:13 [p]Eze 30:13 and Egypt's scepter[p] will pass
away.
12 I will strengthen them in the LORD
10:12 [q]Mic 4:5 and in his name they will walk,[q]"
declares the LORD.

11:1 [r]Eze 31:3 **11** Open your doors, O Lebanon,[r]
so that fire may devour your
cedars!
2 Wail, O pine tree, for the cedar has
fallen;
the stately trees are ruined!
Wail, oaks of Bashan;
11:2 [s]Isa 32:19 the dense forest[s] has been cut
down!
3 Listen to the wail of the shepherds;
their rich pastures are destroyed!
Listen to the roar of the lions;
11:3 the lush thicket of the Jordan is
[t]Jer 2:15; 50:44 ruined![t]

Two Shepherds

4 This is what the LORD my God says:
"Pasture the flock marked for slaughter.
5 Their buyers slaughter them and go
unpunished. Those who sell them say,
'Praise the LORD, I am rich!' Their own
11:5 shepherds do not spare them.[u] 6 For I
[u]Jer 50:7; Eze 34:2-3 will no longer have pity on the people
of the land," declares the LORD. "I
will hand everyone over to his neigh-
11:6 bor[v] and his king. They will oppress the
[v]Zec 14:13 [w]Isa 9:19-21; land, and I will not rescue them from
Jer 13:14; Mic 5:8; 7:2-6 their hands."[w]
7 So I pastured the flock marked for
slaughter, particularly the oppressed of
the flock. Then I took two staffs and
called one Favor and the other Union,
and I pastured the flock. 8 In one month
I got rid of the three shepherds.

The flock detested me, and I grew
weary of them 9 and said, "I will not be
your shepherd. Let the dying die, and 11:9
the perishing perish.[x] Let those who are [x]Jer 15:2;
left eat one another's flesh." 43:11
10 Then I took my staff called Favor[y] 11:10 [y]ver 7
and broke it, revoking[z] the covenant I [z]Ps 89:39;
had made with all the nations. 11 It was Jer 14:21
revoked on that day, and so the afflicted of the flock who were watching me
knew it was the word of the LORD.
12 I told them, "If you think it best,
give me my pay; but if not, keep it." So 11:12 [a]Ex 21:32;
they paid me thirty pieces of silver.[a] Mt 26:15
13 And the LORD said to me, "Throw
it to the potter"—the handsome price
at which they priced me! So I took the
thirty pieces of silver and threw them 11:13
into the house of the LORD to the [b]Mt 27:9-10*;
potter.[b] Ac 1:18-19

GOODNESS

THE SILVER SENTENCE

Zechariah 11:12–13

Judas yearned not for holiness, but for silver. Long eternities before, God had hidden unmined silver in the earth. He was fully aware that men would later mine that silver, fashion it into coins, and use it to buy his only Son—for a purpose more grand than they could ever imagine.

14 Then I broke my second staff called
Union, breaking the brotherhood between Judah and Israel.
15 Then the LORD said to me, "Take
again the equipment of a foolish shepherd. 16 For I am going to raise up a
shepherd over the land who will not
care for the lost, or seek the young, or
heal the injured, or feed the healthy, but
will eat the meat of the choice sheep,
tearing off their hoofs.

17 "Woe to the worthless shepherd,[c] 11:17 [c]Jer 23:1
who deserts the flock! [d]Eze 30:21-22
May the sword strike his arm[d] and [e]Jer 23:1
his right eye!
May his arm be completely
withered,
his right eye totally blinded!"[e]

Jerusalem's Enemies to Be Destroyed

An Oracle

12 This is the word of the LORD
concerning Israel. The LORD,

who stretches out the heavens,[f] who
lays the foundation of the earth,[g] and
who forms the spirit of man[h] within
him, declares: 2“I am going to make Jerusalem a cup[i] that sends all the surrounding peoples reeling.[j] Judah[k] will
be besieged as well as Jerusalem. 3On
that day, when all the nations[l] of the
earth are gathered against her, I will
make Jerusalem an immovable rock[m]
for all the nations. All who try to move
it will injure[n] themselves. 4On that day
I will strike every horse with panic and
its rider with madness,” declares the
LORD. “I will keep a watchful eye over
the house of Judah, but I will blind all
the horses of the nations.[o] 5Then the
leaders of Judah will say in their hearts,
‘The people of Jerusalem are strong, because the LORD Almighty is their God.’
6“On that day I will make the leaders
of Judah like a firepot[p] in a woodpile,
like a flaming torch among sheaves.
They will consume[q] right and left all
the surrounding peoples, but Jerusalem
will remain intact in her place.
7“The LORD will save the dwellings
of Judah first, so that the honor of the
house of David and of Jerusalem’s inhabitants may not be greater than that
of Judah.[r] 8On that day the LORD will
shield[s] those who live in Jerusalem, so
that the feeblest among them will be
like David, and the house of David
will be like God,[t] like the Angel of the
LORD going before[u] them. 9On that
day I will set out to destroy all the nations that attack Jerusalem.[v]

12:1 [f]Isa 42:5; Jer 51:15 [g]Ps 102:25; Heb 1:10 [h]Isa 57:16
12:2 [i]Ps 75:8 [j]Isa 51:23 [k]Zec 14:14
12:3 [l]Zec 14:2 [m]Da 2:34-35 [n]Mt 21:44
12:4 [o]Ps 76:6
12:6 [p]Isa 10:17-18; Zec 11:1 [q]Ob 1:18
12:7 [r]Jer 30:18; Am 9:11
12:8 [s]Joel 3:16; Zec 9:15 [t]Ps 82:6 [u]Mic 7:8
12:9 [v]Zec 14:2-3

Mourning for the One They Pierced

10“And I will pour out on the house
of David and the inhabitants of Jerusalem a spirit[a] of grace and supplication.[w]
They will look on[b] me, the one they
have pierced,[x] and they will mourn
for him as one mourns for an only
child, and grieve bitterly for him as one
grieves for a firstborn son. 11On that
day the weeping in Jerusalem will be
great, like the weeping of Hadad Rimmon in the plain of Megiddo.[y] 12The
land will mourn,[z] each clan by itself,
with their wives by themselves: the clan
of the house of David and their wives,
the clan of the house of Nathan and
their wives, 13the clan of the house of
Levi and their wives, the clan of Shimei
and their wives, 14and all the rest of the
clans and their wives.

12:10 [w]Isa 44:3; Eze 39:29; Joel 2:28-29 [x]Jn 19:34,37*; Rev 1:7
12:11 [y]2Ki 23:29
12:12 [z]Mt 24:30; Rev 1:7

Cleansing From Sin

13 “On that day a fountain[a] will
be opened to the house of Da-
vid and the inhabitants of Jerusalem, to
cleanse[b] them from sin and impurity.
2“On that day, I will banish the
names of the idols[c] from the land, and
they will be remembered no more,” declares the LORD Almighty. “I will remove both the prophets[d] and the spirit
of impurity from the land. 3And if
anyone still prophesies, his father and
mother, to whom he was born, will say
to him, ‘You must die, because you have
told lies in the LORD’s name.’ When
he prophesies, his own parents will stab
him.[e]
4“On that day every prophet will be
ashamed[f] of his prophetic vision. He
will not put on a prophet’s garment[g] of
hair[h] in order to deceive. 5He will say,
‘I am not a prophet. I am a farmer; the
land has been my livelihood since my
youth.[c]’[i] 6If someone asks him, ‘What
are these wounds on your body[d]?’ he
will answer, ‘The wounds I was given at
the house of my friends.’

13:1 [a]Jer 17:13 [b]Ps 51:2; Heb 9:14
13:2 [c]Ex 23:13; Eze 36:25; Hos 2:17 [d]1Ki 22:22; Jer 23:14-15
13:3 [e]Dt 13:6-11; 18:20; Jer 23:34; Eze 14:9
13:4 [f]Jer 6:15; Mic 3:6-7 [g]Mt 3:4 [h]2Ki 1:8; Isa 20:2
13:5 [i]Am 7:14

The Shepherd Struck, the Sheep Scattered

7“Awake, O sword,[j] against my
shepherd,[k]
against the man who is close to
me!”
declares the LORD Almighty.
“Strike the shepherd,
and the sheep will be scattered,[l]
and I will turn my hand against
the little ones.

13:7 [j]Jer 47:6 [k]Isa 40:11; 53:4; Eze 37:24 [l]Mt 26:31*; Mk 14:27*

[a]10 Or *the Spirit* [b]10 Or *to* [c]5 Or *farmer; a man sold me in my youth* [d]6 Or *wounds between your hands*

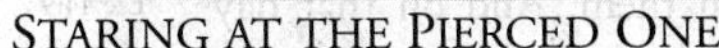

SELF-CONTROL

STARING AT THE PIERCED ONE

Zechariah 12:10

God poured out his Spirit of grace upon the world so that all could look and see that the wounds of Christ are doorways to honest self-appraisal. No one can look upon Christ's wounds and find any satisfaction in unsurrendered living.

8 In the whole land," declares the
LORD,
"two-thirds will be struck down
and perish;
yet one-third will be left in it.[m]
9 This third I will bring into the fire;[n]
I will refine them like silver[o]
and test them like gold.
They will call[p] on my name
and I will answer[q] them;
I will say, 'They are my people,'[r]
and they will say, 'The LORD is
our God.[s]' "

The LORD Comes and Reigns

14 A day of the LORD[t] is coming when your plunder will be divided among you.

2 I will gather all the nations to Jerusalem to fight against it; the city will be captured, the houses ransacked, and the women raped. Half of the city will go into exile, but the rest of the people will not be taken from the city.[u]

3 Then the LORD will go out and fight[v] against those nations, as he fights in the day of battle. 4 On that day his feet will stand on the Mount of Olives,[w] east of Jerusalem, and the Mount of Olives will be split in two from east to west, forming a great valley, with half of the mountain moving north and half moving south. 5 You will flee by my mountain valley, for it will extend to Azel. You will flee as you fled from the earthquake[a][x] in the days of Uzziah king of Judah. Then the LORD my God will come,[y] and all the holy ones with him.[z]

6 On that day there will be no light,[a] no cold or frost. 7 It will be a unique[b] day, without daytime or nighttime[c]—a day known to the LORD. When evening comes, there will be light.[d]

8 On that day living water[e] will flow out from Jerusalem, half to the eastern[f] sea[b] and half to the western sea,[c] in summer and in winter.

9 The LORD will be king over the whole earth.[g] On that day there will be one LORD, and his name the only name.[h]

10 The whole land, from Geba[i] to Rimmon, south of Jerusalem, will become like the Arabah. But Jerusalem will be raised up[j] and remain in its place,[k] from the Benjamin Gate to the site of the First Gate, to the Corner Gate, and from the Tower of Hananel to the royal winepresses. 11 It will be inhabited; never again will it be destroyed. Jerusalem will be secure.[l]

12 This is the plague with which the LORD will strike all the nations that fought against Jerusalem: Their flesh will rot while they are still standing on their feet, their eyes will rot in their sockets, and their tongues will rot in their mouths.[m] 13 On that day men will be stricken by the LORD with great panic. Each man will seize the hand of another, and they will attack each other.[n] 14 Judah[o] too will fight at Jerusalem. The wealth of all the surrounding nations will be collected[p]—great quantities of gold and silver and clothing. 15 A similar plague[q] will strike the horses and mules, the camels and donkeys, and all the animals in those camps.

16 Then the survivors from all the nations that have attacked Jerusalem will go up year after year to worship the King, the LORD Almighty, and to celebrate the Feast of Tabernacles.[r] 17 If any of the peoples of the earth do not go up to Jerusalem to worship[s] the King, the LORD Almighty, they will have no rain. 18 If the Egyptian people do not go up and take part, they will have no rain. The LORD[d] will bring on them the plague he inflicts on the nations that do not go up to celebrate the Feast of Tabernacles.[t] 19 This will be the punishment of Egypt and the punishment of all the nations that do not go up to celebrate the Feast of Tabernacles.

20 On that day HOLY TO THE LORD will be inscribed on the bells of the horses, and the cooking pots[u] in the LORD's house will be like the sacred bowls[v] in front of the altar. 21 Every pot in Jerusalem and Judah will be holy[w] to the LORD Almighty, and all who come to sacrifice will take some of the pots and cook in them. And on that day[x] there will no longer be a Canaanite[e][y] in the house of the LORD Almighty.[z]

[a] 5 Or *5My mountain valley will be blocked and will extend to Azel. It will be blocked as it was blocked because of the earthquake* [b] 8 That is, the Dead Sea [c] 8 That is, the Mediterranean [d] 18 Or *part, then the LORD* [e] 21 Or *merchant*

13:8 [m] Eze 5:2-4,12
13:9 [n] Mal 3:2 [o] Isa 48:10; 1Pe 1:6-7 [p] Ps 50:15 [q] Zec 10:6 [r] Jer 30:22 [s] Jer 29:12
14:1 [t] Isa 13:9; Mal 4:1
14:2 [u] Isa 13:6; Zec 13:8
14:3 [v] Zec 9:14-15
14:4 [w] Eze 11:23
14:5 [x] Am 1:1 [y] Isa 29:6; 66:15-16 [z] Mt 16:27; 25:31
14:6 [a] Isa 13:10; Jer 4:23
14:7 [b] Jer 30:7 [c] Rev 21:23-25; 22:5 [d] Isa 30:26
14:8 [e] Eze 47:1-12; Jn 7:38; Rev 22:1-2 [f] Joel 2:20
14:9 [g] Dt 6:4; Isa 45:24; Rev 11:15 [h] Eph 4:5-6
14:10 [i] 1Ki 15:22 [j] Jer 30:18; Am 9:11 [k] Zec 12:6
14:11 [l] Eze 34:25-28
14:12 [m] Lev 26:16; Dt 28:22
14:13 [n] Zec 11:6
14:14 [o] Zec 12:2 [p] Isa 23:18
14:15 [q] ver 12
14:16 [r] Isa 60:6-9
14:17 [s] Jer 14:4; Am 4:7
14:18 [t] ver 12
14:20 [u] Eze 46:20 [v] Zec 9:15
14:21 [w] Ro 14:6-7; 1Co 10:31 [x] Ne 8:10 [y] Zec 9:8 [z] Eze 44:9

MALACHI

AUTHORSHIP AND DATE

Malachi

c. 430 B.C.

KEY THEMES

Although the Israelites had broken their relationship with God through sin, Malachi preached that forgiveness was still available. Malachi saw that there were still a few persons who loved God and struggled to be faithful in a wayward day. Malachi, like Zechariah, seemed to sense that the finished temple had set the stage for the coming of the Messiah. He closed his book by saying that, before the Messiah would come, God would send Elijah back again to Israel. This is the last statement in the book of Malachi and among the first statements in the books of Mark and John.

FRUIT OF THE SPIRIT IN MALACHI

Faithfulness: Malachi used a rabbinic question-and-answer format in the outline of his book. Five questions were asked to incite Israel to faithfulness.

Question One: How had God loved them (see 1:2)? As a response to this question, Malachi showed the people how God had loved Israel with undeserved grace. This kind of love should have motivated Israel to faithfulness.

Question Two: How had they shown contempt for God's name (see 1:6)? They had shown contempt for God's name by not being faithful in the way they had offered their sacrifices. They had offered only tainted food and crippled animals.

Question Three: How had they wearied God with their words (see 2:17)? They had justified people who mixed their moral values and called evil good.

Question Four: How had they robbed God (see 3:8)? They had robbed God by being unfaithful in their tithes. They had been unfaithful by bringing less than what was required.

Question Five: What had they said against God (see 3:13)? They had spoken against God by saying it was useless to serve him. They had spoken against God by their sour, faithless lifestyles. They had sinned by calling doubt faithfulness.

1:1 [a]Na 1:1 # 1 An oracle:[a] The word[b] of the LORD
[b]1Pe 4:11 to Israel through Malachi.[a]

Jacob Loved, Esau Hated

1:2 [c]Dt 4:37 2“I have loved[c] you,” says the LORD.
[d]Ro 9:13* “But you ask, ‘How have you
loved us?’
“Was not Esau Jacob’s brother?” the
LORD says. “Yet I have loved Jacob,[d]
1:3 3but Esau I have hated, and I have
[e]Isa 34:10 turned his mountains into a wasteland[e]
[f]Eze 35:3-9 and left his inheritance to the desert
jackals.[f]”
4Edom may say, “Though we have
1:4 [g]Isa 9:10 been crushed, we will rebuild[g] the ru-
[h]Eze 25:12-14 ins.”
But this is what the LORD Almighty
says: “They may build, but I will demolish. They will be called the Wicked
Land, a people always under the wrath
of the LORD.[b] 5You will see it with your
1:5 [i]Ps 35:27; own eyes and say, ‘Great[i] is the LORD—
Mic 5:4 [j]Am 1:11-12 even beyond the borders of Israel!’[j]

Blemished Sacrifices

6“A son honors his father, and a servant his master. If I am a father, where
1:6 is the honor due me? If I am a master,
[k]Isa 1:2 where is the respect[k] due me?” says the
[l]Job 5:17 LORD Almighty.[l] “It is you, O priests,
who show contempt for my name.
“But you ask, ‘How have we shown
1:7 contempt for your name?’
[m]ver 12; 7“You place defiled food[m] on my
Lev 21:6 altar.
“But you ask, ‘How have we defiled
you?’
“By saying that the LORD’s table is
contemptible. 8When you bring blind
animals for sacrifice, is that not wrong?
1:8 When you sacrifice crippled or diseased
[n]Lev 22:22; animals,[n] is that not wrong? Try offer-
Dt 15:21 ing them to your governor! Would he
[o]Isa 43:23 be pleased with you? Would he accept
you?” says the LORD Almighty.[o]
1:9 9“Now implore God to be gracious
[p]Lev 23:33-44 to us. With such offerings[p] from your
hands, will he accept you?”—says the
LORD Almighty.
10“Oh, that one of you would shut
the temple doors, so that you would
1:10 not light useless fires on my altar! I am
[q]Hos 5:6 not pleased[q] with you,” says the LORD
[r]Isa 1:11-14; Almighty, “and I will accept no offer-
Jer 14:12 ing[r] from your hands. 11My name will
1:11 be great among the nations, from the
[s]Isa 60:6-7; rising to the setting of the sun. In every
Rev 8:3 place incense[s] and pure offerings will be
brought to my name, because my name
will be great among the nations,” says
the LORD Almighty.
12“But you profane it by saying of
the Lord’s table, ‘It is defiled,’ and of its
food,[t] ‘It is contemptible.’ 13And you 1:12 [t]ver 7
say, ‘What a burden!’[u] and you sniff at
it contemptuously,” says the LORD Al- 1:13 [u]Isa 43:22-24
mighty.
“When you bring injured, crippled
or diseased animals and offer them as
sacrifices, should I accept them from
your hands?” says the LORD. 14“Cursed
is the cheat who has an acceptable male
in his flock and vows to give it, but 1:14
then sacrifices a blemished[v] animal to [v]Lev 22:18-21
the Lord. For I am a great king,[w]” says [w]1Ti 6:15
the LORD Almighty, “and my name is
to be feared among the nations.

Admonition for the Priests

2 “And now this admonition is for 2:1
you, O priests.[x] 2If you do not lis- [x]ver 7
ten, and if you do not set your heart
to honor my name,” says the LORD Almighty, “I will send a curse upon you, 2:2
and I will curse[y] your blessings. Yes, I [y]Dt 28:20
have already cursed them, because you
have not set your heart to honor me.
3“Because of you I will rebuke[b] your
descendants[c]; I will spread on your faces
the offal[z] from your festival sacrifices, 2:3 [z]Ex 29:14
and you will be carried off with it.[a] [a]1Ki 14:10
4And you will know that I have sent
you this admonition so that my covenant with Levi[b] may continue,” says 2:4
the LORD Almighty. 5“My covenant [b]Nu 3:12
was with him, a covenant[c] of life and 2:5 [c]Dt 33:9
peace,[d] and I gave them to him; this [d]Nu 25:12
called for reverence and he revered me
and stood in awe of my name. 6True in- 2:6
struction[e] was in his mouth and nothing [e]Dt 33:10
false was found on his lips. He walked [f]Jer 23:22;
with me in peace and uprightness, and Jas 5:19-20
turned many from sin.[f]
7“For the lips of a priest[g] ought to pre- 2:7 [g]Jer 18:18
serve knowledge, and from his mouth [h]Lev 10:11
men should seek instruction[h]—because [i]Nu 27:21
he is the messenger[i] of the LORD Almighty. 8But you have turned from the
way and by your teaching have caused 2:8
many to stumble;[j] you have violated the [j]Jer 18:15
covenant with Levi,” says the LORD Al-
mighty. 9“So I have caused you to be 2:9
despised[k] and humiliated before all the [k]1Sa 2:30

[a]*1 Malachi* means *my messenger.* [b]*3* Or *cut off* (see Septuagint) [c]*3* Or *will blight your grain*

people, because you have not followed
my ways but have shown partiality in
matters of the law."

Judah Unfaithful

2:10 [l]1Co 8:6 [10]Have we not all one Father[a]?[l] Did
[m]Ex 19:5 not one God create us? Why do we profane the covenant[m] of our fathers by
breaking faith with one another?
[11]Judah has broken faith. A detestable thing has been committed in Israel
and in Jerusalem: Judah has desecrated
2:11 the sanctuary the LORD loves, by mar-
[n]Ne 13:23 rying[n] the daughter of a foreign god.[o]
[o]Ezr 9:1; [12]As for the man who does this, who-
Jer 3:7-9 ever he may be, may the LORD cut
2:12 him off[p] from the tents of Jacob[b]—
[p]Eze 24:21 even though he brings offerings[q] to the
[q]Mal 1:10 LORD Almighty.
[13]Another thing you do: You flood
the LORD's altar with tears. You weep
and wail because he no longer pays at-
2:13 tention[r] to your offerings or accepts
[r]Jer 14:12 them with pleasure from your hands.
[14]You ask, "Why?" It is because the
LORD is acting as the witness between
2:14 you and the wife of your youth,[s] be-
[s]Pr 5:18 cause you have broken faith with her,
though she is your partner, the wife of
your marriage covenant.
[15]Has not ⌊the LORD⌋ made them
2:15 one?[t] In flesh and spirit they are his.
[t]Ge 2:24; And why one? Because he was seeking
Mt 19:4-6 godly offspring.[c][u] So guard yourself in
[u]1Co 7:14 your spirit, and do not break faith with
the wife of your youth.
2:16 [16]"I hate divorce,[v]" says the LORD
[v]Dt 24:1; God of Israel, "and I hate a man's cov-
Mt 5:31-32; ering himself[d] with violence as well as
19:4-9 with his garment," says the LORD Almighty.
So guard yourself in your spirit, and
do not break faith.

The Day of Judgment

2:17 [17]You have wearied[w] the LORD with
[w]Isa 43:24 your words.
"How have we wearied him?" you
ask.
By saying, "All who do evil are good
in the eyes of the LORD, and he is
pleased with them" or "Where is the
God of justice?"
3 "See, I will send my messenger,
3:1 who will prepare the way before
[x]Isa 40:3; me.[x] Then suddenly the Lord you are
Mt 11:10*; seeking will come to his temple; the
Mk 1:2*; Lk 7:27* messenger of the covenant, whom you

FAITHFULNESS

WILDERNESS MAN

Malachi 3:1

This wilderness man named John came like a red chunk of clay from Edom, dressed in camel skins. He did nothing more than tell the truth about Jesus. Many would tell the same truth later, but this man told it first. And so his words were the paving stones that formed God's first causeway to grace.

desire, will come," says the LORD Almighty.
[2]But who can endure[y] the day of his 3:2 [y]Eze 22:14;
coming? Who can stand when he ap- Rev 6:17
pears? For he will be like a refiner's fire[z] [z]Zec 13:9;
or a launderer's soap. [3]He will sit as a Mt 3:10-12
refiner and purifier of silver;[a] he will 3:3 [a]Da 12:10
purify[b] the Levites and refine them like [b]Isa 1:25
gold and silver. Then the LORD will
have men who will bring offerings in 3:4
righteousness, [4]and the offerings[c] of Ju- [c]2Ch 7:12;
dah and Jerusalem will be acceptable to Ps 51:19; Mal 1:11
the LORD, as in days gone by, as in for- [d]2Ch 7:3
mer years.[d]
[5]"So I will come near to you for judgment. I will be quick to testify against 3:5
sorcerers, adulterers and perjurers,[e] [e]Jer 7:9
against those who defraud laborers of [f]Lev 19:13;
their wages,[f] who oppress the widows[g] Jas 5:4 [g]Ex 22:22
and the fatherless, and deprive aliens of
justice, but do not fear me," says the
LORD Almighty.

Robbing God

[6]"I the LORD do not change.[h] So 3:6 [h]Nu 23:19;
you, O descendants of Jacob, are not Jas 1:17
destroyed. [7]Ever since the time of your 3:7
forefathers you have turned away[i] from [i]Jer 7:26;
my decrees and have not kept them. Ac 7:51 [j]Zec 1:3
Return to me, and I will return to
you,"[j] says the LORD Almighty.
"But you ask, 'How are we to return?'
[8]"Will a man rob God? Yet you
rob me.
"But you ask, 'How do we rob you?'
"In tithes[k] and offerings. [9]You are un- 3:8 [k]Ne 13:10-12
der a curse—the whole nation of you—

[a]*10* Or *father* [b]*12* Or *[12]May the LORD cut off from the tents of Jacob anyone who gives testimony in behalf of the man who does this* [c]*15* Or *[15]But the one ⌊who is our father⌋ did not do this, not as long as life remained in him. And what was he seeking? An offspring from God* [d]*16* Or *his wife*

3:10 [l]Ne 13:12 [m]2Ki 7:2
because you are robbing me. [10]Bring
the whole tithe into the storehouse,[l]
that there may be food in my house.
Test me in this," says the LORD Almighty, "and see if I will not throw
open the floodgates[m] of heaven and
pour out so much blessing that you
will not have room enough for it. [11]I
will prevent pests from devouring your
crops, and the vines in your fields will
not cast their fruit," says the LORD Almighty. [12]"Then all the nations will call
you blessed,[n] for yours will be a delight- 3:12 [n]Isa 61:9
ful land,"[o] says the LORD Almighty. [o]Isa 62:4
[13]"You have said harsh things[p] against 3:13 [p]Mal 2:17
me," says the LORD.
"Yet you ask, 'What have we said
against you?'
[14]"You have said, 'It is futile[q] to serve 3:14 [q]Ps 73:13
God. What did we gain by carrying [r]Isa 58:3
out his requirements and going about
like mourners[r] before the LORD Almighty? [15]But now we call the arrogant
blessed. Certainly the evildoers[s] pros- 3:15 [s]Jer 7:10
per, and even those who challenge God
escape.' "
[16]Then those who feared the LORD
talked with each other, and the LORD
listened and heard.[t] A scroll[u] of remem- 3:16 [t]Ps 34:15 [u]Ps 56:8
brance was written in his presence con-
cerning those who feared the LORD
and honored his name.
[17]"They will be mine," says the
LORD Almighty, "in the day when I 3:17 [v]Dt 7:6
make up my treasured possession.[a][v] I [w]Ps 103:13; Isa 26:20
will spare[w] them, just as in compassion
a man spares his son who serves him.
[18]And you will again see the distinction
between the righteous[x] and the wick- 3:18 [x]Ge 18:25
ed, between those who serve God and
those who do not.

The Day of the LORD

4:1 [y]Joel 2:31 [z]Isa 5:24; Ob 1:18
4 "Surely the day is coming;[y] it will
burn like a furnace. All the arrogant and every evildoer will be stubble,[z]
and that day that is coming will set
them on fire," says the LORD Almighty.

[a] 17 Or *Almighty, "my treasured possession, in the day when I act*

DAY 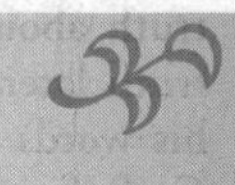 FIVE

▸ SELF-CONTROL AND ITS PLACE IN MY PERSONAL WORSHIP

Malachi 3:8–10

The most certain sign that we are sold out to the indulgent life can be seen in the difference between what we give God and what we keep for ourselves.

In this passage, God tells the people that they are robbing him (see Malachi 3:8–10). Robbing God? What were the Israelites doing with the money they stole from God? They were using it to "feather their own nests." The money we give to God shows how much we love God. The money we withhold from God shows how much we love ourselves. In general, the more we refuse to give sacrificially to God, the more we exhibit our own self-indulgence.

It is better to tithe than not to tithe. But God didn't command tithing so that he could take our little and have much. After all, he owns the world. What could our tithe add to his universal ownership? But God knows that what we hold on to is much more likely to spoil us than what we give. If we keep all that we make for ourselves, we will not be master of all we own, but we will become its slave.

People who cannot give to God destroy themselves. Their grasping miserliness thwarts all greatness in favor of crying, "Mine! Mine!" Those who are too reluctant to give their money to God might be better off burning what they will not give, lest, by keeping it all, they lose control over it and find themselves slaves to what they do own. Ironically, there is little difference between the hedonist and the miser. Both love money supremely, and both have lost control of its power over their lives. The love of it finally owns them.

To begin a study on the topic of Self-Control, Freedom From Permissiveness, turn to the home page on page 452.

▸  JOY

THE SON OF RIGHTEOUSNESS

Malachi 4:2

The sun rises and sets and marks the days that fill our years. But the Son of righteousness has now risen, and the very streaks of dawn's light have written the rosy name of Christ across the pale horizon. He came. The blind marveled at the display, and the deaf at last could hear the trumpets of the morning.

"Not a root or a branch will be left
to them. 2 But for you who revere my
name, the sun of righteousness[a] will
rise with healing[b] in its wings. And you
will go out and leap[c] like calves released
from the stall. 3 Then you will trample[d]
down the wicked; they will be ashes[e]
under the soles of your feet on the day
when I do these things," says the LORD
Almighty.

4:2 [a]Lk 1:78; Eph 5:14 [b]Isa 30:26 [c]Isa 35:6
4:3 [d]Job 40:12 [e]Eze 28:18

4 "Remember the law[f] of my servant
Moses, the decrees and laws I gave him
at Horeb for all Israel.
5 "See, I will send you the prophet
Elijah[g] before that great and dreadful
day of the LORD comes.[h] 6 He will
turn the hearts of the fathers to their
children,[i] and the hearts of the children
to their fathers; or else I will come and
strike[j] the land with a curse."[k]

4:4 [f]Ps 147:19
4:5 [g]Mt 11:14; Lk 1:17 [h]Joel 2:31
4:6 [i]Lk 1:17 [j]Isa 11:4; Rev 19:15 [k]Zec 5:3

NEW TESTAMENT

MATTHEW

AUTHORSHIP AND DATE

Matthew

Probably between A.D. 60 and A.D. 69

KEY THEMES

Matthew was a disciple and former tax collector. His purpose in writing his Gospel was to exhibit Jesus as the Messiah. The book of Matthew is filled with Messianic language, using terms such as "Son of David." It is replete with Old Testament quotes—53 direct quotations and 76 allusions to Old Testament passages. Matthew was careful to show Christ's authority over sickness and his triumph over Satan in the wilderness. Jesus' sacrificial death and his Easter triumph are the powerful conclusion to his biography of Christ. The kingdom of heaven is seen to be Jesus' plan, revealing his universal right to be King of the world. The book falls rather naturally into three divisions:

1. Jesus' genealogy, birth, baptism and temptation (see 1:1—4:11)
2. The Messiah and his message and ministry (see 4:12—25:46)
3. The final events of Jesus' death and resurrection (see 26:1—28:20).

FRUIT OF THE SPIRIT IN MATTHEW

Love: Jesus taught: " 'Love the Lord your God with all your heart and with all your soul and with all your mind.' This is the first and greatest commandment. And the second is like it: 'Love your neighbor as yourself' " (22:37–39). This twofold commandment is so important that if one obeys it, she or he need not be concerned with any other commandments.

Joy: In Matthew 28:8, joy was born in—of all places—a graveyard. There is but one shout of joy that really matters in Scripture. It is the shout: "He has risen!" (28:6). Such delirium happened but once in all of history, for only once has a dead man ever walked out of his grave, never to die again.

Peace: "Peacemakers . . . will be called sons of God," said Jesus (5:9). And why wouldn't they be? The world is anxious and war-filled. A person who induces quarreling people to lay down their swords has taught the world a rare lesson. Peacemakers have seen God descending like a dove onto a battlefield and dying at the hands of human hate. Such a God has every right to call his children to peace.

Patience: "When will all these things happen?" asked the disciples. "When will you come again?" the restless souls asked Jesus (see 24:3). "Patience," said the Son of God. "Get dressed and wait!"

Kindness: Will the meek inherit the earth, or will the kind? Both together, for they are one in the same (see 5:5). Never are the meek unkind, nor do the kind lack humility.

Goodness: Matthew 19:14 tells of an odd wedding: Childish innocence marries adult discernment. Holiness is the natural offspring from such a union. Here is one of heaven's grandest paradoxes: All children must strive for maturity or the world will be managed by loveable people with no discernment. And all adults must become childlike or no one will truly believe or trust in God.

Faithfulness: All our lives we are preparing to go someplace. Each day's schedule presents us with another agenda. Each agenda has its proprieties: How we shall dress, what we shall eat, when we shall get where we need to go. Faithfulness is a matter of leaving the neuroses to God. If God clothes the common grasses and wildflowers with splendor, surely he will take care of all our needs the very moment we commit ourselves to faithfulness (see 6:28–30).

Gentleness: Upon reading Matthew 5:38–39, we are tempted to argue with God: "Turn the other cheek? Lord, this is difficult. I cannot do so without your help. Yet let me obey. Let my assassins see that a gentle reply is a better weapon to fight with for peace than a club. Let my blood call for the end of blood. Give me a cross to spare the world more crucifixions. Let me be like Jesus, dying to keep others from the nails."

Self-Control: Jesus said that the narrow gate is the way to life (see 7:13–14). The path that leads to that gate is a childlike faith in Jesus alone for our salvation. And using the narrow gate as a metaphor for our ongoing walk with Christ, the fruit of self-control is essential. It takes some squeezing to wriggle through the gate. We must leave our gluttony and avarice, our envy and lust, our pride and prejudice. If we want to get through that gate, only our self-control will leave us thin enough to wedge our way into the upper courts of glory.

The Genealogy of Jesus

1 A record of the genealogy of Jesus Christ the son of David,[a] the son of Abraham:[b]

1:1 [a]2Sa 7:12-16; Isa 9:6,7; 11:1; Jer 23:5,6; Mt 9:27; Lk 1:32,69; Ro 1:3; Rev 22:16 [b]Ge 22:18; Gal 3:16

2 Abraham was the father of Isaac,[c]
Isaac the father of Jacob,[d]
Jacob the father of Judah and his brothers,[e]
3 Judah the father of Perez and Zerah, whose mother was Tamar,[f]
Perez the father of Hezron,
Hezron the father of Ram,
4 Ram the father of Amminadab,
Amminadab the father of Nahshon,
Nahshon the father of Salmon,
5 Salmon the father of Boaz, whose mother was Rahab,
Boaz the father of Obed, whose mother was Ruth,
Obed the father of Jesse,
6 and Jesse the father of King David.[g]

1:2 [c]Ge 21:3,12 [d]Ge 25:26 [e]Ge 29:35
1:3 [f]Ge 38:27-30
1:6 [g]1Sa 16:1; 17:12 [h]2Sa 12:24

David was the father of Solomon, whose mother had been Uriah's wife,[h]
7 Solomon the father of Rehoboam,
Rehoboam the father of Abijah,
Abijah the father of Asa,
8 Asa the father of Jehoshaphat,
Jehoshaphat the father of Jehoram,
Jehoram the father of Uzziah,
9 Uzziah the father of Jotham,
Jotham the father of Ahaz,
Ahaz the father of Hezekiah,
10 Hezekiah the father of Manasseh,[i]
Manasseh the father of Amon,
Amon the father of Josiah,
11 and Josiah the father of Jeconiah[a] and his brothers at the time of the exile to Babylon.[j]

1:10 [i]2Ki 20:21
1:11 [j]2Ki 24:14-16; Jer 27:20; Da 1:1,2

12 After the exile to Babylon:
Jeconiah was the father of Shealtiel,[k]
Shealtiel the father of Zerubbabel,[l]
13 Zerubbabel the father of Abiud,
Abiud the father of Eliakim,
Eliakim the father of Azor,
14 Azor the father of Zadok,
Zadok the father of Akim,
Akim the father of Eliud,
15 Eliud the father of Eleazar,
Eleazar the father of Matthan,
Matthan the father of Jacob,
16 and Jacob the father of Joseph, the husband of Mary,[m] of whom was born Jesus, who is called Christ.[n]

1:12 [k]1Ch 3:17 [l]1Ch 3:19; Ezr 3:2
1:16 [m]Lk 1:27 [n]Mt 27:17

17 Thus there were fourteen generations in all from Abraham to David, fourteen from David to the exile to Babylon, and fourteen from the exile to the Christ.[b]

LOVE

GOD'S ONE-FOR-ALL FAMILY OF GRACE

Matthew 1:17

Jesus did not simply fall upon the earth. He came from a family of many generations, listed here by Matthew and going back to Abraham. He issued from a single thread of history—an umbilical cord of grace over 2,000 years in length.

The Birth of Jesus Christ

18 This is how the birth of Jesus
Christ came about: His mother Mary
was pledged to be married to Joseph,
but before they came together, she was
found to be with child through the
Holy Spirit.[o] 19 Because Joseph her hus- 1:18 [o]Lk 1:35
band was a righteous man and did not
want to expose her to public disgrace, 1:19 [p]Dt 24:1
he had in mind to divorce[p] her quietly.
20 But after he had considered this, an
angel of the Lord appeared to him in a
dream and said, "Joseph son of David,
do not be afraid to take Mary home as
your wife, because what is conceived in
her is from the Holy Spirit. 21 She will
give birth to a son, and you are to give 1:21 [q]Lk 1:31 [r]Lk 2:11; Ac 5:31; 13:23,28
him the name Jesus,[c][q] because he will
save his people from their sins."[r]
22 All this took place to fulfill what
the Lord had said through the prophet: 23 "The virgin will be with child and
will give birth to a son, and they will 1:23 [s]Isa 7:14; 8:8,10
call him Immanuel"[d][s]—which means,
"God with us."

[a] *11* That is, Jehoiachin; also in verse 12 [b] *17* Or *Messiah.* "The Christ" (Greek) and "the Messiah" (Hebrew) both mean "the Anointed One."
[c] *21 Jesus* is the Greek form of *Joshua,* which means *the LORD saves.* [d] *23* Isaiah 7:14

▸ KINDNESS

IMMANUEL—GOD IS WITH US, REGARDLESS

Matthew 1:22–23

Love watched the human battle rage,
Then left the throne by love compelled
And woke on straw in Bethlehem—
The infant God, Immanuel.

[24]When Joseph woke up, he did what
the angel of the Lord had commanded
him and took Mary home as his wife.
[25]But he had no union with her until
she gave birth to a son. And he gave
1:25 [t]ver 21 him the name Jesus.[t]

The Visit of the Magi

2 After Jesus was born in Bethlehem
2:1 [u]Lk 2:4-7 [v]Lk 1:5 in Judea,[u] during the time of King
Herod,[v] Magi[a] from the east came to Je-
rusalem [2]and asked, "Where is the one
2:2 [w]Jer 23:5; Mt 27:11; Mk 15:2; Jn 1:49; 18:33-37 [x]Nu 24:17 who has been born king of the Jews?[w]
We saw his star[x] in the east[b] and have
come to worship him."

[3]When King Herod heard this he
was disturbed, and all Jerusalem with
him. [4]When he had called together all
the people's chief priests and teachers
2:5 [y]Jn 7:42 of the law, he asked them where the
Christ[c] was to be born. [5]"In Bethlehem[y] in Judea," they replied, "for this
is what the prophet has written:

[6]" 'But you, Bethlehem, in the land of
Judah,
are by no means least among the
rulers of Judah;
for out of you will come a ruler
2:6 [z]Mic 5:2; 2Sa 5:2 who will be the shepherd of my
people Israel.'[d]"[z]

[7]Then Herod called the Magi secretly and found out from them the exact
time the star had appeared. [8]He sent
them to Bethlehem and said, "Go and
make a careful search for the child. As
soon as you find him, report to me, so
that I too may go and worship him."

[9]After they had heard the king, they
went on their way, and the star they had
seen in the east[e] went ahead of them
until it stopped over the place where
the child was. [10]When they saw the star,
they were overjoyed. [11]On coming to
the house, they saw the child with his
mother Mary, and they bowed down
and worshiped him.[a] Then they opened 2:11 [a]Isa 60:3 [b]Ps 72:10
their treasures and presented him with
gifts[b] of gold and of incense and of 2:12 [c]Heb 11:7 [d]ver 13,19,22; Mt 27:19
myrrh. [12]And having been warned[c] in a
dream[d] not to go back to Herod, they
returned to their country by another
route.

▸ JOY

STAR WALKING

Matthew 2:10–11

No local god, this infant Christ,
Foreign kings came from afar
And traveled to adore a God,
A global child—a global star.

The Escape to Egypt

[13]When they had gone, an angel[e] 2:13 [e]Ac 5:19 [f]ver 12,19,22
of the Lord appeared to Joseph in a
dream.[f] "Get up," he said, "take the
child and his mother and escape to
Egypt. Stay there until I tell you, for
Herod is going to search for the child
to kill him."

[14]So he got up, took the child and
his mother during the night and left for
Egypt, [15]where he stayed until the death
of Herod. And so was fulfilled what
the Lord had said through the prophet: 2:15 [g]Hos 11:1; Ex 4:22,23
"Out of Egypt I called my son."[f][g]

[16]When Herod realized that he had
been outwitted by the Magi, he was furious, and he gave orders to kill all the
boys in Bethlehem and its vicinity who
were two years old and under, in accordance with the time he had learned
from the Magi. [17]Then what was said
through the prophet Jeremiah was fulfilled:

[18]"A voice is heard in Ramah,
weeping and great mourning,
Rachel weeping for her children
and refusing to be comforted,
because they are no more."[g][h] 2:18 [h]Jer 31:15

The Return to Nazareth

[19]After Herod died, an angel of the 2:19 [i]ver 12,13,22
Lord appeared in a dream[i] to Joseph
in Egypt [20]and said, "Get up, take the
child and his mother and go to the land

[a]*1* Traditionally *Wise Men* [b]*2* Or *star when it rose* [c]*4* Or *Messiah* [d]*6* Micah 5:2 [e]*9* Or *seen when it rose* [f]*15* Hosea 11:1 [g]*18* Jer. 31:15

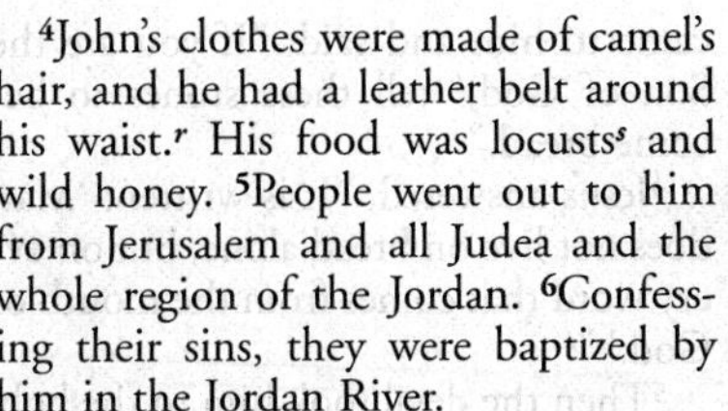

PEACE

RACHEL'S TEARS

Matthew 2:18

Will Rachel ever know peace? Only when the Prince of Peace sets the world right and the only tears will be tears of joy.

Rachel weeps.
Babies massacred by hate
Caused Bethlehem to be a weeping place.
Motherhood is never more costly
Than when its children bleed and die,
And all its lullabies
Are sung to silence.

of Israel, for those who were trying to
take the child's life are dead."
21So he got up, took the child and
his mother and went to the land of Israel. 22But when he heard that Arche-
laus was reigning in Judea in place of
his father Herod, he was afraid to go
2:22 [j]ver 12,13,19; Mt 27:19 [k]Lk 2:39 there. Having been warned in a dream,[j]
he withdrew to the district of Galilee,[k]
23and he went and lived in a town called
2:23 [l]Lk 1:26; Jn 1:45,46 [m]Mt 1:22 [n]Mk 1:24 Nazareth.[l] So was fulfilled[m] what was
said through the prophets: "He will be
called a Nazarene."[n]

John the Baptist Prepares the Way

3:1 [o]Lk 1:13, 57-66; 3:2-19 3 In those days John the Baptist[o]
came, preaching in the Desert of
3:2 [p]Da 2:44; Mt 4:17; 6:10; Lk 11:20; 21:31; Jn 3:3,5; Ac 1:3,6 Judea 2and saying, "Repent, for the kingdom of heaven[p] is near." 3This is he
who was spoken of through the prophet
Isaiah:

"A voice of one calling in the
desert,
3:3 [q]Isa 40:3; Mal 3:1; Lk 1:76; Jn 1:23 'Prepare the way for the Lord,
make straight paths for him.' "[a][q]

PATIENCE

ELIJAH'S MIRROR

Matthew 3:3–4

Elijah, the mystic, lonely desert dweller,
came again—
A trumpet to announce a king.
A wilderness herald came to shake the
sleeping age awake!
The promise, half a millennium in age,
said to all,
"Be patient . . . God keeps his word in
time."

4John's clothes were made of camel's
hair, and he had a leather belt around
his waist.[r] His food was locusts[s] and 3:4 [r]2Ki 1:8 [s]Lev 11:22
wild honey. 5People went out to him
from Jerusalem and all Judea and the
whole region of the Jordan. 6Confess-
ing their sins, they were baptized by
him in the Jordan River.
7But when he saw many of the Pharisees and Sadducees coming to where he
was baptizing, he said to them: "You
brood of vipers![t] Who warned you to 3:7 [t]Mt 12:34; 23:33 [u]Ro 1:18; 1Th 1:10
flee from the coming wrath?[u] 8Produce
fruit in keeping with repentance.[v] 9And
do not think you can say to yourselves, 3:8 [v]Ac 26:20
'We have Abraham as our father.' I tell
you that out of these stones God can
raise up children for Abraham. 10The
ax is already at the root of the trees, and
every tree that does not produce good
fruit will be cut down and thrown into
the fire.[w] 3:10 [w]Mt 7:19; Lk 13:6-9; Jn 15:2,6
11"I baptize you with[b] water for repentance. But after me will come one
who is more powerful than I, whose
sandals I am not fit to carry. He will
baptize you with the Holy Spirit[x] and 3:11 [x]Mk 1:8 [y]Isa 4:4; Ac 2:3,4
with fire.[y] 12His winnowing fork is in
his hand, and he will clear his threshing floor, gathering his wheat into the
barn and burning up the chaff with un- 3:12 [z]Mt 13:30
quenchable fire."[z]

The Baptism of Jesus

13Then Jesus came from Galilee to
the Jordan to be baptized by John.[a] 3:13 [a]Mk 1:4
14But John tried to deter him, saying, "I
need to be baptized by you, and do you
come to me?"
15Jesus replied, "Let it be so now; it
is proper for us to do this to fulfill all
righteousness." Then John consented.
16As soon as Jesus was baptized, he
went up out of the water. At that mo-
ment heaven was opened, and he saw 3:16 [b]Isa 11:2; 42:1
the Spirit of God[b] descending like a
dove and lighting on him. 17And a 3:17 [c]Mt 17:5; Jn 12:28 [d]Ps 2:7; 2Pe 1:17,18 [e]Isa 42:1; Mt 12:18; 17:5; Mk 1:11; 9:7; Lk 9:35
voice from heaven[c] said, "This is my
Son,[d] whom I love; with him I am well
pleased."[e]

The Temptation of Jesus

4 Then Jesus was led by the Spirit
into the desert to be tempted by the
devil. 2After fasting forty days and forty 4:2 [f]Ex 34:28; 1Ki 19:8
nights,[f] he was hungry. 3The tempter[g] 4:3 [g]1Th 3:5

[a]*3* Isaiah 40:3 [b]*11* Or *in*

came to him and said, "If you are the
4:3 [h]Mt 3:17; Jn 5:25; Ac 9:20 Son of God,[h] tell these stones to become bread."
4Jesus answered, "It is written: 'Man
does not live on bread alone, but on ev-
4:4 [i]Dt 8:3 ery word that comes from the mouth of
God.'[a]"[i]
4:5 [j]Ne 11:1; Da 9:24; Mt 27:53 5Then the devil took him to the holy
city[j] and had him stand on the high-
est point of the temple. 6"If you are the
Son of God," he said, "throw yourself
down. For it is written:

"'He will command his angels
concerning you,
and they will lift you up in their
hands,
4:6 [k]Ps 91:11,12 so that you will not strike your foot
against a stone.'[b]"[k]

7Jesus answered him, "It is also writ-
4:7 [l]Dt 6:16 ten: 'Do not put the Lord your God to
the test.'[c]"[l]
8Again, the devil took him to a very
high mountain and showed him all
the kingdoms of the world and their
splendor. 9"All this I will give you," he
said, "if you will bow down and worship me."
4:10 [m]1Ch 21:1 [n]Dt 6:13 10Jesus said to him, "Away from me,
Satan![m] For it is written: 'Worship the
Lord your God, and serve him only.'[d]"[n]
4:11 [o]Mt 26:53; Lk 22:43; Heb 1:14 11Then the devil left him, and angels
came and attended him.[o]

SELF-CONTROL

POWER

Matthew 4:10

Jesus is our mentor in the life of discipline. He denied himself in the wilderness and so made himself believable later when he spoke of self-denial. He modeled what he would teach before he taught it.

Jesus Begins to Preach

12When Jesus heard that John had
4:12 [p]Mt 14:3 [q]Mk 1:14 been put in prison,[p] he returned to
Galilee.[q] 13Leaving Nazareth, he went
4:13 [r]Mk 1:21; Lk 4:23,31; Jn 2:12; 4:46,47 and lived in Capernaum,[r] which was
by the lake in the area of Zebulun and
Naphtali— 14to fulfill what was said
through the prophet Isaiah:
15"Land of Zebulun and land of
Naphtali,
the way to the sea, along the
Jordan,

DAY 2 TWO

JOY AND THE PURPOSE OF GOD IN MY LIFE

Matthew 4:10–11

Joy is a close relative of self-control. Joy is the friend of those who know how and when to say "no" and can say "no" clearly so that it doesn't sound like "maybe."

Joy is the automatic result of the emphatic "no." How the world is missing this single syllable of glory!

The child who wants to stand up for the Biblical truth in a classroom needs the courage to say a good, kingdom-blessed "no."

The executive who is being offered an illegal embezzlement option needs the power of a good, clear "no."

The preacher who faces the temptation to move to a larger and wealthier parish should be motivated by better adjectives than "larger and wealthier" and needs the courage to say "no."

The college student who is looking at the bogus promises of a needle and a syringe, needs the inner strength to say "no."

To any or all who need to say "no," remember that the angels are hovering about, waiting for your response. If you respond as you should, you may be sure that temptations conquered will provide fertile soil for joy.

Consider the words of Joshua 1:9: "Be strong and courageous. Do not be terrified; do not be discouraged, for the LORD your God will be with you wherever you go." When you have stood true, you will not be alone, for you will be standing in the company of proud angels.

To begin a study on the topic of Joy, the Reveling of Angels, turn to the home page on page 700.

Galilee of the Gentiles—
16the people living in darkness
have seen a great light;
on those living in the land of the
shadow of death
a light has dawned."[e][s] 4:16 [s]Isa 9:1,2; Lk 2:32

[a]*4* Deut. 8:3 [b]*6* Psalm 91:11,12 [c]*7* Deut. 6:16
[d]*10* Deut. 6:13 [e]*16* Isaiah 9:1,2

17From that time on Jesus began to preach, "Repent, for the kingdom of heaven[t] is near."

4:17 [t]Mt 3:2

The Calling of the First Disciples

18As Jesus was walking beside the Sea of Galilee,[u] he saw two brothers, Simon called Peter[v] and his brother Andrew. They were casting a net into the lake, for they were fishermen. 19"Come, follow me,"[w] Jesus said, "and I will make you fishers of men." 20At once they left their nets and followed him.

21Going on from there, he saw two other brothers, James son of Zebedee and his brother John.[x] They were in a boat with their father Zebedee, preparing their nets. Jesus called them, 22and immediately they left the boat and their father and followed him.

4:18 [u]Mt 15:29; Mk 7:31; Jn 6:1 [v]Mt 16:17,18
4:19 [w]Mk 10:21,28,52
4:21 [x]Mt 20:20

▸ **FAITHFULNESS**

"THE COMPLEAT ANGLERS"

Matthew 4:19

Fishing faithfully brings life and vitality to Christ's church. The difference between fishing for fish and catching souls is the difference between lunch and the "Hallelujah Chorus."

Jesus Heals the Sick

23Jesus went throughout Galilee,[y] teaching in their synagogues,[z] preaching the good news[a] of the kingdom,[b] and healing every disease and sickness among the people.[c] 24News about him spread all over Syria,[d] and people brought to him all who were ill with various diseases, those suffering severe pain, the demon-possessed,[e] those having seizures,[f] and the paralyzed,[g] and he healed them. 25Large crowds from Galilee, the Decapolis,[a] Jerusalem, Judea and the region across the Jordan followed him.[h]

4:23 [y]Mk 1:39; Lk 4:15,44 [z]Mt 9:35; 13:54; Mk 1:21; Lk 4:15; Jn 6:59 [a]Mk 1:14 [b]Mt 3:2; Ac 20:25 [c]Mt 8:16; 15:30; Ac 10:38
4:24 [d]Lk 2:2 [e]Mt 8:16,28; 9:32; 15:22; Mk 1:32; 5:15,16,18 [f]Mt 17:15 [g]Mt 8:6; 9:2; Mk 2:3
4:25 [h]Mk 3:7,8; Lk 6:17

The Beatitudes

5 Now when he saw the crowds, he went up on a mountainside and sat down. His disciples came to him, 2and he began to teach them, saying:

3 "Blessed are the poor in spirit,
for theirs is the kingdom of heaven.[i]
4 Blessed are those who mourn,
for they will be comforted.[j]

5:3 [i]ver 10,19; Mt 25:34
5:4 [j]Isa 61:2,3; Rev 7:17

▸ **PEACE**

DON'T WORRY, BE HAPPY

Matthew 5:3–10

Blessed are the poor, the grieving and the mistreated.
Keep your eye on them,
You who are rich, indulgent and cruel.
Watch how their poverty has taught them to trust and blessed them with security.

5 Blessed are the meek,
for they will inherit the earth.[k]
6 Blessed are those who hunger and thirst for righteousness,
for they will be filled.[l]
7 Blessed are the merciful,
for they will be shown mercy.
8 Blessed are the pure in heart,[m]
for they will see God.[n]
9 Blessed are the peacemakers,
for they will be called sons of God.[o]
10 Blessed are those who are persecuted because of righteousness,[p]
for theirs is the kingdom of heaven.

5:5 [k]Ps 37:11; Ro 4:13
5:6 [l]Isa 55:1,2
5:8 [m]Ps 24:3,4 [n]Heb 12:14; Rev 22:4
5:9 [o]ver 44,45; Ro 8:14
5:10 [p]1Pe 3:14

11"Blessed are you when people insult you,[q] persecute you and falsely say all kinds of evil against you because of me. 12Rejoice and be glad,[r] because great is your reward in heaven, for in the same way they persecuted the prophets who were before you.[s]

5:11 [q]1Pe 4:14
5:12 [r]Ac 5:41; 1Pe 4:13,16 [s]Mt 23:31,37; Ac 7:52; 1Th 2:15

Salt and Light

13"You are the salt of the earth. But if the salt loses its saltiness, how can it be made salty again? It is no longer good for anything, except to be thrown out and trampled by men.[t]

14"You are the light of the world.[u] A city on a hill cannot be hidden. 15Neither do people light a lamp and put it under a bowl. Instead they put it on its stand, and it gives light to everyone in the house.[v] 16In the same way, let your light shine before men, that they may see your good deeds and praise[w] your Father in heaven.

5:13 [t]Mk 9:50; Lk 14:34,35
5:14 [u]Jn 8:12
5:15 [v]Mk 4:21; Lk 8:16
5:16 [w]Mt 9:8

The Fulfillment of the Law

17"Do not think that I have come to abolish the Law or the Prophets; I have

[a]25 That is, the Ten Cities

not come to abolish them but to fulfill
5:17 [x]Ro 3:31 them.[x] 18I tell you the truth, until heaven
and earth disappear, not the smallest let-
ter, not the least stroke of a pen, will by
any means disappear from the Law un-
5:18 [y]Lk 16:17 til everything is accomplished.[y] 19Any-
5:19 [z]Jas 2:10 one who breaks one of the least of these
commandments[z] and teaches others to
do the same will be called least in the
kingdom of heaven, but whoever practices and teaches these commands will
be called great in the kingdom of heav-
en. 20For I tell you that unless your righteousness surpasses that of the Pharisees
and the teachers of the law, you will certainly not enter the kingdom of heaven.

GOODNESS

BLIND AND BLAND

Matthew 5:16

The blind and bland keep bumping into sightless, tasteless living. Light and salt are the only cures for the blind and bland.

Murder

5:21 [a]Ex 20:13; Dt 5:17 21"You have heard that it was said to
the people long ago, 'Do not murder,[a][a]
and anyone who murders will be sub-
5:22 [b]1Jn 3:15 [c]Mt 26:59 [d]Jas 3:6 ject to judgment.' 22But I tell you that
anyone who is angry with his brother[b]
will be subject to judgment.[b] Again,
anyone who says to his brother, 'Raca,[c]'
is answerable to the Sanhedrin.[c] But
anyone who says, 'You fool!' will be in
danger of the fire of hell.[d]
23"Therefore, if you are offering your
gift at the altar and there remember that
your brother has something against you,
24leave your gift there in front of the altar. First go and be reconciled to your
brother; then come and offer your gift.
25"Settle matters quickly with your
adversary who is taking you to court.
Do it while you are still with him on
the way, or he may hand you over to the
judge, and the judge may hand you over
to the officer, and you may be thrown
into prison. 26I tell you the truth, you
will not get out until you have paid the
last penny.[d]

Adultery

5:27 [e]Ex 20:14; Dt 5:18 27"You have heard that it was said,
'Do not commit adultery.'[e][e] 28But I tell
you that anyone who looks at a woman
lustfully has already committed adul-
tery with her in his heart.[f] 29If your 5:28 [f]Pr 6:25
right eye causes you to sin,[g] gouge it
out and throw it away. It is better for 5:29 [g]Mt 18:6,8,9; Mk 9:42-47

DAY 5 FIVE

KINDNESS AND ITS PLACE IN MY PERSONAL WORSHIP

Matthew 5:23–24

Jesus counseled all quarrelsome worshipers to be reconciled before they came to worship: "Leave your gift there in front of the altar. First go and be reconciled to your brother." Sometimes people come to church and hope to present God a heart of loving admiration while they try to inflate their own personal reputations at the same time.

The church historically has been guilty of what James calls "fights and quarrels" (James 4:1). In your church, when strangers come to worship, do they find members who extend kindness to each other and to the visitor in their midst? Or would visitors be far more likely to find the church embroiled in a cutting, hateful quarrel that would for the most part prevent members from even seeing the stranger?

Grudges and harsh viewpoints not only keep us from seeing the stranger in our midst; they keep us from seeing God. John put it this way, "If anyone says, 'I love God,' yet hates his brother, he is a liar. For anyone who does not love his brother, whom he has seen, cannot love God, whom he has not seen" (1 John 4:20). From what John says, many angry worshipers may come and go to church and never see God at all.

Kind people, on the other hand, enter worship with no human biases against others. Loving all others is the first step of giving uncontaminated love to God. From the high, thin air of exalted worship, these who love can see directly into heaven. Their own kind hearts enable them to see the great God of Isaiah 6. He is for them always high and lifted up. They worship and live in such joy that they never see any contradiction between their own kind nature and the high level of adoration they offer to God. Indeed there is no contradiction.

To begin a study on the topic of Kindness As a Worldview, turn to the home page on page 1058.

[a]*21* Exodus 20:13 [b]*22* Some manuscripts *brother without cause* [c]*22* An Aramaic term of contempt [d]*26* Greek *kodrantes* [e]*27* Exodus 20:14

you to lose one part of your body than for your whole body to be thrown into hell. 30And if your right hand causes you to sin, cut it off and throw it away. It is better for you to lose one part of your body than for your whole body to go into hell.

Divorce

31"It has been said, 'Anyone who divorces his wife must give her a certificate of divorce.'[a][b] 32But I tell you that anyone who divorces his wife, except for marital unfaithfulness, causes her to become an adulteress, and anyone who marries the divorced woman commits adultery.[i]

5:31 [b]Dt 24:1-4
5:32 [i]Lk 16:18

Oaths

33"Again, you have heard that it was said to the people long ago, 'Do not break your oath,[j] but keep the oaths you have made to the Lord.'[k] 34But I tell you, Do not swear at all:[l] either by heaven, for it is God's throne;[m] 35or by the earth, for it is his footstool; or by Jerusalem, for it is the city of the Great King.[n] 36And do not swear by your head, for you cannot make even one hair white or black. 37Simply let your 'Yes' be 'Yes,' and your 'No,' 'No';[o] anything beyond this comes from the evil one.[p]

5:33 [j]Lev 19:12 [k]Nu 30:2; Dt 23:21; Mt 23:16-22
5:34 [l]Jas 5:12 [m]Isa 66:1; Mt 23:22
5:35 [n]Ps 48:2
5:37 [o]Jas 5:12 [p]Mt 6:13; 13:19,38; Jn 17:15; 2Th 3:3; 1Jn 2:13,14; 3:12; 5:18,19

An Eye for an Eye

38"You have heard that it was said, 'Eye for eye, and tooth for tooth.'[b][q] 39But I tell you, Do not resist an evil person. If someone strikes you on the right cheek, turn to him the other also.[r] 40And if someone wants to sue you and take your tunic, let him have your cloak as well. 41If someone forces you to go one mile, go with him two miles. 42Give to the one who asks you, and do not turn away from the one who wants to borrow from you.[s]

5:38 [q]Ex 21:24; Lev 24:20; Dt 19:21
5:39 [r]Lk 6:29; Ro 12:17,19; 1Co 6:7; 1Pe 3:9
5:42 [s]Dt 15:8; Lk 6:30

Love for Enemies

43"You have heard that it was said, 'Love your neighbor[c][t] and hate your enemy.'[u] 44But I tell you: Love your enemies[d] and pray for those who persecute you,[v] 45that you may be sons[w] of your Father in heaven. He causes his sun to rise on the evil and the good, and sends rain on the righteous and the unrighteous.[x] 46If you love those who love you, what reward will you get?[y] Are not even the tax collectors doing that? 47And if you greet only your brothers, what are you doing more than others? Do not even pagans do that? 48Be perfect, therefore, as your heavenly Father is perfect.[z]

5:43 [t]Lev 19:18 [u]Dt 23:6
5:44 [v]Lk 6:27,28; 23:34; Ac 7:60; Ro 12:14; 1Co 4:12; 1Pe 2:23
5:45 [w]ver 9 [x]Job 25:3
5:46 [y]Lk 6:32
5:48 [z]Lev 19:2; 1Pe 1:16

Giving to the Needy

6 "Be careful not to do your 'acts of righteousness' before men, to be seen by them.[a] If you do, you will have no reward from your Father in heaven.

2"So when you give to the needy, do not announce it with trumpets, as the hypocrites do in the synagogues and on the streets, to be honored by men. I tell you the truth, they have received their reward in full. 3But when you give to the needy, do not let your left hand know what your right hand is doing, 4so that your giving may be in secret. Then your Father, who sees what is done in secret, will reward you.[b]

6:1 [a]Mt 23:5
6:4 [b]ver 6,18; Col 3:23,24

Prayer

5"And when you pray, do not be like the hypocrites, for they love to pray standing[c] in the synagogues and on the street corners to be seen by men. I tell you the truth, they have received their reward in full. 6But when you pray, go into your room, close the door and pray to your Father,[d] who is unseen. Then your Father, who sees what is done in secret, will reward you. 7And when you pray, do not keep on babbling[e] like pagans, for they think they will be heard because of their many words.[f] 8Do not be like them, for your Father knows what you need[g] before you ask him.

9"This, then, is how you should pray:

"'Our Father in heaven,
hallowed be your name,
10your kingdom[h] come,
your will be done[i]
on earth as it is in heaven.
11Give us today our daily bread.[j]
12Forgive us our debts,
as we also have forgiven our debtors.[k]
13And lead us not into temptation,[l]
but deliver us from the evil one.[e]'[m]

6:5 [c]Mk 11:25; Lk 18:10-14
6:6 [d]2Ki 4:33
6:7 [e]Ecc 5:2 [f]1Ki 18:26-29
6:8 [g]ver 32
6:10 [h]Mt 3:2 [i]Mt 26:39
6:11 [j]Pr 30:8
6:12 [k]Mt 18:21-35
6:13 [l]Jas 1:13 [m]Mt 5:37

[a] *31* Deut. 24:1 [b] *38* Exodus 21:24; Lev. 24:20; Deut. 19:21 [c] *43* Lev. 19:18 [d] *44* Some late manuscripts *enemies, bless those who curse you, do good to those who hate you* [e] *13* Or *from evil*; some late manuscripts *one, / for yours is the kingdom and the power and the glory forever. Amen.*

GENTLENESS

NOW I LAY ME DOWN TO SLEEP

Matthew 6:9–13

Now I lay me down to sleep
And gentle promises I keep:
Come: His Kingdom
Done: His Will
Thanks: For his provisions offered
Repentance: Begged
The evil one: Excluded from ownership of my life

14 For if you forgive men when they sin
against you, your heavenly Father will
6:14 [n]Mt 18:21-35; also forgive you.[n] 15 But if you do not
Mk 11:25,26; forgive men their sins, your Father will
Eph 4:32; Col 3:13 not forgive your sins.[o]

6:15 [o]Mt 18:35

Fasting

6:16 [p]Isa 58:5 16 "When you fast, do not look somber[p] as the hypocrites do, for they dis-
figure their faces to show men they
are fasting. I tell you the truth, they
have received their reward in full. 17 But
when you fast, put oil on your head
and wash your face, 18 so that it will not
be obvious to men that you are fasting,
but only to your Father, who is unseen;
and your Father, who sees what is done
6:18 [q]ver 4,6 in secret, will reward you.[q]

Treasures in Heaven

19 "Do not store up for yourselves trea-
6:19 [r]Pr 23:4; sures on earth,[r] where moth and rust
Heb 13:5 destroy,[s] and where thieves break in and
[s]Jas 5:2,3 steal. 20 But store up for yourselves trea-
6:20 [t]Mt 19:21; sures in heaven,[t] where moth and rust
Lk 12:33; do not destroy, and where thieves do not
18:22; 1Ti 6:19 break in and steal.[u] 21 For where your
[u]Lk 12:33 treasure is, there your heart will be also.[v]
6:21 [v]Lk 12:34 22 "The eye is the lamp of the body.
If your eyes are good, your whole body
will be full of light. 23 But if your eyes
are bad, your whole body will be full of
darkness. If then the light within you is
darkness, how great is that darkness!
24 "No one can serve two masters. Either he will hate the one and love the
6:24 other, or he will be devoted to the one
[w]Lk 16:13 and despise the other. You cannot serve
6:25 both God and Money.[w]
[x]ver 27,28, 31,34;

Do Not Worry

Lk 10:41; 12:11,22;
Php 4:6; 25 "Therefore I tell you, do not wor-
1Pe 5:7 ry[x] about your life, what you will eat

DAY 3 THREE

JOY AND MY RELATIONSHIP WITH CHRIST

Matthew 6:28–30

When Jesus wanted to teach his disciples the art of depending on his sufficiency, he invited them to consider the lilies of the field. Here the exquisite fashioning of God fell on the tiniest of plants. Jesus used God's creativity in miniature as evidence that God can be trusted to take care of all of our needs. The same God who overwhelms us with the majesty of the ocean can mystify us with a drop of clear, pure dew shaken from the petals of a rose.

To encounter either the wide grandeur or tiny gem-like creativity of God awakens anthems in our soul. Joy is our response to the creation of God. And it is Christ who awakes us to this wonder. It is the Jesus of the wildflowers who calls us to marvel at the lilies and then to contemplate what God's perfect creation means in terms of our ability to depend on him.

We may be prone to forget that Jesus was a man of the outdoors. His entire ministry amounted to a three-year camp-out with his disciples. His miracles of calming the storm, walking on the water or feeding the five thousand are all outside miracles.

Because he had such rapport with the elements and all of nature, it is natural that Christ's sermon illustrations include rain, harvest and wildflowers. Today, many of our hymns focus on the relationship between Christ and the elements:

Fair are the meadows, fairer still the woodlands
Robed in the blooming garb of spring;...
Fair is the sunshine,
Fairer still the moonlight
And all the twinkling starry host;
Jesus shines brighter, Jesus shines purer...

Here's to our "Fairest Lord Jesus." Here's to the Jesus of the wildflowers. Let us look to the lilies, and be reminded through Christ of God's unfailing providence.

To begin a study on the topic of The Joy of Creativity, turn to the home page on page 639.

Jesus Speaks Out *on the Fruit of the Spirit:* Faithfulness

Luke 16:10
Whoever can be trusted with very little can also be trusted with much, and whoever is dishonest with very little will also be dishonest with much.

John 8:31
To the Jews who had believed him, Jesus said, "If you hold to my teaching, you are really my disciples."

John 15:9
As the Father has loved me, so have I loved you. Now remain in my love.

Matthew 19:17
"Why do you ask me about what is good?" Jesus replied. "There is only One who is good. If you want to enter life, obey the commandments."

John 8:51
I tell you the truth, if anyone keeps my word, he will never see death.

John 14:15
If you love me, you will obey what I command.

John 15:10
If you obey my commands, you will remain in my love, just as I have obeyed my Father's commands and remain in his love.

The Final Judgment

When the Son of Man comes in his glory, and all the angels with him, he will sit on his throne in heavenly glory. All the nations will be gathered before him, and he will separate the people one from another as a shepherd separates the sheep from the goats. He will put the sheep on his right and the goats on his left.

Then the King will say to those on his right, "Come, you who are blessed by my Father; take your inheritance, the kingdom prepared for you since the creation of the world. For I was hungry and you gave me something to eat, I was thirsty and you gave me something to drink, I was a stranger and you invited me in, I needed clothes and you clothed me, I was sick and you looked after me, I was in prison and you came to visit me."

Then the righteous will answer him, "Lord, when did we see you hungry and feed you, or thirsty and give you something to drink? When did we see you a stranger and invite you in, or needing clothes and clothe you? When did we see you sick or in prison and go to visit you?"

The King will reply, "I tell you the truth, whatever you did for one of the least of these brothers of mine, you did for me."

Then he will say to those on his left, "Depart from me, you who are cursed, into the eternal fire prepared for the devil and his angels. For I was hungry and you gave me nothing to eat, I was thirsty and you gave me nothing to drink, I was a stranger and you did not invite me in, I needed clothes and you did not clothe me, I was sick and in prison and you did not look after me."

They also will answer, "Lord, when did we see you hungry or thirsty or a stranger or needing clothes or sick or in prison, and did not help you?"

He will reply, "I tell you the truth, whatever you did not do for one of the least of these, you did not do for me."

Then they will go away to eternal punishment, but the righteous to eternal life.

Matthew 25:31–46

Paul Speaks Out *on the Fruit of the Spirit:* Faithfulness

Galatians 5:22

The fruit of the Spirit is love, joy, peace, patience, kindness, goodness, faithfulness.

1 Corinthians 1:9

God, who has called you into fellowship with his Son Jesus Christ our Lord, is faithful.

1 Corinthians 10:13

No temptation has seized you except what is common to man. And God is faithful; he will not let you be tempted beyond what you can bear. But when you are tempted, he will also provide a way out so that you can stand up under it.

1 Timothy 1:12

I thank Christ Jesus our Lord, who has given me strength, that he considered me faithful, appointing me to his service.

Acts 26:1–6

Then Agrippa said to Paul, "You have permission to speak for yourself."

So Paul motioned with his hand and began his defense: "King Agrippa, I consider myself fortunate to stand before you today as I make my defense against all the accusations of the Jews, and especially so because you are well acquainted with all the Jewish customs and controversies. Therefore, I beg you to listen to me patiently.

"The Jews all know the way I have lived ever since I was a child, from the beginning of my life in my own country, and also in Jerusalem. They have known me for a long time and can testify, if they are willing, that according to the strictest sect of our religion, I lived as a Pharisee. And now it is because of my hope in what God has promised our fathers that I am on trial today."

▸ Faithfulness Perseveres

"On one of these journeys I was going to Damascus with the authority and commission of the chief priests. About noon, O king, as I was on the road, I saw a light from heaven, brighter than the sun, blazing around me and my companions. We all fell to the ground, and I heard a voice saying to me in Aramaic, 'Saul, Saul, why do you persecute me? It is hard for you to kick against the goads.'

"Then I asked, 'Who are you, Lord?'

" 'I am Jesus, whom you are persecuting,' the Lord replied. 'Now get up and stand on your feet. I have appeared to you to appoint you as a servant and as a witness of what you have seen of me and what I will show you. I will rescue you from your own people and from the Gentiles. I am sending you to them to open their eyes and turn them from darkness to light, and from the power of Satan to God, so that they may receive forgiveness of sins and a place among those who are sanctified by faith in me.'

"So then, King Agrippa, I was not disobedient to the vision from heaven. First to those in Damascus, then to those in Jerusalem and in all Judea, and to the Gentiles also, I preached that they should repent and turn to God and prove their repentance by their deeds."

Acts 26:12–20

or drink; or about your body, what you
will wear. Is not life more important
than food, and the body more important than clothes? 26 Look at the birds
of the air; they do not sow or reap or
store away in barns, and yet your heav-
6:26 [y]Job 38:41; Ps 147:9 [z]Mt 10:29-31 enly Father feeds them.[y] Are you not
much more valuable than they?[z] 27 Who
of you by worrying can add a single
6:27 [a]Ps 39:5 hour to his life[a]?[a]
28 "And why do you worry about
clothes? See how the lilies of the field
grow. They do not labor or spin. 29 Yet
I tell you that not even Solomon in
all his splendor[b] was dressed like one
6:29 [b]1Ki 10:4-7 of these. 30 If that is how God clothes
the grass of the field, which is here
today and tomorrow is thrown into
6:30 [c]Mt 8:26; 14:31; 16:8 the fire, will he not much more clothe
you, O you of little faith?[c] 31 So do not
worry, saying, 'What shall we eat?' or
'What shall we drink?' or 'What shall
we wear?' 32 For the pagans run after all
6:32 [d]ver 8 these things, and your heavenly Father
knows that you need them.[d] 33 But seek
first his kingdom and his righteousness, and all these things will be given
6:33 [e]Mt 19:29; Mk 10:29-30 to you as well.[e] 34 Therefore do not worry about tomorrow, for tomorrow will
worry about itself. Each day has enough
trouble of its own.

PEACE

WORRY BIRDS

Matthew 6:31

Worry is the foam atop the dither of our lives.
God feeds the birds and clothes the fields with flowers.
Pay heed to birds and honor flowers,
And peace will gild your life with calm and power.

Judging Others

7:1 [f]Lk 6:37; Ro 14:4, 10,13; 1Co 4:5; Jas 4:11,12 7 "Do not judge, or you too will be
judged.[f] 2 For in the same way you
judge others, you will be judged, and
with the measure you use, it will be
7:2 [g]Mk 4:24; Lk 6:38 measured to you.[g]
3 "Why do you look at the speck of
sawdust in your brother's eye and pay
no attention to the plank in your own
eye? 4 How can you say to your brother, 'Let me take the speck out of your
eye,' when all the time there is a plank
in your own eye? 5 You hypocrite, first
take the plank out of your own eye, and
then you will see clearly to remove the
speck from your brother's eye.
6 "Do not give dogs what is sacred;
do not throw your pearls to pigs. If
you do, they may trample them under
their feet, and then turn and tear you to
pieces.

GOODNESS

PEARLS AND PIGS

Matthew 7:6

Pigs treasure swill. The pearls they despise.
Keep holy things on shelves too high for vulgar souls to desecrate.
And give to God those treasures of a heart made intimate.

Ask, Seek, Knock

7 "Ask and it will be given to you;[h] 7:7 [h]Mt 21:22; Mk 11:24; Jn 14:13,14; 15:7,16; 16:23,24; Jas 1:5-8; 4:2,3; 1Jn 3:22; 5:14,15
seek and you will find; knock and the
door will be opened to you. 8 For everyone who asks receives; he who seeks
finds;[i] and to him who knocks, the door 7:8 [i]Pr 8:17; Jer 29:12,13
will be opened.
9 "Which of you, if his son asks for
bread, will give him a stone? 10 Or if he
asks for a fish, will give him a snake? 11 If
you, then, though you are evil, know
how to give good gifts to your children, how much more will your Father
in heaven give good gifts to those who
ask him! 12 So in everything, do to others what you would have them do to
you,[j] for this sums up the Law and the 7:12 [j]Lk 6:31 [k]Ro 13:8-10; Gal 5:14
Prophets.[k]

The Narrow and Wide Gates

13 "Enter through the narrow gate.[l] 7:13 [l]Lk 13:24
For wide is the gate and broad is the
road that leads to destruction, and many
enter through it. 14 But small is the gate
and narrow the road that leads to life,
and only a few find it.

A Tree and Its Fruit

15 "Watch out for false prophets.[m] 7:15 [m]Jer 23:16; Mt 24:24; Mk 13:22; Lk 6:26; 2Pe 2:1; 1Jn 4:1; Rev 16:13 [n]Ac 20:29
They come to you in sheep's clothing,
but inwardly they are ferocious wolves.[n]
16 By their fruit you will recognize them.[o] 7:16 [o]Mt 12:33; Lk 6:44 [p]Jas 3:12
Do people pick grapes from thorn-
bushes, or figs from thistles?[p] 17 Likewise every good tree bears good fruit,

[a]27 Or *single cubit to his height*

but a bad tree bears bad fruit. 18A good
tree cannot bear bad fruit, and a bad tree
cannot bear good fruit. 19Every tree that
does not bear good fruit is cut down
7:19 [q]Mt 3:10 and thrown into the fire.[q] 20Thus, by
their fruit you will recognize them.
7:21 [r]Hos 8:2; Mt 25:11 [s]Ro 2:13; Jas 1:22 21"Not everyone who says to me,
'Lord, Lord,'[r] will enter the kingdom of
heaven, but only he who does the will
7:22 [t]Mt 10:15 [u]1Co 13:1-3 of my Father who is in heaven.[s] 22Many
will say to me on that day,[t] 'Lord, Lord,
did we not prophesy in your name, and
in your name drive out demons and
perform many miracles?'[u] 23Then I will
7:23 [v]Ps 6:8; Mt 25:12,41; Lk 13:25-27 tell them plainly, 'I never knew you.
Away from me, you evildoers!'[v]

The Wise and Foolish Builders

24"Therefore everyone who hears
7:24 [w]Jas 1:22-25 these words of mine and puts them into
practice[w] is like a wise man who built
his house on the rock. 25The rain came
down, the streams rose, and the winds
blew and beat against that house; yet it
did not fall, because it had its foundation on the rock. 26But everyone who
hears these words of mine and does not
put them into practice is like a foolish
man who built his house on sand. 27The
rain came down, the streams rose, and
the winds blew and beat against that
house, and it fell with a great crash."
7:28 [x]Mt 11:1; 13:53; 19:1; 26:1 [y]Mt 13:54; Mk 1:22; 6:2; Lk 4:32; Jn 7:46 28When Jesus had finished saying
these things,[x] the crowds were amazed
at his teaching,[y] 29because he taught as
one who had authority, and not as their
teachers of the law.

The Man With Leprosy

8 When he came down from the
8:2 [z]Lk 5:12 [a]Mt 9:18; 15:25; 18:26; 20:20 mountainside, large crowds followed him. 2A man with leprosy[a][z] came
and knelt before him[a] and said, "Lord,
if you are willing, you can make me
clean."
3Jesus reached out his hand and
touched the man. "I am willing," he
said. "Be clean!" Immediately he was
8:4 [b]Mt 9:30; Mk 5:43; 7:36; 8:30 [c]Lev 14:2-32 cured[b] of his leprosy. 4Then Jesus said
to him, "See that you don't tell anyone.[b]
But go, show yourself to the priest and
offer the gift Moses commanded,[c] as a
testimony to them."

The Faith of the Centurion

5When Jesus had entered Capernaum, a centurion came to him, asking
for help. 6"Lord," he said, "my servant
lies at home paralyzed and in terrible
suffering."
7Jesus said to him, "I will go and heal
him."
8The centurion replied, "Lord, I do
not deserve to have you come under
my roof. But just say the word, and my
servant will be healed.[d] 9For I myself 8:8 [d]Ps 107:20
am a man under authority, with sol-
diers under me. I tell this one, 'Go,'
and he goes; and that one, 'Come,' and
he comes. I say to my servant, 'Do this,'
and he does it."
10When Jesus heard this, he was astonished and said to those following
him, "I tell you the truth, I have not
found anyone in Israel with such great
faith.[e] 11I say to you that many will 8:10 [e]Mt 15:28
come from the east and the west,[f] and 8:11 [f]Ps 107:3; Isa 49:12; 59:19; Mal 1:11 [g]Lk 13:29
will take their places at the feast with
Abraham, Isaac and Jacob in the kingdom of heaven.[g] 12But the subjects of
the kingdom[h] will be thrown outside,
into the darkness, where there will be 8:12 [h]Mt 13:38 [i]Mt 13:42,50; 22:13; 24:51; 25:30; Lk 13:28
weeping and gnashing of teeth."[i]
13Then Jesus said to the centurion,
"Go! It will be done just as you believed
it would."[j] And his servant was healed 8:13 [j]Mt 9:22
at that very hour.

Jesus Heals Many

14When Jesus came into Peter's house,
he saw Peter's mother-in-law lying in
bed with a fever. 15He touched her hand
and the fever left her, and she got up
and began to wait on him.
16When evening came, many who
were demon-possessed were brought to
him, and he drove out the spirits with
a word and healed all the sick.[k] 17This 8:16 [k]Mt 4:23,24
was to fulfill[l] what was spoken through 8:17 [l]Mt 1:22
the prophet Isaiah:

"He took up our infirmities
and carried our diseases."[c][m] 8:18 [m]Isa 53:4 [n]Mk 4:35

The Cost of Following Jesus

18When Jesus saw the crowd around
him, he gave orders to cross to the other
side of the lake.[n] 19Then a teacher of
the law came to him and said, "Teacher,
I will follow you wherever you go."
20Jesus replied, "Foxes have holes and

[a] *2* The Greek word was used for various diseases affecting the skin—not necessarily leprosy.
[b] *3* Greek *made clean* [c] *17* Isaiah 53:4

birds of the air have nests, but the Son
8:20 [o]Da 7:13; Mt 12:8, 32,40; 16:13,27,28; 17:9; 19:28; Mk 2:10; 8:31
of Man[o] has no place to lay his head."
21Another disciple said to him, "Lord,
first let me go and bury my father."
22But Jesus told him, "Follow me,[p]
and let the dead bury their own dead."

8:22 [p]Mt 4:19

Jesus Calms the Storm

23Then he got into the boat and
his disciples followed him. 24Without
warning, a furious storm came up on
the lake, so that the waves swept over
the boat. But Jesus was sleeping. 25The
disciples went and woke him, saying,
8:26 [q]Mt 6:30 [r]Ps 65:7; 89:9; 107:29
"Lord, save us! We're going to drown!"
26He replied, "You of little faith,[q]
why are you so afraid?" Then he got up
and rebuked the winds and the waves,
and it was completely calm.[r]
27The men were amazed and asked,
"What kind of man is this? Even the
winds and the waves obey him!"

GENTLENESS

THE MASTER'S GENTLE STRENGTH

Matthew 8:27

Here is our King of tempest and of wave.
He speaks and storms slink off in shame.
God can order wind.
And, sometimes sooner than his children,
the wind obeys.

The Healing of Two Demon-possessed Men

28When he arrived at the other side
in the region of the Gadarenes,[a] two
8:28 [s]Mt 4:24
demon-possessed[s] men coming from
the tombs met him. They were so violent that no one could pass that way.
8:29 [t]Jdg 11:12; 2Sa 16:10; 1Ki 17:18; Mk 1:24; Lk 4:34; Jn 2:4 [u]2Pe 2:4
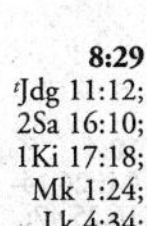
29"What do you want with us,[t] Son of
God?" they shouted. "Have you come
here to torture us before the appointed
time?"[u]
30Some distance from them a large
herd of pigs was feeding. 31The demons
begged Jesus, "If you drive us out, send
us into the herd of pigs."
32He said to them, "Go!" So they
came out and went into the pigs, and
the whole herd rushed down the steep
bank into the lake and died in the water. 33Those tending the pigs ran off,
went into the town and reported all
this, including what had happened to
the demon-possessed men. 34Then the
whole town went out to meet Jesus.
And when they saw him, they pleaded
with him to leave their region.[v]

8:34 [v]Lk 5:8; Ac 16:39

Jesus Heals a Paralytic

9 Jesus stepped into a boat, crossed
over and came to his own town.[w]
9:1 [w]Mt 4:13
2Some men brought to him a paralytic,[x]
9:2 [x]Mt 4:24 [y]ver 22 [z]Jn 16:33 [a]Lk 7:48
lying on a mat. When Jesus saw their
faith,[y] he said to the paralytic, "Take
heart,[z] son; your sins are forgiven."[a]
3At this, some of the teachers of the
9:3 [b]Mt 26:65; Jn 10:33
law said to themselves, "This fellow is
blaspheming!"[b]
4Knowing their thoughts,[c] Jesus said,
9:4 [c]Ps 94:11; Mt 12:25; Lk 6:8; 9:47; 11:17
"Why do you entertain evil thoughts
in your hearts? 5Which is easier: to say,
'Your sins are forgiven,' or to say, 'Get
up and walk'? 6But so that you may
9:6 [d]Mt 8:20
know that the Son of Man[d] has authority on earth to forgive sins . . ." Then he
said to the paralytic, "Get up, take your
mat and go home." 7And the man got
up and went home. 8When the crowd
saw this, they were filled with awe; and
9:8 [e]Mt 5:16; 15:31; Lk 7:16; 13:13; 17:15; 23:47; Jn 15:8; Ac 4:21; 11:18; 21:20
they praised God,[e] who had given such
authority to men.

The Calling of Matthew

9As Jesus went on from there, he saw
a man named Matthew sitting at the
tax collector's booth. "Follow me," he
told him, and Matthew got up and followed him.
10While Jesus was having dinner at
Matthew's house, many tax collectors
and "sinners" came and ate with him
and his disciples. 11When the Pharisees
9:11 [f]Mt 11:19; Lk 5:30; 15:2; Gal 2:15
saw this, they asked his disciples, "Why
does your teacher eat with tax collectors
and 'sinners'?"[f]

GOODNESS

DINNER, ANYONE SINFUL?

Matthew 9:11

Jesus ate with sinners. Sometimes we are known by the company we keep, and sometimes we are changed by it.

12On hearing this, Jesus said, "It is
not the healthy who need a doctor, but
the sick. 13But go and learn what this

[a]*28* Some manuscripts *Gergesenes*; others *Gerasenes*

means: 'I desire mercy, not sacrifice.'[a][g] For I have not come to call the righteous, but sinners."[h]

Jesus Questioned About Fasting

14Then John's disciples came and asked him, "How is it that we and the Pharisees fast,[i] but your disciples do not fast?"

15Jesus answered, "How can the guests of the bridegroom mourn while he is with them?[j] The time will come when the bridegroom will be taken from them; then they will fast.[k]

16"No one sews a patch of unshrunk cloth on an old garment, for the patch will pull away from the garment, making the tear worse. 17Neither do men pour new wine into old wineskins. If they do, the skins will burst, the wine will run out and the wineskins will be ruined. No, they pour new wine into new wineskins, and both are preserved."

A Dead Girl and a Sick Woman

18While he was saying this, a ruler came and knelt before him[l] and said, "My daughter has just died. But come and put your hand on her,[m] and she will live." 19Jesus got up and went with him, and so did his disciples.

20Just then a woman who had been subject to bleeding for twelve years came up behind him and touched the edge of his cloak.[n] 21She said to herself, "If I only touch his cloak, I will be healed."

22Jesus turned and saw her. "Take heart, daughter," he said, "your faith has healed you."[o] And the woman was healed from that moment.[p]

23When Jesus entered the ruler's house and saw the flute players and the noisy crowd,[q] 24he said, "Go away. The girl is not dead[r] but asleep."[s] But they laughed at him. 25After the crowd had been put outside, he went in and took the girl by the hand, and she got up. 26News of this spread through all that region.[t]

Jesus Heals the Blind and Mute

27As Jesus went on from there, two blind men followed him, calling out, "Have mercy on us, Son of David!"[u]

28When he had gone indoors, the blind men came to him, and he asked them, "Do you believe that I am able to do this?"

"Yes, Lord," they replied.

29Then he touched their eyes and said, "According to your faith will it be done to you";[v] 30and their sight was restored. Jesus warned them sternly, "See that no one knows about this."[w] 31But they went out and spread the news about him all over that region.[x]

32While they were going out, a man who was demon-possessed[y] and could not talk[z] was brought to Jesus. 33And when the demon was driven out, the man who had been mute spoke. The crowd was amazed and said, "Nothing like this has ever been seen in Israel."[a]

34But the Pharisees said, "It is by the prince of demons that he drives out demons."[b]

The Workers Are Few

35Jesus went through all the towns and villages, teaching in their synagogues, preaching the good news of the kingdom and healing every disease and sickness.[c] 36When he saw the crowds, he had compassion on them,[d] because they were harassed and helpless, like sheep without a shepherd.[e] 37Then he said to his disciples, "The harvest[f] is plentiful but the workers are few.[g] 38Ask the Lord of the harvest, therefore, to send out workers into his harvest field."

Jesus Sends Out the Twelve

10 He called his twelve disciples to him and gave them authority to drive out evil[b] spirits[h] and to heal every disease and sickness.

2These are the names of the twelve apostles: first, Simon (who is called Peter) and his brother Andrew; James son of Zebedee, and his brother John; 3Philip and Bartholomew; Thomas and Matthew the tax collector; James son of Alphaeus, and Thaddaeus; 4Simon the Zealot and Judas Iscariot, who betrayed him.[i]

5These twelve Jesus sent out with the following instructions: "Do not go among the Gentiles or enter any town of the Samaritans.[j] 6Go rather to the lost sheep of Israel.[k] 7As you go, preach this message: 'The kingdom of heaven[l]

[a]*13* Hosea 6:6 [b]*1* Greek *unclean*

9:13 [g]Hos 6:6; Mic 6:6-8; Mt 12:7 [h]1Ti 1:15
9:14 [i]Lk 18:12
9:15 [j]Jn 3:29 [k]Ac 13:2,3; 14:23
9:18 [l]Mt 8:2 [m]Mk 5:23
9:20 [n]Mt 14:36; Mk 3:10
9:22 [o]Mk 10:52; Lk 7:50; 17:19; 18:42 [p]Mt 15:28
9:23 [q]2Ch 35:25; Jer 9:17,18
9:24 [r]Ac 20:10 [s]Jn 11:11-14
9:26 [t]Mt 4:24
9:27 [u]Mt 15:22; Mk 10:47; Lk 18:38-39
9:29 [v]ver 22
9:30 [w]Mt 8:4
9:31 [x]ver 26; Mk 7:36
9:32 [y]Mt 4:24 [z]Mt 12:22-24
9:33 [a]Mk 2:12
9:34 [b]Mt 12:24; Lk 11:15
9:35 [c]Mt 4:23
9:36 [d]Mt 14:14 [e]Nu 27:17; Eze 34:5,6; Zec 10:2; Mk 6:34
9:37 [f]Jn 4:35 [g]Lk 10:2
10:1 [h]Mk 3:13-15; Lk; 9:1
10:4 [i]Mt 26:14-16,25,47; Jn 13:2,26,27
10:5 [j]2Ki 17:24; Lk 9:52; Jn 4:4-26, 39,40; Ac 8:5,25
10:6 [k]Jer 50:6; Mt 15:24
10:7 [l]Mt 3:2

is near.' 8Heal the sick, raise the dead, cleanse those who have leprosy,[a] drive out demons. Freely you have received, freely give. 9Do not take along any gold or silver or copper in your belts;[m] 10take no bag for the journey, or extra tunic, or sandals or a staff; for the worker is worth his keep.[n]

11"Whatever town or village you enter, search for some worthy person there and stay at his house until you leave. 12As you enter the home, give it your greeting.[o] 13If the home is deserving, let your peace rest on it; if it is not, let your peace return to you. 14If anyone will not welcome you or listen to your words, shake the dust off your feet[p] when you leave that home or town. 15I tell you the truth, it will be more bearable for Sodom and Gomorrah[q] on the day of judgment[r] than for that town.[s] 16I am sending you out like sheep among wolves.[t] Therefore be as shrewd as snakes and as innocent as doves.[u]

10:9 [m]Lk 22:35
10:10 [n]1Ti 5:18
10:12 [o]1Sa 25:6
10:14 [p]Ne 5:13; Lk 10:11; Ac 13:51
10:15 [q]2Pe 2:6 [r]Mt 12:36; 2Pe 2:9; 1Jn 4:17 [s]Mt 11:22,24
10:16 [t]Lk 10:3 [u]Ro 16:19

SELF-CONTROL

LEARNING FROM COBRAS AND PIGEONS

Matthew 10:16

Snakes survive by avoiding footpaths.
Pigeons are paragons of innocence.
Christians survive by keeping out of Satan's way.
It is always right to join the battle for truth,
But seldom wise to start the war.

17"Be on your guard against men; they will hand you over to the local councils[v] and flog you in their synagogues.[w] 18On my account you will be brought before governors and kings[x] as witnesses to them and to the Gentiles. 19But when they arrest you, do not worry about what to say or how to say it.[y] At that time you will be given what to say, 20for it will not be you speaking, but the Spirit of your Father[z] speaking through you.

21"Brother will betray brother to death, and a father his child; children will rebel against their parents[a] and have them put to death. 22All men will hate you because of me, but he who stands firm to the end will be saved.[b] 23When you are persecuted in one place, flee to another. I tell you the truth, you will not finish going through the cities of Israel before the Son of Man comes.

10:17 [v]Mt 5:22 [w]Mt 23:34; Mk 13:9; Ac 5:40; 26:11
10:18 [x]Ac 25:24-26
10:19 [y]Ex 4:12
10:20 [z]Ac 4:8
10:21 [a]ver 35,36; Mic 7:6
10:22 [b]Mt 24:13; Mk 13:13

24"A student is not above his teacher, nor a servant above his master.[c] 25It is enough for the student to be like his teacher, and the servant like his master. If the head of the house has been called Beelzebub,[b] [d] how much more the members of his household!

10:24 [c]Lk 6:40; Jn 13:16; 15:20
10:25 [d]Mk 3:22

LOVE

THE SPARROW CENSUS

Matthew 10:29

If God should forget to count the sparrows on any given day,
The era of grace will have ended.

26"So do not be afraid of them. There is nothing concealed that will not be disclosed, or hidden that will not be made known.[e] 27What I tell you in the dark, speak in the daylight; what is whispered in your ear, proclaim from the roofs. 28Do not be afraid of those who kill the body but cannot kill the soul. Rather, be afraid of the One[f] who can destroy both soul and body in hell. 29Are not two sparrows sold for a penny[c]? Yet not one of them will fall to the ground apart from the will of your Father. 30And even the very hairs of your head are all numbered.[g] 31So don't be afraid; you are worth more than many sparrows.[h]

32"Whoever acknowledges me before men,[i] I will also acknowledge him before my Father in heaven. 33But whoever disowns me before men, I will disown him before my Father in heaven.[j]

34"Do not suppose that I have come to bring peace to the earth. I did not come to bring peace, but a sword. 35For I have come to turn

" 'a man against his father,
a daughter against her mother,
a daughter-in-law against her
mother-in-law[k]—
36 a man's enemies will be the
members of his own
household.'[d] [l]

10:26 [e]Mk 4:22; Lk 8:17
10:28 [f]Isa 8:12,13; Heb 10:31
10:30 [g]1Sa 14:45; 2Sa 14:11; Lk 21:18; Ac 27:34
10:31 [h]Mt; 12:12
10:32 [i]Ro 10:9
10:33 [j]Mk 8:38; 2Ti 2:12
10:35 [k]ver 21
10:36 [l]Mic 7:6

[a]8 The Greek word was used for various diseases affecting the skin—not necessarily leprosy.
[b]25 Greek *Beezeboul* or *Beelzeboul* [c]29 Greek *an assarion* [d]36 Micah 7:6

37"Anyone who loves his father or
mother more than me is not worthy
of me; anyone who loves his son or
10:37 daughter more than me is not worthy
[m]Lk 14:26 of me;[m] 38and anyone who does not
10:38 take his cross and follow me is not wor-
[n]Mt 16:24; Lk 14:27 thy of me.[n] 39Whoever finds his life will
lose it, and whoever loses his life for my 10:39
sake will find it.[o] [o]Lk 17:33;
40"He who receives you receives me,[p] Jn 12:25
and he who receives me receives the 10:40
one who sent me.[q] 41Anyone who re- [p]Mt 18:5;
ceives a prophet because he is a proph- Gal 4:14 [q]Lk 9:48;
et will receive a prophet's reward, and Jn 12:44;
anyone who receives a righteous man 13:20
because he is a righteous man will receive a righteous man's reward. 42And if
anyone gives even a cup of cold water
to one of these little ones because he is
my disciple, I tell you the truth, he will 10:42
certainly not lose his reward."[r] [r]Mt 25:40;
Mk 9:41;
Heb 6:10

DAY 4 FOUR

▸ KINDNESS AND MY SERVICE TO OTHERS

Matthew 10:40–42

Can our service to others be summed up in something so simple as a cup of water? Indeed it can. The water is symbolic of the living water that Christ offers to a dying world. When Jesus talked to a Samaritan woman, he promised that she would have eternal life if she took the water he offered (John 4:13–14). However, it is not the water itself but the kindness of the giver that causes us to notice the universal thirst of the dying world around us.

Samuel Taylor Coleridge laments the fate of the sailors on a ship trapped on a windless sea. Not a hint of breeze created the slightest billow of the sails. The vast sea wore the moss and slime of an English moor. The ocean was a breathless swamp, offering no fresh drinking water. The Mariner laments:

Day after day, day after day,
We stuck, nor breath nor motion;
As idle as a painted ship
Upon a painted ocean.

Water, water everywhere,
And all the boards did shrink;
Water, water every where,
Nor any drop to drink.

Was Coleridge merely lamenting a mythical, fictional ship, or was he talking about a world where the days are dry and any refreshment seems beyond our reach?

The world is thirsty. It is our service to God, our service to others, to offer Christ, the living water, to those who are desperate. We are the water bearers—the Aquarians of life in the vast cultural deserts we have been given charge to save.

To begin a study on the topic of Kindness in the Time of Need, turn to the home page on page 246.

Jesus and John the Baptist

11 After Jesus had finished instructing his twelve disciples,[s] he went 11:1
on from there to teach and preach in [s]Mt 7:28
the towns of Galilee.[a]
2When John heard in prison[t] what 11:2
Christ was doing, he sent his disciples [t]Mt 14:3
3to ask him, "Are you the one who was 11:3
to come,[u] or should we expect someone [u]Ps 118:26;
else?" Jn 11:27; Heb 10:37
4Jesus replied, "Go back and report
to John what you hear and see: 5The
blind receive sight, the lame walk, those
who have leprosy[b] are cured, the deaf
hear, the dead are raised, and the good 11:5
news is preached to the poor.[v] 6Blessed [v]Isa 35:4-6; 61:1;
is the man who does not fall away on Lk 4:18,19
account of me."[w] 11:6
7As John's[x] disciples were leaving, Je- [w]Mt 13:21
sus began to speak to the crowd about 11:7
John: "What did you go out into the [x]Mt 3:1
desert to see? A reed swayed by the
wind? 8If not, what did you go out
to see? A man dressed in fine clothes?
No, those who wear fine clothes are in
kings' palaces. 9Then what did you go 11:9
out to see? A prophet?[y] Yes, I tell you, [y]Mt 21:26;
and more than a prophet. 10This is the Lk 1:76
one about whom it is written:

" 'I will send my messenger ahead of you,
who will prepare your way before you.'[c][z] 11:10 [z]Mal 3:1; Mk 1:2

11I tell you the truth: Among those
born of women there has not risen anyone greater than John the Baptist; yet
he who is least in the kingdom of heav-
en is greater than he. 12From the days

[a]*1* Greek *in their towns* [b]*5* The Greek word was used for various diseases affecting the skin—not necessarily leprosy. [c]*10* Mal. 3:1

of John the Baptist until now, the kingdom of heaven has been forcefully advancing, and forceful men lay hold of
it. 13 For all the Prophets and the Law
prophesied until John. 14 And if you are
willing to accept it, he is the Elijah who
was to come.[a] 15 He who has ears, let
him hear.[b]

16 "To what can I compare this generation? They are like children sitting
in the marketplaces and calling out to
others:

17 " 'We played the flute for you,
and you did not dance;
we sang a dirge,
and you did not mourn.'

18 For John came neither eating[c] nor
drinking,[d] and they say, 'He has a demon.' 19 The Son of Man came eating
and drinking, and they say, 'Here is a
glutton and a drunkard, a friend of tax
collectors and "sinners." '[e] But wisdom
is proved right by her actions."

Woe on Unrepentant Cities

20 Then Jesus began to denounce the
cities in which most of his miracles had
been performed, because they did not
repent. 21 "Woe to you, Korazin! Woe
to you, Bethsaida![f] If the miracles that
were performed in you had been performed in Tyre and Sidon,[g] they would
have repented long ago in sackcloth and
ashes.[h] 22 But I tell you, it will be more
bearable for Tyre and Sidon on the day
of judgment than for you.[i] 23 And you,
Capernaum,[j] will you be lifted up to
the skies? No, you will go down to the
depths.[a][k] If the miracles that were performed in you had been performed in
Sodom, it would have remained to this
day. 24 But I tell you that it will be more
bearable for Sodom on the day of judgment than for you."[l]

Rest for the Weary

25 At that time Jesus said, "I praise
you, Father,[m] Lord of heaven and earth,
because you have hidden these things
from the wise and learned, and revealed
them to little children.[n] 26 Yes, Father,
for this was your good pleasure.

27 "All things have been committed
to me[o] by my Father.[p] No one knows
the Son except the Father, and no one
knows the Father except the Son and
those to whom the Son chooses to reveal him.[q]

28 "Come to me,[r] all you who are
weary and burdened, and I will give
you rest. 29 Take my yoke upon you and
learn from me,[s] for I am gentle and
humble in heart, and you will find rest
for your souls.[t] 30 For my yoke is easy
and my burden is light."[u]

PEACE

LUGGAGE

Matthew 11:28

I am the Christ.
Cast all your cares on me.
Give me life's luggage and let me carry it for you.
There! Doesn't that feel better?
Now rest.
Your burden is eased.

Lord of the Sabbath

12 At that time Jesus went through
the grainfields on the Sabbath.
His disciples were hungry and began to
pick some heads of grain[v] and eat them.
2 When the Pharisees saw this, they said
to him, "Look! Your disciples are doing
what is unlawful on the Sabbath."[w]

3 He answered, "Haven't you read
what David did when he and his companions were hungry?[x] 4 He entered the
house of God, and he and his companions ate the consecrated bread—which
was not lawful for them to do, but only
for the priests.[y] 5 Or haven't you read
in the Law that on the Sabbath the
priests in the temple desecrate the day[z]
and yet are innocent? 6 I tell you that
one[b] greater than the temple is here.[a]
7 If you had known what these words
mean, 'I desire mercy, not sacrifice,'[c][b]
you would not have condemned the innocent. 8 For the Son of Man[c] is Lord of
the Sabbath."

9 Going on from that place, he went
into their synagogue, 10 and a man with
a shriveled hand was there. Looking for
a reason to accuse Jesus, they asked him,
"Is it lawful to heal on the Sabbath?"[d]

11 He said to them, "If any of you
has a sheep and it falls into a pit on

[a] 23 Greek *Hades* [b] 6 Or *something*; also in verses 41 and 42 [c] 7 Hosea 6:6

11:14 [a]Mal 4:5; Mt 17:10-13; Mk 9:11-13; Lk 1:17; Jn 1:21
11:15 [b]Mt 13:9,43; Mk 4:23; Lk 14:35; Rev 2:7
11:18 [c]Mt 3:4 [d]Lk 1:15
11:19 [e]Mt 9:11
11:21 [f]Mk 6:45; Lk 9:10; Jn 12:21 [g]Mt 15:21; Lk 6:17; Ac 12:20 [h]Jnh 3:5-9
11:22 [i]ver 24; Mt 10:15
11:23 [j]Mt 4:13 [k]Isa 14:13-15
11:24 [l]Mt 10:15
11:25 [m]Lk 22:42; Jn 11:41 [n]1Co 1:26-29
11:27 [o]Mt 28:18 [p]Jn 3:35; 13:3; 17:2
11:27 [q]Jn 10:15
11:28 [r]Jn 7:37
11:29 [s]Jn 13:15; Php 2:5; 1Pe 2:21; 1Jn 2:6 [t]Jer 6:16
11:30 [u]1Jn 5:3
12:1 [v]Dt 23:25
12:2 [w]ver 10; Lk 13:14; 14:3; Jn 5:10; 7:23; 9:16
12:3 [x]1Sa 21:6
12:4 [y]Lev 24:5,9
12:5 [z]Nu 28:9,10; Jn 7:22,23
12:6 [a]ver 41,42
12:7 [b]Hos 6:6; Mic 6:6-8; Mt 9:13
12:8 [c]Mt 8:20
12:10 [d]ver 2; Lk 13:14; 14:3; Jn 9:16

the Sabbath, will you not take hold of
12:11 [e]Lk 14:5 it and lift it out?[e] 12How much more
valuable is a man than a sheep![f] There-
12:12 [f]Mt 10:31 fore it is lawful to do good on the Sabbath."
13Then he said to the man, "Stretch
out your hand." So he stretched it out
and it was completely restored, just as
sound as the other. 14But the Pharisees
went out and plotted how they might
12:14 [g]Mt 26:4; 27:1; Mk 3:6; Lk 6:11; Jn 5:18; 11:53 kill Jesus.[g]

God's Chosen Servant

15Aware of this, Jesus withdrew from
12:15 [h]Mt 4:23 that place. Many followed him, and he
healed all their sick,[h] 16warning them
12:16 [i]Mt 8:4 not to tell who he was.[i] 17This was
to fulfill what was spoken through the
prophet Isaiah:

18"Here is my servant whom I have
chosen,
12:18 [j]Mt 3:17 the one I love, in whom I delight;[j]
I will put my Spirit on him,
and he will proclaim justice to the
nations.
19He will not quarrel or cry out;
no one will hear his voice in the
streets.
20A bruised reed he will not break,
and a smoldering wick he will not
snuff out,
till he leads justice to victory.
12:21 [k]Isa 42:1-4 21 In his name the nations will put
their hope."[a] [k]

LOVE

GOD'S ODD FRIENDS

Matthew 12:21

It is so like poor mortals to love only those who are most like themselves. God never loved so narrowly. Pirates, potentates, primitives, pagans, priests and put-ons—God has the most eclectic taste in friends.

Jesus and Beelzebub

22Then they brought him a demon-
possessed man who was blind and mute,
and Jesus healed him, so that he could
12:22 [l]Mt 4:24; 9:32-33 both talk and see.[l] 23All the people were
astonished and said, "Could this be the
12:23 [m]Mt 9:27 Son of David?"[m]
24But when the Pharisees heard this,
12:24 [n]Mk 3:22 they said, "It is only by Beelzebub,[b] [n]
[o]Mt 9:34 the prince of demons, that this fellow
drives out demons."[o]

25Jesus knew their thoughts[p] and 12:25 [p]Mt 9:4
said to them, "Every kingdom divided
against itself will be ruined, and every
city or household divided against itself
will not stand. 26If Satan[q] drives out Sa- 12:26 [q]Mt 4:10
tan, he is divided against himself. How
then can his kingdom stand? 27And if
I drive out demons by Beelzebub, by
whom do your people[r] drive them out? 12:27 [r]Ac 19:13
So then, they will be your judges. 28But
if I drive out demons by the Spirit of
God, then the kingdom of God has
come upon you.
29"Or again, how can anyone enter a
strong man's house and carry off his possessions unless he first ties up the strong
man? Then he can rob his house.
30"He who is not with me is against
me, and he who does not gather with 12:30 [s]Mk 9:40; Lk 11:23
me scatters.[s] 31And so I tell you, every
sin and blasphemy will be forgiven men,
but the blasphemy against the Spirit
will not be forgiven.[t] 32Anyone who 12:31 [t]Mk 3:28,29; Lk 12:10
speaks a word against the Son of Man
will be forgiven, but anyone who speaks
against the Holy Spirit will not be for-
given, either in this age[u] or in the age 12:32 [u]Tit 2:12 [v]Mk 10:30; Lk 20:34,35; Eph 1:21; Heb 6:5
to come.[v]
33"Make a tree good and its fruit will
be good, or make a tree bad and its fruit
will be bad, for a tree is recognized by
its fruit.[w] 34You brood of vipers,[x] how 12:33 [w]Mt 7:16,17; Lk 6:43,44
can you who are evil say anything good? 12:34 [x]Mt 3:7; 23:33 [y]Mt 15:18; Lk 6:45
For out of the overflow of the heart the
mouth speaks.[y] 35The good man brings
good things out of the good stored up
in him, and the evil man brings evil
things out of the evil stored up in him.
36But I tell you that men will have to
give account on the day of judgment
for every careless word they have spoken. 37For by your words you will be
acquitted, and by your words you will
be condemned."

The Sign of Jonah

38Then some of the Pharisees and
teachers of the law said to him, "Teach-
er, we want to see a miraculous sign 12:38 [z]Mt 16:1; Mk 8:11,12; Lk 11:16; Jn 2:18; 6:30; 1Co 1:22
from you."[z]
39He answered, "A wicked and adulterous generation asks for a miraculous
sign! But none will be given it except
the sign of the prophet Jonah.[a] 40For as 12:39 [a]Mt 16:4; Lk 11:29
Jonah was three days and three nights in

[a]*21* Isaiah 42:1-4 [b]*24* Greek *Beezeboul* or *Beelzeboul*; also in verse 27

12:40 [b]Jnh 1:17 [c]Mt 8:20 [d]Mt 16:21
the belly of a huge fish,[b] so the Son of
Man[c] will be three days and three nights
in the heart of the earth.[d] 41The men of
12:41 [e]Jnh 1:2 [f]Jnh 3:5
Nineveh[e] will stand up at the judgment
with this generation and condemn it;
for they repented at the preaching of
Jonah,[f] and now one[a] greater than Jonah is here. 42The Queen of the South
will rise at the judgment with this gen-
12:42 [g]1Ki 10:1; 2Ch 9:1
eration and condemn it; for she came[g]
from the ends of the earth to listen to
Solomon's wisdom, and now one greater than Solomon is here.
43"When an evil[b] spirit comes out of
a man, it goes through arid places seeking rest and does not find it. 44Then it
says, 'I will return to the house I left.'
When it arrives, it finds the house unoccupied, swept clean and put in order. 45Then it goes and takes with it
seven other spirits more wicked than itself, and they go in and live there. And
12:45 [h]2Pe 2:20
the final condition of that man is worse
than the first.[h] That is how it will be
12:46 [i]Mt 1:18; 2:11,13, 14,20; Lk 1:43; 2:33,34, 48,51; Jn 2:1,5; 19:25,26 [j]Mt 13:55; Jn 2:12; 7:3,5; Ac 1:14; 1Co 9:5; Gal 1:19
with this wicked generation."

Jesus' Mother and Brothers

46While Jesus was still talking to
the crowd, his mother[i] and brothers[j]
stood outside, wanting to speak to him.
47Someone told him, "Your mother and
brothers are standing outside, wanting
to speak to you."[c]
48He replied to him, "Who is my
mother, and who are my brothers?"
49Pointing to his disciples, he said,
"Here are my mother and my brothers.
50For whoever does the will of my Fa-
12:50 [k]Jn 15:14
ther in heaven[k] is my brother and sister
and mother."

The Parable of the Sower

13 That same day Jesus went out of
13:1 [l]ver 36; Mt 9:28
the house[l] and sat by the lake.
2Such large crowds gathered around
13:2 [m]Lk 5:3
him that he got into a boat[m] and sat
in it, while all the people stood on the
shore. 3Then he told them many things
in parables, saying: "A farmer went out
to sow his seed. 4As he was scattering
the seed, some fell along the path, and
the birds came and ate it up. 5Some fell
on rocky places, where it did not have
much soil. It sprang up quickly, because
the soil was shallow. 6But when the sun
came up, the plants were scorched, and
they withered because they had no root.
7Other seed fell among thorns, which
grew up and choked the plants. 8Still
other seed fell on good soil, where it
produced a crop—a hundred,[n] sixty or 13:8 [n]Ge 26:12
thirty times what was sown. 9He who
has ears, let him hear."[o] 13:9 [o]Mt 11:15
10The disciples came to him and
asked, "Why do you speak to the people in parables?"
11He replied, "The knowledge of the
secrets of the kingdom of heaven has
been given to you,[p] but not to them. 13:11 [p]Mt 11:25; 16:17; 19:11; Jn 6:65; 1Co 2:10,14; Col 1:27; 1Jn 2:20,27
12Whoever has will be given more, and
he will have an abundance. Whoever
does not have, even what he has will be
taken from him.[q] 13This is why I speak
to them in parables: 13:12 [q]Mt 25:29; Lk 19:26

"Though seeing, they do not see;
though hearing, they do not hear 13:13 [r]Dt 29:4; Jer 5:21; Eze 12:2
or understand.[r]

14In them is fulfilled the prophecy of
Isaiah:

" 'You will be ever hearing but never
understanding;
you will be ever seeing but never
perceiving.
15For this people's heart has become
calloused;
they hardly hear with their ears,
and they have closed their eyes.
Otherwise they might see with their
eyes,
hear with their ears,
understand with their hearts
and turn, and I would heal them.'[d][s] 13:15 [s]Isa 6:9,10; Jn 12:40; Ac 28:26,27; Ro 11:8

16But blessed are your eyes because they
see, and your ears because they hear.[t] 13:16 [t]Mt 16:17
17For I tell you the truth, many proph-
ets and righteous men longed to see
what you see but did not see[u] it, and to 13:17 [u]Jn 8:56; Heb 11:13; 1Pe 1:10-12
hear what you hear but did not hear it.
18"Listen then to what the parable
of the sower means: 19When anyone
hears the message about the kingdom[v] 13:19 [v]Mt 4:23 [w]Mt 5:37
and does not understand it, the evil
one[w] comes and snatches away what
was sown in his heart. This is the seed
sown along the path. 20The one who received the seed that fell on rocky places
is the man who hears the word and at
once receives it with joy. 21But since he
has no root, he lasts only a short time.
When trouble or persecution comes

[a]*41* Or *something;* also in verse 42 [b]*43* Greek *unclean* [c]*47* Some manuscripts do not have verse 47. [d]*15* Isaiah 6:9,10

because of the word, he quickly falls
13:21 [x]Mt 11:6 away.[x] 22The one who received the seed
that fell among the thorns is the man
13:22 [y]Mt 19:23; 1Ti 6:9,10,17 who hears the word, but the worries of
this life and the deceitfulness of wealth[y]
choke it, making it unfruitful. 23But
the one who received the seed that fell
on good soil is the man who hears the
word and understands it. He produces a
crop, yielding a hundred, sixty or thirty
13:23 [z]ver 8 times what was sown."[z]

The Parable of the Weeds

24Jesus told them another parable:
13:24 [a]ver 31,33, 45,47; Mt 18:23; 20:1; 22:2; 25:1; Mk 4:26,30 "The kingdom of heaven is like[a] a
man who sowed good seed in his field.
25But while everyone was sleeping, his
enemy came and sowed weeds among
the wheat, and went away. 26When the
wheat sprouted and formed heads, then
the weeds also appeared.

27"The owner's servants came to him
and said, 'Sir, didn't you sow good seed
in your field? Where then did the weeds
come from?'

28" 'An enemy did this,' he replied.

"The servants asked him, 'Do you
want us to go and pull them up?'

29" 'No,' he answered, 'because while
you are pulling the weeds, you may root
up the wheat with them. 30Let both
grow together until the harvest. At that
time I will tell the harvesters: First collect the weeds and tie them in bundles
13:30 [b]Mt 3:12 to be burned; then gather the wheat
and bring it into my barn.' "[b]

The Parables of the Mustard Seed and the Yeast

13:31 [c]ver 24 [d]Mt 17:20; Lk 17:6 31He told them another parable: "The
kingdom of heaven is like[c] a mustard
seed,[d] which a man took and planted
in his field. 32Though it is the smallest
of all your seeds, yet when it grows, it
is the largest of garden plants and be-
13:32 [e]Ps 104:12; Eze 17:23; 31:6; Da 4:12 comes a tree, so that the birds of the air
come and perch in its branches."[e]

33He told them still another parable:
13:33 [f]ver 24 [g]Ge 18:6 [h]Gal 5:9 "The kingdom of heaven is like[f] yeast
that a woman took and mixed into a
large amount[a] of flour[g] until it worked
all through the dough."[h]

13:34 [i]Mk 4:33; Jn 16:25 34Jesus spoke all these things to the
crowd in parables; he did not say any-
thing to them without using a parable.[i]
35So was fulfilled what was spoken
through the prophet:

"I will open my mouth in parables,
I will utter things hidden since the
creation of the world."[b][j] 13:35 [j]Ps 78:2; Ro 16:25,26; 1Co 2:7; Eph 3:9; Col 1:26

The Parable of the Weeds Explained

36Then he left the crowd and went
into the house. His disciples came to
him and said, "Explain to us the par- 13:36 [k]Mt 15:15
able[k] of the weeds in the field."

37He answered, "The one who sowed 13:37 [l]Mt 8:20
the good seed is the Son of Man.[l] 38The
field is the world, and the good seed 13:38 [m]Jn 8:44,45; 1Jn 3:10
stands for the sons of the kingdom. The
weeds are the sons of the evil one,[m]
39and the enemy who sows them is the 13:39 [n]Joel 3:13 [o]Mt 24:3; 28:20 [p]Rev 14:15
devil. The harvest[n] is the end of the
age,[o] and the harvesters are angels.[p]

PATIENCE

OF SEEDS AND WEEDS

Matthew 13:38

A weed is a plant out of place.
It sins three times:
It takes up space in ground meant to grow usable food;
It steals nourishment intended for the grain;
It produces no good fruit.
Still, tearing it out of the ground can uproot the grain.
Patience is the world's best herbicide.
Let the weeds and grain grow together.
Heaven is on the way.
In time... the harvest.

40"As the weeds are pulled up and
burned in the fire, so it will be at the
end of the age. 41The Son of Man[q] 13:41 [q]Mt 8:20 [r]Mt 24:31
will send out his angels,[r] and they will
weed out of his kingdom everything
that causes sin and all who do evil.
42They will throw them into the fiery
furnace, where there will be weeping 13:42 [s]ver 50; Mt 8:12
and gnashing of teeth.[s] 43Then the righ-
teous will shine like the sun[t] in the 13:43 [t]Da 12:3 [u]Mt 11:15
kingdom of their Father. He who has
ears, let him hear.[u]

The Parables of the Hidden Treasure and the Pearl

44"The kingdom of heaven is like[v] 13:44 [v]ver 24
treasure hidden in a field. When a man

[a] *33* Greek *three satas* (probably about 1/2 bushel or 22 liters) [b] *35* Psalm 78:2

found it, he hid it again, and then in
his joy went and sold all he had and
bought that field.[w]
45"Again, the kingdom of heaven is
like[x] a merchant looking for fine pearls.
46When he found one of great value, he
went away and sold everything he had
and bought it.

The Parable of the Net

47"Once again, the kingdom of heav-
en is like[y] a net that was let down
into the lake and caught all kinds[z] of
fish. 48When it was full, the fishermen
pulled it up on the shore. Then they
sat down and collected the good fish
in baskets, but threw the bad away.
49This is how it will be at the end of
the age. The angels will come and separate the wicked from the righteous[a]
50and throw them into the fiery furnace, where there will be weeping and
gnashing of teeth.[b]
51"Have you understood all these
things?" Jesus asked.
"Yes," they replied.
52He said to them, "Therefore every
teacher of the law who has been instructed about the kingdom of heaven
is like the owner of a house who brings
out of his storeroom new treasures as
well as old."

A Prophet Without Honor

53When Jesus had finished these
parables,[c] he moved on from there.
54Coming to his hometown, he began
teaching the people in their synagogue,[d]
and they were amazed.[e] "Where did
this man get this wisdom and these miraculous powers?" they asked. 55"Isn't
this the carpenter's son?[f] Isn't his mother's[g] name Mary, and aren't his brothers James, Joseph, Simon and Judas?
56Aren't all his sisters with us? Where
then did this man get all these things?"
57And they took offense[h] at him.
But Jesus said to them, "Only in his
hometown and in his own house is a
prophet without honor."[i]
58And he did not do many miracles
there because of their lack of faith.

John the Baptist Beheaded

14 At that time Herod[j] the tetrarch heard the reports about
Jesus,[k] 2and he said to his attendants,

13:44 [w]Isa 55:1; Php 3:7,8
13:45 [x]ver 24
13:47 [y]ver 24 [z]Mt 22:10
13:49 [a]Mt 25:32
13:50 [b]Mt 8:12
13:53 [c]Mt 7:28
13:54 [d]Mt 4:23 [e]Mt 7:28
13:55 [f]Lk 3:23; Jn 6:42 [g]Mt 12:46
13:57 [h]Jn 6:61 [i]Lk 4:24; Jn 4:44
14:1 [j]Mk 8:15; Lk 3:1,19; 13:31; 23:7,8; Ac 4:27; 12:1 [k]Lk 9:7-9

"This is John the Baptist;[l] he has risen
from the dead! That is why miraculous
powers are at work in him."
3Now Herod had arrested John and
bound him and put him in prison[m] because of Herodias, his brother Philip's
wife,[n] 4for John had been saying to him:
"It is not lawful for you to have her."[o]
5Herod wanted to kill John, but he was
afraid of the people, because they considered him a prophet.[p]
6On Herod's birthday the daughter of
Herodias danced for them and pleased
Herod so much 7that he promised with
an oath to give her whatever she asked.
8Prompted by her mother, she said,
"Give me here on a platter the head of
John the Baptist." 9The king was distressed, but because of his oaths and
his dinner guests, he ordered that her
request be granted 10and had John beheaded[q] in the prison. 11His head was
brought in on a platter and given to
the girl, who carried it to her mother.
12John's disciples came and took his
body and buried it.[r] Then they went
and told Jesus.

Jesus Feeds the Five Thousand

13When Jesus heard what had happened, he withdrew by boat privately
to a solitary place. Hearing of this, the
crowds followed him on foot from the
towns. 14When Jesus landed and saw
a large crowd, he had compassion on
them[s] and healed their sick.[t]
15As evening approached, the disciples came to him and said, "This is a remote place, and it's already getting late.
Send the crowds away, so they can go
to the villages and buy themselves some
food."
16Jesus replied, "They do not need
to go away. You give them something
to eat."
17"We have here only five loaves[u] of
bread and two fish," they answered.
18"Bring them here to me," he said.
19And he directed the people to sit down
on the grass. Taking the five loaves and
the two fish and looking up to heaven,
he gave thanks and broke the loaves.[v]
Then he gave them to the disciples, and
the disciples gave them to the people.
20They all ate and were satisfied, and
the disciples picked up twelve basketfuls of broken pieces that were left over.
21The number of those who ate was

14:2 [l]Mt 3:1
14:3 [m]Mt 4:12; 11:2 [n]Lk 3:19,20
14:4 [o]Lev 18:16; 20:21
14:5 [p]Mt 11:9
14:10 [q]Mt 17:12
14:12 [r]Ac 8:2
14:14 [s]Mt 9:36 [t]Mt 4:23
14:17 [u]Mt 16:9
14:19 [v]1Sa 9:13; Mt 26:26; Mk 8:6; Lk 24:30; Ac 2:42; 27:35; 1Ti 4:4

about five thousand men, besides wom-
en and children.

Jesus Walks on the Water

22Immediately Jesus made the disciples get into the boat and go on
ahead of him to the other side, while he
dismissed the crowd. 23After he had dismissed them, he went up on a moun-
14:23 wLk 3:21 tainside by himself to pray.[w] When
evening came, he was there alone, 24but
the boat was already a considerable distance[a] from land, buffeted by the waves
because the wind was against it.
25During the fourth watch of the
night Jesus went out to them, walking
14:26 xLk 24:37 on the lake. 26When the disciples saw
him walking on the lake, they were ter-
14:27 yMt 9:2; Ac 23:11 zDa 10:12; Mt 17:7; 28:10; Lk 1:13,30; 2:10; Ac 18:9; 23:11; Rev 1:17 rified. "It's a ghost,"[x] they said, and
cried out in fear.
27But Jesus immediately said to
them: "Take courage![y] It is I. Don't be
afraid."[z]
28"Lord, if it's you," Peter replied,
"tell me to come to you on the water."

FAITHFULNESS

SEA STROLLING

Matthew 14:28

Anyone can walk on water at Christ's command.
First, be sure he has issued the command;
Then trust and walk.
Don't look down.
Don't doubt.
The sea is as firm as meadowland
For those who trust their Lord's command.

29"Come," he said.
Then Peter got down out of the boat,
walked on the water and came toward
Jesus. 30But when he saw the wind, he
was afraid and, beginning to sink, cried
out, "Lord, save me!"
31Immediately Jesus reached out his
14:31 aMt 6:30 hand and caught him. "You of little
faith,"[a] he said, "why did you doubt?"
32And when they climbed into the
boat, the wind died down. 33Then
those who were in the boat worshiped
14:33 bPs 2:7; Mt 4:3 him, saying, "Truly you are the Son of
God."[b]
34When they had crossed over, they
landed at Gennesaret. 35And when the
men of that place recognized Jesus, they
sent word to all the surrounding country. People brought all their sick to him
36and begged him to let the sick just
touch the edge of his cloak,[c] and all 14:36 cMt 9:20
who touched him were healed.

Clean and Unclean

15 Then some Pharisees and teachers of the law came to Jesus
from Jerusalem and asked, 2"Why do
your disciples break the tradition of the
elders? They don't wash their hands before they eat!"[d] 15:2 dLk 11:38
3Jesus replied, "And why do you break
the command of God for the sake of
your tradition? 4For God said, 'Honor
your father and mother'[b][e] and 'Anyone 15:4 eEx 20:12; Dt 5:16; Eph 6:2 fEx 21:17; Lev 20:9
who curses his father or mother must
be put to death.'[c][f] 5But you say that
if a man says to his father or mother,
'Whatever help you might otherwise
have received from me is a gift devoted
to God,' 6he is not to 'honor his father[d]'
with it. Thus you nullify the word of
God for the sake of your tradition. 7You
hypocrites! Isaiah was right when he
prophesied about you:

8" 'These people honor me with their
lips,
but their hearts are far from me.
9They worship me in vain;
their teachings are but rules taught 15:9 gCol 2:20-22 hIsa 29:13; Mal 2:2
by men.[g]'[e][h]"

10Jesus called the crowd to him and
said, "Listen and understand. 11What
goes into a man's mouth does not make
him 'unclean,'[i] but what comes out of 15:11 iAc 10:14,15 jver 18
his mouth, that is what makes him
'unclean.' "[j]
12Then the disciples came to him and
asked, "Do you know that the Pharisees
were offended when they heard this?"
13He replied, "Every plant that my 15:13 kIsa 60:21; 61:3; Jn 15:2
heavenly Father has not planted[k] will be
pulled up by the roots. 14Leave them; 15:14 lMt 23:16,24; Ro 2:19 mLk 6:39
they are blind guides.[f][l] If a blind man
leads a blind man, both will fall into a
pit."[m]
15Peter said, "Explain the parable 15:15 nMt 13:36
to us."[n]
16"Are you still so dull?"[o] Jesus asked 15:16 oMt 16:9
them. 17"Don't you see that whatever
enters the mouth goes into the stom-

[a]24 Greek *many stadia* [b]4 Exodus 20:12; Deut. 5:16 [c]4 Exodus 21:17; Lev. 20:9 [d]6 Some manuscripts *father or his mother* [e]9 Isaiah 29:13 [f]14 Some manuscripts *guides of the blind*

WEEK 32

KINDNESS

DAY ONE

1 KINDNESS, ALWAYS APPLYING THE GOLDEN RULE

Read Matthew 15:21–28

A Gentile woman in need came to Jesus, a Jewish teacher, to beg a cure for her demon-possessed daughter. Jesus did not consider the woman inferior just because she was a Gentile, although that was the way most Jews of Jesus' day thought of Gentiles. Prejudice blocks the way of those who would like to practice the Golden Rule. There was an old Jewish prayer that said, "God, I thank thee that I am neither a Gentile, a dog, nor a woman." Obviously, this prayer was not popular with dogs, Gentiles or women.

In this passage, Jesus reminds this Canaanite woman that he is a "Jewish Messiah" sent only to the lost sheep of Israel. "It isn't right," said Jesus, "to take the doctrinal bread of authentic, theological Judaism and give it to the dogs (non-Jewish people)." "Yes," said the woman, "but even dogs are welcome to eat the crumbs that fall from the table." Impressed by the woman's faith, Jesus healed her daughter.

Kindness is listening to the hurting even if they are not our kind, or even if they don't adhere to our religion. I was dismayed during the Balkan crisis in the late 1990s to hear "good Christians" in Serbia—and the United States—saying, "It's too bad about the Kosovars; of course, they're Moslem, you know." One does not hear Jesus saying to this woman, "It's too bad about your daughter; of course, she is a Canaanite, you know."

Kindness is applying the Golden Rule to all—even those beyond our sociological or ethnic circle. "Do to others what you would have them to do to you" (Matthew 7:12) is the key to a majestic kindness that changes the world.

MEMORIZE THIS WEEK

MATTHEW 7:12

So in everything, do to others what you would have them do to you, for this sums up the Law and the Prophets.

DAY TWO

2 KINDNESS AND THE PURPOSE OF GOD IN MY LIFE

Caleb had received Hebron because of his faithfulness, but the land was still not subdued. So he issued a challenge to whomever would take it up—"I will give my daughter Acsah in marriage," he said, "to the man who attacks and captures Kiriath Sepher." Later when his daughter asked for a spring of water, Caleb generously gave to her what had already been given to him by God. *Turn to Judges 1:12–15, page 274, for today's study.*

DAY THREE

3 KINDNESS AND MY RELATIONSHIP WITH CHRIST

Sheep without a shepherd—what a pitiable thought! Sheep who have no shepherd must search for food, find shelter from storms and hide from wild animals. They are helpless and alone. What are we, who have a shepherd, to do with these lost sheep? Are we to leave them abandoned? Of course not. We need to invite the lost sheep into the fold. *Turn to Jeremiah 50:6, page 933, for today's study.*

DAY FOUR

4 KINDNESS AND MY SERVICE TO OTHERS

The tribes of Israel were almost to the point of war with each other—over a misunderstanding about an altar. But the flashpoint of conflict was extinguished when the tribes east of the Jordan explained the altar to the western tribes. Those east of the Jordan River were afraid that their separation from the true altar to God would tempt them to stray from their religion; so they had built their own altar to God to remind them of their godly heritage. *Turn to Joshua 22:9–27, page 268, for today's study.*

DAY FIVE

5 KINDNESS AND ITS PLACE IN MY PERSONAL WORSHIP

Jesus counsels us never to go to worship with a broken relationship in our lives (see Matthew 5:23–24). If we try to praise God while we are harboring a grudge against someone, we must leave the worship service, beg our begrudged enemy to forgive our anger and only then, when we are at peace, return to the altar and begin again. Our kindness will have made our worship possible. *Turn to Nahum 1:3, page 1080, for today's study.*

Week 33, Goodness, the Result of Imitating Christ, begins on page 1409, Ephesians 5:1–2.
To begin a topical study on the Fruit of the Spirit, Kindness, turn to the Topical Index, page 1548.

ach and then out of the body? 18But
the things that come out of the mouth
15:18 pMt 12:34; Lk 6:45; Jas 3:6 come from the heart,[p] and these make
a man 'unclean.' 19For out of the heart
come evil thoughts, murder, adultery,
sexual immorality, theft, false testimo-
15:19 qGal 5:19-21 ny, slander.[q] 20These are what make
15:20 rRo 14:14 a man 'unclean';[r] but eating with unwashed hands does not make him 'un-
clean.'"

The Faith of the Canaanite Woman

15:21 sMt 11:21 21Leaving that place, Jesus withdrew
to the region of Tyre and Sidon.[s] 22A
Canaanite woman from that vicinity
came to him, crying out, "Lord, Son of
15:22 tMt 9:27 uMt 4:24 David,[t] have mercy on me! My daughter is suffering terribly from demon-
possession."[u]
23Jesus did not answer a word. So his
disciples came to him and urged him,
"Send her away, for she keeps crying
out after us."
15:24 vMt 10:6,23; Ro 15:8 24He answered, "I was sent only to
the lost sheep of Israel."[v]
15:25 wMt 8:2 25The woman came and knelt before
him.[w] "Lord, help me!" she said.
26He replied, "It is not right to take
the children's bread and toss it to their
dogs."
27"Yes, Lord," she said, "but even the
dogs eat the crumbs that fall from their
masters' table."
28Then Jesus answered, "Woman, you
15:28 xMt 9:22 have great faith![x] Your request is granted." And her daughter was healed from
that very hour.

Jesus Feeds the Four Thousand

29Jesus left there and went along the
Sea of Galilee. Then he went up on
a mountainside and sat down. 30Great
crowds came to him, bringing the lame,
the blind, the crippled, the mute and
many others, and laid them at his feet;
15:30 yMt 4:23 and he healed them.[y] 31The people were
amazed when they saw the mute speak-
ing, the crippled made well, the lame
walking and the blind seeing. And they
15:31 zMt 9:8 praised the God of Israel.[z]
32Jesus called his disciples to him
15:32 aMt 9:36 and said, "I have compassion for these
people;[a] they have already been with
me three days and have nothing to eat.
I do not want to send them away hungry, or they may collapse on the way."
33His disciples answered, "Where
could we get enough bread in this remote place to feed such a crowd?"
34"How many loaves do you have?"
Jesus asked.
"Seven," they replied, "and a few
small fish."
35He told the crowd to sit down on
the ground. 36Then he took the seven
loaves and the fish, and when he had
given thanks, he broke them[b] and gave 15:36 bMt 14:19
them to the disciples, and they in turn
to the people. 37They all ate and were
satisfied. Afterward the disciples picked
up seven basketfuls of broken pieces
that were left over.[c] 38The number of 15:37 cMt 16:10
those who ate was four thousand, be-
sides women and children. 39After Jesus had sent the crowd away, he got
into the boat and went to the vicinity
of Magadan.

PEACE

CROWD CONTROL

Matthew 15:35

Jesus was wise to simply say, "Ladies and gentlemen, please have a seat!" Asking people to be seated peacefully defuses all maddening anger. No army ever took up arms while seated. No crowd ever lost control while sitting on the ground.

The Demand for a Sign

16 The Pharisees and Sadducees[d] 16:1 dAc 4:1 eMt 12:38
came to Jesus and tested him by
asking him to show them a sign from
heaven.[e]
2He replied,[a] "When evening comes,
you say, 'It will be fair weather, for the
sky is red,' 3and in the morning, 'Today it will be stormy, for the sky is red
and overcast.' You know how to interpret the appearance of the sky, but you
cannot interpret the signs of the times.[f] 16:3 fLk 12:54-56
4A wicked and adulterous generation
looks for a miraculous sign, but none
will be given it except the sign of
Jonah."[g] Jesus then left them and went 16:4 gMt 12:39
away.

The Yeast of the Pharisees and Sadducees

5When they went across the lake, the
disciples forgot to take bread. 6"Be care-

[a]*2* Some early manuscripts do not have the rest of verse 2 and all of verse 3.

GENTLENESS

THE WEATHER OF THE HEART

Matthew 16:2–3

As the forecast discloses tomorrow's climate, the weather of the heart will distinguish the true believer.

ful," Jesus said to them. "Be on your
guard against the yeast of the Pharisees
16:6 [h]Lk 12:1 and Sadducees."[h]
7They discussed this among themselves and said, "It is because we didn't
bring any bread."
16:8 [i]Mt 6:30 8Aware of their discussion, Jesus
asked, "You of little faith,[i] why are you
talking among yourselves about having
no bread? 9Do you still not understand?
Don't you remember the five loaves for
16:9 [j]Mt 14:17-21 the five thousand, and how many basketfuls you gathered?[j] 10Or the seven
16:10 [k]Mt 15:34-38 loaves for the four thousand, and how
many basketfuls you gathered?[k] 11How
is it you don't understand that I was
not talking to you about bread? But
be on your guard against the yeast of
the Pharisees and Sadducees." 12Then
they understood that he was not telling
them to guard against the yeast used in
16:12 [l]Ac 4:1 bread, but against the teaching of the
Pharisees and Sadducees.[l]

Peter's Confession of Christ

13When Jesus came to the region of
Caesarea Philippi, he asked his disciples, "Who do people say the Son of
16:14 [m]Mt 3:1; 14:2 [n]Mk 6:15; Jn 1:21 Man is?"
14They replied, "Some say John the
Baptist;[m] others say Elijah; and still oth-
16:16 [o]Mt 4:3; Ps 42:2; Jn 11:27; Ac 14:15; 2Co 6:16; 1Th 1:9; 1Ti 3:15; Heb 10:31; 12:22 ers, Jeremiah or one of the prophets."[n]
15"But what about you?" he asked.
"Who do you say I am?"
16Simon Peter answered, "You are the
Christ,[a] the Son of the living God."[o]
17Jesus replied, "Blessed are you, Simon son of Jonah, for this was not
16:17 [p]1Co 15:50; Gal 1:16; Eph 6:12; Heb 2:14 revealed to you by man,[p] but by my Father in heaven. 18And I tell you that
you are Peter,[b] [q] and on this rock I will
build my church,[r] and the gates of Ha-
16:18 [q]Jn 1:42 [r]Eph 2:20 des[c] will not overcome it.[d] 19I will give
you the keys[s] of the kingdom of heav-
en; whatever you bind on earth will
16:19 [s]Isa 22:22; Rev 3:7 [t]Mt 18:18; Jn 20:23 be[e] bound in heaven, and whatever
you loose on earth will be[e] loosed in
heaven."[t] 20Then he warned his disci-
ples not to tell anyone[u] that he was the 16:20 [u]Mk 8:30
Christ.

Jesus Predicts His Death

21From that time on Jesus began to
explain to his disciples that he must go
to Jerusalem and suffer many things[v] at 16:21 [v]Mk 10:34; Lk 17:25 [w]Jn 2:19 [x]Mt 17:22,23; 27:63; Mk 9:31; Lk 9:22; 18:31-33; 24:6,7
the hands of the elders, chief priests and
teachers of the law, and that he must be
killed and on the third day[w] be raised
to life.[x]
22Peter took him aside and began
to rebuke him. "Never, Lord!" he said.
"This shall never happen to you!"
23Jesus turned and said to Peter, "Get
behind me, Satan![y] You are a stumbling 16:23 [y]Mt 4:10
block to me; you do not have in mind
the things of God, but the things of
men."
24Then Jesus said to his disciples, "If
anyone would come after me, he must
deny himself and take up his cross and 16:24 [z]Mt 10:38; Lk 14:27
follow me.[z] 25For whoever wants to save
his life[f] will lose it, but whoever loses
his life for me will find it.[a] 26What 16:25 [a]Jn 12:25
good will it be for a man if he gains
the whole world, yet forfeits his soul?
Or what can a man give in exchange for
his soul? 27For the Son of Man[b] is go- 16:27 [b]Mt 8:20 [c]Ac 1:11 [d]Job 34:11; Ps 62:12; Jer 17:10; Ro 2:6; 2Co 5:10; Rev 22:12
ing to come[c] in his Father's glory with
his angels, and then he will reward each
person according to what he has done.[d]
28I tell you the truth, some who are
standing here will not taste death before they see the Son of Man coming in
his kingdom."

The Transfiguration

17 After six days Jesus took with
him Peter, James and John the
brother of James, and led them up a
high mountain by themselves. 2There
he was transfigured before them. His
face shone like the sun, and his clothes
became as white as the light. 3Just then
there appeared before them Moses and
Elijah, talking with Jesus.
4Peter said to Jesus, "Lord, it is good
for us to be here. If you wish, I will put
up three shelters—one for you, one for
Moses and one for Elijah."
5While he was still speaking, a bright
cloud enveloped them, and a voice from

[a]*16* Or *Messiah*; also in verse 20 [b]*18 Peter* means *rock*. [c]*18* Or *hell* [d]*18* Or *not prove stronger than it* [e]*19* Or *have been* [f]*25* The Greek word means either *life* or *soul*; also in verse 26.

PATIENCE

When the Heroes of the Ages Meet

Matthew 17:3

Moses lived 600 years before Elijah; and Elijah 900 years before Jesus. Here, on the Mount of Transfiguration, the people of old finally saw the approaching final "exodus" when Christ would deliver all people from their slavery to sin. It was a long wait but well worth it.

the cloud said, "This is my Son, whom
17:5 [e]Mt 3:17; 2Pe 1:17 [f]Ac 3:22,23 I love; with him I am well pleased.[e] Listen to him!"[f]
6When the disciples heard this, they
fell facedown to the ground, terrified.
7But Jesus came and touched them.
17:7 [g]Mt 14:27 "Get up," he said. "Don't be afraid."[g]
8When they looked up, they saw no
one except Jesus.
9As they were coming down the
17:9 [h]Mk 8:30 [i]Mt 8:20 [j]Mt 16:21 mountain, Jesus instructed them, "Don't
tell anyone[h] what you have seen, until
the Son of Man[i] has been raised from
the dead."[j]
10The disciples asked him, "Why
then do the teachers of the law say that
Elijah must come first?"
17:11 [k]Mal 4:6; Lk 1:16,17 11Jesus replied, "To be sure, Elijah
comes and will restore all things.[k] 12But
17:12 [l]Mt 11:14 [m]Mt 14:3,10 [n]Mt 16:21 I tell you, Elijah has already come,[l] and
they did not recognize him, but have
done to him everything they wished.[m]
In the same way the Son of Man is going to suffer[n] at their hands." 13Then the
disciples understood that he was talking
to them about John the Baptist.

The Healing of a Boy With a Demon

14When they came to the crowd, a
man approached Jesus and knelt before
17:15 [o]Mt 4:24 him. 15"Lord, have mercy on my son,"
he said. "He has seizures[o] and is suffering greatly. He often falls into the fire
or into the water. 16I brought him to
your disciples, but they could not heal
him."
17"O unbelieving and perverse generation," Jesus replied, "how long shall I
stay with you? How long shall I put up
with you? Bring the boy here to me."
18Jesus rebuked the demon, and it came
out of the boy, and he was healed from
that moment.
19Then the disciples came to Jesus in
private and asked, "Why couldn't we
drive it out?"
20He replied, "Because you have so
little faith. I tell you the truth, if you
have faith[p] as small as a mustard seed,[q] 17:20 [p]Mt 21:21 [q]Mt 13:31; Mk 11:23; Lk 17:6 [r]1Co 13:2
you can say to this mountain, 'Move
from here to there' and it will move.[r]
Nothing will be impossible for you.[a]"
22When they came together in Gali-
lee, he said to them, "The Son of Man[s] 17:22 [s]Mt 8:20
is going to be betrayed into the hands
of men. 23They will kill him,[t] and on 17:23 [t]Ac 2:23; 3:13 [u]Mt 16:21 [v]Mt 16:21
the third day[u] he will be raised to life."[v]
And the disciples were filled with grief.

The Temple Tax

24After Jesus and his disciples arrived
in Capernaum, the collectors of the
two-drachma tax[w] came to Peter and 17:24 [w]Ex 30:13
asked, "Doesn't your teacher pay the
temple tax[b]?"
25"Yes, he does," he replied.
When Peter came into the house, Jesus was the first to speak. "What do
you think, Simon?" he asked. "From
whom do the kings of the earth collect 17:25 [x]Mt 22:17-21; Ro 13:7
duty and taxes[x]—from their own sons
or from others?"
26"From others," Peter answered.
"Then the sons are exempt," Jesus
said to him. 27"But so that we may not 17:27 [y]Jn 6:61
offend[y] them, go to the lake and throw
out your line. Take the first fish you
catch; open its mouth and you will find
a four-drachma coin. Take it and give it
to them for my tax and yours."

The Greatest in the Kingdom of Heaven

18 At that time the disciples came
to Jesus and asked, "Who is the
greatest in the kingdom of heaven?"
2He called a little child and had him
stand among them. 3And he said: "I tell
you the truth, unless you change and
become like little children,[z] you will 18:3 [z]Mt 19:14; 1Pe 2:2 [a]Mt 3:2
never enter the kingdom of heaven.[a]
4Therefore, whoever humbles himself
like this child is the greatest in the kingdom of heaven.[b] 18:4 [b]Mk 9:35
5"And whoever welcomes a little child
like this in my name welcomes me.[c] 18:5 [c]Mt 10:40
6But if anyone causes one of these little

[a]20 Some manuscripts *you.* [21]*But this kind does not go out except by prayer and fasting.* [b]24 Greek *the two drachmas*

18:6 [d]Mt 5:29; [e]Mk 9:42; Lk 17:2 ones who believe in me to sin,[d] it would
be better for him to have a large mill-
stone hung around his neck and to be
drowned in the depths of the sea.[e]

GENTLENESS

GROW DOWN

Matthew 18:4

Children trust because it is not their nature to toy with falsehood or play with unbelief. No one is readied for heaven by "growing up." Rather, we prepare ourselves for heaven by gently growing down to childlikeness.

7"Woe to the world because of the
things that cause people to sin! Such
18:7 [f]Lk 17:1 things must come, but woe to the man
through whom they come![f] 8If your
18:8 [g]Mt 5:29; Mk 9:43,45 hand or your foot causes you to sin,[g]
cut it off and throw it away. It is better
for you to enter life maimed or crippled than to have two hands or two feet
and be thrown into eternal fire. 9And if
18:9 [h]Mt 5:29 [i]Mt 5:22 your eye causes you to sin,[h] gouge it out
and throw it away. It is better for you
to enter life with one eye than to have
two eyes and be thrown into the fire of
hell.[i]

The Parable of the Lost Sheep

10"See that you do not look down on
one of these little ones. For I tell you
18:10 [j]Ge 48:16; Ps 34:7; Ac 12:11,15; Heb 1:14 that their angels[j] in heaven always see
the face of my Father in heaven.[a]
12"What do you think? If a man owns
a hundred sheep, and one of them wanders away, will he not leave the ninety-nine on the hills and go to look for
the one that wandered off? 13And if he
finds it, I tell you the truth, he is happier about that one sheep than about the
ninety-nine that did not wander off.
14In the same way your Father in heav-
en is not willing that any of these little
ones should be lost.

A Brother Who Sins Against You

18:15 [k]Lev 19:17; Lk 17:3; Gal 6:1; Jas 5:19,20 15"If your brother sins against you,[b]
go and show him his fault,[k] just be-
18:16 [l]Nu 35:30; Dt 17:6; 19:15; Jn 8:17; 2Co 13:1; 1Ti 5:19; Heb 10:28 tween the two of you. If he listens to
you, you have won your brother over.
16But if he will not listen, take one or
two others along, so that 'every matter
may be established by the testimony of
two or three witnesses.'[c][l] 17If he refuses
18:17 [m]1Co 6:1-6 to listen to them, tell it to the church;[m]
and if he refuses to listen even to the
church, treat him as you would a pagan
or a tax collector.[n] 18:17 [n]Ro 16:17; 2Th 3:6,14
18"I tell you the truth, whatever you
bind on earth will be[d] bound in heav-
en, and whatever you loose on earth
will be[d] loosed in heaven.[o] 18:18 [o]Mt 16:19; Jn 20:23
19"Again, I tell you that if two of
you on earth agree about anything you
ask for, it will be done for you[p] by my 18:19 [p]Mt 7:7
Father in heaven. 20For where two or
three come together in my name, there
am I with them."

The Parable of the Unmerciful Servant

21Then Peter came to Jesus and asked,
"Lord, how many times shall I forgive
my brother when he sins against me?[q] 18:21 [q]Mt 6:14 [r]Lk 17:4
Up to seven times?"[r]
22Jesus answered, "I tell you, not sev- 18:22 [s]Ge 4:24
en times, but seventy-seven times.[e][s]

GOODNESS

FORGIVE AND FORGET, FORGIVE AND FORGET, FORGIVE AND . . .

Matthew 18:21–22

How often should you forgive your neighbors? One more time than they ask.

23"Therefore, the kingdom of heaven
is like[t] a king who wanted to settle ac- 18:23 [t]Mt 13:24 [u]Mt 25:19
counts[u] with his servants. 24As he be-
gan the settlement, a man who owed
him ten thousand talents[f] was brought
to him. 25Since he was not able to pay,[v] 18:25 [v]Lk 7:42 [w]Lev 25:39; 2Ki 4:1; Ne 5:5,8
the master ordered that he and his wife
and his children and all that he had be
sold[w] to repay the debt.
26"The servant fell on his knees be-
fore him.[x] 'Be patient with me,' he 18:26 [x]Mt 8:2
begged, 'and I will pay back everything.'
27The servant's master took pity on him,
canceled the debt and let him go.
28"But when that servant went out,
he found one of his fellow servants
who owed him a hundred denarii.[g] He
grabbed him and began to choke him.
'Pay back what you owe me!' he demanded.

[a] *10* Some manuscripts *heaven.* *11The Son of Man came to save what was lost.* [b] *15* Some manuscripts do not have *against you.* [c] *16* Deut. 19:15
[d] *18* Or *have been* [e] *22* Or *seventy times seven*
[f] *24* That is, millions of dollars [g] *28* That is, a few dollars

WEEK 31

PATIENCE

DAY ONE

1 PATIENCE, THE UNHURRIED VIRTUE

Read Matthew 18:21–35

The question, "How many times shall I forgive my brother when he sins against me? Up to seven times?" opened up the issue of patience. Peter felt magnanimous in suggesting seven-fold forgiveness as a worldwide standard. But Jesus reminded him that a better standard would be 77 times. Jesus was not advancing some legalistic rule here. The idea is that when you get to 43 times, you will probably quit counting. You may then become more like God in your willingness to forgive freely—without credits and debits, without a calculator.

Jesus' parable can be paraphrased as follows:

Sue offends Bill.
Sue says, "I'm sorry, Bill, will you forgive me?"
"Certainly, Sue. It was nothing; forget it," says Bill.
Then Sue does the same offensive thing again.
"I'm sorry, Bill, will you forgive me?"
"Certainly, Sue, but try not to do it again."
Then Sue does the same offensive thing again.
"I'm sorry, Bill, will you forgive me?"
"Mmm...uh, okay, but this has got to stop, okay?"
Then Sue does the same offensive thing again.
"I'm sorry, Bill, will you forgive me?"
"Uh...let me think about it, and I'll get back to you."

Patience is an unhurried virtue. Patience waits and forgives and waits and forgives. Meanwhile, Bill, who wishes Sue would get hold of her moral inconsistencies, also sins. It's the same sin he regularly commits against God, and he goes before the Lord and says, "Oh, God, I know I've begged your forgiveness a thousand times for this same sin, but will you forgive me once more?"

And Bill is surprised to hear God's answer: "I don't know, Bill. Did you ever get back to Sue?"

DAY TWO

2 PATIENCE AND THE PURPOSE OF GOD IN MY LIFE

Moses is 120 years old, and his eyes are not dim nor his strength abated. So why is he dying in such vigor without entering Canaan? Because, as we would say today, he "lost his cool" (abandoned his patience) in front of all the people of Israel. Patience is the virtue that demonstrates that we are fully in touch and at ease with the purposes of God in our lives. *Turn to Deuteronomy 34:5–8, page 240, for today's study.*

DAY THREE

3 PATIENCE AND MY RELATIONSHIP WITH CHRIST

Patience is not born by assuming we have all the time we would like in which to accomplish all the goals we would like. The psalmist believed he could make use of the unhurried virtue of patience when he faced God and said, "Show me, O LORD, my life's end and the number of my days." *Turn to Psalm 39:1–5, page 657, for today's study.*

DAY FOUR

4 PATIENCE AND MY SERVICE TO OTHERS

The world's salvation is not an en masse event. God is not in a panic regarding the rate at which people come to him. God knows his kingdom is built one confession at a time. So our service to others lies in confessing Christ, fully believing that our example will bless others and bring them in time to an unhurried and earnest confession of Christ. *Turn to 1 Timothy 6:11–12, page 1442, for today's study.*

DAY FIVE

5 PATIENCE AND ITS PLACE IN MY PERSONAL WORSHIP

The reading aloud of the Word of God has its place in our personal worship. Yet sometimes the church faces a complex travesty: We read the Word of God in a slovenly and boring fashion. Can we not cry honestly, "God is speaking; please, let us not have the world think that God is as boring as our poor attention to reading makes him appear"? When Ezra read the Word of God from daybreak until noon, the Word was all-transforming. *Turn to Nehemiah 8:3–10, page 562, for today's study.*

MEMORIZE THIS WEEK

EXODUS 14:13-14

Moses answered the people, "Do not be afraid. Stand firm and you will see the deliverance the LORD will bring you today. The Egyptians you see today you will never see again. The LORD will fight for you; you need only to be still."

Week 32, Kindness, Always Applying the Golden Rule, begins on page 1141, Matthew 15:21–28. To begin a topical study on the Fruit of the Spirit, Patience, turn to the Topical Index, page 1548.

29“His fellow servant fell to his knees
and begged him, ‘Be patient with me,
and I will pay you back.’
30“But he refused. Instead, he went
off and had the man thrown into prison until he could pay the debt. 31When
the other servants saw what had happened, they were greatly distressed and
went and told their master everything
that had happened.
32“Then the master called the servant
in. ‘You wicked servant,’ he said, ‘I canceled all that debt of yours because you
begged me to. 33Shouldn’t you have had
mercy on your fellow servant just as
I had on you?’ 34In anger his master
turned him over to the jailers to be
tortured, until he should pay back all
he owed.
35“This is how my heavenly Father
will treat each of you unless you forgive
18:35 [y]Mt 6:14; Jas 2:13 your brother from your heart.”[y]

Divorce

19:1 [z]Mt 7:28 **19** When Jesus had finished saying these things,[z] he left Gali-
lee and went into the region of Judea
to the other side of the Jordan. 2Large
crowds followed him, and he healed
19:2 [a]Mt 4:23 them[a] there.
3Some Pharisees came to him to test
19:3 [b]Mt 5:31 him. They asked, “Is it lawful for a man
to divorce his wife[b] for any and every
reason?”

LOVE

ADAM AND EVE—FOR BETTER OR FOR WORSE

Matthew 19:4–6

One man, one woman, one God—this was Eden’s recipe for marriage. It’s still the recipe for paradise.

4“Haven’t you read,” he replied, “that
at the beginning the Creator ‘made
19:4 [c]Ge 1:27; 5:2 them male and female,’[a] [c] 5and said, ‘For
this reason a man will leave his father
and mother and be united to his wife,
19:5 [d]Ge 2:24; 1Co 6:16; Eph 5:31 and the two will become one flesh’[b]?[d]
6So they are no longer two, but one.
Therefore what God has joined together, let man not separate.”
7“Why then,” they asked, “did Mo-
19:7 [e]Dt 24:1-4; Mt 5:31 ses command that a man give his wife
a certificate of divorce and send her
away?”[e]
8Jesus replied, “Moses permitted you
to divorce your wives because your
hearts were hard. But it was not this
way from the beginning. 9I tell you that
anyone who divorces his wife, except
for marital unfaithfulness, and marries
another woman commits adultery.”[f] 19:9 [f]Mt 5:32; Lk 16:18
10The disciples said to him, “If this
is the situation between a husband and
wife, it is better not to marry.”
11Jesus replied, “Not everyone can accept this word, but only those to whom
it has been given.[g] 12For some are eu- 19:11 [g]Mt 13:11; 1Co 7:7-9,17
nuchs because they were born that way;
others were made that way by men;
and others have renounced marriage[c]
because of the kingdom of heaven.
The one who can accept this should accept it.”

The Little Children and Jesus

13Then little children were brought
to Jesus for him to place his hands on
them[h] and pray for them. But the disci- 19:13 [h]Mk 5:23
ples rebuked those who brought them.
14Jesus said, “Let the little children
come to me, and do not hinder them,
for the kingdom of heaven belongs[i] to 19:14 [i]Mt 25:34 [j]Mt 18:3; 1Pe 2:2
such as these.”[j] 15When he had placed
his hands on them, he went on from
there.

The Rich Young Man

16Now a man came up to Jesus and
asked, “Teacher, what good thing must
I do to get eternal life[k]?”[l] 19:16 [k]Mt 25:46 [l]Lk 10:25
17“Why do you ask me about what
is good?” Jesus replied. “There is only
One who is good. If you want to enter
life, obey the commandments.”[m] 19:17 [m]Lev 18:5
18“Which ones?” the man inquired.
Jesus replied, “ ‘Do not murder, do
not commit adultery,[n] do not steal, do 19:18 [n]Jas 2:11
not give false testimony, 19honor your
father and mother,’[d] [o] and ‘love your 19:19 [o]Ex 20:12-16; Dt 5:16-20 [p]Lev 19:18; Mt 5:43
neighbor as yourself.’[e]”[p]
20“All these I have kept,” the young
man said. “What do I still lack?”
21Jesus answered, “If you want to
be perfect,[q] go, sell your possessions 19:21 [q]Mt 5:48 [r]Lk 12:33; Ac 2:45; 4:34-35 [s]Mt 6:20
and give to the poor,[r] and you will
have treasure in heaven.[s] Then come,
follow me.”
22When the young man heard this,

[a]*4* Gen. 1:27 [b]*5* Gen. 2:24 [c]*12* Or *have made themselves eunuchs* [d]*19* Exodus 20:12-16; Deut. 5:16-20 [e]*19* Lev. 19:18

he went away sad, because he had great
wealth.
23Then Jesus said to his disciples, "I
tell you the truth, it is hard for a rich
man[t] to enter the kingdom of heaven.
24Again I tell you, it is easier for a camel
to go through the eye of a needle than
for a rich man to enter the kingdom
of God."

19:23 [t]Mt 13:22; 1Ti 6:9,10

SELF-CONTROL

NEEDLES AND CAMELS

Matthew 19:24

A rich man occasionally manages to drop his gold and cling to the scarred hand of his Savior. So a camel may pass through the eye of a needle, but it is always hard on the camel.

25When the disciples heard this, they
were greatly astonished and asked,
"Who then can be saved?"
26Jesus looked at them and said,
"With man this is impossible, but with
God all things are possible."[u]
27Peter answered him, "We have left
everything to follow you![v] What then
will there be for us?"
28Jesus said to them, "I tell you the
truth, at the renewal of all things, when
the Son of Man sits on his glorious
throne,[w] you who have followed me
will also sit on twelve thrones, judging
the twelve tribes of Israel.[x] 29And everyone who has left houses or brothers
or sisters or father or mother[a] or children or fields for my sake will receive a
hundred times as much and will inherit
eternal life.[y] 30But many who are first
will be last, and many who are last will
be first.[z]

19:26 [u]Ge 18:14; Job 42:2; Jer 32:17; Zec 8:6; Lk 1:37; 18:27; Ro 4:21
19:27 [v]Mt 4:19
19:28 [w]Mt 20:21; 25:31 [x]Lk 22:28-30; Rev 3:21; 4:4; 20:4
19:29 [y]Mt 6:33; 25:46
19:30 [z]Mt 20:16; Mk 10:31; Lk 13:30

The Parable of the Workers in the Vineyard

20 "For the kingdom of heaven is
like[a] a landowner who went out
early in the morning to hire men to
work in his vineyard.[b] 2He agreed to
pay them a denarius for the day and
sent them into his vineyard.
3"About the third hour he went out
and saw others standing in the marketplace doing nothing. 4He told them,
'You also go and work in my vineyard,
and I will pay you whatever is right.'
5So they went.
"He went out again about the sixth
hour and the ninth hour and did the
same thing. 6About the eleventh hour he
went out and found still others standing around. He asked them, 'Why have
you been standing here all day long doing nothing?'
7"'Because no one has hired us,' they
answered.
"He said to them, 'You also go and
work in my vineyard.'
8"When evening came,[c] the owner of
the vineyard said to his foreman, 'Call
the workers and pay them their wages,
beginning with the last ones hired and
going on to the first.'
9"The workers who were hired about
the eleventh hour came and each received a denarius. 10So when those came
who were hired first, they expected to
receive more. But each one of them
also received a denarius. 11When they
received it, they began to grumble[d]
against the landowner. 12'These men
who were hired last worked only one
hour,' they said, 'and you have made
them equal to us who have borne the
burden of the work and the heat[e] of the
day.'
13"But he answered one of them,
'Friend,[f] I am not being unfair to you.
Didn't you agree to work for a denarius? 14Take your pay and go. I want to
give the man who was hired last the
same as I gave you. 15Don't I have the
right to do what I want with my own
money? Or are you envious because I
am generous?'[g]
16"So the last will be first, and the
first will be last."[h]

20:1 [a]Mt 13:24 [b]Mt 21:28,33
20:8 [c]Lev 19:13; Dt 24:15
20:11 [d]Jnh 4:1
20:12 [e]Jnh 4:8; Lk 12:55; Jas 1:11
20:13 [f]Mt 22:12; 26:50
20:15 [g]Dt 15:9; Mk 7:22
20:16 [h]Mt 19:30

Jesus Again Predicts His Death

17Now as Jesus was going up to Jerusalem, he took the twelve disciples aside
and said to them, 18"We are going up
to Jerusalem,[i] and the Son of Man[j] will
be betrayed to the chief priests and the
teachers of the law.[k] They will condemn
him to death 19and will turn him over to
the Gentiles to be mocked and flogged[l]
and crucified.[m] On the third day[n] he
will be raised to life!"[o]

20:18 [i]Lk 9:51 [j]Mt 8:20 [k]Mt 16:21; 27:1,2
20:19 [l]Mt 16:21 [m]Ac 2:23 [n]Mt 16:21 [o]Mt 16:21

A Mother's Request

20Then the mother of Zebedee's sons[p]
came to Jesus with her sons and, kneeling down,[q] asked a favor of him.

20:20 [p]Mt 4:21 [q]Mt 8:2

[a]29 Some manuscripts *mother or wife*

21"What is it you want?" he asked.
She said, "Grant that one of these
two sons of mine may sit at your right
and the other at your left in your
kingdom."[r]

20:21
[r]Mt 19:28

KINDNESS

WHO GETS TO BE VICE PRESIDENT IN HEAVEN?

Matthew 20:21

The original sin is the ultimate sin—
Claim thrones or be gods as you may!
For the last pair alive, like the first pair alive,
Would rather have power than obey.

22"You don't know what you are asking," Jesus said to them. "Can you drink
the cup[s] I am going to drink?"
"We can," they answered.
23Jesus said to them, "You will indeed drink from my cup,[t] but to sit
at my right or left is not for me to
grant. These places belong to those for
whom they have been prepared by my
Father."
24When the ten heard about this, they
were indignant[u] with the two brothers.
25Jesus called them together and said,
"You know that the rulers of the Gentiles lord it over them, and their high
officials exercise authority over them.
26Not so with you. Instead, whoever
wants to become great among you must
be your servant,[v] 27and whoever wants
to be first must be your slave— 28just
as the Son of Man[w] did not come to be
served, but to serve,[x] and to give his life
as a ransom[y] for many."

20:22
[s]Isa 51:17,22; Jer 49:12; Mt 26:39,42; Mk 14:36; Lk 22:42; Jn 18:11

20:23
[t]Ac 12:2; Rev 1:9

20:24
[u]Lk 22:24,25

20:26
[v]Mt 23:11; Mk 9:35

20:28
[w]Mt 8:20
[x]Lk 22:27; Jn 13:13-16; 2Co 8:9; Php 2:7
[y]Isa 53:10; Mt 26:28; 1Ti 2:6; Tit 2:14; Heb 9:28; 1Pe 1:18,19

Two Blind Men Receive Sight

29As Jesus and his disciples were leaving Jericho, a large crowd followed him.
30Two blind men were sitting by the
roadside, and when they heard that Jesus was going by, they shouted, "Lord,
Son of David,[z] have mercy on us!"
31The crowd rebuked them and told
them to be quiet, but they shouted all
the louder, "Lord, Son of David, have
mercy on us!"
32Jesus stopped and called them.
"What do you want me to do for you?"
he asked.
33"Lord," they answered, "we want
our sight."
34Jesus had compassion on them and
touched their eyes. Immediately they
received their sight and followed him.

20:30
[z]Mt 9:27

The Triumphal Entry

21 As they approached Jerusalem
and came to Bethphage on the
Mount of Olives,[a] Jesus sent two disciples, 2saying to them, "Go to the village ahead of you, and at once you will
find a donkey tied there, with her colt
by her. Untie them and bring them to
me. 3If anyone says anything to you,
tell him that the Lord needs them, and
he will send them right away."
4This took place to fulfill what was
spoken through the prophet:

21:1
[a]Mt 24:3; 26:30; Mk 14:26; Lk 19:37; 21:37; 22:39; Jn 8:1; Ac 1:12

5"Say to the Daughter of Zion,
'See, your king comes to you,
gentle and riding on a donkey,
on a colt, the foal of a donkey.' "[a][b]

21:5
[b]Zec 9:9; Isa 62:11

6The disciples went and did as Jesus
had instructed them. 7They brought
the donkey and the colt, placed their
cloaks[c] on them, and Jesus sat on them.
8A very large crowd spread their cloaks
on the road, while others cut branches
from the trees and spread them on the
road. 9The crowds that went ahead of
him and those that followed shouted,

21:8
[c]2Ki 9:13

"Hosanna[b] to the Son of David!"[d]

"Blessed is he who comes in the
name of the Lord!"[c][e]

"Hosanna[b] in the highest!"[f]

21:9
[d]ver 15; Mt 9:27
[e]Ps 118:26; Mt 23:39
[f]Lk 2:14

10When Jesus entered Jerusalem, the
whole city was stirred and asked, "Who
is this?"
11The crowds answered, "This is Jesus, the prophet[g] from Nazareth in Galilee."

21:11
[g]Lk 7:16,39; 24:19; Jn 1:21,25; 6:14; 7:40

Jesus at the Temple

12Jesus entered the temple area and
drove out all who were buying[h] and
selling there. He overturned the tables
of the money changers[i] and the bench-
es of those selling doves.[j] 13"It is written," he said to them, " 'My house will
be called a house of prayer,'[d][k] but you
are making it a 'den of robbers.'[e]"[l]

21:12
[h]Dt 14:26
[i]Ex 30:13
[j]Lev 1:14

21:13
[k]Isa 56:7
[l]Jer 7:11

[a]*5* Zech. 9:9 [b]*9* A Hebrew expression meaning "Save!" which became an exclamation of praise; also in verse 15 [c]*9* Psalm 118:26 [d]*13* Isaiah 56:7
[e]*13* Jer. 7:11

14The blind and the lame came to
him at the temple, and he healed
them.[m] 15But when the chief priests — 21:14 [m]Mt 4:23
and the teachers of the law saw the
wonderful things he did and the chil-
dren shouting in the temple area, "Ho- — 21:15 [n]ver 9; Mt 9:27 [o]Lk 19:39
sanna to the Son of David,"[n] they were
indignant.[o]
16"Do you hear what these children
are saying?" they asked him.
"Yes," replied Jesus, "have you never
read,

DAY 5 FIVE

▸ GENTLENESS AND ITS PLACE IN MY PERSONAL WORSHIP

Matthew 21:14–17

The children want to keep praising Christ on this Palm Sunday, but the priests and teachers of the law won't stand for it. The children have a gentle godliness that comes from innocence—uncorrupted by any ambitious agendas. Children can, indeed, teach us how to worship.

One of my grandsons is from Bangkok. He came to us when he was ten years old, and his religious childhood had been spent as a Buddhist. He was suddenly transplanted into a Christian family and congenially attended our Christian church with us. Upon much reflection, he said after church one day, "Mom, know why I like Jesus better than Buddha?"

"No," replied my daughter. "Why?"

"Well," he explained, "Jesus could say to the storm, 'Quiet! Be still!' and it got still. But Buddha, he don't do nothing but sit there."

This is a child's assessment of adult theology. Yet, as Jesus said in Matthew 11:25, some of the most profound insights are hidden from the scholars and revealed to the children.

But what is best of all is the gentle praise children offer God. It seems as though every Sunday is Palm Sunday to them. They are ever ready to crown Jesus king. So honest and true is their theology that when Karl Barth was asked, "What is the world's most impressive theological truth?" he replied, "Jesus loves me; this I know, for the Bible tells me so."

To begin a study on the topic of Gentleness, Childlike Godliness, turn to the home page on page 315.

"'From the lips of children and
infants
you have ordained praise'[a]?"[p] — 21:16 [p]Ps 8:2

17And he left them and went out of — 21:17 [q]Mt 26:6; Mk 11:1; Lk 24:50; Jn 11:1,18; 12:1
the city to Bethany,[q] where he spent the
night.

The Fig Tree Withers

18Early in the morning, as he was on
his way back to the city, he was hungry. 19Seeing a fig tree by the road, he
went up to it but found nothing on it
except leaves. Then he said to it, "May
you never bear fruit again!" Immediate- — 21:19 [r]Isa 34:4; Jer 8:13
ly the tree withered.[r]
20When the disciples saw this, they
were amazed. "How did the fig tree
wither so quickly?" they asked.
21Jesus replied, "I tell you the truth,
if you have faith and do not doubt,[s] — 21:21 [s]Mt 17:20; Lk 17:6; 1Co 13:2; Jas 1:6
not only can you do what was done to
the fig tree, but also you can say to this
mountain, 'Go, throw yourself into the
sea,' and it will be done. 22If you believe, you will receive whatever you ask
for[t] in prayer." — 21:22 [t]Mt 7:7

The Authority of Jesus Questioned

23Jesus entered the temple courts,
and, while he was teaching, the chief
priests and the elders of the people came
to him. "By what authority[u] are you — 21:23 [u]Ac 4:7; 7:27
doing these things?" they asked. "And
who gave you this authority?"
24Jesus replied, "I will also ask you
one question. If you answer me, I will
tell you by what authority I am doing
these things. 25John's baptism—where
did it come from? Was it from heaven,
or from men?"
They discussed it among themselves
and said, "If we say, 'From heaven,' he
will ask, 'Then why didn't you believe
him?' 26But if we say, 'From men'—we
are afraid of the people, for they all
hold that John was a prophet."[v] — 21:26 [v]Mt 11:9; Mk 6:20
27So they answered Jesus, "We don't
know."
Then he said, "Neither will I tell you
by what authority I am doing these
things.

The Parable of the Two Sons

28"What do you think? There was a
man who had two sons. He went to the

[a]*16* Psalm 8:2

first and said, 'Son, go and work today
21:28 [w]ver 33; Mt 20:1 in the vineyard.'[w]
29" 'I will not,' he answered, but later
he changed his mind and went.
30"Then the father went to the other son and said the same thing. He answered, 'I will, sir,' but he did not go.
31"Which of the two did what his father wanted?"

GOODNESS 

ORPHANS OR SONS AND DAUGHTERS

Matthew 21:31

To obey God gives us the right to call ourselves his children. To disobey is to make the world wonder if we are orphans in the universe.

"The first," they answered.
Jesus said to them, "I tell you the
21:31 [x]Lk 7:29 [y]Lk 7:50 truth, the tax collectors[x] and the prostitutes[y] are entering the kingdom of God
ahead of you. 32For John came to you
21:32 [z]Mt 3:1-12 [a]Lk 3:12,13; 7:29 [b]Lk 7:36-50 [c]Lk 7:30 to show you the way of righteousness,[z]
and you did not believe him, but the
tax collectors[a] and the prostitutes[b] did.
And even after you saw this, you did
not repent[c] and believe him.

The Parable of the Tenants

21:33 [d]Ps 80:8 [e]Isa 5:1-7 [f]Mt 25:14,15 33"Listen to another parable: There
was a landowner who planted[d] a vineyard. He put a wall around it, dug a
winepress in it and built a watchtower.[e]
Then he rented the vineyard to some
farmers and went away on a journey.[f]
34When the harvest time approached,
21:34 [g]Mt 22:3 he sent his servants[g] to the tenants to
collect his fruit.
35"The tenants seized his servants;
21:35 [h]2Ch 24:21; Mt 23:34,37; Heb 11:36,37 they beat one, killed another, and stoned
a third.[h] 36Then he sent other servants[i]
to them, more than the first time, and
21:36 [i]Mt 22:4 the tenants treated them the same way.
37Last of all, he sent his son to them.
'They will respect my son,' he said.
38"But when the tenants saw the son,
21:38 [j]Heb 1:2 [k]Mt 12:14 [l]Ps 2:8 they said to each other, 'This is the
heir.[j] Come, let's kill him[k] and take
his inheritance.'[l] 39So they took him
and threw him out of the vineyard and
killed him.
40"Therefore, when the owner of the
vineyard comes, what will he do to
those tenants?"
41"He will bring those wretches to a
wretched end,"[m] they replied, "and he 21:41 [m]Mt 8:11,12 [n]Ac 13:46; 18:6; 28:28
will rent the vineyard to other tenants,[n]
who will give him his share of the crop
at harvest time."
42Jesus said to them, "Have you never read in the Scriptures:

" 'The stone the builders rejected
has become the capstone[a];
the Lord has done this, 21:42 [o]Ps 118:22,23; Ac 4:11; 1Pe 2:7
and it is marvelous in our eyes'[b]?[o]

43"Therefore I tell you that the kingdom of God will be taken away from
you[p] and given to a people who will 21:43 [p]Mt 8:12
produce its fruit. 44He who falls on this
stone will be broken to pieces, but he
on whom it falls will be crushed."[c][q] 21:44 [q]Lk 2:34
45When the chief priests and the
Pharisees heard Jesus' parables, they
knew he was talking about them. 46They
looked for a way to arrest him, but they
were afraid of the crowd because the
people held that he was a prophet.[r] 21:46 [r]ver 11,26

The Parable of the Wedding Banquet

22 Jesus spoke to them again in
parables, saying: 2"The kingdom of heaven is like[s] a king who pre- 22:2 [s]Mt 13:24
pared a wedding banquet for his son.
3He sent his servants[t] to those who had 22:3 [t]Mt 21:34
been invited to the banquet to tell them
to come, but they refused to come.
4"Then he sent some more servants[u] 22:4 [u]Mt 21:36
and said, 'Tell those who have been
invited that I have prepared my dinner: My oxen and fattened cattle have
been butchered, and everything is ready.
Come to the wedding banquet.'
5"But they paid no attention and
went off—one to his field, another to
his business. 6The rest seized his servants, mistreated them and killed them.
7The king was enraged. He sent his
army and destroyed those murderers[v] 22:7 [v]Lk 19:27
and burned their city.
8"Then he said to his servants, 'The
wedding banquet is ready, but those I
invited did not deserve to come. 9Go
to the street corners[w] and invite to the 22:9 [w]Eze 21:21
banquet anyone you find.' 10So the servants went out into the streets and gathered all the people they could find, both
good and bad,[x] and the wedding hall 22:10 [x]Mt 13:47,48
was filled with guests.

[a]*42* Or *cornerstone* [b]*42* Psalm 118:22,23
[c]*44* Some manuscripts do not have verse 44.

11“But when the king came in to
see the guests, he noticed a man there
who was not wearing wedding clothes.
22:12 ʸMt 20:13; 12‘Friend,’[y] he asked, ‘how did you get
26:50 in here without wedding clothes?’ The
man was speechless.
13“Then the king told the attendants,
‘Tie him hand and foot, and throw
him outside, into the darkness, where
22:13 there will be weeping and gnashing of
ᶻMt 8:12 teeth.’[z]
22:14 14“For many are invited, but few are
ᵃRev 17:14 chosen.”[a]

Paying Taxes to Caesar

15Then the Pharisees went out and
laid plans to trap him in his words.
22:16 16They sent their disciples to him along
ᵇMk 3:6 with the Herodians.[b] “Teacher,” they
said, “we know you are a man of integrity and that you teach the way of God
in accordance with the truth. You aren't
swayed by men, because you pay no attention to who they are. 17Tell us then,
22:17 what is your opinion? Is it right to pay
ᶜMt 17:25 taxes[c] to Caesar or not?”
18But Jesus, knowing their evil intent, said, “You hypocrites, why are you
trying to trap me? 19Show me the coin
used for paying the tax.” They brought
him a denarius, 20and he asked them,
“Whose portrait is this? And whose inscription?”
21“Caesar's,” they replied.
Then he said to them, “Give to Cae-
22:21 ᵈRo 13:7 sar what is Caesar's,[d] and to God what
is God's.”
22When they heard this, they were
22:22 amazed. So they left him and went
ᵉMk 12:12 away.[e]

Marriage at the Resurrection

22:23 ᶠAc 4:1 23That same day the Sadducees,[f] who
ᵍAc 23:8; say there is no resurrection,[g] came to
1Co 15:12 him with a question. 24“Teacher,” they
said, “Moses told us that if a man dies
without having children, his brother
must marry the widow and have chil-
22:24 ʰDt 25:5,6 dren for him.[h] 25Now there were seven
brothers among us. The first one mar-
ried and died, and since he had no children, he left his wife to his brother.
26The same thing happened to the second and third brother, right on down
to the seventh. 27Finally, the woman
died. 28Now then, at the resurrection,
whose wife will she be of the seven,
since all of them were married to her?”

29Jesus replied, “You are in error because you do not know the Scriptures[i] 22:29
or the power of God. 30At the resurrec- ⁱJn 20:9
tion people will neither marry nor be
given in marriage;[j] they will be like the 22:30
angels in heaven. 31But about the resur- ʲMt 24:38
rection of the dead—have you not read
what God said to you, 32‘I am the God
of Abraham, the God of Isaac, and the 22:32
God of Jacob’[a]?[k] He is not the God of ᵏEx 3:6;
the dead but of the living.” Ac 7:32
33When the crowds heard this, they 22:33
were astonished at his teaching.[l] ˡMt 7:28

The Greatest Commandment

34Hearing that Jesus had silenced the 22:34
Sadducees,[m] the Pharisees got together. ᵐAc 4:1
35One of them, an expert in the law,[n] 22:35
tested him with this question: 36“Teach- ⁿLk 7:30;
er, which is the greatest commandment 10:25; 11:45;
in the Law?” 14:3
37Jesus replied: “ ‘Love the Lord your 22:37
God with all your heart and with all ᵒDt 6:5
your soul and with all your mind.’[b][o] 22:39
38This is the first and greatest com- ᵖLev 19:18;
mandment. 39And the second is like it: Mt 5:43;
‘Love your neighbor as yourself.’[c][p] 40All 19:19;
the Law and the Prophets hang on these Gal 5:14
two commandments.”[q] 22:40 ᵠMt 7:12

LOVE

LOVE GOD AND CEASE TO WORRY HOW YOU LIVE

Matthew 22:37

Love God and you will love all those whom God loves.

Love God and you will behave as God desires.

Love God and you will guarantee the world your best.

Whose Son Is the Christ?

41While the Pharisees were gathered
together, Jesus asked them, 42“What do
you think about the Christ[d]? Whose
son is he?”
“The son of David,”[r] they replied. 22:42 ʳMt 9:27
43He said to them, “How is it then
that David, speaking by the Spirit, calls
him ‘Lord’? For he says,
44“ ‘The Lord said to my Lord:
“Sit at my right hand

[a] *32* Exodus 3:6 [b] *37* Deut. 6:5 [c] *39* Lev. 19:18
[d] *42* Or *Messiah*

DAY 4 FOUR

▸ GOODNESS AND MY SERVICE TO OTHERS

Matthew 22:34–40

Jesus grieves over a city that knew the commandments. The people of Jerusalem were good at identifying sin, but they were not good at spotting the Messiah. They could tell when God's law was being violated but not when God himself was in their midst.

What is to be said of the Savior's overcoming love? Does he want to destroy these religious purists who were so good at stamping out sin but so poor at loving others? No, Jesus testifies that he would have gathered them together as a hen gathers her chicks under her wings, but they would not come to him (see Matthew 23:37).

A very fine preacher friend of mine said that when he was a boy, his father gave him a new BB gun for his birthday. They lived on a farm, and he took his new rifle into the barnyard for some target practice. Before long an old mother hen with her brood of little chicks came waddling across the barnyard. He confessed that, without giving it much thought, he pointed his BB gun at the old hen and fired. The air-driven pellet caught her in the neck. The old hen's head flopped oddly to the side as she began to die. But, even as she died, she tucked her little ones under her wings, giving them the last bit of her body's warmth. Her confused little ones huddled there, taking in all the warmth she had to give them.

So it was with Jesus. He desired to gather the great city of Jerusalem under his wings, to impart to its inhabitants his last bit of life. But they were stiff-necked and proud, refusing the life he offered.

Jesus, the sinless Son of God, soon died. His goodness was then made available to them through the cross. Because of Jesus' commitment to the moral requirements of God, our own goodness is a possibility that we may share with others.

To begin a study on the topic of Goodness, a Contentment With the Commandments, turn to the home page on page 1233.

until I put your enemies
under your feet."'[a s]

45If then David calls him 'Lord,' how
can he be his son?" 46No one could
say a word in reply, and from that day
on no one dared to ask him any more
questions.[t]

Seven Woes

23 Then Jesus said to the crowds
and to his disciples: 2"The teachers of the law[u] and the Pharisees sit in
Moses' seat. 3So you must obey them
and do everything they tell you. But do
not do what they do, for they do not
practice what they preach. 4They tie
up heavy loads and put them on men's
shoulders, but they themselves are not
willing to lift a finger to move them.[v]
5"Everything they do is done for men
to see:[w] They make their phylacteries[b x]
wide and the tassels on their garments[y]
long; 6they love the place of honor at
banquets and the most important seats
in the synagogues;[z] 7they love to be
greeted in the marketplaces and to have
men call them 'Rabbi.'[a]
8"But you are not to be called 'Rabbi,' for you have only one Master
and you are all brothers. 9And do not
call anyone on earth 'father,' for you
have one Father,[b] and he is in heaven.
10Nor are you to be called 'teacher,'
for you have one Teacher, the Christ.[c]
11The greatest among you will be your
servant.[c] 12For whoever exalts himself
will be humbled, and whoever humbles
himself will be exalted.[d]
13"Woe to you, teachers of the law
and Pharisees, you hypocrites![e] You shut
the kingdom of heaven in men's faces.
You yourselves do not enter, nor will
you let those enter who are trying to.[d f]
15"Woe to you, teachers of the law
and Pharisees, you hypocrites! You travel over land and sea to win a single convert,[g] and when he becomes one, you
make him twice as much a son of hell[h]
as you are.
16"Woe to you, blind guides![i] You
say, 'If anyone swears by the temple,

[a]*44* Psalm 110:1 [b]*5* That is, boxes containing Scripture verses, worn on forehead and arm
[c]*10* Or *Messiah* [d]*13* Some manuscripts *to.* [14]*Woe to you, teachers of the law and Pharisees, you hypocrites! You devour widows' houses and for a show make lengthy prayers. Therefore you will be punished more severely.*

22:44 [s]Ps 110:1; Ac 2:34,35; 1Co 15:25; Heb 1:13; 10:13
22:46 [t]Mk 12:34; Lk 20:40
23:2 [u]Ezr 7:6,25; Ne 8:4
23:4 [v]Lk 11:46; Ac 15:10; Gal 6:13
23:5 [w]Mt 6:1,2, 5,16 [x]Ex 13:9; Dt 6:8 [y]Nu 15:38; Dt 22:12
23:6 [z]Lk 11:43; 14:7; 20:46
23:7 [a]ver 8; Mk 9:5; 10:51; Jn 1:38,49
23:9 [b]Mal 1:6; Mt 7:11
23:11 [c]Mt 20:26; Mk 9:35
23:12 [d]Lk 14:11
23:13 [e]ver 15,23, 25,27,29 [f]Lk 11:52
23:15 [g]Ac 2:11; 6:5; 13:43 [h]Mt 5:22
23:16 [i]ver 24; Mt 15:14

FAITHFULNESS

MAKE CONVERTS TO GOD AND NOT TO YOUR HANG-UPS

Matthew 23:15

Be sure when you say to sinners "Confess your sins and be like Jesus" that you are not really saying "Get religious and be like me."

Convert the world and build the cause.
With day drive back the night.
But give your converts unto God
And never make them proselytes.

it means nothing; but if anyone swears
by the gold of the temple, he is bound
23:16 [j]Mt 5:33-35 by his oath.'[j] 17You blind fools! Which
is greater: the gold, or the temple that
23:17 [k]Ex 30:29 makes the gold sacred?[k] 18You also say,
'If anyone swears by the altar, it means
nothing; but if anyone swears by the
gift on it, he is bound by his oath.'
19You blind men! Which is greater: the
gift, or the altar that makes the gift
23:19 [l]Ex 29:37 sacred?[l] 20Therefore, he who swears by
the altar swears by it and by everything
on it. 21And he who swears by the temple swears by it and by the one who
23:21 [m]1Ki 8:13; dwells[m] in it. 22And he who swears by
Ps 26:8 heaven swears by God's throne and by
23:22 the one who sits on it.[n]
[n]Ps 11:4; 23"Woe to you, teachers of the law
Mt 5:34 and Pharisees, you hypocrites! You give
23:23 [o]Lev 27:30 a tenth[o] of your spices—mint, dill and
[p]Mic 6:8; cummin. But you have neglected the
Lk 11:42 more important matters of the law—
justice, mercy and faithfulness.[p] You
should have practiced the latter, without neglecting the former. 24You blind
23:24 [q]ver 16 guides![q] You strain out a gnat but swallow a camel.
25"Woe to you, teachers of the law
and Pharisees, you hypocrites! You clean
23:25 [r]Mk 7:4 the outside of the cup and dish,[r] but
[s]Lk 11:39 inside they are full of greed and self-
indulgence.[s] 26Blind Pharisee! First clean
the inside of the cup and dish, and then
the outside also will be clean.
27"Woe to you, teachers of the law
and Pharisees, you hypocrites! You are
23:27 [t]Lk 11:44; like whitewashed tombs,[t] which look
Ac 23:3 beautiful on the outside but on the inside are full of dead men's bones and
everything unclean. 28In the same way,
on the outside you appear to people as
righteous but on the inside you are full
of hypocrisy and wickedness.

29"Woe to you, teachers of the law
and Pharisees, you hypocrites! You build
tombs for the prophets[u] and decorate 23:29 [u]Lk 11:47,48
the graves of the righteous. 30And you
say, 'If we had lived in the days of our
forefathers, we would not have taken
part with them in shedding the blood
of the prophets.' 31So you testify against
yourselves that you are the descendants
of those who murdered the prophets.[v] 23:31 [v]Ac 7:51-52
32Fill up, then, the measure[w] of the sin
of your forefathers! 23:32 [w]1Th 2:16
33"You snakes! You brood of vipers![x] 23:33 [x]Mt 3:7;
How will you escape being condemned 12:34
to hell?[y] 34Therefore I am sending you [y]Mt 5:22
prophets and wise men and teachers. 23:34
Some of them you will kill and crucify;[z] [z]2Ch 36:15,
others you will flog in your synagogues[a] 16; Lk 11:49
and pursue from town to town.[b] 35And [a]Mt 10:17 [b]Mt 10:23
so upon you will come all the righ-
teous blood that has been shed on earth, 23:35
from the blood of righteous Abel[c] to the [c]Ge 4:8;
blood of Zechariah son of Berekiah,[d] Heb 11:4 [d]Zec 1:1
whom you murdered between the tem- [e]2Ch 24:21
ple and the altar.[e] 36I tell you the truth, 23:36
all this will come upon this genera- [f]Mt 10:23;
tion.[f] 24:34
37"O Jerusalem, Jerusalem, you who
kill the prophets and stone those sent to
you,[g] how often I have longed to gather 23:37 [g]2Ch 24:21;
your children together, as a hen gath- Mt 5:12
ers her chicks under her wings, but you
were not willing. 38Look, your house is
left to you desolate.[h] 39For I tell you, 23:38 [h]1Ki 9:7,8; Jer 22:5
you will not see me again until you say,
'Blessed is he who comes in the name 23:39 [i]Ps 118:26;
of the Lord.'[a]"[i] Mt 21:9

Signs of the End of the Age

24 Jesus left the temple and was
walking away when his disciples
came up to him to call his attention
to its buildings. 2"Do you see all these
things?" he asked. "I tell you the truth,
not one stone here will be left on anoth-
er;[j] every one will be thrown down." 24:2 [j]Lk 19:44
3As Jesus was sitting on the Mount of 24:3
Olives,[k] the disciples came to him pri- [k]Mt 21:1
vately. "Tell us," they said, "when will
this happen, and what will be the sign
of your coming and of the end of the
age?"
4Jesus answered: "Watch out that
no one deceives you. 5For many will
come in my name, claiming, 'I am
the Christ,'[b] and will deceive many.[l] 24:5 [l]ver 11,23,24; 1Jn 2:18

[a]*39* Psalm 118:26 [b]*5* Or *Messiah;* also in verse 23

6You will hear of wars and rumors of
wars, but see to it that you are not
alarmed. Such things must happen, but
the end is still to come. 7Nation will rise
against nation, and kingdom against
kingdom.[m] There will be famines[n] and
earthquakes in various places. 8All these
are the beginning of birth pains.
9"Then you will be handed over to be
persecuted[o] and put to death,[p] and you
will be hated by all nations because of
me. 10At that time many will turn away
from the faith and will betray and hate
each other, 11and many false prophets[q]
will appear and deceive many people.
12Because of the increase of wickedness,
the love of most will grow cold, 13but
he who stands firm to the end will be
saved.[r] 14And this gospel of the kingdom[s] will be preached in the whole
world[t] as a testimony to all nations, and
then the end will come.
15"So when you see standing in the
holy place[u] 'the abomination that causes
desolation,'[a][v] spoken of through the
prophet Daniel—let the reader understand— 16then let those who are in
Judea flee to the mountains. 17Let no
one on the roof of his house[w] go down
to take anything out of the house. 18Let
no one in the field go back to get his
cloak. 19How dreadful it will be in those
days for pregnant women and nursing
mothers![x] 20Pray that your flight will
not take place in winter or on the Sabbath. 21For then there will be great distress, unequaled from the beginning
of the world until now—and never to
be equaled again.[y] 22If those days had
not been cut short, no one would survive, but for the sake of the elect[z] those
days will be shortened. 23At that time if
anyone says to you, 'Look, here is the
Christ!' or, 'There he is!' do not believe
it.[a] 24For false Christs and false prophets
will appear and perform great signs and
miracles[b] to deceive even the elect—if
that were possible. 25See, I have told
you ahead of time.
26"So if anyone tells you, 'There he
is, out in the desert,' do not go out;
or, 'Here he is, in the inner rooms,' do
not believe it. 27For as lightning[c] that
comes from the east is visible even in
the west, so will be the coming of the
Son of Man.[d] 28Wherever there is a carcass, there the vultures will gather.[e]
29"Immediately after the distress of
those days

[a]*15* Daniel 9:27; 11:31; 12:11

24:7 [m]Isa 19:2 [n]Ac 11:28
24:9 [o]Mt 10:17 [p]Jn 16:2
24:11 [q]Mt 7:15
24:13 [r]Mt 10:22
24:14 [s]Mt 4:23 [t]Ro 10:18; Col 1:6,23; Lk 2:1; 4:5; Ac 11:28; 17:6; Rev 3:10; 16:14
24:15 [u]Ac 6:13 [v]Da 9:27; 11:31; 12:11
24:17 [w]1Sa 9:25; Mt 10:27; Lk 12:3; Ac 10:9
24:19 [x]Lk 23:29
24:21 [y]Da 12:1; Joel 2:2
24:22 [z]ver 24,31
24:23 [a]Lk 17:23; 1:8
24:24 [b]2Th 2:9-11; Rev 13:13
24:27 [c]Lk 17:24 [d]Mt 8:20
24:28 [e]Lk 17:37

DAY 3 THREE

Faithfulness and My Relationship With Christ

Matthew 24:9–13

We Christians in the West have gotten used to cheap grace. To be a Christian is often to become a part of a prosperous gathering. How safe it is in our day and age to be a Christian. Our attendance at church is never called under threat. But Jesus in this passage of Scripture seems to be saying that we are to be faithful even when our witness is not popular—even when it is dangerous, we are to be openly Christian. Jesus was about to become a martyr himself, so he calls us to be faithful even when our faithfulness will be costly:

When we are to be "handed over to be persecuted and put to death . . ."
When we are "hated by all nations . . ."
When people "will turn away from the faith and will betray and hate each other . . ."
When "many false prophets will appear and deceive many . . ."

In all of these circumstances, we are to be faithful in our relationship with Christ.

But notice the reward of our faithfulness: "He who stands firm to the end will be saved." This passage contains the typical New Testament word for "saved," yet it does not refer to the normal state of salvation. No, this is salvation with a capital *S*. It is that state of final being, face-to-face for eternity with Christ.

The word *saved* sometimes refers to our initial encounter with Christ but at other times indicates an ongoing state of grace in Jesus. But this use of the word *saved* refers to that unending union with Jesus in which we, who have longed to see him and know him with no cloud between us, stand at last in his presence forever. This salvation indeed is the plum of our faithfulness to be plucked from the tree of our obedience.

To begin a study on the topic of God's Blessing on Faithfulness, turn to the home page on page 16.

“ ‘the sun will be darkened,
and the moon will not give its light;
the stars will fall from the sky,
and the heavenly bodies will be shaken.’[a][f]

30“At that time the sign of the Son of Man will appear in the sky, and all the nations of the earth will mourn. They will see the Son of Man coming on the clouds of the sky,[g] with power and great glory. 31And he will send his angels[h] with a loud trumpet call,[i] and they will gather his elect from the four winds, from one end of the heavens to the other.

PATIENCE

THE UNKNOWN HOUR

Matthew 24:36

There is a clock with no hands, no numbers on the dial, no gearbox.
Only God can read its blank face.
When that great clock has reached the hour of glory,
The ages all shall meet.
When will it happen?
Who can say?
God keeps his watch in his pocket.

32“Now learn this lesson from the fig tree: As soon as its twigs get tender and its leaves come out, you know that summer is near. 33Even so, when you see all these things, you know that it[b] is near, right at the door.[j] 34I tell you the truth, this generation[c] will certainly not pass away until all these things have happened.[k] 35Heaven and earth will pass away, but my words will never pass away.[l]

The Day and Hour Unknown

36“No one knows about that day or hour, not even the angels in heaven, nor the Son,[d] but only the Father.[m] 37As it was in the days of Noah,[n] so it will be at the coming of the Son of Man. 38For in the days before the flood, people were eating and drinking, marrying and giving in marriage,[o] up to the day Noah entered the ark; 39and they knew nothing about what would happen until the flood came and took them all away. That is how it will be at the coming of the Son of Man. 40Two men will be in the field; one will be taken and the other left.[p] 41Two women will be grinding with a hand mill; one will be taken and the other left.[q]

42“Therefore keep watch, because you do not know on what day your Lord will come.[r] 43But understand this: If the owner of the house had known at what time of night the thief was coming,[s] he would have kept watch and would not have let his house be broken into. 44So you also must be ready,[t] because the Son of Man will come at an hour when you do not expect him.

45“Who then is the faithful and wise servant,[u] whom the master has put in charge of the servants in his household to give them their food at the proper time? 46It will be good for that servant whose master finds him doing so when he returns.[v] 47I tell you the truth, he will put him in charge of all his possessions.[w] 48But suppose that servant is wicked and says to himself, ‘My master is staying away a long time,’ 49and he then begins to beat his fellow servants and to eat and drink with drunkards.[x] 50The master of that servant will come on a day when he does not expect him and at an hour he is not aware of. 51He will cut him to pieces and assign him a place with the hypocrites, where there will be weeping and gnashing of teeth.[y]

The Parable of the Ten Virgins

25 “At that time the kingdom of heaven will be like[z] ten virgins who took their lamps[a] and went out to meet the bridegroom.[b] 2Five of them were foolish and five were wise.[c] 3The foolish ones took their lamps but did not take any oil with them. 4The wise, however, took oil in jars along with their lamps. 5The bridegroom was a long time in coming, and they all became drowsy and fell asleep.[d]

6“At midnight the cry rang out: ‘Here’s the bridegroom! Come out to meet him!’

7“Then all the virgins woke up and trimmed their lamps. 8The foolish ones said to the wise, ‘Give us some of your oil; our lamps are going out.’[e]

9“ ‘No,’ they replied, ‘there may not

24:29 [f]Isa 13:10; 34:4; Eze 32:7; Joel 2:10,31; Zep 1:15; Rev 6:12,13; 8:12
24:30 [g]Da 7:13; Rev 1:7
24:31 [h]Mt 13:41 [i]Isa 27:13; Zec 9:14; 1Co 15:52; 1Th 4:16; Rev 8:2; 10:7; 11:15
24:33 [j]Jas 5:9
24:34 [k]Mt 16:28; 23:36
24:35 [l]Mt 5:18
24:36 [m]Ac 1:7
24:37 [n]Ge 6:5; 7:6-23
24:38 [o]Mt 22:30
24:40 [p]Lk 17:34
24:41 [q]Lk 17:35
24:42 [r]Mt 25:13; Lk 12:40
24:43 [s]Lk 12:39
24:44 [t]1Th 5:6
24:45 [u]Mt 25:21,23
24:46 [v]Rev 16:15
24:47 [w]Mt 25:21,23
24:49 [x]Lk 21:34
24:51 [y]Mt 8:12
25:1 [z]Mt 13:24 [a]Lk 12:35-38; Ac 20:8; Rev 4:5 [b]Rev 19:7; 21:2
25:2 [c]Mt 24:45
25:5 [d]1Th 5:6
25:8 [e]Lk 12:35

[a] *29* Isaiah 13:10; 34:4 [b] *33* Or *he* [c] *34* Or *race*
[d] *36* Some manuscripts do not have *nor the Son.*

PATIENCE

THE MIDNIGHT CRY

Matthew 25:6

There's a cry that comes but once.
Be ready lest that great shout catch you unprepared.
Keep your lamps trimmed;
Supply yourself with extra oil.
Wait,
For only those with ready light
Shall follow in his retinue.

be enough for both us and you. Instead,
go to those who sell oil and buy some
for yourselves.'
10"But while they were on their way
to buy the oil, the bridegroom arrived.
The virgins who were ready went in
25:10 [f]Rev 19:9 — with him to the wedding banquet.[f] And
the door was shut.
11"Later the others also came. 'Sir!
Sir!' they said. 'Open the door for us!'
12"But he replied, 'I tell you the truth,
I don't know you.'
25:13 [g]Mt 24:42,44; Mk 13:35; Lk 12:40 — 13"Therefore keep watch, because you
do not know the day or the hour.[g]

The Parable of the Talents

25:14 [h]Mt 21:33; Lk 19:12 — 14"Again, it will be like a man going
on a journey,[h] who called his servants
and entrusted his property to them.
15To one he gave five talents[a] of money, to another two talents, and to another one talent, each according to his
25:15 [i]Mt 18:24,25 — ability.[i] Then he went on his journey.
16The man who had received the five
talents went at once and put his money
to work and gained five more. 17So also,
the one with the two talents gained two
more. 18But the man who had received
the one talent went off, dug a hole in
the ground and hid his master's money.
19"After a long time the master of
those servants returned and settled ac-
25:19 [j]Mt 18:23 — counts with them.[j] 20The man who
had received the five talents brought
the other five. 'Master,' he said, 'you
entrusted me with five talents. See, I
have gained five more.'
21"His master replied, 'Well done,
good and faithful servant! You have
been faithful with a few things; I will
25:21 [k]ver 23; Mt 24:45,47; Lk 16:10 — put you in charge of many things.[k]
Come and share your master's happi-
ness!'
22"The man with the two talents also
came. 'Master,' he said, 'you entrusted
me with two talents; see, I have gained
two more.'
23"His master replied, 'Well done,
good and faithful servant! You have
been faithful with a few things; I will
put you in charge of many things.[l] — 25:23 [l]ver 21
Come and share your master's happi-
ness!'
24"Then the man who had received
the one talent came. 'Master,' he said,
'I knew that you are a hard man, harvesting where you have not sown and
gathering where you have not scattered
seed. 25So I was afraid and went out
and hid your talent in the ground. See,
here is what belongs to you.'
26"His master replied, 'You wicked,
lazy servant! So you knew that I harvest where I have not sown and gather
where I have not scattered seed? 27Well
then, you should have put my money
on deposit with the bankers, so that
when I returned I would have received
it back with interest.
28" 'Take the talent from him and
give it to the one who has the ten talents. 29For everyone who has will be
given more, and he will have an abundance. Whoever does not have, even
what he has will be taken from him.[m] — 25:29 [m]Mt 13:12; Mk 4:25; Lk 8:18; 19:26
30And throw that worthless servant out-
side, into the darkness, where there will
be weeping and gnashing of teeth.'[n] — 25:30 [n]Mt 8:12

The Sheep and the Goats

31"When the Son of Man comes[o] in — 25:31 [o]Mt 16:27; Lk 17:30
his glory, and all the angels with him, he
will sit on his throne[p] in heavenly glory. — [p]Mt 19:28
32All the nations will be gathered before
him, and he will separate[q] the people — 25:32 [q]Mal 3:18
one from another as a shepherd sepa- — [r]Eze 34:17,20
rates the sheep from the goats.[r] 33He
will put the sheep on his right and the
goats on his left.
34"Then the King will say to those on — 25:34 [s]Mt 3:2; 5:3,10,19; 19:14; Ac 20:32; 1Co 15:50; Gal 5:21; Jas 2:5
his right, 'Come, you who are blessed
by my Father; take your inheritance, the
kingdom[s] prepared for you since the — [t]Heb 4:3; 9:26; Rev 13:8; 17:8
creation of the world.[t] 35For I was hun-
gry and you gave me something to eat,
I was thirsty and you gave me some- — 25:35 [u]Job 31:32; Isa 58:7; Eze 18:7; Heb 13:2
thing to drink, I was a stranger and you
invited me in,[u] 36I needed clothes and

[a]*15* A talent was worth more than a thousand dollars.

DAY 4 FOUR

▸ FAITHFULNESS AND MY SERVICE TO OTHERS

Matthew 25:31–40

This passage seems in some ways at odds with grace. Here, eternity is offered at first glance to those who have been faithful in serving others. We know from the rest of the New Testament that grace is the free gift of God, given with no strings attached. But this teaching of Jesus suggests that those who know they are heaven bound are so delighted that they cannot help but busy themselves with obedience.

There is a sweet naïveté among the followers of God in this passage. They seem surprised that their commendation should be so wholehearted and overwhelming: "Whenever did we see you hungry or thirsty, a stranger, or naked, or sick, or in prison and minister to you?"

When we minister to any human need, we write the name of Jesus on the very forehead of the person we help. But the ministry we offer is registered in the bookkeeping of heaven as deeds we have done for Jesus alone.

I was in Calcutta at the time of Mother Teresa's death and was among those westerners allowed to visit her as she lay in state. One thing I will never forget: her bare feet protruded from underneath the flag of India. Seeing this tiny woman of such great commitment, her bare feet reminded me of her years of walking into the ghettos of a dismal place and turning even Calcutta into a "City of Joy." I remember her teaching that, when anyone attended to a dying parish, she or he attended the body of Christ himself. Where did she get such an idea? From this very Scripture.

When we meet anyone vile and diseased, we must not think, "poor soul—vile and diseased!" Instead we must pray, "So, dear Christ, it is you. I will attend to you, for I have received heaven from you already, and I refuse to let any of your children endure this human hell without my ministry."

We never cry over any human hurt here on earth without our tears being registered in heaven.

To begin a study on the topic of God's Blessing on Faithfulness, turn to the home page on page 16.

you clothed me,[v] I was sick and you
looked after me,[w] I was in prison and
you came to visit me.'[x]
37"Then the righteous will answer
him, 'Lord, when did we see you hungry and feed you, or thirsty and give
you something to drink? 38When did
we see you a stranger and invite you
in, or needing clothes and clothe you?
39When did we see you sick or in prison
and go to visit you?'
40"The King will reply, 'I tell you the
truth, whatever you did for one of the
least of these brothers of mine, you did
for me.'[y]
41"Then he will say to those on his
left, 'Depart from me,[z] you who are
cursed, into the eternal fire[a] prepared
for the devil and his angels.[b] 42For I was
hungry and you gave me nothing to
eat, I was thirsty and you gave me nothing to drink, 43I was a stranger and you
did not invite me in, I needed clothes
and you did not clothe me, I was sick
and in prison and you did not look after me.'
44"They also will answer, 'Lord, when
did we see you hungry or thirsty or a
stranger or needing clothes or sick or in
prison, and did not help you?'
45"He will reply, 'I tell you the truth,
whatever you did not do for one of the
least of these, you did not do for me.'[c]
46"Then they will go away to eternal
punishment, but the righteous to eternal life."[d][e]

The Plot Against Jesus

26 When Jesus had finished saying
all these things,[f] he said to his
disciples, 2"As you know, the Passover[g]
is two days away—and the Son of Man
will be handed over to be crucified."
3Then the chief priests and the elders of the people assembled[h] in the
palace of the high priest, whose name
was Caiaphas,[i] 4and they plotted to arrest Jesus in some sly way and kill him.[j]
5"But not during the Feast," they said,
"or there may be a riot[k] among the people."

Jesus Anointed at Bethany

6While Jesus was in Bethany[l] in the
home of a man known as Simon the
Leper, 7a woman came to him with an
alabaster jar of very expensive perfume,

25:36 [v]Isa 58:7; Eze 18:7; Jas 2:15,16 [w]Jas 1:27 [x]2Ti 1:16
25:40 [y]Pr 19:17; Mt 10:40,42; Heb 6:10; 13:2
25:41 [z]Mt 7:23 [a]Isa 66:24; Mt 3:12; ; 5:22; Mk 9:43,48; Lk 3:17; Jude 7 [b]2Pe 2:4
25:45 [c]Pr 14:31; 17:5
25:46 [d]Mt 19:29; Jn 3:15,16,36; 17:2,3; Ro 2:7; Gal 6:8; 5:11,13,20 [e]Da 12:2; Jn 5:29; Ac 24:15; Ro 2:7,8; Gal 6:8 [f]Mt 7:28
26:2 [g]Jn 11:55; 13:1
26:3 [h]Ps 2:2 [i]ver 57; Jn 11:47-53; 18:13,14, 24,28
26:4 [j]Mt 12:14
26:5 [k]Mt 27:24
26:6 [l]Mt 21:17

which she poured on his head as he was
reclining at the table.
8When the disciples saw this, they
were indignant. "Why this waste?" they
asked. 9"This perfume could have been
sold at a high price and the money given to the poor."
10Aware of this, Jesus said to them,
"Why are you bothering this woman?
She has done a beautiful thing to me.
11The poor you will always have with
you,[m] but you will not always have me.
12When she poured this perfume on
my body, she did it to prepare me for
burial.[n] 13I tell you the truth, wherever
this gospel is preached throughout the
world, what she has done will also be
told, in memory of her."

26:11 [m]Dt 15:11
26:12 [n]Jn 19:40

DAY 5 FIVE

Goodness and Its Place in My Personal Worship

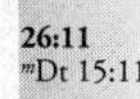

Matthew 26:6–13

Jesus announced to those who would have rebuked this woman that her anointing was a hallmark of history. Whenever anyone spoke of her in years to come, they would remember her not as a wasteful woman who frivolously gave away ministry funds that might have been given to the poor, but rather as an adoring worshiper anointing her Savior at his burial preparation. How rich her gift! She gave the perfume as a precious symbol of her love for the Savior whose own life bore the sweet savor of atonement.

The parallel account in Mark 14:3–9 adds the detail that she broke the jar and then anointed Jesus. Watchman Nee says that our brokenness always releases the sweet aroma of our approval before God. Here was a woman who had no doubt known brokenness. Those who have cried with tears that only God can heal have found that their neediness elicited the pity of God—the healing of God—the outrageous love of God.

Our very brokenness carries the fragrance of God. I have known many Christians who struggled with and later died of cancer. Their prayer struggles, attended by feelings of helpless hopelessness, produced in them a glorious brokenness. And this brokenness ushered them at last into heaven, where its sweet aroma hushed the angels.

The woman who anointed Jesus was good—her goodness was implanted in her life by Jesus himself. But when the goodness that Jesus put there was released, it was yielded up as an offering of love. Every ounce of goodness our Lord places in our lives is passed on for the benefit of those we serve. In the end we must adore him; it is a wonderful pilgrimage from our need to his exaltation.

To begin a study on the topic of Goodness Implanted Into Our Lives Through Christ, turn to the home page on page 1484.

Faithfulness

The Memorial Perfume

Matthew 26:13

She dumped the essence of millions of flowers
Upon the head of Jesus.
It happened long ago,
But the odor sweet that spilled from her obedient heart
Can still be smelled
Wherever air is rank and hellish.
Blessed are those who build memorials with flowers,
For theirs is a legacy perfumed with adoration.

Judas Agrees to Betray Jesus

14Then one of the Twelve—the one
called Judas Iscariot[o]—went to the chief
priests 15and asked, "What are you willing to give me if I hand him over to
you?" So they counted out for him thirty silver coins.[p] 16From then on Judas
watched for an opportunity to hand
him over.

26:14 [o]ver 25,47; Mt 10:4
26:15 [p]Ex 21:32; Zec 11:12

The Lord's Supper

17On the first day of the Feast of Unleavened Bread,[q] the disciples came to
Jesus and asked, "Where do you want
us to make preparations for you to eat
the Passover?"
18He replied, "Go into the city to a
certain man and tell him, 'The Teacher
says: My appointed time[r] is near. I am
going to celebrate the Passover with my
disciples at your house.'" 19So the disciples did as Jesus had directed them and
prepared the Passover.
20When evening came, Jesus was reclining at the table with the Twelve.

26:17 [q]Ex 12:18-20
26:18 [r]Jn 7:6,8,30; 12:23; 13:1; 17:1

21And while they were eating, he said,
“I tell you the truth, one of you will be-
26:21 [s]Lk 22:21-23; Jn 13:21
tray me.”[s]
22They were very sad and began to
say to him one after the other, “Surely
not I, Lord?”
23Jesus replied, “The one who has
dipped his hand into the bowl with me
26:23 [t]Ps 41:9; Jn 13:18
will betray me.[t] 24The Son of Man will
go just as it is written about him.[u] But
26:24 [u]Isa 53; Da 9:26; Mk 9:12; Lk 24:25-27, 46; Ac 17:2,3; 26:22,23
woe to that man who betrays the Son
of Man! It would be better for him if he
had not been born.”
25Then Judas, the one who would betray him, said, “Surely not I, Rabbi?”[v]
Jesus answered, “Yes, it is you.”[a]
26:25 [v]Mt 23:7
26While they were eating, Jesus took
26:26 [w]Mt 14:19; 1Co 10:16
bread, gave thanks and broke it,[w] and
gave it to his disciples, saying, “Take
and eat; this is my body.”
27Then he took the cup, gave thanks
and offered it to them, saying, “Drink
from it, all of you. 28This is my blood
26:28 [x]Ex 24:6-8; Heb 9:20 [y]Mt 20:28; Mk 1:4
of the[b] covenant,[x] which is poured out
for many for the forgiveness of sins.[y]
29I tell you, I will not drink of this fruit
of the vine from now on until that day
26:29 [z]Ac 10:41
when I drink it anew with you[z] in my
Father's kingdom.”
30When they had sung a hymn, they
26:30 [a]Mt 21:1; Mk 14:26
went out to the Mount of Olives.[a]

Jesus Predicts Peter's Denial

31Then Jesus told them, “This very
26:31 [b]Mt 11:6 [c]Zec 13:7; Jn 16:32
night you will all fall away on account
of me,[b] for it is written:

“ ‘I will strike the shepherd,
and the sheep of the flock will be
scattered.’[c][c]

26:32 [d]Mt 28:7, 10,16
32But after I have risen, I will go ahead
of you into Galilee.”[d]
33Peter replied, “Even if all fall away
on account of you, I never will.”
34“I tell you the truth,” Jesus answered, “this very night, before the
rooster crows, you will disown me three
26:34 [e]ver 75; Jn 13:38
times.”[e]
35But Peter declared, “Even if I have
26:35 [f]Jn 13:37
to die with you,[f] I will never disown
you.” And all the other disciples said
the same.

Gethsemane

36Then Jesus went with his disciples
to a place called Gethsemane, and he
said to them, “Sit here while I go over
there and pray.” 37He took Peter and
the two sons of Zebedee[g] along with
26:37 [g]Mt 4:21
him, and he began to be sorrowful and
troubled. 38Then he said to them, “My
26:38 [h]Jn 12:27 [i]ver 40,41
soul is overwhelmed with sorrow[h] to
the point of death. Stay here and keep
watch with me.”[i]
39Going a little farther, he fell with
his face to the ground and prayed, “My
26:39 [j]Mt 20:22 [k]ver 42; Ps 40:6-8; Isa 50:5; Jn 5:30; 6:38
Father, if it is possible, may this cup[j] be
taken from me. Yet not as I will, but as
you will.”[k]
40Then he returned to his disciples
and found them sleeping. “Could you
26:40 [l]ver 38
men not keep watch with me[l] for one
hour?” he asked Peter. 41“Watch and
pray so that you will not fall into
26:41 [m]Mt 6:13
temptation.[m] The spirit is willing, but
the body is weak.”
42He went away a second time and
prayed, “My Father, if it is not possible
for this cup to be taken away unless I
drink it, may your will be done.”
43When he came back, he again
found them sleeping, because their eyes
were heavy. 44So he left them and went
away once more and prayed the third
time, saying the same thing.
45Then he returned to the disciples
and said to them, “Are you still sleeping
26:45 [n]ver 18
and resting? Look, the hour[n] is near,
and the Son of Man is betrayed into the
hands of sinners. 46Rise, let us go! Here
comes my betrayer!”

Jesus Arrested

47While he was still speaking, Judas,
one of the Twelve, arrived. With him
was a large crowd armed with swords
and clubs, sent from the chief priests
and the elders of the people. 48Now
the betrayer had arranged a signal with
them: “The one I kiss is the man; arrest
him.” 49Going at once to Jesus, Judas
26:49 [o]ver 25
said, “Greetings, Rabbi!”[o] and kissed
him.
50Jesus replied, “Friend,[p] do what
26:50 [p]Mt 20:13; 22:12
you came for.”[d]
Then the men stepped forward, seized
Jesus and arrested him. 51With that,
one of Jesus' companions reached for
26:51 [q]Lk 22:36,38 [r]Jn 18:10
his sword,[q] drew it out and struck the
servant of the high priest, cutting off
his ear.[r]
52“Put your sword back in its place,”

[a]25 Or *“You yourself have said it”* [b]28 Some manuscripts *the new* [c]31 Zech. 13:7 [d]50 Or *“Friend, why have you come?”*

Jesus said to him, "for all who draw the sword will die by the sword.[s] 53Do you think I cannot call on my Father, and he will at once put at my disposal more than twelve legions of angels?[t] 54But how then would the Scriptures be fulfilled[u] that say it must happen in this way?"

55At that time Jesus said to the crowd, "Am I leading a rebellion, that you have come out with swords and clubs to capture me? Every day I sat in the temple courts teaching,[v] and you did not arrest me. 56But this has all taken place that the writings of the prophets might be fulfilled."[w] Then all the disciples deserted him and fled.

26:52 [s]Ge 9:6; Rev 13:10
26:53 [t]2Ki 6:17; Da 7:10; Mt 4:11
26:54 [u]ver 24
26:55 [v]Mk 12:35; Lk 21:37; Jn 7:14,28; 18:20
26:56 [w]ver 24

Before the Sanhedrin

57Those who had arrested Jesus took him to Caiaphas,[x] the high priest, where the teachers of the law and the elders had assembled. 58But Peter followed him at a distance, right up to the courtyard of the high priest.[y] He entered and sat down with the guards[z] to see the outcome.

59The chief priests and the whole Sanhedrin[a] were looking for false evidence against Jesus so that they could put him to death. 60But they did not find any, though many false witnesses[b] came forward.

Finally two[c] came forward 61and declared, "This fellow said, 'I am able to destroy the temple of God and rebuild it in three days.' "[d]

62Then the high priest stood up and said to Jesus, "Are you not going to answer? What is this testimony that these men are bringing against you?" 63But Jesus remained silent.[e]

The high priest said to him, "I charge you under oath[f] by the living God:[g] Tell us if you are the Christ,[a] the Son of God."

64"Yes, it is as you say," Jesus replied. "But I say to all of you: In the future you will see the Son of Man sitting at the right hand of the Mighty One[h] and coming on the clouds of heaven."[i]

65Then the high priest tore his clothes[j] and said, "He has spoken blasphemy! Why do we need any more witnesses? Look, now you have heard the blasphemy. 66What do you think?"

"He is worthy of death,"[k] they answered.

26:57 [x]ver 3
26:58 [y]Jn 18:15 [z]Jn 7:32, 45,46
26:59 [a]Mt 5:22
26:60 [b]Ps 27:12; 35:11; Ac 6:13 [c]Dt 19:15
26:61 [d]Jn 2:19
26:63 [e]Mt 27:12,14 [f]Lev 5:1 [g]Mt 16:16
26:64 [h]Ps 110:1 [i]Da 7:13; Rev 1:7
26:65 [j]Mk 14:63
26:66 [k]Lev 24:16; Jn 19:7

67Then they spit in his face and struck him with their fists.[l] Others slapped him 68and said, "Prophesy to us, Christ. Who hit you?"[m]

26:67 [l]Mt 16:21; 27:30
26:68 [m]Lk 22:63-65

Peter Disowns Jesus

69Now Peter was sitting out in the courtyard, and a servant girl came to him. "You also were with Jesus of Galilee," she said.

70But he denied it before them all. "I don't know what you're talking about," he said.

71Then he went out to the gateway, where another girl saw him and said to the people there, "This fellow was with Jesus of Nazareth."

72He denied it again, with an oath: "I don't know the man!"

73After a little while, those standing there went up to Peter and said, "Surely you are one of them, for your accent gives you away."

74Then he began to call down curses on himself and he swore to them, "I don't know the man!"

Immediately a rooster crowed. 75Then Peter remembered the word Jesus had spoken: "Before the rooster crows, you will disown me three times."[n] And he went outside and wept bitterly.

26:75 [n]ver 34; Jn 13:38

Judas Hangs Himself

27 Early in the morning, all the chief priests and the elders of the people came to the decision to put Jesus to death.[o] 2They bound him, led him away and handed him over[p] to Pilate, the governor.[q]

3When Judas, who had betrayed him,[r] saw that Jesus was condemned, he was seized with remorse and returned the thirty silver coins[s] to the chief priests and the elders. 4"I have sinned," he said, "for I have betrayed innocent blood."

"What is that to us?" they replied. "That's your responsibility."[t]

5So Judas threw the money into the temple[u] and left. Then he went away and hanged himself.[v]

6The chief priests picked up the coins and said, "It is against the law to put this into the treasury, since it is blood money." 7So they decided to use the money to buy the potter's field as a burial place for foreigners. 8That is why

27:1 [o]Mt 12:14; Mk 15:1; Lk 22:66
27:2 [p]Mt 20:19 [q]Mk 15:1; Lk 13:1; Ac 3:13; 1Ti 6:13
27:3 [r]Mt 10:4 [s]Mt 26:14,15
27:4 [t]ver 24
27:5 [u]Lk 1:9,21 [v]Ac 1:18

[a]63 Or *Messiah*; also in verse 68

27:8 [w]Ac 1:19 it has been called the Field of Blood[w] to
this day. 9Then what was spoken by Jer-
27:9 [x]Mt 1:22 emiah the prophet was fulfilled:[x] "They
took the thirty silver coins, the price set
on him by the people of Israel, 10and
27:10 [y]Zec 11:12, 13; Jer 32:6-9 they used them to buy the potter's field,
as the Lord commanded me."[a][y]

Jesus Before Pilate

11Meanwhile Jesus stood before the
governor, and the governor asked him,
27:11 [z]Mt 2:2 "Are you the king of the Jews?"[z]
"Yes, it is as you say," Jesus replied.
12When he was accused by the chief
priests and the elders, he gave no
27:12 [a]Mt 26:63; Mk 14:61; Jn 19:9 answer.[a] 13Then Pilate asked him,
"Don't you hear the testimony they
are bringing against you?"[b] 14But Jesus
27:13 [b]Mt 26:62 made no reply,[c] not even to a single
charge—to the great amazement of the
27:14 [c]Mk 14:61 governor.
15Now it was the governor's custom
27:15 [d]Jn 18:39 at the Feast to release a prisoner[d] chosen by the crowd. 16At that time they
had a notorious prisoner, called Barabbas. 17So when the crowd had gathered,
Pilate asked them, "Which one do you
27:17 [e]ver 22; Mt 1:16 want me to release to you: Barabbas, or
Jesus who is called Christ?"[e] 18For he
knew it was out of envy that they had
handed Jesus over to him.
19While Pilate was sitting on the
27:19 [f]Jn 19:13 [g]ver 24 [h]Ge 20:6; Nu 12:6; 1Ki 3:5; Job 33:14-16; Mt 1:20; 2:12,13,19,22 judge's seat,[f] his wife sent him this message: "Don't have anything to do with
that innocent[g] man, for I have suffered
a great deal today in a dream[h] because
of him."
20But the chief priests and the elders
27:20 [i]Ac 3:14 persuaded the crowd to ask for Barabbas and to have Jesus executed.[i]
21"Which of the two do you want me
to release to you?" asked the governor.
"Barabbas," they answered.
22"What shall I do, then, with Jesus
27:22 [j]Mt 1:16 who is called Christ?"[j] Pilate asked.
They all answered, "Crucify him!"
23"Why? What crime has he committed?" asked Pilate.
But they shouted all the louder, "Crucify him!"
24When Pilate saw that he was get-
27:24 [k]Mt 26:5 [l]Ps 26:6 [m]Dt 21:6-8 [n]ver 4 ting nowhere, but that instead an uproar[k] was starting, he took water and
washed his hands[l] in front of the crowd.
"I am innocent of this man's blood,"[m]
he said. "It is your responsibility!"[n]
27:25 [o]Jos 2:19; Ac 5:28 25All the people answered, "Let his
blood be on us and on our children!"[o]

26Then he released Barabbas to them.
But he had Jesus flogged,[p] and handed 27:26 [p]Isa 53:5; Jn 19:1
him over to be crucified.

The Soldiers Mock Jesus

27Then the governor's soldiers took
Jesus into the Praetorium[q] and gathered 27:27 [q]Jn 18:28,33; 19:9
the whole company of soldiers around
him. 28They stripped him and put a
scarlet robe on him,[r] 29and then twist- 27:28 [r]Jn 19:2
ed together a crown of thorns and set
it on his head. They put a staff in his
right hand and knelt in front of him
and mocked him. "Hail, king of the
Jews!" they said.[s] 30They spit on him, 27:29 [s]Isa 53:3; Jn 19:2,3
and took the staff and struck him on
the head again and again.[t] 31After they 27:30 [t]Mt 16:21; 26:67
had mocked him, they took off the robe
and put his own clothes on him. Then 27:31 [u]Isa 53:7
they led him away to crucify him.[u]

PEACE

THE STIGMATA

Matthew 27:31

We must not worry overmuch whether our lives should be lost. After all, Jesus did not ponder some easy plan to save the world that would keep his own flesh free of lesions. He purchased us with wounds of ardent grace.

The Crucifixion

32As they were going out,[v] they met 27:32 [v]Heb 13:12
a man from Cyrene,[w] named Simon, [w]Ac 2:10; 6:9; 11:20; 13:1
and they forced him to carry the cross.[x] [x]Mk 15:21; Lk 23:26
33They came to a place called Gol-
gotha (which means The Place of the
Skull).[y] 34There they offered Jesus wine 27:33 [y]Jn 19:17
to drink, mixed with gall;[z] but after tast-
ing it, he refused to drink it. 35When 27:34 [z]ver 48; Ps 69:21
they had crucified him, they divided up
his clothes by casting lots.[b][a] 36And sit- 27:35 [a]Ps 22:18
ting down, they kept watch[b] over him
there. 37Above his head they placed the 27:36 [b]ver 54
written charge against him: THIS IS
JESUS, THE KING OF THE JEWS. 38Two
robbers were crucified with him,[c] one 27:38 [c]Isa 53:12
on his right and one on his left. 39Those
who passed by hurled insults at him, 27:39 [d]Ps 22:7; 109:25; La 2:15
shaking their heads[d] 40and saying, "You
who are going to destroy the temple

[a] *10* See Zech. 11:12,13; Jer. 19:1-13; 32:6-9.
[b] *35* A few late manuscripts *lots that the word spoken by the prophet might be fulfilled: "They divided my garments among themselves and cast lots for my clothing"* (Psalm 22:18)

and build it in three days,[e] save yourself![f] Come down from the cross, if you are the Son of God!"[g]

41 In the same way the chief priests, the teachers of the law and the elders mocked him. 42 "He saved others," they said, "but he can't save himself! He's the King of Israel![h] Let him come down now from the cross, and we will believe[i] in him. 43 He trusts in God. Let God rescue him[j] now if he wants him, for he said, 'I am the Son of God.'" 44 In the same way the robbers who were crucified with him also heaped insults on him.

The Death of Jesus

45 From the sixth hour until the ninth hour darkness[k] came over all the land. 46 About the ninth hour Jesus cried out in a loud voice, *"Eloi, Eloi,*[a] *lama sabachthani?"*—which means, "My God, my God, why have you forsaken me?"[b][l]

47 When some of those standing there heard this, they said, "He's calling Elijah."

48 Immediately one of them ran and got a sponge. He filled it with wine vinegar,[m] put it on a stick, and offered it to Jesus to drink. 49 The rest said, "Now leave him alone. Let's see if Elijah comes to save him."

50 And when Jesus had cried out again in a loud voice, he gave up his spirit.[n]

51 At that moment the curtain of the temple[o] was torn in two from top to bottom. The earth shook and the rocks split.[p] 52 The tombs broke open and the bodies of many holy people who had died were raised to life. 53 They came out of the tombs, and after Jesus' resurrection they went into the holy city[q] and appeared to many people.

54 When the centurion and those with him who were guarding[r] Jesus saw the earthquake and all that had happened, they were terrified, and exclaimed, "Surely he was the Son[c] of God!"[s]

55 Many women were there, watching from a distance. They had followed Jesus from Galilee to care for his needs.[t] 56 Among them were Mary Magdalene, Mary the mother of James and Joses, and the mother of Zebedee's sons.[u]

The Burial of Jesus

57 As evening approached, there came a rich man from Arimathea, named Joseph, who had himself become a disciple of Jesus. 58 Going to Pilate, he asked for Jesus' body, and Pilate ordered that it be given to him. 59 Joseph took the body, wrapped it in a clean linen cloth, 60 and placed it in his own new tomb[v] that he had cut out of the rock. He rolled a big stone in front of the entrance to the tomb and went away. 61 Mary Magdalene and the other Mary were sitting there opposite the tomb.

The Guard at the Tomb

62 The next day, the one after Preparation Day, the chief priests and the Pharisees went to Pilate. 63 "Sir," they said, "we remember that while he was still alive that deceiver said, 'After three days I will rise again.'[w] 64 So give the order for the tomb to be made secure until the third day. Otherwise, his disciples may come and steal the body and tell the people that he has been raised from the dead. This last deception will be worse than the first."

65 "Take a guard,"[x] Pilate answered. "Go, make the tomb as secure as you know how." 66 So they went and made the tomb secure by putting a seal[y] on the stone[z] and posting the guard.[a]

The Resurrection

28 After the Sabbath, at dawn on the first day of the week, Mary Magdalene and the other Mary[b] went to look at the tomb.

2 There was a violent earthquake,[c] for an angel[d] of the Lord came down from heaven and, going to the tomb, rolled back the stone and sat on it. 3 His appearance was like lightning, and his clothes were white as snow.[e] 4 The guards were so afraid of him that they shook and became like dead men.

5 The angel said to the women, "Do not be afraid,[f] for I know that you are looking for Jesus, who was crucified. 6 He is not here; he has risen, just as he said.[g] Come and see the place where he lay. 7 Then go quickly and tell his disciples: 'He has risen from the dead and is going ahead of you into Galilee.[h] There you will see him.' Now I have told you."

8 So the women hurried away from

27:40 [e]Mt 26:61; Jn 2:19 [f]ver 42 [g]Mt 4:3,6
27:42 [h]Jn 1:49; 12:13 [i]Jn 3:15
27:43 [j]Ps 22:8
27:45 [k]Am 8:9
27:46 [l]Ps 22:1
27:48 [m]ver 34; Ps 69:21
27:50 [n]Jn 19:30
27:51 [o]Ex 26:31-33; Heb 9:3,8 [p]ver 54
27:53 [q]Mt 4:5
27:54 [r]ver 36 [s]Mt 4:3; 17:5
27:55 [t]Lk 8:2,3
27:56 [u]Mk 15:47; Lk 24:10; Jn 19:25
27:60 [v]Mt 27:66; 28:2; Mk 16:4
27:63 [w]Mt 16:21
27:65 [x]ver 66; Mt 28:11
27:66 [y]Da 6:17 [z]ver 60; Mt 28:2 [a]Mt 28:11
28:1 [b]Mt 27:56
28:2 [c]Mt 27:51 [d]Jn 20:12
28:3 [e]Da 10:6; Mk 9:3; Jn 20:12
28:5 [f]ver 10; Mt 14:27
28:6 [g]Mt 16:21
28:7 [h]ver 10,16; Mt 26:32

[a]46 Some manuscripts *Eli, Eli* [b]46 Psalm 22:1
[c]54 Or *a son*

the tomb, afraid yet filled with joy, and
ran to tell his disciples. 9Suddenly Jesus
28:9 [i]Jn 20:14-18 met them.[i] "Greetings," he said. They
came to him, clasped his feet and wor-
28:10 [j]Jn 20:17; Ro 8:29; Heb 2:11-13, 17 shiped him. 10Then Jesus said to them,
"Do not be afraid. Go and tell my
brothers[j] to go to Galilee; there they
will see me."

JOY

GO QUICKLY AND TELL

Matthew 28:7

Good News must be told with joy,
For those who mouth it with a lack of
passion
Make it seem a lie.

The Guards' Report

11While the women were on their
28:11 [k]Mt 27:65,66 way, some of the guards[k] went into the
city and reported to the chief priests
everything that had happened. 12When
the chief priests had met with the elders and devised a plan, they gave the
soldiers a large sum of money, 13telling
them, "You are to say, 'His disciples
came during the night and stole him
away while we were asleep.' 14If this re-
28:14 [l]Mt 27:2 port gets to the governor,[l] we will satisfy him and keep you out of trouble."
15So the soldiers took the money and
did as they were instructed. And this
story has been widely circulated among
28:16 [m]ver 7,10; Mt 26:32 the Jews to this very day.

The Great Commission

28:18 [n]Da 7:13,14; Lk 10:22; Jn 3:35; 17:2; 1Co 15:27; Eph 1:20-22; Php 2:9,10 16Then the eleven disciples went to
Galilee, to the mountain where Jesus
had told them to go.[m] 17When they
saw him, they worshiped him; but
some doubted. 18Then Jesus came to
28:19 [o]Mk 16:15, 16; Lk 24:47; Ac 1:8; 14:21 [p]Ac 2:38; 8:16; Ro 6:3,4 them and said, "All authority in heaven
and on earth has been given to me.[n]
19Therefore go and make disciples of all
nations,[o] baptizing them in[a] the name
of the Father and of the Son and of
28:20 [q]Ac 2:42 [r]Mt 18:20; Ac 18:10 [s]Mt 13:39 the Holy Spirit,[p] 20and teaching[q] them
to obey everything I have commanded
you. And surely I am with you[r] always,
to the very end of the age."[s]

DAY 3 THREE

LOVE AND MY RELATIONSHIP WITH CHRIST

Matthew 28:18–20

My relationship with Christ is secure. He has convinced me that his love for me was real on that day when he died. I never would have known about that day except that Matthew, as well as others, wrote about it in the wonderful Good News biography of Christ. There are several things that make me trust Matthew and the other Gospel writers. First of all, most of the Gospel writers died as martyrs. They died sticking to their stories.

Second, there is another incontrovertible witness to their truth. They all died far from where they had met Jesus. One must ask, "What would cause Matthew and Mark and John to die so far from their homelands? What was it that caused them to abandon dusty, provincial little Galilee?" These men were under an odd compulsion that impelled them to venture far from home and to tell the Good News until they were arrested and martyred. Obviously, they had met in Jesus someone who occupied the core of their belief system and motivated them to leave their families and businesses, never to look back with regret.

God's compassion for the world can be the only reason for their courage and hope. Somehow Jesus managed to forge their bravado into true courage and send them halfway around the world to die as a consequence for telling their life-transforming stories. If Jesus could forge these ordinary souls into such nomadic transformers, I can only conclude that Matthew 28:18–20 must be my calling as well. His will, his call, his commission are mine.

To begin a study on the topic of Love, God's Passion for His World, turn to the home page on page 1253.

[a]*19* Or *into*; see Acts 8:16; 19:5; Romans 6:3; 1 Cor. 1:13; 10:2 and Gal. 3:27.

MARK

AUTHORSHIP AND DATE

Mark

Probably between A.D. 55 and A.D. 65

KEY THEMES

Mark was probably the first Gospel to be written, and it was also likely one of the first books of the New Testament to be written. It is a fast-moving account of the life of Christ, focusing mainly on his journeys and miracles and paying less attention to his teachings than Luke or Matthew. Mark 4 does tell of Jesus' parables, but other teachings are given only briefly and at random. Still, the book is highly significant.

The book of Mark was written to help the Roman world understand who Jesus was and demonstrate beyond a shadow of a doubt that he was the Son of God. While Mark omitted the birth narratives included in Matthew and Luke, his book, like theirs, falls into three divisions:

1. The opening ministry of Jesus (see 1:1–13)
2. His message and ministry (see 1:14—13:37)
3. The final events of Jesus' death and resurrection (see 14:1—16:20).

FRUIT OF THE SPIRIT IN MARK

Love: A woman whose sins had been forgiven came to Jesus and—out of gratitude for all that Jesus had forgiven her—offered her thanks by pouring perfume on Jesus' feet. Some who saw this anointing as a huge waste of money scolded the poor woman. Jesus rebuked them and reminded them that money is only money and that a lavish gratitude of heart should always accompany forgiveness (see 14:1–9).

Peace: Jesus is the Lord of storms (see 4:39). He rebuked the winds, and the world was at peace. All that he worked on the Sea of Galilee he will also work in our hearts. "Quiet! Be still!" (4:39). These words are still a promise for today: Wherever Christ is, the gales that rip and tear our world to tatters are not welcome.

Patience: Sometimes the healing of God takes time. Some who are blind can see the instant they hear the Savior say, "Be healed!" For others, sight comes in two steps. At first they see only people as trees walking (see 8:24); later they receive a second touch and see all things correctly. The distance between step one and step two is called patience.

Kindness: Kindness results from an act of loving your neighbor just as you would love yourself (see 12:33–34). Just as you would never intentionally inflict trouble on yourself, you should also keep your neighbor from pain.

Goodness: "Which is lawful on the Sabbath: to do good or to do evil?" (3:4). Goodness avoids all tedious requirements to keep the Sabbath holy. The Sabbath cannot help but be kept holy when people stop trying to do nothing for one day a week and choose, instead, to do good every day of the week.

Faithfulness: Jesus alleged that the family of God consists of those who do the Father's will. Those who obey all that God says have made God their Father and God's Son their brother (see 3:35).

Gentleness: With a gentle admonition, Jesus said, "Don't be afraid; just believe" (5:36). How kind is the advice that says, "Don't be afraid." This advice is usually not strong enough to make us bold, but if the Counselor who advised us sticks by us with his hand upon our shoulder, then we receive gentleness and are no longer afraid.

Self-Control: Self-denial is self-control. It is difficult to be self-indulgent while lugging around a huge cross. Cross-bearing keeps us from living the capricious life (see 8:34). It causes us to constantly remember that Jesus once traveled the *Via Dolorosa* (road to the cross) with us in mind. Surely we can learn to travel our own *Via Vitae* (road of life) with him in mind.

John the Baptist Prepares the Way

1 The beginning of the gospel about
1:1 [a]Mt 4:3 Jesus Christ, the Son of God.[a] [a]

2 It is written in Isaiah the prophet:
1:2 "I will send my messenger ahead
[b]Mal 3:1; of you,
Mt 11:10; who will prepare your way"[b] [b]—
Lk 7:27 3 "a voice of one calling in the desert,
1:3 'Prepare the way for the Lord,
[c]Isa 40:3; Jn 1:23 make straight paths for him.' "[c] [c]

PATIENCE

A TRUMPET IN THE DESERT

Mark 1:3

John was God's rustic fanfare—a trumpet in the wilderness of the Jordan.
When this cornet had sounded, a thousand years of time stood at attention
And history stretched its neck toward God's redeeming future.
Sure enough, there, in the dim light of this desert, shone a lamp.
A young Messiah could be seen walking calmly toward a busy city.

1:4 4 And so John[d] came, baptizing in the
[d]Mt 3:1 desert region and preaching a baptism
[e]Ac 13:24
[f]Lk 1:77 of repentance[e] for the forgiveness of
sins.[f] 5 The whole Judean countryside
and all the people of Jerusalem went
out to him. Confessing their sins, they
were baptized by him in the Jordan River.
6 John wore clothing made of camel's
1:6 el's hair, with a leather belt around his
[g]Lev 11:22 waist, and he ate locusts[g] and wild honey.
7 And this was his message: "After
me will come one more powerful than
1:7 I, the thongs of whose sandals I am
[h]Ac 13:25 not worthy to stoop down and untie.[h]
1:8 8 I baptize you with[d] water, but he will
[i]Isa 44:3; Joel 2:28; Ac 1:5; 2:4; 11:16; 19:4-6 baptize you with the Holy Spirit."[i]

The Baptism and Temptation of Jesus

9 At that time Jesus came from Naz-
1:9 [j]Mt 2:23 areth[j] in Galilee and was baptized by
John in the Jordan. 10 As Jesus was com-
ing up out of the water, he saw heaven
1:10 being torn open and the Spirit de-
[k]Jn 1:32 scending on him like a dove.[k] 11 And a
voice came from heaven: "You are my
1:11 [l]Mt 3:17 Son,[l] whom I love; with you I am well
pleased."
12 At once the Spirit sent him out into
the desert, 13 and he was in the desert
forty days, being tempted by Satan.[m] 1:13 [m]Mt 4:10
He was with the wild animals, and an-
gels attended him.

The Calling of the First Disciples

14 After John was put in prison, Jesus
went into Galilee,[n] proclaiming the 1:14 [n]Mt 4:12
good news of God.[o] 15 "The time has [o]Mt 4:23
come,"[p] he said. "The kingdom of God 1:15 [p]Gal 4:4;
is near. Repent and believe the good Eph 1:10
news!"[q] [q]Ac 20:21
16 As Jesus walked beside the Sea of
Galilee, he saw Simon and his brother
Andrew casting a net into the lake, for
they were fishermen. 17 "Come, follow
me," Jesus said, "and I will make you
fishers of men." 18 At once they left their
nets and followed him.
19 When he had gone a little farther,
he saw James son of Zebedee and his
brother John in a boat, preparing their
nets. 20 Without delay he called them,
and they left their father Zebedee in
the boat with the hired men and followed him.

Jesus Drives Out an Evil Spirit

21 They went to Capernaum, and
when the Sabbath came, Jesus went 1:21
into the synagogue and began to teach.[r] [r]Mt 4:23;
22 The people were amazed at his teach- Mk 10:1
ing, because he taught them as one who
had authority, not as the teachers of the
law.[s] 23 Just then a man in their syna- 1:22
gogue who was possessed by an evil[e] [s]Mt 7:28,29
spirit cried out, 24 "What do you want
with us,[t] Jesus of Nazareth?[u] Have you 1:24 [t]Mt 8:29
come to destroy us? I know who you [u]Mt 2:23; Lk 24:19;
are—the Holy One of God!"[v] Ac 24:5
25 "Be quiet!" said Jesus sternly. [v]Lk 1:35;
"Come out of him!"[w] 26 The evil spirit Jn 6:69;
shook the man violently and came out Ac 3:14
of him with a shriek.[x] 1:25 [w]ver 34
27 The people were all so amazed[y] that
they asked each other, "What is this? A 1:26 [x]Mk 9:20
new teaching—and with authority! He
even gives orders to evil spirits and they 1:27 [y]Mk 10:24,32
obey him." 28 News about him spread
quickly over the whole region[z] of Gali- 1:28 [z]Mt 9:26
lee.

Jesus Heals Many

29 As soon as they left the synagogue,[a] 1:29
they went with James and John to the [a]ver 21,23

[a]*1* Some manuscripts do not have *the Son of God.*
[b]*2* Mal. 3:1 [c]*3* Isaiah 40:3 [d]*8* Or *in*
[e]*23* Greek *unclean*; also in verses 26 and 27

home of Simon and Andrew. 30 Simon's
mother-in-law was in bed with a fever,
and they told Jesus about her. 31 So he
went to her, took her hand and helped
1:31 [b]Lk 7:14 her up.[b] The fever left her and she began to wait on them.

DAY 3 THREE

Goodness and My Relationship With Christ

Mark 1:21–22

The authority of Christ is the authority we all long for when we seek religious affiliation. After all, there are so many false teachers claiming to have the last word from God. They all seem so sincere. They all seem to be well educated. They all seem to know the truth. We all hunger for someone to say convincingly to us, "This is the absolute truth. This you may depend on." Jesus could do just that!

But where did Jesus get this authority? Well, he was sinless (see 2 Corinthians 5:21, 1 Peter 2:22 and 1 John 3:5). To be free of any error would certainly improve your chances of teaching the dependable truth. But there is even more to it than this. Jesus himself was a teacher steeped in the Word of God. From his knowledge of the Word came his incontrovertible authority.

Jesus knew the Word, but, more than that, he was the Word—the Word made flesh (see John 1:1,14). When God wanted to speak in the past, he spoke through the prophets, but when he wanted to speak to our day, he spoke to us through his Son, "whom he appointed heir of all things, and through whom he made the universe. The Son is the radiance of God's glory and the exact representation of his being, sustaining all things by his powerful word" (Hebrews 1:2–3).

Now if Jesus, being the eternal Word, teaches that the written Word is important for our instruction, perhaps we should allow the written Word to form the basis of our goodness. It is by knowing this written Word that our relationship with Christ, the eternal Word, is made sure.

To begin a study on the topic of Goodness, the Virtue of the Written Word of God, turn to the home page on page 918.

32 That evening after sunset the people brought to Jesus all the sick and
demon-possessed.[c] 33 The whole town 1:32 [c]Mt 4:24
gathered at the door, 34 and Jesus healed
many who had various diseases.[d] He 1:34 [d]Mt 4:23
also drove out many demons, but he [e]Mk 3:12; Ac 16:17,18
would not let the demons speak be-
cause they knew who he was.[e]

Jesus Prays in a Solitary Place

35 Very early in the morning, while
it was still dark, Jesus got up, left the
house and went off to a solitary place,
where he prayed.[f] 36 Simon and his com- 1:35 [f]Lk 3:21
panions went to look for him, 37 and
when they found him, they exclaimed:
"Everyone is looking for you!"
38 Jesus replied, "Let us go somewhere
else—to the nearby villages—so I can
preach there also. That is why I have
come."[g] 39 So he traveled throughout 1:38 [g]Isa 61:1
Galilee, preaching in their synagogues[h] 1:39 [h]Mt 4:23
and driving out demons.[i] [i]Mt 4:24

A Man With Leprosy

40 A man with leprosy[a] came to him
and begged him on his knees,[j] "If you 1:40 [j]Mk 10:17
are willing, you can make me clean."
41 Filled with compassion, Jesus
reached out his hand and touched the
man. "I am willing," he said. "Be clean!"
42 Immediately the leprosy left him and
he was cured.
43 Jesus sent him away at once with
a strong warning: 44 "See that you don't
tell this to anyone.[k] But go, show your- 1:44 [k]Mt 8:4
self to the priest[l] and offer the sacri- [l]Lev 13:49
fices that Moses commanded for your [m]Lev 14:1-32
cleansing,[m] as a testimony to them."
45 Instead he went out and began to
talk freely, spreading the news. As a
result, Jesus could no longer enter a
town openly but stayed outside in lone-
ly places.[n] Yet the people still came to 1:45 [n]Lk 5:15,16
him from everywhere.[o] [o]Mk 2:13; Lk 5:17; Jn 6:2

Jesus Heals a Paralytic

2 A few days later, when Jesus again
entered Capernaum, the people
heard that he had come home. 2 So
many[p] gathered that there was no room 2:1 [p]ver 13; Mk 1:45
left, not even outside the door, and
he preached the word to them. 3 Some
men came, bringing to him a paralytic,[q] 2:3 [q]Mt 4:24
carried by four of them. 4 Since they

[a]*40* The Greek word was used for various diseases affecting the skin—not necessarily leprosy.

could not get him to Jesus because of
the crowd, they made an opening in
the roof above Jesus and, after digging
through it, lowered the mat the paralyzed man was lying on. 5When Jesus
saw their faith, he said to the paralytic,
2:5 “Son, your sins are forgiven.”[r]
[r]Lk 7:48 6Now some teachers of the law were
sitting there, thinking to themselves,
7“Why does this fellow talk like that?
2:7 He's blaspheming! Who can forgive sins
[s]Isa 43:25 but God alone?”[s]
8Immediately Jesus knew in his spirit that this was what they were thinking in their hearts, and he said to them,
“Why are you thinking these things?
9Which is easier: to say to the paralytic, ‘Your sins are forgiven,’ or to say,
‘Get up, take your mat and walk’? 10But
2:10 that you may know that the Son of
[t]Mt 8:20 Man[t] has authority on earth to forgive
sins...” He said to the paralytic, 11“I
tell you, get up, take your mat and go
home.” 12He got up, took his mat and
walked out in full view of them all.
2:12 This amazed everyone and they praised
[u]Mt 9:8 [v]Mt 9:33 God,[u] saying, “We have never seen anything like this!”[v]

▸ JOY

AMAZEMENT ISSUES FORTH PRAISE

Mark 2:11

To behold the Christ and the miracles he performs
Brings stupefaction first.
But as the wonder dies, a song erupts.
And from the music flows healing and enlightenment,
And then a kingdom.

The Calling of Levi

2:13 13Once again Jesus went out beside
[w]Mk 1:45; Lk 5:15; Jn 6:2 the lake. A large crowd came to him,[w]
and he began to teach them. 14As
he walked along, he saw Levi son of
2:14 Alphaeus sitting at the tax collector's
[x]Mt 4:19 booth. “Follow me,”[x] Jesus told him,
and Levi got up and followed him.
15While Jesus was having dinner at
Levi's house, many tax collectors and
“sinners” were eating with him and his
disciples, for there were many who fol-
2:16 lowed him. 16When the teachers of the
[y]Ac 23:9 law who were Pharisees[y] saw him eating
with the “sinners” and tax collectors,
they asked his disciples: “Why does he 2:16
eat with tax collectors and ‘sinners’?”[z] [z]Mt 9:11

▸ GOODNESS

A RABBI'S COMPANY

Mark 2:16

Jesus often ate with “sinners.” But the Pharisees did not. At the least, they never ate with people who sinned more than they did. A lot of assessment went into their dinner invitations. All kinds of pride erupts when more attention is given to how good the guests are, rather than to how good the food is. Measuring other people's sins is a neurotic effort. It works up quite an appetite.

17On hearing this, Jesus said to them,
“It is not the healthy who need a doctor, but the sick. I have not come to call
the righteous, but sinners.”[a] 2:17

Jesus Questioned About Fasting [a]Lk 19:10; 1Ti 1:15

18Now John's disciples and the Phari- 2:18
sees were fasting.[b] Some people came [b]Mt 6:16-18; Ac 13:2
and asked Jesus, “How is it that John's
disciples and the disciples of the Pharisees are fasting, but yours are not?”
19Jesus answered, “How can the
guests of the bridegroom fast while he
is with them? They cannot, so long as
they have him with them. 20But the
time will come when the bridegroom 2:20
will be taken from them,[c] and on that [c]Lk 17:22
day they will fast.
21“No one sews a patch of unshrunk
cloth on an old garment. If he does, the
new piece will pull away from the old,
making the tear worse. 22And no one
pours new wine into old wineskins. If
he does, the wine will burst the skins,
and both the wine and the wineskins
will be ruined. No, he pours new wine
into new wineskins.”

Lord of the Sabbath

23One Sabbath Jesus was going
through the grainfields, and as his disciples walked along, they began to pick
some heads of grain.[d] 24The Pharisees 2:23 [d]Dt 23:25
said to him, “Look, why are they doing
what is unlawful on the Sabbath?”[e] 2:24 [e]Mt 12:2
25He answered, “Have you never read
what David did when he and his companions were hungry and in need? 26In 2:26
the days of Abiathar the high priest,[f] [f]1Ch 24:6; 2Sa 8:17

he entered the house of God and ate
the consecrated bread, which is lawful
2:26 [g]Lev 24:5-9 only for priests to eat.[g] And he also gave
[h]1Sa 21:1-6 some to his companions."[h]
2:27 27Then he said to them, "The Sab-
[i]Ex 23:12; Dt 5:14 bath was made for man,[i] not man for
[j]Col 2:16 the Sabbath.[j] 28So the Son of Man[k] is
2:28 Lord even of the Sabbath."
[k]Mt 8:20 3 Another time he went into the
3:1 synagogue,[l] and a man with a shriv-
[l]Mt 4:23; Mk 1:21 eled hand was there. 2Some of them
were looking for a reason to accuse Je-
3:2 [m]Mt 12:10 sus, so they watched him closely[m] to see
[n]Lk 14:1 if he would heal him on the Sabbath.[n]
3Jesus said to the man with the shriveled hand, "Stand up in front of everyone."
4Then Jesus asked them, "Which is
lawful on the Sabbath: to do good or to
do evil, to save life or to kill?" But they
remained silent.

▸ LOVE

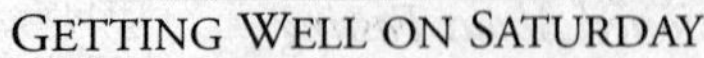

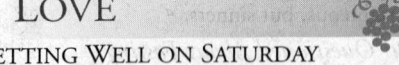

GETTING WELL ON SATURDAY

Mark 3:4

Was it better on the Sabbath for Jesus to rest up or to heal his sick friends? It's a question that only the well debate.

5He looked around at them in anger
and, deeply distressed at their stubborn hearts, said to the man, "Stretch
out your hand." He stretched it out,
and his hand was completely restored.
6Then the Pharisees went out and be-
3:6 [o]Mt 22:16; Mk 12:13 gan to plot with the Herodians[o] how
[p]Mt 12:14 they might kill Jesus.[p]

Crowds Follow Jesus

7Jesus withdrew with his disciples to
the lake, and a large crowd from Gali-
3:7 [q]Mt 4:25 lee followed.[q] 8When they heard all he
was doing, many people came to him
from Judea, Jerusalem, Idumea, and the
regions across the Jordan and around
3:8 [r]Mt 11:21 Tyre and Sidon.[r] 9Because of the crowd
he told his disciples to have a small
boat ready for him, to keep the people
3:10 [s]Mt 4:23 from crowding him. 10For he had healed
[t]Mt 9:20 many,[s] so that those with diseases were
3:11 pushing forward to touch him.[t]
[u]Mt 4:3; Mk 1:23,24 11Whenever the evil[a] spirits saw him,
they fell down before him and cried
3:12 [v]Mt 8:4; out, "You are the Son of God."[u] 12But
Mk 1:24,25, 34; he gave them strict orders not to tell
Ac 16:17,18 who he was.[v]

▸ FAITHFULNESS

FAITHFULNESS AND FOREIGN CEMETERIES

Mark 3:16–19

When Jesus called the Twelve, they had no idea where God's odyssey would take them. Nor could they guess that their obedience would require them to live and die in places far from Galilee. Be careful when you call Christ "Lord." The word is dangerous. For many, it demands a willingness to die away from home.

The Appointing of the Twelve Apostles

13Jesus went up on a mountainside
and called to him those he wanted,
and they came to him.[w] 14He appoint- 3:13 [w]Mt 5:1
ed twelve—designating them apos-
tles[b][x]—that they might be with him 3:14 [x]Mk 6:30
and that he might send them out to
preach 15and to have authority to drive
out demons.[y] 16These are the twelve he 3:15 [y]Mt 10:1
appointed: Simon (to whom he gave
the name Peter);[z] 17James son of Zebe- 3:16 [z]Jn 1:42
dee and his brother John (to them he
gave the name Boanerges, which means
Sons of Thunder); 18Andrew, Philip,
Bartholomew, Matthew, Thomas, James
son of Alphaeus, Thaddaeus, Simon the
Zealot 19and Judas Iscariot, who betrayed him.

Jesus and Beelzebub

20Then Jesus entered a house, and
again a crowd gathered,[a] so that he and 3:20 [a]ver 7
his disciples were not even able to eat.[b] [b]Mk 6:31
21When his family heard about this,
they went to take charge of him, for
they said, "He is out of his mind."[c] 3:21 [c]Jn 10:20; Ac 26:24
22And the teachers of the law who
came down from Jerusalem[d] said, "He is 3:22 [d]Mt 15:1
possessed by Beelzebub[c]![e] By the prince [e]Mt 10:25; 11:18; 12:24;
of demons he is driving out demons."[f] Jn 7:20; 8:48,52;
23So Jesus called them and spoke to 10:20
them in parables:[g] "How can Satan[h] [f]Mt 9:34
drive out Satan? 24If a kingdom is di-
vided against itself, that kingdom can- 3:23 [g]Mk 4:2
not stand. 25If a house is divided against [h]Mt 4:10
itself, that house cannot stand. 26And
if Satan opposes himself and is divided,

[a]*11* Greek *unclean;* also in verse 30 [b]*14* Some manuscripts do not have *designating them apostles.*
[c]*22* Greek *Beezeboul* or *Beelzeboul*

he cannot stand; his end has come. 27In
fact, no one can enter a strong man's
house and carry off his possessions unless he first ties up the strong man.
3:27 [i]Isa 49:24,25 Then he can rob his house.[i] 28I tell you
the truth, all the sins and blasphemies
of men will be forgiven them. 29But
whoever blasphemes against the Holy
Spirit will never be forgiven; he is guilty
3:29 [j]Mt 12:31,32; Lk 12:10 of an eternal sin."[j]
30He said this because they were say-
ing, "He has an evil spirit."

Jesus' Mother and Brothers

3:31 [k]ver 21 31Then Jesus' mother and brothers
arrived.[k] Standing outside, they sent
someone in to call him. 32A crowd was
sitting around him, and they told him,
"Your mother and brothers are outside
looking for you."

KINDNESS

THE FAMILY OF GOD

Mark 3:33

Jesus' family, apparently thinking he was out of his mind, came to take him home.

"Yoo-hoo! Jesus! It's us—your family."

"Then who are these?" asked Jesus, pointing to the crowd.

"These are my family now: the poor, the dispossessed, the unredeemed,

The philosophically decrepit, the outcast leper, the homeless and the broken,

The caste unlovely, the untouchable, the despised . . .

For these I have Good News. I am their brother; God is their Father.

The family will is written; they will inherit palaces of light.

Go home to your poor Nazareth and envy this new family."

33"Who are my mother and my
brothers?" he asked.
34Then he looked at those seated in
a circle around him and said, "Here are
my mother and my brothers! 35Who-
ever does God's will is my brother and
sister and mother."

The Parable of the Sower

4:1 [l]Mk 2:13; 3:7 4 Again Jesus began to teach by the
lake.[l] The crowd that gathered
around him was so large that he got
into a boat and sat in it out on the
lake, while all the people were along the
shore at the water's edge. 2He taught
them many things by parables,[m] and 4:2 [m]ver 11; Mk 3:23
in his teaching said: 3"Listen! A farmer
went out to sow his seed.[n] 4As he was 4:3 [n]ver 26
scattering the seed, some fell along the
path, and the birds came and ate it up.
5Some fell on rocky places, where it
did not have much soil. It sprang up
quickly, because the soil was shallow.
6But when the sun came up, the plants
were scorched, and they withered because they had no root. 7Other seed
fell among thorns, which grew up and
choked the plants, so that they did not
bear grain. 8Still other seed fell on good
soil. It came up, grew and produced a
crop, multiplying thirty, sixty, or even a
hundred times."[o] 4:8 [o]Jn 15:5; Col 1:6
9Then Jesus said, "He who has ears
to hear, let him hear."[p] 4:9 [p]ver 23; Mt 11:15
10When he was alone, the Twelve and
the others around him asked him about
the parables. 11He told them, "The se-
cret of the kingdom of God[q] has been 4:11 [q]Mt 3:2
given to you. But to those on the out- [r]1Co 5:12,13; Col 4:5; 1Th 4:12; 1Ti 3:7
side[r] everything is said in parables 12so
that, [s]Isa 6:9,10; Mt 13:13-15

" 'they may be ever seeing but never
perceiving,
and ever hearing but never
understanding;
otherwise they might turn and be
forgiven!'[a]"[s]

13Then Jesus said to them, "Don't
you understand this parable? How then
will you understand any parable? 14The
farmer sows the word.[t] 15Some people 4:14 [t]Mk 16:20; Lk 1:2; Ac 4:31; 8:4; 16:6; 17:11; Php 1:14
are like seed along the path, where the
word is sown. As soon as they hear it,
Satan[u] comes and takes away the word
that was sown in them. 16Others, like 4:15 [u]Mt 4:10
seed sown on rocky places, hear the
word and at once receive it with joy.
17But since they have no root, they last
only a short time. When trouble or persecution comes because of the word,
they quickly fall away. 18Still others,
like seed sown among thorns, hear the
word; 19but the worries of this life, the 4:19 [v]Mt 19:23; 1Ti 6:9,10,17; 1Jn 2:15-17
deceitfulness of wealth[v] and the desires
for other things come in and choke the
word, making it unfruitful. 20Others,
like seed sown on good soil, hear the
word, accept it, and produce a crop—

[a] *12* Isaiah 6:9,10

thirty, sixty or even a hundred times
what was sown."

A Lamp on a Stand

21He said to them, "Do you bring in
a lamp to put it under a bowl or a bed?
4:21 [w]Mt 5:15 Instead, don't you put it on its stand?[w]
22For whatever is hidden is meant to
be disclosed, and whatever is concealed
is meant to be brought out into the
4:22 [x]Jer 16:17; Mt 10:26; Lk 8:17; 12:2 open.[x] 23If anyone has ears to hear, let
him hear."[y]
24"Consider carefully what you hear,"
4:23 [y]ver 9; Mt 11:15 he continued. "With the measure you
use, it will be measured to you—and
4:24 [z]Mt 7:2; Lk 6:38 even more.[z] 25Whoever has will be giv-
en more; whoever does not have, even
4:25 [a]Mt 13:12; 25:29 what he has will be taken from him."[a]

The Parable of the Growing Seed

4:26 [b]Mt 13:24 26He also said, "This is what the
kingdom of God is like.[b] A man scatters seed on the ground. 27Night and
day, whether he sleeps or gets up, the
seed sprouts and grows, though he does
not know how. 28All by itself the soil
produces grain—first the stalk, then the
head, then the full kernel in the head.
29As soon as the grain is ripe, he puts
the sickle to it, because the harvest has
4:29 [c]Rev 14:15 come."[c]

The Parable of the Mustard Seed

30Again he said, "What shall we say
4:30 [d]Mt 13:24 the kingdom of God is like,[d] or what
parable shall we use to describe it? 31It is
like a mustard seed, which is the smallest seed you plant in the ground. 32Yet
when planted, it grows and becomes
the largest of all garden plants, with
such big branches that the birds of the
air can perch in its shade."
33With many similar parables Jesus
spoke the word to them, as much as
4:33 [e]Jn 16:12 they could understand.[e] 34He did not
4:34 [f]Jn 16:25 say anything to them without using a
parable.[f] But when he was alone with
his own disciples, he explained everything.

Jesus Calms the Storm

35That day when evening came, he
said to his disciples, "Let us go over
to the other side." 36Leaving the crowd
4:36 [g]ver 1; Mk 3:9; 5:2,21; 6:32,45 behind, they took him along, just as he
was, in the boat.[g] There were also other
boats with him. 37A furious squall came
up, and the waves broke over the boat,
so that it was nearly swamped. 38Jesus
was in the stern, sleeping on a cush-
ion. The disciples woke him and said
to him, "Teacher, don't you care if we
drown?"
39He got up, rebuked the wind and
said to the waves, "Quiet! Be still!"
Then the wind died down and it was
completely calm.
40He said to his disciples, "Why are
you so afraid? Do you still have no 4:40 [h]Mt 14:31; Mk 16:14
faith?"[h]
41They were terrified and asked each
other, "Who is this? Even the wind and
the waves obey him!"

The Healing of a Demon-possessed Man

5 They went across the lake to the region of the Gerasenes.[a] 2When Je-
sus got out of the boat,[i] a man with 5:2 [i]Mk 4:1 [j]Mk 1:23
an evil[b] spirit[j] came from the tombs
to meet him. 3This man lived in the
tombs, and no one could bind him any
more, not even with a chain. 4For he
had often been chained hand and foot,
but he tore the chains apart and broke
the irons on his feet. No one was strong
enough to subdue him. 5Night and day
among the tombs and in the hills he
would cry out and cut himself with
stones.
6When he saw Jesus from a distance,
he ran and fell on his knees in front
of him. 7He shouted at the top of his 5:7 [k]Mt 8:29 [l]Mt 4:3; Lk 1:32; 6:35; Ac 16:17; Heb 7:1
voice, "What do you want with me,[k] Je-
sus, Son of the Most High God?[l] Swear
to God that you won't torture me!" 8For
Jesus had said to him, "Come out of
this man, you evil spirit!"
9Then Jesus asked him, "What is
your name?"
"My name is Legion,"[m] he replied, 5:9 [m]ver 15
"for we are many." 10And he begged Jesus again and again not to send them
out of the area.
11A large herd of pigs was feeding
on the nearby hillside. 12The demons
begged Jesus, "Send us among the pigs;
allow us to go into them." 13He gave
them permission, and the evil spirits
came out and went into the pigs. The
herd, about two thousand in number,
rushed down the steep bank into the
lake and were drowned.

[a] *1* Some manuscripts *Gadarenes*; other manuscripts *Gergesenes* [b] *2* Greek *unclean*; also in verses 8 and 13

WEEK 21

PEACE

1 DAY ONE

PEACE, THE EVIDENCE OF CONFIDENCE

Read Mark 4:35–41

Perhaps the most amazing question that Jesus ever asked his disciples was "Why are you so afraid?" One would think his disciples had every right to their fear. After all, the ship was sinking. Wouldn't anyone be afraid in such circumstances?

The question "Why are you so afraid?" gives rise to all kinds of implied questions from the perspective of the disciples: "Is God dead? Has God no power? Is he our Lord?"

Why does Jesus question his disciples? Could it be that the answer can give us some insights into the power of God in our lives?

The disciples are peaceless. Jesus can see that when he awakes from his serene slumber. Perhaps the disciples need to remember who is in control in their world.

There is an old hymn titled "Peace Be Still" which throbs with truth: "No water can swallow the ship where lies the Master of ocean and earth and skies."

Can it be that most of our lives are lived beyond the recognition of the power of God evidenced through the death and resurrection of his Son? Doesn't God have everything in our lives under control? Should not our own security in troubled times come in remembering this? We have God's living Son on board in our lives. We may have confidence, therefore, that in our own stormy situations he will calm the turbulence and give us the confidence of his presence. Then, once our storms have subsided, like his disciples we may remark, "Who is this man Jesus? Even our private tempests are subject to his calm!"

MEMORIZE THIS WEEK

2 TIMOTHY 1:12

That is why I am suffering as I am. Yet I am not ashamed, because I know whom I have believed, and am convinced that he is able to guard what I have entrusted to him for that day.

2 DAY TWO

PEACE AND THE PURPOSE OF GOD IN MY LIFE

Here Eliphaz, one of Job's friends, reminds Job that he preaches peace better than he lives it out. Job had always been good at bringing tranquility to the troubled. But now Job has forgotten his own lessons. It is amazing how the advice we have shared to bring others peace is often neglected in our own lives. Yet God's purpose for our lives always begins with our willingness to believe and apply what we preach to others. *Turn to Job 4:1–6, page 589, for today's study.*

3 DAY THREE

PEACE AND MY RELATIONSHIP WITH CHRIST

Paul tells the Philippians of his confidence: God will not leave them half-grown in their relationship with Christ. Salvation is the first step to growth—but it is not the last step. God will expand on their fledgling faith until it matures into even deeper levels of union with Christ. *Turn to Philippians 1:3–6, page 1414, for today's study.*

4 DAY FOUR

PEACE AND MY SERVICE TO OTHERS

Paul, harboring a runaway slave named Onesimus, begs Philemon to offer peace to the troubled renegade. Our service to others is to preach peace to those who have the power to create it. According to Roman law, Onesimus deserved death for his actions, but his confidence in his master's forgiving grace is great. So he carries Paul's letter, which will bring him either peace or execution. *Turn to Philemon 17–21, page 1457, for today's study.*

5 DAY FIVE

PEACE AND ITS PLACE IN MY PERSONAL WORSHIP

So often when ancient Israel was threatened by military oppressors, the people fled into various military alliances to provide for the national defense. Yet real peace is never political. It is an interior state of confidence that is derived from our love for God. Such indwelling peace is the basis of our personal worship. *Turn to Isaiah 36:4–6, page 830, for today's study.*

Week 22, Patience, Living by God's Timetable, begins on page 593, Job 7:6.
To begin a topical study on the Fruit of the Spirit, Peace, turn to the Topical Index, page 1548.

PEACE

THE DEVIL'S PIGS

Mark 5:12

Come pig . . . Here piggy, piggy!
Please perish in the sea, and take this horde of hell with you,
For God has here a man who has not been welcome in the world.
He needs a herd of pigs to die to teach him who Jesus is.
Not till you've perished in the sea
Will he accept his liberty.

14Those tending the pigs ran off and
reported this in the town and countryside, and the people went out to
see what had happened. 15When they
5:15 came to Jesus, they saw the man who
[n]ver 9 had been possessed by the legion[n] of
[o]ver 16,18; Mt 4:24 demons,[o] sitting there, dressed and in
his right mind; and they were afraid.
16Those who had seen it told the people
what had happened to the demon-possessed man—and told about the pigs as
well. 17Then the people began to plead
with Jesus to leave their region.
18As Jesus was getting into the boat,
the man who had been demon-possessed begged to go with him. 19Jesus
did not let him, but said, "Go home to
5:19 [p]Mt 8:4 your family and tell them[p] how much
the Lord has done for you, and how
he has had mercy on you." 20So the
man went away and began to tell in
5:20 [q]Mt 4:25; Mk 7:31 the Decapolis[a] [q] how much Jesus had
done for him. And all the people were
amazed.

A Dead Girl and a Sick Woman

21When Jesus had again crossed over
5:21 [r]Mt 9:1 by boat to the other side of the lake,[r] a
[s]Mk 4:1 large crowd gathered around him while
he was by the lake.[s] 22Then one of the
5:22 [t]ver 35,36,38; synagogue rulers,[t] named Jairus, came
Lk 13:14; Ac 13:15; 18:8,17 there. Seeing Jesus, he fell at his feet
23and pleaded earnestly with him, "My
little daughter is dying. Please come
5:23 [u]Mt 19:13; and put your hands on[u] her so that she
Mk 6:5; 7:32; 8:23; 16:18; will be healed and live." 24So Jesus went
Lk 4:40; 13:13; Ac 6:6 with him.
A large crowd followed and pressed
around him. 25And a woman was there
5:25 [v]Lev 15:25-30 who had been subject to bleeding[v] for
twelve years. 26She had suffered a great
deal under the care of many doctors
and had spent all she had, yet instead of
getting better she grew worse. 27When
she heard about Jesus, she came up behind him in the crowd and touched his
cloak, 28because she thought, "If I just
touch his clothes,[w] I will be healed." 5:28 [w]Mt 9:20
29Immediately her bleeding stopped and
she felt in her body that she was freed
from her suffering.[x] 5:29 [x]ver 34
30At once Jesus realized that power[y]
had gone out from him. He turned 5:30 [y]Lk 5:17; 6:19
around in the crowd and asked, "Who
touched my clothes?"
31"You see the people crowding
against you," his disciples answered,
"and yet you can ask, 'Who touched
me?'"
32But Jesus kept looking around to
see who had done it. 33Then the woman, knowing what had happened to her,
came and fell at his feet and, trembling
with fear, told him the whole truth.
34He said to her, "Daughter, your faith
has healed you.[z] Go in peace[a] and be 5:34 [z]Mt 9:22
freed from your suffering." [a]Ac 15:33
35While Jesus was still speaking, some
men came from the house of Jairus,
the synagogue ruler.[b] "Your daughter 5:35 [b]ver 22
is dead," they said. "Why bother the
teacher any more?"
36Ignoring what they said, Jesus told
the synagogue ruler, "Don't be afraid;
just believe."
37He did not let anyone follow him
except Peter, James and John the broth- 5:37 [c]Mt 4:21
er of James.[c] 38When they came to
the home of the synagogue ruler,[d] Je- 5:38 [d]ver 22
sus saw a commotion, with people cry-
ing and wailing loudly. 39He went in
and said to them, "Why all this commotion and wailing? The child is not
dead but asleep."[e] 40But they laughed 5:39 [e]Mt 9:24
at him.
After he put them all out, he took
the child's father and mother and the
disciples who were with him, and went
in where the child was. 41He took her
by the hand[f] and said to her, *"Talitha* 5:41 [f]Mk 1:31
koum!" (which means, "Little girl, I say [g]Lk 7:14;
to you, get up!").[g] 42Immediately the Ac 9:40
girl stood up and walked around (she
was twelve years old). At this they were
completely astonished. 43He gave strict
orders not to let anyone know about
this,[h] and told them to give her some- 5:43 [h]Mt 8:4
thing to eat.

[a] *20* That is, the Ten Cities

GENTLENESS

WEEK 44

1 DAY ONE

GENTLENESS, THE HEALING TOUCH OF GOD

Read Mark 5:24–34

Jesus heals a woman who touches his cloak. Gentleness meets urgency in this desperate tale of hope and healing. Gentleness: the feel of linen fabric on desperate, reaching fingertips. Gentleness: Christ feels the power leave his body, but he replies with softness. Behind this gentleness is the frantic need of a woman who has spent all she had on physicians only to be healed by none. When there was no one else to turn to, when every doctor had said no, she sought a gentle healer. These might have been her words:

I struggled just to touch
Him, in my frail attack
Against the crowd so much around.
They shoved me back.

In weakened fury there
I tore the people wall.
I clawed the frenzied air.
The Savior seemed so tall.

Yet through that madding crowd,
I could not seem to probe
The human press. I'd vowed
My hand should touch his robe.

And then the instant came!
The wall gave way. The tide
Fell back. I breathed his name
In freedom at his side.

I fell with hands outstretched
And felt his tunic there.
The crowd moved by a wretch
Who breathed a strange new air.

2 DAY TWO

GENTLENESS AND THE PURPOSE OF GOD IN MY LIFE

David's song of thanksgiving on the day the ark was placed in the tabernacle was a tender reminder of God's guidance in the wilderness. The thundering God of Sinai is not mentioned here. Rather, we hear of the tender God who remembered Israel in the desert. It is this God who watched over them when they were few in number. He stood by them as they lived among the nations. It is this great Yahweh whose gentleness is to be praised henceforward to all generations. *Turn to 1 Chronicles 16:8,19–22, page 482, for today's study.*

3 DAY THREE

GENTLENESS AND MY RELATIONSHIP WITH CHRIST

This account of Jesus giving the Holy Spirit is a gentle description of the commissioning of the apostles to change the world. Jesus but breathes on them, and their worldview is empowered by his gentle act. How we long for the enabling breath of the Savior directly on our lives, for that gentle breath which makes all things new and restores our relationship with both God and our world. *Turn to John 20:21–22, page 1281, for today's study.*

4 DAY FOUR

GENTLENESS AND MY SERVICE TO OTHERS

Two things stand out in this passage. First, Elijah is bold in his demand upon God. Some might think that he is talking somewhat abusively to God ("Have you brought tragedy also upon this widow…by causing her son to die?"). But let it be understood that Elijah is asking boldly. How often, by contrast, we—having no real confidence in our prayers—ask weakly, with little expectation. Second, some prophetic gentleness settles on this story. This fiery man of God is suddenly transformed into a tender healer of bereavement and lost hope. Perhaps this is the sort of gentleness with which we are to serve each other. *Turn to 1 Kings 17:17–24, page 411, for today's study.*

5 DAY FIVE

GENTLENESS AND ITS PLACE IN MY PERSONAL WORSHIP

John writes here with a most gentle spirit. He wants his message to be an honest testimony of those things he saw and knew to be true of Jesus. Still, he declares it gently. John's gentleness establishes the truth he wants to tell the world concerning Jesus. *Turn to 1 John 1:1–4, page 1506, for today's study.*

MEMORIZE THIS WEEK

ISAIAH 11:9

They will neither harm nor destroy
on all my holy mountain,
for the earth will be full of the knowledge of
the LORD
as the waters cover the sea.

Week 45, Self-Control, the Disciplined Life, begins on page 1367, 1 Corinthians 9:24–27.
To begin a topical study on the Fruit of the Spirit, Gentleness, turn to the Topical Index, page 1548.

A Prophet Without Honor

6 Jesus left there and went to his
6:1 [i]Mt 2:23 hometown,[i] accompanied by his
disciples. 2When the Sabbath came,[j] he
6:2 [j]Mk 1:21 began to teach in the synagogue,[k] and
[k]Mt 4:23 many who heard him were amazed.[l]
[l]Mt 7:28 "Where did this man get these
things?" they asked. "What's this wisdom that has been given him, that he
even does miracles! 3Isn't this the carpenter? Isn't this Mary's son and the
6:3 brother of James, Joseph,[a] Judas and
[m]Mt 12:46 Simon?[m] Aren't his sisters here with us?"
[n]Mt 11:6; Jn 6:61 And they took offense at him.[n]

GOODNESS

A Prophet at Home

Mark 6:4

God sometimes comes so near, his very nearness blinds us.
Familiarity sometimes breeds contempt, but it always breeds containment.
Knowing Jesus in little ways prevents our knowing him in greater ways.
Pity most those who study him, yet never really know him—
Scholars who write his life and times, but never feel his nearness.
This affliction stalked the world first in Nazareth.

4Jesus said to them, "Only in his
hometown, among his relatives and in
his own house is a prophet without
honor."[o] 5He could not do any miracles
6:4 [o]Lk 4:24; there, except lay his hands on[p] a few
Jn 4:44 sick people and heal them. 6And he was
6:5 [p]Mk 5:23 amazed at their lack of faith.

Jesus Sends Out the Twelve

Then Jesus went around teaching
6:6 [q]Mt 9:35; from village to village.[q] 7Calling the
Mk 1:39; Twelve to him,[r] he sent them out two
Lk 13:22 by two[s] and gave them authority over
6:7 [r]Mk 3:13 evil[b] spirits.[t]
[s]Dt 17:6; Lk 10:1 8These were his instructions: "Take
[t]Mt 10:1 nothing for the journey except a staff—
no bread, no bag, no money in your
belts. 9Wear sandals but not an extra tunic. 10Whenever you enter a house, stay
there until you leave that town. 11And
6:11 if any place will not welcome you or lis-
[u]Mt 10:14 ten to you, shake the dust off your feet[u]
when you leave, as a testimony against
them."

12They went out and preached that
people should repent.[v] 13They drove 6:12 [v]Lk 9:6
out many demons and anointed many
sick people with oil[w] and healed them. 6:13 [w]Jas 5:14

John the Baptist Beheaded

14King Herod heard about this, for
Jesus' name had become well known.
Some were saying,[c] "John the Baptist[x] 6:14 [x]Mt 3:1
has been raised from the dead, and that
is why miraculous powers are at work
in him."
15Others said, "He is Elijah."[y] 6:15 [y]Mal 4:5 [z]Mt 21:11
And still others claimed, "He is a [a]Mt 16:14;
prophet,[z] like one of the prophets of Mk 8:28
long ago."[a]
16But when Herod heard this, he
said, "John, the man I beheaded, has
been raised from the dead!"
17For Herod himself had given orders
to have John arrested, and he had him 6:17 [b]Mt 4:12;
bound and put in prison.[b] He did this 11:2;
because of Herodias, his brother Philip's Lk 3:19,20
wife, whom he had married. 18For John
had been saying to Herod, "It is not law-
ful for you to have your brother's wife."[c] 6:18 [c]Lev 18:16;
19So Herodias nursed a grudge against 20:21
John and wanted to kill him. But she
was not able to, 20because Herod feared
John and protected him, knowing him
to be a righteous and holy man.[d] When 6:20 [d]Mt 11:9;
Herod heard John, he was greatly puz- 21:26
zled[d]; yet he liked to listen to him.
21Finally the opportune time came. 6:21
On his birthday Herod gave a banquet[e] [e]Est 1:3; 2:18
for his high officials and military com- [f]Lk 3:1
manders and the leading men of Galilee.[f] 22When the daughter of Herodias
came in and danced, she pleased Herod
and his dinner guests.
The king said to the girl, "Ask me
for anything you want, and I'll give it
to you." 23And he promised her with
an oath, "Whatever you ask I will give
you, up to half my kingdom."[g] 6:23 [g]Est 5:3,6; 7:2
24She went out and said to her mother, "What shall I ask for?"
"The head of John the Baptist," she
answered.
25At once the girl hurried in to the
king with the request: "I want you to
give me right now the head of John the
Baptist on a platter."
26The king was greatly distressed, but

[a]3 Greek *Joses*, a variant of *Joseph* [b]7 Greek *unclean* [c]14 Some early manuscripts *He was saying* [d]20 Some early manuscripts *he did many things*

because of his oaths and his dinner
guests, he did not want to refuse her.
27So he immediately sent an executioner with orders to bring John's head. The
man went, beheaded John in the prison, 28and brought back his head on a
platter. He presented it to the girl, and
she gave it to her mother. 29On hearing
of this, John's disciples came and took
his body and laid it in a tomb.

Jesus Feeds the Five Thousand

6:30 [h]Mt 10:2; 30The apostles[h] gathered around Je-
Lk 9:10; 17:5; sus and reported to him all they had
22:14; 24:10; Ac 1:2,26 done and taught.[i] 31Then, because so
[i]Lk 9:10 many people were coming and going
6:31 that they did not even have a chance to
[j]Mk 3:20 eat,[j] he said to them, "Come with me
by yourselves to a quiet place and get
some rest."
32So they went away by themselves in
6:32 [k]ver 45; a boat[k] to a solitary place. 33But many
Mk 4:36 who saw them leaving recognized them
and ran on foot from all the towns and
got there ahead of them. 34When Jesus
landed and saw a large crowd, he had
compassion on them, because they were
6:34 [l]Mt 9:36 like sheep without a shepherd.[l] So he
began teaching them many things.
35By this time it was late in the day,
so his disciples came to him. "This is
a remote place," they said, "and it's already very late. 36Send the people away
so they can go to the surrounding countryside and villages and buy themselves
something to eat."
6:37 37But he answered, "You give them
[m]2Ki 4:42-44 something to eat."[m]
They said to him, "That would take
eight months of a man's wages[a]! Are we
to go and spend that much on bread
and give it to them to eat?"
38"How many loaves do you have?"
he asked. "Go and see."
6:38 When they found out, they said,
[n]Mt 15:34; Mk 8:5 "Five—and two fish."[n]
39Then Jesus directed them to have
all the people sit down in groups on
the green grass. 40So they sat down in
groups of hundreds and fifties. 41Tak-
ing the five loaves and the two fish and
looking up to heaven, he gave thanks
6:41 and broke the loaves.[o] Then he gave
[o]Mt 14:19 them to his disciples to set before the
people. He also divided the two fish
among them all. 42They all ate and were
satisfied, 43and the disciples picked up
twelve basketfuls of broken pieces of
bread and fish. 44The number of the
men who had eaten was five thousand.

Jesus Walks on the Water

45Immediately Jesus made his disci-
ples get into the boat[p] and go on ahead 6:45 [p]ver 32
of him to Bethsaida,[q] while he dis- [q]Mt 11:21
missed the crowd. 46After leaving them, 6:46
he went up on a mountainside to pray.[r] [r]Lk 3:21
47When evening came, the boat was
in the middle of the lake, and he was
alone on land. 48He saw the disciples
straining at the oars, because the wind
was against them. About the fourth
watch of the night he went out to them,
walking on the lake. He was about to
pass by them, 49but when they saw him
walking on the lake, they thought he
was a ghost.[s] They cried out, 50because 6:49
they all saw him and were terrified. [s]Lk 24:37
Immediately he spoke to them and
said, "Take courage! It is I. Don't be
afraid."[t] 51Then he climbed into the 6:50
boat[u] with them, and the wind died [t]Mt 14:27
down.[v] They were completely amazed, 6:51 [u]ver 32
52for they had not understood about the [v]Mk 4:39
loaves; their hearts were hardened.[w] 6:52
53When they had crossed over, they [w]Mk 8:17-21
landed at Gennesaret and anchored
there.[x] 54As soon as they got out of the 6:53 [x]Jn 6:24,25
boat, people recognized Jesus. 55They
ran throughout that whole region and
carried the sick on mats to wherever
they heard he was. 56And wherever he
went—into villages, towns or countryside—they placed the sick in the marketplaces. They begged him to let them
touch even the edge of his cloak,[y] and 6:56
all who touched him were healed. [y]Mt 9:20

Clean and Unclean

7 The Pharisees and some of the
teachers of the law who had come
from Jerusalem gathered around Jesus
and 2saw some of his disciples eating
food with hands that were "unclean,"[z] 7:2
that is, unwashed. 3(The Pharisees and [z]Ac 10:14,28; 11:8;
all the Jews do not eat unless they Ro 14:14
give their hands a ceremonial washing,
holding to the tradition of the elders.[a] 7:3
4When they come from the market- [a]ver 5,8,9,13; Lk 11:38
place they do not eat unless they wash.
And they observe many other traditions, such as the washing of cups, 7:4
pitchers and kettles.[b])[b] [b]Mt 23:25; Lk 11:39

[a]*37* Greek *take two hundred denarii* [b]*4* Some early manuscripts *pitchers, kettles and dining couches*

5So the Pharisees and teachers of the
law asked Jesus, "Why don't your disciples live according to the tradition of
7:5 [c]ver 3; the elders[c] instead of eating their food
Gal 1:14; with 'unclean' hands?"
Col 2:8 6He replied, "Isaiah was right when
he prophesied about you hypocrites; as
it is written:

"'These people honor me with their
lips,
but their hearts are far from me.
7They worship me in vain;
7:7 their teachings are but rules taught
[d]Isa 29:13 by men.'[a][d]

8You have let go of the commands of
7:8 God and are holding on to the tradi-
[e]ver 3 tions of men."[e]
9And he said to them: "You have a
fine way of setting aside the commands
7:9 of God in order to observe[b] your own
[f]ver 3 traditions![f] 10For Moses said, 'Honor
7:10 [g]Ex 20:12; your father and your mother,'[c][g] and,
Dt 5:16 'Anyone who curses his father or moth-
[h]Ex 21:17; Lev 20:9 er must be put to death.'[d][h] 11But
you say[i] that if a man says to his fa-
7:11 [i]Mt 23:16,18 ther or mother: 'Whatever help you
might otherwise have received from
me is Corban' (that is, a gift devoted
to God), 12then you no longer let him
7:13 do anything for his father or mother.
[j]Heb 4:12 13Thus you nullify the word of God[j]
[k]ver 3 by your tradition[k] that you have handed down. And you do many things like
that."
14Again Jesus called the crowd to him
and said, "Listen to me, everyone, and
understand this. 15Nothing outside a
man can make him 'unclean' by going
into him. Rather, it is what comes out
of a man that makes him 'unclean.'[e]"
7:17 17After he had left the crowd and en-
[l]Mk 9:28 tered the house, his disciples asked him[l]
about this parable. 18"Are you so dull?"
he asked. "Don't you see that nothing
that enters a man from the outside can
make him 'unclean'? 19For it doesn't go
into his heart but into his stomach, and
7:19 then out of his body." (In saying this,
[m]Ro 14:1-12; Jesus declared all foods[m] "clean.")[n]
Col 2:16; 1Ti 4:3-5 20He went on: "What comes out of a
[n]Ac 10:15 man is what makes him 'unclean.' 21For
from within, out of men's hearts, come
7:22 evil thoughts, sexual immorality, theft,
[o]Mt 20:15 murder, adultery, 22greed,[o] malice, deceit, lewdness, envy, slander, arrogance
and folly. 23All these evils come from
inside and make a man 'unclean.'"

The Faith of a Syrophoenician Woman

24Jesus left that place and went to the
vicinity of Tyre.[f][p] He entered a house 7:24
and did not want anyone to know it; yet [p]Mt 11:21
he could not keep his presence secret.
25In fact, as soon as she heard about
him, a woman whose little daughter 7:25
was possessed by an evil[g] spirit[q] came [q]Mt 4:24
and fell at his feet. 26The woman was
a Greek, born in Syrian Phoenicia. She
begged Jesus to drive the demon out of
her daughter.
27"First let the children eat all they
want," he told her, "for it is not right to
take the children's bread and toss it to
their dogs."
28"Yes, Lord," she replied, "but even
the dogs under the table eat the children's crumbs."
29Then he told her, "For such a reply,
you may go; the demon has left your
daughter."
30She went home and found her child
lying on the bed, and the demon gone.

The Healing of a Deaf and Mute Man

31Then Jesus left the vicinity of Tyre[r] 7:31 [r]ver 24;
and went through Sidon, down to the Mt 11:21
Sea of Galilee[s] and into the region of [s]Mt 4:18
the Decapolis.[h][t] 32There some people [t]Mt 4:25; Mk 5:20
brought to him a man who was deaf 7:32
and could hardly talk,[u] and they begged [u]Mt 9:32; Lk 11:14
him to place his hand on[v] the man. [v]Mk 5:23
33After he took him aside, away from
the crowd, Jesus put his fingers into the
man's ears. Then he spit[w] and touched 7:33 [w]Mk 8:23
the man's tongue. 34He looked up to
heaven[x] and with a deep sigh[y] said to 7:34 [x]Mk 6:41;
him, *"Ephphatha!"* (which means, "Be Jn 11:41 [y]Mk 8:12
opened!"). 35At this, the man's ears were
opened, his tongue was loosened and
he began to speak plainly.[z] 7:35 [z]Isa 35:5,6
36Jesus commanded them not to tell
anyone.[a] But the more he did so, the 7:36 [a]Mt 8:4
more they kept talking about it. 37Peo-
ple were overwhelmed with amazement.
"He has done everything well," they
said. "He even makes the deaf hear and
the mute speak."

[a]*6,7* Isaiah 29:13 [b]*9* Some manuscripts *set up* [c]*10* Exodus 20:12; Deut. 5:16 [d]*10* Exodus 21:17; Lev. 20:9 [e]*15* Some early manuscripts *'unclean.'* *16If anyone has ears to hear, let him hear.* [f]*24* Many early manuscripts *Tyre and Sidon* [g]*25* Greek *unclean* [h]*31* That is, the Ten Cities

Jesus Feeds the Four Thousand

8 During those days another large
crowd gathered. Since they had
nothing to eat, Jesus called his disci-
8:2 ples to him and said, 2"I have compas-
[b]Mt 9:36 sion for these people;[b] they have already
been with me three days and have noth-
ing to eat. 3If I send them home hungry,
they will collapse on the way, because
some of them have come a long distance."
4His disciples answered, "But where
in this remote place can anyone get
enough bread to feed them?"
5"How many loaves do you have?"
Jesus asked.
"Seven," they replied.
6He told the crowd to sit down on
the ground. When he had taken the
seven loaves and given thanks, he broke
them and gave them to his disciples to
set before the people, and they did so.
7They had a few small fish as well; he
gave thanks for them also and told the
8:7 [c]Mt 14:19 disciples to distribute them.[c] 8The people ate and were satisfied. Afterward the
disciples picked up seven basketfuls of
8:8 [d]ver 20 broken pieces that were left over.[d]
9About four thousand men were present.
And having sent them away, 10he got
into the boat with his disciples and
went to the region of Dalmanutha.
11The Pharisees came and began to
question Jesus. To test him, they asked
8:11 [e]Mt 12:38 him for a sign from heaven.[e] 12He
sighed deeply[f] and said, "Why does this
8:12 [f]Mk 7:34 generation ask for a miraculous sign? I
tell you the truth, no sign will be given
to it." 13Then he left them, got back
into the boat and crossed to the other
side.

The Yeast of the Pharisees and Herod

14The disciples had forgotten to bring
bread, except for one loaf they had with
them in the boat. 15"Be careful," Jesus
8:15 [g]1Co 5:6-8 warned them. "Watch out for the yeast[g]
[h]Lk 12:1 of the Pharisees[h] and that of Herod."[i]
[i]Mt 14:1; Mk 12:13 16They discussed this with one another and said, "It is because we have
no bread."
17Aware of their discussion, Jesus
asked them: "Why are you talking about
having no bread? Do you still not see or
8:17 [j]Isa 6:9,10; Mk 6:52 understand? Are your hearts hardened?[j]
18Do you have eyes but fail to see, and
ears but fail to hear? And don't you remember? 19When I broke the five loaves
for the five thousand, how many basketfuls of pieces did you pick up?"
"Twelve,"[k] they replied. 8:19 [k]Mt 14:20; Mk 6:41-44; Lk 9:17; Jn 6:13
20"And when I broke the seven loaves
for the four thousand, how many basketfuls of pieces did you pick up?"
They answered, "Seven."[l] 8:20 [l]ver 6-9; Mt 15:37
21He said to them, "Do you still not
understand?"[m] 8:21 [m]Mk 6:52

The Healing of a Blind Man at Bethsaida

22They came to Bethsaida,[n] and some 8:22 [n]Mt 11:21
people brought a blind man[o] and begged [o]Mk 10:46; Jn 9:1
Jesus to touch him. 23He took the blind
man by the hand and led him outside
the village. When he had spit[p] on the 8:23 [p]Mk 7:33
man's eyes and put his hands on[q] him, [q]Mk 5:23
Jesus asked, "Do you see anything?"
24He looked up and said, "I see
people; they look like trees walking
around."

▸ PATIENCE

TOUCH . . . TOUCH

Mark 8:24–25

Grace comes as it will. Sometimes Jesus touched the blind once and they were healed. Sometimes he touched them twice. Grace is wonderful however it comes. After all, who's counting?

25Once more Jesus put his hands
on the man's eyes. Then his eyes were
opened, his sight was restored, and
he saw everything clearly. 26Jesus sent
him home, saying, "Don't go into the
village.[a]"

Peter's Confession of Christ

27Jesus and his disciples went on to
the villages around Caesarea Philippi.
On the way he asked them, "Who do
people say I am?"
28They replied, "Some say John the 8:28
Baptist;[r] others say Elijah;[s] and still oth- [r]Mt 3:1 [s]Mal 4:5
ers, one of the prophets."
29"But what about you?" he asked.
"Who do you say I am?"
Peter answered, "You are the 8:29 [t]Jn 6:69;
Christ.[b]"[t] 11:27

[a]26 Some manuscripts *Don't go and tell anyone in the village* [b]29 Or *Messiah*. "The Christ" (Greek) and "the Messiah" (Hebrew) both mean "the Anointed One."

8:30 [u]Mt 8:4; 16:20; 17:9; Mk 9:9; Lk 9:21 30Jesus warned them not to tell anyone about him.[u]

Jesus Predicts His Death

8:31 [v]Mt 8:20 [w]Mt 16:21 [x]Mt 27:1,2 [y]Ac 2:23; 3:13 [z]Mt 16:21 [a]Mt 16:21 31He then began to teach them that
the Son of Man[v] must suffer many
things[w] and be rejected by the elders,
chief priests and teachers of the law,[x] and
that he must be killed[y] and after three
8:32 [b]Jn 18:20 days[z] rise again.[a] 32He spoke plainly[b]
about this, and Peter took him aside
and began to rebuke him.
33But when Jesus turned and looked
at his disciples, he rebuked Peter. "Get
8:33 [c]Mt 4:10 behind me, Satan!"[c] he said. "You do
not have in mind the things of God,
but the things of men."
34Then he called the crowd to him
along with his disciples and said: "If
anyone would come after me, he must
deny himself and take up his cross and
8:34 [d]Mt 10:38; Lk 14:27 follow me.[d] 35For whoever wants to
save his life[a] will lose it, but whoever
8:35 [e]Jn 12:25 loses his life for me and for the gospel
will save it.[e] 36What good is it for a
man to gain the whole world, yet forfeit his soul? 37Or what can a man give
in exchange for his soul? 38If anyone is
ashamed of me and my words in this
adulterous and sinful generation, the
8:38 [f]Mt 8:20 [g]Mt 10:33; Lk 12:9 [h]1Th 2:19 Son of Man[f] will be ashamed of him[g]
when he comes[h] in his Father's glory
with the holy angels."

9 And he said to them, "I tell you the
truth, some who are standing here
9:1 [i]Mk 13:30; Lk 22:18 [j]Mt 24:30; 25:31 will not taste death before they see the
kingdom of God come[i] with power."[j]

The Transfiguration

2After six days Jesus took Peter, James
9:2 [k]Mt 4:21 and John[k] with him and led them up
a high mountain, where they were all
alone. There he was transfigured before them. 3His clothes became daz-
9:3 [l]Mt 28:3 zling white,[l] whiter than anyone in the
world could bleach them. 4And there
appeared before them Elijah and Moses, who were talking with Jesus.
9:5 [m]Mt 23:7 5Peter said to Jesus, "Rabbi,[m] it is
good for us to be here. Let us put up
three shelters—one for you, one for
Moses and one for Elijah." 6(He did not
know what to say, they were so frightened.)
7Then a cloud appeared and enveloped them, and a voice came from the
9:7 [n]Ex 24:16 [o]Mt 3:17 cloud:[n] "This is my Son, whom I love.
Listen to him!"[o]

8Suddenly, when they looked around,
they no longer saw anyone with them
except Jesus.
9As they were coming down the
mountain, Jesus gave them orders not
to tell anyone[p] what they had seen un- 9:9 [p]Mk 8:30 [q]Mt 8:20
til the Son of Man[q] had risen from the
dead. 10They kept the matter to themselves, discussing what "rising from the
dead" meant.
11And they asked him, "Why do the
teachers of the law say that Elijah must
come first?"
12Jesus replied, "To be sure, Elijah
does come first, and restores all things.
Why then is it written that the Son 9:12 [r]Mt 8:20 [s]Mt 16:21 [t]Lk 23:11
of Man[r] must suffer much[s] and be
rejected?[t] 13But I tell you, Elijah has
come,[u] and they have done to him ev- 9:13 [u]Mt 11:14
erything they wished, just as it is writ-
ten about him."

The Healing of a Boy With an Evil Spirit

14When they came to the other disciples, they saw a large crowd around
them and the teachers of the law arguing with them. 15As soon as all the people saw Jesus, they were overwhelmed
with wonder and ran to greet him.
16"What are you arguing with them
about?" he asked.
17A man in the crowd answered,
"Teacher, I brought you my son, who
is possessed by a spirit that has robbed
him of speech. 18Whenever it seizes
him, it throws him to the ground. He
foams at the mouth, gnashes his teeth
and becomes rigid. I asked your disciples to drive out the spirit, but they
could not."
19"O unbelieving generation," Jesus
replied, "how long shall I stay with you?
How long shall I put up with you?
Bring the boy to me."
20So they brought him. When the
spirit saw Jesus, it immediately threw
the boy into a convulsion. He fell to the
ground and rolled around, foaming at
the mouth.[v] 9:20 [v]Mk 1:26
21Jesus asked the boy's father, "How
long has he been like this?"
"From childhood," he answered. 22"It
has often thrown him into fire or water

[a]35 The Greek word means either *life* or *soul*; also in verse 36.

to kill him. But if you can do anything,
take pity on us and help us."
23"'If you can'?" said Jesus. "Everything is possible for him who
believes."[w] 9:23 [w]Mt 21:21; Mk 11:23; Jn 11:40
24Immediately the boy's father exclaimed, "I do believe; help me overcome my unbelief!"

DAY 4 FOUR

▸ SELF-CONTROL AND MY SERVICE TO OTHERS

Mark 9:14–18,29

The disciples in this passage are trying to climb Mount Everest while practicing their spiritual disciplines on an anthill. Jesus tells them that some exercises can only be achieved by those who have conditioned themselves to trust in God for their help. Only those who will allow the lordship of God to rule in their lives will have access to the great power of God.

We are not told whether the disciples were annoyed that their easy-come-easy-go spirituality wouldn't hold up when they were face-to-face with Satan. But their failure should speak clearly to us. The greatest achievements of the saints are always the outgrowth of total commitment.

What are the requirements that make for utter discipline? Paul rehearses the rigors of such discipleship with Timothy: "Endure hardship with us like a good soldier of Christ Jesus" (2 Timothy 2:3). A soldier is one who has trained and prepared for battle. A soldier is familiar with weapons and ready to fight to the death. Does our spiritual walk make us look like boot camp recruits? Or do we find that our discipline has grown soft and ineffectual?

Those who want to achieve great things for God need to practice the great disciplines of spirituality. Jesus said that prayer and devotion to God are the real evidences of a robust inner faith. Self-control is the first step of spiritual discipline. We must practice and prepare ourselves for the coming battles. If we cannot control our appetites, we can hardly be expected to enter into spiritual combat that tries even the souls of those who pray and fast.

To begin a study on the topic of Self-Control, the Path of Coming to Maturity, turn to the home page on page 364.

25When Jesus saw that a crowd was
running to the scene,[x] he rebuked the 9:25 [x]ver 15
evil[a] spirit. "You deaf and mute spirit,"
he said, "I command you, come out of
him and never enter him again."
26The spirit shrieked, convulsed him
violently and came out. The boy looked
so much like a corpse that many said,
"He's dead." 27But Jesus took him by
the hand and lifted him to his feet, and
he stood up.
28After Jesus had gone indoors, his
disciples asked him privately,[y] "Why 9:28 [y]Mk 7:17
couldn't we drive it out?"
29He replied, "This kind can come
out only by prayer.[b]"
30They left that place and passed
through Galilee. Jesus did not want
anyone to know where they were, 31be-
cause he was teaching his disciples. He
said to them, "The Son of Man[z] is go- 9:31 [z]Mt 8:20
ing to be betrayed into the hands of [a]ver 12; Ac 2:23; 3:13
men. They will kill him,[a] and after three [b]Mt 16:21
days[b] he will rise."[c] 32But they did not [c]Mt 16:21
understand what he meant[d] and were 9:32 [d]Lk 2:50; 9:45; 18:34; Jn 12:16
afraid to ask him about it.

Who Is the Greatest?

33They came to Capernaum.[e] When 9:33 [e]Mt 4:13
he was in the house,[f] he asked them, [f]Mk 1:29
"What were you arguing about on the
road?" 34But they kept quiet because on
the way they had argued about who was 9:34 [g]Lk 22:24
the greatest.[g]
35Sitting down, Jesus called the
Twelve and said, "If anyone wants to be
first, he must be the very last, and the
servant of all."[h] 9:35 [h]Mt 18:4; 20:26; Mk 10:43; Lk 22:26
36He took a little child and had him
stand among them. Taking him in his
arms,[i] he said to them, 37"Whoever wel- 9:36 [i]Mk 10:16
comes one of these little children in my
name welcomes me; and whoever welcomes me does not welcome me but
the one who sent me."[j] 9:37 [j]Mt 10:40

Whoever Is Not Against Us Is for Us

38"Teacher," said John, "we saw a
man driving out demons in your name
and we told him to stop, because he 9:38 [k]Nu 11:27-29
was not one of us."[k]
39"Do not stop him," Jesus said. "No
one who does a miracle in my name can
in the next moment say anything bad

[a]25 Greek *unclean* [b]29 Some manuscripts *prayer and fasting*

about me, 40for whoever is not against
9:40 [l]Mt 12:30; Lk 11:23 us is for us.[l] 41I tell you the truth, anyone who gives you a cup of water in my
9:41 [m]Mt 10:42 name because you belong to Christ will
certainly not lose his reward.[m]

Causing to Sin

42"And if anyone causes one of these
9:42 [n]Mt 5:29 [o]Mt 18:6; Lk 17:2 little ones who believe in me to sin,[n] it
would be better for him to be thrown
into the sea with a large millstone tied
around his neck.[o] 43If your hand causes
9:43 [p]Mt 5:29 [q]Mt 5:30; 18:8 [r]Mt 25:41 you to sin,[p] cut it off. It is better for
you to enter life maimed than with two
hands to go into hell,[q] where the fire
never goes out.[a][r] 45And if your foot
9:45 [s]Mt 5:29 [t]Mt 18:8 causes you to sin,[s] cut it off. It is better
for you to enter life crippled than to
have two feet and be thrown into hell.[b][t]
9:47 [u]Mt 5:29 [v]Mt 5:29; 18:9 47And if your eye causes you to sin,[u]
pluck it out. It is better for you to en-
ter the kingdom of God with one eye
than to have two eyes and be thrown
into hell,[v] 48where

9:48 [w]Isa 66:24; Mt 25:41 " 'their worm does not die,
and the fire is not quenched.'[c][w]

LOVE

GEHENNA

Mark 9:47–48

***Gehenna* is the word Jesus used most for hell. Gehenna was the name of the smoldering garbage dump outside Jerusalem. It was a flaming refuse heap, where smoke and flame seemed never to be extinguished. God, having no love for hell, ringed the deep abyss with barriers of love. To get there one must circumvent crucifixion love and crash through barricades of grace.**

9:49 [x]Lev 2:13 49Everyone will be salted[x] with fire.
50"Salt is good, but if it loses its salti-
9:50 [y]Mt 5:13; Lk 14:34,35 [z]Col 4:6 [a]Ro 12:18; 2Co 13:11; 1Th 5:13 ness, how can you make it salty again?[y]
Have salt in yourselves,[z] and be at peace
with each other."[a]

Divorce

10 Jesus then left that place and
10:1 [b]Mk 1:5; Jn 10:40; 11:7 [c]Mt 4:23; Mk 2:13; 4:2; 6:6,34 went into the region of Judea
and across the Jordan.[b] Again crowds of
people came to him, and as was his custom, he taught them.[c]
10:2 [d]Mk 2:16 2Some Pharisees[d] came and tested
him by asking, "Is it lawful for a man
to divorce his wife?"

3"What did Moses command you?"
he replied.
4They said, "Moses permitted a man
to write a certificate of divorce and send
her away."[e] 10:4 [e]Dt 24:1-4; Mt 5:31
5"It was because your hearts were
hard[f] that Moses wrote you this law," 10:5 [f]Ps 95:8; Heb 3:15
Jesus replied. 6"But at the beginning of
creation God 'made them male and fe-
male.'[d][g] 7'For this reason a man will 10:6 [g]Ge 1:27; 5:2
leave his father and mother and be unit-
ed to his wife,[e] 8and the two will be-
come one flesh.'[f][h] So they are no longer 10:8 [h]Ge 2:24; 1Co 6:16
two, but one. 9Therefore what God has
joined together, let man not separate."
10When they were in the house again,
the disciples asked Jesus about this.
11He answered, "Anyone who divorces
his wife and marries another woman
commits adultery against her.[i] 12And if 10:11 [i]Mt 5:32; Lk 16:18
she divorces her husband and marries
another man, she commits adultery."[j] 10:12 [j]Ro 7:3; 1Co 7:10,11

The Little Children and Jesus

13People were bringing little children
to Jesus to have him touch them, but
the disciples rebuked them. 14When Jesus saw this, he was indignant. He said
to them, "Let the little children come
to me, and do not hinder them, for
the kingdom of God belongs to such
as these.[k] 15I tell you the truth, anyone 10:14 [k]Mt 25:34
who will not receive the kingdom of
God like a little child will never enter
it."[l] 16And he took the children in his 10:15 [l]Mt 18:3
arms,[m] put his hands on them and
blessed them. 10:16 [m]Mk 9:36

The Rich Young Man

17As Jesus started on his way, a man
ran up to him and fell on his knees[n] 10:17 [n]Mk 1:40 [o]Lk 10:25; Ac 20:32
before him. "Good teacher," he asked,
"what must I do to inherit eternal
life?"[o]
18"Why do you call me good?" Jesus
answered. "No one is good—except
God alone. 19You know the commandments: 'Do not murder, do not commit
adultery, do not steal, do not give false
testimony, do not defraud, honor your 10:19 [p]Ex 20:12-16; Dt 5:16-20
father and mother.'[g]"[p]

[a]*43* Some manuscripts *out, 44where / " 'their worm does not die, / and the fire is not quenched.'*
[b]*45* Some manuscripts *hell, 46where / " 'their worm does not die, / and the fire is not quenched.'*
[c]*48* Isaiah 66:24 [d]*6* Gen. 1:27 [e]*7* Some early manuscripts do not have *and be united to his wife.*
[f]*8* Gen. 2:24 [g]*19* Exodus 20:12-16; Deut. 5:16-20

52"Go," said Jesus, "your faith has
10:52 [v]Mt 9:22 healed you."[v] Immediately he received
[w]Mt 4:19 his sight and followed[w] Jesus along the
road.

The Triumphal Entry

11 As they approached Jerusalem
and came to Bethphage and
11:1 [x]Mt 21:17 Bethany[x] at the Mount of Olives,[y] Je-
[y]Mt 21:1 sus sent two of his disciples, 2saying to
them, "Go to the village ahead of you,
and just as you enter it, you will find a
11:2 [z]Nu 19:2; colt tied there, which no one has ever
Dt 21:3; ridden.[z] Untie it and bring it here. 3If
1Sa 6:7 anyone asks you, 'Why are you doing
this?' tell him, 'The Lord needs it and
will send it back here shortly.' "
4They went and found a colt outside
11:4 [a]Mk 14:16 in the street, tied at a doorway.[a] As they
untied it, 5some people standing there
asked, "What are you doing, untying
that colt?" 6They answered as Jesus had
told them to, and the people let them
go. 7When they brought the colt to Jesus and threw their cloaks over it, he
sat on it. 8Many people spread their
cloaks on the road, while others spread
branches they had cut in the fields.
9Those who went ahead and those who
followed shouted,

"Hosanna![a]"

11:9 [b]Ps 118:25, 26; Mt 23:39 "Blessed is he who comes in the
name of the Lord!"[b] [b]

10"Blessed is the coming kingdom of
our father David!"

11:10 [c]Lk 2:14 "Hosanna in the highest!"[c]

JOY

HOSANNA!

Mark 11:9

Do you sense that Jesus is in your city? Is he at the portals of your poor heart's door? Is there a word for this? Yes, *Hosanna!*

11Jesus entered Jerusalem and went to
the temple. He looked around at every-
11:11 [d]Mt 21:12,17 thing, but since it was already late, he
went out to Bethany with the Twelve.[d]

Jesus Clears the Temple

12The next day as they were leaving
Bethany, Jesus was hungry. 13Seeing in
the distance a fig tree in leaf, he went
to find out if it had any fruit. When he
reached it, he found nothing but leaves,
because it was not the season for figs.[e] 11:13 [e]Lk 13:6-9
14Then he said to the tree, "May no one
ever eat fruit from you again." And his
disciples heard him say it.
15On reaching Jerusalem, Jesus entered the temple area and began driving out those who were buying and
selling there. He overturned the tables
of the money changers and the bench-
es of those selling doves, 16and would
not allow anyone to carry merchandise
through the temple courts. 17And as he
taught them, he said, "Is it not written:

" 'My house will be called 11:17 [f]Isa 56:7
a house of prayer for all nations'[c]?[f] [g]Jer 7:11

But you have made it 'a den of robbers.'[d]"[g]
18The chief priests and the teachers
of the law heard this and began look-
ing for a way to kill him,[h] for they 11:18 [h]Mt 21:46;
feared him, because the whole crowd Mk 12:12;
was amazed at his teaching.[i] Lk 20:19 [i]Mt 7:28
19When evening came, they[e] went
out of the city.[j] 11:19 [j]Lk 21:37

The Withered Fig Tree

20In the morning, as they went along,
they saw the fig tree withered from the
roots. 21Peter remembered and said to
Jesus, "Rabbi,[k] look! The fig tree you 11:21 [k]Mt 23:7
cursed has withered!"
22"Have[f] faith in God," Jesus answered. 23"I tell you the truth, if anyone
says to this mountain, 'Go, throw yourself into the sea,' and does not doubt in
his heart but believes that what he says
will happen, it will be done for him.[l] 11:23 [l]Mt 21:21
24Therefore I tell you, whatever you ask
for in prayer, believe that you have re-
ceived it, and it will be yours.[m] 25And 11:24 [m]Mt 7:7
when you stand praying, if you hold
anything against anyone, forgive him,
so that your Father in heaven may forgive you your sins.[g]"[n] 11:25 [n]Mt 6:14

The Authority of Jesus Questioned

27They arrived again in Jerusalem,
and while Jesus was walking in the

[a]9 A Hebrew expression meaning "Save!" which became an exclamation of praise; also in verse 10
[b]9 Psalm 118:25,26 [c]*17* Isaiah 56:7 [d]*17* Jer. 7:11
[e]*19* Some early manuscripts *he* [f]*22* Some early manuscripts *If you have* [g]*25* Some manuscripts *sins. 26But if you do not forgive, neither will your Father who is in heaven forgive your sins.*

temple courts, the chief priests, the
teachers of the law and the elders came
to him. 28“By what authority are you
doing these things?” they asked. “And
who gave you authority to do this?”
29Jesus replied, “I will ask you one
question. Answer me, and I will tell
you by what authority I am doing these
things. 30John’s baptism—was it from
heaven, or from men? Tell me!”
31They discussed it among themselves
and said, “If we say, ‘From heaven,’ he
will ask, ‘Then why didn’t you believe
him?’ 32But if we say, ‘From men’ …”
11:32 (They feared the people, for everyone
[o]Mt 11:9 held that John really was a prophet.)[o]
33So they answered Jesus, “We don’t
know.”
Jesus said, “Neither will I tell you
by what authority I am doing these
things.”

The Parable of the Tenants

12 He then began to speak to them
in parables: “A man planted a
12:1 [p]Isa 5:1-7 vineyard.[p] He put a wall around it,
dug a pit for the winepress and built a
watchtower. Then he rented the vineyard to some farmers and went away on
a journey. 2At harvest time he sent a servant to the tenants to collect from them
some of the fruit of the vineyard. 3But
they seized him, beat him and sent him
away empty-handed. 4Then he sent another servant to them; they struck this
man on the head and treated him
shamefully. 5He sent still another, and
that one they killed. He sent many others; some of them they beat, others they
killed.
6“He had one left to send, a son,
12:6 whom he loved. He sent him last of
[q]Heb 1:1-3 all,[q] saying, ‘They will respect my son.’
7“But the tenants said to one anoth-
er, ‘This is the heir. Come, let’s kill
him, and the inheritance will be ours.’
8So they took him and killed him, and
threw him out of the vineyard.
9“What then will the owner of the
vineyard do? He will come and kill
those tenants and give the vineyard to
others. 10Haven’t you read this scripture:

“ ‘The stone the builders rejected
12:10 [r]Ac 4:11 has become the capstone[a];[r]
12:11 11the Lord has done this,
[s]Ps 118:22,23 and it is marvelous in our eyes’[b]?”[s]

JOY

THE CAPSTONE

Mark 12:10

Jesus is the capstone; granite monolith is he.
So let the temple rise secure, a church for all
eternity.

12Then they looked for a way to arrest him because they knew he had spoken the parable against them. But they
were afraid of the crowd;[t] so they left 12:12
him and went away.[u] [t]Mk 11:18 [u]Mt 22:22

Paying Taxes to Caesar

13Later they sent some of the Pharisees and Herodians[v] to Jesus to catch 12:13
him in his words. 14They came to him[w] [v]Mt 22:16; Mk 3:6
and said, “Teacher, we know you are a [w]Mt 12:10
man of integrity. You aren’t swayed by
men, because you pay no attention to
who they are; but you teach the way of
God in accordance with the truth. Is
it right to pay taxes to Caesar or not?
15Should we pay or shouldn’t we?”
But Jesus knew their hypocrisy. “Why
are you trying to trap me?” he asked.
“Bring me a denarius and let me look
at it.” 16They brought the coin, and
he asked them, “Whose portrait is this?
And whose inscription?”
“Caesar’s,” they replied.
17Then Jesus said to them, “Give to
Caesar what is Caesar’s and to God
what is God’s.”[x] 12:17 [x]Ro 13:7
And they were amazed at him.

Marriage at the Resurrection

18Then the Sadducees,[y] who say there 12:18 [y]Ac 4:1
is no resurrection,[z] came to him with a [z]Ac 23:8; 1Co 15:12
question. 19“Teacher,” they said, “Mo-
ses wrote for us that if a man’s brother
dies and leaves a wife but no children,
the man must marry the widow and
have children for his brother.[a] 20Now 12:19 [a]Dt 25:5
there were seven brothers. The first one
married and died without leaving any
children. 21The second one married the
widow, but he also died, leaving no
child. It was the same with the third.
22In fact, none of the seven left any
children. Last of all, the woman died
too. 23At the resurrection[c] whose wife

[a]10 Or *cornerstone* [b]11 Psalm 118:22,23
[c]23 Some manuscripts *resurrection, when men rise from the dead,*

will she be, since the seven were married to her?"

24 Jesus replied, "Are you not in error because you do not know the Scriptures[b] or the power of God? 25 When the dead rise, they will neither marry nor be given in marriage; they will be like the angels in heaven.[c] 26 Now about the dead rising—have you not read in the book of Moses, in the account of the bush, how God said to him, 'I am the God of Abraham, the God of Isaac, and the God of Jacob'[a]?[d] 27 He is not the God of the dead, but of the living. You are badly mistaken!"

The Greatest Commandment

28 One of the teachers of the law[e] came and heard them debating. Noticing that Jesus had given them a good answer, he asked him, "Of all the commandments, which is the most important?"

29 "The most important one," answered Jesus, "is this: 'Hear, O Israel, the Lord our God, the Lord is one.[b] 30 Love the Lord your God with all your heart and with all your soul and with all your mind and with all your strength.'[c][f] 31 The second is this: 'Love your neighbor as yourself.'[d][g] There is no commandment greater than these."

32 "Well said, teacher," the man replied. "You are right in saying that God is one and there is no other but him.[h] 33 To love him with all your heart, with all your understanding and with all your strength, and to love your neighbor as yourself is more important than all burnt offerings and sacrifices."[i]

34 When Jesus saw that he had answered wisely, he said to him, "You are not far from the kingdom of God."[j] And from then on no one dared ask him any more questions.[k]

Whose Son Is the Christ?

35 While Jesus was teaching in the temple courts,[l] he asked, "How is it that the teachers of the law say that the Christ[e] is the son of David?[m] 36 David himself, speaking by the Holy Spirit,[n] declared:

" 'The Lord said to my Lord:
"Sit at my right hand
until I put your enemies
under your feet." '[f][o]

37 David himself calls him 'Lord.' How then can he be his son?"

The large crowd[p] listened to him with delight.

38 As he taught, Jesus said, "Watch out for the teachers of the law. They like to walk around in flowing robes and be greeted in the marketplaces, 39 and have the most important seats in the synagogues and the places of honor at banquets.[q] 40 They devour widows' houses and for a show make lengthy prayers. Such men will be punished most severely."

The Widow's Offering

41 Jesus sat down opposite the place where the offerings were put[r] and watched the crowd putting their money into the temple treasury. Many rich people threw in large amounts. 42 But a poor widow came and put in two very small copper coins,[g] worth only a fraction of a penny.[h]

43 Calling his disciples to him, Jesus said, "I tell you the truth, this poor widow has put more into the treasury than all the others. 44 They all gave out of their wealth; but she, out of her poverty, put in everything—all she had to live on."[s]

Signs of the End of the Age

13 As he was leaving the temple, one of his disciples said to him, "Look, Teacher! What massive stones! What magnificent buildings!"

2 "Do you see all these great buildings?" replied Jesus. "Not one stone here will be left on another; every one will be thrown down."[t]

3 As Jesus was sitting on the Mount of Olives[u] opposite the temple, Peter, James, John[v] and Andrew asked him privately, 4 "Tell us, when will these things happen? And what will be the sign that they are all about to be fulfilled?"

5 Jesus said to them: "Watch out that no one deceives you.[w] 6 Many will come in my name, claiming, 'I am he,' and will deceive many. 7 When you hear of wars and rumors of wars, do not be alarmed. Such things must happen, but

12:24 [b]2Ti 3:15-17
12:25 [c]1Co 15:42, 49,52
12:26 [d]Ex 3:6
12:28 [e]Lk 10:25-28; 20:39
12:30 [f]Dt 6:4,5
12:31 [g]Lev 19:18; Mt 5:43
12:32 [h]Dt 4:35,39; Isa 45:6,14; 46:9
12:33 [i]1Sa 15:22; Hos 6:6; Mic 6:6-8; Heb 10:8
12:34 [j]Mt 3:2 [k]Mt 22:46; Lk 20:40
12:35 [l]Mt 26:55 [m]Mt 9:27
12:36 [n]2Sa 23:2 [o]Ps 110:1; Mt 22:44
12:37 [p]Jn 12:9
12:39 [q]Lk 11:43
12:41 [r]2Ki 12:9; Jn 8:20
12:44 [s]2Co 8:12
13:2 [t]Lk 19:44
13:3 [u]Mt 21:1 [v]Mt 4:21
13:5 [w]ver 22; Jer 29:8; Eph 5:6; 2Th 2:3, 10-12; 1Ti 4:1; 2Ti 3:13; 1Jn 4:6

[a] *26* Exodus 3:6 [b] *29* Or *the Lord our God is one Lord* [c] *30* Deut. 6:4,5 [d] *31* Lev. 19:18 [e] *35* Or *Messiah* [f] *36* Psalm 110:1 [g] *42* Greek *two lepta* [h] *42* Greek *kodrantes*

the end is still to come. 8Nation will rise
against nation, and kingdom against
kingdom. There will be earthquakes in
various places, and famines. These are
the beginning of birth pains.
9"You must be on your guard. You
13:9 will be handed over to the local coun-
[x]Mt 10:17 cils and flogged in the synagogues.[x]
On account of me you will stand be-
fore governors and kings as witnesses
to them. 10And the gospel must first
be preached to all nations. 11Whenever
you are arrested and brought to trial,
do not worry beforehand about what to
say. Just say whatever is given you at the
13:11 time, for it is not you speaking, but the
[y]Mt 10:19,20; Lk 12:11,12 Holy Spirit.[y]
13:12 12"Brother will betray brother to
[z]Mic 7:6; death, and a father his child. Children
Mt 10:21; Lk 12:51-53 will rebel against their parents and have
13:13 them put to death.[z] 13All men will hate
[a]Jn 15:21 you because of me,[a] but he who stands
[b]Mt 10:22 firm to the end will be saved.[b]

SELF-CONTROL

THE ABOMINATION THAT CAUSES DESOLATION

Mark 13:14

During the reign of the Seleucids over Jerusalem, Greek gods were placed in the Jewish temple. Jerusalem was paganized and swine were slaughtered as offerings to Greek deities where El-Shaddai, God Almighty, had once held sway. It was an abomination that causes desolation, a phenomenon of desecration, but also an incident for contemplation.

Apocalypse is triggered by sacrilege. Pity idols and idolaters who never know the size of the God they offend.

14"When you see 'the abomination
13:14 that causes desolation'[a][c] standing where
[c]Da 9:27; 11:31; 12:11 it[b] does not belong—let the reader understand—then let those who are in
Judea flee to the mountains. 15Let no
one on the roof of his house go down
or enter the house to take anything out.
16Let no one in the field go back to
get his cloak. 17How dreadful it will
be in those days for pregnant women
13:17 [d]Lk 23:29 and nursing mothers![d] 18Pray that this
will not take place in winter, 19because
those will be days of distress unequaled
13:19 from the beginning, when God creat-
[e]Mk 10:6 ed the world,[e] until now—and never
to be equaled again.[f] 20If the Lord had 13:19 [f]Da 9:26;
not cut short those days, no one would 12:1;
survive. But for the sake of the elect, Joel 2:2
whom he has chosen, he has shortened
them. 21At that time if anyone says
to you, 'Look, here is the Christ[c]!' or, 13:21
'Look, there he is!' do not believe it.[g] [g]Lk 17:23;
22For false Christs and false prophets[h] 21:8
will appear and perform signs and mir- 13:22
acles[i] to deceive the elect—if that were [h]Mt 7:15 [i]Jn 4:48;
possible. 23So be on your guard;[j] I have 2Th 2:9,10
told you everything ahead of time. 13:23
24"But in those days, following that [j]2Pe 3:17
distress,

" 'the sun will be darkened,
and the moon will not give its
light;
25the stars will fall from the sky,
and the heavenly bodies will be
shaken.'[d][k] 13:25 [k]Isa 13:10;

34:4;
26"At that time men will see the Son Mt 24:29
of Man coming in clouds[l] with great
power and glory. 27And he will send 13:26 [l]Da 7:13;
his angels and gather his elect from the Mt 16:27;
four winds, from the ends of the earth Rev 1:7
to the ends of the heavens.[m] 13:27 [m]Zec 2:6
28"Now learn this lesson from the
fig tree: As soon as its twigs get tender
and its leaves come out, you know that
summer is near. 29Even so, when you
see these things happening, you know
that it is near, right at the door. 30I
tell you the truth, this generation[e][n] will 13:30 [n]Lk 17:25
certainly not pass away until all these [o]Mk 9:1
things have happened.[o] 31Heaven and
earth will pass away, but my words will 13:31
never pass away.[p] [p]Mt 5:18

The Day and Hour Unknown

32"No one knows about that day or
hour, not even the angels in heaven,
nor the Son, but only the Father.[q] 33Be 13:32 [q]Ac 1:7;
on guard! Be alert[f]![r] You do not know 1Th 5:1,2
when that time will come. 34It's like a 13:33
man going away: He leaves his house [r]1Th 5:6
and puts his servants[s] in charge, each 13:34
with his assigned task, and tells the one [s]Mt 25:14
at the door to keep watch.
35"Therefore keep watch because you
do not know when the owner of the
house will come back—whether in the
evening, or at midnight, or when the
rooster crows, or at dawn. 36If he comes

[a] *14* Daniel 9:27; 11:31; 12:11 [b] *14* Or *he*; also in verse 29 [c] *21* Or *Messiah* [d] 25 Isaiah 13:10; 34:4 [e] *30* Or *race* [f] *33* Some manuscripts *alert and pray*

suddenly, do not let him find you sleeping. 37What I say to you, I say to everyone: 'Watch!' "[t]

13:37 [t]Lk 12:35-40

Jesus Anointed at Bethany

14 Now the Passover[u] and the Feast of Unleavened Bread were only two days away, and the chief priests and the teachers of the law were looking for some sly way to arrest Jesus and kill him.[v] 2"But not during the Feast," they said, "or the people may riot."

3While he was in Bethany,[w] reclining at the table in the home of a man known as Simon the Leper, a woman came with an alabaster jar of very expensive perfume, made of pure nard. She broke the jar and poured the perfume on his head.[x]

4Some of those present were saying indignantly to one another, "Why this waste of perfume? 5It could have been sold for more than a year's wages[a] and the money given to the poor." And they rebuked her harshly.

6"Leave her alone," said Jesus. "Why are you bothering her? She has done a beautiful thing to me. 7The poor you will always have with you, and you can help them any time you want.[y] But you will not always have me. 8She did what she could. She poured perfume on my body beforehand to prepare for my burial.[z] 9I tell you the truth, wherever the gospel is preached throughout the world,[a] what she has done will also be told, in memory of her."

10Then Judas Iscariot, one of the Twelve,[b] went to the chief priests to betray Jesus to them.[c] 11They were delighted to hear this and promised to give him money. So he watched for an opportunity to hand him over.

14:1 [u]Jn 11:55; 13:1 [v]Mt 12:14
14:3 [w]Mt 21:17 [x]Lk 7:37-39
14:7 [y]Dt 15:11
14:8 [z]Jn 19:40
14:9 [a]Mt 24:14; Mk 16:15
14:10 [b]Mk 3:16-19 [c]Mt 10:4

The Lord's Supper

12On the first day of the Feast of Unleavened Bread, when it was customary to sacrifice the Passover lamb,[d] Jesus' disciples asked him, "Where do you want us to go and make preparations for you to eat the Passover?"

13So he sent two of his disciples, telling them, "Go into the city, and a man carrying a jar of water will meet you. Follow him. 14Say to the owner of the house he enters, 'The Teacher asks: Where is my guest room, where I may eat the Passover with my disciples?' 15He will show you a large upper room,[e] furnished and ready. Make preparations for us there."

16The disciples left, went into the city and found things just as Jesus had told them. So they prepared the Passover.

17When evening came, Jesus arrived with the Twelve. 18While they were reclining at the table eating, he said, "I tell you the truth, one of you will betray me—one who is eating with me."

19They were saddened, and one by one they said to him, "Surely not I?"

20"It is one of the Twelve," he replied, "one who dips bread into the bowl with me.[f] 21The Son of Man[g] will go just as it is written about him. But woe to that man who betrays the Son of Man! It would be better for him if he had not been born."

22While they were eating, Jesus took bread, gave thanks and broke it,[h] and gave it to his disciples, saying, "Take it; this is my body."

23Then he took the cup, gave thanks and offered it to them, and they all drank from it.[i]

14:12 [d]Ex 12:1-11; Dt 16:1-4; 1Co 5:7
14:15 [e]Ac 1:13
14:20 [f]Jn 13:18-27
14:21 [g]Mt 8:20
14:22 [h]Mt 14:19
14:23 [i]1Co 10:16

▸ LOVE
THE CUP

Mark 14:23

The wine of Maundy Thursday mirrored the thorn-crowned face of love.

What Jesus really says at each Communion is this:

"This is my blood! This is my body! Now, let's talk about your blood and how you spend it.

Let's talk about your body and how you use it.

Calvary was not *my* business; it is *our* business."

24"This is my blood of the[b] covenant,[j] which is poured out for many," he said to them. 25"I tell you the truth, I will not drink again of the fruit of the vine until that day when I drink it anew in the kingdom of God."[k]

26When they had sung a hymn, they went out to the Mount of Olives.[l]

14:24 [j]Mt 26:28
14:25 [k]Mt 3:2
14:26 [l]Mt 21:1

[a]5 Greek *than three hundred denarii* [b]24 Some manuscripts *the new*

Jesus Predicts Peter's Denial

27“You will all fall away,” Jesus told
them, “for it is written:

“ ‘I will strike the shepherd,
14:27 [m]Zec 13:7 and the sheep will be scattered.’[a][m]

14:28 [n]Mk 16:7 28But after I have risen, I will go ahead
of you into Galilee.”[n]
29Peter declared, “Even if all fall away,
I will not.”
30“I tell you the truth,” Jesus answered, “today—yes, tonight—before
14:30 the rooster crows twice[b] you yourself
[o]ver 66-72; will disown me three times.”[o]
Lk 22:34; Jn 13:38 31But Peter insisted emphatically,
14:31 “Even if I have to die with you,[p] I will
[p]Lk 22:33; Jn never disown you.” And all the others
13:37 said the same.

Gethsemane

32They went to a place called Gethsemane, and Jesus said to his disciples,
“Sit here while I pray.” 33He took Peter,
14:33 [q]Mt 4:21 James and John[q] along with him, and
he began to be deeply distressed and
troubled. 34“My soul is overwhelmed
14:34 [r]Jn 12:27 with sorrow to the point of death,”[r]
he said to them. “Stay here and keep
watch.”
35Going a little farther, he fell to the
ground and prayed that if possible the
14:35 [s]ver 41; hour[s] might pass from him. 36*“Abba,*[c]
Mt 26:18 Father,”[t] he said, “everything is possible
14:36 for you. Take this cup[u] from me. Yet
[t]Ro 8:15; Gal 4:6 not what I will, but what you will.”[v]
[u]Mt 20:22 37Then he returned to his disciples
[v]Mt 26:39 and found them sleeping. “Simon,” he
said to Peter, “are you asleep? Could you
not keep watch for one hour? 38Watch
and pray so that you will not fall into
14:38 [w]Mt 6:13 temptation.[w] The spirit is willing, but
[x]Ro 7:22,23 the body is weak.”[x]
39Once more he went away and
prayed the same thing. 40When he came
back, he again found them sleeping, because their eyes were heavy. They did
not know what to say to him.
41Returning the third time, he said
to them, “Are you still sleeping and
14:41 [y]ver 35; resting? Enough! The hour[y] has come.
Mt 26:18 Look, the Son of Man is betrayed into
the hands of sinners. 42Rise! Let us go!
Here comes my betrayer!”

Jesus Arrested

14:43 [z]Mt 10:4 43Just as he was speaking, Judas,[z] one
of the Twelve, appeared. With him was
a crowd armed with swords and clubs,
sent from the chief priests, the teachers
of the law, and the elders.
44Now the betrayer had arranged a
signal with them: “The one I kiss is the
man; arrest him and lead him away under guard.” 45Going at once to Jesus,
Judas said, “Rabbi!”[a] and kissed him. 14:45 [a]Mt 23:7
46The men seized Jesus and arrested
him. 47Then one of those standing near
drew his sword and struck the servant of
the high priest, cutting off his ear.
48“Am I leading a rebellion,” said
Jesus, “that you have come out with
swords and clubs to capture me? 49Ev-
ery day I was with you, teaching in
the temple courts,[b] and you did not 14:49 [b]Mt 26:55
arrest me. But the Scriptures must be [c]Isa 53:7-12; Mt 1:22
fulfilled.”[c] 50Then everyone deserted
him and fled.[d] 14:50 [d]ver 27
51A young man, wearing nothing but
a linen garment, was following Jesus.
When they seized him, 52he fled naked,
leaving his garment behind.

Before the Sanhedrin

53They took Jesus to the high priest,
and all the chief priests, elders and
teachers of the law came together. 54Pe-
ter followed him at a distance, right into
the courtyard of the high priest.[e] There 14:54 [e]Mt 26:3
he sat with the guards and warmed [f]Jn 18:18
himself at the fire.[f]
55The chief priests and the whole
Sanhedrin[g] were looking for evidence 14:55 [g]Mt 5:22
against Jesus so that they could put him
to death, but they did not find any.
56Many testified falsely against him, but
their statements did not agree.
57Then some stood up and gave
this false testimony against him: 58“We
heard him say, ‘I will destroy this man-
made temple and in three days will
build another,[h] not made by man.’ ” 14:58 [h]Mk 15:29; Jn 2:19
59Yet even then their testimony did not
agree.
60Then the high priest stood up before them and asked Jesus, “Are you not
going to answer? What is this testimony that these men are bringing against
you?” 61But Jesus remained silent and 14:61 [i]Isa 53:7; Mt 27:12,14; Mk 15:5; Lk 23:9; Jn 19:9
gave no answer.[i]
Again the high priest asked him, “Are
you the Christ,[d] the Son of the Blessed [j]Mt 16:16; Jn 4:25,26
One?”[j]

[a]*27* Zech. 13:7 [b]*30* Some early manuscripts do not have *twice.* [c]*36* Aramaic for *Father* [d]*61* Or *Messiah*

62"I am," said Jesus. "And you will
see the Son of Man sitting at the right
14:62 hand of the Mighty One and coming
kRev 1:7 on the clouds of heaven."[k]
63The high priest tore his clothes.[l]
14:63 lLev 10:6; "Why do we need any more witnesses?"
21:10; he asked. 64"You have heard the blas-
Nu 14:6; Ac 14:14 phemy. What do you think?"
They all condemned him as worthy
14:64 of death.[m] 65Then some began to spit
mLev 24:16 at him; they blindfolded him, struck
him with their fists, and said, "Prophesy!" And the guards took him and beat
14:65 nMt 16:21 him.[n]

Peter Disowns Jesus

66While Peter was below in the
14:66 courtyard,[o] one of the servant girls of
over 54 the high priest came by. 67When she
14:67 saw Peter warming himself,[p] she looked
pver 54 qMk 1:24 closely at him.
"You also were with that Nazarene,
Jesus,"[q] she said.
68But he denied it. "I don't know
or understand what you're talking
14:68 about,"[r] he said, and went out into the
rver 30,72 entryway.[a]
69When the servant girl saw him
there, she said again to those standing
14:70 around, "This fellow is one of them."
sver 30,68,72 tAc 2:7 70Again he denied it.[s]
After a little while, those standing
near said to Peter, "Surely you are one
of them, for you are a Galilean."[t]
71He began to call down curses on
himself, and he swore to them, "I don't
14:71 uver 30,72 know this man you're talking about."[u]
72Immediately the rooster crowed the
second time.[b] Then Peter remembered
the word Jesus had spoken to him: "Be-
14:72 fore the rooster crows twice[c] you will
vver 30,68 disown me three times."[v] And he broke
down and wept.

Jesus Before Pilate

15 Very early in the morning, the
chief priests, with the elders,
15:1 the teachers of the law[w] and the whole
wMt 27:1; Lk 22:66 Sanhedrin,[x] reached a decision. They
xMt 5:22 yMt 27:2 bound Jesus, led him away and handed
him over to Pilate.[y]
15:2 2"Are you the king of the Jews?"[z]
zver 9,12, 18,26; Mt 2:2 asked Pilate.
"Yes, it is as you say," Jesus replied.
3The chief priests accused him of
many things. 4So again Pilate asked
him, "Aren't you going to answer? See
how many things they are accusing
you of."
5But Jesus still made no reply,[a] and 15:5
Pilate was amazed. aMk 14:61
6Now it was the custom at the Feast
to release a prisoner whom the people
requested. 7A man called Barabbas was
in prison with the insurrectionists who
had committed murder in the uprising.
8The crowd came up and asked Pilate
to do for them what he usually did.
9"Do you want me to release to you 15:9
the king of the Jews?"[b] asked Pilate, bver 2
10knowing it was out of envy that the
chief priests had handed Jesus over to
him. 11But the chief priests stirred up
the crowd to have Pilate release Barab- 15:11
bas[c] instead. cAc 3:14
12"What shall I do, then, with the
one you call the king of the Jews?" Pilate asked them.
13"Crucify him!" they shouted.
14"Why? What crime has he committed?" asked Pilate.
But they shouted all the louder, "Crucify him!"
15Wanting to satisfy the crowd, Pilate
released Barabbas to them. He had Je-
sus flogged,[d] and handed him over to 15:15 dIsa 53:6
be crucified.

The Soldiers Mock Jesus

16The soldiers led Jesus away into the
palace[e] (that is, the Praetorium) and 15:16 eJn 18:28,33;
called together the whole company of 19:9
soldiers. 17They put a purple robe on
him, then twisted together a crown of
thorns and set it on him. 18And they
began to call out to him, "Hail, king 15:18
of the Jews!"[f] 19Again and again they fver 2
struck him on the head with a staff
and spit on him. Falling on their knees,
they paid homage to him. 20And when
they had mocked him, they took off the
purple robe and put his own clothes on
him. Then they led him out[g] to crucify 15:20
him. gHeb 13:12

The Crucifixion

21A certain man from Cyrene,[h] Si- 15:21 hMt 27:32
mon, the father of Alexander and iRo 16:13
Rufus,[i] was passing by on his way in jMt 27:32;
from the country, and they forced him Lk 23:26
to carry the cross.[j] 22They brought

[a]*68* Some early manuscripts *entryway and the rooster crowed* [b]*72* Some early manuscripts do not have *the second time.* [c]*72* Some early manuscripts do not have *twice.*

Jesus to the place called Golgotha
(which means The Place of the Skull).
23Then they offered him wine mixed
15:23 [k]ver 36; Ps 69:21; Pr 31:6 with myrrh,[k] but he did not take it.
24And they crucified him. Dividing up
his clothes, they cast lots[l] to see what
15:24 [l]Ps 22:18 each would get.
25It was the third hour when they
crucified him. 26The written notice of
the charge against him read: THE KING
15:26 [m]ver 2 OF THE JEWS.[m] 27They crucified two
robbers with him, one on his right and
one on his left.[a] 29Those who passed
by hurled insults at him, shaking their
15:29 [n]Ps 22:7; 109:25 [o]Mk 14:58; Jn 2:19 heads[n] and saying, "So! You who are
going to destroy the temple and build
it in three days,[o] 30come down from the
cross and save yourself!"
31In the same way the chief priests
and the teachers of the law mocked
15:31 [p]Ps 22:7 him[p] among themselves. "He saved others," they said, "but he can't save him-
15:32 [q]Mk 14:61 [r]ver 2 self! 32Let this Christ,[b] [q] this King of
Israel,[r] come down now from the cross,
that we may see and believe." Those
crucified with him also heaped insults
on him.

The Death of Jesus

33At the sixth hour darkness came
over the whole land until the ninth
15:33 [s]Am 8:9 hour.[s] 34And at the ninth hour Jesus
cried out in a loud voice, *"Eloi, Eloi,
lama sabachthani?"*—which means,
"My God, my God, why have you for-
15:34 [t]Ps 22:1 saken me?"[c] [t]
35When some of those standing near
heard this, they said, "Listen, he's calling Elijah."
36One man ran, filled a sponge with
15:36 [u]ver 23; Ps 69:21 wine vinegar,[u] put it on a stick, and offered it to Jesus to drink. "Now leave
him alone. Let's see if Elijah comes to
take him down," he said.
37With a loud cry, Jesus breathed his
15:37 [v]Jn 19:30 last.[v]
15:38 [w]Heb 10:19,20 38The curtain of the temple was torn
in two from top to bottom.[w] 39And
15:39 [x]ver 45 [y]Mk 1:1,11; 9:7; Mt 4:3 when the centurion,[x] who stood there
in front of Jesus, heard his cry and[d] saw
how he died, he said, "Surely this man
was the Son[e] of God!"[y]
15:40 [z]Ps 38:11 [a]Mk 16:1; Lk 24:10; Jn 19:25 40Some women were watching from
a distance.[z] Among them were Mary
Magdalene, Mary the mother of James
the younger and of Joses, and Salome.[a]
41In Galilee these women had followed
him and cared for his needs. Many other women who had come up with him
to Jerusalem were also there.[b] 15:41 [b]Mt 27:55,56; Lk 8:2,3

The Burial of Jesus

42It was Preparation Day (that is, the
day before the Sabbath).[c] So as evening 15:42 [c]Mt 27:62; Jn 19:31
approached, 43Joseph of Arimathea, a
prominent member of the Council,[d] 15:43 [d]Mt 5:22 [e]Mt 3:2; Lk 2:25,38
who was himself waiting for the king-
dom of God,[e] went boldly to Pilate and
asked for Jesus' body. 44Pilate was surprised to hear that he was already dead.
Summoning the centurion,[f] he asked 15:45 [f]ver 39
him if Jesus had already died. 45When
he learned from the centurion that it
was so, he gave the body to Joseph. 46So
Joseph bought some linen cloth, took
down the body, wrapped it in the lin-
en, and placed it in a tomb cut out of
rock. Then he rolled a stone against the
entrance of the tomb.[g] 47Mary Magda- 15:46 [g]Mk 16:3
lene and Mary the mother of Joses[h] saw 15:47 [h]ver 40
where he was laid.

KINDNESS

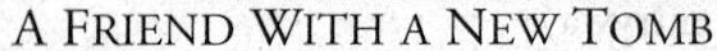

A FRIEND WITH A NEW TOMB

Mark 15:43

In light of the fact that the bodies of crucified criminals were thrown on the garbage dump of the city and set afire, one can imagine that Joseph's plea for Jesus' body must have set the angels singing.

The Resurrection

16 When the Sabbath was over,
Mary Magdalene, Mary the
mother of James, and Salome bought
spices[i] so that they might go to anoint 16:1 [i]Lk 23:56; Jn 19:39,40
Jesus' body. 2Very early on the first day
of the week, just after sunrise, they were
on their way to the tomb 3and they
asked each other, "Who will roll the
stone away from the entrance of the
tomb?"[j] 16:3 [j]Mk 15:46
4But when they looked up, they saw
that the stone, which was very large, had
been rolled away. 5As they entered the
tomb, they saw a young man dressed in
a white robe[k] sitting on the right side, 16:5 [k]Jn 20:12
and they were alarmed.

[a]27 Some manuscripts *left,* [28]*and the scripture was fulfilled which says, "He was counted with the lawless ones"* (Isaiah 53:12) [b]*32* Or *Messiah* [c]*34* Psalm 22:1 [d]*39* Some manuscripts do not have *heard his cry and* [e]*39* Or *a son*

FAITHFULNESS

EASTER LOVE

Mark 16:2

These women got up early. While the eastern sky was aflame and the sun was chasing demons back to hell, the chill of night was dying. Undoubtedly this was the best time to poke around in a tomb, looking for a dead Messiah. He wasn't there, but at least the light was good.

6"Don't be alarmed," he said. "You
16:6 [l]Mk 1:24 are looking for Jesus the Nazarene,[l] who
was crucified. He has risen! He is not
here. See the place where they laid him.
7But go, tell his disciples and Peter,
'He is going ahead of you into Galilee.
16:7 [m]Jn 21:1-23 [n]Mk 14:28 There you will see him,[m] just as he told
you.' "[n]
8Trembling and bewildered, the
women went out and fled from the
tomb. They said nothing to anyone, because they were afraid.

[The earliest manuscripts and some other ancient witnesses do not have Mark 16:9-20.]

9When Jesus rose early on the first
day of the week, he appeared first to
16:9 [o]Jn 20:11-18 Mary Magdalene,[o] out of whom he had
driven seven demons. 10She went and
told those who had been with him
and who were mourning and weeping.
11When they heard that Jesus was alive
and that she had seen him, they did not
believe it.[p] 16:11 [p]ver 13,14; Lk 24:11
12Afterward Jesus appeared in a different form to two of them while they
were walking in the country.[q] 13These 16:12 [q]Lk 24:13-32
returned and reported it to the rest; but
they did not believe them either.
14Later Jesus appeared to the Eleven
as they were eating; he rebuked them
for their lack of faith and their stub- 16:14 [r]Lk 24:36-43
born refusal to believe those who had
seen him after he had risen.[r] 16:15 [s]Mt 28:18-20; Lk 24:47,48
15He said to them, "Go into all the
world and preach the good news to
all creation.[s] 16Whoever believes and 16:16 [t]Jn 3:16,18,36; Ac 16:31
is baptized will be saved, but whoever
does not believe will be condemned.[t]
17And these signs will accompany those 16:17 [u]Mk 9:38; | Lk 10:17; Ac 5:16; 8:7; 16:18; 19:13-16 [v]Ac 2:4; 10:46; 19:6; 1Co 12:10, 28,30
who believe: In my name they will drive
out demons;[u] they will speak in new
tongues;[v] 18they will pick up snakes[w]
with their hands; and when they drink
deadly poison, it will not hurt them at
all; they will place their hands on[x] sick 16:18 [w]Lk 10:19; Ac 28:3-5 [x]Ac 6:6
people, and they will get well."
19After the Lord Jesus had spoken to
them, he was taken up into heaven[y] and 16:19 [y]Lk 24:50,51; Jn 6:62; Ac 1:9-11; 1Ti 3:16 [z]Ps 110:1; Ro 8:34; Col 3:1; Heb 1:3; 12:2
he sat at the right hand of God.[z] 20Then
the disciples went out and preached everywhere, and the Lord worked with
them and confirmed his word by the
signs that accompanied it.

LUKE

AUTHORSHIP AND DATE

The Gospel of Luke gives us a detailed picture of the birth of Christ; it gives information a physician might include when telling the story. While Dr. Luke did not disclose his name in the narrative account, in comparing the prologues of Luke and Acts we can see that both books have the same author; and since Acts contains the famous "we" passages (Acts 16:10–17; 20:5–15), the authorship is easily assigned to Luke.

c. A.D. 60

KEY THEMES

The Gospel of Luke gives us some glimpses of Jesus that are not found in the other Gospels. The events included in the birth narrative are different from those found in Matthew; these incidents include the stories of Simeon, Anna and the birth of John the Baptist. The Gospel of Luke also includes a unique account of Jesus in the temple at age 12. Most scholars agree that this is the most all-inclusive of the Gospels and that the comprehensive scope of the entire life of Christ is better seen here than anywhere else. Luke also gave a prominence not seen in any other Gospel to the women who followed Christ. Since this Gospel, more than any other, contains a "woman's view," some have suggested that Mary may have been among those who helped Luke know of Christ—particularly his early years. The Gospel of Luke focuses on Jesus the Savior and falls rather naturally into three divisions:

1. The birth, temple experience, baptism and temptation of Jesus (see 1:1—4:13)
2. The ministry of Jesus (see 4:14—21:38)
3. The final events of Jesus' death and resurrection (see 22:1—24:53)

FRUIT OF THE SPIRIT IN LUKE

Love: Jesus said, "Love your enemies, do good to those who hate you... If you love those who love you, what credit is that to you? Even 'sinners' love those who love them" (6:27,32). Loving the unlovely is the hard work of grace. Yet that's exactly what Christ did for us when he welcomed us into his kingdom. Having done this himself, it is altogether reasonable that he should require it of us.

Joy: "My soul glorifies the Lord," cried Mary in joy (1:46). Could she really have found such joy after learning the requirements of God? She was about to submit to a pregnancy she could never explain, months of village criticism, and the requirements necessary for her to be the vessel that would bear the Son of God. God gave her a splintering assignment, and she responded to it with joy. It is always the heaviness of the burden that teaches us the best song.

Peace: "Glory to God in the highest," cried the angels, "and on earth peace to men on whom his favor rests" (2:14). The peace of God is not given to those who commit themselves to tyranny and abuse, but to those who receive his grace. Peace to the receivers of grace is as constant as the beating of their hearts.

Patience: The disciples asked Jesus what the sign would be of the end of the age (see 21:7). Jesus dealt with the grand question of every age: "When God? When?" Those who sin in this manner impatiently seek to wrest answers out of God that will supply their every whim. God is never concerned with explaining the "when" of things, only the "why."

Kindness: Kindness arises from gratitude for gifts impossible to repay. Gratitude prompted a woman to anoint Jesus with perfume (see 7:38). Her anointing seemed bold and at the edge of propriety to all those who witnessed it. But Jesus understood that a grateful heart that has received much desires to give some recompense, and kindness is how gratitude gains its voice and says, "Thank you."

Faithfulness: Luke 11:28 defines faithfulness as always doing what God tells us to do, exactly when he tells us to do it.

Gentleness: When the iron was in his flesh and his nervous system was screaming for death, Jesus could not forget the art of gentleness, which he had perfected in better days. And so he turned to the dying, repentant thief and assured him—with no ugly judgmentalism—"Today you will be with me in paradise" (23:43).

Self-Control: The rich young man who came to Jesus wanted what we are all prone to want—great godliness with great riches (see 18:18–23). Unfortunately, we must prioritize and decide which of the two we most cherish. To choose riches means that we will not have either godliness or riches for very long, for riches give only momentary happiness and provide a grand disinheritance at the moment of death. But to choose godliness means that we will receive life everlasting (beginning in that moment) and wealth immeasurable in the life to come.

Introduction

1 Many have undertaken to draw up
an account of the things that have
been fulfilled[a] among us, 2just as they
were handed down to us by those who
from the first[a] were eyewitnesses[b] and
servants of the word.[c] 3Therefore, since I
myself have carefully investigated everything from the beginning, it seemed
good also to me to write an orderly account[d] for you, most excellent[e] Theophilus,[f] 4so that you may know the
certainty of the things you have been
taught.[g]

1:2 [a]Mk 1:1; Jn 15:27; Ac 1:21,22 [b]Heb 2:3; 1Pe 5:1; 2Pe 1:16; 1Jn 1:1 [c]Mk 4:14
1:3 [d]Ac 11:4 [e]Ac 24:3; 26:25 [f]Ac 1:1
1:4 [g]Jn 20:31

FAITHFULNESS

SIGNIFICANCE

Luke 1:3

Luke took time from his medical practice to write to his friend Theophilus. He wanted him to have an orderly and faithful account of the most important life ever lived. *Theophilus* means "friend of God." Luke wanted to make sure his friend lived up to his name.

The Birth of John the Baptist Foretold

5In the time of Herod king of Judea[h]
there was a priest named Zechariah,
who belonged to the priestly division
of Abijah;[i] his wife Elizabeth was also
a descendant of Aaron. 6Both of them
were upright in the sight of God, observing all the Lord's commandments
and regulations blamelessly.[j] 7But they
had no children, because Elizabeth was
barren; and they were both well along
in years.

8Once when Zechariah's division was
on duty and he was serving as priest
before God,[k] 9he was chosen by lot,
according to the custom of the priesthood, to go into the temple of the Lord
and burn incense.[l] 10And when the time
for the burning of incense came, all the
assembled worshipers were praying outside.[m]

11Then an angel[n] of the Lord appeared to him, standing at the right side
of the altar of incense.[o] 12When Zechariah saw him, he was startled and was
gripped with fear.[p] 13But the angel said
to him: "Do not be afraid,[q] Zechariah;
your prayer has been heard. Your wife
Elizabeth will bear you a son, and you
are to give him the name John.[r] 14He
will be a joy and delight to you, and
many will rejoice because of his birth,[s]
15for he will be great in the sight of

1:5 [h]Mt 2:1 [i]1Ch 24:10
1:6 [j]Ge 7:1; 1Ki 9:4
1:8 [k]1Ch 24:19; 2Ch 8:14
1:9 [l]Ex 30:7,8; 1Ch 23:13; 2Ch 29:11
1:10 [m]Lev 16:17
1:11 [n]Ac 5:19 [o]Ex 30:1-10
1:12 [p]Jdg 6:22,23; 13:22
1:13 [q]ver 30; Mt 14:27 [r]ver 60,63
1:14 [s]ver 58

[a]*1* Or *been surely believed*

DAY 2 TWO

PATIENCE AND THE PURPOSE OF GOD IN MY LIFE

Luke 1:5–7,13

For those believers hungry to know and serve God, there may be only one truly important virtue: patience. Oh, how we wish he would hurry his agenda. How we wish he would give us one little peek into that future that is ever so slow in coming. We wish we could pry the calendar from his hand and rip that big watch off his divine wrist. Why are there no clues for tomorrow? Why, when we are so ready to go, is God so late in keeping his appointment with us? God, give us patience, right now!

Zechariah and Elizabeth waited a lifetime. Not until they reached the age when pregnancy appeared a physical impossibility did God bless them with a child.

In one of my children's poems, Sarah—herself in a situation similar to Elizabeth's—finally confesses her pregnancy to Abraham by saying, "I'm gonna have a baby, Abie." The people rejoice with these elderly parents-to-be, but they would have preferred that the baby come earlier. Then when the baby is born, they all smile at Abie and say "Happy Baby!"

The crux of grace is this: God himself smiles down upon "nobody other than Sarah the mother." It was, after all, she who was a living example of the patience of God.

God has a plan for our lives. We all enjoy God's plan and, at least in retrospect, agree that it is just right for us. But it can take years for God to reveal his plan to us, and sometimes—on the front side of all that we wait for—we wish that God would move a little faster. However, from the perspective of hindsight, even Elizabeth and Zechariah would have to agree: Not only is the plan right, but it is well worth our patience.

To begin a study on the topic of Patience, the Slowly Acquired Virtue, turn to the home page on page 565.

the Lord. He is never to take wine or
1:15 [t]Nu 6:3; other fermented drink,[t] and he will be
Jdg 13:4; filled with the Holy Spirit even from
Lk 7:33 [u]Jer 1:5; birth.[a][u] 16Many of the people of Israel
Gal 1:15 will he bring back to the Lord their
1:17 God. 17And he will go on before the
[v]ver 76 Lord,[v] in the spirit and power of Elijah,[w]
[w]Mt 11:14 [x]Mal 4:5,6 to turn the hearts of the fathers to
their children[x] and the disobedient to
the wisdom of the righteous—to make
ready a people prepared for the Lord."
18Zechariah asked the angel, "How
can I be sure of this? I am an old man
1:18 [y]ver 34; and my wife is well along in years."[y]
Ge 17:17 19The angel answered, "I am Gabriel.[z]
1:19 I stand in the presence of God, and I
[z]ver 26; Mt 18:10; have been sent to speak to you and to
Da 8:16; 9:21 tell you this good news. 20And now you
1:20 will be silent and not able to speak[a] un-
[a]Eze 3:26 til the day this happens, because you
did not believe my words, which will
come true at their proper time."
21Meanwhile, the people were waiting for Zechariah and wondering why
he stayed so long in the temple. 22When
he came out, he could not speak to
them. They realized he had seen a vision in the temple, for he kept making
signs[b] to them but remained unable to 1:22 [b]ver 62
speak.
23When his time of service was completed, he returned home. 24After this
his wife Elizabeth became pregnant and
for five months remained in seclusion.
25"The Lord has done this for me," she
said. "In these days he has shown his fa-
vor and taken away my disgrace[c] among 1:25 [c]Ge 30:23;
the people." Isa 4:1

The Birth of Jesus Foretold

1:26 [d]ver 19 [e]Mt 2:23
26In the sixth month, God sent the
angel Gabriel[d] to Nazareth,[e] a town 1:27 [f]Mt
in Galilee, 27to a virgin pledged to be 1:16,18,20;
married to a man named Joseph,[f] a Lk 2:4

[a]15 Or *from his mother's womb*

MARY

Patience, the "Yes, Lord" Mystique (1:1–80)

Patience never argues with God. Back talk is one of the primary indicators of impatience. Gabriel assuaged Mary's fear (see Luke 1:30), but he did not accuse her of impatience. This passage is a testimony to Mary's ordered, unhurried and obedient walk of patience. Gabriel, after all, did give her some pretty astonishing news: First, he told her that she was going to have a baby before she was married (see v. 31). He also told her that this baby would be both the long-awaited Messiah and the Son of God (see vv. 32–33). He then informed her that this child would be conceived supernaturally by the Holy Spirit—a story that would be hard to sell in Nazareth (see v. 35).

But Mary's simple response to this news was obedience: "May it be to me as you have said" (v. 38). It makes us want to ask, "Are you sure, Mary? Can you handle the blitz of gossip that will ensue because of your pregnancy? Can you handle the smirks of disdain when you try to tell others that the child you carry has been conceived by the Holy Spirit?" Mary had one response to those who questioned her for not questioning God: "May it be to me as God has said." And so the greatest story ever told began as the hardest story one might ever have to tell. But patience has a habit of praising God while it waits for miracles to take place, and so Mary sings:

My soul glorifies the Lord
and my spirit rejoices in God my Savior,
for he has been mindful
of the humble state of his servant.
From now on all generations will call me
blessed,
for the Mighty One has done great
things for me—
holy is his name.

(vv. 46–49)

Patience knows that there is never any reason to hurry God to some conclusion that we would like to see him reach by lunchtime. Patience merely says, "May it be to me as God has said," and, of course, it sings while it waits.

descendant of David. The virgin's name
was Mary. 28 The angel went to her and
said, "Greetings, you who are highly favored! The Lord is with you."
29 Mary was greatly troubled at his
words and wondered what kind of greeting this might be. 30 But the angel said
1:30 to her, "Do not be afraid,[g] Mary, you
[g] ver 13; Mt 14:27 have found favor with God. 31 You will
be with child and give birth to a son,
1:31 [h] Isa 7:14; Mt 1:21,25; Lk 2:21 and you are to give him the name Jesus.[h]
32 He will be great and will be called
the Son of the Most High.[i] The Lord
1:32 [i] ver 35,76; Mk 5:7 God will give him the throne of his father David, 33 and he will reign over the
1:33 house of Jacob forever; his kingdom[j]
[j] Mt 28:18 [k] Da 2:44; 7:14,27; Mic 4:7; Heb 1:8 will never end."[k]
34 "How will this be," Mary asked the
angel, "since I am a virgin?"
35 The angel answered, "The Holy
1:35 Spirit will come upon you,[l] and the
[l] Mt 1:18 [m] ver 32,76 [n] Mk 1:24 [o] Mt 4:3 power of the Most High[m] will overshadow you. So the holy one[n] to be
born will be called[a] the Son of God.[o]
36 Even Elizabeth your relative is going
to have a child in her old age, and she
who was said to be barren is in her
sixth month. 37 For nothing is impos-
1:37 [p] Mt 19:26 sible with God."[p]
38 "I am the Lord's servant," Mary
answered. "May it be to me as you have
said." Then the angel left her.

Mary Visits Elizabeth

39 At that time Mary got ready and
hurried to a town in the hill country of
1:39 [q] ver 65 Judea,[q] 40 where she entered Zechariah's
home and greeted Elizabeth. 41 When
Elizabeth heard Mary's greeting, the
baby leaped in her womb, and Elizabeth
was filled with the Holy Spirit. 42 In a
loud voice she exclaimed: "Blessed are
1:42 you among women,[r] and blessed is the
[r] Jdg 5:24 child you will bear! 43 But why am I so
favored, that the mother of my Lord
should come to me? 44 As soon as the
sound of your greeting reached my ears,
the baby in my womb leaped for joy.
45 Blessed is she who has believed that
what the Lord has said to her will be
accomplished!"

Mary's Song

46 And Mary said:

"My soul glorifies the Lord[s] 1:46 [s] Ps 34:2,3
47 and my spirit rejoices in God my
Savior,[t] 1:47 [t] 1Ti 1:1; 2:3
48 for he has been mindful
of the humble state of his servant.[u] 1:48 [u] Ps 138:6
From now on all generations will call [v] Lk 11:27
me blessed,[v]
49 for the Mighty One has done
great things[w] for me— 1:49 [w] Ps 71:19
holy is his name.[x] [x] Ps 111:9
50 His mercy extends to those who fear
him,
from generation to generation.[y] 1:50 [y] Ex 20:6;
51 He has performed mighty deeds with Ps 103:17
his arm;[z] 1:51 [z] Ps 98:1;
he has scattered those who are Isa 40:10
proud in their inmost
thoughts.
52 He has brought down rulers from
their thrones
but has lifted up the humble.
53 He has filled the hungry with good
things[a] 1:53 [a] Ps 107:9
but has sent the rich away empty.
54 He has helped his servant Israel,
remembering to be merciful[b] 1:54 [b] Ps 98:3
55 to Abraham and his descendants[c]
forever, 1:55 [c] Ge 17:19;
even as he said to our fathers." Ps 132:11; Gal 3:16

56 Mary stayed with Elizabeth for
about three months and then returned
home.

The Birth of John the Baptist

57 When it was time for Elizabeth to
have her baby, she gave birth to a son.
58 Her neighbors and relatives heard that
the Lord had shown her great mercy,
and they shared her joy.
59 On the eighth day they came to 1:59
circumcise[d] the child, and they were go- [d] Ge 17:12;
ing to name him after his father Zech- Lev 12:3; Lk 2:21;
ariah, 60 but his mother spoke up and Php 3:5
said, "No! He is to be called John."[e] 1:60
61 They said to her, "There is no [e] ver 13,63

[a] 35 Or *So the child to be born will be called holy,*

FAITHFULNESS

MAGNIFYING GOD

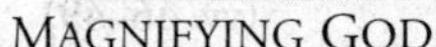

Luke 1:45

Mary discovered that her willingness to believe the seemingly impossible truths of God made God gigantic. Belief magnifies God. Doubt makes him look small. We are called to follow Mary's example and make our praise a magnifying glass.

one among your relatives who has that
name."
1:62 [f]ver 22 — 62 Then they made signs[f] to his father, to find out what he would like to
name the child. 63 He asked for a writing
tablet, and to everyone's astonishment
1:63 [g]ver 13,60 — he wrote, "His name is John."[g] 64 Immediately his mouth was opened and
his tongue was loosed, and he began to
1:64 [h]ver 20 — speak,[h] praising God. 65 The neighbors
were all filled with awe, and throughout
1:65 [i]ver 39 — the hill country of Judea[i] people were
talking about all these things. 66 Every-
one who heard this wondered about it,
asking, "What then is this child going
to be?" For the Lord's hand was with
1:66 [j]Ge 39:2; Ac 11:21 — him.[j]

Zechariah's Song

67 His father Zechariah was filled with
1:67 [k]Joel 2:28 — the Holy Spirit and prophesied:[k]

1:68 [l]Ps 72:18 [m]Ps 111:9; Lk 7:16 — 68 "Praise be to the Lord, the God of Israel,[l]
because he has come and has redeemed his people.[m]
1:69 [n]1Sa 2:1,10; Ps 18:2; 89:17; 132:17; Eze 29:21 [o]Mt 1:1 — 69 He has raised up a horn[a] [n] of salvation for us
in the house of his servant David[o]
1:70 [p]Jer 23:5 — 70 (as he said through his holy prophets of long ago),[p]
71 salvation from our enemies
and from the hand of all who hate us—
1:72 [q]Mic 7:20 [r]Ps 105:8,9; 106:45; Eze 16:60 — 72 to show mercy to our fathers[q]
and to remember his holy covenant,[r]
1:73 [s]Ge 22:16-18 — 73 the oath he swore to our father Abraham:[s]
74 to rescue us from the hand of our enemies,
1:74 [t]Heb 9:14 — and to enable us to serve him[t] without fear
1:75 [u]Eph 4:24 — 75 in holiness and righteousness[u] before him all our days.

1:76 [v]Mt 11:9 [w]ver 32,35 [x]ver 17; Mal 3:1 — 76 And you, my child, will be called a prophet[v] of the Most High;[w]
for you will go on before the Lord to prepare the way for him,[x]
77 to give his people the knowledge of salvation
1:77 [y]Jer 31:34; Mk 1:4 — through the forgiveness of their sins,[y]
78 because of the tender mercy of our God,
1:78 [z]Mal 4:2 — by which the rising sun[z] will come to us from heaven
1:79 [a]Isa 9:2; 59:9; Mt 4:16; Ac 26:18 — 79 to shine on those living in darkness
and in the shadow of death,[a]
to guide our feet into the path of peace."

1:80 [b]Lk 2:40,52 — 80 And the child grew and became
strong in spirit;[b] and he lived in the desert
until he appeared publicly to Israel.

The Birth of Jesus

2:1 [c]Lk 3:1; Mt 22:17 [d]Mt 24:14 [e]Mt 4:24 — **2** In those days Caesar Augustus[c] issued a decree that a census should
be taken of the entire Roman world.[d]
2 (This was the first census that took
place while Quirinius was governor of
Syria.)[e] 3 And everyone went to his own
town to register.
4 So Joseph also went up from the
town of Nazareth in Galilee to Judea,
2:4 [f]Jn 7:42 — to Bethlehem[f] the town of David, because he belonged to the house and
line of David. 5 He went there to register with Mary, who was pledged to
be married to him and was expecting a
child. 6 While they were there, the time
came for the baby to be born, 7 and she
gave birth to her firstborn, a son. She
wrapped him in cloths and placed him
in a manger, because there was no room
for them in the inn.

JOY

A WORKING-CLASS SAVIOR

Luke 2:11

Shepherds also have a Savior! In Christ, God was not offering the world a rich man's religion. Executives may come to faith. Royalty may sip salvation from a silver chalice. But in God's plan farm hands also have a right to joy.

The Shepherds and the Angels

8 And there were shepherds living out
in the fields nearby, keeping watch over
2:9 [g]Lk 1:11; Ac 5:19 — their flocks at night. 9 An angel[g] of the
Lord appeared to them, and the glory
of the Lord shone around them, and
2:10 [h]Mt 14:27 — they were terrified. 10 But the angel said
to them, "Do not be afraid.[h] I bring
2:11 [i]Mt 1:21; Jn 4:42; Ac 5:31 — you good news of great joy that will
be for all the people. 11 Today in the
town of David a Savior[i] has been born

[a] 69 *Horn* here symbolizes strength.

DAY 3 THREE

▸ JOY AND MY RELATIONSHIP WITH CHRIST

Luke 2:13–14

In picturing the Bethlehem angels, I can only imagine how frightening their joy must have been for the shepherds who faced them close up. A sky full of exuberance such as occurred in Luke 2 must have been a paralyzing event. But the shepherds themselves, once the fear had passed, were ready to be filled with joy. The testimony of one of them might have sounded something like this:

"It was just after midnight when the gold broke all around us! The light stung my eyes. It was the worst I've ever felt, I tell you. I choked and gagged. I don't know why—I must have been allergic to all that light. I was terrified. These big, silvery white beings belched out of the skies, like a tangled flock of big geese. Tall as Mount Hermon and big as Philistines. Those bright, big fellows exploded out of the shattered blackness and fell like the sparks from the blacksmith's forge.

My skin started to crawl. My eyes twitched. The hair on my neck prickled and then tried to crawl down my collar.

"Name any fear I've ever felt before this, and I'll deny the force of it. I never in all my life was afraid until that night. The angels did it all. They burst upon me, forcing me into sheer terror . . . It was like the dark nightmares you have as a child, but it was a nightmare with all light. I saw everything, and I trembled.

"All of a sudden the whole flock—or whatever you call a group of angels—started singing, 'Glory to God in the highest and on earth, peace to men on whom his favor rests!'

"Then they were gone, just like that! When all that light and noise was over, things got dark and quiet."

Things may be "dark and quiet" once the joy settles, but, after having praised the Savior, we are never quite the same again. Praise him briefly and live for a day. Praise him regularly and live forever.

To begin a study on the topic of Joy, the Reveling of Angels, turn to the home page on page 700.

to you; he is Christ[a][j] the Lord. 12This
will be a sign[k] to you: You will find a
baby wrapped in cloths and lying in a
manger."
13Suddenly a great company of the
heavenly host appeared with the angel,
praising God and saying,

14"Glory to God in the highest,
and on earth peace[l] to men on
whom his favor rests."

15When the angels had left them and
gone into heaven, the shepherds said
to one another, "Let's go to Bethlehem
and see this thing that has happened,
which the Lord has told us about."
16So they hurried off and found Mary
and Joseph, and the baby, who was lying in the manger. 17When they had
seen him, they spread the word concerning what had been told them about
this child, 18and all who heard it were
amazed at what the shepherds said
to them. 19But Mary treasured up all
these things and pondered them in her
heart.[m] 20The shepherds returned, glorifying and praising God[n] for all the
things they had heard and seen, which
were just as they had been told.

Jesus Presented in the Temple

21On the eighth day, when it was
time to circumcise him,[o] he was named
Jesus, the name the angel had given him
before he had been conceived.[p]
22When the time of their purification according to the Law of Moses[q]
had been completed, Joseph and Mary
took him to Jerusalem to present him
to the Lord 23(as it is written in the Law
of the Lord, "Every firstborn male is to
be consecrated to the Lord"[b]),[r] 24and to
offer a sacrifice in keeping with what is
said in the Law of the Lord: "a pair of
doves or two young pigeons."[c][s]
25Now there was a man in Jerusalem
called Simeon, who was righteous and
devout.[t] He was waiting for the consolation of Israel,[u] and the Holy Spirit
was upon him. 26It had been revealed to
him by the Holy Spirit that he would
not die before he had seen the Lord's
Christ. 27Moved by the Spirit, he went

[a]*11* Or *Messiah.* "The Christ" (Greek) and "the Messiah" (Hebrew) both mean "the Anointed One"; also in verse 26. [b]*23* Exodus 13:2,12 [c]*24* Lev. 12:8

2:11 [j]Mt 1:16; 16:16,20; Jn 11:27; Ac 2:36
2:12 [k]1Sa 2:34; 2Ki 19:29; Isa 7:14
2:14 [l]Lk 1:79; Ro 5:1; Eph 2:14,17
2:19 [m]ver 51
2:20 [n]Mt 9:8
2:21 [o]Lk 1:59 [p]Lk 1:31
2:22 [q]Lev 12:2-8
2:23 [r]Ex 13:2, 12,15; Nu 3:13
2:24 [s]Lev 12:8
2:25 [t]Lk 1:6 [u]ver 38; Isa 52:9; Lk 23:51

PATIENCE

WEEK 49

DAY ONE

PATIENCE, THE WAIT FOR WHAT GOD PROMISES

Read Luke 2:25–32

Old Simeon had waited all his life for a glimpse of the Messiah. Then, in the endless queue of those who have come to offer worship at the temple, the old man sees the baby he has waited all his life to see. It is not often that old men are granted the fulfillment to all their dreams. But Simeon is the recipient of such grace, and he praises God: "Sovereign Lord, as you have promised, you now dismiss your servant in peace."

It is a wonderful thing to die an old man who measured every promise of God and found not a single one of them wanting. God puts the leathery old face of a devout man next to the fresh, new skin of a baby. The contrast between an old, wrinkled visage and the cheek of a newborn child is a picture of how God furnishes every new generation with hope. But in this case, it is more than that. In this case it is confirmation that God always keeps his promises. The old man shows us that God can be depended upon for a lifetime, for God always keeps his promises. But the baby shows us that God will save—and that is what put the sparkle in the old man's eye.

Rabindranath Tagore said, "Every baby comes as proof that God is not yet discouraged of man." The infant Christ tells us, "God is going to change the heart of humankind, and when the change is through, eternity and time will be indistinguishable."

Simeon sings, "My eyes have seen your salvation." In this statement is the realized product of patience. God has many things to show us when the time is right. Until then, the wait itself is wonderful.

DAY TWO

PATIENCE AND THE PURPOSE OF GOD IN MY LIFE

Eagles are the untroubled, unhurried images in this passage. They fly with no suicidal stress in the tension of their wing beats. In fact, there are no wing beats. They simply float a thousand feet above the hurried world of human stress. If we learn how to trust and wait, says the prophet, we shall float above the hassled world and see it as God does. When we do, we will wonder why we did not earlier choose to live the patient life. *Turn to Isaiah 40:30–31, page 836, for today's study.*

DAY THREE

PATIENCE AND MY RELATIONSHIP WITH CHRIST

Here is the verse that settles our destiny: We are awaiting some grand completion. What will we be like? The mirror is too cloudy. We cannot see ourselves. Tomorrow is in the way. But when tomorrow is past, we shall indeed see what we are. Think of this glory: When we finally see how we will be, we will be like Christ. It is hard to wait when we expect such a wonder. Yet waiting with Christ is a pleasant way to bide one's time. *Turn to 1 John 3:2, page 1508, for today's study.*

DAY FOUR

PATIENCE AND MY SERVICE TO OTHERS

The Gershonites are those who are to serve at the tabernacle in menial ways. They are to pack and fold and carry the tabernacle from place to place. It doesn't seem a very auspicious calling when compared to the duties of the Levites. To be in the service of God is to serve in this way: We wait; we take orders, and—no matter how menial our duties—we are thankful to God that we are allowed the privilege of serving him. *Turn to Numbers 4:21–28, page 156, for today's study.*

DAY FIVE

PATIENCE AND ITS PLACE IN MY PERSONAL WORSHIP

It is glorious to walk with God. At every step we remember where we met him, how we first served him and all we still hope for. But the unfolding panoramas of our lives are held together with patience. Abraham returns to Bethel, where he once celebrated this walk of patience. Being certain of the faithfulness of God in the past, he waited with confident patience for the final fulfillment of every divine promise. *Turn to Genesis 13:1–4, page 18, for today's study.*

MEMORIZE THIS WEEK

1 PETER 5:10

And the God of all grace, who called you to his eternal glory in Christ, after you have suffered a little while, will himself restore you and make you strong, firm and steadfast.

Week 50, Goodness, a Contentment With the Commandments, begins on page 1233, Luke 18:18–30. To begin a topical study on the Fruit of the Spirit, Patience, turn to the Topical Index, page 1548.

into the temple courts. When the parents brought in the child Jesus to do
for him what the custom of the Law
2:27 [v]ver 22 required,[v] [28]Simeon took him in his
arms and praised God, saying:

[29]"Sovereign Lord, as you have
2:29 [w]ver 26 promised,[w]
[x]Ac 2:24 you now dismiss[a] your servant in
peace.[x]
[30]For my eyes have seen your
2:30 salvation,[y]
[y]Isa 52:10; Lk 3:6 [31] which you have prepared in the
2:32 sight of all people,
[z]Isa 42:6; [32]a light for revelation to the Gentiles
49:6; and for glory to your people
Ac 13:47; 26:23 Israel."[z]

▸ PATIENCE

NUNC DIMITTIS, NOW DISMISS

Luke 2:29
Simeon had beheld the baby on whose tiny life the ages turned. Now it was all right for Simeon to die. Old men should handle babies and remember Simeon's confidence.

[33]The child's father and mother marveled at what was said about him.
[34]Then Simeon blessed them and said
2:34 [a]Mt 12:46 to Mary, his mother:[a] "This child is
[b]Isa 8:14; Mt 21:44; destined to cause the falling[b] and ris-
1Co 1:23; ing of many in Israel, and to be a sign
2Co 2:16; 1Pe 2:7,8 that will be spoken against, [35]so that
the thoughts of many hearts will be re-
vealed. And a sword will pierce your
own soul too."
2:36 [36]There was also a prophetess,[c] Anna,
[c]Ac 21:9 the daughter of Phanuel, of the tribe of
Asher. She was very old; she had lived
with her husband seven years after her
marriage, [37]and then was a widow until
2:37 she was eighty-four.[b] [d] She never left the
[d]1Ti 5:9 [e]Ac 13:3; temple but worshiped night and day,
14:23; 1Ti 5:5 fasting and praying.[e] [38]Coming up to
them at that very moment, she gave
thanks to God and spoke about the
child to all who were looking forward
2:38 [f]ver 25; to the redemption of Jerusalem.[f]
Isa 40:2; [39]When Joseph and Mary had done
Lk 1:68; 24:21 everything required by the Law of the
2:39 Lord, they returned to Galilee to their
[g]ver 51; Mt 2:23 own town of Nazareth.[g] [40]And the child
grew and became strong; he was filled
2:40 [h]ver 52; with wisdom, and the grace of God was
Lk 1:80 upon him.[h]

The Boy Jesus at the Temple

[41]Every year his parents went to Je-
rusalem for the Feast of the Passover.[i] 2:41 [i]Ex 23:15;
[42]When he was twelve years old, they Dt 16:1-8
went up to the Feast, according to the
custom. [43]After the Feast was over, while
his parents were returning home, the
boy Jesus stayed behind in Jerusalem,
but they were unaware of it. [44]Think-
ing he was in their company, they traveled on for a day. Then they began
looking for him among their relatives
and friends. [45]When they did not find
him, they went back to Jerusalem to
look for him. [46]After three days they
found him in the temple courts, sitting
among the teachers, listening to them
and asking them questions. [47]Everyone
who heard him was amazed[j] at his un- 2:47
derstanding and his answers. [48]When [j]Mt 7:28
his parents saw him, they were aston-
ished. His mother[k] said to him, "Son, 2:48 [k]Mt 12:46
why have you treated us like this? Your [l]Lk 3:23; 4:22
father[l] and I have been anxiously searching for you."
[49]"Why were you searching for me?"
he asked. "Didn't you know I had to be
in my Father's house?"[m] [50]But they did 2:49 [m]Jn 2:16
not understand what he was saying to
them.[n] 2:50 [n]Mk 9:32
[51]Then he went down to Nazareth 2:51
with them[o] and was obedient to them. [o]ver 39;
But his mother treasured all these things Mt 2:23 [p]ver 19
in her heart.[p] [52]And Jesus grew in wis-
dom and stature, and in favor with God 2:52 [q]ver 40;
and men.[q] 1Sa 2:26; Lk 1:80

John the Baptist Prepares the Way

3 In the fifteenth year of the reign
of Tiberius Caesar—when Pontius
Pilate[r] was governor of Judea, Herod[s] 3:1 [r]Mt 27:2
tetrarch of Galilee, his brother Philip [s]Mt 14:1
tetrarch of Iturea and Traconitis, and Ly- 3:2
sanias tetrarch of Abilene—[2]during the [t]Mt 26:3; Jn 18:13;
high priesthood of Annas and Caiaphas,[t] Ac 4:6
the word of God came to John[u] son [u]Mt 3:1 [v]Lk 1:13
of Zechariah[v] in the desert. [3]He went
into all the country around the Jordan,
preaching a baptism of repentance for
the forgiveness of sins.[w] [4]As is written 3:3 [w]ver 16;
in the book of the words of Isaiah the Mk 1:4
prophet:

"A voice of one calling in the desert,
'Prepare the way for the Lord,

[a]29 Or *promised, / now dismiss* [b]37 Or *widow for eighty-four years*

make straight paths for him.
5 Every valley shall be filled in,
every mountain and hill made
low.

DAY 5 FIVE

Goodness and Its Place in My Personal Worship

Luke 3:7–9

John the Baptist may have seemed overly stern in the way he addressed his would-be disciples. To call what would seem to have been perfectly good people a brood of snakes appears to lack the tact and finesse that modern churchgoers require of their pastors. But John's real message is that followers of Jesus must become committed to goodness, for as long as they allow evil and good to coexist in their moral practice, they will lack the basic platform for coming into God's presence.

"Produce fruit in keeping with repentance" is John's advice to those who want to keep God at the center of their worship focus. Repentance is not just getting sin out of our lives; it is a way of viewing God and his requirements for our lives. Those who repent but fail to change the way they live have already confessed that repentance was insignificant to them.

Repentance may be reduced to a formulaic procedure, whereby we take our sins to God and merely confess them in rote fashion. This amounts to a kind of "push-pull, click-click" spiritual reflex that we can do without much emotion or genuine sorrow. What God is after is the kind of confession that amounts to an inner grieving because we have done something that hurt God—something that indeed cost Christ the price of Calvary.

Because our sins hurt God, they should hurt us. Not to allow them to hurt us earns for us John's assessment: a brood of insensitive vipers. But to hurt because of our sins is to be freed from those sins and to see our Savior once again. It is the goodness he imputes on the basis of his perfect sacrifice that allows our personal worship to be rich with sensitivity and divine rapport.

To begin a study on the topic of Goodness, Caring How God Feels About My Morality, turn to the home page on page 51.

The crooked roads shall become
straight,
the rough ways smooth.
6 And all mankind will see God's
salvation.'"[a][x] 3:6 [x]Isa 40:3-5; Ps 98:2; Isa 42:16; 52:10; Lk 2:30
7 John said to the crowds coming out
to be baptized by him, "You brood of
vipers![y] Who warned you to flee from
the coming wrath?[z] 8 Produce fruit in 3:7 [y]Mt 12:34; 23:33 [z]Ro 1:18
keeping with repentance. And do not
begin to say to yourselves, 'We have
Abraham as our father.'[a] For I tell you 3:8 [a]Isa 51:2; Lk 19:9; Jn 8:33,39; Ac 13:26; Ro 4:1,11, 12,16,17; Gal 3:7
that out of these stones God can raise
up children for Abraham. 9 The ax is already at the root of the trees, and every
tree that does not produce good fruit
will be cut down and thrown into the
fire."[b] 3:9 [b]Mt 3:10
10 "What should we do then?"[c] the 3:10 [c]ver 12,14; Ac 2:37; 16:30
crowd asked.
11 John answered, "The man with two
tunics should share with him who has
none, and the one who has food should
do the same."[d] 3:11 [d]Isa 58:7
12 Tax collectors also came to be
baptized.[e] "Teacher," they asked, "what 3:12 [e]Lk 7:29
should we do?"
13 "Don't collect any more than you
are required to,"[f] he told them. 3:13 [f]Lk 19:8
14 Then some soldiers asked him,
"And what should we do?"
He replied, "Don't extort money and
don't accuse people falsely[g]—be con- 3:14 [g]Ex 23:1; Lev 19:11
tent with your pay."
15 The people were waiting expectantly and were all wondering in their hearts
if John[h] might possibly be the Christ.[b][i] 3:15 [h]Mt 3:1 [i]Jn 1:19,20; Ac 13:25
16 John answered them all, "I baptize
you with[c] water.[j] But one more pow-
erful than I will come, the thongs of 3:16 [j]ver 3; Mk 1:4 [k]Jn 1:26,33; Ac 1:5; 11:16; 19:4
whose sandals I am not worthy to un-
tie. He will baptize you with the Holy
Spirit and with fire.[k] 17 His winnowing
fork[l] is in his hand to clear his thresh-
ing floor and to gather the wheat into 3:17 [l]Isa 30:24 [m]Mt 13:30; 25:41
his barn, but he will burn up the chaff
with unquenchable fire."[m] 18 And with
many other words John exhorted the
people and preached the good news to
them.
19 But when John rebuked Herod[n] the 3:19 [n]ver 1
tetrarch because of Herodias, his brother's wife, and all the other evil things he
had done, 20 Herod added this to them 3:20 [o]Mt 14:3,4; Mk 6:17-18
all: He locked John up in prison.[o]

[a]6 Isaiah 40:3-5 [b]15 Or *Messiah* [c]16 Or *in*

The Baptism and Genealogy of Jesus

21When all the people were being
baptized, Jesus was baptized too. And
3:21 [p]Mt 14:23; Mk 1:35; 6:46; Lk 5:16; 6:12; 9:18,28; 11:1
as he was praying,[p] heaven was opened
22and the Holy Spirit descended on
him[q] in bodily form like a dove. And a
voice came from heaven: "You are my
Son,[r] whom I love; with you I am well
3:22 [q]Isa 42:1; Jn 1:32,33; Ac 10:38 [r]Mt 3:17 [s]Mt 3:17
pleased."[s]
23Now Jesus himself was about thirty
years old when he began his ministry.[t]
He was the son, so it was thought, of
3:23 [t]Mt 4:17; Ac 1:1 [u]Lk 1:27
Joseph,[u]

the son of Heli, 24the son of Matthat,
the son of Levi, the son of Melki,
the son of Jannai, the son of Joseph,
25the son of Mattathias, the son of Amos,
the son of Nahum, the son of Esli,
the son of Naggai, 26the son of Maath,
the son of Mattathias, the son of Semein,
the son of Josech, the son of Joda,
3:27 [v]Mt 1:12
27the son of Joanan, the son of Rhesa,
the son of Zerubbabel,[v] the son of Shealtiel,
the son of Neri, 28the son of Melki,
the son of Addi, the son of Cosam,
the son of Elmadam, the son of Er,
29the son of Joshua, the son of Eliezer,
the son of Jorim, the son of Matthat,
the son of Levi, 30the son of Simeon,
the son of Judah, the son of Joseph,
the son of Jonam, the son of Eliakim,
31the son of Melea, the son of Menna,
the son of Mattatha, the son of
3:31 [w]2Sa 5:14; 1Ch 3:5
Nathan,[w]
the son of David, 32the son of Jesse,
the son of Obed, the son of Boaz,
the son of Salmon,[a] the son of Nahshon,
33the son of Amminadab, the son of Ram,[b]
the son of Hezron, the son of Perez,[x]
3:33 [x]Ru 4:18-22; 1Ch 2:10-12
the son of Judah, 34the son of Jacob,
the son of Isaac, the son of Abraham,
the son of Terah, the son of
3:34 [y]Ge 11:24,26
Nahor,[y]
35the son of Serug, the son of Reu,
the son of Peleg, the son of Eber,
the son of Shelah, 36the son of Cainan,
the son of Arphaxad,[z] the son of
3:36 [z]Ge 11:12 [a]Ge 5:28-32
Shem,
the son of Noah, the son of Lamech,[a]
37the son of Methuselah, the son of Enoch,
the son of Jared, the son of Mahalalel,
the son of Kenan, 38the son of Enosh,
the son of Seth, the son of Adam,
3:38 [b]Ge 5:1,2,6-9
the son of God.[b]

The Temptation of Jesus

4:1 [c]ver 14,18 [d]Lk 3:3,21 [e]Lk 2:27
4 Jesus, full of the Holy Spirit,[c] returned from the Jordan[d] and was
led by the Spirit[e] in the desert, 2where
for forty days[f] he was tempted by the
4:2 [f]Ex 34:28; 1Ki 19:8
devil. He ate nothing during those days,
and at the end of them he was hungry.
3The devil said to him, "If you are
the Son of God, tell this stone to become bread."
4Jesus answered, "It is written: 'Man
4:4 [g]Dt 8:3
does not live on bread alone.'[c]"[g]
5The devil led him up to a high place
and showed him in an instant all the
4:5 [h]Mt 24:14
kingdoms of the world.[h] 6And he said
to him, "I will give you all their authority and splendor, for it has been given
4:6 [i]Jn 12:31; 14:30; 1Jn 5:19
to me,[i] and I can give it to anyone I
want to. 7So if you worship me, it will
all be yours."
8Jesus answered, "It is written: 'Worship the Lord your God and serve him
4:8 [j]Dt 6:13
only.'[d]"[j]
9The devil led him to Jerusalem and
had him stand on the highest point
of the temple. "If you are the Son of
God," he said, "throw yourself down
from here. 10For it is written:

[a] *32* Some early manuscripts *Sala* [b] *33* Some manuscripts *Amminadab, the son of Admin, the son of Arni*; other manuscripts vary widely. [c] *4* Deut. 8:3 [d] *8* Deut. 6:13

"'He will command his angels
concerning you
to guard you carefully;
[11]they will lift you up in their hands,
so that you will not strike your
foot against a stone.'[a]"[k]
4:11 [k]Ps 91:11,12 [12]Jesus answered, "It says: 'Do not
put the Lord your God to the test.'[b]"[l]
4:12 [l]Dt 6:16 [13]When the devil had finished all this
tempting,[m] he left him[n] until an oppor-
4:13 [m]Heb 4:15 [n]Jn 14:30 tune time.

Jesus Rejected at Nazareth

4:14 [o]Mt 4:12 [p]Mt 9:26 [14]Jesus returned to Galilee[o] in the
power of the Spirit, and news about him
spread through the whole countryside.[p]
4:15 [q]Mt 4:23 [15]He taught in their synagogues,[q] and
everyone praised him.
[16]He went to Nazareth,[r] where he
4:16 [r]Mt 2:23 [s]Mt 13:54 had been brought up, and on the Sabbath day he went into the synagogue,[s]
as was his custom. And he stood up
to read. [17]The scroll of the prophet Isaiah was handed to him. Unrolling it, he
found the place where it is written:
4:18 [t]Jn 3:34 [18]"The Spirit of the Lord is on me,[t]
because he has anointed me
to preach good news to the poor.
He has sent me to proclaim freedom
for the prisoners
and recovery of sight for the blind,
to release the oppressed,
[19] to proclaim the year of the Lord's
4:19 [u]Isa 61:1,2; Lev 25:10 favor."[c][u]
[20]Then he rolled up the scroll, gave
4:20 [v]ver 17; Mt 26:55 it back to the attendant and sat down.[v]
The eyes of everyone in the synagogue
were fastened on him, [21]and he began
by saying to them, "Today this scripture is fulfilled in your hearing."
[22]All spoke well of him and were
amazed at the gracious words that came
from his lips. "Isn't this Joseph's son?"
4:22 [w]Mt 13:54, 55; Jn 6:42; 7:15 they asked.[w]
[23]Jesus said to them, "Surely you will
quote this proverb to me: 'Physician,
heal yourself! Do here in your home-
4:23 [x]ver 16 [y]Mk 1:21-28; 2:1-12 town[x] what we have heard that you did
in Capernaum.'"[y]
[24]"I tell you the truth," he continued, "no prophet is accepted in his
4:24 [z]Mt 13:57; Jn 4:44 hometown.[z] [25]I assure you that there
were many widows in Israel in Elijah's
time, when the sky was shut for three
and a half years and there was a severe
famine throughout the land.[a] [26]Yet Eli- 4:25 [a]1Ki 17:1; 18:1; Jas 5:17,18
jah was not sent to any of them, but
to a widow in Zarephath in the region
of Sidon.[b] [27]And there were many in Is- 4:26 [b]1Ki 17:8-16; Mt 11:21
rael with leprosy[d] in the time of Elisha
the prophet, yet not one of them was
cleansed—only Naaman the Syrian."[c] 4:27 [c]2Ki 5:1-14
[28]All the people in the synagogue
were furious when they heard this.
[29]They got up, drove him out of the
town,[d] and took him to the brow of the 4:29 [d]Nu 15:35; Ac 7:58; Heb 13:12
hill on which the town was built, in or-
der to throw him down the cliff. [30]But
he walked right through the crowd and 4:30 [e]Jn 8:59; 10:39
went on his way.[e]

GOODNESS

THE HIGH COST OF SELF-UNDERSTANDING

Luke 4:29

Jesus knew who he was, and his proclamation of the truth made enemies of all those who wished him to be just a man. Here began the great divorce. From this time on, the world would be divided between those who wished him to be more and those who wished him to be less.

Jesus Drives Out an Evil Spirit

[31]Then he went down to Caper-
naum,[f] a town in Galilee, and on the 4:31 [f]ver 23; Mt 4:13
Sabbath began to teach the people.
[32]They were amazed at his teaching,[g] 4:32 [g]Mt 7:28 [h]ver 36; Mt 7:29
because his message had authority.[h]
[33]In the synagogue there was a man
possessed by a demon, an evil[e] spirit.
He cried out at the top of his voice,
[34]"Ha! What do you want with us,[i] Je- 4:34 [i]Mt 8:29 [j]Mk 1:24 [k]Jas 2:19 [l]ver 41; Mk 1:24
sus of Nazareth?[j] Have you come to
destroy us? I know who you are[k]—the
Holy One of God!"[l]
[35]"Be quiet!" Jesus said sternly.[m] 4:35 [m]ver 39,41; Mt 8:26; Lk 8:24
"Come out of him!" Then the demon
threw the man down before them all
and came out without injuring him.
[36]All the people were amazed[n] and 4:36 [n]Mt 7:28 [o]ver 32; Mt 7:29; Mt 10:1
said to each other, "What is this teach-
ing? With authority[o] and power he gives
orders to evil spirits and they come
out!" [37]And the news about him spread 4:37 [p]ver 14; Mt 9:26
throughout the surrounding area.[p]

[a]*11* Psalm 91:11,12 [b]*12* Deut. 6:16 [c]*19* Isaiah 61:1,2 [d]*27* The Greek word was used for various diseases affecting the skin—not necessarily leprosy. [e]*33* Greek *unclean;* also in verse 36

Jesus Heals Many

38 Jesus left the synagogue and went
to the home of Simon. Now Simon's
mother-in-law was suffering from a high
fever, and they asked Jesus to help her.
4:39 39 So he bent over her and rebuked[q] the
q ver 35,41 fever, and it left her. She got up at once
and began to wait on them.
40 When the sun was setting, the people brought to Jesus all who had various
kinds of sickness, and laying his hands
4:40 on each one,[r] he healed them.[s] 41 More-
r Mk 5:23 over, demons came out of many people,
s Mt 4:23 shouting, "You are the Son of God!"[t]
4:41 t Mt 4:3 But he rebuked[u] them and would not
u ver 35 v Mt 8:4 allow them to speak,[v] because they knew
he was the Christ.[a]
42 At daybreak Jesus went out to a
solitary place. The people were looking
for him and when they came to where
he was, they tried to keep him from
leaving them. 43 But he said, "I must
preach the good news of the kingdom
4:43 of God[w] to the other towns also, be-
w Mt 3:2 cause that is why I was sent." 44 And he
kept on preaching in the synagogues of
4:44 x Mt 4:23 Judea.[b x]

The Calling of the First Disciples

5 One day as Jesus was standing by
the Lake of Gennesaret,[c] with the
people crowding around him and lis-
5:1 tening to the word of God,[y] 2 he saw at
y Mk 4:14; Heb 4:12 the water's edge two boats, left there by
the fishermen, who were washing their
nets. 3 He got into one of the boats, the
one belonging to Simon, and asked him
to put out a little from shore. Then he
sat down and taught the people from
5:3 z Mt 13:2 the boat.[z]
4 When he had finished speaking, he
said to Simon, "Put out into deep water,
5:4 a Jn 21:6 and let down[d] the nets for a catch."[a]
5:5 5 Simon answered, "Master,[b] we've
b Lk 8:24,45; 9:33,49; 17:13 worked hard all night and haven't caught
anything.[c] But because you say so, I will
c Jn 21:3 let down the nets."
6 When they had done so, they caught
such a large number of fish that their
5:6 d Jn 21:11 nets began to break.[d] 7 So they signaled
their partners in the other boat to come
and help them, and they came and filled
both boats so full that they began to
sink.
8 When Simon Peter saw this, he fell
5:8 e Ge 18:27; Job 42:6; Isa 6:5 at Jesus' knees and said, "Go away from
me, Lord; I am a sinful man!"[e] 9 For
he and all his companions were astonished at the catch of fish they had tak-
en, 10 and so were James and John, the
sons of Zebedee, Simon's partners.
Then Jesus said to Simon, "Don't be
afraid;[f] from now on you will catch 5:10 f Mt 14:27
men." 11 So they pulled their boats up
on shore, left everything and followed
him.[g] 5:11 g ver 28; Mt 4:19

The Man With Leprosy

12 While Jesus was in one of the
towns, a man came along who was cov-
ered with leprosy.[e h] When he saw Jesus, 5:12 h Mt 8:2
he fell with his face to the ground and
begged him, "Lord, if you are willing,
you can make me clean."
13 Jesus reached out his hand and
touched the man. "I am willing," he
said. "Be clean!" And immediately the
leprosy left him.
14 Then Jesus ordered him, "Don't tell
anyone,[i] but go, show yourself to the 5:14 i Mt 8:4 j Lev 14:2-32
priest and offer the sacrifices that Mo-
ses commanded[j] for your cleansing, as
a testimony to them."
15 Yet the news about him spread all
the more,[k] so that crowds of people 5:15 k Mt 9:26
came to hear him and to be healed of
their sicknesses. 16 But Jesus often with-
drew to lonely places and prayed.[l] 5:16 l Mt 14:23; Lk 3:21

Jesus Heals a Paralytic

17 One day as he was teaching, Phar-
isees and teachers of the law,[m] who 5:17 m Mt 15:1; Lk 2:46 n Mk 5:30; Lk 6:19
had come from every village of Galilee
and from Judea and Jerusalem, were sitting there. And the power of the Lord
was present for him to heal the sick.[n]
18 Some men came carrying a paralytic
on a mat and tried to take him into the
house to lay him before Jesus. 19 When
they could not find a way to do this
because of the crowd, they went up on
the roof and lowered him on his mat
through the tiles into the middle of the
crowd, right in front of Jesus.
20 When Jesus saw their faith, he said,
"Friend, your sins are forgiven."[o] 5:20 o Lk 7:48,49
21 The Pharisees and the teachers of
the law began thinking to themselves,
"Who is this fellow who speaks blas-

[a] *41* Or *Messiah* [b] *44* Or *the land of the Jews*; some manuscripts *Galilee* [c] *1* That is, Sea of Galilee [d] *4* The Greek verb is plural. [e] *12* The Greek word was used for various diseases affecting the skin—not necessarily leprosy.

phemy? Who can forgive sins but God
5:21 [p]Isa 43:25 alone?"[p]
22 Jesus knew what they were thinking
and asked, "Why are you thinking these
things in your hearts? 23 Which is easier:
to say, 'Your sins are forgiven,' or to say,
'Get up and walk'? 24 But that you may
5:24 [q]Mt 8:20 know that the Son of Man[q] has authority on earth to forgive sins . . ." He said
to the paralyzed man, "I tell you, get
up, take your mat and go home." 25 Immediately he stood up in front of them,
took what he had been lying on and
went home praising God. 26 Everyone
5:26 [r]Mt 9:8 was amazed and gave praise to God.[r]
They were filled with awe and said, "We
have seen remarkable things today."

The Calling of Levi

27 After this, Jesus went out and saw
5:27 [s]Mt 4:19 a tax collector by the name of Levi sitting at his tax booth. "Follow me,"[s] Je-
5:28 [t]ver 11; Mt 4:19 sus said to him, 28 and Levi got up, left
everything and followed him.[t]

LOVE

TAX COLLECTOR, BIOGRAPHER

Luke 5:27–28

The Pharisees were unable to see the coming of the finished work of Christ: a global kingdom, a church triumphant! They saw only a tax collector, not a biographer of Jesus. Nor could they imagine what wonderful words could come from a tax collector in love with Christ.

29 Then Levi held a great banquet for
Jesus at his house, and a large crowd
5:29 [u]Lk 15:1 of tax collectors[u] and others were eating with them. 30 But the Pharisees and
the teachers of the law who belonged to
5:30 [v]Ac 23:9 [w]Mt 9:11 their sect[v] complained to his disciples,
"Why do you eat and drink with tax
collectors and 'sinners'?"[w]
31 Jesus answered them, "It is not the
healthy who need a doctor, but the sick.
32 I have not come to call the righteous,
5:32 [x]Jn 3:17 but sinners to repentance."[x]

Jesus Questioned About Fasting

5:33 [y]Lk 7:18; Jn 1:35; 3:25,26 33 They said to him, "John's disciples[y]
often fast and pray, and so do the dis-
ciples of the Pharisees, but yours go on
eating and drinking."
34 Jesus answered, "Can you make the
guests of the bridegroom[z] fast while 5:34 [z]Jn 3:29
he is with them? 35 But the time will
come when the bridegroom will be tak-
en from them;[a] in those days they will 5:35 [a]Lk 9:22; 17:22; Jn 16:5-7
fast."
36 He told them this parable: "No one
tears a patch from a new garment and
sews it on an old one. If he does, he
will have torn the new garment, and
the patch from the new will not match
the old. 37 And no one pours new wine
into old wineskins. If he does, the new
wine will burst the skins, the wine will
run out and the wineskins will be ruined. 38 No, new wine must be poured
into new wineskins. 39 And no one after
drinking old wine wants the new, for he
says, 'The old is better.'"

Lord of the Sabbath

6 One Sabbath Jesus was going
through the grainfields, and his disciples began to pick some heads of
grain, rub them in their hands and eat
the kernels.[b] 2 Some of the Pharisees 6:1 [b]Dt 23:25
asked, "Why are you doing what is un-
lawful on the Sabbath?"[c] 6:2 [c]Mt 12:2
3 Jesus answered them, "Have you
never read what David did when he and
his companions were hungry?[d] 4 He en- 6:3 [d]1Sa 21:6
tered the house of God, and taking the
consecrated bread, he ate what is lawful
only for priests to eat.[e] And he also gave 6:4 [e]Lev 24:5,9
some to his companions." 5 Then Jesus
said to them, "The Son of Man[f] is Lord 6:5 [f]Mt 8:20
of the Sabbath."
6 On another Sabbath[g] he went into 6:6 [g]ver 1
the synagogue and was teaching, and a
man was there whose right hand was
shriveled. 7 The Pharisees and the teachers of the law were looking for a reason to accuse Jesus, so they watched
him closely[h] to see if he would heal 6:7 [h]Mt 12:10 [i]Mt 12:2
on the Sabbath.[i] 8 But Jesus knew what
they were thinking[j] and said to the man 6:8 [j]Mt 9:4
with the shriveled hand, "Get up and
stand in front of everyone." So he got
up and stood there.
9 Then Jesus said to them, "I ask you,
which is lawful on the Sabbath: to do
good or to do evil, to save life or to destroy it?"
10 He looked around at them all, and
then said to the man, "Stretch out your
hand." He did so, and his hand was
completely restored. 11 But they were furious[k] and began to discuss with one 6:11 [k]Jn 5:18
another what they might do to Jesus.

The Twelve Apostles

12 One of those days Jesus went out to
a mountainside to pray, and spent the

DAY FIVE

▸ GOODNESS AND ITS PLACE IN MY PERSONAL WORSHIP

Luke 6:12

The account in Luke 6 isn't the only time we read of Jesus praying well into the night.

Your personal adoration of Christ will require that you pray, not because you feel an obligation to pray, but because you are in love with Jesus and strive to imitate his life and goodness. As your Lord has taught you, let your personal worship master this simplicity.

Our Father,
Rejoice! We are not orphans in the universe.
In heaven,
Rejoice! Heaven is as real as Chicago, and you already own real estate there.
Hallowed be your name,
Holy, Holy, Holy! All the saints adore you but never more than I do.
Your kingdom come,
How grateful I am that all earth's corrupt political systems are soon to be renovated.
Your will be done,
Good! Mine was too shabby to matter.
Give us today our daily bread,
And remind us that our hunger is ever your concern.
Forgive us our debts as we also have forgiven our debtors,
This I like best of all—my sin is not counted against me . . . ever.
And lead us not into temptation but deliver us from the evil one,
For yours is the kingdom, power and glory forever.

Yes, Lord, here is the subject matter of Gethsemane—here is the making of a whole night of prayer. Oh, may I imitate you.

To begin a study on the topic of Goodness, the Result of Imitating Christ, turn to the home page on page 1409.

night praying to God.[l] 13 When morn- 6:12 [l]Lk 3:21
ing came, he called his disciples to
him and chose twelve of them, whom
he also designated apostles:[m] 14 Simon 6:13 [m]Mk 6:30
(whom he named Peter), his brother An-
drew, James, John, Philip, Bartholomew,
15 Matthew,[n] Thomas, James son of Al- 6:15 [n]Mt 9:9
phaeus, Simon who was called the Zeal-
ot, 16 Judas son of James, and Judas
Iscariot, who became a traitor.

Blessings and Woes

17 He went down with them and
stood on a level place. A large crowd
of his disciples was there and a great
number of people from all over Judea,
from Jerusalem, and from the coast of
Tyre and Sidon,[o] 18 who had come to 6:17 [o]Mt 4:25; Mt 11:21; Mk 3:7,8
hear him and to be healed of their dis-
eases. Those troubled by evil[a] spirits
were cured, 19 and the people all tried to
touch him,[p] because power was coming 6:19 [p]Mt 9:20 [q]Mt 14:36; Mk 5:30; Lk 5:17
from him and healing them all.[q]
20 Looking at his disciples, he said:

"Blessed are you who are poor,
for yours is the kingdom of God.[r] 6:20 [r]Mt 25:34
21 Blessed are you who hunger now,
for you will be satisfied.[s] 6:21 [s]Isa 55:1,2; Mt 5:6 [t]Isa 61:2,3; Mt 5:4; Rev 7:17
Blessed are you who weep now,
for you will laugh.[t]
22 Blessed are you when men hate you,
when they exclude you[u] and insult you[v] 6:22 [u]Jn 9:22; 16:2 [v]Isa 51:7 [w]Jn 15:21
and reject your name as evil,
because of the Son of Man.[w]

23 "Rejoice in that day and leap for
joy,[x] because great is your reward in 6:23 [x]Mt 5:12 [y]Mt 5:12
heaven. For that is how their fathers
treated the prophets.[y]

24 "But woe to you who are rich,[z] 6:24 [z]Jas 5:1 [a]Lk 16:25
for you have already received your comfort.[a]
25 Woe to you who are well fed now,
for you will go hungry.[b] 6:25 [b]Isa 65:13 [c]Pr 14:13
Woe to you who laugh now,
for you will mourn and weep.[c]
26 Woe to you when all men speak well of you,
for that is how their fathers treated the false prophets.[d] 6:26 [d]Mt 7:15

Love for Enemies

27 "But I tell you who hear me: Love
your enemies, do good to those who

[a]*18* Greek *unclean*

6:27 [e]ver 35; Mt 5:44; Ro 12:20
hate you,[e] 28bless those who curse you,
pray for those who mistreat you.[f] 29If
someone strikes you on one cheek, turn
6:28 [f]Mt 5:44
to him the other also. If someone takes
your cloak, do not stop him from taking your tunic. 30Give to everyone who
asks you, and if anyone takes what be-
6:30 [g]Dt 15:7,8,10; Pr 21:26
longs to you, do not demand it back.[g]
31Do to others as you would have them
6:31 [h]Mt 7:12
do to you.[h]

32"If you love those who love you,
6:32 [i]Mt 5:46
what credit is that to you?[i] Even 'sinners' love those who love them. 33And
if you do good to those who are good
to you, what credit is that to you? Even
'sinners' do that. 34And if you lend to
those from whom you expect repay-
6:34 [j]Mt 5:42
ment, what credit is that to you?[j] Even
'sinners' lend to 'sinners,' expecting to
be repaid in full. 35But love your en-
6:35 [k]ver 27 [l]Ro 8:14 [m]Mk 5:7
emies, do good to them,[k] and lend
to them without expecting to get anything back. Then your reward will be
great, and you will be sons[l] of the Most
High,[m] because he is kind to the un-
6:36 [n]Jas 2:13 [o]Mt 5:48; 6:1; Lk 11:2; 12:32; Ro 8:15; Eph 4:6; 1Pe 1:17; 1Jn 1:3; 3:1
grateful and wicked. 36Be merciful,[n] just
as your Father[o] is merciful.

Judging Others

37"Do not judge, and you will not
be judged.[p] Do not condemn, and you
6:37 [p]Mt 7:1 [q]Mt 6:14
will not be condemned. Forgive, and
you will be forgiven.[q] 38Give, and it
will be given to you. A good measure,
6:38 [r]Ps 79:12; Isa 65:6,7 [s]Mt 7:2; Mk 4:24
pressed down, shaken together and running over, will be poured into your lap.[r]
For with the measure you use, it will be
measured to you."[s]

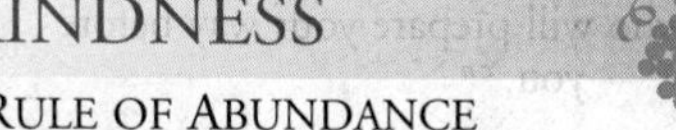

KINDNESS

THE RULE OF ABUNDANCE

Luke 6:38

Stinginess makes God appear a miser.
Stinginess makes grace look poor.
But kindness with a wider brush
Paints portraits of a lavish God.

39He also told them this parable:
"Can a blind man lead a blind man?
6:39 [t]Mt 15:14
Will they not both fall into a pit?[t] 40A
student is not above his teacher, but
everyone who is fully trained will be
6:40 [u]Mt 10:24; Jn 13:16
like his teacher.[u]

41"Why do you look at the speck of
sawdust in your brother's eye and pay
no attention to the plank in your own
eye? 42How can you say to your brother, 'Brother, let me take the speck out
of your eye,' when you yourself fail to
see the plank in your own eye? You
hypocrite, first take the plank out of
your eye, and then you will see clearly
to remove the speck from your brother's eye.

A Tree and Its Fruit

43"No good tree bears bad fruit, nor
does a bad tree bear good fruit. 44Each
tree is recognized by its own fruit.[v] Peo- 6:44 [v]Mt 12:33
ple do not pick figs from thornbushes,
or grapes from briers. 45The good man
brings good things out of the good
stored up in his heart, and the evil man
brings evil things out of the evil stored 6:45 [w]Pr 4:23; Mt 12:34,35; Mk 7:20
up in his heart. For out of the overflow
of his heart his mouth speaks.[w]

FAITHFULNESS

SAY AND OBEY

Luke 6:46

True believers cannot say "No, Lord." The two words cancel each other out. They may be said one at a time, but never together.

The Wise and Foolish Builders

46"Why do you call me, 'Lord, Lord,'[x] 6:46 [x]Jn 13:13 [y]Mal 1:6; Mt 7:21
and do not do what I say?[y] 47I will show
you what he is like who comes to me
and hears my words and puts them into
practice.[z] 48He is like a man building 6:47 [z]Lk 8:21; 11:28; Jas 1:22-25
a house, who dug down deep and laid
the foundation on rock. When a flood
came, the torrent struck that house
but could not shake it, because it was
well built. 49But the one who hears my
words and does not put them into practice is like a man who built a house
on the ground without a foundation.
The moment the torrent struck that
house, it collapsed and its destruction
was complete."

The Faith of the Centurion

7 When Jesus had finished saying all
this[a] in the hearing of the people, 7:1 [a]Mt 7:28
he entered Capernaum. 2There a centu-
rion's servant, whom his master valued
highly, was sick and about to die. 3The
centurion heard of Jesus and sent some
elders of the Jews to him, asking him to
come and heal his servant. 4When they

came to Jesus, they pleaded earnestly
with him, "This man deserves to have
you do this, 5because he loves our nation and has built our synagogue." 6So
Jesus went with them.
He was not far from the house when
the centurion sent friends to say to him:
"Lord, don't trouble yourself, for I do
not deserve to have you come under
my roof. 7That is why I did not even
consider myself worthy to come to you.
But say the word, and my servant will
7:7 [b]Ps 107:20 be healed.[b] 8For I myself am a man under authority, with soldiers under me. I
tell this one, 'Go,' and he goes; and that
one, 'Come,' and he comes. I say to my
servant, 'Do this,' and he does it."
9When Jesus heard this, he was
amazed at him, and turning to the
crowd following him, he said, "I tell
you, I have not found such great faith
even in Israel." 10Then the men who
had been sent returned to the house
and found the servant well.

Jesus Raises a Widow's Son

11Soon afterward, Jesus went to a
town called Nain, and his disciples and
a large crowd went along with him.
12As he approached the town gate, a
dead person was being carried out—the
only son of his mother, and she was
7:13 [c]ver 19; Lk 10:1; 13:15; 17:5; 22:61; 24:34; Jn 11:2 a widow. And a large crowd from the
town was with her. 13When the Lord[c]
saw her, his heart went out to her and
he said, "Don't cry."

KINDNESS

A CRYING WIDOW

Luke 7:13

In Nain Jesus touched a woman who had twice buried her men—first her husband and then her son. Jesus cries with those who weep and his weeping touches sorrow with resurrection—both in Nain and in eternity.

14Then he went up and touched the
7:14 [d]Mt 9:25; Mk 1:31; Lk 8:54; Jn 11:43; Ac 9:40 coffin, and those carrying it stood still.
He said, "Young man, I say to you, get
up!"[d] 15The dead man sat up and began
to talk, and Jesus gave him back to his
mother.
7:16 [e]Lk 1:65 [f]Mt 9:8 [g]ver 39; Mt 21:11 16They were all filled with awe[e] and
praised God.[f] "A great prophet[g] has ap-
peared among us," they said. "God has
come to help his people."[h] 17This news 7:16 [h]Lk 1:68
about Jesus spread throughout Judea[a] 7:17 [i]Mt 9:26
and the surrounding country.[i]

Jesus and John the Baptist

18John's[j] disciples[k] told him about all 7:18 [j]Mt 3:1 [k]Lk 5:33
these things. Calling two of them, 19he
sent them to the Lord to ask, "Are you
the one who was to come, or should we
expect someone else?"
20When the men came to Jesus, they
said, "John the Baptist sent us to you to
ask, 'Are you the one who was to come,
or should we expect someone else?'"
21At that very time Jesus cured many
who had diseases, sicknesses[l] and evil 7:21 [l]Mt 4:23
spirits, and gave sight to many who
were blind. 22So he replied to the messengers, "Go back and report to John
what you have seen and heard: The
blind receive sight, the lame walk, those
who have leprosy[b] are cured, the deaf
hear, the dead are raised, and the good
news is preached to the poor.[m] 23Blessed 7:22 [m]Isa 29:18,19; 35:5,6; 61:1,2; Lk 4:18
is the man who does not fall away on
account of me."
24After John's messengers left, Jesus
began to speak to the crowd about John:
"What did you go out into the desert
to see? A reed swayed by the wind? 25If
not, what did you go out to see? A man
dressed in fine clothes? No, those who
wear expensive clothes and indulge in
luxury are in palaces. 26But what did
you go out to see? A prophet?[n] Yes, I tell 7:26 [n]Mt 11:9
you, and more than a prophet. 27This is
the one about whom it is written:

"'I will send my messenger ahead of
you,
who will prepare your way before
you.'[c][o] 7:27 [o]Mal 3:1; Mt 11:10; Mk 1:2

28I tell you, among those born of wom-
en there is no one greater than John; yet
the one who is least in the kingdom of
God[p] is greater than he." 7:28 [p]Mt 3:2
29(All the people, even the tax collectors, when they heard Jesus' words, ac-
knowledged that God's way was right, 7:29 [q]Mt 21:32; Mk 1:5; Lk 3:12
because they had been baptized by
John.[q] 30But the Pharisees and experts
in the law[r] rejected God's purpose for 7:30 [r]Mt 22:35
themselves, because they had not been
baptized by John.)

[a]*17* Or *the land of the Jews* [b]*22* The Greek word was used for various diseases affecting the skin—not necessarily leprosy. [c]*27* Mal. 3:1

31“To what, then, can I compare the
people of this generation? What are
they like? 32They are like children sitting in the marketplace and calling out
to each other:

“ ‘We played the flute for you,
and you did not dance;
we sang a dirge,
and you did not cry.’

GOODNESS 

CHILDISH GAMES

Luke 7:32
Playing at religion trivializes all God’s dreams.

33For John the Baptist came neither eat-
7:33 [s]Lk 1:15 ing bread nor drinking wine,[s] and you
say, ‘He has a demon.’ 34The Son of
Man came eating and drinking, and
you say, ‘Here is a glutton and a drunkard, a friend of tax collectors and “sin-
7:34 [t]Lk 5:29,30; ners.” ’[t] 35But wisdom is proved right
15:1,2 by all her children.”

Jesus Anointed by a Sinful Woman

36Now one of the Pharisees invited
Jesus to have dinner with him, so he
went to the Pharisee’s house and reclined at the table. 37When a woman
who had lived a sinful life in that town
learned that Jesus was eating at the
Pharisee’s house, she brought an alabaster jar of perfume, 38and as she stood
behind him at his feet weeping, she began to wet his feet with her tears. Then
she wiped them with her hair, kissed
them and poured perfume on them.
39When the Pharisee who had invited him saw this, he said to himself, “If
7:39 [u]ver 16; this man were a prophet,[u] he would
Mt 21:11 know who is touching him and what
kind of woman she is—that she is a sinner.”
40Jesus answered him, “Simon, I have
something to tell you.”
“Tell me, teacher,” he said.
41“Two men owed money to a certain moneylender. One owed him five
hundred denarii,[a] and the other fifty.
42Neither of them had the money to
pay him back, so he canceled the debts
of both. Now which of them will love
him more?”
43Simon replied, “I suppose the one
who had the bigger debt canceled.”

“You have judged correctly,” Jesus
said.
44Then he turned toward the woman
and said to Simon, “Do you see this
woman? I came into your house. You
did not give me any water for my feet,[v] 7:44 [v]Ge 18:4;
but she wet my feet with her tears and 19:2; 43:24;
wiped them with her hair. 45You did not Jdg 19:21; Jn 13:4-14;
give me a kiss,[w] but this woman, from 1Ti 5:10
the time I entered, has not stopped kiss- 7:45 [w]Lk 22:47,48;
ing my feet. 46You did not put oil on Ro 16:16
my head,[x] but she has poured perfume 7:46 [x]Ps 23:5;
on my feet. 47Therefore, I tell you, her Ecc 9:8
many sins have been forgiven—for she
loved much. But he who has been forgiven little loves little.”
48Then Jesus said to her, “Your sins
are forgiven.”[y] 7:48 [y]Mt 9:2
49The other guests began to say
among themselves, “Who is this who
even forgives sins?”
50Jesus said to the woman, “Your
faith has saved you;[z] go in peace.”[a] 7:50 [z]Mt 9:22;

The Parable of the Sower Mk 5:34; Lk 8:48

8 After this, Jesus traveled about from [a]Ac 15:33
one town and village to another,
proclaiming the good news of the kingdom of God.[b] The Twelve were with 8:1 [b]Mt 4:23
him, 2and also some women who had
been cured of evil spirits and diseases:
Mary (called Magdalene)[c] from whom 8:2 [c]Mt 27:55,56
seven demons had come out; 3Joanna
the wife of Cuza, the manager of Her-
od’s[d] household; Susanna; and many 8:3 [d]Mt 14:1
others. These women were helping to
support them out of their own means.
4While a large crowd was gathering
and people were coming to Jesus from
town after town, he told this parable:
5“A farmer went out to sow his seed.
As he was scattering the seed, some fell
along the path; it was trampled on, and
the birds of the air ate it up. 6Some
fell on rock, and when it came up,
the plants withered because they had
no moisture. 7Other seed fell among
thorns, which grew up with it and
choked the plants. 8Still other seed fell
on good soil. It came up and yielded a
crop, a hundred times more than was
sown.”
When he said this, he called out, “He
who has ears to hear, let him hear.”[e] 8:8 [e]Mt 11:15
9His disciples asked him what this par-
able meant. 10He said, “The knowledge

[a]*41* A denarius was a coin worth about a day’s wages.

of the secrets of the kingdom of God has
8:10 [f]Mt 13:11 [g]Isa 6:9; Mt 13:13,14 been given to you,[f] but to others I speak
in parables, so that,

"'though seeing, they may not see;
though hearing, they may not
understand.'[a][g]

11"This is the meaning of the par-
8:11 [h]Heb 4:12 able: The seed is the word of God.[h]
12Those along the path are the ones
who hear, and then the devil comes and
takes away the word from their hearts,
so that they may not believe and be
saved. 13Those on the rock are the ones
who receive the word with joy when
they hear it, but they have no root.
They believe for a while, but in the time
8:13 [i]Mt 11:6 of testing they fall away.[i] 14The seed
that fell among thorns stands for those
who hear, but as they go on their way
8:14 [j]Mt 19:23; 1Ti 6:9,10,17 they are choked by life's worries, riches[j]
and pleasures, and they do not mature.
15But the seed on good soil stands for
those with a noble and good heart, who
hear the word, retain it, and by persevering produce a crop.

A Lamp on a Stand

16"No one lights a lamp and hides it
in a jar or puts it under a bed. Instead,
he puts it on a stand, so that those
8:16 [k]Mt 5:15; Mk 4:21; Lk 11:33 who come in can see the light.[k] 17For
there is nothing hidden that will not be
disclosed, and nothing concealed that
will not be known or brought out into
8:17 [l]Mt 10:26; Mk 4:22; Lk 12:2 the open.[l] 18Therefore consider carefully how you listen. Whoever has will
be given more; whoever does not have,
even what he thinks he has will be tak-
8:18 [m]Mt 13:12; 25:29; Lk 19:26 en from him."[m]

Jesus' Mother and Brothers

19Now Jesus' mother and brothers
came to see him, but they were not able
to get near him because of the crowd.
20Someone told him, "Your mother and
8:20 [n]Jn 7:5 brothers[n] are standing outside, wanting
to see you."

21He replied, "My mother and brothers are those who hear God's word and
8:21 [o]Lk 6:47; 11:28; Jn 14:21 put it into practice."[o]

Jesus Calms the Storm

22One day Jesus said to his disciples,
"Let's go over to the other side of the
lake." So they got into a boat and set
out. 23As they sailed, he fell asleep. A
squall came down on the lake, so that
the boat was being swamped, and they
were in great danger.

24The disciples went and woke him,
saying, "Master, Master,[p] we're going to 8:24 [p]Lk 5:5 [q]Lk 4:35, 39,41 [r]Ps 107:29; Jnh 1:15
drown!"

He got up and rebuked[q] the wind
and the raging waters; the storm subsided, and all was calm.[r] 25"Where is
your faith?" he asked his disciples.

In fear and amazement they asked
one another, "Who is this? He commands even the winds and the water,
and they obey him."

The Healing of a Demon-possessed Man

26They sailed to the region of the Gerasenes,[b] which is across the lake from
Galilee. 27When Jesus stepped ashore,
he was met by a demon-possessed man
from the town. For a long time this
man had not worn clothes or lived in
a house, but had lived in the tombs.
28When he saw Jesus, he cried out and
fell at his feet, shouting at the top of his
voice, "What do you want with me,[s] Je- 8:28 [s]Mt 8:29 [t]Mk 5:7
sus, Son of the Most High God?[t] I beg
you, don't torture me!" 29For Jesus had
commanded the evil[c] spirit to come out
of the man. Many times it had seized
him, and though he was chained hand
and foot and kept under guard, he had
broken his chains and had been driven
by the demon into solitary places.

30Jesus asked him, "What is your
name?"

"Legion," he replied, because many
demons had gone into him. 31And they
begged him repeatedly not to order
them to go into the Abyss.[u] 8:31 [u]Rev 9:1,2,11; 11:7; 17:8; 20:1,3

32A large herd of pigs was feeding
there on the hillside. The demons begged
Jesus to let them go into them, and he
gave them permission. 33When the demons came out of the man, they went
into the pigs, and the herd rushed down
the steep bank into the lake[v] and was 8:33 [v]ver 22,23
drowned.

34When those tending the pigs saw
what had happened, they ran off and
reported this in the town and countryside, 35and the people went out to
see what had happened. When they
came to Jesus, they found the man from

[a]*10* Isaiah 6:9 [b]*26* Some manuscripts *Gadarenes*; other manuscripts *Gergesenes*; also in verse 37
[c]*29* Greek *unclean*

whom the demons had gone out, sitting
8:35 at Jesus' feet,[w] dressed and in his right
[w]Lk 10:39 mind; and they were afraid. 36Those
who had seen it told the people how
8:36 the demon-possessed[x] man had been
[x]Mt 4:24 cured. 37Then all the people of the region of the Gerasenes asked Jesus to
8:37 leave them,[y] because they were over-
[y]Ac 16:39 come with fear. So he got into the boat
and left.
38The man from whom the demons
had gone out begged to go with him,
but Jesus sent him away, saying, 39"Return home and tell how much God has
done for you." So the man went away
and told all over town how much Jesus
had done for him.

A Dead Girl and a Sick Woman

40Now when Jesus returned, a crowd
welcomed him, for they were all expecting him. 41Then a man named Jairus, a
8:41 ruler of the synagogue,[z] came and fell at
[z]ver 49; Jesus' feet, pleading with him to come
Mk 5:22 to his house 42because his only daughter, a girl of about twelve, was dying.
As Jesus was on his way, the crowds
almost crushed him. 43And a woman
was there who had been subject to
8:43 bleeding[a] for twelve years,[a] but no one
[a]Lev 15:25-30 could heal her. 44She came up behind
8:44 him and touched the edge of his cloak,[b]
[b]Mt 9:20 and immediately her bleeding stopped.
45"Who touched me?" Jesus asked.
8:45 When they all denied it, Peter said,
[c]Lk 5:5 "Master,[c] the people are crowding and
pressing against you."
8:46 46But Jesus said, "Someone touched
[d]Mt 14:36; me;[d] I know that power has gone out
Mk 3:10
[e]Lk 5:17; 6:19 from me."[e]

JOY

HIDING OUR CONFESSION

Luke 8:47

"Who touched me?" Jesus asked.
"I did," said the woman sheepishly.
"Then credit God with glory!
Do not cram grace into your purse and run from your obligation to praise.
Heaven does not care for pickpockets."

47Then the woman, seeing that she
could not go unnoticed, came trembling and fell at his feet. In the presence
of all the people, she told why she had
touched him and how she had been instantly healed. 48Then he said to her,
"Daughter, your faith has healed you.[f] 8:48 [f]Mt 9:22
Go in peace."[g] [g]Ac 15:33
49While Jesus was still speaking,
someone came from the house of Jairus,
the synagogue ruler.[h] "Your daughter is 8:49
dead," he said. "Don't bother the teach- [h]ver 41
er any more."
50Hearing this, Jesus said to Jairus,
"Don't be afraid; just believe, and she
will be healed."
51When he arrived at the house of
Jairus, he did not let anyone go in with
him except Peter, John and James,[i] and 8:51
the child's father and mother. 52Mean- [i]Mt 4:21
while, all the people were wailing and
mourning[j] for her. "Stop wailing," Je- 8:52
sus said. "She is not dead but asleep."[k] [j]Lk 23:27 [k]Mt 9:24;
53They laughed at him, knowing that Jn 11:11,13
she was dead. 54But he took her by
the hand and said, "My child, get up!"[l] 8:54
55Her spirit returned, and at once she [l]Lk 7:14
stood up. Then Jesus told them to give
her something to eat. 56Her parents were
astonished, but he ordered them not to 8:56
tell anyone what had happened.[m] [m]Mt 8:4

Jesus Sends Out the Twelve

9 When Jesus had called the Twelve
together, he gave them power and
authority to drive out all demons[n] and 9:1 [n]Mt 10:1
to cure diseases,[o] 2and he sent them out [o]Mt 4:23;
to preach the kingdom of God[p] and Lk 5:17
to heal the sick. 3He told them: "Take 9:2 [p]Mt 3:2
nothing for the journey—no staff, no
bag, no bread, no money, no extra
tunic.[q] 4Whatever house you enter, stay 9:3 [q]Lk 10:4;
there until you leave that town. 5If peo- 22:35
ple do not welcome you, shake the dust
off your feet when you leave their town,
as a testimony against them."[r] 6So they 9:5 [r]Mt 10:14
set out and went from village to village,
preaching the gospel and healing people everywhere.
7Now Herod[s] the tetrarch heard 9:7 [s]Mt 14:1
about all that was going on. And he [t]Mt 3:1
was perplexed, because some were say- [u]ver 19
ing that John[t] had been raised from the
dead,[u] 8others that Elijah had appeared,[v] 9:8 [v]Mt 11:14
and still others that one of the prophets [w]ver 19;
of long ago had come back to life.[w] 9But Jn 1:21
Herod said, "I beheaded John. Who,
then, is this I hear such things about?" 9:9 [x]Lk 23:8
And he tried to see him.[x]

[a]43 Many manuscripts *years, and she had spent all she had on doctors*

Jesus Feeds the Five Thousand

9:10 10When the apostles[y] returned, they
yMk 6:30 zMt 11:21 reported to Jesus what they had done.
Then he took them with him and they
withdrew by themselves to a town called
Bethsaida,[z] 11but the crowds learned
about it and followed him. He welcomed them and spoke to them about
9:11 aver 2; the kingdom of God,[a] and healed those
Mt 3:2 who needed healing.

12Late in the afternoon the Twelve
came to him and said, "Send the crowd
away so they can go to the surrounding
villages and countryside and find food
and lodging, because we are in a remote
place here."

13He replied, "You give them something to eat."

They answered, "We have only five
loaves of bread and two fish—unless we
go and buy food for all this crowd."
14(About five thousand men were
there.)

But he said to his disciples, "Have
them sit down in groups of about fifty
each." 15The disciples did so, and everybody sat down. 16Taking the five loaves
and the two fish and looking up to heav-
en, he gave thanks and broke them.[b]
9:16 bMt 14:19 Then he gave them to the disciples to
set before the people. 17They all ate and
were satisfied, and the disciples picked
up twelve basketfuls of broken pieces
that were left over.

Peter's Confession of Christ

9:18 cLk 3:21 18Once when Jesus was praying[c] in
private and his disciples were with him,
he asked them, "Who do the crowds
say I am?"

19They replied, "Some say John the
9:19 dMt 3:1 Baptist;[d] others say Elijah; and still oth-
ever 7,8 ers, that one of the prophets of long ago
has come back to life."[e]

20"But what about you?" he asked.
"Who do you say I am?"

Peter answered, "The Christ[a] of
9:20 fJn 1:49; 6:66-69; God."[f]
11:27 21Jesus strictly warned them not to
9:21 tell this to anyone.[g] 22And he said,
gMt 16:20; "The Son of Man[h] must suffer many
Mk 8:30 things[i] and be rejected by the elders,
9:22 hMt 8:20 chief priests and teachers of the law,[j]
iMt 16:21 jMt 27:1,2 and he must be killed[k] and on the third
kAc 2:23; 3:13 lMt 16:21 day[l] be raised to life."[m]

mMt 16:21 23Then he said to them all: "If anyone would come after me, he must deny
himself and take up his cross daily and
follow me.[n] 24For whoever wants to save 9:23 nMt 10:38;
his life will lose it, but whoever loses his Lk 14:27
life for me will save it.[o] 25What good is 9:24 oJn 12:25
it for a man to gain the whole world,
and yet lose or forfeit his very self?
26If anyone is ashamed of me and my
words, the Son of Man will be ashamed
of him[p] when he comes in his glory 9:26 pMt 10:33;
and in the glory of the Father and of Lk 12:9; 2Ti 2:12
the holy angels.[q] 27I tell you the truth, qMt 16:27
some who are standing here will not
taste death before they see the kingdom
of God."

The Transfiguration

28About eight days after Jesus said
this, he took Peter, John and James[r] 9:28 rMt 4:21
with him and went up onto a moun- sLk 3:21
tain to pray.[s] 29As he was praying, the
appearance of his face changed, and
his clothes became as bright as a flash
of lightning. 30Two men, Moses and
Elijah, 31appeared in glorious splendor,
talking with Jesus. They spoke about his
departure,[t] which he was about to bring 9:31 t2Pe 1:15
to fulfillment at Jerusalem. 32Peter and
his companions were very sleepy,[u] but 9:32 uMt 26:43
when they became fully awake, they
saw his glory and the two men standing with him. 33As the men were leav-
ing Jesus, Peter said to him, "Master,[v] 9:33 vLk 5:5
it is good for us to be here. Let us put
up three shelters—one for you, one for
Moses and one for Elijah." (He did not
know what he was saying.)

34While he was speaking, a cloud appeared and enveloped them, and they
were afraid as they entered the cloud.
35A voice came from the cloud, saying,
"This is my Son, whom I have chosen;[w] 9:35 wIsa 42:1
listen to him."[x] 36When the voice had xMt 3:17
spoken, they found that Jesus was alone.
The disciples kept this to themselves,
and told no one at that time what they 9:36
had seen.[y] yMt 17:9

The Healing of a Boy With an Evil Spirit

37The next day, when they came
down from the mountain, a large crowd
met him. 38A man in the crowd called
out, "Teacher, I beg you to look at my
son, for he is my only child. 39A spirit
seizes him and he suddenly screams; it
throws him into convulsions so that he

[a]20 Or *Messiah*

foams at the mouth. It scarcely ever
leaves him and is destroying him. 40I
begged your disciples to drive it out,
but they could not."

SELF-CONTROL 

DEALING WITH SATAN

Luke 9:40

Would you encounter the horned defector?
Would you face the devil in all his strength?
Would you wrestle the dragon back to hell?
Then bulk up! Discipline your flabby soul with the muscle of your adoration.
Work out in the closets of confession.
Bench-press the heavy weights of holiness.
Demons make short work of spiritual pip-squeaks.

41"O unbelieving and perverse
9:41 [z]Dt 32:5 generation,"[z] Jesus replied, "how long
shall I stay with you and put up with
you? Bring your son here."
42Even while the boy was coming,
the demon threw him to the ground
in a convulsion. But Jesus rebuked the
evil[a] spirit, healed the boy and gave him
back to his father. 43And they were all
amazed at the greatness of God.
While everyone was marveling at all
that Jesus did, he said to his disciples,
44"Listen carefully to what I am about
to tell you: The Son of Man is going
9:44 [a]ver 22 to be betrayed into the hands of men."[a]
45But they did not understand what
this meant. It was hidden from them,
9:45 [b]Mk 9:32 so that they did not grasp it,[b] and they
were afraid to ask him about it.

Who Will Be the Greatest?

46An argument started among the
disciples as to which of them would
9:46 [c]Lk 22:24 be the greatest.[c] 47Jesus, knowing their
thoughts,[d] took a little child and had
9:47 [d]Mt 9:4 him stand beside him. 48Then he said
to them, "Whoever welcomes this little
child in my name welcomes me; and
whoever welcomes me welcomes the
9:48 [e]Mt 10:40 one who sent me.[e] For he who is least
[f]Mk 9:35 among you all—he is the greatest."[f]
9:49 [g]Lk 5:5 49"Master,"[g] said John, "we saw a
man driving out demons in your name
and we tried to stop him, because he is
not one of us."
9:50 [h]Mt 12:30; Lk 11:23 50"Do not stop him," Jesus said, "for
whoever is not against you is for you."[h]

DAY 3 THREE

SELF-CONTROL AND MY RELATIONSHIP WITH CHRIST

Luke 9:51–56

James and John wanted to call down fire on those who would not readily welcome Jesus into their village. But these "sons of thunder" had missed the point. You don't accept Christ and then kill all unbelievers. Rather, you live like Christ and die for unbelievers.

Christians who bomb abortion clinics, it seems to me, have agreed that the best way to deal with "Samaritans" is to torch them. The best way to torch Samaritans is always to call down fire from heaven—but if heaven won't help out, there's always TNT.

Have you ever known Christians who seemed eager to torch the unbelieving world for the sake of good doctrine? I always wonder what would have happened if Jesus had replied to James and John, "Good idea, let's destroy everybody who won't accept our teachings." James and John would have gone all through life scorching villages, smiling while they burned.

Most people who get "hostile with the gospel" think they are helping out. But the control they should invoke is not on the errant world but on their own errant selves. They shouldn't try to coerce the unbelieving world with thunderbolts. They should try to manage themselves, and once they have made self-control a working principle in their own lives, the Samaritans might warm up to their propositions. Burning villages has never been a good evangelistic technique. On the other hand, burning our egos—our presumed right to control others—has had an amazing effect where it has been tried.

To begin a study on the topic of Self-Control, Managing My Moods, turn to the home page on page 179.

Samaritan Opposition

51As the time approached for him to 9:51 [i]Mk 16:19
be taken up to heaven,[i] Jesus resolutely [j]Lk 13:22; 17:11; 18:31; 19:28
set out for Jerusalem.[j] 52And he sent
messengers on ahead, who went into a
Samaritan[k] village to get things ready 9:52 [k]Mt 10:5

[a]42 Greek *unclean*

for him; 53but the people there did
not welcome him, because he was heading for Jerusalem. 54When the disciples
9:54 [l]Mt 4:21 James and John[l] saw this, they asked,
[m]2Ki 1:10,12 "Lord, do you want us to call fire down
from heaven to destroy them[a]?"[m] 55But
Jesus turned and rebuked them, 56and[b]
they went to another village.

The Cost of Following Jesus

57As they were walking along the
9:57 [n]ver 51 road,[n] a man said to him, "I will follow
you wherever you go."
58Jesus replied, "Foxes have holes and
birds of the air have nests, but the Son
9:58 [o]Mt 8:20 of Man[o] has no place to lay his head."
59He said to another man, "Follow
9:59 [p]Mt 4:19 me."[p]
But the man replied, "Lord, first let
me go and bury my father."
60Jesus said to him, "Let the dead
bury their own dead, but you go and
9:60 [q]Mt 3:2 proclaim the kingdom of God."[q]
61Still another said, "I will follow
you, Lord; but first let me go back and
9:61 [r]1Ki 19:20 say good-by to my family."[r]
62Jesus replied, "No one who puts his
hand to the plow and looks back is fit
for service in the kingdom of God."

Jesus Sends Out the Seventy-two

10:1 [s]Lk 7:13 10 After this the Lord[s] appointed
[t]Lk 9:1,2, 51,52 seventy-two[c] others[t] and sent
[u]Mk 6:7 them two[u] by two ahead of him to
[v]Mt 10:1 every town and place where he was
about to go.[v] 2He told them, "The harvest is plentiful, but the workers are
few. Ask the Lord of the harvest, therefore, to send out workers into his har-
10:2 [w]Mt 9:37,38; vest field.[w] 3Go! I am sending you out
Jn 4:35 like lambs among wolves.[x] 4Do not take
10:3 a purse or bag or sandals; and do not
[x]Mt 10:16 greet anyone on the road.
5"When you enter a house, first say,
'Peace to this house.' 6If a man of peace
is there, your peace will rest on him;
if not, it will return to you. 7Stay in
that house, eating and drinking whatever they give you, for the worker de-
10:7 serves his wages.[y] Do not move around
[y]Mt 10:10; 1Co 9:14; from house to house.
1Ti 5:18 8"When you enter a town and are
10:8 welcomed, eat what is set before you.[z]
[z]1Co 10:27 9Heal the sick who are there and tell
10:9 them, 'The kingdom of God[a] is near
[a]Mt 3:2; 10:7 you.' 10But when you enter a town and
are not welcomed, go into its streets and
say, 11'Even the dust of your town that
sticks to our feet we wipe off against
you.[b] Yet be sure of this: The kingdom 10:11
of God is near.'[c] 12I tell you, it will be [b]Mt 10:14; Mk 6:11
more bearable on that day for Sodom[d] [c]ver 9
than for that town.[e] 10:12
13"Woe to you,[f] Korazin! Woe to [d]Mt 10:15 [e]Mt 11:24
you, Bethsaida! For if the miracles that
were performed in you had been per- 10:13
formed in Tyre and Sidon, they would [f]Lk 6:24-26 [g]Rev 11:3
have repented long ago, sitting in sack-
cloth[g] and ashes. 14But it will be more
bearable for Tyre and Sidon at the
judgment than for you. 15And you,
Capernaum,[h] will you be lifted up to 10:15 [h]Mt 4:13
the skies? No, you will go down to the 10:16
depths.[d] [i]Mt 10:40; Jn 13:20
16"He who listens to you listens to
me; he who rejects you rejects me; but 10:17 [j]ver 1
he who rejects me rejects him who [k]Mk 16:17
sent me."[i]
17The seventy-two[j] returned with joy 10:18 [l]Mt 4:10
and said, "Lord, even the demons sub- [m]Isa 14:12; Rev 9:1;
mit to us in your name."[k] 12:8,9
18He replied, "I saw Satan[l] fall like 10:19
lightning from heaven.[m] 19I have given [n]Mk 16:18; Ac 28:3-5
you authority to trample on snakes[n] 10:20
and scorpions and to overcome all the [o]Ex 32:32;
power of the enemy; nothing will harm Ps 69:28; Da 12:1;
you. 20However, do not rejoice that the Php 4:3; Heb 12:23;
spirits submit to you, but rejoice that Rev 13:8;
your names are written in heaven."[o] 20:12; 21:27

JOY

STROLLING OVER SCORPIONS

Luke 10:19

Believers have authority, but they too seldom use it. If they did, they would see more lightning and less fog in their lives. They would skip through fields of scorpions in open sandals.

21At that time Jesus, full of joy
through the Holy Spirit, said, "I praise
you, Father, Lord of heaven and earth,
because you have hidden these things
from the wise and learned, and revealed
them to little children.[p] Yes, Father, for 10:21 [p]1Co 1:26-29
this was your good pleasure.
22"All things have been committed to 10:22
me by my Father.[q] No one knows who [q]Mt 28:18

[a]54 Some manuscripts *them, even as Elijah did*
[b]55,56 Some manuscripts *them. And he said, "You do not know what kind of spirit you are of, for the Son of Man did not come to destroy men's lives, but to save them." 56And* [c]1 Some manuscripts *seventy*; also in verse 17 [d]15 Greek *Hades*

the Son is except the Father, and no one
knows who the Father is except the Son
and those to whom the Son chooses to
10:22 [r]Jn 1:18 reveal him."[r]
23Then he turned to his disciples and
said privately, "Blessed are the eyes that
see what you see. 24For I tell you that
many prophets and kings wanted to
see what you see but did not see it,
and to hear what you hear but did not
10:24 [s]1Pe 1:10-12 hear it."[s]

The Parable of the Good Samaritan

25On one occasion an expert in the
law stood up to test Jesus. "Teacher,"
he asked, "what must I do to inherit
10:25 [t]Mt 19:16; Lk 18:18 eternal life?"[t]
26"What is written in the Law?" he
replied. "How do you read it?"
27He answered: " 'Love the Lord your
God with all your heart and with all
your soul and with all your strength
10:27 [u]Dt 6:5 [v]Lev 19:18; Mt 5:43 and with all your mind'[a];[u] and, 'Love
your neighbor as yourself.'[b]"[v]
28"You have answered correctly," Jesus
10:28 [w]Lev 18:5; Ro 7:10 replied. "Do this and you will live."[w]
29But he wanted to justify himself,[x]
so he asked Jesus, "And who is my
10:29 [x]Lk 16:15 neighbor?"
30In reply Jesus said: "A man was going down from Jerusalem to Jericho,
when he fell into the hands of robbers.
They stripped him of his clothes, beat
him and went away, leaving him half
dead. 31A priest happened to be going
down the same road, and when he saw
the man, he passed by on the other
10:31 [y]Lev 21:1-3 side.[y] 32So too, a Levite, when he came
to the place and saw him, passed by on
10:33 [z]Mt 10:5 the other side. 33But a Samaritan,[z] as
he traveled, came where the man was;
and when he saw him, he took pity on
him. 34He went to him and bandaged
his wounds, pouring on oil and wine.
Then he put the man on his own donkey, took him to an inn and took care
of him. 35The next day he took out
two silver coins[c] and gave them to the
innkeeper. 'Look after him,' he said,
'and when I return, I will reimburse
you for any extra expense you may
have.'
36"Which of these three do you think
was a neighbor to the man who fell into
the hands of robbers?"
37The expert in the law replied, "The
one who had mercy on him."

Jesus told him, "Go and do likewise."

At the Home of Martha and Mary

38As Jesus and his disciples were on
their way, he came to a village where
a woman named Martha[a] opened her 10:38 [a]Jn 11:1; 12:2
home to him. 39She had a sister called
Mary,[b] who sat at the Lord's feet[c] listen- 10:39 [b]Jn 11:1; 12:3 [c]Lk 8:35
ing to what he said. 40But Martha was
distracted by all the preparations that
had to be made. She came to him and
asked, "Lord, don't you care[d] that my 10:40 [d]Mk 4:38
sister has left me to do the work by my-
self? Tell her to help me!"
41"Martha, Martha," the Lord an-
swered, "you are worried[e] and upset 10:41 [e]Mt 6:25-34; Lk 12:11,22
about many things, 42but only one thing
is needed.[d] [f] Mary has chosen what is 10:42 [f]Ps 27:4
better, and it will not be taken away
from her."

Jesus' Teaching on Prayer

11 One day Jesus was praying[g] in a 11:1 [g]Lk 3:21
certain place. When he finished, [h]Jn 13:13
one of his disciples said to him, "Lord,[h]
teach us to pray, just as John taught his
disciples."
2He said to them, "When you pray,
say:

" 'Father,[e]
hallowed be your name,
your kingdom[i] come.[f] 11:2 [i]Mt 3:2
3Give us each day our daily bread.
4Forgive us our sins,
for we also forgive everyone who 11:4 [j]Mt 18:35; Mk 11:25
sins against us.[g] [j]
And lead us not into temptation.[h]' "[k] [k]Mt 26:41; Jas 1:13

5Then he said to them, "Suppose one
of you has a friend, and he goes to him
at midnight and says, 'Friend, lend me
three loaves of bread, 6because a friend
of mine on a journey has come to me,
and I have nothing to set before him.'
7"Then the one inside answers, 'Don't
bother me. The door is already locked,
and my children are with me in bed.
I can't get up and give you anything.'
8I tell you, though he will not get up

[a] *27* Deut. 6:5 [b] *27* Lev. 19:18 [c] *35* Greek *two denarii* [d] *42* Some manuscripts *but few things are needed—or only one* [e] *2* Some manuscripts *Our Father in heaven* [f] *2* Some manuscripts *come. May your will be done on earth as it is in heaven.* [g] *4* Greek *everyone who is indebted to us* [h] *4* Some manuscripts *temptation but deliver us from the evil one*

DAY 4 FOUR

▸ FAITHFULNESS AND MY SERVICE TO OTHERS

Luke 11:5–8

This parable illustrates the high art of persistence and its efficacy in prayer. Praying faithfully is our willingness to go boldly before the throne and ask what we want from God. And then in faithfulness we will do it again and again.

Notice the high art of persistence in Jesus' parable:

The Requisitioner: **Friend, let me have three loaves of bread. I've had a friend drop in—a hungry friend who eats like a horse—I need three loaves of bread.**

The Groggy Neighbor: **Good grief, man! Do you have any idea what time it is? My kids are in bed; my door is bolted. What do you think I am—an all-night bakery?**

The Requisitioner: **Pretty please, with cream and sugar on it.**

The Groggy Neighbor: **No—be reasonable!**

The Requisitioner: **I'm gonna stand out here and sing the same song—second verse; it could be better, but it's getting worse . . .**

The Groggy Neighbor: **Oh, all right. For pity's sake, quit pounding on my door, and I'll give you the bread and then maybe we'll both get a little sleep.**

Jesus commends the pushy neighbor for acting boldly until he got what he wanted.

Boldness is the key in faithful petitioning. Catherine of Siena became very demanding with God when her brother became ill. "Give me back my brother!" she shouted in her prayer. Some rebuked her for irreverence, but she insisted that the Master told us to claim boldly the desires of our hearts.

To begin a study on the topic of Faithfulness, the High Art of Persistence, turn to the home page on page 635.

and give him the bread because he is his
friend, yet because of the man's bold-
11:8 ˡLk 18:1-6 ness[a] he will get up and give him as
much as he needs.[l]
11:9 ᵐMt 7:7 [9]"So I say to you: Ask and it will be
given to you; seek and you[m] will find;
knock and the door will be opened to
you. [10]For everyone who asks receives;
he who seeks finds; and to him who
knocks, the door will be opened.

▸ FAITHFULNESS

THE WIN-WIN LIFE

Luke 11:11–13

Rocks and scorpions are never God's reply to those who ask for fish and eggs.
Get what you ask for.
Ask for the Spirit.

[11]"Which of you fathers, if your son
asks for[b] a fish, will give him a snake
instead? [12]Or if he asks for an egg,
will give him a scorpion? [13]If you then,
though you are evil, know how to
give good gifts to your children, how
much more will your Father in heaven
give the Holy Spirit to those who ask
him!"

Jesus and Beelzebub

[14]Jesus was driving out a demon that
was mute. When the demon left, the
man who had been mute spoke, and
the crowd was amazed.[n] [15]But some of 11:14 ⁿMt 9:32,33
them said, "By Beelzebub,[c][o] the prince
of demons, he is driving out demons."[p] 11:15 ᵒMk 3:22
[16]Others tested him by asking for a sign ᵖMt 9:34
from heaven.[q]
[17]Jesus knew their thoughts[r] and said 11:16 ᵠMt 12:38
to them: "Any kingdom divided against
itself will be ruined, and a house di- 11:17 ʳMt 9:4
vided against itself will fall. [18]If Satan[s]
is divided against himself, how can his 11:18 ˢMt 4:10
kingdom stand? I say this because you
claim that I drive out demons by Beelzebub. [19]Now if I drive out demons by
Beelzebub, by whom do your followers
drive them out? So then, they will be
your judges. [20]But if I drive out de-
mons by the finger of God,[t] then the 11:20 ᵗEx 8:19
kingdom of God[u] has come to you. ᵘMt 3:2
[21]"When a strong man, fully armed,
guards his own house, his possessions
are safe. [22]But when someone stronger
attacks and overpowers him, he takes
away the armor in which the man trusted and divides up the spoils.
[23]"He who is not with me is against

[a]8 Or *persistence* [b]11 Some manuscripts *for bread, will give him a stone; or if he asks for* [c]15 Greek *Beezeboul* or *Beelzeboul*; also in verses 18 and 19

me, and he who does not gather with
11:23 [v]Mt 12:30; Mk 9:40; Lk 9:50 me, scatters.[v]
24"When an evil[a] spirit comes out of
a man, it goes through arid places seeking rest and does not find it. Then it
says, 'I will return to the house I left.'
25When it arrives, it finds the house
swept clean and put in order. 26Then it
goes and takes seven other spirits more
wicked than itself, and they go in and
live there. And the final condition of
11:26 [w]2Pe 2:20 that man is worse than the first."[w]
27As Jesus was saying these things, a
woman in the crowd called out, "Blessed
is the mother who gave you birth and
11:27 [x]Lk 23:29 nursed you."[x]
28He replied, "Blessed rather are those
11:28 [y]Heb 4:12 [z]Pr 8:32; Lk 6:47; 8:21; Jn 14:21 who hear the word of God[y] and
obey it."[z]

The Sign of Jonah

29As the crowds increased, Jesus said,
"This is a wicked generation. It asks for
11:29 [a]ver 16; Mt 12:38 [b]Jnh 1:17; Mt 16:4 a miraculous sign,[a] but none will be
given it except the sign of Jonah.[b] 30For
as Jonah was a sign to the Ninevites, so
also will the Son of Man be to this generation. 31The Queen of the South will
rise at the judgment with the men of
this generation and condemn them; for
she came from the ends of the earth to
11:31 [c]1Ki 10:1; 2Ch 9:1 listen to Solomon's wisdom,[c] and now
one[b] greater than Solomon is here.
32The men of Nineveh will stand up
at the judgment with this generation
and condemn it; for they repented at
11:32 [d]Jnh 3:5 the preaching of Jonah,[d] and now one
greater than Jonah is here.

The Lamp of the Body

33"No one lights a lamp and puts it
in a place where it will be hidden, or
under a bowl. Instead he puts it on its
stand, so that those who come in may
11:33 [e]Mt 5:15; Mk 4:21; Lk 8:16 see the light.[e] 34Your eye is the lamp of
your body. When your eyes are good,
your whole body also is full of light.
But when they are bad, your body also
is full of darkness. 35See to it, then, that
the light within you is not darkness.
36Therefore, if your whole body is full
of light, and no part of it dark, it will
be completely lighted, as when the light
of a lamp shines on you."

Six Woes

37When Jesus had finished speaking,
a Pharisee invited him to eat with him;
so he went in and reclined at the table.[f] 11:37 [f]Lk 7:36; 14:1
38But the Pharisee, noticing that Jesus
did not first wash before the meal,[g] was 11:38 [g]Mk 7:3,4
surprised.

GOODNESS

The Heart Scrub

Luke 11:38

We never sully God's purposes with dirty hands—only with dirty hearts.

39Then the Lord[h] said to him, "Now 11:39 [h]Lk 7:13 [i]Mt 23:25,26; Mk 7:20-23
then, you Pharisees clean the outside of
the cup and dish, but inside you are full
of greed and wickedness.[i] 40You foolish
people![j] Did not the one who made the 11:40 [j]Lk 12:20; 1Co 15:36
outside make the inside also? 41But give
what is inside ⌊the dish⌋[c] to the poor,[k] 11:41 [k]Lk 12:33 [l]Ac 10:15
and everything will be clean for you.[l]
42"Woe to you Pharisees, because you
give God a tenth[m] of your mint, rue and 11:42 [m]Lk 18:12 [n]Dt 6:5; Mic 6:8 [o]Mt 23:23
all other kinds of garden herbs, but you
neglect justice and the love of God.[n]
You should have practiced the latter
without leaving the former undone.[o] 11:43 [p]Mt 23:6,7; Mk 12:38-39; Lk 14:7; 20:46
43"Woe to you Pharisees, because you
love the most important seats in the
synagogues and greetings in the marketplaces.[p]
44"Woe to you, because you are like
unmarked graves,[q] which men walk over 11:44 [q]Mt 23:27
without knowing it."
45One of the experts in the law[r] an- 11:45 [r]Mt 22:35
swered him, "Teacher, when you say
these things, you insult us also."
46Jesus replied, "And you experts in
the law, woe to you, because you load
people down with burdens they can

[a]*24* Greek *unclean* [b]*31* Or *something*; also in verse 32 [c]*41* Or *what you have*

GOODNESS

Practice First, Preach Later

Luke 11:46

One of the great sins of professional religionists
is that they often require more of their disciples than they do of themselves.
"Come, know God and be better than me" is a valid invitation to grace.
"Come, know God and be better than I care to be" is not.

hardly carry, and you yourselves will
11:46 [s]Mt 23:4 not lift one finger to help them.[s]
47“Woe to you, because you build
tombs for the prophets, and it was your
forefathers who killed them. 48So you
testify that you approve of what your
forefathers did; they killed the proph-
11:48 ets, and you build their tombs.[t] 49Be-
[t]Mt 23:29-32; Ac 7:51-53 cause of this, God in his wisdom[u] said,
‘I will send them prophets and apostles,
11:49 [u]1Co 1:24,30; Col 2:3 some of whom they will kill and others
[v]Mt 23:34 they will persecute.’[v] 50Therefore this
generation will be held responsible for
the blood of all the prophets that has
been shed since the beginning of the
11:51 [w]Ge 4:8 world, 51from the blood of Abel[w] to the
[x]2Ch 24:20, 21 blood of Zechariah,[x] who was killed be-
[y]Mt 23:35,36 tween the altar and the sanctuary. Yes,
I tell you, this generation will be held
responsible for it all.[y]
52“Woe to you experts in the law, because you have taken away the key to
knowledge. You yourselves have not entered, and you have hindered those who
11:52 [z]Mt 23:13 were entering.”[z]
53When Jesus left there, the Pharisees
and the teachers of the law began to
oppose him fiercely and to besiege him
with questions, 54waiting to catch him
11:54 [a]Mt 12:10; Mk 12:13 in something he might say.[a]

Warnings and Encouragements

12 Meanwhile, when a crowd of
many thousands had gathered,
so that they were trampling on one another, Jesus began to speak first to his
disciples, saying: “Be on your guard
against the yeast of the Pharisees, which
12:1 [b]Mt 16:6, 11,12; Mk 8:15 is hypocrisy.[b] 2There is nothing concealed that will not be disclosed, or
hidden that will not be made known.[c]
12:2 [c]Mk 4:22; Lk 8:17 3What you have said in the dark will
be heard in the daylight, and what
you have whispered in the ear in the
inner rooms will be proclaimed from
the roofs.
12:4 [d]Jn 15:14,15 4“I tell you, my friends,[d] do not be
afraid of those who kill the body and
after that can do no more. 5But I will
show you whom you should fear: Fear
him who, after the killing of the body,
has power to throw you into hell. Yes,
12:5 [e]Heb 10:31 I tell you, fear him.[e] 6Are not five sparrows sold for two pennies[a]? Yet not one
of them is forgotten by God. 7Indeed,
the very hairs of your head are all num-
12:7 [f]Mt 10:30 bered.[f] Don't be afraid; you are worth
[g]Mt 12:12 more than many sparrows.[g]
8“I tell you, whoever acknowledges
me before men, the Son of Man will
also acknowledge him before the an-
gels of God.[h] 9But he who disowns me 12:8 [h]Lk 15:10
before men will be disowned[i] before
the angels of God. 10And everyone who 12:9 [i]Mk 8:38; 2Ti 2:12
speaks a word against the Son of Man[j]
will be forgiven, but anyone who blas- 12:10 [j]Mt 8:20
phemes against the Holy Spirit will not [k]Mt 12:31,32; Mk 3:28-29; 1Jn 5:16
be forgiven.[k]
11“When you are brought before synagogues, rulers and authorities, do not
worry about how you will defend your-
selves or what you will say,[l] 12for the 12:11 [l]Mt 10:17,19; Mk 13:11; Lk 21:12,14
Holy Spirit will teach you at that time
what you should say.”[m]

The Parable of the Rich Fool

13Someone in the crowd said to him, 12:12 [m]Ex 4:12; Mt 10:20; Mk 13:11; Lk 21:15
“Teacher, tell my brother to divide the
inheritance with me.”
14Jesus replied, “Man, who appointed me a judge or an arbiter between
you?” 15Then he said to them, “Watch
out! Be on your guard against all kinds
of greed; a man's life does not consist in
the abundance of his possessions.”[n] 12:15 [n]Job 20:20; 31:24; Ps 62:10
16And he told them this parable:
“The ground of a certain rich man produced a good crop. 17He thought to
himself, ‘What shall I do? I have no
place to store my crops.’
18“Then he said, ‘This is what I'll do.
I will tear down my barns and build
bigger ones, and there I will store all my
grain and my goods. 19And I'll say to
myself, “You have plenty of good things
laid up for many years. Take life easy;
eat, drink and be merry.” ’
20“But God said to him, ‘You fool![o] 12:20 [o]Jer 17:11; Lk 11:40
This very night your life will be de- [p]Job 27:8
manded from you.[p] Then who will get [q]Ps 39:6; 49:10
what you have prepared for yourself?’[q]
21“This is how it will be with anyone
who stores up things for himself but is 12:21 [r]ver 33
not rich toward God.”[r]

[a]6 Greek *two assaria*

SELF-CONTROL

BIG BARNS, LARGE FOLLY

Luke 12:20

Get ready for forever.
Tear down your barns
and use the lumber to build a temple.

Do Not Worry

22Then Jesus said to his disciples:
"Therefore I tell you, do not worry
about your life, what you will eat; or

DAY 4 FOUR

▸ PATIENCE AND MY SERVICE TO OTHERS

Luke 12:16–21

Greed alone is an impetus to hurry more and more. The rich man in this parable was possessed by a common notion that he needed to accumulate more "stuff." So he spent his days in a rush to get more. He built bigger barns to certify his future. We are spared many of the details of his barn building, but he seems to have been the kind of man who set deadlines for the builders. No doubt he fidgeted when he saw all that he had to get done, steps always being finished later than he would have liked. Getting rich requires running. And running can consume our lives. William Wordsworth reminds us that, "The world is too much with us; late and soon, Getting and spending, we lay waste our powers." What the rich man did not stop to ask is: "What might I be doing if I were not forever building barns? To what more meaningful activities might I devote my life?"

If we in the 21st century are prone to doubt that greed inspires the hassle, all we have to do is watch the Dow-Jones robots hurrying onto the exchange floor at closing time. A thousand men and women are all clamoring, fidgeting, screening their offers or purchases. Their whole life is devoted to scaling the zigzag inclines of their profit graphs. This is their way of devoting their lives to barn building.

This is how greed inspires the current generation of barn builders. Patience is not the mode of Wall Street. Buy now! Eat fast food! Don't wait on anything! Into this hassled generation comes a quiet word: Slow down, see a needy world and serve it. To serve only yourself is to die on or before the day your barn construction is finished. Then all that is left are barns that will someday be gone. But serve others with your time, and your legacy will live on forever.

To begin a study on the topic of Patience, Living by God's Timetable, turn to the home page on page 593.

about your body, what you will wear.
23Life is more than food, and the body
more than clothes. 24Consider the ravens: They do not sow or reap, they
have no storeroom or barn; yet God
feeds them.[s] And how much more valu- **12:24** [s]Job 38:41; Ps 147:9
able you are than birds! 25Who of you
by worrying can add a single hour to his
life[a]? 26Since you cannot do this very
little thing, why do you worry about
the rest?
27"Consider how the lilies grow. They
do not labor or spin. Yet I tell you, not
even Solomon in all his splendor[t] was **12:27** [t]1Ki 10:4-7
dressed like one of these. 28If that is
how God clothes the grass of the field,
which is here today, and tomorrow is
thrown into the fire, how much more
will he clothe you, O you of little faith![u] **12:28** [u]Mt 6:30
29And do not set your heart on what
you will eat or drink; do not worry
about it. 30For the pagan world runs
after all such things, and your Father[v] **12:30** [v]Lk 6:36
knows that you need them.[w] 31But seek [w]Mt 6:8
his kingdom,[x] and these things will be **12:31** [x]Mt 3:2
given to you as well.[y] [y]Mt 19:29
32"Do not be afraid,[z] little flock, for **12:32** [z]Mt 14:27
your Father has been pleased to give you
the kingdom.[a] 33Sell your possessions [a]Mt 25:34
and give to the poor.[b] Provide purses for **12:33** [b]Mt 19:21; Ac 2:45
yourselves that will not wear out, a trea-
sure in heaven[c] that will not be exhaust- [c]Mt 6:20
ed, where no thief comes near and no [d]Jas 5:2
moth destroys.[d] 34For where your trea-
sure is, there your heart will be also.[e] **12:34** [e]Mt 6:21

Watchfulness

35"Be dressed ready for service and
keep your lamps burning, 36like men
waiting for their master to return from
a wedding banquet, so that when he
comes and knocks they can immediately open the door for him. 37It will be
good for those servants whose master
finds them watching when he comes.[f] **12:37** [f]Mt 24:42,46; 25:13
I tell you the truth, he will dress him- [g]Mt 20:28
self to serve, will have them recline at
the table and will come and wait on
them.[g] 38It will be good for those servants whose master finds them ready,
even if he comes in the second or
third watch of the night. 39But under-
stand this: If the owner of the house **12:39** [h]Mt 6:19;
had known at what hour the thief[h] 1Th 5:2;
was coming, he would not have let his 2Pe 3:10;
house be broken into. 40You also must Rev 3:3; 16:15

[a]25 Or *single cubit to his height*

12:40 [i]Mk 13:33; Lk 21:36 be ready,[i] because the Son of Man will
come at an hour when you do not ex-
pect him."
41Peter asked, "Lord, are you telling
this parable to us, or to everyone?"
12:42 [j]Lk 7:13 42The Lord[j] answered, "Who then is
the faithful and wise manager, whom
the master puts in charge of his servants
to give them their food allowance at the
proper time? 43It will be good for that
servant whom the master finds doing so
when he returns. 44I tell you the truth,
he will put him in charge of all his possessions. 45But suppose the servant says
to himself, 'My master is taking a long
time in coming,' and he then begins to
beat the menservants and maidservants
and to eat and drink and get drunk.
46The master of that servant will come
on a day when he does not expect him
12:46 [k]ver 40 and at an hour he is not aware of.[k] He
will cut him to pieces and assign him a
place with the unbelievers.
47"That servant who knows his master's will and does not get ready or does
not do what his master wants will be
12:47 [l]Dt 25:2 beaten with many blows.[l] 48But the one
who does not know and does things
deserving punishment will be beaten
12:48 [m]Lev 5:17; Nu 15:27-30 with few blows.[m] From everyone who
has been given much, much will be de-
manded; and from the one who has
been entrusted with much, much more
will be asked.

Not Peace but Division

49"I have come to bring fire on the
earth, and how I wish it were already
12:50 [n]Mk 10:38 [o]Jn 19:30 kindled! 50But I have a baptism[n] to undergo, and how distressed I am until it
is completed![o] 51Do you think I came
to bring peace on earth? No, I tell you,
but division. 52From now on there will
be five in one family divided against
each other, three against two and two
against three. 53They will be divided, father against son and son against father,
mother against daughter and daughter
against mother, mother-in-law against
daughter-in-law and daughter-in-law
12:53 [p]Mic 7:6; Mt 10:21 against mother-in-law."[p]

Interpreting the Times

54He said to the crowd: "When you
see a cloud rising in the west, immediately you say, 'It's going to rain,' and
12:54 [q]Mt 16:2 it does.[q] 55And when the south wind
blows, you say, 'It's going to be hot,' and
it is. 56Hypocrites! You know how to interpret the appearance of the earth and
the sky. How is it that you don't know
how to interpret this present time?[r] 12:56 [r]Mt 16:3
57"Why don't you judge for your-
selves what is right? 58As you are going
with your adversary to the magistrate,
try hard to be reconciled to him on
the way, or he may drag you off to the
judge, and the judge turn you over to
the officer, and the officer throw you
into prison.[s] 59I tell you, you will not 12:58 [s]Mt 5:25
get out until you have paid the last
penny.[a]"[t] 12:59 [t]Mt 5:26; Mk 12:42

Repent or Perish

13 Now there were some present at
that time who told Jesus about
the Galileans whose blood Pilate[u] had 13:1 [u]Mt 27:2
mixed with their sacrifices. 2Jesus answered, "Do you think that these Galileans were worse sinners than all the
other Galileans because they suffered 13:2
this way?[v] 3I tell you, no! But unless [v]Jn 9:2,3
you repent, you too will all perish.
4Or those eighteen who died when the
tower in Siloam[w] fell on them—do you 13:4 [w]Jn 9:7,11
think they were more guilty than all the
others living in Jerusalem? 5I tell you,
no! But unless you repent,[x] you too will 13:5 [x]Mt 3:2;
all perish." Ac 2:38
6Then he told this parable: "A man
had a fig tree, planted in his vineyard,
and he went to look for fruit on it, 13:6
but did not find any.[y] 7So he said to [y]Isa 5:2; Jer 8:13;
the man who took care of the vineyard, Mt 21:19
'For three years now I've been coming
to look for fruit on this fig tree and
haven't found any. Cut it down![z] Why 13:7 [z]Mt 3:10
should it use up the soil?'
8" 'Sir,' the man replied, 'leave it alone
for one more year, and I'll dig around
it and fertilize it. 9If it bears fruit next
year, fine! If not, then cut it down.' "

A Crippled Woman Healed on the Sabbath

10On a Sabbath Jesus was teaching in
one of the synagogues,[a] 11and a wom- 13:10 [a]Mt 4:23
an was there who had been crippled
by a spirit for eighteen years.[b] She was 13:11 [b]ver 16
bent over and could not straighten up
at all. 12When Jesus saw her, he called
her forward and said to her, "Woman,
you are set free from your infirmity."
13Then he put his hands on her,[c] and 13:13 [c]Mk 5:23

[a]59 Greek *lepton*

immediately she straightened up and
praised God.
14Indignant because Jesus had healed
13:14 [d]Mt 12:2; Lk 14:3 [e]Mk 5:22 [f]Ex 20:9 on the Sabbath,[d] the synagogue ruler[e]
said to the people, "There are six days
for work.[f] So come and be healed on
those days, not on the Sabbath."
15The Lord answered him, "You hypocrites! Doesn't each of you on the
Sabbath untie his ox or donkey from
the stall and lead it out to give it
13:15 [g]Lk 14:5 water?[g] 16Then should not this woman,
a daughter of Abraham,[h] whom Satan[i]
13:16 [h]Lk 3:8; 19:9 [i]Mt 4:10 has kept bound for eighteen long years,
be set free on the Sabbath day from
what bound her?"
17When he said this, all his oppo-
13:17 [j]Isa 66:5 nents were humiliated,[j] but the people
were delighted with all the wonderful
things he was doing.

The Parables of the Mustard Seed and the Yeast

18Then Jesus asked, "What is the
13:18 [k]Mt 3:2 [l]Mt 13:24 kingdom of God[k] like?[l] What shall I
compare it to? 19It is like a mustard
seed, which a man took and planted in
13:19 [m]Lk 17:6 [n]Mt 13:32 his garden. It grew and became a tree,[m]
and the birds of the air perched in its
branches."[n]
20Again he asked, "What shall I compare the kingdom of God to? 21It is
like yeast that a woman took and mixed
into a large amount[a] of flour until it
13:21 [o]1Co 5:6 worked all through the dough."[o]

The Narrow Door

22Then Jesus went through the towns
and villages, teaching as he made his
13:22 [p]Lk 9:51 way to Jerusalem.[p] 23Someone asked
him, "Lord, are only a few people going
to be saved?"
He said to them, 24"Make every ef-
13:24 [q]Mt 7:13 fort to enter through the narrow door,[q]
because many, I tell you, will try to en-
ter and will not be able to. 25Once the
owner of the house gets up and closes
the door, you will stand outside knocking and pleading, 'Sir, open the door
for us.'
"But he will answer, 'I don't know
13:25 [r]Mt 7:23; 25:10-12 you or where you come from.'[r]
26"Then you will say, 'We ate and
drank with you, and you taught in our
streets.'
27"But he will reply, 'I don't know
13:27 [s]Mt 7:23; 25:41 you or where you come from. Away
from me, all you evildoers!'[s]
28"There will be weeping there, and
gnashing of teeth,[t] when you see Abra-
ham, Isaac and Jacob and all the proph- 13:28 [t]Mt 8:12
ets in the kingdom of God, but you
yourselves thrown out. 29People will
come from east and west[u] and north 13:29 [u]Mt 8:11
and south, and will take their places
at the feast in the kingdom of God.

LOVE

THE OMNI-DIRECTIONAL KINGDOM

Luke 13:29

In Christ's great banquet hall, the room is open on all sides.
The table is international.
Grace is the *lingua franca* (common language) for the meal.
The napkin rings are silver servitude;
The chalices, gold obedience;
The menu, praises set in sapphires;
The entertainment, platinum rapture.
How gained each member of this feast the ticket for admittance?
Each one in separate ages said, "Yes, Lord!"

30Indeed there are those who are last
who will be first, and first who will be
last."[v] 13:30 [v]Mt 19:30

Jesus' Sorrow for Jerusalem

31At that time some Pharisees came
to Jesus and said to him, "Leave this
place and go somewhere else. Herod[w] 13:31 [w]Mt 14:1
wants to kill you."
32He replied, "Go tell that fox, 'I will
drive out demons and heal people today and tomorrow, and on the third
day I will reach my goal.'[x] 33In any case, 13:32 [x]Heb 2:10
I must keep going today and tomorrow
and the next day—for surely no proph-
et[y] can die outside Jerusalem! 13:33 [y]Mt 21:11
34"O Jerusalem, Jerusalem, you who
kill the prophets and stone those sent to
you, how often I have longed to gather
your children together, as a hen gathers
her chicks under her wings,[z] but you 13:34 [z]Mt 23:37
were not willing! 35Look, your house is 13:35 [a]Jer 12:17; 22:5
left to you desolate.[a] I tell you, you will
not see me again until you say, 'Blessed [b]Ps 118:26; Mt 21:9; Lk 19:38
is he who comes in the name of the
Lord.'[b]"[b]

[a]21 Greek *three satas* (probably about 1/2 bushel or 22 liters) [b]35 Psalm 118:26

LOVE

JERUSALEM ENTREATY

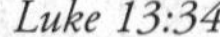

Luke 13:34

A hen, longing to shelter her chicks, will spread her wings and cluck her little ones beneath her feathers. In such a way, love begs the busy world be saved.

Jesus at a Pharisee's House

14 One Sabbath, when Jesus went
to eat in the house of a promi-
14:1 nent Pharisee,[c] he was being carefully
[c]Lk 7:36; 11:37 watched.[d] 2There in front of him was a
[d]Mt 12:10 man suffering from dropsy. 3Jesus asked
14:3 the Pharisees and experts in the law,[e]
[e]Mt 22:35 [f]Mt 12:2 "Is it lawful to heal on the Sabbath
or not?"[f] 4But they remained silent. So
taking hold of the man, he healed him
and sent him away.
5Then he asked them, "If one of you
has a son[a] or an ox that falls into a well
on the Sabbath day, will you not imme-
14:5 diately pull him out?"[g] 6And they had
[g]Lk 13:15 nothing to say.
14:7 7When he noticed how the guests
[h]Lk 11:43 picked the places of honor at the table,[h]
he told them this parable: 8"When
someone invites you to a wedding feast,
do not take the place of honor, for
a person more distinguished than you
may have been invited. 9If so, the host
who invited both of you will come and
say to you, 'Give this man your seat.'
Then, humiliated, you will have to take
the least important place. 10But when
you are invited, take the lowest place,
so that when your host comes, he will
say to you, 'Friend, move up to a better place.' Then you will be honored in
the presence of all your fellow guests.
11For everyone who exalts himself will
14:11 be humbled, and he who humbles him-
[i]Mt 23:12; Lk 18:14 self will be exalted."[i]

GENTLENESS

"SIT HERE—YOU'LL BE COMFORTABLE NEAR THE BACK"

Luke 14:8

Let your heart be ego's usher at every grand occasion. If pride should lure you toward the head table, take another elbow toward a lesser chair. Be gentle. Give better guests the better seats.

12Then Jesus said to his host, "When
you give a luncheon or dinner, do not
invite your friends, your brothers or relatives, or your rich neighbors; if you
do, they may invite you back and so
you will be repaid. 13But when you give
a banquet, invite the poor, the crippled,
the lame, the blind,[j] 14and you will 14:13 [j]ver 21
be blessed. Although they cannot repay
you, you will be repaid at the resurrection of the righteous."[k] 14:14 [k]Ac 24:15

The Parable of the Great Banquet

15When one of those at the table
with him heard this, he said to Jesus,
"Blessed is the man who will eat at the
feast[l] in the kingdom of God."[m] 14:15 [l]Isa 25:6; Mt 26:29; Lk 13:29; Rev 19:9 [m]Mt 3:2
16Jesus replied: "A certain man was
preparing a great banquet and invited
many guests. 17At the time of the banquet he sent his servant to tell those who
had been invited, 'Come, for everything
is now ready.'
18"But they all alike began to make
excuses. The first said, 'I have just
bought a field, and I must go and see it.
Please excuse me.'
19"Another said, 'I have just bought
five yoke of oxen, and I'm on my way
to try them out. Please excuse me.'
20"Still another said, 'I just got married, so I can't come.'
21"The servant came back and reported this to his master. Then the owner
of the house became angry and ordered
his servant, 'Go out quickly into the
streets and alleys of the town and bring
in the poor, the crippled, the blind and
the lame.'[n] 14:21 [n]ver 13
22" 'Sir,' the servant said, 'what you
ordered has been done, but there is still
room.'
23"Then the master told his servant,
'Go out to the roads and country lanes
and make them come in, so that my
house will be full. 24I tell you, not one
of those men who were invited will get
a taste of my banquet.' "[o] 14:24 [o]Mt 21:43; Ac 13:46

The Cost of Being a Disciple

25Large crowds were traveling with Jesus, and turning to them he said: 26"If
anyone comes to me and does not hate
his father and mother, his wife and
children, his brothers and sisters—yes,
even his own life—he cannot be my dis-

[a]5 Some manuscripts *donkey*

14:26 [p]Mt 10:37; Jn 12:25
ciple.[p] 27And anyone who does not carry his cross and follow me cannot be my
14:27 [q]Mt 10:38; Lk 9:23
disciple.[q]
28"Suppose one of you wants to build
a tower. Will he not first sit down and
estimate the cost to see if he has enough
money to complete it? 29For if he lays
the foundation and is not able to finish it, everyone who sees it will ridicule him, 30saying, 'This fellow began
to build and was not able to finish.'

SELF-CONTROL

CRUCIFIXION, ANYONE?

Luke 14:27

It's easy to tell who Christ's disciples really are. Their backs are bent by struggles they've had along the *Via Dolorosa,* the way to the cross. Their hands are chafed by rough wood. They've bled a bit and been crushed beneath the weight of God's requests. Trust such disciples.

31"Or suppose a king is about to go
to war against another king. Will he
not first sit down and consider whether
he is able with ten thousand men to oppose the one coming against him with
twenty thousand? 32If he is not able, he
will send a delegation while the other
is still a long way off and will ask for
terms of peace. 33In the same way, any
of you who does not give up everything
14:33 [r]Php 3:7,8
he has cannot be my disciple.[r]
34"Salt is good, but if it loses its salti-
14:34 [s]Mk 9:50
ness, how can it be made salty again?[s]
35It is fit neither for the soil nor for the
14:35 [t]Mt 5:13 [u]Mt 11:15
manure pile; it is thrown out.[t]
"He who has ears to hear, let him
hear."[u]

The Parable of the Lost Sheep

15:1 [v]Lk 5:29
15 Now the tax collectors[v] and "sinners" were all gathering around
to hear him. 2But the Pharisees and
the teachers of the law muttered, "This
man welcomes sinners and eats with
15:2 [w]Mt 9:11
them."[w]
15:3 [x]Mt 13:3
3Then Jesus told them this parable:[x]
4"Suppose one of you has a hundred
sheep and loses one of them. Does he
not leave the ninety-nine in the open
15:4 [y]Ps 23; 119:176; Jer 31:10; Eze 34:11-16; Lk 5:32; 19:10
country and go after the lost sheep un-
til he finds it?[y] 5And when he finds it,
he joyfully puts it on his shoulders 6and
goes home. Then he calls his friends

DAY 5 FIVE

JOY AND ITS PLACE IN MY PERSONAL WORSHIP

Luke 15:1–7

Joy is the business of heaven. In Luke 15 it is the recovery of something that was lost that brings about that joy. A lost sheep (vv. 4–7), a lost coin (vv. 8–10) and a lost son (vv. 11–32) are all found once again. Jesus remarks in the first two cases (and it is certainly implied in the last case) that the retrieval of that which was lost sets the angels singing.

Over the years I have seen many found who had been spiritually lost. Almost invariably their coming into grace plunged the church into revival. Often it would happen that a whole family would be converted. This would happen person-by-person as the various members of the family—influenced by the uncontainable joy of those who had already found Christ—also came to him.

I recall one woman who had been led to Christ whose husband soon joined her in the faith. Shortly after her husband found Christ, this buoyant new convert asked me whether I would present Christ to her son, who was a city attorney. The young lawyer accepted Christ, and on the Sunday when he came forward to confess his faith, his father came from an opposite corner of the balcony. They were both in tears as they met at the altar.

The testimony of these two men, embracing with tears of joy, was witnessed by the entire church. Joy became so effervescent in our congregation that for the next few months many more came to confess Christ. Joy is inevitably the result of the lost being found. It always sets the angels singing, and it works that same kind of wonder here on earth.

To begin a study on the topic of Joy, the Reveling of Angels, turn to the home page on page 700.

and neighbors together and says, 'Rejoice with me; I have found my lost
sheep.'[z] 7I tell you that in the same way 15:6 [z]ver 9
there will be more rejoicing in heaven
over one sinner who repents than over
ninety-nine righteous persons who do
not need to repent.[a] 15:7 [a]ver 10

LOVE

OUTSIDE THE FLOCK

Luke 15:4

The shepherd has 99 of his sheep. But the one that matters—the one that stirs his longing love—is the one he doesn't have. "It is but a hundredth part, O God! Content yourself! You've nearly all." But God replies, "I take no pleasure in whole numbers. I spend myself on bleeding fractions."

The Parable of the Lost Coin

8"Or suppose a woman has ten silver coins[a] and loses one. Does she
not light a lamp, sweep the house and
search carefully until she finds it? 9And
when she finds it, she calls her friends
and neighbors together and says, 'Rejoice with me; I have found my lost
15:9 [b]ver 6 coin.'[b] 10In the same way, I tell you,
there is rejoicing in the presence of
15:10 the angels of God over one sinner who
[c]ver 7 repents."[c]

FAITHFULNESS

LIGHT THE LAMP, SWEEP THE FLOOR

Luke 15:8

Searching for the lost is the pressing occupation of God.

If you would stop God's searching, stop his love.

If you would stop his love, stop Niagara.

The Parable of the Lost Son

11Jesus continued: "There was a man
15:11 who had two sons.[d] 12The younger one
[d]Mt 21:28 said to his father, 'Father, give me my
15:12 [e]Dt 21:17 share of the estate.'[e] So he divided his
[f]ver 30 property[f] between them.
13"Not long after that, the younger
son got together all he had, set off for
a distant country and there squandered
15:13 [g]ver 30; his wealth[g] in wild living. 14After he
Lk 16:1 had spent everything, there was a severe famine in that whole country, and
he began to be in need. 15So he went
and hired himself out to a citizen of
that country, who sent him to his fields
15:15 to feed pigs.[h] 16He longed to fill his
[h]Lev 11:7 stomach with the pods that the pigs
were eating, but no one gave him anything.
17"When he came to his senses, he
said, 'How many of my father's hired
men have food to spare, and here I am
starving to death! 18I will set out and go
back to my father and say to him: Fa-
ther, I have sinned[i] against heaven and 15:18 [i]Lev 26:40;
against you. 19I am no longer worthy to Mt 3:2
be called your son; make me like one
of your hired men.' 20So he got up and
went to his father.
"But while he was still a long way
off, his father saw him and was filled
with compassion for him; he ran to his
son, threw his arms around him and 15:20
kissed him.[j] [j]Ge 45:14,15;
21"The son said to him, 'Father, I 46:29;
have sinned against heaven and against Ac 20:37
you.[k] I am no longer worthy to be 15:21 [k]Ps 51:4
called your son.[b]'
22"But the father said to his servants,
'Quick! Bring the best robe[l] and put it 15:22
on him. Put a ring on his finger[m] and [l]Zec 3:4; Rev 6:11
sandals on his feet. 23Bring the fattened [m]Ge 41:42
calf and kill it. Let's have a feast and celebrate. 24For this son of mine was dead
and is alive again;[n] he was lost and is 15:24
found.' So they began to celebrate.[o] [n]Eph 2:1,5; 5:14; 1Ti 5:6
25"Meanwhile, the older son was in [o]ver 32
the field. When he came near the house,
he heard music and dancing. 26So he
called one of the servants and asked
him what was going on. 27'Your brother
has come,' he replied, 'and your father
has killed the fattened calf because he
has him back safe and sound.'
28"The older brother became angry[p] 15:28
and refused to go in. So his father went [p]Jnh 4:1
out and pleaded with him. 29But he
answered his father, 'Look! All these
years I've been slaving for you and never disobeyed your orders. Yet you never
gave me even a young goat so I could
celebrate with my friends. 30But when
this son of yours who has squandered
your property[q] with prostitutes[r] comes 15:30 [q]ver 12,13
home, you kill the fattened calf for [r]Pr 29:3
him!'
31"'My son,' the father said, 'you are
always with me, and everything I have
is yours. 32But we had to celebrate and
be glad, because this brother of yours 15:32
was dead and is alive again; he was lost [s]ver 24;
and is found.'"[s] Mal 3:17

[a]*8* Greek *ten drachmas,* each worth about a day's wages [b]*21* Some early manuscripts *son. Make me like one of your hired men.*

WEEK 10

LOVE

DAY ONE

LOVE FORGIVES

Read Luke 15:11–24

The lost son in Luke 15 is a man who has done the most noble of deeds: *He has faced himself.* Perhaps this is the first fearsome work of being forgiven. Here is that courageous moment wherein one actually ascertains that he or she needs forgiveness. The hardest work to be done is to look in the mirror of the Spirit of God and see our failure. At the moment of our confession, we are most unlike the conceited queen in the Grimms's fairy tale, *Snow White*. We know we are not the "fairest of all." The ugliness of our sin is clear to us. We are needy; we have been self-willed; we have hurt others. We have ridden roughshod over a whole field of human emotions. But more than all this, we owe an awesome debt to God. We have hurt our Father in heaven, and this is the savage center of our sin.

We then make a decision about ourselves. We are sinners, and we need to be forgiven. Our forgiveness is available only in one place. We cannot forgive ourselves by ourselves, or we would already have done so. The source of our forgiveness can only be found in the hearts of those our self-will has hurt. Our confession needs to lift its downcast eyes toward God, for he more than anyone has felt the blight of our transgressions. But facing our sin means we have to look back at what we have done and then wait. Will those who need to forgive us actually do it? In that question our agony begins.

In the son's case, he must go home. There and there alone the age-old struggle of justice and mercy will be waged again. If there is life for him, if his heart is ever to beat again, he must be forgiven. And in this case, only his father can do it, for his father is the one most betrayed. Will his father let love rule? Will our Father let love rule in our lives? We know the answers because we know God.

MEMORIZE THIS WEEK

1 JOHN 1:9

If we confess our sins, he is faithful and just and will forgive us our sins and purify us from all unrighteousness.

DAY TWO

LOVE AND THE PURPOSE OF GOD IN MY LIFE

How grateful the psalmist was that God kept no record of his sins. Rather, God had long before revealed a character trait to the psalmist that made holding a grudge impossible. The quality is mercy. Because that quality is a part of God's nature, he keeps no record of our sins. Love has forgiven, and mercy is in place. *Turn to Psalm 130:1–5, page 719, for today's study.*

DAY THREE

LOVE AND MY RELATIONSHIP WITH CHRIST

Paul tells the church in Corinth to forgive those who wound and grieve others. A relationship with God doesn't rest on one's ability to keep the law or to be perfect. The kind of forgiveness Jesus gives cannot be obtained by keeping any kind of moral rules, including the Law of Moses. It comes softly, like love itself, tiptoeing into our lives the moment we say, "I believe." *Turn to 2 Corinthians 2:5–11, page 1380, for today's study.*

DAY FOUR

LOVE AND MY SERVICE TO OTHERS

Jacob, the dying patriarch, leaves a message for his powerful son in Egypt. Joseph is to forgive the horrible atrocities that his brothers committed when they sold him into slavery. Joseph does this, but it may not be his forgiving spirit that is the most beautiful manifestation of love in the passage. It may be that the most beautiful evidence of love comes from old Jacob who loves all his sons and knows that his plea for forgiveness can bring peace to his family. *Turn to Genesis 50:15–21, page 65, for today's study.*

DAY FIVE

LOVE AND ITS PLACE IN MY PERSONAL WORSHIP

The psalmist says that those whose sins are forgiven are blessed. Why blessed? Because those who have carried the wrong have laid down their guilt at last. They have put aside the heavy bundle of self-incrimination. See! They can stand up straight! They run. They fly. They have been given legs and bright new wings by the person who forgave them. Now, without sin, they soar into the presence of God and find their worship sweet. *Turn to Psalm 32:1–2, page 651, for today's study.*

Week 11, Joy, a Positive Attitude, begins on page 358, 2 Samuel 6:14–15.
To begin a topical study on the Fruit of the Spirit, Love, turn to the Topical Index, page 1548.

JOY

REJOICE, THE CHILD IS HOME

Luke 15:32

"We had to celebrate," cried the old father.
There are times when a celebration is a compulsion.
No need to grieve about it.
The angels themselves are obsessed with rescue parties.

The Parable of the Shrewd Manager

16 Jesus told his disciples: "There
was a rich man whose manager
16:1 [t]Lk 15:13,30 was accused of wasting his possessions.[t]
2So he called him in and asked him,
'What is this I hear about you? Give an
account of your management, because
you cannot be manager any longer.'
3"The manager said to himself, 'What
shall I do now? My master is taking
away my job. I'm not strong enough to
dig, and I'm ashamed to beg— 4I know
what I'll do so that, when I lose my job
here, people will welcome me into their
houses.'
5"So he called in each one of his master's debtors. He asked the first, 'How
much do you owe my master?'
6" 'Eight hundred gallons[a] of olive
oil,' he replied.
"The manager told him, 'Take your
bill, sit down quickly, and make it four
hundred.'
7"Then he asked the second, 'And
how much do you owe?'
" 'A thousand bushels[b] of wheat,' he
replied.
"He told him, 'Take your bill and
make it eight hundred.'
8"The master commended the dishonest manager because he had acted
16:8 [u]Ps 17:14 shrewdly. For the people of this world[u]
are more shrewd[v] in dealing with their 16:8 [v]Ps 18:26
own kind than are the people of the [w]Jn 12:36;
light.[w] 9I tell you, use worldly wealth[x] Eph 5:8;
to gain friends for yourselves, so that 1Th 5:5
when it is gone, you will be welcomed 16:9 [x]ver 11,13
into eternal dwellings.[y] [y]Mt 19:21;
Lk 12:33
10"Whoever can be trusted with very
little can also be trusted with much,[z] 16:10 [z]Mt 25:21,23;
and whoever is dishonest with very lit- Lk 19:17
tle will also be dishonest with much.
11So if you have not been trustworthy
in handling worldly wealth,[a] who will 16:11 [a]ver 9,13
trust you with true riches? 12And if you
have not been trustworthy with someone else's property, who will give you
property of your own?
13"No servant can serve two masters.
Either he will hate the one and love the
other, or he will be devoted to the one
and despise the other. You cannot serve
both God and Money."[b] 16:13 [b]ver 9,11;
Mt 6:24
14The Pharisees, who loved money,[c]
heard all this and were sneering at 16:14 [c]1Ti 3:3
Jesus.[d] 15He said to them, "You are the [d]Lk 23:35
ones who justify yourselves[e] in the eyes
of men, but God knows your hearts.[f] 16:15 [e]Lk 10:29
What is highly valued among men is [f]1Sa 16:7;
detestable in God's sight. Rev 2:23

Additional Teachings

16"The Law and the Prophets were
proclaimed until John.[g] Since that time, 16:16 [g]Mt 11:12,13
the good news of the kingdom of God [h]Mt 4:23
is being preached,[h] and everyone is forcing his way into it. 17It is easier for
heaven and earth to disappear than for
the least stroke of a pen to drop out of
the Law.[i] 16:17 [i]Mt 5:18
18"Anyone who divorces his wife and
marries another woman commits adultery, and the man who marries a di-
vorced woman commits adultery.[j] 16:18 [j]Mt 5:31,32;
19:9;
Mk 10:11;
Ro 7:2,3;
1Co 7:10,11

The Rich Man and Lazarus

19"There was a rich man who was
dressed in purple and fine linen and
lived in luxury every day.[k] 20At his gate 16:19 [k]Eze 16:49
was laid a beggar[l] named Lazarus, cov-
ered with sores 21and longing to eat 16:20 [l]Ac 3:2
what fell from the rich man's table.[m] 16:21 [m]Mt 15:27
Even the dogs came and licked his
sores.
22"The time came when the beggar
died and the angels carried him to

PATIENCE

SMART PAGANS: APPLY HERE

Luke 16:8

Smart pagans are sometimes better mentors than foolish believers. Christians schooled in passion often forget to think. It is sometimes wise to ask achieving pagans how they use their resources.

[a]6 Greek *one hundred batous* (probably about 3 kiloliters) [b]7 Greek *one hundred korous* (probably about 35 kiloliters)

DAY 4 FOUR

▸ FAITHFULNESS AND MY SERVICE TO OTHERS

Luke 16:19–26

The Pharisees believed that wealthy people were made rich because of their obedience to God. But here a rich man goes to hell, not for being wealthy, but for refusing to care about those less fortunate than himself.

Hell is haunted! There runs through all its fiery halls the specter of a man who once was rich. He wails from year to year, "Send Lazarus to dip the tip of his finger in water and cool my tongue, because I am in agony in this fire" (Luke 16:24). The cry is continual and eternal, "Send Lazarus, send Lazarus . . . send Lazarus, for I am tormented in this flame."

But who was this Lazarus? He was a man for whom life had been hard. He once lived and begged at the rich man's gate. When the world was generous, he ate. When the world was stingy, he starved. But being hungry was not his passport into heaven. He went to heaven because, whether hungry or full, he was faithful to God.

Those who so often do without in this world must be surprised at the level of their inheritance the moment they enter heaven. There is told a tale of an old, retiring missionary couple. They had spent their lives serving Christ and were returning to America on the same ship with Teddy Roosevelt, who was returning from an African safari. When the ship docked in New York, bands played and crowds amassed to greet the returning president. The old missionary turned to his wife and said, "See! From a single hunting trip, the president returns to ticker tape parades and marching bands; but when we come home, there's no one here to meet us." "My dear," said his wife with a broad grin, "we're not home yet."

Lazarus must have had a welcome in heaven that would make a returning president feel anonymous. Our faithful care for those around us leads us to our ultimate victory—life with Jesus Christ.

To begin a study on the topic of Faithfulness, the Road That Ends in Victory, turn to the home page on page 1540.

Abraham's side. The rich man also died
and was buried. 23In hell,[a] where he
was in torment, he looked up and saw
Abraham far away, with Lazarus by his
side. 24So he called to him, 'Father
Abraham,[n] have pity on me and send — 16:24 [n]ver 30; Lk 3:8 [o]Mt 5:22
Lazarus to dip the tip of his finger in
water and cool my tongue, because I
am in agony in this fire.'[o]
25"But Abraham replied, 'Son, remember that in your lifetime you re-
ceived your good things,[p] while Lazarus — 16:25 [p]Ps 17:14 [q]Lk 6:21, 24,25
received bad things, but now he is com-
forted here and you are in agony.[q] 26And
besides all this, between us and you
a great chasm has been fixed, so that
those who want to go from here to you
cannot, nor can anyone cross over from
there to us.'
27"He answered, 'Then I beg you, father, send Lazarus to my father's house,
28for I have five brothers. Let him warn
them,[r] so that they will not also come — 16:28 [r]Ac 2:40; 20:23; 1Th 4:6
to this place of torment.'
29"Abraham replied, 'They have Mo-
ses[s] and the Prophets;[t] let them listen — 16:29 [s]Lk 24:27,44; Jn 5:45-47; Ac 15:21 [t]Lk 4:17; Jn 1:45
to them.'
30" 'No, father Abraham,'[u] he said,
'but if someone from the dead goes to
them, they will repent.'
31"He said to him, 'If they do not — 16:30 [u]ver 24; Lk 3:8
listen to Moses and the Prophets, they
will not be convinced even if someone
rises from the dead.'"

Sin, Faith, Duty

17 Jesus said to his disciples:
"Things that cause people to — 17:1 [v]Mt 5:29 [w]Mt 18:7
sin[v] are bound to come, but woe to that
person through whom they come.[w] 2It
would be better for him to be thrown
into the sea with a millstone tied around
his neck than for him to cause one — 17:2 [x]Mk 10:24; Lk 10:21 [y]Mt 5:29
of these little ones[x] to sin.[y] 3So watch
yourselves.
"If your brother sins, rebuke him,[z] — 17:3 [z]Mt 18:15 [a]Eph 4:32; Col 3:13
and if he repents, forgive him.[a] 4If he
sins against you seven times in a day,
and seven times comes back to you and — 17:4 [b]Mt 18:21,22
says, 'I repent,' forgive him."[b]
5The apostles[c] said to the Lord,[d] "In- — 17:5 [c]Mk 6:30 [d]Lk 7:13
crease our faith!"
6He replied, "If you have faith as
small as a mustard seed,[e] you can say — 17:6 [e]Mt 13:31; 17:20; Lk 13:19
to this mulberry tree, 'Be uprooted and

[a]23 Greek *Hades*

planted in the sea,’ and it will obey
17:6 [f]Mt 21:21; Mk 9:23 you.[f]
7“Suppose one of you had a servant
plowing or looking after the sheep.
Would he say to the servant when he
comes in from the field, ‘Come along
now and sit down to eat’? 8Would he
not rather say, ‘Prepare my supper, get
17:8 [g]Lk 12:37 yourself ready and wait on me[g] while
I eat and drink; after that you may eat
and drink’? 9Would he thank the servant because he did what he was told to
do? 10So you also, when you have done
everything you were told to do, should
say, ‘We are unworthy servants; we have
17:10 [h]1Co 9:16 only done our duty.’”[h]

Ten Healed of Leprosy

17:11 [i]Lk 9:51 [j]Lk 9:51,52; Jn 4:3,4 11Now on his way to Jerusalem,[i] Jesus traveled along the border between
Samaria and Galilee.[j] 12As he was going
into a village, ten men who had lepro-
17:12 [k]Mt 8:2 [l]Lev 13:45,46 sy[a][k] met him. They stood at a distance[l]
13and called out in a loud voice, “Jesus,
17:13 [m]Lk 5:5 Master,[m] have pity on us!”
14When he saw them, he said, “Go,
17:14 [n]Lev 14:2; Mt 8:4 show yourselves to the priests.”[n] And as
they went, they were cleansed.
15One of them, when he saw he was
17:15 [o]Mt 9:8 healed, came back, praising God[o] in a
loud voice. 16He threw himself at Jesus’
feet and thanked him—and he was a
17:16 [p]Mt 10:5 Samaritan.[p]
17Jesus asked, “Were not all ten
cleansed? Where are the other nine?
18Was no one found to return and give
praise to God except this foreigner?”
19Then he said to him, “Rise and go;
17:19 [q]Mt 9:22 your faith has made you well.”[q]

JOY

THANKFUL SAMARITANS

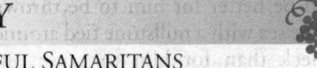

Luke 17:18

One thankful Samaritan better warms the heart of God than do hordes of the ungrateful orthodox. Pride in being right can become a small, cold virtue.

The Coming of the Kingdom of God

20Once, having been asked by the
Pharisees when the kingdom of God
17:20 [r]Mt 3:2 would come,[r] Jesus replied, “The kingdom of God does not come with your
careful observation, 21nor will people
say, ‘Here it is,’ or ‘There it is,’[s] because 17:21 [s]ver 23
the kingdom of God is within[b] you.”
22Then he said to his disciples, “The
time is coming when you will long to
see one of the days of the Son of Man,[t] 17:22 [t]Mt 8:20 [u]Mt 9:15; Lk 5:35
but you will not see it.[u] 23Men will tell
you, ‘There he is!’ or ‘Here he is!’ Do
not go running off after them.[v] 24For 17:23 [v]Mt 24:23; Mk 13:21; Lk 21:8
the Son of Man in his day[c] will be like
the lightning,[w] which flashes and lights
up the sky from one end to the other. 17:24 [w]Mt 24:27
25But first he must suffer many things[x]
and be rejected[y] by this generation.[z] 17:25 [x]Mt 16:21 [y]Lk 9:22; 18:32 [z]Mk 13:30; Lk 21:32
26“Just as it was in the days of Noah,[a]
so also will it be in the days of the Son
of Man. 27People were eating, drink-
ing, marrying and being given in mar- 17:26 [a]Ge 7:6-24
riage up to the day Noah entered the
ark. Then the flood came and destroyed
them all.
28“It was the same in the days of
Lot.[b] People were eating and drinking, 17:28 [b]Ge 19:1-28
buying and selling, planting and build-
ing. 29But the day Lot left Sodom, fire
and sulfur rained down from heaven
and destroyed them all.
30“It will be just like this on the
day the Son of Man is revealed.[c] 31On 17:30 [c]Mt 10:23; 16:27; 24:3,27,37,39; 25:31; 1Co 1:7; 1Th 2:19; 2Th 1:7; 2:8; 2Pe 3:4; Rev 1:7
that day no one who is on the roof
of his house, with his goods inside,
should go down to get them. Likewise,
no one in the field should go back
for anything.[d] 32Remember Lot’s wife![e]
33Whoever tries to keep his life will lose
it, and whoever loses his life will pre- 17:31 [d]Mt 24:17,18; Mk 13:15-16
serve it.[f] 34I tell you, on that night two
people will be in one bed; one will be 17:32 [e]Ge 19:26
taken and the other left. 35Two women
will be grinding grain together; one will 17:33 [f]Jn 12:25
be taken and the other left.[d]”[g]
37“Where, Lord?” they asked. 17:35 [g]Mt 24:41
He replied, “Where there is a dead
body, there the vultures will gather.”[h] 17:37 [h]Mt 24:28

The Parable of the Persistent Widow

18 Then Jesus told his disciples a
parable to show them that they
should always pray and not give up.[i] 18:1 [i]Isa 40:31; Lk 11:5-8; Ac 1:14; Ro 12:12; Eph 6:18; Col 4:2; 1Th 5:17
2He said: “In a certain town there was a
judge who neither feared God nor cared
about men. 3And there was a widow
in that town who kept coming to him

[a] *12* The Greek word was used for various diseases affecting the skin—not necessarily leprosy. [b] *21* Or *among* [c] *24* Some manuscripts do not have *in his day.* [d] *35* Some manuscripts *left.* *36* *Two men will be in the field; one will be taken and the other left.*

18:3 [j]Isa 1:17 with the plea, 'Grant me justice[j] against
my adversary.'
4"For some time he refused. But finally he said to himself, 'Even though
I don't fear God or care about men,
5yet because this widow keeps bothering me, I will see that she gets justice,
18:5 [k]Lk 11:8 so that she won't eventually wear me
out with her coming!' "[k]
18:6 [l]Lk 7:13 6And the Lord[l] said, "Listen to what

DAY 5 FIVE

▸ FAITHFULNESS AND ITS PLACE IN MY PERSONAL WORSHIP

Luke 18:1–8

One of the prayer outlines many are taught to use when they first learn to pray is the ACTS model. This model consists of four parts: *A*doration, *C*ontrition, *T*hanksgiving and *S*upplication. But in the parable in this passage, Jesus adds to our outlines the word *persistence.* It doesn't fit the ACTS acrostic, but persistence indicates the seriousness with which we are to do the work of prayer.

The late Harry Emerson Fosdick said that often our prayers are like a gabby woman who thinks that all her talking has made her a brilliant conversationalist. Persistence in the act of prayer is not verbiage. Persistence is intentionality. It is desire. It *wants* from God. It *hungers* for God. It will not rest until God supplies all that it asks for.

So Jesus tells a parable about a poor widow who persistently pesters a judge. But it is not mere pestering that defines this widow. She is desperate, and it is her desperation that keeps her coming back to the judge. She knows he is the only one who can help her, and she will not cease until she has her way. The judge honors her persistence. In the same way, God also honors persistence in us. He answers those who keep to their agendas, those who will not stop turning to him for fulfillment.

When our persistency in prayer is defined by our desperation to know God, we are assured that we shall hear from heaven and know God's presence.

To begin a study on the topic of Faithfulness, the High Art of Persistence, turn to the home page on page 635.

the unjust judge says. 7And will not
God bring about justice for his chosen
ones, who cry out[m] to him day and 18:7 [m]Ex 22:23; Ps 88:1; Rev 6:10
night? Will he keep putting them off?
8I tell you, he will see that they get justice, and quickly. However, when the
Son of Man[n] comes,[o] will he find faith 18:8 [n]Mt 8:20 [o]Mt 16:27
on the earth?"

The Parable of the Pharisee and the Tax Collector

9To some who were confident of their
own righteousness[p] and looked down 18:9 [p]Lk 16:15 [q]Isa 65:5
on everybody else,[q] Jesus told this para-
ble: 10"Two men went up to the temple
to pray,[r] one a Pharisee and the other 18:10 [r]Ac 3:1
a tax collector. 11The Pharisee stood
up[s] and prayed about[a] himself: 'God, 18:11 [s]Mt 6:5; Mk 11:25
I thank you that I am not like other
men—robbers, evildoers, adulterers—
or even like this tax collector. 12I fast[t] 18:12 [t]Isa 58:3; Mt 9:14
twice a week and give a tenth[u] of all I [u]Mal 3:8; Lk 11:42
get.'
13"But the tax collector stood at a
distance. He would not even look up
to heaven, but beat his breast[v] and said, 18:13 [v]Isa 66:2; Jer 31:19; Lk 23:48
'God, have mercy on me, a sinner.'[w]
14"I tell you that this man, rather [w]Lk 5:32; 1Ti 1:15
than the other, went home justified
before God. For everyone who exalts
himself will be humbled, and he who
humbles himself will be exalted."[x] 18:14 [x]Mt 23:12; Lk 14:11

The Little Children and Jesus

15People were also bringing babies to
Jesus to have him touch them. When
the disciples saw this, they rebuked
them. 16But Jesus called the children
to him and said, "Let the little children come to me, and do not hinder
them, for the kingdom of God belongs
to such as these. 17I tell you the truth,
anyone who will not receive the king-
dom of God like a little child[y] will nev- 18:17 [y]Mt 11:25; 18:3
er enter it."

The Rich Ruler

18A certain ruler asked him, "Good
teacher, what must I do to inherit eternal life?"[z] 18:18 [z]Lk 10:25
19"Why do you call me good?" Jesus
answered. "No one is good—except
God alone. 20You know the commandments: 'Do not commit adultery, do
not murder, do not steal, do not give

[a]*11* Or *to*

18:20 [a]Ex 20:12-16; Dt 5:16-20; Ro 13:9

false testimony, honor your father and
mother.'[a]"[a]
21"All these I have kept since I was a
boy," he said.

DAY 5 FIVE

▸ GENTLENESS AND ITS PLACE IN MY PERSONAL WORSHIP

Luke 18:9–14

Long ago I wrote a poem called "The Pharisee." Listen to its words, and you will see why ego is so hard to displace.

> **Do you see him there? The public square**
> **Is just the place to photograph his face**
> **Etched with earnest lines. He weeps. He**
> **cares.**
> **He thunders recompense, intones his grace.**
> **We must unfold our hands and then**
> **applaud.**
> **And gape at academic piety.**
> **Degrees and robes can make us look like**
> **God,**
> **Festoon us in neon humility.**
>
> **ENCORE! ENCORE! Pray earnestly,**
> **God-friend.**
> **The quadraphonic tone of your *Amen***
> **Will send the curtain flying up again.**
> **The seats are packed with rapt humanity.**
>
> **Kneel closer to the lights so we may see.**
> **Dear God, is this unticketed and free?**

Those who focus on how they look to others are those whose religion is mostly performance. Those who know they are sinners, on the other hand, find their needs too great to imagine that they could achieve actor-status before God.

We must remember that Jesus called the Pharisees hypocrites, and that word means "actor's mask." But gentleness is naked—stripped and vulnerable. It never argues that its face is pretty—only honest. So the tax collector goes home justified because integrity has replaced egotism. Gentleness never appeals to people of power, but it learns worship in the simple acts of openness and integrity.

To begin a study on the topic of Gentleness, the Art of Ego Displacement, turn to the home page on page 1387.

22When Jesus heard this, he said to
him, "You still lack one thing. Sell
everything you have and give to the
poor,[b] and you will have treasure in 18:22 [b]Ac 2:45
heaven.[c] Then come, follow me." [c]Mt 6:20
23When he heard this, he became
very sad, because he was a man of great
wealth. 24Jesus looked at him and said,
"How hard it is for the rich to enter the
kingdom of God![d] 25Indeed, it is easier 18:24 [d]Pr 11:28
for a camel to go through the eye of a
needle than for a rich man to enter the
kingdom of God."
26Those who heard this asked, "Who
then can be saved?"
27Jesus replied, "What is impossible 18:27
with men is possible with God."[e] [e]Mt 19:26
28Peter said to him, "We have left all
we had to follow you!"[f] 18:28 [f]Mt 4:19
29"I tell you the truth," Jesus said
to them, "no one who has left home
or wife or brothers or parents or children for the sake of the kingdom of
God 30will fail to receive many times
as much in this age and, in the age to 18:30
come,[g] eternal life."[h] [g]Mt 12:32 [h]Mt 25:46

Jesus Again Predicts His Death

31Jesus took the Twelve aside and told 18:31
them, "We are going up to Jerusalem,[i] [i]Lk 9:51
and everything that is written by the [j]Ps 22; Isa 53
prophets[j] about the Son of Man[k] will [k]Mt 8:20
be fulfilled. 32He will be handed over
to the Gentiles.[l] They will mock him, 18:32
insult him, spit on him, flog him[m] and [l]Lk 23:1 [m]Mt 16:21
kill him.[n] 33On the third day[o] he will [n]Ac 2:23
rise again."[p] 18:33
34The disciples did not understand [o]Mt 16:21 [p]Mt 16:21
any of this. Its meaning was hidden
from them, and they did not know
what he was talking about.[q] 18:34 [q]Mk 9:32; Lk 9:45

A Blind Beggar Receives His Sight

35As Jesus approached Jericho,[r] a 18:35 [r]Lk 19:1
blind man was sitting by the roadside
begging. 36When he heard the crowd
going by, he asked what was happening. 37They told him, "Jesus of Nazareth is passing by."[s] 18:37 [s]Lk 19:4
38He called out, "Jesus, Son of David,[t]
have mercy[u] on me!" 18:38 [t]ver 39; Mt 9:27
39Those who led the way rebuked [u]Mt 17:15; Lk 18:13
him and told him to be quiet, but he
shouted all the more, "Son of David, 18:39
have mercy on me!"[v] [v]ver 38
40Jesus stopped and ordered the man

[a]*20* Exodus 20:12-16; Deut. 5:16-20

WEEK 50 GOODNESS

1 DAY ONE

Goodness, a Contentment With the Commandments

Read Luke 18:18–30

In most of our lives there is contentment with grace. We needed it so badly when it found us. But having been saved by grace, we spend the rest of our redeemed lives walking around the law. The commandments seem so severe in our thinking.

The "big" commandments—killing, stealing, committing adultery—give us less trouble than the "small" ones—like bearing false testimony and coveting.

We all want to be saved with logic like this and cash in on grace by confessing some general sins while not getting too specific with regard to any of the commandments. Consider the case of the rich young ruler. He was better at avoiding sins of commission (things done wrong) than he was at sins of omission (things he should have been doing but wasn't). He should have been serving the poor. He should have been giving his wealth to feed the hungry. Materialism is not on the "big ten list" unless you group it under covetousness, which the rich young man didn't do.

But one thing must be said to commend this young man. He was comfortable with God's law. *Goodness* is a hard word with which to feel comfortable. Is *anyone* really "good"? Still, if we could keep the commandments, we would be good—or at least we'd be better. But the commandments were not given to help us to be good or better. They were given to make us more righteous so that we could build a relationship with a holy God.

If we are not comfortable with the commandments, are we really comfortable with the idea of wanting to be righteous? If we turn from righteousness, can we ever really relate to the holiness of God?

2 DAY TWO

Goodness and the Purpose of God in My Life

The concepts of laying hold of and keeping God's laws seem most elusive to those who have been raised on "gospel positivism" and high-calorie worship services. By contrast, Judaism has practiced honoring God's laws for years. Judaism has the lowest number of people per capita in prisons and detention centers. Maybe loving God's laws could put a new sense of God's purpose into our lives. *Turn to Proverbs 4:3–4, page 736, for today's study.*

3 DAY THREE

Goodness and My Relationship With Christ

"Since ancient times," said Isaiah, "no one has heard, no ear has perceived, no eye has seen any God besides you, who acts on behalf of those who wait for him." Look at it this way: Jesus is the sinless Son of God. The nearer we live to him, the more his sinless lifestyle will become our own. Walking with Jesus will enhance our love of God's laws. *Turn to Isaiah 64:4–7, page 864, for today's study.*

4 DAY FOUR

Goodness and My Service to Others

Jesus said that we should love the Lord our God with all our hearts and love our neighbors as ourselves. If we love God, we will keep his Sabbath, have no other gods before him and never misuse his name. In short, we will honor the first commandments. If we love our neighbor, we will not lie, covet, steal, kill or commit any sexual sins that would hurt our neighbor. In short, we will honor the last commandments. The key to goodness is not a moral attempt at being good, but a genuine practice of love. *Turn to Matthew 22:34–40, page 1153, for today's study.*

5 DAY FIVE

Goodness and Its Place in My Personal Worship

The most wonderful aspect of goodness—especially the goodness that produces holiness—is experiencing forgiveness, which brings the elation of feeling washed and clean. Goodness comes when God scrubs us up. But sometimes we are like the child who runs from the bathtub because of some childish agenda. But scarlet sins that are washed away leave us white as snow. *Turn to Isaiah 1:18, page 791, for today's study.*

Memorize This Week

Deuteronomy 6:3

Hear, O Israel, and be careful to obey so that it may go well with you and that you may increase greatly in a land flowing with milk and honey, just as the LORD, the God of your fathers, promised you.

Week 51, Faithfulness, the Road That Ends in Victory, begins on page 1540, Revelation 19:11–16.
To begin a topical study on the Fruit of the Spirit, Goodness, turn to the Topical Index, page 1548.

to be brought to him. When he came
near, Jesus asked him, 41"What do you
want me to do for you?"
"Lord, I want to see," he replied.
42Jesus said to him, "Receive your
18:42 [w]Mt 9:22 sight; your faith has healed you."[w] 43Im-
mediately he received his sight and fol-
lowed Jesus, praising God. When all the
18:43 [x]Mt 9:8; Lk 13:17 people saw it, they also praised God.[x]

Zacchaeus the Tax Collector

19:1 [y]Lk 18:35 **19** Jesus entered Jericho[y] and was
passing through. 2A man was
there by the name of Zacchaeus; he was
a chief tax collector and was wealthy.
3He wanted to see who Jesus was, but
being a short man he could not, because of the crowd. 4So he ran ahead
19:4 [z]1Ki 10:27; and climbed a sycamore-fig[z] tree to see
1Ch 27:28; him, since Jesus was coming that way.[a]
Isa 9:10 5When Jesus reached the spot, he
[a]Lk 18:37 looked up and said to him, "Zacchaeus,
come down immediately. I must stay at
your house today." 6So he came down
at once and welcomed him gladly.
7All the people saw this and began to
19:7 mutter, "He has gone to be the guest of
[b]Mt 9:11 a 'sinner.'"[b]
19:8 8But Zacchaeus stood up and said to
[c]Lk 7:13 the Lord,[c] "Look, Lord! Here and now I
[d]Lk 3:12,13 give half of my possessions to the poor,
[e]Ex 22:1; and if I have cheated anybody out of
Lev 6:4,5; Nu 5:7; anything,[d] I will pay back four times
2Sa 12:6 the amount."[e]
19:9 [f]Lk 3:8; 9Jesus said to him, "Today salvation
13:16; has come to this house, because this
Ro 4:16; Gal 3:7 man, too, is a son of Abraham.[f] 10For
19:10 [g]Eze 34:12,16; the Son of Man came to seek and to
Jn 3:17 save what was lost."[g]

GOODNESS

THE COMPASS AND CUP

Luke 19:10

God delights in finding those souls who have no idea why they are on earth. He gives such souls a compass and a jug of water. Then they know where to go and how to help the thirsty whom they meet along the way.

The Parable of the Ten Minas

11While they were listening to this,
he went on to tell them a parable, be-
19:11 cause he was near Jerusalem and the
[h]Mt 3:2 people thought that the kingdom of
[i]Lk 17:20; Ac 1:6 God[h] was going to appear at once.[i]
12He said: "A man of noble birth went
to a distant country to have himself appointed king and then to return. 13So
he called ten of his servants[j] and gave 19:13 [j]Mk 13:34
them ten minas.[a] 'Put this money to
work,' he said, 'until I come back.'
14"But his subjects hated him and
sent a delegation after him to say, 'We
don't want this man to be our king.'
15"He was made king, however, and
returned home. Then he sent for the
servants to whom he had given the
money, in order to find out what they
had gained with it.
16"The first one came and said, 'Sir,
your mina has earned ten more.'
17" 'Well done, my good servant!'[k] his 19:17
master replied. 'Because you have been [k]Pr 27:18
trustworthy in a very small matter, take [l]Lk 16:10
charge of ten cities.'[l]
18"The second came and said, 'Sir,
your mina has earned five more.'
19"His master answered, 'You take
charge of five cities.'
20"Then another servant came and
said, 'Sir, here is your mina; I have
kept it laid away in a piece of cloth.
21I was afraid of you, because you are a
hard man. You take out what you did
not put in and reap what you did not
sow.'[m] 19:21 [m]Mt 25:24
22"His master replied, 'I will judge
you by your own words,[n] you wicked 19:22 [n]2Sa 1:16;
servant! You knew, did you, that I am Job 15:6
a hard man, taking out what I did not [o]Mt 25:26
put in, and reaping what I did not sow?[o]
23Why then didn't you put my money
on deposit, so that when I came back, I
could have collected it with interest?'
24"Then he said to those standing by,
'Take his mina away from him and give
it to the one who has ten minas.'
25" 'Sir,' they said, 'he already has
ten!'
26"He replied, 'I tell you that to everyone who has, more will be given,
but as for the one who has nothing,
even what he has will be taken away.[p] 19:26 [p]Mt 13:12;
27But those enemies of mine who did 25:29;
not want me to be king over them— Lk 8:18
bring them here and kill them in front
of me.' "

The Triumphal Entry

28After Jesus had said this, he went 19:28 [q]Mk 10:32;
on ahead, going up to Jerusalem.[q] 29As Lk 9:51

[a]13 A mina was about three months' wages.

19:29 [r]Mt 21:17 he approached Bethphage and Bethany[r]
[s]Mt 21:1 at the hill called the Mount of Olives,[s]
he sent two of his disciples, saying to
them, 30“Go to the village ahead of you,
and as you enter it, you will find a colt
tied there, which no one has ever ridden. Untie it and bring it here. 31If anyone asks you, ‘Why are you untying it?’
tell him, ‘The Lord needs it.’”
32Those who were sent ahead went
19:32 [t]Lk 22:13 and found it just as he had told them.[t]
33As they were untying the colt, its
owners asked them, “Why are you untying the colt?”
34They replied, “The Lord needs it.”
35They brought it to Jesus, threw
their cloaks on the colt and put Jesus
on it. 36As he went along, people spread
19:36 [u]2Ki 9:13 their cloaks[u] on the road.
37When he came near the place where
the road goes down the Mount of
19:37 [v]Mt 21:1 Olives,[v] the whole crowd of disciples began joyfully to praise God in loud voices
for all the miracles they had seen:

38“Blessed is the king who comes in
19:38 [w]Ps 118:26; Lk 13:35 the name of the Lord!”[a][w]
[x]Lk 2:14 “Peace in heaven and glory in the
highest!”[x]

39Some of the Pharisees in the crowd
said to Jesus, “Teacher, rebuke your
19:39 [y]Mt 21:15,16 disciples!”[y]
40“I tell you,” he replied, “if they
19:40 [z]Hab 2:11 keep quiet, the stones will cry out.”[z]

JOY
THE ROCKS NOW HOLD THEIR TONGUES!

Luke 19:40

The stones always speak at God’s command. They have a limited vocabulary and rarely use it, but rocks know how to shout, “Hosanna!” And, when no one else will shout, they are well able.

41As he approached Jerusalem and
19:41 [a]Isa 22:4; Lk 13:34,35 saw the city, he wept over it[a] 42and said,
“If you, even you, had only known on
this day what would bring you peace—
but now it is hidden from your eyes.
43The days will come upon you when
your enemies will build an embank-
19:43 [b]Isa 29:3; Jer 6:6; Eze 4:2; 26:8; Lk 21:20 ment against you and encircle you and
hem you in on every side.[b] 44They will
dash you to the ground, you and the

DAY 3 THREE
KINDNESS AND MY RELATIONSHIP WITH CHRIST

Luke 19:41–42

Jesus weeping! Jesus wept over the citadel, and the citadel never knew. Tears are the ensigns of kindness. We see some pitiable situation, and we cry. Those who receive our kindness rarely suspect our tears, but they rejoice at our kindness.

It has long haunted me that, years before I was saved, my incognito Lord wept over my condition until at last I came to him. Those in Jerusalem who never suspected the weeping Christ are little different from us. The truth is that God daily laments the fate of all who are lost. He cries over all who are self-serving, who never suspect that there are any larger reasons for which they were given life.

When we become aware of the needs of those around us, we become like Christ in our desire to help others. We who are possessed of such kindness become stalkers of grace. We move into the world serving a wonderful—and sometimes desperate—agenda: “What can I do to serve Christ? What can I do to make the world a better place? What can I do for all of those I see in need?” We don’t actually do for the sake of others; we do as unto Christ.

Little Lord Fauntleroy, in Frances Hodgson Burnett’s famous novel, said, “The world should always be a little better because a man has lived.” This is the motto of every true minister of Christ.

What’s the result of such an attitude? Well, we become more like our Master. I’ve often pondered over those whom Jesus met casually in the way—the blind, for instance, or the lame. In random acts of kindness Jesus gave to the needy for no other reason than that they were children of God. They went home healed.

Kindness—instantaneous and unstoppable—heals our world.

To begin a study on the topic of Kindness As a Worldview, turn to the home page on page 1058.

[a]*38* Psalm 118:26

19:44 [c]Ps 137:9 children within your walls.[c] They will
[d]Mt 24:2; not leave one stone on another,[d] be-
Mk 13:2; cause you did not recognize the time of
Lk 21:6 [e]1Pe 2:12 God's coming[e] to you."

Jesus at the Temple

45Then he entered the temple area
and began driving out those who were
selling. 46"It is written," he said to
them, "'My house will be a house of
19:46 [f]Isa 56:7 prayer'[a];[f] but you have made it 'a den
[g]Jer 7:11 of robbers.'[b]"[g]

GOODNESS

THE PLACE OF PRAYER

Luke 19:45–46

When markets and temples are indistinguishable, God frowns.

19:47 [h]Mt 26:55 47Every day he was teaching at the
[i]Mt 12:14; temple.[h] But the chief priests, the teach-
Mk 11:18 ers of the law and the leaders among
the people were trying to kill him.[i]
48Yet they could not find any way to do
it, because all the people hung on his
words.

The Authority of Jesus Questioned

20 One day as he was teaching the
20:1 [j]Mt 26:55 people in the temple courts[j] and
[k]Lk 8:1 preaching the gospel,[k] the chief priests
and the teachers of the law, together
with the elders, came up to him. 2"Tell
us by what authority you are doing
these things," they said. "Who gave you
20:2 [l]Jn 2:18; this authority?"[l]
Ac 4:7; 7:27 3He replied, "I will also ask you a
question. Tell me, 4John's baptism[m]—
20:4 [m]Mk 1:4 was it from heaven, or from men?"
5They discussed it among themselves
and said, "If we say, 'From heaven,' he
will ask, 'Why didn't you believe him?'
6But if we say, 'From men,' all the peo-
20:6 [n]Lk 7:29 ple[n] will stone us, because they are per-
[o]Mt 11:9 suaded that John was a prophet."[o]
7So they answered, "We don't know
where it was from."
8Jesus said, "Neither will I tell you
by what authority I am doing these
things."

The Parable of the Tenants

9He went on to tell the people this
parable: "A man planted a vineyard,[p]
20:9 [p]Isa 5:1-7 rented it to some farmers and went
[q]Mt 25:14 away for a long time.[q] 10At harvest time
he sent a servant to the tenants so they
would give him some of the fruit of
the vineyard. But the tenants beat him
and sent him away empty-handed. 11He
sent another servant, but that one also
they beat and treated shamefully and
sent away empty-handed. 12He sent still
a third, and they wounded him and
threw him out.
13"Then the owner of the vineyard
said, 'What shall I do? I will send my
son, whom I love;[r] perhaps they will re- 20:13 [r]Mt 3:17
spect him.'
14"But when the tenants saw him,
they talked the matter over. 'This is
the heir,' they said. 'Let's kill him, and
the inheritance will be ours.' 15So they
threw him out of the vineyard and
killed him.
"What then will the owner of the
vineyard do to them? 16He will come
and kill those tenants[s] and give the vine- 20:16 [s]Lk 19:27
yard to others."
When the people heard this, they
said, "May this never be!"
17Jesus looked directly at them and
asked, "Then what is the meaning of
that which is written:

"'The stone the builders rejected
has become the capstone[c]'[d]?[t] 20:17 [t]Ps 118:22; Ac 4:11

18Everyone who falls on that stone will
be broken to pieces, but he on whom it
falls will be crushed."[u] 20:18 [u]Isa 8:14,15
19The teachers of the law and the
chief priests looked for a way to arrest
him[v] immediately, because they knew 20:19 [v]Lk 19:47
he had spoken this parable against them. [w]Mk 11:18
But they were afraid of the people.[w]

Paying Taxes to Caesar

20Keeping a close watch on him, they
sent spies, who pretended to be honest. They hoped to catch Jesus in some-
thing he said[x] so that they might hand 20:20 [x]Mt 12:10
him over to the power and authority of [y]Mt 27:2
the governor.[y] 21So the spies questioned
him: "Teacher, we know that you speak
and teach what is right, and that you do
not show partiality but teach the way
of God in accordance with the truth.[z] 20:21 [z]Jn 3:2
22Is it right for us to pay taxes to Caesar
or not?"
23He saw through their duplicity
and said to them, 24"Show me a denar-

[a]*46* Isaiah 56:7 [b]*46* Jer. 7:11 [c]*17* Or *cornerstone*
[d]*17* Psalm 118:22

ius. Whose portrait and inscription are
on it?"
25"Caesar's," they replied.
He said to them, "Then give to Cae-
20:25 [a]Lk 23:2; sar what is Caesar's,[a] and to God what
Ro 13:7 is God's."
26They were unable to trap him in
what he had said there in public. And
astonished by his answer, they became
silent.

The Resurrection and Marriage

20:27 [b]Ac 4:1 27Some of the Sadducees,[b] who say
[c]Ac 23:8; there is no resurrection,[c] came to Jesus
1Co 15:12 with a question. 28"Teacher," they said,
"Moses wrote for us that if a man's
brother dies and leaves a wife but no
children, the man must marry the wid-
20:28 [d]Dt 25:5 ow and have children for his brother.[d]
29Now there were seven brothers. The
first one married a woman and died
childless. 30The second 31and then the
third married her, and in the same way
the seven died, leaving no children. 32Fi-
nally, the woman died too. 33Now then,
at the resurrection whose wife will she be,
since the seven were married to her?"
34Jesus replied, "The people of this
age marry and are given in marriage.
35But those who are considered worthy
20:35 [e]Mt 12:32 of taking part in that age[e] and in the
resurrection from the dead will neither
marry nor be given in marriage, 36and
they can no longer die; for they are like
20:36 [f]Jn 1:12; the angels. They are God's children,[f]
1Jn 3:1-2 since they are children of the resurrection. 37But in the account of the bush,
even Moses showed that the dead rise,
for he calls the Lord 'the God of Abraham, and the God of Isaac, and the
20:37 [g]Ex 3:6 God of Jacob.'[a][g] 38He is not the God of
the dead, but of the living, for to him
all are alive."
39Some of the teachers of the law responded, "Well said, teacher!" 40And
no one dared to ask him any more
20:40 [h]Mt 22:46; questions.[h]
Mk 12:34

Whose Son Is the Christ?

41Then Jesus said to them, "How is
it that they say the Christ[b] is the Son of
20:41 [i]Mt 1:1 David?[i] 42David himself declares in the
Book of Psalms:

" 'The Lord said to my Lord:
"Sit at my right hand
20:43 [j]Ps 110:1; 43until I make your enemies
Mt 22:44 a footstool for your feet." '[c][j]

44David calls him 'Lord.' How then can
he be his son?"
45While all the people were listening,
Jesus said to his disciples, 46"Beware
of the teachers of the law. They like
to walk around in flowing robes and
love to be greeted in the marketplaces
and have the most important seats in
the synagogues and the places of hon-
or at banquets.[k] 47They devour widows' 20:46 [k]Lk 11:43
houses and for a show make lengthy
prayers. Such men will be punished
most severely."

The Widow's Offering

21 As he looked up, Jesus saw the
rich putting their gifts into the
temple treasury.[l] 2He also saw a poor 21:1 [l]Mt 27:6;
widow put in two very small copper Jn 8:20
coins.[d] 3"I tell you the truth," he said,
"this poor widow has put in more than
all the others. 4All these people gave
their gifts out of their wealth; but she
out of her poverty put in all she had to
live on."[m] 21:4 [m]2Co 8:12

Signs of the End of the Age

5Some of his disciples were remark-
ing about how the temple was adorned
with beautiful stones and with gifts
dedicated to God. But Jesus said, 6"As
for what you see here, the time will
come when not one stone will be left
on another;[n] every one of them will be 21:6 [n]Lk 19:44
thrown down."
7"Teacher," they asked, "when will
these things happen? And what will be
the sign that they are about to take
place?"
8He replied: "Watch out that you
are not deceived. For many will come
in my name, claiming, 'I am he,' and,
'The time is near.' Do not follow them.[o] 21:8 [o]Lk 17:23
9When you hear of wars and revo-
lutions, do not be frightened. These
things must happen first, but the end
will not come right away."
10Then he said to them: "Nation
will rise against nation, and kingdom
against kingdom.[p] 11There will be great 21:10 [p]2Ch 15:6;
earthquakes, famines and pestilences in Isa 19:2
various places, and fearful events and
great signs from heaven.[q] 21:11 [q]Isa 29:6;
12"But before all this, they will lay Joel 2:30
hands on you and persecute you. They

[a]*37* Exodus 3:6 [b]*41* Or *Messiah* [c]*43* Psalm 110:1
[d]*2* Greek *two lepta*

will deliver you to synagogues and prisons, and you will be brought before
kings and governors, and all on account
of my name. 13This will result in your
21:13 [r]Php 1:12 being witnesses to them.[r] 14But make
up your mind not to worry beforehand
21:14 [s]Lk 12:11 how you will defend yourselves.[s] 15For
I will give you[t] words and wisdom that
21:15 [t]Lk 12:12 none of your adversaries will be able to
resist or contradict. 16You will be be-
trayed even by parents, brothers, rela-
21:16 [u]Lk 12:52,53 tives and friends,[u] and they will put
some of you to death. 17All men will
21:17 [v]Jn 15:21 hate you because of me.[v] 18But not a
hair of your head will perish.[w] 19By
21:18 [w]Mt 10:30 standing firm you will gain life.[x]
20"When you see Jerusalem being sur-
21:19 [x]Mt 10:22 rounded by armies,[y] you will know that
its desolation is near. 21Then let those
21:20 [y]Lk 19:43 who are in Judea flee to the mountains,
let those in the city get out, and let
21:21 [z]Lk 17:31 those in the country not enter the city.[z]
22For this is the time of punishment[a]
21:22 [a]Isa 63:4; in fulfillment[b] of all that has been writ-
Da 9:24-27; ten. 23How dreadful it will be in those
Hos 9:7 [b]Mt 1:22 days for pregnant women and nursing
mothers! There will be great distress in
the land and wrath against this people.
24They will fall by the sword and will
be taken as prisoners to all the nations.
21:24 [c]Isa 5:5; Jerusalem will be trampled[c] on by the
63:18; Gentiles until the times of the Gentiles
Da 8:13; are fulfilled.
Rev 11:2 25"There will be signs in the sun,
moon and stars. On the earth, nations
will be in anguish and perplexity at the
21:25 [d]2Pe 3:10,12 roaring and tossing of the sea.[d] 26Men
will faint from terror, apprehensive of
21:26 [e]Mt 24:29 what is coming on the world, for the
heavenly bodies will be shaken.[e] 27At
21:27 [f]Mt 8:20 that time they will see the Son of Man[f]
[g]Rev 1:7 coming in a cloud[g] with power and
great glory. 28When these things begin
to take place, stand up and lift up
21:28 [h]Lk 18:7 your heads, because your redemption is
drawing near."[h]
29He told them this parable: "Look
at the fig tree and all the trees. 30When
they sprout leaves, you can see for yourselves and know that summer is near.
31Even so, when you see these things
happening, you know that the kingdom
21:31 [i]Mt 3:2 of God[i] is near.
32"I tell you the truth, this genera-
21:32 [j]Lk 11:50; 17:25 tion[a][j] will certainly not pass away until
all these things have happened. 33Heav-
21:33 [k]Mt 5:18 en and earth will pass away, but my
words will never pass away.[k]

34"Be careful, or your hearts will be
weighed down with dissipation, drunk-
enness and the anxieties of life,[l] and 21:34 [l]Mk 4:19
that day will close on you unexpected- [m]Lk 12:40,46;
ly[m] like a trap. 35For it will come upon 1Th 5:2-7
all those who live on the face of the
whole earth. 36Be always on the watch,
and pray[n] that you may be able to es- 21:36 [n]Mt 26:41
cape all that is about to happen, and
that you may be able to stand before
the Son of Man."
37Each day Jesus was teaching at the
temple,[o] and each evening he went out[p] 21:37 [o]Mt 26:55
to spend the night on the hill called the [p]Mk 11:19
Mount of Olives,[q] 38and all the people [q]Mt 21:1
came early in the morning to hear him
at the temple.[r] 21:38 [r]Jn 8:2

Judas Agrees to Betray Jesus

22 Now the Feast of Unleavened
Bread, called the Passover, was
approaching,[s] 2and the chief priests and 22:1 [s]Jn 11:55
the teachers of the law were looking
for some way to get rid of Jesus,[t] for 22:2 [t]Mt 12:14
they were afraid of the people. 3Then
Satan[u] entered Judas, called Iscariot,[v] 22:3 [u]Mt 4:10;
one of the Twelve. 4And Judas went Jn 13:2
to the chief priests and the officers of [v]Mt 10:4
the temple guard[w] and discussed with 22:4
them how he might betray Jesus. 5They [w]ver 52; Ac 4:1; 5:24
were delighted and agreed to give him 22:5
money.[x] 6He consented, and watched [x]Zec 11:12
for an opportunity to hand Jesus over
to them when no crowd was present.

The Last Supper

7Then came the day of Unleavened
Bread on which the Passover lamb had
to be sacrificed.[y] 8Jesus sent Peter and 22:7 [y]Ex 12:18-20;
John,[z] saying, "Go and make prepara- Dt 16:5-8;
tions for us to eat the Passover." Mk 14:12
9"Where do you want us to prepare 22:8
for it?" they asked. [z]Ac 3:1,11; 4:13,19; 8:14
10He replied, "As you enter the city,
a man carrying a jar of water will meet
you. Follow him to the house that he
enters, 11and say to the owner of the
house, 'The Teacher asks: Where is the
guest room, where I may eat the Passover with my disciples?' 12He will show
you a large upper room, all furnished.
Make preparations there."
13They left and found things just as
Jesus had told them.[a] So they prepared 22:13
the Passover. [a]Lk 19:32
14When the hour came, Jesus and his

[a]32 Or *race*

22:14 [b]Mk 6:30 apostles[b] reclined at the table.[c] 15 And
[c]Mt 26:20; he said to them, "I have eagerly desired
Mk 14:17,18 to eat this Passover with you before I
22:15 suffer.[d] 16 For I tell you, I will not eat
[d]Mt 16:21 it again until it finds fulfillment in the
22:16 [e]Lk 14:15; kingdom of God."[e]
Rev 19:9 17 After taking the cup, he gave thanks
and said, "Take this and divide it among
you. 18 For I tell you I will not drink
again of the fruit of the vine until the
kingdom of God comes."
19 And he took bread, gave thanks
22:19 [f]Mt 14:19 and broke it,[f] and gave it to them, saying, "This is my body given for you; do
this in remembrance of me."
20 In the same way, after the supper
he took the cup, saying, "This cup is
22:20 the new covenant[g] in my blood, which
[g]Ex 24:8; is poured out for you. 21 But the hand
Isa 42:6; Jer 31:31-34; of him who is going to betray me is
Zec 9:11; 2Co 3:6; with mine on the table.[h] 22 The Son of
Heb 8:6; 9:15 Man[i] will go as it has been decreed,[j]
22:21 but woe to that man who betrays him."
[h]Ps 41:9 23 They began to question among them-
22:22 [i]Mt 8:20 selves which of them it might be who
[j]Ac 2:23; 4:28 would do this.
24 Also a dispute arose among them
as to which of them was considered
22:24 [k]Mk 9:34; to be greatest.[k] 25 Jesus said to them,
Lk 9:46 "The kings of the Gentiles lord it over
them; and those who exercise authority over them call themselves Benefac-
tors. 26 But you are not to be like that.
Instead, the greatest among you should
22:26 be like the youngest,[l] and the one who
[l]1Pe 5:5 rules like the one who serves.[m] 27 For
[m]Mk 9:35; who is greater, the one who is at the
Lk 9:48 table or the one who serves? Is it not
the one who is at the table? But I am
22:27 among you as one who serves.[n] 28 You
[n]Mt 20:28; are those who have stood by me in
Lk 12:37 my trials. 29 And I confer on you a
22:29 [o]Mt 25:34; kingdom,[o] just as my Father conferred
2Ti 2:12 one on me, 30 so that you may eat and
22:30 drink at my table in my kingdom[p] and
[p]Lk 14:15 [q]Mt 19:28 sit on thrones, judging the twelve tribes
of Israel.[q]
22:31 31 "Simon, Simon, Satan has asked[r] to
[r]Job 1:6-12 [s]Am 9:9 sift you[a] as wheat.[s] 32 But I have prayed
22:32 for you,[t] Simon, that your faith may
[t]Jn 17:9,15; not fail. And when you have turned
Ro 8:34 [u]Jn 21:15-17 back, strengthen your brothers."[u]
33 But he replied, "Lord, I am ready to
22:33 go with you to prison and to death."[v]
[v]Jn 11:16 34 Jesus answered, "I tell you, Peter,
before the rooster crows today, you will
deny three times that you know me."
35 Then Jesus asked them, "When I
22:35 [w]Mt 10:9,10; sent you without purse, bag or sandals,[w]
Lk 9:3; 10:4 did you lack anything?"
"Nothing," they answered.
36 He said to them, "But now if you
have a purse, take it, and also a bag; and
if you don't have a sword, sell your cloak
and buy one. 37 It is written: 'And he
22:37 was numbered with the transgressors'[b];[x]
[x]Isa 53:12 and I tell you that this must be fulfilled
in me. Yes, what is written about me is
reaching its fulfillment."
38 The disciples said, "See, Lord, here
are two swords."
"That is enough," he replied.

Jesus Prays on the Mount of Olives

22:39 39 Jesus went out as usual[y] to the
[y]Lk 21:37 [z]Mt 21:1 Mount of Olives,[z] and his disciples followed him. 40 On reaching the place, he
said to them, "Pray that you will not
22:40 fall into temptation."[a] 41 He withdrew
[a]Mt 6:13 about a stone's throw beyond them,
22:41 knelt down[b] and prayed, 42 "Father, if
[b]Lk 18:11 you are willing, take this cup[c] from me;
22:42 [c]Mt 20:22 yet not my will, but yours be done."[d]
[d]Mt 26:39 43 An angel from heaven appeared to
22:43 him and strengthened him.[e] 44 And be-
[e]Mt 4:11; Mk 1:13 ing in anguish, he prayed more earnestly, and his sweat was like drops of blood
falling to the ground.[c]
45 When he rose from prayer and went
back to the disciples, he found them
asleep, exhausted from sorrow. 46 "Why
are you sleeping?" he asked them. "Get
up and pray so that you will not fall
22:46 [f]ver 40 into temptation."[f]

Jesus Arrested

47 While he was still speaking a crowd
came up, and the man who was called

[a]31 The Greek is plural. [b]37 Isaiah 53:12
[c]44 Some early manuscripts do not have verses 43 and 44.

FAITHFULNESS

DOZING IN GETHSEMANE

Luke 22:44–45

What eve of battle found any general in readiness with all his officers asleep?
Still, Jesus knelt and faithfully committed himself to the final struggle.
Blood fell from his brow.
The vise of loneliness closed its jaws upon his heart,
And all his faithless lovers slept.

Judas, one of the Twelve, was leading
them. He approached Jesus to kiss him,
48but Jesus asked him, "Judas, are you
betraying the Son of Man with a kiss?"
49When Jesus' followers saw what
was going to happen, they said, "Lord,
22:49 [g]ver 38 should we strike with our swords?"[g]
50And one of them struck the servant
of the high priest, cutting off his right
ear.
51But Jesus answered, "No more of
this!" And he touched the man's ear and
healed him.
52Then Jesus said to the chief priests,
22:52 [h]ver 4 the officers of the temple guard,[h] and
the elders, who had come for him,
"Am I leading a rebellion, that you have
come with swords and clubs? 53Every
22:53 [i]Mt 26:55 [j]Jn 12:27 [k]Mt 8:12; Jn 1:5; 3:20 day I was with you in the temple courts,[i]
and you did not lay a hand on me.
But this is your hour[j]—when darkness
reigns."[k]

Peter Disowns Jesus

54Then seizing him, they led him
away and took him into the house of
22:54 [l]Mt 26:57; Mk 14:53 [m]Mt 26:58; Mk 14:54; Jn 18:15 the high priest.[l] Peter followed at a
distance.[m] 55But when they had kindled
a fire in the middle of the courtyard
and had sat down together, Peter sat
down with them. 56A servant girl saw
him seated there in the firelight. She
looked closely at him and said, "This
man was with him."
57But he denied it. "Woman, I don't
know him," he said.
58A little later someone else saw him
and said, "You also are one of them."
"Man, I am not!" Peter replied.
59About an hour later another asserted, "Certainly this fellow was with him,
22:59 [n]Lk 23:6 for he is a Galilean."[n]
60Peter replied, "Man, I don't know
what you're talking about!" Just as he
was speaking, the rooster crowed. 61The
Lord[o] turned and looked straight at Pe-
22:61 [o]Lk 7:13 [p]ver 34 ter. Then Peter remembered the word
the Lord had spoken to him: "Before
the rooster crows today, you will disown me three times."[p] 62And he went
outside and wept bitterly.

The Guards Mock Jesus

63The men who were guarding Jesus began mocking and beating him.
64They blindfolded him and demanded, "Prophesy! Who hit you?" 65And
they said many other insulting things 22:65 [q]Mt 16:21
to him.[q]

Jesus Before Pilate and Herod

66At daybreak the council[r] of the el- 22:66 [r]Mt 5:22 [s]Mt 27:1; Mk 15:1
ders of the people, both the chief priests
and teachers of the law, met together,[s]
and Jesus was led before them. 67"If you
are the Christ,[a]" they said, "tell us."
Jesus answered, "If I tell you, you will
not believe me, 68and if I asked you,
you would not answer.[t] 69But from now 22:68 [t]Lk 20:3-8
on, the Son of Man will be seated at the
right hand of the mighty God."[u] 22:69 [u]Mk 16:19
70They all asked, "Are you then the
Son of God?"[v] 22:70 [v]Mt 4:3 [w]Mt 27:11; Lk 23:3
He replied, "You are right in saying
I am."[w]
71Then they said, "Why do we need
any more testimony? We have heard it
from his own lips."

23 Then the whole assembly rose
and led him off to Pilate.[x] 2And 23:1 [x]Mt 27:2; Mk 15:1; Jn 18:28
they began to accuse him, saying, "We
have found this man subverting our
nation.[y] He opposes payment of taxes 23:2 [y]ver 14 [z]Lk 20:22 [a]Jn 19:12
to Caesar[z] and claims to be Christ,[b] a
king."[a]
3So Pilate asked Jesus, "Are you the
king of the Jews?"
"Yes, it is as you say," Jesus replied.
4Then Pilate announced to the chief
priests and the crowd, "I find no basis
for a charge against this man."[b] 23:4 [b]ver 14,22,41; Mt 27:23; Jn 18:38; 1Ti 6:13; 2Co 5:21
5But they insisted, "He stirs up the
people all over Judea[c] by his teaching.
He started in Galilee[c] and has come all
the way here." 23:5 [c]Mk 1:14
6On hearing this, Pilate asked if the
man was a Galilean.[d] 7When he learned 23:6 [d]Lk 22:59
that Jesus was under Herod's jurisdic- 23:7 [e]Mt 14:1; Lk 3:1
tion, he sent him to Herod,[e] who was
also in Jerusalem at that time.
8When Herod saw Jesus, he was
greatly pleased, because for a long time
he had been wanting to see him.[f] From 23:8 [f]Lk 9:9
what he had heard about him, he hoped
to see him perform some miracle. 9He
plied him with many questions, but Je-
sus gave him no answer.[g] 10The chief 23:9 [g]Mk 14:61
priests and the teachers of the law
were standing there, vehemently accus-
ing him. 11Then Herod and his soldiers 23:11 [h]Mk 15:17-19; Jn 19:2,3
ridiculed and mocked him. Dressing
him in an elegant robe,[h] they sent him

[a]67 Or *Messiah* [b]2 Or *Messiah*; also in verses 35 and 39 [c]5 Or *over the land of the Jews*

23:12 back to Pilate. 12That day Herod and
[i]Ac 4:27 Pilate became friends[i]—before this they
had been enemies.
13Pilate called together the chief
priests, the rulers and the people, 14and
said to them, "You brought me this
man as one who was inciting the people to rebellion. I have examined him
in your presence and have found no
23:14 [j]ver 4 basis for your charges against him.[j]
15Neither has Herod, for he sent him
back to us; as you can see, he has done
23:16 nothing to deserve death. 16Therefore,
[k]ver 22; Mt 27:26; I will punish him[k] and then release
Jn 19:1; Ac 16:37; 2Co 11:23,24 him.[a]"
18With one voice they cried out,
"Away with this man! Release Barabbas
23:18 [l]Ac 3:13,14 to us!"[l] 19(Barabbas had been thrown
into prison for an insurrection in the
city, and for murder.)
20Wanting to release Jesus, Pilate
appealed to them again. 21But they
23:22 kept shouting, "Crucify him! Crucify
[m]ver 16 him!"[m]
22For the third time he spoke to
them: "Why? What crime has this man
committed? I have found in him no
grounds for the death penalty. Therefore I will have him punished and then
release him."
23But with loud shouts they insistently demanded that he be crucified,
and their shouts prevailed. 24So Pilate
decided to grant their demand. 25He released the man who had been thrown
into prison for insurrection and murder, the one they asked for, and surrendered Jesus to their will.

The Crucifixion

23:26 [n]Mt 27:32 26As they led him away, they seized
[o]Mk 15:21; Simon from Cyrene,[n] who was on his
Jn 19:17 way in from the country, and put the
cross on him and made him carry it behind Jesus.[o] 27A large number of people
23:27 followed him, including women who
[p]Lk 8:52 mourned and wailed[p] for him. 28Jesus
turned and said to them, "Daughters of
23:28 Jerusalem, do not weep for me; weep
[q]Lk 19:41-44; 21:23,24 for yourselves and for your children.[q]
29For the time will come when you will
say, 'Blessed are the barren women, the
wombs that never bore and the breasts
23:29 [r]Mt 24:19 that never nursed!'[r] 30Then

23:30 [s]Hos 10:8; Isa 2:19; Rev 6:16
" 'they will say to the mountains,
"Fall on us!"
and to the hills, "Cover us!" '[b][s]

31For if men do these things when the
tree is green, what will happen when it
is dry?"[t] 23:31 [t]Eze 20:47
32Two other men, both criminals,
were also led out with him to be
executed.[u] 33When they came to the 23:32 [u]Isa 53:12;
place called the Skull, there they cruci- Mt 27:38; Mk 15:27;
fied him, along with the criminals—one Jn 19:18
on his right, the other on his left. 34Je- 23:34 [v]Mt 11:25
sus said, "Father,[v] forgive them, for they [w]Mt 5:44
do not know what they are doing."[c][w] [x]Ps 22:18
And they divided up his clothes by casting lots.[x]
35The people stood watching, and 23:35
the rulers even sneered at him.[y] They [y]Ps 22:17 [z]Isa 42:1
said, "He saved others; let him save
himself if he is the Christ of God, the
Chosen One."[z]
36The soldiers also came up and
mocked him.[a] They offered him wine 23:36 [a]Ps 22:7
vinegar[b] 37and said, "If you are the king [b]Ps 69:21;
of the Jews,[c] save yourself." Mt 27:48
38There was a written notice above 23:37 [c]Lk 4:3,9
him, which read: THIS IS THE KING
OF THE JEWS.[d] 23:38 [d]Mt 2:2
39One of the criminals who hung
there hurled insults at him: "Aren't you 23:39
the Christ? Save yourself and us!"[e] [e]ver 35,37
40But the other criminal rebuked
him. "Don't you fear God," he said,
"since you are under the same sentence?
41We are punished justly, for we are getting what our deeds deserve. But this
man has done nothing wrong."[f] 23:41 [f]ver 4
42Then he said, "Jesus, remember me
when you come into your kingdom.[d]"[g] 23:42 [g]Mt 16:27
43Jesus answered him, "I tell you the
truth, today you will be with me in 23:43
paradise."[h] [h]2Co 12:3,4; Rev 2:7

Jesus' Death

44It was now about the sixth hour,
and darkness came over the whole land 23:44
until the ninth hour,[i] 45for the sun [i]Am 8:9
stopped shining. And the curtain of 23:45
the temple[j] was torn in two.[k] 46Jesus [j]Ex 26:31-33;
called out with a loud voice,[l] "Father, Heb 9:3,8 [k]Heb 10:19,
into your hands I commit my spirit."[m] 20
When he had said this, he breathed his 23:46
last.[n] [l]Mt 27:50 [m]Ps 31:5; 1Pe 2:23 [n]Jn 19:30
47The centurion, seeing what had
happened, praised God[o] and said, "Surely this was a righteous man." 48When 23:47 [o]Mt 9:8

[a]*16* Some manuscripts *him.*" [17]*Now he was obliged to release one man to them at the Feast.* [b]*30* Hosea 10:8 [c]*34* Some early manuscripts do not have this sentence. [d]*42* Some manuscripts *come with your kingly power*

all the people who had gathered to wit-
23:48 ness this sight saw what took place, they
pLk 18:13 beat their breasts[p] and went away. 49But
all those who knew him, including the
23:49 women who had followed him from
qLk 8:2 Galilee,[q] stood at a distance,[r] watching
rPs 38:11 these things.

GOODNESS

INNOCENCE AT SCAFFOLDS

Luke 23:47

Surely this was the Son of God. Surely.
No one less would smile upon his
executioners
And wish for them a happy Passover.
The Son of God? Surely, surely.

Jesus' Burial

50Now there was a man named Joseph, a member of the Council, a good
and upright man, 51who had not consented to their decision and action. He
came from the Judean town of Ari-
23:51 mathea and he was waiting for the king-
sLk 2:25,38 dom of God.[s] 52Going to Pilate, he
asked for Jesus' body. 53Then he took
it down, wrapped it in linen cloth and
placed it in a tomb cut in the rock, one
in which no one had yet been laid. 54It
23:54 was Preparation Day,[t] and the Sabbath
tMt 27:62 was about to begin.
55The women who had come with
23:55 uver 49 Jesus from Galilee[u] followed Joseph and
saw the tomb and how his body was
23:56 laid in it. 56Then they went home and
vMk 16:1; Lk 24:1 prepared spices and perfumes.[v] But they
wEx 12:16; rested on the Sabbath in obedience to
20:10 the commandment.[w]

The Resurrection

24 On the first day of the week,
very early in the morning, the
women took the spices they had pre-
24:1 xLk 23:56 pared[x] and went to the tomb. 2They
found the stone rolled away from the
tomb, 3but when they entered, they
24:3 did not find the body of the Lord
yver 23,24 Jesus.[y] 4While they were wondering
about this, suddenly two men in clothes
24:4 zJn 20:12 that gleamed like lightning[z] stood beside them. 5In their fright the women
bowed down with their faces to the
ground, but the men said to them,
"Why do you look for the living among
the dead? 6He is not here; he has risen!
Remember how he told you, while he 24:6
was still with you in Galilee:[a] 7'The aMt 17:22,23;
Son of Man[b] must be delivered into Mk 9:30-31;
the hands of sinful men, be crucified Lk 9:22; 24:44
and on the third day be raised again.' "[c] 24:7
8Then they remembered his words.[d] bMt 8:20 cMt 16:21
9When they came back from the
tomb, they told all these things to the 24:8 dJn 2:22
Eleven and to all the others. 10It was
Mary Magdalene, Joanna, Mary the
mother of James, and the others with 24:10 eLk 8:1-3
them[e] who told this to the apostles.[f] fMk 6:30
11But they did not believe[g] the women, 24:11
because their words seemed to them like gMk 16:11
nonsense. 12Peter, however, got up and
ran to the tomb. Bending over, he saw 24:12
the strips of linen lying by themselves,[h] hJn 20:3-7
and he went away,[i] wondering to him- iJn 20:10
self what had happened.

On the Road to Emmaus

13Now that same day two of them were
going to a village called Emmaus, about 24:13
seven miles[a] from Jerusalem.[j] 14They jMk 16:12
were talking with each other about everything that had happened. 15As they
talked and discussed these things with
each other, Jesus himself came up and 24:15
walked along with them;[k] 16but they kver 36
were kept from recognizing him.[l] 24:16
17He asked them, "What are you dis- lJn 20:14; 21:4
cussing together as you walk along?"
They stood still, their faces downcast. 24:18
18One of them, named Cleopas,[m] asked mJn 19:25
him, "Are you only a visitor to Jerusalem and do not know the things that
have happened there in these days?"
19"What things?" he asked. 24:19
"About Jesus of Nazareth,"[n] they re- nMk 1:24
plied. "He was a prophet,[o] powerful in oMt 21:11
word and deed before God and all the
people. 20The chief priests and our rul- 24:20
ers[p] handed him over to be sentenced pLk 23:13
to death, and they crucified him; 21but
we had hoped that he was the one who
was going to redeem Israel.[q] And what 24:21 qLk 1:68;
is more, it is the third day[r] since all this 2:38; 21:28
took place. 22In addition, some of our rMt 16:21
women amazed us.[s] They went to the 24:22
tomb early this morning 23but didn't sver 1-10
find his body. They came and told us
that they had seen a vision of angels,
who said he was alive. 24Then some of
our companions went to the tomb and
found it just as the women had said, 24:24
but him they did not see."[t] tver 12

[a] *13* Greek *sixty stadia* (about 11 kilometers)

PEACE

WEEK 39

1 DAY ONE

PEACE, THE COMPANIONSHIP OF CHRIST

Read Luke 24:13–16,30–35

Charles Spurgeon once said of the all-sufficiency of Christ, "Look to the Living One for life. Look to Jesus for all you need between the gate of hell and the gate of heaven." In Jesus is the ultimate rule of peace.

In 1954 Oberlin College gave Theodore Steinway an honorary degree. At that time, Steinway Pianos had made and sold 342,000 pianos. If you multiply 342,000 (pianos) by 243 (strings in each instrument), and then multiply that number by 40,000 (the pounds of pressure exerted by the strings within each piano), you come to realize that the Steinway Piano Company was filling the world with tension. Yet Theodore Steinway was not given an honorary degree for creating tension in the world. He was given a degree for promoting harmony and beautiful music around the world. Theodore Steinway and his predecessors had created harmony and music out of tension.

Jesus walked along the road to Emmaus with two people who were staggering beneath an immense load of grief. Their hearts were heavy. There was enough tension within each of them to make even a Steinway Piano feel unstressed. Yet their testimony, upon reflection, was, "Were not our hearts burning within us while he talked with us on the road and opened the Scriptures to us?" (Luke 24:32).

When we discuss this passage, not much is made of the fact that Jesus opened the Scriptures, yet how fundamental this is to our inner peace. If the resurrected Christ can bring Scripture into the life of the tormented, God's Word might also serve as a part of our recipe of peace.

2 DAY TWO

PEACE AND THE PURPOSE OF GOD IN MY LIFE

We are to walk with Christ just as we received him: "in the faith." We cannot be saved without exercising faith. Faith in what? Several things: Christ died for us. He really is alive and at the right hand of the Father on high. He will forgive our sins if we but ask. But faith not only begins our walk with him; it is also the purpose of God for all our lives. Peace is derived from our faith by continual companionship with Christ. *Turn to Colossians 2:6–7, page 1423, for today's study.*

3 DAY THREE

PEACE AND MY RELATIONSHIP WITH CHRIST

The Lord gives a sign to King Ahaz, who is troubled by two foreign kings who are threatening to blitz Jerusalem and take his kingdom. The prophet Isaiah assures Ahaz that a child is about to be conceived, and that before this child is grown and "knows enough to reject the wrong and choose the right, the land of the two kings you dread will be laid waste" (Isaiah 7:16). Peace is at the center of this passage both for its long-range promise and for its short-range assurance. *Turn to Isaiah 7:10–17, page 798, for today's study.*

4 DAY FOUR

PEACE AND MY SERVICE TO OTHERS

This prophecy of a promised ruler from Bethlehem ends its celebration of his attributes by saying, "He will be their peace." Service to others is always fraught with struggle and stress. To care for people is to accept their criticisms and inconsistencies, recognizing in the process that we generally have a few things wrong with our own lives. But in this ministry to others, Christ himself is the foundation of our peace. *Turn to Micah 5:4–5, page 1075, for today's study.*

5 DAY FIVE

PEACE AND ITS PLACE IN MY PERSONAL WORSHIP

The returning exiles could see that the temple they had rebuilt lacked the glory of Solomon's earlier temple, and they were depressed about the negative comparison. But God assured them that the glory of the latter house would be greater than that of the former and that, more importantly, God would declare his peace in that place. *Turn to Haggai 2:1–9, page 1095, for today's study.*

MEMORIZE THIS WEEK

1 JOHN 1:7

But if we walk in the light, as he is in the light, we have fellowship with one another, and the blood of Jesus, his Son, purifies us from all sin.

Week 40, Patience, the Slowly Acquired Virtue, begins on page 565, Nehemiah 9:29–31.
To begin a topical study on the Fruit of the Spirit, Peace, turn to the Topical Index, page 1548.

25He said to them, "How foolish
you are, and how slow of heart to believe all that the prophets have spoken!
26Did not the Christ[a] have to suffer
these things and then enter his glory?"[u]
27And beginning with Moses[v] and all
the Prophets,[w] he explained to them
what was said in all the Scriptures concerning himself.[x]
28As they approached the village to
which they were going, Jesus acted as if
he were going farther. 29But they urged
him strongly, "Stay with us, for it is
nearly evening; the day is almost over."
So he went in to stay with them.

24:26 [u]Heb 2:10; 1Pe 1:11
24:27 [v]Ge 3:15; Nu 21:9; Dt 18:15 [w]Isa 7:14; 9:6; 40:10,11; 53; Eze 34:23; Da 9:24; Mic 7:20; Mal 3:1 [x]Jn 1:45

JOY

THE STIGMATA AND THE LOAF

Luke 24:30–31

In the breaking of the bread,
We see the scars of Jesus.
We weep above the loaves—
Our own hands look so good.

30When he was at the table with
them, he took bread, gave thanks, broke
it[y] and began to give it to them. 31Then
their eyes were opened and they recognized him,[z] and he disappeared from
their sight. 32They asked each other,
"Were not our hearts burning within
us[a] while he talked with us on the road
and opened the Scriptures[b] to us?"
33They got up and returned at once
to Jerusalem. There they found the
Eleven and those with them, assembled together 34and saying, "It is true!
The Lord has risen and has appeared to
Simon."[c] 35Then the two told what had
happened on the way, and how Jesus
was recognized by them when he broke
the bread.[d]

24:30 [y]Mt 14:19
24:31 [z]ver 16
24:32 [a]Ps 39:3 [b]ver 27,45
24:34 [c]1Co 15:5
24:35 [d]ver 30,31

Jesus Appears to the Disciples

36While they were still talking about
this, Jesus himself stood among them
and said to them, "Peace be with
you."[e]
37They were startled and frightened,
thinking they saw a ghost.[f] 38He said
to them, "Why are you troubled, and
why do doubts rise in your minds?
39Look at my hands and my feet. It is
I myself! Touch me and see;[g] a ghost
does not have flesh and bones, as you
see I have."
40When he had said this, he showed
them his hands and feet. 41And while
they still did not believe it because of
joy and amazement, he asked them,
"Do you have anything here to eat?"
42They gave him a piece of broiled fish,
43and he took it and ate it in their
presence.[h]
44He said to them, "This is what I
told you while I was still with you:[i] Everything must be fulfilled[j] that is written about me in the Law of Moses,[k] the
Prophets and the Psalms."[l]
45Then he opened their minds so
they could understand the Scriptures.
46He told them, "This is what is written: The Christ will suffer and rise from
the dead on the third day, 47and repentance and forgiveness of sins will be
preached in his name[m] to all nations,[n]
beginning at Jerusalem. 48You are witnesses[o] of these things. 49I am going
to send you what my Father has promised;[p] but stay in the city until you
have been clothed with power from on
high."

24:36 [e]Jn 20:19, 21,26; 14:27
24:37 [f]Mk 6:49
24:39 [g]Jn 20:27; 1Jn 1:1
24:43 [h]Ac 10:41
24:44 [i]Lk 9:45; 18:34 [j]Mt; 16:21; Lk 9:22,44; 18:31-33; 22:37 [k]ver 27 [l]Ps 2; 16; 22; 69; 72; 110; 118
24:47 [m]Ac 5:31; 10:43; 13:38 [n]Mt 28:19
24:48 [o]Ac 1:8; 2:32; 5:32; 13:31; 1Pe 5:1
24:49 [p]Jn 14:16; Ac 1:4

PATIENCE

WAITING IN JERUSALEM

Luke 24:49

Jesus promised Pentecost but ordered his twelve eager friends to wait for its arrival. Pentecost is not just wind and flame. It is waiting, wind and flame. Without the waiting, the flame will never burn, for the fire is snuffed by the whirl of air around our foolish, busy lives.

The Ascension

50When he had led them out to the
vicinity of Bethany,[q] he lifted up his
hands and blessed them. 51While he was
blessing them, he left them and was tak-
en up into heaven.[r] 52Then they worshiped him and returned to Jerusalem
with great joy. 53And they stayed continually at the temple,[s] praising God.

24:50 [q]Mt 21:17
24:51 [r]2Ki 2:11
24:53 [s]Ac 2:46

[a]*26* Or *Messiah*; also in verse 46

JOHN

▸ AUTHORSHIP AND DATE

John the Son of Zebedee

Probably between c. A.D. 85 and A.D. 90

▸ KEY THEMES

The Gospel of John portrays Jesus as God's Son. From chapter to chapter, as the story unfolds, we see this motif fully addressed. The Gospel of John is more an argument for Jesus being the Son of God than it is a chronological telling of Jesus' story. By the time the Gospel of John was written, the Gnostics had likely come on the scene, and John's account of Jesus furnished these heretics with all the information necessary to correct their heresy. Because John argued for the divinity of Christ, he recorded miracles that are sometimes called "sign" miracles—that is, miracles performed as divine proof that Christ was who he said he was. Eight of these miracles are spelled out in John in far more detail than in the other Gospels: (1) the turning of water into wine in 2:1–11, (2) the healing of a boy in 4:46–54, (3) the healing of an invalid at the pool of Bethesda in 5:1–9, (4) the feeding of the 5,000 in 6:1–14, (5) the walk upon the sea in 6:16–21, (6) the healing of a blind man in 9:1–41, (7) the raising of Lazarus in 11:1–44 and (8) the miraculous catch of fish in 21:1–14. The Gospel of John, like the other Gospels, falls rather naturally into three divisions:

1. The introduction of the book (see 1:1—2:11)
2. Jesus' ministry (see 2:12—12:50)
3. The final events of Jesus' death and resurrection (see 13:1—21:25)

▸ FRUIT OF THE SPIRIT IN JOHN

Love: God loved the world to the point of giving Jesus his Son (see 3:16).

Joy: The Triumphal Entry is proof that sometimes joy is as uncontainable as it is fickle (see 12:12–13). It is amazing how quickly people stopped waving palm branches and started waving whips and hammers.

Peace: Jesus is the source of peace (see 14:27). Peace is a gift he gives us—not as a barricade to our darker paths and fearful days, but as an armor of light for the gloom. Such peace comes only from Jesus. His peace is the only peace that keeps company with us through all our future fears. Therefore, considering the force of it all, we should never let our hearts tremble. We should tell fear to spend its fury on those without our Lord.

Kindness: Brutality is the antonym of kindness (see 19:1–5). How odd that Jesus, whose very life was marked by kindness, should suffer brutality from those who failed to profit from his example. The crucifixion is the opposite extreme of how Jesus treated his executioners.

Goodness: The event recorded in John 19:6 brought even a pagan Roman like Pilate to his knees. The Roman governor saw the sinlessness of Christ and cried, "I find no basis for a charge against him."

Faithfulness: Jesus said, "You are my friends if you do what I command" (15:14). Faithfulness is the inscription on the dog tags of our identity. Jesus' friends are those who obey him. All others merely claim a bogus friendship they have never been willing to demonstrate.

Gentleness: "I am the good shepherd," said Jesus (10:14). His sheep know him, and they know that wherever he leads them, it will be for their benefit. They look at his gentle ways and know he is good. When he leads them, his gentleness is less prone to rebuke their waywardness than it is to love them for their infrequent obedience. But then gentleness begets gentleness, and, in time, the virtue of the shepherd becomes the character of the sheep.

Self-Control: Jesus told the man whom he had healed, "See, you are well again. Stop sinning or something worse may happen to you" (5:14). Jesus was telling the man that the key to living free of evil circumstances was to discipline his appetites. It is not always possible to desire what is best, but with Christ's help, we can avoid taking into our lives those things that are destructive to our faith. To "stop sinning" is not altogether possible, but to stop living under its control is.

1:1 [a]Rev 19:13 [b]Jn 17:5; 1Jn 1:2 [c]Php 2:6
1:2 [d]Ge 1:1
1:3 [e]1Co 8:6; Col 1:16; Heb 1:2
1:4 [f]Jn 5:26; 11:25; 14:6 [g]Jn 8:12
1:5 [h]Jn 3:19
1:6 [i]Mt 3:1
1:7 [j]ver 15,19,32

The Word Became Flesh

1 In the beginning was the Word,[a]
and the Word was with God,[b] and
the Word was God. 2 He was with God[c]
in the beginning.[d]
3 Through him all things were made;
without him nothing was made that has
been made.[e] 4 In him was life,[f] and that
life was the light[g] of men. 5 The light
shines in the darkness, but the darkness
has not understood[a] it.[h]
6 There came a man who was sent
from God; his name was John.[i] 7 He
came as a witness to testify[j] concerning that light, so that through him all
men might believe.[k] 8 He himself was
not the light; he came only as a witness
to the light. 9 The true light[l] that gives
light to every man[m] was coming into
the world.[b]
10 He was in the world, and though
the world was made through him,[n] the
world did not recognize him. 11 He came
to that which was his own, but his own
did not receive him. 12 Yet to all who

1:7 [k]ver 12
1:9 [l]1Jn 2:8 [m]Isa 49:6
1:10 [n]Heb 1:2

[a]5 Or *darkness, and the darkness has not overcome*
[b]9 Or *This was the true light that gives light to every man who comes into the world*

JOHN THE BAPTIST

Self-Control, Remembering Who You Are in Relationship to Christ (1:1–51)

John's self-control took the form of rigorous self-denial. He lived in the wilderness when he might have lived in town. He ate locusts and wild honey when he might have had a more normal diet. He dressed in animal skins in an era when tunics and togas were common. Why? Because he understood who he was and what God had called him to do.

But the most godly form of his self-control came when he defined himself to the mob. They asked him who he was, and at any point he could have lied and taken the glory he knew was Christ's alone. But when they asked him their famous "Are you…?" questions, he answered with integrity. We must remember that, at this time in his ministry, John was better known and more popular than the Christ he had come to introduce. Catch this dialogue from John 1:21–23:

"Are you Elijah?"
He said, "I am not."
"Are you the Prophet?"
He answered, "No."
Finally they said, "Who are you? Give us an answer to take back to those who sent us. What do you say about yourself?"
John replied in the words of Isaiah the prophet, "I am the voice of one calling in the desert, 'Make straight the way for the Lord.'"

In response to any of these questions John could have acted to build his own reputation, but at each one he answered truthfully that he was not the Christ or the kind of person the Jews expected to be associated with the coming of the Messiah (see vv. 24–27). His selfless metaphor for explaining his own identity went something like this: "I am a trumpet playing a fanfare for the approach of a king. When you hear the fanfare, you do not ask the name of the man who plays the trumpet; you ask the name of the approaching king. I am a trumpet in the wilderness. Get ready; there is coming a man of fiery baptisms, a man who meets the demands of God himself."

In all of this John practiced self-control, and in every act of self-identification he said very clearly, "Jesus is the big deal, not me. He must increase; I must decrease." John showed us that the essence of self-control is remembering who we are in relationship to Christ.

Self-control is the result of self-denial. Self-denial is the practice of seeing our lives in terms of other people. We were not placed on this earth to be gluttons of God's abundance. We were put here to reclaim the world by denying what we might have enjoyed in order that we may enjoy a kind of abundance that cannot be known until we have denied ourselves. When we utter the words "I renounce," God gives us a trumpet to announce the King.

FAITHFULNESS

REJECTED CLOSE UP

John 1:1

In the beginning was the Word.
It was a good word, a true word, an excellent word.
It was a word that saved, a word that healed, a word that redeemed.
It was easy to pronounce, easy to spell and quite readable.
It was the first word, the last word, the best word.
God took it to the people who knew the Word,
But they refused to put it in their dictionary.
It was a very requiring word.

1:12 [o]ver 7 [p]1Jn 3:23 [q]Gal 3:26 received him, to those who believed[o] in
his name,[p] he gave the right to become
1:13 [r]Jn 3:6; Jas 1:18; 1Pe 1:23; 1Jn 3:9 children of God[q]— 13children born not
of natural descent,[a] nor of human de-
cision or a husband's will, but born of
God.[r]
1:14 [s]Gal 4:4; Php 2:7,8; 1Ti 3:16; Heb 2:14 [t]Jn 14:6 14The Word became flesh[s] and made
his dwelling among us. We have seen
his glory, the glory of the One and
Only,[b] who came from the Father, full
of grace and truth.[t]
1:15 [u]ver 7 [v]ver 30; Mt 3:11 15John testifies[u] concerning him. He
cries out, saying, "This was he of whom
I said, 'He who comes after me has
surpassed me because he was before
1:16 [w]Eph 1:23; Col 1:19 me.' "[v] 16From the fullness[w] of his grace
we have all received one blessing after
1:17 [x]Jn 7:19 [y]ver 14 another. 17For the law was given through
Moses;[x] grace and truth came through
1:18 [z]Ex 33:20; Jn 6:46; Col 1:15; 1Ti 6:16 [a]Jn 3:16,18; 1Jn 4:9 Jesus Christ.[y] 18No one has ever seen
God,[z] but God the One and Only,[b,c][a]
who is at the Father's side, has made
him known.

GOODNESS

THE GLARE OF GLORY

John 1:14

It is an ironic truth that salvation must sometimes be examined in a dim light. Glory, close up, has a holy brightness that bludgeons reason. "The Word became flesh and made his dwelling among us" is high-wattage truth. The glare off this bright truth blurs the vision of those unaccustomed to light.

John the Baptist Denies Being the Christ

19Now this was John's testimony
when the Jews[b] of Jerusalem sent priests 1:19 [b]Jn 2:18; 5:10,16; 6:41,52
and Levites to ask him who he was.
20He did not fail to confess, but con-
fessed freely, "I am not the Christ.[d]"[c] 1:20 [c]Jn 3:28; Lk 3:15,16
21They asked him, "Then who are
you? Are you Elijah?"[d] 1:21 [d]Mt 11:14 [e]Dt 18:15
He said, "I am not."
"Are you the Prophet?"[e]
He answered, "No."
22Finally they said, "Who are you?
Give us an answer to take back to those
who sent us. What do you say about
yourself?"
23John replied in the words of Isaiah
the prophet, "I am the voice of one call- 1:23 [f]Mt 3:1 [g]Isa 40:3
ing in the desert,[f] 'Make straight the
way for the Lord.' "[e][g]
24Now some Pharisees who had been
sent 25questioned him, "Why then do
you baptize if you are not the Christ,
nor Elijah, nor the Prophet?"
26"I baptize with[f] water," John replied, "but among you stands one you
do not know. 27He is the one who 1:27 [h]ver 15,30
comes after me,[h] the thongs of whose
sandals I am not worthy to untie."
28This all happened at Bethany on
the other side of the Jordan,[i] where 1:28 [i]Jn 3:26; 10:40
John was baptizing.

Jesus the Lamb of God

29The next day John saw Jesus coming toward him and said, "Look, the 1:29
Lamb of God,[j] who takes away the sin [j]ver 36;
of the world! 30This is the one I meant Isa 53:7; 1Pe 1:19;
when I said, 'A man who comes after Rev 5:6
me has surpassed me because he was be-
fore me'[k] 31I myself did not know him, 1:30 [k]ver 15,27
but the reason I came baptizing with
water was that he might be revealed to
Israel."
32Then John gave this testimony: "I
saw the Spirit come down from heav- 1:32
en as a dove and remain on him.[l] 33I [l]Mt 3:16; Mk 1:10
would not have known him, except that
the one who sent me to baptize with
water[m] told me, 'The man on whom 1:33 [m]Mk 1:4
you see the Spirit come down and re-
main is he who will baptize with the

[a] *13* Greek *of bloods* [b] *14,18* Or *the Only Begotten* [c] *18* Some manuscripts *but the only* (or *only begotten) Son* [d] *20* Or *Messiah.* "The Christ" (Greek) and "the Messiah" (Hebrew) both mean "the Anointed One"; also in verse 25. [e] *23* Isaiah 40:3 [f] *26* Or *in*; also in verses 31 and 33

1:33 [n]Mt 3:11; Mk 1:8 Holy Spirit.'[n] 34 I have seen and I testify
that this is the Son of God."[o]

1:34 [o]ver 49; Mt 4:3

Jesus' First Disciples

35 The next day John[p] was there again
1:35 [p]Mt 3:1 with two of his disciples. 36 When he
saw Jesus passing by, he said, "Look,
1:36 [q]ver 29 the Lamb of God!"[q]
37 When the two disciples heard him
say this, they followed Jesus. 38 Turning
around, Jesus saw them following and
asked, "What do you want?"
1:38 [r]ver 49; Mt 23:7 They said, "Rabbi"[r] (which means
Teacher), "where are you staying?"
39 "Come," he replied, "and you will
see."
So they went and saw where he was
staying, and spent that day with him. It
was about the tenth hour.
40 Andrew, Simon Peter's brother, was
one of the two who heard what John
had said and who had followed Jesus.
41 The first thing Andrew did was to
find his brother Simon and tell him,
"We have found the Messiah" (that is,
1:41 [s]Jn 4:25 the Christ).[s] 42 And he brought him to
Jesus.
Jesus looked at him and said, "You
1:42 [t]Ge 17:5,15 [u]Mt 16:18 are Simon son of John. You will be
called[t] Cephas" (which, when translated, is Peter[a]).[u]

1:43 [v]Mt 10:3; Jn 6:5-7; 12:21,22; 14:8,9 [w]Mt 4:19

Jesus Calls Philip and Nathanael

43 The next day Jesus decided to leave
for Galilee. Finding Philip,[v] he said to
him, "Follow me."[w]
1:44 [x]Mt 11:21; Jn 12:21 44 Philip, like Andrew and Peter, was
from the town of Bethsaida.[x] 45 Philip
found Nathanael[y] and told him, "We
1:45 [y]Jn 21:2 [z]Lk 24:27 [a]Lk 24:27 [b]Mt 2:23; Mk 1:24 [c]Lk 3:23 have found the one Moses wrote about
in the Law,[z] and about whom the prophets also wrote[a]—Jesus of Nazareth,[b] the
son of Joseph."[c]
1:46 [d]Jn 7:41, 42,52 46 "Nazareth! Can anything good
come from there?"[d] Nathanael asked.
"Come and see," said Philip.

47 When Jesus saw Nathanael approaching, he said of him, "Here is a
true Israelite,[e] in whom there is nothing 1:47 [e]Ro 9:4,6 [f]Ps 32:2
false."[f]
48 "How do you know me?" Nathanael asked.
Jesus answered, "I saw you while you
were still under the fig tree before Philip called you."
49 Then Nathanael declared, "Rabbi,[g] 1:49 [g]ver 38; Mt 23:7 [h]ver 34; Mt 4:3 [i]Mt 2:2; 27:42; Jn 12:13
you are the Son of God;[h] you are the
King of Israel."[i]
50 Jesus said, "You believe[b] because I
told you I saw you under the fig tree.
You shall see greater things than that."
51 He then added, "I tell you[c] the truth, 1:51 [j]Mt 3:16 [k]Ge 28:12 [l]Mt 8:20
you[c] shall see heaven open,[j] and the angels of God ascending and descending[k]
on the Son of Man."[l]

Jesus Changes Water to Wine

2 On the third day a wedding took 2:1 [m]Jn 4:46; 21:2 [n]Mt 12:46
place at Cana in Galilee.[m] Jesus'
mother[n] was there, 2 and Jesus and his
disciples had also been invited to the
wedding. 3 When the wine was gone, Jesus' mother said to him, "They have no
more wine."
4 "Dear woman,[o] why do you involve 2:4 [o]Jn 19:26 [p]Mt 8:29 [q]Mt 26:18; Jn 7:6
me?"[p] Jesus replied. "My time[q] has not
yet come."
5 His mother said to the servants, "Do 2:5 [r]Ge 41:55
whatever he tells you."[r]
6 Nearby stood six stone water jars,
the kind used by the Jews for ceremoni- 2:6 [s]Mk 7:3,4; Jn 3:25
al washing,[s] each holding from twenty
to thirty gallons.[d]
7 Jesus said to the servants, "Fill the
jars with water"; so they filled them to
the brim.
8 Then he told them, "Now draw
some out and take it to the master of
the banquet."
They did so, 9 and the master of the
banquet tasted the water that had been 2:9 [t]Jn 4:46
turned into wine.[t] He did not realize
where it had come from, though the servants who had drawn the water knew.
Then he called the bridegroom aside
10 and said, "Everyone brings out the
choice wine first and then the cheaper
wine after the guests have have had too much
to drink; but you have saved the best
till now."

[a]*42* Both *Cephas* (Aramaic) and *Peter* (Greek) mean *rock.* [b]*50* Or *Do you believe . . . ?* [c]*51* The Greek is plural. [d]*6* Greek *two to three metretes* (probably about 75 to 115 liters)

PATIENCE

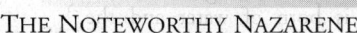

THE NOTEWORTHY NAZARENE

John 1:46

"Jesus of Nazareth"? Why not "Jesus of Damascus"? Because God always waits till those with urban expectations come to see that he is great enough to act in very big ways in very small places.

▸ GOODNESS

THE WINERY OF GOD

John 2:10
"The best wine now?" asked the guest.
"Bring on the water Jesus touched,
And beg the grapes apologize
For their insipid blood."

11This, the first of his miraculous
2:11 [u]ver 23; Jn 3:2; 4:48; 6:2,14,26,30; 12:37; 20:30 [v]Jn 1:14 [w]Ex 14:31 signs,[u] Jesus performed at Cana in Galilee. He thus revealed his glory,[v] and his
disciples put their faith in him.[w]

Jesus Clears the Temple

12After this he went down to Caper-
2:12 [x]Mt 4:13 [y]Mt 12:46 naum[x] with his mother and brothers[y]
and his disciples. There they stayed for
a few days.
13When it was almost time for the
2:13 [z]Jn 11:55 [a]Dt 16:1-6; Lk 2:41 Jewish Passover,[z] Jesus went up to
Jerusalem.[a] 14In the temple courts he
found men selling cattle, sheep and
doves, and others sitting at tables ex-
changing money. 15So he made a whip
out of cords, and drove all from the
temple area, both sheep and cattle; he
scattered the coins of the money changers and overturned their tables. 16To
those who sold doves he said, "Get these
2:16 [b]Lk 2:49 out of here! How dare you turn my Father's house[b] into a market!"
17His disciples remembered that it is
written: "Zeal for your house will con-
2:17 [c]Ps 69:9 sume me."[a] [c]
18Then the Jews demanded of him,
"What miraculous sign can you show us
2:18 [d]Mt 12:38 to prove your authority to do all this?"[d]
19Jesus answered them, "Destroy this
2:19 [e]Mt 26:61; 27:40; Mk 14:58; 15:29 temple, and I will raise it again in three
days."[e]
20The Jews replied, "It has taken for-
ty-six years to build this temple, and

▸ PEACE

HOW TO BUILD A TEMPLE IN THREE DAYS

John 2:19
Want to start a great faith? You have only to take a dead rabbi and place him in a tomb; let him lie there for a single weekend, requiring him to get out on his own. A dead man come alive will make the hair rise on your neck and the Morning Star rise within your heart.

you are going to raise it in three days?"
21But the temple he had spoken of was
his body.[f] 22After he was raised from the 2:21 [f]1Co 6:19
dead, his disciples recalled what he had
said.[g] Then they believed the Scripture 2:22 [g]Lk 24:5-8; Jn 12:16; 14:26
and the words that Jesus had spoken.
23Now while he was in Jerusalem at
the Passover Feast,[h] many people saw 2:23 [h]ver 13
the miraculous signs he was doing and
believed in his name.[b] 24But Jesus would
not entrust himself to them, for he
knew all men. 25He did not need man's
testimony about man, for he knew what 2:25 [i]Mt 9:4; Jn 6:61,64; 13:11
was in a man.[i]

Jesus Teaches Nicodemus

3 Now there was a man of the Phari-
sees named Nicodemus,[j] a member 3:1 [j]Jn 7:50; 19:39 [k]Lk 23:13
of the Jewish ruling council.[k] 2He came
to Jesus at night and said, "Rabbi, we
know you are a teacher who has come
from God. For no one could perform
the miraculous signs[l] you are doing if 3:2 [l]Jn 9:16,33 [m]Ac 2:22; 10:38
God were not with him."[m]
3In reply Jesus declared, "I tell you
the truth, no one can see the kingdom 3:3 [n]Jn 1:13; 1Pe 1:23
of God unless he is born again.[c]"[n]

▸ GENTLENESS

BORN AGAIN

John 3:3
At the end of a long umbilical cord called grace is a new kind of life. Fire cannot burn it. Floods cannot drown it. Weapons cannot harm it. It is gentle but not fragile. It is born in a moment but lives forever. It is a quiet miracle that rearranges the furniture of the heart and redesigns the mind. It is birth sired by our Father in heaven in union with our own submissive wills.

4"How can a man be born when he
is old?" Nicodemus asked. "Surely he
cannot enter a second time into his
mother's womb to be born!"
5Jesus answered, "I tell you the truth,
no one can enter the kingdom of God
unless he is born of water and the
Spirit.[o] 6Flesh gives birth to flesh, but 3:5 [o]Tit 3:5
the Spirit[d] gives birth to spirit.[p] 7You
should not be surprised at my saying, 3:6 [p]Jn 1:13; 1Co 15:50
'You[e] must be born again.' 8The wind

[a]*17* Psalm 69:9 [b]*23* Or *and believed in him* [c]*3* Or *born from above*; also in verse 7 [d]*6* Or *but spirit* [e]*7* The Greek is plural.

blows wherever it pleases. You hear its
sound, but you cannot tell where it
comes from or where it is going. So it is
with everyone born of the Spirit."
9"How can this be?"[q] Nicodemus
asked.
10"You are Israel's teacher,"[r] said Jesus, "and do you not understand these
things? 11I tell you the truth, we speak of
what we know,[s] and we testify to what
we have seen, but still you people do
not accept our testimony.[t] 12I have spoken to you of earthly things and you do
not believe; how then will you believe
if I speak of heavenly things? 13No one
has ever gone into heaven[u] except the
one who came from heaven[v]—the Son
of Man.[a] 14Just as Moses lifted up the
snake in the desert,[w] so the Son of Man
must be lifted up,[x] 15that everyone who
believes[y] in him may have eternal life.[b]

3:9 [q]Jn 6:52,60
3:10 [r]Lk 2:46
3:11 [s]Jn 1:18; 7:16,17 [t]ver 32
3:13 [u]Pr 30:4; Ac 2:34; Eph 4:8-10 [v]Jn 6:38,42
3:14 [w]Nu 21:8,9 [x]Jn 8:28; 12:32
3:15 [y]ver 16,36

LOVE

BRASS SNAKES

John 3:14

Look and live! There is a brazen serpent on a pole.
Refuse to look and die! Admit it is your heart that's brass.

16"For God so loved[z] the world that
he gave his one and only Son,[c] that
whoever believes in him shall not perish
but have eternal life.[a] 17For God did not
send his Son into the world[b] to condemn the world, but to save the world
through him.[c] 18Whoever believes in
him is not condemned,[d] but whoever
does not believe stands condemned already because he has not believed in
the name of God's one and only Son.[d][e]
19This is the verdict: Light[f] has come
into the world, but men loved darkness
instead of light because their deeds were
evil. 20Everyone who does evil hates the
light, and will not come into the light
for fear that his deeds will be exposed.[g]
21But whoever lives by the truth comes
into the light, so that it may be seen
plainly that what he has done has been
done through God."[e]

3:16 [z]Ro 5:8; Eph 2:4; 1Jn 4:9,10 [a]ver 36; Jn 6:29,40; 11:25,26
3:17 [b]Jn 6:29,57; 10:36; 11:42; 17:8,21; 20:21 [c]Jn; 12:47; 1Jn 4:14
3:18 [d]Jn 5:24 [e]1Jn 4:9
3:19 [f]Jn 1:4; 8:12
3:20 [g]Eph 5:11,13

John the Baptist's Testimony About Jesus

22After this, Jesus and his disciples
went out into the Judean countryside,
where he spent some time with them,
and baptized.[h] 23Now John also was
baptizing at Aenon near Salim, because
there was plenty of water, and people
were constantly coming to be baptized.
24(This was before John was put in
prison.)[i] 25An argument developed between some of John's disciples and a
certain Jew[f] over the matter of ceremonial washing.[j] 26They came to John and
said to him, "Rabbi,[k] that man who
was with you on the other side of the
Jordan—the one you testified[l] about—
well, he is baptizing, and everyone is
going to him."
27To this John replied, "A man can
receive only what is given him from
heaven. 28You yourselves can testify that
I said, 'I am not the Christ[g] but am
sent ahead of him.'[m] 29The bride belongs to the bridegroom.[n] The friend
who attends the bridegroom waits and
listens for him, and is full of joy when
he hears the bridegroom's voice. That
joy is mine, and it is now complete.[o]
30He must become greater; I must become less.
31"The one who comes from above[p]
is above all; the one who is from the
earth belongs to the earth, and speaks
as one from the earth.[q] The one who
comes from heaven is above all. 32He
testifies to what he has seen and heard,[r]
but no one accepts his testimony.[s] 33The
man who has accepted it has certified
that God is truthful. 34For the one
whom God has sent[t] speaks the words
of God, for God[h] gives the Spirit[u] without limit. 35The Father loves the Son
and has placed everything in his hands.[v]
36Whoever believes in the Son has eternal life,[w] but whoever rejects the Son
will not see life, for God's wrath remains on him."[i]

Jesus Talks With a Samaritan Woman

4 The Pharisees heard that Jesus was
gaining and baptizing more disciples than John,[x] 2although in fact it
was not Jesus who baptized, but his

3:22 [h]Jn 4:2
3:24 [i]Mt 4:12; 14:3
3:25 [j]Jn 2:6
3:26 [k]Mt 23:7 [l]Jn 1:7
3:28 [m]Jn 1:20,23
3:29 [n]Mt 9:15 [o]Jn 16:24; 17:13; Php 2:2; 1Jn 1:4; 2Jn 12
3:31 [p]ver 13 [q]Jn 8:23; 1Jn 4:5
3:32 [r]Jn 8:26; 15:15 [s]ver 11
3:34 [t]ver 17 [u]Mt 12:18; Lk 4:18; Ac 10:38
3:35 [v]Mt 28:18; Jn 5:20,22; 17:2
3:36 [w]ver 15; Jn 5:24; 6:47
4:1 [x]Jn 3:22,26

[a]*13* Some manuscripts *Man, who is in heaven* [b]*15* Or *believes may have eternal life in him* [c]*16* Or *his only begotten Son* [d]*18* Or *God's only begotten Son* [e]*21* Some interpreters end the quotation after verse 15. [f]*25* Some manuscripts *and certain Jews* [g]*28* Or *Messiah* [h]*34* Greek *he* [i]*36* Some interpreters end the quotation after verse 30.

disciples. 3When the Lord learned of this, he left Judea[y] and went back once more to Galilee.

4Now he had to go through Samaria. 5So he came to a town in Samaria called Sychar, near the plot of ground Jacob had given to his son Joseph.[z] 6Jacob's well was there, and Jesus, tired as he was from the journey, sat down by the well. It was about the sixth hour.

7When a Samaritan woman came to draw water, Jesus said to her, "Will you give me a drink?" 8(His disciples had gone into the town[a] to buy food.)

9The Samaritan woman said to him, "You are a Jew and I am a Samaritan[b] woman. How can you ask me for a drink?" (For Jews do not associate with Samaritans.[a])

10Jesus answered her, "If you knew the gift of God and who it is that asks you for a drink, you would have asked him and he would have given you living water."[c]

11"Sir," the woman said, "you have nothing to draw with and the well is deep. Where can you get this living water? 12Are you greater than our father Jacob, who gave us the well[d] and drank from it himself, as did also his sons and his flocks and herds?"

13Jesus answered, "Everyone who drinks this water will be thirsty again, 14but whoever drinks the water I give him will never thirst.[e] Indeed, the water I give him will become in him a spring of water[f] welling up to eternal life."[g]

15The woman said to him, "Sir, give me this water so that I won't get thirsty[h] and have to keep coming here to draw water."

16He told her, "Go, call your husband and come back."

17"I have no husband," she replied.

Jesus said to her, "You are right when you say you have no husband. 18The fact is, you have had five husbands, and the man you now have is not your husband. What you have just said is quite true."

19"Sir," the woman said, "I can see that you are a prophet.[i] 20Our fathers worshiped on this mountain,[j] but you Jews claim that the place where we must worship is in Jerusalem."[k]

21Jesus declared, "Believe me, woman, a time is coming[l] when you will worship the Father neither on this mountain nor in Jerusalem.[m] 22You Samaritans worship what you do not know;[n] we worship what we do know, for salvation is from the Jews.[o] 23Yet a time is coming and has now come[p] when the true worshipers will worship the Father in spirit[q] and truth, for they are the kind of worshipers the Father seeks. 24God is spirit,[r] and his worshipers must worship in spirit and in truth."

PEACE

THERE IS NO "WHERE" LIKE "EVERYWHERE"

John 4:21

Tell me, where is God's holy land? Where did God touch earth and call it holy? Not in Athens. Not in Jerusalem. Not in Tibet, Mecca or Baghdad. Jesus has come. No single place is sanctified. All lands are his. Every land since his coming is holy.

25The woman said, "I know that Messiah" (called Christ)[s] "is coming. When he comes, he will explain everything to us."

26Then Jesus declared, "I who speak to you am he."[t]

The Disciples Rejoin Jesus

27Just then his disciples returned[u] and were surprised to find him talking with a woman. But no one asked, "What do you want?" or "Why are you talking with her?"

28Then, leaving her water jar, the woman went back to the town and said to the people, 29"Come, see a man who told me everything I ever did.[v] Could this be the Christ[b]?"[w] 30They came out of the town and made their way toward him.

31Meanwhile his disciples urged him, "Rabbi,[x] eat something."

32But he said to them, "I have food to eat[y] that you know nothing about."

33Then his disciples said to each other, "Could someone have brought him food?"

34"My food," said Jesus, "is to do the will[z] of him who sent me and to finish his work.[a] 35Do you not say, 'Four months more and then the harvest'? I

[a]9 Or *do not use dishes Samaritans have used*
[b]29 Or *Messiah*

4:3 [y]Jn 3:22
4:5 [z]Ge 33:19; 48:22; Jos 24:32
4:8 [a]ver 5,39
4:9 [b]Mt 10:5; Lk 9:52,53
4:10 [c]Isa 44:3; Jer 2:13; Zec 14:8; Jn 7:37,38; Rev 21:6; 22:1,17
4:12 [d]ver 6
4:14 [e]Jn 6:35 [f]Jn 7:38 [g]Mt 25:46
4:15 [h]Jn 6:34
4:19 [i]Mt 21:11
4:20 [j]Dt 11:29; Jos 8:33 [k]Lk 9:53
4:21 [l]Jn 5:28; 16:2 [m]Mal 1:11; 1Ti 2:8
4:22 [n]2Ki 17:28-41 [o]Isa 2:3; Ro 3:1,2; 9:4,5
4:23 [p]Jn 5:25; 16:32 [q]Php 3:3
4:24 [r]Php 3:3
4:25 [s]Mt 1:16
4:26 [t]Jn 8:24; 9:35-37
4:27 [u]ver 8
4:29 [v]ver 17,18 [w]Mt 12:23; Jn 7:26,31
4:31 [x]Mt 23:7
4:32 [y]Job 23:12; Mt 4:4; Jn 6:27
4:34 [z]Mt 26:39; Jn 6:38; 17:4; 19:30 [a]Jn 19:30

LOVE

WEEK 28

1 DAY ONE

Love, God's Passion for His World

Read John 4:1–10

God's passion for his world is embedded in earthy things. Observe how God made his entrance into the heart of the Samaritan woman. "Will you give me a drink?" Jesus asked, and with that question, God moved into a mountain village. That small drink of water irrigated the fields of God's harvest.

God is in love with the inhabitants of planet earth. His conquest of love never ceases. Yet he does not storm the planet by conquering continents. Nor does he evangelize it by zip code or precinct. He has no ad campaign that informs the world of his benefits. He is a great God with a small methodology. He unobtrusively shows up among the needy and begins each relationship by asking something of the one he desires to save. He always asks for repentance. Occasionally he asks for something simple, yet obliging.

In Samaria he asked for water—a very common substance. Sixty-two percent of the human body consists of water and three-fourths of the earth is covered with it. He had not asked the Samaritan woman for a cup of diamonds . . . just water. But a diamond—eternal and enduring—was what he gave her in return. Love motivated this diamond-for-water exchange:

"Water," cried her thirsty Lord,
And with reluctance she complied.
He drank, returned the dipper gourd,
She drank. They say she never died.

MEMORIZE THIS WEEK

JOHN 3:16-18

"For God so loved the world that he gave his one and only Son, that whoever believes in him shall not perish but have eternal life. For God did not send his Son into the world to condemn the world, but to save the world through him. Whoever believes in him is not condemned, but whoever does not believe stands condemned already because he has not believed in the name of God's one and only Son."

2 DAY TWO

Love and the Purpose of God in My Life

Jonah met a fish for one reason: Jonah simply didn't want God to love the Ninevites. The Ninevites were hard to love. They pillaged and wrecked havoc with their wars of conquest. They killed the men of a conquered land and made slaves of the women. But what Jonah considered more offensive was the fact that the Ninevites were not Jonah's kind—they were not Jewish. It took a big fish to convince Jonah that God loved a lot of people Jonah didn't care for. *Turn to Jonah 1:1–17, page 1067, for today's study.*

3 DAY THREE

Love and My Relationship With Christ

What we speak of last in life is usually what is most important to us. Jesus' last words were, simply put, "Listen up. God's in love with the people of this planet. Everyone has a right to know that. Go, and as you go, tell the world it has a Lover. The Good News is that people don't have to live or die alone. They don't know this. So get out there and tell them." *Turn to Matthew 28:18–20, page 1164, for today's study.*

4 DAY FOUR

Love and My Service to Others

When Jesus went to his hometown to preach, he chose Isaiah 61 as his text (Luke 4:16–21). Jesus wanted everyone in his hometown to know that God's outrageous grace has been set loose in the world. The poor, who were often the last to hear this Good News, soon discovered they weren't poor any longer! God was dividing up his celestial estate, and all those who wanted their own homes in it could have that if they would but believe in him. *Turn to Isaiah 61:1–3, page 861, for today's study.*

5 DAY FIVE

Love and Its Place in My Personal Worship

What did the people do when they arrived in front of the Lamb? They did what they had done all their lives—they praised God for his salvation. But this celestial victory celebration was really the meeting of lovers who had fallen in love during tougher times on earth. Now they could celebrate their love in better times. *Turn to Revelation 7:9–10, page 1529, for today's study.*

Week 29, Joy, the Reward of Endurance, begins on page 581, Esther 8:15–17.
To begin a topical study on the Fruit of the Spirit, Love, turn to the Topical Index, page 1548.

tell you, open your eyes and look at the
fields! They are ripe for harvest.[b] 36Even
now the reaper draws his wages, even
now he harvests[c] the crop for eternal
life,[d] so that the sower and the reaper
may be glad together. 37Thus the saying
'One sows and another reaps'[e] is true.
38I sent you to reap what you have not
worked for. Others have done the hard
work, and you have reaped the benefits
of their labor."

4:35 [b]Mt 9:37; Lk 10:2
4:36 [c]Ro 1:13 [d]Mt 25:46
4:37 [e]Job 31:8; Mic 6:15

LOVE

HEART HUNGER AND STOMACH HUNGER

John 4:32

Love is the only meal that will satisfy those hungry for eternal things. When this appetite obsesses us, the pangs of lower appetites are overlooked. With a single glimpse of crystal thrones and gold pavilions, we lose our fascination with potatoes.

Many Samaritans Believe

39Many of the Samaritans from that
town[f] believed in him because of the
woman's testimony, "He told me everything I ever did."[g] 40So when the Samaritans came to him, they urged him
to stay with them, and he stayed two
days. 41And because of his words many
more became believers.
42They said to the woman, "We no
longer believe just because of what you
said; now we have heard for ourselves,
and we know that this man really is the
Savior of the world."[h]

4:39 [f]ver 5 [g]ver 29
4:42 [h]Lk 2:11; 1Jn 4:14

Jesus Heals the Official's Son

43After the two days[i] he left for Galilee. 44(Now Jesus himself had pointed
out that a prophet has no honor in his
own country.)[j] 45When he arrived in
Galilee, the Galileans welcomed him.
They had seen all that he had done
in Jerusalem at the Passover Feast,[k] for
they also had been there.
46Once more he visited Cana in Galilee, where he had turned the water into
wine.[l] And there was a certain royal official whose son lay sick at Capernaum.
47When this man heard that Jesus had
arrived in Galilee from Judea,[m] he went
to him and begged him to come and
heal his son, who was close to death.
48"Unless you people see miraculous
signs and wonders,"[n] Jesus told him,
"you will never believe."
49The royal official said, "Sir, come
down before my child dies."
50Jesus replied, "You may go. Your
son will live."
The man took Jesus at his word and
departed. 51While he was still on the
way, his servants met him with the news
that his boy was living. 52When he inquired as to the time when his son got
better, they said to him, "The fever left
him yesterday at the seventh hour."
53Then the father realized that this
was the exact time at which Jesus had
said to him, "Your son will live." So he
and all his household[o] believed.
54This was the second miraculous
sign[p] that Jesus performed, having come
from Judea to Galilee.

4:43 [i]ver 40
4:44 [j]Mt 13:57; Lk 4:24
4:45 [k]Jn 2:23
4:46 [l]Jn 2:1-11
4:47 [m]ver 3,54
4:48 [n]Da 4:2,3; Jn 2:11; Ac 2:43; 14:3; Ro 15:19; 2Co 12:12; Heb 2:4
4:53 [o]Ac 11:14
4:54 [p]ver 48; Jn 2:11

The Healing at the Pool

5 Some time later, Jesus went up to
Jerusalem for a feast of the Jews.
2Now there is in Jerusalem near the
Sheep Gate[q] a pool, which in Aramaic[r]
is called Bethesda[a] and which is surrounded by five covered colonnades.
3Here a great number of disabled people used to lie—the blind, the lame,
the paralyzed.[b] 5One who was there had
been an invalid for thirty-eight years.
6When Jesus saw him lying there and
learned that he had been in this condition for a long time, he asked him, "Do
you want to get well?"
7"Sir," the invalid replied, "I have no
one to help me into the pool when the
water is stirred. While I am trying to
get in, someone else goes down ahead
of me."
8Then Jesus said to him, "Get up!
Pick up your mat and walk."[s] 9At once
the man was cured; he picked up his
mat and walked.
The day on which this took place
was a Sabbath,[t] 10and so the Jews[u] said
to the man who had been healed, "It
is the Sabbath; the law forbids you to
carry your mat."[v]
11But he replied, "The man who

5:2 [q]Ne 3:1; 12:39 [r]Jn 19:13, 17,20; 20:16; Ac 21:40; 22:2; 26:14
5:8 [s]Mt 9:5,6; Mk 2:11; Lk 5:24
5:9 [t]Jn 9:14
5:10 [u]ver 16 [v]Ne 13:15-22; Jer 17:21; Mt 12:2

[a]2 Some manuscripts *Bethzatha;* other manuscripts *Bethsaida* [b]3 Some less important manuscripts *paralyzed—and they waited for the moving of the waters. [4]From time to time an angel of the Lord would come down and stir up the waters. The first one into the pool after each such disturbance would be cured of whatever disease he had.*

made me well said to me, 'Pick up your
mat and walk.'"
12So they asked him, "Who is this
fellow who told you to pick it up and
walk?"
13The man who was healed had no
idea who it was, for Jesus had slipped
away into the crowd that was there.
14Later Jesus found him at the temple and said to him, "See, you are
5:14 well again. Stop sinning[w] or something
[w]Mk 2:5; Jn 8:11 worse may happen to you." 15The man
5:15 went away and told the Jews[x] that it
[x]Jn 1:19 was Jesus who had made him well.

Life Through the Son

16So, because Jesus was doing these
things on the Sabbath, the Jews perse-
5:17 cuted him. 17Jesus said to them, "My
[y]Jn 9:4; 14:10 Father is always at his work[y] to this very
day, and I, too, am working." 18For this
reason the Jews tried all the harder to
5:18 [z]Jn 7:1 kill him;[z] not only was he breaking the
[a]Jn 10:30,33; 19:7 Sabbath, but he was even calling God
his own Father, making himself equal
with God.[a]
19Jesus gave them this answer: "I tell
you the truth, the Son can do nothing
5:19 [b]ver 30; by himself;[b] he can do only what he
Jn 8:28 sees his Father doing, because whatever
the Father does the Son also does. 20For
5:20 [c]Jn 3:35 the Father loves the Son[c] and shows
[d]Jn 14:12 him all he does. Yes, to your amazement he will show him even greater
things than these.[d] 21For just as the Fa-
5:21 [e]Ro 4:17; 8:11 ther raises the dead and gives them life,[e]
[f]Jn 11:25 even so the Son gives life[f] to whom he
is pleased to give it. 22Moreover, the Father judges no one, but has entrusted
5:22 all judgment to the Son,[g] 23that all may
[g]ver 27; Jn 9:39; honor the Son just as they honor the
Ac 10:42; 17:31 Father. He who does not honor the Son
does not honor the Father, who sent
5:23 [h]Lk 10:16; 1Jn 2:23 him.[h]
24"I tell you the truth, whoever hears
my word and believes him who sent
me has eternal life and will not be
5:24 [i]Jn 3:18 condemned;[i] he has crossed over from
[j]1Jn 3:14 death to life.[j] 25I tell you the truth,
5:25 [k]Jn 4:23 a time is coming and has now come[k]
[l]Jn 8:43,47 when the dead will hear[l] the voice of
the Son of God and those who hear will
live. 26For as the Father has life in himself, so he has granted the Son to have
life in himself. 27And he has given him
5:27 [m]ver 22; authority to judge[m] because he is the
Ac 10:42; Son of Man.
17:31 28"Do not be amazed at this, for a

time is coming[n] when all who are in 5:28 [n]Jn 4:21
their graves will hear his voice 29and
come out—those who have done good
will rise to live, and those who have
done evil will rise to be condemned.[o]
30By myself I can do nothing;[p] I judge 5:29 [o]Da 12:2; Mt 25:46
only as I hear, and my judgment is
just,[q] for I seek not to please myself but 5:30 [p]ver 19
him who sent me.[r] [q]Jn 8:16 [r]Mt 26:39; Jn 4:34; 6:38

Testimonies About Jesus

31"If I testify about myself, my testi-
mony is not valid.[s] 32There is another 5:31 [s]Jn 8:14
who testifies in my favor,[t] and I know
that his testimony about me is valid. 5:32 [t]ver 37; Jn 8:18
33"You have sent to John and he has
testified[u] to the truth. 34Not that I ac- 5:33
cept human testimony;[v] but I mention [u]Jn 1:7
it that you may be saved. 35John was 5:34
a lamp that burned and gave light,[w] [v]1Jn 5:9
and you chose for a time to enjoy his 5:35
light. [w]2Pe 1:19
36"I have testimony weightier than
that of John.[x] For the very work that
the Father has given me to finish, and 5:36 [x]1Jn 5:9
which I am doing,[y] testifies that the [y]Jn 14:11; 15:24
Father has sent me.[z] 37And the Father [z]Jn 3:17; 10:25
who sent me has himself testified con-
cerning me.[a] You have never heard his 5:37 [a]Jn 8:18
voice nor seen his form,[b] 38nor does [b]Dt 4:12; 1Ti 1:17; Jn 1:18
his word dwell in you,[c] for you do not
believe the one he sent.[d] 39You diligent-
ly study[a] the Scriptures[e] because you 5:38 [c]1Jn 2:14 [d]Jn 3:17
think that by them you possess eternal
life. These are the Scriptures that testify 5:39 [e]Ro 2:17,18
about me,[f] 40yet you refuse to come to [f]Lk 24:27,44; Ac 13:27
me to have life.
41"I do not accept praise from men,[g] 5:41
42but I know you. I know that you do [g]ver 44
not have the love of God in your hearts.
43I have come in my Father's name, and
you do not accept me; but if someone
else comes in his own name, you will
accept him. 44How can you believe if
you accept praise from one another, yet
make no effort to obtain the praise that
comes from the only God[b]?[h]
45"But do not think I will accuse 5:44 [h]Ro 2:29
you before the Father. Your accuser is 5:45 [i]Jn 9:28
Moses,[i] on whom your hopes are set.[j] [j]Ro 2:17
46If you believed Moses, you would be-
lieve me, for he wrote about me.[k] 47But 5:46 [k]Ge 3:15;
since you do not believe what he wrote, Lk 24:27,44;
how are you going to believe what I Ac 26:22
say?"[l] 5:47 [l]Lk 16:29,31

[a]*39* Or *Study diligently* (the imperative) [b]*44* Some early manuscripts *the Only One*

Jesus Feeds the Five Thousand

6 Some time after this, Jesus crossed
to the far shore of the Sea of Galilee (that is, the Sea of Tiberias), 2 and
a great crowd of people followed him
6:2 because they saw the miraculous signs[m]
[m]Jn 2:11 he had performed on the sick. 3 Then
6:3 Jesus went up on a mountainside[n] and
[n]ver 15 sat down with his disciples. 4 The Jew-
6:4 ish Passover Feast[o] was near.
[o]Jn 2:13; 11:55 5 When Jesus looked up and saw a
great crowd coming toward him, he said

DAY 3 THREE

▸ GENTLENESS AND MY RELATIONSHIP WITH CHRIST

John 6:1–11

One Savior, one servant and one child pulled off the greatest catering feat of all time. The child said, "Here's my lunch." The servant said, "Here's his lunch, but how far will it go among so many?" The Savior said, "Have the crowd sit down." Childlike gentleness appealed to the servant, the servant's obedience appealed to the Savior, and eating appealed to everyone.

The world is about to be amazed at how far a boy's lunch will go. And are we not also amazed that the things we surrender to Jesus—though they seem little in our lives—may be used by God in ways far too impressive for us to imagine?

There is a story long celebrated among Christians of this boy who supplied the meal. The story is that the boy was very proud as the Master took his lunch and began to divide it among the masses. As the boy watched Jesus breaking his loaves, he said, "That's my bread." When Jesus began to pass out his fish to the crowd, the boy said, "That's my fish." But as Jesus kept breaking the bread, and the crowd of thousands kept eating, the little boy said, "That's not my bread and fish anymore."

Gentleness takes our small assets and multiplies them until they serve in wider ways than we could ever imagine. It is amazing how the full surrender of the most trivial offerings can enliven, not just our relationship with Christ, but the whole world.

To begin a study on the topic of Gentleness, Childlike Godliness, turn to the home page on page 315.

to Philip,[p] "Where shall we buy bread 6:5 [p]Jn 1:43
for these people to eat?" 6 He asked this
only to test him, for he already had in
mind what he was going to do.
7 Philip answered him, "Eight months'
wages[a] would not buy enough bread for
each one to have a bite!"
8 Another of his disciples, Andrew, Si-
mon Peter's brother,[q] spoke up, 9 "Here 6:8 [q]Jn 1:40
is a boy with five small barley loaves
and two small fish, but how far will
they go among so many?"[r] 6:9 [r]2Ki 4:43
10 Jesus said, "Have the people sit
down." There was plenty of grass in that
place, and the men sat down, about five
thousand of them. 11 Jesus then took the
loaves, gave thanks,[s] and distributed to 6:11 [s]ver 23; Mt 14:19
those who were seated as much as they
wanted. He did the same with the fish.
12 When they had all had enough to
eat, he said to his disciples, "Gather the
pieces that are left over. Let nothing be
wasted." 13 So they gathered them and
filled twelve baskets with the pieces of
the five barley loaves left over by those
who had eaten.

▸ SELF-CONTROL

THE KING OF FISH

John 6:13

The hungry follow mostly stomach gods. We are prone to worship what fills us up. "Take up my fish and follow me" attracts armies of gluttonous disciples. "Take up my cross" weeds out the lunch-box soldiers.

14 After the people saw the miracu-
lous sign[t] that Jesus did, they began 6:14 [t]Jn 2:11
to say, "Surely this is the Prophet who [u]Dt 18:15,18; Mt 11:3;
is to come into the world."[u] 15 Jesus, 21:11
knowing that they intended to come
and make him king[v] by force, withdrew 6:15 [v]Jn 18:36
again to a mountain by himself.[w] [w]Mt 14:23; Mk 6:46

Jesus Walks on the Water

16 When evening came, his disciples
went down to the lake, 17 where they got
into a boat and set off across the lake
for Capernaum. By now it was dark,
and Jesus had not yet joined them. 18 A
strong wind was blowing and the waters
grew rough. 19 When they had rowed
three or three and a half miles,[b] they

[a] 7 Greek *two hundred denarii* [b] 19 Greek *rowed twenty-five or thirty stadia* (about 5 or 6 kilometers)

saw Jesus approaching the boat, walk-
6:19 [x]Job 9:8 ing on the water;[x] and they were terrified. 20But he said to them, "It is I;
6:20 [y]Mt 14:27 don't be afraid."[y] 21Then they were willing to take him into the boat, and im-
mediately the boat reached the shore
where they were heading.
22The next day the crowd that had
stayed on the opposite shore of the lake[z]
6:22 [z]ver 2 [a]ver 15-21 realized that only one boat had been
there, and that Jesus had not entered
it with his disciples, but that they had
gone away alone.[a] 23Then some boats
6:23 [b]ver 1 [c]ver 11 from Tiberias[b] landed near the place
where the people had eaten the bread af-
ter the Lord had given thanks.[c] 24Once
the crowd realized that neither Jesus nor
his disciples were there, they got into
the boats and went to Capernaum in
search of Jesus.

Jesus the Bread of Life

25When they found him on the other side of the lake, they asked him,
6:25 [d]Mt 23:7 "Rabbi,[d] when did you get here?"
26Jesus answered, "I tell you the truth,
6:26 [e]ver 24 [f]ver 30; Jn 2:11 you are looking for me,[e] not because
you saw miraculous signs[f] but because
you ate the loaves and had your fill.
27Do not work for food that spoils, but
6:27 [g]Isa 55:2 [h]ver 54; Mt 25:46; Jn 4:14 [i]Mt 8:20 [j]Ro 4:11; 1Co 9:2; 2Co 1:22; Eph 1:13; 4:30; 2Ti 2:19; Rev 7:3 for food that endures[g] to eternal life,[h]
which the Son of Man[i] will give you.
On him God the Father has placed his
seal[j] of approval."
28Then they asked him, "What must
we do to do the works God requires?"
29Jesus answered, "The work of God
is this: to believe[k] in the one he has
6:29 [k]1Jn 3:23 [l]Jn 3:17 sent."[l]
30So they asked him, "What miraculous sign[m] then will you give that
6:30 [m]Jn 2:11 [n]Mt 12:38 we may see it and believe you?[n] What
will you do? 31Our forefathers ate the
6:31 [o]Nu 11:7-9 [p]Ex 16:4,15; Ne 9:15; Ps 78:24; 105:40 manna[o] in the desert; as it is written:
'He gave them bread from heaven to
eat.'[a]"[p]
32Jesus said to them, "I tell you the
truth, it is not Moses who has given
you the bread from heaven, but it is
my Father who gives you the true bread
from heaven. 33For the bread of God is
6:33 [q]ver 50 he who comes down from heaven[q] and
gives life to the world."
34"Sir," they said, "from now on give
6:34 [r]Jn 4:15 us this bread."[r]
35Then Jesus declared, "I am the
6:35 [s]ver 48,51 bread of life.[s] He who comes to me will
never go hungry, and he who believes

in me will never be thirsty.[t] 36But as I 6:35 [t]Jn 4:14
told you, you have seen me and still
you do not believe. 37All that the Father
gives me[u] will come to me, and whoev- 6:37 [u]ver 39; Jn 17:2,6,9,24
er comes to me I will never drive away.
38For I have come down from heaven
not to do my will but to do the will
of him who sent me.[v] 39And this is the 6:38 [v]Jn 4:34; 5:30
will of him who sent me, that I shall
lose none of all that he has given me,[w] 6:39 [w]Jn 10:28; 17:12; 18:9 [x]ver 40,44,54
but raise them up at the last day.[x] 40For
my Father's will is that everyone who
looks to the Son and believes in him
shall have eternal life,[y] and I will raise 6:40 [y]Jn 3:15,16
him up at the last day."

FAITHFULNESS

THE BREAD OF LIFE

John 6:35

There is a kind of bread not baked on earth. It is not made from grain and is never toasted. It never grows stale in human larders. Seek this better bread. Eat and never die. But if you trek a less requiring life, there's a common bakery at the corner.

41At this the Jews began to grumble
about him because he said, "I am the
bread that came down from heaven."
42They said, "Is this not Jesus, the son
of Joseph,[z] whose father and mother we 6:42 [z]Lk 4:22 [a]Jn 7:27,28 [b]ver 38,62
know?[a] How can he now say, 'I came
down from heaven'?"[b]
43"Stop grumbling among yourselves," Jesus answered. 44"No one can
come to me unless the Father who sent
me draws him,[c] and I will raise him 6:44 [c]ver 65; Jer 31:3; Jn 12:32
up at the last day. 45It is written in the
Prophets: 'They will all be taught by
God.'[b] [d] Everyone who listens to the Fa- 6:45 [d]Isa 54:13; Jer 31:33,34; Heb 8:10,11; 10:16
ther and learns from him comes to me.
46No one has seen the Father except the
one who is from God;[e] only he has seen
the Father. 47I tell you the truth, he 6:46 [e]Jn 1:18; 5:37; 7:29
who believes has everlasting life. 48I am
the bread of life.[f] 49Your forefathers ate 6:48 [f]ver 35,51
the manna in the desert, yet they died.[g]
50But here is the bread that comes down 6:49 [g]ver 31,58
from heaven,[h] which a man may eat
and not die. 51I am the living bread that 6:50 [h]ver 33
came down from heaven. If anyone eats
of this bread, he will live forever. This
bread is my flesh, which I will give for
the life of the world."[i] 6:51 [i]Heb 10:10

[a] *31* Exodus 16:4; Neh. 9:15; Psalm 78:24,25
[b] *45* Isaiah 54:13

PEACE

THE MANNA EATERS' CEMETERIES

John 6:49

A sea of gravestones marked the exodus. The Israelites ate the manna and boasted regularly of miracles, but they ultimately died and rotted in the sand. Manna made life possible—one starving day at a time. Jesus, "the true bread from heaven" (John 6:32), is the only bread that leaves no tombstones—not even his own.

52Then the Jews began to argue sharp-
6:52 [j]Jn 7:43; 9:16; 10:19 ly among themselves,[j] "How can this
man give us his flesh to eat?"
53Jesus said to them, "I tell you the
truth, unless you eat the flesh of the
6:53 [k]Mt 8:20 Son of Man[k] and drink his blood, you
have no life in you. 54Whoever eats my
flesh and drinks my blood has eternal
life, and I will raise him up at the last
6:54 [l]ver 39 day.[l] 55For my flesh is real food and my
blood is real drink. 56Whoever eats my
flesh and drinks my blood remains in
6:56 [m]Jn 15:4-7; 1Jn 3:24; 4:15 me, and I in him.[m] 57Just as the living
Father sent me[n] and I live because of
the Father, so the one who feeds on me
6:57 [n]Jn 3:17 will live because of me. 58This is the
bread that came down from heaven.
Your forefathers ate manna and died,
but he who feeds on this bread will live
6:58 [o]ver 49-51; Jn 3:36 forever."[o] 59He said this while teaching
in the synagogue in Capernaum.

Many Disciples Desert Jesus

60On hearing it, many of his dis-
6:60 [p]ver 66 ciples[p] said, "This is a hard teaching.
Who can accept it?"
61Aware that his disciples were grumbling about this, Jesus said to them,
6:61 [q]Mt 11:6 "Does this offend you?[q] 62What if you
see the Son of Man ascend to where he
6:62 [r]Mk 16:19; Jn 3:13; 17:5 was before![r] 63The Spirit gives life;[s] the
flesh counts for nothing. The words I
6:63 [s]2Co 3:6 have spoken to you are spirit[a] and they
are life. 64Yet there are some of you who
6:64 [t]Jn 2:25 do not believe." For Jesus had known[t]
from the beginning which of them did
not believe and who would betray him.
65He went on to say, "This is why I told
you that no one can come to me unless
6:65 [u]ver 37,44 the Father has enabled him."[u]
66From this time many of his disci-
6:66 [v]ver 60 ples[v] turned back and no longer followed him.

67"You do not want to leave too, do
you?" Jesus asked the Twelve.[w] 6:67 [w]Mt 10:2
68Simon Peter answered him,[x] "Lord,
to whom shall we go? You have the 6:68 [x]Mt 16:16
words of eternal life. 69We believe and
know that you are the Holy One of
God."[y] 6:69 [y]Mk 8:29; Lk 9:20
70Then Jesus replied, "Have I not
chosen you,[z] the Twelve? Yet one of you 6:70 [z]Jn 15:16,19 [a]Jn 13:27
is a devil!"[a] 71(He meant Judas, the son
of Simon Iscariot, who, though one of
the Twelve, was later to betray him.)

Jesus Goes to the Feast of Tabernacles

7 After this, Jesus went around in Galilee, purposely staying away from
Judea because the Jews[b] there were wait- 7:1 [b]Jn 1:19 [c]Jn 5:18
ing to take his life.[c] 2But when the
Jewish Feast of Tabernacles[d] was near,
3Jesus' brothers[e] said to him, "You ought 7:2 [d]Lev 23:34; Dt 16:16
to leave here and go to Judea, so that
your disciples may see the miracles you 7:3 [e]Mt 12:46
do. 4No one who wants to become a
public figure acts in secret. Since you
are doing these things, show yourself to
the world." 5For even his own brothers
did not believe in him.[f] 7:5 [f]Mk 3:21
6Therefore Jesus told them, "The
right time[g] for me has not yet come; for 7:6 [g]Mt 26:18
you any time is right. 7The world can-
not hate you, but it hates me[h] because 7:7 [h]Jn 15:18,19 [i]Jn 3:19,20
I testify that what it does is evil.[i] 8You
go to the Feast. I am not yet[b] going up
to this Feast, because for me the right
time[j] has not yet come." 9Having said 7:8 [j]ver 6
this, he stayed in Galilee.
10However, after his brothers had left
for the Feast, he went also, not publicly,
but in secret. 11Now at the Feast the
Jews were watching for him[k] and ask- 7:11 [k]Jn 11:56
ing, "Where is that man?"
12Among the crowds there was widespread whispering about him. Some
said, "He is a good man."
Others replied, "No, he deceives the
people."[l] 13But no one would say any- 7:12 [l]ver 40,43
thing publicly about him for fear of 7:13 [m]Jn 9:22; 12:42; 19:38
the Jews.[m]

Jesus Teaches at the Feast

14Not until halfway through the Feast 7:14 [n]ver 28; Mt 26:55
did Jesus go up to the temple courts
and begin to teach.[n] 15The Jews[o] were 7:15 [o]Jn 1:19
amazed and asked, "How did this man

[a]63 Or *Spirit* [b]8 Some early manuscripts do not have *yet.*

7:15 [p]Ac 26:24 get such learning[p] without having
[q]Mt 13:54 studied?"[q]
[16]Jesus answered, "My teaching is not
my own. It comes from him who sent
7:16 me.[r] [17]If anyone chooses to do God's
[r]Jn 3:11; will, he will find out[s] whether my teach-
14:24 7:17 ing comes from God or whether I speak
[s]Ps 25:14; on my own. [18]He who speaks on his
Jn 8:43 own does so to gain honor for himself,[t]
7:18 but he who works for the honor of the
[t]Jn 5:41; one who sent him is a man of truth;
8:50,54 there is nothing false about him. [19]Has
7:19 [u]Jn 1:17 not Moses given you the law?[u] Yet not
[v]ver 1; one of you keeps the law. Why are you
Mt 12:14 trying to kill me?"[v]
7:20 [w]Jn 8:48; [20]"You are demon-possessed,"[w] the
10:20 crowd answered. "Who is trying to kill
you?"
[21]Jesus said to them, "I did one miracle, and you are all astonished. [22]Yet,
7:22 [x]Lev 12:3 because Moses gave you circumcision[x]
[y]Ge 17:10-14 (though actually it did not come from
Moses, but from the patriarchs),[y] you
circumcise a child on the Sabbath.
[23]Now if a child can be circumcised
on the Sabbath so that the law of Moses may not be broken, why are you
angry with me for healing the whole
man on the Sabbath? [24]Stop judging
7:24 by mere appearances, and make a right
[z]Isa 11:3,4; judgment."[z]
Jn 8:15

Is Jesus the Christ?

[25]At that point some of the people
of Jerusalem began to ask, "Isn't this
the man they are trying to kill? [26]Here
he is, speaking publicly, and they are
not saying a word to him. Have the au-
7:26 thorities[a] really concluded that he is the
[a]ver 48 Christ[a]? [27]But we know where this man
7:27 [b]Mt 13:55; is from;[b] when the Christ comes, no
Lk 4:22 one will know where he is from."
[28]Then Jesus, still teaching in the
7:28 [c]ver 14 temple courts,[c] cried out, "Yes, you
[d]Jn 8:14 know me, and you know where I am
[e]Jn 8:26,42 from.[d] I am not here on my own, but
he who sent me is true.[e] You do not
know him, [29]but I know him because I
7:29 [f]Mt 11:27 am from him[f] and he sent me."
[30]At this they tried to seize him, but
7:30 [g]ver 32,44; no one laid a hand on him,[g] because
Jn 10:39 his time had not yet come. [31]Still, many
7:31 in the crowd put their faith in him.[h]
[h]Jn 8:30 They said, "When the Christ comes,
[i]Jn 2:11 will he do more miraculous signs[i] than
this man?"
[32]The Pharisees heard the crowd
whispering such things about him. Then
the chief priests and the Pharisees sent
temple guards to arrest him.
[33]Jesus said, "I am with you for only
a short time,[j] and then I go to the one 7:33
who sent me.[k] [34]You will look for me, [j]Jn 13:33; 16:16
but you will not find me; and where I [k]Jn 16:5,10,
am, you cannot come."[l] 17,28
[35]The Jews said to one another, 7:34
"Where does this man intend to go that [l]Jn 8:21;
we cannot find him? Will he go where 13:33
our people live scattered[m] among the 7:35 [m]Jas 1:1
Greeks,[n] and teach the Greeks? [36]What [n]Jn 12:20;
did he mean when he said, 'You will 1Pe 1:1
look for me, but you will not find me,'
and 'Where I am, you cannot come'?"
[37]On the last and greatest day of
the Feast,[o] Jesus stood and said in a 7:37 [o]Lev 23:36
loud voice, "If anyone is thirsty, let him [p]Isa 55:1;
come to me and drink.[p] [38]Whoever be- Rev 22:17
lieves in me, as[b] the Scripture has said,[q] 7:38
streams of living water[r] will flow from [q]Isa 58:11 [r]Jn 4:10
within him."[s] [39]By this he meant the [s]Jn 4:14
Spirit,[t] whom those who believed in 7:39
him were later to receive.[u] Up to that [t]Joel 2:28;
time the Spirit had not been given, Ac 2:17,33 [u]Jn 20:22
since Jesus had not yet been glorified.[v] [v]Jn 12:23;
[40]On hearing his words, some of the 13:31,32
people said, "Surely this man is the
Prophet."[w] 7:40
[41]Others said, "He is the Christ." [w]Mt 21:11; Jn 1:21
Still others asked, "How can the 7:41
Christ come from Galilee?[x] [42]Does not [x]ver 52;
the Scripture say that the Christ will Jn 1:46
come from David's family[c][y] and from 7:42 [y]Mt 1:1
Bethlehem,[z] the town where David [z]Mic 5:2;
lived?" [43]Thus the people were divid- Mt 2:5,6; Lk 2:4
ed[a] because of Jesus. [44]Some wanted to 7:43
seize him, but no one laid a hand on [a]Jn 9:16;
him.[b] 10:19
7:44 [b]ver 30

Unbelief of the Jewish Leaders

[45]Finally the temple guards went back
to the chief priests and Pharisees, who
asked them, "Why didn't you bring
him in?"
[46]"No one ever spoke the way this 7:46
man does,"[c] the guards declared. [c]Mt 7:28
[47]"You mean he has deceived you 7:47
also?"[d] the Pharisees retorted. [48]"Has [d]ver 12
any of the rulers or of the Pharisees be- 7:48
lieved in him?[e] [49]No! But this mob that [e]Jn 12:42
knows nothing of the law—there is a
curse on them."

[a]*26* Or *Messiah*; also in verses 27, 31, 41 and 42
[b]*37,38* Or / *If anyone is thirsty, let him come to me. / And let him drink,* [38]*who believes in me. / As*
[c]*42* Greek *seed*

7:50 [f]Jn 3:1; 19:39 50Nicodemus,[f] who had gone to Jesus earlier and who was one of their
own number, asked, 51"Does our law
condemn anyone without first hearing
him to find out what he is doing?"
52They replied, "Are you from Galilee, too? Look into it, and you will find
that a prophet[a] does not come out of
7:52 [g]ver 41 Galilee."[g]

[The earliest manuscripts and many
other ancient witnesses do not have
John 7:53–8:11.]

53Then each went to his own home.
8:1 [h]Mt 21:1 8 But Jesus went to the Mount of
Olives.[h] 2At dawn he appeared again
in the temple courts, where all the people gathered around him, and he sat
8:2 [i]ver 20; Mt 26:55 down to teach them.[i] 3The teachers of
the law and the Pharisees brought in a
woman caught in adultery. They made
her stand before the group 4and said to
Jesus, "Teacher, this woman was caught
in the act of adultery. 5In the Law Mo-
8:5 [j]Lev 20:10; Dt 22:22 ses commanded us to stone such wom-
en.[j] Now what do you say?" 6They were
using this question as a trap,[k] in order
8:6 [k]Mt 22:15,18 [l]Mt 12:10 to have a basis for accusing him.[l]
But Jesus bent down and started to
write on the ground with his finger.
7When they kept on questioning him,
he straightened up and said to them, "If
any one of you is without sin, let him
8:7 [m]Dt 17:7 [n]Ro 2:1,22 be the first to throw a stone[m] at her."[n]
8Again he stooped down and wrote on
the ground.
9At this, those who heard began to
go away one at a time, the older ones
first, until only Jesus was left, with
the woman still standing there. 10Jesus
straightened up and asked her, "Woman, where are they? Has no one condemned you?"
11"No one, sir," she said.
8:11 [o]Jn 3:17 [p]Jn 5:14 "Then neither do I condemn you,"[o]
Jesus declared. "Go now and leave your
life of sin."[p]

The Validity of Jesus' Testimony

12When Jesus spoke again to the peo-
8:12 [q]Jn 6:35 [r]Jn 1:4; 12:35 [s]Pr 4:18; Mt 5:14 ple, he said, "I am[q] the light of the
world.[r] Whoever follows me will never
walk in darkness, but will have the light
of life."[s]

13The Pharisees challenged him,
"Here you are, appearing as your own
witness; your testimony is not valid."[t] 8:13 [t]Jn 5:31
14Jesus answered, "Even if I testify
on my own behalf, my testimony is
valid, for I know where I came from
and where I am going.[u] But you have 8:14 [u]Jn 13:3; 16:28 [v]Jn 7:28; 9:29
no idea where I come from[v] or where
I am going. 15You judge by human
standards;[w] I pass judgment on no one.[x] 8:15 [w]Jn 7:24 [x]Jn 3:17
16But if I do judge, my decisions are
right, because I am not alone. I stand
with the Father, who sent me.[y] 17In 8:16 [y]Jn 5:30
your own Law it is written that the tes- 8:17 [z]Dt 17:6; Mt 18:16
timony of two men is valid.[z] 18I am one
who testifies for myself; my other witness is the Father, who sent me."[a] 8:18 [a]Jn 5:37
19Then they asked him, "Where is
your father?"
"You do not know me or my Father,"[b] 8:19 [b]Jn 16:3 [c]Jn 14:7; 1Jn 2:23
Jesus replied. "If you knew me, you
would know my Father also."[c] 20He
spoke these words while teaching[d] in 8:20 [d]Mt 26:55 [e]Mk 12:41 [f]Mt 26:18; Jn 7:30
the temple area near the place where
the offerings were put.[e] Yet no one
seized him, because his time had not
yet come.[f]
21Once more Jesus said to them, "I
am going away, and you will look for
me, and you will die[g] in your sin. Where 8:21 [g]Eze 3:18 [h]Jn 7:34; 13:33
I go, you cannot come."[h]
22This made the Jews ask, "Will he
kill himself? Is that why he says, 'Where
I go, you cannot come'?"
23But he continued, "You are from
below; I am from above. You are of this
world; I am not of this world.[i] 24I told 8:23 [i]Jn 3:31; 17:14
you that you would die in your sins; if
you do not believe that I am ⌊the one
I claim to be⌋,[b][j] you will indeed die in 8:24 [j]Jn 4:26; 13:19
your sins."
25"Who are you?" they asked.
"Just what I have been claiming all
along," Jesus replied. 26"I have much to
say in judgment of you. But he who
sent me is reliable,[k] and what I have 8:26 [k]Jn 7:28 [l]Jn 3:32; 15:15
heard from him I tell the world."[l]
27They did not understand that he
was telling them about his Father. 28So
Jesus said, "When you have lifted up
the Son of Man,[m] then you will know 8:28 [m]Jn 3:14; 5:19; 12:32
that I am ⌊the one I claim to be⌋ and that
I do nothing on my own but speak just
what the Father has taught me. 29The
one who sent me is with me; he has

[a]*52* Two early manuscripts *the Prophet* [b]*24* Or *I am he*; also in verse 28

not left me alone,[n] for I always do what
pleases him."[o] 30Even as he spoke, many
put their faith in him.[p]

The Children of Abraham

31To the Jews who had believed him,
Jesus said, "If you hold to my teaching,[q]
you are really my disciples. 32Then you
will know the truth, and the truth will
set you free."[r]
33They answered him, "We are Abraham's descendants[a][s] and have never
been slaves of anyone. How can you say
that we shall be set free?"
34Jesus replied, "I tell you the truth,
everyone who sins is a slave to sin.[t]
35Now a slave has no permanent place
in the family, but a son belongs to it
forever.[u] 36So if the Son sets you free,
you will be free indeed. 37I know you
are Abraham's descendants. Yet you are
ready to kill me,[v] because you have
no room for my word. 38I am telling
you what I have seen in the Father's
presence,[w] and you do what you have
heard from your father.[b]"
39"Abraham is our father," they
answered.
"If you were Abraham's children,"[x]
said Jesus, "then you would[c] do the
things Abraham did. 40As it is, you are
determined to kill me, a man who has
told you the truth that I heard from
God.[y] Abraham did not do such things.
41You are doing the things your own father does."[z]
"We are not illegitimate children,"
they protested. "The only Father we
have is God himself."[a]

The Children of the Devil

42Jesus said to them, "If God were
your Father, you would love me,[b] for I
came from God[c] and now am here. I
have not come on my own;[d] but he sent
me.[e] 43Why is my language not clear
to you? Because you are unable to hear
what I say. 44You belong to your father,
the devil,[f] and you want to carry out
your father's desire.[g] He was a murderer from the beginning, not holding to
the truth, for there is no truth in him.
When he lies, he speaks his native language, for he is a liar and the father of
lies.[h] 45Yet because I tell the truth,[i] you
do not believe me! 46Can any of you
prove me guilty of sin? If I am telling
the truth, why don't you believe me?

8:29 [n]ver 16; Jn 16:32 [o]Jn 4:34; 5:30; 6:38
8:30 [p]Jn 7:31
8:31 [q]Jn 15:7; 2Jn 9
8:32 [r]Ro 8:2; Jas 2:12
8:33 [s]ver 37,39; Mt 3:9
8:34 [t]Ro 6:16; 2Pe 2:19
8:35 [u]Gal 4:30
8:37 [v]ver 39,40
8:38 [w]Jn 5:19,30; 14:10,24
8:39 [x]ver 37; Ro 9:7; Gal 3:7
8:40 [y]ver 26
8:41 [z]ver 38,44 [a]Isa 63:16; 64:8
8:42 [b]1Jn 5:1 [c]Jn 16:27; 17:8 [d]Jn 7:28 [e]Jn 3:17
8:44 [f]1Jn 3:8 [g]ver 38,41 [h]Ge 3:4
8:45 [i]Jn 18:37

47He who belongs to God hears what
God says.[j] The reason you do not hear
is that you do not belong to God."

The Claims of Jesus About Himself

48The Jews answered him, "Aren't we
right in saying that you are a Samaritan[k] and demon-possessed?"[l]
49"I am not possessed by a demon,"
said Jesus, "but I honor my Father and
you dishonor me. 50I am not seeking
glory for myself;[m] but there is one who
seeks it, and he is the judge. 51I tell you
the truth, if anyone keeps my word, he
will never see death."[n]
52At this the Jews exclaimed, "Now
we know that you are demon-possessed!
Abraham died and so did the prophets,
yet you say that if anyone keeps your
word, he will never taste death. 53Are
you greater than our father Abraham?[o]
He died, and so did the prophets. Who
do you think you are?"
54Jesus replied, "If I glorify myself,[p]
my glory means nothing. My Father,
whom you claim as your God, is the
one who glorifies me.[q] 55Though you
do not know him,[r] I know him.[s] If I
said I did not, I would be a liar like you,
but I do know him and keep his word.[t]
56Your father Abraham[u] rejoiced at the
thought of seeing my day; he saw it[v]
and was glad."
57"You are not yet fifty years old,"
the Jews said to him, "and you have
seen Abraham!"
58"I tell you the truth," Jesus answered, "before Abraham was born,[w] I
am!"[x] 59At this, they picked up stones to
stone him,[y] but Jesus hid himself,[z] slipping away from the temple grounds.

Jesus Heals a Man Born Blind

9 As he went along, he saw a man
blind from birth. 2His disciples
asked him, "Rabbi,[a] who sinned,[b] this
man[c] or his parents,[d] that he was born
blind?"
3"Neither this man nor his parents
sinned," said Jesus, "but this happened
so that the work of God might be displayed in his life.[e] 4As long as it is day,[f]
we must do the work of him who sent

[a]*33* Greek *seed;* also in verse 37 [b]*38* Or *presence. Therefore do what you have heard from the Father.* [c]*39* Some early manuscripts *"If you are Abraham's children," said Jesus, "then*

8:47 [j]Jn 18:37; 1Jn 4:6
8:48 [k]Mt 10:5 [l]ver 52; Jn 7:20
8:50 [m]ver 54; Jn 5:41
8:51 [n]Jn 11:26
8:53 [o]Jn 4:12
8:54 [p]ver 50 [q]Jn 16:14; 17:1,5
8:55 [r]ver 19 [s]Jn 7:28,29 [t]Jn 15:10
8:56 [u]ver 37,39 [v]Mt 13:17; Heb 11:13
8:58 [w]Jn 1:2; 17:5,24 [x]Ex 3:14
8:59 [y]Lev 24:16; Jn 10:31; 11:8 [z]Jn 12:36
9:2 [a]Mt 23:7 [b]ver 34; Lk 13:2; Ac 28:4 [c]Eze 18:20 [d]Ex 20:5; Job 21:19
9:3 [e]Jn 11:4
9:4 [f]Jn 11:9; 12:35

me. Night is coming, when no one can
work. 5While I am in the world, I am
the light of the world."[g]
6Having said this, he spit[h] on the
ground, made some mud with the saliva, and put it on the man's eyes.
7"Go," he told him, "wash in the Pool
of Siloam"[i] (this word means Sent). So
the man went and washed, and came
home seeing.[j]
8His neighbors and those who had
formerly seen him begging asked, "Isn't
this the same man who used to sit and
beg?"[k] 9Some claimed that he was.
Others said, "No, he only looks like
him."
But he himself insisted, "I am the
man."
10"How then were your eyes opened?"
they demanded.
11He replied, "The man they call Jesus made some mud and put it on my
eyes. He told me to go to Siloam and
wash. So I went and washed, and then I
could see."[l]
12"Where is this man?" they asked
him.
"I don't know," he said.

The Pharisees Investigate the Healing

13They brought to the Pharisees the
man who had been blind. 14Now the
day on which Jesus had made the
mud and opened the man's eyes was
a Sabbath.[m] 15Therefore the Pharisees
also asked him how he had received his
sight.[n] "He put mud on my eyes," the
man replied, "and I washed, and now I
see."
16Some of the Pharisees said, "This
man is not from God, for he does not
keep the Sabbath."[o]
But others asked, "How can a sinner
do such miraculous signs?" So they were
divided.[p]
17Finally they turned again to the
blind man, "What have you to say about
him? It was your eyes he opened."
The man replied, "He is a prophet."[q]
18The Jews[r] still did not believe that
he had been blind and had received his
sight until they sent for the man's parents. 19"Is this your son?" they asked.
"Is this the one you say was born blind?
How is it that now he can see?"
20"We know he is our son," the parents answered, "and we know he was
born blind. 21But how he can see now,
or who opened his eyes, we don't know.
Ask him. He is of age; he will speak
for himself." 22His parents said this because they were afraid of the Jews,[s] for
already the Jews had decided that anyone who acknowledged that Jesus was
the Christ[a] would be put out[t] of the
synagogue.[u] 23That was why his parents
said, "He is of age; ask him."[v]
24A second time they summoned the
man who had been blind. "Give glory
to God,[b]"[w] they said. "We know this
man is a sinner."[x]
25He replied, "Whether he is a sinner
or not, I don't know. One thing I do
know. I was blind but now I see!"

PEACE

BEYOND DEFINITION

John 9:25

Christ is peace, surpassing definition.
Taste and see that the Lord is beyond all defining.
Who would wait to understand a melon before enjoying its sweetness?
Enjoy the stars before you take a class in astronomy.
Relish the inner Christ without waiting to understand the incarnation.

26Then they asked him, "What did
he do to you? How did he open your
eyes?"
27He answered, "I have told you already[y] and you did not listen. Why do
you want to hear it again? Do you want
to become his disciples, too?"
28Then they hurled insults at him
and said, "You are this fellow's disciple!
We are disciples of Moses![z] 29We know
that God spoke to Moses, but as for
this fellow, we don't even know where
he comes from."[a]
30The man answered, "Now that is
remarkable! You don't know where he
comes from, yet he opened my eyes.
31We know that God does not listen
to sinners. He listens to the godly man
who does his will.[b] 32Nobody has ever
heard of opening the eyes of a man
born blind. 33If this man were not from
God,[c] he could do nothing."

[a]22 Or *Messiah* [b]24 A solemn charge to tell the truth (see Joshua 7:19)

9:5 [g]Jn 1:4; 8:12; 12:46
9:6 [h]Mk 7:33; 8:23
9:7 [i]ver 11; 2Ki 5:10; Lk 13:4 [j]Isa 35:5; Jn 11:37
9:8 [k]Ac 3:2,10
9:11 [l]ver 7
9:14 [m]Jn 5:9
9:15 [n]ver 10
9:16 [o]Mt 12:2 [p]Jn 6:52; 7:43; 10:19
9:17 [q]Mt 21:11
9:18 [r]Jn 1:19
9:22 [s]Jn 7:13 [t]ver 34; Lk 6:22 [u]Jn 12:42; 16:2
9:23 [v]ver 21
9:24 [w]Jos 7:19 [x]ver 16
9:27 [y]ver 15
9:28 [z]Jn 5:45
9:29 [a]Jn 8:14
9:31 [b]Ge 18:23-32; Ps 34:15,16; 66:18; 145:19,20; Pr 15:29; Isa 1:15; 59:1,2; Jn 15:7; Jas 5:16-18; 1Jn 5:14,15
9:33 [c]ver 16; Jn 3:2

34To this they replied, "You were steeped in sin at birth;[d] how dare you lecture us!" And they threw him out.[e]

Spiritual Blindness

35Jesus heard that they had thrown him out, and when he found him, he said, "Do you believe in the Son of Man?"

36"Who is he, sir?" the man asked. "Tell me so that I may believe in him."[f]

37Jesus said, "You have now seen him; in fact, he is the one speaking with you."[g]

38Then the man said, "Lord, I believe," and he worshiped him.[h]

39Jesus said, "For judgment[i] I have come into this world,[j] so that the blind will see and those who see[k] will become blind."[l]

40Some Pharisees who were with him heard him say this and asked, "What? Are we blind too?"[m]

41Jesus said, "If you were blind, you would not be guilty of sin; but now that you claim you can see, your guilt remains."[n]

The Shepherd and His Flock

10 "I tell you the truth, the man who does not enter the sheep pen by the gate, but climbs in by some other way, is a thief and a robber. 2The man who enters by the gate is the shepherd of his sheep.[o] 3The watchman opens the gate for him, and the sheep listen to his voice.[p] He calls his own sheep by name and leads them out. 4When he has brought out all his own, he goes on ahead of them, and his sheep follow him because they know his voice. 5But they will never follow a stranger; in fact, they will run away from him because they do not recognize a stranger's voice." 6Jesus used this figure of speech,[q] but they did not understand what he was telling them.

7Therefore Jesus said again, "I tell you the truth, I am the gate for the sheep. 8All who ever came before me[r] were thieves and robbers, but the sheep did not listen to them. 9I am the gate; whoever enters through me will be saved.[a] He will come in and go out, and find pasture. 10The thief comes only to steal and kill and destroy; I have come that they may have life, and have it to the full.

11"I am the good shepherd.[s] The good shepherd lays down his life for the sheep.[t] 12The hired hand is not the shepherd who owns the sheep. So when he sees the wolf coming, he abandons the sheep and runs away.[u] Then the wolf attacks the flock and scatters it. 13The man runs away because he is a hired hand and cares nothing for the sheep.

[a]9 Or *kept safe*

9:34 [d]ver 2 [e]ver 22,35; Isa 66:5
9:36 [f]Ro 10:14
9:37 [g]Jn 4:26
9:38 [h]Mt 28:9
9:39 [i]Jn 5:22 [j]Jn 3:19 [k]Lk 4:18 [l]Mt 13:13
9:40 [m]Ro 2:19
9:41 [n]Jn 15:22,24
10:2 [o]ver 11,14
10:3 [p]ver 4,5,14,16,27
10:6 [q]Jn 16:25
10:8 [r]Jer 23:1,2
10:11 [s]ver 14; Isa 40:11; Eze 34:11-16,23; Heb 13:20; 1Pe 5:4; Rev 7:17 [t]Jn 15:13; 1Jn 3:16
10:12 [u]Zec 11:16,17

DAY 3 THREE

Faithfulness and My Relationship With Christ

John 9:24–34

The man who had been born blind had a stubborn commitment to what was right. He had just come into relationship with Christ, and his new relationship was fueled by the fact that he had just been given what he had never had before—sight! Now he is ignited with a stubborn commitment to the two things he knows. He can see, and Jesus' face was the first he ever saw. His is an elementary catechism, but he is fond of celebrating these two realities. Consider the song he might have sung:

I have a gift that makes these
caustic Pharisees seem over-dreary.
I can see the greens and blues of God's
great world better than these men
of God, so long focusing their narrow-
slitted eyes on ink and paper.
It is good to read his word,
and the Pharisees can do it well.
But who would read of God when they
might have him in for dinner?
This is the sin of learned men: They study
in the dim light of sooty rooms,
While God is circling with the white
gulls against the blue-fire dawn of sky.
How poor are they who cannot look up
from dull dogma and see that
God is seated at the very table where
they sit.

To begin a study on the topic of Faithfulness, a Stubborn Commitment to the Right, turn to the home page on page 398.

14“I am the good shepherd;[v] I know my sheep[w] and my sheep know me— 15just as the Father knows me and I know the Father[x]—and I lay down my life for the sheep. 16I have other sheep[y] that are not of this sheep pen. I must bring them also. They too will listen to my voice, and there shall be one flock[z] and one shepherd.[a] 17The reason my Father loves me is that I lay down my life[b]—only to take it up again. 18No one takes it from me, but I lay it down of my own accord.[c] I have authority to lay it down and authority to take it up again. This command I received from my Father.”[d]

19At these words the Jews were again divided.[e] 20Many of them said, “He is demon-possessed[f] and raving mad.[g] Why listen to him?”

21But others said, “These are not the sayings of a man possessed by a demon.[h] Can a demon open the eyes of the blind?”[i]

10:14 [v]ver 11 [w]ver 27
10:15 [x]Mt 11:27
10:16 [y]Isa 56:8 [z]Jn 11:52; Eph 2:11-19 [a]Eze 37:24; 1Pe 2:25
10:17 [b]ver 11,15,18
10:18 [c]Mt 26:53 [d]Jn 15:10; Php 2:8; Heb 5:8
10:19 [e]Jn 7:43; 9:16
10:20 [f]Jn 7:20 [g]Mk 3:21
10:21 [h]Mt 4:24 [i]Ex 4:11; Jn 9:32,33

The Unbelief of the Jews

22Then came the Feast of Dedication[a] at Jerusalem. It was winter, 23and Jesus was in the temple area walking in Solomon's Colonnade.[j] 24The Jews[k] gathered around him, saying, “How long will you keep us in suspense? If you are the Christ,[b] tell us plainly.”[l]

10:23 [j]Ac 3:11; 5:12
10:24 [k]Jn 1:19 [l]Jn 16:25,29

LOVE

CROSS LOVE

John 10:25–26

Do you doubt his love for you? Look upon the bloody wood and stop doubting.

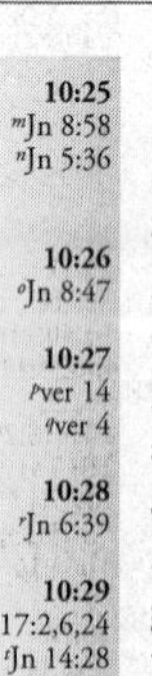

25Jesus answered, “I did tell you,[m] but you do not believe. The miracles I do in my Father's name speak for me,[n] 26but you do not believe because you are not my sheep.[o] 27My sheep listen to my voice; I know them,[p] and they follow me.[q] 28I give them eternal life, and they shall never perish; no one can snatch them out of my hand.[r] 29My Father, who has given them to me,[s] is greater than all[c];[t] no one can snatch them out of my Father's hand. 30I and the Father are one.”[u]

31Again the Jews picked up stones to stone him,[v] 32but Jesus said to them, “I have shown you many great miracles from the Father. For which of these do you stone me?”

33“We are not stoning you for any of these,” replied the Jews, “but for blasphemy, because you, a mere man, claim to be God.”[w]

34Jesus answered them, “Is it not written in your Law,[x] ‘I have said you are gods’[d]?[y] 35If he called them ‘gods,’ to whom the word of God came—and the Scripture cannot be broken— 36what about the one whom the Father set apart[z] as his very own[a] and sent into the world?[b] Why then do you accuse me of blasphemy because I said, ‘I am God's Son’?[c] 37Do not believe me unless I do what my Father does.[d] 38But if I do it, even though you do not believe me, believe the miracles, that you may know and understand that the Father is in me, and I in the Father.”[e] 39Again they tried to seize him,[f] but he escaped their grasp.[g]

40Then Jesus went back across the Jordan[h] to the place where John had been baptizing in the early days. Here he stayed 41and many people came to him. They said, “Though John never performed a miraculous sign,[i] all that John said about this man was true.”[j] 42And in that place many believed in Jesus.[k]

10:25 [m]Jn 8:58 [n]Jn 5:36
10:26 [o]Jn 8:47
10:27 [p]ver 14 [q]ver 4
10:28 [r]Jn 6:39
10:29 [s]Jn 17:2,6,24 [t]Jn 14:28
10:30 [u]Jn 17:21-23
10:31 [v]Jn 8:59
10:33 [w]Lev 24:16; Jn 5:18
10:34 [x]Jn 8:17; Ro 3:19 [y]Ps 82:6
10:36 [z]Jer 1:5 [a]Jn 6:69 [b]Jn 3:17 [c]Jn 5:17,18
10:37 [d]ver 25; Jn 15:24
10:38 [e]Jn 14:10,11, 20; 17:21
10:39 [f]Jn 7:30 [g]Lk 4:30; Jn 8:59
10:40 [h]Jn 1:28
10:41 [i]Jn 2:11; 3:30 [j]Jn 1:26,27, 30,34
10:42 [k]Jn 7:31

The Death of Lazarus

11 Now a man named Lazarus was sick. He was from Bethany,[l] the village of Mary and her sister Martha.[m] 2This Mary, whose brother Lazarus now lay sick, was the same one who poured perfume on the Lord and wiped his feet with her hair.[n] 3So the sisters sent word to Jesus, “Lord, the one you love[o] is sick.”

4When he heard this, Jesus said, “This sickness will not end in death. No, it is for God's glory[p] so that God's Son may be glorified through it.” 5Jesus loved Martha and her sister and Lazarus. 6Yet when he heard that Lazarus was sick, he stayed where he was two more days.

7Then he said to his disciples, “Let us go back to Judea.”[q]

8“But Rabbi,”[r] they said, “a short while ago the Jews tried to stone you,[s] and yet you are going back there?”

11:1 [l]Mt 21:17 [m]Lk 10:38
11:2 [n]Mk 14:3; Lk 7:38; Jn 12:3
11:3 [o]ver 5,36
11:4 [p]ver 40; Jn 9:3
11:7 [q]Jn 10:40
11:8 [r]Mt 23:7 [s]Jn 8:59; 10:31

[a]*22* That is, Hanukkah [b]*24* Or *Messiah* [c]*29* Many early manuscripts *What my Father has given me is greater than all* [d]*34* Psalm 82:6

9 Jesus answered, "Are there not twelve
hours of daylight? A man who walks by
day will not stumble, for he sees by this
11:9 world's light.[t] 10 It is when he walks by
[t]Jn 9:4; 12:35 night that he stumbles, for he has no
light."
11 After he had said this, he went on
11:11 to tell them, "Our friend[u] Lazarus has
[u]ver 3 fallen asleep;[v] but I am going there to
[v]Ac 7:60 wake him up."
12 His disciples replied, "Lord, if he
sleeps, he will get better." 13 Jesus had
been speaking of his death, but his dis-
11:13 ciples thought he meant natural sleep.[w]
[w]Mt 9:24 14 So then he told them plainly, "Lazarus is dead, 15 and for your sake I am
glad I was not there, so that you may
11:16 believe. But let us go to him."
[x]Mt 10:3; Jn 14:5; 16 Then Thomas[x] (called Didymus)
20:24-28; 21:2; said to the rest of the disciples, "Let us
Ac 1:13 also go, that we may die with him."

FAITHFULNESS

URBAN PHOBIA

John 11:16

Thomas was afraid of the city. There public opinion was large, sudden and violent. There, in Jerusalem, Jesus' enemies lay in wait. There was safety outside the city. But redemption rarely walks where things are safe. Those who follow Jesus only when life is safe are more infatuated than in love.

Jesus Comforts the Sisters

17 On his arrival, Jesus found that
Lazarus had already been in the tomb
11:17 for four days.[y] 18 Bethany[z] was less than
[y]ver 6,39 two miles[a] from Jerusalem, 19 and many
11:18 Jews had come to Martha and Mary
[z]ver 1 to comfort them in the loss of their
11:19 brother.[a] 20 When Martha heard that Je-
[a]ver 31; Job 2:11 sus was coming, she went out to meet
him, but Mary stayed at home.[b]
11:20 21 "Lord," Martha said to Jesus, "if
[b]Lk 10:38-42 you had been here, my brother would
11:21 not have died.[c] 22 But I know that even
[c]ver 32,37 now God will give you whatever you
11:22 ask."[d]
[d]ver 41,42; Jn 9:31 23 Jesus said to her, "Your brother will
rise again."
24 Martha answered, "I know he will
11:24 rise again in the resurrection[e] at the
[e]Da 12:2; Jn 5:28,29; Ac 24:15 last day."
25 Jesus said to her, "I am the resur-
11:25 [f]Jn 1:4 rection and the life.[f] He who believes
in me will live, even though he dies;
26 and whoever lives and believes in me
will never die. Do you believe this?"
27 "Yes, Lord," she told him, "I be-
lieve that you are the Christ,[b][g] the Son 11:27 [g]Lk 2:11
of God,[h] who was to come into the [h]Mt 16:16
world."[i] [i]Jn 6:14
28 And after she had said this, she
went back and called her sister Mary
aside. "The Teacher[j] is here," she said, 11:28
"and is asking for you." 29 When Mary [j]Mt 26:18; Jn 13:13
heard this, she got up quickly and went
to him. 30 Now Jesus had not yet entered
the village, but was still at the place
where Martha had met him.[k] 31 When 11:30 [k]ver 20
the Jews who had been with Mary in
the house, comforting her,[l] noticed how 11:31 [l]ver 19
quickly she got up and went out, they
followed her, supposing she was going
to the tomb to mourn there.
32 When Mary reached the place
where Jesus was and saw him, she fell
at his feet and said, "Lord, if you had
been here, my brother would not have
died."[m] 11:32 [m]ver 21
33 When Jesus saw her weeping, and
the Jews who had come along with her
also weeping, he was deeply moved[n] in 11:33 [n]ver 38
spirit and troubled.[o] 34 "Where have you [o]Jn 12:27
laid him?" he asked.
"Come and see, Lord," they replied.
35 Jesus wept.[p] 11:35 [p]Lk 19:41
36 Then the Jews said, "See how he
loved him!"[q] 11:36 [q]ver 3
37 But some of them said, "Could
not he who opened the eyes of the
blind man have kept this man[r] from 11:37 [r]Jn 9:6,7
dying?"[s] [s]ver 21,32

Jesus Raises Lazarus From the Dead

38 Jesus, once more deeply moved,[t] 11:38 [t]ver 33
came to the tomb. It was a cave with a [u]Mt 27:60; Lk 24:2;
stone laid across the entrance.[u] 39 "Take Jn 20:1
away the stone," he said.
"But, Lord," said Martha, the sister
of the dead man, "by this time there
is a bad odor, for he has been there
four days."[v] 11:39 [v]ver 17
40 Then Jesus said, "Did I not tell you
that if you believed,[w] you would see the 11:40 [w]ver 23-25
glory of God?"[x] [x]ver 4
41 So they took away the stone. Then
Jesus looked up[y] and said, "Father,[z] I 11:41 [y]Jn 17:1
thank you that you have heard me. 42 I [z]Mt 11:25

[a] *18* Greek *fifteen stadia* (about 3 kilometers)
[b] *27* Or *Messiah*

KINDNESS

WHAT IS KINDNESS TO A DEAD MAN?

John 11:43

Jesus ordered Lazarus back into the world. Lazarus probably didn't want to come back into this world because the world he would have had to leave was so much better. It is not an act of kindness to be resurrected to a world one would rather not return to. Perhaps that's why Jesus wept. Perhaps Lazarus woke up weeping.

knew that you always hear me, but I
said this for the benefit of the people
11:42 standing here,[a] that they may believe
[a]Jn 12:30 [b]Jn 3:17 that you sent me."[b]
43When he had said this, Jesus called
11:43 [c]Lk 7:14 in a loud voice, "Lazarus, come out!"[c]
44The dead man came out, his hands
11:44 [d]Jn 19:40 and feet wrapped with strips of linen,[d]
[e]Jn 20:7 and a cloth around his face.[e]
Jesus said to them, "Take off the
grave clothes and let him go."

The Plot to Kill Jesus

45Therefore many of the Jews who
11:45 [f]ver 19 had come to visit Mary,[f] and had
[g]Jn 2:23 seen what Jesus did,[g] put their faith
[h]Ex 14:31; Jn 7:31 in him.[h] 46But some of them went to
the Pharisees and told them what Jesus
had done. 47Then the chief priests and
11:47 [i]ver 57 the Pharisees[i] called a meeting[j] of the
[j]Mt 26:3 [k]Mt 5:22 Sanhedrin.[k]
[l]Jn 2:11 "What are we accomplishing?" they
asked. "Here is this man performing
many miraculous signs.[l] 48If we let him
go on like this, everyone will believe in
him, and then the Romans will come
and take away both our place[a] and our
nation."
49Then one of them, named Caia-
11:49 phas,[m] who was high priest that year,[n]
[m]Mt 26:3 [n]ver 51; Jn 18:13,14 spoke up, "You know nothing at all!
50You do not realize that it is better for
you that one man die for the people
11:50 [o]Jn 18:14 than that the whole nation perish."[o]
51He did not say this on his own, but
as high priest that year he prophesied
that Jesus would die for the Jewish nation, 52and not only for that nation but
11:52 [p]Isa 49:6; Jn 10:16 also for the scattered children of God,
to bring them together and make them
11:53 one.[p] 53So from that day on they plot-
[q]Mt 12:14 ted to take his life.[q]

54Therefore Jesus no longer moved
about publicly among the Jews.[r] Instead 11:54 [r]Jn 7:1
he withdrew to a region near the desert,
to a village called Ephraim, where he
stayed with his disciples.
55When it was almost time for the
Jewish Passover,[s] many went up from 11:55 [s]Ex 12:13, 23,27;
the country to Jerusalem for their cer- Mt 26:1,2;
emonial cleansing[t] before the Passover. Mk 14:1;
56They kept looking for Jesus,[u] and as Jn 13:1
they stood in the temple area they asked [t]2Ch 30:17, 18
one another, "What do you think? Isn't
he coming to the Feast at all?" 57But the 11:56 [u]Jn 7:11
chief priests and Pharisees had given or-
ders that if anyone found out where Jesus was, he should report it so that they
might arrest him.

Jesus Anointed at Bethany

12 Six days before the Passover,[v] Je-
sus arrived at Bethany,[w] where 12:1 [v]Jn 11:55 [w]Mt 21:17
Lazarus lived, whom Jesus had raised
from the dead. 2Here a dinner was given 12:2 [x]Lk 10:38-42
in Jesus' honor. Martha served,[x] while
Lazarus was among those reclining at
the table with him. 3Then Mary took
about a pint[b] of pure nard, an expensive
perfume;[y] she poured it on Jesus' feet 12:3 [y]Mk 14:3
and wiped his feet with her hair.[z] And [z]Jn 11:2
the house was filled with the fragrance
of the perfume.
4But one of his disciples, Judas Iscar-
iot, who was later to betray him,[a] ob- 12:4 [a]Mt 10:4
jected, 5"Why wasn't this perfume sold
and the money given to the poor? It
was worth a year's wages.[c]" 6He did not
say this because he cared about the poor
but because he was a thief; as keeper of
the money bag,[b] he used to help him- 12:6 [b]Jn 13:29
self to what was put into it.
7"Leave her alone," Jesus replied. "It
was intended that she should save this
perfume for the day of my burial.[c] 8You 12:7 [c]Jn 19:40
will always have the poor among you,[d]
but you will not always have me." 12:8 [d]Dt 15:11
9Meanwhile a large crowd of Jews
found out that Jesus was there and
came, not only because of him but also
to see Lazarus, whom he had raised
from the dead.[e] 10So the chief priests 12:9 [e]Jn 11:43,44
made plans to kill Lazarus as well, 11for
on account of him[f] many of the Jews 12:11 [f]ver 17,18;
were going over to Jesus and putting Jn 11:45
their faith in him.[g] [g]Jn 7:31

[a]48 Or *temple* [b]3 Greek *a litra* (probably about 0.5 liter) [c]5 Greek *three hundred denarii*

The Triumphal Entry

[12]The next day the great crowd that had come for the Feast heard that Jesus was on his way to Jerusalem. [13]They took palm branches and went out to meet him, shouting,

"Hosanna![a]"

"Blessed is he who comes in the
name of the Lord!"[b h]

"Blessed is the King of Israel!"[i]

12:13 [h]Ps 118:25,26 [i]Jn 1:49

[14]Jesus found a young donkey and sat upon it, as it is written,

[15]"Do not be afraid, O Daughter of
Zion;
see, your king is coming,
seated on a donkey's colt."[c j]

[16]At first his disciples did not understand all this.[k] Only after Jesus was

12:15 [j]Zec 9:9
12:16 [k]Mk 9:32

[a]*13* A Hebrew expression meaning "Save!" which became an exclamation of praise [b]*13* Psalm 118:25,26 [c]*15* Zech. 9:9

MARY OF BETHANY

Joy, the Exhibitionist's Elation (12:1–8)

Mary of Bethany broke a vial of nard and poured this costly perfume on Jesus. After she had anointed his feet, she dried them with her hair. One can only imagine the state of heart that drove her to such exhibitionism. She was obviously a woman deeply in love with Christ.

Joy is hopelessly exhibitionist, for it is not an emotion to be kept in a bottle and released with propriety at a more controlled moment. Mary let go of propriety. Jesus was at hand. Extravagance owned the day. One cannot avoid being flamboyant when near the flame of love.

Didn't Miriam dance and play the tambourine after crossing the Red Sea unharmed (see Exodus 15:20)? Would you have rebuked Miriam and told her to adopt a more reflective kind of worship response? When the ark of the covenant was brought into Jerusalem, David danced before the Lord with all his might (see 2 Samuel 6:14–15). Would you have preferred that David had walked properly into the city, asking those around him to remain in silent prayer? If so, then you misunderstand the nature of joy.

Watch long-separated lovers reuniting in an airport. You may suggest that public embracing is not proper, but the joy of their reunion, not your counsel, dictates their actions. When joy visits us in full force, and we feel the zenith of elation, we may praise to a degree that causes us to break with "proper" behavior. Sometimes we lose the sense of "appropriate" behavior altogether.

Mary was a woman in love with Jesus. She broke the vial of perfume, and the aroma from the broken vial filled the whole house (see John 12:3). Watchman Nee used this Scripture passage to describe the beauty of brokenness. Mary may have been so broken that only her tears could have prompted her to such joy. But whether or not she was broken, there must have been an overwhelming feeling of gratitude in her heart that drove her to express such utter joy in her act of worship.

Her joy is a call to us. How wonderful it is to attend a worship service where the mood is one of unbridled joy. Joy was the delirium of the old-fashioned revivals during which God was so adored that the audience abandoned its sense of propriety in favor of exhilarating praise. This joyful delirium was, in its own special way, an anointing. It was a fragrance of sweet love, given freely and openly. Do you object, feeling that people ought to exercise more control when they praise God? Then read this passage again. When praise is directed toward Jesus as its sole object, it cares little about what anyone else might think. Joy creates its own right to existence. It cares about authenticity, never propriety.

Mary's joy was her anointing. Her action became a memorial for ages to come. It became a testament and symbol of joy. You may say she lacked propriety, and those who mind their manners will agree. But you will convince no one that she was a dour soul with little joy. History still smells the sweetness of her nard. Its aroma still freshens the air centuries later.

glorified[l] did they realize that these things had been written about him and that they had done these things to him.

17 Now the crowd that was with him[m] when he called Lazarus from the tomb and raised him from the dead continued to spread the word. 18 Many people, because they had heard that he had given this miraculous sign,[n] went out to meet him. 19 So the Pharisees said to one another, "See, this is getting us nowhere. Look how the whole world has gone after him!"[o]

Jesus Predicts His Death

20 Now there were some Greeks[p] among those who went up to worship at the Feast. 21 They came to Philip, who was from Bethsaida[q] in Galilee, with a request. "Sir," they said, "we would like to see Jesus." 22 Philip went to tell Andrew; Andrew and Philip in turn told Jesus.

23 Jesus replied, "The hour has come for the Son of Man to be glorified.[r] 24 I tell you the truth, unless a kernel of wheat falls to the ground and dies,[s] it remains only a single seed. But if it dies, it produces many seeds. 25 The man who loves his life will lose it, while the man who hates his life in this world will keep it[t] for eternal life. 26 Whoever serves me must follow me; and where I am, my servant also will be.[u] My Father will honor the one who serves me.

27 "Now my heart is troubled,[v] and what shall I say? 'Father,[w] save me from this hour'?[x] No, it was for this very reason I came to this hour. 28 Father, glorify your name!"

Then a voice came from heaven,[y] "I have glorified it, and will glorify it again." 29 The crowd that was there and heard it said it had thundered; others said an angel had spoken to him.

30 Jesus said, "This voice was for your benefit,[z] not mine. 31 Now is the time for judgment on this world;[a] now the prince of this world[b] will be driven out. 32 But I, when I am lifted up from the earth,[c] will draw all men to myself."[d] 33 He said this to show the kind of death he was going to die.[e]

34 The crowd spoke up, "We have heard from the Law that the Christ[a] will remain forever,[f] so how can you say, 'The Son of Man[g] must be lifted up'?[h] Who is this 'Son of Man'?"

35 Then Jesus told them, "You are going to have the light[i] just a little while longer. Walk while you have the light,[j] before darkness overtakes you.[k] The man who walks in the dark does not know where he is going. 36 Put your trust in the light while you have it, so that you may become sons of light."[l] When he had finished speaking, Jesus left and hid himself from them.[m]

The Jews Continue in Their Unbelief

37 Even after Jesus had done all these miraculous signs[n] in their presence, they still would not believe in him. 38 This was to fulfill the word of Isaiah the prophet:

"Lord, who has believed our message
and to whom has the arm of the
Lord been revealed?"[b][o]

39 For this reason they could not believe, because, as Isaiah says elsewhere:

40 "He has blinded their eyes
and deadened their hearts,
so they can neither see with their
eyes,
nor understand with their hearts,
nor turn—and I would heal
them."[c][p]

41 Isaiah said this because he saw Jesus' glory[q] and spoke about him.[r]

42 Yet at the same time many even among the leaders believed in him.[s] But because of the Pharisees[t] they would not confess their faith for fear they would be put out of the synagogue;[u] 43 for they

12:16 [l]Jn 2:22; 7:39; 14:26
12:17 [m]Jn 11:42
12:18 [n]ver 11
12:19 [o]Jn 11:47,48
12:20 [p]Jn 7:35; Ac 11:20
12:21 [q]Mt 11:21; Jn 1:44
12:23 [r]Jn 13:32; 17:1
12:24 [s]1Co 15:36
12:25 [t]Mt 10:39; Mk 8:35; Lk 14:26
12:26 [u]Jn 14:3; 17:24; 2Co 5:8; 1Th 4:17
12:27 [v]Mt 26:38,39; Jn 11:33,38; 13:21 [w]Mt 11:25 [x]ver 23
12:28 [y]Mt 3:17
12:30 [z]Jn 11:42
12:31 [a]Jn 16:11 [b]Jn 14:30; 16:11; 2Co 4:4; Eph 2:2; 1Jn 4:4
12:32 [c]ver 34; Jn 3:14; 8:28 [d]Jn 6:44
12:33 [e]Jn 18:32
12:34 [f]Ps 110:4; Isa 9:7; Eze 37:25; Da 7:14 [g]Mt 8:20 [h]Jn 3:14
12:35 [i]ver 46 [j]Eph 5:8 [k]1Jn 2:11
12:36 [l]Lk 16:8 [m]Jn 8:59
12:37 [n]Jn 2:11
12:38 [o]Isa 53:1; Ro 10:16
12:40 [p]Isa 6:10; Mt 13:13,15
12:41 [q]Isa 6:1-4 [r]Lk 24:27
12:42 [s]ver 11; Jn 7:48 [t]Jn 7:13 [u]Jn 9:22

LOVE

THE GREAT EITHER/OR OF HISTORY

John 12:27

Jesus could have asked God to save him, which would have seemed reasonable since no one at thirty-three years of age craves execution. Or he could have asked God to save the world, which was reasonable since earth is his love affair. God stood to serve the choice of Christ. Christ chose us. God wept. The seas ran red.

[a] *34* Or *Messiah* [b] *38* Isaiah 53:1 [c] *40* Isaiah 6:10

loved praise from men more than praise
12:43 [v]Jn 5:44 from God.[v]
[44]Then Jesus cried out, "When a man
believes in me, he does not believe in
12:44 [w]Mt 10:40; Jn 5:24 me only, but in the one who sent me.[w]
[45]When he looks at me, he sees the one
12:45 [x]Jn 14:9 who sent me.[x] [46]I have come into the
world as a light,[y] so that no one who
12:46 [y]Jn 1:4; 3:19; 8:12; 9:5 believes in me should stay in darkness.
[47]"As for the person who hears my
words but does not keep them, I do not
judge him. For I did not come to judge
12:47 [z]Jn 3:17 the world, but to save it.[z] [48]There is a
judge for the one who rejects me and
does not accept my words; that very
12:48 [a]Jn 5:45 word which I spoke will condemn him[a]
at the last day. [49]For I did not speak
12:49 [b]Jn 14:31 of my own accord, but the Father who
sent me commanded me[b] what to say
and how to say it. [50]I know that his
command leads to eternal life. So whatever I say is just what the Father has
told me to say."

Jesus Washes His Disciples' Feet

13:1 [c]Jn 11:55 [d]Jn 12:23 [e]Jn 16:28 **13** It was just before the Passover
Feast.[c] Jesus knew that the time
had come[d] for him to leave this world
and go to the Father.[e] Having loved
his own who were in the world, he
now showed them the full extent of his
love.[a]
[2]The evening meal was being served,
and the devil had already prompted
Judas Iscariot, son of Simon, to betray
Jesus. [3]Jesus knew that the Father had
13:3 [f]Mt 28:18 [g]Jn 8:42; 16:27,28,30 put all things under his power,[f] and
that he had come from God[g] and was
returning to God; [4]so he got up from
the meal, took off his outer clothing,
and wrapped a towel around his waist.
[5]After that, he poured water into a basin and began to wash his disciples'
13:5 [h]Lk 7:44 feet,[h] drying them with the towel that
was wrapped around him.
[6]He came to Simon Peter, who said
to him, "Lord, are you going to wash
my feet?"
[7]Jesus replied, "You do not realize
13:7 [i]ver 12 now what I am doing, but later you will
understand."[i]
[8]"No," said Peter, "you shall never
wash my feet."
Jesus answered, "Unless I wash you,
you have no part with me."
[9]"Then, Lord," Simon Peter replied,
"not just my feet but my hands and my
head as well!"

DAY FIVE

LOVE AND ITS PLACE IN MY PERSONAL WORSHIP

John 13:1–17

What would cause the King of heaven to wash the feet of earthlings? One force alone could make this happen: love. If love is the engine of John 13, then humility is the output. Jesus washes the disciples' feet and, in so doing, makes it clear that the servant is not greater than the master; neither is the one who is sent greater than the one who sends.

But what is humility? Is it the ability to put oneself down by sheer self-loathing? No, there is something quite different involved here. Humility isn't making a decision to wash people's feet because we ourselves are contemptible. Humility is not arrived at through some descent of our pride.

I know of only one authentic path to humility. It is to stand next to Christ and see that, by comparison with the King of heaven, we have a lot of reasons to be humble. This means that nothing Christ did could ever be too lowly for us to consider doing. If he could bind his waist with a towel, maybe we could learn the art as well.

Would we, like Peter, object that we could never permit the King of heaven to serve us in this way? Actually it is already too late for that. Jesus has fully redeemed us by purchasing for us a grand liberty, paid for by his own naked execution on the tree.

Now nothing is beneath our dignity. Now we are ready to worship him with our actions and our love. How can we worship? We can stand ready with a basin and towel.

To begin a study on the topic of Love, Permeating All We Do, turn to the home page on page 1372.

[10]Jesus answered, "A person who has
had a bath needs only to wash his feet;
his whole body is clean.[j] And you are 13:10 [j]Jn 15:3
clean, though not every one of you."
[11]For he knew who was going to betray
him, and that was why he said not every one was clean.
[12]When he had finished washing their

[a]1 Or *he loved them to the last*

feet, he put on his clothes and returned
13:13 to his place. "Do you understand what
[k]Jn 11:28 I have done for you?" he asked them.
[l]Lk 6:46; 13"You call me 'Teacher'[k] and 'Lord,'[l]
1Co 12:3; Php 2:11 and rightly so, for that is what I am.
13:14 14Now that I, your Lord and Teacher,
[m]1Pe 5:5 have washed your feet, you also should
13:15 wash one another's feet.[m] 15I have set
[n]Mt 11:29 you an example that you should do
13:16 as I have done for you.[n] 16I tell you
[o]Mt 10:24; Lk 6:40; the truth, no servant is greater than his
Jn 15:20 master,[o] nor is a messenger greater than
13:17 the one who sent him. 17Now that you
[p]Mt 7:24,25; Lk 11:28; know these things, you will be blessed
Jas 1:25 if you do them.[p]

GENTLENESS

THE BASIN AND THE TOWEL

John 13:14

Pride primps upon the stage and treasures cosmetics.
It competes to play kings before others.
Humility passes the theater queue,
Obsessed with a towel and a bowl.

Jesus Predicts His Betrayal

13:18 18"I am not referring to all of you;[q] I
[q]ver 10 know those I have chosen.[r] But this is
[r]Jn 15:16,19 to fulfill the scripture: 'He who shares
[s]Mt 26:23 my bread[s] has lifted up his heel[t] against
[t]Jn 6:70 [u]Ps 41:9 me.'[a][u]
19"I am telling you now before it
happens, so that when it does happen
13:19 you will believe[v] that I am He.[w] 20I tell
[v]Jn 14:29; 16:4 you the truth, whoever accepts anyone
[w]Jn 8:24 I send accepts me; and whoever accepts
me accepts the one who sent me."[x]
13:20 21After he had said this, Jesus was
[x]Mt 10:40; Lk 10:16 troubled in spirit[y] and testified, "I tell
13:21 you the truth, one of you is going to
[y]Jn 12:27 [z]Mt 26:21 betray me."[z]
22His disciples stared at one another,
at a loss to know which of them he
meant. 23One of them, the disciple
13:23 whom Jesus loved,[a] was reclining next
[a]Jn 19:26; 20:2; 21:7,20 to him. 24Simon Peter motioned to this
disciple and said, "Ask him which one
he means."
25Leaning back against Jesus, he asked
13:25 him, "Lord, who is it?"[b]
[b]Jn 21:20 26Jesus answered, "It is the one to
whom I will give this piece of bread
when I have dipped it in the dish."
Then, dipping the piece of bread, he
gave it to Judas Iscariot, son of Simon.
27As soon as Judas took the bread, Satan entered into him.[c] 13:27 [c]Lk 22:3
"What you are about to do, do
quickly," Jesus told him, 28but no one
at the meal understood why Jesus said
this to him. 29Since Judas had charge 13:29
of the money,[d] some thought Jesus was [d]Jn 12:6
telling him to buy what was needed
for the Feast, or to give something to
the poor. 30As soon as Judas had tak-
en the bread, he went out. And it was 13:30
night.[e] [e]Lk 22:53

Jesus Predicts Peter's Denial

31When he was gone, Jesus said, 13:31
"Now is the Son of Man glorified[f] and [f]Jn 7:39
God is glorified in him.[g] 32If God is [g]Jn 14:13; 17:4;
glorified in him,[b] God will glorify the 1Pe 4:11
Son in himself,[h] and will glorify him at 13:32
once. [h]Jn 17:1
33"My children, I will be with you 13:33
only a little longer. You will look for [i]Jn 7:33,34
me, and just as I told the Jews, so I tell 13:34
you now: Where I am going, you can- [j]1Jn 2:7-11; 3:11
not come.[i] [k]Lev 19:18;
34"A new command[j] I give you: Love 1Th 4:9;
one another.[k] As I have loved you, so 1Pe 1:22
you must love one another.[l] 35By this [l]Jn 15:12; Eph 5:2; 1Jn 4:10,11
all men will know that you are my dis-
ciples, if you love one another."[m] 13:35
36Simon Peter asked him, "Lord, [m]1Jn 3:14; 4:20
where are you going?" 13:36
Jesus replied, "Where I am going, [n]ver 33; Jn 14:2
you cannot follow now,[n] but you will [o]Jn 21:18,19;
follow later."[o] 2Pe 1:14

LOVE

ON LOVING THE FAMILY

John 13:35

Quarreling offspring embarrass their parents.
Siblings who scratch at each other's eyes
Suggest that their father is fickle and cruel,
The author of vengeance and lies.

37Peter asked, "Lord, why can't I follow you now? I will lay down my life
for you."
38Then Jesus answered, "Will you
really lay down your life for me? I tell
you the truth, before the rooster crows, 13:38
you will disown me three times![p] [p]Jn 18:27

[a]18 Psalm 41:9 [b]32 Many early manuscripts do not have *If God is glorified in him.*

Jesus Comforts His Disciples

14 "Do not let your hearts be
14:1 [q]ver 27 troubled.[q] Trust in God[a]; trust
also in me. [2]In my Father's house are
many rooms; if it were not so, I would
14:2 [r]Jn 13:33,36 have told you. I am going there[r] to prepare a place for you. [3]And if I go and
prepare a place for you, I will come
back and take you to be with me that
14:3 [s]Jn 12:26 you also may be where I am.[s] [4]You
know the way to the place where I am
going."

Jesus the Way to the Father

14:5 [t]Jn 11:16 [5]Thomas[t] said to him, "Lord, we
don't know where you are going, so
how can we know the way?"
14:6 [u]Jn 10:9 [6]Jesus answered, "I am the way[u] and
[v]Jn 11:25 the truth and the life.[v] No one comes to
the Father except through me. [7]If you
really knew me, you would know[b] my
14:7 [w]Jn 8:19 Father as well.[w] From now on, you do
know him and have seen him."
[8]Philip said, "Lord, show us the Father and that will be enough for us."
[9]Jesus answered: "Don't you know
me, Philip, even after I have been among
you such a long time? Anyone who has
14:9 [x]Jn 12:45; Col 1:15; Heb 1:3 seen me has seen the Father.[x] How can
you say, 'Show us the Father'? [10]Don't
you believe that I am in the Father, and
14:10 [y]Jn 10:38 that the Father is in me?[y] The words I
[z]Jn 5:19 say to you are not just my own.[z] Rather, it is the Father, living in me, who
is doing his work. [11]Believe me when I
14:11 [a]Jn 5:36; 10:38 say that I am in the Father and the Father is in me; or at least believe on the
14:12 [b]Mt 21:21 evidence of the miracles themselves.[a]
[12]I tell you the truth, anyone who has
faith[b] in me will do what I have been
doing.[c] He will do even greater things 14:12 [c]Lk 10:17
than these, because I am going to the
Father. [13]And I will do whatever you
ask[d] in my name, so that the Son may 14:13 [d]Mt 7:7
bring glory to the Father. [14]You may
ask me for anything in my name, and I
will do it.

Jesus Promises the Holy Spirit

[15]"If you love me, you will obey
what I command.[e] [16]And I will ask the 14:15 [e]ver 21,23; Jn 15:10; 1Jn 5:3
Father, and he will give you another
Counselor[f] to be with you forever— 14:16 [f]Jn 15:26; 16:7
[17]the Spirit of truth.[g] The world cannot
accept him,[h] because it neither sees him
nor knows him. But you know him, for 14:17 [g]Jn 15:26; 16:13; 1Jn 4:6 [h]1Co 2:14
he lives with you and will be[c] in you.
[18]I will not leave you as orphans; I will
come to you.[i] [19]Before long, the world 14:18 [i]ver 3,28
will not see me anymore, but you will
see me.[j] Because I live, you also will 14:19 [j]Jn 7:33,34; 16:16 [k]Jn 6:57
live.[k] [20]On that day you will realize that
I am in my Father,[l] and you are in
me, and I am in you. [21]Whoever has 14:20 [l]Jn 10:38
my commands and obeys them, he is
the one who loves me.[m] He who loves 14:21 [m]1Jn 5:3 [n]1Jn 2:5
me will be loved by my Father,[n] and I
too will love him and show myself to
him."
[22]Then Judas[o] (not Judas Iscariot) 14:22 [o]Lk 6:16; Ac 1:13 [p]Ac 10:41
said, "But, Lord, why do you intend
to show yourself to us and not to the
world?"[p]
[23]Jesus replied, "If anyone loves me, 14:23 [q]ver 15 [r]1Jn 2:24; Rev 3:20
he will obey my teaching.[q] My Father
will love him, and we will come to him
and make our home with him.[r] [24]He
who does not love me will not obey my
teaching. These words you hear are not
my own; they belong to the Father who
sent me.[s] 14:24 [s]Jn 7:16
[25]"All this I have spoken while still
with you. [26]But the Counselor,[t] the 14:26 [t]Jn 15:26; 16:7 [u]Ac 2:33 [v]Jn 16:13; 1Jn 2:20,27 [w]Jn 2:22
Holy Spirit, whom the Father will send
in my name,[u] will teach you all things[v]
and will remind you of everything I
have said to you.[w] [27]Peace I leave with
you; my peace I give you.[x] I do not give 14:27 [x]Jn 16:33; Php 4:7; Col 3:15
to you as the world gives. Do not let
your hearts be troubled and do not be
afraid.
[28]"You heard me say, 'I am going
away and I am coming back to you.'[y] If 14:28 [y]ver 2-4,18
you loved me, you would be glad that I

[a]*1* Or *You trust in God* [b]*7* Some early manuscripts *If you really have known me, you would know* [c]*17* Some early manuscripts *and is*

SELF-CONTROL

NAME IT AND ACCLAIM THE NAME

John 14:13

Ask and you shall receive an answer. God will give you what you ask unless he gives you what you didn't know enough to request. When it becomes apparent that you and God want different things, then enroll your appetites in his school of obedience. Want nothing than but to please him, and heaven will dispatch the answer. Be careful though; his pleasure sometimes ends at crosses.

14:28 [z]Jn 5:18 am going to the Father, for the Father[z]
[a]Jn 10:29; is greater than I.[a] 29I have told you now
Php 2:6 before it happens, so that when it does
14:29 happen you will believe.[b] 30I will not
[b]Jn 13:19; speak with you much longer, for the
16:4 prince of this world[c] is coming. He has
14:30 [c]Jn 12:31 no hold on me, 31but the world must
learn that I love the Father and that
14:31 I do exactly what my Father has com-
[d]Jn 10:18; 12:49 manded me.[d]
“Come now; let us leave.

The Vine and the Branches

15:1 [e]Isa 5:1-7 **15** “I am the true vine,[e] and my Father is the gardener. 2He cuts off
every branch in me that bears no fruit,
while every branch that does bear fruit
he prunes[a] so that it will be even more
fruitful. 3You are already clean because
15:3 [f]Jn 13:10; of the word I have spoken to you.[f]
17:17; 4Remain in me, and I will remain in
Eph 5:26 you.[g] No branch can bear fruit by it-
15:4 [g]Jn 6:56; self; it must remain in the vine. Neither
1Jn 2:6 can you bear fruit unless you remain
in me.

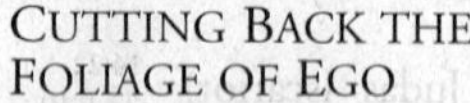

PEACE

CUTTING BACK THE FOLIAGE OF EGO

John 15:1–2

A grapevine is meant to grow grapes. When the vine produces nothing, its very purpose is frustrated. Then comes the pruning knife. It cuts. The vine bleeds. But in giving up its unproductive members, it later hangs heavy with fruit. Pain is the surgeon of the spirit. It amputates dead tissue to bring forth life.

5“I am the vine; you are the branches.
If a man remains in me and I in him,
15:5 [h]ver 16 he will bear much fruit;[h] apart from me
you can do nothing. 6If anyone does
not remain in me, he is like a branch
that is thrown away and withers; such
branches are picked up, thrown into the
15:6 [i]ver 2 fire and burned.[i] 7If you remain in me
and my words remain in you, ask what-
15:7 [j]Mt 7:7 ever you wish, and it will be given you.[j]
8This is to my Father’s glory,[k] that you
15:8 [k]Mt 5:16 bear much fruit, showing yourselves to
[l]Jn 8:31 be my disciples.[l]
9“As the Father has loved me,[m] so
15:9 [m]Jn 17:23, 24,26 have I loved you. Now remain in my
love. 10If you obey my commands,[n] you
15:10 [n]Jn 14:15 will remain in my love, just as I have
obeyed my Father’s commands and re-

PATIENCE

STAY CONNECTED

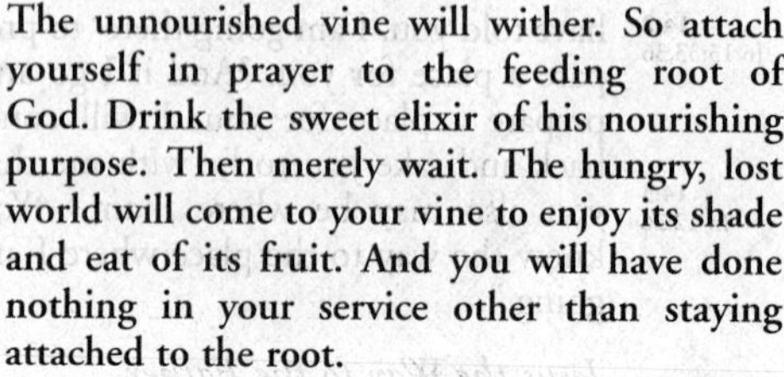

John 15:5

The unnourished vine will wither. So attach yourself in prayer to the feeding root of God. Drink the sweet elixir of his nourishing purpose. Then merely wait. The hungry, lost world will come to your vine to enjoy its shade and eat of its fruit. And you will have done nothing in your service other than staying attached to the root.

main in his love. 11I have told you this
so that my joy may be in you and that
your joy may be complete.[o] 12My com- 15:11 [o]Jn 17:13
mand is this: Love each other as I have
loved you.[p] 13Greater love has no one 15:12 [p]Jn 13:34
than this, that he lay down his life for
his friends.[q] 14You are my friends[r] if 15:13 [q]Jn 10:11;
you do what I command.[s] 15I no lon- Ro 5:7,8
ger call you servants, because a servant 15:14 [r]Lk 12:4
does not know his master’s business. In- [s]Mt 12:50
stead, I have called you friends, for everything that I learned from my Father
I have made known to you.[t] 16You did 15:15 [t]Jn 8:26
not choose me, but I chose you and
appointed you[u] to go and bear fruit— 15:16 [u]Jn 6:70;
fruit that will last. Then the Father 13:18
will give you whatever you ask in my
name. 17This is my command: Love 15:17
each other.[v] [v]ver 12

The World Hates the Disciples

18“If the world hates you,[w] keep in 15:18 [w]1Jn 3:13
mind that it hated me first. 19If you belonged to the world, it would love you
as its own. As it is, you do not belong to 15:19
the world, but I have chosen you[x] out of [x]ver 16
the world. That is why the world hates [y]Jn 17:14
you.[y] 20Remember the words I spoke
to you: ‘No servant is greater than his 15:20
master.’[b][z] If they persecuted me, they [z]Jn 13:16
will persecute you also.[a] If they obeyed [a]2Ti 3:12
my teaching, they will obey yours also.
21They will treat you this way because
of my name,[b] for they do not know the 15:21 [b]Mt; 10:22
One who sent me.[c] 22If I had not come [c]Jn 16:3
and spoken to them, they would not be
guilty of sin. Now, however, they have
no excuse for their sin.[d] 23He who hates 15:22 [d]Jn 9:41;
me hates my Father as well. 24If I had Ro 1:20
not done among them what no one else

[a]2 The Greek for *prunes* also means *cleans.*
[b]20 John 13:16

15:24 [e]Jn 5:36 did,[e] they would not be guilty of sin.
But now they have seen these miracles,
and yet they have hated both me and
my Father. 25But this is to fulfill what
15:25 [f]Ps 35:19; 69:4 is written in their Law: 'They hated me
without reason.'[a][f]

FAITHFULNESS

A SERVANT

John 15:20

A servant with ego is but the slave of arrogance.
A servant who will have no master is but a misnamed renegade.
But a servant who obeys is not greater than his lord.
Faithfulness is but a double-sided cross.
Jesus hangs upon the front;
His disciple, upon the back.

15:26 [g]Jn 14:16 [h]Jn 14:26 [i]Jn 14:17 [j]1Jn 5:7 26"When the Counselor[g] comes,
whom I will send to you from the
Father,[h] the Spirit of truth[i] who goes
out from the Father, he will testify
15:27 [k]Lk 24:48; 1Jn 1:2; 4:14 [l]Lk 1:2 about me.[j] 27And you also must testify,[k]
for you have been with me from the
beginning.[l]
16:1 [m]Jn 15:18-27 [n]Mt 11:6 16 "All this[m] I have told you so that
you will not go astray.[n] 2They
16:2 [o]Jn 9:22 [p]Isa 66:5; Ac 26:9,10; Rev 6:9 will put you out of the synagogue;[o] in
fact, a time is coming when anyone
who kills you will think he is offering
a service to God.[p] 3They will do such
16:3 [q]Jn 15:21; 17:25; 1Jn 3:1 things because they have not known the
Father or me.[q] 4I have told you this, so
16:4 [r]Jn 13:19 that when the time comes you will remember[r] that I warned you. I did not
tell you this at first because I was with
you.

The Work of the Holy Spirit

16:5 [s]Jn 7:33 [t]Jn 13:36; 14:5 5"Now I am going to him who sent
me,[s] yet none of you asks me, 'Where
are you going?'[t] 6Because I have said
these things, you are filled with grief.
7But I tell you the truth: It is for your
16:7 [u]Jn 14:16,26; 15:26 [v]Jn 7:39 good that I am going away. Unless I
go away, the Counselor[u] will not come
to you; but if I go, I will send him to
you.[v] 8When he comes, he will convict
16:9 [w]Jn 15:22 the world of guilt[b] in regard to sin and
righteousness and judgment: 9in regard
16:10 [x]Ac 3:14; 7:52; 1Pe 3:18 to sin,[w] because men do not believe in
me; 10in regard to righteousness,[x] be-
cause I am going to the Father, where

JOY

GIVE ME UP, RECEIVE ME BACK

John 16:7

Ascensions always come ahead of Pentecosts. The "going ups" of God are always just the overtures of his "coming downs." The breeze of his departure stirs the air of his return into gales of fire.

you can see me no longer; 11and in regard to judgment, because the prince of
this world[y] now stands condemned. 16:11 [y]Jn 12:31
12"I have much more to say to you,
more than you can now bear.[z] 13But 16:12 [z]Mk 4:33
when he, the Spirit of truth,[a] comes, he
will guide you into all truth.[b] He will 16:13 [a]Jn 14:17 [b]Jn 14:26
not speak on his own; he will speak only
what he hears, and he will tell you what
is yet to come. 14He will bring glory to
me by taking from what is mine and
making it known to you. 15All that be-
longs to the Father is mine.[c] That is 16:15 [c]Jn 17:10
why I said the Spirit will take from
what is mine and make it known to
you.
16"In a little while[d] you will see me 16:16 [d]Jn 7:33 [e]Jn 14:18-24
no more, and then after a little while
you will see me."[e]

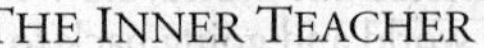

GOODNESS

THE INNER TEACHER

John 16:8

The arrival of the Holy Spirit brought an end to the era during which truth came from lectures. After Pentecost, truth was caught, not taught. It was a contagion of Calvary, a virus of victory that infected the entire world with love.

The Disciples' Grief Will Turn to Joy

17Some of his disciples said to one
another, "What does he mean by saying, 'In a little while you will see me
no more, and then after a little while
you will see me,'[f] and 'Because I am go- 16:17 [f]ver 16
ing to the Father'?"[g] 18They kept ask- [g]ver 5
ing, "What does he mean by 'a little
while'? We don't understand what he is
saying."

[a]25 Psalms 35:19; 69:4 [b]8 Or *will expose the guilt of the world*

19 Jesus saw that they wanted to ask him about this, so he said to them, "Are you asking one another what I meant when I said, 'In a little while you will see me no more, and then after a little while you will see me'? 20 I tell you the truth, you will weep and mourn[h] while the world rejoices. You will grieve, but your grief will turn to joy.[i] 21 A woman giving birth to a child has pain[j] because her time has come; but when her baby is born she forgets the anguish because of her joy that a child is born into the world. 22 So with you: Now is your time of grief,[k] but I will see you again[l] and you will rejoice, and no one will take away your joy. 23 In that day you will no longer ask me anything. I tell you the truth, my Father will give you whatever you ask in my name.[m] 24 Until now you have not asked for anything in my name. Ask and you will receive, and your joy will be complete.[n]

25 "Though I have been speaking figuratively,[o] a time is coming[p] when I will no longer use this kind of language but will tell you plainly about my Father. 26 In that day you will ask in my name.[q] I am not saying that I will ask the Father on your behalf. 27 No, the Father himself loves you because you have loved me[r] and have believed that I came from God. 28 I came from the Father and entered the world; now I am leaving the world and going back to the Father."[s]

29 Then Jesus' disciples said, "Now you are speaking clearly and without figures of speech.[t] 30 Now we can see that you know all things and that you do not even need to have anyone ask you questions. This makes us believe that you came from God."

31 "You believe at last!"[a] Jesus answered. 32 "But a time is coming,[u] and has come, when you will be scattered,[v] each to his own home. You will leave me all alone. Yet I am not alone, for my Father is with me.[w]

33 "I have told you these things, so that in me you may have peace.[x] In this world you will have trouble.[y] But take heart! I have overcome[z] the world."

16:20 [h]Lk 23:27 [i]Jn 20:20
16:21 [j]Isa 26:17; 1Th 5:3
16:22 [k]ver 6 [l]ver 16
16:23 [m]Mt 7:7; Jn 15:16
16:24 [n]Jn 3:29; 15:11
16:25 [o]Mt 13:34; Jn 10:6 [p]ver 2
16:26 [q]ver 23,24
16:27 [r]Jn 14:21,23
16:28 [s]Jn 13:3
16:29 [t]ver 25
16:32 [u]ver 2,25 [v]Mt 26:31 [w]Jn 8:16,29
16:33 [x]Jn 14:27 [y]Jn 15:18-21 [z]Ro 8:37; 1Jn 4:4

LOVE

THE DIALOGUE OF LOVE

John 17:1

The Father: Son, the time has come.
The Son: So soon?
The Father: Do you tremble at my requirement?
The Son: Yes, Father, I tremble.
The Father: In fear?
The Son: No, in the import of my mission.
The Father: The requirement of our loving shall bless the ages.
The Son: I understand. But will the nails hurt?
The Father: Yes—both of us.

Jesus Prays for Himself

17 After Jesus said this, he looked toward heaven[a] and prayed:

"Father, the time has come. Glorify your Son, that your Son may glorify you.[b] 2 For you granted him authority over all people that he might give eternal life to all those you have given him.[c] 3 Now this is eternal life: that they may know you, the only true God, and Jesus Christ, whom you have sent.[d] 4 I have brought you glory[e] on earth by completing the work you gave me to do.[f] 5 And now, Father, glorify me in your presence with the glory I had with you[g] before the world began.[h]

Jesus Prays for His Disciples

6 "I have revealed you[b][i] to those whom you gave me[j] out of the world. They were yours; you gave them to me and they have obeyed your word. 7 Now they know that everything you have given me comes from you. 8 For I gave them the words you gave me[k] and they accepted them. They knew with certainty that I came from you,[l] and they believed that you sent me.[m] 9 I pray for them.[n] I am not praying for the world, but for those you have given me, for they are yours. 10 All I have is yours, and all you have is mine.[o] And glory has come to me through them. 11 I will remain in the world no longer, but they are still in the world,[p] and I am coming to you.[q] Holy Father,

17:1 [a]Jn 11:41 [b]Jn 12:23; 13:31,32
17:2 [c]ver 6,9,24; Da 7:14; Jn 6:37,39
17:3 [d]ver 8,18,21, 23,25; Jn 3:17
17:4 [e]Jn 13:31 [f]Jn 4:34
17:5 [g]Php 2:6 [h]Jn 1:2
17:6 [i]ver 26 [j]ver 2; Jn 6:37,39
17:8 [k]ver 14,26 [l]Jn 16:27 [m]ver 3,18,21, 23,25; Jn 3:17
17:9 [n]Lk 22:32
17:10 [o]Jn 16:15
17:11 [p]Jn 13:1 [q]Jn 7:33

[a] 31 Or *"Do you now believe?"* [b] 6 Greek *your name*; also in verse 26

protect them by the power of your
name—the name you gave me—
so that they may be one[r] as we
are one.[s] 12While I was with them,
I protected them and kept them
safe by that name you gave me.
None has been lost[t] except the one
doomed to destruction[u] so that
Scripture would be fulfilled.
13"I am coming to you now, but
I say these things while I am still
in the world, so that they may
have the full measure of my joy[v]
within them. 14I have given them
your word and the world has hated them,[w] for they are not of the
world any more than I am of the
world.[x] 15My prayer is not that
you take them out of the world
but that you protect them from
the evil one.[y] 16They are not of
the world, even as I am not of
it.[z] 17Sanctify[a] them by the truth;
your word is truth.[a] 18As you sent
me into the world,[b] I have sent
them into the world.[c] 19For them I
sanctify myself, that they too may
be truly sanctified.

17:11 [r]ver 21-23 [s]Jn 10:30
17:12 [t]Jn 6:39 [u]Jn 6:70
17:13 [v]Jn 3:29
17:14 [w]Jn 15:19 [x]Jn 8:23
17:15 [y]Mt 5:37
17:16 [z]ver 14
17:17 [a]Jn 15:3
17:18 [b]ver 3,8,21, 23,25 [c]Jn 20:21

▸ PEACE

CAN PEOPLE SO VERY DIFFERENT BE ONE?

John 17:20–21

The Son: Can people so very different be one?

The Father: If they believe there is a truth greater than their own self-importance, then they may.

The Son: What is this truth so glorious that it overcomes all differences?

The Father: It is a truth that only your dying can illustrate.

The Son: Where will the world find this truth?

The Father: Beyond your naked execution.

Jesus Prays for All Believers

20"My prayer is not for them
alone. I pray also for those who
will believe in me through their
message, 21that all of them may be
one, Father, just as you are in me
and I am in you.[d] May they also be
in us so that the world may believe
that you have sent me.[e] 22I have
given them the glory that you gave
me, that they may be one as we
are one:[f] 23I in them and you in
me. May they be brought to complete unity to let the world know
that you sent me[g] and have loved
them[h] even as you have loved me.
24"Father, I want those you have
given me to be with me where I
am,[i] and to see my glory,[j] the glory you have given me because you
loved me before the creation of the
world.[k]

17:21 [d]Jn 10:38 [e]ver 3,8,18, 23,25; Jn 3:17
17:22 [f]Jn 14:20
17:23 [g]Jn 3:17 [h]Jn 16:27
17:24 [i]Jn 12:26 [j]Jn 1:14 [k]ver 5; Mt 25:34

▸ LOVE

THE PORTRAIT OF GOD

John 17:26

The Son: In 33 brief years I painted your portrait, O God!

The Father: Yes, your brushstrokes were so accurate that everyone knows exactly what love looks like.

The Son: Where was my studio?

The Father: Beyond the city walls, above the garden grave.

The Son: What my colors?

The Father: Your colors, scarlet grace.

The Son: In what resplendent place shall they hang this universal portrait?

The Father: Only the gallery of the heart can house the portrait of my love.

25"Righteous Father, though the
world does not know you,[l] I know
you, and they know that you have
sent me.[m] 26I have made you
known to them,[n] and will continue to make you known in order
that the love you have for me may
be in them[o] and that I myself may
be in them."

17:25 [l]Jn 15:21; 16:3 [m]ver 3,8,18, 21,23; Jn 3:17; 7:29; 16:27
17:26 [n]ver 6 [o]Jn 15:9

Jesus Arrested

18 When he had finished praying,
Jesus left with his disciples and
crossed the Kidron Valley.[p] On the other side there was an olive grove,[q] and he
and his disciples went into it.[r]
2Now Judas, who betrayed him, knew
the place, because Jesus had often met
there with his disciples.[s] 3So Judas came
to the grove, guiding[t] a detachment of

18:1 [p]2Sa 15:23 [q]ver 26 [r]Mt 26:36
18:2 [s]Lk 21:37; 22:39
18:3 [t]Ac 1:16

[a]*17* Greek *hagiazo (set apart for sacred use* or *make holy)*; also in verse 19

soldiers and some officials from the chief
18:3 [u]ver 12 priests and Pharisees.[u] They were carrying torches, lanterns and weapons.
18:4 [v]Jn 6:64; 13:1,11 [w]ver 7 4 Jesus, knowing all that was going to
happen to him,[v] went out and asked
them, "Who is it you want?"[w]

DAY 3 THREE

Kindness and My Relationship With Christ

John 18:10–11

Peter's motive in defense of his Lord may have seemed commendable in his own mind. But because his motives were likely anger and the desire for revenge, Jesus rebuked him and reminded him of the true nature of power and submission.

When it came to military style, Peter made a good fisherman. One might wonder why Peter immediately launched into a swashbuckling foray when not once in three years had Jesus given his disciples any training in the art of warfare. Jesus had, after all, called Peter to fish for men (see Matthew 4:19), not to hack up kingdom opponents. Had poor Malchus not lost an ear, the whole maneuver would have been humorous. Peter should have aimed his sword at something more visceral if he wanted to prove himself a soldier.

This ear-hacking cannot be considered by Malchus to have been kind. It's generally hard to like anyone who hacks off your ear and almost never possible to think of them as kind. But the worst aspect of this sin is that Jesus did not command Peter to do a little swashbuckling to prove his commitment. That was apparently Peter's idea.

Jesus, according to another account, healed Malchus's severed ear (see Luke 22:51), but the incident cannot have made Peter and Malchus best friends. It is hard to evangelize the earless, especially if we have made them so. Kindness leaves the ears intact. One wonders whether, far across the years, Peter didn't stop and laugh at his brash act of aggression. It must have been for him a reminder that, when one acts without Christ's command, he usually succeeds only in some foolish or regrettable conduct.

To begin a study on the topic of Kindness, Anger Washed by Grace, turn to the home page on page 751.

5 "Jesus of Nazareth," they replied.
"I am he," Jesus said. (And Judas the
traitor was standing there with them.)
6 When Jesus said, "I am he," they drew
back and fell to the ground.
7 Again he asked them, "Who is it
you want?"[x] 18:7 [x]ver 4
And they said, "Jesus of Nazareth."
8 "I told you that I am he," Jesus answered. "If you are looking for me, then
let these men go." 9 This happened so
that the words he had spoken would be
fulfilled: "I have not lost one of those
you gave me."[a][y] 18:9 [y]Jn 17:12
10 Then Simon Peter, who had a
sword, drew it and struck the high
priest's servant, cutting off his right ear.
(The servant's name was Malchus.)
11 Jesus commanded Peter, "Put your
sword away! Shall I not drink the cup[z] 18:11 [z]Mt 20:22
the Father has given me?"

Jesus Taken to Annas

12 Then the detachment of soldiers
with its commander and the Jewish of-
ficials[a] arrested Jesus. They bound him 18:12 [a]ver 3
13 and brought him first to Annas, who
was the father-in-law of Caiaphas,[b] the 18:13 [b]ver 24; Mt 26:3
high priest that year. 14 Caiaphas was
the one who had advised the Jews that
it would be good if one man died for 18:14 [c]Jn 11:49-51
the people.[c]

Peter's First Denial

15 Simon Peter and another disciple
were following Jesus. Because this dis- 18:15 [d]Mt 26:3
ciple was known to the high priest,[d] he [e]Mt 26:58;
went with Jesus into the high priest's Mk 14:54;
courtyard,[e] 16 but Peter had to wait out- Lk 22:54
side at the door. The other disciple, who
was known to the high priest, came
back, spoke to the girl on duty there
and brought Peter in.
17 "You are not one of his disciples,
are you?" the girl at the door asked
Peter.
He replied, "I am not."[f] 18:17 [f]ver 25
18 It was cold, and the servants and
officials stood around a fire[g] they had 18:18 [g]Jn 21:9
made to keep warm. Peter also was [h]Mk 14:54,67
standing with them, warming himself.[h]

The High Priest Questions Jesus

19 Meanwhile, the high priest questioned Jesus about his disciples and his
teaching.

[a] 9 John 6:39

20"I have spoken openly to the
world," Jesus replied. "I always taught
18:20 [i]Mt 4:23 in synagogues[i] or at the temple,[j] where
[j]Mt 26:55 all the Jews come together. I said noth-
[k]Jn 7:26 ing in secret.[k] 21Why question me? Ask
those who heard me. Surely they know
what I said."
18:22 22When Jesus said this, one of the of-
[l]ver 3; [m]Mt 16:21; ficials[l] nearby struck him in the face.[m]
Jn 19:3 "Is this the way you answer the high
priest?" he demanded.
23"If I said something wrong," Jesus
replied, "testify as to what is wrong. But
18:23 if I spoke the truth, why did you strike
[n]Mt 5:39; Ac 23:2-5 me?"[n] 24Then Annas sent him, still
18:24 [o]ver 13; bound, to Caiaphas[o] the high priest.[a]
Mt 26:3

Peter's Second and Third Denials

25As Simon Peter stood warming
18:25 [p]ver 18 himself,[p] he was asked, "You are not
[q]ver 17 one of his disciples, are you?"
He denied it, saying, "I am not."[q]
26One of the high priest's servants,
a relative of the man whose ear Peter
18:26 [r]ver 10 had cut off,[r] challenged him, "Didn't I
[s]ver 1 see you with him in the olive grove?"[s]
18:27 [t]Jn 13:38 27Again Peter denied it, and at that moment a rooster began to crow.[t]

Jesus Before Pilate

28Then the Jews led Jesus from Caia-
18:28 [u]Mt 27:2; phas to the palace of the Roman
Mk 15:1; governor.[u] By now it was early morning,
Lk 23:1 [v]ver 33; and to avoid ceremonial uncleanness
Jn 19:9 the Jews did not enter the palace;[v] they
[w]Jn 11:55 wanted to be able to eat the Passover.[w]
29So Pilate came out to them and asked,
"What charges are you bringing against
this man?"
30"If he were not a criminal," they replied, "we would not have handed him
over to you."
31Pilate said, "Take him yourselves
and judge him by your own law."
"But we have no right to execute
anyone," the Jews objected. 32This happened so that the words Jesus had spo-
18:32 [x]Mt 20:19; ken indicating the kind of death he was
26:2; Jn 3:14; 8:28; going to die[x] would be fulfilled.
12:32,33 33Pilate then went back inside the
18:33 [y]ver 28,29; palace,[y] summoned Jesus and asked
Jn 19:9 [z]Lk 23:3; him, "Are you the king of the Jews?"[z]
Mt 2:2 34"Is that your own idea," Jesus asked,
"or did others talk to you about me?"
35"Am I a Jew?" Pilate replied. "It was
your people and your chief priests who
handed you over to me. What is it you
have done?"

36Jesus said, "My kingdom[a] is not 18:36 [a]Mt 3:2
of this world. If it were, my servants [b]Mt 26:53
would fight to prevent my arrest by the [c]Lk 17:21;
Jews.[b] But now my kingdom is from Jn 6:15
another place."[c]
37"You are a king, then!" said Pilate.
Jesus answered, "You are right in saying I am a king. In fact, for this reason
I was born, and for this I came into the 18:37 [d]Jn 3:32
world, to testify to the truth.[d] Everyone [e]Jn 8:47;
on the side of truth listens to me."[e] 1Jn 4:6
38"What is truth?" Pilate asked. With
this he went out again to the Jews and
said, "I find no basis for a charge against 18:38
him.[f] 39But it is your custom for me to [f]Lk 23:4; Jn 19:4,6
release to you one prisoner at the time
of the Passover. Do you want me to release 'the king of the Jews'?"

GOODNESS

THE NO-FAULT SAVIOR

John 18:38

"No fault," said Pilate. "No fault in Jesus!" Pilate, the pagan polytheist, could perceive the sinlessness of Christ. Pilate had worshiped the wrong gods for so long that the right one took no effort at all to recognize.

40They shouted back, "No, not him!
Give us Barabbas!" Now Barabbas had
taken part in a rebellion.[g] 18:40 [g]Ac 3:14

Jesus Sentenced to Be Crucified

19 Then Pilate took Jesus and had
him flogged.[h] 2The soldiers 19:1 [h]Dt 25:3;
twisted together a crown of thorns and Isa 50:6; 53:5;
put it on his head. They clothed him Mt 27:26
in a purple robe 3and went up to him
again and again, saying, "Hail, king of 19:3
the Jews!"[i] And they struck him in the [i]Mt 27:29
face.[j] [j]Jn 18:22
4Once more Pilate came out and
said to the Jews, "Look, I am bringing
him out[k] to you to let you know that 19:4 [k]Jn 18:38
I find no basis for a charge against [l]ver 6;
him."[l] 5When Jesus came out wearing Lk 23:4
the crown of thorns and the purple
robe,[m] Pilate said to them, "Here is the 19:5 [m]ver 2
man!"
6As soon as the chief priests and their
officials saw him, they shouted, "Crucify! Crucify!"
But Pilate answered, "You take him

[a]24 Or *(Now Annas had sent him, still bound, to Caiaphas the high priest.)*

19:6 [n]Ac 3:13 and crucify him.[n] As for me, I find no
[o]ver 4; basis for a charge against him."[o]
Lk 23:4 [7]The Jews insisted, "We have a law,
19:7 and according to that law he must die,[p]
[p]Lev 24:16 because he claimed to be the Son of
[q]Mt 26:63-66; Jn 5:18; 10:33 God."[q]
[8]When Pilate heard this, he was even
19:9 more afraid, [9]and he went back inside
[r]Jn 18:33 the palace.[r] "Where do you come from?"
[s]Mk 14:61 he asked Jesus, but Jesus gave him no
answer.[s] [10]"Do you refuse to speak to
me?" Pilate said. "Don't you realize I
have power either to free you or to crucify you?"
[11]Jesus answered, "You would have
19:11 no power over me if it were not given
[t]Ro 13:1 to you from above.[t] Therefore the one
[u]Jn 18:28-30; Ac 3:13 who handed me over to you[u] is guilty
of a greater sin."
[12]From then on, Pilate tried to set Jesus free, but the Jews kept shouting, "If
you let this man go, you are no friend
19:12 of Caesar. Anyone who claims to be a
[v]Lk 23:2 king[v] opposes Caesar."
19:13 [13]When Pilate heard this, he brought
[w]Mt 27:19 Jesus out and sat down on the judge's
[x]Jn 5:2 seat[w] at a place known as the Stone Pave-
19:14 ment (which in Aramaic[x] is Gabbatha).
[y]Mt 27:62 [z]Mk 15:25 [14]It was the day of Preparation[y] of Pass-
[a]ver 19,21 over Week, about the sixth hour.[z]
"Here is your king,"[a] Pilate said to
the Jews.
[15]But they shouted, "Take him away!
Take him away! Crucify him!"
"Shall I crucify your king?" Pilate
asked.
"We have no king but Caesar," the
chief priests answered.
19:16 [16]Finally Pilate handed him over to
[b]Mt 27:26; Mk 15:15; them to be crucified.[b]
Lk 23:25

The Crucifixion

So the soldiers took charge of Jesus.
19:17 [17]Carrying his own cross,[c] he went out
[c]Ge 22:6; Lk 14:27; to the place of the Skull[d] (which in Ara-
23:26 maic[e] is called Golgotha). [18]Here they
[d]Lk 23:33 [e]Jn 5:2 crucified him, and with him two oth-
19:18 ers[f]—one on each side and Jesus in the
[f]Lk 23:32 middle.
[19]Pilate had a notice prepared and
fastened to the cross. It read: JESUS
19:19 OF NAZARETH,[g] THE KING OF THE
[g]Mk 1:24 [h]ver 14,21 JEWS.[h] [20]Many of the Jews read this
sign, for the place where Jesus was cruci-
19:20 [i]Heb 13:12 fied was near the city,[i] and the sign was
written in Aramaic, Latin and Greek.
[21]The chief priests of the Jews protested
to Pilate, "Do not write 'The King of
the Jews,' but that this man claimed to
be king of the Jews."[j] 19:21 [j]ver 14
[22]Pilate answered, "What I have written, I have written."
[23]When the soldiers crucified Jesus,
they took his clothes, dividing them
into four shares, one for each of them,
with the undergarment remaining. This
garment was seamless, woven in one
piece from top to bottom.

GENTLENESS

DICING AT THE CROSS

John 19:23–24

"You who dice, hold the game!
Do you tear my flesh while trying to keep my robe one piece?
Rather, you should be tearing my robe and leaving my body whole.
Would you wear a dead man's robe?
Better you should clothe yourselves with gentleness
and wear the glory of submission."

[24]"Let's not tear it," they said to one
another. "Let's decide by lot who will
get it."
This happened that the scripture 19:24 [k]ver 28,36,37;
might be fulfilled[k] which said, Mt 1:22 [l]Ps 22:18

"They divided my garments among
them
and cast lots for my clothing."[a] [l]

So this is what the soldiers did. 19:25
[25]Near the cross[m] of Jesus stood his [m]Mt 27:55, 56;
mother,[n] his mother's sister, Mary the Mk 15:40,41;
wife of Clopas, and Mary Magdalene.[o] Lk 23:49 [n]Mt 12:46
[26]When Jesus saw his mother[p] there, [o]Lk 24:18
and the disciple whom he loved[q] stand- 19:26
ing nearby, he said to his mother, "Dear [p]Mt 12:46
woman, here is your son," [27]and to the [q]Jn 13:23
disciple, "Here is your mother." From
that time on, this disciple took her into
his home.

The Death of Jesus

[28]Later, knowing that all was now
completed,[r] and so that the Scripture 19:28
would be fulfilled,[s] Jesus said, "I am [r]ver 30; Jn 13:1
thirsty." [29]A jar of wine vinegar[t] was [s]ver 24,36,37
there, so they soaked a sponge in it, 19:29
put the sponge on a stalk of the hys- [t]Ps 69:21
sop plant, and lifted it to Jesus' lips.

[a]*24* Psalm 22:18

19:30 [u]Lk 12:50; Jn 17:4 30 When he had received the drink, Jesus said, "It is finished."[u] With that, he
bowed his head and gave up his spirit.
19:31 [v]ver 14,42 [w]Dt 21:23; Jos 8:29; 10:26,27 31 Now it was the day of Preparation,[v]
and the next day was to be a special
Sabbath. Because the Jews did not want
the bodies left on the crosses[w] during
the Sabbath, they asked Pilate to have
the legs broken and the bodies taken
down. 32 The soldiers therefore came
and broke the legs of the first man who
had been crucified with Jesus, and then
19:32 [x]ver 18 those of the other.[x] 33 But when they
came to Jesus and found that he was al-
ready dead, they did not break his legs.
19:34 [y]Zec 12:10 [z]1Jn 5:6,8 34 Instead, one of the soldiers pierced[y]
Jesus' side with a spear, bringing a sud-
19:35 [a]Lk 24:48 [b]Jn 15:27; 21:24 den flow of blood and water.[z] 35 The
man who saw it[a] has given testimony,
and his testimony is true.[b] He knows
that he tells the truth, and he testifies
so that you also may believe. 36 These
things happened so that the scripture
19:36 [c]ver 24,28,37; Mt 1:22 [d]Ex 12:46; Nu 9:12; Ps 34:20 would be fulfilled:[c] "Not one of his
bones will be broken,"[a] [d] 37 and, as an-
other scripture says, "They will look on
19:37 [e]Zec 12:10; Rev 1:7 the one they have pierced."[b] [e]

The Burial of Jesus

38 Later, Joseph of Arimathea asked
Pilate for the body of Jesus. Now Joseph was a disciple of Jesus, but secretly
because he feared the Jews. With Pilate's
permission, he came and took the body
away. 39 He was accompanied by Nicodemus, the man who earlier had visited
19:39 [f]Jn 3:1; 7:50 Jesus at night. Nicodemus[f] brought a
mixture of myrrh and aloes, about sev-
enty-five pounds.[c] 40 Taking Jesus' body,
19:40 [g]Lk 24:12; Jn 11:44; 20:5,7 [h]Mt 26:12 the two of them wrapped it, with the
spices, in strips of linen.[g] This was in ac-
cordance with Jewish burial customs.[h]
41 At the place where Jesus was crucified,
there was a garden, and in the garden
a new tomb, in which no one had ever
been laid. 42 Because it was the Jewish
19:42 [i]ver 14,31 [j]ver 20,41 day of Preparation[i] and since the tomb
was nearby,[j] they laid Jesus there.

The Empty Tomb

20 Early on the first day of the
20:1 [k]ver 18; Jn 19:25 [l]Mt 27:60,66 week, while it was still dark,
Mary Magdalene[k] went to the tomb
and saw that the stone had been removed from the entrance.[l] 2 So she came
running to Simon Peter and the other
20:2 [m]Jn 13:23 disciple, the one Jesus loved,[m] and said,
"They have taken the Lord out of the
tomb, and we don't know where they 20:2 [n]ver 13
have put him!"[n]
3 So Peter and the other disciple start- 20:3 [o]Lk 24:12
ed for the tomb.[o] 4 Both were running,
but the other disciple outran Peter and
reached the tomb first. 5 He bent over 20:5 [p]ver 11 [q]Jn 19:40
and looked in[p] at the strips of linen[q]
lying there but did not go in. 6 Then
Simon Peter, who was behind him, arrived and went into the tomb. He saw
the strips of linen lying there, 7 as well as
the burial cloth that had been around
Jesus' head.[r] The cloth was folded up by 20:7 [r]Jn 11:44
itself, separate from the linen. 8 Finally
the other disciple, who had reached the
tomb first,[s] also went inside. He saw 20:8 [s]ver 4
and believed. 9 (They still did not un- 20:9 [t]Mt 22:29; Jn 2:22 [u]Lk 24:26,46
derstand from Scripture[t] that Jesus had
to rise from the dead.)[u]

Jesus Appears to Mary Magdalene

10 Then the disciples went back to
their homes, 11 but Mary stood outside
the tomb crying. As she wept, she bent
over to look into the tomb[v] 12 and saw 20:11 [v]ver 5
two angels in white,[w] seated where Je-
sus' body had been, one at the head and 20:12 [w]Mt 28:2,3; Mk 16:5; Lk 24:4; Ac 5:19
the other at the foot.
13 They asked her, "Woman, why are
you crying?"[x]
"They have taken my Lord away," she 20:13 [x]ver 15 [y]ver 2
said, "and I don't know where they have
put him."[y] 14 At this, she turned around
and saw Jesus standing there,[z] but she 20:14 [z]Mt 28:9; Mk 16:9 [a]Lk 24:16; Jn 21:4
did not realize that it was Jesus.[a]
15 "Woman," he said, "why are you
crying?[b] Who is it you are looking 20:15 [b]ver 13
for?"
Thinking he was the gardener, she

[a]*36* Exodus 12:46; Num. 9:12; Psalm 34:20
[b]*37* Zech. 12:10 [c]*39* Greek *a hundred litrai* (about 34 kilograms)

LOVE

LET GO, TAKE HOLD

John 20:17

"Let go of me, Mary," Jesus seemed to say.
"Do you grasp at me to prove I'm
graspable—no ethereal illusion?
Better I should hold you.
Your life is the illusion!
When you give up your illusions,
You will see that Easter life is the only life
that's real.
The other is too temporal and temporary."

said, "Sir, if you have carried him away,
tell me where you have put him, and I
will get him."
16 Jesus said to her, "Mary."
She turned toward him and cried out
20:16 [c]Jn 5:2 [d]Mt 23:7 in Aramaic,[c] "Rabboni!"[d] (which means
Teacher).
17 Jesus said, "Do not hold on to me,
for I have not yet returned to the Fa-
20:17 [e]Mt 28:10 [f]Jn 7:33 ther. Go instead to my brothers[e] and
tell them, 'I am returning to my Father[f]
and your Father, to my God and your
God.'"
20:18 [g]ver 1 [h]Lk 24:10, 22,23 18 Mary Magdalene[g] went to the
disciples[h] with the news: "I have seen
the Lord!" And she told them that he
had said these things to her.

Jesus Appears to His Disciples 20:19 [i]Jn 7:13 [j]Jn 14:27 [k]ver 21,26; Lk 24:36-39

19 On the evening of that first day of
the week, when the disciples were together, with the doors locked for fear of
the Jews,[i] Jesus came and stood among 20:20 [l]Lk 24:39,40; Jn 19:34 [m]Jn 16:20,22
them and said, "Peace[j] be with you!"[k]
20 After he said this, he showed them
his hands and side.[l] The disciples were 20:21 [n]ver 19 [o]Jn 3:17 [p]Mt 28:19; Jn 17:18
overjoyed[m] when they saw the Lord.
21 Again Jesus said, "Peace be with
you![n] As the Father has sent me,[o] I 20:22 [q]Jn 7:39; Ac 2:38; 8:15-17; 19:2; Gal 3:2
am sending you."[p] 22 And with that he
breathed on them and said, "Receive
the Holy Spirit.[q] 23 If you forgive anyone 20:23 [r]Mt 16:19; 18:18
his sins, they are forgiven; if you do not
forgive them, they are not forgiven."[r]

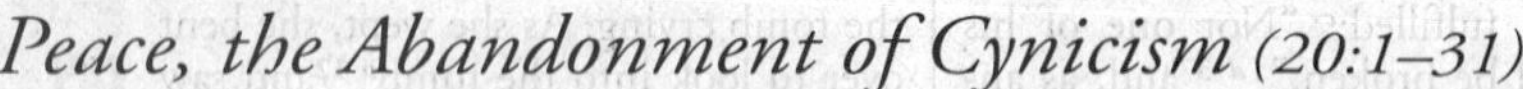

THOMAS

Peace, the Abandonment of Cynicism (20:1–31)

Cynicism is the greatest destroyer of peace. Cynicism is doubt, growing fangs. The more aggressive and evangelistic we become about our doubts, the more peaceless we become. Thomas was not present when Jesus first appeared to the disciples after the resurrection. What a pity! The disciples were "overjoyed when they saw the Lord" (John 20:20).

But Thomas had no joy. While his friends were overcome with elation, he lived in the darkness of doubt. Cynicism broods like a dark serpent on a nest of dead eggs. The apostles' excitement at having seen the Lord alive only added more shadows to Thomas's dark mood. Their joy nettled this poor skeptic. He became angry and scathed them for their credulity: "Unless I see the nail marks in his hands and put my finger where the nails were, and put my hand into his side, I will not believe it" (v. 25).

So the other disciples lived in joy. Their joy gave them peace. But there was no peace for Thomas! No, he elected to be a man at war with himself. He lived a grudge-filled week. He went along his way downcast and propelled by dark anger! A futile, hostile mindset! These were the rank thorns that grew from Thomas's cynicism. A week later Jesus appeared to the disciples again. This time Thomas was there. "Hello there, Thomas. Tada! It's me, Jesus!" the Savior seemed to say. "Put your finger here; see my hands. Reach out your hand and put it into my side. Stop doubting and believe" (v. 27). Then came integrity—and joy! Cynicism and anger died. Dark moods fled before the sunlight. Thomas was healed, and peace overtook him.

All of us have doubts from time to time, but consider this: Did doubt and peace ever occupy joint thrones in your life? No. They cannot rule together. The presence of either one is so odious to the other that one of them must flee. When cynicism is gone, peace may hold sway in our lives, but only then. No wonder the apostle Paul wrote: "Let the peace of Christ rule in your hearts, since as members of one body you were called to peace. And be thankful. Let the word of Christ dwell in you richly as you teach and admonish one another with all wisdom, and as you sing psalms, hymns and spiritual songs with gratitude in your hearts to God" (Colossians 3:15–16).

Thomas could sing only when peace had come to reign in his heart. So it is in our lives as well. Cynicism destroys peace and sets discord into our music. Peace clears the dull floor of our routines and makes a dancing place for joy.

Jesus Appears to Thomas

20:24 [s]Jn 11:16

24 Now Thomas[s] (called Didymus),
one of the Twelve, was not with the disciples when Jesus came. 25 So the other
disciples told him, "We have seen the
Lord!"
But he said to them, "Unless I see
the nail marks in his hands and put
my finger where the nails were, and put
my hand into his side,[t] I will not believe it."[u]
26 A week later his disciples were in
the house again, and Thomas was with
them. Though the doors were locked,
Jesus came and stood among them and
said, "Peace[v] be with you!"[w] 27 Then he
said to Thomas, "Put your finger here;
see my hands. Reach out your hand and
put it into my side. Stop doubting and
believe."[x]
28 Thomas said to him, "My Lord and
my God!"
29 Then Jesus told him, "Because you
have seen me, you have believed;[y]
blessed are those who have not seen and
yet have believed."[z]
30 Jesus did many other miraculous
signs[a] in the presence of his disciples,
which are not recorded in this book.[b]
31 But these are written that you may[a]
believe[c] that Jesus is the Christ, the Son
of God,[d] and that by believing you may
have life in his name.[e]

20:25 [t]ver 20 [u]Mk 16:11
20:26 [v]Jn 14:27 [w]ver 21
20:27 [x]ver 25; Lk 24:40
20:29 [y]Jn 3:15 [z]1Pe 1:8
20:30 [a]Jn 2:11 [b]Jn 21:25
20:31 [c]Jn 3:15; 19:35 [d]Mt 4:3 [e]Mt 25:46

Jesus and the Miraculous Catch of Fish

21 Afterward Jesus appeared again
to his disciples,[f] by the Sea of
Tiberias.[b][g] It happened this way: 2 Simon Peter, Thomas[h] (called Didymus),
Nathanael[i] from Cana in Galilee,[j] the
sons of Zebedee,[k] and two other disciples were together. 3 "I'm going out
to fish," Simon Peter told them, and
they said, "We'll go with you." So they
went out and got into the boat, but that
night they caught nothing.[l]
4 Early in the morning, Jesus stood

21:1 [f]Jn 20:19,26 [g]Jn 6:1
21:2 [h]Jn 11:16 [i]Jn 1:45 [j]Jn 2:1 [k]Mt 4:21
21:3 [l]Lk 5:5

[a]*31* Some manuscripts *may continue to* [b]*1* That is, Sea of Galilee

DAY 3 THREE

Gentleness and My Relationship With Christ

John 20:21–22

One Pentecost long ago I happened to be in Brussels, Belgium. I was there on that very Sunday when the entire world celebrates the coming of the Holy Spirit. The minister read the great passage of Pentecost from Acts. For a moment I felt that awesome unity that makes people of all nationalities one. This first occured on the very day the Spirit first was poured out for all people.

But in John's account of the coming of the Spirit, Jesus breathes on his disciples and then says to them, "receive the Holy Spirit." And they do.

Suddenly, standing there in that great cathedral, I realized: "Pentecost is not merely a day on the church calendar. It is fire and wind that is able to blow at any moment." The elation is inebriating. It comes suddenly, like the wind of which Jesus said, "The wind blows wherever it pleases. You hear its sound, but you cannot tell where it comes from or where it is going. So it is with everyone born of the Spirit" (John 3:8). Like the Jerusalem pilgrims in the book of Acts, our elation must make us appear as though we are drunk on God, and the joy binds the ages.

The gentle breath of God fills us with great power. But more than that, it fills us with an even greater hunger to be breathed upon again and again.

Holy Spirit, breathe on me,
Until my life is clean.
Let sunshine fill its inmost part
With not a cloud between.

To begin a study on the topic of Gentleness, the Healing Touch of God, turn to the home page on page 1175.

Self-Control

Fish on the Starboard Side

John 21:6

Fish show up in abundance where God says fish should be. In this case, 153 obedient bass—or was it perch?—all showed up on the starboard side. A few of them had undoubtedly considered swimming over to the port side but then had decided they'd better not. Fish face their Maker with respect and gather where he tells them to.

WEEK 30

PEACE

DAY ONE

1 PEACE, ACCEPTING A HIGHER WILL

Read John 21:15–19

Peter manages to "fish his way back" from the resurrection hubbub that surrounds Jerusalem. Christ has come back from the dead, but his appearances are infrequent and unpredictable. At the Galilean appearance, Jesus forces Peter to face his unresolved guilt over his denials of Jesus. The turbulence within Peter is called to peace the only way it can be—when Peter abandons his own private agenda (including his attempt to return to fishing) and accepts a higher will for his life.

No believer can ever find peace by posing as a follower of God while remaining dedicated to his or her own will. When the will of God is accepted, real peace becomes possible. Until then our attempts to serve God while having our own way result only in inner turmoil and peacelessness.

R. A. Torrey, the famous evangelist, confessed that he had tried for years to have his own way regarding how he would live his life. While he was doing this, his mother was praying that he would surrender his life to God. Finally, when "life had hit the skids" for him, he found himself contemplating suicide in a lonely hotel room. It was then that he remembered some long-ago maternal advice: "Son, in your darkest hour, call on the name of your mother's God." Torrey confesses that he did not even use the word *Jesus* as he called on the name of God. But, by using the odd nomenclature "my mother's God," he found himself redeemed. Peace was his at once. All his futile plans for his own life were immediately supplanted by a higher will.

MEMORIZE THIS WEEK

ISAIAH 55:10-12

As the rain and the snow
come down from heaven,
and do not return to it
without watering the earth
and making it bud and flourish,
so that it yields seed for the sower and
bread for the eater,
so is my word that goes out from my mouth:
It will not return to me empty,
but will accomplish what I desire
and achieve the purpose for which I
sent it.
You will go out in joy
and be led forth in peace.

DAY TWO

2 PEACE AND THE PURPOSE OF GOD IN MY LIFE

Desiring to do the will of God is the way to peace. We can recognize peace when we see it, but our real problem is that we don't want to do God's will. We are possessed of an odd notion that God's will is no fun and that, if we are forced to do it, we shall be utterly miserable. Psalm 40 contains a better recipe for peace. *Turn to Psalm 40:6–8, page 659, for today's study.*

DAY THREE

3 PEACE AND MY RELATIONSHIP WITH CHRIST

Deep down, Peter probably knew that you didn't have to be a kosher Jew to be a Christian. Yet he most likely thought that Christians who really got into the Mosaic code as he did would be a little more special to God than those who didn't. So God gave him a vision. Afterward, he could see that Christian devotion was wider than he had imagined and that God's peace was available to all. *Turn to Acts 10:9–16, page 1305, for today's study.*

DAY FOUR

4 PEACE AND MY SERVICE TO OTHERS

Paul believed that the peace he had received in Christ was not obtainable from any earthly sources. It had been revealed to him. Peace is the subject of many popular self-help books and the theme of many hot-line telephone numbers. But peace is not to be spoon-fed into our lives like cereal, nor is it instantly derived from our disciplines. Peace is revealed. If God does not show us both its meaning and its source, we will not possess it. *Turn to Galatians 1:10–12, page 1394, for today's study.*

DAY FIVE

5 PEACE AND ITS PLACE IN MY PERSONAL WORSHIP

A monument should have risen in the desert. Saul of Tarsus, while on the road to Damascus, met the Christ he did not believe in. Not only was he changed, but the world itself also reeled under this desert encounter. Not only did Paul find peace for his life, but the world also benefited from the fervor and dedication of a man in love with God. *Turn to Acts 26:9–18, page 1326, for today's study.*

Week 31, Patience, the Unhurried Virtue, begins on page 1146, Matthew 18:21–35.
To begin a topical study on the Fruit of the Spirit, Peace, turn to the Topical Index, page 1548.

DAY 4 FOUR

LOVE AND MY SERVICE TO OTHERS

John 21:15

Every gift bespeaks requirement on the part of the giver. Every gift says to us, "I have come to you because the one who gave me to you loves you very much."

Jesus appeared to the disciples after the resurrection several times, usually without announcement or warning. He must have left them extremely edgy, popping in and out of their lives as he did. Yet each of his appearances to them revealed truths necessary to sustain their faith after his ascension.

In this passage Jesus appears to the disciples at the Sea of Galilee (Tiberias) where he had first met some of them. Peter was one of those who long before had been called from the sea to follow Christ because, as Jesus assured him, Jesus would make him a fisher of men. But following the resurrection, Peter was right back where he had started, fishing for fish.

So Jesus confronts him: "Do you truly love me?"

"Yes, Lord," says the fisher-apostle, "you know that I love you."

"Well, Peter, if you do love me," says Jesus in effect, "act like you love me—feed my sheep. In other words, serve me and those who follow me."

If giving is the number one evidence of love, then serving those who follow Christ is an evidence of love for God as well as for others. I remember a member of my church who was a beautiful Christian but very poor. He wanted to give me a present but had no money. So he came over to my house, audaciously took all my shoes out of my closet and began to polish them. He spent the whole afternoon whistling Christmas carols and polishing my shoes. He loved me. He served me. And I knew of his love.

The generous love of God always motivates us to serve him. Since he has given all, who are we to think that we could ever please him by living self-willed lives void of service? Alas, we cannot. Love like his—giving, never-quitting love—demands our all.

To begin a study on the topic of The Evidence of Love Is Giving, turn to the home page on page 5.

on the shore, but the disciples did not
realize that it was Jesus.[m]
5He called out to them, "Friends,
haven't you any fish?"
"No," they answered.
6He said, "Throw your net on the
right side of the boat and you will find
some." When they did, they were unable
to haul the net in because of the
large number of fish.[n]
7Then the disciple whom Jesus loved[o]
said to Peter, "It is the Lord!" As soon
as Simon Peter heard him say, "It is the
Lord," he wrapped his outer garment
around him (for he had taken it off)
and jumped into the water. 8The other
disciples followed in the boat, towing
the net full of fish, for they were not
far from shore, about a hundred yards.[a]
9When they landed, they saw a fire[p] of
burning coals there with fish on it,[q] and
some bread.
10Jesus said to them, "Bring some of
the fish you have just caught."
11Simon Peter climbed aboard and
dragged the net ashore. It was full
of large fish, 153, but even with so
many the net was not torn. 12Jesus said
to them, "Come and have breakfast."
None of the disciples dared ask him,
"Who are you?" They knew it was the
Lord. 13Jesus came, took the bread and
gave it to them, and did the same with
the fish.[r] 14This was now the third time
Jesus appeared to his disciples[s] after he
was raised from the dead.

Jesus Reinstates Peter

15When they had finished eating, Jesus
said to Simon Peter, "Simon son of
John, do you truly love me more than
these?"
"Yes, Lord," he said, "you know that
I love you."[t]

21:4 [m]Lk 24:16; Jn 20:14
21:6 [n]Lk 5:4-7
21:7 [o]Jn 13:23
21:9 [p]Jn 18:18 [q]ver 10,13
21:13 [r]ver 9
21:14 [s]Jn 20:19,26
21:15 [t]Mt 26:33,35; Jn 13:37

[a]8 Greek *about two hundred cubits* (about 90 meters)

LOVE

FISH OR FAITH?

John 21:15

"Peter, do you love me more than these?" asked Jesus. "These? These boats? These fish? These friends? This way of life?"

"Yes, Lord, I love you more than these," answered Peter.

"Well then, let's talk of sheep, not fish."

21:15 [u]Lk 12:32
Jesus said, "Feed my lambs."[u]
16Again Jesus said, "Simon son of
John, do you truly love me?"
He answered, "Yes, Lord, you know
that I love you."
21:16 [v]Mt 2:6; Ac 20:28; 1Pe 5:2,3
Jesus said, "Take care of my sheep."[v]
17The third time he said to him, "Simon son of John, do you love me?"
Peter was hurt because Jesus asked
21:17 [w]Jn 13:38 [x]Jn 16:30 [y]ver 16
him the third time, "Do you love me?"[w]
He said, "Lord, you know all things;[x]
you know that I love you."
Jesus said, "Feed my sheep.[y] 18I tell
you the truth, when you were younger
you dressed yourself and went where

FAITHFULNESS

"WHAT ABOUT HIM?"

John 21:20–22

Peter received Jesus' prophecy, which implied his martyrdom. He was hoping for some other deal, some better word. "What kind of deal will *he* get?" asked Peter, nodding in John's direction.

"None of your business," Jesus, in effect, said. "You take care of your business, and John will take care of his. Be faithful. Then both of you will be taking care of my business."

you wanted; but when you are old you
will stretch out your hands, and someone else will dress you and lead you
where you do not want to go." 19Jesus
said this to indicate the kind of death[z] 21:19 [z]Jn 12:33; 18:32 [a]2Pe 1:14
by which Peter would glorify God.[a]
Then he said to him, "Follow me!"
20Peter turned and saw that the dis- 21:20 [b]ver 7; Jn 13:23 [c]Jn 13:25
ciple whom Jesus loved[b] was following
them. (This was the one who had leaned
back against Jesus at the supper and
had said, "Lord, who is going to betray you?")[c] 21When Peter saw him, he
asked, "Lord, what about him?"
22Jesus answered, "If I want him to 21:22 [d]Mt 16:27; 1Co 4:5; Rev 2:25 [e]ver 19
remain alive until I return,[d] what is that
to you? You must follow me."[e] 23Be-
cause of this, the rumor spread among 21:23 [f]Ac 1:16
the brothers[f] that this disciple would
not die. But Jesus did not say that he
would not die; he only said, "If I want
him to remain alive until I return, what
is that to you?"
24This is the disciple who testifies to
these things[g] and who wrote them down. 21:24 [g]Jn 15:27 [h]Jn 19:35
We know that his testimony is true.[h]
25Jesus did many other things as well.[i]
If every one of them were written down, 21:25 [i]Jn 20:30
I suppose that even the whole world
would not have room for the books that
would be written.

ACTS

AUTHORSHIP AND DATE

Luke

Probably between A.D. 63 and A.D. 70

KEY THEMES

The book of Acts begins with the story of the coming of the Holy Spirit on Pentecost to empower the newly born church (see 2:1–4). From that point on, the importance of the Spirit cannot be overlooked in Acts. The Spirit is shown to be not only the Creator of the church, but the power and the fire that drives the church's evangelistic appetite. The book of Acts deals with the history of the young church as well as the history of the ongoing ministry of the Holy Spirit. The radical witness of the church was aggressive. But everywhere it met with opposition.

An important transition occurs within the book of Acts. As the Jews increasingly rejected the new church and its Christ-centered teachings, the church increasingly turned toward the Gentiles. A clear division splits the book of Acts. Chapters 1–12 deal with Peter and his leadership of the Jerusalem-centered church. This part of early church history occurred almost totally within Judaism. But beginning with chapter 13, the church, under the leadership of Paul, began to turn toward the Gentiles. The remainder of the book of Acts is dedicated to Paul's missionary journeys as the church moved away from its Jewish moorings centered in Jerusalem.

FRUIT OF THE SPIRIT IN ACTS

Love: As Paul left the Ephesian elders, "they all wept as they embraced him and kissed him" (20:37). Love for fellow servants of Christ is the mark every Christian bears. It is such a definite mark that a saying circulated in the early days of the faith: "Behold how these Christians love one another."

Joy: There is joy wherever heaven touches earth. Where there is wind and fire, there is joy. True joy lacks appropriate deportment. It is not responsible for its propriety. It speaks and sings and exults all at once. Some may call it fanaticism; others may call it foolishness. But none will doubt its existence, for it is as real as the fire and wind that inspire it (see 2:2–4).

Peace: Paul had peace. When the sea was raging and it seemed the world had turned upside down, an angel of the Lord stood beside him (see 27:23). Angels build monuments of peace and bid us lay our anxious beds before them. Then we can sleep in spite of thunder.

Patience: Patience was part of Christ's last command to his church: "Do not leave Jerusalem, but wait" (1:4). Wait for what? Wait for the good stuff—the wind, the fire, the fields of weeping souls. A new world order was about to be born before their eyes. What joy! But they were to wait. It would only be a ten-day wait, but they didn't know that when Jesus gave them his precious promise. We, too, need to wait and be patient. God is at the door. No one knows the exact moment when he will walk through it. Wait and be at ease till the glory comes.

Kindness: Dorcas was a gentle spirit. She was "always doing good and helping the poor." She was also good at needlework and left her surviving friends her arts-and-crafts legacy. After her first death, many displayed her creativity and remembered her kindness (see 9:36–39).

Goodness: Cornelius was a devout and God-fearing man (see 10:1–2). Some unbelievers seem so Christian that Christians wonder why they live more poorly after grace than these unbelieving souls live before it. Still, Cornelius, as good as he was, realized there was a better source of goodness than he possessed. That goodness was bought and paid for by the perfect Son of God.

Faithfulness: Paul was faithful even in prison. In fact his need to be faithful in all likelihood obliterated the "walls" of his prison. Prison is most a prison when those within it find nothing to do but consider the woeful state of their lock-up. Prison is least a prison when those within it live such meaningful lives of faithfulness that their ministry goes on uninterrupted.

Gentleness: The healing of Aeneas was evidence that Christians bathed their compassion in a gentle style that not only healed the sick, but did so gently—as Jesus would have done (see 9:32–35).

Self-Control: The church in Jerusalem sent a letter to the young, largely Gentile church in Antioch, encouraging them to live lives of self-control. We more declare our identity in this world by the things we deny ourselves than by the things we permit ourselves. There is a distinctly Jewish flavor to this letter, but its regard by the Antioch Christians would have signaled to those in Jerusalem that issues of morality and self-control were important to Christians in every realm (see 15:29).

Jesus Taken Up Into Heaven

1:1 [a]Lk 1:1-4 [b]Lk 3:23 1 In my former book,[a] Theophilus,
I wrote about all that Jesus began
1:2 to do and to teach[b] 2until the day he
[c]ver 9,11; Mk 16:19 was taken up to heaven,[c] after giving in-
[d]Mt 28:19,20 structions[d] through the Holy Spirit to
[e]Mk 6:30 [f]Jn 13:18 the apostles[e] he had chosen.[f] 3After his
suffering, he showed himself to these
men and gave many convincing proofs
1:3 [g]Mt 28:17; that he was alive. He appeared to them[g]
Lk 24:34,36; over a period of forty days and spoke
Jn 20:19,26; 21:1,14; about the kingdom of God. 4On one oc-
1Co 15:5-7 casion, while he was eating with them,
he gave them this command: "Do not
1:4 [h]Lk 24:49; leave Jerusalem, but wait for the gift my
Jn 14:16; Father promised, which you have heard
Ac 2:33 me speak about.[h] 5For John baptized
with[a] water, but in a few days you will
be baptized with the Holy Spirit."
6So when they met together, they
asked him, "Lord, are you at this
time going to restore[i] the kingdom to 1:6 [i]Mt 17:11
Israel?"
7He said to them: "It is not for you
to know the times or dates the Father
has set by his own authority.[j] 8But you 1:7 [j]Mt 24:36
will receive power when the Holy Spirit
comes on you;[k] and you will be my wit- 1:8 [k]Ac 2:1-4
nesses[l] in Jerusalem, and in all Judea [l]Lk 24:48
and Samaria,[m] and to the ends of the [m]Ac 8:1-25
earth."[n] [n]Mt 28:19
9After he said this, he was taken up[o] 1:9 [o]ver 2

[a]5 Or *in*

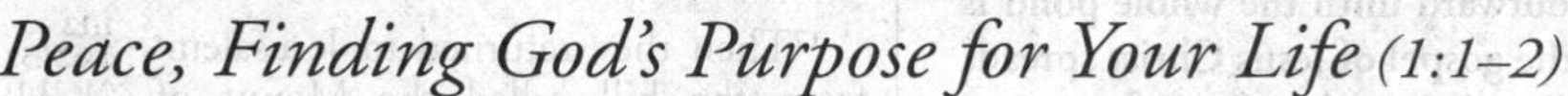

Peace, Finding God's Purpose for Your Life (1:1–2)

Luke wrote two of the most important books of the New Testament—his Gospel and the book of Acts. Without his writings we would lose much of our information about Christ. Many of the parables of Jesus would be unknown without the efforts of this faithful biographer. The birth narrative of Jesus recorded by Luke is completely missing from all of the other Gospels. And the only historical record of the early church found in the Bible was written by Luke. In short, Luke was an obedient chronicler of the life of Christ and the extension of his kingdom, and a man who blessed the world while he himself remained largely anonymous.

Luke included himself in the so-called "we" passages in the book of Acts. By using the pronoun *we* in describing some events, he implied that he was an eyewitness to those episodes. But even in passages where he was involved, he gave little information of how he served with the apostle Paul or what his role was.

In spite of the volume of his writings, we don't know very much about Luke. We do know that he was chosen by God to share the Good News with the world. Luke, like any other Gospel writer, was a man writing under compulsion: "Since I myself have carefully investigated everything from the beginning, it seemed good also to me to write an orderly account for you, most excellent Theophilus, so that you may know the certainty of the things you have been taught" (Luke 1:3–4).

Without focusing on himself, Luke the physician—referred to by Paul as "our dear friend Luke, the doctor" in Colossians 4:14—began his incredible biography of the life of Jesus. It is a tale by a man who, in spite of his demure and self-effacing introduction, knew why he was in the world. He was called by God to write—with the help of the Holy Spirit—a historical account that has lasted over the centuries. The books of Luke and Acts were written by a man of peace. But, of course, people who know why they're in the world and what God has called them to do understand that peace always results from a knowledge of God's will and their obedience to it.

Luke, in saying very little about himself, tells us all we need to know to live in peace and publish it—for his life was dedicated to publishing peace to a peaceless world. Luke tells us of the angels who sang on the night of the Messiah's birth: "Glory to God in the highest, and on earth peace to men on whom his favor rests" (Luke 2:14). The angels, like Luke, are unknown to us. But the peace they published is well celebrated and left for us to remember for all time.

before their very eyes, and a cloud hid
him from their sight.
10They were looking intently up into
1:10 [p]Lk 24:4; Jn 20:12 the sky as he was going, when suddenly
two men dressed in white[p] stood beside
them. 11"Men of Galilee,"[q] they said,
1:11 [q]Ac 2:7 "why do you stand here looking into
the sky? This same Jesus, who has been
taken from you into heaven, will come
back[r] in the same way you have seen 1:11 [r]Mt 16:27
him go into heaven."

DAY 2 TWO

PEACE AND THE PURPOSE OF GOD IN MY LIFE

Acts 1:8

The geography of God is a map of peace. This passage lays out a fourfold strategy to evangelize the world. It speaks of the ever-widening circles of influence that the gospel is to attain. Like a pebble dropped in a pond, causing ripples to sweep outward until the whole pond is in motion, so the gospel of Jesus Christ spreads out in every direction under the influence of the Holy Spirit.

The gospel, like a pin stuck in the middle of a great map, is to be preached from the center outward. Jerusalem, says Jesus, is where the Spirit will arrive. From there the Good News will sweep outward, through Judea and Samaria, until it reaches the ends of the earth. The key is that the gospel starts wherever we are. Keith Green argued that missions is not a matter of "foreign" or "home." After all, everybody is a foreigner to someone. The issue is: Are we missionaries where we are?

"There is no use taking a lamp to Indonesia that won't burn in America," runs the saying. Lost people are no more lost because they live on the other side of an ocean. Nor are we likely to prove to God that we have any real concern about those who live so far away if we have not wept over our own neighborhood.

On giving the Great Commission, Jesus did not say, "Since you all live here in Jerusalem, organize yourselves for mission trips. You'll find that it's easier to promote the saving of lost souls that are an ocean or two away." Christians are always to begin proclaiming peace where they are. If they won't do it there, they won't be successful elsewhere.

To begin a study on the topic of Peace, the Reign of the Holy Spirit, turn to the home page on page 1429.

PEACE

THE LINE OF ADVANCE

Acts 1:8

The kingdom of Christ was to move forward in a seven-step advance. First, the Spirit would come; second, the power would come; third, the witness would begin; fourth, Jerusalem would hear the message; fifth, Judea would hear; sixth, Samaria would hear; and seventh, global witness would be achieved. No step was to be left out; none added. In such an orderly fashion, the entire world would, in time, fly the flag of Christ.

Matthias Chosen to Replace Judas

12Then they returned to Jerusalem[s] 1:12 [s]Lk 24:52
from the hill called the Mount of [t]Mt 21:1
Olives,[t] a Sabbath day's walk[a] from the
city. 13When they arrived, they went
upstairs to the room[u] where they were 1:13 [u]Ac 9:37; 20:8
staying. Those present were Peter, John, [v]Mt 10:2-4; Mk 3:16-19;
James and Andrew; Philip and Thom- Lk 6:14-16
as, Bartholomew and Matthew; James
son of Alphaeus and Simon the Zeal-
ot, and Judas son of James.[v] 14They all 1:14
joined together constantly in prayer,[w] [w]Ac 2:42; 6:4 [x]Lk 23:49,55
along with the women[x] and Mary the [y]Mt 12:46
mother of Jesus, and with his broth-
ers.[y]
15In those days Peter stood up among
the believers[b] (a group numbering about
a hundred and twenty) 16and said,
"Brothers, the Scripture had to be ful-
filled[z] which the Holy Spirit spoke long 1:16 [z]ver 20
ago through the mouth of David con- [a]Jn 13:18
cerning Judas,[a] who served as guide for
those who arrested Jesus— 17he was
one of our number[b] and shared in this 1:17 [b]Jn 6:70,71
ministry."[c] [c]ver 25
18(With the reward[d] he got for his 1:18 [d]Mt 26:14,15
wickedness, Judas bought a field;[e] there [e]Mt 27:3-10
he fell headlong, his body burst open
and all his intestines spilled out. 19Ev-
eryone in Jerusalem heard about this, so
they called that field in their language
Akeldama, that is, Field of Blood.)
20"For," said Peter, "it is written in
the book of Psalms,

[a] *12* That is, about 3/4 mile (about 1,100 meters)
[b] *15* Greek *brothers*

"'May his place be deserted;
let there be no one to dwell
1:20 [f]Ps 69:25 [g]Ps 109:8
in it,'[a][f]
and,

"'May another take his place of
leadership.'[b][g]

21Therefore it is necessary to choose
one of the men who have been with us
the whole time the Lord Jesus went in
1:22 [h]Mk 1:4 [i]ver 8
and out among us, 22beginning from
John's baptism[h] to the time when Jesus
was taken up from us. For one of these
must become a witness[i] with us of his
resurrection."
23So they proposed two men: Joseph
1:24 [j]Ac 6:6; 14:23 [k]1Sa 16:7; Jer 17:10; Ac 15:8; Rev 2:23
called Barsabbas (also known as Justus)
and Matthias. 24Then they prayed,[j]
"Lord, you know everyone's heart.[k]
Show us which of these two you have
chosen 25to take over this apostolic ministry, which Judas left to go where he
belongs." 26Then they cast lots, and the
lot fell to Matthias; so he was added to
1:26 [l]Ac 2:14
the eleven apostles.[l]

The Holy Spirit Comes at Pentecost

2:1 [m]Lev 23:15,16; Ac 20:16 [n]Ac 1:14
2 When the day of Pentecost[m] came,
they were all together[n] in one place.
2Suddenly a sound like the blowing of
a violent wind came from heaven and
filled the whole house where they were
2:2 [o]Ac 4:31
sitting.[o] 3They saw what seemed to be
tongues of fire that separated and came
to rest on each of them. 4All of them
2:4 [p]Mk 16:17; 1Co 12:10
were filled with the Holy Spirit and began to speak in other tongues[c][p] as the
Spirit enabled them.

JOY

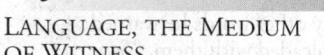

Language, the Medium of Witness

Acts 2:4

In simple nouns and verbs, God's saving message comes.
We hear it and believe, and then we are struck dumb.
To us, beyond the family? Does he offer *us* the name?
It must be so. It must be so. Behold the wind and flame.

5Now there were staying in Jerusalem
2:5 [q]Ac 8:2
God-fearing[q] Jews from every nation
under heaven. 6When they heard this
sound, a crowd came together in bewil-
derment, because each one heard them
speaking in his own language. 7Utterly
2:7 [r]ver 12 [s]Ac 1:11
amazed,[r] they asked: "Are not all these
men who are speaking Galileans?[s] 8Then
how is it that each of us hears them in his
own native language? 9Parthians, Medes
and Elamites; residents of Mesopota-
2:9 [t]1Pe 1:1 [u]Ac 18:2 [v]Ac 16:6; Ro 16:5; 1Co 16:19; 2Co 1:8
mia, Judea and Cappadocia,[t] Pontus[u]
and Asia,[v] 10Phrygia[w] and Pamphylia,[x]
Egypt and the parts of Libya near
Cyrene;[y] visitors from Rome 11(both
Jews and converts to Judaism); Cretans
2:10 [w]Ac 16:6; 18:23 [x]Ac 13:13; 15:38 [y]Mt 27:32
and Arabs—we hear them declaring the
wonders of God in our own tongues!"
12Amazed and perplexed, they asked
one another, "What does this mean?"
13Some, however, made fun of them
2:13 [z]1Co 14:23
and said, "They have had too much
wine.[d]"[z]

Peter Addresses the Crowd

14Then Peter stood up with the Elev-
en, raised his voice and addressed the
crowd: "Fellow Jews and all of you who
live in Jerusalem, let me explain this
to you; listen carefully to what I say.
15These men are not drunk, as you sup-
2:15 [a]1Th 5:7
pose. It's only nine in the morning![a]
16No, this is what was spoken by the
prophet Joel:

JOY

The Oblation

Acts 2:17

God only once lifted this grand censer—this bowl of liquid Spirit.
Then, past the stars and past the grand *aurora borealis* came his intrepid grace.
Streaming down upon the stupefied disciples, it set the world afire.
Two thousand years of Spirit, and the flame yet sears the frost,
Roaring through our pointless lives as fresh as Pentecost.

17"'In the last days, God says,
2:17 [b]Isa 44:3; Jn 7:37-39; Ac 10:45 [c]Ac 21:9
I will pour out my Spirit on all
people.[b]
Your sons and daughters will
prophesy,[c]
your young men will see visions,

[a]*20* Psalm 69:25 [b]*20* Psalm 109:8 [c]*4* Or *languages;* also in verse 11 [d]*13* Or *sweet wine*

your old men will dream dreams.
18 Even on my servants, both men and women,
I will pour out my Spirit in those days,
and they will prophesy.[d]
19 I will show wonders in the heaven above
and signs on the earth below,
blood and fire and billows of smoke.
20 The sun will be turned to darkness
and the moon to blood[e]
before the coming of the great and glorious day of the Lord.
21 And everyone who calls
on the name of the Lord will be saved.'[a][f]

2:18 [d]Ac 21:9-12
2:20 [e]Mt 24:29
2:21 [f]Ro 10:13

22 "Men of Israel, listen to this: Jesus of Nazareth was a man accredited by God to you by miracles, wonders and signs,[g] which God did among you through him,[h] as you yourselves know. 23 This man was handed over to you by God's set purpose and foreknowledge;[i] and you, with the help of wicked men,[b] put him to death by nailing him to the cross.[j] 24 But God raised him from the dead,[k] freeing him from the agony of death, because it was impossible for death to keep its hold on him.[l] 25 David said about him:

" 'I saw the Lord always before me.
Because he is at my right hand,
I will not be shaken.
26 Therefore my heart is glad and my tongue rejoices;
my body also will live in hope,
27 because you will not abandon me to the grave,
nor will you let your Holy One see decay.[m]
28 You have made known to me the paths of life;
you will fill me with joy in your presence.'[c]

2:22 [g]Jn 4:48; Ac 10:38 [h]Jn 3:2
2:23 [i]Lk 22:22; Ac 3:18; 4:28 [j]Lk 24:20; Ac 3:13
2:24 [k]ver 32; 1Co 6:14; 2Co 4:14; Eph 1:20; Col 2:12; Heb 13:20; 1Pe 1:21 [l]Jn 20:9
2:27 [m]ver 31; Ac 13:35

29 "Brothers, I can tell you confidently that the patriarch[n] David died and was buried,[o] and his tomb is here[p] to this day. 30 But he was a prophet and knew that God had promised him on oath that he would place one of his descendants on his throne.[q] 31 Seeing what was ahead, he spoke of the resurrection of the Christ,[d] that he was not abandoned to the grave, nor did his body see decay.[r] 32 God has raised this Jesus to life,[s] and we are all witnesses[t] of the fact. 33 Exalted[u] to the right hand of God,[v] he has received from the Father[w] the promised Holy Spirit[x] and has poured out[y] what you now see and hear. 34 For David did not ascend to heaven, and yet he said,

" 'The Lord said to my Lord:
"Sit at my right hand
35 until I make your enemies
a footstool for your feet." '[e][z]

36 "Therefore let all Israel be assured of this: God has made this Jesus, whom you crucified, both Lord and Christ."[a]

37 When the people heard this, they were cut to the heart and said to Peter and the other apostles, "Brothers, what shall we do?"[b]

38 Peter replied, "Repent and be baptized,[c] every one of you, in the name of Jesus Christ for the forgiveness of your sins.[d] And you will receive the gift of the Holy Spirit. 39 The promise is for you and your children[e] and for all who are far off[f]—for all whom the Lord our God will call."

2:29 [n]Ac 7:8,9 [o]Ac 13:36; 1Ki 2:10 [p]Ne 3:16
2:30 [q]2Sa 7:12; Ps 132:11
2:31 [r]Ps 16:10
2:32 [s]ver 24 [t]Ac 1:8
2:33 [u]Php 2:9 [v]Mk 16:19 [w]Ac 1:4 [x]Jn 7:39; 14:26 [y]Ac 10:45
2:35 [z]Ps 110:1; Mt 22:44
2:36 [a]Lk 2:11
2:37 [b]Lk 3:10, 12,14
2:38 [c]Ac 8:12,16, 36,38; 22:16 [d]Lk 24:47; Ac 3:19
2:39 [e]Isa 44:3 [f]Ac 10:45; Eph 2:13

FAITHFULNESS

CALL CHRIST "LORD" AND WADE OUT INTO THE WATER

Acts 2:38

Let every little soul name Jesus and grow large.
Confess in contrition; cry "Lord" in submission.
Get wise, and get wet!

40 With many other words he warned them; and he pleaded with them, "Save yourselves from this corrupt generation."[g] 41 Those who accepted his message were baptized, and about three thousand were added to their number that day.

2:40 [g]Dt 32:5

The Fellowship of the Believers

42 They devoted themselves to the apostles' teaching and to the fellowship,

[a] *21* Joel 2:28-32 [b] *23* Or *of those not having the law* (that is, Gentiles) [c] *28* Psalm 16:8-11 [d] *31* Or *Messiah.* "The Christ" (Greek) and "the Messiah" (Hebrew) both mean "the Anointed One"; also in verse 36. [e] *35* Psalm 110:1

2:42 [h]Ac 1:14 to the breaking of bread and to prayer.[h]
43Everyone was filled with awe, and
many wonders and miraculous signs
2:43 [i]Ac 5:12 were done by the apostles.[i] 44All the believers were together and had everything
2:44 [j]Ac 4:32 in common.[j] 45Selling their possessions
and goods, they gave to anyone as he
2:45 [k]Mt 19:21 had need.[k] 46Every day they continued
to meet together in the temple courts.[l]
2:46 [l]Lk 24:53; Ac 5:21,42 [m]Ac 20:7 They broke bread[m] in their homes and
ate together with glad and sincere hearts,
47praising God and enjoying the favor
2:47 [n]Ro 14:18 [o]ver 41 Ac 5:14 of all the people.[n] And the Lord added
to their number[o] daily those who were
being saved.

Peter Heals the Crippled Beggar

3:1 [p]Lk 22:8 [q]Ac 2:46 [r]Ps 55:17 3 One day Peter and John[p] were going up to the temple[q] at the time
of prayer—at three in the afternoon.[r]
3:2 [s]Ac 14:8 [t]Lk 16:20 [u]Jn 9:8 2Now a man crippled from birth[s] was
being carried to the temple gate[t] called
Beautiful, where he was put every day
to beg[u] from those going into the temple courts. 3When he saw Peter and
John about to enter, he asked them for
money. 4Peter looked straight at him, as
did John. Then Peter said, "Look at us!"
5So the man gave them his attention,
expecting to get something from them.
6Then Peter said, "Silver or gold I do
3:6 [v]ver 16; Ac 4:10 not have, but what I have I give you. In
the name of Jesus Christ of Nazareth,[v]
walk." 7Taking him by the right hand,
he helped him up, and instantly the
man's feet and ankles became strong.
8He jumped to his feet and began to
walk. Then he went with them into the
3:8 [w]Ac 14:10 temple courts, walking and jumping,[w]
and praising God. 9When all the peo-
ple[x] saw him walking and praising God, 3:9 [x]Ac 4:16,21
10they recognized him as the same man
who used to sit begging at the temple
gate called Beautiful,[y] and they were 3:10 [y]ver 2
filled with wonder and amazement at
what had happened to him.

Peter Speaks to the Onlookers

11While the beggar held on to Peter
and John,[z] all the people were aston- 3:11 [z]Lk 22:8 [a]Jn 10:23; Ac 5:12
ished and came running to them in
the place called Solomon's Colonnade.[a]
12When Peter saw this, he said to them:
"Men of Israel, why does this surprise
you? Why do you stare at us as if by
our own power or godliness we had
made this man walk? 13The God of
Abraham, Isaac and Jacob, the God of
our fathers,[b] has glorified his servant Je- 3:13 [b]Ac 5:30 [c]Mt 27:2 [d]Lk 23:4
sus. You handed him over to be killed,
and you disowned him before Pilate,[c]
though he had decided to let him go.[d] 3:14 [e]Mk 1:24; Ac 4:27 [f]Ac 7:52 [g]Mk 15:11; Lk 23:18-25
14You disowned the Holy[e] and Righ-
teous One[f] and asked that a murderer
be released to you.[g] 15You killed the author of life, but God raised him from
the dead.[h] We are witnesses of this. 16By 3:15 [h]Ac 2:24
faith in the name of Jesus, this man
whom you see and know was made
strong. It is Jesus' name and the faith
that comes through him that has given
this complete healing to him, as you
can all see.
17"Now, brothers, I know that you 3:17 [i]Lk 23:34 [j]Ac 13:27
acted in ignorance,[i] as did your leaders.[j]
18But this is how God fulfilled what he 3:18 [k]Ac 2:23 [l]Lk 24:27 [m]Ac 17:2,3; 26:22,23
had foretold[k] through all the prophets,[l]
saying that his Christ[a] would suffer.[m]
19Repent, then, and turn to God, so that
your sins may be wiped out,[n] that times 3:19 [n]Ac 2:38
of refreshing may come from the Lord,
20and that he may send the Christ, who
has been appointed for you—even Je-
sus. 21He must remain in heaven[o] until 3:21 [o]Ac 1:11 [p]Mt 17:11 [q]Lk 1:70
the time comes for God to restore ev-
erything,[p] as he promised long ago
through his holy prophets.[q] 22For Moses said, 'The Lord your God will raise
up for you a prophet like me from
among your own people; you must lis- 3:22 [r]Dt 18:15,18; Ac 7:37
ten to everything he tells you.[r] 23Any-
one who does not listen to him will
be completely cut off from among his 3:23 [s]Dt 18:19
people.'[b][s]
24"Indeed, all the prophets[t] from 3:24 [t]Lk 24:27

[a]*18* Or *Messiah*; also in verse 20 [b]*23* Deut. 18:15,18,19

JOY

EXUBERANT NUISANCES

Acts 3:6–8

Here is the great giveaway of grace. What's to become of cripples once Christ has healed their legs? They stand and then make exuberant nuisances of themselves, walking and leaping as they do. Sorry, all you who like tradition and ritual. Such joy never stops for church liturgies. When the crippled learn how to walk, watch out! Do not expect them to sit and sing hymns. They are too full of fire now, too noisy and athletic. There is nothing to be done with them except to let them whoop.

Samuel on, as many as have spoken,
3:25 have foretold these days. 25And you are
[u]Ac 2:39 heirs[u] of the prophets and of the cov-
[v]Ro 9:4,5 enant[v] God made with your fathers.
[w]Ge 12:3; He said to Abraham, 'Through your
22:18; 26:4; 28:14 offspring all peoples on earth will be
3:26 blessed.'[a] [w] 26When God raised up[x] his
[x]ver 22; Ac 2:24 servant, he sent him first[y] to you to
[y]Ac 13:46; bless you by turning each of you from
Ro 1:16 your wicked ways."

Peter and John Before the Sanhedrin

4:1 **4** The priests and the captain of the
[z]Lk 22:4 temple guard[z] and the Sadducees[a]
[a]Mt 3:7 came up to Peter and John while they
were speaking to the people. 2They
were greatly disturbed because the apostles were teaching the people and pro-
4:2 claiming in Jesus the resurrection of the
[b]Ac 17:18 dead.[b] 3They seized Peter and John, and
4:3 because it was evening, they put them
[c]Ac 5:18 in jail[c] until the next day. 4But many
4:4 who heard the message believed, and
[d]Ac 2:41 the number of men grew[d] to about five
thousand.
4:5 5The next day the rulers,[e] elders and
[e]Lk 23:13 teachers of the law met in Jerusalem.
4:6 6Annas the high priest was there, and
[f]Mt 26:3; Lk 3:2 so were Caiaphas,[f] John, Alexander and
the other men of the high priest's family.
7They had Peter and John brought before them and began to question them:
"By what power or what name did you
do this?"
8Then Peter, filled with the Holy
4:8 Spirit, said to them: "Rulers and elders
[g]ver 5; Lk 23:13 of the people![g] 9If we are being called
to account today for an act of kind-
4:9 ness shown to a cripple[h] and are asked
[h]Ac 3:6 how he was healed, 10then know this,
you and all the people of Israel: It is
by the name of Jesus Christ of Nazareth, whom you crucified but whom
4:10 God raised from the dead,[i] that this
[i]Ac 2:24 man stands before you healed. 11He is

"'the stone you builders rejected,
which has become the
capstone.'[b] [c] [j] 4:11 [j]Ps 118:22; Isa 28:16; Mt 21:42
12Salvation is found in no one else, for
there is no other name under heaven
given to men by which we must be 4:12
saved."[k] [k]Mt 1:21; Ac 10:43; 1Ti 2:5
13When they saw the courage of Peter
and John[l] and realized that they were 4:13
unschooled, ordinary men,[m] they were [l]Lk 22:8 [m]Mt 11:25
astonished and they took note that these
men had been with Jesus. 14But since
they could see the man who had been
healed standing there with them, there
was nothing they could say. 15So they
ordered them to withdraw from the 4:15
Sanhedrin[n] and then conferred together. [n]Mt 5:22
16"What are we going to do with these
men?"[o] they asked. "Everybody living 4:16 [o]Jn 11:47
in Jerusalem knows they have done an [p]Ac 3:6-10
outstanding miracle,[p] and we cannot
deny it. 17But to stop this thing from
spreading any further among the people, we must warn these men to speak
no longer to anyone in this name."
18Then they called them in again and
commanded them not to speak or teach 4:18
at all in the name of Jesus.[q] 19But Pe- [q]Ac 5:40
ter and John replied, "Judge for yourselves whether it is right in God's sight 4:19
to obey you rather than God.[r] 20For we [r]Ac 5:29
cannot help speaking about what we
have seen and heard."
21After further threats they let them
go. They could not decide how to pun- 4:21
ish them, because all the people[s] were [s]Ac 5:26
praising God[t] for what had happened. [t]Mt 9:8
22For the man who was miraculously
healed was over forty years old.

The Believers' Prayer

23On their release, Peter and John
went back to their own people and reported all that the chief priests and elders had said to them. 24When they
heard this, they raised their voices together in prayer to God. "Sovereign
Lord," they said, "you made the heaven
and the earth and the sea, and everything in them. 25You spoke by the Holy
Spirit through the mouth of your ser- 4:25
vant, our father David:[u] [u]Ac 1:16

"'Why do the nations rage
and the peoples plot in vain?

[a] *25* Gen. 22:18; 26:4 [b] *11* Or *cornerstone*
[c] *11* Psalm 118:22

GENTLENESS

THE PRECIOUS WAY

Acts 4:12

The chasm of sin is deep. The moat between time and eternity is precipitous and wide. There is but one gentle way to span the danger: the bridge called Jesus.

Jesus Speaks Out *on the Fruit of the Spirit:*

Gentleness

Matthew 5:5
Blessed are the meek, for they will inherit the earth.

Matthew 11:29
Take my yoke upon you and learn from me, for I am gentle and humble in heart, and you will find rest for your souls.

Matthew 21:5
Say to the Daughter of Zion,
"See, your king comes to you,
gentle and riding on a donkey,
on a colt, the foal of a donkey."

Matthew 18:1–4
The disciples came to Jesus and asked, "Who is the greatest in the kingdom of heaven?"
He called a little child and had him stand among them. And he said: "I tell you the truth, unless you change and become like little children, you will never enter the kingdom of heaven. Therefore, whoever humbles himself like this child is the greatest in the kingdom of heaven."

Mark 1:41
Filled with compassion, Jesus reached out his hand and touched the man. "I am willing," he said. "Be clean!"

The Good Shepherd

Therefore Jesus said again, "I tell you the truth, I am the gate for the sheep. All who ever came before me were thieves and robbers, but the sheep did not listen to them. I am the gate; whoever enters through me will be saved. He will come in and go out, and find pasture. The thief comes only to steal and kill and destroy; I have come that they may have life, and have it to the full.

"I am the good shepherd. The good shepherd lays down his life for the sheep. The hired hand is not the shepherd who owns the sheep. So when he sees the wolf coming, he abandons the sheep and runs away. Then the wolf attacks the flock and scatters it. The man runs away because he is a hired hand and cares nothing for the sheep.

"I am the good shepherd; I know my sheep and my sheep know me—just as the Father knows me and I know the Father—and I lay down my life for the sheep."

John 10:7–15

Paul Speaks Out *on the Fruit of the Spirit:* Gentleness

2 Corinthians 10:1

By the meekness and gentleness of Christ, I appeal to you—I, Paul, who am "timid" when face to face with you, but "bold" when away!

Ephesians 4:2

Be completely humble and gentle; be patient, bearing with one another in love.

Philippians 4:5

Let your gentleness be evident to all. The Lord is near.

Colossians 3:12

Therefore, as God's chosen people, holy and dearly loved, clothe yourselves with compassion, kindness, humility, gentleness and patience.

1 Corinthians 4:18–21

Some of you have become arrogant, as if I were not coming to you. But I will come to you very soon, if the Lord is willing, and then I will find out not only how these arrogant people are talking, but what power they have. For the kingdom of God is not a matter of talk but of power. What do you prefer? Shall I come to you with a whip, or in love and with a gentle spirit?

Galatians 6:1

Brothers, if someone is caught in a sin, you who are spiritual should restore him gently. But watch yourself, or you also may be tempted.

▸ Gentleness Loves Others

You know, brothers, that our visit to you was not a failure. We had previously suffered and been insulted in Philippi, as you know, but with the help of our God we dared to tell you his gospel in spite of strong opposition. For the appeal we make does not spring from error or impure motives, nor are we trying to trick you. On the contrary, we speak as men approved by God to be entrusted with the gospel. We are not trying to please men but God, who tests our hearts. You know we never used flattery, nor did we put on a mask to cover up greed—God is our witness. We were not looking for praise from men, not from you or anyone else.

As apostles of Christ we could have been a burden to you, but we were gentle among you, like a mother caring for her little children. We loved you so much that we were delighted to share with you not only the gospel of God but our lives as well, because you had become so dear to us. Surely you remember, brothers, our toil and hardship; we worked night and day in order not to be a burden to anyone while we preached the gospel of God to you.

You are witnesses, and so is God, of how holy, righteous and blameless we were among you who believed. For you know that we dealt with each of you as a father deals with his own children, encouraging, comforting and urging you to live lives worthy of God, who calls you into his kingdom and glory.

1 Thessalonians 2:1–12

26 The kings of the earth take their
stand
and the rulers gather together
against the Lord
and against his Anointed One.[a][b][v]
27 Indeed Herod[w] and Pontius Pilate[x]
met together with the Gentiles and the
people[c] of Israel in this city to conspire
against your holy servant Jesus,[y] whom
you anointed. 28 They did what your
power and will had decided beforehand
should happen.[z] 29 Now, Lord, consider
their threats and enable your servants to
speak your word with great boldness.[a]
30 Stretch out your hand to heal and
perform miraculous signs and wonders[b]
through the name of your holy servant
Jesus."[c]
31 After they prayed, the place where
they were meeting was shaken.[d] And
they were all filled with the Holy Spirit
and spoke the word of God boldly.[e]

The Believers Share Their Possessions

32 All the believers were one in heart
and mind. No one claimed that any of
his possessions was his own, but they
shared everything they had.[f] 33 With
great power the apostles continued to
testify[g] to the resurrection[h] of the Lord
Jesus, and much grace was upon them
all. 34 There were no needy persons
among them. For from time to time
those who owned lands or houses sold
them,[i] brought the money from the
sales 35 and put it at the apostles' feet,[j]
and it was distributed to anyone as he
had need.[k]
36 Joseph, a Levite from Cyprus,
whom the apostles called Barnabas[l]
(which means Son of Encouragement),
37 sold a field he owned and brought the
money and put it at the apostles' feet.[m]

Ananias and Sapphira

5 Now a man named Ananias, together with his wife Sapphira, also
sold a piece of property. 2 With his wife's
full knowledge he kept back part of the
money for himself, but brought the rest
and put it at the apostles' feet.[n]
3 Then Peter said, "Ananias, how is it
that Satan[o] has so filled your heart[p] that
you have lied to the Holy Spirit[q] and
have kept for yourself some of the money you received for the land? 4 Didn't it

4:26 [a]Ps 2:1,2; Da 9:25; Lk 4:18; Ac 10:38; Heb 1:9
4:27 [w]Mt 14:1 [x]Mt 27:2; Lk 23:12 [y]ver 30
4:28 [z]Ac 2:23
4:29 [a]ver 13,31; Ac 9:27; 14:3; Php 1:14
4:30 [b]Jn 4:48 [c]ver 27
4:31 [d]Ac 2:2 [e]ver 29
4:32 [f]Ac 2:44
4:33 [g]Lk 24:48 [h]Ac 1:22
4:34 [i]Mt 19:21; Ac 2:45
4:35 [j]ver 37; Ac 5:2 [k]Ac 2:45; 6:1
4:36 [l]Ac 9:27; 1Co 9:6
4:37 [m]ver 35; Ac 5:2
5:2 [n]Ac 4:35,37
5:3 [o]Mt 4:10 [p]Jn 13:2,27 [q]ver 9

belong to you before it was sold? And
after it was sold, wasn't the money at
your disposal? What made you think of
doing such a thing? You have not lied
to men but to God."
5 When Ananias heard this, he fell
down and died.[r] And great fear[s] seized
all who heard what had happened.
6 Then the young men came forward,
wrapped up his body,[t] and carried him
out and buried him.
7 About three hours later his wife
came in, not knowing what had happened. 8 Peter asked her, "Tell me, is this
the price you and Ananias got for the
land?"
"Yes," she said, "that is the price."[u]
9 Peter said to her, "How could you
agree to test the Spirit of the Lord?[v]
Look! The feet of the men who buried
your husband are at the door, and they
will carry you out also."
10 At that moment she fell down at
his feet and died.[w] Then the young men
came in and, finding her dead, carried
her out and buried her beside her husband. 11 Great fear[x] seized the whole
church and all who heard about these
events.

FAITHFULNESS

THE ART OF LYING AND DYING

Acts 5:9

Ananias and Sapphira lied and died. Brief biography—so sad.

The Apostles Heal Many

12 The apostles performed many miraculous signs and wonders[y] among
the people. And all the believers used
to meet together[z] in Solomon's
Colonnade.[a] 13 No one else dared join
them, even though they were highly
regarded by the people.[b] 14 Nevertheless, more and more men and women
believed in the Lord and were added
to their number. 15 As a result, people
brought the sick into the streets and laid
them on beds and mats so that at least
Peter's shadow might fall on some of
them as he passed by.[c] 16 Crowds gathered also from the towns around Jerusalem, bringing their sick and those

5:5 [r]ver 10 [s]ver 11
5:6 [t]Jn 19:40
5:8 [u]ver 2
5:9 [v]ver 3
5:10 [w]ver 5
5:11 [x]ver 5; Ac 19:17
5:12 [y]Ac 2:43 [z]Ac 4:32 [a]Ac 3:11
5:13 [b]Ac 2:47; 4:21
5:15 [c]Ac 19:12

a *26* That is, Christ or Messiah b *26* Psalm 2:1,2
c *27* The Greek is plural.

5:16 tormented by evil[a] spirits, and all of
dMk 16:17 them were healed.[d]

The Apostles Persecuted

17 Then the high priest and all his
5:17 associates, who were members of the
eAc 15:5 party[e] of the Sadducees,[f] were filled
fAc 4:1 with jealousy. 18 They arrested the apos-
5:18 tles and put them in the public jail.[g]
gAc 4:3 19 But during the night an angel[h] of
5:19 the Lord opened the doors of the jail[i]
hMt 1:20; Lk 1:11; and brought them out. 20 "Go, stand in
Ac 8:26; 27:23 the temple courts," he said, "and tell
iAc 16:26 the people the full message of this new
5:20 life."[j]
jJn 6:63,68 21 At daybreak they entered the temple courts, as they had been told, and
began to teach the people.
5:21 When the high priest and his asso-
kAc 4:5,6 lver 27,34,41; ciates[k] arrived, they called together the
Mt 5:22 Sanhedrin[l]—the full assembly of the el-
ders of Israel—and sent to the jail for
the apostles. 22 But on arriving at the
jail, the officers did not find them there.
So they went back and reported, 23 "We
found the jail securely locked, with the
guards standing at the doors; but when
we opened them, we found no one inside." 24 On hearing this report, the captain of the temple guard and the chief
5:24 priests[m] were puzzled, wondering what
mAc 4:1 would come of this.
25 Then someone came and said,
"Look! The men you put in jail are
standing in the temple courts teaching
the people." 26 At that, the captain went
5:26 with his officers and brought the apos-
nAc 4:21 tles. They did not use force, because
5:27 they feared that the people[n] would stone
oMt 5:22 them.
5:28 27 Having brought the apostles, they
pAc 4:18 made them appear before the Sanhe-
qMt 23:35; 27:25; drin[o] to be questioned by the high
Ac 2:23,36; 3:14,15; 7:52 priest. 28 "We gave you strict orders not
5:29 to teach in this name,"[p] he said. "Yet
rAc 4:19 you have filled Jerusalem with your
5:30 teaching and are determined to make
sAc 3:13 us guilty of this man's blood."[q]
tAc 2:24 29 Peter and the other apostles replied:
uAc 10:39; 13:29; "We must obey God rather than men![r]
Gal 3:13; 1Pe 2:24 30 The God of our fathers[s] raised Jesus
5:31 from the dead[t]—whom you had killed
vAc 2:33 wLk 2:11 by hanging him on a tree.[u] 31 God ex-
xMt 1:21; alted him to his own right hand[v] as
Lk 24:47; Ac 2:38 Prince and Savior[w] that he might give
repentance and forgiveness of sins to
5:32 yLk 24:48 Israel.[x] 32 We are witnesses of these
zJn 15:26 things,[y] and so is the Holy Spirit,[z] whom
God has given to those who obey him."
33 When they heard this, they were furious[a] and wanted to put them to death. 5:33
34 But a Pharisee named Gamaliel,[b] a aAc 2:37; 7:54
teacher of the law,[c] who was honored 5:34
by all the people, stood up in the San- bAc 22:3
hedrin and ordered that the men be cLk 2:46
put outside for a little while. 35 Then
he addressed them: "Men of Israel, consider carefully what you intend to do
to these men. 36 Some time ago Theu-
das appeared, claiming to be somebody,
and about four hundred men rallied to
him. He was killed, all his followers
were dispersed, and it all came to nothing. 37 After him, Judas the Galilean ap- 5:37
peared in the days of the census[d] and led dLk 2:1,2
a band of people in revolt. He too was
killed, and all his followers were scattered. 38 Therefore, in the present case I
advise you: Leave these men alone! Let
them go! For if their purpose or activ-
ity is of human origin, it will fail.[e] 39 But 5:38
if it is from God, you will not be able eMt 15:13
to stop these men; you will only find 5:39
yourselves fighting against God."[f] fPr 21:30;
40 His speech persuaded them. They Ac 7:51; 11:17
called the apostles in and had them 5:40
flogged.[g] Then they ordered them not gMt 10:17
to speak in the name of Jesus, and let
them go.
41 The apostles left the Sanhedrin, re- 5:41
joicing[h] because they had been count- hMt 5:12
ed worthy of suffering disgrace for the iJn 15:21
Name.[i] 42 Day after day, in the temple 5:42
courts[j] and from house to house, they jAc 2:46
never stopped teaching and proclaiming
the good news that Jesus is the Christ.[b]

The Choosing of the Seven

6 In those days when the number of 6:1
disciples was increasing,[k] the Gre- kAc 2:41
cian Jews[l] among them complained lAc 9:29 mAc 9:39,41
against the Hebraic Jews because their nAc 4:35
widows[m] were being overlooked in the
daily distribution of food.[n] 2 So the
Twelve gathered all the disciples together and said, "It would not be right
for us to neglect the ministry of the
word of God in order to wait on tables. 3 Brothers,[o] choose seven men from 6:3
among you who are known to be full oAc 1:16
of the Spirit and wisdom. We will turn
this responsibility over to them 4 and
will give our attention to prayer[p] and 6:4
the ministry of the word." pAc 1:14

[a] *16* Greek *unclean* [b] *42* Or *Messiah*

5This proposal pleased the whole group. They chose Stephen,[q] a man full of faith and of the Holy Spirit;[r] also Philip,[s] Procorus, Nicanor, Timon, Parmenas, and Nicolas from Antioch, a convert to Judaism. 6They presented these men to the apostles, who prayed[t] and laid their hands on them.[u]

7So the word of God spread.[v] The number of disciples in Jerusalem increased rapidly, and a large number of priests became obedient to the faith.

Stephen Seized

8Now Stephen, a man full of God's grace and power, did great wonders and miraculous signs[w] among the people. 9Opposition arose, however, from members of the Synagogue of the Freedmen (as it was called)—Jews of Cyrene[x] and Alexandria as well as the provinces of Cilicia[y] and Asia.[z] These men began to argue with Stephen, 10but they could not stand up against his wisdom or the Spirit by whom he spoke.[a]

11Then they secretly[b] persuaded some men to say, "We have heard Stephen speak words of blasphemy against Moses and against God."[c]

12So they stirred up the people and the elders and the teachers of the law. They seized Stephen and brought him before the Sanhedrin.[d] 13They produced false witnesses, who testified, "This fellow never stops speaking against this holy place[e] and against the law. 14For we have heard him say that this Jesus of Nazareth will destroy this place and change the customs Moses handed down to us."[f]

15All who were sitting in the Sanhedrin[g] looked intently at Stephen, and they saw that his face was like the face of an angel.

Stephen's Speech to the Sanhedrin

7 Then the high priest asked him, "Are these charges true?"

2To this he replied: "Brothers and fathers,[h] listen to me! The God of glory[i] appeared to our father Abraham while he was still in Mesopotamia, before he lived in Haran.[j] 3'Leave your country and your people,' God said, 'and go to the land I will show you.'[a][k]

4"So he left the land of the Chaldeans and settled in Haran. After the death of his father, God sent him to this land where you are now living.[l] 5He gave him no inheritance here, not even a foot of ground. But God promised him that he and his descendants after him would possess the land,[m] even though at that time Abraham had no child. 6God spoke to him in this way: 'Your descendants will be strangers in a country not their own, and they will be enslaved and mistreated four hundred years.[n] 7But I will punish the nation they serve as slaves,' God said, 'and afterward they will come out of that country and worship me in this place.'[b][o] 8Then he gave Abraham the covenant of circumcision.[p] And Abraham became the father of Isaac and circumcised him eight days after his birth.[q] Later Isaac became the father of Jacob,[r] and Jacob became the father of the twelve patriarchs.[s]

9"Because the patriarchs were jealous of Joseph,[t] they sold him as a slave into Egypt.[u] But God was with him[v] 10and rescued him from all his troubles. He gave Joseph wisdom and enabled him to gain the goodwill of Pharaoh king of Egypt; so he made him ruler over Egypt and all his palace.[w]

11"Then a famine struck all Egypt and Canaan, bringing great suffering, and our fathers could not find food.[x] 12When Jacob heard that there was grain in Egypt, he sent our fathers on their first visit.[y] 13On their second visit, Joseph told his brothers who he was,[z] and Pharaoh learned about Joseph's family. 14After this, Joseph sent for his father Jacob and his whole family,[a] seventy-five in all.[b] 15Then Jacob went down to Egypt, where he and our fathers died.[c] 16Their bodies were brought back to Shechem and placed in the tomb that Abraham had bought from the sons of Hamor at Shechem for a certain sum of money.[d]

17"As the time drew near for God to fulfill his promise to Abraham, the number of our people in Egypt greatly increased.[e] 18Then another king, who knew nothing about Joseph, became ruler of Egypt.[f] 19He dealt treacherously with our people and oppressed our forefathers by forcing them to throw out their newborn babies so that they would die.[g]

[a]*3* Gen. 12:1 [b]*7* Gen. 15:13,14

6:5 [q]ver 8; Ac 11:19 [r]Ac 11:24 [s]Ac 8:5-40; 21:8
6:6 [t]Ac 1:24; 8:17; 13:3; 2Ti 1:6 [u]Nu 8:10; Ac 9:17; 1Ti 4:14
6:7 [v]Ac 12:24; 19:20
6:8 [w]Jn 4:48
6:9 [x]Mt 27:32 [y]Ac 15:23,41; 22:3; 23:34 [z]Ac 2:9
6:10 [a]Lk 21:15
6:11 [b]1Ki 21:10 [c]Mt 26:59-61
6:12 [d]Mt 5:22
6:13 [e]Ac 21:28
6:14 [f]Ac 15:1; 21:21; 26:3; 28:17
6:15 [g]Mt 5:22
7:2 [h]Ac 22:1 [i]Ps 29:3 [j]Ge 11:31; 15:7
7:3 [k]Ge 12:1
7:4 [l]Ge 12:5
7:5 [m]Ge 12:7; 17:8; 26:3
7:6 [n]Ex 12:40
7:7 [o]Ex 3:12
7:8 [p]Ge 17:9-14 [q]Ge 21:2-4 [r]Ge 25:26 [s]Ge 29:31-35; 30:5-13, 17-24; 35:16-18 22-26
7:9 [t]Ge 37:4,11 [u]Ge 37:28; Ps 105:17 [v]Ge 39:2, 21,23
7:10 [w]Ge 41:37-43
7:11 [x]Ge 41:54
7:12 [y]Ge 42:1,2
7:13 [z]Ge 45:1-4
7:14 [a]Ge 45:9,10 [b]Ge 46:26,27; Ex 1:5; Dt 10:22
7:15 [c]Ge 46:5-7; 49:33; Ex 1:6
7:16 [d]Ge 23:16-20; 33:18,19; 50:13; Jos 24:32
7:17 [e]Ex 1:7; Ps 105:24
7:18 [f]Ex 1:8
7:19 [g]Ex 1:10-22

20“At that time Moses was born, and he was no ordinary child.[a] For three months he was cared for in his father’s house.[h] 21When he was placed outside, Pharaoh’s daughter took him and brought him up as her own son.[i] 22Moses was educated in all the wisdom of the Egyptians[j] and was powerful in speech and action.

23“When Moses was forty years old, he decided to visit his fellow Israelites. 24He saw one of them being mistreated by an Egyptian, so he went to his defense and avenged him by killing the Egyptian. 25Moses thought that his own people would realize that God was using him to rescue them, but they did not. 26The next day Moses came upon two Israelites who were fighting. He tried to reconcile them by saying, ‘Men, you are brothers; why do you want to hurt each other?’

27“But the man who was mistreating the other pushed Moses aside and said, ‘Who made you ruler and judge over us? 28Do you want to kill me as you killed the Egyptian yesterday?’[b] 29When Moses heard this, he fled to Midian, where he settled as a foreigner and had two sons.[k]

30“After forty years had passed, an angel appeared to Moses in the flames of a burning bush in the desert near Mount Sinai. 31When he saw this, he was amazed at the sight. As he went over to look more closely, he heard the Lord’s voice:[l] 32‘I am the God of your fathers, the God of Abraham, Isaac and Jacob.’[c] Moses trembled with fear and did not dare to look.[m]

33“Then the Lord said to him, ‘Take off your sandals; the place where you are standing is holy ground.[n] 34I have indeed seen the oppression of my people in Egypt. I have heard their groaning and have come down to set them free. Now come, I will send you back to Egypt.’[d][o]

35“This is the same Moses whom they had rejected with the words, ‘Who made you ruler and judge?’[p] He was sent to be their ruler and deliverer by God himself, through the angel who appeared to him in the bush. 36He led them out of Egypt[q] and did wonders and miraculous signs in Egypt, at the Red Sea[e][r] and for forty years in the desert.

7:20 [h]Ex 2:2; Heb 11:23
7:21 [i]Ex 2:3-10
7:22 [j]1Ki 4:30; Isa 19:11
7:29 [k]Ex 2:11-15
7:31 [l]Ex 3:1-4
7:32 [m]Ex 3:6
7:33 [n]Ex 3:5; Jos 5:15
7:34 [o]Ex 3:7-10
7:35 [p]ver 27
7:36 [q]Ex 12:41; 33:1 [r]Ex 14:21

37“This is that Moses who told the Israelites, ‘God will send you a prophet like me from your own people.’[f][s] 38He was in the assembly in the desert, with the angel[t] who spoke to him on Mount Sinai, and with our fathers;[u] and he received living words[v] to pass on to us.[w]

39“But our fathers refused to obey him. Instead, they rejected him and in their hearts turned back to Egypt.[x] 40They told Aaron, ‘Make us gods who will go before us. As for this fellow Moses who led us out of Egypt—we don’t know what has happened to him!’[g][y] 41That was the time they made an idol in the form of a calf. They brought sacrifices to it and held a celebration in honor of what their hands had made.[z] 42But God turned away[a] and gave them over to the worship of the heavenly bodies.[b] This agrees with what is written in the book of the prophets:

“ ‘Did you bring me sacrifices and offerings
forty years in the desert, O house of Israel?
43You have lifted up the shrine of Molech
and the star of your god Rephan,
the idols you made to worship.
Therefore I will send you into exile’[h]
[c]beyond Babylon.

44“Our forefathers had the tabernacle of the Testimony[d] with them in the desert. It had been made as God directed Moses, according to the pattern he had seen.[e] 45Having received the tabernacle, our fathers under Joshua brought it with them when they took the land from the nations God drove out before them.[f] It remained in the land until the time of David, 46who enjoyed God’s favor and asked that he might provide a dwelling place for the God of Jacob.[i][g] 47But it was Solomon who built the house for him.

48“However, the Most High does not live in houses made by men.[h] As the prophet says:

49“ ‘Heaven is my throne,
and the earth is my footstool.[i]

7:37 [s]Dt 18:15,18; Ac 3:22
7:38 [t]ver 53 [u]Ex 19:17 [v]Dt 32:45-47; Heb 4:12 [w]Ro 3:2
7:39 [x]Nu 14:3,4
7:40 [y]Ex 32:1,23
7:41 [z]Ex 32:4-6; Ps 106:19,20; Rev 9:20
7:42 [a]Jos 24:20; Isa 63:10 [b]Jer 19:13
7:43 [c]Am 5:25-27
7:44 [d]Ex 38:21 [e]Ex 25:8,9,40
7:45 [f]Jos 3:14-17; 18:1; 23:9; 24:18; Ps 44:2
7:46 [g]2Sa 7:8-16; Ps 132:1-5
7:48 [h]1Ki 8:27; 2Ch 2:6
7:49 [i]Mt 5:34,35

[a]*20* Or *was fair in the sight of God* [b]*28* Exodus 2:14 [c]*32* Exodus 3:6 [d]*34* Exodus 3:5,7,8,10 [e]*36* That is, Sea of Reeds [f]*37* Deut. 18:15 [g]*40* Exodus 32:1 [h]*43* Amos 5:25-27 [i]*46* Some early manuscripts *the house of Jacob*

What kind of house will you build
for me?
says the Lord.
Or where will my resting place be?
50Has not my hand made all these
things?'[a][j]

7:50 [j]Isa 66:1,2

DAY 2 TWO

▸ FAITHFULNESS AND THE PURPOSE OF GOD IN MY LIFE

Acts 7:52–60

The last words of Jesus at his crucifixion invite us to consider the last four statements of Stephen:

#1: "Was there ever a prophet your fathers did not persecute? They even killed those who predicted the coming of the Righteous One. And now you have betrayed and murdered him—you who have received the law that was put into effect through angels but have not obeyed it" (Acts 7:52–53). This blatant telling of the truth was bound to get Stephen into trouble. But faithfulness means that you don't tell the truth just when it's convenient. Stephen told all the truth all the time. This was his definition of faithfulness.

#2: "Look, I see heaven open and the Son of Man standing at the right hand of God" (v. 56). Being faithful is always rewarded by a vision of God. Too great a claim? Not at all, for either in life (as in Stephen's case, during the last moments of his life) or in death, we shall wake to some vision of triumph. Everyone's faithfulness, either in life or in death, will be rewarded by a vision of God.

#3: "Lord Jesus, receive my spirit" (v. 59). Stephen, bleeding from the onslaught of flying stones, confesses his final confidence. Those who have been faithful know such assurance. We who are faithful will find the confidence to greet our eternal Christ without fear.

#4: "Lord, do not hold this sin against them" (v. 60). Faithful men and women are never vindictive, even during their executions. Stephen is modeling his last words after those of Jesus. Jesus was faithful in carrying out all his Father's will without rancor. Stephen, desiring to be like Jesus, could hardly do less.

To begin a study on the topic of Faithfulness: No Compromise, turn to the home page on page 898.

51"You stiff-necked people,[k] with uncircumcised hearts[l] and ears! You are just
like your fathers: You always resist the
Holy Spirit! 52Was there ever a prophet
your fathers did not persecute?[m] They
even killed those who predicted the
coming of the Righteous One. And
now you have betrayed and murdered
him[n]— 53you who have received the
law that was put into effect through angels[o] but have not obeyed it."

The Stoning of Stephen

54When they heard this, they were
furious[p] and gnashed their teeth at him.
55But Stephen, full of the Holy Spirit,
looked up to heaven and saw the glory
of God, and Jesus standing at the right
hand of God.[q] 56"Look," he said, "I
see heaven open[r] and the Son of Man[s]
standing at the right hand of God."
57At this they covered their ears and,
yelling at the top of their voices, they all
rushed at him, 58dragged him out of the
city[t] and began to stone him.[u] Meanwhile, the witnesses laid their clothes[v] at
the feet of a young man named Saul.[w]
59While they were stoning him, Stephen prayed, "Lord Jesus, receive my
spirit."[x] 60Then he fell on his knees[y]
and cried out, "Lord, do not hold this
sin against them."[z] When he had said
this, he fell asleep.

8 And Saul[a] was there, giving approval to his death.

The Church Persecuted and Scattered

On that day a great persecution broke
out against the church at Jerusalem, and

[a]*50* Isaiah 66:1,2

7:51 [k]Ex 32:9; 33:3,5 [l]Lev 26:41; Dt 10:16; Jer 4:4; 9:26
7:52 [m]2Ch 36:16; Mt 5:12 [n]Ac 3:14; 1Th 2:15
7:53 [o]ver 38; Gal 3:19; Heb 2:2
7:54 [p]Ac 5:33
7:55 [q]Mk 16:19
7:56 [r]Mt 3:16 [s]Mt 8:20
7:58 [t]Lk 4:29 [u]Lev 24:14,16; Dt 13:9 [v]Ac 22:20 [w]Ac 8:1
7:59 [x]Ps 31:5; Lk 23:46
7:60 [y]Ac 9:40 [z]Mt 5:44
8:1 [a]Ac 7:58

▸ LOVE

STONE A PROPHET? NO, BUT COULD I HOLD THE COATS OF THOSE WHO DO?

Acts 7:57–58

Saul, the Pharisee, would long remember the day when Stephen died. The stones that took this deacon's life fell heavily upon Saul's own, uncertain soul. What made Saul hold the coats of Stephen's executioners? Orthodoxy. Theologians love being true to "truth." Martyrs, on the other hand, sing mostly of relationships and love.

8:1 [b]Ac 11:19 all except the apostles were scattered[b]
[c]Ac 9:31 throughout Judea and Samaria.[c] 2God-
8:3 ly men buried Stephen and mourned
[d]Ac 7:58 deeply for him. 3But Saul[d] began to de-
[e]Ac 22:4,19; stroy the church.[e] Going from house to
26:10,11; 1Co 15:9; house, he dragged off men and women
Gal 1:13,23; Php 3:6; 1Ti 1:13 and put them in prison.

Philip in Samaria

8:4 [f]ver 1 4Those who had been scattered[f]
[g]Ac 15:35 preached the word wherever they went.[g]
8:5 [h]Ac 6:5 5Philip[h] went down to a city in Samaria and proclaimed the Christ[a] there.
6When the crowds heard Philip and saw
the miraculous signs he did, they all
paid close attention to what he said.
7With shrieks, evil[b] spirits came out of
8:7 [i]Mk 16:17 many,[i] and many paralytics and cripples
[j]Mt 4:24 were healed.[j] 8So there was great joy in
that city.

Simon the Sorcerer

9Now for some time a man named
Simon had practiced sorcery[k] in the city 8:9 [k]Ac 13:6
and amazed all the people of Samaria. [l]Ac 5:36
He boasted that he was someone great,[l]
10and all the people, both high and low,
gave him their attention and exclaimed,
"This man is the divine power known 8:10
as the Great Power."[m] 11They followed [m]Ac 14:11; 28:6
him because he had amazed them for a
long time with his magic. 12But when
they believed Philip as he preached the
good news of the kingdom of God[n] 8:12 [n]Ac 1:3
and the name of Jesus Christ, they were [o]Ac 2:38
baptized,[o] both men and women. 13Si-
mon himself believed and was baptized.
And he followed Philip everywhere, astonished by the great signs and mira- 8:13 [p]ver 6;
cles[p] he saw. Ac 19:11

[a]5 Or *Messiah* [b]7 Greek *unclean*

PHILIP

Joy, the Mark of Revival (8:4–40)

It's amazing what one person can do to bring joy to others. In the life of Philip, we see how his willingness to follow God's plan for his life led him to impact a whole region for God.

Philip was called by God to preach in Samaria. The Jews of Philip's day viewed Samaritans as foreigners and held them in contempt. Yet Philip followed God's call and led a revival in Samaria (see Acts 8:4–8). Great preaching, miracles and exorcisms occurred during his ministry there. The cumulative effect of the revival was that God did business in the lives of a great many people. The single comment about this event in Samaria was: "There was great joy in that city." Great joy is the mark of revival.

Philip continued to preach in Samaria, and his words impacted a well-known sorcerer named Simon (see vv. 9–25). Philip was joined in his outreach by Peter and John, who helped in spreading the Good News to the region.

Philip's joyous kingdom revival continued when he met an Ethiopian eunuch and introduced him to the kingdom of Christ (see vv. 26–40). After the eunuch was baptized, the Spirit of the Lord whisked Philip away, leaving the eunuch alone. But the joy went on and on. As the eunuch left the waters of baptism, he too was filled with elation and went on his way rejoicing (see v. 39).

Philip's work in Samaria is an example of the joy that results from revival. How good it would be to experience that joy throughout our own land. But we must remember that Philip didn't spread the joy simply because he wanted to. The joy came because he wanted to please Christ. When revival renews people's lives with a desire for godly obedience, then joy always follows.

Joy is a standing virtue.
Sitting makes joy fidgety.
Joy calls adrenaline its wine.
Joy calls God its bread.
Joy is not good at silence. Nor can it whisper. It only thrives when it is allowed to sing.

Joy is the love language of those who despise their separation from the ascended Christ and would sing him physically back upon the planet if they could.

14When the apostles in Jerusalem
8:14 [q]ver 1 heard that Samaria[q] had accepted the
[r]Lk 22:8 word of God, they sent Peter and John[r]
to them. 15When they arrived, they
8:15 prayed for them that they might re-
[s]Ac 2:38 ceive the Holy Spirit,[s] 16because the
8:16 Holy Spirit had not yet come upon
[t]Ac 19:2 [u]Mt 28:19; any of them;[t] they had simply been
Ac 2:38 baptized into[a] the name of the Lord
8:17 Jesus.[u] 17Then Peter and John placed
[v]Ac 6:6 their hands on them,[v] and they received
the Holy Spirit.
18When Simon saw that the Spirit
was given at the laying on of the apostles' hands, he offered them money
19and said, "Give me also this ability so
that everyone on whom I lay my hands
may receive the Holy Spirit."
20Peter answered: "May your money
perish with you, because you thought
8:20 you could buy the gift of God with
[w]2Ki 5:16; Da 5:17; money![w] 21You have no part or share
Mt 10:8; in this ministry, because your heart is
Ac 2:38 not right[x] before God. 22Repent of this
8:21 [x]Ps 78:37 wickedness and pray to the Lord. Perhaps he will forgive you for having such
a thought in your heart. 23For I see that
you are full of bitterness and captive to
sin."

GOODNESS

SIMON—BARGAIN SHOPPER

Acts 8:20

How do you get the most out of God with a minimal down payment? This is the number one question of those who try to haggle for cheap grace in the shambles of their pride. Finding that God's power is not for sale, these bargain shoppers often mumble mantras and preach with plastic power. Faith is sold cheaply to those who can't distinguish Pentecost from platitudes.

24Then Simon answered, "Pray to the
8:24 [y]Ex 8:8; Lord for me[y] so that nothing you have
Nu 21:7; said may happen to me."
1Ki 13:6 25When they had testified and proclaimed the word of the Lord, Peter
and John returned to Jerusalem, preach-
8:25 ing the gospel in many Samaritan
[z]ver 40 villages.[z]

Philip and the Ethiopian

8:26 26Now an angel[a] of the Lord said
[a]Ac 5:19 to Philip, "Go south to the road—the
desert road—that goes down from Jerusalem to Gaza." 27So he started out,
and on his way he met an Ethiopian[b][b] 8:27 [b]Ps 68:31;
eunuch,[c] an important official in charge 87:4;
of all the treasury of Candace, queen of Zep 3:10 [c]Isa 56:3-5
the Ethiopians. This man had gone to [d]1Ki 8:41-43;
Jerusalem to worship,[d] 28and on his way Jn 12:20
home was sitting in his chariot reading
the book of Isaiah the prophet. 29The 8:29
Spirit told[e] Philip, "Go to that chariot [e]Ac 10:19; 11:12; 13:2;
and stay near it." 20:23; 21:11
30Then Philip ran up to the chariot
and heard the man reading Isaiah the
prophet. "Do you understand what you
are reading?" Philip asked.
31"How can I," he said, "unless someone explains it to me?" So he invited
Philip to come up and sit with him.
32The eunuch was reading this passage of Scripture:

"He was led like a sheep to the
slaughter,
and as a lamb before the shearer
is silent,
so he did not open his mouth.
33In his humiliation he was deprived
of justice.
Who can speak of his
descendants?
For his life was taken from the 8:33
earth."[c][f] [f]Isa 53:7,8

34The eunuch asked Philip, "Tell me,
please, who is the prophet talking about,
himself or someone else?" 35Then Phil- 8:35
ip began[g] with that very passage of [g]Mt 5:2 [h]Lk 24:27;
Scripture[h] and told him the good news Ac 17:2;
about Jesus. 18:28; 28:23
36As they traveled along the road,
they came to some water and the eunuch said, "Look, here is water. Why
shouldn't I be baptized?"[d][i] 38And he 8:36 [i]Ac 10:47
gave orders to stop the chariot. Then
both Philip and the eunuch went down
into the water and Philip baptized him. 8:39
39When they came up out of the wa- [j]1Ki 18:12;
ter, the Spirit of the Lord suddenly took 2Ki 2:16;
Philip away,[j] and the eunuch did not Eze 3:12,14; 8:3; 11:1,24;
see him again, but went on his way re- 43:5; 2Co 12:2
joicing. 40Philip, however, appeared at 8:40 [k]ver 25
Azotus and traveled about, preaching [l]Ac 10:1,24;
the gospel in all the towns[k] until he 12:19; 21:8,16;
reached Caesarea.[l] 23:23,33; 25:1,4,6,13

[a]*16* Or *in* [b]*27* That is, from the upper Nile region [c]*33* Isaiah 53:7,8 [d]*36* Some late manuscripts *baptized?"* [37]*Philip said, "If you believe with all your heart, you may." The eunuch answered, "I believe that Jesus Christ is the Son of God."*

Saul's Conversion

9 Meanwhile, Saul was still breathing out murderous threats against
9:1 [m]Ac 8:3 the Lord's disciples.[m] He went to the
high priest 2and asked him for letters
to the synagogues in Damascus, so that
if he found any there who belonged to
9:2 [n]Ac 19:9,23; 22:4; 24:14,22 the Way,[n] whether men or women, he
might take them as prisoners to Jeru-
salem. 3As he neared Damascus on his
9:3 [o]1Co 15:8 journey, suddenly a light from heaven
flashed around him.[o] 4He fell to the
ground and heard a voice say to him,
"Saul, Saul, why do you persecute
me?"

PEACE

WHO'S THERE?

Acts 9:5

The Damascus road runs through the desert of our reverie. We hear a voice but cannot distinguish who it is. But, being struck by light and left to grovel on the ground, we might be wise to ask, "Have we met before?" It is then that he might say, "Only briefly—when you held the coats of those who killed a friend of mine." From then on, peace will be impossible till we apologize to God.

5"Who are you, Lord?" Saul asked.
"I am Jesus, whom you are persecuting," he replied. 6"Now get up and go
into the city, and you will be told what
9:6 [p]ver 16 you must do."[p]
7The men traveling with Saul stood
there speechless; they heard the sound[q]
9:7 [q]Jn 12:29 [r]Da 10:7; Ac 22:9 but did not see anyone.[r] 8Saul got up
from the ground, but when he opened
his eyes he could see nothing. So they
led him by the hand into Damascus.
9For three days he was blind, and did
not eat or drink anything.
10In Damascus there was a disciple
named Ananias. The Lord called to him
9:10 [s]Ac 10:3,17,19 in a vision,[s] "Ananias!"
"Yes, Lord," he answered.
11The Lord told him, "Go to the
house of Judas on Straight Street and
9:11 [t]ver 30; Ac 21:39; 22:3 ask for a man from Tarsus[t] named Saul,
for he is praying. 12In a vision he has
seen a man named Ananias come and
9:12 [u]Mk 5:23 place his hands on[u] him to restore his
sight."
13"Lord," Ananias answered, "I have
heard many reports about this man and
all the harm he has done to your saints[v] 9:13 [v]ver 32; Ro 1:7; 16:2,15 [w]Ac 8:3
in Jerusalem.[w] 14And he has come here
with authority from the chief priests[x] to
arrest all who call on your name." 9:14 [x]ver 2,21
15But the Lord said to Ananias, "Go!
This man is my chosen instrument[y] to 9:15 [y]Ac 13:2; Ro 1:1; Gal 1:15 [z]Ro 11:13; 15:15,16; Gal 2:7,8; Eph 3:7,8 [a]Ac 25:22,23; 26:1
carry my name before the Gentiles[z] and
their kings[a] and before the people of Israel. 16I will show him how much he
must suffer for my name."[b]
17Then Ananias went to the house
and entered it. Placing his hands on[c]
Saul, he said, "Brother Saul, the Lord— 9:16 [b]Ac 20:23; 21:11; 2Co 11:23-27
Jesus, who appeared to you on the road
as you were coming here—has sent me
so that you may see again and be filled
with the Holy Spirit." 18Immediately, 9:17 [c]Ac 6:6
something like scales fell from Saul's
eyes, and he could see again. He got
up and was baptized, 19and after taking
some food, he regained his strength.

Saul in Damascus and Jerusalem

Saul spent several days with the disci-
ples[d] in Damascus.[e] 20At once he began 9:19 [d]Ac 11:26 [e]Ac 26:20
to preach in the synagogues[f] that Jesus
is the Son of God.[g] 21All those who 9:20 [f]Ac 13:5,14 [g]Mt 4:3
heard him were astonished and asked,
"Isn't he the man who raised havoc in
Jerusalem among those who call on this
name?[h] And hasn't he come here to take 9:21 [h]Ac 8:3 [i]Gal 1:13,23
them as prisoners to the chief priests?"[i]
22Yet Saul grew more and more powerful and baffled the Jews living in Damascus by proving that Jesus is the
Christ.[a][j] 9:22 [j]Ac 18:5,28
23After many days had gone by, the
Jews conspired to kill him, 24but Saul
learned of their plan.[k] Day and night 9:24 [k]Ac 20:3,19
they kept close watch on the city gates
in order to kill him. 25But his followers took him by night and lowered him
in a basket through an opening in the
wall.[l] 9:25 [l]1Sa 19:12; 2Co 11:32,33
26When he came to Jerusalem,[m] he
tried to join the disciples, but they were 9:26 [m]Ac 22:17; 26:20; Gal 1:17,18
all afraid of him, not believing that he
really was a disciple. 27But Barnabas[n]
took him and brought him to the apostles. He told them how Saul on his
journey had seen the Lord and that the
Lord had spoken to him,[o] and how in 9:27 [n]Ac 4:36 [o]ver 3-6 [p]ver 20,22
Damascus he had preached fearlessly in
the name of Jesus.[p] 28So Saul stayed
with them and moved about freely in
Jerusalem, speaking boldly in the name

[a]22 Or *Messiah*

Week 17 Gentleness

1 Day One

▸ Gentleness, a Way of Winning Others to Christ

Read Acts 9:36–42

Arts and crafts time in Joppa! Dorcas is dead, but all the articles of clothing and needlework that she had done are brought to her deathbed where all celebrate her creativity. Acts 9:36 says that Dorcas was a disciple who was always doing good and helping the poor. But sadly, she became ill and died.

When gentle people pass on, they leave a gaping wound in the center of our lives. When the power-hungry pass on, there is often a feeling of relief. When the miserly and stingy take their leave, there is sometimes a problem making up a funeral party. Remember when the Ghost of Christmas Yet to Come showed old Scrooge his coming funeral and nobody wanted to attend?

Dorcas's life was a testament to her gentleness. Many crowded around her gentle life and held their own little crafts show. They celebrated at her death her giving spirit, so outgoing that she used her creativity to bless others. Dorcas is a role model for all Christian artists. Every creative disciple needs to ask himself or herself, "Have I developed an outgoing gentleness that seeks to use my artistic talents to cause the world to celebrate Jesus?"

Gentleness is a great evangelist. It is the best witness of the gentle living and the best witness of the gentle dead. Gentleness was Christ's gift to Dorcas and Dorcas's best gift to the world. I once heard of an old African man who, upon hearing his first Christian sermon on the gentle Jesus, said, "See there. I always told you there should be a God like that—a gentle God who changes the world so gently that his immense transformations never cause a moment of dread."

In this passage, Dorcas was revived and lived on. Who knows what happened when she died the second time: another arts and crafts party? Another celebration of her gentle life by her gentle converts? No doubt. For gentleness is always celebrated by those around it.

> **Memorize This Week**
>
> **PHILIPPIANS 4:5**
>
> ***Let your gentleness be evident to all. The Lord is near.***

2 Day Two

▸ Gentleness and the Purpose of God in My Life

In our loud days of loud services and loud disciples, the idea that God whispers is most welcome. Sitting before ranks of amplifiers at Christian concerts can make you truly grateful that God still whispers. Gentle is the Almighty—almighty gentle—almighty silent. Ask Elijah. *Turn to 1 Kings 19:11–14, page 415, for today's study.*

3 Day Three

▸ Gentleness and My Relationship With Christ

Gentleness is the great cosmetic that adorns the human spirit. Those who work for hours before their mirror, brushing and creaming and lotioning their way to a supposed loveliness, need to sit quietly before the Spirit. He will seep into their lives and make them truly beautiful. He will supply the unfading gentle spirit that comes neither in creams nor lotions. *Turn to 1 Peter 3:1–6, page 1493, for today's study.*

4 Day Four

▸ Gentleness and My Service to Others

This book is a letter from John to his friend Gaius. It isn't a long letter. Actually, it is more of a thank-you note, rehearsing the great gentleness displayed by this little-known hero of the Bible. It is such a small letter, but there it is, glistening with gentleness and speaking almost entirely on our service to others. *Turn to 3 John 5–11, page 1515, for today's study.*

5 Day Five

▸ Gentleness and Its Place in My Personal Worship

Two hurting women vowed their undying support and offered nothing more to each other than a gentle spirit. Their lesson is driven like a four-chapter wedge into the heavy Hebrew history of the Old Testament, and there it stands—a tale of two loving women. Their gentleness and love placed them in the lineage of Christ and taught the world that life itself is worship. *Turn to Ruth 1:16–17, page 302, for today's study.*

Week 18, Self-Control, the Mark of Obedience, begins on page 1011, Daniel 1:8–17.
To begin a topical study on the Fruit of the Spirit, Gentleness, turn to the Topical Index, page 1548.

of the Lord. 29He talked and debated
9:29 [q]Ac 6:1 with the Grecian Jews,[q] but they tried to
[r]2Co 11:26 kill him.[r] 30When the brothers[s] learned
9:30 of this, they took him down to Caesa-
[s]Ac 1:16 rea[t] and sent him off to Tarsus.[u]
[t]Ac 8:40 [u]ver 11 31Then the church throughout Judea,
Galilee and Samaria[v] enjoyed a time
9:31 [v]Ac 8:1 of peace. It was strengthened; and encouraged by the Holy Spirit, it grew
in numbers, living in the fear of the
Lord.

Aeneas and Dorcas

32As Peter traveled about the country,
9:32 [w]ver 13 he went to visit the saints[w] in Lydda.
33There he found a man named Aeneas,
a paralytic who had been bedridden for
eight years. 34"Aeneas," Peter said to
9:34 [x]Ac 3:6,16; him, "Jesus Christ heals you.[x] Get up
4:10 and take care of your mat." Immedi-
9:35 ately Aeneas got up. 35All those who
[y]1Ch 5:16; 27:29; lived in Lydda and Sharon[y] saw him
Isa 33:9; 35:2; and turned to the Lord.[z]
65:10 [z]Ac 11:21 36In Joppa[a] there was a disciple
named Tabitha (which, when translat-
9:36 [a]Jos 19:46; ed, is Dorcas[a]), who was always doing
2Ch 2:16; Ezr 3:7; good[b] and helping the poor. 37About
Jnh 1:3; that time she became sick and died, and
Ac 10:5 [b]1Ti 2:10; her body was washed and placed in an
Tit 3:8 upstairs room.[c] 38Lydda was near Jop-
9:37 pa; so when the disciples[d] heard that
[c]Ac 1:13 Peter was in Lydda, they sent two men
9:38 to him and urged him, "Please come at
[d]Ac 11:26 once!"
39Peter went with them, and when
9:39 he arrived he was taken upstairs to the
[e]Ac 6:1 room. All the widows[e] stood around
him, crying and showing him the robes
and other clothing that Dorcas had
9:40 made while she was still with them.
[f]Mt 9:25 [g]Lk 22:41; 40Peter sent them all out of the room;[f]
Ac 7:60 then he got down on his knees[g] and
prayed. Turning toward the dead woman, he said, "Tabitha, get up." She
opened her eyes, and seeing Peter she
sat up. 41He took her by the hand and
helped her to her feet. Then he called
the believers and the widows and presented her to them alive. 42This became
known all over Joppa, and many people believed in the Lord. 43Peter stayed
9:43 [h]Ac 10:6 in Joppa for some time with a tanner
named Simon.[h]

Cornelius Calls for Peter

10:1 [i]Ac 8:40 10 At Caesarea[i] there was a man
named Cornelius, a centurion
in what was known as the Italian Regiment. 2He and all his family were
devout and God-fearing;[j] he gave gen- 10:2 [j]ver 22,35;
erously to those in need and prayed to Ac 13:16,26
God regularly. 3One day at about three
in the afternoon[k] he had a vision.[l] He 10:3 [k]Ac 3:1
distinctly saw an angel[m] of God, who [l]Ac 9:10
came to him and said, "Cornelius!" [m]Ac 5:19
4Cornelius stared at him in fear.
"What is it, Lord?" he asked.
The angel answered, "Your prayers
and gifts to the poor have come up as a 10:4
memorial offering[n] before God.[o] 5Now [n]Mt 26:13 [o]Rev 8:4
send men to Joppa[p] to bring back a
man named Simon who is called Peter. 10:5
6He is staying with Simon the tanner,[q] [p]Ac 9:36
whose house is by the sea." 10:6 [q]Ac 9:43
7When the angel who spoke to him
had gone, Cornelius called two of his
servants and a devout soldier who was
one of his attendants. 8He told them
everything that had happened and sent 10:8
them to Joppa.[r] [r]Ac 9:36

Peter's Vision

9About noon the following day as
they were on their journey and approaching the city, Peter went up on the
roof[s] to pray. 10He became hungry and 10:9 [s]Mt 24:17
wanted something to eat, and while the
meal was being prepared, he fell into
a trance.[t] 11He saw heaven opened and 10:10 [t]Ac 22:17
something like a large sheet being let
down to earth by its four corners. 12It
contained all kinds of four-footed animals, as well as reptiles of the earth
and birds of the air. 13Then a voice told
him, "Get up, Peter. Kill and eat."
14"Surely not, Lord!"[u] Peter replied. 10:14 [u]Ac 9:5
"I have never eaten anything impure or [v]Lev 11:4-8,
unclean."[v] 13-20; 20:25; Dt 14:3-20;
15The voice spoke to him a second Eze 4:14
time, "Do not call anything impure that 10:15
God has made clean."[w] [w]Mt 15:11;
16This happened three times, and im- Ro 14:14, 17,20;
mediately the sheet was taken back to 1Co 10:25; 1Ti 4:3,4;
heaven. Tit 1:15
17While Peter was wondering about
the meaning of the vision, the men
sent by Cornelius[x] found out where Si- 10:17 [x]ver 7,8
mon's house was and stopped at the
gate. 18They called out, asking if Simon
who was known as Peter was staying
there.
19While Peter was still thinking about
the vision, the Spirit said[y] to him, "Si- 10:19 [y]Ac 8:29

[a]36 Both *Tabitha* (Aramaic) and *Dorcas* (Greek) mean *gazelle*.

mon, three[a] men are looking for you.
20So get up and go downstairs. Do not
hesitate to go with them, for I have sent
them."[z]

10:20
[z]Ac 15:7-9

DAY 3 THREE

Peace and My Relationship With Christ

Acts 10:9–16

Peter had a vision that defined for him how to abandon prejudice and the narrow peace that Jewish Christians knew in order to find a simpler peace available on a larger scale. How is this vision to be interpreted? What do the various parts mean? Let us examine it piece by piece.

Peter was hungry, and the vision came to him while he was waiting for his dinner to be prepared. Our appetites are so ordinary and so customary, yet eating and drinking use up much of our time. God spoke to Peter just before dinner. Could it be that, through something as trivial as a growling stomach, God wants to speak to us about how to widen our hunger? It is as Jesus said to the disciples in John 4:32, "I have food to eat that you know nothing about." God had delicious meat upon which Peter could sate himself once he got past his old biases.

"Get up, Peter. Kill and eat," cried the voice in the vision. Peter might have obeyed the voice had the things in the sheet been on his list of kosher meats. But they were not, and the order was protested. Peter drew back from the command.

"I have never eaten anything impure or unclean," Peter protested.

"Do not call anything impure that God has made clean," said the voice.

The vision was repeated three times, just in case Peter needed time to think it all through. Finally, Peter saw that he needed to step beyond his prejudicial notions if the gospel were ever to make its way to the Gentiles.

Peter accepted God's higher will. The result was that peace came not only to Peter, but to the entire household of Cornelius as well. This should not surprise us. Peace always comes after accepting a higher will than our own.

To begin a study on the topic of Peace, Accepting a Higher Will, turn to the home page on page 1282.

21Peter went down and said to the
men, "I'm the one you're looking for.
Why have you come?"
22The men replied, "We have come
from Cornelius the centurion. He is a
righteous and God-fearing man,[a] who
is respected by all the Jewish people. A
holy angel told him to have you come to
his house so that he could hear what you
have to say."[b] 23Then Peter invited the
men into the house to be his guests.

10:22
[a]ver 2
[b]Ac 11:14

Peter at Cornelius's House

The next day Peter started out with
them, and some of the brothers[c] from
Joppa went along.[d] 24The following day
he arrived in Caesarea.[e] Cornelius was
expecting them and had called together
his relatives and close friends. 25As Peter
entered the house, Cornelius met him
and fell at his feet in reverence. 26But
Peter made him get up. "Stand up," he
said, "I am only a man myself."[f]
27Talking with him, Peter went inside and found a large gathering of people. 28He said to them: "You are well
aware that it is against our law for a Jew
to associate with a Gentile or visit him.[g]
But God has shown me that I should
not call any man impure or unclean.[h]
29So when I was sent for, I came without raising any objection. May I ask
why you sent for me?"
30Cornelius answered: "Four days ago
I was in my house praying at this hour,
at three in the afternoon. Suddenly a
man in shining clothes stood before me
31and said, 'Cornelius, God has heard
your prayer and remembered your gifts
to the poor. 32Send to Joppa for Simon
who is called Peter. He is a guest in the
home of Simon the tanner, who lives
by the sea.' 33So I sent for you immediately, and it was good of you to come.
Now we are all here in the presence of
God to listen to everything the Lord
has commanded you to tell us."
34Then Peter began to speak: "I now
realize how true it is that God does
not show favoritism[i] 35but accepts men
from every nation who fear him and do
what is right.[j] 36You know the message
God sent to the people of Israel, telling the good news[k] of peace[l] through
Jesus Christ, who is Lord of all.[m] 37You

10:23
[c]Ac 1:16
[d]ver 45;
Ac 11:12

10:24
[e]Ac 8:40

10:26
[f]Ac 14:15;
Rev 19:10

10:28
[g]Jn 4:9;
18:28;
Ac 11:3
[h]Ac 15:8,9

10:34
[i]Dt 10:17;
2Ch 19:7;
Job 34:19;
Ro 2:11;
Gal 2:6;
Eph 6:9;
Col 3:25;
1Pe 1:17

10:35
[j]Ac 15:9

10:36
[k]Ac 13:32
[l]Lk 2:14
[m]Mt 28:18;
Ro 10:12

[a]*19* One early manuscript *two*; other manuscripts do not have the number.

GENTLENESS

THE HAPPY, HUNGRY HEART

Acts 10:33

Cornelius wanted God—all of God, and yet more of God. Jesus was the final step to God. It was a little step, but one Cornelius could not take alone. He needed to be helped by one who knew the way... but even so, gentle people are never far from the kingdom.

know what has happened throughout
Judea, beginning in Galilee after the
baptism that John preached— 38how
10:38 [n]Ac 4:26 God anointed[n] Jesus of Nazareth with
[o]Mt 4:23 [p]Jn 3:2 the Holy Spirit and power, and how he
went around doing good and healing[o]
all who were under the power of the
devil, because God was with him.[p]
10:39 [q]Lk 24:48 39"We are witnesses[q] of everything he
[r]Ac 5:30 did in the country of the Jews and in
Jerusalem. They killed him by hanging
him on a tree,[r] 40but God raised him
10:40 [s]Ac 2:24 from the dead[s] on the third day and
10:41 caused him to be seen. 41He was not
[t]Jn 14:17,22 seen by all the people,[t] but by witnesses
[u]Lk 24:43; Jn 21:13 whom God had already chosen—by us
who ate[u] and drank with him after he
rose from the dead. 42He commanded
10:42 [v]Mt 28:19,20 us to preach to the people[v] and to tes-
[w]Jn 5:22; Ac 17:31; tify that he is the one whom God ap-
Ro 14:9; pointed as judge of the living and the
2Co 5:10; 2Ti 4:1; dead.[w] 43All the prophets testify about
1Pe 4:5 him[x] that everyone[y] who believes in
10:43 him receives forgiveness of sins through
[x]Isa 53:11 [y]Ac 15:9 his name."
44While Peter was still speaking these
10:44 [z]Ac 8:15,16; words, the Holy Spirit came on[z] all
11:15; 15:8 who heard the message. 45The circumcised believers who had come with Pe-
10:45 [a]ver 23 ter[a] were astonished that the gift of
[b]Ac 2:33,38 [c]Ac 11:18 the Holy Spirit had been poured out[b]
even on the Gentiles.[c] 46For they heard
10:46 [d]Mk 16:17 them speaking in tongues[a][d] and praising God.
Then Peter said, 47"Can anyone keep
10:47 these people from being baptized with
[e]Ac 8:36 [f]Ac 11:17 water?[e] They have received the Holy
Spirit just as we have."[f] 48So he ordered
that they be baptized in the name of
10:48 [g]Ac 2:38; 8:16 Jesus Christ.[g] Then they asked Peter to
stay with them for a few days.

Peter Explains His Actions

11:1 [h]Ac 1:16 11 The apostles and the brothers[h]
throughout Judea heard that the
Gentiles also had received the word of
God. 2So when Peter went up to Jeru-
salem, the circumcised believers[i] criti- 11:2 [i]Ac 10:45
cized him 3and said, "You went into the
house of uncircumcised men and ate 11:3
with them."[j] [j]Ac 10:25,28; Gal 2:12
4Peter began and explained everything to them precisely as it had happened: 5"I was in the city of Joppa 11:5
praying, and in a trance I saw a vision.[k] [k]Ac 10:9-32; 9:10
I saw something like a large sheet being
let down from heaven by its four corners, and it came down to where I was.
6I looked into it and saw four-footed
animals of the earth, wild beasts, reptiles, and birds of the air. 7Then I heard
a voice telling me, 'Get up, Peter. Kill
and eat.'
8"I replied, 'Surely not, Lord! Nothing impure or unclean has ever entered
my mouth.'
9"The voice spoke from heaven a second time, 'Do not call anything impure 11:9
that God has made clean.'[l] 10This hap- [l]Ac 10:15
pened three times, and then it was all
pulled up to heaven again.
11"Right then three men who had
been sent to me from Caesarea stopped
at the house where I was staying. 12The 11:12
Spirit told[m] me to have no hesitation [m]Ac 8:29 [n]Ac 15:9;
about going with them.[n] These six Ro 3:22
brothers also went with me, and we
entered the man's house. 13He told us
how he had seen an angel appear in
his house and say, 'Send to Joppa for
Simon who is called Peter. 14He will
bring you a message through which you
and all your household[o] will be saved.' 11:14 [o]Jn 4:53;
15"As I began to speak, the Holy Spir- Ac 16:15, 31-34;
it came on[p] them as he had come on 1Co 1:11,16
us at the beginning.[q] 16Then I remem- 11:15
bered what the Lord had said: 'John [p]Ac 10:44 [q]Ac 2:4
baptized with[b] water, but you will be 11:16
baptized with the Holy Spirit.'[r] 17So [r]Mk 1:8;
if God gave them the same gift as he Ac 1:5
gave us,[s] who believed in the Lord Jesus 11:17
Christ, who was I to think that I could [s]Ac 10:45,47
oppose God?"
18When they heard this, they had
no further objections and praised God,
saying, "So then, God has granted even 11:18
the Gentiles repentance unto life."[t] [t]Ro 10:12,13; 2Co 7:10

The Church in Antioch

19Now those who had been scattered
by the persecution in connection with

[a]46 Or *other languages* [b]16 Or *in*

Stephen[u] traveled as far as Phoenicia,
Cyprus and Antioch,[v] telling the message only to Jews. 20Some of them, however, men from Cyprus[w] and Cyrene,[x]
went to Antioch and began to speak
to Greeks also, telling them the good
news about the Lord Jesus. 21The Lord's
hand was with them,[y] and a great number of people believed and turned to
the Lord.[z]
22News of this reached the ears of
the church at Jerusalem, and they sent
Barnabas[a] to Antioch. 23When he arrived and saw the evidence of the grace
of God,[b] he was glad and encouraged
them all to remain true to the Lord with
all their hearts.[c] 24He was a good man,
full of the Holy Spirit and faith, and a
great number of people were brought
to the Lord.[d]
25Then Barnabas went to Tarsus[e] to
look for Saul, 26and when he found
him, he brought him to Antioch. So
for a whole year Barnabas and Saul
met with the church and taught great
numbers of people. The disciples[f] were
called Christians first[g] at Antioch.
27During this time some prophets[h]
came down from Jerusalem to Antioch.
28One of them, named Agabus,[i] stood
up and through the Spirit predicted
that a severe famine would spread over
the entire Roman world.[j] (This happened during the reign of Claudius.)[k]
29The disciples,[l] each according to his
ability, decided to provide help[m] for the
brothers[n] living in Judea. 30This they
did, sending their gift to the elders[o] by
Barnabas and Saul.[p]

Peter's Miraculous Escape From Prison

12 It was about this time that King
Herod arrested some who belonged to the church, intending to persecute them. 2He had James, the brother
of John,[q] put to death with the sword.
3When he saw that this pleased the
Jews,[r] he proceeded to seize Peter also.
This happened during the Feast of Unleavened Bread.[s] 4After arresting him,
he put him in prison, handing him over
to be guarded by four squads of four
soldiers each. Herod intended to bring
him out for public trial after the Passover.
5So Peter was kept in prison, but the
church was earnestly praying to God
for him.[t]
6The night before Herod was to bring
him to trial, Peter was sleeping between
two soldiers, bound with two chains,[u]
and sentries stood guard at the entrance.
7Suddenly an angel[v] of the Lord appeared and a light shone in the cell. He
struck Peter on the side and woke him
up. "Quick, get up!" he said, and the
chains fell off Peter's wrists.[w]
8Then the angel said to him, "Put
on your clothes and sandals." And Peter
did so. "Wrap your cloak around you
and follow me," the angel told him. 9Pe-
ter followed him out of the prison, but
he had no idea that what the angel was
doing was really happening; he thought
he was seeing a vision.[x] 10They passed
the first and second guards and came
to the iron gate leading to the city. It
opened for them by itself,[y] and they
went through it. When they had walked
the length of one street, suddenly the
angel left him.
11Then Peter came to himself[z] and
said, "Now I know without a doubt
that the Lord sent his angel and rescued me[a] from Herod's clutches and
from everything the Jewish people were
anticipating."
12When this had dawned on him, he
went to the house of Mary the mother
of John, also called Mark,[b] where many
people had gathered and were praying.[c]
13Peter knocked at the outer entrance,
and a servant girl named Rhoda came
to answer the door.[d] 14When she recognized Peter's voice, she was so overjoyed[e] she ran back without opening it
and exclaimed, "Peter is at the door!"
15"You're out of your mind," they
told her. When she kept insisting that
it was so, they said, "It must be his
angel."[f]
16But Peter kept on knocking, and
when they opened the door and saw
him, they were astonished. 17Peter motioned with his hand[g] for them to be
quiet and described how the Lord had
brought him out of prison. "Tell James[h]
and the brothers[i] about this," he said,
and then he left for another place.
18In the morning, there was no small
commotion among the soldiers as to
what had become of Peter. 19After
Herod had a thorough search made for
him and did not find him, he cross-

11:19 [u]Ac 8:1,4 [v]ver 26,27; Ac 13:1; 18:22; Gal 2:11
11:20 [w]Ac 4:36 [x]Mt 27:32
11:21 [y]Lk 1:66 [z]Ac 2:47
11:22 [a]Ac 4:36
11:23 [b]Ac 13:43; 14:26; 20:24 [c]Ac 14:22
11:24 [d]ver 21; Ac 5:14
11:25 [e]Ac 9:11
11:26 [f]Ac 6:1,2; 13:52 [g]Ac 26:28; 1Pe 4:16
11:27 [h]Ac 13:1; 15:32; 1Co 12:28, 29; Eph 4:11
11:28 [i]Ac 21:10 [j]Mt 24:14 [k]Ac 18:2
11:29 [l]ver 26 [m]Ro 15:26; 2Co 9:2 [n]Ac 1:16
11:30 [o]Ac 14:23 [p]Ac 12:25
12:2 [q]Mt 4:21
12:3 [r]Ac 24:27 [s]Ex 12:15; 23:15
12:5 [t]Eph 6:18
12:6 [u]Ac 21:33
12:7 [v]Ac 5:19 [w]Ac 16:26
12:9 [x]Ac 9:10
12:10 [y]Ac 5:19; 16:26
12:11 [z]Lk 15:17 [a]Ps 34:7; Da 3:28; 6:22; 2Co 1:10; 2Pe 2:9
12:12 [b]ver 25; Ac 15:37,39; Col 4:10; Phm 24; 1Pe 5:13 [c]ver 5
12:13 [d]Jn 18:16,17
12:14 [e]Lk 24:41
12:15 [f]Mt 18:10
12:17 [g]Ac 13:16; 19:33; 21:40 [h]Ac 15:13 [i]Ac 1:16

examined the guards and ordered that
12:19 [j]Ac 16:27 they be executed.[j]
[k]Ac 8:40

Herod's Death

Then Herod went from Judea to Caesarea[k] and stayed there a while. 20He had
12:20 been quarreling with the people of Tyre
[l]Mt 11:21 and Sidon;[l] they now joined together
[m]1Ki 5:9,11; Eze 27:17 and sought an audience with him. Having secured the support of Blastus, a
trusted personal servant of the king,
they asked for peace, because they depended on the king's country for their
food supply.[m]
21On the appointed day Herod, wearing his royal robes, sat on his throne
and delivered a public address to the
people. 22They shouted, "This is the
voice of a god, not of a man." 23Im-
mediately, because Herod did not give
12:23 praise to God, an angel of the Lord
[n]1Sa 25:38; 2Sa 24:16,17 struck him down,[n] and he was eaten by
worms and died.
12:24 24But the word of God continued to
[o]Ac 6:7; 19:20 increase and spread.[o]
12:25 25When Barnabas[p] and Saul had
[p]Ac 4:36 [q]Ac 11:30 finished their mission,[q] they returned
from[a] Jerusalem, taking with them John,
[r]ver 12 also called Mark.[r]

Barnabas and Saul Sent Off

13:1 [s]Ac 11:19 13 In the church at Antioch[s] there
[t]Ac 11:27 were prophets[t] and teachers:
[u]Ac 4:36; 11:22-26 Barnabas,[u] Simeon called Niger, Lu-
[v]Mt 14:1 cius of Cyrene, Manaen (who had been
brought up with Herod[v] the tetrarch)
and Saul. 2While they were worshiping
the Lord and fasting, the Holy Spirit
13:2 [w]Ac 8:29 said,[w] "Set apart for me Barnabas and
[x]Ac 14:26 Saul for the work[x] to which I have
[y]Ac 22:21 called them."[y] 3So after they had fasted
13:3 [z]Ac 6:6 and prayed, they placed their hands on
[a]Ac 14:26 them[z] and sent them off.[a]

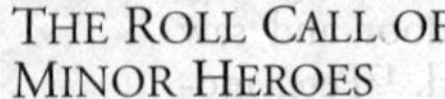

FAITHFULNESS

THE ROLL CALL OF
MINOR HEROES

Acts 13:1–2

These fine men fasted and prayed for Christ to send out missionaries. Imagine their surprise when he sent them.

On Cyprus

4The two of them, sent on their way
13:4 [b]ver 2,3 by the Holy Spirit,[b] went down to Se-
[c]Ac 4:36 leucia and sailed from there to Cyprus.[c]
5When they arrived at Salamis, they
proclaimed the word of God in the Jew-
ish synagogues.[d] John[e] was with them 13:5 [d]Ac 9:20
as their helper. [e]Ac 12:12
6They traveled through the whole island until they came to Paphos. There 13:6
they met a Jewish sorcerer[f] and false [f]Ac 8:9
prophet[g] named Bar-Jesus, 7who was [g]Mt 7:15
an attendant of the proconsul,[h] Sergius 13:7 [h]ver 8,12;
Paulus. The proconsul, an intelligent Ac 19:38
man, sent for Barnabas and Saul because he wanted to hear the word of
God. 8But Elymas the sorcerer[i] (for 13:8 [i]Ac 8:9
that is what his name means) opposed [j]ver 7
them and tried to turn the proconsul[j] [k]Ac 6:7
from the faith.[k] 9Then Saul, who was
also called Paul, filled with the Holy 13:9
Spirit,[l] looked straight at Elymas and [l]Ac 4:8
said, 10"You are a child of the devil[m] and 13:10 [m]Mt 13:38;
an enemy of everything that is right! Jn 8:44
You are full of all kinds of deceit and [n]Hos 14:9
trickery. Will you never stop perverting
the right ways of the Lord?[n] 11Now the 13:11
hand of the Lord is against you.[o] You [o]Ex 9:3;
are going to be blind, and for a time 1Sa 5:6,7;
you will be unable to see the light of the Ps 32:4
sun."
Immediately mist and darkness came
over him, and he groped about, seeking someone to lead him by the hand. 13:12
12When the proconsul[p] saw what had [p]ver 7
happened, he believed, for he was
amazed at the teaching about the Lord.

In Pisidian Antioch

13From Paphos,[q] Paul and his com- 13:13 [q]ver 6
panions sailed to Perga in Pamphylia, [r]Ac 12:12
where John[r] left them to return to Jerusalem. 14From Perga they went on to 13:14
Pisidian Antioch.[s] On the Sabbath[t] they [s]Ac 14:19,21
entered the synagogue[u] and sat down. [t]Ac 16:13
15After the reading from the Law[v] and [u]Ac 9:20
the Prophets, the synagogue rulers sent 13:15
word to them, saying, "Brothers, if you [v]Ac 15:21
have a message of encouragement for
the people, please speak."
16Standing up, Paul motioned with 13:16
his hand[w] and said: "Men of Israel and [w]Ac 12:17
you Gentiles who worship God, listen
to me! 17The God of the people of Israel chose our fathers; he made the people 13:17
prosper during their stay in Egypt, with [x]Ex 6:6,7;
mighty power he led them out of that Dt 7:6-8
country,[x] 18he endured their conduct[b][y] 13:18
for about forty years in the desert,[z] 19he [y]Dt 1:31 [z]Ac 7:36

[a]*25* Some manuscripts *to* [b]*18* Some manuscripts *and cared for them*

overthrew seven nations in Canaan[a] and
13:19 [a]Dt 7:1 [b]Jos 19:51 gave their land to his people[b] as their
inheritance. 20All this took about 450
13:20 [c]Jdg 2:16 [d]1Sa 3:19,20 years.
“After this, God gave them judges[c]
until the time of Samuel the prophet.[d]
13:21 [e]1Sa 8:5,19 [f]1Sa 10:1 [g]1Sa 9:1,2 21Then the people asked for a king,[e]
and he gave them Saul[f] son of Kish, of
the tribe of Benjamin,[g] who ruled forty
13:22 [h]1Sa 15:23,26 [i]1Sa 16:13; Ps 89:20 [j]1Sa 13:14 years. 22After removing Saul,[h] he made
David their king.[i] He testified concern-
ing him: ‘I have found David son of
Jesse a man after my own heart;[j] he will
do everything I want him to do.’
13:23 [k]Mt 1:1 [l]Lk 2:11 [m]Mt 1:21 [n]ver 32 23“From this man's descendants[k] God
has brought to Israel the Savior[l] Jesus,[m]
as he promised.[n] 24Before the coming
of Jesus, John preached repentance and
13:24 [o]Mk 1:4 baptism to all the people of Israel.[o] 25As
John was completing his work,[p] he said:
13:25 [p]Ac 20:24 [q]Jn 1:20 [r]Mt 3:11; Jn 1:27 ‘Who do you think I am? I am not
that one.[q] No, but he is coming after
me, whose sandals I am not worthy to
untie.’[r]
26“Brothers, children of Abraham,
13:26 [s]Ac 4:12 and you God-fearing Gentiles, it is to
us that this message of salvation[s] has
been sent. 27The people of Jerusalem
13:27 [t]Ac 3:17 [u]Lk 24:27 and their rulers did not recognize Jesus,[t]
yet in condemning him they fulfilled
the words of the prophets[u] that are read
every Sabbath. 28Though they found
13:28 [v]Mt 27:20-25; Ac 3:14 no proper ground for a death sentence,
they asked Pilate to have him executed.[v]
13:29 [w]Lk 18:31 [x]Ac 5:30 [y]Lk 23:53 29When they had carried out all that
was written about him,[w] they took him
down from the tree[x] and laid him in
13:30 [z]Mt 28:6; Ac 2:24 a tomb.[y] 30But God raised him from
the dead,[z] 31and for many days he was
seen by those who had traveled with
13:31 [a]Mt 28:16 [b]Lk 24:48 him from Galilee to Jerusalem.[a] They
are now his witnesses[b] to our people.
32“We tell you the good news:[c] What
13:32 [c]Ac 5:42 [d]Ac 26:6; Ro 4:13 God promised our fathers[d] 33he has fulfilled for us, their children, by raising
up Jesus. As it is written in the second
Psalm:

“ ‘You are my Son;
13:33 [e]Ps 2:7 today I have become your
Father.’[a][b][e]

34The fact that God raised him from
the dead, never to decay, is stated in
these words:

“ ‘I will give you the holy and
13:34 [f]Isa 55:3 sure blessings promised to
David.’[c][f]

35So it is stated elsewhere:

“ ‘You will not let your Holy One see
decay.’[d][g] 13:35 [g]Ps 16:10; Ac 2:27

36“For when David had served God's
purpose in his own generation, he fell
asleep; he was buried with his fathers[h] 13:36 [h]1Ki 2:10; Ac 2:29
and his body decayed. 37But the one
whom God raised from the dead did
not see decay.
38“Therefore, my brothers, I want
you to know that through Jesus the for- 13:38 [i]Lk 24:47; Ac 2:38
giveness of sins is proclaimed to you.[i]
39Through him everyone who believes
is justified from everything you could
not be justified from by the law of Mo-
ses.[j] 40Take care that what the prophets 13:39 [j]Ro 3:28
have said does not happen to you:

41“ ‘Look, you scoffers,
wonder and perish,
for I am going to do something in
your days
that you would never believe,
even if someone told you.’[e]”[k] 13:41 [k]Hab 1:5

42As Paul and Barnabas were leaving
the synagogue,[l] the people invited them 13:42 [l]ver 14
to speak further about these things on
the next Sabbath. 43When the congregation was dismissed, many of the Jews
and devout converts to Judaism followed Paul and Barnabas, who talked
with them and urged them to continue 13:43 [m]Ac 11:23; 14:22
in the grace of God.[m]
44On the next Sabbath almost the
whole city gathered to hear the word
of the Lord. 45When the Jews saw the
crowds, they were filled with jealousy
and talked abusively[n] against what Paul 13:45 [n]Ac 18:6; 1Pe 4:4; Jude 10 [o]1Th 2:16
was saying.[o]
46Then Paul and Barnabas answered
them boldly: “We had to speak the 13:46 [p]ver 26; Ac 3:26 [q]Ac 18:6; 22:21; 28:28
word of God to you first.[p] Since you
reject it and do not consider yourselves
worthy of eternal life, we now turn to
the Gentiles.[q] 47For this is what the
Lord has commanded us:

“ ‘I have made you[f] a light for the
Gentiles,[r] 13:47 [r]Lk 2:32 [s]Isa 49:6
that you[f] may bring salvation to
the ends of the earth.’[g]”[s]

48When the Gentiles heard this, they
were glad and honored the word of the

[a] *33* Or *have begotten you* [b] *33* Psalm 2:7
[c] *34* Isaiah 55:3 [d] *35* Psalm 16:10 [e] *41* Hab. 1:5
[f] *47* The Greek is singular. [g] *47* Isaiah 49:6

Lord; and all who were appointed for eternal life believed.

49The word of the Lord spread through the whole region. 50But the Jews incited the God-fearing women of high standing and the leading men of the city. They stirred up persecution against Paul and Barnabas, and expelled them from their region.[t] 51So they shook the dust from their feet[u] in protest against them and went to Iconium.[v] 52And the disciples were filled with joy and with the Holy Spirit.

13:50 [t]1Th 2:16
13:51 [u]Mt 10:14; Ac 18:6 [v]Ac 14:1, 19,21; 2Ti 3:11

In Iconium

14 At Iconium[w] Paul and Barnabas went as usual into the Jewish synagogue. There they spoke so effectively that a great number of Jews and Gentiles believed. 2But the Jews who refused to believe stirred up the Gentiles and poisoned their minds against the brothers. 3So Paul and Barnabas spent considerable time there, speaking boldly[x] for the Lord, who confirmed the message of his grace by enabling them to do miraculous signs and wonders.[y] 4The people of the city were divided; some sided with the Jews, others with the apostles.[z] 5There was a plot afoot among the Gentiles and Jews, together with their leaders, to mistreat them and stone them.[a] 6But they found out about it and fled[b] to the Lycaonian cities of Lystra and Derbe and to the surrounding country, 7where they continued to preach[c] the good news.[d]

14:1 [w]Ac 13:51
14:3 [x]Ac 4:29 [y]Jn 4:48; Heb 2:4
14:4 [z]Ac 17:4,5
14:5 [a]ver 19
14:6 [b]Mt 10:23
14:7 [c]Ac 16:10 [d]ver 15,21

In Lystra and Derbe

8In Lystra there sat a man crippled in his feet, who was lame from birth[e] and had never walked. 9He listened to Paul as he was speaking. Paul looked directly at him, saw that he had faith to be healed[f] 10and called out, "Stand up on your feet!" At that, the man jumped up and began to walk.[g]

11When the crowd saw what Paul had done, they shouted in the Lycaonian language, "The gods have come down to us in human form!"[h] 12Barnabas they called Zeus, and Paul they called Hermes because he was the chief speaker. 13The priest of Zeus, whose temple was just outside the city, brought bulls and wreaths to the city gates because he and the crowd wanted to offer sacrifices to them.

14:8 [e]Ac 3:2
14:9 [f]Mt 9:28,29
14:10 [g]Ac 3:8
14:11 [h]Ac 8:10; 28:6

14But when the apostles Barnabas and Paul heard of this, they tore their clothes[i] and rushed out into the crowd, shouting: 15"Men, why are you doing this? We too are only men,[j] human like you. We are bringing you good news,[k] telling you to turn from these worthless things[l] to the living God,[m] who made heaven and earth[n] and sea and everything in them.[o] 16In the past, he let[p] all nations go their own way.[q] 17Yet he has not left himself without testimony:[r] He has shown kindness by giving you rain from heaven and crops in their seasons;[s] he provides you with plenty of food and fills your hearts with joy." 18Even with these words, they had difficulty keeping the crowd from sacrificing to them.

19Then some Jews[t] came from Antioch and Iconium[u] and won the crowd over. They stoned Paul[v] and dragged him outside the city, thinking he was dead. 20But after the disciples[w] had gathered around him, he got up and went back into the city. The next day he and Barnabas left for Derbe.

14:14 [i]Mk 14:63
14:15 [j]Ac 10:26; Jas 5:17 [k]ver 7,21; Ac 13:32 [l]1Sa 12:21; 1Co 8:4; 1Th 1:9 [m]Mt 16:16 [n]Ge 1:1; Jer 14:22 [o]Ps 146:6; Rev 14:7
14:16 [p]Ac 17:30 [q]Ps 81:12; Mic 4:5
14:17 [r]Ac 17:27; Ro 1:20 [s]Dt 11:14; Job 5:10; Ps 65:10
14:19 [t]Ac 13:45 [u]Ac 13:51 [v]2Co 11:25; 2Ti 3:11
14:20 [w]ver 22,28; Ac 11:26

The Return to Antioch in Syria

21They preached the good news in that city and won a large number of disciples. Then they returned to Lystra, Iconium[x] and Antioch, 22strengthening the disciples and encouraging them to remain true to the faith.[y] "We must go through many hardships[z] to enter the kingdom of God," they said. 23Paul and Barnabas appointed elders[a][a] for them in each church and, with prayer and fasting,[b] committed them to the Lord,[c] in whom they had put their trust. 24After going through Pisidia, they came into Pamphylia, 25and when they had preached the word in Perga, they went down to Attalia.

26From Attalia they sailed back to Antioch,[d] where they had been committed to the grace of God[e] for the work they had now completed.[f] 27On arriving there, they gathered the church together and reported all that God had done through them[g] and how he had opened the door[h] of faith to the Gentiles. 28And they stayed there a long time with the disciples.

14:21 [x]Ac 13:51
14:22 [y]Ac 11:23; 13:43 [z]Jn 16:33; 1Th 3:3; 2Ti 3:12
14:23 [a]Ac 11:30; Tit 1:5 [b]Ac 13:3 [c]Ac 20:32
14:26 [d]Ac 11:19 [e]Ac 15:40 [f]Ac 13:1,3
14:27 [g]Ac 15:4,12; 21:19 [h]1Co 16:9; 2Co 2:12; Col 4:3; Rev 3:8

[a]23 Or *Barnabas ordained elders*; or *Barnabas had elders elected*

The Council at Jerusalem

15:1 [i]ver 24; Gal 2:12 [j]ver 5; Gal 5:2,3 [k]Ac 6:14 15 Some men[i] came down from
Judea to Antioch and were
teaching the brothers: "Unless you are
circumcised,[j] according to the custom
taught by Moses,[k] you cannot be saved."
2This brought Paul and Barnabas into
sharp dispute and debate with them.
So Paul and Barnabas were appointed,
15:2 [l]Gal 2:2 [m]Ac 11:30 along with some other believers, to go
up to Jerusalem[l] to see the apostles
and elders[m] about this question. 3The
church sent them on their way, and
as they traveled through Phoenicia and
15:3 [n]Ac 14:27 Samaria, they told how the Gentiles
had been converted.[n] This news made
all the brothers very glad. 4When they
came to Jerusalem, they were welcomed
by the church and the apostles and el-
15:4 [o]ver 12; Ac 14:27 ders, to whom they reported everything
God had done through them.[o]
5Then some of the believers who belonged to the party of the Pharisees
stood up and said, "The Gentiles must
be circumcised and required to obey
the law of Moses."
6The apostles and elders met to consider this question. 7After much discussion, Peter got up and addressed them:
"Brothers, you know that some time
ago God made a choice among you that
the Gentiles might hear from my lips
15:8 [p]Ac 1:24 [q]Ac 10:44,47 the message of the gospel and believe.
8God, who knows the heart,[p] showed
that he accepted them by giving the
Holy Spirit to them,[q] just as he did to
15:9 [r]Ac 10:28,34; 11:12 [s]Ac 10:43 us. 9He made no distinction between us
and them,[r] for he purified their hearts
by faith.[s] 10Now then, why do you try
15:10 [t]Mt 23:4; Gal 5:1 to test God by putting on the necks
of the disciples a yoke[t] that neither
we nor our fathers have been able to
15:11 [u]Ro 3:24; Eph 2:5-8 bear? 11No! We believe it is through the
grace[u] of our Lord Jesus that we are
saved, just as they are."
12The whole assembly became silent
as they listened to Barnabas and Paul
15:12 [v]Jn 4:48 [w]Ac 14:27 telling about the miraculous signs and
wonders[v] God had done among the
Gentiles through them.[w] 13When they
15:13 [x]Ac 12:17 finished, James[x] spoke up: "Brothers,
listen to me. 14Simon[a] has described to
us how God at first showed his concern
by taking from the Gentiles a people
for himself. 15The words of the prophets are in agreement with this, as it is
written:

16" 'After this I will return
and rebuild David's fallen tent.
Its ruins I will rebuild,
and I will restore it,
17that the remnant of men may seek
the Lord,
and all the Gentiles who bear my
name,
says the Lord, who does these
things'[b][y] 15:17 [y]Am 9:11,12
18 that have been known for ages.[c]

19"It is my judgment, therefore, that
we should not make it difficult for the
Gentiles who are turning to God. 20In-
stead we should write to them, telling
them to abstain from food polluted by 15:20 [z]1Co 8:7-13; 10:14-28; Rev 2:14,20 [a]1Co 10:7,8 [b]ver 29; Ge 9:4; Lev 3:17; Dt 12:16,23
idols,[z] from sexual immorality,[a] from
the meat of strangled animals and from
blood.[b] 21For Moses has been preached
in every city from the earliest times
and is read in the synagogues on every
Sabbath."[c] 15:21 [c]Ac 13:15; 2Co 3:14,15

The Council's Letter to Gentile Believers

22Then the apostles and elders, with
the whole church, decided to choose
some of their own men and send them
to Antioch with Paul and Barnabas.
They chose Judas (called Barsabbas) 15:22 [d]ver 27,32,40
and Silas,[d] two men who were leaders
among the brothers. 23With them they
sent the following letter:

The apostles and elders, your brothers,

To the Gentile believers in An- 15:23 [e]ver 1 [f]ver 41 [g]Ac 23:25,26; Jas 1:1
tioch,[e] Syria and Cilicia:[f]

Greetings.[g]

24We have heard that some went
out from us without our autho-
rization and disturbed you, trou-
bling your minds by what they 15:24 [h]ver 1; Gal 1:7; 5:10
said.[h] 25So we all agreed to choose
some men and send them to you
with our dear friends Barnabas
and Paul— 26men who have risked 15:26 [i]Ac 9:23-25; 14:19
their lives[i] for the name of our
Lord Jesus Christ. 27Therefore we
are sending Judas and Silas to confirm by word of mouth what we
are writing. 28It seemed good to

[a]*14* Greek *Simeon*, a variant of *Simon*; that is, Peter
[b]*17* Amos 9:11,12 [c]*17,18* Some manuscripts *things'— / 18known to the Lord for ages is his work*

DAY 4 FOUR 

SELF-CONTROL AND MY SERVICE TO OTHERS

Acts 15:36–41

The conflict at the end of Acts 15 may have been more of a personal crisis than we have heretofore imagined. Paul and Barnabas actually parted company over John Mark, whom Paul felt was a quitter and not dependable when hard times came. Barnabas disagreed, feeling that John Mark had matured since his earlier defection and should be given a second chance. By the end of his life (or at least his ministry), in the last letter Paul wrote, the apostle seems to have changed his mind about John Mark (see 2 Timothy 4:11).

Managing our moods and getting our feelings about our viewpoints under control is very important in our service to others. I have come to believe that there is only one real handicap that keeps us from serving others: our undisciplined lives. The major detriment to the success of our evangelism is our own frail discipleship.

Sir Walter Scott was lame.
Fyodor Dostoyevsky was epileptic.
Abraham Lincoln grew up in utter poverty.
Lord Byron had a clubfoot.
Franklin D. Roosevelt was partially paralyzed.
Ludwig van Beethoven had a hearing impairment and eventually became deaf.
Helen Keller was blind and deaf.

These people faced difficult personal challenges, yet they astounded the world with achievements that only their personal discipline can explain. The truly disabled are those whose moods are uncontrollable. Those who try to serve Christ without disciplining their lives end up making their faith a kind of religious romance in which they indulge every week or so. But those who can control their moods and manage their tempers demonstrate that the kingdom of God is a believable, desirable place to seek.

To begin a study on the topic of Self-Control, Managing My Moods, turn to the home page on page 179.

the Holy Spirit[j] and to us not 15:28 [j]Ac 5:32
to burden you with anything be-
yond the following requirements:
29You are to abstain from food sacrificed to idols, from blood, from
the meat of strangled animals and 15:29 [k]ver 20; Ac 21:25
from sexual immorality.[k] You will
do well to avoid these things.

Farewell.

30The men were sent off and went
down to Antioch, where they gathered
the church together and delivered the
letter. 31The people read it and were
glad for its encouraging message. 32Ju-
das and Silas, who themselves were
prophets, said much to encourage and
strengthen the brothers. 33After spending some time there, they were sent
off by the brothers with the blessing 15:33 [l]Mk 5:34; Ac 16:36; 1Co 16:11
of peace[l] to return to those who had
sent them.[a] 35But Paul and Barnabas
remained in Antioch, where they and 15:35 [m]Ac 8:4
many others taught and preached[m] the
word of the Lord.

Disagreement Between Paul and Barnabas

36Some time later Paul said to Bar- 15:36 [n]Ac 13:4,13, 14,51; 14:1,6, 24,25
nabas, "Let us go back and visit the
brothers in all the towns[n] where we
preached the word of the Lord and see
how they are doing." 37Barnabas want- 15:37 [o]Ac 12:12
ed to take John, also called Mark,[o] with
them, 38but Paul did not think it wise
to take him, because he had deserted 15:38 [p]Ac 13:13
them[p] in Pamphylia and had not con-
tinued with them in the work. 39They
had such a sharp disagreement that
they parted company. Barnabas took
Mark and sailed for Cyprus, 40but Paul

[a]33 Some manuscripts *them,* [34]*but Silas decided to remain there*

KINDNESS 

WHEN CHRISTIANS DISAGREE

Acts 15:38

Christ can use even dissonance to widen the gospel's advance. Barnabas and Paul argued, broke up their team and formed two teams. Because of their separation, the gospel flew in two directions. No one knows whether their argument was kind. But God orchestrated the end result.

chose Silas[q] and left, commended by
the brothers to the grace of the Lord.[r]
41 He went through Syria[s] and Cilicia,[t]
strengthening the churches.[u]

Timothy Joins Paul and Silas

16 He came to Derbe and then to
Lystra,[v] where a disciple named
Timothy[w] lived, whose mother was a
Jewess and a believer, but whose father
was a Greek. 2 The brothers[x] at Lystra
and Iconium[y] spoke well of him. 3 Paul
wanted to take him along on the journey, so he circumcised him because of
the Jews who lived in that area, for
they all knew that his father was a
Greek.[z] 4 As they traveled from town
to town, they delivered the decisions
reached by the apostles and elders[a] in
Jerusalem[b] for the people to obey.[c] 5 So
the churches were strengthened[d] in the
faith and grew daily in numbers.

Paul's Vision of the Man of Macedonia

6 Paul and his companions traveled
throughout the region of Phrygia[e] and
Galatia,[f] having been kept by the Holy
Spirit from preaching the word in the
province of Asia.[g] 7 When they came to
the border of Mysia, they tried to enter
Bithynia, but the Spirit of Jesus[h] would
not allow them to. 8 So they passed by
Mysia and went down to Troas.[i] 9 During the night Paul had a vision[j] of a
man of Macedonia standing and begging him, "Come over to Macedonia[k]
and help us." 10 After Paul had seen the
vision, we[l] got ready at once to leave
for Macedonia, concluding that God
had called us to preach the gospel[m] to
them.

15:40 [q]ver 22 [r]Ac 11:23
15:41 [s]ver 23 [t]Ac 6:9 [u]Ac 16:5
16:1 [v]Ac 14:6 [w]Ac 17:14; 18:5; 19:22; Ro 16:21; 1Co 4:17; 2Co 1:1,19; 1Th 3:2,6; 1Ti 1:2,18; 2Ti 1:2,5,6
16:2 [x]ver 40 [y]Ac 13:51
16:3 [z]Gal 2:3
16:4 [a]Ac 11:30 [b]Ac 15:2 [c]Ac 15:28,29
16:5 [d]Ac 9:31; 15:41
16:6 [e]Ac 18:23 [f]Ac 18:23; Gal 1:2; 3:1 [g]Ac 2:9
16:7 [h]Ro 8:9; Gal 4:6
16:8 [i]ver 11; 2Co 2:12; 2Ti 4:13
16:9 [j]Ac 9:10 [k]Ac 20:1,3
16:10 [l]ver 10-17 [m]Ac 14:7

LOVE

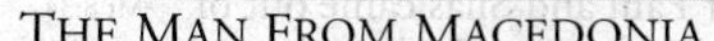

THE MAN FROM MACEDONIA

Acts 16:9

In a quandary about where to go to preach Christ, Paul had a vision. He set sail for the Roman province of Macedonia, and Europe heard the gospel, making it another day, another continent, another conquest by a God-called vagabond. How nice it is that foot soldiers dream. Continents are wrapped up in the package of their vision.

Lydia's Conversion in Philippi

11 From Troas[n] we put out to sea and
sailed straight for Samothrace, and the
next day on to Neapolis. 12 From there
we traveled to Philippi,[o] a Roman colony and the leading city of that district
of Macedonia.[p] And we stayed there
several days.

13 On the Sabbath[q] we went outside
the city gate to the river, where we expected to find a place of prayer. We sat
down and began to speak to the women
who had gathered there. 14 One of those
listening was a woman named Lydia, a
dealer in purple cloth from the city of
Thyatira,[r] who was a worshiper of God.
The Lord opened her heart[s] to respond
to Paul's message. 15 When she and the
members of her household[t] were baptized, she invited us to her home. "If
you consider me a believer in the Lord,"
she said, "come and stay at my house."
And she persuaded us.

Paul and Silas in Prison

16 Once when we were going to the
place of prayer,[u] we were met by a slave
girl who had a spirit[v] by which she predicted the future. She earned a great
deal of money for her owners by fortune-telling. 17 This girl followed Paul
and the rest of us, shouting, "These
men are servants of the Most High
God,[w] who are telling you the way to
be saved." 18 She kept this up for many
days. Finally Paul became so troubled
that he turned around and said to the
spirit, "In the name of Jesus Christ I
command you to come out of her!" At
that moment the spirit left her.[x]

19 When the owners of the slave girl
realized that their hope of making money[y] was gone, they seized Paul and Silas[z]
and dragged[a] them into the marketplace
to face the authorities. 20 They brought
them before the magistrates and said,
"These men are Jews, and are throwing
our city into an uproar[b] 21 by advocating customs unlawful for us Romans[c]
to accept or practice."[d]

22 The crowd joined in the attack
against Paul and Silas, and the magistrates ordered them to be stripped and
beaten.[e] 23 After they had been severely
flogged, they were thrown into prison,
and the jailer[f] was commanded to guard
them carefully. 24 Upon receiving such

16:11 [n]ver 8
16:12 [o]Ac 20:6; Php 1:1; 1Th 2:2 [p]ver 9
16:13 [q]Ac 13:14
16:14 [r]Rev 1:11 [s]Lk 24:45
16:15 [t]Ac 11:14
16:16 [u]ver 13 [v]Dt 18:11; 1Sa 28:3,7
16:17 [w]Mk 5:7
16:18 [x]Mk 16:17
16:19 [y]ver 16; Ac 19:25,26 [z]Ac 15:22 [a]Ac 8:3; 17:6; 21:30; Jas 2:6
16:20 [b]Ac 17:6
16:21 [c]ver 12 [d]Est 3:8
16:22 [e]2Co 11:25; 1Th 2:2
16:23 [f]ver 27,36

orders, he put them in the inner cell
and fastened their feet in the stocks.[g]
25 About midnight Paul and Silas were
praying and singing hymns[h] to God,
and the other prisoners were listening
to them. 26 Suddenly there was such a
violent earthquake that the foundations
of the prison were shaken.[i] At once all
the prison doors flew open,[j] and everybody's chains came loose.[k] 27 The jailer
woke up, and when he saw the prison
doors open, he drew his sword and was
about to kill himself because he thought
the prisoners had escaped.[l] 28 But Paul
shouted, "Don't harm yourself! We are
all here!"
29 The jailer called for lights, rushed
in and fell trembling before Paul and
Silas. 30 He then brought them out
and asked, "Sirs, what must I do to be
saved?"[m]
31 They replied, "Believe in the Lord
Jesus, and you will be saved—you and
your household."[n] 32 Then they spoke
the word of the Lord to him and to
all the others in his house. 33 At that
hour of the night[o] the jailer took them
and washed their wounds; then immediately he and all his family were baptized. 34 The jailer brought them into
his house and set a meal before them;
he[p] was filled with joy because he had
come to believe in God—he and his
whole family.
35 When it was daylight, the magistrates sent their officers to the jailer with
the order: "Release those men." 36 The
jailer[q] told Paul, "The magistrates have
ordered that you and Silas be released.
Now you can leave. Go in peace."[r]
37 But Paul said to the officers: "They
beat us publicly without a trial, even
though we are Roman citizens,[s] and
threw us into prison. And now do they
want to get rid of us quietly? No! Let
them come themselves and escort us
out."
38 The officers reported this to the
magistrates, and when they heard that
Paul and Silas were Roman citizens,
they were alarmed.[t] 39 They came to appease them and escorted them from the
prison, requesting them to leave the
city.[u] 40 After Paul and Silas came out of
the prison, they went to Lydia's house,[v]
where they met with the brothers[w] and
encouraged them. Then they left.

In Thessalonica

17 When they had passed through
Amphipolis and Apollonia, they
came to Thessalonica,[x] where there was
a Jewish synagogue. 2 As his custom was,
Paul went into the synagogue,[y] and on
three Sabbath[z] days he reasoned with

16:24 gJob 13:27; 33:11; Jer 20:2,3; 29:26
16:25 hEph 5:19
16:26 iAc 4:31 jAc 12:10 kAc 12:7
16:27 lAc 12:19
16:30 mAc 2:37
16:31 nAc 11:14
16:33 over 25
16:34 pAc 11:14
16:36 qver 23,27 rAc 15:33
16:37 sAc 22:25-29
16:38 tAc 22:29
16:39 uMt 8:34
16:40 vver 14 wver 2; Ac 1:16
17:1 xver 11,13; Php 4:16; 1Th 1:1; 2Th 1:1; 2Ti 4:10
17:2 yAc 9:20 zAc 13:14

DAY 2 TWO

JOY AND THE PURPOSE OF GOD IN MY LIFE

Acts 16:22–26

Tears have a way of sifting and refining our praise. The best music is produced when we sing through our tears. Paul and Silas sang in a jail cell. They were incarcerated because of honoring God's purpose in their lives. Their praise came from honest joy—joy obtained by standing true when standing was most difficult.

Joy is a frequent reward of endurance. Trials and singing fit together better than one might think. We can trace the journey from trial to joy in this way: First, we face the trial. Second, God enables us with power beyond ourselves. Third, we trust and win—or at least we survive. Fourth, we praise the Lord.

Joy results from facing Satan and triumphing over him. Remember the disciples in Luke 10:17? They returned from their preaching and healing tour in great joy. "Lord," they exulted, "even the demons submit to us in your name." One wonders whether they were not close to song even as the joy of their triumph swept over them.

Martin Luther felt the same elation of triumph over Satan when he wrote:

And though this world, with devils filled,
should threaten to undo us,
We will not fear, for God has willed His
truth to triumph through us:
The Prince of Darkness grim, we tremble
not for him;
His rage we can endure, for, lo his doom
is sure,
One little word shall fell him.

Luther's steadfastness illustrates the point: Endurance and triumph produce joy.

To begin a study on the topic of Joy, the Reward of Endurance, turn to the home page on page 581.

17:2 [a]Ac 8:35 — them from the Scriptures,[a] 3explaining
and proving that the Christ[a] had to
17:3 [b]Lk 24:26; Ac 3:18 [c]Lk 24:46 [d]Ac 9:22; 18:28 — suffer[b] and rise from the dead.[c] "This
Jesus I am proclaiming to you is the
Christ,[a]"[d] he said. 4Some of the Jews
were persuaded and joined Paul and
17:4 [e]Ac 15:22 — Silas,[e] as did a large number of God-
fearing Greeks and not a few promi-
nent women.

5But the Jews were jealous; so they
rounded up some bad characters from
the marketplace, formed a mob and
17:5 [f]ver 13; 1Th 2:16 [g]Ro 16:21 — started a riot in the city.[f] They rushed
to Jason's[g] house in search of Paul and
Silas in order to bring them out to the
crowd.[b] 6But when they did not find
17:6 [h]Ac 16:19 [i]Mt 24:14 [j]Ac 16:20 — them, they dragged[h] Jason and some
other brothers before the city officials,
shouting: "These men who have caused
trouble all over the world[i] have now
come here,[j] 7and Jason has welcomed
them into his house. They are all defy-
17:7 [k]Lk 23:2; Jn 19:12 — ing Caesar's decrees, saying that there is
another king, one called Jesus."[k] 8When
they heard this, the crowd and the
city officials were thrown into turmoil.
17:9 [l]ver 5 — 9Then they made Jason[l] and the others
post bond and let them go.

In Berea

17:10 [m]ver 13; Ac 20:4 — 10As soon as it was night, the brothers sent Paul and Silas away to Berea.[m]
On arriving there, they went to the
Jewish synagogue. 11Now the Bereans
17:11 [n]ver 1 [o]Lk 16:29; Jn 5:39 — were of more noble character than the
Thessalonians,[n] for they received the
message with great eagerness and examined the Scriptures[o] every day to see
if what Paul said was true. 12Many of
the Jews believed, as did also a number
of prominent Greek women and many
Greek men.

13When the Jews in Thessalonica
learned that Paul was preaching the
word of God at Berea, they went there
too, agitating the crowds and stirring
17:14 [p]Ac 15:22 [q]Ac 16:1 — them up. 14The brothers immediately
sent Paul to the coast, but Silas[p] and
Timothy[q] stayed at Berea. 15The men
17:15 [r]ver 16,21,22; Ac 18:1; 1Th 3:1 [s]Ac 18:5 — who escorted Paul brought him to Athens[r] and then left with instructions for
Silas and Timothy to join him as soon
as possible.[s]

In Athens

16While Paul was waiting for them
in Athens, he was greatly distressed to
see that the city was full of idols. 17So
he reasoned in the synagogue[t] with the — 17:17 [t]Ac 9:20
Jews and the God-fearing Greeks, as
well as in the marketplace day by day
with those who happened to be there.
18A group of Epicurean and Stoic philosophers began to dispute with him.
Some of them asked, "What is this babbler trying to say?" Others remarked,
"He seems to be advocating foreign
gods." They said this because Paul was
preaching the good news about Jesus
and the resurrection.[u] 19Then they took — 17:18 [u]ver 31,32; Ac 4:2
him and brought him to a meeting of
the Areopagus,[v] where they said to him, — 17:19 [v]ver 22 [w]Mk 1:27
"May we know what this new teaching[w]
is that you are presenting? 20You are
bringing some strange ideas to our ears,
and we want to know what they mean."
21(All the Athenians and the foreigners
who lived there spent their time doing
nothing but talking about and listening
to the latest ideas.)

22Paul then stood up in the meeting
of the Areopagus and said: "Men of
Athens! I see that in every way you are
very religious. 23For as I walked around
and looked carefully at your objects of
worship, I even found an altar with this
inscription: TO AN UNKNOWN GOD.
Now what you worship as something — 17:23 [x]Jn 4:22
unknown[x] I am going to proclaim to
you.

24"The God who made the world — 17:24 [y]Isa 42:5; Ac 14:15 [z]Dt 10:14; Mt 11:25 [a]Ac 7:48
and everything in it[y] is the Lord of
heaven and earth[z] and does not live in
temples built by hands.[a] 25And he is not
served by human hands, as if he needed anything, because he himself gives
all men life and breath and everything — 17:25 [b]Ps 50:10-12; Isa 42:5
else.[b] 26From one man he made every
nation of men, that they should inhabit
the whole earth; and he determined the
times set for them and the exact places
where they should live.[c] 27God did this — 17:26 [c]Dt 32:8; Job 12:23
so that men would seek him and per-
haps reach out for him and find him, — 17:27 [d]Dt 4:7; Jer 23:23,24; Ac 14:17
though he is not far from each one of
us.[d] 28'For in him we live and move and
have our being.'[e] As some of your own — 17:28 [e]Job 12:10; Da 5:23
poets have said, 'We are his offspring.'

29"Therefore since we are God's off-
spring, we should not think that the — 17:29 [f]Isa 40:18-20; Ro 1:23
divine being is like gold or silver or
stone—an image made by man's de- — 17:30 [g]Ac 14:16; Ro 3:25 [h]ver 23; 1Pe 1:14
sign and skill.[f] 30In the past God over-
looked[g] such ignorance,[h] but now he

[a]3 Or *Messiah* [b]5 Or *the assembly of the people*

commands all people everywhere to repent.[i] 31For he has set a day when he will judge[j] the world with justice[k] by the man he has appointed.[l] He has given proof of this to all men by raising him from the dead."[m]

32When they heard about the resurrection of the dead,[n] some of them sneered, but others said, "We want to hear you again on this subject." 33At that, Paul left the Council. 34A few men became followers of Paul and believed. Among them was Dionysius, a member of the Areopagus,[o] also a woman named Damaris, and a number of others.

In Corinth

18 After this, Paul left Athens[p] and went to Corinth.[q] 2There he met a Jew named Aquila, a native of Pontus, who had recently come from Italy with his wife Priscilla,[r] because Claudius[s] had ordered all the Jews to leave Rome. Paul went to see them, 3and because he was a tentmaker as they were, he stayed and worked with them.[t] 4Every Sabbath[u] he reasoned in the synagogue, trying to persuade Jews and Greeks.

17:30 [i]Lk 24:47; Tit 2:11,12
17:31 [j]Mt 10:15 [k]Ps 9:8; 96:13; 98:9 [l]Ac 10:42 [m]Ac 2:24
17:32 [n]ver 18,31
17:34 [o]ver 19,22
18:1 [p]Ac 17:15 [q]Ac 19:1; 1Co 1:2; 2Co 1:1,23; 2Ti 4:20
18:2 [r]Ro 16:3; 1Co 16:19; 2Ti 4:19 [s]Ac 11:28
18:3 [t]Ac 20:34; 1Co 4:12; 1Th 2:9; 2Th 3:8
18:4 [u]Ac 13:14

JOY

TENTS: PRICED TO SELL!

Acts 18:2–3

Paul was a tentmaker, and with his needle he stitched two continents together. Priscilla and Aquila also worked with canvas. Thus did an earthly trio serve their heavenly Trinity. In making tents, they stitched their pagan world into a tabernacle of joy.

5When Silas[v] and Timothy[w] came from Macedonia,[x] Paul devoted himself exclusively to preaching, testifying to the Jews that Jesus was the Christ.[a][y] 6But when the Jews opposed Paul and became abusive,[z] he shook out his clothes in protest and said to them, "Your blood be on your own heads![a] I am clear of my responsibility.[b] From now on I will go to the Gentiles."[c]

7Then Paul left the synagogue and went next door to the house of Titius Justus, a worshiper of God.[d] 8Crispus,[e] the synagogue ruler,[f] and his entire household[g] believed in the Lord; and many of the Corinthians who heard him believed and were baptized.

9One night the Lord spoke to Paul in a vision: "Do not be afraid; keep on speaking, do not be silent. 10For I am with you,[h] and no one is going to attack and harm you, because I have many people in this city." 11So Paul stayed for a year and a half, teaching them the word of God.

12While Gallio was proconsul of Achaia,[i] the Jews made a united attack on Paul and brought him into court. 13"This man," they charged, "is persuading the people to worship God in ways contrary to the law."

14Just as Paul was about to speak, Gallio said to the Jews, "If you Jews were making a complaint about some misdemeanor or serious crime, it would be reasonable for me to listen to you. 15But since it involves questions about words and names and your own law[j]—settle the matter yourselves. I will not be a judge of such things." 16So he had them ejected from the court. 17Then they all turned on Sosthenes[k] the synagogue ruler and beat him in front of the court. But Gallio showed no concern whatever.

Priscilla, Aquila and Apollos

18Paul stayed on in Corinth for some time. Then he left the brothers[l] and sailed for Syria, accompanied by Priscilla and Aquila. Before he sailed, he had his hair cut off at Cenchrea[m] because of a vow he had taken.[n] 19They arrived at Ephesus,[o] where Paul left Priscilla and Aquila. He himself went into the synagogue and reasoned with the Jews. 20When they asked him to spend more time with them, he declined. 21But as he left, he promised, "I will come back if it is God's will."[p] Then he set sail from Ephesus. 22When he landed at Caesarea,[q] he went up and greeted the church and then went down to Antioch.[r]

23After spending some time in Antioch, Paul set out from there and traveled from place to place throughout the region of Galatia[s] and Phrygia, strengthening all the disciples.[t]

24Meanwhile a Jew named Apollos,[u] a native of Alexandria, came to Ephesus.

18:5 [v]Ac 15:22 [w]Ac 16:1 [x]Ac 16:9; 17:14,15 [y]ver 28; Ac 17:3
18:6 [z]Ac 13:45 [a]2Sa 1:16; Eze 18:13; 33:4 [b]Ac 20:26 [c]Ac 13:46
18:7 [d]Ac 16:14
18:8 [e]1Co 1:14 [f]Mk 5:22 [g]Ac 11:14
18:10 [h]Mt 28:20
18:12 [i]ver 27
18:15 [j]Ac 23:29; 25:11,19
18:17 [k]1Co 1:1
18:18 [l]Ac 1:16 [m]Ro 16:1 [n]Nu 6:2,5,18; Ac 21:24
18:19 [o]ver 21,24; 1Co 15:32
18:21 [p]Ro 1:10; 1Co 4:19; Jas 4:15
18:22 [q]Ac 8:40 [r]Ac 11:19
18:23 [s]Ac 16:6 [t]Ac 14:22; 15:32,41
18:24 [u]Ac 19:1; 1Co 1:12; 3:5,6,22; 4:6; 16:12; Tit 3:13

[a]5 Or *Messiah;* also in verse 28

DAY 3 THREE

Gentleness and My Relationship With Christ

Acts 18:24–26

Apollos was a great communicator. Acts 18:25 says that he preached the Word of God "with great fervor." It was not easy to fall asleep during his sermons. But from the standpoint of the incomplete message he spoke, it would have been better if those who heard him had fallen asleep. Bad doctrine in the hands of great communicators represents a kind of double threat.

But this must be said for Apollos: He was open to the truth. And when Priscilla and Aquila took him home for a few lessons in Bible doctrine, his teaching improved. Both the teachers and the student are to be commended for focusing on the work of Christ, thus bringing a life-changing message to many who came to hear great preaching.

A popular cable evangelist in our day began teaching that the Trinity should be enlarged to include the "seven spirits" that minister before the throne mentioned in Revelation 4:5. Some faithful, more theological souls were able to take him aside and teach him how to expound the Word in keeping with sound doctrine. As in the case of Apollos, the errant evangelist corrected his doctrine and was properly commended.

False teachers can sometimes be reclaimed, but it is never done better than when we approach them with a gentle spirit—that means displacing our own sense of ego with a serving spirit. The church must strive to retain a pure message and focus on Christ. The lives of gentle and teachable leaders and followers are the guarantee that the church does not lose its focus.

To begin a study on the topic of Gentleness, the Art of Ego Displacement, turn to the home page on page 1387.

He was a learned man, with a thorough
knowledge of the Scriptures. 25He had
been instructed in the way of the Lord,
18:25 and he spoke with great fervor[a][v] and
[v]Ro 12:11 taught about Jesus accurately, though
[w]Ac 19:3 he knew only the baptism of John.[w]
26He began to speak boldly in the synagogue.
When Priscilla and Aquila heard
him, they invited him to their home
and explained to him the way of God
more adequately.
27When Apollos wanted to go to
Achaia,[x] the brothers[y] encouraged him 18:27
and wrote to the disciples there to wel- [x]ver 12
come him. On arriving, he was a great [y]ver 18
help to those who by grace had believed. 28For he vigorously refuted the
Jews in public debate, proving from the 18:28
Scriptures[z] that Jesus was the Christ.[a] [z]Ac 17:2 [a]ver 5; Ac 9:22

Paul in Ephesus

19 While Apollos was at Corinth,[b] 19:1 [b]Ac 18:1
Paul took the road through the [c]Ac 18:19
interior and arrived at Ephesus.[c] There
he found some disciples 2and asked
them, "Did you receive the Holy Spirit
when[b] you believed?"
They answered, "No, we have not
even heard that there is a Holy Spirit."
3So Paul asked, "Then what baptism
did you receive?"
"John's baptism," they replied.
4Paul said, "John's baptism was a baptism of repentance. He told the people
to believe in the one coming after him, 19:4 [d]Jn 1:7;
that is, in Jesus."[d] 5On hearing this, Ac 13:24,25
they were baptized into[c] the name of
the Lord Jesus. 6When Paul placed his 19:6
hands on them,[e] the Holy Spirit came [e]Ac 6:6; 8:17
on them,[f] and they spoke in tongues[d][g] [f]Ac 2:4 [g]Mk 16:17;
and prophesied. 7There were about Ac 10:46
twelve men in all. 19:8
8Paul entered the synagogue[h] and [h]Ac 9:20
spoke boldly there for three months, ar- [i]Ac 1:3; 28:23
guing persuasively about the kingdom
of God.[i] 9But some of them[j] became 19:9
obstinate; they refused to believe and [j]Ac 14:4
publicly maligned the Way.[k] So Paul [k]ver 23; Ac 9:2
left them. He took the disciples[l] with [l]ver 30; Ac 11:26
him and had discussions daily in the
lecture hall of Tyrannus. 10This went
on for two years,[m] so that all the Jews 19:10 [m]Ac 20:31
and Greeks who lived in the province of [n]ver 22,26,27
Asia[n] heard the word of the Lord.
11God did extraordinary miracles[o] 19:11 [o]Ac 8:13
through Paul, 12so that even handker-
chiefs and aprons that had touched him
were taken to the sick, and their illness- 19:12
es were cured[p] and the evil spirits left [p]Ac 5:15
them.
13Some Jews who went around driv- 19:13
ing out evil spirits[q] tried to invoke the [q]Mt 12:27
name of the Lord Jesus over those who

[a]25 Or *with fervor in the Spirit* [b]2 Or *after*
[c]5 Or *in* [d]6 Or *other languages*

19:13 were demon-possessed. They would say,
rMk 9:38 “In the name of Jesus,[r] whom Paul
preaches, I command you to come out.”
14Seven sons of Sceva, a Jewish chief
priest, were doing this. 15⌞One day⌟ the
evil spirit answered them, “Jesus I know,
and I know about Paul, but who are
you?” 16Then the man who had the evil
spirit jumped on them and overpowered them all. He gave them such a
beating that they ran out of the house
naked and bleeding.

FAITHFULNESS

THE SONS OF SCEVA

Acts 19:13–15

Know Jesus before you use his name to confront the devil. Satan can always tell a Christian sympathizer from a true Christian.

19:17 17When this became known to the
sAc 18:19 Jews and Greeks living in Ephesus,[s] they
tAc 5:5,11 were all seized with fear,[t] and the name
of the Lord Jesus was held in high hon-
or. 18Many of those who believed now
came and openly confessed their evil
deeds. 19A number who had practiced
sorcery brought their scrolls together
and burned them publicly. When they
calculated the value of the scrolls, the
total came to fifty thousand drachmas.[a]
19:20 20In this way the word of the Lord
uAc 6:7; 12:24 spread widely and grew in power.[u]
19:21 21After all this had happened, Paul
vAc 20:16,22; decided to go to Jerusalem,[v] passing
Ro 15:25 wAc 16:9 through Macedonia[w] and Achaia.[x] “Af-
xAc 18:12 ter I have been there,” he said, “I must
yRo 15:24,28 visit Rome also.”[y] 22He sent two of
19:22 zAc 13:5 his helpers,[z] Timothy[a] and Erastus,[b] to
aAc 16:1 Macedonia, while he stayed in the prov-
bRo 16:23; 2Ti 4:20 ince of Asia[c] a little longer.
cver 10,26,27

The Riot in Ephesus

19:23 23About that time there arose a great
dAc 9:2 disturbance about the Way.[d] 24A silversmith named Demetrius, who made sil-
ver shrines of Artemis, brought in no
little business for the craftsmen. 25He
called them together, along with the
workmen in related trades, and said:
19:25 “Men, you know we receive a good in-
eAc 16:16, 19,20 come from this business.[e] 26And you
see and hear how this fellow Paul has
19:26 convinced and led astray large numbers
fAc 18:19 of people here in Ephesus[f] and in prac-
tically the whole province of Asia. He
says that man-made gods are no gods
at all.[g] 27There is danger not only that 19:26
our trade will lose its good name, but gDt 4:28; Ps 115:4;
also that the temple of the great god- Isa 44:10-20;
dess Artemis will be discredited, and Jer 10:3-5; Ac 17:29;
the goddess herself, who is worshiped 1Co 8:4; Rev 9:20
throughout the province of Asia and
the world, will be robbed of her divine
majesty.”
28When they heard this, they were
furious and began shouting: “Great is 19:28
Artemis of the Ephesians!”[h] 29Soon the hAc 18:19
whole city was in an uproar. The people
seized Gaius[i] and Aristarchus,[j] Paul’s 19:29
traveling companions from Macedonia,[k] iAc 20:4; Ro 16:23;
and rushed as one man into the the- 1Co 1:14 jAc 20:4;
ater. 30Paul wanted to appear before the 27:2;
crowd, but the disciples would not let Col 4:10; Phm 24
him. 31Even some of the officials of kAc 16:9
the province, friends of Paul, sent him
a message begging him not to venture
into the theater.
32The assembly was in confusion:
Some were shouting one thing, some 19:32
another.[l] Most of the people did not lAc 21:34
even know why they were there. 33The
Jews pushed Alexander to the front, and
some of the crowd shouted instructions 19:33
to him. He motioned[m] for silence in or- mAc 12:17
der to make a defense before the peo-
ple. 34But when they realized he was
a Jew, they all shouted in unison for
about two hours: “Great is Artemis of
the Ephesians!”
35The city clerk quieted the crowd 19:35
and said: “Men of Ephesus,[n] doesn’t all nAc 18:19
the world know that the city of Ephesus
is the guardian of the temple of the great
Artemis and of her image, which fell
from heaven? 36Therefore, since these
facts are undeniable, you ought to be
quiet and not do anything rash. 37You
have brought these men here, though
they have neither robbed temples[o] nor 19:37
blasphemed our goddess. 38If, then, De- oRo 2:22
metrius and his fellow craftsmen have
a grievance against anybody, the courts
are open and there are proconsuls.[p] 19:38 pAc 13:7,8,12
They can press charges. 39If there is anything further you want to bring up, it
must be settled in a legal assembly. 40As
it is, we are in danger of being charged
with rioting because of today’s events.
In that case we would not be able to account for this commotion, since there

[a] *19* A drachma was a silver coin worth about a day’s wages.

is no reason for it." 41After he had said
this, he dismissed the assembly.

Through Macedonia and Greece

20 When the uproar had ended,
20:1 [q]Ac 11:26 Paul sent for the disciples[q] and,
[r]Ac 16:9 after encouraging them, said good-by
and set out for Macedonia.[r] 2He traveled through that area, speaking many
words of encouragement to the people,
and finally arrived in Greece, 3where he
stayed three months. Because the Jews
20:3 [s]ver 19; made a plot against him[s] just as he was
Ac 9:23,24; 23:12,15,30; about to sail for Syria, he decided to go
25:3; back through Macedonia.[t] 4He was ac-
2Co 11:26 [t]Ac 16:9 companied by Sopater son of Pyrrhus
from Berea, Aristarchus[u] and Secundus
20:4 [u]Ac 19:29 from Thessalonica,[v] Gaius[w] from Der-
[v]Ac 17:1 [w]Ac 19:29 be, Timothy[x] also, and Tychicus[y] and
[x]Ac 16:1 [y]Eph 6:21; Trophimus[z] from the province of Asia.
Col 4:7; 5These men went on ahead and waited
2Ti 4:12; Tit 3:12 for us[a] at Troas.[b] 6But we sailed from
[z]Ac 21:29; Philippi[c] after the Feast of Unleavened
2Ti 4:20 Bread, and five days later joined the
20:5 others at Troas,[d] where we stayed seven
[a]Ac 16:10 [b]Ac 16:8 days.

20:6 [c]Ac 16:12 *Eutychus Raised From the Dead*
[d]Ac 16:8 *at Troas*

20:7 [e]1Co 16:2; 7On the first day of the week[e] we
Rev 1:10 came together to break bread. Paul
spoke to the people and, because he
intended to leave the next day, kept
20:8 on talking until midnight. 8There were
[f]Ac 1:13 many lamps in the upstairs room[f] where
we were meeting. 9Seated in a window
was a young man named Eutychus, who
was sinking into a deep sleep as Paul
talked on and on. When he was sound
asleep, he fell to the ground from the
third story and was picked up dead.
20:10 [g]1Ki 17:21; 10Paul went down, threw himself on the
2Ki 4:34 young man[g] and put his arms around
[h]Mt 9:23,24 him. "Don't be alarmed," he said. "He's
20:11 alive!"[h] 11Then he went upstairs again
[i]ver 7 and broke bread[i] and ate. After talking
until daylight, he left. 12The people
took the young man home alive and
were greatly comforted.

Paul's Farewell to the Ephesian Elders

13We went on ahead to the ship and
sailed for Assos, where we were going to
take Paul aboard. He had made this ar-
rangement because he was going there
on foot. 14When he met us at Assos, we
took him aboard and went on to Mity-
lene. 15The next day we set sail from
there and arrived off Kios. The day after
that we crossed over to Samos, and on
the following day arrived at Miletus.[j] 20:15 [j]ver 17;
16Paul had decided to sail past Ephesus[k] 2Ti 4:20
to avoid spending time in the province 20:16 [k]Ac 18:19
of Asia, for he was in a hurry to reach [l]Ac 19:21
Jerusalem,[l] if possible, by the day of [m]Ac 2:1;
Pentecost.[m] 1Co 16:8
17From Miletus, Paul sent to Ephesus 20:17
for the elders[n] of the church. 18When [n]Ac 11:30
they arrived, he said to them: "You
know how I lived the whole time I was 20:18 [o]Ac 18:19-21;
with you,[o] from the first day I came 19:1-41
into the province of Asia. 19I served
the Lord with great humility and with
tears, although I was severely tested by 20:19
the plots of the Jews.[p] 20You know that [p]ver 3
I have not hesitated to preach anything[q] 20:20
that would be helpful to you but have [q]ver 27
taught you publicly and from house to 20:21
house. 21I have declared to both Jews[r] [r]Ac 18:5 [s]Ac 2:38
and Greeks that they must turn to God [t]Ac 24:24; 26:18;
in repentance[s] and have faith in our Eph 1:15; Col 2:5;
Lord Jesus.[t] Phm 5
22"And now, compelled by the Spir-
it, I am going to Jerusalem,[u] not know- 20:22
ing what will happen to me there. 23I [u]ver 16
only know that in every city the Holy 20:23
Spirit warns me[v] that prison and hard- [v]Ac 21:4
ships are facing me.[w] 24However, I con- [w]Ac 9:16
sider my life worth nothing to me,[x] if 20:24 [x]Ac 21:13
only I may finish the race and com- [y]2Co 4:1 [z]Gal 1:1;
plete the task[y] the Lord Jesus has given Tit 1:3
me[z]—the task of testifying to the gospel of God's grace.
25"Now I know that none of you
among whom I have gone about preach-
ing the kingdom will ever see me again.[a] 20:25 [a]ver 38
26Therefore, I declare to you today that
I am innocent of the blood of all men.[b] 20:26 [b]Ac 18:6
27For I have not hesitated to proclaim 20:27
to you the whole will of God.[c] 28Keep [c]ver 20
watch over yourselves and all the flock
of which the Holy Spirit has made you
overseers.[a][d] Be shepherds of the church 20:28 [d]1Pe 5:2
of God,[b] which he bought with his own
blood. 29I know that after I leave, sav-
age wolves[e] will come in among you 20:29 [e]Mt 7:15
and will not spare the flock.[f] 30Even [f]ver 28
from your own number men will arise
and distort the truth in order to draw 20:30
away disciples[g] after them. 31So be on [g]Ac 11:26
your guard! Remember that for three

[a]28 Traditionally *bishops* [b]28 Many manuscripts *of the Lord*

years[h] I never stopped warning each of you night and day with tears.[i]

32"Now I commit you to God[j] and to the word of his grace, which can build you up and give you an inheritance[k] among all those who are sanctified.[l] 33I have not coveted anyone's silver or gold or clothing.[m] 34You yourselves know that these hands of mine have supplied my own needs and the needs of my companions.[n] 35In everything I did, I showed you that by this kind of hard work we must help the weak, remembering the words the Lord Jesus himself said: 'It is more blessed to give than to receive.' "

36When he had said this, he knelt down with all of them and prayed.[o] 37They all wept as they embraced him and kissed him.[p] 38What grieved them most was his statement that they would never see his face again.[q] Then they accompanied him to the ship.

On to Jerusalem

21 After we[r] had torn ourselves away from them, we put out to sea and sailed straight to Cos. The next day we went to Rhodes and from there to Patara. 2We found a ship crossing over to Phoenicia,[s] went on board and set sail. 3After sighting Cyprus and passing to the south of it, we sailed on to Syria. We landed at Tyre, where our ship was to unload its cargo. 4Finding the disciples[t] there, we stayed with them seven days. Through the Spirit[u] they urged Paul not to go on to Jerusalem. 5But when our time was up, we left and continued on our way. All the disciples and their wives and children accompanied us out of the city, and there on the beach we knelt to pray.[v] 6After saying good-by to each other, we went aboard the ship, and they returned home.

7We continued our voyage from Tyre[w] and landed at Ptolemais, where we greeted the brothers[x] and stayed with them for a day. 8Leaving the next day, we reached Caesarea[y] and stayed at the house of Philip[z] the evangelist,[a] one of the Seven. 9He had four unmarried daughters who prophesied.[b]

10After we had been there a number of days, a prophet named Agabus[c] came down from Judea. 11Coming over to us, he took Paul's belt, tied his own hands and feet with it and said, "The Holy Spirit says, 'In this way the Jews of Jerusalem will bind[d] the owner of this belt and will hand him over to the Gentiles.' "[e]

12When we heard this, we and the people there pleaded with Paul not to go up to Jerusalem. 13Then Paul answered, "Why are you weeping and breaking my heart? I am ready not only to be bound, but also to die[f] in Jerusalem for the name of the Lord Jesus."[g] 14When he would not be dissuaded, we gave up and said, "The Lord's will be done."

15After this, we got ready and went up to Jerusalem. 16Some of the disciples from Caesarea[h] accompanied us and brought us to the home of Mnason, where we were to stay. He was a man from Cyprus[i] and one of the early disciples.

Paul's Arrival at Jerusalem

17When we arrived at Jerusalem, the brothers received us warmly.[j] 18The next day Paul and the rest of us went to see James,[k] and all the elders[l] were present. 19Paul greeted them and reported in detail what God had done among the Gentiles[m] through his ministry.[n]

20When they heard this, they praised God. Then they said to Paul: "You see, brother, how many thousands of Jews have believed, and all of them are zealous[o] for the law.[p] 21They have been informed that you teach all the Jews who live among the Gentiles to turn away from Moses,[q] telling them not to circumcise their children[r] or live according to our customs.[s] 22What shall we do? They will certainly hear that you have come, 23so do what we tell you. There are four men with us who have made a vow.[t] 24Take these men, join in their purification rites[u] and pay their expenses, so that they can have their heads shaved.[v] Then everybody will know there is no truth in these reports about you, but that you yourself are living in obedience to the law. 25As for the Gentile believers, we have written to them our decision that they should abstain from food sacrificed to idols, from blood, from the meat of strangled animals and from sexual immorality."[w]

26The next day Paul took the men and purified himself along with them.

20:31 [h]Ac 19:10 [i]ver 19
20:32 [j]Ac 14:23 [k]Eph 1:14; Col 1:12; 3:24; Heb 9:15; 1Pe 1:4 [l]Ac 26:18
20:33 [m]1Sa 12:3; 1Co 9:12; 2Co 7:2; 11:9; 12:14-17
20:34 [n]Ac 18:3
20:36 [o]Lk 22:41; Ac 21:5
20:37 [p]Lk 15:20
20:38 [q]ver 25
21:1 [r]Ac 16:10
21:2 [s]Ac 11:19
21:4 [t]Ac 11:26 [u]ver 11; Ac 20:23
21:5 [v]Ac 20:36
21:7 [w]Ac 12:20 [x]Ac 1:16
21:8 [y]Ac 8:40 [z]Ac 6:5; 8:5-40 [a]Eph 4:11; 2Ti 4:5
21:9 [b]Lk 2:36; Ac 2:17
21:10 [c]Ac 11:28
21:11 [d]ver 33 [e]1Ki 22:11
21:13 [f]Ac 20:24 [g]Ac 9:16
21:16 [h]Ac 8:40 [i]ver 3,4
21:17 [j]Ac 15:4
21:18 [k]Ac 15:13 [l]Ac 11:30
21:19 [m]Ac 14:27 [n]Ac 1:17
21:20 [o]Ac 22:3; Ro 10:2; Gal 1:14 [p]Ac 15:1,5
21:21 [q]ver 28 [r]Ac 15:19-21; 1Co 7:18,19 [s]Ac 6:14
21:23 [t]Ac 18:18
21:24 [u]ver 26; Ac 24:18 [v]Ac 18:18
21:25 [w]Ac 15:20,29

Then he went to the temple to give notice of the date when the days of purification would end and the offering would be made for each of them.[x]

Paul Arrested

27When the seven days were nearly over, some Jews from the province of Asia saw Paul at the temple. They stirred up the whole crowd and seized him,[y] 28shouting, "Men of Israel, help us! This is the man who teaches all men everywhere against our people and our law and this place. And besides, he has brought Greeks into the temple area and defiled this holy place."[z] 29(They had previously seen Trophimus[a] the Ephesian[b] in the city with Paul and assumed that Paul had brought him into the temple area.)

30The whole city was aroused, and the people came running from all directions. Seizing Paul,[c] they dragged him[d] from the temple, and immediately the gates were shut. 31While they were trying to kill him, news reached the commander of the Roman troops that the whole city of Jerusalem was in an uproar. 32He at once took some officers and soldiers and ran down to the crowd. When the rioters saw the commander and his soldiers, they stopped beating Paul.[e]

33The commander came up and arrested him and ordered him to be bound[f] with two[g] chains.[h] Then he asked who he was and what he had done. 34Some in the crowd shouted one thing and some another,[i] and since the commander could not get at the truth because of the uproar, he ordered that Paul be taken into the barracks.[j] 35When Paul reached the steps,[k] the violence of the mob was so great he had to be carried by the soldiers. 36The crowd that followed kept shouting, "Away with him!"[l]

Paul Speaks to the Crowd

37As the soldiers were about to take Paul into the barracks,[m] he asked the commander, "May I say something to you?"

"Do you speak Greek?" he replied. 38"Aren't you the Egyptian who started a revolt and led four thousand terrorists out into the desert[n] some time ago?"[o]

39Paul answered, "I am a Jew, from Tarsus[p] in Cilicia,[q] a citizen of no ordinary city. Please let me speak to the people."

40Having received the commander's permission, Paul stood on the steps and motioned[r] to the crowd. When they were all silent, he said to them in Aramaic[a]:[s]

22 1"Brothers and fathers,[t] listen now to my defense."

2When they heard him speak to them in Aramaic,[u] they became very quiet.

Then Paul said: 3"I am a Jew,[v] born in Tarsus[w] of Cilicia, but brought up in this city. Under[x] Gamaliel[y] I was thoroughly trained in the law of our fathers[z] and was just as zealous[a] for God as any of you are today. 4I persecuted[b] the followers of this Way to their death, arresting both men and women and throwing them into prison,[c] 5as also the high priest and all the Council[d] can testify. I even obtained letters from them to their brothers[e] in Damascus,[f] and went there to bring these people as prisoners to Jerusalem to be punished.

6"About noon as I came near Damascus, suddenly a bright light from heaven flashed around me.[g] 7I fell to the ground and heard a voice say to me, 'Saul! Saul! Why do you persecute me?'

8"'Who are you, Lord?' I asked.

"'I am Jesus of Nazareth, whom you are persecuting,' he replied. 9My companions saw the light,[h] but they did not understand the voice[i] of him who was speaking to me.

10"'What shall I do, Lord?' I asked.

"'Get up,' the Lord said, 'and go into Damascus. There you will be told all that you have been assigned to do.'[j] 11My companions led me by the hand into Damascus, because the brilliance of the light had blinded me.[k]

12"A man named Ananias came to see me.[l] He was a devout observer of the law and highly respected by all the Jews living there.[m] 13He stood beside me and said, 'Brother Saul, receive your sight!' And at that very moment I was able to see him.

14"Then he said: 'The God of our fathers[n] has chosen you to know his will and to see[o] the Righteous One[p] and to hear words from his mouth. 15You will be his witness[q] to all men of what you have seen and heard. 16And now what

[a]40 Or possibly *Hebrew*; also in 22:2

21:26 [x]Nu 6:13-20; Ac 24:18
21:27 [y]Ac 24:18; 26:21
21:28 [z]Mt 24:15; Ac 24:5,6
21:29 [a]Ac 20:4 [b]Ac 18:19
21:30 [c]Ac 26:21 [d]Ac 16:19
21:32 [e]Ac 23:27
21:33 [f]ver 11 [g]Ac 12:6 [h]Ac 20:23; Eph 6:20; 2Ti 2:9
21:34 [i]Ac 19:32 [j]ver 37; Ac 23:10, 16,32
21:35 [k]ver 40
21:36 [l]Lk 23:18; Jn 19:15; Ac 22:22
21:37 [m]ver 34
21:38 [n]Mt 24:26 [o]Ac 5:36
21:39 [p]Ac 9:11 [q]Ac 22:3
21:40 [r]Ac 12:17 [s]Jn 5:2
22:1 [t]Ac 7:2
22:2 [u]Ac 21:40
22:3 [v]Ac 21:39 [w]Ac 9:11 [x]Lk 10:39 [y]Ac 5:34 [z]Ac 26:5 [a]Ac 21:20
22:4 [b]Ac 8:3 [c]ver 19,20
22:5 [d]Lk 22:66 [e]Ac 13:26 [f]Ac 9:2
22:6 [g]Ac 9:3
22:9 [h]Ac 26:13 [i]Ac 9:7
22:10 [j]Ac 16:30
22:11 [k]Ac 9:8
22:12 [l]Ac 9:17 [m]Ac 10:22
22:14 [n]Ac 3:13 [o]1Co 9:1; 15:8 [p]Ac 7:52
22:15 [q]Ac 23:11; 26:16

are you waiting for? Get up, be bap-
22:16 [r]Ac 2:38 tized[r] and wash your sins away,[s] calling
[s]Heb 10:22 on his name.’[t]
[t]Ro 10:13 17“When I returned to Jerusalem[u]
22:17 and was praying at the temple, I fell
[u]Ac 9:26 [v]Ac 10:10 into a trance[v] 18and saw the Lord speaking. ‘Quick!’ he said to me. ‘Leave Je-
rusalem immediately, because they will
not accept your testimony about me.’
19“ ‘Lord,’ I replied, ‘these men know
22:19 that I went from one synagogue to an-
[w]ver 4; Ac 8:3 other to imprison[w] and beat[x] those who
[x]Mt 10:17 believe in you. 20And when the blood of
your martyr[a] Stephen was shed, I stood
there giving my approval and guarding
22:20 the clothes of those who were killing
[y]Ac 7:57-60; 8:1 him.’[y]
21“Then the Lord said to me, ‘Go;
22:21 I will send you far away to the Gen-
[z]Ac 9:15; 13:46 tiles.’ ”[z]

Paul the Roman Citizen

22The crowd listened to Paul until he
said this. Then they raised their voices
22:22 [a]Ac 21:36 and shouted, “Rid the earth of him![a]
[b]Ac 25:24 He’s not fit to live!”[b]
22:23 23As they were shouting and throw-
[c]Ac 7:58 ing off their cloaks[c] and flinging dust
[d]2Sa 16:13 into the air,[d] 24the commander ordered
22:24 [e]Ac 21:34 Paul to be taken into the barracks.[e] He
[f]ver 29 directed[f] that he be flogged and questioned in order to find out why the people were shouting at him like this. 25As
they stretched him out to flog him, Paul
said to the centurion standing there, “Is
22:25 it legal for you to flog a Roman citizen
[g]Ac 16:37 who hasn’t even been found guilty?”[g]
26When the centurion heard this, he
went to the commander and reported
it. “What are you going to do?” he
asked. “This man is a Roman citizen.”
27The commander went to Paul and
asked, “Tell me, are you a Roman citizen?”
“Yes, I am,” he answered.
28Then the commander said, “I had
to pay a big price for my citizenship.”
“But I was born a citizen,” Paul replied.
29Those who were about to question
him withdrew immediately. The commander himself was alarmed when he
22:29 realized that he had put Paul, a Roman
[h]ver 24,25; Ac 16:38 citizen,[h] in chains.

Before the Sanhedrin

30The next day, since the commander
wanted to find out exactly why Paul was
being accused by the Jews,[i] he released 22:30 [i]Ac 23:28
him[j] and ordered the chief priests and [j]Ac 21:33
all the Sanhedrin[k] to assemble. Then he [k]Mt 5:22
brought Paul and had him stand before
them.

23 Paul looked straight at the San- 23:1
hedrin[l] and said, “My brothers,[m] [l]Ac 22:30 [m]Ac 22:5
I have fulfilled my duty to God in all [n]Ac 24:16; 1Co 4:4;
good conscience[n] to this day.” 2At this 2Co 1:12; 2Ti 1:3;
the high priest Ananias[o] ordered those Heb 13:18
standing near Paul to strike him on the 23:2
mouth.[p] 3Then Paul said to him, “God [o]Ac 24:1
will strike you, you whitewashed wall![q] [p]Jn 18:22
You sit there to judge me according to 23:3
the law, yet you yourself violate the law [q]Mt 23:27 [r]Lev 19:15; Dt 25:1,2;
by commanding that I be struck!”[r] Jn 7:51
4Those who were standing near Paul
said, “You dare to insult God’s high
priest?”
5Paul replied, “Brothers, I did not realize that he was the high priest; for it
is written: ‘Do not speak evil about the
ruler of your people.’[b]”[s] 23:5 [s]Ex 22:28
6Then Paul, knowing that some of
them were Sadducees and the others
Pharisees, called out in the Sanhedrin,
“My brothers,[t] I am a Pharisee,[u] the son 23:6 [t]Ac 22:5
of a Pharisee. I stand on trial because [u]Ac 26:5; Php 3:5
of my hope in the resurrection of the [v]Ac 24:15,21;
dead.”[v] 7When he said this, a dispute 26:8
broke out between the Pharisees and
the Sadducees, and the assembly was
divided. 8(The Sadducees say that there
is no resurrection,[w] and that there are 23:8
neither angels nor spirits, but the Phari- [w]Mt 22:23
sees acknowledge them all.)
9There was a great uproar, and some
of the teachers of the law who were 23:9
Pharisees[x] stood up and argued vigor- [x]Mk 2:16
ously. “We find nothing wrong with [y]ver 29; Ac 25:25;
this man,”[y] they said. “What if a spirit 26:31
or an angel has spoken to him?”[z] 10The [z]Ac 22:7, 17,18
dispute became so violent that the com-
mander was afraid Paul would be torn
to pieces by them. He ordered the
troops to go down and take him away
from them by force and bring him into 23:10
the barracks.[a] [a]Ac 21:34
11The following night the Lord stood
near Paul and said, “Take courage![b] As 23:11 [b]Ac 18:9
you have testified about me in Jerusa- [c]Ac 19:21;
lem, so you must also testify in Rome.”[c] 28:23

The Plot to Kill Paul

12The next morning the Jews formed
a conspiracy and bound themselves with

[a]20 Or *witness* [b]5 Exodus 22:28

an oath not to eat or drink until they
23:12 [d]ver 14,21,30; Ac 25:3
had killed Paul.[d] 13 More than forty men
were involved in this plot. 14 They went
to the chief priests and elders and said,
"We have taken a solemn oath not to
23:14 [e]ver 12
eat anything until we have killed Paul.[e]
23:15 [f]ver 1; Ac 22:30
15 Now then, you and the Sanhedrin[f]
petition the commander to bring him
before you on the pretext of wanting
more accurate information about his
case. We are ready to kill him before he
gets here."
16 But when the son of Paul's sister
23:16 [g]ver 10; Ac 21:34
heard of this plot, he went into the barracks[g] and told Paul.
17 Then Paul called one of the centu-
rions and said, "Take this young man
to the commander; he has something to
tell him." 18 So he took him to the commander.
23:18 [h]Eph 3:1
The centurion said, "Paul, the
prisoner,[h] sent for me and asked me to
bring this young man to you because he
has something to tell you."
19 The commander took the young
man by the hand, drew him aside
and asked, "What is it you want to
tell me?"
20 He said: "The Jews have agreed to
23:20 [i]ver 1 [j]ver 14,15
ask you to bring Paul before the Sanhedrin[i] tomorrow on the pretext of wanting more accurate information about
him.[j] 21 Don't give in to them, because
23:21 [k]ver 13 [l]ver 12,14
more than forty[k] of them are waiting
in ambush for him. They have taken an
oath not to eat or drink until they have
killed him.[l] They are ready now, waiting for your consent to their request."
22 The commander dismissed the
young man and cautioned him, "Don't
tell anyone that you have reported this
to me."

Paul Transferred to Caesarea

23 Then he called two of his centu-
rions and ordered them, "Get ready a
detachment of two hundred soldiers,
23:23 [m]Ac 8:40 [n]ver 33
seventy horsemen and two hundred
spearmen[a] to go to Caesarea[m] at nine
tonight.[n] 24 Provide mounts for Paul so
23:24 [o]ver 26,33; Ac 24:1-3,10; 25:14
that he may be taken safely to Governor Felix."[o]
25 He wrote a letter as follows:

26 Claudius Lysias,

23:26 [p]Lk 1:3; Ac 24:3; 26:25
To His Excellency,[p] Governor Felix:

23:26 [q]Ac 15:23
Greetings.[q]

27 This man was seized by the
Jews and they were about to kill
23:27 [r]Ac 21:32 [s]Ac 21:33 [t]Ac 22:25-29
him,[r] but I came with my troops
and rescued him,[s] for I had learned
that he is a Roman citizen.[t] 28 I
wanted to know why they were accusing him, so I brought him to
23:28 [u]Ac 22:30
their Sanhedrin.[u] 29 I found that the
accusation had to do with ques-
23:29 [v]Ac 18:15; 25:19 [w]ver 9; Ac 26:31
tions about their law,[v] but there
was no charge against him[w] that
deserved death or imprisonment.
23:30 [x]ver 20,21 [y]Ac 20:3 [z]ver 35; Ac 24:19; 25:16
30 When I was informed[x] of a plot[y]
to be carried out against the man,
I sent him to you at once. I also
ordered his accusers[z] to present to
you their case against him.

31 So the soldiers, carrying out their
orders, took Paul with them during the
night and brought him as far as Antipa-
23:32 [a]ver 23 [b]Ac 21:34
tris. 32 The next day they let the cavalry[a]
go on with him, while they returned to
23:33 [c]ver 23,24 [d]Ac 8:40 [e]ver 26
the barracks.[b] 33 When the cavalry[c] arrived in Caesarea,[d] they delivered the
letter to the governor[e] and handed Paul
over to him. 34 The governor read the
letter and asked what province he was
23:34 [f]Ac 6:9; 21:39
from. Learning that he was from Cilicia,[f] 35 he said, "I will hear your case
23:35 [g]ver 30; Ac 24:19; 25:16 [h]Ac 24:27
when your accusers[g] get here." Then he
ordered that Paul be kept under guard[h]
in Herod's palace.

The Trial Before Felix

24 Five days later the high priest
24:1 [i]Ac 23:2 [j]Ac 23:30,35 [k]Ac 23:24
Ananias[i] went down to Caesa-
rea with some of the elders and a lawyer named Tertullus, and they brought
their charges[j] against Paul before the
governor.[k] 2 When Paul was called in,
Tertullus presented his case before Felix: "We have enjoyed a long period of
peace under you, and your foresight has
brought about reforms in this nation.
3 Everywhere and in every way, most ex-
24:3 [l]Lk 1:3; Ac 23:26; 26:25
cellent[l] Felix, we acknowledge this with
profound gratitude. 4 But in order not
to weary you further, I would request
that you be kind enough to hear us
briefly.
5 "We have found this man to be a
24:5 [m]Ac 16:20; 17:6
troublemaker, stirring up riots[m] among

[a] *23* The meaning of the Greek for this word is uncertain.

the Jews[n] all over the world. He is a ringleader of the Nazarene[o] sect[p] 6and even tried to desecrate the temple;[q] so we seized him. 8By[a] examining him yourself you will be able to learn the truth about all these charges we are bringing against him."

9The Jews joined in the accusation,[r] asserting that these things were true.

10When the governor[s] motioned for him to speak, Paul replied: "I know that for a number of years you have been a judge over this nation; so I gladly make my defense. 11You can easily verify that no more than twelve days[t] ago I went up to Jerusalem to worship. 12My accusers did not find me arguing with anyone at the temple,[u] or stirring up a crowd[v] in the synagogues or anywhere else in the city. 13And they cannot prove to you the charges they are now making against me.[w] 14However, I admit that I worship the God of our fathers[x] as a follower of the Way,[y] which they call a sect.[z] I believe everything that agrees with the Law and that is written in the Prophets,[a] 15and I have the same hope in God as these men, that there will be a resurrection[b] of both the righteous and the wicked.[c] 16So I strive always to keep my conscience clear[d] before God and man.

17"After an absence of several years, I came to Jerusalem to bring my people gifts for the poor[e] and to present offerings. 18I was ceremonially clean[f] when they found me in the temple courts doing this. There was no crowd with me, nor was I involved in any disturbance.[g] 19But there are some Jews from the province of Asia, who ought to be here before you and bring charges if they have anything against me.[h] 20Or these who are here should state what crime they found in me when I stood before the Sanhedrin— 21unless it was this one thing I shouted as I stood in their presence: 'It is concerning the resurrection of the dead that I am on trial before you today.' "[i]

22Then Felix, who was well acquainted with the Way, adjourned the proceedings. "When Lysias the commander comes," he said, "I will decide your case." 23He ordered the centurion to keep Paul under guard[j] but to give him some freedom[k] and permit his friends to take care of his needs.[l]

24Several days later Felix came with his wife Drusilla, who was a Jewess. He sent for Paul and listened to him as he spoke about faith in Christ Jesus.[m] 25As Paul discoursed on righteousness, self-control[n] and the judgment[o] to come, Felix was afraid and said, "That's enough for now! You may leave. When I find it convenient, I will send for you." 26At the same time he was hoping that Paul would offer him a bribe, so he sent for him frequently and talked with him.

27When two years had passed, Felix was succeeded by Porcius Festus,[p] but because Felix wanted to grant a favor to the Jews,[q] he left Paul in prison.[r]

The Trial Before Festus

25 Three days after arriving in the province, Festus went up from Caesarea[s] to Jerusalem, 2where the chief priests and Jewish leaders appeared before him and presented the charges against Paul.[t] 3They urgently requested Festus, as a favor to them, to have Paul transferred to Jerusalem, for they were preparing an ambush to kill him along the way. 4Festus answered, "Paul is being held[u] at Caesarea, and I myself am going there soon. 5Let some of your leaders come with me and press charges against the man there, if he has done anything wrong."

6After spending eight or ten days with them, he went down to Caesarea, and the next day he convened the court[v] and ordered that Paul be brought before him. 7When Paul appeared, the Jews

24:5 [n]Ac 21:28 [o]Mk 1:24 [p]ver 14; Ac 26:5; 28:22
24:6 [q]Ac 21:28
24:9 [r]1Th 2:16
24:10 [s]Ac 23:24
24:11 [t]Ac 21:27; ver 1
24:12 [u]Ac 25:8; 28:17 [v]ver 18
24:13 [w]Ac 25:7
24:14 [x]Ac 3:13 [y]Ac 9:2 [z]ver 5 [a]Ac 26:6,22; 28:23
24:15 [b]Ac 23:6; 28:20 [c]Da 12:2; Jn 5:28,29
24:16 [d]Ac 23:1
24:17 [e]Ac 11:29,30; Ro 15:25-28, 31; 1Co 16:1-4, 15; 2Co 8:1-4; Gal 2:10
24:18 [f]Ac 21:26 [g]ver 12
24:19 [h]Ac 23:30
24:21 [i]Ac 23:6
24:23 [j]Ac 23:35 [k]Ac 28:16 [l]Ac 23:16; 27:3
24:24 [m]Ac 20:21
24:25 [n]Gal 5:23; 2Pe 1:6 [o]Ac 10:42
24:27 [p]Ac 25:1,4, 9,14 [q]Ac 12:3; 25:9 [r]Ac 23:35; 25:14
25:1 [s]Ac 8:40
25:2 [t]ver 15; Ac 24:1
25:4 [u]Ac 24:23
25:6 [v]ver 17

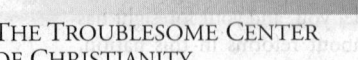

FAITHFULNESS

THE TROUBLESOME CENTER OF CHRISTIANITY

Acts 24:20–21

The resurrection is a difficult doctrine—a stone in the path of those who want a logical way to faith. If Christ is really alive, who knows what he might require of potential converts? So some skeptics must keep Christ at bay. It is easier to doubt the resurrection than to put yourself at risk by following a living Savior.

[a]6-8 Some manuscripts *him and wanted to judge him according to our law. 7But the commander, Lysias, came and with the use of much force snatched him from our hands 8and ordered his accusers to come before you. By*

who had come down from Jerusalem
stood around him, bringing many seri-
25:7 [w]Mk 15:3; Lk 23:2,10; Ac 24:5,6 [x]Ac 24:13 ous charges against him,[w] which they
could not prove.[x]
8Then Paul made his defense: "I have
done nothing wrong against the law
25:8 [y]Ac 6:13; 24:12; 28:17 of the Jews or against the temple[y] or
against Caesar."
25:9 [z]Ac 24:27 [a]ver 20 9Festus, wishing to do the Jews a
favor,[z] said to Paul, "Are you willing to
go up to Jerusalem and stand trial before me there on these charges?"[a]
10Paul answered: "I am now standing before Caesar's court, where I ought
to be tried. I have not done any wrong
to the Jews, as you yourself know very
well. 11If, however, I am guilty of doing anything deserving death, I do not
refuse to die. But if the charges brought
25:11 [b]ver 21,25; Ac 26:32; 28:19 against me by these Jews are not true,
no one has the right to hand me over to
them. I appeal to Caesar!"[b]

SELF-CONTROL

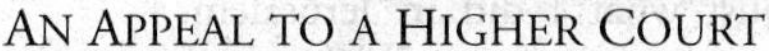

AN APPEAL TO A HIGHER COURT

Acts 25:10–11

This appeal eventually took Paul, a Roman citizen, to the center of the empire. There, under house arrest, perhaps chained constantly to a guard, he wrote letters that the courts could not judge and that the world must obey. He preached the cross while struggling with crosses of his own. Who's glad he had to bear the pain? None of us. Yet had he not suffered to tell the world of Christ, would we have found him quite so convincing? Would he have believed as firmly had God required less of him?

12After Festus had conferred with his
council, he declared: "You have appealed
to Caesar. To Caesar you will go!"

Festus Consults King Agrippa

13A few days later King Agrippa and
25:13 [c]Ac 8:40 Bernice arrived at Caesarea[c] to pay their
respects to Festus. 14Since they were
spending many days there, Festus discussed Paul's case with the king. He
25:14 [d]Ac 24:27 said: "There is a man here whom Felix
left as a prisoner.[d] 15When I went to Je-
25:15 [e]ver 2; Ac 24:1 rusalem, the chief priests and elders of
the Jews brought charges against him[e]
and asked that he be condemned.
16"I told them that it is not the Roman custom to hand over any man
before he has faced his accusers and
has had an opportunity to defend him-
self against their charges.[f] 17When they 25:16 [f]ver 4,5; Ac 23:30
came here with me, I did not delay
the case, but convened the court the
next day and ordered the man to be
brought in.[g] 18When his accusers got up 25:17 [g]ver 6,10
to speak, they did not charge him with
any of the crimes I had expected. 19In- 25:19 [h]Ac 18:15; 23:29 [i]Ac 17:22
stead, they had some points of dispute[h]
with him about their own religion[i] and
about a dead man named Jesus who
Paul claimed was alive. 20I was at a loss
how to investigate such matters; so I
asked if he would be willing to go to
Jerusalem and stand trial there on these
charges.[j] 21When Paul made his appeal 25:20 [j]ver 9
to be held over for the Emperor's deci-
sion, I ordered him held until I could 25:21 [k]ver 11,12
send him to Caesar."[k]
22Then Agrippa said to Festus, "I
would like to hear this man myself."
He replied, "Tomorrow you will hear 25:22 [l]Ac 9:15
him."[l]

Paul Before Agrippa

23The next day Agrippa and Bernice[m] 25:23 [m]ver 13; Ac 26:30
came with great pomp and entered the
audience room with the high ranking
officers and the leading men of the city.
At the command of Festus, Paul was
brought in. 24Festus said: "King Agrippa, and all who are present with us,
you see this man! The whole Jewish 25:24 [n]ver 2,3,7 [o]Ac 22:22
community[n] has petitioned me about
him in Jerusalem and here in Caesarea,
shouting that he ought not to live any
longer.[o] 25I found he had done noth-
ing deserving of death,[p] but because he 25:25 [p]Ac 23:9 [q]ver 11
made his appeal to the Emperor[q] I de-
cided to send him to Rome. 26But I
have nothing definite to write to His
Majesty about him. Therefore I have
brought him before all of you, and especially before you, King Agrippa, so
that as a result of this investigation I
may have something to write. 27For I
think it is unreasonable to send on a
prisoner without specifying the charges
against him."
26 Then Agrippa said to Paul, "You
have permission to speak for 26:1 [r]Ac 9:15; 25:22
yourself."[r]
So Paul motioned with his hand and
began his defense: 2"King Agrippa, I
consider myself fortunate to stand before you today as I make my defense

DAY 5 FIVE

▸ PEACE AND ITS PLACE IN MY PERSONAL WORSHIP

Acts 26:9–18

Paul met Jesus on the Damascus road, and the world was never the same again—because Paul was forever changed. Paul had been a devout Jew, and there can be no question about his devotion to his religious tradition. But the question is: "How did the nature of his personal worship change after he met Jesus?"

Before his conversion, Paul was undoubtedly committed to God, as well as to Judaism with all its attributes and traditions. He must have entered the temple with a deep love for God and a fervor for all Jewish truths. So fervent was he, in fact, that he gave himself to the purpose of destroying Christianity. He believed God wanted Judaism to be unrivaled by any new "ism." He must have surveyed the temple with pride, adored the Pentateuch, and kept the feasts and observances in utter sincerity.

Then Paul met Jesus! Suddenly his adoration took on a very personal tone. From the beginning of his new life in Christ, he must have realized that he had finally discovered a way of worship that focused on truth, for truth resides in the person of Christ, the fountain of all truth. Now Paul began to worship in truth, and the result of that worship was a sweet peace that centered on Jesus.

There can be no doubt that Christianity is a religion of relationships. Like Paul, we worship truth insofar as that truth adheres to the person of Christ and to his teaching. We were born again because we became related to Christ. We sing "What a Friend we have in Jesus," not "What a friend we have in doctrine." We do not go to church to exalt the six rules of peace, the eight principles of grace, or even the Ten Commandments. We are concerned with dogma only because Jesus has called us to God's truth, to righteous living and to clear thinking. But our worship is reserved for God and God alone. When that attitude of worship is in place, we live and walk in an atmosphere of peace.

To begin a study on the topic of Peace, Accepting a Higher Will, turn to the home page on page 1282.

against all the accusations of the Jews,
3and especially so because you are well
acquainted with all the Jewish customs[s]
and controversies.[t] Therefore, I beg you
to listen to me patiently.
4"The Jews all know the way I have
lived ever since I was a child,[u] from the
beginning of my life in my own country, and also in Jerusalem. 5They have
known me for a long time[v] and can
testify, if they are willing, that according to the strictest sect of our religion,
I lived as a Pharisee.[w] 6And now it is
because of my hope[x] in what God has
promised our fathers[y] that I am on trial
today. 7This is the promise our twelve
tribes[z] are hoping to see fulfilled as they
earnestly serve God day and night.[a]
O king, it is because of this hope that
the Jews are accusing me.[b] 8Why should
any of you consider it incredible that
God raises the dead?[c]
9"I too was convinced[d] that I ought
to do all that was possible to oppose[e]
the name of Jesus of Nazareth.[f] 10And
that is just what I did in Jerusalem.
On the authority of the chief priests
I put many of the saints[g] in prison,[h]
and when they were put to death, I cast
my vote against them.[i] 11Many a time
I went from one synagogue to another
to have them punished,[j] and I tried to
force them to blaspheme. In my obses-
sion against them, I even went to foreign cities to persecute them.
12"On one of these journeys I was
going to Damascus with the authority
and commission of the chief priests.
13About noon, O king, as I was on the
road, I saw a light from heaven, brighter than the sun, blazing around me and
my companions. 14We all fell to the
ground, and I heard a voice[k] saying to
me in Aramaic,[a] 'Saul, Saul, why do
you persecute me? It is hard for you to
kick against the goads.'
15"Then I asked, 'Who are you,
Lord?'
"'I am Jesus, whom you are persecuting,' the Lord replied. 16'Now get up
and stand on your feet.[l] I have appeared
to you to appoint you as a servant and
as a witness of what you have seen of
me and what I will show you.[m] 17I will
rescue you[n] from your own people and
from the Gentiles.[o] I am sending you

[a]14 Or *Hebrew*

26:3 [s]ver 7; Ac 6:14 [t]Ac 25:19
26:4 [u]Gal 1:13,14; Php 3:5
26:5 [v]Ac 22:3 [w]Ac 23:6; Php 3:5
26:6 [x]Ac 23:6; 24:15; 28:20 [y]Ac 13:32; Ro 15:8
26:7 [z]Jas 1:1 [a]1Th 3:10; 1Ti 5:5 [b]ver 2
26:8 [c]Ac 23:6
26:9 [d]1Ti 1:13 [e]Jn 16:2 [f]Jn 15:21
26:10 [g]Ac 9:13 [h]Ac 8:3; 9:2,14,21 [i]Ac 22:20
26:11 [j]Mt 10:17
26:14 [k]Ac 9:7
26:16 [l]Eze 2:1; Da 10:11 [m]Ac 22:14,15
26:17 [n]Jer 1:8,19 [o]Ac 9:15

26:18 [p]Isa 35:5 [q]Isa 42:7,16; Eph 5:8; Col 1:13; 1Pe 2:9 [r]Lk 24:47; Ac 2:38 [s]Ac 20:21,32
26:20 [t]Ac 9:19-25 [u]Ac 9:26-29; 22:17-20 [v]Ac 9:15; 13:46 [w]Ac 3:19 [x]Mt 3:8; Lk 3:8
26:21 [y]Ac 21:27,30 [z]Ac 21:31
26:22 [a]Lk 24:27,44; Ac 10:43; 24:14
26:23 [b]1Co 15:20, 23; Col 1:18; Rev 1:5 [c]Lk 2:32
26:24 [d]Jn 10:20; 1Co 4:10 [e]Jn 7:15
26:25 [f]Ac 23:26
26:26 [g]ver 3
26:28 [h]Ac 11:26
26:29 [i]Ac 21:33
26:30 [j]Ac 25:23

to them [18]to open their eyes[p] and turn them from darkness to light,[q] and from the power of Satan to God, so that they may receive forgiveness of sins[r] and a place among those who are sanctified by faith in me.'[s]

[19]"So then, King Agrippa, I was not disobedient to the vision from heaven. [20]First to those in Damascus,[t] then to those in Jerusalem[u] and in all Judea, and to the Gentiles[v] also, I preached that they should repent[w] and turn to God and prove their repentance by their deeds.[x] [21]That is why the Jews seized me[y] in the temple courts and tried to kill me.[z] [22]But I have had God's help to this very day, and so I stand here and testify to small and great alike. I am saying nothing beyond what the prophets and Moses said would happen[a]— [23]that the Christ[a] would suffer and, as the first to rise from the dead,[b] would proclaim light to his own people and to the Gentiles."[c]

[24]At this point Festus interrupted Paul's defense. "You are out of your mind,[d] Paul!" he shouted. "Your great learning[e] is driving you insane."

[25]"I am not insane, most excellent[f] Festus," Paul replied. "What I am saying is true and reasonable. [26]The king is familiar with these things,[g] and I can speak freely to him. I am convinced that none of this has escaped his notice, because it was not done in a corner. [27]King Agrippa, do you believe the prophets? I know you do."

[28]Then Agrippa said to Paul, "Do you think that in such a short time you can persuade me to be a Christian?"[h]

[29]Paul replied, "Short time or long—I pray God that not only you but all who are listening to me today may become what I am, except for these chains."[i]

[30]The king rose, and with him the governor and Bernice[j] and those sitting with them. [31]They left the room, and while talking with one another, they said, "This man is not doing anything that deserves death or imprisonment."[k]

[32]Agrippa said to Festus, "This man could have been set free[l] if he had not appealed to Caesar."[m]

Paul Sails for Rome

27 When it was decided that we[n] would sail for Italy,[o] Paul and some other prisoners were handed over to a centurion named Julius, who belonged to the Imperial Regiment.[p] [2]We boarded a ship from Adramyttium about to sail for ports along the coast of the province of Asia,[q] and we put out to sea. Aristarchus,[r] a Macedonian[s] from Thessalonica,[t] was with us.

[3]The next day we landed at Sidon;[u] and Julius, in kindness to Paul,[v] allowed him to go to his friends so they might provide for his needs.[w] [4]From there we put out to sea again and passed to the lee of Cyprus because the winds were against us.[x] [5]When we had sailed across the open sea off the coast of Cilicia[y] and Pamphylia, we landed at Myra in Lycia. [6]There the centurion found an Alexandrian ship[z] sailing for Italy[a] and put us on board. [7]We made slow headway for many days and had difficulty arriving off Cnidus. When the wind did not allow us to hold our course,[b] we sailed to the lee of Crete,[c] opposite Salmone. [8]We moved along the coast with difficulty and came to a place called Fair Havens, near the town of Lasea.

[9]Much time had been lost, and sailing had already become dangerous because by now it was after the Fast.[b][d] So Paul warned them, [10]"Men, I can see that our voyage is going to be disastrous and bring great loss to ship and cargo, and to our own lives also."[e] [11]But the centurion, instead of listening to what Paul said, followed the advice of the pilot and of the owner of the ship. [12]Since the harbor was unsuitable to winter in, the majority decided that we should sail on, hoping to reach Phoenix and winter there. This was a harbor in Crete, facing both southwest and northwest.

The Storm

[13]When a gentle south wind began to blow, they thought they had obtained

[a]*23* Or *Messiah* [b]*9* That is, the Day of Atonement (Yom Kippur)

26:31 [k]Ac 23:9
26:32 [l]Ac 28:18 [m]Ac 25:11
27:1 [n]Ac 16:10 [o]Ac 18:2; 25:12,25 [p]Ac 10:1
27:2 [q]Ac 2:9 [r]Ac 19:29 [s]Ac 16:9 [t]Ac 17:1
27:3 [u]Mt 11:21 [v]ver 43 [w]Ac 24:23; 28:16
27:4 [x]ver 7
27:5 [y]Ac 6:9
27:6 [z]Ac 28:11 [a]ver 1
27:7 [b]ver 4 [c]ver 12,13,21
27:9 [d]Lev 16:29-31; 23:27-29; Nu 29:7
27:10 [e]ver 21

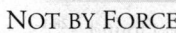

GENTLENESS

NOT BY FORCE

Acts 26:26–28

Nothing can force people to receive Christ. Yet Christ died openly, against a hostile sky, so publicly that none can pretend they haven't heard.

what they wanted; so they weighed anchor and sailed along the shore of Crete.
14Before very long, a wind of hurricane
27:14 [f]Mk 4:37 force,[f] called the “northeaster,” swept
down from the island. 15The ship was
caught by the storm and could not head
into the wind; so we gave way to it
and were driven along. 16As we passed
to the lee of a small island called Cau-
da, we were hardly able to make the
lifeboat secure. 17When the men had
hoisted it aboard, they passed ropes under the ship itself to hold it together.
27:17 [g]ver 26,39 Fearing that they would run aground[g]
on the sandbars of Syrtis, they lowered
the sea anchor and let the ship be driv-
en along. 18We took such a violent battering from the storm that the next
27:18 [h]ver 19,38; Jnh 1:5 day they began to throw the cargo
overboard.[h] 19On the third day, they
threw the ship's tackle overboard with
their own hands. 20When neither sun
nor stars appeared for many days and
the storm continued raging, we finally
gave up all hope of being saved.

21After the men had gone a long
time without food, Paul stood up before
them and said: “Men, you should have
27:21 [i]ver 10 [j]ver 7 taken my advice[i] not to sail from Crete;[j]
then you would have spared yourselves
this damage and loss. 22But now I urge
27:22 [k]ver 25,36 you to keep up your courage,[k] because
not one of you will be lost; only the ship
27:23 [l]Ac 5:19 [m]Ro 1:9 [n]Ac 18:9; 23:11; 2Ti 4:17 will be destroyed. 23Last night an angel[l]
of the God whose I am and whom
I serve[m] stood beside me[n] 24and said,
‘Do not be afraid, Paul. You must stand
27:24 [o]Ac 23:11 [p]ver 44 trial before Caesar;[o] and God has graciously given you the lives of all who sail
with you.’[p] 25So keep up your courage,[q]
27:25 [q]ver 22,36 [r]Ro 4:20,21 men, for I have faith in God that it will
happen just as he told me.[r] 26Never-
27:26 [s]ver 17,39 [t]Ac 28:1 theless, we must run aground[s] on some
island.”[t]

The Shipwreck

27On the fourteenth night we were
still being driven across the Adriatic[a]
Sea, when about midnight the sailors
sensed they were approaching land.
28They took soundings and found that
the water was a hundred and twenty
feet[b] deep. A short time later they took
soundings again and found it was ninety
feet[c] deep. 29Fearing that we would be
dashed against the rocks, they dropped
four anchors from the stern and prayed
for daylight. 30In an attempt to escape
from the ship, the sailors let the lifeboat[u] down into the sea, pretending 27:30 [u]ver 16
they were going to lower some anchors
from the bow. 31Then Paul said to
the centurion and the soldiers, “Unless
these men stay with the ship, you can-
not be saved.”[v] 32So the soldiers cut the 27:31 [v]ver 24
ropes that held the lifeboat and let it
fall away.

33Just before dawn Paul urged them
all to eat. “For the last fourteen days,”
he said, “you have been in constant suspense and have gone without food—
you haven't eaten anything. 34Now I
urge you to take some food. You need
it to survive. Not one of you will lose 27:34 [w]Mt 10:30
a single hair from his head.”[w] 35After
he said this, he took some bread and
gave thanks to God in front of them 27:35 [x]Mt 14:19
all. Then he broke it[x] and began to
eat. 36They were all encouraged[y] and 27:36 [y]ver 22,25
ate some food themselves. 37Altogether
there were 276 of us on board. 38When
they had eaten as much as they wanted,
they lightened the ship by throwing the 27:38 [z]ver 18; Jnh 1:5
grain into the sea.[z]

39When daylight came, they did not
recognize the land, but they saw a bay
with a sandy beach,[a] where they decided 27:39 [a]Ac 28:1
to run the ship aground if they could.
40Cutting loose the anchors,[b] they left 27:40 [b]ver 29
them in the sea and at the same time
untied the ropes that held the rudders.
Then they hoisted the foresail to the
wind and made for the beach. 41But the
ship struck a sandbar and ran aground.
The bow stuck fast and would not
move, and the stern was broken to 27:41 [c]2Co 11:25
pieces by the pounding of the surf.[c]

42The soldiers planned to kill the
prisoners to prevent any of them from
swimming away and escaping. 43But the
centurion wanted to spare Paul's life[d] 27:43 [d]ver 3
and kept them from carrying out their
plan. He ordered those who could swim
to jump overboard first and get to land.
44The rest were to get there on planks
or on pieces of the ship. In this way everyone reached land in safety.[e] 27:44 [e]ver 22,31

Ashore on Malta

28 Once safely on shore, we[f] found 28:1 [f]Ac 16:10 [g]Ac 27:26,39
out that the island[g] was called
Malta. 2The islanders showed us un-

[a]*27* In ancient times the name referred to an area extending well south of Italy. [b]*28* Greek *twenty orguias* (about 37 meters) [c]*28* Greek *fifteen orguias* (about 27 meters)

usual kindness. They built a fire and
welcomed us all because it was raining
and cold. 3Paul gathered a pile of brush-
wood and, as he put it on the fire, a
viper, driven out by the heat, fastened
itself on his hand. 4When the islanders
28:4 saw the snake hanging from his hand,[h]
[h]Mk 16:18 [i]Lk 13:2,4 they said to each other, "This man must
be a murderer; for though he escaped
from the sea, Justice has not allowed
him to live."[i] 5But Paul shook the snake
off into the fire and suffered no ill ef-
28:5 [j]Lk 10:19 fects.[j] 6The people expected him to
swell up or suddenly fall dead, but after
waiting a long time and seeing nothing
28:6 [k]Ac 14:11 unusual happen to him, they changed
their minds and said he was a god.[k]

GOODNESS

WHEN SNAKES BITE APOSTLES

Acts 28:5

Who can say why the snake, while fleeing from the campfire, sunk its fangs into such a noble hand? The watching crowd thought it was because Paul was a bad man. After all, bad snakes don't bite good people, do they? But Paul did not die. In surviving the snakebite, he became an enigma to the local islanders. Since he had their attention, he used it to speak of how Christ came to deal with the writhing evil at the center of their lives.

7There was an estate nearby that belonged to Publius, the chief official of
the island. He welcomed us to his home
and for three days entertained us hospitably. 8His father was sick in bed, suffering from fever and dysentery. Paul
28:8 [l]Jas 5:14,15 went in to see him and, after prayer,[l]
[m]Ac 9:40 placed his hands on him and healed
him.[m] 9When this had happened, the
rest of the sick on the island came and
were cured. 10They honored us in many
ways and when we were ready to sail,
they furnished us with the supplies we
needed.

Arrival at Rome

11After three months we put out to
sea in a ship that had wintered in the is-
28:11 [n]Ac 27:6 land. It was an Alexandrian ship[n] with
the figurehead of the twin gods Castor
and Pollux. 12We put in at Syracuse and
stayed there three days. 13From there
we set sail and arrived at Rhegium. The
next day the south wind came up, and
on the following day we reached Pute-
oli. 14There we found some brothers[o] 28:14 [o]Ac 1:16
who invited us to spend a week with
them. And so we came to Rome. 15The
brothers[p] there had heard that we were 28:15 [p]Ac 1:16
coming, and they traveled as far as the
Forum of Appius and the Three Taverns
to meet us. At the sight of these men
Paul thanked God and was encouraged.
16When we got to Rome, Paul was al-
lowed to live by himself, with a soldier 28:16 [q]Ac 24:23; 27:3
to guard him.[q]

Paul Preaches at Rome Under Guard

17Three days later he called together 28:17 [r]Ac 25:2 [s]Ac 22:5 [t]Ac 25:8 [u]Ac 6:14
the leaders of the Jews.[r] When they
had assembled, Paul said to them: "My
brothers,[s] although I have done nothing
against our people[t] or against the customs of our ancestors,[u] I was arrested in
Jerusalem and handed over to the Ro-
mans. 18They examined me[v] and want- 28:18 [v]Ac 22:24 [w]Ac 26:31,32 [x]Ac 23:9
ed to release me,[w] because I was not
guilty of any crime deserving death.[x]
19But when the Jews objected, I was 28:19 [y]Ac 25:11
compelled to appeal to Caesar[y]—not
that I had any charge to bring against
my own people. 20For this reason I have
asked to see you and talk with you. It is
because of the hope of Israel[z] that I am 28:20 [z]Ac 26:6,7 [a]Ac 21:33
bound with this chain."[a]
21They replied, "We have not received any letters from Judea concern-
ing you, and none of the brothers[b] who 28:21 [b]Ac 22:5
have come from there has reported or
said anything bad about you. 22But we
want to hear what your views are, for
we know that people everywhere are
talking against this sect."[c] 28:22 [c]Ac 24:5,14
23They arranged to meet Paul on a
certain day, and came in even larger
numbers to the place where he was
staying. From morning till evening he
explained and declared to them the 28:23 [d]Ac 19:8 [e]Ac 17:3 [f]Ac 8:35
kingdom of God[d] and tried to convince
them about Jesus[e] from the Law of
Moses and from the Prophets.[f] 24Some
were convinced by what he said, but 28:24 [g]Ac 14:4
others would not believe.[g] 25They disagreed among themselves and began to
leave after Paul had made this final
statement: "The Holy Spirit spoke the
truth to your forefathers when he said
through Isaiah the prophet:

26" 'Go to this people and say,

"You will be ever hearing but never
understanding;
you will be ever seeing but never
perceiving."
28:27 [b]Ps 119:70 [i]Isa 6:9,10
27 For this people's heart has become
calloused;[b]
they hardly hear with their ears,
and they have closed their eyes.
Otherwise they might see with their
eyes,
hear with their ears,
understand with their hearts
and turn, and I would heal them.'[a][i]

28:28 [j]Lk 2:30 [k]Ac 13:46
28 "Therefore I want you to know that
God's salvation[j] has been sent to the
Gentiles,[k] and they will listen!"[b]
30 For two whole years Paul stayed
there in his own rented house and welcomed all who came to see him. 31 Boldly and without hindrance he preached
the kingdom of God[l] and taught about
the Lord Jesus Christ.
28:31 [l]ver 23; Mt 4:23

[a]27 Isaiah 6:9,10 [b]28 Some manuscripts *listen!"* *29After he said this, the Jews left, arguing vigorously among themselves.*

▸ PATIENCE

AWAITING TRIAL

Acts 28:30–31

Paul spent two years in his own rented house. He was patient in his waiting. Those 730 days were his, and each day was marked with a sermon confirming that Paul was not a prisoner of Caesar but a prisoner of the glorious reality that God was in Christ reconciling the world to himself.

ROMANS

AUTHORSHIP AND DATE

Paul

c. A.D. 57

KEY THEMES

Paul wrote this letter to the Christians at Rome, whom he had not yet visited, but—by his own testimony—whom he longed to see (see 15:23–24). He confessed that his long-desired visit must be put off, for it had become necessary that he visit Jerusalem (see 15:25). The book of Romans deals specifically with sin and salvation, the ministry of the saints and God's sovereignty over the world. In his introduction to Romans, Paul talks about the worldwide task of spreading the gospel. He closes the first chapter of Romans by looking at the depravity of sin, and the consequences of serving idols made in the image of created things, rather than serving the Creator himself.

FRUIT OF THE SPIRIT IN ROMANS

Love: Loving God includes an extraordinary benefit: We find that the world makes more sense as we learn to love God. When we view the horrible circumstances of our lives through the single lens of loving God—in light of time and perspective—we see that all things occur in life to give God glory (see 8:28).

Joy: Theologians who study God, defining him for the world, are rarely credible unless they sing. Paul was the first great theologian, and he was trusted because his doxologies (glory songs) were ever erupting within his treatises. See 11:33–36 for one of Paul's joyous songs.

Peace: Peace is a matter of having a mind controlled by the Spirit (see 8:6).

Patience: Trials have a way of taming our impatience until we learn to sit quietly, waiting on some sign that God understands the pain we are enduring. Not only does pain produce patience, it ultimately produces character and hope (see 5:3–5).

Kindness: Kindness marks the Christian; it is the warm sleeve of grace in a wintry world, and Christians give it freely to each other (see 12:10).

Goodness: Goodness is not natural in our lives (see 3:10–12). Everyone sins, and goodness only comes when we realize we can never achieve goodness through personal effort. Then we can begin trusting God to supply it from the treasure house of Christ's sinlessness.

Faithfulness: Abraham believed God; he was faithful. God took his faithfulness, and with transforming grace, changed it instantly to righteousness (see 4:23). Jesus is heaven's great gift of atonement for earth's inability to live morally. When God sees us being faithful to trust in him rather than in our own efforts, he is faithful in return to credit us with righteousness (see vv. 23–24).

Self-Control: Our own self-control was made possible by Christ. Adam was the first bungler of this virtue, but Christ repaired it all: "For just as through the disobedience of the one man the many were made sinners, so also through the obedience of the one man the many will be made righteous" (5:19).

1

1 Paul, a servant of Christ Jesus,
1:1 [a]1Co 1:1 called to be an apostle[a] and set
[b]Ac 9:15 apart[b] for the gospel of God[c]— 2the
[c]2Co 11:7 gospel he promised beforehand through
1:2 his prophets in the Holy Scriptures[d]
[d]Gal 3:8 3regarding his Son, who as to his hu-
1:3 man nature[e] was a descendant of Da-
[e]Jn 1:14 vid, 4and who through the Spirit[a] of
holiness was declared with power to be
the Son of God[b] by his resurrection
from the dead: Jesus Christ our Lord.
5Through him and for his name's sake,
1:5 we received grace and apostleship to call
[f]Ac 9:15 people from among all the Gentiles[f] to
[g]Ac 6:7 the obedience that comes from faith.[g]
1:6 6And you also are among those who are
[h]Rev 17:14 called to belong to Jesus Christ.[h]

JOY

JESUS THE VICTOR

Romans 1:1–4

Are you weak? Do you feel inadequate? Have your outer circumstances forced you into some shadowy corner of terror? Look inward. Ordinary people explode with joy as they see their potential in Christ. Bless your own weaknesses. Exalt your own need. Then rejoice at what your life contains. He is the winner!

7To all in Rome who are loved by
1:7 [i]Ro 8:39 God[i] and called to be saints:
[j]1Co 1:3 Grace and peace to you from God
our Father and from the Lord Jesus
Christ.[j]

Paul's Longing to Visit Rome

1:8 8First, I thank my God through Jesus
[k]1Co 1:4 Christ for all of you,[k] because your faith
[l]Ro 16:19 is being reported all over the world.[l]
1:9 9God, whom I serve[m] with my whole
[m]2Ti 1:3 heart in preaching the gospel of his Son,
[n]Php 1:8 is my witness[n] how constantly I remember you 10in my prayers at all times; and
I pray that now at last by God's will the
way may be opened for me to come to
1:10 [o]Ro 15:32 you.[o]
11I long to see you[p] so that I may im-
1:11 [p]Ro 15:23 part to you some spiritual gift to make
you strong— 12that is, that you and I
may be mutually encouraged by each
other's faith. 13I do not want you to be
unaware, brothers, that I planned many
times to come to you (but have been
1:13 prevented from doing so until now)[q]
[q]Ro 15:22,23 in order that I might have a harvest
among you, just as I have had among
the other Gentiles.
14I am obligated[r] both to Greeks and 1:14
non-Greeks, both to the wise and the [r]1Co 9:16
foolish. 15That is why I am so eager to
preach the gospel also to you who are at 1:15
Rome.[s] [s]Ro 15:20

GOODNESS

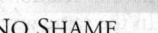

NO SHAME

Romans 1:16

He once hung naked on a cross so that we might be clothed in grace. Perfect goodness spent its sinless blood where it most mattered. Could we ever be ashamed? Surely not. To blush to speak his name is to forget the price he paid.

16I am not ashamed of the gospel,[t] 1:16 [t]2Ti 1:8
because it is the power of God[u] for [u]1Co 1:18
the salvation of everyone who believes: [v]Ac 3:26
first for the Jew,[v] then for the Gentile.[w] [w]Ro 2:9,10
17For in the gospel a righteousness from
God is revealed,[x] a righteousness that 1:17 [x]Ro 3:21
is by faith from first to last,[c] just as it [y]Hab 2:4;
is written: "The righteous will live by Gal 3:11;
faith."[d][y] Heb 10:38

God's Wrath Against Mankind

1:18 [z]Eph 5:6;
18The wrath of God[z] is being revealed Col 3:6
from heaven against all the godlessness
and wickedness of men who suppress
the truth by their wickedness, 19since
what may be known about God is plain
to them, because God has made it plain
to them.[a] 20For since the creation of 1:19 [a]Ac 14:17
the world God's invisible qualities—his
eternal power and divine nature—have
been clearly seen, being understood 1:20
from what has been made,[b] so that men [b]Ps 19:1-6
are without excuse.
21For although they knew God, they
neither glorified him as God nor gave
thanks to him, but their thinking be- 1:21
came futile and their foolish hearts were [c]Jer 2:5;
darkened.[c] 22Although they claimed to Eph 4:17,18
be wise, they became fools[d] 23and ex- 1:22 [d]1Co 1:20,27
changed the glory of the immortal God
for images[e] made to look like mortal 1:23 [e]Ps 106:20; Jer
man and birds and animals and rep- 2:11; Ac
tiles. 17:29
24Therefore God gave them over[f] in 1:24 [f]Eph 4:19

[a]4 Or *who as to his spirit* [b]4 Or *was appointed to be the Son of God with power* [c]17 Or *is from faith to faith* [d]17 Hab. 2:4

the sinful desires of their hearts to sexual impurity for the degrading of their
bodies with one another.[g] 25They exchanged the truth of God for a lie,[h] and
worshiped and served created things[i]
rather than the Creator—who is forever
praised.[j] Amen.
26Because of this, God gave them
over[k] to shameful lusts.[l] Even their
women exchanged natural relations for
unnatural ones.[m] 27In the same way the
men also abandoned natural relations
with women and were inflamed with
lust for one another. Men committed
indecent acts with other men, and received in themselves the due penalty for
their perversion.[n]
28Furthermore, since they did not
think it worthwhile to retain the knowledge of God, he gave them over[o] to a
depraved mind, to do what ought not
to be done. 29They have become filled
with every kind of wickedness, evil,
greed and depravity. They are full of
envy, murder, strife, deceit and malice.
They are gossips,[p] 30slanderers, God-
haters, insolent, arrogant and boastful;
they invent ways of doing evil; they disobey their parents;[q] 31they are senseless,
faithless, heartless,[r] ruthless. 32Although
they know God's righteous decree that
those who do such things deserve death,[s]
they not only continue to do these very
things but also approve[t] of those who
practice them.

1:24 [g]1Pe 4:3
1:25 [h]Isa 44:20 [i]Jer 10:14 [j]Ro 9:5
1:26 [k]ver 24,28 [l]1Th 4:5 [m]Lev 18:22,23
1:27 [n]Lev 18:22; 20:13
1:28 [o]ver 24,26
1:29 [p]2Co 12:20
1:30 [q]2Ti 3:2
1:31 [r]2Ti 3:3
1:32 [s]Ro 6:23 [t]Ps 50:18; Lk 11:48; Ac 8:1; 22:20

DAY 3 THREE

► KINDNESS AND MY RELATIONSHIP WITH CHRIST

Romans 2:3–4

God is kind, not in order to lead people to repentance, God is kind because it is his nature to be kind. He could not be unkind and retain his nature as a loving, perfect God. But this kindness has a huge fringe benefit. It draws us into relationship with Christ.

God loved the world so much that his kindness was spent to the very last drop of Christ's blood. Sinful humanity must ask, "Was this self-concerned planet worth it?" Theologians sometimes refer to this question as "the burden of God." God created humanity to glorify him, and yet humans sinned and did not glorify God. In fact human rebellion required God to answer humanity's sin with the life of his Son.

The mother of the Singer in my parable titled "A Symphony in Sand" stands at the foot of the gallows that will claim the life of her son and asks:

"O Son, was the planet worth all this?"
She gestured to His hanging form,
"Should love bleed out its last for worlds
Too self-concerned to pity all its whispers
When it has lost the volume of its voice?
You loved but have no lovers.
Where are all those for whom this price is paid?"

The kindness of God leads the world to repentance. What a heavy penalty must be levied against all those who see the kindness of Calvary and walk past it unchanged.

To begin a study on the topic of Kindness in the Time of Need, turn to the home page on page 246.

God's Righteous Judgment

2 You, therefore, have no excuse,[u] you
who pass judgment on someone
else, for at whatever point you judge
the other, you are condemning yourself, because you who pass judgment
do the same things.[v] 2Now we know
that God's judgment against those who
do such things is based on truth. 3So
when you, a mere man, pass judgment
on them and yet do the same things,
do you think you will escape God's
judgment? 4Or do you show contempt
for the riches[w] of his kindness,[x] tolerance[y] and patience,[z] not realizing
that God's kindness leads you toward
repentance?[a]
5But because of your stubbornness
and your unrepentant heart, you are
storing up wrath against yourself for
the day of God's wrath, when his righteous judgment[b] will be revealed. 6God
"will give to each person according to
what he has done."[a c] 7To those who by
persistence in doing good seek glory,
honor[d] and immortality,[e] he will give
eternal life. 8But for those who are self-
seeking and who reject the truth and
follow evil,[f] there will be wrath and anger. 9There will be trouble and distress
for every human being who does evil:

2:1 [u]Ro 1:20 [v]2Sa 12:5-7; Mt 7:1,2
2:4 [w]Ro 9:23; Eph 1:7,18; 2:7 [x]Ro 11:22 [y]Ro 3:25 [z]Ex 34:6 [a]2Pe 3:9
2:5 [b]Jude 6
2:6 [c]Ps 62:12; Mt 16:27
2:7 [d]ver 10 [e]1Co 15:53,54
2:8 [f]2Th 2:12

[a]6 Psalm 62:12; Prov. 24:12

2:9 first for the Jew, then for the Gentile;[g]
[g]1Pe 4:17 10but glory, honor and peace for every-
2:10 one who does good: first for the Jew,
[h]ver 9 then for the Gentile.[h] 11For God does
2:11 not show favoritism.[i]
[i]Ac 10:34 12All who sin apart from the law will
2:12 also perish apart from the law, and all
[j]Ro 3:19; who sin under the law[j] will be judged
1Co 9:20,21 by the law. 13For it is not those who
2:13 hear the law who are righteous in God's
[k]Jas 1:22, sight, but it is those who obey[k] the law
23,25 who will be declared righteous. 14(Indeed, when Gentiles, who do not have
2:14 the law, do by nature things required by
[l]Ac 10:35 the law,[l] they are a law for themselves,
even though they do not have the law,
15since they show that the requirements
of the law are written on their hearts,
their consciences also bearing witness,
and their thoughts now accusing, now
even defending them.) 16This will take
2:16 place on the day when God will judge
[m]Ecc 12:14 men's secrets[m] through Jesus Christ,[n] as
[n]Ac 10:42 [o]Ro 16:25 my gospel[o] declares.

FAITHFULNESS

SECRETS

Romans 2:16

Dare you hide any petty sins in an unswept closet of your conscience? Take care. All things hidden and unconfessed must yet be faced. Someday he will exhume such smoldering corruption, exposing all with brighter light than you can imagine.

The Jews and the Law

17Now you, if you call yourself a
Jew; if you rely on the law and brag
2:17 [p]ver 23; about your relationship to God;[p] 18if
Mic 3:11; you know his will and approve of what
Ro 9:4 is superior because you are instructed
by the law; 19if you are convinced that
you are a guide for the blind, a light
for those who are in the dark, 20an instructor of the foolish, a teacher of infants, because you have in the law the
embodiment of knowledge and truth—
21you, then, who teach others, do you
not teach yourself? You who preach
2:21 [q]Mt 23:3,4 against stealing, do you steal?[q] 22You
2:22 who say that people should not commit
[r]Ac 19:37 adultery, do you commit adultery? You
2:23 who abhor idols, do you rob temples?[r]
[s]ver 17 23You who brag about the law,[s] do you
dishonor God by breaking the law? 24As
it is written: "God's name is blasphemed

among the Gentiles because of you."[a][t] 2:24 [t]Isa 52:5;
25Circumcision has value if you ob- Eze 36:22
serve the law, but if you break the 2:25
law,[u] you have become as though you [u]Gal 5:3
had not been circumcised.[v] 26If those [v]Jer 4:4
who are not circumcised keep the law's 2:26
requirements,[w] will they not be regard- [w]Ro 8:4
ed as though they were circumcised?[x] [x]1Co 7:19
27The one who is not circumcised physically and yet obeys the law will con- 2:27
demn you[y] who, even though you have [y]Mt 12:41,42
the[b] written code and circumcision, are 2:28
a lawbreaker. [z]Mt 3:9;
28A man is not a Jew if he is only one Jn 8:39; Ro 9:6,7
outwardly,[z] nor is circumcision merely [a]Gal 6:15
outward and physical.[a] 29No, a man is a 2:29
Jew if he is one inwardly; and circumci- [b]Php 3:3; Col 2:11
sion is circumcision of the heart, by the [c]Ro 7:6
Spirit,[b] not by the written code.[c] Such a [d]Jn 5:44; 1Co 4:5;
man's praise is not from men, but from 2Co 10:18; 1Th 2:4;
God.[d] 1Pe 3:4

God's Faithfulness

3 What advantage, then, is there in
being a Jew, or what value is there
in circumcision? 2Much in every way!
First of all, they have been entrusted 3:2 [e]Dt 4:8;
with the very words of God.[e] Ps 147:19
3What if some did not have faith?[f] 3:3
Will their lack of faith nullify God's [f]Heb 4:2
faithfulness?[g] 4Not at all! Let God be [g]2Ti 2:13
true,[h] and every man a liar.[i] As it is 3:4 [h]Jn 3:33
written: [i]Ps 116:11 [j]Ps 51:4

"So that you may be proved right
when you speak
and prevail when you judge."[c][j]

5But if our unrighteousness brings
out God's righteousness more clearly,
what shall we say? That God is unjust
in bringing his wrath on us? (I am using 3:5
a human argument.)[k] 6Certainly not! If [k]Ro 6:19; Gal 3:15
that were so, how could God judge the 3:6
world?[l] 7Someone might argue, "If my [l]Ge 18:25
falsehood enhances God's truthfulness 3:7
and so increases his glory,[m] why am I [m]ver 4
still condemned as a sinner?" 8Why not
say—as we are being slanderously reported as saying and as some claim
that we say—"Let us do evil that good 3:8
may result"?[n] Their condemnation is [n]Ro 6:1
deserved.

No One Is Righteous

9What shall we conclude then? Are
we any better[d]? Not at all! We have

[a]*24* Isaiah 52:5; Ezek. 36:22 [b]*27* Or *who, by means of a* [c]*4* Psalm 51:4 [d]*9* Or *worse*

already made the charge that Jews and
3:9 [o]ver 19,23; Gentiles alike are all under sin.[o] 10As it
Gal 3:22 is written:

"There is no one righteous, not even
one;
11 there is no one who understands,
no one who seeks God.
12All have turned away,
they have together become
worthless;
3:12 there is no one who does good,
[p]Ps 14:1-3 not even one."[a][p]
3:13 13"Their throats are open graves;
[q]Ps 5:9 their tongues practice deceit."[b][q]
[r]Ps 140:3 "The poison of vipers is on their
lips."[c][r]
3:14 14 "Their mouths are full of cursing
[s]Ps 10:7 and bitterness."[d][s]
15"Their feet are swift to shed blood;
16 ruin and misery mark their ways,
17and the way of peace they do not
know."[e]
3:18 18 "There is no fear of God before
[t]Ps 36:1 their eyes."[f][t]

3:19 19Now we know that whatever the
[u]Jn 10:34 law says,[u] it says to those who are under
[v]Ro 2:12 the law,[v] so that every mouth may be
silenced and the whole world held accountable to God. 20Therefore no one
3:20 will be declared righteous in his sight
[w]Ac 13:39; by observing the law;[w] rather, through
Gal 2:16 [x]Ro 7:7 the law we become conscious of sin.[x]

Righteousness Through Faith

21But now a righteousness from
3:21 [y]Ro 1:17; 9:30 God,[y] apart from law, has been made
[z]Ac 10:43 known, to which the Law and the
3:22 Prophets testify.[z] 22This righteousness
[a]Ro 9:30 from God comes through faith[a] in Je-

PEACE

THE GREAT BUYBACK

Romans 3:23–24

Once the devil bought your soul for pennies.
The coins of your small successes were not enough to buy your freedom back.
Then came God, rich with heavy currency gathered from the olive trees of Maundy Thursday.
He laid the red-soaked coins before the registers of hell and bought you back.
It was a happy day for God.
How do *you* remember it?

sus Christ to all who believe. There is
no difference,[b] 23for all have sinned and 3:22 [b]Ro 10:12;
fall short of the glory of God, 24and Gal 3:28;
are justified freely by his grace[c] through Col 3:11
the redemption[d] that came by Christ 3:24
Jesus. 25God presented him as a sacri- [c]Ro 4:16;
fice of atonement,[g][e] through faith in his Eph 2:8 [d]Eph 1:7,14;
blood.[f] He did this to demonstrate his Col 1:14; Heb 9:12
justice, because in his forbearance he 3:25
had left the sins committed beforehand [e]1Jn 4:10 [f]Heb 9:12,14
unpunished[g]— 26he did it to demon- [g]Ac 17:30
strate his justice at the present time, so
as to be just and the one who justifies
those who have faith in Jesus.
27Where, then, is boasting?[h] It is ex- 3:27 [h]Ro 2:17,23;
cluded. On what principle? On that of 4:2;
observing the law? No, but on that of 1Co 1:29-31;
faith. 28For we maintain that a man is Eph 2:9
justified by faith apart from observing
the law.[i] 29Is God the God of Jews only? 3:28
Is he not the God of Gentiles too? Yes, [i]ver 20,21; Ac 13:39;
of Gentiles too,[j] 30since there is only Eph 2:9
one God, who will justify the circum- 3:29
cised by faith and the uncircumcised [j]Ro 9:24
through that same faith.[k] 31Do we, then, 3:30 [k]Gal 3:8
nullify the law by this faith? Not at all!
Rather, we uphold the law.

Abraham Justified by Faith

4 What then shall we say that Abraham, our forefather, discovered in
this matter? 2If, in fact, Abraham was
justified by works, he had something
to boast about—but not before God.[l] 4:2 [l]1Co 1:31
3What does the Scripture say? "Abra-
ham believed God, and it was credited
to him as righteousness."[h][m] 4:3
4Now when a man works, his wages [m]ver 5,9,22; Ge 15:6;
are not credited to him as a gift,[n] but Gal 3:6; Jas 2:23
as an obligation. 5However, to the man
who does not work but trusts God who 4:4 [n]Ro 11:6
justifies the wicked, his faith is credited
as righteousness. 6David says the same
thing when he speaks of the blessedness
of the man to whom God credits righteousness apart from works:

7"Blessed are they
whose transgressions are forgiven,
whose sins are covered.
8Blessed is the man
whose sin the Lord will never 4:8
count against him."[i][o] [o]Ps 32:1,2; 2Co 5:19

[a]*12* Psalms 14:1-3; 53:1-3; Eccles. 7:20
[b]*13* Psalm 5:9 [c]*13* Psalm 140:3 [d]*14* Psalm 10:7
[e]*17* Isaiah 59:7,8 [f]*18* Psalm 36:1 [g]*25* Or *as the one who would turn aside his wrath, taking away sin*
[h]*3* Gen. 15:6; also in verse 22 [i]*8* Psalm 32:1,2

9Is this blessedness only for the
circumcised, or also for the uncircumcised?[p] We have been saying that
Abraham's faith was credited to him as
righteousness.[q] 10Under what circumstances was it credited? Was it after he
was circumcised, or before? It was not
after, but before! 11And he received the
sign of circumcision, a seal of the righteousness that he had by faith while he
was still uncircumcised.[r] So then, he
is the father[s] of all who believe[t] but
have not been circumcised, in order
that righteousness might be credited to
them. 12And he is also the father of the
circumcised who not only are circumcised but who also walk in the footsteps
of the faith that our father Abraham
had before he was circumcised.

13It was not through law that Abraham and his offspring received the
promise[u] that he would be heir of the
world,[v] but through the righteousness
that comes by faith. 14For if those who
live by law are heirs, faith has no value
and the promise is worthless,[w] 15because
law brings wrath.[x] And where there is
no law there is no transgression.[y]

16Therefore, the promise comes by
faith, so that it may be by grace[z] and
may be guaranteed[a] to all Abraham's
offspring—not only to those who are of
the law but also to those who are of the
faith of Abraham. He is the father of
us all. 17As it is written: "I have made
you a father of many nations."[a][b] He is
our father in the sight of God, in whom
he believed—the God who gives life[c] to
the dead and calls[d] things that are not[e]
as though they were.

18Against all hope, Abraham in hope
believed and so became the father of
many nations,[f] just as it had been said
to him, "So shall your offspring be."[b][g]
19Without weakening in his faith, he
faced the fact that his body was as good
as dead[h]—since he was about a hundred years old[i]—and that Sarah's womb
was also dead.[j] 20Yet he did not waver
through unbelief regarding the promise of God, but was strengthened in
his faith and gave glory to God,[k] 21be-
ing fully persuaded that God had power to do what he had promised.[l] 22This
is why "it was credited to him as
righteousness."[m] 23The words "it was
credited to him" were written not for
him alone, 24but also for us,[n] to whom
God will credit righteousness—for us
who believe in him[o] who raised Jesus

[a]17 Gen. 17:5 [b]18 Gen. 15:5

4:9 [p]Ro 3:30
4:9 [q]ver 3
4:11 [r]Ge 17:10,11 [s]ver 16,17; Lk 19:9 [t]Ro 3:22
4:13 [u]Gal 3:16,29 [v]Ge 17:4-6
4:14 [w]Gal 3:18
4:15 [x]Ro 7:7-25; 1Co 15:56; 2Co 3:7; Gal 3:10; Ro 7:12 [y]Ro 3:20; 7:7
4:16 [z]Ro 3:24 [a]Ro 15:8
4:17 [b]Ge 17:5 [c]Jn 5:21 [d]Isa 48:13 [e]1Co 1:28
4:18 [f]ver 17 [g]Ge 15:5
4:19 [h]Heb 11:11,12 [i]Ge 17:17 [j]Ge 18:11
4:20 [k]Mt 9:8
4:21 [l]Ge 18:14; Heb 11:19
4:22 [m]ver 3
4:24 [n]Ro 15:4; 1Co 9:10; 10:11 [o]Ro 10:9

DAY 3 THREE

LOVE AND MY RELATIONSHIP WITH CHRIST

Romans 4:7–8

Love is the trumpet of the morning, the sentinel of midnight, the loaf of bread at noon. Love is the pathway through the wilderness of our fears. There is one grand basis for the Christian's peace: Our sins have been forgiven once and for all. Romans 4:8 says, "Blessed is the man whose sin the Lord will never count against him."

In *The Pilgrim's Progress,* John Bunyan's character Christian is on his way up the hill to the cross and is bent by the weight of his sin. This sin is symbolized by a huge bundle under which he has staggered all his life. When Christian arrives at the cross, his burden of sin is released. The bundle "fell from off his back, and began to tumble."

The burden that has bent Christian low all his life rolls off and is gone. It rolls down the hill of Calvary and is swallowed up in the mouth of the open sepulchre, which Christ left empty when he rose again.

Now Christian is free! His unrighteousness is forgiven! His sin is covered! His condition is ever as the psalmist says, "As far as the east is from the west, so far has he removed our transgressions from us" (Psalm 103:12).

There is no more wonderful evidence of God's giving love than the lightness of being we discover when we stand up straight for the first time in our lives, knowing that God has completely forgiven all our sins. The greatest gift of God's giving love is to be free of the curse of our sins forever. Small wonder the hymnist wrote:

Free from the law, O happy condition,
Jesus has bled and there is remission,
Cursed by the law and bruised by the fall,
Grace hath redeemed us once for all.

To begin a study on the topic of The Evidence of Love Is Giving, turn to the home page on page 5.

DAY 3 THREE

▸ LOVE AND MY RELATIONSHIP WITH CHRIST

Romans 5:5–8

Was there ever love like the love that Jesus has for us? In his dying we were cemented to that love, which fixes us forever in the beloved.

The story exists in several forms, but the one I like best tells of a little boy carrying a light bag across his shoulder. The bag was full of strange flutterings, which could not escape the notice of an old man who passed him on a narrow bridge. The old man had nearly passed by when intrigue overcame him, and he spoke to the boy quite abruptly, "Whatcha got in that bag, Sonny?"

"Nothin' but a bag full of sparrows," replied the boy.

"Whatcha gonna do with those birds?" probed the old man.

"I'm gonna torture them, pull out all their feathers and then, when they can't fly anymore, I'll feed them to the cat."

"How much would you take for all of them?"

"Oh, 'bout two dollars," replied the boy.

The old man reached in his pocket and pulled out two dollars. "Here," he said. The boy took the money and handed over the sack of sparrows. The old man opened the bag and all the birds bolted in a flash of thrashing feathers into the sunlight.

It happened that God met Satan on the bridge between worlds. Satan had a sack on his back, and God said, "What's in the sack, Satan?"

"Humanity," Satan replied.

"What are you gonna do with them?" God asked.

"I'm going to force them to live lifetimes of brutality and pain, and then, when they're all worn out, I'm going to throw them into hell."

"What will you take for them?" asked God.

"Just the life of your Son," Satan replied.

"Done!" said God and, as the hammer rang out upon the nails, God opened the bag and set humanity free.

To begin a study on the topic of Love, the Unconditional Longing of God, turn to the home page on page 89.

our Lord from the dead.[p] 25He was delivered over to death for our sins[q] and
was raised to life for our justification.

Peace and Joy

5 Therefore, since we have been justified through faith,[r] we[a] have peace
with God through our Lord Jesus
Christ, 2through whom we have gained
access[s] by faith into this grace in which
we now stand.[t] And we[a] rejoice in the
hope[u] of the glory of God. 3Not only so,
but we[a] also rejoice in our sufferings,[v]
because we know that suffering produces perseverance;[w] 4perseverance, character; and character, hope. 5And hope[x]
does not disappoint us, because God
has poured out his love into our hearts
by the Holy Spirit,[y] whom he has giv-
en us.
6You see, at just the right time,[z] when
we were still powerless, Christ died for
the ungodly.[a] 7Very rarely will anyone
die for a righteous man, though for a
good man someone might possibly dare
to die. 8But God demonstrates his own
love for us in this: While we were still
sinners, Christ died for us.[b]
9Since we have now been justified by
his blood,[c] how much more shall we be
saved from God's wrath[d] through him!
10For if, when we were God's enemies,[e]
we were reconciled[f] to him through the
death of his Son, how much more, having been reconciled, shall we be saved
through his life![g] 11Not only is this so,
but we also rejoice in God through our
Lord Jesus Christ, through whom we
have now received reconciliation.

Death Through Adam, Life Through Christ

12Therefore, just as sin entered the
world through one man,[h] and death
through sin,[i] and in this way death
came to all men, because all sinned—
13for before the law was given, sin was
in the world. But sin is not taken into
account when there is no law.[j] 14Nev-
ertheless, death reigned from the time
of Adam to the time of Moses, even
over those who did not sin by breaking
a command, as did Adam, who was a
pattern of the one to come.[k]
15But the gift is not like the trespass.

4:24 [p]Ac 2:24
4:25 [q]Isa 53:5,6; Ro 5:6,8
5:1 [r]Ro 3:28
5:2 [s]Eph 2:18 [t]1Co 15:1 [u]Heb 3:6
5:3 [v]Mt 5:12 [w]Jas 1:2,3
5:5 [x]Php 1:20 [y]Ac 2:33
5:6 [z]Gal 4:4 [a]Ro 4:25
5:8 [b]Jn 15:13; 1Pe 3:18
5:9 [c]Ro 3:25 [d]Ro 1:18
5:10 [e]Ro 11:28; Col 1:21 [f]2Co 5:18,19; Col 1:20,22 [g]Ro 8:34
5:12 [h]ver 15,16,17; 1Co 15:21,22 [i]Ge 2:17; 3:19; Ro 6:23
5:13 [j]Ro 4:15
5:14 [k]1Co 15:22,45

[a]1,2,3 Or *let us*

For if the many died by the trespass
5:15 [l]ver 12,18,19 of the one man,[l] how much more did
[m]Ac 15:11 God's grace and the gift that came by
the grace of the one man, Jesus Christ,[m]
overflow to the many! 16 Again, the gift
of God is not like the result of the
one man's sin: The judgment followed
one sin and brought condemnation, but
the gift followed many trespasses and
brought justification. 17 For if, by the
5:17 [n]ver 12 trespass of the one man, death[n] reigned
through that one man, how much more
will those who receive God's abundant
provision of grace and of the gift of
righteousness reign in life through the
one man, Jesus Christ.

18 Consequently, just as the result of
one trespass was condemnation for all
5:18 [o]ver 12 men,[o] so also the result of one act
[p]Ro 4:25 of righteousness was justification[p] that
brings life for all men. 19 For just as
through the disobedience of the one
5:19 [q]ver 12 man[q] the many were made sinners, so
[r]Php 2:8 also through the obedience[r] of the one
man the many will be made righteous.

▸ PATIENCE

TWO BOYS: FIRST ADAM AND SECOND ADAM

Romans 5:19

God had two boys.
Adam had full confidence but could not master self-denial.
In one small moment, he gave up heaven's greatest word: *Father*.
But see what God's other boy achieved in time.
He denied himself, died and gave new meaning to the word *Father*, passing it on to us.

20 The law was added so that the tres-
5:20 [s]Ro 7:7,8; Gal 3:19 pass might increase.[s] But where sin increased, grace increased all the more,[t]
[t]1Ti 1:13,14 21 so that, just as sin reigned in death,[u]
5:21 [u]ver 12,14 so also grace might reign through righteousness to bring eternal life through
Jesus Christ our Lord.

Dead to Sin, Alive in Christ

6 What shall we say, then? Shall we
6:1 [v]ver 15; Ro 3:5,8 go on sinning so that grace may
increase?[v] 2 By no means! We died to
6:2 [w]Col 3:3,5; 1Pe 2:24 sin;[w] how can we live in it any longer?
3 Or don't you know that all of us who
were baptized[x] into Christ Jesus were 6:3 [x]Mt 28:19
baptized into his death? 4 We were therefore buried with him through baptism
into death in order that, just as Christ 6:4 [y]Col 2:12 [z]Ro 7:6; Gal 6:15; Eph 4:22-24; Col 3:10
was raised from the dead[y] through the
glory of the Father, we too may live a
new life.[z]

▸ FAITHFULNESS

THE SYMBOL GRAND

Romans 6:4

Do you believe Jesus once was buried?
Then allow yourself to be buried in baptism and declare it.
Do you believe Jesus came up out of the grave?
Keep silent no longer.
Rise from the water.
Let the world know.

5 If we have been united with him like
this in his death, we will certainly also
be united with him in his resurrection.[a] 6:5 [a]2Co 4:10; Php 3:10,11
6 For we know that our old self[b] was
crucified with him[c] so that the body of 6:6 [b]Eph 4:22; Col 3:9 [c]Gal 2:20; Col 2:12,20 [d]Ro 7:24
sin[d] might be done away with,[a] that we
should no longer be slaves to sin— 7 because anyone who has died has been
freed from sin.
8 Now if we died with Christ, we believe that we will also live with him.
9 For we know that since Christ was
raised from the dead,[e] he cannot die 6:9 [e]Ac 2:24 [f]Rev 1:18
again; death no longer has mastery over
him.[f] 10 The death he died, he died to 6:10 [g]ver 2
sin[g] once for all; but the life he lives, he
lives to God.

▸ SELF-CONTROL

DIE AND LIVE

Romans 6:11

The dead have conquered all temptation.
The dead don't sin.
So when temptation crooks its finger and gives you its beguiling smile, play dead.

11 In the same way, count yourselves
dead to sin[h] but alive to God in Christ 6:11 [h]ver 2
Jesus. 12 Therefore do not let sin reign
in your mortal body so that you obey

[a]6 Or *be rendered powerless*

DAY 3 THREE

▸ SELF-CONTROL AND MY RELATIONSHIP WITH CHRIST

Romans 6:19–23

Being set free from our excessive freedoms is a gift of God. I rarely meet a person who is so free that his or her "freedoms" are leading to destruction. But here and there I meet a person like Harry. When Harry was a high school student, he began to overeat. He loved food—all food—but particularly junk food. Harry loved life and good times and, even though he claimed to be a Christian, Harry would rationalize, "Well, Jesus wants us to enjoy life." By the time Harry was out of high school, he weighed 250 pounds. The next time I saw him, he was in his mid-twenties and weighed 400 pounds. His lack of self-control had brought his indulgences to excess.

The last time I visited Harry, he was living in a mobile home. I entered his home and wondered how Harry had gotten into the mobile home. I felt sure it could not have been through the same narrow door I had used. When I saw him, spread across the width of an entire sofa, I smiled, and we conversed congenially. As we spoke he was eating cherry pie filling directly from the can. Was Harry free, free to eat anything he wanted? Of course not. Harry was enslaved.

Paul says that self-control is being set free from the sin of too much freedom. Then we voluntarily opt to place our overindulgences directly into the hands of Christ. As we surrender our old, self-serving lifestyles, we are set free from our destructive freedoms and given charge of a glorious new freedom—self-control used in obedience to the Lord.

The moment we are saved, we are empowered—not to control the world, but to control ourselves. When we are in charge of our own lives, we realize that we have been given the greatest of all gifts—freedom from a destructive permissiveness.

To begin a study on the topic of Self-Control, Freedom From Permissiveness, turn to the home page on page 452.

its evil desires. 13 Do not offer the parts
of your body to sin, as instruments
of wickedness,[i] but rather offer yourselves to God, as those who have been
brought from death to life; and offer
the parts of your body to him as instruments of righteousness.[j] 14 For sin shall
not be your master, because you are not
under law,[k] but under grace.[l]

6:13 [i]ver 16,19; Ro 7:5 [j]Ro 12:1; 1Pe 2:24
6:14 [k]Gal 5:18 [l]Ro 3:24

▸ SELF-CONTROL 

CHRIST, NOT APPETITE, MUST REIGN

Romans 6:14

Self-denial is the twin of self-control. Remember, addictions are never born fully grown. They are nurtured in the warm, dark nests of our illicit preferences. Feed addictions and they grow strong. Starve them and they wither and die. The best time to kill a giant is in its infancy.

Slaves to Righteousness

15 What then? Shall we sin because
we are not under law but under grace?
By no means! 16 Don't you know that
when you offer yourselves to someone
to obey him as slaves, you are slaves
to the one whom you obey—whether
you are slaves to sin,[m] which leads to
death,[n] or to obedience, which leads
to righteousness? 17 But thanks be to
God[o] that, though you used to be slaves
to sin, you wholeheartedly obeyed the
form of teaching[p] to which you were
entrusted. 18 You have been set free from
sin[q] and have become slaves to righteousness.
19 I put this in human terms[r] because
you are weak in your natural selves. Just
as you used to offer the parts of your
body in slavery to impurity and to ever-
increasing wickedness, so now offer
them in slavery to righteousness leading
to holiness. 20 When you were slaves to
sin,[s] you were free from the control of
righteousness.[t] 21 What benefit did you
reap at that time from the things you
are now ashamed of? Those things result in death![u] 22 But now that you have
been set free from sin[v] and have become slaves to God,[w] the benefit you
reap leads to holiness, and the result is
eternal life. 23 For the wages of sin is

6:16 [m]Jn 8:34; 2Pe 2:19 [n]ver 23
6:17 [o]Ro 1:8; 2Co 2:14 [p]2Ti 1:13
6:18 [q]ver 7,22; Ro 8:2
6:19 [r]Ro 3:5
6:20 [s]ver 13 [t]ver 16
6:21 [u]ver 23
6:22 [v]ver 18 [w]1Co 7:22; 1Pe 2:16

death,[x] but the gift of God is eternal life[y] in[a] Christ Jesus our Lord.

An Illustration From Marriage

7 Do you not know, brothers[z]—for I am speaking to men who know the law—that the law has authority over a man only as long as he lives? 2For example, by law a married woman is bound to her husband as long as he is alive, but if her husband dies, she is released from the law of marriage.[a] 3So then, if she marries another man while her husband is still alive, she is called an adulteress. But if her husband dies, she is released from that law and is not an adulteress, even though she marries another man.

4So, my brothers, you also died to the law[b] through the body of Christ,[c] that you might belong to another, to him who was raised from the dead, in order that we might bear fruit to God. 5For when we were controlled by the sinful nature,[b] the sinful passions aroused by the law[d] were at work in our bodies,[e] so that we bore fruit for death. 6But now, by dying to what once bound us, we have been released from the law so that we serve in the new way of the Spirit, and not in the old way of the written code.[f]

Struggling With Sin

7What shall we say, then? Is the law sin? Certainly not! Indeed I would not have known what sin was except through the law.[g] For I would not have known what coveting really was if the law had not said, "Do not covet."[c][h] 8But sin, seizing the opportunity afforded by the commandment,[i] produced in me every kind of covetous desire. For apart from law, sin is dead.[j] 9Once I was alive apart from law; but when the commandment came, sin sprang to life and I died. 10I found that the very commandment that was intended to bring life[k] actually brought death. 11For sin, seizing the opportunity afforded by the commandment, deceived me,[l] and through the commandment put me to death. 12So then, the law is holy, and the commandment is holy, righteous and good.[m]

13Did that which is good, then, become death to me? By no means! But in order that sin might be recognized as sin, it produced death in me through what was good, so that through the commandment sin might become utterly sinful.

14We know that the law is spiritual; but I am unspiritual,[n] sold[o] as a slave to sin. 15I do not understand what I do. For what I want to do I do not do, but what I hate I do.[p] 16And if I do what I do not want to do, I agree that the law is good.[q] 17As it is, it is no longer I myself who do it, but it is sin living in me.[r] 18I know that nothing good lives in me, that is, in my sinful nature.[d][s] For I have the desire to do what is good, but I cannot carry it out. 19For what I do is not the good I want to do; no, the evil I do not want to do—this I keep on doing.[t] 20Now if I do what I do not want to do, it is no longer I who do it, but it is sin living in me that does it.[u]

6:23 [x]Ge 2:17; Ro 5:12; Gal 6:7,8; Jas 1:15 [y]Mt 25:46
7:1 [z]Ro 1:13
7:2 [a]1Co 7:39
7:4 [b]Ro 8:2; Gal 2:19 [c]Col 1:22
7:5 [d]Ro 7:7-11 [e]Ro 6:13
7:6 [f]Ro 2:29; 2Co 3:6
7:7 [g]Ro 3:20; 4:15 [h]Ex 20:17; Dt 5:21
7:8 [i]ver 11 [j]Ro 4:15; 1Co 15:56
7:10 [k]Lev 18:5; Lk 10:26-28; Ro 10:5; Gal 3:12
7:11 [l]Ge 3:13
7:12 [m]1Ti 1:8
7:14 [n]1Co 3:1 [o]1Ki 21:20, 25; 2Ki 17:17
7:15 [p]ver 19; Gal 5:17
7:16 [q]ver 12
7:17 [r]ver 20
7:18 [s]ver 25
7:19 [t]ver 15
7:20 [u]ver 17

GOODNESS

THE UNIVERSAL STRUGGLE

Romans 7:19

Good and evil both vie to stain our wills.
What color wins?
Whichever one you choose.
You alone control the color of your heart.

21So I find this law at work:[v] When I want to do good, evil is right there with me. 22For in my inner being[w] I delight in God's law;[x] 23but I see another law at work in the members of my body, waging war[y] against the law of my mind and making me a prisoner of the law of sin at work within my members. 24What a wretched man I am! Who will rescue me from this body of death?[z] 25Thanks be to God—through Jesus Christ our Lord!

So then, I myself in my mind am a slave to God's law, but in the sinful nature a slave to the law of sin.

Life Through the Spirit

8 Therefore, there is now no condemnation[a] for those who are in Christ Jesus,[e][b] 2because through Christ

7:21 [v]ver 23,25
7:22 [w]Eph 3:16 [x]Ps 1:2
7:23 [y]Gal 5:17; Jas 4:1; 1Pe 2:11
7:24 [z]Ro 6:6; 8:2
8:1 [a]ver 34 [b]ver 39; Ro 16:3

[a]23 Or *through* [b]5 Or *the flesh*; also in verse 25
[c]7 Exodus 20:17; Deut. 5:21 [d]18 Or *my flesh*
[e]1 Some later manuscripts *Jesus, who do not live according to the sinful nature but according to the Spirit,*

Jesus the law of the Spirit of life[c] set me
free[d] from the law of sin[e] and death.
3 For what the law was powerless[f] to do
in that it was weakened by the sinful

8:2 [c]1Co 15:45 [d]Ro 6:18 [e]Ro 7:4
8:3 [f]Ac 13:39; Heb 7:18

DAY 3 THREE

Peace and My Relationship With Christ

Romans 8:5–8

Why does the mind controlled by the Spirit naturally result in peace? Because the Spirit of God champions in our lives the things that promote peace. He sees the battles that cannot be won in human terms. He causes us to pace our lives so that when we get to those battles, we have already made peace with the outcome.

Maybe you have heard the "Serenity Prayer." It goes: "Lord, help me to change the things that can be changed, accept the things that cannot be changed and have the wisdom to know the difference." It is the Holy Spirit who teaches us this wisdom.

I have written a children's poem called "Leonardo Lobster" in which an old lobster offers his son this advice:

If ever you enter a trap, Leonardo, you don't have
To find yourself stewed, baked, and dead.
You can't fight the trap, my two-pinchered son,
By charging the steel that lies out ahead.

How true this is. The Spirit helps us to see where it is better to accept the steel out ahead than to struggle to do what cannot be done.

The second thing that the Holy Spirit does to promote peace is to place the responsibility for any outcome in the hands of God. When we have been obedient to the Lord in any endeavor, the outcome is not our responsibility. So our whole affair with Jesus is promoted beyond the level of "try and acquiesce." It has become a lifestyle of "trust and celebrate." This second approach brings contentment regardless of the siuation. Best of all, there is no failure and no guilt, no trauma or lingering recriminations! All that is left to us is peace.

To begin a study on the topic of Peace, the Reign of the Holy Spirit, turn to the home page on page 1429.

nature,[a] God did by sending his own
Son in the likeness of sinful man[g] to be
a sin offering.[b][h] And so he condemned
sin in sinful man,[c] 4 in order that the
righteous requirements of the law might
be fully met in us, who do not live according to the sinful nature but according to the Spirit.[i]
5 Those who live according to the sinful nature have their minds set on what
that nature desires;[j] but those who live
in accordance with the Spirit have their
minds set on what the Spirit desires.[k]
6 The mind of sinful man[d] is death,
but the mind controlled by the Spirit
is life[l] and peace; 7 the sinful mind[e] is
hostile to God.[m] It does not submit
to God's law, nor can it do so. 8 Those
controlled by the sinful nature cannot
please God.
9 You, however, are controlled not by
the sinful nature but by the Spirit, if the
Spirit of God lives in you.[n] And if anyone does not have the Spirit of Christ,[o]
he does not belong to Christ. 10 But if
Christ is in you,[p] your body is dead
because of sin, yet your spirit is alive
because of righteousness. 11 And if the
Spirit of him who raised Jesus from the
dead[q] is living in you, he who raised
Christ from the dead will also give life
to your mortal bodies[r] through his Spirit, who lives in you.
12 Therefore, brothers, we have an
obligation—but it is not to the sinful
nature, to live according to it. 13 For if
you live according to the sinful nature,
you will die; but if by the Spirit you
put to death the misdeeds of the body,
you will live,[s] 14 because those who are
led by the Spirit of God[t] are sons of
God.[u] 15 For you did not receive a spirit that makes you a slave again to
fear,[v] but you received the Spirit of
sonship.[f] And by him we cry, *"Abba,*[g]
Father."[w] 16 The Spirit himself testifies
with our spirit[x] that we are God's children. 17 Now if we are children, then
we are heirs[y]—heirs of God and co-
heirs with Christ, if indeed we share in
his sufferings in order that we may also
share in his glory.[z]

8:3 [g]Php 2:7 [h]Heb 2:14,17
8:4 [i]Gal 5:16
8:5 [j]Gal 5:19-21 [k]Gal 5:22-25
8:6 [l]Gal 6:8
8:7 [m]Jas 4:4
8:9 [n]1Co 6:19; Gal 4:6 [o]Jn 14:17; 1Jn 4:13
8:10 [p]Gal 2:20; Eph 3:17; Col 1:27
8:11 [q]Ac 2:24 [r]Jn 5:21
8:13 [s]Gal 6:8
8:14 [t]Gal 5:18 [u]Jn 1:12; Rev 21:7
8:15 [v]2Ti 1:7; Heb 2:15 [w]Mk 14:36; Gal 4:5,6
8:16 [x]Eph 1:13
8:17 [y]Ac 20:32; Gal 4:7 [z]1Pe 4:13

[a]3 Or *the flesh;* also in verses 4, 5, 8, 9, 12 and 13 [b]3 Or *man, for sin* [c]3 Or *in the flesh* [d]6 Or *mind set on the flesh* [e]7 Or *the mind set on the flesh* [f]15 Or *adoption* [g]15 Aramaic for *Father*

Future Glory

8:18 [a]2Co 4:17; 1Pe 4:13

[18]I consider that our present sufferings are not worth comparing with the
glory that will be revealed in us.[a] [19]The

DAY 5 FIVE

PATIENCE AND ITS PLACE IN MY PERSONAL WORSHIP

Romans 8:18–25

Perhaps the place to begin examining this passage is in Romans 8:25: "But if we hope for what we do not yet have, we wait for it patiently." Patience is the grand interpreter of so many of the unfathomable events of our lives. What unfathomable events? Romans 8:18–25 is filled with an inordinate number of unfathomable events. Here are three events over which we must wrestle and for which we usually have no really satisfactory explanation:

1. Our present sufferings (v. 18). These sometimes afflict us with such seemingly unreasonable pain that we have no idea why God is permitting such things to happen to us. Paul offers no real answer except to assure us that present suffering is not worthy to be compared with the glory that shall be.

2. The creation is in bondage to decay (v. 21). Why does the world die around us? If Paul asked this question, are we, too, justified in asking it? On a regular basis whole species die and pass into extinction. Why this senseless corruption of creation? Humankind itself seems to be responsible. Paul says that we await the Redeemer's resolution to the problem.

3. We ourselves are groaning as we wait for God to redeem our bodies (v. 23). Like the creation itself, we are eager for God to finish his work in us and bring us to completion in himself. This is a kind of patience, agrees the apostle, but it is a groaning patience, and we find it difficult to wait.

Yet this impatient patience results in a kind of delicious agony at the center of our worship. We wait and groan, but we wait nonetheless, and as we wait, we anticipate. The anticipation is our response of joy to the certain hope that God has given us.

To begin a study on the topic of Patience, the Slowly Acquired Virtue, turn to the home page on page 565.

creation waits in eager expectation for
the sons of God to be revealed. [20]For
the creation was subjected to frustration, not by its own choice, but by
the will of the one who subjected it,[b] 8:20 [b]Ge 3:17-19
in hope [21]that[a] the creation itself will
be liberated from its bondage to decay[c] 8:21 [c]Ac 3:21; 2Pe 3:13; Rev 21:1
and brought into the glorious freedom
of the children of God.

GENTLENESS

BECOMING ADOPTED

Romans 8:15

Orphans and homeless:
Take heart. Behold the gentleness of God!
You have a Father, God.
You have a Brother, Jesus.
You have a family, the redeemed of all the ages.
Your adoption papers are signed in red—
The most indelible color in heaven.

[22]We know that the whole creation 8:22 [d]Jer 12:4
has been groaning[d] as in the pains of
childbirth right up to the present time.
[23]Not only so, but we ourselves, who 8:23 [e]2Co 5:5 [f]2Co 5:2,4 [g]Gal 5:5
have the firstfruits of the Spirit,[e] groan[f]
inwardly as we wait eagerly[g] for our
adoption as sons, the redemption of
our bodies. [24]For in this hope we were
saved.[h] But hope that is seen is no hope 8:24 [h]1Th 5:8
at all. Who hopes for what he already
has? [25]But if we hope for what we do
not yet have, we wait for it patiently.
[26]In the same way, the Spirit helps us
in our weakness. We do not know what
we ought to pray for, but the Spirit him-
self intercedes for us[i] with groans that 8:26 [i]Eph 6:18
words cannot express. [27]And he who
searches our hearts[j] knows the mind of 8:27 [j]Rev 2:23
the Spirit, because the Spirit intercedes

[a]20,21 Or *subjected it in hope.* [21]*For*

KINDNESS

JOINT HEIRS WITH CHRIST

Romans 8:17

Hear the only will and testament of God, a testament of kindness:
I, God, being of sound mind and possessed of all power, do hereby
bequeath to my son Jesus and to all of his brothers and sisters the universe itself.

for the saints in accordance with God's
will.

More Than Conquerors

28And we know that in all things
God works for the good of those who
8:28 [k]1Co 1:9; love him,[a] who[b] have been called[k] ac-
2Ti 1:9 cording to his purpose. 29For those
8:29 God foreknew[l] he also predestined[m] to
[l]Ro 11:2 be conformed to the likeness of his
[m]Eph 1:5,11 [n]1Co 15:49; Son,[n] that he might be the firstborn
2Co 3:18; Php 3:21; among many brothers. 30And those he
1Jn 3:2 predestined,[o] he also called; those he
8:30 called, he also justified;[p] those he justi-
[o]Eph 1:5,11 [p]1Co 6:11 fied, he also glorified.[q]
[q]Ro 9:23 31What, then, shall we say in response
8:31 to this?[r] If God is for us, who can be
[r]Ro 4:1 against us?[s] 32He who did not spare his
[s]Ps 118:6 own Son,[t] but gave him up for us all—
8:32 [t]Jn 3:16; how will he not also, along with him,
Ro 4:25; 5:8 graciously give us all things? 33Who will
8:33 bring any charge[u] against those whom
[u]Isa 50:8,9 God has chosen? It is God who justifies. 34Who is he that condemns? Christ
8:34 [v]Ro 5:6-8 Jesus, who died[v]—more than that, who
[w]Mk 16:19 was raised to life—is at the right hand
[x]Heb 7:25; 9:24; of God[w] and is also interceding for us.[x]
1Jn 2:1 35Who shall separate us from the love
of Christ? Shall trouble or hardship or
8:35 persecution or famine or nakedness or
[y]1Co 4:11 danger or sword?[y] 36As it is written:

"For your sake we face death all day
long;
8:36 we are considered as sheep to be
[z]Ps 44:22; 2Co 4:11 slaughtered."[c z]

8:37 37No, in all these things we are more
[a]1Co 15:57 [b]Gal 2:20; than conquerors[a] through him who
Rev 1:5; 3:9 loved us.[b] 38For I am convinced that
neither death nor life, neither angels
8:38 nor demons,[d] neither the present nor
[c]Eph 1:21; 1Pe 3:22 the future, nor any powers,[c] 39neither
height nor depth, nor anything else in
all creation, will be able to separate us
8:39 [d]Ro 5:8 from the love of God[d] that is in Christ
Jesus our Lord.

LOVE

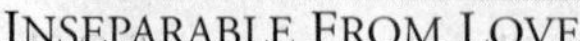

INSEPARABLE FROM LOVE

Romans 8:35

"I am God. Are you plagued by fears of my abandonment? I will only leave you when there are waterless seas, windless hurricanes, painless crucifixions and powerless resurrections."

God's Sovereign Choice

9 I speak the truth in Christ—I am 9:1
not lying,[e] my conscience confirms[f] [e]2Co 11:10;
it in the Holy Spirit— 2I have great sor- Gal 1:20; 1Ti 2:7
row and unceasing anguish in my heart. [f]Ro 1:9

LOVE

THE LONGING OF LOVE

Romans 9:3

Love is at its apex when a gallant person volunteers for the guillotine. To go willingly to hell to make heaven a possibility for the guilty is to love like love's Inventor.

3For I could wish that I myself[g] were 9:3
cursed[h] and cut off from Christ for the [g]Ex 32:32
sake of my brothers, those of my own [h]1Co 12:3; 16:22
race,[i] 4the people of Israel. Theirs is [i]Ro 11:14
the adoption as sons;[j] theirs the divine 9:4
glory, the covenants,[k] the receiving of [j]Ex 4:22 [k]Ge 17:2;
the law,[l] the temple worship[m] and the Ac 3:25;
promises.[n] 5Theirs are the patriarchs, Eph 2:12 [l]Ps 147:19
and from them is traced the human an- [m]Heb 9:1
cestry of Christ,[o] who is God over all,[p] [n]Ac 13:32
forever praised![e q] Amen. 9:5 [o]Mt 1:1-16
6It is not as though God's word had [p]Jn 1:1
failed. For not all who are descended [q]Ro 1:25
from Israel are Israel.[r] 7Nor because they 9:6 [r]Ro 2:28,29;
are his descendants are they all Abra- Gal 6:16
ham's children. On the contrary, "It is
through Isaac that your offspring will
be reckoned."[f s] 8In other words, it is 9:7
not the natural children who are God's [s]Ge 21:12;
children,[t] but it is the children of the Heb 11:18
promise who are regarded as Abraham's 9:8
offspring. 9For this was how the promise [t]Ro 8:14
was stated: "At the appointed time I will
return, and Sarah will have a son."[g u] 9:9 [u]Ge 18:10,14
10Not only that, but Rebekah's chil-
dren had one and the same father, our
father Isaac.[v] 11Yet, before the twins 9:10 [v]Ge 25:21
were born or had done anything good
or bad—in order that God's purpose[w] 9:11 [w]Ro 8:28
in election might stand: 12not by works
but by him who calls—she was told,
"The older will serve the younger."[h x] 9:12 [x]Ge 25:23
13Just as it is written: "Jacob I loved,
but Esau I hated."[i y] 9:13 [y]Mal 1:2,3

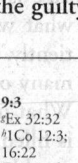

[a]*28* Some manuscripts *And we know that all things work together for good to those who love God* [b]*28* Or *works together with those who love him to bring about what is good—with those who* [c]*36* Psalm 44:22 [d]*38* Or *nor heavenly rulers* [e]*5* Or *Christ, who is over all. God be forever praised!* Or *Christ. God who is over all be forever praised!* [f]*7* Gen. 21:12 [g]*9* Gen. 18:10,14 [h]*12* Gen. 25:23 [i]*13* Mal. 1:2,3

9:14 14What then shall we say? Is God un-
[z]2Ch 19:7 just? Not at all![z] 15For he says to Moses,

"I will have mercy on whom I have
mercy,
9:15 and I will have compassion on
[a]Ex 33:19 whom I have compassion."[a][a]

9:16 16It does not, therefore, depend on man's
[b]Eph 2:8 desire or effort, but on God's mercy.[b]
17For the Scripture says to Pharaoh: "I
raised you up for this very purpose, that
I might display my power in you and
9:17 that my name might be proclaimed in all
[c]Ex 9:16 the earth."[b][c] 18Therefore God has mercy
9:18 on whom he wants to have mercy, and
[d]Ex 4:21 he hardens whom he wants to harden.[d]
9:19 19One of you will say to me:[e] "Then
[e]Ro 11:19 why does God still blame us? For who
[f]2Ch 20:6; Da 4:35 resists his will?"[f] 20But who are you,
O man, to talk back to God? "Shall
what is formed say to him who formed
9:20 it,[g] 'Why did you make me like this?' "[c][h]
[g]Isa 64:8 [h]Isa 29:16 21Does not the potter have the right
to make out of the same lump of clay
9:21 some pottery for noble purposes and
[i]2Ti 2:20 some for common use?[i]
22What if God, choosing to show
his wrath and make his power known,
9:22 bore with great patience[j] the objects
[j]Ro 2:4 of his wrath—prepared for destruction?
23What if he did this to make the riches
9:23 of his glory[k] known to the objects of
[k]Ro 2:4 [l]Ro 8:30 his mercy, whom he prepared in advance for glory[l]— 24even us, whom he
9:24 also called,[m] not only from the Jews but
[m]Ro 8:28 [n]Ro 3:29 also from the Gentiles?[n] 25As he says in
Hosea:

"I will call them 'my people' who are
not my people;
9:25 and I will call her 'my loved one'
[o]Hos 2:23; 1Pe 2:10 who is not my loved one,"[d][o]

26and,

"It will happen that in the very place
where it was said to them,
'You are not my people,'
they will be called 'sons of the living
9:26 God.' "[e][p]
[p]Hos 1:10

27Isaiah cries out concerning Israel:

"Though the number of the
Israelites be like the sand by
9:27 the sea,[q]
[q]Ge 22:17; Hos 1:10 [r]Ro 11:5 only the remnant will be saved.[r]
28For the Lord will carry out
9:28 his sentence on earth with speed
[s]Isa 10:22,23 and finality."[f][s]

29It is just as Isaiah said previously:

9:29 "Unless the Lord Almighty[t]
[t]Jas 5:4 had left us descendants,
[u]Isa 1:9; Dt 29:23; Isa 13:19; Jer 50:40 we would have become like
Sodom,
we would have been like
Gomorrah."[g][u]

Israel's Unbelief

30What then shall we say? That the
Gentiles, who did not pursue righteousness, have obtained it, a righteousness
9:30 that is by faith;[v] 31but Israel, who pur-
[v]Ro 1:17; 10:6; Gal 2:16; Php 3:9; Heb 11:7 sued a law of righteousness,[w] has not
attained it.[x] 32Why not? Because they
pursued it not by faith but as if it
9:31 were by works. They stumbled over the
[w]Isa 51:1; Ro 10:2,3 [x]Gal 5:4 "stumbling stone."[y] 33As it is written:

"See, I lay in Zion a stone that
9:32 causes men to stumble
[y]1Pe 2:8 and a rock that makes them fall,
9:33 and the one who trusts in him will
[z]Isa 28:16; Ro 10:11 never be put to shame."[h][z]

FAITHFULNESS

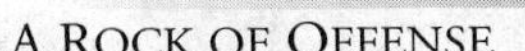

A Rock of Offense

Romans 9:33

Cornerstones are stumbling stones to those unskilled at building. So is Christ the very place where atheists trip but wise men lay the foundations of their lives.

10

Brothers, my heart's desire and
prayer to God for the Israelites
is that they may be saved. 2For I can
10:2 testify about them that they are zealous[a]
[a]Ac 21:20 for God, but their zeal is not based on
knowledge. 3Since they did not know
the righteousness that comes from God
10:3 and sought to establish their own, they
[b]Ro 1:17 did not submit to God's righteousness.[b]
10:4 4Christ is the end of the law[c] so that
[c]Gal 3:24; Ro 7:1-4 there may be righteousness for every-
[d]Ro 3:22 one who believes.[d]
10:5 5Moses describes in this way the
[e]Lev 18:5; Ne 9:29; Eze 20:11, 13,21; Ro 7:10 righteousness that is by the law: "The
man who does these things will live
by them."[i][e] 6But the righteousness that
10:6 is by faith[f] says: "Do not say in your
[f]Ro 9:30 heart, 'Who will ascend into heaven?' "[j]

a*15* Exodus 33:19 b*17* Exodus 9:16
c*20* Isaiah 29:16; 45:9 d*25* Hosea 2:23
e*26* Hosea 1:10 f*28* Isaiah 10:22,23
g*29* Isaiah 1:9 h*33* Isaiah 8:14; 28:16
i*5* Lev. 18:5 j*6* Deut. 30:12

10:7 (that is, to bring Christ down) 7“or
[g]Dt 30:12 ‘Who will descend into the deep?’[a]”[g]
(that is, to bring Christ up from the
dead). 8But what does it say? “The
10:8 word is near you; it is in your mouth
[h]Dt 30:14 and in your heart,”[b][h] that is, the word

DAY 4 FOUR

▸ GOODNESS AND MY SERVICE TO OTHERS

Romans 10:12–15

Preaching is telling. Preaching is seen in the Bible as the critical mouthpiece of the church. When Biblical preaching is in place, the church remains informed about its calling, sinners are saved and the saved behave better.

The apostle Paul has a kind of “this is the house that Jack built” progressive argument going here. Remember the nursery rhyme:

This is the house that Jack built.

This is the malt
That lay in the house that Jack built.

This is the rat
That ate the malt
That lived in the house that Jack built.

This is the cat
That killed the rat . . .
And so on.

Paul says:
This is Jesus who is Lord of all.
These are the ones who believe in the One who is Jesus who is Lord of all.
These are the preachers who tell the ones who believe in the One who is called Jesus who is Lord of all.

Then at the end of this argument for the importance of preaching, Paul says in essence, “Blessed are all who are called to inform the world that Jesus is Lord of all. Blessed are the preachers.” Then he quotes Isaiah—“How beautiful are the feet of those who bring good news!”

The telling of the news is our calling. Telling is glorious work. Telling is bringing the world to a new center—the lordship of Christ.

To begin a study on the topic of Goodness Implanted Into Our Lives Through Christ, turn to the home page on page 1484.

of faith we are proclaiming: 9That if
you confess[i] with your mouth, “Jesus is 10:9 [i]Mt 10:32;
Lord,” and believe in your heart that Lk 12:8
God raised him from the dead,[j] you [j]Ac 2:24
will be saved. 10For it is with your heart
that you believe and are justified, and
it is with your mouth that you confess
and are saved. 11As the Scripture says,
“Anyone who trusts in him will never be 10:11 [k]Isa 28:16;
put to shame.”[c][k] 12For there is no dif- Ro 9:33
ference between Jew and Gentile[l]—the 10:12 [l]Ro 3:22,29
same Lord is Lord of all[m] and richly [m]Ac 10:36
blesses all who call on him, 13for, “Everyone who calls on the name of the 10:13 [n]Ac 2:21
Lord[n] will be saved.”[d][o] [o]Joel 2:32

▸ FAITHFULNESS

THE GRAND CONFESSION

Romans 10:9

Two planks form the approach of eternity. Neither plank will serve alone. One is called confession; the other, faith.

14How, then, can they call on the one
they have not believed in? And how can
they believe in the one of whom they
have not heard? And how can they hear
without someone preaching to them?
15And how can they preach unless they
are sent? As it is written, “How beauti-
ful are the feet of those who bring good 10:15 [p]Isa 52:7;
news!”[e][p] Na 1:15
16But not all the Israelites accepted
the good news. For Isaiah says, “Lord, 10:16 [q]Isa 53:1;
who has believed our message?”[f][q] Jn 12:38
17Consequently, faith comes from hear-
ing the message,[r] and the message is 10:17 [r]Gal 3:2,5
heard through the word of Christ.[s] [s]Col 3:16
18But I ask: Did they not hear? Of
course they did:

“Their voice has gone out into all
the earth,
their words to the ends of the 10:18 [t]Ps 19:4;
world.”[g][t] Mt 24:14; Col 1:6,23; 1Th 1:8

19Again I ask: Did Israel not understand? First, Moses says,

“I will make you envious[u] by those 10:19 [u]Ro 11:11,14
who are not a nation; [v]Dt 32:21
I will make you angry by a nation
that has no understanding.”[h][v]

20And Isaiah boldly says,

[a]*7* Deut. 30:13 [b]*8* Deut. 30:14 [c]*11* Isaiah 28:16 [d]*13* Joel 2:32 [e]*15* Isaiah 52:7 [f]*16* Isaiah 53:1 [g]*18* Psalm 19:4 [h]*19* Deut. 32:21

"I was found by those who did not
seek me;
I revealed myself to those who did
10:20 [w]Isa 65:1; Ro 9:30
not ask for me."[a][w]
21But concerning Israel he says,
"All day long I have held out my
hands
to a disobedient and obstinate
10:21 [x]Isa 65:2
people."[b][x]

The Remnant of Israel

11:1 [y]1Sa 12:22; Jer 31:37 [z]2Co 11:22 [a]Php 3:5
11 I ask then: Did God reject his
people? By no means![y] I am
an Israelite myself, a descendant of
Abraham,[z] from the tribe of Benjamin.[a]
11:2 [b]Ro 8:29
2God did not reject his people, whom
he foreknew.[b] Don't you know what the
Scripture says in the passage about Elijah—how he appealed to God against
Israel: 3"Lord, they have killed your
prophets and torn down your altars; I
am the only one left, and they are trying
11:3 [c]1Ki 19:10,14
to kill me"[c]?[c] 4And what was God's answer to him? "I have reserved for myself
seven thousand who have not bowed
11:4 [d]1Ki 19:18
the knee to Baal."[d][d] 5So too, at the
present time there is a remnant[e] chosen
11:5 [e]Ro 9:27
by grace. 6And if by grace, then it is
no longer by works;[f] if it were, grace
11:6 [f]Ro 4:4
would no longer be grace.[e]
11:7 [g]Ro 9:31 [h]ver 25; Ro 9:18
7What then? What Israel sought so
earnestly it did not obtain,[g] but the
elect did. The others were hardened,[h]
8as it is written:

"God gave them a spirit of stupor,
eyes so that they could not see
11:8 [i]Mt 13:13-15 [j]Dt 29:4; Isa 29:10
and ears so that they could not
hear,[i]
to this very day."[f][j]
9And David says:

"May their table become a snare and
a trap,
a stumbling block and a
retribution for them.
10May their eyes be darkened so they
cannot see,
11:10 [k]Ps 69:22,23
and their backs be bent forever."[g][k]

Ingrafted Branches

11Again I ask: Did they stumble so
as to fall beyond recovery? Not at
11:11 [l]ver 1 [m]Ac 13:46 [n]Ro 10:19
all![l] Rather, because of their transgression, salvation has come to the Gentiles[m] to make Israel envious.[n] 12But if
their transgression means riches for the
11:12 [o]ver 25
world, and their loss means riches for
the Gentiles,[o] how much greater riches
will their fullness bring!
11:13 [p]Ac 9:15
13I am talking to you Gentiles. Inas-
much as I am the apostle to the Gentiles,[p] I make much of my ministry 14in
11:14 [q]ver 11; Ro 10:19 [r]1Co 1:21; 1Ti 2:4; Tit 3:5
the hope that I may somehow arouse
my own people to envy[q] and save[r] some
of them. 15For if their rejection is the
reconciliation[s] of the world, what will
their acceptance be but life from the
11:15 [s]Ro 5:10 [t]Lk 15:24,32
dead?[t] 16If the part of the dough offered
as firstfruits[u] is holy, then the whole
11:16 [u]Lev 23:10,17; Nu 15:18-21
batch is holy; if the root is holy, so are
the branches.
17If some of the branches have been
11:17 [v]Jer 11:16; Jn 15:2 [w]Ac 2:39; Eph 2:11-13
broken off,[v] and you, though a wild olive shoot, have been grafted in among
the others[w] and now share in the nourishing sap from the olive root, 18do not
boast over those branches. If you do,
consider this: You do not support the
11:18 [x]Jn 4:22
root, but the root supports you.[x] 19You
will say then, "Branches were broken off
so that I could be grafted in." 20Grant-
11:20 [y]1Co 10:12; 2Co 1:24 [z]Ro 12:16; 1Ti 6:17 [a]1Pe 1:17
ed. But they were broken off because of
unbelief, and you stand by faith.[y] Do
not be arrogant,[z] but be afraid.[a] 21For if
God did not spare the natural branches,
he will not spare you either.
11:22 [b]Ro 2:4 [c]1Co 15:2; Heb 3:6 [d]Jn 15:2
22Consider therefore the kindness[b]
and sternness of God: sternness to those
who fell, but kindness to you, provided that you continue[c] in his kindness.
Otherwise, you also will be cut off.[d]
23And if they do not persist in unbelief,
they will be grafted in, for God is able
11:23 [e]2Co 3:16
to graft them in again.[e] 24After all, if
you were cut out of an olive tree that is
wild by nature, and contrary to nature
were grafted into a cultivated olive tree,
how much more readily will these, the
natural branches, be grafted into their
own olive tree!

All Israel Will Be Saved

11:25 [f]Ro 1:13 [g]Ro 16:25 [h]Ro 12:16 [i]ver 7; Ro 9:18 [j]Lk 21:24
25I do not want you to be ignorant[f]
of this mystery,[g] brothers, so that you
may not be conceited:[h] Israel has experienced a hardening[i] in part until the
full number of the Gentiles has come
in.[j] 26And so all Israel will be saved, as
it is written:

[a] *20* Isaiah 65:1 [b] *21* Isaiah 65:2 [c] *3* 1 Kings 19:10,14 [d] *4* 1 Kings 19:18 [e] *6* Some manuscripts *by grace. But if by works, then it is no longer grace; if it were, work would no longer be work.* [f] *8* Deut. 29:4; Isaiah 29:10 [g] *10* Psalm 69:22,23

DAY 5 FIVE

Self-Control and Its Place in My Personal Worship

Romans 12:1–2

J.B. Phillips translated Romans 12:2, "Don't let the world squeeze you into its mold." You hold the key to the final form your Christianity takes. You alone decide just how far you will conform to the world's image of *the real man, the independent woman, the powerful executive.* Finding an image to conform to is easy for the believer. Hang a picture of Jesus in the mental gallery of your life, and do all you can at each waking moment to look like that picture.

There is a fable of a Persian prince who was born a hunchback. The prince realized that one day he would become the caliph who would rule the realm and that his twisted form would not command respect from his people. In fact, it did not even demand his own respect. So as he advanced toward adolescence, he had the royal sculptor carve a stone statue of himself just as he would look when he became a grown man—if he were not hunchbacked. Soon the statue was finished and set up in the courtyard just outside his bedroom.

Then every day the prince performed a strange ritual. He would go to the statue, remove his shirt from his deformed back and stand back to back with his perfect alter ego. Then he would strain in what seemed a comical mode to throw his own twisted shoulders against the stately shoulders of the marble statue. At first people laughed at this comical ritual. But day by day—year by year—it seemed to the entire world that the prince's back was becoming straighter and straighter. Then one day, just before his coronation as caliph, he backed up to his statue and felt the thrilling touch of its cold marble shoulders against his own. He had become what he had striven to be.

The goal of our own personal worship is to make us like Jesus. He is like the great marble statue whose image we would bear. Our calling in worship is to become like him alone. No other standard will suffice.

To begin a study on the topic of Self-Control, the Mark of Obedience, turn to the home page on page 1011.

"The deliverer will come from Zion;
he will turn godlessness away from Jacob.
27 And this is[a] my covenant with them
when I take away their sins."[b][k]

28 As far as the gospel is concerned, they are enemies[l] on your account; but as far as election is concerned, they are loved on account of the patriarchs,[m] 29 for God's gifts and his call[n] are irrevocable.[o] 30 Just as you who were at one time disobedient[p] to God have now received mercy as a result of their disobedience, 31 so they too have now become disobedient in order that they too may now[c] receive mercy as a result of God's mercy to you. 32 For God has bound all men over to disobedience[q] so that he may have mercy on them all.

Doxology

33 Oh, the depth of the riches[r] of the
wisdom and[d] knowledge of God![s]
How unsearchable his judgments,
and his paths beyond tracing out![t]
34 "Who has known the mind of the Lord?
Or who has been his counselor?"[e][u]
35 "Who has ever given to God,
that God should repay him?"[f][v]
36 For from him and through him and
to him are all things.[w]
To him be the glory forever!
Amen.[x]

Living Sacrifices

12 Therefore, I urge you,[y] brothers, in view of God's mercy, to offer your bodies as living sacrifices,[z] holy and pleasing to God—this is your spiritual[g] act of worship. 2 Do not conform[a] any longer to the pattern of this world,[b] but be transformed by the renewing of your mind.[c] Then you will be able to test and approve what God's will is[d]—his good, pleasing and perfect will.

3 For by the grace given me[e] I say to every one of you: Do not think of yourself more highly than you ought, but rather think of yourself with sober judgment, in accordance with the mea-

11:27 [k]Isa 27:9; Heb 8:10,12
11:28 [l]Ro 5:10 [m]Dt 7:8; 10:15; Ro 9:5
11:29 [n]Ro 8:28 [o]Heb 7:21
11:30 [p]Eph 2:2
11:32 [q]Ro 3:9
11:33 [r]Ro 2:4 [s]Ps 92:5 [t]Job 11:7
11:34 [u]Isa 40:13,14; Job 15:8; 36:22; 1Co 2:16
11:35 [v]Job 35:7
11:36 [w]1Co 8:6; Col 1:16; Heb 2:10 [x]Ro 16:27
12:1 [y]Eph 4:1 [z]Ro 6:13, 16,19; 1Pe 2:5
12:2 [a]1Pe 1:14 [b]1Jn 2:15 [c]Eph 4:23 [d]Eph 5:17
12:3 [e]Ro 15:15; Gal 2:9; Eph 4:7

[a]*27* Or *will be* [b]*27* Isaiah 59:20,21; 27:9; Jer. 31:33,34 [c]*31* Some manuscripts do not have *now.* [d]*33* Or *riches and the wisdom and the* [e]*34* Isaiah 40:13 [f]*35* Job 41:11 [g]*1* Or *reasonable*

sure of faith God has given you. 4Just
as each of us has one body with many
members, and these members do not all
have the same function,[f] 5so in Christ
we who are many form one body,[g] and
each member belongs to all the others.
6We have different gifts,[h] according to
the grace given us. If a man's gift is
prophesying, let him use it in proportion to his[a] faith.[i] 7If it is serving, let
him serve; if it is teaching, let him
teach;[j] 8if it is encouraging, let him
encourage;[k] if it is contributing to the
needs of others, let him give generously;[l]
if it is leadership, let him govern diligently; if it is showing mercy, let him
do it cheerfully.

Love

9Love must be sincere.[m] Hate what
is evil; cling to what is good. 10Be devoted to one another in brotherly love.[n]
Honor one another above yourselves.[o]
11Never be lacking in zeal, but keep your
spiritual fervor,[p] serving the Lord. 12Be
joyful in hope,[q] patient in affliction,[r]
faithful in prayer. 13Share with God's
people who are in need. Practice hospitality.[s]

14Bless those who persecute you;[t]
bless and do not curse. 15Rejoice with
those who rejoice; mourn with those
who mourn.[u] 16Live in harmony with
one another.[v] Do not be proud, but be
willing to associate with people of low
position.[b] Do not be conceited.[w]

17Do not repay anyone evil for evil.[x]
Be careful to do what is right in the
eyes of everybody.[y] 18If it is possible, as
far as it depends on you, live at peace
with everyone.[z] 19Do not take revenge,[a]
my friends, but leave room for God's
wrath, for it is written: "It is mine to
avenge; I will repay,"[c] [b]says the Lord.
20On the contrary:

"If your enemy is hungry, feed him;
if he is thirsty, give him something
to drink.
In doing this, you will heap burning
coals on his head."[d] [c]

21Do not be overcome by evil, but overcome evil with good.

12:4 [f]1Co 12:12-14; Eph 4:16
12:5 [g]1Co 10:17
12:6 [h]1Co 7:7; 12:4,8-10 [i]1Pe 4:10,11
12:7 [j]Eph 4:11
12:8 [k]Ac 15:32 [l]2Co 9:5-13
12:9 [m]1Ti 1:5
12:10 [n]Heb 13:1 [o]Php 2:3
12:11 [p]Ac 18:25
12:12 [q]Ro 5:2 [r]Heb 10:32,36
12:13 [s]1Ti 3:2
12:14 [t]Mt 5:44
12:15 [u]Job 30:25
12:16 [v]Ro 15:5 [w]Jer 45:5; Ro 11:25
12:17 [x]Pr 20:22 [y]2Co 8:21
12:18 [z]Mk 9:50; Ro 14:19
12:19 [a]Lev 19:18; Pr 20:22; 24:29 [b]Dt 32:35
12:20 [c]Pr 25:21,22; Mt 5:44; Lk 6:27

Submission to the Authorities

13 Everyone must submit himself
to the governing authorities,[d]
for there is no authority except that
which God has established.[e] The authorities that exist have been established
by God. 2Consequently, he who rebels
against the authority is rebelling against
what God has instituted, and those who
do so will bring judgment on themselves. 3For rulers hold no terror for
those who do right, but for those who
do wrong. Do you want to be free from
fear of the one in authority? Then do
what is right and he will commend
you.[f] 4For he is God's servant to do
you good. But if you do wrong, be
afraid, for he does not bear the sword
for nothing. He is God's servant, an
agent of wrath to bring punishment on
the wrongdoer.[g] 5Therefore, it is necessary to submit to the authorities, not
only because of possible punishment
but also because of conscience.

6This is also why you pay taxes, for
the authorities are God's servants, who
give their full time to governing. 7Give
everyone what you owe him: If you owe
taxes,[h] pay taxes; if revenue, then revenue; if respect, then respect; if honor,
then honor.

Love, for the Day Is Near

8Let no debt remain outstanding, except the continuing debt to love one
another, for he who loves his fellowman
has fulfilled the law.[i] 9The commandments, "Do not commit adultery," "Do
not murder," "Do not steal," "Do not
covet,"[e] [j] and whatever other commandment there may be, are summed up in
this one rule: "Love your neighbor as
yourself."[f] [k] 10Love does no harm to its
neighbor. Therefore love is the fulfillment of the law.[l]

11And do this, understanding the
present time. The hour has come[m] for
you to wake up from your slumber,[n] because our salvation is nearer now than
when we first believed. 12The night is
nearly over; the day is almost here.[o] So
let us put aside the deeds of darkness[p]
and put on the armor[q] of light. 13Let
us behave decently, as in the daytime,
not in orgies and drunkenness, not in
sexual immorality and debauchery, not
in dissension and jealousy.[r] 14Rather,
clothe yourselves with the Lord Jesus

[a]*6* Or *in agreement with the* [b]*16* Or *willing to do menial work* [c]*19* Deut. 32:35 [d]*20* Prov. 25:21,22
[e]*9* Exodus 20:13-15,17; Deut. 5:17-19,21
[f]*9* Lev. 19:18

13:1 [d]Tit 3:1; 1Pe 2:13,14
13:1 [e]Da 2:21; Jn 19:11
13:3 [f]1Pe 2:14
13:4 [g]1Th 4:6
13:7 [h]Mt 17:25; 22:17,21; Lk 23:2
13:8 [i]ver 10; Jn 13:34; Gal 5:14; Col 3:14
13:9 [j]Ex 20:13-15, 17; Dt 5:17-19, 21 [k]Lev 19:18; Mt 19:19
13:10 [l]ver 8; Mt 22:39,40
13:11 [m]1Co 7:29-31; 10:11 [n]Eph 5:14; 1Th 5:5,6
13:12 [o]1Jn 2:8 [p]Eph 5:11 [q]Eph 6:11,13
13:13 [r]Gal 5:20,21

GOODNESS

DRESSED WITH A NEW WORLDVIEW

Romans 13:14

We are saved by a holiness we did not perfect, dressed in goodness we did not achieve. Still we have put on the Lord Jesus Christ, heaven's uniform of the day.

13:14 [s]Gal 3:27; 5:16; Eph 4:24 Christ,[s] and do not think about how to
gratify the desires of the sinful nature.[a]

The Weak and the Strong

14:1 [t]Ro 15:1; 1Co 8:9-12 14 Accept him whose faith is weak,[t]
without passing judgment on
disputable matters. 2One man's faith allows him to eat everything, but another
man, whose faith is weak, eats only vegetables. 3The man who eats everything
14:3 [u]Lk 18:9 [v]Col 2:16 must not look down on him[u] who does
not, and the man who does not eat ev-
erything must not condemn[v] the man
who does, for God has accepted him.
4Who are you to judge someone else's
14:4 [w]Jas 4:12 servant?[w] To his own master he stands
or falls. And he will stand, for the Lord
is able to make him stand.
5One man considers one day more
14:5 [x]Gal 4:10 sacred than another;[x] another man considers every day alike. Each one should
be fully convinced in his own mind.
6He who regards one day as special,
does so to the Lord. He who eats meat,
eats to the Lord, for he gives thanks to
14:6 [y]Mt 14:19; 1Co 10:30, 31; 1Ti 4:3,4 God;[y] and he who abstains, does so to
the Lord and gives thanks to God. 7For
none of us lives to himself alone[z] and
14:7 [z]2Co 5:15; Gal 2:20 none of us dies to himself alone. 8If we
live, we live to the Lord; and if we die,
we die to the Lord. So, whether we live
14:8 [a]Php 1:20 or die, we belong to the Lord.[a]
9For this very reason, Christ died and
14:9 [b]Rev 1:18 returned to life[b] so that he might be the
[c]2Co 5:15 Lord of both the dead and the living.[c]
10You, then, why do you judge your
brother? Or why do you look down on
your brother? For we will all stand be-
14:10 [d]2Co 5:10 fore God's judgment seat.[d] 11It is written:

"'As surely as I live,' says the Lord,
'every knee will bow before me;
every tongue will confess to
14:11 [e]Isa 45:23; Php 2:10,11 God.'"[b][e]

14:12 [f]Mt 12:36; 1Pe 4:5 12So then, each of us will give an account of himself to God.[f]

13Therefore let us stop passing judg-
ment[g] on one another. Instead, make 14:13 [g]Mt 7:1
up your mind not to put any stumbling
block or obstacle in your brother's way.
14As one who is in the Lord Jesus, I
am fully convinced that no food[c] is un-
clean in itself.[h] But if anyone regards 14:14 [h]Ac 10:15
something as unclean, then for him it is [i]1Co 8:7
unclean.[i] 15If your brother is distressed
because of what you eat, you are no
longer acting in love.[j] Do not by your 14:15 [j]Eph 5:2
eating destroy your brother for whom [k]1Co 8:11
Christ died.[k] 16Do not allow what you
consider good to be spoken of as evil.[l] 14:16 [l]1Co 10:30
17For the kingdom of God is not a mat- 14:17
ter of eating and drinking,[m] but of righ- [m]1Co 8:8
teousness, peace and joy in the Holy [n]Ro 15:13
Spirit,[n] 18because anyone who serves
Christ in this way is pleasing to God
and approved by men.[o] 14:18 [o]2Co 8:21

LOVE

VOTING FOR LOVE

Romans 14:15

If ever you are torn between conviction and compassion, cast your vote for love.

19Let us therefore make every effort 14:19
to do what leads to peace[p] and to mu- [p]Ps 34:14; Ro 12:18; Heb 12:14
tual edification.[q] 20Do not destroy the [q]Ro 15:2; 2Co 12:19
work of God for the sake of food.[r] All
food is clean, but it is wrong for a man
to eat anything that causes someone else 14:20 [r]ver 15
to stumble.[s] 21It is better not to eat meat [s]1Co 8:9-12
or drink wine or to do anything else
that will cause your brother to fall.[t] 14:21 [t]1Co 8:13
22So whatever you believe about these
things keep between yourself and God.
Blessed is the man who does not con-
demn[u] himself by what he approves. 14:22 [u]1Jn 3:21
23But the man who has doubts[v] is con- 14:23
demned if he eats, because his eating [v]ver 5
is not from faith; and everything that
does not come from faith is sin.

15 We who are strong ought to bear
with the failings of the weak[w] 15:1 [w]Ro 14:1; Gal 6:1,2; 1Th 5:14
and not to please ourselves. 2Each of
us should please his neighbor for his
good,[x] to build him up.[y] 3For even 15:2 [x]1Co 10:33
Christ did not please himself[z] but, as [y]Ro 14:19
it is written: "The insults of those who
insult you have fallen on me."[d][a] 4For 15:3 [z]2Co 8:9 [a]Ps 69:9
everything that was written in the past

[a]*14* Or *the flesh* [b]*11* Isaiah 45:23
[c]*14* Or *that nothing* [d]*3* Psalm 69:9

15:4 was written to teach us,[b] so that through
[b]Ro 4:23,24 endurance and the encouragement of
the Scriptures we might have hope.
[5]May the God who gives endurance
and encouragement give you a spirit of
15:5 unity[c] among yourselves as you follow
[c]Ro 12:16; 1Co 1:10 Christ Jesus, [6]so that with one heart
15:6 and mouth you may glorify the God
[d]Rev 1:6 and Father[d] of our Lord Jesus Christ.
15:7 [7]Accept one another,[e] then, just as
[e]Ro 14:1 Christ accepted you, in order to bring
15:8 praise to God. [8]For I tell you that Christ
[f]Mt 15:24; Ac 3:25,26 has become a servant of the Jews[a][f] on
[g]2Co 1:20 behalf of God's truth, to confirm the
promises[g] made to the patriarchs [9]so
15:9 [h]Ro 3:29 that the Gentiles[h] may glorify God[i] for
[i]Mt 9:8 his mercy, as it is written:
[j]2Sa 22:50; Ps 18:49

> "Therefore I will praise you among
> the Gentiles;
> I will sing hymns to your
> name."[b][j]

[10]Again, it says,

15:10 [k]Dt 32:43
> "Rejoice, O Gentiles, with his
> people."[c][k]

[11]And again,

15:11 [l]Ps 117:1
> "Praise the Lord, all you Gentiles,
> and sing praises to him, all you
> peoples."[d][l]

[12]And again, Isaiah says,

15:12 [m]Rev 5:5 [n]Isa 11:10; Mt 12:21
> "The Root of Jesse[m] will spring up,
> one who will arise to rule over the
> nations;
> the Gentiles will hope in him."[e][n]

15:13 [13]May the God of hope fill you with
[o]Ro 14:17 [p]ver 19; all joy and peace[o] as you trust in him,
1Co 2:4; so that you may overflow with hope by
1Th 1:5 the power of the Holy Spirit.[p]

Paul the Minister to the Gentiles

[14]I myself am convinced, my brothers, that you yourselves are full of
15:14 [q]Eph 5:9 goodness,[q] complete in knowledge[r] and
[r]2Pe 1:12 competent to instruct one another. [15]I
have written you quite boldly on some
points, as if to remind you of them
15:15 [s]Ro 12:3 again, because of the grace God gave
me[s] [16]to be a minister of Christ Jesus
15:16 to the Gentiles[t] with the priestly duty
[t]Ac 9:15; Ro 11:13 of proclaiming the gospel of God,[u] so
[u]Ro 1:1 that the Gentiles might become an of-
[v]Isa 66:20 fering[v] acceptable to God, sanctified by
the Holy Spirit.
15:17 [w]Php 3:3 [17]Therefore I glory in Christ Jesus[w]
[x]Heb 2:17 in my service to God.[x] [18]I will not venture to speak of anything except what
Christ has accomplished through me in
leading the Gentiles[y] to obey God[z] by 15:18
what I have said and done— [19]by the [y]Ac 15:12; 21:19; Ro 1:5
power of signs and miracles,[a] through [z]Ro 16:26
the power of the Spirit.[b] So from Jeru-
salem[c] all the way around to Illyricum, 15:19 [a]Jn 4:48; Ac 19:11
I have fully proclaimed the gospel of [b]ver 13
Christ. [20]It has always been my ambi- [c]Ac 22:17-21
tion to preach the gospel where Christ
was not known, so that I would not be
building on someone else's foundation.[d] 15:20 [d]2Co 10:15, 16
[21]Rather, as it is written:

> "Those who were not told about
> him will see,
> and those who have not heard will 15:21 [e]Isa 52:15
> understand."[f][e]

[22]This is why I have often been hin- 15:22
dered from coming to you.[f] [f]Ro 1:13

Kindness

The Frontiersman for Christ

Romans 15:19–20

Christ in the believer is a compass fixed on the North Star. In the ancient world, Spain was the farthest possible point from Antioch. So Paul believed that when Spain knew of Christ (vv. 23–24), the kingdom would have been preached throughout the entire world.

Paul's Plan to Visit Rome

[23]But now that there is no more place
for me to work in these regions, and
since I have been longing for many years
to see you,[g] [24]I plan to do so when I 15:23
go to Spain.[h] I hope to visit you while [g]Ac 19:21; Ro 1:10,11
passing through and to have you assist
me on my journey there, after I have en- 15:24 [h]ver 28
joyed your company for a while. [25]Now,
however, I am on my way to Jerusalem[i] 15:25 [i]Ac 19:21
in the service[j] of the saints there. [26]For [j]Ac 24:17
Macedonia[k] and Achaia[l] were pleased 15:26
to make a contribution for the poor [k]Ac 16:9; 2Co 8:1
among the saints in Jerusalem. [27]They [l]Ac 18:12
were pleased to do it, and indeed they
owe it to them. For if the Gentiles have
shared in the Jews' spiritual blessings,
they owe it to the Jews to share with 15:27
them their material blessings.[m] [28]So af- [m]1Co 9:11
ter I have completed this task and have
made sure that they have received this

[a]*8* Greek *circumcision* [b]*9* 2 Samuel 22:50; Psalm 18:49 [c]*10* Deut. 32:43 [d]*11* Psalm 117:1 [e]*12* Isaiah 11:10 [f]*21* Isaiah 52:15

15:29 [n]Ro 1:10,11
15:30 [o]Gal 5:22 [p]2Co 1:11; Col 4:12
15:31 [q]2Th 3:2
15:32 [r]Ac 18:21 [s]Ro 1:10,13 [t]1Co 16:18
15:33 [u]Ro 16:20; 2Co 13:11; Php 4:9; 1Th 5:23; Heb 13:20

fruit, I will go to Spain and visit you on
the way. 29 I know that when I come to
you,[n] I will come in the full measure of
the blessing of Christ.

30 I urge you, brothers, by our Lord
Jesus Christ and by the love of the
Spirit,[o] to join me in my struggle by
praying to God for me.[p] 31 Pray that I
may be rescued[q] from the unbelievers in
Judea and that my service in Jerusalem
may be acceptable to the saints there,
32 so that by God's will[r] I may come to
you[s] with joy and together with you be
refreshed.[t] 33 The God of peace[u] be with
you all. Amen.

Personal Greetings

16 I commend[v] to you our sister
Phoebe, a servant[a] of the church
in Cenchrea.[w] 2 I ask you to receive her
in the Lord[x] in a way worthy of the
saints and to give her any help she
may need from you, for she has been
a great help to many people, including me.

3 Greet Priscilla[b] and Aquila,[y] my fellow workers in Christ Jesus.[z] 4 They

16:1 [v]2Co 3:1 [w]Ac 18:18
16:2 [x]Php 2:29
16:3 [y]Ac 18:2 [z]ver 7,9,10

[a]*1* Or *deaconess* [b]*3* Greek *Prisca,* a variant of *Priscilla*

PRISCILLA & AQUILA

Kindness, the Root of Hospitality (16:3–5)

Priscilla and Aquila are mentioned several times in Acts 18 and three times in other books of the New Testament, and in almost every instance they are practicing hospitality. In four passages their home is mentioned as a center of hospitality. During the New Testament era, travelers often relied on the kindness of families for shelter and provisions. Couples like Priscilla and Aquila were most appreciated for their constancy and kindness in offering their home to those in need. Consider these passages:

"After this, Paul left Athens and went to Corinth. There he met a Jew named Aquila, a native of Pontus, who had recently come from Italy with his wife Priscilla, because Claudius had ordered all the Jews to leave Rome. Paul went to see them, and because he was a tent-maker as they were, he stayed and worked with them" (vv. 1–3). This is the first recorded instance of Aquila and Priscilla showing kindness by opening their home to others.

"Paul stayed on in Corinth for some time. Then he left the brothers and sailed for Syria, accompanied by Priscilla and Aquila" (v. 18). Here the couple serves as the apostle's traveling companions.

"Meanwhile a Jew named Apollos, a native of Alexandria, came to Ephesus. He was a learned man, with a thorough knowledge of the Scriptures. He had been instructed in the way of the Lord, and he spoke with great fervor and taught about Jesus accurately, though he knew only the baptism of John. He began to speak boldly in the synagogue. When Priscilla and Aquila heard him, they invited him to their home and explained to him the way of God more adequately" (vv. 24–26). Here this kind and hospitable couple invited a traveling preacher into their home for some doctrinal lessons.

"Greet Priscilla and Aquila, my fellow workers in Christ Jesus. They risked their lives for me. Not only I but all the churches of the Gentiles are grateful to them. Greet also the church that meets at their house" (Romans 16:3–5). Here the hospitality of this couple took a grand leap of self-sacrifice for the apostle. Notice that Priscilla and Aquila, who had so often opened up their home to practice kindness to others, had now opened their home as a place for a new church to meet.

Blessed be Priscilla and Aquila! We know nothing of their abilities in public speaking. We know nothing of their abilities in evangelism or church administration. We only know that they were used by God to be kind, and for their service the apostles bowed their heads in thanks.

WEEK 3 PEACE

DAY ONE

1 PEACE, A TRUCE WITH GOD TO END MY ALIENATION FROM HIM

Read Romans 16:20

God's grace affords those who long to serve him the power to triumph in the realm of spiritual struggle. Satan is the author of all such struggle, so Paul makes it clear that God is going to crush Satan under the heel of those who rely on the strength of God for their hope.

Once Satan is defeated, our turmoil is gone, and we can fulfill God's plans for our lives. Nothing is more beautiful than to exalt God and achieve in Christ an inner serenity free of all turbulence. After Jesus was victorious over Satan in the wilderness, angels came to Jesus and ministered to him. After the reign of Satan is over in our own lives, peace will be born, and we will serve God without distraction.

Alienation is always the by-product of evil. Just as God draws us to himself, Satan drives wedges into that holy relationship. The devil actively works at trying to limit the number of God's friends.

The God of peace will crush Satan under his feet. What a great promise this is! When we were lost in sin, Satan kept us in turmoil. He agitated our troubled minds with hatred, self-will and ambition. He left us weeping in despair, helpless before our hopelessness. The evil one is the author of our identity crisis, the breaker of our hope. He always comes shod in the muddy boots that stomp our desire for clean morality into unwholesome pleasures.

But when Jesus reigns, our old enemy is crushed. We are free to live and serve God in peace.

DAY TWO

2 PEACE AND THE PURPOSE OF GOD IN MY LIFE

When God acts to save us, his peace seeks us out in our world of stress and confusion. We realize that there is a better way to live, a way of life that spreads peace and resolves contentions. Our conversion brings us to a new level of peace, and we then share God's peace with others through our changed lives. *Turn to Titus 3:3–11, page 1454, for today's study.*

DAY THREE

3 PEACE AND MY RELATIONSHIP WITH CHRIST

The human heart is subject to turmoil, but Jesus enters our hearts to save us, and a calm falls over all our agitation like oil falls on water. Jesus and turmoil cannot coexist for long within any human heart. Where Jesus is, there is peace. *Turn to Colossians 3:15, page 1424, for today's study.*

DAY FOUR

4 PEACE AND MY SERVICE TO OTHERS

The blessing of Aaron is our sign of peace. Moses, at the command of God, gives Aaron a benediction with which he is always to bless Israel. The last word of this benediction is *peace*. Christians ought to frame this benediction and hang it in the gallery of their hearts. Such a benediction paves the way for peace in all our dealings with others. Aaron blessed Israel 3,000 years ago. The three millennia since then have only added new force to this old benediction. *Turn to Numbers 6:22–26, page 159, for today's study.*

DAY FIVE

5 PEACE AND ITS PLACE IN MY PERSONAL WORSHIP

God's peace is a promise of truce. When we see a rainbow, we are reminded of God's truce with the descendants of Noah. That truce extends to all of us through one of Noah's descendants, Jesus. When we worship the Prince of Peace, his peace will give us joy in the face of an uncertain world. *Turn to Genesis 9:8–17, page 13, for today's study.*

MEMORIZE THIS WEEK

JOHN 14:27

Peace I leave with you; my peace I give you. I do not give to you as the world gives. Do not let your hearts be troubled and do not be afraid.

Week 4, Patience, the Art of Waiting on God, begins on page 1500, 2 Peter 3:8–9.
To begin a topical study on the Fruit of the Spirit, Peace, turn to the Topical Index, page 1548.

risked their lives for me. Not only
I but all the churches of the Gentiles are grateful to them.

16:5 [a]1Co 16:19; Col 4:15; Phm 2 [b]1Co 16:15

5 Greet also the church that meets at
their house.[a]
Greet my dear friend Epenetus, who
was the first convert[b] to Christ in
the province of Asia.
6 Greet Mary, who worked very hard
for you.
7 Greet Andronicus and Junias, my rel-

16:7 [c]ver 11,21

atives[c] who have been in prison
with me. They are outstanding
among the apostles, and they were
in Christ before I was.
8 Greet Ampliatus, whom I love in the
Lord.
9 Greet Urbanus, our fellow worker

16:9 [d]ver 3

in Christ,[d] and my dear friend
Stachys.
10 Greet Apelles, tested and approved in
Christ.
Greet those who belong to the house-
hold of Aristobulus.

16:11 [e]ver 7,21

11 Greet Herodion, my relative.[e]
Greet those in the household of Nar-
cissus who are in the Lord.
12 Greet Tryphena and Tryphosa, those
women who work hard in the
Lord.
Greet my dear friend Persis, another
woman who has worked very hard
in the Lord.
13 Greet Rufus, chosen in the Lord, and
his mother, who has been a mother to me, too.
14 Greet Asyncritus, Phlegon, Hermes,

16:15 [f]ver 2 [g]ver 14

Patrobas, Hermas and the brothers
with them.
15 Greet Philologus, Julia, Nereus and

16:16 [h]1Co 16:20; 2Co 13:12; 1Th 5:26

his sister, and Olympas and all the
saints[f] with them.[g]
16 Greet one another with a holy kiss.[h]
All the churches of Christ send greetings.
17 I urge you, brothers, to watch out
for those who cause divisions and put
obstacles in your way that are contrary

16:17 [i]Gal 1:8,9; 1Ti 1:3; 6:3 [j]2Th 3:6,14; 2Jn 10

to the teaching you have learned.[i] Keep
away from them.[j] 18 For such people are
not serving our Lord Christ, but their
own appetites.[k] By smooth talk and flat-

16:18 [k]Php 3:19 [l]Col 2:4

tery they deceive[l] the minds of naive people. 19 Everyone has heard[m] about your

16:19 [m]Ro 1:8 [n]Mt 10:16; 1Co 14:20

obedience, so I am full of joy over you;
but I want you to be wise about what is
good, and innocent about what is evil.[n]

16:20 [o]Ro 15:33 [p]Ge 3:15 [q]1Th 5:28

20 The God of peace[o] will soon crush[p]
Satan under your feet.
The grace of our Lord Jesus be with
you.[q]
21 Timothy,[r] my fellow worker, sends

16:21 [r]Ac 16:1 [s]Ac 13:1 [t]Ac 17:5 [u]ver 7,11

his greetings to you, as do Lucius,[s] Jason[t] and Sosipater, my relatives.[u]
22 I, Tertius, who wrote down this letter, greet you in the Lord.
23 Gaius, whose hospitality I and the
whole church here enjoy, sends you his
greetings.

16:23 [v]Ac 19:22

Erastus,[v] who is the city's director of
public works, and our brother Quartus
send you their greetings.[a]

16:25 [w]Eph 3:20 [x]Ro 2:16 [y]Eph 1:9; Col 1:26,27

25 Now to him who is able[w] to establish you by my gospel[x] and the proclamation of Jesus Christ, according to
the revelation of the mystery[y] hidden
for long ages past, 26 but now revealed
and made known through the prophetic
writings by the command of the eternal
God, so that all nations might believe
and obey him— 27 to the only wise God

16:27 [z]Ro 11:36

be glory forever through Jesus Christ!
Amen.[z]

[a]23 Some manuscripts *their greetings.* [24] *May the grace of our Lord Jesus Christ be with all of you. Amen.*

1 Corinthians

Authorship and Date

Paul

c. A.D. 55

Key Themes

First Corinthians was one of the first books of the New Testament to be written. It was written by Paul after he heard of all the troubles that plagued the Corinthian church. It is easy to tell from even a surface reading that Paul had to address many problems within the Corinthian fellowship. The large number of recent converts and the immaturity of these new believers likely caused the difficulties within the group. Point by point, Paul addressed the following issues:

1. Loyalty and unity: The people of the Corinthian congregation were split over which of their particular religious heroes were admirable enough to deserve their allegiance (see 1:10—4:21).
2. A need for excommunication (see 5:1–13).
3. Christians in the courts: Should Christians sue each other (see 6:1–8)?
4. The many sexual sins rampant within the church (see 6:9–20).
5. Questions and problems related to marriage (see 7:1–40).
6. Meat offered to idols, and the consciences of weaker brothers (see 8:1—11:2).
7. Worship propriety, the Lord's Supper and the proper respect for, and use of, spiritual gifts (see 11:3—14:40).
8. The resurrection (see 15:1–58).

Chapter 16 then covers Paul's concluding remarks. This letter is full of stern corrections as well as an admonition for piety to be the central goal of the believer. Love is the path of unity (see chapter 13); righteousness and holy living aid believers in the avoidance of the excesses of disunity and idolatry.

Fruit of the Spirit in 1 Corinthians

Love: To be multilingual and yet be without love is to be an unintelligible, clanging gong. To be prophetic and understand distant things far away and yet be without love is to be meaningless. To have powers of faith that move the world and yet be without love is to be an invalid. To be philanthropic and yet be without love for the needy is to have gained nothing. To possess all virtues and yet be without love is to have passed through the world without having been in it (see 13:1–13).

Joy: The ultimate joy will be the final celebration that will come to every Christian when death, the great and final terror, is seen for what it is—a paper tiger. Then, as the graves gape and the cemeteries apologize for all the tears they have caused, we will shout, "Death has been swallowed up in victory . . . Where, O death, is your sting?" (15:54–55).

Kindness: Paul reminded the Corinthians that some persons had traded kindness for haughtiness because they thought they would never have to reckon with the apostle again (see 4:18). Kindness should be a lifestyle, not an act coerced by fear. Meanness that is merely cloaked with kindness for fear of rebuke has not reckoned honestly with the cross.

Goodness: After naming a gallery of evil traits—idolatry, prostitution, perversion, drunkenness, libel and scandal—Paul reminded the Corinthians that they had received the goodness of God: "But you were washed, you were sanctified, you were justified in the name of the Lord Jesus Christ and by the Spirit of our God" (6:11). Goodness is a bath, a court reprieve, a christening at which time we are named after Jesus.

Faithfulness: Faithfulness is our response to grace. We were bought and paid for with Christ's blood. God purchased us at Calvary, drop by drop, in strangling torture. There, where he spent everything, we found Christmas, rich and eternal—packaged in the shroud of Good Friday. Now we live every moment looking for the chance to be worthy of the price (see 6:20).

Self-Control: The best way to avoid returning to old addictions is to stay away from old addicts. Separating ourselves from sin makes sin-free living easier (see 5:9). Those who wish to give up hot fudge sundaes should keep away from ice cream parlors.

1:1 [a]Ro 1:1; Eph 1:1 [b]2Co 1:1 [c]Ac 18:17

1 Paul, called to be an apostle[a] of
Christ Jesus by the will of God,[b]
and our brother Sosthenes,[c]

1:2 [d]Ac 18:1 [e]Ro 1:7

2To the church of God in Corinth,[d]
to those sanctified in Christ Jesus and
called[e] to be holy, together with all those
everywhere who call on the name of
our Lord Jesus Christ—their Lord and
ours:

DAY 2 TWO

▸ PATIENCE AND THE PURPOSE OF GOD IN MY LIFE

1 Corinthians 1:4–9

Will God ask us to do something and then leave us? Of course not! Yet when we are called to wait, what can possibly keep us from becoming impatient? Haven't we all at some point sat in a waiting room while a doctor treats others? Haven't we sat in a traffic jam for hours, waiting for something—anything—to move? But waiting for Jesus is the ultimate and truly worthwhile wait. We wait for his coming to set all things right in our world. We wait for his coming to show us perfection. We wait for his coming to herald that our future is here. One day we will be with God, the lover of our souls.

So how to wait with patience? Simple. We know our purpose, and we are equipped by God to accomplish that purpose. Our purpose is to remain strong until the end. We are called to be faithful, modeling ourselves after the One we follow. As God is faithful, so should we be faithful.

And we are equipped. God has given us blessings abounding. He has given us the gifts we need to accomplish his purpose for us. Later in this letter, we find a listing of some specific gifts. And we find that the ultimate gift, the Holy Spirit, administers these gifts for us (1 Corinthians 12).

God has called us to wait. So we practice patience. But God has given us gifts to equip us to fulfill his purposes as we wait. Through his graciousness, we learn patience, and through our exercise of that patience, we fulfill his purposes.

To begin a study on the topic of Patience, the Art of Waiting on God, turn to the home page on page 1500.

3Grace and peace to you from God
our Father and the Lord Jesus Christ.[f] 1:3 [f]Ro 1:7

Thanksgiving

4I always thank God for you[g] because 1:4 [g]Ro 1:8
of his grace given you in Christ Jesus.
5For in him you have been enriched[h] 1:5 [h]2Co 9:11
in every way—in all your speaking and [i]2Co 8:7
in all your knowledge[i]— 6because our
testimony[j] about Christ was confirmed 1:6 [j]Rev 1:2
in you. 7Therefore you do not lack any
spiritual gift as you eagerly wait for our
Lord Jesus Christ to be revealed.[k] 8He 1:7 [k]Php 3:20; Tit 2:13; 2Pe 3:12
will keep you strong to the end, so that
you will be blameless[l] on the day of our
Lord Jesus Christ. 9God, who has called 1:8 [l]1Th 3:13
you into fellowship with his Son Jesus
Christ our Lord,[m] is faithful.[n] 1:9 [m]1Jn 1:3 [n]Isa 49:7; 1Th 5:24

Divisions in the Church

10I appeal to you, brothers, in the
name of our Lord Jesus Christ, that
all of you agree with one another so
that there may be no divisions among
you and that you may be perfectly united in mind and thought. 11My brothers, some from Chloe's household have
informed me that there are quarrels
among you. 12What I mean is this:
One of you says, "I follow Paul";[o] an- 1:12 [o]1Co 3:4,22
other, "I follow Apollos";[p] another, "I [p]Ac 18:24
follow Cephas[a]";[q] still another, "I fol- [q]Jn 1:42
low Christ."

▸ GOODNESS

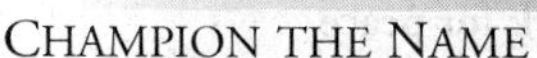

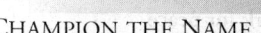

CHAMPION THE NAME

1 Corinthians 1:12

Some "heroes" of the gospel claim the light that God has set to fall on Christ alone. Follow no one whose name on the marquee is larger than the name of Christ.

13Is Christ divided? Was Paul crucified for you? Were you baptized into[b]
the name of Paul?[r] 14I am thankful that 1:13 [r]Mt 28:19
I did not baptize any of you except
Crispus[s] and Gaius,[t] 15so no one can say 1:14 [s]Ac 18:8; Ro 16:23 [t]Ac 19:29
that you were baptized into my name.
16(Yes, I also baptized the household
of Stephanas;[u] beyond that, I don't re- 1:16 [u]1Co 16:15
member if I baptized anyone else.) 17For
Christ did not send me to baptize,[v] but 1:17 [v]Jn 4:2
to preach the gospel—not with words

[a]*12* That is, Peter [b]*13* Or *in*; also in verse 15

1:17 [w]1Co 2:1,4,13

of human wisdom,[w] lest the cross of
Christ be emptied of its power.

Christ the Wisdom and Power of God

18 For the message of the cross is foolishness to those who are perishing,[x] but
to us who are being saved it is the power of God.[y] 19 For it is written:

1:18 [x]2Co 2:15 [y]Ro 1:16

"I will destroy the wisdom of the wise;

DAY 3 THREE

▸ FAITHFULNESS AND MY RELATIONSHIP WITH CHRIST

1 Corinthians 1:20–25

James A. Harnish asks the question, "Where do we find the power to be a disciple?" The answer is Jesus. It is Christ who supplies the recipe for the relationship. Faithfully he has stood by, supplying us with the power to stand for him. So once again, where do we find that living water, which refreshes us by his faithfulness?

Where do we find the power to hang in there in this world?
Where do we find the power to keep going when the going really gets tough?
Where do we find the power to continue to believe in love in a world that is filled with hate?
Where do we find the power to continue to work for peace in a world that is addicted to violence?
Where do we find the power to continue to believe in good in a world that is filled with so much evil?
Where do we find the power to continue to believe that ultimately God's kingdom will come and God's will, as revealed in Jesus, will be done in all of the creation?
Where do you find the power to be a disciple of Jesus in this world?

This kind of power can be found in our faithfulness—there or nowhere!

To begin a study on the topic of Faithfulness: No Compromise, turn to the home page on page 898.

the intelligence of the intelligent I will frustrate."[a][z]

1:19 [z]Isa 29:14

20 Where is the wise man?[a] Where is
the scholar? Where is the philosopher
of this age? Has not God made foolish[b]
the wisdom of the world? 21 For since in
the wisdom of God the world through
its wisdom did not know him, God was
pleased through the foolishness of what
was preached to save those who believe. 22 Jews demand miraculous signs[c]
and Greeks look for wisdom, 23 but we
preach Christ crucified: a stumbling
block[d] to Jews and foolishness[e] to Gentiles, 24 but to those whom God has
called,[f] both Jews and Greeks, Christ
the power of God and the wisdom of
God.[g] 25 For the foolishness[h] of God
is wiser than man's wisdom, and the
weakness[i] of God is stronger than man's
strength.

1:20 [a]Isa 19:11,12 [b]Job 12:17; Ro 1:22
1:22 [c]Mt 12:38
1:23 [d]Lk 2:34; Gal 5:11 [e]1Co 2:14
1:24 [f]Ro 8:28 [g]ver 30; Col 2:3
1:25 [h]ver 18 [i]2Co 13:4

▸ GENTLENESS

THE FOLLY MAGNIFICENT

1 Corinthians 1:18

Preaching is sometimes an art in question. Some say it is boring and scoff at it. But consider the product of this oft-despised calling: The entire kingdom of God has been formed by the folly of this gentle art.

26 Brothers, think of what you were
when you were called. Not many of
you were wise by human standards; not
many were influential; not many were
of noble birth. 27 But God chose[j] the
foolish[k] things of the world to shame
the wise; God chose the weak things
of the world to shame the strong. 28 He
chose the lowly things of this world and
the despised things—and the things
that are not[l]—to nullify the things
that are, 29 so that no one may boast
before him.[m] 30 It is because of him
that you are in Christ Jesus, who has
become for us wisdom from God—
that is, our righteousness,[n] holiness and
redemption.[o] 31 Therefore, as it is written: "Let him who boasts boast in the
Lord."[b][p]

1:27 [j]Jas 2:5 [k]ver 20
1:28 [l]Ro 4:17
1:29 [m]Eph 2:9
1:30 [n]Jer 23:5,6; 2Co 5:21 [o]Ro 3:24; Eph 1:7,14
1:31 [p]Jer 9:23,24; 2Co 10:17

2 When I came to you, brothers, I
did not come with eloquence or su-

[a]*19* Isaiah 29:14 [b]*31* Jer. 9:24

2:1 perior wisdom[q] as I proclaimed to you
[q]1Co 1:17 the testimony about God.[a] 2For I resolved to know nothing while I was
with you except Jesus Christ and him
2:2 [r]Gal 6:14; crucified.[r] 3I came to you[s] in weakness
1Co 1:23 and fear, and with much trembling.
2:3 4My message and my preaching were
[s]Ac 18:1-18 not with wise and persuasive words,
but with a demonstration of the Spirit's
2:4 [t]Ro 15:19 power,[t] 5so that your faith might not
rest on men's wisdom, but on God's
2:5 [u]2Co 4:7; 6:7 power.[u]

FAITHFULNESS

THE FOCUS

1 Corinthians 2:2

Narrow your preaching.
Do you preach Jesus, the cross and being as nice as you can be?
Drop "nice as you can be."
Serve one grand simplicity: Jesus Christ and him crucified.

Wisdom From the Spirit

6We do, however, speak a message of
2:6 [v]Eph 4:13; wisdom among the mature,[v] but not
Php 3:15; the wisdom of this age[w] or of the rulers
Heb 5:14 [w]1Co 1:20 of this age, who are coming to nothing.
7No, we speak of God's secret wisdom,
a wisdom that has been hidden and
that God destined for our glory before
time began. 8None of the rulers of this
age understood it, for if they had, they
would not have crucified the Lord of
2:8 [x]Ac 7:2; glory.[x] 9However, as it is written:
Jas 2:1

"No eye has seen,
no ear has heard,
2:9 [y]Isa 64:4; 65:17 no mind has conceived
what God has prepared for those
who love him"[b][y]—

2:10 [z]Mt 13:11; Eph 3:3,5 [a]Jn 14:26
10but God has revealed[z] it to us by his
Spirit.[a]

PEACE

THE DEPTHS OF KNOWLEDGE

1 Corinthians 2:10–12

Would you know the ocean? Then seek it at its depths, for, deep in the ocean, silence will bludgeon you dumb, and wondrous stillness will crush you with its vast reality. God is oceanlike, yet larger. God is wonder, only multiplied.

The Spirit searches all things, even
the deep things of God. 11For who
among men knows the thoughts of a
man[b] except the man's spirit[c] within 2:11 [b]Jer 17:9
him? In the same way no one knows [c]Pr 20:27
the thoughts of God except the Spirit
of God. 12We have not received the
spirit[d] of the world[e] but the Spirit who 2:12 [d]Ro 8:15
is from God, that we may understand [e]1Co 1:20,27
what God has freely given us. 13This is
what we speak, not in words taught us
by human wisdom[f] but in words taught 2:13 [f]1Co 1:17
by the Spirit, expressing spiritual truths
in spiritual words.[c] 14The man without
the Spirit does not accept the things
that come from the Spirit of God, for
they are foolishness[g] to him, and he 2:14 [g]1Co 1:18
cannot understand them, because they
are spiritually discerned. 15The spiritual
man makes judgments about all things,
but he himself is not subject to any
man's judgment:

16"For who has known the mind of the
Lord
that he may instruct him?"[d][h] 2:16 [h]Isa 40:13
But we have the mind of Christ.[i] [i]Jn 15:15

LOVE

BABIES BY CHOICE

1 Corinthians 3:1

It's natural to love the early, easy wonder of salvation.
Babies thrive on immaturity.
They are in the world but never much in charge of it.
They live without changing it.
They require ministry without giving it.
Jesus dreamed of a kingdom with fewer infants and
More soldiers.

On Divisions in the Church

3 Brothers, I could not address you 3:1 [j]1Co 2:15
as spiritual[j] but as worldly[k]—mere [k]Ro 7:14;
infants[l] in Christ. 2I gave you milk, not 1Co 2:14 [l]Heb 5:13
solid food,[m] for you were not yet ready 3:2 [m]Heb
for it.[n] Indeed, you are still not ready. 5:12-14;
3You are still worldly. For since there 1Pe 2:2
is jealousy and quarreling[o] among you, [n]Jn 16:12
are you not worldly? Are you not act- 3:3 [o]1Co 1:11;
ing like mere men? 4For when one says, Gal 5:20

[a]1 Some manuscripts *as I proclaimed to you God's mystery* [b]9 Isaiah 64:4 [c]13 Or *Spirit, interpreting spiritual truths to spiritual men* [d]16 Isaiah 40:13

GOODNESS

FOUNDATIONS

1 Corinthians 3:4

"I was baptized by a cardinal."
"I was baptized by a priest."
"I was baptized by a holy soul
Who studied in the East."

Tell me not who poured the water.
Let us call one Shepherd good.
Let us gaze through fields of martyrs;
Honor Christ who spilt his blood.

"I follow Paul," and another, "I follow
3:4 Apollos,"[p] are you not mere men?
[p]1Co 1:12 5What, after all, is Apollos? And what
is Paul? Only servants, through whom
you came to believe—as the Lord has
assigned to each his task. 6I planted
3:6 the seed,[q] Apollos watered it, but God
[q]Ac 18:4-11 made it grow. 7So neither he who plants
nor he who waters is anything, but only
God, who makes things grow. 8The
man who plants and the man who waters have one purpose, and each will be
3:8 rewarded according to his own labor.[r]
[r]Ps 62:12 9For we are God's fellow workers;[s] you
3:9 [s]2Co 6:1 are God's field,[t] God's building.[u]
[t]Isa 61:3 10By the grace God has given me,[v] I
[u]Eph 2:20-22; laid a foundation[w] as an expert build-
1Pe 2:5 er, and someone else is building on it.
3:10 [v]Ro 12:3 But each one should be careful how he
[w]Ro 15:20 builds. 11For no one can lay any foundation other than the one already laid,
3:11 which is Jesus Christ.[x] 12If any man
[x]Isa 28:16; builds on this foundation using gold,
Eph 2:20 silver, costly stones, wood, hay or straw,
13his work will be shown for what it is,[y]
3:13 [y]1Co 4:5 because the Day[z] will bring it to light.
[z]2Th 1:7-10 It will be revealed with fire, and the fire
will test the quality of each man's work.
14If what he has built survives, he will
receive his reward. 15If it is burned up,
he will suffer loss; he himself will be
saved, but only as one escaping through
3:15 [a]Jude 23 the flames.[a]
16Don't you know that you yourselves
3:16 [b]1Co 6:19; are God's temple[b] and that God's Spirit
2Co 6:16 lives in you? 17If anyone destroys God's
temple, God will destroy him; for God's
temple is sacred, and you are that temple.
18Do not deceive yourselves. If any
3:18 [c]Isa 5:21; one of you thinks he is wise[c] by the
1Co 8:2 standards of this age, he should become a "fool" so that he may become
wise. 19For the wisdom of this world
is foolishness[d] in God's sight. As it is 3:19 [d]1Co 1:20,27
written: "He catches the wise in their [e]Job 5:13
craftiness"[a];[e] 20and again, "The Lord
knows that the thoughts of the wise
are futile."[b][f] 21So then, no more boast- 3:20 [f]Ps 94:11
ing about men![g] All things are yours,[h]
22whether Paul or Apollos or Cephas[c][i] 3:21 [g]1Co 4:6
or the world or life or death or the [h]Ro 8:32
present or the future[j]—all are yours, 3:22 [i]1Co 1:12
23and you are of Christ,[k] and Christ is [j]Ro 8:38
of God.

Apostles of Christ 3:23 [k]1Co 15:23; 2Co 10:7; Gal 3:29

4 So then, men ought to regard us as
servants of Christ and as those en-
trusted[l] with the secret things[m] of God. 4:1 [l]1Co 9:17; Tit 1:7
2Now it is required that those who have [m]Ro 16:25
been given a trust must prove faithful.
3I care very little if I am judged by
you or by any human court; indeed,
I do not even judge myself. 4My conscience is clear, but that does not make
me innocent.[n] It is the Lord who judges 4:4 [n]Ro 2:13
me. 5Therefore judge nothing[o] before
the appointed time; wait till the Lord 4:5 [o]Mt 7:1,2;
comes. He will bring to light what is Ro 2:1
hidden in darkness and will expose the [p]Ro 2:29
motives of men's hearts. At that time
each will receive his praise from God.[p]
6Now, brothers, I have applied these
things to myself and Apollos for your
benefit, so that you may learn from us
the meaning of the saying, "Do not
go beyond what is written."[q] Then you 4:6 [q]1Co 1:19,31;
will not take pride in one man over 3:19,20
against another.[r] 7For who makes you [r]1Co 1:12
different from anyone else? What do
you have that you did not receive?[s] And 4:7 [s]Jn 3:27;
if you did receive it, why do you boast Ro 12:3,6
as though you did not?
8Already you have all you want! Al-
ready you have become rich![t] You have 4:8 [t]Rev 3:17,18
become kings—and that without us!
How I wish that you really had become
kings so that we might be kings with
you! 9For it seems to me that God has
put us apostles on display at the end
of the procession, like men condemned 4:9
to die[u] in the arena. We have been [u]Ro 8:36
made a spectacle[v] to the whole uni- [v]Heb 10:33
verse, to angels as well as to men. 10We 4:10
are fools[w] for Christ, but you are so [w]1Co 1:18;
wise in Christ![x] We are weak, but you Ac 17:18 [x]1Co 3:18
are strong![y] You are honored, we are [y]1Co 2:3
dishonored! 11To this very hour we go

[a]*19* Job 5:13 [b]*20* Psalm 94:11 [c]*22* That is, Peter

hungry and thirsty, we are in rags, we
4:11 [z]Ro 8:35; are brutally treated, we are homeless.[z]
2Co 11:23-27 12We work hard with our own hands.[a]
When we are cursed, we bless;[b] when
4:12 [a]Ac 18:3 we are persecuted, we endure it; 13when
[b]1Pe 3:9 we are slandered, we answer kindly. Up
to this moment we have become the
4:13 [c]La 3:45 scum of the earth, the refuse[c] of the
world.
14I am not writing this to shame you,
4:14 [d]1Th 2:11 but to warn you, as my dear children.[d]
15Even though you have ten thousand
guardians in Christ, you do not have
many fathers, for in Christ Jesus I be-
4:15 came your father through the gospel.[e]
[e]1Co 9:12,14, 18,23 16Therefore I urge you to imitate me.[f]
17For this reason I am sending to you
4:16 [f]1Co 11:1; Timothy, my son[g] whom I love, who
Php 3:17; is faithful in the Lord. He will remind
1Th 1:6; 2Th 3:7,9 you of my way of life in Christ Jesus,
which agrees with what I teach every-
4:17 [g]1Ti 1:2 where in every church.[h]
[h]1Co 7:17 18Some of you have become arrogant,
as if I were not coming to you. 19But
4:19 I will come to you very soon,[i] if the
[i]2Co 1:15,16 Lord is willing,[j] and then I will find
[j]Ac 18:21 out not only how these arrogant people are talking, but what power they
have. 20For the kingdom of God is not
a matter of talk but of power. 21What
do you prefer? Shall I come to you with
4:21 a whip,[k] or in love and with a gentle
[k]2Co 1:23; 13:2,10 spirit?

Expel the Immoral Brother!

5 It is actually reported that there
is sexual immorality among you,
and of a kind that does not occur even
among pagans: A man has his father's
5:1 [l]Lev 18:8; wife.[l] 2And you are proud! Shouldn't
Dt 22:30 you rather have been filled with grief[m]
5:2 and have put out of your fellowship the
[m]2Co 7:7-11 man who did this? 3Even though I am
not physically present, I am with you in
5:3 spirit.[n] And I have already passed judg-
[n]Col 2:5 ment on the one who did this, just as
if I were present. 4When you are assem-
5:4 [o]2Th 3:6 bled in the name of our Lord Jesus[o] and
I am with you in spirit, and the power
of our Lord Jesus is present, 5hand this
5:5 [p]1Ti 1:20 man over[p] to Satan, so that the sinful
nature[a] may be destroyed and his spirit
saved on the day of the Lord.
5:6 6Your boasting is not good.[q] Don't
[q]Jas 4:16 you know that a little yeast[r] works
[r]Mt 16:6,12 through the whole batch of dough?[s]
[s]Gal 5:9 7Get rid of the old yeast that you may
be a new batch without yeast—as you
really are. For Christ, our Passover lamb,
has been sacrificed.[t] 8Therefore let us 5:7 [t]Mk 14:12;
keep the Festival, not with the old yeast, 1Pe 1:19
the yeast of malice and wickedness, but
with bread without yeast,[u] the bread of 5:8 [u]Ex 12:14,15;
sincerity and truth. Dt 16:3
9I have written you in my letter not
to associate[v] with sexually immoral peo- 5:9 [v]Eph 5:11;
ple— 10not at all meaning the people 2Th 3:6,14
of this world[w] who are immoral, or 5:10
the greedy and swindlers, or idolaters. [w]1Co 10:27
In that case you would have to leave
this world. 11But now I am writing you
that you must not associate with anyone who calls himself a brother but is
sexually immoral or greedy, an idolater[x] 5:11 [x]1Co 10:7,14
or a slanderer, a drunkard or a swindler.
With such a man do not even eat.
12What business is it of mine to judge
those outside[y] the church? Are you not 5:12 [y]Mk 4:11
to judge those inside?[z] 13God will judge [z]ver 3-5; 1Co 6:1-4
those outside. "Expel the wicked man
from among you."[b][a] 5:13 [a]Dt 13:5

Lawsuits Among Believers

6 If any of you has a dispute with
another, dare he take it before the
ungodly for judgment instead of be-
fore the saints?[b] 2Do you not know that 6:1 [b]Mt 18:17
the saints will judge the world?[c] And if 6:2 [c]Mt 19:28;
you are to judge the world, are you not Lk 22:30
competent to judge trivial cases? 3Do
you not know that we will judge angels?
How much more the things of this life!
4Therefore, if you have disputes about
such matters, appoint as judges even
men of little account in the church![c] 5I
say this to shame you.[d] Is it possible that 6:5 [d]1Co 4:14
there is nobody among you wise enough [e]Ac 1:15
to judge a dispute between believers?[e]
6But instead, one brother goes to law
against another—and this in front of
unbelievers![f] 6:6 [f]2Co 6:14,15
7The very fact that you have lawsuits among you means you have been
completely defeated already. Why not
rather be wronged? Why not rather be
cheated?[g] 8Instead, you yourselves cheat 6:7 [g]Mt 5:39,40
and do wrong, and you do this to your
brothers.[h] 6:8 [h]1Th 4:6
9Do you not know that the wicked
will not inherit the kingdom of God?[i] 6:9 [i]Gal 5:21
Do not be deceived:[j] Neither the sexu- [j]1Co 15:33;
ally immoral nor idolaters nor adulterers Jas 1:16

[a]5 Or *that his body*; or *that the flesh*
[b]*13* Deut. 17:7; 19:19; 21:21; 22:21,24; 24:7
[c]*4* Or *matters, do you appoint as judges men of little account in the church?*

nor male prostitutes nor homosexual offenders 10 nor thieves nor the greedy nor
drunkards nor slanderers nor swindlers
will inherit the kingdom of God. 11 And
6:11 that is what some of you were.[k] But
[k]Eph 2:2 you were washed,[l] you were sanctified,[m]
[l]Ac 22:16 [m]1Co 1:2 you were justified in the name of the

DAY 4 FOUR

Self-Control and My Service to Others

1 Corinthians 6:12–13

Do we have such liberty in the Lord that we can be a Christian and still be as immoral as we please? Some Corinthians thought so, and Paul addresses such attitudes by saying that we can love Jesus and do anything we *want* to, but the wonderful thing is that Jesus has changed all our *want tos*. The questions we have to face with every moral decision are two:

First: Is what I am deciding to do beneficial? In other words, what are the long-term benefits or consequences of this action? Self-control mandates that we take the long look at our every moral or immoral deed. In this way we will use good, sound reason to make our choices.

Second: Is what I'm about to do just one little step in surrendering my long-term liberty? I will never forget an alcoholic who bragged, as alcoholics are prone to do, "Liquor? Oh, I can take it or leave it. I just stop off at a bar every night on the way home and have two small martinis. I am not an alcoholic; I can stop any time I want to." I challenged him to come straight home three nights in a row and prove to me, God and his family that he could take it or leave it. He discovered to his dismay that he was truly chemically dependent.

Paul said, "I will honor self-control in my life, for I will not be mastered by anything." When we are truly free of the control of any appetite on our life, then we are truly free to minister to others. But if we try to serve Christ and any other single appetite, we risk having something besides Jesus become the lord of our lives. When that happens, our usefulness to Christ is over.

To begin a study on the topic of Self-Control, Saying No to Our Appetites, turn to the home page on page 105.

Goodness

Kingdom People

1 Corinthians 6:9–10

In the footprints of Christ's wounded feet walk cleanliness and purity of heart. Beware the prophet who cries, "Receive Christ and remain as you are." Beware those who sing "Just as I Am" but, having seen Christ, remain just as they were.

Lord Jesus Christ and by the Spirit of
our God.

Sexual Immorality

12 "Everything is permissible for
me"—but not everything is beneficial.[n] 6:12 [n]1Co 10:23
"Everything is permissible for me"—
but I will not be mastered by anything.
13 "Food for the stomach and the stomach for food"—but God will destroy
them both.[o] The body is not meant for 6:13 [o]Col 2:22
sexual immorality, but for the Lord, and
the Lord for the body. 14 By his power
God raised the Lord from the dead,
and he will raise us also.[p] 15 Do you not 6:14 [p]Ro 6:5;
know that your bodies are members of Eph 1:19,20
Christ himself?[q] Shall I then take the 6:15
members of Christ and unite them with [q]Ro 12:5
a prostitute? Never! 16 Do you not know
that he who unites himself with a prostitute is one with her in body? For it is
said, "The two will become one flesh."[a][r] 6:16
17 But he who unites himself with the [r]Ge 2:24;
Lord is one with him in spirit.[s] Mt 19:5; Eph 5:31
18 Flee from sexual immorality.[t] All 6:17
other sins a man commits are outside [s]Jn 17:21-23; Gal 2:20
his body, but he who sins sexually sins 6:18
against his own body.[u] 19 Do you not [t]2Co 12:21;
know that your body is a temple[v] of 1Th 4:3,4;
the Holy Spirit, who is in you, whom Heb 13:4 [u]Ro 6:12
you have received from God? You are 6:19
not your own;[w] 20 you were bought at a [v]Jn 2:21 [w]Ro 14:7,8

[a] *16* Gen. 2:24

Self-Control

The Price and the Reputation

1 Corinthians 6:20

To be faithful requires but one great motivation. Think of what Christ paid to purchase you, and then endeavor to be worth the purchase price.

6:20 [x]Ac 20:28; 1Co 7:23; 1Pe 1:18,19; Rev 5:9 price.[x] Therefore honor God with your
body.

Marriage

7 Now for the matters you wrote
about: It is good for a man not to
7:1 [y]ver 8,26 marry.[a][y] 2But since there is so much immorality, each man should have his own
wife, and each woman her own husband. 3The husband should fulfill his
7:3 [z]Ex 21:10; 1Pe 3:7 marital duty to his wife,[z] and likewise
the wife to her husband. 4The wife's
body does not belong to her alone but
also to her husband. In the same way,
the husband's body does not belong to
him alone but also to his wife. 5Do not
deprive each other except by mutual
7:5 [a]Ex 19:15; 1Sa 21:4,5 [b]Mt 4:10 [c]1Th 3:5 consent and for a time,[a] so that you
may devote yourselves to prayer. Then
come together again so that Satan[b] will
not tempt[c] you because of your lack
of self-control. 6I say this as a conces-
7:6 [d]2Co 8:8 sion, not as a command.[d] 7I wish that
7:7 [e]ver 8; 1Co 9:5 [f]Mt 19:11,12; Ro 12:6; 1Co 12:4,11 all men were as I am.[e] But each man
has his own gift from God; one has this
gift, another has that.[f]
8Now to the unmarried and the widows I say: It is good for them to stay
7:8 [g]ver 1,26 unmarried, as I am.[g] 9But if they cannot
control themselves, they should marry,[h]
7:9 [h]1Ti 5:14 for it is better to marry than to burn
with passion.
10To the married I give this command (not I, but the Lord): A wife must
7:10 [i]Mal 2:14-16; Mt 5:32; 19:3-9; Mk 10:11; Lk 16:18 not separate from her husband.[i] 11But
if she does, she must remain unmarried
or else be reconciled to her husband.
And a husband must not divorce his
wife.
12To the rest I say this (I, not the
7:12 [j]ver 6,10; 2Co 11:17 Lord):[j] If any brother has a wife who
is not a believer and she is willing to
live with him, he must not divorce
her. 13And if a woman has a husband
who is not a believer and he is willing
to live with her, she must not divorce
him. 14For the unbelieving husband has
been sanctified through his wife, and
the unbelieving wife has been sanctified
through her believing husband. Otherwise your children would be unclean,
7:14 [k]Mal 2:15 but as it is, they are holy.[k]
15But if the unbeliever leaves, let him
7:15 [l]Ro 14:19; 1Co 14:33 do so. A believing man or woman is
not bound in such circumstances; God
has called us to live in peace.[l] 16How
7:16 [m]Ro 11:14 [n]1Pe 3:1 do you know, wife, whether you will
save[m] your husband?[n] Or, how do you
know, husband, whether you will save
your wife?
17Nevertheless, each one should retain the place in life that the Lord assigned to him and to which God has
called him.[o] This is the rule I lay down 7:17 [o]Ro 12:3 [p]1Co 4:17; 14:33; 2Co 8:18; 11:28
in all the churches.[p] 18Was a man al-
ready circumcised when he was called?
He should not become uncircumcised.
Was a man uncircumcised when he was
called? He should not be circumcised.[q] 7:18 [q]Ac 15:1,2
19Circumcision is nothing and uncir-
cumcision is nothing.[r] Keeping God's 7:19 [r]Ro 2:25-27; Gal 5:6; 6:15; Col 3:11
commands is what counts. 20Each one
should remain in the situation which he
was in when God called him.[s] 21Were 7:20 [s]ver 24
you a slave when you were called? Don't
let it trouble you—although if you can
gain your freedom, do so. 22For he
who was a slave when he was called
by the Lord is the Lord's freedman;[t] 7:22 [t]Jn 8:32,36; Phm 16 [u]Eph 6:6
similarly, he who was a free man when
he was called is Christ's slave.[u] 23You
were bought at a price;[v] do not become 7:23 [v]1Co 6:20
slaves of men. 24Brothers, each man, as
responsible to God, should remain in
the situation God called him to.[w] 7:24 [w]ver 20
25Now about virgins: I have no com-
mand from the Lord,[x] but I give a judg- 7:25 [x]ver 6; 2Co 8:8 [y]2Co 4:1; 1Ti 1:13,16
ment as one who by the Lord's mercy[y]
is trustworthy. 26Because of the present
crisis, I think that it is good for you to
remain as you are.[z] 27Are you married? 7:26 [z]ver 1,8
Do not seek a divorce. Are you unmar-
ried? Do not look for a wife. 28But if
you do marry, you have not sinned; and
if a virgin marries, she has not sinned.
But those who marry will face many
troubles in this life, and I want to spare
you this.
29What I mean, brothers, is that the
time is short.[a] From now on those who 7:29 [a]ver 31; Ro 13:11,12
have wives should live as if they had
none; 30those who mourn, as if they
did not; those who are happy, as if they
were not; those who buy something, as
if it were not theirs to keep; 31those
who use the things of the world, as if
not engrossed in them. For this world
in its present form is passing away.[b] 7:31 [b]1Jn 2:17
32I would like you to be free from
concern. An unmarried man is con-
cerned about the Lord's affairs[c]—how 7:32 [c]1Ti 5:5
he can please the Lord. 33But a mar-
ried man is concerned about the affairs

[a]*1* Or "*It is good for a man not to have sexual relations with a woman.*"

of this world—how he can please his
wife— 34and his interests are divided.
An unmarried woman or virgin is concerned about the Lord's affairs: Her aim
is to be devoted to the Lord in both
body and spirit.[d] But a married wom- 7:34
an is concerned about the affairs of this [d]Lk 2:37
world—how she can please her hus-
band. 35I am saying this for your own
good, not to restrict you, but that you
may live in a right way in undivided[e] 7:35
devotion to the Lord. [e]Ps 86:11
36If anyone thinks he is acting im-
properly toward the virgin he is engaged to, and if she is getting along in
years and he feels he ought to marry, he
should do as he wants. He is not sinning.[f] They should get married. 37But 7:36
the man who has settled the matter in [f]ver 28
his own mind, who is under no compulsion but has control over his own
will, and who has made up his mind not
to marry the virgin—this man also does
the right thing. 38So then, he who marries the virgin does right,[g] but he who 7:38
does not marry her does even better.[a] [g]Heb 13:4
39A woman is bound to her husband
as long as he lives.[h] But if her husband 7:39
dies, she is free to marry anyone she [h]Ro 7:2,3
wishes, but he must belong to the Lord.[i] [i]2Co 6:14
40In my judgment,[j] she is happier if she 7:40
stays as she is—and I think that I too [j]ver 25
have the Spirit of God.

Food Sacrificed to Idols

8 Now about food sacrificed to idols:[k] 8:1
We know that we all possess knowl- [k]Ac 15:20
edge.[b] [l] Knowledge puffs up, but love [l]Ro 15:14
builds up. 2The man who thinks he 8:2
knows something[m] does not yet know [m]1Co 3:18 [n]1Co 13:8,9,12; 1Ti 6:4
as he ought to know.[n] 3But the man 8:3
who loves God is known by God.[o] [o]Ro 8:29; Gal 4:9
4So then, about eating food sacrificed 8:4
to idols:[p] We know that an idol is noth- [p]ver 1,7,10
ing at all in the world[q] and that there [q]1Co 10:19
is no God but one.[r] 5For even if there [r]Dt 6:4; Eph 4:6
are so-called gods,[s] whether in heaven 8:5
or on earth (as indeed there are many [s]2Th 2:4
"gods" and many "lords"), 6yet for us 8:6
there is but one God, the Father,[t] from [t]Mal 2:10

[a]*36-38* Or *36If anyone thinks he is not treating his daughter properly, and if she is getting along in years, and he feels she ought to marry, he should do as he wants. He is not sinning. He should let her get married. 37But the man who has settled the matter in his own mind, who is under no compulsion but has control over his own will, and who has made up his mind to keep the virgin unmarried—this man also does the right thing. 38So then, he who gives his virgin in marriage does right, but he who does not give her in marriage does even better.*
[b]*1* Or *"We all possess knowledge," as you say*

DAY 4 FOUR

Self-Control and My Service to Others

1 Corinthians 8:9–13

Our liberty is immense in Christ. Yet we are to rein in the wide latitudes of our choices. We must be free in Christ to select all that he permits us. If Jesus approves any appetite for our enjoyment, it is ours to enjoy—with one exception. There may be something that Jesus approves for us, but if someone else saw us doing it, they might accuse us of being superficial or worldly. Then for the sake of those whom our liberty might injure, Christ asks us to desist from that activity.

How are we to think of activities which are permitted by Christ and yet a possible stumbling block to a weaker individual? For years after I began pastoring my first church, I refused to go to a restaurant on Sunday. While other church members regularly ate out after worship services, our family did not. It was not that our family considered it to be wrong, but there were a few in our congregation who considered it to be ungodly. So to avoid wounding their weak consciences, we ate at home. During those years I had to learn to balance between what was sometimes just griping Christians and those who truly had convictions about eating out on Sunday. Needless to say, it was a great relief to all when even the grudging Christians began going to the cafeteria on the Lord's day. All too soon, it was these same Christians who began complaining that my sermons were so long they that allowed the Methodists to beat the Baptists to the cafeteria.

Still, Paul establishes the principle in 1 Corinthians 8:12, "When you sin against your brothers in this way and wound their weak conscience, you sin against Christ." So when you cannot tell whether you're offending a sincere, weaker brother or just a griper, it is more Christlike to live your life so as not to sin against anyone else's conscience.

To begin a study on the topic of Self-Control, the Mark of Obedience, turn to the home page on page 1011.

8:6 [u]Ro 11:36 [v]Eph 4:5 [w]Jn 1:3 whom all things came[u] and for whom
we live; and there is but one Lord,[v]
Jesus Christ, through whom all things
came[w] and through whom we live.
7But not everyone knows this. Some
people are still so accustomed to idols
that when they eat such food they think
of it as having been sacrificed to an idol,
and since their conscience is weak,[x] it
8:7 [x]Ro 14:14; 1Co 10:28 is defiled. 8But food does not bring us
near to God;[y] we are no worse if we do
8:8 [y]Ro 14:17 not eat, and no better if we do.
9Be careful, however, that the exercise of your freedom does not become
8:9 [z]Gal 5:13 [a]Ro 14:1 a stumbling block[z] to the weak.[a] 10For
if anyone with a weak conscience sees
you who have this knowledge eating
in an idol's temple, won't he be em-
boldened to eat what has been sacrificed to idols? 11So this weak brother,
8:11 [b]Ro 14:15,20 for whom Christ died, is destroyed[b]
by your knowledge. 12When you sin
8:12 [c]Mt 18:6 against your brothers[c] in this way and
wound their weak conscience, you sin
against Christ. 13Therefore, if what I
eat causes my brother to fall into sin, I
will never eat meat again, so that I will
8:13 [d]Ro 14:21 not cause him to fall.[d]

The Rights of an Apostle

9:1 [e]2Co 12:12 [f]1Co 15:8 [g]1Co 3:6; 4:15 9 Am I not free? Am I not an apostle?[e]
Have I not seen Jesus our Lord?[f]
Are you not the result of my work in
the Lord?[g] 2Even though I may not be
an apostle to others, surely I am to you!
9:2 [h]2Co 3:2,3 For you are the seal[h] of my apostleship
in the Lord.

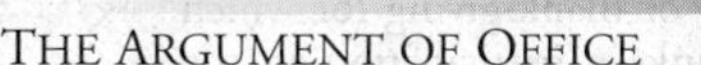

GENTLENESS

THE ARGUMENT OF OFFICE

1 Corinthians 9:1

The apostle Paul did not believe that low self-esteem and humility were the same thing. Low self-esteem is in a sense a kind of mental illness. Humility is understanding who you are in terms of the greatness of Christ. It is no sin to think well of yourself. It is a sin to *need* to think well of yourself.

3This is my defense to those who sit
in judgment on me. 4Don't we have
9:4 [i]1Th 2:6 the right to food and drink?[i] 5Don't we
have the right to take a believing wife[j]
9:5 [j]1Co 7:7,8 [k]Mt 12:46 along with us, as do the other apostles
and the Lord's brothers[k] and Cephas[a]?

6Or is it only I and Barnabas[l] who must 9:6 [l]Ac 4:36
work for a living?
7Who serves as a soldier at his own
expense? Who plants a vineyard[m] and 9:7 [m]Dt 20:6; Pr 27:18
does not eat of its grapes? Who tends a
flock and does not drink of the milk?
8Do I say this merely from a human
point of view? Doesn't the Law say the
same thing? 9For it is written in the
Law of Moses: "Do not muzzle an ox
while it is treading out the grain."[b][n] Is 9:9 [n]Dt 25:4; 1Ti 5:18 [o]Dt 22:1-4
it about oxen that God is concerned?[o]
10Surely he says this for us, doesn't
he? Yes, this was written for us,[p] be- 9:10 [p]Ro 4:23,24 [q]2Ti 2:6
cause when the plowman plows and the
thresher threshes, they ought to do so
in the hope of sharing in the harvest.[q]
11If we have sown spiritual seed among
you, is it too much if we reap a material
harvest from you?[r] 12If others have this 9:11 [r]Ro 15:27
right of support from you, shouldn't we
have it all the more?
But we did not use this right.[s] On 9:12 [s]Ac 18:3 [t]2Co 11:7-12
the contrary, we put up with anything
rather than hinder[t] the gospel of Christ.
13Don't you know that those who work
in the temple get their food from the
temple, and those who serve at the altar
share in what is offered on the altar?[u] 9:13 [u]Lev 6:16,26; Dt 18:1
14In the same way, the Lord has com-
manded that those who preach the gos- 9:14 [v]Mt 10:10; 1Ti 5:18
pel should receive their living from the
gospel.[v]

SELF-CONTROL

THE "WOE POINT"

1 Corinthians 9:16

Your "woe point" must be determined if you are to define clearly what God has set out for you to do. How do you find your "woe point"? Say "Woe to me if I do not ________" (finish in 25 words or less). What came to your mind? Isolate your "woe point" and you will name that compulsion whose fulfillment in your life will bring pleasure to God.

15But I have not used any of these 9:15 [w]Ac 18:3 [x]2Co 11:9,10
rights.[w] And I am not writing this in
the hope that you will do such things
for me. I would rather die than have
anyone deprive me of this boast.[x] 16Yet
when I preach the gospel, I cannot
boast, for I am compelled to preach.[y] 9:16 [y]Ro 1:14; Ac 9:15
Woe to me if I do not preach the

[a]5 That is, Peter [b]9 Deut. 25:4

gospel! 17If I preach voluntarily, I have
9:17 a reward;[z] if not voluntarily, I am sim-
[z]1Co 3:8,14 ply discharging the trust committed to
[a]Gal 2:7; Col 1:25 me.[a] 18What then is my reward? Just
this: that in preaching the gospel I may
9:18 offer it free of charge,[b] and so not make
[b]2Co 11:7; 12:13 use of my rights in preaching it.
9:19 19Though I am free[c] and belong to no
[c]ver 1 [d]Gal 5:13 man, I make myself a slave to everyone,[d]
[e]Mt 18:15; 1Pe 3:1 to win as many as possible.[e] 20To the
Jews I became like a Jew, to win the
9:20 Jews.[f] To those under the law I became
[f]Ac 16:3; 21:20-26; like one under the law (though I my-
Ro 11:14 self am not under the law), so as to
win those under the law. 21To those not
9:21 [g]Ro 2:12,14 having the law[g] I became like one not
having the law (though I am not free
from God's law but am under Christ's
law), so as to win those not having the
law. 22To the weak I became weak, to
win the weak. I have become all things
9:22 to all men[h] so that by all possible means
[h]1Co 10:33 [i]Ro 11:14 I might save some.[i] 23I do all this for
the sake of the gospel, that I may share
in its blessings.

GOODNESS

All Things to All People for the One Christ

1 Corinthians 9:22

Do you have some friend you would like to love to Christ? Before that friend will want to be like Christ, he or she will likely want to be like you. We rarely make converts by "selling" Jesus. What we "sell" is Jesus packaged in our lives.

24Do you not know that in a race all
the runners run, but only one gets the
9:24 prize? Run[j] in such a way as to get the
[j]Gal 2:2; 2Ti 4:7; prize. 25Everyone who competes in the
Heb 12:1 games goes into strict training. They do
it to get a crown that will not last; but
we do it to get a crown that will last
9:25 [k]Jas 1:12; forever.[k] 26Therefore I do not run like
Rev 2:10 a man running aimlessly; I do not fight
like a man beating the air. 27No, I beat
9:27 my body[l] and make it my slave so that
[l]Ro 8:13 after I have preached to others, I myself
will not be disqualified for the prize.

Warnings From Israel's History

10 For I do not want you to be
ignorant of the fact, brothers,
10:1 that our forefathers were all under the
[m]Ex 13:21 cloud[m] and that they all passed through
the sea.[n] 2They were all baptized into 10:1 [n]Ex 14:22,29
Moses in the cloud and in the sea.
3They all ate the same spiritual food
4and drank the same spiritual drink; 10:4
for they drank from the spiritual rock[o] [o]Ex 17:6;
that accompanied them, and that rock Nu 20:11;
was Christ. 5Nevertheless, God was not Ps 78:15
pleased with most of them; their bodies
were scattered over the desert.[p] 10:5
6Now these things occurred as exam- [p]Nu 14:29;
ples[a] to keep us from setting our hearts Heb 3:17
on evil things as they did. 7Do not be
idolaters,[q] as some of them were; as it 10:7 [q]ver 14
is written: "The people sat down to eat [r]Ex 32:4,6,19
and drink and got up to indulge in pa-
gan revelry."[b][r] 8We should not commit sexual immorality, as some of them
did—and in one day twenty-three thou- 10:8
sand of them died.[s] 9We should not test [s]Nu 25:1-9
the Lord, as some of them did—and
were killed by snakes.[t] 10And do not 10:9
grumble, as some of them did[u]—and [t]Nu 21:5,6
were killed[v] by the destroying angel.[w] 10:10 [u]Nu 16:41
11These things happened to them as [v]Nu 16:49
examples and were written down as [w]Ex 12:23
warnings for us, on whom the fulfill- 10:11
ment of the ages has come.[x] 12So, if you [x]Ro 13:11
think you are standing firm,[y] be careful 10:12
that you don't fall! 13No temptation has [y]Ro 11:20
seized you except what is common to
man. And God is faithful;[z] he will not 10:13
let you be tempted beyond what you [z]1Co 1:9
can bear.[a] But when you are tempted, [a]2Pe 2:9
he will also provide a way out so that
you can stand up under it.

Idol Feasts and the Lord's Supper

14Therefore, my dear friends, flee
from idolatry. 15I speak to sensible people; judge for yourselves what I say. 16Is
not the cup of thanksgiving for which
we give thanks a participation in the
blood of Christ? And is not the bread
that we break a participation in the
body of Christ?[b] 17Because there is one 10:16 [b]Mt 26:26-28
loaf, we, who are many, are one body,[c]
for we all partake of the one loaf. 10:17 [c]Ro 12:5;
18Consider the people of Israel: Do 1Co 12:27
not those who eat the sacrifices[d] partici- 10:18
pate in the altar? 19Do I mean then that [d]Lev
a sacrifice offered to an idol is anything, 7:6,14,15
or that an idol is anything?[e] 20No, but 10:19
the sacrifices of pagans are offered to [e]1Co 8:4
demons,[f] not to God, and I do not 10:20
want you to be participants with de- [f]Dt 32:17; Ps 106:37;
mons. 21You cannot drink the cup of Rev 9:20

[a]6 Or *types*; also in verse 11 [b]7 Exodus 32:6

WEEK 45 SELF-CONTROL

1 DAY ONE

SELF-CONTROL, THE DISCIPLINED LIFE

Read 1 Corinthians 9:24–27

Bring me my bow of purest gold—
Bring me my arrows of desire—
Bring me my harp oh clouds unfold—
Bring me my chariots of fire.

These are the words of William Blake, and this image from the movie *Chariots of Fire* remains a striking symbol of discipline. The movie portrays athletes charging down the cinder lanes, legs driving like pistons, arms pumping like jackhammers, lungs gasping for oxygen, hoping for enough strength to finish the race. The athletes are able to compete only because they have practiced and trained for the race.

Discipline is a synonym for self-control. Paul reminds the Corinthians that they are to run and to run and to run. "Run," says the apostle, "in such a way as to get the prize." But this is more than a mere athletic contest. Athletes are in the business of gold medals. What a narrow goal of life! An athlete's effective years of competition are seldom more than ten. If he or she has not won the medal by that time, others who are just emerging from adolescence will be banging at the doors of success, ready to claim their prizes.

But I believe Paul noticed as he got older that certain areas of Christian discipline became harder for him. He testified that he had to beat his body to contain and keep up the rigors of Christian discipline. What can he mean when he refers to beating his body? Just this: As we get older, we find that the old bones are heavier with past achievements. The old muscles are weaker from years of service.

Francis of Assisi had a way of personalizing God's creation by calling things "brother" this or "sister" that. He called his body "brother donkey." A donkey is a balky animal that has to be convinced from time to time that he must move. A strong smack is sometimes necessary to convince a donkey to move. He will, otherwise, lock his legs, plant his hooves in the sand and refuse to budge.

So Paul asserted that he intended to be self-controlled, disciplined—lest after he had preached to others he himself should be disqualified.

MEMORIZE THIS WEEK

EPHESIANS 4:1

As a prisoner for the Lord, then, I urge you to live a life worthy of the calling you have received.

2 DAY TWO

SELF-CONTROL AND THE PURPOSE OF GOD IN MY LIFE

Proverbs 1:2–3 states that the proverbs were written, in part, to enable those who honored them to live a disciplined life. But self-control alone is never God's purpose for our lives. Simply to be disciplined for discipline's sake is no great reason to live. But to discipline our lives to allow us to become effective ministers to others is the enabling power of ministry. *Turn to Proverbs 1:1–6, page 733, for today's study.*

3 DAY THREE

SELF-CONTROL AND MY RELATIONSHIP WITH CHRIST

Time is the one commodity we all could use more of. We cannot hold on to life forever. Every heartbeat brings us closer to some finale. Jesus is coming, a reality which ought to make us more disciplined, more serious about the issue of productive living. *Turn to 1 Peter 4:7, page 1494, for today's study.*

4 DAY FOUR

SELF-CONTROL AND MY SERVICE TO OTHERS

A great gift was given to Timothy at the laying on of hands. This gift was so special that it could only have come from God. Still, it was a gift in the rough. It was an unplowed field. It could be rendered useful only if Timothy worked to improve the gift, determined never to neglect the gift that lived inside him. *Turn to 1 Timothy 4:13–16, page 1440, for today's study.*

5 DAY FIVE

SELF-CONTROL AND ITS PLACE IN MY PERSONAL WORSHIP

In some of the apostle Paul's earliest writing, he seems to be expressing the belief that he will be alive for Christ's second coming. But in 2 Timothy, Paul's last book, he seems to be thinking of death instead of the second coming. He is ready to be offered, and he now realizes that a crown is the final reward of self-control. The disciplined life always ends in victory. *Turn to 2 Timothy 4:6–8, page 1449, for today's study.*

Week 46, Love, Permeating All We Do, begins on page 1372, 1 Corinthians 13:1–13.
To begin a topical study on the Fruit of the Spirit, Self-Control, turn to the Topical Index, page 1548.

the Lord and the cup of demons too;
you cannot have a part in both the
Lord's table and the table of demons.[g]

10:21 [g]2Co 6:15,16

DAY 4 FOUR

▸ GOODNESS AND MY SERVICE TO OTHERS

1 Corinthians 10:23—11:1

Paul argues here for issues of right and wrong. The simple thing that Paul is trying to say is that goodness always seeks to maintain a balance between conviction and compassion. While we need to strive for holiness, at the same time we need to be certain that our desire to help others remains unimpeded by our beliefs. Paul was convinced that meat that had been sacrificed to the Roman gods and later sold in the market was acceptable to eat.

But there were others who felt that meat offered to Zeus should never be eaten by Christians. So Paul's advice to those who felt as he did was that they should go ahead and eat the meat, for it was perfectly good. But he warned the Corinthians not to press the rightness of their position to the point it compromised their compassion.

In other words if we come to the place where we are torn between conviction and compassion and must take one course or the other, it is better to emphasize compassion.

An evangelist found himself trying to win a scantily dressed woman to Christ. "Sister, if you'll put on some clothes, I'd like to tell you about Jesus." He was surprised when she slammed the door in his face. He should not have been. His intentions may have been right, but they were hidden by his lack of sensitivity.

One of the early Christian "desert fathers" left his hermitage and went into town to reclaim his niece who had become a prostitute. He did not agree that a man of God should frequent brothels, but he abandoned his convictions and entered. There he confronted his niece and reclaimed her for God.

Remember that Jesus was accused of fraternizing with sinners, and so he did. He did not admire their lifestyles, but he felt their need. With such goodness, we build a bridge to others.

To begin a study on the topic of Goodness and the Desire for Holiness, turn to the home page on page 790.

22Are we trying to arouse the Lord's
jealousy?[h] Are we stronger than he?[i]

10:22 [h]Dt 32:16,21 [i]Ecc 6:10; Isa 45:9

The Believer's Freedom

23"Everything is permissible"—but
not everything is beneficial.[j] "Everything is permissible"—but not everything is constructive. 24Nobody should
seek his own good, but the good of
others.[k]
25Eat anything sold in the meat
market without raising questions of
conscience,[l] 26for, "The earth is the
Lord's, and everything in it."[a][m]
27If some unbeliever invites you to
a meal and you want to go, eat whatever is put before you[n] without raising
questions of conscience. 28But if anyone says to you, "This has been offered
in sacrifice," then do not eat it, both
for the sake of the man who told you
and for conscience' sake[b][o]— 29the other
man's conscience, I mean, not yours.
For why should my freedom[p] be judged
by another's conscience? 30If I take part
in the meal with thankfulness, why am
I denounced because of something I
thank God for?[q]

10:23 [j]1Co 6:12
10:24 [k]ver 33; Ro 15:1,2; 1Co 13:5; Php 2:4,21
10:25 [l]Ac 10:15; 1Co 8:7
10:26 [m]Ps 24:1
10:27 [n]Lk 10:7
10:28 [o]1Co 8:7,10-12
10:29 [p]Ro 14:16; 1Co 9:1,19
10:30 [q]Ro 14:6

▸ SELF-CONTROL

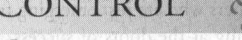

SANCTIFYING LIFE

1 Corinthians 10:31

Do you do something, eat something or drink something that does not honor Christ? Do you love him? Then stop doing it; stop eating it; stop drinking it!

31So whether you eat or drink or
whatever you do, do it all for the glory
of God.[r] 32Do not cause anyone to
stumble,[s] whether Jews, Greeks or the
church of God[t]— 33even as I try to
please everybody in every way.[u] For
I am not seeking my own good but
the good of many, so that they may
11 be saved.[v] 1Follow my example,
as I follow the example[w] of
Christ.

10:31 [r]Col 3:17; 1Pe 4:11
10:32 [s]Ac 24:16 [t]Ac 20:28
10:33 [u]Ro 15:2; 1Co 9:22 [v]Ro 11:14
11:1 [w]1Co 4:16

Propriety in Worship

2I praise you[x] for remembering me
in everything[y] and for holding to the

11:2 [x]ver 17,22 [y]1Co 4:17

[a]26 Psalm 24:1 [b]28 Some manuscripts *conscience' sake, for "the earth is the Lord's and everything in it"*

11:2 [z]1Co 15:2,3; 2Th 2:15

teachings,[a] just as I passed them on to you.[z]

11:3 [a]Eph 1:22 [b]Ge 3:16; Eph 5:23 [c]1Co 3:23

3 Now I want you to realize that the head of every man is Christ,[a] and the head of the woman is man,[b] and the head of Christ is God.[c] 4 Every man who prays or prophesies with his head covered dishonors his head. 5 And every woman who prays or prophesies[d] with her head uncovered dishonors her head—it is just as though her head were shaved.[e] 6 If a woman does not cover her head, she should have her hair cut off; and if it is a disgrace for a woman to have her hair cut or shaved off, she should cover her head. 7 A man ought not to cover his head,[b] since he is the image[f] and glory of God; but the woman is the glory of man. 8 For man did not come from woman, but woman from man;[g] 9 neither was man created for woman, but woman for man.[h] 10 For this reason, and because of the angels, the woman ought to have a sign of authority on her head.

11:5 [d]Ac 21:9 [e]Dt 21:12

11:7 [f]Ge 1:26; Jas 3:9

11:8 [g]Ge 2:21-23; 1Ti 2:13

11:9 [h]Ge 2:18

11 In the Lord, however, woman is not independent of man, nor is man independent of woman. 12 For as woman came from man, so also man is born of woman. But everything comes from God.[i] 13 Judge for yourselves: Is it proper for a woman to pray to God with her head uncovered? 14 Does not the very nature of things teach you that if a man has long hair, it is a disgrace to him, 15 but that if a woman has long hair, it is her glory? For long hair is given to her as a covering. 16 If anyone wants to be contentious about this, we have no other practice—nor do the churches of God.[j]

11:12 [i]Ro 11:36

11:16 [j]1Co 7:17

The Lord's Supper

17 In the following directives I have no praise for you,[k] for your meetings do more harm than good. 18 In the first place, I hear that when you come together as a church, there are divisions[l] among you, and to some extent I believe it. 19 No doubt there have to be differences among you to show which of you have God's approval.[m] 20 When you come together, it is not the Lord's Supper you eat, 21 for as you eat, each of you goes ahead without waiting for anybody else.[n] One remains hungry, anoth-

11:17 [k]ver 2,22

11:18 [l]1Co 1:10-12; 3:3

11:19 [m]1Jn 2:19

11:21 [n]2Pe 2:13; Jude 12

[a]2 Or *traditions* [b]4-7 Or *4Every man who prays or prophesies with long hair dishonors his head. 5And every woman who prays or prophesies with no covering ⌞of hair⌟ on her head dishonors her head—she is just like one of the "shorn women." 6If a woman has no covering, let her be for now with short hair, but since it is a disgrace for a woman to have her hair shorn or shaved, she should grow it again. 7A man ought not to have long hair*

DAY 2 TWO

▸ SELF-CONTROL AND THE PURPOSE OF GOD IN MY LIFE

1 Corinthians 10:31

Whatever we do—eating or drinking—let us do all for the glory of God. This simple statement is the most positive of all guides to self-control. We often try to learn self-control by making a big list of do's and don'ts and then make ourselves miserable trying to become great believers by all the things we deny ourselves. This is not to play down self-denial, but it is better to focus on what we can enjoy in Christ rather than focusing on the things we are trying to avoid.

What is the purpose of God in your life? Well, as simply as it can be put, it is to glorify God. How do you glorify him—by posting a list of no-no's and trying to be good by your negations? Never! You merely ask yourself at every juncture of life whether what you are about to do does indeed glorify God. If not, don't do it. Again, the rule is simple: Whatever you do, do it all for the glory of God.

But will it work? Let's take something as practical as dieting. Aren't many of us trying to let the thinner us, trapped within the thicker us, get out? My friend was 50 pounds overweight all his life. He had tried liquid diets, solid diets, lettuce diets, banana and spinach diets. He stayed 50 pounds overweight, resolving after every Saturday night pizza party that next week he'd really lose weight. What delivered him was that he wrote out 1 Corinthians 10:31 on a little white card. Then before every meal he took the card out and set it by his plate. Self-control was his. Gluttony was gone. He discovered that 1 Corinthians 10:31 worked so well that he didn't have to wait for heaven to get a little closer to having his glorified body. Self-control provided the key to his victory.

To begin a study on the topic of Self-Control, the Mark of Obedience, turn to the home page on page 1011.

er gets drunk. 22Don't you have homes
to eat and drink in? Or do you despise
11:22 [o]1Co 10:32 the church of God[o] and humiliate those
[p]Jas 2:6 who have nothing?[p] What shall I say to
[q]ver 2,17 you? Shall I praise you[q] for this? Certainly not!
11:23 23For I received from the Lord[r] what
[r]Gal 1:12 I also passed on to you:[s] The Lord Je-
[s]1Co 15:3 sus, on the night he was betrayed, took
bread, 24and when he had given thanks,
he broke it and said, "This is my body,
which is for you; do this in remembrance of me." 25In the same way, after
supper he took the cup, saying, "This
11:25 [t]Lk 22:20 cup is the new covenant[t] in my blood;[u]
[u]1Co 10:16 do this, whenever you drink it, in remembrance of me." 26For whenever
you eat this bread and drink this cup,
you proclaim the Lord's death until he
comes.

PATIENCE

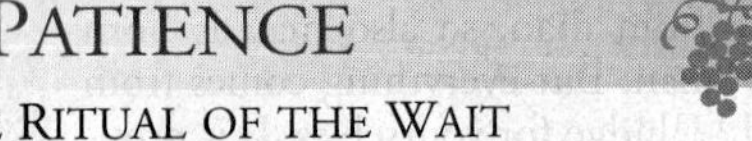

THE RITUAL OF THE WAIT

1 Corinthians 11:26

All Christians live in anticipation of the second coming. What shall we do till he comes? We shall break the bread and drink the wine and remember that he who will come the second time bought us by bleeding when he came the first time.

27Therefore, whoever eats the bread
or drinks the cup of the Lord in an unworthy manner will be guilty of sinning against the body and blood of the
11:27 [v]Heb 10:29 Lord.[v] 28A man ought to examine him-
11:28 self[w] before he eats of the bread and
[w]2Co 13:5 drinks of the cup. 29For anyone who
eats and drinks without recognizing the
body of the Lord eats and drinks judgment on himself. 30That is why many
among you are weak and sick, and a
number of you have fallen asleep. 31But
11:31 if we judged ourselves, we would not
[x]Ps 32:5; 1Jn 1:9 come under judgment.[x] 32When we are
judged by the Lord, we are being dis-
11:32 [y]Ps 94:12; ciplined[y] so that we will not be con-
Heb 12:7-10; Rev 3:19 demned with the world.
33So then, my brothers, when you
11:34 come together to eat, wait for each
[z]ver 21 other. 34If anyone is hungry,[z] he should
[a]ver 22 eat at home,[a] so that when you meet
[b]1Co 4:19 together it may not result in judgment.
And when I come[b] I will give further
directions.

Spiritual Gifts

12 Now about spiritual gifts,[c] 12:1
brothers, I do not want you to [c]Ro 1:11; 1Co 14:1,37
be ignorant. 2You know that when you
were pagans,[d] somehow or other you 12:2 [d]Eph 2:11,12;
were influenced and led astray to mute 1Pe 4:3
idols.[e] 3Therefore I tell you that no one [e]Ps 115:5; Jer 10:5;
who is speaking by the Spirit of God Hab 2:18,19;
says, "Jesus be cursed,"[f] and no one can 1Th 1:9
say, "Jesus is Lord,"[g] except by the Holy 12:3 [f]Ro 9:3
Spirit.[h] [g]Jn 13:13 [h]1Jn 4:2,3
4There are different kinds of gifts,
but the same Spirit.[i] 5There are differ- 12:4 [i]Ro 12:4-8;
ent kinds of service, but the same Lord. Eph 4:11; Heb 2:4
6There are different kinds of working,
but the same God[j] works all of them in 12:6
all men. [j]Eph 4:6
7Now to each one the manifestation
of the Spirit is given for the common
good.[k] 8To one there is given through 12:7 [k]Eph 4:12
the Spirit the message of wisdom,[l] to
another the message of knowledge[m] by 12:8 [l]1Co 2:6
means of the same Spirit, 9to another [m]2Co 8:7
faith[n] by the same Spirit, to another 12:9 [n]Mt 17:19,20;
gifts of healing[o] by that one Spirit, 10to 2Co 4:13
another miraculous powers,[p] to anoth- [o]ver 28,30
er prophecy, to another distinguishing 12:10
between spirits,[q] to another speaking in [p]Gal 3:5 [q]1Jn 4:1
different kinds of tongues,[a][r] and to still [r]Mk 16:17
another the interpretation of tongues.[a]
11All these are the work of one and the 12:11
same Spirit,[s] and he gives them to each [s]ver 4
one, just as he determines.

One Body, Many Parts

12The body is a unit, though it is
made up of many parts; and though all
its parts are many, they form one body.[t] 12:12
So it is with Christ.[u] 13For we were [t]Ro 12:5 [u]ver 27
all baptized by[b] one Spirit[v] into one 12:13
body—whether Jews or Greeks, slave or [v]Eph 2:18
free[w]—and we were all given the one [w]Gal 3:28; Col 3:11
Spirit to drink.[x] [x]Jn 7:37-39
14Now the body is not made up of
one part but of many. 15If the foot
should say, "Because I am not a hand,
I do not belong to the body," it would
not for that reason cease to be part of
the body. 16And if the ear should say,
"Because I am not an eye, I do not
belong to the body," it would not for
that reason cease to be part of the body.
17If the whole body were an eye, where
would the sense of hearing be? If the
whole body were an ear, where would

[a]*10* Or *languages;* also in verse 28 [b]*13* Or *with;* or *in*

the sense of smell be? 18But in fact God
12:18 [y]ver 28 has arranged[y] the parts in the body,
[z]ver 11 every one of them, just as he wanted
them to be.[z] 19If they were all one part,
12:20 where would the body be? 20As it is,
[a]ver 12,14 there are many parts, but one body.[a]
21The eye cannot say to the hand,
"I don't need you!" And the head cannot say to the feet, "I don't need you!"
22On the contrary, those parts of the
body that seem to be weaker are indispensable, 23and the parts that we think
are less honorable we treat with special
honor. And the parts that are unpre-
sentable are treated with special modesty, 24while our presentable parts need
no special treatment. But God has combined the members of the body and has
given greater honor to the parts that
lacked it, 25so that there should be no
division in the body, but that its parts
should have equal concern for each other. 26If one part suffers, every part suffers with it; if one part is honored, every
12:27 part rejoices with it.
[b]Eph 1:23; 27Now you are the body of Christ,[b]
4:12; and each one of you is a part of it.[c]
Col 1:18,24 28And in the church[d] God has appoint-
[c]Ro 12:5 ed first of all apostles,[e] second prophets,
12:28 [d]1Co 10:32 third teachers, then workers of miracles,
[e]Eph 4:11 also those having gifts of healing,[f] those
[f]ver 9 [g]Ro 12:6-8 able to help others, those with gifts
[h]ver 10 of administration,[g] and those speaking
in different kinds of tongues.[h] 29Are
all apostles? Are all prophets? Are all
teachers? Do all work miracles? 30Do all
have gifts of healing? Do all speak in
12:30 [i]ver 10 tongues[a]?[i] Do all interpret? 31But ea-
12:31 gerly desire[b][j] the greater gifts.
[j]1Co 14:1,39

Love

And now I will show you the most
excellent way.

13:1 [k]ver 8 13 If I speak in the tongues[c][k] of
men and of angels, but have not
love, I am only a resounding gong or
a clanging cymbal. 2If I have the gift
of prophecy and can fathom all myster-
13:2 [l]1Co 14:2 ies[l] and all knowledge, and if I have a
[m]1Co 12:9 [n]Mt 17:20; faith[m] that can move mountains,[n] but
21:21 have not love, I am nothing. 3If I give
13:3 [o]Mt 6:2 all I possess to the poor[o] and surrender
[p]Da 3:28 my body to the flames,[d][p] but have not
love, I gain nothing.
13:4 [q]1Th 5:14 4Love is patient,[q] love is kind. It does
not envy, it does not boast, it is not
13:5 proud. 5It is not rude, it is not self-
[r]1Co 10:24 seeking,[r] it is not easily angered, it keeps
no record of wrongs. 6Love does not de-
light in evil[s] but rejoices with the truth.[t] 13:6 [s]2Th 2:12
7It always protects, always trusts, always [t]2Jn 4;
hopes, always perseveres. 3Jn 3,4
8Love never fails. But where there are
prophecies,[u] they will cease; where there 13:8 [u]ver 2
are tongues,[v] they will be stilled; where [v]ver 1
there is knowledge, it will pass away.
9For we know in part[w] and we prophesy 13:9 [w]ver 12;
in part, 10but when perfection comes,[x] 1Co 8:2
the imperfect disappears. 11When I was 13:10
a child, I talked like a child, I thought [x]Php 3:12
like a child, I reasoned like a child.
When I became a man, I put childish
ways behind me. 12Now we see but a
poor reflection as in a mirror; then we 13:12
shall see face to face.[y] Now I know in [y]Ge 32:30; 2Co 5:7;
part; then I shall know fully, even as I 1Jn 3:2 [z]1Co 8:3
am fully known.[z]
13And now these three remain: faith, 13:13
hope and love.[a] But the greatest of these [a]Gal 5:5,6
is love.[b] [b]1Co 16:14

LOVE

THE SUPREME GIFT

1 Corinthians 13:13

Love is the simple gift that matters when other gifts become too showy, too pricey, too self-serving.

Love heals when other gifts injure.

Love listens when other gifts get gabby.

Love serves when other gifts are pushy.

Love has two wonderful friends: faith and hope. When all three are welcome in the heart, wisdom is resident.

Gifts of Prophecy and Tongues

14 Follow the way of love[c] and 14:1 [c]1Co 16:14
eagerly desire[d] spiritual gifts,[e] [d]ver 39;
especially the gift of prophecy. 2For 1Co 12:31 [e]1Co 12:1
anyone who speaks in a tongue[e][f] does 14:2
not speak to men but to God. Indeed, [f]Mk 16:17
no one understands him; he utters [g]1Co 13:2
mysteries[g] with his spirit.[f] 3But everyone who prophesies speaks to men
for their strengthening,[h] encouragement 14:3
and comfort. 4He who speaks in a [h]ver 4,5,12,17,26;
tongue[i] edifies himself, but he who Ro 14:19
prophesies[j] edifies the church. 5I would 14:4 [i]Mk 16:17
like every one of you to speak in [j]1Co 13:2

[a]*30* Or *other languages* [b]*31* Or *But you are eagerly desiring* [c]*1* Or *languages* [d]*3* Some early manuscripts *body that I may boast* [e]*2* Or *another language*; also in verses 4, 13, 14, 19, 26 and 27
[f]*2* Or *by the Spirit*

WEEK 46

LOVE

1 DAY ONE
LOVE, PERMEATING ALL WE DO

Read 1 Corinthians 13:1–13

Two of the greatest passages for the Christian's development are Galatians 5:22–24 and 1 Corinthians 13. What is so interesting about these two passages is that one is completely contained in the other. In uniting the fruit of the Spirit passage with the love chapter of the Bible, a flawless guide is obtained to the Christian's inner life. Consider the similar messages of these two wonderful passages.

Galatians 5:22–23	1 Corinthians 13:1–13
1. Love	Love will never cease giving; the greatest of these is love.
2. Joy	Love does not delight in evil but rejoices with the truth.
3. Peace	Love is not easily angered, it keeps no record of wrongs.
4. Patience	Love is patient; it always hopes.
5. Kindness	Love is kind; it does not envy.
6. Goodness	Love always protects, always trusts.
7. Faithfulness	Love never fails; it always perseveres.
8. Gentleness	Love does not boast; it is not proud.
9. Self-control	Love is not self-seeking; it is not rude.

Love is the first characteristic of the fruit of the Spirit. It is well placed at the head of the list, for it permeates all the rest of the attributes. Somehow, if we live a life of love, the other virtues will attend us all the days of our lives. Love is the key that unlocks the entire fruit basket of Galatians 5:22–23, as well as permeating 1 Corinthians 13.

2 DAY TWO
LOVE AND THE PURPOSE OF GOD IN MY LIFE

Remembering the scope of God's world and his love for those who exist beyond our own little world is a purpose of God. The familiar theme of the sojourn in Egypt is again mentioned in this passage. The treatment of foreigners in our midst bears the specific command to love. We are to love aliens because we remember those times when we were foreigners and needed love. Somehow when we remember our own needy times, it encourages us to reach out to those in need. *Turn to Leviticus 19:33–34, page 137, for today's study.*

3 DAY THREE
LOVE AND MY RELATIONSHIP WITH CHRIST

Because of God's great love for us, it pleased him to send his Son Jesus, in whom all the fullness of the Deity dwells in bodily form. He permitted this incarnation because he desired to end our alienation from himself. So Jesus came, fully God and fully man, to make one perfect sacrifice. When God became a man, human beings became more than human. God had destined them for the throne. *Turn to Colossians 1:19–23, page 1421, for today's study.*

4 DAY FOUR
LOVE AND MY SERVICE TO OTHERS

God was indeed in Christ reconciling the world unto himself. But the story gets even better: Christ has committed to us his reconciling office. Here Paul suggests that we are to go as far as we can in redeeming a lost world. How far should we go? Well, the sinless Son of God agreed to become the bearer of all sins so that when his dying was complete, reconciliation could reach its redeeming arms around the world. *Turn to 2 Corinthians 5:17–21, page 1382, for today's study.*

5 DAY FIVE
LOVE AND ITS PLACE IN MY PERSONAL WORSHIP

Foot washing is the service Jesus rendered on the night before he died. In doing this he showed us that nothing is beneath our dignity. Since that night when Christ displayed his servanthood, we have only to ask God, "What do you want done? Where is it to be done? When?" There are no further questions. We carry his basin. We have his towel around our waist. *Turn to John 13:1–17, page 1269, for today's study.*

MEMORIZE THIS WEEK

GALATIANS 4:4-5

But when the time had fully come, God sent his Son, born of a woman, born under law, to redeem those under law, that we might receive the full rights of sons.

Week 47, Joy, the Reveling of Angels, begins on page 700, Psalm 103:20–22.
To begin a topical study on the Fruit of the Spirit, Love, turn to the Topical Index, page 1548.

tongues,[a] but I would rather have you
14:5 [k]Nu 11:29
prophesy.[k] He who prophesies is greater
than one who speaks in tongues,[a] unless
he interprets, so that the church may be
edified.
6Now, brothers, if I come to you and
speak in tongues, what good will I be
to you, unless I bring you some revela-
14:6 [l]ver 26; Eph 1:17 [m]Ro 6:17
tion[l] or knowledge or prophecy or word
of instruction?[m] 7Even in the case of
lifeless things that make sounds, such
as the flute or harp, how will anyone
know what tune is being played unless
there is a distinction in the notes?
8Again, if the trumpet does not sound a
14:8 [n]Nu 10:9; Jer 4:19
clear call, who will get ready for battle?[n]
9So it is with you. Unless you speak intelligible words with your tongue, how
will anyone know what you are saying?
You will just be speaking into the air.
10Undoubtedly there are all sorts of languages in the world, yet none of them
is without meaning. 11If then I do not
grasp the meaning of what someone is
saying, I am a foreigner to the speaker,
and he is a foreigner to me. 12So it is
with you. Since you are eager to have
spiritual gifts, try to excel in gifts that
build up the church.
13For this reason anyone who speaks
in a tongue should pray that he may
interpret what he says. 14For if I pray
in a tongue, my spirit prays, but my
mind is unfruitful. 15So what shall I do?
I will pray with my spirit, but I will
14:15 [o]Eph 5:19; Col 3:16
also pray with my mind; I will sing[o]
with my spirit, but I will also sing with
my mind. 16If you are praising God
with your spirit, how can one who finds
himself among those who do not un-
14:16 [p]Dt 27:15-26; 1Ch 16:36; Ne 8:6; Ps 106:48; Rev 5:14; 7:12 [q]1Co 11:24
derstand[b] say "Amen"[p] to your
thanksgiving,[q] since he does not know
what you are saying? 17You may be giving thanks well enough, but the other
man is not edified.
18I thank God that I speak in tongues
more than all of you. 19But in the
church I would rather speak five intelligible words to instruct others than ten
thousand words in a tongue.
20Brothers, stop thinking like chil-
14:20 [r]Eph 4:14; Heb 5:12,13; 1Pe 2:2 [s]Ro 16:19
dren.[r] In regard to evil be infants,[s] but
in your thinking be adults. 21In the
Law[t] it is written:
14:21 [t]Jn 10:34

"Through men of strange tongues
and through the lips of foreigners
I will speak to this people,
but even then they will not listen
14:21 [u]Isa 28:11,12
to me,"[c][u]
says the Lord.

22Tongues, then, are a sign, not for
14:22 [v]ver 1
believers but for unbelievers; prophecy,[v]
however, is for believers, not for unbelievers. 23So if the whole church
comes together and everyone speaks in
tongues, and some who do not understand[d] or some unbelievers come in, will
they not say that you are out of your
14:23 [w]Ac 2:13
mind?[w] 24But if an unbeliever or someone who does not understand[e] comes in
while everybody is prophesying, he will
be convinced by all that he is a sinner
and will be judged by all, 25and the secrets of his heart will be laid bare. So
14:25 [x]Isa 45:14; Zec 8:23
he will fall down and worship God, ex-
claiming, "God is really among you!"[x]

SELF-CONTROL

EXCESS WITHIN CONTROL

1 Corinthians 14:23

Enjoy God in freedom. But be sure your freedom does not make God appear foolish. Be spontaneous. Spontaneity has vitality. But do not make God appear the champion of some lunacy that only runs and leaps, having forgotten how to think.

Orderly Worship

26What then shall we say, brothers?
14:26 [y]1Co 12:7-10 [z]Eph 5:19 [a]ver 6 [b]Ro 14:19
When you come together, everyone[y]
has a hymn,[z] or a word of instruction,[a]
a revelation, a tongue or an interpretation. All of these must be done for
the strengthening[b] of the church. 27If
anyone speaks in a tongue, two—or at
the most three—should speak, one at
a time, and someone must interpret.
28If there is no interpreter, the speaker
should keep quiet in the church and
speak to himself and God.
29Two or three prophets should speak,
and the others should weigh carefully
14:29 [c]1Co 12:10
what is said.[c] 30And if a revelation
comes to someone who is sitting down,
the first speaker should stop. 31For you
can all prophesy in turn so that everyone may be instructed and encouraged.

[a]*5* Or *other languages*; also in verses 6, 18, 22, 23 and 39 [b]*16* Or *among the inquirers*
[c]*21* Isaiah 28:11,12 [d]*23* Or *some inquirers*
[e]*24* Or *or some inquirer*

32The spirits of prophets are subject to
14:32 [d]1Jn 4:1 the control of prophets.[d] 33For God is
14:33 [e]ver 40 not a God of disorder[e] but of peace.
[f]Ac 9:13 As in all the congregations of the
saints,[f] 34women should remain silent
in the churches. They are not allowed
14:34 [g]1Ti 2:11,12 to speak, but must be in submission,[g]
[h]Ge 3:16 as the Law says.[h] 35If they want to inquire about something, they should ask
their own husbands at home; for it is
disgraceful for a woman to speak in the
church.
36Did the word of God originate with
you? Or are you the only people it has
reached? 37If anybody thinks he is a
14:37 [i]2Co 10:7 prophet[i] or spiritually gifted, let him
[j]1Jn 4:6 acknowledge that what I am writing to
you is the Lord's command.[j] 38If he ig-
14:39 [k]1Co 12:31 nores this, he himself will be ignored.[a]
39Therefore, my brothers, be eager[k]
to prophesy, and do not forbid speaking in tongues. 40But everything should
14:40 [l]ver 33 be done in a fitting and orderly[l] way.

The Resurrection of Christ

15:1 [m]Ro 2:16 **15** Now, brothers, I want to remind
15:2 [n]Ro 1:16 [o]Ro 11:22 you of the gospel[m] I preached to
you, which you received and on which
you have taken your stand. 2By this gos-
15:3 [p]Gal 1:12 pel you are saved,[n] if you hold firmly[o]
[q]1Co 11:23 to the word I preached to you. Other-
[r]Isa 53:5; 1Pe 2:24 wise, you have believed in vain.
[s]Lk 24:27; Ac 26:22,23 3For what I received[p] I passed on
to you[q] as of first importance[b]: that
15:4 [t]Ac 2:24 Christ died for our sins[r] according to
[u]Mt 16:21 the Scriptures,[s] 4that he was buried,
[v]Ac 2:25,30,31 that he was raised[t] on the third day[u]
according to the Scriptures,[v] 5and that
15:5 [w]Lk 24:34 he appeared to Peter,[c][w] and then to
[x]Mk 16:14 the Twelve.[x] 6After that, he appeared to

▸ FAITHFULNESS

THE LIST OF THOSE WHO SAW

1 Corinthians 15:5-8

Peter saw him,
Then the Twelve,
Then five hundred all at once.
Then James, his half brother,
Then all of the apostles,
Then Saul of Tarsus.

Five hundred and fourteen people are mentioned in this list of witnesses. Many died a martyr's death, insisting that they had seen the living Christ. If they died to say he lives, perhaps they should be heard.

more than five hundred of the brothers at the same time, most of whom
are still living, though some have fall-
en asleep. 7Then he appeared to James,
then to all the apostles,[y] 8and last of all 15:7 [y]Lk 24:33, 36,37; Ac 1:3,4
he appeared to me also,[z] as to one ab-
normally born. 15:8 [z]Ac 9:3-6,17; 1Co 9:1
9For I am the least of the apostles[a]
and do not even deserve to be called
an apostle, because I persecuted[b] the 15:9 [a]Eph 3:8; 1Ti 1:15 [b]Ac 8:3
church of God. 10But by the grace of
God I am what I am, and his grace
to me[c] was not without effect. No, I 15:10 [c]Ro 12:3
worked harder than all of them[d]—yet [d]2Co 11:23
not I, but the grace of God that was [e]Php 2:13
with me.[e] 11Whether, then, it was I or
they, this is what we preach, and this is
what you believed.

▸ PEACE

THE HORRIBLE HYPOTHESIS

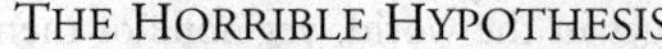

1 Corinthians 15:14

If Christ is not risen... O horrible hypothesis!
If Christ be not risen... humankind is but a species of zoology.
Villains and vicars are equal in eternity—
Life is a madhouse without scheme or key—
We are all orphans in the universe if Christ is not risen.

The Resurrection of the Dead

12But if it is preached that Christ has
been raised from the dead, how can
some of you say that there is no res- 15:12 [f]Ac 17:32; 23:8; 2Ti 2:18
urrection of the dead?[f] 13If there is no
resurrection of the dead, then not even
Christ has been raised. 14And if Christ
has not been raised,[g] our preaching is 15:14 [g]1Th 4:14
useless and so is your faith. 15More than
that, we are then found to be false witnesses about God, for we have testified
about God that he raised Christ from
the dead.[h] But he did not raise him if 15:15 [h]Ac 2:24
in fact the dead are not raised. 16For if
the dead are not raised, then Christ has
not been raised either. 17And if Christ
has not been raised, your faith is futile;
you are still in your sins.[i] 18Then those 15:17 [i]Ro 4:25
also who have fallen asleep in Christ are
lost. 19If only for this life we have hope
in Christ, we are to be pitied more than
all men.[j] 15:19 [j]1Co 4:9

[a]38 Some manuscripts *If he is ignorant of this, let him be ignorant* [b]3 Or *you at the first* [c]5 Greek *Cephas*

[20]But Christ has indeed been raised from the dead,[k] the firstfruits[l] of those who have fallen asleep.[m] [21]For since death came through a man,[n] the resurrection of the dead comes also through a man. [22]For as in Adam all die, so in Christ all will be made alive.[o] [23]But each in his own turn: Christ, the firstfruits;[p] then, when he comes,[q] those who belong to him. [24]Then the end will come, when he hands over the kingdom[r] to God the Father after he has destroyed all dominion, authority and power.[s] [25]For he must reign until he has put all his enemies under his feet.[t] [26]The last enemy to be destroyed is death.[u] [27]For he "has put everything under his feet."[a][v] Now when it says that "everything" has been put under him, it is clear that this does not include God himself, who put everything under Christ.[w] [28]When he has done this, then the Son himself will be made subject to him who put everything under him,[x] so that God may be all in all.[y]

[29]Now if there is no resurrection, what will those do who are baptized for the dead? If the dead are not raised at all, why are people baptized for them? [30]And as for us, why do we endanger ourselves every hour?[z] [31]I die every day[a]—I mean that, brothers—just as surely as I glory over you in Christ Jesus our Lord. [32]If I fought wild beasts[b] in Ephesus[c] for merely human reasons, what have I gained? If the dead are not raised,

> "Let us eat and drink,
> for tomorrow we die."[b][d]

[33]Do not be misled: "Bad company corrupts good character." [34]Come back to your senses as you ought, and stop sinning; for there are some who are ignorant of God—I say this to your shame.

The Resurrection Body

[35]But someone may ask,[e] "How are the dead raised? With what kind of body will they come?"[f] [36]How foolish![g] What you sow does not come to life unless it dies.[h] [37]When you sow, you do not plant the body that will be, but just a seed, perhaps of wheat or of something else. [38]But God gives it a body as he has determined, and to each kind of seed he gives its own body.[i] [39]All flesh is not the same: Men have one kind of flesh, animals have another, birds another and fish another. [40]There are also heavenly bodies and there are earthly bodies; but the splendor of the heavenly bodies is one kind, and the splendor of the earthly bodies is another. [41]The sun has one kind of splendor, the moon another and the stars another; and star differs from star in splendor.

[42]So will it be[j] with the resurrection of the dead. The body that is sown is perishable, it is raised imperishable; [43]it is sown in dishonor, it is raised in glory;[k] it is sown in weakness, it is raised in power; [44]it is sown a natural body, it is raised a spiritual body.[l]

If there is a natural body, there is also a spiritual body. [45]So it is written: "The first man Adam became a living being"[c];[m] the last Adam,[n] a life-giving spirit.[o] [46]The spiritual did not come first, but the natural, and after that the spiritual. [47]The first man was of the dust of the earth,[p] the second man from heaven.[q] [48]As was the earthly man, so are those who are of the earth; and as is the man from heaven, so also are those who are of heaven.[r] [49]And just as we have borne the likeness of the earthly man,[s] so shall we[d] bear the likeness of the man from heaven.[t]

[50]I declare to you, brothers, that flesh and blood[u] cannot inherit the kingdom of God, nor does the perishable inherit the imperishable. [51]Listen, I tell you a mystery:[v] We will not all sleep, but we will all be changed[w]— [52]in a flash, in the twinkling of an eye, at the last trumpet. For the trumpet will sound,[x]

15:20 [k]1Pe 1:3 [l]ver 23; Ac 26:23; Rev 1:5 [m]ver 6,18
15:21 [n]Ro 5:12
15:22 [o]Ro 5:14-18
15:23 [p]ver 20 [q]ver 52
15:24 [r]Da 7:14,27 [s]Ro 8:38
15:25 [t]Ps 110:1; Mt 22:44
15:26 [u]2Ti 1:10; Rev 20:14; 21:4
15:27 [v]Ps 8:6 [w]Mt 28:18
15:28 [x]Php 3:21 [y]1Co 3:23
15:30 [z]2Co 11:26
15:31 [a]Ro 8:36
15:32 [b]2Co 1:8 [c]Ac 18:19 [d]Isa 22:13; Lk 12:19
15:35 [e]Ro 9:19 [f]Eze 37:3
15:36 [g]Lk 11:40 [h]Jn 12:24
15:38 [i]Ge 1:11
15:42 [j]Da 12:3; Mt 13:43
15:43 [k]Php 3:21; Col 3:4
15:44 [l]ver 50
15:45 [m]Ge 2:7 [n]Ro 5:14 [o]Jn 5:21; Ro 8:2
15:47 [p]Ge 2:7; 3:19 [q]Jn 3:13,31
15:48 [r]Php 3:20,21
15:49 [s]Ge 5:3 [t]Ro 8:29
15:50 [u]Jn 3:3,5
15:51 [v]1Co 13:2 [w]Php 3:21
15:52 [x]Mt 24:31

[a]*27* Psalm 8:6 [b]*32* Isaiah 22:13 [c]*45* Gen. 2:7
[d]*49* Some early manuscripts *so let us*

PATIENCE

FIRST MENTION OF THE LAST TRUMPET

1 Corinthians 15:51–52

Some in Corinth had lost family members to death and had despaired at their passing, for Christ had not yet come. But here was the apostle's solace: Remember, all you who grieve, there is a horn in heaven—a trumpet will sound in time. Just wait. God will plow earth's cemeteries, and they, ashamed of all their shallow graves, shall open and surrender their contents to the Christ, who first taught graves to yield.

15:52 [y]Jn 5:25 the dead[y] will be raised imperishable,
and we will be changed. 53 For the
perishable must clothe itself with the
15:53 imperishable,[z] and the mortal with im-
[z]2Co 5:2,4 mortality. 54 When the perishable has
been clothed with the imperishable,
and the mortal with immortality, then
the saying that is written will come
15:54 true: "Death has been swallowed up in
[a]Isa 25:8; Rev 20:14 victory."[a] [a]

15:55 [b]Hos 13:14 55 "Where, O death, is your victory?
Where, O death, is your sting?"[b] [b]

15:56 [c]Ro 5:12 56 The sting of death is sin,[c] and the
[d]Ro 4:15 power of sin is the law.[d] 57 But thanks
15:57 [e]2Co 2:14 be to God![e] He gives us the victory
[f]Ro 8:37 through our Lord Jesus Christ.[f]
58 Therefore, my dear brothers, stand
firm. Let nothing move you. Always
give yourselves fully to the work of the
15:58 Lord,[g] because you know that your la-
[g]1Co 16:10 bor in the Lord is not in vain.

The Collection for God's People

16:1 [h]Ac 24:17 16 Now about the collection[h] for
[i]Ac 9:13 God's people:[i] Do what I told
[j]Ac 16:6 the Galatian[j] churches to do. 2 On the
16:2 [k]Ac 20:7 first day of every week,[k] each one of
[l]2Co 9:4,5 you should set aside a sum of money in
keeping with his income, saving it up,
so that when I come no collections will
have to be made.[l] 3 Then, when I arrive,
I will give letters of introduction to the
16:3 [m]2Co 8:18,19 men you approve[m] and send them with
your gift to Jerusalem. 4 If it seems ad-
visable for me to go also, they will accompany me.

Personal Requests

5 After I go through Macedonia, I
16:5 [n]1Co 4:19 will come to you[n]—for I will be going
[o]Ac 19:21 through Macedonia.[o] 6 Perhaps I will
stay with you awhile, or even spend the
winter, so that you can help me on my
journey,[p] wherever I go. 7 I do not want 16:6 [p]Ro 15:24
to see you now and make only a pass-
ing visit; I hope to spend some time 16:7
with you, if the Lord permits.[q] 8 But I [q]Ac 18:21
will stay on at Ephesus[r] until Pentecost,[s] 16:8
9 because a great door for effective work [r]Ac 18:19
has opened to me,[t] and there are many [s]Ac 2:1
who oppose me. 16:9
10 If Timothy[u] comes, see to it that [t]Ac 14:27
he has nothing to fear while he is with 16:10
you, for he is carrying on the work of [u]Ac 16:1
the Lord,[v] just as I am. 11 No one, then, [v]1Co 15:58
should refuse to accept him.[w] Send him 16:11
on his way in peace[x] so that he may re- [w]1Ti 4:12
turn to me. I am expecting him along [x]Ac 15:33
with the brothers.
12 Now about our brother Apollos:[y] I 16:12
strongly urged him to go to you with [y]Ac 18:24; 1Co 1:12
the brothers. He was quite unwilling to
go now, but he will go when he has the
opportunity.
13 Be on your guard; stand firm[z] in 16:13
the faith; be men of courage; be strong.[a] [z]Gal 5:1;
14 Do everything in love.[b] Php 1:27; 1Th 3:8;
15 You know that the household of 2Th 2:15 [a]Eph 6:10
Stephanas[c] were the first converts[d] in
Achaia,[e] and they have devoted them- 16:14 [b]1Co 14:1
selves to the service of the saints. I urge 16:15
you, brothers, 16 to submit[f] to such as [c]1Co 1:16 [d]Ro 16:5
these and to everyone who joins in the [e]Ac 18:12
work, and labors at it. 17 I was glad when 16:16
Stephanas, Fortunatus and Achaicus ar- [f]Heb 13:17
rived, because they have supplied what
was lacking from you.[g] 18 For they re- 16:17 [g]2Co 11:9;
freshed[h] my spirit and yours also. Such Php 2:30
men deserve recognition.[i] 16:18 [h]Phm 7 [i]Php 2:29

Final Greetings

19 The churches in the province of
Asia send you greetings. Aquila and
Priscilla[c][j] greet you warmly in the Lord, 16:19 [j]Ac 18:2
and so does the church that meets at [k]Ro 16:5
their house.[k] 20 All the brothers here
send you greetings. Greet one another 16:20
with a holy kiss.[l] [l]Ro 16:16
21 I, Paul, write this greeting in my 16:21
own hand.[m] [m]Gal 6:11; Col 4:18
22 If anyone does not love the
Lord[n]—a curse[o] be on him. Come, 16:22 [n]Eph 6:24
O Lord[d]![p] [o]Ro 9:3 [p]Rev 22:20
23 The grace of the Lord Jesus be with
you.[q] 16:23 [q]Ro 16:20
24 My love to all of you in Christ Jesus. Amen.[e]

[a]*54* Isaiah 25:8 [b]*55* Hosea 13:14 [c]*19* Greek *Prisca,* a variant of *Priscilla* [d]*22* In Aramaic the expression *Come, O Lord* is *Marana tha.* [e]*24* Some manuscripts do not have *Amen.*

► LOVE

SYSTEMATIC GENEROSITY

1 Corinthians 16:2

Give generously,
and you will be the best of church members.
Give everything,
and you will be deeply Christian.
Give everything without counting the cost,
and you will be like Christ.

2 CORINTHIANS

AUTHORSHIP AND DATE

Paul

Between A.D. 55 and A.D. 57

KEY THEMES

Paul founded the Corinthian church on one of his missionary journeys, and his letters to them give us a glimpse of his relationship with them. Many scholars believe that Paul wrote at least four letters to the Corinthian church, the first and third of which were lost (note 1 Corinthians 5:9–11; 2 Corinthians 2:6–9; 7:12). What we call 1 Corinthians was actually his second letter to the church, and what we call 2 Corinthians was really his fourth letter. While 1 Corinthians was written to rebuke the people for their disunity, idolatry and sexual improprieties, 2 Corinthians was written by Paul to defend himself against the many false teachers who had twisted his teaching and abused his reputation. In the process of his defense, Paul talks about his suffering and trials (chapters 10–13), and in chapter 12 he deals with his "thorn in the flesh." He concludes the book by discussing the collection that he was gathering for the impoverished Christians in Jerusalem—a subject with which he ended other letters and a cause which dominated his vision (as described in the book of Acts).

FRUIT OF THE SPIRIT IN 2 CORINTHIANS

Love: Love gone one step further is grace. God's grace is not only more love than we deserve, it is love that is all-sufficient. Paul had a "thorn in [his] flesh" (12:7). The Greek word for this phrase is *skolops,* which was really more of an impaling stake than a simple thorn. Paul's affliction was deep enough, hurtful enough and personal enough that Paul would not confess to his readers what it was. But even though God would not take it away, God's overwhelming, all-sufficient, undeserved love made it possible for Paul to live with it. Jesus told Paul, "My grace is sufficient for you, for my power is made perfect in weakness" (12:9). As long as grace was in the world—and it evermore would be—Paul would delight in his weakness, for it revealed God's almighty, undeserved, all-sufficient love. Weakness, dressed with such love, is strength in disguise (see 12:10).

Peace: Peace is the daily work of God in this world. God wants peace, not enmity. So from daybreak to daybreak, century after century, God has encouraged our troubled world toward reconciliation. And God's inner heart of peace has proclaimed us to be ambassadors who call to the entire world, "Our God is a God of peace, and we are called to the highest work there is: making peace. Please, poor hating, angry world—be reconciled to God" (see 5:17–20).

Kindness: As Paul faced his weakness (see 11:30), he became kind. As he became kind, he ministered to others. His weakness led, not to arrogant testimonials, but to a kind confession.

Goodness: We arrive at goodness by discipline, by demolishing "arguments and every pretension that sets itself up against the knowledge of God, and we take captive every thought to make it obedient to Christ" (10:5). To police the rebel mind with grace is to arrive at goodness by taking the shortest route.

Faithfulness: Paul listed the dangers that he had undergone to prove himself faithful (see 11:22–30). He confessed, somewhat sheepishly, that such a list of conquered trials might make him appear boastful, but he chose to let his faithfulness serve his weakness. Weakness produces need, and need seeks after the strength that is found only in God.

Gentleness: Grace, the most enduring quality in the world, is placed in the center of our lives. But it has for its lodging place the most fragile home: our mortal bodies and tentative intentions. We have a glorious treasure in a porcelain jar. One thing cannot be doubted: The jars are temporary and expendable, but God's grace endures forever (see 4:7–12). The life-changing value of the treasure reminds us to preach to a dying world. The fragile nature of our lives and testimonies requires us to do it gently.

Self-Control: Self-control leads to a voluntary separation from the world (see 6:17–18). Self-control means that we separate ourselves from idolaters—those who serve other gods, such as ego desires and personal gratification. The desire for separation comes from setting the all-powerful Christ next to the tinseled altars of those idolaters who have nothing at the center of their lives.

1 Paul, an apostle of Christ Jesus by
1:1 [a]1Co 1:1; the will of God,[a] and Timothy our
Eph 1:1; Col 1:1; brother,
2Ti 1:1 [b]1Co 10:32 To the church of God[b] in Corinth,
[c]Ac 18:12 together with all the saints throughout
Achaia:[c]
2Grace and peace to you from God
1:2 [d]Ro 1:7 our Father and the Lord Jesus Christ.[d]

The God of All Comfort

3Praise be to the God and Father of
1:3 [e]Eph 1:3; our Lord Jesus Christ,[e] the Father of
1Pe 1:3 compassion and the God of all comfort,
1:4 [f]2Co 7:6,7,13 4who comforts us[f] in all our troubles,
so that we can comfort those in any
trouble with the comfort we ourselves
have received from God. 5For just as
1:5 the sufferings of Christ flow over into
[g]2Co 4:10; Col 1:24 our lives,[g] so also through Christ our
comfort overflows. 6If we are distressed,
1:6 [h]2Co 4:15 it is for your comfort and salvation;[h] if
we are comforted, it is for your com-
fort, which produces in you patient
endurance of the same sufferings we
suffer. 7And our hope for you is firm,
because we know that just as you share
1:7 [i]Ro 8:17 in our sufferings,[i] so also you share in
our comfort.
8We do not want you to be uninformed, brothers, about the hardships
1:8 [j]1Co 15:32 we suffered[j] in the province of Asia.
We were under great pressure, far be-
yond our ability to endure, so that we
despaired even of life. 9Indeed, in our
hearts we felt the sentence of death. But
this happened that we might not rely
1:9 [k]Jer 17:5,7 on ourselves but on God,[k] who raises
the dead. 10He has delivered us from
1:10 [l]Ro 15:31 such a deadly peril,[l] and he will deliver
us. On him we have set our hope that
he will continue to deliver us, 11as you
1:11 [m]Ro 15:30; help us by your prayers.[m] Then many
Php 1:19 [n]2Co 4:15 will give thanks[n] on our[a] behalf for the
gracious favor granted us in answer to
the prayers of many.

Paul's Change of Plans

12Now this is our boast: Our con-
1:12 [o]Ac 23:1 science[o] testifies that we have conducted
[p]2Co 2:17 [q]1Co 2:1,4,13 ourselves in the world, and especially in
our relations with you, in the holiness
and sincerity[p] that are from God. We
have done so not according to worldly
wisdom[q] but according to God's grace.
13For we do not write you anything you
cannot read or understand. And I hope
that, 14as you have understood us in
part, you will come to understand fully that you can boast of us just as we
will boast of you in the day of the Lord 1:14
Jesus.[r] [r]1Co 1:8
15Because I was confident of this, I 1:15
planned to visit you[s] first so that you [s]1Co 4:19
might benefit twice.[t] 16I planned to vis- [t]Ro 1:11,13; 15:29
it you on my way[u] to Macedonia and 1:16
to come back to you from Macedonia, [u]1Co 16:5-7
and then to have you send me on my
way to Judea. 17When I planned this,
did I do it lightly? Or do I make my
plans in a worldly manner[v] so that in 1:17 [v]2Co 10:2,3
the same breath I say, "Yes, yes" and
"No, no"?
18But as surely as God is faithful,[w] 1:18 [w]1Co 1:9
our message to you is not "Yes" and
"No." 19For the Son of God, Jesus
Christ, who was preached among you
by me and Silas[b] and Timothy, was not
"Yes" and "No," but in him it has al-
ways been[x] "Yes." 20For no matter how 1:19 [x]Heb 13:8
many promises[y] God has made, they 1:20
are "Yes" in Christ. And so through him [y]Ro 15:8
the "Amen"[z] is spoken by us to the glo- [z]1Co 14:16
ry of God. 21Now it is God who makes
both us and you stand firm in Christ. 1:21 [a]1Jn 2:20,27
He anointed[a] us, 22set his seal of ownership on us, and put his Spirit in our 1:22 [b]2Co 5:5
hearts as a deposit, guaranteeing what is
to come.[b] 1:23 [c]Ro 1:9;
23I call God as my witness[c] that it Gal 1:20 [d]1Co 4:21;
was in order to spare you[d] that I did not 2Co 2:1,3; 13:2,10
return to Corinth. 24Not that we lord it
over[e] your faith, but we work with you 1:24 [e]1Pe 5:3
for your joy, because it is by faith you [f]Ro 11:20; 1Co 15:1
2 stand firm.[f] 1So I made up my mind
that I would not make another pain- 2:1 [g]2Co 1:23
ful visit to you.[g] 2For if I grieve you,[h]
who is left to make me glad but you 2:2 [h]2Co 7:8
whom I have grieved? 3I wrote as I did[i]
so that when I came I should not be dis- 2:3 [i]2Co 7:8,12
tressed[j] by those who ought to make me [j]2Co 12:21
rejoice. I had confidence[k] in all of you, [k]2Co 8:22; Gal 5:10
that you would all share my joy. 4For I
wrote you[l] out of great distress and an- 2:4 [l]2Co 7:8,12
guish of heart and with many tears, not
to grieve you but to let you know the
depth of my love for you.

Forgiveness for the Sinner

5If anyone has caused grief,[m] he has 2:5 [m]1Co 5:1,2
not so much grieved me as he has
grieved all of you, to some extent—not
to put it too severely. 6The punishment[n] 2:6 [n]1Co 5:4,5

[a]*11* Many manuscripts *your* [b]*19* Greek *Silvanus,* a variant of *Silas*

inflicted on him by the majority is sufficient for him. 7Now instead, you ought
to forgive and comfort him,[o] so that he
will not be overwhelmed by excessive
sorrow. 8I urge you, therefore, to reaffirm your love for him. 9The reason I
wrote you was to see if you would stand
the test and be obedient in everything.[p]
10If you forgive anyone, I also forgive
him. And what I have forgiven—if there
was anything to forgive—I have forgiv-
en in the sight of Christ for your sake,
11in order that Satan[q] might not outwit us. For we are not unaware of his
schemes.[r]

2:7 [o]Gal 6:1; Eph 4:32
2:9 [p]2Co 10:6
2:11 [q]Mt 4:10 [r]Lk 22:31; 2Co 4:4; 1Pe 5:8,9

DAY 3 THREE

Love and My Relationship With Christ

2 Corinthians 2:5–11

The word *gospel* means "Good News." There are many reasons why the news is good. It is good because it is all about grace, eternal life and union with Christ. But the best thing about the Good News is that forgiveness for sin was immensely simplified when Jesus took upon himself the sacrificial work of Golgotha.

It is for this reason that Paul exhorts the believers to forgive others. Haven't they been forgiven through the finished work of Christ on the cross? The Law of Moses did not misunderstand the seriousness of sin, but it did make forgiveness a complex matter involving the taking of an animal to the temple and having it slain. But now Jesus has removed the effort from the process of obtaining God's loving forgiveness. Jesus has died and risen again, and we are forgiven merely for the asking. The blood atonement is still required, but Jesus took care of it once and for all on the cross.

We sing the hymn "Nearer My God to Thee." It is a wonderful song, but its truth is marred by the distance we put into our relationship with Christ by unconfessed sin. Unconfessed sin can only sing, "Farther My God from Thee." All sin moves us in the direction of this cold remoteness to God. We can only be brought near to God by a genuine plea for forgiveness. Then we in turn can be free to forgive others.

To begin a study on the topic of Love Forgives, turn to the home page on page 1227.

Ministers of the New Covenant

12Now when I went to Troas[s] to
preach the gospel of Christ[t] and found
that the Lord had opened a door[u] for
me, 13I still had no peace of mind,[v] because I did not find my brother Titus[w]
there. So I said good-by to them and
went on to Macedonia.

2:12 [s]Ac 16:8 [t]Ro 1:1 [u]Ac 14:27
2:13 [v]2Co 7:5 [w]2Co 7:6,13; 12:18

Patience

Faithful at Doorways

2 Corinthians 2:12

Life is a patient corridor of years, and along life's hallway are a thousand doors. Never force one of them open. Wait and pray. If no door seems to open, check the windows.

14But thanks be to God,[x] who always leads us in triumphal procession
in Christ and through us spreads everywhere the fragrance[y] of the knowledge
of him. 15For we are to God the aroma
of Christ among those who are being
saved and those who are perishing.[z]
16To the one we are the smell of death;[a]
to the other, the fragrance of life. And
who is equal to such a task?[b] 17Unlike
so many, we do not peddle the word
of God for profit.[c] On the contrary,
in Christ we speak before God with
sincerity,[d] like men sent from God.[e]

3 Are we beginning to commend ourselves[f] again? Or do we need, like
some people, letters of recommenda-
tion[g] to you or from you? 2You yourselves are our letter, written on our
hearts, known and read by everybody.[h]
3You show that you are a letter from
Christ, the result of our ministry, written not with ink but with the Spirit of
the living God, not on tablets of stone[i]
but on tablets of human hearts.[j]
4Such confidence[k] as this is ours
through Christ before God. 5Not that
we are competent in ourselves to claim
anything for ourselves, but our competence comes from God.[l] 6He has made
us competent as ministers of a new covenant[m]—not of the letter but of the
Spirit; for the letter kills, but the Spirit
gives life.[n]

2:14 [x]Ro 6:17 [y]Eph 5:2; Php 4:18
2:15 [z]1Co 1:18
2:16 [a]Lk 2:34 [b]2Co 3:5,6
2:17 [c]2Co 4:2 [d]1Co 5:8 [e]2Co 1:12
3:1 [f]2Co 5:12; 12:11 [g]Ac 18:27
3:2 [h]1Co 9:2
3:3 [i]Ex 24:12 [j]Pr 3:3; Jer 31:33; Eze 11:19
3:4 [k]Eph 3:12
3:5 [l]1Co 15:10
3:6 [m]Lk 22:20 [n]Jn 6:63

The Glory of the New Covenant

7Now if the ministry that brought
death, which was engraved in letters on

stone, came with glory, so that the Israelites could not look steadily at the
3:7 face of Moses because of its glory,[o] fad-
[o]Ex 34:29-35 ing though it was, 8will not the minis-
3:9 try of the Spirit be even more glorious?
[p]ver 7 9If the ministry that condemns men[p]
[q]Ro 1:17; is glorious, how much more glorious is
3:21,22 the ministry that brings righteousness![q]
10For what was glorious has no glory
now in comparison with the surpassing
glory. 11And if what was fading away
came with glory, how much greater is
the glory of that which lasts!
12Therefore, since we have such a
3:12 hope, we are very bold.[r] 13We are not
[r]Eph 6:19 like Moses, who would put a veil over
3:13 his face[s] to keep the Israelites from
[s]ver 7; Ex 34:33 gazing at it while the radiance was fading away. 14But their minds were made
3:14 dull,[t] for to this day the same veil re-
[t]Ro 11:7,8 [u]Ac 13:15 mains when the old covenant[u] is read.[v]
[v]ver 6 It has not been removed, because only
in Christ is it taken away. 15Even to
this day when Moses is read, a veil cov-
3:16 ers their hearts. 16But whenever any-
[w]Ro 11:23 [x]Ex 34:34 one turns to the Lord,[w] the veil is taken
3:17 away.[x] 17Now the Lord is the Spirit,[y]
[y]Isa 61:1,2 and where the Spirit of the Lord is, there
[z]Jn 8:32 is freedom.[z] 18And we, who with un-
3:18 veiled faces all reflect[a][a] the Lord's glory,[b]
[a]1Co 13:12 [b]2Co 4:4,6 are being transformed into his likeness[c]
[c]Ro 8:29 with ever-increasing glory, which comes
from the Lord, who is the Spirit.

KINDNESS

THE LIBERTY OF CHRIST

2 Corinthians 3:17

Are you bound in the misery of your small, uninformed career plans? Are you manacled to stingy dreams that focus only on your happiness? Stop. Wash your eyes, stare at the horizon and search for his coming.

See, there he comes—the Spirit with a shining gift. The gift is liberty! The giver is pure love. You are free.

Treasures in Jars of Clay

4:1 4 Therefore, since through God's
[d]1Co 7:25 mercy[d] we have this ministry, we
do not lose heart. 2Rather, we have re-
4:2 nounced secret and shameful ways;[e] we
[e]1Co 4:5 [f]2Co 2:17 do not use deception, nor do we distort the word of God.[f] On the contrary,
by setting forth the truth plainly we
commend ourselves to every man's con-
science[g] in the sight of God. 3And even 4:2 [g]2Co 5:11
if our gospel[h] is veiled,[i] it is veiled to
those who are perishing.[j] 4The god[k] of 4:3 [h]2Co 2:12
this age has blinded[l] the minds of unbe- [i]2Co 3:14
lievers, so that they cannot see the light [j]1Co 1:18
of the gospel of the glory of Christ, 4:4
who is the image of God. 5For we do [k]Jn 12:31 [l]2Co 3:14
not preach ourselves,[m] but Jesus Christ
as Lord, and ourselves as your servants[n] 4:5 [m]1Co 1:13
for Jesus' sake. 6For God, who said, "Let [n]1Co 9:19
light shine out of darkness,"[b][o] made 4:6
his light shine in our hearts[p] to give us [o]Ge 1:3 [p]2Pe 1:19
the light of the knowledge of the glory
of God in the face of Christ.

GENTLENESS

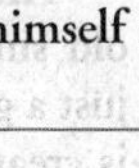

TREASURE IN CLAY JARS

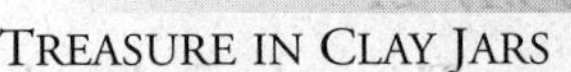

2 Corinthians 4:7

Here is the diamond at the center of your faith: the living Son of God, packaged in the drab mortality of your swift-passing life. Is it not wonderful that God would hide himself in such a cramped, unworthy place?

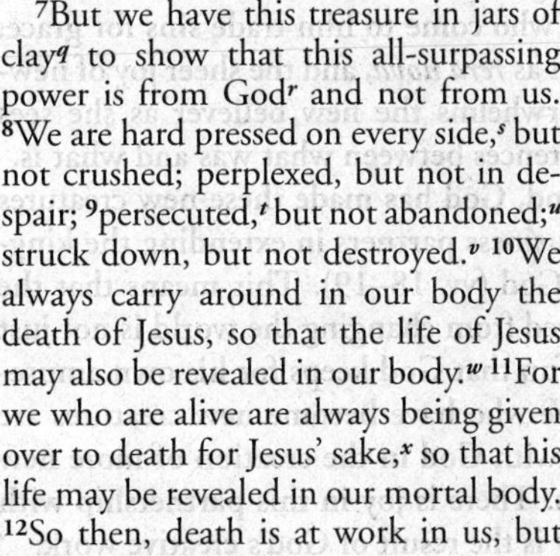

7But we have this treasure in jars of 4:7
clay[q] to show that this all-surpassing [q]Job 4:19; 2Co 5:1
power is from God[r] and not from us. [r]1Co 2:5
8We are hard pressed on every side,[s] but 4:8
not crushed; perplexed, but not in de- [s]2Co 7:5
spair; 9persecuted,[t] but not abandoned;[u]
struck down, but not destroyed.[v] 10We 4:9 [t]Jn 15:20
always carry around in our body the [u]Heb 13:5
death of Jesus, so that the life of Jesus [v]Ps 37:24
may also be revealed in our body.[w] 11For 4:10 [w]Ro 6:5
we who are alive are always being given
over to death for Jesus' sake,[x] so that his 4:11 [x]Ro 8:36
life may be revealed in our mortal body.
12So then, death is at work in us, but
life is at work in you.[y] 4:12 [y]2Co 13:9
13It is written: "I believed; therefore 4:13
I have spoken."[c][z] With that same spirit [z]Ps 116:10
of faith we also believe and therefore
speak, 14because we know that the one
who raised the Lord Jesus from the dead
will also raise us with Jesus[a] and present 4:14 [a]1Th 4:14
us with you in his presence.[b] 15All this [b]Eph 5:27
is for your benefit, so that the grace that
is reaching more and more people may
cause thanksgiving[c] to overflow to the 4:15
glory of God. [c]2Co 1:11
16Therefore we do not lose heart.
Though outwardly we are wasting away, 4:16
yet inwardly[d] we are being renewed[e] [d]Ro 7:22 [e]Col 3:10

[a]18 Or *contemplate* [b]6 Gen. 1:3
[c]13 Psalm 116:10

day by day. 17For our light and momentary troubles are achieving for us an
eternal glory that far outweighs them
all.[f] 18So we fix our eyes not on what is
seen, but on what is unseen.[g] For what
is seen is temporary, but what is unseen
is eternal.

4:17 [f]Ro 8:18; 1Pe 1:6,7
4:18 [g]Ro 8:24; Heb 11:1

Our Heavenly Dwelling

5 Now we know that if the earthly[h]
tent[i] we live in is destroyed, we have

5:1 [h]1Co 15:47 [i]2Pe 1:13,14

DAY 4 FOUR

Love and My Service to Others

2 Corinthians 5:17–21

Ambassador status: This is the final work of love. God is recreating the world by the sheer force of love. Here are the steps toward this status:

First, God is making new creatures out of old sinners (2 Corinthians 5:17). This is not just a giant, celestial retreading operation. God is creating a species that has never existed before. All who come to him trade sins for grace, come out as *rera nova,* and the sheer joy of newness overwhelms the new believer as she sees the differences between what was and what is.

Second, God has made these new creatures fellow business partners in extending the kingdom of God (vv. 18–19). This means that the joy derived from changing the world is not just a lot of fun that God keeps for his own amusement. We who have become new creatures are to work with God in the creation of more new creatures. There is joy in this partnership with God. Joy is the result of God's creative work.

Third, we gained ambassador status when we were made new (v. 20). Ambassadors are those who live in one realm while representing the business of another. Our home address is now one realm away, and we are here in God's beloved world, working with him to claim it before both realms become one. We are citizens of heaven, working to make earth look a little more like heaven before history is concluded. So we have an obligation to reconcile the world to God, and the joy of this immense calling makes every sunrise brighter.

To begin a study on the topic of Love, Permeating All We Do, turn to the home page on page 1372.

a building from God, an eternal house
in heaven, not built by human hands.
2Meanwhile we groan,[j] longing to be
clothed with our heavenly dwelling,[k]
3because when we are clothed, we will
not be found naked. 4For while we are
in this tent, we groan and are burdened,
because we do not wish to be unclothed
but to be clothed with our heavenly
dwelling,[l] so that what is mortal may be
swallowed up by life. 5Now it is God
who has made us for this very purpose
and has given us the Spirit as a deposit,
guaranteeing what is to come.[m]
6Therefore we are always confident
and know that as long as we are at home
in the body we are away from the Lord.
7We live by faith, not by sight.[n] 8We are
confident, I say, and would prefer to be
away from the body and at home with
the Lord.[o] 9So we make it our goal to
please him,[p] whether we are at home
in the body or away from it. 10For we
must all appear before the judgment
seat of Christ, that each one may receive what is due him[q] for the things
done while in the body, whether good
or bad.

5:2 [j]ver 4; Ro 8:23 [k]1Co 15:53, 54
5:4 [l]1Co 15:53,54
5:5 [m]Ro 8:23; 2Co 1:22
5:7 [n]1Co 13:12
5:8 [o]Php 1:23
5:9 [p]Ro 14:18
5:10 [q]Mt 16:27; Ro 14:10; Eph 6:8

Faithfulness

The Reckoning

2 Corinthians 5:10

"I met you long ago," says Jesus. "I called you friend. I have kept unending counsel with you. I have never left your side. Are you surprised to see me on the final throne of judgment? I, your lifelong friend, am at last your magistrate. Do not despair; you have been faithful."

The Ministry of Reconciliation

11Since, then, we know what it is to
fear the Lord,[r] we try to persuade men.
What we are is plain to God, and I hope
it is also plain to your conscience.[s] 12We
are not trying to commend ourselves to
you again,[t] but are giving you an opportunity to take pride in us,[u] so that
you can answer those who take pride in
what is seen rather than in what is in
the heart. 13If we are out of our mind,[v]
it is for the sake of God; if we are in our
right mind, it is for you. 14For Christ's
love compels us, because we are convinced that one died for all, and therefore all died.[w] 15And he died for all,

5:11 [r]Heb 10:31; Jude 23 [s]2Co 4:2
5:12 [t]2Co 3:1 [u]2Co 1:14
5:13 [v]2Co 11:1,16,17
5:14 [w]Gal 2:20

that those who live should no longer
5:15 live for themselves[x] but for him who
[x]Ro 14:7-9 died for them and was raised again.

PEACE

THE DEFINITION

> *2 Corinthians 5:18–19*
>
> **There is Good News: The chasm of hell has been bridged. God in Christ was making friends with a world that never thought friendship with God all that important.**

5:16 16So from now on we regard no one
[y]2Co 11:18 from a worldly[y] point of view. Though
we once regarded Christ in this way, we
5:17 do so no longer. 17Therefore, if anyone
[z]Gal 6:15 is in Christ, he is a new creation;[z] the
[a]Isa 65:17; Rev 21:4,5 old has gone, the new has come![a] 18All
5:18 this is from God, who reconciled us to
[b]Ro 5:10; Col 1:20 himself through Christ[b] and gave us the
ministry of reconciliation: 19that God
was reconciling the world to himself in
5:19 Christ, not counting men's sins against
[c]Ro 4:8 them.[c] And he has committed to us
5:20 the message of reconciliation. 20We
[d]2Co 6:1; Eph 6:20 are therefore Christ's ambassadors,[d] as
though God were making his appeal
through us. We implore you on Christ's
5:21 behalf: Be reconciled to God. 21God
[e]Heb 4:15; 1Pe 2:22,24; 1Jn 3:5 made him who had no sin[e] to be sin[a]
for us, so that in him we might become
[f]Ro 1:17 the righteousness of God.[f]
6:1 6 As God's fellow workers[g] we urge
[g]1Co 3:9; 2Co 5:20 you not to receive God's grace in
vain. 2For he says,

"In the time of my favor I heard you,
6:2 and in the day of salvation I
[h]Isa 49:8 helped you."[b][h]

I tell you, now is the time of God's favor, now is the day of salvation.

Paul's Hardships

6:3 3We put no stumbling block in any-
[i]Ro 14:13,20; 1Co 9:12; 10:32 one's path,[i] so that our ministry will
not be discredited. 4Rather, as servants
of God we commend ourselves in every
way: in great endurance; in troubles,
6:5 hardships and distresses; 5in beatings,
[j]2Co 11:23-25 imprisonments[j] and riots; in hard work,
[k]1Co 4:11 sleepless nights and hunger;[k] 6in puri-
6:6 ty, understanding, patience and kind-
[l]1Th 1:5 ness; in the Holy Spirit[l] and in sincere
6:7 love; 7in truthful speech[m] and in the
[m]2Co 4:2 power of God; with weapons of righ-
[n]2Co 10:4; Eph 6:10-18 teousness[n] in the right hand and in the
left; 8through glory and dishonor,[o] bad 6:8
report and good report; genuine, yet re- [o]1Co 4:10
garded as impostors;[p] 9known, yet re- [p]Mt 27:63
garded as unknown; dying,[q] and yet 6:9
we live on;[r] beaten, and yet not killed; [q]Ro 8:36
10sorrowful, yet always rejoicing;[s] poor, [r]2Co 1:8-10; 4:10,11
yet making many rich;[t] having nothing, 6:10
and yet possessing everything.[u] [s]2Co 7:4
11We have spoken freely to you, Cor- [t]2Co 8:9
inthians, and opened wide our hearts [u]Ro 8:32; 1Co 3:21
to you.[v] 12We are not withholding our 6:11
affection from you, but you are with- [v]2Co 7:3
holding yours from us. 13As a fair
exchange—I speak as to my children[w]— 6:13
open wide your hearts also. [w]1Co 4:14

Do Not Be Yoked With Unbelievers

14Do not be yoked together[x] with 6:14
unbelievers. For what do righteousness [x]1Co 5:9,10
and wickedness have in common? Or [y]Eph 5:7,11; 1Jn 1:6
what fellowship can light have with
darkness?[y] 15What harmony is there between Christ and Belial[c]? What does a
believer[z] have in common with an un- 6:15
believer? 16What agreement is there be- [z]Ac 5:14
tween the temple of God and idols? For
we are the temple[a] of the living God. As 6:16
God has said: "I will live with them and [a]1Co 3:16
walk among them, and I will be their [b]Lev 26:12;
God, and they will be my people."[d][b] Jer 32:38; Eze 37:27

17"Therefore come out from them[c] 6:17
and be separate, [c]Rev 18:4
says the Lord. [d]Isa 52:11
Touch no unclean thing,
and I will receive you."[e][d]
18"I will be a Father to you,
and you will be my sons and
daughters,[e] 6:18
says the Lord Almighty."[f] [e]Isa 43:6

7 Since we have these promises,[f] dear 7:1
friends, let us purify ourselves from [f]2Co 6:17,18
everything that contaminates body and
spirit, perfecting holiness out of reverence for God.

Paul's Joy

2Make room for us in your hearts.[g] 7:2
We have wronged no one, we have cor- [g]2Co 6:12,13
rupted no one, we have exploited no
one. 3I do not say this to condemn
you; I have said before that you have 7:3
such a place in our hearts[h] that we [h]2Co 6:11,12

[a]*21* Or *be a sin offering* [b]*2* Isaiah 49:8
[c]*15* Greek *Beliar*, a variant of *Belial*
[d]*16* Lev. 26:12; Jer. 32:38; Ezek. 37:27
[e]*17* Isaiah 52:11; Ezek. 20:34,41
[f]*18* 2 Samuel 7:14; 7:8

would live or die with you. 4I have great
confidence in you; I take great pride in
you. I am greatly encouraged; in all our
troubles my joy knows no bounds.[i]
5For when we came into Macedonia,[j]
this body of ours had no rest, but we
were harassed at every turn[k]—conflicts
on the outside, fears within.[l] 6But God,
who comforts the downcast,[m] comforted us by the coming of Titus,[n] 7and
not only by his coming but also by the
comfort you had given him. He told us
about your longing for me, your deep
sorrow, your ardent concern for me, so
that my joy was greater than ever.
8Even if I caused you sorrow by my
letter,[o] I do not regret it. Though I did
regret it—I see that my letter hurt you,
but only for a little while— 9yet now I
am happy, not because you were made
sorry, but because your sorrow led you
to repentance. For you became sorrowful as God intended and so were not
harmed in any way by us. 10Godly
sorrow brings repentance that leads to
salvation[p] and leaves no regret, but
worldly sorrow brings death. 11See what
this godly sorrow has produced in you:
what earnestness, what eagerness to
clear yourselves, what indignation, what
alarm, what longing, what concern,[q]
what readiness to see justice done. At
every point you have proved yourselves
to be innocent in this matter. 12So even
though I wrote to you,[r] it was not on
account of the one who did the wrong[s]
or of the injured party, but rather that
before God you could see for yourselves
how devoted to us you are. 13By all this
we are encouraged.

In addition to our own encouragement, we were especially delighted to
see how happy Titus[t] was, because his
spirit has been refreshed by all of you.
14I had boasted to him about you,[u] and
you have not embarrassed me. But just
as everything we said to you was true,
so our boasting about you to Titus[v] has
proved to be true as well. 15And his affection for you is all the greater when he
remembers that you were all obedient,[w]
receiving him with fear and trembling.[x]
16I am glad I can have complete confidence in you.[y]

7:4 [i]2Co 6:10
7:5 [j]2Co 2:13 [k]2Co 4:8 [l]Dt 32:25
7:6 [m]2Co 1:3,4 [n]ver 13; 2Co 2:13
7:8 [o]2Co 2:2,4
7:10 [p]Ac 11:18
7:11 [q]ver 7
7:12 [r]ver 8; 2Co 2:3,9 [s]1Co 5:1,2
7:13 [t]ver 6; 2Co 2:13
7:14 [u]ver 4 [v]ver 6
7:15 [w]2Co 2:9 [x]Php 2:12
7:16 [y]2Co 2:3

Generosity Encouraged

8 And now, brothers, we want you
to know about the grace that God
has given the Macedonian[z] churches.
2Out of the most severe trial, their overflowing joy and their extreme poverty
welled up in rich generosity. 3For I testify that they gave as much as they
were able,[a] and even beyond their ability. Entirely on their own, 4they urgently pleaded with us for the privilege of
sharing in this service[b] to the saints.[c]
5And they did not do as we expected,
but they gave themselves first to the
Lord and then to us in keeping with
God's will. 6So we urged[d] Titus,[e] since
he had earlier made a beginning, to
bring also to completion[f] this act of
grace on your part. 7But just as you excel in everything[g]—in faith, in speech,
in knowledge,[h] in complete earnestness
and in your love for us[a]—see that you
also excel in this grace of giving.
8I am not commanding you,[i] but I
want to test the sincerity of your love
by comparing it with the earnestness
of others. 9For you know the grace of
our Lord Jesus Christ,[j] that though he
was rich, yet for your sakes he became
poor,[k] so that you through his poverty
might become rich.
10And here is my advice[l] about what
is best for you in this matter: Last year
you were the first not only to give but
also to have the desire to do so.[m] 11Now
finish the work, so that your eager willingness[n] to do it may be matched by
your completion of it, according to your
means. 12For if the willingness is there,
the gift is acceptable according to what
one has,[o] not according to what he does
not have.

13Our desire is not that others might
be relieved while you are hard pressed,
but that there might be equality. 14At
the present time your plenty will supply
what they need,[p] so that in turn their
plenty will supply what you need. Then
there will be equality, 15as it is written:
"He who gathered much did not have
too much, and he who gathered little
did not have too little."[b][q]

Titus Sent to Corinth

16I thank God,[r] who put into the
heart[s] of Titus[t] the same concern I have
for you. 17For Titus not only welcomed
our appeal, but he is coming to you

[a]*7* Some manuscripts *in our love for you*
[b]*15* Exodus 16:18

8:1 [z]Ac 16:9
8:3 [a]1Co 16:2
8:4 [b]Ac 24:17 [c]Ro 15:25; 2Co 9:1
8:6 [d]ver 17; 2Co 12:18 [e]ver 16,23 [f]ver 10,11
8:7 [g]2Co 9:8 [h]1Co 1:5
8:8 [i]1Co 7:6
8:9 [j]2Co 13:14 [k]Mt 20:28; Php 2:6-8
8:10 [l]1Co 7:25,40 [m]1Co 16:2,3; 2Co 9:2
8:11 [n]2Co 9:2
8:12 [o]Mk 12:43, 44; Lk 21:3
8:14 [p]2Co 9:12
8:15 [q]Ex 16:18
8:16 [r]2Co 2:14 [s]Rev 17:17 [t]2Co 2:13

with much enthusiasm and on his own
initiative.[u] 18And we are sending along
with him the brother[v] who is praised by
all the churches[w] for his service to the
gospel.[x] 19What is more, he was chosen
by the churches to accompany us[y] as we
carry the offering, which we administer
in order to honor the Lord himself and
to show our eagerness to help.[z] 20We
want to avoid any criticism of the way
we administer this liberal gift. 21For we
are taking pains to do what is right, not
only in the eyes of the Lord but also in
the eyes of men.[a]
22In addition, we are sending with
them our brother who has often proved
to us in many ways that he is zealous,
and now even more so because of his
great confidence in you. 23As for Titus,
he is my partner[b] and fellow worker[c]
among you; as for our brothers,[d] they
are representatives of the churches and
an honor to Christ. 24Therefore show
these men the proof of your love and
the reason for our pride in you,[e] so that
the churches can see it.

9 There is no need[f] for me to write to
you about this service to the saints.[g]
2For I know your eagerness to help, and
I have been boasting[h] about it to the
Macedonians, telling them that since
last year[i] you in Achaia[j] were ready to
give; and your enthusiasm has stirred
most of them to action. 3But I am sending the brothers in order that our boasting about you in this matter should not
prove hollow, but that you may be ready,
as I said you would be.[k] 4For if any
Macedonians[l] come with me and find
you unprepared, we—not to say anything about you—would be ashamed of
having been so confident. 5So I thought
it necessary to urge the brothers to visit
you in advance and finish the arrange-
ments for the generous gift you had
promised. Then it will be ready as a
generous gift,[m] not as one grudgingly
given.[n]

Sowing Generously

6Remember this: Whoever sows sparingly will also reap sparingly, and whoever sows generously will also reap
generously.[o] 7Each man should give
what he has decided in his heart to give,[p]
not reluctantly or under compulsion,[q]
for God loves a cheerful giver.[r] 8And
God is able[s] to make all grace abound

8:17 [u]ver 6
8:18 [v]2Co 12:18 [w]1Co 7:17 [x]2Co 2:12
8:19 [y]1Co 16:3,4 [z]ver 11,12
8:21 [a]Ro 12:17; 14:18
8:23 [b]Phm 17 [c]Php 2:25 [d]ver 18,22
8:24 [e]2Co 7:4,14; 9:2
9:1 [f]1Th 4:9 [g]2Co 8:4
9:2 [h]2Co 7:4,14 [i]2Co 8:10 [j]Ac 18:12
9:3 [k]1Co 16:2
9:4 [l]Ro 15:26
9:5 [m]Php 4:17 [n]2Co 12:17, 18
9:6 [o]Pr 11:24,25; 22:9; Gal 6:7,9
9:7 [p]Ex 25:2; 2Co 8:12 [q]Dt 15:10 [r]Ro 12:8
9:8 [s]Eph 3:20

to you, so that in all things at all
times, having all that you need,[t] you
will abound in every good work. 9As it
is written:

> "He has scattered abroad his gifts to
> the poor;
> his righteousness endures
> forever."[a][u]

10Now he who supplies seed to the
sower and bread for food[v] will also
supply and increase your store of seed
and will enlarge the harvest of your
righteousness.[w] 11You will be made rich[x]
in every way so that you can be generous on every occasion, and through us
your generosity will result in thanksgiving to God.[y]
12This service that you perform is
not only supplying the needs[z] of God's
people but is also overflowing in many
expressions of thanks to God.[a] 13Be-
cause of the service[b] by which you
have proved yourselves, men will praise
God[c] for the obedience that accompanies your confession of the gospel of
Christ,[d] and for your generosity in sharing with them and with everyone else.
14And in their prayers for you their
hearts will go out to you, because of
the surpassing grace God has given you.
15Thanks be to God[e] for his indescribable gift![f]

▸ LOVE

GRATITUDE

2 Corinthians 9:15

Thanks be to God for his indescribable gift. Indescribable? Yes. There are gifts so majestic that they forbid our compliment. The gift of God's own Son is so majestic that it defies description. It lays the finger of God on our lips and says, "Quiet, please."

Paul's Defense of His Ministry

10 By the meekness and gentleness[g]
of Christ, I appeal to you—I,
Paul,[h] who am "timid" when face to
face with you, but "bold" when away!
2I beg you that when I come I may not
have to be as bold[i] as I expect to be toward some people who think that we
live by the standards of this world. 3For

[a]9 Psalm 112:9

9:8 [t]Php 4:19
9:9 [u]Ps 112:9
9:10 [v]Isa 55:10 [w]Hos 10:12
9:11 [x]1Co 1:5 [y]2Co 1:11
9:12 [z]2Co 8:14 [a]2Co 1:11
9:13 [b]2Co 8:4 [c]Mt 9:8 [d]2Co 2:12
9:15 [e]2Co 2:14 [f]Ro 5:15,16
10:1 [g]Mt 11:29 [h]Gal 5:2
10:2 [i]1Co 4:21; 2Co 13:2,10

though we live in the world, we do not
wage war as the world does. 4The weapons we fight with[j] are not the weapons of the world. On the contrary,
they have divine power[k] to demolish
strongholds.[l] 5We demolish arguments
and every pretension that sets itself
up against the knowledge of God,[m]
and we take captive every thought to
make it obedient[n] to Christ. 6And we
will be ready to punish every act of
disobedience, once your obedience is
complete.[o]

10:4 [j]2Co 6:7 [k]1Co 2:5 [l]Jer 1:10; 2Co 13:10
10:5 [m]Isa 2:11,12; 1Co 1:19 [n]2Co 9:13
10:6 [o]2Co 2:9; 7:15

SELF-CONTROL

EVERY THOUGHT MUST SERVE GOD

2 Corinthians 10:5

Do not think that the conscious mind is a broad ocean. It is not. It is but a narrow trickle of awareness, allowing one thought at a time to pass through its channel. Every thought may pass through this narrow stricture only with permission. So take every thought captive. Allow only those thoughts that honor Christ to pass through.

7You are looking only on the surface
of things.[a][p] If anyone is confident that
he belongs to Christ,[q] he should consider again that we belong to Christ just
as much as he.[r] 8For even if I boast
somewhat freely about the authority the
Lord gave us for building you up rather than pulling you down,[s] I will not
be ashamed of it. 9I do not want to
seem to be trying to frighten you with
my letters. 10For some say, "His letters
are weighty and forceful, but in person
he is unimpressive[t] and his speaking
amounts to nothing."[u] 11Such people

10:7 [p]Jn 7:24 [q]1Co 1:12; 3:23; 14:37 [r]2Co 11:23
10:8 [s]2Co 13:10
10:10 [t]1Co 2:3; Gal 4:13,14 [u]1Co 1:17

KINDNESS

CUTTING REMARKS

2 Corinthians 10:10

The Corinthians had refused to build Paul up. They had been free with criticism. It is so easy to take up the scissors of gossip and cut a heart to ribbons. Blessed, rather, are those who, with the thread of affirmation, stitch back together the shredded souls of those whom hate has abused.

should realize that what we are in our
letters when we are absent, we will be
in our actions when we are present.
12We do not dare to classify or compare ourselves with some who commend themselves.[v] When they measure
themselves by themselves and compare
themselves with themselves, they are
not wise. 13We, however, will not boast
beyond proper limits, but will confine
our boasting to the field God has assigned to us,[w] a field that reaches even
to you. 14We are not going too far in
our boasting, as would be the case if we
had not come to you, for we did get as
far as you[x] with the gospel of Christ.[y]
15Neither do we go beyond our limits
by boasting of work done by others.[b][z]
Our hope is that, as your faith continues to grow,[a] our area of activity among
you will greatly expand, 16so that we
can preach the gospel in the regions
beyond you.[b] For we do not want to
boast about work already done in another man's territory. 17But, "Let him
who boasts boast in the Lord."[c][c] 18For it
is not the one who commends himself[d]
who is approved, but the one whom the
Lord commends.[e]

10:12 [v]2Co 3:1
10:13 [w]ver 15,16
10:14 [x]1Co 3:6 [y]2Co 2:12
10:15 [z]Ro 15:20 [a]2Th 1:3
10:16 [b]Ac 19:21
10:17 [c]Jer 9:24; 1Co 1:31
10:18 [d]ver 12 [e]Ro 2:29; 1Co 4:5

Paul and the False Apostles

11 I hope you will put up with[f] a
little of my foolishness;[g] but you
are already doing that. 2I am jealous for
you with a godly jealousy. I promised
you to one husband,[h] to Christ, so that
I might present you[i] as a pure virgin to
him. 3But I am afraid that just as Eve
was deceived by the serpent's cunning,[j]
your minds may somehow be led astray
from your sincere and pure devotion to
Christ. 4For if someone comes to you
and preaches a Jesus other than the Jesus we preached,[k] or if you receive a
different spirit[l] from the one you received, or a different gospel[m] from the
one you accepted, you put up with it
easily enough. 5But I do not think I
am in the least inferior to those "su-
per-apostles."[n] 6I may not be a trained

11:1 [f]ver 4,19,20; Mt 17:17 [g]ver 16,17,21; 2Co 5:13
11:2 [h]Hos 2:19; Eph 5:26,27 [i]2Co 4:14
11:3 [j]Ge 3:1-6,13; Jn 8:44; 1Ti 2:14; Rev 12:9
11:4 [k]1Co 3:11 [l]Ro 8:15 [m]Gal 1:6-9
11:5 [n]2Co 12:11; Gal 2:6

[a]7 Or *Look at the obvious facts* [b]*13-15* Or *13We, however, will not boast about things that cannot be measured, but we will boast according to the standard of measurement that the God of measure has assigned us—a measurement that relates even to you. 14 . . . 15Neither do we boast about things that cannot be measured in regard to the work done by others.* [c]*17* Jer. 9:24

WEEK 26

GENTLENESS

1 DAY ONE
Gentleness, the Art of Ego Displacement

Read 2 Corinthians 10:1–6

The fine art of ego displacement only matters when we make a decision about what we are going to displace our ego with, and the only acceptable answer is Jesus Christ. In this passage Paul suggests how we are to bring our lives under the power of Jesus. We are fighting a war for the control of the world, and the battlefield is our minds. The world can only be transformed if we understand that we are not fighting with ordinary military weapons but with our thoughts. We are not fighting *hard.* We are fighting *smart!*

We are called to make Jesus Lord of our gray matter. When we have let Christ's mind dwell in us, our minds will achieve a new dynamic. This dynamic will enable us to be the most creative and achieving people in the world.

Christianity has always been involved in warfare of the mind. It is with our minds that we have power to out-think and out-pray the sinister forces of Satan, the god of this world. So our intentions are our broadswords. Our dreams of the kingdom are our tanks and rifles. And our minds are the bunkers where we deploy the powerful winning strategy that will not be overcome.

But how does all this war-like verbiage promote ego displacement? We will show the world that arrogant armaments cannot stand before the innocent power of gentleness. And we will arrive at this gentleness by taking every thought captive and making it obedient to Christ. This means that, between the time we think a thought and the time we turn it into words, we have transformed it into something that Jesus would say. Will such a battle tactic work? Can such disciplined gentleness win? Let us wait for his appearing, and we shall see.

2 DAY TWO
Gentleness and the Purpose of God in My Life

God has a way of teaching humility to those whose towering egos have never desired to learn the art of gentleness. Unfortunately, the lessons of ego displacement are usually hard to bear. So this passage is a reminder that the people who desire peace may have to face the tread of combat boots on their own soil to learn God's way of gentleness. *Turn to Isaiah 8:6–8, page 801, for today's study.*

3 DAY THREE
Gentleness and My Relationship With Christ

This passage speaks of one of the hardest of errors to correct: doctrinal error. The focus of the church on spreading the gospel of Christ must be preserved and protected. But people are very sensitive about what they believe—whether or not it is biblical. So to correct them requires the most sensitive of approaches. Aquila and Priscilla seemed to have this ability. Perhaps their own gentle spirits were the true enablers. *Turn to Acts 18:24–26, page 1317, for today's study.*

4 DAY FOUR
Gentleness and My Service to Others

Those who lust for power bring hurt and pain to those around them. When anyone makes ego the prime focus of life, others will naturally get left out, left behind or trampled in the process. David learned that lesson through the bitterest of circumstances. *Turn to 2 Samuel 18:1–5, page 373, for today's study.*

5 DAY FIVE
Gentleness and Its Place in My Personal Worship

This passage illustrates why most of us would rather deal with an honest sinner than an ego-driven church member. Tax collectors have had the good fortune to be discovered in their sin, and since everyone knows who and what they are, they are much easier to live with. Pharisees, however, are harder to live with because they have a religious reputation to defend, and reputation and ego pass so close that it's hard to tell whom Pharisees really serve. *Turn to Luke 18:9–14, page 1232, for today's study.*

Memorize This Week

EPHESIANS 4:2

Be completely humble and gentle; be patient, bearing with one another in love.

Week 27, Self-Control, Saying No to Our Appetites, begins on page 105, Exodus 32:19–26.
To begin a topical study on the Fruit of the Spirit, Gentleness, turn to the Topical Index, page 1548.

11:6 [o]1Co 1:17 [p]Eph 3:4
speaker,[o] but I do have knowledge.[p] We
have made this perfectly clear to you in
every way.
11:7 [q]2Co 12:13 [r]1Co 9:18
7Was it a sin[q] for me to lower myself
in order to elevate you by preaching the
gospel of God to you free of charge?[r]
8I robbed other churches by receiving
support from them[s] so as to serve you. 11:8 [s]Php 4:15,18
9And when I was with you and needed
something, I was not a burden to anyone, for the brothers who came from
Macedonia supplied what I needed. I
have kept myself from being a burden 11:9 [t]2Co 12:13, 14,16
to you[t] in any way, and will continue

PAUL

Self-Control, the Foundation of the Christian Faith (11:1–33)

The apostle Paul enumerated his hardships, blow by blow, only once in the Scriptures. This passage lists all he had undergone so that the name of Christ might be established in the world. To any who think they have denied themselves excessively, the apostle would say: "I have worked much harder, been in prison more frequently, been flogged more severely, and been exposed to death again and again. Five times I received from the Jews forty lashes minus one. Three times I was beaten with rods, once I was stoned, three times I was shipwrecked, I spent a night and a day in the open sea, I have been constantly on the move. I have been in danger from rivers, in danger from bandits, in danger from my own countrymen, in danger from the Gentiles; in danger in the city, in danger in the country, in danger at sea; and in danger from false brothers. I have labored and toiled and have often gone without sleep; I have known hunger and thirst and have often gone without food; I have been cold and naked. Besides everything else, I face daily the pressure of my concern for all the churches" (2 Corinthians 11:23–28).

But these hardships are summed up by the apostle under a single and simple rule: "I have been crucified with Christ and I no longer live, but Christ lives in me. The life I live in the body, I live by faith in the Son of God, who loved me and gave himself for me" (Galatians 2:20). Self-control and self-crucifixion amounted to the same thing to the apostle. If he could nail his ego to the cross, his selfish desires would be all the easier to manage. Paul believed that self-control is an essential part of the wonderful new life we have been given to enjoy in Christ.

Paul realized that our management of life is in direct relationship to our management of ourselves. This is true in a spiritual sense as well. Just as Christ gained mastery over death by dying, we too can gain mastery over all the world of temptation and sin by dying to ourselves. "In the same way, count yourselves dead to sin but alive to God in Christ Jesus. Therefore do not let sin reign in your mortal body so that you obey its evil desires. Do not offer the parts of your body to sin, as instruments of wickedness, but rather offer yourselves to God, as those who have been brought from death to life; and offer the parts of your body to him as instruments of righteousness. For sin shall not be your master, because you are not under law, but under grace" (Romans 6:11–14).

Self-control is dying to sin. But self-control is so much more than that: It is endurance, the kind of endurance that the apostle lived so that the kingdom of God might become a reality in the world. All that Paul enumerated in 2 Corinthians 11—all that he suffered—he endured through the discipline of self-control. This strong endurance, this powerful self-control, enabled him to write almost half the New Testament and to plant the gospel in Europe. To control the self is to offer Christ a soul free of any other master. To control the self is to stand beyond the soft life and offer God the studied life. It is to say no to our appetites because we have "food to eat that [those who don't know Christ] know nothing about" (John 4:32). It is to pour out the wine of our addictions because the water of life in Christ is better nectar.

11:10 [u]Ro 9:1 [v]Ac 18:12 [w]1Co 9:15
to do so. 10As surely as the truth of
Christ is in me,[u] nobody in the regions
of Achaia[v] will stop this boasting[w] of
mine. 11Why? Because I do not love
11:11 [x]2Co 12:15
you? God knows I do![x] 12And I will
keep on doing what I am doing in order to cut the ground from under those
who want an opportunity to be considered equal with us in the things they
boast about.

11:13 [y]2Pe 2:1 [z]Tit 1:10 [a]Rev 2:2
13For such men are false apostles,[y]
deceitful[z] workmen, masquerading as
apostles of Christ.[a] 14And no wonder,
for Satan himself masquerades as an angel of light. 15It is not surprising, then,
if his servants masquerade as servants of
righteousness. Their end will be what
11:15 [b]Php 3:19
their actions deserve.[b]

Paul Boasts About His Sufferings

16I repeat: Let no one take me for a
11:16 [c]ver 1
fool.[c] But if you do, then receive me just
as you would a fool, so that I may do
a little boasting. 17In this self-confident
boasting I am not talking as the Lord
11:17 [d]1Co 7:12,25
would,[d] but as a fool. 18Since many are
boasting in the way the world does,
11:18 [e]Php 3:3,4
I too will boast.[e] 19You gladly put up
with fools since you are so wise![f] 20In
11:19 [f]1Co 4:10
fact, you even put up with anyone who
enslaves you[g] or exploits you or takes
11:20 [g]Gal 2:4
advantage of you or pushes himself forward or slaps you in the face. 21To my
11:21 [h]2Co 10:1,10 [i]Php 3:4
shame I admit that we were too weak[h]
for that!

What anyone else dares to boast
about—I am speaking as a fool—I also
11:22 [j]Php 3:5 [k]Ro 9:4
dare to boast about.[i] 22Are they Hebrews? So am I.[j] Are they Israelites? So
am I.[k] Are they Abraham's descendants?
So am I. 23Are they servants of Christ?
(I am out of my mind to talk like this.)
11:23 [l]1Co 15:10 [m]Ac 16:23; 2Co 6:4,5
I am more. I have worked much harder,[l]
been in prison more frequently,[m] been
flogged more severely, and been exposed
to death again and again. 24Five times I
11:24 [n]Dt 25:3
received from the Jews the forty lashes[n]
minus one. 25Three times I was beaten
11:25 [o]Ac 16:22 [p]Ac 14:19
with rods,[o] once I was stoned,[p] three
times I was shipwrecked, I spent a night
and a day in the open sea, 26I have
been constantly on the move. I have
been in danger from rivers, in danger
from bandits, in danger from my own
11:26 [q]Ac 9:23; 14:5 [r]Ac 21:31 [s]Gal 2:4
countrymen,[q] in danger from Gentiles;
in danger in the city,[r] in danger in the
country, in danger at sea; and in danger
from false brothers.[s] 27I have labored
and toiled and have often gone without
sleep; I have known hunger and thirst
and have often gone without food;[t] I 11:27 [t]1Co 4:11,12; 2Co 6:5
have been cold and naked. 28Besides everything else, I face daily the pressure of
my concern for all the churches. 29Who
is weak, and I do not feel weak? Who
is led into sin, and I do not inwardly
burn?

30If I must boast, I will boast of the
things that show my weakness.[u] 31The 11:30 [u]1Co 2:3
God and Father of the Lord Jesus, who
is to be praised forever,[v] knows that I 11:31 [v]Ro 9:5
am not lying. 32In Damascus the governor under King Aretas had the city
of the Damascenes guarded in order to
arrest me.[w] 33But I was lowered in a 11:32 [w]Ac 9:24
basket from a window in the wall and
slipped through his hands.[x] 11:33 [x]Ac 9:25

Paul's Vision and His Thorn

12 I must go on boasting.[y] Although there is nothing to be 12:1 [y]2Co 11:16, 30 [z]ver 7
gained, I will go on to visions and
revelations from the Lord.[z] 2I know a
man in Christ who fourteen years ago 12:2 [a]Ac 8:39 [b]Eph 4:10 [c]2Co 11:11
was caught up[a] to the third heaven.[b]
Whether it was in the body or out of
the body I do not know—God knows.[c]
3And I know that this man—whether
in the body or apart from the body I
do not know, but God knows— 4was 12:4 [d]Lk 23:43; Rev 2:7
caught up to paradise.[d] He heard inexpressible things, things that man is not
permitted to tell. 5I will boast about a
man like that, but I will not boast about
myself, except about my weaknesses.
6Even if I should choose to boast, I 12:6 [e]2Co 11:16
would not be a fool,[e] because I would
be speaking the truth. But I refrain, so
no one will think more of me than is
warranted by what I do or say.

7To keep me from becoming conceited because of these surpassingly great
revelations, there was given me a thorn

PEACE

FERTILE THORNS

2 Corinthians 12:9

Do you bear a hurt so ripping that its pain, like an incision left unsutured, cannot be healed? Give it to Christ. Then stand back and watch the thorns that tore your flesh grow fruit. See! What you thought was a thicket of thorns was but the orchard of your God.

in my flesh,[f] a messenger of Satan, to
torment me. 8Three times I pleaded
with the Lord to take it away from

12:7 [f]Nu 33:55

DAY 5 FIVE

▸ JOY AND ITS PLACE IN MY PERSONAL WORSHIP

2 Corinthians 12:1–10

Paul speaks here of his religious experience. He has seen Christ! He saw him as Isaiah did: "raised and lifted up" (52:13). Paul found the exact form of his religious experience hard to describe. "Whether it was in the body or out of the body," Paul wasn't sure. Perhaps that's the danger of religious experiences. We may experience great feelings of religious transport, but we are at a loss later to tell the exact nature of what transpired.

Worship, too, is a religious experience. How poor we would be without it. What aspects of Paul's life-changing vision should we desire to characterize our own walk with Christ?

1. He was "caught up" (2 Corinthians 12:2). We should desire that same sense of transport, a lifting of our lives above the commonplace and the mundane.

2. Paul didn't know whether he was "in the body or out of the body" (vv. 2–3). We ought to understand that if we have a vital affair with Christ, it will come to us within the context of such overwhelming mystery that we will likely be unable to understand it ourselves—let alone explain it to others. Yet we need that very kind of experience. For a God who cannot encounter us with mysteries too wonderful for us, would be too much like us to be of any real use to us.

3. "He heard inexpressible things, things that man is not permitted to tell" (v. 4). This is the delicious case of all our "prayer-closet experiences." We delve deeply into a relationship with Christ and the intimacy is glorious. But intimacy—physical or spiritual—is the language of two, and it cannot really be communicated to a group. Our personal worship will, from time to time, provide us with such a warm camaraderie that we will feel at a loss to define it.

To begin a study on the topic of Joy, Focusing on a Higher Reality, turn to the home page on page 413.

me.[g] 9But he said to me, "My grace
is sufficient for you, for my power[h] is
made perfect in weakness." Therefore I
will boast all the more gladly about my
weaknesses, so that Christ's power may
rest on me. 10That is why, for Christ's
sake, I delight in weaknesses, in insults,
in hardships,[i] in persecutions,[j] in difficulties. For when I am weak, then I am
strong.[k]

Paul's Concern for the Corinthians

11I have made a fool of myself,[l] but
you drove me to it. I ought to have
been commended by you, for I am
not in the least inferior to the "super-
apostles,"[m] even though I am nothing.[n]
12The things that mark an apostle—
signs, wonders and miracles[o]—were
done among you with great perseverance. 13How were you inferior to the
other churches, except that I was never
a burden to you?[p] Forgive me this
wrong![q]
14Now I am ready to visit you for the
third time,[r] and I will not be a burden
to you, because what I want is not your
possessions but you. After all, children
should not have to save up for their
parents,[s] but parents for their children.[t]
15So I will very gladly spend for you everything I have and expend myself as
well.[u] If I love you more, will you love
me less? 16Be that as it may, I have not
been a burden to you.[v] Yet, crafty fellow that I am, I caught you by trickery! 17Did I exploit you through any of
the men I sent you? 18I urged[w] Titus to
go to you and I sent our brother[x] with
him. Titus did not exploit you, did he?
Did we not act in the same spirit and
follow the same course?
19Have you been thinking all along
that we have been defending ourselves
to you? We have been speaking in the
sight of God[y] as those in Christ; and
everything we do, dear friends, is for
your strengthening.[z] 20For I am afraid
that when I come[a] I may not find you
as I want you to be, and you may not
find me as you want me to be.[b] I fear
that there may be quarreling,[c] jealousy,
outbursts of anger, factions,[d] slander,
gossip,[e] arrogance and disorder.[f] 21I am
afraid that when I come again my God
will humble me before you, and I will
be grieved[g] over many who have sinned
earlier[h] and have not repented of the

12:8 [g]Mt 26:39,44
12:9 [h]Php 4:13
12:10 [i]2Co 6:4 [j]Ro 5:3; 2Th 1:4 [k]2Co 13:4
12:11 [l]2Co 11:1 [m]2Co 11:5 [n]1Co 15:9,10
12:12 [o]Jn 4:48
12:13 [p]1Co 9:12,18 [q]2Co 11:7
12:14 [r]2Co 13:1 [s]1Co 4:14,15 [t]Pr 19:14
12:15 [u]Php 2:17; 1Th 2:8
12:16 [v]2Co 11:9
12:18 [w]2Co 8:6,16 [x]2Co 8:18
12:19 [y]Ro 9:1 [z]2Co 10:8
12:20 [a]2Co 2:1-4 [b]1Co 4:21 [c]1Co 1:11; 3:3 [d]Gal 5:20 [e]Ro 1:29 [f]1Co 14:33
12:21 [g]2Co 2:1,4 [h]2Co 13:2

impurity, sexual sin and debauchery in which they have indulged.

Final Warnings

13 This will be my third visit to you.[i] "Every matter must be established by the testimony of two or three witnesses."[a][j] 2I already gave you a warning when I was with you the second time. I now repeat it while absent: On my return I will not spare[k] those who sinned earlier[l] or any of the others, 3since you are demanding proof that Christ is speaking through me.[m] He is not weak in dealing with you, but is powerful among you. 4For to be sure, he was crucified in weakness,[n] yet he lives by God's power.[o] Likewise, we are weak[p] in him, yet by God's power we will live with him to serve you.

5Examine yourselves[q] to see whether you are in the faith; test yourselves.[r] Do you not realize that Christ Jesus is in you[s]—unless, of course, you fail the test? 6And I trust that you will discover that we have not failed the test. 7Now we pray to God that you will not do anything wrong. Not that people will see that we have stood the test but that you will do what is right even though we may seem to have failed. 8For we cannot do anything against the truth, but only for the truth. 9We are glad whenever we are weak but you are strong; and our prayer is for your perfection.[t] 10This is why I write these things when I am absent, that when I come I may not have to be harsh in my use of authority—the authority the Lord gave me for building you up, not for tearing you down.[u]

Final Greetings

11Finally, brothers,[v] good-by. Aim for perfection, listen to my appeal, be of one mind, live in peace.[w] And the God of love and peace[x] will be with you.

12Greet one another with a holy kiss.[y] 13All the saints send their greetings.[z]

14May the grace of the Lord Jesus Christ,[a] and the love of God,[b] and the fellowship of the Holy Spirit[c] be with you all.

[a] *1* Deut. 19:15

13:1 [i]2Co 12:14 [j]Dt 19:15; Mt 18:16
13:2 [k]2Co 1:23 [l]2Co 12:21
13:3 [m]Mt 10:20; 1Co 5:4
13:4 [n]Php 2:7,8; 1Pe 3:18 [o]Ro 1:4; 6:4 [p]ver 9
13:5 [q]1Co 11:28 [r]Jn 6:6 [s]Ro 8:10
13:9 [t]ver 11
13:10 [u]2Co 10:8
13:11 [v]1Th 4:1; 2Th 3:1 [w]Mk 9:50 [x]Ro 15:33; Eph 6:23
13:12 [y]Ro 16:16
13:13 [z]Php 4:22
13:14 [a]Ro 16:20; 2Co 8:9 [b]Ro 5:5; Jude 21 [c]Php 2:1

GALATIANS

Authorship and Date

Paul

Depending on to whom Paul wrote this letter, it was written either c. A.D. 49 or c. A.D. 55.

Key Themes

The book of Galatians was written to combat the deadly heresy of the Judaizers. The Judaizers believed that one could only be a Christian by keeping all the Jewish laws and ordinances. Galatians was written to announce that in Christ all believers had been set free from the demands of the Mosaic system. Salvation is by grace through faith—plus nothing else. Paul was anxious to emphasize the total freedom we have in Christ. The major themes of the book are—as you would then expect—faith, freedom and the Holy Spirit.

In Galatians 5:22–23 the fruit of the Spirit are named and identified. These brief verses outline the virtues introduced in this Bible. The studies in this Bible are designed to pull the entire Bible into a single-themed wholeness around these pivotal verses. The fruit of the Spirit listed in these verses are set in sharp contrast to vices introduced in 5:19–21. For those who are free in Christ, the fruit of the Spirit is the glorious treasure of righteous living.

Fruit of the Spirit in Galatians

Love: "The only thing that counts is faith expressing itself through love" (5:6). Paul made this statement in the midst of a doctrinal debate about whether or not circumcision was important or unimportant with regard to faith in Christ. Paul was not trying to downplay the importance of good doctrine, but rather he was trying to play up love, the chief virtue of saving faith.

Peace: Paul lamented quarreling over caste by reminding his readers that in Christ there has been a great leveling of humanity (see 3:26–29). Peace comes because no one has power over another in the kingdom of God: "There is neither Jew nor Greek, slave nor free, male nor female, for you are all one in Christ Jesus" (v. 28).

Kindness: There is one resolution that will deliver us forever from pride: "May I never boast except in the cross of our Lord Jesus Christ" (6:14). When we have given up pride, we will suddenly become interested in others. From that point on, we will be nice to those we might have overlooked when we were more self-involved.

Faithfulness: Paul's faithfulness extended to the point of, in a sense, self-crucifixion. Paul had put to death his desire to pursue selfish ends, and when the old self had perished on the cross, the new self came to experience a resurrection, crying, "I no longer live, but Christ lives in me. The life I live in the body, I live by faith in the Son of God, who loved me and gave himself for me" (2:20). Self-crucifixion is the first great step toward living the faithful life.

Gentleness: There has been much speculation as to whether or not Paul had vision problems. Galatians 4:15 ("If you could have done so, you would have torn out your eyes and given them to me") and 6:11 ("See what large letters I use as I write to you with my own hand") are verses some use to support their belief that Paul had trouble with his eyesight. Whether or not this may be inferred is academic, for, in some ways, even if Paul was only using a popular cliché of the day in Galatians 4:15, it only makes it more certain that the Galatians were servant-oriented. They understood that gentle ministry is Christlike ministry, and they lavished their gentleness on the apostle.

Self-Control: Self-control is best achieved when the Holy Spirit is in complete charge of our lives. When he is in control, all self-indulgence is put far away, and we are unlikely to be found acting in our own self-interest. It is even as Paul counseled the Galatians: "Live by the Spirit, and you will not gratify the desires of the sinful nature" (5:16).

1 Paul, an apostle—sent not from
1:1 men nor by man, but by Jesus
[a]Ac 9:15 Christ[a] and God the Father, who raised
[b]Ac 2:24 him from the dead[b]— 2and all the
1:2 brothers with me,[c]
[c]Php 4:21
[d]Ac 16:6; 1Co 16:1 To the churches in Galatia:[d]

1:3 3Grace and peace to you from God
[e]Ro 1:7 our Father and the Lord Jesus Christ,[e]
1:4 4who gave himself for our sins[f] to res-
[f]Mt 20:28; cue us from the present evil age, accord-
Ro 4:25; Gal 2:20 ing to the will of our God and Father,[g]
[g]Php 4:2
1:5 5to whom be glory for ever and ever.
[h]Ro 11:36 Amen.[h]

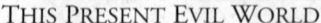

JOY

THIS PRESENT EVIL WORLD

Galatians 1:3–4

We struggled in the quicksand of this present evil world. We thought all was lost and then—joy! Christ taught us to fly.

Earth holds a strange power that ties feet
to the dust,
So that ponderous people are held to her
crust.
But the wind whispers tales of a force in
the sky,
And those with the courage to scorn dust
can fly.

No Other Gospel

6I am astonished that you are so
1:6 quickly deserting the one who called[i]
[i]Gal 5:8 you by the grace of Christ and are turn-
[j]2Co 11:4 ing to a different gospel[j]— 7which is
really no gospel at all. Evidently some
1:7 people are throwing you into confu-
[k]Ac 15:24; Gal 5:10 sion[k] and are trying to pervert the gospel of Christ. 8But even if we or an
angel from heaven should preach a gos-
1:8 pel other than the one we preached to
[l]2Co 11:4 you,[l] let him be eternally condemned![m]
[m]Ro 9:3 9As we have already said, so now I say
1:9 again: If anybody is preaching to you a
[n]Ro 16:17 gospel other than what you accepted,[n]
let him be eternally condemned!
10Am I now trying to win the approval of men, or of God? Or am I try-
1:10 ing to please men?[o] If I were still trying
[o]Ro 2:29; 1Th 2:4 to please men, I would not be a servant
of Christ.

Paul Called by God

1:11 11I want you to know, brothers,[p] that
[p]1Co 15:1 the gospel I preached is not something
that man made up. 12I did not receive
it from any man,[q] nor was I taught it; 1:12
rather, I received it by revelation[r] from [q]ver 1 [r]ver 16
Jesus Christ.

DAY FOUR

PEACE AND MY SERVICE TO OTHERS

Galatians 1:10–12

Consider the verses in today's reading and ask yourself, "What did Paul's acceptance of a higher will really mean in relationship to his service to others?" It meant this: Paul could really minister to others once the turmoil from his own heart and life had been removed. Notice his testimony in the verses that immediately follow.

"For you have heard of my previous way of life in Judaism, how intensely I persecuted the church of God and tried to destroy it... But when God, who set me apart from birth and called me by his grace, was pleased to reveal his Son in me so that I might preach him among the Gentiles, I did not consult any man, nor did I go up to Jerusalem to see those who were apostles before I was, but I went immediately into Arabia and later returned to Damascus" (Galatians 1:13,15–17).

We need to remember that the voice that spoke to Paul on the Damascus road said to him, "It is hard for you to kick against the goads" (Acts 26:14). The implication here seems to be that Paul's conscience was far from settled with regard to his persecution of Christians. Into his troubled thoughts God spoke, and Paul finally found peace.

Great ideas gain acceptance very slowly in stubborn hearts. Peace comes equally slowly. In fact, peace usually gets a little blood on its tranquility before trowelled hearts come to acceptance.

Peace is ours when we have accepted a higher will. When Paul accepted the call of God, he began to minister in ways he might never have imagined. He was freed to bring peace to others out of his own peace. When we focus on the will of God in our lives, we find peace, and we find that we can spread that peace to others.

To begin a study on the topic of Peace, Accepting a Higher Will, turn to the home page on page 1282.

13For you have heard of my previous
way of life in Judaism,[s] how intensely I
persecuted the church of God and tried
to destroy it.[t] 14I was advancing in Judaism beyond many Jews of my own
age and was extremely zealous for the
traditions of my fathers.[u] 15But when
God, who set me apart from birth[a][v] and
called me[w] by his grace, was pleased
16to reveal his Son in me so that I might
preach him among the Gentiles,[x] I did
not consult any man,[y] 17nor did I go
up to Jerusalem to see those who were
apostles before I was, but I went immediately into Arabia and later returned to
Damascus.
18Then after three years,[z] I went up
to Jerusalem[a] to get acquainted with
Peter[b] and stayed with him fifteen days.
19I saw none of the other apostles—
only James,[b] the Lord's brother. 20I assure you before God that what I am
writing you is no lie.[c] 21Later I went
to Syria and Cilicia.[d] 22I was personally
unknown to the churches of Judea[e] that
are in Christ. 23They only heard the
report: "The man who formerly persecuted us is now preaching the faith[f]
he once tried to destroy." 24And they
praised God[g] because of me.

Paul Accepted by the Apostles

2 Fourteen years later I went up again
to Jerusalem,[h] this time with Barnabas. I took Titus along also. 2I went in
response to a revelation and set before
them the gospel that I preach among
the Gentiles.[i] But I did this privately
to those who seemed to be leaders, for
fear that I was running or had run my
race[j] in vain. 3Yet not even Titus,[k] who
was with me, was compelled to be circumcised, even though he was a Greek.[l]
4This matter arose⌞ because some false
brothers[m] had infiltrated our ranks to
spy on[n] the freedom[o] we have in Christ
Jesus and to make us slaves. 5We did
not give in to them for a moment, so
that the truth of the gospel[p] might remain with you.
6As for those who seemed to be important[q]—whatever they were makes no
difference to me; God does not judge by
external appearance[r]—those men added nothing to my message. 7On the
contrary, they saw that I had been entrusted with the task[s] of preaching the
gospel to the Gentiles,[c][t] just as Peter[u]

1:13 [s]Ac 26:4,5 [t]Ac 8:3
1:14 [u]Mt 15:2
1:15 [v]Isa 49:1,5; Jer 1:5 [w]Ac 9:15
1:16 [x]Gal 2:9 [y]Mt 16:17
1:18 [z]Ac 9:22,23 [a]Ac 9:26,27
1:19 [b]Mt 13:55
1:20 [c]Ro 9:1
1:21 [d]Ac 6:9
1:22 [e]1Th 2:14
1:23 [f]Ac 6:7
1:24 [g]Mt 9:8
2:1 [h]Ac 15:2
2:2 [i]Ac 15:4,12 [j]1Co 9:24; Php 2:16
2:3 [k]2Co 2:13 [l]Ac 16:3; 1Co 9:21
2:4 [m]2Co 11:26 [n]Jude 4 [o]Ac 15:1; Gal 5:1,13
2:5 [p]ver 14
2:6 [q]Gal 6:3 [r]Ac 10:34
2:7 [s]1Th 2:4; 1Ti 1:11 [t]Ac 9:15 [u]ver 9,11,14

had been to the Jews.[d] 8For God, who
was at work in the ministry of Peter
as an apostle[v] to the Jews, was also at
work in my ministry as an apostle to
the Gentiles. 9James, Peter[e][w] and John,
those reputed to be pillars,[x] gave me and
Barnabas[y] the right hand of fellowship
when they recognized the grace given to
me.[z] They agreed that we should go to
the Gentiles, and they to the Jews. 10All
they asked was that we should continue
to remember the poor,[a] the very thing I
was eager to do.

Paul Opposes Peter

11When Peter[b] came to Antioch,[c] I
opposed him to his face, because he was
clearly in the wrong. 12Before certain
men came from James, he used to eat
with the Gentiles.[d] But when they arrived, he began to draw back and separate himself from the Gentiles because
he was afraid of those who belonged
to the circumcision group.[e] 13The other Jews joined him in his hypocrisy, so
that by their hypocrisy even Barnabas[f]
was led astray.
14When I saw that they were not acting in line with the truth of the gospel,[g]
I said to Peter[h] in front of them all,
"You are a Jew, yet you live like a Gentile and not like a Jew.[i] How is it, then,
that you force Gentiles to follow Jewish
customs?
15"We who are Jews by birth[j] and not
'Gentile sinners'[k] 16know that a man is
not justified by observing the law, but
by faith in Jesus Christ.[l] So we, too,
have put our faith in Christ Jesus that
we may be justified by faith in Christ
and not by observing the law, because
by observing the law no one will be justified.
17"If, while we seek to be justified in
Christ, it becomes evident that we ourselves are sinners,[m] does that mean that
Christ promotes sin? Absolutely not![n]
18If I rebuild what I destroyed, I prove
that I am a lawbreaker. 19For through
the law[o] I died to the law so that I
might live for God.[p] 20I have been crucified with Christ[q] and I no longer live,
but Christ lives in me.[r] The life I live in
the body, I live by faith in the Son of

2:8 [v]Ac 1:25
2:9 [w]ver 7,11,14 [x]1Ti 3:15 [y]Ac 4:36 [z]Ro 12:3
2:10 [a]Ac 24:17
2:11 [b]ver 7,9,14 [c]Ac 11:19
2:12 [d]Ac 11:3 [e]Ac 11:2
2:13 [f]ver 1; Ac 4:36
2:14 [g]ver 5 [h]ver 7,9,11 [i]Ac 10:28
2:15 [j]Php 3:4,5 [k]1Sa 15:18
2:16 [l]Ac 13:39; Ro 9:30
2:17 [m]ver 15 [n]Gal 3:21
2:19 [o]Ro 7:4 [p]Ro 6:10, 11,14; 2Co 5:15
2:20 [q]Ro 6:6 [r]1Pe 4:2

[a]15 Or *from my mother's womb* [b]18 Greek *Cephas* [c]7 Greek *uncircumcised* [d]7 Greek *circumcised*; also in verses 8 and 9 [e]9 Greek *Cephas*; also in verses 11 and 14

PEACE

DYING FIRST, LIVING LATER

Galatians 2:20

The words *dead* and *risen* were the bookends of a single weekend in Jesus' life. Jesus could not own the second adjective until he agreed to wear the first. Nor can we. Those who crucify themselves begin to live the very moment they agree to die. The greatest paradox of Christianity is that crosses are the birthing places of life, the porches of resurrection.

God,[s] who loved me[t] and gave himself
for me.[u] 21 I do not set aside the grace
of God, for if righteousness could be
gained through the law,[v] Christ died for
nothing!"[a]

2:20 [s]Mt 4:3 [t]Ro 8:37 [u]Gal 1:4
2:21 [v]Gal 3:21

Faith or Observance of the Law

3 You foolish Galatians! Who has bewitched you?[w] Before your very eyes
Jesus Christ was clearly portrayed as
crucified.[x] 2 I would like to learn just

3:1 [w]Gal 5:7 [x]1Co 1:23

[a]*21* Some interpreters end the quotation after verse 14.

BARNABAS

Gentleness, the Art of Encouragement (2:1–9)

We know that Barnabas was among the first of the generous patrons of the church. He sold a field and brought the money to the apostles, laying it at their feet. He gave in a gentle and unobtrusive way that may have encouraged the more self-seeking and less gentle Ananias and Sapphira to give in Acts 5. Barnabas's name means "Son of Encouragement."

How exalted is the virtue of encouragement! We live in a world where criticism is customary and a good word of support is rare. But Barnabas was an encourager, and he distinguished himself in life by practicing the art. Who knows what role he may have played in the very creation of the New Testament, for he was the traveling companion of both John Mark and the apostle Paul. Encouragement is a gentle art, one that often provides a kind word to those who need it.

Acts 11:19–24 describes an example of Barnabas's encouragement to the early church. The early church was a multicultural affair. In this passage the thumbscrews of persecution had begun to tighten down upon the church in the Jewish community, following the martyrdom of Stephen. As the pressure became intense, Jewish Christians left the Jerusalem area and scattered "as far as Phoenicia, Cyprus and Antioch" (v. 19). This meant that those who were scattered began to evangelize Gentiles; previously they had evangelized only Jews. "The Lord's hand was with them, and a great number of people believed and turned to the Lord" (v. 21). One can only imagine the stress caused by both persecution and multicultural revival. It was a day when encouragement was severely needed.

But Barnabas was there. "When he arrived and saw the evidence of the grace of God, he was glad and encouraged them all to remain true to the Lord with all their hearts" (v. 23). Barnabas used some good old-fashioned affirmation to strengthen those who had been saved.

But there was another advantage of Barnabas's gentle approach. Gentleness itself is a soul-winner. This passage says that Barnabas was "a good man, full of the Holy Spirit and faith, and a great number of people were brought to the Lord" (v. 24). Gentleness is the tool that encouragement uses to evangelize. Most people are not led to the Lord by carefully crafted, hard-core arguments. Most people are brought to the Lord by gentle listening and support. People who feel affirmed and encouraged often rush into the arms of a Savior they are not afraid of. Barnabas encouraged such faith. Gentleness was his method.

Would you win your world to Christ? Open your clenched, doubled fists. Ask the Spirit to soften your hardened face, and make it a point to smile at those who need Jesus. Don't try to argue souls into the kingdom of God; "listen" them into the church. Give up your wintry efficiency and become a gentle rain that touches arid ground with hope.

one thing from you: Did you receive
3:2 the Spirit by observing the law, or by
[y]Ro 10:17 believing what you heard?[y] 3Are you so
foolish? After beginning with the Spirit,
are you now trying to attain your goal
by human effort? 4Have you suffered so
much for nothing—if it really was for
3:5 nothing? 5Does God give you his Spirit
[z]1Co 12:10 and work miracles[z] among you because
you observe the law, or because you believe what you heard?

FAITHFULNESS

FAITH FIRST, FAITH SECOND

Galatians 3:3

We are held in faith by the same force that gave us faith. Self-reliance is not a theme in the course on faith. It is instead a rhetoric of code and cliché: "Please God, I'd rather do it myself... After all, God helps those who help themselves... If it is to be, it's up to me." Self-reliance most often comes from crowing egos. It is a worthless virtue in heaven. It keeps grace at arm's length and chops at the waves to provide its own salvation.

6Consider Abraham: "He believed
3:6 God, and it was credited to him as righ-
[a]Ge 15:6; Ro 4:3 teousness."[a][a] 7Understand, then, that
those who believe[b] are children of Abra-
3:7 [b]ver 9 ham. 8The Scripture foresaw that God
would justify the Gentiles by faith, and
3:8 [c]Ge 12:3; announced the gospel in advance to
Ac 3:25 Abraham: "All nations will be blessed
3:9 through you."[b][c] 9So those who have
[d]ver 7; faith[d] are blessed along with Abraham,
Ro 4:16 the man of faith.
10All who rely on observing the law
are under a curse, for it is written:
"Cursed is everyone who does not con-
3:10 tinue to do everything written in the
[e]Dt 27:26; Book of the Law."[c][e] 11Clearly no one is
Jer 11:3 justified before God by the law, because,
3:11 "The righteous will live by faith."[d][f]
[f]Hab 2:4; 12The law is not based on faith; on
Gal 2:16; Heb 10:38 the contrary, "The man who does these
3:12 things will live by them."[e][g] 13Christ re-
[g]Lev 18:5; Ro 10:5 deemed us from the curse of the law[h] by
3:13 becoming a curse for us, for it is writ-
[h]Gal 4:5 ten: "Cursed is everyone who is hung
[i]Dt 21:23; Ac 5:30 on a tree."[f][i] 14He redeemed us in or-
3:14 der that the blessing given to Abraham
[j]Ro 4:9,16 might come to the Gentiles through
[k]ver 2; Joel 2:28; Christ Jesus,[j] so that by faith we might
Ac 2:33 receive the promise of the Spirit.[k]

GOODNESS

SHAME ON THE BLESSED ONE

Galatians 3:13

The goodness of Christ has vanquished our sinful nature.

Jesus, the cursed One, purchased for us the blessing of God.

Jesus, the shamed One, earned us the glorification.

Jesus, the dying One, brought us life.

Confidently entering hell, Christ swung open the gates of heaven.

The Law and the Promise

15Brothers, let me take an example
from everyday life. Just as no one can
set aside or add to a human covenant
that has been duly established, so it is
in this case. 16The promises were spoken to Abraham and to his seed.[l] The 3:16
Scripture does not say "and to seeds," [l]Lk 1:55; Ro 4:13,16
meaning many people, but "and to your
seed,"[g] meaning one person, who is
Christ. 17What I mean is this: The law, 3:17
introduced 430 years[m] later, does not [m]Ge 15:13,14; Ex 12:40
set aside the covenant previously estab-
lished by God and thus do away with
the promise. 18For if the inheritance depends on the law, then it no longer
depends on a promise;[n] but God in 3:18
his grace gave it to Abraham through a [n]Ro 4:14
promise.
19What, then, was the purpose of
the law? It was added because of trans- 3:19
gressions[o] until the Seed[p] to whom the [o]Ro 5:20
promise referred had come. The law [p]ver 16
was put into effect through angels[q] by a [q]Ac 7:53 [r]Ex 20:19
mediator.[r] 20A mediator,[s] however, does 3:20
not represent just one party; but God is [s]Heb 8:6; 9:15; 12:24
one.
21Is the law, therefore, opposed to the
promises of God? Absolutely not![t] For 3:21
if a law had been given that could im- [t]Gal 2:17 [u]Gal 2:21
part life, then righteousness would cer-
tainly have come by the law.[u] 22But the
Scripture declares that the whole world
is a prisoner of sin,[v] so that what was 3:22
promised, being given through faith in [v]Ro 3:9-19; 11:32
Jesus Christ, might be given to those
who believe.
23Before this faith came, we were held

[a]*6* Gen. 15:6 [b]*8* Gen. 12:3; 18:18; 22:18
[c]*10* Deut. 27:26 [d]*11* Hab. 2:4 [e]*12* Lev. 18:5
[f]*13* Deut. 21:23 [g]*16* Gen. 12:7; 13:15; 24:7

GENTLENESS

FIRST PRIDE, THEN PREJUDICE

Galatians 3:28

Avoid pride. Acknowledge the price Christ paid to redeem us all—male and female, Jew and Greek, slave and free. Be honest; God loves everyone else as much as he loves you. Treat everyone gently. Live free of superiority. All prejudice is nourished in the soil of pride. It rests on a grand fallacy: "If only my enemies were more like me, I wouldn't feel myself superior." Then this assessment gives way to hate, and hate opens the door to a more dangerous fallacy: "If only I could eliminate all my enemies, all that would be left would be my friends." The first fallacy sponsors snobbery and social division; the second, genocide.

3:23 prisoners[w] by the law, locked up until
[w]Ro 11:32 faith should be revealed. 24So the law
3:24 was put in charge to lead us to Christ[a][x]
[x]Ro 10:4 [y]Gal 2:16 that we might be justified by faith.[y]
25Now that faith has come, we are no
longer under the supervision of the law.

Sons of God

3:26 [z]Ro 8:14 26You are all sons of God[z] through
faith in Christ Jesus, 27for all of you
3:27 [a]Mt 28:19; Ro 6:3 who were baptized into Christ[a] have
[b]Ro 13:14 clothed yourselves with Christ.[b] 28There
is neither Jew nor Greek, slave nor free,[c]
3:28 [c]Col 3:11 male nor female, for you are all one in
[d]Jn 10:16; 17:11; Christ Jesus.[d] 29If you belong to Christ,[e]
Eph 2:14,15 then you are Abraham's seed, and heirs
according to the promise.[f]
3:29 [e]1Co 3:23 [f]ver 16 4 What I am saying is that as long as
the heir is a child, he is no differ-
ent from a slave, although he owns the
whole estate. 2He is subject to guardians and trustees until the time set by
his father. 3So also, when we were chil-

PATIENCE

KAIROS—THE FULLNESS OF TIME

Galatians 4:4

Jesus came when the clock of history was running down. The big hand was on hope and the little hand was on desperation. The time was full. There was a star in the east, and a baby cried as God stepped down from crystal safety to bloody reconciliation.

dren, we were in slavery[g] under the ba- 4:3 [g]Gal 2:4
sic principles of the world.[h] 4But when [h]Col 2:8,20
the time had fully come,[i] God sent his
Son, born of a woman,[j] born under 4:4 [i]Mk 1:15;
law,[k] 5to redeem those under law, that Eph 1:10
we might receive the full rights[l] of sons. [j]Jn 1:14 [k]Lk 2:27
6Because you are sons, God sent the 4:5
Spirit of his Son into our hearts,[m] the [l]Jn 1:12
Spirit who calls out, "Abba,[b] Father."[n] 4:6
7So you are no longer a slave, but a son; [m]Ro 5:5 [n]Ro 8:15,16
and since you are a son, God has made
you also an heir.[o] 4:7 [o]Ro 8:17

KINDNESS

THE SLAVES AND SONS OF KINDNESS

Galatians 4:7

"What am I to bid for all these souls?" cried Satan. God saw him gloat as though he had the power to cause the races to die in hopelessness.

"I bid Calvary!" cried God.

"Sold!" cried Satan.

Jesus died and two millennia of needy sinners walked into heaven and heard God use a strange and glorious new word: *children*.

Paul's Concern for the Galatians

8Formerly, when you did not know 4:8
God,[p] you were slaves to those who [p]1Co 1:21;
by nature are not gods.[q] 9But now that Eph 2:12; 1Th 4:5
you know God—or rather are known [q]2Ch 13:9; Isa 37:19
by God[r]—how is it that you are turn-
ing back to those weak and miserable 4:9 [r]1Co 8:3
principles? Do you wish to be enslaved[s] [s]ver 3
by them all over again?[t] 10You are ob- [t]Col 2:20
serving special days and months and
seasons and years![u] 11I fear for you, that 4:10 [u]Ro 14:5
somehow I have wasted my efforts on
you.[v] 4:11 [v]1Th 3:5
12I plead with you, brothers,[w] be-
come like me, for I became like you. 4:12 [w]Gal 6:18
You have done me no wrong. 13As you
know, it was because of an illness[x] that I 4:13 [x]1Co 2:3
first preached the gospel to you. 14Even
though my illness was a trial to you,
you did not treat me with contempt or
scorn. Instead, you welcomed me as if
I were an angel of God, as if I were
Christ Jesus himself.[y] 15What has hap- 4:14 [y]Mt 10:40
pened to all your joy? I can testify that,
if you could have done so, you would

[a]24 Or *charge until Christ came* [b]6 Aramaic for *Father*

have torn out your eyes and given them
4:16 to me. 16Have I now become your en-
[z]Am 5:10 emy by telling you the truth?[z]
17Those people are zealous to win
you over, but for no good. What they
want is to alienate you ⌞from us⌟, so
that you may be zealous for them. 18It
is fine to be zealous, provided the pur-
4:18 pose is good, and to be so always and
[a]ver 13,14 not just when I am with you.[a] 19My
4:19 dear children,[b] for whom I am again in
[b]1Co 4:15 the pains of childbirth until Christ is
[c]Eph 4:13 formed in you,[c] 20how I wish I could
be with you now and change my tone,
because I am perplexed about you!

Hagar and Sarah

21Tell me, you who want to be under the law, are you not aware of what
the law says? 22For it is written that
Abraham had two sons, one by the
4:22 [d]Ge 16:15 slave woman[d] and the other by the free
[e]Ge 21:2 woman.[e] 23His son by the slave woman
4:23 was born in the ordinary way;[f] but his
[f]Ro 9:7,8 son by the free woman was born as the
[g]Ge 18:10-14; Heb 11:11 result of a promise.[g]
24These things may be taken figuratively, for the women represent two covenants. One covenant is from Mount
Sinai and bears children who are to
be slaves: This is Hagar. 25Now Hagar
stands for Mount Sinai in Arabia and
corresponds to the present city of Jerusalem, because she is in slavery with
4:26 her children. 26But the Jerusalem that
[h]Heb 12:22; is above[h] is free, and she is our mother.
Rev 3:12 27For it is written:

"Be glad, O barren woman,
who bears no children;
break forth and cry aloud,
you who have no labor pains;
because more are the children of the
desolate woman
4:27 [i]Isa 54:1 than of her who has a husband."[a][i]

28Now you, brothers, like Isaac, are
children of promise. 29At that time the
4:29 [j]ver 23 son born in the ordinary way[j] persecut-
[k]Ge 21:9 ed the son born by the power of the
Spirit.[k] It is the same now. 30But what
does the Scripture say? "Get rid of the
slave woman and her son, for the slave
woman's son will never share in the in-
4:30 heritance with the free woman's son."[b][l]
[l]Ge 21:10 31Therefore, brothers, we are not children of the slave woman, but of the free
woman.

Freedom in Christ

5 It is for freedom that Christ has set 5:1
us free.[m] Stand firm,[n] then, and do [m]Jn 8:32
not let yourselves be burdened again by [n]1Co 16:13 [o]Ac 15:10;
a yoke of slavery.[o] Gal 2:4
2Mark my words! I, Paul, tell you
that if you let yourselves be circum- 5:2
cised,[p] Christ will be of no value to you [p]Ac 15:1
at all. 3Again I declare to every man
who lets himself be circumcised that
he is obligated to obey the whole law.[q] 5:3 [q]Gal 3:10
4You who are trying to be justified by
law have been alienated from Christ;
you have fallen away from grace.[r] 5But 5:4 [r]Heb 12:15;
by faith we eagerly await through the 2Pe 3:17
Spirit the righteousness for which we
hope.[s] 6For in Christ Jesus neither cir- 5:5
cumcision nor uncircumcision has any [s]Ro 8:23,24
value.[t] The only thing that counts is
faith expressing itself through love.[u] 5:6 [t]1Co 7:19 [u]1Th 1:3
7You were running a good race.[v] Who
cut in on you[w] and kept you from obey- 5:7 [v]1Co 9:24
ing the truth? 8That kind of persuasion [w]Gal 3:1
does not come from the one who calls
you.[x] 9"A little yeast works through the 5:8 [x]Ro 8:28;
whole batch of dough."[y] 10I am confi- Gal 1:6
dent[z] in the Lord that you will take no 5:9 [y]1Co 5:6
other view.[a] The one who is throwing
you into confusion[b] will pay the pen- 5:10 [z]2Co 2:3
alty, whoever he may be. 11Brothers, if [a]Php 3:15
I am still preaching circumcision, why [b]Gal 1:7
am I still being persecuted?[c] In that case 5:11 [c]Gal 4:29;
the offense[d] of the cross has been abol- 6:12
ished. 12As for those agitators,[e] I wish [d]1Co 1:23
they would go the whole way and emas- 5:12 [e]ver 10
culate themselves!
13You, my brothers, were called to be
free. But do not use your freedom to 5:13
indulge the sinful nature[c];[f] rather, serve [f]1Co 8:9; 1Pe 2:16
one another[g] in love. 14The entire law [g]1Co 9:19;
is summed up in a single command: Eph 5:21
"Love your neighbor as yourself."[d][h] 15If 5:14 [h]Lev 19:18;
you keep on biting and devouring each Mt 22:39
other, watch out or you will be destroyed by each other.

Life by the Spirit

16So I say, live by the Spirit,[i] and 5:16 [i]Ro 8:2,4-6,
you will not gratify the desires of the 9,14
sinful nature.[j] 17For the sinful nature [j]ver 24
desires what is contrary to the Spirit,
and the Spirit what is contrary to the
sinful nature.[k] They are in conflict with 5:17 [k]Ro 8:5-8
each other, so that you do not do what

[a] *27* Isaiah 54:1 [b] *30* Gen. 21:10 [c] *13* Or *the flesh*; also in verses 16, 17, 19 and 24 [d] *14* Lev. 19:18

5:17 [l]Ro 7:15-23 you want.[l] 18But if you are led by the
Spirit, you are not under law.[m]
19The acts of the sinful nature are
obvious: sexual immorality,[n] impurity 5:18 [m]Ro 6:14; 1Ti 1:9
and debauchery; 20idolatry and witch-
craft; hatred, discord, jealousy, fits of 5:19 [n]1Co 6:18
rage, selfish ambition, dissensions, fac-
tions 21and envy; drunkenness, orgies,
and the like.[o] I warn you, as I did be- 5:21 [o]Ro 13:13
fore, that those who live like this will
not inherit the kingdom of God.
22But the fruit[p] of the Spirit is love,[q] 5:22 [p]Mt 7:16-20; Eph 5:9 [q]Col 3:12-15
joy, peace, patience, kindness, good-
ness, faithfulness, 23gentleness and self-
control.[r] Against such things there is no 5:23 [r]Ac 24:25
law. 24Those who belong to Christ Jesus 5:24 [s]Ro 6:6 [t]ver 16,17
have crucified the sinful nature[s] with its
passions and desires.[t] 25Since we live by
the Spirit, let us keep in step with the
Spirit. 26Let us not become conceited,[u] 5:26 [u]Php 2:3
provoking and envying each other.

DAY 3 THREE

Self-Control and My Relationship With Christ

Galatians 5:16,19–21

In this passage Paul offers us a four-word antidote to indulging ourselves in our appetites. It is not a message of negativity. It is instead a proactive approach that each individual believer both initiates and completes. What is this four-word recipe for success in a life of self-control? It is this: *Live by the Spirit!* When we live by the Spirit, says the apostle, we will not indulge ourselves in the never-ending clamor of all those appetites that beg our indulgence.

What are these horrible flings into indulgence? See Galatians 5:19–21. To read this list at first may seem like we are reading of sins so terrible that we ourselves could never be guilty of them. But don't believe it. It is nothing more than the grace of God that keeps us from falling into these sins at any given moment.

Remember, too, indulgence never jumps into great crimes on the first leap. The truth is that we move into great sin through baby steps of compromise. Consider this list:

Sexual immorality begins in simple office flirtations.
Impurity and debauchery starts with pornography.
Ambition begins with buttering up the boss.
Drunkenness begins with one simple drink.

So it is through the little bargains we strike with Satan by which we lose our usefulness to Christ. Jesus has given us the power to overcome our appetites and to defeat Satan. Before he left earth, Christ promised to send a helper to his followers. This helper is our key to living for Christ. This helper gives us the strength to resist any compromise. For it is through such minor concessions that we fail to live by the Spirit, the One sent to help us become holy and grow in our relationship with Jesus.

To begin a study on the topic of Self-Control, Saying No to Our Appetites, turn to the home page on page 105.

Love

Fruit of the Spirit

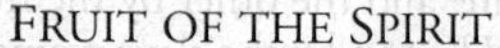

Galatians 5:22–23

There is an orchard whose fruit is lush.
Love is the definition of God.
Joy is the response of those who brush the sleeve of love.
Peace is the result of having all our conflicts washed in love.
Patience is the art that never hurries love.
Kindness is love's application.
Goodness is the life grown moral by seeking love's pleasure.
Faithfulness is love's servant.
Gentleness is love's method.
Self-control is love's submission to integrity.
Grace is the tree on which such fruit hangs.
Its nutrition is eternal life.

Doing Good to All

6 Brothers, if someone is caught in a 6:1 [v]1Co 2:15
sin, you who are spiritual[v] should
restore him gently. But watch yourself,
or you also may be tempted. 2Carry
each other's burdens, and in this way 6:2 [w]Ro 15:1; Jas 2:8
you will fulfill the law of Christ.[w] 3If
anyone thinks he is something[x] when
he is nothing, he deceives himself. 4Each 6:3 [x]Ro 12:3; 1Co 8:2
one should test his own actions. Then
he can take pride in himself, without
comparing himself to somebody else,
5for each one should carry his own
load.
6Anyone who receives instruction in

KINDNESS

BAGGAGE HANDLERS: APPLY AT THE CROSS

Galatians 6:2

So many carry so much. Are you strong enough to lift their cares? Kindness volunteers to carry all that crushes the human spirit. When you see the burdened, ask yourself, "Is he crushed beneath a cross that I could lift?"

6:6 [y]1Co 9:11,14 the word must share all good things
with his instructor.[y]
6:7 [z]1Co 6:9 [a]2Co 9:6 7Do not be deceived:[z] God cannot be
mocked. A man reaps what he sows.[a]
8The one who sows to please his sinful
nature, from that nature[a] will reap
6:8 [b]Job 4:8; Hos 8:7 [c]Jas 3:18 destruction;[b] the one who sows to please
the Spirit, from the Spirit will reap eter-
nal life.[c] 9Let us not become weary in
6:9 [d]1Co 15:58 [e]Rev 2:10 doing good,[d] for at the proper time we
will reap a harvest if we do not give up.[e]
10Therefore, as we have opportunity, let
6:10 [f]Pr 3:27 [g]Eph 2:19 us do good[f] to all people, especially to
those who belong to the family[g] of be-
lievers.

Not Circumcision but a New Creation

6:11 [h]1Co 16:21 11See what large letters I use as I write
to you with my own hand![h]

12Those who want to make a good
impression outwardly are trying to com-
pel you to be circumcised.[i] The only 6:12 [i]Ac 15:1 [j]Gal 5:11
reason they do this is to avoid being
persecuted[j] for the cross of Christ.
13Not even those who are circumcised
obey the law,[k] yet they want you to be 6:13 [k]Ro 2:25 [l]Php 3:3
circumcised that they may boast about
your flesh.[l] 14May I never boast except
in the cross of our Lord Jesus Christ,
through which[b] the world has been cru-
cified to me, and I to the world.[m] 15Nei- 6:14 [m]Ro 6:2,6
ther circumcision nor uncircumcision
means anything;[n] what counts is a new 6:15 [n]1Co 7:19 [o]2Co 5:17
creation.[o] 16Peace and mercy to all who
follow this rule, even to the Israel of
God.

17Finally, let no one cause me trou- 6:17 [p]Isa 44:5; 2Co 1:5
ble, for I bear on my body the marks[p]
of Jesus.

18The grace of our Lord Jesus Christ[q] 6:18 [q]Ro 16:20 [r]2Ti 4:22
be with your spirit,[r] brothers. Amen.

[a]8 Or *his flesh, from the flesh* [b]14 Or *whom*

LOVE

MARKED BY DEVOTION

Galatians 6:17

Have you scars you earned in loving Jesus? How wonderful! He has scars he earned in loving you.

EPHESIANS

AUTHORSHIP AND DATE

Paul

c. A.D. 60

KEY THEMES

Ephesians was not written—as the book of Galatians was—to deal with any problems or to correct any heresies. But the book of Ephesians abounds with warm encouragement and the clarification of basic concepts that God has ordained to be lived out in his church. The book can be broken down as follows:

1. God directed his cosmic plan of salvation before the world began (see 1:3–14).
2. Jesus is seated at God's right hand in glory and is head over everything in the church (see 1:15–23).
3. We have been saved and given a superior existence in Jesus Christ (see ch. 2).
4. Paul's celebration of his own calling (see ch. 3).
5. The unity of the church, its doctrine and commission (see 4:1–16).
6. How to live as children of light (see 4:17—5:21).
7. Paul's celebrated double metaphor of Christ's love for the church and human love within the family (see 5:22—6:4).
8. Spiritual warfare and how serious this invisible but real conflict is (see 6:10–20).

All in all, the book calls us to put Christ at the center of the church and all our relationships. As we do this, we will be living out God's purposes in our lives.

FRUIT OF THE SPIRIT IN EPHESIANS

Love: The first aspect of God's love that we meet is grace. This expression of love cannot be earned or even initiated. Grace saves us through faith and leaves us so ecstatic that we cry out to the Father in our gratitude. Grace is by definition "first love." This love is "gift love," and it is the most significant love we will ever know (see 2:8–9).

Joy: Ephesians 1:3–6 gives us four reasons to praise God: "Praise be to the God and Father of our Lord Jesus Christ, who [1] has blessed us in the heavenly realms with every spiritual blessing in Christ. [2] For he chose us in him before the creation of the world to be holy and blameless in his sight. [3] In love he predestined us to be adopted as his sons through Jesus Christ, in accordance with his pleasure and will—[4] to the praise of his glorious grace, which he has freely given us in the One he loves."

Peace: God went to great lengths to make peace with humanity. Paul describes this peace as bringing us "near through the blood of Christ" (2:13). God's reconciling work is the work of bringing us near. To reinforce this concept, Paul employed a metaphor of a wall that separates Jews from Gentiles. There was an actual wall in the temple, which separated the court of Israel (the court of the Jews) from the court of the Gentiles. As a Gentile advanced into the temple, he or she could not advance beyond the separating wall (*mesotoikon* in Greek) into the court of Israel. But with Christ's coming, God smashed the separating wall, and all people, regardless of ethnic background, may now come into his presence (see 2:14–18).

Kindness: Paul asserts that our faith in Jesus allows us to approach God with confidence. It is because of this confidence that Paul encouraged the Ephesians not to despair because of his imprisonment and suffering (see 3:12–13). This confidence protected Paul from despair; it did not drive Paul into pride. He said, "For this reason I kneel before the Father" (v. 14). Kneeling is the posture of meekness, and meekness is the forerunner of kindness.

Goodness: The secret of arriving at goodness is not moral struggle and earnest intent. We become good when we are clothed with Christ's righteousness—a righteousness that is absolutely sinless. It is placed around us like a new garment. It replaces our old value system and makes us new in the attitude of our minds (see 4:22–24).

Faithfulness: We are encouraged to dress ourselves in power for the spiritual war that rages all around us. The armor of the Christian knight is described in Ephesians 6:10–18. Armor exists to protect the warrior and each piece is important. Still, the shield of faith (see v. 16) is a reminder that our faith protects us from the arrows and spears of our enemy. To be faithful is to stand—protected by the armor, without any possibility of being wounded.

Self-Control: Paul spoke of the fruit of the Spirit in Galatians 5:22–23. In Ephesians 5:8–10 he speaks of the fruit of the light: "For you were once darkness, but now you are light in the Lord. Live as children of the light (for the fruit of the light consists in all goodness, righteousness and truth) and find out what pleases the Lord." Self-control is born in our desire to find out what pleases the Lord. When we discover what pleases God, we have also found the key to self-control.

1:1 [a]1Co1:1 1 Paul, an apostle[a] of Christ Jesus by
[b]2Co 1:1 [c]Col 1:2 the will of God,[b]

To the saints in Ephesus,[a] the faithful[b][c] in Christ Jesus:

[2]Grace and peace to you from God
1:2 [d]Ro 1:7 our Father and the Lord Jesus Christ.[d]

Spiritual Blessings in Christ

[3]Praise be to the God and Father of
1:3 [e]2Co 1:3 our Lord Jesus Christ,[e] who has blessed
[f]Eph 2:6; us in the heavenly realms[f] with every
3:10; 6:12 spiritual blessing in Christ. [4]For he
1:4 chose us in him before the creation of
[g]Eph 5:27; the world to be holy and blameless[g] in
Col 1:22 [h]Eph his sight. In love[h] [5]he[c] predestined[i] us
4:2,15,16 to be adopted as his sons through Jesus
1:5 [i]Ro 8:29,30 Christ, in accordance with his pleasure[j]
[j]1Co 1:21 and will— [6]to the praise of his glori-
1:6 ous grace, which he has freely given us
[k]Mt 3:17 in the One he loves.[k] [7]In him we have
1:7 redemption[l] through his blood, the for-
[l]Ro 3:24 giveness of sins, in accordance with the
riches of God's grace [8]that he lavished
on us with all wisdom and understanding. [9]And he[d] made known to us the
1:9 mystery[m] of his will according to his
[m]Ro 16:25 good pleasure, which he purposed in
Christ, [10]to be put into effect when
the times will have reached their fulfill-
1:10 [n]Gal 4:4 ment[n]—to bring all things in heaven
[o]Col 1:20 and on earth together under one head,
even Christ.[o]

LOVE

HAND-PICKED FOR LOVE

Ephesians 1:4–5

God, while the universe cooled, saw the world where you would one day live. It was then that he wrote your name in fire across new space. Do not think you stumbled into love. God planned to love you before the world began its spin about the sun.

[11]In him we were also chosen,[e] having been predestined according to the
plan of him who works out everything
1:11 [p]Eph 3:11; in conformity with the purpose[p] of his
Heb 6:17 will, [12]in order that we, who were the
first to hope in Christ, might be for the
1:12 [q]ver 6,14 praise of his glory.[q] [13]And you also were
included in Christ when you heard the
1:13 [r]Col 1:5 word of truth,[r] the gospel of your salva-
[s]Eph 4:30 tion. Having believed, you were marked
in him with a seal,[s] the promised Holy
Spirit, [14]who is a deposit guaranteeing
our inheritance[t] until the redemption 1:14 [t]Ac 20:32
of those who are God's possession—to
the praise of his glory.

GENTLENESS

THE POWER AT THE CENTER OF YOUR SOUL IS THE POWER AT THE CENTER OF THE UNIVERSE

Ephesians 1:18–21

Jesus is the cosmic pilot, driving galaxies with the same precision he used to save your soul. Yet his vast dominion is never domineering. He is as gentle at saving souls as he is at celestial engineering.

Thanksgiving and Prayer

[15]For this reason, ever since I heard
about your faith in the Lord Jesus and 1:15 [u]Col 1:4
your love for all the saints,[u] [16]I have
not stopped giving thanks for you,[v] re- 1:16 [v]Ro 1:8
membering you in my prayers. [17]I keep
asking that the God of our Lord Jesus
Christ, the glorious Father,[w] may give 1:17 [w]Jn 20:17
you the Spirit[f] of wisdom[x] and revela- [x]Col 1:9
tion, so that you may know him bet-
ter. [18]I pray also that the eyes of your
heart may be enlightened[y] in order that 1:18 [y]Ac 26:18;
you may know the hope to which he 2Co 4:6
has called you, the riches of his glorious inheritance in the saints, [19]and his
incomparably great power for us who
believe. That power[z] is like the work- 1:19 [z]Col 1:29
ing of his mighty strength,[a] [20]which he [a]Eph 6:10
exerted in Christ when he raised him 1:20
from the dead[b] and seated him at his [b]Ac 2:24
right hand in the heavenly realms, [21]far
above all rule and authority, power and
dominion, and every title[c] that can be 1:21
given, not only in the present age but [c]Php 2:9,10
also in the one to come. [22]And God
placed all things under his feet[d] and ap- 1:22 [d]Mt 28:18
pointed him to be head[e] over everything [e]Eph 4:15;
for the church, [23]which is his body, the 5:23
fullness of him who fills everything in
every way.

Made Alive in Christ

2 As for you, you were dead in your 2:1 [f]ver 5;
transgressions and sins,[f] [2]in which Col 2:13
you used to live[g] when you followed 2:2 [g]Col 3:7

[a]*1* Some early manuscripts do not have *in Ephesus.* [b]*1* Or *believers who are* [c]*4,5* Or *sight in love. [5]He* [d]*8,9* Or *us. With all wisdom and understanding, [9]he* [e]*11* Or *were made heirs* [f]*17* Or *a spirit*

the ways of this world and of the ruler
2:2 [h]Jn 12:31; of the kingdom of the air,[h] the spirit
Eph 6:12 who is now at work in those who are
[i]Eph 5:6 disobedient.[i] 3All of us also lived among
them at one time, gratifying the crav-
2:3 [j]Gal 5:16 ings of our sinful nature[a][j] and following its desires and thoughts. Like the
rest, we were by nature objects of wrath.
4But because of his great love for us,
God, who is rich in mercy, 5made us
alive with Christ even when we were
2:5 [k]ver 1 dead in transgressions[k]—it is by grace
[l]ver 8; you have been saved.[l] 6And God raised
Ac 15:11 us up with Christ and seated us with
2:6 [m]Eph 1:20 him[m] in the heavenly realms[n] in Christ
[n]Eph 1:3 Jesus, 7in order that in the coming ages
he might show the incomparable riches
2:7 [o]Tit 3:4 of his grace, expressed in his kindness[o]
2:8 to us in Christ Jesus. 8For it is by grace
[p]ver 5 you have been saved,[p] through faith—

DAY FIVE

▸ KINDNESS AND ITS PLACE IN MY PERSONAL WORSHIP

Ephesians 2:6–10

This passage must be the epitome in correlating kindness, grace and saving faith—three great attributes that are bound together inseparably in this passage. This concept is too lovely for prosaic discussion, so allow me to set it in verse:

God raised up Christ and seated him above
In places so majestic we but wonder
"Is there any edge to heaven's love?
Is there any realm of grace above or under
Where he might now or in some part
of space
Reveal to us the reason for such grace?"
Kindness came, and dressed in rich
humility
It drew eternity toward my time,
And I stare bewildered that it all is free,
And Christ, the cosmic Lord, is friends
with me.

Saved by faith, by grace and naught of me.
Yet purchased as a present from love's sea—
So wide and deep and free I marvel yet
At love that bled and saved without regret.

To begin a study on the topic of Kindness, the Approach to Grace, turn to the home page on page 343.

and this not from yourselves, it is the
gift of God— 9not by works,[q] so that 2:9 [q]2Ti 1:9
no one can boast.[r] 10For we are God's [r]1Co 1:29
workmanship, created[s] in Christ Jesus 2:10 [s]Eph 4:24
to do good works,[t] which God prepared [t]Tit 2:14
in advance for us to do.

▸ PATIENCE

THE STATUARY OF THE MASTER SCULPTOR

Ephesians 2:10

God works like Michelangelo when creating every Christian. Does the chisel hurt? Welcome it. He's sculpting you into a work of grace. Be content to receive the form he gives you; glory in the image that you wear. We are his poetry, his canvas, his sculpture, his glory. His creations are never hurried. Celebrate his finishing of your life, however long it takes him to complete you.

One in Christ

11Therefore, remember that formerly you who are Gentiles by birth and
called "uncircumcised" by those who
call themselves "the circumcision" (that
done in the body by the hands of
men)[u]— 12remember that at that time 2:11 [u]Col 2:11
you were separate from Christ, excluded
from citizenship in Israel and foreign-
ers to the covenants of the promise,[v] 2:12 [v]Gal 3:17
without hope[w] and without God in [w]1Th 4:13
the world. 13But now in Christ Jesus
you who once were far away have been
brought near[x] through the blood of 2:13 [x]ver 17;
Christ.[y] Ac 2:39 [y]Col 1:20
14For he himself is our peace, who
has made the two one[z] and has de- 2:14 [z]1Co 12:13
stroyed the barrier, the dividing wall of
hostility, 15by abolishing in his flesh[a] 2:15 [a]Col 1:21,22
the law with its commandments and [b]Col 2:14
regulations.[b] His purpose was to create

[a]3 Or *our flesh*

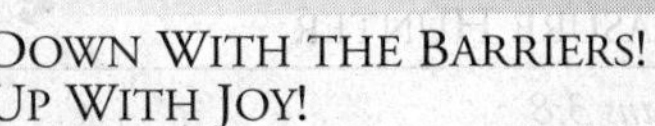

▸ PEACE

DOWN WITH THE BARRIERS! UP WITH JOY!

Ephesians 2:14

There was once a wall in an ancient temple. It divided Jews from Gentiles, the chosen from those not chosen. Now all are chosen. Grace doesn't care much for walls.

2:15 [c]Gal 3:28 in himself one[c] new man out of the
two, thus making peace, 16and in this
2:16 one body to reconcile both of them to
[d]Col 1:20,22 God through the cross,[d] by which he
2:17 put to death their hostility. 17He came
[e]Ps 148:14; and preached peace to you who were
Isa 57:19 far away and peace to those who were
2:18 [f]Eph 3:12 near.[e] 18For through him we both have
[g]Col 1:12 access[f] to the Father[g] by one Spirit.[h]
[h]1Co 12:13 19Consequently, you are no longer
2:19 [i]ver 12 foreigners and aliens,[i] but fellow citi-
[j]Php 3:20 zens[j] with God's people and members of
[k]Gal 6:10 God's household,[k] 20built on the foun-
2:20 dation[l] of the apostles and prophets,
[l]Mt 16:18; Rev 21:14 with Christ Jesus himself as the chief
[m]1Pe 2:4-8 cornerstone.[m] 21In him the whole building is joined together and rises to be-
2:21 [n]1Co 3:16,17 come a holy temple[n] in the Lord. 22And
in him you too are being built togeth-
er to become a dwelling in which God
lives by his Spirit.

Paul the Preacher to the Gentiles

3 For this reason I, Paul, the prison-
3:1 [o]Ac 23:18; er[o] of Christ Jesus for the sake of
Eph 4:1 you Gentiles—
2Surely you have heard about the ad-
3:2 ministration of God's grace that was
[p]Col 1:25 given to me[p] for you, 3that is, the mys-
3:3 tery[q] made known to me by revelation,[r]
[q]Ro 16:25 [r]1Co 2:10 as I have already written briefly. 4In
reading this, then, you will be able to
3:4 [s]2Co 11:6 understand my insight[s] into the mystery of Christ, 5which was not made
known to men in other generations as
it has now been revealed by the Spirit
3:5 to God's holy apostles and prophets.[t]
[t]Ro 16:26 6This mystery is that through the gos-
3:6 pel the Gentiles are heirs[u] together with
[u]Gal 3:29 [v]Eph 2:15,16 Israel, members together of one body,[v]
and sharers together in the promise in
Christ Jesus.
3:7 7I became a servant of this gospel[w]
[w]1Co 3:5 by the gift of God's grace given me
[x]Eph 1:19 through the working of his power.[x] 8Al-
though I am less than the least of all
God's people,[y] this grace was given me: 3:8
to preach to the Gentiles the unsearch- [y]1Co 15:9
able riches of Christ, 9and to make
plain to everyone the administration
of this mystery,[z] which for ages past 3:9 [z]Ro 16:25
was kept hidden in God, who created
all things. 10His intent was that now,
through the church, the manifold wisdom of God[a] should be made known[b] 3:10
to the rulers and authorities[c] in the [a]1Co 2:7
heavenly realms, 11according to his eter- [b]1Pe 1:12 [c]Eph 1:21
nal purpose which he accomplished in
Christ Jesus our Lord. 12In him and
through faith in him we may approach
God[d] with freedom and confidence.[e] 3:12 [d]Eph 2:18
13I ask you, therefore, not to be dis- [e]Heb 4:16
couraged because of my sufferings for
you, which are your glory.

A Prayer for the Ephesians

14For this reason I kneel[f] before the 3:14
Father, 15from whom his whole fami- [f]Php 2:10
ly[a] in heaven and on earth derives its
name. 16I pray that out of his glorious
riches he may strengthen you with pow- 3:16
er[g] through his Spirit in your inner [g]Col 1:11
being,[h] 17so that Christ may dwell in [h]Ro 7:22
your hearts[i] through faith. And I pray 3:17 [i]Jn 14:23
that you, being rooted[j] and established [j]Col 1:23
in love, 18may have power, together
with all the saints, to grasp how wide
and long and high and deep[k] is the love 3:18 [k]Job 11:8,9
of Christ, 19and to know this love that
surpasses knowledge—that you may be
filled[l] to the measure of all the fullness 3:19
of God.[m] [l]Col 2:10 [m]Eph 1:23
20Now to him who is able[n] to do 3:20
immeasurably more than all we ask or [n]Ro 16:25
imagine, according to his power that is
at work within us, 21to him be glory in
the church and in Christ Jesus throughout all generations, for ever and ever! 3:21
Amen.[o] [o]Ro 11:36

Unity in the Body of Christ

4 As a prisoner[p] for the Lord, then, 4:1 [p]Eph 3:1
I urge you to live a life worthy[q] [q]Php 1:27; Col 1:10
of the calling you have received. 2Be
completely humble and gentle; be pa- 4:2
tient, bearing with one another[r] in love.[s] [r]Col 3:12,13 [s]Eph 1:4
3Make every effort to keep the unity[t] of 4:3
the Spirit through the bond of peace. [t]Col 3:14
4There is one body and one Spirit[u]— 4:4
just as you were called to one hope [u]1Co 12:13
when you were called— 5one Lord, one

[a]15 Or *whom all fatherhood*

GOODNESS

THE TREASURE HUNTER

Ephesians 3:8

It is a selfish thing to look for treasure unless, once found, you give it to the poor. It is a selfish thing to seek the love of Christ unless, once found, you give it to the lonely and despised.

faith, one baptism; 6one God and Fa-
4:6 ther of all, who is over all and through
vRo 11:36 all and in all.[v]
4:7 7But to each one of us[w] grace has
w1Co 12:7,11 been given[x] as Christ apportioned it.
xRo 12:3 8This is why it[a] says:

DAY 4 FOUR

PEACE AND MY SERVICE TO OTHERS

Ephesians 4:3–6

Keeping the unity of the Spirit through the bond of peace is the basis for all our service to others. Why? No one would want a peaceless, argumentative minister to become his or her guide to the deeper life.

The plea for unity in this passage is backed up by the evidence of such oneness throughout the entire kingdom of God. *Unity* comes from the Latin *unus*, meaning "one." This must indeed be God's favorite number. Look at the glorious things the number one promotes in the church (Ephesians 4:3–6):

One body—consider the alternative: a quarrelsome cacophony of differing viewpoints and neurotic church members.
One Spirit—whose permeation of each heart produces our great commonality.
One hope—all believers have but one future. Jesus' second coming should be hope enough to make the church one.
One Lord—glory of glories, the Spirit bears witness that we all know and serve one Lord.
One faith—there is but one true, universal church, which Jesus left to serve him in this world. Those who insist on belonging to Jesus but won't belong to his church are simply hirelings.
One baptism—celebrating Jesus from one worldwide confession of his lordship.
One God and Father of all—all believers have the same Creator and Father.

With all this harmony, peace is as certain as sunrise. Accepting the unity of God's favorite number allows us to live in peace with others.

To begin a study on the topic of Peace, the Reign of the Holy Spirit, turn to the home page on page 1429.

"When he ascended on high, 4:8
he led captives[y] in his train yCol 2:15
and gave gifts to men."[b][z] zPs 68:18

9(What does "he ascended" mean except that he also descended to the lower,
earthly regions[c]? 10He who descended
is the very one who ascended higher
than all the heavens, in order to fill the
whole universe.) 11It was he who gave
some to be apostles,[a] some to be proph- 4:11 a1Co 12:28
ets, some to be evangelists,[b] and some bAc 21:8
to be pastors and teachers, 12to prepare
God's people for works of service, so 4:12
that the body of Christ[c] may be built c1Co 12:27
up 13until we all reach unity[d] in the 4:13 dver 3,5
faith and in the knowledge of the Son eCol 1:28
of God and become mature,[e] attaining
to the whole measure of the fullness of
Christ.
14Then we will no longer be infants,[f] 4:14 f1Co 14:20
tossed back and forth by the waves,[g] gJas 1:6
and blown here and there by every hEph 6:11
wind of teaching and by the cunning
and craftiness of men in their deceitful
scheming.[h] 15Instead, speaking the truth
in love, we will in all things grow up
into him who is the Head,[i] that is, 4:15 iEph 1:22
Christ. 16From him the whole body,
joined and held together by every sup-
porting ligament, grows[j] and builds it- 4:16 jCol 2:19
self up in love, as each part does its
work.

Living as Children of Light

17So I tell you this, and insist on it
in the Lord, that you must no longer
live as the Gentiles do, in the futility
of their thinking.[k] 18They are darkened 4:17 kRo 1:21
in their understanding[l] and separated 4:18
from the life of God[m] because of the ig- lRo 1:21 mEph 2:12
norance that is in them due to the hard- n2Co 3:14
ening of their hearts.[n] 19Having lost all 4:19
sensitivity,[o] they have given themselves o1Ti 4:2
over[p] to sensuality[q] so as to indulge in pRo 1:24 qCol 3:5
every kind of impurity, with a continu-
al lust for more.

20You, however, did not come to
know Christ that way. 21Surely you
heard of him and were taught in him
in accordance with the truth that is in
Jesus. 22You were taught, with regard 4:22
to your former way of life, to put off[r] r1Pe 2:1
your old self,[s] which is being corrupt- sRo 6:6
ed by its deceitful desires; 23to be made

[a]8 Or *God* [b]8 Psalm 68:18 [c]9 Or *the depths of the earth*

4:23 [t]Col 3:10 new in the attitude of your minds;[t]
4:24 [u]Ro 6:4 24and to put on the new self,[u] created to
[v]Eph 2:10 be like God in true righteousness and
holiness.[v]

FAITHFULNESS

THE MOMENTARY WORK OF MIND RENEWAL

Ephesians 4:22–24

Is your mind antique?
Does its teaching value other days?
Haul down your rotted ego.
Clean away corrupt philosophies.
Renew your mind.
Honor Christ!

25Therefore each of you must put off
4:25 [w]Zec 8:16 falsehood and speak truthfully[w] to his
[x]Ro 12:5 neighbor, for we are all members of one
body.[x] 26"In your anger do not sin"[a]:
Do not let the sun go down while you
are still angry, 27and do not give the
devil a foothold. 28He who has been
stealing must steal no longer, but must
4:28 [y]Ac 20:35 work,[y] doing something useful with his
[z]1Th 4:11 own hands,[z] that he may have some-
[a]Lk 3:11 thing to share with those in need.[a]
29Do not let any unwholesome talk
4:29 [b]Col 3:8 come out of your mouths,[b] but only
what is helpful for building others up
according to their needs, that it may
benefit those who listen. 30And do not
4:30 [c]1Th 5:19 grieve the Holy Spirit of God,[c] with
[d]Ro 8:23 whom you were sealed for the day of
redemption.[d] 31Get rid of all bitterness,
rage and anger, brawling and slander,
4:31 [e]Col 3:8 along with every form of malice.[e] 32Be
kind and compassionate to one anoth-
er, forgiving each other, just as in Christ
4:32 [f]Mt 6:14,15 God forgave you.[f]
5:1 [g]Lk 6:36 5 Be imitators of God,[g] therefore, as
dearly loved children 2and live a life
5:2 [h]Gal 1:4 of love, just as Christ loved us and gave
[i]2Co 2:15; Heb 7:27 himself up for us[h] as a fragrant offering
and sacrifice to God.[i]
3But among you there must not be
even a hint of sexual immorality, or of
5:3 [j]Col 3:5 any kind of impurity, or of greed,[j] because these are improper for God's holy
people. 4Nor should there be obscenity,
foolish talk or coarse joking, which are
5:4 [k]ver 20 out of place, but rather thanksgiving.[k]
5For of this you can be sure: No im-
moral, impure or greedy person—such
5:5 [l]Col 3:5 a man is an idolater[l]—has any inheritance in the kingdom of Christ and of
God.[b][m] 6Let no one deceive you with 5:5 [m]1Co 6:9
empty words, for because of such things
God's wrath[n] comes on those who are 5:6 [n]Ro 1:18
disobedient. 7Therefore do not be partners with them.
8For you were once[o] darkness, but 5:8 [o]Eph 2:2
now you are light in the Lord. Live as [p]Lk 16:8
children of light[p] 9(for the fruit[q] of the 5:9 [q]Gal 5:22
light consists in all goodness, righteous-
ness and truth) 10and find out what
pleases the Lord. 11Have nothing to do
with the fruitless deeds of darkness, but
rather expose them. 12For it is shameful
even to mention what the disobedient
do in secret. 13But everything exposed
by the light[r] becomes visible, 14for it 5:13 [r]Jn 3:20,21
is light that makes everything visible.
This is why it is said:

"Wake up, O sleeper,[s] 5:14 [s]Ro 13:11
rise from the dead,[t] [t]Jn 5:25
and Christ will shine on you."[u] [u]Isa 60:1

15Be very careful, then, how you
live—not as unwise but as wise, 16mak- 5:16 [v]Col 4:5
ing the most of every opportunity,[v] be- [w]Eph 6:13
cause the days are evil.[w] 17Therefore do
not be foolish, but understand what the 5:17 [x]Ro 12:2; 1Th 4:3
Lord's will is.[x] 18Do not get drunk on
wine,[y] which leads to debauchery. In- 5:18 [y]Pr 20:1
stead, be filled with the Spirit.[z] 19Speak [z]Lk 1:15
to one another with psalms, hymns and
spiritual songs.[a] Sing and make music 5:19 [a]Ac 16:25; Col 3:16
in your heart to the Lord, 20always giv-
ing thanks[b] to God the Father for ev- 5:20 [b]Ps 34:1
erything, in the name of our Lord Jesus
Christ.

PATIENCE

TIME IS A GIFT

Ephesians 5:15–16

The days are evil, but time itself is a gift of God. Use every silver minute set in every hour of gold to serve the purposes of God. Make every second of your life a present set in platinum, and offer it to him for whom a thousand years are but a day.

21Submit to one another[c] out of rev- 5:21 [c]Gal 5:13
erence for Christ.

Wives and Husbands

22Wives, submit to your husbands[d] 5:22 [d]Ge 3:16; 1Pe 3:1,5,6
as to the Lord.[e] 23For the husband is the [e]Eph 6:5

[a]*26* Psalm 4:4 [b]*5* Or *kingdom of the Christ and God*

GOODNESS

WEEK 33

1 DAY ONE

▸ GOODNESS, THE RESULT OF IMITATING CHRIST

Read Ephesians 5:1–2

In Ephesians 5:1–2, Paul says that Jesus was poured out as a "fragrant offering" for our salvation. But in Philippians 2:17, Paul says that he sees his own life poured out as a "drink offering." Paul was in an uncertain situation. He was in prison and did not know whether he would live or die. But in Paul's mind, he was already a sacrifice through his ministry to others. What a wonderful way to be poured out—serving Jesus by serving others. Being poured out was the best way Paul could use his life. Even in the face of prison, hardship or death, Paul could rejoice.

In Ephesians 5:1–2, Paul says that we are to pattern ourselves after Christ. In Philippians 2:6–7, he says that Jesus emptied himself of his divine prerogatives in order to become one of us. He emptied himself of his cosmic power and omnipresence. He poured out his thunderbolt-Jehovah self to become both God and man. The emptying process resulted in Jesus' incarnation—he became flesh and blood for the purpose of redeeming us.

How are we to imitate the grand actions of Christ? How can we imitate the ultimate goodness that affected all people in all generations? Perhaps it is a start to pour out our lives for others—to show goodness to those around us. Perhaps, at the same time, we will be pouring out self-will and petty ambition. Perhaps, in this process, we will imitate something of Christ.

2 DAY TWO

▸ GOODNESS AND THE PURPOSE OF GOD IN MY LIFE

We are called by God to fulfill a purpose. What an incredible feeling for any Christian—to know that we are called to good. When Christ is glorified in us, when we live our lives for him, we are fulfilling the great purposes of God. We are living out goodness in our lives. *Turn to 2 Thessalonians 1:11–12, page 1433, for today's study.*

3 DAY THREE

▸ GOODNESS AND MY RELATIONSHIP WITH CHRIST

Enoch had a relatively short life compared to Methuselah, but the Scriptures note that he walked with God. Goodness is always the result of walking with God. "Enoch walked with God" and "then he was no more, because God took him away." He was "raptured"—snatched away—because of his closeness to God. The walk of faith with Christ is an inherent delight—an ecstasy that may very well culminate in rapture. *Turn to Genesis 5:21–24, page 9, for today's study.*

4 DAY FOUR

▸ GOODNESS AND MY SERVICE TO OTHERS

Elisha modeled his life after his friend and mentor, Elijah. How do we determine the person we will become? Who will we model ourselves after? In ministering to others, there is no greater example to follow than that of the one who was the friend of the poor and humble—Jesus. *Turn to 2 Kings 2:6–15, page 424, for today's study.*

5 DAY FIVE

▸ GOODNESS AND ITS PLACE IN MY PERSONAL WORSHIP

Christ prayed all night and, by his example, he gives us an illustration of personal worship—one well worth imitating. Would it not be wonderful to say that our spiritual director was Jesus? But why did he spend the entire night in prayer? He was hungry for relationship with his Father and eager to know and pursue his Father's will. May these two things be said of our prayer life as well. *Turn to Luke 6:12, page 1208, for today's study.*

MEMORIZE THIS WEEK

3 JOHN 11

Dear friend, do not imitate what is evil but what is good. Anyone who does what is good is from God. Anyone who does what is evil has not seen God.

Week 34, Faithfulness, a Stubborn Commitment to the Right, begins on page 398, 1 Kings 8:54–61. To begin a topical study on the Fruit of the Spirit, Goodness, turn to the Topical Index, page 1548.

head of the wife as Christ is the head of
5:23 [f]1Co 11:3; Eph 1:22 the church,[f] his body, of which he is the
Savior. 24Now as the church submits to
Christ, so also wives should submit to
their husbands in everything.

JOY

THANK YOU, THANK YOU, THANK YOU!

Ephesians 5:20

When you wake, say "Thank You!"
When you fall asleep, say "Thank You!"
When pain is yours, say "Thank You!"
When laughter ripples through the corridors of your affairs, say "Thank You!"
Say "Thank you" when you mean it.
Say "Thank you" when you don't mean it till, in time, you do mean it.
Say "Thank you" when life says, "You're welcome."
Say "Thank you" when none say, "You're welcome."
Say "Thank you" as the unending litany of your grateful life:
"Thank you, thank you, thank you!"

5:25 [g]Col 3:19 [h]ver 2 25Husbands, love your wives,[g] just as
Christ loved the church and gave him-
5:26 [i]Ac 22:16 self up for her[h] 26to make her holy,
cleansing[a] her by the washing[i] with water through the word, 27and to present
her to himself as a radiant church, with-
5:27 [j]Eph 1:4; Col 1:22 out stain or wrinkle or any other blemish, but holy and blameless.[j] 28In this
5:28 [k]ver 25 same way, husbands ought to love their
wives[k] as their own bodies. He who
loves his wife loves himself. 29After all,
no one ever hated his own body, but
he feeds and cares for it, just as Christ
does the church— 30for we are mem-
5:30 [l]1Co 12:27 bers of his body.[l] 31"For this reason a
man will leave his father and mother
and be united to his wife, and the two
5:31 [m]Ge 2:24; Mt 19:5; 1Co 6:16 will become one flesh."[b][m] 32This is a
profound mystery—but I am talking
about Christ and the church. 33How-
5:33 [n]ver 25 ever, each one of you also must love his
wife[n] as he loves himself, and the wife
must respect her husband.

Children and Parents

6:1 [o]Col 3:20 6 Children, obey your parents in the
Lord, for this is right.[o] 2"Honor
your father and mother"—which is the
first commandment with a promise—
3"that it may go well with you and
that you may enjoy long life on the 6:3 [p]Ex 20:12
earth."[c][p]
4Fathers, do not exasperate your 6:4 [q]Col 3:21 [r]Ge 18:19; Dt 6:7
children;[q] instead, bring them up in the
training and instruction of the Lord.[r]

[a]26 Or *having cleansed* [b]31 Gen. 2:24
[c]3 Deut. 5:16

DAY 4 FOUR

FAITHFULNESS AND MY SERVICE TO OTHERS

Ephesians 6:10–18

We are to take our stand, says the apostle. But our stand against what, or rather, against whom? Remember, the Lord's Prayer says, "Deliver us from the evil one" (Matthew 6:13). The evil one is that ever present, ever challenging force that daily strives to destroy our faithfulness. You may be sure that if Satan had his way, all our intentions to stand true would crumble. So Paul urges us to dress for the onslaught. We have to wear the armor, clothing ourselves for the fray. If Satan had his way, God's intentions for us would die in self-concern and wishy-washy commitments. How can we serve others? The answer lies in standing firm in our commitment to do right.

You will notice that, of the full panoply of armor, only in Ephesians 6:17 do we come across the single piece that is offensive in nature. All the other pieces of armor mentioned are for our defense; only the sword of the Spirit is given for our offense. With the faithful protection of God's armor, we are ready to go to battle. We are sent out to be faithful in our warfare with Satan. He is called by many names: the evil one (Matthew 13:19), a murderer (John 8:44), the devil (Ephesians 6:11), our enemy (1 Peter 5:8), the great dragon or ancient serpent (Revelation 12:9), and the accuser (Revelation 12:10). But by whatever name we meet him, we are to employ God's armor for our protection and the sword of the Spirit for our faithful advance as we fulfill God's calling to serve him.

To begin a study on the topic of Faithfulness: No Compromise, turn to the home page on page 898.

Slaves and Masters

5 Slaves, obey your earthly masters
6:5 with respect[s] and fear, and with sincer-
[s]1Ti 6:1 [t]Col 3:22 ity of heart,[t] just as you would obey
[u]Eph 5:22 Christ.[u] 6 Obey them not only to win
their favor when their eye is on you,
but like slaves of Christ, doing the will
of God from your heart. 7 Serve wholeheartedly, as if you were serving the
6:7 Lord, not men,[v] 8 because you know
[v]Col 3:23 that the Lord will reward everyone for
6:8 whatever good he does,[w] whether he is
[w]Col 3:24 slave or free.

9 And masters, treat your slaves in the
same way. Do not threaten them, since
you know that he who is both their
6:9 Master and yours[x] is in heaven, and
[x]Job 31:13,14 there is no favoritism with him.

The Armor of God

6:10 [y]1Co 16:13 10 Finally, be strong in the Lord[y] and
[z]Eph 1:19 in his mighty power.[z] 11 Put on the full
6:11 [a]Ro 13:12 armor of God[a] so that you can take your
stand against the devil's schemes. 12 For
our struggle is not against flesh and
blood, but against the rulers, against
6:12 [b]Eph 1:21 the authorities,[b] against the powers[c] of
[c]Ro 8:38 this dark world and against the spiritual
[d]Eph 1:3 forces of evil in the heavenly realms.[d]
13 Therefore put on the full armor of
God, so that when the day of evil
comes, you may be able to stand your
ground, and after you have done everything, to stand. 14 Stand firm then, with
the belt of truth buckled around your
waist,[e] with the breastplate of righteous- 6:14 [e]Isa 11:5
ness in place,[f] 15 and with your feet fit- [f]Isa 59:17
ted with the readiness that comes from 6:15
the gospel of peace.[g] 16 In addition to all [g]Isa 52:7
this, take up the shield of faith,[h] with 6:16 [h]1Jn 5:4
which you can extinguish all the flam-
ing arrows of the evil one. 17 Take the
helmet of salvation[i] and the sword of 6:17 [i]Isa 59:17
the Spirit, which is the word of God.[j] [j]Heb 4:12
18 And pray in the Spirit on all occa- 6:18
sions[k] with all kinds of prayers and [k]Lk 18:1
requests.[l] With this in mind, be alert [l]Mt 26:41; Php 1:4
and always keep on praying for all the
saints.

19 Pray also for me,[m] that whenever I 6:19 [m]1Th 5:25
open my mouth, words may be given [n]Ac 4:29; 2Co 3:12
me so that I will fearlessly[n] make known
the mystery of the gospel, 20 for which I
am an ambassador[o] in chains.[p] Pray that 6:20 [o]2Co 5:20
I may declare it fearlessly, as I should. [p]Ac 21:33

Final Greetings

21 Tychicus,[q] the dear brother and 6:21 [q]Ac 20:4
faithful servant in the Lord, will tell
you everything, so that you also may
know how I am and what I am doing.
22 I am sending him to you for this very
purpose, that you may know how we
are,[r] and that he may encourage you. 6:22 [r]Col 4:7-9

23 Peace[s] to the brothers, and love 6:23
with faith from God the Father and the [s]Gal 6:16; 1Pe 5:14
Lord Jesus Christ. 24 Grace to all who
love our Lord Jesus Christ with an undying love.

PHILIPPIANS

AUTHORSHIP AND DATE

Paul

c. A.D. 61

KEY THEMES

Philippians, like each of the other prison epistles (Ephesians, Colossians and Galatians), was written from Rome during that period of time when Paul was incarcerated, awaiting his appeal before Nero. The book of Philippians is perhaps the most tender and joyous of all Paul's letters. Paul rehearses his love of Christ for the Philippian church. He celebrates with thanksgiving the chains he wore, for they brought him additional opportunities to share the gospel (see 1:15–18). He was settled about Christ's control, and, whether he lived or died, he knew it would all be to God's glory (see 1:19–30).

Chapter 2 is a call to emulate Christ's humility, which was demonstrated by Christ's descent into flesh. This is, doubtless, the strongest Christological passage in the Bible. It is climaxed by a call to be gallant in character, as were Paul's beloved traveling companions Timothy and Epaphroditus (see vv. 12–30). The remaining two chapters of the book celebrate the overcoming Christ (see 3:7–11) and encourage the believers to keep pressing on to know Christ's all-surpassing excellence (see 3:12–21). There is a strong plea to purge the mind of all sin and devote it to virtue (see 4:8). There is also a reminder of the confidence we have in Christ, who makes all things possible (see 4:13) and supplies us with strength to accomplish all he asks (see 4:19).

FRUIT OF THE SPIRIT IN PHILIPPIANS

Love: There is perhaps no deeper love than the love between Christians who together serve Jesus in the trenches. A. W. Tozer used to talk about frontline and rearguard fellowship as he defined the Greek word *koinonia*, which is translated *fellowship*. He said that those Christians who best understood the word *fellowship* were not generals who planned battles safely from the rear, but infantry Christians who lived dangerously on the frontline in "foxhole discipleship" that required life-and-death commitment. Paul seems to assert this truth when he said, "It is right for me to feel this way about all of you, since I have you in my heart; for whether I am in chains or defending and confirming the gospel, all of you share in God's grace with me" (1:7).

Joy: Paul had found that, even in chains, joy smashed through his incarceration with real liberty in Christ. As long as Christ was being magnified, Paul was willing for God to use anything, even his chains, to bring him joy (see 1:17–18).

Kindness: Jesus Christ set an example for all to follow. Jesus, "being in very nature God, did not consider equality with God something to be grasped, but made himself nothing, taking the very nature of a servant, being made in human likeness. And being found in appearance as a man, he humbled himself and became obedient to death—even death on a cross!" (2:6–8). In this voluntary surrender of his divine rights and prerogatives, Jesus made humility, not power, a conscious choice. Kindness is a volitional choice to treat others as Jesus would treat them. Kindness is willing to live for others, having found living for self to be too small a reason.

Goodness: Goodness, like meekness, is to be a choice in our lives. We are to decide to be good and then pursue goodness to the glory of God. "Do everything without complaining or arguing, so that you may become blameless and pure, children of God without fault in a crooked and depraved generation" (2:14–15).

Faithfulness: Faithfulness produces a longing to be completely identified with Christ. It hungers to know what it means that Christ died for us, lived for us and was raised to make our own lives possible. Paul hungered for such identification. His zeal for faithfulness led him to take the last step—the hunger for complete union: "I want to know Christ and the power of his resurrection and the fellowship of sharing in his sufferings, becoming like him in his death, and so, somehow, to attain to the resurrection from the dead" (3:10–11).

Gentleness: "Let your gentleness be evident to all. The Lord is near" (4:5). Gentleness is rarely an exhibitionist virtue, as pride is. Still, in Paul's opinion, gentleness is a virtue that should be obvious to those around us. For all the dangers that lie in being an exhibitionist about our gentleness, the apostle said it is a virtue worth publishing. So, work hard to be gentle, and if you are honestly gentle, then let it be obvious in the church. Gentleness: If you've honestly got it—flaunt it!

1:1 [a]Ac 16:1; 2Co 1:1 [b]Ac 9:13 [c]Ac 16:12 [d]1Ti 3:1 [e]1Ti 3:8
1 Paul and Timothy,[a] servants of
Christ Jesus,
To all the saints[b] in Christ Jesus at
Philippi,[c] together with the overseers[a][d]
and deacons:[e]

1:2 [f]Ro 1:7
2Grace and peace to you from God
our Father and the Lord Jesus Christ.[f]

Thanksgiving and Prayer

1:3 [g]Ro 1:8
3I thank my God every time I re-
1:4 [h]Ro 1:10
member you.[g] 4In all my prayers for all
1:5 [i]Ac 2:42; Php 4:15 [j]Ac 16:12-40
of you, I always pray[h] with joy 5because
of your partnership[i] in the gospel from
the first day[j] until now, 6being confi-
1:6 [k]ver 10; 1Co 1:8
dent of this, that he who began a good
work in you will carry it on to completion until the day of Christ Jesus.[k]

PATIENCE

FINISHING SCHOOL

Philippians 1:6

Who would criticize a painting before the artist had finished painting it? Grace is the artist, and you are God's in-process canvas. Say to all who would criticize you, "Please be patient with me; God is not finished with me yet."

1:7 [l]2Pe 1:13 [m]2Co 7:3 [n]ver 13,14,17; Ac 21:33 [o]ver 16
7It is right[l] for me to feel this way
about all of you, since I have you in my
heart;[m] for whether I am in chains[n] or
defending[o] and confirming the gospel,
all of you share in God's grace with me.
1:8 [p]Ro 1:9
8God can testify[p] how I long for all of
you with the affection of Christ Jesus.
9And this is my prayer: that your
1:9 [q]1Th 3:12
love[q] may abound more and more in
knowledge and depth of insight, 10so
that you may be able to discern what
1:10 [r]ver 6; 1Co 1:8
is best and may be pure and blameless
until the day of Christ,[r] 11filled with
1:11 [s]Jas 3:18
the fruit of righteousness[s] that comes
through Jesus Christ—to the glory and
praise of God.

Paul's Chains Advance the Gospel

12Now I want you to know, brothers, that what has happened to me has
really served to advance the gospel. 13As
a result, it has become clear throughout
1:13 [t]ver 7,14,17
the whole palace guard[b] and to everyone else that I am in chains[t] for Christ.
1:14 [u]ver 7,13,17
14Because of my chains,[u] most of the
brothers in the Lord have been encour-

[a] *1* Traditionally *bishops* [b] *13* Or *whole palace*

DAY THREE

PEACE AND MY RELATIONSHIP WITH CHRIST

Philippians 1:3–6

The initial joy we each embrace upon discovering Christ sometimes seems absent in the first real crisis we face following our conversion. This crisis may also prompt feelings of abandonment by God, feelings that steal our peace and rob us of confidence.

But God makes it clear that we are to remember that all his promises remain in place—even during our seasons of doubt. Peace is always as near as our confidence in the promise in Philippians 1:6. He who started a good work in us will not walk off and leave the job half finished. He will perform his work right up until the time Jesus comes again.

Our relationship with Jesus stimulates our confidence in God's finishing work in us. God spent the blood of his Son to purchase our salvation, and he is committed to our continuing maturity. He longs to see in every new Christian the same thing every good mother wants to see in her babies: growth.

A good mother wants her babies to grow. She—like our loving heavenly Father—will love those babies whether they grow or not, but she longs to see them come to maturity as responsible adults. I know a mother whose second son was born mentally impaired. Unlike her first son who matured, went to school and obtained a good job and independent life, her second son remained dependent all of his life. He was never able to feed himself, and he never outgrew diapers. The mother spent equal amounts of love on both sons, yet was never rewarded by maturity in her second. She experienced the child's love in other ways that brought her joy, but she never knew the joy of watching him grow up.

God longs for us to grow up. We are his children, heirs with his Son. He wants our confidence to bring us peace in any circumstance. Our maturity brings joy to God and peacefulness to our own lives.

To begin a study on the topic of Peace, the Evidence of Confidence, turn to the home page on page 1173.

aged to speak the word of God more
courageously and fearlessly.
15It is true that some preach Christ
out of envy and rivalry, but others out
of goodwill. 16The latter do so in love,
knowing that I am put here for the
1:16 [v]ver 7,12 defense of the gospel.[v] 17The former
1:17 preach Christ out of selfish ambition,[w]
[w]Php 2:3 not sincerely, supposing that they can
[x]ver 7,13,14 stir up trouble for me while I am in
chains.[a][x] 18But what does it matter?
The important thing is that in every
way, whether from false motives or true,
Christ is preached. And because of this
I rejoice.

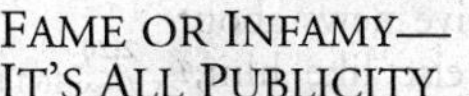

JOY

FAME OR INFAMY— IT'S ALL PUBLICITY

Philippians 1:18

The name of Jesus has been spread through both evangelism and controversy. Yet Jesus' name itself brings a sweet benediction to both unbelief and antagonism. "Jesus" is the name whose music heals cacophonies and enriches symphonies. Say his name and stand back. The world will either sing praise or condemn the name in song. Either way there is music.

1:19 Yes, and I will continue to rejoice,
[y]2Co 1:11 19for I know that through your prayers[y]
[z]Ac 16:7 and the help given by the Spirit of Jesus
Christ,[z] what has happened to me will
turn out for my deliverance.[b] 20I eagerly
1:20 [a]Ro 8:19 expect[a] and hope that I will in no way
[b]ver 14 be ashamed, but will have sufficient
[c]1Co 6:20 courage[b] so that now as always Christ
[d]Ro 14:8 will be exalted in my body,[c] whether by
life or by death.[d] 21For to me, to live is
1:21 [e]Gal 2:20 Christ[e] and to die is gain. 22If I am to
go on living in the body, this will mean

LOVE

LIVING'S GOOD, DYING'S BETTER

Philippians 1:21

To be a Christian is to live at the fork in the road. One of those beautiful roads is physical life with Christ. The other is eternal union with Christ. One road must be taken. Neither road is a mistake. Either road knows his companionship. Both end at the uninterrupted togetherness of lovers.

fruitful labor for me. Yet what shall I
choose? I do not know! 23I am torn between the two: I desire to depart[f] and 1:23
be with Christ,[g] which is better by far; [f]2Ti 4:6 [g]Jn 12:26;
24but it is more necessary for you that 2Co 5:8
I remain in the body. 25Convinced of
this, I know that I will remain, and I
will continue with all of you for your
progress and joy in the faith, 26so that
through my being with you again your
joy in Christ Jesus will overflow on account of me.
27Whatever happens, conduct your-
selves in a manner worthy[h] of the gos- 1:27 [h]Eph 4:1
pel of Christ. Then, whether I come [i]1Co 16:13
and see you or only hear about you [j]Jude 3
in my absence, I will know that you
stand firm[i] in one spirit, contending[j]
as one man for the faith of the gospel
28without being frightened in any way
by those who oppose you. This is a sign
to them that they will be destroyed,
but that you will be saved—and that
by God. 29For it has been granted to 1:29 [k]Mt 5:11,12
you[k] on behalf of Christ not only to [l]Ac 14:22
believe on him, but also to suffer[l] for
him, 30since you are going through the 1:30 [m]Col 2:1; 1Th
same struggle[m] you saw[n] I had, and now 2:2 [n]Ac 16:19-40
hear[o] that I still have. [o]ver 13

Imitating Christ's Humility

2 If you have any encouragement
from being united with Christ, if
any comfort from his love, if any fellow- 2:1 [p]2Co 13:14
ship with the Spirit,[p] if any tenderness [q]Col 3:12
and compassion,[q] 2then make my joy 2:2
complete[r] by being like-minded,[s] hav- [r]Jn 3:29
ing the same love, being one[t] in spirit [s]Php 4:2 [t]Ro 12:16
and purpose. 3Do nothing out of self- 2:3
ish ambition or vain conceit,[u] but in [u]Gal 5:26
humility consider others better than [v]Ro 12:10;
yourselves.[v] 4Each of you should look 1Pe 5:5
not only to your own interests, but also
to the interests of others.
5Your attitude should be the same as 2:5
that of Christ Jesus:[w] [w]Mt 11:29

6Who, being in very nature[c] God,[x] 2:6 [x]Jn 1:1
did not consider equality with [y]Jn 5:18
God[y] something to be
grasped,
7but made himself nothing,
taking the very nature[d] of a 2:7 [z]Mt 20:28
servant,[z] [a]Jn 1:14;
being made in human likeness.[a] Heb 2:17

[a]*16,17* Some late manuscripts have verses 16 and 17 in reverse order. [b]*19* Or *salvation* [c]*6* Or *in the form of* [d]*7* Or *the form*

KINDNESS

THE MIND OF CHRIST

Philippians 2:5

To have the mind of Christ is to let Christ supplant your awareness with his divine consciousness. Then all your thoughts will originate in him, and your every deed will consciously serve the world he loves.

8 And being found in appearance as a
man,
2:8 [b]Mt 26:39; Jn 10:18; Heb 5:8 he humbled himself
and became obedient to death[b]—
even death on a cross!
2:9 [c]Ac 2:33; Heb 2:9 [d]Eph 1:20,21 9 Therefore God exalted him[c] to the
highest place
and gave him the name that is
above every name,[d]
10 that at the name of Jesus every knee
2:10 [e]Ro 14:11 [f]Mt 28:18 should bow,[e]
in heaven and on earth and under
the earth,[f]
11 and every tongue confess that Jesus
2:11 [g]Jn 13:13 Christ is Lord,[g]
to the glory of God the Father.

Shining as Stars

12 Therefore, my dear friends, as you
have always obeyed—not only in my
presence, but now much more in my
2:12 [h]2Co 7:15 absence—continue to work out your
salvation with fear and trembling,[h] 13 for
2:13 [i]Ezr 1:5 it is God who works in you[i] to will and
to act according to his good purpose.
14 Do everything without complain-

PATIENCE

THE DISCIPLE'S DISCIPLINE

Philippians 2:12

Working *out* your salvation is not working *for* your salvation—salvation is a gift Christ already paid for.

Working *out* your salvation is not working *on* your salvation—salvation is complete the moment you receive it.

Working *out* your salvation is *developing your discipleship* so that each successive stage of salvation's completion leaves you ever more usable to God. It is as though you were given a huge raw diamond the moment you were saved, and you must spend all the rest of your life cutting the facets to release its brilliance.

ing[j] or arguing, 15 so that you may be- 2:14 [j]1Co 10:10; 1Pe 4:9
come blameless and pure, children of
God[k] without fault in a crooked and de- 2:15 [k]Mt 5:45,48; Eph 5:1 [l]Ac 2:40
praved generation,[l] in which you shine
like stars in the universe 16 as you hold
out[a] the word of life—in order that I
may boast on the day of Christ that 2:16 [m]1Th 2:19
I did not run or labor for nothing.[m]
17 But even if I am being poured out 2:17 [n]2Ti 4:6 [o]Ro 15:16
like a drink offering[n] on the sacrifice[o]
and service coming from your faith, I
am glad and rejoice with all of you.
18 So you too should be glad and rejoice
with me.

Timothy and Epaphroditus

19 I hope in the Lord Jesus to send
Timothy to you soon,[p] that I also may 2:19 [p]ver 23
be cheered when I receive news about
you. 20 I have no one else like him,[q] 2:20 [q]1Co 16:10
who takes a genuine interest in your
welfare. 21 For everyone looks out for 2:21 [r]1Co 10:24; 13:5
his own interests,[r] not those of Jesus
Christ. 22 But you know that Timothy
has proved himself, because as a son 2:22 [s]1Co 4:17; 1Ti 1:2
with his father[s] he has served with me
in the work of the gospel. 23 I hope,
therefore, to send him as soon as I see
how things go with me.[t] 24 And I am 2:23 [t]ver 19
confident[u] in the Lord that I myself will 2:24 [u]Php 1:25
come soon.
25 But I think it is necessary to send
back to you Epaphroditus, my brother,
fellow worker[v] and fellow soldier,[w] who 2:25 [v]Php 4:3 [w]Phm 2 [x]Php 4:18
is also your messenger, whom you sent
to take care of my needs.[x] 26 For he longs
for all of you[y] and is distressed because 2:26 [y]Php 1:8
you heard he was ill. 27 Indeed he was
ill, and almost died. But God had mercy on him, and not on him only but
also on me, to spare me sorrow upon
sorrow. 28 Therefore I am all the more
eager to send him, so that when you see
him again you may be glad and I may
have less anxiety. 29 Welcome him in the
Lord with great joy, and honor men
like him,[z] 30 because he almost died for 2:29 [z]1Co 16:18; 1Ti 5:17
the work of Christ, risking his life to
make up for the help you could not 2:30 [a]1Co 16:17
give me.[a]

No Confidence in the Flesh

3 Finally, my brothers, rejoice in the
Lord! It is no trouble for me to
write the same things to you again, and
it is a safeguard for you.

[a] *16* Or *hold on to*

2Watch out for those dogs,[b] those
men who do evil, those mutilators of
the flesh. 3For it is we who are the
circumcision,[c] we who worship by the
Spirit of God, who glory in Christ Jesus, and who put no confidence in the
flesh— 4though I myself have reasons
for such confidence.

If anyone else thinks he has reasons
to put confidence in the flesh, I have
more: 5circumcised[d] on the eighth day,
of the people of Israel,[e] of the tribe of
Benjamin,[f] a Hebrew of Hebrews; in
regard to the law, a Pharisee;[g] 6as for
zeal, persecuting the church;[h] as for legalistic righteousness,[i] faultless.

7But whatever was to my profit I now
consider loss[j] for the sake of Christ.
8What is more, I consider everything a
loss compared to the surpassing greatness of knowing[k] Christ Jesus my Lord,
for whose sake I have lost all things.
I consider them rubbish, that I may
gain Christ 9and be found in him, not
having a righteousness of my own that
comes from the law,[l] but that which is
through faith in Christ—the righteousness that comes from God and is by
faith.[m] 10I want to know Christ and the
power of his resurrection and the fellowship of sharing in his sufferings,[n]
becoming like him in his death,[o] 11and
so, somehow, to attain to the resurrection[p] from the dead.

3:2 [b]Ps 22:16,20
3:3 [c]Ro 2:28,29; Gal 6:15; Col 2:11
3:5 [d]Lk 1:59 [e]2Co 11:22 [f]Ro 11:1 [g]Ac 23:6
3:6 [h]Ac 8:3 [i]Ro 10:5
3:7 [j]Mt 13:44; Lk 14:33
3:8 [k]Eph 4:13; 2Pe 1:2
3:9 [l]Ro 10:5 [m]Ro 9:30
3:10 [n]Ro 8:17 [o]Ro 6:3-5
3:11 [p]Rev 20:5,6

JOY

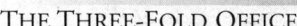

THE THREE-FOLD OFFICE

Philippians 3:10

First, know him.

Second, hunger to understand the things he suffered, even to the point of suffering them yourself.

Third, wake every morning and shout, "He is risen!" The victory will cover your failures with power and infuse your whole world with light.

Pressing on Toward the Goal

12Not that I have already obtained all
this, or have already been made perfect,[q]
but I press on to take hold[r] of that for
which Christ Jesus took hold of me.[s]
13Brothers, I do not consider myself yet
to have taken hold of it. But one thing
I do: Forgetting what is behind[t] and
straining toward what is ahead, 14I press
on[u] toward the goal to win the prize for
which God has called[v] me heavenward
in Christ Jesus.

15All of us who are mature[w] should
take such a view of things.[x] And if on
some point you think differently, that
too God will make clear to you. 16Only
let us live up to what we have already
attained.

17Join with others in following my
example,[y] brothers, and take note of
those who live according to the pattern we gave you. 18For, as I have often
told you before and now say again even
with tears,[z] many live as enemies of the
cross of Christ.[a] 19Their destiny is destruction, their god is their stomach,[b]
and their glory is in their shame.[c] Their
mind is on earthly things.[d] 20But our
citizenship[e] is in heaven.[f] And we eagerly await a Savior from there, the
Lord Jesus Christ,[g] 21who, by the power[h] that enables him to bring everything
under his control, will transform our
lowly bodies[i] so that they will be like
his glorious body.[j]

4 Therefore, my brothers, you whom
I love and long for,[k] my joy and
crown, that is how you should stand
firm[l] in the Lord, dear friends!

Exhortations

2I plead with Euodia and I plead with
Syntyche to agree with each other[m] in
the Lord. 3Yes, and I ask you, loyal yokefellow,[a] help these women who have
contended at my side in the cause of
the gospel, along with Clement and the
rest of my fellow workers, whose names
are in the book of life.

4Rejoice in the Lord always. I will say
it again: Rejoice![n] 5Let your gentleness
be evident to all. The Lord is near.[o] 6Do
not be anxious about anything,[p] but in
everything, by prayer and petition, with
thanksgiving, present your requests to
God.[q] 7And the peace of God,[r] which
transcends all understanding, will guard
your hearts and your minds in Christ
Jesus.

8Finally, brothers, whatever is true,
whatever is noble, whatever is right,
whatever is pure, whatever is lovely,
whatever is admirable—if anything is
excellent or praiseworthy—think about

[a]3 Or *loyal Syzygus*

3:12 [q]1Co 13:10 [r]1Ti 6:12 [s]Ac 9:5,6
3:13 [t]Lk 9:62
3:14 [u]Heb 6:1 [v]Ro 8:28
3:15 [w]1Co 2:6 [x]Gal 5:10
3:17 [y]1Co 4:16; 1Pe 5:3
3:18 [z]Ac 20:31 [a]Gal 6:12
3:19 [b]Ro 16:18 [c]Ro 6:21 [d]Ro 8:5,6
3:20 [e]Eph 2:19 [f]Col 3:1 [g]1Co 1:7
3:21 [h]Eph 1:19 [i]1Co 15:43-53 [j]Col 3:4
4:1 [k]Php 1:8 [l]1Co 16:13; Php 1:27
4:2 [m]Php 2:2
4:4 [n]Ro 12:12; Php 3:1
4:5 [o]Heb 10:37; Jas 5:8,9
4:6 [p]Mt 6:25-34 [q]Eph 6:18
4:7 [r]Isa 26:3; Jn 14:27; Col 3:15

such things. [9]Whatever you have learned
or received or heard from me, or seen in
4:9 me—put it into practice.[s] And the God
[s]Php 3:17 [t]Ro 15:33 of peace[t] will be with you.

Thanks for Their Gifts

[10]I rejoice greatly in the Lord that at
last you have renewed your concern for
4:10 me.[u] Indeed, you have been concerned,
[u]2Co 11:9 but you had no opportunity to show it.
4:11 [11]I am not saying this because I am in
[v]1Ti 6:6,8 need, for I have learned to be content[v]
whatever the circumstances. [12]I know
what it is to be in need, and I know
what it is to have plenty. I have learned
4:12 the secret of being content in any and
[w]1Co 4:11 [x]2Co 11:9 every situation, whether well fed or
4:13 hungry,[w] whether living in plenty or in
[y]2Co 12:9 want.[x] [13]I can do everything through
4:14 him who gives me strength.[y]
[z]Php 1:7 [14]Yet it was good of you to share[z] in
my troubles. [15]Moreover, as you Philip- 4:15
pians know, in the early days[a] of your [a]Php 1:5
acquaintance with the gospel, when I set [b]2Co 11:8,9
out from Macedonia, not one church
shared with me in the matter of giving
and receiving, except you only;[b] [16]for
even when I was in Thessalonica,[c] you 4:16
sent me aid again and again when I was [c]Ac 17:1
in need.[d] [17]Not that I am looking for [d]1Th 2:9
a gift, but I am looking for what may
be credited to your account.[e] [18]I have 4:17
received full payment and even more; [e]1Co 9:11,12
I am amply supplied, now that I have
received from Epaphroditus[f] the gifts 4:18
you sent. They are a fragrant[g] offering, [f]Php 2:25 [g]2Co 2:14
an acceptable sacrifice, pleasing to God. 4:19
[19]And my God will meet all your needs[h] [h]Ps 23:1;
according to his glorious riches[i] in 2Co 9:8
Christ Jesus. [i]Ro 2:4
[20]To our God and Father[j] be glory 4:20
for ever and ever. Amen.[k] [j]Gal 1:4 [k]Ro 11:36

Final Greetings

[21]Greet all the saints in Christ Jesus. 4:21
The brothers who are with me[l] send [l]Gal 1:2
greetings. [22]All the saints[m] send you 4:22
greetings, especially those who belong [m]Ac 9:13
to Caesar's household.
[23]The grace of the Lord Jesus Christ[n] 4:23
be with your spirit. Amen.[a] [n]Ro 16:20

[a]23 Some manuscripts do not have *Amen.*

PEACE

ROLLING WITH THE PUNCHES

Philippians 4:12

Contentment does not come from having pleasant circumstances. Contentment comes from knowing that, even when life caves in, God is in the darkness.

COLOSSIANS

AUTHORSHIP AND DATE

Paul

c. A.D. 60

KEY THEMES

Paul wrote this book to refute what has been called the "Colossian heresy." Although we don't know exactly what it was, it seems to have included some of these ideas:

1. A kind of ritual taboo system that had attached itself to the gospel, causing the Colossians to enforce certain religious holidays as a form of Christian doctrine (see 2:16–17). The Jewish believers went so far as to make circumcision a requirement of Christianity.
2. The worship of angels (see 2:18).
3. Published legalistic prohibitions, which included: "Do not handle! Do not taste! Do not touch!" (2:21).

The believers of the New Testament era were constantly besieged by renegade teachers and mystics who tried to augment the simple gospel with innovations of their own. Paul realized this was not freedom but slavery, and he cautioned the Colossians, "So then, just as you received Christ Jesus as Lord, continue to live in him, rooted and built up in him, strengthened in the faith as you were taught, and overflowing with thankfulness. See to it that no one takes you captive through hollow and deceptive philosophy" (2:6–8).

FRUIT OF THE SPIRIT IN COLOSSIANS

Joy: Joy is to be a lifestyle (see 1:11–12). In some ways, this seems an insensitive way to live. On any given Sunday in the church, there are people who are carrying great stress. They are experiencing joblessness, illness or bereavement. Should the church always be joyous? Yes. We are called to be a people who are confident that God has everything under control. This is to give us joy, even though some in the church are undergoing deep heartaches. Still, joy is to mark our lives. Resiliency is a necessary attribute for Christians who desire to make a difference in the troubled world in which they live their victorious lives.

Peace: God is in the business of making peace by reconciling all lost men and women to himself. But his peacemaking goes even further than conversion peace. Within the heart of God lives a principle that will not tolerate any enmities that make war on each other in his great universe. God wants to call every quarreling atom within the cosmos to a truce, till the entire universe is filled with his peace. "For God was pleased to have all his fullness dwell in [Jesus], and through him to reconcile to himself all things, whether things on earth or things in heaven, by making peace through his blood, shed on the cross" (1:19–20). Jesus, in time, will have the world joined in one grand unity and harmony of grace.

Faithfulness: Faithfulness is the very definition of the Christian life: "So then, just as you received Christ Jesus as Lord, continue to live in him, rooted and built up in him, strengthened in the faith as you were taught, and overflowing with thankfulness" (2:6–7).

1:1 [a]1Co 1:1 [b]2Co 1:1

1 Paul, an apostle[a] of Christ Jesus by
the will of God,[b] and Timothy our
brother,

2To the holy and faithful[a] brothers in
Christ at Colosse:

DAY 3 THREE

Love and My Relationship With Christ

Colossians 1:19–23

This passage contains the grand interrogatives of God's saving work in Jesus Christ. Read these verses and watch them unfold.

Who is the keeper of this grand force, the incarnation? It is God who, in his own wonderful imagination, conceived of something so powerful. God was willing that all the Deity should dwell bodily in Christ (see Colossians 2:9).

Why would God put such celestial and redeeming machinery into place? Because God was in love with people who didn't love him in return. To overcome the problem of human disinterest in his love, he came to make peace. Many who didn't love him were reconciled to him, and their reconciliation was the entire reason for this "divine romance." God's Son died, and with every drop of blood that fell, God said, "I love you; I love you; I love you."

When did God effect this great redeeming plan? At the very time when we were in need, when we were alienated, indeed when we were even his enemies—at that time he set his plan into motion. Galatians 4:4 says that God sent his Son when the time was exactly right, *in plenitudo temporis.*

For what purpose did God do all this? His goal was to present us as completely holy in his sight, without blemish and free from every accusation. Isn't it wonderful that Jesus lived a completely sinless life? God has arranged it so that we appear in our moral lives just like Jesus because of his work on the cross. The architect of this wonderful reconciliation is love. Love is the stuff of God. Love is the very definition of God. And we look like love when we accept Christ.

To begin a study on the topic of Love, Permeating All We Do, turn to the home page on page 1372.

Grace[c] and peace to you from God
our Father.[b][d]

Thanksgiving and Prayer

3We always thank God,[e] the Father
of our Lord Jesus Christ, when we pray
for you, 4because we have heard of your
faith in Christ Jesus and of the love[f]
you have for all the saints[g]— 5the faith
and love that spring from the hope[h]
that is stored up for you in heaven[i] and
that you have already heard about in
the word of truth, the gospel 6that has
come to you. All over the world[j] this
gospel is bearing fruit[k] and growing,
just as it has been doing among you
since the day you heard it and understood God's grace in all its truth. 7You
learned it from Epaphras,[l] our dear fellow servant, who is a faithful minister[m]
of Christ on our[c] behalf, 8and who also
told us of your love in the Spirit.[n]
9For this reason, since the day we
heard about you,[o] we have not stopped
praying for you and asking God to
fill you with the knowledge of his
will[p] through all spiritual wisdom and
understanding.[q] 10And we pray this in
order that you may live a life worthy[r] of
the Lord and may please him in every
way: bearing fruit in every good work,
growing in the knowledge of God, 11be-
ing strengthened with all power[s] according to his glorious might so that
you may have great endurance and
patience,[t] and joyfully 12giving thanks
to the Father,[u] who has qualified you[d]
to share in the inheritance[v] of the saints
in the kingdom of light. 13For he has
rescued us from the dominion of darkness[w] and brought us into the kingdom[x] of the Son he loves,[y] 14in whom
we have redemption,[e][z] the forgiveness
of sins.[a]

The Supremacy of Christ

15He is the image[b] of the invisible
God,[c] the firstborn over all creation.
16For by him all things were created:[d]
things in heaven and on earth, visible
and invisible, whether thrones or powers or rulers or authorities;[e] all things
were created by him and for him.[f] 17He
is before all things,[g] and in him all

[a]2 Or *believing* [b]2 Some manuscripts *Father and the Lord Jesus Christ* [c]7 Some manuscripts *your* [d]12 Some manuscripts *us* [e]14 A few late manuscripts *redemption through his blood*

1:2 [c]Col 4:18 [d]Ro 1:7
1:3 [e]Ro 1:8
1:4 [f]Gal 5:6 [g]Eph 1:15
1:5 [h]1Th 5:8; Tit 1:2 [i]1Pe 1:4
1:6 [j]Ro 10:18 [k]Jn 15:16
1:7 [l]Phm 23 [m]Col 4:7
1:8 [n]Ro 15:30
1:9 [o]Eph 1:15 [p]Eph 5:17 [q]Eph 1:17
1:10 [r]Eph 4:1
1:11 [s]Eph 3:16 [t]Eph 4:2
1:12 [u]Eph 5:20 [v]Ac 20:32
1:13 [w]Ac 26:18 [x]Eph 6:12; 2Pe 1:11 [y]Mt 3:17
1:14 [z]Ro 3:24 [a]Eph 1:7
1:15 [b]2Co 4:4 [c]Jn 1:18
1:16 [d]Jn 1:3 [e]Eph 1:20,21 [f]Ro 11:36
1:17 [g]Jn 1:2

LOVE

THE CENTER OF THE CENTER— THE FARTHEST EDGE OF THE FARTHEST EDGE

Colossians 1:16

Name any star. God lives there.

Name any desert on any moon of Jupiter. God lives there.

The farthest point in space is but a corner of his living room,

Yet he who keeps a summer palace in the middle of Andromeda

Still craves a throne in the center of your heart.

things hold together. 18And he is the
1:18 [h]Eph 1:22 head[h] of the body, the church; he is
[i]Ac 26:23; the beginning and the firstborn from
Rev 1:5 among the dead,[i] so that in everything
he might have the supremacy. 19For
1:19 [j]Eph 1:5 God was pleased[j] to have all his fullness[k]
[k]Jn 1:16 dwell in him, 20and through him to rec-
1:20 [l]2Co 5:18 oncile[l] to himself all things, whether
[m]Eph 1:10 things on earth or things in heaven,[m]
[n]Eph 2:13 by making peace through his blood,[n]
shed on the cross.
21Once you were alienated from God
1:21 [o]Ro 5:10 and were enemies[o] in your minds[p] be-
[p]Eph 2:3 cause of[a] your evil behavior. 22But now
he has reconciled you by Christ's physi-
1:22 [q]Ro 7:4 cal body[q] through death to present you
[r]Eph 5:27 holy in his sight, without blemish and
free from accusation[r]— 23if you contin-
1:23 [s]Eph 3:17 ue in your faith, established[s] and firm,
[t]ver 5 not moved from the hope[t] held out in
[u]Ro 10:18 the gospel. This is the gospel that you
[v]ver 25; heard and that has been proclaimed to
1Co 3:5 every creature under heaven,[u] and of
which I, Paul, have become a servant.[v]

Paul's Labor for the Church

24Now I rejoice in what was suffered
for you, and I fill up in my flesh what
is still lacking in regard to Christ's af-
1:24 [w]2Co 1:5 flictions,[w] for the sake of his body,
which is the church. 25I have become its
1:25 [x]ver 23 servant[x] by the commission God gave
[y]Eph 3:2 me[y] to present to you the word of God
1:26 [z]Ro 16:25 in its fullness— 26the mystery[z] that has
been kept hidden for ages and genera-
tions, but is now disclosed to the saints.
27To them God has chosen to make
1:27 [a]Mt 13:11 known[a] among the Gentiles the glorious riches of this mystery, which is
Christ in you, the hope of glory.

28We proclaim him, admonishing[b] 1:28 [b]Col 3:16
and teaching everyone with all wisdom,[c] [c]1Co 2:6,7
so that we may present everyone per- [d]Eph 5:27
fect[d] in Christ. 29To this end I labor,[e] 1:29 [e]1Co 15:10
struggling[f] with all his energy, which so [f]Col 2:1
powerfully works in me.[g] [g]Eph 1:19

2 I want you to know how much
I am struggling[h] for you and for 2:1 [h]Col 1:29;
those at Laodicea,[i] and for all who have 4:12
not met me personally. 2My purpose is [i]Rev 1:11
that they may be encouraged in heart[j] 2:2 [j]Col 4:8
and united in love, so that they may
have the full riches of complete understanding, in order that they may know
the mystery of God, namely, Christ, 3in
whom are hidden all the treasures of
wisdom and knowledge.[k] 4I tell you this 2:3 [k]Ro 11:33;
so that no one may deceive you by fine- 1Co 1:24,30
sounding arguments.[l] 5For though I am 2:4
absent from you in body, I am present [l]Ro 16:18
with you in spirit[m] and delight to see 2:5 [m]1Th 2:17
how orderly[n] you are and how firm[o] [n]1Co 14:40
your faith in Christ is. [o]1Pe 5:9

Freedom From Human Regulations Through Life With Christ

6So then, just as you received Christ
Jesus as Lord,[p] continue to live in him, 2:6 [p]Col 1:10
7rooted[q] and built up in him, strength- 2:7
ened in the faith as you were taught, [q]Eph 3:17
and overflowing with thankfulness.
8See to it that no one takes you
captive through hollow and deceptive
philosophy,[r] which depends on human 2:8 [r]1Ti 6:20
tradition and the basic principles of this [s]Gal 4:3
world[s] rather than on Christ.

JOY

DON'T REPLACE RELATIONSHIP WITH REGULATIONS

Colossians 2:8

When first Christ entered your life, the joy of his love occupied you night and day. Have you now left your celebration to study dull books that major on the doctrines of the church? It is a sin to marry for romance only to spend the rest of your life lecturing on the authenticity of the wedding certificate.

9For in Christ all the fullness of
the Deity lives in bodily form, 10and
you have been given fullness in Christ,
who is the head[t] over every power 2:10 [t]Eph 1:22
and authority. 11In him you were also

[a]21 Or *minds, as shown by*

2:11 [u]Ro 2:29; circumcised,[u] in the putting off of the
Php 3:3 sinful nature,[a][v] not with a circumcision
[v]Gal 5:24 done by the hands of men but with the
circumcision done by Christ, [12]having
been buried with him in baptism and
2:12 raised with him[w] through your faith in
[w]Ro 6:5 [x]Ac 2:24 the power of God, who raised him from
the dead.[x]
2:13 [13]When you were dead in your sins[y]
[y]Eph 2:1,5 and in the uncircumcision of your sinful nature,[b] God made you[c] alive with
Christ. He forgave us all our sins, [14]hav-
ing canceled the written code, with its
regulations,[z] that was against us and that 2:14 [z]Eph 2:15
stood opposed to us; he took it away, [a]1Pe 2:24
nailing it to the cross.[a] [15]And having 2:15
disarmed the powers and authorities,[b] [b]Eph 6:12
he made a public spectacle of them,[c] [c]Lk 10:18
triumphing over them by the cross.[d]
[16]Therefore do not let anyone judge 2:16
you[d] by what you eat or drink,[e] or with [d]Ro 14:3,4 [e]Ro 14:17
regard to a religious festival,[f] a New [f]Ro 14:5 [g]1Ch 23:31
Moon celebration[g] or a Sabbath day.[h] [h]Gal 4:10
[17]These are a shadow of the things that
were to come;[i] the reality, however, is 2:17
found in Christ. [18]Do not let anyone [i]Heb 8:5
who delights in false humility[j] and the 2:18
worship of angels disqualify you for the [j]ver 23 [k]Php 3:14
prize.[k] Such a person goes into great de-
tail about what he has seen, and his unspiritual mind puffs him up with idle
notions. [19]He has lost connection with
the Head,[l] from whom the whole body, 2:19
supported and held together by its liga- [l]Eph 1:22
ments and sinews, grows as God causes [m]Eph 4:16
it to grow.[m]
[20]Since you died with Christ to the
basic principles of this world,[n] why, 2:20
as though you still belonged to it, do [n]Gal 4:3,9 [o]ver 14,16
you submit to its rules:[o] [21]"Do not
handle! Do not taste! Do not touch!"?
[22]These are all destined to perish[p] with 2:22
use, because they are based on human [p]1Co 6:13 [q]Isa 29:13;
commands and teachings.[q] [23]Such reg- Mt 15:9;
ulations indeed have an appearance of Tit 1:14
wisdom, with their self-imposed worship, their false humility and their harsh
treatment of the body, but they lack
any value in restraining sensual indulgence.

Rules for Holy Living

3 Since, then, you have been raised
with Christ, set your hearts on
things above, where Christ is seated at
the right hand of God. [2]Set your minds 3:2
on things above, not on earthly things.[r] [r]Php 3:19,20
[3]For you died,[s] and your life is now hid- 3:3 [s]Ro 6:2;
den with Christ in God. [4]When Christ, 2Co 5:14
who is your[e] life, appears,[t] then you 3:4 [t]1Co 1:7
also will appear with him in glory.[u] [u]1Pe 1:13;
[5]Put to death, therefore, whatever be- 1Jn 3:2
longs to your earthly nature: sexual immorality, impurity, lust, evil desires and 3:5 [v]Eph 5:3
greed,[v] which is idolatry.[w] [6]Because of [w]Eph 5:5

[a]*11* Or *the flesh* [b]*13* Or *your flesh* [c]*13* Some manuscripts *us* [d]*15* Or *them in him*
[e]*4* Some manuscripts *our*

DAY 2 TWO

▸ PEACE AND THE PURPOSE OF GOD IN MY LIFE

Colossians 2:6–7

A sure outline for finding the way to peace leaps from this passage and grips our minds. Consider it: Peace is a faith proposition. Just as we have received, so are we to walk. We cannot be saved without a confident faith. Faith appropriates eternity. Faith makes us friends with God. Faith hands us the key to the safety deposit box of all God's promises, and we are instant heirs of all that Christ will inherit (see Romans 8:17).

Continuing in Christ—our ongoing relationship with him—is also a peace proposition. No one can be endowed with a spirit of continual inner harmony unless that person has a steadfast continuance in Christ. Being rooted in Christ is faith and peace. Being rooted in Christ is more than just walking; it is going deeper in our knowledge and understanding as a result of our desire. Faith and peace do not spring spontaneously from a shallow preoccupation with religious things. Unless we desire ever-greater levels of devotion, the foundations of our peace will crumble under the weight of our own growing spiritual disinterest.

Thankfulness is our overflowing response to the blessings of faith and peace. In this attitude we walk with joy, and our peace is published by our very demeanor. In short, all is gained when we walk by the same force by which we have been saved. That is God's will. Then peace marks our lives, and the picture of grace we paint transforms the world.

To begin a study on the topic of Peace, the Companionship of Christ, turn to the home page on page 1243.

3:6 [x]Ro 1:18 these, the wrath of God[x] is coming.[a]
3:7 7You used to walk in these ways, in
[y]Eph 2:2 the life you once lived.[y] 8But now you
3:8 must rid yourselves[z] of all such things as
[z]Eph 4:22 [a]Eph 4:31 these: anger, rage, malice, slander,[a] and
[b]Eph 4:29 filthy language from your lips.[b] 9Do not
3:9 lie to each other,[c] since you have taken
[c]Eph 4:22,25 off your old self with its practices 10and
3:10 [d]Ro 12:2; have put on the new self, which is being
Eph 4:23 renewed[d] in knowledge in the image of

DAY 3 THREE

▸ Peace and My Relationship With Christ

Colossians 3:15

The glorious thing about peace is that it constitutes the soul of our relationship with Christ. We relate to Christ, we converse with Christ, we experience and grow in Christ only when his peace is the very atmosphere that shelters our ongoing relationship with him. The word *rule* in Colossians 3:15 means to "umpire" or "arbitrate" the struggles and disquietudes of our lives.

One prominent twentieth-century philosopher rejected traditional Christianity because he concluded that its fierce doctrinal nature inspired quarrels over truth that divided the Christian world into angry, isolated denominations. He claimed that Christian doctrine had spawned bloodshed, ethnic cleansing, wars and crusades. One can argue that much of the history of the church has been that of quarreling Christians, championing viewpoints rather than celebrating their great commonalties in peace. But Paul suggests that each Christian needs to let the peace of Christ arbitrate in his or her own soul. When the peace of Christ rules the inner life of the individual, it is freed to begin its purifying work in the church universal.

Disputes over doctrines have often brought about the fiercest of clashes within Christianity. And why? If Christ rules from the throne of our hearts, surely we can trust each other to love all that he loves. Let us allow Christ the rule of our hearts so that unity within the church may bring others to know about him and be changed by that peace and love.

To begin a study on the topic of Peace, a Truce With God to End My Alienation From Him, turn to the home page on page 1353.

its Creator.[e] 11Here there is no Greek 3:10 [e]Eph 2:10
or Jew,[f] circumcised or uncircumcised,
barbarian,[g] Scythian, slave or free,[h] but 3:11 [f]Ro 10:12
Christ is all,[i] and is in all. [g]1Co 7:19
12Therefore, as God's chosen people, [h]Gal 3:28 [i]Eph 1:23
holy and dearly loved, clothe yourselves 3:12
with compassion, kindness, humility,[j] [j]Php 2:3
gentleness and patience.[k] 13Bear with [k]2Co 6:6; Gal 5:22,23
each other[l] and forgive whatever griev-
ances you may have against one an- 3:13 [l]Eph 4:2
other. Forgive as the Lord forgave you.[m] [m]Eph 4:32
14And over all these virtues put on love,[n] 3:14
which binds them all together in per- [n]1Co 13:1-13 [o]Eph 4:3
fect unity.[o]
15Let the peace of Christ[p] rule in 3:15
your hearts, since as members of one [p]Jn 14:27
body you were called to peace. And
be thankful. 16Let the word of Christ[q] 3:16
dwell in you richly as you teach and ad- [q]Ro 10:17 [r]Col 1:28
monish one another with all wisdom,[r] [s]Eph 5:19
and as you sing psalms, hymns and
spiritual songs with gratitude in your
hearts to God.[s] 17And whatever you do,[t] 3:17
whether in word or deed, do it all in the [t]1Co 10:31 [u]Eph 5:20
name of the Lord Jesus, giving thanks[u]
to God the Father through him.

▸ PEACE

A Referee Invoking Peace

Colossians 3:15

Neurosis is your choice. It takes over only when you let it.

Stress has a conqueror—it is the Savior.

Turmoil has a referee—it is peace.

Rules for Christian Households

18Wives, submit to your husbands,[v] 3:18 [v]Eph 5:22
as is fitting in the Lord.
19Husbands, love your wives and do
not be harsh with them.
20Children, obey your parents in everything, for this pleases the Lord.
21Fathers, do not embitter your children, or they will become discouraged.
22Slaves, obey your earthly masters in
everything; and do it, not only when
their eye is on you and to win their favor, but with sincerity of heart and reverence for the Lord. 23Whatever you do,
work at it with all your heart, as working for the Lord, not for men, 24since
you know that you will receive an in-

[a]6 Some early manuscripts *coming on those who are disobedient*

heritance[w] from the Lord as a reward. It is the Lord Christ you are serving. 25 Anyone who does wrong will be repaid for his wrong, and there is no favoritism.[x]

4 Masters, provide your slaves with what is right and fair, because you know that you also have a Master in heaven.

3:24 [w]Ac 20:32
3:25 [x]Ac 10:34

Further Instructions

2 Devote yourselves to prayer,[y] being watchful and thankful. 3 And pray for us, too, that God may open a door[z] for our message, so that we may proclaim the mystery of Christ, for which I am in chains.[a] 4 Pray that I may proclaim it clearly, as I should. 5 Be wise[b] in the way you act toward outsiders;[c] make the most of every opportunity.[d] 6 Let your conversation be always full of grace,[e] seasoned with salt,[f] so that you may know how to answer everyone.[g]

4:2 [y]Lk 18:1
4:3 [z]Ac 14:27 [a]Eph 6:19,20
4:5 [b]Eph 5:15 [c]Mk 4:11 [d]Eph 5:16
4:6 [e]Eph 4:29 [f]Mk 9:50 [g]1Pe 3:15

KINDNESS

DIPLOMACY BECOMES THE DIPLOMAT

Colossians 4:6

Think of how to answer all your antagonists so as to lighten their lives. To learn the art of holy love, you must care about unpleasant people as much as God does. Jesus didn't die just for the people you think of as "nice."

Final Greetings

7 Tychicus[h] will tell you all the news about me. He is a dear brother, a faithful minister and fellow servant[i] in the Lord. 8 I am sending him to you for the express purpose that you may know about our[a] circumstances and that he may encourage your hearts.[j] 9 He is coming with Onesimus,[k] our faithful and dear brother, who is one of you. They will tell you everything that is happening here.

10 My fellow prisoner Aristarchus[l] sends you his greetings, as does Mark, the cousin of Barnabas.[m] (You have received instructions about him; if he comes to you, welcome him.) 11 Jesus, who is called Justus, also sends greetings. These are the only Jews among my fellow workers for the kingdom of God, and they have proved a comfort to me. 12 Epaphras,[n] who is one of you and a servant of Christ Jesus, sends greetings. He is always wrestling in prayer for you,[o] that you may stand firm in all the will of God, mature[p] and fully assured. 13 I vouch for him that he is working hard for you and for those at Laodicea[q] and Hierapolis. 14 Our dear friend Luke,[r] the doctor, and Demas[s] send greetings. 15 Give my greetings to the brothers at Laodicea, and to Nympha and the church in her house.[t]

16 After this letter has been read[u] to you, see that it is also read in the church of the Laodiceans and that you in turn read the letter from Laodicea.

17 Tell Archippus:[v] "See to it that you complete the work you have received in the Lord."[w]

18 I, Paul, write this greeting in my own hand.[x] Remember[y] my chains. Grace be with you.[z]

[a]8 Some manuscripts *that he may know about your*

4:7 [h]Ac 20:4 [i]Eph 6:21,22
4:8 [j]Eph 6:21,22
4:9 [k]Phm 10
4:10 [l]Ac 19:29 [m]Ac 4:36
4:12 [n]Col 1:7; Phm 23 [o]Ro 15:30 [p]1Co 2:6
4:13 [q]Col 2:1
4:14 [r]2Ti 4:11; Phm 24 [s]2Ti 4:10
4:15 [t]Ro 16:5
4:16 [u]2Th 3:14
4:17 [v]Phm 2 [w]2Ti 4:5
4:18 [x]1Co 16:21 [y]Heb 13:3 [z]1Ti 6:21; 2Ti 4:22; Tit 3:15; Heb 13:25

1 THESSALONIANS

AUTHORSHIP AND DATE

Paul

A.D. 51

KEY THEMES

Paul opens this letter with a volley of thanksgiving and then moves into the second chapter to talk about the apostolic lifestyle and requirement—defending them before the Thessalonians. In chapter 4, the apostle discusses how we ought to live in order to please God (see 4:1–12) and presents the heart of the argument concerning the Lord's second coming (see vv. 13–18). Paul spoke first to those whose loved ones had died, assuring them that their loved ones' deaths would in no way hinder the second coming, nor would their loved ones miss out on Christ's coming merely because they had died (see 4:14–18). In chapter 5, he discusses the secretive nature of the second coming and the kind of behavior we ought to exhibit as we prepare for it (see vv. 1–11). He ends the chapter with general counsel to love and esteem each other and live lives of love and common support in Christ, having respect for prophecies, holding to the good and avoiding every kind of evil (see vv. 12–22).

FRUIT OF THE SPIRIT IN 1 THESSALONIANS

Love: Witnesses share Christ with others because they are in love with the people for whom Christ died. If we love people, we will share with them the whole gospel. One often hears certain Christians say, "I just love Bill and Sue, but I don't think I could ever find the courage to talk to them about God." Paul saw things quite the other way: "We loved you so much that we were delighted to share with you not only the gospel of God but our lives as well, because you had become so dear to us" (2:8).

Joy: Joy is to be our constant demeanor. Crabby Christians rarely make good evangelists. On the contrary, there ought to be a passion in our vibrancy. We should "be joyful always; pray continually; give thanks in all circumstances" (5:16–18). Joy draws the disconsolate to Christ like no magnet ever drew steel.

Kindness: Kindness is really a decision we make. Paul amplified this when he said, "Make it your ambition to lead a quiet life, to mind your own business" (4:11). Paul seems to be saying, "Get ambitious about your humility." This may seem like an oxymoron—like saying, "Why aren't you more proud of being humble?" Still, we should be possessed of a passion to be humble. When we have successfully stopped putting ourselves in the center of our lives, we will see the needs of others, and we will be kind, knowing this is what Jesus would have done.

Goodness: Goodness and holiness lie in the imitation of Christ (see 1:6). It is foolish to assume that all we have to do to be holy is to stop sinning. That would be hard work indeed. It is far easier to fall in love with Christ and simply let your love conform you to his likeness. Imitating the Savior will produce goodness as its by-product.

Self-Control: First Thessalonians 5:6 encourages us to practice self-control as a way of getting ready for the second coming of Christ. Preachers used to ask congregations what they wanted to be doing when Jesus came again. What they really were asking was, "Do you want to be caught living an indulgent life of sin, or would you rather be practicing self-control at the time of his blessed coming?" It's a fair question.

1:1 [a]Ac 16:1; 2Th 1:1 [b]Ac 17:1 [c]Ro 1:7 **1** Paul, Silas[a] and Timothy,[a]

To the church of the Thessalonians[b]
in God the Father and the Lord Jesus
Christ:

Grace and peace to you.[b][c]

Thanksgiving for the Thessalonians' Faith

2We always thank God for all of
1:2 [d]Ro 1:8 you,[d] mentioning you in our prayers.
3We continually remember before our
God and Father your work produced
1:3 [e]2Th 1:11 by faith,[e] your labor prompted by love,
and your endurance inspired by hope
in our Lord Jesus Christ.

4For we know, brothers loved by God,
that he has chosen you, 5because our
1:5 [f]2Th 2:14 gospel[f] came to you not simply with
words, but also with power, with the
Holy Spirit and with deep conviction.
You know how we lived among you
for your sake. 6You became imitators
1:6 [g]1Co 4:16 [h]Ac 17:5-10 [i]Ac 13:52 of us[g] and of the Lord; in spite of severe suffering,[h] you welcomed the mes-
sage with the joy given by the Holy
Spirit.[i] 7And so you became a model
to all the believers in Macedonia and
Achaia. 8The Lord's message rang out
from you not only in Macedonia and
Achaia—your faith in God has become
1:8 [j]Ro 1:8; 10:18 known everywhere.[j] Therefore we do
not need to say anything about it, 9for
they themselves report what kind of re-
ception you gave us. They tell how you
turned to God from idols[k] to serve the
1:9 [k]1Co 12:2; Gal 4:8 living and true God, 10and to wait for
his Son from heaven, whom he raised
1:10 [l]Ac 2:24 [m]Ro 5:9 from the dead[l]—Jesus, who rescues us
from the coming wrath.[m]

Paul's Ministry in Thessalonica

2:1 [n]1Th 1:5,9 **2** You know, brothers, that our visit
to you[n] was not a failure. 2We had
previously suffered[o] and been insulted 2:2 [o]Ac 16:22; Php 1:30
in Philippi, as you know, but with the
help of our God we dared to tell you
his gospel in spite of strong opposition. 3For the appeal we make does not
spring from error or impure motives,[p] 2:3 [p]2Co 2:17
nor are we trying to trick you. 4On the
contrary, we speak as men approved by
God to be entrusted with the gospel.[q] 2:4 [q]Gal 2:7 [r]Gal 1:10
We are not trying to please men[r] but
God, who tests our hearts. 5You know
we never used flattery, nor did we put
on a mask to cover up greed[s]—God is 2:5 [s]Ac 20:33 [t]Ro 1:9
our witness.[t] 6We were not looking for
praise from men, not from you or anyone else.

As apostles[u] of Christ we could have 2:6 [u]1Co 9:1,2
been a burden to you, 7but we were
gentle among you, like a mother car-
ing for her little children.[v] 8We loved 2:7 [v]ver 11
you so much that we were delighted to
share with you not only the gospel of
God but our lives as well,[w] because you 2:8 [w]2Co 12:15; 1Jn 3:16
had become so dear to us. 9Surely you
remember, brothers, our toil and hard-
ship; we worked[x] night and day in or- 2:9 [x]Ac 18:3 [y]2Th 3:8
der not to be a burden to anyone[y] while
we preached the gospel of God to you.

10You are witnesses,[z] and so is God, 2:10 [z]1Th 1:5 [a]2Co 1:12
of how holy,[a] righteous and blameless
we were among you who believed. 11For
you know that we dealt with each of you
as a father deals with his own children,[b] 2:11 [b]ver 7; 1Co 4:14
12encouraging, comforting and urging
you to live lives worthy[c] of God, who 2:12 [c]Eph 4:1
calls you into his kingdom and glory.

13And we also thank God continu-
ally[d] because, when you received the 2:13 [d]1Th 1:2 [e]Heb 4:12
word of God,[e] which you heard from
us, you accepted it not as the word
of men, but as it actually is, the word
of God, which is at work in you who
believe. 14For you, brothers, became
imitators of God's churches in Judea,[f] 2:14 [f]Gal 1:22 [g]Ac 17:5; 2Th 1:4
which are in Christ Jesus: You suffered
from your own countrymen[g] the same
things those churches suffered from the
Jews, 15who killed the Lord Jesus[h] and 2:15 [h]Ac 2:23 [i]Mt 5:12
the prophets[i] and also drove us out.
They displease God and are hostile to
all men 16in their effort to keep us from
speaking to the Gentiles[j] so that they 2:16 [j]Ac 13:45,50 [k]Mt 23:32
may be saved. In this way they always
heap up their sins to the limit.[k] The

[a]*1* Greek *Silvanus,* a variant of *Silas* [b]*1* Some early manuscripts *you from God our Father and the Lord Jesus Christ*

PATIENCE

SOON AND VERY SOON

1 Thessalonians 1:10

Sometimes pressures may wake you up.
Sometimes a robin committed to the springtime may do the job.
But think of going to sleep on earth
And being roused a universe away.
Celebrate that coming morning when your alarm clock will be a silver trumpet.

WEEK 48

PEACE

1 DAY ONE

PEACE, THE REIGN OF THE HOLY SPIRIT

Read 1 Thessalonians 1:4–10

How did Paul know the Thessalonian believers were chosen by God? The gospel had come to them with power—power from the Holy Spirit. The message had come by the Spirit, and the result was changed lives. The Holy Spirit is a great gift from heaven; to have the Spirit is to have a great blessing. What are the wonders of the Spirit, and what is it that he does in our lives?

Come, let us journey to the day of Pentecost, the day the Holy Spirit was poured out on the believers. Those who had been anointed by wind and fire moved into the streets of Jerusalem with such mystical elation that they were accused of being drunk on wine. With the coming of the Spirit came reason for celebration. How often do we encounter worship that owns such compelling mystery? How wonderful it would be if current congregations were accused of being drunk on God. All too often they appear dead, void of any touch from the inebriating God.

Into these accusations of drunken belief come the words of Joel, spoken by Peter: "In the last days, God says, I will pour out my Spirit on all people. Your sons and daughters will prophesy, your young men will see visions, your old men will dream dreams . . . And everyone who calls on the name of the Lord will be saved" (Acts 2:17,21).

What is the grand legacy of all this fire and wind? Peace! Reconciliation with God is God's aim in this stressed-out world. The answer is never to try to unstress things. The answer is to confess Christ, receive the Holy Spirit and enjoy the peace.

2 DAY TWO

PEACE AND THE PURPOSE OF GOD IN MY LIFE

Jesus' final words should be heeded because Jesus, like so many great persons of history, said last the things most strategic. "Power is on the way," said Jesus. "This power will enable you to change the world. Get ready for the power. The Holy Spirit will settle on you like a sweet, warm rain, and your arid lives will be productive once again." *Turn to Acts 1:8, page 1288, for today's study.*

3 DAY THREE

PEACE AND MY RELATIONSHIP WITH CHRIST

The sinful nature leads to idolatry and abasement; the Spirit leads to the grand affirmation that Christ is the Lord. So whenever you hear God glorified, Christ exalted and the kingdom of God proclaimed, you may be sure that the Holy Spirit is at work. That is one of the Spirit's purposes in the world, one of the reasons he is in our lives. He's the source of every valuable word that escapes our lips. *Turn to Romans 8:5–8, page 1342, for today's study.*

4 DAY FOUR

PEACE AND MY SERVICE TO OTHERS

The Spirit is the seeker of unity. However, be sure that unity is not bought at any price. The only member of the Trinity to wear an adjective is the Spirit. His adjective is "Holy." The Spirit is interested in integrity and truth and right doctrine. There is no point in trying to harmonize truth and error. But after truth occupies the center of our fellowship, unity is his second great agenda. *Turn to Ephesians 4:3–6, page 1407, for today's study.*

5 DAY FIVE

PEACE AND ITS PLACE IN MY PERSONAL WORSHIP

Ezekiel prophesied one of the greatest of all God's promises: "I will give you a new heart and put a new spirit in you" (36:26). Peace is the result of this heart transplant. We cannot, by trying to reform, do enough to "re-moralize" our depravity. We must rely on God to give us a new heart. *Turn to Ezekiel 36:24–28, page 992, for today's study.*

MEMORIZE THIS WEEK

PSALM 51:10-12

Create in me a pure heart, O God,
and renew a steadfast spirit within me.
Do not cast me from your presence
or take your Holy Spirit from me.
Restore to me the joy of your salvation
and grant me a willing spirit, to sustain me.

Week 49, Patience, the Wait for What God Promises, begins on page 1201, Luke 2:25–32.
To begin a topical study on the Fruit of the Spirit, Peace, turn to the Topical Index, page 1548.

wrath of God has come upon them at last.[a]

Paul's Longing to See the Thessalonians

17But, brothers, when we were torn away from you for a short time (in person, not in thought),[l] out of our intense longing we made every effort to see you.[m] 18For we wanted to come to you—certainly I, Paul, did, again and again—but Satan[n] stopped us.[o] 19For what is our hope, our joy, or the crown[p] in which we will glory[q] in the presence of our Lord Jesus when he comes?[r] Is it not you? 20Indeed, you are our glory[s] and joy.

3 So when we could stand it no longer,[t] we thought it best to be left by ourselves in Athens.[u] 2We sent Timothy, who is our brother and God's fellow worker[b] in spreading the gospel of Christ, to strengthen and encourage you in your faith, 3so that no one would be unsettled by these trials. You know quite well that we were destined for them.[v] 4In fact, when we were with you, we kept telling you that we would be persecuted. And it turned out that way, as you well know.[w] 5For this reason, when I could stand it no longer,[x] I sent to find out about your faith. I was afraid that in some way the tempter[y] might have tempted you and our efforts might have been useless.[z]

Timothy's Encouraging Report

6But Timothy has just now come to us from you[a] and has brought good news about your faith and love.[b] He has told us that you always have pleasant memories of us and that you long to see us, just as we also long to see you. 7Therefore, brothers, in all our distress and persecution we were encouraged about you because of your faith. 8For now we really live, since you are standing firm[c] in the Lord. 9How can we thank God enough for you[d] in return for all the joy we have in the presence of our God because of you? 10Night and day we pray[e] most earnestly that we may see you again[f] and supply what is lacking in your faith.

11Now may our God and Father himself and our Lord Jesus clear the way for us to come to you. 12May the Lord make your love increase and overflow for each other[g] and for everyone else, just as ours does for you. 13May he strengthen your hearts so that you will be blameless[h] and holy in the presence of our God and Father when our Lord Jesus comes[i] with all his holy ones.

Living to Please God

4 Finally, brothers,[j] we instructed you how to live in order to please God,[k] as in fact you are living. Now we ask you and urge you in the Lord Jesus to do this more and more. 2For you know what instructions we gave you by the authority of the Lord Jesus.

3It is God's will that you should be sanctified: that you should avoid sexual immorality;[l] 4that each of you should learn to control his own body[c][m] in a way that is holy and honorable, 5not in passionate lust[n] like the heathen,[o] who do not know God; 6and that in this matter no one should wrong his brother or take advantage of him.[p] The Lord will punish men for all such sins,[q] as we have already told you and warned you. 7For God did not call us to be impure, but to live a holy life.[r] 8Therefore, he who rejects this instruction does not reject man but God, who gives you his Holy Spirit.[s]

9Now about brotherly love[t] we do not need to write to you,[u] for you yourselves have been taught by God to love each other.[v] 10And in fact, you do love all the brothers throughout Macedonia.[w] Yet we urge you, brothers, to do so more and more.[x]

11Make it your ambition to lead a quiet life, to mind your own business and to work with your hands,[y] just as we told you, 12so that your daily life may win the respect of outsiders[z] and so that you will not be dependent on anybody.

[a]16 Or *them fully* [b]2 Some manuscripts *brother and fellow worker*; other manuscripts *brother and God's servant* [c]4 Or *learn to live with his own wife*; or *learn to acquire a wife*

2:17 [l]1Co 5:3; Col 2:5 [m]1Th 3:10
2:18 [n]Mt 4:10 [o]Ro 1:13; 15:22
2:19 [p]Php 4:1 [q]2Co 1:14 [r]Mt 16:27; 1Th 3:13
2:20 [s]2Co 1:14
3:1 [t]ver 5 [u]Ac 17:15
3:3 [v]Ac 9:16; 14:22
3:4 [w]1Th 2:14
3:5 [x]ver 1 [y]Mt 4:3 [z]Gal 2:2; Php 2:16
3:6 [a]Ac 18:5 [b]1Th 1:3
3:8 [c]1Co 16:13
3:9 [d]1Th 1:2
3:10 [e]2Ti 1:3 [f]1Th 2:17
3:12 [g]1Th 4:9,10
3:13 [h]1Co 1:8 [i]1Th 2:19
4:1 [j]2Co 13:11 [k]2Co 5:9
4:3 [l]1Co 6:18
4:4 [m]1Co 7:2,9
4:5 [n]Ro 1:26 [o]Eph 4:17
4:6 [p]1Co 6:8 [q]Heb 13:4
4:7 [r]Lev 11:44; 1Pe 1:15
4:8 [s]Ro 5:5; Gal 4:6
4:9 [t]Ro 12:10 [u]1Th 5:1 [v]Jn 13:34
4:10 [w]1Th 1:7 [x]1Th 3:12
4:11 [y]Eph 4:28; 2Th 3:10-12
4:12 [z]Mk 4:11

▸ FAITHFULNESS

JESUS IS COMING!

1 Thessalonians 4:14

Have you lost a Christian loved one to death? The second coming is God's lost and found department.

The Coming of the Lord

13Brothers, we do not want you to be
ignorant about those who fall asleep, or
to grieve like the rest of men, who have
4:13 [a]Eph 2:12 no hope.[a] 14We believe that Jesus died
and rose again and so we believe that
God will bring with Jesus those who
4:14 [b]1Co 15:18 have fallen asleep in him.[b] 15According
to the Lord's own word, we tell you
that we who are still alive, who are
left till the coming of the Lord, will
certainly not precede those who have
4:15 [c]1Co 15:52 fallen asleep.[c] 16For the Lord himself
will come down from heaven, with a
loud command, with the voice of the
archangel and with the trumpet call of
4:16 God,[d] and the dead in Christ will rise
[d]Mt 24:31 [e]1Co 15:23; first.[e] 17After that, we who are still alive
2Th 2:1 and are left[f] will be caught up together
4:17 with them in the clouds[g] to meet the
[f]1Co 15:52 Lord in the air. And so we will be with
[g]Ac 1:9; Rev 11:12 the Lord[h] forever. 18Therefore encour-
[h]Jn 12:26 age each other with these words.

5 Now, brothers, about times and
5:1 [i]Ac 1:7 dates[i] we do not need to write to
[j]1Th 4:9 you,[j] 2for you know very well that
5:2 the day of the Lord[k] will come like a
[k]1Co 1:8 thief in the night.[l] 3While people are
[l]2Pe 3:10 saying, "Peace and safety," destruction
will come on them suddenly, as labor
pains on a pregnant woman, and they
will not escape.

GENTLENESS

A THIEF IN THE NIGHT

1 Thessalonians 5:2

An odd metaphor of the second coming is this:

Stealth is the gentle issue.
Quiet comes as the spoiler of a rich man's fortune.
Quiet comes as the thief of souls.
Was Jesus here?
He must have been, for we are not.

4But you, brothers, are not in dark-
5:4 [m]Ac 26:18; ness[m] so that this day should surprise
1Jn 2:8 you like a thief. 5You are all sons of the
light and sons of the day. We do not
belong to the night or to the darkness.
6So then, let us not be like others, who
are asleep,[n] but let us be alert and self- 5:6 [n]Ro 13:11
controlled. 7For those who sleep, sleep
at night, and those who get drunk, get
drunk at night.[o] 8But since we belong 5:7 [o]Ac 2:15;
to the day, let us be self-controlled, put- 2Pe 2:13
ting on faith and love as a breastplate,[p] 5:8
and the hope of salvation[q] as a helmet.[r] [p]Eph 6:14 [q]Ro 8:24
9For God did not appoint us to suffer [r]Eph 6:17
wrath but to receive salvation through 5:9
our Lord Jesus Christ.[s] 10He died for [s]2Th 2:13,14
us so that, whether we are awake or
asleep, we may live together with him.[t] 5:10
11Therefore encourage one another and [t]2Co 5:15
build each other up, just as in fact you
are doing.

Final Instructions

12Now we ask you, brothers, to respect those who work hard among you,
who are over you in the Lord[u] and 5:12 [u]1Ti 5:17;
who admonish you. 13Hold them in Heb 13:17
the highest regard in love because of
their work. Live in peace with each
other.[v] 14And we urge you, brothers, 5:13 [v]Mk 9:50
warn those who are idle,[w] encourage
the timid, help the weak,[x] be patient 5:14 [w]2Th 3:6,7,11
with everyone. 15Make sure that no- [x]Ro 14:1
body pays back wrong for wrong,[y] but 5:15
always try to be kind to each other[z] and [y]1Pe 3:9 [z]Gal 6:10;
to everyone else. Eph 4:32
16Be joyful always;[a] 17pray continu- 5:16
ally; 18give thanks in all circumstances, [a]Php 4:4
for this is God's will for you in Christ
Jesus.
19Do not put out the Spirit's fire;[b] 5:19 [b]Eph 4:30
20do not treat prophecies[c] with con-
tempt. 21Test everything.[d] Hold on to 5:20 [c]1Co 14:1-40
the good. 22Avoid every kind of evil. 5:21
23May God himself, the God of [d]1Co 14:29; 1Jn 4:1
peace,[e] sanctify you through and
through. May your whole spirit, soul 5:23 [e]Ro 15:33
and body be kept blameless at the com-
ing of our Lord Jesus Christ. 24The one 5:24
who calls you is faithful[f] and he will [f]1Co 1:9
do it. 5:25 [g]Eph 6:19
25Brothers, pray for us.[g] 26Greet all 5:26
the brothers with a holy kiss.[h] 27I charge [h]Ro 16:16
you before the Lord to have this letter 5:27
read to all the brothers.[i] [i]Col 4:16
28The grace of our Lord Jesus Christ 5:28
be with you.[j] [j]Ro 16:20

2 THESSALONIANS

AUTHORSHIP AND DATE

Paul

A.D. 51–52

KEY THEMES

Paul begins this letter in his customary way and then offers both a general thanksgiving and a specific thanksgiving regarding the second coming. This opening is one of the strongest in Paul's letters and includes a dramatic picture of the day of Christ. Paul then addresses the reasons for the persecution of the Thessalonian church, which had led many members to conclude that the time of the end was near. Paul had given the impression in his first letter that the second coming could occur any time; therefore, many of the believers had actually quit their jobs and were idle. Paul was firm with these idle persons, saying that if they would not work, those in the church who continued to work should not feed them (see 3:10). Yet Paul closes the letter with an admonition to love and care for each other.

FRUIT OF THE SPIRIT IN 2 THESSALONIANS

Peace: Paul asked the Lord of peace to give the Thessalonians peace (see 3:16). This congregation was most troubled over the persecutions that had befallen them and over their own neurotic wrangling about when Jesus would come again. So the Thessalonians needed peace. Paul reminded them that Jesus is the Lord of peace and that spending consecrated time in his presence would increase their peace. The truth of this is most obvious; we cannot be overly uptight while we are living close to the Lord of peace. It just isn't possible. Our peace or peacelessness is a direct indicator of the closeness of our relationship with him.

Faithfulness: Paul reminded the Thessalonians that he was boasting far and wide about their ability to be faithful under persecution (see 1:4). There is no certain way to measure the depth of our faithfulness without trial. Faithfulness is never sure of itself until it has stared hardship in the face and asked itself just how much it believes.

1 Paul, Silas[a] and Timothy,[a]
To the church of the Thessalonians
in God our Father and the Lord Jesus
Christ:

1:1 [a]Ac 16:1; 1Th 1:1

DAY 2 TWO

▸ GOODNESS AND THE PURPOSE OF GOD IN MY LIFE

2 Thessalonians 1:11–12

How is Jesus glorified in us and we in him? As we read this passage, we should ask ourselves, "How do we imitate Christ?" Is it not by asking him to cut out of our lives all that does not look like him? Think of yourself as a block of marble out of which Christ, the artist, is fashioning a replica of himself. Then invite Jesus, your artist, to create you by chipping away at all those bulges of ugly rock that distract from the statue's beauty. Cry out to him:

Come Master sculptor,
Urge the marble,
Cut the ugly rock away,
Chisel off the faulty stone that
Doesn't look like Jesus.
Trim away the calloused edges
Of my hard, unyielding mind,
Cut the stony cysts of incompassion
From my heart.
Wound my hands with steel and
Hang me on the wood of April,
That I may know you, Lord,
And the power of your resurrection
And the fellowship of your suffering.
Being made conformable to your death
For
Lord, I would be crucified
With you that I might live,
Yet not my poor miserable life,
But your great life living out of me.

The process of becoming the finished work of Christ is furthered by longing to be like him, rather than by trying to be good. Goodness is always the result of our passion to imitate Christ; in so doing, we fulfill the good purposes of God.

To begin a study on the topic of Goodness, the Result of Imitating Christ, turn to the home page on page 1409.

2Grace and peace to you from God
the Father and the Lord Jesus Christ.[b]

Thanksgiving and Prayer

3We ought always to thank God for
you, brothers, and rightly so, because
your faith is growing more and more,
and the love every one of you has
for each other is increasing.[c] 4Therefore,
among God's churches we boast[d]
about your perseverance and faith[e] in
all the persecutions and trials you are
enduring.[f]
5All this is evidence[g] that God's judgment
is right, and as a result you will
be counted worthy of the kingdom of
God, for which you are suffering. 6God
is just: He will pay back trouble to
those who trouble you[h] 7and give relief
to you who are troubled, and to us as
well. This will happen when the Lord
Jesus is revealed from heaven in blazing
fire with his powerful angels.[i] 8He will
punish those who do not know God[j]
and do not obey the gospel of our Lord
Jesus.[k] 9They will be punished with everlasting
destruction[l] and shut out from
the presence of the Lord and from the
majesty of his power[m] 10on the day[n] he
comes to be glorified[o] in his holy people
and to be marveled at among all
those who have believed. This includes
you, because you believed our testimony
to you.[p]

1:2 [b]Ro 1:7
1:3 [c]1Th 3:12
1:4 [d]2Co 7:14 [e]1Th 1:3 [f]1Th 2:14
1:5 [g]Php 1:28
1:6 [h]Col 3:25; Rev 6:10
1:7 [i]1Th 4:16; Jude 14
1:8 [j]Gal 4:8 [k]Ro 2:8
1:9 [l]Php 3:19; 2Pe 3:7 [m]2Th 2:8
1:10 [n]1Co 3:13 [o]Jn 17:10 [p]1Co 1:6

▸ FAITHFULNESS

THE FINALE OF FIRE

2 Thessalonians 1:6–7

God indeed made promises to earth.
He pledged earth his rainbow sign.
"You have my word, my seal and worth.
No more floods, the fire next time."

11With this in mind, we constantly
pray for you, that our God may count
you worthy[q] of his calling, and that by
his power he may fulfill every good purpose
of yours and every act prompted
by your faith.[r] 12We pray this so that
the name of our Lord Jesus may be glorified
in you,[s] and you in him, according
to the grace of our God and the
Lord Jesus Christ.[b]

1:11 [q]ver 5 [r]1Th 1:3
1:12 [s]Php 2:9-11

[a]*1* Greek *Silvanus,* a variant of *Silas* [b]*12* Or *God and Lord, Jesus Christ*

The Man of Lawlessness

2 Concerning the coming of our Lord
Jesus Christ and our being gathered
2:1 to him,[t] we ask you, brothers, 2not to
tMk 13:27; 1Th 4:15-17 become easily unsettled or alarmed by
some prophecy, report or letter[u] sup-
2:2 u2Th 3:17 posed to have come from us, saying
v1Co 1:8 that the day of the Lord[v] has already
2:3 come. 3Don't let anyone deceive you[w]
wEph 5:6-8 xDa 7:25; in any way, for ⌞that day will not
8:25; 11:36; Rev 13:5,6 come⌟ until the rebellion occurs and
the man of lawlessness[a] is revealed,[x]
the man doomed to destruction. 4He
will oppose and will exalt himself over
2:4 everything that is called God[y] or is wor-
y1Co 8:5 zIsa 14:13,14; shiped, so that he sets himself up in
Eze 28:2 God's temple, proclaiming himself to
be God.[z]

PATIENCE

FIRST APOSTASY, THEN APOCALYPSE

2 Thessalonians 2:3

Some will fall away
In smug denials of the faith.
Then will come the Lord of their incredulity
and say, "Surprise!"

5Don't you remember that when I
was with you I used to tell you these
things? 6And now you know what is
holding him back, so that he may be
revealed at the proper time. 7For the secret power of lawlessness is already at
work; but the one who now holds it
back will continue to do so till he is tak-
en out of the way. 8And then the lawless
one will be revealed, whom the Lord
Jesus will overthrow with the breath of
2:8 his mouth[a] and destroy by the splen-
aIsa 11:4; Rev 19:15 dor of his coming. 9The coming of
the lawless one will be in accordance
with the work of Satan displayed in all
kinds of counterfeit miracles, signs and

GOODNESS

CHRIST AND ANTICHRIST

2 Thessalonians 2:4

Consider him who stands against God's only Son
And bids the masses doubt their only hope.
Who can this devil be but the antichrist?

wonders,[b] 10and in every sort of evil that 2:9
deceives those who are perishing.[c] They bMt 24:24; Jn 4:48
perish because they refused to love the
truth and so be saved. 11For this reason 2:10 c1Co 1:18
God sends them[d] a powerful delusion 2:11
so that they will believe the lie 12and dRo 1:28
so that all will be condemned who have
not believed the truth but have delight- 2:12
ed in wickedness.[e] eRo 1:32

Stand Firm

13But we ought always to thank God
for you, brothers loved by the Lord, because from the beginning God chose
you[b][f] to be saved[g] through the sancti- 2:13 fEph 1:4
fying work of the Spirit[h] and through g1Th 5:9 h1Pe 1:2
belief in the truth. 14He called you to
this through our gospel, that you might
share in the glory of our Lord Jesus
Christ. 15So then, brothers, stand firm[i] 2:15 i1Co 16:13
and hold to the teachings[c] we passed on j1Co 11:2
to you,[j] whether by word of mouth or
by letter.
16May our Lord Jesus Christ himself
and God our Father, who loved us[k] and 2:16 kJn 3:16
by his grace gave us eternal encourage-
ment and good hope, 17encourage[l] your 2:17 l1Th 3:2
hearts and strengthen[m] you in every m2Th 3:3
good deed and word.

Request for Prayer

3 Finally, brothers,[n] pray for us[o] that 3:1 n1Th 4:1
the message of the Lord[p] may spread o1Th 5:25
rapidly and be honored, just as it was p1Th 1:8
with you. 2And pray that we may be delivered from wicked and evil men,[q] for 3:2 qRo 15:31
not everyone has faith. 3But the Lord
is faithful,[r] and he will strengthen and 3:3 r1Co 1:9
protect you from the evil one.[s] 4We sMt 5:37
have confidence[t] in the Lord that you 3:4
are doing and will continue to do the t2Co 2:3
things we command. 5May the Lord di-
rect your hearts[u] into God's love and 3:5 u1Ch 29:18
Christ's perseverance.

Warning Against Idleness

6In the name of the Lord Jesus
Christ,[v] we command you, brothers, to 3:6 v1Co 5:4
keep away from[w] every brother who is wRo 16:17
idle[x] and does not live according to the xver 7,11 y1Co 11:2
teaching[d] you received from us.[y] 7For
you yourselves know how you ought to
follow our example.[z] We were not idle 3:7 z1Co 4:16
when we were with you, 8nor did we eat

[a]3 Some manuscripts *sin* [b]13 Some manuscripts *because God chose you as his firstfruits* [c]15 Or *traditions* [d]6 Or *tradition*

PATIENCE

WAITING PATIENTLY

2 Thessalonians 3:5

Even if you think Christ will come tomorrow, plant that apple tree today. Even if you think Christ will come tomorrow, do not get dressed in white and go to the mountains to await him.

Study and learn from those who, through the years, have gathered on hilltops, dressed in white, impatiently waiting. They all had "special understanding," which they tried to use as a lever to pry open the heavens. When the day came and Jesus didn't, they stumbled back to the lowlands, where the hungry still needed feeding and the grieving still needed consolation.

anyone's food without paying for it. On
3:8 [a]Ac 18:3; Eph 4:28 the contrary, we worked[a] night and day,
laboring and toiling so that we would
not be a burden to any of you. [9]We
did this, not because we do not have
3:9 [b]1Co 9:4-14 [c]ver 7 the right to such help,[b] but in order
to make ourselves a model for you to
3:10 [d]1Th 3:4 [e]1Th 4:11 follow.[c] [10]For even when we were with
you,[d] we gave you this rule: "If a man
will not work,[e] he shall not eat."
3:11 [f]ver 6,7; 1Ti 5:13 [11]We hear that some among you are
idle. They are not busy; they are busy-
3:12 [g]1Th 4:1 bodies.[f] [12]Such people we command
and urge in the Lord Jesus Christ[g] to

FAITHFULNESS

PUNCH THE TIME CLOCK AND AVOID MOUNTAIN TOPS

2 Thessalonians 3:10

Many quit their jobs, believing that Jesus' second coming would occur before their next paycheck came. Then, of course, the "faithless" working Christians were expected to feed the fiery unemployed. Watch, but keep your job—even pay into your retirement fund.

settle down and earn the bread they
eat.[h] [13]And as for you, brothers, never 3:12 [h]1Th 4:11; Eph 4:28
tire of doing what is right.[i]
[14]If anyone does not obey our in- 3:13 [i]Gal 6:9
struction in this letter, take special note
of him. Do not associate with him,[j] in 3:14 [j]ver 6
order that he may feel ashamed. [15]Yet
do not regard him as an enemy, but 3:15 [k]Gal 6:1; 1Th 5:14
warn him as a brother.[k]

Final Greetings

[16]Now may the Lord of peace[l] him- 3:16 [l]Ro 15:33 [m]Ru 2:4
self give you peace at all times and
in every way. The Lord be with all of
you.[m]
[17]I, Paul, write this greeting in my
own hand,[n] which is the distinguishing 3:17 [n]1Co 16:21
mark in all my letters. This is how I
write.
[18]The grace of our Lord Jesus Christ 3:18 [o]Ro 16:20
be with you all.[o]

1 TIMOTHY

AUTHORSHIP AND DATE

Paul

c. A.D. 64

KEY THEMES

The letters to Timothy and Titus are called the Pastoral Letters because they were written to give counsel and instruction to two pastors, Timothy and Titus. Most scholars believe that Paul was released from his first Roman imprisonment (described in Acts 28) in A.D. 62–63. He was then free to complete a fourth missionary journey, during which time the Pastoral Letters were written. During these travels, he left Titus in charge of the church in Crete and Timothy in charge of the Ephesian congregation. When the persecutions began under Nero, Paul was again taken to prison (in A.D. 66–67). This imprisonment was vastly different from his earlier, more congenial incarceration. Instead of being in his own rented house, he was likely imprisoned in the Mamertine Prison in Rome, where he awaited his death. While 1 Timothy and Titus were written during his years of freedom between imprisonments, 2 Timothy was written during his final imprisonment. Paul may actually have been dead by the time Timothy received his second letter.

The themes of 1 Timothy abound with pastoral counsel. The book is composed of "how to's":

1. How to deal with false teachers (see 1:3–11)
2. How to deal with worship issues (see 2:1–15)
3. How to develop good leaders (see 3:1–16)
4. Additional information on how to recognize and deal with false teachers (see 4:1–16)
5. How to deal with the matters of a pastoral ministry as well as various age groups in the church (see 5:1—6:2)
6. How to stand true in the faith and develop an impeccable lifestyle (see 6:3–16).

FRUIT OF THE SPIRIT IN 1 TIMOTHY

Love: Paul reminded Timothy that he was to command the false teachers to teach the truth. The goal of this was to promote good doctrine, which would promote love and a sincere faith (see 1:3–5). This may seem like a circuitous way to move from honest doctrine to love, but love only looks real in the middle of false teaching, and pretense is hypocrisy.

Peace: There are two ingredients for peace in the church: godliness and contentment (see 6:6). Contentment without godliness is spurious peace that has nothing to offer the truly troubled. Godliness without contentment is spurious as well, for it has an aura of holiness but is troubled and peaceless.

Patience: Paul recommended patience in the laying on of hands (see 5:22). Those who were set apart to serve God would benefit from having a time during which they were observed. Waiting to see how their faith actually endured was most important. Perhaps the sins that have caused so many ordained men and women to fall from ministry could have been avoided if someone, somewhere, had not been so impatient for his or her ordination.

Self-Control: Paul's advice to his young son in the ministry was this: "Fight the good fight of the faith. Take hold of the eternal life to which you were called when you made your good confession in the presence of many witnesses" (6:12). It is good when older ministers can serve as mentors to those who are younger and can remind them that a good reputation always requires a fight. This is the best way to learn.

1:1 [a]Tit 1:3 [b]Col 1:27

1

Paul, an apostle of Christ Jesus by the command of God[a] our Savior and of Christ Jesus our hope,[b]

DAY 3 THREE

▸ PATIENCE AND MY RELATIONSHIP WITH CHRIST

1 Timothy 1:15–16

How do we view ourselves through the eyes of Christ? Grace is the antidote for our own self-love. The blatant fact is that we are sinners, but grace takes into account our need for cleansing and washes us clean. Paul was, in his own eyes, the chief of sinners, but Christ is the chief of grace. Grace comes to us as he wills—at God's speed, slowly it seems to us, yet always in time to include us in the beloved.

Would you, with Paul, say, "I am the worst of sinners"? If so, then all is well, for grace is working in you; be as patient in your waiting for it as God is in his coming to you. John Bunyan wrote long ago: "O Son of God, grace was in all thy tears; grace came bubbling out of thy side with thy blood; grace came forth with every word of thy sweet mouth; grace came out where the whip smote thee, where the thorns pricked thee, where the nails and spears pierced thee. O blessed Son of God, here is grace indeed! unsearchable riches of grace! unthought of riches of grace! grace to make angels wonder, grace to make sinners happy, grace to astonish devils!"

God wants us to revel in the joy of seeing his plan lived out in our lives. He sees all things from the beginning and knows exactly how everything will work out. But he wants us to see it as well. I know of no happier Christians than those who can see what God has in mind to do with their lives and enjoy watching it happen. Such observant disciples infect their world with joy.

The crux of God's patient grace appears in 1 Timothy 1:16: "But for that very reason I was shown mercy so that in me, the worst of sinners, Christ Jesus might display his unlimited patience as an example for those who would believe on him and receive eternal life."

To begin a study on the topic of Patience, the Slowly Acquired Virtue, turn to the home page on page 565.

2To Timothy[c] my true son[d] in the 1:2
faith: [c]Ac 16:1 [d]2Ti 1:2; Tit 1:4

Grace, mercy and peace from God
the Father and Christ Jesus our Lord.

Warning Against False Teachers of the Law

3As I urged you when I went into
Macedonia, stay there in Ephesus[e] so 1:3
that you may command certain men [e]Ac 18:19
not to teach false doctrines[f] any longer [f]Gal 1:6,7
4nor to devote themselves to myths[g] 1:4
and endless genealogies. These promote [g]1Ti 4:7; Tit 1:14
controversies[h] rather than God's work— [h]1Ti 6:4
which is by faith. 5The goal of this
command is love, which comes from a
pure heart[i] and a good conscience and 1:5
a sincere faith.[j] 6Some have wandered [i]2Ti 2:22
away from these and turned to mean- [j]2Ti 1:5
ingless talk. 7They want to be teachers
of the law, but they do not know what
they are talking about or what they so
confidently affirm.

8We know that the law is good[k] if 1:8
one uses it properly. 9We also know that [k]Ro 7:12
law[a] is made not for the righteous but
for lawbreakers and rebels,[l] the ungodly 1:9
and sinful, the unholy and irreligious; [l]Gal 3:19
for those who kill their fathers or mothers, for murderers, 10for adulterers and
perverts, for slave traders and liars and
perjurers—and for whatever else is contrary to the sound doctrine[m] 11that 1:10
conforms to the glorious gospel of [m]2Ti 4:3; Tit 1:9
the blessed God, which he entrusted
to me.[n] 1:11 [n]Gal 2:7

The Lord's Grace to Paul

12I thank Christ Jesus our Lord, who
has given me strength,[o] that he con- 1:12 [o]Php 4:13
sidered me faithful, appointing me to
his service. 13Even though I was once a
blasphemer and a persecutor[p] and a vi- 1:13 [p]Ac 8:3
olent man, I was shown mercy because I [q]Ac 26:9
acted in ignorance and unbelief.[q] 14The
grace of our Lord was poured out on
me abundantly,[r] along with the faith 1:14 [r]Ro 5:20
and love that are in Christ Jesus.[s] [s]2Ti 1:13

15Here is a trustworthy saying[t] that 1:15
deserves full acceptance: Christ Jesus [t]1Ti 3:1; 2Ti 2:11; Tit 3:8
came into the world to save sinners—of
whom I am the worst. 16But for that
very reason I was shown mercy[u] so that 1:16 [u]ver 13
in me, the worst of sinners, Christ Jesus
might display his unlimited patience as

[a]9 Or *that the law*

GOODNESS

THE EGO IS THE CHIEF
RENOVATING SITE OF CHRIST

1 Timothy 1:15

Those who feel they have no sin, sin regularly with pride.

Those who feel they are chief of sinners draw near to reasonable righteousness.

Why do those most innocent feel their sin to be the blackest?

Could it be that the closer we stand to light, the darker falls our shadow?

an example for those who would believe on him and receive eternal life.
1:17 [v]Rev 15:3 17Now to the King[v] eternal, immortal,
[w]Col 1:15 invisible,[w] the only God, be honor and
[x]Ro 11:36 glory for ever and ever. Amen.[x]
18Timothy, my son, I give you this
instruction in keeping with the proph-
1:18 [y]1Ti 4:14 ecies once made about you,[y] so that
[z]2Ti 2:3 by following them you may fight the
good fight,[z] 19holding on to faith and
a good conscience. Some have rejected
these and so have shipwrecked their
1:19 [a]1Ti 6:21 faith.[a] 20Among them are Hymenaeus[b]
and Alexander,[c] whom I have handed
1:20 [b]2Ti 2:17 over to Satan[d] to be taught not to blas-
[c]2Ti 4:14 [d]1Co 5:5 pheme.

Instructions on Worship

2 I urge, then, first of all, that requests, prayers, intercession and
2:2 [e]Ezr 6:10; Ro 13:1 thanksgiving be made for everyone—
2for kings and all those in authority,[e]
that we may live peaceful and quiet
2:4 [f]Eze 18:23,32 lives in all godliness and holiness. 3This
[g]Tit 2:11 is good, and pleases God our Savior,
[h]2Ti 2:25 4who wants[f] all men[g] to be saved and to
2:5 [i]Ro 3:29,30 come to a knowledge of the truth.[h] 5For
[j]Gal 3:20 there is one God[i] and one mediator[j]

FAITHFULNESS

THE ARBITER

1 Timothy 2:5

Are you in danger of being accused by God of sin too horrible to forgive?

It might be true, except that you have for your attorney Jesus Christ.

This arbiter is known in the highest court. Rest easy.

Your counselor has never lost a case.

between God and men, the man Christ
Jesus, 6who gave himself as a ransom
for all men—the testimony[k] given in 2:6 [k]1Co 1:6
its proper time.[l] 7And for this purpose [l]1Ti 6:15
I was appointed a herald and an apos-
tle—I am telling the truth, I am not ly-
ing—and a teacher[m] of the true faith to 2:7 [m]2Ti 1:11
the Gentiles.[n] [n]Ac 9:15; Eph 3:7,8
8I want men everywhere to lift up
holy hands[o] in prayer, without anger or 2:8 [o]Ps 134:2; Lk 24:50
disputing.
9I also want women to dress modestly, with decency and propriety, not
with braided hair or gold or pearls
or expensive clothes,[p] 10but with good 2:9 [p]1Pe 3:3
deeds, appropriate for women who pro-
fess to worship God.
11A woman should learn in quietness
and full submission.[q] 12I do not per- 2:11 [q]1Co 14:34
mit a woman to teach or to have au-
thority over a man; she must be silent.
13For Adam was formed first, then Eve.[r] 2:13 [r]Ge 2:7,22; 1Co 11:8
14And Adam was not the one deceived;
it was the woman who was deceived
and became a sinner.[s] 15But women[a] 2:14 [s]Ge 3:1-6,13; 2Co 11:3
will be saved[b] through childbearing—if
they continue in faith, love[t] and holi- 2:15 [t]1Ti 1:14
ness with propriety.

Overseers and Deacons

3 Here is a trustworthy saying:[u] If 3:1 [u]1Ti 1:15
anyone sets his heart on being an [v]Ac 20:28
overseer,[c][v] he desires a noble task. 2Now
the overseer must be above reproach,[w] 3:2 [w]Tit 1:6-8
the husband of but one wife, temperate, [x]Ro 12:13
self-controlled, respectable, hospitable,[x] [y]2Ti 2:24
able to teach,[y] 3not given to drunk- 3:3 [z]2Ti 2:24
enness, not violent but gentle, not [a]Heb 13:5; 1Pe 5:2
quarrelsome,[z] not a lover of money.[a]
4He must manage his own family well
and see that his children obey him with
proper respect.[b] 5(If anyone does not 3:4 [b]Tit 1:6
know how to manage his own family,
how can he take care of God's church?)[c] 3:5 [c]1Co 10:32
6He must not be a recent convert, or
he may become conceited[d] and fall un- 3:6 [d]1Ti 6:4
der the same judgment as the devil. 7He
must also have a good reputation with
outsiders, so that he will not fall into
disgrace and into the devil's trap.[e] 3:7 [e]2Ti 2:26
8Deacons,[f] likewise, are to be men
worthy of respect, sincere, not indulg- 3:8 [f]Php 1:1
ing in much wine,[g] and not pursuing [g]Tit 2:3
dishonest gain. 9They must keep hold
of the deep truths of the faith with

[a] *15* Greek *she* [b] *15* Or *restored* [c] *1* Traditionally *bishop*; also in verse 2

DAY 4 FOUR

Self-Control and My Service to Others

1 Timothy 4:13–16

Pauls recommends to Timothy the preacher's task: public reading of the Scripture, preaching, teaching and developing the special gift.

It's this "special gift" that is the key focus of our disciplines. Paul says that it was given to Timothy at the laying on of hands. Somehow we all want to appreciate those innate gifts that are given to us through DNA. Talent is another way of defining those gifts. We all have some of these talents because our genes have split and split until our bodies are filled with the genetic footprints of our abilities. These gifts made Caruso sing, Cassatt paint, and Hemingway write.

But I am interested in Timothy's special gift. It wasn't inborn. It came to him when the elders laid their hands on him, and there—on the spot—God gave him a gift that would be utilized only by God for the advancement of his kingdom.

Still, Timothy would have to work out this special calling, to "fan into flame the gift of God" (2 Timothy 1:6). Then he would be better able to serve because he would have taken this beautiful thing God had given him and developed it to the point that he could use it all for God's glory.

Paul names spiritual gifts in three different passages: Romans 12, 1 Corinthians 12 and Ephesians 4. These gifts have been given by God specifically to enlarge his church and make it more effective. These gifts are not given in the fullest state of their development. God gives them as "diamonds in the rough." We spend the rest of our lives developing and improving our gifts and working them out (see Philippians 2:12–13).

God's mandate of self-control is that we never neglect improving the gifts that God has conferred on us as his Spirit entered us. Then our lives will be always under renovation and the church will be furnished for its work in the world.

To begin a study on the topic of Self-Control, the Disciplined Life, turn to the home page on page 1367.

a clear conscience.[h] 10 They must first be tested; and then if there is nothing against them, let them serve as deacons.

11 In the same way, their wives[a] are to be women worthy of respect, not malicious talkers[i] but temperate and trustworthy in everything.

12 A deacon must be the husband of but one wife and must manage his children and his household well.[j] 13 Those who have served well gain an excellent standing and great assurance in their faith in Christ Jesus.

14 Although I hope to come to you soon, I am writing you these instructions so that, 15 if I am delayed, you will know how people ought to conduct themselves in God's household, which is the church[k] of the living God, the pillar and foundation of the truth. 16 Beyond all question, the mystery[l] of godliness is great:

He[b] appeared in a body,[c][m]
  was vindicated by the Spirit,
was seen by angels,
  was preached among the nations,[n]
was believed on in the world,
  was taken up in glory.[o]

Instructions to Timothy

4 The Spirit[p] clearly says that in later times[q] some will abandon the faith and follow deceiving spirits[r] and things taught by demons. 2 Such teachings come through hypocritical liars, whose consciences have been seared as with a hot iron.[s] 3 They forbid people to marry[t] and order them to abstain from certain foods,[u] which God created[v] to be received with thanksgiving[w] by those who believe and who know the truth. 4 For everything God created is good,[x] and nothing is to be rejected if it is received with thanksgiving, 5 because it is consecrated by the word of God and prayer.

6 If you point these things out to the brothers, you will be a good minister of Christ Jesus, brought up in the truths of the faith[y] and of the good teaching that you have followed. 7 Have nothing to do with godless myths and old wives' tales;[z] rather, train yourself to be godly.

3:9 [h]1Ti 1:19
3:11 [i]2Ti 3:3; Tit 2:3
3:12 [j]ver 4
3:15 [k]ver 5; Eph 2:21
3:16 [l]Ro 16:25 [m]Jn 1:14 [n]Col 1:23 [o]Mk 16:19
4:1 [p]Jn 16:13 [q]2Ti 3:1 [r]2Th 2:3
4:2 [s]Eph 4:19
4:3 [t]Heb 13:4 [u]Col 2:16 [v]Ge 1:29 [w]Ro 14:6
4:4 [x]Ro 14:14-18
4:6 [y]1Ti 1:10
4:7 [z]2Ti 2:16

[a] *11* Or *way, deaconesses* [b] *16* Some manuscripts *God* [c] *16* Or *in the flesh*

8For physical training is of some value,
but godliness has value for all things,[a]
holding promise for both the present
life[b] and the life to come.
9This is a trustworthy saying[c] that deserves full acceptance 10(and for this we
labor and strive), that we have put our
hope in the living God, who is the Savior of all men, and especially of those
who believe.
11Command and teach these things.[d]
12Don't let anyone look down on you
because you are young, but set an example[e] for the believers in speech, in
life, in love, in faith[f] and in purity.
13Until I come, devote yourself to the
public reading of Scripture, to preaching and to teaching. 14Do not neglect
your gift, which was given you through
a prophetic message[g] when the body of
elders laid their hands on you.[h]

4:8 [a]1Ti 6:6 [b]Ps 37:9,11; Mk 10:29,30
4:9 [c]1Ti 1:15
4:11 [d]1Ti 5:7; 6:2
4:12 [e]Tit 2:7; 1Pe 5:3 [f]1Ti 1:14
4:14 [g]1Ti 1:18 [h]Ac 6:6; 2Ti 1:6

KINDNESS

ORDINATION: SANCTIFIED BY GOD'S KINDNESS

1 Timothy 4:14

Ordination is not a church certificate. It is a gift that Christians give one another. Ordination is two things, really. First, it is a godly faith made warm by human touch. Second, the laying on of hands affirms God's high-voltage power at work in low-wattage believers. The Spirit's current electrifies the gift that makes God's power usable in the one who is touched.

15Be diligent in these matters; give
yourself wholly to them, so that everyone may see your progress. 16Watch
your life and doctrine closely. Persevere
in them, because if you do, you will
save both yourself and your hearers.

Advice About Widows, Elders and Slaves

5 Do not rebuke an older man[i] harshly,[j] but exhort him as if he were
your father. Treat younger men[k] as
brothers, 2older women as mothers, and
younger women as sisters, with absolute purity.
3Give proper recognition to those
widows who are really in need.[l] 4But
if a widow has children or grandchildren, these should learn first of all to
put their religion into practice by caring for their own family and so repaying their parents and grandparents,[m] for
this is pleasing to God.[n] 5The widow
who is really in need[o] and left all alone
puts her hope in God[p] and continues
night and day to pray[q] and to ask God
for help. 6But the widow who lives for
pleasure is dead even while she lives.[r]
7Give the people these instructions,[s]
too, so that no one may be open to
blame. 8If anyone does not provide for
his relatives, and especially for his immediate family, he has denied[t] the faith
and is worse than an unbeliever.
9No widow may be put on the list
of widows unless she is over sixty, has
been faithful to her husband,[a] 10and is
well known for her good deeds,[u] such
as bringing up children, showing hospitality, washing the feet[v] of the saints,
helping those in trouble[w] and devoting
herself to all kinds of good deeds.
11As for younger widows, do not put
them on such a list. For when their
sensual desires overcome their dedication to Christ, they want to marry.
12Thus they bring judgment on themselves, because they have broken their
first pledge. 13Besides, they get into the
habit of being idle and going about
from house to house. And not only do
they become idlers, but also gossips and
busybodies,[x] saying things they ought
not to. 14So I counsel younger widows
to marry,[y] to have children, to manage
their homes and to give the enemy no
opportunity for slander.[z] 15Some have
in fact already turned away to follow
Satan.[a]
16If any woman who is a believer has
widows in her family, she should help
them and not let the church be burdened with them, so that the church
can help those widows who are really in
need.[b]
17The elders[c] who direct the affairs of
the church well are worthy of double
honor,[d] especially those whose work is
preaching and teaching. 18For the Scripture says, "Do not muzzle the ox while
it is treading out the grain,"[b][e] and "The
worker deserves his wages."[c][f] 19Do not
entertain an accusation against an elder[g] unless it is brought by two or three
witnesses.[h] 20Those who sin are to be

5:1 [i]Tit 2:2 [j]Lev 19:32 [k]Tit 2:6
5:3 [l]ver 5,16
5:4 [m]Eph 6:1,2 [n]1Ti 2:3
5:5 [o]ver 3,16 [p]1Co 7:34; 1Pe 3:5 [q]Lk 2:37
5:6 [r]Lk 15:24
5:7 [s]1Ti 4:11
5:8 [t]2Pe 2:1; Jude 4; Tit 1:16
5:10 [u]Ac 9:36; 1Ti 6:18; 1Pe 2:12 [v]Lk 7:44 [w]ver 16
5:13 [x]2Th 3:11
5:14 [y]1Co 7:9 [z]1Ti 6:1
5:15 [a]Mt 4:10
5:16 [b]ver 3-5
5:17 [c]Ac 11:30 [d]Php 2:29; 1Th 5:12
5:18 [e]Dt 25:4; 1Co 9:7-9 [f]Lk 10:7; Lev 19:13; Dt 24:14,15; Mt 10:10; 1Co 9:14
5:19 [g]Ac 11:30 [h]Mt 18:16

[a]9 Or *has had but one husband* [b]*18* Deut. 25:4
[c]*18* Luke 10:7

rebuked[i] publicly, so that the others
may take warning.[j]
21I charge you, in the sight of God
and Christ Jesus[k] and the elect angels,
to keep these instructions without partiality, and to do nothing out of favoritism.
22Do not be hasty in the laying on of

5:20 [i]2Ti 4:2; Tit 1:13 [j]Dt 13:11
5:21 [k]1Ti 6:13; 2Ti 4:1

DAY 4 FOUR

PATIENCE AND MY SERVICE TO OTHERS

1 Timothy 6:11–12

Confession is the glorious calling of the church. It is the church's great ministry of compassion, for it allows those perishing beyond God's love to accept an eternity of grace. Confession is a ministry of identity, for it allows men and women to identify with the church by openly naming Jesus as their Lord. Confession furnishes the joy of worship as people in the congregation openly talk about the central love affair of their lives.

There is urgency in our confession, for if people do not find Christ, they will perish. But there is also to be a well-paced preaching that takes the necessary time to explain the gospel to the unsaved. We must advance steadily into the world, taking time to teach and preach thoroughly the confession of the church.

Jesus says in Matthew 10:32–36 that professing his name will in some sense be the most nerve-racking element of our work. Why? Because the very word *Jesus,* whose confession brings glory to the church, is at the same time a word that is not everywhere welcome. Even some families have been divided over the issue of who Jesus is and what his rightful place in their lives should be. Some confessions result in applause, some martyrdom.

But let the unhurried virtue of patience steadily advance the preaching of the grand truth to all those who will receive it. And may we who preach the confessional life be patient, always ready to be kind to those who will not receive the truth, treating them as Christ himself would treat them.

To begin a study on the topic of Patience, the Unhurried Virtue, turn to the home page on page 1146.

hands,[l] and do not share in the sins of
others.[m] Keep yourself pure.
23Stop drinking only water, and use
a little wine[n] because of your stomach
and your frequent illnesses.
24The sins of some men are obvious,
reaching the place of judgment ahead
of them; the sins of others trail behind
them. 25In the same way, good deeds
are obvious, and even those that are not
cannot be hidden.

5:22 [l]Ac 6:6 [m]Eph 5:11
5:23 [n]1Ti 3:8

6 All who are under the yoke of slavery should consider their masters
worthy of full respect,[o] so that God's
name and our teaching may not be
slandered.[p] 2Those who have believing
masters are not to show less respect
for them because they are brothers.[q]
Instead, they are to serve them even
better, because those who benefit from
their service are believers, and dear to
them. These are the things you are to
teach and urge on them.[r]

6:1 [o]Eph 6:5; Tit 2:9; 1Pe 2:18 [p]Tit 2:5,8
6:2 [q]Phm 16 [r]1Ti 4:11

Love of Money

3If anyone teaches false doctrines[s] and
does not agree to the sound instruction[t]
of our Lord Jesus Christ and to godly
teaching, 4he is conceited and understands nothing. He has an unhealthy
interest in controversies and quarrels
about words[u] that result in envy, strife,
malicious talk, evil suspicions 5and constant friction between men of corrupt
mind, who have been robbed of the
truth[v] and who think that godliness is a
means to financial gain.
6But godliness with contentment[w] is
great gain.[x] 7For we brought nothing
into the world, and we can take nothing out of it.[y] 8But if we have food and
clothing, we will be content with that.[z]
9People who want to get rich[a] fall into
temptation and a trap[b] and into many
foolish and harmful desires that plunge
men into ruin and destruction. 10For
the love of money[c] is a root of all kinds
of evil. Some people, eager for money,
have wandered from the faith[d] and
pierced themselves with many griefs.

6:3 [s]1Ti 1:3 [t]1Ti 1:10
6:4 [u]2Ti 2:14
6:5 [v]Tit 1:15
6:6 [w]Php 4:11; Heb 13:5 [x]1Ti 4:8
6:7 [y]Job 1:21; Ecc 5:15
6:8 [z]Heb 13:5
6:9 [a]Pr 15:27 [b]1Ti 3:7
6:10 [c]1Ti 3:3 [d]Jas 5:19

Paul's Charge to Timothy

11But you, man of God,[e] flee from
all this, and pursue righteousness, godliness, faith, love,[f] endurance and gentleness. 12Fight the good fight[g] of the
faith. Take hold of[h] the eternal life to
which you were called when you made

6:11 [e]2Ti 3:17 [f]2Ti 2:22
6:12 [g]1Co 9:25,26; 1Ti 1:18 [h]Php 3:12

your good confession in the presence of
many witnesses. **13**In the sight of God,
who gives life to everything, and of
Christ Jesus, who while testifying before
6:13 [i]Jn 18:33-37 Pontius Pilate[i] made the good confes-
[j]1Ti 5:21 sion, I charge you[j] **14**to keep this command without spot or blame until the
appearing of our Lord Jesus Christ,
15which God will bring about in his own
6:15 [k]1Ti 1:11 time—God, the blessed[k] and only Ruler,[l]
[l]1Ti 1:17 the King of kings and Lord of lords,[m]
[m]Rev 17:14; 19:16 **16**who alone is immortal[n] and who lives
in unapproachable light, whom no one
6:16 [n]1Ti 1:17 has seen or can see.[o] To him be honor
[o]Jn 1:18 and might forever. Amen.

17Command those who are rich in
this present world not to be arrogant
nor to put their hope in wealth,[p] which 6:17 [p]Lk 12:20,21
is so uncertain, but to put their hope [q]1Ti 4:10
in God,[q] who richly provides us with [r]Ac 14:17
everything for our enjoyment.[r] **18**Command them to do good, to be rich in
good deeds,[s] and to be generous and 6:18 [s]1Ti 5:10
willing to share.[t] **19**In this way they will [t]Ro 12:8,13
lay up treasure for themselves[u] as a firm 6:19
foundation for the coming age, so that [u]Mt 6:20
they may take hold of the life that is
truly life.

20Timothy, guard what has been en-
trusted[v] to your care. Turn away from 6:20 [v]2Ti 1:12,14
godless chatter[w] and the opposing ideas [w]2Ti 2:16
of what is falsely called knowledge,
21which some have professed and in so 6:21
doing have wandered from the faith.[x] [x]2Ti 2:18
Grace be with you.[y] [y]Col 4:18

2 TIMOTHY

Authorship and Date

Paul

c. A.D. 67–68

Key Themes

This book is perhaps the most warm and needy of all of Paul's letters. It was certainly the last letter he wrote before his death. It was written out of Paul's loneliness, for he readily confessed that many of his friends had abandoned him (see 4:9–10).

In spite of the fact that Paul believed he would be executed (see 4:6), the book abounds with incredible teachings on boldness and steadfast adherence to the gospel (see 4:1–3). The times were desperate, and the evidence of the last days called for a commitment to the truths that define the gospel (see 3:1–17). There is a summons to steadfast commitment all through the book. This summons appears in dynamic metaphors of commitment and service (see 2:1–21). Most of all, the book resonates with an emotive and tender sense of parting. Paul loved Timothy, his son in the faith. Like any father, Paul wanted all he had taught and lived to be entrusted to his son. Paul's expectation that he would be alive for Jesus' second coming (see 1 Corinthians 15:51) had now given way to the realistic expectation that he would be killed and given a crown of righteousness (see 4:6–8). But the victory of commitment hangs about the book in a sweet aroma of impending martyrdom. Glory is the final end of those whose faith never wavers.

Fruit of the Spirit in 2 Timothy

Joy: "Recalling your tears, I long to see you, so that I may be filled with joy" (1:4). This is most descriptive of the joy that accompanies truly great Christian friendships. What joy there is in finding brothers and sisters who long to see us and be a part of our lives! Paul had found in Timothy someone with whom to entrust his teaching and ministry. He knew that his calling would yield fruit into the next generation. It is quite possible that Paul had no idea to what extent his letters would become the literature of the ages. Not knowing the future brought even more joy into the relationship he shared with Timothy, to whom he gave his legacy of passion.

Faithfulness: There are times in life when we may feel forsaken and alone. In Paul's case, he didn't just feel alone; he was alone. He confessed that Demas had deserted him, for Demas had loved this present world. Other friends had been called away either on business or for the sake of the gospel. Luke, the blessed physician, alone was with him as a faithful friend (see 4:10–11). Even more than the faithfulness of Luke, Paul could honestly say, "But the Lord stood at my side and gave me strength" (4:17). God calls us to faithfulness, but the best part is that he always proves himself faithful, promising that he will never leave us nor forsake us (see Hebrews 13:5).

Gentleness: Paul painted a picture of the gentle minister of Christ: that person "must not quarrel; instead, he must be kind to everyone, able to teach, not resentful. Those who oppose him he must gently instruct" (2:24–25). Perhaps the greatest quality of the gentle minister is that of love—even to opponents. This minister makes no one afraid. All in the church feel free to come to such a pastor and never fear embarrassment, abuse or rejection.

Self-Control: Paul used two striking metaphors to show the importance of voluntarily submitting ourselves to the rigors of Christian discipline: that of a soldier and of an athlete (see 2:4–5). Those who discipline themselves to obey build a life of honor based on the virtue of self-control.

1 Paul, an apostle of Christ Jesus by
1:1 [a]2Co 1:1 the will of God,[a] according to the
[b]Eph 3:6; 1Ti 6:19 promise of life that is in Christ Jesus,[b]

1:2 [c]Ac 16:1 2To Timothy,[c] my dear son:[d]

[d]1Ti 1:2 Grace, mercy and peace from God
the Father and Christ Jesus our Lord.

Encouragement to Be Faithful

1:3 [e]Ro 1:8 3I thank God,[e] whom I serve, as my
[f]Ro 1:10 forefathers did, with a clear conscience,
as night and day I constantly remem-
ber you in my prayers.[f] 4Recalling your
1:4 [g]Ac 20:37 tears,[g] I long to see you,[h] so that I may
[h]2Ti 4:9 be filled with joy. 5I have been remind-
1:5 ed of your sincere faith,[i] which first
[i]1Ti 1:5 lived in your grandmother Lois and in
[j]Ac 16:1 your mother Eunice[j] and, I am persuaded, now lives in you also. 6For this
reason I remind you to fan into flame
the gift of God, which is in you through
1:6 the laying on of my hands.[k] 7For God
[k]1Ti 4:14 did not give us a spirit of timidity,[l] but
1:7 a spirit of power, of love and of self-
[l]Ro 8:15 discipline.

FAITHFULNESS

FAITH OF OUR MOTHERS

2 Timothy 1:5

Faith of our mothers, holy faith…
We will be true to thee till death.

8So do not be ashamed[m] to testify
1:8 [m]Mk 8:38; about our Lord, or ashamed of me his
Ro 1:16 prisoner.[n] But join with me in suffering
[n]Eph 3:1 [o]2Ti 2:3,9; 4:5 for the gospel,[o] by the power of God,
9who has saved us and called[p] us to a
1:9 [p]Ro 8:28 holy life—not because of anything we
have done but because of his own pur-
pose and grace. This grace was given us
in Christ Jesus before the beginning of
1:10 [q]Eph 1:9 time, 10but it has now been revealed[q]
[r]1Co 15:26, 54 through the appearing of our Savior,
Christ Jesus, who has destroyed death[r]
and has brought life and immortality to
light through the gospel. 11And of this
gospel I was appointed a herald and an
1:11 apostle and a teacher.[s] 12That is why
[s]1Ti 2:7 I am suffering as I am. Yet I am not
ashamed, because I know whom I have
believed, and am convinced that he is
1:12 [t]1Ti 6:20 able to guard[t] what I have entrusted to
[u]ver 18 him for that day.[u]
1:13 13What you heard from me, keep[v]
[v]Tit 1:9 as the pattern of sound teaching, with
[w]1Ti 1:14 faith and love in Christ Jesus.[w] 14Guard
the good deposit that was entrusted to
you—guard it with the help of the Holy
Spirit who lives in us.[x] 1:14 [x]Ro 8:9
15You know that everyone in the
province of Asia has deserted me,[y] in- 1:15 [y]2Ti 4:10,11,16
cluding Phygelus and Hermogenes.
16May the Lord show mercy to the
household of Onesiphorus,[z] because he 1:16 [z]2Ti 4:19
often refreshed me and was not ashamed
of my chains. 17On the contrary, when
he was in Rome, he searched hard for
me until he found me. 18May the Lord
grant that he will find mercy from the
Lord on that day! You know very well
in how many ways he helped me[a] in 1:18 [a]Heb 6:10
Ephesus.

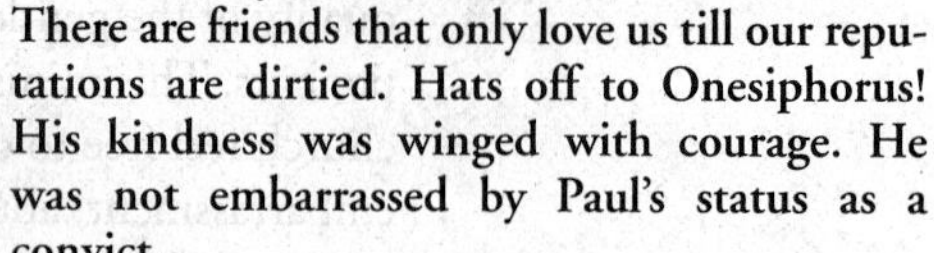

KINDNESS

CHAINS AND SHAME

2 Timothy 1:16

There are friends that only love us till our reputations are dirtied. Hats off to Onesiphorus! His kindness was winged with courage. He was not embarrassed by Paul's status as a convict.

2 You then, my son, be strong[b] in the 2:1 [b]Eph 6:10
grace that is in Christ Jesus. 2And
the things you have heard me say[c] in 2:2 [c]2Ti 1:13
the presence of many witnesses[d] entrust [d]1Ti 6:12
to reliable men who will also be quali-
fied to teach others. 3Endure hardship
with us like a good soldier[e] of Christ 2:3 [e]1Ti 1:18
Jesus. 4No one serving as a soldier gets
involved in civilian affairs—he wants to
please his commanding officer. 5Simi-
larly, if anyone competes as an athlete,
he does not receive the victor's crown[f] 2:5 [f]1Co 9:25
unless he competes according to the
rules. 6The hardworking farmer should
be the first to receive a share of the
crops. 7Reflect on what I am saying, for

SELF-CONTROL

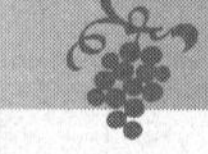

SOLDIERS

2 Timothy 2:3

Soldiers do not grumble when they are asked to live outdoors in storms and when hunger is a constant companion. Soldiers enlist for the long haul. Christians, on the other hand, have been known to grumble over the smallest inconvenience. They enlist, but their commitment is often shorter than the bivouac.

the Lord will give you insight into all
this.
2:8 [g]Ac 2:24 [h]Mt 1:1 [i]Ro 2:16 [8]Remember Jesus Christ, raised from
the dead,[g] descended from David.[h] This
is my gospel,[i] [9]for which I am suffer-
2:9 [j]Ac 9:16 ing[j] even to the point of being chained
like a criminal. But God's word is not
2:10 [k]Col 1:24 chained. [10]Therefore I endure everything[k] for the sake of the elect, that
they too may obtain the salvation that
is in Christ Jesus, with eternal glory.[l] 2:10 [l]2Co 4:17
[11]Here is a trustworthy saying:

If we died with him,
we will also live with him;[m] 2:11 [m]Ro 6:2-11
[12]if we endure,
we will also reign with him.[n] 2:12 [n]Ro 8:17; 1Pe 4:13
If we disown him,

TIMOTHY

Goodness, the Benefit of Righteous Mentoring (1:1–18)

Paul believed that Timothy's goodness was a result of the influence of the many mentors in his life. His mentors didn't just tell him to live a good life; they modeled the good life and lived it out in such a way as to make it both attractive and desirable to Timothy.

Timothy's first mentors were his grandmother Lois and his mother Eunice, both of whom were models of "sincere faith" (2 Timothy 1:5). There was no pretense in the genuine goodness that Timothy learned at home. Eunice and Lois were incapable of being anything other than who they appeared to be.

Paul was also Timothy's mentor. "For this reason," said Paul, "I remind you to fan into flame the gift of God, which is in you through the laying on of my hands" (v. 6). Then Paul rehearsed the counsel that came from his own life: "So do not be ashamed to testify about our Lord, or ashamed of me his prisoner. But join with me in suffering for the gospel, by the power of God, who has saved us and called us to a holy life" (vv. 8–9). Paul's example was Timothy's calling to a holy life. It was the apostle's summons to continue to live a good life, for goodness elevated one small step toward God is holiness.

But if these reminders were not enough, Paul emphasized once more the value of that goodness to which God had called Timothy and which his mentors had demonstrated for him. "What you heard from me, keep as the pattern of sound teaching, with faith and love in Christ Jesus. Guard the good deposit that was entrusted to you—guard it with the help of the Holy Spirit who lives in us" (vv. 13–14). The words *good deposit* might just as well read "the deposit of goodness," for goodness had been introduced into Timothy's life by his mentors.

In a very real sense we are the creation of those who went before us. We are all indebted to our mentors, just as Timothy was. "Do your best to present yourself to God as one approved, a workman who does not need to be ashamed and who correctly handles the word of truth" (2:15). Live a good life, Paul said, as a man who never needs to apologize for either his lifestyle or his teaching.

Paul's life was almost over, and he was saying to his young son in the faith, "For I am already being poured out like a drink offering" (4:6). When one gives the best offering possible, it is an offering of value. The quality of Paul's life was considered a near-perfect offering given to God. He wanted Timothy to be able to say the same thing. Paul confessed as the curtain was closing on his life, "I have fought the good fight" (v. 7). Paul had indeed lived a good life, and the goodness he lived he passed on to Timothy. Timothy had been shown what goodness looked like. Now he was to spend his life becoming what he had been shown.

In our own lives, we can look to those godly people who model Jesus to us. But we can build a statue of Jesus in the center of our lives and wake each morning determined to be like the Christ we behold. Imitating Christ—through the example of others or of Christ himself—is the simplest recipe for goodness.

PATIENCE

MISUNDERSTOOD NOBILITY

2 Timothy 2:12

If we endure, we shall reign. This is a simple rule for all who are waiting to be a part of Christ's everlasting triumph. Reigning with Christ is the crown forged on an anvil of gold with hammers of silver.

2:12 [o]Mt 10:33 he will also disown us;[o]
13if we are faithless,
2:13 [p]Nu 23:19; Ro 3:3 he will remain faithful,[p]
for he cannot disown himself.

A Workman Approved by God

14Keep reminding them of these
things. Warn them before God against
2:14 [q]1Ti 6:4 quarreling about words;[q] it is of no value, and only ruins those who listen.
15Do your best to present yourself to
God as one approved, a workman who
does not need to be ashamed and who
2:15 [r]Eph 1:13; Jas 1:18 correctly handles the word of truth.[r]
16Avoid godless chatter,[s] because those
who indulge in it will become more
2:16 [s]Tit 3:9 and more ungodly. 17Their teaching will
spread like gangrene. Among them are
2:17 [t]1Ti 1:20 Hymenaeus[t] and Philetus, 18who have
wandered away from the truth. They
say that the resurrection has already
taken place, and they destroy the faith
2:18 [u]1Ti 1:19 of some.[u] 19Nevertheless, God's solid
foundation stands firm,[v] sealed with
2:19 [v]Isa 28:16 [w]Jn 10:14 [x]1Co 1:2 this inscription: "The Lord knows those
who are his,"[a][w] and, "Everyone who
confesses the name of the Lord[x] must
turn away from wickedness."
20In a large house there are articles
not only of gold and silver, but also of
wood and clay; some are for noble pur-

GENTLENESS

DEBATE ONLY THE ESSENTIAL ISSUES

2 Timothy 2:23

Rhetoric is the sport of the comfortable.

Debate is the contest of egos seeking to outdo each other.

Service is the joy of those who know they must listen the lost to Christ,

For it is impossible to argue the world into heaven.

poses and some for ignoble.[y] 21If a man 2:20 [y]Ro 9:21
cleanses himself from the latter, he will
be an instrument for noble purposes,
made holy, useful to the Master and
prepared to do any good work.[z] 2:21 [z]2Ti 3:17
22Flee the evil desires of youth, and
pursue righteousness, faith, love[a] and 2:22 [a]1Ti 1:14; 6:11
peace, along with those who call on the
Lord out of a pure heart.[b] 23Don't have [b]1Ti 1:5
anything to do with foolish and stupid
arguments, because you know they produce quarrels. 24And the Lord's servant
must not quarrel; instead, he must be
kind to everyone, able to teach, not
resentful.[c] 25Those who oppose him he 2:24 [c]1Ti 3:2,3
must gently instruct, in the hope that 2:25
God will grant them repentance lead- [d]1Ti 2:4
ing them to a knowledge of the truth,[d] 2:26
26and that they will come to their senses [e]1Ti 3:7
and escape from the trap of the devil,[e]
who has taken them captive to do his
will.

Godlessness in the Last Days

3 But mark this: There will be terri-
ble times in the last days.[f] 2People 3:1 [f]1Ti 4:1
will be lovers of themselves, lovers of
money,[g] boastful, proud[h], abusive, dis- 3:2 [g]1Ti 3:3
obedient to their parents,[i] ungrateful, [h]Ro 1:30
unholy, 3without love, unforgiving, slan- [i]Ro 1:30
derous, without self-control, brutal, not
lovers of the good, 4treacherous, rash,
conceited,[j] lovers of pleasure rather than 3:4 [j]1Ti 3:6
lovers of God— 5having a form of god-
liness but denying its power. Have nothing to do with them.

GOODNESS

GOODNESS IS A FORM OF GODLINESS

2 Timothy 3:2–5

There are some who know everything about God as a doctrine, yet they have nothing to do with him as the owner of their lives.

6They are the kind who worm their
way[k] into homes and gain control over 3:6 [k]Jude 4
weak-willed women, who are loaded
down with sins and are swayed by all
kinds of evil desires, 7always learning
but never able to acknowledge the truth.
8Just as Jannes and Jambres opposed 3:8
Moses,[l] so also these men oppose[m] the [l]Ex 7:11 [m]Ac 13:8
truth—men of depraved minds,[n] who, [n]1Ti 6:5

[a]*19* Num. 16:5 (see Septuagint)

as far as the faith is concerned, are rejected. 9But they will not get very far
3:9 because, as in the case of those men,[o]
[o]Ex 7:12 their folly will be clear to everyone.

Paul's Charge to Timothy

10You, however, know all about my
3:10 teaching,[p] my way of life, my purpose,
[p]1Ti 4:6 faith, patience, love, endurance, 11per-
secutions, sufferings—what kinds of
3:11 things happened to me in Antioch,[q]
[q]Ac 13:14,50 Iconium and Lystra, the persecutions
[r]2Co 11:23-27 I endured.[r] Yet the Lord rescued me
[s]Ps 34:19 from all of them.[s] 12In fact, everyone
who wants to live a godly life in Christ
3:12 Jesus will be persecuted,[t] 13while evil
[t]Ac 14:22 men and impostors will go from bad to
3:13 worse,[u] deceiving and being deceived.
[u]2Ti 2:16 14But as for you, continue in what you
have learned and have become con-
vinced of, because you know those
3:14 from whom you learned it,[v] 15and how
[v]2Ti 1:13 from infancy[w] you have known the holy
3:15 Scriptures,[x] which are able to make
[w]2Ti 1:5 [x]Jn 5:39 you wise[y] for salvation through faith
[y]Ps 119:98,99 in Christ Jesus. 16All Scripture is God-
3:16 breathed[z] and is useful for teaching,[a]
[z]2Pe 1:20,21 [a]Ro 4:23,24 rebuking, correcting and training in
righteousness, 17so that the man of
3:17 God[b] may be thoroughly equipped for
[b]1Ti 6:11 [c]2Ti 2:21 every good work.[c]

FAITHFULNESS

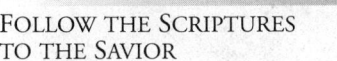

FOLLOW THE SCRIPTURES TO THE SAVIOR

2 Timothy 3:14–15

There is one road map that leads to the
author of eternal life—
It is the Book.
Our God can write!
He lifts his starry quill,
And the ages beg for paper.
A thousand pages
Of Adam's sad biography,
And on each one
The grace-drawn portrait of his Son.

4 In the presence of God and of
Christ Jesus, who will judge the
4:1 living and the dead,[d] and in view of
[d]Ac 10:42 [e]1Ti 5:21 his appearing and his kingdom, I give
4:2 you this charge:[e] 2Preach[f] the Word;[g] be
[f]1Ti 4:13 [g]Gal 6:6 prepared in season and out of season;
[h]1Ti 5:20; Tit 1:13; 2:15 correct, rebuke[h] and encourage—with
great patience and careful instruction.
3For the time will come when men will
not put up with sound doctrine.[i] In- 4:3 [i]1Ti 1:10
stead, to suit their own desires, they
will gather around them a great number of teachers to say what their itching
ears want to hear. 4They will turn their
ears away from the truth and turn aside 4:4
to myths.[j] 5But you, keep your head in [j]1Ti 1:4
all situations, endure hardship,[k] do the 4:5
work of an evangelist,[l] discharge all the [k]2Ti 1:8 [l]Ac 21:8
duties of your ministry.

DAY 5 FIVE

SELF-CONTROL AND ITS PLACE IN MY PERSONAL WORSHIP

2 Timothy 4:6–8

Personal discipline over a lifetime always wins the crown of righteousness. But self-control is not the kind of discipline that hurries us from one holy agenda to the next. The key is pacing. Those who pace their self-control tend to live longer, and their longevity presents to God effective, faithful years of service instead of hurried, neurotic-driven good deeds. So Paul arrives in heaven, having penned nearly half of the books of the New Testament and having started dozens of churches over the course of three missionary journeys. He didn't get to heaven as soon as he might have wished, but he took many others with him.

Pacing our lives should never bypass joy. One is always reminded of those two very old women who died and went to heaven and were amazed at the beauty of the place. "Just think, Mabel," said one of glory's new émigrés, "we could have been here a lot sooner if we hadn't eaten all that oat bran." Our discipline is not to be one of grieving and grudging. The joy of our discipline ought to possess us from day to day and manifest itself in our worship.

To begin a study on the topic of Self-Control, the Disciplined Life, turn to the home page on page 1367.

6For I am already being poured out 4:6
like a drink offering,[m] and the time [m]Php 2:17
has come for my departure.[n] 7I have [n]Php 1:23 4:7
fought the good fight,[o] I have finished [o]1Ti 1:18
the race,[p] I have kept the faith. 8Now [p]1Co 9:24 4:8
there is in store for me[q] the crown of [q]Col 1:5

PEACE

THE FINAL CONFIDENCE

2 Timothy 4:6

Paul was confident that when he closed his eyes in this world, he would open them in the next. He considered execution only a momentary stopover between worlds.

righteousness, which the Lord, the righ-
4:8 teous Judge, will award to me on that
[r]2Ti 1:12 day[r]—and not only to me, but also to
all who have longed for his appearing.

Personal Remarks

9 Do your best to come to me quick-
4:10 ly, 10 for Demas,[s] because he loved this
[s]Col 4:14 [t]1Jn 2:15 world,[t] has deserted me and has gone
[u]Ac 16:6 to Thessalonica. Crescens has gone to
Galatia,[u] and Titus to Dalmatia. 11 Only
4:11 Luke[v] is with me.[w] Get Mark[x] and bring
[v]Col 4:14 [w]2Ti 1:15 him with you, because he is helpful to
[x]Ac 12:12 me in my ministry. 12 I sent Tychicus[y] to
4:12 Ephesus. 13 When you come, bring the
[y]Ac 20:4 cloak that I left with Carpus at Troas,
and my scrolls, especially the parch-
4:14 ments.
[z]Ac 19:33 14 Alexander[z] the metalworker did me
a great deal of harm. The Lord will re-
pay him for what he has done.[a] 15 You 4:14 [a]Ro 12:19
too should be on your guard against
him, because he strongly opposed our
message.

16 At my first defense, no one came to
my support, but everyone deserted me.
May it not be held against them.[b] 17 But 4:16
the Lord stood at my side[c] and gave me [b]Ac 7:60
strength, so that through me the mes- 4:17
sage might be fully proclaimed and all [c]Ac 23:11 [d]Ac 9:15
the Gentiles might hear it.[d] And I was
delivered from the lion's mouth. 18 The
Lord will rescue me from every evil attack[e] and will bring me safely to his 4:18
heavenly kingdom. To him be glory for [e]Ps 121:7 [f]Ro 11:36
ever and ever. Amen.[f]

Final Greetings

19 Greet Priscilla[a] and Aquila[g] and the 4:19
household of Onesiphorus. 20 Erastus[h] [g]Ac 18:2
stayed in Corinth, and I left Trophi- 4:20
mus[i] sick in Miletus. 21 Do your best to [h]Ac 19:22 [i]Ac 20:4
get here before winter.[j] Eubulus greets 4:21
you, and so do Pudens, Linus, Claudia [j]ver 9
and all the brothers. 4:22

22 The Lord be with your spirit.[k] [k]Gal 6:18; Phm 25
Grace be with you.[l] [l]Col 4:18

[a] *19* Greek *Prisca,* a variant of *Priscilla*

TITUS

AUTHORSHIP AND DATE

Paul

c. A.D. 64

KEY THEMES

Paul defined for Titus the nature of salvation (see 3:5). The grace factor was always a key theme with the apostle. As in the other Pastoral Letters, Paul spent a great deal of time talking about the church: How it was to develop leaders—particularly elders (see 1:5–9)—and how it was to lead other groups in the church (see 2:1–14). Paul wanted to be sure that the Cretans, for all their other faults (see 1:12), were responsible citizens (see 3:1–2) and lived godly lives free from spiritual error (see 3:1–11). The Roman Empire was building quite a case against Christians, and anti-Christian sentiment was growing. Perhaps Paul was beginning to recognize that worldwide persecution was on the way. His many admonitions to be good citizens were likely in the interest of giving the Romans no more grist for their mills of persecution.

As in the book of 1 Timothy, Paul had much to say about recognizing and dealing with false teachers (see 1:10–16). As Paul grew older, he no doubt wanted to be sure that the church identified false teaching and continued fearlessly preaching the truth. This was especially important until the canon of the New Testament became fixed.

FRUIT OF THE SPIRIT IN TITUS

Goodness: "An overseer [pastor, bishop]," said the apostle, "must be blameless—not overbearing, not quick-tempered, not given to drunkenness, not violent, not pursuing dishonest gain. Rather he must be hospitable, one who loves what is good, who is self-controlled, upright, holy and disciplined" (1:7–8). Why would Paul set such high standards for pastors? The world needs to be able to see that the goodness that Christians forever talk about is as accessible as the nearest pastor, whose appetites are controlled by godly volition. Such a pastor says, "It is safe to imitate me, for I am bound up in imitating Christ."

Self-Control: "Encourage the young men to be self-controlled," said the apostle (2:6). Self-denial and self-control are harder habits to master during the younger years, when the fever of appetites rages within us. Still, those young people who master their appetites in youth have fewer defeats to challenge their walk with Christ in later years. Lessons learned young stabilize us throughout life. So it is with self-control.

1:1 [a]Ro 1:1 **1** Paul, a servant of God[a] and an
[b]1Ti 2:4 apostle of Jesus Christ for the faith
of God's elect and the knowledge of the
truth[b] that leads to godliness— **2**a faith
and knowledge resting on the hope of
1:2 eternal life,[c] which God, who does not
[c]2Ti 1:1 [d]2Ti 1:9 lie, promised before the beginning of
1:3 time,[d] **3**and at his appointed season[e] he
[e]1Ti 2:6 brought his word to light[f] through the
[f]2Ti 1:10 [g]1Ti 1:11 preaching entrusted to me[g] by the com-
[h]Lk 1:47 mand of God our Savior,[h]

1:4 **4**To Titus,[i] my true son in our com-
[i]2Co 2:13 mon faith:

Grace and peace from God the Father and Christ Jesus our Savior.

Titus's Task on Crete

1:5 **5**The reason I left you in Crete[j] was
[j]Ac 27:7 that you might straighten out what was
[k]Ac 11:30 left unfinished and appoint[a] elders[k] in
every town, as I directed you. **6**An elder
1:6 must be blameless,[l] the husband of but
[l]1Ti 3:2 one wife, a man whose children believe
and are not open to the charge of being
wild and disobedient. **7**Since an over-
1:7 seer[b][m] is entrusted with God's work,[n]
[m]1Ti 3:1 [n]1Co 4:1 he must be blameless—not overbear-
[o]1Ti 3:3,8 ing, not quick-tempered, not given to
drunkenness, not violent, not pursuing
dishonest gain.[o] **8**Rather he must be hos-
1:8 pitable,[p] one who loves what is good,[q]
[p]1Ti 3:2 [q]2Ti 3:3 who is self-controlled, upright, holy and
disciplined. **9**He must hold firmly[r] to
1:9 the trustworthy message as it has been
[r]1Ti 1:19 [s]1Ti 1:10 taught, so that he can encourage others by sound doctrine[s] and refute those
who oppose it.
10For there are many rebellious peo-
1:10 ple, mere talkers[t] and deceivers, espe-
[t]1Ti 1:6 [u]1:12 cially those of the circumcision group.[u]
11They must be silenced, because they
1:11 are ruining whole households[v] by teach-
[v]2Ti 3:6 ing things they ought not to teach—
and that for the sake of dishonest gain.
12Even one of their own prophets[w] has
1:12 [w]Ac 17:28 said, "Cretans[x] are always liars, evil
[x]Ac 2:11 brutes, lazy gluttons." **13**This testimony
1:13 is true. Therefore, rebuke[y] them sharp-
[y]2Co 13:10 [z]Tit 2:2 ly, so that they will be sound in the
faith[z] **14**and will pay no attention to
1:14 Jewish myths[a] or to the commands[b] of
[a]1Ti 1:4 [b]Col 2:22 those who reject the truth. **15**To the
pure, all things are pure, but to those
who are corrupted and do not believe,
nothing is pure.[c] In fact, both their
1:15 [c]Ro 14:14,23 minds and consciences are corrupted.
16They claim to know God, but by their

actions they deny him.[d] They are de- 1:16 [d]1Jn 2:4
testable, disobedient and unfit for do-
ing anything good.

What Must Be Taught to Various Groups

2 You must teach what is in accord
with sound doctrine.[e] **2**Teach the 2:1 [e]1Ti 1:10
older men to be temperate, worthy of
respect, self-controlled, and sound in
faith,[f] in love and in endurance. 2:2 [f]Tit 1:13
3Likewise, teach the older women to
be reverent in the way they live, not
to be slanderers or addicted to much
wine,[g] but to teach what is good. **4**Then 2:3 [g]1Ti 3:8
they can train the younger women to
love their husbands and children, **5**to
be self-controlled and pure, to be busy
at home, to be kind, and to be subject
to their husbands,[h] so that no one will 2:5 [h]Eph 5:22
malign the word of God.[i] [i]1Ti 6:1
6Similarly, encourage the young men[j] 2:6
to be self-controlled. **7**In everything set [j]1Ti 5:1
them an example[k] by doing what is 2:7 [k]1Ti 4:12
good. In your teaching show integrity,
seriousness **8**and soundness of speech
that cannot be condemned, so that
those who oppose you may be ashamed
because they have nothing bad to say
about us.[l] 2:8 [l]1Pe 2:12
9Teach slaves to be subject to their
masters in everything,[m] to try to please 2:9 [m]Eph 6:5
them, not to talk back to them, **10**and
not to steal from them, but to show
that they can be fully trusted, so that in
every way they will make the teaching
about God our Savior attractive.[n] 2:10
11For the grace of God that brings [n]Mt 5:16
salvation has appeared to all men.[o] **12**It 2:11 [o]1Ti 2:4
teaches us to say "No" to ungodliness
and worldly passions,[p] and to live self- 2:12 [p]Tit 3:3
controlled, upright and godly lives[q] in [q]2Ti 3:12
this present age, **13**while we wait for

[a]5 Or *ordain* [b]7 Traditionally *bishop*

▸ PATIENCE

The Glorious Impending

Titus 2:13

As we grow in our love for Christ, a glorious sense of anticipation begins to occupy us. It is as though something undefined but wonderful is written on the dial of every mundane clock. The word *Maranatha* ("Come, O Lord!") swings unseen on every pendulum.

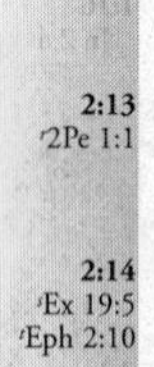

the blessed hope—the glorious appearing of our great God and Savior, Jesus 2:13
Christ,[r] 14who gave himself for us to [r]2Pe 1:1
redeem us from all wickedness and to
purify for himself a people that are his 2:14
very own,[s] eager to do what is good.[t] [s]Ex 19:5
15These, then, are the things you [t]Eph 2:10
should teach. Encourage and rebuke
with all authority. Do not let anyone
despise you.

Doing What Is Good

3 Remind the people to be subject to
rulers and authorities,[u] to be obe- 3:1 [u]Ro 13:1
dient, to be ready to do whatever is [v]2Ti 2:21
good,[v] 2to slander no one,[w] to be peace- 3:2 [w]Eph 4:31;
able and considerate, and to show true 2Ti 2:24
humility toward all men.
3At one time we too were foolish,
disobedient, deceived and enslaved by
all kinds of passions and pleasures. We
lived in malice and envy, being hated
and hating one another. 4But when the
kindness[x] and love of God our Savior 3:4 [x]Eph 2:7
appeared,[y] 5he saved us, not because of [y]Tit 2:11
righteous things we had done,[z] but be- 3:5 [z]Eph 2:9
cause of his mercy. He saved us through [a]Ro 12:2
the washing of rebirth and renewal[a] by
the Holy Spirit, 6whom he poured out
on us[b] generously through Jesus Christ 3:6 [b]Ro 5:5
our Savior, 7so that, having been jus-
tified by his grace,[c] we might become 3:7
heirs[d] having the hope[e] of eternal life.[f] [c]Ro 3:24
8This is a trustworthy saying.[g] And I [d]Ro 8:17 [e]Ro 8:24
want you to stress these things, so that [f]Tit 1:2
those who have trusted in God may be 3:8 [g]1Ti 1:15
careful to devote themselves to doing [h]Tit 2:14
what is good.[h] These things are excellent and profitable for everyone.

DAY 2 TWO

▸ PEACE AND THE PURPOSE OF GOD IN MY LIFE

Titus 3:3–11

This passage in Titus describes the peaceless lives we once lived. We were foolish, disobedient and deceived by all kinds of passions and pleasures. We lived in envy and were full of malice. Then into our turmoil walked the peace of Christ. God saved us, and the Holy Spirit raised the white flag over all our turmoil. When God called us to salvation, we were called to peace.

At our conversion our troubled spirits heard the words, "Be still!" (see Mark 4:39)—and we were ashamed of the pointless noise we had once allowed to live in the center of our souls. Can you remember where his "be still" found you? The storms of meaninglessness raged all about you. The winds of indecision buffeted you. The tides of turmoil raged. You knew not who you were. You found no pier of support in all the turbulence. Then he came with his peace.

The result of this new peace is suggested in Titus 3:9–11. From now on those Christians who once loved argument now avoid controversy and despise their foolish quarrels. Christ's peace counsels those who love divisive behavior to put their quarrelsome natures aside and enjoy the quiet.

So living in peace and making peace become the purpose of God in our lives. Having learned peace through our conversion, we begin to publish it as evidence of our salvation. We came upon that grace that saved us not because of righteous things we had done but because of his mercy. Now we model his grace, and in the process others discover his salvation.

To begin a study on the topic of Peace, a Truce With God to End My Alienation From Him, turn to the home page on page 1353.

▸ KINDNESS

SAVED BY THE KINDNESS OF GOD

Titus 3:4–5

Would you be saved? Seek grace. Do not list your virtues on the back of your old baptism certificate. Jesus died high against the sky—his shoulders taut against the bloody wood—to keep you from such nonsense.

9But avoid foolish controversies and
genealogies and arguments and quar-
rels[i] about the law, because these are 3:9 [i]1Ti 1:4;
unprofitable and useless. 10Warn a divi- 2Ti 2:14
sive person once, and then warn him a
second time. After that, have nothing
to do with him.[j] 11You may be sure that 3:10 [j]Ro 16:17
such a man is warped and sinful; he is
self-condemned.

Final Remarks

12As soon as I send Artemas or Tychicus[k] to you, do your best to come 3:12
to me at Nicopolis, because I have de- [k]Ac 20:4

3:12 [l]2Ti 4:9,21 cided to winter there.[l] [13]Do everything
you can to help Zenas the lawyer and
3:13 [m]Ac 18:24 Apollos[m] on their way and see that they
have everything they need. [14]Our peo-
3:14 ple must learn to devote themselves to
[n]ver 8 doing what is good,[n] in order that they
may provide for daily necessities and
not live unproductive lives.
[15]Everyone with me sends you greetings. Greet those who love us in the 3:15
faith.[o] [o]1Ti 1:2
Grace be with you all.[p] [p]Col 4:18

PHILEMON

AUTHORSHIP AND DATE

Paul

c. A.D. 60

KEY THEMES

This letter was written to ask Philemon to forgive Onesimus, his runaway slave. It was, in some ways, a stern fist of negotiation wrapped in the velvet glove of love. Paul asked Philemon not to prosecute his runaway slave in a time when prosecution was the customary thing to do. Further, he asked Philemon to forgive Onesimus and reinstate him fully in Christian love. Many of the early Christians were slaves, so this letter establishes a precedent for loving relationships between slaves and free people in the early church. In the Roman Empire, there were more slaves than free people. Slaves were seen as a necessary part of the economy, and the rebellion of Spartacus left Romans apprehensive about showing any kindness or compassion toward renegade slaves. Any insolence or attempts to escape were to be met with sternness. So in this letter the strongest of animosities were addressed, and a new rule of relationship—love—was established.

FRUIT OF THE SPIRIT IN PHILEMON

Love: In Philemon 5, Paul handed this first-century Christian the greatest of compliments. Philemon loved all the Christians he knew. It is no trick to love God, for God is loving. But loving the people of God can, at times, be a hefty challenge. There is an old jingle which reads:

> To live above with saints we love,
> Oh that will be the glory!
> But to live below, with saints we know—
> Well, that's a different story.

Perhaps people like Philemon love all the saints by remembering one precept: God loves everyone else just as much as he loves us. It may, at times, appear that God must not love very wisely if he loves everyone the same, but perhaps we haven't looked in a mirror recently.

1:1 [1]Paul, a prisoner[a] of Christ Jesus, and
[a]ver 9,23; Eph 3:1 [b]2Co 1:1 Timothy our brother,[b]
[c]Php 2:25 To Philemon our dear friend and fel-
1:2 low worker,[c] [2]to Apphia our sister, to
[d]Col 4:17 [e]Php 2:25 Archippus[d] our fellow soldier[e] and to
[f]Ro 16:5 the church that meets in your home:[f]

DAY 4 FOUR

PEACE AND MY SERVICE TO OTHERS

Philemon 17–21

Paul declares in this letter that he has a confidence that Philemon will forgive his renegade slave, Onesimus. The apostle believes that his own inner turmoil, as well as Onesimus's, will be rewarded by peace when Philemon offers forgiveness to his errant slave.

We do not know the outcome of this story, but even as we read this letter, the shortest of all Paul's letters, we feel Paul's confidence that Philemon will indeed forgive and reinstate Onesimus. The tone of Paul's plea is confidence. And confidence itself is the grand porch before God's Holy Mansion of Peace. Philemon could not serve those to whom God had called him until he lived up to Paul's positive expectation. Then peace would be evident to all who were watching.

It is a good thing to desire to live up to the expectations of other believers. Others count on us. They believe in us. We see God's expectations a little at a time, but we do know what others expect of us. And in our good example to them, we will have gone a long way toward pleasing God.

Place this longing to fulfill the positive expectations of others in the center of your own life. The good things they expect of you can be accomplished. When you are living peacefully and as a good example before others, then you will find it easier to minister to others, for it is hard to serve when your own life is in turmoil. The way to a life of joyous service is to surrender the turmoil, embrace the peace of Christ and move confidently into the ministry to which God has called you.

To begin a study on the topic of Peace, the Evidence of Confidence, turn to the home page on page 1173.

[3]Grace to you and peace from God
our Father and the Lord Jesus Christ.

Thanksgiving and Prayer

[4]I always thank my God[g] as I remem- 1:4 [g]Ro 1:8
ber you in my prayers, [5]because I hear
about your faith in the Lord Jesus and
your love for all the saints.[h] [6]I pray 1:5 [h]Eph 1:15; Col 1:4
that you may be active in sharing your
faith, so that you will have a full understanding of every good thing we have
in Christ. [7]Your love has given me great
joy and encouragement,[i] because you, 1:7 [i]2Co 7:4,13
brother, have refreshed[j] the hearts of [j]ver 20
the saints.

Paul's Plea for Onesimus

[8]Therefore, although in Christ I
could be bold and order you to do what
you ought to do, [9]yet I appeal to you
on the basis of love. I then, as Paul—
an old man and now also a prisoner[k] 1:9 [k]ver 1,23
of Christ Jesus— [10]I appeal to you for 1:10
my son[l] Onesimus,[a][m] who became my [l]1Co 4:15
son while I was in chains. [11]Formerly [m]Col 4:9
he was useless to you, but now he has
become useful both to you and to me.
[12]I am sending him—who is my very
heart—back to you. [13]I would have
liked to keep him with me so that he
could take your place in helping me
while I am in chains for the gospel.
[14]But I did not want to do anything
without your consent, so that any favor you do will be spontaneous and not
forced.[n] [15]Perhaps the reason he was 1:14 [n]2Co 9:7;
separated from you for a little while 1Pe 5:2
was that you might have him back for
good— [16]no longer as a slave, but bet- 1:16 [o]Mt 23:8;
ter than a slave, as a dear brother.[o] He is 1Ti 6:2
very dear to me but even dearer to you,

[a]*10 Onesimus* means *useful.*

GENTLENESS

BELOVED RENEGADE

Philemon 15–16

Dear Philemon:
Onesimus did not run away.
He left you for a season
That you might receive him forever.
As Christ owned you and set you free,
Give this, your slave, his liberty.
Besides, you owe me one.
Love, Paul

both as a man and as a brother in the
Lord.
1:17 [p]2Co 8:23 [17]So if you consider me a partner,[p]
welcome him as you would welcome
me. [18]If he has done you any wrong
or owes you anything, charge it to me.
[19]I, Paul, am writing this with my own
hand. I will pay it back—not to mention that you owe me your very self.
[20]I do wish, brother, that I may have
1:20 [q]ver 7 some benefit from you in the Lord;
1:21 [r]2Co 2:3 refresh[q] my heart in Christ. [21]Confi-
dent[r] of your obedience, I write to you,
knowing that you will do even more
than I ask.
[22]And one thing more: Prepare a
guest room for me, because I hope to 1:22
be[s] restored to you in answer to your [s]Php 1:25; 2:24
prayers.[t] [t]2Co 1:11

1:23
[23]Epaphras,[u] my fellow prisoner in [u]Col 1:7
Christ Jesus, sends you greetings. [24]And 1:24
so do Mark,[v] Aristarchus,[w] Demas[x] and [v]Ac 12:12 [w]Ac 19:29
Luke, my fellow workers. [x]Col 4:14
[25]The grace of the Lord Jesus Christ 1:25
be with your spirit.[y] [y]2Ti 4:22

HEBREWS

▸ AUTHORSHIP AND DATE

A number of people have been suggested as the author: The writer calls Timothy his brother (see 13:23), and authorship was, for that reason, assigned to Paul for centuries. But this seems unlikely, for the writing styles are very different. Paul would also have been more likely to refer to Timothy as a son rather than as a brother. Other persons suggested as the possible writer of the book: Priscilla, Barnabas, Apollos and Philip. The leading candidates for authorship are Barnabas and Apollos.

Probably written before the destruction of the temple in A.D. 70, for the book speaks of the temple sacrificial system as though it was still in force.

▸ KEY THEMES

Hebrews was written to the Christian Jews of the *diaspora* (dispersion)—Jews all across the Roman Empire who had become Christians. In Hebrews we encounter the first of the universal or catholic Epistles. This group of letters was meant to be widely read, passing from church to church, to strengthen and encourage the entire Christian world.

Hebrews 1–10 contains an argument for the greatness of Christ and demonstrates that Christ is superior in every way to the values and heroes of the Old Testament. Line by line, Christ is shown to be superior to the old covenant (see 1:5—7:28), angels (see 1:5—2:18), Moses (see 3:1—4:13) and the Levitical priesthood (see 4:14—7:28). The writer of Hebrews went on to show how Jesus, our high priest, is superior to all priests in his sacrificial work (see 8:1—10:18). After much encouraging counsel (see 10:19–39), Hebrews deals with faith, its heroes and its methods (see 11:1—12:29). Finally, the conclusion of the book contains many practical suggestions for Christian living, as well as personal remarks, prayer requests and a blessing (see ch. 13). Hebrews is an exalted look at the high and powerful place Jesus is to hold in our lives.

▸ FRUIT OF THE SPIRIT IN HEBREWS

Love: "Keep on loving each other as brothers. Do not forget to entertain strangers, for by so doing some people have entertained angels without knowing it" (13:1–2). Hospitality is a gracious expression of love we offer Christ, and those who know how to wield it as a weapon of godly love find that it causes even strangers to fall fast in love with God. Those who know how to offer hospitality effectively open their arms and homes—their own tiny realms of sanctity and love—to others. No act is more sacred. Surely hospitality is an expression of love born in heaven and placed directly on earth by God himself.

Joy: According to Hebrews 2:6–8, we are clothed with glory and honor. We are at the center of undeserved grace, and we bask in a love won for us by another. Surely thanklessness must be the most universal attitude. No wonder Shakespeare's King Lear said, "How sharper than a serpent's tooth it is to have a thankless child." If the children of God have no song, the world itself will never learn to sing.

Peace: Mechizedek was the king of Salem *(shalom)*, the king of peace. Jesus is a priest forever after the order of Mechizedek. He is the King of peace who calls his subjects to publish his monarchy.

Patience: Abraham and Sarah learned the fine art of trusting God for the long haul. Waiting for a son seemed tedious to them at times, but no promise of God ever went begging. Patience is our way of trusting the long-term pledges of God (see 11:11).

Goodness: There is no doctrine so important as the sinlessness of Christ. If Christ be only generous enough to die for us, but not perfect enough to save us, his death is noble but of little consequence. Only if Jesus is perfect in every way, can we look to him who never sinned as a hope for those of us who constantly sin. Will his sinlessness redeem us? "How much more, then, will the blood of Christ, who through the eternal Spirit offered himself unblemished to God, cleanse our consciences from acts that lead to death, so that we may serve the living God!" (9:14).

Faithfulness: Faithfulness spawns confidence. The more we serve God in the tough times, the more we notice that he never fails. This confidence leads us to boldness in prayer, and then, being bold in prayer, we "approach the throne of grace with confidence, so that we may receive mercy and find grace to help us in our time of need" (4:16).

Self-Control: Each of us is to show confidence in God and persevere, taking complete charge of our lives. This kind of self-control will give us victory over immorality and make our hope sure (see 6:11).

The Son Superior to Angels

1 In the past God spoke[a] to our forefathers through the prophets[b] at many times and in various ways,[c] [2]but in these last days he has spoken to us by his Son, whom he appointed heir[d] of all things, and through whom[e] he made the universe. [3]The Son is the radiance of God's glory[f] and the exact representation of his being, sustaining all things[g] by his powerful word. After he had provided purification for sins,[h] he sat down at the right hand of the Majesty in heaven.[i] [4]So he became as much superior to the angels as the name he has inherited is superior to theirs.[j]

1:1 [a]Jn 9:29; Heb 2:2,3 [b]Ac 2:30 [c]Nu 12:6,8
1:2 [d]Ps 2:8 [e]Jn 1:3
1:3 [f]Jn 1:14 [g]Col 1:17 [h]Heb 7:27 [i]Mk 16:19
1:4 [j]Eph 1:21; Php 2:9,10

LOVE

WHEN GOD SPOKE BEST

Hebrews 1:1–2

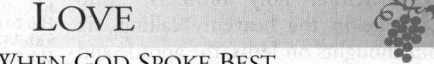

When God began to call all rebels to return to love,
He shouted his reality in nature—but it was not enough.
He cried his reality through all the Decalogue—but it was not enough.
He begged the race return to him through the prophets—but it was not enough.
Finally, he sent his Son.
That was more than enough.

[5]For to which of the angels did God ever say,

"You are my Son;
today I have become your Father[a]"[b]?[k]

Or again,

"I will be his Father,
and he will be my Son"[c]?[l]

[6]And again, when God brings his firstborn into the world,[m] he says,

"Let all God's angels worship him."[d][n]

[7]In speaking of the angels he says,

"He makes his angels winds,
his servants flames of fire."[e][o]

[8]But about the Son he says,

"Your throne, O God, will last for ever and ever,
and righteousness will be the scepter of your kingdom.
[9]You have loved righteousness and hated wickedness;
therefore God, your God, has set you above your companions[p]
by anointing you with the oil[q] of joy."[f]

[10]He also says,

"In the beginning, O Lord, you laid the foundations of the earth,
and the heavens are the work of your hands.
[11]They will perish, but you remain;
they will all wear out like a garment.[r]
[12]You will roll them up like a robe;
like a garment they will be changed.
But you remain the same,[s]
and your years will never end."[g][t]

[13]To which of the angels did God ever say,

"Sit at my right hand
until I make your enemies
a footstool[u] for your feet"[h]?[v]

[14]Are not all angels ministering spirits[w] sent to serve those who will inherit salvation?[x]

1:5 [k]Ps 2:7 [l]2Sa 7:14
1:6 [m]Heb 10:5 [n]Dt 32:43 (LXX and DSS); Ps 97:7
1:7 [o]Ps 104:4
1:9 [p]Php 2:9 [q]Isa 61:1,3
1:11 [r]Isa 34:4
1:12 [s]Heb 13:8 [t]Ps 102:25-27
1:13 [u]Jos 10:24; Heb 10:13 [v]Ps 110:1
1:14 [w]Ps 103:20 [x]Heb 5:9

Warning to Pay Attention

2 We must pay more careful attention, therefore, to what we have heard, so that we do not drift away. [2]For if the message spoken[y] by angels[z] was binding, and every violation and disobedience received its just punishment,[a] [3]how shall we escape if we ignore such a great salvation?[b] This salvation, which was first announced by the Lord,[c] was confirmed to us by those who heard him.[d] [4]God also testified to it by signs, wonders and various miracles,[e] and gifts of the Holy Spirit[f] distributed according to his will.[g]

2:2 [y]Heb 1:1 [z]Dt 33:2; Ac 7:53 [a]Heb 10:28
2:3 [b]Heb 10:29 [c]Heb 1:2 [d]Lk 1:2
2:4 [e]Jn 4:48 [f]1Co 12:4 [g]Eph 1:5

Jesus Made Like His Brothers

[5]It is not to angels that he has subjected the world to come, about which we are speaking. [6]But there is a place where someone has testified:

[a]5 Or *have begotten you* [b]5 Psalm 2:7 [c]5 2 Samuel 7:14; 1 Chron. 17:13 [d]6 Deut. 32:43 (see Dead Sea Scrolls and Septuagint) [e]7 Psalm 104:4 [f]9 Psalm 45:6,7 [g]12 Psalm 102:25-27 [h]13 Psalm 110:1

"What is man that you are mindful
of him,
the son of man that you care for
2:6 [h]Job 7:17
him?[h]
7 You made him a little[a] lower than
the angels;
you crowned him with glory and
honor
8 and put everything under his
2:8 [i]Ps 8:4-6; 1Co 15:25
feet."[b][i]

In putting everything under him, God
left nothing that is not subject to him.
Yet at present we do not see everything
subject to him. 9 But we see Jesus, who
was made a little lower than the angels,
2:9 [j]Ac 2:33; 3:13; Php 2:9 [k]Php 2:7-9 [l]Jn 3:16; 2Co 5:15
now crowned with glory and honor[j]
because he suffered death,[k] so that by
the grace of God he might taste death
for everyone.[l]

PEACE

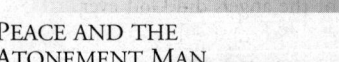

PEACE AND THE ATONEMENT MAN

Hebrews 2:9

Is *atonement* "at-one-ment"?
Yes.
Is *history* "his-story"?
Yes.
Is *justification*
"Just-as-if-I-had never sinned"? Yes.
The best word games
Are harbingers of life.

10 In bringing many sons to glory,
it was fitting that God, for whom
2:10 [m]Ro 11:36 [n]Lk 24:26; Heb 7:28
and through whom everything exists,[m]
should make the author of their salvation perfect through suffering.[n] 11 Both
the one who makes men holy and those
2:11 [o]Heb 10:10 [p]Mt 28:10; Jn 20:17
who are made holy[o] are of the same
family. So Jesus is not ashamed to call
them brothers.[p] 12 He says,

"I will declare your name to my
brothers;
in the presence of the congregation
2:12 [q]Ps 22:22
I will sing your praises."[c][q]

13 And again,
2:13 [r]Isa 8:17 [s]Isa 8:18; Jn 10:29
"I will put my trust in him."[d][r]

And again he says,

"Here am I, and the children God
has given me."[e][s]

14 Since the children have flesh and
2:14 [t]Jn 1:14
blood, he too shared in their humanity[t]
so that by his death he might destroy[u]
him who holds the power of death—
that is, the devil[v]— 15 and free those
who all their lives were held in slavery
by their fear[w] of death. 16 For surely it is
not angels he helps, but Abraham's descendants. 17 For this reason he had to
be made like his brothers[x] in every way,
in order that he might become a merciful[y] and faithful high priest[z] in service to God,[a] and that he might make
atonement for[f] the sins of the people.
18 Because he himself suffered when he
was tempted, he is able to help those
who are being tempted.[b]

2:14 [u]1Co 15:54-57; 2Ti 1:10 [v]1Jn 3:8
2:15 [w]2Ti 1:7
2:17 [x]Php 2:7 [y]Heb 5:2 [z]Heb 4:14,15; 7:26,28 [a]Heb 5:1
2:18 [b]Heb 4:15

Jesus Greater Than Moses

3 Therefore, holy brothers,[c] who
share in the heavenly calling, fix
your thoughts on Jesus, the apostle and
high priest[d] whom we confess.[e] 2 He was
faithful to the one who appointed him,
just as Moses was faithful in all God's
house.[f] 3 Jesus has been found worthy
of greater honor than Moses, just as the
builder of a house has greater honor
than the house itself. 4 For every house is
built by someone, but God is the builder of everything. 5 Moses was faithful as
a servant[g] in all God's house,[h] testifying to what would be said in the future.
6 But Christ is faithful as a son[i] over
God's house. And we are his house,[j]
if we hold on[k] to our courage and the
hope[l] of which we boast.

3:1 [c]Heb 2:11 [d]Heb 2:17 [e]Heb 4:14
3:2 [f]Nu 12:7
3:5 [g]Ex 14:31 [h]ver 2; Nu 12:7
3:6 [i]Heb 1:2 [j]1Co 3:16 [k]Ro 11:22 [l]Ro 5:2

Warning Against Unbelief

7 So, as the Holy Spirit says:[m]

3:7 [m]Heb 9:8

"Today, if you hear his voice,
8 do not harden your hearts
as you did in the rebellion,
during the time of testing in the
desert,
9 where your fathers tested and tried
me
and for forty years saw what I
did.[n]
10 That is why I was angry with that
generation,
and I said, 'Their hearts are always
going astray,
and they have not known my
ways.'

3:9 [n]Ac 7:36

[a] *7* Or *him for a little while*; also in verse 9
[b] *8* Psalm 8:4-6 [c] *12* Psalm 22:22 [d] *13* Isaiah 8:17
[e] *13* Isaiah 8:18 [f] *17* Or *and that he might turn aside God's wrath, taking away*

11 So I declared on oath in my anger,
'They shall never enter my
3:11 [o]Heb 4:3,5 [p]Ps 95:7-11 rest.'[o]"[a][p]

12 See to it, brothers, that none of
you has a sinful, unbelieving heart that
turns away from the living God. 13 But
3:13 [q]Heb 10:24,25 [r]Eph 4:22 encourage one another daily,[q] as long as
it is called Today, so that none of you
may be hardened by sin's deceitfulness.[r]
14 We have come to share in Christ if we
3:14 [s]ver 6 hold firmly[s] till the end the confidence
we had at first. 15 As has just been said:

3:15 [t]ver 7,8; Ps 95:7,8 "Today, if you hear his voice,
do not harden your hearts
as you did in the rebellion."[b][t]

FAITHFULNESS

CLINGING IS THE EVIDENCE

Hebrews 3:14

Cling to the person of Christ. Are your hands too weak for such a grand endeavor? Take heart. Your salvation is not determined by *your* grasp, but by *his*. When you reached out to God, his love took hold of you. No one ever wriggles from the iron grip of grace.

16 Who were they who heard and rebelled? Were they not all those Moses
3:16 [u]Nu 14:2 led out of Egypt?[u] 17 And with whom
was he angry for forty years? Was it not
with those who sinned, whose bodies
3:17 [v]Nu 14:29; Ps 106:26 fell in the desert?[v] 18 And to whom did
God swear that they would never enter
3:18 [w]Nu 14:20-23 [x]Heb 4:6 his rest[w] if not to those who disobeyed[c]?[x]
19 So we see that they were not able to
3:19 [y]Jn 3:36 enter, because of their unbelief.[y]

A Sabbath-Rest for the People of God

4 Therefore, since the promise of entering his rest still stands, let us be
careful that none of you be found to
4:1 [z]Heb 12:15 have fallen short of it.[z] 2 For we also
have had the gospel preached to us, just
as they did; but the message they heard
was of no value to them, because those
who heard did not combine it with
4:2 [a]1Th 2:13 faith.[d][a] 3 Now we who have believed enter that rest, just as God has said,

"So I declared on oath in my anger,
'They shall never enter my
4:3 [b]Ps 95:11; Heb 3:11 rest.'"[e][b]

And yet his work has been finished
since the creation of the world. 4 For
somewhere he has spoken about the
seventh day in these words: "And on
the seventh day God rested from all
his work."[f][c] 5 And again in the passage 4:4 [c]Ge 2:2,3; Ex 20:11
above he says, "They shall never enter
my rest."[d]
6 It still remains that some will enter 4:5 [d]Ps 95:11
that rest, and those who formerly had
the gospel preached to them did not
go in, because of their disobedience.[e] 4:6 [e]Heb 3:18
7 Therefore God again set a certain day,
calling it Today, when a long time later
he spoke through David, as was said before:

"Today, if you hear his voice,
do not harden your hearts."[g][f] 4:7 [f]Ps 95:7,8; Heb 3:7,8,15

8 For if Joshua had given them rest,[g] God
would not have spoken[h] later about 4:8 [g]Jos 22:4 [h]Heb 1:1
another day. 9 There remains, then, a
Sabbath-rest for the people of God;
10 for anyone who enters God's rest also
rests from his own work, just as God
did from his.[i] 11 Let us, therefore, make 4:10 [i]ver 4
every effort to enter that rest, so that no
one will fall by following their example 4:11 [j]Heb 3:18
of disobedience.[j]
12 For the word of God[k] is living and 4:12 [k]1Pe 1:23 [l]Jer 23:29 [m]Eph 6:17; Rev 1:16 [n]1Co 14:24, 25
active.[l] Sharper than any double-edged
sword,[m] it penetrates even to dividing
soul and spirit, joints and marrow; it
judges the thoughts and attitudes of
the heart.[n] 13 Nothing in all creation is
hidden from God's sight.[o] Everything 4:13 [o]Ps 33:13-15
is uncovered and laid bare before the
eyes of him to whom we must give account.

[a] *11* Psalm 95:7-11 [b] *15* Psalm 95:7,8
[c] *18* Or *disbelieved* [d] *2* Many manuscripts *because they did not share in the faith of those who obeyed*
[e] *3* Psalm 95:11; also in verse 5 [f] *4* Gen. 2:2
[g] *7* Psalm 95:7,8

GENTLENESS

THE GENTLE COMMONER

Hebrews 4:15

The great deed of divinity came when Jesus opted for humanity. He inhabited flesh so convincingly that the people of his day questioned his divinity more than his humanity. He was so thoroughly human that
he could die like someone else
for the sake of everyone else
and look pretty much like anyone else.

Jesus the Great High Priest

14Therefore, since we have a great high priest who has gone through the
heavens,[a] [p] Jesus the Son of God, let
us hold firmly to the faith we profess.[q]
15For we do not have a high priest
who is unable to sympathize with our
weaknesses, but we have one who has
been tempted in every way, just as we
are[r]—yet was without sin.[s] 16Let us
then approach the throne of grace with
confidence, so that we may receive mercy and find grace to help us in our time
of need.

4:14 [p]Heb 6:20 [q]Heb 3:1

4:15 [r]Heb 2:18 [s]2Co 5:21

DAY 2 TWO

▸ GOODNESS AND THE PURPOSE OF GOD IN MY LIFE

Hebrews 4:12

"The word of God is living." How different God's Word is from other weaker words. Other books are full of "inky" words, written on paper. They have no more life than the ink and paper give them. But God's Word is alive.

God's word is "active." It holds the exclusive power to blast into our everyday morality with higher requirements. It possesses the raw energy to change us from self-serving individuals to dedicated men and women of God.

"Sharper than any double-edged sword." The word for "sword" here is *machaira*. This type of sword had a short, 18-inch blade, and with it Rome conquered the world. When their enemies saw the Romans coming with their very short swords, they must have felt very secure. But the truth is that these swords were sharp on both sides and were short enough to work very well in close battle. And that's how the Romans fought—close in. Thus the *machaira* enabled them to defeat their enemies and conquer the world. And so God's Word will enable us.

"It penetrates even to dividing soul and spirit, joints and marrow." The Word of God operates deep within our souls. It is medicine for our bad psychology, our bad sociology, our distorted self-image and our irrational arrogance. It corrects our lives from deep within our inner thoughts—where only God knows us. Down where we most need surgery, the Word performs "idea-ectomies" until we are living the lives of goodness that God has always known were possible.

"It judges the thoughts and attitudes of the heart." We are always better for its judgments. There, in the center of our beings, the Word keeps us in touch with God's purposes for our lives.

To begin a study on the topic of Goodness, the Virtue of the Written Word of God, turn to the home page on page 918.

▸ LOVE

LOVE: THE BOLD APPROACH

Hebrews 4:16

Do you have a need? Bring it boldly to your Father. Run to him like a child crying after a fall. Be bold with God. Do not shrink back from towering glass and crystal seas. Do not let the elders and living creatures who surround his austere holiness make you tremble. Charge into the throne room unafraid. Claim his love; state your case.

5 Every high priest is selected from
among men and is appointed to
represent them in matters related to
God, to offer gifts and sacrifices[t] for
sins.[u] 2He is able to deal gently with
those who are ignorant and are going
astray,[v] since he himself is subject to
weakness.[w] 3This is why he has to offer
sacrifices for his own sins, as well as for
the sins of the people.[x]
4No one takes this honor upon himself; he must be called by God, just as
Aaron was.[y] 5So Christ also did not take
upon himself the glory[z] of becoming a
high priest. But God said[a] to him,

"You are my Son;
 today I have become your
 Father.[b]"[c] [b]

6And he says in another place,

"You are a priest forever,
 in the order of Melchizedek."[d] [c]

7During the days of Jesus' life on
earth, he offered up prayers and petitions with loud cries and tears[d] to the
one who could save him from death,
and he was heard because of his reverent submission.[e] 8Although he was a

5:1 [t]Heb 8:3 [u]Heb 7:27

5:2 [v]Heb 2:18 [w]Heb 7:28

5:3 [x]Heb 7:27; 9:7

5:4 [y]Ex 28:1

5:5 [z]Jn 8:54 [a]Heb 1:1 [b]Ps 2:7

5:6 [c]Ps 110:4; Heb 7:17,21

5:7 [d]Mt 27:46,50 [e]Mk 14:36

[a]14 Or *gone into heaven* [b]5 Or *have begotten you*
[c]5 Psalm 2:7 [d]6 Psalm 110:4

son, he learned obedience from what he
5:8 [f]Php 2:8 suffered[f] 9and, once made perfect,[g] he
5:9 [g]Heb 2:10 became the source of eternal salvation
for all who obey him 10and was desig-
5:10 [h]ver 5 [i]ver 6 nated by God to be high priest[h] in the
order of Melchizedek.[i]

DAY 4 FOUR

▸ GENTLENESS AND MY SERVICE TO OTHERS

Hebrews 5:1–3

This passage is a reminder to all Christians that every person has been saved from a life of sin and alienation from God. Even the priests of the Old Testament, those who were called by God, were subject to the same temptations and moral weaknesses as any other people. Such knowledge keeps those who minister to others gentle in all their dealings. They know how close they are to being the one ministered to instead of the one ministering.

The difference between those who are members of God's family and those who are still bound to sin lies in their appropriation of the work of Jesus. He alone allows us to approach our world with gentleness. *Gentle* is what happens to *fierce* when Jesus touches it with *grace.*

I will never get over the effect of God's saving transformation on people's lives. People who were lost in sin, filled with anger and bitterness, give up their hatred and become approachable. That is, of course, why we minister to others. Those of us who minister are not people to whom gentleness comes naturally. We are all people who have been remodeled by grace. We thankfully leave our old natures far behind as we embrace gentleness in our treatment of others.

When we consider that we are all sinners, saved by grace, our ministry to others becomes gentle. We understand where we came from—a world of hopeless despair without Christ. We also understand where we are going—to a bright future with God forever. In the meantime, we gently bring hope to others, so that they will find us approachable. Only then we will have opportunity to share the grace of God with them.

To begin a study on the topic of Gentleness, the Approachable Life, turn to the home page on page 306.

Warning Against Falling Away

11We have much to say about this,
but it is hard to explain because you are
slow to learn. 12In fact, though by this
time you ought to be teachers, you need
someone to teach you the elementary
truths[j] of God's word all over again. You 5:12 [j]Heb 6:1
need milk, not solid food![k] 13Anyone [k]1Co 3:2; 1Pe 2:2
who lives on milk, being still an infant,[l]
is not acquainted with the teaching 5:13 [l]1Co 14:20
about righteousness. 14But solid food is
for the mature,[m] who by constant use 5:14 [m]1Co 2:6
have trained themselves to distinguish [n]Isa 7:15
good from evil.[n]

6 Therefore let us leave[o] the elemen- 6:1 [o]Php 3:12-14
tary teachings[p] about Christ and [p]Heb 5:12
go on to maturity, not laying again the [q]Heb 9:14
foundation of repentance from acts that
lead to death,[a][q] and of faith in God,
2instruction about baptisms,[r] the lay- 6:2 [r]Jn 3:25
ing on of hands,[s] the resurrection of the [s]Ac 6:6
dead,[t] and eternal judgment. 3And God [t]Ac 17:18,32
permitting,[u] we will do so. 6:3 [u]Ac 18:21

▸ JOY

THE ABCS OF GRADUATE DISCIPLES

Hebrews 6:1–2

The ABCs must be learned. They are the foundation of commerce and education. Treasure them. The alphabet is the friend of God. Treasure each simple letter, for each was used to form the mighty paragraphs of God's Word.

4It is impossible for those who have
once been enlightened,[v] who have tast- 6:4 [v]Heb 10:32
ed the heavenly gift,[w] who have shared [w]Eph 2:8
in the Holy Spirit,[x] 5who have tasted [x]Gal 3:2
the goodness of the word of God and
the powers of the coming age, 6if they
fall away, to be brought back to repen-
tance,[y] because[b] to their loss they are 6:6 [y]2Pe 2:21; 1Jn 5:16
crucifying the Son of God all over again
and subjecting him to public disgrace.
7Land that drinks in the rain often
falling on it and that produces a crop
useful to those for whom it is farmed
receives the blessing of God. 8But land
that produces thorns and thistles is
worthless and is in danger of being 6:8
cursed.[z] In the end it will be burned. [z]Ge 3:17,18; Isa 5:6
9Even though we speak like this,
dear friends,[a] we are confident of bet- 6:9 [a]1Co 10:14
ter things in your case—things that

[a]1 Or *from useless rituals* [b]6 Or *repentance while*

accompany salvation. 10God is not unjust; he will not forget your work and the love you have shown him as you have helped his people and continue to help them.[b] 11We want each of you to show this same diligence to the very end, in order to make your hope[c] sure. 12We do not want you to become lazy, but to imitate[d] those who through faith and patience[e] inherit what has been promised.[f]

6:10 [b]Mt 10:40,42; 25:40; 1Th 1:3
6:11 [c]Heb 3:6
6:12 [d]Heb 13:7 [e]2Th 1:4; Jas 1:3; Rev 13:10 [f]Heb 10:36

DAY 3 THREE

▸ PEACE AND MY RELATIONSHIP WITH CHRIST

Hebrews 7:1–3

Is your heart a prayer room? Visualize your heart as the place where you meet with Christ, the ultimate king of peace. I have written on this very metaphor in a book called *Table of Inwardness*. In this small book I pictured myself in concord with Jesus, sitting at a table set for two. The setting of my prayer rendezvous with Christ is always a garden of peace.

If there are things in my life that bring turmoil to the setting, I ask him to clear away the busy noise of my self-important agenda so that we can meet in peace. But how do we get rid of that busy inner noise that produces a restlessness in our hearts? This is difficult indeed. All of our lives, from the time we are first able to think, we talk to ourselves inside our minds. We live all our lives in this never-ending stream of conversation. Our minds are chatty, never stopping to rest. We talk, talk, talk inside ourselves. To complicate the matter, "inside ourselves" is the address we give to God, for here amid the chatter lives the Holy Spirit, always trying to get a word in edgewise. I have called this never-ending inner dialogue "roof-brain" chatter, a term I borrowed from Joseph Chilton Pearce.

This unending stream of mental commentary needs to come to a halt if Christ is ever to commune with us. I suggest focusing on Christ himself until we call the noise to silence. Then we can press on to learn the art of listening prayer.

At this point, peace is born in our lives. Into this new calm that we establish by silencing our busy minds, Christ makes his entry and is ours. He is ours for fellowship and ours for instruction. He is ours for friendship and commission. He is ours for the moderated life, ours for the life of peace.

To begin a study on the topic of Peace and the Prince of Peace, turn to the home page on page 19.

The Certainty of God's Promise

13When God made his promise to Abraham, since there was no one greater for him to swear by, he swore by himself,[g] 14saying, "I will surely bless you and give you many descendants."[a][h] 15And so after waiting patiently, Abraham received what was promised.[i]

16Men swear by someone greater than themselves, and the oath confirms what is said and puts an end to all argument.[j] 17Because God wanted to make the unchanging[k] nature of his purpose very clear to the heirs of what was promised,[l] he confirmed it with an oath. 18God did this so that, by two unchangeable things in which it is impossible for God to lie,[m] we who have fled to take hold of the hope[n] offered to us may be greatly encouraged. 19We have this hope as an anchor for the soul, firm and secure. It enters the inner sanctuary behind the curtain,[o] 20where Jesus, who went before us, has entered on our behalf.[p] He has become a high priest[q] forever, in the order of Melchizedek.[r]

6:13 [g]Ge 22:16; Lk 1:73
6:14 [h]Ge 22:17
6:15 [i]Ge 21:5
6:16 [j]Ex 22:11
6:17 [k]Ps 110:4 [l]Heb 11:9
6:18 [m]Nu 23:19; Tit 1:2 [n]Heb 3:6
6:19 [o]Lev 16:2; Heb 9:2,3,7
6:20 [p]Heb 4:14 [q]Heb 2:17 [r]Heb 5:6

Melchizedek the Priest

7 This Melchizedek was king of Salem and priest of God Most High.[s] He met Abraham returning from the defeat of the kings and blessed him,[t] 2and Abraham gave him a tenth of everything. First, his name means "king of righteousness"; then also, "king of Salem" means "king of peace." 3Without father or mother, without genealogy,[u] without beginning of days or end of life, like the Son of God[v] he remains a priest forever.

4Just think how great he was: Even the patriarch[w] Abraham gave him a tenth of the plunder![x] 5Now the law requires the descendants of Levi who become priests to collect a tenth from the people[y]—that is, their brothers—even though their brothers are descended from Abraham. 6This man, however, did not trace his descent from Levi, yet

7:1 [s]Mk 5:7 [t]Ge 14:18-20
7:3 [u]ver 6 [v]Mt 4:3
7:4 [w]Ac 2:29 [x]Ge 14:20
7:5 [y]Nu 18:21,26

[a]*14* Gen. 22:17

7:6 [z]Ge 14:19,20 [a]Ro 4:13 he collected a tenth from Abraham and
blessed[z] him who had the promises.[a]
7And without doubt the lesser person is
blessed by the greater. 8In the one case,
the tenth is collected by men who die;
but in the other case, by him who is de-
7:8 [b]Heb 5:6; 6:20 clared to be living.[b] 9One might even
say that Levi, who collects the tenth,
paid the tenth through Abraham, 10be-
cause when Melchizedek met Abraham,
Levi was still in the body of his ancestor.

Jesus Like Melchizedek

11If perfection could have been attained through the Levitical priesthood
(for on the basis of it the law was given
7:11 [c]ver 18,19; Heb 8:7 [d]Heb 10:1 [e]ver 17 to the people),[c] why was there still need
for another priest to come[d]—one in the
order of Melchizedek,[e] not in the order
of Aaron? 12For when there is a change
of the priesthood, there must also be a
change of the law. 13He of whom these
7:13 [f]ver 11 [g]ver 14 things are said belonged to a different
tribe,[f] and no one from that tribe has
7:14 [h]Isa 11:1; Mt 1:3; Lk 3:33 ever served at the altar.[g] 14For it is clear
that our Lord descended from Judah,[h]
and in regard to that tribe Moses said
nothing about priests. 15And what we
have said is even more clear if another
priest like Melchizedek appears, 16one
who has become a priest not on the basis of a regulation as to his ancestry but
on the basis of the power of an indestructible life. 17For it is declared:

7:15 [i]Ps 110:4; ver 21; Heb 5:6 "You are a priest forever,
in the order of Melchizedek."[a][i]

7:18 [j]Ro 8:3 18The former regulation is set aside
because it was weak and useless[j] 19(for
7:19 [k]Ac 13:39; Ro 3:20; Heb 9:9 [l]Heb 4:16 the law made nothing perfect),[k] and a
better hope is introduced, by which we
draw near to God.[l]
20And it was not without an oath!
Others became priests without any oath,
21but he became a priest with an oath
when God said to him:

"The Lord has sworn
7:21 [m]1Sa 15:29 [n]Ps 110:4 and will not change his mind:[m]
'You are a priest forever.' "[a][n]

22Because of this oath, Jesus has become
7:22 [o]Heb 8:6 the guarantee of a better covenant.[o]
23Now there have been many of those
priests, since death prevented them from
continuing in office; 24but because Je-
7:24 [p]ver 28 sus lives forever, he has a permanent
priesthood.[p] 25Therefore he is able to
save completely[b] those who come to 7:25 [q]ver 19 [r]Ro 8:34
God[q] through him, because he always
lives to intercede for them.[r]

FAITHFULNESS

SAVED AND KEPT

Hebrews 7:25

At first I accepted the Christ who made promises.
Then I accepted the Christ who inhabited his promises.
Then I accepted the Christ who was a promise.
Then I realized I could not distinguish among the three.

26Such a high priest meets our need—
one who is holy, blameless, pure, set 7:26 [s]2Co 5:21 [t]Heb 4:14
apart from sinners,[s] exalted above the
heavens.[t] 27Unlike the other high priests,
he does not need to offer sacrifices[u] day 7:27 [u]Heb 5:1 [v]Heb 5:3 [w]Heb 9:12,26,28 [x]Eph 5:2; Heb 9:14,28
after day, first for his own sins,[v] and
then for the sins of the people. He sacrificed for their sins once for all[w] when he
offered himself.[x] 28For the law appoints
as high priests men who are weak;[y] but 7:28 [y]Heb 5:2 [z]Heb 1:2 [a]Heb 2:10
the oath, which came after the law, ap-
pointed the Son,[z] who has been made
perfect[a] forever.

The High Priest of a New Covenant

8 The point of what we are saying
is this: We do have such a high
priest,[b] who sat down at the right hand 8:1 [b]Heb 2:17
of the throne of the Majesty in heaven,
2and who serves in the sanctuary, the
true tabernacle[c] set up by the Lord, not 8:2 [c]Heb 9:11,24
by man.
3Every high priest is appointed to of- 8:3 [d]Heb 5:1 [e]Heb 9:14
fer both gifts and sacrifices,[d] and so
it was necessary for this one also to
have something to offer.[e] 4If he were
on earth, he would not be a priest, for
there are already men who offer the
gifts prescribed by the law.[f] 5They serve 8:4 [f]Heb 5:1
at a sanctuary that is a copy[g] and shad- 8:5 [g]Heb 9:23 [h]Col 2:17; Heb 10:1 [i]Heb 11:7; 12:25 [j]Ex 25:40
ow[h] of what is in heaven. This is why
Moses was warned[i] when he was about
to build the tabernacle: "See to it that
you make everything according to the
pattern shown you on the mountain."[c][j]

[a]17,21 Psalm 110:4 [b]25 Or *forever*
[c]5 Exodus 25:40

6But the ministry Jesus has received is as superior to theirs as the covenant[k] of which he is mediator[l] is superior to the old one, and it is founded on better promises.

7For if there had been nothing wrong with that first covenant, no place would have been sought for another.[m] 8But God found fault with the people and said[a]:

"The time is coming, declares the Lord,
when I will make a new covenant[n]
with the house of Israel
and with the house of Judah.
9It will not be like the covenant
I made with their forefathers[o]
when I took them by the hand
to lead them out of Egypt,
because they did not remain faithful
to my covenant,
and I turned away from them,
declares the Lord.
10This is the covenant I will make with
the house of Israel
after that time, declares the Lord.
I will put my laws in their minds
and write them on their hearts.[p]
I will be their God,
and they will be my people.[q]
11No longer will a man teach his
neighbor,
or a man his brother, saying,
'Know the Lord,'
because they will all know me,[r]
from the least of them to the
greatest.
12For I will forgive their wickedness
and will remember their sins no
more."[s][b][t]

13By calling this covenant "new," he has made the first one obsolete;[u] and what is obsolete and aging will soon disappear.

8:6 [k]Lk 22:20 [l]Heb 7:22
8:7 [m]Heb 7:11,18
8:8 [n]Jer 31:31
8:9 [o]Ex 19:5,6
8:10 [p]2Co 3:3; Heb 10:16 [q]Zec 8:8
8:11 [r]Isa 54:13; Jn 6:45
8:12 [s]Heb 10:17 [t]Ro 11:27
8:13 [u]2Co 5:17

Worship in the Earthly Tabernacle

9 Now the first covenant had regulations for worship and also an earthly sanctuary.[v] 2A tabernacle[w] was set up. In its first room were the lampstand,[x] the table[y] and the consecrated bread;[z] this was called the Holy Place. 3Behind the second curtain was a room called the Most Holy Place,[a] 4which had the golden altar of incense[b] and the gold-covered ark of the covenant.[c] This ark contained the gold jar of manna,[d] Aaron's staff that had budded,[e] and the stone tablets of the covenant. 5Above the ark were the cherubim of the Glory,[f] overshadowing the atonement cover.[c] But we cannot discuss these things in detail now.

6When everything had been arranged like this, the priests entered regularly[g] into the outer room to carry on their ministry. 7But only the high priest entered[h] the inner room, and that only once a year,[i] and never without blood, which he offered for himself[j] and for the sins the people had committed in ignorance. 8The Holy Spirit was showing[k] by this that the way[l] into the Most Holy Place had not yet been disclosed as long as the first tabernacle was still standing. 9This is an illustration for the present time, indicating that the gifts and sacrifices being offered[m] were not able to clear the conscience of the worshiper. 10They are only a matter of food[n] and drink[o] and various ceremonial washings—external regulations[p] applying until the time of the new order.

9:1 [v]Ex 25:8
9:2 [w]Ex 25:8,9 [x]Ex 25:31-39 [y]Ex 25:23-29 [z]Lev 24:5-8
9:3 [a]Ex 26:31-33
9:4 [b]Ex 30:1-5 [c]Ex 25:10-22 [d]Ex 16:32,33

The Blood of Christ

11When Christ came as high priest[q] of the good things that are already here,[d][r] he went through the greater and more perfect tabernacle[s] that is not man-made, that is to say, not a part of this creation. 12He did not enter by means of the blood of goats and calves;[t] but he entered the Most Holy Place[u] once for all[v] by his own blood, having obtained eternal redemption. 13The blood of goats and bulls and the ashes of a heifer[w] sprinkled on those who are ceremonially unclean sanctify them so that they are outwardly clean. 14How much more, then, will the blood of Christ, who through the eternal Spirit[x] offered himself unblemished to God, cleanse our consciences[y] from acts that lead to death,[e][z] so that we may serve the living God!

15For this reason Christ is the mediator[a] of a new covenant, that those who are called may receive the promised eternal inheritance—now that he has died as a ransom to set them free

9:4 [e]Nu 17:10
9:5 [f]Ex 25:17-19
9:6 [g]Nu 28:3
9:7 [h]Lev 16:11-19 [i]Lev 16:34 [j]Heb 5:2,3
9:8 [k]Heb 3:7 [l]Jn 14:6; Heb 10:19,20
9:9 [m]Heb 5:1
9:10 [n]Lev 11:2-23 [o]Col 2:16 [p]Heb 7:16
9:11 [q]Heb 2:17 [r]Heb 10:1 [s]Heb 8:2
9:12 [t]Heb 10:4 [u]ver 24 [v]Heb 7:27
9:13 [w]Nu 19:9,17,18
9:14 [x]1Pe 3:18 [y]Tit 2:14; Heb 10:2,22 [z]Heb 6:1
9:15 [a]1Ti 2:5

[a]8 Some manuscripts may be translated *fault and said to the people.* [b]12 Jer. 31:31-34
[c]5 Traditionally *the mercy seat* [d]11 Some early manuscripts *are to come* [e]14 Or *from useless rituals*

from the sins committed under the first
9:15 covenant.[b]
[b]Heb 7:22 16 In the case of a will,[a] it is necessary
to prove the death of the one who made
it, 17 because a will is in force only when
somebody has died; it never takes effect while the one who made it is living.
18 This is why even the first covenant
9:18 was not put into effect without blood.[c]
[c]Ex 24:6-8 19 When Moses had proclaimed every
commandment of the law to all the people, he took the blood of calves, together with water, scarlet wool and branches
of hyssop, and sprinkled the scroll and
9:19 all the people.[d] 20 He said, "This is the
[d]Ex 24:6-8 blood of the covenant, which God has
9:20 [e]Ex 24:8; Mt commanded you to keep."[b][e] 21 In the
26:28 same way, he sprinkled with the blood
both the tabernacle and everything used
in its ceremonies. 22 In fact, the law requires that nearly everything be cleansed
9:22 [f]Lev 8:15 with blood,[f] and without the shedding
[g]Lev 17:11 of blood there is no forgiveness.[g]

KINDNESS

THE KINDNESS OF GOD AND THE BLOOD OF NECESSITY

Hebrews 9:22

My biography's a snap to comprehend: Jesus bled; I was washed. The End.

23 It was necessary, then, for the cop-
9:23 ies[h] of the heavenly things to be purified
[h]Heb 8:5 with these sacrifices, but the heavenly
things themselves with better sacrifices
than these. 24 For Christ did not enter
a man-made sanctuary that was only a
9:24 copy of the true one;[i] he entered heav-
[i]Heb 8:2 en itself, now to appear for us in God's
presence. 25 Nor did he enter heaven to
offer himself again and again, the way
the high priest enters the Most Holy
9:25 Place[j] every year with blood that is not
[j]Heb 10:19 his own.[k] 26 Then Christ would have
[k]ver 7,8 had to suffer many times since the cre-
9:26 ation of the world.[l] But now he has ap-
[l]Heb 4:3 peared once for all[m] at the end of the
[m]Heb 7:27 ages to do away with sin by the sacrifice of himself. 27 Just as man is des-
9:27 tined to die once,[n] and after that to face
[n]Ge 3:19 [o]2Co 5:10 judgment,[o] 28 so Christ was sacrificed
once to take away the sins of many peo-
9:28 ple; and he will appear a second time,[p]
[p]Tit 2:13 [q]1Pe 2:24 not to bear sin,[q] but to bring salvation
[r]1Co 1:7 to those who are waiting for him.[r]

Christ's Sacrifice Once for All

10 The law is only a shadow[s] of the 10:1 [s]Heb 8:5
good things[t] that are coming— [t]Heb 9:11
not the realities themselves.[u] For this [u]Heb 9:23 [v]Heb 7:19
reason it can never, by the same sacri-
fices repeated endlessly year after year,
make perfect[v] those who draw near to
worship. 2 If it could, would they not
have stopped being offered? For the
worshipers would have been cleansed
once for all, and would no longer have
felt guilty for their sins. 3 But those sacrifices are an annual reminder of sins,[w] 10:3 [w]Heb 9:7
4 because it is impossible for the blood 10:4
of bulls and goats[x] to take away sins. [x]Heb 9:12,13
5 Therefore, when Christ came into
the world,[y] he said: 10:5 [y]Heb 1:6

"Sacrifice and offering you did not [z]1Pe 2:24
desire,
but a body you prepared for me;[z]
6 with burnt offerings and sin
offerings
you were not pleased.
7 Then I said, 'Here I am—it is
written about me in the
scroll[a]— 10:7 [a]Jer 36:2
I have come to do your will, [b]Ps 40:6-8
O God.'"[c][b]

8 First he said, "Sacrifices and offerings,
burnt offerings and sin offerings you
did not desire, nor were you pleased 10:8 [c]ver 5,6; Mk
with them"[c] (although the law required 12:33
them to be made). 9 Then he said, "Here 10:9
I am, I have come to do your will."[d] He [d]ver 7
sets aside the first to establish the second. 10 And by that will, we have been
made holy[e] through the sacrifice of the 10:10 [e]Jn 17:19
body[f] of Jesus Christ once for all.[g] [f]Heb 2:14; 1Pe 2:24
11 Day after day every priest stands [g]Heb 7:27
and performs his religious duties; again 10:11
and again he offers the same sacrifices,[h] [h]Heb 5:1
which can never take away sins.[i] 12 But [i]ver 1,4
when this priest had offered for all time
one sacrifice for sins, he sat down at the
right hand of God. 13 Since that time
he waits for his enemies to be made his 10:13
footstool,[j] 14 because by one sacrifice he [j]Heb 1:13
has made perfect[k] forever those who are 10:14
being made holy. [k]ver 1
15 The Holy Spirit also testifies[l] to us 10:15 [l]Heb 3:7
about this. First he says:

16 "This is the covenant I will make
with them

[a]*16* Same Greek word as *covenant*; also in verse 17
[b]*20* Exodus 24:8 [c]*7* Psalm 40:6-8 (see Septuagint)

DAY 5 FIVE

▸ FAITHFULNESS AND ITS PLACE IN MY PERSONAL WORSHIP

Hebrews 10:25

The church: It's always there—sometimes interesting, many times not. There's virtue in attending church, for there we meet with God and those who love him. Why is this meeting time so special? Here are ten reasons for going to church.

1. There is one place that constantly reminds us that heaven exists—it's the church.

2. God's house is a constant reminder to the nation that the nation ought to be more like God's house.

3. God's house is a place of worship, and worship is the hassle-stopper.

4. Those who constantly run without stopping for God eventually become all legs and no heart.

5. Church is the place for teaching our children the life of faith. It is a place where they are ever in training to become tomorrow's moral giants.

6. There we live in a community of need—our brothers and sisters, like ourselves, have many needs. We can lift them up as they lift us.

7. There is praise there, and praise keeps us from living in a world where despair is common.

8. The Bible is read in church. Just to hear these living words of God gives us the power to triumph over our momentary problems.

9. The gospel is preached there, and where the gospel is preached, people come to Christ.

10. Jesus is exalted there, and anywhere that Christ is exalted is a place where our own spirits soar.

Hebrews 10:25 is a call not just to worship, but to worship in a specific place, where altars are central, and where God can be expected to show up.

To begin a study on the topic of Faithfulness, the Road That Ends in Victory, turn to the home page on page 1540.

after that time, says the Lord.
I will put my laws in their hearts,
and I will write them on their
minds."[a][m] 10:16 mJer 31:33; Heb 8:10
17 Then he adds:

"Their sins and lawless acts
I will remember no more."[b][n] 10:17 nHeb 8:12

18 And where these have been forgiven,
there is no longer any sacrifice for sin.

A Call to Persevere

19 Therefore, brothers, since we have 10:19 oEph 2:18; Heb 9:8,12,25
confidence to enter the Most Holy
Place[o] by the blood of Jesus, 20 by a new
and living way[p] opened for us through 10:20 pHeb 9:8 qHeb 9:3
the curtain,[q] that is, his body, 21 and
since we have a great priest[r] over the
house of God, 22 let us draw near to 10:21 rHeb 2:17
God[s] with a sincere heart in full assur- 10:22 sHeb 7:19 tEze 36:25; Heb 9:14
ance of faith, having our hearts sprin-
kled to cleanse us from a guilty
conscience[t] and having our bodies
washed with pure water. 23 Let us hold
unswervingly to the hope[u] we profess, 10:23 uHeb 3:6 v1Co 1:9
for he who promised is faithful.[v] 24 And
let us consider how we may spur one
another on toward love and good deeds.
25 Let us not give up meeting together,[w] 10:25 wAc 2:42 xHeb 3:13
as some are in the habit of doing, but
let us encourage one another[x]—and all
the more as you see the Day approaching.

26 If we deliberately keep on sinning[y] 10:26 yNu 15:30; 2Pe 2:20
after we have received the knowledge
of the truth, no sacrifice for sins is left,
27 but only a fearful expectation of judg-
ment and of raging fire[z] that will con- 10:27 zIsa 26:11; 2Th 1:7; Heb 9:27
sume the enemies of God. 28 Anyone
who rejected the law of Moses died
without mercy on the testimony of two

[a] *16* Jer. 31:33 [b] *17* Jer. 31:34

▸ PATIENCE

THE GRATEFUL LIVING

Hebrews 10:25

Assemble and wait!
The church is the keeper of saving truth.
The church is the place where worship springs from all the grateful saved.
Go to church.
Wait.
He comes where expectant believers assemble.

10:28 [a]Dt 17:6,7; Heb 2:2
or three witnesses.[a] 29How much more
severely do you think a man deserves
10:29 [b]Heb 6:6 [c]Mt 26:28 [d]Eph 4:30; Heb 6:4 [e]Heb 2:3
to be punished who has trampled the
Son of God under foot,[b] who has treated as an unholy thing the blood of the
covenant[c] that sanctified him, and who
has insulted the Spirit[d] of grace?[e] 30For
10:30 [f]Dt 32:35; Ro 12:19 [g]Dt 32:36
we know him who said, "It is mine to
avenge; I will repay,"[a][f] and again, "The
Lord will judge his people."[b][g] 31It is a
dreadful thing to fall into the hands of
10:31 [h]Mt 16:16
the living God.[h]
32Remember those earlier days after
10:32 [i]Heb 6:4 [j]Php 1:29,30
you had received the light,[i] when you
stood your ground in a great contest
in the face of suffering.[j] 33Sometimes
you were publicly exposed to insult and
10:33 [k]1Co 4:9 [l]Php 4:14; 1Th 2:14
persecution;[k] at other times you stood
side by side with those who were so
treated.[l] 34You sympathized with those
10:34 [m]Heb 13:3 [n]Heb 11:16
in prison[m] and joyfully accepted the
confiscation of your property, because
you knew that you yourselves had better and lasting possessions.[n]
35So do not throw away your confidence; it will be richly rewarded. 36You
10:36 [o]Lk 21:19; Heb 12:1
need to persevere[o] so that when you
have done the will of God, you will receive what he has promised. 37For in
just a very little while,

10:37 [p]Mt 11:3 [q]Rev 22:20
"He who is coming[p] will come and
will not delay.[q]
10:38 [r]Ro 1:17; Gal 3:11
38 But my righteous one[c] will live by
faith.[r]
And if he shrinks back,
I will not be pleased with him."[d]

39But we are not of those who shrink
back and are destroyed, but of those
who believe and are saved.

By Faith

11:1 [s]Ro 8:24; 2Co 4:18
11 Now faith is being sure of what
we hope for and certain of what
we do not see.[s] 2This is what the an-
11:2 [t]ver 4,39
cients were commended for.[t]
3By faith we understand that the uni-
11:3 [u]Ge 1; Jn 1:3; 2Pe 3:5
verse was formed at God's command,[u]
so that what is seen was not made out
of what was visible.
4By faith Abel offered God a better
sacrifice than Cain did. By faith he was
commended as a righteous man, when
11:4 [v]Ge 4:4; 1Jn 3:12 [w]Heb 12:24
God spoke well of his offerings.[v] And
by faith he still speaks, even though he
is dead.[w]
5By faith Enoch was taken from this
life, so that he did not experience death;

FAITHFULNESS

The Substance of Hope

Hebrews 11:1

Faith is being sure of what we hope for.
It is the evidence of things unseen.
Faith is the substance of things surreal.
It is
Intangible yet touching,
Invisible but visionary,
Inaudible but full of trumpets.
It is a grasping after what cannot be held
Till finally it holds us.

he could not be found, because God
had taken him away.[x] For before he was 11:5 [x]Ge 5:21-24
taken, he was commended as one who
pleased God. 6And without faith it is
impossible to please God, because any-
one who comes to him[y] must believe 11:6 [y]Heb 7:19
that he exists and that he rewards those
who earnestly seek him.
7By faith Noah, when warned about
things not yet seen, in holy fear built
an ark[z] to save his family.[a] By his faith 11:7 [z]Ge 6:13-22 [a]1Pe 3:20
he condemned the world and became
heir of the righteousness that comes by
faith.
8By faith Abraham, when called to
go to a place he would later receive
as his inheritance,[b] obeyed and went,[c] 11:8 [b]Ge 12:7 [c]Ge 12:1-4; Ac 7:2-4
even though he did not know where he
was going. 9By faith he made his home
in the promised land[d] like a stranger 11:9 [d]Ac 7:5 [e]Ge 12:8; 18:1,9 [f]Heb 6:17
in a foreign country; he lived in tents,[e]
as did Isaac and Jacob, who were heirs
with him of the same promise.[f] 10For
he was looking forward to the city[g] 11:10 [g]Heb 12:22; 13:14 [h]Rev 21:2,14
with foundations,[h] whose architect and
builder is God.
11By faith Abraham, even though he
was past age—and Sarah herself was 11:11 [i]Ge 17:17-19; 18:11-14 [j]Ge 21:2
barren[i]—was enabled to become a fa-
ther[j] because he[e] considered him faithful who had made the promise. 12And
so from this one man, and he as good as
dead,[k] came descendants as numerous 11:12 [k]Ro 4:19 [l]Ge 22:17
as the stars in the sky and as countless
as the sand on the seashore.[l]
13All these people were still living by
faith when they died. They did not re- 11:13 [m]ver 39
ceive the things promised;[m] they only

[a]30 Deut. 32:35 [b]30 Deut. 32:36; Psalm 135:14
[c]38 One early manuscript *But the righteous*
[d]38 Hab. 2:3,4 [e]11 Or *By faith even Sarah, who was past age, was enabled to bear children because she*

saw them and welcomed them from
a distance.[n] And they admitted that 11:13 [n]Mt 13:17
they were aliens and strangers on earth.[o] [o]Ge 23:4;
14People who say such things show that Ps 39:12;
they are looking for a country of their 1Pe 1:17
own. 15If they had been thinking of the
country they had left, they would have
had opportunity to return.[p] 16Instead, 11:15 [p]Ge 24:6-8
they were longing for a better coun-
try—a heavenly one.[q] Therefore God is 11:16 [q]2Ti 4:18
not ashamed[r] to be called their God,[s] [r]Mk 8:38 [s]Ex 3:6,15
for he has prepared a city[t] for them. [t]Heb 13:14
17By faith Abraham, when God test-
ed him, offered Isaac as a sacrifice.[u] 11:17 [u]Ge 22:1-10;
He who had received the promises was Jas 2:21
about to sacrifice his one and only son,
18even though God had said to him,
"It is through Isaac that your offspring[a] 11:18 [v]Ge 21:12;
will be reckoned."[b][v] 19Abraham rea- Ro 9:7
soned that God could raise the dead,[w] 11:19 [w]Ro 4:21
and figuratively speaking, he did receive
Isaac back from death.
20By faith Isaac blessed Jacob and 11:20 [x]Ge 27:27-29,
Esau in regard to their future.[x] 39,40
21By faith Jacob, when he was dying, 11:21 [y]Ge 48:1,8-22
blessed each of Joseph's sons,[y] and worshiped as he leaned on the top of his
staff.
22By faith Joseph, when his end was
near, spoke about the exodus of the Is-
raelites from Egypt and gave instruc- 11:22 [z]Ge 50:24,25;
tions about his bones.[z] Ex 13:19
23By faith Moses' parents hid him
for three months after he was born,[a] 11:23 [a]Ex 2:2
because they saw he was no ordinary [b]Ex 1:16,22
child, and they were not afraid of the
king's edict.[b]
24By faith Moses, when he had grown
up, refused to be known as the son 11:24
of Pharaoh's daughter.[c] 25He chose to [c]Ex 2:10,11
be mistreated[d] along with the people 11:25
of God rather than to enjoy the plea- [d]ver 37
sures of sin for a short time. 26He re-
garded disgrace[e] for the sake of Christ 11:26 [e]Heb 13:13
as of greater value than the treasures of [f]Heb 10:35
Egypt, because he was looking ahead to
his reward.[f] 27By faith he left Egypt,[g] 11:27 [g]Ex 12:50,51
not fearing the king's anger; he perse-
vered because he saw him who is invisible. 28By faith he kept the Passover and
the sprinkling of blood, so that the destroyer of the firstborn would not touch
the firstborn of Israel.[h] 11:28 [h]Ex 12:21-23
29By faith the people passed through
the Red Sea[c] as on dry land; but when
the Egyptians tried to do so, they were
drowned.[i] 11:29 [i]Ex 14:21-31
30By faith the walls of Jericho fell,
after the people had marched around
them for seven days.[j] 11:30 [j]Jos 6:12-20
31By faith the prostitute Rahab,

[a]*18* Greek *seed* [b]*18* Gen. 21:12 [c]*29* That is, Sea of Reeds

DAY 5 FIVE

Faithfulness and Its Place in My Personal Worship

Hebrews 11:8–12

This passage contains the record of Abraham's reward for his faithfulness. Here he is honored and upheld as a model for all generations. Abraham is not remembered because he celebrated God's faithfulness after he saw God's plans come to pass. Abraham is honored because he recognized God as Lord before he ever knew the fulfillment of God's plan for his descendants. In Genesis 12 Abraham first received the promise that God would make his descendants into a great nation. Time is compacted in this chapter, and a scant five verses later Abraham enters Canaan, where "he built an altar to the LORD and called on the name of LORD" (v. 8).

Abraham built the altar near Bethel, which means "house of God," and the very word suggests that this would be a place to return to again and again as Abraham trusted in the faithfulness of God. It is right to worship God for the promises he has already fulfilled, but it is a mark of real faith to worship while we wait for that fulfillment. In this passage in Hebrews Abraham was said to worship while he looked forward to a city from God.

Have you learned the art of worshiping the Christ who has promised you he will come? He has not as yet kept that promise, but be faithful and worship him. Somewhere in time, all will be done exactly as he has said. He is the promise keeper. He has saved you to worship him with unwavering confidence in his promises.

Sing to your Lord each morning, "Jesus, if I do not see your promises fulfilled today, I will set my alarm extra early tomorrow morning."

To begin a study on the topic of God's Blessing on Faithfulness, turn to the home page on page 16.

Jesus Speaks Out *on the Fruit of the Spirit:* Self-Control

Matthew 4:8–11

The devil took [Jesus] to a very high mountain and showed him all the kingdoms of the world and their splendor. "All this I will give you," he said, "if you will bow down and worship me."

Jesus said to him, "Away from me, Satan! For it is written: 'Worship the Lord your God, and serve him only.' "

Then the devil left him, and angels came and attended him.

Luke 9:23

If anyone would come after me, he must deny himself and take up his cross daily and follow me.

Mark 14:36

"Abba, Father," [Jesus] said, "everything is possible for you. Take this cup from me. Yet not what I will, but what you will."

John 13:37–38

Peter asked, "Lord, why can't I follow you now? I will lay down my life for you."

Jesus answered, "Will you really lay down your life for me? I tell you the truth, before the rooster crows, you will disown me three times!"

Matthew 19:17

"Why do you ask me about what is good?" Jesus replied. "There is only One who is good. If you want to enter life, obey the commandments."

▸ The Ten Bridesmaids

The kingdom of heaven will be like ten virgins who took their lamps and went out to meet the bridegroom. Five of them were foolish and five were wise. The foolish ones took their lamps but did not take any oil with them. The wise, however, took oil in jars along with their lamps. The bridegroom was a long time in coming, and they all became drowsy and fell asleep.

At midnight the cry rang out: "Here's the bridegroom! Come out to meet him!"

Then all the virgins woke up and trimmed their lamps. The foolish ones said to the wise, "Give us some of your oil; our lamps are going out."

"No," they replied, "there may not be enough for both us and you. Instead, go to those who sell oil and buy some for yourselves."

But while they were on their way to buy the oil, the bridegroom arrived. The virgins who were ready went in with him to the wedding banquet. And the door was shut.

Later the others also came. "Sir! Sir!" they said. "Open the door for us!"

But he replied, "I tell you the truth, I don't know you."

Therefore keep watch, because you do not know the day or the hour.

Matthew 25:1–13

Paul Speaks Out *on the Fruit of the Spirit:* Self-Control

1 Thessalonians 5:6

Let us not be like others, who are asleep, but let us be alert and self-controlled.

1 Thessalonians 5:8

Since we belong to the day, let us be self-controlled, putting on faith and love as a breastplate, and the hope of salvation as a helmet.

2 Timothy 1:7

God did not give us a spirit of timidity, but a spirit of power, of love and of self-discipline.

Titus 2:11–12

The grace of God that brings salvation has appeared to all men. It teaches us to say "No" to ungodliness and worldly passions, and to live self-controlled, upright and godly lives in this present age.

Self-Control Seeks God

The wrath of God is being revealed from heaven against all the godlessness and wickedness of men who suppress the truth by their wickedness, since what may be known about God is plain to them, because God has made it plain to them. For since the creation of the world God's invisible qualities—his eternal power and divine nature—have been clearly seen, being understood from what has been made, so that men are without excuse.

For although they knew God, they neither glorified him as God nor gave thanks to him, but their thinking became futile and their foolish hearts were darkened. Although they claimed to be wise, they became fools and exchanged the glory of the immortal God for images made to look like mortal man and birds and animals and reptiles.

Therefore God gave them over in the sinful desires of their hearts to sexual impurity for the degrading of their bodies with one another. They exchanged the truth of God for a lie, and worshiped and served created things rather than the Creator—who is forever praised. Amen.

Because of this, God gave them over to shameful lusts. Even their women exchanged natural relations for unnatural ones. In the same way the men also abandoned natural relations with women and were inflamed with lust for one another. Men committed indecent acts with other men, and received in themselves the due penalty for their perversion.

Furthermore, since they did not think it worthwhile to retain the knowledge of God, he gave them over to a depraved mind, to do what ought not to be done. They have become filled with every kind of wickedness, evil, greed and depravity. They are full of envy, murder, strife, deceit and malice. They are gossips, slanderers, God-haters, insolent, arrogant and boastful; they invent ways of doing evil; they disobey their parents; they are senseless, faithless, heartless, ruthless. Although they know God's righteous decree that those who do such things deserve death, they not only continue to do these very things but also approve of those who practice them.

Romans 1:18–32

because she welcomed the spies, was not
killed with those who were disobedient.[a][k]
32And what more shall I say? I do not
have time to tell about Gideon, Barak,[l]
Samson, Jephthah, David,[m] Samuel[n]
and the prophets, 33who through faith
conquered kingdoms,[o] administered
justice, and gained what was promised; who shut the mouths of lions,[p]
34quenched the fury of the flames, and
escaped the edge of the sword; whose
weakness was turned to strength;[q] and
who became powerful in battle and
routed foreign armies.[r] 35Women received back their dead, raised to life
again.[s] Others were tortured and refused to be released, so that they might
gain a better resurrection. 36Some faced
jeers and flogging,[t] while still others
were chained and put in prison.[u] 37They
were stoned[b];[v] they were sawed in two;
they were put to death by the sword.[w]
They went about in sheepskins and
goatskins,[x] destitute, persecuted and
mistreated— 38the world was not worthy of them. They wandered in deserts
and mountains, and in caves[y] and holes
in the ground.
39These were all commended[z] for
their faith, yet none of them received
what had been promised.[a] 40God had
planned something better for us so that
only together with us would they be
made perfect.

11:31 [k]Jos 2:1,9-14; 6:22-25; Jas 2:25
11:32 [l]Jdg 4-5 [m]1Sa 16:1,13 [n]1Sa 1:20
11:33 [o]2Sa 7:11; 8:1-3 [p]Da 6:22
11:34 [q]2Ki 20:7 [r]Jdg 15:8
11:35 [s]1Ki 17:22,23
11:36 [t]Jer 20:2 [u]Ge 39:20
11:37 [v]2Ch 24:21 [w]1Ki 19:10 [x]2Ki 1:8
11:38 [y]1Ki 18:4
11:39 [z]ver 2,4 [a]ver 13

God Disciplines His Sons

12 Therefore, since we are surrounded by such a great cloud
of witnesses, let us throw off everything
that hinders and the sin that so easily
entangles, and let us run[b] with perseverance[c] the race marked out for us.
2Let us fix our eyes on Jesus, the author
and perfecter of our faith, who for the
joy set before him endured the cross,[d]
scorning its shame,[e] and sat down at
the right hand of the throne of God.
3Consider him who endured such opposition from sinful men, so that you
will not grow weary[f] and lose heart.
4In your struggle against sin, you
have not yet resisted to the point of
shedding your blood.[g] 5And you have
forgotten that word of encouragement
that addresses you as sons:

"My son, do not make light of the
Lord's discipline,
and do not lose heart when he
rebukes you,
6because the Lord disciplines those he
loves,[h]
and he punishes everyone he
accepts as a son."[c][i]

7Endure hardship as discipline; God
is treating you as sons.[j] For what son
is not disciplined by his father? 8If you
are not disciplined (and everyone undergoes discipline),[k] then you are illegitimate children and not true sons.
9Moreover, we have all had human fathers who disciplined us and we respected them for it. How much more should
we submit to the Father of our spirits[l]
and live![m] 10Our fathers disciplined us
for a little while as they thought best;
but God disciplines us for our good,
that we may share in his holiness.[n] 11No
discipline seems pleasant at the time,
but painful. Later on, however, it produces a harvest of righteousness and
peace[o] for those who have been trained
by it.
12Therefore, strengthen your feeble
arms and weak knees.[p] 13"Make level
paths for your feet,"[d][q] so that the
lame may not be disabled, but rather
healed.[r]

Warning Against Refusing God

14Make every effort to live in peace
with all men[s] and to be holy;[t] without
holiness no one will see the Lord.[u] 15See
to it that no one misses the grace of
God[v] and that no bitter root grows up
to cause trouble and defile many. 16See
that no one is sexually immoral, or is
godless like Esau, who for a single meal
sold his inheritance rights as the oldest
son.[w] 17Afterward, as you know, when
he wanted to inherit this blessing, he

12:1 [b]1Co 9:24 [c]Heb 10:36
12:2 [d]Php 2:8,9 [e]Heb 13:13
12:3 [f]Gal 6:9
12:4 [g]Heb 10:32-34
12:6 [h]Ps 94:12; Rev 3:19 [i]Pr 3:11,12
12:7 [j]Dt 8:5
12:8 [k]1Pe 5:9
12:9 [l]Nu 16:22 [m]Isa 38:16
12:10 [n]2Pe 1:4
12:11 [o]Isa 32:17; Jas 3:17,18
12:12 [p]Isa 35:3
12:13 [q]Pr 4:26 [r]Gal 6:1
12:14 [s]Ro 14:19 [t]Ro 6:22 [u]Mt 5:8
12:15 [v]Gal 5:4; Heb 3:12
12:16 [w]Ge 25:29-34

[a]31 Or *unbelieving* [b]37 Some early manuscripts *stoned; they were put to the test;* [c]6 Prov. 3:11,12 [d]13 Prov. 4:26

GOODNESS

THE FAR TREK

Hebrews 12:2

Jesus suffered and died, pioneering the first trek of any mortal into the uncharted territories of eternity. Best of all, he came back with road maps.

PATIENCE

WEEK 13

DAY ONE

1 Patience Brings the Blessing of God

Read Hebrews 11:35–40

One of the most tender verses in the Bible is Hebrews 11:38. After recounting many hideous deaths of early followers of God, this wonderful verse says, "the world was not worthy of them."

Those faithful saints who were killed for their beliefs are here honored. Ironically, many of those who have held the matches or wielded the implements of torture throughout time were people who claimed allegiance to God and who believed that they were doing God's service by burning inferior disciples.

Arrogance alone lights such heinous fires.

How many a martyr died feeling that God was disinterested or uncaring in this time of need? Yet, here in a tender exposé of faithfulness, the writer of Hebrews says, "These were all commended for their faith, yet none of them received what had been promised." Their patience and perseverance ended in more waiting. What is the plan that God has prepared for us? What is the "something better"? Who can say for sure? His purpose will not be entirely consummated until Jesus splits the skies and history is finished. And then we will know the end of all truth. God never lies; all that he has promised will come to be after we have waited long enough. Patience will at last expose us to glory immeasurable, for patience is the key to the final blessing of God.

DAY TWO

2 Patience and the Purpose of God in My Life

Here is Peter's word to slaves on how they were to respond to abuse from their masters. Peter is addressing the question, "Why do bad things happen to good people?" or in this case, "Why do beatings and afflictions come to noble slaves?" Like Job, Peter has no answer to this riddle of pain. But Peter does say that unjust suffering raises our consciousness of God, shifts our focus to God and gilds our hurt with Christlikeness, for Christ himself also suffered unjustly (1 Peter 2:21–23). Therefore, suffering is a direct route to the blessings of God. *Turn to 1 Peter 2:18–20, page 1492, for today's study.*

DAY THREE

3 Patience and My Relationship With Christ

Christ reminds the church of Philadelphia that patient endurance under trial is the key to God's special protection. There comes a time when God says of those who have endured so much pain, "Enough is enough! I will not permit you to suffer anymore." Let this passage remind us that Jesus notices our pain. He weeps when we weep, and he longs to take those he loves out of harm's way. *Turn to Revelation 3:10, page 1525, for today's study.*

DAY FOUR

4 Patience and My Service to Others

"A hot-tempered man stirs up dissension, but a patient man calms a quarrel," says the wisdom writer. Celebrate all those who act like Jesus in church council meetings and congregational conferences! They have learned the art of patience, the godliness in saying, "I will be patient with others, for I see Jesus in their needs." *Turn to Proverbs 15:18, page 749, for today's study.*

DAY FIVE

5 Patience and Its Place in My Personal Worship

What is our response to answers to prayer? We ask of God and believe in his mercy. When Hannah received her long-awaited answer, she couldn't help but give back to God. In the face of God's goodness and plentitude, Hannah responded with gifts and worship. Our patience brings blessings, and our response is to return gifts to the blessing-bearer. *Turn to 1 Samuel 1:9–28, page 311, for today's study.*

Memorize This Week

ROMANS 12:12

Be joyful in hope, patient in affliction, faithful in prayer.

Week 14, Kindness in the Time of Need, begins on page 246, Joshua 2:8–14.
To begin a topical study on the Fruit of the Spirit, Patience, turn to the Topical Index, page 1548.

was rejected. He could bring about no
12:17 [x]Ge 27:30-40 change of mind, though he sought the
blessing with tears.[x]
12:18 [18]You have not come to a mountain
[y]Ex 19:12-22; Dt 4:11 that can be touched and that is burning with fire; to darkness, gloom and
12:19 [z]Ex 20:18 storm;[y] [19]to a trumpet blast[z] or to such
a voice speaking words that those who

DAY 4 FOUR

▸ JOY AND MY SERVICE TO OTHERS

Hebrews 13:2

Entertaining angels without knowing it! Remember Sarah's experience of cooking for a trio of vagabonds and then discovering that she had been providing hospitality for a delegation from heaven:

The LORD appeared to Abraham near the great trees of Mamre while he was sitting at the entrance to his tent in the heat of the day. Abraham looked up and saw three men standing nearby. When he saw them, he hurried from the entrance of his tent to meet them and bowed low to the ground . . .

So Abraham hurried into the tent to Sarah. "Quick," he said, "get three seahs of fine flour and knead it and bake some bread."

Then he ran to the herd and selected a choice, tender calf and gave it to a servant, who hurried to prepare it. He then brought some curds and milk and the calf that had been prepared, and set these before them. While they ate, he stood near them under a tree.

"Where is your wife Sarah?" they asked him.

"There, in the tent," he said.

Then the LORD said, "I will surely return to you about this time next year, and Sarah your wife will have a son."

(Genesis 18:1–2,6–10)

Angels are often subtle. When Abraham first saw his visitors, did it occur to him that they might be angels? Did Sarah wonder who they were as she baked bread for them? It is good to take strangers seriously. Angels are all about us, and we just never know…

To begin a study on the topic of Joy, the Reveling of Angels, turn to the home page on page 700.

heard it begged that no further word be
spoken to them,[a] [20]because they could 12:19 [a]Ex 20:19; Dt 5:5,25
not bear what was commanded: "If
even an animal touches the mountain,
it must be stoned."[a][b] [21]The sight was so 12:20
terrifying that Moses said, "I am trem- [b]Ex 19:12,13
bling with fear."[b]
[22]But you have come to Mount Zion,
to the heavenly Jerusalem,[c] the city[d] 12:22 [c]Gal 4:26
of the living God. You have come to [d]Heb 11:10
thousands upon thousands of angels in
joyful assembly, [23]to the church of the
firstborn, whose names are written in
heaven.[e] You have come to God, the 12:23 [e]Lk 10:20
judge of all men,[f] to the spirits of righ- [f]Ps 94:2
teous men made perfect,[g] [24]to Jesus the [g]Php 3:12
mediator of a new covenant, and to
the sprinkled blood that speaks a better
word than the blood of Abel.[h] 12:24 [h]Ge 4:10; Heb 11:4
[25]See to it that you do not refuse
him who speaks. If they did not escape
when they refused him who warned[i] 12:25 [i]Heb 8:5; 11:7
them on earth, how much less will we, [j]Heb 2:2,3
if we turn away from him who warns us
from heaven?[j] [26]At that time his voice
shook the earth,[k] but now he has prom- 12:26 [k]Ex 19:18
ised, "Once more I will shake not only [l]Hag 2:6
the earth but also the heavens."[c][l] [27]The
words "once more" indicate the remov-
ing of what can be shaken[m]—that is, 12:27 [m]1Co 7:31;
created things—so that what cannot be 2Pe 3:10
shaken may remain.
[28]Therefore, since we are receiving a
kingdom that cannot be shaken,[n] let us 12:28 [n]Da 2:44
be thankful, and so worship God ac- [o]Heb 13:15
ceptably with reverence and awe,[o] [29]for
our "God is a consuming fire."[d][p] 12:29 [p]Dt 4:24

Concluding Exhortations 13:1 [q]Ro 12:10; 1Pe 1:22

13 Keep on loving each other as
brothers[q]. [2]Do not forget to en- 13:2 [r]Mt 25:35
tertain strangers,[r] for by so doing some [s]Ge 18:1-33
people have entertained angels without
knowing it.[s] [3]Remember those in pris- 13:3 [t]Mt 25:36;
on[t] as if you were their fellow prisoners, Col 4:18
and those who are mistreated as if you
yourselves were suffering.
[4]Marriage should be honored by all,
and the marriage bed kept pure, for
God will judge the adulterer and all the
sexually immoral.[u] [5]Keep your lives free 13:4 [u]1Co 6:9
from the love of money and be content
with what you have,[v] because God has 13:5 [v]Php 4:11
said,

[a]*20* Exodus 19:12,13 [b]*21* Deut. 9:19
[c]*26* Haggai 2:6 [d]*29* Deut. 4:24

13:5 [a]Dt 31:6,8; Jos 1:5

"Never will I leave you;
never will I forsake you."[a][w]
6So we say with confidence,

"The Lord is my helper; I will not
be afraid.
What can man do to me?"[b]

7Remember your leaders,[x] who spoke
the word of God to you. Consider the
outcome of their way of life and imitate[y] their faith. 8Jesus Christ is the
same yesterday and today and forever.[z]
9Do not be carried away by all kinds
of strange teachings.[a] It is good for our
hearts to be strengthened[b] by grace,
not by ceremonial foods,[c] which are of
no value to those who eat them. 10We
have an altar from which those who
minister at the tabernacle have no right
to eat.[d]
11The high priest carries the blood of
animals into the Most Holy Place as a
sin offering, but the bodies are burned
outside the camp.[e] 12And so Jesus also
suffered outside the city gate[f] to make
the people holy through his own blood.
13Let us, then, go to him outside the
camp, bearing the disgrace he bore.[g]
14For here we do not have an enduring
city, but we are looking for the city that
is to come.[h]
15Through Jesus, therefore, let us
continually offer to God a sacrifice[i] of
praise—the fruit of lips[j] that confess
his name. 16And do not forget to do
good and to share with others,[k] for with
such sacrifices[l] God is pleased.
17Obey your leaders and submit to
their authority. They keep watch over
you[m] as men who must give an account.
Obey them so that their work will be a
joy, not a burden, for that would be of
no advantage to you.
18Pray for us.[n] We are sure that we
have a clear conscience[o] and desire to
live honorably in every way. 19I particu-

[a]5 Deut. 31:6 [b]6 Psalm 118:6,7

13:7 [x]ver 17,24 [y]Heb 6:12
13:8 [z]Heb 1:12
13:9 [a]Eph 4:14 [b]Col 2:7 [c]Col 2:16
13:10 [d]1Co 9:13; 10:18
13:11 [e]Ex 29:14; Lev 16:27
13:12 [f]Jn 19:17
13:13 [g]Heb 11:26
13:14 [h]Php 3:20; Heb 12:22
13:15 [i]1Pe 2:5 [j]Hos 14:2
13:16 [k]Ro 12:13 [l]Php 4:18
13:17 [m]Isa 62:6; Ac 20:28
13:18 [n]1Th 5:25 [o]Ac 23:1

DAY 3 THREE

▸ Faithfulness and My Relationship With Christ

Hebrews 13:5–8

God's Word never soars higher in its defense of Christ than in the book of Hebrews, which has built into it a kind of weeping conscience for those who are persecuted. People all around the writer of this noble letter were suffering for their faith (Hebrews 10:32–34). The writer knew this, and his tears spilled out in some of the most elegant writing of the New Testament. Hebrews 13:5 voices the promise of glory—God will never forsake us. Verse 8 is the definition of Christ's role in the life of the believer: "He is the same yesterday and today and forever."

Hebrews 13:5 says that Christ will never abandon us—ever! What comfort this must have been to those undergoing persecution. Is this why they found voice for high praise in the midst of their suffering?

Hebrews 13:8 says that Jesus is the same yesterday, today and forever. It is around this dynamic truth that we one day will meet him. There at last will be gathered the church universal: those of the first century who were persecuted for him; those of the Middle Ages who woke to great themes of reformation; those of the twentieth century who linked hands around the globe for the evangelization of the continents. No matter how the various ages and cultures dress, no matter their languages—Jesus is the same for all ages. No wonder the hymnist wrote:

**People and realms of every tongue
Dwell in his love with sweet accord
While other nations own their lord
And other worlds attend God's word.**

He is ours—the unchanging Christ—the Lord of our souls! He is ours, and through him we learn to become ever more faithful to him.

For the next study of Faithfulness, the Habit of Spiritual Dependency, turn to the home page on page 260.

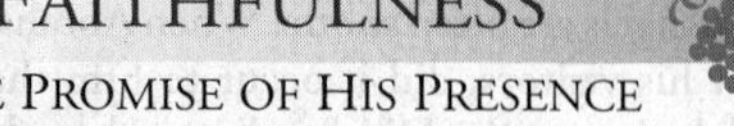

▸ Faithfulness

The Promise of His Presence

Hebrews 13:5
**He will never leave you.
He will never forsake you.
His presence is his promise.
Descend into despair if you must;
He will stay with you during your descent.
Always there, always strong, always Jesus.**

larly urge you to pray so that I may be
restored to you soon.[p]
20May the God of peace,[q] who
through the blood of the eternal covenant[r] brought back from the dead[s]
our Lord Jesus, that great Shepherd of
the sheep,[t] 21equip you with everything
good for doing his will, and may he
work in us[u] what is pleasing to him,[v]
through Jesus Christ, to whom be glory
for ever and ever. Amen.[w]

22Brothers, I urge you to bear with
my word of exhortation, for I have written you only a short letter.[x]
23I want you to know that our brother Timothy[y] has been released. If he arrives soon, I will come with him to see
you.
24Greet all your leaders[z] and all God's
people. Those from Italy[a] send you their
greetings.
25Grace be with you all.[b]

13:19 [p]Phm 22
13:20 [q]Ro 15:33 [r]Isa 55:3; Eze 37:26; Zec 9:11 [s]Ac 2:24 [t]Jn 10:11
13:21 [u]Php 2:13 [v]1Jn 3:22 [w]Ro 11:36
13:22 [x]1Pe 5:12
13:23 [y]Ac 16:1
13:24 [z]ver 7,17 [a]Ac 18:2
13:25 [b]Col 4:18

JAMES

AUTHORSHIP AND DATE

There were four leaders in the early church named James. James the son of Zebedee might have been a likely candidate to have written this letter except he was martyred by Herod in A.D. 44, and he therefore died too early to have written it. Neither of the other two—James the Less and James the son of Alphaeus—had the leadership stature to have written this book. Therefore, James the brother of Jesus and the leader of the Jerusalem church is the man most scholars believe to be the author.

The book was written between c. A.D. 50 and A.D. 60.

KEY THEMES

The book of James deals with practical matters of faith. It lacks the high Christology of many of Paul's writings and of the book of Hebrews, and, for that reason, Martin Luther regarded it as a fluffy set of moralisms, lacking the Christ-driven punch of much of the rest of the New Testament. Nevertheless, it abounds in practical instruction in the following eight areas:

1. Trials and temptations (see 1:2–18)
2. Stop listening and start acting (see 1:19–27)
3. Avoid playing favorites and building cliques in the church (see 2:1–13)
4. Relating faith and works (see 2:14–26)
5. Taming the tongue (see 3:1–12)
6. Discerning heavenly wisdom; a warning against worldliness (see 3:13—4:17)
7. How rich people ought to behave (see 5:1–6)
8. Developing patience in suffering; power in prayer (see 5:7–20).

FRUIT OF THE SPIRIT IN JAMES

Joy: James opens his letter with an odd exhortation to joy: "Consider it pure joy, my brothers, whenever you face trials of many kinds, because you know that the testing of your faith develops perseverance" (1:2–3). It is hard to rejoice in the hard times, and the book of James is not really asking us to do that. It is asking us to rejoice that we are allowed to have hard times. James and Paul saw trials in the same way. Paul's "thorn in [the] flesh" became an occasion of thankfulness in his life (see 2 Corinthians 12:7–10). The apostle found that trials produced a need in his life, and that need caused him to seek Jesus, who then came to abide with him through the ordeal. It was this abiding that brought the hallelujahs for the pain. Without the pain, there was no need; without the need, no Jesus. Hallelujah!

Kindness: "God opposes the proud but gives grace to the humble" (4:6). Humility wins the laurel, the gold medal in God's Olympiad. It is won by those who long jump over pride, hurdle over compliments and pole vault over their own ambitions. On the gold medal of these athletes is written: "I have a Lord. He has treated me with undeserved kindness. Therefore, I will treat others as I have been treated."

Goodness: Goodness, for James, had a very simple recipe: "Get rid of all moral filth" (1:21).

Faithfulness: Faithfulness is a virtue steeled in the furnace of trial. It has known the pressure of the vise and the heat of the furnace. It has become tempered, tough, resistant. It has been through the fire so often that it faces flame without fear. It demonstrates its steadfastness by its certain, measured tread as it advances through the cobra's den. James offered such steadfast souls this benediction: "Blessed is the man who perseveres under trial, because when he has stood the test, he will receive the crown of life that God has promised to those who love him" (1:12).

1:1 [a]Ac 15:13 [b]Tit 1:1 [c]Ac 26:7 [d]Dt 32:26; Jn 7:35; 1Pe 1:1

1 James,[a] a servant of God[b] and of
the Lord Jesus Christ,

To the twelve tribes[c] scattered[d] among
the nations:

Greetings.

GENTLENESS

JESUS' BROTHER

James 1:1

Jesus had a brother.
Funny his brother wouldn't mention it.
Funny his brother wouldn't brag about it.
Funny he wouldn't sell tickets to his lectures at the family reunion.
Funny he wouldn't write a best-seller called *Growing Up With Jesus.*
Funny he preferred calling himself a "servant" rather than pressing his family connections.
Funny!

Trials and Temptations

2Consider it pure joy, my brothers,
whenever you face trials of many kinds,[e]
3because you know that the testing of
your faith develops perseverance. 4Per-
severance must finish its work so that
you may be mature and complete, not
lacking anything. 5If any of you lacks
wisdom, he should ask God,[f] who gives
generously to all without finding fault,
and it will be given to him.[g] 6But when
he asks, he must believe and not doubt,[h]
because he who doubts is like a wave of
the sea, blown and tossed by the wind.
7That man should not think he will receive anything from the Lord; 8he is a
double-minded man,[i] unstable in all he
does.
9The brother in humble circumstances ought to take pride in his high
position. 10But the one who is rich
should take pride in his low position,
because he will pass away like a wild
flower.[j] 11For the sun rises with scorching heat and withers[k] the plant; its blossom falls and its beauty is destroyed.[l]
In the same way, the rich man will fade
away even while he goes about his business.
12Blessed is the man who perseveres
under trial, because when he has stood
the test, he will receive the crown of
life[m] that God has promised to those
who love him.[n]
13When tempted, no one should say,
"God is tempting me." For God cannot be tempted by evil, nor does he
tempt anyone; 14but each one is tempted when, by his own evil desire, he is
dragged away and enticed. 15Then, after desire has conceived, it gives birth
to sin;[o] and sin, when it is full-grown,
gives birth to death.[p]
16Don't be deceived,[q] my dear
brothers.[r] 17Every good and perfect gift
is from above,[s] coming down from the
Father of the heavenly lights, who does
not change[t] like shifting shadows. 18He
chose to give us birth[u] through the
word of truth, that we might be a kind
of firstfruits[v] of all he created.

1:2 [e]Mt 5:12; 1Pe 1:6
1:5 [f]1Ki 3:9,10; Pr 2:3-6 [g]Mt 7:7
1:6 [h]Mk 11:24
1:8 [i]Jas 4:8
1:10 [j]1Co 7:31; 1Pe 1:24
1:11 [k]Ps 102:4,11 [l]Isa 40:6-8
1:12 [m]1Co 9:25 [n]Jas 2:5
1:15 [o]Job 15:35; Ps 7:14 [p]Ro 6:23
1:16 [q]1Co 6:9 [r]ver 19
1:17 [s]Jn 3:27 [t]Nu 23:19; Mal 3:6
1:18 [u]Jn 1:13 [v]Eph 1:12; Rev 14:4

Listening and Doing

19My dear brothers, take note of this:
Everyone should be quick to listen,
slow to speak[w] and slow to become angry, 20for man's anger does not bring
about the righteous life that God desires. 21Therefore, get rid of[x] all moral
filth and the evil that is so prevalent
and humbly accept the word planted in
you,[y] which can save you.
22Do not merely listen to the word,
and so deceive yourselves. Do what it
says. 23Anyone who listens to the word
but does not do what it says is like
a man who looks at his face in a mirror 24and, after looking at himself, goes
away and immediately forgets what he
looks like. 25But the man who looks
intently into the perfect law that gives
freedom,[z] and continues to do this, not
forgetting what he has heard, but doing it—he will be blessed in what he
does.[a]
26If anyone considers himself religious and yet does not keep a tight
rein on his tongue,[b] he deceives himself and his religion is worthless. 27Re-
ligion that God our Father accepts as
pure and faultless is this: to look after[c]
orphans and widows[d] in their distress
and to keep oneself from being polluted by the world.[e]

1:19 [w]Pr 10:19
1:21 [x]Eph 4:22 [y]Eph 1:13
1:25 [z]Jas 2:12 [a]Jn 13:17
1:26 [b]Ps 34:13; 1Pe 3:10
1:27 [c]Mt 25:36 [d]Isa 1:17,23 [e]Ro 12:2

Favoritism Forbidden

2 My brothers, as believers in our glorious[f] Lord Jesus Christ, don't show
favoritism.[g] 2Suppose a man comes into
your meeting wearing a gold ring and

2:1 [f]1Co 2:8 [g]Lev 19:15

GENTLENESS

DON'T RATE THE RACE

James 2:1

Are you hard on the world around you?
Jesus was gentle.
Do you treat some people better than others?
Jesus didn't.
Do you look for people with connections to pick as your friends?
Jesus didn't.
Be glad; he might not have picked you.

fine clothes, and a poor man in shabby
clothes also comes in. 3If you show special attention to the man wearing fine
clothes and say, "Here's a good seat for
you," but say to the poor man, "You
stand there" or "Sit on the floor by
my feet," 4have you not discriminated
2:4 among yourselves and become judges[h]
[h]Jn 7:24 with evil thoughts?
2:5 5Listen, my dear brothers:[i] Has not
[i]Jas 1:16,19 God chosen those who are poor in the
[j]1Co 1:26-28 [k]Lk 12:21 eyes of the world[j] to be rich in faith[k]
[l]Jas 1:12 and to inherit the kingdom he prom-
ised those who love him?[l] 6But you have
2:6 insulted the poor.[m] Is it not the rich
[m]1Co 11:22 who are exploiting you? Are they not
[n]Ac 8:3 the ones who are dragging you into
court?[n] 7Are they not the ones who are
slandering the noble name of him to
whom you belong?
8If you really keep the royal law found
in Scripture, "Love your neighbor as
2:8 yourself,"[a] [o] you are doing right. 9But if
[o]Lev 19:18 you show favoritism,[p] you sin and are
2:9 convicted by the law as lawbreakers.[q]
[p]ver 1 [q]Dt 1:17 10For whoever keeps the whole law and
yet stumbles at just one point is guilty
2:10 of breaking all of it.[r] 11For he who said,
[r]Mt 5:19; Gal 3:10 "Do not commit adultery,"[b] [s] also said,
2:11 "Do not murder."[c] [t] If you do not com-
[s]Ex 20:14; Dt 5:18 mit adultery but do commit murder,
[t]Ex 20:13; Dt 5:17 you have become a lawbreaker.
12Speak and act as those who are go-
ing to be judged by the law that gives
2:12 freedom,[u] 13because judgment without
[u]Jas 1:25 mercy will be shown to anyone who
2:13 has not been merciful.[v] Mercy triumphs
[v]Mt 5:7; 18:32-35 over judgment!

Faith and Deeds

14What good is it, my brothers, if
a man claims to have faith but has
no deeds?[w] Can such faith save him? 2:14 [w]Mt 7:26; Jas 1:22-25
15Suppose a brother or sister is without
clothes and daily food.[x] 16If one of you 2:15 [x]Mt 25:35,36
says to him, "Go, I wish you well; keep

[a]*8* Lev. 19:18 [b]*11* Exodus 20:14; Deut. 5:18
[c]*11* Exodus 20:13; Deut. 5:17

DAY 4 FOUR

JOY AND MY SERVICE TO OTHERS

James 2:14–17

Joy is the uncontainable expression of our faith. But joy is not something God gives us just so that we can experience a spiritual high. Joy is the consistent response of lives lived in the presence of God's salvation. We have been investigating the joy that results from seeing the creativity of God. But God also wants to use our own lives to create a better life for those around us. Joy is a direct result of our willing service to others.

When we see anyone in need of our ministry and fail to help that person, we lose the opportunity to experience joy. The fullest joy comes to us when we know that we have been the agents of God in creating a better life for those needy souls whom God has placed in our way.

We are God's crown of creation. But it is still natural for us to get hungry and thirsty, to grow tired and cold. To celebrate our humanity fully, we must not only seek to take care of our own needs, but to care in the same way for the needs of others. This is our ministry to the world—to care, and care genuinely.

God creates life—our lives and the lives of those needy souls to whom he calls us to minister. But the joy that belongs to us cannot develop until we learn to take those lives God has created and give them a better quality of life. Only after we will have taken the time to care will we have earned an honest joy. Caring and healing as Jesus himself did is the shortest path to joy. Such service reminds us that we are partners with God in extending his kingdom by blessing his hurting world with our own commitment to Christ.

To begin a study on the topic of The Joy of Creativity, turn to the home page on page 639.

WEEK 24

GOODNESS

1 DAY ONE
Goodness Implanted Into Our Lives Through Christ

Read James 2:20–24

Abraham believed God, and it was credited to him as righteousness. Laws tell us how to behave. Jesus told us not how to behave, but what to believe. For what we believe determines how we behave. In this way faith will always precede ethics because faith always defines ethics. It is interesting to watch a godless culture try to determine what's right or wrong. Having abandoned faith, the only determinants of morality can degenerate to this question: "Does this hurt someone else?" Abraham didn't ask such questions. He followed God and, in the process, lived a life that brought good to the entire world.

But beyond the fact that belief instructs behavior, belief actually imparts the moral life that we ourselves did not live. It is as though we "pinch off" righteousness from Jesus' holy and perfect life and place that "pinch of perfection" in the center of our lives, where it approves us to God. In other words, Jesus paid the price, and we're living off the change returned from his Calvary transaction.

This is a mighty theme of the apostle Paul: Faith is credited as righteousness (see Romans 4). The goodness that Jesus gives us supplants our own sinful lives the moment we believe. Then of course we reap the benefits of goodness in our lives and share that goodness with others.

We are Christ's. We benefit from his perfect sacrifice, and that perfect sacrifice will one day present us faultless before our Father (see Jude 24), and our faith will be credited as righteousness forever.

Memorize This Week

ROMANS 3:21-22

But now a righteousness from God, apart from law, has been made known, to which the Law and the Prophets testify. This righteousness from God comes through faith in Jesus Christ to all who believe.

2 DAY TWO
Goodness and the Purpose of God in My Life

Abraham followed God's plan for his life. He followed God even when he didn't understand the purpose of God's calling. His obedience is an example to us of faith in God, and it is a foreshadowing of God's ultimate sacrifice and Christ's ultimate obedience on the hill at Calvary. *Turn to Genesis 22:1–2,6–14, page 29, for today's study.*

3 DAY THREE
Goodness and My Relationship With Christ

The young man wanted eternal life and appeared to be satisfied with what he perceived as required to go to heaven. So Jesus reiterated the commandments, and the man—highly self-congratulatory—said he had kept all these things from his youth. Jesus replied that being good is not a mere legal affair. There is one more thing required. There is the matter of committing oneself to the greatest cause known—the kingdom of God. *Turn to Mark 10:17–22, page 1184, for today's study.*

4 DAY FOUR
Goodness and My Service to Others

Goodness has for its final plateau a concern for all the unevangelized. Paul challenges the good to demonstrate their goodness by sharing with everyone the Good News of salvation. After all, when can a person more fully experience goodness than when he or she offers the sinless, indwelling Christ to another? *Turn to Romans 10:12–15, page 1346, for today's study.*

5 DAY FIVE
Goodness and Its Place in My Personal Worship

Goodness is honoring the glorious lordship of Jesus Christ. The woman who anointed Jesus is doing just that. This anointing is her response of love. She could think of no other way to let the goodness of her life celebrate the goodness of his. But where did she acquire this goodness? If we could ask her, she would testify that all the goodness she found within herself had been planted there by Christ himself. *Turn to Matthew 26:6–13, page 1159, for today's study.*

Week 25, Faithfulness, the Habit of Spiritual Dependency, begins on page 260, Joshua 14:13–14.
To begin a topical study on the Fruit of the Spirit, Goodness, turn to the Topical Index, page 1548.

warm and well fed," but does nothing
about his physical needs, what good is
2:16 it?[y] 17 In the same way, faith by itself,
[y]1Jn 3:17,18 if it is not accompanied by action, is
dead.
18 But someone will say, "You have
faith; I have deeds."
2:18 Show me your faith without deeds,[z]
[z]Ro 3:28 and I will show you my faith by what
[a]Jas 3:13 I do.[a] 19 You believe that there is one
2:19 God.[b] Good! Even the demons believe
[b]Dt 6:4 that[c]—and shudder.
[c]Mt 8:29; Lk 4:34 20 You foolish man, do you want evidence that faith without deeds is use-
2:20 less?[a][d] 21 Was not our ancestor Abraham
[d]ver 17,26 considered righteous for what he did
when he offered his son Isaac on the
2:21 altar?[e] 22 You see that his faith and his
[e]Ge 22:9,12 actions were working together,[f] and his
2:22 faith was made complete by what he
[f]Heb 11:17 did.[g] 23 And the scripture was fulfilled
[g]1Th 1:3 that says, "Abraham believed God, and
it was credited to him as righteous-
2:23 ness,"[b][h] and he was called God's friend.[i]
[h]Ge 15:6; Ro 4:3 24 You see that a person is justified by
[i]2Ch 20:7; Isa 41:8 what he does and not by faith alone.
25 In the same way, was not even Ra-
hab the prostitute considered righteous
for what she did when she gave lodging
to the spies and sent them off in a dif-
2:25 ferent direction?[j] 26 As the body with-
[j]Heb 11:31 out the spirit is dead, so faith without
2:26 deeds is dead.[k]
[k]ver 17,20

Taming the Tongue

3 Not many of you should presume
to be teachers, my brothers, because you know that we who teach will
be judged more strictly. 2 We all stum-
3:2 ble[l] in many ways. If anyone is never at
[l]1Ki 8:46; Jas 2:10 fault in what he says,[m] he is a perfect
[m]1Pe 3:10 [n]Mt 12:37 man,[n] able to keep his whole body in
[o]Jas 1:26 check.[o]
3 When we put bits into the mouths
of horses to make them obey us, we
3:3 can turn the whole animal.[p] 4 Or take
[p]Ps 32:9 ships as an example. Although they are
so large and are driven by strong winds,
they are steered by a very small rudder
wherever the pilot wants to go. 5 Likewise the tongue is a small part of the
3:5 body, but it makes great boasts.[q] Con-
[q]Ps 12:3,4 sider what a great forest is set on fire
by a small spark. 6 The tongue also is a
3:6 fire,[r] a world of evil among the parts of
[r]Pr 16:27 [s]Mt 15:11,18,19 the body. It corrupts the whole person,[s]
sets the whole course of his life on fire,
and is itself set on fire by hell.

7 All kinds of animals, birds, reptiles
and creatures of the sea are being tamed
and have been tamed by man, 8 but no
man can tame the tongue. It is a restless
evil, full of deadly poison.[t] 3:8
9 With the tongue we praise our Lord [t]Ps 140:3; Ro 3:13
and Father, and with it we curse men, 3:9
who have been made in God's likeness.[u] [u]Ge 1:26,27; 1Co 11:7
10 Out of the same mouth come praise
and cursing. My brothers, this should
not be. 11 Can both fresh water and

[a]20 Some early manuscripts *dead* [b]23 Gen. 15:6

DAY 4 FOUR

Gentleness and My Service to Others

James 3:13–18

Wisdom from heaven is gentle and kind, says James in this passage. Gentleness is the greatest asset for those who want to minister to others. The renowned Phillips Brooks was a great pastor because he practiced childlike gentleness.

On one occasion a young mother in his congregation had a baby—her first—and the baby was born dead. The poor woman suffered from a kind of dementia and would not face the fact of the child's death. She clung to her dead baby, cowering in the corner of her room in a rocking chair. When anyone tried to take the baby away from her, she clung all the more fiercely to the dead child. The more they tried to wrench the baby from her arms, the more she clung to it. It finally became clear that if they were to pry the baby out of her arms, they were going to have to tear it forcefully from her. The harshness of such an action would have been brutal. But God rescued the desperate situation.

Enter the gentle servant Brooks.

He walked to her rocking chair, smiled kindly at her and said, "What a beautiful child. Would you mind if I rocked her a while?"

So kind was he that the woman extended the child to him, and to the surprise of all, Dr. Brooks took her seat in the rocker and tenderly rocked her baby.

An ugly crisis had been resolved by a wise and gentle spirit.

To begin a study on the topic of Gentleness, Childlike Godliness, turn to the home page on page 315.

salt[a] water flow from the same spring?
12My brothers, can a fig tree bear olives,
3:12 [v]Mt 7:16 or a grapevine bear figs?[v] Neither can a
salt spring produce fresh water.

DAY 2 TWO

▸ PEACE AND THE PURPOSE OF GOD IN MY LIFE

James 3:18

James says that we are to be peacemakers who sow peace. In this he sounds like his half-brother Jesus, who taught, "Blessed are the peacemakers." The church in every generation is hungry for people who will honor their calling to make peace.

How do we become peacemakers who sow in peace and reap a harvest of righteousness? One of the most exciting aspects of our lives in Christ is that we are called to evangelize with a ministry of peace. The world is a troubled place, and most lives have never heard the right prescription for peace. Jesus is that medicine, and we are the apothecaries of peace.

Our purpose in the world and the church is to publish peace. The church is made up of individuals with differing viewpoints and ideas. In virtually every congregation, there are enough devisive individual differences to blow the body apart were it not for the moderating qualities of those who are called to peace.

Many atheistic philosophers have looked at quarrelling churches and decided that their own peacelessness could not risk serving a Christ who, in their minds, could promote such a warlike faith. The church—how pitiably true—often seems to be a hangout for grudges. In the book of Philippians, Paul confronts two quarreling women, Euodia and Syntyche (see 4:2), to bring their quarreling spirits into calm, and he actually asks one of those who would receive the letter to play the role of peacemaker in adjudicating their argument. This passage should remind us that the church in every age is well served by those who pray and bless their churches into harmony.

With the admonitions of James, Jesus and Paul, how can we not pursue peace in the church and throughout our world?

To begin a study on the topic of Peace and the Prince of Peace, turn to the home page on page 19.

Two Kinds of Wisdom

13Who is wise and understanding
among you? Let him show it[w] by his 3:13 [w]Jas 2:18
good life, by deeds done in the humility
that comes from wisdom. 14But if you
harbor bitter envy and selfish ambition[x] 3:14 [x]ver 16
in your hearts, do not boast about it or [y]Jas 5:19
deny the truth.[y] 15Such "wisdom" does
not come down from heaven[z] but is 3:15 [z]Jas 1:17
earthly, unspiritual, of the devil.[a] 16For [a]1Ti 4:1
where you have envy and selfish ambition, there you find disorder and every
evil practice.
17But the wisdom that comes from
heaven[b] is first of all pure; then peace- 3:17 [b]1Co 2:6
loving, considerate, submissive, full of [c]Lk 6:36
mercy[c] and good fruit, impartial and [d]Ro 12:9
sincere.[d] 18Peacemakers who sow in
peace raise a harvest of righteousness.[e] 3:18 [e]Pr 11:18; Isa 32:17

Submit Yourselves to God

4 What causes fights and quarrels[f] 4:1 [f]Tit 3:9
among you? Don't they come from [g]Ro 7:23
your desires that battle[g] within you?
2You want something but don't get it.
You kill and covet, but you cannot have
what you want. You quarrel and fight.
You do not have, because you do not
ask God. 3When you ask, you do not
receive,[h] because you ask with wrong 4:3 [h]Ps 18:41
motives,[i] that you may spend what you [i]1Jn 3:22; 5:14
get on your pleasures.
4You adulterous people, don't you 4:4 [j]Jas 1:27
know that friendship with the world[j] [k]1Jn 2:15
is hatred toward God?[k] Anyone who [l]Jn 15:19
chooses to be a friend of the world
becomes an enemy of God.[l] 5Or do you
think Scripture says without reason that
the spirit he caused to live in us envies
intensely?[b] 6But he gives us more grace.
That is why Scripture says:

> "God opposes the proud
> but gives grace to the humble."[c][m] 4:6 [m]Ps 138:6; Pr 3:34; Mt 23:12

7Submit yourselves, then, to God.
Resist the devil,[n] and he will flee from 4:7 [n]Eph 4:27; 1Pe 5:6-9
you. 8Come near to God and he will
come near to you.[o] Wash your hands,[p] 4:8 [o]2Ch 15:2
you sinners, and purify your hearts, you [p]Isa 1:16
double-minded.[q] 9Grieve, mourn and [q]Jas 1:8
wail. Change your laughter to mourn-
ing and your joy to gloom.[r] 10Humble 4:9 [r]Lk 6:25

[a]*11* Greek *bitter* (see also verse 14) [b]*5* Or *that God jealously longs for the spirit that he made to live in us;* or *that the Spirit he caused to live in us longs jealously* [c]*6* Prov. 3:34

yourselves before the Lord, and he will lift you up.

11Brothers, do not slander one another.[s] Anyone who speaks against his brother or judges him[t] speaks against the law and judges it. When you judge the law, you are not keeping it,[u] but sitting in judgment on it. 12There is only one Lawgiver and Judge, the one who is able to save and destroy.[v] But you—who are you to judge your neighbor?[w]

Boasting About Tomorrow

13Now listen, you who say, "Today or tomorrow we will go to this or that city, spend a year there, carry on business and make money."[x] 14Why, you do not even know what will happen tomorrow. What is your life? You are a mist that appears for a little while and then vanishes.[y] 15Instead, you ought to say, "If it is the Lord's will,[z] we will live and do this or that." 16As it is, you boast and brag. All such boasting is evil.[a] 17Anyone, then, who knows the good he ought to do and doesn't do it, sins.[b]

Warning to Rich Oppressors

5 Now listen, you rich people,[c] weep and wail because of the misery that is coming upon you. 2Your wealth has rotted, and moths have eaten your clothes.[d] 3Your gold and silver are corroded. Their corrosion will testify against you and eat your flesh like fire. You have hoarded wealth in the last days.[e] 4Look! The wages you failed to pay the workmen[f] who mowed your fields are crying out against you. The cries[g] of the harvesters have reached the ears of the Lord Almighty.[h] 5You have lived on earth in luxury and self-indulgence. You have fattened yourselves[i] in the day of slaughter.[a][j] 6You have condemned and murdered innocent men,[k] who were not opposing you.

Patience in Suffering

7Be patient, then, brothers, until the Lord's coming. See how the farmer waits for the land to yield its valuable crop and how patient he is for the autumn and spring rains.[l] 8You too, be patient and stand firm, because the Lord's coming is near.[m] 9Don't grumble against each other, brothers,[n] or you will be judged. The Judge[o] is standing at the door![p]

10Brothers, as an example of patience in the face of suffering, take the prophets[q] who spoke in the name of the Lord. 11As you know, we consider blessed[r] those who have persevered. You have heard of Job's perseverance[s] and have seen what the Lord finally brought about.[t] The Lord is full of compassion and mercy.[u]

12Above all, my brothers, do not swear—not by heaven or by earth or by anything else. Let your "Yes" be yes, and your "No," no, or you will be condemned.[v]

The Prayer of Faith

13Is any one of you in trouble? He should pray.[w] Is anyone happy? Let him sing songs of praise.[x] 14Is any one of you sick? He should call the elders of the church to pray over him and anoint him with oil[y] in the name of the Lord. 15And the prayer offered in faith will make the sick person well; the Lord will raise him up. If he has sinned, he will be forgiven. 16Therefore confess your sins[z] to each other and pray for each other so that you may be healed.[a] The prayer of a righteous man is powerful and effective.[b]

17Elijah was a man just like us.[c] He prayed earnestly that it would not rain, and it did not rain on the land for three and a half years.[d] 18Again he prayed, and the heavens gave rain, and the earth produced its crops.[e]

19My brothers, if one of you should wander from the truth[f] and someone should bring him back,[g] 20remember this: Whoever turns a sinner from the error of his way will save[h] him from death and cover over a multitude of sins.[i]

[a]5 Or *yourselves as in a day of feasting*

4:11 [s]1Pe 2:1 [t]Mt 7:1 [u]Jas 1:22
4:12 [v]Mt 10:28 [w]Ro 14:4
4:13 [x]Pr 27:1
4:14 [y]Job 7:7; Ps 102:3
4:15 [z]Ac 18:21
4:16 [a]1Co 5:6
4:17 [b]Lk 12:47; Jn 9:41
5:1 [c]Lk 6:24
5:2 [d]Job 13:28; Mt 6:19,20
5:3 [e]ver 7,8
5:4 [f]Lev 19:13 [g]Dt 24:15 [h]Ro 9:29
5:5 [i]Am 6:1 [j]Jer 12:3; 25:34
5:6 [k]Heb 10:38
5:7 [l]Dt 11:14; Jer 5:24
5:8 [m]Ro 13:11; 1Pe 4:7
5:9 [n]Jas 4:11 [o]1Co 4:5; 1Pe 4:5 [p]Mt 24:33
5:10 [q]Mt 5:12
5:11 [r]Mt 5:10 [s]Job 1:21,22; 2:10 [t]Job 42:10, 12-17 [u]Nu 14:18
5:12 [v]Mt 5:34-37
5:13 [w]Ps 50:15 [x]Col 3:16
5:14 [y]Mk 6:13
5:16 [z]Mt 3:6 [a]1Pe 2:24 [b]Jn 9:31
5:17 [c]Ac 14:15 [d]1Ki 17:1; Lk 4:25
5:18 [e]1Ki 18:41-45
5:19 [f]Jas 3:14 [g]Mt 18:15
5:20 [h]Ro 11:14 [i]1Pe 4:8

1 PETER

AUTHORSHIP AND DATE

Peter

c. A.D. 62–64

KEY THEMES

Peter pictured salvation as a gift of grace: Jesus died for us and provided a wonderful new life for us to enjoy. Peter discussed what persecution brings us as we learn the art of suffering and as we receive its meaning. He not only discussed what a privilege it is to belong to God's greater family, but he described how each individual family unit ought to operate and how husbands and wives are to find the best kind of marriage relationship. Peter discussed how each of us is to praise God for salvation and seek the discipline of the holy life. He encouraged the believers to stand fast in the faith and said that the holy life is not only possible, but it is also the most desirable way to live.

FRUIT OF THE SPIRIT IN 1 PETER

Love: How can we tell that we are loved by God? We know that we are loved because we are "a chosen people, a royal priesthood, a holy nation, a people belonging to God, that [we] may declare the praises of him who called [us] out of darkness into his wonderful light" (2:9). One of the surest signs of God's love: He has given us undeserved status wrapped in a package of grace.

Joy: Praise should be offered to the One who provides the most important and precious things in our lives! So Peter opened his letter with joy: "Praise be to the God and Father of our Lord Jesus Christ! In his great mercy he has given us new birth into a living hope through the resurrection of Jesus Christ from the dead" (1:3). Every sunrise ought to help us recall Easter; therefore, praising God for the resurrection ought to be our habit each sunrise.

Peace: Peter gave a most unique summons to peace: "Finally, all of you, live in harmony with one another; be sympathetic, love as brothers, be compassionate and humble" (3:8). If this simple recipe were lettered on the cornerstone of the

United Nations building, the building could be made into a "museum of wars that used to be."

Patience: "The end of all things is near. Therefore be clear minded and self-controlled so that you can pray" (4:7). Is it logical to say, "Doomsday will be tomorrow at noon, so relax"? Yes! The big deadlines remind us that God is in charge and that all our impatience will not hurry the Almighty along.

Goodness: Jesus' sinlessness is mentor enough to sinners who will never conquer the problem of sin in their lives. But then, Christ suffered for us, leaving us an example that we "should follow in his steps" (2:21). Goodness has a standard, and those who stand for Christ honor it.

Faithfulness: Since Satan is a roaring lion on the prowl, desiring to devour our lives, we should learn the art of faithfulness to God. Such an image of our enemy ought to call us to "resist him, standing firm in the faith" (5:9) because we know that Satan's persecution of the church is universal. Satan fears our faithfulness. Faithfulness is the mighty weapon of the meek; it makes all of us lion slayers.

Gentleness: Practice gentleness by showing proper respect to everyone, by loving other believers, by fearing God and by being good citizens (see 2:17). In such a world, God's people will seem wholesome and worthy of emulation.

Self-Control: A life in Christ has learned to behave itself. A life without self-control is a life out of control (see 4:3).

1:1 a2Pe 1:1; bMt 24:22; cAc 16:7 1 Peter, an apostle of Jesus Christ,[a]
To God's elect,[b] strangers in the
world, scattered throughout Pontus, Galatia, Cappadocia, Asia and Bithynia,[c]
2who have been chosen according to
1:2 dRo 8:29; e2Th 2:13; fHeb 10:22; 12:24 the foreknowledge[d] of God the Father,
through the sanctifying work of the
Spirit,[e] for obedience to Jesus Christ
and sprinkling by his blood:[f]

Grace and peace be yours in abundance.

Praise to God for a Living Hope

3Praise be to the God and Father
1:3 g2Co 1:3; Eph 1:3; hTit 3:5; Jas 1:18; i1Co 15:20 of our Lord Jesus Christ![g] In his great
mercy[h] he has given us new birth into
a living hope through the resurrection
of Jesus Christ from the dead,[i] 4and
into an inheritance that can never perish, spoil or fade—kept in heaven for
1:4 jCol 1:5 you,[j] 5who through faith are shielded
by God's power[k] until the coming of
1:5 kJn 10:28 the salvation that is ready to be revealed
in the last time. 6In this you greatly
1:6 lRo 5:2; m1Pe 5:10; nJas 1:2 rejoice,[l] though now for a little while[m]
you may have had to suffer grief in
all kinds of trials.[n] 7These have come
1:7 oJob 23:10; Ps 66:10; Pr 17:3; pJas 1:3; qRo 2:7 so that your faith—of greater worth
than gold, which perishes even though
refined by fire[o]—may be proved genuine[p] and may result in praise, glory and
honor when Jesus Christ is revealed.[q]
8Though you have not seen him, you
love him; and even though you do not
1:8 rJn 20:29 see him now, you believe in him[r] and
are filled with an inexpressible and glorious joy, 9for you are receiving the
goal of your faith, the salvation of your
1:9 sRo 6:22 souls.[s]
10Concerning this salvation, the
1:10 tMt 26:24; uMt 13:17 prophets, who spoke[t] of the grace that
was to come to you, searched intently
and with the greatest care,[u] 11trying to
find out the time and circumstances to
1:11 v2Pe 1:21 which the Spirit of Christ[v] in them was
pointing when he predicted the suf-
ferings of Christ and the glories that
would follow. 12It was revealed to them
that they were not serving themselves
but you, when they spoke of the things
that have now been told you by those
1:12 wver 25 who have preached the gospel to you[w]
by the Holy Spirit sent from heaven.
Even angels long to look into these
things.

Be Holy

13Therefore, prepare your minds for
action; be self-controlled; set your hope
fully on the grace to be given you when
Jesus Christ is revealed. 14As obedient
children, do not conform[x] to the evil 1:14 xRo 12:2; yEph 4:18
desires you had when you lived in ig-
norance.[y] 15But just as he who called
you is holy, so be holy in all you do;[z] 1:15 z2Co 7:1; 1Th 4:7
16for it is written: "Be holy, because I
am holy."[a][a]
17Since you call on a Father who 1:16 aLev 11:44,45
judges each man's work impartially,[b] live 1:17 bAc 10:34; cHeb 12:28
your lives as strangers here in reverent
fear.[c] 18For you know that it was not
with perishable things such as silver or
gold that you were redeemed[d] from the 1:18 dMt 20:28; 1Co 6:20
empty way of life handed down to you
from your forefathers, 19but with the
precious blood of Christ, a lamb[e] with- 1:19 eJn 1:29; fEx 12:5
out blemish or defect.[f] 20He was cho-
sen before the creation of the world,[g]
but was revealed in these last times[h] for 1:20 gEph 1:4; hHeb 9:26
your sake. 21Through him you believe
in God,[i] who raised him from the dead 1:21 iRo 4:24
and glorified him, and so your faith and
hope are in God.

LOVE

BOUGHT AT GOD'S EXPENSE

1 Peter 1:18–19

You were not purchased with cheap silver coinage—
God is rich with silver.
You were not redeemed with ingots of gold—
Heaven is paved with the stuff.
You were bought with the only currency that can impoverish God—
The blood of his one and only Son.

22Now that you have purified[j] your- 1:22 jJas 4:8; kJn 13:34; Heb 13:1
selves by obeying the truth so that you
have sincere love for your brothers, love
one another deeply,[k] from the heart.[b]
23For you have been born again,[l] not 1:23 lJn 1:13; mHeb 4:12
of perishable seed, but of imperishable,
through the living and enduring word
of God.[m] 24For,

"All men are like grass,
and all their glory is like the
flowers of the field;
the grass withers and the flowers fall,

[a] *16* Lev. 11:44,45; 19:2; 20:7 [b] *22* Some early manuscripts *from a pure heart*

1:25 [n]Isa 40:6-8
25 but the word of the Lord stands
forever."[a][n]

And this is the word that was preached
to you.

2:1 [o]Eph 4:22 [p]Jas 4:11
2 Therefore, rid yourselves[o] of all malice and all deceit, hypocrisy, envy,
and slander[p] of every kind. 2Like new-
2:2 [q]1Co 3:2 [r]Eph 4:15,16
born babies, crave pure spiritual milk,[q]
so that by it you may grow up[r] in your
salvation, 3now that you have tasted
2:3 [s]Heb 6:5
that the Lord is good.[s]

The Living Stone and a Chosen People

4As you come to him, the living
2:4 [t]ver 7
Stone[t]—rejected by men but chosen
by God and precious to him— 5you
2:5 [u]1Co 3:9 [v]1Ti 3:15 [w]Isa 61:6 [x]Php 4:18; Heb 13:15
also, like living stones, are being built[u]
into a spiritual house[v] to be a holy
priesthood,[w] offering spiritual sacrifices
acceptable to God through Jesus Christ.[x]
6For in Scripture it says:

"See, I lay a stone in Zion,
a chosen and precious
2:6 [y]Eph 2:20 [z]Isa 28:16
cornerstone,[y]
and the one who trusts in him
will never be put to shame."[b][z]

7Now to you who believe, this stone
is precious. But to those who do not
2:7 [a]2Co 2:16 [b]Ps 118:22
believe,[a]

"The stone the builders rejected
has become the capstone,[c]"[d][b]

8and,

"A stone that causes men to stumble
2:8 [c]Isa 8:14; 1Co 1:23
and a rock that makes them
fall."[e][c]

[a]*25* Isaiah 40:6-8 [b]*6* Isaiah 28:16 [c]*7* Or *cornerstone* [d]*7* Psalm 118:22 [e]*8* Isaiah 8:14

JOY

THE JOYOUS WORK OF THE SPECIAL PEOPLE

1 Peter 2:9–10

The flags of all empires dip their colors
before the scarlet flag of God's kingdom.
The angels have a serenade for all believers:
You are a special people;
You are a royal priesthood;
Each of you is a story of mercy.

DAY THREE

JOY AND MY RELATIONSHIP WITH CHRIST

1 Peter 2:9

We are indeed a "royal priesthood." And what is it that priests do? They are mediators—go-betweens—those who intercede between God and his world. Priests inform the world what God expects and help the world get better acquainted with God.

But notice what kind of priests Peter says we have become: praising priests. We are called to wake the world to wonder—for we have been called "out of darkness into his wonderful light."

Praising priests! Jesus is called a priest in the book of Hebrews. And Jesus is the ultimate reason for praise. How can we keep silent about the glorious future that awaits us because of all that Jesus has done?

Our praise should lighten our load and bring others hope in their hour of need. It should transport us from a "Sad Sack" mentality to "The Hallelujah Chorus." But does praise really heal us to this extent?

Have you ever gotten up on Sunday morning, feeling beaten by life, and told yourself that you just didn't feel like going to church? Do not be deceived by your low mood. It is at just such times that you need to go! Crawl on in, low as a reptile in your joyless world. Then wait for the praise to begin. It will overwhelm you. It will force your chin up. It will lift your face toward the colored glass. Soon, your heart will rebuke you. What's this? You're clapping? Now you're dancing? Praise has done it again. We who know Christ are the choir leaders of the kingdom. We are the healers of the gloom-chained. We are the priests of praise!

And once the praising has begun, the world itself is mystified by the energy and power of it all. Why? Because praise transforms all it touches. It transforms the "praiser" first, and bit by bit it changes the entire world. Praise changes everything in time and shows the world Christ in us.

To begin a study on the topic of Joy, the Infallible Proof of the Presence of God, turn to the home page on page 1086.

2:8 [d]Ro 9:22

They stumble because they disobey the message—which is also what they were destined for.[d]

DAY 2 TWO

▸ PATIENCE AND THE PURPOSE OF GOD IN MY LIFE

1 Peter 2:18–20

One cannot read this passage without being reminded that in Philippians 3:10 Paul promises us that we will become spiritually mature by sharing in the fellowship of Christ's suffering. Likewise, here Peter attempts to help slaves find some meaning in the severity of their abuses. He assures them that questions about their pain can be a reminder that suffering brings our focus on God, and that focus will steady us in the painful walk through the valley of our travails.

Pain! How we turn from it. When we are under its muddy gloom, we rarely find the strength to "give thanks in all circumstances" (1 Thessalonians 5:18). Yet once we are past the hurt and struggle we realize that had it not been for the pain, we would not have gained such a clear picture of Christ.

The suffering is never ours alone. I remember a time when our village doctor had to stitch up a gash in the forehead of our little girl. What I could not help but notice was that as the doctor did his work, our daughter fixed her eyes on her mother's, and the interlocking of their gazes resulted in a sharing that made her pain bearable.

This is something like the lesson that Peter is giving those who have suffered for no apparent reason. "Fix your eyes on the eyes of God," he says, and although the pain will still be there, gazing patiently at your Father in heaven will make your hurt a season of blessing in your life. In time you will see it as such a blessing that, if you had your whole life to live over again, you would not leave out this painful season. For your suffering will have meaning like that of Christ: "When they hurled their insults at him, he did not retaliate; when he suffered, he made no threats. Instead, he entrusted himself to him who judges justly" (1 Peter 2:23).

To begin a study on the topic of Patience Brings the Blessing of God, turn to the home page on page 1476.

9But you are a chosen people,[e] a royal
priesthood, a holy nation,[f] a people belonging to God, that you may declare
the praises of him who called you out
of darkness into his wonderful light.[g]
10Once you were not a people, but now
you are the people of God;[h] once you
had not received mercy, but now you
have received mercy.
11Dear friends, I urge you, as aliens
and strangers in the world, to abstain
from sinful desires,[i] which war against
your soul.[j] 12Live such good lives among
the pagans that, though they accuse
you of doing wrong, they may see your
good deeds[k] and glorify God[l] on the
day he visits us.

Submission to Rulers and Masters

13Submit yourselves for the Lord's
sake to every authority[m] instituted
among men: whether to the king, as
the supreme authority, 14or to governors, who are sent by him to punish
those who do wrong[n] and to commend
those who do right.[o] 15For it is God's
will[p] that by doing good you should silence the ignorant talk of foolish men.[q]
16Live as free men,[r] but do not use your
freedom as a cover-up for evil; live as
servants of God.[s] 17Show proper respect
to everyone: Love the brotherhood of
believers,[t] fear God, honor the king.[u]
18Slaves, submit yourselves to your
masters with all respect,[v] not only to
those who are good and considerate,[w]
but also to those who are harsh. 19For it
is commendable if a man bears up under the pain of unjust suffering because
he is conscious of God.[x] 20But how is
it to your credit if you receive a beating for doing wrong and endure it? But
if you suffer for doing good and you
endure it, this is commendable before
God.[y] 21To this[z] you were called, because Christ suffered for you, leaving
you an example,[a] that you should follow in his steps.

22"He committed no sin,
and no deceit was found in his
mouth."[a][b]

23When they hurled their insults at
him, he did not retaliate; when he suffered, he made no threats.[c] Instead, he
entrusted himself[d] to him who judges

[a]22 Isaiah 53:9

2:9 [e]Dt 10:15 [f]Isa 62:12 [g]Ac 26:18
2:10 [h]Hos 1:9,10
2:11 [i]Gal 5:16 [j]Jas 4:1
2:12 [k]Php 2:15; 1Pe 3:16 [l]Mt 5:16; 9:8
2:13 [m]Ro 13:1
2:14 [n]Ro 13:4 [o]Ro 13:3
2:15 [p]1Pe 3:17 [q]ver 12
2:16 [r]Jn 8:32 [s]Ro 6:22
2:17 [t]Ro 12:10 [u]Ro 13:7
2:18 [v]Eph 6:5 [w]Jas 3:17
2:19 [x]1Pe 3:14,17
2:20 [y]1Pe 3:17
2:21 [z]Ac 14:22 [a]Mt 16:24
2:22 [b]Isa 53:9
2:23 [c]Isa 53:7 [d]Lk 23:46

DAY 3 THREE

▸ Gentleness and My Relationship With Christ

1 Peter 3:1–6

The gospel of Christ has immensely liberated women, and how grateful all of us are to Jesus for that freedom. But it was not always so. In the first century women were often at the mercy of their husbands in every realm of life from the social to the political. But many women came to Christ without the approval of their husbands. And although their husbands might have not approved, they longed to somehow bring their mates to Christ. Since they were under the control of their husbands, many women could not tell those men about their conversion experiences. They could not explain their beliefs, debate their theology or even share their newfound joy and peace.

Peter gives advice to women in this restrictive situation. They could show their husbands their new faith without words. They could live lives of submission and gentleness. Peter explains that a quiet spirit can speak volumes.

Sometimes words get in the way of evangelizing. Rather than telling others about our faith, a gentle spirit can show others what we believe. How does a gentle spirit witness?

It majors on the purity of the inner life.

It has unfading beauty.

It has history. It was the way that holy people of the past made themselves beautiful.

Let's not assume that Peter was telling women to entirely disregard their appearance. For both men and women, looking clean and attractive is a positive goal. However, emphasizing outward beauty and neglecting one's inward state of being impede our ability to effectively minister to others. No matter how attractive we may appear, people will not be drawn to Christ if we are cruel, dishonest or unkind.

Loveliness is essentially an inward matter. The lack of it cannot be compensated for by mere cosmetics. Peter reminds us all that the best way of spreading God's love is to have a beautiful, gentle spirit.

To begin a study on the topic of Gentleness, a Way of Winning Others to Christ, turn to the home page on page 1303.

justly. 24 He himself bore our sins[e] in
his body on the tree, so that we might
die to sins[f] and live for righteousness;
by his wounds you have been healed.[g]
25 For you were like sheep going astray,[h]
but now you have returned to the Shepherd[i] and Overseer of your souls.

Wives and Husbands

3 Wives, in the same way be submissive[j] to your husbands[k] so that, if
any of them do not believe the word,
they may be won over[l] without words
by the behavior of their wives, 2 when
they see the purity and reverence of
your lives. 3 Your beauty should not
come from outward adornment, such
as braided hair and the wearing of gold
jewelry and fine clothes.[m] 4 Instead, it
should be that of your inner self,[n] the
unfading beauty of a gentle and quiet
spirit, which is of great worth in God's
sight. 5 For this is the way the holy
women of the past who put their hope
in God[o] used to make themselves beautiful. They were submissive to their
own husbands, 6 like Sarah, who obeyed
Abraham and called him her master.[p]
You are her daughters if you do what is
right and do not give way to fear.
7 Husbands,[q] in the same way be considerate as you live with your wives, and
treat them with respect as the weaker
partner and as heirs with you of the
gracious gift of life, so that nothing will
hinder your prayers.

Suffering for Doing Good

8 Finally, all of you, live in harmony
with one another; be sympathetic, love
as brothers,[r] be compassionate and
humble.[s] 9 Do not repay evil with evil[t]
or insult with insult,[u] but with blessing,
because to this[v] you were called so that
you may inherit a blessing.[w] 10 For,

"Whoever would love life
and see good days
must keep his tongue from evil
and his lips from deceitful speech.
11 He must turn from evil and do
good;
he must seek peace and pursue it.
12 For the eyes of the Lord are on the
righteous
and his ears are attentive to their
prayer,

2:24 [e]Heb 9:28 [f]Ro 6:2 [g]Isa 53:5; Heb 12:13; Jas 5:16
2:25 [h]Isa 53:6 [i]Jn 10:11
3:1 [j]1Pe 2:18 [k]Eph 5:22 [l]1Co 7:16; 9:19
3:3 [m]Isa 3:18-23; 1Ti 2:9
3:4 [n]Ro 7:22
3:5 [o]1Ti 5:5
3:6 [p]Ge 18:12
3:7 [q]Eph 5:25-33
3:8 [r]Ro 12:10 [s]1Pe 5:5
3:9 [t]Ro 12:17 [u]1Pe 2:23 [v]1Pe 2:21 [w]Heb 6:14

DAY 3 THREE

Self-Control and My Relationship With Christ

1 Peter 4:7

"The end of all things is near." The world is in dress rehearsal for the grand event at the end of time.

The Cromwellian government in England knew the fiery Adventism of the Fifth Monarchists. They believed that the execution of Charles I was precedent to the coming of Christ.

In 1844 the Millerites assembled in white to await the second coming.

The Jehovah's Witnesses believed that Jesus was coming soon and had various dates set for the event.

The rise of Hitler led American evangelists to believe that he was the antichrist and that Jesus would soon be coming again.

The Cuban Missile Crisis had evangelical preachers everywhere preaching the proximity of the second coming.

Hal Lindsay's bestseller, *The Late Great Planet Earth,* explained how the European Common Market was another evidence of the Savior's approaching return.

And at the end of the twentieth century, the threat of the Y2K computer bug incited more talk of the second coming.

Peter reminded us that time is short, and yet he wrote this nearly twenty centuries before our current scholars have issued the same warning. So then who is correct? Peter or the later theorists?

Well, both should prompt us to self-control and holy living. Peter said it best in his second letter: "Since everything will be destroyed in this way, what kind of people ought you to be? You ought to live holy and godly lives as you look forward to the day of God and speed its coming" (3:11–12).

The calendar is approaching its final page. The sand is all but through the hourglass. The time has come to take charge of our lives.

To begin a study on the topic of Self-Control, the Disciplined Life, turn to the home page on page 1367.

but the face of the Lord is against
those who do evil."[a x] 3:12 [x]Ps 34:12-16

13 Who is going to harm you if you
are eager to do good?[y] 14 But even if you 3:13 [y]Pr 16:7
should suffer for what is right, you are
blessed.[z] "Do not fear what they fear[b]; 3:14 [z]1Pe 2:19,20;
do not be frightened."[c a] 15 But in your 4:15,16
hearts set apart Christ as Lord. Always [a]Isa 8:12,13
be prepared to give an answer[b] to every- 3:15
one who asks you to give the reason [b]Col 4:6
for the hope that you have. But do this
with gentleness and respect, 16 keeping
a clear conscience,[c] so that those who 3:16 [c]Heb 13:18
speak maliciously against your good be- [d]1Pe 2:12,15
havior in Christ may be ashamed of
their slander.[d] 17 It is better, if it is God's
will,[e] to suffer for doing good[f] than for 3:17 [e]1Pe 2:15
doing evil. 18 For Christ died for sins[g] [f]1Pe 2:20
once for all, the righteous for the un- 3:18
righteous, to bring you to God. He was [g]1Pe 2:21
put to death in the body[h] but made [h]Col 1:22; 1Pe 4:1
alive by the Spirit,[i] 19 through whom[d] [i]1Pe 4:6
also he went and preached to the spir-
its in prison[j] 20 who disobeyed long ago
when God waited patiently in the days 3:19 [j]1Pe 4:6
of Noah while the ark was being built.[k]
In it only a few people, eight in all, were 3:20 [k]Ge 6:3,5,13,14
saved[l] through water, 21 and this water [l]Heb 11:7
symbolizes baptism that now saves you[m]
also—not the removal of dirt from the 3:21 [m]Tit 3:5
body but the pledge[e] of a good con- [n]1Pe 1:3
science toward God. It saves you by
the resurrection of Jesus Christ,[n] 22 who
has gone into heaven and is at God's
right hand[o]—with angels, authorities 3:22 [o]Mk 16:19
and powers in submission to him.[p] [p]Ro 8:38

Living for God

4 Therefore, since Christ suffered in
his body, arm yourselves also with
the same attitude, because he who has
suffered in his body is done with sin.
2 As a result, he does not live the rest of
his earthly life for evil human desires,[q] 4:2 [q]Ro 6:2
but rather for the will of God. 3 For
you have spent enough time in the past[r] 4:3 [r]Eph 2:2
doing what pagans choose to do—living
in debauchery, lust, drunkenness, orgies, carousing and detestable idolatry.
4 They think it strange that you do not
plunge with them into the same flood
of dissipation, and they heap abuse on
you.[s] 5 But they will have to give ac- 4:4 [s]1Pe 3:16

[a] *12* Psalm 34:12-16 [b] *14* Or *not fear their threats*
[c] *14* Isaiah 8:12 [d] *18,19* Or *alive in the spirit, 19 through which* [e] *21* Or *response*

count to him who is ready to judge the
4:5 [t]Ac 10:42; 2Ti 4:1 living and the dead.[t] 6For this is the
reason the gospel was preached even to
4:6 [u]1Pe 3:19 those who are now dead,[u] so that they
might be judged according to men in
regard to the body, but live according
to God in regard to the spirit.

7The end of all things is near.[v] There-
4:7 [v]Ro 13:11 fore be clear minded and self-controlled
so that you can pray. 8Above all, love
4:8 [w]1Pe 1:22 [x]Pr 10:12 each other deeply,[w] because love covers
over a multitude of sins.[x] 9Offer hos-
4:9 [y]Php 2:14 pitality to one another without grumbling.[y] 10Each one should use whatever
4:10 [z]Ro 12:6,7 [a]1Co 4:2 gift he has received to serve others,[z]
faithfully[a] administering God's grace in
its various forms. 11If anyone speaks,
he should do it as one speaking the
very words of God. If anyone serves,
he should do it with the strength God
4:11 [b]Eph 6:10 [c]1Co 10:31 provides,[b] so that in all things God may
be praised[c] through Jesus Christ. To
him be the glory and the power for ever
and ever. Amen.

PEACE

TREASURE THE TRIALS

1 Peter 4:12–14

Trials are not what they seem.
They are not ordeals of pain and stress—
They are enticements delicious,
Luring us to remember
The true state of things:
Our lover is incomparable;
Our destiny, inescapable;
Our life, unthreatenable.

Suffering for Being a Christian

12Dear friends, do not be surprised
4:12 [d]1Pe 1:6,7 at the painful trial you are suffering,[d]
as though something strange were hap-
pening to you. 13But rejoice that you
participate in the sufferings of Christ,
so that you may be overjoyed when his
4:13 [e]Ro 8:17 glory is revealed.[e] 14If you are insulted
because of the name of Christ, you are
4:14 [f]Mt 5:11 blessed,[f] for the Spirit of glory and of
God rests on you. 15If you suffer, it
should not be as a murderer or thief
or any other kind of criminal, or even
as a meddler. 16However, if you suffer
4:16 [g]Ac 5:41 as a Christian, do not be ashamed, but
praise God that you bear that name.[g]
4:17 [h]Jer 25:29 17For it is time for judgment to begin
with the family of God;[h] and if it be-
gins with us, what will the outcome be
for those who do not obey the gospel of
God?[i] 18And, 4:17 [i]2Th 1:8

"If it is hard for the righteous to be
saved,
what will become of the ungodly 4:18 [j]Pr 11:31; Lk 23:31
and the sinner?"[a][j]

19So then, those who suffer according
to God's will should commit themselves
to their faithful Creator and continue
to do good.

To Elders and Young Men

5 To the elders among you, I appeal as 5:1 [k]Ac 11:30
a fellow elder,[k] a witness[l] of Christ's [l]Lk 24:48
sufferings and one who also will share [m]1Pe 1:5,7; Rev 1:9
in the glory to be revealed:[m] 2Be shep-
herds of God's flock[n] that is under your 5:2 [n]Jn 21:16
care, serving as overseers—not because [o]1Ti 3:3
you must, but because you are willing,
as God wants you to be; not greedy for
money,[o] but eager to serve; 3not lording 5:3 [p]Eze 34:4
it over[p] those entrusted to you, but be- [q]Php 3:17
ing examples[q] to the flock. 4And when
the Chief Shepherd appears, you will 5:4 [r]1Co 9:25
receive the crown of glory[r] that will
never fade away.

5Young men, in the same way be sub-
missive[s] to those who are older. All of 5:5 [s]Eph 5:21 [t]Pr 3:34;
you, clothe yourselves with humility to- Jas 4:6
ward one another, because,

"God opposes the proud
but gives grace to the humble."[b][t]

6Humble yourselves, therefore, under 5:6 [u]Jas 4:10
God's mighty hand, that he may lift 5:7 [v]Ps 37:5; Mt 6:25
you up in due time.[u] 7Cast all your anx- [w]Heb 13:5
iety on him[v] because he cares for you.[w]

[a]18 Prov. 11:31 [b]5 Prov. 3:34

KINDNESS

ATLAS AND JESUS

1 Peter 5:7

The foolish Greeks taught that Atlas carried the leaden world upon his shoulders. Poor Atlas—anemic, weak, a nonexistent soul!

Jesus carried the sins of the entire world. Yours too! He still carries all you find too crushing to endure. And in the hard times, he gently carries even you.

5:8 [x]Job 1:7
5:9 [y]Jas 4:7 [z]Col 2:5 [a]Ac 14:22

8Be self-controlled and alert. Your
enemy the devil prowls around[x] like
a roaring lion looking for someone to
devour. 9Resist him,[y] standing firm
in the faith,[z] because you know that
your brothers throughout the world
are undergoing the same kind of
sufferings.[a]
10And the God of all grace, who
called you to his eternal glory[b] in
Christ, after you have suffered a little
while, will himself restore you and
make you strong,[c] firm and steadfast.
11To him be the power for ever and
ever. Amen.[d]

5:10 [b]2Co 4:17
5:10 [c]2Th 2:17
5:11 [d]Ro 11:36

[a]12 Greek *Silvanus,* a variant of *Silas*

JOHN MARK

Gentleness, the Winning Characteristic of a Missionary Witness (5:1–14)

Any thorough discussion of the life of John Mark will require a gleaning of various passages from the New Testament. It would seem that the young man who fled naked from Gethsemane was John Mark (Mark 14:51), the author of the Gospel of Mark, and that the Last Supper may have been eaten in his home earlier that same evening. By examining eight different passages, we can piece together a biography of sorts:

After Paul and Barnabas had delivered a gift from the church in Antioch to the believers in Jerusalem, they brought John Mark with them when they returned to the city of Antioch (Acts 12:25). It was from there that the missionary journeys of Paul originated.

When Paul and Barnabas began their first missionary journey, John Mark was their traveling companion and helper (13:4–5).

John Mark left the missionaries in Perga of Pamphylia for unknown reasons (v. 13). But it seems the apostle Paul considered John Mark to be a quitter.

In preparation for the second missionary journey, Paul and Barnabas broke into a fierce quarrel over John Mark. Barnabas wanted to take him on the second missionary journey, but Paul did not. So John Mark and Barnabas formed their own missionary team and went to Cyprus to evangelize, while Paul chose Silas and returned to Asia Minor (15:36–41).

Colossians 4:10 reveals that Barnabas and John Mark were cousins. This would make some sense in light of the fact that the church in Jerusalem met at John Mark's house (Acts 12:12), and Barnabas had an early connection with that church (4:36).

Both Colossians 4:10 and Philemon 24 show that Paul later had a friendly attitude toward John Mark, suggesting that the two had come to some kind of reconciliation.

Near the end of his life, Paul even confessed that he wanted to see John Mark, because John Mark was very helpful to him in his ministry (2 Timothy 4:11).

The first epistle of Peter connected John Mark with Peter (1 Peter 5:13). This is a noble reference, for it is generally believed that John Mark's Gospel narrative was derived from the teachings of Peter, who was an eyewitness of the life of Christ. This connection gives John Mark's Gospel its apostolic authority.

All in all, Mark was a key figure of the New Testament. Although he is often remembered as the man whom Paul didn't want on his missionary journey and the one who caused a rift between Paul and Barnabas, it seems that John Mark overcame his initial rocky start in ministry. He may have felt discouraged or angry about some of the events in his life, but he overcame difficult relationships. Perhaps his gentle spirit led to the reconciliation between himself and Paul. In any case, Mark's gentle spirit influenced others and witnessed to the gentle Christ in a way history could not forget.

FAITHFULNESS

THE ROAR OF THE ENEMY

1 Peter 5:8

I met a lion in the way and trembled at his roar. Yet when I looked closer, I could see that his fangs and claws were gone. And I rejoiced in knowing that Jesus had met my enemy before I had gotten there.

Final Greetings

12With the help of Silas,[a] [e] whom I
regard as a faithful brother, I have written to you briefly,[f] encouraging you
and testifying that this is the true grace
of God. Stand fast in it.
13She who is in Babylon, chosen together with you, sends you her greetings, and so does my son Mark.[g] 14Greet
one another with a kiss of love.[h]
Peace[i] to all of you who are in Christ.

5:12 [e]2Co 1:19
5:12 [f]Heb 13:22
5:13 [g]Ac 12:12
5:14 [h]Ro 16:16 [i]Eph 6:23

2 PETER

▸ AUTHORSHIP AND DATE

Peter

Between A.D. 65 and A.D. 68

▸ KEY THEMES

Second Peter addresses three main themes:

1. Instructions on how to live and grow in Christ (see 1:1–11)
2. How to combat false teachings (see 2:1–22)
3. Encouragement to be watchful in lieu of the unknown hour of Christ's second coming (see 3:1–16)
4. In 2 Peter 1:12–21, Peter told the believers that his purpose in writing was to remind them of these things and encourage them to remember that his own direct, eyewitness account of the life of Christ was apostolic and should be respected (see 1:16–18). He also reminded them that the Holy Spirit was the source of divine inspiration (see 1:19–21).

▸ FRUIT OF THE SPIRIT IN 2 PETER

Patience: Patience becomes possible if we remember that our watches are calibrated in seconds, but God's watch is calibrated in centuries. It gets easier to wait if you remember: "With the Lord a day is like a thousand years" (3:8). Slower watches have a way of making better-paced, more pleasant lives.

Kindness: Peter discussed teachers whose boldness and arrogance caused them to turn from meekness (see 2:10). They were not good at taking orders. And those who are not good at taking orders are not overly adept at having a Lord, nor do they easily arrive at a meaningful life. The only meaningful life is based on Christlikeness, and Christlikeness is that kind of meekness that results in kindness.

Goodness: Goodness is the foundation of many other virtues: "For this very reason, make every effort to add to your faith goodness; and to goodness, knowledge; and to knowledge, self-control; and to self-control, perseverance; and to perseverance, godliness; and to godliness, brotherly kindness; and to brotherly kindness, love" (1:5–7).

1:1 [a]Ro 1:1 1 Simon Peter, a servant[a] and apostle
[b]1Pe 1:1 [c]Ro 3:21-26 of Jesus Christ,[b]

[d]Tit 2:13 To those who through the righteousness[c] of our God and Savior Jesus
Christ[d] have received a faith as precious
as ours:

2Grace and peace be yours in abundance through the knowledge of God
1:2 [e]Php 3:8 and of Jesus our Lord.[e]

Making One's Calling and Election Sure

1:3 3His divine power[f] has given us ev-
[f]1Pe 1:5 [g]1Th 2:12 erything we need for life and godliness
through our knowledge of him who
called us[g] by his own glory and goodness. 4Through these he has given us
1:4 his very great and precious promises,[h]
[h]2Co 7:1 [i]Eph 4:24; so that through them you may partic-
Heb 12:10; 1Jn 3:2 ipate in the divine nature[i] and escape
[j]2Pe 2:18-20 the corruption in the world caused by
evil desires.[j]

5For this very reason, make every
effort to add to your faith goodness;
1:5 [k]Col 2:3 and to goodness, knowledge;[k] 6and to
knowledge, self-control;[l] and to self-
1:6 [l]Ac 24:25 control, perseverance; and to perse-
[m]ver 3 verance, godliness;[m] 7and to godliness,
brotherly kindness; and to brotherly
1:7 [n]1Th 3:12 kindness, love.[n] 8For if you possess these
qualities in increasing measure, they
1:8 will keep you from being ineffective
[o]Jn 15:2; Tit 3:14 and unproductive[o] in your knowledge
of our Lord Jesus Christ. 9But if anyone
1:9 does not have them, he is nearsighted
[p]1Jn 2:11 [q]Eph 5:26 and blind,[p] and has forgotten that he
has been cleansed from his past sins.[q]

10Therefore, my brothers, be all the
more eager to make your calling and
1:10 election sure. For if you do these things,
[r]2Pe 3:17 you will never fall,[r] 11and you will receive a rich welcome into the eternal
kingdom of our Lord and Savior Jesus
Christ.

Prophecy of Scripture

1:12 12So I will always remind you of these
[s]Php 3:1; 1Jn 2:21 things,[s] even though you know them
and are firmly established in the truth
you now have. 13I think it is right to
1:13 refresh your memory as long as I live
[t]2Co 5:1,4 in the tent of this body,[t] 14because I
1:14 know that I will soon put it aside,[u] as
[u]2Ti 4:6 our Lord Jesus Christ has made clear to
[v]Jn 21:18,19 me.[v] 15And I will make every effort to
1:15 see that after my departure[w] you will al-
[w]Lk 9:31 ways be able to remember these things.

16We did not follow cleverly invented stories when we told you about the
power and coming of our Lord Jesus
Christ, but we were eyewitnesses of his
majesty.[x] 17For he received honor and 1:16 [x]Mt 17:1-8
glory from God the Father when the
voice came to him from the Majestic
Glory, saying, "This is my Son, whom 1:17
I love; with him I am well pleased."[a][y] [y]Mt 3:17
18We ourselves heard this voice that
came from heaven when we were with 1:18
him on the sacred mountain.[z] [z]Mt 17:6

19And we have the word of the prophets made more certain, and you will do
well to pay attention to it, as to a light[a] 1:19 [a]Ps 119:105
shining in a dark place, until the day [b]Rev 22:16
dawns and the morning star[b] rises in
your hearts. 20Above all, you must understand that no prophecy of Scripture
came about by the prophet's own interpretation. 21For prophecy never had
its origin in the will of man, but men
spoke from God[c] as they were carried 1:21 [c]2Ti 3:16
along by the Holy Spirit.[d] [d]2Sa 23:2; Ac 1:16; 1Pe 1:11

False Teachers and Their Destruction

2 But there were also false prophets[e] 2:1 [e]Dt 13:1-3
among the people, just as there will [f]1Ti 4:1 [g]Jude 4
be false teachers among you.[f] They will [h]1Co 6:20
secretly introduce destructive heresies,
even denying the sovereign Lord[g] who
bought them[h]—bringing swift destruction on themselves. 2Many will follow
their shameful ways and will bring the
way of truth into disrepute. 3In their 2:3
greed these teachers will exploit you[i] [i]2Co 2:17;
with stories they have made up. Their 1Th 2:5
condemnation has long been hanging
over them, and their destruction has
not been sleeping.

4For if God did not spare angels
when they sinned, but sent them to
hell,[b] putting them into gloomy dun- 2:4
geons[c] to be held for judgment;[j] 5if he [j]Jude 6;
did not spare the ancient world[k] when Rev 20:1,2
he brought the flood on its ungodly 2:5
people, but protected Noah, a preacher [k]2Pe 3:6 [l]Heb 11:7;
of righteousness, and seven others;[l] 6if 1Pe 3:20
he condemned the cities of Sodom and
Gomorrah by burning them to ashes,[m] 2:6 [m]Ge 19:24,25
and made them an example[n] of what is [n]Nu 26:10;
going to happen to the ungodly; 7and Jude 7
if he rescued Lot,[o] a righteous man, 2:7 [o]Ge 19:16

[a] *17* Matt. 17:5; Mark 9:7; Luke 9:35 [b] *4* Greek *Tartarus* [c] *4* Some manuscripts *into chains of darkness*

WEEK 4

PATIENCE

1 DAY ONE

PATIENCE, THE ART OF WAITING ON GOD

Read 2 Peter 3:8–9

In his brief but significant letter, Peter reminds us that lack of patience is a frequent problem in our lives. God has a big clock, whose slow-moving hands tick off centuries. We have only small clocks, whose twirling second-hands sweep out the hurried seconds of our lives. Time! Peter says in this passage that God's clocks have no second-hands. His days are millennia.

A thousand years are but a day; with such a clock God never gets neurotic. There are no pressing deadlines in eternity. God rules; the ages dawdle in. No hurry—such impediments as speed and time limits are only for those who wear watches and keep appointment books.

In the stretch between our small, short lives and the never-ending life of the Great God, we fidget and grow impatient. The answer is for us to move in close to God and dwell in his everlasting light; only there will we find contentment with no impatience.

There is an art required in patience. The art consists in the alignment of our finite watches with God's eternal clock. We do not have unlimited time to accomplish his plan for our lives. Therefore we must, as the psalmist suggests, "number our days aright" (Psalm 90:12). What does he mean by this? We are never to forget that our lives are fleeting and—especially by the reckoning of God's great clock—coming to a swift end. Therefore, we must do two things: First, we must pace ourselves so that we do not live frantically, and then we must schedule the appointments of our lives so that every earthly moment yields some heavenly product.

MEMORIZE THIS WEEK

PSALM 37:3-4

Trust in the LORD and do good;
dwell in the land and enjoy safe pasture.
Delight yourself in the LORD
and he will give you the desires of your heart.

2 DAY TWO

PATIENCE AND THE PURPOSE OF GOD IN MY LIFE

Our purpose is patience. God calls us to wait. But notice that God equips us for our wait. We do not have to wait alone and unprepared. God gives us what we need to minister. Paul reminds us that God is faithful to those he calls. He will not ask something of us and then not give us what we need to accomplish that task. *Turn to 1 Corinthians 1:4–9, page 1357, for today's study.*

3 DAY THREE

PATIENCE AND MY RELATIONSHIP WITH CHRIST

The psalmist seems quite passive about finding himself in the most desperate of situations. In a slimy, mire-filled pit he waits. God acts. He is freed! Following his quicksand liberation is a life of praise. Our salvation experiences are no less miraculous. We look to Christ our Savior and rest in his calm because we know he is able to overcome everything to set us free. *Turn to Psalm 40:1–3, page 658, for today's study.*

4 DAY FOUR

PATIENCE AND MY SERVICE TO OTHERS

Do not oppress anyone who is still in the same spiritual state where you once were before Christ found you. Think back. Remember the days of hopelessness? Remember the hours of fear? Some still live with those burdens. Those who do not know Christ as Savior have a destiny so dreadful that Christians dare not add any criticism to the weight the lost already carry. *Turn to Exodus 23:9, page 94, for today's study.*

5 DAY FIVE

PATIENCE AND ITS PLACE IN MY PERSONAL WORSHIP

The key to the psalmist's personal power is that he has "stilled and quieted" his soul. The essence of arriving at a state of patience is the ability to take all our "inner noise," all our endless chatter, and order it to be quiet. A noisy inner life is offensive to our Christ, for he has entered the throne room of our hearts and expects that our focus be on him. *Turn to Psalm 131:1–3, page 720, for today's study.*

Week 5, Kindness As a Worldview, begins on page 1058, Amos 5:11–13.
To begin a topical study on the Fruit of the Spirit, Patience, turn to the Topical Index, page 1548.

who was distressed by the filthy lives of
2:7 p2Pe 3:17 lawless men[p] [8](for that righteous man,
living among them day after day, was
tormented in his righteous soul by the
lawless deeds he saw and heard)— [9]if
this is so, then the Lord knows how
to rescue godly men from trials[q] and
2:9 q1Co 10:13 to hold the unrighteous for the day
of judgment, while continuing their
2:10 punishment.[a] [10]This is especially true of
r2Pe 3:3 those who follow the corrupt desire[r] of
sJude 8 the sinful nature[b] and despise authority.

Bold and arrogant, these men are not
afraid to slander celestial beings;[s] [11]yet
even angels, although they are stronger
and more powerful, do not bring slanderous accusations against such beings
2:11 tJude 9 in the presence of the Lord.[t] [12]But these
men blaspheme in matters they do not
understand. They are like brute beasts,
creatures of instinct, born only to be
caught and destroyed, and like beasts
2:12 uJude 10 they too will perish.[u]

[13]They will be paid back with harm
for the harm they have done. Their
idea of pleasure is to carouse in broad
2:13 vRo 13:13 daylight.[v] They are blots and blemishes,
w1Co 11:20, 21; reveling in their pleasures while they
Jude 12 feast with you.[c][w] [14]With eyes full of
adultery, they never stop sinning; they
2:14 xver 18 seduce[x] the unstable; they are experts
yver 3 in greed[y]—an accursed brood![z] [15]They
zEph 2:3 have left the straight way and wan-
2:15 dered off to follow the way of Balaam[a]
aNu 22:4-20; Jude 11 son of Beor, who loved the wages of
wickedness. [16]But he was rebuked for
his wrongdoing by a donkey—a beast
without speech—who spoke with a
man's voice and restrained the prophet's
2:16 bNu 22:21-30 madness.[b]

[17]These men are springs without wa-
2:17 cJude 12 ter[c] and mists driven by a storm. Black-
dJude 13 est darkness is reserved for them.[d] [18]For
2:18 eJude 16 they mouth empty, boastful words[e] and,
by appealing to the lustful desires of
sinful human nature, they entice people
who are just escaping from those who
live in error. [19]They promise them freedom, while they themselves are slaves of
2:19 depravity—for a man is a slave to what-
fJn 8:34; Ro 6:16 ever has mastered him.[f] [20]If they have
escaped the corruption of the world by
2:20 g2Pe 1:2 knowing[g] our Lord and Savior Jesus
hMt 12:45 Christ and are again entangled in it and
overcome, they are worse off at the end
than they were at the beginning.[h] [21]It
would have been better for them not
to have known the way of righteousness, than to have known it and then
to turn their backs on the sacred com- 2:21
mand that was passed on to them.[i] [22]Of iHeb 6:4-6
them the proverbs are true: "A dog re-
turns to its vomit,"[d][j] and, "A sow that 2:22
is washed goes back to her wallowing in jPr 26:11
the mud."

The Day of the Lord

3 Dear friends, this is now my second
letter to you. I have written both of 3:1
them as reminders[k] to stimulate you to k2Pe 1:13
wholesome thinking. [2]I want you to recall the words spoken in the past by the
holy prophets and the command given
by our Lord and Savior through your
apostles.

[3]First of all, you must understand 3:3
that in the last days scoffers[l] will come, l1Ti 4:1 m2Pe 2:10;
scoffing and following their own evil Jude 18
desires.[m] [4]They will say, "Where is this 3:4
'coming' he promised?[n] Ever since our nIsa 5:19;
fathers died, everything goes on as it Eze 12:22; Mt 24:48
has since the beginning of creation."[o] oMk 10:6
[5]But they deliberately forget that long 3:5
ago by God's word[p] the heavens exist- pGe 1:6,9;
ed and the earth was formed out of wa- Heb 11:3
ter and by water.[q] [6]By these waters also qPs 24:2
the world of that time was deluged and
destroyed.[r] [7]By the same word the pres- 3:6 rGe 7:21,22
ent heavens and earth are reserved for 3:7
fire,[s] being kept for the day of judg- sver 10,12; 2Th 1:7
ment and destruction of ungodly men.

PATIENCE

THE DOUBT DELUSION

2 Peter 3:4

Where is the promise of his coming?

Stare down at the dial of your watch. Which of those small, black numbers will soon align with heaven's clock? Sing with those of the ages:

"He comes in power; rejoice, the hour of jubilee is here.
Lift up the cry, before we die, Our Savior will appear."

[8]But do not forget this one thing,
dear friends: With the Lord a day is like
a thousand years, and a thousand years 3:8
are like a day.[t] [9]The Lord is not slow in tPs 90:4

[a]9 Or *unrighteous for punishment until the day of judgment* [b]10 Or *the flesh* [c]13 Some manuscripts *in their love feasts* [d]22 Prov. 26:11

3:9 [u]Hab 2:3; Heb 10:37 [v]Ro 2:4 [w]1Ti 2:4

keeping his promise,[u] as some understand slowness. He is patient[v] with you, not wanting anyone to perish, but everyone to come to repentance.[w]

3:10 [x]Lk 12:39; 1Th 5:2 [y]Mt 24:35; Rev 21:1

[10]But the day of the Lord will come like a thief.[x] The heavens will disappear with a roar; the elements will be destroyed by fire, and the earth and everything in it will be laid bare.[a][y]

PATIENCE

GOD'S CLOCK

2 Peter 3:9

When will he come?
Look not to prophets bearing placards.
Trust not those blaring sermons that make the world tremble.
History will end when every soul who will be saved has been saved.
Evangelize if you would hurry heaven.

3:12 [z]1Co 1:7 [a]Ps 50:3 [b]ver 10

3:13 [c]Isa 65:17; 66:22; Rev 21:1

3:14 [d]1Th 3:13

[11]Since everything will be destroyed in this way, what kind of people ought you to be? You ought to live holy and godly lives [12]as you look forward[z] to the day of God and speed its coming.[b][a] That day will bring about the destruction of the heavens by fire, and the elements will melt in the heat.[b] [13]But in keeping with his promise we are looking forward to a new heaven and a new earth,[c] the home of righteousness.

[14]So then, dear friends, since you are looking forward to this, make every effort to be found spotless, blameless[d] and at peace with him. [15]Bear in mind

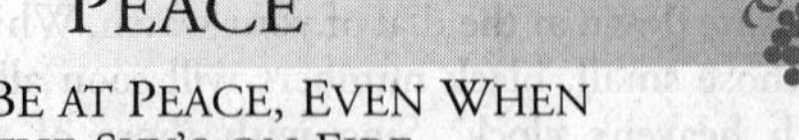

PEACE

BE AT PEACE, EVEN WHEN THE SKY'S ON FIRE

2 Peter 3:12

When the earth burns and the sky's on fire, Jesus will be back.

When the elements melt and molten manganese flows in the same riverbeds that once held God's forgiving stream, Jesus will be back.

Behind the last great wall of fire will come our King astride a steed.
We shall wave palm branches noncombustible
to welcome in the age nonflammable.

3:15 [e]Ro 2:4 [f]ver 9 [g]Eph 3:3

that our Lord's patience[e] means salvation,[f] just as our dear brother Paul also wrote you with the wisdom that God gave him.[g] [16]He writes the same way in all his letters, speaking in them of these matters. His letters contain some things

[a]*10* Some manuscripts *be burned up* [b]*12* Or *as you wait eagerly for the day of God to come*

DAY 4 FOUR

PEACE AND MY SERVICE TO OTHERS

2 Peter 3:14

Peter encourages us to make every effort to be "spotless, blameless and at peace." How would such a personal resolve improve our service to others? Such a resolution, if carried out, would keep people open to the ministry God has called us to perform.

Christians who live in inner conflict do not attract converts. Our own private battles often keep us from even seeing those around us who are in need. Indeed we must call these inner wars to peace before we can see either Christ or our world.

The truth is that people who are at peace make excellent ministers. Peacemakers have no personal agenda. They have no desire to use other people to further their own goals. Peacemakers create an attitude, a mood, an atmosphere that makes other people unafraid. In fact, the very appearance of a peacemaker into anyone's company says, "Don't be afraid. Forget your anxieties. Let's sit down and talk together." This effect reminds us of the appearance of angels in the Bible. Take, for instance, their appearance to the frightened shepherds in Luke's nativity account. The angels cry, "Do not be afraid!" It was probably a bit too late, for seeing an angel does tend to cause apoplexy. But the word of the angels is one that publishes peace.

If there is any ministry that must bring joy to God, it has to be that of giving the terrified a little security. We who love Christ are to reveal the peace he offers to a world of frightened children.

To begin a study on the topic of Peace and the Prince of Peace, turn to the home page on page 19.

that are hard to understand, which ignorant and unstable[h] people distort, as
they do the other Scriptures,[i] to their
own destruction.
17Therefore, dear friends, since you
already know this, be on your guard[j]
so that you may not be carried away by
the error[k] of lawless men and fall from
your secure position.[l] 18But grow in the
grace and knowledge of our Lord and
Savior Jesus Christ.[m] To him be glory
both now and forever! Amen.

3:16 [h]2Pe 2:14 [i]ver 2
3:17 [j]1Co 10:12
3:17 [k]2Pe 2:18 [l]Rev 2:5
3:18 [m]2Pe 1:11

1 JOHN

AUTHORSHIP AND DATE

John

Between A.D. 85 and A.D. 95

KEY THEMES

Gnosticism was the heresy that occasioned the necessity of this letter (and indeed flavored the apologetic tone of all of John's letters). John attacked the many facets of gnosticism. First, Gnostics believed that all matter was evil and all spirit was good. This led them to say that the body was evil.

Second, they believed that persons are not saved so much by grace as by knowledge (the Greek word *gnosis*—knowledge—became their label of faith). This view led to twisted beliefs about Christ: Some held that Christ only seemed to have a body, hence some of them were called Docetists (from *dokeo,* the Greek word for "to seem"). Others said that the Spirit of Christ became joined to his body at his baptism but left his body before the crucifixion.

Third, they held that—since the body and spirit were separate—it didn't matter much what the body did; this view, of course, led people to indulge in all sorts of immorality with no sense of guilt because they believed the body was by nature evil and unredeemable.

In 1 John, as well as in John's other writings, John attacked these false teachings even as he wrote to give believers an understanding of their salvation and its assurance.

FRUIT OF THE SPIRIT IN 1 JOHN

Love: A great theologian defined God as "the ground of all being." Another philosopher defined God as all that is more important than yourself. Psalm 19 defines God with glory. But 1 John 4:8 defines God in only three words: God is love. As protoplasm is the stuff of cell life, or as wood is the stuff of trees, so love is the stuff of God. If God, who is pure spirit (see John 4:24), could be dissected, the inside of him would be love and the outside of him would be love. Love is the skin of God, the viscera of God, the heart of God. Love is all of God, inside and outside, topside and downside, God in definition and fact.

Joy: John confessed to writing this letter to preach what he had seen and heard about Jesus. In the very writing of it, his joy was made complete (see 1:4). Why? Because there is joy in mouthing what our hearts will not keep quiet about. No virtue longs to "blab it all" quite so much as joy. Joy is not good at keeping secrets. It talks too loudly because it finds no release in whispering. Joy is a show-off who finds its exhibitionism sweet.

Peace: Peace is a simple matter of walking in the light (see 1:7). When you walk along with Jesus, you can never do so with clenched teeth. No one ever walked along the road to Emmaus thinking, "Grrrrr! I'm gonna get even with the world as soon as I wriggle out from under the lordship of Christ." Jesus himself makes our fellowship sweet wherever we go. We can never totally think darkly of the human race when we're anywhere within the proximity of his light.

Kindness: All of John's literature is marked by a single and wonderful diminishment: We are the children of God. To be a believer is not to welcome yourself to divine peerage, making yourself equal with the Father. No, God is the grand adult, the unequaled Father. We come into his presence small, needy and dependent. We are his children—and happy to be so (see 3:1). Our security depends upon God being bigger and wiser and more powerful than we are. Such children relish the word *Father*, remembering his kindness.

Faithfulness: "This is love for God: to obey his commands" (5:3). Love knows only a single yardstick: faithfulness. If you want to know how great love is, you have but to measure the size of the obedience it inspires.

Self-Control: "Whoever claims to live in him must walk as Jesus did" (2:6). And how did Jesus walk? He gave up every right to walk in his own selfish direction. He walked paths that pleased his Father, paths that led to destinations that made all of heaven rejoice. He denied all he might have had to complete all that God called him to do. He submitted himself to heaven. "No servant is greater than his master, nor is a messenger greater than the one who sent him" (John 13:16). Stay in charge of yourself, for only then will you be able to walk as Jesus did.

The Word of Life

1 That which was from the begin-
1:1 ning,[a] which we have heard, which
aJn 1:2 bJn 1:14; we have seen with our eyes,[b] which
2Pe 1:16 we have looked at and our hands have
cJn 20:27 touched[c]—this we proclaim concerning
the Word of life. 2The life appeared;[d]
1:2 dJn 1:1-4; we have seen it and testify to it, and we
1Ti 3:16 proclaim to you the eternal life, which
was with the Father and has appeared
to us. 3We proclaim to you what we
have seen and heard, so that you also
may have fellowship with us. And our
fellowship is with the Father and with
his Son, Jesus Christ.[e] 4We write this[f] 1:3 e1Co 1:9
to make our[a] joy complete.[g] 1:4 f1Jn 2:1 gJn 3:29

Walking in the Light

5This is the message we have heard[h] 1:5
from him and declare to you: God is h1Jn 3:11
light; in him there is no darkness at
all. 6If we claim to have fellowship with 1:6
him yet walk in the darkness,[i] we lie i2Co 6:14
and do not live by the truth.[j] 7But if we jJn 3:19-21
walk in the light, as he is in the light,
we have fellowship with one another,
and the blood of Jesus, his Son, purifies 1:7
us from all[b] sin.[k] kHeb 9:14; Rev 1:5
8If we claim to be without sin,[l] we
deceive ourselves and the truth is not in 1:8 lPr 20:9;
us.[m] 9If we confess our sins, he is faith- Jas 3:2
ful and just and will forgive us our sins[n] m1Jn 2:4
and purify us from all unrighteousness. 1:9 nPs 32:5; 51:2
10If we claim we have not sinned, we
make him out to be a liar[o] and his word 1:10 o1Jn 5:10
has no place in our lives.[p] p1Jn 2:14

DAY 5 FIVE

▸ Gentleness and Its Place in My Personal Worship

1 John 1:1–4

The sensate feeling in this passage is too real to be denied. John's books were written at a time when gnosticism was rampant. One of the chief gnostic heresies was docetism (from the Greek *dokeo*, "to seem"). Docetists taught that Jesus wasn't really a man, but that he only appeared or seemed to be so. In their view he was only a ghostly messiah who never really became flesh and blood.

John wanted to combat this notion. Notice the sensuous ways in which he speaks of how the church, himself included, had actually encountered the living Christ. Notice the very physical qualities of this Christ.

Christ, whom "we have heard";
Christ, whom "we have seen with our eyes";
Christ, whom "our hands have touched."

Here is Jesus whose gentle being is reported with gentle honesty. This brand of gentleness is powerful enough to blast the church into the church age.

Notice the epigram to the apostle's testimony. This hearable, seeable, touchable Christ is real; his demeanor is gentle and approachable, and he is the vitality of the victorious church.

Sunday by Sunday as we come to worship, we may have confidence that the Bible is true. John and the other witnesses have certified it. May we be as gentle in our ministry of certainty as John is in his reporting of it.

To begin a study on the topic of Gentleness, the Healing Touch of God, turn to the home page on page 1175.

▸ JOY

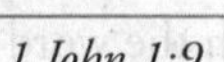

ALL

1 John 1:9

Shall I receive this blessing?
Yes, all!
If I confess the sins I can remember, will he forgive the sins I have forgotten?
Yes, all.
All my sins forgiven forever—remembered no more?
Yes, all.

2 My dear children,[q] I write this to 2:1
you so that you will not sin. But qver 12,13,28
if anybody does sin, we have one who rRo 8:34;
speaks to the Father in our defense[r]— Heb 7:25
Jesus Christ, the Righteous One. 2He is
the atoning sacrifice for our sins,[s] and 2:2 sRo 3:25
not only for ours but also for[c] the sins
of the whole world.
3We know that we have come to know
him if we obey his commands.[t] 4The 2:3 tJn 14:15
man who says, "I know him," but does
not do what he commands is a liar, and
the truth is not in him.[u] 5But if anyone 2:4 u1Jn 1:6,8

a4 Some manuscripts *your* b7 Or *every*
c2 Or *He is the one who turns aside God's wrath, taking away our sins, and not only ours but also*

2:5 [v]Jn 14:21,23 obeys his word,[v] God's love[a] is truly
[w]1Jn 4:12 made complete in him.[w] This is how we
know we are in him: 6Whoever claims
2:6 [x]Mt 11:29; to live in him must walk as Jesus did.[x]
1Pe 2:21 7Dear friends, I am not writing you
2:7 a new command but an old one, which
[y]1Jn 3:11,23; you have had since the beginning.[y] This
2Jn 5,6 old command is the message you have
heard. 8Yet I am writing you a new
2:8 [z]Jn 13:34 command;[z] its truth is seen in him and
[a]Ro 13:12 you, because the darkness is passing[a]
[b]Jn 1:9 [c]Eph 5:8; and the true light[b] is already shining.[c]
1Th 5:5 9Anyone who claims to be in the
light but hates his brother is still in the
2:10 darkness. 10Whoever loves his brother
[d]1Jn 3:14 lives in the light,[d] and there is nothing
in him[b] to make him stumble. 11But
whoever hates his brother is in the darkness and walks around in the darkness;
he does not know where he is going,
2:11 [e]Jn 12:35 because the darkness has blinded him.[e]

12I write to you, dear children,
because your sins have been
forgiven on account of his
name.
13I write to you, fathers,
because you have known him who
is from the beginning.
I write to you, young men,
because you have overcome the
2:13 [f]ver 14 evil one.[f]
I write to you, dear children,
because you have known the Father.
14I write to you, fathers,
because you have known him who
is from the beginning.
I write to you, young men,
2:14 [g]Eph 6:10 because you are strong,[g]
[h]Jn 5:38; 1Jn 1:10 and the word of God lives in you,[h]
[i]ver 13 and you have overcome the evil
one.[i]

Do Not Love the World

15Do not love the world or anything
2:15 [j]Ro 12:2 in the world.[j] If anyone loves the world,
[k]Jas 4:4 the love of the Father is not in him.[k]
16For everything in the world—the crav-
2:16 ings of sinful man,[l] the lust of his eyes[m]
[l]Ro 13:14 and the boasting of what he has and
[m]Pr 27:20 does—comes not from the Father but
from the world. 17The world and its de-
2:17 sires pass away,[n] but the man who does
[n]1Co 7:31 the will of God lives forever.

Warning Against Antichrists

18Dear children, this is the last hour;
and as you have heard that the anti-
christ is coming,[o] even now many an- 2:18 [o]ver 22;
tichrists have come.[p] This is how we 1Jn 4:3;
know it is the last hour. 19They went 2Jn 7 [p]1Jn 4:1
out from us,[q] but they did not really
belong to us. For if they had belonged 2:19 [q]Ac 20:30
to us, they would have remained with [r]1Co 11:19
us; but their going showed that none of
them belonged to us.[r]
20But you have an anointing[s] from 2:20 [s]2Co 1:21
the Holy One,[t] and all of you know [t]Mk 1:24
the truth.[c][u] 21I do not write to you be- [u]Jn 14:26
cause you do not know the truth, but 2:21 [v]2Pe 1:12;
because you do know it[v] and because Jude 5
no lie comes from the truth. 22Who
is the liar? It is the man who denies
that Jesus is the Christ. Such a man
is the antichrist—he denies the Father 2:22
and the Son.[w] 23No one who denies the [w]2Jn 7
Son has the Father; whoever acknowl-
edges the Son has the Father also.[x] 2:23 [x]Jn 8:19;
24See that what you have heard from 1Jn 4:15
the beginning remains in you. If it does,
you also will remain in the Son and 2:24
in the Father.[y] 25And this is what he [y]Jn 14:23
promised us—even eternal life.
26I am writing these things to you
about those who are trying to lead you
astray.[z] 27As for you, the anointing[a] you 2:26 [z]2Jn 7
received from him remains in you, and
you do not need anyone to teach you. 2:27 [a]ver 20
But as his anointing teaches you about
all things and as that anointing is real,
not counterfeit—just as it has taught
you, remain in him.

Children of God

28And now, dear children,[b] continue 2:28 [b]ver 1
in him, so that when he appears[c] we [c]1Jn 3:2
may be confident[d] and unashamed be- [d]1Jn 4:17
fore him at his coming.[e] [e]1Th 2:19
29If you know that he is righteous,[f] 2:29 [f]1Jn 3:7
you know that everyone who does what
is right has been born of him.

3 How great is the love[g] the Father 3:1 [g]Jn 3:16
has lavished on us, that we should [h]Jn 1:12
be called children of God![h] And that [i]Jn 16:3
is what we are! The reason the world
does not know us is that it did not
know him.[i] 2Dear friends, now we are
children of God, and what we will be
has not yet been made known. But we
know that when he appears,[d] we shall 3:2 [j]Ro 8:29;
be like him,[j] for we shall see him as 2Pe 1:4
he is.[k] 3Everyone who has this hope [k]2Co 3:18

[a]5 Or *word, love for God* [b]*10* Or *it* [c]*20* Some manuscripts *and you know all things* [d]*2* Or *when it is made known*

KINDNESS 

TO SEE IS TO BE

1 John 3:2

We who are the children of God are sustained by a vision. We have seen the Christ—high and lifted up—holy and in love with his Father. Like a child intrigued by an athlete, we cannot quit thinking about Jesus. The glory is ours, for we cannot help becoming what we cannot quit thinking about.

3:3 [l]2Co 7:1; in him purifies himself,[l] just as he is
2Pe 3:13,14 pure.
3:4 [4]Everyone who sins breaks the law;
[m]1Jn 5:17 in fact, sin is lawlessness.[m] [5]But you
know that he appeared so that he might
3:5 take away our sins. And in him is no
[n]2Co 5:21 sin.[n] [6]No one who lives in him keeps on
3:6 sinning.[o] No one who continues to sin
[o]ver 9 [p]3Jn 11 has either seen him[p] or known him.[q]
[q]1Jn 2:4 [7]Dear children,[r] do not let anyone
3:7 lead you astray.[s] He who does what is
[r]1Jn 2:1 right is righteous, just as he is righteous.[t]
[s]1Jn 2:26 [t]1Jn 2:29 [8]He who does what is sinful is of the
3:8 [u]Jn 8:44 devil,[u] because the devil has been sinning from the beginning. The reason
the Son of God appeared was to destroy the devil's work. [9]No one who is
3:9 [v]Jn 1:13 born of God[v] will continue to sin,[w] be-
[w]1Jn 5:18 [x]1Pe 1:23 cause God's seed[x] remains in him; he
cannot go on sinning, because he has
been born of God. [10]This is how we
know who the children of God are and
who the children of the devil are: Anyone who does not do what is right is
3:10 not a child of God; nor is anyone who
[y]1Jn 4:8 does not love[y] his brother.

Love One Another

3:11 [z]1Jn 1:5 [11]This is the message you heard[z] from
[a]Jn 13:34,35; the beginning: We should love one
2Jn 5 another.[a] [12]Do not be like Cain, who
3:12 belonged to the evil one and murdered
[b]Ge 4:8 his brother.[b] And why did he murder
him? Because his own actions were evil
and his brother's were righteous. [13]Do
3:13 not be surprised, my brothers, if the
[c]Jn 15:18,19; world hates you.[c] [14]We know that we
17:14 have passed from death to life,[d] because
3:14 [d]Jn 5:24 we love our brothers. Anyone who does
[e]1Jn 2:9 not love remains in death.[e] [15]Anyone
3:15 who hates his brother is a murderer,[f]
[f]Mt 5:21,22; and you know that no murderer has
Jn 8:44 [g]Gal 5:20,21 eternal life in him.[g]
[16]This is how we know what love is:

DAY 3 THREE 

PATIENCE AND MY RELATIONSHIP WITH CHRIST

1 John 3:2

We who follow Christ daily await the finished picture of ourselves. We shall be like him, and we shall appear as he appears. Such a prospect is enough to make our waiting glorious.

Francis Fenelon said long ago that patience itself works hand in hand with love, and that love in turn makes everything easy.

Jesus Christ said to all Christians without exception, "Let him who would be my disciple carry his cross, and follow me." The broad way leads to perdition. We must follow the narrow way which few enter. We must be born again, renounce ourselves, hate ourselves, become a child, be poor in spirit, weep to be comforted, and not be of the world which is cursed because of its scandals.

These truths frighten many people, and this is because they only know what religion exacts without knowing what it offers, and they ignore the spirit of love which makes everything easy. They do not know that it leads to the highest perfection by a feeling of peace and love which sweetens all the struggle.

Those who are wholly God's are always happy. They know by experience that the yoke of the Lord is "easy and light," that we find in him "rest for the soul," and that he comforts those who are weary and overburdened, as he himself has said.

To begin a study on the topic of Patience, the Wait for What God Promises, turn to the home page on page 1201.

Jesus Christ laid down his life for us.
And we ought to lay down our lives 3:16 [h]Jn 15:13
for our brothers.[h] [17]If anyone has material possessions and sees his brother 3:17
in need but has no pity on him,[i] how [i]Dt 15:7,8
can the love of God be in him?[j] [18]Dear [j]1Jn 4:20
children,[k] let us not love with words or 3:18 [k]1Jn 2:1
tongue but with actions and in truth.[l] [l]Eze 33:31;
[19]This then is how we know that we be- Ro 12:9
long to the truth, and how we set our
hearts at rest in his presence [20]whenev-

er our hearts condemn us. For God is
greater than our hearts, and he knows
everything.
[21]Dear friends, if our hearts do not
condemn us, we have confidence before
God[m] [22]and receive from him anything
we ask,[n] because we obey his commands
and do what pleases him.[o] [23]And this is
his command: to believe[p] in the name
of his Son, Jesus Christ, and to love one
another as he commanded us.[q] [24]Those
who obey his commands live in him,[r]
and he in them. And this is how we
know that he lives in us: We know it by
the Spirit he gave us.[s]

3:21 [m]1Jn 5:14
3:22 [n]Mt 7:7 [o]Jn 8:29
3:23 [p]Jn 6:29 [q]Jn 13:34
3:24 [r]1Jn 2:6 [s]1Jn 4:13

Test the Spirits

4 Dear friends, do not believe every
spirit, but test the spirits to see
whether they are from God, because
many false prophets have gone out into
the world.[t] [2]This is how you can recognize the Spirit of God: Every spirit
that acknowledges that Jesus Christ has
come in the flesh[u] is from God,[v] [3]but
every spirit that does not acknowledge
Jesus is not from God. This is the spirit of the antichrist,[w] which you have
heard is coming and even now is already in the world.
[4]You, dear children, are from God

4:1 [t]2Pe 2:1; 1Jn 2:18
4:2 [u]Jn 1:14; 1Jn 2:23 [v]1Co 12:3
4:3 [w]1Jn 2:22; 2Jn 7

JOHN

Unforsaking, Life-long Love (4:1–21)

Yesterday his love was there. Today it meets us at every moment of our need. Tomorrow he will wait for us at sunrise to walk us through the day. We are always kept by Christ's unforsaking, life-long love.

John is, presumably, often called the disciple whom Jesus loved (see John 13:23; 20:2). This is not to imply that Jesus thought less of the other disciples. We can only suspect that his love for John was his personal response to John's love for him. Christ's love for John was constant across many decades. But the constancy of Christ's love doesn't mean that John was perfect and deserved such love. John and his brother James once suggested they be allowed to call down fire on some inhospitable Samaritans (Luke 9:54). And another time they asked Jesus for seats of power and prestige in Jesus' kingdom (see Mark 10:35–37). Jesus nicknamed these brothers "Sons of Thunder" for their fiery flights of temper and longings for power (see 3:17).

But despite glaring weaknesses and mistakes, John was above all else a lover—a life-long lover. When he was an old man on the island of Patmos, his great love came to fruition. John saw Jesus—his great, unforsaking lover—one last time. He exulted in this love, proclaiming Jesus as the One "who loves us and has freed us from our sins by his blood, and has made us to be a kingdom and priests to serve his God and Father" (Revelation 1:5–6).

John continued to celebrate the extent of Christ's love in Revelation 1:9. In this verse John claimed to be so in love with Christ that his love could only be fully demonstrated by the persecution he was undergoing. "I, John, your brother and companion in the suffering and kingdom and patient endurance that are ours in Jesus, was on the island of Patmos because of the word of God and the testimony of Jesus." John loved Christ from the time he first met him, and he rejoiced in the gospel, the real reason for this love. John had been captured by Jesus' "crossly" love and was ever after a captive of the heart. John's love was stretched to the limits and ultimately grew so large that he defined God himself as love (1 John 4:8).

God's love was the air he breathed—air
that gave him his voice of praise.
God's love was the water he drank—
And the fire that warmed his existence in
icy storms of hateful persecution.
God's love was God himself—
Constant as the stars—
Warm as the sun—
Steady as the testimony John bore to his
world.

and have overcome them, because the
one who is in you[x] is greater than the
one who is in the world.[y] 5They are
from the world[z] and therefore speak
from the viewpoint of the world, and
the world listens to them. 6We are from
God, and whoever knows God listens
to us; but whoever is not from God
does not listen to us.[a] This is how we
recognize the Spirit[a] of truth[b] and the
spirit of falsehood.

God's Love and Ours

7Dear friends, let us love one another,[c]
for love comes from God. Everyone
who loves has been born of God and
knows God.[d] 8Whoever does not love
does not know God, because God is
love.[e] 9This is how God showed his love
among us: He sent his one and only
Son[b] into the world that we might live
through him.[f] 10This is love: not that
we loved God, but that he loved us[g]
and sent his Son as an atoning sacrifice for[c] our sins.[h] 11Dear friends, since
God so loved us,[i] we also ought to love
one another. 12No one has ever seen
God;[j] but if we love one another, God
lives in us and his love is made complete in us.[k]

13We know that we live in him and
he in us, because he has given us of his
Spirit.[l] 14And we have seen and testify[m]
that the Father has sent his Son to be
the Savior of the world.[n] 15If anyone
acknowledges that Jesus is the Son of
God,[o] God lives in him and he in God.
16And so we know and rely on the love
God has for us.

God is love.[p] Whoever lives in love
lives in God, and God in him.[q] 17In
this way, love is made complete[r] among
us so that we will have confidence on
the day of judgment, because in this
world we are like him. 18There is no
fear in love. But perfect love drives out
fear,[s] because fear has to do with punishment. The one who fears is not made
perfect in love.

19We love because he first loved us.[t]
20If anyone says, "I love God," yet hates
his brother,[u] he is a liar.[v] For anyone
who does not love his brother, whom
he has seen,[w] cannot love God, whom
he has not seen.[x] 21And he has given
us this command: Whoever loves God
must also love his brother.[y]

4:4 [x]Ro 8:31 [y]Jn 12:31
4:5 [z]Jn 15:19
4:6 [a]Jn 8:47 [b]Jn 14:17
4:7 [c]1Jn 3:11 [d]1Jn 2:4
4:8 [e]ver 7,16
4:9 [f]Jn 3:16,17; 1Jn 5:11
4:10 [g]Ro 5:8,10 [h]1Jn 2:2
4:11 [i]Jn 3:16
4:12 [j]Jn 1:18; 1Ti 6:16 [k]1Jn 2:5
4:13 [l]1Jn 3:24
4:14 [m]Jn 15:27 [n]Jn 3:17
4:15 [o]Ro 10:9
4:16 [p]ver 8 [q]1Jn 3:24
4:17 [r]1Jn 2:5
4:18 [s]Ro 8:15
4:19 [t]ver 10
4:20 [u]1Jn 2:9 [v]1Jn 2:4 [w]1Jn 3:17 [x]ver 12
4:21 [y]Mt 5:43

Faith in the Son of God

5 Everyone who believes that Jesus is
the Christ[z] is born of God,[a] and
everyone who loves the father loves
his child as well.[b] 2This is how we
know that we love the children of God:
by loving God and carrying out his
commands.[c] 3This is love for God: to
obey his commands. And his commands are not burdensome,[d] 4for everyone born of God overcomes[e] the world.
This is the victory that has overcome
the world, even our faith. 5Who is it
that overcomes the world? Only he who
believes that Jesus is the Son of God.

6This is the one who came by water
and blood[f]—Jesus Christ. He did not
come by water only, but by water and
blood. And it is the Spirit who testifies, because the Spirit is the truth.[g]
7For there are three[h] that testify: 8the[d]
Spirit, the water and the blood; and
the three are in agreement. 9We accept
man's testimony,[i] but God's testimony
is greater because it is the testimony
of God,[j] which he has given about his
Son. 10Anyone who believes in the Son
of God has this testimony in his heart.[k]
Anyone who does not believe God has
made him out to be a liar,[l] because
he has not believed the testimony God
has given about his Son. 11And this is
the testimony: God has given us eternal
life, and this life is in his Son.[m] 12He
who has the Son has life; he who does
not have the Son of God does not have
life.[n]

Concluding Remarks

13I write these things to you who believe in the name of the Son of God[o]
so that you may know that you have
eternal life.[p] 14This is the confidence[q]
we have in approaching God: that if
we ask anything according to his will,
he hears us.[r] 15And if we know that he
hears us—whatever we ask—we know[s]
that we have what we asked of him.

16If anyone sees his brother commit
a sin that does not lead to death, he

5:1 [z]1Jn 2:22 [a]Jn 1:13; 1Jn 2:23 [b]Jn 8:42
5:2 [c]Jn 14:15; 2Jn 6
5:3 [d]Mt 11:30
5:4 [e]Jn 16:33
5:6 [f]Jn 19:34 [g]Jn 14:17
5:7 [h]Mt 18:16
5:9 [i]Jn 5:34 [j]Mt 3:16,17; Jn 8:17,18
5:10 [k]Ro 8:16; Gal 4:6 [l]Jn 3:33
5:11 [m]Jn 1:4; 1Jn 2:25
5:12 [n]Jn 3:15,16,36
5:13 [o]1Jn 3:23 [p]Jn 20:31; 1Jn 1:1,2
5:14 [q]1Jn 3:21 [r]Mt 7:7
5:15 [s]ver 18,19,20

[a]*6* Or *spirit* [b]*9* Or *his only begotten Son* [c]*10* Or *as the one who would turn aside his wrath, taking away* [d]*7,8* Late manuscripts of the Vulgate *testify in heaven: the Father, the Word and the Holy Spirit, and these three are one. 8And there are three that testify on earth: the* (not found in any Greek manuscript before the sixteenth century)

5:16 [t]Jas 5:15 should pray and God will give him life.[t]
[u]Heb 6:4-6; 10:26 I refer to those whose sin does not lead
[v]Jer 7:16 to death.[u] There is a sin that leads to
death. I am not saying that he should
pray about that.[v] 17All wrongdoing is
5:17 [w]1Jn 3:4 sin,[w] and there is sin that does not lead
[x]1Jn 2:1 to death.[x]
18We know that anyone born of God
does not continue to sin; the one who
5:18 was born of God keeps him safe, and
[y]Jn 14:30 the evil one cannot harm him.[y] 19We
know that we are children of God,[z] and 5:19 [z]1Jn 4:6
that the whole world is under the con- [a]Gal 1:4
trol of the evil one.[a] 20We know also
that the Son of God has come and
has given us understanding,[b] so that we 5:20 [b]Lk 24:45
may know him who is true.[c] And we are [c]Jn 17:3
in him who is true—even in his Son Je- [d]ver 11
sus Christ. He is the true God and eternal life.[d]
21Dear children, keep yourselves from 5:21 [e]1Co 10:14;
idols.[e] 1Th 1:9

2 JOHN

Authorship and Date

John

Between A.D. 85 and A.D. 95

Key Themes

This brief book has two purposes: First, to warn the believers to watch out for false teachers (see vv. 1–11); and second, to warmly inform believers that John hoped to visit them so that his joy might be made full (see vv. 12–13). This book was written to a double audience: to "the chosen lady and her children" (either an unknown Christian woman and her family or a figurative designation for a specific church) and to "all who know the truth" (v. 1). It is a short but firm word on watchfulness and love.

Fruit of the Spirit in 2 John

Patience: Impatience spawns error. When we get in a hurry, we make mistakes in every area, including doctrine. "Anyone who runs ahead and does not continue in the teaching of Christ does not have God" (v. 9). Running ahead does, indeed, keep us from prizing the steady, unchanging Word of God. Patience is a word of grace that is offered like a benediction on all our study of truth.

1 The elder,[a]

To the chosen[b] lady and her children, whom I love in the truth—and
not I only, but also all who know the
truth[c]— 2 because of the truth,[d] which
lives in us[e] and will be with us forever:

3 Grace, mercy and peace from God
the Father and from Jesus Christ,[f] the
Father's Son, will be with us in truth
and love.

4 It has given me great joy to find
some of your children walking in the
truth,[g] just as the Father commanded
us. 5 And now, dear lady, I am not writing you a new command but one we
have had from the beginning.[h] I ask
that we love one another. 6 And this is
love:[i] that we walk in obedience to his
commands. As you have heard from the
beginning, his command is that you
walk in love.

1:1 [a]3Jn 1 [b]Ro 16:13 [c]Jn 8:32
1:2 [d]2Pe 1:12 [e]1Jn 1:8
1:3 [f]Ro 1:7
1:4 [g]3Jn 3,4
1:5 [h]1Jn 2:7; 3:11
1:6 [i]1Jn 2:5

7 Many deceivers, who do not acknowledge Jesus Christ[j] as coming in
the flesh, have gone out into the world.[k]
Any such person is the deceiver and the
antichrist.[l] 8 Watch out that you do not
lose what you have worked for, but that
you may be rewarded fully.[m] 9 Anyone
who runs ahead and does not continue
in the teaching of Christ does not have
God; whoever continues in the teaching has both the Father and the Son.[n]
10 If anyone comes to you and does
not bring this teaching, do not take
him into your house or welcome him.[o]
11 Anyone who welcomes him shares[p]
in his wicked work.

12 I have much to write to you, but I
do not want to use paper and ink. Instead, I hope to visit you and talk with
you face[q] to face, so that our joy may be
complete.

13 The children of your chosen[r] sister
send their greetings.

1:7 [j]1Jn 2:22; 4:2,3 [k]1Jn 4:1 [l]1Jn 2:18
1:8 [m]1Co 3:8
1:9 [n]1Jn 2:23
1:10 [o]Ro 16:17
1:11 [p]1Ti 5:22
1:12 [q]3Jn 13,14
1:13 [r]ver 1

3 JOHN

AUTHORSHIP AND DATE

John

Between A.D. 85 and A.D. 95

KEY THEMES

The book of 3 John was written by the same writer of all the books that bear his name: John the son of Zebedee. At the time of this writing, he was an old man—apparently the only apostle who was not martyred at a young age. John's main message is faithfulness. John once more holds up the standard of faith that we are to follow.

FRUIT OF THE SPIRIT IN 3 JOHN

Joy: John said that it gave him joy to hear the report that his disciples were standing true through the hard times (see v. 3). There is no greater joy than to know there are people who won't buckle under when things are tight, but are tougher than the times they are asked to live in. No one likes to see a martyr die, but in heaven joy erupts because someone was willing to take truth to its most costly end.

Self-Control: Self-control practices a short creed: "Do not imitate what is evil but what is good" (v. 11).

1:1 [a]2Jn 1 [1]The elder,[a]

To my dear friend Gaius, whom I
love in the truth.

[2]Dear friend, I pray that you may
enjoy good health and that all may go
well with you, even as your soul is get-
1:3 ting along well. [3]It gave me great joy
[b]ver 5,10 to have some brothers[b] come and tell
[c]2Jn 4 about your faithfulness to the truth and
how you continue to walk in the truth.[c]
1:4 [4]I have no greater joy than to hear that
[d]1Co 4:15; 1Jn 2:1 my children[d] are walking in the truth.
[5]Dear friend, you are faithful in what
1:5 you are doing for the brothers, even
[e]Ro 12:13; Heb 13:2 though they are strangers to you.[e] [6]They
have told the church about your love.
You will do well to send them on their
1:7 way in a manner worthy of God. [7]It
[f]Jn 15:21 was for the sake of the Name[f] that they
[g]Ac 20:33,35 went out, receiving no help from the
pagans.[g] [8]We ought therefore to show
hospitality to such men so that we may
work together for the truth.
[9]I wrote to the church, but Diotrephes, who loves to be first, will have
1:10 [h]2Jn 12 nothing to do with us. [10]So if I come,[h]
[i]ver 5 [j]Jn 9:22,34 I will call attention to what he is doing,
gossiping maliciously about us. Not sat-
isfied with that, he refuses to welcome
the brothers.[i] He also stops those who
want to do so and puts them out of the
church.[j]
1:11 [11]Dear friend, do not imitate what
[k]Ps 37:27 is evil but what is good.[k] Anyone who
[l]1Jn 2:29 [m]1Jn 3:6,9,10 does what is good is from God.[l] Anyone who does what is evil has not seen
1:12 God.[m] [12]Demetrius is well spoken of by
[n]1Ti 3:7 everyone[n]—and even by the truth it-
[o]Jn 21:24 self. We also speak well of him, and you
know that our testimony is true.[o]
[13]I have much to write you, but I do
not want to do so with pen and ink. [14]I
1:14 hope to see you soon, and we will talk
[p]2Jn 12 face to face.[p]

Peace to you. The friends here send
their greetings. Greet the friends there 1:14
by name.[q] [q]Jn 10:3

DAY 4 FOUR

▸ GENTLENESS AND MY SERVICE TO OTHERS

3 John 5–11

This letter is gentle—from a gentle pen, addressed to the gentle Gaius. Yet it throbs with purpose. Although this book is short, barely enough verses to contrast the gentility of Gaius with the cruelty of Diotrephes, it contains an excellent example of Christian tenderness in action. Consider the contrast between the two men mentioned in this book.

Gaius continues to walk in the truth (v. 3), leads others to walk in the truth (v. 4), and is gentle to strangers (v. 5). Gaius is the very picture of a winning gentleness that serves others and draws them to Christ.

Now consider Diotrephes (vv. 10–11). He is ambitious and craves power. He is a malicious gossip. He is inhospitable, even to good people, and is hasty in throwing people out of the church.

The writer of this brief letter gives us a positive role model in Gaius. Gentleness reaches out to others. It does not reside undisturbed within a person. Gentleness gets its feet wet. Gentleness gets its hands dirty. The hard work of ministering is often done by the most compassionate of souls.

We can imitate the gentle life by working for Christ and his kingdom. What a great reminder for the church—those who minister with gentleness will win others and please God.

To begin a study on the topic of Gentleness, a Way of Winning Others to Christ, turn to the home page on page 1303.

JUDE

Authorship and Date

Jude, the brother of Jesus

Probably c. A.D. 65

Key Themes

The themes of this book are very similar to those of 2 Peter. This book was likely written before 2 Peter, and therefore it seems that Peter picked up and amplified the themes first addressed here in the book of Jude. It was not uncommon for ancient writers to quote other writers whom they felt paralleled their own beliefs, as in the Synoptic Gospels. The themes of the book are these:

1. All believers should contend for the faith once entrusted to the saints (see v. 3).
2. Steer clear of falsehood and immorality (see vv. 4–16).
3. Stand true and build yourselves up in the faith during these horrible last days (see vv. 17–23).
4. A benediction for all time (see vv. 24–25).

Jude is a powerful study in the triumph of the gospel over falsehood. It contains the strongest of challenges to live up to the faith with which we have been entrusted.

Fruit of the Spirit in Jude

Love: Jude said that it was not the food that corrupted the believers at church dinners, rather the false teachers were the blemishes on their love feasts (see v. 12). They, like Balaam in the Old Testament, were masters of devious compromise (see v. 11). They took a beautiful meal and turned it into shameful indulgence and blasphemed the word love. Love ceases being love when it becomes self-love. But self-love was the only kind of love these false teachers knew.

Patience: Jude's advice was that we should not hurry as we build ourselves up, but we should wait for the mercy of Christ. Christ will put the final, eternal touches of mercy on our lives (see vv. 20–21). Why, in reality, would we want to "hurry up and try to be like Jesus"? The truth is that the building of the holy life requires a lifetime of emulation. To look like Jesus does not require a seven-step, hurry-up course. It requires the patient spending of our days.

Goodness: Goodness is on the way. At the end of each day's moral effort, we may sigh and say, "How poorly did I live my faith today." But when God is completely finished with us, we will be so much like Jesus that we will be indistinguishable from him. Someday, God our Savior, who is able to keep us from falling, will present us faultless before his throne (see v. 24). Then the goodness that eluded us all our lives will be worn like a cloak, thrown across our shoulders by the sinless Son of God. In reality, indwelling goodness never is a struggle for us. Jesus won it on the cross and is holding it, like a butler holds the cloak of a guest, readying it for its final presentation at our homecoming.

1Jude,[a] a servant of Jesus Christ and a brother of James,

To those who have been called,[b] who are loved by God the Father and kept by[a] Jesus Christ:[c]

2Mercy, peace and love be yours in abundance.[d]

The Sin and Doom of Godless Men

3Dear friends, although I was very eager to write to you about the salvation we share,[e] I felt I had to write and urge you to contend[f] for the faith that was once for all entrusted to the saints. 4For certain men whose condemnation was written about[b] long ago have secretly slipped in among you.[g] They are godless men, who change the grace of our God into a license for immorality and deny Jesus Christ our only Sovereign and Lord.[h]

5Though you already know all this, I want to remind you that the Lord[c] delivered his people out of Egypt, but later destroyed those who did not believe.[i] 6And the angels who did not keep their positions of authority but abandoned their own home—these he has kept in darkness, bound with everlasting chains for judgment on the great Day.[j] 7In a similar way, Sodom and Gomorrah and the surrounding towns[k] gave themselves up to sexual immorality and perversion. They serve as an example of those who suffer the punishment of eternal fire.[l]

8In the very same way, these dreamers pollute their own bodies, reject authority and slander celestial beings.[m] 9But even the archangel Michael,[n] when he was disputing with the devil about the body of Moses, did not dare to bring a slanderous accusation against him, but said, "The Lord rebuke you!"[o] 10Yet these men speak abusively against whatever they do not understand; and what things they do understand by instinct, like unreasoning animals—these are the very things that destroy them.[p]

11Woe to them! They have taken the way of Cain;[q] they have rushed for profit into Balaam's error;[r] they have been destroyed in Korah's rebellion.[s]

12These men are blemishes at your love feasts,[t] eating with you without the slightest qualm—shepherds who feed only themselves. They are clouds without rain,[u] blown along by the wind;[v] autumn trees, without fruit and uprooted[w]—twice dead. 13They are wild waves of the sea,[x] foaming up their shame;[y] wandering stars, for whom blackest darkness has been reserved forever.[z]

14Enoch,[a] the seventh from Adam, prophesied about these men: "See, the Lord is coming with thousands upon thousands of his holy ones[b] 15to judge[c] everyone, and to convict all the ungodly of all the ungodly acts they have done in the ungodly way, and of all the harsh words ungodly sinners have spoken against him."[d] 16These men are grumblers and faultfinders; they follow their own evil desires; they boast[e] about themselves and flatter others for their own advantage.

A Call to Persevere

17But, dear friends, remember what the apostles of our Lord Jesus Christ foretold.[f] 18They said to you, "In the last times[g] there will be scoffers who will follow their own ungodly desires."[h] 19These are the men who divide you, who follow mere natural instincts and do not have the Spirit.[i]

20But you, dear friends, build yourselves up[j] in your most holy faith and pray in the Holy Spirit.[k] 21Keep yourselves in God's love as you wait[l] for the mercy of our Lord Jesus Christ to bring you to eternal life.

22Be merciful to those who doubt; 23snatch others from the fire and save them;[m] to others show mercy, mixed

1:1 [a]Mt 13:55; Ac 1:13 [b]Ro 1:6,7 [c]Jn 17:12
1:2 [d]2Pe 1:2
1:3 [e]Tit 1:4 [f]1Ti 6:12
1:4 [g]Gal 2:4 [h]Tit 1:16; 2Pe 2:1
1:5 [i]Nu 14:29; Ps 106:26
1:6 [j]2Pe 2:4,9
1:7 [k]Dt 29:23 [l]2Pe 2:6
1:8 [m]2Pe 2:10
1:9 [n]Da 10:13,21 [o]Zec 3:2
1:10 [p]2Pe 2:12
1:11 [q]Ge 4:3-8; 1Jn 3:12 [r]2Pe 2:15 [s]Nu 16:1-3, 31-35
1:12 [t]2Pe 2:13; 1Co 11:20-22
1:12 [u]Pr 25:14; 2Pe 2:17 [v]Eph 4:14 [w]Mt 15:13
1:13 [x]Isa 57:20 [y]Php 3:19 [z]2Pe 2:17
1:14 [a]Ge 5:18,21-24 [b]Dt 33:2; Da 7:10
1:15 [c]2Pe 2:6-9 [d]1Ti 1:9
1:16 [e]2Pe 2:18
1:17 [f]2Pe 3:2
1:18 [g]1Ti 4:1 [h]2Pe 2:1
1:19 [i]1Co 2:14,15
1:20 [j]Col 2:7 [k]Eph 6:18
1:21 [l]Tit 2:13; 2Pe 3:12
1:23 [m]Am 4:11; Zec 3:2-5

[a] *1* Or *for;* or *in* [b] *4* Or *men who were marked out for condemnation* [c] *5* Some early manuscripts *Jesus*

PEACE

PEACE FROM HIM WHO KEEPS US FROM FALLING

Jude 24

We must be like a child, wisely clinging to our Father's hand as we walk the ledges of desperation.

"Come play along the precipice.
Don't worry that the cliff is steep.
The little flowers along the brink
Are daisies but their roots grow deep."
Cling! Cling! Cling!

with fear—hating even the clothing
1:23 [n]Rev 3:4 stained by corrupted flesh.[n]

Doxology

1:24 [o]Ro 16:25 24 To him who is able[o] to keep you
from falling and to present you before
his glorious presence[p] without fault[q]
and with great joy— 25 to the only God[r]
our Savior be glory, majesty, power
and authority, through Jesus Christ our
Lord, before all ages, now and forevermore![s] Amen.[t]

1:24 [p]2Co 4:14 [q]Col 1:22

1:25 [r]Jn 5:44; 1Ti 1:17 [s]Heb 13:8 [t]Ro 11:36

REVELATION

AUTHORSHIP AND DATE

John the son of Zebedee

c. A.D. 95

KEY THEMES

After a brief introduction (see ch. 1), Revelation falls rather naturally into two broad divisions: the letters to the seven churches (see 2:1—3:22) and the account of the various visions regarding events that lead to the end of time (see 4:1—22:21). The doxologies of the book are among the most notable in the Bible, and they have worked their way into such beautiful works of art as Handel's Messiah. The issues of praise and glory come bound together with a sense of judgment and finality. In spite of its stern pictures of the end of all flesh, the book abounds with the pathos of those who suffer unjustly and those who will find a strong recompense for all their hurts in the justice of God. The images of the reign of Christ paint a picture of final union with Christ in the most enticing of colors. The new Jerusalem and the new heaven and the new earth are portrayed as beautiful places where every tear is wiped away and where joy is forever the business of the saints.

FRUIT OF THE SPIRIT IN REVELATION

Love: Revelation 2:2–4 is a weeping bit of counsel to the church of Ephesus, which had lost its first love. Nothing is so exciting as first love. It thrills and changes our entire being. Yet how quickly what once thrilled us can become "business as usual." Sheldon Van Auken spoke of the dangers of a "creeping separateness" in love. Love is a flame that is extinguished by neglect. John told the Ephesians, "Don't let it happen to you!"

Joy: Revelation 5:2 is a sad lament: "Who is worthy to break the seals and open the scroll?" None were found. Then the Lamb of God came into the scene and the elders proclaimed him worthy; all of heaven erupted with joy as the caroling angels exulted: "You are worthy to take the scroll and to open its seals" (5:9).

Peace: The new Jerusalem will be a place of peace—there will be no wars. But peace is more than the absence of war, it is the presence of Christ. Here in this city is a river, clear as crystal. On each side of the river is the tree of life. Its leaves are for the healing of the nations (see 22:2). In such a world we will be forever united with Christ, and that union is the very definition of peace.

Patience: John is given a vision that begs us to be patient and wait. But the waiting is hard. It is hard because Christ's return will not occur at our bidding. But, wait! "Look, he is coming in the clouds, and every eye will see him" (1:7).

Kindness: Under the altar were the martyrs (see 6:9). These witnesses had been slain for their faithfulness to the testimony they bore. But their humility in dying had not gone unnoticed. God will, in time, reward the meek with flamboyant, outrageous justice. One senses in this passage that those under the altar gave kindness to the world, only to reap its abuse. But kindness, in time, always wins over abuse.

Goodness: What metaphor could possibly describe complete and pure goodness? Goodness can only be pictured as something wedding-white, holy and without blemish. This ultimate goodness is a goodness to end all goodness: "For the wedding of the Lamb has come, and his bride has made herself ready. Fine linen, bright and clean, was given to her to wear" (19:7–8).

Faithfulness: Faithfulness will have its great reward. Those who never stop believing and acting on the name of Christ will find that God rewards, at last, what they thought had gone unnoticed. For indeed he says to all, as he said to those in Smyrna, "Be faithful, even to the point of death, and I will give you the crown of life" (2:10).

Gentleness: The gentle Jesus of the Gospels is now in armor, and his fury will trample out the vintage where the grapes of wrath are stored. Gentleness is never God-gone-soft. Gentleness must allow the Christ who rode the donkey into Jerusalem to come in splendor. He will ride the splitting skies of judgment. See this gentle Jesus now: "His head and hair [are] white like wool . . . his eyes [are] like blazing fire . . . his voice [is] like the sound of rushing waters . . . and out of his mouth [comes] a sharp double-edged sword" (1:14–16).

Self-Control: Revelation is a book of great contrasts. It sets meek martyrs (see ch. 6) alongside Jezebel, the self-indulgent prophetess (see 2:20). There are many who go to church but don't live out their Christian principles. These persons always defame the church as a place of hypocrisy and shame. Jezebel represents sexual indulgence and idolatry, standing in the midst of the committed people of God who prize self-control and holiness.

Prologue

1 The revelation of Jesus Christ,
which God gave him to show his
servants what must soon take place. He
1:1 [a]Rev 22:16 made it known by sending his angel[a]
to his servant John, 2 who testifies to
everything he saw—that is, the word
of God and the testimony of Jesus
1:2 [b]1Co 1:6; Rev 12:17 Christ.[b] 3 Blessed is the one who reads
the words of this prophecy, and blessed
are those who hear it and take to heart
1:3 [c]Lk 11:28 what is written in it,[c] because the time
is near.

Greetings and Doxology

4 John,

To the seven churches in the province of Asia:

Grace and peace to you from him
who is, and who was, and who is to
1:4 [d]Rev 3:1; 4:5 come, and from the seven spirits[a][d] before his throne, 5 and from Jesus Christ,
1:5 [e]Rev 3:14 [f]Col 1:18 [g]Rev 17:14 who is the faithful witness,[e] the firstborn from the dead,[f] and the ruler of
the kings of the earth.[g]

To him who loves us and has freed
us from our sins by his blood, 6 and has
1:6 [h]1Pe 2:5 [i]Ro 11:36 made us to be a kingdom and priests[h]
to serve his God and Father—to him
be glory and power for ever and ever!
Amen.[i]

7 Look, he is coming with the
1:7 [j]Da 7:13 clouds,[j]
and every eye will see him,
even those who pierced him;
and all the peoples of the earth
will mourn[k] because of him. 1:7 [k]Zec 12:10
So shall it be! Amen.

8 "I am the Alpha and the Omega,"[l] 1:8 [l]Rev 21:6 [m]Rev 4:8
says the Lord God, "who is, and who
was, and who is to come, the
Almighty."[m]

[a]4 Or *the sevenfold Spirit*

FAITHFULNESS

THE BOOKENDS OF HISTORY

Revelation 1:8

I am Jesus,
Faithful and true through all time!
When chaos yearned to be, I was there.
When primeval oceans fell on empty coasts, I was there.
When Adam stood naked, proud in Eden, I was there.
I am Jesus.
I am before clocks and after calendars.
I am the start and finish of time;
I am the once upon a time and the happily ever after;
I am the bookends of history.

DAY 3 THREE

JOY AND MY RELATIONSHIP WITH CHRIST

Revelation 1:12–16

The mood of the book of Revelation is a curious intermingling of joy and apocalyptic portent. The reigning Christ is presented in a tale of futurism and conquering saints. Yet the songs of joy that arise from the book are truly inspiring.

Consider the traditional hymn "Holy, Holy, Holy":
"Holy, Holy, Holy . . . Lord God Almighty"
(see Revelation 4:8).

Consider Handel's "Messiah":
"The kingdom of the world has become
the kingdom of our Lord and of his Christ,
and he will reign for ever and ever"
(see Revelation 11:15).

And yet another Handel text:
"Hallelujah!
For the Lord God Almighty reigns"
(see Revelation 19:6).

Consider, also, Julia Ward Howe's "Battle Hymn of the Republic":
"Mine eyes have seen the glory of the
coming of the Lord;
He is trampling out the vintage where the
grapes of wrath are stored; . . .
He treads the winepress of the fury
of Almighty God"
(see Revelation 19:15).

The great book of Revelation focuses on the joy that emanates from a rich, deep encounter with God.

To begin a study on the topic of Joy, Focusing on a Higher Reality, turn to the home page on page 413.

One Like a Son of Man

9I, John, your brother and companion in the suffering[n] and kingdom and patient endurance[o] that are ours in Jesus, was on the island of Patmos because of the word of God and the testimony of Jesus. 10On the Lord's Day I was in the Spirit,[p] and I heard behind me a loud voice like a trumpet,[q] 11which said: "Write on a scroll what you see and send it to the seven churches:[r] to Ephesus, Smyrna, Pergamum, Thyatira, Sardis,[s] Philadelphia and Laodicea."

12I turned around to see the voice that was speaking to me. And when I turned I saw seven golden lampstands,[t] 13and among the lampstands was someone "like a son of man,"[a][u] dressed in a robe reaching down to his feet and with a golden sash around his chest.[v] 14His head and hair were white like wool, as white as snow, and his eyes were like blazing fire.[w] 15His feet were like bronze glowing in a furnace,[x] and his voice was like the sound of rushing waters.[y] 16In his right hand he held seven stars,[z] and out of his mouth came a sharp double-edged sword.[a] His face was like the sun shining in all its brilliance.

17When I saw him, I fell at his feet[b] as though dead. Then he placed his right hand on me and said: "Do not be afraid. I am the First and the Last.[c] 18I am the Living One; I was dead,[d] and behold I am alive for ever and ever![e] And I hold the keys of death and Hades.[f]

19"Write, therefore, what you have seen, what is now and what will take place later. 20The mystery of the seven stars that you saw in my right hand and of the seven golden lampstands[g] is this: The seven stars are the angels[b] of the seven churches,[h] and the seven lampstands are the seven churches.[i]

1:9 [n]Php 4:14 [o]2Ti 2:12
1:10 [p]Rev 4:2 [q]Rev 4:1
1:11 [r]ver 4,20 [s]Rev 3:1
1:12 [t]Ex 25:31-40; Zec 4:2
1:13 [u]Eze 1:26; Da 7:13; 10:16 [v]Da 10:5; Rev 15:6
1:14 [w]Da 7:9; 10:6; Rev 19:12
1:15 [x]Da 10:6 [y]Eze 43:2; Rev 14:2
1:16 [z]Rev 2:1; 3:1 [a]Isa 49:2; Heb 4:12; Rev 2:12,16
1:17 [b]Eze 1:28; Da 8:17,18 [c]Isa 41:4; 44:6; 48:12; Rev 22:13
1:18 [d]Ro 6:9 [e]Rev 4:9,10 [f]Rev 20:1
1:20 [g]Zec 4:2 [h]ver 4,11 [i]Mt 5:14,15

To the Church in Ephesus

2 "To the angel[c] of the church in Ephesus write:

These are the words of him who holds the seven stars in his right hand[j] and walks among the seven golden lampstands:[k] 2I know your deeds,[l] your hard work and your perseverance. I know that you cannot tolerate wicked men, that you have tested[m] those who claim to be apostles but are not, and have found them false.[n] 3You have persevered and have endured hardships for my name,[o] and have not grown weary.

4Yet I hold this against you: You have forsaken your first love.[p] 5Remember the height from which you have fallen! Repent[q] and do the things you did at first. If you do not repent, I will come to you and remove your lampstand[r] from its place. 6But you have this in your favor: You hate the practices of the Nicolaitans,[s] which I also hate.

7He who has an ear, let him hear[t] what the Spirit says to the churches. To him who overcomes, I will give the right to eat from the tree of life,[u] which is in the paradise[v] of God.

To the Church in Smyrna

8"To the angel of the church in Smyrna[w] write:

These are the words of him who is the First and the Last,[x] who died and came to life again.[y] 9I know your afflictions and your poverty—yet you are rich![z] I know the slander of those who say they are Jews and are not,[a] but are a synagogue of Satan.[b] 10Do not be afraid of what you are about to suffer. I tell you, the devil will put some of you in prison to test you,[c] and you will suffer persecution for ten days.[d] Be faithful,[e] even to the point of death, and I will give you the crown of life.

11He who has an ear, let him hear what the Spirit says to the churches. He who overcomes will not be hurt at all by the second death.[f]

To the Church in Pergamum

12"To the angel of the church in Pergamum[g] write:

These are the words of him who has the sharp, double-edged sword.[h] 13I know where you live—

2:1 [j]Rev 1:16 [k]Rev 1:12,13
2:2 [l]Rev 3:1,8,15 [m]1Jn 4:1 [n]2Co 11:13
2:3 [o]Jn 15:21
2:4 [p]Mt 24:12
2:5 [q]ver 16,22 [r]Rev 1:20
2:6 [s]ver 15
2:7 [t]Mt 11:15; Rev 3:6,13,22 [u]Ge 2:9; Rev 22:2, 14,19 [v]Lk 23:43
2:8 [w]Rev 1:11 [x]Rev 1:17 [y]Rev 1:18
2:9 [z]Jas 2:5 [a]Rev 3:9 [b]Mt 4:10
2:10 [c]Rev 3:10 [d]Da 1:12,14 [e]ver 13
2:11 [f]Rev 20:6,14; 21:8
2:12 [g]Rev 1:11 [h]Rev 1:16

[a]*13* Daniel 7:13 [b]*20* Or *messengers*
[c]*1* Or *messenger*; also in verses 8, 12 and 18

where Satan has his throne. Yet you remain true to my name. You did not renounce your faith in me,[i] even in the days of Antipas, my faithful witness, who was put to death in your city—where Satan lives.[j]

14Nevertheless, I have a few things against you:[k] You have people there who hold to the teaching of Balaam,[l] who taught Balak to entice the Israelites to sin by eating food sacrificed to idols and by committing sexual immorality.[m] 15Likewise you also have those who hold to the teaching of the Nicolaitans.[n] 16Repent therefore! Otherwise, I will soon come to you and will fight against them with the sword of my mouth.[o]

17He who has an ear, let him hear what the Spirit says to the churches. To him who overcomes, I will give some of the hidden manna.[p] I will also give him a white stone with a new name[q] written on it, known only to him who receives it.[r]

To the Church in Thyatira

18"To the angel of the church in Thyatira[s] write:

These are the words of the Son of God, whose eyes are like blazing fire and whose feet are like burnished bronze.[t] 19I know your deeds,[u] your love and faith, your service and perseverance, and that you are now doing more than you did at first.

20Nevertheless, I have this against you: You tolerate that woman Jezebel,[v] who calls herself a prophetess. By her teaching she misleads my servants into sexual immorality and the eating of food sacrificed to idols. 21I have given her time[w] to repent of her immorality, but she is unwilling.[x] 22So I will cast her on a bed of suffering, and I will make those who commit adultery[y] with her suffer intensely, unless they repent of her ways. 23I will strike her children dead. Then all the churches will know that I am he who searches hearts and minds,[z] and I will repay each of you according to your deeds. 24Now I say to the rest of you in Thyatira, to you who do not hold to her teaching and have not learned Satan's so-called deep secrets (I will not impose any other burden on you):[a] 25Only hold on to what you have[b] until I come.

26To him who overcomes and

2:13 [i]Rev 14:12 [j]ver 9,24
2:14 [k]ver 20 [l]2Pe 2:15 [m]1Co 6:13
2:15 [n]ver 6
2:16 [o]2Th 2:8; Rev 1:16
2:17 [p]Jn 6:49,50 [q]Isa 62:2 [r]Rev 19:12
2:18 [s]Rev 1:11 [t]Rev 1:14,15
2:19 [u]ver 2
2:20 [v]1Ki 16:31; 21:25; 2Ki 9:7
2:21 [w]Ro 2:4 [x]Rev 9:20
2:22 [y]Rev 17:2; 18:9
2:23 [z]1Sa 16:7; Jer 11:20; Ac 1:24; Ro 8:27
2:24 [a]Ac 15:28
2:25 [b]Rev 3:11

DAY 5 FIVE

▸ Faithfulness and Its Place in My Personal Worship

Revelation 2:10

"Be faithful, even to the point of death, and I will give you the crown of life," said the risen Christ to the church at Smyrna. Will we ever tire of the testimonies of martyrs who affirmed this truth? Consider the expressions of this philosophy from the pens of those who testify:

Remember Dietrich Bonhoeffer's translation of Luke 9:23: "Take up [your] cross and follow me"? Bonhoeffer said that what this invitation really meant was, "Come with me and die."

Or think of Jim Elliot, whose philosophy was, "He is no fool who gives what he cannot keep to gain what he cannot lose."

Or remember Lottie Moon, whose epitaph reads, "Faithful unto death."

Or Martin Luther King, whose tombstone reads, "Let justice roll down like water and righteousness as an ever-flowing stream (Amos 5:24)."

Faithfulness is our spiritual worship that calls us all to answer the question posed by the familiar, old hymn:

Must I be carried through the skies
On flowery beds of ease
While others fought to win the prize
And sailed through bloody seas?

Faithfulness is the currency of martyrs, and when they have spent it all, they will then spend their very blood. They know only one word that brings terror. It is the word *disobedience.*

To begin a study on the topic of Faithfulness, the Habit of Spiritual Dependency, turn to the home page on page 260.

does my will to the end, I will give
2:26 [c]Ps 2:8; Rev 3:21 authority over the nations[c]—
27'He will rule them with an iron
2:27 [d]Rev 12:5 [e]Isa 30:14; Jer 19:11 scepter;[d]
he will dash them to
pieces like pottery'[a][e]—
just as I have received authority
from my Father. 28I will also give
2:28 [f]Rev 22:16 him the morning star.[f] 29He who
has an ear, let him hear[g] what the
2:29 [g]ver 7 Spirit says to the churches.

To the Church in Sardis

3 "To the angel[b] of the church in
Sardis write:

These are the words of him who
3:1 [h]Rev 1:4 [i]Rev 1:16 [j]Rev 2:2 [k]1Ti 5:6 holds the seven spirits[c][h] of God
and the seven stars.[i] I know your
deeds;[j] you have a reputation of being alive, but you are dead.[k] 2Wake
up! Strengthen what remains and is
about to die, for I have not found
your deeds complete in the sight
of my God. 3Remember, therefore,
what you have received and heard;
3:3 [l]Rev 2:5 [m]2Pe 3:10 obey it, and repent.[l] But if you do
not wake up, I will come like a
thief,[m] and you will not know at
what time I will come to you.
4Yet you have a few people in
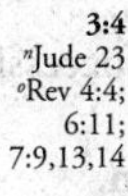
3:4 [n]Jude 23 [o]Rev 4:4; 6:11; 7:9,13,14 Sardis who have not soiled their
clothes.[n] They will walk with me,
dressed in white,[o] for they are worthy. 5He who overcomes will, like
them, be dressed in white. I will
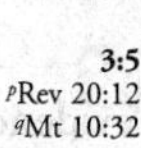
3:5 [p]Rev 20:12 [q]Mt 10:32 never blot out his name from the
book of life,[p] but will acknowledge
his name before my Father[q] and
his angels. 6He who has an ear, let
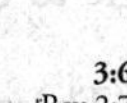
3:6 [r]Rev 2:7 him hear[r] what the Spirit says to
the churches.

SELF-CONTROL

DRESSED FOR THE LAST MILE

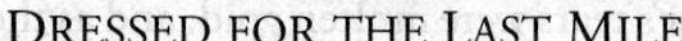

Revelation 3:4

Heaven loves white.
Its gates swing wide at such a noble color.

To the Church in Philadelphia

7"To the angel of the church in Phila-
3:7 [s]Rev 1:11 [t]1Jn 5:20 [u]Isa 22:22; Mt 16:19 delphia[s] write:

These are the words of him who
is holy and true,[t] who holds the
key of David.[u] What he opens no

DAY 3 THREE

PATIENCE AND MY RELATIONSHIP WITH CHRIST

Revelation 3:10

This passage, like the one in 1 Peter, makes the point that those who endure hurt with patience are behaving like Christ. Not only does he notice their pain, but he also walks with them through every step of the suffering. Just as God the Father felt every pain of his Son, so our Savior feels our hurt and suffers with us every step of the way.

In the 1992 Barcelona Olympics, Derek Redmond ripped a hamstring as he raced in the semifinals of the 400-meter track and field event. The tendon's snap was so loud that it sounded like rifle fire to those around the athlete. Young Redmond collapsed in pain on the track. Although he had trained all of his life for this big race, he would not place. But he determined to try to finish the race. As he hobbled along the last 250 meters, a tall gentleman made his way down onto the track. It was Derek's father. He couldn't help Derek win, for the race was now over. But he could help him make it through the last painful meters. As Derek steadied himself on his father's strong frame, he and his dad limped across the finish line together.

Was Redmond disappointed? Of course. Yet of all the competitions of that Olympics, the event most of us will remember best was Derek Redmond leaning on his father, whose love made it possible for his son to finish the race.

Dear Christian, the race is not ours. We are running only the course Christ's love demands. And his accompaniment is sure. The finish line is also not ours. But our Father guarantees us that, whatever sacrifice the race demands, we will not finish it alone.

Patience! The blessing of God is on the way. You may not receive the gold medal in the race of life, but you have his guarantee that you will not have to cross the finish line alone.

To begin a study on the topic of Patience Brings the Blessing of God, turn to the home page on page 1476.

[a]*27* Psalm 2:9 [b]*1* Or *messenger*; also in verses 7 and 14 [c]*1* Or *the sevenfold Spirit*

one can shut, and what he shuts no
one can open. 8I know your deeds.
See, I have placed before you an
3:8 [v]Ac 14:27 open door[v] that no one can shut. I
[w]Rev 2:13 know that you have little strength,
yet you have kept my word and
have not denied my name.[w] 9I will
make those who are of the syna-
3:9 [x]Rev 2:9 gogue of Satan,[x] who claim to be
[y]Isa 49:23 Jews though they are not, but are
[z]Isa 43:4 liars—I will make them come and
fall down at your feet[y] and acknowledge that I have loved you.[z]
10Since you have kept my command to endure patiently, I will
3:10 [a]2Pe 2:9 also keep you[a] from the hour of
[b]Rev 2:10 trial that is going to come upon
[c]Rev 6:10; 17:8 the whole world to test[b] those who
live on the earth.[c]
11I am coming soon. Hold on
3:11 [d]Rev 2:25 to what you have,[d] so that no one
[e]Rev 2:10 will take your crown.[e] 12Him who
3:12 [f]Gal 2:9 overcomes I will make a pillar[f]
[g]Rev 14:1; 22:4 in the temple of my God. Never
[h]Rev 21:2,10 again will he leave it. I will write
on him the name of my God[g] and
the name of the city of my God,
the new Jerusalem,[h] which is coming down out of heaven from my
God; and I will also write on him
my new name. 13He who has an
ear, let him hear what the Spirit
says to the churches.

To the Church in Laodicea

14"To the angel of the church in Laodicea write:

These are the words of the
Amen, the faithful and true wit-
3:14 [i]Col 1:16,18 ness, the ruler of God's creation.[i]
15I know your deeds, that you are
3:15 [j]Ro 12:11 neither cold nor hot.[j] I wish you
were either one or the other! 16So,
because you are lukewarm—neither hot nor cold—I am about to
spit you out of my mouth. 17You
3:17 [k]Hos 12:8; say, 'I am rich; I have acquired
1Co 4:8 wealth and do not need a thing.'[k]
But you do not realize that you are
wretched, pitiful, poor, blind and
naked. 18I counsel you to buy from
me gold refined in the fire, so you
can become rich; and white clothes
to wear, so you can cover your
3:18 [l]Rev 16:15 shameful nakedness;[l] and salve to
put on your eyes, so you can see.
19Those whom I love I rebuke

DAY 3 THREE

FAITHFULNESS AND MY RELATIONSHIP WITH CHRIST

Revelation 3:21

This is Christ's promise to the Laodicean church: "To him who overcomes, I will give the right to sit with me on my throne." We are, as Paul Bilheimer suggests, destined for the throne. But there are a few trials we need to undergo before we achieve this destiny. This is the Laodicean progression: faithfulness, then triumph!

The Laodicean church was powerful and wealthy. But power and wealth often breed complacency and a reluctance to practice self-denial. While members of this congregation lived such a complacent life, there were others who were suffering and dying under intense waves of persecution. In verse 20 Jesus reminds the Laodicean church that he is standing at the door of history and is about to reenter time for the grand reckoning. He urges its members to resist compromise so that they may triumph.

According to a popular story, when Jesus reentered heaven after his resurrection, God asked him, "Son, have you redeemed the world I sent you forth to save?"

"I have," said the Son.

"Son," said the Father, "were you successful in redeeming the world?"

"Some were saved," replied the Son.

"Some?" asked the Father.

"Twelve or so," said the Son.

"What, no more? Have you any evidence that your mission was a serious struggle to redeem?"

At this the Son held out his hands. "These," he said, "I gained in loving earth. I have no other evidence but these."

The Father gazed upon his hands and wept. The Father's tears were molten gold, and as they fell, they collected into a circlet of bright light, and then he took the crown fashioned from his tears and set it on the Savior's head.

All heaven stood in silence before this simple truth: Tears are the stuff of which all crowns are made.

To begin a study on the topic of Faithfulness, the Road That Ends in Victory, turn to the home page on page 1540.

3:19 [m]Pr 3:12; and discipline.[m] So be earnest, and
Heb 12:5,6 repent.[n] 20 Here I am! I stand at the
[n]Rev 2:5 door[o] and knock. If anyone hears
3:20 my voice and opens the door,[p] I
[o]Mt 24:33 [p]Lk 12:36 will come in[q] and eat with him,
[q]Jn 14:23 and he with me.

PEACE

AT THE DOOR

> *Revelation 3:20*
> **Christ is at the door of time.**
> **There's a sweet meal to be shared,**
> **A Savior to be enjoyed.**

21 To him who overcomes, I will
give the right to sit with me on my
3:21 throne,[r] just as I overcame[s] and
[r]Mt 19:28 sat down with my Father on his
[s]Rev 5:5 throne. 22 He who has an ear, let
3:22 him hear[t] what the Spirit says to
[t]Rev 2:7 the churches."

The Throne in Heaven

4 After this I looked, and there before me was a door standing open
in heaven. And the voice I had first
4:1 heard speaking to me like a trumpet[u]
[u]Rev 1:10 [v]Rev 11:12 said, "Come up here,[v] and I will show
[w]Rev 1:19 you what must take place after this."[w]
4:2 2 At once I was in the Spirit,[x] and there
[x]Rev 1:10 [y]Isa 6:1; before me was a throne in heaven[y] with
Eze 1:26-28; someone sitting on it. 3 And the one
Da 7:9 who sat there had the appearance of jas-
4:3 per and carnelian. A rainbow,[z] resem-
[z]Eze 1:28 bling an emerald, encircled the throne.
4 Surrounding the throne were twenty-
four other thrones, and seated on them
4:4 were twenty-four elders.[a] They were
[a]Rev 11:16 [b]Rev 3:4,5 dressed in white[b] and had crowns of
gold on their heads. 5 From the throne
came flashes of lightning, rumblings
4:5 [c]Rev 8:5; and peals of thunder.[c] Before the throne,
16:18 seven lamps[d] were blazing. These are
[d]Zec 4:2 [e]Rev 1:4 the seven spirits[a][e] of God. 6 Also before
4:6 the throne there was what looked like a
[f]Rev 15:2 sea of glass,[f] clear as crystal.
[g]Eze 1:5 In the center, around the throne,
were four living creatures,[g] and they
were covered with eyes, in front and in
back. 7 The first living creature was like
a lion, the second was like an ox, the
third had a face like a man, the fourth
4:7 was like a flying eagle.[h] 8 Each of the
[h]Eze 1:10; 10:14 four living creatures had six wings[i] and
was covered with eyes all around, even
4:8 [i]Isa 6:2 under his wings. Day and night they
never stop saying:

"Holy, holy, holy
is the Lord God Almighty,[j] 4:8 [j]Isa 6:3;
who was, and is, and is to come."[k] Rev 1:8 [k]Rev 1:4

9 Whenever the living creatures give glory, honor and thanks to him who sits on
the throne[l] and who lives for ever and 4:9 [l]Ps 47:8
ever, 10 the twenty-four elders[m] fall down 4:10
before him[n] who sits on the throne,[o] [m]ver 4 [n]Rev 5:8,14
and worship him who lives for ever and [o]ver 2
ever. They lay their crowns before the
throne and say:

11 "You are worthy, our Lord and God,
to receive glory and honor and
power,[p] 4:11 [p]Rev 5:12
for you created all things, [q]Rev 10:6
and by your will they were created
and have their being."[q]

JOY

AT THE CENTER OF HEAVEN'S ADORATION

> *Revelation 4:11*
> **He is worthy! Glory is his! Honor is his!**
> **He is our Creator, our Savior, the Lamb.**
> **The Creator is waiting for his creation to say "Thank you."**
> **The Lamb is waiting for a world to acknowledge his wounds.**
> **The King is waiting for a world to bow down.**
> **Majesty is enchanted with humility.**
> **Divinity is enthralled with humanity.**
> **Love is in love with faith.**

The Scroll and the Lamb

5 Then I saw in the right hand of him
who sat on the throne[r] a scroll with 5:1 [r]ver 7,13
writing on both sides[s] and sealed[t] with [s]Eze 2:9,10
seven seals. 2 And I saw a mighty angel [t]Isa 29:11; Da 12:4
proclaiming in a loud voice, "Who is
worthy to break the seals and open the
scroll?" 3 But no one in heaven or on
earth or under the earth could open the
scroll or even look inside it. 4 I wept and
wept because no one was found who
was worthy to open the scroll or look
inside. 5 Then one of the elders said to
me, "Do not weep! See, the Lion[u] of 5:5 [u]Ge 49:9
the tribe of Judah, the Root of David,[v] [v]Isa 11:1,10;
has triumphed. He is able to open the Ro 15:12;
scroll and its seven seals." Rev 22:16
6 Then I saw a Lamb,[w] looking as if 5:6 [w]Jn 1:29

[a]5 Or *the sevenfold Spirit*

it had been slain, standing in the center of the throne, encircled by the four living creatures and the elders. He had seven horns and seven eyes,[x] which are the seven spirits[a] of God sent out into all the earth. 7He came and took the scroll from the right hand of him who sat on the throne.[y] 8And when he had taken it, the four living creatures and the twenty-four elders fell down before the Lamb. Each one had a harp[z] and they were holding golden bowls full of incense, which are the prayers[a] of the saints. 9And they sang a new song:[b]

"You are worthy[c] to take the scroll
and to open its seals,
because you were slain,
and with your blood[d] you
purchased[e] men for God
from every tribe and language and
people and nation.
10You have made them to be a
kingdom and priests[f] to
serve our God,
and they will reign on the earth."

5:6 [x]Zec 4:10
5:7 [y]ver 1
5:8 [z]Rev 14:2 [a]Ps 141:2
5:9 [b]Ps 40:3 [c]Rev 4:11 [d]Heb 9:12 [e]1Co 6:20
5:10 [f]1Pe 2:5

GOODNESS

Goodness Is Holiness and Holiness, a Worthy Servant

Revelation 5:9

When the great scroll of final things was about to be broken open and the world was about to be seared by celestial fires, only someone of great sacrifice was counted worthy to open the book. It was he who had redeemed all nations with his blood. None in heaven doubted his worthiness.

11Then I looked and heard the voice of many angels, numbering thousands upon thousands, and ten thousand times ten thousand.[g] They encircled the throne and the living creatures and the elders. 12In a loud voice they sang:

"Worthy is the Lamb, who was slain,
to receive power and wealth and
wisdom and strength
and honor and glory and praise!"[h]

13Then I heard every creature in heaven and on earth and under the earth[i] and on the sea, and all that is in them, singing:

"To him who sits on the throne and
to the Lamb[j]
be praise and honor and glory and
power,
for ever and ever!"[k]

14The four living creatures said, "Amen,"[l] and the elders fell down and worshiped.[m]

5:11 [g]Da 7:10; Heb 12:22
5:12 [h]Rev 4:11
5:13 [i]ver 3; Php 2:10 [j]Rev 6:16
5:13 [k]1Ch 29:11
5:14 [l]Rev 4:9 [m]Rev 4:10; 19:4

The Seals

6 I watched as the Lamb[n] opened the first of the seven seals.[o] Then I heard one of the four living creatures[p] say in a voice like thunder,[q] "Come!" 2I looked, and there before me was a white horse![r] Its rider held a bow, and he was given a crown,[s] and he rode out as a conqueror bent on conquest.[t]

3When the Lamb opened the second seal, I heard the second living creature[u] say, "Come!" 4Then another horse came out, a fiery red one.[v] Its rider was given power to take peace from the earth[w] and to make men slay each other. To him was given a large sword.

5When the Lamb opened the third seal, I heard the third living creature[x] say, "Come!" I looked, and there before me was a black horse![y] Its rider was holding a pair of scales in his hand. 6Then I heard what sounded like a voice among the four living creatures,[z] saying, "A quart[b] of wheat for a day's wages,[c] and three quarts of barley for a day's wages,[c] and do not damage[a] the oil and the wine!"

7When the Lamb opened the fourth seal, I heard the voice of the fourth living creature[b] say, "Come!" 8I looked, and there before me was a pale horse![c] Its rider was named Death, and Hades[d] was following close behind him. They were given power over a fourth of the earth to kill by sword, famine and plague, and by the wild beasts of the earth.[e]

9When he opened the fifth seal, I saw under the altar[f] the souls of those who had been slain[g] because of the word of God and the testimony they had maintained. 10They called out in a loud voice, "How long,[h] Sovereign Lord, holy and true,[i] until you judge the inhabitants of the earth and avenge our blood?"[j] 11Then each of them was given a white robe,[k] and they were told to wait a little longer, until the num-

6:1 [n]Rev 5:6 [o]Rev 5:1 [p]Rev 4:6,7 [q]Rev 14:2; 19:6
6:2 [r]Zec 6:3; Rev 19:11 [s]Zec 6:11; Rev 14:14 [t]Ps 45:4
6:3 [u]Rev 4:7
6:4 [v]Zec 6:2 [w]Mt 10:34
6:5 [x]Rev 4:7 [y]Zec 6:2
6:6 [z]Rev 4:6,7 [a]Rev 9:4
6:7 [b]Rev 4:7
6:8 [c]Zec 6:3 [d]Hos 13:14 [e]Jer 15:2,3; Eze 5:12,17
6:9 [f]Rev 14:18; 16:7 [g]Rev 20:4
6:10 [h]Zec 1:12 [i]Rev 3:7 [j]Rev 19:2
6:11 [k]Rev 3:4

[a]6 Or *the sevenfold Spirit* [b]6 Greek *a choinix* (probably about a liter) [c]6 Greek *a denarius*

ber of their fellow servants and brothers
6:11 [l]Heb 11:40 who were to be killed as they had been
was completed.[l]

PATIENCE

FAITHFULNESS: AWAITING THE FINAL CRY

Revelation 6:11

When you complain that God is moving too slowly to satisfy your pace, your impatience is but one more evidence of your unwillingness to trust. "Wait" is the grand instruction. Never hurry past your impatience to see whether God can be coaxed into joining your neuroses. Just wait. History is on the rails. God's rendezvous with final things is right on schedule. Your impatience embarrasses the angels, who never burst into the overture before the maestro's downbeat.

6:12 [m]Rev 16:18 [n]Mt 24:29 12 I watched as he opened the sixth
seal. There was a great earthquake.[m] The
sun turned black[n] like sackcloth made
of goat hair, the whole moon turned
blood red, 13 and the stars in the sky fell
6:13 [o]Mt 24:29; Rev 8:10; 9:1 [p]Isa 34:4 to earth,[o] as late figs drop from a fig
tree[p] when shaken by a strong wind.
14 The sky receded like a scroll, rolling
6:14 [q]Jer 4:24; Rev 16:20 up, and every mountain and island was
removed from its place.[q]
15 Then the kings of the earth, the
princes, the generals, the rich, the
mighty, and every slave and every free
6:15 [r]Isa 2:10, 19,21 man hid in caves and among the rocks
of the mountains.[r] 16 They called to the
mountains and the rocks, "Fall on us[s]
6:16 [s]Hos 10:8; Lk 23:30 and hide us from the face of him who
sits on the throne and from the wrath of
the Lamb! 17 For the great day[t] of their
6:17 [t]Zep 1:14,15; Rev 16:14 [u]Ps 76:7 wrath has come, and who can stand?"[u]

144,000 Sealed

7 After this I saw four angels standing at the four corners of the earth,
7:1 [v]Da 7:2 holding back the four winds[v] of the
earth to prevent any wind from blow-
ing on the land or on the sea or on any
tree. 2 Then I saw another angel coming up from the east, having the seal of
the living God. He called out in a loud
voice to the four angels who had been
given power to harm the land and the
sea: 3 "Do not harm[w] the land or the sea
7:3 [w]Rev 6:6 [x]Eze 9:4; Rev 22:4 or the trees until we put a seal on the
foreheads[x] of the servants of our God."

4 Then I heard the number[y] of those 7:4 [y]Rev 9:16 [z]Rev 14:1,3
who were sealed: 144,000[z] from all the
tribes of Israel.

5 From the tribe of Judah 12,000
were sealed,
from the tribe of Reuben 12,000,
from the tribe of Gad 12,000,

DAY 5 FIVE

LOVE AND ITS PLACE IN MY PERSONAL WORSHIP

Revelation 7:9–10

The union of time and eternity has come! God is love, and those of all ages who are redeemed are in love with him. The divine romance has come to fruition. Notice what the redeemed of all ages do when they enter the celestial presence: They praise. Those who find no joy in adoration here on earth will likely not enjoy heaven much. Worship is the business of heaven. The second coming is the downbeat for an eternity of praise. In my book *The Finale*, the second coming brings forth praise:

The long-awaited Prince had come...
The liberated prisoners sang . . .

The Golden Age has dawned upon the
grave of time
And we are free!
We lay aside the chains of our humanity.
The Singer comes to save the remnant of
the age.
The gates fling wide!
The banner waves above the Troubadour
of Life
Astride a steed of light!
He comes! He comes!
The blind can see!
The halt march perfectly!
The prisoners are free!

With such love watching the borders of eternity is there any reason that our personal worship should not join the adulation of those in Revelation who stand in his glory at last, overwhelmed by his grace forever? Praise is the very least we can offer.

To begin a study on the topic of Love, God's Passion for His World, turn to the home page on page 1253.

[6]from the tribe of Asher 12,000,
from the tribe of Naphtali 12,000,
from the tribe of Manasseh 12,000,
[7]from the tribe of Simeon 12,000,
from the tribe of Levi 12,000,
from the tribe of Issachar 12,000,
[8]from the tribe of Zebulun 12,000,
from the tribe of Joseph 12,000,
from the tribe of Benjamin 12,000.

The Great Multitude in White Robes

[9]After this I looked and there before
me was a great multitude that no one
could count, from every nation, tribe,
people and language,[a] standing before 7:9 [a]Rev 5:9 [b]ver 15
the throne[b] and in front of the Lamb.
They were wearing white robes and
were holding palm branches in their
hands. [10]And they cried out in a loud
voice:

"Salvation belongs to our God,[c] 7:10 [c]Ps 3:8; Rev 12:10; 19:1
who sits on the throne,
and to the Lamb."

[11]All the angels were standing around 7:11 [d]Rev 4:4 [e]Rev 4:6 [f]Rev 4:10
the throne and around the elders[d] and
the four living creatures.[e] They fell
down on their faces[f] before the throne
and worshiped God, [12]saying:

"Amen!
Praise and glory
and wisdom and thanks and honor
and power and strength
be to our God for ever and ever. 7:12 [g]Rev 5:12-14
Amen!"[g]

[13]Then one of the elders asked me,
"These in white robes—who are they,
and where did they come from?"
[14]I answered, "Sir, you know."
And he said, "These are they who
have come out of the great tribulation; 7:14 [h]Rev 22:14 [i]Heb 9:14; 1Jn 1:7
they have washed their robes[h] and made
them white in the blood of the Lamb.[i]

DAY 3 THREE
JOY AND MY RELATIONSHIP WITH CHRIST

Revelation 7:13–17

Joy is the mood of heaven. These who sing in Revelation 7 have come out of great trial. Their robes have been made white, having been dipped in the cleansing blood of the Lamb. Their simple song is recorded in Revelation 7:10: "Salvation belongs to our God, who sits on the throne, and to the Lamb." It was probably similar to the songs that those who had been slain had sung during their martyrdoms. Many of these saints had likely sung their way into heaven from flaming stakes, and they undoubtably kept the music going when they got there.

It was customary during the Middle Ages to blind canaries by sticking hot needles in their eyes in order to make them sing for their owners. The cruelty done to these tiny creatures left them in darkness. They knew of no way to affirm their existence but to sing. So the birds sang. Night was all they knew or would ever know, and the only punctuation for their unending night was the melody they themselves created.

Could it be that joy is our only sensible response in the face of evil? When we hurt and can find no light in our endless nights of hopelessness, we sing. Singing of our joy and commitment to Jesus may be the only response hurting Christians can make to a seemingly senseless world.

The martyrs of Revelation 7 knew only a dark world. Yet, in that darkness, they remained faithful. They died singing. And after death they sang because singing is the business of heaven.

To begin a study on the topic of Joy, the Reward of Endurance, turn to the home page on page 581.

JOY

THE MARTYRS' TRIUMPH

Revelation 7:14

Every age has a cadre of those who paid for faith with their blood. Is there a baptism of desire? There must be. Those who long to be obedient are washed by their longing.

Is there a baptism of fire? Yes, those who bleed and are washed by martyrdom receive their robes—pure and clean. Let your faith join with those in every age whose blood was their witness.

15 Therefore,

"they are before the throne of God[j]
and serve him[k] day and night in
his temple;[l]
and he who sits on the throne will
spread his tent over them.[m]
16 Never again will they hunger;
never again will they thirst.
The sun will not beat upon them,
nor any scorching heat.[n]
17 For the Lamb at the center of
the throne will be their
shepherd;[o]
he will lead them to springs of
living water.
And God will wipe away every tear
from their eyes."[p]

7:15 [j]ver 9 [k]Rev 22:3 [l]Rev 11:19 [m]Isa 4:5,6; Rev 21:3
7:16 [n]Isa 49:10
7:17 [o]Ps 23:1; Jn 10:11 [p]Isa 25:8; Rev 21:4

KINDNESS

THE GREAT CONSOLATION

Revelation 7:17

God is a Father whose heart is torn when his children weep. He has built heaven with grand acoustics. Joy will swell until all crying is erased. Crying may seem serious on earth, but it is really only a temporary reaction that eternity can't tolerate.

The Seventh Seal and the Golden Censer

8 When he opened the seventh seal,[q]
there was silence in heaven for
about half an hour.
2 And I saw the seven angels[r] who
stand before God, and to them were
given seven trumpets.
3 Another angel,[s] who had a golden
censer, came and stood at the altar. He
was given much incense to offer, with
the prayers of all the saints,[t] on the
golden altar[u] before the throne. 4 The
smoke of the incense, together with the
prayers of the saints, went up before
God[v] from the angel's hand. 5 Then the
angel took the censer, filled it with fire
from the altar,[w] and hurled it on the
earth; and there came peals of thunder,[x]
rumblings, flashes of lightning and an
earthquake.[y]

8:1 [q]Rev 6:1
8:2 [r]ver 6-13; Rev 9:1,13; 11:15
8:3 [s]Rev 7:2 [t]Rev 5:8 [u]Ex 30:1-6; Heb 9:4; Rev 9:13
8:4 [v]Ps 141:2
8:5 [w]Lev 16:12,13 [x]Rev 4:5 [y]Rev 6:12

The Trumpets

6 Then the seven angels who had
the seven trumpets[z] prepared to sound
them.
7 The first angel sounded his trumpet,
and there came hail and fire[a] mixed
with blood, and it was hurled down
upon the earth. A third[b] of the earth
was burned up, a third of the trees were
burned up, and all the green grass was
burned up.[c]
8 The second angel sounded his
trumpet, and something like a huge
mountain,[d] all ablaze, was thrown into
the sea. A third[e] of the sea turned into
blood,[f] 9 a third[g] of the living creatures
in the sea died, and a third of the ships
were destroyed.
10 The third angel sounded his trumpet,
and a great star, blazing like a torch,
fell from the sky[h] on a third of the
rivers and on the springs of water[i]—
11 the name of the star is Wormwood.[a]
A third[j] of the waters turned bitter, and
many people died from the waters that
had become bitter.[k]
12 The fourth angel sounded his trumpet,
and a third of the sun was struck,
a third of the moon, and a third[l] of
the stars, so that a third of them turned
dark.[m] A third of the day was without
light, and also a third of the night.
13 As I watched, I heard an eagle that
was flying in midair[n] call out in a loud
voice: "Woe! Woe! Woe[o] to the inhabitants
of the earth, because of the trumpet
blasts about to be sounded by the
other three angels!"

9 The fifth angel sounded his trumpet,
and I saw a star that had fallen
from the sky to the earth.[p] The star
was given the key to the shaft of the
Abyss.[q] 2 When he opened the Abyss,
smoke rose from it like the smoke from
a gigantic furnace.[r] The sun and sky
were darkened[s] by the smoke from the
Abyss. 3 And out of the smoke locusts[t]
came down upon the earth and were
given power like that of scorpions[u] of
the earth. 4 They were told not to harm[v]
the grass of the earth or any plant
or tree,[w] but only those people who
did not have the seal of God on their
foreheads.[x] 5 They were not given power
to kill them, but only to torture them
for five months.[y] And the agony they
suffered was like that of the sting of a
scorpion[z] when it strikes a man. 6 During
those days men will seek death, but
will not find it; they will long to die,
but death will elude them.[a]

[a] *11* That is, Bitterness

8:6 [z]ver 2
8:7 [a]Eze 38:22 [b]ver 7-12; Rev 9:15,18; 12:4 [c]Rev 9:4
8:8 [d]Jer 51:25 [e]ver 7 [f]Rev 16:3
8:9 [g]ver 7
8:10 [h]Isa 14:12; Rev 6:13; 9:1 [i]Rev 14:7; 16:4
8:11 [j]ver 7 [k]Jer 9:15; 23:15
8:12 [l]ver 7 [m]Ex 10:21-23; Rev 6:12,13
8:13 [n]Rev 14:6; 19:17 [o]Rev 9:12; 11:14
9:1 [p]Rev 8:10 [q]ver 2,11; Lk 8:31
9:2 [r]Ge 19:28; Ex 19:18 [s]Joel 2:2,10
9:3 [t]Ex 10:12-15 [u]ver 5,10
9:4 [v]Rev 6:6 [w]Rev 8:7 [x]Rev 7:2,3
9:5 [y]ver 10 [z]ver 3
9:6 [a]Job 3:21; Jer 8:3; Rev 6:16

9:7 7The locusts looked like horses
[b]Joel 2:4 prepared for battle.[b] On their heads
[c]Da 7:8 they wore something like crowns of
gold, and their faces resembled human
9:8 faces.[c] 8Their hair was like women's hair,
[d]Joel 1:6 and their teeth were like lions' teeth.[d]
9They had breastplates like breastplates
of iron, and the sound of their wings
9:9 was like the thundering of many horses
[e]Joel 2:5 and chariots rushing into battle.[e] 10They
had tails and stings like scorpions, and
9:10 in their tails they had power to torment
[f]ver 3,5,19 people for five months.[f] 11They had as
9:11 king over them the angel of the Abyss,[g]
[g]ver 1,2 whose name in Hebrew is Abaddon,
and in Greek, Apollyon.[a]
9:12 12The first woe is past; two other
[h]Rev 8:13 woes are yet to come.[h]
13The sixth angel sounded his trum-
9:13 pet, and I heard a voice coming from
[i]Ex 30:1-3 the horns[b][i] of the golden altar that is
[j]Rev 8:3 before God.[j] 14It said to the sixth angel
who had the trumpet, "Release the four
9:14 angels who are bound at the great river
[k]Rev 16:12 Euphrates."[k] 15And the four angels who
had been kept ready for this very hour
9:15 and day and month and year were re-
[l]ver 18 leased to kill a third of mankind.[l] 16The
number of the mounted troops was
9:16 two hundred million. I heard their
[m]Rev 5:11; 7:4 number.[m]
17The horses and riders I saw in my
vision looked like this: Their breastplates were fiery red, dark blue, and yellow as sulfur. The heads of the horses
9:17 resembled the heads of lions, and out
[n]Rev 11:5 of their mouths[n] came fire, smoke and
[o]ver 18 sulfur.[o] 18A third of mankind was killed[p]
9:18 by the three plagues of fire, smoke and
[p]ver 15 [q]ver 17 sulfur[q] that came out of their mouths.
19The power of the horses was in their
mouths and in their tails; for their tails
were like snakes, having heads with
which they inflict injury.
20The rest of mankind that were not
9:20 killed by these plagues still did not re-
[r]Dt 31:29 pent of the work of their hands;[r] they
[s]1Co 10:20 did not stop worshiping demons,[s] and
[t]Ps 115:4-7; 135:15-17; Da 5:23 idols of gold, silver, bronze, stone and
wood—idols that cannot see or hear or
9:21 walk.[t] 21Nor did they repent[u] of their
[u]Rev 2:21 [v]Rev 18:23 murders, their magic arts,[v] their sexual
[w]Rev 17:2,5 immorality[w] or their thefts.

The Angel and the Little Scroll

10 Then I saw another mighty an-
10:1 [x]Rev 5:2 gel[x] coming down from heaven.
He was robed in a cloud, with a rainbow above his head; his face was like
the sun,[y] and his legs were like fiery 10:1 [y]Mt 17:2;
pillars.[z] 2He was holding a little scroll, Rev 1:16 [z]Rev 1:15
which lay open in his hand. He planted
his right foot on the sea and his left foot
on the land, 3and he gave a loud shout
like the roar of a lion. When he shout- 10:3
ed, the voices of the seven thunders[a] [a]Rev 4:5
spoke. 4And when the seven thunders
spoke, I was about to write; but I heard
a voice from heaven say, "Seal up what
the seven thunders have said and do 10:4 [b]Da 8:26;
not write it down."[b] 12:4,9; Rev 22:10
5Then the angel I had seen standing
on the sea and on the land raised his 10:5
right hand to heaven.[c] 6And he swore [c]Da 12:7
by him who lives for ever and ever, who
created the heavens and all that is in
them, the earth and all that is in it, 10:6 [d]Rev 4:11;
and the sea and all that is in it,[d] and 14:7 [e]Rev 16:17
said, "There will be no more delay![e]
7But in the days when the seventh angel is about to sound his trumpet, the 10:7
mystery[f] of God will be accomplished, [f]Ro 16:25
just as he announced to his servants the
prophets."
8Then the voice that I had heard 10:8
from heaven[g] spoke to me once more: [g]ver 4
"Go, take the scroll that lies open in the
hand of the angel who is standing on
the sea and on the land."
9So I went to the angel and asked him
to give me the little scroll. He said to
me, "Take it and eat it. It will turn your 10:9
stomach sour, but in your mouth it will [h]Jer 15:16;
be as sweet as honey."[h] 10I took the little Eze 2:8-3:3
scroll from the angel's hand and ate it. It
tasted as sweet as honey in my mouth,
but when I had eaten it, my stomach
turned sour. 11Then I was told, "You 10:11
must prophesy[i] again about many peo- [i]Eze 37:4,9
ples, nations, languages and kings."

The Two Witnesses

11 I was given a reed like a measuring rod[j] and was told, "Go 11:1
and measure the temple of God and the [j]Eze 40:3; Rev 21:15
altar, and count the worshipers there.
2But exclude the outer court;[k] do not 11:2
measure it, because it has been given [k]Eze 40:17,20 [l]Lk 21:24
to the Gentiles.[l] They will trample on [m]Rev 21:2 [n]Da 7:25;
the holy city[m] for 42 months.[n] 3And I Rev 13:5
will give power to my two witnesses,[o]
and they will prophesy for 1,260 days, 11:3 [o]Rev 1:5
clothed in sackcloth."[p] 4These are the [p]Ge 37:34

[a]*11 Abaddon* and *Apollyon* mean *Destroyer.*
[b]*13* That is, projections

11:4 [q]Ps 52:8; Jer 11:16; Zec 4:3,11 [r]Zec 4:14 two olive trees[q] and the two lampstands
that stand before the Lord of the earth.[r]
5If anyone tries to harm them, fire
comes from their mouths and devours
11:5 [s]2Ki 1:10; Jer 5:14 [t]Nu 16:29,35 their enemies.[s] This is how anyone who
wants to harm them must die.[t] 6These
men have power to shut up the sky so
that it will not rain during the time
they are prophesying; and they have
11:6 [u]Ex 7:17,19 power to turn the waters into blood[u]
and to strike the earth with every kind
of plague as often as they want.
7Now when they have finished their
11:7 [v]Rev 13:1-4 [w]Da 7:21 testimony, the beast[v] that comes up
from the Abyss will attack them,[w] and
overpower and kill them. 8Their bodies will lie in the street of the great city,
11:8 [x]Isa 1:9 [y]Heb 13:12 which is figuratively called Sodom[x] and
Egypt, where also their Lord was cruci-
fied.[y] 9For three and a half days men
from every people, tribe, language and
nation will gaze on their bodies and re-
11:9 [z]Ps 79:2,3 fuse them burial.[z] 10The inhabitants of
the earth[a] will gloat over them and will
11:10 [a]Rev 3:10 [b]Est 9:19,22 celebrate by sending each other gifts,[b]
because these two prophets had tor-
mented those who live on the earth.
11But after the three and a half days a
11:11 [c]Eze 37:5,9,10,14 breath of life from God entered them,[c]
and they stood on their feet, and ter-
ror struck those who saw them. 12Then
they heard a loud voice from heaven
11:12 [d]Rev 4:1 [e]2Ki 2:11; Ac 1:9 saying to them, "Come up here."[d] And
they went up to heaven in a cloud,[e]
while their enemies looked on.
13At that very hour there was a severe earthquake and a tenth of the city
11:13 [f]Rev 6:12 [g]Rev 14:7 [h]Rev 16:11 collapsed. Seven thousand people were
killed in the earthquake,[f] and the sur-
vivors were terrified and gave glory[g] to
the God of heaven.[h]
14The second woe has passed; the
11:14 [i]Rev 8:13 third woe is coming soon.[i]

The Seventh Trumpet

15The seventh angel sounded his
11:15 [j]Rev 10:7 [k]Rev 16:17; 19:1 [l]Rev 12:10 [m]Da 2:44; 7:14,27 trumpet,[j] and there were loud voices[k]
in heaven, which said:

"The kingdom of the world has
become the kingdom of our
Lord and of his Christ,[l]
and he will reign for ever and
ever."[m]

11:16 [n]Rev 4:4 16And the twenty-four elders,[n] who were
seated on their thrones before God,
fell on their faces and worshiped God,
17saying:

"We give thanks to you, Lord God
Almighty,[o] 11:17 [o]Rev 1:8 [p]Rev 19:6
the One who is and who was,
because you have taken your great
power
and have begun to reign.[p]
18The nations were angry;[q] 11:18 [q]Ps 2:1 [r]Rev 10:7 [s]Rev 19:5
and your wrath has come.
The time has come for judging the
dead,
and for rewarding your servants
the prophets[r]
and your saints and those who
reverence your name,
both small and great[s]—
and for destroying those who destroy
the earth."

19Then God's temple[t] in heaven was 11:19 [t]Rev 15:5,8 [u]Rev 16:21
opened, and within his temple was seen
the ark of his covenant. And there came
flashes of lightning, rumblings, peals
of thunder, an earthquake and a great
hailstorm.[u]

The Woman and the Dragon

12 A great and wondrous sign appeared in heaven: a woman
clothed with the sun, with the moon
under her feet and a crown of twelve
stars on her head. 2She was pregnant and
cried out in pain[v] as she was about to 12:2 [v]Gal 4:19
give birth. 3Then another sign appeared
in heaven: an enormous red dragon with
seven heads and ten horns[w] and seven 12:3 [w]Da 7:7,20; Rev 13:1 [x]Rev 19:12
crowns[x] on his heads. 4His tail swept a
third[y] of the stars out of the sky and
flung them to the earth.[z] The dragon 12:4 [y]Rev 8:7 [z]Da 8:10 [a]Mt 2:16
stood in front of the woman who was
about to give birth, so that he might devour her child[a] the moment it was born.
5She gave birth to a son, a male child,
who will rule all the nations with an iron 12:5 [b]Ps 2:9; Rev 2:27
scepter.[b] And her child was snatched up
to God and to his throne. 6The woman
fled into the desert to a place prepared
for her by God, where she might be tak-
en care of for 1,260 days.[c] 12:6 [c]Rev 11:2
7And there was war in heaven. Michael and his angels fought against the
dragon,[d] and the dragon and his angels 12:7 [d]ver 3
fought back. 8But he was not strong
enough, and they lost their place in
heaven. 9The great dragon was hurled 12:9 [e]Ge 3:1-7 [f]Mt 25:41 [g]Rev 20:3,8,10 [h]Lk 10:18; Jn 12:31
down—that ancient serpent[e] called the
devil,[f] or Satan, who leads the whole
world astray.[g] He was hurled to the
earth,[h] and his angels with him.

10 Then I heard a loud voice in heaven[i] say:

"Now have come the salvation and
the power and the kingdom
of our God,
and the authority of his Christ.
For the accuser of our brothers,[j]
who accuses them before our God
day and night,
has been hurled down.
11 They overcame him
by the blood of the Lamb[k]
and by the word of their
testimony;[l]
they did not love their lives so much
as to shrink from death.[m]
12 Therefore rejoice, you heavens[n]
and you who dwell in them!
But woe[o] to the earth and the sea,[p]
because the devil has gone down
to you!
He is filled with fury,
because he knows that his time is
short."

12:10 [i]Rev 11:15 [j]Job 1:9-11; Zec 3:1
12:11 [k]Rev 7:14 [l]Rev 6:9 [m]Lk 14:26
12:12 [n]Ps 96:11; Isa 49:13; Rev 18:20 [o]Rev 8:13 [p]Rev 10:6

GENTLENESS

LAMB AND CONQUEROR

Revelation 12:11

There are castles of light in canyons of glass,
In glittering empires that dreamers achieve.
There's a king I've been told, on a dais of gold
Whose treasures are given to those who believe.

13 When the dragon[q] saw that he had been hurled to the earth, he pursued the woman who had given birth to the male child.[r] 14 The woman was given the two wings of a great eagle,[s] so that she might fly to the place prepared for her in the desert, where she would be taken care of for a time, times and half a time,[t] out of the serpent's reach. 15 Then from his mouth the serpent spewed water like a river, to overtake the woman and sweep her away with the torrent. 16 But the earth helped the woman by opening its mouth and swallowing the river that the dragon had spewed out of his mouth. 17 Then the dragon was enraged at the woman and went off to make war[u] against the rest of her offspring[v]—those who obey God's commandments[w] and hold to the testimony of Jesus.[x]

12:13 [q]ver 3 [r]ver 5
12:14 [s]Ex 19:4 [t]Da 7:25
12:17 [u]Rev 11:7 [v]Ge 3:15 [w]Rev 14:12 [x]Rev 1:2

13

1 And the dragon[a] stood on the shore of the sea.

The Beast out of the Sea

And I saw a beast coming out of the sea.[y] He had ten horns and seven heads,[z] with ten crowns on his horns, and on each head a blasphemous name.[a] 2 The beast I saw resembled a leopard,[b] but had feet like those of a bear[c] and a mouth like that of a lion.[d] The dragon gave the beast his power and his throne and great authority.[e] 3 One of the heads of the beast seemed to have had a fatal wound, but the fatal wound had been healed.[f] The whole world was astonished[g] and followed the beast. 4 Men worshiped the dragon because he had given authority to the beast, and they also worshiped the beast and asked, "Who is like[h] the beast? Who can make war against him?"

5 The beast was given a mouth to utter proud words and blasphemies[i] and to exercise his authority for forty-two months.[j] 6 He opened his mouth to blaspheme God, and to slander his name and his dwelling place and those who live in heaven.[k] 7 He was given power to make war[l] against the saints and to conquer them. And he was given authority over every tribe, people, language and nation.[m] 8 All inhabitants of the earth[n] will worship the beast—all whose names have not been written in the book of life[o] belonging to the Lamb that was slain from the creation of the world.[b] [p]

9 He who has an ear, let him hear.[q]

10 If anyone is to go into captivity,
into captivity he will go.
If anyone is to be killed[c] with the
sword,
with the sword he will be killed.[r]

This calls for patient endurance and faithfulness[s] on the part of the saints.[t]

The Beast out of the Earth

11 Then I saw another beast, coming out of the earth. He had two horns like a lamb, but he spoke like a drag-

13:1 [y]Da 7:1-6; Rev 15:2 [z]Rev 12:3 [a]Da 11:36; Rev 17:3
13:2 [b]Da 7:6 [c]Da 7:5 [d]Da 7:4 [e]Rev 16:10
13:3 [f]ver 12,14 [g]Rev 17:8
13:4 [h]Ex 15:11
13:5 [i]Da 7:8,11,20,25; 11:36; 2Th 2:4 [j]Rev 11:2
13:6 [k]Rev 12:12
13:7 [l]Da 7:21; Rev 11:7 [m]Rev 5:9
13:8 [n]Rev 3:10 [o]Rev 3:5; 20:12 [p]Mt 25:34
13:9 [q]Rev 2:7
13:10 [r]Jer 15:2; 43:11 [s]Heb 6:12 [t]Rev 14:12

[a] *1* Some late manuscripts *And I* [b] *8* Or *written from the creation of the world in the book of life belonging to the Lamb that was slain* [c] *10* Some manuscripts *anyone kills*

on. 12 He exercised all the authority[u] of
the first beast on his behalf,[v] and made
the earth and its inhabitants worship
the first beast,[w] whose fatal wound had
been healed.[x] 13 And he performed great
and miraculous signs,[y] even causing fire
to come down from heaven[z] to earth
in full view of men. 14 Because of the
signs[a] he was given power to do on
behalf of the first beast, he deceived[b]
the inhabitants of the earth. He ordered
them to set up an image in honor of the
beast who was wounded by the sword
and yet lived. 15 He was given power
to give breath to the image of the first
beast, so that it could speak and cause
all who refused to worship the image
to be killed.[c] 16 He also forced everyone,
small and great,[d] rich and poor, free
and slave, to receive a mark on his right
hand or on his forehead,[e] 17 so that no
one could buy or sell unless he had the
mark,[f] which is the name of the beast
or the number of his name.[g]

18 This calls for wisdom.[h] If anyone
has insight, let him calculate the number of the beast, for it is man's number.[i]
His number is 666.

The Lamb and the 144,000

14 Then I looked, and there before me was the Lamb,[j] standing on Mount Zion,[k] and with him
144,000[l] who had his name and his
Father's name[m] written on their foreheads. 2 And I heard a sound from heav-
en like the roar of rushing waters[n] and
like a loud peal of thunder. The sound
I heard was like that of harpists playing their harps.[o] 3 And they sang a new
song[p] before the throne and before the
four living creatures and the elders. No
one could learn the song except the
144,000[q] who had been redeemed from
the earth. 4 These are those who did not
defile themselves with women, for they
kept themselves pure.[r] They follow the
Lamb wherever he goes. They were purchased from among men[s] and offered as
firstfruits[t] to God and the Lamb. 5 No
lie was found in their mouths;[u] they are
blameless.[v]

The Three Angels

6 Then I saw another angel flying in
midair,[w] and he had the eternal gospel
to proclaim to those who live on the
earth[x]—to every nation, tribe, language
and people.[y] 7 He said in a loud voice,
"Fear God[z] and give him glory,[a] because
the hour of his judgment has come.
Worship him who made the heavens,
the earth, the sea and the springs of
water."[b]

8 A second angel followed and said,
"Fallen! Fallen is Babylon the Great[c],
which made all the nations drink the
maddening wine of her adulteries."[d]

9 A third angel followed them and
said in a loud voice: "If anyone worships the beast and his image[e] and receives his mark on the forehead or on
the hand, 10 he, too, will drink of the
wine of God's fury,[f] which has been
poured full strength into the cup of
his wrath.[g] He will be tormented with
burning sulfur in the presence of the
holy angels and of the Lamb. 11 And the
smoke of their torment rises for ever
and ever.[h] There is no rest day or night
for those who worship the beast and
his image, or for anyone who receives
the mark of his name." 12 This calls for
patient endurance on the part of the
saints[i] who obey God's commandments
and remain faithful to Jesus.

13 Then I heard a voice from heaven
say, "Write: Blessed are the dead who
die in the Lord[j] from now on."

"Yes," says the Spirit, "they will rest
from their labor, for their deeds will follow them."

The Harvest of the Earth

14 I looked, and there before me was
a white cloud, and seated on the cloud
was one "like a son of man"[a][k] with a
crown[l] of gold on his head and a sharp
sickle in his hand. 15 Then another angel came out of the temple and called in
a loud voice to him who was sitting on
the cloud, "Take your sickle[m] and reap,
because the time to reap has come, for
the harvest[n] of the earth is ripe." 16 So
he who was seated on the cloud swung
his sickle over the earth, and the earth
was harvested.

17 Another angel came out of the temple in heaven, and he too had a sharp
sickle. 18 Still another angel, who had
charge of the fire, came from the altar
and called in a loud voice to him who
had the sharp sickle, "Take your sharp
sickle and gather the clusters of grapes

[a] *14* Daniel 7:13

13:12 [u] ver 4 [v] ver 14 [w] Rev 14:9,11 [x] ver 3
13:13 [y] Mt 24:24 [z] 1Ki 18:38; Rev 20:9
13:14 [a] 2Th 2:9,10 [b] Rev 12:9
13:15 [c] Da 3:3-6
13:16 [d] Rev 19:5 [e] Rev 14:9
13:17 [f] Rev 14:9 [g] Rev 14:11; 15:2
13:18 [h] Rev 17:9 [i] Rev 15:2; 21:17
14:1 [j] Rev 5:6 [k] Ps 2:6 [l] Rev 7:4 [m] Rev 3:12
14:2 [n] Rev 1:15 [o] Rev 5:8
14:3 [p] Rev 5:9 [q] ver 1
14:4 [r] 2Co 11:2; Rev 3:4 [s] Rev 5:9 [t] Jas 1:18
14:5 [u] Ps 32:2; Zep 3:13 [v] Eph 5:27
14:6 [w] Rev 8:13 [x] Rev 3:10
14:6 [y] Rev 13:7
14:7 [z] Rev 15:4 [a] Rev 11:13 [b] Rev 8:10
14:8 [c] Isa 21:9; Jer 51:8 [d] Rev 17:2,4; 18:3,9
14:9 [e] Rev 13:14
14:10 [f] Isa 51:17; Jer 25:15 [g] Rev 18:6
14:11 [h] Isa 34:10; Rev 19:3
14:12 [i] Rev 13:10
14:13 [j] 1Co 15:18; 1Th 4:16
14:14 [k] Da 7:13; Rev 1:13 [l] Rev 6:2
14:15 [m] Joel 3:13 [n] Jer 51:33

from the earth's vine, because its grapes
are ripe." 19The angel swung his sickle
on the earth, gathered its grapes and
threw them into the great winepress of
14:19 [o]Rev 19:15 God's wrath.[o] 20They were trampled in
the winepress[p] outside the city,[q] and
14:20 [p]Isa 63:3 [q]Heb 13:12; Rev 11:8 blood flowed out of the press, rising as
high as the horses' bridles for a distance
of 1,600 stadia.[a]

Seven Angels With Seven Plagues

15:1 [r]Rev 12:1,3 [s]Rev 16:1 [t]Lev 26:21 15 I saw in heaven another great
and marvelous sign:[r] seven an-
gels[s] with the seven last plagues[t]—last,
because with them God's wrath is completed. 2And I saw what looked like a
15:2 [u]Rev 4:6 [v]Rev 13:14 sea of glass[u] mixed with fire and, standing beside the sea, those who had been
victorious over the beast and his image[v]
and over the number of his name. They
15:3 [w]Ex 15:1; Dt 32:4 [x]Ps 111:2 [y]Ps 145:17 held harps given them by God 3and
sang the song of Moses[w] the servant of
God and the song of the Lamb:

"Great and marvelous are your
deeds,[x]
Lord God Almighty.
Just and true are your ways,[y]
King of the ages.
15:4 [z]Jer 10:7 [a]Isa 66:23 4Who will not fear you, O Lord,[z]
and bring glory to your name?
For you alone are holy.
All nations will come
and worship before you,[a]
for your righteous acts have been
revealed."

15:5 [b]Rev 11:19 [c]Nu 1:50 5After this I looked and in heaven
the temple,[b] that is, the tabernacle of
the Testimony,[c] was opened. 6Out of the
15:6 [d]Rev 14:15 [e]ver 1 [f]Rev 1:13 temple[d] came the seven angels with the
seven plagues.[e] They were dressed in
clean, shining linen and wore golden
sashes around their chests.[f] 7Then one
15:7 [g]Rev 4:6 of the four living creatures[g] gave to the
seven angels seven golden bowls filled
with the wrath of God, who lives for
ever and ever. 8And the temple was
15:8 [h]Isa 6:4 [i]Ex 40:34,35; 1Ki 8:10,11; 2Ch 5:13,14 filled with smoke[h] from the glory of
God and from his power, and no one
could enter the temple[i] until the seven
plagues of the seven angels were completed.

The Seven Bowls of God's Wrath

16 Then I heard a loud voice from
the temple saying to the seven
16:1 [j]Rev 15:1 angels,[j] "Go, pour out the seven bowls
of God's wrath on the earth."

2The first angel went and poured out
his bowl on the land,[k] and ugly and 16:2 [k]Rev 8:7 [l]Ex 9:9-11 [m]Rev 13:15-17
painful sores[l] broke out on the people
who had the mark of the beast and worshiped his image.[m]
3The second angel poured out his
bowl on the sea, and it turned into
blood like that of a dead man, and ev- 16:3 [n]Ex 7:17-21; Rev 8:8,9
ery living thing in the sea died.[n]
4The third angel poured out his bowl
on the rivers and springs of water,[o] and 16:4 [o]Rev 8:10 [p]Ex 7:17-21
they became blood.[p] 5Then I heard the
angel in charge of the waters say:

"You are just in these judgments,[q] 16:5 [q]Rev 15:3 [r]Rev 1:4 [s]Rev 15:4
you who are and who were,[r] the
Holy One,[s]
because you have so judged;
6for they have shed the blood of your
saints and prophets,
and you have given them blood to 16:6 [t]Isa 49:26; Rev 17:6
drink[t] as they deserve."

7And I heard the altar[u] respond: 16:7 [u]Rev 6:9 [v]Rev 15:3; 19:2

"Yes, Lord God Almighty,
true and just are your
judgments."[v]

8The fourth angel[w] poured out his 16:8 [w]Rev 8:12 [x]Rev 14:18
bowl on the sun, and the sun was giv-
en power to scorch people with fire.[x]
9They were seared by the intense heat 16:9 [y]ver 11,21 [z]Rev 2:21 [a]Rev 11:13
and they cursed the name of God,[y] who
had control over these plagues, but they
refused to repent[z] and glorify him.[a]
10The fifth angel poured out his bowl 16:10 [b]Rev 13:2 [c]Rev 9:2
on the throne of the beast,[b] and his
kingdom was plunged into darkness.[c]
Men gnawed their tongues in agony 16:11 [d]ver 9,21 [e]Rev 11:13 [f]ver 2 [g]Rev 2:21
11and cursed[d] the God of heaven[e] be-
cause of their pains and their sores,[f] but
they refused to repent of what they had
done.[g]
12The sixth angel poured out his bowl 16:12 [h]Rev 9:14 [i]Isa 41:2
on the great river Euphrates,[h] and its
water was dried up to prepare the way
for the kings from the East.[i] 13Then I
saw three evil[b] spirits that looked like
frogs; they came out of the mouth of 16:13 [j]Rev 12:3 [k]Rev 13:1 [l]Rev 19:20
the dragon,[j] out of the mouth of the
beast[k] and out of the mouth of the false
prophet.[l] 14They are spirits of demons[m] 16:14 [m]1Ti 4:1 [n]Rev 17:14
performing miraculous signs, and they
go out to the kings of the whole world,
to gather them for the battle[n] on the
great day of God Almighty.

[a]*20* That is, about 180 miles (about 300 kilometers)
[b]*13* Greek *unclean*

15"Behold, I come like a thief! Blessed
16:15 is he who stays awake[o] and keeps his
[o]Lk 12:37 clothes with him, so that he may not go
naked and be shamefully exposed."
16Then they gathered the kings to-
16:16 [p]Rev 9:11 gether to the place that in Hebrew[p] is
[q]2Ki 23:29,30 called Armageddon.[q]

PEACE

ARMAGEDDON

Revelation 16:16

There is a coming battlefield
Where evil will hang its
Dull black banners before its long gray lines of hate.
But watch the hosts of light.
Their trenches flow with
Light invincible and with peace everlasting.

16:17 17The seventh angel poured out his
[r]Eph 2:2 bowl into the air,[r] and out of the tem-
[s]Rev 14:15 [t]Rev 11:15 ple[s] came a loud voice[t] from the throne,
[u]Rev 21:6 saying, "It is done!"[u] 18Then there came
16:18 flashes of lightning, rumblings, peals of
[v]Rev 4:5 [w]Rev 6:12 thunder[v] and a severe earthquake. No
[x]Da 12:1 earthquake[w] like it has ever occurred
since man has been on earth,[x] so tre-
16:19 mendous was the quake. 19The great
[y]Rev 17:18 city[y] split into three parts, and the cities
[z]Rev 18:5 [a]Rev 14:8 of the nations collapsed. God remem-
[b]Rev 14:10 bered[z] Babylon the Great[a] and gave
her the cup filled with the wine of the
fury of his wrath.[b] 20Every island fled
16:20 away and the mountains could not be
[c]Rev 6:14 found.[c] 21From the sky huge hailstones[d]
16:21 of about a hundred pounds each fell
[d]Rev 11:19 [e]Ex 9:23-25 upon men. And they cursed God on account of the plague of hail,[e] because the
plague was so terrible.

The Woman on the Beast

17:1 [f]Rev 15:1 **17** One of the seven angels[f] who
[g]Rev 21:9 [h]Rev 16:19 had the seven bowls[g] came and
[i]Rev 19:2 said to me, "Come, I will show you the
[j]Jer 51:13 punishment[h] of the great prostitute,[i]
who sits on many waters.[j] 2With her
the kings of the earth committed adultery and the inhabitants of the earth
17:2 [k]Rev 14:8; 18:3 were intoxicated with the wine of her
adulteries."[k]
3Then the angel carried me away in
17:3 [l]Rev 12:6,14 the Spirit into a desert.[l] There I saw a
[m]Rev 13:1 [n]Rev 12:3 woman sitting on a scarlet beast that
was covered with blasphemous names[m]
and had seven heads and ten horns.[n]
4The woman was dressed in purple and
scarlet, and was glittering with gold,
precious stones and pearls.[o] She held a 17:4 [o]Rev 18:16
golden cup[p] in her hand, filled with [p]Jer 51:7; Rev 18:6
abominable things and the filth of her
adulteries. 5This title was written on
her forehead:

MYSTERY
BABYLON THE GREAT[q] 17:5 [q]Rev 14:8
THE MOTHER OF PROSTITUTES
AND OF THE ABOMINATIONS OF
THE EARTH.

6I saw that the woman was drunk with 17:6
the blood of the saints,[r] the blood of [r]Rev 18:24
those who bore testimony to Jesus.
When I saw her, I was greatly astonished. 7Then the angel said to me:
"Why are you astonished? I will explain 17:7
to you the mystery[s] of the woman and [s]ver 5
of the beast she rides, which has the [t]ver 3
seven heads and ten horns.[t] 8The beast,
which you saw, once was, now is not,
and will come up out of the Abyss and 17:8
go to his destruction.[u] The inhabitants [u]Rev 13:10
of the earth[v] whose names have not [v]Rev 3:10 [w]Rev 13:8
been written in the book of life[w] from [x]Rev 13:3
the creation of the world will be astonished[x] when they see the beast, because
he once was, now is not, and yet will
come.
9"This calls for a mind with wisdom.[y] 17:9 [y]Rev 13:18
The seven heads are seven hills on which
the woman sits. 10They are also seven
kings. Five have fallen, one is, the other has not yet come; but when he does
come, he must remain for a little while.
11The beast who once was, and now is 17:11
not,[z] is an eighth king. He belongs to [z]ver 8
the seven and is going to his destruction.
12"The ten horns[a] you saw are ten 17:12 [a]Rev 12:3
kings who have not yet received a king- [b]Rev 18:10,17,19
dom, but who for one hour[b] will re-
ceive authority as kings along with the
beast. 13They have one purpose and will
give their power and authority to the 17:13
beast.[c] 14They will make war[d] against [c]ver 17
the Lamb, but the Lamb will overcome 17:14
them because he is Lord of lords and [d]Rev 16:14 [e]1Ti 6:15;
King of kings[e]—and with him will be Rev 19:16 [f]Mt 22:14
his called, chosen[f] and faithful follow-
ers."
15Then the angel said to me, "The
waters[g] you saw, where the prostitute 17:15
sits, are peoples, multitudes, nations [g]Isa 8:7 [h]Rev 13:7
and languages.[h] 16The beast and the ten
horns you saw will hate the prostitute. 17:16
They will bring her to ruin[i] and leave [i]Rev 18:17,19

17:16 [j]Eze 16:37,39 [k]Rev 19:18 [l]Rev 18:8
17:17 [m]Rev 10:7
17:18 [n]Rev 16:19

her naked;[j] they will eat her flesh[k] and
burn her with fire.[l] 17For God has put
it into their hearts to accomplish his
purpose by agreeing to give the beast
their power to rule, until God's words
are fulfilled.[m] 18The woman you saw is
the great city[n] that rules over the kings
of the earth."

The Fall of Babylon

18:1 [o]Rev 17:1 [p]Rev 10:1 [q]Eze 43:2

18 After this I saw another angel[o]
coming down from heaven.[p] He
had great authority, and the earth was
illuminated by his splendor.[q] 2With a
mighty voice he shouted:

18:2 [r]Rev 14:8 [s]Isa 13:21,22; Jer 50:39

"Fallen! Fallen is Babylon the Great![r]
She has become a home for
demons
and a haunt for every evil[a] spirit,
a haunt for every unclean and
detestable bird.[s]
3For all the nations have drunk
the maddening wine of her
adulteries.[t]
The kings of the earth committed
adultery with her,[u]
and the merchants of the earth
grew rich[v] from her excessive
luxuries."[w]

18:3 [t]Rev 14:8 [u]Rev 17:2 [v]Eze 27:9-25 [w]ver 7,9

4Then I heard another voice from
heaven say:

18:4 [x]Isa 48:20; Jer 50:8; 2Co 6:17

"Come out of her, my people,[x]
so that you will not share in her
sins,
so that you will not receive any of
her plagues;
5for her sins are piled up to heaven,[y]
and God has remembered[z] her
crimes.
6Give back to her as she has given;
pay her back[a] double for what she
has done.
Mix her a double portion from
her own cup.[b]
7Give her as much torture and grief
as the glory and luxury she gave
herself.[c]
In her heart she boasts,
'I sit as queen; I am not a widow,
and I will never mourn.'[d]
8Therefore in one day[e] her plagues
will overtake her:
death, mourning and famine.
She will be consumed by fire,[f]
for mighty is the Lord God who
judges her.

18:5 [y]Jer 51:9 [z]Rev 16:19
18:6 [a]Ps 137:8; Jer 50:15,29 [b]Rev 14:10; 16:19
18:7 [c]Eze 28:2-8 [d]Isa 47:7,8; Zep 2:15
18:8 [e]ver 10; Isa 47:9; Jer 50:31,32 [f]Rev 17:16

9"When the kings of the earth who
committed adultery with her[g] and
shared her luxury see the smoke of her
burning,[h] they will weep and mourn
over her.[i] 10Terrified at her torment,
they will stand far off[j] and cry:

18:9 [g]Rev 17:2,4 [h]ver 18; Rev 19:3 [i]Eze 26:17,18
18:10 [j]ver 15,17 [k]ver 16,19 [l]Rev 17:12

" 'Woe! Woe, O great city,[k]
O Babylon, city of power!
In one hour[l] your doom has come!'

11"The merchants[m] of the earth will
weep and mourn over her because no
one buys their cargoes any more[n]—
12cargoes of gold, silver, precious stones
and pearls; fine linen, purple, silk and
scarlet cloth; every sort of citron wood,
and articles of every kind made of ivory,
costly wood, bronze, iron and marble;[o]
13cargoes of cinnamon and spice, of incense, myrrh and frankincense, of wine
and olive oil, of fine flour and wheat;
cattle and sheep; horses and carriages;
and bodies and souls of men.[p]
14"They will say, 'The fruit you
longed for is gone from you. All your
riches and splendor have vanished, never to be recovered.' 15The merchants
who sold these things and gained their
wealth from her[q] will stand far off, terrified at her torment. They will weep
and mourn[r] 16and cry out:

18:11 [m]Eze 27:27 [n]ver 3
18:12 [o]Rev 17:4
18:13 [p]Eze 27:13; 1Ti 1:10
18:15 [q]ver 3 [r]Eze 27:31

" 'Woe! Woe, O great city,
dressed in fine linen, purple and
scarlet,
and glittering with gold, precious
stones and pearls![s]
17In one hour[t] such great wealth has
been brought to ruin!'[u]

18:16 [s]Rev 17:4
18:17 [t]ver 10 [u]Rev 17:16 [v]Eze 27:28-30

"Every sea captain, and all who travel
by ship, the sailors, and all who earn
their living from the sea,[v] will stand far
off. 18When they see the smoke of her
burning, they will exclaim, 'Was there
ever a city like this great city?'[w] 19They
will throw dust on their heads,[x] and
with weeping and mourning cry out:

18:18 [w]Eze 27:32; Rev 13:4
18:19 [x]Jos 7:6; Eze 27:30 [y]Rev 17:16

" 'Woe! Woe, O great city,
where all who had ships on the
sea
became rich through her wealth!
In one hour she has been brought to
ruin![y]
20Rejoice over her, O heaven![z]
Rejoice, saints and apostles and
prophets!

18:20 [z]Jer 51:48; Rev 12:12

[a]2 Greek *unclean*

18:20 [a]Rev 19:2
God has judged her for the way she
treated you.' "[a]

18:21 [b]Rev 5:2 [c]Jer 51:63
[21]Then a mighty angel[b] picked up a
boulder the size of a large millstone and
threw it into the sea,[c] and said:

"With such violence
the great city of Babylon will be
thrown down,
never to be found again.
[22]The music of harpists and musicians,
flute players and trumpeters,
will never be heard in you again.[d]
No workman of any trade
will ever be found in you again.
The sound of a millstone
will never be heard in you again.[e]
[23]The light of a lamp
will never shine in you again.
The voice of bridegroom and bride
will never be heard in you again.[f]
Your merchants were the world's
great men.[g]
By your magic spell[h] all the
nations were led astray.
[24]In her was found the blood of
prophets and of the saints,[i]
and of all who have been killed on
the earth."[j]

18:22 [d]Isa 24:8; Eze 26:13 [e]Jer 25:10
18:23 [f]Jer 7:34; 16:9; 25:10 [g]Isa 23:8 [h]Na 3:4
18:24 [i]Rev 16:6; 17:6 [j]Jer 51:49

Hallelujah!

19 After this I heard what sounded like the roar of a great multitude[k] in heaven shouting:

19:1 [k]Rev 11:15 [l]Rev 7:10 [m]Rev 4:11

"Hallelujah!
Salvation[l] and glory and power[m]
belong to our God,
[2] for true and just are his judgments.
He has condemned the great
prostitute
who corrupted the earth by her
adulteries.
He has avenged on her the blood of
his servants."[n]

19:2 [n]Dt 32:43; Rev 6:10

[3]And again they shouted:

"Hallelujah!
The smoke from her goes up for ever
and ever."[o]

19:3 [o]Isa 34:10; Rev 14:11

[4]The twenty-four elders[p] and the
four living creatures[q] fell down[r] and
worshiped God, who was seated on the
throne. And they cried:

19:4 [p]Rev 4:4 [q]Rev 4:6 [r]Rev 5:14

"Amen, Hallelujah!"

[5]Then a voice came from the throne,
saying:

"Praise our God,
all you his servants,[s]
you who fear him,
both small and great!"[t]

19:5 [s]Ps 134:1 [t]Rev 11:18; 20:12

[6]Then I heard what sounded like a
great multitude,[u] like the roar of rushing waters and like loud peals of thunder, shouting:

19:6 [u]Rev 11:15

"Hallelujah!
For our Lord God Almighty
reigns.
[7]Let us rejoice and be glad
and give him glory!
For the wedding of the Lamb[v] has
come,
and his bride[w] has made herself
ready.
[8]Fine linen, bright and clean,
was given her to wear."
(Fine linen stands for the righteous acts[x]
of the saints.)

19:7 [v]Mt 22:2; 25:10; Eph 5:32 [w]Rev 21:2,9
19:8 [x]Rev 15:4

[9]Then the angel said to me,[y] "Write:[z]
'Blessed are those who are invited to the
wedding supper of the Lamb!' "[a] And
he added, "These are the true words of
God."[b]

19:9 [y]ver 10 [z]Rev 1:19 [a]Lk 14:15 [b]Rev 21:5; 22:6

JOY

The Marriage Supper of the Lamb

Revelation 19:9

See the banquet table. See the ancient, golden goblets filled with the wine of triumph. See those of all ages meet! They stand behind their gilded chairs and raise their glasses to the Lamb of God.

[10]At this I fell at his feet to worship
him.[c] But he said to me, "Do not do
it! I am a fellow servant with you and
with your brothers who hold to the
testimony of Jesus. Worship God![d] For
the testimony of Jesus[e] is the spirit of
prophecy."

19:10 [c]Rev 22:8 [d]Ac 10:25,26; Rev 22:9 [e]Rev 12:17

The Rider on the White Horse

[11]I saw heaven standing open and
there before me was a white horse,
whose rider[f] is called Faithful and True.[g]
With justice he judges and makes war.[h]
[12]His eyes are like blazing fire,[i] and
on his head are many crowns.[j] He has
a name written on him that no one
knows but he himself.[k] [13]He is dressed

19:11 [f]Rev 6:2 [g]Rev 3:14 [h]Isa 11:4
19:12 [i]Rev 1:14 [j]Rev 6:2 [k]Rev 2:17

WEEK 51 FAITHFULNESS

1 DAY ONE

Faithfulness, the Road That Ends in Victory

Read Revelation 19:11–16

The final triumph of the Apocalypse is the appearance of the rider on a white horse. On his robe and on his thigh is written—King of Kings and Lord of Lords. The rider is Jesus, but his name in this account is Faithful and True. Jesus is God's Son, and he patiently endured the cross so that he might finish what his Father had given him to do. If there is any doubt that faithfulness is the road that leads to victory, we have but to look at this account to prove it true.

"Be faithful, even to the point of death, and I will give you the crown of life," said Jesus to the church at Smyrna (Revelation 2:10). Faithfulness always ends in victory. How complete is this victory? Here are ten facets of the victory that faithfulness produces.

The dwelling of God will be with humankind (Revelation 21:3).
God will wipe away all tears (v. 4).
There will be no more death (v. 4).
There will be no more pain (v. 4).
Everything will be made new (v. 5).
Anyone thirsty may drink from the spring of the water of life (v. 6).
The faithful will be in the presence of the celestial wedding party (v. 9).
The faithful will live in a jewel-encrusted, new city (vv. 15–21).
Nothing impure will enter the city (v. 27).
All those whose names are written in the Lamb's book of life will be there (v. 27).

The second coming is a celebration of the faithful. All that they have endured ends now in victory. Revelation 19:6 reminds us that the faithful will sing with the innumerable hosts: "Hallelujah! For our Lord God Almighty reigns."

Memorize This Week

1 SAMUEL 26:23

The LORD rewards every man for his righteousness and faithfulness. The LORD delivered you into my hands today, but I would not lay a hand on the LORD's anointed.

2 DAY TWO

Faithfulness and the Purpose of God in My Life

God requires faithfulness. When we are making difficult decisions, when our future is at stake, we can rest assured that God will guide us when we are faithful. Jehoshaphat was faithful, and God worked in his life. Faithfulness, even in difficult times, brings victory. *Turn to 2 Chronicles 20:20–30, page 517, for today's study.*

3 DAY THREE

Faithfulness and My Relationship With Christ

Jesus promises that he will give all those who overcome the trials of their faith the right to rule with him on his throne. One of the faith's great missionaries gave her own food supply to the starving Chinese of her parish. As a result, she died of malnutrition. Her death derived from her faithfulness, and her faithfulness ended in victory. On her tombstone are the words "Faithful unto death." *Turn to Revelation 3:21, page 1526, for today's study.*

4 DAY FOUR

Faithfulness and My Service to Others

Jesus does not condemn the rich man because he is rich. The rich man's condemnation came because his wealth gave him a smug self-sufficiency that blinded him to the needs of those around him. The beggar Lazarus is not to be commended for being poor but for being faithful. Because he was faithful, when he died he was carried to Abraham's bosom. Faithfulness always ends in victory. *Turn to Luke 16:19–26, page 1229, for today's study.*

5 DAY FIVE

Faithfulness and Its Place in My Personal Worship

Faithfulness in personal worship is the jewel in the soul of the believer. Here is the New Testament's only specific challenge to attend local worship services on a regular basis. Faithfulness is all the more urgent, says the writer of Hebrews, because we can see the Day approaching. What day is the writer referring to? The day when our Lord comes for us. Then we shall behold him face to face and the necessity for us to go to church to adore him will be over. *Turn to Hebrews 10:25, page 1470, for today's study.*

Week 52, Self-Control, Freedom From Permissiveness, begins on page 452, 2 Kings 21:1–9.
To begin a topical study on the Fruit of the Spirit, Faithfulness, turn to the Topical Index, page 1548.

▸ FAITHFULNESS 

JESUS, FAITHFUL AND TRUE

Revelation 19:11

Christ is Victor! It is he who rides the white horse and holds the title "King of kings and Lord of lords."

19:13 [l]Isa 63:2,3 in a robe dipped in blood,[l] and his
[m]Jn 1:1 name is the Word of God.[m] 14The
armies of heaven were following him,
riding on white horses and dressed in
19:14 [n]ver 8 fine linen,[n] white and clean. 15Out of
19:15 his mouth comes a sharp sword[o] with
[o]Rev 1:16 which to strike down[p] the nations. "He
[p]Isa 11:4; 2Th 2:8 will rule them with an iron scepter."[a][q]
[q]Ps 2:9; Rev 2:27 He treads the winepress[r] of the fury of
[r]Rev 14:20 the wrath of God Almighty. 16On his
19:16 robe and on his thigh he has this name
[s]ver 12 [t]Rev 17:14 written:[s]

KING OF KINGS AND LORD OF LORDS.[t]

17And I saw an angel standing in the
sun, who cried in a loud voice to all
19:17 [u]ver 21 the birds[u] flying in midair,[v] "Come,[w]
[v]Rev 8:13 [w]Eze 39:17 gather together for the great supper of
God, 18so that you may eat the flesh
of kings, generals, and mighty men, of
horses and their riders, and the flesh
19:18 [x]Eze 39:18-20 of all people,[x] free and slave, small and
great."
19Then I saw the beast and the kings
19:19 [y]Rev 16:14,16 of the earth[y] and their armies gathered
together to make war against the rider
on the horse and his army. 20But the
19:20 beast was captured, and with him the
[z]Rev 16:13 false prophet[z] who had performed the
[a]Rev 13:12 miraculous signs on his behalf.[a] With
[b]Da 7:11; Rev 20:10, 14,15; 21:8 these signs he had deluded those who
[c]Rev 14:10 had received the mark of the beast and
worshiped his image. The two of them
were thrown alive into the fiery lake[b]
19:21 of burning sulfur.[c] 21The rest of them
[d]ver 15 were killed with the sword[d] that came
[e]ver 11,19 out of the mouth of the rider on the
[f]ver 17 horse,[e] and all the birds[f] gorged themselves on their flesh.

The Thousand Years

20 And I saw an angel coming
down out of heaven,[g] having the
20:1 [g]Rev 10:1 key[h] to the Abyss and holding in his
[h]Rev 1:18 hand a great chain. 2He seized the drag-
20:2 on, that ancient serpent, who is the
[i]Rev 12:9 [j]2Pe 2:4 devil, or Satan,[i] and bound him for a
thousand years.[j] 3He threw him into 20:3 [k]Da 6:17
the Abyss, and locked and sealed[k] it [l]Rev 12:9
over him, to keep him from deceiving
the nations[l] anymore until the thousand years were ended. After that, he 20:4
must be set free for a short time. [m]Da 7:9
4I saw thrones[m] on which were seated [n]Rev 6:9
those who had been given authority to [o]Rev 13:12
judge. And I saw the souls of those who [p]Rev 13:16
had been beheaded[n] because of their
testimony for Jesus and because of the
word of God. They had not worshiped
the beast[o] or his image and had not
received his mark on their foreheads
or their hands.[p] They came to life and
reigned with Christ a thousand years.
5(The rest of the dead did not come 20:5
to life until the thousand years were [q]Lk 14:14; Php 3:11
ended.) This is the first resurrection.[q]
6Blessed[r] and holy are those who have 20:6 [r]Rev 14:13
part in the first resurrection. The sec- [s]Rev 2:11
ond death[s] has no power over them, [t]Rev 1:6
but they will be priests[t] of God and of [u]ver 4
Christ and will reign with him[u] for a
thousand years.

▸ LOVE 

THE MARTYRS' REIGN OF LOVE

Revelation 20:4

Those who endured the battle to its fearsome end are now made kings. Is it not time for them to reign? They knew the pain of dying—claw and fang, flame and stake. But blade and rope are past. The martyrs are now monarchs. Their suffering is swallowed up in symphonies.

Satan's Doom

7When the thousand years are over,[v] 20:7 [v]ver 2
Satan will be released from his prison
8and will go out to deceive the nations[w] 20:8 [w]ver 3,10
in the four corners of the earth—Gog [x]Eze 38:2; 39:1
and Magog[x]—to gather them for [y]Rev 16:14
battle.[y] In number they are like the [z]Heb 11:12
sand on the seashore.[z] 9They marched
across the breadth of the earth and sur- 20:9
rounded[a] the camp of God's people, the [a]Eze 38:9,16
city he loves. But fire came down from [b]Eze 38:22; 39:6
heaven[b] and devoured them. 10And the
devil, who deceived them,[c] was thrown 20:10 [c]Rev 19:20
into the lake of burning sulfur, where [d]Rev 14:10,11
the beast and the false prophet had been
thrown. They will be tormented day
and night for ever and ever.[d]

[a] *15* Psalm 2:9

The Dead Are Judged

[11]Then I saw a great white throne[e] and him who was seated on it. Earth and sky fled from his presence, and there was no place for them. [12]And I saw the dead, great and small, standing before the throne, and books were opened.[f] Another book was opened, which is the book of life.[g] The dead were judged according to what they had done[h] as recorded in the books. [13]The sea gave up the dead that were in it, and death and Hades[i] gave up the dead[j] that were in them, and each person was judged according to what he had done. [14]Then death[k] and Hades were thrown into the lake of fire. The lake of fire is the second death. [15]If anyone's name was not found written in the book of life,[l] he was thrown into the lake of fire.

20:11 [e]Rev 4:2
20:12 [f]Da 7:10 [g]Rev 3:5 [h]Jer 17:10; Mt 16:27; Rev 2:23
20:13 [i]Rev 6:8 [j]Isa 26:19
20:14 [k]1Co 15:26
20:15 [l]ver 12

The New Jerusalem

21 Then I saw a new heaven and a new earth,[m] for the first heaven and the first earth had passed away, and there was no longer any sea. [2]I saw the Holy City, the new Jerusalem, coming down out of heaven from God,[n] prepared as a bride beautifully dressed for her husband. [3]And I heard a loud voice from the throne saying, "Now the dwelling of God is with men, and he will live with them. They will be his people, and God himself will be with them and be their God.[o] [4]He will wipe every tear from their eyes.[p] There will be no more death[q] or mourning or crying or pain,[r] for the old order of things has passed away."

[5]He who was seated on the throne[s] said, "I am making everything new!" Then he said, "Write this down, for these words are trustworthy and true."[t]

[6]He said to me: "It is done.[u] I am the Alpha and the Omega,[v] the Beginning and the End. To him who is thirsty I will give to drink without cost from the spring of the water of life.[w] [7]He who overcomes will inherit all this, and I will be his God and he will be my son. [8]But the cowardly, the unbelieving, the vile, the murderers, the sexually immoral, those who practice magic arts, the idolaters and all liars[x]—their place will be in the fiery lake of burning sulfur. This is the second death."[y]

21:1 [m]Isa 65:17; 2Pe 3:13
21:2 [n]Heb 11:10; 12:22; Rev 3:12
21:3 [o]2Co 6:16
21:4 [p]Rev 7:17 [q]1Co 15:26; Rev 20:14 [r]Isa 35:10; 65:19
21:5 [s]Rev 4:9; 20:11 [t]Rev 19:9
21:6 [u]Rev 16:17 [v]Rev 1:8; 22:13 [w]Jn 4:10
21:8 [x]1Co 6:9 [y]Rev 2:11

[9]One of the seven angels who had the seven bowls full of the seven last plagues[z] came and said to me, "Come, I will show you the bride,[a] the wife of the Lamb." [10]And he carried me away[b] in the Spirit[c] to a mountain great and high, and showed me the Holy City, Jerusalem, coming down out of heaven from God. [11]It shone with the glory of God,[d] and its brilliance was like that of a very precious jewel, like a jasper, clear as crystal.[e] [12]It had a great, high wall with twelve gates, and with twelve angels at the gates. On the gates were written the names of the twelve tribes of Israel.[f] [13]There were three gates on the east, three on the north, three on the south and three on the west. [14]The wall of the city had twelve foundations, and on them were the names of the twelve apostles of the Lamb.

[15]The angel who talked with me had a measuring rod[g] of gold to measure the city, its gates and its walls. [16]The city was laid out like a square, as long as it was wide. He measured the city with the rod and found it to be 12,000 stadia[a] in length, and as wide and high as it is long. [17]He measured its wall and it was 144 cubits[b] thick,[c] by man's measurement, which the angel was using. [18]The wall was made of jasper,[h] and the city of pure gold, as pure as glass.[i] [19]The foundations of the city walls were decorated with every kind of precious stone.[j] The first foundation was jasper, the second sapphire, the third chalcedony, the fourth emerald, [20]the fifth sardonyx, the sixth carnelian,[k] the seventh chrysolite, the eighth beryl, the ninth topaz, the tenth chrysoprase, the eleventh jacinth, and the twelfth amethyst.[d] [21]The twelve gates were twelve pearls, each gate made of a single pearl. The great street of the city was of pure gold, like transparent glass.[l]

[22]I did not see a temple[m] in the city, because the Lord God Almighty[n] and the Lamb[o] are its temple. [23]The city does not need the sun or the moon to shine on it, for the glory of God gives it light,[p] and the Lamb is its lamp. [24]The nations will walk by its light, and the

21:9 [z]Rev 15:1,6,7 [a]Rev 19:7
21:10 [b]Rev 17:3 [c]Rev 1:10
21:11 [d]Rev 15:8; 22:5 [e]Rev 4:6
21:12 [f]Eze 48:30-34
21:15 [g]Rev 11:1
21:18 [h]ver 11 [i]ver 21
21:19 [j]Isa 54:11,12
21:20 [k]Rev 4:3
21:21 [l]ver 18
21:22 [m]Jn 4:21,23 [n]Rev 1:8 [o]Rev 5:6
21:23 [p]Isa 24:23; 60:19,20; Rev 22:5

[a] *16* That is, about 1,400 miles (about 2,200 kilometers) [b] *17* That is, about 200 feet (about 65 meters) [c] *17* Or *high* [d] *20* The precise identification of some of these precious stones is uncertain.

kings of the earth will bring their splendor into it.[q] 25On no day will its gates ever be shut,[r] for there will be no night there.[s] 26The glory and honor of the nations will be brought into it. 27Nothing impure will ever enter it, nor will anyone who does what is shameful or deceitful,[t] but only those whose names are written in the Lamb's book of life.

21:24 [q]Isa 60:3,5
21:25 [r]Isa 60:11 [s]Zec 14:7; Rev 22:5
21:27 [t]Isa 52:1; Joel 3:17; Rev 22:14,15

The River of Life

22 Then the angel showed me the river of the water of life, as clear as crystal,[u] flowing[v] from the throne of God and of the Lamb 2down the middle of the great street of the city. On each side of the river stood the tree of life,[w] bearing twelve crops of fruit, yielding its fruit every month. And the leaves of the tree are for the healing of the nations.[x] 3No longer will there be any curse.[y] The throne of God and of the Lamb will be in the city, and his servants will serve him.[z] 4They will see his face,[a] and his name will be on their foreheads.[b] 5There will be no more night.[c] They will not need the light of a lamp or the light of the sun, for the Lord God will give them light.[d] And they will reign for ever and ever.[e]

6The angel said to me,[f] "These words are trustworthy and true.[g] The Lord, the God of the spirits of the prophets,[h] sent his angel[i] to show his servants the things that must soon take place."

22:1 [u]Rev 4:6 [v]Eze 47:1; Zec 14:8
22:2 [w]Rev 2:7 [x]Eze 47:12
22:3 [y]Zec 14:11 [z]Rev 7:15
22:4 [a]Mt 5:8 [b]Rev 14:1
22:5 [c]Rev 21:25 [d]Rev 21:23 [e]Da 7:27; Rev 20:4
22:6 [f]Rev 1:1 [g]Rev 19:9; 21:5 [h]Heb 12:9 [i]ver 16

Jesus Is Coming

7"Behold, I am coming soon![j] Blessed[k] is he who keeps the words of the prophecy in this book."

8I, John, am the one who heard and saw these things.[l] And when I had heard and seen them, I fell down to worship at the feet[m] of the angel who had been showing them to me. 9But he said to me, "Do not do it! I am a fellow servant with you and with your brothers the prophets and of all who keep the words of this book.[n] Worship God!"[o]

10Then he told me, "Do not seal up[p] the words of the prophecy of this book, because the time is near.[q] 11Let him who does wrong continue to do wrong; let him who is vile continue to be vile; let him who does right continue to do right; and let him who is holy continue to be holy."[r]

22:7 [j]Rev 3:11 [k]Rev 1:3
22:8 [l]Rev 1:1 [m]Rev 19:10
22:9 [n]ver 10,18,19 [o]Rev 19:10
22:10 [p]Da 8:26; Rev 10:4 [q]Rev 1:3
22:11 [r]Eze 3:27; Da 12:10

12"Behold, I am coming soon![s] My reward is with me,[t] and I will give to everyone according to what he has done. 13I am the Alpha and the Omega,[u] the First and the Last,[v] the Beginning and the End.[w]

22:12 [s]ver 7,20 [t]Isa 40:10
22:13 [u]Rev 1:8 [v]Rev 1:17 [w]Rev 21:6

PATIENCE

CLOCK-WATCHING

Revelation 22:12

He is coming soon.
Watch not to speed the clock,
But heed the skies, when the sun torches the horizon:
There are vistas where wind blows the stars.
There are ledges where daring may dare.
There are crags only claimed in abandon
By those unafraid of thin air.

14"Blessed are those who wash their robes, that they may have the right to the tree of life[x] and may go through the gates[y] into the city.[z] 15Outside[a] are the dogs,[b] those who practice magic arts, the sexually immoral, the murderers, the idolaters and everyone who loves and practices falsehood.

16"I, Jesus,[c] have sent my angel to give you[a] this testimony for the churches.[d] I am the Root[e] and the Offspring of David, and the bright Morning Star."[f]

17The Spirit[g] and the bride say, "Come!" And let him who hears say, "Come!" Whoever is thirsty, let him come; and whoever wishes, let him take the free gift of the water of life.

18I warn everyone who hears the words of the prophecy of this book: If anyone adds anything to them,[h] God will add to him the plagues described in this book.[i] 19And if anyone takes words away[j] from this book of prophecy, God will take away from him his share in the tree of life and in the holy city, which are described in this book.

20He who testifies to these things[k] says, "Yes, I am coming soon."

Amen. Come, Lord Jesus.[l]

21The grace of the Lord Jesus be with God's people.[m] Amen.

22:14 [x]Rev 2:7 [y]Rev 21:12 [z]Rev 21:27
22:15 [a]1Co 6:9,10; Gal 5:19-21; Col 3:5,6 [b]Php 3:2
22:16 [c]Rev 1:1 [d]Rev 1:4 [e]Rev 5:5 [f]2Pe 1:19; Rev 2:28
22:17 [g]Rev 2:7
22:18 [h]Dt 4:2; Pr 30:6 [i]Rev 15:6-16:21
22:19 [j]Dt 4:2
22:20 [k]Rev 1:2 [l]1Co 16:22
22:21 [m]Ro 16:20

[a]16 The Greek is plural.

STUDY HELPS

WEIGHTS AND MEASURES

The figures of the table are calculated on the basis of a shekel equaling 11.5 grams, a cubit equaling 18 inches, and an ephah equaling 22 liters. The quart referred to is either a dry quart (slightly larger than a liter) or a liquid quart (slightly smaller than a liter), whichever is applicable. The ton referred to in the footnotes is the American ton of 2,000 pounds.

This table is based upon the best available information, but it is not intended to be mathematically precise; like the measurement equivalents in the footnotes, it merely gives approximate amounts and distances. Weights and measures differed somewhat at various times and places in the ancient world. There is uncertainty particularly about the ephah and the bath; further discoveries may shed more light on these units of capacity.

	Biblical Unit		*Approximate American Equivalent*	*Approximate Metric Equivalent*
WEIGHTS	talent	(60 minas)	75 pounds	34 kilograms
	mina	(50 shekels)	1 1/4 pounds	0.6 kilogram
	shekel	(2 bekas)	2/5 ounce	11.5 grams
	pim	(2/3 shekel)	1/3 ounce	7.6 grams
	beka	(10 gerahs)	1/5 ounce	5.5 grams
	gerah		1/50 ounce	0.6 gram
LENGTH	cubit		18 inches	0.5 meter
	span		9 inches	23 centimeters
	handbreadth		3 inches	8 centimeters
CAPACITY				
Dry Measure	cor [homer]	(10 ephahs)	6 bushels	220 liters
	lethek	(5 ephahs)	3 bushels	110 liters
	ephah	(10 omers)	3/5 bushel	22 liters
	seah	(1/3 ephah)	7 quarts	7.3 liters
	omer	(1/10 ephah)	2 quarts	2 liters
	cab	(1/18 ephah)	1 quart	1 liter
Liquid Measure	bath	(1 ephah)	6 gallons	22 liters
	hin	(1/6 bath)	4 quarts	4 liters
	log	(1/72 bath)	1/3 quart	0.3 liter

CHARACTER PROFILE INDEX 

The following index lists all of the character profiles of the individuals who are highlighted in this Bible. They are arranged in alphabetical order within the Testaments.

OLD TESTAMENT

NEW TESTAMENT

Topical Index

The first section of this topical index has been designed as a quick-reference guide to what this Bible has to say about each particular fruit of the Spirit. For each fruit, this section lists the week numbers and their topics and home page locations, as well as the locations of the character profiles scattered throughout the Bible that relate to the particular fruit of the Spirit and the "Jesus Speaks Out . . ." and "Paul Speaks Out . . ." pages.

The second section lists issues of interest other than the fruit of the Spirit as they appear in the daily readings and character profiles.

Love

Home Pages

Character Profiles

Jesus and Paul Speak Out on the Fruit of the Spirit: Love

Joy

Home Pages

Character Profiles

Jesus and Paul Speak Out on the Fruit of the Spirit: Joy

Peace

Home Pages

Character Profiles

Jesus and Paul Speak Out on the Fruit of the Spirit: Peace

Patience

Home Pages

Character Profiles

Jesus and Paul Speak Out on the Fruit of the Spirit: Self-Control

Acknowledgments

Page 5. From *Two Gentlemen of Verona,* by William Shakespeare.

Page 18. Joseph Bayley, as quoted in *The Book of Jesus,* edited by Calvin Miller. Copyright 1996 by Simon & Schuster Publishers, New York, NY, pp. 247–248.

Page 83. "Amazing Grace," words by John Newton, 1779.

Page 89. From "The Hound of Heaven," by Francis Thompson, 1859–1907.

Page 97. "Holy, Holy, Holy," words by Reginald Heber, 1826.

Page 97. "I Need Thee Every Hour," words by Annie Sherwood Hawks, 1872.

Page 125. "Draw Me Nearer," words by Francis Jane (Fanny) Crosby, in *Brightest and Best.* Copyright 1875 by Biglow & Main, NewYork, NY.

Page 139. "More About Jesus," words by Eliza Edmunds Stiles Hewitt, in *Glad Hallelujahs,* 1887.

Page 180. "Holy, Holy, Holy," words by Reginald Heber, 1826.

Page 180. "What a Friend We Have in Jesus," words by Joseph Mendlicott Scriven, 1855.

Page 302. *Steel Magnolias,* by Robert Harling. Copyright 1995 by Dramatists Play Service.

Page 306. "Gentle Jesus, Meek and Mild," words by Charles Wesley, in *Hymns and Sacred Poems,* 1742.

Page 343. Martin Luther, as quoted in *The Book of Jesus,* edited by Calvin Miller. Copyright 1996 by Simon & Schuster Publishers, New York, NY, pp. 577.

Page 432. From "Paradise Lost," by John Milton.

Page 465. From *Othello,* by William Shakespeare.

Page 524. From *A Tale of Three Kings,* by Gene Edwards. Copyright 1992 by Tyndale House Publishers, Carol Stream, IL.

Page 545. Martin Luther, as quoted in *The Book of Jesus,* ed. by Calvin Miller. Copyright 1996 by Simon & Schuster Publishers, New York, NY, pp. 285.

Page 581. From *Star Riders of Ren,* by Calvin Miller. Copyright 1983 by Harper & Row, San Francisco, CA, p. 165.

Page 634. From "The Hound of Heaven," by Francis Thompson, 1859–1907.

Page 635. "The Imitation of Christ," by Thomas à Kempis, as quoted in *The Book of Jesus,* ed. by Calvin Miller. Copyright 1996 by Simon & Schuster Publishers, New York, NY, pp. 337.

Page 649. "O How I Love Jesus," words by Frederick Whitfield, 1849.

Page 658. From *The Pilgrim's Progress,* by John Bunyan.

Page 713. From *An Owner's Manual for the Unfinished Soul,* by Calvin Miller. Copyright 1997 by Harold Shaw Publishers, Wheaton, IL, pp. 41,43–45.

Page 723. From *Through the Valley of the Kwai: From Death Camp Despair to Spiritual Triumph,* by Ernest Gordan. Copyright 1997 by Wipf & Stock Publishers.

Page 724. From "The Hound of Heaven," by Francis Thompson, 1859–1907.

Page 749. From *No Exit,* by Jean Paul Sartre. Copyright 1944.

Page 749. "When We All Get to Heaven," words by Eliza Edmunds Stites Hewitt in *Pentecostal Praises* by William Kirkpatrick and Henry Gilmour, 1898.

Page 790. From *The Merchant of Venice,* by William Shakespeare.

Page 791. "Are You Washed in the Blood?" words by Elisha Albright Hoffman, in *Spiritual Songs for Gospel Meetings and the Sunday School.* Copyright 1878 by Barker & Smellie, Cleveland, OH.

Page 798. From *A Symphony in Sand,* by Calvin Miller. Copyright 1990 by Word Publishing, Waco, TX, 1990, p. 7.

Page 827. From *The Fear of God: The Christian Book of Mystical Verse,* ed. by A.W. Tozer. Copyright 1963 by Christian Publications, Harrisburg, PA, pp. 18–20.

Page 848. "The Coventry Carol," words by Robert Croo. Published by Simon & Schuster, New York, NY, 1996, pp. 158–159.

Page 863. From *An Owner's Manual for the Unfinished Soul,* by Calvin Miller. Copyright 1997 by Harold Shaw Publishers, Wheaton, IL, p. 86.

Page 898. From *Once Upon a Tree,* by Calvin Miller. Copyright 1967 by Baker Book House, Grand Rapids, MI.

Page 971. "When First I Reckoned with His Love," by Calvin Miller, from *An Owner's Manual for the Unfinished Soul,* by Calvin Miller. Copyright 1997 by Harold Shaw Publishers, Wheaton, IL, p. 65.

Page 1039. "O Come All Ye Faithful (Adeste Fideles)," words by John Francis Wade, 1743. Trans. To English by Frederick Oakely, 1841.

Page 1040. From "The Hound of Heaven," by Francis Thompson, 1859–1907.

Page 1047. From "The Hound of Heaven," by Francis Thompson, 1859–1907.

Page 1096. From *An Owner's Manual for the Unfinished Soul,* by Calvin Miller. Copyright 1997 by Harold Shaw Publishers, Wheaton, IL, pp. 88–90.

Page 1126. "Fairest Lord Jesus," trans. by Joseph August Seiss, 1873.

Page 1134. From "The Rime of the Ancient Mariner," Part II, by Samuel Coleridge, 1797.

Page 1175. From *An Owner's Manual for the Unfinished Soul,* by Calvin Miller. Copyright 1997 by Harold Shaw Publishers, Wheaton, IL, pp. 96.

Page 1196. "I'm Gonna Have a Baby, Abie!" from *When the Aardvark Parked on the Ark,* by Calvin Miller. Copyright 1984, by Harper & Row, San Francisco, CA, p. 44.

Page 1200. From *An Owner's Manual for the Unfinished Soul,* by Calvin Miller. Copyright 1997 by Harold Shaw Publishers, Wheaton, IL, pp. 157–158.

Page 1221. From *Miscellaneous Sonnets. Part i. xxxiii.* by William Wordsworth, 1770–1850.

Page 1227. From *Little Snow White,* by Jacob and Wilhelm Grimm, 1812.

Page 1232. "The Pharisee" from *An Owner's Manual for the Unfinished Soul,* by Calvin Miller. Copyright 1997 by Harold Shaw Publishers, Wheaton, IL, p. 107.

Page 1235. From *Little Lord Fauntleroy,* by Frances Hodgson Burnett.

Page 1281. From *An Owner's Manual for the Unfinished Soul,* by Calvin Miller. Copyright 1997 by Harold Shaw Publishers, Wheaton, IL, pp. 93–94.

Page 1303. From *A Christmas Carol,* by Charles Dickens.

Page 1314. "A Mighty Fortress Is Our God," by Martin Luther, 1529. Trans. to English by Frederic Henry Hedge, 1853.

Page 1326. "What a Friend We Have in Jesus," words by Joseph Mendlicott Scriven, 1855.

Page 1334. From *A Symphony in Sand,* by Calvin Miller. Copyright 1990 by Word Publishing, Waco, TX, 1990, pp. 100–101.

Page 1337. From *Pilgrim's Progress,* by John Bunyan.

Page 1337. "Free From the Law," words by Philip Paul Bliss, 1873.

Page 1342. "Leonardo Lobster," from *When the Aardvark Parked on the Ark,* by Calvin Miller. Copyright 1984, by Harper & Row, San Francisco, CA, p. 8.

Page 1348. From *The New Testament in Modern English,* by John B. Phillips. Copyright 1972 by Macmillan Publishing Company, Inc., 1972.

Page 1358. James A. Harnish, as quoted in *A Cup*

of Coffee at the Soul Café, by Leonard Sweet. Copyright 1998 by Broadman & Holman, Nashville, TN, p. 50.

Page 1362. "Just As I Am," words by Charlotte Elliott, 1835.

Page 1380. "Nearer, My God, to Thee," words by Sarah Fuller Flower Adams, in *Hymns and Anthems,* by William Johnson Fox, 1841.

Page 1438. John Bunyan, as quoted in *The Book of Jesus,* ed. by Calvin Miller. Copyright 1996 by Simon & Schuster Publishers, New York, NY, pp. 244.

Page 1460. From *King Lear,* by William Shakespeare.

Page 1466. From *Table of Inwardness,* by Calvin Miller. Copyright 1984 by InterVarsity Press, Downers Grove, IL, p. 9.

Page 1466. From *Cracking the Cosmic Egg,* by Joseph Chilton Pearce.

Page 1508. Francois Fenelon, as quoted in *The Book of Jesus,* edited by Calvin Miller. Copyright 1996 by Simon & Schuster Publishers, New York, NY, p. 350–351.

Page 1522. "Holy, Holy, Holy," by Reginald Heber, 1826.

Page 1522. "Messiah," by George Frederick Handel.

Page 1522. "Battle Hymn of the Republic," by Julia Ward Howe, 1861.

Page 1524. "Must Jesus Bear the Cross Alone?" words by: Stanza 1: Thomas Shepherd, *Penitential Cries,* 1693, alt. Stanza 2: from a missionary collection published in Norwich, England, early 19th century. Stanza 3: *The Oberlin Social and Sabbath School Hymn Book,* by George Nelson Allen, 1844. Stanzas 4–5: *Plymouth Collection of Hymns and Tunes,* by Henry Ward Beecher, 1855, by AMS. Barnes and Burr, New York, NY.

Page 1529. From *The Finale,* by Calvin Miller. Copyright 1979 by InterVarsity Press, Downers Grove, IL, pp. 145–147.

Every effort has been made to trace the ownership of copyright items in this collection and to obtain permission for their use. The publisher would appreciate notification of, and copyright details for, any instances where further acknowledgment is due, so that adjustments may be made in a future reprint.

NIV CONCORDANCE

An Introduction

This NIV Concordance is a condensation of *The NIV Complete Concordance*, taking over 35,000 references from the latter's 250,000. These 35,000 references have been selected as the most helpful for the average Bible student or layperson.

When determining whether or not to include a verse reference, we gave careful consideration to the passage in which the verse is located. We also encourage you to always consider the larger context of the passage, giving special attention to the flow of the thought from beginning to end. Whenever you look up a verse, your goal should be to discover the intended meaning of the verse in context. Do not use this concordance, or any concordance, merely as a *verse-finder*; it should also be used as a *passage-finder*. The contexts surrounding each entry are longer than those usually found in concordances; but even so, the context excerpts are too brief for study purposes. They serve only to help you locate familiar verses.

In some cases the usual short contextual phrases are ineffective in helping you locate a passage. This is especially true in studying key events in a Bible character's life. Therefore, we have incorporated 260 "block entries" in which we use descriptive phrases that mark the breadth of a passage containing episodes of that person's life. The descriptive phrases replace the brief context surrounding each occurrence of the name.

Often more than one Bible character has the same name. For example, there are more than thirty Zechariahs in the Bible. In these cases we have given the name a block entry, assigning each person a number (1), (2), etc., and have included a descriptive phrase to distinguish each. Insignificant names are not included.

In this concordance there are 1,239 key word entries that have an exhaustive list of every appearance of that word. When this occurs, the word or block entry is marked with an asterisk (*).

This mini-concordance includes some words not found in *The NIV Complete Concordance.* These words include: *boy, boy's, boys, daughter, daughters, girl, man, man's, men, men's, people, peoples, woman,* and *women.*

Since this concordance can only serve one translation—the New International Version—it is difficult for readers familiar with the Authorized Version to make the transition from its older, more archaic language to that of the NIV. We have tried, therefore, to make this transition a bit easier by including some forty-four prominent Authorized Version words and linking them to NIV words that have taken their place. We wish to thank Dr. Daniel E. Sauerwein of Multnomah Bible College for supplying the data for these additional words.

We pray that this concordance will be used by NIV readers to introduce them to the full scope of God's truth in every book of the Bible.

John R. Kohlenberger III
Edward W. Goodrick

CONCORDANCE

AARON

Genealogy of (Ex 6:16–20; Jos 21:4, 10; 1Ch 6:3–15).

Priesthood of (Ex 28:1; Nu 17; Heb 5:1–4; 7), garments (Ex 28; 39), consecration (Ex 29), ordination (Lev 8).

Spokesman for Moses (Ex 4:14–16, 27–31; 7:1–2). Supported Moses' hands in battle (Ex 17:8–13). Built golden calf (Ex 32; Dt 9:20). Talked against Moses (Nu 12). Priesthood opposed (Nu 16); staff budded (Nu 17). Forbidden to enter land (Nu 20:1–12). Death (Nu 20:22–29; 33:38–39).

ABADDON*

Rev 9:11 whose name in Hebrew is *A,*

ABANDON (ABANDONED)

Dt 4:31 he will not *a* or destroy you
1Ki 6:13 and will not *a* my people Israel."
Ne 9:19 compassion you did not *a* them
9:31 an end to them or *a* them,
Ps 16:10 you will not *a* me to the grave,
Ac 2:27 you will not *a* me to the grave,
1Ti 4: 1 in later times some will *a* the faith

ABANDONED (ABANDON)

Ge 24:27 who has not *a* his kindness
2Co 4: 9 persecuted, but not *a;* struck down,

ABBA*

Mk 14:36 "*A,* Father," he said, "everything is
Ro 8:15 And by him we cry, "*A,* Father."
Gal 4: 6 the Spirit who calls out, "*A,* Father

ABEDNEGO

Deported to Babylon with Daniel (Da 1:1–6). Name changed from Azariah (Da 1:7). Refused defilement by food (Da 1:8–20). Refused idol worship (Da 3:1–12); saved from furnace (Da 3:13–30).

ABEL

Second son of Adam (Ge 4:2). Offered proper sacrifice (Ge 4:4; Heb 11:4). Murdered by Cain (Ge 4:8; Mt 23:35; Lk 11:51; 1Jn 3:12).

ABHOR (ABHORS)

Lev 26:30 of your idols, and I will *a* you.
Dt 7:26 Utterly *a* and detest it,
Ps 26: 5 I *a* the assembly of evildoers
119:163 I hate and *a* falsehood
139:21 and *a* those who rise up against you
Am 6: 8 "I *a* the pride of Jacob
Ro 2:22 You who *a* idols, do you rob

ABHORS (ABHOR)

Pr 11: 1 The LORD *a* dishonest scales,

ABIATHAR

High priest in days of Saul and David (1Sa 22; 2Sa 15; 1Ki 1–2; Mk 2:26). Escaped Saul's slaughter of priests (1Sa 22:18–23). Supported David in Absalom's revolt (2Sa 15:24–29). Supported Adonijah (1Ki 1:7–42); deposed by Solomon (1Ki 2:22–35; cf. 1Sa 2:31–35).

ABIGAIL

1. Sister of David (1Ch 2:16–17).

2. Wife of Nabal (1Sa 25:30); pled for his life with David (1Sa 25:14–35). Became David's wife after Nabal's death (1Sa 25:36–42); bore him Kileab (2Sa 3:3) also known as Daniel (1Ch 3:1).

ABIHU

Son of Aaron (Ex 6:23; 24:1, 9); killed for offering unauthorized fire (Lev 10; Nu 3:2–4; 1Ch 24:1–2).

ABIJAH

1. Second son of Samuel (1Ch 6:28); a corrupt judge (1Sa 8:1–5).

2. An Aaronic priest (1Ch 24:10; Lk 1:5).

3. Son of Jeroboam I of Israel; died as prophesied by Ahijah (1Ki 14:1–18).

4. Son of Rehoboam; king of Judah who fought Jeroboam I attempting to reunite the kingdom (1Ki 14:31–15:8; 2Ch 12:16–14:1; Mt 1:7).

ABILITY (ABLE)

Ex 35:34 tribe of Dan, the *a* to teach others.
Dt 8:18 for it is he who gives you the *a*
Ezr 2:69 According to their *a* they gave
Mt 25:15 one talent, each according to his *a.*
Ac 11:29 disciples, each according to his *a,*
2Co 1: 8 far beyond our *a* to endure,
8: 3 were able, and even beyond their *a.*

ABIMELECH

1. King of Gerar who took Abraham's wife Sarah, believing her to be his sister (Ge 20). Later made a covenant with Abraham (Ge 21:22–33).

2. King of Gerar who took Isaac's wife Rebekah, believing her to be his sister (Ge 26:1–11). Later made a covenant with Isaac (Ge 26:12–31).

3. Son of Gideon (Jdg 8:31). Attempted to make himself king (Jdg 9).

ABISHAG*

Shunammite virgin; attendant of David in his old age (1Ki 1:1–15; 2:17–22).

ABISHAI

Son of Zeruiah, David's sister (1Sa 26:6; 1Ch 2:16). One of David's chief warriors (1Ch 11:15–21): against Edom (1Ch 18:12–13), Ammon (2Sa 10), Absalom (2Sa 18), Sheba (2Sa 20). Wanted to kill Saul (1Sa 26), killed Abner (2Sa 2:18–27; 3:22–39), wanted to kill Shimei (2Sa 16:5–13; 19:16–23).

ABLE (ABILITY ENABLE ENABLED ENABLES ENABLING)

Nu 14:16 'The LORD was not *a*
1Ch 29:14 that we should be *a* to give
2Ch 2: 6 who is *a* to build a temple for him,
Eze 7:19 and gold will not be *a* to save them
Da 3:17 the God we serve is *a* to save us
4:37 walk in pride he is *a* to humble.
Mt 9:28 "Do you believe that I am *a*
Lk 13:24 will try to enter and will not be *a* to
14:30 to build and was not *a* to finish.'
21:15 none of your adversaries will be *a*
21:36 and that you may be *a* to stand
Ac 5:39 you will not be *a* to stop these men;
Ro 8:39 will be *a* to separate us
14: 4 for the Lord is *a* to make him stand
16:25 to him who is *a* to establish you
2Co 9: 8 God is *a* to make all grace abound
Eph 3:20 him who is *a* to do immeasurably
6:13 you may be *a* to stand your ground,
1Ti 3: 2 respectable, hospitable, *a* to teach,
2Ti 1:12 and am convinced that he is *a*
2:24 kind to everyone, *a* to teach,
3:15 which are *a* to make you wise
Heb 2:18 he is *a* to help those who are being
7:25 he is *a* to save completely
Jas 3: 2 *a* to keep his whole body in check.
Jude :24 To him who is *a* to keep you
Rev 5: 5 He is *a* to open the scroll

ABNER

Cousin of Saul and commander of his army (1Sa 14:50; 17:55–57; 26). Made Ish-Bosheth king after Saul (2Sa 2:8–10), but later defected to David (2Sa 3:6–21). Killed Asahel (2Sa 2:18–32), for which he was killed by Joab and Abishai (2Sa 3:22–39).

ABOLISH (ABOLISHED ABOLISHING)

Hos 2:18 I will *a* from the land,
Mt 5:17 that I have come to *a* the Law

ABOLISHED (ABOLISH)

Gal 5:11 the offense of the cross has been *a.*

ABOLISHING* (ABOLISH)

Eph 2:15 by *a* in his flesh the law

ABOMINATION*

Da 11:31 set up the *a* that causes desolation.
12:11 *a* that causes desolation is set up,
Mt 24:15 the holy place 'the *a* that causes
Mk 13:14 you see 'the *a* that causes

ABOUND (ABOUNDING)

2Co 9: 8 able to make all grace *a* to you,
9: 8 you will *a* in every good work.
Php 1: 9 that your love may *a* more

ABOUNDING (ABOUND)

Ex 34: 6 slow to anger, *a* in love
Nu 14:18 *a* in love and forgiving sin
Ne 9:17 slow to anger and *a* in love.
Ps 86: 5 *a* in love to all who call to you.
86:15 slow to anger, *a* in love
103: 8 slow to anger, *a* in love.
Joel 2:13 slow to anger and *a* in love,
Jnh 4: 2 slow to anger and *a* in love,

ABRAHAM

Abram, son of Terah (Ge 11:26–27), husband of Sarah (Ge 11:29).

Covenant relation with the LORD (Ge 12:1–3; 13:14–17; 15; 17; 22:15–18; Ex 2:24; Ne 9:8; Ps 105; Mic 7:20; Lk 1:68–75; Ro 4; Heb 6:13–15).

Called from Ur, via Haran, to Canaan (Ge 12:1; Ac 7:2–4; Heb 11:8–10). Moved to Egypt, nearly lost Sarah to Pharoah (Ge 12:10–20). Divided the land with Lot; settled in Hebron (Ge 13). Saved Lot from four kings (Ge 14:1–16); blessed by Melchizedek (Ge 14:17–20; Heb 7:1–20). Declared righteous by faith (Ge 15:6; Ro 4:3; Gal 3:6–9). Fathered Ishmael by Hagar (Ge 16).

Name changed from Abram (Ge 17:5; Ne 9:7). Circumcised (Ge 17; Ro 4:9–12). Entertained three visitors (Ge 18); promised a son by Sarah (Ge 18:9–15; 17:16). Questioned destruction of Sodom and Gomorrah (Ge 18:16–33). Moved to Gerar; nearly lost Sarah to Abimelech (Ge 20).

Fathered Isaac by Sarah (Ge 21:1–7; Ac 7:8; Heb 11:11–12); sent away Hagar and Ishmael (Ge 21:8–21; Gal 4:22–30). Covenant with Abimelech (Ge 21:22–32). Tested by offering Isaac (Ge 22; Heb 11:17–19; Jas 2:21–24). Sarah died; bought field of Ephron for burial (Ge 23). Secured wife for Isaac (Ge 24). Fathered children by Keturah (Ge 25:1–6; 1Ch 1:32–33). Death (Ge 25:7–11).

Called servant of God (Ge 26:24), friend of God (2Ch 20:7; Isa 41:8; Jas 2:23), prophet (Ge 20:7), father of Israel (Ex 3:15; Isa 51:2; Mt 3:9; Jn 8:39–58).

ABSALOM

Son of David by Maacah (2Sa 3:3; 1Ch 3:2). Killed Amnon for rape of his sister Tamar; banished by David (2Sa 13). Returned to Jerusalem; received by David (2Sa 14). Rebelled against David; siezed kingdom (2Sa 15–17). Killed (2Sa 18).

ABSENT
Col 2: 5 though I am *a* from you in body,

ABSOLUTE*
1Ti 5: 2 women as sisters, with *a* purity.

ABSTAIN (ABSTAINS)
Ex 19:15 *A* from sexual relations."
Nu 6: 3 he must *a* from wine and other
Ac 15:20 them to *a* from food polluted
1Pe 2:11 to *a* from sinful desires,

ABSTAINS* (ABSTAIN)
Ro 14: 6 thanks to God; and he who *a,*

ABUNDANCE (ABUNDANT)
Ge 41:29 Seven years of great *a* are coming
Job 36:31 and provides food in *a.*
Ps 66:12 but you brought us to a place of *a.*
Ecc 5:12 but the *a* of a rich man
Isa 66:11 and delight in her overflowing *a."*
Jer 2:22 and use an *a* of soap,
Mt 13:12 given more, and he will have an *a.*
25:29 given more, and he will have an *a.*
Lk 12:15 consist in the *a* of his possessions."
1Pe 1: 2 Grace and peace be yours in *a.*
2Pe 1: 2 yours in *a* through the knowledge
Jude : 2 peace and love be yours in *a.*

ABUNDANT (ABUNDANCE)
Dt 28:11 will grant you *a* prosperity—
32: 2 like *a* rain on tender plants.
Job 36:28 and *a* showers fall on mankind.
Ps 68: 9 You gave *a* showers, O God;
78:15 gave them water as *a* as the seas;
132:15 I will bless her with *a* provisions;
145: 7 will celebrate your *a* goodness
Pr 12:11 works his land will have *a* food,
28:19 works his land will have *a* food,
Jer 33: 9 and will tremble at the *a* prosperity
Ro 5:17 who receive God's *a* provision

ABUSIVE
2Ti 3: 2 *a,* disobedient to their parents,

ABYSS*
Lk 8:31 not to order them to go into the *A.*
Rev 9: 1 the key to the shaft of the *A.*
9: 2 When he opened the *A,* smoke rose
9: 2 darkened by the smoke from the *A.*
9:11 king over them the angel of the *A,*
11: 7 up from the *A* will attack them,
17: 8 and will come up out of the *A*
20: 1 having the key to the *A*
20: 3 He threw him into the *A,*

ACCEPT (ACCEPTABLE ACCEPTANCE ACCEPTED ACCEPTS)
Ex 23: 8 "Do not *a* a bribe,
Dt 16:19 Do not *a* a bribe, for a bribe blinds
Job 42: 8 and I will *a* his prayer and not deal
Pr 10: 8 The wise in heart *a* commands,
Pr 19:20 Listen to advice and *a* instruction,
Ro 15: 7 *A* one another, then, just
Jas 1:21 humbly *a* the word planted in you,

ACCEPTABLE (ACCEPT)
Pr 21: 3 is more *a* to the LORD

ACCEPTANCE* (ACCEPT)
Ro 11:15 what will their *a* be but life
1Ti 1:15 saying that deserves full *a:*
4: 9 saying that deserves full *a*

ACCEPTED (ACCEPT)
Ge 4: 7 will you not be *a?* But if you do not
Job 42: 9 and the LORD *a* Job's prayer.
Lk 4:24 "no prophet is *a* in his hometown.
Gal 1: 9 you a gospel other than what you *a,*

ACCEPTS (ACCEPT)
Ps 6: 9 the LORD *a* my prayer.
Jn 13:20 whoever *a* anyone I send *a* me;
13:20 whoever *a* me *a* the one who sent

ACCESS
Ro 5: 2 through whom we have gained *a*
Eph 2:18 For through him we both have *a*

ACCOMPANIED (ACCOMPANY)
1Co 10: 4 from the spiritual rock that *a* them,
Jas 2:17 if it is not *a* by action, is dead.

ACCOMPANIES (ACCOMPANY)
2Co 9:13 obedience that *a* your confession

ACCOMPANY (ACCOMPANIED ACCOMPANIES)
Dt 28: 2 *a* you if you obey the LORD your
Mk 16:17 these signs will *a* those who believe
Heb 6: 9 your case—things that *a* salvation.

ACCOMPLISH
Ecc 2: 2 And what does pleasure *a?"*
Isa 44:28 and will *a* all that I please;
55:11 but will *a* what I desire

ACCORD
Nu 24:13 not do anything of my own *a,*
Jn 10:18 but I lay it down of my own *a.*
12:49 For I did not speak of my own *a,*

ACCOUNT (ACCOUNTABLE)
Ge 2: 4 This is the *a* of the heavens
5: 1 This is the written *a* of Adam's line
6: 9 This is the *a* of Noah.
10: 1 This is the *a* of Shem, Ham
11:10 This is the *a* of Shem.
11:27 This is the *a* of Terah.
25:12 This is the *a* of Abraham's son
25:19 This is the *a* of Abraham's son
36: 1 This is the *a* of Esau (that is, Edom
36: 9 This is the *a* of Esau the father
37: 2 This is the *a* of Jacob.
Mt 12:36 to give *a* on the day of judgment
Lk 16: 2 Give an *a* of your management,
Ro 14:12 each of us will give an *a* of himself
Heb 4:13 of him to whom we must give *a.*

ACCOUNTABLE* (ACCOUNT)
Eze 3:18 and I will hold you *a* for his blood.
3:20 and I will hold you *a* for his blood.
33: 6 but I will hold the watchman *a*
33: 8 and I will hold you *a* for his blood.
34:10 and will hold them *a* for my flock.
Da 6: 2 The satraps were made *a* to them
Jnh 1:14 Do not hold us *a* for killing
Ro 3:19 and the whole world held *a* to God.

ACCURATE
Dt 25:15 You must have *a* and honest
Pr 11: 1 but *a* weights are his delight.

ACCURSED (CURSE)
2Pe 2:14 experts in greed—an *a* brood!

ACCUSATION (ACCUSE)
1Ti 5:19 Do not entertain an *a*

ACCUSATIONS (ACCUSE)
2Pe 2:11 do not bring slanderous *a*

ACCUSE (ACCUSATION ACCUSATIONS ACCUSER ACCUSES ACCUSING)
Pr 3:30 Do not *a* a man for no reason—
Lk 3:14 and don't *a* people falsely—

ACCUSER (ACCUSE)
Jn 5:45 Your *a* is Moses, on whom your
Rev 12:10 For the *a* of our brothers,

ACCUSES (ACCUSE)
Job 40: 2 Let him who *a* God answer him!"
Rev 12:10 who *a* them before our God day

ACCUSING (ACCUSE)
Ro 2:15 and their thoughts now *a,*

ACHAN*

Sin at Jericho caused defeat at Ai; stoned (Jos 7; 22:20; 1Ch 2:7).

ACHE*
Pr 14:13 Even in laughter the heart may *a,*

ACHIEVE
Isa 55:11 *a* the purpose for which I sent it.

ACHISH

King of Gath before whom David feigned insanity (1Sa 21:10–15). Later "ally" of David (2Sa 27–29).

ACKNOWLEDGE (ACKNOWLEDGED ACKNOWLEDGES)
Pr 3: 6 in all your ways *a* him,
Jer 3:13 Only *a* your guilt—
Hos 6: 3 let us press on to *a* him.
Mt 10:32 *a* him before my Father in heaven.
Lk 12: 8 *a* him before the angels of God.
1Jn 4: 3 spirit that does not *a* Jesus is not

ACKNOWLEDGED (ACKNOWLEDGE)
Lk 7:29 *a* that God's way was right,

ACKNOWLEDGES* (ACKNOWLEDGE)
Ps 91:14 for he *a* my name.
Mt 10:32 "Whoever *a* me before men,
Lk 12: 8 whoever *a* me before men,
1Jn 2:23 whoever *a* the Son has the Father
4: 2 Every spirit that *a* that Jesus Christ
4:15 If anyone *a* that Jesus is the Son

ACQUIRES (ACQUIRING)
Pr 18:15 of the discerning *a* knowledge;

ACQUIRING* (ACQUIRES)
Pr 1: 3 for *a* a disciplined and prudent life,

ACQUIT (ACQUITTING)
Ex 23: 7 to death, for I will not *a* the guilty.

ACQUITTING* (ACQUIT)
Dt 25: 1 *a* the innocent and condemning
Pr 17:15 *A* the guilty and condemning

ACT (ACTION ACTIONS ACTIVE ACTIVITY ACTS)
Ps 119:126 It is time for you to *a,* O LORD;

ACTION (ACT)
2Co 9: 2 has stirred most of them to *a.*
Jas 2:17 if it is not accompanied by *a,*
1Pe 1:13 minds for *a;* be self-controlled;

ACTIONS (ACT)
Mt 11:19 wisdom is proved right by her *a."*
Gal 6: 4 Each one should test his own *a.*
Tit 1:16 but by their *a* they deny him.

ACTIVE* (ACT)
Phm :6 I pray that you may be *a*
Heb 4:12 For the word of God is living and *a*

ACTIVITY (ACT)
Ecc 3:1 a season for every *a* under heaven:
3:17 for there will be a time for every *a*,

ACTS (ACT)
1Ch 16:9 tell of all his wonderful *a*.
Ps 71:16 proclaim your mighty *a*,
71:24 tell of your righteous *a*
105:2 tell of all his wonderful *a*.
106:2 Who can proclaim the mighty *a*
145:4 they will tell of your mighty *a*.
145:12 all men may know of your mighty *a*
150:2 Praise him for his *a* of power;
Isa 64:6 all our righteous *a* are like filthy
Mt 6:1 not to do your '*a* of righteousness'

ADAM
1. First man (Ge 1:26–2:25; Ro 5:14; 1Ti 2:13). Sin of (Ge 3; Hos 6:7; Ro 5:12–21). Children of (Ge 4:1–5:5). Death of (Ge 5:5; Ro 5:12–21; 1Co 15:22).
2. City (Jos 3:16).

ADD (ADDED)
Dt 4:2 Do not *a* to what I command you
12:32 do not *a* to it or take away from it.
Pr 1:5 let the wise listen and *a*
9:9 he will *a* to his learning.
30:6 Do not *a* to his words,
Mt 6:27 by worrying can *a* a single hour
Lk 12:25 by worrying can *a* a single hour
Rev 22:18 God will *a* to him the plagues

ADDED (ADD)
Ecc 3:14 nothing can be *a* to it and nothing
Ac 2:47 Lord *a* to their number daily those
Ro 5:20 The law was *a* so that the trespass
Gal 3:19 It was *a* because of transgressions

ADDICTED*
Tit 2:3 to be slanderers or *a* to much wine,

ADMINISTRATION*
1Co 12:28 with gifts of *a*, and those speaking
Eph 3:2 Surely you have heard about the *a*
3:9 to everyone the *a* of this mystery,

ADMIRABLE*
Php 4:8 whatever is lovely, whatever is *a*—

ADMIT
Hos 5:15 until they *a* their guilt.

ADMONISH* (ADMONISHING)
Col 3:16 and *a* one another with all wisdom,
1Th 5:12 you in the Lord and who *a* you.

ADMONISHING* (ADMONISH)
Col 1:28 *a* and teaching everyone

ADONIJAH
1. Son of David by Haggith (2Sa 3:4; 1Ch 3:2). Attempted to be king after David; killed by Solomon's order (1Ki 1–2).
2. Levite; teacher of the Law (2Ch 17:8).

ADOPTED (ADOPTION)
Eph 1:5 In love he predestined us to be *a*

ADOPTION* (ADOPTED)
Ro 8:23 as we wait eagerly for our *a* as sons,
9:4 Theirs is the *a* as sons; theirs

ADORE*
SS 1:4 How right they are to *a* you!

ADORNMENT* (ADORNS)
1Pe 3:3 should not come from outward *a*,

ADORNS* (ADORNMENT)
Ps 93:5 holiness *a* your house
Isa 61:10 as a bride *a* herself with her jewels.
61:10 bridegroom *a* his head like a priest,

ADULTERER (ADULTERY)
Lev 20:10 both the *a* and the adulteress must
Heb 13:4 for God will judge the *a*

ADULTERERS (ADULTERY)
1Co 6:9 idolaters nor *a* nor male prostitutes
1Ti 1:10 for murderers, for *a* and perverts,

ADULTERESS (ADULTERY)
Hos 3:1 she is loved by another and is an *a*.

ADULTERIES (ADULTERY)
Jer 3:8 sent her away because of all her *a*.

ADULTEROUS (ADULTERY)
Mk 8:38 in this *a* and sinful generation,
Jas 4:4 You *a* people, don't you know that

ADULTERY (ADULTERER ADULTERERS ADULTERESS ADULTERIES ADULTEROUS)
Ex 20:14 "You shall not commit *a*.
Dt 5:18 "You shall not commit *a*.
Mt 5:27 that it was said, 'Do not commit *a*.'
5:28 lustfully has already committed *a*
5:32 the divorced woman commits *a*.
15:19 murder, *a*, sexual immorality, theft
19:9 marries another woman commits *a*
19:18 do not commit *a*, do not steal,
Mk 7:21 theft, murder, *a*, greed, malice,
10:11 marries another woman commits *a*
10:12 another man, she commits *a*."
10:19 do not commit *a*, do not steal,
Lk 16:18 a divorced woman commits *a*.
16:18 marries another woman commits *a*
18:20 'Do not commit *a*, do not murder,
Jn 8:4 woman was caught in the act of *a*.
Rev 18:3 of the earth committed *a* with her,

ADULTS*
1Co 14:20 but in your thinking be *a*.

ADVANCE (ADVANCED)
Ps 18:29 With your help I can *a*
Php 1:12 has really served to *a* the gospel.

ADVANCED (ADVANCE)
Job 32:7 *a* years should teach wisdom.'

ADVANTAGE
Ex 22:22 "Do not take *a* of a widow
Dt 24:14 Do not take *a* of a hired man who is
Ro 3:1 What *a*, then, is there
2Co 11:20 or exploits you or takes *a* of you
1Th 4:6 should wrong his brother or take *a*

ADVERSITY*
Pr 17:17 and a brother is born for *a*.
Isa 30:20 the Lord gives you the bread of *a*

ADVICE (ADVISERS)
1Ki 12:8 rejected the *a* the elders
12:14 he followed the *a* of the young men
2Ch 10:8 rejected the *a* the elders
Pr 12:5 but the *a* of the wicked is deceitful.
12:15 but a wise man listens to *a*.
19:20 Listen to *a* and accept instruction,
20:18 Make plans by seeking *a*;

ADVISERS (ADVICE)
Pr 11:14 but many *a* make victory sure.

ADVOCATE*
Job 16:19 my *a* is on high.

AFFLICTED (AFFLICTION)
Job 2:7 and *a* Job with painful sores
36:6 but gives the *a* their rights.
Ps 9:12 he does not ignore the cry of the *a*.
9:18 nor the hope of the *a* ever perish.
119:67 Before I was *a* I went astray,
119:71 It was good for me to be *a*
119:75 and in faithfulness you have *a* me.
Isa 49:13 will have compassion on his *a* ones.
53:4 smitten by him, and *a*.
53:7 He was oppressed and *a*,
Na 1:12 Although I have *a* you, O Judah,

AFFLICTION (AFFLICTED AFFLICTIONS)
Dt 16:3 bread of *a*, because you left Egypt
Ps 107:41 he lifted the needy out of their *a*
Isa 30:20 of adversity and the water of *a*,
48:10 in the furnace of *a*.
La 3:33 For he does not willingly bring *a*
Ro 12:12 patient in *a*, faithful in prayer.

AFFLICTIONS (AFFLICTION)
Col 1:24 lacking in regard to Christ's *a*,

AFRAID (FEAR)
Ge 3:10 and I was *a* because I was naked;
26:24 Do not be *a*, for I am with you;
Ex 2:14 Then Moses was *a* and thought,
3:6 because he was *a* to look at God.
Dt 1:21 Do not be *a*; do not be discouraged
1:29 "Do not be terrified; do not be *a*
20:1 do not be *a* of them,
20:3 Do not be fainthearted or *a*;
2Ki 25:24 "Do not be *a* of the Babylonian
1Ch 13:12 David was *a* of God that day
Ps 27:1 of whom shall I be *a*?
56:3 When I am *a*, / I will trust in you.
56:4 in God I trust; I will not be *a*.
Pr 3:24 lie down, you will not be *a*;
Isa 10:24 do not be *a* of the Assyrians,
12:2 I will trust and not be *a*.
44:8 Do not tremble, do not be *a*.
Jer 1:8 Do not be *a* of them, for I am
Mt 8:26 You of little faith, why are you so *a*
10:28 be *a* of the One who can destroy
10:31 So don't be *a*; you are worth more
Mk 5:36 "Don't be *a*; just believe."
Lk 9:34 and they were *a* as they entered
Jn 14:27 hearts be troubled and do not be *a*.
Ac 27:24 beside me and said, 'Do not be *a*,
Ro 11:20 Do not be arrogant, but be *a*.
Heb 13:6 Lord is my helper; I will not be *a*.

AGAG (AGAGITE)
King of Amalekites not killed by Saul (1Sa 15).

AGAGITE (AGAG)
Est 8:3 to the evil plan of Haman the *A*,

AGED (AGES)
Job 12:12 Is not wisdom found among the *a*?
Pr 17:6 children are a crown to the *a*,

AGES (AGED)
Ro 16:25 the mystery hidden for long *a* past,
Eph 2:7 that in the coming *a* he might show
3:9 which for *a* past was kept hidden
Col 1:26 that has been kept hidden for *a*
Rev 15:3 King of the *a*.

AGONY
Lk 16:24 because I am in *a* in this fire.'
Rev 16:10 Men gnawed their tongues in *a*

AGREE (AGREEMENT AGREES)
Mt 18:19 on earth *a* about anything you ask
Ro 7:16 want to do, I *a* that the law is good.
Php 4:2 with Syntyche to *a* with each other

AGREEMENT (AGREE)
2Co 6:16 What *a* is there between the temple

AGREES* (AGREE)
Ac 7:42 This *a* with what is written
24:14 I believe everything that *a*
1Co 4:17 which *a* with what I teach

AGRIPPA*

Descendant of Herod; king before whom Paul pled his case in Caesarea (Ac 25:13–26:32).

AHAB

1. Son of Omri; king of Israel (1Ki 16:28–22:40), husband of Jezebel (1Ki 16:31). Promoted Baal worship (1Ki 16:31–33); opposed by Elijah (1Ki 17:1; 18; 21), a prophet (1Ki 20:35–43), Micaiah (1Ki 22:1–28). Defeated Ben-Hadad (1Ki 20). Killed for failing to kill Ben-Hadad and for murder of Naboth (1Ki 20:35–21:40).

2. A false prophet (Jer 29:21–22).

AHAZ

1. Son of Jotham; king of Judah, (2Ki 16; 2Ch 28). Idolatry of (2Ki 16:3–4, 10–18; 2Ch 28:1–4, 22–25). Defeated by Aram and Israel (2Ki 16:5–6; 2Ch 28:5–15). Sought help from Assyria rather than the LORD (2Ki 16:7–9; 2Ch 28:16–21; Isa 7).

2. Benjamite, descendant of Saul (1Ch 8:35–36).

AHAZIAH

1. Son of Ahab; king of Israel (1Ki 22:51–2Ki 1:18; 2Ch 20:35–37). Made an unsuccessful alliance with Jehoshaphat of Judah (2Ch 20:35–37). Died for seeking Baal rather than the LORD (2Ki 1).

2. Son of Jehoram; king of Judah (2Ki 8:25–29; 9:14–29), also called Jehoahaz (2Ch 21:17–22:9; 25:23). Killed by Jehu while visiting Joram (2Ki 9:14–29; 2Ch 22:1–9).

AHIJAH

1Sa 14:18 Saul said to *A,* "Bring the ark
1Ki 14: 2 *A* the prophet is there—the one

AHIMELECH

1. Priest who helped David in his flight from Saul (1Sa 21–22).

2. One of David's warriors (1Sa 26:6).

AHITHOPHEL

One of David's counselors who sided with Absalom (2Sa 15:12, 31–37; 1Ch 27:33–34); committed suicide when his advice was ignored (2Sa 16:15–17:23).

AI

Jos 7: 4 they were routed by the men of *A,*
8:28 So Joshua burned *A* and made it

AID

Isa 38:14 troubled; O Lord, come to my *a!"*
Php 4:16 you sent me *a* again and again

AIM

1Co 7:34 Her *a* is to be devoted to the Lord
2Co 13:11 *A* for perfection, listen

AIR

Mt 8:20 and birds of the *a* have nests,
Lk 9:58 and birds of the *a* have nests,
1Co 9:26 not fight like a man beating the *a.*
14: 9 You will just be speaking into the *a*
Eph 2: 2 of the ruler of the kingdom of the *a,*
1Th 4:17 clouds to meet the Lord in the *a.*

ALABASTER*

Mt 26: 7 came to him with an *a* jar
Mk 14: 3 a woman came with an *a* jar
Lk 7:37 she brought an *a* jar of perfume,

ALARM (ALARMED)

2Co 7:11 indignation, what *a,* what longing,

ALARMED (ALARM)

Mk 13: 7 and rumors of wars, do not be *a.*
2Th 2: 2 not to become easily unsettled or *a*

ALERT*

Jos 8: 4 All of you be on the *a.*
Ps 17:11 with eyes *a,* to throw me
Isa 21: 7 let him be *a,* / fully *a."*
Mk 13:33 Be *a!* You do not know
Eph 6:18 be *a* and always keep on praying
1Th 5: 6 but let us be *a* and self-controlled.
1Pe 5: 8 Be self-controlled and *a.*

ALIEN (ALIENATED ALIENS)

Ex 22:21 "Do not mistreat an *a*
Lev 24:22 are to have the same law for the *a*
Ps 146: 9 The LORD watches over the *a*

ALIENATED (ALIEN)

Gal 5: 4 by law have been *a* from Christ;
Col 1:21 Once you were *a* from God

ALIENS (ALIEN)

Ex 23: 9 know how it feels to be *a,*
1Pe 2:11 as *a* and strangers in the world,

ALIVE (LIVE)

1Sa 2: 6 LORD brings death and makes *a;*
Lk 24:23 vision of angels, who said he was *a.*
Ac 1: 3 convincing proofs that he was *a.*
Ro 6:11 but *a* to God in Christ Jesus.
1Co 15:22 so in Christ all will be made *a.*
Eph 2: 5 made us *a* with Christ

ALMIGHTY (MIGHT)

Ge 17: 1 "I am God *A;* walk before me
Ex 6: 3 to Isaac and to Jacob as God *A,*
Ru 1:20 the *A* has made my life very bitter.
Job 11: 7 Can you probe the limits of the *A?*
33: 4 the breath of the *A* gives me life.
Ps 89: 8 O LORD God *A,* who is like you?
91: 1 will rest in the shadow of the *A.*
Isa 6: 3 "Holy, holy, holy is the LORD *A;*
45:13 says the LORD *A."*
47: 4 the LORD *A* is his name—
48: 2 the LORD *A* is his name:
51:15 the LORD *A* is his name.
54: 5 the LORD *A* is his name—
Am 5:14 the LORD God *A* will be with you,
5:15 the LORD God *A* will have mercy
Rev 4: 8 holy is the Lord God *A,* who was,
19: 6 For our Lord God *A* reigns.

ALPHA*

Rev 1: 8 "I am the *A* and the Omega,"
21: 6 I am the *A* and the Omega,
22:13 I am the *A* and the Omega,

ALTAR

Ge 8:20 Then Noah built an *a* to the LORD
12: 7 So he built an *a* there to the LORD
13:18 where he built an *a* to the LORD.
22: 9 Abraham built an *a* there
22: 9 his son Isaac and laid him on the *a,*
26:25 Isaac built an *a* there and called
35: 1 and build an *a* there to God,
Ex 17:15 Moses built an *a* and called it
27: 1 "Build an *a* of acacia wood,
30: 1 "Make an *a* of acacia wood
37:25 They made the *a* of incense out
Dt 27: 5 an *a* to the LORD your God, an *a*
Jos 8:30 on Mount Ebal an *a* to the LORD,
22:10 built an imposing *a* there
Jdg 6:24 So Gideon built an *a* to the LORD
21: 4 the next day the people built an *a*
1Sa 7:17 he built an *a* there to the LORD.
14:35 Then Saul built an *a* to the LORD;
2Sa 24:25 David built an *a* to the LORD
1Ki 12:33 sacrifices on the *a* he had built
13: 2 "O *a, a!* This is what the LORD
16:32 He set up an *a* for Baal
18:30 and he repaired the *a* of the LORD
2Ki 16:11 So Uriah the priest built an *a*
1Ch 21:26 David built an *a* to the LORD
2Ch 4: 1 made a bronze *a* twenty cubits
4:19 the golden *a;* the tables
15: 8 He repaired the *a* of the LORD
32:12 'You must worship before one *a*
33:16 he restored the *a* of the LORD
Ezr 3: 2 to build the *a* of the God of Israel
Isa 6: 6 taken with tongs from the *a.*
Eze 40:47 the *a* was in front of the temple.
Mt 5:23 if you are offering your gift at the *a*
Ac 17:23 found an *a* with this inscription:
Heb 13:10 We have an *a* from which those
Rev 6: 9 I saw under the *a* the souls

ALTER*

Ps 89:34 or *a* what my lips have uttered.

ALWAYS

Dt 15:11 There will *a* be poor people
Ps 16: 8 I have set the LORD *a* before me.
51: 3 and my sin is *a* before me.
Pr 23: 7 who is *a* thinking about the cost.
Mt 26:11 The poor you will *a* have with you,
28:20 And surely I am with you *a,*
Mk 14: 7 The poor you will *a* have with you,
Jn 12: 8 You will *a* have the poor
1Co 13: 7 *a* protects, *a* trusts, *a* hopes, *a*
Php 4: 4 Rejoice in the Lord *a.*
1Pe 3:15 *A* be prepared to give an answer

AMALEKITES

Ex 17: 8 *A* came and attacked the Israelites
1Sa 15: 2 'I will punish the *A*

AMASA

Nephew of David (1Ch 2:17). Commander of Absalom's forces (2Sa 17:24–27). Returned to David (2Sa 19:13). Killed by Joab (2Sa 20:4–13).

AMASSES*

Pr 28: 8 *a* it for another, who will be kind

AMAZED

Mt 7:28 the crowds were *a* at his teaching,
Mk 6: 6 And he was *a* at their lack of faith.
10:24 The disciples were *a* at his words.
Ac 2: 7 Utterly *a,* they asked: "Are not all
13:12 for he was *a* at the teaching about

AMAZIAH

1. Son of Joash; king of Judah (2Ki 14; 2Ch 25). Defeated Edom (2Ki 14:7; 2Ch 25:5–13); defeated by Israel for worshiping Edom's gods (2Ki 14:8–14; 2Ch 25:14–24).

2. Idolatrous priest who opposed Amos (Am 7:10–17).

AMBASSADOR* (AMBASSADORS)

Eph 6:20 for which I am an *a* in chains.

AMBASSADORS (AMBASSADOR)

2Co 5:20 We are therefore Christ's *a,*

AMBITION*

Ro 15:20 It has always been my *a*
Gal 5:20 fits of rage, selfish *a,* dissensions,
Php 1:17 preach Christ out of selfish *a,*
2: 3 Do nothing out of selfish *a*
1Th 4:11 Make it your *a* to lead a quiet life,
Jas 3:14 and selfish *a* in your hearts,
3:16 where you have envy and selfish *a,*

AMENDS

Pr 14: 9 Fools mock at making *a* for sin,

AMNON

Firstborn of David (2Sa 3:2; 1Ch 3:1). Killed by Absalom for raping his sister Tamar (2Sa 13).

AMON

1. Son of Manasseh; king of Judah (2Ki 21:18–26; 1Ch 3:14; 2Ch 33:21–25).

2. Ruler of Samaria under Ahab (1Ki 22:26; 2Ch 18:25).

AMOS
1. Prophet from Tekoa (Am 1:1; 7:10–17).
2. Ancestor of Jesus (Lk 3:25).

ANAK (ANAKITES)
Nu 13:28 even saw descendants of *A* there.

ANAKITES (ANAK)
Dt 1:28 We even saw the *A* there.' "
2:10 and numerous, and as tall as the *A.*
9: 2 "Who can stand up against the *A?*"

ANANIAS
1. Husband of Sapphira; died for lying to God (Ac 5:1–11).
2. Disciple who baptized Saul (Ac 9:10–19).
3. High priest at Paul's arrest (Ac 22:30–24:1).

ANCESTORS (ANCESTRY)
1Ki 19: 4 I am no better than my *a.*"

ANCESTRY (ANCESTORS)
Ro 9: 5 from them is traced the human *a*

ANCHOR
Heb 6:19 We have this hope as an *a*

ANCIENT
Da 7: 9 and the *A* of Days took his seat.
7:13 He approached the *A* of Days
7:22 until the *A* of Days came

ANDREW*
Apostle; brother of Simon Peter (Mt 4:18; 10:2; Mk 1:16–18, 29; 3:18; 13:3; Lk 6:14; Jn 1:35–44; 6:8–9; 12:22; Ac 1:13).

ANGEL (ANGELS ARCHANGEL)
Ge 16: 7 The *a* of the LORD found Hagar
22:11 But the *a* of the LORD called out
Ex 23:20 I am sending an *a* ahead of you
Nu 22:23 When the donkey saw the *a*
Jdg 2: 1 The *a* of the LORD went up
6:22 Gideon realized that it was the *a*
13:15 Manoah said to the *a* of the LORD
2Sa 24:16 The *a* of the LORD was then
1Ki 19: 7 The *a* of the LORD came back
2Ki 19:35 That night the *a* of the LORD went
Ps 34: 7 The *a* of the LORD encamps
Hos 12: 4 He struggled with the *a*
Mt 2:13 an *a* of the Lord appeared
28: 2 for an *a* of the Lord came
Lk 1:26 God sent the *a* Gabriel
2: 9 An *a* of the Lord appeared to them,
22:43 An *a* from heaven appeared to him
Ac 6:15 his face was like the face of an *a.*
12: 7 Suddenly an *a* of the Lord
2Co 11:14 Satan himself masquerades as an *a*
Gal 1: 8 or an *a* from heaven should preach

ANGELS (ANGEL)
Ps 91:11 command his *a* concerning you
Mt 4: 6 command his *a* concerning you,
13:39 of the age, and the harvesters are *a.*
13:49 The *a* will come and separate
18:10 For I tell you that their *a*
25:41 prepared for the devil and his *a.*
Lk 4:10 command his *a* concerning you
20:36 for they are like the *a.*
1Co 6: 3 you not know that we will judge *a?*
13: 1 in the tongues of men and of *a,*
Col 2:18 and the worship of *a* disqualify you
Heb 1: 4 as much superior to the *a*
1: 6 "Let all God's *a* worship him."
1: 7 "He makes his *a* winds,
1:14 Are not all *a* ministering spirits
2: 7 made him a little lower than the *a;*
2: 9 was made a little lower than the *a,*
13: 2 some people have entertained *a*
1Pe 1:12 Even *a* long to look
2Pe 2: 4 For if God did not spare *a*
Jude : 6 *a* who did not keep their positions

ANGER (ANGERED ANGRY)
Ex 15: 7 You unleashed your burning *a;*
22:24 My *a* will be aroused, and I will kill
32:10 alone so that my *a* may burn
32:11 "why should your *a* burn
32:12 Turn from your fierce *a;* relent
32:19 his *a* burned and he threw
34: 6 slow to *a,* abounding in love
Lev 26:28 then in my *a* I will be hostile
Nu 14:18 slow to *a,* abounding in love
25:11 has turned my *a* away
32:10 LORD's *a* was aroused that day
32:13 The LORD's *a* burned
Dt 9:19 I feared the *a* and wrath
29:28 In furious *a* and in great wrath
Jdg 14:19 Burning with *a,* he went up
2Sa 12: 5 David burned with *a*
2Ki 22:13 Great is the LORD's *a* that burns
Ne 9:17 slow to *a* and abounding in love.
Ps 30: 5 For his *a* lasts only a moment,
78:38 Time after time he restrained his *a*
86:15 slow to *a,* abounding in love
90: 7 We are consumed by your *a*
103: 8 slow to *a,* abounding in love.
Pr 15: 1 but a harsh word stirs up *a.*
29:11 A fool gives full vent to his *a,*
30:33 so stirring up *a* produces strife."
Jnh 4: 2 slow to *a* and abounding in love,
Eph 4:26 "In your *a* do not sin": Do not let
Jas 1:20 for man's *a* does not bring about

ANGERED (ANGER)
Pr 22:24 do not associate with one easily *a,*
1Co 13: 5 it is not easily *a,* it keeps no record

ANGRY (ANGER)
Ps 2:12 Kiss the Son, lest he be *a*
95:10 For forty years I was *a*
Pr 29:22 An *a* man stirs up dissension,
Mt 5:22 But I tell you that anyone who is *a*
Jas 1:19 slow to speak and slow to become *a*

ANGUISH
Ps 118: 5 In my *a* I cried to the LORD,
Jer 4:19 Oh, my *a,* my *a!*
Zep 1:15 a day of distress and *a,*
Lk 21:25 nations will be in *a* and perplexity
22:44 in *a,* he prayed more earnestly,
Ro 9: 2 and unceasing *a* in my heart.

ANIMALS
Ge 1:24 wild *a,* each according to its kind."
7:16 The *a* going in were male
Dt 14: 4 These are the *a* you may eat: the ox
Job 12: 7 ask the *a,* and they will teach you,
Isa 43:20 The wild *a* honor me,

ANNOUNCE (ANNOUNCED)
Mt 6: 2 give to the needy, do not *a* it

ANNOUNCED (ANNOUNCE)
Isa 48: 5 before they happened I *a* them
Gal 3: 8 and *a* the gospel in advance

ANNOYANCE*
Pr 12:16 A fool shows his *a* at once,

ANNUAL*
Ex 30:10 This *a* atonement must be made
Jdg 21:19 there is the *a* festival of the LORD
1Sa 1:21 family to offer the *a* sacrifice
2:19 husband to offer the *a* sacrifice.
20: 6 an *a* sacrifice is being made there
2Ch 8:13 New Moons and the three *a* feasts
Heb 10: 3 those sacrifices are an *a* reminder

ANOINT (ANOINTED ANOINTING)
Ex 30:26 use it to *a* the Tent of Meeting,
30:30 "*A* Aaron and his sons
1Sa 9:16 *A* him leader over my people Israel
15: 1 to *a* you king over his people Israel;
2Ki 9: 3 what the LORD says: I *a* you king
Ps 23: 5 You *a* my head with oil;
Da 9:24 prophecy and to *a* the most holy.
Jas 5:14 and *a* him with oil in the name

ANOINTED (ANOINT)
1Ch 16:22 "Do not touch my *a* ones;
Ps 105:15 "Do not touch my *a* ones;
Isa 61: 1 because the LORD has *a* me
Da 9:26 the *A* One will be cut off
Lk 4:18 because he has *a* me
Ac 10:38 how God *a* Jesus of Nazareth

ANOINTING (ANOINT)
Lev 8:12 some of the *a* oil on Aaron's head
1Ch 29:22 *a* him before the LORD to be ruler
Ps 45: 7 by *a* you with the oil of joy.
Heb 1: 9 by *a* you with the oil of joy."
1Jn 2:20 you have an *a* from the Holy One,
2:27 about all things and as that *a* is real,

ANT* (ANTS)
Pr 6: 6 Go to the *a,* you sluggard;

ANTICHRIST* (ANTICHRISTS)
1Jn 2:18 have heard that the *a* is coming,
2:22 a man is the *a*— he denies
4: 3 of the *a,* which you have heard is
2Jn : 7 person is the deceiver and the *a.*

ANTICHRISTS* (ANTICHRIST)
1Jn 2:18 even now many *a* have come.

ANTIOCH
Ac 11:26 were called Christians first at *A.*

ANTS* (ANT)
Pr 30:25 *A* are creatures of little strength,

ANXIETIES* (ANXIOUS)
Lk 21:34 drunkenness and the *a* of life,

ANXIETY (ANXIOUS)
1Pe 5: 7 Cast all your *a* on him

ANXIOUS (ANXIETIES ANXIETY)
Pr 12:25 An *a* heart weighs a man down,
Php 4: 6 Do not be *a* about anything,

APOLLOS*
Christian from Alexandria, learned in the Scriptures; instructed by Aquila and Priscilla (Ac 18:24–28). Ministered at Corinth (Ac 19:1; 1Co 1:12; 3; Tit 3:13).

APOLLYON*
Rev 9:11 is Abaddon, and in Greek, *A.*

APOSTLE (APOSTLES APOSTLES')
Ro 11:13 as I am the *a* to the Gentiles,
1Co 9: 1 Am I not an *a?* Have I not seen
2Co 12:12 The things that mark an *a*— signs,
Gal 2: 8 of Peter as an *a* to the Jews,
1Ti 2: 7 was appointed a herald and an *a*—
2Ti 1:11 I was appointed a herald and an *a*
Heb 3: 1 *a* and high priest whom we confess.

APOSTLES (APOSTLE)
See also Andrew, Bartholomew, James, John, Judas, Matthew, Matthias, Nathanael, Paul, Peter, Philip, Simon, Thaddaeus, Thomas.
Mk 3:14 twelve—designating them *a*—
Lk 11:49 'I will send them prophets and *a,*
Ac 1:26 so he was added to the eleven *a.*
2:43 signs were done by the *a.*
1Co 12:28 God has appointed first of all *a,*
15: 9 For I am the least of the *a*
2Co 11:13 masquerading as *a* of Christ.
Eph 2:20 built on the foundation of the *a*
4:11 It was he who gave some to be *a,*
Rev 21:14 names of the twelve *a* of the Lamb.

APOSTLES' (APOSTLE)
Ac 5: 2 the rest and put it at the *a'* feet.

Ac 8:18 at the laying on of the *a'* hands,

APPEAL
Ac 25:11 I *a* to Caesar!" After Festus had
Phm : 9 yet I *a* to you on the basis of love.

APPEAR (APPEARANCE APPEARANCES APPEARED APPEARING APPEARS)
Ge 1: 9 to one place, and let dry ground *a."*
Lev 16: 2 I *a* in the cloud over the atonement
Mt 24:30 of the Son of Man will *a* in the sky,
Mk 13:22 false prophets will *a* and perform
Lk 19:11 of God was going to *a* at once.
2Co 5:10 we must all *a* before the judgment
Col 3: 4 also will *a* with him in glory.
Heb 9:24 now to *a* for us in God's presence.
9:28 and he will *a* a second time,

APPEARANCE (APPEAR)
1Sa 16: 7 Man looks at the outward *a,*
Isa 52:14 his *a* was so disfigured beyond that
53: 2 in his *a* that we should desire him.
Gal 2: 6 God does not judge by external *a*—

APPEARANCES* (APPEAR)
Jn 7:24 Stop judging by mere *a,*

APPEARED (APPEAR)
Nu 14:10 glory of the LORD *a* at the Tent
Mt 1:20 an angel of the Lord *a* to him
Lk 2: 9 An angel of the Lord *a* to them,
1Co 15: 5 and that he *a* to Peter,
Heb 9:26 now he has *a* once for all at the end

APPEARING (APPEAR)
1Ti 6:14 until the *a* of our Lord Jesus Christ,
2Ti 1:10 through the *a* of our Savior,
4: 8 to all who have longed for his *a.*
Tit 2:13 the glorious *a* of our great God

APPEARS (APPEAR)
Mal 3: 2 Who can stand when he *a?*
Col 3: 4 When Christ, who is your life, *a,*
1Pe 5: 4 And when the Chief Shepherd *a,*
1Jn 3: 2 But we know that when he *a,*

APPETITE
Pr 16:26 The laborer's *a* works for him;
Ecc 6: 7 yet his *a* is never satisfied.
Jer 50:19 his *a* will be satisfied

APPLES
Pr 25:11 is like *a* of gold in settings of silver.

APPLY (APPLYING)
Pr 22:17 *a* your heart to what I teach,
23:12 *A* your heart to instruction

APPLYING (APPLY)
Pr 2: 2 and *a* your heart to understanding,

APPOINT (APPOINTED)
Ps 61: 7 *a* your love and faithfulness
1Th 5: 9 For God did not *a* us
Tit 1: 5 and *a* elders in every town,

APPOINTED (APPOINT)
Dt 1:15 *a* them to have authority over you
Pr 8:23 I was *a* from eternity,
Da 11:27 an end will still come at the *a* time.
Hab 2: 3 For the revelation awaits an *a* time;
Jn 15:16 Chose you and *a* you to go
Ro 9: 9 "At the *a* time I will return,

APPROACH (APPROACHING)
Ex 24: 2 but Moses alone is to *a* the LORD;
Eph 3:12 in him we may *a* God with freedom
Heb 4:16 Let us then *a* the throne of grace

APPROACHING (APPROACH)
Heb 10:25 all the more as you see the Day *a.*
1Jn 5:14 is the confidence we have in *a* God:

APPROPRIATE
1Ti 2:10 *a* for women who profess

APPROVAL (APPROVE)
Jdg 18: 6 Your journey has the LORD's *a."*
Jn 6:27 the Father has placed his seal of *a."*
1Co 11:19 to show which of you have God's *a*
Gal 1:10 trying to win the *a* of men,

APPROVE (APPROVAL APPROVED APPROVES)
Ro 2:18 if you know his will and *a*
12: 2 and *a* what God's will is—

APPROVED* (APPROVE)
Ro 14:18 pleasing to God and *a* by men.
16:10 Greet Apelles, tested and *a*
2Co 10:18 who commends himself who is *a,*
1Th 2: 4 as men *a* by God to be entrusted
2Ti 2:15 to present yourself to God as one *a,*

APPROVES* (APPROVE)
Ro 14:22 not condemn himself by what he *a.*

APT*
Pr 15:23 A man finds joy in giving an *a* reply

AQUILA*
Husband of Priscilla; co-worker with Paul, instructor of Apollos (Ac 18; Ro 16:3; 1Co 16:19; 2Ti 4:19).

ARABIA
Gal 1:17 but I went immediately into *A*
4:25 Hagar stands for Mount Sinai in *A*

ARARAT
Ge 8: 4 came to rest on the mountains of *A.*

ARAUNAH
2Sa 24:16 threshing floor of *A* the Jebusite.

ARBITER* (ARBITRATE)
Lk 12:14 who appointed me a judge or an *a*

ARBITRATE* (ARBITER)
Job 9:33 If only there were someone to *a*

ARCHANGEL* (ANGEL)
1Th 4:16 with the voice of the *a*
Jude : 9 *a* Michael, when he was disputing

ARCHER
Pr 26:10 Like an *a* who wounds at random

ARCHIPPUS*
Col 4:17 Tell *A:* "See to it that you complete
Phm : 2 to *A* our fellow soldier

ARCHITECT*
Heb 11:10 whose *a* and builder is God.

AREOPAGUS*
Ac 17:19 brought him to a meeting of the *A,*
17:22 up in the meeting of the *A*
17:34 of the *A,* also a woman named

ARGUE (ARGUMENT ARGUMENTS)
Job 13: 3 and to *a* my case with God.
13: 8 Will you *a* the case for God?
Pr 25: 9 If you *a* your case with a neighbor,

ARGUMENT (ARGUE)
Heb 6:16 is said and puts an end to all *a.*

ARGUMENTS (ARGUE)
Isa 41:21 "Set forth your *a,"* says Jacob's
Col 2: 4 you by fine-sounding *a.*
2Ti 2:23 to do with foolish and stupid *a,*
Tit 3: 9 and *a* and quarrels about the law,

ARK
Ge 6:14 So make yourself an *a*
Ex 25:21 and put in the *a* the Testimony,
Dt 10: 5 put the tablets in the *a* I had made,
1Sa 4:11 The *a* of God was captured,
7: 2 that the *a* remained at Kiriath
2Sa 6:17 They brought the *a* of the LORD
1Ki 8: 9 There was nothing in the *a*
1Ch 13: 9 out his hand to steady the *a,*
2Ch 35: 3 "Put the sacred *a* in the temple that
Heb 9: 4 This *a* contained the gold jar
11: 7 in holy fear built an *a*
Rev 11:19 within his temple was seen the *a*

ARM (ARMY)
Nu 11:23 "Is the LORD's *a* too short?
Dt 4:34 hand and an outstretched *a,*
7:19 mighty hand and outstretched *a,*
Ps 44: 3 it was your right hand, your *a,*
98: 1 his right hand and his holy *a*
Jer 27: 5 outstretched *a* I made the earth
1Pe 4: 1 *a* yourselves also with the same

ARMAGEDDON*
Rev 16:16 that in Hebrew is called *A.*

ARMIES (ARMY)
1Sa 17:26 Philistine that he should defy the *a*
Rev 19:14 *a* of heaven were following him,

ARMOR (ARMY)
1Ki 20:11 on his *a* should not boast like one
Jer 46: 4 put on your *a!*
Ro 13:12 deeds of darkness and put on the *a*
Eph 6:11 Put on the full *a* of God
6:13 Therefore put on the full *a* of God,

ARMS (ARMY)
Dt 33:27 underneath are the everlasting *a.*
Ps 18:32 It is God who *a* me with strength
Pr 31:17 her *a* are strong for her tasks.
31:20 She opens her *a* to the poor
Isa 40:11 He gathers the lambs in his *a*
Mk 10:16 And he took the children in his *a,*
Heb 12:12 strengthen your feeble *a*

ARMY (ARM ARMIES ARMOR ARMS)
Ps 33:16 No king is saved by the size of his *a*
Joel 2: 2 a large and mighty *a* comes,
2: 5 like a mighty *a* drawn up for battle.
2:11 thunders at the head of his *a;*
Rev 19:19 the rider on the horse and his *a.*

AROMA
Ge 8:21 The LORD smelled the pleasing *a*
Ex 29:18 a pleasing *a,* an offering made
Lev 3:16 made by fire, a pleasing *a.*
2Co 2:15 For we are to God the *a* of Christ

AROUSE (AROUSED)
Ro 11:14 I may somehow *a* my own people

AROUSED (AROUSE)
Ps 78:58 they *a* his jealousy with their idols.

ARRANGED
1Co 12:18 But in fact God has *a* the parts

ARRAYED*
Ps 110: 3 *A* in holy majesty,
Isa 61:10 and *a* me in a robe of righteousness

ARREST
Mt 10:19 But when they *a* you, do not worry

ARROGANCE (ARROGANT)
1Sa 2: 3 or let your mouth speak such *a,*
Pr 8:13 I hate pride and *a,*
Mk 7:22 lewdness, envy, slander, *a* and folly
2Co 12:20 slander, gossip, *a* and disorder.

ARROGANT (ARROGANCE)
Ps 5: 5 The *a* cannot stand
119:78 May the *a* be put to shame
Pr 17: 7 *A* lips are unsuited to a fool—
21:24 *a* man—"Mocker" is his name;

Ro 1:30 God-haters, insolent, *a*
11:20 Do not be *a,* but be afraid.
1Ti 6:17 in this present world not to be *a*

ARROW (ARROWS)
Ps 91: 5 nor the *a* that flies by day,
Pr 25:18 Like a club or a sword or a sharp *a*

ARROWS (ARROW)
Ps 64: 3 and aim their words like deadly *a.*
64: 7 But God will shoot them with *a;*
127: 4 Like *a* in the hands of a warrior
Pr 26:18 firebrands or deadly *a*
Eph 6:16 you can extinguish all the flaming *a*

ARTAXERXES
King of Persia; allowed rebuilding of temple under Ezra (Ezr 4; 7), and of walls of Jerusalem under his cupbearer Nehemiah (Ne 2; 5:14; 13:6).

ARTEMIS
Ac 19:28 "Great is *A* of the Ephesians!"

ASA
King of Judah (1Ki 15:8–24; 1Ch 3:10; 2Ch 14–16). Godly reformer (2Ch 15); in later years defeated Israel with help of Aram, not the LORD (1Ki 15:16–22; 2Ch 16).

ASAHEL
1. Nephew of David, one of his warriors (2Sa 23:24; 1Ch 2:16; 11:26; 27:7). Killed by Abner (2Sa 2); avenged by Joab (2Sa 3:22–39).
2. Levite; teacher (2Ch 17:8).

ASAPH
1. Recorder to Hezekiah (2Ki 18:18, 37; Isa 36:3, 22).
2. Levitical musician (1Ch 6:39; 15:17–19; 16:4–7, 37). Sons of (1Ch 25; 2Ch 5:12; 20:14; 29:13; 35:15; Ezr 2:41; 3:10; Ne 7:44; 11:17; 12:27–47). Psalms of (2Ch 29:30; Ps 50; 73–83).

ASCEND* (ASCENDED ASCENDING)
Dt 30:12 "Who will *a* into heaven to get it
Ps 24: 3 Who may *a* the hill of the LORD?
Isa 14:13 "I will *a* to heaven;
14:14 I will *a* above the tops of the clouds
Jn 6:62 of Man *a* to where he was before!
Ac 2:34 For David did not *a* to heaven,
Ro 10: 6 'Who will *a* into heaven?' " (that is,

ASCENDED (ASCEND)
Ps 68:18 When you *a* on high,
Eph 4: 8 "When he *a* on high,

ASCENDING (ASCEND)
Ge 28:12 and the angels of God were *a*
Jn 1:51 and the angels of God *a*

ASCRIBE*
1Ch 16:28 *A* to the LORD, O families
16:28 *a* to the LORD glory and strength,
16:29 *a* to the LORD the glory due his
Job 36: 3 I will *a* justice to my Maker.
Ps 29: 1 *A* to the LORD, O mighty ones,
29: 1 *a* to the LORD glory and strength.
29: 2 *A* to the LORD the glory due his
96: 7 *A* to the LORD, O families
96: 7 *a* to the LORD glory and strength.
96: 8 *A* to the LORD the glory due his

ASHAMED (SHAME)
Mk 8:38 If anyone is *a* of me and my words
Lk 9:26 If anyone is *a* of me and my words,
Ro 1:16 I am not *a* of the gospel,
2Ti 1: 8 So do not be *a* to testify about our
2:15 who does not need to be *a*

ASHER
Son of Jacob by Zilpah (Ge 30:13; 35:26; 46:17; Ex 1:4; 1Ch 2:2). Tribe of blessed (Ge 49:20; Dt 33:24–25), numbered (Nu 1:40–41; 26:44–47), allotted land (Jos 10:24–31; Eze 48:2), failed to fully possess (Jdg 1:31–32), failed to support Deborah (Jdg 5:17), supported Gideon (Jdg 6:35; 7:23) and David (1Ch 12:36), 12,000 from (Rev 7:6).

ASHERAH (ASHERAHS)
Ex 34:13 and cut down their *A* poles.
1Ki 18:19 the four hundred prophets of *A,*

ASHERAHS* (ASHERAH)
Jdg 3: 7 and served the Baals and the *A.*

ASHES
Job 42: 6 and repent in dust and *a.*"
Mt 11:21 ago in sackcloth and *a.*

ASHTORETHS
Jdg 2:13 and served Baal and the *A.*
1Sa 7: 4 put away their Baals and *A,*

ASLEEP (SLEEP)
1Co 15:18 who have fallen *a* in Christ are lost.
1Th 4:13 be ignorant about those who fall *a,*

ASSEMBLY
Ps 1: 5 nor sinners in the *a* of the righteous
35:18 I will give you thanks in the great *a*
82: 1 God presides in the great *a;*
149: 1 his praise in the *a* of the saints.

ASSIGNED
1Ki 7:14 and did all the work *a* to him.
Mk 13:34 with his *a* task, and tells the one
1Co 3: 5 as the Lord has *a* to each his task.
7:17 place in life that the Lord *a* to him
2Co 10:13 to the field God has *a* to us,

ASSOCIATE
Pr 22:24 do not *a* with one easily angered,
Jn 4: 9 (For Jews do not *a* with Samaritans
Ac 10:28 law for a Jew to *a* with a Gentile
Ro 12:16 but be willing to *a* with people
1Co 5: 9 to *a* with sexually immoral people
5:11 am writing you that you must not *a*
2Th 3:14 Do not *a* with him,

ASSURANCE (ASSURED)
Heb 10:22 with a sincere heart in full *a* of faith

ASSURED (ASSURANCE)
Col 4:12 the will of God, mature and fully *a.*

ASTRAY
Ps 119:67 Before I was afflicted I went *a,*
Pr 10:17 ignores correction leads others *a.*
20: 1 whoever is led *a* by them is not
Isa 53: 6 We all, like sheep, have gone *a,*
Jer 50: 6 their shepherds have led them *a*
Jn 16: 1 you so that you will not go *a.*
1Pe 2:25 For you were like sheep going *a,*
1Jn 3: 7 do not let anyone lead you *a.*

ASTROLOGERS
Isa 47:13 Let your *a* come forward,
Da 2: 2 *a* to tell him what he had dreamed.

ATE (EAT)
Ge 3: 6 wisdom, she took some and *a* it.
27:25 Jacob brought it to him and he *a;*
2Sa 9:11 Mephibosheth *a* at David's table
Ps 78:25 Men *a* the bread of angels;
Jer 15:16 When your words came, I *a* them;
Eze 3: 3 So I *a* it, and it tasted as sweet
Mt 14:20 They all *a* and were satisfied,
15:37 They all *a* and were satisfied.
Mk 6:42 They all *a* and were satisfied,
Lk 9:17 They all *a* and were satisfied,

ATHALIAH
Granddaughter of Omri; wife of Jehoram and mother of Ahaziah; encouraged their evil ways (2Ki 8:18, 27; 2Ch 22:2). At death of Ahaziah she made herself queen, killing all his sons but Joash (2Ki 11:1–3; 2Ch 22:10–12); killed six years later when Joash was revealed (2Ki 11:4–16; 2Ch 23:1–15).

ATHLETE*
2Ti 2: 5 if anyone competes as an *a,*

ATONE* (ATONEMENT)
Ex 30:15 to the LORD to *a* for your lives.
2Ch 29:24 for a sin offering to *a* for all Israel,
Da 9:24 an end to sin, to *a* for wickedness,

ATONED* (ATONEMENT)
Dt 21: 8 And the bloodshed will be *a* for.
1Sa 3:14 guilt of Eli's house will never be *a*
Pr 16: 6 faithfulness sin is *a* for;
Isa 6: 7 guilt is taken away and your sin *a*
22:14 your dying day this sin will not be *a*
27: 9 then, will Jacob's guilt be *a* for,

ATONEMENT (ATONE ATONED)
Ex 25:17 "Make an *a* cover of pure gold—
30:10 Once a year Aaron shall make *a*
Lev 17:11 it is the blood that makes *a*
23:27 this seventh month is the Day of *A.*
Nu 25:13 and made *a* for the Israelites."
Ro 3:25 presented him as a sacrifice of *a,*
Heb 2:17 that he might make *a* for the sins

ATTACK
Ps 109: 3 they *a* me without cause.

ATTAINED
Php 3:16 up to what we have already *a.*
Heb 7:11 If perfection could have been *a*

ATTENTION (ATTENTIVE)
Pr 4: 1 pay *a* and gain understanding.
4:20 My son, pay *a* to what I say;
5: 1 My son, pay *a* to my wisdom,
7:24 pay *a* to what I say.
22:17 Pay *a* and listen to the sayings
Ecc 7:21 Do not pay *a* to every word people
Isa 42:20 many things, but have paid no *a;*
Tit 1:14 and will pay no *a* to Jewish myths
Heb 2: 1 We must pay more careful *a,*

ATTENTIVE (ATTENTION)
Ne 1:11 let your ear be *a* to the prayer
1Pe 3:12 and his ears are *a* to their prayer,

ATTITUDE (ATTITUDES)
Eph 4:23 new in the *a* of your minds;
Php 2: 5 Your *a* should be the same
1Pe 4: 1 yourselves also with the same *a,*

ATTITUDES (ATTITUDE)
Heb 4:12 it judges the thoughts and *a*

ATTRACTIVE
Tit 2:10 teaching about God our Savior *a.*

AUDIENCE
Pr 29:26 Many seek an *a* with a ruler,

AUTHORITIES (AUTHORITY)
Ro 13: 1 *a* that exist have been established
13: 5 it is necessary to submit to the *a,*
13: 6 for the *a* are God's servants,
Eph 3:10 and *a* in the heavenly realms,
6:12 but against the rulers, against the *a,*
Col 1:16 thrones or powers or rulers or *a;*
2:15 having disarmed the powers and *a,*
Tit 3: 1 people to be subject to rulers and *a,*
1Pe 3:22 *a* and powers in submission to him.

AUTHORITY (AUTHORITIES)
Mt 7:29 because he taught as one who had *a*
9: 6 the Son of Man has *a* on earth
28:18 "All *a* in heaven and on earth has
Mk 1:22 he taught them as one who had *a,*
2:10 the Son of Man has *a* on earth

Lk 4:32 because his message had *a.*
5:24 the Son of Man has *a* on earth
Jn 10:18 *a* to lay it down and *a*
Ac 1: 7 the Father has set by his own *a.*
Ro 7: 1 that the law has *a* over a man only
13: 1 for there is no *a* except that which
13: 2 rebels against the *a* is rebelling
1Co 11:10 to have a sign of *a* on her head.
15:24 he has destroyed all dominion, *a*
1Ti 2: 2 for kings and all those in *a,*
2:12 to teach or to have *a* over a man;
Tit 2:15 Encourage and rebuke with all *a.*
Heb 13:17 your leaders and submit to their *a.*

AUTUMN*
Dt 11:14 both *a* and spring rains,
Ps 84: 6 the *a* rains also cover it with pools.
Jer 5:24 who gives *a* and spring rains
Joel 2:23 both *a* and spring rains, as before.
Jas 5: 7 and how patient he is for the *a*
Jude :12 blown along by the wind; *a* trees,

AVENGE (VENGEANCE)
Lev 26:25 sword upon you to *a* the breaking
Dt 32:35 It is mine to *a;* I will repay.
32:43 for he will *a* the blood
Ro 12:19 "It is mine to *a;* I will repay,"
Heb 10:30 "It is mine to *a;* I will repay,"
Rev 6:10 of the earth and *a* our blood?"

AVENGER (VENGEANCE)
Nu 35:27 the *a* of blood may kill the accused
Jos 20: 3 find protection from the *a* of blood.
Ps 8: 2 to silence the foe and the *a.*

AVENGES (VENGEANCE)
Ps 94: 1 O LORD, the God who *a,*

AVENGING (VENGEANCE)
1Sa 25:26 and from *a* yourself with your own
Na 1: 2 The LORD is a jealous and *a* God;

AVOID (AVOIDS)
Pr 4:15 *A* it, do not travel on it;
20: 3 It is to a man's honor to *a* strife,
20:19 so *a* a man who talks too much.
Ecc 7:18 who fears God will *a* all ›extremes‹.
1Th 4: 3 you should *a* sexual immorality;
5:22 *A* every kind of evil.
2Ti 2:16 *A* godless chatter, because those
Tit 3: 9 But *a* foolish controversies

AVOIDS* (AVOID)
Pr 16: 6 of the LORD a man *a* evil.
16:17 The highway of the upright *a* evil;

AWAITS (WAIT)
Pr 15:10 Stern discipline *a* him who leaves
28:22 and is unaware that poverty *a* him.

AWAKE (WAKE)
Ps 17:15 when I *a,* I will be satisfied
Pr 6:22 when you *a,* they will speak to you.

AWARD*
2Ti 4: 8 will *a* to me on that day—

AWARE
Ex 34:29 he was not *a* that his face was
Mt 24:50 and at an hour he is not *a* of.
Lk 12:46 and at an hour he is not *a* of.

AWE* (AWESOME OVERAWED)
1Sa 12:18 So all the people stood in *a*
1Ki 3:28 they held the king in *a,*
Job 25: 2 "Dominion and *a* belong to God;
Ps 119:120 I stand in *a* of your laws.
Ecc 5: 7 Therefore stand in *a* of God.
Isa 29:23 will stand in *a* of the God of Israel.
Jer 2:19 and have no *a* of me,"
33: 9 they will be in *a* and will tremble
Hab 3: 2 I stand in *a* of your deeds,
Mal 2: 5 and stood in *a* of my name.
Mt 9: 8 they were filled with *a;*
Lk 1:65 The neighbors were all filled with *a*
5:26 They were filled with *a* and said,
7:16 They were all filled with *a*
Ac 2:43 Everyone was filled with *a,*
Heb 12:28 acceptably with reverence and *a,*

AWESOME* (AWE)
Ge 28:17 and said, "How *a* is this place!
Ex 15:11 *a* in glory,
34:10 among will see how *a* is the work
Dt 4:34 or by great and *a* deeds,
7:21 is among you, is a great and *a* God.
10:17 the great God, mighty and *a,*
10:21 and *a* wonders you saw
28:58 revere this glorious and *a* name—
34:12 performed the *a* deeds that Moses
Jdg 13: 6 like an angel of God, very *a.*
2Sa 7:23 *a* wonders by driving out nations
1Ch 17:21 *a* wonders by driving out nations
Ne 1: 5 of heaven, the great and *a* God,
4:14 and *a,* and fight for your brothers,
9:32 the great, mighty and *a* God,
Job 10:16 again display your *a* power
37:22 God comes in *a* majesty.
Ps 45: 4 let your right hand display *a* deeds.
47: 2 How *a* is the LORD Most High,
65: 5 us with *a* deeds of righteousness,
66: 3 to God, "How *a* are your deeds!
66: 5 how *a* his works in man's behalf!
68:35 You are *a,* O God,
89: 7 he is more *a* than all who surround
99: 3 praise your great and *a* name—
106:22 and *a* deeds by the Red Sea.
111: 9 holy and *a* is his name.
145: 6 of the power of your *a* works,
Isa 64: 3 when you did *a* things that we did
Eze 1:18 Their rims were high and *a,*
1:22 expanse, sparkling like ice, and *a.*
Da 2:31 dazzling statue, *a* in appearance.
9: 4 "O Lord, the great and *a* God,
Zep 2:11 The LORD will be *a* to them

AX
Mt 3:10 The *a* is already at the root
Lk 3: 9 The *a* is already at the root

BAAL
Jdg 6:25 Tear down your father's altar to *B*
1Ki 16:32 *B* in the temple of *B* that he built
18:25 Elijah said to the prophets of *B,*
19:18 knees have not bowed down to *B*
2Ki 10:28 Jehu destroyed *B* worship in Israel.
Jer 19: 5 places of *B* to burn their sons
Ro 11: 4 have not bowed the knee to *B.*"

BAASHA
King of Israel (1Ki 15:16–16:7; 2Ch 16:1–6).

BABBLER* (BABBLING)
Ac 17:18 "What is this *b* trying to say?"

BABBLING* (BABBLER)
Mt 6: 7 do not keep on *b* like pagans,

BABIES* (BABY)
Ge 25:22 The *b* jostled each other within her
Ex 2: 6 "This is one of the Hebrew *b,*"
Lk 18:15 also bringing *b* to Jesus
Ac 7:19 them to throw out their newborn *b*
1Pe 2: 2 Like newborn *b,* crave pure

BABY* (BABIES BABY'S)
Ex 2: 6 She opened it and saw the *b.*
2: 7 women to nurse the *b* for you?"
2: 9 So the woman took the *b*
2: 9 "Take this *b* and nurse him for me,
1Ki 3:17 I had a *b* while she was there
3:18 was born, this woman also had a *b.*
3:26 give her the living *b!* Don't kill him
3:27 Give the living *b* to the first woman
Isa 49:15 "Can a mother forget the *b*
Lk 1:41 the *b* leaped in her womb,
1:44 the *b* in my womb leaped for joy.
1:57 time for Elizabeth to have her *b,*
2: 6 the time came for the *b* to be born,
2:12 You will find a *b* wrapped in strips
2:16 the *b,* who was lying in the manger.
Jn 16:21 but when her *b* is born she forgets

BABY'S* (BABY)
Ex 2: 8 the girl went and got the *b* mother.

BABYLON
Ps 137: 1 By the rivers of *B* we sat and wept
Jer 29:10 seventy years are completed for *B,*
51:37 *B* will be a heap of ruins,
Rev 14: 8 "Fallen! Fallen is *B* the Great,
17: 5 MYSTERY *B* THE GREAT

BACKS
2Pe 2:21 and then to turn their *b*

BACKSLIDING* (BACKSLIDINGS)
Jer 2:19 your *b* will rebuke you.
3:22 I will cure you of *b.*"
14: 7 For our *b* is great;
15: 6 "You keep on *b.*
Eze 37:23 them from all their sinful *b,*

BACKSLIDINGS* (BACKSLIDING)
Jer 5: 6 and their *b* many.

BALAAM
Prophet who attempted to curse Israel (Nu 22–24; Dt 23:4–5; 2Pe 2:15; Jude 11). Killed in Israel's vengeance on Midianites (Nu 31:8; Jos 13:22).

BALAK
Moabite king who hired Balaam to curse Israel (Nu 22–24; Jos 24:9).

BALDHEAD
2Ki 2:23 "Go on up, you *b!*" they said.

BALM
Jer 8:22 Is there no *b* in Gilead?

BANISH (BANISHED)
Jer 25:10 I will *b* from them the sounds of joy

BANISHED (BANISH)
Dt 30: 4 Even if you have been *b*

BANNER
Ex 17:15 and called it The LORD is my *B.*
SS 2: 4 and his *b* over me is love.
Isa 11:10 the Root of Jesse will stand as a *b*

BANQUET
SS 2: 4 He has taken me to the *b* hall,
Lk 14:13 when you give a *b,* invite the poor,

BAPTISM* (BAPTIZE)
Mt 21:25 John's *b*— where did it come from?
Mk 1: 4 and preaching a *b* of repentance
10:38 baptized with the *b* I am baptized
10:39 baptized with the *b* I am baptized
11:30 John's *b*— was it from heaven,
Lk 3: 3 preaching a *b* of repentance
12:50 But I have a *b* to undergo,
20: 4 John's *b*— was it from heaven,
Ac 1:22 beginning from John's *b*
10:37 after the *b* that John preached—
13:24 and *b* to all the people of Israel.
18:25 though he knew only the *b* of John.
19: 3 did you receive?" "John's *b,*"
19: 3 "Then what *b* did you receive?"
19: 4 "John's *b* was a *b* of repentance.
Ro 6: 4 with him through *b* into death
Eph 4: 5 one Lord, one faith, one *b;*
Col 2:12 having been buried with him in *b*
1Pe 3:21 this water symbolizes *b* that now

BAPTISMS* (BAPTIZE)
Heb 6: 2 instruction about *b*, the laying

BAPTIZE* (BAPTISM BAPTISMS BAPTIZED BAPTIZING)
Mt 3:11 He will *b* you with the Holy Spirit
3:11 "I *b* you with water for repentance.
Mk 1: 8 I *b* you with water, but he will
1: 8 he will *b* you with the Holy Spirit."
Lk 3:16 He will *b* you with the Holy Spirit
3:16 John answered them all, "I *b* you
Jn 1:25 "Why then do you *b*
1:26 nor the Prophet?" "I *b* with water,"
1:33 and remain is he who will *b*
1:33 me to *b* with water told me,
1Co 1:14 I am thankful that I did not *b* any
1:17 For Christ did not send me to *b*,

BAPTIZED* (BAPTIZE)
Mt 3: 6 they were *b* by him in the Jordan
3:13 to the Jordan to be *b* by John.
3:14 saying, "I need to be *b* by you,
3:16 as Jesus was *b*, he went up out
Mk 1: 5 they were *b* by him in the Jordan
1: 9 and was *b* by John in the Jordan.
10:38 or be *b* with the baptism I am
10:38 with the baptism I am *b* with?"
10:39 and be *b* with the baptism I am
10:39 with the baptism I am *b* with,
16:16 believes and is *b* will be saved,
Lk 3: 7 to the crowds coming out to be *b*
3:12 Tax collectors also came to be *b*.
3:21 were being *b*, Jesus was *b* too.
7:29 because they had been *b* by John.
7:30 they had not been *b* by John.)
Jn 3:22 spent some time with them, and *b*.
3:23 were constantly coming to be *b*.
4: 2 in fact it was not Jesus who *b*,
Ac 1: 5 For John *b* with water,
1: 5 but in a few days you will be *b*
2:38 Repent and be *b*, every one of you,
2:41 who accepted his message were *b*,
8:12 they were *b*, both men and women.
8:13 Simon himself believed and was *b*.
8:16 they had simply been *b*
8:36 Why shouldn't I be *b*?"
8:38 into the water and Philip *b* him.
9:18 was *b*, and after taking some food,
10:47 people from being *b* with water?
10:48 So he ordered that they be *b*
11:16 what the Lord had said, 'John *b*
11:16 you will be *b* with the Holy Spirit.'
16:15 members of her household were *b*,
16:33 he and all his family were *b*.
18: 8 heard him believed and were *b*.
19: 5 they were *b* into the name
22:16 be *b* and wash your sins away,
Ro 6: 3 *b* into Christ Jesus were *b*
1Co 1:13 Were you *b* into the name of Paul?
1:15 so no one can say that you were *b*
1:16 I also *b* the household of Stephanas
1:16 I don't remember if I *b* anyone else
10: 2 They were all *b* into Moses
12:13 For we were all *b* by one Spirit
15:29 what will those do who are *b*
15:29 why are people *b* for them?
Gal 3:27 all of you who were *b*

BAPTIZING* (BAPTIZE)
Mt 3: 7 coming to where he was *b*,
28:19 *b* them in the name of the Father
Mk 1: 4 *b* in the desert region
Jn 1:28 of the Jordan, where John was *b*.
1:31 but the reason I came *b*
3:23 also was *b* at Aenon near Salim,
3:26 he is *b*, and everyone is going
4: 1 and *b* more disciples than John,
10:40 to the place where John had been *b*

BAR-JESUS*
Ac 13: 6 and false prophet named *B*,

BARABBAS
Mt 27:26 Then he released *B* to them.

BARAK*
Judge who fought with Deborah against Canaanites (Jdg 4–5; 1Sa 12:11; Heb 11:32).

BARBARIAN*
Col 3:11 circumcised or uncircumcised, *b*,

BARBS*
Nu 33:55 allow to remain will become *b*

BARE
Hos 2: 3 as *b* as on the day she was born;
Heb 4:13 and laid *b* before the eyes of him

BARNABAS*
Disciple, originally Joseph (Ac 4:36), prophet (Ac 13:1), apostle (Ac 14:14). Brought Paul to apostles (Ac 9:27), Antioch (Ac 11:22–29; Gal 2:1–13), on the first missionary journey (Ac 13–14). Together at Jerusalem Council, they separated over John Mark (Ac 15). Later co-workers (1Co 9:6; Col 4:10).

BARREN
Ge 11:30 Sarai was *b*; she had no children.
29:31 her womb, but Rachel was *b*.
Ps 113: 9 He settles the *b* woman
Isa 54: 1 "Sing, O *b* woman,
Lk 1: 7 children, because Elizabeth was *b*;
Gal 4:27 "Be glad, O *b* woman,
Heb 11:11 and Sarah herself was *b*—

BARTHOLOMEW*
Apostle (Mt 10:3; Mk 3:18; Lk 6:14; Ac 1:13). Possibly also known as Nathanael (Jn 1:45–49; 21:2).

BARUCH
Jeremiah's secretary (Jer 32:12–16; 36; 43:1–6; 45:1–2).

BARZILLAI
1. Gileadite who aided David during Absalom's revolt (2Sa 17:27; 19:31–39).
2. Son-in-law of 1. (Ezr 2:61; Ne 7:63).

BASHAN
Jos 22: 7 Moses had given land in *B*,
Ps 22:12 strong bulls of *B* encircle me.

BASIN
Ex 30:18 "Make a bronze *b*,

BASKET
Ex 2: 3 she got a papyrus *b* for him
Ac 9:25 him in a *b* through an opening
2Co 11:33 I was lowered in a *b* from a window

BATCH*
Ro 11:16 then the whole *b* is holy;
1Co 5: 6 through the whole *b* of dough?
5: 7 old yeast that you may be a new *b*
Gal 5: 9 through the whole *b* of dough."

BATH (BATHING)
Jn 13:10 person who has had a *b* needs only

BATHING (BATH)
2Sa 11: 2 From the roof he saw a woman *b*.

BATHSHEBA*
Wife of Uriah who committed adultery with and became wife of David (2Sa 11), mother of Solomon (2Sa 12:24; 1Ki 1–2; 1Ch 3:5).

BATTLE (BATTLES)
1Sa 17:47 for the *b* is the LORD's,
2Ch 20:15 For the *b* is not yours, but God's.
Ps 24: 8 the LORD mighty in *b*.
Ecc 9:11 or the *b* to the strong,
Isa 31: 4 down to do *b* on Mount Zion
Eze 13: 5 in the *b* on the day of the LORD.
Rev 16:14 them for the *b* on the great day
20: 8 and Magog—to gather them for *b*.

BATTLES* (BATTLE)
1Sa 8:20 to go out before us and fight our *b*."
18:17 and fight the *b* of the LORD."
25:28 because he fights the LORD's *b*.
2Ch 32: 8 God to help us and to fight our *b*."

BEAR (BEARING BEARS BIRTH BIRTHRIGHT BORE BORN CHILDBEARING CHILDBIRTH FIRSTBORN NEWBORN REBIRTH)
Ge 4:13 punishment is more than I can *b*.
Ps 38: 4 like a burden too heavy to *b*.
Isa 11: 7 The cow will feed with the *b*,
53:11 and he will *b* their iniquities.
Da 7: 5 beast, which looked like a *b*.
Mt 7:18 A good tree cannot *b* bad fruit,
Jn 15: 2 branch that does *b* fruit he prunes
15: 8 glory, that you *b* much fruit,
15:16 appointed you to go and *b* fruit—
Ro 7: 4 in order that we might *b* fruit
15: 1 ought to *b* with the failings
1Co 10:13 tempted beyond what you can *b*.
Col 3:13 *B* with each other and forgive

BEARD
Lev 19:27 or clip off the edges of your *b*.
Isa 50: 6 to those who pulled out my *b*;

BEARING (BEAR)
Eph 4: 2 *b* with one another in love.
Col 1:10 *b* fruit in every good work,
Heb 13:13 outside the camp, *b* the disgrace he

BEARS (BEAR)
1Ki 8:43 house I have built *b* your Name.
Ps 68:19 who daily *b* our burdens.

BEAST (BEASTS)
Rev 13:18 him calculate the number of the *b*,
16: 2 people who had the mark of the *b*
19:20 who had received the mark of the *b*

BEASTS (BEAST)
Da 7: 3 Four great *b*, each different
1Co 15:32 If I fought wild *b* in Ephesus

BEAT (BEATEN BEATING BEATINGS)
Isa 2: 4 They will *b* their swords
Joel 3:10 *B* your plowshares into swords
Mic 4: 3 They will *b* their swords
1Co 9:27 I *b* my body and make it my slave

BEATEN (BEAT)
Lk 12:47 do what his master wants will be *b*
12:48 deserving punishment will be *b*
2Co 11:25 Three times I was *b* with rods,

BEATING (BEAT)
1Co 9:26 I do not fight like a man *b* the air.
1Pe 2:20 if you receive a *b* for doing wrong

BEATINGS (BEAT)
Pr 19:29 and *b* for the backs of fools.

BEAUTIFUL* (BEAUTY)
Ge 6: 2 that the daughters of men were *b*,
12:11 "I know what a *b* woman you are.
12:14 saw that she was a very *b* woman.
24:16 The girl was very *b*, a virgin;
26: 7 of Rebekah, because she is *b*."
29:17 Rachel was lovely in form, and *b*.
49:21 that bears *b* fawns.
Nu 24: 5 "How *b* are your tents, O Jacob,
Dt 21:11 among the captives a *b* woman
Jos 7:21 saw in the plunder a *b* robe
1Sa 25: 3 was an intelligent and *b* woman,
2Sa 11: 2 The woman was very *b*,

2Sa 13: 1 the *b* sister of Absalom son
14:27 and she became a *b* woman.
1Ki 1: 3 throughout Israel for a *b* girl
1: 4 The girl was very *b;* she took care
Est 2: 2 for *b* young virgins for the king.
2: 3 realm to bring all these *b* girls
Job 38:31 "Can you bind the *b* Pleiades?
42:15 land were there found women as *b*
Ps 48: 2 It is *b* in its loftiness,
Pr 11:22 is a *b* woman who shows no
24: 4 filled with rare and *b* treasures.
Ecc 3:11 He has made everything *b*
SS 1: 8 *Lover* If you do not know, most *b*
1:10 Your cheeks are *b* with earrings,
1:15 Oh, how *b!*
1:15 *Lover* How *b* you are, my darling!
2:10 my *b* one, and come with me.
2:13 my *b* one, come with me."
4: 1 How *b* you are, my darling!
4: 1 Oh, how *b!*
4: 7 All *b* you are, my darling;
5: 9 most *b* of women?
6: 1 most *b* of women?
6: 4 *Lover* You are *b,* my darling,
7: 1 How *b* your sandaled feet,
7: 6 How *b* you are and how pleasing,
Isa 4: 2 of the LORD will be *b*
28: 5 a *b* wreath
52: 7 How *b* on the mountains
Jer 3:19 the most *b* inheritance
6: 2 so *b* and delicate.
11:16 with fruit *b* in form.
46:20 "Egypt is a *b* heifer,
Eze 7:20 They were proud of their *b* jewelry
16: 7 and became the most *b* of jewels.
16:12 and a *b* crown on your head.
16:13 You became very *b* and rose
20: 6 and honey, the most *b* of all lands.
20:15 and honey, most *b* of all lands—
23:42 and *b* crowns on their heads.
27:24 traded with you *b* garments,
31: 3 with *b* branches overshadowing
31: 9 I made it *b*
33:32 who sings love songs with a *b* voice
Da 4:12 Its leaves were *b,* its fruit abundant
4:21 with *b* leaves and abundant fruit,
8: 9 to the east and toward the *B* Land.
11:16 will establish himself in the *B* Land
11:41 He will also invade the *B* Land.
11:45 the seas at the *b* holy mountain.
Zec 9:17 How attractive and *b* they will be!
Mt 23:27 which look *b* on the outside
26:10 She has done a *b* thing to me.
Mk 14: 6 She has done a *b* thing to me.
Lk 21: 5 temple was adorned with *b* stones
Ac 3: 2 carried to the temple gate called *B,*
3:10 at the temple gate called *B,*
Ro 10:15 "How *b* are the feet
1Pe 3: 5 in God used to make themselves *b.*

BEAUTY* (BEAUTIFUL)
Est 1:11 order to display her *b* to the people
2: 3 let *b* treatments be given to them.
2: 9 her with her *b* treatments
2:12 months of *b* treatments prescribed
Ps 27: 4 to gaze upon the *b* of the LORD
37:20 LORD's enemies will be like the *b*
45:11 The king is enthralled by your *b;*
50: 2 From Zion, perfect in *b,*
Pr 6:25 lust in your heart after her *b*
31:30 is deceptive, and *b* is fleeting;
Isa 3:24 instead of *b,* branding.
28: 1 to the fading flower, his glorious *b,*
28: 4 That fading flower, his glorious *b,*
33:17 Your eyes will see the king in his *b*
53: 2 He had no *b* or majesty
61: 3 to bestow on them a crown of *b*
La 2:15 the perfection of *b,*
Eze 16:14 had given you made your *b* perfect,
16:14 the nations on account of your *b,*
16:15 passed by and your *b* became his.
16:15 " 'But you trusted in your *b*
16:25 lofty shrines and degraded your *b,*
27: 3 "I am perfect in *b."*
27: 4 your builders brought your *b*
27:11 they brought your *b* to perfection.
28: 7 draw their swords against your *b*
28:12 full of wisdom and perfect in *b.*
28:17 proud on account of your *b,*
31: 7 It was majestic in *b,*
31: 8 could match its *b.*
Jas 1:11 blossom falls and its *b* is destroyed.
1Pe 3: 3 Your *b* should not come
3: 4 the unfading *b* of a gentle

BED (SICKBED)
Isa 28:20 The *b* is too short to stretch out on,
Lk 11: 7 and my children are with me in *b.*
17:34 night two people will be in one *b;*
Heb 13: 4 and the marriage *b* kept pure,

BEELZEBUB*
Mt 10:25 of the house has been called *B,*
12:24 "It is only by *B,* the prince
12:27 And if I drive out demons by *B,*
Mk 3:22 possessed by *B!* By the prince
Lk 11:15 "By *B,* the prince of demons,
11:18 claim that I drive out demons by *B.*
11:19 Now if I drive out demons by *B,*

BEER
Pr 20: 1 Wine is a mocker and *b* a brawler;

BEERSHEBA
Ge 21:14 and wandered in the desert of *B.*
Jdg 20: 1 all the Israelites from Dan to *B*
1Sa 3:20 to *B* recognized that Samuel was
2Sa 3:10 and Judah from Dan to *B."*
17:11 Let all Israel, from Dan to *B*—
24: 2 the tribes of Israel from Dan to *B*
24:15 of the people from Dan to *B* died.
1Ki 4:25 from Dan to *B,* lived in safety,
1Ch 21: 2 count the Israelites from *B* to Dan.
2Ch 30: 5 throughout Israel, from *B* to Dan,

BEFALLS*
Pr 12:21 No harm *b* the righteous,

BEGGING
Ps 37:25 or their children *b* bread.
Ac 16: 9 of Macedonia standing and *b* him,

BEGINNING
Ge 1: 1 In the *b* God created the heavens
Ps 102:25 In the *b* you laid the foundations
111:10 of the LORD is the *b* of wisdom;
Pr 1: 7 of the LORD is the *b* of knowledge
9:10 of the LORD is the *b* of wisdom,
Ecc 3:11 fathom what God has done from *b*
Isa 40:21 Has it not been told you from the *b*
46:10 I make known the end from the *b,*
Mt 24: 8 All these are the *b* of birth pains.
Lk 1: 3 investigated everything from the *b,*
Jn 1: 1 In the *b* was the Word,
1Jn 1: 1 That which was from the *b,*
Rev 21: 6 and the Omega, the *B* and the End.
22:13 and the Last, the *B* and the End.

BEHAVE (BEHAVIOR)
Ro 13:13 Let us *b* decently, as in the daytime

BEHAVIOR (BEHAVE)
1Pe 3: 1 without words by the *b* of their wives,
3:16 maliciously against your good *b*

BEHEMOTH*
Job 40:15 "Look at the *b,*

BELIEVE (BELIEVED BELIEVER BELIEVERS BELIEVES BELIEVING)
Ex 4: 1 "What if they do not *b* me
1Ki 10: 7 I did not *b* these things until I came
2Ch 9: 6 But I did not *b* what they said
Ps 78:32 of his wonders, they did not *b.*
Hab 1: 5 that you would not *b,*
Mt 18: 6 one of these little ones who *b* in me
21:22 If you *b,* you will receive whatever
27:42 from the cross, and we will *b* in him
Mk 1:15 Repent and *b* the good news!"
5:36 ruler, "Don't be afraid; just *b."*
9:24 "I do *b;* help me overcome my
9:42 one of these little ones who *b* in me
11:24 *b* that you have received it,
15:32 the cross, that we may see and *b."*
16:16 but whoever does not *b* will be
16:17 signs will accompany those who *b:*
Lk 8:12 so that they may not *b* and be saved.
8:13 They *b* for a while, but in the time
8:50 just *b,* and she will be healed."
22:67 you will not *b* me,
24:25 to *b* all that the prophets have
Jn 1: 7 that through him all men might *b.*
3:18 does not *b* stands condemned
4:42 "We no longer *b* just
5:38 for you do not *b* the one he sent.
5:46 believed Moses, you would *b* me,
6:29 to *b* in the one he has sent."
6:69 We *b* and know that you are
7: 5 his own brothers did not *b* in him.
8:24 if you do not *b* that I am ›the one I
9:35 "Do you *b* in the Son of Man?"
9:36 "Tell me so that I may *b* in him."
9:38 "Lord, I *b,"* and he worshiped him.
10:26 you do not *b* because you are not
10:37 Do not *b* me unless I do what my
10:38 you do not *b* me, *b* the miracles,
11:27 "I *b* that you are the Christ,
12:37 they still would not *b* in him.
12:39 For this reason they could not *b,*
12:44 in me, he does not *b* in me only,
13:19 does happen you will *b* that I am
14:10 Don't you *b* that I am in the Father
14:11 *B* me when I say that I am
14:11 or at least *b* on the evidence
16:30 This makes us *b* that you came
16:31 "You *b* at last!" Jesus answered.
17:21 that the world may *b* that you have
19:35 he testifies so that you also may *b.*
20:27 Stop doubting and *b."*
20:31 written that you may *b* that Jesus is
Ac 16:31 They replied, "*B* in the Lord Jesus,
19: 4 the people to *b* in the one coming
24:14 I *b* everything that agrees
26:27 Agrippa, do you *b* the prophets?
Ro 3:22 faith in Jesus Christ to all who *b.*
4:11 he is the father of all who *b*
10: 9 *b* in your heart that God raised him
10:10 For it is with your heart that you *b*
10:14 And how can they *b* in the one
16:26 so that all nations might *b*
1Co 1:21 preached to save those who *b.*
Gal 3:22 might be given to those who *b.*
Php 1:29 of Christ not only to *b* on him,
1Th 4:14 We *b* that Jesus died and rose again
2Th 2:11 delusion so that they will *b* the lie
1Ti 4:10 and especially of those who *b.*
Tit 1: 6 a man whose children *b*
Heb 11: 6 comes to him must *b* that he exists
Jas 1: 6 But when he asks, he must *b*
2:19 Even the demons *b* that—
2:19 You *b* that there is one God.
1Pe 2: 7 to you who *b,* this stone is precious
1Jn 3:23 to *b* in the name of his Son,
4: 1 Dear friends, do not *b* every spirit,
5:13 things to you who *b* in the name

BELIEVED (BELIEVE)
Ge 15: 6 Abram *b* the LORD, and he
Ex 4:31 signs before the people, and they *b.*
Isa 53: 1 Who has *b* our message
Jnh 3: 5 The Ninevites *b* God.
Lk 1:45 is she who has *b* that what the Lord

Jn 1:12 to those who *b* in his name,
2:22 Then they *b* the Scripture
3:18 because he has not *b* in the name
5:46 If you *b* Moses, you would believe
7:39 whom those who *b*
11:40 "Did I not tell you that if you *b*,
12:38 "Lord, who has *b* our message
20: 8 He saw and *b*.
20:29 who have not seen and yet have *b*."
Ac 13:48 were appointed for eternal life *b*.
19: 2 the Holy Spirit when you *b*?"
Ro 4: 3 Scripture say? "Abraham *b* God,
10:14 call on the one they have not *b* in?
10:16 "Lord, who has *b* our message?"
1Co 15: 2 Otherwise, you have *b* in vain.
Gal 3: 6 Consider Abraham: "He *b* God,
2Th 2:12 who have not *b* the truth
1Ti 3:16 was *b* on in the world,
2Ti 1:12 because I know whom I have *b*,
Jas 2:23 that says, "Abraham *b* God,

BELIEVER* (BELIEVE)
1Ki 18: 3 (Obadiah was a devout *b*
Ac 16: 1 whose mother was a Jewess and a *b*
16:15 "If you consider me a *b* in the Lord
1Co 7:12 brother has a wife who is not a *b*
7:13 has a husband who is not a *b*
2Co 6:15 What does a *b* have in common
1Ti 5:16 any woman who is a *b* has widows

BELIEVERS* (BELIEVE)
Jn 4:41 of his words many more became *b*.
Ac 1:15 among the *b* (a group numbering
2:44 All the *b* were together
4:32 All the *b* were one in heart
5:12 And all the *b* used to meet together
9:41 he called the *b* and the widows
10:45 The circumcised *b* who had come
11: 2 the circumcised *b* criticized him
15: 2 along with some other *b*,
15: 5 Then some of the *b* who belonged
15:23 To the Gentile *b* in Antioch,
21:25 for the Gentile *b*, we have written
1Co 6: 5 to judge a dispute between *b*?
14:22 is for *b*, not for unbelievers.
14:22 not for *b* but for unbelievers;
Gal 6:10 who belong to the family of *b*.
1Th 1: 7 a model to all the *b* in Macedonia
1Ti 4:12 set an example for the *b* in speech,
6: 2 benefit from their service are *b*,
Jas 2: 1 *b* in our glorious Lord Jesus Christ,
1Pe 2:17 Love the brotherhood of *b*,

BELIEVES* (BELIEVE)
Pr 14:15 A simple man *b* anything,
Mk 9:23 is possible for him who *b*."
11:23 *b* that what he says will happen,
16:16 Whoever *b* and is baptized will be
Jn 3:15 that everyone who *b*
3:16 that whoever *b* in him shall not
3:18 Whoever *b* in him is not
3:36 Whoever *b* in the Son has eternal
5:24 *b* him who sent me has eternal life
6:35 and he who *b* in me will never be
6:40 and *b* in him shall have eternal life,
6:47 he who *b* has everlasting life.
7:38 Whoever *b* in me, as the Scripture
11:25 He who *b* in me will live, even
11:26 and *b* in me will never die.
12:44 Jesus cried out, "When a man *b*
12:46 so that no one who *b*
Ac 10:43 about him that everyone who *b*
13:39 him everyone who *b* is justified
Ro 1:16 for the salvation of everyone who *b*
10: 4 righteousness for everyone who *b*.
1Jn 5: 1 Everyone who *b* that Jesus is
5: 5 Only he who *b* that Jesus is the Son
5:10 Anyone who *b* in the Son

BELIEVING* (BELIEVE)
Jn 20:31 and that by *b* you may have life

Ac 9:26 not *b* that he really was a disciple.
1Co 7:14 sanctified through her *b* husband.
7:15 A *b* man or woman is not bound
9: 5 right to take a *b* wife along with us,
Gal 3: 2 or by *b* what you heard? Are you
1Ti 6: 2 Those who have *b* masters are not

BELLY
Ge 3:14 You will crawl on your *b*
Da 2:32 its *b* and thighs of bronze,
Mt 12:40 three nights in the *b* of a huge fish,

BELONG (BELONGING BELONGS)
Ge 40: 8 "Do not interpretations *b* to God?
Lev 25:55 for the Israelites *b* to me
Dt 10:14 LORD your God *b* the heavens,
29:29 The secret things *b*
Job 12:13 "To God *b* wisdom and power;
12:16 To him *b* strength and victory;
25: 2 "Dominion and awe *b* to God;
Ps 47: 9 for the kings of the earth *b* to God;
95: 4 and the mountain peaks *b* to him.
115:16 The highest heavens *b*
Jer 5:10 for these people do not *b*
Jn 8:44 You *b* to your father, the devil,
15:19 As it is, you do not *b* to the world,
Ro 1: 6 called to *b* to Jesus Christ.
7: 4 that you might *b* to another,
8: 9 of Christ, he does not *b* to Christ.
14: 8 we live or die, we *b* to the Lord.
1Co 7:39 but he must *b* to the Lord.
15:23 when he comes, those who *b*
Gal 3:29 If you *b* to Christ, then you are
5:24 Those who *b* to Christ Jesus have
1Th 5: 5 We do not *b* to the night
5: 8 But since we *b* to the day, let us be
1Jn 3:19 then is how we know that we *b*

BELONGING (BELONG)
1Pe 2: 9 a holy nation, a people *b* to God,

BELONGS (BELONG)
Lev 27:30 *b* to the LORD; it is holy
Dt 1:17 of any man, for judgment *b* to God.
Job 41:11 Everything under heaven *b* to me.
Ps 22:28 for dominion *b* to the LORD
89:18 Indeed, our shield *b* to the LORD,
111:10 To him *b* eternal praise.
Eze 18: 4 For every living soul *b* to me,
Jn 8:47 He who *b* to God hears what God
Ro 12: 5 each member *b* to all the others.
Rev 7:10 "Salvation *b* to our God,

BELOVED* (LOVE)
Dt 33:12 "Let the *b* of the LORD rest secure
SS 5: 9 How is your *b* better than others,
5: 9 *Friends* How is your *b* better
Jer 11:15 "What is my *b* doing in my temple

BELSHAZZAR
King of Babylon in days of Daniel (Da 5).

BELT
Ex 12:11 with your cloak tucked into your *b*,
1Ki 18:46 and, tucking his cloak into his *b*,
2Ki 4:29 "Tuck your cloak into your *b*,
9: 1 "Tuck your cloak into your *b*,
Isa 11: 5 Righteousness will be his *b*
Eph 6:14 with the *b* of truth buckled

BENEFICIAL* (BENEFIT)
1Co 6:12 for me"—but not everything is *b*.
10:23 but not everything is *b*.

BENEFIT (BENEFICIAL BENEFITS)
Job 22: 2 "Can a man be of *b* to God?
Isa 38:17 Surely it was for my *b*
Ro 6:22 the *b* you reap leads to holiness,
2Co 4:15 All this is for your *b*,

BENEFITS (BENEFIT)
Ps 103: 2 and forget not all his *b*.

Jn 4:38 you have reaped the *b* of their labor

BENJAMIN
Twelfth son of Jacob by Rachel (Ge 35:16–24; 46:19–21; 1Ch 2:2). Jacob refused to send him to Egypt, but relented (Ge 42–45). Tribe of blessed (Ge 49:27; Dt 33:12), numbered (Nu 1:37; 26:41), allotted land (Jos 18:11–28; Eze 48:23), failed to fully possess (Jdg 1:21), nearly obliterated (Jdg 20–21), sided with Ish-Bosheth (2Sa 2), but turned to David (1Ch 12:2, 29). 12,000 from (Rev 7:8).

BEREANS*
Ac 17:11 the *B* were of more noble character

BESTOWING* (BESTOWS)
Pr 8:21 *b* wealth on those who love me

BESTOWS (BESTOWING)
Ps 84:11 the LORD *b* favor and honor;

BETHANY
Mk 11: 1 and *B* at the Mount of Olives,

BETHEL
Ge 28:19 He called that place *B*,

BETHLEHEM
Ru 1:19 went on until they came to *B*.
1Sa 16: 1 I am sending you to Jesse of *B*.
2Sa 23:15 from the well near the gate of *B*!"
Mic 5: 2 "But you, *B* Ephrathah,
Mt 2: 1 After Jesus was born in *B* in Judea,
2: 6 " 'But you, *B*, in the land of Judah,

BETHPHAGE
Mt 21: 1 came to *B* on the Mount of Olives,

BETHSAIDA
Jn 12:21 who was from *B* in Galilee,

BETRAY (BETRAYED BETRAYS)
Ps 89:33 nor will I ever *b* my faithfulness.
Pr 25: 9 do not *b* another man's confidence,
Mt 10:21 "Brother will *b* brother to death,
26:21 the truth, one of you will *b* me."

BETRAYED (BETRAY)
Mt 27: 4 "for I have *b* innocent blood."

BETRAYS (BETRAY)
Pr 11:13 A gossip *b* a confidence,
20:19 A gossip *b* a confidence;

BEULAH*
Isa 62: 4 and your land *B*;

BEWITCHED*
Gal 3: 1 foolish Galatians! Who has *b* you?

BEZALEL
Judahite craftsman in charge of building the tabernacle (Ex 31:1–11; 35:30–39:31).

BIDDING*
Ps 103:20 you mighty ones who do his *b*,
148: 8 stormy winds that do his *b*,

BILDAD
One of Job's friends (Job 8; 18; 25).

BILHAH
Servant of Rachel, mother of Jacob's sons Dan and Naphtali (Ge 30:1–7; 35:25; 46:23–25).

BIND (BINDS BOUND)
Dt 6: 8 and *b* them on your foreheads.
Pr 3: 3 *b* them around your neck,
6:21 *B* them upon your heart forever;
7: 3 *B* them on your fingers;
Isa 61: 1 me to *b* up the brokenhearted,
Mt 16:19 whatever you *b* on earth will be

BINDS (BIND)
Ps 147: 3 and *b* up their wounds.
Isa 30:26 when the LORD *b* up the bruises

BIRD (BIRDS)
Pr 27: 8 Like a *b* that strays from its nest
Ecc 10:20 a *b* of the air may carry your words,

BIRDS (BIRD)
Mt 8:20 and *b* of the air have nests,
Lk 9:58 and *b* of the air have nests,

BIRTH (BEAR)
Ps 51: 5 Surely I was sinful at *b*,
58: 3 Even from *b* the wicked go astray;
Isa 26:18 but we gave *b* to wind.
Mt 1:18 This is how the *b* of Jesus Christ
24: 8 these are the beginning of *b* pains.
Jn 3: 6 Flesh gives *b* to flesh, but the Spirit
1Pe 1: 3 great mercy he has given us new *b*

BIRTHRIGHT (BEAR)
Ge 25:34 So Esau despised his *b*.

BITTEN
Nu 21: 8 anyone who is *b* can look at it

BITTER (BITTERNESS EMBITTER)
Ex 12: 8 along with *b* herbs, and bread made
Pr 27: 7 what is *b* tastes sweet.

BITTERNESS (BITTER)
Pr 14:10 Each heart knows its own *b*,
17:25 and *b* to the one who bore him.
Ro 3:14 full of cursing and *b*."
Eph 4:31 Get rid of all *b*, rage and anger,

BLACK
Zec 6: 6 The one with the *b* horses is going
Rev 6: 5 and there before me was a *b* horse!

BLAMELESS* (BLAMELESSLY)
Ge 6: 9 *b* among the people of his time,
17: 1 walk before me and be *b*.
Dt 18:13 You must be *b* before the LORD
2Sa 22:24 I have been *b* before him
22:26 to the *b* you show yourself *b*,
Job 1: 1 This man was *b* and upright;
1: 8 one on earth like him; he is *b*
2: 3 one on earth like him; he is *b*
4: 6 and your *b* ways your hope?
8:20 God does not reject a *b* man
9:20 if I were *b*, it would pronounce me
9:21 "Although I am *b*,
9:22 'He destroys both the *b*
12: 4 though righteous and *b*!
22: 3 gain if your ways were *b*?
31: 6 and he will know that I am *b*—
Ps 15: 2 He whose walk is *b*
18:23 I have been *b* before him
18:25 to the *b* you show yourself *b*,
19:13 Then will I be *b*,
26: 1 for I have led a *b* life;
26:11 But I lead a *b* life;
37:18 The days of the *b* are known
37:37 Consider the *b*, observe the upright
84:11 from those whose walk is *b*.
101: 2 I will be careful to lead a *b* life—
101: 2 house with *b* heart.
101: 6 he whose walk is *b*
119: 1 Blessed are they whose ways are *b*,
119:80 May my heart be *b*
Pr 2: 7 a shield to those whose walk is *b*,
2:21 and the *b* will remain in it;
11: 5 of the *b* makes a straight way
11:20 in those whose ways are *b*.
19: 1 Better a poor man whose walk is *b*
20: 7 The righteous man leads a *b* life;
28: 6 Better a poor man whose walk is *b*
28:10 *b* will receive a good inheritance.
28:18 He whose walk is *b* is kept safe,
Eze 28:15 You were *b* in your ways
1Co 1: 8 so that you will be *b* on the day
Eph 1: 4 world to be holy and *b* in his sight.
5:27 any other blemish, but holy and *b*.
Php 1:10 and *b* until the day of Christ,
2:15 so that you may become *b* and pure
1Th 2:10 and *b* we were among you who
3:13 hearts so that you will be *b*
5:23 and body be kept *b* at the coming
Tit 1: 6 An elder must be *b*, the husband of
1: 7 he must be *b*— not overbearing,
Heb 7:26 *b*, pure, set apart from sinners,
2Pe 3:14 effort to be found spotless, *b*
Rev 14: 5 found in their mouths; they are *b*.

BLAMELESSLY* (BLAMELESS)
Lk 1: 6 commandments and regulations *b*.

BLASPHEME* (BLASPHEMED BLASPHEMER BLASPHEMES BLASPHEMIES BLASPHEMING BLASPHEMOUS BLASPHEMY)
Ex 22:28 "Do not *b* God or curse the ruler
Ac 26:11 and I tried to force them to *b*.
1Ti 1:20 over to Satan to be taught not to *b*.
2Pe 2:12 these men *b* in matters they do not
Rev 13: 6 He opened his mouth to *b* God,

BLASPHEMED* (BLASPHEME)
Lev 24:11 of the Israelite woman *b* the Name
2Ki 19: 6 of the king of Assyria have *b* me.
19:22 Who is it you have insulted and *b*?
Isa 37: 6 of the king of Assyria have *b* me.
37:23 Who is it you have insulted and *b*?
52: 5 my name is constantly *b*.
Eze 20:27 your fathers *b* me by forsaking me:
Ac 19:37 robbed temples nor *b* our goddess.
Ro 2:24 name is *b* among the Gentiles

BLASPHEMER* (BLASPHEME)
Lev 24:14 "Take the *b* outside the camp.
24:23 they took the *b* outside the camp
1Ti 1:13 I was once a *b* and a persecutor

BLASPHEMES* (BLASPHEME)
Lev 24:16 anyone who *b* the name
24:16 native-born, when he *b* the Name,
Nu 15:30 native-born or alien, *b* the LORD,
Mk 3:29 whoever *b* against the Holy Spirit
Lk 12:10 but anyone who *b* against the Holy

BLASPHEMIES* (BLASPHEME)
Ne 9:18 or when they committed awful *b*.
9:26 to you; they committed awful *b*.
Mk 3:28 and *b* of men will be forgiven them.
Rev 13: 5 and *b* and to exercise his authority

BLASPHEMING* (BLASPHEME)
Mt 9: 3 "This fellow is *b*!" Knowing their
Mk 2: 7 He's *b*! Who can forgive sins

BLASPHEMOUS* (BLASPHEME)
Rev 13: 1 and on each head a *b* name.
17: 3 that was covered with *b* names

BLASPHEMY* (BLASPHEME)
Mt 12:31 and *b* will be forgiven men,
12:31 the *b* against the Spirit will not be
26:65 Look, now you have heard the *b*.
26:65 "He has spoken *b*! Why do we
Mk 14:64 "You have heard the *b*.
Lk 5:21 "Who is this fellow who speaks *b*?
Jn 10:33 replied the Jews, "but for *b*,
10:36 Why then do you accuse me of *b*
Ac 6:11 words of *b* against Moses

BLAST*
Ex 15: 8 By the *b* of your nostrils
19:13 horn sounds a long *b* may they go
19:16 and a very loud trumpet *b*.
Nu 10: 5 When a trumpet *b* is sounded,
10: 6 At the sounding of a second *b*,
10: 6 The *b* will be the signal
Nu 10: 9 sound a *b* on the trumpets.
Jos 6: 5 you hear them sound a long *b*
6:16 the priests sounded the trumpet *b*,
2Sa 22:16 at the *b* of breath from his nostrils.
Job 4: 9 at the *b* of his anger they perish.
39:25 At the *b* of the trumpet he snorts,
Ps 18:15 the *b* of breath from your nostrils.
98: 6 and the *b* of the ram's horn—
147:17 Who can withstand his icy *b*?
Isa 27: 8 with his fierce *b* he drives her out,
Eze 22:20 a furnace to melt it with a fiery *b*,
Am 2: 2 tumult amid war cries and the *b*
Heb 12:19 to a trumpet *b* or to such a voice

BLEATING*
1Sa 15:14 "What then is this *b* of sheep

BLEMISH (BLEMISHES)
Lev 22:21 be without defect or *b*
Eph 5:27 or wrinkle or any other *b*,
Col 1:22 without *b* and free from accusation
1Pe 1:19 a lamb without *b* or defect.

BLEMISHES* (BLEMISH)
2Pe 2:13 and *b*, reveling in their pleasures
Jude :12 These men are *b* at your love feasts

BLESS (BLESSED BLESSES BLESSING BLESSINGS)
Ge 12: 3 I will *b* those who *b* you,
32:26 not let you go unless you *b* me."
Dt 7:13 He will love you and *b* you
33:11 *B* all his skills, O LORD,
Ps 72:15 and *b* him all day long.
Ro 12:14 Bless those who persecute you; *b*

BLESSED (BLESS)
Ge 1:22 God *b* them and said, "Be fruitful
2: 3 And God *b* the seventh day
22:18 nations on earth will be *b*,
Nu 24: 9 "May those who bless you be *b*
1Ch 17:27 have *b* it, and it will be *b* forever."
Ps 1: 1 *B* is the man
2:12 *B* are all who take refuge in him.
32: 2 *B* is the man
33:12 *B* is the nation whose God is
40: 4 *B* is the man
41: 1 *B* is he who has regard for the weak
84: 5 *B* are those whose strength is
89:15 *B* are those who have learned
94:12 *B* is the man you discipline,
106: 3 *B* are they who maintain justice,
112: 1 *B* is the man who fears the LORD,
118:26 *B* is he who comes in the name
119: 1 *B* are they whose ways are
119: 2 *B* are they who keep his statutes
127: 5 *B* is the man
Pr 3:13 *B* is the man who finds wisdom,
8:34 *B* is the man who listens to me,
28:20 A faithful man will be richly *b*,
29:18 but *b* is he who keeps the law.
31:28 Her children arise and call her *b*;
Isa 30:18 *B* are all who wait for him!
Mal 3:12 Then all the nations will call you *b*,
3:15 But now we call the arrogant *b*.
Mt 5: 3 saying: "*B* are the poor in spirit,
5: 4 *B* are those who mourn,
5: 5 *B* are the meek,
5: 6 *B* are those who hunger
5: 7 *B* are the merciful,
5: 8 *B* are the pure in heart,
5: 9 *B* are the peacemakers,
5:10 *B* are those who are persecuted
5:11 "*B* are you when people insult you,
Lk 1:48 on all generations will call me *b*,
Jn 12:13 "*B* is he who comes in the name
Ac 20:35 'It is more *b* to give than to receive
Tit 2:13 while we wait for the *b* hope—
Jas 1:12 *B* is the man who perseveres
Rev 1: 3 *B* is the one who reads the words
22: 7 *B* is he who keeps the words

Rev 22:14 "*B* are those who wash their robes,

BLESSES (BLESS)
Ps 29:11 the LORD *b* his people with peace.
Ro 10:12 and richly *b* all who call on him,

BLESSING (BLESS)
Ge 27: 4 so that I may give you my *b*
Dt 23: 5 turned the curse into a *b* for you,
33: 1 This is the *b* that Moses the man
Pr 10:22 The *b* of the LORD brings wealth,
Eze 34:26 there will be showers of *b*.

BLESSINGS (BLESS)
Dt 11:29 proclaim on Mount Gerizim the *b*,
Jos 8:34 all the words of the law—the *b*
Pr 10: 6 *B* crown the head of the righteous,
Ro 15:27 shared in the Jews' spiritual *b*,

BLIND (BLINDED)
Mt 15:14 a *b* man leads a *b* man, both will fall
23:16 "Woe to you, *b* guides! You say,
Mk 10:46 a *b* man, Bartimaeus (that is,
Lk 6:39 "Can a *b* man lead a *b* man?
Jn 9:25 I was *b* but now I see!"

BLINDED (BLIND)
Jn 12:40 elsewhere: "He has *b* their eyes
2Co 4: 4 The god of this age has *b* the minds

BLOOD (BLOODSHED BLOODTHIRSTY)
Ge 4:10 Your brother's *b* cries out to me
9: 6 "Whoever sheds the *b* of man,
Ex 12:13 and when I see the *b*, I will pass
24: 8 "This is the *b* of the covenant that
Lev 16:15 and take its *b* behind the curtain
17:11 For the life of a creature is in the *b*,
Dt 12:23 eat the *b*, because the *b* is the life,
Ps 72:14 for precious is their *b* in his sight.
Pr 6:17 hands that shed innocent *b*,
Isa 1:11 pleasure in the *b* of bulls and lambs
Mt 26:28 This is my *b* of the covenant,
27:24 "I am innocent of this man's *b*,"
Mk 14:24 "This is my *b* of the covenant,
Lk 22:44 drops of *b* falling to the ground.
Jn 6:53 of the Son of Man and drink his *b*,
Ac 15:20 of strangled animals and from *b*.
20:26 innocent of the *b* of all men.
Ro 3:25 of atonement, through faith in his *b*
5: 9 have now been justified by his *b*,
1Co 11:25 cup is the new covenant in my *b*;
Eph 1: 7 we have redemption through his *b*,
2:13 near through the *b* of Christ.
Col 1:20 by making peace through his *b*,
Heb 9: 7 once a year, and never without *b*,
9:12 once for all by his own *b*,
9:20 "This is the *b* of the covenant,
9:22 of *b* there is no forgiveness.
12:24 word than the *b* of Abel.
1Pe 1:19 but with the precious *b* of Christ,
1Jn 1: 7 and the *b* of Jesus, his Son,
Rev 1: 5 has freed us from our sins by his *b*,
5: 9 with your *b* you purchased men
7:14 white in the *b* of the Lamb.
12:11 him by the *b* of the Lamb
19:13 He is dressed in a robe dipped in *b*,

BLOODSHED (BLOOD)
Jer 48:10 on him who keeps his sword from *b*
Eze 35: 6 did not hate *b*, *b* will pursue you.
Hab 2:12 to him who builds a city with *b*

BLOODTHIRSTY* (BLOOD)
Ps 5: 6 *b* and deceitful men
26: 9 my life with *b* men,
55:23 *b* and deceitful men
59: 2 and save me from *b* men.
139:19 Away from me, you *b* men!
Pr 29:10 *B* men hate a man of integrity

BLOSSOM
Isa 35: 1 the wilderness will rejoice and *b*.

BLOT (BLOTS)
Ex 32:32 then *b* me out of the book you have
Ps 51: 1 *b* out my transgressions.
Rev 3: 5 I will never *b* out his name

BLOTS (BLOT)
Isa 43:25 "I, even I, am he who *b* out

BLOWN
Eph 4:14 and *b* here and there by every wind
Jas 1: 6 doubts is like a wave of the sea, *b*
Jude :12 without rain, *b* along by the wind;

BLUSH
Jer 6:15 they do not even know how to *b*.

BOAST (BOASTS)
1Ki 20:11 armor should not *b* like one who
Ps 34: 2 My soul will *b* in the LORD;
44: 8 In God we make our *b* all day long,
Pr 27: 1 Do not *b* about tomorrow,
Jer 9:23 or the rich man *b* of his riches,
1Co 1:31 Let him who boasts *b* in the Lord."
2Co 10:17 Let him who boasts *b* in the Lord."
11:30 I do not inwardly burn? If I must *b*,
Gal 6:14 May I never *b* except in the cross
Eph 2: 9 not by works, so that no one can *b*.

BOASTS (BOAST)
Jer 9:24 but let him who *b* boast about this:

BOAZ
Wealthy Bethlehemite who showed favor to Ruth (Ru 2), married her (Ru 4). Ancestor of David (Ru 4:18–22; 1Ch 2:12–15), Jesus (Mt 1:5–16; Lk 3:23–32).

BODIES (BODY)
Isa 26:19 their *b* will rise.
Ro 12: 1 to offer your *b* as living sacrifices,
1Co 6:15 not know that your *b* are members
Eph 5:28 to love their wives as their own *b*.

BODILY (BODY)
Col 2: 9 of the Deity lives in *b* form,

BODY (BODIES BODILY EMBODIMENT)
Zec 13: 6 What are these wounds on your *b*?'
Mt 10:28 afraid of those who kill the *b*
26:26 saying, "Take and eat; this is my *b*
26:41 spirit is willing, but the *b* is weak."
Mk 14:22 saying, "Take it; this is my *b*."
Lk 22:19 saying, "This is my *b* given for you;
Jn 13:10 wash his feet; his whole *b* is clean.
Ro 6:13 Do not offer the parts of your *b*
12: 4 us has one *b* with many members,
1Co 6:19 not know that your *b* is a temple
6:20 Therefore honor God with your *b*.
11:24 "This is my *b*, which is for you;
12:12 The *b* is a unit, though it is made up
12:13 baptized by one Spirit into one *b*—
15:44 a natural *b*, it is raised a spiritual *b*.
Eph 1:23 which is his *b*, the fullness
4:25 for we are all members of one *b*.
5:30 for we are members of his *b*.
Php 1:20 Christ will be exalted in my *b*,
Col 1:24 sake of his *b*, which is the church.

BOLD (BOLDNESS)
Ps 138: 3 you made me *b* and stouthearted.
Pr 21:29 A wicked man puts up a *b* front,
28: 1 but the righteous are as *b* as a lion.

BOLDNESS* (BOLD)
Lk 11: 8 of the man's *b* he will get up
Ac 4:29 to speak your word with great *b*.

BONDAGE
Ezr 9: 9 God has not deserted us in our *b*.

BONES
Ge 2:23 "This is now bone of my *b*
Ps 22:14 and all my *b* are out of joint.
22:17 I can count all my *b*;
Eze 37: 1 middle of a valley; it was full of *b*.
Jn 19:36 "Not one of his *b* will be broken,"

BOOK (BOOKS)
Ex 32:33 against me I will blot out of my *b*.
Jos 1: 8 Do not let this *B* of the Law depart
2Ki 22: 8 "I have found the *B* of the Law
2Ch 34:15 "I have found the *B* of the Law
Ne 8: 8 They read from the *B* of the Law
Ps 69:28 May they be blotted out of the *b*
Da 12: 1 name is found written in the *b*—
Jn 20:30 which are not recorded in this *b*.
Php 4: 3 whose names are in the *b* of life.
Rev 3: 5 never blot out his name from the *b*
20:12 *b* was opened, which is the *b*
20:15 was not found written in the *b*
21:27 written in the Lamb's *b* of life.
22:18 him the plagues described in this *b*.

BOOKS* (BOOK)
Ecc 12:12 Of making many *b* there is no end,
Da 7:10 and the *b* were opened.
Jn 21:25 for the *b* that would be written.
Rev 20:12 the throne, and *b* were opened.
20:12 they had done as recorded in the *b*.

BORE (BEAR)
Isa 53:12 For he *b* the sin of many,
1Pe 2:24 He himself *b* our sins in his body

BORN (BEAR)
Ecc 3: 2 a time to be *b* and a time to die,
Isa 9: 6 For to us a child is *b*,
66: 8 Can a country be *b* in a day
Lk 2:11 of David a Savior has been *b* to you
Jn 3: 3 see the kingdom of God unless he is *b* again.
3: 4 How can a man be *b* when he is old
3: 5 unless he is *b* of water
3: 7 at my saying, 'You must be *b* again
3: 8 it is with everyone *b* of the Spirit."
1Pe 1:23 For you have been *b* again,
1Jn 3: 9 because he has been *b* of God.
4: 7 Everyone who loves has been *b*
5: 1 believes that Jesus is the Christ is *b*
5: 4 for everyone *b* of God overcomes
5:18 We know that anyone *b*

BORROWER
Pr 22: 7 and the *b* is servant to the lender.

BOTHER (BOTHERING)
Lk 11: 7 one inside answers, 'Don't *b* me.

BOTHERING (BOTHER)
Lk 18: 5 yet because this widow keeps *b* me,

BOUGHT (BUY)
Ac 20:28 which he *b* with his own blood.
1Co 6:20 You are not your own; you were *b*
7:23 You were *b* at a price; do not
2Pe 2: 1 the sovereign Lord who *b* them—

BOUND (BIND)
Is 56: 3 Let no foreigner who has *b* himself
Mt 16:19 bind on earth will be *b* in heaven,
18:18 bind on earth will be *b* in heaven,
Ro 7: 2 by law a married woman is *b*
1Co 7:39 A woman is *b* to her husband
Jude : 6 *b* with everlasting chains
Rev 20: 2 and *b* him for a thousand years.

BOUNDARY (BOUNDS)
Nu 34: 3 your southern *b* will start
Pr 23:10 Do not move an ancient *b* stone
Hos 5:10 who move *b* stones.

BOUNDS (BOUNDARY)
2Co 7: 4 all our troubles my joy knows no *b*.

BOUNTY*
Ge 49:26 than the *b* of the age-old hills.
Dt 28:12 heavens, the storehouse of his *b*,
1Ki 10:13 he had given her out of his royal *b*.
Ps 65:11 You crown the year with your *b*,
68:10 from your *b*, O God, you provided
Jer 31:12 rejoice in the *b* of the LORD—
31:14 my people will be filled with my *b*

BOW (BOWED BOWS)
Dt 5: 9 You shall not *b* down to them
1Ki 22:34 But someone drew his *b* at random
Ps 5: 7 in reverence will I *b* down
44: 6 I do not trust in my *b*,
95: 6 Come, let us *b* down in worship,
138: 2 I will *b* down toward your holy
Isa 44:19 Shall I *b* down to a block of wood?"
45:23 Before me every knee will *b*;
Ro 14:11 'every knee will *b* before me;
Php 2:10 name of Jesus every knee should *b*,

BOWED (BOW)
Ps 145:14 and lifts up all who are *b* down.
146: 8 the LORD lifts up those who are *b*

BOWS (BOW)
Isa 44:15 he makes an idol and *b* down to it.
44:17 he *b* down to it and worships.

BOY (BOY'S BOYS)
Ge 21:17 God heard the *b* crying,
22:12 not lay a hand on the *b*
Jdg 13: 5 *b* is to be a Nazirite,
1Sa 2:11 *b* ministered before the LORD.
3: 8 the LORD was calling the *b*.
Isa 7:16 before the *b* knows enough
Mt 17:18 demon, and it came out of the *b*
Lk 2:43 the *b* Jesus stayed behind

BOY'S (BOY)
1Ki 17:22 the *b* life returned to him
2Ki 4:34 the *b* body grew warm

BOYS (BOY)
Ge 25:24 twin *b* in her womb
Ex 1:18 they let the *b* live.

BRACE*
Job 38: 3 *B* yourself like a man;
40: 7 out of the storm: "*B* yourself like
Na 2: 1 *b* yourselves,

BRAG*
Am 4: 5 and *b* about your freewill offerings
Ro 2:17 *b* about your relationship to God;
2:23 temples? You who *b* about the law,
Jas 4:16 As it is, you boast and *b*.

BRAIDED
1Ti 2: 9 not with *b* hair or gold or pearls
1Pe 3: 3 as *b* hair and the wearing

BRANCH (BRANCHES)
Isa 4: 2 In that day the *B* of the LORD will
Jer 23: 5 up to David a righteous *B*,
33:15 I will make a righteous *B* sprout
Zec 3: 8 going to bring my servant, the *B*.
6:12 is the man whose name is the *B*,
Jn 15: 2 while every *b* that does bear fruit
15: 4 No *b* can bear fruit by itself;

BRANCHES (BRANCH)
Jn 15: 5 "I am the vine; you are the *b*.
Ro 11:21 if God did not spare the natural *b*,

BRAVE
2Sa 2: 7 Now then, be strong and *b*,
13:28 you this order? Be strong and *b*."

BREACH (BREAK)
Ps 106:23 stood in the *b* before him

BREACHING (BREAK)
Pr 17:14 Starting a quarrel is like *b* a dam;

BREAD
Ex 12: 8 and *b* made without yeast.
23:15 the Feast of Unleavened *B*;
25:30 Put the *b* of the Presence
Dt 8: 3 that man does not live on *b* alone
Ps 78:25 Men ate the *b* of angels;
Pr 30: 8 but give me only my daily *b*.
Ecc 11: 1 Cast your *b* upon the waters,
Isa 55: 2 Why spend money on what is not *b*
Mt 4: 3 tell these stones to become *b*."
4: 4 'Man does not live on *b* alone,
6:11 Give us today our daily *b*.
26:26 Jesus took *b*, gave thanks
Mk 14:22 Jesus took *b*, gave thanks
Lk 4: 3 tell this stone to become *b*."
4: 4 'Man does not live on *b* alone.' "
9:13 "We have only five loaves of *b*
11: 3 Give us each day our daily *b*.
22:19 And he took *b*, gave thanks
Jn 6:33 For the *b* of God is he who comes
6:35 Jesus declared, "I am the *b* of life.
6:41 "I am the *b* that came
6:48 I am the *b* of life.
6:51 I am the living *b* that came
6:51 This *b* is my flesh, which I will give
21:13 took the *b* and gave it to them,
1Co 10:16 And is not the *b* that we break
11:23 took *b*, and when he had given
11:26 For whenever you eat this *b*

BREAK (BREACH BREACHING BREAKERS BREAKING BREAKS BROKE BROKEN BROKENNESS)
Nu 30: 2 he must not *b* his word
Jdg 2: 1 'I will never *b* my covenant
Pr 25:15 and a gentle tongue can *b* a bone.
Isa 42: 3 A bruised reed he will not *b*,
Mal 2:15 and do not *b* faith with the wife
Mt 12:20 A bruised reed he will not *b*,
Ac 20: 7 week we came together to *b* bread.
1Co 10:16 the bread that we *b* a participation
Rev 5: 2 "Who is worthy to *b* the seals

BREAKERS* (BREAK)
Ps 42: 7 all your waves and *b*
93: 4 mightier than the *b* of the sea—
Jnh 2: 3 all your waves and *b*

BREAKING (BREAK)
Jos 9:20 fall on us for *b* the oath we swore
Eze 16:59 oath by *b* the covenant.
17:18 the oath by *b* the covenant.
Ac 2:42 to the *b* of bread and to prayer.
Jas 2:10 at just one point is guilty of *b* all

BREAKS (BREAK)
Jer 23:29 "and like a hammer that *b* a rock
1Jn 3: 4 Everyone who sins *b* the law;

BREASTPIECE (BREASTPLATE)
Ex 28:15 Fashion a *b* for making decisions—

BREASTPLATE* (BREASTPIECE)
Isa 59:17 He put on righteousness as his *b*,
Eph 6:14 with the *b* of righteousness in place
1Th 5: 8 putting on faith and love as a *b*,

BREASTS
La 4: 3 Even jackals offer their *b*

BREATH (BREATHED GOD-BREATHED)
Ge 2: 7 into his nostrils the *b* of life,

BREATHED (BREATH)
Ge 2: 7 *b* into his nostrils the breath of life,
Mk 15:37 With a loud cry, Jesus *b* his last.
Jn 20:22 And with that he *b* on them

BREEDS*
Pr 13:10 Pride only *b* quarrels,

BRIBE
Ex 23: 8 "Do not accept a *b*,
Dt 16:19 for a *b* blinds the eyes of the wise
27:25 "Cursed is the man who accepts a *b*
Pr 6:35 will refuse the *b*, however great it

BRIDE
Isa 62: 5 as a bridegroom rejoices over his *b*,
Rev 19: 7 and his *b* has made herself ready.
21: 2 as a *b* beautifully dressed
21: 9 I will show you the *b*, the wife
22:17 The Spirit and the *b* say, "Come!"

BRIDEGROOM
Ps 19: 5 which is like a *b* coming forth
Mt 25: 1 and went out to meet the *b*.
25: 5 The *b* was a long time in coming,

BRIGHTENS* (BRIGHTNESS)
Pr 16:15 When a king's face *b*, it means life;
Ecc 8: 1 Wisdom *b* a man's face

BRIGHTER (BRIGHTNESS)
Pr 4:18 shining ever *b* till the full light

BRIGHTNESS* (BRIGHTENS BRIGHTER)
2Sa 22:13 Out of the *b* of his presence
23: 4 like the *b* after rain
Ps 18:12 of the *b* of his presence clouds
Isa 59: 9 for *b*, but we walk in deep shadows.
60: 3 and kings to the *b* of your dawn.
60:19 will the *b* of the moon shine on you
Da 12: 3 who are wise will shine like the *b*
Am 5:20 pitch-dark, without a ray of *b*?

BRILLIANCE* (BRILLIANT)
Ac 22:11 the *b* of the light had blinded me.
Rev 1:16 was like the sun shining in all its *b*.
21:11 its *b* was like that of a very precious

BRILLIANT* (BRILLIANCE)
Ecc 9:11 or wealth to the *b*
Eze 1: 4 and surrounded by *b* light.
1:27 and *b* light surrounded him.

BRINK*
Pr 5:14 I have come to the *b* of utter ruin

BRITTLE
Da 2:42 will be partly strong and partly *b*.

BROAD
Mt 7:13 and *b* is the road that leads

BROKE (BREAK)
Mt 26:26 took bread, gave thanks and *b* it,
Mk 14:22 took bread, gave thanks and *b* it,
Ac 2:46 They *b* bread in their homes
20:11 he went upstairs again and *b* bread
1Co 11:24 when he had given thanks, he *b* it

BROKEN (BREAK)
Ps 34:20 not one of them will be *b*.
51:17 The sacrifices of God are a *b* spirit;
Ecc 4:12 of three strands is not quickly *b*.
Lk 20:18 on that stone will be *b* to pieces,
Jn 7:23 the law of Moses may not be *b*,
10:35 and the Scripture cannot be *b*—
19:36 "Not one of his bones will be *b*,"
Ro 11:20 they were *b* off because of unbelief,

BROKENHEARTED* (HEART)
Ps 34:18 The LORD is close to the *b*
109:16 and the needy and the *b*.
147: 3 He heals the *b*
Isa 61: 1 He has sent me to bind up the *b*,

BROKENNESS* (BREAK)
Isa 65:14 and wail in *b* of spirit.

BRONZE
Ex 27: 2 and overlay the altar with *b.*
30:18 "Make a *b* basin, with its *b* stand,
Nu 21: 9 So Moses made a *b* snake
Da 2:32 and thighs of *b,* its legs of iron,
10: 6 legs like the gleam of burnished *b,*
Rev 1:15 His feet were like *b* glowing
2:18 whose feet are like burnished *b.*

BROTHER (BROTHER'S BROTHERHOOD BROTHERLY BROTHERS)
Pr 17:17 and a *b* is born for adversity.
18:24 a friend who sticks closer than a *b.*
27:10 neighbor nearby than a *b* far away.
Mt 5:24 and be reconciled to your *b;*
18:15 "If your *b* sins against you,
Mk 3:35 Whoever does God's will is my *b*
Lk 17: 3 "If your *b* sins, rebuke him,
Ro 14:15 not by your eating destroy your *b*
14:21 anything else that will cause your *b*
1Co 8:13 if what I eat causes my *b* to fall
2Th 3: 6 away from every *b* who is idle
3:15 as an enemy, but warn him as a *b.*
Phm :16 but better than a slave, as a dear *b.*
Jas 2:15 Suppose a *b* or sister is
4:11 Anyone who speaks against his *b*
1Jn 2: 9 hates his *b* is still in the darkness.
2:10 Whoever loves his *b* lives
2:11 But whoever hates his *b* is
3:10 is anyone who does not love his *b.*
3:15 who hates his *b* is a murderer,
3:17 material possessions and sees his *b*
4:20 For anyone who does not love his *b*
4:20 yet hates his *b,* he is a liar.
4:21 loves God must also love his *b.*
5:16 If anyone sees his *b* commit a sin

BROTHER'S (BROTHER)
Ge 4: 9 "Am I my *b* keeper?" The LORD
Mt 7: 5 remove the speck from your *b* eye.
Ro 14:13 or obstacle in your *b* way.

BROTHERHOOD (BROTHER)
1Pe 2:17 Love the *b* of believers, fear God,

BROTHERLY* (BROTHER)
Ro 12:10 devoted to one another in *b* love.
1Th 4: 9 Now about *b* love we do not need
2Pe 1: 7 and to godliness, *b* kindness;
1: 7 kindness; and to *b* kindness,

BROTHERS (BROTHER)
Jos 1:14 You are to help your *b*
Ps 133: 1 is when *b* live together in unity!
Pr 6:19 who stirs up dissension among *b.*
Mt 12:49 "Here are my mother and my *b.*
19:29 everyone who has left houses or *b*
25:40 one of the least of these *b* of mine,
Mk 3:33 "Who are my mother and my *b?"*
10:29 or *b* or sisters or mother or father
Lk 21:16 will be betrayed even by parents, *b,*
22:32 turned back, strengthen your *b."*
Jn 7: 5 his own *b* did not believe in him.
Ac 15:32 to encourage and strengthen the *b.*
Ro 9: 3 off from Christ for the sake of my *b*
1Co 8:12 sin against your *b* in this way
2Co 11:26 and in danger from false *b.*
Gal 2: 4 some false *b* had infiltrated our
1Th 4:10 you do love all the *b*
5:26 Greet all the *b* with a holy kiss.
1Ti 6: 2 for them because they are *b.*
Heb 2:11 Jesus is not ashamed to call them *b.*
2:17 to be made like his *b* in every way,
13: 1 Keep on loving each other as *b.*
1Pe 1:22 you have sincere love for your *b,*
3: 8 be sympathetic, love as *b,*
1Jn 3:14 death to life, because we love our *b.*
3:16 to lay down our lives for our *b.*
3Jn :10 he refuses to welcome the *b.*
Rev 12:10 For the accuser of our *b,*

BROW
Ge 3:19 By the sweat of your *b*

BRUISED (BRUISES)
Isa 42: 3 A *b* reed he will not break,
Mt 12:20 A *b* reed he will not break,

BRUISES (BRUISED)
Isa 30:26 when the LORD binds up the *b*

BRUTAL (BRUTE)
2Ti 3: 3 slanderous, without self-control, *b,*

BRUTE* (BRUTAL)
Ps 73:22 I was a *b* beast before you.
2Pe 2:12 They are like *b* beasts, creatures

BUBBLING*
Pr 18: 4 the fountain of wisdom is a *b* brook
Isa 35: 7 the thirsty ground *b* springs.

BUCKET*
Isa 40:15 the nations are like a drop in a *b;*

BUCKLED* (BUCKLER)
Eph 6:14 belt of truth *b* around your waist,

BUCKLER* (BUCKLED)
Ps 35: 2 Take up shield and *b;*

BUD (BUDDED)
Isa 27: 6 Israel will *b* and blossom

BUDDED (BUD)
Heb 9: 4 Aaron's staff that had *b,*

BUILD (BUILDER BUILDERS BUILDING BUILDS BUILT REBUILD REBUILT)
2Sa 7: 5 Are you the one to *b* me a house
1Ki 6: 1 he began to *b* the temple
Ecc 3: 3 a time to tear down and a time to *b,*
Mt 16:18 and on this rock I will *b* my church,
Ac 20:32 which can *b* you up and give you
Ro 15: 2 neighbor for his good, to *b* him up.
1Co 14:12 excel in gifts that *b* up the church.
1Th 5:11 one another and *b* each other up,
Jude :20 *b* yourselves up in your most holy

BUILDER* (BUILD)
1Co 3:10 I laid a foundation as an expert *b,*
Heb 3: 3 the *b* of a house has greater honor
3: 4 but God is the *b* of everything.
11:10 whose architect and *b* is God.

BUILDERS (BUILD)
Ps 118:22 The stone the *b* rejected
Mt 21:42 " 'The stone the *b* rejected
Mk 12:10 " 'The stone the *b* rejected
Lk 20:17 " 'The stone the *b* rejected
Ac 4:11 " 'the stone you *b* rejected,
1Pe 2: 7 "The stone the *b* rejected

BUILDING (BUILD)
Ezr 3: 8 to supervise the *b* of the house
Ne 4:17 of Judah who were *b* the wall.
Ro 15:20 so that I would not be *b*
1Co 3: 9 you are God's field, God's *b.*
2Co 5: 1 we have a *b* from God, an eternal
10: 8 us for *b* you up rather
13:10 the Lord gave me for *b* you up,
Eph 2:21 him the whole *b* is joined together
4:29 helpful for *b* others up according

BUILDS (BUILD)
Ps 127: 1 Unless the LORD *b* the house,
Pr 14: 1 The wise woman *b* her house,
1Co 3:10 one should be careful how he *b.*
3:12 If any man *b* on this foundation
8: 1 Knowledge puffs up, but love *b* up.
Eph 4:16 grows and *b* itself up in love,

BUILT (BUILD)
1Ki 6:14 So Solomon *b* the temple
Mt 7:24 is like a wise man who *b* his house
Lk 6:49 is like a man who *b* a house
Ac 17:24 does not live in temples *b* by hands.
1Co 3:14 If what he has *b* survives, he will
2Co 5: 1 in heaven, not *b* by human hands.
Eph 2:20 *b* on the foundation of the apostles
4:12 the body of Christ may be *b* up
Col 2: 7 live in him, rooted and *b* up in him,
1Pe 2: 5 are being *b* into a spiritual house

BULL (BULLS)
Lev 4: 3 bring to the LORD a young *b*

BULLS (BULL)
1Ki 7:25 The Sea stood on twelve *b,*
Heb 10: 4 it is impossible for the blood of *b*

BURDEN (BURDENED BURDENS BURDENSOME)
Ps 38: 4 like a *b* too heavy to bear.
Ecc 1:13 What a heavy *b* God has laid
Mt 11:30 my yoke is easy and my *b* is light."
Ac 15:28 to us not to *b* you with anything
2Co 11: 9 from being a *b* to you in any way,
12:14 and I will not be a *b* to you,
1Th 2: 9 day in order not to be a *b* to anyone
2Th 3: 8 so that we would not be a *b* to any
Heb 13:17 not a *b,* for that would be

BURDENED* (BURDEN)
Isa 43:23 have not *b* you with grain offerings
43:24 But you have *b* me with your sins
Mic 6: 3 How have I *b* you? Answer me.
Mt 11:28 all you who are weary and *b,*
2Co 5: 4 are in this tent, we groan and are *b,*
Gal 5: 1 do not let yourselves be *b* again
1Ti 5:16 not let the church be *b* with them,

BURDENS (BURDEN)
Ps 68:19 who daily bears our *b.*
Lk 11:46 down with *b* they can hardly carry,
Gal 6: 2 Carry each other's *b,*

BURDENSOME (BURDEN)
1Jn 5: 3 And his commands are not *b,*

BURIED (BURY)
Ru 1:17 die I will die, and there I will be *b.*
Ro 6: 4 *b* with him through baptism
1Co 15: 4 that he was *b,* that he was raised
Col 2:12 having been *b* with him in baptism

BURN (BURNING BURNT)
Dt 7: 5 and *b* their idols in the fire.
Ps 79: 5 long will your jealousy *b* like fire?
1Co 7: 9 to marry than to *b* with passion.

BURNING (BURN)
Ex 27:20 so that the lamps may be kept *b.*
Lev 6: 9 the fire must be kept *b* on the altar.
Ps 18:28 You, O LORD, keep my lamp *b;*
Pr 25:22 you will heap *b* coals on his head,
Ro 12:20 you will heap *b* coals on his head."
Rev 19:20 alive into the fiery lake of *b* sulfur.

BURNISHED*
1Ki 7:45 of the LORD were of *b* bronze.
Eze 1: 7 and gleamed like *b* bronze.
Da 10: 6 and legs like the gleam of *b* bronze,
Rev 2:18 and whose feet are like *b* bronze.

BURNT (BURN)
Ge 8:20 he sacrificed *b* offerings on it.
22: 2 as a *b* offering on one
Ex 10:25 and *b* offerings to present
18:12 brought a *b* offering and other
40: 6 Place the altar of *b* offering in front
Lev 1: 3 " 'If the offering is a *b* offering
Jos 8:31 offered to the LORD *b* offerings
Jdg 6:26 offer the second bull as a *b* offering
13:16 But if you prepare a *b* offering,
1Ki 3: 4 offered a thousand *b* offerings

1Ki 9:25 year Solomon sacrificed *b* offerings
10: 5 and the *b* offerings he made
Ezr 3: 2 Israel to sacrifice *b* offerings on it,
Eze 43:18 for sacrificing *b* offerings

BURST
Ps 98: 4 *b* into jubilant song with music;
Isa 44:23 *B* into song, you mountains,
49:13 *b* into song, O mountains!
52: 9 *B* into songs of joy together,
54: 1 *b* into song, shout for joy,
55:12 will *b* into song before you,

BURY (BURIED)
Mt 8:22 and let the dead *b* their own dead."
Lk 9:60 "Let the dead *b* their own dead,

BUSH
Ex 3: 2 the *b* was on fire it did not burn up.
Mk 12:26 the account of the *b*, how God said
Lk 20:37 But in the account of the *b*,
Ac 7:35 who appeared to him in the *b*.

BUSINESS
Ecc 4: 8 a miserable *b!*
Da 8:27 and went about the king's *b*.
1Co 5:12 What *b* is it of mine to judge those
1Th 4:11 to mind your own *b* and to work
Jas 1:11 even while he goes about his *b*.

BUSY*
1Ki 18:27 Perhaps he is deep in thought, or *b*,
20:40 While your servant was *b* here
Isa 32: 6 his mind is *b* with evil:
Hag 1: 9 of you is *b* with his own house.
2Th 3:11 They are not *b;* they are
Tit 2: 5 to be *b* at home, to be kind,

BUSYBODIES*
2Th 3:11 They are not busy; they are *b*.
1Ti 5:13 *b*, saying things they ought not to.

BUY (BOUGHT BUYS)
Pr 23:23 *B* the truth and do not sell it;
Isa 55: 1 Come, *b* wine and milk
Rev 13:17 so that no one could *b* or sell

BUYS (BUY)
Pr 31:16 She considers a field and *b* it;

BYWORD (WORD)
1Ki 9: 7 Israel will then become a *b*
Ps 44:14 You have made us a *b*
Joel 2:17 a *b* among the nations.

CAESAR
Mt 22:21 "Give to *C* what is Caesar's,

CAIN
Firstborn of Adam (Ge 4:1), murdered brother Abel (Ge 4:1–16; 1Jn 3:12).

CAKE
Hos 7: 8 Ephraim is a flat *c* not turned over.

CALEB
Judahite who spied out Canaan (Nu 13:6); allowed to enter land because of faith (Nu 13:30–14:38; Dt 1:36). Possessed Hebron (Jos 14:6–15:19).

CALF
Ex 32: 4 into an idol cast in the shape of a *c*,
Pr 15:17 than a fattened *c* with hatred.
Lk 15:23 Bring the fattened *c* and kill it.
Ac 7:41 made an idol in the form of a *c*.

CALL (CALLED CALLING CALLS)
1Ki 18:24 I will *c* on the name of the LORD.
2Ki 5:11 *c* on the name of the LORD his
1Ch 16: 8 to the LORD, *c* on his name;
Ps 105: 1 to the LORD, *c* on his name;
116:13 and *c* on the name of the LORD.
Ps 116:17 and *c* on the name of the LORD.
145:18 near to all who *c* on him,
Pr 31:28 children arise and *c* her blessed;
Isa 5:20 Woe to those who *c* evil good
12: 4 to the LORD, *c* on his name;
55: 6 *c* on him while he is near.
65:24 Before they *c* I will answer;
Jer 33: 3 '*C* to me and I will answer you
Zep 3: 9 that all of them may *c* on the name
Zec 13: 9 They will *c* on my name
Mt 9:13 come to *c* the righteous,
Mk 2:17 I have not come to *c* the righteous,
Lk 5:32 I have not come to *c* the righteous,
Ac 2:39 all whom the Lord our God will *c*."
9:14 to arrest all who *c* on your name."
9:21 among those who *c* on this name?
Ro 10:12 and richly blesses all who *c* on him,
11:29 gifts and his *c* are irrevocable.
1Co 1: 2 with all those everywhere who *c*
1Th 4: 7 For God did not *c* us to be impure,
2Ti 2:22 along with those who *c*

CALLED (CALL)
Ge 2:23 she shall be *c* 'woman,'
5: 2 he blessed them and *c* them "man
12: 8 and *c* on the name of the LORD.
21:33 and there he *c* upon the name
26:25 and *c* on the name of the LORD.
1Sa 3: 5 and said, "Here I am; you *c* me."
2Ch 7:14 if my people, who are *c*
Ps 34: 6 This poor man *c*, and the LORD
116: 4 Then I *c* on the name of the LORD
Isa 56: 7 for my house will be *c*
La 3:55 I *c* on your name, O LORD,
Hos 11: 1 and out of Egypt I *c* my son.
Mt 1:16 was born Jesus, who is *c* Christ.
2:15 "Out of Egypt I *c* my son."
21:13 " 'My house will be *c* a house
Mk 11:17 " 'My house will be *c*
Lk 1:32 will be *c* the Son of the Most High.
1:35 to be born will be *c* the Son of God.
Ro 1: 1 *c* to be an apostle and set apart
1: 6 among those who are *c* to belong
1: 7 loved by God and *c* to be saints:
8:28 who have been *c* according
8:30 And those he predestined, he also *c*
1Co 1: 1 *c* to be an apostle of Christ Jesus
1: 2 in Christ Jesus and *c* to be holy,
1:24 but to those whom God has *c*,
1:26 of what you were when you were *c*.
7:15 God has *c* us to live in peace.
7:17 and to which God has *c* him.
Gal 1: 6 deserting the one who *c* you
1:15 from birth and *c* me by his grace,
5:13 You, my brothers, were *c* to be free
Eph 1:18 the hope to which he has *c* you,
4: 4 as you were *c* to one hope
Col 3:15 of one body you were *c* to peace.
2Th 2:14 He *c* you to this through our gospel
1Ti 6:12 life to which you were *c*
2Ti 1: 9 who has saved us and *c* us
Heb 9:15 that those who are *c* may receive
1Pe 1:15 But just as he who *c* you is holy,
2: 9 of him who *c* you out of darkness
3: 9 to this you were *c* so that you may
5:10 who *c* you to his eternal glory
2Pe 1: 3 of him who *c* us by his own glory
Jude : 1 To those who have been *c*,

CALLING (CALL)
Isa 40: 3 A voice of one *c:*
Mt 3: 3 "A voice of one *c* in the desert,
Mk 1: 3 "a voice of one *c* in the desert,
10:49 Cheer up! On your feet! He's *c* you
Lk 3: 4 "A voice of one *c* in the desert,
Jn 1:23 I am the voice of one *c* in the desert
Ac 22:16 wash your sins away, *c* on his name
Eph 4: 1 worthy of the *c* you have received.
2Th 1:11 may count you worthy of his *c*,
2Pe 1:10 all the more eager to make your *c*

CALLOUS* (CALLOUSED)
Ps 17:10 They close up their *c* hearts,
73: 7 From their *c* hearts comes iniquity;
119:70 Their hearts are *c* and unfeeling,

CALLOUSED* (CALLOUS)
Isa 6:10 Make the heart of this people *c;*
Mt 13:15 this people's heart has become *c;*
Ac 28:27 this people's heart has become *c;*

CALLS (CALL)
Ps 147: 4 and *c* them each by name.
Isa 40:26 and *c* them each by name.
Joel 2:32 And everyone who *c*
Mt 22:43 speaking by the Spirit, *c* him 'Lord
Jn 10: 3 He *c* his own sheep by name
Ac 2:21 And everyone who *c*
Ro 10:13 "Everyone who *c* on the name
1Th 2:12 who *c* you into his kingdom
5:24 The one who *c* you is faithful

CALM (CALMS)
Ps 107:30 They were glad when it grew *c*,
Isa 7: 4 keep *c* and don't be afraid.
Eze 16:42 I will be *c* and no longer angry.

CALMS* (CALM)
Pr 15:18 but a patient man *c* a quarrel.

CAMEL
Mt 19:24 it is easier for a *c* to go
23:24 strain out a gnat but swallow a *c*.
Mk 10:25 It is easier for a *c* to go
Lk 18:25 it is easier for a *c* to go

CAMP (ENCAMPS)
Heb 13:13 outside the *c*, bearing the disgrace

CANAAN (CANAANITE CANAANITES)
Ge 10:15 *C* was the father of Sidon his
Lev 14:34 "When you enter the land of *C*,
25:38 of Egypt to give you the land of *C*
Nu 13: 2 men to explore the land of *C*,
33:51 'When you cross the Jordan into *C*,
Jdg 4: 2 a king of *C*, who reigned in Hazor.
1Ch 16:18 "To you I will give the land of *C*
Ps 105:11 "To you I will give the land of *C*
Ac 13:19 he overthrew seven nations in *C*

CANAANITE (CANAAN)
Ge 10:18 Later the *C* clans scattered
28: 1 "Do not marry a *C* woman.
Jos 5: 1 all the *C* kings along the seacoast
Jdg 1:32 lived among the *C* inhabitants

CANAANITES (CANAAN)
Ex 33: 2 before you and drive out the *C*,

CANCEL (CANCELED)
Dt 15: 1 seven years you must *c* debts.

CANCELED (CANCEL)
Mt 18:27 pity on him, *c* the debt
Lk 7:42 so he *c* the debts of both.
Col 2:14 having *c* the written code,

CANDLESTICKS see LAMPSTANDS

CANOPY*
2Sa 22:12 He made darkness his *c*
2Ki 16:18 away the Sabbath *c* that had been
Ps 18:11 made darkness his covering, his *c*
Isa 4: 5 over all the glory will be a *c*.
40:22 stretches out the heavens like a *c*,
Jer 43:10 he will spread his royal *c*

CAPERNAUM
Mt 4:13 Nazareth, he went and lived in *C*,
Jn 6:59 teaching in the synagogue in *C*.

CAPITAL
Dt 21:22 guilty of a *c* offense is put to death

CAPSTONE* (STONE)
Ps 118:22 has become the *c*;
Zec 4: 7 he will bring out the *c* to shouts
Mt 21:42 has become the *c*;
Mk 12:10 has become the *c*;
Lk 20:17 has become the *c*?
Ac 4:11 which has become the *c*.'
1Pe 2: 7 has become the *c*,"

CAPTIVATE* (CAPTIVE)
Pr 6:25 or let her *c* you with her eyes,

CAPTIVATED* (CAPTIVE)
Pr 5:19 may you ever be *c* by her love.
5:20 Why be *c*, my son, by an adulteress

CAPTIVE (CAPTIVATE CAPTIVATED CAPTIVES CAPTIVITY CAPTURED)
Ac 8:23 full of bitterness and *c* to sin."
2Co 10: 5 and we take *c* every thought
Col 2: 8 See to it that no one takes you *c*
2Ti 2:26 who has taken them *c* to do his will.

CAPTIVES (CAPTIVE)
Ps 68:18 you led *c* in your train;
Isa 61: 1 to proclaim freedom for the *c*
Eph 4: 8 he led *c* in his train

CAPTIVITY (CAPTIVE)
Dt 28:41 because they will go into *c*.
2Ki 25:21 So Judah went into *c*, away
Jer 30: 3 Israel and Judah back from *c*
52:27 So Judah went into *c*, away
Eze 29:14 I will bring them back from *c*

CAPTURED (CAPTIVE)
1Sa 4:11 The ark of God was *c*,
2Sa 5: 7 David *c* the fortress of Zion,
2Ki 17: 6 the king of Assyria *c* Samaria

CARCASS
Jdg 14: 9 taken the honey from the lion's *c*.
Mt 24:28 there is a *c*, there the vultures

CARE (CAREFUL CARES CARING)
Ps 8: 4 the son of man that you *c* for him?
65: 9 You *c* for the land and water it;
144: 3 what is man that you *c* for him,
Pr 29: 7 The righteous *c* about justice
Mk 5:26 deal under the *c* of many doctors
Lk 10:34 him to an inn and took *c* of him.
18: 4 I don't fear God or *c* about men,
Jn 21:16 Jesus said, "Take *c* of my sheep."
1Ti 3: 5 how can he take *c* of God's church
6:20 what has been entrusted to your *c*.
Heb 2: 6 the son of man that you *c* for him?
1Pe 5: 2 of God's flock that is under your *c*,

CAREFUL* (CARE)
Ge 31:24 "Be *c* not to say anything to Jacob,
31:29 'Be *c* not to say anything to Jacob,
Ex 19:12 'Be *c* that you do not go up
23:13 "Be *c* to do everything I have said
34:12 Be *c* not to make a treaty
34:15 "Be *c* not to make a treaty
Lev 18: 4 and be *c* to follow my decrees.
25:18 " 'Follow my decrees and be *c*
26: 3 and are *c* to obey my commands,
Dt 2: 4 afraid of you, but be very *c*.
4: 9 before you today? Only be *c*,
4:23 Be *c* not to forget the covenant
5:32 So be *c* to do what the LORD your
6: 3 be *c* to obey so that it may go well
6:12 be *c* that you do not forget
6:25 And if we are *c* to obey all this law
7:12 attention to these laws and are *c*
8: 1 Be *c* to follow every command I am
8:11 Be *c* that you do not forget
11:16 Be *c*, or you will be enticed
12: 1 and laws you must be *c* to follow
12:13 Be *c* not to sacrifice your burnt
12:19 Be *c* not to neglect the Levites
Dt 12:28 Be *c* to obey all these regulations I
12:30 be *c* not to be ensnared
15: 5 are *c* to follow all these commands
15: 9 Be *c* not to harbor this wicked
17:10 Be *c* to do everything they direct
24: 8 cases of leprous diseases be very *c*
Jos 1: 7 Be *c* to obey all the law my servant
1: 8 so that you may be *c*
22: 5 But be very *c* to keep
23: 6 be *c* to obey all that is written
23:11 be very *c* to love the LORD your
1Ki 8:25 if only your sons are *c* in all they do
2Ki 10:31 Yet Jehu was not *c* to keep the law
17:37 You must always be *c*
21: 8 if only they will be *c*
1Ch 22:13 if you are *c* to observe the decrees
28: 8 Be *c* to follow all the commands
2Ch 6:16 if only your sons are *c* in all they do
33: 8 if only they will be *c*
Ezr 4:22 Be *c* not to neglect this matter.
Job 36:18 Be *c* that no one entices you
Ps 101: 2 I will be *c* to lead a blameless life—
Pr 13:24 he who loves him is *c*
27:23 give *c* attention to your herds;
Isa 7: 4 Be *c*, keep calm and don't be afraid.
Jer 17:21 Be *c* not to carry a load
17:24 But if you are *c* to obey me,
22: 4 For if you are *c* to carry out these
Eze 11:20 will follow my decrees and be *c*
18:19 has been *c* to keep all my decrees,
20:19 follow my decrees and be *c*
20:21 they were not *c* to keep my laws—
36:27 you to follow my decrees and be *c*
37:24 and be *c* to keep my decrees.
Mic 7: 5 be *c* of your words.
Hag 1: 5 "Give *c* thought to your ways.
1: 7 "Give *c* thought to your ways.
2:15 give *c* thought to this from this day
2:18 Give *c* thought: Is there yet any
2:18 give *c* thought to the day
Mt 2: 8 and make a *c* search for the child.
6: 1 "Be *c* not to do your 'acts
16: 6 "Be *c*," Jesus said to them.
Mk 8:15 "Be *c*," Jesus warned them.
Lk 21:34 Be *c*, or your hearts will be weighed
Ro 12:17 Be *c* to do what is right in the eyes
1Co 3:10 each one should be *c* how he builds
8: 9 Be *c*, however, that the exercise
10:12 standing firm, be *c* that you don't
Eph 5:15 Be very *c*, then, how you live—
2Ti 4: 2 great patience and *c* instruction.
Tit 3: 8 may be *c* to devote themselves
Heb 2: 1 We must pay more *c* attention,
4: 1 let us be *c* that none

CARELESS*
Mt 12:36 for every *c* word they have spoken.

CARES* (CARE)
Dt 11:12 It is a land the LORD your God *c*
Job 39:16 she *c* not that her labor was in vain,
Ps 55:22 Cast your *c* on the LORD
142: 4 no one *c* for my life.
Pr 12:10 A righteous man *c* for the needs
Ecc 5: 3 when there are many *c*,
Jer 12:11 because there is no one who *c*.
30:17 Zion for whom no one *c*.'
Na 1: 7 He *c* for those who trust in him,
Jn 10:13 and *c* nothing for the sheep.
Eph 5:29 but he feeds and *c* for it, just
1Pe 5: 7 on him because he *c* for you.

CARING* (CARE)
1Th 2: 7 like a mother *c* for her little
1Ti 5: 4 practice by *c* for their own family

CARPENTER (CARPENTER'S)
Mk 6: 3 does miracles! Isn't this the *c*?

CARPENTER'S* (CARPENTER)
Mt 13:55 "Isn't this the *c* son? Isn't his

CARRIED (CARRY)
Ex 19: 4 and how I *c* you on eagles' wings
Dt 1:31 how the LORD your God *c* you,
Isa 53: 4 and *c* our sorrows,
63: 9 he lifted them up and *c* them
Mt 8:17 and *c* our diseases."
Heb 13: 9 Do not be *c* away by all kinds
2Pe 1:21 as they were *c* along by the Holy
3:17 so that you may not be *c* away

CARRIES (CARRY)
Dt 32:11 and *c* them on its pinions.
Isa 40:11 and *c* them close to his heart;

CARRY (CARRIED CARRIES CARRYING)
Lev 16:22 goat will *c* on itself all their sins
26:15 and fail to *c* out all my commands
Isa 46: 4 I have made you and I will *c* you;
Lk 14:27 anyone who does not *c* his cross
Gal 6: 2 *C* each other's burdens,
6: 5 for each one should *c* his own load.

CARRYING (CARRY)
Jn 19:17 *C* his own cross, he went out
1Jn 5: 2 loving God and *c* out his

CARVED (CARVES)
Nu 33:52 Destroy all their *c* images
Mic 5:13 I will destroy your *c* images

CARVES* (CARVED)
Dt 27:15 "Cursed is the man who *c* an image

CASE
Pr 18:17 to present his *c* seems right,
22:23 for the LORD will take up their *c*
23:11 he will take up their *c* against you.

CAST (CASTING)
Ex 34:17 "Do not make *c* idols.
Lev 16: 8 He is to *c* lots for the two goats—
Ps 22:18 and *c* lots for my clothing.
55:22 *C* your cares on the LORD
Pr 16:33 The lot is *c* into the lap,
Ecc 11: 1 *C* your bread upon the waters,
Jn 19:24 and *c* lots for my clothing."
1Pe 5: 7 *C* all your anxiety on him

CASTING (CAST)
Pr 18:18 *C* the lot settles disputes
Mt 27:35 divided up his clothes by *c* lots.

CATCH (CATCHES CAUGHT)
Lk 5: 4 and let down the nets for a *c*."
5:10 from now on you will *c* men."

CATCHES (CATCH)
Job 5:13 He *c* the wise in their craftiness,
1Co 3:19 "He *c* the wise in their craftiness";

CATTLE
Ps 50:10 and the *c* on a thousand hills.

CAUGHT (CATCH)
Ge 22:13 there in a thicket he saw a ram *c*
2Co 12: 2 who fourteen years ago was *c* up
1Th 4:17 and are left will be *c* up together with them

CAUSE (CAUSES)
Pr 24:28 against your neighbor without *c*,
Ecc 8: 3 Do not stand up for a bad *c*,
Mt 18: 7 of the things that *c* people to sin!
Ro 14:21 else that will *c* your brother
1Co 10:32 Do not *c* anyone to stumble,

CAUSES (CAUSE)
Ps 7:16 The trouble he *c* recoils on himself;
Isa 8:14 a stone that *c* men to stumble
Mt 5:29 If your right eye *c* you to sin,
5:30 And if your right hand *c* you to sin,
18: 6 if anyone *c* one of these little ones
18: 8 or your foot *c* you to sin,

Ro 14:20 to eat anything that *c* someone else
1Co 8:13 if what I eat *c* my brother to fall
1Pe 2: 8 "A stone that *c* men to stumble

CAUTIOUS**
Pr 12:26 A righteous man is *c* in friendship,

CEASE
Ps 46: 9 He makes wars *c* to the ends

CELEBRATE**
Ex 10: 9 we are to *c* a festival to the LORD
12:14 generations to come you shall *c* it
12:17 *C* this day as a lasting ordinance
12:17 "*C* the Feast of Unleavened Bread,
12:47 community of Israel must *c* it.
12:48 to *c* the LORD's Passover must
23:14 are to *c* a festival to me.
23:15 "*C* the Feast of Unleavened Bread;
23:16 "*C* the Feast of Harvest
23:16 "*C* the Feast of Ingathering
34:18 "*C* the Feast of Unleavened Bread.
34:22 "*C* the Feast of Weeks
Lev 23:39 *c* the festival to the LORD
23:41 *C* this as a festival to the LORD
23:41 for the generations to come; *c* it
Nu 9: 2 "Have the Israelites *c* the Passover
9: 3 *C* it at the appointed time,
9: 4 told the Israelites to *c* the Passover,
9: 6 of them could not *c* the Passover
9:10 they may still *c* the LORD's
9:11 are to *c* it on the fourteenth day
9:12 When they *c* the Passover,
9:13 on a journey fails to *c* the Passover,
9:14 to *c* the LORD's Passover must do
29:12 *C* a festival to the LORD
Dt 16: 1 *c* the Passover of the LORD your
16:10 Then *c* the Feast of Weeks
16:13 *C* the Feast of Tabernacles
16:15 For seven days *c* the Feast
Jdg 16:23 to Dagon their god and to *c*,
2Sa 6:21 the LORD's people Israel—I will *c*
2Ki 23:21 "*C* the Passover to the LORD your
2Ch 30: 1 and *c* the Passover to the LORD,
30: 2 decided to *c* the Passover
30: 3 able to *c* it at the regular time
30: 5 and *c* the Passover to the LORD,
30:13 in Jerusalem to *c* the Feast
30:23 to *c* the festival seven more days;
Ne 8:12 of food and to *c* with great joy,
12:27 to *c* joyfully the dedication
Est 9:21 to have them *c* annually
Ps 145: 7 They will *c* your abundant
Isa 30:29 as on the night you *c* a holy festival
Na 1:15 *C* your festivals, O Judah,
Zec 14:16 and to *c* the Feast of Tabernacles.
14:18 up to *c* the Feast of Tabernacles.
14:19 up to *c* the Feast of Tabernacles.
Mt 26:18 I am going to *c* the Passover
Lk 15:23 Let's have a feast and *c*.
15:24 So they began to *c*.
15:29 goat so I could *c* with my friends.
15:32 But we had to *c* and be glad,
Rev 11:10 will *c* by sending each other gifts,

CELESTIAL**
2Pe 2:10 afraid to slander *c* beings;
Jude : 8 authority and slander *c* beings.

CENSER (CENSERS)
Lev 16:12 is to take a *c* full of burning coals
Rev 8: 3 Another angel, who had a golden *c*,

CENSERS (CENSER)
Nu 16: 6 Take *c* and tomorrow put fire

CENTURION
Mt 8: 5 had entered Capernaum, a *c* came
27:54 When the *c* and those
Mk 15:39 And when the *c*, who stood there
Lk 7: 3 The *c* heard of Jesus and sent some
Lk 23:47 The *c*, seeing what had happened,
Ac 10: 1 a *c* in what was known
27: 1 handed over to a *c* named Julius,

CEPHAS** (PETER)
Jn 1:42 You will be called *C*" (which,
1Co 1:12 another, "I follow *C*"; still another,
3:22 Paul or Apollos or *C* or the world
9: 5 and the Lord's brothers and *C*?

CEREMONIAL** (CEREMONY)
Lev 14: 2 at the time of his *c* cleansing,
15:13 off seven days for his *c* cleansing;
Mk 7: 3 they give their hands a *c* washing,
Jn 2: 6 used by the Jews for *c* washing,
3:25 Jew over the matter of *c* washing.
11:55 to Jerusalem for their *c* cleansing
18:28 to avoid *c* uncleanness the Jews did
Heb 9:10 drink and various *c* washings—
13: 9 not by *c* foods, which are

CEREMONIALLY** (CEREMONY)
Lev 4:12 outside the camp to a place *c* clean,
5: 2 touches anything *c* unclean—
6:11 the camp to a place that is *c* clean.
7:19 anyone *c* clean may eat it.
7:19 touches anything *c* unclean must
10:14 Eat them in a *c* clean place;
11: 4 not have a split hoof; it is *c* unclean
12: 2 birth to a son will be *c* unclean
12: 7 and then she will be *c* clean
13: 3 he shall pronounce him *c* unclean.
14: 8 with water; then he will be *c* clean.
15:28 and after that she will be *c* clean.
15:33 lies with a woman who is *c* unclean.
17:15 he will be *c* unclean till evening.
21: 1 must not make himself *c* unclean
22: 3 of your descendants is *c* unclean
27:11 he vowed is a *c* unclean animal—
Nu 5: 2 who is *c* unclean because of a dead
6: 7 must not make himself *c* unclean
8: 6 Israelites and make them *c* clean.
9: 6 they were *c* unclean on account
9:13 But if a man who is *c* clean
18:11 household who is *c* clean may eat
18:13 household who is *c* clean may eat
19: 7 but he will be *c* unclean till evening
19: 9 and put them in a *c* clean place
19:18 Then a man who is *c* clean is
Dt 12:15 Both the *c* unclean and the clean
12:22 Both the *c* unclean and the clean
14: 7 they are *c* unclean for you.
15:22 Both the *c* unclean and the clean
1Sa 20:26 to David to make him *c* unclean—
2Ch 13:11 the bread on the *c* clean table
30:17 for all those who were not *c* clean
Ezr 6:20 themselves and were all *c* clean.
Ne 12:30 Levites had purified themselves *c*,
Isa 66:20 of the LORD in *c* clean vessels.
Eze 22:10 period, when they are *c* unclean.
Ac 24:18 I was *c* clean when they found me
Heb 9:13 those who are *c* unclean sanctify

CEREMONY** (CEREMONIAL CEREMONIALLY)
Ge 50:11 Egyptians are holding a solemn *c*
Ex 12:25 as he promised, observe this *c*.
12:26 'What does this *c* mean to you?'
13: 5 are to observe this *c* in this month:

CERTAIN (CERTAINTY)
2Pe 1:19 word of the prophets made more *c*,

CERTAINTY** (CERTAIN)
Lk 1: 4 so that you may know the *c*
Jn 17: 8 They knew with *c* that I came

CERTIFICATE** (CERTIFIED)
Dt 24: 1 and he writes her a *c* of divorce,
24: 3 and writes her a *c* of divorce,
Isa 50: 1 "Where is your mother's *c*
Jer 3: 8 I gave faithless Israel her *c*
Mt 5:31 divorces his wife must give her a *c*
19: 7 that a man give his wife a *c*
Mk 10: 4 a man to write a *c* of divorce

CERTIFIED** (CERTIFICATE)
Jn 3:33 has accepted it has *c* that God is

CHAFF
Ps 1: 4 They are like *c*
35: 5 May they be like *c* before the wind,
Da 2:35 became like *c* on a threshing floor
Mt 3:12 up the *c* with unquenchable fire."

CHAINED (CHAINS)
2Ti 2: 9 But God's word is not *c*.

CHAINS (CHAINED)
Eph 6:20 for which I am an ambassador in *c*.
Col 4:18 Remember my *c*.
2Ti 1:16 and was not ashamed of my *c*.
Jude : 6 with everlasting *c* for judgment

CHAMPION
Ps 19: 5 like a *c* rejoicing to run his course.

CHANCE
Ecc 9:11 but time and *c* happen to them all.

CHANGE (CHANGED)
1Sa 15:29 of Israel does not lie or *c* his mind;
Ps 110: 4 and will not *c* his mind:
Jer 7: 5 If you really *c* your ways
Mal 3: 6 "I the LORD do not *c*.
Mt 18: 3 unless you *c* and become like little
Heb 7:21 and will not *c* his mind:
Jas 1:17 who does not *c* like shifting

CHANGED (CHANGE)
1Sa 10: 6 you will be *c* into a different person
Hos 11: 8 My heart is *c* within me;
1Co 15:51 but we will all be *c*— in a flash,

CHARACTER**
Ru 3:11 that you are a woman of noble *c*.
Pr 12: 4 of noble *c* is her husband's crown,
31:10 A wife of noble *c* who can find?
Ac 17:11 noble *c* than the Thessalonians,
Ro 5: 4 perseverance, *c*; and *c*, hope.
1Co 15:33 "Bad company corrupts good *c*."

CHARGE (CHARGES)
Job 34:13 him in *c* of the whole world?
Ro 8:33 Who will bring any *c*
1Co 9:18 the gospel I may offer it free of *c*,
2Co 11: 7 the gospel of God to you free of *c*?
2Ti 4: 1 I give you this *c*: Preach the Word;
Phm :18 or owes you anything, *c* it to me.

CHARGES (CHARGE)
Isa 50: 8 Who then will bring *c* against me?

CHARIOT (CHARIOTS)
2Ki 2:11 suddenly a *c* of fire and horses
Ps 104: 3 He makes the clouds his *c*
Ac 8:28 sitting in his *c* reading the book

CHARIOTS (CHARIOT)
2Ki 6:17 and *c* of fire all around Elisha.
Ps 20: 7 Some trust in *c* and some in horses,
68:17 The *c* of God are tens of thousands

CHARM** (CHARMING)
Pr 17: 8 bribe is a *c* to the one who gives it;
31:30 *C* is deceptive, and beauty is

CHARMING** (CHARM)
Pr 26:25 his speech is *c*, do not believe
SS 1:16 Oh, how *c*!

CHASE (CHASES)
Lev 26: 8 Five of you will *c* a hundred,

CHASES* (CHASE)
Pr 12:11 he who *c* fantasies lacks judgment.
28:19 one who *c* fantasies will have his

CHASM*
Lk 16:26 and you a great *c* has been fixed,

CHATTER* (CHATTERING)
1Ti 6:20 Turn away from godless *c*
2Ti 2:16 Avoid godless *c*, because those

CHATTERING* (CHATTER)
Pr 10: 8 but a *c* fool comes to ruin.
10:10 and a *c* fool comes to ruin.

CHEAT* (CHEATED CHEATING CHEATS)
Mal 1:14 "Cursed is the *c* who has
1Co 6: 8 you yourselves *c* and do wrong,

CHEATED* (CHEAT)
Ge 31: 7 yet your father has *c* me
1Sa 12: 3 Whom have I *c*? Whom have I
12: 4 "You have not *c* or oppressed us,"
Lk 19: 8 if I have *c* anybody out of anything,
1Co 6: 7 Why not rather be *c*? Instead,

CHEATING* (CHEAT)
Am 8: 5 and *c* with dishonest scales,

CHEATS* (CHEAT)
Lev 6: 2 or if he *c* him, or if he finds lost

CHEEK (CHEEKS)
Mt 5:39 someone strikes you on the right *c*,
Lk 6:29 If someone strikes you on one *c*,

CHEEKS (CHEEK)
Isa 50: 6 my *c* to those who pulled out my

CHEERFUL* (CHEERS)
Pr 15:13 A happy heart makes the face *c*,
15:15 but the *c* heart has a continual feast
15:30 A *c* look brings joy to the heart,
17:22 A *c* heart is good medicine,
2Co 9: 7 for God loves a *c* giver.

CHEERS (CHEERFUL)
Pr 12:25 but a kind word *c* him up.

CHEMOSH
2Ki 23:13 for *C* the vile god of Moab,

CHERISH (CHERISHED CHERISHES)
Ps 17:14 You still the hunger of those you *c*;

CHERISHED (CHERISH)
Ps 66:18 If I had *c* sin in my heart,

CHERISHES* (CHERISH)
Pr 19: 8 he who *c* understanding prospers.

CHERUB (CHERUBIM)
Ex 25:19 Make one *c* on one end
Eze 28:14 You were anointed as a guardian *c*,

CHERUBIM (CHERUB)
Ge 3:24 side of the Garden of Eden *c*
1Sa 4: 4 who is enthroned between the *c*.
2Sa 6: 2 enthroned between the *c* that are
22:11 He mounted the *c* and flew;
1Ki 6:23 a pair of *c* of olive wood,
2Ki 19:15 of Israel, enthroned between the *c*,
1Ch 13: 6 who is enthroned between the *c*—
Ps 18:10 He mounted the *c* and flew;
80: 1 who sit enthroned between the *c*,
99: 1 he sits enthroned between the *c*,
Isa 37:16 of Israel, enthroned between the *c*,
Eze 10: 1 was over the heads of the *c*.

CHEST
Ex 25:10 "Have them make a *c*
2Ki 12: 9 Jehoiada the priest took a *c*
Da 2:32 its *c* and arms of silver, its belly
Rev 1:13 with a golden sash around his *c*.

CHEWS
Lev 11: 3 divided and that *c* the cud.

CHIEF
1Pe 5: 4 And when the *C* Shepherd appears,

CHILD (CHILDISH CHILDREN CHILDREN'S GRANDCHILDREN)
Pr 20:11 Even a *c* is known by his actions,
22: 6 Train a *c* in the way he should go,
22:15 Folly is bound up in the heart of a *c*
23:13 not withhold discipline from a *c*;
29:15 *c* left to himself disgraces his mother.
Isa 7:14 The virgin will be with *c*
9: 6 For to us a *c* is born,
11: 6 and a little *c* will lead them.
66:13 As a mother comforts her *c*,
Mt 1:23 "The virgin will be with *c*
18: 2 He called a little *c* and had him
Lk 1:42 and blessed is the *c* you will bear!
1:80 And the *c* grew and became strong
1Co 13:11 When I was a *c*, I talked like a *c*,
1Jn 5: 1 who loves the father loves his *c*

CHILDBEARING (BEAR)
Ge 3:16 greatly increase your pains in *c*;

CHILDBIRTH (BEAR)
Gal 4:19 the pains of *c* until Christ is formed

CHILDISH* (CHILD)
1Co 13:11 When I became a man, I put *c* ways

CHILDREN (CHILD)
Ex 20: 5 punishing the *c* for the sin
Dt 4: 9 Teach them to your *c*
6: 7 Impress them on your *c*.
11:19 them to your *c*, talking about them
14: 1 You are the *c* of the LORD your
24:16 nor *c* put to death for their fathers;
30:19 so that you and your *c* may live
32:46 so that you may command your *c*
Job 1: 5 "Perhaps my *c* have sinned
Ps 8: 2 From the lips of *c* and infants
78: 5 forefathers to teach their *c*,
Pr 17: 6 Children's *c* are a crown
20: 7 blessed are his *c* after him.
31:28 Her *c* arise and call her blessed;
Joel 1: 3 Tell it to your *c*,
Mal 4: 6 the hearts of the fathers to their *c*,
Mt 7:11 how to give good gifts to your *c*,
11:25 and revealed them to little *c*.
18: 3 you change and become like little *c*
19:14 "Let the little *c* come to me,
21:16 " 'From the lips of *c* and infants
Mk 9:37 one of these little *c* in my name
10:14 "Let the little *c* come to me,
10:16 And he took the *c* in his arms,
13:12 *C* will rebel against their parents
Lk 10:21 and revealed them to little *c*.
18:16 "Let the little *c* come to me,
Jn 1:12 the right to become *c* of God—
Ac 2:39 The promise is for you and your *c*
Ro 8:16 with our spirit that we are God's *c*.
1Co 14:20 Brothers, stop thinking like *c*.
2Co 12:14 parents, but parents for their *c*.
Eph 6: 1 *C*, obey your parents in the Lord,
6: 4 do not exasperate your *c*; instead,
Col 3:20 *C*, obey your parents in everything,
3:21 Fathers, do not embitter your *c*,
1Ti 3: 4 and see that his *c* obey him
3:12 and must manage his *c* and his
5:10 bringing up *c*, showing hospitality,
Heb 2:13 and the *c* God has given me."
1Jn 3: 1 that we should be called *c* of God!

CHILDREN'S (CHILD)
Isa 54:13 and great will be your *c* peace.

CHOKE
Mk 4:19 come in and *c* the word,

CHOOSE (CHOOSES CHOSE CHOSEN)
Dt 30:19 Now *c* life, so that you
Jos 24:15 then *c* for yourselves this day
Pr 8:10 *C* my instruction instead of silver,
16:16 to *c* understanding rather
Jn 15:16 You did not *c* me, but I chose you

CHOOSES (CHOOSE)
Mt 11:27 to whom the Son *c* to reveal him.
Lk 10:22 to whom the Son *c* to reveal him."
Jn 7:17 If anyone *c* to do God's will,

CHOSE (CHOOSE)
Ge 13:11 So Lot *c* for himself the whole plain
Ps 33:12 the people he *c* for his inheritance.
Jn 15:16 but I *c* you and appointed you to go
1Co 1:27 But God *c* the foolish things
Eph 1: 4 he *c* us in him before the creation
2Th 2:13 from the beginning God *c* you

CHOSEN (CHOOSE)
Isa 41: 8 Jacob, whom I have *c*,
Mt 22:14 For many are invited, but few are *c*
Lk 10:42 Mary has *c* what is better,
23:35 the Christ of God, the *C* One."
Jn 15:19 but I have *c* you out of the world.
1Pe 1:20 He was *c* before the creation
2: 9 But you are a *c* people, a royal

CHRIST (CHRIST'S CHRISTIAN CHRISTIANS CHRISTS)
Mt 1:16 was born Jesus, who is called *C*.
16:16 Peter answered, "You are the *C*,
22:42 "What do you think about the *C*?
Mk 1: 1 of the gospel about Jesus *C*,
8:29 Peter answered, "You are the *C*."
14:61 "Are you the *C*, the Son
Lk 9:20 Peter answered, "The *C* of God."
Jn 1:41 found the Messiah" (that is, the *C*).
20:31 you may believe that Jesus is the *C*,
Ac 2:36 you crucified, both Lord and *C*."
5:42 the good news that Jesus is the *C*.
9:22 by proving that Jesus is the *C*.
9:34 said to him, "Jesus *C* heals you.
17: 3 proving that the *C* had to suffer
18:28 the Scriptures that Jesus was the *C*.
26:23 that the *C* would suffer and,
Ro 1: 4 from the dead: Jesus *C* our Lord.
3:22 comes through faith in Jesus *C*
5: 1 God through our Lord Jesus *C*,
5: 6 we were still powerless, *C* died
5: 8 While we were still sinners, *C* died
5:11 in God through our Lord Jesus *C*,
5:17 life through the one man, Jesus *C*.
6: 4 as *C* was raised from the dead
6: 9 that since *C* was raised
6:23 life in *C* Jesus our Lord.
7: 4 to the law through the body of *C*,
8: 1 for those who are in *C* Jesus,
8: 9 Spirit of *C*, he does not belong to *C*.
8:17 heirs of God and co-heirs with *C*,
8:34 Who is he that condemns? *C* Jesus,
8:35 us from the love of *C*?
9: 5 is traced the human ancestry of *C*,
10: 4 *C* is the end of the law
12: 5 so in *C* we who are many form one
13:14 yourselves with the Lord Jesus *C*,
14: 9 *C* died and returned to life
15: 3 For even *C* did not please himself
15: 5 yourselves as you follow *C* Jesus,
15: 7 then, just as *C* accepted you,
16:18 people are not serving our Lord *C*,
1Co 1: 2 to those sanctified in *C* Jesus
1: 7 for our Lord Jesus *C* to be revealed.
1:13 Is *C* divided? Was Paul crucified
1:17 For *C* did not send me to baptize,
1:23 but we preach *C* crucified:
1:30 of him that you are in *C* Jesus,

1Co 2: 2 except Jesus *C* and him crucified.
3:11 one already laid, which is Jesus *C.*
5: 7 For *C,* our Passover lamb,
6:15 bodies are members of *C* himself?
8: 6 and there is but one Lord, Jesus *C,*
8:12 conscience, you sin against *C.*
10: 4 them, and that rock was *C.*
11: 1 as I follow the example of *C.*
11: 3 the head of every man is *C,*
12:27 Now you are the body of *C,*
15: 3 that *C* died for our sins according
15:14 And if *C* has not been raised,
15:22 so in *C* all will be made alive.
15:57 victory through our Lord Jesus *C.*
2Co 1: 5 as the sufferings of *C* flow
2:14 us in triumphal procession in *C*
3: 3 show that you are a letter from *C,*
3:14 because only in *C* is it taken away.
4: 4 light of the gospel of the glory of *C,*
4: 5 not preach ourselves, but Jesus *C*
4: 6 of the glory of God in the face of *C.*
5:10 before the judgment seat of *C,*
5:17 Therefore, if anyone is in *C,*
6:15 What harmony is there between *C*
10: 1 the meekness and gentleness of *C,*
11: 2 you to one husband, to *C,*
Gal 1: 7 are trying to pervert the gospel of *C*
2: 4 on the freedom we have in *C* Jesus
2:16 but by faith in Jesus *C.*
2:17 does that mean that *C* promotes sin
2:20 I have been crucified with *C*
2:21 *C* died for nothing!" You foolish
3:13 *C* redeemed us from the curse
3:16 meaning one person, who is *C.*
3:26 of God through faith in *C* Jesus,
4:19 of childbirth until *C* is formed
5: 1 for freedom that *C* has set us free.
5: 4 by law have been alienated from *C;*
5:24 to *C* Jesus have crucified the sinful
6:14 in the cross of our Lord Jesus *C,*
Eph 1: 3 with every spiritual blessing in *C.*
1:10 together under one head, even *C.*
1:20 which he exerted in *C*
2: 5 made us alive with *C*
2:10 created in *C* Jesus
2:12 time you were separate from *C,*
2:20 with *C* Jesus himself as the chief
3: 8 the unsearchable riches of *C,*
3:17 so that *C* may dwell in your hearts
4: 7 has been given as *C* apportioned it.
4:13 measure of the fullness of *C.*
4:15 into him who is the Head, that is, *C*
4:32 just as in *C* God forgave you.
5: 2 as *C* loved us and gave himself up
5:21 out of reverence for *C.*
5:23 as *C* is the head of the church,
5:25 just as *C* loved the church
Php 1:18 motives or true, *C* is preached.
1:21 to live is *C* and to die is gain.
1:23 I desire to depart and be with *C,*
1:27 worthy of the gospel of *C.*
1:29 on behalf of *C* not only to believe
2: 5 be the same as that of *C* Jesus:
3: 7 now consider loss for the sake of *C.*
3:10 I want to know *C* and the power
3:18 as enemies of the cross of *C.*
4:19 to his glorious riches in *C* Jesus.
Col 1: 4 heard of your faith in *C* Jesus
1:27 which is *C* in you, the hope of glory
1:28 may present everyone perfect in *C.*
2: 2 the mystery of God, namely, *C,*
2: 6 as you received *C* Jesus as Lord,
2: 9 For in *C* all the fullness
2:13 God made you alive with *C.*
2:17 the reality, however, is found in *C.*
3: 1 then, you have been raised with *C,*
3: 3 and your life is now hidden with *C*
3:15 Let the peace of *C* rule
1Th 5: 9 through our Lord Jesus *C.*
2Th 2: 1 the coming of our Lord Jesus *C*
2Th 2:14 in the glory of our Lord Jesus *C.*
1Ti 1:12 I thank *C* Jesus our Lord, who has
1:15 *C* Jesus came into the world
1:16 *C* Jesus might display his unlimited
2: 5 the man *C* Jesus, who gave himself
2Ti 1: 9 us in *C* Jesus before the beginning
1:10 appearing of our Savior, *C* Jesus,
2: 1 in the grace that is in *C* Jesus.
2: 3 us like a good soldier of *C* Jesus.
2: 8 Remember Jesus *C,* raised
2:10 the salvation that is in *C* Jesus,
3:12 life in *C* Jesus will be persecuted,
3:15 salvation through faith in *C* Jesus.
4: 1 presence of God and of *C* Jesus,
Tit 2:13 our great God and Savior, Jesus *C,*
Heb 3: 6 But *C* is faithful as a son
3:14 to share in *C* if we hold firmly
5: 5 So *C* also did not take
6: 1 the elementary teachings about *C*
9:11 When *C* came as high priest
9:14 more, then, will the blood of *C,*
9:15 For this reason *C* is the mediator
9:24 For *C* did not enter a man-made
9:26 Then *C* would have had
9:28 so *C* was sacrificed once
10:10 of the body of Jesus *C* once for all.
13: 8 Jesus *C* is the same yesterday
1Pe 1: 2 for obedience to Jesus *C*
1: 3 of Jesus *C* from the dead,
1:11 he predicted the sufferings of *C*
1:19 but with the precious blood of *C,*
2:21 because *C* suffered for you,
3:15 in your hearts set apart *C* as Lord.
3:18 For *C* died for sins once for all,
3:21 you by the resurrection of Jesus *C,*
4:13 participate in the sufferings of *C,*
4:14 insulted because of the name of *C,*
2Pe 1: 1 and Savior Jesus *C* have received
1:16 and coming of our Lord Jesus *C,*
1Jn 2: 1 Jesus *C,* the Righteous One.
2:22 man who denies that Jesus is the *C.*
3:16 Jesus *C* laid down his life for us.
3:23 in the name of his Son, Jesus *C,*
4: 2 that Jesus *C* has come
5: 1 believes that Jesus is the *C* is born
5:20 even in his Son Jesus *C.*
2Jn : 9 teaching of *C* does not have God;
Jude : 4 deny Jesus *C* our only Sovereign
Rev 1: 1 The revelation of Jesus *C,*
1: 5 from Jesus *C,* who is the faithful
11:15 kingdom of our Lord and of his *C,*
20: 4 reigned with *C* a thousand years.
20: 6 they will be priests of God and of *C*

CHRIST'S (CHRIST)
1Co 9:21 from God's law but am under *C* law
2Co 5:14 For *C* love compels us,
5:20 We are therefore *C* ambassadors,
12: 9 so that *C* power may rest on me.
Col 1:22 by *C* physical body through death

CHRISTIAN* (CHRIST)
Ac 26:28 you can persuade me to be a *C?*"
1Pe 4:16 as a *C,* do not be ashamed,

CHRISTIANS* (CHRIST)
Ac 11:26 The disciples were called *C* first

CHRISTS* (CHRIST)
Mt 24:24 For false *C* and false prophets will
Mk 13:22 For false *C* and false prophets will

CHURCH
Mt 16:18 and on this rock I will build my *c,*
18:17 if he refuses to listen even to the *c,*
Ac 20:28 Be shepherds of the *c* of God,
1Co 5:12 of mine to judge those outside the *c*
14: 4 but he who prophesies edifies the *c.*
14:12 to excel in gifts that build up the *c.*
14:26 done for the strengthening of the *c.*
15: 9 because I persecuted the *c* of God.
Gal 1:13 how intensely I persecuted the *c*
Eph 5:23 as Christ is the head of the *c,*
Col 1:18 he is the head of the body, the *c;*
1:24 the sake of his body, which is the *c.*

CHURNING
Pr 30:33 For as *c* the milk produces butter,

CIRCLE
Isa 40:22 enthroned above the *c* of the earth,

CIRCUMCISE (CIRCUMCISED CIRCUMCISION)
Dt 10:16 *C* your hearts, therefore,

CIRCUMCISED (CIRCUMCISE)
Ge 17:10 Every male among you shall be *c.*
17:12 who is eight days old must be *c,*
Jos 5: 3 and *c* the Israelites at Gibeath
Gal 5: 2 that if you let yourselves be *c,*

CIRCUMCISION (CIRCUMCISE)
Ro 2:25 *C* has value if you observe the law,
2:29 and *c* is *c* of the heart, by the Spirit,
1Co 7:19 *C* is nothing and uncircumcision is

CIRCUMSTANCES
Php 4:11 to be content whatever the *c.*
1Th 5:18 continually; give thanks in all *c,*

CITIES (CITY)
Lk 19:17 small matter, take charge of ten *c.'*
19:19 'You take charge of five *c.'*

CITIZENS (CITIZENSHIP)
Eph 2:19 but fellow *c* with God's people

CITIZENSHIP* (CITIZENS)
Ac 22:28 "I had to pay a big price for my *c.*"
Eph 2:12 excluded from *c* in Israel
Php 3:20 But our *c* is in heaven.

CITY (CITIES)
Mt 5:14 A *c* on a hill cannot be hidden.
Ac 18:10 I have many people in this *c.*"
Heb 13:14 here we do not have an enduring *c,*
Rev 21: 2 saw the Holy *C,* the new

CIVILIAN*
2Ti 2: 4 a soldier gets involved in *c* affairs—

CLAIM (CLAIMS RECLAIM)
Pr 25: 6 do not *c* a place among great men;
1Jn 1: 6 If we *c* to have fellowship
1: 8 If we *c* to be without sin, we
1:10 If we *c* we have not sinned,

CLAIMS (CLAIM)
Jas 2:14 if a man *c* to have faith
1Jn 2: 6 Whoever *c* to live in him must walk
2: 9 Anyone who *c* to be in the light

CLANGING*
1Co 13: 1 a resounding gong or a *c* cymbal.

CLAP* (CLAPPED CLAPS)
Job 21: 5 *c* your hand over your mouth.
Ps 47: 1 *C* your hands, all you nations;
98: 8 Let the rivers *c* their hands,
Pr 30:32 *c* your hand over your mouth!
Isa 55:12 will *c* their hands.
La 2:15 *c* their hands at you;

CLAPPED* (CLAP)
2Ki 11:12 and the people *c* their hands
Eze 25: 6 Because you have *c* your hands

CLAPS* (CLAP)
Job 27:23 It *c* its hands in derision
34:37 scornfully he *c* his hands among us
Na 3:19 *c* his hands at your fall,

COMFORTER* (COMFORT)
Ecc 4: 1 and they have no *c;*
4: 1 and they have no *c.*
Jer 8:18 O my *C* in sorrow,

COMFORTERS* (COMFORT)
Job 16: 2 miserable *c* are you all!
Ps 69:20 for *c,* but I found none.

COMFORTING* (COMFORT)
Isa 66:11 satisfied at her *c* breasts;
Zec 1:13 *c* words to the angel who talked
Jn 11:31 *c* her, noticed how quickly she got
1Th 2:12 *c* and urging you to live lives

COMFORTS* (COMFORT)
Job 29:25 I was like one who *c* mourners.
Isa 49:13 For the LORD *c* his people
51:12 "I, even I, am he who *c* you.
66:13 As a mother *c* her child,
2Co 1: 4 who *c* us in all our troubles,
7: 6 But God, who *c* the downcast,

COMMAND (COMMANDED COMMANDING COMMANDMENT COMMANDMENTS COMMANDS)
Ex 7: 2 You are to say everything I *c* you,
Nu 14:41 are you disobeying the LORD's *c?*
24:13 to go beyond the *c* of the LORD—
Dt 4: 2 Do not add to what I *c* you
8: 1 to follow every *c* I am giving you
12:32 See that you do all I *c* you;
15:11 I *c* you to be openhanded
30:16 For I *c* you today to love
32:46 so that you may *c* your children
Ps 91:11 For he will *c* his angels concerning
Pr 13:13 but he who respects a *c* is rewarded
Ecc 8: 2 Obey the king's *c,* I say,
Jer 1: 7 you to and say whatever I *c* you.
1:17 and say to them whatever I *c* you.
7:23 Walk in all the ways I *c* you,
11: 4 Obey me and do everything I *c* you
26: 2 Tell them everything I *c* you;
Joel 2:11 mighty are those who obey his *c.*
Mt 4: 6 He will *c* his angels concerning you
15: 3 why do you break the *c* of God
Lk 4:10 " 'He will *c* his angels concerning
Jn 14:15 love me, you will obey what I *c.*
15:12 My *c* is this: Love each other
15:14 friends if you do what I *c.*
15:17 This is my *c:* Love each other.
1Co 14:37 writing to you is the Lord's *c.*
Gal 5:14 law is summed up in a single *c:*
1Ti 1: 5 goal of this *c* is love, which comes
6:14 to you keep this *c* without spot
6:17 *C* those who are rich
Heb 11: 3 universe was formed at God's *c,*
2Pe 2:21 on the sacred *c* that was passed
3: 2 and the *c* given by our Lord
1Jn 2: 7 I am not writing you a new *c*
3:23 this is his *c:* to believe in the name
4:21 And he has given us this *c:*
2Jn : 6 his *c* is that you walk in love.

COMMANDED (COMMAND)
Ge 2:16 And the LORD God *c* the man,
7: 5 Noah did all that the LORD *c* him.
50:12 Jacob's sons did as he had *c* them:
Ex 7: 6 did just as the LORD *c* them.
19: 7 all the words the LORD had *c* him
Dt 4: 5 laws as the LORD my God *c* me,
6:24 The LORD *c* us to obey all these
Jos 1: 9 Have I not *c* you? Be strong
1:16 Whatever you have *c* us we will do,
2Sa 5:25 So David did as the LORD *c* him,
2Ki 17:13 the entire Law that I *c* your fathers
21: 8 careful to do everything I *c* them
2Ch 33: 8 do everything I *c* them concerning
Ps 33: 9 he *c,* and it stood firm.
78: 5 which he *c* our forefathers
148: 5 for he *c* and they were created.
Mt 28:20 to obey everything I have *c* you.
1Co 9:14 Lord has *c* that those who preach
1Jn 3:23 and to love one another as he *c* us.
2Jn : 4 in the truth, just as the Father *c* us.

COMMANDING (COMMAND)
2Ti 2: 4 he wants to please his *c* officer.

COMMANDMENT* (COMMAND)
Jos 22: 5 But be very careful to keep the *c*
Mt 22:36 which is the greatest *c* in the Law?"
22:38 This is the first and greatest *c.*
Mk 12:31 There is no *c* greater than these."
Lk 23:56 the Sabbath in obedience to the *c.*
Jn 13:34 "A new *c* I give you: Love one
Ro 7: 8 the opportunity afforded by the *c,*
7: 9 when the *c* came, sin sprang to life
7:10 that the very *c* that was intended
7:11 and through the *c* put me to death.
7:11 the opportunity afforded by the *c,*
7:12 and the *c* is holy, righteous
7:13 through the *c* sin might become
13: 9 and whatever other *c* there may be,
Eph 6: 2 which is the first *c* with a promise
Heb 9:19 Moses had proclaimed every *c*

COMMANDMENTS* (COMMAND)
Ex 20: 6 who love me and keep my *c.*
34:28 of the covenant—the Ten *C.*
Dt 4:13 to you his covenant, the Ten *C,*
5:10 who love me and keep my *c.*
5:22 These are the *c* the LORD
6: 6 These *c* that I give you today are
9:10 were all the *c* the LORD
10: 4 The Ten *C* he had proclaimed
Ecc 12:13 Fear God and keep his *c,*
Mt 5:19 one of the least of these *c*
19:17 If you want to enter life, obey the *c*
22:40 the Prophets hang on these two *c."*
Mk 10:19 You know the *c:* 'Do not murder,
12:28 "Of all the *c,* which is the most
Lk 1: 6 observing all the Lord's *c*
18:20 You know the *c:* 'Do not commit
Ro 13: 9 The *c,* "Do not commit adultery,"
Eph 2:15 in his flesh the law with its *c*
Rev 12:17 those who obey God's *c*
14:12 part of the saints who obey God's *c*

COMMANDS (COMMAND)
Ex 24:12 and *c* I have written for their
25:22 give you all my *c* for the Israelites.
34:32 gave them all the *c* the LORD had
Lev 22:31 "Keep my *c* and follow them.
Nu 15:39 and so you will remember all the *c*
Dt 7: 9 those who love him and keep his *c.*
7:11 Therefore, take care to follow the *c*
11: 1 decrees, his laws and his *c* always.
11:27 the blessing if you obey the *c*
28: 1 carefully follow all his *c* I give you
30:10 LORD your God and keep his *c*
Jos 22: 5 to walk in all his ways, to obey his *c*
1Ki 2: 3 and keep his decrees and *c,*
8:58 in all his ways and to keep the *c,*
8:61 to live by his decrees and obey his *c*
1Ch 28: 7 unswerving in carrying out my *c*
29:19 devotion to keep your *c,*
2Ch 31:21 in obedience to the law and the *c,*
Ne 1: 5 those who love him and obey his *c,*
Ps 78: 7 but would keep his *c.*
112: 1 who finds great delight in his *c.*
119:10 do not let me stray from your *c.*
119:32 I run in the path of your *c,*
119:35 Direct me in the path of your *c,*
119:47 for I delight in your *c*
119:48 I lift up my hands to your *c,*
119:73 me understanding to learn your *c.*
119:86 All your *c* are trustworthy;
119:96 but your *c* are boundless.
119:98 Your *c* make me wiser
119:115 that I may keep the *c* of my God!
119:127 Because I love your *c*
Ps 119:131 longing for your *c.*
119:143 but your *c* are my delight.
119:151 and all your *c* are true.
119:172 for all your *c* are righteous.
119:176 for I have not forgotten your *c.*
Pr 2: 1 and store up my *c* within you,
3: 1 but keep my *c* in your heart,
6:23 For these *c* are a lamp,
10: 8 The wise in heart accept *c,*
Isa 48:18 you had paid attention to my *c,*
Da 9: 4 all who love him and obey his *c,*
Mt 5:19 teaches these *c* will be called great
Mk 7: 8 You have let go of the *c* of God
7: 9 way of setting aside the *c* of God
Jn 14:21 Whoever has my *c* and obeys them,
15:10 If you obey my *c,* you will remain
Ac 17:30 but now he *c* all people everywhere
1Co 7:19 Keeping God's *c* is what counts.
1Jn 2: 3 come to know him if we obey his *c.*
2: 4 but does not do what he *c* is a liar,
3:22 we obey his *c* and do what pleases
3:24 Those who obey his *c* live in him,
5: 2 loving God and carrying out his *c.*
5: 3 And his *c* are not burdensome,
5: 3 This is love for God: to obey his *c.*
2Jn : 6 that we walk in obedience to his *c.*

COMMEMORATE
Ex 12:14 "This is a day you are to *c;*

COMMEND* (COMMENDABLE COMMENDED COMMENDS)
Ps 145: 4 One generation will *c* your works
Ecc 8:15 So I *c* the enjoyment of life,
Ro 13: 3 do what is right and he will *c* you.
16: 1 I *c* to you our sister Phoebe,
2Co 3: 1 beginning to *c* ourselves again?
4: 2 the truth plainly we *c* ourselves
5:12 trying to *c* ourselves to you again,
6: 4 as servants of God we *c* ourselves
10:12 with some who *c* themselves.
1Pe 2:14 and to *c* those who do right.

COMMENDABLE* (COMMEND)
1Pe 2:19 For it is *c* if a man bears up
2:20 you endure it, this is *c* before God.

COMMENDED* (COMMEND)
Ne 11: 2 The people *c* all the men who
Job 29:11 and those who saw me *c* me,
Lk 16: 8 master *c* the dishonest manager
Ac 15:40 *c* by the brothers to the grace
2Co 12:11 I ought to have been *c* by you,
Heb 11: 2 This is what the ancients were *c* for
11: 4 By faith he was *c* as a righteous
11: 5 he was *c* as one who pleased God.
11:39 These were all *c* for their faith,

COMMENDS* (COMMEND)
Pr 15: 2 of the wise *c* knowledge,
2Co 10:18 but the one whom the Lord *c.*
10:18 not the one who *c* himself who is

COMMIT (COMMITS COMMITTED)
Ex 20:14 "You shall not *c* adultery.
Dt 5:18 "You shall not *c* adultery.
1Sa 7: 3 and *c* yourselves to the LORD
Ps 31: 5 Into your hands I *c* my spirit;
37: 5 *C* your way to the LORD;
Pr 16: 3 *C* to the LORD whatever you do,
Mt 5:27 that it was said, 'Do not *c* adultery.'
5:32 causes her to *c* adultery,
19:18 do not *c* adultery, do not steal,
Mk 10:19 do not *c* adultery, do not steal,
Lk 18:20 'Do not *c* adultery, do not murder,
23:46 into your hands I *c* my spirit."
Ac 20:32 I *c* you to God and to the word
Ro 2:22 do you *c* adultery? You who abhor
2:22 that people should not *c* adultery,
13: 9 "Do not *c* adultery,"
1Co 10: 8 We should not *c* sexual immorality,

Jas 2:11 do not *c* adultery but do *c* murder,
1Pe 4:19 to God's will should *c* themselves
Rev 2:22 I will make those who *c* adultery

COMMITS (COMMIT)
Pr 6:32 man who *c* adultery lacks
29:22 a hot-tempered one *c* many sins.
Ecc 8:12 a wicked man *c* a hundred crimes
Eze 18:12 He *c* robbery.
18:14 who sees all the sins his father *c*,
18:24 from his righteousness and *c* sin
18:26 from his righteousness and *c* sin,
22:11 you one man *c* a detestable offense
Mt 5:32 the divorced woman *c* adultery.
19: 9 marries another woman *c* adultery
Mk 10:11 marries another woman *c* adultery
10:12 another man, she *c* adultery."
Lk 16:18 a divorced woman *c* adultery.
16:18 marries another woman *c* adultery,

COMMITTED (COMMIT)
Nu 5: 7 and must confess the sin he has *c*.
1Ki 8:61 But your hearts must be fully *c*
15:14 Asa's heart was fully *c*
2Ch 16: 9 those whose hearts are fully *c*
Mt 5:28 lustfully has already *c* adultery
11:27 "All things have been *c* to me
Lk 10:22 "All things have been *c* to me
Ac 14:23 *c* them to the Lord,
14:26 where they had been *c* to the grace
1Co 9:17 I am simply discharging the trust *c*
2Co 5:19 And he has *c* to us the message
1Pe 2:22 "He *c* no sin,
Rev 17: 2 the kings of the earth *c* adultery
18: 3 of the earth *c* adultery with her,
18: 9 kings of the earth who *c* adultery

COMMON
Ge 11: 1 had one language and a *c* speech.
Lev 10:10 between the holy and the *c*,
Pr 22: 2 Rich and poor have this in *c*:
29:13 the oppressor have this in *c*:
Ac 2:44 together and had everything in *c*.
1Co 10:13 has seized you except what is *c*
2Co 6:14 and wickedness have in *c*?

COMPANION (COMPANIONS)
Ps 55:13 my *c*, my close friend,
55:20 My *c* attacks his friends;
Pr 13:20 but a *c* of fools suffers harm.
28: 7 a *c* of gluttons disgraces his father.
29: 3 *c* of prostitutes squanders his
Rev 1: 9 your brother and *c* in the suffering

COMPANIONS (COMPANION)
Ps 45: 7 your God, has set you above your *c*
Pr 18:24 A man of many *c* may come to ruin
Heb 1: 9 your God, has set you above your *c*

COMPANY
Ps 14: 5 present in the *c* of the righteous.
Pr 21:16 comes to rest in the *c* of the dead.
24: 1 do not desire their *c*;
Jer 15:17 I never sat in the *c* of revelers,
1Co 15:33 "Bad *c* corrupts good character."

COMPARE* (COMPARED COMPARING COMPARISON)
Job 28:17 Neither gold nor crystal can *c*
28:19 The topaz of Cush cannot *c* with it;
39:13 but they cannot *c* with the pinions
Ps 86: 8 no deeds can *c* with yours.
89: 6 skies above can *c* with the LORD?
Pr 3:15 nothing you desire can *c* with her.
8:11 nothing you desire can *c* with her.
Isa 40:18 To whom, then, will you *c* God?
40:18 What image will you *c* him to?
40:25 "To whom will you *c* me?
46: 5 "To whom will you *c* me
La 2:13 With what can I *c* you,
Eze 31: 8 *c* with its branches—
Da 1:13 Then *c* our appearance with that
Mt 11:16 "To what can I *c* this generation?
Lk 7:31 I *c* the people of this generation?
13:18 What shall I *c* it to? It is like
13:20 What shall I *c* the kingdom of God
2Co 10:12 and *c* themselves with themselves,
10:12 or *c* ourselves with some who

COMPARED* (COMPARE)
Jdg 8: 2 What have I accomplished *c* to you
8: 3 What was I able to do *c* to you?"
Isa 46: 5 you liken me that we may be *c*?
Eze 31: 2 Who can be *c* with you in majesty?
31:18 the trees of Eden can be *c* with you
Php 3: 8 I consider everything a loss *c*

COMPARING* (COMPARE)
Ro 8:18 present sufferings are not worth *c*
2Co 8: 8 the sincerity of your love by *c* it
Gal 6: 4 without *c* himself to somebody else

COMPARISON* (COMPARE)
2Co 3:10 now in *c* with the surpassing glory.

COMPASSION* (COMPASSIONATE COMPASSIONS)
Ex 33:19 I will have *c* on whom I will have *c*.
Dt 13:17 he will show you mercy, have *c*
28:54 man among you will have no *c*
30: 3 restore your fortunes and have *c*
32:36 and have *c* on his servants
Jdg 2:18 for the LORD had *c* on them
1Ki 3:26 son was alive was filled with *c*
2Ki 13:23 and had *c* and showed concern
2Ch 30: 9 and your children will be shown *c*
Ne 9:19 of your great *c* you did not
9:27 and in your great *c* you gave them
9:28 in your *c* you delivered them time
Ps 51: 1 according to your great *c*
77: 9 Has he in anger withheld his *c*?"
90:13 Have *c* on your servants.
102:13 You will arise and have *c* on Zion,
103: 4 and crowns you with love and *c*.
103:13 As a father has *c* on his children,
103:13 so the LORD has *c*
116: 5 our God is full of *c*.
119:77 Let your *c* come to me that I may
119:156 Your *c* is great, O LORD;
135:14 and have *c* on his servants.
145: 9 he has *c* on all he has made.
Isa 13:18 will they look with *c* on children.
14: 1 The LORD will have *c* on Jacob;
27:11 so their Maker has no *c* on them,
30:18 he rises to show you *c*.
49:10 He who has *c* on them will guide
49:13 and will have *c* on his afflicted ones
49:15 and have no *c* on the child she has
51: 3 and will look with *c* on all her ruins
54: 7 with deep *c* I will bring you back.
54: 8 I will have *c* on you,"
54:10 says the LORD, who has *c* on you.
60:10 in favor I will show you *c*.
63: 7 to his *c* and many kindnesses.
63:15 and *c* are withheld from us.
Jer 12:15 I will again have *c* and will bring
13:14 *c* to keep me from destroying them
15: 6 I can no longer show *c*.
21: 7 show them no mercy or pity or *c*.'
30:18 and have *c* on his dwellings;
31:20 I have great *c* for him,"
33:26 restore their fortunes and have *c*
42:12 I will show you *c* so that he will
42:12 so that he will have *c* on you
La 3:32 he brings grief, he will show *c*,
Eze 9: 5 without showing pity or *c*.
16: 5 or had *c* enough to do any
39:25 and will have *c* on all the people
Hos 2:19 in love and *c*.
11: 8 all my *c* is aroused.
13:14 "I will have no *c*,
14: 3 for in you the fatherless find *c*."
Am 1:11 stifling all *c*,
Jnh 3: 9 with *c* turn from his fierce anger
3:10 he had *c* and did not bring
Mic 7:19 You will again have *c* on us;
Zec 7: 9 show mercy and *c* to one another.
10: 6 because I have *c* on them.
Mal 3:17 as in *c* a man spares his son who
Mt 9:36 When he saw the crowds, he had *c*
14:14 he had *c* on them and healed their
15:32 "I have *c* for these people;
20:34 Jesus had *c* on them and touched
Mk 1:41 with *c*, Jesus reached out his hand
6:34 and saw a large crowd, he had *c*
8: 2 "I have *c* for these people;
Lk 15:20 and was filled with *c* for him;
Ro 9:15 and I will have *c* on whom I have *c*
2Co 1: 3 the Father of *c* and the God
Php 2: 1 and *c*, then make my joy complete
Col 3:12 clothe yourselves with *c*, kindness,
Jas 5:11 The Lord is full of *c* and mercy.

COMPASSIONATE* (COMPASSION)
Ex 22:27 out to me, I will hear, for I am *c*.
34: 6 the LORD, the *c* and gracious God
2Ch 30: 9 LORD your God is gracious and *c*.
Ne 9:17 gracious and *c*, slow to anger
Ps 86:15 O Lord, are a *c* and gracious God,
103: 8 The LORD is *c* and gracious,
111: 4 the LORD is gracious and *c*.
112: 4 the gracious and *c* and righteous
145: 8 The LORD is gracious and *c*,
La 4:10 With their own hands *c* women
Joel 2:13 for he is gracious and *c*,
Jnh 4: 2 that you are a gracious and *c* God,
Eph 4:32 Be kind and *c* to one another,
1Pe 3: 8 love as brothers, be *c* and humble.

COMPASSIONS* (COMPASSION)
La 3:22 for his *c* never fail.

COMPELLED (COMPULSION)
Ac 20:22 "And now, *c* by the Spirit,
1Co 9:16 I cannot boast, for I am *c* to preach.

COMPELS (COMPULSION)
Job 32:18 and the spirit within me *c* me;
2Co 5:14 For Christ's love *c* us, because we

COMPETENCE* (COMPETENT)
2Co 3: 5 but our *c* comes from God.

COMPETENT* (COMPETENCE)
Ro 15:14 and *c* to instruct one another.
1Co 6: 2 are you not *c* to judge trivial cases?
2Co 3: 5 Not that we are *c* in ourselves to claim
3: 6 He has made us *c* as ministers

COMPETES*
1Co 9:25 Everyone who *c* in the games goes
2Ti 2: 5 Similarly, if anyone *c* as an athlete,
2: 5 unless he *c* according to the rules.

COMPLACENCY* (COMPLACENT)
Pr 1:32 and the *c* of fools will destroy them
Eze 30: 9 ships to frighten Cush out of her *c*.

COMPLACENT* (COMPLACENCY)
Isa 32: 9 You women who are so *c*,
32:11 Tremble, you *c* women;
Am 6: 1 Woe to you who are *c* in Zion,
Zep 1:12 and punish those who are *c*,

COMPLAINING*
Php 2:14 Do everything without *c* or arguing

COMPLETE
Dt 16:15 your hands, and your joy will be *c*.
Jn 3:29 That joy is mine, and it is now *c*.
15:11 and that your joy may be *c*.
16:24 will receive, and your joy will be *c*.
17:23 May they be brought to *c* unity

CONFESSING* (CONFESS)
Ezr 10: 1 While Ezra was praying and *c,*
Da 9:20 *c* my sin and the sin
Mt 3: 6 *C* their sins, they were baptized
Mk 1: 5 *C* their sins, they were baptized

CONFESSION* (CONFESS)
Ezr 10:11 Now make *c* to the LORD,
Ne 9: 3 and spent another quarter in *c*
2Co 9:13 obedience that accompanies your *c*
1Ti 6:12 called when you made your good *c*
6:13 Pontius Pilate made the good *c,*

CONFIDENCE* (CONFIDENT)
Jdg 9:26 and its citizens put their *c* in him.
2Ki 18:19 On what are you basing this *c*
2Ch 32: 8 And the people gained *c*
32:10 On what are you basing your *c,*
Job 4: 6 Should not your piety be your *c*
Ps 71: 5 my *c* since my youth.
Pr 3:26 for the LORD will be your *c*
3:32 but takes the upright into his *c.*
11:13 A gossip betrays a *c,*
20:19 A gossip betrays a *c;*
25: 9 do not betray another man's *c,*
31:11 Her husband has full *c* in her
Isa 32:17 will be quietness and *c* forever.
36: 4 On what are you basing this *c*
Jer 17: 7 whose *c* is in him.
49:31 which lives in *c,"*
Eze 29:16 a source of *c* for the people of Israel
Mic 7: 5 put no *c* in a friend.
2Co 2: 3 I had *c* in all of you, that you would
3: 4 Such *c* as this is ours
7: 4 I have great *c* in you; I take great
7:16 I am glad I can have complete *c*
8:22 so because of his great *c* in you.
Eph 3:12 God with freedom and *c.*
Php 3: 3 and who put no *c* in the flesh—
3: 4 I myself have reasons for such *c.*
3: 4 reasons to put *c* in the flesh,
2Th 3: 4 We have *c* in the Lord that you are
Heb 3:14 till the end the *c* we had at first.
4:16 the throne of grace with *c,*
10:19 since we have *c* to enter the Most
10:35 So do not throw away your *c;*
13: 6 So we say with *c,*
1Jn 3:21 we have *c* before God and receive
4:17 us so that we will have *c* on the day
5:14 This is the *c* we have

CONFIDENT* (CONFIDENCE)
Job 6:20 because they had been *c;*
Ps 27: 3 even then will I be *c.*
27:13 I am still *c* of this:
Lk 18: 9 To some who were *c*
2Co 1:15 Because I was *c* of this, I planned
5: 6 Therefore we are always *c*
5: 8 We are *c,* I say, and would prefer
9: 4 ashamed of having been so *c.*
10: 7 If anyone is *c* that he belongs
Gal 5:10 I am *c* in the Lord that you will
Php 1: 6 day until now, being *c* of this,
2:24 I am *c* in the Lord that I myself will
Phm :21 *C* of your obedience, I write to you,
Heb 6: 9 we are *c* of better things
1Jn 2:28 that when he appears we may be *c*

CONFIDES*
Ps 25:14 The LORD *c* in those who fear him

CONFORM* (CONFORMED CONFORMITY CONFORMS)
Ro 12: 2 Do not *c* any longer to the pattern
1Pe 1:14 do not *c* to the evil desires you had

CONFORMED* (CONFORM)
Eze 5: 7 *c* to the standards of the nations
11:12 but have *c* to the standards
Ro 8:29 predestined to be *c* to the likeness

CONFORMITY* (CONFORM)
Eph 1:11 in *c* with the purpose of his will,

CONFORMS* (CONFORM)
1Ti 1:11 to the sound doctrine that *c*

CONQUEROR* (CONQUERORS)
Mic 1:15 I will bring a *c* against you
Rev 6: 2 he rode out as a *c* bent on conquest.

CONQUERORS (CONQUEROR)
Ro 8:37 than *c* through him who loved us.

CONSCIENCE* (CONSCIENCE-STRICKEN CONSCIENCES CONSCIENTIOUS)
Ge 20: 5 I have done this with a clear *c*
20: 6 I know you did this with a clear *c,*
1Sa 25:31 have on his *c* the staggering burden
Job 27: 6 my *c* will not reproach me as long
Ac 23: 1 to God in all good *c* to this day."
24:16 to keep my *c* clear before God
Ro 9: 1 my *c* confirms it in the Holy Spirit
13: 5 punishment but also because of *c.*
1Co 4: 4 My *c* is clear, but that does not
8: 7 since their *c* is weak, it is defiled.
8:10 with a weak *c* sees you who have
8:12 in this way and wound their weak *c*
10:25 without raising questions of *c,*
10:27 you without raising questions of *c.*
10:28 man who told you and for *c'* sake—
10:29 freedom be judged by another's *c?*
10:29 the other man's *c,* I mean,
2Co 1:12 Our *c* testifies that we have
4: 2 to every man's *c* in the sight of God
5:11 and I hope it is also plain to your *c.*
1Ti 1: 5 and a good *c* and a sincere faith.
1:19 holding on to faith and a good *c.*
3: 9 truths of the faith with a clear *c.*
2Ti 1: 3 as my forefathers did, with a clear *c*
Heb 9: 9 able to clear the *c* of the worshiper.
10:22 to cleanse us from a guilty *c*
13:18 We are sure that we have a clear *c*
1Pe 3:16 and respect, keeping a clear *c,*
3:21 the pledge of a good *c* toward God.

CONSCIENCE-STRICKEN* (CONSCIENCE)
1Sa 24: 5 David was *c* for having cut
2Sa 24:10 David was *c* after he had counted

CONSCIENCES* (CONSCIENCE)
Ro 2:15 their *c* also bearing witness,
1Ti 4: 2 whose *c* have been seared
Tit 1:15 their minds and *c* are corrupted.
Heb 9:14 cleanse our *c* from acts that lead

CONSCIENTIOUS* (CONSCIENCE)
2Ch 29:34 for the Levites had been more *c*

CONSCIOUS*
Ro 3:20 through the law we become *c* of sin
1Pe 2:19 of unjust suffering because he is *c*

CONSECRATE (CONSECRATED)
Ex 13: 2 "*C* to me every firstborn male.
40: 9 *c* it and all its furnishings,
Lev 20: 7 " '*C* yourselves and be holy,
25:10 *C* the fiftieth year and proclaim
1Ch 15:12 fellow Levites are to *c* yourselves

CONSECRATED (CONSECRATE)
Ex 29:43 and the place will be *c* by my glory.
Lev 8:30 So he *c* Aaron and his garments
2Ch 7:16 *c* this temple so that my Name may
Lk 2:23 is to be *c* to the Lord"),
1Ti 4: 5 because it is *c* by the word of God

CONSENT
1Co 7: 5 except by mutual *c* and for a time,

CONSIDER (CONSIDERATE CONSIDERED CONSIDERS)
1Sa 12:24 *c* what great things he has done
16: 7 "Do not *c* his appearance
2Ch 19: 6 "*C* carefully what you do,
Job 37:14 stop and *c* God's wonders.
Ps 8: 3 When I *c* your heavens,
77:12 and *c* all your mighty deeds.
107:43 and *c* the great love of the LORD.
143: 5 and *c* what your hands have done.
Pr 6: 6 *c* its ways and be wise!
20:25 and only later to *c* his vows.
Ecc 7:13 *C* what God has done:
Lk 12:24 *C* the ravens: They do not sow
12:27 about the rest? "*C* how the lilies
Php 2: 3 but in humility *c* others better
3: 8 I *c* everything a loss compared
Heb 10:24 And let us *c* how we may spur one
Jas 1: 2 *C* it pure joy, my brothers,

CONSIDERATE* (CONSIDER)
Tit 3: 2 to be peaceable and *c,*
Jas 3:17 then peace-loving, *c,* submissive,
1Pe 2:18 only to those who are good and *c,*
3: 7 in the same way be *c* as you live

CONSIDERED (CONSIDER)
Job 1: 8 "Have you *c* my servant Job?
2: 3 "Have you *c* my servant Job?
Ps 44:22 we are *c* as sheep to be slaughtered.
Isa 53: 4 yet we *c* him stricken by God,
Ro 8:36 we are *c* as sheep to be slaughtered

CONSIDERS (CONSIDER)
Pr 31:16 She *c* a field and buys it;
Ro 14: 5 One man *c* one day more sacred
Jas 1:26 If anyone *c* himself religious

CONSIST (CONSISTS)
Lk 12:15 a man's life does not *c*

CONSISTS (CONSIST)
Eph 5: 9 fruit of the light *c* in all goodness,

CONSOLATION
Ps 94:19 your *c* brought joy to my soul.

CONSPIRE
Ps 2: 1 Why do the nations *c*

CONSTANT
Dt 28:66 You will live in *c* suspense,
Pr 19:13 wife is like a *c* dripping.
27:15 a *c* dripping on a rainy day;
Ac 27:33 "you have been in *c* suspense
Heb 5:14 by *c* use have trained themselves

CONSTRUCTIVE*
1Co 10:23 but not everything is *c.*

CONSULT
Pr 15:12 he will not *c* the wise.
Gal 1:16 I did not *c* any man, nor did I go up

CONSUME (CONSUMES CONSUMING)
Jn 2:17 "Zeal for your house will *c* me."

CONSUMES (CONSUME)
Ps 69: 9 for zeal for your house *c* me,

CONSUMING (CONSUME)
Dt 4:24 For the LORD your God is a *c* fire,
Heb 12:29 and awe, for our "God is a *c* fire."

CONTAIN* (CONTAINED CONTAINS)
1Ki 8:27 the highest heaven, cannot *c* you.
2Ch 2: 6 the highest heavens, cannot *c* him?
6:18 the highest heavens, cannot *c* you.
Ecc 8: 8 power over the wind to *c* it;
2Pe 3:16 His letters *c* some things that are

CONTAINED (CONTAIN)
Heb 9: 4 This ark *c* the gold jar of manna,

CONTAINS (CONTAIN)
Pr 15: 6 of the righteous *c* great treasure,

CONTAMINATES*
2Co 7: 1 from everything that *c* body

CONTEMPT
Pr 14:31 He who oppresses the poor shows *c*
17: 5 He who mocks the poor shows *c*
18: 3 When wickedness comes, so does *c*
Da 12: 2 others to shame and everlasting *c.*
Mal 1: 6 O priests, who show *c* for my name.
Ro 2: 4 Or do you show *c* for the riches
Gal 4:14 you did not treat me with *c*
1Th 5:20 do not treat prophecies with *c.*

CONTEND (CONTENDED CONTENDING CONTENTIOUS)
Ge 6: 3 "My Spirit will not *c*
Ps 35: 1 *C,* O LORD, with those who
Isa 49:25 I will *c* with those who *c* with you,
Jude : 3 you to *c* for the faith that was once

CONTENDED (CONTEND)
Php 4: 3 help these women who have *c*

CONTENDING* (CONTEND)
Php 1:27 *c* as one man for the faith

CONTENT* (CONTENTMENT)
Jos 7: 7 If only we had been *c* to stay
Pr 13:25 The righteous eat to their hearts' *c,*
19:23 one rests *c,* untouched by trouble.
Ecc 4: 8 yet his eyes were not *c*
Lk 3:14 don't accuse people falsely—be *c*
Php 4:11 to be *c* whatever the circumstances
4:12 I have learned the secret of being *c*
1Ti 6: 8 and clothing, we will be *c* with that.
Heb 13: 5 and be *c* with what you have,

CONTENTIOUS* (CONTEND)
1Co 11:16 If anyone wants to be *c* about this,

CONTENTMENT* (CONTENT)
Job 36:11 and their years in *c.*
SS 8:10 like one bringing *c.*
1Ti 6: 6 But godliness with *c* is great gain.

CONTEST*
Heb 10:32 in a great *c* in the face of suffering.

CONTINUAL (CONTINUE)
Pr 15:15 but the cheerful heart has a *c* feast.
Eph 4:19 of impurity, with a *c* lust for more.

CONTINUE (CONTINUAL CONTINUES CONTINUING)
1Ki 8:23 servants who *c* wholeheartedly
2Ch 6:14 servants who *c* wholeheartedly
Ps 36:10 *C* your love to those who know you
Ac 13:43 urged them to *c* in the grace of God
Ro 11:22 provided that you *c* in his kindness.
Gal 3:10 Cursed is everyone who does not *c*
Php 2:12 *c* to work out your salvation
Col 1:23 if you *c* in your faith, established
2: 6 received Christ Jesus as Lord, *c*
1Ti 2:15 if they *c* in faith, love and holiness
2Ti 3:14 *c* in what you have learned
1Jn 2:28 And now, dear children, *c* in him,
3: 9 born of God will *c* to sin,
5:18 born of God does not *c* to sin;
2Jn : 9 and does not *c* in the teaching
Rev 22:11 and let him who is holy *c* to be holy
22:11 let him who does right *c* to do right;

CONTINUES (CONTINUE)
Ps 100: 5 *c* through all generations.
119:90 Your faithfulness *c*
2Co 10:15 Our hope is that, as your faith *c*
1Jn 3: 6 No one who *c* to sin has

CONTINUING (CONTINUE)
Ro 13: 8 the *c* debt to love one another,

CONTRIBUTION (CONTRIBUTIONS)
Ro 15:26 pleased to make a *c* for the poor

CONTRIBUTIONS (CONTRIBUTION)
2Ch 24:10 all the people brought their *c* gladly
31:12 they faithfully brought in the *c,*

CONTRITE*
Ps 51:17 a broken and *c* heart,
Isa 57:15 also with him who is *c* and lowly
57:15 and to revive the heart of the *c.*
66: 2 he who is humble and *c* in spirit,

CONTROL (CONTROLLED CONTROLS SELF-CONTROL SELF-CONTROLLED)
Pr 29:11 a wise man keeps himself under *c.*
1Co 7: 9 But if they cannot *c* themselves,
7:37 but has *c* over his own will,
1Th 4: 4 you should learn to *c* his own body

CONTROLLED (CONTROL)
Ps 32: 9 but must be *c* by bit and bridle
Ro 8: 6 but the mind *c* by the Spirit is life
8: 8 Those *c* by the sinful nature cannot

CONTROLS* (CONTROL)
Job 37:15 you know how God *c* the clouds
Pr 16:32 a man who *c* his temper

CONTROVERSIES*
Ac 26: 3 with all the Jewish customs and *c.*
1Ti 1: 4 These promote *c* rather
6: 4 He has an unhealthy interest in *c*
Tit 3: 9 But avoid foolish *c* and genealogies

CONVERSATION
Col 4: 6 Let your *c* be always full of grace,

CONVERT
1Ti 3: 6 He must not be a recent *c,*

CONVICT (CONVICTION)
Pr 24:25 with those who *c* the guilty,
Jn 16: 8 he will *c* the world of guilt in regard
Jude :15 and to *c* all the ungodly

CONVICTION* (CONVICT)
1Th 1: 5 the Holy Spirit and with deep *c.*

CONVINCE* (CONVINCED CONVINCING)
Ac 28:23 and tried to *c* them about Jesus

CONVINCED* (CONVINCE)
Ge 45:28 "I'm *c!* My son Joseph is still alive.
Lk 16:31 will not be *c* even if someone rises
Ac 19:26 and hear how this fellow Paul has *c*
26: 9 "I too was *c* that I ought
26:26 I am *c* that none of this has escaped
28:24 Some were *c* by what he said,
Ro 2:19 if you are *c* that you are a guide
8:38 For I am *c* that neither death
14: 5 Each one should be fully *c*
14:14 I am fully *c* that no food is unclean
15:14 I myself am *c,* my brothers,
1Co 14:24 he will be *c* by all that he is a sinner
2Co 5:14 we are *c* that one died for all,
Php 1:25 *C* of this, I know that I will remain,
2Ti 1:12 and am *c* that he is able
3:14 have learned and have become *c*

CONVINCING* (CONVINCE)
Ac 1: 3 and gave many *c* proofs that he was

COOLNESS*
Pr 25:13 Like the *c* of snow at harvest time

COPIES (COPY)
Heb 9:23 for the *c* of the heavenly things

COPY (COPIES)
Dt 17:18 for himself on a scroll a *c* of this law
Heb 8: 5 They serve at a sanctuary that is a *c*
9:24 sanctuary that was only a *c*

CORBAN*
Mk 7:11 received from me is *C'* (that is,

CORD (CORDS)
Jos 2:18 you have tied this scarlet *c*
Ecc 4:12 *c* of three strands is not quickly

CORDS (CORD)
Pr 5:22 the *c* of his sin hold him fast.
Isa 54: 2 lengthen your *c,*
Hos 11: 4 them with *c* of human kindness,

CORINTH
Ac 18: 1 Paul left Athens and went to *C.*
1Co 1: 2 To the church of God in *C,*
2Co 1: 1 To the church of God in *C,*

CORNELIUS*
Roman to whom Peter preached; first Gentile Christian (Ac 10).

CORNER (CORNERS)
Ru 3: 9 "Spread the *c* of your garment
Pr 21: 9 Better to live on a *c* of the roof
25:24 Better to live on a *c* of the roof
Ac 26:26 because it was not done in a *c.*

CORNERS (CORNER)
Mt 6: 5 on the street *c* to be seen by men.
22: 9 Go to the street *c* and invite

CORNERSTONE* (STONE)
Job 38: 6 or who laid its *c*—
Isa 28:16 a precious *c* for a sure foundation;
Jer 51:26 rock will be taken from you for a *c,*
Zec 10: 4 From Judah will come the *c,*
Eph 2:20 Christ Jesus himself as the chief *c.*
1Pe 2: 6 a chosen and precious *c,*

CORRECT* (CORRECTED CORRECTING CORRECTION CORRECTIONS CORRECTS)
Job 6:26 Do you mean to *c* what I say,
40: 2 contends with the Almighty *c* him?
Jer 10:24 *C* me, LORD, but only with justice
2Ti 4: 2 *c,* rebuke and encourage—

CORRECTED* (CORRECT)
Pr 29:19 A servant cannot be *c*

CORRECTING* (CORRECT)
2Ti 3:16 *c* and training in righteousness,

CORRECTION* (CORRECT)
Lev 26:23 things you do not accept my *c*
Job 36:10 He makes them listen to *c*
Pr 5:12 How my heart spurned *c!*
10:17 whoever ignores *c* leads others
12: 1 but he who hates *c* is stupid.
13:18 but whoever heeds *c* is honored.
15: 5 whoever heeds *c* shows prudence.
15:10 he who hates *c* will die.
15:12 A mocker resents *c;*
15:32 whoever heeds *c* gains
29:15 The rod of *c* imparts wisdom,
Jer 2:30 they did not respond to *c.*
5: 3 crushed them, but they refused *c.*
7:28 LORD its God or responded to *c.*
Zep 3: 2 she accepts no *c.*
3: 7 you will fear me / and accept *c!'*

CORRECTIONS* (CORRECT)
Pr 6:23 and the *c* of discipline

CORRECTS* (CORRECT)
Job 5:17 "Blessed is the man whom God *c;*
Pr 9: 7 Whoever *c* a mocker invites insult;

CORRUPT (CORRUPTED CORRUPTION CORRUPTS)
Ge 6:11 Now the earth was *c* in God's sight

Dt 5:21 "You shall not *c* your neighbor's
7:25 Do not *c* the silver and gold
Mic 2: 2 They *c* fields and seize them,
Ro 7: 7 if the law had not said, "Do not *c.*"
13: 9 "Do not steal," "Do not *c,*"
Jas 4: 2 *c,* but you cannot have what you

COVETED* (COVET)
Jos 7:21 weighing fifty shekels, I *c* them
Ac 20:33 I have not *c* anyone's silver or gold

COVETING
Ro 7: 7 what *c* really was if the law

COVETOUS* (COVET)
Ro 7: 8 in me every kind of *c* desire.

COWARDLY*
Rev 21: 8 But the *c,* the unbelieving, the vile,

COWS
Ge 41: 2 of the river there came up seven *c,*
Ex 25: 5 skins dyed red and hides of sea *c;*
Nu 4: 6 are to cover this with hides of sea *c,*
1Sa 6: 7 Hitch the *c* to the cart,

CRAFTINESS* (CRAFTY)
Job 5:13 He catches the wise in their *c,*
1Co 3:19 "He catches the wise in their *c*";
Eph 4:14 and *c* of men in their deceitful

CRAFTSMAN
Pr 8:30 Then I was the *c* at his side.

CRAFTY* (CRAFTINESS)
Ge 3: 1 the serpent was more *c* than any
1Sa 23:22 They tell me he is very *c.*
Job 5:12 He thwarts the plans of the *c,*
15: 5 you adopt the tongue of the *c.*
Pr 7:10 like a prostitute and with *c* intent.
12: 2 but the LORD condemns a *c* man.
14:17 and a *c* man is hated.
2Co 12:16 *c* fellow that I am, I caught you

CRAVE* (CRAVED CRAVES CRAVING CRAVINGS)
Nu 11: 4 with them began to *c* other food,
Dt 12:20 you *c* meat and say, "I would like
Pr 23: 3 Do not *c* his delicacies,
23: 6 do not *c* his delicacies;
31: 4 not for rulers to *c* beer,
Mic 7: 1 none of the early figs that I *c.*
1Pe 2: 2 newborn babies, *c* pure spiritual

CRAVED* (CRAVE)
Nu 11:34 the people who had *c* other food.
Ps 78:18 by demanding the food they *c.*
78:29 for he had given them what they *c.*
78:30 turned from the food they *c,*

CRAVES* (CRAVE)
Pr 13: 4 The sluggard *c* and gets nothing,
21:10 The wicked man *c* evil;
21:26 All day long he *c* for more,

CRAVING* (CRAVE)
Job 20:20 he will have no respite from his *c;*
Ps 106:14 In the desert they gave in to their *c;*
Pr 10: 3 but he thwarts the *c* of the wicked.
13: 2 the unfaithful have a *c* for violence.
21:25 The sluggard's *c* will be the death
Jer 2:24 sniffing the wind in her *c*—

CRAVINGS* (CRAVE)
Ps 10: 3 He boasts of the *c* of his heart;
Eph 2: 3 gratifying the *c* of our sinful nature
1Jn 2:16 in the world—the *c* of sinful man,

CRAWL
Ge 3:14 You will *c* on your belly

CREATE* (CREATED CREATES CREATING CREATION CREATOR)
Ps 51:10 *C* in me a pure heart, O God,
Isa 4: 5 Then the LORD will *c* over all
45: 7 I bring prosperity and *c* disaster;
45: 7 I form the light and *c* darkness,
45:18 he did not *c* it to be empty,
65:17 "Behold, I will *c* / new heavens
65:18 for I will *c* Jerusalem to be a delight
65:18 forever in what I will *c,*
Jer 31:22 The LORD will *c* a new thing
Mal 2:10 one Father? Did not one God *c* us?
Eph 2:15 His purpose was to *c*

CREATED* (CREATE)
Ge 1: 1 In the beginning God *c* the heavens
1:21 God *c* the great creatures of the sea
1:27 So God *c* man in his own image,
1:27 in the image of God he *c* him;
1:27 male and female he *c* them.
2: 4 and the earth when they were *c.*
5: 1 When God *c* man, he made him
5: 2 He *c* them male and female
5: 2 when they were *c,* he called them
6: 7 whom I have *c,* from the face
Dt 4:32 from the day God *c* man
Ps 89:12 You *c* the north and the south;
89:47 what futility you have *c* all men!
102:18 a people not yet *c* may praise
104:30 you send your Spirit, / they are *c,*
139:13 For you *c* my inmost being;
148: 5 for he commanded and they were *c*
Isa 40:26 Who *c* all these?
41:20 that the Holy One of Israel has *c* it.
42: 5 he who *c* the heavens and stretched
43: 1 he who *c* you, O Jacob,
43: 7 whom I *c* for my glory,
45: 8 I, the LORD, have *c* it.
45:12 and *c* mankind upon it.
45:18 he who *c* the heavens,
48: 7 They are *c* now, and not long ago;
54:16 And it is I who have *c* the destroyer
54:16 "See, it is I who *c* the blacksmith
57:16 the breath of man that I have *c.*
Eze 21:30 In the place where you were *c,*
28:13 the day you were *c* they were
28:15 ways from the day you were *c*
Mk 13:19 when God *c* the world, until now—
Ro 1:25 and served *c* things rather
1Co 11: 9 neither was man *c* for woman,
Eph 2:10 *c* in Christ Jesus to do good works,
3: 9 hidden in God, who *c* all things.
4:24 *c* to be like God in true
Col 1:16 For by him all things were *c:*
1:16 all things were *c* by him
1Ti 4: 3 which God *c* to be received
4: 4 For everything God *c* is good,
Heb 12:27 *c* things—so that what cannot be
Jas 1:18 a kind of firstfruits of all he *c.*
Rev 4:11 and by your will they were *c*
4:11 for you *c* all things,
10: 6 who *c* the heavens and all that is

CREATES* (CREATE)
Am 4:13 *c* the wind,

CREATING* (CREATE)
Ge 2: 3 the work of *c* that he had done.
Isa 57:19 *c* praise on the lips of the mourners

CREATION* (CREATE)
Hab 2:18 he who makes it trusts in his own *c;*
Mt 13:35 hidden since the *c* of the world."
25:34 for you since the *c* of the world.
Mk 10: 6 of *c* God 'made them male
16:15 and preach the good news to all *c.*
Jn 17:24 me before the *c* of the world.
Ro 1:20 For since the *c* of the world God's
8:19 The *c* waits in eager expectation
8:20 For the *c* was subjected
8:21 in hope that the *c* itself will be
8:22 that the whole *c* has been groaning
8:39 depth, nor anything else in all *c,*
2Co 5:17 he is a new *c;* the old has gone,
Gal 6:15 anything; what counts is a new *c.*
Eph 1: 4 us in him before the *c* of the world
Col 1:15 God, the firstborn over all *c.*
Heb 4: 3 finished since the *c* of the world.
4:13 Nothing in all *c* is hidden
9:11 that is to say, not a part of this *c.*
9:26 times since the *c* of the world.
1Pe 1:20 chosen before the *c* of the world,
2Pe 3: 4 as it has since the beginning of *c.*"
Rev 3:14 true witness, the ruler of God's *c.*
13: 8 slain from the *c* of the world.
17: 8 life from the *c* of the world will be

CREATOR* (CREATE)
Ge 14:19 *C* of heaven and earth.
14:22 God Most High, *C* of heaven
Dt 32: 6 Is he not your Father, your *C,*
Ecc 12: 1 Remember your *C*
Isa 27:11 and their *C* shows them no favor.
40:28 the *C* of the ends of the earth.
43:15 Israel's *C,* your King."
Mt 19: 4 the beginning the *C* 'made them
Ro 1:25 created things rather than the *C*—
Col 3:10 in knowledge in the image of its *C.*
1Pe 4:19 themselves to their faithful *C*

CREATURE (CREATURES)
Lev 17:11 For the life of a *c* is in the blood,
17:14 the life of every *c* is its blood.
Ps 136:25 and who gives food to every *c.*
Eze 1:15 beside each *c* with its four faces.
Rev 4: 7 The first living *c* was like a lion,

CREATURES (CREATURE)
Ge 6:19 bring into the ark two of all living *c,*
8:21 again will I destroy all living *c,*
Ps 104:24 the earth is full of your *c.*
Eze 1: 5 was what looked like four living *c.*

CREDIT (CREDITED CREDITOR CREDITS)
Lk 6:33 what *c* is that to you? Even
Ro 4:24 to whom God will *c* righteousness
1Pe 2:20 it to your *c* if you receive a beating

CREDITED (CREDIT)
Ge 15: 6 and he *c* it to him as righteousness.
Ps 106:31 This was *c* to him as righteousness
Eze 18:20 of the righteous man will be *c*
Ro 4: 3 and it was *c* to him as righteousness
4: 4 his wages are not *c* to him as a gift,
4: 5 his faith is *c* as righteousness.
4: 9 saying that Abraham's faith was *c*
4:23 The words "it was *c*
Gal 3: 6 and it was *c* to him as righteousness
Php 4:17 for what may be *c* to your account.
Jas 2:23 and it was *c* to him as righteousness

CREDITOR (CREDIT)
Dt 15: 2 Every *c* shall cancel the loan he has

CREDITS (CREDIT)
Ro 4: 6 whom God *c* righteousness apart

CRETANS (CRETE)
Tit 1:12 "*C* are always liars, evil brutes,

CRETE (CRETANS)
Ac 27:12 harbor in *C,* facing both southwest

CRIED (CRY)
Ex 2:23 groaned in their slavery and *c* out,
14:10 They were terrified and *c* out
Nu 20:16 but when we *c* out to the LORD,
Jos 24: 7 But they *c* to the LORD for help,
Jdg 3: 9 But when they *c* out to the LORD,
3:15 Again the Israelites *c* out
4: 3 they *c* to the LORD for help.
6: 6 the Israelites that they *c* out

Jdg 10:12 Maonites oppressed you and you *c*
1Sa 7: 9 He *c* out to the LORD
12: 8 they *c* to the LORD for help,
12:10 They *c* out to the LORD and said,
Ps 18: 6 I *c* to my God for help.

CRIMINALS
Lk 23:32 both *c*, were also led out with him

CRIMSON
Isa 1:18 though they are red as *c*,
63: 1 with his garments stained *c*?

CRIPPLED
2Sa 9: 3 of Jonathan; he is *c* in both feet."
Mk 9:45 better for you to enter life *c*

CRISIS*
1Co 7:26 of the present *c*, I think that it is

CRITICISM*
2Co 8:20 We want to avoid any *c*

CROOKED*
Dt 32: 5 but a warped and *c* generation.
2Sa 22:27 to the *c* you show yourself shrewd.
Ps 18:26 to the *c* you show yourself shrewd.
125: 5 But those who turn to *c* ways
Pr 2:15 whose paths are *c*
5: 6 her paths are *c*, but she knows it
8: 8 none of them is *c* or perverse.
10: 9 he who takes *c* paths will be found
Ecc 7:13 what he has made *c*?
Isa 59: 8 have turned them into *c* roads;
La 3: 9 he has made my paths *c*.
Lk 3: 5 The *c* roads shall become straight,
Php 2:15 children of God without fault in a *c*

CROP (CROPS)
Mt 13: 8 where it produced a *c*— a hundred,
21:41 share of the *c* at harvest time."

CROPS (CROP)
Pr 3: 9 with the firstfruits of all your *c*;
10: 5 He who gathers *c* in summer is
28: 3 like a driving rain that leaves no *c*.
2Ti 2: 6 the first to receive a share of the *c*.

CROSS (CROSSED CROSSING)
Dt 4:21 swore that I would not *c* the Jordan
12:10 But you will *c* the Jordan
Mt 10:38 and anyone who does not take his *c*
16:24 and take up his *c* and follow me.
Mk 8:34 and take up his *c* and follow me.
Lk 9:23 take up his *c* daily and follow me.
14:27 anyone who does not carry his *c*
Jn 19:17 Carrying his own *c*, he went out
Ac 2:23 to death by nailing him to the *c*.
1Co 1:17 lest the *c* of Christ be emptied
1:18 the message of the *c* is foolishness
Gal 5:11 offense of the *c* has been abolished.
6:12 persecuted for the *c* of Christ.
6:14 in the *c* of our Lord Jesus Christ,
Eph 2:16 both of them to God through the *c*,
Php 2: 8 even death on a *c*!
3:18 as enemies of the *c* of Christ.
Col 1:20 through his blood, shed on the *c*.
2:14 he took it away, nailing it to the *c*.
2:15 triumphing over them by the *c*.
Heb 12: 2 set before him endured the *c*,

CROSSED (CROSS)
Jos 4: 7 When it *c* the Jordan, the waters
Jn 5:24 he has *c* over from death to life.

CROSSING (CROSS)
Ge 48:14 he was the younger, and *c* his arms,

CROSSROADS (ROAD)
Jer 6:16 "Stand at the *c* and look;

CROUCHING
Ge 4: 7 sin is *c* at your door; it desires

CROWD (CROWDS)
Ex 23: 2 Do not follow the *c* in doing wrong.

CROWDS (CROWD)
Mt 9:36 he saw the *c*, he had compassion

CROWED (CROWS)
Mt 26:74 the man!" Immediately a rooster *c*.

CROWN (CROWNED CROWNS)
Pr 4: 9 present you with a *c* of splendor."
10: 6 Blessings *c* the head
12: 4 noble character is her husband's *c*,
16:31 Gray hair is a *c* of splendor;
17: 6 Children's children are a *c*
Isa 35:10 everlasting joy will *c* their heads.
51:11 everlasting joy will *c* their heads.
61: 3 to bestow on them a *c* of beauty
62: 3 You will be a *c* of splendor
Eze 16:12 and a beautiful *c* on your head.
Zec 9:16 like jewels in a *c*.
Mt 27:29 and then twisted together a *c* of thorns
Mk 15:17 then twisted together a *c* of thorns
Jn 19: 2 The soldiers twisted together a *c*
19: 5 When Jesus came out wearing the *c*
1Co 9:25 it to get a *c* that will last forever.
9:25 it to get a *c* that will not last;
Php 4: 1 and long for, my joy and *c*,
1Th 2:19 or the *c* in which we will glory
2Ti 2: 5 he does not receive the victor's *c*
4: 8 store for me the *c* of righteousness,
Jas 1:12 he will receive the *c*
1Pe 5: 4 you will receive the *c*
Rev 2:10 and I will give you the *c* of life.
3:11 so that no one will take your *c*.
14:14 a son of man" with a *c* of gold

CROWNED* (CROWN)
Ps 8: 5 and *c* him with glory and honor.
Pr 14:18 the prudent are *c* with knowledge.
SS 3:11 crown with which his mother *c* him
Heb 2: 7 you *c* him with glory and honor
2: 9 now *c* with glory and honor

CROWNS (CROWN)
Ps 103: 4 and *c* me with love and compassion
149: 4 he *c* the humble with salvation.
Pr 11:26 blessing *c* him who is willing to sell.
Rev 4: 4 and had *c* of gold on their heads.
4:10 They lay their *c* before the throne
12: 3 ten horns and seven *c* on his heads.
19:12 and on his head are many *c*.

CROWS (CROWED)
Mt 26:34 this very night, before the rooster *c*

CRUCIFIED* (CRUCIFY)
Mt 20:19 to be mocked and flogged and *c*.
26: 2 of Man will be handed over to be *c*
27:26 and handed him over to be *c*.
27:35 When they had *c* him, they divided
27:38 Two robbers were *c* with him,
27:44 same way the robbers who were *c*
28: 5 looking for Jesus, who was *c*.
Mk 15:15 and handed him over to be *c*.
15:24 And they *c* him.
15:25 the third hour when they *c* him.
15:27 They *c* two robbers with him,
15:32 Those *c* with him also heaped
16: 6 for Jesus the Nazarene, who was *c*.
Lk 23:23 insistently demanded that he be *c*,
23:33 *c* him, along with the criminals—
24: 7 be *c* and on the third day be raised
24:20 sentenced to death, and they *c* him;
Jn 19:16 him over to them to be *c*.
19:18 Here they *c* him, and with him two
19:20 for the place where Jesus was *c* was
19:23 When the soldiers *c* Jesus,
19:32 of the first man who had been *c*
19:41 At the place where Jesus was *c*,
Ac 2:36 whom you *c*, both Lord and Christ
4:10 whom you *c* but whom God raised
Ro 6: 6 For we know that our old self was *c*
1Co 1:13 Is Christ divided? Was Paul *c*
1:23 but we preach Christ *c*: a stumbling
2: 2 except Jesus Christ and him *c*.
2: 8 they would not have *c* the Lord
2Co 13: 4 to be sure, he was *c* in weakness,
Gal 2:20 I have been *c* with Christ
3: 1 Christ was clearly portrayed as *c*.
5:24 Christ Jesus have *c* the sinful
6:14 which the world has been *c*
Rev 11: 8 where also their Lord was *c*.

CRUCIFY* (CRUCIFIED CRUCIFYING)
Mt 23:34 Some of them you will kill and *c*;
27:22 They all answered, "*C* him!" "Why
27:23 they shouted all the louder, "*C* him
27:31 Then they led him away to *c* him.
Mk 15:13 "*C* him!" they shouted.
15:14 they shouted all the louder, "*C* him
15:20 Then they led him out to *c* him.
Lk 23:21 they kept shouting, "*C* him! *C* him
Jn 19: 6 they shouted, "*C*! *C*!"
19: 6 "You take him and *c* him.
19:10 either to free you or to *c* you?"
19:15 Crucify him!" "Shall I *c* your king
19:15 away! Take him away! *C* him!"

CRUCIFYING* (CRUCIFY)
Heb 6: 6 to their loss they are *c* the Son

CRUSH (CRUSHED)
Ge 3:15 he will *c* your head,
Isa 53:10 it was the LORD's will to *c* him
Ro 16:20 The God of peace will soon *c* Satan

CRUSHED (CRUSH)
Ps 34:18 and saves those who are *c* in spirit.
Pr 17:22 but a *c* spirit dries up the bones.
18:14 but a *c* spirit who can bear?
Isa 53: 5 he was *c* for our iniquities;
2Co 4: 8 not *c*; perplexed, but not in despair;

CRY (CRIED)
Ex 2:23 *c* for help because of their slavery
Ps 5: 2 Listen to my *c* for help,
34:15 and his ears are attentive to their *c*;
40: 1 he turned to me and heard my *c*.
130: 1 Out of the depths I *c* to you,
Pr 21:13 to the *c* of the poor,
La 2:18 *c* out to the Lord.
Hab 2:11 The stones of the wall will *c* out,
Lk 19:40 keep quiet, the stones will *c* out."

CUNNING
2Co 11: 3 deceived by the serpent's *c*,
Eph 4:14 and by the *c* and craftiness of men

CUP
Ps 23: 5 my *c* overflows.
Isa 51:22 from that *c*, the goblet of my wrath,
51:22 the *c* that made you stagger;
Mt 10:42 if anyone gives even a *c* of cold water
20:22 "Can you drink the *c* I am going
23:25 You clean the outside of the *c*
23:26 First clean the inside of the *c*
26:27 Then he took the *c*, gave thanks
26:39 may this *c* be taken from me.
26:42 possible for this *c* to be taken away
Mk 9:41 anyone who gives you a *c* of water
10:38 "Can you drink the *c* I drink
10:39 "You will drink the *c* I drink
14:23 Then he took the *c*, gave thanks
14:36 Take this *c* from me.
Lk 11:39 Pharisees clean the outside of the *c*
22:17 After taking the *c*, he gave thanks
22:20 after the supper he took the *c*,
22:20 "This *c* is the new covenant

Lk 22:42 if you are willing, take this *c*
Jn 18:11 I not drink the *c* the Father has
1Co 10:16 Is not the *c* of thanksgiving
10:21 the *c* of the Lord and the *c*
11:25 after supper he took the *c*, saying,
11:25 "This *c* is the new covenant

CUPBEARER
Ge 40: 1 the *c* and the baker of the king
Ne 1:11 I was *c* to the king.

CURE (CURED)
Jer 17: 9 and beyond *c*.
30:15 your pain that has no *c*?
Hos 5:13 But he is not able to *c* you,
Lk 9: 1 out all demons and to *c* diseases,

CURED (CURE)
Mt 11: 5 those who have leprosy are *c*,
Lk 6:18 troubled by evil spirits were *c*,

CURSE (ACCURSED CURSED CURSES CURSING)
Ge 4:11 Now you are under a *c*
8:21 "Never again will I *c* the ground
12: 3 and whoever curses you I will *c*;
Dt 11:26 before you today a blessing and a *c*
11:28 the *c* if you disobey the commands
21:23 hung on a tree is under God's *c*.
23: 5 turned the *c* into a blessing for you,
Job 1:11 he will surely *c* you to your face."
2: 5 he will surely *c* you to your face."
2: 9 *C* God and die!" He replied,
Ps 109:28 They may *c*, but you will bless;
Pr 3:33 The LORD's *c* is on the house
24:24 peoples will *c* him and nations
Mal 2: 2 and I will *c* your blessings.
Lk 6:28 bless those who *c* you, pray
Ro 12:14 persecute you; bless and do not *c*.
Gal 3:10 on observing the law are under a *c*,
3:13 of the law by becoming a *c* for us,
Jas 3: 9 with it we *c* men, who have been
Rev 22: 3 No longer will there be any *c*.

CURSED (CURSE)
Ge 3:17 "*C* is the ground because of you;
Dt 27:15 "*C* is the man who carves an image
27:16 "*C* is the man who dishonors his
27:17 "*C* is the man who moves his
27:18 "*C* is the man who leads the blind
27:19 *C* is the man who withholds justice
27:20 "*C* is the man who sleeps
27:21 "*C* is the man who has sexual
27:22 "*C* is the man who sleeps
27:23 "*C* is the man who sleeps
27:24 "*C* is the man who kills his
27:25 "*C* is the man who accepts a bribe
27:26 "*C* is the man who does not uphold
Jer 17: 5 "*C* is the one who trusts in man,
Mal 1:14 "*C* is the cheat who has
Ro 9: 3 I could wish that I myself were *c*
1Co 4:12 When we are *c*, we bless;
12: 3 "Jesus be *c*," and no one can say,
Gal 3:10 "*C* is everyone who does not
3:13 *C* is everyone who is hung on a tree

CURSES (CURSE)
Ex 21:17 "Anyone who *c* his father
Lev 20: 9 " 'If anyone *c* his father or mother,
Nu 5:23 is to write these *c* on a scroll
Jos 8:34 the blessings and the *c*— just
Pr 20:20 If a man *c* his father or mother,
28:27 to them receives many *c*.
Mt 15: 4 and 'Anyone who *c* his father
Mk 7:10 and, 'Anyone who *c* his father

CURSING (CURSE)
Ps 109:18 He wore *c* as his garment;
Ro 3:14 "Their mouths are full of *c*
Jas 3:10 the same mouth come praise and *c*.

CURTAIN
Ex 26:31 "Make a *c* of blue, purple
26:33 The *c* will separate the Holy Place
Mt 27:51 At that moment the *c*
Mk 15:38 The *c* of the temple was torn in two
Lk 23:45 the *c* of the temple was torn in two.
Heb 6:19 the inner sanctuary behind the *c*,
9: 3 Behind the second *c* was a room
10:20 opened for us through the *c*,

CUSTOM
Job 1: 5 This was Job's regular *c*.
Mk 10: 1 and as was his *c*, he taught them.
Lk 4:16 into the synagogue, as was his *c*.
Ac 17: 2 As his *c* was, Paul went

CUT
Lev 19:27 " 'Do not *c* the hair at the sides
21: 5 of their beards or *c* their bodies.
1Ki 3:25 "*C* the living child in two
Isa 51: 1 to the rock from which you were *c*
53: 8 For he was *c* off from the land
Da 2:45 of the rock *c* out of a mountain,
9:26 the Anointed One will be *c* off
Mt 3:10 not produce good fruit will be *c*
24:22 If those days had not been *c* short,
1Co 11: 6 for a woman to have her hair *c*

CYMBAL* (CYMBALS)
1Co 13: 1 a resounding gong or a clanging *c*.

CYMBALS (CYMBAL)
1Ch 15:16 instruments: lyres, harps and *c*.
2Ch 5:12 dressed in fine linen and playing *c*,
Ps 150: 5 praise him with resounding *c*.

CYRUS
Persian king who allowed exiles to return (2Ch 36:22–Ezr 1:8), to rebuild temple (Ezr 5:13–6:14), as appointed by the LORD (Isa 44:28–45:13).

DAGON
Jdg 16:23 offer a great sacrifice to *D* their god
1Sa 5: 2 Dagon's temple and set it beside *D*.

DAMASCUS
Ac 9: 3 As he neared *D* on his journey,

DAN
1. Son of Jacob by Bilhah (Ge 30:4–6; 35:25; 46:23). Tribe of blessed (Ge 49:16–17; Dt 33:22), numbered (Nu 1:39; 26:43), allotted land (Jos 19:40–48; Eze 48:1), failed to fully possess (Jdg 1:34–35), failed to support Deborah (Jdg 5:17), possessed Laish/Dan (Jdg 18).
2. Northernmost city in Israel (Ge 14:14; Jdg 18; 20:1).

DANCE (DANCED DANCING)
Ecc 3: 4 a time to mourn and a time to *d*,
Mt 11:17 and you did not *d*;

DANCED (DANCE)
2Sa 6:14 *d* before the LORD
Mk 6:22 of Herodias came in and *d*,

DANCING (DANCE)
Ps 30:11 You turned my wailing into *d*;
149: 3 Let them praise his name with *d*

DANGER
Pr 22: 3 A prudent man sees *d*
27:12 The prudent see *d* and take refuge,
Mt 5:22 will be in *d* of the fire of hell.
Ro 8:35 famine or nakedness or *d* or sword?
2Co 11:26 I have been in *d* from rivers,

DANIEL
1. Hebrew exile to Babylon, name changed to Belteshazzar (Da 1:6–7). Refused to eat unclean food (Da 1:8–21). Interpreted Nebuchadnezzar's dreams (Da 2; 4), writing on the wall (Da 5). Thrown into lion's den (Da 6). Visions of (Da 7–12).
2. Son of David (1Ch 3:1).

DARIUS
1. King of Persia (Ezr 4:5), allowed rebuilding of temple (Ezr 5–6).
2. Mede who conquered Babylon (Da 5:31).

DARK (DARKENED DARKENS DARKNESS)
Job 34:22 There is no *d* place, no deep
Ps 18: 9 *d* clouds were under his feet.
Pr 31:15 She gets up while it is still *d*;
SS 1: 6 Do not stare at me because I am *d*,
Jn 12:35 in the *d* does not know where he is
Ro 2:19 a light for those who are in the *d*,
2Pe 1:19 as to a light shining in a *d* place,

DARKENED (DARK)
Joel 2:10 the sun and moon are *d*,
Mt 24:29 " 'the sun will be *d*,
Ro 1:21 and their foolish hearts were *d*.
Eph 4:18 They are *d* in their understanding

DARKENS (DARK)
Job 38: 2 "Who is this that *d* my counsel

DARKNESS (DARK)
Ge 1: 2 *d* was over the surface of the deep,
1: 4 he separated the light from the *d*.
Ex 10:22 and total *d* covered all Egypt
20:21 approached the thick *d* where God
2Sa 22:29 the LORD turns my *d* into light.
Ps 18:28 my God turns my *d* into light.
91: 6 the pestilence that stalks in the *d*,
112: 4 Even in *d* light dawns
139:12 even the *d* will not be dark to you;
Pr 4:19 the way of the wicked is like deep *d*
Isa 5:20 and light for *d*,
42:16 I will turn the *d* into light
45: 7 I form the light and create *d*,
58:10 then your light will rise in the *d*,
61: 1 and release from *d*,
Joel 2:31 The sun will be turned to *d*
Mt 4:16 the people living in *d*
6:23 how great is that *d*! "No one can
Lk 11:34 are bad, your body also is full of *d*.
23:44 and *d* came over the whole land
Jn 1: 5 The light shines in the *d*,
3:19 but men loved *d* instead of light
Ac 2:20 The sun will be turned to *d*
2Co 4: 6 who said, "Let light shine out of *d*
6:14 fellowship can light have with *d*?
Eph 5: 8 For you were once *d*, but now you
5:11 to do with the fruitless deeds of *d*,
1Pe 2: 9 out of *d* into his wonderful light.
2Pe 2:17 Blackest *d* is reserved for them.
1Jn 1: 5 in him there is no *d* at all.
2: 9 but hates his brother is still in the *d*.
Jude : 6 in *d*, bound with everlasting chains
:13 for whom blackest *d* has been

DASH
Ps 2: 9 you will *d* them to pieces like

DAUGHTER (DAUGHTERS)
Ex 1:10 she took him to Pharaoh's *d*
Jdg 11:40 to commemorate the *d* of Jephthah
Est 2: 7 Mordecai had taken her as his own *d*
Ps 9:14 praises in the gates of the *D* of Zion
137: 8 O *D* of Babylon, doomed
Isa 62:11 "Say to the *D* of Zion,
Zec 9: 9 Shout, *D* of Jerusalem!
Mk 5:34 "*D*, your faith has healed you.
7:29 the demon has left your *d*.

DAUGHTERS (DAUGHTER)
Ge 6: 2 the *d* of men were beautiful,
19:36 Lot's *d* became pregnant
Nu 36:10 Zelophehad's *d* did as the LORD
Joel 2:28 sons and *d* will prophesy,

DAVID

Son of Jesse (Ru 4:17–22; 1Ch 2:13–15), ancestor of Jesus (Mt 1:1–17; Lk 3:31). Wives and children (1Sa 18; 25:39–44; 2Sa 3:2–5; 5:13–16; 11:27; 1Ch 3:1–9).

Anointed king by Samuel (1Sa 16:1–13). Musician to Saul (1Sa 16:14–23; 18:10). Killed Goliath (1Sa 17). Relation with Jonathan (1Sa 18:1–4; 19–20; 23:16–18; 2Sa 1). Disfavor of Saul (1Sa 18:6–23:29). Spared Saul's life (1Sa 24; 26). Among Philistines (1Sa 21:10–14; 27–30). Lament for Saul and Jonathan (2Sa 1).

Anointed king of Judah (2Sa 2:1–11). Conflict with house of Saul (2Sa 2–4). Anointed king of Israel (2Sa 5:1–4; 1Ch 11:1–3). Conquered Jerusalem (2Sa 5:6–10; 1Ch 11:4–9). Brought ark to Jerusalem (2Sa 6; 1Ch 13; 15–16). The LORD promised eternal dynasty (2Sa 7; 1Ch 17; Ps 132). Showed kindness to Mephibosheth (2Sa 9). Adultery with Bathsheba, murder of Uriah (2Sa 11–12). Son Amnon raped daughter Tamar; killed by Absalom (2Sa 13). Absalom's revolt (2Sa 14–17); death (2Sa 18). Sheba's revolt (2Sa 20). Victories: Philistines (2Sa 5:17–25; 1Ch 14:8–17; 2Sa 21:15–22; 1Ch 20:4–8), Ammonites (2Sa 10; 1Ch 19), various (2Sa 8; 1Ch 18). Mighty men (2Sa 23:8–39; 1Ch 11–12). Punished for numbering army (2Sa 24; 1Ch 21). Appointed Solomon king (1Ki 1:28–2:9). Prepared for building of temple (1Ch 22–29). Last words (2Sa 23:1–7). Death (1Ki 2:10–12; 1Ch 29:28).

Psalmist (Mt 22:43–45), musician (Am 6:5), prophet (2Sa 23:2–7; Ac 1:16; 2:30).

Psalms of: 2 (Ac 4:25), 3–32, 34–41, 51–65, 68–70, 86, 95 (Heb 4:7), 101, 103, 108–110, 122, 124, 131, 133, 138–145.

DAWN (DAWNED DAWNS)

Ps 37: 6 your righteousness shine like the *d*,
Pr 4:18 is like the first gleam of *d*,
Isa 14:12 O morning star, son of the *d!*
Am 4:13 he who turns *d* to darkness,
5: 8 who turns blackness into *d*

DAWNED (DAWN)

Isa 9: 2 a light has *d*.
Mt 4:16 a light has *d*."

DAWNS* (DAWN)

Ps 65: 8 where morning *d* and evening
112: 4 in darkness light *d* for the upright,
Hos 10:15 When that day *d*,
2Pe 1:19 until the day *d* and the morning

DAY (DAYS)

Ge 1: 5 God called the light "*d*,"
1: 5 and there was morning—the first *d*
1: 8 there was morning—the second *d*.
1:13 there was morning—the third *d*.
1:19 there was morning—the fourth *d*.
1:23 there was morning—the fifth *d*.
1:31 there was morning—the sixth *d*.
2: 2 so on the seventh *d* he rested
8:22 *d* and night
Ex 16:30 the people rested on the seventh *d*.
20: 8 "Remember the Sabbath *d*
Lev 16:30 on this *d* atonement will be made
23:28 because it is the *D* of Atonement,
Nu 14:14 before them in a pillar of cloud by *d*
Jos 1: 8 meditate on it *d* and night,
2Ki 7: 9 This is a *d* of good news
25:30 *D* by *d* the king gave Jehoiachin
1Ch 16:23 proclaim his salvation *d* after *d*.
Ne 8:18 *D* after *d*, from the first *d*
Ps 84:10 Better is one *d* in your courts
96: 2 proclaim his salvation *d* after *d*.
118:24 This is the *d* the LORD has made;
Pr 27: 1 not know what a *d* may bring forth.
Isa 13: 9 a cruel *d*, with wrath and fierce
Jer 46:10 But that *d* belongs to the Lord,
50:31 "for your *d* has come,
Eze 30: 2 "Alas for that *d!*"
Joel 1:15 "Alas for that *d!*
2:31 and dreadful *d* of the LORD.
Am 3:14 On the *d* I punish Israel for her sins
5:20 Will not the *d* of the LORD be
Ob :15 "The *d* of the LORD is near
Zep 1:14 The great *d* of the LORD is near—
Zec 2:11 joined with the LORD in that *d*
14: 1 A *d* of the LORD is coming
14: 7 It will be a unique *d*,
Mal 4: 5 dreadful *d* of the LORD comes.
Mt 24:38 up to the *d* Noah entered the ark;
Lk 11: 3 Give us each *d* our daily bread.
17:24 in his *d* will be like the lightning,
Ac 5:42 *D* after *d*, in the temple courts
17:11 examined the Scriptures every *d*
17:17 as in the marketplace *d* by *d*
Ro 14: 5 man considers every *d* alike.
1Co 5: 5 his spirit saved on the *d* of the Lord
2Co 4:16 we are being renewed *d* by *d*.
11:25 I spent a night and a *d*
1Th 5: 2 for you know very well that the *d*
5: 4 so that this *d* should surprise you
2Th 2: 2 saying that the *d* of the Lord has
Heb 7:27 need to offer sacrifices *d* after *d*,
2Pe 3: 8 With the Lord a *d* is like
3:10 *d* of the Lord will come like a thief.
Rev 6:17 For the great *d* of their wrath has
16:14 on the great *d* of God Almighty.

DAYS (DAY)

Dt 17:19 he is to read it all the *d* of his life
32: 7 Remember the *d* of old;
Ps 23: 6 all the *d* of my life,
34:12 and desires to see many good *d*,
39: 5 have made my *d* a mere
90:10 The length of our *d* is seventy years
90:12 Teach us to number our *d* aright,
103:15 As for man, his *d* are like grass,
128: 5 all the *d* of your life;
Pr 31:12 all the *d* of her life.
Ecc 9: 9 all the *d* of this meaningless life
12: 1 Creator in the *d* of your youth,
Isa 38:20 all the *d* of our lives
Da 7: 9 and the Ancient of *D* took his seat.
7:13 He approached the Ancient of *D*
7:22 until the Ancient of *D* came
Hos 3: 5 and to his blessings in the last *d*.
Joel 2:29 I will pour out my Spirit in those *d*.
Mic 4: 1 In the last *d*
Lk 19:43 The *d* will come upon you
Ac 2:17 by the prophet Joel: " 'In the last *d*,
2Ti 3: 1 will be terrible times in the last *d*.
Heb 1: 2 in these last *d* he has spoken to us
2Pe 3: 3 that in the last *d* scoffers will come,

DAZZLING*

Da 2:31 *d* statue, awesome in appearance.
Mk 9: 3 His clothes became *d* white,

DEACON* (DEACONS)

1Ti 3:12 A *d* must be the husband of

DEACONS* (DEACON)

Php 1: 1 together with the overseers and *d*:
1Ti 3: 8 *D*, likewise, are to be men worthy
3:10 against them, let them serve as *d*.

DEAD (DIE)

Lev 17:15 who eats anything found *d*
Dt 18:11 or spiritist or who consults the *d*.
Isa 8:19 Why consult the *d* on behalf
Mt 8:22 and let the *d* bury their own *d*."
28: 7 'He has risen from the *d*
Lk 15:24 For this son of mine was *d*
24:46 rise from the *d* on the third day,
Ro 6:11 count yourselves *d* to sin
1Co 15:29 do who are baptized for the *d*?
Eph 2: 1 you were *d* in your transgressions
1Th 4:16 and the *d* in Christ will rise first.
Jas 2:17 is not accompanied by action, is *d*.
Jas 2:26 so faith without deeds is *d*.
Rev 14:13 Blessed are the *d* who die
20:12 And I saw the *d*, great and small,

DEADENED* (DIE)

Jn 12:40 and *d* their hearts,

DEAR* (DEARER)

2Sa 1:26 you were very *d* to me.
Ps 102:14 For her stones are *d*
Jer 31:20 Is not Ephraim my *d* son,
Jn 2: 4 "*D* woman, why do you involve me
19:26 he said to his mother, "*D* woman,
Ac 15:25 to you with our *d* friends Barnabas
Ro 16: 5 Greet my *d* friend Epenetus,
16: 9 in Christ, and my *d* friend Stachys.
16:12 Greet my *d* friend Persis, another
1Co 4:14 but to warn you, as my *d* children.
10:14 my *d* friends, flee from idolatry.
15:58 Therefore, my *d* brothers,
2Co 7: 1 we have these promises, *d* friends,
12:19 and everything we do, *d* friends,
Gal 4:19 My *d* children, for whom I am
Eph 6:21 the *d* brother and faithful servant
Php 2:12 my *d* friends, as you have always
4: 1 firm in the Lord, *d* friends!
Col 1: 7 Epaphras, our *d* fellow servant,
4: 7 He is a *d* brother, a faithful
4: 9 our faithful and *d* brother,
4:14 Our *d* friend Luke, the doctor,
1Th 2: 8 because you had become so *d* to us.
1Ti 6: 2 their service are believers, and *d*
2Ti 1: 2 To Timothy, my *d* son: Grace,
Phm : 1 To Philemon our *d* friend
:16 He is very *d* to me but
:16 better than a slave, as a *d* brother.
Heb 6: 9 we speak like this, *d* friends,
Jas 1:16 Don't be deceived, my *d* brothers.
1:19 My *d* brothers, take note of this:
2: 5 thoughts? Listen, my *d* brothers:
1Pe 2:11 *D* friends, I urge you, as aliens
4:12 *D* friends, do not be surprised
2Pe 3: 1 *D* friends, this is now my second
3: 8 not forget this one thing, *d* friends:
3:14 *d* friends, since you are looking
3:15 just as our *d* brother Paul
3:17 *d* friends, since you already know
1Jn 2: 1 My *d* children, I write this to you
2: 7 *D* friends, I am not writing you
2:12 I write to you, *d* children,
2:13 I write to you, *d* children,
2:18 *D* children, this is the last hour;
2:28 *d* children, continue in him,
3: 2 *D* friends, now we are children
3: 7 *D* children, do not let anyone lead
3:18 love of God be in him? *D* children,
3:21 *D* friends, if our hearts do not
4: 1 *D* friends, do not believe every
4: 4 *d* children, are from God
4: 7 *D* friends, let us love one another,
4:11 *D* friends, since God so loved us,
5:21 *D* children, keep yourselves
2Jn : 5 *d* lady, I am not writing you a new
3Jn : 1 The elder, To my *d* friend Gaius,
: 2 *D* friend, I pray that you may enjoy
: 5 *D* friend, you are faithful
:11 *D* friend, do not imitate what is evil
Jude : 3 *D* friends, although I was very
:17 But, *d* friends, remember what
:20 *d* friends, build yourselves up

DEARER* (DEAR)

Phm :16 dear to me but even *d* to you,

DEATH (DIE)

Ex 21:12 kills him shall surely be put to *d*.
Nu 35:16 the murderer shall be put to *d*.
Dt 30:19 set before you life and *d*,
Ru 1:17 if anything but *d* separates you
2Ki 4:40 O man of God, there is *d* in the pot
Job 26: 6 *D* is naked before God;

Ps 23: 4 the valley of the shadow of *d*,
44:22 for your sake we face *d* all day long
89:48 What man can live and not see *d*,
116:15 is the *d* of his saints.
Pr 8:36 all who hate me love *d*."
11:19 he who pursues evil goes to his *d*.
14:12 but in the end it leads to *d*.
15:11 *D* and Destruction lie open
16:25 but in the end it leads to *d*.
18:21 tongue has the power of life and *d*,
19:18 do not be a willing party to his *d*.
23:14 and save his soul from *d*.
Ecc 7: 2 for *d* is the destiny of every man;
Isa 25: 8 he will swallow up *d* forever.
53:12 he poured out his life unto *d*,
Eze 18:23 pleasure in the *d* of the wicked?
18:32 pleasure in the *d* of anyone,
33:11 pleasure in the *d* of the wicked,
Hos 13:14 Where, O *d*, are your plagues?
Jn 5:24 he has crossed over from *d* to life.
Ro 4:25 delivered over to *d* for our sins
5:12 and in this way *d* came to all men,
5:14 *d* reigned from the time of Adam
6: 3 Jesus were baptized into his *d*?
6:23 For the wages of sin is *d*,
7:24 me from this body of *d*?
8:13 put to *d* the misdeeds of the body,
8:36 your sake we face *d* all day long;
1Co 15:21 For since *d* came through a man,
15:26 The last enemy to be destroyed is *d*
15:55 Where, O *d*, is your sting?"
2Ti 1:10 who has destroyed *d* and has
Heb 2:14 him who holds the power of *d*—
1Jn 5:16 There is a sin that leads to *d*.
Rev 1:18 And I hold the keys of *d* and Hades
2:11 hurt at all by the second *d*.
20: 6 The second *d* has no power
20:14 The lake of fire is the second *d*.
20:14 Then *d* and Hades were thrown
21: 4 There will be no more *d*
21: 8 This is the second *d*."

DEBAUCHERY*
Ro 13:13 not in sexual immorality and *d*,
2Co 12:21 and *d* in which they have indulged.
Gal 5:19 impurity and *d*; idolatry
Eph 5:18 drunk on wine, which leads to *d*.
1Pe 4: 3 living in *d*, lust, drunkenness,

DEBORAH*
1. Prophetess who led Israel to victory over Canaanites (Jdg 4–5).
2. Rebekah's nurse (Ge 35:8).

DEBT* (DEBTOR DEBTORS DEBTS)
Dt 15: 3 must cancel any *d* your brother
24: 6 the upper one—as security for a *d*,
1Sa 22: 2 or in *d* or discontented gathered
Job 24: 9 of the poor is seized for a *d*.
Mt 18:25 that he had be sold to repay the *d*.
18:27 canceled the *d* and let him go.
18:30 into prison until he could pay the *d*.
18:32 'I canceled all that *d* of yours
Lk 7:43 who had the bigger *d* canceled."
Ro 13: 8 Let no *d* remain outstanding,
13: 8 continuing *d* to love one another,

DEBTOR* (DEBT)
Isa 24: 2 for *d* as for creditor.

DEBTORS* (DEBT)
Hab 2: 7 Will not your *d* suddenly arise?
Mt 6:12 as we also have forgiven our *d*.
Lk 16: 5 called in each one of his master's *d*.

DEBTS* (DEBT)
Dt 15: 1 seven years you must cancel *d*.
15: 2 time for canceling *d* has been
15: 9 the year for canceling *d*, is near,"
31:10 in the year for canceling *d*,
2Ki 4: 7 "Go, sell the oil and pay your *d*.
Ne 10:31 the land and will cancel all *d*.
Pr 22:26 or puts up security for *d*;
Mt 6:12 Forgive us our *d*,
Lk 7:42 so he canceled the *d* of both.

DECAY*
Ps 16:10 will you let your Holy One see *d*.
49: 9 and not see *d*.
49:14 their forms will *d* in the grave,
Pr 12: 4 a disgraceful wife is like *d*
Isa 5:24 so their roots will *d*
Hab 3:16 *d* crept into my bones,
Ac 2:27 will you let your Holy One see *d*.
2:31 to the grave, nor did his body see *d*.
13:34 never to *d*, is stated in these words:
13:35 will not let your Holy One see *d*.'
13:37 raised from the dead did not see *d*.
Ro 8:21 liberated from its bondage to *d*

DECEIT (DECEIVE)
Ps 5: 9 with their tongue they speak *d*.
Isa 53: 9 nor was any *d* in his mouth.
Da 8:25 He will cause *d* to prosper,
Zep 3:13 nor will *d* be found in their mouths.
Mk 7:22 greed, malice, *d*, lewdness, envy,
Ac 13:10 You are full of all kinds of *d*
Ro 1:29 murder, strife, *d* and malice.
3:13 their tongues practice *d*."
1Pe 2: 1 yourselves of all malice and all *d*,
2:22 and no *d* was found in his mouth."

DECEITFUL (DECEIVE)
Jer 17: 9 The heart is *d* above all things
Hos 10: 2 Their heart is *d*,
2Co 11:13 men are false apostles, *d* workmen,
Eph 4:14 of men in their *d* scheming.
4:22 is being corrupted by its *d* desires;
1Pe 3:10 and his lips from *d* speech.
Rev 21:27 who does what is shameful or *d*,

DECEITFULNESS* (DECEIVE)
Ps 119:118 for their *d* is in vain.
Mt 13:22 and the *d* of wealth choke it,
Mk 4:19 the *d* of wealth and the desires
Heb 3:13 of you may be hardened by sin's *d*.

DECEIVE (DECEIT DECEITFUL DECEITFULNESS DECEIVED DECEIVER DECEIVERS DECEIVES DECEIVING DECEPTION DECEPTIVE)
Lev 19:11 " 'Do not *d* one another.
Pr 14: 5 A truthful witness does not *d*,
24:28 or use your lips to *d*.
Jer 37: 9 Do not *d* yourselves, thinking,
Zec 13: 4 garment of hair in order to *d*.
Mt 24: 5 'I am the Christ,' and will *d* many.
24:11 will appear and *d* many people.
24:24 and miracles to *d* even the elect—
Mk 13: 6 'I am he,' and will *d* many.
13:22 and miracles to *d* the elect—
Ro 16:18 and flattery they *d* the minds
1Co 3:18 Do not *d* yourselves.
Eph 5: 6 Let no one *d* you with empty words
Col 2: 4 this so that no one may *d* you
2Th 2: 3 Don't let anyone *d* you in any way,
Jas 1:22 to the word, and so *d* yourselves.
1Jn 1: 8 we *d* ourselves and the truth is not
Rev 20: 8 and will go out to *d* the nations

DECEIVED (DECEIVE)
Ge 3:13 "The serpent *d* me, and I ate."
Lk 21: 8 "Watch out that you are not *d*.
1Co 6: 9 the kingdom of God? Do not be *d*:
2Co 11: 3 Eve was *d* by the serpent's cunning
Gal 6: 7 Do not be *d*: God cannot be
1Ti 2:14 And Adam was not the one *d*;
2Ti 3:13 to worse, deceiving and being *d*.
Tit 3: 3 *d* and enslaved by all kinds
Jas 1:16 Don't be *d*, my dear brothers.
Rev 13:14 he *d* the inhabitants of the earth.
20:10 And the devil, who *d* them,

DECEIVER (DECEIVE)
Mt 27:63 while he was still alive that *d* said,
2Jn : 7 Any such person is the *d*

DECEIVERS* (DECEIVE)
Ps 49: 5 when wicked *d* surround me—
Tit 1:10 and *d*, especially those
2Jn : 7 Many *d*, who do not acknowledge

DECEIVES (DECEIVE)
Pr 26:19 is a man who *d* his neighbor
Mt 24: 4 "Watch out that no one *d* you.
Mk 13: 5 "Watch out that no one *d* you.
Gal 6: 3 when he is nothing, he *d* himself.
2Th 2:10 sort of evil that *d* those who are
Jas 1:26 he *d* himself and his religion is

DECEIVING* (DECEIVE)
Lev 6: 2 by *d* his neighbor about something
1Ti 4: 1 follow *d* spirits and things taught
2Ti 3:13 go from bad to worse, *d*
Rev 20: 3 him from *d* the nations anymore

DECENCY* (DECENTLY)
1Ti 2: 9 women to dress modestly, with *d*

DECENTLY* (DECENCY)
Ro 13:13 Let us behave *d*, as in the daytime,

DECEPTION (DECEIVE)
Pr 14: 8 but the folly of fools is *d*.
26:26 His malice may be concealed by *d*,
Mt 27:64 This last *d* will be worse
2Co 4: 2 we do not use *d*, nor do we distort

DECEPTIVE (DECEIVE)
Pr 11:18 The wicked man earns *d* wages,
31:30 Charm is *d*, and beauty is fleeting;
Jer 7: 4 Do not trust in *d* words and say,
Col 2: 8 through hollow and *d* philosophy,

DECIDED (DECISION)
2Co 9: 7 man should give what he has *d*

DECISION (DECIDED)
Ex 28:29 heart on the breastpiece of *d*
Joel 3:14 multitudes in the valley of *d*!

DECLARE (DECLARED DECLARING)
1Ch 16:24 *D* his glory among the nations,
Ps 19: 1 The heavens *d* the glory of God;
96: 3 *D* his glory among the nations,
Isa 42: 9 and new things I *d*;

DECLARED (DECLARE)
Mk 7:19 Jesus *d* all foods "clean.")
Ro 2:13 the law who will be *d* righteous.
3:20 no one will be *d* righteous

DECLARING (DECLARE)
Ps 71: 8 *d* your splendor all day long.
Ac 2:11 we hear them *d* the wonders

DECREE (DECREED DECREES)
Ex 15:25 There the LORD made a *d*
1Ch 16:17 He confirmed it to Jacob as a *d*,
Ps 2: 7 I will proclaim the *d* of the LORD:
7: 6 Awake, my God; *d* justice.
81: 4 this is a *d* for Israel,
148: 6 he gave a *d* that will never pass
Da 4:24 and this is the *d* the Most High has
Lk 2: 1 Augustus issued a *d* that a census
Ro 1:32 know God's righteous *d* that those

DECREED (DECREE)
Ps 78: 5 He *d* statutes for Jacob
Jer 40: 2 LORD your God *d* this disaster
La 3:37 happen if the Lord has not *d* it?
Da 9:24 "Seventy 'sevens' are *d*
9:26 and desolations have been *d*.
Lk 22:22 Son of Man will go as it has been *d*,

DECREES (DECREE)
Ge 26: 5 my commands, my *d* and my laws
Ex 15:26 to his commands and keep all his *d,*
18:16 inform them of God's *d* and laws."
18:20 Teach them the *d* and laws,
Lev 10:11 Israelites all the *d* the LORD has
18: 4 and be careful to follow my *d.*
18: 5 Keep my *d* and laws,
18:26 you must keep my *d* and my laws.
Ps 119:12 teach me your *d.*
119:16 I delight in your *d;*
119:48 and I meditate on your *d.*
119:112 My heart is set on keeping your *d*

DEDICATE (DEDICATED DEDICATION)
Nu 6:12 He must *d* himself to the LORD
Pr 20:25 for a man to *d* something rashly

DEDICATED (DEDICATE)
Lev 21:12 he has been *d* by the anointing oil
Nu 6: 9 thus defiling the hair he has *d,*
6:18 shave off the hair that he *d.*
18: 6 *d* to the LORD to do the work
1Ki 8:63 and all the Israelites *d* the temple
2Ch 29:31 "You have now *d* yourselves
Ne 3: 1 They *d* it and set its doors in place,

DEDICATION (DEDICATE)
Nu 6:19 shaved off the hair of his *d,*
Jn 10:22 came the Feast of *D* at Jerusalem.
1Ti 5:11 sensual desires overcome their *d*

DEED (DEEDS)
Jer 32:10 and sealed the *d,* had it witnessed,
32:16 After I had given the *d* of purchase
Col 3:17 you do, whether in word or *d,*
2Th 2:17 and strengthen you in every good *d*

DEEDS (DEED)
Dt 3:24 or on earth who can do the *d*
4:34 or by great and awesome *d,*
34:12 the awesome *d* that Moses
1Sa 2: 3 and by him *d* are weighed.
1Ch 16:24 his marvelous *d* among all peoples.
Job 34:25 Because he takes note of their *d,*
Ps 26: 7 and telling of all your wonderful *d.*
45: 4 right hand display awesome *d.*
65: 5 with awesome *d* of righteousness,
66: 3 "How awesome are your *d!*
71:17 day I declare your marvelous *d.*
72:18 who alone does marvelous *d.*
73:28 I will tell of all your *d.*
75: 1 men tell of your wonderful *d.*
77:11 I will remember the *d* of the LORD
77:12 and consider all your mighty *d.*
78: 4 the praiseworthy *d* of the LORD,
78: 7 and would not forget his *d*
86: 8 no *d* can compare with yours.
86:10 you are great and do marvelous *d;*
88:12 or your righteous *d* in the land
90:16 May your *d* be shown
92: 4 For you make me glad by your *d,*
96: 3 his marvelous *d* among all peoples.
107: 8 and his wonderful *d* for men,
107:15 and his wonderful *d* for men,
107:21 and his wonderful *d* for men.
107:24 his wonderful *d* in the deep.
107:31 and his wonderful *d* for men.
111: 3 Glorious and majestic are his *d,*
145: 6 and I will proclaim your great *d.*
Jer 32:19 purposes and mighty are your *d.*
Hab 3: 2 I stand in awe of your *d,* O LORD.
Mt 5:16 that they may see your good *d*
Lk 1:51 He has performed mighty *d*
23:41 we are getting what our *d* deserve.
Ac 26:20 prove their repentance by their *d.*
1Ti 6:18 rich in good *d,* and to be generous
Heb 10:24 on toward love and good *d.*
Jas 2:14 claims to have faith but has no *d?*
2:18 Show me your faith without *d,*
2:20 faith without *d* is useless?
Jas 2:26 so faith without *d* is dead.
1Pe 2:12 they may see your good *d*
Rev 2:19 I know your *d,* your love and faith,
2:23 each of you according to your *d.*
3: 1 I know your *d;* you have
3: 2 I have not found your *d* complete
3: 8 I know your *d.*
3:15 I know your *d,* that you are neither
14:13 for their *d* will follow them."
15: 3 "Great and marvelous are your *d,*

DEEP (DEPTH DEPTHS)
Ge 1: 2 was over the surface of the *d,*
8: 2 Now the springs of the *d*
Ps 42: 7 *D* calls to *d*
Lk 5: 4 to Simon, "Put out into *d* water,
1Co 2:10 all things, even the *d* things
1Ti 3: 9 hold of the *d* truths of the faith

DEER
Ps 42: 1 As the *d* pants for streams of water,

DEFAMED*
Isa 48:11 How can I let myself be *d?*

DEFEATED
1Co 6: 7 have been completely *d* already.

DEFEND (DEFENDED DEFENDER DEFENDING DEFENDS DEFENSE)
Ps 72: 4 He will *d* the afflicted
74:22 Rise up, O God, and *d* your cause;
82: 2 "How long will you *d* the unjust
82: 3 *D* the cause of the weak
119:154 *D* my cause and redeem me;
Pr 31: 9 *d* the rights of the poor and needy
Isa 1:17 *D* the cause of the fatherless,
1:23 They do not *d* the cause
Jer 5:28 they do not *d* the rights of the poor.
50:34 He will vigorously *d* their cause

DEFENDED (DEFEND)
Jer 22:16 He *d* the cause of the poor

DEFENDER (DEFEND)
Ex 22: 2 the *d* is not guilty of bloodshed;
Ps 68: 5 to the fatherless, a *d* of widows,
Pr 23:11 for their *D* is strong;

DEFENDING (DEFEND)
Ps 10:18 *d* the fatherless and the oppressed,
Ro 2:15 now accusing, now even *d* them.)
Php 1: 7 or *d* and confirming the gospel,

DEFENDS* (DEFEND)
Dt 10:18 He *d* the cause of the fatherless
33: 7 With his own hands he *d* his cause.
Isa 51:22 your God, who *d* his people:

DEFENSE (DEFEND)
Ps 35:23 Awake, and rise to my *d!*
Php 1:16 here for the *d* of the gospel.
1Jn 2: 1 speaks to the Father in our *d*—

DEFERRED*
Pr 13:12 Hope *d* makes the heart sick,

DEFIED
1Sa 17:45 armies of Israel, whom you have *d.*
1Ki 13:26 the man of God who *d* the word

DEFILE (DEFILED)
Da 1: 8 Daniel resolved not to *d* himself
Rev 14: 4 are those who did not *d* themselves

DEFILED (DEFILE)
Isa 24: 5 The earth is *d* by its people;

DEFRAUD
Lev 19:13 Do not *d* your neighbor or rob him.
Mk 10:19 do not *d,* honor your father

DEITY*
Col 2: 9 of the *D* lives in bodily form,

DELAY
Ecc 5: 4 vow to God, do not *d* in fulfilling it.
Isa 48: 9 my own name's sake I *d* my wrath;
Heb 10:37 is coming will come and will not *d.*
Rev 10: 6 and said, "There will be no more *d!*

DELICACIES
Ps 141: 4 let me not eat of their *d.*
Pr 23: 3 Do not crave his *d,*
23: 6 do not crave his *d;*

DELICIOUS*
Pr 9:17 food eaten in secret is *d!*"

DELIGHT* (DELIGHTED DELIGHTFUL DELIGHTING DELIGHTS)
Lev 26:31 and I will take no *d* in the pleasing
Dt 30: 9 The LORD will again *d* in you
1Sa 2: 1 for I *d* in your deliverance.
15:22 "Does the LORD *d*
Ne 1:11 the prayer of your servants who *d*
Job 22:26 Surely then you will find *d*
27:10 Will he find *d* in the Almighty?
Ps 1: 2 But his *d* is in the law of the LORD
16: 3 in whom is all my *d.*
35: 9 and *d* in his salvation.
35:27 those who *d* in my vindication
37: 4 *D* yourself in the LORD
43: 4 to God, my joy and my *d.*
51:16 You do not *d* in sacrifice,
51:19 whole burnt offerings to *d* you;
62: 4 they take *d* in lies.
68:30 Scatter the nations who *d* in war.
111: 2 by all who *d* in them.
112: 1 who finds great *d* in his commands.
119:16 I *d* in your decrees;
119:24 Your statutes are my *d;*
119:35 for there I find *d.*
119:47 for I *d* in your commands
119:70 but I *d* in your law.
119:77 for your law is my *d.*
119:92 If your law had not been my *d,*
119:143 but your commands are my *d.*
119:174 and your law is my *d.*
147:10 nor his *d* in the legs of a man;
149: 4 For the LORD takes *d*
Pr 1:22 How long will mockers *d*
2:14 who *d* in doing wrong
8:30 I was filled with *d* day after day,
11: 1 but accurate weights are his *d.*
29:17 he will bring *d* to your soul.
Ecc 2:10 My heart took *d* in all my work,
SS 1: 4 We rejoice and *d* in you;
2: 3 I *d* to sit in his shade,
Isa 5: 7 are the garden of his *d.*
11: 3 he will *d* in the fear of the LORD.
13:17 and have no *d* in gold.
32:14 the *d* of donkeys, a pasture
42: 1 my chosen one in whom I *d;*
55: 2 and your soul will *d* in the richest
58:13 if you call the Sabbath a *d*
61:10 I *d* greatly in the LORD;
62: 4 for the LORD will take *d* in you,
65:18 for I will create Jerusalem to be a *d*
65:19 and take *d* in my people;
66: 3 their souls *d* in their abominations;
66:11 *d* in her overflowing abundance."
Jer 9:24 for in these I *d,*"
15:16 they were my joy and my heart's *d,*
31:20 the child in whom I *d?*
49:25 the town in which I *d?*
Eze 24:16 away from you the *d* of your eyes.
24:21 in which you take pride, the *d*
24:25 and glory, the *d* of their eyes,
Hos 7: 3 *d* the king with their wickedness,
Mic 1:16 for the children in whom you *d;*
7:18 but *d* to show mercy.
Zep 3:17 He will take great *d* in you,

Mt 12:18 the one I love, in whom I *d;*
Mk 12:37 large crowd listened to him with *d.*
Lk 1:14 He will be a joy and *d* to you,
Ro 7:22 in my inner being I *d* in God's law;
1Co 13: 6 Love does not *d* in evil
2Co 12:10 for Christ's sake, I *d* in weaknesses,
Col 2: 5 and *d* to see how orderly you are

DELIGHTED (DELIGHT)
2Sa 22:20 he rescued me because he *d* in me.
1Ki 10: 9 who has *d* in you and placed you
2Ch 9: 8 who has *d* in you and placed you
Ps 18:19 he rescued me because he *d* in me.
Lk 13:17 but the people were *d* with all

DELIGHTFUL* (DELIGHT)
Ps 16: 6 surely I have a *d* inheritance.
SS 1: 2 for your love is more *d* than wine.
4:10 How *d* is your love, my sister,
Mal 3:12 for yours will be a *d* land,"

DELIGHTING* (DELIGHT)
Pr 8:31 and *d* in mankind.

DELIGHTS (DELIGHT)
Est 6: 6 for the man the king *d* to honor?"
Ps 22: 8 since he *d* in him."
35:27 who *d* in the well-being
36: 8 from your river of *d.*
37:23 if the LORD *d* in a man's way
147:11 the LORD *d* in those who fear him,
Pr 3:12 as a father the son he *d* in.
10:23 of understanding *d* in wisdom.
11:20 he *d* in those whose ways are
12:22 but he *d* in men who are truthful.
14:35 A king *d* in a wise servant,
18: 2 but *d* in airing his own opinions.
23:24 he who has a wise son *d* in him.
Col 2:18 Do not let anyone who *d*

DELILAH*
Woman who betrayed Samson (Jdg 16:4–22).

DELIVER (DELIVERANCE DELIVERED DELIVERER DELIVERS)
Dt 32:39 and no one can *d* out of my hand.
Ps 22: 8 Let him *d* him,
72:12 For he will *d* the needy who cry out
79: 9 *d* us and forgive our sins
109:21 of the goodness of your love, *d* me.
119:170 *d* me according to your promise.
Mt 6:13 but *d* us from the evil one.'
2Co 1:10 hope that he will continue to *d* us,

DELIVERANCE (DELIVER)
1Sa 2: 1 for I delight in your *d.*
Ps 3: 8 From the LORD comes *d.*
32: 7 and surround me with songs of *d.*
33:17 A horse is a vain hope for *d;*
Ob :17 But on Mount Zion will be *d;*

DELIVERED (DELIVER)
Ps 34: 4 he *d* me from all my fears.
107: 6 and he *d* them from their distress.
116: 8 have *d* my soul from death,
Da 12: 1 written in the book—will be *d.*
Ro 4:25 He was *d* over to death for our sins

DELIVERER* (DELIVER)
Jdg 3: 9 for them a *d,* Othniel son of Kenaz,
3:15 and he gave them a *d*— Ehud,
2Sa 22: 2 is my rock, my fortress and my *d;*
2Ki 13: 5 The LORD provided a *d* for Israel,
Ps 18: 2 is my rock, my fortress and my *d;*
40:17 You are my help and my *d;*
70: 5 You are my help and my *d;*
140: 7 O Sovereign LORD, my strong *d,*
144: 2 my stronghold and my *d,*
Ac 7:35 sent to be their ruler and *d*
Ro 11:26 "The *d* will come from Zion;

DELIVERS (DELIVER)
Ps 34:17 he *d* them from all their troubles.
34:19 but the LORD *d* him from them all
37:40 The LORD helps them and *d* them
37:40 he *d* them from the wicked

DELUSION*
2Th 2:11 God sends them a powerful *d*

DEMAND (DEMANDED)
Lk 6:30 belongs to you, do not *d* it back.

DEMANDED (DEMAND)
Lk 12:20 This very night your life will be *d*
12:48 been given much, much will be *d;*

DEMETRIUS
Ac 19:24 A silversmith named *D,* who made

DEMON* (DEMONS)
Mt 9:33 And when the *d* was driven out,
11:18 and they say, 'He has a *d.*'
17:18 Jesus rebuked the *d,* and it came
Mk 7:26 to drive the *d* out of her daughter.
7:29 the *d* has left your daughter."
7:30 lying on the bed, and the *d* gone.
Lk 4:33 there was a man possessed by a *d,*
4:35 Then the *d* threw the man
7:33 wine, and you say, 'He has a *d.*'
8:29 driven by the *d* into solitary places.
9:42 the *d* threw him to the ground
11:14 When the *d* left, the man who had
11:14 was driving out a *d* that was mute.
Jn 8:49 "I am not possessed by a *d,*"
10:21 Can a *d* open the eyes of the blind
10:21 sayings of a man possessed by a *d.*

DEMON-POSSESSED* (DEMON-POSSESSION)
Mt 4:24 those suffering severe pain, the *d,*
8:16 many who were *d* were brought
8:28 two *d* men coming
8:33 what had happened to the *d* men.
9:32 man who was *d* and could not talk
12:22 they brought him a *d* man who was
Mk 1:32 brought to Jesus all the sick and *d.*
5:16 what had happened to the *d* man—
5:18 the man who had been *d* begged
Lk 8:27 met by a *d* man from the town.
8:36 the people how the *d* man had been
Jn 7:20 "You are *d,*" the crowd answered.
8:48 that you are a Samaritan and *d?*"
8:52 "Now we know that you are *d!*
10:20 Many of them said, "He is *d*
Ac 19:13 Jesus over those who were *d.*

DEMON-POSSESSION* (DEMON-POSSESSED)
Mt 15:22 is suffering terribly from *d.*"

DEMONS* (DEMON)
Dt 32:17 to *d,* which are not God—
Ps 106:37 and their daughters to *d.*
Mt 7:22 and in your name drive out *d*
8:31 *d* begged Jesus, "If you drive us
9:34 prince of *d* that he drives out *d.*"
10: 8 who have leprosy, drive out *d.*
12:24 of *d,* that this fellow drives out
12:24 that this fellow drives out *d.*"
12:27 And if I drive out *d* by Beelzebub,
12:28 if I drive out *d* by the Spirit of God,
Mk 1:34 He also drove out many *d,*
1:34 but he would not let the *d* speak
1:39 their synagogues and driving out *d.*
3:15 to have authority to drive out *d.*
3:22 the prince of *d* he is driving out *d.*"
5:12 The *d* begged Jesus, "Send us
5:15 possessed by the legion of *d,*
6:13 They drove out many *d*
9:38 "we saw a man driving out *d*
16: 9 out of whom he had driven seven *d*
16:17 In my name they will drive out *d;*
Lk 4:41 *d* came out of many people,
8: 2 from whom seven *d* had come out;
8:30 because many *d* had gone into him.
8:32 The *d* begged Jesus to let them go
8:33 When the *d* came out of the man,
8:35 from whom the *d* had gone out,
8:38 from whom the *d* had gone out
9: 1 and authority to drive out all *d*
9:49 "we saw a man driving out *d*
10:17 the *d* submit to us in your name."
11:15 the prince of *d,* he is driving out *d.*"
11:18 you claim that I drive out *d*
11:19 Now if I drive out *d* by Beelzebub,
11:20 if I drive out *d* by the finger of God,
13:32 'I will drive out *d* and heal people
Ro 8:38 neither angels nor *d,* neither
1Co 10:20 of pagans are offered to *d,*
10:20 you to be participants with *d.*
10:21 of the Lord and the cup of *d* too;
10:21 the Lord's table and the table of *d.*
1Ti 4: 1 spirits and things taught by *d.*
Jas 2:19 Good! Even the *d* believe that—
Rev 9:20 they did not stop worshiping *d,*
16:14 of *d* performing miraculous signs,
18: 2 She has become a home for *d*

DEMONSTRATE* (DEMONSTRATES DEMONSTRATION)
Ro 3:25 He did this to *d* his justice,
3:26 he did it to *d* his justice

DEMONSTRATES* (DEMONSTRATE)
Ro 5: 8 God *d* his own love for us in this:

DEMONSTRATION* (DEMONSTRATE)
1Co 2: 4 but with a *d* of the Spirit's power,

DEN
Da 6:16 and threw him into the lions' *d.*
Mt 21:13 you are making it a '*d* of robbers.' "
Mk 11:17 you have made it 'a *d* of robbers.' "
Lk 19:46 but you have made it 'a *d* of robbers

DENARII* (DENARIUS)
Mt 18:28 who owed him a hundred *d.*
Lk 7:41 One owed him five hundred *d,*

DENARIUS (DENARII)
Mt 20: 2 agreed to pay them a *d* for the day
Mk 12:15 Bring me a *d* and let me look at it."

DENIED (DENY)
Mt 26:70 But he *d* it before them all.
Mk 14:68 But he *d* it.
Lk 22:57 But he *d* it.
Jn 18:25 He *d* it, saying, "I am not."
1Ti 5: 8 he has *d* the faith and is worse
Rev 3: 8 my word and have not *d* my name.

DENIES (DENY)
1Jn 2:22 It is the man who *d* that Jesus is
2:23 No one who *d* the Son has

DENY (DENIED DENIES DENYING)
Ex 23: 6 "Do not *d* justice to your poor
Job 27: 5 till I die, I will not *d* my integrity.
Isa 5:23 but *d* justice to the innocent.
La 3:35 to *d* a man his rights
Am 2: 7 and *d* justice to the oppressed.
Mt 16:24 he must *d* himself and take up his
Mk 8:34 he must *d* himself and take up his
Lk 9:23 he must *d* himself and take up his
22:34 you will *d* three times that you
Ac 4:16 miracle, and we cannot *d* it.
Tit 1:16 but by their actions they *d* him.
Jas 3:14 do not boast about it or *d* the truth.
Jude : 4 *d* Jesus Christ our only Sovereign

DENYING* (DENY)
Eze 22:29 mistreat the alien, *d* them justice.
2Ti 3: 5 a form of godliness but *d* its power.
2Pe 2: 1 *d* the sovereign Lord who bought

DEPART (DEPARTED DEPARTS DEPARTURE)
Ge 49:10 The scepter will not *d* from Judah,
Job 1:21 and naked I will *d*.
Mt 25:41 '*D* from me, you who are cursed,
Php 1:23 I desire to *d* and be with Christ,

DEPARTED (DEPART)
1Sa 4:21 "The glory has *d* from Israel"—
Ps 119:102 I have not *d* from your laws,

DEPARTS (DEPART)
Ecc 5:15 and as he comes, so he *d*.

DEPARTURE (DEPART)
Lk 9:31 spoke about his *d*, which he was
2Ti 4: 6 and the time has come for my *d*.
2Pe 1:15 after my *d* you will always be able

DEPEND
Ps 62: 7 My salvation and my honor *d*

DEPOSES*
Da 2:21 he sets up kings and *d* them.

DEPOSIT
Mt 25:27 money on *d* with the bankers,
Lk 19:23 didn't you put my money on *d*,
2Co 1:22 put his Spirit in our hearts as a *d*,
5: 5 and has given us the Spirit as a *d*,
Eph 1:14 who is a *d* guaranteeing our
2Ti 1:14 Guard the good *d* that was

DEPRAVED* (DEPRAVITY)
Eze 16:47 ways you soon became more *d*
23:11 and prostitution she was more *d*
Ro 1:28 he gave them over to a *d* mind,
Php 2:15 fault in a crooked and *d* generation,
2Ti 3: 8 oppose the truth—men of *d* minds,

DEPRAVITY* (DEPRAVED)
Ro 1:29 of wickedness, evil, greed and *d*.
2Pe 2:19 they themselves are slaves of *d*—

DEPRIVE
Dt 24:17 Do not *d* the alien or the fatherless
Pr 18: 5 or to *d* the innocent of justice.
31: 5 *d* all the oppressed of their rights.
Isa 10: 2 to *d* the poor of their rights
29:21 with false testimony *d* the innocent
La 3:36 to *d* a man of justice—
1Co 7: 5 Do not *d* each other
9:15 die than have anyone *d* me

DEPTH (DEEP)
Ro 8:39 any powers, neither height nor *d*,
11:33 the *d* of the riches of the wisdom

DEPTHS (DEEP)
Ps 130: 1 Out of the *d* I cry to you, O LORD;

DERIDES*
Pr 11:12 who lacks judgment *d* his neighbor,

DERIVES*
Eph 3:15 in heaven and on earth *d* its name.

DESCEND (DESCENDED DESCENDING)
Ro 10: 7 "or 'Who will *d* into the deep?' "

DESCENDED (DESCEND)
Eph 4: 9 except that he also *d* to the lower,
Heb 7:14 For it is clear that our Lord *d*

DESCENDING (DESCEND)
Ge 28:12 of God were ascending and *d* on it.
Mt 3:16 the Spirit of God *d* like a dove
Mk 1:10 and the Spirit *d* on him like a dove.
Jn 1:51 and *d* on the Son of Man."

DESECRATING*
Ne 13:17 you are doing—*d* the Sabbath day?
13:18 against Israel by *d* the Sabbath."
Isa 56: 2 who keeps the Sabbath without *d* it
56: 6 who keep the Sabbath without *d* it
Eze 44: 7 *d* my temple while you offered me

DESERT
Nu 32:13 wander in the *d* forty years,
Dt 8:16 He gave you manna to eat in the *d*,
29: 5 years that I led you through the *d*,
Ne 9:19 you did not abandon them in the *d*.
Ps 78:19 "Can God spread a table in the *d*?
78:52 led them like sheep through the *d*.
Pr 21:19 Better to live in a *d*
Isa 32: 2 like streams of water in the *d*
32:15 and the *d* becomes a fertile field,
35: 6 and streams in the *d*.
43:20 because I provide water in the *d*
Mk 1: 3 "a voice of one calling in the *d*,
1:13 and he was in the *d* forty days,
Rev 12: 6 fled into the *d* to a place prepared

DESERTED (DESERTS)
Ezr 9: 9 our God has not *d* us
Mt 26:56 all the disciples *d* him and fled.
2Ti 1:15 in the province of Asia has *d* me,

DESERTING (DESERTS)
Gal 1: 6 are so quickly *d* the one who called

DESERTS (DESERTED DESERTING)
Zec 11:17 who *d* the flock!

DESERVE* (DESERVED DESERVES)
Ge 40:15 to *d* being put in a dungeon."
Lev 26:21 times over, as your sins *d*.
Jdg 20:10 it can give them what they *d*
1Sa 26:16 you and your men *d* to die,
1Ki 2:26 You *d* to die, but I will not put you
Ps 28: 4 bring back upon them what they *d*.
94: 2 pay back to the proud what they *d*.
103:10 he does not treat us as our sins *d*
Pr 3:27 from those who *d* it,
Ecc 8:14 men who get what the righteous *d*,
8:14 men who get what the wicked *d*,
Isa 66: 6 repaying his enemies all they *d*.
Jer 14:16 out on them the calamity they *d*.
17:10 according to what his deeds *d*."
21:14 I will punish you as your deeds *d*,
32:19 to his conduct and as his deeds *d*.
49:12 "If those who do not *d*
La 3:64 Pay them back what they *d*,
Eze 16:59 I will deal with you as you *d*,
Zec 1: 6 to us what our ways and practices *d*
Mt 8: 8 I do not *d* to have you come
22: 8 those I invited did not *d* to come.
Lk 7: 6 for I do not *d* to have you come
23:15 he has done nothing to *d* death.
23:41 for we are getting what our deeds *d*
Ro 1:32 those who do such things *d* death,
1Co 15: 9 even *d* to be called an apostle,
16:18 Such men *d* recognition.
2Co 11:15 end will be what their actions *d*.
Rev 16: 6 blood to drink as they *d*."

DESERVED* (DESERVE)
2Sa 19:28 descendants *d* nothing
Ezr 9:13 less than our sins have *d*
Job 33:27 but I did not get what I *d*.
Ac 23:29 charge against him that *d* death
Ro 3: 8 Their condemnation is *d*.

DESERVES* (DESERVE)
Nu 35:31 the life of a murderer, who *d* to die.
Dt 25: 2 If the guilty man *d* to be beaten,
25: 2 the number of lashes his crime *d*,
Jdg 9:16 and if you have treated him as he *d*
2Sa 12: 5 the man who did this *d* to die!
Job 34:11 upon him what his conduct *d*.
Jer 51: 6 he will pay her what she *d*.
Lk 7: 4 "This man *d* to have you do this,
10: 7 for the worker *d* his wages.
Ac 26:31 is not doing anything that *d* death
1Ti 1:15 saying that *d* full acceptance:
4: 9 saying that *d* full acceptance
5:18 and "The worker *d* his wages."
Heb 10:29 severely do you think a man *d*

DESIGNATED
Lk 6:13 also *d* apostles: Simon (whom he
Heb 5:10 and was *d* by God to be high priest

DESIRABLE* (DESIRE)
Ge 3: 6 and also *d* for gaining wisdom,
Pr 22: 1 A good name is more *d*
Jer 3:19 and give you a *d* land,

DESIRE* (DESIRABLE DESIRED DESIRES)
Ge 3:16 Your *d* will be for your husband,
Dt 5:21 You shall not set your *d*
1Sa 9:20 to whom is all the *d* of Israel turned
2Sa 19:38 anything you *d* from me I will do
23: 5 and grant me my every *d*?
1Ch 29:18 keep this *d* in the hearts
2Ch 1:11 "Since this is your heart's *d*
9: 8 and his *d* to uphold them forever,
Job 13: 3 But I *d* to speak to the Almighty
21:14 We have no *d* to know your ways.
Ps 10:17 O LORD, the *d* of the afflicted;
20: 4 May he give you the *d*
21: 2 You have granted him the *d*
27:12 me over to the *d* of my foes,
40: 6 Sacrifice and offering you did not *d*
40: 8 I *d* to do your will, O my God;
40:14 may all who *d* my ruin
41: 2 him to the *d* of his foes.
51: 6 Surely you *d* truth
70: 2 may all who *d* my ruin
73:25 earth has nothing I *d* besides you
Pr 3:15 nothing you *d* can compare
8:11 and nothing you *d* can compare
10:24 what the righteous *d* will be
11:23 The *d* of the righteous ends only
12:12 The wicked *d* the plunder
17:16 since he has no *d* to get wisdom?
24: 1 do not *d* their company;
Ecc 12: 5 and *d* no longer is stirred.
SS 6:12 my *d* set me among the royal
7:10 and his *d* is for me.
Isa 26: 8 are the *d* of our hearts.
53: 2 appearance that we should *d* him.
55:11 but will accomplish what I *d*
Eze 24:25 delight of their eyes, their heart's *d*,
Hos 6: 6 For I *d* mercy, not sacrifice,
Mic 7: 3 the powerful dictate what they *d*—
Mal 3: 1 whom you *d*, will come," says
Mt 9:13 learn what this means: 'I *d* mercy,
12: 7 what these words mean, 'I *d* mercy,
Jn 8:44 want to carry out your father's *d*.
Ro 7: 8 in me every kind of covetous *d*.
7:18 For I have the *d* to do what is good,
9:16 depend on man's *d* or effort,
10: 1 my heart's *d* and prayer to God
1Co 12:31 But eagerly *d* the greater gifts.
14: 1 and eagerly *d* spiritual gifts,
2Co 8:10 but also to have the *d* to do so.
8:13 Our *d* is not that others might be
Php 1:23 I *d* to depart and be with Christ,
Heb 10: 5 Sacrifice and offering you did not *d*
10: 8 and sin offerings you did not *d*,
13:18 *d* to live honorably in every way.
Jas 1:14 by his own evil *d*, he is dragged
1:15 Then, after *d* has conceived,
2Pe 2:10 of those who follow the corrupt *d*

DESIRED (DESIRE)
Hag 2: 7 and the *d* of all nations will come,
Lk 22:15 "I have eagerly *d* to eat this

DESIRES* (DESIRE)
Ge 4: 7 at your door; it *d* to have you,
41:16 will give Pharaoh the answer he *d*."
2Sa 3:21 rule over all that your heart *d*."
1Ki 11:37 rule over all that your heart *d*;

Job 17:11 and so are the *d* of my heart.
31:16 "If I have denied the *d* of the poor
Ps 34:12 and *d* to see many good days,
37: 4 he will give you the *d* of your heart.
103: 5 who satisfies your *d* with good things,
140: 8 do not grant the wicked their *d*,
145:16 satisfy the *d* of every living thing.
145:19 He fulfills the *d* of those who fear
Pr 11: 6 the unfaithful are trapped by evil *d*.
13: 4 *d* of the diligent are fully satisfied.
19:22 What a man *d* is unfailing love;
Ecc 6: 2 so that he lacks nothing his heart *d*,
SS 2: 7 or awaken love / until it so *d*.
3: 5 or awaken love / until it so *d*.
8: 4 or awaken love / until it so *d*.
Hab 2: 4 his *d* are not upright—
Mk 4:19 and the *d* for other things come in
Ro 1:24 over in the sinful *d* of their hearts
6:12 body so that you obey its evil *d*.
8: 5 set on what that nature *d*;
8: 5 set on what the Spirit *d*.
13:14 to gratify the *d* of the sinful nature.
Gal 5:16 and you will not gratify the *d*
5:17 the sinful nature *d* what is contrary
5:24 nature with its passions and *d*.
Eph 2: 3 and following its *d* and thoughts.
4:22 being corrupted by its deceitful *d*;
Col 3: 5 impurity, lust, evil *d* and greed,
1Ti 3: 1 an overseer, he *d* a noble task.
5:11 their sensual *d* overcome their
6: 9 and harmful *d* that plunge men
2Ti 2:22 Flee the evil *d* of youth,
3: 6 are swayed by all kinds of evil *d*,
4: 3 Instead, to suit their own *d*,
Jas 1:20 about the righteous life that God *d*.
4: 1 from your *d* that battle within you?
1Pe 1:14 conform to the evil *d* you had
2:11 to abstain from sinful *d*, which war
4: 2 of his earthly life for evil human *d*,
2Pe 1: 4 in the world caused by evil *d*.
2:18 to the lustful *d* of sinful human
3: 3 and following their own evil *d*.
1Jn 2:17 The world and its *d* pass away,
Jude :16 they follow their own evil *d*;
:18 will follow their own ungodly *d*."

DESOLATE (DESOLATION)
Isa 54: 1 are the children of the *d* woman
Gal 4:27 are the children of the *d* woman

DESOLATION (DESOLATE)
Da 11:31 up the abomination that causes *d*.
12:11 abomination that causes *d* is set up,
Mt 24:15 'the abomination that causes *d*,'

DESPAIR (DESPAIRED)
Isa 61: 3 instead of a spirit of *d*.
2Co 4: 8 perplexed, but not in *d*; persecuted,

DESPAIRED* (DESPAIR)
2Co 1: 8 ability to endure, so that we *d*

DESPERATE*
2Sa 12:18 He may do something *d*."
Ps 60: 3 have shown your people *d* times;
79: 8 for we are in *d* need.
142: 6 for I am in *d* need;

DESPISE (DESPISED DESPISES)
2Sa 12: 9 Why did you *d* the word
Job 5:17 so do not *d* the discipline
36: 5 God is mighty, but does not *d* men;
42: 6 Therefore I *d* myself
Ps 51:17 O God, you will not *d*.
102:17 he will not *d* their plea.
Pr 1: 7 but fools *d* wisdom and discipline.
3:11 do not *d* the LORD's discipline
6:30 Men do not *d* a thief if he steals
23:22 do not *d* your mother
Jer 14:21 of your name do not *d* us;
Am 5:10 and *d* him who tells the truth.
Am 5:21 "I hate, I *d* your religious feasts;
Mt 6:24 devoted to the one and *d* the other.
Lk 16:13 devoted to the one and *d* the other.
1Co 11:22 Or do you *d* the church of God
Tit 2:15 Do not let anyone *d* you.
2Pe 2:10 of the sinful nature and *d* authority.

DESPISED (DESPISE)
Ge 25:34 So Esau *d* his birthright.
Ps 22: 6 by men and *d* by the people.
Pr 12: 8 but men with warped minds are *d*.
Isa 53: 3 He was *d* and rejected by men,
53: 3 he was *d*, and we esteemed him not
1Co 1:28 of this world and the *d* things—

DESPISES (DESPISE)
Pr 14:21 He who *d* his neighbor sins,
15:20 but a foolish man *d* his mother.
15:32 who ignores discipline *d* himself,
Zec 4:10 "Who *d* the day of small things?

DESTINED (DESTINY)
Lk 2:34 "This child is *d* to cause the falling
1Co 2: 7 and that God *d* for our glory
Col 2:22 These are all *d* to perish with use,
1Th 3: 3 know quite well that we were *d*
Heb 9:27 Just as man is *d* to die once,
1Pe 2: 8 which is also what they were *d* for.

DESTINY* (DESTINED PREDESTINED)
Job 8:13 Such is the *d* of all who forget God;
Ps 73:17 then I understood their final *d*.
Ecc 7: 2 for death is the *d* of every man;
9: 2 share a common *d*— the righteous
9: 3 the sun: The same *d* overtakes all.
Isa 65:11 and fill bowls of mixed wine for *D*,
Php 3:19 Their *d* is destruction, their god is

DESTITUTE
Ps 102:17 to the prayer of the *d*;
Pr 31: 8 for the rights of all who are *d*.
Heb 11:37 *d*, persecuted and mistreated—

DESTROY (DESTROYED DESTROYING DESTROYS DESTRUCTION DESTRUCTIVE)
Ge 6:17 floodwaters on the earth to *d* all life
9:11 will there be a flood to *d* the earth."
Pr 1:32 complacency of fools will *d* them;
Mt 10:28 of the One who can *d* both soul
Mk 14:58 'I will *d* this man-made temple
Lk 4:34 to *d* us? I know who you are—
Jn 10:10 only to steal and kill and *d*;
Ac 8: 3 But Saul began to *d* the church.
Rev 11:18 destroying those who *d* the earth."

DESTROYED (DESTROY)
Dt 8:19 you today that you will surely be *d*.
Job 19:26 And after my skin has been *d*,
Pr 6:15 he will suddenly be *d*—
11: 3 the unfaithful are *d*
21:28 listens to him will be *d* forever.
29: 1 will suddenly be *d*—
Isa 55:13 which will not be *d*."
Da 2:44 up a kingdom that will never be *d*,
6:26 his kingdom will not be *d*,
1Co 5: 5 so that the sinful nature may be *d*
8:11 for whom Christ died, is *d*
15:24 Father after he has *d* all dominion,
15:26 The last enemy to be *d* is death.
2Co 4: 9 abandoned; struck down, but not *d*.
5: 1 if the earthly tent we live in is *d*,
Gal 5:15 or you will be *d* by each other.
Eph 2:14 the two one and has *d* the barrier,
2Ti 1:10 who has *d* death and has brought
Heb 10:39 of those who shrink back and are *d*,
2Pe 2:12 born only to be caught and *d*,
3:10 the elements will be *d* by fire,
3:11 Since everything will be *d*
Jude : 5 later *d* those who did not believe.
:11 have been *d* in Korah's rebellion.

DESTROYING (DESTROY)
Jer 23: 1 "Woe to the shepherds who are *d*

DESTROYS (DESTROY)
Pr 6:32 whoever does so *d* himself.
11: 9 mouth the godless *d* his neighbor,
18: 9 is brother to one who *d*.
28:24 he is partner to him who *d*.
Ecc 9:18 but one sinner *d* much good.
1Co 3:17 If anyone *d* God's temple,

DESTRUCTION (DESTROY)
Nu 32:15 and you will be the cause of their *d*
Pr 16:18 Pride goes before *d*,
17:19 he who builds a high gate invites *d*.
24:22 for those two will send sudden *d*
Hos 13:14 Where, O grave, is your *d*?
Mt 7:13 broad is the road that leads to *d*,
Lk 6:49 it collapsed and its *d* was complete
Jn 17:12 except the one doomed to *d*
Ro 9:22 of his wrath—prepared for *d*?
Gal 6: 8 from that nature will reap *d*;
Php 3:19 Their destiny is *d*, their god is their
1Th 5: 3 *d* will come on them suddenly,
2Th 1: 9 punished with everlasting *d*
2: 3 is revealed, the man doomed to *d*.
1Ti 6: 9 that plunge men into ruin and *d*.
2Pe 2: 1 bringing swift *d* on themselves.
2: 3 and their *d* has not been sleeping.
3: 7 of judgment and *d* of ungodly men.
3:12 That day will bring about the *d*
3:16 other Scriptures, to their own *d*.
Rev 17: 8 out of the Abyss and go to his *d*.
17:11 to the seven and is going to his *d*.

DESTRUCTIVE (DESTROY)
2Pe 2: 1 will secretly introduce *d* heresies,

DETERMINED (DETERMINES)
Job 14: 5 Man's days are *d*;
Isa 14:26 This is the plan *d* for the whole
Da 11:36 for what has been *d* must take place
Ac 17:26 and he *d* the times set for them

DETERMINES* (DETERMINED)
Ps 147: 4 He *d* the number of the stars
Pr 16: 9 but the LORD *d* his steps.
1Co 12:11 them to each one, just as he *d*.

DETEST (DETESTABLE DETESTED DETESTS)
Lev 11:10 in the water—you are to *d*.
Pr 8: 7 for my lips *d* wickedness.
13:19 but fools *d* turning from evil.
16:12 Kings *d* wrongdoing,
24: 9 and men *d* a mocker.
29:27 The righteous *d* the dishonest;
29:27 the wicked *d* the upright.

DETESTABLE (DETEST)
Pr 6:16 seven that are *d* to him:
21:27 The sacrifice of the wicked is *d*—
28: 9 even his prayers are *d*.
Isa 1:13 Your incense is *d* to me.
41:24 he who chooses you is *d*.
44:19 Shall I make a *d* thing
Jer 44: 4 'Do not do this *d* thing that I hate!'
Eze 8:13 doing things that are even more *d*."
Lk 16:15 among men is *d* in God's sight.
Tit 1:16 They are *d*, disobedient
1Pe 4: 3 orgies, carousing and *d* idolatry.

DETESTED* (DETEST)
Zec 11: 8 The flock *d* me, and I grew weary

DETESTS* (DETEST)
Dt 22: 5 LORD your God *d* anyone who
23:18 the LORD your God *d* them both.
25:16 LORD your God *d* anyone who
Pr 3:32 for the LORD *d* a perverse man
11:20 The LORD *d* men
12:22 The LORD *d* lying lips,

Pr 15: 8 The LORD *d* the sacrifice
15: 9 The LORD *d* the way
15:26 The LORD *d* the thoughts
16: 5 The LORD *d* all the proud of heart
17:15 the LORD *d* them both.
20:10 the LORD *d* them both.
20:23 The LORD *d* differing weights,

DEVIATE**
2Ch 8:15 They did not *d* from the king's

DEVICES**
Ps 81:12 to follow their own *d.*

DEVIL** (DEVIL'S)
Mt 4: 1 the desert to be tempted by the *d.*
4: 5 the *d* took him to the holy city
4: 8 *d* took him to a very high mountain
4:11 the *d* left him, and angels came
13:39 the enemy who sows them is the *d.*
25:41 the eternal fire prepared for the *d*
Lk 4: 2 forty days he was tempted by the *d.*
4: 3 *d* said to him, "If you are the Son
4: 5 The *d* led him up to a high place
4: 9 The *d* led him to Jerusalem
4:13 When the *d* had finished all this
8:12 then the *d* comes and takes away
Jn 6:70 of you is a *d!"* (He meant Judas,
8:44 You belong to your father, the *d,*
13: 2 the *d* had already prompted Judas
Ac 10:38 were under the power of the *d,*
13:10 "You are a child of the *d*
Eph 4:27 and do not give the *d* a foothold.
1Ti 3: 6 under the same judgment as the *d.*
2Ti 2:26 and escape from the trap of the *d,*
Heb 2:14 the *d*— and free those who all their
Jas 3:15 but is earthly, unspiritual, of the *d.*
4: 7 Resist the *d,* and he will flee
1Pe 5: 8 Your enemy the *d* prowls
1Jn 3: 8 because the *d* has been sinning
3: 8 who does what is sinful is of the *d,*
3:10 and who the children of the *d* are:
Jude : 9 with the *d* about the body of Moses
Rev 2:10 the *d* will put some of you in prison
12: 9 that ancient serpent called the *d*
12:12 the *d* has gone down to you!
20: 2 that ancient serpent, who is the *d,*
20:10 And the *d,* who deceived them,

DEVIL'S** (DEVIL)
Eph 6:11 stand against the *d* schemes.
1Ti 3: 7 into disgrace and into the *d* trap.
1Jn 3: 8 was to destroy the *d* work.

DEVIOUS**
Pr 2:15 and who are *d* in their ways.
14: 2 he whose ways are *d* despises him.
21: 8 The way of the guilty is *d,*

DEVOTE** (DEVOTED DEVOTING DEVOTION DEVOUT)
1Ch 22:19 Now *d* your heart and soul
2Ch 31: 4 Levites so they could *d* themselves
Job 11:13 "Yet if you *d* your heart to him
Jer 30:21 for who is he who will *d* himself
Mic 4:13 You will *d* their ill-gotten gains
1Co 7: 5 so that you may *d* yourselves
Col 4: 2 *D* yourselves to prayer, being
1Ti 1: 4 nor to *d* themselves to myths
4:13 *d* yourself to the public reading
Tit 3: 8 may be careful to *d* themselves
3:14 people must learn to *d* themselves

DEVOTED (DEVOTE)
1Ki 11: 4 and his heart was not fully *d*
Ezr 7:10 For Ezra had *d* himself to the study
Ps 86: 2 Guard my life, for I am *d* to you.
Mt 6:24 or he will be *d* to the one
Mk 7:11 from me is Corban' (that is, a gift *d*
Ac 2:42 They *d* themselves
18: 5 Paul *d* himself exclusively
Ro 12:10 Be *d* to one another
1Co 7:34 Her aim is to be *d* to the Lord
16:15 and they have *d* themselves
2Co 7:12 for yourselves how *d* to us you are.

DEVOTING** (DEVOTE)
1Ti 5:10 *d* herself to all kinds of good deeds.

DEVOTION** (DEVOTE)
2Ki 20: 3 and with wholehearted *d* and have
1Ch 28: 9 and serve him with wholehearted *d*
29: 3 in my *d* to the temple
29:19 son Solomon the wholehearted *d*
2Ch 32:32 and his acts of *d* are written
35:26 of Josiah's reign and his acts of *d,*
Job 6:14 despairing man should have the *d*
15: 4 and hinder *d* to God.
Isa 38: 3 and with wholehearted *d* and have
Jer 2: 2 " 'I remember the *d* of your youth,
Eze 33:31 With their mouths they express *d,*
1Co 7:35 way in undivided *d* to the Lord.
2Co 11: 3 from your sincere and pure *d*

DEVOUR (DEVOURED DEVOURING DEVOURS)
2Sa 2:26 "Must the sword *d* forever?
Mk 12:40 They *d* widows' houses
1Pe 5: 8 lion looking for someone to *d.*

DEVOURED (DEVOUR)
Jer 30:16 But all who devour you will be *d;*

DEVOURING (DEVOUR)
Gal 5:15 keep on biting and *d* each other,

DEVOURS (DEVOUR)
2Sa 11:25 the sword *d* one as well as another.
Pr 21:20 but a foolish man *d* all he has.

DEVOUT** (DEVOTE)
1Ki 18: 3 (Obadiah was a *d* believer
Isa 57: 1 *d* men are taken away,
Lk 2:25 Simeon, who was righteous and *d.*
Ac 10: 2 his family were *d* and God-fearing;
10: 7 a *d* soldier who was one of his attendants
13:43 and *d* converts to Judaism followed
22:12 He was a *d* observer of the law

DEW
Jdg 6:37 If there is *d* only on the fleece

DICTATED
Jer 36: 4 and while Jeremiah *d* all the words

DIE (DEAD DEADENED DEATH DIED DIES DYING)
Ge 2:17 when you eat of it you will surely *d*
3: 3 you must not touch it, or you will *d*
3: 4 will not surely *d,"* the serpent said
Ex 11: 5 Every firstborn son in Egypt will *d,*
Ru 1:17 Where you *d* I will *d,* and there I
2Ki 14: 6 each is to *d* for his own sins."
Job 2: 9 Curse God and *d!"* He replied,
Pr 5:23 He will *d* for lack of discipline,
10:21 but fools *d* for lack of judgment.
15:10 he who hates correction will *d.*
23:13 with the rod, he will not *d.*
Ecc 3: 2 a time to be born and a time to *d,*
Isa 22:13 "for tomorrow we *d!"*
66:24 their worm will not *d,* nor will their
Jer 31:30 everyone will *d* for his own sin;
Eze 3:18 that wicked man will *d* for his sin,
3:19 he will *d* for his sin; but you will
3:20 block before him, he will *d.*
18: 4 soul who sins is the one who will *d.*
18:20 soul who sins is the one who will *d.*
18:31 Why will you *d,* O house of Israel?
33: 8 'O wicked man, you will surely *d,'*
Mt 26:52 "for all who draw the sword will *d*
Mk 9:48 " 'their worm does not *d,*
Jn 8:21 and you will *d* in your sin.
Jn 11:26 and believes in me will never *d.*
Ro 5: 7 Very rarely will anyone *d*
14: 8 and if we *d,* we *d* to the Lord.
1Co 15:22 in Adam all *d,* so in Christ all will
15:31 I *d* every day—I mean that,
15:32 for tomorrow we *d."*
Php 1:21 to live is Christ and to *d* is gain.
Heb 9:27 Just as man is destined to *d* once,
1Pe 2:24 so that we might *d* to sins
Rev 14:13 Blessed are the dead who *d*

DIED (DIE)
1Ki 16:18 So he *d,* because of the sins he had
1Ch 1:51 Hadad also *d.*
10:13 Saul *d* because he was unfaithful
Lk 16:22 "The time came when the beggar *d*
Ro 5: 6 we were still powerless, Christ *d*
5: 8 we were still sinners, Christ *d*
6: 2 By no means! We *d* to sin;
6: 7 anyone who has *d* has been freed
6: 8 if we *d* with Christ, we believe that
6:10 The death he *d,* he *d* to sin once
14: 9 Christ *d* and returned to life
14:15 brother for whom Christ *d.*
1Co 8:11 for whom Christ *d,* is destroyed
15: 3 that Christ *d* for our sins according
2Co 5:14 *d* for all, and therefore all *d.*
5:15 he *d* for all, that those who live
Col 2:20 Since you *d* with Christ
3: 3 For you *d,* and your life is now
1Th 4:14 We believe that Jesus *d*
5:10 He *d* for us so that, whether we are
2Ti 2:11 If we *d* with him,
Heb 9:15 now that he has *d* as a ransom
9:17 in force only when somebody has *d*
1Pe 3:18 For Christ *d* for sins once for all,
Rev 2: 8 who *d* and came to life again.

DIES (DIE)
Job 14:14 If a man *d,* will he live again?
Pr 11: 7 a wicked man *d,* his hope perishes;
26:20 without gossip a quarrel *d* down.
Jn 11:25 in me will live, even though he *d;*
12:24 But if it *d,* it produces many seeds.
Ro 7: 2 but if her husband *d,* she is released
14: 7 and none of us *d* to himself alone.
1Co 7:39 But if her husband *d,* she is free
15:36 does not come to life unless it *d.*

DIFFERENCE** (DIFFERENT)
2Sa 19:35 Can I tell the *d* between what is
2Ch 12: 8 so that they may learn the *d*
Eze 22:26 they teach that there is no *d*
44:23 are to teach my people the *d*
Ro 3:22 There is no *d,* for all have sinned
10:12 For there is no *d* between Jew
Gal 2: 6 whatever they were makes no *d*

DIFFERENCES** (DIFFERENT)
1Co 11:19 to be *d* among you to show which

DIFFERENT** (DIFFERENCE DIFFERENCES DIFFERING DIFFERS)
Lev 19:19 " 'Do not mate *d* kinds of animals.
Nu 14:24 my servant Caleb has a *d* spirit
1Sa 10: 6 you will be changed into a *d* person
Est 1: 7 each one *d* from the other,
3: 8 whose customs are *d* from those
Da 7: 3 Four great beasts, each *d*
7: 7 It was *d* from all the former beasts,
7:19 which was *d* from all the others
7:23 It will be *d* from all the other
7:24 them another king will arise, *d*
11:29 but this time the outcome will be *d*
Mk 16:12 Jesus appeared in a *d* form
Ro 12: 6 We have *d* gifts, according
1Co 4: 7 For who makes you *d*
12: 4 There are *d* kinds of gifts,
12: 5 There are *d* kinds of service,
12: 6 There are *d* kinds of working,
12:10 speaking in *d* kinds of tongues,

1Co 12:28 and those speaking in *d* kinds
2Co 11: 4 or a *d* gospel from the one you
11: 4 or if you receive a *d* spirit
Gal 1: 6 and are turning to a *d* gospel—
4: 1 he is no *d* from a slave,
Heb 7:13 are said belonged to a *d* tribe,
Jas 2:25 and sent them off in a *d* direction?

DIFFERING* (DIFFERENT)
Dt 25:13 Do not have two *d* weights
25:14 Do not have two *d* measures
Pr 20:10 Differing weights and *d* measures
20:10 *D* weights and differing measures
20:23 The LORD detests *d* weights,

DIFFERS* (DIFFERENT)
1Co 15:41 and star *d* from star in splendor.

DIFFICULT (DIFFICULTIES)
Ex 18:22 but have them bring every *d* case
Dt 30:11 commanding you today is not too *d*
2Ki 2:10 "You have asked a *d* thing,"
Eze 3: 5 of obscure speech and *d* language,
Ac 15:19 that we should not make it *d*

DIFFICULTIES* (DIFFICULT)
Dt 31:17 and *d* will come upon them,
31:21 when many disasters and *d* come
2Co 12:10 in hardships, in persecutions, in *d*.

DIGNITY
Pr 31:25 She is clothed with strength and *d*;

DIGS
Pr 26:27 If a man *d* a pit, he will fall into it;

DILIGENCE (DILIGENT)
Ezr 5: 8 The work is being carried on with *d*
Heb 6:11 to show this same *d* to the very end

DILIGENT (DILIGENCE)
Pr 10: 4 but *d* hands bring wealth.
12:24 *D* hands will rule,
12:27 the *d* man prizes his possessions.
13: 4 of the *d* are fully satisfied.
21: 5 The plans of the *d* lead to profit
1Ti 4:15 Be *d* in these matters; give yourself

DINAH*
Only daughter of Jacob, by Leah (Ge 30:21; 46:15). Raped by Shechem; avenged by Simeon and Levi (Ge 34).

DINE
Pr 23: 1 When you sit to *d* with a ruler,

DIOTREPHES*
3Jn : 9 but *D*, who loves to be first,

DIRECT (DIRECTED DIRECTIVES DIRECTS)
Ge 18:19 so that he will *d* his children
Dt 17:10 to do everything they *d* you to do.
Ps 119:35 *D* me in the path of your
119:133 *D* my footsteps according
Jer 10:23 it is not for man to *d* his steps.
2Th 3: 5 May the Lord *d* your hearts
1Ti 5:17 The elders who *d* the affairs

DIRECTED (DIRECT)
Ge 24:51 master's son, as the LORD has *d*."
Nu 16:40 as the LORD *d* him through Moses
Dt 2: 1 Sea, as the LORD had *d* me.
6: 1 laws the LORD your God *d* me
Jos 11: 9 did to them as the LORD had *d*:
11:23 just as the LORD had *d* Moses,
Pr 20:24 A man's steps are *d* by the LORD.
Jer 13: 2 as the LORD *d*, and put it
Ac 7:44 It had been made as God *d* Moses,
Tit 1: 5 elders in every town, as I *d* you.

DIRECTIVES* (DIRECT)
1Co 11:17 In the following *d* I have no praise

DIRECTS (DIRECT)
Ps 42: 8 By day the LORD *d* his love,
Isa 48:17 who *d* you in the way you should

DIRGE*
Mt 11:17 we sang a *d*,
Lk 7:32 we sang a *d*,

DISABLED*
Jn 5: 3 number of *d* people used to lie—
Heb 12:13 so that the lame may not be *d*,

DISAGREEMENT*
Ac 15:39 had such a sharp *d* that they parted

DISAPPEAR (DISAPPEARED DISAPPEARS)
Mt 5:18 will by any means *d* from the Law
Lk 16:17 earth to *d* than for the least stroke
Heb 8:13 is obsolete and aging will soon *d*.
2Pe 3:10 The heavens will *d* with a roar;

DISAPPEARED (DISAPPEAR)
1Ki 20:40 busy here and there, the man *d*."

DISAPPEARS (DISAPPEAR)
1Co 13:10 perfection comes, the imperfect *d*.

DISAPPOINT* (DISAPPOINTED)
Ro 5: 5 And hope does not *d* us,

DISAPPOINTED (DISAPPOINT)
Ps 22: 5 in you they trusted and were not *d*.

DISAPPROVE*
Pr 24:18 or the LORD will see and *d*

DISARMED*
Col 2:15 And having *d* the powers

DISASTER
Ex 32:12 and do not bring *d* on your people.
Ps 57: 1 wings until the *d* has passed.
Pr 1:26 I in turn will laugh at your *d*;
3:25 Have no fear of sudden *d*
6:15 Therefore *d* will overtake him
16: 4 even the wicked for a day of *d*.
17: 5 over *d* will not go unpunished.
27:10 house when *d* strikes you—
Isa 45: 7 I bring prosperity and create *d*;
Jer 17:17 you are my refuge in the day of *d*.
Eze 7: 5 An unheard-of *d* is coming.

DISCERN (DISCERNED DISCERNING DISCERNMENT)
Ps 19:12 Who can *d* his errors?
139: 3 You *d* my going out and my lying
Php 1:10 you may be able to *d* what is best

DISCERNED (DISCERN)
1Co 2:14 because they are spiritually *d*.

DISCERNING (DISCERN)
1Ki 3: 9 So give your servant a *d* heart
3:12 I will give you a wise and *d* heart,
Pr 1: 5 and let the *d* get guidance—
8: 9 To the *d* all of them are right;
10:13 on the lips of the *d*,
14: 6 knowledge comes easily to the *d*.
14:33 in the heart of the *d*
15:14 The *d* heart seeks knowledge,
16:21 The wise in heart are called *d*,
17:24 A *d* man keeps wisdom in view,
17:28 and *d* if he holds his tongue.
18:15 heart of the *d* acquires knowledge;
19:25 rebuke a *d* man, and he will gain
28: 7 He who keeps the law is a *d* son,

DISCERNMENT (DISCERN)
Ps 119:125 I am your servant; give me *d*
Pr 3:21 preserve sound judgment and *d*,
17:10 A rebuke impresses a man of *d*
28:11 a poor man who has *d* sees

DISCHARGED* (DISCHARGING)
Ecc 8: 8 As no one is *d* in time of war,

DISCHARGING* (DISCHARGED)
1Co 9:17 I am simply *d* the trust committed

DISCIPLE (DISCIPLES DISCIPLES')
Mt 10:42 these little ones because he is my *d*,
Lk 14:26 his own life—he cannot be my *d*.
14:27 and follow me cannot be my *d*.
14:33 everything he has cannot be my *d*.
Jn 13:23 of them, the *d* whom Jesus loved,
19:26 and the *d* whom he loved standing
21: 7 Then the *d* whom Jesus loved said
21:20 saw that the *d* whom Jesus loved

DISCIPLES (DISCIPLE)
Mt 10: 1 He called his twelve *d* to him
26:56 Then all the *d* deserted him
28:19 Therefore go and make *d*
Mk 3: 7 withdrew with his *d* to the lake,
16:20 Then the *d* went out and preached
Lk 6:13 he called his *d* to him and chose
Jn 2:11 and his *d* put their faith in him.
6:66 many of his *d* turned back
8:31 to my teaching, you are really my *d*
12:16 At first his *d* did not understand all
13:35 men will know that you are my *d*
15: 8 showing yourselves to be my *d*.
20:20 The *d* were overjoyed
Ac 6: 1 the number of *d* was increasing,
11:26 The *d* were called Christians first
14:22 strengthening the *d*
18:23 Phrygia, strengthening all the *d*.

DISCIPLES' (DISCIPLE)
Jn 13: 5 and began to wash his *d* feet,

DISCIPLINE* (DISCIPLINED DISCIPLINES SELF-DISCIPLINE)
Dt 4:36 made you hear his voice to *d* you.
11: 2 and experienced the *d*
21:18 listen to them when they *d* him,
Job 5:17 so do not despise the *d*
Ps 6: 1 or *d* me in your wrath.
38: 1 or *d* me in your wrath.
39:11 You rebuke and *d* men for their sin;
94:12 Blessed is the man you *d*, O LORD
Pr 1: 2 for attaining wisdom and *d*;
1: 7 but fools despise wisdom and *d*.
3:11 do not despise the LORD's *d*
5:12 You will say, "How I hated *d*!
5:23 He will die for lack of *d*,
6:23 and the corrections of *d*
10:17 He who heeds *d* shows the way
12: 1 Whoever loves *d* loves knowledge,
13:18 He who ignores *d* comes to poverty
13:24 who loves him is careful to *d* him.
15: 5 A fool spurns his father's *d*,
15:10 Stern *d* awaits him who leaves
15:32 He who ignores *d* despises himself,
19:18 *D* your son, for in that there is hope
22:15 the rod of *d* will drive it far
23:13 Do not withhold *d* from a child;
23:23 get wisdom, *d* and understanding.
29:17 *D* your son, and he will give you
Jer 17:23 would not listen or respond to *d*.
30:11 I will *d* you but only with justice;
32:33 would not listen or respond to *d*.
46:28 I will *d* you but only with justice;
Hos 5: 2 I will *d* all of them.
Heb 12: 5 do not make light of the Lord's *d*,
12: 7 as *d*; God is treating you
12: 8 (and everyone undergoes *d*),
12:11 No *d* seems pleasant at the time,
Rev 3:19 Those whom I love I rebuke and *d*.

DISCIPLINED* (DISCIPLINE)
Pr 1: 3 for acquiring a *d* and prudent life,
Isa 26:16 when you *d* them,
Jer 31:18 and I have been *d*.

Jas 1: 6 he must believe and not *d,*
Jude :22 Be merciful to those who *d;*

DOUBTING* (DOUBT)
Jn 20:27 Stop *d* and believe."

DOUBTS* (DOUBT)
Lk 24:38 and why do *d* rise in your minds?
Ro 14:23 the man who has *d* is condemned
Jas 1: 6 he who *d* is like a wave of the sea,

DOVE (DOVES)
Ge 8: 8 Then he sent out a *d* to see
Mt 3:16 Spirit of God descending like a *d*

DOVES (DOVE)
Lev 12: 8 is to bring two *d* or two young
Mt 10:16 as snakes and as innocent as *d.*
Lk 2:24 "a pair of *d* or two young pigeons."

DOWNCAST
Ps 42: 5 Why are you *d,* O my soul?
2Co 7: 6 But God, who comforts the *d,*

DOWNFALL
Hos 14: 1 Your sins have been your *d!*

DRAGON
Rev 12: 7 and his angels fought against the *d,*
13: 2 The *d* gave the beast his power
20: 2 He seized the *d,* that ancient

DRAW (DRAWING DRAWS)
Mt 26:52 "for all who *d* the sword will die
Jn 12:32 up from the earth, will *d* all men
Heb 10:22 let us *d* near to God

DRAWING (DRAW)
Lk 21:28 because your redemption is *d* near

DRAWS (DRAW)
Jn 6:44 the Father who sent me *d* him,

DREAD (DREADFUL)
Ps 53: 5 they were, overwhelmed with *d,*

DREADFUL (DREAD)
Mt 24:19 How *d* it will be in those days
Heb 10:31 It is a *d* thing to fall into the hands

DREAM
Joel 2:28 your old men will *d* dreams,
Ac 2:17 your old men will *d* dreams.

DRESS
1Ti 2: 9 I also want women to *d* modestly,

DRIFT*
Heb 2: 1 so that we do not *d* away.

DRINK (DRINKING DRINKS DRUNK DRUNKARD DRUNKARD'S DRUNKARDS DRUNKENNESS)
Ex 29:40 of a hin of wine as a *d* offering.
Nu 6: 3 He must not *d* grape juice
Jdg 7: 5 from those who kneel down to *d."*
2Sa 23:15 that someone would get me a *d*
Pr 5:15 *D* water from your own cistern,
Mt 20:22 "Can you *d* the cup I am going to *d*
26:27 saying, "*D* from it, all of you.
Mk 16:18 and when they *d* deadly poison,
Lk 12:19 Take life easy; eat, *d* and be merry
Jn 7:37 let him come to me and *d.*
18:11 Shall I not *d* the cup the Father has
1Co 10: 4 and drank the same spiritual *d;*
12:13 were all given the one Spirit to *d.*
Php 2:17 being poured out like a *d* offering
2Ti 4: 6 being poured out like a *d* offering,
Rev 14:10 too, will *d* of the wine of God's fury
21: 6 to *d* without cost from the spring

DRINKING (DRINK)
Ro 14:17 God is not a matter of eating and *d,*

DRINKS (DRINK)
Isa 5:22 and champions at mixing *d,*
Jn 4:13 "Everyone who *d* this water will be
6:54 and *d* my blood has eternal life,
1Co 11:27 or *d* the cup of the Lord

DRIPPING
Pr 19:13 wife is like a constant *d.*
27:15 a constant *d* on a rainy day;

DRIVE (DRIVES)
Ex 23:30 Little by little I will *d* them out
Nu 33:52 *d* out all the inhabitants of the land
Jos 13:13 Israelites did not *d* out the people
23:13 will no longer *d* out these nations
Pr 22:10 *D* out the mocker, and out goes
Mt 10: 1 authority to *d* out evil spirits
Jn 6:37 comes to me I will never *d* away.

DRIVES (DRIVE)
Mt 12:26 If Satan *d* out Satan, he is divided
1Jn 4:18 But perfect love *d* out fear,

DROP (DROPS)
Pr 17:14 so *d* the matter before a dispute
Isa 40:15 Surely the nations are like a *d*

DROPS (DROP)
Lk 22:44 his sweat was like *d* of blood falling

DROSS
Ps 119:119 of the earth you discard like *d;*
Pr 25: 4 Remove the *d* from the silver,

DROUGHT
Jer 17: 8 It has no worries in a year of *d*

DROWNED
Ex 15: 4 are *d* in the Red Sea.
Mt 18: 6 and to be *d* in the depths of the sea.
Heb 11:29 tried to do so, they were *d.*

DROWSINESS*
Pr 23:21 and *d* clothes them in rags.

DRUNK (DRINK)
1Sa 1:13 Eli thought she was *d* and said
Ac 2:15 men are not *d,* as you suppose.
Eph 5:18 Do not get *d* on wine, which leads

DRUNKARD (DRINK)
Mt 11:19 and a *d,* a friend of tax collectors
1Co 5:11 or a slanderer, a *d* or a swindler.

DRUNKARD'S* (DRINK)
Pr 26: 9 Like a thornbush in a *d* hand

DRUNKARDS (DRINK)
Pr 23:21 for *d* and gluttons become poor,
1Co 6:10 nor the greedy nor *d* nor slanderers

DRUNKENNESS (DRINK)
Lk 21:34 weighed down with dissipation, *d*
Ro 13:13 and *d,* not in sexual immorality
Gal 5:21 factions and envy; *d,* orgies,
1Ti 3: 3 not given to *d,* not violent
1Pe 4: 3 living in debauchery, lust, *d,* orgies,

DRY
Ge 1: 9 place, and let *d* ground appear."
Ex 14:16 go through the sea on *d* ground.
Jos 3:17 the crossing on *d* ground.
Isa 53: 2 and like a root out of *d* ground.
Eze 37: 4 '*D* bones, hear the word

DULL
Isa 6:10 make their ears *d*
2Co 3:14 But their minds were made *d,*

DUST
Ge 2: 7 man from the *d* of the ground
3:19 for *d* you are
Job 42: 6 and repent in *d* and ashes."
Ps 22:15 you lay me in the *d* of death.
103:14 he remembers that we are *d.*
Ecc 3:20 all come from *d,* and to *d* all return.
Mt 10:14 shake the *d* off your feet
1Co 15:47 was of the *d* of the earth,

DUTIES (DUTY)
2Ti 4: 5 discharge all the *d* of your ministry

DUTY (DUTIES)
Ecc 12:13 for this is the whole *d* of man.
Ac 23: 1 I have fulfilled my *d* to God
1Co 7: 3 husband should fulfill his marital *d*

DWELL (DWELLING DWELLINGS DWELLS DWELT)
Ex 25: 8 for me, and I will *d* among them.
2Sa 7: 5 the one to build me a house to *d* in?
1Ki 8:27 "But will God really *d* on earth?
Ps 23: 6 I will *d* in the house of the LORD
37: 3 *d* in the land and enjoy safe pasture
61: 4 I long to *d* in your tent forever
Pr 8:12 wisdom, *d* together with prudence;
Isa 33:14 of us can *d* with the consuming fire
43:18 do not *d* on the past.
Jn 5:38 nor does his word *d* in you,
Eph 3:17 so that Christ may *d* in your hearts
Col 1:19 to have all his fullness *d* in him,
3:16 the word of Christ *d* in you richly

DWELLING (DWELL)
Lev 26:11 I will put my *d* place among you,
Dt 26:15 from heaven, your holy *d* place,
Ps 90: 1 Lord, you have been our *d* place
2Co 5: 2 to be clothed with our heavenly *d,*
Eph 2:22 to become a *d* in which God lives

DWELLINGS (DWELL)
Lk 16: 9 will be welcomed into eternal *d.*

DWELLS (DWELL)
Ps 46: 4 holy place where the Most High *d.*
91: 1 He who *d* in the shelter

DWELT (DWELL)
Dt 33:16 of him who *d* in the burning bush.

DYING (DIE)
Ro 7: 6 by *d* to what once bound us,
2Co 6: 9 yet regarded as unknown; *d,*

EAGER
Pr 31:13 and works with *e* hands.
Ro 8:19 The creation waits in *e* expectation
1Co 14:12 Since you are *e* to have spiritual
14:39 my brothers, be *e* to prophesy,
Tit 2:14 a people that are his very own, *e*
1Pe 5: 2 greedy for money, but *e* to serve;

EAGLE (EAGLE'S EAGLES)
Dt 32:11 like an *e* that stirs up its nest
Eze 1:10 each also had the face of an *e.*
Rev 4: 7 the fourth was like a flying *e.*
12:14 given the two wings of a great *e,*

EAGLE'S (EAGLE)
Ps 103: 5 your youth is renewed like the *e.*

EAGLES (EAGLE)
Isa 40:31 They will soar on wings like *e;*

EAR (EARS)
Ex 21: 6 and pierce his *e* with an awl.
Ps 5: 1 Give *e* to my words, O LORD,
Pr 2: 2 turning your *e* to wisdom
1Co 2: 9 no *e* has heard,
12:16 if the *e* should say, "Because I am
Rev 2: 7 He who has an *e,* let him hear what

EARN (EARNED EARNINGS)
2Th 3:12 down and *e* the bread they eat.

EARNED (EARN)
Pr 31:31 Give her the reward she has *e,*

EARNESTNESS
2Co 7:11 what *e,* what eagerness
8: 7 in complete *e* and in your love

EARNINGS (EARN)
Pr 31:16 out of her *e* she plants a vineyard.

EARRING (EARRINGS)
Pr 25:12 Like an *e* of gold or an ornament

EARRINGS (EARRING)
Ex 32: 2 Take off the gold *e* that your wives,

EARS (EAR)
Job 42: 5 My *e* had heard of you
Ps 34:15 and his *e* are attentive to their cry;
Pr 21:13 If a man shuts his *e* to the cry
26:17 Like one who seizes a dog by the *e*
Isa 6:10 hear with their *e,*
Mt 11:15 He who has *e,* let him hear.
2Ti 4: 3 to say what their itching *e* want
1Pe 3:12 his *e* are attentive to their prayer,

EARTH (EARTH'S EARTHLY)
Ge 1: 1 God created the heavens and the *e.*
1: 2 Now the *e* was formless and empty,
7:24 The waters flooded the *e*
14:19 Creator of heaven and *e.*
1Ki 8:27 "But will God really dwell on *e?*
Job 26: 7 he suspends the *e* over nothing.
Ps 24: 1 *e* is the LORD's, and everything
46: 6 he lifts his voice, the *e* melts.
90: 2 or you brought forth the *e*
97: 5 before the Lord of all the *e.*
102:25 you laid the foundations of the *e,*
108: 5 and let your glory be over all the *e.*
Pr 8:26 before he made the *e* or its fields
Isa 6: 3 the whole *e* is full of his glory."
24:20 The *e* reels like a drunkard,
37:16 You have made heaven and *e.*
40:22 enthroned above the circle of the *e,*
51: 6 the *e* will wear out like a garment
54: 5 he is called the God of all the *e.*
55: 9 the heavens are higher than the *e,*
65:17 new heavens and a new *e.*
66: 1 and the *e* is my footstool.
Jer 10:10 When he is angry, the *e* trembles;
23:24 "Do not I fill heaven and *e?"*
33:25 and the fixed laws of heaven and *e,*
Hab 2:20 let all the *e* be silent before him."
Mt 5: 5 for they will inherit the *e.*
5:35 or by the *e,* for it is his footstool;
6:10 done on *e* as it is in heaven.
16:19 bind on *e* will be bound
24:35 Heaven and *e* will pass away,
28:18 and on *e* has been given to me.
Lk 2:14 on *e* peace to men
Jn 12:32 when I am lifted up from the *e,*
Ac 4:24 "you made the heaven and the *e*
7:49 and the *e* is my footstool.
1Co 10:26 The *e* is the Lord's, and everything
Eph 3:15 in heaven and on *e* derives its name
Php 2:10 in heaven and on *e* and under the *e,*
Heb 1:10 you laid the foundations of the *e,*
2Pe 3:13 to a new heaven and a new *e,*
Rev 8: 7 A third of the *e* was burned up,
12:12 But woe to the *e* and the sea,
20:11 *E* and sky fled from his presence,
21: 1 I saw a new heaven and a new *e,*
21: 1 and the first *e* had passed away,

EARTH'S (EARTH)
Job 38: 4 when I laid the *e* foundation?

EARTHENWARE
Pr 26:23 Like a coating of glaze over *e*

EARTHLY (EARTH)
Eph 4: 9 descended to the lower, *e* regions?
Php 3:19 Their mind is on *e* things.
Col 3: 2 on things above, not on *e* things.
3: 5 whatever belongs to your *e* nature:

EARTHQUAKE (EARTHQUAKES)
Eze 38:19 at that time there shall be a great *e*
Mt 28: 2 There was a violent *e,* for an angel
Rev 6:12 There was a great *e.*

EARTHQUAKES (EARTHQUAKE)
Mt 24: 7 There will be famines and *e*

EASE
Pr 1:33 and be at *e,* without fear of harm."

EASIER (EASY)
Lk 16:17 It is *e* for heaven and earth
18:25 it is *e* for a camel to go

EAST
Ge 2: 8 God had planted a garden in the *e,*
Ps 103:12 as far as the *e* is from the west,
Eze 43: 2 God of Israel coming from the *e.*
Mt 2: 1 Magi from the *e* came to Jerusalem
2: 2 We saw his star in the *e*

EASY (EASIER)
Mt 11:30 For my yoke is *e* and my burden is

EAT (ATE EATEN EATER EATING EATS)
Ge 2:16 "You are free to *e* from any tree
2:17 but you must not *e* from the tree
3:19 you will *e* your food
Ex 12:11 *E* it in haste; it is the LORD's
Lev 11: 2 these are the ones you may *e:*
17:12 "None of you may *e* blood,
Dt 8:16 He gave you manna to *e*
14: 4 These are the animals you may *e:*
Jdg 14:14 "Out of the eater, something to *e;*
2Sa 9: 7 and you will always *e* at my table."
Pr 31:27 and does not *e* the bread of idleness
Isa 55: 1 come, buy and *e!*
65:25 and the lion will *e* straw like the ox,
Eze 3: 1 *e* what is before you, *e* this scroll;
Mt 14:16 You give them something to *e."*
15: 2 wash their hands before they *e!"*
26:26 "Take and *e;* this is my body."
Mk 14:14 where I may *e* the Passover
Lk 10: 8 and are welcomed, *e* what is set
12:19 Take life easy; *e,* drink
12:22 what you will *e;* or about your body
Jn 4:32 to *e* that you know nothing about."
6:31 bread from heaven to *e.'"*
6:52 can this man give us his flesh to *e?"*
Ac 10:13 Kill and *e."*
Ro 14: 2 faith allows him to *e* everything,
14:15 is distressed because of what you *e,*
14:20 to *e* anything that causes someone
14:21 It is better not to *e* meat
1Co 5:11 With such a man do not even *e.*
8:13 if what I *e* causes my brother to fall
10:25 *E* anything sold in the meat market
10:27 *e* whatever is put before you
10:31 So whether you *e* or drink
11:26 For whenever you *e* this bread
2Th 3:10 man will not work, he shall not *e."*
Rev 2: 7 the right to *e* from the tree of life,
3:20 I will come in and *e* with him,

EATEN (EAT)
Ge 3:11 Have you *e* from the tree that I
Ac 10:14 "I have never *e* anything impure
Rev 10:10 when I had *e* it, my stomach turned

EATER (EAT)
Isa 55:10 for the sower and bread for the *e,*

EATING (EAT)
Ex 34:28 and forty nights without *e* bread
Ro 14:15 not by your *e* destroy your brother
14:17 kingdom of God is not a matter of *e*
14:23 because his *e* is not from faith;
1Co 8: 4 about *e* food sacrificed to idols:
8:10 you who have this knowledge *e*
Jude :12 *e* with you without the slightest

EATS (EAT)
1Sa 14:24 "Cursed be any man who *e* food
Lk 15: 2 "This man welcomes sinners and *e*
Jn 6:51 If anyone *e* of this bread, he will live
6:54 Whoever *e* my flesh and drinks my
Ro 14: 2 faith is weak, *e* only vegetables.
14: 3 man who *e* everything must not
14: 6 He who *e* meat, *e* to the Lord,
14:23 has doubts is condemned if he *e,*
1Co 11:27 whoever *e* the bread or drinks

EBAL
Dt 11:29 and on Mount *E* the curses.
Jos 8:30 Joshua built on Mount *E* an altar

EBENEZER
1Sa 7:12 He named it *E,* saying, "Thus far

EDEN
Ge 2: 8 in *E;* and there he put the man
Eze 28:13 You were in *E,*

EDGE (DOUBLE-EDGED)
Mt 9:20 and touched the *e* of his cloak.

EDICT
Heb 11:23 they were not afraid of the king's *e.*

EDIFICATION (EDIFIED EDIFIES)
Ro 14:19 leads to peace and to mutual *e.*

EDIFIED* (EDIFICATION)
1Co 14: 5 so that the church may be *e.*
14:17 but the other man is not *e.*

EDIFIES* (EDIFICATION)
1Co 14: 4 but he who prophesies *e* the church
14: 4 speaks in a tongue *e* himself,

EDOM
Ge 36: 1 the account of Esau (that is, *E).*
36: 8 *E)* settled in the hill country of Seir
Isa 63: 1 Who is this coming from *E,*
Ob : 1 Sovereign LORD says about *E—*

EDUCATED*
Ac 7:22 Moses was *e* in all the wisdom

EFFECT* (EFFECTIVE)
Job 41:26 sword that reaches him has no *e,*
Isa 32:17 *e* of righteousness will be quietness
Ac 7:53 put into *e* through angels
1Co 15:10 his grace to me was not without *e.*
Gal 3:19 put into *e* through angels
Eph 1:10 put into *e* when the times will have
Heb 9:17 it never takes *e* while the one who
9:18 put into *e* without blood.

EFFECTIVE* (EFFECT)
1Co 16: 9 a great door for *e* work has opened
Jas 5:16 a righteous man is powerful and *e.*

EFFORT*
Ecc 2:19 into which I have poured my *e*
Da 6:14 and made every *e* until sundown
Lk 13:24 "Make every *e* to enter
Jn 5:44 yet make no *e* to obtain the praise
Ro 9:16 depend on man's desire or *e,*
14:19 make every *e* to do what leads
Gal 3: 3 to attain your goal by human *e?*
Eph 4: 3 Make every *e* to keep the unity
1Th 2:16 to all men in their *e* to keep us
2:17 intense longing we made every *e*
Heb 4:11 make every *e* to enter that rest,
12:14 Make every *e* to live in peace
2Pe 1: 5 make every *e* to add
1:15 And I will make every *e* to see that
3:14 make every *e* to be found spotless,

EGG
Lk 11:12 for an *e,* will give him a scorpion?

EGLON
1. Fat king of Moab killed by Ehud (Jdg 3:12–30).
2. City in Canaan (Jos 10).

EGYPT (EGYPTIANS)
Ge 12:10 went down to *E* to live there
37:28 Ishmaelites, who took him to *E.*
42: 3 went down to buy grain from *E.*
45:20 the best of all *E* will be yours.' "
46: 6 and all his offspring went to *E.*
47:27 Now the Israelites settled in *E*
Ex 3:11 and bring the Israelites out of *E?"*
12:40 lived in *E* was 430 years.
12:41 all the LORD's divisions left *E.*
32: 1 Moses who brought us up out of *E,*
Nu 11:18 We were better off in *E!"*
14: 4 choose a leader and go back to *E."*
24: 8 "God brought them out of *E;*
Dt 6:21 "We were slaves of Pharaoh in *E,*
1Ki 4:30 greater than all the wisdom of *E.*
10:28 horses were imported from *E*
11:40 but Jeroboam fled to *E,*
14:25 king of *E* attacked Jerusalem.
2Ch 35:20 Neco king of *E* went up to fight
36: 3 The king of *E* dethroned him
Isa 19:23 a highway from *E* to Assyria.
Hos 11: 1 and out of *E* I called my son.
Mt 2:15 "Out of *E* I called my son."
Heb 11:27 By faith he left *E,* not fearing
Rev 11: 8 is figuratively called Sodom and *E,*

EGYPTIANS (EGYPT)
Nu 14:13 "Then the *E* will hear about it!

EHUD
Left-handed judge who delivered Israel from Moabite king, Eglon (Jdg 3:12–30).

EKRON
1Sa 5:10 So they sent the ark of God to *E.*

ELAH
Son of Baasha; king of Israel (1Ki 16:6–14).

ELATION
Pr 28:12 righteous triumph, there is great *e;*

ELDER* (ELDERLY ELDERS)
Isa 3: 2 the soothsayer and *e,*
1Ti 5:19 an accusation against an *e*
Tit 1: 6 *e* must be blameless, the husband
1Pe 5: 1 among you, I appeal as a fellow *e,*
2Jn : 1 The *e,* To the chosen lady
3Jn : 1 The *e,* To my dear friend Gaius,

ELDERLY* (ELDER)
Lev 19:32 show respect for the *e*

ELDERS (ELDER)
1Ki 12: 8 rejected the advice the *e* gave him
Mt 15: 2 break the tradition of the *e?*
Mk 7: 3 holding to the tradition of the *e.*
7: 5 to the tradition of the *e* instead
Ac 11:30 gift to the *e* by Barnabas
14:23 and Barnabas appointed *e* for them
15: 2 the apostles and *e* about this
15: 4 the church and the apostles and *e,*
15: 6 and *e* met to consider this question.
15:22 and *e,* with the whole church,
15:23 The apostles and *e,* your brothers,
16: 4 and *e* in Jerusalem for the people
20:17 to Ephesus for the *e* of the church.
21:18 and all the *e* were present.
23:14 They went to the chief priests and *e*
24: 1 to Caesarea with some of the *e*
1Ti 4:14 when the body of *e* laid their hands
5:17 The *e* who direct the affairs
Tit 1: 5 and appoint *e* in every town,
Jas 5:14 He should call the *e* of the church
1Pe 5: 1 To the *e* among you, I appeal
Rev 4: 4 seated on them were twenty-four *e.*
4:10 the twenty-four *e* fall

ELEAZAR
Third son of Aaron (Ex 6:23–25). Succeeded Aaron as high priest (Nu 20:26; Dt 10:6). Allotted land to tribes (Jos 14:1). Death (Jos 24:33).

ELECT* (ELECTION)
Mt 24:22 the sake of the *e* those days will be
24:24 miracles to deceive even the *e*—
24:31 and they will gather his *e*
Mk 13:20 sake of the *e,* whom he has chosen,
13:22 and miracles to deceive the *e*—
13:27 gather his *e* from the four winds,
Ro 11: 7 it did not obtain, but the *e* did.
1Ti 5:21 and Christ Jesus and the *e* angels,
2Ti 2:10 everything for the sake of the *e,*
Tit 1: 1 Christ for the faith of God's *e*
1Pe 1: 1 To God's *e,* strangers in the world,

ELECTION* (ELECT)
Ro 9:11 God's purpose in *e* might stand:
11:28 but as far as *e* is concerned,
2Pe 1:10 to make your calling and *e* sure.

ELEMENTARY* (ELEMENTS)
Heb 5:12 someone to teach you the *e* truths
6: 1 us leave the *e* teachings about

ELEMENTS* (ELEMENTARY)
2Pe 3:10 the *e* will be destroyed by fire,
3:12 and the *e* will melt in the heat.

ELEVATE*
2Co 11: 7 to *e* you by preaching the gospel

ELI
High priest in youth of Samuel (1Sa 1–4). Blessed Hannah (1Sa 1:12–18); raised Samuel (1Sa 2:11–26). Prophesied against because of wicked sons (1Sa 2:27–36). Death of Eli and sons (1Sa 4:11–22).

ELIHU
One of Job's friends (Job 32–37).

ELIJAH
Prophet; predicted famine in Israel (1Ki 17:1; Jas 5:17). Fed by ravens (1Ki 17:2–6). Raised Sidonian widow's son (1Ki 17:7–24). Defeated prophets of Baal at Carmel (1Ki 18:16–46). Ran from Jezebel (1Ki 19:1–9). Prophesied death of Azariah (2Ki 1). Succeeded by Elishah (1Ki 19:19–21; 2Ki 2:1–18). Taken to heaven in whirlwind (2Ki 2:11–12).
Return prophesied (Mal 4:5–6); equated with John the Baptist (Mt 17:9–13; Mk 9:9–13; Lk 1:17). Appeared with Moses in transfiguration of Jesus (Mt 17:1–8; Mk 9:1–8).

ELIMELECH
Ru 1: 3 Now *E,* Naomi's husband, died,

ELIPHAZ
1. Firstborn of Esau (Ge 36).
2. One of Job's friends (Job 4–5; 15; 22).

ELISHA
Prophet; successor of Elijah (1Ki 19:16–21); inherited his cloak (2Ki 2:1–18). Purified bad water (2Ki 2:19–22). Cursed young men (2Ki 2:23–25). Aided Israel's defeat of Moab (2Ki 3). Provided widow with oil (2Ki 4:1–7). Raised Shunammite woman's son (2Ki 4:8–37). Purified food (2Ki 4:38–41). Fed 100 men (2Ki 4:42–44). Healed Naaman's leprosy (2Ki 5). Made axhead float (2Ki 6:1–7). Captured Arameans (2Ki 6:8–23). Political adviser to Israel (2Ki 6:24–8:6; 9:1–3; 13:14–19), Damascus (2Ki 8:7–15). Death (2Ki 13:20).

ELIZABETH*
Mother of John the Baptist, relative of Mary (Lk 1:5–58).

ELKANAH
Husband of Hannah, father of Samuel (1Sa 1–2).

ELOI*
Mt 27:46 *"E, E, lama sabachthani?"—*
Mk 15:34 *"E, E, lama sabachthani?"—*

ELOQUENCE* (ELOQUENT)
1Co 2: 1 come with *e* or superior wisdom

ELOQUENT* (ELOQUENCE)
Ex 4:10 "O Lord, I have never been *e,*

ELYMAS
Ac 13: 8 *E* the sorcerer (for that is what his

EMBEDDED*
Ecc 12:11 sayings like firmly *e* nails—

EMBERS
Pr 26:21 As charcoal to *e* and as wood to fire

EMBITTER* (BITTER)
Col 3:21 Fathers, do not *e* your children,

EMBODIMENT* (BODY)
Ro 2:20 have in the law the *e* of knowledge

EMPTIED (EMPTY)
1Co 1:17 the cross of Christ be *e* of its power.

EMPTY (EMPTIED)
Ge 1: 2 Now the earth was formless and *e,*
Job 26: 7 the northern ›skiesſ over *e* space;
Isa 45:18 he did not create it to be *e,*
55:11 It will not return to me *e,*
Jer 4:23 and it was formless and *e;*
Lk 1:53 but has sent the rich away *e.*
Eph 5: 6 no one deceive you with *e* words,
1Pe 1:18 from the *e* way of life handed
2Pe 2:18 For they mouth *e,* boastful words

ENABLE (ABLE)
Lk 1:74 to *e* us to serve him without fear
Ac 4:29 *e* your servants to speak your word

ENABLED* (ABLE)
Lev 26:13 *e* you to walk with heads held high.
Ru 4:13 And the LORD *e* her to conceive,
Jn 6:65 unless the Father has *e* him."
Ac 2: 4 other tongues as the Spirit *e* them.
7:10 and *e* him to gain the goodwill
Heb 11:11 was *e* to become a father

ENABLES (ABLE)
Php 3:21 by the power that *e* him

ENABLING* (ABLE)
Ac 14: 3 the message of his grace by *e* them

ENCAMPS* (CAMP)
Ps 34: 7 The angel of the LORD *e*

ENCOURAGE* (ENCOURAGED ENCOURAGEMENT ENCOURAGES ENCOURAGING)
Dt 1:38 *E* him, because he will lead Israel
3:28 and *e* and strengthen him,
2Sa 11:25 Say this to *e* Joab."
19: 7 Now go out and *e* your men.
Job 16: 5 But my mouth would *e* you;
Ps 10:17 you *e* them, and you listen
64: 5 They *e* each other in evil plans,
Isa 1:17 *e* the oppressed.
Jer 29: 8 to the dreams you *e* them to have.
Ac 15:32 to *e* and strengthen the brothers.
Ro 12: 8 if it is encouraging, let him *e;*
Eph 6:22 how we are, and that he may *e* you.

Col 4: 8 and that he may *e* your hearts.
1Th 3: 2 to strengthen and *e* you
4:18 Therefore *e* each other
5:11 Therefore *e* one another
5:14 those who are idle, *e* the timid,
2Th 2:17 *e* your hearts and strengthen you
2Ti 4: 2 rebuke and *e*— with great patience
Tit 1: 9 so that he can *e* others
2: 6 *e* the young men to be
2:15 *E* and rebuke with all authority.
Heb 3:13 But *e* one another daily, as long
10:25 but let us *e* one another—

ENCOURAGED* (ENCOURAGE)
Jdg 7:11 you will be *e* to attack the camp."
20:22 But the men of Israel *e* one another
2Ch 22: 3 for his mother *e* him
32: 6 and *e* them with these words:
35: 2 and *e* them in the service
Eze 13:22 you *e* the wicked not to turn
Ac 9:31 It was strengthened; and *e*
11:23 and *e* them all to remain true
16:40 met with the brothers and *e* them.
18:27 the brothers *e* him and wrote
27:36 They were all *e* and ate some food
28:15 men Paul thanked God and was *e*.
Ro 1:12 and I may be mutually *e*
1Co 14:31 everyone may be instructed and *e*.
2Co 7: 4 I am greatly *e;* in all our troubles
7:13 By all this we are *e*.
Php 1:14 brothers in the Lord have been *e*
Col 2: 2 My purpose is that they may be *e*
1Th 3: 7 persecution we were *e* about you
Heb 6:18 offered to us may be greatly *e*.

ENCOURAGEMENT* (ENCOURAGE)
Ac 4:36 Barnabas (which means Son of *E*),
13:15 a message of *e* for the people,
20: 2 speaking many words of *e*
Ro 15: 4 *e* of the Scriptures we might have
15: 5 and *e* give you a spirit of unity
1Co 14: 3 to men for their strengthening, *e*
2Co 7:13 to our own *e*, we were especially
Php 2: 1 If you have any *e* from being united
2Th 2:16 and by his grace gave us eternal *e*
Phm : 7 love has given me great joy and *e*,
Heb 12: 5 word of *e* that addresses you

ENCOURAGES* (ENCOURAGE)
Isa 41: 7 The craftsman *e* the goldsmith,

ENCOURAGING* (ENCOURAGE)
Ac 14:22 *e* them to remain true to the faith.
15:31 and were glad for its *e* message.
20: 1 for the disciples and, after *e* them,
Ro 12: 8 if it is *e*, let him encourage;
1Th 2:12 *e*, comforting and urging you
1Pe 5:12 *e* you and testifying that this is

ENCROACH
Pr 23:10 or *e* on the fields of the fatherless,

END (ENDS)
Ps 119:33 then I will keep them to the *e*.
119:112 to the very *e*.
Pr 1:19 Such is the *e* of all who go
5: 4 but in the *e* she is bitter as gall,
5:11 At the *e* of your life you will groan,
14:12 but in the *e* it leads to death.
14:13 and joy may *e* in grief.
16:25 but in the *e* it leads to death.
19:20 and in the *e* you will be wise.
20:21 will not be blessed at the *e*.
23:32 In the *e* it bites like a snake
25: 8 for what will you do in the *e*
28:23 in the *e* gain more favor
29:21 he will bring grief in the *e*.
Ecc 3:11 done from beginning to *e*.
7: 8 The *e* of a matter is better
12:12 making many books there is no *e*,
Eze 7: 2 The *e!* The *e* has come

Mt 10:22 firm to the *e* will be saved.
24:13 firm to the *e* will be saved.
24:14 nations, and then the *e* will come.
Lk 21: 9 but the *e* will not come right away
Ro 10: 4 Christ is the *e* of the law
1Co 15:24 the *e* will come, when he hands
Rev 21: 6 Omega, the Beginning and the *E*.
22:13 the Last, the Beginning and the *E*.

ENDS (END)
Ps 19: 4 their words to the *e* of the world.
Pr 20:17 he *e* up with a mouth full of gravel.
Isa 49: 6 salvation to the *e* of the earth."
62:11 proclamation to the *e* of the earth:
Ac 13:47 salvation to the *e* of the earth.' "
Ro 10:18 their words to the *e* of the world."

ENDURANCE* (ENDURE)
Ro 15: 4 through *e* and the encouragement
15: 5 May the God who gives *e*
2Co 1: 6 which produces in you patient *e*
6: 4 in great *e;* in troubles, hardships
Col 1:11 might so that you may have great *e*
1Th 1: 3 and your *e* inspired by hope
1Ti 6:11 faith, love, *e* and gentleness.
2Ti 3:10 patience, love, *e*, persecutions,
Tit 2: 2 and sound in faith, in love and in *e*.
Rev 1: 9 and patient *e* that are ours in Jesus,
13:10 This calls for patient *e*
14:12 This calls for patient *e* on the part

ENDURE (ENDURANCE ENDURED ENDURES ENDURING)
Ps 72:17 May his name *e* forever;
Pr 12:19 Truthful lips *e* forever,
27:24 for riches do not *e* forever,
Ecc 3:14 everything God does will *e* forever;
Da 2:44 to an end, but it will itself *e* forever.
Mal 3: 2 who can *e* the day of his coming?
1Co 4:12 when we are persecuted, we *e* it;
2Co 1: 8 far beyond our ability to *e*,
2Ti 2: 3 *E* hardship with us like a good
2:10 Therefore I *e* everything
2:12 if we *e*, / we will also reign
4: 5 head in all situations, *e* hardship,
Heb 12: 7 *E* hardship as discipline; God is
1Pe 2:20 a beating for doing wrong and *e* it?
2:20 suffer for doing good and you *e* it,
Rev 3:10 kept my command to *e* patiently,

ENDURED* (ENDURE)
Ps 123: 3 for we have *e* much contempt.
123: 4 We have *e* much ridicule
132: 1 and all the hardships he *e*.
Ac 13:18 and *e* their conduct forty years
2Ti 3:11 and Lystra, the persecutions I *e*.
Heb 12: 2 set before him *e* the cross,
12: 3 him who *e* such opposition
Rev 2: 3 and have *e* hardships for my name,

ENDURES (ENDURE)
Ps 102:12 renown *e* through all generations.
112: 9 his righteousness *e* forever;
136: 1 *His love e forever.*
Da 9:15 made for yourself a name that *e*
2Co 9: 9 his righteousness *e* forever."

ENDURING (ENDURE)
2Th 1: 4 persecutions and trials you are *e*.
1Pe 1:23 through the living and *e* word

ENEMIES (ENEMY)
Ps 23: 5 in the presence of my *e*.
110: 1 hand until I make your *e*
Pr 16: 7 his *e* live at peace with him.
Isa 59:18 wrath to his *e*
Mic 7: 6 a man's *e* are the members
Mt 5:44 Love your *e* and pray
10:36 a man's *e* will be the members
Lk 6:27 Love your *e*, do good
6:35 But love your *e*, do good to them,

Lk 20:43 hand until I make your *e*
Ro 5:10 For if, when we were God's *e*,
1Co 15:25 reign until he has put all his *e*
Php 3:18 many live as *e* of the cross of Christ
Heb 1:13 hand until I make your *e*
10:13 for his *e* to be made his footstool,

ENEMY (ENEMIES ENMITY)
Pr 24:17 Do not gloat when your *e* falls;
25:21 If your *e* is hungry, give him food
27: 6 but an *e* multiplies kisses.
29:24 of a thief is his own *e;*
Lk 10:19 to overcome all the power of the *e;*
Ro 12:20 "If your *e* is hungry, feed him;
1Co 15:26 The last *e* to be destroyed is death.
1Ti 5:14 and to give the *e* no opportunity
1Pe 5: 8 Your *e* the devil prowls

ENERGY*
Col 1:29 struggling with all his *e*, which

ENGRAVED
Isa 49:16 I have *e* you on the palms
2Co 3: 7 which was *e* in letters on stone,

ENHANCES*
Ro 3: 7 my falsehood *e* God's truthfulness

ENJOY (JOY)
Dt 6: 2 and so that you may *e* long life.
Ps 37: 3 dwell in the land and *e* safe pasture.
Pr 28:16 ill-gotten gain will *e* a long life.
Ecc 3:22 better for a man than to *e* his work,
Eph 6: 3 and that you may *e* long life
Heb 11:25 rather than to *e* the pleasures of sin
3Jn : 2 I pray that you may *e* good health

ENJOYMENT (JOY)
Ecc 4: 8 and why am I depriving myself of *e*
1Ti 6:17 us with everything for our *e*.

ENLARGE (ENLARGES)
2Co 9:10 *e* the harvest of your righteousness.

ENLARGES (ENLARGE)
Dt 33:20 Blessed is he who *e* Gad's domain!

ENLIGHTENED* (LIGHT)
Eph 1:18 that the eyes of your heart may be *e*
Heb 6: 4 for those who have once been *e*,

ENMITY* (ENEMY)
Ge 3:15 And I will put *e*

ENOCH
1. Son of Cain (Ge 4:17–18).
2. Descendant of Seth; walked with God and taken by him (Ge 5:18–24; Heb 11:5). Prophet (Jude 14).

ENSLAVED (SLAVE)
Gal 4: 9 Do you wish to be *e* by them all
Tit 3: 3 and *e* by all kinds of passions

ENSNARE (SNARE)
Pr 5:22 of a wicked man *e* him;
Ecc 7:26 but the sinner she will *e*.

ENSNARED* (SNARE)
Dt 7:25 for yourselves, or you will be *e* by it
12:30 be careful not to be *e*
Ps 9:16 the wicked are *e* by the work
Pr 6: 2 *e* by the words of your mouth,
22:25 and get yourself *e*.

ENTANGLED (ENTANGLES)
2Pe 2:20 and are again *e* in it and overcome,

ENTANGLES* (ENTANGLED)
Heb 12: 1 and the sin that so easily *e*,

ENTER (ENTERED ENTERING ENTERS ENTRANCE)
Ps 95:11 “They shall never *e* my rest.”
100: 4 *E* his gates with thanksgiving
Pr 2:10 For wisdom will *e* your heart,
Mt 5:20 will certainly not *e* the kingdom
7:13 *“E* through the narrow gate.
7:21 Lord,’ will *e* the kingdom of heaven
18: 3 you will never *e* the kingdom
18: 8 It is better for you to *e* life maimed
19:17 to *e* life, obey the commandments
19:23 man to *e* the kingdom of heaven.
Mk 9:43 It is better for you to *e* life maimed
9:45 It is better for you to *e* life crippled
9:47 for you to *e* the kingdom of God
10:15 like a little child will never *e* it.”
10:23 is for the rich to *e* the kingdom
Lk 13:24 will try to *e* and will not be able to.
13:24 “Make every effort to *e*
18:17 like a little child will never *e* it.”
18:24 is for the rich to *e* the kingdom
Jn 3: 5 no one can *e* the kingdom of God.
Heb 3:11 ‘They shall never *e* my rest.’ ”
4:11 make every effort to *e* that rest,

ENTERED (ENTER)
Ps 73:17 me till I *e* the sanctuary of God;
Eze 4:14 meat has ever *e* my mouth.”
Ac 11: 8 or unclean has ever *e* my mouth.’
Ro 5:12 as sin *e* the world through one man,
Heb 9:12 but he *e* the Most Holy Place once

ENTERING (ENTER)
Mt 21:31 the prostitutes are *e* the kingdom
Lk 11:52 have hindered those who were *e.*”
Heb 4: 1 the promise of *e* his rest still stands,

ENTERS (ENTER)
Mk 7:18 you see that nothing that *e* a man
Jn 10: 2 The man who *e* by the gate is

ENTERTAIN* (ENTERTAINED ENTERTAINMENT)
Jdg 16:25 “Bring out Samson to *e* us.”
Mt 9: 4 “Why do you *e* evil thoughts
1Ti 5:19 Do not *e* an accusation
Heb 13: 2 Do not forget to *e* strangers,

ENTERTAINED* (ENTERTAIN)
Ac 28: 7 and for three days *e* us hospitably.
Heb 13: 2 so doing some people have *e* angels

ENTERTAINMENT* (ENTERTAIN)
Da 6:18 without any *e* being brought to him

ENTHRALLED*
Ps 45:11 The king is *e* by your beauty;

ENTHRONED* (THRONE)
1Sa 4: 4 who is *e* between the cherubim.
2Sa 6: 2 who is *e* between the cherubim that
2Ki 19:15 of Israel, *e* between the cherubim,
1Ch 13: 6 who is *e* between the cherubim—
Ps 2: 4 The One *e* in heaven laughs;
9:11 to the LORD, *e* in Zion;
22: 3 Yet you are *e* as the Holy One;
29:10 The LORD sits *e* over the flood;
29:10 the LORD is *e* as King forever.
55:19 God, who is *e* forever,
61: 7 May he be *e* in God’s presence
80: 1 who sit *e* between the cherubim,
99: 1 he sits *e* between the cherubim,
102:12 But you, O LORD, sit *e* forever;
113: 5 the One who sits *e* on high,
132:14 here I will sit *e,* for I have desired it
Isa 14:13 I will sit *e* on the mount
37:16 of Israel, *e* between the cherubim,
40:22 He sits *e* above the circle
52: 2 rise up, sit *e,* O Jerusalem.

ENTHRONES* (THRONE)
Job 36: 7 he *e* them with kings

ENTHUSIASM*
2Co 8:17 he is coming to you with much *e*
9: 2 and your *e* has stirred most of them

ENTICE* (ENTICED ENTICES)
Pr 1:10 My son, if sinners *e* you,
2Pe 2:18 they *e* people who are just escaping
Rev 2:14 who taught Balak to *e* the Israelites

ENTICED* (ENTICE)
Dt 4:19 do not be *e* into bowing
11:16 or you will be *e* to turn away
2Ki 17:21 Jeroboam *e* Israel away
Job 31: 9 If my heart has been *e* by a woman,
31:27 so that my heart was secretly *e*
Jas 1:14 desire, he is dragged away and *e.*

ENTICES* (ENTICE)
Dt 13: 6 your closest friend secretly *e* you,
Job 36:18 Be careful that no one *e* you
Pr 16:29 A violent man *e* his neighbor

ENTIRE
Gal 5:14 The *e* law is summed up

ENTRANCE (ENTER)
Mt 27:60 stone in front of the *e* to the tomb
Mk 15:46 a stone against the *e* of the tomb.
16: 3 away from the *e* of the tomb?”
Jn 11:38 cave with a stone laid across the *e.*
20: 1 had been removed from the *e.*

ENTRUST (TRUST)
Jn 2:24 Jesus would not *e* himself to them,
2Ti 2: 2 the presence of many witnesses *e*

ENTRUSTED (TRUST)
Jer 13:20 Where is the flock that was *e* to you
Jn 5:22 but has *e* all judgment to the Son,
Ro 3: 2 they have been *e* with the very
6:17 of teaching to which you were *e.*
1Co 4: 1 as those *e* with the secret things
1Th 2: 4 by God to be *e* with the gospel.
1Ti 1:11 of the blessed God, which he *e*
6:20 guard what has been *e* to your care.
2Ti 1:12 able to guard what I have *e* to him
1:14 Guard the good deposit that was *e*
Tit 1: 3 light through the preaching *e* to me
1: 7 Since an overseer is *e*
1Pe 2:23 he *e* himself to him who judges
5: 3 not lording it over those *e* to you,
Jude : 3 once for all *e* to the saints.

ENVIES
Jas 4: 5 spirit he caused to live in us *e*

ENVIOUS (ENVY)
Dt 32:21 I will make them *e*
Pr 24:19 or be *e* of the wicked,
Ro 10:19 “I will make you *e*

ENVOY
Pr 13:17 but a trustworthy *e* brings healing.

ENVY (ENVIOUS ENVYING)
Pr 3:31 Do not *e* a violent man
14:30 but *e* rots the bones.
23:17 Do not let your heart *e* sinners,
24: 1 Do not *e* wicked men,
Mk 7:22 malice, deceit, lewdness, *e,* slander
Ro 1:29 They are full of *e,* murder, strife,
11:14 arouse my own people to *e*
1Co 13: 4 It does not *e,* it does not boast,
Gal 5:21 factions and *e;* drunkenness, orgies
Php 1:15 that some preach Christ out of *e*
1Ti 6: 4 and quarrels about words that result in *e,*
Tit 3: 3 lived in malice and *e,* being hated
Jas 3:14 But if you harbor bitter *e*
3:16 where you have *e* and selfish
1Pe 2: 1 *e,* and slander of every kind.

ENVYING* (ENVY)
Gal 5:26 provoking and *e* each other.

EPHAH
Eze 45:11 The *e* and the bath are

EPHESUS
Ac 18:19 at *E,* where Paul left Priscilla
19: 1 the interior and arrived at *E.*
Eph 1: 1 To the saints in *E,* the faithful
Rev 2: 1 the angel of the church in *E* write:

EPHRAIM

1. Second son of Joseph (Ge 41:52; 46:20). Blessed as firstborn by Jacob (Ge 48). Tribe of numbered (Nu 1:33; 26:37), blessed (Dt 33:17), allotted land (Jos 16:4–9; Eze 48:5), failed to fully possess (Jos 16:10; Jdg 1:29).

2. Synonymous with Northern Kingdom (Isa 7:17; Hos 5).

EQUAL (EQUALITY EQUITY)
Dt 33:25 and your strength will *e* your days.
1Sa 9: 2 without *e* among the Israelites—
Isa 40:25 who is my *e?*” says the Holy One.
46: 5 you compare me or count me *e?*
Da 1:19 and he found none *e* to Daniel,
Jn 5:18 making himself *e* with God.
1Co 12:25 that its parts should have *e* concern
2Co 2:16 And who is *e* to such a task?

EQUALITY* (EQUAL)
2Co 8:13 pressed, but that there might be *e.*
8:14 Then there will be *e,* as it is written:
Php 2: 6 did not consider *e*

EQUIP* (EQUIPPED)
Heb 13:21 *e* you with everything good

EQUIPPED (EQUIP)
2Ti 3:17 man of God may be thoroughly *e*

EQUITY* (EQUAL)
Ps 96:10 he will judge the peoples with *e.*
98: 9 and the peoples with *e.*
99: 4 you have established *e;*

ERODES*
Job 14:18 “But as a mountain *e* and crumbles

ERROR (ERRORS)
Jas 5:20 Whoever turns a sinner from the *e*
2Pe 2:18 escaping from those who live in *e.*

ERRORS* (ERROR)
Ps 19:12 Who can discern his *e?*
Ecc 10: 4 calmness can lay great *e* to rest.

ESAU

Firstborn of Isaac, twin of Jacob (Ge 25:21–26). Also called Edom (Ge 25:30). Sold Jacob his birthright (Ge 25:29–34); lost blessing (Gen 27). Married Hittites (Ge 26:34), Ishmaelites (Ge 28:6–9). Reconciled to Jacob (Gen 33). Genealogy (Ge 36). The LORD chose Jacob over Esau (Mal 1:2–3), but gave Esau land (Dt 2:2–12). Descendants eventually obliterated (Ob 1–21; Jer 49:7–22).

ESCAPE (ESCAPED ESCAPES ESCAPING)
Ps 68:20 from the Sovereign LORD comes *e*
Pr 11: 9 through knowledge the righteous *e.*
Ro 2: 3 think you will *e* God’s judgment?
1Th 5: 3 woman, and they will not *e.*
2Ti 2:26 and *e* from the trap of the devil,
Heb 2: 3 how shall we *e* if we ignore such
12:25 If they did not *e* when they refused
2Pe 1: 4 and *e* the corruption in the world

ESCAPED (ESCAPE)
2Pe 2:20 If they have *e* the corruption

ESCAPES (ESCAPE)
Pr 12:13 but a righteous man *e* trouble.

ESCAPING (ESCAPE)
1Co 3:15 only as one *e* through the flames.
2Pe 2:18 they entice people who are just *e*

ESTABLISH (ESTABLISHED ESTABLISHES)
Ge 6:18 But I will *e* my covenant with you,
17:21 But my covenant I will *e* with Isaac
2Sa 7:11 the LORD himself will *e* a house
1Ki 9: 5 I will *e* your royal throne
1Ch 28: 7 I will *e* his kingdom forever
Ps 90:17 *e* the work of our hands for us—
Isa 26:12 LORD, you *e* peace for us;
Ro 10: 3 God and sought to *e* their own,
16:25 able to *e* you by my gospel
Heb 10: 9 sets aside the first to *e* the second.

ESTABLISHED (ESTABLISH)
Ge 9:17 the sign of the covenant I have *e*
Ex 6: 4 also *e* my covenant with them
Pr 16:12 a throne is *e* through righteousness.

ESTABLISHES (ESTABLISH)
Job 25: 2 he *e* order in the heights of heaven.
Isa 42: 4 till he *e* justice on earth.

ESTATE
Ps 136:23 who remembered us in our low *e*

ESTEEMED
Pr 22: 1 to be *e* is better than silver or gold.
Isa 53: 3 he was despised, and we *e* him not.

ESTHER
Jewess, originally named Hadassah, who lived in Persia; cousin of Mordecai (Est 2:7). Chosen queen of Xerxes (Est 2:8–18). Persuaded by Mordecai to foil Haman's plan to exterminate the Jews (Est 3–4). Revealed Haman's plans to Xerxes, resulting in Haman's death (Est 7), the Jews' preservation (Est 8–9), Mordecai's exaltation (Est 8:15; 9:4; 10). Decreed celebration of Purim (Est 9:18–32).

ETERNAL* (ETERNALLY ETERNITY)
Ge 21:33 the name of the LORD, the *E* God.
Dt 33:27 The *e* God is your refuge,
1Ki 10: 9 of the LORD's *e* love for Israel,
Ps 16:11 with *e* pleasures at your right hand.
21: 6 you have granted him *e* blessings
111:10 To him belongs *e* praise.
119:89 Your word, O LORD, is *e*;
119:160 all your righteous laws are *e*.
Ecc 12: 5 Then man goes to his *e* home
Isa 26: 4 LORD, the LORD, is the Rock *e*.
47: 7 the *e* queen!'
Jer 10:10 he is the living God, the *e* King.
Da 4: 3 His kingdom is an *e* kingdom;
4:34 His dominion is an *e* dominion;
Hab 3: 6 His ways are *e*.
Mt 18: 8 two feet and be thrown into *e* fire.
19:16 good thing must I do to get *e* life?"
19:29 as much and will inherit *e* life.
25:41 into the *e* fire prepared for the devil
25:46 but the righteous to *e* life."
25:46 they will go away to *e* punishment,
Mk 3:29 be forgiven; he is guilty of an *e* sin."
10:17 "what must I do to inherit *e* life?"
10:30 and in the age to come, *e* life.
Lk 10:25 "what must I do to inherit *e* life?"
16: 9 will be welcomed into *e* dwellings.
18:18 what must I do to inherit *e* life?"
18:30 and, in the age to come, *e* life."
Jn 3:15 believes in him may have *e* life.
3:16 him shall not perish but have *e* life.
3:36 believes in the Son has *e* life,
4:14 spring of water welling up to *e* life."
4:36 now he harvests the crop for *e* life,
5:24 believes him who sent me has *e* life
5:39 that by them you possess *e* life.
6:27 but for food that endures to *e* life,
Jn 6:40 believes in him shall have *e* life,
6:54 and drinks my blood has *e* life,
6:68 You have the words of *e* life.
10:28 I give them *e* life, and they shall
12:25 in this world will keep it for *e* life.
12:50 that his command leads to *e* life.
17: 2 all people that he might give *e* life
17: 3 this is *e* life: that they may know
Ac 13:46 yourselves worthy of *e* life,
13:48 were appointed for *e* life believed.
Ro 1:20 his *e* power and divine nature—
2: 7 and immortality, he will give *e* life.
5:21 righteousness to bring *e* life
6:22 to holiness, and the result is *e* life.
6:23 but the gift of God is *e* life
16:26 by the command of the *e* God,
2Co 4:17 for us an *e* glory that far outweighs
4:18 temporary, but what is unseen is *e*.
5: 1 from God, an *e* house in heaven,
Gal 6: 8 from the Spirit will reap *e* life.
Eph 3:11 to his *e* purpose which he
2Th 2:16 his grace gave us *e* encouragement
1Ti 1:16 believe on him and receive *e* life.
1:17 Now to the King *e*, immortal,
6:12 Take hold of the *e* life
2Ti 2:10 is in Christ Jesus, with *e* glory.
Tit 1: 2 resting on the hope of *e* life,
3: 7 heirs having the hope of *e* life.
Heb 5: 9 he became the source of *e* salvation
6: 2 of the dead, and *e* judgment.
9:12 having obtained *e* redemption.
9:14 through the *e* Spirit offered himself
9:15 the promised *e* inheritance—
13:20 of the *e* covenant brought back
1Pe 5:10 you to his *e* glory in Christ,
2Pe 1:11 into the *e* kingdom of our Lord
1Jn 1: 2 and we proclaim to you the *e* life,
2:25 what he promised us—even *e* life.
3:15 know that no murderer has *e* life
5:11 God has given us *e* life,
5:13 you may know that you have *e* life.
5:20 He is the true God and *e* life.
Jude : 7 who suffer the punishment of *e* fire.
:21 Christ to bring you to *e* life.
Rev 14: 6 and he had the *e* gospel to proclaim

ETERNALLY* (ETERNAL)
Gal 1: 8 let him be *e* condemned! As we
1: 9 let him be *e* condemned! Am I now

ETERNITY* (ETERNAL)
Ps 93: 2 you are from all *e*.
Pr 8:23 I was appointed from *e*,
Ecc 3:11 also set *e* in the hearts of men;

ETHIOPIAN*
Jer 13:23 Can the *E* change his skin
Ac 8:27 and on his way he met an *E* eunuch

EUNUCH (EUNUCHS)
Ac 8:27 on his way he met an Ethiopian *e*,

EUNUCHS (EUNUCH)
Isa 56: 4 "To the *e* who keep my Sabbaths,
Mt 19:12 For some are *e* because they were

EUTYCHUS*
Ac 20: 9 was a young man named *E*,

EVANGELIST* (EVANGELISTS)
Ac 21: 8 stayed at the house of Philip the *e*,
2Ti 4: 5 hardship, do the work of an *e*,

EVANGELISTS* (EVANGELIST)
Eph 4:11 some to be prophets, some to be *e*,

EVE*
Ge 3:20 Adam named his wife *E*,
4: 1 Adam lay with his wife *E*,
2Co 11: 3 as *E* was deceived by the serpent's
1Ti 2:13 For Adam was formed first, then *E*

EVEN-TEMPERED* (TEMPER)
Pr 17:27 and a man of understanding is *e*.

EVENING
Ge 1: 5 there was *e*, and there was morning

EVER (EVERLASTING FOREVER FOREVERMORE)
Ex 15:18 LORD will reign for *e* and *e*."
Dt 8:19 If you *e* forget the LORD your
1Ki 3:12 anyone like you, nor will there *e* be.
Job 4: 7 were the upright *e* destroyed?
Ps 5:11 let them *e* sing for joy.
10:16 The LORD is King for *e* and *e*;
21: 4 length of days, for *e* and *e*.
25: 3 will *e* be put to shame,
25:15 My eyes are *e* on the LORD,
26: 3 for your love is *e* before me,
45: 6 O God, will last for *e* and *e*;
45:17 nations will praise you for *e* and *e*.
48:14 For this God is our God for *e* and *e*;
52: 8 God's unfailing love for *e* and *e*.
61: 8 will I *e* sing praise to your name
71: 6 I will *e* praise you.
84: 4 they are *e* praising you.
89:33 nor will I *e* betray my faithfulness.
111: 8 They are steadfast for *e* and *e*,
119:44 your law, for *e* and *e*.
119:98 for they are *e* with me.
132:12 sit on your throne for *e* and *e*."
145: 1 I will praise your name for *e* and *e*.
145: 2 and extol your name for *e* and *e*.
145:21 his holy name for *e* and *e*.
Pr 4:18 shining *e* brighter till the full light
5:19 may you *e* be captivated
Isa 66: 8 Who has *e* heard of such a thing?
66: 8 Who has *e* seen such things?
Jer 7: 7 I gave your forefathers for *e* and *e*.
25: 5 and your fathers for *e* and *e*.
31:36 the descendants of Israel *e* cease
Da 2:20 be to the name of God for *e* and *e*;
7:18 it forever—yes, for *e* and *e*.'
12: 3 like the stars for *e* and *e*.
Mic 4: 5 our God for *e* and *e*.
Mt 13:14 you will be *e* seeing but never
13:14 " 'You will be *e* hearing
Mk 4:12 *e* hearing but never understanding;
Jn 1:18 No one has *e* seen God,
Gal 1: 5 to whom be glory for *e* and *e*.
Eph 3:21 all generations, for *e* and *e*!
Php 4:20 and Father be glory for *e* and *e*.
1Ti 1:17 be honor and glory for *e* and *e*.
2Ti 4:18 To him be glory for *e* and *e*.
Heb 1: 8 O God, will last for *e* and *e*,
13:21 to whom be glory for *e* and *e*.
1Pe 4:11 the glory and the power for *e* and *e*.
5:11 To him be the power for *e* and *e*.
1Jn 4:12 No one has *e* seen God;
Rev 1: 6 him be glory and power for *e* and *e*!
1:18 and behold I am alive for *e* and *e*!
21:27 Nothing impure will *e* enter it,
22: 5 And they will reign for *e* and *e*.

EVER-INCREASING* (INCREASE)
Ro 6:19 to impurity and to *e* wickedness,
2Co 3:18 into his likeness with *e* glory,

EVERLASTING* (EVER)
Ge 9:16 and remember the *e* covenant
17: 7 an *e* covenant between me and you
17: 8 I will give as an *e* possession to you
17:13 in your flesh is to be an *e* covenant.
17:19 an *e* covenant for his descendants
48: 4 *e* possession to your descendants
Nu 18:19 It is an *e* covenant of salt
Dt 33:15 and the fruitfulness of the *e* hills;
33:27 and underneath are the *e* arms.
2Sa 23: 5 made with me an *e* covenant,
1Ch 16:17 to Israel as an *e* covenant:
16:36 from *e* to *e*.
29:10 from *e* to *e*.

Ezr 9:12 to your children as an *e* inheritance
Ne 9: 5 your God, who is from *e* to *e*."
Ps 41:13 from *e* to *e*.
52: 5 God will bring you down to *e* ruin:
74: 3 toward these *e* ruins,
78:66 he put them to *e* shame.
90: 2 from *e* to *e* you are God.
103:17 But from *e* to *e*
105:10 to Israel as an *e* covenant:
106:48 from *e* to *e*.
119:142 Your righteousness is *e*
139:24 and lead me in the way *e*.
145:13 Your kingdom is an *e* kingdom,
Isa 9: 6 *E* Father, Prince of Peace.
24: 5 and broken the *e* covenant.
30: 8 it may be an *e* witness.
33:14 Who of us can dwell with *e* burning
35:10 *e* joy will crown their heads.
40:28 The LORD is the *e* God,
45:17 the LORD with an *e* salvation;
45:17 to ages *e*.
51:11 *e* joy will crown their heads.
54: 8 but with *e* kindness
55: 3 I will make an *e* covenant with you,
55:13 for an *e* sign,
56: 5 I will give them an *e* name
60:15 I will make you the *e* pride
60:19 for the LORD will be your *e* light,
60:20 the LORD will be your *e* light,
61: 7 and *e* joy will be theirs.
61: 8 and make an *e* covenant with them.
63:12 to gain for himself *e* renown,
Jer 5:22 an *e* barrier it cannot cross.
23:40 I will bring upon you *e* disgrace—
23:40 *e* shame that will not be forgotten."
25: 9 of horror and scorn, and an *e* ruin.
31: 3 "I have loved you with an *e* love;
32:40 I will make an *e* covenant
50: 5 the LORD in an *e* covenant
Eze 16:60 and I will establish an *e* covenant
37:26 with them; it will be an *e* covenant.
Da 7:14 dominion is an *e* dominion that will
7:27 His kingdom will be an *e* kingdom,
9:24 to bring in *e* righteousness,
12: 2 others to shame and *e* contempt.
12: 2 some to *e* life, others to shame
Mic 6: 2 you *e* foundations of the earth.
Hab 1:12 O LORD, are you not from *e*?
Jn 6:47 the truth, he who believes has *e* life.
2Th 1: 9 punished with *e* destruction
Jude : 6 bound with *e* chains for judgment

EVER-PRESENT*
Ps 46: 1 an *e* help in trouble

EVIDENCE (EVIDENT)
Jn 14:11 on the *e* of the miracles themselves.
Ac 11:23 and saw the *e* of the grace of God,
2Th 1: 5 All this is *e* that God's judgment is
Jas 2:20 do you want *e* that faith

EVIDENT (EVIDENCE)
Php 4: 5 Let your gentleness be *e* to all.

EVIL (EVILDOER EVILDOERS EVILS)
Ge 2: 9 of the knowledge of good and *e*.
3: 5 be like God, knowing good and *e*."
6: 5 of his heart was only *e* all the time.
Ex 32:22 how prone these people are to *e*.
Jdg 2:11 Then the Israelites did *e* in the eyes
3: 7 The Israelites did *e* in the eyes
3:12 Once again the Israelites did *e*
4: 1 the Israelites once again did *e*
6: 1 Again the Israelites did *e*
10: 6 Again the Israelites did *e*
13: 1 Again the Israelites did *e*
1Ki 11: 6 So Solomon did *e* in the eyes
16:25 But Omri did *e* in the eyes
2Ki 15:24 Pekahiah did *e* in the eyes
Job 1: 1 he feared God and shunned *e*.
1: 8 a man who fears God and shuns *e*."
Job 34:10 Far be it from God to do *e*,
36:21 Beware of turning to *e*,
Ps 5: 4 not a God who takes pleasure in *e*;
23: 4 I will fear no *e*,
34:13 keep your tongue from *e*
34:14 Turn from *e* and do good;
34:16 is against those who do *e*,
37: 1 Do not fret because of *e* men
37: 8 do not fret—it leads only to *e*.
37:27 Turn from *e* and do good;
49: 5 fear when *e* days come,
51: 4 and done what is *e* in your sight,
97:10 those who love the LORD hate *e*,
101: 4 I will have nothing to do with *e*.
141: 4 not my heart be drawn to what is *e*,
Pr 4:27 keep your foot from *e*.
8:13 To fear the LORD is to hate *e*;
10:23 A fool finds pleasure in *e* conduct,
11:19 he who pursues *e* goes to his death.
11:27 *e* comes to him who searches for it.
14:16 man fears the LORD and shuns *e*,
17:13 If a man pays back *e* for good,
20:30 Blows and wounds cleanse away *e*,
24:19 Do not fret because of *e* men
24:20 for the *e* man has no future hope,
26:23 are fervent lips with an *e* heart.
28: 5 *E* men do not understand justice,
29: 6 An *e* man is snared by his own sin,
Ecc 12:14 whether it is good or *e*.
Isa 5:20 Woe to those who call *e* good
13:11 I will punish the world for its *e*,
55: 7 and the *e* man his thoughts.
Jer 4:14 wash the *e* from your heart
18: 8 nation I warned repents of its *e*,
18:11 So turn from your *e* ways,
Eze 33:11 Turn! Turn from your *e* ways!
33:13 he will die for the *e* he has done.
33:15 and does no *e*, he will surely live;
Am 5:13 for the times are *e*.
Hab 1:13 Your eyes are too pure to look on *e*;
Zec 8:17 do not plot *e* against your neighbor,
Mt 5:45 He causes his sun to rise on the *e*
6:13 but deliver us from the *e* one.'
7:11 If you, then, though you are *e*,
12:34 you who are *e* say anything good?
12:35 and the *e* man brings *e* things out
12:35 out of the *e* stored up in him.
12:43 "When an *e* spirit comes out
15:19 out of the heart come *e* thoughts,
Mk 7:21 come *e* thoughts, sexual
Lk 6:45 and the *e* man brings *e* things out
11:13 If you then, though you are *e*,
Jn 3:19 of light because their deeds were *e*.
3:20 Everyone who does *e* hates
17:15 you protect them from the *e* one.
Ro 1:30 they invent ways of doing *e*;
2: 8 who reject the truth and follow *e*,
2: 9 for every human being who does *e*:
3: 8 "Let us do *e* that good may result"?
6:12 body so that you obey its *e* desires.
7:19 no, the *e* I do not want to do—
7:21 to do good, *e* is right there with me.
12: 9 Hate what is *e*; cling
12:17 Do not repay anyone *e* for *e*.
12:21 Do not be overcome by *e*,
14:16 good to be spoken of as *e*.
16:19 and innocent about what is *e*.
1Co 13: 6 Love does not delight in *e*
14:20 In regard to *e* be infants,
Eph 5:16 because the days are *e*.
6:12 forces of *e* in the heavenly realms.
6:16 all the flaming arrows of the *e* one.
Col 3: 5 impurity, lust, *e* desires and greed,
1Th 5:22 Avoid every kind of *e*.
2Th 3: 3 and protect you from the *e* one.
1Ti 6:10 of money is a root of all kinds of *e*.
2Ti 2:22 Flee the *e* desires of youth,
3: 6 are swayed by all kinds of *e* desires,
3:13 while *e* men and impostors will go
Heb 5:14 to distinguish good from *e*.
Jas 1:13 For God cannot be tempted by *e*,
1:21 and the *e* that is so prevalent,
3: 6 a world of *e* among the parts
3: 8 It is a restless *e*, full
1Pe 2:16 your freedom as a cover-up for *e*;
3: 9 Do not repay *e* with *e* or insult
3:10 must keep his tongue from *e*
3:17 for doing good than for doing *e*.
1Jn 2:13 you have overcome the *e* one.
2:14 and you have overcome the *e* one.
3:12 who belonged to the *e* one
5:18 and the *e* one cannot harm him.
5:19 is under the control of the *e* one.
3Jn :11 do not imitate what is *e*

EVILDOER* (EVIL)
2Sa 3:39 the LORD repay the *e* according
Ps 101: 8 I will cut off every *e*
Mal 4: 1 and every *e* will be stubble,

EVILDOERS* (EVIL)
1Sa 24:13 saying goes, 'From *e* come evil
Job 8:20 or strengthen the hands of *e*.
34: 8 He keeps company with *e*;
34:22 where *e* can hide.
Ps 14: 4 Will *e* never learn—
14: 6 You *e* frustrate the plans
26: 5 I abhor the assembly of *e*
36:12 See how the *e* lie fallen—
53: 4 Will the *e* never learn—
59: 2 Deliver me from *e*
64: 2 from that noisy crowd of *e*.
92: 7 and all *e* flourish,
92: 9 all *e* will be scattered.
94: 4 all the *e* are full of boasting.
94:16 will take a stand for me against *e*?
119:115 Away from me, you *e*,
125: 5 the LORD will banish with the *e*.
141: 4 deeds with men who are *e*;
141: 5 ever against the deeds of *e*;
141: 9 from the traps set by *e*.
Pr 21:15 but terror to *e*.
Isa 1: 4 a brood of *e*,
31: 2 against those who help *e*.
Jer 23:14 They strengthen the hands of *e*,
Hos 10: 9 the *e* in Gibeah?
Mal 3:15 Certainly the *e* prosper, and
Mt 7:23 you *e*!' "Therefore everyone who
Lk 13:27 Away from me, all you *e*!'
18:11 *e*, adulterers—or even like this tax

EVILS* (EVIL)
Mk 7:23 All these *e* come from inside

EWE
2Sa 12: 3 one little *e* lamb he had bought.

EXACT*
Ge 43:21 the *e* weight—in the mouth
Est 4: 7 including the *e* amount
Mt 2: 7 from them the *e* time the star had
Jn 4:53 realized that this was the *e* time
Ac 17:26 the *e* places where they should live.
Heb 1: 3 the *e* representation of his being,

EXALT* (EXALTED EXALTS)
Ex 15: 2 my father's God, and I will *e* him.
Jos 3: 7 begin to *e* you in the eyes
1Sa 2:10 and *e* the horn of his anointed."
1Ch 25: 5 the promises of God to *e* him.
29:12 power to *e* and give strength to all.
Job 19: 5 If indeed you would *e* yourselves
Ps 30: 1 I will *e* you, O LORD,
34: 3 let us *e* his name together.
35:26 may all who *e* themselves over me
37:34 He will *e* you to inherit the land;
38:16 *e* themselves over me
75: 6 or from the desert can *e* a man.
89:17 and by your favor you *e* our horn.
99: 5 *E* the LORD our God
99: 9 *E* the LORD our God

EXPLOIT* (EXPLOITED EXPLOITING EXPLOITS)
Pr 22:22 Do not *e* the poor because they are
Isa 58: 3 and *e* all your workers.
2Co 12:17 Did I *e* you through any
12:18 Titus did not *e* you, did he?
2Pe 2: 3 greed these teachers will *e* you

EXPLOITED* (EXPLOIT)
2Co 7: 2 no one, we have *e* no one.

EXPLOITING* (EXPLOIT)
Jas 2: 6 Is it not the rich who are *e* you?

EXPLOITS (EXPLOIT)
2Co 11:20 or *e* you or takes advantage of you

EXPLORE
Nu 13: 2 "Send some men to *e* the land

EXPOSE (EXPOSED)
1Co 4: 5 will *e* the motives of men's hearts.
Eph 5:11 of darkness, but rather *e* them.

EXPOSED (EXPOSE)
Jn 3:20 for fear that his deeds will be *e.*
Eph 5:13 everything *e* by the light becomes

EXPRESS (EXPRESSING)
Ro 8:26 us with groans that words cannot *e.*

EXPRESSING* (EXPRESS)
1Co 2:13 *e* spiritual truths in spiritual words.
Gal 5: 6 thing that counts is faith *e* itself

EXTENDS (EXTENT)
Pr 31:20 and *e* her hands to the needy.
Lk 1:50 His mercy *e* to those who fear him,

EXTENT (EXTENDS)
Jn 13: 1 he now showed them the full *e*

EXTERNAL
Gal 2: 6 judge by *e* appearance—

EXTINGUISH (EXTINGUISHED)
Eph 6:16 which you can *e* all the flaming

EXTINGUISHED (EXTINGUISH)
2Sa 21:17 the lamp of Israel will not be *e.*"

EXTOL*
Job 36:24 Remember to *e* his work,
Ps 34: 1 I will *e* the LORD at all times;
68: 4 *e* him who rides on the clouds—
95: 2 and *e* him with music and song.
109:30 mouth I will greatly *e* the LORD;
111: 1 I will *e* the LORD with all my heart
115:18 it is we who *e* the LORD,
117: 1 *e* him, all you peoples.
145: 2 and *e* your name for ever and ever.
145:10 your saints will *e* you.
147:12 *E* the LORD, O Jerusalem;

EXTORT*
Lk 3:14 "Don't *e* money and don't accuse

EXTRAORDINARY*
Ac 19:11 God did *e* miracles through Paul,

EXTREME (EXTREMES)
2Co 8: 2 and their *e* poverty welled up

EXTREMES* (EXTREME)
Ecc 7:18 who fears God will avoid all *e*.

EXULT
Ps 89:16 they *e* in your righteousness.
Isa 45:25 will be found righteous and will *e.*

EYE (EYES)
Ge 3: 6 good for food and pleasing to the *e,*
Ex 21:24 you are to take life for life, *e* for *e,*
Dt 19:21 life for life, *e* for *e,* tooth for tooth,
Ps 94: 9 Does he who formed the *e* not see?
Mt 5:29 If your right *e* causes you to sin,
5:38 *'E* for *e,* and tooth for tooth.'
6:22 "The *e* is the lamp of the body.
7: 3 of sawdust in your brother's *e*
1Co 2: 9 "No *e* has seen,
12:16 I am not an *e,* I do not belong
15:52 of an *e,* at the last trumpet.
Eph 6: 6 favor when their *e* is on you,
Col 3:22 not only when their *e* is on you
Rev 1: 7 and every *e* will see him,

EYES (EYE)
Nu 15:39 the lusts of your own hearts and *e.*
33:55 remain will become barbs in your *e*
Dt 11:12 the *e* of the LORD your God are
12:25 right in the *e* of the LORD.
16:19 for a bribe blinds the *e* of the wise
Jos 23:13 on your backs and thorns in your *e,*
1Sa 15:17 you were once small in your own *e,*
1Ki 10: 7 I came and saw with my own *e.*
2Ki 9:30 heard about it, she painted her *e,*
2Ch 16: 9 For the *e* of the LORD range
Job 31: 1 "I made a covenant with my *e*
36: 7 He does not take his *e*
Ps 25:15 My *e* are ever on the LORD,
36: 1 God before his *e.*
101: 6 My *e* will be on the faithful
118:23 and it is marvelous in our *e.*
119:18 Open my *e* that I may see
119:37 my *e* away from worthless things;
121: 1 I lift up my *e* to the hills—
123: 1 I lift up my *e* to you,
139:16 your *e* saw my unformed body.
141: 8 But my *e* are fixed on you,
Pr 3: 7 Do not be wise in your own *e;*
4:25 Let your *e* look straight ahead,
15: 3 The *e* of the LORD are everywhere
17:24 a fool's *e* wander to the ends
Isa 6: 5 and my *e* have seen the King,
33:17 Your *e* will see the king
42: 7 to open *e* that are blind,
Jer 24: 6 My *e* will watch over them
Hab 1:13 Your *e* are too pure to look on evil;
Mt 6:22 If your *e* are good, your whole
21:42 and it is marvelous in our *e*?
Lk 16:15 ones who justify yourselves in the *e*
24:31 Then their *e* were opened
Jn 4:35 open your *e* and look at the fields!
Ac 1: 9 he was taken up before their very *e,*
2Co 4:18 So we fix our *e* not on what is seen,
8:21 not only in the *e* of the Lord but
Eph 1:18 also that the *e* of your heart may be
Heb 12: 2 Let us fix our *e* on Jesus, the author
Jas 2: 5 poor in the *e* of the world to be rich
1Pe 3:12 For the *e* of the Lord are
Rev 7:17 wipe away every tear from their *e.*"
21: 4 He will wipe every tear from their *e*

EYEWITNESSES* (WITNESS)
Lk 1: 2 by those who from the first were *e*
2Pe 1:16 but we were *e* of his majesty.

EZEKIEL*
Priest called to be prophet to the exiles (Eze 1–3). Symbolically acted out destruction of Jerusalem (Eze 4–5; 12; 24).

EZRA*
Priest and teacher of the Law who led a return of exiles to Israel to reestablish temple and worship (Ezr 7–8). Corrected intermarriage of priests (Ezr 9–10). Read Law at celebration of Feast of Tabernacles (Ne 8). Participated in dedication of Jerusalem's walls (Ne 12).

FACE (FACES)
Ge 32:30 "It is because I saw God *f* to *f,*
Ex 3: 6 Moses hid his *f,* because he was
33:11 would speak to Moses *f* to *f,*
33:20 But," he said, "you cannot see my *f*
Ex 34:29 was not aware that his *f* was radiant
Nu 6:25 the LORD make his *f* shine
12: 8 With him I speak *f* to *f,*
14:14 O LORD, have been seen *f* to *f,*
Dt 5: 4 The LORD spoke to you *f* to *f* out
31:17 I will hide my *f* from them,
34:10 whom the LORD knew *f* to *f,*
Jdg 6:22 the angel of the LORD *f* to *f!*"
2Ki 14: 8 challenge: "Come, meet me *f* to *f.*"
1Ch 16:11 seek his *f* always.
2Ch 7:14 and seek my *f* and turn
25:17 of Israel: "Come, meet me *f* to *f.*"
Ezr 9: 6 and disgraced to lift up my *f* to you,
Ps 4: 6 Let the light of your *f* shine upon us
27: 8 Your *f,* LORD, I will seek.
31:16 Let your *f* shine on your servant;
44: 3 and the light of your *f,*
44:22 Yet for your sake we *f* death all day
51: 9 Hide your *f* from my sins
67: 1 and make his *f* shine upon us; *Selah*
80: 3 make your *f* shine upon us,
105: 4 seek his *f* always.
119:135 Make your *f* shine
SS 2:14 and your *f* is lovely.
Isa 50: 7 Therefore have I set my *f* like flint,
50: 8 Let us *f* each other!
54: 8 I hid my *f* from you for a moment,
Jer 32: 4 and will speak with him *f* to *f*
34: 3 and he will speak with you *f* to *f.*
Eze 1:10 Each of the four had the *f* of a man,
20:35 *f* to *f,* I will execute judgment
Mt 17: 2 His *f* shone like the sun,
18:10 angels in heaven always see the *f*
Lk 9:29 the appearance of his *f* changed,
Ro 8:36 "For your sake we *f* death all day
1Co 13:12 mirror; then we shall see *f* to *f.*
2Co 3: 7 could not look steadily at the *f*
4: 6 the glory of God in the *f* of Christ.
10: 1 who am "timid" when *f* to *f*
1Pe 3:12 but the *f* of the Lord is
2Jn :12 to visit you and talk with you *f* to *f,*
3Jn :14 see you soon, and we will talk *f* to *f.*
Rev 1:16 His *f* was like the sun shining
22: 4 They will see his *f,* and his name

FACES (FACE)
2Co 3:18 who with unveiled *f* all reflect

FACTIONS
2Co 12:20 outbursts of anger, *f,* slander,
Gal 5:20 selfish ambition, dissensions, *f*

FADE (FADING)
Jas 1:11 the rich man will *f* away
1Pe 5: 4 of glory that will never *f* away.

FADING (FADE)
2Co 3: 7 *f* though it was, will not
3:11 if what was *f* away came with glory,
3:13 at it while the radiance was *f* away.

FAIL (FAILED FAILING FAILINGS FAILS FAILURE)
Lev 26:15 and *f* to carry out all my commands
1Ki 2: 4 you will never *f* to have a man
1Ch 28:20 He will not *f* you or forsake you
2Ch 34:33 they did not *f* to follow the LORD,
Ps 89:28 my covenant with him will never *f.*
Pr 15:22 Plans *f* for lack of counsel,
Isa 51: 6 my righteousness will never *f.*
La 3:22 for his compassions never *f.*
Lk 22:32 Simon, that your faith may not *f.*
2Co 13: 5 unless, of course, you *f* the test?

FAILED (FAIL)
Jos 23:14 has been fulfilled; not one has *f.*
1Ki 8:56 Not one word has *f*
Ps 77: 8 Has his promise *f* for all time?
Ro 9: 6 as though God's word had *f.*
2Co 13: 6 discover that we have not *f* the test.

FAILING (FAIL)
1Sa 12:23 sin against the LORD by *f* to pray

FAILINGS (FAIL)
Ro 15: 1 ought to bear with the *f* of the weak

FAILS (FAIL)
Jer 14: 6 their eyesight *f*
Joel 1:10 the oil *f*.
1Co 13: 8 Love never *f*.

FAILURE* (FAIL)
1Th 2: 1 that our visit to you was not a *f*.

FAINT
Isa 40:31 they will walk and not be *f*.

FAINTHEARTED* (HEART)
Dt 20: 3 Do not be *f* or afraid; do not be
20: 8 shall add, "Is any man afraid or *f*?

FAIR (FAIRNESS)
Pr 1: 3 doing what is right and just and *f*;
Col 4: 1 slaves with what is right and *f*,

FAIRNESS* (FAIR)
Pr 29:14 If a king judges the poor with *f*,

FAITH* (FAITHFUL FAITHFULLY FAITHFULNESS FAITHLESS)
Ex 21: 8 because he has broken *f* with her.
Dt 32:51 both of you broke *f* with me
Jos 22:16 'How could you break *f*
Jdg 9:16 and in good *f* when you made
9:19 and in good *f* toward Jerub-Baal
1Sa 14:33 "You have broken *f*," he said.
2Ch 20:20 Have *f* in the LORD your God
20:20 have *f* in his prophets and you will
Isa 7: 9 If you do not stand firm in your *f*,
26: 2 the nation that keeps *f*.
Hab 2: 4 but the righteous will live by his *f*—
Mal 2:10 by breaking *f* with one another?
2:11 one another? Judah has broken *f*.
2:14 because you have broken *f* with her
2:15 and do not break *f* with the wife
2:16 in your spirit, and do not break *f*.
Mt 6:30 O you of little *f*? So do not worry,
8:10 anyone in Israel with such great *f*.
8:26 He replied, "You of little *f*,
9: 2 When Jesus saw their *f*, he said
9:22 he said, "your *f* has healed you."
9:29 According to your *f* will it be done
13:58 there because of their lack of *f*.
14:31 of little *f*," he said, "why did you
15:28 "Woman, you have great *f*!
16: 8 Jesus asked, "You of little *f*,
17:20 if you have *f* as small as a mustard
17:20 "Because you have so little *f*.
21:21 if you have *f* and do not doubt,
24:10 many will turn away from the *f*
Mk 2: 5 When Jesus saw their *f*, he said
4:40 still have no *f*?" They were
5:34 "Daughter, your *f* has healed you.
6: 6 he was amazed at their lack of *f*.
10:52 said Jesus, "your *f* has healed you."
11:22 "Have *f* in God," Jesus answered.
16:14 he rebuked them for their lack of *f*
Lk 5:20 When Jesus saw their *f*, he said,
7: 9 I have not found such great *f*
7:50 the woman, "Your *f* has saved you;
8:25 "Where is your *f*?" he asked his
8:48 "Daughter, your *f* has healed you.
12:28 will he clothe you, O you of little *f*!
17: 5 "Increase our *f*!" He replied,
17: 6 "If you have *f* as small
17:19 your *f* has made you well."
18: 8 will he find *f* on the earth?"
18:42 your sight; your *f* has healed you."
22:32 Simon, that your *f* may not fail.
Jn 2:11 and his disciples put their *f* in him.
7:31 in the crowd put their *f* in him.
8:30 he spoke, many put their *f* in him.
Jn 11:45 had seen what Jesus did, put their *f*
12:11 to Jesus and putting their *f* in him.
12:42 they would not confess their *f*
14:12 anyone who has *f* in me will do
Ac 3:16 By *f* in the name of Jesus, this man
3:16 *f* that comes through him that has
6: 5 full of *f* and of the Holy Spirit;
6: 7 of priests became obedient to the *f*.
11:24 full of the Holy Spirit and *f*,
13: 8 to turn the proconsul from the *f*.
14: 9 saw that he had *f* to be healed
14:22 them to remain true to the *f*.
14:27 the door of *f* to the Gentiles.
15: 9 for he purified their hearts by *f*.
16: 5 were strengthened in the *f*
20:21 and have *f* in our Lord Jesus.
24:24 as he spoke about *f* in Christ Jesus.
26:18 those who are sanctified by *f*
27:25 for I have *f* in God that it will
Ro 1: 5 to the obedience that comes from *f*.
1: 8 because your *f* is being reported all
1:12 encouraged by each other's *f*.
1:17 is by *f* from first to last,
1:17 "The righteous will live by *f*."
3: 3 What if some did not have *f*?
3: 3 lack of *f* nullify God's faithfulness?
3:22 comes through *f* in Jesus Christ
3:25 a sacrifice of atonement, through *f*
3:26 one who justifies those who have *f*
3:27 the law? No, but on that of *f*.
3:28 by *f* apart from observing the law.
3:30 through that same *f*.
3:30 will justify the circumcised by *f*
3:31 nullify the law by this *f*? Not at all!
4: 5 his *f* is credited as righteousness.
4: 9 that Abraham's *f* was credited
4:11 had by *f* while he was still
4:12 of the *f* that our father Abraham
4:13 the righteousness that comes by *f*.
4:14 *f* has no value and the promise is
4:16 Therefore, the promise comes by *f*,
4:16 are of the *f* of Abraham.
4:19 Without weakening in his *f*,
4:20 but was strengthened in his *f*
5: 1 we have been justified through *f*,
5: 2 access by *f* into this grace
9:30 a righteousness that is by *f*;
9:32 Because they pursued it not by *f*
10: 6 the righteousness that is by *f* says:
10: 8 the word of *f* we are proclaiming:
10:17 *f* comes from hearing the message,
11:20 of unbelief, and you stand by *f*.
12: 3 measure of *f* God has given you.
12: 6 let him use it in proportion to his *f*.
14: 1 Accept him whose *f* is weak,
14: 2 One man's *f* allows him
14: 2 but another man, whose *f* is weak,
14:23 because his eating is not from *f*;
14:23 that does not come from *f* is sin.
1Co 2: 5 so that your *f* might not rest
12: 9 to another *f* by the same Spirit,
13: 2 and if I have a *f* that can move
13:13 And now these three remain: *f*,
15:14 is useless and so is your *f*.
15:17 has not been raised, your *f* is futile;
16:13 stand firm in the *f*; be men
2Co 1:24 Not that we lord it over your *f*,
1:24 because it is by *f* you stand firm.
4:13 With that same spirit of *f* we
5: 7 We live by *f*, not by sight.
8: 7 in *f*, in speech, in knowledge,
10:15 as your *f* continues to grow,
13: 5 to see whether you are in the *f*;
Gal 1:23 now preaching the *f* he once tried
2:16 Jesus that we may be justified by *f*
2:16 but by *f* in Jesus Christ.
2:16 have put our *f* in Christ Jesus that
2:20 I live by *f* in the Son of God,
3: 8 would justify the Gentiles by *f*,
3: 9 So those who have *f* are blessed
Gal 3: 9 along with Abraham, the man of *f*.
3:11 "The righteous will live by *f*."
3:12 based on *f*; on the contrary,
3:14 by *f* we might receive the promise
3:22 being given through *f*
3:23 Before this *f* came, we were held
3:23 up until *f* should be revealed.
3:24 that we might be justified by *f*.
3:25 that *f* has come, we are no longer
3:26 of God through *f* in Christ Jesus,
5: 5 But by *f* we eagerly await
5: 6 that counts is *f* expressing itself
Eph 1:15 ever since I heard about your *f*
2: 8 through *f*— and this not
3:12 through *f* in him we may approach
3:17 dwell in your hearts through *f*.
4: 5 one Lord, one *f*, one baptism;
4:13 up until we all reach unity in the *f*
6:16 to all this, take up the shield of *f*,
6:23 love with *f* from God the Father
Php 1:25 for your progress and joy in the *f*,
1:27 as one man for the *f* of the gospel
2:17 and service coming from your *f*,
3: 9 comes from God and is by *f*.
3: 9 that which is through *f* in Christ—
Col 1: 4 heard of your *f* in Christ Jesus
1: 5 the *f* and love that spring
1:23 continue in your *f*, established
2: 5 and how firm your *f* in Christ is.
2: 7 in the *f* as you were taught,
2:12 him through your *f* in the power
1Th 1: 3 Father your work produced by *f*,
1: 8 your *f* in God has become known
3: 2 and encourage you in your *f*,
3: 5 I sent to find out about your *f*.
3: 6 brought good news about your *f*
3: 7 about you because of your *f*.
3:10 supply what is lacking in your *f*.
5: 8 on *f* and love as a breastplate,
2Th 1: 3 because your *f* is growing more
1: 4 and *f* in all the persecutions
1:11 and every act prompted by your *f*.
3: 2 evil men, for not everyone has *f*.
1Ti 1: 2 To Timothy my true son in the *f*:
1: 4 than God's work—which is by *f*.
1: 5 a good conscience and a sincere *f*.
1:14 along with the *f* and love that are
1:19 and so have shipwrecked their *f*.
1:19 on to *f* and a good conscience.
2: 7 of the true *f* to the Gentiles.
2:15 if they continue in *f*, love
3: 9 of the *f* with a clear conscience.
3:13 assurance in their *f* in Christ Jesus.
4: 1 later times some will abandon the *f*
4: 6 brought up in the truths of the *f*
4:12 in life, in love, in *f* and in purity.
5: 8 he has denied the *f* and is worse
6:10 have wandered from the *f*
6:11 pursue righteousness, godliness, *f*,
6:12 Fight the good fight of the *f*.
6:21 so doing have wandered from the *f*.
2Ti 1: 5 been reminded of your sincere *f*,
1:13 with *f* and love in Christ Jesus.
2:18 and they destroy the *f* of some.
2:22 and pursue righteousness, *f*,
3: 8 as far as the *f* is concerned,
3:10 my purpose, *f*, patience, love,
3:15 wise for salvation through *f*
4: 7 finished the race, I have kept the *f*.
Tit 1: 1 Christ for the *f* of God's elect
1: 2 a *f* and knowledge resting
1: 4 my true son in our common *f*:
1:13 so that they will be sound in the *f*
2: 2 self-controlled, and sound in *f*,
3:15 Greet those who love us in the *f*.
Phm : 5 because I hear about your *f*
: 6 may be active in sharing your *f*,
Heb 4: 2 heard did not combine it with *f*.
4:14 firmly to the *f* we profess.
6: 1 and of *f* in God, instruction about

Hab 6:12 but to imitate those who through f
10:22 heart in full assurance of f,
10:38 But my righteous one will live by f.
11: 1 f is being sure of what we hope for
11: 3 By f we understand that
11: 4 And by f he still speaks, even
11: 4 By f Abel offered God a better
11: 4 By f he was commended
11: 5 By f Enoch was taken from this life
11: 6 And without f it is impossible
11: 7 By his f he condemned the world
11: 7 By f Noah, when warned about
11: 7 the righteousness that comes by f.
11: 8 By f Abraham, when called to go
11: 9 By f he made his home
11:11 By f Abraham, even though he was
11:13 living by f when they died.
11:17 By f Abraham, when God tested
11:20 By f Isaac blessed Jacob
11:21 By f Jacob, when he was dying,
11:22 By f Joseph, when his end was near
11:23 By f Moses' parents hid him
11:24 By f Moses, when he had grown up
11:27 By f he left Egypt, not fearing
11:28 By f he kept the Passover
11:29 By f the people passed
11:30 By f the walls of Jericho fell,
11:31 By f the prostitute Rahab,
11:33 through f conquered kingdoms,
11:39 were all commended for their f,
12: 2 the author and perfecter of our f,
13: 7 way of life and imitate their f.
Jas 1: 3 of your f develops perseverance.
2: 5 the eyes of the world to be rich in f
2:14 has no deeds? Can such f save him?
2:14 if a man claims to have f
2:17 In the same way, f by itself,
2:18 I will show you my f by what I do.
2:18 Show me your f without deeds,
2:18 "You have f; I have deeds."
2:20 do you want evidence that f
2:22 You see that his f and his actions
2:22 and his f was made complete
2:24 by what he does and not by f alone.
2:26 so f without deeds is dead.
5:15 in f will make the sick person well;
1Pe 1: 5 who through f are shielded
1: 7 These have come so that your f—
1: 9 you are receiving the goal of your f,
1:21 and so your f and hope are in God.
5: 9 Resist him, standing firm in the f,
2Pe 1: 1 Jesus Christ have received a f
1: 5 effort to add to your f goodness;
1Jn 5: 4 overcome the world, even our f.
Jude : 3 to contend for the f that was once
:20 up in your most holy f
Rev 2:13 You did not renounce your f in me,
2:19 your love and f, your service

FAITHFUL* (FAITH)
Nu 12: 7 he is f in all my house.
Dt 7: 9 your God is God; he is the f God,
32: 4 A f God who does no wrong,
1Sa 2:35 I will raise up for myself a f priest,
2Sa 20:19 We are the peaceful and f in Israel.
22:26 "To the f you show yourself f,
1Ki 3: 6 because he was f to you
2Ch 31:18 were f in consecrating themselves.
31:20 and f before the LORD his God.
Ne 9: 8 You found his heart f to you,
Ps 12: 1 the f have vanished
18:25 To the f you show yourself f,
25:10 of the LORD are loving and f
31:23 The LORD preserves the f,
33: 4 he is f in all he does.
37:28 and will not forsake his f ones.
78: 8 whose spirits were not f to him.
78:37 they were not f to his covenant.
89:19 to your f people you said:
89:24 My f love will be with him,
89:37 the f witness in the sky."
97:10 for he guards the lives of his f ones
101: 6 My eyes will be on the f in the land,
111: 7 The works of his hands are f
145:13 The LORD is f to all his promises
146: 6 the LORD, who remains f forever.
Pr 2: 8 and protects the way of his f ones.
20: 6 but a f man who can find?
28:20 A f man will be richly blessed,
31:26 and f instruction is on her tongue.
Isa 1:21 See how the f city has become
1:26 the F City."
49: 7 because of the LORD, who is f,
55: 3 my f love promised to David.
Jer 42: 5 f witness against us if we do not act
Eze 43:11 so that they may be f to its design
48:11 who were f in serving me
Hos 11:12 even against the f Holy One.
Zec 8: 8 I will be f and righteous to them
Mt 24:45 Who then is the f and wise servant,
25:21 'Well done, good and f servant!
25:21 You have been f with a few things;
25:23 You have been f with a few things;
25:23 'Well done, good and f servant!
Lk 12:42 then is the f and wise manager,
Ro 12:12 patient in affliction, f in prayer.
1Co 1: 9 his Son Jesus Christ our Lord, is f.
4: 2 been given a trust must prove f.
4:17 my son whom I love, who is f
10:13 And God is f; he will not let you be
2Co 1:18 no"? But as surely as God is f,
Eph 1: 1 in Ephesus, the f in Christ Jesus:
6:21 the dear brother and f servant
Col 1: 2 and f brothers in Christ at Colosse:
1: 7 who is a f minister of Christ
4: 7 a f minister and fellow servant
4: 9 He is coming with Onesimus, our f
1Th 5:24 The one who calls you is f
2Th 3: 3 the Lord is f, and he will strengthen
1Ti 1:12 he considered me f, appointing me
5: 9 has been f to her husband,
2Ti 2:13 he will remain f,
Heb 2:17 and f high priest in service to God,
3: 2 He was f to the one who appointed
3: 2 as Moses was f in all God's house.
3: 5 Moses was f as a servant
3: 6 But Christ is f as a son
8: 9 because they did not remain f
10:23 for he who promised is f.
11:11 he considered him f who had made
1Pe 4:19 themselves to their f Creator
5:12 whom I regard as a f brother,
1Jn 1: 9 he is f and just and will forgive us
3Jn : 5 you are f in what you are doing
Rev 1: 5 who is the f witness, the firstborn
2:10 Be f, even to the point of death,
2:13 the days of Antipas, my f witness,
3:14 the words of the Amen, the f
14:12 commandments and remain f
17:14 his called, chosen and f followers."
19:11 whose rider is called F and True.

FAITHFULLY* (FAITH)
Dt 11:13 if you f obey the commands I am
Jos 2:14 f when the LORD gives us the land
1Sa 12:24 and serve him f with all your heart;
1Ki 2: 4 and if they walk f before me
2Ki 20: 3 how I have walked before you f
22: 7 because they are acting f."
2Ch 19: 9 must serve f and wholeheartedly
31:12 they f brought in the contributions,
31:15 and Shecaniah assisted him f
32: 1 all that Hezekiah had so f done,
34:12 The men did the work f.
Ne 9:33 you have acted f, while we did
13:14 so f done for the house of my God
Isa 38: 3 how I have walked before you f
Jer 23:28 one who has my word speak it f.
Eze 18: 9 and f keeps my laws.
44:15 and who f carried out the duties
1Pe 4:10 f administering God's grace

FAITHFULNESS* (FAITH)
Ge 24:27 not abandoned his kindness and f
24:49 if you will show kindness and f
32:10 and f you have shown your servant.
47:29 you will show me kindness and f.
Ex 34: 6 f, maintaining love to thousands,
Jos 24:14 the LORD and serve him with all f.
1Sa 26:23 man for his righteousness and f.
2Sa 2: 6 now show you kindness and f,
15:20 May kindness and f be with you."
Ps 30: 9 Will it proclaim your f?
36: 5 your f to the skies.
40:10 I speak of your f and salvation.
54: 5 in your f destroy them.
57: 3 God sends his love and his f.
57:10 your f reaches to the skies.
61: 7 appoint your love and f
71:22 the harp for your f, O my God;
85:10 Love and f meet together;
85:11 F springs forth from the earth,
86:15 to anger, abounding in love and f.
88:11 your f in Destruction?
89: 1 mouth I will make your f known
89: 2 that you established your f
89: 5 your f too, in the assembly
89: 8 and your f surrounds you.
89:14 love and f go before you.
89:33 nor will I ever betray my f.
89:49 which in your f you swore to David
91: 4 his f will be your shield
92: 2 and your f at night,
98: 3 and his f to the house of Israel;
100: 5 f continues through all
108: 4 your f reaches to the skies.
111: 8 done in f and uprightness.
115: 1 because of your love and f.
117: 2 the f of the LORD endures forever.
119:75 and in f you have afflicted me.
119:90 f continues through all
138: 2 name for your love and your f,
143: 1 in your f and righteousness
Pr 3: 3 Let love and f never leave you;
14:22 plan what is good find love and f.
16: 6 Through love and f sin is atoned for
20:28 Love and f keep a king safe;
Isa 11: 5 and f the sash around his waist.
16: 5 in f a man will sit on it—
25: 1 for in perfect f
38:18 cannot hope for your f.
38:19 about your f.
42: 3 In f he will bring forth justice;
61: 8 In my f I will reward them
La 3:23 great is your f.
Hos 2:20 I will betroth you in f,
4: 1 "There is no f, no love,
Mt 23:23 of the law—justice, mercy and f.
Ro 3: 3 lack of faith nullify God's f?
Gal 5:22 patience, kindness, goodness, f,
3Jn : 3 and tell about your f to the truth
Rev 13:10 and f on the part of the saints.

FAITHLESS* (FAITH)
Ps 78:57 fathers they were disloyal and f,
101: 3 The deeds of f men I hate;
119:158 I look on the f with loathing,
Pr 14:14 The f will be fully repaid
Jer 3: 6 you seen what f Israel has done?
3: 8 I gave f Israel her certificate
3:11 "F Israel is more righteous
3:12 f Israel,' declares the LORD,
3:14 f people," declares the LORD,
3:22 "Return, f people;
12: 1 Why do all the f live at ease?
Ro 1:31 they are senseless, f, heartless,
2Ti 2:13 if we are f,

FALL (FALLEN FALLING FALLS)
Ps 37:24 though he stumble, he will not f,
55:22 he will never let the righteous f.

Ps 69: 9 of those who insult you *f* on me.
145:14 The LORD upholds all those who *f*
Pr 11:28 Whoever trusts in his riches will *f*,
Isa 40: 7 The grass withers and the flowers *f*,
Mt 7:25 yet it did not *f*, because it had its
Lk 10:18 "I saw Satan *f* like lightning
11:17 a house divided against itself will *f*.
23:30 say to the mountains, "*F* on us!"
Ro 3:23 and *f* short of the glory of God,
Heb 6: 6 if they *f* away, to be brought back

FALLEN (FALL)
2Sa 1:19 How the mighty have *f*!
Isa 14:12 How you have *f* from heaven,
1Co 11:30 and a number of you have *f* asleep.
15: 6 though some have *f* asleep.
15:18 who have *f* asleep in Christ are lost.
15:20 of those who have *f* asleep.
Gal 5: 4 you have *f* away from grace.
1Th 4:15 precede those who have *f* asleep.

FALLING (FALL)
Jude :24 able to keep you from *f*

FALLS (FALL)
Pr 11:14 For lack of guidance a nation *f*,
24:17 Do not gloat when your enemy *f*;
28:14 he who hardens his heart *f*
Mt 13:21 of the word, he quickly *f* away.
21:44 He who *f* on this stone will be
Jn 12:24 a kernel of wheat *f* to the ground
Ro 14: 4 To his own master he stands or *f*.

FALSE (FALSEHOOD FALSELY)
Ex 20:16 "You shall not give *f* testimony
23: 1 "Do not spread *f* reports.
23: 7 Have nothing to do with a *f* charge
Dt 5:20 "You shall not give *f* testimony
Pr 12:17 but a *f* witness tells lies.
13: 5 The righteous hate what is *f*,
14: 5 but a *f* witness pours out lies.
14:25 but a *f* witness is deceitful.
19: 5 A *f* witness will not go unpunished,
19: 9 A *f* witness will not go unpunished,
21:28 A *f* witness will perish,
25:18 is the man who gives *f* testimony
Isa 44:25 who foils the signs of *f* prophets
Jer 23:16 they fill you with *f* hopes.
Mt 7:15 "Watch out for *f* prophets.
15:19 theft, *f* testimony, slander.
19:18 not steal, do not give *f* testimony,
24:11 and many *f* prophets will appear
24:24 For *f* Christs and *f* prophets will
Mk 10:19 do not give *f* testimony, do not
13:22 For *f* Christs and *f* prophets will
Lk 6:26 their fathers treated the *f* prophets.
18:20 not steal, do not give *f* testimony,
Jn 1:47 in whom there is nothing *f*."
1Co 15:15 found to be *f* witnesses about God,
2Co 11:13 For such men are *f* apostles,
11:26 and in danger from *f* brothers.
Gal 2: 4 some *f* brothers had infiltrated our
Php 1:18 whether from *f* motives or true,
Col 2:18 anyone who delights in *f* humility
2:23 their *f* humility and their harsh
1Ti 1: 3 not to teach *f* doctrines any longer
6: 3 If anyone teaches *f* doctrines
2Pe 2: 1 also *f* prophets among the people,
2: 1 there will be *f* teachers among you.
1Jn 4: 1 many *f* prophets have gone out
Rev 16:13 out of the mouth of the *f* prophet.
19:20 with him the *f* prophet who had
20:10 and the *f* prophet had been thrown.

FALSEHOOD* (FALSE)
Job 21:34 left of your answers but *f*!"
31: 5 "If I have walked in *f*
Ps 52: 3 *f* rather than speaking the truth.
119:163 I hate and abhor *f*
Pr 30: 8 Keep *f* and lies far from me;
Isa 28:15 and *f* our hiding place."

Ro 3: 7 "If my *f* enhances God's
Eph 4:25 each of you must put off *f*
1Jn 4: 6 Spirit of truth and the spirit of *f*.
Rev 22:15 everyone who loves and practices *f*

FALSELY (FALSE)
Lev 19:12 " 'Do not swear *f* by my name
Mt 5:11 *f* say all kinds of evil against you
Lk 3:14 and don't accuse people *f*—
1Ti 6:20 ideas of what is *f* called knowledge,

FALTER*
Pr 24:10 If you *f* in times of trouble,
Isa 42: 4 he will not *f* or be discouraged

FAME
Jos 9: 9 of the *f* of the LORD your God.
Isa 66:19 islands that have not heard of my *f*
Hab 3: 2 LORD, I have heard of your *f*;

FAMILIES (FAMILY)
Ps 68: 6 God sets the lonely in *f*,

FAMILY (FAMILIES)
Pr 15:27 greedy man brings trouble to his *f*,
31:15 she provides food for her *f*
Mk 5:19 to your *f* and tell them how much
Lk 9:61 go back and say good-by to my *f*."
12:52 in one *f* divided against each other,
Ac 10: 2 He and all his *f* were devout
16:33 and all his *f* were baptized.
16:34 he and his whole *f*.
1Ti 3: 4 He must manage his own *f* well
3: 5 how to manage his own *f*,
5: 4 practice by caring for their own *f*
5: 8 and especially for his immediate *f*,

FAMINE
Ge 12:10 Now there was a *f* in the land,
26: 1 Now there was a *f* in the land—
41:30 seven years of *f* will follow them.
Ru 1: 1 the judges ruled, there was a *f*
1Ki 18: 2 Now the *f* was severe in Samaria,
Am 8:11 but a *f* of hearing the words
Ro 8:35 or persecution or *f* or nakedness

FAN*
2Ti 1: 6 you to *f* into flame the gift of God,

FANTASIES*
Ps 73:20 you will despise them as *f*.
Pr 12:11 but he who chases *f* lacks judgment
28:19 one who chases *f* will have his fill

FAST (FASTING)
Dt 10:20 Hold *f* to him and take your oaths
11:22 in all his ways and to hold *f* to him
13: 4 serve him and hold *f* to him.
30:20 to his voice, and hold *f* to him.
Jos 22: 5 to hold *f* to him and to serve him
23: 8 to hold *f* to the LORD your God,
2Ki 18: 6 He held *f* to the LORD
Ps 119:31 I hold *f* to your statutes, O LORD;
139:10 your right hand will hold me *f*.
Mt 6:16 "When you *f*, do not look somber
1Pe 5:12 Stand *f* in it.

FASTING (FAST)
Ps 35:13 and humbled myself with *f*.
Ac 13: 2 were worshiping the Lord and *f*,
14:23 and *f*, committed them to the Lord

FATHER (FATHER'S FATHERED FATHERLESS FATHERS FOREFATHERS)
Ge 2:24 this reason a man will leave his *f*
17: 4 You will be the *f* of many nations.
Ex 20:12 "Honor your *f* and your mother,
21:15 "Anyone who attacks his *f*
21:17 "Anyone who curses his *f*
Lev 18: 7 " 'Do not dishonor your *f*
19: 3 you must respect his mother and *f*,
20: 9 " 'If anyone curses his *f* or mother,

Dt 1:31 carried you, as a *f* carries his son,
5:16 "Honor your *f* and your mother,
21:18 son who does not obey his *f*
32: 6 Is he not your *F*, your Creator,
2Sa 7:14 I will be his *f*, and he will be my son
1Ch 17:13 I will be his *f*, and he will be my son
22:10 will be my son, and I will be his *f*.
28: 6 to be my son, and I will be his *f*.
Job 38:28 Does the rain have a *f*?
Ps 2: 7 today I have become your *F*.
27:10 Though my *f* and mother forsake
68: 5 A *f* to the fatherless, a defender
89:26 to me, 'You are my *F*,
103:13 As a *f* has compassion
Pr 3:12 as a *f* the son he delights in.
10: 1 A wise son brings joy to his *f*,
17:21 there is no joy for the *f* of a fool.
17:25 A foolish son brings grief to his *f*
23:22 Listen to your *f*, who gave you life,
23:24 *f* of a righteous man has great joy;
28: 7 of gluttons disgraces his *f*.
28:24 He who robs his *f* or mother
29: 3 loves wisdom brings joy to his *f*,
Isa 9: 6 Everlasting *F*, Prince of Peace.
45:10 Woe to him who says to his *f*,
63:16 But you are our *F*,
Jer 2:27 They say to wood, 'You are my *f*,'
3:19 I thought you would call me '*F*'
31: 9 because I am Israel's *f*,
Eze 18:19 the son not share the guilt of his *f*?'
Mic 7: 6 For a son dishonors his *f*,
Mal 1: 6 If I am a *f*, where is the honor due
2:10 we not all one *F*? Did not one God
Mt 3: 9 'We have Abraham as our *f*.'
5:16 and praise your *F* in heaven.
6: 9 " 'Our *F* in heaven,
6:26 yet your heavenly *F* feeds them.
10:37 "Anyone who loves his *f*
11:27 no one knows the *F* except the Son
15: 4 'Honor your *f* and mother'
18:10 the face of my *F* in heaven.
19: 5 this reason a man will leave his *f*
19:19 honor your *f* and mother,'
19:29 or brothers or sisters or *f* or mother
23: 9 And do not call anyone on earth '*f*,'
Mk 7:10 'Honor your *f* and your mother,' and,
Lk 9:59 "Lord, first let me go and bury my *f*
12:53 *f* against son and son against *f*,
14:26 and does not hate his *f* and mother,
18:20 honor your *f* and mother.' "
23:34 Jesus said, "*F*, forgive them,
Jn 3:35 The *F* loves the Son and has placed
4:21 you will worship the *F* neither
5:17 "My *F* is always at his work
5:18 he was even calling God his own *F*,
5:20 For the *F* loves the Son
6:44 the *F* who sent me draws him,
6:46 No one has seen the *F*
8:19 "You do not know me or my *F*,"
8:28 speak just what the *F* has taught me
8:41 The only *F* we have is God himself
8:42 God were your *F*, you would love
8:44 You belong to your *f*, the devil,
10:17 reason my *F* loves me is that I lay
10:30 I and the *F* are one."
10:38 and understand that the *F* is in me,
14: 6 No one comes to the *F*
14: 9 who has seen me has seen the *F*.
14:28 for the *F* is greater than I.
15: 9 "As the *F* has loved me,
15:23 He who hates me hates my *F*
20:17 'I am returning to my *F* and your *F*,
Ac 13:33 today I have become your *F*.'
Ro 4:11 he is the *f* of all who believe
4:16 He is the *f* of us all.
8:15 And by him we cry, "*Abba*, *F*."
1Co 4:15 for in Christ Jesus I became your *f*
2Co 6:18 "I will be a *F* to you,
Eph 5:31 this reason a man will leave his *f*
6: 2 "Honor your *f* and mother"—

Php 2:11 to the glory of God the *F.*
Heb 1: 5 today I have become your *F*"?
12: 7 what son is not disciplined by his *f?*
1Jn 1: 3 And our fellowship is with the *F*
2:15 the love of the *F* is not in him.
2:22 he denies the *F* and the Son.

FATHER'S (FATHER)
Pr 13: 1 A wise son heeds his *f* instruction,
15: 5 A fool spurns his *f* discipline,
19:13 A foolish son is his *f* ruin,
Mt 16:27 going to come in his *F* glory
Lk 2:49 had to be in my *F* house?"
Jn 2:16 How dare you turn my *F* house
10:29 can snatch them out of my *F* hand.
14: 2 In my *F* house are many rooms;
15: 8 to my *F* glory, that you bear much

FATHERED (FATHER)
Dt 32:18 You deserted the Rock, who *f* you;

FATHERLESS (FATHER)
Dt 10:18 He defends the cause of the *f*
14:29 the *f* and the widows who live
24:17 Do not deprive the alien or the *f*
24:19 Leave it for the alien, the *f*
26:12 the alien, the *f* and the widow,
Ps 68: 5 A father to the *f,* a defender
82: 3 Defend the cause of the weak and *f*
Pr 23:10 or encroach on the fields of the *f,*

FATHERS (FATHER)
Ex 20: 5 for the sin of the *f* to the third
Jer 31:29 'The *f* have eaten sour grapes,
Mal 4: 6 the hearts of the children to their *f;*
Lk 1:17 the hearts of the *f* to their children
11:11 "Which of you *f,* if your son asks
Jn 4:20 Our *f* worshiped on this mountain,
1Co 4:15 you do not have many *f,*
Eph 6: 4 *F,* do not exasperate your children;
Col 3:21 *F,* do not embitter your children,
Heb 12: 9 all had human *f* who disciplined us

FATHOM* (FATHOMED)
Job 11: 7 "Can you *f* the mysteries of God?
Ps 145: 3 his greatness no one can *f.*
Ecc 3:11 yet they cannot *f* what God has
Isa 40:28 and his understanding no one can *f*
1Co 13: 2 and can *f* all mysteries and all

FATHOMED* (FATHOM)
Job 5: 9 performs wonders that cannot be *f,*
9:10 performs wonders that cannot be *f,*

FATTENED
Pr 15:17 than a *f* calf with hatred.
Lk 15:23 Bring the *f* calf and kill it.

FAULT (FAULTS)
1Sa 29: 3 I have found no *f* in him."
Mt 18:15 and show him his *f,* just
Php 2:15 of God without *f* in a crooked
Jas 1: 5 generously to all without finding *f,*
Jude :24 his glorious presence without *f*

FAULTFINDERS*
Jude :16 These men are grumblers and *f;*

FAULTLESS*
Pr 8: 9 they are *f* to those who have
Php 3: 6 as for legalistic righteousness, *f.*
Jas 1:27 Father accepts as pure and *f* is this:

FAULTS* (FAULT)
Job 10: 6 that you must search out my *f*
Ps 19:12 Forgive my hidden *f.*

FAVOR (FAVORITISM)
Ge 4: 4 The LORD looked with *f* on Abel
6: 8 But Noah found *f* in the eyes
Ex 33:12 and you have found *f* with me.'
34: 9 if I have found *f* in your eyes,"
Lev 26: 9 " 'I will look on you with *f*
Nu 11:15 if I have found *f* in your eyes—
Jdg 6:17 "If now I have found *f* in your eyes,
1Sa 2:26 in *f* with the LORD and with men.
2Sa 2: 6 and I too will show you the same *f*
2Ki 13: 4 Jehoahaz sought the LORD's *f,*
2Ch 33:12 In his distress he sought the *f*
Est 7: 3 "If I have found *f* with you, O king,
Ps 90:17 May the *f* of the Lord our God rest
Pr 8:35 and receives *f* from the LORD.
18:22 and receives *f* from the LORD.
19: 6 Many curry *f* with a ruler,
Isa 61: 2 proclaim the year of the LORD's *f*
Zec 11: 7 called one *F* and the other Union,
Lk 1:30 Mary, you have found *f* with God.
2:14 to men on whom his *f* rests."
2:52 and in *f* with God and men.
4:19 to proclaim the year of the Lord's *f*
2Co 6: 2 now is the time of God's *f,*

FAVORITISM* (FAVOR)
Ex 23: 3 and do not show *f* to a poor man
Lev 19:15 to the poor or *f* to the great,
Ac 10:34 true it is that God does not show *f*
Ro 2:11 For God does not show *f.*
Eph 6: 9 and there is no *f* with him.
Col 3:25 for his wrong, and there is no *f.*
1Ti 5:21 and to do nothing out of *f.*
Jas 2: 1 Lord Jesus Christ, don't show *f.*
2: 9 But if you show *f,* you sin

FEAR (AFRAID FEARED FEARS FRIGHTENED GOD-FEARING)
Dt 6:13 *F* the LORD your God, serve him
10:12 but to *f* the LORD your God,
31:12 and learn to *f* the LORD your God
31:13 and learn to *f* the LORD your God
Jos 4:24 you might always *f* the LORD
24:14 "Now *f* the LORD and serve him
1Sa 12:14 If you *f* the LORD and serve
12:24 But be sure to *f* the LORD
2Sa 23: 3 when he rules in the *f* of God,
2Ch 19: 7 let the *f* of the LORD be upon you.
26: 5 who instructed him in the *f* of God.
Job 1: 9 "Does Job *f* God for nothing?"
Ps 2:11 Serve the LORD with *f*
19: 9 The *f* of the LORD is pure,
23: 4 I will *f* no evil,
27: 1 whom shall I *f?*
33: 8 Let all the earth *f* the LORD;
34: 7 around those who *f* him,
34: 9 *F* the LORD, you his saints,
46: 2 Therefore we will not *f,*
86:11 that I may *f* your name.
90:11 great as the *f* that is due you.
91: 5 You will not *f* the terror of night,
111:10 *f* of the LORD is the beginning
118: 4 Let those who *f* the LORD say:
128: 1 Blessed are all who *f* the LORD,
145:19 of those who *f* him;
147:11 delights in those who *f* him,
Pr 1: 7 *f* of the LORD is the beginning
1:33 and be at ease, without *f* of harm."
8:13 To *f* the LORD is to hate evil;
9:10 *f* of the LORD is the beginning
10:27 The *f* of the LORD adds length
14:27 The *f* of the LORD is a fountain
15:33 *f* of the LORD teaches a man
16: 6 through the *f* of the LORD a man
19:23 The *f* of the LORD leads to life:
22: 4 Humility and the *f* of the LORD
29:25 *F* of man will prove to be a snare,
31:21 she has no *f* for her household;
Ecc 12:13 *F* God and keep his
Isa 11: 3 delight in the *f* of the LORD.
33: 6 the *f* of the LORD is the key
35: 4 "Be strong, do not *f;*
41:10 So do not *f,* for I am with you;
41:13 and says to you, Do not *f;*
43: 1 "*F* not, for I have redeemed you;
51: 7 Do not *f* the reproach of men
Isa 54:14 you will have nothing to *f.*
Jer 17: 8 It does not *f* when heat comes;
Lk 12: 5 I will show you whom you should *f:*
2Co 5:11 we know what it is to *f* the Lord,
Php 2:12 to work out your salvation with *f*
1Jn 4:18 But perfect love drives out *f,*
Jude :23 to others show mercy, mixed with *f*
Rev 14: 7 "*F* God and give him glory,

FEARED (FEAR)
Job 1: 1 he *f* God and shunned evil.
Ps 76: 7 You alone are to be *f.*
Mal 3:16 those who *f* the LORD talked

FEARS (FEAR)
Job 1: 8 a man who *f* God and shuns evil."
2: 3 a man who *f* God and shuns evil.
Ps 34: 4 he delivered me from all my *f.*
112: 1 is the man who *f* the LORD,
Pr 14:16 A wise man *f* the LORD
14:26 He who *f* the LORD has a secure
31:30 a woman who *f* the LORD is
2Co 7: 5 conflicts on the outside, *f* within.
1Jn 4:18 The one who *f* is not made perfect

FEAST (FEASTING FEASTS)
Pr 15:15 the cheerful heart has a continual *f.*
2Pe 2:13 pleasures while they *f* with you.

FEASTING (FEAST)
Pr 17: 1 than a house full of *f,* with strife.

FEASTS (FEAST)
Am 5:21 "I hate, I despise your religious *f;*
Jude :12 men are blemishes at your love *f,*

FEATHERS
Ps 91: 4 He will cover you with his *f,*

FEEBLE
Job 4: 3 you have strengthened *f* hands.
Isa 35: 3 Strengthen the *f* hands,
Heb 12:12 strengthen your *f* arms

FEED (FEEDS)
Jn 21:15 Jesus said, "*F* my lambs."
21:17 Jesus said, "*F* my sheep.
Ro 12:20 "If your enemy is hungry, *f* him;
Jude :12 shepherds who *f* only themselves.

FEEDS (FEED)
Pr 15:14 but the mouth of a fool *f* on folly.
Mt 6:26 yet your heavenly Father *f* them.
Jn 6:57 so the one who *f* on me will live

FEEL
Jdg 16:26 me where I can *f* the pillars that
Ps 115: 7 they have hands, but cannot *f,*

FEET (FOOT)
Ru 3: 8 discovered a woman lying at his *f.*
Ps 8: 6 you put everything under his *f:*
22:16 have pierced my hands and my *f.*
40: 2 he set my *f* on a rock
56:13 and my *f* from stumbling,
66: 9 and kept our *f* from slipping.
73: 2 as for me, my *f* had almost slipped;
110: 1 a footstool for your *f.*"
119:105 Your word is a lamp to my *f*
Pr 4:26 Make level paths for your *f*
Isa 52: 7 are the *f* of those who bring good
Da 2:33 its *f* partly of iron and partly
Na 1:15 the *f* of one who brings good news,
Mt 10:14 shake the dust off your *f*
22:44 enemies under your *f.*" '
Lk 1:79 to guide our *f* into the path of peace
20:43 a footstool for your *f.*" '
24:39 Look at my hands and my *f.*
Jn 13: 5 and began to wash his disciples' *f,*
13:14 also should wash one another's *f.*
Ro 3:15 "Their *f* are swift to shed blood;
10:15 "How beautiful are the *f*

Ro 16:20 will soon crush Satan under your *f.*
1Co 12:21 And the head cannot say to the *f,*
15:25 has put all his enemies under his *f.*
Eph 1:22 God placed all things under his *f*
1Ti 5:10 washing the *f* of the saints,
Heb 1:13 a footstool for your *f*"?
2: 8 and put everything under his *f.*"
12:13 "Make level paths for your *f,*"
Rev 1:15 His *f* were like bronze glowing

FELIX

Governor before whom Paul was tried (Ac 23:23–24:27).

FELLOWSHIP
Ex 20:24 burnt offerings and *f* offerings,
Lev 3: 1 If someone's offering is a *f* offering,
1Co 1: 9 who has called you into *f*
5: 2 out of your *f* the man who did this?
2Co 6:14 what *f* can light have with darkness
13:14 and the *f* of the Holy Spirit be
Gal 2: 9 and Barnabas the right hand of *f*
Php 2: 1 if any *f* with the Spirit,
3:10 the *f* of sharing in his sufferings,
1Jn 1: 3 And our *f* is with the Father
1: 3 so that you also may have *f* with us.
1: 6 claim to have *f* with him yet walk
1: 7 we have *f* with one another,

FEMALE
Ge 1:27 male and *f* he created them.
5: 2 He created them male and *f*
Mt 19: 4 Creator 'made them male and *f,*'
Mk 10: 6 God 'made them male and *f.*'
Gal 3:28 *f,* for you are all one in Christ Jesus

FEROCIOUS
Mt 7:15 but inwardly they are *f* wolves.

FERTILE (FERTILIZE)
Isa 32:15 and the desert becomes a *f* field,
Jer 2: 7 I brought you into a *f* land

FERTILIZE* (FERTILE)
Lk 13: 8 and I'll dig around it and *f* it.

FERVOR*
Ac 18:25 and he spoke with great *f*
Ro 12:11 but keep your spiritual *f,* serving

FESTIVAL
1Co 5: 8 Therefore let us keep the *F,*
Col 2:16 or with regard to a religious *f,*

FESTUS

Successor of Felix; sent Paul to Caesar (Ac 25–26).

FEVER
Job 30:30 my body burns with *f.*
Mt 8:14 mother-in-law lying in bed with a *f.*
Lk 4:38 was suffering from a high *f,*
Jn 4:52 "The *f* left him yesterday
Ac 28: 8 suffering from *f* and dysentery.

FIELD (FIELDS)
Ge 4: 8 Abel, "Let's go out to the *f.*"
Lev 19: 9 reap to the very edges of your *f*
19:19 Do not plant your *f* with two kinds
Pr 31:16 She considers a *f* and buys it;
Isa 40: 6 glory is like the flowers of the *f.*
Mt 6:28 See how the lilies of the *f* grow.
6:30 how God clothes the grass of the *f,*
13:38 *f* is the world, and the good seed
13:44 is like treasure hidden in a *f.*
Lk 14:18 I have just bought a *f,* and I must go
1Co 3: 9 you are God's *f,* God's building.
1Pe 1:24 glory is like the flowers of the *f;*

FIELDS (FIELD)
Ru 2: 2 go to the *f* and pick up the leftover
Lk 2: 8 were shepherds living out in the *f*
Jn 4:35 open your eyes and look at the *f!*

FIG (FIGS SYCAMORE-FIG)
Ge 3: 7 so they sewed *f* leaves together
Jdg 9:10 "Next, the trees said to the *f* tree,
1Ki 4:25 man under his own vine and *f* tree.
Pr 27:18 He who tends a *f* tree will eat its
Mic 4: 4 and under his own *f* tree,
Zec 3:10 to sit under his vine and *f* tree,'
Mt 21:19 Seeing a *f* tree by the road,
Lk 13: 6 "A man had a *f* tree, planted
Jas 3:12 brothers, can a *f* tree bear olives,
Rev 6:13 drop from a *f* tree when shaken

FIGHT (FIGHTING FIGHTS FOUGHT)
Ex 14:14 The LORD will *f* for you; you need
Dt 1:30 going before you, will *f* for you,
3:22 the LORD your God himself will *f*
Ne 4:20 Our God will *f* for us!"
Ps 35: 1 *f* against those who *f* against me.
Jn 18:36 my servants would *f*
1Co 9:26 I do not *f* like a man beating the air.
2Co 10: 4 The weapons we *f*
1Ti 1:18 them you may *f* the good *f,*
6:12 Fight the good *f* of the faith.
2Ti 4: 7 fought the good *f,* I have finished

FIGHTING (FIGHT)
Jos 10:14 Surely the LORD was *f* for Israel!

FIGHTS (FIGHT)
Jos 23:10 the LORD your God *f* for you,
1Sa 25:28 because he *f* the LORD's battles.
Jas 4: 1 What causes *f* and quarrels

FIGS (FIG)
Lk 6:44 People do not pick *f*
Jas 3:12 grapevine bear *f?* Neither can a salt

FILL (FILLED FILLING FILLS FULL FULLNESS FULLY)
Ge 1:28 and increase in number; *f* the earth
Ps 16:11 you will *f* me with joy
81:10 wide your mouth and I will *f* it.
Pr 28:19 who chases fantasies will have his *f*
Hag 2: 7 and I will *f* this house with glory,'
Jn 6:26 you ate the loaves and had your *f.*
Ac 2:28 you will *f* me with joy
Ro 15:13 the God of hope *f* you with all joy

FILLED (FILL)
Ex 31: 3 I have *f* him with the Spirit of God,
35:31 he has *f* him with the Spirit of God,
Dt 34: 9 son of Nun was *f* with the spirit
1Ki 8:10 the cloud *f* the temple
8:11 glory of the LORD *f* his temple.
2Ch 5:14 of the LORD *f* the temple of God.
7: 1 the glory of the LORD *f* the temple
Ps 72:19 may the whole earth be *f*
119:64 The earth is *f* with your love,
Isa 6: 4 and the temple was *f* with smoke.
Eze 10: 3 and a cloud *f* the inner court.
10: 4 The cloud *f* the temple,
43: 5 the glory of the LORD *f* the temple
Hab 2:14 For the earth will be *f*
3: 3 and his praise *f* the earth.
Mt 5: 6 for they will be *f.*
Lk 1:15 and he will be *f* with the Holy Spirit
1:41 and Elizabeth was *f* with the Holy
1:67 His father Zechariah was *f*
2:40 and became strong; he was *f*
Jn 12: 3 the house was *f* with the fragrance
Ac 2: 2 *f* the whole house where they were
2: 4 All of them were *f*
4: 8 Then Peter, *f* with the Holy Spirit,
4:31 they were all *f* with the Holy Spirit
9:17 and be *f* with the Holy Spirit."
13: 9 called Paul, *f* with the Holy Spirit,
Eph 5:18 Instead, be *f* with the Spirit.
Php 1:11 *f* with the fruit of righteousness
Rev 15: 8 And the temple was *f* with smoke

FILLING (FILL)
Eze 44: 4 the glory of the LORD *f* the temple

FILLS (FILL)
Nu 14:21 of the LORD *f* the whole earth,
Ps 107: 9 and *f* the hungry with good things.
Eph 1:23 fullness of him who *f* everything

FILTH (FILTHY)
Isa 4: 4 The Lord will wash away the *f*
Jas 1:21 rid of all moral *f* and the evil that is

FILTHY (FILTH)
Isa 64: 6 all our righteous acts are like *f* rags;
Col 3: 8 and *f* language from your lips.
2Pe 2: 7 by the *f* lives of lawless men

FINAL (FINALITY)
Ps 73:17 then I understood their *f* destiny.

FINALITY* (FINAL)
Ro 9:28 on earth with speed and *f.*"

FINANCIAL*
1Ti 6: 5 that godliness is a means to *f* gain.

FIND (FINDS FOUND)
Nu 32:23 be sure that your sin will *f* you out.
Dt 4:29 you will *f* him if you look for him
1Sa 23:16 and helped him *f* strength in God.
Job 23: 3 If only I knew where to *f* him;
Ps 36: 7 *f* refuge in the shadow
62: 5 *F* rest, O my soul, in God alone;
91: 4 under his wings you will *f* refuge;
Pr 8:17 and those who seek me *f* me.
14:22 those who plan what is good *f* love
20: 6 but a faithful man who can *f?*
24:14 if you *f* it, there is a future hope
31:10 A wife of noble character who can *f*
Jer 6:16 and you will *f* rest for your souls.
29:13 and *f* me when you seek me
Mt 7: 7 seek and you will *f;* knock
11:29 and you will *f* rest for your souls.
16:25 loses his life for me will *f* it.
22: 9 invite to the banquet anyone you *f.*'
Lk 11: 9 seek and you will *f;* knock
18: 8 will he *f* faith on the earth?"
Jn 10: 9 come in and go out, and *f* pasture.

FINDS (FIND)
Ps 62: 1 My soul *f* rest in God alone;
112: 1 who *f* great delight
119:162 like one who *f* great spoil.
Pr 3:13 Blessed is the man who *f* wisdom,
8:35 For whoever *f* me *f* life
11:27 He who seeks good *f* good will,
18:22 He who *f* a wife *f* what is good
Mt 7: 8 he who seeks *f;* and to him who
10:39 Whoever *f* his life will lose it,
Lk 11:10 he who seeks *f;* and to him who
12:37 whose master *f* them watching
12:43 servant whom the master *f* doing
15: 4 go after the lost sheep until he *f* it?
15: 8 and search carefully until she *f* it?

FINE-SOUNDING* (SOUND)
Col 2: 4 may deceive you by *f* arguments.

FINGER
Ex 8:19 to Pharaoh, "This is the *f* of God."
31:18 of stone inscribed by the *f* of God.
Dt 9:10 two stone tablets inscribed by the *f*
Lk 11:20 But if I drive out demons by the *f*
16:24 to dip the tip of his *f* in water
Jn 8: 6 to write on the ground with his *f.*
20:25 and put my *f* where the nails were,

FINISH (FINISHED)
Jn 4:34 him who sent me and to *f* his work.
5:36 that the Father has given me to *f,*
Ac 20:24 if only I may *f* the race
2Co 8:11 Now *f* the work, so that your eager

Jas 1: 4 Perseverance must *f* its work

FINISHED (FINISH)
Ge 2: 2 seventh day God had *f* the work he
Jn 19:30 the drink, Jesus said, "It is *f*."
2Ti 4: 7 I have *f* the race, I have kept

FIRE
Ex 3: 2 in flames of *f* from within a bush.
13:21 in a pillar of *f* to give them light,
Lev 6:12 *f* on the altar must be kept burning;
9:24 *F* came out from the presence
1Ki 18:38 Then the *f* of the LORD fell
2Ki 2:11 suddenly a chariot of *f*
Isa 5:24 as tongues of *f* lick up straw
30:27 and his tongue is a consuming *f*.
Jer 23:29 my word like *f*," declares
Da 3:25 four men walking around in the *f*,
Zec 3: 2 stick snatched from the *f*?"
Mal 3: 2 For he will be like a refiner's *f*
Mt 3:11 you with the Holy Spirit and with *f*.
3:12 the chaff with unquenchable *f*."
5:22 will be in danger of the *f* of hell.
18: 8 and be thrown into eternal *f*.
25:41 into the eternal *f* prepared
Mk 9:43 where the *f* never goes out.
9:48 and the *f* is not quenched.'
9:49 Everyone will be salted with *f*.
Lk 3:16 you with the Holy Spirit and with *f*.
12:49 I have come to bring *f* on the earth,
Ac 2: 3 to be tongues of *f* that separated
1Co 3:13 It will be revealed with *f*,
1Th 5:19 Do not put out the Spirit's *f*;
Heb 12:29 for our "God is a consuming *f*."
Jas 3: 5 set on *f* by a small spark.
3: 6 also is a *f*, a world of evil
2Pe 3:10 the elements will be destroyed by *f*,
Jude : 7 suffer the punishment of eternal *f*.
:23 snatch others from the *f*
Rev 1:14 and his eyes were like blazing *f*.
20:14 The lake of *f* is the second death.

FIRM*
Ex 14:13 Stand *f* and you will see
15: 8 surging waters stood *f* like a wall;
Jos 3:17 the covenant of the LORD stood *f*
2Ch 20:17 stand *f* and see the deliverance
Ezr 9: 8 giving us a *f* place in his sanctuary,
Job 11:15 you will stand *f* and without fear.
36: 5 he is mighty, and *f* in his purpose.
41:23 they are *f* and immovable.
Ps 20: 8 but we rise up and stand *f*.
30: 7 you made my mountain stand *f*;
33: 9 he commanded, and it stood *f*.
33:11 of the LORD stand *f* forever,
37:23 he makes his steps *f*;
40: 2 and gave me a *f* place to stand.
75: 3 it is I who hold its pillars *f*.
78:13 made the water stand *f* like a wall.
89: 2 that your love stands *f* forever,
89: 4 and make your throne *f*
93: 5 Your statutes stand *f*;
119:89 it stands *f* in the heavens.
Pr 4:26 and take only ways that are *f*.
10:25 but the righteous stand *f* forever.
12: 7 the house of the righteous stands *f*.
Isa 7: 9 If you do not stand *f* in your faith,
22:17 about to take *f* hold of you
22:23 drive him like a peg into a *f* place;
22:25 into the *f* place will give way;
Eze 13: 5 so that it will stand *f* in the battle
Zec 8:23 nations will take *f* hold of one Jew
Mt 10:22 he who stands *f* to the end will be
24:13 he who stands *f* to the end will be
Mk 13:13 he who stands *f* to the end will be
Lk 21:19 By standing *f* you will gain life.
1Co 10:12 So, if you think you are standing *f*,
15:58 my dear brothers, stand *f*.
16:13 on your guard; stand *f* in the faith;
2Co 1: 7 for you is *f*, because we know that
1:21 who makes both us and you stand *f*
2Co 1:24 because it is by faith you stand *f*.
Gal 5: 1 Stand *f*, then, and do not let
Eph 6:14 Stand *f* then, with the belt
Php 1:27 I will know that you stand *f*
4: 1 that is how you should stand *f*
Col 1:23 in your faith, established and *f*,
2: 5 and how *f* your faith in Christ is.
4:12 that you may stand *f* in all the will
1Th 3: 8 since you are standing *f* in the Lord
2Th 2:15 stand *f* and hold to the teachings
1Ti 6:19 a *f* foundation for the coming age,
2Ti 2:19 God's solid foundation stands *f*,
Heb 6:19 an anchor for the soul, *f* and secure
Jas 5: 8 You too, be patient and stand *f*,
1Pe 5: 9 Resist him, standing *f* in the faith,
5:10 make you strong, *f* and steadfast.

FIRST
Ge 1: 5 and there was morning—the *f* day.
13: 4 and where he had *f* built an altar.
Ex 34:19 *f* offspring of every womb belongs
1Ki 22: 5 "*F* seek the counsel of the LORD."
Pr 18:17 *f* to present his case seems right,
Isa 44: 6 I am the *f* and I am the last;
48:12 I am the *f* and I am the last.
Mt 5:24 *F* go and be reconciled
6:33 But seek *f* his kingdom
7: 5 *f* take the plank out
19:30 But many who are *f* will be last,
20:16 last will be *f*, and the *f* will be last."
20:27 wants to be *f* must be your slave—
22:38 This is the *f* and greatest
23:26 *F* clean the inside of the cup
Mk 9:35 to be *f*, he must be the very last,
10:31 are *f* will be last, and the last *f*."
10:44 wants to be *f* must be slave
13:10 And the gospel must *f* be preached
Lk 13:30 will be *f*, and *f* who will be last."
Jn 8: 7 let him be the *f* to throw a stone
Ac 11:26 disciples were called Christians *f*
Ro 1:16 *f* for the Jew, then for the Gentile.
1:17 is by faith from *f* to last,
2: 9 *f* for the Jew, then for the Gentile;
2:10 *f* for the Jew, then for the Gentile.
1Co 12:28 in the church God has appointed *f*
15:45 "The *f* man Adam became a living
2Co 8: 5 they gave themselves *f* to the Lord
Eph 6: 2 which is the *f* commandment
1Th 4:16 and the dead in Christ will rise *f*.
1Ti 2:13 For Adam was formed *f*, then Eve.
Heb 10: 9 He sets aside the *f*
Jas 3:17 comes from heaven is *f* of all pure;
1Jn 4:19 We love because he *f* loved us.
3Jn : 9 but Diotrephes, who loves to be *f*,
Rev 1:17 I am the *F* and the Last.
2: 4 You have forsaken your *f* love.
22:13 and the Omega, the *F* and the Last,

FIRSTBORN (BEAR)
Ex 11: 5 Every *f* son in Egypt will die,
34:20 Redeem all your *f* sons.
Ps 89:27 I will also appoint him my *f*,
Lk 2: 7 and she gave birth to her *f*, a son.
Ro 8:29 that he might be the *f*
Col 1:15 image of the invisible God, the *f*
1:18 and the *f* from among the dead,
Heb 1: 6 when God brings his *f*
12:23 of the *f*, whose names are written
Rev 1: 5 who is the faithful witness, the *f*

FIRSTFRUITS
Ex 23:16 the Feast of Harvest with the *f*
23:19 "Bring the best of the *f* of your soil
Ro 8:23 who have the *f* of the Spirit,
1Co 15:23 Christ, the *f*; then, when he comes,
Rev 14: 4 offered as *f* to God and the Lamb.

FISH (FISHERS)
Ge 1:26 let them rule over the *f* of the sea
Jnh 1:17 But the LORD provided a great *f*
Mt 7:10 asks for a *f*, will give him a snake?
Mt 12:40 three nights in the belly of a huge *f*,
14:17 loaves of bread and two *f*,"
Mk 6:38 they said, "Five—and two *f*."
Lk 5: 6 of *f* that their nets began to break.
9:13 loaves of bread and two *f*—
Jn 6: 9 small barley loaves and two small *f*,
21: 5 haven't you any *f*?" "No,"
21:11 It was full of large *f*, 153, but

FISHERMEN
Mk 1:16 a net into the lake, for they were *f*.

FISHERS (FISH)
Mt 4:19 "and I will make you *f* of men."
Mk 1:17 "and I will make you *f* of men."

FISHHOOK*
Job 41: 1 pull in the leviathan with a *f*

FISTS
Mt 26:67 and struck him with their *f*.

FIT (FITTING)
Jdg 17: 6 no king; everyone did as he saw *f*.
21:25 no king; everyone did as he saw *f*.

FITTING* (FIT)
Ps 33: 1 it is *f* for the upright to praise him.
147: 1 how pleasant and *f* to praise him!
Pr 10:32 of the righteous know what is *f*,
19:10 It is not *f* for a fool to live in luxury
26: 1 honor is not *f* for a fool.
1Co 14:40 everything should be done in a *f*
Col 3:18 to your husbands, as is *f* in the Lord
Heb 2:10 sons to glory, it was *f* that God,

FIX* (FIXED)
Dt 11:18 *F* these words of mine
Job 14: 3 Do you *f* your eye on such a one?
Pr 4:25 *f* your gaze directly before you.
Isa 46: 8 "Remember this, *f* it in mind,
Am 9: 4 I will *f* my eyes upon them
2Co 4:18 we *f* our eyes not on what is seen,
Heb 3: 1 heavenly calling, *f* your thoughts
12: 2 Let us *f* our eyes on Jesus,

FIXED* (FIX)
2Ki 8:11 stared at him with a *f* gaze
Job 38:10 when I *f* limits for it
Ps 141: 8 my eyes are *f* on you, O Sovereign
Pr 8:28 *f* securely the fountains of the deep
Jer 33:25 and night and the *f* laws of heaven
Lk 16:26 and you a great chasm has been *f*,

FLAME (FLAMES FLAMING)
2Ti 1: 6 you to fan into *f* the gift of God,

FLAMES (FLAME)
1Co 3:15 only as one escaping through the *f*.
13: 3 and surrender my body to the *f*,

FLAMING (FLAME)
Eph 6:16 you can extinguish all the *f* arrows

FLANK
Eze 34:21 Because you shove with *f*

FLASH
1Co 15:52 in a *f*, in the twinkling of an eye,

FLATTER* (FLATTERING FLATTERS FLATTERY)
Job 32:21 nor will I *f* any man;
Ps 78:36 But then they would *f* him
Jude :16 *f* others for their own advantage.

FLATTERING* (FLATTER)
Ps 12: 2 their *f* lips speak with deception.
12: 3 May the LORD cut off all *f* lips
Pr 26:28 and a *f* mouth works ruin.
28:23 than he who has a *f* tongue.
Eze 12:24 or *f* divinations among the people

FLATTERS* (FLATTER)
Ps 36: 2 For in his own eyes he *f* himself
Pr 29: 5 Whoever *f* his neighbor

FLATTERY* (FLATTER)
Job 32:22 for if I were skilled in *f*,
Da 11:32 With *f* he will corrupt those who
Ro 16:18 and *f* they deceive the minds
1Th 2: 5 You know we never used *f*,

FLAWLESS*
2Sa 22:31 the word of the LORD is *f*.
Job 11: 4 You say to God, 'My beliefs are *f*
Ps 12: 6 And the words of the LORD are *f*,
18:30 the word of the LORD is *f*.
Pr 30: 5 "Every word of God is *f*;
SS 5: 2 my dove, my *f* one.

FLEE (FLEES)
Ps 139: 7 Where can I *f* from your presence?
1Co 6:18 *F* from sexual immorality.
10:14 my dear friends, *f* from idolatry.
1Ti 6:11 But you, man of God, *f* from all this
2Ti 2:22 *F* the evil desires of youth,
Jas 4: 7 Resist the devil, and he will *f*

FLEECE
Jdg 6:37 I will place a wool *f*

FLEES (FLEE)
Pr 28: 1 The wicked man *f* though no one

FLEETING*
Job 14: 2 like a *f* shadow, he does not endure
Ps 39: 4 let me know how *f* is my life.
89:47 Remember how *f* is my life.
144: 4 his days are like a *f* shadow.
Pr 21: 6 is a *f* vapor and a deadly snare.
31:30 Charm is deceptive, and beauty is *f*

FLESH
Ge 2:23 and *f* of my *f*;
2:24 and they will become one *f*.
2Ch 32: 8 With him is only the arm of *f*,
Job 19:26 yet in my *f* I will see God;
Eze 11:19 of stone and give them a heart of *f*.
36:26 of stone and give you a heart of *f*.
Mt 19: 5 and the two will become one *f*'?
Mk 10: 8 and the two will become one *f*.'
Jn 1:14 The Word became *f* and made his
6:51 This bread is my *f*, which I will give
1Co 6:16 "The two will become one *f*."
15:39 All *f* is not the same: Men have one
Eph 5:31 and the two will become one *f*."
6:12 For our struggle is not against *f*
Php 3: 2 do evil, those mutilators of the *f*.
1Jn 4: 2 come in the *f* is from God,
Jude :23 the clothing stained by corrupted *f*.

FLIGHT
Dt 32:30 or two put ten thousand to *f*,

FLINT
Isa 50: 7 Therefore have I set my face like *f*,
Zec 7:12 They made their hearts as hard as *f*

FLIRTING*
Isa 3:16 *f* with their eyes,

FLOCK (FLOCKS)
Ps 77:20 You led your people like a *f*
78:52 he brought his people out like a *f*;
95: 7 the *f* under his care.
Isa 40:11 He tends his *f* like a shepherd:
Jer 10:21 and all their *f* is scattered.
23: 2 "Because you have scattered my *f*
31:10 watch over his *f* like a shepherd.'
Eze 34: 2 not shepherds take care of the *f*?
Zec 11:17 who deserts the *f*!
Mt 26:31 the sheep of the *f* will be scattered.'
Lk 12:32 little *f*, for your Father has been
Jn 10:16 shall be one *f* and one shepherd.
Ac 20:28 all the *f* of which the Holy Spirit
1Co 9: 7 Who tends a *f* and does not drink
1Pe 5: 2 Be shepherds of God's *f* that is
5: 3 but being examples to the *f*.

FLOCKS (FLOCK)
Lk 2: 8 keeping watch over their *f* at night.

FLOG (FLOGGED FLOGGING)
Pr 19:25 *F* a mocker, and the simple will
Ac 22:25 to *f* a Roman citizen who hasn't

FLOGGED (FLOG)
Jn 19: 1 Pilate took Jesus and had him *f*.
Ac 5:40 the apostles in and had them *f*.
16:23 After they had been severely *f*,
2Co 11:23 frequently, been *f* more severely,

FLOGGING (FLOG)
Heb 11:36 *f*, while still others were chained

FLOOD (FLOODGATES)
Ge 7: 7 ark to escape the waters of the *f*.
Mal 2:13 You *f* the LORD's altar with tears.
Mt 24:38 For in the days before the *f*,
2Pe 2: 5 world when he brought the *f*

FLOODGATES (FLOOD)
Ge 7:11 the *f* of the heavens were opened.
Mal 3:10 see if I will not throw open the *f*

FLOOR
Jas 2: 3 or "Sit on the *f* by my feet,"

FLOUR
Lev 2: 1 his offering is to be of fine *f*.
Nu 7:13 filled with fine *f* mixed with oil
28: 9 of an ephah of fine *f* mixed with oil.

FLOURISH (FLOURISHES FLOURISHING)
Ps 72: 7 In his days the righteous will *f*;
92: 7 and all evildoers *f*,
92:12 The righteous will *f* like a palm tree
Pr 14:11 but the tent of the upright will *f*.

FLOURISHES (FLOURISH)
Pr 12:12 but the root of the righteous *f*.

FLOURISHING (FLOURISH)
Ps 52: 8 *f* in the house of God;

FLOW (FLOWING)
Nu 13:27 and it does *f* with milk and honey!
Jn 7:38 streams of living water will *f*

FLOWER (FLOWERS)
Job 14: 2 up like a *f* and withers away;
Ps 103:15 he flourishes like a *f* of the field;
Jas 1:10 he will pass away like a wild *f*.

FLOWERS (FLOWER)
Isa 40: 6 and all their glory is like the *f*
40: 7 The grass withers and the *f* fall,
1Pe 1:24 and all their glory is like the *f*

FLOWING (FLOW)
Ex 3: 8 a land *f* with milk and honey—
33: 3 Go up to the land *f* with milk
Nu 16:14 us into a land *f* with milk
Jos 5: 6 a land *f* with milk and honey.
Ps 107:33 *f* springs into thirsty ground,
107:35 the parched ground into *f* springs;
Jer 32:22 a land *f* with milk and honey.
Eze 20: 6 a land *f* with milk and honey,
Rev 22: 1 *f* from the throne of God

FLUTE
Ps 150: 4 praise him with the strings and *f*,
Mt 11:17 " 'We played the *f* for you,
1Co 14: 7 that make sounds, such as the *f*

FOAL*
Zec 9: 9 on a colt, the *f* of a donkey.
Mt 21: 5 on a colt, the *f* of a donkey.' "

FOILS*
Ps 33:10 The LORD *f* the plans
Isa 44:25 who *f* the signs of false prophets

FOLDING* (FOLDS)
Pr 6:10 a little *f* of the hands to rest—
24:33 a little *f* of the hands to rest—

FOLDS (FOLDING)
Ecc 4: 5 The fool *f* his hands

FOLLOW (FOLLOWED FOLLOWING FOLLOWS)
Ex 23: 2 Do not *f* the crowd in doing wrong.
Lev 18: 4 and be careful to *f* my decrees.
Dt 5: 1 Learn them and be sure to *f* them.
17:19 *f* carefully all the words of this law
1Ki 11: 6 he did not *f* the LORD completely,
2Ch 34:33 they did not fail to *f* the LORD,
Ps 23: 6 Surely goodness and love will *f* me
119:166 and I *f* your commands.
Mt 4:19 *f* me," Jesus said, "and I will make
8:19 I will *f* you wherever you go."
8:22 But Jesus told him, "*F* me,
16:24 and take up his cross and *f* me.
19:27 "We have left everything to *f* you!
Lk 9:23 take up his cross daily and *f* me.
9:61 Still another said, "I will *f* you,
Jn 10: 4 his sheep *f* him because they know
10: 5 But they will never *f* a stranger;
10:27 I know them, and they *f* me.
12:26 Whoever serves me must *f* me;
21:19 Then he said to him, "*F* me!"
1Co 1:12 One of you says, "I *f* Paul";
11: 1 *F* my example, as I follow
14: 1 *F* the way of love and eagerly
2Th 3: 9 ourselves a model for you to *f*.
1Pe 2:21 that you should *f* in his steps.
Rev 14: 4 They *f* the Lamb wherever he goes.

FOLLOWED (FOLLOW)
Nu 32:11 they have not *f* me wholeheartedly,
Dt 1:36 he *f* the LORD wholeheartedly."
Jos 14:14 he *f* the LORD, the God of Israel,
2Ch 10:14 he *f* the advice of the young men
Mt 4:20 once they left their nets and *f* him.
9: 9 and Matthew got up and *f* him.
26:58 But Peter *f* him at a distance,
Lk 18:43 he received his sight and *f* Jesus,

FOLLOWING (FOLLOW)
Ps 119:14 I rejoice in *f* your statutes
Php 3:17 Join with others in *f* my example,
1Ti 1:18 by *f* them you may fight the good

FOLLOWS (FOLLOW)
Jn 8:12 Whoever *f* me will never walk

FOLLY (FOOL)
Pr 14:29 a quick-tempered man displays *f*.
19: 3 A man's own *f* ruins his life,
Ecc 10: 1 so a little *f* outweighs wisdom
Mk 7:22 envy, slander, arrogance and *f*.
2Ti 3: 9 their *f* will be clear to everyone.

FOOD (FOODS)
Ge 1:30 I give every green plant for *f*."
Pr 12: 9 to be somebody and have no *f*.
12:11 his land will have abundant *f*,
20:13 you will have *f* to spare.
20:17 *F* gained by fraud tastes sweet
21:20 of the wise are stores of choice *f*
22: 9 for he shares his *f* with the poor.
23: 3 for that *f* is deceptive.
23: 6 Do not eat the *f* of a stingy man,
25:21 If your enemy is hungry, give him *f*
31:14 bringing her *f* from afar.
31:15 she provides *f* for her family
Isa 58: 7 not to share your *f* with the hungry
Eze 18: 7 but gives his *f* to the hungry

Da 1: 8 to defile himself with the royal *f*
Mt 3: 4 His *f* was locusts and wild honey.
6:25 Is not life more important than *f*,
Jn 4:32 "I have *f* to eat that you know
4:34 have brought him *f*?" "My *f*,"
6:27 Do not work for *f* that spoils,
6:55 my flesh is real *f* and my blood is
Ac 15:20 to abstain from *f* polluted by idols,
Ro 14:14 fully convinced that no *f* is unclean
1Co 8: 1 Now about *f* sacrificed to idols:
8: 8 But *f* does not bring us near to God
2Co 11:27 and have often gone without *f*;
1Ti 6: 8 But if we have *f* and clothing,
Heb 5:14 But solid *f* is for the mature,
Jas 2:15 sister is without clothes and daily *f*.

FOODS (FOOD)
Mk 7:19 Jesus declared all *f* "clean.")

FOOL (FOLLY FOOL'S FOOLISH FOOLISHNESS FOOLS)
1Sa 25:25 his name is *F*, and folly goes
Ps 14: 1 The *f* says in his heart,
Pr 10:10 and a chattering *f* comes to ruin.
10:18 and whoever spreads slander is a *f*.
12:15 The way of a *f* seems right to him,
12:16 A *f* shows his annoyance at once,
14:16 but a *f* is hotheaded and reckless.
15: 5 A *f* spurns his father's discipline,
17:12 than a *f* in his folly.
17:16 use is money in the hand of a *f*,
17:21 To have a *f* for a son brings grief;
17:28 Even a *f* is thought wise
18: 2 A *f* finds no pleasure
20: 3 but every *f* is quick to quarrel.
23: 9 Do not speak to a *f*,
24: 7 Wisdom is too high for a *f*;
26: 4 Do not answer a *f* according
26: 5 Answer a *f* according to his folly,
26: 7 is a proverb in the mouth of a *f*.
26:11 so a *f* repeats his folly.
26:12 for a *f* than for him.
27:22 Though you grind a *f* in a mortar,
28:26 He who trusts in himself is a *f*,
29:11 A *f* gives full vent to his anger,
29:20 for a *f* than for him.
Mt 5:22 But anyone who says, 'You *f*!'
Lk 12:20 "But God said to him, 'You *f*!
1Co 3:18 he should become a "*f*"
2Co 11:21 I am speaking as a *f*—I

FOOL'S (FOOL)
Pr 14: 3 A *f* talk brings a rod to his back,
18: 7 A *f* mouth is his undoing,

FOOLISH (FOOL)
Pr 10: 1 but a *f* son grief to his mother.
14: 1 her own hands the *f* one tears hers
15:20 but a *f* man despises his mother.
17:25 A *f* son brings grief to his father
19:13 A *f* son is his father's ruin,
Mt 7:26 practice is like a *f* man who built
25: 2 of them were *f* and five were wise.
Lk 11:40 You *f* people! Did not the one who
24:25 He said to them, "How *f* you are,
1Co 1:20 Has not God made *f* the wisdom
1:27 God chose the *f* things of the world
Gal 3: 1 died for nothing!" You *f* Galatians!
Eph 5: 4 should there be obscenity, *f* talk
5:17 Therefore do not be *f*,
Tit 3: 9 But avoid *f* controversies

FOOLISHNESS (FOOL)
1Co 1:18 of the cross is *f* to those who are
1:21 through the *f* of what was preached
1:23 block to Jews and *f* to Gentiles,
1:25 For the *f* of God is wiser
2:14 for they are *f* to him, and he cannot
3:19 of this world is *f* in God's sight.

FOOLS (FOOL)
Pr 1: 7 but *f* despise wisdom and discipline
3:35 but *f* he holds up to shame.
12:23 but the heart of *f* blurts out folly.
13:19 but *f* detest turning from evil.
13:20 but a companion of *f* suffers harm.
14: 9 *F* mock at making amends for sin,
14:24 but the folly of *f* yields folly.
Ecc 7: 5 than to listen to the song of *f*.
7: 6 so is the laughter of *f*.
10: 6 *F* are put in many high positions,
Mt 23:17 You blind *f*! Which is greater:
Ro 1:22 they became *f* and exchanged
1Co 4:10 We are *f* for Christ, but you are

FOOT (FEET FOOTHOLD)
Jos 1: 3 every place where you set your *f*,
Ps 121: 3 He will not let your *f* slip—
Pr 3:23 and your *f* will not stumble;
4:27 keep your *f* from evil.
25:17 Seldom set *f* in your neighbor's
Isa 1: 6 From the sole of your *f* to the top
Mt 18: 8 or your *f* causes you to sin,
Lk 4:11 so that you will not strike your *f*
1Co 12:15 If the *f* should say, "Because I am
Rev 10: 2 He planted his right *f* on the sea

FOOTHOLD* (FOOT)
Ps 69: 2 where there is no *f*.
73: 2 I had nearly lost my *f*.
Eph 4:27 and do not give the devil a *f*.

FOOTSTEPS (STEP)
Ps 119:133 Direct my *f* according

FOOTSTOOL
Ps 99: 5 and worship at his *f*;
110: 1 a *f* for your feet."
Isa 66: 1 and the earth is my *f*.
Mt 5:35 for it is his *f*; or by Jerusalem,
Ac 7:49 and the earth is my *f*.
Heb 1:13 a *f* for your feet"?
10:13 for his enemies to be made his *f*,

FORBEARANCE*
Ro 3:25 because in his *f* he had left the sins

FORBID
1Co 14:39 and do not *f* speaking in tongues.
1Ti 4: 3 They *f* people to marry

FORCE (FORCED FORCEFUL FORCES FORCING)
Jn 6:15 to come and make him king by *f*,
Ac 26:11 and I tried to *f* them to blaspheme.
Gal 2:14 that you *f* Gentiles

FORCED (FORCE)
Mt 27:32 and they *f* him to carry the cross.
Phm :14 do will be spontaneous and not *f*.

FORCEFUL* (FORCE)
Mt 11:12 forcefully advancing, and *f* men lay
2Co 10:10 "His letters are weighty and *f*,

FORCES (FORCE)
Mt 5:41 If someone *f* you to go one mile,
Eph 6:12 and against the spiritual *f* of evil

FORCING (FORCE)
Lk 16:16 and everyone is *f* his way into it.

FOREFATHERS (FATHER)
Heb 1: 1 spoke to our *f* through the prophets
1Pe 1:18 handed down to you from your *f*,

FOREHEAD (FOREHEADS)
Ex 13: 9 a reminder on your *f* that the law
13:16 on your *f* that the LORD brought
1Sa 17:49 and struck the Philistine on the *f*.
Rev 13:16 a mark on his right hand or on his *f*,

FOREHEADS (FOREHEAD)
Dt 6: 8 hands and bind them on your *f*.
Rev 9: 4 not have the seal of God on their *f*.
14: 1 his Father's name written on their *f*

FOREIGN (FOREIGNER FOREIGNERS)
Ge 35: 2 "Get rid of the *f* gods you have
2Ch 14: 3 He removed the *f* altars
33:15 He got rid of the *f* gods
Isa 28:11 with *f* lips and strange tongues

FOREIGNER (FOREIGN)
Lk 17:18 give praise to God except this *f*?"
1Co 14:11 I am a *f* to the speaker,

FOREIGNERS (FOREIGN)
Eph 2:12 *f* to the covenants of the promise,
2:19 you are no longer *f* and aliens,

FOREKNEW* (KNOW)
Ro 8:29 For those God *f* he
11: 2 not reject his people, whom he *f*.

FOREKNOWLEDGE* (KNOW)
Ac 2:23 to you by God's set purpose and *f*;
1Pe 1: 2 to the *f* of God the Father,

FORESAW*
Gal 3: 8 Scripture *f* that God would justify

FOREST
Jas 3: 5 Consider what a great *f* is set

FOREVER (EVER)
Ge 3:22 the tree of life and eat, and live *f*."
6: 3 Spirit will not contend with man *f*,
Ex 3:15 This is my name *f*, the name
2Sa 7:26 so that your name will be great *f*.
1Ki 2:33 may there be the LORD's peace *f*."
9: 3 by putting my Name there *f*.
1Ch 16:15 He remembers his covenant *f*,
16:34 his love endures *f*.
16:41 "for his love endures *f*."
17:24 and that your name will be great *f*.
2Ch 5:13 his love endures *f*."
20:21 for his love endures *f*."
Ps 9: 7 The LORD reigns *f*;
23: 6 dwell in the house of the LORD *f*.
28: 9 be their shepherd and carry them *f*.
29:10 the LORD is enthroned as King *f*.
33:11 the plans of the LORD stand firm *f*
37:28 They will be protected *f*,
44: 8 and we will praise your name *f*.
61: 4 I long to dwell in your tent *f*
72:19 Praise be to his glorious name *f*;
73:26 and my portion *f*.
77: 8 Has his unfailing love vanished *f*?
79:13 will praise you *f*;
81:15 and their punishment would last *f*.
86:12 I will glorify your name *f*.
89: 1 of the LORD's great love *f*;
92: 8 But you, O LORD, are exalted *f*.
100: 5 is good and his love endures *f*;
102:12 But you, O LORD, sit enthroned *f*;
104:31 of the LORD endure *f*;
107: 1 his love endures *f*.
110: 4 "You are a priest *f*,
111: 3 and his righteousness endures *f*.
112: 6 man will be remembered *f*.
117: 2 of the LORD endures *f*.
118: 1 his love endures *f*.
119:111 Your statutes are my heritage *f*;
119:152 that you established them to last *f*.
136: 1 *His love endures* f.
146: 6 the LORD, who remains faithful *f*.
Pr 10:25 but the righteous stand firm *f*.
27:24 for riches do not endure *f*,
Isa 25: 8 he will swallow up death *f*.
26: 4 Trust in the LORD *f*,
32:17 will be quietness and confidence *f*.
40: 8 but the word of our God stands *f*."
51: 6 But my salvation will last *f*,

Isa 51: 8 But my righteousness will last *f,*
57:15 he who lives *f,* whose name is holy:
59:21 from this time on and *f,"*
Jer 33:11 his love endures *f."*
Eze 37:26 put my sanctuary among them *f.*
Da 2:44 to an end, but it will itself endure *f.*
3: 9 live *f!* You have issued a decree,
Jn 6:51 eats of this bread, he will live *f.*
14:16 Counselor to be with you *f—*
Ro 9: 5 who is God over all, *f* praised!
16:27 to the only wise God be glory *f*
1Co 9:25 it to get a crown that will last *f.*
1Th 4:17 And so we will be with the Lord *f.*
Heb 5: 6 "You are a priest *f,*
7:17 "You are a priest *f,*
7:24 Jesus lives *f,* he has a permanent
13: 8 same yesterday and today and *f.*
1Pe 1:25 but the word of the Lord stands *f."*
1Jn 2:17 who does the will of God lives *f.*
2Jn : 2 lives in us and will be with us *f:*

FOREVERMORE (EVER)
Ps 113: 2 both now and *f.*

FORFEIT
Mk 8:36 the whole world, yet *f* his soul?
Lk 9:25 and yet lose or *f* his very self?

FORGAVE (FORGIVE)
Ps 32: 5 and you *f*
65: 3 you *f* our transgressions
78:38 you *f* their iniquities
Eph 4:32 just as in Christ God *f* you.
Col 2:13 He *f* us all our sins, having
3:13 Forgive as the Lord *f* you.

FORGET (FORGETS FORGETTING FORGOT FORGOTTEN)
Dt 4:23 Be careful not to *f* the covenant
6:12 that you do not *f* the LORD,
2Ki 17:38 Do not *f* the covenant I have made
Ps 9:17 all the nations that *f* God.
10:12 Do not *f* the helpless.
50:22 "Consider this, you who *f* God,
78: 7 and would not *f* his deeds
103: 2 and *f* not all his benefits.
119:93 I will never *f* your precepts,
137: 5 may my right hand *f* its skill.
Pr 3: 1 My son, do not *f* my teaching,
4: 5 do not *f* my words or swerve
Isa 49:15 "Can a mother *f* the baby
51:13 that you *f* the LORD your Maker,
Jer 2:32 Does a maiden *f* her jewelry,
23:39 I will surely *f* you and cast you out
Heb 6:10 he will not *f* your work
13: 2 Do not *f* to entertain strangers,
13:16 And do not *f* to do good
2Pe 3: 8 But do not *f* this one thing,

FORGETS (FORGET)
Jn 16:21 her baby is born she *f* the anguish
Jas 1:24 immediately *f* what he looks like.

FORGETTING* (FORGET)
Php 3:13 *F* what is behind and straining
Jas 1:25 to do this, not *f* what he has heard,

FORGIVE* (FORGAVE FORGIVENESS FORGIVES FORGIVING)
Ge 50:17 I ask you to *f* your brothers the sins
50:17 please *f* the sins of the servants
Ex 10:17 Now *f* my sin once more
23:21 he will not *f* your rebellion,
32:32 But now, please *f* their sin—
34: 9 *f* our wickedness and our sin,
Nu 14:19 with your great love, *f* the sin
Dt 29:20 will never be willing to *f* him;
Jos 24:19 He will not *f* your rebellion
1Sa 15:25 *f* my sin and come back with me,
25:28 Please *f* your servant's offense,
1Ki 8:30 place, and when you hear, *f.*
8:34 and *f* the sin of your people Israel
8:36 and *f* the sin of your servants,
8:39 *F* and act; deal with each man
8:50 *f* all the offenses they have
8:50 *f* your people, who have sinned
2Ki 5:18 But may the LORD *f* your servant
5:18 may the LORD *f* your servant
24: 4 and the LORD was not willing to *f.*
2Ch 6:21 place; and when you hear, *f.*
6:25 and *f* the sin of your people Israel
6:27 and *f* the sin of your servants,
6:30 *F,* and deal with each man
6:39 *f* your people, who have sinned
7:14 will *f* their sin and will heal their
Job 7:21 and *f* my sins?
Ps 19:12 *F* my hidden faults.
25:11 *f* my iniquity, though it is great.
79: 9 deliver us and *f* our sins
Isa 2: 9 do not *f* them.
Jer 5: 1 I will *f* this city.
5: 7 "Why should I *f* you?
18:23 Do not *f* their crimes
31:34 "For I will *f* their wickedness
33: 8 and will *f* all their sins of rebellion
36: 3 then I will *f* their wickedness
50:20 for I will *f* the remnant I spare.
Da 9:19 O Lord, listen! O Lord, *f!* O Lord,
Hos 1: 6 that I should at all *f* them.
14: 2 "*F* all our sins
Am 7: 2 *f!* How can Jacob survive?
Mt 6:12 *F* us our debts,
6:14 For if you *f* men when they sin
6:14 heavenly Father will also *f* you.
6:15 But if you do not *f* men their sins,
6:15 your Father will not *f* your sins.
9: 6 authority on earth to *f* sins..
18:21 many times shall I *f* my brother
18:35 you *f* your brother from your heart
Mk 2: 7 Who can *f* sins but God alone?"
2:10 authority on earth to *f* sins
11:25 anything against anyone, *f* him,
11:25 in heaven may *f* you your sins."
Lk 5:21 Who can *f* sins but God alone?"
5:24 authority on earth to *f* sins..
6:37 *F,* and you will be forgiven.
11: 4 *F* us our sins,
11: 4 *f* everyone who sins against us.
17: 3 rebuke him, and if he repents, *f* him
17: 4 and says, 'I repent,' *f* him."
23:34 Jesus said, "Father, *f* them,
Jn 20:23 If you *f* anyone his sins, they are
20:23 if you do not *f* them, they are not
Ac 8:22 Perhaps he will *f* you
2Co 2: 7 you ought to *f* and comfort him,
2:10 If you *f* anyone, I also *f* him.
2:10 if there was anything to *f—*
12:13 a burden to you? *F* me this wrong!
Col 3:13 and *f* whatever grievances you may
3:13 *F* as the Lord forgave you.
Heb 8:12 For I will *f* their wickedness
1Jn 1: 9 and just and will *f* us our sins

FORGIVENESS* (FORGIVE)
Ps 130: 4 But with you there is *f;*
Mt 26:28 out for many for the *f* of sins.
Mk 1: 4 of repentance for the *f* of sins.
Lk 1:77 salvation through the *f* of their sins,
3: 3 of repentance for the *f* of sins.
24:47 and *f* of sins will be preached
Ac 5:31 that he might give repentance and *f*
10:43 believes in him receives *f* of sins
13:38 that through Jesus the *f*
26:18 so that they may receive *f* of sins
Eph 1: 7 through his blood, the *f* of sins,
Col 1:14 in whom we have redemption, the *f*
Heb 9:22 the shedding of blood there is no *f.*

FORGIVES* (FORGIVE)
Ps 103: 3 He *f* all my sins
Mic 7:18 pardons sin and *f* the transgression
Lk 7:49 "Who is this who even *f* sins?"

FORGIVING* (FORGIVE)
Ex 34: 7 and *f* wickedness, rebellion and sin.
Nu 14:18 abounding in love and *f* sin
Ne 9:17 But you are a *f* God, gracious
Ps 86: 5 You are *f* and good, O Lord,
99: 8 you were to Israel a *f* God,
Da 9: 9 The Lord our God is merciful and *f*
Eph 4:32 to one another, *f* each other,

FORGOT (FORGET)
Dt 32:18 you *f* the God who gave you birth.
Ps 78:11 They *f* what he had done,
106:13 But they soon *f* what he had done

FORGOTTEN (FORGET)
Job 11: 6 God has even *f* some of your sin.
Ps 44:20 If we had *f* the name of our God
Isa 17:10 You have *f* God your Savior;
Hos 8:14 Israel has *f* his Maker
Lk 12: 6 Yet not one of them is *f* by God.
2Pe 1: 9 and has *f* that he has been cleansed

FORM (FORMED)
Isa 52:14 *f* marred beyond human likeness—
2Ti 3: 5 having a *f* of godliness

FORMED (FORM)
Ge 2: 7 —the LORD God *f* the man
2:19 Now the LORD God had *f* out
Ps 103:14 for he knows how we are *f,*
Ecc 11: 5 or how the body is *f* in a mother's
Isa 29:16 Shall what is *f* say to him who *f* it,
45:18 but *f* it to be inhabited—
49: 5 he who *f* me in the womb
Jer 1: 5 "Before I *f* you in the womb I knew
Ro 9:20 "Shall what is *f* say to him who *f* it,
Gal 4:19 of childbirth until Christ is *f* in you,
1Ti 2:13 For Adam was *f* first, then Eve.
Heb 11: 3 understand that the universe was *f*
2Pe 3: 5 and the earth was *f* out of water

FORMLESS*
Ge 1: 2 Now the earth was *f* and empty,
Jer 4:23 and it was *f* and empty;

FORSAKE (FORSAKEN)
Dt 31: 6 he will never leave you nor *f* you."
Jos 1: 5 I will never leave you nor *f* you.
24:16 "Far be it from us to *f* the LORD
2Ch 15: 2 but if you *f* him, he will *f* you.
Ps 27:10 Though my father and mother *f* me
94:14 he will never *f* his inheritance.
Isa 55: 7 Let the wicked *f* his way
Heb 13: 5 never will I *f* you."

FORSAKEN (FORSAKE)
Ps 22: 1 my God, why have you *f* me?
37:25 I have never seen the righteous *f*
Mt 27:46 my God, why have you *f* me?"
Rev 2: 4 You have *f* your first love.

FORTRESS
2Sa 22: 2 "The LORD is my rock, my *f*
Ps 18: 2 The LORD is my rock, my *f*
31: 2 a strong *f* to save me.
59:16 for you are my *f,*
71: 3 for you are my rock and my *f.*
Pr 14:26 who fears the LORD has a secure *f,*

FORTUNE-TELLING*
Ac 16:16 deal of money for her owners by *f.*

FORTY
Ge 7: 4 on the earth for *f* days and *f* nights,
18:29 "What if only *f* are found there?"
Ex 16:35 The Israelites ate manna *f* years,
24:18 on the mountain *f* days and *f* nights
Nu 14:34 For *f* years—one year for each
Jos 14: 7 I was *f* years old when Moses
1Sa 4:18 He had led Israel *f* years.
2Sa 5: 4 king, and he reigned *f* years.
1Ki 19: 8 he traveled *f* days and *f* nights

2Ki 12: 1 and he reigned in Jerusalem *f* years
2Ch 9:30 in Jerusalem over all Israel *f* years.
Eze 29:12 her cities will lie desolate *f* years
Jnh 3: 4 "*F* more days and Nineveh will be
Mt 4: 2 After fasting *f* days and *f* nights,

FOUGHT (FIGHT)
1Co 15:32 If I *f* wild beasts in Ephesus
2Ti 4: 7 I have *f* the good fight, I have

FOUND (FIND)
2Ki 22: 8 "I have *f* the Book of the Law
1Ch 28: 9 If you seek him, he will be *f* by you;
2Ch 15:15 sought God eagerly, and he was *f*
Isa 55: 6 Seek the LORD while he may be *f*;
65: 1 I was *f* by those who did not seek
Da 5:27 on the scales and *f* wanting.
Mt 1:18 she was *f* to be with child
Lk 15: 6 with me; I have *f* my lost sheep.'
15: 9 with me; I have *f* my lost coin.'
15:24 is alive again; he was lost and is *f*.'
Ac 4:12 Salvation is *f* in no one else,
Ro 10:20 "I was *f* by those who did not seek
Jas 2: 8 If you really keep the royal law *f*
Rev 5: 4 no one was *f* who was worthy

FOUNDATION (FOUNDATIONS FOUNDED)
Isa 28:16 a precious cornerstone for a sure *f*;
Mt 7:25 because it had its *f* on the rock.
Lk 14:29 For if he lays the *f* and is not able
Ro 15:20 building on someone else's *f*.
1Co 3:10 I laid a *f* as an expert builder,
3:11 For no one can lay any *f* other
Eph 2:20 built on the *f* of the apostles
1Ti 3:15 the pillar and *f* of the truth.
2Ti 2:19 God's solid *f* stands firm,
Heb 6: 1 not laying again the *f* of repentance

FOUNDATIONS (FOUNDATION)
Ps 102:25 In the beginning you laid the *f*
Heb 1:10 O Lord, you laid the *f* of the earth,

FOUNDED (FOUNDATION)
Jer 10:12 he *f* the world by his wisdom
Heb 8: 6 and it is *f* on better promises.

FOUNTAIN
Ps 36: 9 For with you is the *f* of life;
Pr 14:27 The fear of the LORD is a *f* of life,
18: 4 the *f* of wisdom is a bubbling brook.
Zec 13: 1 "On that day a *f* will be opened

FOX (FOXES)
Lk 13:32 He replied, "Go tell that *f*,

FOXES (FOX)
SS 2:15 the little *f*
Mt 8:20 "*F* have holes and birds

FRAGRANCE (FRAGRANT)
Ex 30:38 it to enjoy its *f* must be cut
Jn 12: 3 filled with the *f* of the perfume.
2Co 2:14 us spreads everywhere the *f*
2:16 of death; to the other, the *f* of life.

FRAGRANT (FRAGRANCE)
Eph 5: 2 as a *f* offering and sacrifice to God.
Php 4:18 They are a *f* offering, an acceptable

FREE (FREED FREEDOM FREELY)
Ge 2:16 "You are *f* to eat from any tree
Ps 118: 5 and he answered by setting me *f*.
119:32 for you have set my heart *f*.
146: 7 The LORD sets prisoners *f*,
Pr 6: 3 then do this, my son, to *f* yourself,
Jn 8:32 and the truth will set you *f*."
8:36 if the Son sets you *f*, you will be *f*
Ro 6:18 You have been set *f* from sin
8: 2 of life set me *f* from the law of sin
1Co 12:13 whether Jews or Greeks, slave or *f*
Gal 3:28 slave nor *f*, male nor female,
Gal 5: 1 for freedom that Christ has set us *f*.
1Pe 2:16 *f* men, but do not use your freedom

FREED (FREE)
Ps 116:16 you have *f* me from my chains.
Ro 6: 7 anyone who has died has been *f*
Rev 1: 5 has *f* us from our sins by his blood,

FREEDOM (FREE)
Ps 119:45 I will walk about in *f*,
Isa 61: 1 to proclaim *f* for the captives
Lk 4:18 me to proclaim *f* for the prisoners
Ro 8:21 into the glorious *f* of the children
1Co 7:21 although if you can gain your *f*,
2Co 3:17 the Spirit of the Lord is, there is *f*.
Gal 2: 4 ranks to spy on the *f* we have
5:13 But do not use your *f* to indulge
Jas 1:25 into the perfect law that gives *f*,
1Pe 2:16 but do not use your *f* as a cover-up

FREELY (FREE)
Isa 55: 7 and to our God, for he will *f* pardon
Mt 10: 8 Freely you have received, *f* give.
Ro 3:24 and are justified *f* by his grace
Eph 1: 6 which he has *f* given us

FRESH
Jas 3:11 Can both *f* water and salt water

FRET*
Ps 37: 1 Do not *f* because of evil men
37: 7 do not *f* when men succeed
37: 8 do not *f*— it leads only to evil.
Pr 24:19 Do not *f* because of evil men

FRICTION
1Ti 6: 5 and constant *f* between men

FRIEND (FRIENDS FRIENDSHIP)
Ex 33:11 as a man speaks with his *f*.
2Ch 20: 7 descendants of Abraham your *f*?
Pr 17:17 A *f* loves at all times,
18:24 there is a *f* who sticks closer
27: 6 Wounds from a *f* can be trusted
27:10 Do not forsake your *f* and the *f*
Isa 41: 8 you descendants of Abraham my *f*,
Mt 11:19 a *f* of tax collectors and "sinners." '
Lk 11: 8 him the bread because he is his *f*,
Jn 19:12 "If you let this man go, you are no *f*
Jas 2:23 and he was called God's *f*.
4: 4 Anyone who chooses to be a *f*

FRIENDS (FRIEND)
Pr 16:28 and a gossip separates close *f*.
17: 9 the matter separates close *f*.
Zec 13: 6 given at the house of my *f*.'
Jn 15:13 that he lay down his life for his *f*.
15:14 You are my *f* if you do what I

FRIENDSHIP (FRIEND)
Jas 4: 4 don't you know that *f*

FRIGHTENED (FEAR)
Php 1:28 gospel without being *f* in any way.
1Pe 3:14 fear what they fear; do not be *f*."

FROGS
Ex 8: 2 plague your whole country with *f*.
Rev 16:13 three evil spirits that looked like *f*;

FRUIT (FRUITFUL)
Jdg 9:11 'Should I give up my *f*, so good
Ps 1: 3 which yields its *f* in season
Pr 11:30 The *f* of the righteous is a tree
12:14 From the *f* of his lips a man is filled
27:18 He who tends a fig tree will eat its *f*
Isa 11: 1 from his roots a Branch will bear *f*.
27: 6 and fill all the world with *f*.
32:17 The *f* of righteousness will be peace
Jer 17: 8 and never fails to bear *f*."
Hos 10:12 reap the *f* of unfailing love,
14: 2 that we may offer the *f* of our lips.
Am 8: 1 showed me: a basket of ripe *f*.
Mt 3: 8 Produce *f* in keeping
3:10 does not produce good *f* will be cut
7:16 By their *f* you will recognize them.
7:17 good *f*, but a bad tree bears bad *f*.
7:20 by their *f* you will recognize them.
12:33 a tree good and its *f* will be good,
Lk 3: 9 does not produce good *f* will be cut
6:43 nor does a bad tree bear good *f*.
13: 6 and he went to look for *f* on it,
Jn 15: 2 branch in me that bears no *f*,
15:16 and bear *f*—*f* that will last.
Ro 7: 4 in order that we might bear *f*
Gal 5:22 But the *f* of the Spirit is love, joy,
Php 1:11 with the *f* of righteousness that
Col 1:10 bearing *f* in every good work,
Heb 13:15 the *f* of lips that confess his name.
Jas 3:17 and good *f*, impartial and sincere.
Jude :12 autumn trees, without *f*
Rev 22: 2 of *f*, yielding its *f* every month.

FRUITFUL (FRUIT)
Ge 1:22 "Be *f* and increase in number
9: 1 "Be *f* and increase in number
35:11 be *f* and increase in number.
Ex 1: 7 the Israelites were *f* and multiplied
Ps 128: 3 Your wife will be like a *f* vine
Jn 15: 2 prunes so that it will be even more *f*.
Php 1:22 this will mean *f* labor for me.

FRUITLESS*
Eph 5:11 to do with the *f* deeds of darkness,

FRUSTRATION
Ro 8:20 For the creation was subjected to *f*,

FUEL
Isa 44:19 "Half of it I used for *f*;

FULFILL (FULFILLED FULFILLMENT FULFILLS)
Nu 23:19 Does he promise and not *f*?
Ps 61: 8 and *f* my vows day after day.
116:14 I will *f* my vows to the LORD
138: 8 The LORD will *f* his purpose
Ecc 5: 5 than to make a vow and not *f* it.
Isa 46:11 far-off land, a man to *f* my purpose.
Jer 33:14 'when I will *f* the gracious promise
Mt 1:22 place to *f* what the Lord had said
3:15 us to do this to *f* all righteousness."
4:14 *f* what was said
5:17 come to abolish them but to *f* them.
8:17 This was to *f* what was spoken
12:17 This was to *f* what was spoken
21: 4 place to *f* what was spoken
Jn 12:38 This was to *f* the word
13:18 But this is to *f* the scripture:
15:25 But this is to *f* what is written
1Co 7: 3 husband should *f* his marital duty

FULFILLED (FULFILL)
Jos 21:45 of Israel failed; every one was *f*.
23:14 Every promise has been *f*;
Pr 13:12 but a longing *f* is a tree of life.
13:19 A longing *f* is sweet to the soul,
Mt 2:15 so was *f* what the Lord had said
2:17 the prophet Jeremiah was *f*:
2:23 So was *f* what was said
13:14 In them is *f* the prophecy of Isaiah:
13:35 So was *f* what was spoken
26:54 would the Scriptures be *f* that say it
26:56 of the prophets might be *f*."
27: 9 by Jeremiah the prophet was *f*:
Mk 13: 4 that they are all about to be *f*?"
14:49 But the Scriptures must be *f*."
Lk 4:21 "Today this scripture is *f*
18:31 about the Son of Man will be *f*.
24:44 Everything must be *f* that is
Jn 18: 9 words he had spoken would be *f*:
19:24 the Scripture might be *f* which said,
19:28 and so that the Scripture would be *f*

Jn 19:36 so that the Scripture would be *f:*
Ac 1:16 to be *f* which the Holy Spirit spoke
Ro 13: 8 loves his fellowman has *f* the law.
Jas 2:23 And the scripture was *f* that says,

FULFILLMENT (FULFILL)
Ro 13:10 Therefore love is the *f* of the law.

FULFILLS (FULFILL)
Ps 57: 2 to God, who *f* his purpose for me.
145:19 He *f* the desires of those who fear

FULL (FILL)
2Ch 24:10 them into the chest until it was *f.*
Ps 127: 5 whose quiver is *f* of them.
Pr 27: 7 He who is *f* loathes honey,
31:11 Her husband has *f* confidence
Isa 6: 3 the whole earth is *f* of his glory."
11: 9 for the earth will be *f*
Lk 4: 1 Jesus, *f* of the Holy Spirit,
Jn 10:10 may have life, and have it to the *f.*
Ac 6: 3 known to be *f* of the Spirit
6: 5 a man *f* of faith and of the Holy
7:55 But Stephen, *f* of the Holy Spirit,
11:24 *f* of the Holy Spirit and faith,

FULL-GROWN* (GROW)
Jas 1:15 when it is *f,* gives birth to death.

FULLNESS* (FILL)
Dt 33:16 gifts of the earth and its *f*
Jn 1:16 From the *f* of his grace we have all
Ro 11:12 greater riches will their *f* bring!
Eph 1:23 the *f* of him who fills everything
3:19 to the measure of all the *f* of God.
4:13 to the whole measure of the *f*
Col 1:19 to have all his *f* dwell in him,
1:25 to you the word of God in its *f*—
2: 9 in Christ all the *f* of the Deity lives
2:10 and you have been given *f* in Christ

FULLY (FILL)
1Ki 8:61 your hearts must be *f* committed
2Ch 16: 9 whose hearts are *f* committed
Ps 119: 4 that are to be *f* obeyed.
119:138 they are *f* trustworthy.
Pr 13: 4 of the diligent are *f* satisfied.
Lk 6:40 everyone who is *f* trained will be
Ro 4:21 being *f* persuaded that God had
14: 5 Each one should be *f* convinced
1Co 13:12 shall know *f,* even as I am *f* known.
15:58 Always give yourselves *f*
2Ti 4:17 the message might be *f* proclaimed

FURIOUS (FURY)
Dt 29:28 In *f* anger and in great wrath
Jer 32:37 where I banish them in my *f* anger

FURNACE
Isa 48:10 in the *f* of affliction.
Da 3: 6 be thrown into a blazing *f.*"
Mt 13:42 will throw them into the fiery *f,*

FURY (FURIOUS)
Isa 14: 6 and in *f* subdued nations
Jer 21: 5 and a mighty arm in anger and *f*
Rev 14:10 will drink of the wine of God's *f,*
16:19 with the wine of the *f* of his wrath.
19:15 the winepress of the *f* of the wrath

FUTILE (FUTILITY)
Mal 3:14 You have said, 'It is *f* to serve God.
1Co 3:20 that the thoughts of the wise are *f.*"

FUTILITY (FUTILE)
Eph 4:17 in the *f* of their thinking.

FUTURE
Ps 37:37 there is a *f* for the man of peace.
Pr 23:18 There is surely a *f* hope for you,
Ecc 7:14 anything about his *f.*
8: 7 Since no man knows the *f,*
Jer 29:11 plans to give you hope and a *f.*
31:17 So there is hope for your *f,*"
Ro 8:38 neither the present nor the *f,*
1Co 3:22 life or death or the present or the *f*

GABRIEL*
Angel who interpreted Daniel's visions (Da 8:16–26; 9:20–27); announced births of John (Lk 1:11–20), Jesus (Lk 1:26–38).

GAD
1. Son of Jacob by Zilpah (Ge 30:9–11; 35:26; 1Ch 2:2). Tribe of blessed (Ge 49:19; Dt 33:20–21), numbered (Nu 1:25; 26:18), allotted land east of the Jordan (Nu 32; 34:14; Jos 18:7; 22), west (Eze 48:27–28), 12,000 from (Rev 7:5).
2. Prophet; seer of David (1Sa 22:5; 2Sa 24:11–19; 1Ch 29:29).

GAIN (GAINED GAINS)
Ex 14:17 And I will *g* glory through Pharaoh
Ps 60:12 With God we will *g* the victory,
Pr 4: 1 pay attention and *g* understanding.
8: 5 You who are simple, *g* prudence;
28:16 he who hates ill-gotten *g* will enjoy
28:23 in the end *g* more favor
Isa 63:12 to *g* for himself everlasting renown
Da 2: 8 that you are trying to *g* time,
Mk 8:36 it for a man to *g* the whole world,
Lk 9:25 it for a man to *g* the whole world,
21:19 standing firm you will *g* life.
1Co 13: 3 but have not love, I *g* nothing.
Php 1:21 to live is Christ and to die is *g.*
3: 8 that I may *g* Christ and be found
1Ti 3:13 have served well *g* an excellent
6: 5 godliness is a means to financial *g.*
6: 6 with contentment is great *g.*

GAINED (GAIN)
Jer 32:20 have *g* the renown that is still yours
Ro 5: 2 through whom we have *g* access

GAINS (GAIN)
Pr 3:13 the man who *g* understanding,
11:16 A kindhearted woman *g* respect,
15:32 heeds correction *g* understanding.
29:23 but a man of lowly spirit *g* honor.
Mt 16:26 for a man if he *g* the whole world,

GALILEE
Isa 9: 1 but in the future he will honor *G*
Mt 4:15 *G* of the Gentiles—
26:32 I will go ahead of you into *G.*"
28:10 Go and tell my brothers to go to *G;*

GALL
Mt 27:34 mixed with *g;* but after tasting it,

GALLIO
Ac 18:12 While *G* was proconsul of Achaia,

GALLOWS
Est 7:10 Haman on the *g* he had prepared

GAMALIEL
Ac 5:34 But a Pharisee named *G,* a teacher

GAMES
1Co 9:25 in the *g* goes into strict training.

GAP
Eze 22:30 stand before me in the *g* on behalf

GAPE*
Ps 35:21 They *g* at me and say, "Aha! Aha!

GARDEN (GARDENER)
Ge 2: 8 the LORD God had planted a *g*
2:15 put him in the *G* of Eden to work it
SS 4:12 You are a *g* locked up, my sister,
Isa 58:11 You will be like a well-watered *g,*
Jer 31:12 They will be like a well-watered *g,*
Eze 28:13 the *g* of God;
31: 9 Eden in the *g* of God.

GARDENER (GARDEN)
Jn 15: 1 true vine, and my Father is the *g.*

GARLAND*
Pr 1: 9 They will be a *g* to grace your head
4: 9 She will set a *g* of grace

GARMENT (GARMENTS)
Ps 102:26 they will all wear out like a *g.*
Isa 50: 9 They will all wear out like a *g;*
51: 6 the earth will wear out like a *g*
61: 3 and a *g* of praise
Mt 9:16 of unshrunk cloth on an old *g,*
Jn 19:23 This *g* was seamless, woven
Heb 1:11 they will all wear out like a *g.*

GARMENTS (GARMENT)
Ge 3:21 The LORD God made *g* of skin
Ex 28: 2 Make sacred *g* for your brother
Lev 16:23 and take off the linen *g* he put
16:24 holy place and put on his regular *g.*
Isa 61:10 me with *g* of salvation
63: 1 with his *g* stained crimson?
Joel 2:13 and not your *g.*
Zec 3: 4 and I will put rich *g* on you."
Jn 19:24 "They divided my *g* among them

GATE (GATES)
Ps 118:20 This is the *g* of the LORD
Pr 31:23 husband is respected at the city *g,*
31:31 works bring her praise at the city *g.*
Mt 7:13 For wide is the *g* and broad is
7:13 "Enter through the narrow *g.*
Jn 10: 1 not enter the sheep pen by the *g,*
10: 2 enters by the *g* is the shepherd
10: 7 "I tell you the truth, I am the *g*
10: 9 I am the *g;* whoever enters
Heb 13:12 also suffered outside the city *g*
Rev 21:21 each *g* made of a single pearl.

GATES (GATE)
Ps 24: 7 Lift up your heads, O you *g;*
24: 9 Lift up your heads, O you *g;*
100: 4 Enter his *g* with thanksgiving
118:19 Open for me the *g* of righteousness
Isa 60:11 Your *g* will always stand open,
60:18 and your *g* Praise.
62:10 Pass through, pass through the *g!*
Mt 16:18 the *g* of Hades will not overcome it
Rev 21:12 On the *g* were written the names
21:21 The twelve *g* were twelve pearls,
21:25 On no day will its *g* ever be shut,
22:14 may go through the *g* into the city.

GATH
1Sa 17:23 the Philistine champion from *G,*
2Sa 1:20 "Tell it not in *G,*
Mic 1:10 Tell it not in *G;*

GATHER (GATHERED GATHERS)
Ps 106:47 and *g* us from the nations,
Isa 11:12 and *g* the exiles of Israel;
Jer 3:17 and all nations will *g* in Jerusalem
23: 3 "I myself will *g* the remnant
31:10 who scattered Israel will *g* them
Zep 2: 1 *G* together, *g* together,
3:20 At that time I will *g* you;
Zec 14: 2 I will *g* all the nations to Jerusalem
Mt 12:30 he who does not *g* with me scatters
13:30 then *g* the wheat and bring it
23:37 longed to *g* your children together,
24:31 and they will *g* his elect
25:26 *g* where I have not scattered seed?
Mk 13:27 and *g* his elect from the four winds,
Lk 3:17 and to *g* the wheat into his barn,
11:23 and he who does not *g* with me,
13:34 longed to *g* your children together,

GATHERED (GATHER)
Ex 16:18 and he who *g* little did not have too

Pr 30: 4 Who has *g* up the wind
Mt 25:32 All the nations will be *g* before him
2Co 8:15 and he who *g* little did not have too
2Th 2: 1 Lord Jesus Christ and our being *g*
Rev 16:16 Then they *g* the kings together

GATHERS (GATHER)
Ps 147: 2 he *g* the exiles of Israel.
Pr 10: 5 He who *g* crops in summer is a wise
Isa 40:11 He *g* the lambs in his arms
Mt 23:37 a hen *g* her chicks under her wings,

GAVE (GIVE)
Ge 2:20 man *g* names to all the livestock,
3: 6 She also *g* some to her husband,
14:20 Abram *g* him a tenth of everything.
28: 4 the land God *g* to Abraham."
35:12 The land I *g* to Abraham
39:23 *g* him success in whatever he did.
47:11 *g* them property in the best part
Ex 4:11 to him, "Who *g* man his mouth?
31:18 he *g* him the two tablets
Dt 2:12 did in the land the LORD *g* them
2:36 The LORD our God *g* us all
3:12 I *g* the Reubenites and the Gadites
3:13 I *g* to the half tribe of Manasseh.
3:15 And I *g* Gilead to Makir.
3:16 Gadites I *g* the territory extending
8:16 He *g* you manna to eat in the desert
26: 9 us to this place and *g* us this land,
32: 8 the Most High *g* the nations their
Jos 11:23 and he *g* it as an inheritance
13:14 tribe of Levi he *g* no inheritance,
14:13 *g* him Hebron as his inheritance.
21:44 The LORD *g* them rest
24:13 I *g* you a land on which you did not
1Sa 27: 6 So on that day Achish *g* him Ziklag
2Sa 12: 8 I *g* you the house of Israel
1Ki 4:29 God *g* Solomon wisdom
5:12 The LORD *g* Solomon wisdom,
Ezr 2:69 According to their ability they *g*
Ne 9:15 In their hunger you *g* them bread
9:20 You *g* your good Spirit
9:22 You *g* them kingdoms and nations,
9:27 compassion you *g* them deliverers,
Job 1:21 LORD *g* and the LORD has taken
42:10 prosperous again and *g* him twice
Ps 69:21 and *g* me vinegar for my thirst.
135:12 he *g* their land as an inheritance,
Ecc 12: 7 the spirit returns to God who *g* it.
Eze 3: 2 and he *g* me the scroll to eat.
Mt 1:25 And he *g* him the name Jesus.
25:35 and you *g* me something to drink,
25:42 and you *g* me nothing to drink,
26:26 Jesus took bread, *g* thanks
27:50 in a loud voice, he *g* up his spirit.
Mk 6: 7 *g* them authority over evil spirits.
Jn 1:12 he *g* the right to become children
3:16 so loved the world that he *g* his one
17: 4 by completing the work you *g* me
17: 6 you *g* them to me and they have
19:30 bowed his head and *g* up his spirit.
Ac 1: 3 *g* many convincing proofs that he
2:45 they *g* to anyone as he had need.
11:17 *g* them the same gift as he *g* us,
Ro 1:24 Therefore God *g* them
1:26 God *g* them over to shameful lusts.
1:28 he *g* them over to a depraved mind,
8:32 not spare his own Son, but *g* him up
2Co 5:18 *g* us the ministry of reconciliation:
8: 3 For I testify that they *g* as much
8: 5 they *g* themselves first to the Lord
Gal 1: 4 who *g* himself for our sins
2:20 who loved me and *g* himself for me
Eph 4: 8 and *g* gifts to men."
5: 2 as Christ loved us and *g* himself up
5:25 and *g* himself up for her
2Th 2:16 and by his grace *g* us eternal
1Ti 2: 6 who *g* himself as a ransom
Tit 2:14 who *g* himself for us to redeem us
1Jn 3:24 We know it by the Spirit he *g* us.

GAZE
Ps 27: 4 to *g* upon the beauty of the LORD
Pr 4:25 fix your *g* directly before you.

GEDALIAH
Governor of Judah appointed by Nebuchadnezzar (2Ki 25:22–26; Jer 39–41).

GEHAZI*
Servant of Elisha (2Ki 4:12–5:27; 8:4–5).

GENEALOGIES
1Ti 1: 4 themselves to myths and endless *g*.
Tit 3: 9 avoid foolish controversies and *g*

GENERATION (GENERATIONS)
Ex 3:15 am to be remembered from *g* to *g*.
Nu 32:13 until the whole *g* of those who had
Dt 1:35 of this evil *g* shall see the good land
Jdg 2:10 After that whole *g* had been
Ps 24: 6 Such is the *g* of those who seek him
48:13 tell of them to the next *g*.
71:18 I declare your power to the next *g*,
78: 4 we will tell the next *g*
102:18 Let this be written for a future *g*,
112: 2 the *g* of the upright will be blessed
145: 4 One *g* will commend your works
La 5:19 your throne endures from *g* to *g*.
Da 4: 3 his dominion endures from *g* to *g*.
4:34 his kingdom endures from *g* to *g*.
Joel 1: 3 and their children to the next *g*.
Mt 12:39 adulterous *g* asks for a miraculous
17:17 "O unbelieving and perverse *g*,"
23:36 all this will come upon this *g*.
24:34 this *g* will certainly not pass away
Mk 9:19 "O unbelieving *g*," Jesus replied,
13:30 this *g* will certainly not pass away
Lk 1:50 who fear him, from *g* to *g*.
11:29 Jesus said, "This is a wicked *g*.
11:30 will the Son of Man be to this *g*.
11:50 Therefore this *g* will be held
21:32 this *g* will certainly not pass away
Ac 2:40 Save yourselves from this corrupt *g*
Php 2:15 fault in a crooked and depraved *g*,

GENERATIONS (GENERATION)
Ge 9:12 a covenant for all *g* to come:
17: 7 after you for the *g* to come,
17: 9 after you for the *g* to come.
Ex 20: 6 a thousand *g* of those
31:13 and you for the *g* to come,
Dt 7: 9 covenant of love to a thousand *g*
32: 7 consider the *g* long past.
1Ch 16:15 he commanded, for a thousand *g*,
Job 8: 8 "Ask the former *g*
Ps 22:30 future *g* will be told about the Lord
33:11 of his heart through all *g*.
45:17 your memory through all *g*;
89: 1 faithfulness known through all *g*.
90: 1 throughout all *g*.
100: 5 continues through all *g*.
102:12 your renown endures through all *g*.
105: 8 he commanded, for a thousand *g*,
119:90 continues through all *g*;
135:13 renown, O LORD, through all *g*.
145:13 dominion endures through all *g*.
146:10 your God, O Zion, for all *g*.
Pr 27:24 and a crown is not secure for all *g*.
Isa 41: 4 forth the *g* from the beginning?
51: 8 my salvation through all *g*."
Lk 1:48 now on all *g* will call me blessed,
Eph 3: 5 not made known to men in other *g*
3:21 in Christ Jesus throughout all *g*,
Col 1:26 been kept hidden for ages and *g*,

GENEROSITY* (GENEROUS)
2Co 8: 2 poverty welled up in rich *g*.
9:11 and through us your *g* will result
9:13 and for your *g* in sharing with them

GENEROUS* (GENEROSITY)
Ps 37:26 They are always *g* and lend freely;
112: 5 Good will come to him who is *g*
Pr 11:25 A *g* man will prosper;
22: 9 A *g* man will himself be blessed,
Mt 20:15 Or are you envious because I am *g*
2Co 9: 5 Then it will be ready as a *g* gift,
9: 5 for the *g* gift you had promised.
9:11 way so that you can be *g*
1Ti 6:18 and to be *g* and willing to share.

GENTILE (GENTILES)
Ac 21:25 As for the *G* believers, we have
Ro 1:16 first for the Jew, then for the *G*.
2: 9 first for the Jew, then for the *G*;
2:10 first for the Jew, then for the *G*.
10:12 difference between Jew and *G*—

GENTILES (GENTILE)
Isa 42: 6 and a light for the *G*,
49: 6 also make you a light for the *G*,
49:22 "See, I will beckon to the *G*,
Lk 2:32 a light for revelation to the *G*
21:24 on by the *G* until the times
Ac 9:15 to carry my name before the *G*
10:45 been poured out even on the *G*.
11:18 granted even the *G* repentance unto
13:16 and you *G* who worship God,
13:46 of eternal life, we now turn to the *G*
13:47 I have made you a light for the *G*,
14:27 opened the door of faith to the *G*.
15:14 by taking from the *G* a people
18: 6 From now on I will go to the *G*."
22:21 I will send you far away to the *G*.' "
26:20 and in all Judea, and to the *G* also,
28:28 salvation has been sent to the *G*,
Ro 2:14 when *G*, who do not have the law,
3: 9 and *G* alike are all under sin.
3:29 Is he not the God of *G* too? Yes,
9:24 from the Jews but also from the *G*?
11:11 to the *G* to make Israel envious.
11:12 their loss means riches for the *G*,
11:13 as I am the apostle to the *G*,
15: 9 I will praise you among the *G*;
15: 9 so that the *G* may glorify God
1Co 1:23 block to Jews and foolishness to *G*,
Gal 1:16 I might preach him among the *G*,
2: 2 gospel that I preach among the *G*.
2: 8 my ministry as an apostle to the *G*.
2: 9 agreed that we should go to the *G*,
3: 8 that God would justify the *G*
3:14 to the *G* through Christ Jesus,
Eph 3: 6 the gospel the *G* are heirs together
3: 8 to the *G* the unsearchable riches
Col 1:27 among the *G* the glorious riches
1Ti 2: 7 a teacher of the true faith to the *G*.
2Ti 4:17 and all the *G* might hear it.

GENTLE* (GENTLENESS)
Dt 28:54 Even the most *g* and sensitive man
28:56 The most *g* and sensitive woman
28:56 and *g* that she would not venture
2Sa 18: 5 Be *g* with the young man Absalom
1Ki 19:12 And after the fire came a *g* whisper
Job 41: 3 Will he speak to you with *g* words?
Pr 15: 1 A *g* answer turns away wrath,
25:15 and a *g* tongue can break a bone.
Jer 11:19 I had been like a *g* lamb led
Zec 9: 9 *g* and riding on a donkey,
Mt 11:29 for I am *g* and humble in heart,
21: 5 *g* and riding on a donkey,
Ac 27:13 When a *g* south wind began
1Co 4:21 or in love and with a *g* spirit?
Eph 4: 2 Be completely humble and *g*;
1Th 2: 7 but we were *g* among you,
1Ti 3: 3 not violent but *g*, not quarrelsome,
1Pe 3: 4 the unfading beauty of a *g*

GENTLENESS* (GENTLE)
2Co 10: 1 By the meekness and *g* of Christ,
Gal 5:23 faithfulness, *g* and self-control.

Php 4: 5 Let your *g* be evident to all.
Col 3:12 kindness, humility, *g* and patience.
1Ti 6:11 faith, love, endurance and *g*.
1Pe 3:15 But do this with *g* and respect,

GENUINE*
2Co 6: 8 *g*, yet regarded as impostors;
Php 2:20 who takes a *g* interest
1Pe 1: 7 may be proved *g* and may result

GERIZIM
Dt 27:12 on Mount *G* to bless the people:

GERSHOM
Ex 2:22 and Moses named him *G*, saying,

GETHSEMANE*
Mt 26:36 disciples to a place called *G*,
Mk 14:32 They went to a place called *G*,

GHOST see also SPIRIT
Lk 24:39 a *g* does not have flesh and bones,

GIBEON
Jos 10:12 "O sun, stand still over *G*,

GIDEON*
Judge, also called Jerub-Baal; freed Israel from Midianites (Jdg 6–8; Heb 11:32). Given sign of fleece (Jdg 6:36–40).

GIFT (GIFTED GIFTS)
Pr 18:16 A *g* opens the way for the giver
21:14 A *g* given in secret soothes anger,
Ecc 3:13 in all his toil—this is the *g* of God.
Mt 5:23 if you are offering your *g*
Jn 4:10 "If you knew the *g* of God
Ac 1: 4 wait for the *g* my Father promised,
2:38 And you will receive the *g*
11:17 So if God gave them the same *g*
Ro 6:23 but the *g* of God is eternal life
12: 6 If a man's *g* is prophesying,
1Co 7: 7 each man has his own *g* from God;
2Co 8:12 the *g* is acceptable according
9:15 be to God for his indescribable *g!*
Eph 2: 8 it is the *g* of God—not by works,
1Ti 4:14 not neglect your *g*, which was
2Ti 1: 6 you to fan into flame the *g* of God,
Heb 6: 4 who have tasted the heavenly *g*,
Jas 1:17 and perfect *g* is from above,
1Pe 3: 7 with you of the gracious *g* of life,
4:10 should use whatever *g* he has
Rev 22:17 let him take the free *g* of the water

GIFTED* (GIFT)
1Co 14:37 he is a prophet or spiritually *g*,

GIFTS (GIFT)
Ps 76:11 bring *g* to the One to be feared.
112: 9 He has scattered abroad his *g*
Pr 25:14 of *g* he does not give.
Mt 2:11 and presented him with *g* of gold
7:11 Father in heaven give good *g*
7:11 to give good *g* to your children,
Lk 11:13 to give good *g* to your children,
Ac 10: 4 and *g* to the poor have come up
Ro 11:29 for God's *g* and his call are
12: 6 We have different *g*, according
1Co 12: 1 Now about spiritual *g*, brothers,
12: 4 There are different kinds of *g*,
12:28 those with *g* of administration,
12:30 all work miracles? Do all have *g*
12:31 But eagerly desire the greater *g*.
14: 1 and eagerly desire spiritual *g*,
14:12 eager to have spiritual *g*,
14:12 excel in *g* that build up the church.
2Co 9: 9 "He has scattered abroad his *g*
Eph 4: 8 and gave *g* to men."
Heb 2: 4 and *g* of the Holy Spirit distributed
9: 9 indicating that the *g* and sacrifices

GILEAD
1Ch 27:21 the half-tribe of Manasseh in *G*:
Jer 8:22 Is there no balm in *G?*
46:11 "Go up to *G* and get balm,

GILGAL
Jos 5: 9 So the place has been called *G*

GIRD*
Ps 45: 3 *G* your sword upon your side,

GIRL
Ge 24:16 *g* was very beautiful, a virgin;
2Ki 5: 2 a young *g* from Israel.
Mk 5:41 Little *g*, I say to you, get up!

GIVE (GAVE GIVEN GIVER GIVES GIVING LIFE-GIVING)
Ge 28: 4 you and your descendants the blessing *g* to Abraham
28:22 that you *g* me I will *g* you a tenth."
Ex 20:16 "You shall not *g* false testimony
30:15 The rich are not to *g* more
Nu 6:26 and *g* you peace." '
Dt 5:20 "You shall not *g* false testimony
15:10 *G* generously to him and do
15:14 *G* to him as the LORD your God
1Sa 1:11 then I will *g* him to the LORD
1:28 So now I *g* him to the LORD.
2Ch 15: 7 be strong and do not *g* up,
Pr 21:26 but the righteous *g* without sparing
23:26 My son, *g* me your heart
25:21 if he is thirsty, *g* him water to drink
30: 8 but *g* me only my daily bread.
31:31 *G* her the reward she has earned,
Ecc 3: 6 a time to search and a time to *g* up,
Isa 42: 8 I will not *g* my glory to another
Eze 36:26 I will *g* you a new heart
Mt 6:11 *G* us today our daily bread.
7:11 know how to *g* good gifts
10: 8 Freely you have received, freely *g*.
16:19 I will *g* you the keys
22:21 "*G* to Caesar what is Caesar's,
Mk 8:37 Or what can a man *g* in exchange
10:19 not steal, do not *g* false testimony,
Lk 6:38 *G*, and it will be given to you.
11: 3 *G* us each day our daily bread.
11:13 Father in heaven *g* the Holy Spirit
14:33 who does not *g* up everything he
Jn 10:28 I *g* them eternal life, and they shall
13:34 "A new commandment I *g* you:
14:16 he will *g* you another Counselor
14:27 I do not *g* to you as the world gives.
14:27 leave with you; my peace I *g* you.
17: 2 people that he might *g* eternal life
Ac 20:35 blessed to *g* than to receive.' "
Ro 2: 7 immortality, he will *g* eternal life.
8:32 with him, graciously *g* us all things
12: 8 let him *g* generously;
13: 7 *G* everyone what you owe him:
14:12 each of us will *g* an account
2Co 9: 7 Each man should *g* what he has
Gal 2: 5 We did not *g* in to them
6: 9 reap a harvest if we do not *g* up.
Heb 10:25 Let us not *g* up meeting together,
Rev 14: 7 "Fear God and *g* him glory,

GIVEN (GIVE)
Nu 8:16 are to be *g* wholly to me.
Dt 26:11 things the LORD your God has *g*
Job 3:23 Why is life *g* to a man
Ps 115:16 but the earth he has *g* to man.
Isa 9: 6 to us a son is *g*,
Mt 6:33 and all these things will be *g* to you
7: 7 "Ask and it will be *g* to you;
13:12 Whoever has will be *g* more,
22:30 people will neither marry nor be *g*
25:29 everyone who has will be *g* more,
Lk 6:38 Give, and it will be *g* to you.
8:10 kingdom of God has been *g* to you,
11: 9 Ask and it will be *g* to you;
Lk 22:19 saying, "This is my body *g* for you;
Jn 3:27 man can receive only what is *g* him
15: 7 you wish, and it will be *g* you.
17:24 I want those you have *g* me to be
17:24 the glory you have *g* me
18:11 the cup the Father has *g* me?"
Ac 5:32 whom God has *g* to those who
20:24 the task the Lord Jesus has *g* me—
Ro 5: 5 the Holy Spirit, whom he has *g* us.
1Co 4: 2 those who have been *g* a trust must
11:24 and when he had *g* thanks,
12:13 we were all *g* the one Spirit to drink
2Co 5: 5 and has *g* us the Spirit as a deposit,
Eph 1: 6 which he has freely *g* us
4: 7 to each one of us grace has been *g*
1Ti 4:14 was *g* you through a prophetic
1Jn 4:13 because he has *g* us of his Spirit.

GIVER* (GIVE)
Pr 18:16 A gift opens the way for the *g*
2Co 9: 7 for God loves a cheerful *g*.

GIVES (GIVE)
Job 35:10 who *g* songs in the night,
Ps 119:130 The unfolding of your words *g* light;
Pr 3:34 but *g* grace to the humble.
11:24 One man *g* freely, yet gains
14:30 A heart at peace *g* life to the body,
15:30 good news *g* health to the bones.
19: 6 of a man who *g* gifts.
25:26 is a righteous man who *g* way
28:27 He who *g* to the poor will lack
29: 4 justice a king *g* a country stability,
Isa 40:29 He *g* strength to the weary
Hab 2:15 "Woe to him who *g* drink
Mt 10:42 if anyone *g* even a cup of cold water
Jn 5:21 even so the Son *g* life to whom he is
6:63 The Spirit *g* life; the flesh counts
1Co 15:57 He *g* us the victory
2Co 3: 6 the letter kills, but the Spirit *g* life.
1Th 4: 8 who *g* you his Holy Spirit.
Jas 1:25 into the perfect law that *g* freedom,
4: 6 but *g* grace to the humble."
1Pe 5: 5 but *g* grace to the humble."

GIVING (GIVE)
Ne 8: 8 *g* the meaning so that the people
Est 9:19 a day for *g* presents to each other.
Ps 19: 8 *g* joy to the heart.
Pr 15:23 A man finds joy in *g* an apt reply—
Mt 6: 4 so that your *g* may be in secret.
24:38 marrying and *g* in marriage,
Ac 15: 8 them by *g* the Holy Spirit to them,
2Co 8: 7 also excel in this grace of *g*.
Php 4:15 shared with me in the matter of *g*

GLAD* (GLADDENS GLADNESS)
Ex 4:14 his heart will be *g* when he sees you
Jos 22:33 They were *g* to hear the report
Jdg 8:25 "We'll be *g* to give them."
18:20 household?" Then the priest was *g*.
1Sa 19: 5 and you saw it and were *g*.
2Sa 1:20 daughters of the Philistines be *g*,
1Ki 8:66 *g* in heart for all the good things
1Ch 16:31 heavens rejoice, let the earth be *g*;
2Ch 7:10 and *g* in heart for the good things
Ps 5:11 let all who take refuge in you be *g*;
9: 2 I will be *g* and rejoice in you;
14: 7 let Jacob rejoice and Israel be *g!*
16: 9 Therefore my heart is *g*
21: 6 made him *g* with the joy
31: 7 I will be *g* and rejoice in your love,
32:11 Rejoice in the LORD and be *g*,
40:16 rejoice and be *g* in you;
45: 8 music of the strings makes you *g*.
46: 4 whose streams make *g* the city
48:11 the villages of Judah are *g*
53: 6 let Jacob rejoice and Israel be *g!*
58:10 The righteous will be *g*
67: 4 May the nations be *g* and sing
68: 3 But may the righteous be *g*

Ps 69:32 The poor will see and be *g*—
70: 4 rejoice and be *g* in you;
90:14 for joy and be *g* all our days.
90:15 Make us *g* for as many days
92: 4 For you make me *g* by your deeds,
96:11 heavens rejoice, let the earth be *g;*
97: 1 LORD reigns, let the earth be *g;*
97: 8 and the villages of Judah are *g*
105:38 Egypt was *g* when they left,
107:30 They were *g* when it grew calm,
118:24 let us rejoice and be *g* in it.
149: 2 of Zion be *g* in their King.
Pr 23:15 then my heart will be *g;*
23:25 May your father and mother be *g;*
29: 6 a righteous one can sing and be *g.*
Ecc 8:15 sun than to eat and drink and be *g.*
Isa 25: 9 let us rejoice and be *g*
35: 1 and the parched land will be *g;*
65:18 But be *g* and rejoice forever
66:10 with Jerusalem and be *g* for her,
Jer 20:15 who made him very *g,* saying,
31:13 Then maidens will dance and be *g,*
41:13 were with him, they were *g.*
50:11 "Because you rejoice and are *g,*
La 4:21 be *g,* O Daughter of Edom,
Joel 2:21 be *g* and rejoice.
2:23 Be *g,* O people of Zion,
Hab 1:15 and so he rejoices and is *g.*
Zep 3:14 Be *g* and rejoice with all your heart
Zec 2:10 and be *g,* O Daughter of Zion.
8:19 will become joyful and *g* occasions
10: 7 their hearts will be *g* as with wine.
Mt 5:12 be *g,* because great is your reward
Lk 15:32 But we had to celebrate and be *g,*
Jn 4:36 and the reaper may be *g* together.
8:56 my day; he saw it and was *g.*"
11:15 for your sake I am *g* I was not there
14:28 you would be *g* that I am going
Ac 2:26 Therefore my heart is *g*
2:46 together with *g* and sincere hearts,
11:23 he was *g* and encouraged them all
13:48 they were *g* and honored the word
15: 3 news made all the brothers very *g.*
15:31 were *g* for its encouraging message.
1Co 16:17 was *g* when Stephanas, Fortunatus
2Co 2: 2 who is left to make me *g*
7:16 I am *g* I can have complete
13: 9 We are *g* whenever we are weak
Gal 4:27 "Be *g,* O barren woman,
Php 2:17 I am *g* and rejoice with all of you.
2:18 So you too should be *g* and rejoice
2:28 you see him again you may be *g*
Rev 19: 7 Let us rejoice and be *g*

GLADDENS* (GLAD)
Ps 104:15 wine that *g* the heart of man,

GLADNESS* (GLAD)
2Ch 29:30 So they sang praises with *g*
Est 8:16 a time of happiness and joy, *g*
8:17 there was joy and *g*
Job 3:22 who are filled with *g*
Ps 35:27 shout for joy and *g;*
45:15 They are led in with joy and *g;*
51: 8 Let me hear joy and *g;*
65:12 the hills are clothed with *g.*
100: 2 Worship the LORD with *g;*
Ecc 5:20 God keeps him occupied with *g*
9: 7 Go, eat your food with *g,*
Isa 16:10 *g* are taken away from the orchards
35:10 *G* and joy will overtake them,
51: 3 Joy and *g* will be found in her,
51:11 *G* and joy will overtake them,
61: 3 the oil of *g* / instead of mourning,
Jer 7:34 and *g* and to the voices of bride
16: 9 and *g* and to the voices of bride
25:10 from them the sounds of joy and *g,*
31:13 I will turn their mourning into *g;*
33:11 once more the sounds of joy and *g,*
48:33 Joy and *g* are gone
Joel 1:16 joy and *g*

GLAZE*
Pr 26:23 of *g* over earthenware

GLEAM*
Pr 4:18 of the righteous is like the first *g*
Da 10: 6 legs like the *g* of burnished bronze,

GLOAT (GLOATS)
Pr 24:17 Do not *g* when your enemy falls;

GLOATS* (GLOAT)
Pr 17: 5 whoever *g* over disaster will not go

GLORIES* (GLORY)
1Pe 1:11 and the *g* that would follow.

GLORIFIED* (GLORY)
Isa 66: 5 'Let the LORD be *g,*
Eze 39:13 day I am *g* will be a memorable day
Da 4:34 and *g* him who lives forever.
Jn 7:39 since Jesus had not yet been *g.*
11: 4 glory so that God's Son may be *g*
12:16 after Jesus was *g* did they realize
12:23 come for the Son of Man to be *g.*
12:28 "I have *g* it, and will glorify it again
13:31 Son of Man *g* and God is *g* in him.
13:32 If God is *g* in him, God will glorify
Ac 3:13 our fathers, has *g* his servant Jesus.
Ro 1:21 they neither *g* him as God
8:30 those he justified, he also *g.*
2Th 1:10 comes to be *g* in his holy people
1:12 of our Lord Jesus may be *g* in you,
1Pe 1:21 him from the dead and *g* him,

GLORIFIES* (GLORY)
Lk 1:46 My soul *g* the Lord
Jn 8:54 as your God, is the one who *g* me.

GLORIFY* (GLORY)
Ps 34: 3 *G* the LORD with me;
63: 3 my lips will *g* you.
69:30 and *g* him with thanksgiving.
86:12 I will *g* your name forever.
Isa 60:13 and I will *g* the place of my feet.
Da 4:37 and exalt and *g* the King of heaven,
Jn 8:54 Jesus replied, "If I *g* myself,
12:28 glorified it, and will *g* it again."
12:28 *g* your name!" Then a voice came
13:32 God will *g* the Son in himself,
13:32 in himself, and will *g* him at once.
17: 1 *G* your Son, that your Son may
17: 1 your Son, that your Son may *g* you.
17: 5 *g* me in your presence
21:19 death by which Peter would *g* God.
Ro 15: 6 and mouth you may *g* the God
15: 9 so that the Gentiles may *g* God
1Pe 2:12 and *g* God on the day he visits us.
Rev 16: 9 they refused to repent and *g* him.

GLORIFYING* (GLORY)
Lk 2:20 *g* and praising God

GLORIOUS* (GLORY)
Dt 28:58 not revere this *g* and awesome
33:29 and your *g* sword.
1Ch 29:13 and praise your *g* name.
Ne 9: 5 "Blessed be your *g* name,
Ps 16: 3 they are the *g* ones
45:13 All *g* is the princess
66: 2 make his praise *g.*
72:19 Praise be to his *g* name forever;
87: 3 *G* things are said of you,
111: 3 *G* and majestic are his deeds,
145: 5 of the *g* splendor of your majesty,
145:12 the *g* splendor of your kingdom.
Isa 3: 8 defying his *g* presence.
4: 2 the LORD will be beautiful and *g,*
11:10 and his place of rest will be *g.*
12: 5 for he has done *g* things;
28: 1 to the fading flower, his *g* beauty,
28: 4 That fading flower, his *g* beauty,
28: 5 will be a *g* crown,
Isa 42:21 to make his law great and *g.*
60: 7 and I will adorn my *g* temple.
63:12 who sent his *g* arm of power
63:14 to make for yourself a *g* name.
63:15 from your lofty throne, holy and *g.*
64:11 *g* temple, where our fathers praised
Jer 13:18 for your *g* crowns
14:21 do not dishonor your *g* throne.
17:12 A *g* throne, exalted
48:17 how broken the *g* staff!'
Mt 19:28 the Son of Man sits on his *g* throne,
Lk 9:31 appeared in *g* splendor, talking
Ac 2:20 of the great and *g* day of the Lord.
Ro 8:21 and brought into the *g* freedom
2Co 3: 8 of the Spirit be even more *g?*
3: 9 how much more *g* is the ministry
3: 9 ministry that condemns men is *g,*
3:10 For what was *g* has no glory now
Eph 1: 6 to the praise of his *g* grace,
1:17 *g* Father, may give you the Spirit
1:18 the riches of his *g* inheritance
3:16 of his *g* riches he may strengthen
Php 3:21 so that they will be like his *g* body.
4:19 to his *g* riches in Christ Jesus.
Col 1:11 all power according to his *g* might
1:27 among the Gentiles the *g* riches
1Ti 1:11 to the *g* gospel of the blessed God,
Tit 2:13 the *g* appearing of our great God
Jas 2: 1 believers in our *g* Lord Jesus Christ
1Pe 1: 8 with an inexpressible and *g* joy,
Jude :24 before his *g* presence without fault

GLORIOUSLY* (GLORY)
Isa 24:23 and before its elders, *g.*

GLORY (GLORIES GLORIFIED GLORIFIES GLORIFY GLORIFYING GLORIOUS GLORIOUSLY)
Ex 14: 4 But I will gain *g* for myself
14:17 And I will gain *g* through Pharaoh
15:11 awesome in *g,*
16:10 and there was the *g* of the LORD
24:16 and the *g* of the LORD settled
33:18 Moses said, "Now show me your *g*
40:34 and the *g* of the LORD filled
Nu 14:21 the *g* of the LORD fills the whole
Dt 5:24 LORD our God has shown us his *g*
Jos 7:19 "My son, give *g* to the LORD,
1Sa 4:21 "The *g* has departed from Israel"—
1Ch 16:10 *G* in his holy name;
16:24 Declare his *g* among the nations,
16:28 ascribe to the LORD *g*
29:11 and the *g* and the majesty
Ps 8: 1 You have set your *g*
8: 5 and crowned him with *g* and honor
19: 1 The heavens declare the *g* of God;
24: 7 that the King of *g* may come in.
26: 8 the place where your *g* dwells.
29: 1 ascribe to the LORD *g*
29: 9 And in his temple all cry, *"G!"*
57: 5 let your *g* be over all the earth.
66: 2 Sing the *g* of his name;
72:19 the whole earth be filled with his *g.*
96: 3 Declare his *g* among the nations,
102:15 of the earth will revere your *g.*
108: 5 and let your *g* be over all the earth.
149: 9 This is the *g* of all his saints.
Pr 19:11 it is to his *g* to overlook an offense.
25: 2 It is the *g* of God to conceal
Isa 4: 5 over all the *g* will be a canopy.
6: 3 the whole earth is full of his *g.*"
24:16 *"G* to the Righteous One."
26:15 You have gained *g* for yourself;
35: 2 they will see the *g* of the LORD,
40: 5 the *g* of the LORD will be revealed
42: 8 I will not give my *g* to another
42:12 Let them give *g* to the LORD
43: 7 whom I created for my *g,*
44:23 he displays his *g* in Israel.
48:11 I will not yield my *g* to another.
66:18 and they will come and see my *g.*

Isa 66:19 They will proclaim my *g*
Eze 1:28 the likeness of the *g* of the LORD.
10: 4 the radiance of the *g* of the LORD.
43: 2 and the land was radiant with his *g*.
44: 4 and saw the *g* of the LORD filling
Hab 2:14 knowledge of the *g* of the LORD,
3: 3 His *g* covered the heavens
Zec 2: 5 'and I will be its *g* within.'
Mt 16:27 in his Father's *g* with his angels,
24:30 of the sky, with power and great *g*.
25:31 sit on his throne in heavenly *g*.
25:31 the Son of Man comes in his *g*,
Mk 8:38 in his Father's *g* with the holy
13:26 in clouds with great power and *g*.
Lk 2: 9 and the *g* of the Lord shone
2:14 saying, "*G* to God in the highest,
9:26 and in the *g* of the Father
9:26 of him when he comes in his *g*
9:32 they saw his *g* and the two men
19:38 in heaven and *g* in the highest!"
21:27 in a cloud with power and great *g*.
24:26 these things and then enter his *g*?"
Jn 1:14 We have seen his *g*, the *g* of the One
2:11 He thus revealed his *g*,
8:50 I am not seeking *g* for myself;
8:54 myself, my *g* means nothing.
11: 4 for God's *g* so that God's Son may
11:40 you would see the *g* of God?"
12:41 he saw Jesus' *g* and spoke about
14:13 so that the Son may bring *g*
15: 8 is to my Father's *g*, that you bear
16:14 He will bring *g* to me by taking
17: 4 I have brought you *g* on earth
17: 5 presence with the *g* I had with you
17:10 *g* has come to me through them.
17:22 given them the *g* that you gave
17:24 to see my *g*, the *g* you have given
Ac 7: 2 The God of *g* appeared
7:55 up to heaven and saw the *g* of God,
Ro 1:23 exchanged the *g* of the immortal
2: 7 by persistence in doing good seek *g*
2:10 then for the Gentile; but *g*,
3: 7 truthfulness and so increases his *g*,
3:23 and fall short of the *g* of God,
4:20 in his faith and gave *g* to God,
8:17 that we may also share in his *g*.
8:18 with the *g* that will be revealed
9: 4 theirs the divine *g*, the covenants,
9:23 riches of his *g* known to the objects
9:23 whom he prepared in advance for *g*
11:36 To him be the *g* forever! Amen.
15:17 Therefore I *g* in Christ Jesus
16:27 to the only wise God be *g* forever
1Co 2: 7 for our *g* before time began.
10:31 whatever you do, do it all for the *g*
11: 7 but the woman is the *g* of man.
11: 7 since he is the image and *g* of God;
11:15 it is her *g*? For long hair is given
15:43 it is raised in *g*; it is sown
2Co 1:20 spoken by us to the *g* of God.
3: 7 in letters on stone, came with *g*,
3: 7 the face of Moses because of its *g*,
3:10 comparison with the surpassing *g*.
3:10 what was glorious has no *g* now
3:11 how much greater is the *g*
3:11 what was fading away came with *g*,
3:18 faces all reflect the Lord's *g*,
3:18 likeness with ever-increasing *g*,
4: 4 of the gospel of the *g* of Christ,
4: 6 of the knowledge of the *g* of God
4:15 to overflow to the *g* of God.
4:17 us an eternal *g* that far outweighs
Gal 1: 5 to whom be *g* for ever and ever.
Eph 1:12 might be for the praise of his *g*.
1:14 to the praise of his *g*.
3:13 for you, which are your *g*.
3:21 to him be *g* in the church
Php 1:11 to the *g* and praise of God.
2:11 to the *g* of God the Father.
3: 3 of God, who *g* in Christ Jesus,
Php 4:20 and Father be *g* for ever and ever.
Col 1:27 Christ in you, the hope of *g*.
3: 4 also will appear with him in *g*.
1Th 2:12 you into his kingdom and *g*.
2:19 in which we will *g* in the presence
2:20 Indeed, you are our *g* and joy.
2Th 2:14 in the *g* of our Lord Jesus Christ.
1Ti 1:17 be honor and *g* for ever and ever.
3:16 was taken up in *g*.
2Ti 2:10 is in Christ Jesus, with eternal *g*.
4:18 To him be *g* for ever and ever.
Heb 1: 3 The Son is the radiance of God's *g*
2: 7 you crowned him with *g* and honor
2: 9 now crowned with *g* and honor
2:10 In bringing many sons to *g*,
5: 5 take upon himself the *g*
9: 5 the ark were the cherubim of the *G*,
13:21 to whom be *g* for ever and ever.
1Pe 1: 7 *g* and honor when Jesus Christ is
1:24 and all their *g* is like the flowers
4:11 To him be the *g* and the power
4:13 overjoyed when his *g* is revealed.
4:14 for the Spirit of *g* and of God rests
5: 1 will share in the *g* to be revealed:
5: 4 of *g* that will never fade away.
5:10 you to his eternal *g* in Christ,
2Pe 1: 3 of him who called us by his own *g*
1:17 and *g* from God the Father
1:17 came to him from the Majestic *G*,
3:18 To him be *g* both now and forever!
Jude :25 to the only God our Savior be *g*,
Rev 1: 6 to him be *g* and power for ever
4: 9 the living creatures give *g*,
4:11 to receive *g* and honor and power,
5:12 and honor and *g* and praise!"
5:13 and honor and *g* and power,
7:12 Praise and *g*
11:13 and gave *g* to the God of heaven.
14: 7 "Fear God and give him *g*,
15: 4 and bring *g* to your name?
15: 8 with smoke from the *g* of God
19: 1 *g* and power belong to our God,
19: 7 and give him *g*!
21:11 It shone with the *g* of God,
21:23 for the *g* of God gives it light,
21:26 *g* and honor of the nations will be

GLOWING
Eze 8: 2 was as bright as *g* metal.
Rev 1:15 His feet were like bronze *g*

GLUTTONS* (GLUTTONY)
Pr 23:21 for drunkards and *g* become poor,
28: 7 of *g* disgraces his father.
Tit 1:12 always liars, evil brutes, lazy *g*."

GLUTTONY* (GLUTTONS)
Pr 23: 2 throat if you are given to *g*.

GNASHING
Mt 8:12 where there will be weeping and *g*

GNAT* (GNATS)
Mt 23:24 You strain out a *g* but swallow

GNATS (GNAT)
Ex 8:16 of Egypt the dust will become *g*."

GOADS
Ecc 12:11 The words of the wise are like *g*,
Ac 26:14 hard for you to kick against the *g*.'

GOAL*
Lk 13:32 on the third day I will reach my *g*.'
2Co 5: 9 So we make it our *g* to please him,
Gal 3: 3 to attain your *g* by human effort?
Php 3:14 on toward the *g* to win the prize
1Ti 1: 5 The *g* of this command is love,
1Pe 1: 9 for you are receiving the *g*

GOAT (GOATS SCAPEGOAT)
Ge 15: 9 "Bring me a heifer, a *g* and a ram,
Ge 30:32 and every spotted or speckled *g*.
37:31 slaughtered a *g* and dipped
Ex 26: 7 Make curtains of *g* hair for the tent
Lev 16: 9 shall bring the *g* whose lot falls
Nu 7:16 one male *g* for a sin offering;
Isa 11: 6 the leopard will lie down with the *g*
Da 8: 5 suddenly a *g* with a prominent

GOATS (GOAT)
Nu 7:17 five male *g* and five male lambs
Mt 25:32 separates the sheep from the *g*.
Heb 10: 4 of bulls and *g* to take away sins.

GOD (GOD'S GODLINESS GODLY GODS)
Ge 1: 1 In the beginning *G* created
1: 2 and the Spirit of *G* was hovering
1: 3 And *G* said, "Let there be light,"
1: 7 So *G* made the expanse
1: 9 And *G* said, "Let the water
1:11 Then *G* said, "Let the land produce
1:20 And *G* said, "Let the water teem
1:21 So *G* created the great creatures
1:25 *G* made the wild animals according
1:26 Then *G* said, "Let us make man
1:27 So *G* created man in his own image
1:31 *G* saw all that he had made,
2: 3 And *G* blessed the seventh day
2: 7 And the LORD *G* formed the man
2: 8 the LORD *G* had planted a garden
2:18 The LORD *G* said, "It is not good
2:22 Then the LORD *G* made a woman
3: 1 to the woman, "Did *G* really say,
3: 5 you will be like *G*, knowing good
3: 8 from the LORD *G* among the trees
3: 9 But the LORD *G* called to the man
3:21 The LORD *G* made garments
3:22 LORD *G* said, "The man has now
3:23 So the LORD *G* banished him
5: 1 When *G* created man, he made him
5:22 Enoch walked with *G* 300 years
5:24 because *G* took him away.
6: 2 sons of *G* saw that the daughters
6: 9 of his time, and he walked with *G*.
6:12 *G* saw how corrupt the earth had
8: 1 But *G* remembered Noah
9: 1 Then *G* blessed Noah and his sons,
9: 6 for in the image of *G*
9:16 everlasting covenant between *G*
14:18 He was priest of *G* Most High,
14:19 Blessed be Abram by *G* Most High,
16:13 "You are the *G* who sees me,"
17: 1 "I am *G* Almighty; walk before me
17: 7 to be your *G* and the *G*
21: 4 him, as *G* commanded him.
21: 6 "*G* has brought me laughter,
21:20 *G* was with the boy as he grew up.
21:22 *G* is with you in everything you do.
21:33 name of the LORD, the Eternal *G*.
22: 1 Some time later *G* tested Abraham.
22: 8 "*G* himself will provide the lamb
22:12 Now I know that you fear *G*,
25:11 Abraham's death, *G* blessed his
28:12 and the angels of *G* were ascending
28:17 other than the house of *G*;
31:42 But *G* has seen my hardship
31:50 remember that *G* is a witness
32: 1 and the angels of *G* met him.
32:28 because you have struggled with *G*
32:30 "It is because I saw *G* face to face,
33:11 for *G* has been gracious to me
35: 1 and build an altar there to *G*,
35: 5 and the terror of *G* fell
35:10 *G* said to him, "Your name is Jacob
35:11 *G* said to him, "I am *G* Almighty;
41:51 *G* has made me forget all my
41:52 *G* has made me fruitful in the land
50:20 but *G* intended it for good
50:24 But *G* will surely come to your aid
Ex 2:24 *G* heard their groaning
3: 5 "Do not come any closer," *G* said.
3: 6 because he was afraid to look at *G*.

Ex 3:12 And *G* said, "I will be with you.
3:14 what shall I tell them?" *G* said
4:27 he met Moses at the mountain of *G*
6: 7 own people, and I will be your *G*.
8:10 is no one like the LORD our *G*.
10:16 sinned against the LORD your *G*
13:18 So *G* led the people
15: 2 He is my *G*, and I will praise him,
16:12 that I am the LORD your *G*.'"
17: 9 with the staff of *G* in my hands."
18: 5 camped near the mountain of *G*.
19: 3 Then Moses went up to *G*,
20: 1 And *G* spoke all these words:
20: 2 the LORD your *G*, who brought
20: 5 the LORD your *G*, am a jealous *G*,
20: 7 the name of the LORD your *G*,
20:10 a Sabbath to the LORD your *G*.
20:12 the LORD your *G* is giving you.
20:19 But do not have *G* speak to us
20:20 the fear of *G* will be with you
22:20 "Whoever sacrifices to any *g* other
22:28 "Do not blaspheme *G*
23:19 to the house of the LORD your *G*.
31:18 inscribed by the finger of *G*.
34: 6 the compassionate and gracious *G*,
34:14 name is Jealous, is a jealous *G*.
Lev 2:13 salt of the covenant of your *G* out
11:44 the LORD your *G*; consecrate
18:21 not profane the name of your *G*.
19: 2 the LORD your *G*, am holy.
20: 7 because I am the LORD your *G*.
21: 6 They must be holy to their *G*
22:33 out of Egypt to be your *G*.
26:12 walk among you and be your *G*,
Nu 15:40 and will be consecrated to your *G*.
22:18 the command of the LORD my *G*.
22:38 I must speak only what *G* puts
23:19 *G* is not a man, that he should lie,
25:13 zealous for the honor of his *G*
Dt 1:17 for judgment belongs to *G*.
1:21 the LORD your *G* has given you
1:30 The LORD your *G*, who is going
3:22 LORD your *G* himself will fight
3:24 For what *g* is there in heaven
4:24 is a consuming fire, a jealous *G*.
4:29 there you seek the LORD your *G*,
4:31 the LORD your *G* is a merciful *G*;
4:39 heart this day that the LORD is *G*
5: 9 the LORD your *G*, am a jealous *G*,
5:11 the name of the LORD your *G*,
5:12 the LORD your *G* has commanded
5:14 a Sabbath to the LORD your *G*.
5:15 the LORD your *G* brought you out
5:16 the LORD your *G* has commanded
5:16 the LORD your *G* is giving you.
5:24 LORD our *G* has shown us his
5:26 of the living *G* speaking out of fire,
6: 2 them may fear the LORD your *G*
6: 4 LORD our *G*, the LORD is one.
6: 5 Love the LORD your *G*
6:13 the LORD your *G*, serve him only
6:16 Do not test the LORD your *G*
7: 6 holy to the LORD your *G*.
7: 9 your *G* is *G*; he is the faithful *G*,
7:12 the LORD your *G* will keep his
7:19 LORD your *G* will do the same
7:21 is a great and awesome *G*.
8: 5 the LORD your *G* disciplines you.
8:11 do not forget the LORD your *G*,
8:18 But remember the LORD your *G*,
9:10 inscribed by the finger of *G*.
10:12 but to fear the LORD your *G*,
10:14 the LORD your *G* belong
10:17 For the LORD your *G* is *G* of gods
10:21 He is your praise; he is your *G*,
11: 1 Love the LORD your *G*
11:13 to love the LORD your *G*
12:12 rejoice before the LORD your *G*,
12:28 in the eyes of the LORD your *G*.
13: 3 The LORD your *G* is testing you

Dt 13: 4 the LORD your *G* you must
15: 6 the LORD your *G* will bless you
15:19 the LORD your *G* every firstborn
16:11 rejoice before the LORD your *G*
16:17 the LORD your *G* has blessed you.
18:13 before the LORD your *G*.
18:15 The LORD your *G* will raise up
19: 9 to love the LORD your *G*
22: 5 the LORD your *G* detests anyone
23: 5 the LORD your *G* loves you.
23:14 the LORD your *G* moves about
23:21 a vow to the LORD your *G*,
25:16 the LORD your *G* detests anyone
26: 5 declare before the LORD your *G*:
29:13 that he may be your *G*
29:29 belong to the LORD our *G*,
30: 2 return to the LORD your *G*
30: 4 the LORD your *G* will gather you
30: 6 The LORD your *G* will circumcise
30:16 today to love the LORD your *G*,
30:20 you may love the LORD your *G*,
31: 6 for the LORD your *G* goes
32: 3 Oh, praise the greatness of our *G*!
32: 4 A faithful *G* who does no wrong,
33:27 The eternal *G* is your refuge,
Jos 1: 9 for the LORD your *G* will be
14: 8 the LORD my *G* wholeheartedly.
14: 9 the LORD my *G* wholeheartedly.'
14:14 the *G* of Israel, wholeheartedly.
22: 5 to love the LORD your *G*,
22:22 The Mighty One, *G*, the LORD!
22:34 Between Us that the LORD is *G*.
23: 8 to hold fast to the LORD your *G*,
23:11 careful to love the LORD your *G*.
23:14 the LORD your *G* gave you has
23:15 of the LORD your *G* has come true
24:19 He is a holy *G*; he is a jealous *G*.
24:23 to the LORD, the *G* of Israel."
Jdg 5: 3 to the LORD, the *G* of Israel.
16:28 O *G*, please strengthen me just
Ru 1:16 be my people and your *G* my *G*.
2:12 by the LORD, the *G* of Israel,
1Sa 2: 2 there is no Rock like our *G*.
2: 3 for the LORD is a *G* who knows,
2:25 another man, *G* may mediate
10:26 men whose hearts *G* had touched.
12:12 the LORD your *G* was your king.
16:15 spirit from *G* is tormenting you.
17:26 defy the armies of the living *G*?"
17:36 defied the armies of the living *G*.
17:45 the *G* of the armies of Israel,
17:46 world will know that there is a *G*
23:16 and helped him find strength in *G*.
28:15 and *G* has turned away from me.
30: 6 strength in the LORD his *G*.
2Sa 7:22 and there is no *G* but you,
7:23 on earth that *G* went out to redeem
14:14 But *G* does not take away life;
21:14 *G* answered prayer in behalf
22: 3 my *G* is my rock, in whom I take
22:31 "As for *G*, his way is perfect;
22:32 And who is the Rock except our *G*
22:33 It is *G* who arms me with strength
22:47 Exalted be *G*, the Rock, my Savior!
1Ki 2: 3 what the LORD your *G* requires:
4:29 *G* gave Solomon wisdom
5: 5 for the Name of the LORD my *G*,
8:23 there is no *G* like you in heaven
8:27 "But will *G* really dwell on earth?
8:60 may know that the LORD is *G*
8:61 committed to the LORD our *G*,
10:24 to hear the wisdom *G* had put
15:30 he provoked the LORD, the *G*
18:21 If the LORD is *G*, follow him;
18:36 it be known today that you are *G*
18:37 are *G*, and that you are turning
20:28 a *g* of the hills and not a *g*
2Ki 5:15 "Now I know that there is no *G*
18: 5 in the LORD, the *G* of Israel.
19:15 *G* of Israel, enthroned

2Ki 19:19 Now, O LORD our *G*, deliver us
1Ch 12:18 for your *G* will help you."
13: 2 if it is the will of the LORD our *G*,
16:35 Cry out, "Save us, O *G* our Savior;
17:20 and there is no *G* but you,
17:24 the *G* over Israel, is Israel's *G*!'
21: 8 said to *G*, "I have sinned greatly
22: 1 house of the LORD *G* is to be here,
22:19 soul to seeking the LORD your *G*.
28: 2 for the footstool of our *G*,
28: 9 acknowledge the *G* of your father,
28:20 for the LORD *G*, my *G*, is with you
29: 1 not for man but for the LORD *G*.
29: 2 provided for the temple of my *G*—
29: 3 of my *G* I now give my personal
29:10 *G* of our father Israel,
29:13 Now, our *G*, we give you thanks,
29:16 O LORD our *G*, as for all this
29:17 my *G*, that you test the heart
29:18 *G* of our fathers Abraham,
2Ch 2: 4 for the Name of the LORD my *G*
5:14 of the LORD filled the temple of *G*
6: 4 be to the LORD, the *G* of Israel,
6:14 there is no *G* like you in heaven
6:18 "But will *G* really dwell on earth
10:15 for this turn of events was from *G*,
13:12 *G* is with us; he is our leader.
15: 3 was without the true *G*,
15:12 the *G* of their fathers,
15:15 They sought *G* eagerly,
18:13 I can tell him only what my *G* says
19: 3 have set your heart on seeking *G*."
19: 7 with the LORD our *G* there is no
20: 6 are you not the *G* who is in heaven?
20:20 Have faith in the LORD your *G*
25: 8 for *G* has the power to help
26: 5 sought the LORD, *G* gave him
30: 9 for the LORD your *G* is gracious
30:19 who sets his heart on seeking *G*—
31:21 he sought his *G* and worked
32:31 *G* left him to test him
33:12 the favor of the LORD his *G*
34:33 fail to follow the LORD, the *G*
Ezr 6:21 to seek the LORD, the *G* of Israel.
7:18 accordance with the will of your *G*.
7:23 Whatever the *G* of heaven has
8:22 "The gracious hand of our *G* is
8:31 The hand of our *G* was on us,
9: 6 "O my *G*, I am too ashamed
9: 9 our *G* has not deserted us
9:13 our *G*, you have punished us less
9:15 *G* of Israel, you are righteous!
Ne 1: 5 the great and awesome *G*,
5: 9 fear of our *G* to avoid the reproach
5:15 for *G* I did not act like that.
7: 2 feared *G* more than most men do.
8: 8 from the Book of the Law of *G*,
8:18 from the Book of the Law of *G*.
9: 5 and praise the LORD your *G*,
9:17 But you are a forgiving *G*,
9:31 you are a gracious and merciful *G*.
9:32 the great, mighty and awesome *G*,
10:29 oath to follow the Law of *G* given
10:39 not neglect the house of our *G*."
12:43 *G* had given them great joy.
13:11 Why is the house of *G* neglected?"
13:26 He was loved by his *G*,
13:31 Remember me with favor, O my *G*.
Job 1: 1 he feared *G* and shunned evil.
1:22 by charging *G* with wrongdoing.
2:10 Shall we accept good from *G*,
4:17 a mortal be more righteous than *G*?
5:17 is the man whom *G* corrects;
8: 3 Does *G* pervert justice?
8:20 "Surely *G* does not reject
9: 2 a mortal be righteous before *G*?
11: 7 Can you fathom the mysteries of *G*
12:13 "To *G* belong wisdom and power;
16: 7 Surely, O *G*, you have worn me out
19:26 yet in my flesh I will see *G*;

Job 21:19 '*G* stores up a man's punishment
21:22 Can anyone teach knowledge to *G*,
22:12 "Is not *G* in the heights of heaven?
22:13 Yet you say, 'What does *G* know?
22:21 "Submit to *G* and be at peace
25: 2 "Dominion and awe belong to *G*;
25: 4 can a man be righteous before *G*?
26: 6 Death is naked before *G*;
30:20 O *G*, but you do not answer;
31: 6 let *G* weigh me in honest scales
31:14 do when *G* confronts me?
32:13 let *G* refute him, not man.'
33: 6 I am just like you before *G*;
33:14 For *G* does speak—now one way,
33:26 He prays to *G* and finds favor
34:10 Far be it from *G* to do evil,
34:12 is unthinkable that *G* would do
34:23 *G* has no need to examine men
34:33 Should *G* then reward you
36: 5 "*G* is mighty, but does not despise
36:26 is *G*— beyond our understanding!
37:22 *G* comes in awesome majesty.
Ps 5: 4 You are not a *G* who takes pleasure
7:11 *G* is a righteous judge,
10:14 O *G*, do see trouble and grief;
14: 5 for *G* is present in the company
18: 2 my *G* is my rock, in whom I take
18:28 my *G* turns my darkness into light.
18:30 As for *G*, his way is perfect;
18:31 And who is the Rock except our *G*
18:32 It is *G* who arms me with strength
18:46 Exalted be *G* my Savior!
19: 1 The heavens declare the glory of *G*;
22: 1 *G*, my *G*, why have you forsaken
22:10 womb you have been my *G*.
27: 9 O *G* my Savior.
29: 3 the *G* of glory thunders,
31: 5 redeem me, O LORD, the *G*
31:14 I say, "You are my *G*."
33:12 the nation whose *G* is the LORD,
35:24 righteousness, O LORD my *G*;
37:31 The law of his *G* is in his heart;
40: 3 a hymn of praise to our *G*.
40: 8 I desire to do your will, O my *G*;
42: 1 so my soul pants for you, O *G*.
42: 2 thirsts for *G*, for the living *G*.
42: 5 Put your hope in *G*,
42: 8 a prayer to the *G* of my life.
42:11 Put your hope in *G*,
43: 4 to *G*, my joy and my delight.
44: 8 In *G* we make our boast all day
45: 6 O *G*, will last for ever and ever;
45: 7 therefore *G*, your *G*, has set you
46: 1 *G* is our refuge and strength,
46: 5 *G* will help her at break of day.
46:10 "Be still, and know that I am *G*;
47: 1 shout to *G* with cries of joy.
47: 6 Sing praises to *G*, sing praises;
47: 7 For *G* is the King of all the earth;
48: 9 Within your temple, O *G*,
49: 7 or give to *G* a ransom for him—
50: 2 *G* shines forth.
50: 3 Our *G* comes and will not be silent;
51: 1 Have mercy on me, O *G*,
51:10 Create in me a pure heart, O *G*,
51:17 O *G*, you will not despise.
53: 2 any who seek *G*.
54: 4 Surely *G* is my help;
55:19 *G*, who is enthroned forever,
56: 4 In *G*, whose word I praise,
56:10 In *G*, whose word I praise,
56:13 that I may walk before *G*
57: 3 *G* sends his love and his
57: 7 My heart is steadfast, O *G*,
59:17 are my fortress, my loving *G*.
62: 1 My soul finds rest in *G* alone;
62: 7 my honor depend on *G*;
62: 8 for *G* is our refuge.
62:11 One thing *G* has spoken,
63: 1 O *G*, you are my *G*,

Ps 65: 5 O *G* our Savior,
66: 1 Shout with joy to *G*, all the earth!
66: 3 Say to *G*, "How awesome are your
66: 5 Come and see what *G* has done,
66:16 listen, all you who fear *G*;
66:20 Praise be to *G*,
68: 4 Sing to *G*, sing praise to his name,
68: 6 *G* sets the lonely in families,
68:20 Our *G* is a *G* who saves;
68:24 has come into view, O *G*,
68:35 You are awesome, O *G*,
69: 5 You know my folly, O *G*;
70: 1 Hasten, O *G*, to save me;
70: 4 "Let *G* be exalted!"
70: 5 come quickly to me, O *G*.
71:17 my youth, O *G*, you have taught
71:18 do not forsake me, O *G*,
71:19 reaches to the skies, O *G*,
71:22 harp for your faithfulness, O my *G*;
73:17 me till I entered the sanctuary of *G*;
73:26 but *G* is the strength of my heart
76:11 Make vows to the LORD your *G*
77:13 What *g* is so great as our God?
77:14 You are the *G* who performs
78:19 Can *G* spread a table in the desert?
79: 9 Help us, O *G* our Savior,
81: 1 Sing for joy to *G* our strength;
82: 1 *G* presides in the great assembly;
84: 2 out for the living *G*.
84:10 a doorkeeper in the house of my *G*
84:11 For the LORD *G* is a sun
86:12 O Lord my *G*, with all my heart;
86:15 a compassionate and gracious *G*,
87: 3 O city of *G*: *Selah*
89: 7 of the holy ones *G* is greatly feared;
90: 2 to everlasting you are *G*.
91: 2 my *G*, in whom I trust."
94:22 my *G* the rock in whom I take
95: 7 for he is our *G*
99: 8 you were to Israel a forgiving *G*,
99: 9 Exalt the LORD our *G*
100: 3 Know that the LORD is *G*.
108: 1 My heart is steadfast, O *G*;
113: 5 Who is like the LORD our *G*,
115: 3 Our *G* is in heaven;
116: 5 our *G* is full of compassion.
123: 2 look to the LORD our *G*,
136: 2 Give thanks to the *G* of gods.
136:26 Give thanks to the *G* of heaven.
139:17 to me are your thoughts, O *G*!
139:23 Search me, O *G*, and know my
143:10 for you are my *G*;
144: 2 He is my loving *G* and my fortress,
147: 1 is to sing praises to our *G*,
Pr 3: 4 in the sight of *G* and man.
14:31 to the needy honors *G*.
25: 2 of *G* to conceal a matter;
30: 5 "Every word of *G* is flawless;
Ecc 2:26 *G* gives wisdom, knowledge
3:11 cannot fathom what *G* has done
3:13 in all his toil—this is the gift of *G*.
3:14 *G* does it so that men will revere him.
5: 4 When you make a vow to *G*,
5:19 in his work—this is a gift of *G*.
8:12 who are reverent before *G*.
11: 5 cannot understand the work of *G*,
12: 7 the spirit returns to *G* who gave it.
12:13 Fear *G* and keep his
Isa 5:16 the holy *G* will show himself holy
9: 6 Wonderful Counselor, Mighty *G*,
12: 2 Surely *G* is my salvation;
25: 9 "Surely this is our *G*;
28:11 *G* will speak to this people,
29:23 will stand in awe of the *G* of Israel.
30:18 For the LORD is a *G* of justice.
35: 4 your *G* will come,
37:16 you alone are *G* over all
40: 1 says your *G*.
40: 3 a highway for our *G*.
40: 8 the word of our *G* stands forever."

Isa 40:18 then, will you compare *G*?
40:28 The LORD is the everlasting *G*,
41:10 not be dismayed, for I am your *G*.
41:13 For I am the LORD, your *G*,
43:10 Before me no *g* was formed,
44: 6 apart from me there is no *G*.
44:15 he also fashions a *g* and worships it;
45:18 he is *G*;
48:17 "I am the LORD your *G*,
52: 7 "Your *G* reigns!"
52:12 *G* of Israel will be your rear guard.
55: 7 to our *G*, for he will freely pardon.
57:21 says my *G*, "for the wicked."
59: 2 you from your *G*;
60:19 and your *G* will be your glory.
61: 2 and the day of vengeance of our *G*,
61:10 my soul rejoices in my *G*.
62: 5 so will your *G* rejoice over you.
Jer 7:23 I will be your *G* and you will be my
10:10 But the LORD is the true *G*;
10:12 But *G* made the earth by his power;
23:23 "Am I only a *G* nearby,"
23:36 distort the words of the living *G*,
31:33 I will be their *G*,
32:27 "I am the LORD, the *G*
42: 6 for we will obey the LORD our *G*."
51:10 what the LORD our *G* has done.'
51:56 For the LORD is a *G* of retribution
Eze 28:13 the garden of *G*;
34:31 and I am your *G*, declares
Da 2:28 there is a *G* in heaven who reveals
3:17 the *G* we serve is able to save us
3:29 for no other *g* can save in this way
6:16 "May your *G*, whom you serve
9: 4 O Lord, the great and awesome *G*,
10:12 to humble yourself before your *G*,
11:36 things against the *G* of gods.
Hos 1: 9 my people, and I am not your *G*.
1:10 will be called 'sons of the living *G*.'
4: 6 you have ignored the law of your *G*
6: 6 acknowledgment of *G* rather
9: 8 The prophet, along with my *G*,
12: 6 and wait for your *G* always.
Joel 2:13 Return to the LORD your *G*,
2:23 rejoice in the LORD your *G*,
Am 4:12 prepare to meet your *G*, O Israel."
4:13 the LORD *G* Almighty is his name
Jnh 1: 6 Get up and call on your *g*!
4: 2 a gracious and compassionate *G*,
Mic 6: 8 and to walk humbly with your *G*.
7: 7 I wait for *G* my Savior;
7:18 Who is a *G* like you,
Na 1: 2 LORD is a jealous and avenging *G*;
Hab 3:18 I will be joyful in *G* my Savior.
Zep 3:17 The LORD your *G* is with you,
Zec 14: 5 Then the LORD my *G* will come,
Mal 2:10 Father? Did not one *G* create us?
2:16 says the LORD *G* of Israel,
3: 8 Will a man rob *G*? Yet you rob me.
Mt 1:23 which means, "*G* with us."
4: 4 comes from the mouth of *G*.'"
4: 7 'Do not put the Lord your *G*
4:10 'Worship the Lord your *G*,
5: 8 for they will see *G*.
6:24 You cannot serve both *G*
19: 6 Therefore what *G* has joined
19:26 but with *G* all things are possible."
22:21 and to *G* what is God's."
22:32 He is not the *G* of the dead
22:37 "'Love the Lord your *G*
27:46 which means, "My *G*, my *G*,
Mk 2: 7 Who can forgive sins but *G* alone?"
7:13 Thus you nullify the word of *G*
10: 6 of creation *G* 'made them male
10: 9 Therefore what *G* has joined
10:18 "No one is good—except *G* alone.
10:27 all things are possible with *G*."
11:22 "Have faith in *G*," Jesus answered.
12:17 and to *G* what is God's."
12:29 the Lord our *G*, the Lord is one.

Mk 12:30 Love the Lord your *G*
15:34 which means, "My *G*, my *G*,
16:19 and he sat at the right hand of *G*.
Lk 1:30 Mary, you have found favor with *G*
1:37 For nothing is impossible with *G*."
1:47 my spirit rejoices in *G* my Savior,
2:14 "Glory to *G* in the highest,
2:52 and in favor with *G* and men.
4: 8 'Worship the Lord your *G*
5:21 Who can forgive sins but *G* alone?"
8:39 tell how much *G* has done for you."
10: 9 'The kingdom of *G* is near you.'
10:27 " 'Love the Lord your *G*
13:18 "What is the kingdom of *G* like?
18:19 "No one is good—except *G* alone.
18:27 with men is possible with *G*."
20:25 and to *G* what is God's."
20:38 He is not the *G* of the dead,
22:69 at the right hand of the mighty *G*."
Jn 1: 1 was with *G*, and the Word was *G*.
1:18 ever seen *G*, but *G* the One and Only,
1:29 Lamb of *G*, who takes away the sin
3:16 "For *G* so loved the world that he
3:34 the one whom *G* has sent speaks
4:24 *G* is spirit, and his worshipers must
5:44 praise that comes from the only *G*?
6:29 answered, "The work of *G* is this:
7:17 my teaching comes from *G* or
8:42 to them, "If *G* were your Father,
8:47 belongs to *G* hears what *G* says.
11:40 you would see the glory of *G*?"
13: 3 from *G* and was returning to *G*;
13:31 of Man glorified and *G* is glorified
14: 1 Trust in *G*; trust also in me.
17: 3 the only true *G*, and Jesus Christ,
20:17 your Father, to my *G* and your *G*
20:28 "My Lord and my *G*!"
20:31 the Son of *G*, and that
Ac 2:11 wonders of *G* in our own tongues!"
2:24 But *G* raised him from the dead,
2:33 Exalted to the right hand of *G*,
2:36 *G* has made this Jesus, whom you
3:15 but *G* raised him from the dead.
3:19 Repent, then, and turn to *G*,
4:31 and spoke the word of *G* boldly.
5: 4 You have not lied to men but to *G*
5:29 "We must obey *G* rather than men!
5:31 *G* exalted him to his own right
5:32 whom *G* has given
7:55 to heaven and saw the glory of *G*,
8:21 your heart is not right before *G*.
11: 9 anything impure that *G* has made
12:24 But the word of *G* continued
13:32 What *G* promised our fathers he
15:10 to test *G* by putting on the necks
17:23 TO AN UNKNOWN *G*.
17:30 In the past *G* overlooked such
20:27 to you the whole will of *G*.
20:32 "Now I commit you to *G*
24:16 keep my conscience clear before *G*
Ro 1:16 the power of *G* for the salvation
1:17 a righteousness from *G* is revealed,
1:18 The wrath of *G* is being revealed
1:24 Therefore *G* gave them
1:26 *G* gave them over to shameful lusts
2:11 For *G* does not show favoritism.
2:16 when *G* will judge men's secrets
3: 4 Let *G* be true, and every man a liar.
3:19 world held accountable to *G*.
3:23 and fall short of the glory of *G*,
3:29 Is *G* the *G* of Jews only? Is he not
4: 3 say? "Abraham believed *G*,
4: 6 to whom *G* credits righteousness
4:17 the *G* who gives life to the dead
4:24 to whom *G* will credit
5: 1 we have peace with *G*
5: 5 because *G* has poured out his love
5: 8 *G* demonstrates his own love for us
6:22 and have become slaves to *G*,
Ro 6:23 but the gift of *G* is eternal life
8: 7 the sinful mind is hostile to *G*.
8:17 heirs of *G* and co-heirs with Christ,
8:28 in all things *G* works for the good
9:14 What then shall we say? Is *G* unjust
9:18 Therefore *G* has mercy
10: 9 in your heart that *G* raised him
11: 2 *G* did not reject his people,
11:22 the kindness and sternness of *G*:
11:32 For *G* has bound all men
13: 1 exist have been established by *G*.
14:12 give an account of himself to *G*.
16:20 *G* of peace will soon crush Satan
1Co 1:18 are being saved it is the power of *G*.
1:20 Has not *G* made foolish
1:25 For the foolishness of *G* is wiser
1:27 But *G* chose the foolish things
2: 9 what *G* has prepared
2:11 of *G* except the Spirit of *G*.
3: 6 watered it, but *G* made it grow.
3:17 God's temple, *G* will destroy
6:20 Therefore honor *G* with your body.
7: 7 each man has his own gift from *G*;
7:15 *G* has called us to live in peace.
7:20 was in when *G* called him.
7:24 each man, as responsible to *G*,
8: 3 man who loves *G* is known by *G*.
8: 8 food does not bring us near to *G*;
10:13 *G* is faithful; he will not let you be
10:31 do it all for the glory of *G*.
12:24 But *G* has combined the members
14:33 For *G* is not a *G* of disorder
15:24 over the kingdom to *G* the Father
15:28 so that *G* may be all in all.
15:34 are some who are ignorant of *G*—
15:57 be to *G*! He gives us the victory
2Co 1: 9 rely on ourselves but on *G*,
2:14 be to *G*, who always leads us
2:15 For we are to *G* the aroma of Christ
2:17 we do not peddle the word of *G*
3: 5 but our competence comes from *G*.
4: 2 nor do we distort the word of *G*.
4: 7 this all-surpassing power is from *G*
5: 5 Now it is *G* who has made us
5:19 that *G* was reconciling the world
5:20 though *G* were making his appeal
5:21 *G* made him who had no sin
6:16 we are the temple of the living *G*.
9: 7 for *G* loves a cheerful giver.
9: 8 *G* is able to make all grace abound
10:13 to the field *G* has assigned to us,
Gal 2: 6 *G* does not judge by external
3: 5 Does *G* give you his Spirit
3: 6 Abraham: "He believed *G*,
3:11 justified before *G* by the law,
3:26 You are all sons of *G* through faith
6: 7 not be deceived: *G* cannot be
Eph 1:22 *G* placed all things under his feet
2: 8 it is the gift of *G*— not by works,
2:10 which *G* prepared in advance for us
2:22 in which *G* lives by his Spirit.
4: 6 one baptism; one *G* and Father
4:24 to be like *G* in true righteousness
5: 1 Be imitators of *G*, therefore,
6: 6 doing the will of *G* from your heart.
Php 2: 6 Who, being in very nature *G*,
2: 9 Therefore *G* exalted him
2:13 for it is *G* who works in you to will
4: 7 peace of *G*, which transcends all
4:19 And my *G* will meet all your needs
Col 1:19 For *G* was pleased
2:13 *G* made you alive with Christ.
1Th 2: 4 trying to please men but *G*,
2:13 but as it actually is, the word of *G*,
3: 9 How can we thank *G* enough
4: 7 For *G* did not call us to be impure,
4: 9 taught by *G* to love each other.
5: 9 For *G* did not appoint us
1Ti 2: 5 one mediator between *G* and men,
4: 4 For everything *G* created is good,
1Ti 5: 4 for this is pleasing to *G*.
2Ti 1: 6 you to fan into flame the gift of *G*,
Tit 1: 2 which *G*, who does not lie,
2:13 glorious appearing of our great *G*
Heb 1: 1 In the past *G* spoke
3: 4 but *G* is the builder of everything.
4: 4 "And on the seventh day *G* rested
4:12 For the word of *G* is living
6:10 *G* is not unjust; he will not forget
6:18 in which it is impossible for *G* to lie
7:19 by which we draw near to *G*.
7:25 come to *G* through him,
10:22 draw near to *G* with a sincere heart
10:31 to fall into the hands of the living *G*
11: 5 commended as one who pleased *G*.
11: 6 faith it is impossible to please *G*,
12: 7 as discipline; *G* is treating you
12:10 but *G* disciplines us for our good,
12:29 for our "*G* is a consuming fire."
13:15 offer to *G* a sacrifice of praise—
Jas 1:12 crown of life that *G* has promised
1:13 For *G* cannot be tempted by evil,
1:27 Religion that *G* our Father accepts
2:19 You believe that there is one *G*.
2:23 "Abraham believed *G*,
4: 4 the world becomes an enemy of *G*.
4: 6 "*G* opposes the proud
4: 8 Come near to *G* and he will come
1Pe 1:23 the living and enduring word of *G*.
2:20 this is commendable before *G*.
3:18 the unrighteous, to bring you to *G*.
4:11 it with the strength *G* provides,
5: 5 because, "*G* opposes the proud
2Pe 1:21 but men spoke from *G*
2: 4 For if *G* did not spare angels
1Jn 1: 5 *G* is light; in him there is no
2:17 the will of *G* lives forever.
3: 1 we should be called children of *G*!
3: 9 born of *G* will continue to sin,
3:10 we know who the children of *G* are
3:20 For *G* is greater than our hearts,
4: 7 for love comes from *G*.
4: 8 not know *G*, because *G* is love.
4: 9 This is how *G* showed his love
4:11 Dear friends, since *G* so loved us,
4:12 No one has ever seen *G*;
4:15 *G* lives in him and he in *G*.
4:16 *G* is love.
4:20 "I love *G*," yet hates his brother,
4:21 Whoever loves *G* must
5: 2 that we love the children of *G*:
5: 3 love for *G*: to obey his commands.
5: 4 born of *G* overcomes the world.
5:10 does not believe *G* has made him
5:14 have in approaching *G*:
5:18 born of *G* does not continue to sin;
Rev 4: 8 holy is the Lord *G* Almighty,
7:12 be to our *G* for ever and ever.
7:17 *G* will wipe away every tear
11:16 fell on their faces and worshiped *G*,
15: 3 Lord *G* Almighty.
17:17 For *G* has put it into their hearts
19: 6 For our Lord *G* Almighty reigns.
21: 3 Now the dwelling of *G* is with men,
21:23 for the glory of *G* gives it light,

GOD-BREATHED* (BREATH)
2Ti 3:16 All Scripture is *G* and is useful

GOD-FEARING* (FEAR)
Ecc 8:12 that it will go better with *G* men,
Ac 2: 5 staying in Jerusalem *G* Jews
10: 2 all his family were devout and *G*;
10:22 He is a righteous and *G* man,
13:26 of Abraham, and you *G* Gentiles,
13:50 But the Jews incited the *G* women
17: 4 as did a large number of *G* Greeks
17:17 with the Jews and the *G* Greeks,

GOD-HATERS* (HATE)
Ro 1:30 They are gossips, slanderers, *G*,

GOD'S (GOD)
2Ch 20:15 For the battle is not yours, but *G.*
Job 37:14 stop and consider *G* wonders.
Ps 52: 8 I trust in *G* unfailing love
69:30 I will praise *G* name in song
Mk 3:35 Whoever does *G* will is my brother
Jn 7:17 If anyone chooses to do *G* will,
10:36 'I am *G* Son'? Do not believe me
Ro 2: 3 think you will escape *G* judgment?
2: 4 not realizing that *G* kindness leads
3: 3 lack of faith nullify *G* faithfulness?
7:22 in my inner being I delight in *G* law
9:16 or effort, but on *G* mercy.
11:29 for *G* gifts and his call are
12: 2 and approve what *G* will is—
12:13 Share with *G* people who are
13: 6 for the authorities are *G* servants,
1Co 7:19 Keeping *G* commands is what
2Co 6: 2 now is the time of *G* favor,
Eph 1: 7 riches of *G* grace that he lavished
1Th 4: 3 It is *G* will that you should be sanctified;
5:18 for this is *G* will for you
1Ti 6: 1 so that *G* name and our teaching
2Ti 2:19 *G* solid foundation stands firm,
Tit 1: 7 overseer is entrusted with *G* work,
Heb 1: 3 The Son is the radiance of *G* glory
9:24 now to appear for us in *G* presence.
11: 3 was formed at *G* command,
1Pe 2:15 For it is *G* will that
3: 4 which is of great worth in *G* sight.
1Jn 2: 5 *G* love is truly made complete

GODLESS
Job 20: 5 the joy of the *g* lasts but a moment.
1Ti 6:20 Turn away from *g* chatter

GODLINESS (GOD)
1Ti 2: 2 and quiet lives in all *g* and holiness.
4: 8 but *g* has value for all things,
6: 5 and who think that *g* is a means
6: 6 *g* with contentment is great gain.
6:11 and pursue righteousness, *g,* faith,
2Pe 1: 6 and to perseverance, *g;*

GODLY (GOD)
Ps 4: 3 that the LORD has set apart the *g*
2Co 7:10 *G* sorrow brings repentance that
11: 2 jealous for you with a *g* jealousy.
2Ti 3:12 everyone who wants to live a *g* life
2Pe 3:11 You ought to live holy and *g* lives

GODS (GOD)
Ex 20: 3 "You shall have no other *g*
Dt 5: 7 "You shall have no other *g*
1Ch 16:26 For all the *g* of the nations are idols
Ps 82: 6 "I said, 'You are "*g*";
Jn 10:34 have said you are *g*'? If he called
Ac 19:26 He says that man-made *g* are no *g*

GOG
Eze 38:18 When *G* attacks the land of Israel,
Rev 20: 8 *G* and Magog—to gather them

GOLD
1Ki 20: 3 'Your silver and *g* are mine,
Job 22:25 then the Almighty will be your *g,*
23:10 tested me, I will come forth as *g.*
28:15 cannot be bought with the finest *g,*
31:24 "If I have put my trust in *g*
Ps 19:10 They are more precious than *g,*
119:127 more than *g,* more than pure *g,*
Pr 3:14 and yields better returns than *g.*
22: 1 esteemed is better than silver or *g.*
Hag 2: 8 The silver is mine and the *g* is mine
Mt 2:11 and presented him with gifts of *g*
Rev 3:18 to buy from me *g* refined in the fire,

GOLGOTHA*
Mt 27:33 to a place called *G* (which means
Mk 15:22 to the place called *G* (which means
Jn 19:17 (which in Aramaic is called *G*).

GOLIATH
Philistine giant killed by David (1Sa 17; 21:9).

GOMORRAH
Ge 19:24 sulfur on Sodom and *G*—
Mt 10:15 and *G* on the day of judgment
2Pe 2: 6 and *G* by burning them to ashes,
Jude : 7 *G* and the surrounding towns gave

GOOD
Ge 1: 4 God saw that the light was *g,*
1:10 And God saw that it was *g.*
1:12 And God saw that it was *g.*
1:18 And God saw that it was *g.*
1:21 And God saw that it was *g.*
1:25 And God saw that it was *g.*
1:31 he had made, and it was very *g.*
2: 9 and the tree of the knowledge of *g*
2: 9 pleasing to the eye and *g* for food.
2:18 "It is not *g* for the man to be alone.
3:22 become like one of us, knowing *g*
50:20 but God intended it for *g*
2Ch 7: 3 "He is *g;* / his love endures
31:20 doing what was *g* and right
Job 2:10 Shall we accept *g* from God,
Ps 14: 1 there is no one who does *g.*
34: 8 Taste and see that the LORD is *g;*
34:14 Turn from evil and do *g;*
37: 3 Trust in the LORD and do *g;*
37:27 Turn from evil and do *g;*
52: 9 for your name is *g.*
53: 3 there is no one who does *g,*
84:11 no *g* thing does he withhold
86: 5 You are forgiving and *g,* O Lord
100: 5 For the LORD is *g* and his love
103: 5 satisfies your desires with *g* things,
112: 5 *G* will come to him who is
119:68 You are *g,* and what you do is *g;*
133: 1 How *g* and pleasant it is
145: 9 The LORD is *g* to all;
147: 1 How *g* it is to sing praises
Pr 3: 4 you will win favor and a *g* name
3:27 Do not withhold *g*
11:27 He who seeks *g* finds *g* will,
13:22 A *g* man leaves an inheritance
14:22 those who plan what is *g* find love
15: 3 on the wicked and the *g.*
15:23 and how *g* is a timely word!
15:30 *g* news gives health to the bones.
17:22 A cheerful heart is *g* medicine,
18:22 He who finds a wife finds what is *g*
19: 2 It is not *g* to have zeal
22: 1 A *g* name is more desirable
31:12 She brings him *g,* not harm,
Ecc 12:14 whether it is *g* or evil.
Isa 5:20 Woe to those who call evil *g*
40: 9 You who bring *g* tidings
52: 7 the feet of those who bring *g* news,
61: 1 me to preach *g* news to the poor.
Jer 6:16 ask where the *g* way is,
13:23 Neither can you do *g*
32:39 the *g* of their children after them.
Eze 34:14 I will tend them in a *g* pasture,
Mic 6: 8 has showed you, O man, what is *g.*
Na 1:15 the feet of one who brings *g* news,
Mt 5:45 sun to rise on the evil and the *g,*
7:11 Father in heaven give *g* gifts
7:17 Likewise every *g* tree bears *g* fruit,
7:18 A *g* tree cannot bear bad fruit,
12:35 The *g* man brings *g* things out
13: 8 Still other seed fell on *g* soil,
13:24 is like a man who sowed *g* seed
13:48 and collected the *g* fish in baskets,
19:17 "There is only One who is *g.*
22:10 both *g* and bad, and the wedding
25:21 'Well done, *g* and faithful servant!
Mk 1:15 Repent and believe the *g* news!"
3: 4 lawful on the Sabbath: to do *g*
4: 8 Still other seed fell on *g* soil.
8:36 What *g* is it for a man
10:18 "No one is *g*— except God alone.
16:15 preach the *g* news to all creation.
Lk 2:10 I bring you *g* news
3: 9 does not produce *g* fruit will be
6:27 do *g* to those who hate you,
6:43 nor does a bad tree bear *g* fruit.
6:45 The *g* man brings *g* things out
8: 8 Still other seed fell on *g* soil.
9:25 What *g* is it for a man
14:34 "Salt is *g,* but if it loses its saltiness,
18:19 "No one is *g*— except God alone.
19:17 " 'Well done, my *g* servant!'
Jn 10:11 "I am the *g* shepherd.
Ro 3:12 there is no one who does *g,*
7:12 is holy, righteous and *g.*
7:16 want to do, I agree that the law is *g.*
7:18 I have the desire to do what is *g,*
8:28 for the *g* of those who love him,
10:15 feet of those who bring *g* news!"
12: 2 his *g,* pleasing and perfect will.
12: 9 Hate what is evil; cling to what is *g.*
13: 4 For he is God's servant to do you *g*
16:19 you to be wise about what is *g,*
1Co 7: 1 It is *g* for a man not to marry.
10:24 should seek his own *g,* but the *g*
15:33 Bad company corrupts *g* character
2Co 9: 8 you will abound in every *g* work.
Gal 4:18 provided the purpose is *g,*
6: 9 us not become weary in doing *g,*
6:10 as we have opportunity, let us do *g*
Eph 2:10 in Christ Jesus to do *g* works,
6: 8 everyone for whatever *g* he does,
Php 1: 6 that he who began a *g* work
Col 1:10 bearing fruit in every *g* work,
1Th 5:21 Hold on to the *g.*
1Ti 3: 7 have a *g* reputation with outsiders,
4: 4 For everything God created is *g,*
6:12 Fight the *g* fight of the faith.
6:18 them to do *g,* to be rich in *g* deeds,
2Ti 3:17 equipped for every *g* work.
4: 7 I have fought the *g* fight, I have
Tit 1: 8 loves what is *g,* who is
2: 7 an example by doing what is *g.*
2:14 his very own, eager to do what is *g.*
Heb 5:14 to distinguish *g* from evil.
10:24 on toward love and *g* deeds.
12:10 but God disciplines us for our *g,*
13:16 do not forget to do *g* and to share
Jas 4:17 who knows the *g* he ought to do
1Pe 2: 3 you have tasted that the Lord is *g.*
2:12 Live such *g* lives among the pagans
2:18 not only to those who are *g*
3:17 to suffer for doing *g*

GOODS
Ecc 5:11 As *g* increase,

GORGE
Pr 23:20 or *g* themselves on meat,

GOSHEN
Ge 45:10 You shall live in the region of *G*
Ex 8:22 differently with the land of *G,*

GOSPEL
Ro 1:16 I am not ashamed of the *g,*
15:16 duty of proclaiming the *g* of God,
15:20 to preach the *g* where Christ was
1Co 1:17 to preach the *g*— not with words
9:12 rather than hinder the *g* of Christ.
9:14 who preach the *g* should receive
9:16 Woe to me if I do not preach the *g!*
15: 1 you of the *g* I preached to you,
15: 2 By this *g* you are saved,
2Co 4: 4 light of the *g* of the glory of Christ,
9:13 your confession of the *g*
Gal 1: 7 a different *g*— which is really no *g*
Eph 6:15 comes from the *g* of peace.
Php 1:27 in a manner worthy of the *g*
Col 1:23 This is the *g* that you heard

1Th 2: 4 by God to be entrusted with the *g*.
2Th 1: 8 do not obey the *g* of our Lord Jesus
2Ti 1:10 immortality to light through the *g*.
Rev 14: 6 he had the eternal *g* to proclaim

GOSSIP*
Pr 11:13 A *g* betrays a confidence,
16:28 and a *g* separates close friends.
18: 8 of a *g* are like choice morsels;
20:19 A *g* betrays a confidence;
26:20 without *g* a quarrel dies down.
26:22 of a *g* are like choice morsels;
2Co 12:20 slander, *g*, arrogance and disorder.

GOVERN (GOVERNMENT)
Ge 1:16 the greater light to *g* the day
Job 34:17 Can he who hates justice *g*?
Ro 12: 8 it is leadership, let him *g* diligently;

GOVERNMENT (GOVERN)
Isa 9: 6 and the *g* will be on his shoulders.

GRACE* (GRACIOUS)
Ps 45: 2 lips have been anointed with *g*,
Pr 1: 9 will be a garland to *g* your head
3:22 an ornament to *g* your neck.
3:34 but gives *g* to the humble.
4: 9 She will set a garland of *g*
Isa 26:10 Though *g* is shown to the wicked,
Jnh 2: 8 forfeit the *g* that could be theirs.
Zec 12:10 of Jerusalem a spirit of *g*
Lk 2:40 and the *g* of God was upon him.
Jn 1:14 who came from the Father, full of *g*
1:16 of his *g* we have all received one
1:17 *g* and truth came through Jesus
Ac 4:33 and much *g* was upon them all.
6: 8 a man full of God's *g* and power,
11:23 saw the evidence of the *g* of God,
13:43 them to continue in the *g* of God.
14: 3 message of his *g* by enabling them
14:26 they had been committed to the *g*
15:11 We believe it is through the *g*
15:40 by the brothers to the *g* of the Lord
18:27 to those who by *g* had believed.
20:24 testifying to the gospel of God's *g*.
20:32 to God and to the word of his *g*,
Ro 1: 5 we received *g* and apostleship
1: 7 *G* and peace to you
3:24 and are justified freely by his *g*
4:16 be by *g* and may be guaranteed
5: 2 access by faith into this *g*
5:15 came by the *g* of the one man,
5:15 how much more did God's *g*
5:17 God's abundant provision of *g*
5:20 where sin increased, *g* increased all
5:21 also *g* might reign
6: 1 on sinning so that *g* may increase?
6:14 you are not under law, but under *g*.
6:15 we are not under law but under *g*?
11: 5 there is a remnant chosen by *g*.
11: 6 if by *g*, then it is no longer by works
11: 6 if it were, *g* would no longer be *g*.
12: 3 For by the *g* given me I say
12: 6 according to the *g* given us.
15:15 because of the *g* God gave me
16:20 The *g* of our Lord Jesus be
1Co 1: 3 *G* and peace to you
1: 4 of his *g* given you in Christ Jesus.
3:10 By the *g* God has given me,
15:10 But by the *g* of God I am what I am
15:10 but the *g* of God that was with me.
15:10 his *g* to me was not without effect.
16:23 The *g* of the Lord Jesus be with you
2Co 1: 2 *G* and peace to you
1:12 wisdom but according to God's *g*.
4:15 so that the *g* that is reaching more
6: 1 not to receive God's *g* in vain.
8: 1 to know about the *g* that God has
8: 6 also to completion this act of *g*
8: 7 also excel in this *g* of giving.
8: 9 For you know the *g*
2Co 9: 8 able to make all *g* abound to you,
9:14 of the surpassing *g* God has given
12: 9 "My *g* is sufficient for you,
13:14 May the *g* of the Lord Jesus Christ,
Gal 1: 3 *G* and peace to you
1: 6 the one who called you by the *g*
1:15 from birth and called me by his *g*,
2: 9 when they recognized the *g* given
2:21 I do not set aside the *g* of God,
3:18 God in his *g* gave it to Abraham
5: 4 you have fallen away from *g*.
6:18 The *g* of our Lord Jesus Christ be
Eph 1: 2 *G* and peace to you
1: 6 to the praise of his glorious *g*,
1: 7 riches of God's *g* that he lavished
2: 5 it is by *g* you have been saved.
2: 7 the incomparable riches of his *g*,
2: 8 For it is by *g* you have been saved,
3: 2 of God's *g* that was given to me
3: 7 by the gift of God's *g* given me
3: 8 God's people, this *g* was given me:
4: 7 to each one of us *g* has been given
6:24 *G* to all who love our Lord Jesus
Php 1: 2 *G* and peace to you
1: 7 all of you share in God's *g* with me.
4:23 The *g* of the Lord Jesus Christ be
Col 1: 2 *G* and peace to you
1: 6 understood God's *g* in all its truth.
4: 6 conversation be always full of *g*,
4:18 *G* be with you.
1Th 1: 1 and the Lord Jesus Christ: *G*
5:28 The *g* of our Lord Jesus Christ be
2Th 1: 2 *G* and peace to you
1:12 according to the *g* of our God
2:16 and by his *g* gave us eternal
3:18 The *g* of our Lord Jesus Christ be
1Ti 1: 2 my true son in the faith: *G*,
1:14 The *g* of our Lord was poured out
6:21 *G* be with you.
2Ti 1: 2 To Timothy, my dear son: *G*,
1: 9 This *g* was given us in Christ Jesus
1: 9 because of his own purpose and *g*.
2: 1 be strong in the *g* that is
4:22 *G* be with you.
Tit 1: 4 *G* and peace from God the Father
2:11 For the *g* of God that brings
3: 7 having been justified by his *g*,
3:15 *G* be with you all.
Phm : 3 *G* to you and peace
:25 The *g* of the Lord Jesus Christ be
Heb 2: 9 that by the *g* of God he might taste
4:16 find *g* to help us in our time of need
4:16 the throne of *g* with confidence,
10:29 and who has insulted the Spirit of *g*
12:15 See to it that no one misses the *g*
13: 9 hearts to be strengthened by *g*,
13:25 *G* be with you all.
Jas 4: 6 but gives *g* to the humble."
4: 6 But he gives us more *g*. That is why
1Pe 1: 2 *G* and peace be yours in abundance
1:10 who spoke of the *g* that was
1:13 fully on the *g* to be given you
4:10 faithfully administering God's *g*
5: 5 but gives *g* to the humble."
5:10 the God of all *g*, who called you
5:12 and testifying that this is the true *g*
2Pe 1: 2 *G* and peace be yours in abundance
3:18 But grow in the *g* and knowledge
2Jn : 3 and will be with us forever: *G*,
Jude : 4 who change the *g* of our God
Rev 1: 4 *G* and peace to you
22:21 The *g* of the Lord Jesus be

GRACIOUS (GRACE)
Ex 34: 6 the compassionate and *g* God,
Nu 6:25 and be *g* to you;
Ne 9:17 But you are a forgiving God, *g*
Ps 67: 1 May God be *g* to us and bless us
Pr 22:11 a pure heart and whose speech is *g*
Isa 30:18 Yet the LORD longs to be *g* to you

GRAIN
Lev 2: 1 When someone brings a *g* offering
Lk 17:35 women will be grinding *g* together;
1Co 9: 9 ox while it is treading out the *g*."

GRANDCHILDREN (CHILD)
1Ti 5: 4 But if a widow has children or *g*,

GRANDMOTHER (MOTHER)
2Ti 1: 5 which first lived in your *g* Lois

GRANT (GRANTED)
Ps 20: 5 May the LORD *g* all your requests
51:12 *g* me a willing spirit, to sustain me.

GRANTED (GRANT)
Pr 10:24 what the righteous desire will be *g*.
Mt 15:28 great faith! Your request is *g*."
Php 1:29 For it has been *g* to you on behalf

GRAPES
Nu 13:23 branch bearing a single cluster of *g*.
Jer 31:29 'The fathers have eaten sour *g*,
Eze 18: 2 " 'The fathers eat sour *g*,
Mt 7:16 Do people pick *g* from thornbushes
Rev 14:18 and gather the clusters of *g*

GRASPED
Php 2: 6 with God something to be *g*,

GRASS
Ps 103:15 As for man, his days are like *g*,
Isa 40: 6 "All men are like *g*,
Mt 6:30 If that is how God clothes the *g*
1Pe 1:24 "All men are like *g*,

GRASSHOPPERS
Nu 13:33 We seemed like *g* in our own eyes,

GRATIFY* (GRATITUDE)
Ro 13:14 think about how to *g* the desires
Gal 5:16 and you will not *g* the desires

GRATITUDE (GRATIFY)
Col 3:16 and spiritual songs with *g*

GRAVE (GRAVES)
Nu 19:16 who touches a human bone or a *g*,
Dt 34: 6 day no one knows where his *g* is.
Ps 5: 9 Their throat is an open *g*;
49:15 will redeem my life from the *g*;
Pr 7:27 Her house is a highway to the *g*,
Hos 13:14 Where, O *g*, is your destruction?
Jn 11:44 "Take off the *g* clothes
Ac 2:27 you will not abandon me to the *g*,

GRAVES (GRAVE)
Eze 37:12 I am going to open your *g*
Jn 5:28 are in their *g* will hear his voice
Ro 3:13 "Their throats are open *g*;

GRAY
Pr 16:31 *G* hair is a crown of splendor;
20:29 *g* hair the splendor of the old.

GREAT (GREATER GREATEST GREATNESS)
Ge 12: 2 I will make your name *g*,
12: 2 "I will make you into a *g* nation
Ex 32:11 out of Egypt with *g* power
Nu 14:19 In accordance with your *g* love,
Dt 4:32 so *g* as this ever happened,
10:17 the *g* God, mighty and awesome,
29:28 in *g* wrath the LORD uprooted
Jos 7: 9 do for your own *g* name?"
Jdg 16: 5 you the secret of his *g* strength
2Sa 7:22 "How *g* you are, O Sovereign
22:36 you stoop down to make me *g*.
24:14 for his mercy is *g*; but do not let me
1Ch 17:19 made known all these *g* promises.
Ps 18:35 you stoop down to make me *g*.
19:11 in keeping them there is *g* reward.
47: 2 the *g* King over all the earth!

Ps 57:10 For *g* is your love, reaching
68:11 and *g* was the company
89: 1 of the LORD's *g* love forever;
103:11 so *g* is his love for those who fear
107:43 consider the *g* love of the LORD.
108: 4 For *g* is your love, higher
117: 2 For *g* is his love toward us,
119:165 *G* peace have they who love your
145: 3 *G* is the LORD and most worthy
Pr 22: 1 is more desirable than *g* riches;
23:24 of a righteous man has *g* joy;
Isa 42:21 to make his law *g* and glorious.
Jer 27: 5 With my *g* power and outstretched
32:19 *g* are your purposes and mighty are
La 3:23 *g* is your faithfulness.
Da 9: 4 "O Lord, the *g* and awesome God,
Joel 2:11 The day of the LORD is *g*;
2:20 Surely he has done *g* things.
Zep 1:14 "The *g* day of the LORD is near—
Mal 1:11 My name will be *g*
4: 5 the prophet Elijah before that *g*
Mt 20:26 whoever wants to become *g*
Mk 10:43 whoever wants to become *g*
Lk 6:23 because *g* is your reward in heaven.
6:35 Then your reward will be *g*,
21:27 in a cloud with power and *g* glory.
Eph 1:19 and his incomparably *g* power
2: 4 But because of his *g* love for us,
1Ti 6: 6 with contentment is *g* gain.
Tit 2:13 glorious appearing of our *g* God
Heb 2: 3 if we ignore such a *g* salvation?
1Jn 3: 1 How *g* is the love the Father has
Rev 6:17 For the *g* day of their wrath has
20:11 Then I saw a *g* white throne

GREATER (GREAT)
Mt 11:11 there has not risen anyone *g*
12: 6 I tell you that one *g*
12:41 and now one *g* than Jonah is here.
12:42 now one *g* than Solomon is here.
Mk 12:31 There is no commandment *g*
Jn 1:50 You shall see *g* things than that."
3:30 He must become *g*; I must become
14:12 He will do even *g* things than these
15:13 *G* love has no one than this,
1Co 12:31 But eagerly desire the *g* gifts.
2Co 3:11 how much *g* is the glory
Heb 3: 3 the builder of a house has *g* honor
3: 3 worthy of *g* honor than Moses,
7: 7 lesser person is blessed by the *g*.
11:26 as of *g* value than the treasures
1Jn 3:20 For God is *g* than our hearts,
4: 4 is in you is *g* than the one who is

GREATEST (GREAT)
Mt 22:38 is the first and *g* commandment.
23:11 *g* among you will be your servant.
Lk 9:48 least among you all—he is the *g*."
1Co 13:13 But the *g* of these is love.

GREATNESS* (GREAT)
Ex 15: 7 In the *g* of your majesty
Dt 3:24 to show to your servant your *g*
32: 3 Oh, praise the *g* of our God!
1Ch 29:11 O LORD, is the *g* and the power
2Ch 9: 6 half the *g* of your wisdom was told
Est 10: 2 account of the *g* of Mordecai
Ps 145: 3 his *g* no one can fathom.
150: 2 praise him for his surpassing *g*.
Isa 63: 1 forward in the *g* of his strength?
Eze 38:23 I will show my *g* and my holiness,
Da 4:22 your *g* has grown until it reaches
5:18 and *g* and glory and splendor.
7:27 and *g* of the kingdoms
Mic 5: 4 will live securely, for then his *g*
Lk 9:43 And they were all amazed at the *g*
Php 3: 8 compared to the surpassing *g*

GREED (GREEDY)
Lk 12:15 on your guard against all kinds of *g*
Ro 1:29 kind of wickedness, evil, *g*
Eph 5: 3 or of any kind of impurity, or of *g*,
Col 3: 5 evil desires and *g*, which is idolatry
2Pe 2:14 experts in *g*— an accursed brood!

GREEDY (GREED)
Pr 15:27 A *g* man brings trouble
1Co 6:10 nor thieves nor the *g* nor drunkards
Eph 5: 5 No immoral, impure or *g* person—
1Pe 5: 2 not *g* for money, but eager to serve;

GREEK (GREEKS)
Gal 3:28 There is neither Jew nor *G*,
Col 3:11 Here there is no *G* or Jew,

GREEKS (GREEK)
1Co 1:22 miraculous signs and *G* look

GREEN
Ps 23: 2 makes me lie down in *g* pastures,

GREW (GROW)
Lk 1:80 And the child *g* and became strong
2:52 And Jesus *g* in wisdom and stature,
Ac 9:31 by the Holy Spirit, it *g* in numbers,
16: 5 in the faith and *g* daily in numbers.

GRIEF (GRIEFS GRIEVANCES GRIEVE GRIEVED)
Ps 10:14 O God, do see trouble and *g*;
Pr 10: 1 but a foolish son *g* to his mother.
14:13 and joy may end in *g*.
17:21 To have a fool for a son brings *g*;
Ecc 1:18 the more knowledge, the more *g*.
La 3:32 Though he brings *g*, he will show
Jn 16:20 but your *g* will turn to joy.
1Pe 1: 6 had to suffer *g* in all kinds of trials.

GRIEFS* (GRIEF)
1Ti 6:10 pierced themselves with many *g*.

GRIEVANCES* (GRIEF)
Col 3:13 forgive whatever *g* you may have

GRIEVE (GRIEF)
Eph 4:30 do not *g* the Holy Spirit of God,
1Th 4:13 or to *g* like the rest of men,

GRIEVED (GRIEF)
Isa 63:10 and *g* his Holy Spirit.

GRINDING
Lk 17:35 women will be *g* grain together;

GROAN (GROANING GROANS)
Ro 8:23 *g* inwardly as we wait eagerly
2Co 5: 4 For while we are in this tent, we *g*

GROANING (GROAN)
Ex 2:24 God heard their *g* and he
Eze 21: 7 'Why are you *g*?' you shall say,
Ro 8:22 that the whole creation has been *g*

GROANS (GROAN)
Ro 8:26 with *g* that words cannot express.

GROUND
Ge 1:10 God called the dry *g* "land,"
3:17 "Cursed is the *g* because of you;
4:10 blood cries out to me from the *g*.
Ex 3: 5 where you are standing is holy *g*."
15:19 walked through the sea on dry *g*.
Isa 53: 2 and like a root out of dry *g*.
Mt 10:29 fall to the *g* apart from the will
25:25 and hid your talent in the *g*.
Jn 8: 6 to write on the *g* with his finger.
Eph 6:13 you may be able to stand your *g*,

GROW (FULL-GROWN GREW GROWING GROWS)
Pr 13:11 by little makes it *g*.
20:13 not love sleep or you will *g* poor;
Isa 40:31 they will run and not *g* weary,
Mt 6:28 See how the lilies of the field *g*.
1Co 3: 6 watered it, but God made it *g*.
2Pe 3:18 But *g* in the grace and knowledge

GROWING (GROW)
Col 1: 6 this gospel is bearing fruit and *g*,
1:10 *g* in the knowledge of God,
2Th 1: 3 your faith is *g* more and more,

GROWS (GROW)
Eph 4:16 *g* and builds itself up in love,
Col 2:19 *g* as God causes it to grow.

GRUMBLE (GRUMBLED GRUMBLERS GRUMBLING)
1Co 10:10 And do not *g*, as some of them did
Jas 5: 9 Don't *g* against each other,

GRUMBLED (GRUMBLE)
Ex 15:24 So the people *g* against Moses,
Nu 14:29 and who has *g* against me.

GRUMBLERS* (GRUMBLE)
Jude :16 These men are *g* and faultfinders;

GRUMBLING (GRUMBLE)
Jn 6:43 "Stop *g* among yourselves,"
1Pe 4: 9 to one another without *g*.

GUARANTEE (GUARANTEEING)
Heb 7:22 Jesus has become the *g*

GUARANTEEING* (GUARANTEE)
2Co 1:22 as a deposit, *g* what is to come.
5: 5 as a deposit, *g* what is to come.
Eph 1:14 who is a deposit *g* our inheritance

GUARD (GUARDS)
1Sa 2: 9 He will *g* the feet of his saints,
Ps 141: 3 Set a *g* over my mouth, O LORD;
Pr 2:11 and understanding will *g* you.
4:13 *g* it well, for it is your life.
4:23 Above all else, *g* your heart,
7: 2 *g* my teachings as the apple
Isa 52:12 the God of Israel will be your rear *g*
Mk 13:33 Be on *g*! Be alert! You do not know
Lk 12: 1 "Be on your *g* against the yeast
12:15 Be on your *g* against all kinds
Ac 20:31 So be on your *g*! Remember that
1Co 16:13 Be on your *g*; stand firm in the faith
Php 4: 7 will *g* your hearts and your minds
1Ti 6:20 *g* what has been entrusted
2Ti 1:14 *G* the good deposit that was

GUARDS (GUARD)
Pr 13: 3 He who *g* his lips *g* his life,
19:16 who obeys instructions *g* his life,
21:23 He who *g* his mouth and his tongue
22: 5 he who *g* his soul stays far

GUIDANCE (GUIDE)
Pr 1: 5 and let the discerning get *g*—
11:14 For lack of *g* a nation falls,
24: 6 for waging war you need *g*,

GUIDE (GUIDANCE GUIDED GUIDES)
Ex 13:21 of cloud to *g* them on their way
15:13 In your strength you will *g* them
Ne 9:19 cease to *g* them on their path,
Ps 25: 5 *g* me in your truth and teach me,
43: 3 let them *g* me;
48:14 he will be our *g* even to the end.
67: 4 and *g* the nations of the earth.
73:24 You *g* me with your counsel,
139:10 even there your hand will *g* me,
Pr 4:11 I *g* you in the way of wisdom
6:22 When you walk, they will *g* you;
Isa 58:11 The LORD will *g* you always;
Jn 16:13 comes, he will *g* you into all truth.

GUIDED (GUIDE)
Ps 107:30 he *g* them to their desired haven.

GUIDES (GUIDE)
Ps 23: 3 He *g* me in paths of righteousness
25: 9 He *g* the humble in what is right
Pr 11: 3 The integrity of the upright *g* them,
16:23 A wise man's heart *g* his mouth,
Mt 23:16 "Woe to you, blind *g*! You say,
23:24 You blind *g*! You strain out a gnat

GUILT (GUILTY)
Lev 5:15 It is a *g* offering.
Ps 32: 5 the *g* of my sin.
38: 4 My *g* has overwhelmed me
Isa 6: 7 your *g* is taken away and your sin
Jer 2:22 the stain of your *g* is still before me
Eze 18:19 'Why does the son not share the *g*

GUILTY (GUILT)
Ex 34: 7 does not leave the *g* unpunished;
Mk 3:29 Spirit will never be forgiven; he is *g*
Jn 8:46 Can any of you prove me *g* of sin?
1Co 11:27 in an unworthy manner will be *g*
Heb 10: 2 and would no longer have felt *g*
10:22 to cleanse us from a *g* conscience
Jas 2:10 at just one point is *g* of breaking all

HABAKKUK*
Prophet to Judah (Hab 1:1; 3:1).

HABIT
1Ti 5:13 they get into the *h* of being idle
Heb 10:25 as some are in the *h* of doing,

HADAD
Edomite adversary of Solomon (1Ki 11:14–25).

HADES*
Mt 16:18 the gates of *H* will not overcome it.
Rev 1:18 And I hold the keys of death and *H*
6: 8 *H* was following close behind him.
20:13 and *H* gave up the dead that were
20:14 *H* were thrown into the lake of fire.

HAGAR
Servant of Sarah, wife of Abraham, mother of Ishmael (Ge 16:1–6; 25:12). Driven away by Sarah while pregnant (Ge 16:5–16); after birth of Isaac (Ge 21:9–21; Gal 4:21–31).

HAGGAI*
Post-exilic prophet who encouraged rebuilding of the temple (Ezr 5:1; 6:14; Hag 1–2).

HAIL
Ex 9:19 the *h* will fall on every man
Rev 8: 7 and there came *h* and fire mixed

HAIR (HAIRS HAIRY)
Lev 19:27 " 'Do not cut the *h* at the sides
Nu 6: 5 he must let the *h* of his head grow
Pr 16:31 Gray *h* is a crown of splendor;
20:29 gray *h* the splendor of the old.
Lk 7:44 and wiped them with her *h*.
21:18 But not a *h* of your head will perish
Jn 11: 2 and wiped his feet with her *h*.
12: 3 and wiped his feet with her *h*.
1Co 11: 6 for a woman to have her *h* cut
11: 6 she should have her *h* cut off;
11:14 that if a man has long *h*,
11:15 For long *h* is given to her
11:15 but that if a woman has long *h*,
1Ti 2: 9 not with braided *h* or gold or pearls
1Pe 3: 3 as braided *h* and the wearing
Rev 1:14 and *h* were white like wool,

HAIRS (HAIR)
Mt 10:30 even the very *h* of your head are all
Lk 12: 7 the very *h* of your head are all

HAIRY (HAIR)
Ge 27:11 "But my brother Esau is a *h* man,

HALF
Ex 30:13 This *h* shekel is an offering
Jos 8:33 *H* of the people stood in front
1Ki 3:25 give *h* to one and *h* to the other."
10: 7 Indeed, not even *h* was told me;
Est 5: 3 Even up to *h* the kingdom,
Da 7:25 him for a time, times and *h* a time.
Mk 6:23 up to *h* my kingdom."

HALF-TRIBE (TRIBE)
Nu 32:33 and the *h* of Manasseh son

HALLELUJAH*
Rev 19: 1, 3, 4, 6.

HALLOWED* (HOLY)
Mt 6: 9 *h* be your name,
Lk 11: 2 *h* be your name,

HALT
Job 38:11 here is where your proud waves *h*?

HALTER*
Pr 26: 3 for the horse, a *h* for the donkey,

HAM
Son of Noah (Ge 5:32; 1Ch 1:4), father of Canaan (Ge 9:18; 10:6–20; 1Ch 1:8–16). Saw Noah's nakedness (Ge 9:20–27).

HAMAN
Agagite nobleman honored by Xerxes (Est 3:1–2). Plotted to exterminate the Jews because of Mordecai (Est 3:3–15). Forced to honor Mordecai (Est 5–6). Plot exposed by Esther (Est 5:1–8; 7:1–8). Hanged (Est 7:9–10).

HAMPERED*
Pr 4:12 you walk, your steps will not be *h*;

HAND (HANDED HANDFUL HANDS OPENHANDED)
Ge 24: 2 "Put your *h* under my thigh.
47:29 put your *h* under my thigh
Ex 13: 3 out of it with a mighty *h*.
15: 6 Your right *h*, O LORD,
33:22 and cover you with my *h*
Dt 12: 7 in everything you have put your *h*
1Ki 8:42 and your mighty *h* and your
13: 4 But the *h* he stretched out
1Ch 29:14 you only what comes from your *h*.
29:16 it comes from your *h*, and all
2Ch 6:15 with your *h* you have fulfilled it—
Ne 4:17 materials did their work with one *h*
Job 40: 4 I put my *h* over my mouth.
Ps 16: 8 Because he is at my right *h*,
32: 4 your *h* was heavy upon me;
37:24 the LORD upholds him with his *h*.
44: 3 it was your right *h*, your arm,
45: 9 at your right *h* is the royal bride
63: 8 your right *h* upholds me.
75: 8 In the *h* of the LORD is a cup
91: 7 ten thousand at your right *h*,
98: 1 his right *h* and his holy arm
109:31 at the right *h* of the needy one,
110: 1 "Sit at my right *h*
137: 5 may my right *h* forget its skill.
139:10 even there your *h* will guide me,
145:16 You open your *h*
Pr 27:16 or grasping oil with the *h*.
Ecc 5:15 that he can carry in his *h*.
9:10 Whatever your *h* finds to do,
Isa 11: 8 the young child put his *h*
40:12 the waters in the hollow of his *h*,
41:13 who takes hold of your right *h*
44: 5 still another will write on his *h*,
48:13 My own *h* laid the foundations
64: 8 we are all the work of your *h*.
La 3: 3 he has turned his *h* against me
Da 10:10 *h* touched me and set me trembling
Jnh 4:11 people who cannot tell their right *h*
Hab 3: 4 rays flashed from his *h*,
Mt 5:30 if your right *h* causes you to sin,
6: 3 know what your right *h* is doing,
12:10 a man with a shriveled *h* was there.
18: 8 If your *h* or your foot causes you
22:44 "Sit at my right *h*
26:64 at the right *h* of the Mighty One
Mk 3: 1 a man with a shriveled *h* was there.
9:43 If your *h* causes you to sin, cut it off
12:36 "Sit at my right *h*
16:19 and he sat at the right *h* of God.
Lk 6: 6 there whose right *h* was shriveled.
20:42 "Sit at my right *h*
22:69 at the right *h* of the mighty God."
Jn 10:28 one can snatch them out of my *h*.
20:27 Reach out your *h* and put it
Ac 7:55 Jesus standing at the right *h* of God
1Co 12:15 I am not a *h*, I do not belong
Heb 1:13 "Sit at my right *h*
Rev 13:16 to receive a mark on his right *h*

HANDED (HAND)
Da 7:25 The saints will be *h* over to him
1Ti 1:20 whom I have *h* over to Satan

HANDFUL (HAND)
Ecc 4: 6 Better one *h* with tranquillity

HANDLE (HANDLES)
Col 2:21 "Do not *h*! Do not taste! Do not

HANDLES (HANDLE)
2Ti 2:15 who correctly *h* the word of truth.

HANDS (HAND)
Ge 27:22 but the *h* are the *h* of Esau."
Ex 17:11 As long as Moses held up his *h*,
29:10 his sons shall lay their *h* on its head
Dt 6: 8 Tie them as symbols on your *h*
Jdg 7: 6 lapped with their *h* to their mouths.
2Ki 11:12 and the people clapped their *h*
2Ch 6: 4 who with his *h* has fulfilled what he
Ps 22:16 they have pierced my *h*
24: 4 He who has clean *h* and a pure
31: 5 Into your *h* I commit my spirit;
31:15 My times are in your *h*;
47: 1 Clap your *h*, all you nations;
63: 4 and in your name I will lift up my *h*
Pr 10: 4 Lazy *h* make a man poor,
21:25 because his *h* refuse to work.
31:13 and works with eager *h*.
31:20 and extends her *h* to the needy.
Ecc 10:18 if his *h* are idle, the house leaks.
Isa 35: 3 Strengthen the feeble *h*,
49:16 you on the palms of my *h*;
55:12 will clap their *h*.
65: 2 All day long I have held out my *h*
La 3:41 Let us lift up our hearts and our *h*
Lk 23:46 into your *h* I commit my spirit."
Ac 6: 6 who prayed and laid their *h*
8:18 at the laying on of the apostles' *h*,
13: 3 they placed their *h* on them
19: 6 When Paul placed his *h* on them,
28: 8 placed his *h* on him and healed him
1Th 4:11 and to work with your *h*,
1Ti 2: 8 to lift up holy *h* in prayer,
4:14 body of elders laid their *h* on you.
5:22 hasty in the laying on of *h*,
2Ti 1: 6 you through the laying on of my *h*.
Heb 6: 2 the laying on of *h*, the resurrection

HANDSOME*
Ge 39: 6 Now Joseph was well-built and *h*,
1Sa 16:12 a fine appearance and *h* features.
17:42 ruddy and *h*, and he despised him.
2Sa 14:25 praised for his *h* appearance
1Ki 1: 6 also very *h* and was born next
SS 1:16 *Beloved* How *h* you are, my lover!
Eze 23: 6 all of them *h* young men,
23:12 horsemen, all *h* young men.
23:23 with them, *h* young men,
Da 1: 4 without any physical defect, *h*,

Zec 11:13 the *h* price at which they priced me

HANG (HANGED HANGING HUNG)
Mt 22:40 and the Prophets *h* on these two

HANGED (HANG)
Mt 27: 5 Then he went away and *h* himself.

HANGING (HANG)
Ac 10:39 They killed him by *h* him on a tree,

HANNAH*
Wife of Elkanah, mother of Samuel (1Sa 1). Prayer at dedication of Samuel (1Sa 2:1–10). Blessed (1Sa 2:18–21).

HAPPIER (HAPPY)
Mt 18:13 he is *h* about that one sheep
1Co 7:40 she is *h* if she stays as she is—

HAPPINESS* (HAPPY)
Dt 24: 5 bring *h* to the wife he has married.
Est 8:16 For the Jews it was a time of *h*
Job 7: 7 my eyes will never see *h* again.
Ecc 2:26 gives wisdom, knowledge and *h,*
Mt 25:21 Come and share your master's *h!'*
25:23 Come and share your master's *h!'*

HAPPY* (HAPPIER HAPPINESS)
Ge 30:13 The women will call me *h.*"
30:13 Then Leah said, "How *h* I am!
1Ki 4:20 they drank and they were *h.*
10: 8 How *h* your men must be!
10: 8 men must be! How *h* your officials,
2Ch 9: 7 How *h* your men must be!
9: 7 men must be! How *h* your officials,
Est 5: 9 Haman went out that day *h*
5:14 the king to the dinner and be *h.*"
Ps 10: 6 I'll always be *h* and never have
68: 3 may they be *h* and joyful.
113: 9 as a *h* mother of children.
137: 8 *h* is he who repays you
Pr 15:13 A *h* heart makes the face cheerful,
Ecc 3:12 better for men than to be *h*
5:19 to accept his lot and be *h*
7:14 When times are good, be *h;*
11: 9 Be *h,* young man, while you are
Jnh 4: 6 Jonah was very *h* about the vine.
Zec 8:19 and glad occasions and *h* festivals
1Co 7:30 those who are *h,* as if they were not
2Co 7: 9 yet now I am *h,* not because you
7:13 delighted to see how *h* Titus was,
Jas 5:13 Is anyone *h?* Let him sing songs

HARD (HARDEN HARDENED HARDENING HARDENS HARDER HARDSHIP HARDSHIPS)
Ge 18:14 Is anything too *h* for the LORD?
1Ki 10: 1 came to test him with *h* questions.
Pr 14:23 All *h* work brings a profit,
Jer 32:17 Nothing is too *h* for you.
Zec 7:12 They made their hearts as *h* as flint
Mt 19:23 it is *h* for a rich man
Mk 10: 5 your hearts were *h* that Moses
Jn 6:60 disciples said, "This is a *h* teaching.
Ac 20:35 of *h* work we must help the weak,
26:14 It is *h* for you to kick
Ro 16:12 woman who has worked very *h*
1Co 4:12 We work *h* with our own hands.
2Co 6: 5 imprisonments and riots; in *h* work
1Th 5:12 to respect those who work *h*
Rev 2: 2 your *h* work and your

HARDEN (HARD)
Ex 4:21 I will *h* his heart so that he will not
Ps 95: 8 do not *h* your hearts as you did
Ro 9:18 he hardens whom he wants to *h.*
Heb 3: 8 do not *h* your hearts

HARDENED (HARD)
Ex 10:20 But the LORD *h* Pharaoh's heart,

HARDENING* (HARD)
Ro 11:25 Israel has experienced a *h* in part
Eph 4:18 in them due to the *h* of their hearts.

HARDENS* (HARD)
Pr 28:14 he who *h* his heart falls into trouble
Ro 9:18 and he *h* whom he wants to harden.

HARDER (HARD)
1Co 15:10 No, I worked *h* than all of them—
2Co 11:23 I have worked much *h,* been

HARDHEARTED* (HEART)
Dt 15: 7 do not be *h* or tightfisted

HARDSHIP (HARD)
Ro 8:35 Shall trouble or *h* or persecution
2Ti 2: 3 Endure *h* with us like a good
4: 5 endure *h,* do the work
Heb 12: 7 Endure *h* as discipline; God is

HARDSHIPS (HARD)
Ac 14:22 go through many *h* to enter
2Co 6: 4 in troubles, *h* and distresses;
12:10 in insults, in *h,* in persecutions,
Rev 2: 3 and have endured *h* for my name,

HARM (HARMS)
1Ch 16:22 do my prophets no *h.*"
Ps 105:15 do my prophets no *h.*"
121: 6 the sun will not *h* you by day,
Pr 3:29 not plot *h* against your neighbor,
12:21 No *h* befalls the righteous,
31:12 She brings him good, not *h,*
Jer 10: 5 they can do no *h*
29:11 to prosper you and not to *h* you,
Ro 13:10 Love does no *h* to its neighbor.
1Co 11:17 for your meetings do more *h*
1Jn 5:18 the evil one cannot *h* him.

HARMONY*
Zec 6:13 there will be *h* between the two.'
Ro 12:16 Live in *h* with one another.
2Co 6:15 What *h* is there between Christ
1Pe 3: 8 live in *h* with one another;

HARMS* (HARM)
Pr 8:36 whoever fails to find me *h* himself;

HARP (HARPS)
Ge 4:21 the father of all who play the *h*
1Sa 16:23 David would take his *h* and play.
Ps 33: 2 Praise the LORD with the *h;*
98: 5 with the *h* and the sound of singing
150: 3 praise him with the *h* and lyre,
Rev 5: 8 Each one had a *h* and they were

HARPS (HARP)
Ps 137: 2 we hung our *h,*

HARSH
Pr 15: 1 but a *h* word stirs up anger.
Col 2:23 and their *h* treatment of the body,
3:19 and do not be *h* with them.
1Pe 2:18 but also to those who are *h.*
Jude :15 of all the *h* words ungodly sinners

HARVEST (HARVESTERS)
Ge 8:22 seedtime and *h,*
Ex 23:16 the Feast of *H* with the firstfruits
Dt 16:15 God will bless you in all your *h*
Pr 10: 5 during *h* is a disgraceful son.
Jer 8:20 "The *h* is past,
Joel 3:13 for the *h* is ripe.
Mt 9:37 *h* is plentiful but the workers are
Lk 10: 2 He told them, "The *h* is plentiful,
Jn 4:35 at the fields! They are ripe for *h.*
1Co 9:11 if we reap a material *h* from you?
2Co 9:10 the *h* of your righteousness.
Gal 6: 9 at the proper time we will reap a *h*
Heb 12:11 it produces a *h* of righteousness
Jas 3:18 in peace raise a *h* of righteousness.
Rev 14:15 for the *h* of the earth is ripe."

HARVESTERS (HARVEST)
Ru 2: 3 to glean in the fields behind the *h.*

HASTE (HASTEN HASTY)
Ex 12:11 it in *h;* it is the LORD's Passover.
Pr 21: 5 as surely as *h* leads to poverty.
29:20 Do you see a man who speaks in *h?*

HASTEN (HASTE)
Ps 70: 1 *H,* O God, to save me;
119:60 I will *h* and not delay

HASTY* (HASTE)
Pr 19: 2 nor to be *h* and miss the way.
Ecc 5: 2 do not be *h* in your heart
1Ti 5:22 Do not be *h* in the laying

HATE (GOD-HATERS HATED HATES HATING HATRED)
Lev 19:17 " 'Do not *h* your brother
Ps 5: 5 you *h* all who do wrong.
36: 2 too much to detect or *h* his sin.
45: 7 righteousness and *h* wickedness;
97:10 those who love the LORD *h* evil,
119:104 therefore I *h* every wrong path.
119:163 I *h* and abhor falsehood
139:21 Do I not *h* those who *h* you,
Pr 8:13 To fear the LORD is to *h* evil;
9: 8 rebuke a mocker or he will *h* you;
13: 5 The righteous *h* what is false,
25:17 too much of you, and he will *h* you.
29:10 Bloodthirsty men *h* a man
Ecc 3: 8 a time to love and a time to *h,*
Isa 61: 8 I *h* robbery and iniquity.
Eze 35: 6 Since you did not *h* bloodshed,
Am 5:15 *H* evil, love good;
Mal 2:16 "I *h* divorce," says the LORD God
Mt 5:43 your neighbor and *h* your enemy.'
10:22 All men will *h* you because of me,
Lk 6:22 Blessed are you when men *h* you,
6:27 do good to those who *h* you,
14:26 does not *h* his father and mother,
Ro 12: 9 *H* what is evil; cling to what is good

HATED (HATE)
Mal 1: 3 loved Jacob, but Esau I have *h,*
Jn 15:18 keep in mind that it *h* me first.
Ro 9:13 "Jacob I loved, but Esau I *h.*"
Eph 5:29 no one ever *h* his own body,
Heb 1: 9 righteousness and *h* wickedness;

HATES (HATE)
Pr 6:16 There are six things the LORD *h,*
13:24 He who spares the rod *h* his son,
15:27 but he who *h* bribes will live.
26:28 A lying tongue *h* those it hurts,
Jn 3:20 Everyone who does evil *h* the light,
12:25 while the man who *h* his life
1Jn 2: 9 *h* his brother is still in the darkness.
4:20 "I love God," yet *h* his brother,

HATING (HATE)
Jude :23 *h* even the clothing stained

HATRED (HATE)
Pr 10:12 *H* stirs up dissension,
15:17 than a fattened calf with *h.*
Jas 4: 4 with the world is *h* toward God?

HAUGHTY
Pr 6:17 detestable to him: / *h* eyes,
16:18 a *h* spirit before a fall.

HAVEN
Ps 107:30 he guided them to their desired *h.*

HAY
1Co 3:12 costly stones, wood, *h* or straw,

HEAD (HEADS HOTHEADED)
Ge 3:15 he will crush your *h*,
Nu 6: 5 no razor may be used on his *h*.
Jdg 16:17 If my *h* were shaved, my strength
1Sa 9: 2 a *h* taller than any of the others.
2Sa 18: 9 Absalom's *h* got caught in the tree.
Ps 23: 5 You anoint my *h* with oil;
133: 2 is like precious oil poured on the *h*,
Pr 10: 6 Blessings crown the *h*
25:22 will heap burning coals on his *h*,
Isa 59:17 and the helmet of salvation on his *h*
Eze 33: 4 his blood will be on his own *h*.
Mt 8:20 of Man has no place to lay his *h*."
Jn 19: 2 crown of thorns and put it on his *h*.
Ro 12:20 will heap burning coals on his *h*."
1Co 11: 3 and the *h* of Christ is God.
11: 5 her *h* uncovered dishonors her *h*—
12:21 And the *h* cannot say to the feet,
Eph 1:22 him to be *h* over everything
5:23 For the husband is the *h* of the wife
Col 1:18 And he is the *h* of the body,
2Ti 4: 5 keep your *h* in all situations,
Rev 14:14 with a crown of gold on his *h*
19:12 and on his *h* are many crowns.

HEADS (HEAD)
Lev 26:13 you to walk with *h* held high.
Ps 22: 7 they hurl insults, shaking their *h*:
24: 7 Lift up your *h*, O you gates;
Isa 35:10 everlasting joy will crown their *h*.
51:11 everlasting joy will crown their *h*.
Mt 27:39 shaking their *h* and saying,
Lk 21:28 stand up and lift up your *h*,
Ac 18: 6 "Your blood be on your own *h*!
Rev 4: 4 and had crowns of gold on their *h*.

HEAL* (HEALED HEALING HEALS)
Nu 12:13 please *h* her!" The LORD replied
Dt 32:39 I have wounded and I will *h*,
2Ki 20: 5 and seen your tears; I will *h* you.
20: 8 the sign that the LORD will *h* me
2Ch 7:14 their sin and will *h* their land.
Job 5:18 he injures, but his hands also *h*.
Ps 6: 2 *h* me, for my bones are in agony.
41: 4 *h* me, for I have sinned against you
Ecc 3: 3 a time to kill and a time to *h*,
Isa 19:22 he will strike them and *h* them.
19:22 respond to their pleas and *h* them.
57:18 seen his ways, but I will *h* him;
57:19 "And I will *h* them."
Jer 17:14 *H* me, O LORD, and I will be
30:17 and *h* your wounds,'
33: 6 I will *h* my people and will let them
La 2:13 Who can *h* you?
Hos 5:13 not able to *h* your sores.
6: 1 but he will *h* us;
7: 1 whenever I would *h* Israel,
14: 4 "I will *h* their waywardness
Na 3:19 Nothing can *h* your wound;
Zec 11:16 or seek the young, or *h* the injured,
Mt 8: 7 said to him, "I will go and *h* him."
10: 1 to *h* every disease and sickness.
10: 8 *H* the sick, raise the dead,
12:10 "Is it lawful to *h* on the Sabbath?"
13:15 and turn, and I would *h* them.'
17:16 but they could not *h* him."
Mk 3: 2 if he would *h* him on the Sabbath.
6: 5 on a few sick people and *h* them.
Lk 4:23 to me: 'Physician, *h* yourself!
5:17 present for him to *h* the sick.
6: 7 to see if he would *h* on the Sabbath.
7: 3 him to come and *h* his servant.
8:43 years, but no one could *h* her.
9: 2 kingdom of God and to *h* the sick.
10: 9 *H* the sick who are there
13:32 and *h* people today and tomorrow,
14: 3 "Is it lawful to *h* on the Sabbath
Jn 4:47 begged him to come and *h* his son,
12:40 nor turn—and I would *h* them."
Ac 4:30 Stretch out your hand to *h*
28:27 and turn, and I would *h* them.'

HEALED* (HEAL)
Ge 20:17 to God, and God *h* Abimelech,
Ex 21:19 and see that he is completely *h*.
Lev 13:37 hair has grown in it, the itch is *h*.
14: 3 If the person has been *h*
Jos 5: 8 were in camp until they were *h*.
1Sa 6: 3 you will be *h*, and you will know
2Ki 2:21 LORD says: 'I have *h* this water.
2Ch 30:20 heard Hezekiah and *h* the people.
Ps 30: 2 and you *h* me.
107:20 He sent forth his word and *h* them;
Isa 6:10 and turn and be *h*."
53: 5 and by his wounds we are *h*.
Jer 14:19 us so that we cannot be *h*?
17:14 Heal me, O LORD, and I will be *h*;
51: 8 perhaps she can be *h*.
51: 9 but she cannot be *h*;
51: 9 " 'We would have *h* Babylon,
Eze 34: 4 the weak or *h* the sick
Hos 11: 3 it was I who *h* them.
Mt 4:24 and the paralyzed, and he *h* them.
8: 8 the word, and my servant will be *h*.
8:13 his servant was *h* at that very hour.
8:16 with a word and *h* all the sick.
9:21 If I only touch his cloak, I will be *h*
9:22 he said, "your faith has *h* you."
9:22 woman was *h* from that moment.
12:15 him, and he *h* all their sick,
12:22 Jesus *h* him, so that he could both
14:14 on them and *h* their sick.
14:36 and all who touched him were *h*.
15:28 And her daughter was *h*
15:30 laid them at his feet; and he *h* them
17:18 and he was *h* from that moment.
19: 2 followed him, and he *h* them there.
21:14 to him at the temple, and he *h* them
Mk 1:34 and Jesus *h* many who had various
3:10 For he had *h* many, so that those
5:23 hands on her so that she will be *h*
5:28 If I just touch his clothes, I will be *h*
5:34 "Daughter, your faith has *h* you.
6:13 people with oil and *h* them.
6:56 and all who touched him were *h*.
10:52 said Jesus, "your faith has *h* you."
Lk 4:40 hands on each one, he *h* them.
5:15 and to be *h* of their sicknesses.
6:18 and to be *h* of their diseases.
7: 7 the word, and my servant will be *h*.
8:47 and how she had been instantly *h*.
8:48 "Daughter, your faith has *h* you.
8:50 just believe, and she will be *h*."
9:11 and *h* those who needed healing.
9:42 *h* the boy and gave him back
13:14 Jesus had *h* on the Sabbath,
13:14 So come and be *h* on those days,
14: 4 he *h* him and sent him away.
17:15 when he saw he was *h*, came back,
18:42 your sight; your faith has *h* you."
22:51 touched the man's ear and *h* him.
Jn 5:10 said to the man who had been *h*,
5:13 man who was *h* had no idea who it
Ac 4: 9 and are asked how he was *h*,
4:10 stands before you *h*.
4:14 who had been *h* standing there
4:22 man who was miraculously *h* was
5:16 evil spirits, and all of them were *h*.
8: 7 paralytics and cripples were *h*.
14: 9 saw that he had faith to be *h*
28: 8 placed his hands on him and *h* him.
Heb 12:13 may not be disabled, but rather *h*.
Jas 5:16 for each other so that you may be *h*
1Pe 2:24 by his wounds you have been *h*.
Rev 13: 3 but the fatal wound had been *h*.
13:12 whose fatal wound had been *h*.

HEALING* (HEAL)
2Ch 28:15 food and drink, and *h* balm.
Pr 12:18 but the tongue of the wise brings *h*.
13:17 but a trustworthy envoy brings *h*.
15: 4 The tongue that brings *h* is a tree
16:24 sweet to the soul and *h* to the bones
Isa 58: 8 and your *h* will quickly appear;
Jer 8:15 for a time of *h*
8:22 Why then is there no *h*
14:19 for a time of *h*
30:12 your injury beyond *h*.
30:13 no *h* for you.
33: 6 I will bring health and *h* to it;
46:11 there is no *h* for you.
Eze 30:21 It has not been bound up for *h*
47:12 for food and their leaves for *h*."
Mal 4: 2 rise with *h* in its wings.
Mt 4:23 and *h* every disease and sickness
9:35 and *h* every disease and sickness.
Lk 6:19 coming from him and *h* them all.
9: 6 gospel and *h* people everywhere.
9:11 and healed those who needed *h*.
Jn 7:23 angry with me for *h* the whole man
Ac 3:16 him that has given this complete *h*
10:38 *h* all who were under the power
1Co 12: 9 to another gifts of *h*
12:28 also those having gifts of *h*,
12:30 Do all have gifts of *h*? Do all speak
Rev 22: 2 are for the *h* of the nations.

HEALS* (HEAL)
Ex 15:26 for I am the LORD, who *h* you."
Lev 13:18 a boil on his skin and it *h*,
Ps 103: 3 and *h* all your diseases;
147: 3 He *h* the brokenhearted
Isa 30:26 and *h* the wounds he inflicted.
Ac 9:34 said to him, "Jesus Christ *h* you.

HEALTH* (HEALTHIER HEALTHY)
1Sa 25: 6 And good *h* to all that is yours!
25: 6 Good *h* to you and your household
Ps 38: 3 of your wrath there is no *h*
38: 7 there is no *h* in my body.
Pr 3: 8 This will bring *h* to your body
4:22 and *h* to a man's whole body.
15:30 and good news gives *h* to the bones
Isa 38:16 You restored me to *h*
Jer 30:17 But I will restore you to *h*
33: 6 I will bring *h* and healing to it;
3Jn : 2 I pray that you may enjoy good *h*

HEALTHIER* (HEALTH)
Da 1:15 end of the ten days they looked *h*

HEALTHY* (HEALTH)
Ge 41: 5 Seven heads of grain, *h* and good,
41: 7 of grain swallowed up the seven *h*,
Ps 73: 4 their bodies are *h* and strong.
Zec 11:16 or heal the injured, or feed the *h*,
Mt 9:12 "It is not the *h* who need a doctor,
Mk 2:17 "It is not the *h* who need a doctor,
Lk 5:31 "It is not the *h* who need a doctor,

HEAP
Pr 25:22 you will *h* burning coals
Ro 12:20 you will *h* burning coals

HEAR (HEARD HEARING HEARS)
Ex 15:14 The nations will *h* and tremble;
22:27 I will *h*, for I am compassionate.
Nu 14:13 Then the Egyptians will *h* about it!
Dt 1:16 *H* the disputes between your
4:36 heaven he made you *h* his voice
6: 4 *H*, O Israel: The LORD our God,
19:20 The rest of the people will *h* of this
31:13 must *h* it and learn
Jos 7: 9 of the country will *h* about this
1Ki 8:30 *H* the supplication of your servant
2Ki 19:16 O LORD, and *h*; open your eyes,
2Ch 7:14 then will I *h* from heaven
Job 31:35 ("Oh, that I had someone to *h* me!
Ps 94: 9 he who implanted the ear not *h*?
95: 7 Today, if you *h* his voice,
Ecc 7:21 or you may *h* your servant cursing
Isa 21: 3 I am staggered by what I *h*,
29:18 that day the deaf will *h* the words

Isa 30:21 your ears will *h* a voice behind you,
51: 7 *H* me, you who know what is right,
59: 1 nor his ear too dull to *h*.
65:24 while they are still speaking I will *h*
Jer 5:21 who have ears but do not *h*:
Eze 33: 7 so *h* the word I speak and give
37: 4 'Dry bones, *h* the word
Mt 11: 5 the deaf *h*, the dead are raised,
11:15 He who has ears, let him *h*.
13:17 and to *h* what you *h* but did not *h* it
Mk 12:29 answered Jesus, "is this: '*H*,
Lk 7:22 the deaf *h*, the dead are raised,
Jn 8:47 reason you do not *h* is that you do
Ac 13: 7 he wanted to *h* the word of God.
13:44 gathered to *h* the word of the Lord.
17:32 "We want to *h* you again
Ro 2:13 is not those who *h* the law who are
10:14 they *h* without someone preaching
2Ti 4: 3 what their itching ears want to *h*.
Heb 3: 7 "Today, if you *h* his voice,
Rev 1: 3 and blessed are those who *h* it

HEARD (HEAR)
Ex 2:24 God *h* their groaning and he
Dt 4:32 has anything like it ever been *h* of?
2Sa 7:22 as we have *h* with our own ears.
Job 42: 5 My ears had *h* of you
Isa 40:21 Have you not *h*?
40:28 Have you not *h*?
66: 8 Who has ever *h* of such a thing?
Jer 18:13 Who has ever *h* anything like this?
Da 10:12 your words were *h*, and I have
12: 8 I *h*, but I did not understand.
Hab 3:16 I *h* and my heart pounded,
Mt 5:21 "You have *h* that it was said
5:27 "You have *h* that it was said,
5:33 you have *h* that it was said
5:38 "You have *h* that it was said,
5:43 "You have *h* that it was said,
Lk 12: 3 in the dark will be *h* in the daylight,
Jn 8:26 and what I have *h* from him I tell
Ac 2: 6 because each one *h* them speaking
1Co 2: 9 no ear has *h*,
2Co 12: 4 He *h* inexpressible things,
1Th 2:13 word of God, which you *h* from us,
2Ti 1:13 What you *h* from me, keep
Jas 1:25 not forgetting what he has *h*,
Rev 22: 8 am the one who *h* and saw these

HEARING (HEAR)
Isa 6: 9 Be ever *h*, but never understanding
Mt 13:14 will be ever *h* but never
Mk 4:12 ever *h* but never understanding;
Ac 28:26 will be ever *h* but never
Ro 10:17 faith comes from *h* the message,
1Co 12:17 where would the sense of *h* be?

HEARS (HEAR)
Jn 5:24 whoever *h* my word and believes
1Jn 5:14 according to his will, he *h* us.
Rev 3:20 If anyone *h* my voice and opens

HEART (BROKENHEARTED FAINT-HEARTED HARDHEARTED HEART'S HEARTACHE HEARTS KINDHEARTED SIMPLEHEARTED STOUTHEARTED WHOLEHEARTED WHOLEHEARTEDLY)
Ge 6: 5 of his *h* was only evil all the time.
Ex 4:21 But I will harden his *h*
25: 2 each man whose *h* prompts him
35:21 and whose *h* moved him came
Lev 19:17 Do not hate your brother in your *h*.
Dt 4: 9 or let them slip from your *h* as long
4:29 if you look for him with all your *h*
6: 5 LORD your God with all your *h*
10:12 LORD your God with all your *h*
11:13 and to serve him with all your *h*
13: 3 you love him with all your *h*
15:10 and do so without a grudging *h*;
26:16 observe them with all your *h*
29:18 you today whose *h* turns away
Dt 30: 2 and obey him with all your *h*
30: 6 you may love him with all your *h*
30:10 LORD your God with all your *h*
Jos 22: 5 and to serve him with all your *h*
23:14 You know with all your *h*
1Sa 10: 9 God changed Saul's *h*,
12:20 serve the LORD with all your *h*.
12:24 serve him faithfully with all your *h*;
13:14 sought out a man after his own *h*
14: 7 I am with you *h* and soul."
16: 7 but the LORD looks at the *h*."
17:32 "Let no one lose *h* on account
1Ki 2: 4 faithfully before me with all their *h*
3: 9 So give your servant a discerning *h*
3:12 give you a wise and discerning *h*,
8:48 back to you with all their *h*
9: 3 and my *h* will always be there.
9: 4 walk before me in integrity of *h*
10:24 the wisdom God had put in his *h*.
11: 4 and his *h* was not fully devoted
14: 8 and followed me with all his *h*,
15:14 Asa's *h* was fully committed
2Ki 22:19 Because your *h* was responsive
23: 3 with all his *h* and all his soul,
1Ch 28: 9 for the LORD searches every *h*
2Ch 6:38 back to you with all their *h*
7:16 and my *h* will always be there.
15:12 of their fathers, with all their *h*
15:17 Asa's *h* was fully committed
17: 6 His *h* was devoted to the ways
22: 9 sought the LORD with all his *h*."
34:31 with all his *h* and all his soul,
36:13 stiff-necked and hardened his *h*
Ezr 1: 5 everyone whose *h* God had moved
Ne 4: 6 the people worked with all their *h*.
Job 19:27 How my *h* yearns within me!
22:22 and lay up his words in your *h*.
37: 1 "At this my *h* pounds
Ps 9: 1 you, O LORD, with all my *h*;
14: 1 The fool says in his *h*,
16: 9 Therefore my *h* is glad
19:14 and the meditation of my *h*
20: 4 he give you the desire of your *h*
24: 4 who has clean hands and a pure *h*,
26: 2 examine my *h* and my mind;
37: 4 will give you the desires of your *h*.
37:31 The law of his God is in his *h*;
44:21 since he knows the secrets of the *h*
45: 1 My *h* is stirred by a noble theme
51:10 Create in me a pure *h*, O God,
51:17 a broken and contrite *h*,
53: 1 The fool says in his *h*,
66:18 If I had cherished sin in my *h*,
73: 1 to those who are pure in *h*.
73:26 My flesh and my *h* may fail,
86:11 give me an undivided *h*,
90:12 that we may gain a *h* of wisdom.
97:11 and joy on the upright in *h*.
108: 1 My *h* is steadfast, O God;
109:22 and my *h* is wounded within me.
111: 1 will extol the LORD with all my *h*
112: 7 his *h* is steadfast, trusting
112: 8 His *h* is secure, he will have no fear
119: 2 and seek him with all their *h*.
119:10 I seek you with all my *h*;
119:11 I have hidden your word in my *h*
119:30 I have set my *h* on your laws.
119:32 for you have set my *h* free.
119:34 and obey it with all my *h*.
119:36 Turn my *h* toward your statutes
119:58 sought your face with all my *h*;
119:69 I keep your precepts with all my *h*.
119:111 they are the joy of my *h*.
119:112 My *h* is set on keeping your
119:145 I call with all my *h*; answer me,
125: 4 to those who are upright in *h*.
138: 1 you, O LORD, with all my *h*;
139:23 Search me, O God, and know my *h*
Pr 2: 2 applying your *h* to understanding,
3: 1 but keep my commands in your *h*,
Pr 3: 3 write them on the tablet of your *h*.
3: 5 Trust in the LORD with all your *h*
4: 4 hold of my words with all your *h*;
4:21 keep them within your *h*;
4:23 Above all else, guard your *h*,
6:21 Bind them upon your *h* forever;
7: 3 write them on the tablet of your *h*.
10: 8 The wise in *h* accept commands,
13:12 Hope deferred makes the *h* sick,
14:13 Even in laughter the *h* may ache,
14:30 A *h* at peace gives life to the body,
15:13 A happy *h* makes the face cheerful,
15:15 the cheerful *h* has a continual feast.
15:28 *h* of the righteous weighs its
15:30 A cheerful look brings joy to the *h*,
16:23 A wise man's *h* guides his mouth,
17:22 A cheerful *h* is good medicine,
20: 9 can say, "I have kept my *h* pure;
22:11 He who loves a pure *h*
22:17 apply your *h* to what I teach,
22:18 when you keep them in your *h*
23:15 My son, if your *h* is wise,
23:19 and keep your *h* on the right path.
23:26 My son, give me your *h*
24:17 stumbles, do not let your *h* rejoice,
27:19 so a man's *h* reflects the man.
Ecc 5: 2 do not be hasty in your *h*
8: 5 wise *h* will know the proper time
11:10 banish anxiety from your *h*
SS 3: 1 I looked for the one my *h* loves;
4: 9 You have stolen my *h*, my sister,
5: 2 *Beloved* I slept but my *h* was awake
5: 4 my *h* began to pound for him.
8: 6 Place me like a seal over your *h*,
Isa 6:10 Make the *h* of this people calloused
40:11 and carries them close to his *h*;
57:15 and to revive the *h* of the contrite.
66:14 you see this, your *h* will rejoice
Jer 3:15 give you shepherds after my own *h*,
4:14 wash the evil from your *h*
9:26 of Israel is uncircumcised in *h*."
17: 9 The *h* is deceitful above all things
20: 9 is in my *h* like a fire,
24: 7 I will give them a *h* to know me,
29:13 when you seek me with all your *h*.
32:39 I will give them singleness of *h*
32:41 them in this land with all my *h*
51:46 Do not lose *h* or be afraid
Eze 11:19 I will give them an undivided *h*
18:31 and get a new *h* and a new spirit.
36:26 I will give you a new *h*
44: 7 foreigners uncircumcised in *h*
Da 7: 4 and the *h* of a man was given to it.
Joel 2:12 "return to me with all your *h*,
2:13 Rend your *h*
Zep 3:14 Be glad and rejoice with all your *h*,
Mt 5: 8 Blessed are the pure in *h*,
5:28 adultery with her in his *h*.
6:21 treasure is, there your *h* will be
11:29 for I am gentle and humble in *h*,
12:34 of the *h* the mouth speaks.
13:15 For this people's *h* has become
15:18 out of the mouth come from the *h*,
15:19 For out of the *h* come evil thoughts
18:35 forgive your brother from your *h*."
22:37 the Lord your God with all your *h*
Mk 11:23 and does not doubt in his *h*
12:30 the Lord your God with all your *h*
12:33 To love him with all your *h*,
Lk 2:19 and pondered them in her *h*.
2:51 treasured all these things in her *h*.
6:45 out of the good stored up in his *h*,
6:45 overflow of his *h* his mouth speaks.
8:15 for those with a noble and good *h*,
10:27 the Lord your God with all your *h*
12:34 treasure is, there your *h* will be
Jn 12:27 "Now my *h* is troubled,
Ac 1:24 "Lord, you know everyone's *h*.
2:37 they were cut to the *h*
4:32 All the believers were one in *h*

Ac 8:21 your *h* is not right before God.
15: 8 who knows the *h,* showed that he
16:14 The Lord opened her *h* to respond
28:27 For this people's *h* has become
Ro 1: 9 with my whole *h* in preaching
2:29 is circumcision of the *h,*
10: 9 in your *h* that God raised him
10:10 is with your *h* that you believe
15: 6 with one *h* and mouth you may
1Co 14:25 the secrets of his *h* will be laid bare.
2Co 2: 4 anguish of *h* and with many tears,
4: 1 this ministry, we do not lose *h.*
4:16 Therefore we do not lose *h.*
9: 7 give what he has decided in his *h*
Eph 1:18 eyes of your *h* may be enlightened
5:19 make music in your *h* to the Lord,
6: 5 and with sincerity of *h,* just
6: 6 doing the will of God from your *h.*
Php 1: 7 since I have you in my *h;* for
Col 2: 2 is that they may be encouraged in *h*
3:22 but with sincerity of *h*
3:23 work at it with all your *h,*
1Ti 1: 5 which comes from a pure *h*
3: 1 If anyone sets his *h*
2Ti 2:22 call on the Lord out of a pure *h.*
Phm :12 who is my very *h*— back to you.
:20 in the Lord; refresh my *h* in Christ.
Heb 4:12 the thoughts and attitudes of the *h.*
1Pe 1:22 one another deeply, from the *h.*

HEART'S* (HEART)
2Ch 1:11 "Since this is your *h* desire
Jer 15:16 they were my joy and my *h* delight,
Eze 24:25 delight of their eyes, their *h* desire,
Ro 10: 1 my *h* desire and prayer to God

HEARTACHE* (HEART)
Pr 15:13 but *h* crushes the spirit.

HEARTLESS*
La 4: 3 but my people have become *h*
Ro 1:31 they are senseless, faithless, *h,*

HEARTS (HEART)
Lev 26:41 their uncircumcised *h* are humbled
Dt 6: 6 are to be upon your *h.*
10:16 Circumcise your *h,* therefore,
11:18 Fix these words of mine in your *h*
30: 6 your God will circumcise your *h*
Jos 11:20 himself who hardened their *h*
24:23 and yield your *h* to the LORD,
1Sa 7: 3 to the LORD with all your *h,*
10:26 valiant men whose *h* God had
2Sa 15: 6 and so he stole the *h* of the men
1Ki 8:39 for you alone know the *h* of all men
8:61 your *h* must be fully committed
18:37 are turning their *h* back again."
1Ch 29:18 and keep their *h* loyal to you.
2Ch 6:30 (for you alone know the *h* of men),
11:16 tribe of Israel who set their *h*
29:31 all whose *h* were willing brought
Ps 7: 9 who searches minds and *h,*
33:21 In him our *h* rejoice,
62: 8 pour out your *h* to him,
95: 8 do not harden your *h* as you did
Ecc 3:11 also set eternity in the *h* of men;
Isa 26: 8 are the desire of our *h.*
29:13 but their *h* are far from me.
35: 4 say to those with fearful *h,*
51: 7 people who have my law in your *h:*
63:17 harden our *h* so we do not revere
65:14 out of the joy of their *h,*
Jer 4: 4 circumcise your *h,*
12: 2 but far from their *h.*
17: 1 on the tablets of their *h*
31:33 and write it on their *h.*
Mal 4: 6 He will turn the *h* of the fathers
Mt 15: 8 but their *h* are far from me.
Mk 6:52 the loaves; their *h* were hardened.
7: 6 but their *h* are far from me.
7:21 out of men's *h,* come evil thoughts,
Lk 1:17 to turn the *h* of the fathers
16:15 of men, but God knows your *h.*
24:32 "Were not our *h* burning within us
Jn 5:42 not have the love of God in your *h.*
14: 1 "Do not let your *h* be troubled.
14:27 Do not let your *h* be troubled
Ac 7:51 with uncircumcised *h* and ears!
11:23 true to the Lord with all their *h.*
15: 9 for he purified their *h* by faith.
28:27 understand with their *h*
Ro 1:21 and their foolish *h* were darkened.
2:15 of the law are written on their *h,*
5: 5 love into our *h* by the Holy Spirit,
8:27 who searches our *h* knows
1Co 4: 5 will expose the motives of men's *h.*
2Co 1:22 put his Spirit in our *h* as a deposit,
3: 2 written on our *h,* known
3: 3 but on tablets of human *h.*
4: 6 shine in our *h* to give us the light
6:11 and opened wide our *h* to you.
6:13 to my children—open wide your *h*
7: 2 Make room for us in your *h.*
Gal 4: 6 the Spirit of his Son into our *h,*
Eph 3:17 dwell in your *h* through faith.
Php 4: 7 will guard your *h* and your minds
Col 3: 1 set your *h* on things above,
3:15 the peace of Christ rule in your *h,*
3:16 with gratitude in your *h* to God.
1Th 2: 4 men but God, who tests our *h.*
3:13 May he strengthen your *h*
2Th 2:17 encourage your *h* and strengthen
Phm : 7 have refreshed the *h* of the saints.
Heb 3: 8 do not harden your *h*
8:10 and write them on their *h.*
10:16 I will put my laws in their *h,*
10:22 having our *h* sprinkled
Jas 4: 8 purify your *h,* you double-minded.
2Pe 1:19 the morning star rises in your *h.*
1Jn 3:20 For God is greater than our *h,*

HEAT
Ps 19: 6 nothing is hidden from its *h.*
2Pe 3:12 and the elements will melt in the *h.*

HEAVEN (HEAVENLY HEAVENS HEAVENWARD)
Ge 14:19 Creator of *h* and earth.
28:12 with its top reaching to *h,*
Ex 16: 4 rain down bread from *h* for you.
20:22 that I have spoken to you from *h:*
Dt 26:15 from *h,* your holy dwelling place,
30:12 "Who will ascend into *h* to get it
1Ki 8:27 the highest *h,* cannot contain you.
8:30 Hear from *h,* your dwelling place,
22:19 the host of *h* standing around him
2Ki 2: 1 up to *h* in a whirlwind,
19:15 You have made *h* and earth.
2Ch 7:14 then will I hear from *h*
Isa 14:12 How you have fallen from *h,*
66: 1 "*H* is my throne,
Da 7:13 coming with the clouds of *h.*
Mt 3: 2 for the kingdom of *h* is near."
3:16 At that moment *h* was opened,
4:17 for the kingdom of *h* is near."
5:12 because great is your reward in *h,*
5:19 great in the kingdom of *h.*
6: 9 " 'Our Father in *h,*
6:10 done on earth as it is in *h.*
6:20 up for yourselves treasures in *h,*
7:21 Lord,' will enter the kingdom of *h,*
16:19 bind on earth will be bound in *h,*
18: 3 will never enter the kingdom of *h.*
18:18 bind on earth will be bound in *h,*
19:14 the kingdom of *h* belongs to such
19:21 and you will have treasure in *h.*
19:23 man to enter the kingdom of *h.*
23:13 the kingdom of *h* in men's faces.
24:35 *H* and earth will pass away,
26:64 and coming on the clouds of *h.*"
28:18 "All authority in *h*
Mk 1:10 he saw *h* being torn open
10:21 and you will have treasure in *h.*
13:31 *H* and earth will pass away,
14:62 and coming on the clouds of *h.*"
16:19 he was taken up into *h*
Lk 3:21 *h* was opened and the Holy Spirit
10:18 saw Satan fall like lightning from *h.*
10:20 that your names are written in *h.*"
12:33 in *h* that will not be exhausted,
15: 7 in *h* over one sinner who repents
18:22 and you will have treasure in *h.*
21:33 *H* and earth will pass away,
24:51 left them and was taken up into *h.*
Jn 3:13 No one has ever gone into *h*
6:38 down from *h* not to do my will
12:28 Then a voice came from *h,*
Ac 1:11 has been taken from you into *h,*
7:49 the prophet says: " '*H* is my
7:55 looked up to *h* and saw the glory
9: 3 a light from *h* flashed around him.
26:19 disobedient to the vision from *h.*
Ro 10: 6 'Who will ascend into *h?*' " (that is,
1Co 15:47 the earth, the second man from *h.*
2Co 5: 1 an eternal house in *h,* not built
12: 2 ago was caught up to the third *h.*
Eph 1:10 to bring all things in *h*
Php 2:10 *h* and on earth and under the earth,
3:20 But our citizenship is in *h.*
Col 1:16 things in *h* and on earth, visible
4: 1 that you also have a Master in *h.*
1Th 1:10 and to wait for his Son from *h,*
4:16 himself will come down from *h,*
Heb 1: 3 hand of the Majesty in *h.*
8: 5 and shadow of what is in *h.*
9:24 he entered *h* itself, now to appear
12:23 whose names are written in *h.*
1Pe 1: 4 spoil or fade—kept in *h* for you,
3:22 who has gone into *h* and is
2Pe 3:13 we are looking forward to a new *h*
Rev 5:13 Then I heard every creature in *h*
11:19 God's temple in *h* was opened,
12: 7 And there was war in *h.*
15: 5 this I looked and in *h* the temple,
19: 1 of a great multitude in *h* shouting:
19:11 I saw *h* standing open and there
21: 1 Then I saw a new *h* and a new earth
21:10 coming down out of *h* from God.

HEAVENLY (HEAVEN)
Ps 8: 5 him a little lower than the *h* beings
2Co 5: 2 to be clothed with our *h* dwelling,
Eph 1: 3 in the *h* realms with every spiritual
1:20 at his right hand in the *h* realms,
2Ti 4:18 bring me safely to his *h* kingdom.
Heb 12:22 to the *h* Jerusalem, the city

HEAVENS (HEAVEN)
Ge 1: 1 In the beginning God created the *h*
11: 4 with a tower that reaches to the *h,*
Dt 33:26 who rides on the *h* to help you
1Ki 8:27 The *h,* even the highest heaven,
2Ch 2: 6 since the *h,* even the highest
Ezr 9: 6 and our guilt has reached to the *h.*
Ne 9: 6 You made the *h,* even the highest
Job 11: 8 They are higher than the *h*—
38:33 Do you know the laws of the *h?*
Ps 8: 3 When I consider your *h,*
19: 1 The *h* declare the glory of God;
33: 6 of the LORD were the *h* made,
57: 5 Be exalted, O God, above the *h;*
102:25 the *h* are the work of your hands.
103:11 as high as the *h* are above the earth,
108: 4 is your love, higher than the *h;*
115:16 The highest *h* belong to the LORD
119:89 it stands firm in the *h.*
135: 6 in the *h* and on the earth,
139: 8 If I go up to the *h,* you are there;
148: 1 Praise the LORD from the *h,*
Isa 40:26 Lift your eyes and look to the *h:*
45: 8 "You *h* above, rain
51: 6 Lift up your eyes to the *h,*
55: 9 "As the *h* are higher than the earth,

HIGHWAY
Isa 40: 3 a *h* for our God.

HILL (HILLS)
Ps 24: 3 ascend the *h* of the LORD?
Isa 40: 4 every mountain and *h* made low;
Mt 5:14 A city on a *h* cannot be hidden.
Lk 3: 5 every mountain and *h* made low.

HILLS (HILL)
1Ki 20:23 "Their gods are gods of the *h*.
Ps 50:10 and the cattle on a thousand *h*.
121: 1 I lift up my eyes to the *h*—
Hos 10: 8 and to the *h*, "Fall on us!"
Lk 23:30 and to the *h*, "Cover us!" '
Rev 17: 9 The seven heads are seven *h*

HINDER (HINDERED HINDERS)
1Sa 14: 6 Nothing can *h* the LORD
Mt 19:14 come to me, and do not *h* them,
1Co 9:12 anything rather than *h* the gospel
1Pe 3: 7 so that nothing will *h* your prayers.

HINDERED (HINDER)
Lk 11:52 and you have *h* those who were

HINDERS (HINDER)
Heb 12: 1 let us throw off everything that *h*

HINT*
Eph 5: 3 even a *h* of sexual immorality,

HIP
Ge 32:32 socket of Jacob's *h* was touched

HIRAM
King of Tyre; helped David build his palace (2Sa 5:11–12; 1Ch 14:1); helped Solomon build the temple (1Ki 5; 2Ch 2) and his navy (1Ki 9:10–27; 2Ch 8).

HIRED
Lk 15:15 and *h* himself out to a citizen
Jn 10:12 *h* hand is not the shepherd who

HOARDED (HOARDS)
Ecc 5:13 wealth *h* to the harm of its owner,
Jas 5: 3 You have *h* wealth in the last days.

HOARDS (HOARDED)
Pr 11:26 People curse the man who *h* grain,

HOLD (HELD HOLDS)
Ex 20: 7 LORD will not *h* anyone guiltless
Lev 19:13 " 'Do not *h* back the wages
Dt 5:11 LORD will not *h* anyone guiltless
11:22 in all his ways and to *h* fast to him
13: 4 serve him and *h* fast to him.
30:20 listen to his voice, and *h* fast to him
Jos 22: 5 to *h* fast to him and to serve him
2Ki 4:16 "you will *h* a son in your arms."
Ps 18:16 from on high and took *h* of me;
73:23 you *h* me by my right hand.
Pr 4: 4 "Lay *h* of my words
Isa 41:13 who takes *h* of your right hand
54: 2 do not *h* back;
Eze 3:18 and I will *h* you accountable
3:20 and I will *h* you accountable
33: 6 I will *h* the watchman accountable
Zec 8:23 nations will take firm *h* of one Jew
Mk 11:25 if you *h* anything against anyone,
Jn 20:17 Jesus said, "Do not *h* on to me,
Php 2:16 as you *h* out the word of life—
3:12 but I press on to take *h* of that
Col 1:17 and in him all things *h* together.
1Th 5:21 *H* on to the good.
1Ti 6:12 Take *h* of the eternal life
Heb 10:23 Let us *h* unswervingly

HOLDS (HOLD)
Pr 10:19 but he who *h* his tongue is wise.
17:28 and discerning if he *h* his tongue.

HOLES
Hag 1: 6 to put them in a purse with *h* in it."
Mt 8:20 "Foxes have *h* and birds

HOLINESS* (HOLY)
Ex 15:11 majestic in *h*,
Dt 32:51 because you did not uphold my *h*
1Ch 16:29 the LORD in the splendor of his *h*.
2Ch 20:21 him for the splendor of his *h*
Ps 29: 2 in the splendor of his *h*.
89:35 Once for all, I have sworn by my *h*
93: 5 *h* adorns your house
96: 9 in the splendor of his *h*;
Isa 29:23 they will acknowledge the *h*
35: 8 it will be called the Way of *H*.
Eze 36:23 I will show the *h* of my great name,
38:23 I will show my greatness and my *h*,
Am 4: 2 LORD has sworn by his *h*:
Lk 1:75 fear in *h* and righteousness
Ro 1: 4 the Spirit of *h* was declared
6:19 to righteousness leading to *h*.
6:22 the benefit you reap leads to *h*,
1Co 1:30 our righteousness, *h*
2Co 1:12 in the *h* and sincerity that are
7: 1 perfecting *h* out of reverence
Eph 4:24 God in true righteousness and *h*.
1Ti 2: 2 quiet lives in all godliness and *h*.
2:15 love and *h* with propriety.
Heb 12:10 that we may share in his *h*.
12:14 without *h* no one will see the Lord.

HOLY (HALLOWED HOLINESS)
Ge 2: 3 the seventh day and made it *h*,
Ex 3: 5 you are standing is *h* ground."
16:23 a *h* Sabbath to the LORD.
19: 6 kingdom of priests and a *h* nation.'
20: 8 the Sabbath day by keeping it *h*.
26:33 Place from the Most *H* Place.
26:33 curtain will separate the *H* Place
28:36 seal: *H* TO THE LORD.
29:37 Then the altar will be most *h*,
30:10 It is most *h* to the LORD."
30:29 them so they will be most *h*,
31:13 I am the LORD, who makes you *h*.
40: 9 all its furnishings, and it will be *h*.
Lev 10: 3 I will show myself *h*;
10:10 must distinguish between the *h*
10:13 in a *h* place, because it is your share
11:44 and be *h*, because I am *h*.
11:45 therefore be *h*, because I am *h*.
19: 2 'Be *h* because I, the LORD your
19: 8 he has desecrated what is *h*
19:24 the fourth year all its fruit will be *h*,
20: 3 and profaned my *h* name.
20: 7 " 'Consecrate yourselves and be *h*,
20: 8 I am the LORD, who makes you *h*.
20:26 You are to be *h* to me because I,
21: 6 They must be *h* to their God
21: 8 Consider them *h*, because I
22: 9 am the LORD, who makes them *h*.
22:32 Do not profane my *h* name.
25:12 For it is a jubilee and is to be *h*
27: 9 given to the LORD becomes *h*.
Nu 4:15 they must not touch the *h* things
6: 5 He must be *h* until the period
20:12 as *h* in the sight of the Israelites,
20:13 and where he showed himself *h*
Dt 5:12 the Sabbath day by keeping it *h*,
23:14 Your camp must be *h*,
26:15 from heaven, your *h* dwelling place
33: 2 He came with myriads of *h* ones
Jos 5:15 place where you are standing is *h*."
24:19 He is a *h* God; he is a jealous God.
1Sa 2: 2 "There is no one *h* like the LORD;
6:20 of the LORD, this *h* God?
21: 5 even on missions that are not *h*.
2Ki 4: 9 often comes our way is a *h* man
1Ch 16:10 Glory in his *h* name;
16:35 may give thanks to your *h* name,
29: 3 I have provided for this *h* temple:
2Ch 30:27 heaven, his *h* dwelling place.
Ezr 9: 2 and have mingled the *h* race
Ne 11: 1 the *h* city, while the remaining nine
Job 6:10 not denied the words of the *H* One.
Ps 2: 6 King on Zion, my *h* hill."
11: 4 The LORD is in his *h* temple;
16:10 will you let your *H* One see decay.
22: 3 you are enthroned as the *H* One;
24: 3 Who may stand in his *h* place?
30: 4 praise his *h* name.
77:13 Your ways, O God, are *h*.
78:54 to the border of his *h* land,
99: 3 he is *h*.
99: 5 he is *h*.
99: 9 for the LORD our God is *h*.
105: 3 Glory in his *h* name;
111: 9 *h* and awesome is his name.
Pr 9:10 of the *H* One is understanding.
Isa 5:16 the *h* God will show himself *h*
6: 3 *H*, *h*, *h* is the LORD Almighty;
8:13 is the one you are to regard as *h*,
29:23 they will keep my name *h*;
40:25 who is my equal?" says the *H* One.
43: 3 the *H* One of Israel, your Savior;
54: 5 *H* One of Israel is your Redeemer;
57:15 who lives forever, whose name is *h*:
58:13 and the LORD's *h* day honorable,
Jer 17:22 but keep the Sabbath day *h*,
Eze 20:41 I will show myself *h* among you
22:26 to my law and profane my *h* things;
28:22 and show myself *h* within her.
28:25 I will show myself *h* among them
36:20 nations they profaned my *h* name,
38:16 when I show myself *h* through you
44:23 the difference between the *h*
Da 9:24 prophecy and to anoint the most *h*.
Hab 2:20 But the LORD is in his *h* temple;
Zec 14: 5 and all the *h* ones with him.
14:20 On that day *H* TO THE LORD
Mt 24:15 in the *h* place 'the abomination
Mk 1:24 the *H* One of God!" "Be quiet!"
Lk 1:35 the *h* one to be born will be called
1:49 *h* is his name.
4:34 the *H* One of God!" "Be quiet!"
Jn 6:69 and know that you are the *H* One
Ac 2:27 will you let your *H* One see decay.
13:35 will not let your *H* One see decay.'
Ro 1: 2 prophets in the *H* Scriptures
7:12 and the commandment is *h*,
11:16 if the root is *h*, so are the branches.
12: 1 as living sacrifices, *h* and pleasing
1Co 1: 2 in Christ Jesus and called to be *h*,
7:14 be unclean, but as it is, they are *h*.
Eph 1: 4 the creation of the world to be *h*
2:21 and rises to become a *h* temple
3: 5 by the Spirit to God's *h* apostles
5: 3 improper for God's *h* people.
5:26 up for her to make her *h*,
Col 1:22 death to present you *h* in his sight,
1Th 2:10 and so is God, of how *h*,
3:13 and *h* in the presence of our God
3:13 comes with all his *h* ones.
4: 7 us to be impure, but to live a *h* life.
2Th 1:10 to be glorified in his *h* people
1Ti 2: 8 to lift up *h* hands in prayer,
2Ti 1: 9 saved us and called us to a *h* life—
2:21 for noble purposes, made *h*,
3:15 you have known the *h* Scriptures,
Tit 1: 8 upright, *h* and disciplined.
Heb 2:11 Both the one who makes men *h*
7:26 one who is *h*, blameless, pure,
10:10 we have been made *h*
10:14 those who are being made *h*.
10:19 to enter the Most *H* Place
12:14 in peace with all men and to be *h*;
13:12 gate to make the people *h*
1Pe 1:15 But just as he who called you is *h*,
1:16 is written: "Be *h*, because I am *h*."
2: 5 house to be a *h* priesthood,
2: 9 a royal priesthood, a *h* nation,
3: 5 For this is the way the *h* women

2Pe 3:11 You ought to live *h* and godly lives
Jude :14 upon thousands of his *h* ones
Rev 3: 7 are the words of him who is *h*
4: 8 *"H, h, h* is the Lord God
15: 4 For you alone are *h*.
20: 6 and *h* are those who have part
22:11 let him who is *h* continue to be *h*."

HOME (HOMES)
Dt 6: 7 Talk about them when you sit at *h*
11:19 about them when you sit at *h*
20: 5 Let him go *h*, or he may die
24: 5 is to be free to stay at *h*
Ru 1:11 "Return *h*, my daughters.
2Sa 7:10 them so that they can have a *h*
1Ch 16:43 and David returned *h* to bless his
Ps 84: 3 Even the sparrow has found a *h*,
113: 9 settles the barren woman in her *h*
Pr 3:33 but he blesses the *h* of the righteous
27: 8 is a man who strays from his *h*.
Ecc 12: 5 Then man goes to his eternal *h*
Eze 36: 8 for they will soon come *h*.
Mic 2: 2 They defraud a man of his *h*,
Mt 1:24 and took Mary *h* as his wife.
Mk 10:29 "no one who has left *h* or brothers
Lk 10:38 named Martha opened her *h*
Jn 14:23 to him and make our *h* with him.
19:27 this disciple took her into his *h*.
Ac 16:15 baptized, she invited us to her *h*.
Tit 2: 5 to be busy at *h*, to be kind,

HOMELESS*
1Co 4:11 we are brutally treated, we are *h*.

HOMES (HOME)
Ne 4:14 daughters, your wives and your *h*."
Isa 32:18 in secure *h*,
Mk 10:30 as much in this present age (*h*,
1Ti 5:14 to manage their *h* and to give

HOMETOWN
Mt 13:57 "Only in his *h*
Lk 4:24 "no prophet is accepted in his *h*.

HOMOSEXUAL*
1Co 6: 9 male prostitutes nor *h* offenders

HONEST (HONESTY)
Lev 19:36 Use *h* scales and *h* weights,
Dt 25:15 and *h* weights and measures,
Job 31: 6 let God weigh me in *h* scales
Pr 12:17 truthful witness gives *h* testimony,

HONESTY (HONEST)
2Ki 12:15 they acted with complete *h*.

HONEY (HONEYCOMB)
Ex 3: 8 a land flowing with milk and *h*—
Jdg 14: 8 a swarm of bees and some *h*,
1Sa 14:26 they saw the *h* oozing out,
Ps 19:10 than *h* from the comb.
119:103 sweeter than *h* to my mouth!
Pr 25:16 If you find *h*, eat just enough—
SS 4:11 milk and *h* are under your tongue.
Isa 7:15 and *h* when he knows enough
Eze 3: 3 it tasted as sweet as *h* in my mouth.
Mt 3: 4 His food was locusts and wild *h*.
Rev 10: 9 mouth it will be as sweet as *h*."

HONEYCOMB (HONEY)
SS 4:11 Your lips drop sweetness as the *h*,
5: 1 I have eaten my *h* and my honey;

HONOR (HONORABLE HONORABLY HONORED HONORS)
Ex 20:12 *"H* your father and your mother,
Nu 20:12 trust in me enough to *h* me
25:13 he was zealous for the *h* of his God
Dt 5:16 *"H* your father and your mother,
Jdg 4: 9 going about this, the *h* will not be
1Sa 2: 8 and has them inherit a throne of *h*.
2:30 Those who *h* me I will *h*,
1Ch 29:12 Wealth and *h* come from you;
2Ch 1:11 or *h*, nor for the death
18: 1 had great wealth and *h*,
Est 6: 6 for the man the king delights to *h*
Ps 8: 5 and crowned him with glory and *h*.
45:11 *h* him, for he is your lord.
84:11 the LORD bestows favor and *h*;
Pr 3: 9 *H* the LORD with your wealth,
3:35 The wise inherit *h*,
15:33 and humility comes before *h*.
18:12 but humility comes before *h*.
20: 3 It is to a man's *h* to avoid strife,
25:27 is it honorable to seek one's own *h*.
Isa 29:13 and *h* me with their lips,
Jer 33: 9 and *h* before all nations
Mt 13:57 own house is a prophet without *h*."
15: 4 *'H* your father and mother'
15: 8 These people *h* me with their lips,
19:19 *h* your father and mother,'
23: 6 they love the place of *h* at banquets
Mk 6: 4 own house is a prophet without *h*."
Lk 14: 8 do not take the place of *h*,
Jn 5:23 that all may *h* the Son just
7:18 does so to gain *h* for himself,
12:26 My Father will *h* the one who
Ro 12:10 *H* one another above yourselves.
1Co 6:20 Therefore *h* God with your body.
Eph 6: 2 *"H* your father and mother"—
1Ti 5:17 well are worthy of double *h*,
Heb 2: 7 you crowned him with glory and *h*
Rev 4: 9 *h* and thanks to him who sits

HONORABLE (HONOR)
1Th 4: 4 body in a way that is holy and *h*,

HONORABLY (HONOR)
Heb 13:18 and desire to live *h* in every way.

HONORED (HONOR)
Ps 12: 8 when what is vile is *h* among men.
Pr 13:18 but whoever heeds correction is *h*.
Da 4:34 I *h* and glorified him who lives
1Co 12:26 if one part is *h*, every part rejoices
Heb 13: 4 Marriage should be *h* by all,

HONORS (HONOR)
Ps 15: 4 but *h* those who fear the LORD,
Pr 14:31 to the needy *h* God.

HOOF
Ex 10:26 not a *h* is to be left behind.

HOOKS
Isa 2: 4 and their spears into pruning *h*.
Joel 3:10 and your pruning *h* into spears.
Mic 4: 3 and their spears into pruning *h*.

HOPE (HOPES)
Job 13:15 Though he slay me, yet will I *h*
Ps 25: 3 No one whose *h* is in you
33:17 A horse is a vain *h* for deliverance;
33:18 on those whose *h* is
42: 5 Put your *h* in God,
62: 5 my *h* comes from him.
119:74 for I have put my *h* in your word.
130: 5 and in his word I put my *h*.
130: 7 O Israel, put your *h* in the LORD,
146: 5 whose *h* is in the LORD his God,
147:11 who put their *h* in his unfailing love
Pr 13:12 *H* deferred makes the heart sick,
23:18 There is surely a future *h* for you,
Isa 40:31 but those who *h* in the LORD
Jer 29:11 plans to give you *h* and a future.
La 3:21 and therefore I have *h*:
Zec 9:12 to your fortress, O prisoners of *h*;
Ro 5: 4 character; and character, *h*.
8:20 in *h* that the creation itself will be
8:24 But *h* that is seen is no *h* at all.
8:25 if we *h* for what we do not yet have,
12:12 Be joyful in *h*, patient in affliction,
15: 4 of the Scriptures we might have *h*.
15:13 May the God of *h* fill you
1Co 13:13 now these three remain: faith, *h*
15:19 for this life we have *h* in Christ,
Eph 2:12 without *h* and without God
Col 1:27 Christ in you, the *h* of glory.
1Th 1: 3 and your endurance inspired by *h*
5: 8 and the *h* of salvation as a helmet.
1Ti 4:10 that we have put our *h*
6:17 but to put their *h* in God,
Tit 1: 2 resting on the *h* of eternal life,
2:13 while we wait for the blessed *h*—
Heb 6:19 We have this *h* as an anchor
10:23 unswervingly to the *h* we profess,
11: 1 faith is being sure of what we *h* for
1Jn 3: 3 Everyone who has this *h*

HOPES (HOPE)
1Co 13: 7 always *h*, always perseveres.

HORN (HORNS)
Ex 19:13 when the ram's *h* sounds a long
27: 2 Make a *h* at each of the four
Da 7: 8 This *h* had eyes like the eyes

HORNS (HORN)
Da 7:24 ten *h* are ten kings who will come
Rev 5: 6 He had seven *h* and seven eyes,
12: 3 and ten *h* and seven crowns
13: 1 He had ten *h* and seven heads,
17: 3 and had seven heads and ten *h*.

HORRIBLE (HORROR)
Jer 5:30 "A *h* and shocking thing

HORROR (HORRIBLE)
Jer 2:12 and shudder with great *h*,"

HORSE
Ps 147:10 not in the strength of the *h*,
Pr 26: 3 A whip for the *h*, a halter
Zec 1: 8 before me was a man riding a red *h*
Rev 6: 2 and there before me was a white *h!*
6: 4 Come!" Then another *h* came out,
6: 5 and there before me was a black *h!*
6: 8 and there before me was a pale *h!*
19:11 and there before me was a white *h*,

HOSANNA
Mt 21: 9 *"H* in the highest!"
Mk 11: 9 *"H!"*
Jn 12:13 *"H!"*

HOSEA
Prophet whose wife and family pictured the unfaithfulness of Israel (Hos 1–3).

HOSHEA (JOSHUA)
1. Original name of Joshua (Nu 13:16).
2. Last king of Israel (2Ki 15:30; 17:1–6).

HOSPITABLE* (HOSPITALITY)
1Ti 3: 2 self-controlled, respectable, *h*,
Tit 1: 8 Rather he must be *h*, one who loves

HOSPITABLY* (HOSPITALITY)
Ac 28: 7 and for three days entertained us *h*.

HOSPITALITY* (HOSPITABLE HOSPITABLY)
Ro 12:13 Practice *h*.
16:23 whose *h* I and the whole church
1Ti 5:10 as bringing up children, showing *h*,
1Pe 4: 9 Offer *h* to one another
3Jn : 8 therefore to show *h* to such men

HOSTILE (HOSTILITY)
Ro 8: 7 the sinful mind is *h* to God.

HOSTILITY (HOSTILE)
Eph 2:14 wall of *h*, by abolishing
2:16 by which he put to death their *h*.

HOT
1Ti 4: 2 have been seared as with a *h* iron.
Rev 3:15 that you are neither cold nor *h.*

HOT-TEMPERED (TEMPER)
Pr 15:18 A *h* man stirs up dissension,
19:19 A *h* man must pay the penalty;
22:24 Do not make friends with a *h* man,
29:22 and a *h* one commits many sins.

HOTHEADED (HEAD)
Pr 14:16 but a fool is *h* and reckless.

HOUR
Ecc 9:12 knows when his *h* will come:
Mt 6:27 you by worrying can add a single *h*
Lk 12:40 the Son of Man will come at an *h*
Jn 12:23 The *h* has come for the Son of Man
12:27 for this very reason I came to this *h*

HOUSE (HOUSEHOLD HOUSEHOLDS HOUSES STOREHOUSE)
Ex 12:22 the door of his *h* until morning.
20:17 shall not covet your neighbor's *h.*
Nu 12: 7 he is faithful in all my *h.*
Dt 5:21 desire on your neighbor's *h*
2Sa 7:11 LORD himself will establish a *h*
1Ch 17:23 and his *h* be established forever.
Ne 10:39 "We will not neglect the *h*
Ps 23: 6 I will dwell in the *h* of the LORD
27: 4 dwell in the *h* of the LORD
69: 9 for zeal for your *h* consumes me,
84:10 a doorkeeper in the *h* of my God
122: 1 "Let us go to the *h* of the LORD."
127: 1 Unless the LORD builds the *h,*
Pr 7:27 Her *h* is a highway to the grave,
21: 9 than share a *h* with a quarrelsome
Isa 56: 7 a *h* of prayer for all nations."
Jer 7:11 Has this *h,* which bears my Name,
18: 2 "Go down to the potter's *h,*
Eze 33: 7 made you a watchman for the *h*
Joel 3:18 will flow out of the LORD's *h*
Zec 13: 6 given at the *h* of my friends.'
Mt 7:24 is like a wise man who built his *h*
10:11 and stay at his *h* until you leave.
12:29 can anyone enter a strong man's *h*
21:13 My *h* will be called a *h* of prayer,'
Mk 3:25 If a *h* is divided against itself,
11:17 " 'My *h* will be called
Lk 6:48 He is like a man building a *h,*
10: 7 Do not move around from *h* to *h.*
11:17 a *h* divided against itself will fall.
11:24 'I will return to the *h* I left.'
15: 8 sweep the *h* and search carefully
19: 9 Today salvation has come to this *h,*
Jn 2:16 How dare you turn my Father's *h*
2:17 "Zeal for your *h* will consume me."
12: 3 the *h* was filled with the fragrance
14: 2 In my Father's *h* are many rooms;
Ac 20:20 you publicly and from *h* to *h.*
Ro 16: 5 the church that meets at their *h.*
Heb 3: 3 the builder of a *h* has greater honor
1Pe 2: 5 built into a spiritual *h* to be a holy

HOUSEHOLD (HOUSE)
Ex 12: 3 lamb for his family, one for each *h.*
Jos 24:15 my *h,* we will serve the LORD."
Pr 31:21 it snows, she has no fear for her *h;*
31:27 over the affairs of her *h*
Mic 7: 6 are the members of his own *h.*
Mt 10:36 will be the members of his own *h.*'
12:25 or *h* divided against itself will not
Ac 16:31 you will be saved—you and your *h*
Eph 2:19 people and members of God's *h,*
1Ti 3:12 manage his children and his *h* well.
3:15 to conduct themselves in God's *h,*

HOUSEHOLDS (HOUSE)
Tit 1:11 because they are ruining whole *h*

HOUSES (HOUSE)
Ex 12:27 passed over the *h* of the Israelites
Mt 19:29 everyone who has left *h* or brothers

HOVERING* (HOVERS)
Ge 1: 2 of God was *h* over the waters.
Isa 31: 5 Like birds *h* overhead,

HOVERS* (HOVERING)
Dt 32:11 and *h* over its young,

HULDAH*
Prophetess inquired by Hilkiah for Josiah (2Ki 22; 2Ch 34:14–28).

HUMAN (HUMANITY)
Lev 24:17 If anyone takes the life of a *h* being,
Isa 52:14 his form marred beyond *h* likeness
Jn 8:15 You judge by *h* standards;
Ro 1: 3 as to his *h* nature was a descendant
9: 5 from them is traced the *h* ancestry
1Co 1:17 not with words of *h* wisdom,
1:26 of you were wise by *h* standards;
2:13 not in words taught us by *h* wisdom
2Co 3: 3 of stone but on tablets of *h* hearts.
Gal 3: 3 to attain your goal by *h* effort?
2Pe 2:18 lustful desires of sinful *h* nature,

HUMANITY* (HUMAN)
Heb 2:14 he too shared in their *h* so that

HUMBLE (HUMBLED HUMBLES HUMILIATE HUMILIATED HUMILITY)
Nu 12: 3 (Now Moses was a very *h* man,
2Ch 7:14 will *h* themselves and pray
Ps 18:27 You save the *h*
25: 9 He guides the *h* in what is right
149: 4 he crowns the *h* with salvation.
Pr 3:34 but gives grace to the *h.*
Isa 66: 2 he who is *h* and contrite in spirit,
Mt 11:29 for I am gentle and *h* in heart,
Eph 4: 2 Be completely *h* and gentle;
Jas 4: 6 but gives grace to the *h.*"
4:10 *H* yourselves before the Lord,
1Pe 5: 5 but gives grace to the *h.*"
5: 6 *H* yourselves,

HUMBLED (HUMBLE)
Mt 23:12 whoever exalts himself will be *h,*
Lk 14:11 who exalts himself will be *h,*
Php 2: 8 he *h* himself

HUMBLES* (HUMBLE)
1Sa 2: 7 he *h* and he exalts.
Isa 26: 5 He *h* those who dwell on high,
Mt 18: 4 whoever *h* himself like this child is
23:12 whoever *h* himself will be exalted.
Lk 14:11 he who *h* himself will be exalted."
18:14 he who *h* himself will be exalted."

HUMILIATE* (HUMBLE)
Pr 25: 7 than for him to *h* you
1Co 11:22 and *h* those who have nothing?

HUMILIATED (HUMBLE)
Jer 31:19 I was ashamed and *h*
Lk 14: 9 *h,* you will have to take the least

HUMILITY* (HUMBLE)
Ps 45: 4 of truth, *h* and righteousness;
Pr 11: 2 but with *h* comes wisdom.
15:33 and *h* comes before honor.
18:12 but *h* comes before honor.
22: 4 *H* and the fear of the LORD
Zep 2: 3 Seek righteousness, seek *h;*
Ac 20:19 I served the Lord with great *h*
Php 2: 3 but in *h* consider others better
Col 2:18 let anyone who delights in false *h*
2:23 their false *h* and their harsh
3:12 *h,* gentleness and patience.
Tit 3: 2 and to show true *h* toward all men.
Jas 3:13 in the *h* that comes from wisdom.

1Pe 5: 5 clothe yourselves with *h*

HUNG (HANG)
Dt 21:23 anyone who is *h* on a tree is
Mt 18: 6 him to have a large millstone *h*
Lk 19:48 all the people *h* on his words.
Gal 3:13 "Cursed is everyone who is *h*

HUNGER (HUNGRY)
Ne 9:15 In their *h* you gave them bread
Pr 6:30 to satisfy his *h* when he is starving.
Mt 5: 6 Blessed are those who *h*
Lk 6:21 Blessed are you who *h* now,
2Co 6: 5 sleepless nights and *h;* in purity,
11:27 I have known *h* and thirst
Rev 7:16 Never again will they *h;*

HUNGRY (HUNGER)
Job 24:10 carry the sheaves, but still go *h.*
Ps 107: 9 and fills the *h* with good things.
146: 7 and gives food to the *h.*
Pr 19:15 and the shiftless man goes *h.*
25:21 If your enemy is *h,* give him food
27: 7 to the *h* even what is bitter tastes
Isa 58: 7 not to share your food with the *h*
58:10 spend yourselves in behalf of the *h*
Eze 18: 7 but gives his food to the *h*
18:16 but gives his food to the *h*
Mt 15:32 I do not want to send them away *h,*
25:35 For I was *h* and you gave me
25:42 For I was *h* and you gave me
Lk 1:53 He has filled the *h* with good things
Jn 6:35 comes to me will never go *h,*
Ro 12:20 "If your enemy is *h,* feed him;
1Co 4:11 To this very hour we go *h*
Php 4:12 whether well fed or *h,*

HUR
Ex 17:12 Aaron and *H* held his hands up—

HURL
Mic 7:19 *h* all our iniquities into the depths

HURT (HURTS)
Ecc 8: 9 it over others to his own *h.*
Mk 16:18 deadly poison, it will not *h* them
Rev 2:11 He who overcomes will not be *h*

HURTS* (HURT)
Ps 15: 4 even when it *h,*
Pr 26:28 A lying tongue hates those it *h,*

HUSBAND (HUSBAND'S HUSBANDS)
Pr 31:11 Her *h* has full confidence in her
31:23 Her *h* is respected at the city gate,
31:28 her *h* also, and he praises her:
Isa 54: 5 For your Maker is your *h*—
Jer 3:14 the LORD, "for I am your *h.*
3:20 like a woman unfaithful to her *h,*
Jn 4:17 "I have no *h,*" she replied.
Ro 7: 2 a married woman is bound to her *h*
1Co 7: 2 and each woman her own *h.*
7: 3 The *h* should fulfill his marital duty
7:10 wife must not separate from her *h.*
7:11 And a *h* must not divorce his wife.
7:13 And if a woman has a *h* who is not
7:14 For the unbelieving *h* has been
7:39 A woman is bound to her *h* as long
7:39 But if her *h* dies, she is free
2Co 11: 2 I promised you to one *h,* to Christ,
Gal 4:27 woman than of her who has a *h.*"
Eph 5:23 For the *h* is the head of the wife
5:33 and the wife must respect her *h.*
1Ti 3: 2 the *h* of but one wife, temperate,
3:12 A deacon must be the *h* of
5: 9 has been faithful to her *h,*
Tit 1: 6 An elder must be blameless, the *h*

HUSBANDMAN see **GARDENER**

HUSBAND'S (HUSBAND)
Dt 25: 5 Her *h* brother shall take her

Pr 12: 4 of noble character is her *h* crown,
1Co 7: 4 the *h* body does not belong

HUSBANDS (HUSBAND)
Eph 5:22 submit to your *h* as to the Lord.
5:25 *H,* love your wives, just
5:28 *h* ought to love their wives
Col 3:18 submit to your *h,* as is fitting
3:19 *H,* love your wives and do not be
Tit 2: 4 the younger women to love their *h*
2: 5 and to be subject to their *h,*
1Pe 3: 1 same way be submissive to your *h*
3: 7 *H,* in the same way be considerate

HUSHAI
Wise man of David who frustrated Ahithophel's advice and foiled Absalom's revolt (2Sa 15:32–37; 16:15–17:16; 1Ch 27:33).

HYMN* (HYMNS)
Ps 40: 3 a *h* of praise to our God.
Mt 26:30 they had sung a *h,* they went out
Mk 14:26 they had sung a *h,* they went out
1Co 14:26 everyone has a *h,* or a word

HYMNS* (HYMN)
Ac 16:25 Silas were praying and singing *h*
Ro 15: 9 I will sing *h* to your name."
Eph 5:19 to one another with psalms, *h*
Col 3:16 *h* and spiritual songs with gratitude

HYPOCRISY* (HYPOCRITE HYPOCRITES HYPOCRITICAL)
Mt 23:28 but on the inside you are full of *h*
Mk 12:15 we?" But Jesus knew their *h.*
Lk 12: 1 yeast of the Pharisees, which is *h.*
Gal 2:13 The other Jews joined him in his *h,*
2:13 by their *h* even Barnabas was led
1Pe 2: 1 *h,* envy, and slander of every kind.

HYPOCRITE* (HYPOCRISY)
Mt 7: 5 You *h,* first take the plank out
Lk 6:42 You *h,* first take the plank out

HYPOCRITES* (HYPOCRISY)
Ps 26: 4 nor do I consort with *h;*
Mt 6: 2 as the *h* do in the synagogues
6: 5 when you pray, do not be like the *h*
6:16 do not look somber as the *h* do,
15: 7 You *h!* Isaiah was right
22:18 their evil intent, said, "You *h,*
23:13 of the law and Pharisees, you *h!*
23:15 of the law and Pharisees, you *h!*
23:23 of the law and Pharisees, you *h!*
23:25 of the law and Pharisees, you *h!*
23:27 you *h!* You are like whitewashed
23:29 of the law and Pharisees, you *h!*
24:51 and assign him a place with the *h,*
Mk 7: 6 when he prophesied about you *h;*
Lk 12:56 *H!* You know how
13:15 The Lord answered him, "You *h!*

HYPOCRITICAL* (HYPOCRISY)
1Ti 4: 2 teachings come through *h* liars,

HYSSOP
Ex 12:22 Take a bunch of *h,* dip it
Ps 51: 7 with *h,* and I will be clean;
Jn 19:29 the sponge on a stalk of the *h* plant,

ICHABOD
1Sa 4:21 She named the boy *I,* saying,

IDLE* (IDLENESS IDLERS)
Dt 32:47 They are not just *i* words for you—
Job 11: 3 Will your *i* talk reduce men
Ecc 10:18 if his hands are *i,* the house leaks.
11: 6 at evening let not your hands be *i,*
Isa 58:13 as you please or speaking *i* words,
Col 2:18 mind puffs him up with *i* notions.
1Th 5:14 those who are *i,* encourage
2Th 3: 6 away from every brother who is *i*
3: 7 We were not *i* when we were
3:11 We hear that some among you are *i*
1Ti 5:13 they get into the habit of being *i*

IDLENESS* (IDLE)
Pr 31:27 and does not eat the bread of *i.*

IDLERS* (IDLE)
1Ti 5:13 And not only do they become *i,*

IDOL (IDOLATER IDOLATERS IDOLATRY IDOLS)
Ex 20: 4 make for yourself an *i* in the form
32: 4 made it into an *i* cast in the shape
Isa 40:19 As for an *i,* a craftsman casts it,
41: 7 He nails down the *i*
44:15 he makes an *i* and bows down to it.
44:17 From the rest he makes a god, his *i;*
Hab 2:18 "Of what value is an *i,*
1Co 8: 4 We know that an *i* is nothing at all

IDOLATER* (IDOL)
1Co 5:11 an *i* or a slanderer, a drunkard
Eph 5: 5 greedy person—such a man is an *i*

IDOLATERS (IDOL)
1Co 5:10 or the greedy and swindlers, or *i.*
6: 9 Neither the sexually immoral nor *i*

IDOLATRY (IDOL)
1Sa 15:23 and arrogance like the evil of *i.*
1Co 10:14 my dear friends, flee from *i.*
Gal 5:20 and debauchery; *i* and witchcraft;
Col 3: 5 evil desires and greed, which is *i.*
1Pe 4: 3 orgies, carousing and detestable *i.*

IDOLS (IDOL)
Dt 32:16 angered him with their detestable *i.*
Ps 78:58 aroused his jealousy with their *i.*
Isa 44: 9 All who make *i* are nothing,
Eze 23:39 sacrificed their children to their *i,*
Ac 15:20 to abstain from food polluted by *i,*
21:25 abstain from food sacrificed to *i,*
1Co 8: 1 Now about food sacrificed to *i:*
1Jn 5:21 children, keep yourselves from *i.*
Rev 2:14 to sin by eating food sacrificed to *i*

IGNORANT (IGNORE)
1Co 15:34 for there are some who are *i* of God
Heb 5: 2 to deal gently with those who are *i*
1Pe 2:15 good you should silence the *i* talk
2Pe 3:16 which *i* and unstable people distort

IGNORE (IGNORANT IGNORED IGNORES)
Dt 22: 1 do not *i* it but be sure
Ps 9:12 he does not *i* the cry of the afflicted
Heb 2: 3 if we *i* such a great salvation?

IGNORED (IGNORE)
Hos 4: 6 you have *i* the law of your God,
1Co 14:38 he ignores this, he himself will be *i.*

IGNORES* (IGNORE)
Pr 10:17 whoever *i* correction leads others
13:18 He who *i* discipline comes
15:32 He who *i* discipline despises
1Co 14:38 If he *i* this, he himself will be

ILL (ILLNESS)
Mt 4:24 brought to him all who were *i*

ILL-GOTTEN
Pr 1:19 the end of all who go after *i* gain;
10: 2 *I* treasures are of no value,

ILL-TEMPERED* (TEMPER)
Pr 21:19 than with a quarrelsome and *i* wife.

ILLEGITIMATE
Heb 12: 8 then you are *i* children

ILLNESS (ILL)
2Ki 8: 9 'Will I recover from this *i?*' "
2Ch 16:12 even in his *i* he did not seek help
Ps 41: 3 and restore him from his bed of *i.*
Isa 38: 9 king of Judah after his *i*

ILLUMINATED*
Rev 18: 1 and the earth was *i* by his splendor.

IMAGE (IMAGES)
Ge 1:26 "Let us make man in our *i,*
1:27 So God created man in his own *i,*
9: 6 for in the *i* of God
Dt 27:15 "Cursed is the man who carves an *i*
Isa 40:18 What *i* will you compare him to?
Da 3: 1 King Nebuchadnezzar made an *i*
1Co 11: 7 since he is the *i* and glory of God;
2Co 4: 4 glory of Christ, who is the *i* of God.
Col 1:15 He is the *i* of the invisible God,
3:10 in knowledge in the *i* of its Creator.
Rev 13:14 them to set up an *i* in honor

IMAGES (IMAGE)
Ps 97: 7 All who worship *i* are put to shame,
Jer 10:14 His *i* are a fraud;
Ro 1:23 of the immortal God for *i* made

IMAGINATION (IMAGINE)
Eze 13: 2 who prophesy out of their own *i:*

IMAGINE (IMAGINATION)
Eph 3:20 more than all we ask or *i,*

IMITATE (IMITATORS)
1Co 4:16 Therefore I urge you to *i* me.
Heb 6:12 but to *i* those who through faith
13: 7 of their way of life and *i* their faith.
3Jn :11 do not *i* what is evil but what is

IMITATORS* (IMITATE)
Eph 5: 1 Be *i* of God, therefore,
1Th 1: 6 You became *i* of us and of the Lord
2:14 became *i* of God's churches

IMMANUEL*
Isa 7:14 birth to a son, and will call him *I.*
8: 8 O *I!*"
Mt 1:23 and they will call him *I*"—

IMMORAL* (IMMORALITY)
Pr 6:24 keeping you from the *i* woman,
1Co 5: 9 to associate with sexually *i* people
5:10 the people of this world who are *i,*
5:11 but is sexually *i* or greedy,
6: 9 Neither the sexually *i* nor idolaters
Eph 5: 5 No *i,* impure or greedy person—
Heb 12:16 See that no one is sexually *i,*
13: 4 the adulterer and all the sexually *i.*
Rev 21: 8 the murderers, the sexually *i,*
22:15 the sexually *i,* the murderers,

IMMORALITY* (IMMORAL)
Nu 25: 1 in sexual *i* with Moabite women,
Jer 3: 9 Because Israel's *i* mattered so little
Mt 15:19 murder, adultery, sexual *i,* theft,
Mk 7:21 sexual *i,* theft, murder, adultery,
Ac 15:20 from sexual *i,* from the meat
15:29 animals and from sexual *i.*
21:25 animals and from sexual *i.*"
Ro 13:13 not in sexual *i* and debauchery,
1Co 5: 1 reported that there is sexual *i*
6:13 The body is not meant for sexual *i,*
6:18 Flee from sexual *i.*
7: 2 But since there is so much *i,*
10: 8 We should not commit sexual *i,*
Gal 5:19 sexual *i,* impurity and debauchery;
Eph 5: 3 must not be even a hint of sexual *i,*
Col 3: 5 sexual *i,* impurity, lust, evil desires
1Th 4: 3 that you should avoid sexual *i;*
Jude : 4 grace of our God into a license for *i*
: 7 gave themselves up to sexual *i*
Rev 2:14 and by committing sexual *i.*

Rev 2:20 misleads my servants into sexual *i*
2:21 given her time to repent of her *i,*
9:21 their sexual *i* or their thefts.

IMMORTAL* (IMMORTALITY)
Ro 1:23 glory of the *i* God for images made
1Ti 1:17 Now to the King eternal, *i,*
6:16 who alone is *i* and who lives

IMMORTALITY* (IMMORTAL)
Pr 12:28 along that path is *i.*
Ro 2: 7 honor and *i,* he will give eternal life
1Co 15:53 and the mortal with *i.*
15:54 with *i,* then the saying that is
2Ti 1:10 and *i* to light through the gospel.

IMPARTIAL*
Jas 3:17 and good fruit, *i* and sincere.

IMPARTS*
Pr 29:15 The rod of correction *i* wisdom,

IMPERFECT*
1Co 13:10 perfection comes, the *i* disappears.

IMPERISHABLE
1Co 15:42 it is raised *i;* it is sown in dishonor,
15:50 nor does the perishable inherit the *i*
1Pe 1:23 not of perishable seed, but of *i,*

IMPLANTED*
Ps 94: 9 Does he who *i* the ear not hear?

IMPLORE*
Mal 1: 9 "Now *i* God to be gracious to us.
2Co 5:20 We *i* you on Christ's behalf:

IMPORTANCE* (IMPORTANT)
1Co 15: 3 passed on to you as of first *i:*

IMPORTANT (IMPORTANCE)
Mt 6:25 Is not life more *i* than food,
23:23 have neglected the more *i* matters
Mk 12:29 "The most *i* one," answered Jesus,
12:33 as yourself is more *i* than all burnt
Php 1:18 The *i* thing is that in every way,

IMPOSSIBLE
Mt 17:20 Nothing will be *i* for you."
19:26 "With man this is *i,*
Mk 10:27 "With man this is *i,* but not
Lk 1:37 For nothing is *i* with God."
18:27 "What is *i* with men is possible
Ac 2:24 it was *i* for death to keep its hold
Heb 6: 4 It is *i* for those who have once been
6:18 things in which it is *i* for God to lie,
10: 4 because it is *i* for the blood of bulls
11: 6 without faith it is *i* to please God,

IMPOSTORS
2Ti 3:13 and *i* will go from bad to worse,

IMPRESS* (IMPRESSES)
Dt 6: 7 *I* them on your children.

IMPRESSES* (IMPRESS)
Pr 17:10 A rebuke *i* a man of discernment

IMPROPER*
Eph 5: 3 these are *i* for God's holy people.

IMPURE (IMPURITY)
Ac 10:15 not call anything *i* that God has
Eph 5: 5 No immoral, *i* or greedy person—
1Th 2: 3 spring from error or *i* motives,
4: 7 For God did not call us to be *i,*
Rev 21:27 Nothing *i* will ever enter it,

IMPURITY (IMPURE)
Ro 1:24 hearts to sexual *i* for the degrading
Gal 5:19 sexual immorality, *i*
Eph 4:19 as to indulge in every kind of *i,*
5: 3 or of any kind of *i,* or of greed,

Col 3: 5 *i,* lust, evil desires and greed,

INCENSE
Ex 30: 1 altar of acacia wood for burning *i.*
40: 5 Place the gold altar of *i* in front
Ps 141: 2 my prayer be set before you like *i;*
Mt 2:11 him with gifts of gold and of *i*
Heb 9: 4 which had the golden altar of *i*
Rev 5: 8 were holding golden bowls full of *i,*
8: 4 The smoke of the *i,* together

INCLINATION (INCLINES)
Ge 6: 5 and that every *i* of the thoughts

INCLINES* (INCLINATION)
Ecc 10: 2 The heart of the wise *i* to the right,

INCOME
Ecc 5:10 wealth is never satisfied with his *i.*
1Co 16: 2 sum of money in keeping with his *i,*

INCOMPARABLE*
Eph 2: 7 ages he might show the *i* riches

INCREASE (EVER-INCREASING INCREASED INCREASES INCREASING)
Ge 1:22 "Be fruitful and *i* in number
3:16 "I will greatly *i* your pains
8:17 be fruitful and *i* in number upon it
Ps 62:10 though your riches *i,*
Pr 22:16 oppresses the poor to *i* his wealth
Isa 9: 7 Of the *i* of his government
Mt 24:12 Because of the *i* of wickedness,
Lk 17: 5 said to the Lord, "*I* our faith!"
Ac 12:24 But the word of God continued to *i*
Ro 5:20 added so that the trespass might *i.*
1Th 3:12 May the Lord make your love *i*

INCREASED (INCREASE)
Ac 6: 7 of disciples in Jerusalem *i* rapidly,
Ro 5:20 But where sin *i,* grace *i* all the more

INCREASES (INCREASE)
Pr 24: 5 and a man of knowledge *i* strength;

INCREASING (INCREASE)
Ac 6: 1 when the number of disciples was *i,*
2Th 1: 3 one of you has for each other is *i.*
2Pe 1: 8 these qualities in *i* measure,

INCREDIBLE*
Ac 26: 8 of you consider it *i* that God raises

INDECENT
Ro 1:27 Men committed *i* acts

INDEPENDENT*
1Co 11:11 however, woman is not *i* of man,
11:11 of man, nor is man *i* of woman.

INDESCRIBABLE*
2Co 9:15 Thanks be to God for his *i* gift!

INDESTRUCTIBLE*
Heb 7:16 on the basis of the power of an *i* life

INDIGNANT
Mk 10:14 When Jesus saw this, he was *i.*

INDISPENSABLE*
1Co 12:22 seem to be weaker are *i,*

INEFFECTIVE*
2Pe 1: 8 they will keep you from being *i*

INEXPRESSIBLE*
2Co 12: 4 He heard *i* things, things that man
1Pe 1: 8 are filled with an *i* and glorious joy,

INFANCY* (INFANTS)
2Ti 3:15 from *i* you have known the holy

INFANTS (INFANCY)
Ps 8: 2 From the lips of children and *i*

Mt 21:16 " 'From the lips of children and *i*
1Co 3: 1 but as worldly—mere *i* in Christ.
14:20 In regard to evil be *i,*
Eph 4:14 Then we will no longer be *i,*

INFIRMITIES*
Isa 53: 4 Surely he took up our *i*
Mt 8:17 "He took up our *i*

INFLAMED
Ro 1:27 were *i* with lust for one another.

INFLUENTIAL*
1Co 1:26 not many were *i;* not many were

INHABITANTS (INHABITED)
Nu 33:55 " 'But if you do not drive out the *i*
Rev 8:13 Woe! Woe to the *i* of the earth,

INHABITED (INHABITANTS)
Isa 45:18 but formed it to be *i*—

INHERIT (CO-HEIRS HEIR HEIRS HERITAGE INHERITANCE)
Dt 1:38 because he will lead Israel to *i* it.
Jos 1: 6 people to *i* the land I swore
Ps 37:11 But the meek will *i* the land
37:29 the righteous will *i* the land
Zec 2:12 The LORD will *i* Judah
Mt 5: 5 for they will *i* the earth.
19:29 as much and will *i* eternal life.
Mk 10:17 "what must I do to *i* eternal life?"
Lk 10:25 "what must I do to *i* eternal life?"
18:18 what must I do to *i* eternal life?"
1Co 6: 9 the wicked will not *i* the kingdom
15:50 blood cannot *i* the kingdom of God
Rev 21: 7 He who overcomes will *i* all this,

INHERITANCE (INHERIT)
Lev 20:24 I will give it to you as an *i,*
Dt 4:20 to be the people of his *i,*
10: 9 the LORD is their *i,* as the LORD
Jos 14: 3 two-and-a-half tribes their *i* east
Ps 16: 6 surely I have a delightful *i.*
33:12 the people he chose for his *i.*
136:21 and gave their land as an *i,*
Pr 13:22 A good man leaves an *i*
Mt 25:34 blessed by my Father; take your *i,*
Eph 1:14 who is a deposit guaranteeing our *i*
5: 5 has any *i* in the kingdom of Christ
Col 1:12 you to share in the *i* of the saints
3:24 you know that you will receive an *i*
Heb 9:15 receive the promised eternal *i*—
1Pe 1: 4 and into an *i* that can never perish,

INIQUITIES (INIQUITY)
Ps 78:38 he forgave their *i*
103:10 or repay us according to our *i.*
Isa 53: 5 he was crushed for our *i;*
53:11 and he will bear their *i.*
59: 2 But your *i* have separated
Mic 7:19 and hurl all our *i* into the depths

INIQUITY (INIQUITIES)
Ps 25:11 forgive my *i,* though it is great.
32: 5 and did not cover up my *i.*
51: 2 Wash away all my *i*
51: 9 and blot out all my *i.*
Isa 53: 6 the *i* of us all.

INJURED
Eze 34:16 will bind up the *i* and strengthen
Zec 11:16 or heal the *i,* or feed the healthy,

INJUSTICE
2Ch 19: 7 the LORD our God there is no *i*

INK
2Co 3: 3 not with *i* but with the Spirit

INN*
Lk 2: 7 there was no room for them in the *i*

Lk 10:34 took him to an *i* and took care

INNOCENT
Ex 23: 7 do not put an *i* or honest person
Dt 25: 1 acquitting the *i* and condemning
Pr 6:17 hands that shed *i* blood,
17:26 It is not good to punish an *i* man,
Mt 10:16 shrewd as snakes and as *i* as doves.
27: 4 "for I have betrayed *i* blood."
27:24 I am *i* of this man's blood," he said.
Ac 20:26 declare to you today that I am *i*
Ro 16:19 what is good, and *i* about what is
1Co 4: 4 but that does not make me *i.*

INQUIRE
Isa 8:19 should not a people *i* of their God?

INSCRIPTION
Mt 22:20 And whose *i?*" "Caesar's,"
2Ti 2:19 with this *i:* "The Lord knows those

INSIGHT
1Ki 4:29 Solomon wisdom and very great *i,*
Ps 119:99 I have more *i* than all my teachers,
Pr 5: 1 listen well to my words of *i,*
21:30 There is no wisdom, no *i,* no plan
Php 1: 9 more in knowledge and depth of *i,*
2Ti 2: 7 for the Lord will give you *i*

INSOLENT
Ro 1:30 God-haters, *i,* arrogant

INSPIRED*
Hos 9: 7 the *i* man a maniac.
1Th 1: 3 and your endurance *i* by hope

INSTALLED
Ps 2: 6 "I have *i* my King

INSTINCT* (INSTINCTS)
2Pe 2:12 are like brute beasts, creatures of *i,*
Jude :10 things they do understand by *i,*

INSTINCTS* (INSTINCT)
Jude :19 who follow mere natural *i*

INSTITUTED
Ro 13: 2 rebelling against what God has *i,*
1Pe 2:13 to every authority *i* among men:

INSTRUCT (INSTRUCTED INSTRUCTION INSTRUCTIONS INSTRUCTOR)
Ps 32: 8 I will *i* you and teach you
105:22 to *i* his princes as he pleased
Pr 9: 9 *I* a wise man and he will be wiser
Ro 15:14 and competent to *i* one another.
1Co 2:16 that he may *i* him?"
14:19 to *i* others than ten thousand words
2Ti 2:25 who oppose him he must gently *i,*

INSTRUCTED (INSTRUCT)
2Ch 26: 5 who *i* him in the fear of God.
Pr 21:11 a wise man is *i,* he gets knowledge.
Isa 50: 4 LORD has given me an *i* tongue,
Mt 13:52 who has been *i* about the kingdom
1Co 14:31 in turn so that everyone may be *i*

INSTRUCTION (INSTRUCT)
Pr 1: 8 Listen, my son, to your father's *i*
4: 1 Listen, my sons, to a father's *i;*
4:13 Hold on to *i,* do not let it go;
8:10 Choose my *i* instead of silver,
8:33 Listen to my *i* and be wise;
13: 1 A wise son heeds his father's *i,*
13:13 He who scorns *i* will pay for it,
16:20 Whoever gives heed to *i* prospers,
16:21 and pleasant words promote *i.*
19:20 Listen to advice and accept *i,*
23:12 Apply your heart to *i*
1Co 14: 6 or prophecy or word of *i?*
14:26 or a word of *i,* a revelation,
Eph 6: 4 up in the training and *i* of the Lord.
1Th 4: 8 he who rejects this *i* does not reject
2Th 3:14 If anyone does not obey our *i*
1Ti 1:18 I give you this *i* in keeping
6: 3 to the sound *i* of our Lord Jesus
2Ti 4: 2 with great patience and careful *i.*

INSTRUCTIONS (INSTRUCT)
1Ti 3:14 I am writing you these *i* so that,

INSTRUCTOR (INSTRUCT)
Gal 6: 6 share all good things with his *i.*

INSTRUMENT* (INSTRUMENTS)
Eze 33:32 beautiful voice and plays an *i* well,
Ac 9:15 This man is my chosen *i*
2Ti 2:21 he will be an *i* for noble purposes,

INSTRUMENTS (INSTRUMENT)
Ro 6:13 as *i* of wickedness, but rather offer

INSULT (INSULTED INSULTS)
Pr 9: 7 corrects a mocker invites *i;*
12:16 but a prudent man overlooks an *i.*
Mt 5:11 Blessed are you when people *i* you,
Lk 6:22 when they exclude you and *i* you
1Pe 3: 9 evil with evil or *i* with *i,*

INSULTED (INSULT)
Heb 10:29 and who has *i* the Spirit of grace?
Jas 2: 6 love him? But you have *i* the poor.
1Pe 4:14 If you are *i* because of the name

INSULTS (INSULT)
Ps 22: 7 they hurl *i,* shaking their heads:
69: 9 the *i* of those who insult you fall
Pr 22:10 quarrels and *i* are ended.
Mk 15:29 passed by hurled *i* at him,
Jn 9:28 Then they hurled *i* at him and said,
Ro 15: 3 "The *i* of those who insult you have
2Co 12:10 in *i,* in hardships, in persecutions,
1Pe 2:23 When they hurled their *i* at him,

INTEGRITY*
Dt 9: 5 or your *i* that you are going
1Ki 9: 4 if you walk before me in *i* of heart
1Ch 29:17 the heart and are pleased with *i.*
Ne 7: 2 because he was a man of *i*
Job 2: 3 And he still maintains his *i,*
2: 9 "Are you still holding on to your *i?*
6:29 reconsider, for my *i* is at stake.
27: 5 till I die, I will not deny my *i.*
Ps 7: 8 according to my *i,* O Most High.
25:21 May *i* and uprightness protect me,
41:12 In my *i* you uphold me
78:72 David shepherded them with *i*
Pr 10: 9 The man of *i* walks securely,
11: 3 The *i* of the upright guides them,
13: 6 Righteousness guards the man of *i,*
17:26 or to flog officials for their *i.*
29:10 Bloodthirsty men hate a man of *i*
Isa 45:23 my mouth has uttered in all *i*
59: 4 no one pleads his case with *i.*
Mt 22:16 "we know you are a man of *i*
Mk 12:14 we know you are a man of *i.*
Tit 2: 7 your teaching show *i,* seriousness

INTELLIGENCE (INTELLIGENT)
Isa 29:14 the *i* of the intelligent will vanish."
1Co 1:19 *i* of the intelligent I will frustrate."

INTELLIGENT (INTELLIGENCE)
Isa 29:14 the intelligence of the *i* will vanish

INTELLIGIBLE
1Co 14:19 I would rather speak five *i* words

INTENDED
Ge 50:20 place of God? You *i* to harm me,

INTENSE
1Th 2:17 out of our *i* longing we made every
Rev 16: 9 They were seared by the *i* heat

INTERCEDE (INTERCEDES INTERCEDING INTERCESSION INTERCESSOR)
Heb 7:25 he always lives to *i* for them.

INTERCEDES* (INTERCEDE)
Ro 8:26 but the Spirit himself *i* for us
8:27 because the Spirit *i* for the saints

INTERCEDING* (INTERCEDE)
Ro 8:34 hand of God and is also *i* for us.

INTERCESSION* (INTERCEDE)
Isa 53:12 and made *i* for the transgressors.
1Ti 2: 1 *i* and thanksgiving be made

INTERCESSOR* (INTERCEDE)
Job 16:20 My *i* is my friend

INTEREST (INTERESTS)
Lev 25:36 Do not take *i* of any kind from him,
Dt 23:20 You may charge a foreigner *i,*
Mt 25:27 would have received it back with *i.*
Php 2:20 who takes a genuine *i*

INTERESTS (INTEREST)
1Co 7:34 his wife—and his *i* are divided.
Php 2: 4 only to your own *i,* but also to the *i*
2:21 everyone looks out for his own *i,*

INTERFERE*
Ezr 6: 7 Do not *i* with the work

INTERMARRY (MARRY)
Dt 7: 3 Do not *i* with them.
Ezr 9:14 and *i* with the peoples who commit

INTERPRET (INTERPRETATION INTERPRETER INTERPRETS)
Ge 41:15 "I had a dream, and no one can *i* it.
Mt 16: 3 you cannot *i* the signs of the times.
1Co 12:30 Do all *i?* But eagerly desire
14:13 pray that he may *i* what he says.
14:27 one at a time, and someone must *i.*

INTERPRETATION (INTERPRET)
1Co 12:10 and to still another the *i* of tongues.
14:26 a revelation, a tongue or an *i.*
2Pe 1:20 about by the prophet's own *i.*

INTERPRETER (INTERPRET)
1Co 14:28 If there is no *i,* the speaker should

INTERPRETS (INTERPRET)
1Co 14: 5 he *i,* so that the church may be

INVADED
2Ki 17: 5 king of Assyria *i* the entire land,
24: 1 king of Babylon *i* the land,

INVENT* (INVENTED)
Ro 1:30 boastful; they *i* ways of doing evil;

INVENTED* (INVENT)
2Pe 1:16 We did not follow cleverly *i* stories

INVESTIGATED
Lk 1: 3 I myself have carefully *i* everything

INVISIBLE*
Ro 1:20 of the world God's *i* qualities—
Col 1:15 He is the image of the *i* God,
1:16 and on earth, visible and *i,*
1Ti 1:17 immortal, *i,* the only God,
Heb 11:27 because he saw him who is *i.*

INVITE (INVITED INVITES)
Mt 22: 9 *i* to the banquet anyone you find.'
25:38 did we see you a stranger and *i* you
Lk 14:12 do not *i* your friends, your brothers
14:13 you give a banquet, *i* the poor,

INVITED (INVITE)
Zep 1: 7 he has consecrated those he has *i.*
Mt 22:14 For many are *i,* but few are chosen
25:35 I was a stranger and you *i* me in,
Lk 14:10 But when you are *i,* take the lowest
Rev 19: 9 'Blessed are those who are *i*

INVITES (INVITE)
Pr 18: 6 and his mouth *i* a beating.
1Co 10:27 If some unbeliever *i* you to a meal

INVOLVED
2Ti 2: 4 a soldier gets *i* in civilian affairs—

IRON
2Ki 6: 6 threw it there, and made the *i* float.
Ps 2: 9 will rule them with an *i* scepter;
Pr 27:17 As *i* sharpens *i,*
Da 2:33 and thighs of bronze, its legs of *i,*
1Ti 4: 2 have been seared as with a hot *i.*
Rev 2:27 He will rule them with an *i* scepter;
12: 5 all the nations with an *i* scepter.
19:15 He will rule them with an *i* scepter

IRRELIGIOUS*
1Ti 1: 9 and sinful, the unholy and *i;*

IRREVOCABLE*
Ro 11:29 for God's gifts and his call are *i.*

ISAAC
Son of Abraham by Sarah (Ge 17:19; 21:1–7; 1Ch 1:28). Abrahamic covenant perpetuated through (Ge 17:21; 26:2–5). Offered up by Abraham (Ge 22; Heb 11:17–19). Rebekah taken as wife (Ge 24). Inherited Abraham's estate (Ge 25:5). Fathered Esau and Jacob (Ge 25:19–26; 1Ch 1:34). Nearly lost Rebekah to Abimelech (Ge 26:1–11). Covenant with Abimelech (Ge 26:12–31). Tricked into blessing Jacob (Ge 27). Death (Ge 35:27–29). Father of Israel (Ex 3:6; Dt 29:13; Ro 9:10).

ISAIAH
Prophet to Judah (Isa 1:1). Called by the LORD (Isa 6). Announced judgment to Ahaz (Isa 7), deliverance from Assyria to Hezekiah (2Ki 19; Isa 36–37), deliverance from death to Hezekiah (2Ki 20:1–11; Isa 38). Chronicler of Judah's history (2Ch 26:22; 32:32).

ISH-BOSHETH*
Son of Saul who attempted to succeed him as king (2Sa 2:8–4:12; 1Ch 8:33).

ISHMAEL
Son of Abraham by Hagar (Ge 16; 1Ch 1:28). Blessed, but not son of covenant (Ge 17:18–21; Gal 4:21–31). Sent away by Sarah (Ge 21:8–21). Children (Ge 25:12–18; 1Ch 1:29–31). Death (Ge 25:17).

ISLAND
Rev 1: 9 was on the *i* of Patmos
16:20 Every *i* fled away

ISRAEL (ISRAEL'S ISRAELITE ISRAELITES)
1. Name given to Jacob (see JACOB).
2. Corporate name of Jacob's descendants; often specifically Northern Kingdom.
Ex 28:11 Engrave the names of the sons of *I*
28:29 of the sons of *I* over his heart
Nu 24:17 a scepter will rise out of *I.*
Dt 6: 4 Hear, O *I:* The LORD our God,
10:12 O *I,* what does the LORD your
Jos 4:22 *I* crossed the Jordan on dry ground
Jdg 17: 6 In those days *I* had no king;
Ru 2:12 of *I,* under whose wings you have
1Sa 3:20 *I* from Dan to Beersheba
4:21 "The glory has departed from *I*"—
14:23 So the LORD rescued *I* that day,
15:26 has rejected you as king over *I!*"
1Sa 17:46 will know that there is a God in *I.*
18:16 But all *I* and Judah loved David,
2Sa 5: 2 'You will shepherd my people *I,*
5: 3 they anointed David king over *I.*
14:25 In all *I* there was not a man
1Ki 1:35 I have appointed him ruler over *I*
10: 9 of the LORD's eternal love for *I,*
18:17 "Is that you, you troubler of *I?*"
19:18 Yet I reserve seven thousand in *I*—
2Ki 5: 8 know that there is a prophet in *I.*"
1Ch 17:22 made your people *I* your very own
21: 1 incited David to take a census of *I.*
29:25 Solomon in the sight of all *I*
2Ch 9: 8 of the love of your God for *I*
Ps 73: 1 Surely God is good to *I,*
81: 8 if you would but listen to me, O *I!*
98: 3 his faithfulness to the house of *I;*
99: 8 you were to *I* a forgiving God,
Isa 11:12 and gather the exiles of *I;*
27: 6 *I* will bud and blossom
44:21 O *I,* I will not forget you.
46:13 my splendor to *I.*
Jer 2: 3 *I* was holy to the LORD,
23: 6 and *I* will live in safety.
31: 2 I will come to give rest to *I.*"
31:10 'He who scattered *I* will gather
31:31 covenant with the house of *I*
33:17 sit on the throne of the house of *I,*
Eze 3:17 you a watchman for the house of *I;*
33: 7 you a watchman for the house of *I;*
34: 2 prophesy against the shepherds of *I*
37:28 that I the LORD make *I* holy,
39:23 of *I* went into exile for their sin,
Da 9:20 my sin and the sin of my people *I*
Hos 11: 1 "When *I* was a child, I loved him,
Am 4:12 prepare to meet your God, O *I.*"
7:11 and *I* will surely go into exile,
8: 2 "The time is ripe for my people *I;*
9:14 I will bring back my exiled people *I*
Mic 5: 2 one who will be ruler over *I,*
Zep 3:13 The remnant of *I* will do no wrong;
Zec 11:14 brotherhood between Judah and *I.*
Mal 1: 5 even beyond the borders of *I!*'
Mt 2: 6 be the shepherd of my people *I.*' "
10: 6 Go rather to the lost sheep of *I.*
15:24 only to the lost sheep of *I.*"
Mk 12:29 'Hear, O *I,* the Lord our God,
Lk 22:30 judging the twelve tribes of *I.*
Ac 1: 6 going to restore the kingdom to *I?*"
9:15 and before the people of *I.*
Ro 9: 4 of my own race, the people of *I.*
9: 6 all who are descended from *I* are *I.*
9:31 but *I,* who pursued a law
11: 7 What *I* sought so earnestly it did
11:26 And so all *I* will be saved,
Gal 6:16 who follow this rule, even to the *I*
Eph 2:12 excluded from citizenship in *I*
3: 6 Gentiles are heirs together with *I,*
Heb 8: 8 covenant with the house of *I*
Rev 7: 4 144,000 from all the tribes of *I.*
21:12 the names of the twelve tribes of *I.*

ISRAEL'S (ISRAEL)
Jdg 10:16 he could bear *I* misery no longer.
2Sa 23: 1 *I* singer of songs:
Isa 44: 6 *I* King and Redeemer, the LORD
Jer 3: 9 Because *I* immorality mattered
31: 9 because I am *I* father,
Jn 3:10 "You are *I* teacher," said Jesus,

ISRAELITE (ISRAEL)
Ex 16: 1 The whole *I* community set out
35:29 All the *I* men and women who
Nu 8:16 offspring from every *I* woman.
20: 1 the whole *I* community arrived
20:22 The whole *I* community set out
Jn 1:47 "Here is a true *I,* in whom there is
Ro 11: 1 I am an *I* myself, a descendant

ISRAELITES (ISRAEL)
Ex 1: 7 the *I* were fruitful and multiplied
2:23 The *I* groaned in their slavery
3: 9 the cry of the *I* has reached me,
12:35 The *I* did as Moses instructed
12:37 The *I* journeyed from Rameses
14:22 and the *I* went through the sea
16:12 I have heard the grumbling of the *I.*
16:35 The *I* ate manna forty years,
24:17 To the *I* the glory of the LORD
28:30 decisions for the *I* over his heart
29:45 Then I will dwell among the *I*
31:16 The *I* are to observe the Sabbath,
33: 5 "Tell the *I,* 'You are a stiff-necked
39:42 The *I* had done all the work just
Lev 22:32 be acknowledged as holy by the *I.*
25:46 rule over your fellow *I* ruthlessly.
25:55 for the *I* belong to me as servants.
Nu 2:32 These are the *I,* counted according
6:23 'This is how you are to bless the *I.*
9: 2 "Have the *I* celebrate the Passover
9:17 the *I* set out; wherever the cloud
10:12 Then the *I* set out from the Desert
14: 2 All the *I* grumbled against Moses
20:12 as holy in the sight of the *I,*
21: 6 they bit the people and many *I* died
26:65 had told those *I* they would surely
27:12 and see the land I have given the *I.*
33: 3 The *I* set out from Rameses
35:10 "Speak to the *I* and say to them:
Dt 33: 1 on the *I* before his death.
Jos 1: 2 about to give to them—to the *I.*
5: 6 The *I* had moved about
7: 1 the *I* acted unfaithfully in regard
8:32 There in the presence of the *I,*
18: 1 of the *I* gathered at Shiloh
21: 3 the *I* gave the Levites the following
22: 9 of Manasseh left the *I* at Shiloh
Jdg 2:11 Then the *I* did evil in the eyes
3:12 Once again the *I* did evil
4: 1 the *I* once again did evil in the eyes
6: 1 Again the *I* did evil in the eyes
10: 6 Again the *I* did evil in the eyes
13: 1 Again the *I* did evil in the eyes
1Sa 17: 2 Saul and the *I* assembled
1Ki 8:63 and all the *I* dedicated the temple
9:22 did not make slaves of any of the *I;*
12: 1 for all the *I* had gone there
12:17 But as for the *I* who were living
2Ki 17:24 towns of Samaria to replace the *I.*
1Ch 9: 2 in their own towns were some *I,*
10: 1 fought against Israel; the *I* fled
11: 4 and all the *I* marched to Jerusalem,
2Ch 7: 6 and all the *I* were standing.
Ne 1: 6 the sins we *I,* including myself
Jer 16:14 who brought the *I* up out of Egypt,'
Hos 1:10 "Yet the *I* will be like the sand
3: 1 Love her as the LORD loves the *I,*
Am 4: 5 boast about them, you *I,*
Mic 5: 3 return to join the *I.*
Ro 9:27 the number of the *I* be like the sand
10: 1 for the *I* is that they may be saved.
10:16 But not all the *I* accepted the good
2Co 11:22 Are they *I?* So am I.

ISSACHAR
Son of Jacob by Leah (Ge 30:18; 35:23; 1Ch 2:1). Tribe of blessed (Ge 49:14–15; Dt 33:18–19), numbered (Nu 1:29; 26:25), allotted land (Jos 19:17–23; Eze 48:25), assisted Deborah (Jdg 5:15), 12,000 from (Rev 7:7).

ISSUING*
Da 9:25 From the *i* of the decree to restore

ITALY
Ac 27: 1 decided that we would sail for *I,*
Heb 13:24 from *I* send you their greetings.

ITCHING*
2Ti 4: 3 to say what their *i* ears want to hear

ITHAMAR

Son of Aaron (Ex 6:23; 1Ch 6:3). Duties at tabernacle (Ex 38:21; Nu 4:21–33; 7:8).

ITTAI

2Sa 15:19 The king said to *I* the Gittite,

IVORY

1Ki 10:22 silver and *i*, and apes and baboons.
22:39 the palace he built and inlaid with *i*

JABBOK

Ge 32:22 and crossed the ford of the *J*.
Dt 3:16 and out to the *J* River,

JABESH

1Sa 11: 1 And all the men of *J* said to him,
31:12 wall of Beth Shan and went to *J*,
1Ch 10:12 and his sons and brought them to *J*.

JABESH GILEAD

Jdg 21: 8 that no one from *J* had come to
2Sa 2: 4 the men of *J* who had buried Saul,
1Ch 10:11 the inhabitants of *J* heard

JACOB

Second son of Isaac, twin of Esau (Ge 26:21–26; 1Ch 1:34). Bought Esau's birthright (Ge 26:29–34); tricked Isaac into blessing him (Ge 27:1–37). Fled to Haran (Ge 28:1–5). Abrahamic covenant perpetuated through (Ge 28:13–15; Mal 1:2). Vision at Bethel (Ge 28:10–22). Served Laban for Rachel and Leah (Ge 29:1–30). Children (Ge 29:31–30:24; 35:16–26; 1Ch 2–9). Flocks increased (Ge 30:25–43). Returned to Canaan (Ge 31). Wrestled with God; name changed to Israel (Ge 32:22–32). Reconciled to Esau (Ge 33). Returned to Bethel (Ge 35:1–15). Favored Joseph (Ge 37:3). Sent sons to Egypt during famine (Ge 42–43). Settled in Egypt (Ge 46). Blessed Ephraim and Manasseh (Ge 48). Blessed sons (Ge 49:1–28; Heb 11:21). Death (Ge 49:29–33). Burial (Ge 50:1–14).

JAEL*

Woman who killed Canaanite general, Sisera (Jdg 4:17–22; 5:24–27).

JAIR

Judge from Gilead (Jdg 10:3–5).

JAIRUS*

Synagogue ruler whose daughter Jesus raised (Mk 5:22–43; Lk 8:41–56).

JAMES

1. Apostle; brother of John (Mt 4:21–22; 10:2; Mk 3:17; Lk 5:1–10). At transfiguration (Mt 17:1–13; Mk 9:1–13; Lk 9:28–36). Killed by Herod (Ac 12:2).

2. Apostle; son of Alphaeus (Mt 10:3; Mk 3:18; Lk 6:15).

3. Brother of Jesus (Mt 13:55; Mk 6:3; Lk 24:10; Gal 1:19) and Judas (Jude 1). With believers before Pentecost (Ac 1:13). Leader of church at Jerusalem (Ac 12:17; 15; 21:18; Gal 2:9, 12). Author of epistle (Jas 1:1).

JAPHETH

Son of Noah (Ge 5:32; 1Ch 1:4–5). Blessed (Ge 9:18–28). Sons of (Ge 10:2–5).

JAR (JARS)

Ge 24:14 let down your *j* that I may have
1Ki 17:14 'The *j* of flour will not be used up
Jer 19: 1 "Go and buy a clay *j* from a potter.
Lk 8:16 hides it in a *j* or puts it under a bed.

JARS (JAR)

Jn 2: 6 Nearby stood six stone water *j*,
2Co 4: 7 we have this treasure in *j* of clay

JASPER

Ex 28:20 row a chrysolite, an onyx and a *j*.
Eze 28:13 chrysolite, onyx and *j*,
Rev 4: 3 sat there had the appearance of *j*
21:19 The first foundation was *j*,

JAVELIN

1Sa 17:45 me with sword and spear and *j*,

JAWBONE

Jdg 15:15 Finding a fresh *j* of a donkey,

JEALOUS (JEALOUSY)

Ex 20: 5 the LORD your God, am a *j* God,
34:14 whose name is Jealous, is a *j* God.
Dt 4:24 God is a consuming fire, a *j* God.
6:15 is a *j* God and his anger will burn
32:21 They made me *j* by what is no god
Jos 24:19 He is a holy God; he is a *j* God.
Eze 16:38 of my wrath and *j* anger.
16:42 my *j* anger will turn away from you
23:25 I will direct my *j* anger against you,
36: 6 in my *j* wrath because you have
Joel 2:18 the LORD will be *j* for his land
Na 1: 2 LORD is a *j* and avenging God;
Zep 3: 8 consumed by the fire of my *j* anger.
Zec 1:14 I am very *j* for Jerusalem and Zion,
8: 2 "I am very *j* for Zion; I am burning
2Co 11: 2 I am *j* for you with a godly jealousy

JEALOUSY (JEALOUS)

Ps 79: 5 How long will your *j* burn like fire?
Pr 6:34 for *j* arouses a husband's fury,
27: 4 but who can stand before *j*?
SS 8: 6 its *j* unyielding as the grave.
Zep 1:18 In the fire of his *j*
Zec 8: 2 I am burning with *j* for her."
Ro 13:13 debauchery, not in dissension and *j*
1Co 3: 3 For since there is *j* and quarreling
10:22 trying to arouse the Lord's *j*?
2Co 11: 2 I am jealous for you with a godly *j*.
12:20 *j*, outbursts of anger, factions,
Gal 5:20 hatred, discord, *j*, fits of rage,

JEERS*

Heb 11:36 Some faced *j* and flogging,

JEHOAHAZ

1. Son of Jehu; king of Israel (2Ki 13:1–9).

2. Son of Josiah; king of Judah (2Ki 23:31–34; 2Ch 36:1–4).

JEHOASH

1. See JOASH.

2. Son of Jehoahaz; king of Israel. Defeat of Aram prophesied by Elisha (2Ki 13:10–25). Defeated Amaziah in Jerusalem (2Ki 14:1–16; 2Ch 25:17–24).

JEHOIACHIN

Son of Jehoiakim; king of Judah exiled by Nebuchadnezzar (2Ki 24:8–17; 2Ch 36:8–10; Jer 22:24–30; 24:1). Raised from prisoner status (2Ki 25:27–30; Jer 52:31–34).

JEHOIADA

Priest who sheltered Joash from Athaliah (2Ki 11–12; 2Ch 22:11–24:16).

JEHOIAKIM

Son of Josiah; made king of Judah by Pharaoh Neco (2Ki 23:34–24:6; 2Ch 36:4–8; Jer 22:18–23). Burned scroll of Jeremiah's prophecies (Jer 36).

JEHORAM

1. Son of Jehoshaphat; king of Judah (2Ki 8:16–24). Prophesied against by Elijah; killed by the LORD (2Ch 21).

2. See JORAM.

JEHOSHAPHAT

Son of Asa; king of Judah. Strengthened his kingdom (2Ch 17). Joined with Ahab against Aram (2Ki 22; 2Ch 18). Established judges (2Ch 19). Joined with Joram against Moab (2Ki 3; 2Ch 20).

JEHU

1. Prophet against Baasha (2Ki 16:1–7).

2. King of Israel. Anointed by Elijah to obliterate house of Ahab (1Ki 19:16–17); anointed by servant of Elisha (2Ki 9:1–13). Killed Joram and Ahaziah (2Ki 9:14–29; 2Ch 22:7–9), Jezebel (2Ki 9:30–37), relatives of Ahab (2Ki 10:1–17), ministers of Baal (2Ki 10:18–29). Death (2Ki 10:30–36).

JEPHTHAH

Judge from Gilead who delivered Israel from Ammon (Jdg 10:6–12:7). Made rash vow concerning his daughter (Jdg 11:30–40).

JEREMIAH

Prophet to Judah (Jer 1:1–3). Called by the LORD (Jer 1). Put in stocks (Jer 20:1–3). Threatened for prophesying (Jer 11:18–23; 26). Opposed by Hananiah (Jer 28). Scroll burned (Jer 36). Imprisoned (Jer 37). Thrown into cistern (Jer 38). Forced to Egypt with those fleeing Babylonians (Jer 43).

JERICHO

Nu 22: 1 along the Jordan across from *J*.
Jos 3:16 the people crossed over opposite *J*.
5:10 camped at Gilgal on the plains of *J*,
Lk 10:30 going down from Jerusalem to *J*,
Heb 11:30 By faith the walls of *J* fell,

JEROBOAM

1. Official of Solomon; rebelled to become first king of Israel (1Ki 11:26–40; 12:1–20; 2Ch 10). Idolatry (1Ki 12:25–33); judgment for (1Ki 13–14; 2Ch 13).

2. Son of Jehoash; king of Israel (1Ki 14:23–29).

JERUSALEM

Jos 10: 1 of *J* heard that Joshua had taken Ai
15: 8 of the Jebusite city (that is, *J*).
Jdg 1: 8 The men of Judah attacked *J* also
1Sa 17:54 head and brought it to *J*,
2Sa 5: 5 and in *J* he reigned over all Israel
5: 6 and his men marched to *J*
9:13 And Mephibosheth lived in *J*,
11: 1 But David remained in *J*.
15:29 took the ark of God back to *J*
24:16 stretched out his hand to destroy *J*,
1Ki 3: 1 the LORD, and the wall around *J*.
9:15 the wall of *J*, and Hazor, Megiddo
9:19 whatever he desired to build in *J*,
10:26 cities and also with him in *J*.
10:27 as common in *J* as stones,
11: 7 of *J*, Solomon built a high place
11:13 my servant and for the sake of *J*,
11:36 always have a lamp before me in *J*,
11:42 Solomon reigned in *J*
12:27 at the temple of the LORD in *J*,
14:21 and he reigned seventeen years in *J*
14:25 Shishak king of Egypt attacked *J*.
15: 2 and he reigned in *J* three years.
15:10 and he reigned in *J* forty-one years.
22:42 he reigned in *J* twenty-five years.
2Ki 8:17 and he reigned in *J* eight years.
8:26 and he reigned in *J* one year.
12: 1 and he reigned in *J* forty years.
12:17 Then he turned to attack *J*.
14: 2 he reigned in *J* twenty-nine years.
14:13 Then Jehoash went to *J*
15: 2 and he reigned in *J* fifty-two years.
15:33 and he reigned in *J* sixteen years.
16: 2 and he reigned in *J* sixteen years.
16: 5 Israel marched up to fight against *J*
18: 2 he reigned in *J* twenty-nine years.

2Ki 18:17 Lachish to King Hezekiah at *J.*
19:31 For out of *J* will come a remnant,
21: 1 and he reigned in *J* fifty-five years.
21:12 going to bring such disaster on *J*
21:19 and he reigned in *J* two years.
22: 1 he reigned in *J* thirty-one years.
23:27 and I will reject *J,* the city I chose,
23:31 and he reigned in *J* three months.
23:36 and he reigned in *J* eleven years.
24: 8 and he reigned in *J* three months.
24:10 king of Babylon advanced on *J*
24:14 He carried into exile all *J:*
24:18 and he reigned in *J* eleven years.
24:20 anger that all this happened to *J*
25: 1 king of Babylon marched against *J*
25: 9 royal palace and all the houses of *J.*
1Ch 11: 4 and all the Israelites marched to *J,*
21:16 sword in his hand extended over *J.*
2Ch 1: 4 he had pitched a tent for it in *J.*
3: 1 the LORD in *J* on Mount Moriah,
6: 6 now I have chosen *J* for my Name
9: 1 she came to *J* to test him
20:15 and all who live in Judah and *J!*
20:27 and *J* returned joyfully to *J,*
29: 8 LORD has fallen on Judah and *J;*
36:19 and broke down the wall of *J;*
Ezr 1: 2 a temple for him at *J* in Judah.
2: 1 to Babylon (they returned to *J*
3: 1 people assembled as one man in *J.*
4:12 up to us from you have gone to *J*
4:24 of God in *J* came to a standstill
6:12 or to destroy this temple in *J.*
7: 8 Ezra arrived in *J* in the fifth month
9: 9 a wall of protection in Judah and *J.*
10: 7 for all the exiles to assemble in *J.*
Ne 1: 2 the exile, and also about *J.*
1: 3 The wall of *J* is broken down,
2:11 to *J,* and after staying there three
2:17 Come, let us rebuild the wall of *J,*
2:20 you have no share in *J* or any claim
3: 8 They restored *J* as far as the Broad
4: 8 fight against *J* and stir up trouble
11: 1 leaders of the people settled in *J,*
12:27 At the dedication of the wall of *J,*
12:43 in *J* could be heard far away.
Ps 51:18 build up the walls of *J.*
79: 1 they have reduced *J* to rubble.
122: 2 in your gates, O *J.*
122: 3 *J* is built like a city
122: 6 Pray for the peace of *J:*
125: 2 As the mountains surround *J,*
128: 5 may you see the prosperity of *J,*
137: 5 If I forget you, O *J,*
147: 2 The LORD builds up *J;*
147:12 Extol the LORD, O *J;*
SS 6: 4 lovely as *J,*
Isa 1: 1 and *J* that Isaiah son of Amoz saw
2: 1 saw concerning Judah and *J:*
3: 1 is about to take from *J* and Judah
3: 8 *J* staggers,
4: 3 recorded among the living in *J.*
8:14 And for the people of *J* he will be
27:13 LORD on the holy mountain in *J.*
31: 5 the LORD Almighty will shield *J;*
33:20 your eyes will see *J,*
40: 2 Speak tenderly to *J,*
40: 9 You who bring good tidings to *J,*
52: 1 O *J,* the holy city.
52: 2 rise up, sit enthroned, O *J.*
62: 6 on your walls, O *J;*
62: 7 give him no rest till he establishes *J*
65:18 for I will create *J* to be a delight
Jer 2: 2 and proclaim in the hearing of *J:*
3:17 time they will call *J* The Throne
4: 5 and proclaim in *J* and say:
4:14 O *J,* wash the evil from your heart
5: 1 "Go up and down the streets of *J,*
6: 6 and build siege ramps against *J.*
8: 5 Why does *J* always turn away?
9:11 "I will make *J* a heap of ruins,
Jer 13:27 Woe to you, O *J!*
23:14 And among the prophets of *J*
24: 1 into exile from *J* to Babylon
26:18 *J* will become a heap of rubble,
32: 2 of Babylon was then besieging *J,*
33:10 the streets of *J* that are deserted,
39: 1 This is how *J* was taken: In
51:50 and think on *J.*"
52:14 broke down all the walls around *J.*
La 1: 7 *J* remembers all the treasures
Eze 14:21 send against *J* my four dreadful
16: 2 confront *J* with her detestable
Da 6:10 the windows opened toward *J.*
9: 2 of *J* would last seventy years.
9:12 done like what has been done to *J.*
9:25 and rebuild *J* until the Anointed
Joel 3: 1 restore the fortunes of Judah and *J,*
3:16 and thunder from *J;*
3:17 *J* will be holy;
Am 2: 5 will consume the fortresses of *J.*"
Ob :11 and cast lots for *J,*
Mic 1: 5 Is it not *J?*
4: 2 the word of the LORD from *J.*
Zep 3:16 On that day they will say to *J,*
Zec 1:14 'I am very jealous for *J* and Zion,
1:17 comfort Zion and choose *J.*'"
2: 2 He answered me, "To measure *J,*
2: 4 '*J* will be a city without walls
8: 3 I will return to Zion and dwell in *J.*
8: 8 I will bring them back to live in *J;*
8:15 determined to do good again to *J*
8:22 powerful nations will come to *J*
9: 9 Shout, Daughter of *J!*
9:10 and the war-horses from *J,*
12: 3 I will make *J* an immovable rock
12:10 the inhabitants of *J* a spirit of grace
14: 2 the nations to *J* to fight against it;
14: 8 living water will flow out from *J,*
14:16 that have attacked *J* will go up
Mt 16:21 to his disciples that he must go to *J*
20:18 said to them, "We are going up to *J*
21:10 When Jesus entered *J,* the whole
23:37 "O *J, J,* you who kill the prophets
Mk 10:33 "We are going up to *J,*" he said,
Lk 2:22 Mary took him to *J* to present him
2:41 Every year his parents went to *J*
2:43 the boy Jesus stayed behind in *J,*
4: 9 The devil led him to *J*
9:31 about to bring to fulfillment at *J.*
9:51 Jesus resolutely set out for *J,*
13:34 die outside *J!* "O *J, J,*
18:31 told them, "We are going up to *J,*
19:41 As he approached *J* and saw
21:20 "When you see *J* being surrounded
21:24 *J* will be trampled
24:47 name to all nations, beginning at *J.*
Jn 4:20 where we must worship is in *J.*"
Ac 1: 4 this command: "Do not leave *J,*
1: 8 and you will be my witnesses in *J,*
6: 7 of disciples in *J* increased rapidly,
20:22 by the Spirit, I am going to *J,*
23:11 As you have testified about me in *J*
Ro 15:19 So from *J* all the way
Gal 4:25 corresponds to the present city of *J*
4:26 But the *J* that is above is free,
Heb 12:22 to the heavenly *J,* the city
Rev 3:12 the new *J,* which is coming
21: 2 I saw the Holy City, the new *J,*
21:10 and showed me the Holy City, *J,*

JESSE

Father of David (Ru 4:17–22; 1Sa 16; 1Ch 2:12–17).

JESUS

LIFE: Genealogy (Mt 1:1–17; Lk 3:21–37). Birth announced (Mt 1:18–25; Lk 1:26–45). Birth (Mt 2:1–12; Lk 2:1–40). Escape to Egypt (Mt 2:13–23). As a boy in the temple (Lk 2:41–52). Baptism (Mt 3:13–17; Mk 1:9–11; Lk 3:21–22; Jn 1:32–34). Temptation (Mt 4:1–11; Mk 1:12–13; Lk 4:1–13). Ministry in Galilee (Mt 4:12–18:35; Mk 1:14–9:50; Lk 4:14–13:9; Jn 1:35–2:11; 4; 6), Transfiguration (Mt 17:1–8; Mk 9:2–8; Lk 9:28–36), on the way to Jerusalem (Mt 19–20; Mk 10; Lk 13:10–19:27), in Jerusalem (Mt 21–25; Mk 11–13; Lk 19:28–21:38; Jn 2:12–3:36; 5; 7–12). Last supper (Mt 26:17–35; Mk 14:12–31; Lk 22:1–38; Jn 13–17). Arrest and trial (Mt 26:36–27:31; Mk 14:43–15:20; Lk 22:39–23:25; Jn 18:1–19:16). Crucifixion (Mt 27:32–66; Mk 15:21–47; Lk 23:26–55; Jn 19:28–42). Resurrection and appearances (Mt 28; Mk 16; Lk 24; Jn 20–21; Ac 1:1–11; 7:56; 9:3–6; 1Co 15:1–8; Rev 1:1–20).

MIRACLES. Healings: official's son (Jn 4:43–54), demoniac in Capernaum (Mk 1:23–26; Lk 4:33–35), Peter's mother-in-law (Mt 8:14–17; Mk 1:29–31; Lk 4:38–39), leper (Mt 8:2–4; Mk 1:40–45; Lk 5:12–16), paralytic (Mt 9:1–8; Mk 2:1–12; Lk 5:17–26), cripple (Jn 5:1–9), shriveled hand (Mt 12:10–13; Mk 3:1–5; Lk 6:6–11), centurion's servant (Mt 8:5–13; Lk 7:1–10), widow's son raised (Lk 7:11–17), demoniac (Mt 12:22–23; Lk 11:14), Gadarene demoniacs (Mt 8:28–34; Mk 5:1–20; Lk 8:26–39), woman's bleeding and Jairus' daughter (Mt 9:18–26; Mk 5:21–43; Lk 8:40–56), blind man (Mt 9:27–31), mute man (Mt 9:32–33), Canaanite woman's daughter (Mt 15:21–28; Mk 7:24–30), deaf man (Mk 7:31–37), blind man (Mk 8:22–26), demoniac boy (Mt 17:14–18; Mk 9:14–29; Lk 9:37–43), ten lepers (Lk 17:11–19), man born blind (Jn 9:1–7), Lazarus raised (Jn 11), crippled woman (Lk 13:11–17), man with dropsy (Lk 14:1–6), two blind men (Mt 20:29–34; Mk 10:46–52; Lk 18:35–43), Malchus' ear (Lk 22:50–51). Other Miracles: water to wine (Jn 2:1–11), catch of fish (Lk 5:1–11), storm stilled (Mt 8:23–27; Mk 4:37–41; Lk 8:22–25), 5,000 fed (Mt 14:15–21; Mk 6:35–44; Lk 9:10–17; Jn 6:1–14), walking on water (Mt 14:25–33; Mk 6:48–52; Jn 6:15–21), 4,000 fed (Mt 15:32–39; Mk 8:1–9), money from fish (Mt 17:24–27), fig tree cursed (Mt 21:18–22; Mk 11:12–14), catch of fish (Jn 21:1–14).

MAJOR TEACHING: Sermon on the Mount (Mt 5–7; Lk 6:17–49), to Nicodemus (Jn 3), to Samaritan woman (Jn 4), Bread of Life (Jn 6:22–59), at Feast of Tabernacles (Jn 7–8), woes to Pharisees (Mt 23; Lk 11:37–54), Good Shepherd (Jn 10:1–18), Olivet Discourse (Mt 24–25; Mk 13; Lk 21:5–36), Upper Room Discourse (Jn 13–16).

PARABLES: Sower (Mt 13:3–23; Mk 4:3–25; Lk 8:5–18), seed's growth (Mk 4:26–29), wheat and weeds (Mt 13:24–30, 36–43), mustard seed (Mt 13:31–32; Mk 4:30–32), yeast (Mt 13:33; Lk 13:20–21), hidden treasure (Mt 13:44), valuable pearl (Mt 13:45–46), net (Mt 13:47–51), house owner (Mt 13:52), good Samaritan (Lk 10:25–37), unmerciful servant (Mt 18:15–35), lost sheep (Mt 18:10–14; Lk 15:4–7), lost coin (Lk 15:8–10), lost son (Lk 15:11–32), dishonest manager (Lk 16:1–13), rich man and Lazarus (Lk 16:19–31), persistent widow (Lk 18:1–8), Pharisee and tax collector (Lk 18:9–14), payment of workers (Mt 20:1–16), tenants and the vineyard (Mt 21:28–46; Mk 12:1–12; Lk 20:9–19), wedding banquet (Mt 22:1–14), faithful servant (Mt 24:45–51), ten virgins (Mt 25:1–13), talents (Mt 25:1–30; Lk 19:12–27).

DISCIPLES see APOSTLES. Call of (Jn 1:35–51; Mt 4:18–22; 9:9; Mk 1:16–20; 2:13–14; Lk 5:1–11, 27–28). Named Apostles (Mk 3:13–19; Lk 6:12–16). Twelve sent out (Mt 10; Mk 6:7–11; Lk 9:1–5). Seventy sent out (Lk 10:1–24). Defection of (Jn 6:60–71; Mt 26:56; Mk 14:50–52). Final commission (Mt 28:16–20; Jn 21:15–23; Ac 1:3–8).

Ac 2:32 God has raised this *J* to life,
9: 5 "I am *J,* whom you are persecuting
9:34 said to him, "*J* Christ heals you.

Ac 15:11 of our Lord *J* that we are saved,
16:31 "Believe in the Lord *J*,
20:24 the task the Lord *J* has given me—
Ro 3:24 redemption that came by Christ *J*.
5:17 life through the one man, *J* Christ.
8: 1 for those who are in Christ *J*,
1Co 1: 7 for our Lord *J* Christ to be revealed
2: 2 except *J* Christ and him crucified.
6:11 in the name of the Lord *J* Christ
8: 6 and there is but one Lord, *J* Christ,
12: 3 and no one can say, "*J* is Lord,"
2Co 4: 5 not preach ourselves, but *J* Christ
13: 5 Do you not realize that Christ *J* is
Gal 2:16 but by faith in *J* Christ.
3:28 for you are all one in Christ *J*.
5: 6 in Christ *J* neither circumcision
6:17 bear on my body the marks of *J*.
Eph 1: 5 as his sons through *J* Christ,
2:10 created in Christ *J*
2:20 with Christ *J* himself as the chief
Php 1: 6 until the day of Christ *J*.
2: 5 be the same as that of Christ *J*:
2:10 name of *J* every knee should bow,
Col 3:17 do it all in the name of the Lord *J*,
1Th 1:10 whom he raised from the dead—*J*,
4:14 We believe that *J* died
5:23 at the coming of our Lord *J* Christ.
2Th 1: 7 when the Lord *J* is revealed
2: 1 the coming of our Lord *J* Christ
1Ti 1:15 Christ *J* came into the world
2Ti 1:10 appearing of our Savior, Christ *J*,
2: 3 us like a good soldier of Christ *J*.
3:12 life in Christ *J* will be persecuted,
Tit 2:13 our great God and Savior, *J* Christ,
Heb 2: 9 But we see *J*, who was made a little
2:11 So *J* is not ashamed to call them
3: 1 fix your thoughts on *J*, the apostle
3: 3 *J* has been found worthy
4:14 through the heavens, *J* the Son
6:20 where *J*, who went before us,
7:22 *J* has become the guarantee
7:24 but because *J* lives forever,
8: 6 But the ministry *J* has received is
12: 2 Let us fix our eyes on *J*, the author
12:24 to *J* the mediator of a new
1Pe 1: 3 the resurrection of *J* Christ
2Pe 1:16 and coming of our Lord *J* Christ,
1Jn 1: 7 and the blood of *J*, his Son,
2: 1 *J* Christ, the Righteous One.
2: 6 to live in him must walk as *J* did.
4:15 anyone acknowledges that *J* is
Rev 1: 1 The revelation of *J* Christ,
22:16 *J*, have sent my angel
22:20 Come, Lord *J*.

JETHRO

Father-in-law and adviser of Moses (Ex 3:1; 18). Also known as Reuel (Ex 2:18).

JEW (JEWS JEWS' JUDAISM)
Est 2: 5 of Susa a *J* of the tribe of Benjamin,
Zec 8:23 of one *J* by the hem of his robe
Ac 21:39 "I am a *J*, from Tarsus in Cilicia,
Ro 1:16 first for the *J*, then for the Gentile.
2:28 A man is not a *J* if he is only one
10:12 there is no difference between *J*
1Co 9:20 To the Jews I became like a *J*,
Gal 2:14 "You are a *J*, yet you live like
3:28 There is neither *J* nor Greek,
Col 3:11 Here there is no Greek or *J*,

JEWEL (JEWELRY JEWELS)
Pr 20:15 that speak knowledge are a rare *j*.
SS 4: 9 with one *j* of your necklace.
Rev 21:11 that of a very precious *j*,

JEWELRY (JEWEL)
Ex 35:22 and brought gold *j* of all kinds:
Jer 2:32 Does a maiden forget her *j*,
Eze 16:11 you with *j*: I put bracelets
1Pe 3: 3 wearing of gold *j* and fine clothes.

JEWELS (JEWEL)
Isa 54:12 your gates of sparkling *j*,
61:10 as a bride adorns herself with her *j*.
Zec 9:16 like *j* in a crown.

JEWS (JEW)
Ne 4: 1 He ridiculed the *J*,
Est 3:13 kill and annihilate all the *J*—
4:14 and deliverance for the *J* will arise
Mt 2: 2 who has been born king of the *J*?
27:11 "Are you the king of the *J*?" "Yes,
Jn 4: 9 (For *J* do not associate
4:22 for salvation is from the *J*.
19: 3 saying, "Hail, king of the *J*!"
Ac 20:21 I have declared to both *J*
Ro 3:29 Is God the God of *J* only?
9:24 not only from the *J* but
15:27 they owe it to the *J* to share
1Co 1:22 *J* demand miraculous signs
9:20 To the *J* I became like a Jew,
12:13 whether *J* or Greeks, slave or free
Gal 2: 8 of Peter as an apostle to the *J*,
Rev 2: 9 slander of those who say they are *J*
3: 9 claim to be *J* though they are not,

JEWS' (JEW)
Ro 15:27 shared in the *J* spiritual blessings,

JEZEBEL

Sidonian wife of Ahab (1Ki 16:31). Promoted Baal worship (1Ki 16:32–33). Killed prophets of the LORD (1Ki 18:4, 13). Opposed Elijah (1Ki 19:1–2). Had Naboth killed (1Ki 21). Death prophesied (1Ki 21:17–24). Killed by Jehu (2Ki 9:30–37).

JEZREEL
2Ki 9:36 at *J* dogs will devour Jezebel's flesh
10: 7 and sent them to Jehu in *J*.
Hos 1: 4 house of Jehu for the massacre at *J*,

JOAB

Nephew of David (1Ch 2:16). Commander of his army (2Sa 8:16). Victorious over Ammon (2Sa 10; 1Ch 19), Rabbah (2Sa 11; 1Ch 20), Jerusalem (1Ch 11:6), Absalom (2Sa 18), Sheba (2Sa 20). Killed Abner (2Sa 3:22–39), Amasa (2Sa 20:1–13). Numbered David's army (2Sa 24; 1Ch 21). Sided with Adonijah (1Ki 1:17, 19). Killed by Benaiah (1Ki 2:5–6, 28–35).

JOASH

Son of Ahaziah; king of Judah. Sheltered from Athaliah by Jehoiada (2Ki 11; 2Ch 22:10–23:21). Repaired temple (2Ki 12; 2Ch 24).

JOB

Wealthy man from Uz; feared God (Job 1:1–5). Righteousness tested by disaster (Job 1:6–22), personal affliction (Job 2). Maintained innocence in debate with three friends (Job 3–31), Elihu (Job 32–37). Rebuked by the LORD (Job 38–41). Vindicated and restored to greater stature by the LORD (Job 42). Example of righteousness (Eze 14:14, 20).

JOCHEBED*

Mother of Moses and Aaron (Ex 6:20; Nu 26:59).

JOEL

Prophet (Joel 1:1; Ac 2:16).

JOHN

1. Son of Zechariah and Elizabeth (Lk 1). Called the Baptist (Mt 3:1–12; Mk 1:2–8). Witness to Jesus (Mt 3:11–12; Mk 1:7–8; Lk 3:15–18; Jn 1:6–35; 3:27–30; 5:33–36). Doubts about Jesus (Mt 11:2–6; Lk 7:18–23). Arrest (Mt 4:12; Mk 1:14). Execution (Mt 14:1–12; Mk 6:14–29; Lk 9:7–9). Ministry compared to Elijah (Mt 11:7–19; Mk 9:11–13; Lk 7:24–35).

2. Apostle; brother of James (Mt 4:21–22; 10:2; Mk 3:17; Lk 5:1–10). At transfiguration (Mt 17:1–13; Mk 9:1–13; Lk 9:28–36). Desire to be greatest (Mk 10:35–45). Leader of church at Jerusalem (Ac 4:1–3; Gal 2:9). Elder who wrote epistles (2Jn 1; 3Jn 1). Prophet who wrote Revelation (Rev 1:1; 22:8).

3. Cousin of Barnabas, co-worker with Paul, (Ac 12:12–13:13; 15:37), see MARK.

JOIN (JOINED JOINS)
Ne 10:29 all these now *j* their brothers
Pr 23:20 Do not *j* those who drink too much
24:21 and do not *j* with the rebellious,
Jer 3:18 of Judah will *j* the house of Israel,
Eze 37:17 *J* them together into one stick
Da 11:34 who are not sincere will *j* them.
Ro 15:30 to *j* me in my struggle by praying
2Ti 1: 8 *j* with me in suffering for the gospel

JOINED (JOIN)
Zec 2:11 "Many nations will be *j*
Mt 19: 6 Therefore what God has *j* together,
Mk 10: 9 Therefore what God has *j* together,
Ac 1:14 They all *j* together constantly
Eph 2:21 him the whole building is *j* together
4:16 *j* and held together

JOINS (JOIN)
1Co 16:16 and to everyone who *j* in the work,

JOINT (JOINTS)
Ps 22:14 and all my bones are out of *j*.

JOINTS (JOINT)
Heb 4:12 even to dividing soul and spirit, *j*

JOKING*
Ge 19:14 his sons-in-law thought he was *j*.
Pr 26:19 and says, "I was only *j*!"
Eph 5: 4 or coarse *j*, which are out of place,

JONAH

Prophet in days of Jeroboam II (2Ki 14:25). Called to Nineveh; fled to Tarshish (Jnh 1:1–3). Cause of storm; thrown into sea (Jnh 1:4–16). Swallowed by fish (Jnh 1:17). Prayer (Jnh 2). Preached to Nineveh (Jnh 3). Attitude reproved by the LORD (Jnh 4). Sign of (Mt 12:39–41; Lk 11:29–32).

JONATHAN

Son of Saul (1Sa 13:16; 1Ch 8:33). Valiant warrior (1Sa 13–14). Relation to David (1Sa 18:1–4; 19–20; 23:16–18). Killed at Gilboa (1Sa 31). Mourned by David (2Sa 1).

JOPPA
Ezr 3: 7 logs by sea from Lebanon to *J*,
Jnh 1: 3 to *J*, where he found a ship bound
Ac 9:43 Peter stayed in *J* for some time

JORAM

1. Son of Ahab; king of Israel. Fought with Jehoshaphat against Moab (2Ki 3). Killed with Ahaziah by Jehu (2Ki 8:25–29; 9:14–26; 2Ch 22:5–9).

2. See JEHORAM.

JORDAN
Ge 13:10 plain of the *J* was well watered,
Nu 22: 1 and camped along the *J*
34:12 boundary will go down along the *J*
Dt 3:27 you are not going to cross this *J*.
Jos 1: 2 get ready to cross the *J* River
3:11 go into the *J* ahead of you.
3:17 ground in the middle of the *J*,
4:22 Israel crossed the *J* on dry ground.'
2Ki 2: 7 and Elisha had stopped at the *J*.
2:13 and stood on the bank of the *J*.
5:10 wash yourself seven times in the *J*,
6: 4 They went to the *J* and began

Ps 114: 3 the *J* turned back;
Isa 9: 1 along the *J*— The people walking
Jer 12: 5 manage in the thickets by the *J*?
Mt 3: 6 baptized by him in the *J* River.
4:15 the way to the sea, along the *J*,
Mk 1: 9 and was baptized by John in the *J*.

JOSEPH

1. Son of Jacob by Rachel (Ge 30:24; 1Ch 2:2). Favored by Jacob, hated by brothers (Ge 37:3–4). Dreams (Ge 37:5–11). Sold by brothers (Ge 37:12–36). Served Potiphar; imprisoned by false accusation (Ge 39). Interpreted dreams of Pharaoh's servants (Ge 40), of Pharaoh (Ge 41:4–40). Made greatest in Egypt (Ge 41:41–57). Sold grain to brothers (Ge 42–45). Brought Jacob and sons to Egypt (Ge 46–47). Sons Ephraim and Manasseh blessed (Ge 48). Blessed (Ge 49:22–26; Dt 33:13–17). Death (Ge 50:22–26; Ex 13:19; Heb 11:22). 12,000 from (Rev 7:8).

2. Husband of Mary, mother of Jesus (Mt 1:16–24; 2:13–19; Lk 1:27; 2; Jn 1:45).

3. Disciple from Arimathea, who gave his tomb for Jesus' burial (Mt 27:57–61; Mk 15:43–47; Lk 24:50–52).

4. Original name of Barnabas (Ac 4:36).

JOSHUA (HOSHEA)

1. Son of Nun; name changed from Hoshea (Nu 13:8, 16; 1Ch 7:27). Fought Amalekites under Moses (Ex 17:9–14). Servant of Moses on Sinai (Ex 24:13; 32:17). Spied Canaan (Nu 13). With Caleb, allowed to enter land (Nu 14:6, 30). Succeeded Moses (Dt 1:38; 31:1–8; 34:9).

Charged Israel to conquer Canaan (Jos 1). Crossed Jordan (Jos 3–4). Circumcised sons of wilderness wanderings (Jos 5). Conquered Jericho (Jos 6), Ai (Jos 7–8), five kings at Gibeon (Jos 10:1–28), southern Canaan (Jos 10:29–43), northern Canaan (Jos 11–12). Defeated at Ai (Jos 7). Deceived by Gibeonites (Jos 9). Renewed covenant (Jos 8:30–35; 24:1–27). Divided land among tribes (Jos 13–22). Last words (Jos 23). Death (Jos 24:28–31).

2. High priest during rebuilding of temple (Hag 1–2; Zec 3:1–9; 6:11).

JOSIAH

Son of Amon; king of Judah (2Ki 21:26; 1Ch 3:14). Prophesied (1Ki 13:2). Book of Law discovered during his reign (2Ki 22; 2Ch 34:14–31). Reforms (2Ki 23:1–25; 2Ch 34:1–13; 35:1–19). Killed by Pharaoh Neco (2Ki 23:29–30; 2Ch 35:20–27).

JOTHAM

1. Son of Gideon (Jdg 9).

2. Son of Azariah (Uzziah); king of Judah (2Ki 15:32–38; 2Ch 26:21–27:9).

JOURNEY

Dt 1:33 who went ahead of you on your *j*,
2: 7 over your *j* through this vast desert
Jdg 18: 6 Your *j* has the LORD's approval."
Ezr 8:21 and ask him for a safe *j* for us
Job 16:22 before I go on the *j* of no return.
Isa 35: 8 The unclean will not *j* on it;
Mt 25:14 it will be like a man going on a *j*,
Ro 15:24 to have you assist me on my *j* there

JOY* (ENJOY ENJOYMENT JOYFUL JOYOUS OVERJOYED REJOICE REJOICES REJOICING)

Ge 31:27 so I could send you away with *j*
Lev 9:24 shouted for *j* and fell facedown.
Dt 16:15 and your *j* will be complete.
Jdg 9:19 may Abimelech be your *j*,
1Ch 12:40 and sheep, for there was *j* in Israel.
16:27 strength and *j* in his dwelling place.
16:33 sing for *j* before the LORD,
29:17 with *j* how willingly your people
1Ch 29:22 drank with great *j* in the presence
2Ch 30:26 There was great *j* in Jerusalem,
Ezr 3:12 while many others shouted for *j*.
3:13 of the shouts of *j* from the sound
6:16 of the house of God with *j*.
6:22 with *j* by changing the attitude
6:22 *j* the Feast of Unleavened Bread,
Ne 8:10 for the *j* of the LORD is your
8:12 and to celebrate with great *j*,
8:17 And their *j* was very great.
12:43 God had given them great *j*.
Est 8:16 a time of happiness and *j*,
8:17 there was *j* and gladness
9:17 and made it a day of feasting and *j*.
9:18 and made it a day of feasting and *j*.
9:19 as a day of *j* and feasting,
9:22 and *j* and giving presents of food
9:22 their sorrow was turned into *j*
Job 3: 7 may no shout of *j* be heard in it.
6:10 my *j* in unrelenting pain—
8:21 and your lips with shouts of *j*.
9:25 they fly away without a glimpse of *j*
10:20 from me so I can have a moment's *j*
20: 5 the *j* of the godless lasts
33:26 he sees God's face and shouts for *j*;
38: 7 and all the angels shouted for *j*?
Ps 4: 7 have filled my heart with greater *j*
5:11 let them ever sing for *j*.
16:11 me with *j* in your presence,
19: 8 giving *j* to the heart.
20: 5 We will shout for *j*
21: 1 How great is his *j* in the victories
21: 6 with the *j* of your presence.
27: 6 will I sacrifice with shouts of *j*;
28: 7 My heart leaps for *j*
30:11 sackcloth and clothed me with *j*,
33: 3 play skillfully, and shout for *j*.
35:27 shout for *j* and gladness;
42: 4 with shouts of *j* and thanksgiving
43: 4 to God, my *j* and my delight.
45: 7 by anointing you with the oil of *j*.
45:15 They are led in with *j* and gladness;
47: 1 shout to God with cries of *j*.
47: 5 God has ascended amid shouts of *j*,
48: 2 the *j* of the whole earth.
51: 8 Let me hear *j* and gladness;
51:12 to me the *j* of your salvation
65: 8 you call forth songs of *j*.
65:13 they shout for *j* and sing.
66: 1 Shout with *j* to God, all the earth!
67: 4 the nations be glad and sing for *j*,
71:23 My lips will shout for *j*
81: 1 Sing for *j* to God our strength;
86: 4 Bring *j* to your servant,
89:12 Hermon sing for *j* at your name.
90:14 for *j* and be glad all our days.
92: 4 I sing for *j* at the works
94:19 your consolation brought *j*
95: 1 let us sing for *j* to the LORD;
96:12 the trees of the forest will sing for *j*;
97:11 and *j* on the upright in heart.
98: 4 for *j* to the LORD, all the earth,
98: 6 shout for *j* before the LORD,
98: 8 the mountains sing together for *j*;
100: 1 for *j* to the LORD, all the earth.
105:43 his chosen ones with shouts of *j*;
106: 5 share in the *j* of your nation
107:22 and tell of his works with songs of *j*
118:15 Shouts of *j* and victory
119:111 they are the *j* of my heart.
126: 2 our tongues with songs of *j*.
126: 3 and we are filled with *j*.
126: 5 will reap with songs of *j*.
126: 6 will return with songs of *j*,
132: 9 may your saints sing for *j*."
132:16 and her saints will ever sing for *j*.
137: 3 tormentors demanded songs of *j*;
137: 6 my highest *j*.
149: 5 and sing for *j* on their beds.
Pr 10: 1 A wise son brings *j* to his father,
Pr 10:28 The prospect of the righteous is *j*,
11:10 wicked perish, there are shouts of *j*.
12:20 but *j* for those who promote peace.
14:10 and no one else can share its *j*.
14:13 and *j* may end in grief.
15:20 A wise son brings *j* to his father,
15:23 A man finds *j* in giving an apt reply
15:30 A cheerful look brings *j*
17:21 there is no *j* for the father of a fool.
21:15 it brings *j* to the righteous
23:24 of a righteous man has great *j*;
27: 9 incense bring *j* to the heart,
27:11 my son, and bring *j* to my heart;
29: 3 A man who loves wisdom brings *j*
Ecc 8:15 Then *j* will accompany him
11: 9 let your heart give you *j* in the days
Isa 9: 3 and increased their *j*;
12: 3 With *j* you will draw water
12: 6 Shout aloud and sing for *j*,
16: 9 shouts of *j* over your ripened fruit
16:10 *J* and gladness are taken away
22:13 But see, there is *j* and revelry,
24:11 all *j* turns to gloom,
24:14 raise their voices, they shout for *j*;
26:19 wake up and shout for *j*.
35: 2 will rejoice greatly and shout for *j*.
35: 6 the mute tongue shout for *j*.
35:10 Gladness and *j* will overtake them,
35:10 everlasting *j* will crown their heads
42:11 Let the people of Sela sing for *j*;
44:23 Sing for *j*, O heavens,
48:20 Announce this with shouts of *j*
49:13 Shout for *j*, O heavens;
51: 3 *J* and gladness will be found in her,
51:11 Gladness and *j* will overtake them,
51:11 everlasting *j* will crown their heads
52: 8 together they shout for *j*.
52: 9 Burst into songs of *j* together,
54: 1 burst into song, shout for *j*,
55:12 You will go out in *j*
56: 7 give them *j* in my house of prayer.
58:14 then you will find your *j*
60: 5 heart will throb and swell with *j*;
60:15 and the *j* of all generations.
61: 7 and everlasting *j* will be theirs.
65:14 out of the *j* of their hearts,
65:18 and its people a *j*.
66: 5 that we may see your *j*!'
Jer 7:34 will bring an end to the sounds of *j*
15:16 they were my *j* and my heart's
16: 9 will bring an end to the sounds of *j*
25:10 banish from them the sounds of *j*
31: 7 "Sing with *j* for Jacob;
31:12 shout for *j* on the heights of Zion;
31:13 give them comfort and *j* instead
33: 9 this city will bring me renown, *j*,
33:11 be heard once more the sounds of *j*
48:33 *J* and gladness are gone
48:33 no one treads them with shouts of *j*
48:33 they are not shouts of *j*.
51:48 will shout for *j* over Babylon,
La 2:15 the *j* of the whole earth?"
5:15 *J* is gone from our hearts;
Eze 7: 7 not *j*, upon the mountains.
24:25 their *j* and glory, the delight
Joel 1:12 Surely the *j* of mankind
1:16 *j* and gladness
Mt 13:20 and at once receives it with *j*.
13:44 in his *j* went and sold all he had
28: 8 afraid yet filled with *j*,
Mk 4:16 and at once receive it with *j*.
Lk 1:14 He will be a *j* and delight to you,
1:44 the baby in my womb leaped for *j*.
1:58 great mercy, and they shared her *j*.
2:10 news of great *j* that will be
6:23 "Rejoice in that day and leap for *j*,
8:13 the word with *j* when they hear it,
10:17 The seventy-two returned with *j*
10:21 full of *j* through the Holy Spirit,
24:41 still did not believe it because of *j*

Lk 24:52 returned to Jerusalem with great *j.*
Jn 3:29 That *j* is mine, and it is now
3:29 full of *j* when he hears
15:11 and that your *j* may be complete.
15:11 this so that my *j* may be in you
16:20 but your grief will turn to *j.*
16:21 because of her *j* that a child is born
16:22 and no one will take away your *j.*
16:24 and your *j* will be complete.
17:13 measure of my *j* within them.
Ac 2:28 with *j* in your presence.'
8: 8 So there was great *j* in that city.
13:52 And the disciples were filled with *j*
14:17 and fills your hearts with *j.*"
16:34 he was filled with *j* because he had come
Ro 14:17 peace and *j* in the Holy Spirit,
15:13 the God of hope fill you with all *j*
15:32 will I may come to you with *j*
16:19 so I am full of *j* over you;
2Co 1:24 but we work with you for your *j,*
2: 3 that you would all share my *j.*
7: 4 our troubles my *j* knows no
7: 7 so that my *j* was greater than ever.
8: 2 their overflowing *j* and their
Gal 4:15 What has happened to all your *j?*
5:22 *j,* peace, patience, kindness,
Php 1: 4 I always pray with *j*
1:25 for your progress and *j* in the faith,
1:26 being with you again your *j*
2: 2 then make my *j* complete
2:29 him in the Lord with great *j,*
4: 1 and long for, my *j* and crown,
1Th 1: 6 with the *j* given by the Holy Spirit.
2:19 For what is our hope, our *j,*
2:20 Indeed, you are our glory and *j.*
3: 9 you in return for all the *j* we have
2Ti 1: 4 so that I may be filled with *j.*
Phm : 7 Your love has given me great *j*
Heb 1: 9 by anointing you with the oil of *j.*"
12: 2 for the *j* set before him endured
13:17 them so that their work will be a *j,*
Jas 1: 2 Consider it pure *j,* my brothers,
4: 9 to mourning and your *j* to gloom.
1Pe 1: 8 with an inexpressible and glorious *j*
1Jn 1: 4 this to make our *j* complete.
2Jn : 4 It has given me great *j* to find some
:12 so that our *j* may be complete.
3Jn : 3 It gave me great *j* to have some
: 4 I have no greater *j*
Jude :24 without fault and with great *j*—

JOYFUL* (JOY)
Dt 16:14 Be *j* at your Feast—you, your sons
1Sa 18: 6 with *j* songs and with tambourines
1Ki 8:66 *j* and glad in heart
1Ch 15:16 as singers to sing *j* songs,
2Ch 7:10 *j* and glad in heart
Ps 68: 3 may they be happy and *j.*
100: 2 come before him with *j* songs.
Ecc 9: 7 and drink your wine with a *j* heart,
Isa 24: 8 the *j* harp is silent.
Jer 31: 4 and go out to dance with the *j.*
Hab 3:18 I will be *j* in God my Savior.
Zec 8:19 and tenth months will become *j*
10: 7 Their children will see it and be *j;*
Ro 12:12 Be *j* in hope, patient in affliction,
1Th 5:16 Be *j* always; pray continually;
Heb 12:22 thousands of angels in *j* assembly,

JOYOUS* (JOY)
Est 8:15 the city of Susa held a *j* celebration.

JUBILANT
Ps 96:12 let the fields be *j,* and everything
98: 4 burst into *j* song with music;

JUBILEE
Lev 25:11 The fiftieth year shall be a *j* for you;

JUDAH (JUDEA)
1. Son of Jacob by Leah (Ge 29:35; 35:23; 1Ch 2:1). Did not want to kill Joseph (Ge 37:26–27). Among Canaanites, fathered Perez by Tamar (Ge 38). Tribe of blessed as ruling tribe (Ge 49:8–12; Dt 33:7), numbered (Nu 1:27; 26:22), allotted land (Jos 15; Eze 48:7), failed to fully possess (Jos 15:63; Jdg 1:1–20).
2. Name used for people and land of Southern Kingdom.
Ru 1: 7 take them back to the land of *J.*
2Sa 2: 4 king over the house of *J.*
Isa 1: 1 The vision concerning *J*
3: 8 *J* is falling;
Jer 13:19 All *J* will be carried into exile,
30: 3 bring my people Israel and *J* back
Hos 1: 7 I will show love to the house of *J;*
Zec 10: 4 From *J* will come the cornerstone,
Mt 2: 6 least among the rulers of *J;*
Heb 7:14 that our Lord descended from *J,*
8: 8 and with the house of *J.*
Rev 5: 5 of the tribe of *J,* the Root of David,

JUDAISM (JEW)
Ac 13:43 devout converts to *J* followed Paul
Gal 1:13 of my previous way of life in *J,*
1:14 advancing in *J* beyond many Jews

JUDAS
1. Apostle; son of James (Lk 6:16; Jn 14:22; Ac 1:13). Probably also called Thaddaeus (Mt 10:3; Mk 3:18).
2. Brother of James and Jesus (Mt 13:55; Mk 6:3), also called Jude (Jude 1).
3. Christian prophet (Ac 15:22–32).
4. Apostle, also called Iscariot, who betrayed Jesus (Mt 10:4; 26:14–56; Mk 3:19; 14:10–50; Lk 6:16; 22:3–53; Jn 6:71; 12:4; 13:2–30; 18:2–11). Suicide of (Mt 27:3–5; Ac 1:16–25).

JUDEA (JUDAH)
Mt 2: 1 born in Bethlehem in *J,*
24:16 are in *J* flee to the mountains.
Lk 3: 1 Pontius Pilate was governor of *J,*
Ac 1: 8 and in all *J* and Samaria,
9:31 Then the church throughout *J,*
1Th 2:14 imitators of God's churches in *J,*

JUDGE (JUDGED JUDGES JUDGING JUDGMENT JUDGMENTS)
Ge 16: 5 May the LORD *j* between you
18:25 Will not the *J* of all the earth do
Lev 19:15 but *j* your neighbor fairly.
Dt 1:16 between your brothers and *j* fairly,
17:12 man who shows contempt for the *j*
32:36 The LORD will *j* his people
Jdg 2:18 Whenever the LORD raised up a *j*
1Sa 2:10 the LORD will *j* the ends
3:13 that I would *j* his family forever
7:15 *j* over Israel all the days of his life.
24:12 May the LORD *j* between you
1Ki 8:32 *J* between your servants,
1Ch 16:33 for he comes to *j* the earth.
2Ch 6:23 *J* between your servants, repaying
19: 7 *J* carefully, for with the LORD our
Job 9:15 plead with my *J* for mercy.
Ps 7: 8 *J* me, O LORD, according
7: 8 let the LORD *j* the peoples.
7:11 God is a righteous *j,*
9: 8 He will *j* the world in righteousness
50: 6 for God himself is *j.*
51: 4 and justified when you *j.*
75: 2 it is I who *j* uprightly.
76: 9 when you, O God, rose up to *j,*
82: 8 Rise up, O God, *j* the earth,
94: 2 Rise up, O *J* of the earth;
96:10 he will *j* the peoples with equity.
96:13 He will *j* the world in righteousness
98: 9 He will *j* the world in righteousness
110: 6 He will *j* the nations, heaping up
Pr 31: 9 Speak up and *j* fairly;
Isa 2: 4 He will *j* between the nations
3:13 he rises to *j* the people.
11: 3 He will not *j* by what he sees
33:22 For the LORD is our *j,*
Jer 11:20 Almighty, you who *j* righteously
Eze 7: 3 I will *j* you according
7:27 by their own standards I will *j* them
18:30 O house of Israel, I will *j* you,
20:36 so I will *j* you, declares
22: 2 "Son of man, will you *j* her?
34:17 I will *j* between one sheep
Joel 3:12 sit to *j* all the nations on every side.
Mic 3:11 Her leaders *j* for a bribe,
4: 3 He will *j* between many peoples
Mt 7: 1 Do not *j,* or you too will be judged.
Lk 6:37 "Do not *j,* and you will not be
18: 2 there was a *j* who neither feared
Jn 5:27 And he has given him authority to *j*
5:30 By myself I can do nothing; I *j* only
8:16 But if I do *j,* my decisions are right,
12:47 For I did not come to *j* the world,
12:48 There is a *j* for the one who rejects
Ac 10:42 as *j* of the living and the dead.
17:31 a day when he will *j* the world
Ro 2:16 day when God will *j* men's secrets
3: 6 how could God *j* the world?
14:10 then, why do you *j* your brother?
1Co 4: 3 indeed, I do not even *j* myself.
4: 5 Therefore *j* nothing
6: 2 And if you are to *j* the world,
6: 2 that the saints will *j* the world?
Gal 2: 6 not *j* by external appearance—
Col 2:16 Therefore do not let anyone *j* you
2Ti 4: 1 who will *j* the living and the dead,
4: 8 which the Lord, the righteous *J,*
Heb 10:30 "The Lord will *j* his people."
12:23 come to God, the *j* of all men,
13: 4 for God will *j* the adulterer
Jas 4:12 There is only one Lawgiver and *J,*
4:12 who are you to *j* your neighbor?
1Pe 4: 5 to him who is ready to *j* the living
Rev 20: 4 who had been given authority to *j.*

JUDGED (JUDGE)
Mt 7: 1 "Do not judge, or you too will be *j.*
1Co 4: 3 I care very little if I am *j* by you
10:29 For why should my freedom be *j*
11:31 But if we *j* ourselves, we would not
14:24 all that he is a sinner and will be *j*
Jas 3: 1 who teach will be *j* more strictly.
Rev 20:12 The dead were *j* according

JUDGES (JUDGE)
Jdg 2:16 Then the LORD raised up *j,*
Job 9:24 he blindfolds its *j.*
Ps 58:11 there is a God who *j* the earth."
75: 7 But it is God who *j:*
Pr 29:14 If a king *j* the poor with fairness,
Jn 5:22 Moreover, the Father *j* no one,
1Co 4: 4 It is the Lord who *j* me.
Heb 4:12 it *j* the thoughts and attitudes
1Pe 1:17 on a Father who *j* each man's work
2:23 himself to him who *j* justly.
Rev 19:11 With justice he *j* and makes war.

JUDGING (JUDGE)
Ps 9: 4 on your throne, *j* righteously.
Pr 24:23 To show partiality in *j* is not good:
Isa 16: 5 one who in *j* seeks justice
Mt 19:28 *j* the twelve tribes of Israel.
Jn 7:24 Stop *j* by mere appearances,

JUDGMENT (JUDGE)
Nu 33: 4 for the LORD had brought *j*
Dt 1:17 of any man, for *j* belongs to God.
32:41 and my hand grasps it in *j,*
1Sa 25:33 May you be blessed for your good *j*
Ps 1: 5 the wicked will not stand in the *j,*
9: 7 he has established his throne for *j.*
76: 8 From heaven you pronounced *j,*
82: 1 he gives *j* among the "gods":

JUDGMENTS (JUDGE)

JUG

JUST* (JUSTICE JUSTIFICATION JUSTIFIED JUSTIFIES JUSTIFY JUSTIFYING JUSTLY)

JUSTICE* (JUST)

Am 5: 7 You who turn *j* into bitterness
5:12 and you deprive the poor of *j*
5:15 maintain *j* in the courts.
5:24 But let *j* roll on like a river,
6:12 But you have turned *j* into poison
Mic 3: 1 Should you not know *j*,
3: 8 and with *j* and might,
3: 9 who despise *j*
Hab 1: 4 and *j* never prevails.
1: 4 so that *j* is perverted.
Zep 3: 5 by morning he dispenses his *j*,
Zec 7: 9 'Administer true *j*; show mercy
Mal 2:17 or "Where is the God of *j*?"
3: 5 and deprive aliens of *j*,
Mt 12:18 he will proclaim *j* to the nations.
12:20 till he leads *j* to victory.
23:23 important matters of the law—*j*,
Lk 11:42 you neglect *j* and the love of God.
18: 3 'Grant me *j* against my adversary.'
18: 5 I will see that she gets *j*,
18: 7 And will not God bring about *j*
18: 8 he will see that they get *j*,
Ac 8:33 humiliation he was deprived of *j*.
17:31 with *j* by the man he has appointed.
28: 4 *J* has not allowed him to live."
Ro 3:25 He did this to demonstrate his *j*,
3:26 it to demonstrate his *j*
2Co 7:11 what readiness to see *j* done.
Heb 11:33 administered *j*, and gained what
Rev 19:11 With *j* he judges and makes war.

JUSTIFICATION* (JUST)
Eze 16:52 for you have furnished some *j*
Ro 4:25 and was raised to life for our *j*.
5:16 many trespasses and brought *j*.
5:18 of righteousness was *j* that brings

JUSTIFIED* (JUST)
Ps 51: 4 and *j* when you judge.
Lk 18:14 rather than the other, went home *j*
Ac 13:39 from everything you could not be *j*
13:39 him everyone who believes is *j*
Ro 3:24 and are *j* freely by his grace
3:28 For we maintain that a man is *j*
4: 2 If, in fact, Abraham was *j* by works,
5: 1 since we have been *j* through faith,
5: 9 Since we have now been *j*
8:30 those he called, he also *j*; those he *j*,
10:10 heart that you believe and are *j*,
1Co 6:11 you were *j* in the name
Gal 2:16 in Christ Jesus that we may be *j*
2:16 observing the law no one will be *j*.
2:16 sinners' know that a man is not *j*
2:17 "If, while we seek to be *j* in Christ,
3:11 Clearly no one is *j* before God
3:24 to Christ that we might be *j* by faith
5: 4 to be *j* by law have been alienated
Tit 3: 7 so that, having been *j* by his grace,
Jas 2:24 You see that a person is *j*

JUSTIFIES* (JUST)
Ro 3:26 one who *j* those who have faith
4: 5 but trusts God who *j* the wicked,
8:33 God has chosen? It is God who *j*.

JUSTIFY* (JUST)
Est 7: 4 such distress would *j* disturbing
Job 40: 8 you condemn me to *j* yourself?
Isa 53:11 my righteous servant will *j* many,
Lk 10:29 But he wanted to *j* himself,
16:15 "You are the ones who *j* yourselves
Ro 3:30 who will *j* the circumcised by faith
Gal 3: 8 that God would *j* the Gentiles

JUSTIFYING* (JUST)
Job 32: 2 angry with Job for *j* himself rather

JUSTLY* (JUST)
Ps 58: 1 Do you rulers indeed speak *j*?
67: 4 for you rule the peoples *j*
Jer 7: 5 and deal with each other *j*,
Mic 6: 8 To act *j* and to love mercy
Lk 23:41 We are punished *j*,
1Pe 2:23 himself to him who judges *j*.

KADESH
Nu 20: 1 of Zin, and they stayed at *K*.
Dt 1:46 And so you stayed in *K* many days

KADESH BARNEA
Nu 32: 8 I sent them from *K* to look over

KEBAR
Eze 1: 1 among the exiles by the *K* River,

KEDORLAOMER
Ge 14:17 Abram returned from defeating *K*

KEEP (KEEPER KEEPING KEEPS KEPT)
Ge 31:49 "May the LORD *k* watch
Ex 15:26 his commands and *k* all his
20: 6 and *k* my commandments.
Lev 15:31 You must *k* the Israelites separate
Nu 6:24 and *k* you;
Dt 4: 2 but *k* the commands of the LORD
6:17 Be sure to *k* the commands
7: 9 who love him and *k* his commands.
7:12 your God will *k* his covenant
11: 1 your God and *k* his requirements,
13: 4 *K* his commands and obey him;
30:10 your God and *k* his commands
30:16 and to *k* his commands, decrees
Jos 22: 5 careful to *k* the commandment
1Ki 8:58 and to *k* the commands,
2Ki 17:19 Judah did not *k* the commands
23: 3 the LORD and *k* his commands,
1Ch 29:18 and *k* their hearts loyal to you.
2Ch 6:14 you who *k* your covenant of love
34:31 the LORD and *k* his commands,
Job 14:16 but not *k* track of my sin.
Ps 18:28 You, O LORD, *k* my lamp burning
19:13 *K* your servant also from willful
78:10 they did not *k* God's covenant
119: 2 Blessed are they who *k* his statutes
119: 9 can a young man *k* his way pure?
121: 7 The LORD will *k* you
141: 3 *k* watch over the door of my lips.
Pr 4:21 *k* them within your heart;
4:24 *k* corrupt talk far from your lips.
30: 8 *K* falsehood and lies far from me;
Ecc 3: 6 a time to *k* and a time
12:13 and *k* his commandments,
Isa 26: 3 You will *k* in perfect peace
42: 6 I will *k* you and will make you
58:13 "If you *k* your feet
Jer 16:11 forsook me and did not *k* my law.
Eze 20:19 and be careful to *k* my laws.
Mt 10:10 for the worker is worth his *k*.
Lk 12:35 and *k* your lamps burning,
17:33 tries to *k* his life will lose it,
Jn 10:24 How long will you *k* us in suspense
12:25 in this world will *k* it for eternal life
Ac 2:24 for death to *k* its hold on him.
18: 9 "Do not be afraid; *k* on speaking,
Ro 7:19 want to do—this I *k* on doing.
12:11 but *k* your spiritual fervor,
14:22 you believe about these things *k*
16:17 *K* away from them.
1Co 1: 8 He will *k* you strong to the end,
2Co 12: 7 To *k* me from becoming conceited
Gal 5:25 let us *k* in step with the Spirit.
Eph 4: 3 Make every effort to *k* the unity
2Th 3: 6 to *k* away from every brother who
1Ti 5:22 *K* yourself pure.
2Ti 4: 5 *k* your head in all situations,
Heb 9:20 God has commanded you to *k*."
13: 5 *K* your lives free from the love
Jas 1:26 and yet does not *k* a tight rein
2: 8 If you really *k* the royal law found
3: 2 able to *k* his whole body in check.
2Pe 1: 8 will *k* you from being ineffective
Jude :21 *K* yourselves in God's love
Jude :24 able to *k* you from falling
Rev 3:10 also *k* you from the hour
22: 9 of all who *k* the words of this book.

KEEPER (KEEP)
Ge 4: 9 I my brother's *k*?" The LORD

KEEPING (KEEP)
Ex 20: 8 the Sabbath day by *k* it holy.
Dt 5:12 the Sabbath day by *k* it holy,
13:18 *k* all his commands that I am
Ps 19:11 in *k* them there is great reward.
119:112 My heart is set on *k* your decrees
Pr 15: 3 *k* watch on the wicked
Mt 3: 8 Produce fruit in *k* with repentance.
Lk 2: 8 *k* watch over their flocks at night.
1Co 7:19 *K* God's commands is what counts.
2Co 8: 5 and then to us in *k* with God's will.
Jas 4:11 you are not *k* it, but sitting
1Pe 3:16 and respect, *k* a clear conscience,
2Pe 3: 9 Lord is not slow in *k* his promise,

KEEPS (KEEP)
Ne 1: 5 who *k* his covenant of love
Ps 15: 4 who *k* his oath
Pr 12:23 A prudent man *k* his knowledge
15:21 of understanding *k* a straight
17:28 a fool is thought wise if he *k* silent,
29:11 a wise man *k* himself under control
Isa 56: 2 who *k* the Sabbath
Da 9: 4 who *k* his covenant of love
Am 5:13 Therefore the prudent man *k* quiet
Jn 7:19 Yet not one of you *k* the law.
8:51 if anyone *k* my word, he will never
1Co 13: 5 is not easily angered, it *k* no record
Jas 2:10 For whoever *k* the whole law
Rev 22: 7 Blessed is he who *k* the words

KEILAH
1Sa 23:13 that David had escaped from *K*,

KEPT (KEEP)
Ex 12:42 Because the LORD *k* vigil that
Dt 7: 8 and *k* the oath he swore
2Ki 18: 6 he *k* the commands the LORD had
Ne 9: 8 You have *k* your promise
Ps 130: 3 If you, O LORD, *k* a record of sins,
Isa 38:17 In your love you *k* me
Mt 19:20 these I have *k*," the young man
2Co 11: 9 I have *k* myself from being
2Ti 4: 7 finished the race, I have *k* the faith.
1Pe 1: 4 spoil or fade—*k* in heaven for you,

KERNEL
Mk 4:28 then the full *k* in the head.
Jn 12:24 a *k* of wheat falls to the ground

KEY (KEYS)
Isa 33: 6 the fear of the LORD is the *k*
Rev 20: 1 having the *k* to the Abyss

KEYS* (KEY)
Mt 16:19 I will give you the *k* of the kingdom
Rev 1:18 And I hold the *k* of death

KICK*
Ac 26:14 for you to *k* against the goads.'

KILL (KILLED KILLS)
Ecc 3: 3 a time to *k* and a time to heal,
Mt 10:28 *k* the body but cannot *k* the soul.
17:23 They will *k* him, and on the third
Mk 9:31 will *k* him, and after three days
10:34 spit on him, flog him and *k* him.

KILLED (KILL)
Ge 4: 8 his brother Abel and *k* him.
Ex 2:12 he *k* the Egyptian and hid him
13:15 the LORD *k* every firstborn
Nu 35:11 who has *k* someone accidentally
1Sa 17:50 down the Philistine and *k* him.
Ne 9:26 They *k* your prophets, who had

Hos 6: 5 I *k* you with the words
Lk 11:48 they *k* the prophets, and you build
Ac 3:15 You *k* the author of life,

KILLS (KILL)
Ex 21:12 *k* him shall surely be put to death.
Lev 24:21 but whoever *k* a man must be put
2Co 3: 6 for the letter *k*, but the Spirit gives

KIND (KINDNESS KINDNESSES KINDS)
Ge 1:24 animals, each according to its *k*."
2Ch 10: 7 "If you will be *k* to these people
Pr 11:17 A *k* man benefits himself,
12:25 but a *k* word cheers him up.
14:21 blessed is he who is *k* to the needy.
14:31 whoever is *k* to the needy honors
19:17 He who is *k* to the poor lends
Da 4:27 by being *k* to the oppressed.
Lk 6:35 because he is *k* to the ungrateful
1Co 13: 4 Love is patient, love is *k*.
15:35 With what *k* of body will they
Eph 4:32 Be *k* and compassionate
1Th 5:15 but always try to be *k* to each other
2Ti 2:24 instead, he must be *k* to everyone,
Tit 2: 5 to be busy at home, to be *k*,

KINDHEARTED* (HEART)
Pr 11:16 A *k* woman gains respect,

KINDNESS (KIND)
Ge 24:12 and show *k* to my master Abraham
32:10 I am unworthy of all the *k*
39:21 he showed him *k* and granted him
Jdg 8:35 failed to show *k* to the family
Ru 2:20 has not stopped showing his *k*
2Sa 9: 3 to whom I can show God's *k*?"
22:51 he shows unfailing *k*
Ps 18:50 he shows unfailing *k*
141: 5 righteous man strike me—it is a *k*;
Isa 54: 8 but with everlasting *k*
Jer 9:24 I am the LORD, who exercises *k*,
Hos 11: 4 I led them with cords of human *k*,
Ac 14:17 He has shown *k* by giving you rain
Ro 11:22 Consider therefore the *k*
2Co 6: 6 understanding, patience and *k*;
Gal 5:22 peace, patience, *k*, goodness,
Eph 2: 7 expressed in his *k* to us
Col 3:12 yourselves with compassion, *k*,
Tit 3: 4 But when the *k* and love
2Pe 1: 7 brotherly *k*; and to brotherly *k*,

KINDNESSES* (KIND)
Ps 106: 7 did not remember your many *k*,
Isa 63: 7 I will tell of the *k* of the LORD,
63: 7 to his compassion and many *k*.

KINDS (KIND)
Ge 1:12 bearing seed according to their *k*
1Co 12: 4 There are different *k* of gifts,
1Ti 6:10 of money is a root of all *k* of evil.
1Pe 1: 6 had to suffer grief in all *k* of trials.

KING (KING'S KINGDOM KINGDOMS KINGS)

1. Kings of Judah and Israel: see Saul, David, Solomon.

2. Kings of Judah: see Rehoboam, Abijah, Asa, Jehoshaphat, Jehoram, Ahaziah, Athaliah (Queen), Joash, Amaziah, Azariah (Uzziah), Jotham, Ahaz, Hezekiah, Manasseh, Amon, Josiah, Jehoahaz, Jehoiakim, Jehoiachin, Zedekiah.

3. Kings of Israel: see Jeroboam I, Nadab, Baasha, Elah, Zimri, Tibni, Omri, Ahab, Ahaziah, Joram, Jehu, Jehoahaz, Jehoash, Jeroboam II, Zechariah, Shallum, Menahem, Pekah, Pekahiah, Hoshea.

Ex 1: 8 a new *k*, who did not know about
Dt 17:14 "Let us set a *k* over us like all
Jdg 17: 6 In those days Israel had no *k*;
1Sa 8: 5 now appoint a *k* to lead us,
11:15 as *k* in the presence of the LORD.
1Sa 12:12 the LORD your God was your *k*.
2Sa 2: 4 and there they anointed David *k*
1Ki 1:30 Solomon your son shall be *k*
Ps 2: 6 "I have installed my *K*
24: 7 that the *K* of glory may come in.
44: 4 You are my *K* and my God,
47: 7 For God is the *K* of all the earth;
Isa 32: 1 See, a *k* will reign in righteousness
Jer 30: 9 and David their *k*,
Hos 3: 5 their God and David their *k*.
Mic 2:13 *k* will pass through before them,
Zec 9: 9 See, your *k* comes to you,
Mt 2: 2 is the one who has been born *k*
27:11 "Are you the *k* of the Jews?" "Yes,
Lk 19:38 "Blessed is the *k* who comes
23: 3 "Are you the *k* of the Jews?" "Yes,
23:38 THE *K* OF THE JEWS.
Jn 1:49 of God; you are the *K* of Israel."
12:13 "Blessed is the *K* of Israel!"
Ac 17: 7 saying that there is another *k*,
1Ti 1:17 Now to the *K* eternal, immortal,
6:15 the *K* of kings and Lord of lords,
Heb 7: 1 This Melchizedek was *k* of Salem
1Pe 2:13 to the *k*, as the supreme authority,
2:17 of believers, fear God, honor the *k*.
Rev 15: 3 *K* of the ages.
17:14 he is Lord of lords and *K* of kings—
19:16 *K* OF KINGS AND LORD

KING'S (KING)
Pr 21: 1 The *k* heart is in the hand
Ecc 8: 3 in a hurry to leave the *k* presence.

KINGDOM (KING)
Ex 19: 6 you will be for me a *k* of priests
Dt 17:18 When he takes the throne of his *k*,
2Sa 7:12 body, and I will establish his *k*.
1Ki 11:31 to tear the *k* out of Solomon's hand
1Ch 17:11 own sons, and I will establish his *k*.
29:11 Yours, O LORD, is the *k*;
Ps 45: 6 justice will be the scepter of your *k*.
103:19 and his *k* rules over all.
145:11 They will tell of the glory of your *k*
Eze 29:14 There they will be a lowly *k*.
Da 2:39 "After you, another *k* will rise,
4: 3 His *k* is an eternal *k*;
7:27 His *k* will be an everlasting *k*,
Ob :21 And the *k* will be the LORD's.
Mt 3: 2 Repent, for the *k* of heaven is near
4:17 Repent, for the *k* of heaven is near
4:23 preaching the good news of the *k*,
5: 3 for theirs is the *k* of heaven.
5:10 for theirs is the *k* of heaven.
5:19 great in the *k* of heaven.
5:19 least in the *k* of heaven,
5:20 you will certainly not enter the *k*
6:10 your *k* come,
6:33 But seek first his *k* and his
7:21 Lord,' will enter the *k* of heaven,
8:11 Isaac and Jacob in the *k* of heaven.
8:12 the subjects of the *k* will be thrown
9:35 preaching the good news of the *k*
10: 7 preach this message: 'The *k*
11:11 least in the *k* of heaven is greater
11:12 the *k* of heaven has been forcefully
12:25 "Every *k* divided against itself will
12:26 How then can his *k* stand?
12:28 then the *k* of God has come
13:11 knowledge of the secrets of the *k*
13:19 hears the message about the *k*
13:24 "The *k* of heaven is like a man who
13:31 *k* of heaven is like a mustard seed,
13:33 "The *k* of heaven is like yeast that
13:38 stands for the sons of the *k*.
13:41 of his *k* everything that causes sin
13:43 the sun in the *k* of their Father.
13:44 *k* of heaven is like treasure hidden
13:45 the *k* of heaven is like a merchant
13:47 *k* of heaven is like a net that was let
13:52 has been instructed about the *k*
16:19 the keys of the *k* of heaven;
Mt 16:28 the Son of Man coming in his *k*."
18: 1 the greatest in the *k* of heaven?"
18: 3 you will never enter the *k*
18: 4 the greatest in the *k* of heaven.
18:23 the *k* of heaven is like a king who
19:12 because of the *k* of heaven.
19:14 for the *k* of heaven belongs to such
19:23 man to enter the *k* of heaven.
19:24 for a rich man to enter the *k* of God
20: 1 "For the *k* of heaven is like
20:21 the other at your left in your *k*."
21:31 the prostitutes are entering the *k*
21:43 "Therefore I tell you that the *k*
22: 2 "The *k* of heaven is like a king who
23:13 You shut the *k* of heaven
24: 7 rise against nation, and *k* against *k*.
24:14 gospel of the *k* will be preached
25: 1 "At that time the *k*
25:34 the *k* prepared for you
26:29 anew with you in my Father's *k*."
Mk 1:15 "The *k* of God is near.
3:24 If a *k* is divided against itself,
3:24 against itself, that *k* cannot stand.
4:11 "The secret of the *k*
4:26 "This is what the *k* of God is like.
4:30 "What shall we say the *k*
6:23 I will give you, up to half my *k*."
9: 1 before they see the *k* of God come
9:47 better for you to enter the *k* of God
10:14 for the *k* of God belongs to such
10:15 anyone who will not receive the *k*
10:23 for the rich to enter the *k* of God!"
10:24 how hard it is to enter the *k* of God
10:25 for a rich man to enter the *k* of God
11:10 "Blessed is the coming *k*
12:34 "You are not far from the *k* of God
13: 8 rise against nation, and *k* against *k*.
14:25 day when I drink it anew in the *k*
15:43 who was himself waiting for the *k*
Lk 1:33 Jacob forever; his *k* will never
4:43 of the *k* of God to the other towns
6:20 for yours is the *k* of God.
7:28 in the *k* of God is greater than he."
8: 1 proclaiming the good news of the *k*
8:10 knowledge of the secrets of the *k*
9: 2 out to preach the *k* of God
9:11 spoke to them about the *k* of God,
9:27 before they see the *k* of God."
9:60 you go and proclaim the *k* of God
9:62 fit for service in the *k* of God."
10: 9 'The *k* of God is near you.'
10:11 sure of this: The *k* of God is near.'
11: 2 your *k* come.
11:17 "Any *k* divided against itself will
11:18 himself, how can his *k* stand?
11:20 then the *k* of God has come to you.
12:31 seek his *k*, and these things will be
12:32 has been pleased to give you the *k*.
13:18 "What is the *k* of God like?
13:20 What shall I compare the *k* of God
13:28 all the prophets in the *k* of God,
13:29 places at the feast in the *k* of God.
14:15 eat at the feast in the *k* of God."
16:16 the good news of the *k*
17:20 when the *k* of God would come,
17:20 *k* of God does not come with careful
17:21 because the *k* of God is within you
18:16 for the *k* of God belongs to such
18:17 anyone who will not receive the *k*
18:24 for the rich to enter the *k* of God!
18:25 for a rich man to enter the *k* of God
18:29 for the sake of the *k* of God will fail
19:11 and the people thought that the *k*
21:10 rise against nation, and *k* against *k*.
21:31 you know that the *k* of God is near.
22:16 until it finds fulfillment in the *k*
22:18 the vine until the *k* of God comes."
22:29 And I confer on you a *k*, just
22:30 and drink at my table in my *k*
23:42 me when you come into your *k*."

Lk 23:51 he was waiting for the *k* of God.
Jn 3: 3 no one can see the *k* of God.
3: 5 no one can enter the *k* of God.
18:36 now my *k* is from another place."
18:36 "My *k* is not of this world.
Ac 1: 3 and spoke about the *k* of God.
1: 6 going to restore the *k* to Israel?"
8:12 he preached the good news of the *k*
14:22 hardships to enter the *k* of God,"
19: 8 arguing persuasively about the *k*
20:25 about preaching the *k* will ever see
28:23 and declared to them the *k* of God
28:31 hindrance he preached the *k*
Ro 14:17 For the *k* of God is not a matter
1Co 4:20 For the *k* of God is not a matter
6: 9 the wicked will not inherit the *k*
6:10 swindlers will inherit the *k* of God.
15:24 hands over the *k* to God the Father
15:50 blood cannot inherit the *k* of God,
Gal 5:21 live like this will not inherit the *k*
Eph 2: 2 and of the ruler of the *k* of the air,
5: 5 has any inheritance in the *k*
Col 1:12 of the saints in the *k* of light.
1:13 and brought us into the *k*
4:11 among my fellow workers for the *k*
1Th 2:12 who calls you into his *k* and glory.
2Th 1: 5 will be counted worthy of the *k*
2Ti 4: 1 in view of his appearing and his *k*,
4:18 bring me safely to his heavenly *k*.
Heb 1: 8 will be the scepter of your *k*.
12:28 we are receiving a *k* that cannot be
Jas 2: 5 to inherit the *k* he promised those
2Pe 1:11 into the eternal *k* of our Lord
Rev 1: 6 has made us to be a *k* and priests
1: 9 companion in the suffering and *k*
5:10 You have made them to be a *k*
11:15 of the world has become the *k*
11:15 "The *k* of the world has become
12:10 the power and the *k* of our God,
16:10 his *k* was plunged into darkness.
17:12 who have not yet received a *k*,

KINGDOMS (KING)
2Ki 19:15 God over all the *k* of the earth.
19:19 so that all *k* on earth may know
2Ch 20: 6 rule over all the *k* of the nations.
Ps 68:32 Sing to God, O *k* of the earth,
Isa 37:16 God over all the *k* of the earth.
37:20 so that all *k* on earth may know
Eze 29:15 It will be the lowliest of *k*
37:22 or be divided into two *k*.
Da 4:17 Most High is sovereign over the *k*
7:17 great beasts are four *k* that will rise
Zep 3: 8 to gather the *k*

KINGS (KING)
Ps 2: 2 The *k* of the earth take their stand
47: 9 for the *k* of the earth belong to God
68:29 *k* will bring you gifts.
72:11 All *k* will bow down to him
110: 5 he will crush *k* on the day
149: 8 to bind their *k* with fetters,
Pr 16:12 *K* detest wrongdoing,
Isa 24:21 and the *k* on the earth below.
52:15 and *k* will shut their mouths
60:11 their *k* led in triumphal procession.
Da 2:21 he sets up *k* and deposes them.
7:24 ten horns are ten *k* who will come
Lk 21:12 and you will be brought before *k*
1Co 4: 8 You have become *k*—
1Ti 2: 2 for *k* and all those in authority,
6:15 the King of *k* and Lord of lords,
Rev 1: 5 and the ruler of the *k* of the earth.
17:14 he is Lord of lords and King of *k*—
19:16 KING OF *K* AND LORD

KINSMAN-REDEEMER (REDEEM)
Ru 3: 9 over me, since you are a *k*."
4:14 day has not left you without a *k*.

KISS (KISSED KISSES)
Ps 2:12 *K* the Son, lest he be angry
Pr 24:26 is like a *k* on the lips.
SS 1: 2 *Beloved* Let him *k* me
8: 1 I would *k* you,
Lk 22:48 the Son of Man with a *k*?"
Ro 16:16 Greet one another with a holy *k*.
1Co 16:20 Greet one another with a holy *k*.
2Co 13:12 Greet one another with a holy *k*.
1Th 5:26 Greet all the brothers with a holy *k*
1Pe 5:14 Greet one another with a *k* of love.

KISSED (KISS)
Mk 14:45 Judas said, "Rabbi!" and *k* him.
Lk 7:38 *k* them and poured perfume

KISSES* (KISS)
Pr 27: 6 but an enemy multiplies *k*.
SS 1: 2 with the *k* of his mouth—

KNEE (KNEES)
Isa 45:23 Before me every *k* will bow;
Ro 14:11 'every *k* will bow before me;
Php 2:10 name of Jesus every *k* should bow,

KNEEL (KNELT)
Est 3: 2 But Mordecai would not *k* down
Ps 95: 6 let us *k* before the LORD our
Eph 3:14 For this reason I *k*

KNEES (KNEE)
1Ki 19:18 all whose *k* have not bowed
Isa 35: 3 steady the *k* that give way;
Da 6:10 times a day he got down on his *k*
Lk 5: 8 he fell at Jesus' *k* and said,
Heb 12:12 your feeble arms and weak *k*.

KNELT* (KNEEL)
1Ki 1:16 Bathsheba bowed low and *k*
2Ch 6:13 and then *k* down before the whole
7: 3 they *k* on the pavement
29:29 everyone present with him *k* down
Est 3: 2 officials at the king's gate *k* down
Mt 8: 2 and *k* before him and said,
9:18 a ruler came and *k* before him
15:25 The woman came and *k* before him
17:14 a man approached Jesus and *k*
27:29 *k* in front of him and mocked him.
Lk 22:41 *k* down and prayed, "Father,
Ac 20:36 he *k* down with all of them
21: 5 there on the beach we *k* to pray.

KNEW (KNOW)
2Ch 33:13 Manasseh *k* that the LORD is God
Job 23: 3 If only I *k* where to find him;
Pr 24:12 "But we *k* nothing about this,"
Jer 1: 5 you in the womb I *k* you,
Jnh 4: 2 I *k* that you are a gracious
Mt 7:23 tell them plainly, 'I never *k* you.
12:25 Jesus *k* their thoughts
Jn 2:24 himself to them, for he *k* all men.
14: 7 If you really *k* me, you would know

KNIFE
Ge 22:10 and took the *k* to slay his son.
Pr 23: 2 and put a *k* to your throat

KNOCK* (KNOCKS)
Mt 7: 7 *k* and the door will be opened
Lk 11: 9 *k* and the door will be opened
Rev 3:20 I am! I stand at the door and *k*.

KNOCKS (KNOCK)
Mt 7: 8 and to him who *k*, the door will be

KNOW (FOREKNEW FOREKNOWLEDGE KNEW KNOWING KNOWLEDGE KNOWN KNOWS)
Ge 22:12 Now I *k* that you fear God,
Ex 6: 7 you will *k* that I am the LORD
14: 4 and the Egyptians will *k* that I am
33:13 teach me your ways so I may *k* you
Dt 7: 9 *K* therefore that the LORD your
18:21 "How can we *k* when a message
Jos 4:24 of the earth might *k* that the hand
23:14 You *k* with all your heart
1Sa 17:46 the whole world will *k* that there is
1Ki 8:39 heart (for you alone *k* the hearts
Job 11: 6 *K* this: God has even forgotten
19:25 I *k* that my Redeemer lives,
42: 3 things too wonderful for me to *k*.
Ps 9:10 Those who *k* your name will trust
46:10 "Be still, and *k* that I am God;
100: 3 *K* that the LORD is God.
139: 1 and you *k* me.
139:23 Search me, O God, and *k* my heart;
145:12 so that all men may *k*
Pr 27: 1 for you do not *k* what a day may
30: 4 Tell me if you *k*!
Ecc 8: 5 wise heart will *k* the proper time
Isa 29:15 "Who sees us? Who will *k*?"
40:21 Do you not *k*?
Jer 6:15 they do not even *k* how to blush.
22:16 Is that not what it means to *k* me?"
24: 7 I will give them a heart to *k* me,
31:34 his brother, saying, '*K* the LORD,'
33: 3 unsearchable things you do not *k*.'
Eze 2: 5 they will *k* that a prophet has been
6:10 they will *k* that I am the LORD;
Da 11:32 people who *k* their God will firmly
Mt 6: 3 let your left hand *k* what your right
7:11 *k* how to give good gifts
9: 6 But so that you may *k* that the Son
22:29 you do not *k* the Scriptures
24:42 you do not *k* on what day your
26:74 "I don't *k* the man!" Immediately
Mk 12:24 you do not *k* the Scriptures
Lk 1: 4 so that you may *k* the certainty
11:13 *k* how to give good gifts
12:48 But the one who does not *k*
13:25 'I don't *k* you or where you come
21:31 you *k* that the kingdom of God is
23:34 for they do not *k* what they are
Jn 1:26 among you stands one you do not *k*
3:11 we speak of what we *k*,
4:22 we worship what we do *k*,
4:42 and we *k* that this man really is
6:69 and *k* that you are the Holy One
7:28 You do not *k* him, but I *k* him
8:14 for I *k* where I came from
8:19 "You do not *k* me or my Father,"
8:32 Then you will *k* the truth,
8:55 Though you do not *k* him, I *k* him.
9:25 One thing I do *k*.
10: 4 him because they *k* his voice.
10:14 I *k* my sheep and my sheep *k* me—
10:27 I *k* them, and they follow me.
12:35 the dark does not *k* where he is
13:17 Now that you *k* these things,
13:35 all men will *k* that you are my
14:17 you *k* him, for he lives with you
15:21 for they do not *k* the One who sent
16:30 we can see that you *k* all things
17: 3 that they may *k* you, the only true
17:23 to let the world *k* that you sent me
21:15 he said, "you *k* that I love you."
21:24 We *k* that his testimony is true.
Ac 1: 7 "It is not for you to *k* the times
1:24 "Lord, you *k* everyone's heart.
Ro 3:17 and the way of peace they do not *k*
6: 3 Or don't you *k* that all
6: 6 For we *k* that our old self was
6:16 Don't you *k* that when you offer
7:14 We *k* that the law is spiritual;
7:18 I *k* that nothing good lives in me,
8:22 We *k* that the whole creation has
8:26 We do not *k* what we ought to pray
8:28 we *k* that in all things God works
1Co 1:21 through its wisdom did not *k* him,
2: 2 For I resolved to *k* nothing
3:16 Don't you *k* that you yourselves
5: 6 Don't you *k* that a little yeast

1Co 6: 2 Do you not *k* that the saints will
6:15 Do you not *k* that your bodies are
6:16 Do you not *k* that he who unites
6:19 Do you not *k* that your body is
7:16 How do you *k*, wife, whether you
8: 2 does not yet *k* as he ought to *k*.
9:13 Don't you *k* that those who work
9:24 Do you not *k* that
13: 9 For we *k* in part and we prophesy
13:12 Now I *k* in part; then I shall *k* fully,
15:58 because you *k* that your labor
2Co 5: 1 we *k* that if the earthly tent we live
5:11 we *k* what it is to fear the Lord,
8: 9 For you *k* the grace
Gal 1:11 you to *k*, brothers, that the gospel I
2:16 not 'Gentile sinners' *k* that a man
Eph 1:17 so that you may *k* him better.
1:18 in order that you may *k* the hope
6: 8 you *k* that the Lord will reward
6: 9 since you *k* that he who is both
Php 3:10 I want to *k* Christ and the power
4:12 I *k* what it is to be in need,
Col 2: 2 order that they may *k* the mystery
4: 1 because you *k* that you
4: 6 so that you may *k* how
1Th 3: 3 You *k* quite well that we were
5: 2 for you *k* very well that the day
2Th 1: 8 punish those who do not *k* God
1Ti 1: 7 they do not *k* what they are talking
3: 5 (If anyone does not *k* how
3:15 you will *k* how people ought
2Ti 1:12 because I *k* whom I have believed,
2:23 you *k* they produce quarrels.
3:14 you *k* those from whom you
Heb 8:11 because they will all *k* me,
11: 8 he did not *k* where he was going.
Jas 1: 3 because you *k* that the testing
3: 1 you *k* that we who teach will be
4: 4 don't you *k* that friendship
4:14 *k* what will happen tomorrow.
1Pe 1:18 For you *k* that it was not
2Pe 1:12 even though you *k* them
1Jn 2: 3 We *k* that we have come
2: 4 The man who says, "I *k* him,"
2: 5 This is how we *k* we are in him:
2:11 he does not *k* where he is going,
2:20 and all of you *k* the truth.
2:29 you *k* that everyone who does
3: 1 not *k* us is that it did not *k* him.
3: 2 But we *k* that when he appears,
3:10 This is how we *k* who the children
3:14 We *k* that we have passed
3:16 This is how we *k* what love is:
3:19 then is how we *k* that we belong
3:24 We *k* it by the Spirit he gave us.
4: 8 does not love does not *k* God,
4:13 We *k* that we live in him
4:16 so we *k* and rely on the love God
5: 2 This is how we *k* that we love
5:13 so that you may *k* that you have
5:15 And if we *k* that he hears us—
5:18 We *k* that anyone born
5:20 We *k* also that the Son
Rev 2: 2 I *k* your deeds, your hard work
2: 9 I *k* your afflictions and your
2:19 I *k* your deeds, your love and faith,
3: 3 you will not *k* at what time I will
3:15 I *k* your deeds, that you are neither

KNOWING (KNOW)
Ge 3: 5 and you will be like God, *k* good
3:22 now become like one of us, *k* good
Jn 19:28 *k* that all was now completed,
Php 3: 8 of *k* Christ Jesus my Lord,
Phm :21 *k* that you will do even more
Heb 13: 2 entertained angels without *k* it.

KNOWLEDGE (KNOW)
Ge 2: 9 the tree of the *k* of good and evil.
2:17 eat from the tree of the *k* of good
2Ch 1:10 and *k*, that I may lead this people,
Job 21:22 "Can anyone teach *k* to God,
38: 2 counsel with words without *k*?
42: 3 obscures my counsel without *k*?'
Ps 19: 2 night after night they display *k*.
73:11 Does the Most High have *k*?"
94:10 Does he who teaches man lack *k*?
119:66 Teach me *k* and good judgment,
139: 6 Such *k* is too wonderful for me,
Pr 1: 4 *k* and discretion to the young—
1: 7 of the LORD is the beginning of *k*,
2: 5 and find the *k* of God.
2: 6 from his mouth come *k*
2:10 and *k* will be pleasant to your soul.
3:20 by his *k* the deeps were divided,
8:10 *k* rather than choice gold,
8:12 I possess *k* and discretion.
9:10 *k* of the Holy One is understanding
10:14 Wise men store up *k*,
12: 1 Whoever loves discipline loves *k*,
12:23 A prudent man keeps his *k*
13:16 Every prudent man acts out of *k*,
14: 6 *k* comes easily to the discerning.
15: 7 The lips of the wise spread *k*;
15:14 The discerning heart seeks *k*,
17:27 A man of *k* uses words
18:15 heart of the discerning acquires *k*;
19: 2 to have zeal without *k*,
19:25 discerning man, and he will gain *k*.
20:15 lips that speak *k* are a rare jewel.
23:12 and your ears to words of *k*.
24: 4 through *k* its rooms are filled
Ecc 7:12 but the advantage of *k* is this:
Isa 11: 2 the Spirit of *k* and of the fear
11: 9 full of the *k* of the LORD
40:14 Who was it that taught him *k*
Jer 3:15 who will lead you with *k*
Hos 4: 6 are destroyed from lack of *k*.
Hab 2:14 filled with the *k* of the glory
Mal 2: 7 lips of a priest ought to preserve *k*,
Mt 13:11 The *k* of the secrets of the kingdom
Lk 8:10 The *k* of the secrets of the kingdom
11:52 you have taken away the key to *k*.
Ac 18:24 with a thorough *k* of the Scriptures
Ro 1:28 worthwhile to retain the *k* of God,
10: 2 but their zeal is not based on *k*.
11:33 riches of the wisdom and *k* of God!
1Co 8: 1 *K* puffs up, but love builds up.
8:11 Christ died, is destroyed by your *k*.
12: 8 to another the message of *k*
13: 2 can fathom all mysteries and all *k*,
13: 8 where there is *k*, it will pass away.
2Co 2:14 everywhere the fragrance of the *k*
4: 6 light of the *k* of the glory of God
8: 7 in *k*, in complete earnestness
11: 6 a trained speaker, but I do have *k*.
Eph 3:19 to know this love that surpasses *k*
4:13 and in the *k* of the Son of God
Php 1: 9 and more in *k* and depth of insight,
Col 1: 9 God to fill you with the *k* of his will
1:10 every good work, growing in the *k*
2: 3 all the treasures of wisdom and *k*.
3:10 which is being renewed in *k*
1Ti 2: 4 and to come to a *k* of the truth.
6:20 ideas of what is falsely called *k*,
Tit 1: 1 and the *k* of the truth that leads
Heb 10:26 after we have received the *k*
2Pe 1: 5 and to goodness, *k*; and to *k*,
3:18 grow in the grace and *k* of our Lord

KNOWN (KNOW)
Ex 6: 3 the LORD I did not make myself *k*
Ps 16:11 You have made *k* to me the path
89: 1 I will make your faithfulness *k*
98: 2 LORD has made his salvation *k*
105: 1 make *k* among the nations what he
119:168 for all my ways are *k* to you.
Pr 20:11 Even a child is *k* by his actions,
Isa 12: 4 make *k* among the nations what he
46:10 *k* the end from the beginning,
61: 9 Their descendants will be *k*
Eze 38:23 I will make myself *k* in the sight
39: 7 " 'I will make *k* my holy name
Mt 10:26 or hidden that will not be made *k*.
24:43 of the house had *k* at what time
Lk 19:42 had only *k* on this day what would
Jn 15:15 from my Father I have made *k*
16:14 from what is mine and making it *k*
17:26 I have made you *k* to them,
Ac 2:28 You have made *k* to me the paths
Ro 1:19 since what may be *k* about God is
3:21 apart from law, has been made *k*,
9:22 his wrath and make his power *k*,
11:34 "Who has *k* the mind of the Lord?
15:20 the gospel where Christ was not *k*,
16:26 and made *k* through the prophetic
1Co 2:16 "For who has *k* the mind
8: 3 But the man who loves God is *k*
13:12 know fully, even as I am fully *k*.
2Co 3: 2 written on our hearts, *k*
Gal 4: 9 or rather are *k* by God—
Eph 3: 5 which was not made *k* to men
6:19 will fearlessly make *k* the mystery
2Ti 3:15 infancy you have *k* the holy
2Pe 2:21 than to have *k* it and then

KNOWS (KNOW)
1Sa 2: 3 for the LORD is a God who *k*,
Est 4:14 And who *k* but that you have come
Job 23:10 But he *k* the way that I take;
Ps 44:21 since he *k* the secrets of the heart?
94:11 The LORD *k* the thoughts of man;
103:14 for he *k* how we are formed,
Ecc 8: 7 Since no man *k* the future,
8:17 Even if a wise man claims he *k*,
9:12 no man *k* when his hour will come:
Isa 29:16 "He *k* nothing"?
Jer 9:24 that he understands and *k* me,
Mt 6: 8 for your Father *k* what you need
11:27 No one *k* the Son
24:36 "No one *k* about that day or hour,
Lk 12:47 "That servant who *k* his master's
16:15 of men, but God *k* your hearts.
Ac 15: 8 who *k* the heart, showed that he
Ro 8:27 who searches our hearts *k* the mind
1Co 2:11 who among men *k* the thoughts
8: 2 who thinks he *k* something does
2Ti 2:19 The Lord *k* those who are his," and
Jas 4:17 who *k* the good he ought to do
1Jn 4: 6 and whoever *k* God listens to us;
4: 7 born of God and *k* God.

KOHATHITE (KOHATHITES)
Nu 3:29 The *K* clans were to camp

KOHATHITES (KOHATHITE)
Nu 3:28 The *K* were responsible
4:15 *K* are to carry those things that are

KORAH
Levite who led rebellion against Moses and Aaron (Nu 16; Jude 11).

KORAZIN
Mt 11:21 "Woe to you, *K*! Woe to you,

LABAN
Brother of Rebekah (Ge 24:29), father of Rachel and Leah (Ge 29:16). Received Abraham's servant (Ge 24:29–51). Provided daughters as wives for Jacob in exchange for Jacob's service (Ge 29:1–30). Provided flocks for Jacob's service (Ge 30:25–43). After Jacob's departure, pursued and covenanted with him (Ge 31).

LABOR (LABORING)
Ex 1:11 to oppress them with forced *l*,
20: 9 Six days you shall *l* and do all your
Dt 5:13 Six days you shall *l* and do all your
Ps 127: 1 its builders *l* in vain.
128: 2 You will eat the fruit of your *l*;
Pr 12:24 but laziness ends in slave *l*.

Isa 54: 1 you who were never in *l*;
55: 2 and your *l* on what does not satisfy
Mt 6:28 They do not *l* or spin.
Jn 4:38 have reaped the benefits of their *l*."
1Co 3: 8 rewarded according to his own *l*.
15:58 because you know that your *l*
Gal 4:27 you who have no *l* pains;
Php 2:16 day of Christ that I did not run or *l*
Rev 14:13 "they will rest from their *l*,

LABORING* (LABOR)
2Th 3: 8 *l* and toiling so that we would not

LACK (LACKED LACKING LACKS)
Ps 34: 9 for those who fear him *l* nothing.
Pr 5:23 He will die for *l* of discipline,
10:21 but fools die for *l* of judgment.
11:14 For *l* of guidance a nation falls,
15:22 Plans fail for *l* of counsel,
28:27 to the poor will *l* nothing,
Mk 6: 6 he was amazed at their *l* of faith.
16:14 he rebuked them for their *l* of faith
Ro 3: 3 Will their *l* of faith nullify God's
1Co 1: 7 you do not *l* any spiritual gift
7: 5 because of your *l* of self-control.
Col 2:23 *l* any value in restraining sensual

LACKED (LACK)
Dt 2: 7 and you have not *l* anything.
Ne 9:21 them in the desert; they *l* nothing,
1Co 12:24 honor to the parts that *l* it,

LACKING (LACK)
Pr 17:18 A man *l* in judgment strikes hands
Ro 12:11 Never be *l* in zeal, but keep your
Jas 1: 4 and complete, not *l* anything.

LACKS (LACK)
Pr 6:32 who commits adultery *l* judgment;
11:12 man who *l* judgment derides his
12:11 he who chases fantasies *l* judgment
15:21 delights a man who *l* judgment,
24:30 of the man who *l* judgment;
25:28 is a man who *l* self-control.
28:16 A tyrannical ruler *l* judgment,
31:11 and *l* nothing of value.
Eze 34: 8 because my flock *l* a shepherd
Jas 1: 5 any of you *l* wisdom, he should ask

LAID (LAY)
Isa 53: 6 and the LORD has *l* on him
Mk 6:29 took his body and *l* it in a tomb.
Lk 6:48 and *l* the foundation on rock.
Ac 6: 6 and *l* their hands on them.
1Co 3:11 other than the one already *l*,
1Ti 4:14 body of elders *l* their hands on you.
1Jn 3:16 Jesus Christ *l* down his life for us.

LAKE
Mt 8:24 a furious storm came up on the *l*,
14:25 out to them, walking on the *l*.
Mk 4: 1 into a boat and sat in it out on the *l*,
Lk 8:33 down the steep bank into the *l*
Jn 6:25 him on the other side of the *l*,
Rev 19:20 into the fiery *l* of burning sulfur.
20:14 The *l* of fire is the second death.

LAMB (LAMB'S LAMBS)
Ge 22: 8 "God himself will provide the *l*
Ex 12:21 and slaughter the Passover *l*.
Nu 9:11 are to eat the *l*, together
2Sa 12: 4 he took the ewe *l* that belonged
Isa 11: 6 The wolf will live with the *l*,
53: 7 he was led like a *l* to the slaughter,
Mk 14:12 to sacrifice the Passover *l*,
Jn 1:29 *L* of God, who takes away the sin
Ac 8:32 as a *l* before the shearer is silent,
1Co 5: 7 our Passover *l*, has been sacrificed.
1Pe 1:19 a *l* without blemish or defect.
Rev 5: 6 Then I saw a *L*, looking
5:12 "Worthy is the *L*, who was slain,
7:14 white in the blood of the *L*.
14: 4 They follow the *L* wherever he
15: 3 of God and the song of the *L*:
17:14 but the *L* will overcome them
19: 9 to the wedding supper of the *L*!' "
21:23 gives it light, and the *L* is its lamp.

LAMB'S (LAMB)
Rev 21:27 written in the *L* book of life.

LAMBS (LAMB)
Lk 10: 3 I am sending you out like *l*
Jn 21:15 Jesus said, "Feed my *l*."

LAME
Isa 33:23 even the *l* will carry off plunder.
35: 6 Then will the *l* leap like a deer,
Mt 11: 5 The blind receive sight, the *l* walk,
15:31 the *l* walking and the blind seeing.
Lk 14:21 the crippled, the blind and the *l*.'

LAMENT
2Sa 1:17 took up this *l* concerning Saul
Eze 19: 1 Take up a *l* concerning the princes

LAMP (LAMPS LAMPSTAND LAMPSTANDS)
2Sa 22:29 You are my *l*, O LORD;
Ps 18:28 You, O LORD, keep my *l* burning;
119:105 Your word is a *l* to my feet
132:17 and set up a *l* for my anointed one.
Pr 6:23 For these commands are a *l*,
20:27 *l* of the LORD searches the spirit
31:18 and her *l* does not go out at night.
Mt 6:22 "The eye is the *l* of the body.
Lk 8:16 "No one lights a *l* and hides it
Rev 21:23 gives it light, and the Lamb is its *l*.
22: 5 They will not need the light of a *l*

LAMPS (LAMP)
Mt 25: 1 be like ten virgins who took their *l*
Lk 12:35 for service and keep your *l* burning,
Rev 4: 5 the throne, seven *l* were blazing.

LAMPSTAND (LAMP)
Ex 25:31 "Make a *l* of pure gold
Zec 4: 2 "I see a solid gold *l* with a bowl
4:11 on the right and the left of the *l*?"
Heb 9: 2 In its first room were the *l*,
Rev 2: 5 and remove your *l* from its place.

LAMPSTANDS (LAMP)
2Ch 4: 7 He made ten gold *l* according
Rev 1:12 when I turned I saw seven golden *l*,
1:20 and of the seven golden *l* is this:

LAND (LANDS)
Ge 1:10 God called the dry ground "*l*,"
1:11 "Let the *l* produce vegetation:
1:24 "Let the *l* produce living creatures
12: 1 and go to the *l* I will show you.
12: 7 To your offspring I will give this *l*."
13:15 All the *l* that you see I will give
15:18 "To your descendants I give this *l*,
50:24 out of this *l* to the *l* he promised
Ex 3: 8 a *l* flowing with milk and honey—
6: 8 to the *l* I swore with uplifted hand
33: 3 Go up to the *l* flowing with milk
Lev 25:23 *l* must not be sold permanently,
Nu 14: 8 us into that *l*, a *l* flowing with milk
35:33 Do not pollute the *l* where you are.
Dt 1: 8 See, I have given you this *l*.
8: 7 God is bringing you into a good *l*—
11:10 The *l* you are entering to take
28:21 you from the *l* you are entering
29:19 will bring disaster on the watered *l*
34: 1 LORD showed him the whole *l*—
Jos 13: 2 "This is the *l* that remains:
14: 4 Levites received no share of the *l*
14: 9 *l* on which your feet have walked
2Sa 21:14 answered prayer in behalf of the *l*.
2Ki 17: 5 of Assyria invaded the entire *l*,
24: 1 king of Babylon invaded the *l*,
25:21 into captivity, away from her *l*.
2Ch 7:14 their sin and will heal their *l*.
7:20 then I will uproot Israel from my *l*,
36:21 The *l* enjoyed its sabbath rests;
Ezr 9:11 entering to possess is a *l* polluted
Ne 9:36 in the *l* you gave our forefathers
Ps 37:11 But the meek will inherit the *l*
37:29 the righteous will inherit the *l*
136:21 and gave their *l* as an inheritance,
142: 5 my portion in the *l* of the living."
Pr 2:21 For the upright will live in the *l*,
12:11 who works his *l* will have abundant
Isa 6:13 though a tenth remains in the *l*,
53: 8 cut off from the *l* of the living;
Jer 2: 7 But you came and defiled my *l*
Eze 36:24 and bring you back into your own *l*.

LANDS (LAND)
Ps 111: 6 giving them the *l* of other nations.
Eze 20: 6 honey, the most beautiful of all *l*.
Zec 10: 9 in distant *l* they will remember me.

LANGUAGE (LANGUAGES)
Ge 11: 1 Now the whole world had one *l*
11: 9 there the LORD confused the *l*
Ps 19: 3 There is no speech or *l*
Jn 8:44 When he lies, he speaks his native *l*
Ac 2: 6 heard them speaking in his own *l*.
Col 3: 8 slander, and filthy *l* from your lips.
Rev 5: 9 from every tribe and *l* and people
7: 9 every nation, tribe, people and *l*,
14: 6 to every nation, tribe, *l* and people.

LANGUAGES (LANGUAGE)
Zec 8:23 "In those days ten men from all *l*

LAODICEA
Rev 3:14 the angel of the church in *L* write:

LAP
Jdg 7: 5 "Separate those who *l* the water

LASHES
Pr 17:10 more than a hundred *l* a fool.
2Co 11:24 from the Jews the forty *l* minus one

LAST (LASTING LASTS LATTER)
Ex 14:24 During the *l* watch of the night
2Sa 23: 1 These are the *l* words of David:
Isa 2: 2 and Jerusalem: In the *l* days
41: 4 and with the *l*— I am he."
44: 6 I am the first and I am the *l*;
48:12 I am the first and I am the *l*.
Hos 3: 5 and to his blessings in the *l* days.
Mic 4: 1 In the *l* days
Mt 19:30 But many who are first will be *l*,
20: 8 beginning with the *l* ones hired
21:37 *L* of all, he sent his son to them.
Mk 9:35 must be the very *l*, and the servant
10:31 are first will be *l*, and the *l* first."
15:37 a loud cry, Jesus breathed his *l*.
Jn 6:40 and I will raise him up at the *l* day."
15:16 and bear fruit—fruit that will *l*.
Ac 2:17 " 'In the *l* days, God says,
Ro 1:17 is by faith from first to *l*,
1Co 15:26 *l* enemy to be destroyed is death.
15:52 of an eye, at the *l* trumpet.
2Ti 3: 1 will be terrible times in the *l* days.
2Pe 3: 3 in the *l* days scoffers will come,
Jude :18 "In the *l* times there will be
Rev 1:17 I am the First and the *L*.
22:13 the First and the *L*, the Beginning

LASTING (LAST)
Ex 12:14 to the LORD—a *l* ordinance.
Lev 24: 8 of the Israelites, as a *l* covenant.
Nu 25:13 have a covenant of a *l* priesthood,
Heb 10:34 had better and *l* possessions.

LASTS (LAST)
Ps 30: 5 For his anger *l* only a moment,
2Co 3:11 greater is the glory of that which *l*!

LATTER (LAST)
Job 42:12 The LORD blessed the *l* part
Mt 23:23 You should have practiced the *l*,
Php 1:16 *l* do so in love, knowing that I am

LAUGH (LAUGHED LAUGHS LAUGHTER)
Ps 59: 8 But you, O LORD, *l* at them;
Pr 31:25 she can *l* at the days to come.
Ecc 3: 4 a time to weep and a time to *l*,
Lk 6:21 for you will *l*.
6:25 Woe to you who *l* now,

LAUGHED (LAUGH)
Ge 17:17 Abraham fell facedown; he *l*
18:12 So Sarah *l* to herself as she thought,

LAUGHS (LAUGH)
Ps 2: 4 The One enthroned in heaven *l*;
37:13 but the Lord *l* at the wicked,

LAUGHTER (LAUGH)
Ge 21: 6 Sarah said, "God has brought me *l*,
Ps 126: 2 Our mouths were filled with *l*,
Pr 14:13 Even in *l* the heart may ache,
Jas 4: 9 Change your *l* to mourning

LAVISHED
Eph 1: 8 of God's grace that he *l* on us
1Jn 3: 1 great is the love the Father has *l*

LAW (LAWFUL LAWGIVER LAWS)
Lev 24:22 are to have the same *l* for the alien
Nu 6:13 " 'Now this is the *l* for the Nazirite
Dt 1: 5 Moses began to expound this *l*,
6:25 to obey all this *l* before the LORD
27:26 of this *l* by carrying them out."
31:11 you shall read this *l* before them
31:26 "Take this Book of the *L*
Jos 1: 7 to obey all the *l* my servant Moses
1: 8 of the *L* depart from your mouth;
22: 5 and the *l* that Moses the servant
2Ki 22: 8 of the *L* in the temple of the LORD
2Ch 6:16 walk before me according to my *l*,
17: 9 the Book of the *L* of the LORD;
34:14 of the *L* of the LORD that had
Ezr 7: 6 versed in the *L* of Moses,
Ne 8: 2 Ezra the priest brought the *L*
8: 8 from the Book of the *L* of God,
Ps 1: 2 and on his *l* he meditates day
19: 7 The *l* of the LORD is perfect,
37:31 The *l* of his God is in his heart;
40: 8 your *l* is within my heart."
119:18 wonderful things in your *l*.
119:70 but I delight in your *l*.
119:72 *l* from your mouth is more precious
119:77 for your *l* is my delight.
119:97 Oh, how I love your *l*!
119:163 but I love your *l*.
119:165 peace have they who love your *l*,
Pr 28: 9 If anyone turns a deaf ear to the *l*,
29:18 but blessed is he who keeps the *l*.
Isa 2: 3 The *l* will go out from Zion,
8:20 To the *l* and to the testimony!
42:21 to make his *l* great and glorious.
Jer 2: 8 deal with the *l* did not know me;
8: 8 for we have the *l* of the LORD,"
31:33 "I will put my *l* in their minds
Mic 4: 2 The *l* will go out from Zion,
Hab 1: 7 they are a *l* to themselves
Zec 7:12 as flint and would not listen to the *l*
Mt 5:17 that I have come to abolish the *L*
7:12 sums up the *L* and the Prophets.
22:36 greatest commandment in the *L*?"
22:40 All the *L* and the Prophets hang
23:23 more important matters of the *l*—
Lk 11:52 "Woe to you experts in the *l*,
16:17 stroke of a pen to drop out of the *L*.
24:44 me in the *L* of Moses,
Jn 1:17 For the *l* was given through Moses;
Ac 13:39 justified from by the *l* of Moses.
Ro 2:12 All who sin apart from the *l* will
2:15 of the *l* are written on their hearts,
2:20 you have in the *l* the embodiment
2:25 value if you observe the *l*,
3:19 we know that whatever the *l* says,
3:20 in his sight by observing the *l*;
3:21 apart from *l*, has been made known
3:28 by faith apart from observing the *l*.
3:31 Not at all! Rather, we uphold the *l*.
4:13 It was not through *l* that Abraham
4:15 worthless, because *l* brings wrath.
4:16 not only to those who are of the *l*
5:13 for before the *l* was given,
5:20 *l* was added so that the trespass
6:14 because you are not under *l*,
6:15 we are not under *l* but under grace?
7: 1 that the *l* has authority
7: 4 also died to the *l* through the body
7: 5 aroused by the *l* were at work
7: 6 released from the *l* so that we serve
7: 7 then? Is the *l* sin? Certainly not!
7: 8 For apart from *l*, sin is dead.
7:12 *l* is holy, and the commandment is
7:14 We know that the *l* is spiritual;
7:22 my inner being I delight in God's *l*;
7:25 in my mind am a slave to God's *l*,
8: 2 because through Christ Jesus the *l*
8: 3 For what the *l* was powerless to do
8: 4 of the *l* might be fully met in us,
8: 7 It does not submit to God's *l*,
9: 4 covenants, the receiving of the *l*,
9:31 who pursued a *l* of righteousness,
10: 4 Christ is the end of the *l*
13: 8 his fellowman has fulfilled the *l*.
13:10 love is the fulfillment of the *l*.
1Co 6: 6 goes to *l* against another—
9: 9 For it is written in the *L* of Moses:
9:20 the *l* I became like one under the *l*
9:21 I became like one not having the *l*
15:56 and the power of sin is the *l*.
Gal 2:16 justified by observing the *l*,
2:19 For through the *l* I died to the *l*
3: 2 the Spirit by observing the *l*,
3: 5 you because you observe the *l*,
3:10 on observing the *l* are under a curse
3:11 justified before God by the *l*,
3:13 curse of the *l* by becoming a curse
3:17 The *l*, introduced 430 years later,
3:19 then, was the purpose of the *l*?
3:21 Is the *l*, therefore, opposed
3:23 we were held prisoners by the *l*,
3:24 So the *l* was put in charge to lead us
4:21 you who want to be under the *l*,
5: 3 obligated to obey the whole *l*.
5: 4 justified by *l* have been alienated
5:14 The entire *l* is summed up
5:18 by the Spirit, you are not under *l*.
6: 2 and in this way you will fulfill the *l*
Eph 2:15 flesh the *l* with its commandments
Php 3: 9 of my own that comes from the *l*,
1Ti 1: 8 We know that the *l* is good
Heb 7:12 there must also be a change of the *l*.
7:19 (for the *l* made nothing perfect),
10: 1 The *l* is only a shadow
Jas 1:25 intently into the perfect *l* that gives
2: 8 If you really keep the royal *l* found
2:10 For whoever keeps the whole *l*
4:11 or judges him speaks against the *l*
1Jn 3: 4 Everyone who sins breaks the *l*;

LAWFUL (LAW)
Mt 12:12 Therefore it is *l* to do good

LAWGIVER* (LAW)
Isa 33:22 the LORD is our *l*,
Jas 4:12 There is only one *L* and Judge,

LAWLESS (LAWLESSNESS)
2Th 2: 8 And then the *l* one will be revealed
Heb 10:17 "Their sins and *l* acts

LAWLESSNESS* (LAWLESS)
2Th 2: 3 and the man of *l* is revealed,
2: 7 power of *l* is already at work;
1Jn 3: 4 sins breaks the law; in fact, sin is *l*.

LAWS (LAW)
Ex 21: 1 "These are the *l* you are to set
Lev 25:18 and be careful to obey my *l*,
Dt 4: 1 and *l* I am about to teach you.
30:16 decrees and *l*; then you will live
Ps 119:30 I have set my heart on your *l*.
119:43 for I have put my hope in your *l*.
119:120 I stand in awe of your *l*.
119:164 for your righteous *l*.
119:175 and may your *l* sustain me.
Eze 36:27 and be careful to keep my *l*.
Heb 8:10 I will put my *l* in their minds
10:16 I will put my *l* in their hearts,

LAWSUITS
Hos 10: 4 therefore *l* spring up
1Co 6: 7 The very fact that you have *l*

LAY (LAID LAYING LAYS)
Ex 29:10 and his sons shall *l* their hands
Lev 1: 4 He is to *l* his hand on the head
4:15 the community are to *l* their hands
Nu 8:10 the Israelites are to *l* their hands
27:18 whom is the spirit, and *l* your hand
1Sa 26: 9 Who can *l* a hand on the LORD's
Job 1:12 on the man himself do not *l* a finger
22:22 and *l* up his words in your heart.
Ecc 10: 4 calmness can *l* great errors to rest.
Isa 28:16 "See, I *l* a stone in Zion,
Mt 8:20 of Man has no place to *l* his head."
28: 6 Come and see the place where he *l*.
Mk 6: 5 *l* his hands on a few sick people
Lk 9:58 of Man has no place to *l* his head."
Jn 10:15 and I *l* down my life for the sheep.
10:18 but I *l* it down of my own accord.
15:13 that he *l* down his life
Ac 8:19 on whom I *l* my hands may receive
Ro 9:33 I *l* in Zion a stone that causes men
1Co 3:11 no one can *l* any foundation other
1Pe 2: 6 "See, I *l* a stone in Zion,
1Jn 3:16 And we ought to *l* down our lives
Rev 4:10 They *l* their crowns

LAYING (LAY)
Lk 4:40 and *l* his hands on each one,
Ac 8:18 at the *l* on of the apostles' hands,
1Ti 5:22 Do not be hasty in the *l* on of hands
2Ti 1: 6 is in you through the *l*
Heb 6: 1 not *l* again the foundation
6: 2 instruction about baptisms, the *l*

LAYS (LAY)
Jn 10:11 The good shepherd *l* down his life

LAZARUS
1. Poor man in Jesus' parable (Lk 16:19–31).
2. Brother of Mary and Martha whom Jesus raised from the dead (Jn 11:1–12:19).

LAZINESS* (LAZY)
Pr 12:24 but *l* ends in slave labor.
19:15 *L* brings on deep sleep,

LAZY* (LAZINESS)
Ex 5: 8 They are *l*; that is why they are
5:17 Pharaoh said, "*L*, that's what you
5:17 "Lazy, that's what you are—*l*!
Pr 10: 4 *L* hands make a man poor,
12:27 The *l* man does not roast his game,
26:15 he is too *l* to bring it back
Ecc 10:18 If a man is *l*, the rafters sag;
Mt 25:26 replied, 'You wicked, *l* servant!
Tit 1:12 liars, evil brutes, *l* gluttons."
Heb 6:12 We do not want you to become *l*,

LEAD (LEADER LEADERS LEADERSHIP LEADS LED)
Ex 15:13 "In your unfailing love you will *l*
Nu 14: 8 with us, he will *l* us into that land,
Dt 31: 2 and I am no longer able to *l* you.
Jos 1: 6 because you will *l* these people
1Sa 8: 5 now appoint a king to *l* us,
2Ch 1:10 knowledge, that I may *l* this people
Ps 27:11 *l* me in a straight path
61: 2 *l* me to the rock that is higher
139:24 and *l* me in the way everlasting.
143:10 *l* me on level ground.
Pr 4:11 and *l* you along straight paths.
Ecc 5: 6 Do not let your mouth *l* you
Isa 11: 6 and a little child will *l* them.
49:10 and *l* them beside springs of water.
Da 12: 3 those who *l* many to righteousness,
Mt 6:13 And *l* us not into temptation,
Lk 11: 4 And *l* us not into temptation.' "
Gal 3:24 So the law was put in charge to *l* us
1Th 4:11 it your ambition to *l* a quiet life,
1Jn 3: 7 do not let anyone *l* you astray.
Rev 7:17 he will *l* them to springs

LEADER (LEAD)
1Sa 7: 6 Samuel was *l* of Israel at Mizpah.
10: 1 Has not the LORD anointed you *l*
12: 2 I have been your *l* from my youth
13:14 and appointed him *l* of his people,

LEADERS (LEAD)
Heb 13: 7 Remember your *l*, who spoke
13:17 Obey your *l* and submit

LEADERSHIP* (LEAD)
Nu 33: 1 by divisions under the *l* of Moses
Ps 109: 8 may another take his place of *l*.
Ac 1:20 " 'May another take his place of *l*.'
Ro 12: 8 if it is *l*, let him govern diligently;

LEADS (LEAD)
Dt 27:18 is the man who *l* the blind astray
Ps 23: 2 he *l* me beside quiet waters,
37: 8 do not fret—it *l* only to evil.
68: 6 he *l* forth the prisoners
Pr 2:18 For her house *l* down to death
10:17 ignores correction *l* others astray.
14:23 but mere talk *l* only to poverty.
16:25 but in the end it *l* to death.
19:23 The fear of the LORD *l* to life:
20: 7 righteous man *l* a blameless life;
21: 5 as surely as haste *l* to poverty.
Isa 40:11 he gently *l* those that have young.
Mt 7:13 and broad is the road that *l*
12:20 till he *l* justice to victory.
15:14 If a blind man *l* a blind man,
Jn 10: 3 sheep by name and *l* them out.
Ro 6:16 which *l* to death, or to obedience,
6:22 the benefit you reap *l* to holiness,
14:19 effort to do what *l* to peace
2Co 2:14 always *l* us in triumphal procession
7:10 sorrow brings repentance that *l*
Tit 1: 1 of the truth that *l* to godliness—

LEAH
Wife of Jacob (Ge 29:16–30); bore six sons and one daughter (Ge 29:31–30:21; 34:1; 35:23).

LEAN (LEANED)
Pr 3: 5 *l* not on your own understanding;

LEANED (LEAN)
Ge 47:31 as he *l* on the top of his staff.
Jn 21:20 (This was the one who had *l* back
Heb 11:21 as he *l* on the top of his staff.

LEAP (LEAPED LEAPS)
Isa 35: 6 Then will the lame *l* like a deer,
Mal 4: 2 *l* like calves released from the stall.
Lk 6:23 "Rejoice in that day and *l* for joy,

LEAPED (LEAP)
Lk 1:41 heard Mary's greeting, the baby *l*

LEAPS (LEAP)
Ps 28: 7 My heart *l* for joy

LEARN (LEARNED LEARNING LEARNS)
Dt 4:10 so that they may *l* to revere me
5: 1 *L* them and be sure to follow them.
31:12 and *l* to fear the LORD your God
Ps 119: 7 as I *l* your righteous laws.
Isa 1:17 *l* to do right!
26: 9 of the world *l* righteousness.
Mt 11:29 yoke upon you and *l* from me,
Jn 14:31 world must *l* that I love the Father
1Th 4: 4 that each of you should *l*
1Ti 2:11 A woman should *l* in quietness
5: 4 these should *l* first of all

LEARNED (LEARN)
Ps 119:152 Long ago I *l* from your statutes
Mt 11:25 things from the wise and *l*,
Php 4: 9 Whatever you have *l* or received
4:11 for I have *l* to be content whatever
2Ti 3:14 continue in what you have *l*
Heb 5: 8 he *l* obedience from what he

LEARNING (LEARN)
Pr 1: 5 let the wise listen and add to their *l*,
9: 9 man and he will add to his *l*.
Isa 44:25 who overthrows the *l* of the wise
Jn 7:15 "How did this man get such *l*
2Ti 3: 7 always *l* but never able

LEARNS (LEARN)
Jn 6:45 and *l* from him comes to me.

LEATHER
2Ki 1: 8 and with a *l* belt around his waist."
Mt 3: 4 and he had a *l* belt around his waist

LEAVES
Ge 3: 7 so they sewed fig *l* together
Eze 47:12 for food and their *l* for healing."
Rev 22: 2 the *l* of the tree are for the healing

LEBANON
Dt 11:24 from the desert to *L*,
1Ki 4:33 from the cedar of *L*

LED (LEAD)
Ex 3: 1 and he *l* the flock to the far side
Dt 8: 2 the LORD your God *l* you all
1Ki 11: 3 and his wives *l* him astray.
2Ch 26:16 his pride *l* to his downfall.
Ne 13:26 he was *l* into sin by foreign women.
Ps 68:18 you *l* captives in your train;
78:52 he *l* them like sheep
Pr 7:21 persuasive words she *l* him astray;
20: 1 whoever is *l* astray
Isa 53: 7 he was *l* like a lamb to the slaughter
Jer 11:19 I had been like a gentle lamb *l*
Am 2:10 and I *l* you forty years in the desert
Mt 4: 1 Then Jesus was *l* by the Spirit
27:31 they *l* him away to crucify him.
Lk 4: 1 was *l* by the Spirit in the desert,
Ac 8:32 "He was *l* like a sheep
Ro 8:14 those who are *l* by the Spirit
2Co 7: 9 your sorrow *l* you to repentance.
Gal 5:18 But if you are *l* by the Spirit,
Eph 4: 8 he *l* captives in his train

LEEKS*
Nu 11: 5 melons, *l*, onions and garlic.

LEFT
Dt 28:14 or to the *l*, following other gods
Jos 1: 7 turn from it to the right or to the *l*,
23: 6 aside to the right or to the *l*.
2Ki 22: 2 aside to the right or to the *l*.
Pr 4:27 Do not swerve to the right or the *l*;
Isa 30:21 turn to the right or to the *l*,
Mt 6: 3 do not let your *l* hand know what
25:33 on his right and the goats on his *l*.

LEGALISTIC*
Php 3: 6 as for *l* righteousness, faultless.

LEGION
Mk 5: 9 "My name is *L*," he replied,

LEND (LENDER LENDS MONEYLENDER)
Lev 25:37 You must not *l* him money
Dt 15: 8 freely *l* him whatever he needs.
Ps 37:26 are always generous and *l* freely;
Eze 18: 8 He does not *l* at usury
Lk 6:34 if you *l* to those from whom you

LENDER (LEND)
Pr 22: 7 and the borrower is servant to the *l*.
Isa 24: 2 for borrower as for *l*,

LENDS (LEND)
Ps 15: 5 who *l* his money without usury
112: 5 to him who is generous and *l* freely,
Pr 19:17 to the poor *l* to the LORD,

LENGTH (LONG)
Ps 90:10 The *l* of our days is seventy years—
Pr 10:27 The fear of the LORD adds *l* to life

LENGTHY* (LONG)
Mk 12:40 and for a show make *l* prayers.
Lk 20:47 and for a show make *l* prayers.

LEOPARD
Isa 11: 6 the *l* will lie down with the goat,
Da 7: 6 beast, one that looked like a *l*.
Rev 13: 2 The beast I saw resembled a *l*,

LEPROSY (LEPROUS)
Nu 12:10 toward her and saw that she had *l*;
2Ki 5: 1 was a valiant soldier, but he had *l*.
7: 3 men with *l* at the entrance
2Ch 26:21 King Uzziah had *l*
Mt 11: 5 those who have *l* are cured,
Lk 17:12 ten men who had *l* met him.

LEPROUS (LEPROSY)
Ex 4: 6 and when he took it out, it was *l*,

LETTER (LETTERS)
Mt 5:18 not the smallest *l*, not the least
2Co 3: 2 You yourselves are our *l*, written
3: 6 for the *l* kills, but the Spirit gives
2Th 3:14 not obey our instruction in this *l*,

LETTERS (LETTER)
2Co 3: 7 which was engraved in *l* on stone,
10:10 "His *l* are weighty and forceful,
2Pe 3:16 His *l* contain some things that are

LEVEL
Ps 143:10 lead me on *l* ground.
Pr 4:26 Make *l* paths for your feet
Isa 26: 7 The path of the righteous is *l*;
40: 4 the rough ground shall become *l*,
Jer 31: 9 on a *l* path where they will not
Heb 12:13 "Make *l* paths for your feet,"

LEVI (LEVITE LEVITES LEVITICAL)
1. Son of Jacob by Leah (Ge 29:34; 46:11; 1Ch 2:1). With Simeon avenged rape of Dinah (Ge 34). Tribe of blessed (Ge 49:5–7; Dt 33:8–11), chosen as priests (Nu 3–4), numbered (Nu 3:39; 26:62), allotted cities, but not land (Nu 18; 35; Dt 10:9; Jos 13:14; 21), land (Eze 48:8–22), 12,000 from (Rev 7:7).
2. See MATTHEW.

LEVIATHAN
Job 41: 1 pull in the *l* with a fishhook
Ps 74:14 you who crushed the heads of *L*
Isa 27: 1 *L* the gliding serpent,

LEVITE (LEVI)
Dt 26:12 you shall give it to the *L*, the alien,
Jdg 19: 1 a *L* who lived in a remote area

LEVITES (LEVI)
Nu 1:53 The *L* are to be responsible
3:12 "I have taken the *L*
8: 6 "Take the *L* from among the other
18:21 I give to the *L* all the tithes in Israel
35: 7 must give the *L* forty-eight towns,
2Ch 31: 2 assigned the priests and *L*
Mal 3: 3 he will purify the *L* and refine them

LEVITICAL (LEVI)
Heb 7:11 attained through the *L* priesthood

LEWDNESS
Mk 7:22 malice, deceit, *l*, envy, slander,

LIAR* (LIE)
Dt 19:18 and if the witness proves to be a *l*,
Job 34: 6 I am considered a *l*;
Pr 17: 4 *l* pays attention to a malicious
19:22 better to be poor than a *l*.
30: 6 will rebuke you and prove you a *l*.
Mic 2:11 If a *l* and deceiver comes and says,
Jn 8:44 for he is a *l* and the father of lies.
8:55 I did not, I would be a *l* like you,
Ro 3: 4 Let God be true, and every man a *l*.
1Jn 1:10 we make him out to be a *l*
2: 4 not do what he commands is a *l*,
2:22 Who is the *l*? It is the man who
4:20 yet hates his brother, he is a *l*.
5:10 God has made him out to be a *l*,

LIARS* (LIE)
Ps 63:11 the mouths of *l* will be silenced.
116:11 "All men are *l*."
Isa 57: 4 the offspring of *l*?
Mic 6:12 her people are *l*
1Ti 1:10 for slave traders and *l* and perjurers
4: 2 come through hypocritical *l*,
Tit 1:12 "Cretans are always *l*, evil brutes,
Rev 3: 9 though they are not, but are *l*—
21: 8 magic arts, the idolaters and all *l*—

LIBERATED*
Ro 8:21 that the creation itself will be *l*

LICENSE
Jude : 4 of our God into a *l* for immorality

LICK
Ps 72: 9 and his enemies will *l* the dust.
Isa 49:23 they will *l* the dust at your feet.
Mic 7:17 They will *l* dust like a snake,

LIE (LIAR LIARS LIED LIES LYING)
Lev 18:22 " 'Do not *l* with a man
19:11 " 'Do not *l*.
Nu 23:19 God is not a man, that he should *l*,
Dt 6: 7 when you *l* down and when you get
25: 2 the judge shall make him *l* down
1Sa 15:29 the Glory of Israel does not *l*
Ps 4: 8 I will *l* down and sleep in peace,
23: 2 me *l* down in green pastures,
89:35 and I will not *l* to David—
Pr 3:24 when you *l* down, you will not be
Isa 11: 6 leopard will *l* down with the goat,
28:15 for we have made a *l* our refuge
Jer 9: 5 They have taught their tongues to *l*
23:14 They commit adultery and live a *l*.
Eze 13: 6 are false and their divinations a *l*.
34:14 they will *l* down in good grazing
Ro 1:25 exchanged the truth of God for a *l*,
Col 3: 9 Do not *l* to each other,
2Th 2:11 so that they will believe the *l*
Tit 1: 2 which God, who does not *l*,
Heb 6:18 which it is impossible for God to *l*,
1Jn 2:21 because no *l* comes from the truth.
Rev 14: 5 No *l* was found in their mouths;

LIED (LIE)
Ac 5: 4 You have not *l* to men but to God."

LIES (LIE)
Lev 6: 3 finds lost property and *l* about it,
Ps 5: 6 You destroy those who tell *l*;
10: 7 His mouth is full of curses and *l*
12: 2 Everyone *l* to his neighbor;
34:13 and your lips from speaking *l*.
58: 3 they are wayward and speak *l*.
144: 8 whose mouths are full of *l*,
Pr 6:19 a false witness who pours out *l*
12:17 but a false witness tells *l*.
19: 5 he who pours out *l* will not go free.
19: 9 and he who pours out *l* will perish.
29:12 If a ruler listens to *l*,
30: 8 Keep falsehood and *l* far from me;
Isa 59: 3 Your lips have spoken *l*,
Jer 5:31 The prophets prophesy *l*,
9: 3 like a bow, to shoot *l*;
14:14 "The prophets are prophesying *l*
Hos 11:12 Ephraim has surrounded me with *l*,
Jn 8:44 for he is a liar and the father of *l*.

LIFE (LIVE)
Ge 1:30 everything that has the breath of *l*
2: 7 into his nostrils the breath of *l*,
2: 9 of the garden were the tree of *l*
6:17 to destroy all *l* under the heavens,
9: 5 for the *l* of his fellow man.
9:11 Never again will all *l* be cut
Ex 21: 6 Then he will be his servant for *l*.
21:23 you are to take *l* for *l*, eye for eye,
23:26 I will give you a full *l* span.
Lev 17:14 the *l* of every creature is its blood.
24:17 " 'If anyone takes the *l*
24:18 must make restitution—*l* for *l*.
Nu 35:31 a ransom for the *l* of a murderer,
Dt 4:42 one of these cities and save his *l*.
12:23 because the blood is the *l*,
19:21 Show no pity: *l* for *l*, eye for eye,
30:15 I set before you today *l*
30:19 Now choose *l*, so that you
30:20 For the LORD is your *l*,
32:39 I put to death and I bring to *l*,
32:47 words for you—they are your *l*.
1Sa 19: 5 He took his *l* in his hands
Job 2: 6 hands; but you must spare his *l*."
33: 4 of the Almighty gives me *l*.
33:30 that the light of *l* may shine on him.
Ps 16:11 known to me the path of *l*;
17:14 this world whose reward is in this *l*.
23: 6 all the days of my *l*,
27: 1 LORD is the stronghold of my *l*—
34:12 Whoever of you loves *l*
36: 9 For with you is the fountain of *l*;
39: 4 let me know how fleeting is my *l*.
41: 2 will protect him and preserve his *l*;
49: 7 No man can redeem the *l*
49: 8 the ransom for a *l* is costly,
63: 3 Because your love is better than *l*,
69:28 they be blotted out of the book of *l*
91:16 With long *l* will I satisfy him
104:33 I will sing to the LORD all my *l*;
119:25 preserve my *l* according to your word
Pr 1: 3 a disciplined and prudent *l*,
3: 2 will prolong your *l* many years
3:18 of *l* to those who embrace her;
4:23 for it is the wellspring of *l*.
6:23 are the way to *l*,
6:26 adulteress preys upon your very *l*.
7:23 little knowing it will cost him his *l*.
8:35 For whoever finds me finds *l*
10:11 of the righteous is a fountain of *l*,
10:27 of the LORD adds length to *l*,
11:30 of the righteous is a tree of *l*,
13: 3 He who guards his lips guards his *l*,
13:12 but a longing fulfilled is a tree of *l*.
13:14 of the wise is a fountain of *l*,
14:27 of the LORD is a fountain of *l*,
15: 4 that brings healing is a tree of *l*,
Pr 16:22 Understanding is a fountain of *l*
19: 3 A man's own folly ruins his *l*,
19:23 The fear of the LORD leads to *l*:
21:21 finds *l*, prosperity and honor.
Isa 53:10 LORD makes his *l* a guilt offering,
53:11 he will see the light of *l*
53:12 he poured out his *l* unto death,
Jer 10:23 that a man's *l* is not his own;
La 3:58 you redeemed my *l*.
Eze 18:27 and right, he will save his *l*.
37: 5 enter you, and you will come to *l*.
Da 12: 2 some to everlasting *l*, others
Jnh 2: 6 you brought my *l* up from the pit,
Mal 2: 5 a covenant of *l* and peace,
Mt 6:25 Is not *l* more important than food,
7:14 and narrow the road that leads to *l*,
10:39 Whoever finds his *l* will lose it,
16:21 and on the third day be raised to *l*.
16:25 wants to save his *l* will lose it,
18: 8 better for you to enter *l* maimed
19:16 thing must I do to get eternal *l*?"
19:29 as much and will inherit eternal *l*.
20:28 to give his *l* as a ransom for many."
25:46 but the righteous to eternal *l*."
Mk 8:35 but whoever loses his *l* for me
9:43 better for you to enter *l* maimed
10:17 "what must I do to inherit eternal *l*
10:30 and in the age to come, eternal *l*.
10:45 to give his *l* as a ransom for many."
Lk 6: 9 to save *l* or to destroy it?"
9:22 and on the third day be raised to *l*."
9:24 wants to save his *l* will lose it,
12:15 a man's *l* does not consist
12:22 do not worry about your *l*,
12:25 can add a single hour to his *l*?
14:26 even his own *l*— he cannot be my
17:33 tries to keep his *l* will lose it,
21:19 standing firm you will gain *l*.
Jn 1: 4 In him was *l*, and that *l* was
3:15 believes in him may have eternal *l*.
3:36 believes in the Son has eternal *l*,
4:14 of water welling up to eternal *l*."
5:21 raises the dead and gives them *l*,
5:24 him who sent me has eternal *l*
5:26 For as the Father has *l* in himself,
5:39 that by them you possess eternal *l*.
5:40 refuse to come to me to have *l*.
6:27 for food that endures to eternal *l*,
6:33 down from heaven and gives *l*
6:35 Jesus declared, "I am the bread of *l*
6:40 believes in him shall have eternal *l*,
6:47 he who believes has everlasting *l*.
6:48 I am the bread of *l*.
6:51 give for the *l* of the world."
6:53 and drink his blood, you have no *l*
6:63 The Spirit gives *l*; the flesh counts
6:68 You have the words of eternal *l*.
8:12 but will have the light of *l*."
10:10 I have come that they may have *l*,
10:15 and I lay down my *l* for the sheep.
10:17 loves me is that I lay down my *l*—
10:28 I give them eternal *l*, and they shall
11:25 "I am the resurrection and the *l*.
12:25 The man who loves his *l* will lose it,
12:50 his command leads to eternal *l*.
13:37 I will lay down my *l* for you."
14: 6 am the way and the truth and the *l*.
15:13 lay down his *l* for his friends.
17: 2 people that he might give eternal *l*
17: 3 Now this is eternal *l*: that they may
20:31 that by believing you may have *l*
Ac 2:32 God has raised this Jesus to *l*,
3:15 You killed the author of *l*,
11:18 the Gentiles repentance unto *l*."
13:48 appointed for eternal *l* believed.
Ro 2: 7 immortality, he will give eternal *l*.
4:25 was raised to *l* for our justification.
5:10 shall we be saved through his *l*!
5:18 was justification that brings *l*
5:21 righteousness to bring eternal *l*

Ro 6: 4 the Father, we too may live a new *l.*
6:13 have been brought from death to *l;*
6:22 holiness, and the result is eternal *l.*
6:23 but the gift of God is eternal *l*
8: 6 mind controlled by the Spirit is *l*
8:11 also give *l* to your mortal bodies
8:38 convinced that neither death nor *l,*
1Co 15:19 If only for this *l* we have hope
15:36 What you sow does not come to *l*
2Co 2:16 to the other, the fragrance of *l.*
3: 6 letter kills, but the Spirit gives *l.*
4:10 so that the *l* of Jesus may
5: 4 is mortal may be swallowed up by *l.*
Gal 2:20 The *l* I live in the body, I live
3:21 had been given that could impart *l,*
6: 8 from the Spirit will reap eternal *l.*
Eph 4: 1 I urge you to live a *l* worthy
Php 2:16 as you hold out the word of *l*—
4: 3 whose names are in the book of *l.*
Col 1:10 order that you may live a *l* worthy
3: 3 your *l* is now hidden with Christ
1Th 4:12 so that your daily *l* may win
1Ti 1:16 on him and receive eternal *l.*
4: 8 for both the present *l* and the *l*
4:12 in *l,* in love, in faith and in purity.
4:16 Watch your *l* and doctrine closely.
6:12 Take hold of the eternal *l*
6:19 hold of the *l* that is truly *l.*
2Ti 1: 9 saved us and called us to a holy *l*—
1:10 destroyed death and has brought *l*
3:12 to live a godly *l* in Christ Jesus will
Tit 1: 2 resting on the hope of eternal *l,*
3: 7 heirs having the hope of eternal *l.*
Heb 7:16 of the power of an indestructible *l.*
Jas 1:12 crown of *l* that God has promised
3:13 Let him show it by his good *l,*
1Pe 3: 7 with you of the gracious gift of *l,*
3:10 "Whoever would love *l*
4: 2 rest of his earthly *l* for evil human
2Pe 1: 3 given us everything we need for *l*
1Jn 1: 1 proclaim concerning the Word of *l.*
2:25 he promised us—even eternal *l.*
3:14 we have passed from death to *l,*
3:16 Jesus Christ laid down his *l* for us.
5:11 has given us eternal *l,* and this *l* is
5:20 He is the true God and eternal *l.*
Jude :21 Christ to bring you to eternal *l.*
Rev 2: 7 the right to eat from the tree of *l,*
2: 8 who died and came to *l* again.
2:10 and I will give you the crown of *l.*
3: 5 name from the book of *l,*
13: 8 written in the book of *l* belonging
17: 8 in the book of *l* from the creation
20:12 was opened, which is the book of *l.*
20:15 not found written in the book of *l,*
21: 6 from the spring of the water of *l.*
21:27 written in the Lamb's book of *l.*
22: 1 me the river of the water of *l,*
22: 2 side of the river stood the tree of *l,*
22:14 may have the right to the tree of *l*
22:17 take the free gift of the water of *l.*
22:19 from him his share in the tree of *l*

LIFE-GIVING (GIVE)
Pr 15:31 He who listens to a *l* rebuke
1Co 15:45 being"; the last Adam, a *l* spirit.

LIFETIME (LIVE)
Ps 30: 5 but his favor lasts a *l;*
Lk 16:25 in your *l* you received your good

LIFT (LIFTED LIFTING LIFTS)
Ps 3: 3 you bestow glory on me and *l*
28: 2 as I *l* up my hands
63: 4 in your name I will *l* up my hands.
91:12 they will *l* you up in their hands,
121: 1 I *l* up my eyes to the hills—
123: 1 I *l* up my eyes to you,
134: 2 *L* up your hands in the sanctuary
143: 8 for to you I *l* up my soul.
Isa 40: 9 *l* up your voice with a shout,
La 2:19 *L* up your hands to him
3:41 Let us *l* up our hearts and our
Mt 4: 6 they will *l* you up in their hands,
Lk 21:28 stand up and *l* up your heads,
1Ti 2: 8 everywhere to *l* up holy hands
Jas 4:10 the Lord, and he will *l* you up.
1Pe 5: 6 that he may *l* you up in due time.

LIFTED (LIFT)
Ne 8: 6 and all the people *l* their hands
Ps 24: 7 be *l* up, you ancient doors,
40: 2 He *l* me out of the slimy pit,
41: 9 has *l* up his heel against me.
Isa 52:13 *l* up and highly exalted.
63: 9 he *l* them up and carried them
Jn 3:14 Moses *l* up the snake in the desert,
8:28 "When you have *l* up the Son
12:32 when I am *l* up from the earth,
12:34 'The Son of Man must be *l* up'?
13:18 shares my bread has *l* up his heel

LIFTING (LIFT)
Ps 141: 2 may the *l* up of my hands be like

LIFTS (LIFT)
Ps 113: 7 and *l* the needy from the ash heap;

LIGAMENT* (LIGAMENTS)
Eph 4:16 held together by every supporting *l*

LIGAMENTS* (LIGAMENT)
Col 2:19 held together by its *l* and sinews,

LIGHT (ENLIGHTENED LIGHTS)
Ge 1: 3 "Let there be *l,*" and there was *l.*
Ex 13:21 in a pillar of fire to give them *l,*
25:37 it so that they *l* the space in front
2Sa 22:29 LORD turns my darkness into *l.*
Job 38:19 "What is the way to the abode of *l?*
Ps 4: 6 Let the *l* of your face shine upon us
18:28 my God turns my darkness into *l.*
19: 8 giving *l* to the eyes.
27: 1 LORD is my *l* and my salvation—
36: 9 in your *l* we see *l.*
56:13 God in the *l* of life.
76: 4 You are resplendent with *l,*
89:15 who walk in the *l* of your presence,
104: 2 He wraps himself in *l*
119:105 and a *l* for my path.
119:130 The unfolding of your words gives *l;*
139:12 for darkness is as *l* to you.
Pr 4:18 till the full *l* of day.
Isa 2: 5 let us walk in the *l* of the LORD.
9: 2 have seen a great *l;*
42: 6 and a *l* for the Gentiles,
45: 7 I form the *l* and create darkness,
49: 6 also make you a *l* for the Gentiles,
53:11 he will see the *l* of life
60: 1 "Arise, shine, for your *l* has come,
60:19 LORD will be your everlasting *l,*
Eze 1:27 and brilliant *l* surrounded him.
Mic 7: 8 the LORD will be my *l.*
Mt 4:16 have seen a great *l;*
5:14 "You are the *l* of the world.
5:15 it gives *l* to everyone in the house.
5:16 let your *l* shine before men,
6:22 your whole body will be full of *l.*
11:30 yoke is easy and my burden is *l.*"
17: 2 his clothes became as white as the *l*
24:29 and the moon will not give its *l;*
Mk 13:24 and the moon will not give its *l;*
Lk 2:32 a *l* for revelation to the Gentiles
8:16 those who come in can see the *l.*
11:33 those who come in may see the *l.*
Jn 1: 4 and that life was the *l* of men.
1: 5 The *l* shines in the darkness,
1: 7 witness to testify concerning that *l,*
1: 9 The true *l* that gives *l*
3:19 but men loved darkness instead of *l*
3:20 Everyone who does evil hates the *l,*
8:12 he said, "I am the *l* of the world.
Jn 9: 5 in the world, I am the *l* of the world
12:35 Walk while you have the *l,*
12:46 I have come into the world as a *l,*
Ac 13:47 " 'I have made you a *l*
Ro 13:12 darkness and put on the armor of *l.*
2Co 4: 6 made his *l* shine in our hearts
6:14 Or what fellowship can *l* have
11:14 masquerades as an angel of *l.*
Eph 5: 8 but now you are *l* in the Lord.
1Th 5: 5 You are all sons of the *l*
1Ti 6:16 and who lives in unapproachable *l,*
1Pe 2: 9 of darkness into his wonderful *l.*
2Pe 1:19 as to a *l* shining in a dark place,
1Jn 1: 5 God is *l;* in him there is no
1: 7 But if we walk in the *l,*
2: 9 Anyone who claims to be in the *l*
Rev 21:23 for the glory of God gives it *l,*
22: 5 for the Lord God will give them *l.*

LIGHTNING
Ex 9:23 and *l* flashed down to the ground.
20:18 and *l* and heard the trumpet
Ps 18:12 with hailstones and bolts of *l.*
Eze 1:13 it was bright, and *l* flashed out of it.
Da 10: 6 his face like *l,* his eyes like flaming
Mt 24:27 For as the *l* that comes from the east
28: 3 His appearance was like *l,*
Lk 10:18 "I saw Satan fall like *l* from heaven.
Rev 4: 5 From the throne came flashes of *l,*

LIGHTS (LIGHT)
Ge 1:14 "Let there be *l* in the expanse
Lk 8:16 No one *l* a lamp and hides it in a jar

LIKE-MINDED* (MIND)
Php 2: 2 make my joy complete by being *l,*

LIKENESS
Ge 1:26 man in our image, in our *l,*
Ps 17:15 I will be satisfied with seeing your *l*
Isa 52:14 his form marred beyond human *l*—
Ro 8: 3 Son in the *l* of sinful man
8:29 to be conformed to the *l* of his Son,
2Co 3:18 his *l* with ever-increasing glory,
Php 2: 7 being made in human *l.*
Jas 3: 9 who have been made in God's *l.*

LILIES (LILY)
Lk 12:27 "Consider how the *l* grow.

LILY (LILIES)
SS 2: 1 a *l* of the valleys.
2: 2 *Lover* Like a *l* among thorns

LIMIT
Ps 147: 5 his understanding has no *l.*
Jn 3:34 for God gives the Spirit without *l.*

LINEN
Lev 16: 4 He is to put on the sacred *l* tunic,
Pr 31:22 she is clothed in fine *l* and purple.
31:24 She makes *l* garments
Mk 15:46 So Joseph bought some *l* cloth,
Jn 20: 6 He saw the strips of *l* lying there,
Rev 15: 6 shining *l* and wore golden sashes
19: 8 Fine *l,* bright and clean,

LINGER
Hab 2: 3 Though it *l,* wait for it;

LION (LION'S LIONS')
Jdg 14: 6 power so that he tore the *l* apart
1Sa 17:34 When a *l* or a bear came
Isa 11: 7 and the *l* will eat straw like the ox.
65:25 and the *l* will eat straw like the ox,
Eze 1:10 right side each had the face of a *l,*
10:14 the third the face of a *l,*
Da 7: 4 "The first was like a *l,*
1Pe 5: 8 around like a roaring *l* looking
Rev 4: 7 The first living creature was like a *l*
5: 5 See, the *L* of the tribe of Judah,

LION'S (LION)
Ge 49: 9 You are a *l* cub, O Judah;

LIONS' (LION)
Da 6: 7 shall be thrown into the *l* den.

LIPS
Ps 8: 2 From the *l* of children and infants
34: 1 his praise will always be on my *l.*
40: 9 I do not seal my *l,*
63: 3 my *l* will glorify you.
119:171 May my *l* overflow with praise,
140: 3 the poison of vipers is on their *l.*
141: 3 keep watch over the door of my *l.*
Pr 10:13 on the *l* of the discerning,
10:18 who conceals his hatred has lying *l,*
10:32 *l* of the righteous know what is
12:22 The LORD detests lying *l,*
13: 3 He who guards his *l* guards his life,
14: 7 will not find knowledge on his *l.*
24:26 is like a kiss on the *l.*
26:23 are fervent *l* with an evil heart.
27: 2 someone else, and not your own *l.*
Isa 6: 5 For I am a man of unclean *l,*
28:11 with foreign *l* and strange tongues
29:13 and honor me with their *l,*
Mal 2: 7 "For the *l* of a priest ought
Mt 15: 8 These people honor me with their *l*
21:16 " 'From the *l* of children
Lk 4:22 words that came from his *l.*
Ro 3:13 "The poison of vipers is on their *l.*"
Col 3: 8 and filthy language from your *l.*
Heb 13:15 the fruit of *l* that confess his name.
1Pe 3:10 and his *l* from deceitful speech.

LISTEN (LISTENED LISTENING LISTENS)
Dt 18:15 You must *l* to him.
30:20 *l* to his voice, and hold fast to him.
1Ki 4:34 came to *l* to Solomon's wisdom,
2Ki 21: 9 But the people did not *l.*
Pr 1: 5 let the wise *l* and add
Ecc 5: 1 Go near to *l* rather
Eze 2: 5 And whether they *l* or fail to *l*—
Mt 12:42 earth to *l* to Solomon's wisdom,
Mk 9: 7 *L* to him!" Suddenly,
Jn 10:27 My sheep *l* to my voice; I know
Ac 3:22 you must *l* to everything he tells
Jas 1:19 Everyone should be quick to *l,*
1:22 Do not merely *l* to the word,
1Jn 4: 6 not from God does not *l* to us.

LISTENED (LISTEN)
Ne 8: 3 And all the people *l* attentively
Isa 66: 4 when I spoke, no one *l.*
Da 9: 6 We have not *l* to your servants

LISTENING (LISTEN)
1Sa 3: 9 Speak, LORD, for your servant is *l*
Pr 18:13 He who answers before *l*—
Lk 10:39 at the Lord's feet *l* to what he said.

LISTENS (LISTEN)
Pr 12:15 but a wise man *l* to advice.
Lk 10:16 "He who *l* to you *l*
1Jn 4: 6 and whoever knows God *l* to us;

LIVE (ALIVE LIFE LIFETIME LIVES LIVING)
Ge 3:22 tree of life and eat, and *l* forever."
Ex 20:12 so that you may *l* long
33:20 for no one may see me and *l.*"
Nu 21: 8 who is bitten can look at it and *l.*"
Dt 5:24 we have seen that a man can *l*
6: 2 as you *l* by keeping all his decrees
8: 3 to teach you that man does not *l*
Job 14:14 If a man dies, will he *l* again?
Ps 15: 1 Who may *l* on your holy hill?
24: 1 the world, and all who *l* in it;
26: 8 I love the house where you *l,*
119:175 Let me *l* that I may praise you,
Pr 21: 9 Better to *l* on a corner of the roof
21:19 Better to *l* in a desert
Ecc 9: 4 a *l* dog is better off than a dead lion
Isa 26:19 But your dead will *l;*
55: 3 hear me, that your soul may *l.*
Eze 17:19 LORD says: As surely as I *l,*
20:11 for the man who obeys them will *l*
37: 3 can these bones *l?*" I said,
Am 5: 6 Seek the LORD and *l,*
Hab 2: 4 but the righteous will *l* by his faith
Zec 2:11 I will *l* among you and you will
Mt 4: 4 'Man does not *l* on bread alone,
Lk 4: 4 'Man does not *l* on bread alone.' "
Jn 14:19 Because I *l,* you also will *l.*
Ac 17:24 does not *l* in temples built by hands
17:28 'For in him we *l* and move
Ro 1:17 "The righteous will *l* by faith."
2Co 5: 7 We *l* by faith, not by sight.
6:16 "I will *l* with them and walk
Gal 2:20 The life I *l* in the body, I *l* by faith
3:11 "The righteous will *l* by faith."
5:25 Since we *l* by the Spirit, let us keep
Eph 4:17 that you must no longer *l*
Php 1:21 to *l* is Christ and to die is gain.
Col 1:10 order that you may *l* a life worthy
1Th 4: 1 we instructed you how to *l* in order
5:13 *L* in peace with each other.
1Ti 2: 2 that we may *l* peaceful
2Ti 3:12 who wants to *l* a godly life
Tit 2:12 and to *l* self-controlled, upright
Heb 10:38 But my righteous one will *l* by faith
12:14 Make every effort to *l* in peace
1Pe 1:17 *l* your lives as strangers here
3: 8 *l* in harmony with one another;

LIVES (LIVE)
Ge 45: 7 and to save your *l* by a great
Job 19:25 I know that my Redeemer *l,*
Pr 1:19 it takes away the *l*
Isa 57:15 he who *l* forever, whose name is
Da 3:28 to give up their *l* rather than serve
Jn 14:17 for he *l* with you and will be in you.
Ro 6:10 but the life he *l,* he *l* to God.
7:18 I know that nothing good *l* in me,
8: 9 if the Spirit of God *l* in you.
14: 7 For none of us *l* to himself alone
1Co 3:16 and that God's Spirit *l* in you?
Gal 2:20 I no longer live, but Christ *l* in me.
1Th 2: 8 only the gospel of God but our *l*
1Ti 2: 2 quiet *l* in all godliness and holiness.
Tit 2:12 and godly *l* in this present age,
Heb 7:24 but because Jesus *l* forever,
13: 5 Keep your *l* free from the love
1Pe 3: 2 the purity and reverence of your *l.*
2Pe 3:11 You ought to live holy and godly *l*
1Jn 3:16 to lay down our *l* for our brothers.
4:16 Whoever *l* in love *l* in God,

LIVING (LIVE)
Ge 2: 7 and the man became a *l* being.
1Sa 17:26 defy the armies of the *l* God?"
Isa 53: 8 cut off from the land of the *l;*
Jer 2:13 the spring of *l* water,
Eze 1: 5 what looked like four *l* creatures.
Zec 14: 8 On that day *l* water will flow out
Mt 22:32 the God of the dead but of the *l.*"
Jn 4:10 he would have given you *l* water."
6:51 I am the *l* bread that came
7:38 streams of *l* water will flow
Ro 8:11 Jesus from the dead is *l* in you,
12: 1 to offer your bodies as *l* sacrifices,
1Co 9:14 the gospel should receive their *l*
Heb 4:12 For the word of God is *l* and active.
10:20 and *l* way opened for us
10:31 to fall into the hands of the *l* God.
1Pe 1:23 through the *l* and enduring word
Rev 1:18 I am the *L* One; I was dead,
4: 6 the throne, were four *l* creatures,
7:17 to springs of *l* water.

LOAD (LOADS)
Gal 6: 5 for each one should carry his own *l.*

LOADS (LOAD)
Mt 23: 4 They tie up heavy *l* and put them

LOAF (LOAVES)
1Co 10:17 for we all partake of the one *l.*

LOAVES (LOAF)
Mk 6:41 Taking the five *l* and the two fish
8: 6 When he had taken the seven *l*
Lk 11: 5 'Friend, lend me three *l* of bread,

LOCKED
Jn 20:26 the doors were *l,* Jesus came
Gal 3:23 *l* up until faith should be revealed.

LOCUSTS
Ex 10: 4 I will bring *l* into your country
Joel 2:25 you for the years the *l* have eaten—
Mt 3: 4 His food was *l* and wild honey.
Rev 9: 3 And out of the smoke *l* came

LOFTY
Ps 139: 6 too *l* for me to attain.
Isa 57:15 is what the high and *l* One says—

LONELY
Ps 68: 6 God sets the *l* in families,
Lk 5:16 Jesus often withdrew to *l* places

LONG (LENGTH LENGTHY LONGED LONGING LONGINGS LONGS)
Ex 17:11 As *l* as Moses held up his hands,
Nu 6: 5 the hair of his head grow *l.*
1Ki 18:21 "How *l* will you waver
Ps 119:97 I meditate on it all day *l.*
119:174 I *l* for your salvation, O LORD,
Hos 7:13 I *l* to redeem them
Am 5:18 Why do you *l* for the day
Mt 25: 5 The bridegroom was a *l* time
Jn 9: 4 As *l* as it is day, we must do
1Co 11:14 that if a man has *l* hair,
Eph 3:18 to grasp how wide and *l* and high
Php 1: 8 God can testify how I *l* for all
1Pe 1:12 Even angels *l* to look

LONGED (LONG)
Mt 13:17 righteous men *l* to see what you see
23:37 how often I have *l*
Lk 13:34 how often I have *l*
2Ti 4: 8 to all who have *l* for his appearing.

LONGING* (LONG)
Dt 28:65 with *l,* and a despairing heart.
Job 7: 2 Like a slave *l* for the evening
Ps 119:20 My soul is consumed with *l*
119:81 with *l* for your salvation,
119:131 *l* for your commands.
143: 7 my spirit faints with *l.*
Pr 13:12 but a *l* fulfilled is a tree of life.
13:19 A *l* fulfilled is sweet to the soul,
Eze 23:27 look on these things with *l*
Lk 16:21 and *l* to eat what fell from the rich
Ro 15:23 since I have been *l* for many years
2Co 5: 2 *l* to be clothed with our heavenly
7: 7 He told us about your *l* for me,
7:11 what alarm, what *l,* what concern,
1Th 2:17 out of our intense *l* we made every
Heb 11:16 they were *l* for a better country—

LONGINGS* (LONG)
Ps 38: 9 All my *l* lie open before you,
112:10 the *l* of the wicked will come

LONGS* (LONG)
Ps 63: 1 my body *l* for you,
Isa 26: 9 in the morning my spirit *l* for you.
30:18 Yet the LORD *l* to be gracious
Php 2:26 For he *l* for all of you and is

LOOK (LOOKED LOOKING LOOKS)
Ge 19:17 "Flee for your lives! Don't *l* back,
Ex 3: 6 because he was afraid to *l* at God.

Nu 21: 8 anyone who is bitten can *l* at it
32: 8 Kadesh Barnea to *l* over the land.
Dt 4:29 you will find him if you *l* for him
1Sa 16: 7 The LORD does not *l*
Job 31: 1 not to *l* lustfully at a girl.
Ps 34: 5 Those who *l* to him are radiant;
105: 4 *L* to the LORD and his strength;
113: 6 who stoops down to *l*
123: 2 As the eyes of slaves *l* to the hand
Pr 1:28 they will *l* for me but will not find
4:25 Let your eyes *l* straight ahead,
15:30 A cheerful *l* brings joy to the heart,
Isa 17: 7 In that day men will *l*
31: 1 do not *l* to the Holy One of Israel,
40:26 Lift your eyes and *l* to the heavens:
60: 5 Then you will *l* and be radiant,
Jer 3: 3 Yet you have the brazen *l*
6:16 "Stand at the crossroads and *l*;
Eze 34:11 for my sheep and *l* after them.
Hab 1:13 Your eyes are too pure to *l* on evil;
Zec 12:10 They will *l* on me, the one they
Mt 18:10 "See that you do not *l* down on one
18:12 go to *l* for the one that wandered
23:27 which *l* beautiful on the outside
Mk 13:21 '*L*, here is the Christ!' or, '*L*,
Lk 6:41 "Why do you *l* at the speck
24:39 *L* at my hands and my feet.
Jn 1:36 he said, "*L*, the Lamb of God!"
4:35 open your eyes and *l* at the fields!
19:37 "They will *l* on the one they have
Ro 14:10 why do you *l* down on your brother
Php 2: 4 Each of you should *l* not only
1Ti 4:12 Don't let anyone *l* down on you
Jas 1:27 to *l* after orphans and widows
1Pe 1:12 long to *l* into these things.
2Pe 3:12 as you *l* forward to the day of God

LOOKED (LOOK)
Ge 19:26 Lot's wife *l* back, and she became
Ex 2:25 So God *l* on the Israelites
1Sa 6:19 because they had *l* into the ark
SS 3: I *l* for the one my heart loves;
Eze 22:30 "I *l* for a man among them who
34: 6 and no one searched or *l* for them.
44: 4 I *l* and saw the glory
Da 7: 9 "As I *l*,
10: 5 I *l* up and there before me was
Hab 3: 6 he *l*, and made the nations tremble.
Mt 25:36 I was sick and you *l* after me,
Lk 18: 9 and *l* down on everybody else,
22:61 The Lord turned and *l* straight
1Jn 1: 1 which we have *l* at and our hands

LOOKING (LOOK)
Ps 69: 3 *l* for my God.
119:82 My eyes fail, *l* for your promise;
119:123 My eyes fail, *l* for your salvation,
Mk 16: 6 "You are *l* for Jesus the Nazarene,
2Co 10: 7 You are *l* only on the surface
Php 4:17 Not that I am *l* for a gift,
1Th 2: 6 We were not *l* for praise from men,
2Pe 3:13 with his promise we are *l* forward
Rev 5: 6 I saw a Lamb, *l* as if it had been

LOOKS (LOOK)
1Sa 16: 7 Man *l* at the outward appearance,
Ezr 8:22 is on everyone who *l* to him,
Ps 104:32 who *l* at the earth, and it trembles;
138: 6 on high, he *l* upon the lowly,
Pr 27:18 he who *l* after his master will be
Eze 34:12 As a shepherd *l* after his scattered
Mt 5:28 But I tell you that anyone who *l*
16: 4 and adulterous generation *l*
Lk 9:62 and *l* back is fit for service
Jn 6:40 Father's will is that everyone who *l*
12:45 When he *l* at me, he sees the one
Php 2:21 For everyone *l* out
Jas 1:25 But the man who *l* intently

LOOSE
Isa 33:23 Your rigging hangs *l*:

Mt 16:19 and whatever you *l* on earth will be
18:18 and whatever you *l* on earth will be

LORD† (= Lord in the NIV. See also LORD'S† LORDED LORDING)
Ge 18:27 been so bold as to speak to the *L*,
Ex 15:17 O *L*, your hands established.
Nu 16:13 now you also want to *l* it over us?
Dt 10:17 God of gods and *L* of lords,
Jos 3:13 the *L* of all the earth—set foot
1Ki 3:10 *L* was pleased that Solomon had
Ne 4:14 Remember the *L*, who is great
Job 28:28 'The fear of the *L*— that is wisdom,
Ps 37:13 but the *L* laughs at the wicked,
38:22 O *L* my Savior.
54: 4 the *L* is the one who sustains me.
62:12 and that you, O *L*, are loving.
69: 6 O *L*, the LORD Almighty;
86: 5 You are forgiving and good, O *L*,
86: 8 gods there is none like you, O *L*;
89:49 O *L*, where is your former great
110: 1 The LORD says to my *L*:
110: 5 The *L* is at your right hand;
130: 3 O *L*, who could stand?
135: 5 that our *L* is greater than all gods.
136: 3 Give thanks to the *L* of lords:
147: 5 Great is our *L* and mighty in power
Isa 6: 1 I saw the *L* seated on a throne,
Da 2:47 and the *L* of kings and a revealer
9: 4 "O *L*, the great and awesome God,
9: 7 "*L*, you are righteous,
9: 9 The *L* our God is merciful
9:19 O *L*, listen! O *L*, forgive! O *L*,
Mt 3: 3 'Prepare the way for the *L*,
4: 7 'Do not put the *L* your God
4:10 'Worship the *L* your God,
7:21 "Not everyone who says to me, '*L*,
9:38 Ask the *L* of the harvest, therefore,
12: 8 Son of Man is *L* of the Sabbath."
20:25 of the Gentiles *l* it over them,
21: 9 comes in the name of the *L*!"
22:37 " 'Love the *L* your God
22:44 For he says, " 'The *L* said to my *L*:
23:39 comes in the name of the *L*.' "
Mk 1: 3 'Prepare the way for the *L*,
12:11 the *L* has done this,
12:29 the *L* our God, the *L* is one.
12:30 Love the *L* your God
Lk 2: 9 glory of the *L* shone around them,
6: 5 The Son of Man is *L* of the Sabbath
6:46 "Why do you call me, '*L*, *L*,'
10:27 " 'Love the *L* your God
11: 1 one of his disciples said to him, "*L*,
24:34 The *L* has risen and has appeared
Jn 1:23 'Make straight the way for the *L*.' "
Ac 2:21 on the name of the *L* will be saved.'
2:25 " 'I saw the *L* always before me.
2:34 " 'The *L* said to my *L*:
8:16 into the name of the *L* Jesus.
9: 5 "Who are you, *L*?" Saul asked.
10:36 through Jesus Christ, who is *L*
11:23 true to the *L* with all their hearts.
16:31 replied, "Believe in the *L* Jesus,
Ro 4:24 in him who raised Jesus our *L*
5:11 in God through our *L* Jesus Christ,
6:23 life in Christ Jesus our *L*.
8:39 of God that is in Christ Jesus our *L*.
10: 9 with your mouth, "Jesus is *L*,"
10:13 on the name of the *L* will be saved
10:16 *L*, who has believed our message?"
11:34 Who has known the mind of the *L*?
12:11 your spiritual fervor, serving the *L*.
13:14 yourselves with the *L* Jesus Christ,
14: 4 for the *L* is able to make him stand.
14: 8 we live to the *L*; and if we die,
1Co 1:31 Let him who boasts boast in the *L*."
3: 5 the *L* has assigned to each his task.
4: 5 time; wait till the *L* comes.
6:13 for the *L*, and the *L* for the body.
6:14 By his power God raised the *L*
7:32 affairs—how he can please the *L*.

1Co 7:34 to be devoted to the *L* in both body
7:35 in undivided devotion to the *L*.
7:39 but he must belong to the *L*.
8: 6 and there is but one *L*, Jesus Christ,
10: 9 We should not test the *L*,
11:23 For I received from the *L* what I
12: 3 "Jesus is *L*," except by the Holy
15:57 victory through our *L* Jesus Christ.
15:58 fully to the work of the *L*,
16:22 If anyone does not love the *L*—
2Co 1:24 Not that we *l* it over your faith,
2:12 found that the *L* had opened a door
3:17 Now the *L* is the Spirit,
4: 5 but Jesus Christ as *L*, and ourselves
5: 6 in the body we are away from the *L*
8: 5 they gave themselves first to the *L*
8:21 not only in the eyes of the *L* but
10:17 Let him who boasts boast in the *L*."
10:18 but the one whom the *L* commends
13:10 the authority the *L* gave me
Gal 6:14 in the cross of our *L* Jesus Christ,
Eph 4: 5 one *L*, one faith, one baptism;
5: 8 but now you are light in the *L*.
5:10 and find out what pleases the *L*.
5:19 make music in your heart to the *L*,
5:22 submit to your husbands as to the *L*
6: 1 obey your parents in the *L*,
6: 7 as if you were serving the *L*,
6: 8 know that the *L* will reward
6:10 in the *L* and in his mighty power.
Php 2:11 confess that Jesus Christ is *L*,
3: 1 my brothers, rejoice in the *L*!
3: 8 of knowing Christ Jesus my *L*,
4: 1 you should stand firm in the *L*,
4: 4 Rejoice in the *L* always.
4: 5 The *L* is near.
Col 1:10 you may live a life worthy of the *L*
2: 6 as you received Christ Jesus as *L*,
3:13 Forgive as the *L* forgave you.
3:17 do it all in the name of the *L* Jesus,
3:18 your husbands, as is fitting in the *L*.
3:20 in everything, for this pleases the *L*
3:23 as working for the *L*, not for men,
3:24 It is the *L* Christ you are serving.
3:24 receive an inheritance from the *L*
4:17 work you have received in the *L*."
1Th 3: 8 since you are standing firm in the *L*
3:12 May the *L* make your love increase
4: 1 and urge you in the *L* Jesus
4: 6 The *L* will punish men
4:15 who are left till the coming of the *L*
5: 2 day of the *L* will come like a thief
5:23 at the coming of our *L* Jesus Christ.
2Th 1: 7 when the *L* Jesus is revealed
1:12 of our *L* Jesus may be glorified
2: 1 the coming of our *L* Jesus Christ
2: 8 whom the *L* Jesus will overthrow
3: 3 *L* is faithful, and he will strengthen
3: 5 May the *L* direct your hearts
1Ti 6:15 the King of kings and *L* of lords,
2Ti 1: 8 ashamed to testify about our *L*,
2:19 "The *L* knows those who are his,"
4: 8 which the *L*, the righteous Judge,
4:17 But the *L* stood at my side
Heb 1:10 O *L*, you laid the foundations
10:30 "The *L* will judge his people."
12:14 holiness no one will see the *L*.
13: 6 *L* is my helper; I will not be afraid.
Jas 3: 9 With the tongue we praise our *L*
4:10 Humble yourselves before the *L*,
5:11 The *L* is full of compassion
1Pe 1:25 the word of the *L* stands forever."
2: 3 you have tasted that the *L* is good.
3:12 eyes of the *L* are on the righteous
3:15 in your hearts set apart Christ as *L*.
2Pe 1:11 into the eternal kingdom of our *L*
1:16 and coming of our *L* Jesus Christ,
2: 1 the sovereign *L* who bought
2: 9 then the *L* knows how
3: 9 The *L* is not slow in keeping his

Pr 3: 5 Trust in the *L* with all your heart
3: 7 fear the *L* and shun evil.
3: 9 Honor the *L* with your wealth,
3:12 the *L* disciplines those he loves,
3:19 By wisdom the *L* laid the earth's
5:21 are in full view of the *L*,
6:16 There are six things the *L* hates,
8:13 To fear the *L* is to hate evil;
9:10 "The fear of the *L* is the beginning
10:27 The fear of the *L* adds length to life
11: 1 The *L* abhors dishonest scales,
12:22 The *L* detests lying lips,
14: 2 whose walk is upright fears the *L*,
14:26 He who fears the *L* has a secure
14:27 The fear of the *L* is a fountain
15: 3 The eyes of the *L* are everywhere,
15:16 Better a little with the fear of the *L*
15:33 of the *L* teaches a man wisdom,
16: 2 but motives are weighed by the *L*.
16: 3 Commit to the *L* whatever you do,
16: 4 The *L* works out everything
16: 5 The *L* detests all the proud of heart
16: 9 but the *L* determines his steps.
16:33 but its every decision is from the *L*.
18:10 The name of the *L* is a strong tower
18:22 and receives favor from the *L*.
19:14 but a prudent wife is from the *L*.
19:17 to the poor lends to the *L*,
19:23 The fear of the *L* leads to life:
20:10 the *L* detests them both.
21: 2 but the *L* weighs the heart.
21: 3 to the *L* than sacrifice.
21:30 that can succeed against the *L*.
21:31 but victory rests with the *L*.
22: 2 The *L* is the Maker of them all.
22:23 for the *L* will take up their case
23:17 for the fear of the *L*.
24:18 or the *L* will see and disapprove
24:21 Fear the *L* and the king, my son,
25:22 and the *L* will reward you.
28:14 is the man who always fears the *L*,
29:26 from the *L* that man gets justice.
30: 7 "Two things I ask of you, O *L*;
31:30 a woman who fears the *L* is
Isa 2: 3 up to the mountain of the *L*,
2:10 the ground from dread of the *L*
3:17 the *L* will make their scalps bald."
4: 2 of the *L* will be beautiful
5:16 the *L* Almighty will be exalted
6: 3 holy, holy is the *L* Almighty;
9: 7 The zeal of the *L* Almighty
11: 2 The Spirit of the *L* will rest on him
11: 9 full of the knowledge of the *L*
12: 2 The *L*, the *L*, is my strength
18: 7 of the Name of the *L* Almighty.
24: 1 the *L* is going to lay waste the earth
25: 1 O *L*, you are my God;
25: 6 this mountain the *L* Almighty will
25: 8 The Sovereign *L* will wipe away
26: 4 Trust in the *L* forever,
26: 8 *L*, walking in the way of your laws,
26:13 O *L*, our God, other lords
26:21 the *L* is coming out of his dwelling
27: 1 the *L* will punish with his sword,
27:12 In that day the *L* will thresh
28: 5 In that day the *L* Almighty
29: 6 the *L* Almighty will come
29:15 to hide their plans from the *L*,
30:18 For the *L* is a God of justice.
30:26 when the *L* binds up the bruises
30:27 the Name of the *L* comes from afar
30:30 The *L* will cause men
33: 2 O *L*, be gracious to us;
33: 6 the fear of the *L* is the key
33:22 For the *L* is our judge,
34: 2 The *L* is angry with all nations;
35: 2 they will see the glory of the *L*,
35:10 the ransomed of the *L* will return.
38: 7 to you that the *L* will do what he
40: 3 the way for the *L*;
Isa 40: 5 the glory of the *L* will be revealed,
40: 7 the breath of the *L* blows on them.
40:10 the Sovereign *L* comes with power,
40:14 Whom did the *L* consult
40:28 The *L* is the everlasting God,
40:31 but those who hope in the *L*
41:14 will help you," declares the *L*,
41:20 that the hand of the *L* has done this
42: 6 the *L*, have called you
42: 8 "I am the *L*; that is my name!
42:13 The *L* will march out like a mighty
42:21 It pleased the *L*
43: 3 For I am the *L*, your God,
43:11 I, even I, am the *L*,
44: 6 "This is what the *L* says—
44:24 I am the *L*,
45: 5 I am the *L*, and there is no other;
45: 7 I, the *L*, do all these things.
45:21 Was it not I, the *L*?
48:17 "I am the *L* your God,
50: 4 Sovereign *L* has given me
50:10 Who among you fears the *L*
51: 1 and who seek the *L*:
51:11 The ransomed of the *L* will return.
51:15 the *L* Almighty is his name.
53: 1 the arm of the *L* been revealed?
53: 6 and the *L* has laid on him
53:10 and the will of the *L* will prosper
54: 5 the *L* Almighty is his name—
55: 6 Seek the *L* while he may be found;
55: 7 to the *L*, and he will have mercy
56: 6 who bind themselves to the *L*
58: 8 of the *L* will be your rear guard.
58:11 The *L* will guide you always;
59: 1 the arm of the *L* is not too short
60: 1 the glory of the *L* rises upon you.
60:16 Then you will know that I, the *L*,
60:20 the *L* will be your everlasting light,
61: 1 Spirit of the Sovereign *L* is on me,
61: 3 a planting of the *L*
61:10 I delight greatly in the *L*;
61:11 so the Sovereign *L* will make
62: 4 for the *L* will take delight in you,
63: 7 I will tell of the kindnesses of the *L*,
64: 8 Yet, O *L*, you are our Father.
66:15 See, the *L* is coming with fire,
Jer 1: 9 Then the *L* reached out his hand
2:19 when you forsake the *L* your God
3:25 sinned against the *L* our God,
4: 4 Circumcise yourselves to the *L*,
8: 7 the requirements of the *L*.
9:24 I am the *L*, who exercises kindness,
10: 6 No one is like you, O *L*;
10:10 But the *L* is the true God;
12: 1 You are always righteous, O *L*,
14: 7 O *L*, do something for the sake
14:20 O *L*, we acknowledge our
16:15 will say, 'As surely as the *L* lives,
16:19 O *L*, my strength and my fortress,
17: 7 is the man who trusts in the *L*,
17:10 "I the *L* search the heart
20:11 *L* is with me like a mighty warrior;
23: 6 The *L* Our Righteousness.
24: 7 heart to know me, that I am the *L*.
28: 9 as one truly sent by the *L* only
31:11 For the *L* will ransom Jacob
31:22 The *L* will create a new thing
31:34 his brother, saying, 'Know the *L*,'
32:27 I am the *L*, the God of all mankind.
33:16 The *L* Our Righteousness.'
36: 6 the words of the *L* that you wrote
40: 3 now the *L* has brought it about;
42: 3 Pray that the *L* your God will tell
42: 4 I will tell you everything the *L* says
42: 6 we will obey the *L* our God,
50: 4 go in tears to seek the *L* their God.
51:10 " 'The *L* has vindicated us;
51:56 For the *L* is a God of retribution;
La 3:24 to myself, "The *L* is my portion;
3:25 *L* is good to those whose hope is
La 3:40 and let us return to the *L*.
Eze 1: 3 the word of the *L* came
1:28 of the likeness of the glory of the *L*.
4:14 Sovereign *L*! I have never defiled
10: 4 Then the glory of the *L* rose
15: 7 you will know that I am the *L*.
30: 3 the day of the *L* is near—
36:23 nations will know that I am the *L*,
37: 4 'Dry bones, hear the word of the *L*!
43: 4 glory of the *L* entered the temple
44: 4 LORD filling the temple of the *L*,
Da 9: 2 to the word of the *L* given
Hos 1: 7 horsemen, but by the *L* their God."
2:20 and you will acknowledge the *L*.
3: 1 as the *L* loves the Israelites,
3: 5 They will come trembling to the *L*
6: 1 "Come, let us return to the *L*.
6: 3 Let us acknowledge the *L*;
10:12 for it is time to seek the *L*,
12: 5 the *L* is his name of renown!
14: 1 O Israel, to the *L* your God.
Joel 1: 1 The word of the *L* that came
1:15 For the day of the *L* is near;
2: 1 for the day of the *L* is coming.
2:11 The day of the *L* is great;
2:13 Return to the *L* your God,
2:23 rejoice in the *L* your God,
2:31 the great and dreadful day of the *L*.
2:32 on the name of the *L* will be saved;
3:14 For the day of the *L* is near
3:16 the *L* will be a refuge for his people,
Am 4:13 the *L* God Almighty is his name.
5: 6 Seek the *L* and live,
5:15 Perhaps the *L* God Almighty will
5:18 long for the day of the *L*?
7:15 *L* took me from tending the flock
8:12 searching for the word of the *L*,
9: 5 The Lord, the *L* Almighty,
Ob :15 "The day of the *L* is near
Jnh 1: 3 But Jonah ran away from the *L*
1: 4 the *L* sent a great wind on the sea,
1:17 But the *L* provided a great fish
2: 9 Salvation comes from the *L*."
4: 2 He prayed to the *L*, "O *L*,
4: 6 Then the *L* God provided a vine
Mic 1: 1 The word of the *L* that came to Micah
4: 2 up to the mountain of the *L*,
5: 4 flock in the strength of the *L*,
6: 2 For the *L* has a case
6: 8 And what does the *L* require of you
7: 7 as for me, I watch in hope for the *L*,
Na 1: 2 The *L* takes vengeance on his foes
1: 3 The *L* is slow to anger
Hab 2:14 knowledge of the glory of the *L*,
2:20 But the *L* is in his holy temple;
3: 2 I stand in awe of your deeds, O *L*.
Zep 1: 1 The word of the *L* that came
1: 7 for the day of the *L* is near.
3:17 The *L* your God is with you,
Hag 1: 1 the word of the *L* came
1: 8 and be honored," says the *L*.
2:23 that day,' declares the *L* Almighty,
Zec 1: 1 the word of the *L* came
1:17 and the *L* will again comfort Zion
3: 1 standing before the angel of the *L*,
4: 6 by my Spirit,' says the *L* Almighty.
6:12 and build the temple of the *L*.
8:21 the *L* and seek the *L* Almighty.
9:16 The *L* their God will save them
14: 5 Then the *L* my God will come,
14: 9 The *L* will be king
14:16 the *L* Almighty, and to celebrate
Mal 1: 1 The word of the *L* to Israel
3: 6 "I the *L* do not change.
4: 5 and dreadful day of the *L* comes.

LORD'S‡ (= LORD's in the NIV. See also LORD‡)
Ex 4:14 the *L* anger burned against Moses
12:11 Eat it in haste; it is the *L* Passover.

Ex 34:34 he entered the *L* presence
Lev 23: 4 " 'These are the *L* appointed feasts,
Nu 9:23 At the *L* command they encamped
14:41 you disobeying the *L* command?
32:13 The *L* anger burned against Israel
Dt 6:18 is right and good in the *L* sight,
10:13 and to observe the *L* commands
32: 9 For the *L* portion is his people,
Jos 21:45 Not one of all the *L* good promises
1Sa 24:10 because he is the *L* anointed.'
1Ki 10: 9 Because of the *L* eternal love
Ps 24: 1 The earth is the *L*, and everything
32:10 but the *L* unfailing love
89: 1 of the *L* great love forever;
103:17 *L* love is with those who fear him,
118:15 "The *L* right hand has done mighty
Pr 3:11 do not despise the *L* discipline
19:21 but it is the *L* purpose that prevails.
Isa 24:14 west they acclaim the *L* majesty.
30: 9 to listen to the *L* instruction.
49: 4 Yet what is due me is in the *L* hand
53:10 Yet it was the *L* will to crush him
55:13 This will be for the *L* renown,
61: 2 to proclaim the year of the *L* favor
62: 3 of splendor in the *L* hand,
Jer 25:17 So I took the cup from the *L* hand
48:10 lax in doing the *L* work!
51: 7 was a gold cup in the *L* hand;
La 3:22 of the *L* great love we are not
Eze 7:19 them in the day of the *L* wrath.
Joel 3:18 will flow out of the *L* house
Ob :21 And the kingdom will be the *L*.
Mic 4: 1 of the *L* temple will be established
6: 2 O mountains, the *L* accusation;
Hab 2:16 from the *L* right hand is coming
Zep 2: 3 sheltered on the day of the *L* anger.

LOSE (LOSES LOSS LOST)
Dt 1:28 Our brothers have made us *l* heart.
1Sa 17:32 "Let no one *l* heart on account
Isa 7: 4 Do not *l* heart because of these two
Mt 10:39 Whoever finds his life will *l* it,
Lk 9:25 and yet *l* or forfeit his very self?
Jn 6:39 that I shall *l* none of all that he has
2Co 4: 1 this ministry, we do not *l* heart.
4:16 Therefore we do not *l* heart.
Heb 12: 3 will not grow weary and *l* heart.
12: 5 do not *l* heart when he rebukes you
2Jn : 8 that you do not *l* what you have

LOSES (LOSE)
Mt 5:13 But if the salt *l* its saltiness,
Lk 15: 4 you has a hundred sheep and *l* one
15: 8 has ten silver coins and *l* one.

LOSS (LOSE)
Ro 11:12 and their *l* means riches
1Co 3:15 he will suffer *l*; he himself will be
Php 3: 8 I consider everything a *l* compared

LOST (LOSE)
Ps 73: 2 I had nearly *l* my foothold.
Jer 50: 6 "My people have been *l* sheep;
Eze 34: 4 the strays or searched for the *l*.
34:16 for the *l* and bring back the strays.
Mt 18:14 any of these little ones should be *l*.
Lk 15: 4 go after the *l* sheep until he finds it?
15: 6 with me; I have found my *l* sheep.'
15: 9 with me; I have found my *l* coin.'
15:24 is alive again; he was *l* and is found
19:10 to seek and to save what was *l*."
Php 3: 8 for whose sake I have *l* all things.

LOT (LOTS)
Nephew of Abraham (Ge 11:27; 12:5). Chose to live in Sodom (Ge 13). Rescued from four kings (Ge 14). Rescued from Sodom (Ge 19:1–29; 2Pe 2:7). Fathered Moab and Ammon by his daughters (Ge 19:30–38).
Est 3: 7 the *l*) in the presence of Haman
9:24 the *l*) for their ruin and destruction.
Pr 16:33 The *l* is cast into the lap,
18:18 Casting the *l* settles disputes
Ecc 3:22 his work, because that is his *l*.
Ac 1:26 Then they cast lots, and the *l* fell

LOTS (LOT)
Jos 18:10 Joshua then cast *l* for them
Ps 22:18 and cast *l* for my clothing.
Joel 3: 3 They cast *l* for my people
Ob :11 and cast *l* for Jerusalem,
Mt 27:35 divided up his clothes by casting *l*.
Ac 1:26 Then they cast *l*, and the lot fell

LOVE* (BELOVED LOVED LOVELY LOVER LOVER'S LOVERS LOVES LOVING LOVING-KINDNESS)
Ge 20:13 'This is how you can show your *l*
22: 2 your only son, Isaac, whom you *l*,
29:18 Jacob was in *l* with Rachel and said
29:20 days to him because of his *l* for her.
29:32 Surely my husband will *l* me now."
Ex 15:13 "In your unfailing *l* you will lead
20: 6 showing *l* to a thousand generations
20: 6 of those who *l* me
21: 5 'I *l* my master and my wife
34: 6 abounding in *l* and faithfulness,
34: 7 maintaining *l* to thousands,
Lev 19:18 but *l* your neighbor as yourself.
19:34 *L* him as yourself,
Nu 14:18 abounding in *l* and forgiving sin
14:19 In accordance with your great *l*,
Dt 5:10 showing *l* to a thousand generations
5:10 of those who *l* me
6: 5 *L* the LORD your God
7: 9 generations of those who *l* him
7: 9 keeping his covenant of *l*
7:12 God will keep his covenant of *l*
7:13 He will *l* you and bless you
10:12 to walk in all his ways, to *l* him,
10:19 you are to *l* those who are aliens,
11: 1 *L* the LORD your God
11:13 to *l* the LORD your God
11:22 to *l* the LORD your God,
13: 3 you *l* him with all your heart
13: 6 wife you *l*, or your closest friend
19: 9 to *l* the LORD your God
21:15 the son of the wife he does not *l*,
21:16 the son of the wife he does not *l*.
30: 6 so that you may *l* him
30:16 today to *l* the LORD your God,
30:20 and that you may *l* the LORD your
33: 3 Surely it is you who *l* the people;
Jos 22: 5 to *l* the LORD your God, to walk
23:11 careful to *l* the LORD your God.
Jdg 5:31 may they who *l* you be like the sun
14:16 You hate me! You don't really *l* me
16: 4 he fell in *l* with a woman
16:15 "How can you say, 'I *l* you,'
1Sa 18:20 Saul's daughter Michal was in *l*
20:17 had David reaffirm his oath out of *l*
2Sa 1:26 Your *l* for me was wonderful,
7:15 But my *l* will never be taken away
13: 1 son of David fell in *l* with Tamar,
13: 4 said to him, "I'm in *l* with Tamar,
16:17 "Is this the *l* you show your friend?
19: 6 You *l* those who hate you
19: 6 hate you and hate those who *l* you.
1Ki 3: 3 Solomon showed his *l*
8:23 you who keep your covenant of *l*
10: 9 of the LORD's eternal *l* for Israel,
11: 2 Solomon held fast to them in *l*.
1Ch 16:34 his *l* endures forever.
16:41 "for his *l* endures forever."
17:13 I will never take my *l* away
2Ch 5:13 his *l* endures forever."
6:14 you who keep your covenant of *l*
6:42 Remember the great *l* promised
7: 3 his *l* endures forever."
7: 6 saying, "His *l* endures forever."
9: 8 Because of the *l* of your God
19: 2 and *l* those who hate the LORD?
2Ch 20:21 for his *l* endures forever."
Ezr 3:11 his *l* to Israel endures forever."
Ne 1: 5 covenant of *l* with those who *l* him
9:17 slow to anger and abounding in *l*.
9:32 who keeps his covenant of *l*,
13:22 to me according to your great *l*.
Job 15:34 of those who *l* bribes.
19:19 those I *l* have turned against me.
37:13 or to water his earth and show his *l*.
Ps 4: 2 How long will you *l* delusions
5:11 that those who *l* your name may
6: 4 save me because of your unfailing *l*.
11: 5 wicked and those who *l* violence
13: 5 But I trust in your unfailing *l*;
17: 7 Show the wonder of your great *l*,
18: 1 I *l* you, O LORD, my strength.
21: 7 through the unfailing *l*
23: 6 Surely goodness and *l* will follow
25: 6 O LORD, your great mercy and *l*,
25: 7 according to your *l* remember me,
26: 3 for your *l* is ever before me,
26: 8 I *l* the house where you live,
31: 7 I will be glad and rejoice in your *l*,
31:16 save me in your unfailing *l*.
31:21 for he showed his wonderful *l*
31:23 *L* the LORD, all his saints!
32:10 but the LORD's unfailing *l*
33: 5 the earth is full of his unfailing *l*.
33:18 whose hope is in his unfailing *l*,
33:22 May your unfailing *l* rest upon us,
36: 5 Your *l*, O LORD, reaches
36: 7 How priceless is your unfailing *l*!
36:10 Continue your *l* to those who know
40:10 I do not conceal your *l*
40:11 may your *l* and your truth always
40:16 may those who *l* your salvation
42: 8 By day the LORD directs his *l*,
44:26 of your unfailing *l*.
45: 7 You *l* righteousness and hate
48: 9 we meditate on your unfailing *l*.
51: 1 according to your unfailing *l*;
52: 3 You *l* evil rather than good,
52: 4 You *l* every harmful word,
52: 8 I trust in God's unfailing *l*
57: 3 God sends his *l* and his faithfulness
57:10 For great is your *l*, reaching
59:16 in the morning I will sing of your *l*;
60: 5 that those you *l* may be delivered.
61: 7 appoint your *l* and faithfulness
63: 3 Because your *l* is better than life,
66:20 or withheld his *l* from me!
69:13 in your great *l*, O God,
69:16 out of the goodness of your *l*;
69:36 and those who *l* his name will dwell
70: 4 may those who *l* your salvation
77: 8 Has his unfailing *l* vanished forever
85: 7 Show us your unfailing *l*, O LORD
85:10 *L* and faithfulness meet together;
86: 5 abounding in *l* to all who call
86:13 For great is your *l* toward me;
86:15 abounding in *l* and faithfulness.
88:11 Is your *l* declared in the grave,
89: 1 of the LORD's great *l* forever;
89: 2 declare that your *l* stands firm
89:14 *l* and faithfulness go before you.
89:24 My faithful *l* will be with him,
89:28 I will maintain my *l* to him forever,
89:33 but I will not take my *l* from him,
89:49 where is your former great *l*,
90:14 with your unfailing *l*,
92: 2 to proclaim your *l* in the morning
94:18 your *l*, O LORD, supported me.
97:10 Let those who *l* the LORD hate
98: 3 He has remembered his *l*
100: 5 is good and his *l* endures forever;
101: 1 I will sing of your *l* and justice;
103: 4 crowns you with *l* and compassion.
103: 8 slow to anger, abounding in *l*.
103:11 so great is his *l* for those who fear
103:17 LORD's *l* is with those who fear

Ps 106: 1 his *l* endures forever.
106:45 and out of his great *l* he relented.
107: 1 his *l* endures forever.
107: 8 to the LORD for his unfailing *l*
107:15 to the LORD for his unfailing *l*
107:21 to the LORD for his unfailing *l*
107:31 to the LORD for his unfailing *l*
107:43 consider the great *l* of the LORD.
108: 4 For great is your *l*, higher
108: 6 that those you *l* may be delivered.
109:21 out of the goodness of your *l*,
109:26 save me in accordance with your *l*.
115: 1 because of your *l* and faithfulness.
116: 1 I *l* the LORD, for he heard my
117: 2 For great is his *l* toward us,
118: 1 his *l* endures forever.
118: 2 "His *l* endures forever."
118: 3 "His *l* endures forever."
118: 4 "His *l* endures forever."
118:29 his *l* endures forever.
119:41 May your unfailing *l* come to me,
119:47 because I *l* them.
119:48 to your commands, which I *l*,
119:64 The earth is filled with your *l*,
119:76 May your unfailing *l* be my
119:88 my life according to your *l*,
119:97 Oh, how I *l* your law!
119:113 but I *l* your law.
119:119 therefore I *l* your statutes.
119:124 your servant according to your *l*
119:127 Because I *l* your commands
119:132 to those who *l* your name.
119:149 in accordance with your *l*;
119:159 O LORD, according to your *l*.
119:159 See how I *l* your precepts;
119:163 but I *l* your law.
119:165 peace have they who *l* your law,
119:167 for I *l* them greatly.
122: 6 "May those who *l* you be secure.
130: 7 for with the LORD is unfailing *l*
136: 1 *-26 His l endures forever.*
138: 2 for your *l* and your faithfulness,
138: 8 your *l*, O LORD, endures forever
143: 8 of your unfailing *l*,
143:12 In your unfailing *l*, silence my
145: 8 slow to anger and rich in *l*.
145:20 over all who *l* him,
147:11 who put their hope in his unfailing *l*
Pr 1:22 you simple ones *l* your simple
3: 3 Let *l* and faithfulness never leave
4: 6 *l* her, and she will watch over you.
5:19 you ever be captivated by her *l*.
7:18 let's drink deep of *l* till morning;
7:18 let's enjoy ourselves with *l*!
8:17 I *l* those who *l* me,
8:21 wealth on those who *l* me
8:36 all who hate me *l* death."
9: 8 rebuke a wise man and he will *l* you
10:12 but *l* covers over all wrongs.
14:22 those who plan what is good find *l*
15:17 of vegetables where there is *l*
16: 6 Through *l* and faithfulness sin is
17: 9 over an offense promotes *l*,
18:21 and those who *l* it will eat its fruit.
19:22 What a man desires is unfailing *l*;
20: 6 claims to have unfailing *l*,
20:13 Do not *l* sleep or you will grow
20:28 *L* and faithfulness keep a king safe;
20:28 through *l* his throne is made secure
21:21 who pursues righteousness and *l*
27: 5 rebuke than hidden *l*.
Ecc 3: 8 a time to *l* and a time to hate,
9: 1 but no man knows whether *l*
9: 6 Their *l*, their hate
9: 9 life with your wife, whom you *l*,
SS 1: 2 for your *l* is more delightful
1: 3 No wonder the maidens *l* you!
1: 4 we will praise your *l* more
1: 7 you whom I *l*, where you graze
2: 4 and his banner over me is *l*.
SS 2: 5 for I am faint with *l*.
2: 7 Do not arouse or awaken *l*
3: 5 Do not arouse or awaken *l*
4:10 How delightful is your *l*, my sister,
4:10 How much more pleasing is your *l*
5: 8 Tell him I am faint with *l*.
7: 6 O *l*, with your delights!
7:12 there I will give you my *l*.
8: 4 Do not arouse or awaken *l*
8: 6 for *l* is as strong as death,
8: 7 Many waters cannot quench *l*;
8: 7 all the wealth of his house for *l*,
Isa 1:23 they all *l* bribes
5: 1 I will sing for the one I *l*
16: 5 In *l* a throne will be established;
38:17 In your *l* you kept me
43: 4 and because I *l* you,
54:10 yet my unfailing *l* for you will not
55: 3 my faithful *l* promised to David.
56: 6 to *l* the name of the LORD,
56:10 they *l* to sleep.
57: 8 a pact with those whose beds you *l*,
61: 8 "For I, the LORD, *l* justice;
63: 9 In his *l* and mercy he redeemed
66:10 all you who *l* her;
Jer 2:25 I *l* foreign gods,
2:33 How skilled you are at pursuing *l*!
5:31 and my people *l* it this way.
12: 7 I will give the one I *l*
14:10 "They greatly *l* to wander;
16: 5 my *l* and my pity from this people
31: 3 you with an everlasting *l*;
32:18 You show *l* to thousands
33:11 his *l* endures forever."
La 3:22 of the LORD's great *l* we are not
3:32 so great is his unfailing *l*.
Eze 16: 8 saw that you were old enough for *l*,
23:17 of *l*, and in their lust they defiled
33:32 more than one who sings *l* songs
Da 9: 4 covenant of *l* with all who *l* him
Hos 1: 6 for I will no longer show *l*
1: 7 Yet I will show *l* to the house
2: 4 I will not show my *l* to her children
2:19 in *l* and compassion.
2:23 I will show my *l* to the one I called
3: 1 Go, show your *l* to your wife again,
3: 1 and *l* the sacred raisin cakes."
3: 1 *L* her as the LORD loves
4: 1 "There is no faithfulness, no *l*,
4:18 their rulers dearly *l* shameful ways.
6: 4 Your *l* is like the morning mist,
9: 1 you *l* the wages of a prostitute
9:15 I will no longer *l* them;
10:12 reap the fruit of unfailing *l*,
11: 4 with ties of *l*;
12: 6 maintain *l* and justice,
14: 4 and *l* them freely,
Joel 2:13 slow to anger and abounding in *l*,
Am 4: 5 for this is what you *l* to do,"
5:15 Hate evil, *l* good;
Jnh 4: 2 slow to anger and abounding in *l*,
Mic 3: 2 you who hate good and *l* evil;
6: 8 To act justly and to *l* mercy
Zep 3:17 he will quiet you with his *l*,
Zec 8:17 and do not *l* to swear falsely.
8:19 Therefore *l* truth and peace."
Mt 3:17 "This is my Son, whom I *l*;
5:43 '*L* your neighbor and hate your
5:44 *L* your enemies and pray
5:46 you *l* those who *l* you, what reward
6: 5 for they *l* to pray standing
6:24 he will hate the one and *l* the other,
12:18 the one I *l*, in whom I delight;
17: 5 "This is my Son, whom I *l*;
19:19 and '*l* your neighbor as yourself.' "
22:37 " '*L* the Lord your God
22:39 '*L* your neighbor as yourself.'
23: 6 they *l* the place of honor
23: 7 they *l* to be greeted
24:12 the *l* of most will grow cold,
Mk 1:11 "You are my Son, whom I *l*;
9: 7 "This is my Son, whom I *l*.
12:30 *L* the Lord your God
12:31 '*L* your neighbor as yourself.'
12:33 To *l* him with all your heart,
12:33 and to *l* your neighbor
Lk 3:22 "You are my Son, whom I *l*;
6:27 you who hear me: *L* your enemies,
6:32 Even 'sinners' *l* those who *l* them.
6:32 you *l* those who *l* you, what credit
6:35 *l* your enemies, do good to them,
7:42 which of them will *l* him more?"
10:27 and, '*L* your neighbor as yourself
10:27 " '*L* the Lord your God
11:42 you neglect justice and the *l* of God
11:43 you *l* the most important seats
16:13 he will hate the one and *l* the other,
20:13 whom I *l*; perhaps they will respect
20:46 *l* to be greeted in the marketplaces
Jn 5:42 I know that you do not have the *l*
8:42 were your Father, you would *l* me,
11: 3 "Lord, the one you *l* is sick."
13: 1 them the full extent of his *l*.
13:34 I give you: *L* one another.
13:34 so you must *l* one another.
13:35 disciples, if you *l* one another."
14:15 "If you *l* me, you will obey what I
14:21 I too will *l* him and show myself
14:23 My Father will *l* him, and we will
14:24 He who does not *l* me will not obey
14:31 world must learn that I *l* the Father
15: 9 Now remain in my *l*.
15:10 commands and remain in his *l*.
15:10 you will remain in my *l*,
15:12 *L* each other as I have loved you.
15:13 Greater *l* has no one than this,
15:17 This is my command: *L* each other.
15:19 to the world, it would *l* you
17:26 known in order that the *l* you have
21:15 do you truly *l* me more than these
21:15 he said, "you know that I *l* you."
21:16 Yes, Lord, you know that I *l* you."
21:16 do you truly *l* me?" He answered,
21:17 all things; you know that I *l* you."
21:17 "Do you *l* me?" He said, "Lord,
21:17 "Simon son of John, do you *l* me?"
Ro 5: 5 because God has poured out his *l*
5: 8 God demonstrates his own *l* for us
8:28 for the good of those who *l* him,
8:35 us from the *l* of Christ?
8:39 us from the *l* of God that is
12: 9 *L* must be sincere.
12:10 to one another in brotherly *l*.
13: 8 continuing debt to *l* one another,
13: 9 "*L* your neighbor as yourself."
13:10 Therefore *l* is the fulfillment
13:10 *L* does no harm to its neighbor.
14:15 you are no longer acting in *l*.
15:30 and by the *l* of the Spirit,
16: 8 Greet Ampliatus, whom I *l*
1Co 2: 9 prepared for those who *l* him"—
4:17 my son whom I *l*, who is faithful
4:21 or in *l* and with a gentle spirit?
8: 1 Knowledge puffs up, but *l* builds up
13: 1 have not *l*, I am only a resounding
13: 2 but have not *l*, I am nothing.
13: 3 but have not *l*, I gain nothing.
13: 4 Love is patient, *l* is kind.
13: 4 *L* is patient, love is kind.
13: 6 *L* does not delight in evil
13: 8 *L* never fails.
13:13 But the greatest of these is *l*.
13:13 three remain: faith, hope and *l*.
14: 1 way of *l* and eagerly desire spiritual
16:14 Do everything in *l*.
16:22 If anyone does not *l* the Lord—
16:24 My *l* to all of you in Christ Jesus.
2Co 2: 4 to let you know the depth of my *l*
2: 8 therefore, to reaffirm your *l* for him
5:14 For Christ's *l* compels us,

2Co 6: 6 in the Holy Spirit and in sincere *l*;
8: 7 complete earnestness and in your *l*
8: 8 sincerity of your *l* by comparing it
8:24 show these men the proof of your *l*
11:11 Why? Because I do not *l* you?
12:15 If I *l* you more, will you *l* me less?
13:11 And the God of *l* and peace will be
13:14 of the Lord Jesus Christ, and the *l*
Gal 5: 6 is faith expressing itself through *l*.
5:13 rather, serve one another in *l*.
5:14 "*L* your neighbor as yourself."
5:22 But the fruit of the Spirit is *l*, joy,
Eph 1: 4 In *l* he predestined us
1:15 and your *l* for all the saints,
2: 4 But because of his great *l* for us,
3:17 being rooted and established in *l*,
3:18 and high and deep is the *l* of Christ,
3:19 and to know this *l* that surpasses
4: 2 bearing with one another in *l*.
4:15 Instead, speaking the truth in *l*,
4:16 grows and builds itself up in *l*,
5: 2 loved children and live a life of *l*,
5:25 *l* your wives, just as Christ loved
5:28 husbands ought to *l* their wives
5:33 each one of you also must *l* his wife
6:23 *l* with faith from God the Father
6:24 Christ with an undying *l*.
6:24 to all who *l* our Lord Jesus Christ
Php 1: 9 that your *l* may abound more
1:16 so in *l*, knowing that I am put here
2: 1 from his *l*, if any fellowship
2: 2 having the same *l*, being one
4: 1 you whom I *l* and long for,
Col 1: 4 of the *l* you have for all the saints—
1: 5 *l* that spring from the hope that is
1: 8 also told us of your *l* in the Spirit.
2: 2 in heart and united in *l*,
3:14 And over all these virtues put on *l*,
3:19 *l* your wives and do not be harsh
1Th 1: 3 your labor prompted by *l*,
3: 6 good news about your faith and *l*.
3:12 May the Lord make your *l* increase
4: 9 about brotherly *l* we do not need
4: 9 taught by God to *l* each other.
4:10 you do *l* all the brothers
5: 8 on faith and *l* as a breastplate,
5:13 them in the highest regard in *l*
2Th 1: 3 and the *l* every one of you has
2:10 because they refused to *l* the truth
3: 5 direct your hearts into God's *l*
1Ti 1: 5 The goal of this command is *l*,
1:14 and *l* that are in Christ Jesus.
2:15 *l* and holiness with propriety.
4:12 in life, in *l*, in faith and in purity.
6:10 For the *l* of money is a root
6:11 faith, *l*, endurance and gentleness.
2Ti 1: 7 of power, of *l* and of self-discipline.
1:13 with faith and *l* in Christ Jesus.
2:22 and pursue righteousness, faith, *l*
3: 3 unholy, without *l*, unforgiving,
3:10 faith, patience, *l*, endurance,
Tit 2: 2 in faith, in *l* and in endurance.
2: 4 women to *l* their husbands
3: 4 and *l* of God our Savior appeared,
3:15 Greet those who *l* us in the faith.
Phm : 5 and your *l* for all the saints.
: 7 Your *l* has given me great joy
: 9 yet I appeal to you on the basis of *l*.
Heb 6:10 and the *l* you have shown him
10:24 may spur one another on toward *l*
13: 5 free from the *l* of money
Jas 1:12 promised to those who *l* him.
2: 5 he promised those who *l* him?
2: 8 "*L* your neighbor as yourself,"
1Pe 1: 8 you have not seen him, you *l* him;
1:22 the truth so that you have sincere *l*
1:22 *l* one another deeply,
2:17 *L* the brotherhood of believers,
3: 8 be sympathetic, *l* as brothers,
3:10 "Whoever would *l* life
1Pe 4: 8 Above all, *l* each other deeply,
4: 8 *l* covers over a multitude of sins.
5:14 Greet one another with a kiss of *l*.
2Pe 1: 7 and to brotherly kindness, *l*.
1:17 "This is my Son, whom I *l*;
1Jn 2: 5 God's *l* is truly made complete
2:15 Do not *l* the world or anything
2:15 the *l* of the Father is not in him.
3: 1 How great is the *l* the Father has
3:10 anyone who does not *l* his brother.
3:11 We should *l* one another.
3:14 Anyone who does not *l* remains
3:14 because we *l* our brothers.
3:16 This is how we know what *l* is:
3:17 how can the *l* of God be in him?
3:18 let us not *l* with words or tongue
3:23 to *l* one another as he commanded
4: 7 Dear friends, let us *l* one another,
4: 7 for *l* comes from God.
4: 8 Whoever does not *l* does not know
4: 8 not know God, because God is *l*.
4: 9 This is how God showed his *l*
4:10 This is *l*: not that we loved God,
4:11 we also ought to *l* one another.
4:12 seen God; but if we *l* one another,
4:12 and his *l* is made complete in us.
4:16 God is *l*.
4:16 Whoever lives in *l* lives in God,
4:16 and rely on the *l* God has for us.
4:17 *l* is made complete among us
4:18 But perfect *l* drives out fear,
4:18 There is no fear in *l*.
4:18 who fears is not made perfect in *l*.
4:19 We *l* because he first loved us.
4:20 If anyone says, "I *l* God,"
4:20 anyone who does not *l* his brother,
4:20 whom he has seen, cannot *l* God,
4:21 loves God must also *l* his brother.
5: 2 we know that we *l* the children
5: 3 This is *l* for God: to obey his
2Jn : 1 whom I *l* in the truth—
: 3 will be with us in truth and *l*.
: 5 I ask that we *l* one another.
: 6 his command is that you walk in *l*.
: 6 this is *l*: that we walk in obedience
3Jn : 1 To my dear friend Gaius, whom I *l*
: 6 have told the church about your *l*.
Jude : 2 peace and *l* be yours in abundance.
:12 men are blemishes at your *l* feasts,
:21 Keep yourselves in God's *l*
Rev 2: 4 You have forsaken your first *l*.
2:19 I know your deeds, your *l* and faith
3:19 Those whom I *l* I rebuke
12:11 they did not *l* their lives so much

LOVED* (LOVE)
Ge 24:67 she became his wife, and he *l* her;
25:28 *l* Esau, but Rebekah *l* Jacob.
29:30 and he *l* Rachel more than Leah.
29:31 the LORD saw that Leah was not *l*,
29:33 the LORD heard that I am not *l*,
34: 3 and he *l* the girl and spoke tenderly
37: 3 Now Israel *l* Joseph more than any
37: 4 saw that their father *l* him more
Dt 4:37 Because he *l* your forefathers
7: 8 But it was because the LORD *l* you
10:15 on your forefathers and *l* them,
1Sa 1: 5 a double portion because he *l* her,
18: 1 in spirit with David, and he *l* him
18: 3 with David because he *l* him
18:16 But all Israel and Judah *l* David,
18:28 that his daughter Michal *l* David,
20:17 because he *l* him as he *l* himself.
2Sa 1:23 in life they were *l* and gracious,
12:24 The LORD *l* him; and
12:25 and because the LORD *l* him,
13:15 hated her more than he had *l* her.
1Ki 11: 1 *l* many foreign women
2Ch 11:21 Rehoboam *l* Maacah daughter
26:10 in the fertile lands, for he *l* the soil.
Ne 13:26 He was *l* by his God, and God
Ps 44: 3 light of your face, for you *l* them.
47: 4 the pride of Jacob, whom he *l*.
78:68 Mount Zion, which he *l*.
88:18 taken my companions and *l* ones
109:17 He *l* to pronounce a curse—
Isa 5: 1 My *l* one had a vineyard
Jer 2: 2 how as a bride you *l* me
8: 2 which they have *l* and served
31: 3 "I have *l* you with an everlasting
Eze 16:37 those you *l* as well as those you
Hos 2: 1 and of your sisters, 'My *l* one.'
2:23 to the one I called 'Not my *l* one.'
3: 1 though she is *l* by another
9:10 became as vile as the thing they *l*.
11: 1 "When Israel was a child, I *l* him,
Mal 1: 2 "But you ask, 'How have you *l* us?'
1: 2 "I have *l* you," says the LORD.
1: 2 "Yet I have *l* Jacob, but Esau I
Mk 10:21 Jesus looked at him and *l* him.
12: 6 left to send, a son, whom he *l*.
Lk 7:47 been forgiven—for she *l* much.
16:14 The Pharisees, who *l* money,
Jn 3:16 so *l* the world that he gave his one
3:19 but men *l* darkness instead of light
11: 5 Jesus *l* Martha and her sister
11:36 "See how he *l* him!" But some
12:43 for they *l* praise from men more
13: 1 Having *l* his own who were
13:23 the disciple whom Jesus *l*,
13:34 As I have *l* you, so you must love
14:21 He who loves me will be *l*
14:28 If you *l* me, you would be glad that
15: 9 the Father has *l* me, so have I *l* you.
15:12 Love each other as I have *l* you.
16:27 loves you because you have *l* me
17:23 have *l* them even as you have *l* me.
17:24 you *l* me before the creation
19:26 the disciple whom he *l* standing
20: 2 one Jesus *l*, and said, "They have
21: 7 the disciple whom Jesus *l* said
21:20 whom Jesus *l* was following
Ro 1: 7 To all in Rome who are *l* by God
8:37 conquerors through him who *l* us.
9:13 "Jacob I *l*, but Esau I hated."
9:25 her 'my *l* one' who is not my *l* one,"
11:28 they are *l* on account
Gal 2:20 who *l* me and gave himself for me.
Eph 5: 1 as dearly *l* children and live a life
5: 2 as Christ *l* us and gave himself up
5:25 just as Christ *l* the church
Col 3:12 and dearly *l*, clothe yourselves
1Th 1: 4 For we know, brothers *l* by God,
2: 8 We *l* you so much that we were
2Th 2:13 for you, brothers *l* by the Lord,
2:16 who *l* us and by his grace gave us
2Ti 4:10 for Demas, because he *l* this world,
Heb 1: 9 You have *l* righteousness
2Pe 2:15 who *l* the wages of wickedness.
1Jn 4:10 This is love: not that we *l* God,
4:10 but that he *l* us and sent his Son
4:11 Dear friends, since God so *l* us,
4:19 We love because he first *l* us.
Jude : 1 who are *l* by God the Father
Rev 3: 9 and acknowledge that I have *l* you.

LOVELY* (LOVE)
Ge 29:17 but Rachel was *l* in form,
Est 1:11 and nobles, for she was *l* to look at.
2: 7 was *l* in form and features,
Ps 84: 1 How *l* is your dwelling place,
SS 1: 5 Dark am I, yet *l*,
2:14 and your face is *l*.
4: 3 your mouth is *l*.
5:16 he is altogether *l*.
6: 4 *l* as Jerusalem,
Am 8:13 *l* young women and strong young
Php 4: 8 whatever is *l*, whatever is

LOVER* (LOVE)
SS 1:13 My *l* is to me a sachet of myrrh

SS 1:14 My *l* is to me a cluster
1:16 How handsome you are, my *l!*
2: 3 is my *l* among the young men.
2: 8 Listen! My *l!*
2: 9 My *l* is like a gazelle or a young
2:10 My *l* spoke and said to me,
2:16 *Beloved* My *l* is mine and I am his;
2:17 turn, my *l,*
4:16 Let my *l* come into his garden
5: 2 Listen! My *l* is knocking:
5: 4 My *l* thrust his hand
5: 5 I arose to open for my *l,*
5: 6 I opened for my *l,*
5: 6 but my *l* had left; he was gone.
5: 8 if you find my *l,*
5:10 *Beloved* My *l* is radiant and ruddy,
5:16 This is my *l,* this my friend,
6: 1 Where has your *l* gone,
6: 1 Which way did your *l* turn,
6: 2 *Beloved* My *l* has gone
6: 3 I am my lover's and my *l* is mine;
7: 9 May the wine go straight to my *l,*
7:10 I belong to my *l,*
7:11 my *l,* let us go to the countryside,
7:13 that I have stored up for you, my *l.*
8: 5 leaning on her *l?*
8:14 *Beloved* Come away, my *l,*
1Ti 3: 3 not quarrelsome, not a *l* of money.

LOVER'S* (LOVE)
SS 6: 3 I am my *l* and my lover is mine;

LOVERS* (LOVE)
SS 5: 1 drink your fill, O *l.*
Jer 3: 1 as a prostitute with many *l*—
3: 2 the roadside you sat waiting for *l,*
4:30 Your *l* despise you;
La 1: 2 Among all her *l*
Eze 16:33 but you give gifts to all your *l,*
16:36 in your promiscuity with your *l,*
16:37 I am going to gather all your *l,*
16:39 Then I will hand you over to your *l,*
16:41 and you will no longer pay your *l.*
23: 5 she lusted after her *l,* the Assyrians
23: 9 I handed her over to her *l,*
23:20 There she lusted after her *l,*
23:22 I will stir up your *l* against you,
Hos 2: 5 She said, 'I will go after my *l,*
2: 7 She will chase after her *l*
2:10 lewdness before the eyes of her *l;*
2:12 she said were her pay from her *l;*
2:13 and went after her *l,*
8: 9 Ephraim has sold herself to *l.*
2Ti 3: 2 People will be *l* of themselves,
3: 2 *l* of money, boastful, proud,
3: 3 without self-control, brutal, not *l*
3: 4 *l* of pleasure rather than *l* of God—

LOVES* (LOVE)
Ge 44:20 sons left, and his father *l* him.'
Dt 10:18 and *l* the alien, giving him food
15:16 because he *l* you and your family
21:15 and he *l* one but not the other,
21:16 son of the wife he *l* in preference
23: 5 because the LORD your God *l* you
28:54 wife he *l* or his surviving children,
28:56 will begrudge the husband she *l*
33:12 and the one the LORD *l* rests
Ru 4:15 who *l* you and who is better to you
2Ch 2:11 "Because the LORD *l* his people,
Ps 11: 7 he *l* justice;
33: 5 The LORD *l* righteousness
34:12 Whoever of you *l* life
37:28 For the LORD *l* the just
87: 2 the LORD *l* the gates of Zion
91:14 Because he *l* me," says the LORD,
99: 4 The King is mighty, he *l* justice—
119:140 and your servant *l* them.
127: 2 for he grants sleep to those he *l.*
146: 8 the LORD *l* the righteous.
Pr 3:12 the LORD disciplines those he *l,*
Pr 12: 1 Whoever *l* discipline *l* knowledge,
13:24 he who *l* him is careful
15: 9 he *l* those who pursue
17:17 A friend *l* at all times,
17:19 He who *l* a quarrel *l* sin;
19: 8 He who gets wisdom *l* his own soul
21:17 He who *l* pleasure will become
21:17 whoever *l* wine and oil will never
22:11 He who *l* a pure heart and whose
29: 3 A man who *l* wisdom brings joy
Ecc 5:10 Whoever *l* money never has
5:10 whoever *l* wealth is never satisfied
SS 3: 1 I looked for the one my heart *l;*
3: 2 I will search for the one my heart *l.*
3: 3 "Have you seen the one my heart *l*
3: 4 when I found the one my heart *l.*
Hos 3: 1 as the LORD *l* the Israelites,
10:11 that *l* to thresh;
12: 7 he *l* to defraud.
Mal 2:11 the sanctuary the LORD *l,*
Mt 10:37 anyone who *l* his son or daughter
10:37 "Anyone who *l* his father
Lk 7: 5 because he *l* our nation
7:47 has been forgiven little *l* little."
Jn 3:35 Father *l* the Son and has placed
5:20 For the Father *l* the Son
10:17 reason my Father *l* me is that I lay
12:25 The man who *l* his life will lose it,
14:21 He who *l* me will be loved
14:21 obeys them, he is the one who *l* me.
14:23 Jesus replied, "If anyone *l* me,
16:27 the Father himself *l* you
Ro 13: 8 for he who *l* his fellowman has
1Co 8: 3 But the man who *l* God is known
2Co 9: 7 for God *l* a cheerful giver.
Eph 1: 6 has freely given us in the One he *l.*
5:28 He who *l* his wife *l* himself.
5:33 must love his wife as he *l* himself,
Col 1:13 us into the kingdom of the Son he *l,*
Tit 1: 8 one who *l* what is good, who is
Heb 12: 6 the Lord disciplines those he *l,*
1Jn 2:10 Whoever *l* his brother lives
2:15 If anyone *l* the world, the love
4: 7 Everyone who *l* has been born
4:21 Whoever *l* God must also love his
5: 1 who *l* the father *l* his child
3Jn : 9 but Diotrephes, who *l* to be first,
Rev 1: 5 To him who *l* us and has freed us
20: 9 camp of God's people, the city he *l.*
22:15 and everyone who *l* and practices

LOVING* (LOVE)
Ps 25:10 All the ways of the LORD are *l*
59:10 my *l* God.
59:17 O God, are my fortress, my *l* God.
62:12 and that you, O Lord, are *l.*
144: 2 He is my *l* God and my fortress,
145:13 and *l* toward all he has made.
145:17 and *l* toward all he has made.
Pr 5:19 A *l* doe, a graceful deer—
Heb 13: 1 Keep on *l* each other as brothers.
1Jn 5: 2 by *l* God and carrying out his

LOVING-KINDNESS* (LOVE)
Jer 31: 3 I have drawn you with *l.*

LOWER
Ps 8: 5 You made him a little *l*
2Co 11: 7 a sin for me to *l* myself in order
Heb 2: 7 You made him a little *l*

LOWING
1Sa 15:14 What is this *l* of cattle that I hear?"

LOWLY
Job 5:11 The *l* he sets on high,
Ps 138: 6 on high, he looks upon the *l,*
Pr 29:23 but a man of *l* spirit gains honor.
Isa 57:15 also with him who is contrite and *l*
Eze 21:26 *l* will be exalted and the exalted
1Co 1:28 He chose the *l* things of this world

LOYAL
1Ch 29:18 and keep their hearts *l* to you.
Ps 78: 8 whose hearts were not *l* to God,

LUKE*
Co-worker with Paul (Col 4:14; 2Ti 4:11; Phm 24).

LUKEWARM*
Rev 3:16 So, because you are *l*— neither hot

LUST (LUSTED LUSTS)
Pr 6:25 Do not *l* in your heart
Eze 20:30 and *l* after their vile images?
Col 3: 5 sexual immorality, impurity, *l,*
1Th 4: 5 not in passionate *l* like the heathen,
1Pe 4: 3 in debauchery, *l,* drunkenness,
1Jn 2:16 the *l* of his eyes and the boasting

LUSTED (LUST)
Eze 23: 5 she *l* after her lovers, the Assyrians

LUSTS* (LUST)
Nu 15:39 yourselves by going after the *l*
Ro 1:26 God gave them over to shameful *l.*

LUXURY
Jas 5: 5 You have lived on earth in *l*

LYDIA'S*
Ac 16:40 went to *L* house, where they met

LYING (LIE)
Pr 6:17 a *l* tongue,
12:22 The LORD detests *l* lips,
21: 6 A fortune made by a *l* tongue
26:28 A *l* tongue hates those it hurts,

MACEDONIA
Ac 16: 9 "Come over to *M* and help us."

MAD
Dt 28:34 The sights you see will drive you *m*

MADE (MAKE)
Ge 1: 7 So God *m* the expanse
1:16 God *m* two great lights—
1:16 He also *m* the stars.
1:25 God *m* the wild animals according
1:31 God saw all that he had *m,*
2:22 Then the LORD God *m* a woman
6: 6 was grieved that he had *m* man
9: 6 has God *m* man.
15:18 that day the LORD *m* a covenant
Ex 20:11 six days the LORD *m* the heavens
20:11 the Sabbath day and *m* it holy.
24: 8 the covenant that the LORD has *m*
32: 4 *m* it into an idol cast in the shape
Lev 16:34 Atonement is to be *m* once a year
Dt 32: 6 who *m* you and formed you?
Jos 24:25 On that day Joshua *m* a covenant
2Ki 19:15 You have *m* heaven and earth.
2Ch 2:12 the God of Israel, who *m* heaven
Ne 9: 6 You *m* the heavens,
9:10 You *m* a name for yourself,
Ps 33: 6 of the LORD were the heavens *m,*
95: 5 The sea is his, for he *m* it,
96: 5 but the LORD *m* the heavens.
100: 3 It is he who *m* us, and we are his;
118:24 This is the day the LORD has *m;*
136: 7 who *m* the great lights—
139:14 I am fearfully and wonderfully *m;*
Ecc 3:11 He has *m* everything beautiful
Isa 43: 7 whom I formed and *m."*
45:12 It is I who *m* the earth
45:18 he who fashioned and *m* the earth,
66: 2 Has not my hand *m* all these things
Jer 10:12 But God *m* the earth by his power;
27: 5 and outstretched arm I *m* the earth
32:17 you have *m* the heavens
33: 2 LORD says, he who *m* the earth,
51:15 "He *m* the earth by his power;

Eze 3:17 I have *m* you a watchman
33: 7 I have *m* you a watchman
Am 5: 8 (he who *m* the Pleiades and Orion,
Jnh 1: 9 who *m* the sea and the land."
Mk 2:27 "The Sabbath was *m* for man,
Jn 1: 3 Through him all things were *m;*
Ac 17:24 "The God who *m* the world
1Co 3: 6 watered it, but God *m* it grow.
Heb 1: 2 through whom he *m* the universe.
Jas 3: 9 who have been *m* in God's likeness
Rev 14: 7 Worship him who *m* the heavens,

MAGDALENE
Lk 8: 2 Mary (called *M)* from whom seven

MAGI
Mt 2: 1 *M* from the east came to Jerusalem

MAGIC (MAGICIANS)
Eze 13:20 I am against your *m* charms
Rev 21: 8 those who practice *m* arts,
22:15 those who practice *m* arts,

MAGICIANS (MAGIC)
Ex 7:11 the Egyptian *m* also did the same
Da 2: 2 So the king summoned the *m,*

MAGNIFICENCE* (MAGNIFICENT)
1Ch 22: 5 for the LORD should be of great *m*

MAGNIFICENT (MAGNIFICENCE)
1Ki 8:13 I have indeed built a *m* temple
Isa 28:29 in counsel and *m* in wisdom.
Mk 13: 1 stones! What *m* buildings!"

MAGOG
Eze 38: 2 of the land of *M,* the chief prince
39: 6 I will send fire on *M*
Rev 20: 8 and *M*— to gather them for battle.

MAIDEN (MAIDENS)
Pr 30:19 and the way of a man with a *m.*
Isa 62: 5 As a young man marries a *m,*
Jer 2:32 Does a *m* forget her jewelry,

MAIDENS (MAIDEN)
SS 1: 3 No wonder the *m* love you!

MAIMED
Mt 18: 8 It is better for you to enter life *m*

MAINTAIN (MAINTAINING)
Ps 82: 3 *m* the rights of the poor
106: 3 Blessed are they who *m* justice,
Hos 12: 6 *m* love and justice,
Am 5:15 *m* justice in the courts.
Ro 3:28 For we *m* that a man is justified

MAINTAINING* (MAINTAIN)
Ex 34: 7 faithfulness, *m* love to thousands,

MAJESTIC* (MAJESTY)
Ex 15: 6 was *m* in power.
15:11 *m* in holiness,
Job 37: 4 he thunders with his *m* voice.
Ps 8: 1 how *m* is your name in all the earth
8: 9 how *m* is your name in all the earth
29: 4 the voice of the LORD is *m.*
68:15 of Bashan are *m* mountains;
76: 4 more *m* than mountains rich
111: 3 Glorious and *m* are his deeds,
SS 6: 4 *m* as troops with banners.
6:10 *m* as the stars in procession?
Isa 30:30 men to hear his *m* voice
Eze 31: 7 It was *m* in beauty,
2Pe 1:17 came to him from the *M* Glory,

MAJESTY* (MAJESTIC)
Ex 15: 7 In the greatness of your *m*
Dt 5:24 has shown us his glory and his *m,*
11: 2 his *m,* his mighty hand, his
33:17 In *m* he is like a firstborn bull;
33:26 and on the clouds in his *m.*
1Ch 16:27 Splendor and *m* are before him;
29:11 and the *m* and the splendor,
Est 1: 4 the splendor and glory of his *m.*
7: 3 if it pleases your *m,* grant me my
Job 37:22 God comes in awesome *m.*
40:10 and clothe yourself in honor and *m*
Ps 21: 5 on him splendor and *m.*
45: 3 with splendor and *m.*
45: 4 In your *m* ride forth victoriously
68:34 whose *m* is over Israel,
93: 1 The LORD reigns, he is robed in *m*
93: 1 the LORD is robed in *m*
96: 6 Splendor and *m* are before him;
104: 1 clothed with splendor and *m.*
110: 3 Arrayed in holy *m,*
145: 5 of the glorious splendor of your *m,*
Isa 2:10 and the splendor of his *m!*
2:19 and the splendor of his *m,*
2:21 and the splendor of his *m,*
24:14 west they acclaim the LORD's *m.*
26:10 and regard not the *m* of the LORD.
53: 2 or *m* to attract us to him,
Eze 31: 2 can be compared with you in *m?*
31:18 with you in splendor and *m?*
Da 4:30 and for the glory of my *m?"*
Mic 5: 4 in the *m* of the name
Zec 6:13 and he will be clothed with *m*
Ac 19:27 will be robbed of her divine *m."*
25:26 to write to His *M* about him.
2Th 1: 9 and from the *m* of his power
Heb 1: 3 hand of the *M* in heaven.
8: 1 of the throne of the *M* in heaven,
2Pe 1:16 but we were eyewitnesses of his *m.*
Jude :25 only God our Savior be glory, *m,*

MAKE (MADE MAKER MAKERS MAKES MAKING MAN-MADE)
Ge 1:26 "Let us *m* man in our image,
2:18 I will *m* a helper suitable for him."
6:14 *m* yourself an ark of cypress wood;
12: 2 "I will *m* you into a great nation
Ex 22: 3 thief must certainly *m* restitution,
25: 9 *M* this tabernacle and all its
25:40 See that you *m* them according
Nu 6:25 the LORD *m* his face shine
2Sa 7: 9 Now I will *m* your name great,
Job 7:17 "What is man that you *m* so much
Ps 4: 8 *m* me dwell in safety.
20: 4 and *m* all your plans succeed.
108: 1 *m* music with all my soul.
110: 1 hand until I *m* your enemies
119:165 and nothing can *m* them stumble.
Pr 3: 6 and he will *m* your paths straight.
4:26 *M* level paths for your feet
20:18 *M* plans by seeking advice;
Isa 14:14 I will *m* myself like the Most High
29:16 "He did not *m* me"?
55: 3 I will *m* an everlasting covenant
61: 8 and *m* an everlasting covenant
Jer 31:31 "when I will *m* a new covenant
Eze 37:26 I will *m* a covenant of peace
Mt 3: 3 *m* straight paths for him.'"
28:19 and *m* disciples of all nations,
Mk 1:17 "and I will *m* you fishers of men."
Lk 13:24 "*M* every effort to enter
14:23 country lanes and *m* them come in,
Ro 14:19 *m* every effort to do what leads
2Co 5: 9 So we *m* it our goal to please him,
Eph 4: 3 *M* every effort to keep the unity
Col 4: 5 *m* the most of every opportunity.
1Th 4:11 *M* it your ambition
Heb 4:11 *m* every effort to enter that rest,
8: 5 it that you *m* everything according
12:14 *M* every effort to live in peace
2Pe 1: 5 *m* every effort to add
3:14 *m* every effort to be found spotless,

MAKER* (MAKE)
Job 4:17 Can a man be more pure than his *M*
9: 9 He is the *M* of the Bear and Orion,
32:22 my *M* would soon take me away.
Job 35:10 no one says, 'Where is God my *M,*
36: 3 I will ascribe justice to my *M.*
40:19 yet his *M* can approach him
Ps 95: 6 kneel before the LORD our *M;*
115:15 the *M* of heaven and earth.
121: 2 the *M* of heaven and earth.
124: 8 the *M* of heaven and earth.
134: 3 the *M* of heaven and earth,
146: 6 the *M* of heaven and earth,
149: 2 Let Israel rejoice in their *M;*
Pr 14:31 poor shows contempt for their *M,*
17: 5 poor shows contempt for their *M;*
22: 2 The LORD is the *M* of them all.
Ecc 11: 5 the *M* of all things.
Isa 17: 7 that day men will look to their *M*
27:11 so their *M* has no compassion
45: 9 to him who quarrels with his *M,*
45:11 the Holy One of Israel, and its *M:*
51:13 that you forget the LORD your *M,*
54: 5 For your *M* is your husband—
Jer 10:16 for he is the *M* of all things,
51:19 for he is the *M* of all things,
Hos 8:14 Israel has forgotten his *M*

MAKERS* (MAKE)
Isa 45:16 All the *m* of idols will be put

MAKES (MAKE)
Ps 23: 2 *m* me lie down in green pastures,
Pr 13:12 Hope deferred *m* the heart sick,
1Co 3: 7 but only God, who *m* things grow.

MAKING (MAKE)
Ps 19: 7 *m* wise the simple.
Ecc 12:12 Of *m* many books there is no end,
Jn 5:18 *m* himself equal with God.
Eph 5:16 *m* the most of every opportunity,

MALACHI*
Mal 1: 1 of the LORD to Israel through *M.*

MALE
Ge 1:27 *m* and female he created them.
Ex 13: 2 to me every firstborn *m.*
Nu 8:16 the first *m* offspring
Mt 19: 4 the Creator 'made them *m*
Gal 3:28 slave nor free, *m* nor female,

MALICE (MALICIOUS)
Mk 7:22 adultery, greed, *m,* deceit,
Ro 1:29 murder, strife, deceit and *m.*
1Co 5: 8 the yeast of *m* and wickedness,
Eph 4:31 along with every form of *m.*
Col 3: 8 *m,* slander, and filthy language
1Pe 2: 1 rid yourselves of all *m*

MALICIOUS (MALICE)
Pr 26:24 A *m* man disguises himself
1Ti 3:11 not *m* talkers but temperate
6: 4 *m* talk, evil suspicions

MALIGN
Tit 2: 5 so that no one will *m* the word

MAN (MAN'S MANKIND MEN MEN'S WOMAN WOMEN)
Ge 1:26 "Let us make *m* in our image,
2: 7 God formed the *m* from the dust
2: 8 *m* became a living being
2:15 God took the *m* and put
2:18 for the *m* to be alone
2:20 *m* gave names to all the
2:23 she was taken out of *m.*
2:25 *m* and his wife were both
3: 9 God called to the *m,*
3:22 *m* has now become like
4: 1 I have brought forth a *m.*
6: 3 not contend with *m* forever,
6: 6 grieved that he had made *m*
9: 6 Whoever sheds the blood of *m,*
Dt 8: 3 *m* does not live on bread
1Sa 13:14 a *m* after his own heart

1Sa 15:29 he is not a *m* that he
16: 7 at the things *m* looks at.
Job 14: 1 *M* born of woman is of few
14:14 If a *m* dies, will he live
Ps 1: 1 Blessed is the *m* who does
8: 4 what is *m* that you are
32: 2 Blessed is the *m* whose sin
40: 4 Blessed is the *m* who makes
84:12 blessed is the *m* who trusts
103:15 As for *m*, his days are
112: 1 Blessed is the *m* who fears
119: 9 can a young *m* keep his
127: 5 Blessed is the *m* whose quiver
144: 3 what is *m* that you care
Pr 3:13 Blessed is the *m* who finds
9: 9 Instruct a wise *m*
14:12 that seems right to a *m*,
30:19 way of a *m* with a maiden.
Isa 53: 3 a *m* of sorrows,
Jer 17: 5 the one who trusts in *m*,
17: 7 blessed is the *m* who trusts
Eze 22:30 I looked for a *m*
Mt 4: 4 *M* does not live on bread
19: 5 a *m* will leave his father
Mk 8:36 What good is it for a *m*
Lk 4: 4 '*M* does not live on bread
Ro 5:12 entered the world through one *m*
1Co 2:15 spiritual *m* makes judgments
3:12 If any *m* builds on this
7: 1 good for a *m* not to marry.
7: 2 each *m* should have his own
11: 3 head of every *m* is Christ,
11: 3 head of woman is *m*
13:11 When I became a *m*,
15:21 death came through a *m*,
15:45 first *m* Adam became a
15:47 the second *m* from heaven
2Co 12: 2 I know a *m* in Christ
Eph 2:15 create in himself one new *m*
5:31 a *m* will leave his father
Php 2: 8 found in appearance as a *m*,
1Ti 2: 5 the *m* Christ Jesus,
2:11 have authority over a *m*;
2Ti 3:17 that the *m* of God may be
Heb 2: 6 what is *m* that you are
9:27 as *m* is destined to die

MAN'S (MAN)
Pr 20:24 A *m* steps are directed by
Jer 10:23 a *m* life is not his own;
1Co 1:25 is wiser than *m* wisdom,

MAN-MADE (MAKE)
Heb 9:11 perfect tabernacle that is not *m*,
9:24 not enter a *m* sanctuary that was

MANAGE (MANAGER)
Jer 12: 5 how will you *m* in the thickets
1Ti 3: 4 He must *m* his own family well
3:12 one wife and must *m* his children
5:14 to *m* their homes and to give

MANAGER (MANAGE)
Lk 12:42 Who then is the faithful and wise *m*
16: 1 a rich man whose *m* was accused

MANASSEH
1. Firstborn of Joseph (Ge 41:51; 46:20). Blessed by Jacob but not firstborn (Ge 48). Tribe of blessed (Dt 33:17), numbered (Nu 1:35; 26:34), half allotted land east of Jordan (Nu 32; Jos 13:8–33), half west (Jos 17; Eze 48:4), failed to fully possess (Jos 17:12–13; Jdg 1:27), 12,000 from (Rev 7:6).
2. Son of Hezekiah; king of Judah (2Ki 21:1–18; 2Ch 33:1–20). Judah exiled for his detestable sins (2Ki 21:10–15). Repentance (2Ch 33:12–19).

MANDRAKES
Ge 30:14 give me some of your son's *m*."

MANGER
Lk 2:12 in strips of cloth and lying in a *m*."

MANIFESTATION*
1Co 12: 7 to each one the *m* of the Spirit is

MANKIND (MAN)
Ge 6: 7 I will wipe *m*, whom I have created
Ps 33:13 and sees all *m*;
Pr 8:31 and delighting in *m*.
Ecc 7:29 God made *m* upright,
Isa 40: 5 and all *m* together will see it.
45:12 and created *m* upon it.
Jer 32:27 "I am the LORD, the God of all *m*.
Zec 2:13 Be still before the LORD, all *m*,
Lk 3: 6 And all *m* will see God's salvation

MANNA
Ex 16:31 people of Israel called the bread *m*.
Dt 8:16 He gave you *m* to eat in the desert,
Jn 6:49 Your forefathers ate the *m*
Rev 2:17 I will give some of the hidden *m*.

MANNER
1Co 11:27 in an unworthy *m* will be guilty
Php 1:27 conduct yourselves in a *m* worthy

MANSIONS*
Ps 49:14 far from their princely *m*.
Isa 5: 9 the fine *m* left without occupants.
Am 3:15 and the *m* will be demolished,"
5:11 though you have built stone *m*,

MARCH
Jos 6: 4 *m* around the city seven times,
Isa 42:13 LORD will *m* out like a mighty

MARITAL* (MARRY)
Ex 21:10 of her food, clothing and *m* rights.
Mt 5:32 except for *m* unfaithfulness,
19: 9 except for *m* unfaithfulness,
1Co 7: 3 husband should fulfill his *m* duty

MARK (MARKS)
Cousin of Barnabas (Col 4:10; 2Ti 4:11; Phm 24; 1Pe 5:13), see JOHN.
Ge 4:15 Then the LORD put a *m* on Cain
Rev 13:16 to receive a *m* on his right hand

MARKET (MARKETPLACE MARKETPLACES)
Jn 2:16 turn my Father's house into a *m*!"

MARKETPLACE (MARKET)
Lk 7:32 are like children sitting in the *m*

MARKETPLACES (MARKET)
Mt 23: 7 they love to be greeted in the *m*

MARKS (MARK)
Jn 20:25 Unless I see the nail *m* in his hands
Gal 6:17 bear on my body the *m* of Jesus.

MARRED
Isa 52:14 his form *m* beyond human likeness

MARRIAGE (MARRY)
Mt 22:30 neither marry nor be given in *m*;
24:38 marrying and giving in *m*,
Ro 7: 2 she is released from the law of *m*.
Heb 13: 4 by all, and the *m* bed kept pure,

MARRIED (MARRY)
Dt 24: 5 happiness to the wife he has *m*.
Ezr 10:10 you have *m* foreign women,
Pr 30:23 an unloved woman who is *m*,
Mt 1:18 pledged to be *m* to Joseph,
Mk 12:23 since the seven were *m* to her?"
Ro 7: 2 by law a *m* woman is bound
1Co 7:27 Are you *m*? Do not seek a divorce.
7:33 But a *m* man is concerned about
7:36 They should get *m*.

MARRIES (MARRY)
Mt 5:32 anyone who *m* the divorced woman
19: 9 and *m* another woman commits
Lk 16:18 the man who *m* a divorced woman

MARROW
Heb 4:12 joints and *m*; it judges the thoughts

MARRY (INTERMARRY MARITAL MARRIAGE MARRIED MARRIES)
Dt 25: 5 brother shall take her and *m* her
Mt 22:30 resurrection people will neither *m*
1Co 7: 1 It is good for a man not to *m*.
7: 9 control themselves, they should *m*,
7:28 if you do *m*, you have not sinned;
1Ti 4: 3 They forbid people to *m*
5:14 So I counsel younger widows to *m*,

MARTHA*
Sister of Mary and Lazarus (Lk 10:38–42; Jn 11; 12:2).

MARVELED* (MARVELOUS)
Lk 2:33 mother *m* at what was said about
2Th 1:10 and to be *m* at among all those who

MARVELING* (MARVELOUS)
Lk 9:43 While everyone was *m*

MARVELOUS* (MARVELED MARVELING)
1Ch 16:24 his *m* deeds among all peoples.
Job 37: 5 God's voice thunders in *m* ways;
Ps 71:17 to this day I declare your *m* deeds.
72:18 who alone does *m* deeds.
86:10 For you are great and do *m* deeds;
96: 3 his *m* deeds among all peoples.
98: 1 for he has done *m* things;
118:23 and it is *m* in our eyes.
Isa 25: 1 you have done *m* things,
Zec 8: 6 but will it seem *m* to me?"
8: 6 "It may seem *m* to the remnant
Mt 21:42 and it is *m* in our eyes'?
Mk 12:11 and it is *m* in our eyes'?"
Rev 15: 1 in heaven another great and *m* sign
15: 3 "Great and *m* are your deeds,

MARY
1. Mother of Jesus (Mt 1:16–25; Lk 1:27–56; 2:1–40). With Jesus at temple (Lk 2:41–52), at the wedding in Cana (Jn 2:1–5), questioning his sanity (Mk 3:21), at the cross (Jn 19:25–27). Among disciples after Ascension (Ac 1:14).
2. Magdalene; former demoniac (Lk 8:2). Helped support Jesus' ministry (Lk 8:1–3). At the cross (Mt 27:56; Mk 15:40; Jn 19:25), burial (Mt 27:61; Mk 15:47). Saw angel after resurrection (Mt 28:1–10; Mk 16:1–9; Lk 24:1–12); also Jesus (Jn 20:1–18).
3. Sister of Martha and Lazarus (Jn 11). Washed Jesus' feet (Jn 12:1–8).

MASQUERADES*
2Co 11:14 for Satan himself *m* as an angel

MASTER (MASTER'S MASTERED MASTERS MASTERY)
Ge 4: 7 to have you, but you must *m* it."
Hos 2:16 you will no longer call me 'my *m*.'
Mal 1: 6 If I am a *m*, where is the respect
Mt 10:24 nor a servant above his *m*.
23: 8 for you have only one *M*
24:46 that servant whose *m* finds him
25:21 "His *m* replied, 'Well done,
25:23 "His *m* replied, 'Well done,
Ro 6:14 For sin shall not be your *m*,
14: 4 To his own *m* he stands or falls.
Col 4: 1 you know that you also have a *M*
2Ti 2:21 useful to the *M* and prepared

MASTER'S (MASTER)
Mt 25:21 Come and share your *m* happiness

MASTERED* (MASTER)
1Co 6:12 but I will not be *m* by anything.
2Pe 2:19 a slave to whatever has *m* him.

MASTERS (MASTER)
Pr 25:13 he refreshes the spirit of his *m*.
Mt 6:24 "No one can serve two *m*.
Lk 16:13 "No servant can serve two *m*.
Eph 6: 5 obey your earthly *m* with respect
6: 9 And *m*, treat your slaves
Col 3:22 obey your earthly *m* in everything;
4: 1 *M*, provide your slaves
1Ti 6: 1 should consider their *m* worthy
6: 2 who have believing *m* are not
Tit 2: 9 subject to their *m* in everything,
1Pe 2:18 to your *m* with all respect,

MASTERY* (MASTER)
Ro 6: 9 death no longer has *m* over him.

MAT
Mk 2: 9 'Get up, take your *m* and walk'?
Ac 9:34 Get up and take care of your *m*."

MATCHED*
2Co 8:11 do it may be *m* by your completion

MATTHEW*
Apostle; former tax collector (Mt 9:9–13; 10:3; Mk 3:18; Lk 6:15; Ac 1:13). Also called Levi (Mk 2:14–17; Lk 5:27–32).

MATTHIAS
Ac 1:26 the lot fell to *M;* so he was added

MATURE* (MATURITY)
Lk 8:14 and pleasures, and they do not *m*.
1Co 2: 6 a message of wisdom among the *m*,
Eph 4:13 of the Son of God and become *m*,
Php 3:15 of us who are *m* should take such
Col 4:12 firm in all the will of God, *m*
Heb 5:14 But solid food is for the *m*,
Jas 1: 4 work so that you may be *m*

MATURITY* (MATURE)
Heb 6: 1 about Christ and go on to *m*,

MEAL
Pr 15:17 Better a *m* of vegetables where
1Co 10:27 some unbeliever invites you to a *m*
Heb 12:16 for a single *m* sold his inheritance

MEANING
Ne 8: 8 and giving the *m* so that the people

MEANINGLESS
Ecc 1: 2 "*M! M!*" says the Teacher.
1Ti 1: 6 from these and turned to *m* talk.

MEANS
1Co 9:22 by all possible *m* I might save some

MEASURE (MEASURED MEASURES)
Ps 71:15 though I know not its *m*.
Eze 45: 3 In the sacred district, *m*
Zec 2: 2 He answered me, "To *m* Jerusalem
Lk 6:38 A good *m*, pressed
Eph 3:19 to the *m* of all the fullness of God.
4:13 to the whole *m* of the fullness
Rev 11: 1 "Go and *m* the temple of God

MEASURED (MEASURE)
Isa 40:12 Who has *m* the waters
Jer 31:37 if the heavens above can be *m*

MEASURES (MEASURE)
Dt 25:14 Do not have two differing *m*
Pr 20:10 Differing weights and differing *m*

MEAT
Pr 23:20 or gorge themselves on *m*,
Ro 14: 6 He who eats *m*, eats to the Lord,
14:21 It is better not to eat *m*
1Co 8:13 I will never eat *m* again,
10:25 *m* market without raising questions

MEDDLER* (MEDDLES)
1Pe 4:15 kind of criminal, or even as a *m*.

MEDDLES* (MEDDLER)
Pr 26:17 is a passer-by who *m*

MEDIATOR
1Ti 2: 5 and one *m* between God and men,
Heb 8: 6 of which he is *m* is superior
9:15 For this reason Christ is the *m*
12:24 to Jesus the *m* of a new covenant,

MEDICINE*
Pr 17:22 A cheerful heart is good *m*,

MEDITATE* (MEDITATED MEDITATES MEDITATION)
Ge 24:63 out to the field one evening to *m*,
Jos 1: 8 from your mouth; *m* on it day
Ps 48: 9 we *m* on your unfailing love.
77:12 I will *m* on all your works
119:15 I *m* on your precepts
119:23 your servant will *m*
119:27 then I will *m* on your wonders.
119:48 and I *m* on your decrees.
119:78 but I will *m* on your precepts.
119:97 I *m* on it all day long.
119:99 for I *m* on your statutes.
119:148 that I may *m* on your promises.
143: 5 I *m* on all your works
145: 5 I will *m* on your wonderful works.

MEDITATED* (MEDITATE)
Ps 39: 3 and as I *m*, the fire burned;

MEDITATES* (MEDITATE)
Ps 1: 2 and on his law he *m* day and night.

MEDITATION* (MEDITATE)
Ps 19:14 of my mouth and the *m* of my heart
104:34 May my *m* be pleasing to him,

MEDIUM
Lev 20:27 " 'A man or woman who is a *m*

MEEK* (MEEKNESS)
Ps 37:11 But the *m* will inherit the land
Zep 3:12 the *m* and humble,
Mt 5: 5 Blessed are the *m*,

MEEKNESS* (MEEK)
2Co 10: 1 By the *m* and gentleness of Christ,

MEET (MEETING MEETINGS MEETS)
Ps 42: 2 When can I go and *m* with God?
85:10 Love and faithfulness *m* together;
Am 4:12 prepare to *m* your God, O Israel."
1Co 11:34 when you *m* together it may not
1Th 4:17 them in the clouds to *m* the Lord

MEETING (MEET)
Ex 40:34 the cloud covered the Tent of *M*,
Heb 10:25 Let us not give up *m* together,

MEETINGS* (MEET)
1Co 11:17 for your *m* do more harm

MEETS (MEET)
Heb 7:26 Such a high priest *m* our need—

MELCHIZEDEK
Ge 14:18 *M* king of Salem brought out bread
Ps 110: 4 in the order of *M*."
Heb 7:11 in the order of *M*, not in the order

MELT (MELTS)
2Pe 3:12 and the elements will *m* in the heat.

MELTS (MELT)
Am 9: 5 he who touches the earth and it *m*,

MEMBER (MEMBERS)
Ro 12: 5 each *m* belongs to all the others.

MEMBERS (MEMBER)
Mic 7: 6 a man's enemies are the *m*
Mt 10:36 a man's enemies will be the *m*
Ro 7:23 law at work in the *m* of my body,
12: 4 of us has one body with many *m*,
1Co 6:15 not know that your bodies are *m*
12:24 But God has combined the *m*
Eph 3: 6 *m* together of one body,
4:25 for we are all *m* of one body.
5:30 for we are *m* of his body.
Col 3:15 as *m* of one body you were called

MEMORABLE* (MEMORY)
Eze 39:13 day I am glorified will be a *m* day

MEMORIES* (MEMORY)
1Th 3: 6 us that you always have pleasant *m*

MEMORY (MEMORABLE MEMORIES)
Pr 10: 7 *m* of the righteous will be
Mt 26:13 she has done will also be told, in *m*

MEN (MAN)
Ge 6: 2 daughter of *m* were beautiful,
6: 4 heroes of old, *m* of renown
Ps 9:20 nations know they are but *m*.
11: 4 He observes the sons of *m;*
Mt 4:19 will make you fishers of *m*
5:16 your light shine before *m*
6:14 if you forgive *m* when
10:32 acknowledges me before *m*
12:31 blasphemy will be forgiven *m*,
12:36 *m* will have to give account
23: 5 is done for *m* to see:
Mk 7: 7 are but rules taught by *m*.
Lk 6:22 Blessed are you when *m*
6:26 Woe to you when all *m*
Jn 1: 4 life was the light of *m*.
2:24 for he knew all *m*.
3:19 *m* loved darkness instead
12:32 will draw all *m* to myself
13:35 all *m* will know that you
Ac 5:29 obey God rather than *m!*
Ro 1:18 wickedness of *m*
1:27 indecent acts with other *m*,
5:12 death came to all *m*,
1Co 2:11 among *m* knows the thoughts
3: 3 acting like mere *m?*
3:21 no more boasting about *m!*
9:22 all things to all *m*
13: 1 tongues of *m* and of angels
16:13 be *m* of courage;
16:18 Such *m* deserve recognition.
2Co 5:11 we try to persuade *m*.
8:21 but also in the eyes of *m*.
Gal 1: 1 sent not from *m* nor
1:10 to win approval of *m*, or
Eph 4: 8 and gave gifts to *m*.
1Th 2: 4 as *m* approved by God
2:13 not as the word of *m*,
1Ti 2: 4 wants all *m* to be saved
2: 6 as a ransom for all *m*—
4:10 the Savior of all *m*
5: 2 younger *m* as brothers
2Ti 2: 2 entrust to reliable *m*
Tit 2:11 has appeared to all *m*.
Heb 5: 1 is selected from among *m*
7:28 high priests *m* who are weak;
2Pe 1:21 but *m* spoke from God
Rev 21: 3 dwelling of God is with *m*,

MEN'S (MAN)
2Ki 19:18 fashioned by *m* hands.
2Ch 32:19 the work of *m* hands.
1Co 2: 5 not rest on *m* wisdom,

MENAHEM*
King of Israel (2Ki 15:17–22).

MENE
Da 5:25 that was written: *M, M,*

MEPHIBOSHETH
Son of Jonathan shown kindness by David (2Sa 4:4; 9; 21:7). Accused of siding with Absalom (2Sa 16:1–4; 19:24–30).

MERCHANT
Pr 31:14 She is like the *m* ships,
Mt 13:45 of heaven is like a *m* looking

MERCIFUL (MERCY)
Dt 4:31 the LORD your God is a *m* God;
Ne 9:31 for you are a gracious and *m* God.
Ps 77: 9 Has God forgotten to be *m?*
78:38 Yet he was *m;*
Jer 3:12 for I am *m,*' declares the LORD,
Da 9: 9 The Lord our God is *m*
Mt 5: 7 Blessed are the *m,*
Lk 1:54 remembering to be *m*
6:36 Be *m,* just as your Father is *m.*
Heb 2:17 in order that he might become a *m*
Jas 2:13 to anyone who has not been *m.*
Jude :22 Be *m* to those who doubt; snatch

MERCY (MERCIFUL)
Ex 33:19 *m* on whom I will have *m,*
2Sa 24:14 of the LORD, for his *m* is great;
1Ch 21:13 for his *m* is very great;
Ne 9:31 But in your great *m* you did not put
Ps 25: 6 O LORD, your great *m* and love,
28: 6 for he has heard my cry for *m.*
57: 1 Have *m* on me, O God, have *m*
Pr 28:13 renounces them finds *m.*
Isa 63: 9 and *m* he redeemed them;
Da 9:18 but because of your great *m.*
Hos 6: 6 For I desire *m,* not sacrifice,
Am 5:15 LORD God Almighty will have *m*
Mic 6: 8 To act justly and to love *m*
7:18 but delight to show *m.*
Hab 3: 2 in wrath remember *m.*
Zec 7: 9 show *m* and compassion
Mt 5: 7 for they will be shown *m.*
9:13 learn what this means: 'I desire *m,*
12: 7 'I desire *m,* not sacrifice,' you
18:33 Shouldn't you have had *m*
23:23 justice, *m* and faithfulness.
Lk 1:50 His *m* extends to those who fear
Ro 9:15 "I will have *m* on whom I have *m,*
9:18 Therefore God has *m*
11:32 so that he may have *m* on them all.
12: 1 brothers, in view of God's *m,*
12: 8 if it is showing *m,* let him do it
Eph 2: 4 who is rich in *m,* made us alive
1Ti 1:13 I was shown *m* because I acted
1:16 for that very reason I was shown *m*
Tit 3: 5 we had done, but because of his *m.*
Heb 4:16 so that we may receive *m*
Jas 2:13 judgment without *m* will be shown
2:13 *M* triumphs over judgment!
3:17 submissive, full of *m* and good fruit
5:11 full of compassion and *m.*
1Pe 1: 3 In his great *m* he has given us new
2:10 once you had not received *m,*
Jude :23 to others show *m,* mixed with fear

MERRY
Lk 12:19 Take life easy; eat, drink and be *m*

MESHACH
Hebrew exiled to Babylon; name changed from Mishael (Da 1:6–7). Refused defilement by food (Da 1:8–20). Refused to worship idol (Da 3:1–18); saved from furnace (Da 3:19–30).

MESSAGE (MESSENGER)
Isa 53: 1 Who has believed our *m*
Jn 12:38 "Lord, who has believed our *m*
Ac 5:20 "and tell the people the full *m*
10:36 You know the *m* God sent
Ac 17:11 for they received the *m*
Ro 10:16 who has believed our *m?"*
10:17 faith comes from hearing the *m,*
1Co 1:18 For the *m* of the cross is
2: 4 My *m* and my preaching were not
2Co 5:19 to us the *m* of reconciliation.
2Th 3: 1 pray for us that the *m*
Tit 1: 9 firmly to the trustworthy *m*
Heb 4: 2 the *m* they heard was of no value
1Pe 2: 8 because they disobey the *m*—

MESSENGER (MESSAGE)
Pr 25:13 is a trustworthy *m*
Mal 3: 1 I will send my *m,* who will prepare
Mt 11:10 " 'I will send my *m* ahead of you,
2Co 12: 7 a *m* of Satan, to torment me.

MESSIAH*
Jn 1:41 "We have found the *M"* (that is,
4:25 "I know that *M"* (called Christ) "is

METHUSELAH
Ge 5:27 Altogether, *M* lived 969 years,

MICAH
1. Idolater from Ephraim (Jdg 17–18).
2. Prophet from Moresheth (Jer 26:18–19; Mic 1:1).

MICAIAH
Prophet of the LORD who spoke against Ahab (1Ki 22:1–28; 2Ch 18:1–27).

MICHAEL
Archangel (Jude 9); warrior in angelic realm, protector of Israel (Da 10:13, 21; 12:1; Rev 12:7).

MICHAL
Daughter of Saul, wife of David (1Sa 14:49; 18:20–28). Warned David of Saul's plot (1Sa 19). Saul gave her to Paltiel (1Sa 25:44); David retrieved her (2Sa 3:13–16). Criticized David for dancing before the ark (2Sa 6:16–23); 1Ch 15:29).

MIDIAN
Ex 2:15 Pharaoh and went to live in *M,*
Jdg 7: 2 me to deliver *M* into their hands.

MIDWIVES
Ex 1:17 The *m,* however, feared God

MIGHT (ALMIGHTY MIGHTIER MIGHTY)
Jdg 16:30 Then he pushed with all his *m,*
2Sa 6: 5 with all their *m* before the LORD,
6:14 before the LORD with all his *m,*
2Ch 20: 6 Power and *m* are in your hand,
Ps 21:13 we will sing and praise your *m.*
54: 1 vindicate me by your *m.*
Isa 63:15 Where are your zeal and your *m?*
Mic 3: 8 and with justice and *m,*
Zec 4: 6 'Not by *m* nor by power,
Col 1:11 power according to his glorious *m*
1Ti 6:16 To him be honor and *m* forever.

MIGHTIER (MIGHT)
Ps 93: 4 *M* than the thunder

MIGHTY (MIGHT)
Ge 49:24 of the hand of the *M* One of Jacob,
Ex 6: 1 of my *m* hand he will drive them
13: 3 out of it with a *m* hand.
Dt 5:15 out of there with a *m* hand
7: 8 he brought you out with a *m* hand
10:17 the great God, *m* and awesome,
34:12 one has ever shown the *m* power
2Sa 1:19 How the *m* have fallen!
23: 8 the names of David's *m* men:
Ne 9:32 the great, *m* and awesome God,
Job 36: 5 God is *m,* but does not despise men
Ps 24: 8 The LORD strong and *m,*
45: 3 upon your side, O *m* one;
50: 1 The *M* One, God, the LORD,
Ps 62: 7 he is my *m* rock, my refuge.
68:33 who thunders with *m* voice.
71:16 proclaim your *m* acts,
77:12 and consider all your *m* deeds.
77:15 With your *m* arm you redeemed
89: 8 You are *m,* O LORD,
93: 4 the LORD on high is *m.*
99: 4 The King is *m,* he loves justice—
110: 2 LORD will extend your *m* scepter
118:15 right hand has done *m* things!
136:12 with a *m* hand and outstretched
145: 4 they will tell of your *m* acts.
145:12 all men may know of your *m* acts
147: 5 Great is our Lord and *m* in power;
SS 8: 6 like a *m* flame.
Isa 9: 6 Wonderful Counselor, *M* God,
60:16 your Redeemer, the *M* One
63: 1 *m* to save."
Jer 10: 6 and your name is *m* in power.
20:11 with me like a *m* warrior;
32:19 your purposes and *m* are your
Eze 20:33 I will rule over you with a *m* hand
Zep 3:17 he is *m* to save.
Mt 26:64 at the right hand of the *M* One
Eph 1:19 like the working of his *m* strength,
6:10 in the Lord and in his *m* power.
1Pe 5: 6 therefore, under God's *m* hand,

MILE*
Mt 5:41 If someone forces you to go one *m,*

MILK
Ex 3: 8 a land flowing with *m* and honey—
23:19 a young goat in its mother's *m.*
Pr 30:33 as churning the *m* produces butter,
Isa 55: 1 Come, buy wine and *m*
1Co 3: 2 I gave you *m,* not solid food,
Heb 5:12 You need *m,* not solid food!
1Pe 2: 2 babies, crave pure spiritual *m,*

MILLSTONE (STONE)
Lk 17: 2 sea with a *m* tied around his neck

MIND (DOUBLE-MINDED LIKE-MINDED MINDED MINDFUL MINDS)
Nu 23:19 that he should change his *m.*
Dt 28:65 LORD will give you an anxious *m,*
1Sa 15:29 Israel does not lie or change his *m;*
1Ch 28: 9 devotion and with a willing *m,*
2Ch 30:12 the people to give them unity of *m*
Ps 26: 2 examine my heart and my *m;*
110: 4 and will not change his *m:*
Isa 26: 3 him whose *m* is steadfast,
Jer 17:10 and examine the *m,*
Mt 22:37 all your soul and with all your *m.'*
Mk 12:30 with all your *m* and with all your
Lk 10:27 your strength and with all your *m';*
Ac 4:32 believers were one in heart and *m.*
Ro 1:28 he gave them over to a depraved *m*
7:25 I myself in my *m* am a slave
8: 6 The *m* of sinful man is death,
8: 7 the sinful *m* is hostile to God.
12: 2 by the renewing of your *m.*
14:13 make up your *m* not
1Co 1:10 you may be perfectly united in *m*
2: 9 no *m* has conceived
14:14 spirit prays, but my *m* is unfruitful.
2Co 13:11 be of one *m,* live in peace.
Php 3:19 Their *m* is on earthly things.
Col 2:18 and his unspiritual *m* puffs him up
1Th 4:11 to *m* your own business
Heb 7:21 and will not change his *m:*

MINDED* (MIND)
1Pe 4: 7 be clear *m* and self-controlled

MINDFUL* (MIND)
Ps 8: 4 what is man that you are *m* of him,
Lk 1:48 God my Savior, for he has been *m*
Heb 2: 6 What is man that you are *m* of him,

MINDS (MIND)
Dt 11:18 of mine in your hearts and *m;*
Ps 7: 9 who searches *m* and hearts,
Jer 31:33 "I will put my law in their *m*
Lk 24:38 and why do doubts rise in your *m?*
24:45 Then he opened their *m*
Ro 8: 5 to the sinful nature have their *m* set
2Co 4: 4 god of this age has blinded the *m*
Eph 4:23 new in the attitude of your *m;*
Col 3: 2 Set your *m* on things above,
Heb 8:10 I will put my laws in their *m*
10:16 and I will write them on their *m."*
1Pe 1:13 prepare your *m* for action;
Rev 2:23 I am he who searches hearts and *m,*

MINISTER (MINISTERING MINISTERS MINISTRY)
Ps 101: 6 will *m* to me.
1Ti 4: 6 you will be a good *m*

MINISTERING (MINISTER)
Heb 1:14 Are not all angels *m* spirits sent

MINISTERS (MINISTER)
2Co 3: 6 as *m* of a new covenant—

MINISTRY (MINISTER)
Ac 6: 4 to prayer and the *m* of the word."
Ro 11:13 I make much of my *m*
2Co 4: 1 God's mercy we have this *m,*
5:18 gave us the *m* of reconciliation:
6: 3 so that our *m* will not be
Gal 2: 8 who was at work in the *m* of Peter
2Ti 4: 5 discharge all the duties of your *m.*
Heb 8: 6 But the *m* Jesus has received is

MIRACLE* (MIRACLES MIRACULOUS)
Ex 7: 9 'Perform a *m,'* then say to Aaron,
Mk 9:39 "No one who does a *m*
Lk 23: 8 hoped to see him perform some *m.*
Jn 7:21 "I did one *m,* and you are all
Ac 4:16 they have done an outstanding *m,*

MIRACLES* (MIRACLE)
1Ch 16:12 his *m,* and the judgments he
Ne 9:17 to remember the *m* you performed
Job 5: 9 *m* that cannot be counted.
9:10 *m* that cannot be counted.
Ps 77:11 I will remember your *m* of long ago
77:14 You are the God who performs *m;*
78:12 He did *m* in the sight
105: 5 his *m,* and the judgments he
106: 7 they gave no thought to your *m;*
106:22 *m* in the land of Ham
Mt 7:22 out demons and perform many *m?'*
11:20 most of his *m* had been performed,
11:21 If the *m* that were performed
11:23 If the *m* that were performed
13:58 And he did not do many *m* there
24:24 and perform great signs and *m*
Mk 6: 2 does *m!* Isn't this the carpenter?
6: 5 He could not do any *m* there,
13:22 and *m* to deceive the elect—
Lk 10:13 For if the *m* that were performed
19:37 for all the *m* they had seen:
Jn 7: 3 disciples may see the *m* you do.
10:25 *m* I do in my Father's name speak
10:32 "I have shown you many great *m*
10:38 do not believe me, believe the *m,*
14:11 the evidence of the *m* themselves.
15:24 But now they have seen these *m,*
Ac 2:22 accredited by God to you by *m,*
8:13 by the great signs and *m* he saw.
19:11 God did extraordinary *m*
Ro 15:19 by the power of signs and *m,*
1Co 12:28 third teachers, then workers of *m,*
12:29 Are all teachers? Do all work *m?*
2Co 12:12 and *m*— were done among you
Gal 3: 5 work *m* among you because you
2Th 2: 9 in all kinds of counterfeit *m,*
Heb 2: 4 it by signs, wonders and various *m,*

MIRACULOUS (MIRACLE)
Dt 13: 1 and announces to you a *m* sign
Mt 12:39 generation asks for a *m* sign!
13:54 this wisdom and these *m* powers?"
Jn 2:11 This, the first of his *m* signs,
2:23 people saw the *m* signs he was
3: 2 could perform the *m* signs you are
4:48 "Unless you people see *m* signs
7:31 will he do more *m* signs
9:16 "How can a sinner do such *m* signs
12:37 Jesus had done all these *m* signs
20:30 Jesus did many other *m* signs
Ac 2:43 *m* signs were done by the apostles.
5:12 apostles performed many *m* signs
1Co 1:22 Jews demand *m* signs and Greeks
12:10 to another *m* powers,

MIRE
Ps 40: 2 out of the mud and *m;*
Isa 57:20 whose waves cast up *m* and mud.

MIRIAM
Sister of Moses and Aaron (Nu 26:59). Led dancing at Red Sea (Ex 15:20–21). Struck with leprosy for criticizing Moses (Nu 12). Death (Nu 20:1).

MIRROR
1Co 13:12 but a poor reflection as in a *m;*
Jas 1:23 a man who looks at his face in a *m*

MISDEEDS*
Ps 99: 8 though you punished their *m.*
Ro 8:13 put to death the *m* of the body,

MISERY
Ex 3: 7 "I have indeed seen the *m*
Jdg 10:16 he could bear Israel's *m* no longer.
Hos 5:15 in their *m* they will earnestly seek
Ro 3:16 ruin and *m* mark their ways,
Jas 5: 1 of the *m* that is coming upon you.

MISFORTUNE
Ob :12 brother in the day of his *m,*

MISLEAD (MISLED)
Isa 47:10 wisdom and knowledge *m* you

MISLED (MISLEAD)
1Co 15:33 Do not be *m:* "Bad company

MISS (MISSES)
Pr 19: 2 nor to be hasty and *m* the way.

MISSES (MISS)
Heb 12:15 See to it that no one *m* the grace

MIST
Hos 6: 4 Your love is like the morning *m,*
Jas 4:14 You are a *m* that appears for a little

MISTREAT (MISTREATED)
Ex 22:21 "Do not *m* an alien or oppress him,
Eze 22:29 and needy and *m* the alien,
Lk 6:28 pray for those who *m* you.

MISTREATED (MISTREAT)
Eze 22: 7 *m* the fatherless and the widow.
Heb 11:25 to be *m* along with the people
11:37 destitute, persecuted and *m*—
13: 3 who are *m* as if you yourselves

MISUSE* (MISUSES)
Ex 20: 7 "You shall not *m* the name
Dt 5:11 "You shall not *m* the name
Ps 139:20 your adversaries *m* your name.

MISUSES* (MISUSE)
Ex 20: 7 anyone guiltless who *m* his name.
Dt 5:11 anyone guiltless who *m* his name.

MIXED (MIXING)
Da 2:41 even as you saw iron *m* with clay.

MIXING (MIXED)
Isa 5:22 and champions at *m* drinks,

MOAB (MOABITESS)
Ge 19:37 she named him *M;* he is the father
Dt 34: 6 He buried him in *M,* in the valley
Ru 1: 1 live for a while in the country of *M.*
Isa 15: 1 An oracle concerning *M:*
Jer 48:16 "The fall of *M* is at hand;
Am 2: 1 "For three sins of *M,*

MOABITESS (MOAB)
Ru 1:22 accompanied by Ruth the *M,*

MOAN
Ps 90: 9 we finish our years with a *m.*

MOCK (MOCKED MOCKER MOCKERS MOCKING MOCKS)
Ps 22: 7 All who see me *m* me;
119:51 The arrogant *m* me
Pr 1:26 I will *m* when calamity overtakes
14: 9 Fools *m* at making amends for sin,
Mk 10:34 who will *m* him and spit on him,

MOCKED (MOCK)
Ps 89:51 with which they have *m* every step
Mt 27:29 knelt in front of him and *m* him.
27:41 of the law and the elders *m* him.
Gal 6: 7 not be deceived: God cannot be *m.*

MOCKER (MOCK)
Pr 9: 7 corrects a *m* invites insult;
9:12 if you are a *m,* you alone will suffer
20: 1 Wine is a *m* and beer a brawler;
22:10 Drive out the *m,* and out goes strife

MOCKERS (MOCK)
Ps 1: 1 or sit in the seat of *m.*
Pr 29: 8 *M* stir up a city,

MOCKING (MOCK)
Isa 50: 6 face from *m* and spitting.

MOCKS (MOCK)
Pr 17: 5 He who *m* the poor shows
30:17 "The eye that *m* a father,

MODEL*
Eze 28:12 " 'You were the *m* of perfection,
1Th 1: 7 And so you became a *m*
2Th 3: 9 to make ourselves a *m* for you

MODESTY*
1Co 12:23 are treated with special *m,*

MOLDED*
Job 10: 9 Remember that you *m* me like clay

MOLDY
Jos 9: 5 of their food supply was dry and *m.*

MOLECH
Lev 20: 2 of his children to *M* must be put
1Ki 11:33 and *M* the god of the Ammonites,

MOMENT (MOMENTARY)
Job 20: 5 the joy of the godless lasts but a *m.*
Ps 2:12 for his wrath can flare up in a *m.*
30: 5 For his anger lasts only a *m,*
Pr 12:19 but a lying tongue lasts only a *m.*
Isa 54: 7 "For a brief *m* I abandoned you,
66: 8 or a nation be brought forth in a *m?*
Gal 2: 5 We did not give in to them for a *m,*

MOMENTARY* (MOMENT)
2Co 4:17 and *m* troubles are achieving

MONEY
Pr 13:11 Dishonest *m* dwindles away,
Ecc 5:10 Whoever loves *m* never has *m*
Isa 55: 1 and you who have no *m,*
Mt 6:24 You cannot serve both God and *M.*

Mt 27: 5 Judas threw the *m* into the temple
Lk 3:14 "Don't extort *m* and don't accuse
9: 3 no bread, no *m*, no extra tunic.
16:13 You cannot serve both God and *M*
Ac 5: 2 part of the *m* for himself,
1Co 16: 2 set aside a sum of *m* in keeping
1Ti 3: 3 not quarrelsome, not a lover of *m*.
6:10 For the love of *m* is a root
2Ti 3: 2 lovers of *m*, boastful, proud,
Heb 13: 5 free from the love of *m*
1Pe 5: 2 not greedy for *m*, but eager to serve

MONEYLENDER* (LEND)
Ex 22:25 not be like a *m;* charge him no
Lk 7:41 men owed money to a certain *m*.

MONTH (MONTHS)
Ex 12: 2 "This *m* is to be for you the first
Eze 47:12 Every *m* they will bear,
Rev 22: 2 of fruit, yielding its fruit every *m*.

MONTHS (MONTH)
Gal 4:10 and *m* and seasons and years!
Rev 11: 2 trample on the holy city for 42 *m*.
13: 5 his authority for forty-two *m*.

MOON
Jos 10:13 and the *m* stopped,
Ps 8: 3 the *m* and the stars,
74:16 you established the sun and *m*.
89:37 be established forever like the *m*,
104:19 The *m* marks off the seasons,
121: 6 nor the *m* by night.
136: 9 the *m* and stars to govern the night;
148: 3 Praise him, sun and *m*,
SS 6:10 fair as the *m*, bright as the sun,
Joel 2:31 and the *m* to blood
Hab 3:11 and *m* stood still in the heavens
Mt 24:29 and the *m* will not give its light;
Ac 2:20 and the *m* to blood
1Co 15:41 *m* another and the stars another;
Col 2:16 a New *M* celebration or a Sabbath
Rev 6:12 the whole *m* turned blood red,
21:23 city does not need the sun or the *m*

MORAL*
Jas 1:21 rid of all *m* filth and the evil that is

MORDECAI
Benjamite exile who raised Esther (Est 2:5–15). Exposed plot to kill Xerxes (Est 2:19–23). Refused to honor Haman (Est 3:1–6; 5:9–14). Charged Esther to foil Haman's plot against the Jews (Est 4). Xerxes forced Haman to honor Mordecai (Est 6). Mordecai exalted (Est 8–10). Established Purim (Est 9:18–32).

MORIAH*
Ge 22: 2 and go to the region of *M*.
2Ch 3: 1 LORD in Jerusalem on Mount *M*,

MORNING
Ge 1: 5 and there was *m*— the first day.
Dt 28:67 In the *m* you will say, "If only it
2Sa 23: 4 he is like the light of *m* at sunrise
Ps 5: 3 In the *m*, O LORD,
Pr 27:14 blesses his neighbor early in the *m*,
Isa 14:12 O *m* star, son of the dawn!
La 3:23 They are new every *m;*
2Pe 1:19 and the *m* star rises in your hearts.
Rev 2:28 I will also give him the *m* star.
22:16 of David, and the bright *M* Star."

MORTAL
Ge 6: 3 for he is *m;* his days will be
Job 10: 4 Do you see as a *m* sees?
Ro 8:11 also give life to your *m* bodies
1Co 15:53 and the *m* with immortality.
2Co 5: 4 that what is *m* may be swallowed

MOSES
Levite; brother of Aaron (Ex 6:20; 1Ch 6:3). Put in basket into Nile; discovered and raised by Pharaoh's daughter (Ex 2:1–10). Fled to Midian after killing Egyptian (Ex 2:11–15). Married to Zipporah, fathered Gershom (Ex 2:16–22).

Called by the LORD to deliver Israel (Ex 3–4). Pharaoh's resistance (Ex 5). Ten plagues (Ex 7–11). Passover and Exodus (Ex 12–13). Led Israel through Red Sea (Ex 14). Song of deliverance (Ex 15:1–21). Brought water from rock (Ex 17:1–7). Raised hands to defeat Amalekites (Ex 17:8–16). Delegated judges (Ex 18; Dt 1:9–18).

Received Law at Sinai (Ex 19–23; 25–31; Jn 1:17). Announced Law to Israel (Ex 19:7–8; 24; 35). Broke tablets because of golden calf (Ex 32; Dt 9). Saw glory of the LORD (Ex 33–34). Supervised building of tabernacle (Ex 36–40). Set apart Aaron and priests (Lev 8–9). Numbered tribes (Nu 1–4; 26). Opposed by Aaron and Miriam (Nu 12). Sent spies into Canaan (Nu 13). Announced forty years of wandering for failure to enter land (Nu 14). Opposed by Korah (Nu 16). Forbidden to enter land for striking rock (Nu 20:1–13; Dt 1:37). Lifted bronze snake for healing (Nu 21:4–9; Jn 3:14). Final address to Israel (Dt 1–33). Succeeded by Joshua (Nu 27:12–23; Dt 34). Death (Dt 34:5–12).

"Law of Moses" (1Ki 2:3; Ezr 3:2; Mk 12:26; Lk 24:44). "Book of Moses" (2Ch 25:12; Ne 13:1). "Song of Moses" (Ex 15:1–21; Rev 15:3). "Prayer of Moses" (Ps 90).

MOTH
Mt 6:19 where *m* and rust destroy,

MOTHER (GRANDMOTHER MOTHER-IN-LAW MOTHER'S)
Ge 2:24 and *m* and be united to his wife,
3:20 because she would become the *m*
Ex 20:12 "Honor your father and your *m*,
Lev 20: 9 " 'If anyone curses his father or *m*,
Dt 5:16 "Honor your father and your *m*,
21:18 who does not obey his father and *m*
27:16 who dishonors his father or his *m*."
Jdg 5: 7 arose a *m* in Israel.
1Sa 2:19 Each year his *m* made him a little
Ps 113: 9 as a happy *m* of children.
Pr 10: 1 but a foolish son grief to his *m*.
23:22 do not despise your *m*
23:25 May your father and *m* be glad;
29:15 a child left to himself disgraces his *m*.
30:17 that scorns obedience to a *m*,
31: 1 an oracle his *m* taught him:
Isa 49:15 "Can a *m* forget the baby
66:13 As a *m* comforts her child,
Jer 20:17 with my *m* as my grave,
Mic 7: 6 a daughter rises up against her *m*,
Mt 10:35 a daughter against her *m*,
10:37 or *m* more than me is not worthy
12:48 He replied to him, "Who is my *m*,
15: 4 'Honor your father and *m*'
19: 5 and *m* and be united to his wife,
19:19 honor your father and *m*,'
Mk 7:10 'Honor your father and your *m*,' and,
10:19 honor your father and *m*.' "
Lk 11:27 "Blessed is the *m* who gave you
12:53 daughter and daughter against *m*,
18:20 honor your father and *m*.' "
Jn 19:27 to the disciple, "Here is your *m*."
Gal 4:26 is above is free, and she is our *m*.
Eph 5:31 and *m* and be united to his wife,
6: 2 "Honor your father and *m*"—
1Th 2: 7 like a *m* caring for her little
2Ti 1: 5 and in your *m* Eunice and,

MOTHER-IN-LAW (MOTHER)
Ru 2:19 Ruth told her *m* about the one
Mt 10:35 a daughter-in-law against her *m*—

MOTHER'S (MOTHER)
Job 1:21 "Naked I came from my *m* womb,
Pr 1: 8 and do not forsake your *m* teaching
Ecc 5:15 from his *m* womb,
11: 5 the body is formed in a *m* womb,
Jn 3: 4 time into his *m* womb to be born!"

MOTIVE* (MOTIVES)
1Ch 28: 9 and understands every *m*

MOTIVES* (MOTIVE)
Pr 16: 2 but *m* are weighed by the LORD.
1Co 4: 5 will expose the *m* of men's hearts.
Php 1:18 whether from false *m* or true,
1Th 2: 3 spring from error or impure *m*,
Jas 4: 3 because you ask with wrong *m*,

MOUNT (MOUNTAIN MOUNTAINS MOUNTAINTOPS)
Ps 89: 9 when its waves *m* up, you still them
Isa 14:13 enthroned on the *m* of assembly,
Eze 28:14 You were on the holy *m* of God;
Zec 14: 4 stand on the *M* of Olives,

MOUNTAIN (MOUNT)
Ge 22:14 "On the *m* of the LORD it will be
Ex 24:18 And he stayed on the *m* forty days
Dt 5: 4 face to face out of the fire on the *m*.
Job 14:18 "But as a *m* erodes and crumbles
Ps 48: 1 in the city of our God, his holy *m*.
Isa 40: 4 every *m* and hill made low;
Mic 4: 2 let us go up to the *m* of the LORD,
Mt 4: 8 the devil took him to a very high *m*
17:20 say to this *m*, 'Move from here
Mk 9: 2 with him and led them up a high *m*,
Lk 3: 5 every *m* and hill made low.
Jn 4:21 the Father neither on this *m*
2Pe 1:18 were with him on the sacred *m*.

MOUNTAINS (MOUNT)
Ps 36: 6 righteousness is like the mighty *m*,
46: 2 the *m* fall into the heart of the sea,
90: 2 Before the *m* were born
Isa 52: 7 How beautiful on the *m*
54:10 Though the *m* be shaken
55:12 the *m* and hills
Eze 34: 6 My sheep wandered over all the *m*
Mt 24:16 are in Judea flee to the *m*.
Lk 23:30 they will say to the *m*, "Fall on us!"
1Co 13: 2 if I have a faith that can move *m*,
Rev 6:16 They called to the *m* and the rocks,

MOUNTAINTOPS (MOUNT)
Isa 42:11 let them shout from the *m*.

MOURN (MOURNING MOURNS)
Ecc 3: 4 a time to *m* and a time to dance,
Isa 61: 2 to comfort all who *m*,
Mt 5: 4 Blessed are those who *m*,
Ro 12:15 *m* with those who *m*.

MOURNING (MOURN)
Isa 61: 3 instead of *m*,
Jer 31:13 I will turn their *m* into gladness;
Rev 21: 4 There will be no more death or *m*

MOURNS (MOURN)
Zec 12:10 as one *m* for an only child,

MOUTH (MOUTHS)
Nu 22:38 only what God puts in my *m*."
Dt 8: 3 comes from the *m* of the LORD.
18:18 I will put my words in his *m*,
30:14 it is in your *m* and in your heart
Jos 1: 8 of the Law depart from your *m;*
2Ki 4:34 *m* to *m*, eyes to eyes, hands
Ps 10: 7 His *m* is full of curses and lies
17: 3 resolved that my *m* will not sin.
19:14 May the words of my *m*
37:30 *m* of the righteous man utters
40: 3 He put a new song in my *m*,
71: 8 My *m* is filled with your praise,
119:103 sweeter than honey to my *m!*
141: 3 Set a guard over my *m*, O LORD;
Pr 2: 6 and from his *m* come knowledge

Pr 4:24 Put away perversity from your *m;*
10:11 The *m* of the righteous is a fountain
10:31 *m* of the righteous brings forth
16:23 A wise man's heart guides his *m,*
26:28 and a flattering *m* works ruin.
27: 2 praise you, and not your own *m;*
Ecc 5: 2 Do not be quick with your *m,*
SS 1: 2 with the kisses of his *m*—
5:16 His *m* is sweetness itself;
Isa 29:13 come near to me with their *m*
40: 5 For the *m* of the LORD has spoken
45:23 my *m* has uttered in all integrity
51:16 I have put my words in your *m*
53: 7 so he did not open his *m.*
55:11 my word that goes out from my *m:*
59:21 *m* will not depart from your *m,*
Eze 3: 2 So I opened my *m,* and he gave me
Mal 2: 7 and from his *m* men should seek
Mt 4: 4 comes from the *m* of God.' "
12:34 overflow of the heart the *m* speaks.
15:11 into a man's *m* does not make him
15:18 out of the *m* come from the heart,
Lk 6:45 overflow of his heart his *m* speaks.
Ro 10: 9 That if you confess with your *m,*
15: 6 and *m* you may glorify the God
1Pe 2:22 and no deceit was found in his *m.*"
Rev 1:16 and out of his *m* came a sharp
2:16 them with the sword of my *m.*
3:16 I am about to spit you out of my *m.*
19:15 Out of his *m* comes a sharp sword

MOUTHS (MOUTH)
Ps 78:36 would flatter him with their *m,*
Eze 33:31 With their *m* they express devotion
Ro 3:14 "Their *m* are full of cursing
Eph 4:29 talk come out of your *m,*
Jas 3: 3 bits into the *m* of horses

MOVE (MOVED MOVES)
Dt 19:14 Do not *m* your neighbor's
Pr 23:10 Do not *m* an ancient boundary
Ac 17:28 and *m* and have our being.'
1Co 13: 2 have a faith that can *m* mountains,
15:58 Let nothing *m* you.

MOVED (MOVE)
Ex 35:21 and whose heart *m* him came
2Ch 36:22 the LORD *m* the heart
Ezr 1: 5 everyone whose heart God had *m*
Ps 93: 1 it cannot be *m.*
Jn 11:33 he was deeply *m* in spirit
Col 1:23 not *m* from the hope held out

MOVES (MOVE)
Dt 23:14 For the LORD your God *m* about

MUD (MUDDIED)
Ps 40: 2 out of the *m* and mire;
Isa 57:20 whose waves cast up mire and *m.*
Jn 9: 6 made some *m* with the saliva,
2Pe 2:22 back to her wallowing in the *m.*"

MUDDIED (MUD)
Pr 25:26 Like a *m* spring or a polluted well
Eze 32:13 or *m* by the hoofs of cattle.

MULBERRY*
Lk 17: 6 you can say to this *m* tree,

MULTITUDE (MULTITUDES)
Isa 31: 1 who trust in the *m* of their chariots
Jas 5:20 and cover over a *m* of sins.
1Pe 4: 8 love covers over a *m* of sins.
Rev 7: 9 me was a great *m* that no one could
19: 1 of a great *m* in heaven shouting:

MULTITUDES (MULTITUDE)
Ne 9: 6 and the *m* of heaven worship you.
Da 12: 2 *M* who sleep in the dust
Joel 3:14 *M, m* in the valley of decision!

MURDER (MURDERED MURDERER MURDERERS)
Ex 20:13 "You shall not *m.*
Dt 5:17 "You shall not *m.*
Pr 28:17 A man tormented by the guilt of *m*
Mt 5:21 'Do not *m,* and anyone who
15:19 *m,* adultery, sexual immorality,
Ro 1:29 *m,* strife, deceit and malice.
13: 9 "Do not *m,*" "Do not steal,"
Jas 2:11 adultery," also said, "Do not *m.*"

MURDERED (MURDER)
Mt 23:31 of those who *m* the prophets.
Ac 7:52 now you have betrayed and *m* him
1Jn 3:12 to the evil one and *m* his brother.

MURDERER (MURDER)
Nu 35:16 he is a *m;* the *m* shall be put
Jn 8:44 He was a *m* from the beginning,
1Jn 3:15 who hates his brother is a *m,*

MURDERERS (MURDER)
1Ti 1: 9 for *m,* for adulterers and perverts,
Rev 21: 8 the *m,* the sexually immoral,
22:15 the sexually immoral, the *m,*

MUSIC* (MUSICAL MUSICIAN MUSICIANS)
Ge 31:27 singing to the *m* of tambourines
Jdg 5: 3 I will make *m* to the LORD,
1Ch 6:31 put in charge of the *m* in the house
6:32 They ministered with *m*
25: 6 fathers for the *m* of the temple
25: 7 and skilled in *m* for the LORD—
Ne 12:27 and with the *m* of cymbals,
Job 21:12 They sing to the *m* of tambourine
Ps 27: 6 and make *m* to the LORD.
33: 2 make *m* to him on the ten-stringed
45: 8 the *m* of the strings makes you glad
57: 7 I will sing and make *m.*
81: 2 Begin the *m,* strike the tambourine,
87: 7 As they make *m* they will sing,
92: 1 and make *m* to your name,
92: 3 to the *m* of the ten-stringed lyre
95: 2 and extol him with *m* and song.
98: 4 burst into jubilant song with *m;*
98: 5 make *m* to the LORD
108: 1 make *m* with all my soul.
144: 9 the ten-stringed lyre I will make *m*
147: 7 make *m* to our God on the harp.
149: 3 make *m* to him with tambourine
Isa 30:32 will be to the *m* of tambourines
La 5:14 young men have stopped their *m.*
Eze 26:13 *m* of your harps will be heard no
Da 3: 5 lyre, harp, pipes and all kinds of *m,*
3: 7 and all kinds of *m,* all the peoples,
3:10 and all kinds of *m* must fall down
3:15 lyre, harp, pipes and all kinds of *m,*
Am 5:23 to the *m* of your harps.
Hab 3:19 For the director of *m.*
Lk 15:25 came near the house, he heard *m*
Eph 5:19 make *m* in your heart to the Lord,
Rev 18:22 The *m* of harpists and musicians,

MUSICAL* (MUSIC)
1Ch 15:16 accompanied by *m* instruments:
23: 5 with the *m* instruments I have
2Ch 7: 6 with the LORD's *m* instruments,
23:13 with *m* instruments were leading
34:12 skilled in playing *m* instruments—
Ne 12:36 with *m* instruments prescribed
Am 6: 5 and improvise on *m* instruments.

MUSICIAN* (MUSIC)
1Ch 6:33 Heman, the *m,* the son of Joel,

MUSICIANS* (MUSIC)
1Ki 10:12 to make harps and lyres for the *m.*
1Ch 9:33 Those who were *m,* heads
15:19 The *m* Heman, Asaph
2Ch 5:12 All the Levites who were *m*—
9:11 to make harps and lyres for the *m.*
35:15 The *m,* the descendants of Asaph,
Ps 68:25 are the singers, after them the *m;*
Rev 18:22 The music of harpists and *m,*

MUSTARD
Mt 13:31 kingdom of heaven is like a *m* seed,
17:20 you have faith as small as a *m* seed,
Mk 4:31 It is like a *m* seed, which is

MUTILATORS*
Php 3: 2 those men who do evil, those *m*

MUTUAL* (MUTUALLY)
Ro 14:19 leads to peace and to *m* edification.
1Co 7: 5 by *m* consent and for a time,

MUTUALLY* (MUTUAL)
Ro 1:12 and I may be *m* encouraged

MUZZLE*
Dt 25: 4 Do not *m* an ox while it is treading
Ps 39: 1 I will put a *m* on my mouth
1Co 9: 9 "Do not *m* an ox while it is
1Ti 5:18 "Do not *m* the ox while it is

MYRRH
Ps 45: 8 All your robes are fragrant with *m*
SS 1:13 My lover is to me a sachet of *m*
Mt 2:11 of gold and of incense and of *m.*
Mk 15:23 offered him wine mixed with *m,*
Jn 19:39 Nicodemus brought a mixture of *m*
Rev 18:13 of incense, *m* and frankincense,

MYSTERIES* (MYSTERY)
Job 11: 7 "Can you fathom the *m* of God?
Da 2:28 a God in heaven who reveals *m.*
2:29 of *m* showed you what is going
2:47 Lord of kings and a revealer of *m,*
1Co 13: 2 can fathom all *m* and all knowledge
14: 2 he utters *m* with his spirit.

MYSTERY* (MYSTERIES)
Da 2:18 God of heaven concerning this *m,*
2:19 the night the *m* was revealed
2:27 to the king the *m* he has asked
2:30 this *m* has been revealed to me,
2:47 for you were able to reveal this *m.*"
4: 9 and no *m* is too difficult for you.
Ro 11:25 you to be ignorant of this *m,*
16:25 to the revelation of the *m* hidden
1Co 15:51 I tell you a *m:* We will not all sleep,
Eph 1: 9 to us the *m* of his will according
3: 3 the *m* made known to me
3: 4 insight into the *m* of Christ,
3: 6 This *m* is that through the gospel
3: 9 the administration of this *m,*
5:32 This is a profound *m*—
6:19 I will fearlessly make known the *m*
Col 1:26 the *m* that has been kept hidden
1:27 the glorious riches of this *m,*
2: 2 in order that they may know the *m*
4: 3 so that we may proclaim the *m*
1Ti 3:16 the *m* of godliness is great:
Rev 1:20 *m* of the seven stars that you saw
10: 7 the *m* of God will be accomplished,
17: 5 written on her forehead: *M*
17: 7 explain to you the *m* of the woman

MYTHS*
1Ti 1: 4 nor to devote themselves to *m*
4: 7 Have nothing to do with godless *m*
2Ti 4: 4 from the truth and turn aside to *m.*
Tit 1:14 will pay no attention to Jewish *m*

NAAMAN
Aramean general whose leprosy was cleansed by Elisha (2Ki 5).

NABAL
Wealthy Carmelite the LORD killed for refusing

to help David (1Sa 25). David married Abigail, his widow (1Sa 25:39–42).

NABOTH*

Jezreelite killed by Jezebel for his vineyard (1Ki 21). Ahab's family destroyed for this (1Ki 21:17–24; 2Ki 9:21–37).

NADAB

1. Firstborn of Aaron (Ex 6:23); killed with Abihu for offering unauthorized fire (Lev 10; Nu 3:4).

2. Son of Jeroboam I; king of Israel (1Ki 15:25–32).

NAHUM

Prophet against Nineveh (Na 1:1).

NAIL* (NAILING)

Jn 20:25 "Unless I see the *n* marks

NAILING* (NAIL)

Ac 2:23 him to death by *n* him to the cross.
Col 2:14 he took it away, *n* it to the cross.

NAIVE

Ro 16:18 they deceive the minds of *n* people.

NAKED

Ge 2:25 The man and his wife were both *n*,
Job 1:21 *N* I came from my mother's womb,
Isa 58: 7 when you see the *n*, to clothe him,
2Co 5: 3 are clothed, we will not be found *n*.

NAME (NAMES)

Ge 2:19 man to see what he would *n* them;
4:26 to call on the *n* of the LORD.
11: 4 so that we may make a *n*
12: 2 I will make your *n* great,
32:29 Jacob said, "Please tell me your *n*."
Ex 3:15 This is my *n* forever, the *n*
20: 7 "You shall not misuse the *n*
34:14 for the LORD, whose *n* is Jealous,
Lev 24:11 Israelite woman blasphemed the *N*
Dt 5:11 "You shall not misuse the *n*
12:11 choose as a dwelling for his *N*—
18: 5 minister in the LORD's *n* always.
25: 6 carry on the *n* of the dead brother
28:58 this glorious and awesome *n*—
Jos 7: 9 do for your own great *n*?"
Jdg 13:17 "What is your *n*, so that we may
1Sa 12:22 of his great *n* the LORD will not
2Sa 6: 2 which is called by the *N*, the name
7: 9 Now I will make your *n* great,
1Ki 5: 5 will build the temple for my *N*.'
8:29 you said, 'My *N* shall be there,'
1Ch 17: 8 I will make your *n* like the names
2Ch 7:14 my people, who are called by my *n*,
Ne 9:10 You made a *n* for yourself,
Ps 8: 1 how majestic is your *n*
9:10 Those who know your *n* will trust
20: 7 in the *n* of the LORD our God.
29: 2 to the LORD the glory due his *n*;
34: 3 let us exalt his *n* together.
44:20 If we had forgotten the *n*
66: 2 Sing the glory of his *n*;
68: 4 Sing to God, sing praise to his *n*,
79: 9 for the glory of your *n*;
96: 8 to the LORD the glory due his *n*;
103: 1 my inmost being, praise his holy *n*.
115: 1 but to your *n* be the glory,
138: 2 your *n* and your word.
145: 1 I will praise your *n* for ever
147: 4 and calls them each by *n*.
Pr 3: 4 you will win favor and a good *n*
18:10 *n* of the LORD is a strong tower;
22: 1 A good *n* is more desirable
30: 4 What is his *n*, and the *n* of his son?
Ecc 7: 1 A good *n* is better
SS 1: 3 your *n* is like perfume poured out.
Isa 12: 4 thanks to the LORD, call on his *n*;
26: 8 your *n* and renown
40:26 and calls them each by *n*.
42: 8 "I am the LORD; that is my *n*!
56: 5 I will give them an everlasting *n*
57:15 who lives forever, whose *n* is holy:
63:14 to make for yourself a glorious *n*.
Jer 14: 7 do something for the sake of your *n*
15:16 for I bear your *n*,
Eze 20: 9 of my *n* I did what would keep it
20:14 of my *n* I did what would keep it
20:22 of my *n* I did what would keep it
Da 12: 1 everyone whose *n* is found written
Hos 12: 5 the LORD is his *n* of renown!
Joel 2:32 on the *n* of the LORD will be saved
Mic 5: 4 in the majesty of the *n*
Zep 3: 9 call on the *n* of the LORD
Zec 6:12 is the man whose *n* is the Branch,
14: 9 one LORD, and his *n* the only *n*.
Mal 1: 6 O priests, who show contempt for my *n*.
Mt 1:21 and you are to give him the *n* Jesus,
6: 9 hallowed be your *n*,
18:20 or three come together in my *n*,
24: 5 For many will come in my *n*,
28:19 them in the *n* of the Father
Mk 9:41 gives you a cup of water in my *n*
Lk 11: 2 hallowed be your *n*,
Jn 10: 3 He calls his own sheep by *n*
14:13 I will do whatever you ask in my *n*,
16:24 asked for anything in my *n*.
Ac 2:21 on the *n* of the Lord will be saved.'
4:12 for there is no other *n*
Ro 10:13 "Everyone who calls on the *n*
Php 2: 9 him the *n* that is above every *n*,
2:10 at the *n* of Jesus every knee should
Col 3:17 do it all in the *n* of the Lord Jesus,
Heb 1: 4 as the *n* he has inherited is superior
Jas 5:14 him with oil in the *n* of the Lord.
1Jn 5:13 believe in the *n* of the Son of God
Rev 2:17 stone with a new *n* written on it,
3: 5 I will never blot out his *n*
3:12 I will also write on him my new *n*.
19:13 and his *n* is the Word of God.
20:15 If anyone's *n* was not found written

NAMES (NAME)

Ex 28: 9 engrave on them the *n* of the sons
Lk 10:20 but rejoice that your *n* are written
Php 4: 3 whose *n* are in the book of life.
Heb 12:23 whose *n* are written in heaven.
Rev 21:27 but only those whose *n* are written

NAOMI

Wife of Elimelech, mother-in-law of Ruth (Ru 1:2, 4). Left Bethlehem for Moab during famine (Ru 1:1). Returned a widow, with Ruth (Ru 1:6–22). Advised Ruth to seek marriage with Boaz (Ru 2:17–3:4). Cared for Ruth's son Obed (Ru 4:13–17).

NAPHTALI

Son of Jacob by Bilhah (Ge 30:8; 35:25; 1Ch 2:2). Tribe of blessed (Ge 49:21; Dt 33:23), numbered (Nu 1:43; 26:50), allotted land (Jos 19:32–39; Eze 48:3), failed to fully possess (Jdg 1:33), supported Deborah (Jdg 4:10; 5:18), David (1Ch 12:34), 12,000 from (Rev 7:6).

NARROW

Mt 7:13 "Enter through the *n* gate.
7:14 and *n* the road that leads to life,

NATHAN

Prophet and chronicler of Israel's history (1Ch 29:29; 2Ch 9:29). Announced the Davidic covenant (2Sa 7; 1Ch 17). Denounced David's sin with Bathsheba (2Sa 12). Supported Solomon (1Ki 1).

NATHANAEL*

Apostle (Jn 1:45–49; 21:2). Probably also called Bartholomew (Mt 10:3).

NATION (NATIONS)

Ge 12: 2 "I will make you into a great *n*
Ex 19: 6 a kingdom of priests and a holy *n*.'
Dt 4: 7 What other *n* is so great
Jos 5: 8 And after the whole *n* had been
2Sa 7:23 one *n* on earth that God went out
Ps 33:12 Blessed is the *n* whose God is
Pr 11:14 For lack of guidance a *n* falls,
14:34 Righteousness exalts a *n*,
Isa 2: 4 *N* will not take up sword
26: 2 that the righteous *n* may enter,
60:12 For the *n* or kingdom that will not
65: 1 To a *n* that did not call on my name
66: 8 a *n* be brought forth in a moment?
Mic 4: 3 *N* will not take up sword
Mt 24: 7 *N* will rise against *n*,
Mk 13: 8 *N* will rise against *n*,
1Pe 2: 9 a royal priesthood, a holy *n*,
Rev 5: 9 and language and people and *n*.
7: 9 from every *n*, tribe, people
14: 6 to every *n*, tribe, language

NATIONS (NATION)

Ge 17: 4 You will be the father of many *n*.
18:18 and all *n* on earth will be blessed
Ex 19: 5 of all *n* you will be my treasured
Lev 20:26 apart from the *n* to be my own.
Dt 7: 1 drives out before you many *n*—
15: 6 You will rule over many *n*
Jdg 3: 1 These are the *n* the LORD left
2Ch 20: 6 rule over all the kingdoms of the *n*.
Ne 1: 8 I will scatter you among the *n*,
Ps 2: 1 Why do the *n* conspire
2: 8 I will make the *n* your inheritance,
9: 5 You have rebuked the *n*
22:28 and he rules over the *n*.
46:10 I will be exalted among the *n*,
47: 8 God reigns over the *n*;
66: 7 his eyes watch the *n*—
67: 2 your salvation among all *n*.
68:30 Scatter the *n* who delight in war.
72:17 All *n* will be blessed through him,
96: 3 Declare his glory among the *n*,
99: 2 he is exalted over all the *n*.
106:35 but they mingled with the *n*
110: 6 He will judge the *n*, heaping up
113: 4 The LORD is exalted over all the *n*
Isa 2: 2 and all *n* will stream to it.
11:10 the *n* will rally to him,
12: 4 among the *n* what he has done,
40:15 Surely the *n* are like a drop
42: 1 and he will bring justice to the *n*.
51: 4 justice will become a light to the *n*.
52:15 so will he sprinkle many *n*,
56: 7 a house of prayer for all *n*."
60: 3 *N* will come to your light,
66:18 and gather all *n* and tongues,
Jer 1: 5 you as a prophet to the *n*."
3:17 and all *n* will gather in Jerusalem
31:10 "Hear the word of the LORD, O *n*;
33: 9 and honor before all *n*
46:28 I completely destroy all the *n*
Eze 22: 4 you an object of scorn to the *n*
34:13 I will bring them out from the *n*
36:23 *n* will know that I am the LORD,
37:22 and they will never again be two *n*
39:21 I will display my glory among the *n*
Hos 7: 8 "Ephraim mixes with the *n*;
Joel 2:17 a byword among the *n*.
3: 2 I will gather all *n*
Am 9:12 and all the *n* that bear my name,"
Zep 3: 8 I have decided to assemble the *n*,
Hag 2: 7 and the desired of all *n* will come,
Zec 8:13 an object of cursing among the *n*,
8:23 *n* will take firm hold of one Jew
9:10 He will proclaim peace to the *n*.
14: 2 I will gather all the *n* to Jerusalem
Mt 12:18 he will proclaim justice to the *n*.
24: 9 and you will be hated by all *n*
24:14 whole world as a testimony to all *n*,

Mt 25:32 All the *n* will be gathered
28:19 and make disciples of all *n*,
Mk 11:17 a house of prayer for all *n*?
Ac 4:25 " 'Why do the *n* rage
Ro 15:12 who will arise to rule over the *n*;
Gal 3: 8 All *n* will be blessed through you."
1Ti 3:16 was preached among the *n*,
Rev 15: 4 All *n* will come
21:24 The *n* will walk by its light,
22: 2 are for the healing of the *n*.

NATURAL (NATURE)
Ro 6:19 you are weak in your *n* selves.
1Co 15:44 If there is a *n* body, there is

NATURE (NATURAL)
Ro 1:20 his eternal power and divine *n*—
7:18 lives in me, that is, in my sinful *n*.
8: 4 do not live according to the sinful *n*
8: 5 to the sinful *n* have their minds set
8: 8 by the sinful *n* cannot please God.
13:14 to gratify the desires of the sinful *n*.
Gal 5:13 freedom to indulge the sinful *n*;
5:19 The acts of the sinful *n* are obvious:
5:24 Jesus have crucified the sinful *n*
Php 2: 6 Who, being in very *n* God,
Col 3: 5 whatever belongs to your earthly *n*
2Pe 1: 4 you may participate in the divine *n*

NAZARENE* (NAZARETH)
Mt 2:23 prophets: "He will be called a *N.*"
Mk 14:67 "You also were with that *N*, Jesus,"
16: 6 "You are looking for Jesus the *N*,
Ac 24: 5 He is a ringleader of the *N* sect and

NAZARETH (NAZARENE)
Mt 4:13 Leaving *N*, he went and lived
Lk 4:16 to *N*, where he had been brought
Jn 1:46 "*N*! Can anything good come

NAZIRITE
Nu 6: 2 of separation to the LORD as a *N*,
Jdg 13: 7 because the boy will be a *N* of God

NEBO
Dt 34: 1 Then Moses climbed Mount *N*

NEBUCHADNEZZAR
Babylonian king. Subdued and exiled Judah (2Ki 24–25; 2Ch 36; Jer 39). Dreams interpreted by Daniel (Da 2; 4). Worshiped God (Da 3:28–29; 4:34–37).

NECESSARY*
Ac 1:21 Therefore it is *n* to choose one
Ro 13: 5 it is *n* to submit to the authorities,
2Co 9: 5 I thought it *n* to urge the brothers
Php 1:24 it is more *n* for you that I remain
2:25 But I think it is *n* to send back
Heb 8: 3 and so it was *n* for this one
9:16 it is *n* to prove the death
9:23 It was *n*, then, for the copies

NECK (STIFF-NECKED)
Pr 3:22 an ornament to grace your *n*.
6:21 fasten them around your *n*.
Mt 18: 6 a large millstone hung around his *n*

NECO
Pharaoh who killed Josiah (2Ki 23:29–30; 2Ch 35:20–22), deposed Jehoahaz (2Ki 23:33–35; 2Ch 36:3–4).

NEED (NEEDS NEEDY)
1Ki 8:59 Israel according to each day's *n*,
Ps 79: 8 for we are in desperate *n*.
116: 6 when I was in great *n*, he saved me.
142: 6 for I am in desperate *n*;
Mt 6: 8 for your Father knows what you *n*
Lk 15:14 country, and he began to be in *n*.
Ac 2:45 they gave to anyone as he had *n*.
Ro 12:13 with God's people who are in *n*.
1Co 12:21 say to the hand, "I don't *n* you!"
Eph 4:28 something to share with those in *n*.
1Ti 5: 3 to those widows who are really in *n*
Heb 4:16 grace to help us in our time of *n*.
1Jn 3:17 sees his brother in *n* but has no pity

NEEDLE
Mt 19:24 go through the eye of a *n*

NEEDS (NEED)
Isa 58:11 he will satisfy your *n*
Php 2:25 sent to take care of my *n*.
4:19 God will meet all your *n* according
Jas 2:16 does nothing about his physical *n*,

NEEDY (NEED)
Dt 15:11 toward the poor and *n* in your land.
1Sa 2: 8 and lifts the *n* from the ash heap;
Ps 35:10 and *n* from those who rob them."
69:33 The LORD hears the *n*
72:12 he will deliver the *n* who cry out,
140:12 and upholds the cause of the *n*.
Pr 14:21 blessed is he who is kind to the *n*.
14:31 to the *n* honors God.
22:22 and do not crush the *n* in court,
31: 9 defend the rights of the poor and *n*
31:20 and extends her hands to the *n*.
Mt 6: 2 "So when you give to the *n*,

NEGLECT* (NEGLECTED)
Dt 12:19 Be careful not to *n* the Levites
14:27 And do not *n* the Levites living
Ezr 4:22 Be careful not to *n* this matter.
Ne 10:39 We will not *n* the house of our God
Est 6:10 Do not *n* anything you have
Ps 119:16 I will not *n* your word.
Lk 11:42 you *n* justice and the love of God.
Ac 6: 2 for us to *n* the ministry of the word
1Ti 4:14 Do not *n* your gift, which was

NEGLECTED (NEGLECT)
Mt 23:23 But you have *n* the more important

NEHEMIAH
Cupbearer of Artaxerxes (Ne 2:1); governor of Israel (Ne 8:9). Returned to Jerusalem to rebuild walls (Ne 2–6). With Ezra, reestablished worship (Ne 8). Prayer confessing nation's sin (Ne 9). Dedicated wall (Ne 12).

NEIGHBOR (NEIGHBOR'S)
Ex 20:16 give false testimony against your *n*.
20:17 or anything that belongs to your *n*
Lev 19:13 Do not defraud your *n* or rob him.
19:17 Rebuke your *n* frankly
19:18 but love your *n* as yourself.
Ps 15: 3 who does his *n* no wrong
Pr 3:29 Do not plot harm against your *n*,
11:12 who lacks judgment derides his *n*,
14:21 He who despises his *n* sins,
16:29 A violent man entices his *n*
24:28 against your *n* without cause,
25:18 gives false testimony against his *n*.
27:10 better a *n* nearby than a brother far
27:14 If a man loudly blesses his *n*
29: 5 Whoever flatters his *n*
Jer 31:34 No longer will a man teach his *n*,
Zec 8:17 do not plot evil against your *n*,
Mt 5:43 Love your *n* and hate your enemy.'
19:19 and 'love your *n* as yourself.' "
Mk 12:31 The second is this: 'Love your *n*
Lk 10:27 and, 'Love your *n* as yourself.' "
10:29 who is my *n*?" In reply Jesus said:
Ro 13: 9 "Love your *n* as yourself."
13:10 Love does no harm to its *n*.
15: 2 Each of us should please his *n*
Gal 5:14 "Love your *n* as yourself."
Eph 4:25 and speak truthfully to his *n*,
Heb 8:11 No longer will a man teach his *n*,
Jas 2: 8 "Love your *n* as yourself,"

NEIGHBOR'S (NEIGHBOR)
Ex 20:17 You shall not covet your *n* wife,
Dt 5:21 not set your desire on your *n* house
19:14 not move your *n* boundary stone
27:17 who moves his *n* boundary stone."
Pr 25:17 Seldom set foot in your *n* house—

NESTS
Mt 8:20 and birds of the air have *n*,

NET (NETS)
Pr 1:17 How useless to spread a *n*
Hab 1:15 he catches them in his *n*,
Mt 13:47 of heaven is like a *n* that was let
Jn 21: 6 "Throw your *n* on the right side

NETS (NET)
Ps 141:10 Let the wicked fall into their own *n*
Mt 4:20 At once they left their *n*
Lk 5: 4 and let down the *n* for a catch."

NEVER-FAILING*
Am 5:24 righteousness like a *n* stream!

NEW
Ps 40: 3 He put a *n* song in my mouth,
98: 1 Sing to the LORD a *n* song,
Ecc 1: 9 there is nothing *n* under the sun.
Isa 42: 9 and *n* things I declare;
62: 2 you will be called by a *n* name
65:17 *n* heavens and a *n* earth.
66:22 "As the *n* heavens and the *n* earth
Jer 31:31 "when I will make a *n* covenant
La 3:23 They are *n* every morning;
Eze 11:19 undivided heart and put a *n* spirit
18:31 and get a *n* heart and a *n* spirit.
36:26 give you a *n* heart and put a *n* spirit
Zep 3: 5 and every *n* day he does not fail,
Mt 9:17 Neither do men pour *n* wine
Mk 16:17 they will speak in *n* tongues;
Lk 5:39 after drinking old wine wants the *n*
22:20 "This cup is the *n* covenant
Jn 13:34 "A *n* commandment I give you:
Ac 5:20 the full message of this *n* life."
Ro 6: 4 the Father, we too may live a *n* life.
1Co 5: 7 old yeast that you may be a *n* batch
11:25 "This cup is the *n* covenant
2Co 3: 6 as ministers of a *n* covenant—
5:17 he is a *n* creation; the old has gone,
Gal 6:15 what counts is a *n* creation.
Eph 4:23 to be made *n* in the attitude
4:24 and to put on the *n* self, created
Col 3:10 and have put on the *n* self,
Heb 8: 8 when I will make a *n* covenant
9:15 is the mediator of a *n* covenant,
10:20 by a *n* and living way opened for us
12:24 Jesus the mediator of a *n* covenant,
1Pe 1: 3 great mercy he has given us *n* birth
2Pe 3:13 to a *n* heaven and a *n* earth,
1Jn 2: 8 Yet I am writing you a *n* command;
Rev 2:17 stone with a *n* name written on it,
3:12 the *n* Jerusalem, which is coming
21: 1 I saw a *n* heaven and a *n* earth,

NEWBORN (BEAR)
1Pe 2: 2 Like *n* babies, crave pure spiritual

NEWS
2Ki 7: 9 This is a day of good *n*
Ps 112: 7 He will have no fear of bad *n*;
Pr 15:30 good *n* gives health to the bones.
25:25 is good *n* from a distant land.
Isa 52: 7 the feet of those who bring good *n*,
61: 1 me to preach good *n* to the poor.
Na 1:15 the feet of one who brings good *n*,
Mt 4:23 preaching the good *n*
9:35 preaching the good *n*
11: 5 the good *n* is preached to the poor.
Mk 1:15 Repent and believe the good *n*!"
16:15 preach the good *n* to all creation.
Lk 1:19 and to tell you this good *n*.

Lk 2:10 I bring you good *n*
3:18 and preached the good *n* to them.
4:43 "I must preach the good *n*
8: 1 proclaiming the good *n*
16:16 the good *n* of the kingdom
Ac 5:42 proclaiming the good *n* that Jesus
10:36 telling the good *n* of peace
14: 7 continued to preach the good *n*.
14:21 They preached the good *n*
17:18 preaching the good *n* about Jesus
Ro 10:15 feet of those who bring good *n*!"

NICODEMUS*

Pharisee who visited Jesus at night (Jn 3). Argued fair treatment of Jesus (Jn 7:50–52). With Joseph, prepared Jesus for burial (Jn 19:38–42).

NIGHT (NIGHTS NIGHTTIME)
Ge 1: 5 and the darkness he called "*n*."
1:16 and the lesser light to govern the *n*.
Ex 13:21 and by *n* in a pillar of fire
14:24 During the last watch of the *n*.
Dt 28:66 filled with dread both *n* and day,
Jos 1: 8 and *n*, so that you may be careful
Job 35:10 who gives songs in the *n*,
Ps 1: 2 on his law he meditates day and *n*.
19: 2 *n* after *n* they display knowledge.
42: 8 at *n* his song is with me—
63: 6 of you through the watches of the *n*
77: 6 I remembered my songs in the *n*.
90: 4 or like a watch in the *n*.
91: 5 You will not fear the terror of *n*,
119:148 through the watches of the *n*,
121: 6 nor the moon by *n*.
136: 9 the moon and stars to govern the *n*;
Pr 31:18 and her lamp does not go out at *n*.
Isa 21:11 Watchman, what is left of the *n*?"
58:10 and your *n* will become like
Jer 33:20 and my covenant with the *n*,
Lk 2: 8 watch over their flocks at *n*.
6:12 and spent the *n* praying to God.
Jn 3: 2 He came to Jesus at *n* and said,
9: 4 *N* is coming, when no one can work
1Th 5: 2 Lord will come like a thief in the *n*.
5: 5 We do not belong to the *n*
Rev 21:25 for there will be no *n* there.

NIGHTS (NIGHT)
Jnh 1:17 the fish three days and three *n*.
Mt 4: 2 After fasting forty days and forty *n*
12:40 three *n* in the belly of a huge fish,
2Co 6: 5 in hard work, sleepless *n*

NIGHTTIME* (NIGHT)
Zec 14: 7 or *n*— a day known to the LORD.

NIMROD
Ge 10: 9 "Like *N*, a mighty hunter

NINEVEH
Jnh 1: 2 "Go to the great city of *N*
Na 1: 1 An oracle concerning *N*.
Mt 12:41 The men of *N* will stand up

NOAH

Righteous man (Eze 14:14, 20) called to build ark (Ge 6–8; Heb 11:7; 1Pe 3:20; 2Pe 2:5). God's covenant with (Ge 9:1–17). Drunkenness of (Ge 9:18–23). Blessed sons, cursed Canaan (Ge 9:24–27).

NOBLE
Ru 3:11 you are a woman of *n* character.
Ps 45: 1 My heart is stirred by a *n* theme
Pr 12: 4 of *n* character is her husband's
31:10 A wife of *n* character who can find?
31:29 "Many women do *n* things,
Isa 32: 8 But the *n* man makes *n* plans,
Lk 8:15 good soil stands for those with a *n*
Ro 9:21 of clay some pottery for *n* purposes
Php 4: 8 whatever is *n*, whatever is right,
2Ti 2:20 some are for *n* purposes

NOSTRILS
Ge 2: 7 and breathed into his *n* the breath
Ex 15: 8 By the blast of your *n*
Ps 18:15 at the blast of breath from your *n*.

NOTE
Ac 4:13 and they took *n* that these men had
Php 3:17 take *n* of those who live according

NOTHING
2Sa 24:24 offerings that cost me *n*."
Ne 9:21 in the desert; they lacked *n*,
Ps 73:25 earth has *n* I desire besides you
Jer 32:17 *N* is too hard for you
Jn 15: 5 apart from me you can do *n*.

NOURISH
Pr 10:21 The lips of the righteous *n* many,

NULLIFY
Mt 15: 6 Thus you *n* the word of God
Ro 3:31 Do we, then, *n* the law by this faith

OATH
Ex 33: 1 up to the land I promised on *o*
Nu 30: 2 or takes an *o* to obligate himself
Dt 6:18 promised on *o* to your forefathers,
7: 8 and kept the *o* he swore
29:12 you this day and sealing with an *o*,
Ps 95:11 So I declared on *o* in my anger,
119:106 I have taken an *o* and confirmed it,
132:11 The LORD swore an *o* to David,
Ecc 8: 2 because you took an *o* before God.
Mt 5:33 'Do not break your *o*, but keep
Heb 7:20 And it was not without an *o*!

OBADIAH

1. Believer who sheltered 100 prophets from Jezebel (1Ki 18:1–16).

2. Prophet against Edom (Ob 1).

OBEDIENCE* (OBEY)
Ge 49:10 and the *o* of the nations is his.
Jdg 2:17 of *o* to the LORD's commands.
1Ch 21:19 So David went up in *o*
2Ch 31:21 in *o* to the law and the commands,
Pr 30:17 that scorns *o* to a mother,
Lk 23:56 Sabbath in *o* to the commandment.
Ac 21:24 but that you yourself are living in *o*
Ro 1: 5 to the *o* that comes from faith.
5:19 also through the *o* of the one man
6:16 to *o*, which leads to righteousness?
16:19 Everyone has heard about your *o*,
2Co 9:13 for the *o* that accompanies your
10: 6 once your *o* is complete.
Phm :21 Confident of your *o*, I write to you,
Heb 5: 8 he learned *o* from what he suffered
1Pe 1: 2 for *o* to Jesus Christ and sprinkling
2Jn : 6 that we walk in *o* to his commands.

OBEDIENT* (OBEY)
Dt 30:17 heart turns away and you are not *o*,
Isa 1:19 If you are willing and *o*,
Lk 2:51 with them and was *o* to them.
Ac 6: 7 of priests became *o* to the faith.
2Co 2: 9 if you would stand the test and be *o*
7:15 he remembers that you were all *o*,
10: 5 thought to make it *o* to Christ.
Php 2: 8 and became *o* to death—
Tit 3: 1 to be *o*, to be ready
1Pe 1:14 As *o* children, do not conform

OBEY (OBEDIENCE OBEDIENT OBEYED OBEYING OBEYS)
Ex 12:24 "*O* these instructions as a lasting
19: 5 Now if you *o* me fully and keep my
24: 7 the LORD has said; we will *o*."
Lev 18: 4 You must *o* my laws and be careful
25:18 and be careful to *o* my laws,
Nu 15:40 remember to *o* all my commands
Dt 5:27 We will listen and *o*."
6: 3 careful to *o* so that it may go well
6:24 us to *o* all these decrees
11:13 if you faithfully *o* the commands I
12:28 to *o* all these regulations I am
13: 4 Keep his commands and *o* him;
21:18 son who does not *o* his father
28: 1 If you fully *o* the LORD your God
28:15 if you do not *o* the LORD your
30: 2 and *o* him with all your heart
30:10 if you *o* the LORD your God
30:14 and in your heart so you may *o* it.
32:46 children to *o* carefully all the words
Jos 1: 7 to *o* all the law my servant Moses
22: 5 in all his ways, to *o* his commands,
24:24 the LORD our God and *o* him."
1Sa 15:22 To *o* is better than sacrifice,
1Ki 8:61 by his decrees and *o* his commands
2Ki 17:13 that I commanded your fathers to *o*
2Ch 34:31 and to *o* the words of the covenant
Ne 1: 5 who love him and *o* his commands,
Ps 103:18 and remember to *o* his precepts.
103:20 who *o* his word.
119:17 I will *o* your word.
119:34 and *o* it with all my heart.
119:57 I have promised to *o* your words.
119:67 but now I *o* your word.
119:100 for I *o* your precepts.
119:129 therefore I *o* them.
119:167 I *o* your statutes,
Pr 5:13 I would not *o* my teachers
Jer 7:23 I gave them this command: *O* me,
11: 4 '*O* me and do everything I
11: 7 and again, saying, "*O* me."
42: 6 we will *o* the LORD our God,
Da 9: 4 who love him and *o* his commands,
Mt 8:27 the winds and the waves *o* him!"
19:17 to enter life, *o* the commandments
28:20 to *o* everything I have commanded
Lk 11:28 hear the word of God and *o* it."
Jn 14:15 you will *o* what I command.
14:23 loves me, he will *o* my teaching.
14:24 not love me will not *o* my teaching.
15:10 If you *o* my commands, you will
Ac 5:29 "We must *o* God rather than men!
5:32 given to those who *o* him."
Ro 2:13 it is those who *o* the law who will
6:12 body so that you *o* its evil desires.
6:16 slaves to the one whom you *o*—
6:16 yourselves to someone to *o* him
15:18 in leading the Gentiles to *o* God
16:26 nations might believe and *o* him—
Gal 5: 3 obligated to *o* the whole law.
Eph 6: 1 *o* your parents in the Lord,
6: 5 *o* your earthly masters with respect
Col 3:20 *o* your parents in everything,
3:22 *o* your earthly masters
2Th 3:14 anyone does not *o* our instruction
1Ti 3: 4 and see that his children *o* him
Heb 5: 9 eternal salvation for all who *o* him
13:17 *O* your leaders and submit
1Pe 4:17 for those who do not *o* the gospel
1Jn 3:24 Those who *o* his commands live
5: 3 love for God: to *o* his commands.
Rev 12:17 those who *o* God's commandments
14:12 the saints who *o* God's

OBEYED (OBEY)
Ge 22:18 blessed, because you have *o* me."
Jos 1:17 we fully *o* Moses, so we will obey
Ps 119: 4 that are to be fully *o*.
Da 9:10 we have not *o* the LORD our God
Jnh 3: 3 Jonah *o* the word of the LORD
Mic 5:15 the nations that have not *o* me."
Jn 15:10 as I have *o* my Father's commands
15:20 If they *o* my teaching, they will
17: 6 and they have *o* your word.
Ac 7:53 through angels but have not *o* it."
Ro 6:17 you wholeheartedly *o* the form
Php 2:12 as you have always *o*— not only
Heb 11: 8 *o* and went, even though he did not
1Pe 3: 6 who *o* Abraham and called him her

OBEYING (OBEY)
1Sa 15:22 as in *o* the voice of the LORD?
Ps 119: 5 steadfast in *o* your decrees!
Gal 5: 7 and kept you from *o* the truth?
1Pe 1:22 purified yourselves by *o* the truth

OBEYS (OBEY)
Lev 18: 5 for the man who *o* them will live
Pr 19:16 He who *o* instructions guards his
Eze 20:11 for the man who *o* them will live
Jn 14:21 has my commands and *o* them,
Ro 2:27 and yet *o* the law will condemn you
1Jn 2: 5 if anyone *o* his word, God's love is

OBLIGATED (OBLIGATION)
Ro 1:14 I am *o* both to Greeks
Gal 5: 3 himself be circumcised that he is *o*

OBLIGATION (OBLIGATED)
Ro 8:12 Therefore, brothers, we have an *o*

OBSCENITY*
Eph 5: 4 Nor should there be *o,* foolish talk

OBSCURES*
Job 42: 3 'Who is this that *o* my counsel

OBSERVE (OBSERVING)
Ex 31:13 'You must *o* my Sabbaths.
Lev 25: 2 the land itself must *o* a sabbath
Dt 4: 6 *O* them carefully, for this will show
5:12 "*O* the Sabbath day
8: 6 *O* the commands of the LORD
11:22 If you carefully *o* all these
26:16 carefully *o* them with all your heart
Ps 37:37 the blameless, *o* the upright;

OBSERVING (OBSERVE)
Ro 3:27 principle? On that of *o* the law?
Gal 2:16 a man is not justified by *o* the law,
3: 2 you receive the Spirit by *o* the law,
3:10 All who rely on *o* the law are

OBSOLETE
Heb 8:13 he has made the first one *o;*

OBSTACLE* (OBSTACLES)
Ro 14:13 or *o* in your brother's way.

OBSTACLES (OBSTACLE)
Ro 16:17 put *o* in your way that are contrary

OBSTINATE
Isa 65: 2 hands to an *o* people,
Ro 10:21 to a disobedient and *o* people."

OBTAIN (OBTAINED OBTAINS)
Ro 11: 7 sought so earnestly it did not *o,*
2Ti 2:10 they too may *o* the salvation that

OBTAINED (OBTAIN)
Ro 9:30 not pursue righteousness, have *o* it,
Php 3:12 Not that I have already *o* all this,
Heb 9:12 having *o* eternal redemption.

OBTAINS* (OBTAIN)
Pr 12: 2 A good man *o* favor

OBVIOUS*
Mt 6:18 so that it will not be *o*
Gal 5:19 The acts of the sinful nature are *o:*
1Ti 5:24 The sins of some men are *o,*
5:25 In the same way, good deeds are *o,*

OCCASIONS
Eph 6:18 in the Spirit on all *o* with all kinds

OFFENDED (OFFENSE)
Pr 18:19 An *o* brother is more unyielding

OFFENDERS* (OFFENSE)
1Co 6: 9 nor homosexual *o* nor thieves

OFFENSE (OFFENDED OFFENDERS OFFENSES OFFENSIVE)
Pr 17: 9 over an *o* promotes love,
19:11 it is to his glory to overlook an *o.*
Gal 5:11 In that case the *o* of the cross has

OFFENSES (OFFENSE)
Isa 44:22 swept away your *o* like a cloud,
59:12 For our *o* are many in your sight,
Eze 18:30 Repent! Turn away from all your *o;*
33:10 "Our *o* and sins weigh us down,

OFFENSIVE (OFFENSE)
Ps 139:24 See if there is any *o* way in me,

OFFER (OFFERED OFFERING OFFERINGS OFFERS)
Ps 4: 5 *O* right sacrifices
Ro 6:13 Do not *o* the parts of your body
12: 1 to *o* your bodies as living sacrifices,
Heb 9:25 he enter heaven to *o* himself again
13:15 therefore, let us continually *o*

OFFERED (OFFER)
Isa 50: 6 I *o* my back to those who beat me,
1Co 9:13 share in what is *o* on the altar?
10:20 of pagans are *o* to demons,
Heb 7:27 once for all when he *o* himself.
9:14 the eternal Spirit *o* himself
11: 4 By faith Abel *o* God a better
11:17 when God tested him, *o* Isaac
Jas 5:15 prayer *o* in faith will make the sick

OFFERING (OFFER)
Ge 4: 3 of the soil as an *o* to the LORD.
22: 2 a burnt *o* on one of the mountains I
22: 8 provide the lamb for the burnt *o,*
Ex 29:24 before the LORD as a wave *o.*
29:40 quarter of a hin of wine as a drink *o.*
Lev 1: 3 If the *o* is a burnt *o* from the herd,
2: 4 " 'If you bring a grain *o* baked
3: 1 " 'If someone's *o* is a fellowship *o,*
4: 3 a sin *o* for the sin he has committed
5:15 It is a guilt *o.*
7:37 ordination *o* and the fellowship *o,*
9:24 and consumed the burnt *o*
22:18 to fulfill a vow or as a freewill *o,*
22:21 a special vow or as a freewill *o,*
1Sa 13: 9 And Saul offered up the burnt *o.*
1Ch 21:26 from heaven on the altar of burnt *o.*
2Ch 7: 1 and consumed the burnt *o*
Ps 40: 6 Sacrifice and *o* you did not desire,
116:17 I will sacrifice a thank *o* to you
Isa 53:10 the LORD makes his life a guilt *o,*
Mt 5:23 if you are *o* your gift at the altar
Ro 8: 3 likeness of sinful man to be a sin *o.*
Eph 5: 2 as a fragrant *o* and sacrifice to God.
Php 2:17 I am being poured out like a drink *o*
4:18 are a fragrant *o,* an acceptable
2Ti 4: 6 being poured out like a drink *o,*
Heb 10: 5 "Sacrifice and *o* you did not desire,
1Pe 2: 5 *o* spiritual sacrifices acceptable

OFFERINGS (OFFER)
1Sa 15:22 Does the LORD delight in burnt *o*
2Ch 35: 7 and goats for the Passover *o,*
Isa 1:13 Stop bringing meaningless *o!*
Hos 6: 6 of God rather than burnt *o.*
Mal 3: 8 do we rob you?' "In tithes and *o.*
Mk 12:33 is more important than all burnt *o*
Heb 10: 8 First he said, "Sacrifices and *o,*

OFFERS (OFFER)
Heb 10:11 and again he *o* the same sacrifices,

OFFICER (OFFICIALS)
2Ti 2: 4 wants to please his commanding *o.*

OFFICIALS (OFFICER)
Ex 5:21 a stench to Pharaoh and his *o.*
Pr 17:26 or to flog *o* for their integrity.
29:12 all his *o* become wicked.

OFFSPRING
Ge 3:15 and between your *o* and hers;
12: 7 "To your *o* I will give this land."
13:16 I will make your *o* like the dust
26: 4 and through your *o* all nations
28:14 blessed through you and your *o.*
Ex 13: 2 The first *o* of every womb
Ru 4:12 Through the *o* the LORD gives
Isa 44: 3 I will pour out my Spirit on your *o,*
53:10 he will see his *o* and prolong his
Ac 3:25 'Through your *o* all peoples
17:28 own poets have said, 'We are his *o.*'
17:29 "Therefore since we are God's *o,*
Ro 4:18 said to him, "So shall your *o* be."
9: 8 who are regarded as Abraham's *o.*

OG
Nu 21:33 *O* king of Bashan and his whole
Ps 136:20 and *O* king of Bashan—

OIL
Ex 29: 7 Take the anointing *o* and anoint
30:25 It will be the sacred anointing *o.*
Dt 14:23 tithe of your grain, new wine and *o,*
1Sa 10: 1 Then Samuel took a flask of *o*
16:13 So Samuel took the horn of *o*
1Ki 17:16 and the jug of *o* did not run dry,
2Ki 4: 6 Then the *o* stopped flowing.
Ps 23: 5 You anoint my head with *o;*
45: 7 by anointing you with the *o* of joy.
104:15 *o* to make his face shine,
133: 2 It is like precious *o* poured
Pr 21:17 loves wine and *o* will never be
Isa 1: 6 or soothed with *o.*
61: 3 the *o* of gladness
Mt 25: 3 but did not take any *o* with them.
Heb 1: 9 by anointing you with the *o* of joy."

OLIVE (OLIVES)
Ge 8:11 beak was a freshly plucked *o* leaf!
Jdg 9: 8 said to the *o* tree, 'Be our king.'
Jer 11:16 LORD called you a thriving *o* tree
Zec 4: 3 Also there are two *o* trees by it,
Ro 11:17 and you, though a wild *o* shoot,
11:24 of an *o* tree that is wild by nature,
Rev 11: 4 These are the two *o* trees

OLIVES (OLIVE)
Zec 14: 4 stand on the Mount of *O,*
Mt 24: 3 sitting on the Mount of *O,*
Jas 3:12 a fig tree bear *o,* or a grapevine bear

OMEGA*
Rev 1: 8 "I am the Alpha and the *O,*"
21: 6 I am the Alpha and the *O,*
22:13 I am the Alpha and the *O,*

OMIT*
Jer 26: 2 I command you; do not *o* a word.

OMRI
King of Israel (1Ki 16:21–26).

ONESIMUS*
Col 4: 9 He is coming with *O,* our faithful
Phm :10 I appeal to you for my son *O,*

ONESIPHORUS*
2Ti 1:16 mercy to the household of *O,*
4:19 Aquila and the household of *O.*

ONIONS*
Nu 11: 5 melons, leeks, *o* and garlic.

ONYX
Ex 28: 9 "Take two *o* stones and engrave
28:20 in the fourth row a chrysolite, an *o*

OPENHANDED* (HAND)
Dt 15: 8 Rather be *o* and freely lend him
15:11 you to be *o* toward your brothers

OPINIONS*
1Ki 18:21 will you waver between two *o?*
Pr 18: 2 but delights in airing his own *o.*

OPPONENTS (OPPOSE)
Pr 18:18 and keeps strong *o* apart.

OPPORTUNE (OPPORTUNITY)
Lk 4:13 he left him until an *o* time.

OPPORTUNITY* (OPPORTUNE)
1Sa 18:21 "Now you have a second *o*
Jer 46:17 he has missed his *o.*'
Mt 26:16 watched for an *o* to hand him over.
Mk 14:11 So he watched for an *o* to hand him
Lk 22: 6 and watched for an *o* to hand Jesus
Ac 25:16 and has had an *o* to defend himself
Ro 7: 8 seizing the *o* afforded
7:11 seizing the *o* afforded
1Co 16:12 but he will go when he has the *o.*
2Co 5:12 are giving you an *o* to take pride
11:12 from under those who want an *o*
Gal 6:10 as we have *o,* let us do good
Eph 5:16 making the most of every *o,*
Php 4:10 but you had no *o* to show it.
Col 4: 5 make the most of every *o.*
1Ti 5:14 to give the enemy no *o* for slander.
Heb 11:15 they would have had *o* to return.

OPPOSE (OPPONENTS OPPOSED OPPOSES OPPOSING OPPOSITION)
Ex 23:22 and will *o* those who *o* you.
1Sa 2:10 those who *o* the LORD will be
Job 23:13 he stands alone, and who can *o* him
Ac 11:17 I to think that I could *o* God?"
2Ti 2:25 Those who *o* him he must gently
Tit 1: 9 doctrine and refute those who *o* it.
2: 8 so that those who *o* you may be

OPPOSED (OPPOSE)
Gal 2:11 to Antioch, I *o* him to his face,
3:21 therefore, *o* to the promises of God

OPPOSES (OPPOSE)
Jas 4: 6 "God *o* the proud
1Pe 5: 5 because, "God *o* the proud

OPPOSING (OPPOSE)
1Ti 6:20 the *o* ideas of what is falsely called

OPPOSITION (OPPOSE)
Heb 12: 3 Consider him who endured such *o*

OPPRESS (OPPRESSED OPPRESSES OPPRESSION OPPRESSOR)
Ex 1:11 masters over them to *o* them
22:21 "Do not mistreat an alien or *o* him,
Isa 3: 5 People will *o* each other—
Eze 22:29 they *o* the poor and needy
Da 7:25 the Most High and *o* his saints
Am 5:12 You *o* the righteous and take bribes
Zec 7:10 Do not *o* the widow
Mal 3: 5 who *o* the widows

OPPRESSED (OPPRESS)
Jdg 2:18 as they groaned under those who *o*
Ps 9: 9 The LORD is a refuge for the *o,*
82: 3 the rights of the poor and *o.*
146: 7 He upholds the cause of the *o*
Pr 16:19 in spirit and among the *o*
31: 5 and deprive all the *o* of their rights.
Isa 1:17 encourage the *o.*
53: 7 He was *o* and afflicted,
58:10 and satisfy the needs of the *o,*
Zec 10: 2 *o* for lack of a shepherd.
Lk 4:18 to release the *o,*

OPPRESSES (OPPRESS)
Pr 14:31 He who *o* the poor shows contempt
22:16 He who *o* the poor
Eze 18:12 He *o* the poor and needy.

OPPRESSION (OPPRESS)
Ps 12: 5 "Because of the *o* of the weak
72:14 He will rescue them from *o*
119:134 Redeem me from the *o* of men,
Isa 53: 8 By *o* and judgment he was taken
58: 9 "If you do away with the yoke of *o,*

OPPRESSOR (OPPRESS)
Ps 72: 4 he will crush the *o.*
Isa 51:13 For where is the wrath of the *o?*
Jer 22: 3 hand of his *o* the one who has been

ORDAINED
Ps 8: 2 you have *o* praise
111: 9 he *o* his covenant forever—
139:16 All the days *o* for me
Eze 28:14 for so I *o* you.
Hab 1:12 you have *o* them to punish.
Mt 21:16 you have *o* praise'?"

ORDER (ORDERLY ORDERS)
Nu 9:23 They obeyed the LORD's *o,*
Ps 110: 4 in the *o* of Melchizedek."
Heb 5:10 priest in the *o* of Melchizedek.
9:10 until the time of the new *o.*
Rev 21: 4 for the old *o* of things has passed

ORDERLY (ORDER)
1Co 14:40 done in a fitting and *o* way.
Col 2: 5 and delight to see how *o* you are

ORDERS (ORDER)
Mk 1:27 He even gives *o* to evil spirits
3:12 But he gave them strict *o* not
9: 9 Jesus gave them *o* not

ORDINARY
Ac 4:13 that they were unschooled, *o* men,

ORGIES*
Ro 13:13 not in *o* and drunkenness,
Gal 5:21 drunkenness, *o,* and the like.
1Pe 4: 3 *o,* carousing and detestable

ORIGIN (ORIGINATE ORIGINS)
2Pe 1:21 For prophecy never had its *o*

ORIGINATE* (ORIGIN)
1Co 14:36 Did the word of God *o* with you?

ORIGINS* (ORIGIN)
Mic 5: 2 whose *o* are from of old,

ORNAMENT* (ORNAMENTED)
Pr 3:22 an *o* to grace your neck.
25:12 of gold or an *o* of fine gold

ORNAMENTED (ORNAMENT)
Ge 37: 3 and he made a richly *o* robe for him

ORPHAN* (ORPHANS)
Ex 22:22 advantage of a widow or an *o.*

ORPHANS (ORPHAN)
Jn 14:18 will not leave you as *o;* I will come
Jas 1:27 to look after *o* and widows

OTHNIEL
Nephew of Caleb (Jos 15:15–19; Jdg 1:12–15). Judge who freed Israel from Aram (Jdg 3:7–11).

OUTBURSTS*
2Co 12:20 jealousy, *o* of anger, factions,

OUTCOME
Heb 13: 7 Consider the *o* of their way of life
1Pe 4:17 what will the *o* be for those who do

OUTNUMBER
Ps 139:18 they would *o* the grains of sand.

OUTSIDERS*
Col 4: 5 wise in the way you act toward *o;*
1Th 4:12 daily life may win the respect of *o*
1Ti 3: 7 also have a good reputation with *o,*

OUTSTANDING
SS 5:10 *o* among ten thousand.
Ro 13: 8 no debt remain *o,*

OUTSTRETCHED
Ex 6: 6 and will redeem you with an *o* arm
Dt 4:34 by a mighty hand and an *o* arm,
5:15 with a mighty hand and an *o* arm.
1Ki 8:42 your mighty hand and your *o* arm
Ps 136:12 with a mighty hand and *o* arm;
Jer 27: 5 and *o* arm I made the earth
32:17 by your great power and *o* arm.
Eze 20:33 an *o* arm and with outpoured wrath

OUTWEIGHS (WEIGH)
2Co 4:17 an eternal glory that far *o* them all.

OUTWIT*
2Co 2:11 in order that Satan might not *o* us.

OVERAWED* (AWE)
Ps 49:16 Do not be *o* when a man grows rich

OVERBEARING*
Tit 1: 7 not *o,* not quick-tempered,

OVERCAME (OVERCOME)
Rev 3:21 as I *o* and sat down with my Father
12:11 They *o* him

OVERCOME (OVERCAME OVERCOMES)
Mt 16:18 and the gates of Hades will not *o* it.
Mk 9:24 I do believe; help me *o* my unbelief
Lk 10:19 to *o* all the power of the enemy;
Jn 16:33 But take heart! I have *o* the world."
Ro 12:21 Do not be *o* by evil, but *o* evil
2Pe 2:20 and are again entangled in it and *o,*
1Jn 2:13 because you have *o* the evil one.
4: 4 are from God and have *o* them,
5: 4 is the victory that has *o* the world,
Rev 17:14 but the Lamb will *o* them

OVERCOMES* (OVERCOME)
1Jn 5: 4 born of God *o* the world.
5: 5 Who is it that *o* the world?
Rev 2: 7 To him who *o,* I will give the right
2:11 He who *o* will not be hurt at all
2:17 To him who *o,* I will give some
2:26 To him who *o* and does my will
3: 5 He who *o* will, like them, be
3:12 Him who *o* I will make a pillar
3:21 To him who *o,* I will give the right
21: 7 He who *o* will inherit all this,

OVERFLOW (OVERFLOWING OVERFLOWS)
Ps 65:11 and your carts *o* with abundance.
119:171 May my lips *o* with praise,
La 1:16 and my eyes *o* with tears.
Mt 12:34 out of the *o* of the heart the mouth
Lk 6:45 out of the *o* of his heart his mouth
Ro 5:15 Jesus Christ, *o* to the many! Again,
15:13 so that you may *o* with hope
2Co 4:15 to *o* to the glory of God.
1Th 3:12 *o* for each other and for everyone

OVERFLOWING (OVERFLOW)
Pr 3:10 then your barns will be filled to *o,*
2Co 8: 2 their *o* joy and their extreme
9:12 *o* in many expressions of thanks
Col 2: 7 as you were taught, and *o*

OVERFLOWS* (OVERFLOW)
Ps 23: 5 my cup *o.*
2Co 1: 5 also through Christ our comfort *o.*

OVERJOYED* (JOY)
Da 6:23 The king was *o* and gave orders
Mt 2:10 they saw the star, they were *o.*

Jn 20:20 The disciples were *o*
Ac 12:14 she was so *o* she ran back
1Pe 4:13 so that you may be *o*

OVERLOOK
Pr 19:11 it is to his glory to *o* an offense.

OVERSEER* (OVERSEERS)
Pr 6: 7 no *o* or ruler,
1Ti 3: 1 anyone sets his heart on being an *o*,
3: 2 Now the *o* must be above reproach,
Tit 1: 7 Since an *o* is entrusted
1Pe 2:25 returned to the Shepherd and *O*

OVERSEERS* (OVERSEER)
Ac 20:28 the Holy Spirit has made you *o*.
Php 1: 1 together with the *o* and deacons:
1Pe 5: 2 as *o*— not because you must,

OVERSHADOW* (OVERSHADOWING)
Lk 1:35 power of the Most High will *o* you.

OVERSHADOWING (OVERSHADOW)
Ex 25:20 wings spread upward, *o* the cover
Heb 9: 5 the glory, *o* the atonement cover.

OVERTHROW (OVERTHROWS)
2Th 2: 8 whom the Lord Jesus will *o*

OVERTHROWS (OVERTHROW)
Pr 13: 6 but wickedness *o* the sinner.
Isa 44:25 who *o* the learning of the wise

OVERWHELMED (OVERWHELMING)
2Sa 22: 5 the torrents of destruction *o* me.
1Ki 10: 5 temple of the LORD, she was *o*.
Ps 38: 4 My guilt has *o* me
65: 3 When we were *o* by sins,
Mt 26:38 "My soul is *o* with sorrow
Mk 7:37 People were *o* with amazement.
9:15 they were *o* with wonder
2Co 2: 7 so that he will not be *o*

OVERWHELMING (OVERWHELMED)
Pr 27: 4 Anger is cruel and fury *o*,
Isa 10:22 *o* and righteous.
28:15 When an *o* scourge sweeps by,

OWE
Ro 13: 7 If you *o* taxes, pay taxes; if revenue
Phm :19 to mention that you *o* me your very

OWNER'S (OWNERSHIP)
Isa 1: 3 the donkey his *o* manger,

OWNERSHIP* (OWNER'S)
2Co 1:22 He anointed us, set his seal of *o*

OX (OXEN)
Dt 25: 4 Do not muzzle an *o*
Isa 11: 7 and the lion will eat straw like the *o*
Eze 1:10 and on the left the face of an *o*;
Lk 13:15 of you on the Sabbath untie his *o*
1Co 9: 9 "Do not muzzle an *o*
1Ti 5:18 "Do not muzzle the *o*
Rev 4: 7 second was like an *o*, the third had

OXEN (OX)
1Ki 19:20 Elisha then left his *o* and ran
Lk 14:19 'I have just bought five yoke of *o*,

PAGAN (PAGANS)
Mt 18:17 as you would a *p* or a tax collector.
Lk 12:30 For the *p* world runs

PAGANS* (PAGAN)
Isa 2: 6 and clasp hands with *p*.
Mt 5:47 Do not even *p* do that? Be perfect,
6: 7 do not keep on babbling like *p*,
6:32 For the *p* run after all these things,
1Co 5: 1 that does not occur even among *p*:
10:20 but the sacrifices of *p* are offered
12: 2 You know that when you were *p*,
1Pe 2:12 such good lives among the *p* that,
4: 3 in the past doing what *p* choose
3Jn : 7 receiving no help from the *p*.

PAID (PAY)
Isa 40: 2 that her sin has been *p* for,
Zec 11:12 So they *p* me thirty pieces of silver.

PAIN (PAINFUL PAINS)
Ge 3:16 with *p* you will give birth
6: 6 and his heart was filled with *p*.
Job 6:10 my joy in unrelenting *p*—
33:19 may be chastened on a bed of *p*
Jer 4:19 I writhe in *p*.
15:18 Why is my *p* unending
Mt 4:24 suffering severe *p*,
Jn 16:21 woman giving birth to a child has *p*
1Pe 2:19 up under the *p* of unjust suffering
Rev 21: 4 or mourning or crying or *p*,

PAINFUL (PAIN)
Ge 3:17 through *p* toil you will eat of it
5:29 and *p* toil of our hands caused
Job 6:25 How *p* are honest words!
Eze 28:24 neighbors who are *p* briers
2Co 2: 1 I would not make another *p* visit
Heb 12:11 seems pleasant at the time, but *p*.
1Pe 4:12 at the *p* trial you are suffering,

PAINS (PAIN)
Ge 3:16 "I will greatly increase your *p*
Mt 24: 8 these are the beginning of birth *p*.
Ro 8:22 as in the *p* of childbirth right up
Gal 4:19 again in the *p* of childbirth
1Th 5: 3 as labor *p* on a pregnant woman,

PAIRS
Ge 7: 8 *P* of clean and unclean animals,

PALACE (PALACES)
2Sa 7: 2 "Here I am, living in a *p* of cedar,
Jer 22: 6 is what the LORD says about the *p*
22:13 "Woe to him who builds his *p*

PALACES (PALACE)
Mt 11: 8 wear fine clothes are in kings' *p*.
Lk 7:25 and indulge in luxury are in *p*.

PALE
Isa 29:22 no longer will their faces grow *p*.
Jer 30: 6 every face turned deathly *p*?
Da 10: 8 my face turned deathly *p*
Rev 6: 8 and there before me was a *p* horse!

PALM (PALMS)
Jn 12:13 They took *p* branches and went out
Rev 7: 9 and were holding *p* branches

PALMS (PALM)
Isa 49:16 you on the *p* of my hands;

PAMPERS*
Pr 29:21 If a man *p* his servant from youth,

PANIC
Dt 20: 3 or give way to *p* before them.
1Sa 14:15 It was a *p* sent by God.
Eze 7: 7 there is *p*, not joy,
Zec 14:13 by the LORD with great *p*.

PANTS
Ps 42: 1 As the deer *p* for streams of water,

PARABLES
See also JESUS: PARABLES
Ps 78: 2 I will open my mouth in *p*,
Mt 13:35 "I will open my mouth in *p*,
Lk 8:10 but to others I speak in *p*, so that,

PARADISE*
Lk 23:43 today you will be with me in *p*."
2Co 12: 4 God knows—was caught up to *p*.
Rev 2: 7 of life, which is in the *p* of God.

PARALYTIC
Mt 9: 2 Some men brought to him a *p*,
Mk 2: 3 bringing to him a *p*, carried by four
Ac 9:33 a *p* who had been bedridden

PARCHED
Ps 143: 6 my soul thirsts for you like a *p* land.

PARCHMENTS*
2Ti 4:13 and my scrolls, especially the *p*.

PARDON* (PARDONED PARDONS)
2Ch 30:18 *p* everyone who sets his heart
Job 7:21 Why do you not *p* my offenses
Isa 55: 7 and to our God, for he will freely *p*.
Joel 3:21 I will *p*."

PARDONED* (PARDON)
Nu 14:19 as you have *p* them from the time
Joel 3:21 bloodguilt, which I have not *p*,

PARDONS* (PARDON)
Mic 7:18 who *p* sin and forgives

PARENTS
Pr 17: 6 and *p* are the pride of their children
19:14 wealth are inherited from *p*,
Mt 10:21 children will rebel against their *p*
Lk 18:29 left home or wife or brothers or *p*
21:16 You will be betrayed even by *p*, brothers,
Jn 9: 3 Neither this man nor his *p* sinned,"
Ro 1:30 they disobey their *p*; they are
2Co 12:14 for their *p*, but *p* for their children.
Eph 6: 1 Children, obey your *p* in the Lord,
Col 3:20 obey your *p* in everything,
1Ti 5: 4 repaying their *p* and grandparents,
2Ti 3: 2 disobedient to their *p*, ungrateful,

PARTAKE*
1Co 10:17 for we all *p* of the one loaf.

PARTIAL* (PARTIALITY)
Pr 18: 5 It is not good to be *p* to the wicked

PARTIALITY (PARTIAL)
Lev 19:15 do not show *p* to the poor,
Dt 1:17 Do not show *p* in judging;
10:17 who shows no *p* and accepts no
16:19 Do not pervert justice or show *p*.
2Ch 19: 7 our God there is no injustice or *p*
Job 32:21 I will show *p* to no one,
34:19 who shows no *p* to princes
Pr 24:23 To show *p* in judging is not good:
Mal 2: 9 have shown *p* in matters of the law
Lk 20:21 and that you do not show *p*
1Ti 5:21 keep these instructions without *p*,

PARTICIPANTS (PARTICIPATE)
1Co 10:20 you to be *p* with demons.

PARTICIPATE (PARTICIPANTS PARTICIPATION)
1Pe 4:13 rejoice that you *p* in the sufferings
2Pe 1: 4 that through them you may *p*

PARTICIPATION (PARTICIPATE)
1Co 10:16 is not the bread that we break a *p*

PARTNER (PARTNERS PARTNERSHIP)
Pr 2:17 who has left the *p* of her youth
Mal 2:14 though she is your *p*, the wife
1Pe 3: 7 them with respect as the weaker *p*

PARTNERS (PARTNER)
Eph 5: 7 Therefore do not be *p* with them.

PARTNERSHIP* (PARTNER)
Php 1: 5 because of your *p* in the gospel

PASS (PASSED PASSER-BY PASSING)
Ex 12:13 and when I see the blood, I will *p*
33:19 goodness to *p* in front of you,

1Ki 9: 8 all who *p* by will be appalled
19:11 for the LORD is about to *p* by."
Ps 90:10 for they quickly *p*, and we fly away.
105:19 till what he foretold came to *p*,
Isa 31: 5 he will '*p* over' it and will rescue it
43: 2 When you *p* through the waters,
62:10 *P* through, *p* through the gates!
Jer 22: 8 "People from many nations will *p*
La 1:12 to you, all you who *p* by?
Da 7:14 dominion that will not *p* away,
Am 5:17 for I will *p* through your midst,"
Mt 24:34 will certainly not *p* away
24:35 Heaven and earth will *p* away,
Mk 13:31 Heaven and earth will *p* away,
Lk 21:33 Heaven and earth will *p* away,
1Co 13: 8 there is knowledge, it will *p* away.
Jas 1:10 he will *p* away like a wild flower.
1Jn 2:17 The world and its desires *p* away,

PASSED (PASS)
Ge 15:17 a blazing torch appeared and *p*
Ex 33:22 you with my hand until I have *p* by.
2Ch 21:20 He *p* away, to no one's regret,
Ps 57: 1 wings until the disaster has *p*.
Lk 10:32 saw him, *p* by on the other side.
1Co 15: 3 For what I received I *p* on to you
Heb 11:29 By faith the people *p*

PASSER-BY* (PASS)
Pr 26:10 is he who hires a fool or any *p*.
26:17 is a *p* who meddles

PASSING (PASS)
1Co 7:31 world in its present form is *p* away.
1Jn 2: 8 because the darkness is *p*

PASSION* (PASSIONATE PASSIONS)
Hos 7: 6 Their *p* smolders all night;
1Co 7: 9 better to marry than to burn with *p*.

PASSIONATE* (PASSION)
1Th 4: 5 not in *p* lust like the heathen,

PASSIONS* (PASSION)
Ro 7: 5 the sinful *p* aroused
Gal 5:24 crucified the sinful nature with its *p*
Tit 2:12 to ungodliness and worldly *p*,
3: 3 and enslaved by all kinds of *p*

PASSOVER
Ex 12:11 Eat it in haste; it is the LORD's *P*.
Nu 9: 2 Have the Israelites celebrate the *P*
Dt 16: 1 celebrate the *P* of the LORD your
Jos 5:10 the Israelites celebrated the *P*.
2Ki 23:21 "Celebrate the *P* to the LORD
Ezr 6:19 the exiles celebrated the *P*.
Mk 14:12 customary to sacrifice the *P* lamb,
Lk 22: 1 called the *P*, was approaching,
1Co 5: 7 our *P* lamb, has been sacrificed.
Heb 11:28 he kept the *P* and the sprinkling

PAST
Isa 43:18 do not dwell on the *p*.
65:16 For the *p* troubles will be forgotten
Ro 15: 4 in the *p* was written to teach us,
16:25 the mystery hidden for long ages *p*,
Eph 3: 9 which for ages *p* was kept hidden
Heb 1: 1 In the *p* God spoke

PASTORS*
Eph 4:11 and some to be *p* and teachers,

PASTURE (PASTURES)
Ps 37: 3 dwell in the land and enjoy safe *p*.
95: 7 and we are the people of his *p*,
100: 3 we are his people, the sheep of his *p*
Jer 50: 7 against the LORD, their true *p*,
Eze 34:13 I will *p* them on the mountains
Zec 11: 4 "*P* the flock marked for slaughter.
Jn 10: 9 come in and go out, and find *p*.

PASTURES (PASTURE)
Ps 23: 2 He makes me lie down in green *p*,

PATCH
Jer 10: 5 Like a scarecrow in a melon *p*,
Mt 9:16 No one sews a *p* of unshrunk cloth

PATH (PATHS)
Ps 16:11 known to me the *p* of life;
27:11 lead me in a straight *p*
119:32 I run in the *p* of your commands,
119:105 and a light for my *p*.
Pr 2: 9 and fair—every good *p*.
12:28 along that *p* is immortality.
15:10 awaits him who leaves the *p*;
15:19 the *p* of the upright is a highway.
15:24 The *p* of life leads upward
21:16 from the *p* of understanding
Isa 26: 7 The *p* of the righteous is level;
Jer 31: 9 on a level *p* where they will not
Mt 13: 4 fell along the *p*, and the birds came
Lk 1:79 to guide our feet into the *p* of peace
2Co 6: 3 no stumbling block in anyone's *p*,

PATHS (PATH)
Ps 23: 3 He guides me in *p* of righteousness
25: 4 teach me your *p*;
Pr 2:13 who leave the straight *p*
3: 6 and he will make your *p* straight.
4:11 and lead you along straight *p*.
4:26 Make level *p* for your feet
5:21 and he examines all his *p*.
8:20 along the *p* of justice,
22: 5 In the *p* of the wicked lie thorns
Isa 2: 3 so that we may walk in his *p*."
Jer 6:16 ask for the ancient *p*,
Mic 4: 2 so that we may walk in his *p*."
Mt 3: 3 make straight *p* for him.'"
Ac 2:28 to me the *p* of life;
Ro 11:33 and his *p* beyond tracing out!
Heb 12:13 "Make level *p* for your feet,"

PATIENCE* (PATIENT)
Pr 19:11 A man's wisdom gives him *p*;
25:15 Through *p* a ruler can be persuaded
Ecc 7: 8 and *p* is better than pride.
Isa 7:13 Is it not enough to try the *p* of men?
7:13 Will you try the *p* of my God also?
Ro 2: 4 and *p*, not realizing that God's
9:22 bore with great *p* the objects
2Co 6: 6 understanding, *p* and kindness;
Gal 5:22 joy, peace, *p*, kindness, goodness,
Col 1:11 may have great endurance and *p*,
3:12 humility, gentleness and *p*.
1Ti 1:16 Jesus might display his unlimited *p*
2Ti 3:10 my purpose, faith, *p*, love,
4: 2 with great *p* and careful instruction
Heb 6:12 *p* inherit what has been promised.
Jas 5:10 as an example of *p* in the face
2Pe 3:15 that our Lord's *p* means salvation,

PATIENT* (PATIENCE PATIENTLY)
Ne 9:30 For many years you were *p*
Job 6:11 What prospects, that I should be *p*?
Pr 14:29 A *p* man has great understanding,
15:18 but a *p* man calms a quarrel.
16:32 Better a *p* man than a warrior,
Mt 18:26 'Be *p* with me,' he begged,
18:29 'Be *p* with me, and I will pay you
Ro 12:12 Be joyful in hope, *p* in affliction,
1Co 13: 4 Love is *p*, love is kind.
2Co 1: 6 produces in you *p* endurance
Eph 4: 2 humble and gentle; be *p*,
1Th 5:14 help the weak, be *p* with everyone.
Jas 5: 7 Be *p*, then, brothers,
5: 7 and how *p* he is for the autumn
5: 8 You too, be *p* and stand firm,
2Pe 3: 9 He is *p* with you, not wanting
Rev 1: 9 *p* endurance that are ours in Jesus,
13:10 This calls for *p* endurance
14:12 This calls for *p* endurance

PATIENTLY* (PATIENT)
Ps 37: 7 still before the LORD and wait *p*
40: 1 I waited *p* for the LORD;
Isa 38:13 I waited *p* till dawn,
Hab 3:16 Yet I will wait *p* for the day
Ac 26: 3 I beg you to listen to me *p*.
Ro 8:25 we do not yet have, we wait for it *p*.
Heb 6:15 after waiting *p*, Abraham received
1Pe 3:20 ago when God waited *p* in the days
Rev 3:10 kept my command to endure *p*,

PATTERN
Ex 25:40 according to the *p* shown you
Ro 5:14 who was a *p* of the one to come.
12: 2 longer to the *p* of this world,
2Ti 1:13 keep as the *p* of sound teaching,
Heb 8: 5 according to the *p* shown you

PAUL

Also called Saul (Ac 13:9). Pharisee from Tarsus (Ac 9:11; Php 3:5). Apostle (Gal 1). At stoning of Stephen (Ac 8:1). Persecuted Church (Ac 9:1–2; Gal 1:13). Vision of Jesus on road to Damascus (Ac 9:4–9; 26:12–18). In Arabia (Gal 1:17). Preached in Damascus; escaped death through the wall in a basket (Ac 9:19–25). In Jerusalem; sent back to Tarsus (Ac 9:26–30).

Brought to Antioch by Barnabas (Ac 11:22–26). First missionary journey to Cyprus and Galatia (Ac 13–14). Stoned at Lystra (Ac 14:19–20). At Jerusalem council (Ac 15). Split with Barnabas over Mark (Ac 15:36–41).

Second missionary journey with Silas (Ac 16–20). Called to Macedonia (Ac 16:6–10). Freed from prison in Philippi (Ac 16:16–40). In Thessalonica (Ac 17:1–9). Speech in Athens (Ac 17:16–33). In Corinth (Ac 18). In Ephesus (Ac 19). Return to Jerusalem (Ac 20). Farewell to Ephesian elders (Ac 20:13–38). Arrival in Jerusalem (Ac 21:1–26). Arrested (Ac 21:27–36). Addressed crowds (Ac 22), Sanhedrin (Ac 23:1–11). Transferred to Caesarea (Ac 23:12–35). Trial before Felix (Ac 24), Festus (Ac 25:1–12). Before Agrippa (Ac 25:13–26:32). Voyage to Rome; shipwreck (Ac 27). Arrival in Rome (Ac 28).

Epistles: Romans, 1 and 2 Corinthians, Galatians, Ephesians, Philippians, Colossians, 1 and 2 Thessalonians, 1 and 2 Timothy, Titus, Philemon.

PAVEMENT
Jn 19:13 as the Stone *P* (which

PAY (PAID PAYMENT PAYS REPAID REPAY REPAYING)
Lev 26:43 They will *p* for their sins
Dt 7:12 If you *p* attention to these laws
Pr 4: 1 *p* attention and gain understanding
4:20 My son, *p* attention to what I say;
5: 1 My son, *p* attention to my wisdom,
6:31 if he is caught, he must *p* sevenfold,
19:19 man must *p* the penalty;
22:17 *P* attention and listen
24:29 I'll *p* that man back for what he did
Eze 40: 4 and *p* attention to everything I am
Zec 11:12 give me my *p*; but if not, keep it."
Mt 20: 2 He agreed to *p* them a denarius
22:16 you *p* no attention to who they are.
22:17 Is it right to *p* taxes to Caesar
Lk 3:14 falsely—be content with your *p*."
19: 8 I will *p* back four times the amount
Ro 13: 6 This is also why you *p* taxes,
2Pe 1:19 you will do well to *p* attention to it,

PAYMENT (PAY)
Ps 49: 8 no *p* is ever enough—
Php 4:18 I have received full *p* and

PAYS (PAY)
Pr 17:13 If a man *p* back evil for good,
1Th 5:15 sure that nobody *p* back wrong

PEACE (PEACEABLE PEACEFUL PEACEMAKERS)
Lev 26: 6 " 'I will grant *p* in the land,
Nu 6:26 and give you *p*." '
25:12 him I am making my covenant of *p*
Dt 20:10 make its people an offer of *p*.
Jdg 3:11 So the land had *p* for forty years,
3:30 and the land had *p* for eighty years.
5:31 Then the land had *p* forty years.
6:24 and called it The LORD is *P*.
8:28 the land enjoyed *p* forty years.
1Sa 7:14 And there was *p* between Israel
2Sa 10:19 they made *p* with the Israelites
1Ki 2:33 may there be the LORD's *p* forever
22:44 also at *p* with the king of Israel.
2Ki 9:17 come in *p*?' " The horseman rode
1Ch 19:19 they made *p* with David
22: 9 and I will grant Israel *p*
2Ch 14: 1 and in his days the country was at *p*
20:30 kingdom of Jehoshaphat was at *p*,
Job 3:26 I have no *p*, no quietness;
22:21 to God and be at *p* with him;
Ps 29:11 LORD blesses his people with *p*.
34:14 seek *p* and pursue it.
37:11 and enjoy great *p*.
37:37 there is a future for the man of *p*.
85:10 righteousness and *p* kiss each other
119:165 Great *p* have they who love your
120: 7 I am a man of *p*;
122: 6 Pray for the *p* of Jerusalem:
147:14 He grants *p* to your borders
Pr 12:20 but joy for those who promote *p*.
14:30 A heart at *p* gives life to the body,
16: 7 his enemies live at *p* with him.
17: 1 Better a dry crust with *p* and quiet
Ecc 3: 8 a time for war and a time for *p*.
Isa 9: 6 Everlasting Father, Prince of *P*.
14: 7 All the lands are at rest and at *p*;
26: 3 You will keep in perfect *p*
32:17 The fruit of righteousness will be *p*;
48:18 your *p* would have been like a river,
48:22 "There is no *p*," says the LORD,
52: 7 who proclaim *p*,
53: 5 punishment that brought us *p* was
54:10 nor my covenant of *p* be removed,"
55:12 and be led forth in *p*;
57: 2 enter into *p*;
57:19 *P*, *p*, to those far and near,"
57:21 "There is no *p*," says my God,
59: 8 The way of *p* they do not know;
Jer 6:14 '*P*, *p*,' they say,
8:11 "*P*, *p*," . . . there is no *p*.
30:10 Jacob will again have *p*
46:27 Jacob will again have *p*
Eze 13:10 "*P*," when there is no *p*,
34:25 " 'I will make a covenant of *p*
37:26 I will make a covenant of *p*
Mic 5: 5 And he will be their *p*.
Zec 8:19 Therefore love truth and *p*."
9:10 He will proclaim *p* to the nations.
Mal 2: 5 a covenant of life and *p*,
2: 6 He walked with me in *p*
Mt 10:34 I did not come to bring *p*,
Mk 9:50 and be at *p* with each other."
Lk 1:79 to guide our feet into the path of *p*
2:14 on earth *p* to men on whom his
19:38 "*P* in heaven and glory
Jn 14:27 *P* I leave with you; my *p*
16:33 so that in me you may have *p*.
Ro 1: 7 and *p* to you from God our Father
2:10 and *p* for everyone who does good:
5: 1 we have *p* with God
8: 6 by the Spirit is life and *p*;
12:18 on you, live at *p* with everyone.
14:19 effort to do what leads to *p*
1Co 7:15 God has called us to live in *p*.
14:33 a God of disorder but of *p*.
2Co 13:11 be of one mind, live in *p*.
Gal 5:22 joy, *p*, patience, kindness,
Eph 2:14 he himself is our *p*, who has made
Eph 2:15 thus making *p*, and in this one body
2:17 and *p* to those who were near.
6:15 comes from the gospel of *p*.
Php 4: 7 the *p* of God, which transcends all
Col 1:20 by making *p* through his blood,
3:15 Let the *p* of Christ rule
3:15 of one body you were called to *p*.
1Th 5: 3 While people are saying, "*P*
5:13 Live in *p* with each other.
5:23 the God of *p*, sanctify you through
2Th 3:16 the Lord of *p* himself give you *p*
2Ti 2:22 righteousness, faith, love and *p*,
Heb 7: 2 "king of Salem" means "king of *p*."
12:11 *p* for those who have been trained
12:14 effort to live in *p* with all men
13:20 May the God of *p*, who
1Pe 3:11 he must seek *p* and pursue it.
2Pe 3:14 blameless and at *p* with him.
Rev 6: 4 power to take *p* from the earth

PEACEABLE* (PEACE)
Tit 3: 2 to slander no one, to be *p*

PEACEFUL (PEACE)
1Ti 2: 2 that we may live *p* and quiet lives

PEACE-LOVING
Jas 3:17 then *p*, considerate

PEACEMAKERS* (PEACE)
Mt 5: 9 Blessed are the *p*,
Jas 3:18 *P* who sow in peace raise a harvest

PEARL* (PEARLS)
Rev 21:21 each gate made of a single *p*.

PEARLS (PEARL)
Mt 7: 6 do not throw your *p* to pigs.
13:45 like a merchant looking for fine *p*.
1Ti 2: 9 or gold or *p* or expensive clothes,
Rev 21:21 The twelve gates were twelve *p*,

PEDDLE*
2Co 2:17 we do not *p* the word of God

PEG
Jdg 4:21 She drove the *p* through his temple

PEKAH
King of Israel (2Ki 15:25–31; Isa 7:1).

PEKAHIAH*
Son of Menahem; king of Israel (2Ki 15:22–26).

PEN
Ps 45: 1 my tongue is the *p*
Mt 5:18 letter, not the least stroke of a *p*,
Jn 10: 1 who does not enter the sheep *p*

PENETRATES*
Heb 4:12 it *p* even to dividing soul and spirit,

PENNIES* (PENNY)
Lk 12: 6 not five sparrows sold for two *p*?

PENNY* (PENNIES)
Mt 5:26 out until you have paid the last *p*.
10:29 Are not two sparrows sold for a *p*?
Mk 12:42 worth only a fraction of a *p*.
Lk 12:59 out until you have paid the last *p*."

PENTECOST*
Ac 2: 1 of *P* came, they were all together
20:16 if possible, by the day of *P*.
1Co 16: 8 I will stay on at Ephesus until *P*.

PEOPLE (PEOPLES)
Ge 11: 6 as one *p* speaking the same
Ex 5: 1 Let my *p* go,
6: 7 take you as my own *p*,
8:23 between my *p* and your *p*.
15:13 the *p* you have redeemed.
19: 8 The *p* all responded together,
Ex 24: 3 Moses went and told the *p*
32: 1 When the *p* saw that Moses
32: 9 they are a stiff-necked *p*.
33:13 this nation is your *p*.
Lev 9: 7 for yourself and the *p*;
16:24 the burnt offering for the *p*,
26:12 and you will be my *p*.
Nu 11:11 burden of all these *p* on
14:11 *p* treat me with contempt?
14:19 forgive the sin of these *p*,
22: 5 A *p* has come out of Egypt
Dt 4: 6 a wise and understanding *p*.
4:20 the *p* of his inheritance,
5:28 what this *p* said to you.
7: 6 a *p* holy to the LORD
26:18 that you are his *p*,
31: 7 you must go with this *p*
31:16 these *p* will soon prostitute
32: 9 the LORD's portion is his *p*,
32:43 atonement for his land and *p*.
33:29 a *p* saved by the LORD?
Jos 1: 6 you will lead this *p*
24:24 the *p* said to Joshua,
Jdg 2: 7 *p* served the LORD throughout
Ru 1:16 Your *p* will be my *p*
1Sa 8: 7 the *p* are saying to you;
12:22 LORD will not reject his *p*,
2Sa 5: 2 will shepherd my *p* Israel
7:10 provide a place for my *p* Israel
1Ki 3: 8 among the *p* you have chosen,
8:30 your *p* Israel when they pray
8:56 has given rest to his *p*
18:39 when all the *p* saw this,
2Ki 23: 3 all the *p* pledged themselves
1Ch 17:21 to redeem *p* for himself
29:17 how willingly your *p* who are
2Ch 2:11 Because the LORD loves his *p*,
7: 5 *p* dedicated the temple
7:14 if my *p*, who are called
30: 6 "*P* of Israel, return to
36:16 was aroused against his *p*
Ezr 2: 1 These are the *p* of the
3: 1 *p* assembled as one man
Ne 1:10 your *p*, whom you redeemed
4: 6 *p* worked with all their heart
8: 1 *p* assembled as one man
Est 3: 6 to destroy all Mordecai's *p*,
Job 12: 2 Doubtless you are the *p*,
Ps 29:11 gives strength to his *p*;
33:12 *p* he chose for his inheritance
50: 4 that he may judge his *p*
53: 6 restores the fortunes of his *p*,
81:13 If my *p* would but listen
94:14 LORD will not reject his *p*;
95: 7 we are the *p* of his pasture,
95:10 a *p* whose hearts go astray,
125: 2 the LORD surrounds his *p*
135:14 LORD will vindicate his *p*
144:15 *p* whose God is the LORD.
Pr 14:34 sin is a disgrace to any *p*.
29: 2 righteous thrive, the *p* rejoice
29:18 the *p* cast off restraint
Isa 1: 3 my *p* do not understand.
1: 4 a *p* loaded with guilt,
5:13 my *p* will go into exile
6:10 the heart of this *p* calloused;
9: 2 the *p* walking in darkness
12:12 will assemble the scattered *p*
19:25 Blessed be Egypt my *p*,
25: 8 remove the disgrace of his *p*
29:13 These *p* come near to me
40: 1 Comfort, comfort my *p*
40: 7 Surely the *p* are grass.
42: 6 a covenant for the *p*
49:13 the LORD comforts his *p*
51: 4 "Listen to me, my *p*;
52: 6 my *p* will know my name;
53: 8 for the transgression of my *p*
60:21 will all your *p* be righteous
62:12 will be called the Holy *P*,

Isa 65:23 they will be a *p* blessed
Jer 2:11 my *p* have exchanged their
2:13 *p* have committed two sins:
2:32 my *p* have forgotten me,
4:22 My *p* are fools;
5:14 Because the *p* have spoken
5:31 my *p* love it this way
7:16 do not pray for this *p*
7:23 you will be my *p*,
18:15 my *p* have forgotten me;
30: 3 I will bring my *p* Israel
Eze 13:23 I will save my *p* from
36: 8 fruit for my *p* Israel,
36:28 you will be my *p*,
36:38 be filled with flocks of *p*.
37:13 Then you, my *p*, will know
38:14 *p* Israel are living in safety
39: 7 name among my *p* Israel.
Da 7:27 saints, the *p* of the Most High.
8:24 mighty men and the holy *p*
9:19 your *p* bear your name
9:24 are decreed for your *p*
9:26 *p* of the ruler who will come
10:14 will happen to your *p*
11:32 *p* who know their God will
12: 1 prince who protects your *p*.
Hos 1:10 'You are not my *p*,'
2:23 'You are my *p*';
4:14 a *p* without understanding
Joel 2:18 and take pity on his *p*.
3:16 be a refuge for his *p*,
Am 9:14 back my exiled *p* Israel;
Mic 6: 2 a case against his *p*;
7:14 Shepherd your *p* with
Hag 1:12 remnant of the *p* obeyed
Zec 2:11 and will become my *p*.
8: 7 I will save my *p*
13: 9 will say, 'They are my *p*,'
Mk 7: 6 *p* honor me with their lips
8:27 "Who do *p* say I am?"
Lk 1:17 make ready a *p* prepared
1:68 and has redeemed his *p*.
2:10 joy that will be for all the *p*.
21:23 and wrath against this *p*.
Jn 11:50 one man die for the *p*
18:14 if one man died for the *p*.
Ac 15:14 from the Gentiles a *p*.
18:10 have many *p* in this city.
Ro 9:25 will call them 'my *p*.'
11: 1 Did God reject his *p*?
15:10 O Gentiles, with his *p*."
2Co 6:16 and they will be my *p*."
Tit 2:14 a *p* that are his very own,
Heb 2:17 for the sins of the *p*.
4: 9 a Sabbath-rest for the *p*
5: 3 for the sins of the *p*.
10:30 Lord will judge his *p*.
11:25 mistreated along with the *p*
13:12 to make the *p* holy
1Pe 2: 9 you are a chosen *p*,
2:10 Once you were not a *p*,
2:10 you are the *p* of God;
2Pe 2: 1 false prophets among the *p*,
3:11 kind of *p* ought you to be?
Rev 18: 4 "Come out of her, my *p*,
21: 3 They will be his *p*,

PEOPLES (PEOPLE)
Ge 17:16 kings of *p* will come from her
25:23 two *p* from within you will
27:29 and *p* bow down to you
28: 3 become a community of *p*.
48: 4 you a community of *p*.
Dt 14: 2 of all the *p* on the face of
28:10 Then all the *p* on earth
32: 8 set up boundaries for the *p*
Jos 4:24 all the *p* of the earth might
1Ki 8:43 all the *p* of the earth may
2Ch 7:20 of ridicule among all *p*.
Ps 9: 8 he will govern the *p*
Ps 67: 5 may all the *p* praise you.
87: 6 in the register of the *p*:
96:10 he will judge the *p*
Isa 2: 4 settle disputes for many *p*.
17:12 Oh, the uproar of the *p*—
25: 6 of rich food for all *p*,
34: 1 pay attention, you *p*!
55: 4 him a witness to the *p*,
Jer 10: 3 customs of the *p* are worthless
Da 7:14 all *p*, nations and men
Mic 4: 1 and *p* will stream to it.
4: 3 will judge between many *p*
5: 7 in the midst of many *p*
Zep 3: 9 purify the lips of the *p*,
3:20 among all the *p* of the
Zec 8:20 Many *p* and the inhabitants
12: 2 all the surrounding *p* reeling.
Rev 10:11 prophesy again about many *p*,
17:15 the prostitute sits, are *p*,

PEOR
Nu 25: 3 joined in worshiping the Baal of *P*.
Dt 4: 3 who followed the Baal of *P*.

PERCEIVE (PERCEIVING)
Ps 139: 2 you *p* my thoughts from afar.
Pr 24:12 not he who weighs the heart *p* it?

PERCEIVING* (PERCEIVE)
Isa 6: 9 be ever seeing, but never *p*.'
Mt 13:14 you will be ever seeing but never *p*.
Mk 4:12 may be ever seeing but never *p*,
Ac 28:26 you will be ever seeing but never *p*

PERFECT* (PERFECTER PERFECTING PERFECTION)
Dt 32: 4 He is the Rock, his works are *p*,
2Sa 22:31 "As for God, his way is *p*;
22:33 and makes my way *p*.
Job 36: 4 one *p* in knowledge is with you.
37:16 of him who is *p* in knowledge?
Ps 18:30 As for God, his way is *p*;
18:32 and makes my way *p*.
19: 7 The law of the LORD is *p*,
50: 2 From Zion, *p* in beauty,
64: 6 "We have devised a *p* plan!"
SS 6: 9 but my dove, my *p* one, is unique,
Isa 25: 1 for in *p* faithfulness
26: 3 You will keep in *p* peace
Eze 16:14 had given you made your beauty *p*,
27: 3 "I am *p* in beauty."
28:12 full of wisdom and *p* in beauty.
Mt 5:48 Do not even pagans do that? Be *p*,
5:48 as your heavenly Father is *p*.
19:21 answered, "If you want to be *p*,
Ro 12: 2 his good, pleasing and *p* will.
2Co 12: 9 for my power is made *p*
Php 3:12 or have already been made *p*,
Col 1:28 so that we may present everyone *p*
3:14 binds them all together in *p* unity.
Heb 2:10 the author of their salvation *p*
5: 9 what he suffered and, once made *p*,
7:19 useless (for the law made nothing *p*
7:28 who has been made *p* forever.
9:11 and more *p* tabernacle that is not
10: 1 make *p* those who draw
10:14 he has made *p* forever those who
11:40 with us would they be made *p*.
12:23 spirits of righteous men made *p*,
Jas 1:17 Every good and *p* gift is from above
1:25 into the *p* law that gives freedom,
3: 2 he is a *p* man, able
1Jn 4:18 But *p* love drives out fear,
4:18 The one who fears is not made *p*

PERFECTER* (PERFECT)
Heb 12: 2 the author and *p* of our faith,

PERFECTING* (PERFECT)
2Co 7: 1 *p* holiness out of reverence for God

PERFECTION* (PERFECT)
Ps 119:96 To all *p* I see a limit;
La 2:15 the *p* of beauty,
Eze 27: 4 builders brought your beauty to *p*.
27:11 they brought your beauty to *p*.
28:12 " 'You were the model of *p*,
1Co 13:10 but when *p* comes, the imperfect
2Co 13: 9 and our prayer is for your *p*.
13:11 Aim for *p*, listen to my appeal,
Heb 7:11 If *p* could have been attained

PERFORM (PERFORMED PERFORMS)
Ex 3:20 with all the wonders that I will *p*
2Sa 7:23 to *p* great and awesome wonders
Jn 3: 2 no one could *p* the miraculous

PERFORMED (PERFORM)
Mt 11:21 If the miracles that were *p*
Jn 10:41 John never *p* a miraculous

PERFORMS (PERFORM)
Ps 77:14 You are the God who *p* miracles;

PERFUME
Ecc 7: 1 A good name is better than fine *p*,
SS 1: 3 your name is like *p* poured out.
Mk 14: 3 jar of very expensive *p*,

PERIL
2Co 1:10 us from such a deadly *p*,

PERISH (PERISHABLE PERISHED PERISHES PERISHING)
Ge 6:17 Everything on earth will *p*.
Est 4:16 And if I *p*, I *p*."
Ps 1: 6 but the way of the wicked will *p*.
37:20 But the wicked will *p*:
73:27 Those who are far from you will *p*;
102:26 They will *p*, but you remain;
Pr 11:10 when the wicked *p*, there are
19: 9 and he who pours out lies will *p*.
21:28 A false witness will *p*,
28:28 when the wicked *p*, the righteous
Isa 1:28 who forsake the LORD will *p*.
29:14 the wisdom of the wise will *p*,
60:12 that will not serve you will *p*;
Zec 11: 9 the dying die, and the perishing *p*.
Lk 13: 3 unless you repent, you too will all *p*
13: 5 unless you repent, you too will all *p*
21:18 But not a hair of your head will *p*.
Jn 3:16 whoever believes in him shall not *p*
10:28 eternal life, and they shall never *p*;
Ro 2:12 apart from the law will also *p* apart
Col 2:22 These are all destined to *p* with use,
2Th 2:10 They *p* because they refused
Heb 1:11 They will *p*, but you remain;
1Pe 1: 4 into an inheritance that can never *p*
2Pe 3: 9 not wanting anyone to *p*,

PERISHABLE (PERISH)
1Co 15:42 The body that is sown is *p*,
1Pe 1:18 not with *p* things such
1:23 not of *p* seed, but of imperishable,

PERISHED (PERISH)
Ps 119:92 I would have *p* in my affliction.

PERISHES (PERISH)
Job 8:13 so *p* the hope of the godless.
1Pe 1: 7 which *p* even though refined by fire

PERISHING (PERISH)
1Co 1:18 foolishness to those who are *p*,
2Co 2:15 being saved and those who are *p*.
4: 3 it is veiled to those who are *p*.

PERJURERS* (PERJURY)
Mal 3: 5 and *p*, against those who defraud
1Ti 1:10 for slave traders and liars and *p*—

PERJURY* (PERJURERS)
Jer 7: 9 murder, commit adultery and *p*,

PERMANENT
Heb 7:24 lives forever, he has a *p* priesthood.

PERMISSIBLE (PERMIT)
1Co 6:12 "Everything is *p* for me"—
10:23 "Everything is *p*"— but not

PERMIT (PERMISSIBLE PERMITTED)
Hos 5: 4 "Their deeds do not *p* them
1Ti 2:12 I do not *p* a woman to teach

PERMITTED (PERMIT)
Mt 19: 8 Moses *p* you to divorce your wives
2Co 12: 4 things that man is not *p* to tell.

PERSECUTE (PERSECUTED PERSECUTION PERSECUTIONS)
Ps 119:86 for men *p* me without cause.
Mt 5:11 *p* you and falsely say all kinds
5:44 and pray for those who *p* you,
Jn 15:20 they persecuted me, they will *p* you
Ac 9: 4 why do you *p* me?" "Who are you,
Ro 12:14 Bless those who *p* you; bless

PERSECUTED (PERSECUTE)
Mt 5:10 Blessed are those who are *p*
5:12 same way they *p* the prophets who
Jn 15:20 If they *p* me, they will persecute
1Co 4:12 when we are *p*, we endure it;
15: 9 because I *p* the church of God.
2Co 4: 9 in despair; *p*, but not abandoned;
1Th 3: 4 kept telling you that we would be *p*.
2Ti 3:12 life in Christ Jesus will be *p*,
Heb 11:37 destitute, *p* and mistreated—

PERSECUTION (PERSECUTE)
Mt 13:21 When trouble or *p* comes
Ro 8:35 or hardship or *p* or famine

PERSECUTIONS (PERSECUTE)
Mk 10:30 and with them, *p*) and in the age
2Co 12:10 in hardships, in *p*, in difficulties.
2Th 1: 4 faith in all the *p* and trials you are
2Ti 3:11 love, endurance, *p*, sufferings—

PERSEVERANCE* (PERSEVERE)
Ro 5: 3 we know that suffering produces *p*;
5: 4 *p*, character; and character, hope.
2Co 12:12 were done among you with great *p*.
2Th 1: 4 churches we boast about your *p*
3: 5 into God's love and Christ's *p*.
Heb 12: 1 run with *p* the race marked out
Jas 1: 3 the testing of your faith develops *p*.
1: 4 *P* must finish its work
5:11 You have heard of Job's *p*
2Pe 1: 6 *p*; and to *p*, godliness;
Rev 2: 2 your hard work and your *p*.
2:19 and faith, your service and *p*,

PERSEVERE* (PERSEVERANCE PERSEVERED PERSEVERES PERSEVERING)
1Ti 4:16 *P* in them, because if you do,
Heb 10:36 You need to *p* so that

PERSEVERED* (PERSEVERE)
Heb 11:27 he *p* because he saw him who is
Jas 5:11 consider blessed those who have *p*.
Rev 2: 3 You have *p* and have endured

PERSEVERES* (PERSEVERE)
1Co 13: 7 trusts, always hopes, always *p*.
Jas 1:12 Blessed is the man who *p*

PERSEVERING* (PERSEVERE)
Lk 8:15 retain it, and by *p* produce a crop.

PERSIANS
Da 6:15 law of the Medes and *P* no decree

PERSISTENCE*
Ro 2: 7 To those who by *p*

PERSUADE (PERSUADED PERSUASIVE)
Ac 18: 4 trying to *p* Jews and Greeks.
2Co 5:11 is to fear the Lord, we try to *p* men.

PERSUADED (PERSUADE)
Ro 4:21 being fully *p* that God had power

PERSUASIVE (PERSUADE)
1Co 2: 4 not with wise and *p* words,

PERVERSION* (PERVERT)
Lev 18:23 sexual relations with it; that is a *p*.
20:12 What they have done is a *p*;
Ro 1:27 the due penalty for their *p*.
Jude : 7 up to sexual immorality and *p*.

PERVERT (PERVERSION PERVERTED PERVERTS)
Ex 23: 2 do not *p* justice by siding
Dt 16:19 Do not *p* justice or show partiality.
Job 34:12 that the Almighty would *p* justice.
Pr 17:23 to *p* the course of justice.
Gal 1: 7 are trying to *p* the gospel of Christ.

PERVERTED (PERVERT)
1Sa 8: 3 and accepted bribes and *p* justice.

PERVERTS* (PERVERT)
1Ti 1:10 for murderers, for adulterers and *p*,

PESTILENCE (PESTILENCES)
Ps 91: 6 nor the *p* that stalks in the darkness

PESTILENCES (PESTILENCE)
Lk 21:11 famines and *p* in various places,

PETER
Apostle, brother of Andrew, also called Simon (Mt 10:2; Mk 3:16; Lk 6:14; Ac 1:13), and Cephas (Jn 1:42). Confession of Christ (Mt 16:13–20; Mk 8:27–30; Lk 9:18–27). At transfiguration (Mt 17:1–8; Mk 9:2–8; Lk 9:28–36; 2Pe 1:16–18). Caught fish with coin (Mt 17:24–27). Denial of Jesus predicted (Mt 26:31–35; Mk 14:27–31; Lk 22:31–34; Jn 13:31–38). Denied Jesus (Mt 26:69–75; Mk 14:66–72; Lk 22:54–62; Jn 18:15–27). Commissioned by Jesus to shepherd his flock (Jn 21:15–23).

Speech at Pentecost (Ac 2). Healed beggar (Ac 3:1–10). Speech at temple (Ac 3:11–26), before Sanhedrin (Ac 4:1–22). In Samaria (Ac 8:14–25). Sent by vision to Cornelius (Ac 10). Announced salvation of Gentiles in Jerusalem (Ac 11; 15). Freed from prison (Ac 12). Inconsistency at Antioch (Gal 2:11–21). At Jerusalem Council (Ac 15).

Epistles: 1–2 Peter.

PETITION (PETITIONS)
1Ch 16: 4 to make *p*, to give thanks,
Php 4: 6 by prayer and *p*, with thanksgiving,

PETITIONS (PETITION)
Heb 5: 7 he offered up prayers and *p*

PHANTOM*
Ps 39: 6 Man is a mere *p* as he goes to

PHARAOH (PHARAOH'S)
Ge 12:15 her to *P*, and she was taken
41:14 So *P* sent for Joseph, and he was
Ex 14: 4 glory for myself through *P*
14:17 And I will gain glory through *P*

PHARAOH'S (PHARAOH)
Ex 7: 3 But I will harden *P* heart, and

PHARISEE (PHARISEES)
Ac 23: 6 brothers, I am a *P*, the son of a *P*.
Php 3: 5 in regard to the law, a *P*; as for zeal,

PHARISEES (PHARISEE)
Mt 5:20 surpasses that of the *P*
16: 6 guard against the yeast of the *P*
23:13 of the law and *P*, you hypocrites!
Jn 3: 1 a man of the *P* named Nicodemus,

PHILADELPHIA
Rev 3: 7 the angel of the church in *P* write:

PHILEMON*
Phm : 1 To *P* our dear friend and fellow

PHILIP
1. Apostle (Mt 10:3; Mk 3:18; Lk 6:14; Jn 1:43–48; 14:8; Ac 1:13).
2. Deacon (Ac 6:1–7); evangelist in Samaria (Ac 8:4–25), to Ethiopian (Ac 8:26–40).

PHILIPPI
Ac 16:12 From there we traveled to *P*,
Php 1: 1 To all the saints in Christ Jesus at *P*

PHILISTINE (PHILISTINES)
Jos 13: 3 of the five *P* rulers in Gaza,
1Sa 14: 1 let's go over to the *P* outpost
17:26 is this uncircumcised *P* that he
17:37 me from the hand of this *P*."

PHILISTINES (PHILISTINE)
Jdg 10: 7 them into the hands of the *P*
13: 1 the hands of the *P* for forty years.
16: 5 The rulers of the *P* went to her
1Sa 4: 1 at Ebenezer, and the *P* at Aphek.
5: 8 together all the rulers of the *P*
13:23 a detachment of *P* had gone out
17: 1 the *P* gathered their forces for war
23: 1 the *P* are fighting against Keilah
27: 1 is to escape to the land of the *P*.
31: 1 Now the *P* fought against Israel;
2Sa 5:17 When the *P* heard that David had
8: 1 David defeated the *P* and subdued
21:15 there was a battle between the *P*
2Ki 18: 8 he defeated the *P*, as far as Gaza
Am 1: 8 Ekron till the last of the *P* is dead,"

PHILOSOPHER* (PHILOSOPHY)
1Co 1:20 Where is the *p* of this age?

PHILOSOPHY* (PHILOSOPHER)
Col 2: 8 through hollow and deceptive *p*,

PHINEHAS
Nu 25: 7 When *P* son of Eleazar, the son
Ps 106:30 But *P* stood up and intervened,

PHOEBE*
Ro 16: 1 I commend to you our sister *P*,

PHYLACTERIES*
Mt 23: 5 They make their *p* wide

PHYSICAL
Ro 2:28 merely outward and *p*.
Col 1:22 by Christ's *p* body through death
1Ti 4: 8 For *p* training is of some value,
Jas 2:16 but does nothing about his *p* needs,

PICK (PICKED)
Mk 16:18 they will *p* up snakes

PICKED (PICK)
Lk 14: 7 noticed how the guests *p* the places
Jn 5: 9 he *p* up his mat and walked.

PIECE (PIECES)
Jn 19:23 woven in one *p* from top to bottom.

PIECES (PIECE)
Ge 15:17 and passed between the *p*.
Jer 34:18 and then walked between its *p*.
Zec 11:12 So they paid me thirty *p* of silver.
Mt 14:20 of broken *p* that were left over.

PIERCE (PIERCED)
Ex 21: 6 and *p* his ear with an awl.

Pr 12:18 Reckless words *p* like a sword,
Lk 2:35 a sword will *p* your own soul too."

PIERCED (PIERCE)
Ps 22:16 they have *p* my hands and my feet.
40: 6 but my ears you have *p*;
Isa 53: 5 But he was *p* for our transgressions,
Zec 12:10 look on me, the one they have *p*,
Jn 19:37 look on the one they have *p*."
Rev 1: 7 even those who *p* him;

PIG'S (PIGS)
Pr 11:22 Like a gold ring in a *p* snout

PIGEONS
Lev 5:11 afford two doves or two young *p*,
Lk 2:24 "a pair of doves or two young *p*."

PIGS (PIG'S)
Mt 7: 6 do not throw your pearls to *p*.
Mk 5:11 A large herd of *p* was feeding on

PILATE
Governor of Judea. Questioned Jesus (Mt 27:1–26; Mk 15:15; Lk 22:66–23:25; Jn 18:28–19:16); sent him to Herod (Lk 23:6–12); consented to his crucifixion when crowds chose Barabbas (Mt 27:15–26; Mk 15:6–15; Lk 23:13–25; Jn 19:1–10).

PILLAR (PILLARS)
Ge 19:26 and she became a *p* of salt.
Ex 13:21 ahead of them in a *p* of cloud
1Ti 3:15 the *p* and foundation of the truth.
Rev 3:12 who overcomes I will make a *p*

PILLARS (PILLAR)
Gal 2: 9 and John, those reputed to be *p*,

PINIONS
Dt 32:11 and carries them on its *p*.

PISGAH
Dt 3:27 Go up to the top of *P* and look west

PIT
Ps 7:15 falls into the *p* he has made.
40: 2 He lifted me out of the slimy *p*,
103: 4 who redeems your life from the *p*
Pr 23:27 for a prostitute is a deep *p*
26:27 If a man digs a *p*, he will fall into it;
Isa 24:17 Terror and *p* and snare await you,
38:17 me from the *p* of destruction;
Mt 15:14 a blind man, both will fall into a *p*."

PITCH
Ge 6:14 and coat it with *p* inside and out.
Ex 2: 3 and coated it with tar and *p*.

PITIED (PITY)
1Co 15:19 we are to be *p* more than all men.

PITY (PITIED)
Ps 72:13 He will take *p* on the weak
Ecc 4:10 But *p* the man who falls
Lk 10:33 when he saw him, he took *p* on him

PLAGUE (PLAGUED PLAGUES)
2Ch 6:28 "When famine or *p* comes
Ps 91: 6 nor the *p* that destroys at midday.

PLAGUED* (PLAGUE)
Ps 73: 5 they are not *p* by human ills.
73:14 All day long I have been *p*;

PLAGUES (PLAGUE)
Hos 13:14 Where, O death, are your *p*?
Rev 21: 9 full of the seven last *p* came
22:18 to him the *p* described in this book.

PLAIN
Isa 40: 4 the rugged places a *p*.
Ro 1:19 what may be known about God is *p*

PLAN (PLANNED PLANS)
Ex 26:30 according to the *p* shown you
Job 42: 2 no *p* of yours can be thwarted.
Pr 14:22 those who *p* what is good find love
21:30 is no wisdom, no insight, no *p*
Am 3: 7 nothing without revealing his *p*
Eph 1:11 predestined according to the *p*

PLANK
Mt 7: 3 attention to the *p* in your own eye?
Lk 6:41 attention to the *p* in your own eye?

PLANNED (PLAN)
Ps 40: 5 The things you *p* for us
Isa 14:24 "Surely, as I have *p*, so it will be,
23: 9 The LORD Almighty *p* it,
46:11 what I have *p*, that will I do.
Heb 11:40 God had *p* something better for us

PLANS (PLAN)
Ps 20: 4 and make all your *p* succeed.
33:11 *p* of the LORD stand firm forever,
Pr 15:22 *P* fail for lack of counsel,
16: 3 and your *p* will succeed.
19:21 Many are the *p* in a man's heart,
20:18 Make *p* by seeking advice;
Isa 29:15 to hide their *p* from the LORD,
30: 1 those who carry out *p* that are not
32: 8 But the noble man makes noble *p*,
2Co 1:17 Or do I make my *p* in a worldly

PLANT (PLANTED PLANTING PLANTS)
Am 9:15 I will *p* Israel in their own land,
Mt 15:13 "Every *p* that my heavenly Father

PLANTED (PLANT)
Ge 2: 8 the LORD God had *p* a garden
Ps 1: 3 He is like a tree *p* by streams
Jer 17: 8 He will be like a tree *p* by the water
Mt 15:13 Father has not *p* will be pulled
21:33 was a landowner who *p* a vineyard.
Lk 13: 6 "A man had a fig tree, *p*
1Co 3: 6 I *p* the seed, Apollos watered it,
Jas 1:21 humbly accept the word *p* in you,

PLANTING (PLANT)
Isa 61: 3 a *p* of the LORD

PLANTS (PLANT)
Pr 31:16 out of her earnings she *p* a vineyard
1Co 3: 7 So neither he who *p* nor he who
9: 7 Who *p* a vineyard and does not eat

PLATTER
Mk 6:25 head of John the Baptist on a *p*."

PLAY (PLAYED)
1Sa 16:23 David would take his harp and *p*.
Isa 11: 8 The infant will *p* near the hole

PLAYED (PLAY)
Lk 7:32 " 'We *p* the flute for you,
1Co 14: 7 anyone know what tune is being *p*

PLEA (PLEAD PLEADED PLEADS)
1Ki 8:28 to your servant's prayer and his *p*
Ps 102:17 he will not despise their *p*.
La 3:56 You heard my *p*: "Do not close

PLEAD (PLEA)
Isa 1:17 *p* the case of the widow.

PLEADED (PLEA)
2Co 12: 8 Three times I *p* with the Lord

PLEADS (PLEA)
Job 16:21 on behalf of a man he *p* with God

PLEASANT (PLEASE)
Ge 49:15 and how *p* is his land,
Ps 16: 6 for me in *p* places;
133: 1 How good and *p* it is
135: 3 sing praise to his name, for that is *p*
147: 1 how *p* and fitting to praise him!
Pr 2:10 knowledge will be *p* to your soul.
3:17 Her ways are *p* ways,
16:21 and *p* words promote instruction.
16:24 *P* words are a honeycomb,
Isa 30:10 Tell us *p* things,
1Th 3: 6 that you always have *p* memories
Heb 12:11 No discipline seems *p* at the time,

PLEASANTNESS* (PLEASE)
Pr 27: 9 the *p* of one's friend springs

PLEASE (PLEASANT PLEASANTNESS PLEASED PLEASES PLEASING PLEASURE PLEASURES)
Ps 69:31 This will *p* the LORD more
Pr 20:23 and dishonest scales do not *p* him.
Isa 46:10 and I will do all that I *p*.
Jer 6:20 your sacrifices do not *p* me."
27: 5 and I give it to anyone I *p*.
Jn 5:30 for I seek not to *p* myself
Ro 8: 8 by the sinful nature cannot *p* God.
15: 1 of the weak and not to *p* ourselves.
15: 2 Each of us should *p* his neighbor
1Co 7:32 affairs—how he can *p* the Lord.
10:33 I try to *p* everybody in every way.
2Co 5: 9 So we make it our goal to *p* him,
Gal 1:10 or of God? Or am I trying to *p* men
6: 8 the one who sows to *p* the Spirit,
Col 1:10 and may *p* him in every way:
1Th 2: 4 We are not trying to *p* men
4: 1 how to live in order to *p* God,
2Ti 2: 4 wants to *p* his commanding officer.
Tit 2: 9 to try to *p* them, not to talk back
Heb 11: 6 faith it is impossible to *p* God,

PLEASED (PLEASE)
Dt 28:63 as it *p* the LORD to make you
1Sa 12:22 LORD was *p* to make you his own.
1Ki 3:10 The Lord was *p* that Solomon had
1Ch 29:17 that you test the heart and are *p*
Mic 6: 7 Will the LORD be *p*
Mal 1:10 I am not *p* with you," says
Mt 3:17 whom I love; with him I am well *p*
17: 5 whom I love; with him I am well *p*.
Mk 1:11 whom I love; with you I am well *p*
Lk 3:22 whom I love; with you I am well *p*
1Co 1:21 God was *p* through the foolishness
Col 1:19 For God was *p* to have all his
Heb 10: 6 you were not *p*.
10: 8 nor were you *p* with them"
10:38 I will not be *p* with him."
11: 5 commended as one who *p* God.
13:16 for with such sacrifices God is *p*.
2Pe 1:17 whom I love; with him I am well *p*

PLEASES (PLEASE)
Job 23:13 He does whatever he *p*.
Ps 115: 3 he does whatever *p* him.
135: 6 The LORD does whatever *p* him,
Pr 15: 8 but the prayer of the upright *p* him.
21: 1 it like a watercourse wherever he *p*.
Ecc 2:26 To the man who *p* him, God gives
7:26 man who *p* God will escape her,
Da 4:35 He does as he *p*
Jn 3: 8 The wind blows wherever it *p*.
8:29 for I always do what *p* him."
Eph 5:10 truth) and find out what *p* the Lord
Col 3:20 in everything, for this *p* the Lord.
1Ti 2: 3 This is good, and *p* God our Savior,
1Jn 3:22 his commands and do what *p* him.

PLEASING (PLEASE)
Ge 2: 9 trees that were *p* to the eye
Lev 1: 9 an aroma *p* to the LORD.
Ps 19:14 be *p* in your sight,
104:34 May my meditation be *p* to him,
Pr 15:26 but those of the pure are *p* to him.
16: 7 When a man's ways are *p*
SS 1: 3 *P* is the fragrance of your perfumes
4:10 How much more *p* is your love

SS 7: 6 How beautiful you are and how *p*,
Ro 12: 1 *p* to God—this is your spiritual
14:18 Christ in this way is *p* to God
Php 4:18 an acceptable sacrifice, *p* to God.
1Ti 5: 4 grandparents, for this is *p* to God.
Heb 13:21 may he work in us what is *p* to him,

PLEASURE (PLEASE)
Ps 5: 4 You are not a God who takes *p*
51:16 you do not take *p* in burnt offerings
147:10 His *p* is not in the strength
Pr 10:23 A fool finds *p* in evil conduct,
18: 2 A fool finds no *p* in understanding
21:17 He who loves *p* will become poor;
Isa 1:11 I have no *p*
Jer 6:10 they find no *p* in it.
Eze 18:23 Do I take any *p* in the death
18:32 For I take no *p* in the death
33:11 I take no *p* in the death
Lk 10:21 Father, for this was your good *p*.
Eph 1: 5 in accordance with his *p* and will—
1: 9 of his will according to his good *p*,
1Ti 5: 6 the widow who lives for *p* is dead
2Ti 3: 4 lovers of *p* rather than lovers
2Pe 2:13 Their idea of *p* is to carouse

PLEASURES* (PLEASE)
Ps 16:11 with eternal *p* at your right hand.
Lk 8:14 and *p*, and they do not mature.
Tit 3: 3 by all kinds of passions and *p*.
Heb 11:25 rather than to enjoy the *p* of sin
Jas 4: 3 may spend what you get on your *p*.
2Pe 2:13 reveling in their *p* while they feast

PLEDGE
Dt 24:17 take the cloak of the widow as a *p*.
1Pe 3:21 but the *p* of a good conscience

PLEIADES
Job 38:31 "Can you bind the beautiful *P*?
Am 5: 8 (he who made the *P* and Orion,

PLENTIFUL (PLENTY)
Mt 9:37 harvest is *p* but the workers are
Lk 10: 2 harvest is *p*, but the workers are

PLENTY (PLENTIFUL)
2Co 8:14 the present time your *p* will supply
Php 4:12 whether living in *p* or in want.

PLOT (PLOTS)
Est 2:22 Mordecai found out about the *p*
Ps 2: 1 and the peoples *p* in vain?
Pr 3:29 not *p* harm against your neighbor,
Zec 8:17 do not *p* evil against your neighbor,
Ac 4:25 and the peoples *p* in vain?

PLOTS (PLOT)
Pr 6:14 who *p* evil with deceit in his heart

PLOW (PLOWMAN PLOWSHARES)
Lk 9:62 "No one who puts his hand to the *p*

PLOWMAN (PLOW)
1Co 9:10 because when the *p* plows

PLOWSHARES (PLOW)
1Sa 13:20 to the Philistines to have their *p*,
Isa 2: 4 They will beat their swords into *p*
Joel 3:10 Beat your *p* into swords
Mic 4: 3 They will beat their swords into *p*

PLUCK
Mk 9:47 your eye causes you to sin, *p* it out.

PLUNDER (PLUNDERED)
Ex 3:22 And so you will *p* the Egyptians."
Est 3:13 of Adar, and to *p* their goods.
8:11 to *p* the property of their enemies.
9:10 did not lay their hands on the *p*.
Pr 22:23 and will *p* those who *p* them.
Isa 3:14 the *p* from the poor is

PLUNDERED (PLUNDER)
Eze 34: 8 lacks a shepherd and so has been *p*

PLUNGE
1Ti 6: 9 and harmful desires that *p* men
1Pe 4: 4 think it strange that you do not *p*

PODS
Lk 15:16 with the *p* that the pigs were eating,

POINT
Mt 4: 5 on the highest *p* of the temple.
26:38 with sorrow to the *p* of death.
Jas 2:10 yet stumbles at just one *p* is guilty
Rev 2:10 Be faithful, even to the *p* of death,

POISON
Ps 140: 3 the *p* of vipers is on their lips.
Mk 16:18 and when they drink deadly *p*,
Ro 3:13 "The *p* of vipers is on their lips."
Jas 3: 8 It is a restless evil, full of deadly *p*.

POLE (POLES)
Nu 21: 8 "Make a snake and put it up on a *p*;
Dt 16:21 not set up any wooden Asherah *p*

POLES (POLE)
Ex 25:13 Then make *p* of acacia wood

POLISHED
Isa 49: 2 he made me into a *p* arrow

POLLUTE* (POLLUTED POLLUTES)
Nu 35:33 " 'Do not *p* the land where you are.
Jude : 8 these dreamers *p* their own bodies,

POLLUTED* (POLLUTE)
Ezr 9:11 entering to possess is a land *p*
Pr 25:26 Like a muddied spring or a *p* well
Ac 15:20 to abstain from food *p* by idols,
Jas 1:27 oneself from being *p* by the world.

POLLUTES* (POLLUTE)
Nu 35:33 Bloodshed *p* the land,

PONDER (PONDERED)
Ps 64: 9 and *p* what he has done.
119:95 but I will *p* your statutes.

PONDERED (PONDER)
Ps 111: 2 they are *p* by all who delight
Lk 2:19 up all these things and *p* them

POOR (POVERTY)
Lev 19:10 Leave them for the *p* and the alien.
23:22 Leave them for the *p* and the alien.
27: 8 If anyone making the vow is too *p*
Dt 15: 4 there should be no *p* among you,
15: 7 is a *p* man among your brothers
15:11 There will always be *p* people
24:12 If the man is *p*, do not go to sleep
24:14 advantage of a hired man who is *p*
Job 5:16 So the *p* have hope,
24: 4 force all the *p* of the land
Ps 14: 6 frustrate the plans of the *p*,
34: 6 This *p* man called, and the LORD
35:10 You rescue the *p* from those too
40:17 Yet I am *p* and needy;
68:10 O God, you provided for the *p*.
82: 3 maintain the rights of the *p*
112: 9 scattered abroad his gifts to the *p*,
113: 7 He raises the *p* from the dust
140:12 the LORD secures justice for the *p*
Pr 10: 4 Lazy hands make a man *p*,
13: 7 to be *p*, yet has great wealth.
14:20 The *p* are shunned
14:31 oppresses the *p* shows contempt
17: 5 who mocks the *p* shows contempt
19: 1 Better a *p* man whose walk is
19:17 to the *p* lends to the LORD,
19:22 better to be *p* than a liar.
20:13 not love sleep or you will grow *p*;
21:13 to the cry of the *p*,
21:17 who loves pleasure will become *p*;
22: 2 Rich and *p* have this in common:
22: 9 for he shares his food with the *p*.
22:22 not exploit the *p* because they are *p*
28: 6 Better a *p* man whose walk is
28:27 to the *p* will lack nothing,
29: 7 care about justice for the *p*,
31: 9 defend the rights of the *p*
31:20 She opens her arms to the *p*
Ecc 4:13 Better a *p* but wise youth
Isa 3:14 the plunder from the *p* is
10: 2 to deprive the *p* of their rights
14:30 of the *p* will find pasture,
25: 4 You have been a refuge for the *p*,
32: 7 schemes to destroy the *p* with lies,
61: 1 me to preach good news to the *p*.
Jer 22:16 He defended the cause of the *p*
Eze 18:12 He oppresses the *p* and needy.
Am 2: 7 They trample on the heads of the *p*
4: 1 you women who oppress the *p*
5:11 You trample on the *p*
Zec 7:10 or the fatherless, the alien or the *p*.
Mt 5: 3 saying: "Blessed are the *p* in spirit,
11: 5 the good news is preached to the *p*.
19:21 your possessions and give to the *p*,
26:11 The *p* you will always have
Mk 12:42 But a *p* widow came and put
14: 7 The *p* you will always have
Lk 4:18 me to preach good news to the *p*.
6:20 "Blessed are you who are *p*,
11:41 is inside ⸤the dish⸥ to the *p*,
14:13 invite the *p*, the crippled, the lame,
21: 2 also saw a *p* widow put
Jn 12: 8 You will always have the *p*
Ac 9:36 doing good and helping the *p*.
10: 4 and gifts to the *p* have come up
24:17 to bring my people gifts for the *p*
Ro 15:26 for the *p* among the saints
1Co 13: 3 If I give all I possess to the *p*
2Co 6:10 sorrowful, yet always rejoicing; *p*,
8: 9 yet for your sakes he became *p*,
Gal 2:10 continue to remember the *p*,
Jas 2: 2 and a *p* man in shabby clothes
2: 5 not God chosen those who are *p*
2: 6 But you have insulted the *p*.

POPULATION*
Pr 14:28 A large *p* is a king's glory,

PORTION
Nu 18:29 as the LORD's *p* the best
Dt 32: 9 For the LORD's *p* is his people,
1Sa 1: 5 But to Hannah he gave a double *p*
2Ki 2: 9 "Let me inherit a double *p*
Ps 73:26 and my *p* forever.
119:57 You are my *p*, O LORD;
Isa 53:12 Therefore I will give him a *p*
Jer 10:16 He who is the *P* of Jacob is not like
La 3:24 to myself, "The LORD is my *p*;
Zec 2:12 LORD will inherit Judah as his *p*

PORTRAIT
Lk 20:24 Whose *p* and inscription are on it?"

PORTRAYED
Gal 3: 1 very eyes Jesus Christ was clearly *p*

POSITION (POSITIONS)
Ro 12:16 to associate with people of low *p*.
Jas 1: 9 ought to take pride in his high *p*.
2Pe 3:17 and fall from your secure *p*.

POSITIONS (POSITION)
2Ch 20:17 Take up your *p*; stand firm
Jude : 6 the angels who did not keep their *p*

POSSESS (POSSESSED POSSESSING POSSESSION POSSESSIONS)
Nu 33:53 for I have given you the land to *p*.
Dt 4:14 you are crossing the Jordan to *p*.

PRACTICES (PRACTICE)
Ps 101: 7 No one who *p* deceit
Mt 5:19 but whoever *p* and teaches these
Col 3: 9 taken off your old self with its *p*

PRAISE (PRAISED PRAISES PRAISEWORTHY PRAISING)
Ex 15: 2 He is my God, and I will *p* him,
Dt 10:21 He is your *p;* he is your God,
26:19 declared that he will set you in *p,*
32: 3 Oh, *p* the greatness of our God!
Ru 4:14 said to Naomi: "*P* be to the LORD,
2Sa 22: 4 to the LORD, who is worthy of *p,*
22:47 The LORD lives! *P* be to my Rock
1Ch 16:25 is the LORD and most worthy of *p;*
16:35 that we may glory in your *p.*"
23: 5 four thousand are to *p* the LORD
29:10 "*P* be to you, O LORD,
2Ch 5:13 they raised their voices in *p*
20:21 and to *p* him for the splendor
29:30 to *p* the LORD with the words
Ezr 3:10 took their places to *p* the LORD,
Ne 9: 5 and *p* the LORD your God,
Ps 8: 2 you have ordained *p*
9: 1 I will *p* you, O LORD,
16: 7 I will *p* the LORD, who counsels
26: 7 proclaiming aloud your *p*
30: 4 *p* his holy name.
33: 1 it is fitting for the upright to *p* him.
34: 1 his *p* will always be on my lips.
40: 3 a hymn of *p* to our God.
42: 5 for I will yet *p* him,
43: 5 for I will yet *p* him,
45:17 the nations will *p* you for ever
47: 7 sing to him a psalm of *p.*
48: 1 the LORD, and most worthy of *p,*
51:15 and my mouth will declare your *p.*
56: 4 In God, whose word I *p,*
57: 9 I will *p* you, O Lord,
63: 4 I will *p* you as long as I live,
65: 1 *P* awaits you, O God, in Zion;
66: 2 make his *p* glorious.
66: 8 *P* our God, O peoples,
68:19 *P* be to the Lord, to God our Savior
68:26 *p* the LORD in the assembly
69:30 I will *p* God's name in song
69:34 Let heaven and earth *p* him,
71: 8 My mouth is filled with your *p,*
71:14 I will *p* you more and more.
71:22 I will *p* you with the harp
74:21 the poor and needy *p* your name.
86:12 I will *p* you, O Lord my God,
89: 5 The heavens *p* your wonders,
92: 1 It is good to *p* the LORD
96: 2 Sing to the LORD, *p* his name;
100: 4 and his courts with *p;*
101: 1 to you, O LORD, I will sing *p.*
102:18 not yet created may *p* the LORD:
103: 1 *P* the LORD, O my soul;
103:20 *P* the LORD, you his angels,
104: 1 *P* the LORD, O my soul.
105: 2 Sing to him, sing *p* to him;
106: 1 *P* the LORD.
108: 3 I will *p* you, O LORD,
111: 1 *P* the LORD.
113: 1 *P* the LORD.
117: 1 *P* the LORD, all you nations;
119:175 Let me live that I may *p* you,
135: 1 *P* the LORD.
135:20 you who fear him, *p* the LORD.
138: 1 I will *p* you, O LORD,
139:14 I *p* you because I am fearfully
144: 1 *P* be to the LORD my Rock,
145: 3 is the LORD and most worthy of *p;*
145:10 All you have made will *p* you,
145:21 Let every creature *p* his holy name
146: 1 *P* the LORD, O my soul.
147: 1 how pleasant and fitting to *p* him!
148: 1 *P* the LORD from the heavens,
148:13 Let them *p* the name of the LORD,
Ps 149: 1 his *p* in the assembly of the saints.
149: 6 May the *p* of God be
149: 9 *P* the LORD.
150: 2 *p* him for his surpassing greatness.
150: 6 that has breath *p* the LORD.
Pr 27: 2 Let another *p* you, and not your
27:21 man is tested by the *p* he receives.
31:31 let her works bring her *p*
SS 1: 4 we will *p* your love more than wine
Isa 12: 1 "I will *p* you, O LORD.
42:10 his *p* from the ends of the earth,
61: 3 and a garment of *p*
Jer 33: 9 *p* and honor before all nations
Da 2:20 "*P* be to the name of God for ever
4:37 *p* and exalt and glorify the King
Mt 5:16 and *p* your Father in heaven.
21:16 you have ordained *p*?"
Lk 19:37 to *p* God in loud voices
Jn 5:44 effort to obtain the *p* that comes
12:43 for they loved *p* from men more
Ro 2:29 Such a man's *p* is not from men,
15: 7 in order to bring *p* to God.
2Co 1: 3 *P* be to the God and Father
Eph 1: 3 *P* be to the God and Father
1: 6 to the *p* of his glorious grace,
1:12 might be for the *p* of his glory.
1:14 to the *p* of his glory.
1Th 2: 6 We were not looking for *p*
Heb 13:15 offer to God a sacrifice of *p*—
Jas 3: 9 With the tongue we *p* our Lord
5:13 happy? Let him sing songs of *p.*
Rev 5:13 be *p* and honor and glory
7:12 *P* and glory

PRAISED (PRAISE)
1Ch 29:10 David *p* the LORD in the presence
Ne 8: 6 Ezra *p* the LORD, the great God;
Job 1:21 may the name of the LORD be *p.*"
Ps 113: 2 Let the name of the LORD be *p,*
Pr 31:30 who fears the LORD is to be *p.*
Isa 63: 7 the deeds for which he is to be *p,*
Da 2:19 Then Daniel *p* the God of heaven
4:34 Then I *p* the Most High; I honored
Lk 18:43 the people saw it, they also *p* God.
23:47 seeing what had happened, *p* God
Ro 9: 5 who is God over all, forever *p!*
Gal 1:24 And they *p* God because of me.
1Pe 4:11 that in all things God may be *p*

PRAISES (PRAISE)
2Sa 22:50 I will sing *p* to your name.
Ps 18:49 I will sing *p* to your name.
47: 6 Sing *p* to God, sing *p;*
147: 1 How good it is to sing *p* to our God,
Pr 31:28 her husband also, and he *p* her:
1Pe 2: 9 that you may declare the *p*

PRAISEWORTHY* (PRAISE)
Ps 78: 4 the *p* deeds of the LORD,
Php 4: 8 if anything is excellent or *p*—

PRAISING (PRAISE)
Lk 2:13 *p* God and saying, "Glory to God
2:20 *p* God for all the things they had
Ac 2:47 *p* God and enjoying the favor
10:46 speaking in tongues and *p* God.
1Co 14:16 If you are *p* God with your spirit,

PRAY (PRAYED PRAYER PRAYERS PRAYING PRAYS)
Dt 4: 7 is near us whenever we *p* to him?
1Sa 12:23 the LORD by failing to *p* for you.
1Ki 8:30 when they *p* toward this place.
2Ch 7:14 will humble themselves and *p*
Ezr 6:10 and *p* for the well-being of the king
Job 42: 8 My servant Job will *p* for you,
Ps 5: 2 for to you I *p.*
32: 6 let everyone who is godly *p*
122: 6 *P* for the peace of Jerusalem:
Jer 29: 7 *P* to the LORD for it,
29:12 upon me and come and *p* to me,
Jer 42: 3 *P* that the LORD your God will
Mt 5:44 and *p* for those who persecute you,
6: 5 "And when you *p,* do not be like
6: 9 "This, then, is how you should *p:*
14:23 up on a mountainside by himself to *p.*
19:13 hands on them and *p* for them.
26:36 Sit here while I go over there and *p*
Lk 6:28 *p* for those who mistreat you.
11: 1 us to *p,* just as John taught his
18: 1 them that they should always *p*
22:40 "*P* that you will not fall
Jn 17:20 I *p* also for those who will believe
Ro 8:26 do not know what we ought to *p* for,
1Co 14:13 in a tongue should *p* that he may
Eph 1:18 I *p* also that the eyes
3:16 I *p* that out of his glorious riches he
6:18 And *p* in the Spirit on all occasions
Col 1:10 we *p* this in order that you may live
4: 3 *p* for us, too, that God may open
1Th 5:17 Be joyful always; *p* continually;
2Th 1:11 in mind, we constantly *p* for you,
Jas 5:13 one of you in trouble? He should *p.*
5:16 *p* for each other so that you may be
1Pe 4: 7 self-controlled so that you can *p.*
Jude :20 up in your most holy faith and *p*

PRAYED (PRAY)
1Sa 1:27 I *p* for this child, and the LORD
1Ki 18:36 Elijah stepped forward and *p:*
19: 4 under it and *p* that he might die.
2Ki 6:17 And Elisha *p,* "O LORD,
2Ch 30:18 But Hezekiah *p* for them, saying,
Ne 4: 9 we *p* to our God and posted a guard
Job 42:10 After Job had *p* for his friends,
Da 6:10 got down on his knees and *p,*
9: 4 I *p* to the LORD my God
Jnh 2: 1 From inside the fish Jonah *p*
Mt 26:39 with his face to the ground and *p,*
Mk 1:35 off to a solitary place, where he *p.*
14:35 *p* that if possible the hour might
Lk 22:41 knelt down and *p,* "Father,
Jn 17: 1 he looked toward heaven and *p:*
Ac 4:31 After they *p,* the place where they
6: 6 who *p* and laid their hands on them
8:15 they *p* for them that they might
13: 3 So after they had fasted and *p,*

PRAYER (PRAY)
2Ch 30:27 for their *p* reached heaven,
Ezr 8:23 about this, and he answered our *p.*
Ps 4: 1 be merciful to me and hear my *p.*
6: 9 the LORD accepts my *p.*
17: 1 Give ear to my *p*—
17: 6 give ear to me and hear my *p.*
65: 2 O you who hear *p,*
66:20 who has not rejected my *p*
86: 6 Hear my *p,* O LORD;
Pr 15: 8 but the *p* of the upright pleases him
15:29 but he hears the *p* of the righteous.
Isa 56: 7 a house of *p* for all nations."
Mt 21:13 house will be called a house of *p,*'
21:22 receive whatever you ask for in *p.*"
Mk 9:29 This kind can come out only by *p.*"
11:24 whatever you ask for in *p,*
Jn 17:15 My *p* is not that you take them out
Ac 1:14 all joined together constantly in *p,*
2:42 to the breaking of bread and to *p.*
6: 4 and will give our attention to *p*
10:31 has heard your *p* and remembered
16:13 expected to find a place of *p.*
Ro 12:12 patient in affliction, faithful in *p.*
1Co 7: 5 you may devote yourselves to *p.*
2Co 13: 9 and our *p* is for your perfection.
Php 1: 9 this is my *p:* that your love may
4: 6 but in everything, by *p* and petition
Col 4: 2 yourselves to *p,* being watchful
1Ti 2: 8 to lift up holy hands in *p,*
4: 5 by the word of God and *p.*
Jas 5:15 *p* offered in faith will make the sick
1Pe 3:12 and his ears are attentive to their *p,*

PRAYERS (PRAY)
1Ch 5:20 He answered their *p*, because they
Isa 1:15 even if you offer many *p*,
Mk 12:40 and for a show make lengthy *p*.
2Co 1:11 as you help us by your *p*.
Eph 6:18 on all occasions with all kinds of *p*
1Ti 2: 1 then, first of all, that requests, *p*,
1Pe 3: 7 so that nothing will hinder your *p*.
Rev 5: 8 which are the *p* of the saints.
8: 3 with the *p* of all the saints,

PRAYING (PRAY)
Ge 24:45 "Before I finished *p* in my heart,
1Sa 1:12 As she kept on *p* to the LORD,
Mk 11:25 And when you stand *p*,
Lk 3:21 as he was *p*, heaven was opened
6:12 and spent the night *p* to God.
9:29 As he was *p*, the appearance
Jn 17: 9 I am not *p* for the world,
Ac 9:11 from Tarsus named Saul, for he is *p*
16:25 and Silas were *p* and singing hymns
Ro 15:30 in my struggle by *p* to God for me.
Eph 6:18 always keep on *p* for all the saints.

PRAYS (PRAY)
1Co 14:14 my spirit *p*, but my mind is

PREACH (PREACHED PREACHING)
Isa 61: 1 me to *p* good news to the poor.
Mt 10: 7 As you go, *p* this message:
23: 3 they do not practice what they *p*.
Mk 16:15 and *p* the good news to all creation.
Lk 4:18 me to *p* good news to the poor.
Ac 9:20 At once he began to *p*
16:10 us to *p* the gospel to them.
Ro 1:15 am so eager to *p* the gospel
10:15 how can they *p* unless they are sent
15:20 to *p* the gospel where Christ was
1Co 1:17 to *p* the gospel—not with words
1:23 wisdom, but we *p* Christ crucified:
9:14 that those who *p* the gospel should
9:16 Woe to me if I do not *p* the gospel!
2Co 4: 5 For we do not *p* ourselves,
10:16 so that we can *p* the gospel
Gal 1: 8 from heaven should *p* a gospel
2Ti 4: 2 I give you this charge: *P* the Word;

PREACHED (PREACH)
Mt 24:14 gospel of the kingdom will be *p*
Mk 6:12 and *p* that people should repent.
13:10 And the gospel must first be *p*
14: 9 wherever the gospel is *p*
Ac 8: 4 had been scattered *p* the word
28:31 hindrance he *p* the kingdom
1Co 9:27 so that after I have *p* to others,
15: 1 you of the gospel I *p* to you,
2Co 11: 4 other than the Jesus we *p*,
Gal 1: 8 other than the one we *p* to you,
Eph 2:17 *p* peace to you who were far away
Php 1:18 false motives or true, Christ is *p*.
1Ti 3:16 was *p* among the nations,
1Pe 1:25 this is the word that was *p* to you.
3:19 and *p* to the spirits in prison who

PREACHING (PREACH)
Lk 9: 6 *p* the gospel and healing people
Ac 18: 5 devoted himself exclusively to *p*,
Ro 10:14 hear without someone *p* to them?
1Co 2: 4 and my *p* were not with wise
9:18 in *p* the gospel I may offer it free
Gal 1: 9 If anybody is *p* to you a gospel
1Ti 4:13 the public reading of Scripture, to *p*
5:17 especially those whose work is *p*

PRECEDE*
1Th 4:15 will certainly not *p* those who have

PRECEPTS*
Dt 33:10 He teaches your *p* to Jacob
Ps 19: 8 The *p* of the LORD are right,
103:18 and remember to obey his *p*.
Ps 105:45 that they might keep his *p*
111: 7 all his *p* are trustworthy.
111:10 who follow his *p* have good
119: 4 You have laid down *p*
119:15 I meditate on your *p*
119:27 understand the teaching of your *p*;
119:40 How I long for your *p*!
119:45 for I have sought out your *p*.
119:56 I obey your *p*.
119:63 to all who follow your *p*.
119:69 I keep your *p* with all my heart.
119:78 but I will meditate on your *p*.
119:87 but I have not forsaken your *p*.
119:93 I will never forget your *p*,
119:94 I have sought out your *p*.
119:100 for I obey your *p*.
119:104 I gain understanding from your *p*;
119:110 but I have not strayed from your *p*.
119:128 because I consider all your *p* right,
119:134 that I may obey your *p*.
119:141 I do not forget your *p*.
119:159 See how I love your *p*;
119:168 I obey your *p* and your statutes,
119:173 for I have chosen your *p*.

PRECIOUS
Ps 19:10 They are more *p* than gold,
72:14 for *p* is their blood in his sight.
116:15 *P* in the sight of the LORD
119:72 from your mouth is more *p* to me
139:17 How *p* to me are your thoughts,
Pr 8:11 for wisdom is more *p* than rubies,
Isa 28:16 a *p* cornerstone for a sure
1Pe 1:19 but with the *p* blood of Christ,
2: 4 but chosen by God and *p* to him—
2: 6 a chosen and *p* cornerstone,
2Pe 1: 1 Christ have received a faith as *p*
1: 4 us his very great and *p* promises,

PREDESTINED* (DESTINY)
Ro 8:29 *p* to be conformed to the likeness
8:30 And those he *p*, he also called;
Eph 1: 5 In love he *p* us to be adopted
1:11 having been *p* according

PREDICTED (PREDICTION)
1Sa 28:17 The LORD has done what he *p*
Ac 7:52 killed those who *p* the coming
1Pe 1:11 when he *p* the sufferings of Christ

PREDICTION* (PREDICTED PREDICTIONS)
Jer 28: 9 only if his *p* comes true."

PREDICTIONS (PREDICTION)
Isa 44:26 and fulfills the *p* of his messengers,

PREGNANT
Ex 21:22 who are fighting hit a *p* woman
Mt 24:19 be in those days for *p* women
1Th 5: 3 as labor pains on a *p* woman,

PREPARE (PREPARED)
Ps 23: 5 You *p* a table before me
Isa 25: 6 the LORD Almighty will *p*
40: 3 "In the desert *p*
Am 4:12 *p* to meet your God, O Israel."
Mal 3: 1 who will *p* the way before me.
Mt 3: 3 '*P* the way for the Lord,
Jn 14: 2 there to *p* a place for you.
Eph 4:12 to *p* God's people for works
1Pe 1:13 Therefore, *p* your minds for action;

PREPARED (PREPARE)
Ex 23:20 to bring you to the place I have *p*.
Mt 25:34 the kingdom *p* for you
Ro 9:22 of his wrath—*p* for destruction?
1Co 2: 9 what God has *p* for those who love
Eph 2:10 which God *p* in advance for us
2Ti 2:21 and *p* to do any good work.
4: 2 be *p* in season and out of season;
1Pe 3:15 Always be *p* to give an answer

PRESCRIBED
Ezr 7:23 Whatever the God of heaven has *p*,

PRESENCE (PRESENT)
Ex 25:30 Put the bread of the *P* on this table
33:14 The LORD replied, "My *P* will go
Nu 4: 7 "Over the table of the *P* they are
1Sa 6:20 in the *p* of the LORD, this
21: 6 of the *P* that had been removed
2Sa 22:13 Out of the brightness of his *p*
2Ki 17:23 LORD removed them from his *p*,
23:27 also from my *p* as I removed Israel,
Ezr 9:15 one of us can stand in your *p*."
Ps 16:11 you will fill me with joy in your *p*,
21: 6 with the joy of your *p*.
23: 5 in the *p* of my enemies.
31:20 the shelter of your *p* you hide them
41:12 and set me in your *p* forever.
51:11 Do not cast me from your *p*
52: 9 in the *p* of your saints.
89:15 who walk in the light of your *p*,
90: 8 our secret sins in the light of your *p*
114: 7 O earth, at the *p* of the Lord,
139: 7 Where can I flee from your *p*?
Isa 26:17 so were we in your *p*, O LORD.
Jer 5:22 "Should you not tremble in my *p*?
Eze 38:20 of the earth will tremble at my *p*.
Hos 6: 2 that we may live in his *p*.
Na 1: 5 The earth trembles at his *p*,
Mal 3:16 in his *p* concerning those who
Ac 2:28 you will fill me with joy in your *p*.'
1Th 3: 9 have in the *p* of our God
3:13 and holy in the *p* of our God
2Th 1: 9 and shut out from the *p* of the Lord
Heb 9:24 now to appear for us in God's *p*.
1Jn 3:19 rest in his *p* whenever our hearts
Jude :24 before his glorious *p* without fault

PRESENT (PRESENCE)
1Co 3:22 life or death or the *p* or the future—
7:26 of the *p* crisis, I think that it is good
2Co 11: 2 so that I might *p* you as a pure
Eph 5:27 and to *p* her to himself
1Ti 4: 8 holding promise for both the *p* life
2Ti 2:15 Do your best to *p* yourself to God
Jude :24 and to *p* you before his glorious

PRESERVE
Lk 17:33 and whoever loses his life will *p* it.

PRESERVES
Ps 1 19:50 Your promise *p* my life.

PRESS (PRESSED PRESSURE)
Php 3:12 but I *p* on to take hold of that
3:14 I *p* on toward the goal

PRESSED (PRESS)
Lk 6:38 *p* down, shaken together

PRESSURE (PRESS)
2Co 1: 8 We were under great *p*, far
11:28 I face daily the *p* of my concern

PRETENDED
1Sa 21:13 So he *p* to be insane

PREVAILS
1Sa 2: 9 "It is not by strength that one *p*;
Pr 19:21 but it is the LORD's purpose that *p*

PRICE (PRICELESS)
Job 28:18 the *p* of wisdom is beyond rubies.
1Co 6:20 your own; you were bought at a *p*.
7:23 bought at a *p*; do not become slaves

PRICELESS* (PRICE)
Ps 36: 7 How *p* is your unfailing love!

PRIDE (PROUD)
Pr 8:13 I hate *p* and arrogance,
11: 2 When *p* comes, then comes

Pr 13:10 *P* only breeds quarrels,
16:18 *P* goes before destruction,
29:23 A man's *p* brings him low,
Isa 25:11 God will bring down their *p*
Da 4:37 And those who walk in *p* he is able
Am 8: 7 The LORD has sworn by the *P*
2Co 5:12 giving you an opportunity to take *p*
7: 4 in you; I take great *p* in you.
8:24 and the reason for our *p* in you,
Gal 6: 4 Then he can take *p* in himself,
Jas 1: 9 ought to take *p* in his high position.

PRIEST (PRIESTHOOD PRIESTLY PRIESTS)
Ge 14:18 He was *p* of God Most High,
Nu 5:10 to the *p* will belong to the *p*.'"
2Ch 13: 9 and seven rams may become a *p*
Ps 110: 4 "You are a *p* forever,
Heb 2:17 faithful high *p* in service to God,
3: 1 and high *p* whom we confess.
4:14 have a great high *p* who has gone
4:15 do not have a high *p* who is unable
5: 6 "You are a *p* forever,
6:20 He has become a high *p* forever,
7: 3 Son of God he remains a *p* forever.
7:15 clear if another *p* like Melchizedek
7:26 Such a high *p* meets our need—
8: 1 We do have such a high *p*,
10:11 Day after day every *p* stands
13:11 The high *p* carries the blood

PRIESTHOOD (PRIEST)
Heb 7:24 lives forever, he has a permanent *p*.
1Pe 2: 5 into a spiritual house to be a holy *p*,
2: 9 you are a chosen people, a royal *p*,

PRIESTLY (PRIEST)
Ro 15:16 to the Gentiles with the *p* duty

PRIESTS (PRIEST)
Ex 19: 6 you will be for me a kingdom of *p*
Lev 21: 1 "Speak to the *p*, the sons of Aaron,
Eze 42:13 where the *p* who approach
46: 2 *p* are to sacrifice his burnt offering
Mal 1: 6 O *p*, who show contempt for my name.
Rev 5:10 to be a kingdom and *p*
20: 6 but they will be *p* of God

PRIME
Isa 38:10 recovery: I said, "In the *p* of my life

PRINCE (PRINCES PRINCESS)
Isa 9: 6 Everlasting Father, *P* of Peace.
Eze 34:24 and my servant David will be *p*
37:25 my servant will be their *p* forever.
Da 8:25 stand against the *P* of princes.
Jn 12:31 now the *p* of this world will be
Ac 5:31 as *P* and Savior that he might give

PRINCES (PRINCE)
Ps 118: 9 than to trust in *p*.
148:11 you *p* and all rulers on earth,
Isa 40:23 He brings *p* to naught

PRINCESS* (PRINCE)
Ps 45:13 All glorious is the *p*

PRISCILLA*
Wife of Aquila; co-worker with Paul (Ac 18; Ro 16:3; 1Co 16:19; 2Ti 4:19); instructor of Apollos (Ac 18:24–28).

PRISON (PRISONER PRISONERS)
Ps 66:11 You brought us into *p*
142: 7 Set me free from my *p*,
Isa 42: 7 to free captives from *p*
Mt 25:36 I was in *p* and you came to visit me
2Co 11:23 been in *p* more frequently,
Heb 11:36 others were chained and put in *p*.
13: 3 Remember those in *p*
1Pe 3:19 spirits in *p* who disobeyed long ago
Rev 20: 7 Satan will be released from his *p*

PRISONER (PRISON)
Ro 7:23 and making me a *p* of the law of sin
Gal 3:22 declares that the whole world is a *p*
Eph 3: 1 the *p* of Christ Jesus for the sake

PRISONERS (PRISON)
Ps 68: 6 he leads forth the *p* with singing;
79:11 groans of the *p* come before you;
107:10 *p* suffering in iron chains,
146: 7 The LORD sets *p* free,
Zec 9:12 to your fortress, O *p* of hope;
Lk 4:18 me to proclaim freedom for the *p*
Gal 3:23 we were held *p* by the law,

PRIVILEGE*
2Co 8: 4 pleaded with us for the *p* of sharing

PRIZE*
1Co 9:24 Run in such a way as to get the *p*.
9:24 but only one gets the *p*? Run
9:27 will not be disqualified for the *p*.
Php 3:14 on toward the goal to win the *p*
Col 2:18 of angels disqualify you for the *p*.

PROBE
Job 11: 7 Can you *p* the limits
Ps 17: 3 Though you *p* my heart

PROCEDURE
Ecc 8: 6 For there is a proper time and *p*

PROCESSION
Ps 68:24 Your *p* has come into view, O God,
118:27 boughs in hand, join in the festal *p*
1Co 4: 9 on display at the end of the *p*,
2Co 2:14 us in triumphal *p* in Christ

PROCLAIM (PROCLAIMED PROCLAIMING PROCLAIMS PROCLAMATION)
Ex 33:19 and I will *p* my name, the LORD,
Lev 25:10 and *p* liberty throughout the land
Dt 30:12 and *p* it to us so we may obey it?"
2Sa 1:20 *p* it not in the streets of Ashkelon,
1Ch 16:23 *p* his salvation day after day.
Ne 8:15 and that they should *p* this word
Ps 2: 7 I will *p* the decree of the LORD:
9:11 *p* among the nations what he has
19: 1 the skies *p* the work of his hands.
22:31 They will *p* his righteousness
40: 9 I *p* righteousness in the great
50: 6 the heavens *p* his righteousness,
64: 9 they will *p* the works of God
68:34 *P* the power of God,
71:16 I will come and *p* your mighty acts,
92: 2 to *p* your love in the morning
96: 2 *p* his salvation day after day.
97: 6 The heavens *p* his righteousness,
106: 2 Who can *p* the mighty acts
118:17 will *p* what the LORD has done.
145: 6 and I will *p* your great deeds.
Isa 12: 4 and *p* that his name is exalted.
42:12 and *p* his praise in the islands.
52: 7 who *p* salvation,
61: 1 to *p* freedom for the captives
66:19 They will *p* my glory
Jer 7: 2 house and there *p* this message:
50: 2 lift up a banner and *p* it;
Hos 5: 9 I *p* what is certain.
Zec 9:10 He will *p* peace to the nations.
Mt 10:27 in your ear, *p* from the roofs.
12:18 and he will *p* justice to the nations.
Lk 4:18 me to *p* freedom for the prisoners
9:60 you go and *p* the kingdom of God."
Ac 17:23 unknown I am going to *p*
20:27 hesitated to *p* to you the whole will
1Co 11:26 you *p* the Lord's death
Col 1:28 We *p* him, admonishing
4: 4 Pray that I may *p* it clearly,
1Jn 1: 1 this we *p* concerning the Word

PROCLAIMED (PROCLAIM)
Ex 9:16 and that my name might be *p*
Ex 34: 5 there with him and *p* his name,
Ps 68:11 was the company of those who *p* it:
Ro 15:19 I have fully *p* the gospel of Christ.
Col 1:23 that has been *p* to every creature
2Ti 4:17 me the message might be fully *p*

PROCLAIMING (PROCLAIM)
Ps 26: 7 *p* aloud your praise
92:15 *p*, "The LORD is upright;
Ac 5:42 and *p* the good news that Jesus is
Ro 10: 8 the word of faith we are *p*:

PROCLAIMS (PROCLAIM)
Dt 18:22 If what a prophet *p* in the name

PROCLAMATION (PROCLAIM)
Isa 62:11 The LORD has made *p*

PRODUCE (PRODUCES)
Mt 3: 8 *P* fruit in keeping with repentance.
3:10 tree that does not *p* good fruit will

PRODUCES (PRODUCE)
Pr 30:33 so stirring up anger *p* strife."
Ro 5: 3 that suffering *p* perseverance;
Heb 12:11 it *p* a harvest of righteousness

PROFANE (PROFANED)
Lev 19:12 and so *p* the name of your God.
22:32 Do not *p* my holy name.
Mal 2:10 Why do we *p* the covenant

PROFANED (PROFANE)
Eze 36:20 the nations they *p* my holy name,

PROFESS*
1Ti 2:10 for women who *p* to worship God.
Heb 4:14 let us hold firmly to the faith we *p*.
10:23 unswervingly to the hope we *p*,

PROFIT (PROFITABLE)
Pr 14:23 All hard work brings a *p*,
21: 5 The plans of the diligent lead to *p*
Isa 44:10 which can *p* him nothing?
2Co 2:17 not peddle the word of God for *p*.
Php 3: 7 was to my *p* I now consider loss

PROFITABLE* (PROFIT)
Pr 3:14 for she is more *p* than silver
31:18 She sees that her trading is *p*,
Tit 3: 8 These things are excellent and *p*

PROFOUND
Job 9: 4 His wisdom is *p*, his power is vast.
Ps 92: 5 how *p* your thoughts!
Eph 5:32 This is a *p* mystery—but I am

PROGRESS
Php 1:25 continue with all of you for your *p*
1Ti 4:15 so that everyone may see your *p*.

PROLONG*
Dt 5:33 *p* your days in the land that you
Ps 85: 5 Will you *p* your anger
Pr 3: 2 for they will *p* your life many years
Isa 53:10 will see his offspring and *p* his days,
La 4:22 he will not *p* your exile.

PROMISE (PROMISED PROMISES)
Nu 23:19 Does he *p* and not fulfill?
Jos 23:14 Every *p* has been fulfilled;
2Sa 7:25 keep forever the *p* you have made
1Ki 8:20 The LORD has kept the *p* he made
8:24 You have kept your *p*
Ne 5:13 man who does not keep this *p*.
9: 8 have kept your *p* because you are
Ps 77: 8 Has his *p* failed for all time?
119:41 your salvation according to your *p*;
119:50 Your *p* preserves my life.
119:58 to me according to your *p*.
119:162 I rejoice in your *p*
Ac 2:39 The *p* is for you and your children
Ro 4:13 offspring received the *p* that he

Ro 4:20 unbelief regarding the *p* of God,
Gal 3:14 that by faith we might receive the *p*
Eph 2:12 foreigners to the covenants of the *p*
1Ti 4: 8 holding *p* for both the present life
Heb 6:13 When God made his *p* to Abraham
11:11 him faithful who had made the *p*.
2Pe 3: 9 Lord is not slow in keeping his *p*,
3:13 with his *p* we are looking forward

PROMISED (PROMISE)
Ge 21: 1 did for Sarah what he had *p*.
24: 7 who spoke to me and *p* me on oath,
Ex 3:17 And I have *p* to bring you up out
Nu 10:29 for the LORD has *p* good things
Dt 15: 6 your God will bless you as he has *p*,
26:18 his treasured possession as he *p*,
2Sa 7:28 and you have *p* these good things
1Ki 9: 5 I *p* David your father when I said,
2Ch 6:15 with your mouth you have *p*
Ps 119:57 I have *p* to obey your words.
Lk 24:49 to send you what my Father has *p*;
Ac 1: 4 but wait for the gift my Father *p*,
13:32 What God *p* our fathers he has
Ro 4:21 power to do what he had *p*.
Tit 1: 2 *p* before the beginning of time,
Heb 10:23 for he who *p* is faithful.
10:36 you will receive what he has *p*.
Jas 1:12 the crown of life that God has *p*
2: 5 the kingdom he *p* those who love
2Pe 3: 4 "Where is this 'coming' he *p*?
1Jn 2:25 And this is what he *p* us—

PROMISES (PROMISE)
Jos 21:45 one of all the LORD's good *p*
23:14 of all the good *p* the LORD your
1Ki 8:56 failed of all the good *p* he gave
1Ch 17:19 and made known all these great *p*.
Ps 85: 8 he *p* peace to his people, his saints
106:12 Then they believed his *p*
119:140 Your *p* have been thoroughly
119:148 that I may meditate on your *p*.
145:13 The LORD is faithful to all his *p*
Ro 9: 4 the temple worship and the *p*.
2Co 1:20 matter how many *p* God has made,
7: 1 Since we have these *p*, dear friends,
Heb 8: 6 and it is founded on better *p*.
2Pe 1: 4 us his very great and precious *p*,

PROMOTE (PROMOTES)
Pr 12:20 but joy for those who *p* peace.
16:21 and pleasant words *p* instruction.
1Ti 1: 4 These *p* controversies rather

PROMOTES (PROMOTE)
Pr 17: 9 over an offense *p* love,

PROMPTED
1Th 1: 3 your labor *p* by love, and your
2Th 1:11 and every act *p* by your faith.

PRONOUNCE (PRONOUNCED)
1Ch 23:13 to *p* blessings in his name forever.

PRONOUNCED (PRONOUNCE)
1Ch 16:12 miracles, and the judgments he *p*,

PROOF (PROVE)
Ac 17:31 He has given *p* of this to all men
2Co 8:24 Therefore show these men the *p*

PROPER
Ps 104:27 give them their food at the *p* time.
145:15 give them their food at the *p* time.
Ecc 5:18 Then I realized that it is good and *p*
8: 5 the wise heart will know the *p* time
Mt 24:45 give them their food at the *p* time?
Lk 1:20 which will come true at their *p* time
1Co 11:13 Is it *p* for a woman to pray to God
Gal 6: 9 at the *p* time we will reap a harvest
1Ti 2: 6 the testimony given in its *p* time.
1Pe 2:17 Show *p* respect to everyone:

PROPERTY
Heb 10:34 the confiscation of your *p*,

PROPHECIES (PROPHESY)
1Co 13: 8 where there are *p*, they will cease;
1Th 5:20 do not treat *p* with contempt.

PROPHECY (PROPHESY)
Da 9:24 to seal up vision and *p*
1Co 12:10 miraculous powers, to another *p*,
13: 2 of *p* and can fathom all mysteries
14: 1 gifts, especially the gift of *p*.
14: 6 or *p* or word of instruction?
14:22 *p*, however, is for believers,
2Pe 1:20 you must understand that no *p*
Rev 22:18 the words of the *p* of this book:

PROPHESIED (PROPHESY)
Nu 11:25 the Spirit rested on them, they *p*,
1Sa 19:24 and also *p* in Samuel's presence.
Jn 11:51 that year he *p* that Jesus would
Ac 19: 6 and they spoke in tongues and *p*.
21: 9 four unmarried daughters who *p*.

PROPHESIES (PROPHESY)
Jer 28: 9 the prophet who *p* peace will be
Eze 12:27 and he *p* about the distant future.'
1Co 11: 4 *p* with his head covered dishonors
14: 3 But everyone who *p* speaks to men

PROPHESY (PROPHECIES PROPHECY PROPHESIED PROPHESIES PROPHESYING PROPHET PROPHET'S PROPHETESS PROPHETS)
1Sa 10: 6 and you will *p* with them;
Eze 13: 2 Say to those who *p* out
13:17 daughters of your people who *p* out
34: 2 *p* against the shepherds of Israel;
37: 4 "*P* to these bones and say to them,
Joel 2:28 Your sons and daughters will *p*,
Mt 7:22 Lord, did we not *p* in your name,
Ac 2:17 Your sons and daughters will *p*,
1Co 13: 9 know in part and we *p* in part,
14:39 my brothers, be eager to *p*,
Rev 11: 3 and they will *p* for 1,260 days,

PROPHESYING (PROPHESY)
1Ch 25: 1 and Jeduthun for the ministry of *p*,
Ro 12: 6 If a man's gift is *p*, let him use it

PROPHET (PROPHESY)
Ex 7: 1 your brother Aaron will be your *p*.
Nu 12: 6 "When a *p* of the LORD is
Dt 13: 1 If a *p*, or one who foretells
18:18 up for them a *p* like you
18:22 If what a *p* proclaims in the name
1Sa 3:20 that Samuel was attested as a *p*
9: 9 because the *p* of today used
1Ki 1: 8 son of Jehoiada, Nathan the *p*,
18:36 the *p* Elijah stepped forward
2Ki 5: 8 and he will know that there is a *p*
6:12 "but Elisha, the *p* who is in Israel,
20: 1 The *p* Isaiah son of Amoz went
2Ch 35:18 since the days of the *p* Samuel;
36:12 himself before Jeremiah the *p*,
Ezr 5: 1 Haggai the *p* and Zechariah the *p*,
Eze 2: 5 they will know that a *p* has been
33:33 they will know that a *p* has been
Hos 9: 7 the *p* is considered a fool,
Am 7:14 "I was neither a *p* nor a prophet's
Hab 1: 1 that Habakkuk the *p* received.
Hag 1: 1 came through the *p* Haggai
Zec 1: 1 to the *p* Zechariah son of Berekiah,
13: 4 that day every *p* will be ashamed
Mal 4: 5 I will send you the *p* Elijah
Mt 10:41 Anyone who receives a *p*
11: 9 what did you go out to see? A *p*?
12:39 except the sign of the *p* Jonah.
Lk 1:76 will be called a *p* of the Most High;
4:24 "no *p* is accepted in his hometown.
7:16 A great *p* has appeared among us,"
24:19 "He was a *p*, powerful in word
Jn 1:21 "Are you the *P*?" He answered,
Ac 7:37 'God will send you a *p* like me
21:10 a *p* named Agabus came
1Co 14:37 If anybody thinks he is a *p*
Rev 16:13 and out of the mouth of the false *p*.

PROPHET'S (PROPHESY)
2Pe 1:20 about by the *p* own interpretation.

PROPHETESS (PROPHESY)
Ex 15:20 Then Miriam the *p*, Aaron's sister,
Jdg 4: 4 a *p*, the wife of Lappidoth,
Isa 8: 3 I went to the *p*, and she conceived
Lk 2:36 a *p*, Anna, the daughter of Phanuel,

PROPHETS (PROPHESY)
Nu 11:29 that all the LORD's people were *p*
1Sa 10:11 Is Saul also among the *p*?"
28: 6 him by dreams or Urim or *p*.
1Ki 19:10 put your *p* to death with the sword.
1Ch 16:22 do my *p* no harm."
Ps 105:15 do my *p* no harm."
Jer 23: 9 Concerning the *p*:
23:30 "I am against the *p* who steal
Eze 13: 2 prophesy against the *p*
Mt 5:17 come to abolish the Law or the *P*;
7:12 for this sums up the Law and the *P*.
7:15 "Watch out for false *p*.
22:40 and the *P* hang on these two
23:37 you who kill the *p* and stone those
24:24 false Christs and false *p* will appear
26:56 of the *p* might be fulfilled."
Lk 10:24 For I tell you that many *p*
11:49 'I will send them *p* and apostles,
24:25 believe all that the *p* have spoken!
24:44 me in the Law of Moses, the *P*
Ac 3:24 "Indeed, all the *p* from Samuel on,
10:43 All the *p* testify about him that
13: 1 the church at Antioch there were *p*
26:22 nothing beyond what the *p*
28:23 the Law of Moses and from the *P*.
Ro 1: 2 through his *p* in the Holy
3:21 to which the Law and the *P* testify.
11: 3 they have killed your *p*
1Co 12:28 second *p*, third teachers, then
12:29 Are all *p*? Are all teachers?
14:32 The spirits of *p* are subject
Eph 2:20 foundation of the apostles and *p*,
3: 5 Spirit to God's holy apostles and *p*.
4:11 some to be *p*, some
Heb 1: 1 through the *p* at many times
1Pe 1:10 Concerning this salvation, the *p*,
2Pe 1:19 word of the *p* made more certain,
3: 2 spoken in the past by the holy *p*
1Jn 4: 1 because many false *p* have gone out
Rev 11:10 these two *p* had tormented those
18:20 Rejoice, saints and apostles and *p*!

PROPORTION
Dt 16:10 by giving a freewill offering in *p*
16:17 Each of you must bring a gift in *p*

PROPRIETY*
1Ti 2: 9 with decency and *p*,
2:15 in faith, love and holiness with *p*.

PROSPECT*
Pr 10:28 The *p* of the righteous is joy,

PROSPER (PROSPERED PROSPERITY PROSPEROUS PROSPERS)
Dt 5:33 so that you may live and *p*
28:63 pleased the LORD to make you *p*
29: 9 that you may *p* in everything you
1Ki 2: 3 so that you may *p* in all you do
Ezr 6:14 and *p* under the preaching
Pr 11:10 When the righteous *p*, the city
11:25 A generous man will *p*;
17:20 A man of perverse heart does not *p*
28:13 who conceals his sins does not *p*,

Pr 28:25 he who trusts in the LORD will *p*.
Isa 53:10 of the LORD will *p* in his hand.
Jer 12: 1 Why does the way of the wicked *p*?

PROSPERED (PROSPER)
Ge 39: 2 was with Joseph and he *p*,
2Ch 14: 7 So they built and *p*.
31:21 And so he *p*.

PROSPERITY (PROSPER)
Dt 28:11 will grant you abundant *p*—
30:15 I set before you today life and *p*,
Job 36:11 will spend the rest of their days in *p*
Ps 73: 3 when I saw the *p* of the wicked.
122: 9 I will seek your *p*.
128: 2 blessings and *p* will be yours.
Pr 3: 2 and bring you *p*.
13:21 but *p* is the reward of the righteous.
21:21 finds life, *p* and honor.
Isa 45: 7 I bring *p* and create disaster;

PROSPEROUS (PROSPER)
Dt 30: 9 your God will make you most *p*
Jos 1: 8 Then you will be *p* and successful.
Job 42:10 the LORD made him *p* again

PROSPERS (PROSPER)
Ps 1: 3 Whatever he does *p*.
Pr 16:20 gives heed to instruction *p*,
19: 8 he who cherishes understanding *p*.

PROSTITUTE (PROSTITUTES PROSTITUTION)
Lev 20: 6 and spiritists to *p* himself
Nu 15:39 and not *p* yourselves by going
Jos 2: 1 the house of a *p* named Rahab
Pr 6:26 for the *p* reduces you to a loaf
7:10 like a *p* and with crafty intent.
23:27 for a *p* is a deep pit
Eze 16:15 and used your fame to become a *p*.
23: 7 a *p* to all the elite of the Assyrians
Hos 3: 3 you must not be a *p* or be intimate
1Co 6:15 of Christ and unite them with a *p*?
6:16 with a *p* is one with her in body?
Rev 17: 1 you the punishment of the great *p*,

PROSTITUTES (PROSTITUTE)
Pr 29: 3 of *p* squanders his wealth.
Mt 21:31 and the *p* are entering the kingdom
Lk 15:30 property with *p* comes home,
1Co 6: 9 male *p* nor homosexual offenders

PROSTITUTION (PROSTITUTE)
Eze 16:16 where you carried on your *p*.
23: 3 engaging in *p* from their youth.
Hos 4:10 engage in *p* but not increase,

PROSTRATE
Dt 9:18 again I fell *p* before the LORD
1Ki 18:39 they fell *p* and cried, "The LORD

PROTECT (PROTECTED PROTECTION PROTECTS)
Dt 23:14 about in your camp to *p* you
Ps 25:21 integrity and uprightness *p* me,
32: 7 you will *p* me from trouble
40:11 your truth always *p* me.
41: 2 The LORD will *p* him
91:14 I will *p* him, for he acknowledges
140: 1 *p* me from men of violence,
Pr 2:11 Discretion will *p* you,
4: 6 forsake wisdom, and she will *p* you;
Jn 17:11 *p* them by the power of your name
17:15 that you *p* them from the evil one.
2Th 3: 3 and *p* you from the evil one.

PROTECTED (PROTECT)
Jos 24:17 He *p* us on our entire journey
1Sa 30:23 He has *p* us and handed
Ps 37:28 They will be *p* forever,
Jn 17:12 I *p* them and kept them safe

PROTECTION (PROTECT)
Ezr 9: 9 he has given us a wall of *p* in Judah
Ps 5:11 Spread your *p* over them,

PROTECTS (PROTECT)
Ps 116: 6 The LORD *p* the simplehearted;
Pr 2: 8 and *p* the way of his faithful ones.
1Co 13: 7 It always *p*, always trusts,

PROUD (PRIDE)
Ps 31:23 but the *p* he pays back in full.
101: 5 has haughty eyes and a *p* heart,
138: 6 but the *p* he knows from afar.
Pr 3:34 He mocks *p* mockers
16: 5 The LORD detests all the *p*
16:19 than to share plunder with the *p*.
18:12 his downfall a man's heart is *p*,
21: 4 Haughty eyes and a *p* heart,
Isa 2:12 store for all the *p* and lofty,
Ro 12:16 Do not be *p*, but be willing
1Co 13: 4 it does not boast, it is not *p*.
2Ti 3: 2 lovers of money, boastful, *p*,
Jas 4: 6 "God opposes the *p*
1Pe 5: 5 because, "God opposes the *p*

PROVE (PROOF PROVED PROVING)
Pr 29:25 Fear of man will *p* to be a snare,
Jn 8:46 Can any of you *p* me guilty of sin?
Ac 26:20 *p* their repentance by their deeds.
1Co 4: 2 been given a trust must *p* faithful.

PROVED (PROVE)
Ps 51: 4 so that you are *p* right
Mt 11:19 wisdom is *p* right by her actions."
Ro 3: 4 "So that you may be *p* right
1Pe 1: 7 may be *p* genuine and may result

PROVIDE (PROVIDED PROVIDES PROVISION)
Ge 22: 8 "God himself will *p* the lamb
22:14 that place "The LORD will *P*."
Isa 43:20 because I *p* water in the desert
61: 3 and *p* for those who grieve in Zion
1Co 10:13 *p* a way out so that you can stand
1Ti 5: 8 If anyone does not *p*
Tit 3:14 in order that they may *p*

PROVIDED (PROVIDE)
Ps 68:10 O God, you *p* for the poor.
111: 9 He *p* redemption for his people;
Jnh 1:17 But the LORD *p* a great fish
4: 6 Then the LORD God *p* a vine
4: 7 dawn the next day God *p* a worm,
4: 8 God *p* a scorching east wind,
Gal 4:18 to be zealous, *p* the purpose is good
Heb 1: 3 After he had *p* purification for sins,

PROVIDES (PROVIDE)
Ps 111: 5 He *p* food for those who fear him;
Pr 31:15 she *p* food for her family
Eze 18: 7 and *p* clothing for the naked.
1Ti 6:17 who richly *p* us with everything
1Pe 4:11 it with the strength God *p*,

PROVING* (PROVE)
Ac 9:22 by *p* that Jesus is the Christ.
17: 3 and *p* that the Christ had to suffer
18:28 *p* from the Scriptures that Jesus

PROVISION (PROVIDE)
Ro 5:17 who receive God's abundant *p*

PROVOKED
Ecc 7: 9 Do not be quickly *p* in your spirit,
Jer 32:32 Judah have *p* me by all the evil they

PROWLS
1Pe 5: 8 Your enemy the devil *p*

PRUDENCE* (PRUDENT)
Pr 1: 4 for giving *p* to the simple,
8: 5 You who are simple, gain *p*;
8:12 "I, wisdom, dwell together with *p*;
15: 5 whoever heeds correction shows *p*.
19:25 and the simple will learn *p*;

PRUDENT* (PRUDENCE)
Pr 1: 3 acquiring a disciplined and *p* life,
12:16 but a *p* man overlooks an insult.
12:23 A *p* man keeps his knowledge
13:16 Every *p* man acts out of knowledge
14: 8 The wisdom of the *p* is
14:15 a *p* man gives thought to his steps.
14:18 the *p* are crowned with knowledge.
19:14 but a *p* wife is from the LORD.
22: 3 *p* man sees danger and takes
27:12 The *p* see danger and take refuge,
Jer 49: 7 Has counsel perished from the *p*?
Am 5:13 Therefore the *p* man keeps quiet

PRUNES (PRUNING)
Jn 15: 2 that does bear fruit he *p*

PRUNING (PRUNES)
Isa 2: 4 and their spears into *p* hooks.
Joel 3:10 and your *p* hooks into spears.

PSALMS
Eph 5:19 Speak to one another with *p*,
Col 3:16 and as you sing *p*, hymns

PUBLICLY
Ac 20:20 have taught you *p* and from house
1Ti 5:20 Those who sin are to be rebuked *p*,

PUFFS
1Co 8: 1 Knowledge *p* up, but love builds up

PULLING
2Co 10: 8 building you up rather than *p* you

PUNISH (PUNISHED PUNISHES PUNISHMENT)
Ge 15:14 But I will *p* the nation they serve
Ex 32:34 I will *p* them for their sin."
Pr 17:26 It is not good to *p* an innocent man,
23:13 if you *p* him with the rod, he will
Isa 13:11 I will *p* the world for its evil,
Jer 2:19 Your wickedness will *p* you;
21:14 I will *p* you as your deeds deserve,
Zep 1:12 and *p* those who are complacent,
Ac 7: 7 But I will *p* the nation they serve
2Th 1: 8 He will *p* those who do not know
1Pe 2:14 by him to *p* those who do wrong

PUNISHED (PUNISH)
Ezr 9:13 you have *p* us less than our sins
Ps 99: 8 though you *p* their misdeeds.
La 3:39 complain when *p* for his sins?
Mk 12:40 Such men will be *p* most severely."
Lk 23:41 the same sentence? We are *p* justly,
2Th 1: 9 be *p* with everlasting destruction
Heb 10:29 to be *p* who has trampled the Son

PUNISHES (PUNISH)
Heb 12: 6 and he *p* everyone he accepts

PUNISHMENT (PUNISH)
Isa 53: 5 the *p* that brought us peace was
Jer 4:18 This is your *p*.
Mt 25:46 Then they will go away to eternal *p*
Lk 12:48 and does things deserving *p* will be
21:22 For this is the time of *p*
Ro 13: 4 wrath to bring *p* on the wrongdoer.
Heb 2: 2 disobedience received its just *p*,
2Pe 2: 9 while continuing their *p*.

PURCHASED
Ps 74: 2 Remember the people you *p* of old,
Rev 5: 9 with your blood you *p* men for God

PURE (PURIFICATION PURIFIED PURIFIES PURIFY PURITY)
2Sa 22:27 to the *p* you show yourself *p*,

Job 14: 4 Who can bring what is *p*
Ps 19: 9 The fear of the LORD is *p*,
24: 4 who has clean hands and a *p* heart,
51:10 Create in me a *p* heart, O God,
119: 9 can a young man keep his way *p*?
Pr 15:26 those of the *p* are pleasing to him.
20: 9 can say, "I have kept my heart *p*;
Isa 52:11 Come out from it and be *p*,
Hab 1:13 Your eyes are too *p* to look on evil;
Mt 5: 8 Blessed are the *p* in heart,
2Co 11: 2 I might present you as a *p* virgin
Php 4: 8 whatever is *p*, whatever is lovely,
1Ti 1: 5 which comes from a *p* heart
5:22 Keep yourself *p*.
2Ti 2:22 call on the Lord out of a *p* heart.
Tit 1:15 To the *p*, all things are *p*,
2: 5 to be self-controlled and *p*,
Heb 7:26 blameless, *p*, set apart from sinners
13: 4 and the marriage bed kept *p*,
Jas 1:27 that God our Father accepts as *p*
3:17 comes from heaven is first of all *p*;
1Jn 3: 3 him purifies himself, just as he is *p*.

PURGE
Pr 20:30 and beatings *p* the inmost being.

PURIFICATION (PURE)
Heb 1: 3 After he had provided *p* for sins,

PURIFIED (PURE)
Ac 15: 9 for he *p* their hearts by faith.
1Pe 1:22 Now that you have *p* yourselves

PURIFIES* (PURE)
1Jn 1: 7 of Jesus, his Son, *p* us from all sin.
3: 3 who has this hope in him *p* himself,

PURIFY (PURE)
Nu 19:12 He must *p* himself with the water
2Co 7: 1 us *p* ourselves from everything that
Tit 2:14 to *p* for himself a people that are
Jas 4: 8 you sinners, and *p* your hearts,
1Jn 1: 9 and *p* us from all unrighteousness.

PURIM
Est 9:26 Therefore these days were called *P*

PURITY* (PURE)
Hos 8: 5 long will they be incapable of *p*?
2Co 6: 6 in *p*, understanding, patience
1Ti 4:12 in life, in love, in faith and in *p*.
5: 2 as sisters, with absolute *p*.
1Pe 3: 2 when they see the *p* and reverence

PURPLE
Pr 31:22 she is clothed in fine linen and *p*.
Mk 15:17 They put a *p* robe on him, then

PURPOSE (PURPOSED PURPOSES)
Ex 9:16 I have raised you up for this very *p*,
Job 36: 5 he is mighty, and firm in his *p*.
Pr 19:21 but it is the LORD's *p* that prevails
Isa 46:10 I say: My *p* will stand,
55:11 and achieve the *p* for which I sent it
Ac 2:23 handed over to you by God's set *p*
Ro 8:28 have been called according to his *p*.
9:11 in order that God's *p*
9:17 "I raised you up for this very *p*,
1Co 3: 8 the man who waters have one *p*,
2Co 5: 5 who has made us for this very *p*
Gal 4:18 be zealous, provided the *p* is good,
Eph 1:11 in conformity with the *p* of his will,
3:11 according to his eternal *p* which he
Php 2: 2 love, being one in spirit and *p*.
2:13 and to act according to his good *p*.
2Ti 1: 9 but because of his own *p* and grace.

PURPOSED (PURPOSE)
Isa 14:24 and as I have *p*, so it will stand.
14:27 For the LORD Almighty has *p*,
Eph 1: 9 which he *p* in Christ, to be put

PURPOSES (PURPOSE)
Ps 33:10 he thwarts the *p* of the peoples.
Jer 23:20 the *p* of his heart.
32:19 great are your *p* and mighty are

PURSE (PURSES)
Hag 1: 6 to put them in a *p* with holes in it."
Lk 10: 4 Do not take a *p* or bag or sandals;
22:36 "But now if you have a *p*, take it,

PURSES (PURSE)
Lk 12:33 Provide *p* for yourselves that will

PURSUE (PURSUES)
Ps 34:14 seek peace and *p* it.
Pr 15: 9 he loves those who *p* righteousness
Ro 9:30 who did not *p* righteousness,
1Ti 6:11 and *p* righteousness, godliness,
2Ti 2:22 and *p* righteousness, faith,
1Pe 3:11 he must seek peace and *p* it.

PURSUES (PURSUE)
Pr 21:21 He who *p* righteousness and love
28: 1 wicked man flees though no one *p*,

QUAIL
Ex 16:13 That evening *q* came and covered
Nu 11:31 and drove *q* in from the sea.

QUALITIES* (QUALITY)
Da 6: 3 by his exceptional *q* that the king
Ro 1:20 of the world God's invisible *q*—
2Pe 1: 8 For if you possess these *q*

QUALITY (QUALITIES)
1Co 3:13 and the fire will test the *q*

QUARREL (QUARRELING QUARRELS QUARRELSOME)
Pr 15:18 but a patient man calms a *q*.
17:14 Starting a *q* is like breaching a dam;
17:19 He who loves a *q* loves sin;
20: 3 but every fool is quick to *q*.
26:17 in a *q* not his own.
26:20 without gossip a *q* dies down.
2Ti 2:24 And the Lord's servant must not *q*;
Jas 4: 2 You *q* and fight.

QUARRELING (QUARREL)
1Co 3: 3 For since there is jealousy and *q*
2Ti 2:14 before God against *q* about words;

QUARRELS (QUARREL)
Pr 13:10 Pride only breeds *q*,
Isa 45: 9 Woe to him who *q* with his Maker,
2Ti 2:23 because you know they produce *q*.
Jas 4: 1 What causes fights and *q*

QUARRELSOME (QUARREL)
Pr 19:13 a *q* wife is like a constant dripping.
21: 9 than share a house with a *q* wife.
26:21 so is a *q* man for kindling strife.
1Ti 3: 3 not violent but gentle, not *q*,

QUEEN
1Ki 10: 1 When the *q* of Sheba heard about
2Ch 9: 1 When the *q* of Sheba heard
Mt 12:42 The *Q* of the South will rise

QUENCH (QUENCHED)
SS 8: 7 Many waters cannot *q* love;

QUENCHED (QUENCH)
Isa 66:24 nor will their fire be *q*,
Mk 9:48 and the fire is not *q*.'

QUICK-TEMPERED* (TEMPER)
Pr 14:17 A *q* man does foolish things,
14:29 but a *q* man displays folly.
Tit 1: 7 not *q*, not given to drunkenness,

QUIET (QUIETNESS)
Ps 23: 2 he leads me beside *q* waters,
Pr 17: 1 Better a dry crust with peace and *q*
Ecc 9:17 The *q* words of the wise are more
Am 5:13 Therefore the prudent man keeps *q*
Zep 3:17 he will *q* you with his love,
Lk 19:40 he replied, "if they keep *q*,
1Th 4:11 it your ambition to lead a *q* life,
1Ti 2: 2 we may live peaceful and *q* lives
1Pe 3: 4 beauty of a gentle and *q* spirit,

QUIETNESS (QUIET)
Isa 30:15 in *q* and trust is your strength,
32:17 the effect of righteousness will be *q*
1Ti 2:11 A woman should learn in *q*

QUIVER
Ps 127: 5 whose *q* is full of them.

RACE
Ecc 9:11 The *r* is not to the swift
Ac 20:24 if only I may finish the *r*
1Co 9:24 that in a *r* all the runners run,
Gal 2: 2 that I was running or had run my *r*
5: 7 You were running a good *r*.
2Ti 4: 7 I have finished the *r*, I have kept
Heb 12: 1 perseverance the *r* marked out

RACHEL
Daughter of Laban (Ge 29:16); wife of Jacob (Ge 29:28); bore two sons (Ge 30:22–24; 35:16–24; 46:19). Stole Laban's gods (Ge 31:19, 32–35). Death (Ge 35:19–20).

RADIANCE (RADIANT)
Eze 1:28 so was the *r* around him.
Heb 1: 3 The Son is the *r* of God's glory

RADIANT (RADIANCE)
Ex 34:29 he was not aware that his face was *r*
Ps 34: 5 Those who look to him are *r*;
SS 5:10 *Beloved* My lover is *r* and ruddy,
Isa 60: 5 Then you will look and be *r*,
Eph 5:27 her to himself as a *r* church,

RAGE
Ac 4:25 " 'Why do the nations *r*
Col 3: 8 *r*, malice, slander, and filthy

RAGS
Isa 64: 6 our righteous acts are like filthy *r*;

RAHAB
Prostitute of Jericho who hid Israelite spies (Jos 2; 6:22–25; Heb 11:31; Jas 2:25). Mother of Boaz (Mt 1:5).

RAIN (RAINBOW)
Ge 7: 4 from now I will send *r* on the earth
1Ki 17: 1 nor *r* in the next few years
18: 1 and I will send *r* on the land."
Mt 5:45 and sends *r* on the righteous
Jas 5:17 it did not *r* on the land for three
Jude :12 They are clouds without *r*,

RAINBOW (RAIN)
Ge 9:13 I have set my *r* in the clouds,

RAISE (RISE)
Jn 6:39 but *r* them up at the last day.
1Co 15:15 he did not *r* him if in fact the dead

RAISED (RISE)
Isa 52:13 he will be *r* and lifted up
Mt 17:23 on the third day he will be *r* to life
Lk 7:22 the deaf hear, the dead are *r*,
Ac 2:24 But God *r* him from the dead,
Ro 4:25 was *r* to life for our justification.
6: 4 as Christ was *r* from the dead
8:11 And if the Spirit of him who *r* Jesus
10: 9 in your heart that God *r* him
1Co 15: 4 that he was *r* on the third day
15:20 But Christ has indeed been *r*

RALLY*
Isa 11:10 the nations will *r* to him,

RAM (RAMS)
Ge 22:13 there in a thicket he saw a *r* caught
Da 8: 3 before me was a *r* with two horns,

RAMPART*
Ps 91: 4 will be your shield and *r*.

RAMS (RAM)
1Sa 15:22 to heed is better than the fat of *r*.
Mic 6: 7 pleased with thousands of *r*,

RAN (RUN)
Jnh 1: 3 But Jonah *r* away from the LORD

RANSOM (RANSOMED)
Isa 50: 2 Was my arm too short to *r* you?
Hos 13:14 "I will *r* them from the power
Mt 20:28 and to give his life as a *r* for many."
Mk 10:45 and to give his life as a *r* for many."
1Ti 2: 6 who gave himself as a *r* for all men
Heb 9:15 as a *r* to set them free

RANSOMED (RANSOM)
Isa 35:10 and the *r* of the LORD will return.

RARE
Pr 20:15 that speak knowledge are a *r* jewel.

RAVEN (RAVENS)
Ge 8: 7 made in the ark and sent out a *r*,
Job 38:41 Who provides food for the *r*

RAVENS (RAVEN)
1Ki 17: 6 The *r* brought him bread
Ps 147: 9 and for the young *r* when they call.
Lk 12:24 Consider the *r*: They do not sow

READ (READING READS)
Dt 17:19 he is to *r* it all the days of his life
Jos 8:34 Joshua *r* all the words of the law—
2Ki 23: 2 He *r* in their hearing all the words
Ne 8: 8 They *r* from the Book of the Law
Jer 36: 6 and *r* to the people from the scroll
2Co 3: 2 known and *r* by everybody.

READING (READ)
1Ti 4:13 to the public *r* of Scripture,

READS (READ)
Rev 1: 3 Blessed is the one who *r* the words

REAFFIRM
2Co 2: 8 therefore, to *r* your love for him.

REAL* (REALITIES REALITY)
Jn 6:55 is *r* food and my blood is *r* drink.
1Jn 2:27 all things and as that anointing is *r*,

REALITIES* (REAL)
Heb 10: 1 are coming—not the *r* themselves.

REALITY* (REAL)
Col 2:17 the *r*, however, is found in Christ.

REALM (REALMS)
Hab 2: 9 "Woe to him who builds his *r*

REALMS (REALM)
Eph 1: 3 the heavenly *r* with every spiritual
2: 6 in the heavenly *r* in Christ Jesus,

REAP (REAPER REAPS)
Job 4: 8 and those who sow trouble *r* it.
Ps 126: 5 will *r* with songs of joy.
Hos 8: 7 and *r* the whirlwind.
10:12 *r* the fruit of unfailing love,
Jn 4:38 you to *r* what you have not worked
Ro 6:22 the benefit you *r* leads to holiness,
2Co 9: 6 generously will also *r* generously.
Gal 6: 8 from that nature will *r* destruction;

REAPER (REAP)
Jn 4:36 and the *r* may be glad together.

REAPS (REAP)
Pr 11:18 who sows righteousness *r* a sure
22: 8 He who sows wickedness *r* trouble,
Gal 6: 7 A man *r* what he sows.

REASON (REASONED)
Ge 2:24 For this *r* a man will leave his
Isa 1:18 "Come now, let us *r* together,"
Mt 19: 5 'For this *r* a man will leave his
Jn 12:27 it was for this very *r* I came
15:25 'They hated me without *r*.'
1Pe 3:15 to give the *r* for the hope that you
2Pe 1: 5 For this very *r*, make every effort

REASONED (REASON)
1Co 13:11 thought like a child, I *r* like a child.

REBEKAH
Sister of Laban, secured as bride for Isaac (Ge 24). Mother of Esau and Jacob (Ge 25:19–26). Taken by Abimelech as sister of Isaac; returned (Ge 26:1–11). Encouraged Jacob to trick Isaac out of blessing (Ge 27:1–17).

REBEL (REBELLED REBELLION REBELS)
Nu 14: 9 Only do not *r* against the LORD.
1Sa 12:14 and do not *r* against his commands,
Mt 10:21 children will *r* against their parents

REBELLED (REBEL)
Ps 78:56 and *r* against the Most High;
Isa 63:10 Yet they *r*

REBELLION (REBEL)
Ex 34: 7 and forgiving wickedness, *r* and sin
Nu 14:18 in love and forgiving sin and *r*.
1Sa 15:23 For *r* is like the sin of divination,
2Th 2: 3 will not come! until the *r* occurs

REBELS (REBEL)
Ro 13: 2 he who *r* against the authority is
1Ti 1: 9 but for lawbreakers and *r*,

REBIRTH* (BEAR)
Tit 3: 5 us through the washing of *r*

REBUILD (BUILD)
Ezr 5: 2 set to work to *r* the house of God
Ne 2:17 let us *r* the wall of Jerusalem,
Ps 102:16 For the LORD will *r* Zion
Da 9:25 and *r* Jerusalem until the Anointed
Am 9:14 they will *r* the ruined cities
Ac 15:16 Its ruins I will *r*,

REBUILT (BUILD)
Zec 1:16 and there my house will be *r*.

REBUKE (REBUKED REBUKES REBUKING)
Lev 19:17 *R* your neighbor frankly
Ps 141: 5 let him *r* me—it is oil on my head.
Pr 3:11 and do not resent his *r*,
9: 8 *r* a wise man and he will love you.
15:31 He who listens to a life-giving *r*
17:10 A *r* impresses a man
19:25 *r* a discerning man, and he will gain
25:12 is a wise man's *r* to a listening ear.
27: 5 Better is open *r*
30: 6 or he will *r* you and prove you a liar
Ecc 7: 5 It is better to heed a wise man's *r*
Isa 54: 9 never to *r* you again.
Jer 2:19 your backsliding will *r* you.
Lk 17: 3 "If your brother sins, *r* him,
1Ti 5: 1 Do not *r* an older man harshly,
2Ti 4: 2 correct, *r* and encourage—
Tit 1:13 Therefore, *r* them sharply,
2:15 Encourage and *r* with all authority.
Rev 3:19 Those whom I love I *r*

REBUKED (REBUKE)
Mk 16:14 he *r* them for their lack of faith
1Ti 5:20 Those who sin are to be *r* publicly,

REBUKES (REBUKE)
Job 22: 4 "Is it for your piety that he *r* you
Pr 28:23 He who *r* a man will
29: 1 remains stiff-necked after many *r*
Heb 12: 5 do not lose heart when he *r* you,

REBUKING (REBUKE)
2Ti 3:16 *r*, correcting and training

RECEIVE (RECEIVED RECEIVES)
Mt 10:41 a righteous man will *r* a righteous
Mk 10:15 anyone who will not *r* the kingdom
Jn 20:22 and said, "*R* the Holy Spirit.
Ac 1: 8 you will *r* power when the Holy
2:38 you will *r* the gift of the Holy Spirit
19: 2 "Did you *r* the Holy Spirit
20:35 'It is more blessed to give than to *r*
1Co 9:14 the gospel should *r* their living
2Co 6:17 and I will *r* you."
1Ti 1:16 believe on him and *r* eternal life.
Jas 1: 7 should not think he will *r* anything
2Pe 1:11 and you will *r* a rich welcome
1Jn 3:22 and *r* from him anything we ask,
Rev 4:11 to *r* glory and honor and power,
5:12 to *r* power and wealth and wisdom

RECEIVED (RECEIVE)
Mt 6: 2 they have *r* their reward in full.
10: 8 Freely you have *r*, freely give.
Mk 11:24 believe that you have *r* it,
Jn 1:12 Yet to all who *r* him,
1:16 his grace we have all *r* one blessing
Ac 8:17 and they *r* the Holy Spirit.
10:47 They have *r* the Holy Spirit just
Ro 8:15 but you *r* the Spirit of sonship.
1Co 11:23 For I *r* from the Lord what I
2Co 1: 4 the comfort we ourselves have *r*
Col 2: 6 just as you *r* Christ Jesus as Lord,
1Pe 4:10 should use whatever gift he has *r*

RECEIVES (RECEIVE)
Pr 18:22 and *r* favor from the LORD.
27:21 but man is tested by the praise he *r*.
Mt 7: 8 everyone who asks *r*; he who seeks
10:40 he who *r* me *r* the one who sent me.
10:40 "He who *r* you *r* me, and he who
Ac 10:43 believes in him *r* forgiveness of sins

RECITE
Ps 45: 1 as I *r* my verses for the king;

RECKLESS
Pr 12:18 *R* words pierce like a sword,
14:16 but a fool is hotheaded and *r*.

RECKONING
Isa 10: 3 What will you do on the day of *r*,
Hos 9: 7 the days of *r* are at hand.

RECLAIM* (CLAIM)
Isa 11:11 time to *r* the remnant that is left

RECOGNITION (RECOGNIZE)
1Co 16:18 Such men deserve *r*.
1Ti 5: 3 Give proper *r* to those widows who

RECOGNIZE (RECOGNITION RECOGNIZED)
Mt 7:16 By their fruit you will *r* them.
1Jn 4: 2 This is how you can *r* the Spirit
4: 6 This is how we *r* the Spirit of truth

RECOGNIZED (RECOGNIZE)
Mt 12:33 for a tree is *r* by its fruit.
Ro 7:13 in order that sin might be *r* as sin,

RECOMPENSE*
Isa 40:10 and his *r* accompanies him.

Isa 62:11 and his *r* accompanies him.' "

RECONCILE* (RECONCILED RECONCILIATION RECONCILING)
Ac 7:26 He tried to *r* them by saying, 'Men,
Eph 2:16 in this one body to *r* both of them
Col 1:20 him to *r* to himself all things,

RECONCILED* (RECONCILE)
Mt 5:24 First go and be *r* to your brother;
Lk 12:58 try hard to be *r* to him on the way,
Ro 5:10 how much more, having been *r,*
5:10 we were *r* to him through the death
1Co 7:11 or else be *r* to her husband.
2Co 5:18 who *r* us to himself through Christ
5:20 you on Christ's behalf: Be *r* to God.
Col 1:22 he has *r* you by Christ's physical

RECONCILIATION* (RECONCILE)
Ro 5:11 whom we have now received *r.*
11:15 For if their rejection is the *r*
2Co 5:18 and gave us the ministry of *r:*
5:19 committed to us the message of *r.*

RECONCILING* (RECONCILE)
2Co 5:19 that God was *r* the world to himself

RECORD (RECORDED)
Ps 130: 3 If you, O LORD, kept a *r* of sins,
Hos 13:12 his sins are kept on *r.*
1Co 13: 5 is not easily angered, it keeps no *r*

RECORDED (RECORD)
Job 19:23 "Oh, that my words were *r,*
Jn 20:30 which are not *r* in this book.

RECOUNT*
Ps 40: 5 no one can *r* to you;
79:13 we will *r* your praise.
119:13 With my lips I *r*

RED
Ex 15: 4 are drowned in the *R* Sea.
Ps 106: 9 He rebuked the *R* Sea,
Pr 23:31 Do not gaze at wine when it is *r,*
Isa 1:18 though they are *r* as crimson,

REDEEM (KINSMAN-REDEEMER REDEEMED REDEEMER REDEEMS REDEMPTION)
Ex 6: 6 will *r* you with an outstretched arm
2Sa 7:23 on earth that God went out to *r*
Ps 44:26 *r* us because of your unfailing love.
49: 7 No man can *r* the life of another
49:15 God will *r* my life from the grave;
130: 8 He himself will *r* Israel
Hos 13:14 I will *r* them from death.
Gal 4: 5 under law, to *r* those under law,
Tit 2:14 for us to *r* us from all wickedness

REDEEMED (REDEEM)
Job 33:28 He *r* my soul from going
Ps 71:23 I, whom you have *r.*
107: 2 Let the *r* of the LORD say this—
Isa 35: 9 But only the *r* will walk there,
63: 9 In his love and mercy he *r* them;
Gal 3:13 Christ *r* us from the curse
1Pe 1:18 or gold that you were *r*

REDEEMER (REDEEM)
Job 19:25 I know that my *R* lives,
Ps 19:14 O LORD, my Rock and my *R.*
Isa 44: 6 and *R,* the LORD Almighty:
48:17 your *R,* the Holy One of Israel:
59:20 "The *R* will come to Zion,

REDEEMS (REDEEM)
Ps 34:22 The LORD *r* his servants;
103: 4 he *r* my life from the pit

REDEMPTION (REDEEM)
Ps 130: 7 and with him is full *r.*
Lk 21:28 because your *r* is drawing near."
Ro 3:24 grace through the *r* that came
8:23 as sons, the *r* of our bodies.
1Co 1:30 our righteousness, holiness and *r.*
Eph 1: 7 In him we have *r* through his blood
1:14 until the *r* of those who are God's
4:30 you were sealed for the day of *r.*
Col 1:14 in whom we have *r,* the forgiveness
Heb 9:12 having obtained eternal *r.*

REED
Isa 42: 3 A bruised *r* he will not break,
Mt 12:20 A bruised *r* he will not break,

REFINE*
Jer 9: 7 "See, I will *r* and test them,
Zec 13: 9 I will *r* them like silver
Mal 3: 3 and *r* them like gold and silver.

REFLECT (REFLECTS)
2Co 3:18 unveiled faces all *r* the Lord's

REFLECTS (REFLECT)
Pr 27:19 As water *r* a face,

REFRESH (REFRESHED REFRESHING)
Phm :20 in the Lord; *r* my heart in Christ.

REFRESHED (REFRESH)
Pr 11:25 refreshes others will himself be *r.*

REFRESHING* (REFRESH)
Ac 3:19 that times of *r* may come

REFUGE
Nu 35:11 towns to be your cities of *r,*
Dt 33:27 The eternal God is your *r,*
Jos 20: 2 to designate the cities of *r,*
Ru 2:12 wings you have come to take *r.*"
2Sa 22: 3 God is my rock, in whom I take *r,*
22:31 a shield for all who take *r* in him.
Ps 2:12 Blessed are all who take *r* in him.
5:11 But let all who take *r* in you be glad
9: 9 The LORD is a *r* for the oppressed,
16: 1 for in you I take *r.*
17: 7 those who take *r* in you
18: 2 God is my rock, in whom I take *r.*
31: 2 be my rock of *r,*
34: 8 blessed is the man who takes *r*
36: 7 find *r* in the shadow of your wings.
46: 1 God is our *r* and strength,
62: 8 for God is our *r.*
71: 1 In you, O LORD, I have taken *r;*
91: 2 "He is my *r* and my fortress,
144: 2 my shield, in whom I take *r,*
Pr 14:26 and for his children it will be a *r.*
30: 5 a shield to those who take *r* in him.
Na 1: 7 a *r* in times of trouble.

REFUSE (REFUSED)
Jn 5:40 yet you *r* to come to me to have life

REFUSED (REFUSE)
2Th 2:10 because they *r* to love the truth
Rev 16: 9 but they *r* to repent and glorify him

REGARD (REGARDS)
1Th 5:13 Hold them in the highest *r* in love

REGARDS (REGARD)
Ro 14:14 But if anyone *r* something

REGRET
2Co 7:10 leads to salvation and leaves no *r,*

REHOBOAM

Son of Solomon (1Ki 11:43; 1Ch 3:10). Harsh treatment of subjects caused divided kingdom (1Ki 12:1–24; 14:21–31; 2Ch 10–12).

REIGN (REIGNED REIGNS)
Ex 15:18 The LORD will *r*
Ps 68:16 mountain where God chooses to *r,*
Isa 9: 7 He will *r* on David's throne
24:23 for the LORD Almighty will *r*
32: 1 See, a king will *r* in righteousness
Jer 23: 5 a King who will *r* wisely
Lk 1:33 and he will *r* over the house
Ro 6:12 Therefore do not let sin *r*
1Co 15:25 For he must *r* until he has put all
2Ti 2:12 we will also *r* with him.
Rev 11:15 and he will *r* for ever and ever."
20: 6 will *r* with him for a thousand years
22: 5 And they will *r* for ever and ever.

REIGNED (REIGN)
Ro 5:21 so that, just as sin *r* in death,
Rev 20: 4 and *r* with Christ a thousand years.

REIGNS (REIGN)
Ps 9: 7 The LORD *r* forever;
47: 8 God *r* over the nations;
93: 1 The LORD *r,* he is robed
96:10 among the nations, "The LORD *r*
97: 1 The LORD *r,* let the earth be glad;
99: 1 The LORD *r,* / let the nations tremble;
146:10 The LORD *r* forever,
Isa 52: 7 "Your God *r!*"
Rev 19: 6 For our Lord God Almighty *r.*

REIN
Jas 1:26 and yet does not keep a tight *r*

REJECT (REJECTED REJECTION REJECTS)
Ps 94:14 For the LORD will not *r* his people
Ro 11: 1 I ask then: Did God *r* his people?

REJECTED (REJECT)
1Sa 8: 7 it is not you they have *r,*
1Ki 19:10 The Israelites have *r* your covenant
2Ki 17:15 They *r* his decrees
Ps 66:20 who has not *r* my prayer
118:22 The stone the builders *r*
Isa 5:24 for they have *r* the law
41: 9 chosen you and have not *r* you.
53: 3 He was despised and *r* by men,
Jer 8: 9 Since they have *r* the word
Mt 21:42 " 'The stone the builders *r*
1Ti 4: 4 nothing is to be *r* if it is received
1Pe 2: 4 *r* by men but chosen by God
2: 7 "The stone the builders *r*

REJECTION* (REJECT)
Ro 11:15 For if their *r* is the reconciliation

REJECTS (REJECT)
Lk 10:16 but he who *r* me *r* him who sent me
Jn 3:36 whoever *r* the Son will not see life,
1Th 4: 8 he who *r* this instruction does not

REJOICE (JOY)
Dt 12: 7 shall *r* in everything you have put
1Ch 16:10 of those who seek the LORD *r.*
16:31 Let the heavens *r,* let the earth be
Ps 2:11 and *r* with trembling.
5:11 those who love your name may *r*
9:14 and there *r* in your salvation.
34: 2 let the afflicted hear and *r.*
63:11 But the king will *r* in God;
66: 6 come, let us *r* in him.
68: 3 and *r* before God;
105: 3 of those who seek the LORD *r.*
118:24 let us *r* and be glad in it.
119:14 I *r* in following your statutes
119:162 I *r* in your promise
149: 2 Let Israel *r* in their Maker;
Pr 5:18 may you *r* in the wife of your youth
23:25 may she who gave you birth *r!*
24:17 stumbles, do not let your heart *r,*
Isa 9: 3 as men *r*
35: 1 the wilderness will *r* and blossom.
61: 7 they will *r* in their inheritance;
62: 5 so will your God *r* over you.
Jer 31:12 they will *r* in the bounty

Zep 3:17 he will *r* over you with singing."
Zec 9: 9 *R* greatly, O Daughter of Zion!
Lk 6:23 "*R* in that day and leap for joy,
10:20 but *r* that your names are written
15: 6 '*R* with me; I have found my lost
15: 9 '*R* with me; I have found my lost
Ro 5: 2 And we *r* in the hope of the glory
12:15 Rejoice with those who *r;* mourn
Php 2:17 I am glad and *r* with all of you.
3: 1 Finally, my brothers, *r* in the Lord!
4: 4 *R* in the Lord always.
1Pe 4:13 But *r* that you participate
Rev 19: 7 Let us *r* and be glad

REJOICES (JOY)
Ps 13: 5 my heart *r* in your salvation.
16: 9 my heart is glad and my tongue *r;*
Isa 61:10 my soul *r* in my God.
62: 5 as a bridegroom *r* over his bride,
Lk 1:47 and my spirit *r* in God my Savior,
Ac 2:26 my heart is glad and my tongue *r;*
1Co 12:26 if one part is honored, every part *r*
13: 6 delight in evil but *r* with the truth.

REJOICING (JOY)
2Sa 6:12 to the City of David with *r.*
Ne 12:43 *r* because God had given them
Ps 30: 5 but *r* comes in the morning.
Lk 15: 7 in the same way there will be more *r*
Ac 5:41 *r* because they had been counted
2Co 6:10 sorrowful, yet always *r;* poor,

RELATIVES
Pr 19: 7 A poor man is shunned by all his *r*
Mk 6: 4 among his *r* and in his own house is
Lk 21:16 betrayed even by parents, brothers, *r*
1Ti 5: 8 If anyone does not provide for his *r*

RELEASE (RELEASED)
Isa 61: 1 and *r* from darkness,
Lk 4:18 to *r* the oppressed,

RELEASED (RELEASE)
Ro 7: 6 we have been *r* from the law
Rev 20: 7 Satan will be *r* from his prison

RELENTED (RELENTS)
Ex 32:14 the LORD *r* and did not bring
Ps 106:45 and out of his great love he *r.*

RELENTS* (RELENTED)
Joel 2:13 and he *r* from sending calamity.
Jnh 4: 2 a God who *r* from sending calamity

RELIABLE (RELY)
Pr 22:21 teaching you true and *r* words,
Jn 8:26 But he who sent me is *r,*
2Ti 2: 2 witnesses entrust to *r* men who will

RELIANCE* (RELY)
Pr 25:19 is *r* on the unfaithful in times

RELIED (RELY)
2Ch 13:18 were victorious because they *r*
16: 8 Yet when you *r* on the LORD,
Ps 71: 6 From birth I have *r* on you;

RELIEF
Job 35: 9 they plead for *r* from the arm
Ps 94:13 you grant him *r* from days
143: 1 come to my *r.*
La 3:49 without *r,*
3:56 to my cry for *r.*"
2Th 1: 7 and give *r* to you who are troubled,

RELIGION* (RELIGIOUS)
Ac 25:19 dispute with him about their own *r*
26: 5 to the strictest sect of our *r,*
1Ti 5: 4 all to put their *r* into practice
Jas 1:26 himself and his *r* is worthless.
1:27 *R* that God our Father accepts

RELIGIOUS (RELIGION)
Jas 1:26 If anyone considers himself *r*

RELY (RELIABLE RELIANCE RELIED)
Isa 50:10 and *r* on his God.
Eze 33:26 you then possess the land? You *r*
2Co 1: 9 this happened that we might not *r*
Gal 3:10 All who *r* on observing the law are
1Jn 4:16 and *r* on the love God has for us.

REMAIN (REMAINS)
Nu 33:55 allow to *r* will become barbs
Ps 102:27 But you *r* the same,
Jn 1:32 from heaven as a dove and *r* on him
15: 4 *R* in me, and I will *r* in you.
15: 7 If you *r* in me and my words
15: 9 Now *r* in my love.
Ro 13: 8 Let no debt *r* outstanding,
1Co 13:13 And now these three *r:* faith,
2Ti 2:13 he will *r* faithful,
Heb 1:11 They will perish, but you *r;*
1Jn 2:27 just as it has taught you, *r* in him.

REMAINS (REMAIN)
Ps 146: 6 the LORD, who *r* faithful forever.
Heb 7: 3 Son of God he *r* a priest forever.

REMEDY
Isa 3: 7 "I have no *r.*

REMEMBER (REMEMBERED REMEMBERS REMEMBRANCE)
Ge 9:15 I will *r* my covenant between me
Ex 20: 8 "*R* the Sabbath day
33:13 *R* that this nation is your people."
Dt 5:15 *R* that you were slaves in Egypt
1Ch 16:12 *R* the wonders he has done,
Job 36:24 *R* to extol his work,
Ps 25: 6 *R,* O LORD, your great mercy
63: 6 On my bed I *r* you;
74: 2 *R* the people you purchased of old,
77:11 I will *r* the deeds of the LORD;
Ecc 12: 1 *R* your Creator
Isa 46: 8 "*R* this, fix it in mind,
Jer 31:34 and will *r* their sins no more."
Hab 3: 2 in wrath *r* mercy.
Lk 1:72 and to *r* his holy covenant,
Gal 2:10 we should continue to *r* the poor,
Php 1: 3 I thank my God every time I *r* you.
2Ti 2: 8 *R* Jesus Christ, raised
Heb 8:12 and will *r* their sins no more."

REMEMBERED (REMEMBER)
Ex 2:24 he *r* his covenant with Abraham,
3:15 am to be *r* from generation
Ps 98: 3 He has *r* his love
106:45 for their sake he *r* his covenant
111: 4 He has caused his wonders to be *r;*
136:23 to the One who *r* us
Isa 65:17 The former things will not be *r,*
Eze 18:22 offenses he has committed will be *r*
33:13 things he has done will be *r;*

REMEMBERS (REMEMBER)
Ps 103:14 he *r* that we are dust.
111: 5 he *r* his covenant forever.
Isa 43:25 and *r* your sins no more.

REMEMBRANCE (REMEMBER)
Lk 22:19 given for you; do this in *r* of me."
1Co 11:24 which is for you; do this in *r* of me
11:25 whenever you drink it, in *r* of me."

REMIND
Jn 14:26 will *r* you of everything I have said
2Pe 1:12 I will always *r* you of these things,

REMNANT
Ezr 9: 8 has been gracious in leaving us a *r*
Isa 11:11 time to reclaim the *r* that is left
Jer 23: 3 "I myself will gather the *r*
Zec 8:12 inheritance to the *r* of this people.

Ro 11: 5 the present time there is a *r* chosen

REMOVED
Ps 30:11 you *r* my sackcloth and clothed me
103:12 so far has he *r* our transgressions
Jn 20: 1 and saw that the stone had been *r*

REND
Joel 2:13 *R* your heart

RENEW (RENEWAL RENEWED RENEWING)
Ps 51:10 and *r* a steadfast spirit within me.
Isa 40:31 will *r* their strength.

RENEWAL (RENEW)
Isa 57:10 You found *r* of your strength,
Tit 3: 5 of rebirth and *r* by the Holy Spirit,

RENEWED (RENEW)
Ps 103: 5 that your youth is *r* like the eagle's.
2Co 4:16 yet inwardly we are being *r* day

RENEWING* (RENEW)
Ro 12: 2 transformed by the *r* of your mind.

RENOUNCE (RENOUNCED RENOUNCES)
Da 4:27 *R* your sins by doing what is right,

RENOUNCED (RENOUNCE)
2Co 4: 2 we have *r* secret and shameful

RENOUNCES (RENOUNCE)
Pr 28:13 confesses and *r* them finds

RENOWN*
Ge 6: 4 were the heroes of old, men of *r.*
Ps 102:12 *r* endures through all generations.
135:13 *r,* O LORD, through all
Isa 26: 8 your name and *r*
55:13 This will be for the LORD's *r,*
63:12 to gain for himself everlasting *r,*
Jer 13:11 to be my people for my *r* and praise
32:20 have gained the *r* that is still yours.
33: 9 Then this city will bring me *r,* joy,
49:25 the city of *r* not been abandoned,
Eze 26:17 How you are destroyed, O city of *r,*
Hos 12: 5 the LORD is his name of *r!*

REPAID (PAY)
Lk 6:34 to 'sinners,' expecting to be *r* in full
14:14 you will be *r* at the resurrection
Col 3:25 Anyone who does wrong will be *r*

REPAY (PAY)
Dt 7:10 But those who hate him he will *r*
32:35 It is mine to avenge; I will *r.*
Ru 2:12 May the LORD *r* you
Ps 103:10 or *r* us according to our iniquities.
116:12 How can I *r* the LORD
Jer 25:14 I will *r* them according
Ro 12:17 Do not *r* anyone evil for evil.
12:19 "It is mine to avenge; I will *r,*"
1Pe 3: 9 Do not *r* evil with evil

REPAYING (PAY)
2Ch 6:23 *r* the guilty by bringing
1Ti 5: 4 so *r* their parents and grandparents

REPEATED
Heb 10: 1 the same sacrifices *r* endlessly year

REPENT (REPENTANCE REPENTED REPENTS)
1Ki 8:47 *r* and plead with you in the land
Job 36:10 commands them to *r* of their evil.
42: 6 and *r* in dust and ashes."
Jer 15:19 "If you *r,* I will restore you
Eze 18:30 *R!* Turn away from all your
18:32 *R* and live! "Take up a lament
Mt 3: 2 "*R,* for the kingdom of heaven is
4:17 "*R,* for the kingdom of heaven is
Mk 6:12 and preached that people should *r.*

Lk 13: 3 unless you *r,* you too will all perish.
Ac 2:38 Peter replied, "*R* and be baptized,
3:19 *R,* then, and turn to God,
17:30 all people everywhere to *r.*
26:20 also, I preached that they should *r*
Rev 2: 5 *R* and do the things you did at first.

REPENTANCE (REPENT)
Isa 30:15 "In *r* and rest is your salvation,
Mt 3: 8 Produce fruit in keeping with *r.*
Mk 1: 4 a baptism of *r* for the forgiveness
Lk 3: 8 Produce fruit in keeping with *r.*
5:32 call the righteous, but sinners to *r.*"
24:47 and *r* and forgiveness of sins will be
Ac 20:21 that they must turn to God in *r*
26:20 and prove their *r* by their deeds.
Ro 2: 4 kindness leads you toward *r?*
2Co 7:10 Godly sorrow brings *r* that leads
2Pe 3: 9 but everyone to come to *r.*

REPENTED (REPENT)
Mt 11:21 they would have *r* long ago

REPENTS (REPENT)
Lk 15: 7 in heaven over one sinner who *r*
15:10 of God over one sinner who *r.*"
17: 3 rebuke him, and if he *r,* forgive him

REPORTS
Ex 23: 1 "Do not spread false *r.*

REPOSES*
Pr 14:33 Wisdom *r* in the heart

REPRESENTATION*
Heb 1: 3 and the exact *r* of his being,

REPROACH
Job 27: 6 my conscience will not *r* me
Isa 51: 7 Do not fear the *r* of men
1Ti 3: 2 Now the overseer must be above *r,*

REPUTATION
1Ti 3: 7 also have a good *r* with outsiders,

REQUESTS
Ps 20: 5 May the LORD grant all your *r.*
Php 4: 6 with thanksgiving, present your *r*

REQUIRE (REQUIRED REQUIRES)
Mic 6: 8 And what does the LORD *r* of you

REQUIRED (REQUIRE)
1Co 4: 2 it is *r* that those who have been

REQUIRES (REQUIRE)
1Ki 2: 3 what the LORD your God *r:*
Heb 9:22 the law *r* that nearly everything be

RESCUE (RESCUED RESCUES)
Ps 22: 8 let the LORD *r* him.
31: 2 come quickly to my *r;*
69:14 *R* me from the mire,
91:14 says the LORD, "I will *r* him;
143: 9 *R* me from my enemies, O LORD,
Da 6:20 been able to *r* you from the lions?"
Ro 7:24 Who will *r* me from this body
Gal 1: 4 himself for our sins to *r* us
2Pe 2: 9 how to *r* godly men from trials

RESCUED (RESCUE)
Ps 18:17 He *r* me from my powerful enemy,
Pr 11: 8 The righteous man is *r*
Col 1:13 For he has *r* us from the dominion

RESCUES (RESCUE)
Da 6:27 He *r* and he saves;
1Th 1:10 who *r* us from the coming wrath.

RESENT* (RESENTFUL RESENTS)
Pr 3:11 and do not *r* his rebuke,

RESENTFUL* (RESENT)
2Ti 2:24 to everyone, able to teach, not *r.*

RESENTS* (RESENT)
Pr 15:12 A mocker *r* correction;

RESERVE (RESERVED)
1Ki 19:18 Yet I *r* seven thousand in Israel—

RESERVED (RESERVE)
Ro 11: 4 "I have *r* for myself seven

RESIST (RESISTED RESISTS)
Da 11:32 know their God will firmly *r* him.
Mt 5:39 I tell you, Do not *r* an evil person.
Lk 21:15 of your adversaries will be able to *r*
Jas 4: 7 *R* the devil, and he will flee
1Pe 5: 9 *R* him, standing firm in the faith,

RESISTED (RESIST)
Job 9: 4 Who has *r* him and come out

RESISTS* (RESIST)
Ro 9:19 For who *r* his will?" But who are

RESOLVED
Ps 17: 3 I have *r* that my mouth will not sin.
Da 1: 8 But Daniel *r* not to defile himself
1Co 2: 2 For I *r* to know nothing while I was

RESOUNDING*
Ps 150: 5 praise him with *r* cymbals.
1Co 13: 1 I am only a *r* gong or a clanging

RESPECT (RESPECTABLE RESPECTED RESPECTS)
Lev 19: 3 " 'Each of you must *r* his mother
19:32 show *r* for the elderly and revere
Pr 11:16 A kindhearted woman gains *r,*
Mal 1: 6 where is the *r* due me?" says
Eph 5:33 and the wife must *r* her husband.
6: 5 obey your earthly masters with *r*
1Th 4:12 so that your daily life may win the *r*
5:12 to *r* those who work hard
1Ti 3: 4 children obey him with proper *r.*
3: 8 are to be men worthy of *r,* sincere,
3:11 are to be women worthy of *r,*
6: 1 their masters worthy of full *r,*
Tit 2: 2 worthy of *r,* self-controlled,
1Pe 2:17 Show proper *r* to everyone:
3: 7 them with *r* as the weaker partner
3:16 But do this with gentleness and *r,*

RESPECTABLE* (RESPECT)
1Ti 3: 2 self-controlled, *r,* hospitable,

RESPECTED (RESPECT)
Pr 31:23 Her husband is *r* at the city gate,

RESPECTS (RESPECT)
Pr 13:13 he who *r* a command is rewarded.

RESPLENDENT*
Ps 76: 4 You are *r* with light,
132:18 but the crown on his head will be *r*

RESPOND
Ps 102:17 He will *r* to the prayer
Hos 2:21 "I will *r* to the skies,

RESPONSIBILITY (RESPONSIBLE)
Ac 18: 6 your own heads! I am clear of my *r.*

RESPONSIBLE (RESPONSIBILITY)
Nu 1:53 The Levites are to be *r* for the care
1Co 7:24 Brothers, each man, as *r* to God,

REST (RESTED RESTS SABBATH-REST)
Ex 31:15 the seventh day is a Sabbath of *r,*"
33:14 go with you, and I will give you *r.*"
Lev 25: 5 The land is to have a year of *r.*
Dt 31:16 going to *r* with your fathers,
Jos 14:15 Then the land had *r* from war.
Jos 21:44 The LORD gave them *r*
1Ki 5: 4 The LORD my god has given me *r*
1Ch 22: 9 who will be a man of peace and *r,*
Job 3:17 and there the weary are at *r.*
Ps 16: 9 my body also will *r* secure,
33:22 May your unfailing love *r* upon us,
62: 1 My soul finds *r* in God alone;
62: 5 Find *r,* O my soul, in God alone;
90:17 of the Lord our God *r* upon us;
91: 1 will *r* in the shadow
95:11 "They shall never enter my *r.*"
Pr 6:10 a little folding of the hands to *r*—
Isa 11: 2 Spirit of the LORD will *r* on him—
11:10 and his place of *r* will be glorious.
30:15 "In repentance and *r* is your
32:18 in undisturbed places of *r.*
57:20 which cannot *r,*
Jer 6:16 and you will find *r* for your souls.
47: 6 'how long till you *r?*
Mt 11:28 and burdened, and I will give you *r.*
2Co 12: 9 so that Christ's power may *r* on me
Heb 3:11 'They shall never enter my *r.*' "
4: 3 'They shall never enter my *r.*' "
4:10 for anyone who enters God's *r*
Rev 14:13 "they will *r* from their labor,

RESTED (REST)
Ge 2: 2 so on the seventh day he *r*
Heb 4: 4 "And on the seventh day God *r*

RESTITUTION
Ex 22: 3 "A thief must certainly make *r,*
Lev 6: 5 He must make *r* in full, add a fifth
Nu 5: 8 the *r* belongs to the LORD

RESTORE (RESTORES)
Ps 51:12 *R* to me the joy of your salvation
80: 3 *R* us, O God;
126: 4 *R* our fortunes, O LORD,
Jer 31:18 *R* me, and I will return,
La 5:21 *R* us to yourself, O LORD,
Da 9:25 From the issuing of the decree to *r*
Na 2: 2 The LORD will *r* the splendor
Gal 6: 1 are spiritual should *r* him gently.
1Pe 5:10 will himself *r* you and make you

RESTORES (RESTORE)
Ps 23: 3 he *r* my soul.

RESTRAINED (RESTRAINT)
Ps 78:38 Time after time he *r* his anger

RESTRAINING (RESTRAINT)
Pr 27:16 *r* her is like *r* the wind
Col 2:23 value in *r* sensual indulgence.

RESTRAINT (RESTRAINED RESTRAINING)
Pr 17:27 of knowledge uses words with *r,*
23: 4 have the wisdom to show *r.*
29:18 no revelation, the people cast off *r;*

RESTS (REST)
Dt 33:12 and the one the LORD loves *r*
Pr 19:23 one *r* content, untouched
Lk 2:14 to men on whom his favor *r.*"

RESULT
Lk 21:13 This will *r* in your being witnesses
Ro 6:22 to holiness, and the *r* is eternal life.
11:31 as a *r* of God's mercy to you.
2Co 3: 3 from Christ, the *r* of our ministry,
2Th 1: 5 as a *r* you will be counted worthy
1Pe 1: 7 may be proved genuine and may *r*

RESURRECTION*
Mt 22:23 who say there is no *r,* came to him
22:28 at the *r,* whose wife will she be
22:30 At the *r* people will neither marry
22:31 But about the *r* of the dead—
27:53 and after Jesus' *r* they went
Mk 12:18 who say there is no *r,* came to him
12:23 At the *r* whose wife will she be,

Lk 14:14 repaid at the *r* of the righteous."
20:27 who say there is no *r*, came to Jesus
20:33 at the *r* whose wife will she be,
20:35 in the *r* from the dead will neither
20:36 since they are children of the *r*.
Jn 11:24 again in the *r* at the last day."
11:25 Jesus said to her, "I am the *r*
Ac 1:22 become a witness with us of his *r*."
2:31 he spoke of the *r* of the Christ,
4: 2 in Jesus the *r* of the dead.
4:33 to testify to the *r* of the Lord Jesus,
17:18 good news about Jesus and the *r*.
17:32 When they heard about the *r*
23: 6 of my hope in the *r* of the dead."
23: 8 Sadducees say that there is no *r*,
24:15 that there will be a *r*
24:21 'It is concerning the *r*
Ro 1: 4 Son of God by his *r* from the dead:
6: 5 also be united with him in his *r*.
1Co 15:12 some of you say that there is no *r*
15:13 If there is no *r* of the dead,
15:21 the *r* of the dead comes
15:29 if there is no *r*, what will those do
15:42 So will it be with the *r* of the dead.
Php 3:10 power of his *r* and the fellowship
3:11 to attain to the *r* from the dead.
2Ti 2:18 say that the *r* has already taken
Heb 6: 2 on of hands, the *r* of the dead,
11:35 so that they might gain a better *r*.
1Pe 1: 3 hope through the *r* of Jesus Christ
3:21 It saves you by the *r* of Jesus Christ
Rev 20: 5 This is the first *r*.
20: 6 those who have part in the first *r*.

RETALIATE*
1Pe 2:23 he did not *r*; when he suffered,

RETRIBUTION
Ps 69:22 may it become *r* and a trap.
Jer 51:56 For the LORD is a God of *r*;
Ro 11: 9 a stumbling block and a *r* for them.

RETURN (RETURNED RETURNS)
Ge 3:19 and to dust you will *r*."
2Sa 12:23 go to him, but he will not *r* to me."
2Ch 30: 9 If you *r* to the LORD, then your
Ne 1: 9 but if you *r* to me and obey my
Job 10:21 joy before I go to the place of no *r*,
16:22 before I go on the journey of no *r*.
22:23 If you *r* to the Almighty, you will
Ps 80:14 *R* to us, O God Almighty!
126: 6 will *r* with songs of joy,
Isa 10:21 A remnant will *r*, a remnant
35:10 the ransomed of the LORD will *r*.
55:11 It will not *r* to me empty,
Jer 24: 7 for they will *r* to me
31: 8 a great throng will *r*.
La 3:40 and let us *r* to the LORD.
Hos 6: 1 "Come, let us *r* to the LORD.
12: 6 But you must *r* to your God;
14: 1 *R*, O Israel, to the LORD your
Joel 2:12 "*r* to me with all your heart,
Zec 1: 3 '*R* to me,' declares the LORD
10: 9 and they will *r*.

RETURNED (RETURN)
Ps 35:13 When my prayers *r*
Am 4: 6 yet you have not *r* to me,"
1Pe 2:25 now you have *r* to the Shepherd

RETURNS (RETURN)
Pr 3:14 and yields better *r* than gold.
Isa 52: 8 When the LORD *r* to Zion,
Mt 24:46 finds him doing so when he *r*.

REUBEN
Firstborn of Jacob by Leah (Ge 29:32; 46:8; 1Ch 2:1). Attempted to rescue Joseph (Ge 37:21–30). Lost birthright for sleeping with Bilhah (Ge 35:22; 49:4). Tribe of blessed (Ge 49:3–4; Dt 33:6), numbered (Nu 1:21; 26:7), allotted land east of Jordan (Nu 32; 34:14; Jos 13:15), west (Eze 48:6), failed to help Deborah (Jdg 5:15–16), supported David (1Ch 12:37), 12,000 from (Rev 7:5).

REVEAL (REVEALED REVEALS REVELATION REVELATIONS)
Mt 11:27 to whom the Son chooses to *r* him.
Gal 1:16 was pleased to *r* his Son in me

REVEALED (REVEAL)
Dt 29:29 but the things *r* belong to us
Isa 40: 5 the glory of the LORD will be *r*,
43:12 I have *r* and saved and proclaimed
53: 1 the arm of the LORD been *r*?
65: 1 I *r* myself to those who did not ask
Mt 11:25 and *r* them to little children.
Jn 12:38 the arm of the Lord been *r*?"
17: 6 "I have *r* you to those whom you
Ro 1:17 a righteousness from God is *r*,
8:18 with the glory that will be *r* in us.
10:20 I *r* myself to those who did not ask
16:26 but now *r* and made known
1Co 2:10 but God has *r* it to us by his Spirit.
2Th 1: 7 happen when the Lord Jesus is *r*
2: 3 and the man of lawlessness is *r*,
1Pe 1: 7 and honor when Jesus Christ is *r*.
1:20 but was *r* in these last times
4:13 overjoyed when his glory is *r*.

REVEALS* (REVEAL)
Nu 23: 3 Whatever he *r* to me I will tell you
Job 12:22 He *r* the deep things of darkness
Da 2:22 He *r* deep and hidden things;
2:28 a God in heaven who *r* mysteries.
Am 4:13 and *r* his thoughts to man,

REVELATION* (REVEAL)
2Sa 7:17 David all the words of this entire *r*.
1Ch 17:15 David all the words of this entire *r*.
Pr 29:18 Where there is no *r*, the people cast
Da 10: 1 a *r* was given to Daniel (who was
Hab 2: 2 "Write down the *r*
2: 3 For the *r* awaits an appointed time;
Lk 2:32 a light for *r* to the Gentiles
Ro 16:25 according to the *r*
1Co 14: 6 I bring you some *r* or knowledge
14:26 a *r*, a tongue or an interpretation.
14:30 And if a *r* comes to someone who is
Gal 1:12 I received it by *r* from Jesus Christ.
2: 2 I went in response to a *r*
Eph 1:17 you the Spirit of wisdom and *r*,
3: 3 mystery made known to me by *r*,
Rev 1: 1 *r* of Jesus Christ, which God gave

REVELATIONS* (REVEAL)
2Co 12: 1 on to visions and *r* from the Lord.
12: 7 of these surpassingly great *r*,

REVELED* (REVELRY)
Ne 9:25 they *r* in your great goodness.

REVELRY (REVELED)
Ex 32: 6 drink and got up to indulge in *r*.
1Co 10: 7 and got up to indulge in pagan *r*."

REVENGE (VENGEANCE)
Lev 19:18 " 'Do not seek *r* or bear a grudge
Ro 12:19 Do not take *r*, my friends,

REVERE* (REVERENCE REVERENT REVERING)
Lev 19:32 for the elderly and *r* your God.
Dt 4:10 so that they may learn to *r* me
13: 4 must follow, and him you must *r*.
14:23 to *r* the LORD your God always.
17:19 learn to *r* the LORD his God
28:58 and do not *r* this glorious
Job 37:24 Therefore, men *r* him,
Ps 22:23 *R* him, all you descendants
33: 8 let all the people of the world *r* him
102:15 of the earth will *r* your glory.
Ecc 3:14 God does it so that men will *r* him.
Isa 25: 3 cities of ruthless nations will *r* you.
59:19 of the sun, they will *r* his glory.
63:17 hearts so we do not *r* you?
Jer 10: 7 Who should not *r* you,
Hos 10: 3 because we did not *r* the LORD.
Mal 4: 2 But for you who *r* my name,

REVERENCE (REVERE)
Lev 19:30 and have *r* for my sanctuary.
Ne 5:15 of *r* for God I did not act like that.
Ps 5: 7 in *r* will I bow down
Da 6:26 people must fear and *r* the God
2Co 7: 1 perfecting holiness out of *r* for God
Eph 5:21 to one another out of *r* for Christ.
Col 3:22 of heart and *r* for the Lord.
1Pe 3: 2 when they see the purity and *r*
Rev 11:18 and those who *r* your name,

REVERENT* (REVERE)
Ecc 8:12 with God-fearing men, who are *r*
Tit 2: 3 women to be *r* in the way they live,
Heb 5: 7 because of his *r* submission.
1Pe 1:17 as strangers here in *r* fear.

REVERING* (REVERE)
Dt 8: 6 walking in his ways and *r* him.
Ne 1:11 who delight in *r* your name.

REVERSE*
Isa 43:13 When I act, who can *r* it?"

REVIVE* (REVIVING)
Ps 80:18 *r* us, and we will call on your name.
85: 6 Will you not *r* us again,
Isa 57:15 and to *r* the heart of the contrite.
57:15 to *r* the spirit of the lowly
Hos 6: 2 After two days he will *r* us;

REVIVING* (REVIVE)
Ps 19: 7 *r* the soul.

REVOKED
Isa 45:23 a word that will not be *r*:

REWARD (REWARDED REWARDING REWARDS)
Ge 15: 1 your very great *r*."
1Sa 24:19 May the LORD *r* you well
Ps 19:11 in keeping them there is great *r*.
62:12 Surely you will *r* each person
127: 3 children a *r* from him.
Pr 9:12 are wise, your wisdom will *r* you;
11:18 sows righteousness reaps a sure *r*.
13:21 prosperity is the *r* of the righteous.
19:17 he will *r* him for what he has done.
25:22 and the LORD will *r* you.
31:31 Give her the *r* she has earned,
Isa 40:10 See, his *r* is with him,
49: 4 and my *r* is with my God."
61: 8 In my faithfulness I will *r* them
62:11 See, his *r* is with him,
Jer 17:10 to *r* a man according to his conduct
32:19 you *r* everyone according
Mt 5:12 because great is your *r* in heaven,
6: 1 you will have no *r*
6: 5 they have received their *r* in full.
10:41 a prophet will receive a prophet's *r*,
16:27 and then he will *r* each person
Lk 6:23 because great is your *r* in heaven.
6:35 Then your *r* will be great,
1Co 3:14 built survives, he will receive his *r*.
Eph 6: 8 know that the Lord will *r* everyone
Col 3:24 an inheritance from the Lord as a *r*.
Heb 11:26 he was looking ahead to his *r*.
Rev 22:12 I am coming soon! My *r* is with me

REWARDED (REWARD)
Ru 2:12 May you be richly *r* by the LORD,
2Sa 22:21 of my hands he has *r* me.
2Ch 15: 7 for your work will be *r*."
Ps 18:24 The LORD has *r* me according

Pr 13:13 he who respects a command is *r.*
14:14 and the good man *r* for his.
Jer 31:16 for your work will be *r,"*
1Co 3: 8 and each will be *r* according
Heb 10:35 your confidence; it will be richly *r.*
2Jn : 8 but that you may be *r* fully.

REWARDING* (REWARD)
Rev 11:18 for *r* your servants the prophets

REWARDS (REWARD)
1Sa 26:23 The LORD *r* every man
Pr 12:14 the work of his hands *r* him.
Heb 11: 6 that he *r* those who earnestly seek

RIBS
Ge 2:21 he took one of the man's *r*

RICH (RICHES RICHEST)
Job 34:19 does not favor the *r* over the poor,
Ps 49:16 overawed when a man grows *r,*
145: 8 slow to anger and *r* in love.
Pr 21:17 loves wine and oil will never be *r.*
22: 2 *R* and poor have this in common:
23: 4 Do not wear yourself out to get *r;*
28: 6 than a *r* man whose ways are
28:20 to get *r* will not go unpunished.
28:22 A stingy man is eager to get *r*
Ecc 5:12 but the abundance of a *r* man
Isa 33: 6 a *r* store of salvation and wisdom
53: 9 and with the *r* in his death,
Jer 9:23 or the *r* man boast of his riches,
Zec 3: 4 and I will put *r* garments on you."
Mt 19:23 it is hard for a *r* man
Lk 1:53 but has sent the *r* away empty.
6:24 "But woe to you who are *r,*
12:21 for himself but is not *r* toward God
16: 1 "There was a *r* man whose
21: 1 Jesus saw the *r* putting their gifts
2Co 6:10 yet making many *r;* having nothing
8: 2 poverty welled up in *r* generosity.
8: 9 he was *r,* yet for your sakes he
9:11 You will be made *r* in every way
Eph 2: 4 love for us, God, who is *r* in mercy,
1Ti 6: 9 want to get *r* fall into temptation
6:17 Command those who are *r*
6:18 to do good, to be *r* in good deeds,
Jas 1:10 the one who is *r* should take pride
2: 5 the eyes of the world to be *r* in faith
5: 1 you *r* people, weep and wail
Rev 2: 9 and your poverty—yet you are *r!*
3:18 you can become *r;* and white

RICHES (RICH)
Job 36:18 that no one entices you by *r;*
Ps 49: 6 and boast of their great *r?*
49:12 despite his *r,* does not endure;
62:10 though your *r* increase,
119:14 as one rejoices in great *r.*
Pr 3:16 in her left hand are *r* and honor.
11:28 Whoever trusts in his *r* will fall,
22: 1 is more desirable than great *r;*
27:24 for *r* do not endure forever,
30: 8 give me neither poverty nor *r,*
Isa 10: 3 Where will you leave your *r?*
60: 5 to you the *r* of the nations will
Jer 9:23 or the rich man boast of his *r,*
Lk 8:14 *r* and pleasures, and they do not
Ro 9:23 to make the *r* of his glory known
11:33 the depth of the *r* of the wisdom
Eph 2: 7 he might show the incomparable *r*
3: 8 to the Gentiles the unsearchable *r*
Col 1:27 among the Gentiles the glorious *r*
2: 2 so that they may have the full *r*

RICHEST (RICH)
Isa 55: 2 and your soul will delight in the *r*

RID
Ge 21:10 "Get *r* of that slave woman
1Co 5: 7 Get *r* of the old yeast that you may
Gal 4:30 "Get *r* of the slave woman

RIDE (RIDER RIDING)
Ps 45: 4 In your majesty *r* forth victoriously

RIDER (RIDE)
Rev 6: 2 was a white horse! Its *r* held a bow,
19:11 whose *r* is called Faithful and True.

RIDING (RIDE)
Zec 9: 9 gentle and *r* on a donkey,
Mt 21: 5 gentle and *r* on a donkey,

RIGGING
Isa 33:23 Your *r* hangs loose:

RIGHT (RIGHTS)
Ge 4: 7 But if you do not do what is *r,*
18:19 of the LORD by doing what is *r*
18:25 the Judge of all the earth do *r?"*
48:13 on his left toward Israel's *r* hand,
Ex 15: 6 Your *r* hand, O LORD,
15:26 and do what is *r* in his eyes,
Dt 5:32 do not turn aside to the *r*
6:18 Do what is *r* and good
13:18 and doing what is *r* in his eyes.
Jos 1: 7 do not turn from it to the *r*
1Sa 12:23 you the way that is good and *r.*
1Ki 3: 9 to distinguish between *r* and wrong
15: 5 For David had done what was *r*
2Ki 7: 9 to each other, "We're not doing *r.*
Ne 9:13 and laws that are just and *r,*
Ps 16: 8 Because he is at my *r* hand,
16:11 eternal pleasures at your *r* hand.
17: 7 you who save by your *r* hand
18:35 and your *r* hand sustains me;
19: 8 The precepts of the LORD are *r,*
25: 9 He guides the humble in what is *r*
33: 4 For the word of the LORD is *r*
44: 3 it was your *r* hand, your arm,
45: 4 let your *r* hand display awesome
51: 4 so that you are proved *r*
63: 8 your *r* hand upholds me.
73:23 you hold me by my *r* hand.
91: 7 ten thousand at your *r* hand,
98: 1 his *r* hand and his holy arm
106: 3 who constantly do what is *r.*
110: 1 "Sit at my *r* hand
118:15 LORD's *r* hand has done mighty
119:144 Your statutes are forever *r;*
137: 5 may my *r* hand forget ›its skill‹.
139:10 your *r* hand will hold me fast.
Pr 1: 3 doing what is *r* and just and fair;
4:27 Do not swerve to the *r* or the left;
14:12 There is a way that seems *r*
18:17 The first to present his case seems *r*
Ecc 7:20 who does what is *r* and never sins.
SS 1: 4 How *r* they are to adore you!
Isa 1:17 learn to do *r!*
7:15 reject the wrong and choose the *r.*
30:10 us no more visions of what is *r!*
30:21 Whether you turn to the *r*
41:10 you with my righteous *r* hand.
41:13 who takes hold of your *r* hand
48:13 my *r* hand spread out the heavens;
64: 5 to the help of those who gladly do *r*
Jer 23: 5 and do what is just and *r* in the land
Eze 18: 5 who does what is just and *r.*
18:21 and does what is just and *r,*
33:14 and does what is just and *r*—
Hos 14: 9 The ways of the LORD are *r;*
Mt 5:29 If your *r* eye causes you to sin,
6: 3 know what your *r* hand is doing,
22:44 "Sit at my *r* hand
25:33 He will put the sheep on his *r*
Jn 1:12 he gave the *r* to become children
Ac 2:34 "Sit at my *r* hand
7:55 Jesus standing at the *r* hand of God
Ro 3: 4 "So that you may be proved *r*
8:34 is at the *r* hand of God and is
9:21 Does not the potter have the *r*
Ro 12:17 careful to do what is *r* in the eyes
1Co 9: 4 Don't we have the *r* to food
2Co 8:21 we are taking pains to do what is *r,*
Eph 1:20 and seated him at his *r* hand
6: 1 parents in the Lord, for this is *r.*
Php 4: 8 whatever is *r,* whatever is pure,
2Th 3:13 never tire of doing what is *r.*
Heb 1: 3 down at the *r* hand of the Majesty
Jas 2: 8 as yourself," you are doing *r.*
1Pe 3:14 if you should suffer for what is *r,*
1Jn 2:29 who does what is *r* has been born
Rev 2: 7 I will give the *r* to eat from the tree
3:21 I will give the *r* to sit with me
22:11 let him who does *r* continue to do *r*

RIGHTEOUS (RIGHTEOUSLY RIGHTEOUSNESS)
Ge 6: 9 Noah was a *r* man, blameless
18:23 "Will you sweep away the *r*
Nu 23:10 Let me die the death of the *r,*
Ne 9: 8 your promise because you are *r.*
Job 36: 7 He does not take his eyes off the *r;*
Ps 1: 5 nor sinners in the assembly of the *r.*
5:12 O LORD, you bless the *r;*
11: 7 For the LORD is *r,*
15: 2 and who does what is *r,*
34:15 The eyes of the LORD are on the *r*
37:16 Better the little that the *r* have
37:21 but the *r* give generously;
37:25 yet I have never seen the *r* forsaken
37:30 of the *r* man utters wisdom,
55:22 he will never let the *r* fall.
64:10 Let the *r* rejoice in the LORD
68: 3 But may the *r* be glad
112: 4 compassionate and *r* man.
118:20 through which the *r* may enter.
119: 7 as I learn your *r* laws.
119:137 *R* are you, O LORD,
140:13 Surely the *r* will praise your name
143: 2 for no one living is *r* before you.
145:17 The LORD is *r* in all his ways
Pr 3:33 but he blesses the home of the *r.*
4:18 of the *r* is like the first gleam
10: 7 of the *r* will be a blessing,
10:11 The mouth of the *r* is a fountain
10:16 The wages of the *r* bring them life,
10:20 The tongue of the *r* is choice silver,
10:24 what the *r* desire will be granted.
10:28 The prospect of the *r* is joy,
10:32 of the *r* know what is fitting,
11:23 The desire of the *r* ends only
11:30 The fruit of the *r* is a tree of life,
12:10 A *r* man cares for the needs
12:21 No harm befalls the *r,*
13: 9 The light of the *r* shines brightly,
15:28 of the *r* weighs its answers,
15:29 but he hears the prayer of the *r.*
16:31 it is attained by a *r* life.
18:10 the *r* run to it and are safe.
20: 7 The *r* man leads a blameless life;
21:15 justice is done, it brings joy to the *r*
23:24 The father of a *r* man has great joy;
28: 1 but the *r* are as bold as a lion.
29: 6 but a *r* one can sing and be glad.
29: 7 The *r* care about justice
29:27 The *r* detest the dishonest;
Ecc 7:20 There is not a *r* man on earth
Isa 26: 7 The path of the *r* is level;
41:10 you with my *r* right hand.
45:21 a *r* God and a Savior;
53:11 his knowledge my *r* servant will
64: 6 and all our *r* acts are like filthy rags
Jer 23: 5 up to David a *r* Branch,
Eze 3:20 when a *r* man turns
18: 5 "Suppose there is a *r* man
18:20 of the *r* man will be credited
33:12 The *r* man, if he sins, will not be
Da 9:18 requests of you because we are *r,*
Hab 2: 4 but the *r* will live by his faith—
Zec 9: 9 *r* and having salvation,

Mal 3:18 see the distinction between the *r*
Mt 5:45 rain on the *r* and the unrighteous.
9:13 For I have not come to call the *r*,
10:41 and anyone who receives a *r* man
13:43 Then the *r* will shine like the sun
13:49 and separate the wicked from the *r*
25:37 "Then the *r* will answer him, 'Lord,
25:46 to eternal punishment, but the *r*
Ac 24:15 will be a resurrection of both the *r*
Ro 1:17 as it is written: "The *r* will live
2: 5 when his *r* judgment will be
2:13 the law who will be declared *r*.
3:10 "There is no one *r*, not even one;
3:20 Therefore no one will be declared *r*
5:19 one man the many will be made *r*.
Gal 3:11 because, "The *r* will live by faith."
1Ti 1: 9 that law is made not for the *r*
2Ti 4: 8 which the Lord, the *r* Judge,
Tit 3: 5 because of *r* things we had done,
Heb 10:38 But my *r* one will live by faith.
Jas 5:16 The prayer of a *r* man is powerful
1Pe 3:12 the eyes of the Lord are on the *r*
3:18 the *r* for the unrighteous,
4:18 "If it is hard for the *r* to be saved,
1Jn 2: 1 defense—Jesus Christ, the *R* One.
3: 7 does what is right is *r*, just as he is *r*.
Rev 19: 8 stands for the *r* acts of the saints.)

RIGHTEOUSLY* (RIGHTEOUS)
Ps 9: 4 on your throne, judging *r*.
Isa 33:15 He who walks *r*
Jer 11:20 LORD Almighty, you who judge *r*

RIGHTEOUSNESS (RIGHTEOUS)
Ge 15: 6 and he credited it to him as *r*.
Dt 9: 4 of this land because of my *r*."
1Sa 26:23 LORD rewards every man for his *r*
1Ki 10: 9 to maintain justice and *r*."
Job 37:23 great *r*, he does not oppress.
Ps 7:17 to the LORD because of his *r*
9: 8 He will judge the world in *r*;
17:15 And I—in *r* I will see your face;
23: 3 He guides me in paths of *r*
33: 5 The LORD loves *r* and justice;
35:28 My tongue will speak of your *r*
36: 6 Your *r* is like the mighty
37: 6 He will make your *r* shine like
40: 9 I proclaim *r* in the great assembly;
45: 4 in behalf of truth, humility and *r*;
45: 7 You love *r* and hate wickedness;
48:10 your right hand is filled with *r*.
65: 5 us with awesome deeds of *r*,
71: 2 Rescue me and deliver me in your *r*
71:15 My mouth will tell of your *r*,
71:19 Your *r* reaches to the skies, O God,
85:10 *r* and peace kiss each other.
89:14 *R* and justice are the foundation
96:13 He will judge the world in *r*
98: 9 He will judge the world in *r*
103: 6 The LORD works *r*
103:17 his *r* with their children's children
106:31 This was credited to him as *r*
111: 3 and his *r* endures forever.
118:19 Open for me the gates of *r*;
132: 9 May your priests be clothed with *r*;
145: 7 and joyfully sing of your *r*.
Pr 11: 5 *r* of the blameless makes a straight
11:18 he who sows *r* reaps a sure reward.
13: 6 *R* guards the man of integrity,
14:34 *R* exalts a nation,
16: 8 Better a little with *r*
16:12 a throne is established through *r*.
21:21 He who pursues *r* and love
Isa 5:16 will show himself holy by his *r*.
9: 7 it with justice and *r*
11: 4 but with *r* he will judge the needy,
16: 5 and speeds the cause of *r*.
26: 9 the people of the world learn *r*.
32:17 The fruit of *r* will be peace;
42: 6 "I, the LORD, have called you in *r*;
42:21 the LORD for the sake of his *r*
Isa 45: 8 "You heavens above, rain down *r*;
51: 1 "Listen to me, you who pursue *r*
51: 6 my *r* will never fail.
51: 8 But my *r* will last forever,
58: 8 then your *r* will go before you,
59:17 He put on *r* as his breastplate,
61:10 and arrayed me in a robe of *r*,
63: 1 "It is I, speaking in *r*,
Jer 9:24 justice and *r* on earth,
23: 6 The LORD Our *R*.
Eze 3:20 a righteous man turns from his *r*
14:20 save only themselves by their *r*.
18:20 The *r* of the righteous man will be
33:12 *r* of the righteous man will not save
Da 9:24 to bring in everlasting *r*,
12: 3 and those who lead many to *r*,
Hos 10:12 Sow for yourselves *r*,
Am 5:24 *r* like a never-failing stream!
Mic 7: 9 I will see his *r*.
Zep 2: 3 Seek *r*, seek humility;
Mal 4: 2 the sun of *r* will rise with healing
Mt 5: 6 those who hunger and thirst for *r*,
5:10 who are persecuted because of *r*,
5:20 unless your *r* surpasses that
6: 1 to do your 'acts of *r*' before men,
6:33 But seek first his kingdom and his *r*
Jn 16: 8 world of guilt in regard to sin and *r*
Ac 24:25 Paul discoursed on *r*, self-control
Ro 1:17 For in the gospel a *r* from God is
3: 5 brings out God's *r* more clearly,
3:22 This *r* from God comes
4: 3 and it was credited to him as *r*."
4: 5 wicked, his faith is credited as *r*.
4: 6 man to whom God credits *r* apart
4: 9 faith was credited to him as *r*.
4:13 through the *r* that comes by faith.
4:22 why "it was credited to him as *r*."
5:18 of *r* was justification that brings life
6:13 body to him as instruments of *r*.
6:16 or to obedience, which leads to *r*?
6:18 and have become slaves to *r*.
6:19 in slavery to *r* leading to holiness.
8:10 yet your spirit is alive because of *r*.
9:30 did not pursue *r*, have obtained it,
10: 3 they did not know the *r* that comes
14:17 but of *r*, peace and joy
1Co 1:30 our *r*, holiness and redemption.
2Co 3: 9 is the ministry that brings *r*!
5:21 that in him we might become the *r*
6: 7 with weapons of *r* in the right hand
6:14 For what do *r* and wickedness have
9: 9 his *r* endures forever."
Gal 2:21 for if *r* could be gained
3: 6 and it was credited to him as *r*."
3:21 then *r* would certainly have come
Eph 4:24 created to be like God in true *r*
5: 9 *r* and truth) and find out what
6:14 with the breastplate of *r* in place,
Php 1:11 filled with the fruit of *r* that comes
3: 6 as for legalistic *r*, faultless.
3: 9 not having a *r* of my own that
1Ti 6:11 and pursue *r*, godliness, faith, love,
2Ti 2:22 and pursue *r*, faith, love and peace,
3:16 correcting and training in *r*,
4: 8 is in store for me the crown of *r*,
Heb 1: 8 and *r* will be the scepter
5:13 with the teaching about *r*.
7: 2 his name means "king of *r*";
11: 7 became heir of the *r* that comes
12:11 it produces a harvest of *r*
Jas 2:23 and it was credited to him as *r*,"
3:18 sow in peace raise a harvest of *r*.
1Pe 2:24 die to sins and live for *r*;
2Pe 2:21 not to have known the way of *r*,
3:13 and a new earth, the home of *r*.

RIGHTS (RIGHT)
Ps 82: 3 maintain the *r* of the poor
Pr 31: 8 for the *r* of all who are destitute.
Isa 10: 2 to deprive the poor of their *r*
La 3:35 to deny a man his *r*
Gal 4: 5 that we might receive the full *r*

RING
Pr 11:22 Like a gold *r* in a pig's snout
Lk 15:22 Put a *r* on his finger and sandals

RIOTS
2Co 6: 5 imprisonments and *r*; in hard work,

RIPE
Joel 3:13 for the harvest is *r*.
Am 8: 1 showed me: a basket of *r* fruit.
Jn 4:35 at the fields! They are *r* for harvest.
Rev 14:15 for the harvest of the earth is *r*."

RISE (RAISE RAISED RISEN ROSE)
Lev 19:32 " '*R* in the presence of the aged,
Nu 24:17 a scepter will *r* out of Israel.
Isa 26:19 their bodies will *r*.
Mal 4: 2 of righteousness will *r* with healing
Mt 27:63 'After three days I will *r* again.'
Mk 8:31 and after three days *r* again.
Lk 18:33 On the third day he will *r* again."
Jn 5:29 those who have done good will *r*
20: 9 had to *r* from the dead.)
Ac 17: 3 had to suffer and *r* from the dead.
1Th 4:16 and the dead in Christ will *r* first.

RISEN (RISE)
Mt 28: 6 He is not here; he has *r*, just
Mk 16: 6 He has *r*! He is not here.
Lk 24:34 The Lord has *r* and has appeared

RIVER (RIVERS)
Ps 46: 4 There is a *r* whose streams make
Isa 66:12 "I will extend peace to her like a *r*,
Eze 47:12 grow on both banks of the *r*.
Rev 22: 1 Then the angel showed me the *r*

RIVERS (RIVER)
Ps 137: 1 By the *r* of Babylon we sat

ROAD (CROSSROADS ROADS)
Mt 7:13 and broad is the *r* that leads

ROADS (ROAD)
Lk 3: 5 crooked *r* shall become straight,

ROARING
1Pe 5: 8 prowls around like a *r* lion looking

ROB (ROBBERS ROBBERY ROBS)
Mal 3: 8 "Will a man *r* God? Yet you *r* me.

ROBBERS (ROB)
Jer 7:11 become a den of *r* to you?
Mk 15:27 They crucified two *r* with him,
Lk 19:46 but you have made it 'a den of *r*.' "
Jn 10: 8 came before me were thieves and *r*,

ROBBERY (ROB)
Isa 61: 8 I hate *r* and iniquity.

ROBE (ROBED ROBES)
Ge 37: 3 and he made a richly ornamented *r*
Isa 6: 1 the train of his *r* filled the temple.
61:10 arrayed me in a *r* of righteousness,
Rev 6:11 each of them was given a white *r*,

ROBED (ROBE)
Ps 93: 1 the LORD is *r* in majesty
Isa 63: 1 Who is this, *r* in splendor,

ROBES (ROBE)
Ps 45: 8 All your *r* are fragrant with myrrh
Rev 7:13 "These in white *r*— who are they,

ROBS* (ROB)
Pr 19:26 He who *r* his father and drives out
28:24 He who *r* his father or mother

ROCK
Ge 49:24 of the Shepherd, the *R* of Israel,
Ex 17: 6 Strike the *r,* and water will come
Nu 20: 8 Speak to that *r* before their eyes
Dt 32: 4 He is the *R,* his works are perfect,
32:13 him with honey from the *r,*
2Sa 22: 2 "The LORD is my *r,* my fortress
Ps 18: 2 The LORD is my *r,* my fortress
19:14 O LORD, my *R* and my Redeemer
40: 2 he set my feet on a *r*
61: 2 lead me to the *r* that is higher
92:15 he is my *R,* and there is no
Isa 26: 4 the LORD, is the *R* eternal.
51: 1 to the *r* from which you were cut
Da 2:34 you were watching, a *r* was cut out,
Mt 7:24 man who built his house on the *r.*
16:18 and on this *r* I will build my church
Ro 9:33 and a *r* that makes them fall,
1Co 10: 4 the spiritual *r* that accompanied
1Pe 2: 8 and a *r* that makes them fall."

ROD (RODS)
2Sa 7:14 I will punish him with the *r* of men,
Ps 23: 4 your *r* and your staff,
Pr 13:24 He who spares the *r* hates his son,
22:15 the *r* of discipline will drive it far
23:13 if you punish him with the *r,*
29:15 *r* of correction imparts wisdom,
Isa 11: 4 the earth with the *r* of his mouth;

RODS (ROD)
2Co 11:25 Three times I was beaten with *r,*

ROLL (ROLLED)
Mk 16: 3 "Who will *r* the stone away

ROLLED (ROLL)
Lk 24: 2 They found the stone *r* away

ROMAN
Ac 16:37 even though we are *R* citizens,
22:25 you to flog a *R* citizen who hasn't

ROOF (ROOFS)
Pr 21: 9 Better to live on a corner of the *r*

ROOFS
Mt 10:27 in your ear, proclaim from the *r.*

ROOM (ROOMS)
Mt 6: 6 But when you pray, go into your *r,*
Mk 14:15 He will show you a large upper *r,*
Lk 2: 7 there was no *r* for them in the inn.
Jn 8:37 because you have no *r* for my word
21:25 the whole world would not have *r*
2Co 7: 2 Make *r* for us in your hearts.

ROOMS (ROOM)
Jn 14: 2 In my Father's house are many *r;*

ROOSTER
Mt 26:34 this very night, before the *r* crows,

ROOT (ROOTED ROOTS)
Isa 11:10 In that day the *R* of Jesse will stand
53: 2 and like a *r* out of dry ground.
Mt 3:10 already at the *r* of the trees,
13:21 But since he has no *r,* he lasts only
Ro 11:16 if the *r* is holy, so are the branches.
15:12 "The *R* of Jesse will spring up,
1Ti 6:10 of money is a *r* of all kinds of evil.
Rev 5: 5 the *R* of David, has triumphed.
22:16 I am the *R* and the Offspring

ROOTED (ROOT)
Eph 3:17 being *r* and established in love,

ROOTS (ROOT)
Isa 11: 1 from his *r* a Branch will bear fruit.

ROSE (RISE)
SS 2: 1 I am a *r* of Sharon,
1Th 4:14 believe that Jesus died and *r* again

ROTS
Pr 14:30 but envy *r* the bones.

ROUGH
Isa 42:16 and make the *r* places smooth.
Lk 3: 5 the *r* ways smooth.

ROUND
Ecc 1: 6 *r* and *r* it goes,

ROYAL
Ps 45: 9 at your right hand is the *r* bride
Da 1: 8 not to defile himself with the *r* food
Jas 2: 8 If you really keep the *r* law found
1Pe 2: 9 a *r* priesthood, a holy nation,

RUBBISH*
Php 3: 8 I consider them *r,* that I may gain

RUBIES
Job 28:18 the price of wisdom is beyond *r.*
Pr 3:15 She is more precious than *r;*
8:11 for wisdom is more precious than *r,*
31:10 She is worth far more than *r.*

RUDDER*
Jas 3: 4 by a very small *r* wherever the pilot

RUDDY
1Sa 16:12 He was *r,* with a fine appearance
SS 5:10 *Beloved* My lover is radiant and *r,*

RUDE*
1Co 13: 5 It is not *r,* it is not self-seeking,

RUIN (RUINED RUINING RUINS)
Pr 10: 8 but a chattering fool comes to *r.*
10:10 and a chattering fool comes to *r.*
10:14 but the mouth of a fool invites *r.*
10:29 but it is the *r* of those who do evil.
18:24 many companions may come to *r,*
19:13 A foolish son is his father's *r,*
26:28 and a flattering mouth works *r.*
SS 2:15 that *r* the vineyards,
Eze 21:27 A *r!* A *r!* I will make it a *r!*
1Ti 6: 9 desires that plunge men into *r*

RUINED (RUIN)
Isa 6: 5 "I am *r!* For I am a man
Mt 9:17 and the wineskins will be *r.*
12:25 divided against itself will be *r,*

RUINING* (RUIN)
Tit 1:11 they are *r* whole households

RUINS (RUIN)
Pr 19: 3 A man's own folly *r* his life,
Ecc 4: 5 and *r* himself.
2Ti 2:14 and only *r* those who listen.

RULE (RULER RULERS RULES)
Ge 1:26 let them *r* over the fish of the sea
3:16 and he will *r* over you."
Jdg 8:22 said to Gideon, "*R* over us—
1Sa 12:12 'No, we want a king to *r* over us'—
Ps 2: 9 You will *r* them with an iron
67: 4 for you *r* the peoples justly
119:133 let no sin *r* over me.
Pr 17: 2 A wise servant will *r*
Isa 28:10 *r* on *r,* *r* on *r;*
Eze 20:33 I will *r* over you with a mighty
Zec 6:13 and will sit and *r* on his throne.
9:10 His *r* will extend from sea to sea
Ro 13: 9 are summed up in this one *r:*
15:12 arise to *r* over the nations;
1Co 7:17 This is the *r* I lay down in all
Gal 6:16 and mercy to all who follow this *r,*
Eph 1:21 far above all *r* and authority,
Col 3:15 the peace of Christ *r* in your hearts,
2Th 3:10 we gave you this *r:* "If a man will
Rev 2:27 He will *r* them with an iron scepter;
12: 5 who will *r* all the nations
19:15 He will *r* them with an iron scepter

RULER (RULE)
Ps 8: 6 You made him *r* over the works
Pr 19: 6 Many curry favor with a *r,*
23: 1 When you sit to dine with a *r,*
25:15 Through patience a *r* can be
29:26 Many seek an audience with a *r,*
Isa 60:17 and righteousness your *r.*
Da 9:25 the *r,* comes, there will be seven
Mic 5: 2 one who will be *r* over Israel,
Mt 2: 6 for out of you will come a *r*
Eph 2: 2 of the *r* of the kingdom of the air,
1Ti 6:15 God, the blessed and only *R,*
Rev 1: 5 and the *r* of the kings of the earth.

RULERS (RULE)
Ps 2: 2 and the *r* gather together
119:161 *R* persecute me without cause,
Isa 40:23 reduces the *r* of this world
Da 7:27 and all *r* will worship and obey him
Mt 20:25 "You know that the *r*
Ac 13:27 and their *r* did not recognize Jesus,
Ro 13: 3 For *r* hold no terror
1Co 2: 6 of this age or of the *r* of this age,
Eph 3:10 should be made known to the *r*
6:12 the *r,* against the authorities,
Col 1:16 or powers or *r* or authorities;

RULES (RULE)
Nu 15:15 is to have the same *r* for you
2Sa 23: 3 when he *r* in the fear of God,
Ps 22:28 and he *r* over the nations.
66: 7 He *r* forever by his power,
103:19 and his kingdom *r* over all.
Isa 29:13 is made up only of *r* taught by men.
40:10 and his arm *r* for him.
Mt 15: 9 their teachings are but *r* taught
Lk 22:26 one who *r* like the one who serves.
2Ti 2: 5 he competes according to the *r.*

RUMORS
Jer 51:46 afraid when *r* are heard in the land;
Mt 24: 6 You will hear of wars and *r* of wars,

RUN (RAN RUNNERS RUNNING RUNS)
Ps 19: 5 champion rejoicing to *r* his course.
Pr 4:12 when you *r,* you will not stumble.
18:10 the righteous *r* to it and are safe.
Isa 10: 3 To whom will you *r* for help?
40:31 they will *r* and not grow weary,
Joel 3:18 ravines of Judah will *r* with water.
Hab 2: 2 so that a herald may *r* with it.
1Co 9:24 *R* in such a way as to get the prize.
Gal 2: 2 that I was running or had *r* my race
Php 2:16 on the day of Christ that I did not *r*
Heb 12: 1 let us *r* with perseverance the race

RUNNERS* (RUN)
1Co 9:24 that in a race all the *r* run,

RUNNING (RUN)
Ps 133: 2 *r* down on Aaron's beard,
Lk 17:23 Do not go *r* off after them.
1Co 9:26 I do not run like a man *r* aimlessly;
Gal 5: 7 You were *r* a good race.

RUNS (RUN)
Jn 10:12 he abandons the sheep and *r* away.

RUSH
Pr 1:16 for their feet *r* into sin,
6:18 feet that are quick to *r* into evil,
Isa 59: 7 Their feet *r* into sin;

RUST
Mt 6:19 where moth and *r* destroy,

RUTH*
Moabitess; widow who went to Bethlehem with mother-in-law Naomi (Ru 1). Gleaned in field of Boaz; shown favor (Ru 2). Proposed marriage to

Boaz (Ru 3). Married (Ru 4:1–12); bore Obed, ancestor of David (Ru 4:13–22), Jesus (Mt 1:5).

RUTHLESS
Pr 11:16 but *r* men gain only wealth.
Ro 1:31 are senseless, faithless, heartless, *r.*

SABBATH (SABBATHS)
Ex 20: 8 "Remember the *S* day
31:14 " 'Observe the *S,* because it is holy
Lev 25: 2 the land itself must observe a *s*
Dt 5:12 "Observe the *S* day
Isa 56: 2 keeps the *S* without desecrating it,
56: 6 all who keep the *S*
58:13 if you call the *S* a delight
Jer 17:21 not to carry a load on the *S* day
Mt 12: 1 through the grainfields on the *S.*
Lk 13:10 On a *S* Jesus was teaching in one
Col 2:16 a New Moon celebration or a *S* day

SABBATH-REST* (REST)
Heb 4: 9 then, a *S* for the people of God;

SABBATHS (SABBATH)
2Ch 2: 4 evening and on *S* and New Moons
Eze 20:12 Also I gave them my *S*

SACKCLOTH
Ps 30:11 you removed my *s* and clothed me
Da 9: 3 in fasting, and in *s* and ashes.
Mt 11:21 would have repented long ago in *s*

SACRED
Lev 23: 2 are to proclaim as *s* assemblies.
Mt 7: 6 "Do not give dogs what is *s;*
Ro 14: 5 One man considers one day more *s*
1Co 3:17 for God's temple is *s,* and you are
2Pe 1:18 were with him on the *s* mountain.
2:21 on the *s* command that was

SACRIFICE (SACRIFICED SACRIFICES)
Ge 22: 2 *S* him there as a burnt offering
Ex 12:27 'It is the Passover *s* to the LORD,
1Sa 15:22 To obey is better than *s,*
1Ki 18:38 the LORD fell and burned up the *s,*
1Ch 21:24 or *s* a burnt offering that costs me
Ps 40: 6 *S* and offering you did not desire,
50:14 *S* thank offerings to God,
51:16 You do not delight in *s,*
54: 6 I will *s* a freewill offering to you;
107:22 Let them *s* thank offerings
141: 2 of my hands be like the evening *s.*
Pr 15: 8 The LORD detests the *s*
21: 3 to the LORD than *s.*
Da 9:27 the 'seven' he will put an end to *s*
12:11 time that the daily *s* is abolished
Hos 6: 6 For I desire mercy, not *s,*
Mt 9:13 this means: 'I desire mercy, not *s.'*
Ro 3:25 God presented him as a *s*
Eph 5: 2 as a fragrant offering and *s* to God.
Php 4:18 an acceptable *s,* pleasing to God.
Heb 9:26 away with sin by the *s* of himself.
10: 5 "*S* and offering you did not desire,
10:10 holy through the *s* of the body
10:14 by one *s* he has made perfect
10:18 there is no longer any *s* for sin.
11: 4 faith Abel offered God a better *s*
13:15 offer to God a *s* of praise—
1Jn 2: 2 He is the atoning *s* for our sins,
4:10 as an atoning *s* for our sins.

SACRIFICED (SACRIFICE)
Ac 15:29 are to abstain from food *s* to idols,
1Co 5: 7 our Passover lamb, has been *s.*
8: 1 Now about food *s* to idols:
Heb 7:27 He *s* for their sins once for all
9:28 so Christ was *s* once

SACRIFICES (SACRIFICE)
Ps 51:17 The *s* of God are a broken spirit;
Mk 12:33 than all burnt offerings and *s."*
Ro 12: 1 to offer your bodies as living *s,*
Heb 9:23 with better *s* than these.
13:16 for with such *s* God is pleased.
1Pe 2: 5 offering spiritual *s* acceptable

SAD
Lk 18:23 he heard this, he became very *s,*

SADDUCEES
Mt 16: 6 the yeast of the Pharisees and *S."*
Mk 12:18 *S,* who say there is no resurrection,
Ac 23: 8 *S* say that there is no resurrection,

SAFE (SAVE)
Ps 27: 5 he will keep me *s* in his dwelling;
37: 3 in the land and enjoy *s* pasture.
Pr 18:10 the righteous run to it and are *s.*
28:26 he who walks in wisdom is kept *s.*
29:25 in the LORD is kept *s.*
Jer 12: 5 If you stumble in *s* country,
Jn 17:12 kept them *s* by that name you gave
1Jn 5:18 born of God keeps him *s,*

SAFETY (SAVE)
Ps 4: 8 make me dwell in *s.*
Hos 2:18 so that all may lie down in *s.*
1Th 5: 3 people are saying, "Peace and *s,"*

SAINTS
1Sa 2: 9 He will guard the feet of his *s,*
Ps 16: 3 As for the *s* who are in the land,
30: 4 Sing to the LORD, you *s* of his;
31:23 Love the LORD, all his *s!*
34: 9 Fear the LORD, you his *s,*
116:15 is the death of his *s.*
149: 1 his praise in the assembly of the *s.*
149: 5 Let the *s* rejoice in this honor
Da 7:18 the *s* of the Most High will receive
Ro 8:27 intercedes for the *s* in accordance
1Co 6: 2 not know that the *s* will judge
Eph 1:15 Jesus and your love for all the *s,*
1:18 of his glorious inheritance in the *s,*
6:18 always keep on praying for all the *s*
Phm : 7 have refreshed the hearts of the *s.*
Rev 5: 8 which are the prayers of the *s.*
19: 8 for the righteous acts of the *s.)*

SAKE (SAKES)
1Sa 12:22 For the *s* of his great name
Ps 23: 3 righteousness for his name's *s.*
44:22 Yet for your *s* we face death all day
106: 8 Yet he saved them for his name's *s,*
Isa 42:21 for the *s* of his righteousness
43:25 your transgressions, for my own *s,*
48: 9 For my own name's *s* I delay my
48:11 For my own *s,* for my own *s,*
Jer 14: 7 for the *s* of your name.
14:21 For the *s* of your name do not
Eze 20: 9 But for the *s* of my name I did what
20:14 But for the *s* of my name I did what
20:22 and for the *s* of my name I did what
36:22 but for the *s* of my holy name,
Da 9:17 For your *s,* O Lord, look with favor
Mt 10:39 life for my *s* will find it.
19:29 for my *s* will receive a hundred
1Co 9:23 I do all this for the *s* of the gospel,
2Co 12:10 for Christ's *s,* I delight
Php 3: 7 loss for the *s* of Christ.
Heb 11:26 He regarded disgrace for the *s*
1Pe 2:13 for the Lord's *s* to every authority
3Jn : 7 was for the *s* of the Name that they

SAKES* (SAKE)
2Co 8: 9 yet for your *s* he became poor,

SALEM
Ge 14:18 king of *S* brought out bread
Heb 7: 2 "king of *S"* means "king of peace."

SALT
Ge 19:26 and she became a pillar of *s.*
Nu 18:19 covenant of *s* before the LORD
Mt 5:13 "You are the *s* of the earth.
Col 4: 6 with *s,* so that you may know how
Jas 3:11 *s* water flow from the same spring?

SALVATION* (SAVE)
Ex 15: 2 he has become my *s.*
2Sa 22: 3 my shield and the horn of my *s.*
23: 5 Will he not bring to fruition my *s*
1Ch 16:23 proclaim his *s* day after day.
2Ch 6:41 O LORD God, be clothed with *s,*
Ps 9:14 and there rejoice in your *s.*
13: 5 my heart rejoices in your *s.*
14: 7 that *s* for Israel would come out
18: 2 is my shield and the horn of my *s,*
27: 1 The LORD is my light and my *s*—
28: 8 a fortress of *s* for his anointed one.
35: 3 "I am your *s."*
35: 9 and delight in his *s.*
37:39 The *s* of the righteous comes
40:10 I speak of your faithfulness and *s.*
40:16 those who love your *s* always say,
50:23 way so that I may show him the *s*
51:12 Restore to me the joy of your *s*
53: 6 that *s* for Israel would come out
62: 1 my *s* comes from him.
62: 2 He alone is my rock and my *s;*
62: 6 He alone is my rock and my *s;*
62: 7 My *s* and my honor depend
67: 2 your *s* among all nations.
69:13 answer me with your sure *s.*
69:27 do not let them share in your *s.*
69:29 may your *s,* O God, protect me.
70: 4 those who love your *s* always say,
71:15 of your *s* all day long,
74:12 you bring *s* upon the earth.
85: 7 and grant us your *s.*
85: 9 Surely his *s* is near those who fear
91:16 and show him my *s."*
95: 1 to the Rock of our *s.*
96: 2 proclaim his *s* day after day.
98: 1 have worked *s* for him.
98: 2 The LORD has made his *s* known
98: 3 the *s* of our God.
116:13 I will lift up the cup of *s*
118:14 he has become my *s.*
118:21 you have become my *s.*
119:41 your *s* according to your promise;
119:81 with longing for your *s,*
119:123 My eyes fail, looking for your *s,*
119:155 *S* is far from the wicked,
119:166 I wait for your *s,* O LORD,
119:174 I long for your *s,* O LORD,
132:16 I will clothe her priests with *s,*
149: 4 he crowns the humble with *s.*
Isa 12: 2 Surely God is my *s;*
12: 2 he has become my *s."*
12: 3 from the wells of *s.*
25: 9 let us rejoice and be glad in his *s."*
26: 1 God makes *s*
26:18 We have not brought *s* to the earth;
30:15 "In repentance and rest is your *s,*
33: 2 our *s* in time of distress.
33: 6 a rich store of *s* and wisdom
45: 8 let *s* spring up,
45:17 the LORD with an everlasting *s;*
46:13 I will grant *s* to Zion,
46:13 and my *s* will not be delayed.
49: 6 that you may bring my *s*
49: 8 and in the day of *s* I will help you;
51: 5 my *s* is on the way,
51: 6 But my *s* will last forever,
51: 8 my *s* through all generations."
52: 7 who proclaim *s,*
52:10 the *s* of our God.
56: 1 for my *s* is close at hand
59:16 so his own arm worked *s* for him,
59:17 and the helmet of *s* on his head;
60:18 but you will call your walls *S*
61:10 me with garments of *s*
62: 1 her *s* like a blazing torch.
63: 5 so my own arm worked *s* for me,

Jer 3:23 is the *s* of Israel.
La 3:26 quietly for the *s* of the LORD.
Jnh 2: 9 *S* comes from the LORD."
Zec 9: 9 righteous and having *s*,
Lk 1:69 He has raised up a horn of *s* for us
1:71 of long ago), *s* from our enemies
1:77 give his people the knowledge of *s*
2:30 For my eyes have seen your *s*,
3: 6 And all mankind will see God's *s*
19: 9 "Today *s* has come to this house,
Jn 4:22 for *s* is from the Jews.
Ac 4:12 *S* is found in no one else,
13:26 message of *s* has been sent.
13:47 that you may bring *s* to the ends
28:28 to know that God's *s* has been sent
Ro 1:16 for the *s* of everyone who believes:
11:11 *s* has come to the Gentiles
13:11 because our *s* is nearer now
2Co 1: 6 it is for your comfort and *s*;
6: 2 and in the day of *s* I helped you."
6: 2 of God's favor, now is the day of *s*.
7:10 brings repentance that leads to *s*
Eph 1:13 word of truth, the gospel of your *s*.
6:17 Take the helmet of *s* and the sword
Php 2:12 to work out your *s* with fear
1Th 5: 8 and the hope of *s* as a helmet.
5: 9 to receive *s* through our Lord Jesus
2Ti 2:10 they too may obtain the *s* that is
3:15 wise for *s* through faith
Tit 2:11 of God that brings *s* has appeared
Heb 1:14 to serve those who will inherit *s*?
2: 3 This *s*, which was first announced
2: 3 escape if we ignore such a great *s*?
2:10 of their *s* perfect through suffering.
5: 9 of eternal *s* for all who obey him
6: 9 case—things that accompany *s*.
9:28 to bring *s* to those who are waiting
1Pe 1: 5 the coming of the *s* that is ready
1: 9 of your faith, the *s* of your souls.
1:10 Concerning this *s*, the prophets,
2: 2 by it you may grow up in your *s*,
2Pe 3:15 that our Lord's patience means *s*,
Jude : 3 to write to you about the *s* we share
Rev 7:10 "*S* belongs to our God,
12:10 have come the *s* and the power
19: 1 *S* and glory and power belong

SAMARIA (SAMARITAN)
1Ki 16:24 He bought the hill of *S*
2Ki 17: 6 the king of Assyria captured *S*
Jn 4: 4 Now he had to go through *S*.
4: 5 came to a town in *S* called Sychar,

SAMARITAN (SAMARIA)
Lk 10:33 But a *S*, as he traveled, came where
17:16 and thanked him—and he was a *S*.
Jn 4: 7 When a *S* woman came

SAMSON
Danite judge. Birth promised (Jdg 13). Married to Philistine, but wife given away (Jdg 14). Vengeance on Philistines (Jdg 15). Betrayed by Delilah (Jdg 16:1–22). Death (Jdg 16:23–31). Feats of strength: killed lion (Jdg 14:6), 30 Philistines (Jdg 14:19), 1,000 Philistines with jawbone (Jdg 15:13–17), carried off gates of Gaza (Jdg 16:3), pushed down temple of Dagon (Jdg 16:25–30).

SAMUEL
Ephraimite judge and prophet (Heb 11:32). Birth prayed for (1Sa 1:10–18). Dedicated to temple by Hannah (1Sa 1:21–28). Raised by Eli (1Sa 2:11, 18–26). Called as prophet (1Sa 3). Led Israel to victory over Philistines (1Sa 7). Asked by Israel for a king (1Sa 8). Anointed Saul as king (1Sa 9–10). Farewell speech (1Sa 12). Rebuked Saul for sacrifice (1Sa 13). Announced rejection of Saul (1Sa 15). Anointed David as king (1Sa 16). Protected David from Saul (1Sa 19:18–24). Death (1Sa 25:1). Returned from dead to condemn Saul (1Sa 28).

SANBALLAT
Led opposition to Nehemiah's rebuilding of Jerusalem (Ne 2:10, 19; 4; 6).

SANCTIFIED* (SANCTIFY)
Jn 17:19 that they too may be truly *s*.
Ac 20:32 among all those who are *s*.
26:18 among those who are *s* by faith
Ro 15:16 to God, *s* by the Holy Spirit.
1Co 1: 2 to those *s* in Christ Jesus
6:11 But you were washed, you were *s*,
7:14 and the unbelieving wife has been *s*
7:14 the unbelieving husband has been *s*
1Th 4: 3 It is God's will that you should be *s*
Heb 10:29 blood of the covenant that *s* him,

SANCTIFY* (SANCTIFIED SANCTIFYING)
Jn 17:17 *S* them by the truth; your word is
17:19 For them I *s* myself, that they too
1Th 5:23 *s* you through and through.
Heb 9:13 are ceremonially unclean *s* them

SANCTIFYING* (SANCTIFY)
2Th 2:13 through the *s* work of the Spirit
1Pe 1: 2 through the *s* work of the Spirit,

SANCTUARY
Ex 25: 8 "Then have them make a *s* for me,
Lev 19:30 and have reverence for my *s*,
Ps 15: 1 LORD, who may dwell in your *s*?
63: 2 I have seen you in the *s*
68:24 of my God and King into the *s*.
68:35 are awesome, O God, in your *s*;
73:17 me till I entered the *s* of God;
102:19 looked down from his *s* on high,
134: 2 Lift up your hands in the *s*
150: 1 Praise God in his *s*;
Eze 37:26 I will put my *s* among them forever
41: 1 the man brought me to the outer *s*
Da 9:26 will destroy the city and the *s*.
Heb 6:19 It enters the inner *s*
8: 2 in the *s*, the true tabernacle set up
8: 5 They serve at a *s* that is a copy
9:24 enter a man-made *s* that was only

SAND
Ge 22:17 and as the *s* on the seashore.
Mt 7:26 man who built his house on *s*.

SANDAL (SANDALS)
Ru 4: 7 one party took off his *s*

SANDALS (SANDAL)
Ex 3: 5 off your *s*, for the place where you
Dt 25: 9 take off one of his *s*, spit in his face
Jos 5:15 off your *s*, for the place where you
Mt 3:11 whose *s* I am not fit to carry.

SANG (SING)
Ex 15: 1 and the Israelites *s* this song
15:21 Miriam *s* to them:
Nu 21:17 Then Israel *s* this song:
Jdg 5: 1 Barak son of Abinoam *s* this song:
1Sa 18: 7 As they danced, they *s*:
2Sa 22: 1 David *s* to the LORD the words
2Ch 5:13 in praise to the LORD and *s*:
29:30 So they *s* praises with gladness
Ezr 3:11 thanksgiving they *s* to the LORD:
Job 38: 7 while the morning stars *s* together
Ps 106:12 and *s* his praise.
Rev 5: 9 And they *s* a new song:
5:12 In a loud voice they *s*:
14: 3 they *s* a new song before the throne
15: 3 and *s* the song of Moses the servant

SAP
Ro 11:17 share in the nourishing *s*

SAPPHIRA*
Ac 5: 1 together with his wife *S*,

SARAH
Wife of Abraham, originally named Sarai; barren (Ge 11:29–31; 1Pe 3:6). Taken by Pharaoh as Abraham's sister; returned (Ge 12:10–20). Gave Hagar to Abraham; sent her away in pregnancy (Ge 16). Name changed; Isaac promised (Ge 17:15–21; 18:10–15; Heb 11:11). Taken by Abimelech as Abraham's sister; returned (Ge 20). Isaac born; Hagar and Ishmael sent away (Ge 21:1–21; Gal 4:21–31). Death (Ge 23).

SARDIS
Rev 3: 1 the angel of the church in *S* write:

SASH (SASHES)
Rev 1:13 with a golden *s* around his chest.

SASHES (SASH)
Rev 15: 6 wore golden *s* around their chests.

SAT (SIT)
Ps 137: 1 By the rivers of Babylon we *s*
Mk 16:19 and he *s* at the right hand of God.
Lk 10:39 who *s* at the Lord's feet listening
Heb 1: 3 he *s* down at the right hand
8: 1 who *s* down at the right hand
10:12 he *s* down at the right hand of God.
12: 2 and *s* down at the right hand

SATAN
Job 1: 6 and *S* also came with them.
Zec 3: 2 said to *S*, "The LORD rebuke you,
Mt 12:26 If *S* drives out *S*, he is divided
16:23 *S*! You are a stumbling block to me;
Mk 4:15 *S* comes and takes away the word
Lk 10:18 "I saw *S* fall like lightning
22: 3 *S* entered Judas, called Iscariot,
Ro 16:20 The God of peace will soon crush *S*
1Co 5: 5 is present, hand this man over to *S*,
2Co 11:14 for *S* himself masquerades
12: 7 a messenger of *S*, to torment me.
1Ti 1:20 handed over to *S* to be taught not
Rev 12: 9 serpent called the devil, or *S*,
20: 2 or *S*, and bound him for a thousand
20: 7 *S* will be released from his prison

SATISFIED (SATISFY)
Ps 17:15 I will be *s* with seeing your likeness
22:26 The poor will eat and be *s*;
63: 5 My soul will be *s* as with the richest
104:28 they are *s* with good things.
105:40 *s* them with the bread of heaven.
Pr 13: 4 the desires of the diligent are fully *s*
30:15 are three things that are never *s*,
Ecc 5:10 whoever loves wealth is never *s*
Isa 53:11 he will see the light ›of life‹ and be *s*
Mt 14:20 They all ate and were *s*,
Lk 6:21 for you will be *s*.

SATISFIES* (SATISFY)
Ps 103: 5 who *s* your desires with good things,
107: 9 for he *s* the thirsty
147:14 and *s* you with the finest of wheat.

SATISFY (SATISFIED SATISFIES)
Ps 90:14 *S* us in the morning
145:16 *s* the desires of every living thing.
Pr 5:19 may her breasts *s* you always,
Isa 55: 2 and your labor on what does not *s*?
58:10 and *s* the needs of the oppressed,

SAUL
1. Benjamite; anointed by Samuel as first king of Israel (1Sa 9–10). Defeated Ammonites (1Sa 11). Rebuked for offering sacrifice (1Sa 13:1–15). Defeated Philistines (1Sa 14). Rejected as king for failing to annihilate Amalekites (1Sa 15). Soothed from evil spirit by David (1Sa 16:14–23). Sent David against Goliath (1Sa 17). Jealousy and

attempted murder of David (1Sa 18:1–11). Gave David Michal as wife (1Sa 18:12–30). Second attempt to kill David (1Sa 19). Anger at Jonathan (1Sa 20:26–34). Pursued David: killed priests at Nob (1Sa 22), went to Keilah and Ziph (1Sa 23), life spared by David at En Gedi (1Sa 24) and in his tent (1Sa 26). Rebuked by Samuel's spirit for consulting witch at Endor (1Sa 28). Wounded by Philistines; took his own life (1Sa 31; 1Ch 10). Lamented by David (2Sa 1:17–27). Children (1Sa 14:49–51; 1Ch 8).

2. See PAUL

SAVAGE

Ac 20:29 *s* wolves will come in among you

SAVE (SAFE SAFETY SALVATION SAVED SAVES SAVIOR)

Ge 45: 5 to *s* lives that God sent me ahead
1Ch 16:35 Cry out, "*S* us, O God our Savior;
Job 40:14 that your own right hand can *s* you.
Ps 17: 7 you who *s* by your right hand
18:27 You *s* the humble
28: 9 *S* your people and bless your
31:16 *s* me in your unfailing love.
69:35 for God will *s* Zion
71: 2 turn your ear to me and *s* me.
72:13 and *s* the needy from death.
89:48 or *s* himself from the power
91: 3 Surely he will *s* you
109:31 to *s* his life from those who
146: 3 in mortal men, who cannot *s*.
Pr 2:16 will *s* you also from the adulteress,
Isa 35: 4 he will come to *s* you."
38:20 The LORD will *s* me,
46: 7 it cannot *s* him from his troubles.
59: 1 of the LORD is not too short to *s*,
63: 1 mighty to *s*."
Jer 17:14 *s* me and I will be saved,
Eze 3:18 ways in order to *s* his life,
7:19 able to *s* them in the day
14:14 they could *s* only themselves
33:12 of the righteous man will not *s* him
34:22 I will *s* my flock, and they will no
Da 3:17 the God we serve is able to *s* us
Hos 1: 7 and I will *s* them—not by bow,
Zep 1:18 will be able to *s* them
3:17 he is mighty to *s*.
Zec 8: 7 "I will *s* my people
Mt 1:21 he will *s* his people from their sins
16:25 wants to *s* his life will lose it,
Lk 19:10 to seek and to *s* what was lost."
Jn 3:17 but to *s* the world through him.
12:47 come to judge the world, but to *s* it.
Ro 11:14 people to envy and *s* some of them.
1Co 7:16 whether you will *s* your husband?
1Ti 1:15 came into the world to *s* sinners—
Heb 7:25 to *s* completely those who come
Jas 5:20 of his way will *s* him from death
Jude :23 others from the fire and *s* them;

SAVED (SAVE)

Ps 22: 5 They cried to you and were *s*;
33:16 No king is *s* by the size of his army;
34: 6 he *s* him out of all his troubles.
106:21 They forgot the God who *s* them,
116: 6 when I was in great need, he *s* me.
Isa 25: 9 we trusted in him, and he *s* us.
45:22 "Turn to me and be *s*,
64: 5 How then can we be *s*?
Jer 4:14 from your heart and be *s*.
8:20 and we are not *s*."
Eze 3:19 but you will have *s* yourself.
33: 5 warning, he would have *s* himself.
Joel 2:32 on the name of the LORD will be *s*;
Mt 10:22 firm to the end will be *s*.
24:13 firm to the end will be *s*.
Mk 13:13 firm to the end will be *s*.
16:16 believes and is baptized will be *s*,
Jn 10: 9 enters through me will be *s*.
Ac 2:21 on the name of the Lord will be *s*.'
2:47 daily those who were being *s*.
4:12 to men by which we must be *s*."
15:11 of our Lord Jesus that we are *s*,
16:30 do to be *s*?" They replied,
Ro 5: 9 how much more shall we be *s*
9:27 only the remnant will be *s*.
10: 1 the Israelites is that they may be *s*.
10: 9 him from the dead, you will be *s*.
10:13 on the name of the Lord will be *s*."
11:26 so all Israel will be *s*, as it is written:
1Co 1:18 to us who are being *s* it is the power
3:15 will suffer loss; he himself will be *s*,
5: 5 his spirit *s* on the day of the Lord.
10:33 of many, so that they may be *s*.
15: 2 By this gospel you are *s*,
Eph 2: 5 it is by grace you have been *s*.
2: 8 For it is by grace you have been *s*,
2Th 2:13 you to be *s* through the sanctifying
1Ti 2: 4 who wants all men to be *s*
2:15 But women will be *s*
2Ti 1: 9 who has *s* us and called us
Tit 3: 5 He *s* us through the washing
Heb 10:39 but of those who believe and are *s*.

SAVES (SAVE)

Ps 7:10 who *s* the upright in heart.
68:20 Our God is a God who *s*;
145:19 he hears their cry and *s* them.
1Pe 3:21 It *s* you by the resurrection

SAVIOR* (SAVE)

Dt 32:15 and rejected the Rock his *S*.
2Sa 22: 3 stronghold, my refuge and my *s*—
22:47 Exalted be God, the Rock, my *S*!
1Ch 16:35 Cry out, "Save us, O God our *S*;
Ps 18:46 Exalted be God my *S*!
24: 5 and vindication from God his *S*.
25: 5 for you are God my *S*,
27: 9 O God my *S*.
38:22 O Lord my *S*.
42: 5 my *S* and
42:11 my *S* and my God.
43: 5 my *S* and my God.
65: 5 O God our *S*,
68:19 Praise be to the Lord, to God our *S*,
79: 9 Help us, O God our *S*,
85: 4 Restore us again, O God our *S*,
89:26 my God, the Rock my *S*.'
Isa 17:10 You have forgotten God your *S*;
19:20 he will send them a *s* and defender,
43: 3 the Holy One of Israel, your *S*;
43:11 and apart from me there is no *s*.
45:15 O God and *S* of Israel.
45:21 a righteous God and a *S*;
49:26 that I, the LORD, am your *S*,
60:16 know that I, the LORD, am your *S*,
62:11 'See, your *S* comes!
63: 8 and so he became their *S*.
Jer 14: 8 its *S* in times of distress,
Hos 13: 4 no *S* except me.
Mic 7: 7 I wait for God my *S*;
Hab 3:18 I will be joyful in God my *S*.
Lk 1:47 and my spirit rejoices in God my *S*,
2:11 of David a *S* has been born to you;
Jn 4:42 know that this man really is the *S*
Ac 5:31 *S* that he might give repentance
13:23 God has brought to Israel the *S*
Eph 5:23 his body, of which he is the *S*.
Php 3:20 we eagerly await a *S* from there,
1Ti 1: 1 by the command of God our *S*
2: 3 This is good, and pleases God our *S*
4:10 who is the *S* of all men,
2Ti 1:10 through the appearing of our *S*,
Tit 1: 3 me by the command of God our *S*,
1: 4 the Father and Christ Jesus our *S*.
2:10 about God our *S* attractive.
2:13 appearing of our great God and *S*,
3: 4 and love of God our *S* appeared,
3: 6 through Jesus Christ our *S*,
2Pe 1: 1 *S* Jesus Christ have received a faith
1:11 eternal kingdom of our Lord and *S*
2:20 and *S* Jesus Christ and are again
3: 2 and *S* through your apostles.
3:18 and knowledge of our Lord and *S*
1Jn 4:14 Son to be the *S* of the world.
Jude :25 to the only God our *S* be glory,

SCALE (SCALES)

Ps 18:29 with my God I can *s* a wall.

SCALES (SCALE)

Lev 11: 9 may eat any that have fins and *s*.
19:36 Use honest *s* and honest weights,
Pr 11: 1 The LORD abhors dishonest *s*,
Da 5:27 You have been weighed on the *s*
Rev 6: 5 Its rider was holding a pair of *s*

SCAPEGOAT (GOAT)

Lev 16:10 by sending it into the desert as a *s*.

SCARECROW*

Jer 10: 5 Like a *s* in a melon patch,

SCARLET

Jos 2:21 she tied the *s* cord in the window.
Isa 1:18 "Though your sins are like *s*,
Mt 27:28 They stripped him and put a *s* robe

SCATTER (SCATTERED SCATTERS)

Dt 4:27 The LORD will *s* you
Ne 1: 8 I will *s* you among the nations,
Jer 9:16 I will *s* them among nations that
30:11 the nations among which I *s* you,
Zec 10: 9 I *s* them among the peoples,

SCATTERED (SCATTER)

Isa 11:12 he will assemble the *s* people
Jer 31:10 'He who *s* Israel will gather them
Zec 2: 6 "for I have *s* you to the four winds
13: 7 and the sheep will be *s*,
Mt 26:31 and the sheep of the flock will be *s*.'
Jn 11:52 but also for the *s* children of God,
Ac 8: 4 who had been *s* preached the word
Jas 1: 1 To the twelve tribes *s*
1Pe 1: 1 *s* throughout Pontus, Galatia,

SCATTERS (SCATTER)

Mt 12:30 he who does not gather with me *s*.

SCEPTER

Ge 49:10 The *s* will not depart from Judah,
Nu 24:17 a *s* will rise out of Israel.
Ps 2: 9 You will rule them with an iron *s*;
45: 6 a *s* of justice will be the *s*
Heb 1: 8 and righteousness will be the *s*
Rev 2:27 'He will rule them with an iron *s*;
12: 5 rule all the nations with an iron *s*.
19:15 "He will rule them with an iron *s*."

SCHEMES

Pr 6:18 a heart that devises wicked *s*,
24: 9 The *s* of folly are sin,
2Co 2:11 For we are not unaware of his *s*.
Eph 6:11 stand against the devil's *s*.

SCHOLAR*

1Co 1:20 Where is the *s*? Where is

SCOFFERS

2Pe 3: 3 that in the last days *s* will come,

SCORN (SCORNED SCORNING SCORNS)

Ps 69: 7 For I endure *s* for your sake,
69:20 *S* has broken my heart
89:41 he has become the *s*
109:25 I am an object of *s* to my accusers;
119:22 Remove from me *s* and contempt,
Mic 6:16 you will bear the *s* of the nations."

SCORNED (SCORN)

Ps 22: 6 *s* by men and despised

SCORNING (SCORN)

Heb 12: 2 him endured the cross, *s* its shame,

SCORNS (SCORN)
Pr 13:13 He who *s* instruction will pay for it,
30:17 that *s* obedience to a mother,

SCORPION
Lk 11:12 will give him a *s*? If you then,
Rev 9: 5 sting of a *s* when it strikes a man.

SCOUNDREL
Pr 6:12 A *s* and villain,

SCRIPTURE (SCRIPTURES)
Jn 2:22 Then they believed the *S*
7:42 Does not the *S* say that the Christ
10:35 and the *S* cannot be broken—
Ac 8:32 was reading this passage of *S*:
1Ti 4:13 yourself to the public reading of *S*,
2Ti 3:16 All *S* is God-breathed
2Pe 1:20 that no prophecy of *S* came about

SCRIPTURES (SCRIPTURE)
Mt 22:29 because you do not know the *S*
Lk 24:27 said in all the *S* concerning himself.
24:45 so they could understand the *S*.
Jn 5:39 These are the *S* that testify about
Ac 17:11 examined the *S* every day to see
2Ti 3:15 you have known the holy *S*,
2Pe 3:16 as they do the other *S*,

SCROLL
Ps 40: 7 it is written about me in the *s*.
Isa 34: 4 and the sky rolled up like a *s*;
Eze 3: 1 eat what is before you, eat this *s*;
Heb 10: 7 it is written about me in the *s*—
Rev 6:14 The sky receded like a *s*, rolling up,
10: 8 take the *s* that lies open in the hand

SCUM
1Co 4:13 this moment we have become the *s*

SEA (SEASHORE)
Ex 14:16 go through the *s* on dry ground.
Dt 30:13 "Who will cross the *s* to get it
1Ki 7:23 He made the *S* of cast metal,
Job 11: 9 and wider than the *s*.
Ps 93: 4 mightier than the breakers of the *s*
95: 5 The *s* is his, for he made it,
Ecc 1: 7 All streams flow into the *s*,
Isa 57:20 the wicked are like the tossing *s*,
Jnh 1: 4 LORD sent a great wind on the *s*,
Mic 7:19 iniquities into the depths of the *s*.
Hab 2:14 as the waters cover the *s*.
Zec 9:10 His rule will extend from *s* to *s*
Mt 18: 6 drowned in the depths of the *s*.
1Co 10: 1 that they all passed through the *s*.
Jas 1: 6 who doubts is like a wave of the *s*,
Jude :13 They are wild waves of the *s*,
Rev 10: 2 He planted his right foot on the *s*
13: 1 I saw a beast coming out of the *s*.
20:13 The *s* gave up the dead that were
21: 1 and there was no longer any *s*.

SEAL (SEALED SEALS)
Ps 40: 9 I do not *s* my lips,
SS 8: 6 Place me like a *s* over your heart,
Da 12: 4 and *s* the words of the scroll
Jn 6:27 God the Father has placed his *s*
1Co 9: 2 For you are the *s* of my apostleship
2Co 1:22 set his *s* of ownership on us,
Eph 1:13 you were marked in him with a *s*,
Rev 6: 3 the Lamb opened the second *s*,
6: 5 When the Lamb opened the third *s*,
6: 7 the Lamb opened the fourth *s*,
6: 9 When he opened the fifth *s*,
6:12 I watched as he opened the sixth *s*.
8: 1 When he opened the seventh *s*,
9: 4 people who did not have the *s*
22:10 "Do not *s* up the words

SEALED (SEAL)
Eph 4:30 with whom you were *s* for the day
2Ti 2:19 solid foundation stands firm, *s*
Rev 5: 1 on both sides and *s* with seven seals

SEALS (SEAL)
Rev 5: 2 "Who is worthy to break the *s*
6: 1 opened the first of the seven *s*.

SEAMLESS*
Jn 19:23 This garment was *s*, woven

SEARCH (SEARCHED SEARCHES SEARCHING)
Ps 4: 4 *s* your hearts and be silent.
139:23 *S* me, O God, and know my heart;
Pr 2: 4 and *s* for it as for hidden treasure,
25: 2 to *s* out a matter is the glory
SS 3: 2 I will *s* for the one my heart loves.
Jer 17:10 "I the LORD *s* the heart
Eze 34:11 I myself will *s* for my sheep
34:16 I will *s* for the lost and bring back
Lk 15: 8 and *s* carefully until she finds it?

SEARCHED (SEARCH)
Ps 139: 1 O LORD, you have *s* me
Ecc 12:10 The Teacher *s* to find just the right
1Pe 1:10 *s* intently and with the greatest

SEARCHES (SEARCH)
1Ch 28: 9 for the LORD *s* every heart
Ps 7: 9 who *s* minds and hearts,
Pr 11:27 but evil comes to him who *s* for it.
20:27 The lamp of the LORD *s* the spirit
Ro 8:27 And he who *s* our hearts knows
1Co 2:10 The Spirit *s* all things,
Rev 2:23 will know that I am he who *s* hearts

SEARCHING (SEARCH)
Jdg 5:15 there was much *s* of heart.
Am 8:12 *s* for the word of the LORD,

SEARED
1Ti 4: 2 whose consciences have been *s*

SEASHORE (SEA)
Jos 11: 4 as numerous as the sand on the *s*.
1Ki 4:29 as measureless as the sand on the *s*.

SEASON (SEASONED SEASONS)
Lev 26: 4 I will send you rain in its *s*,
Ps 1: 3 which yields its fruit in *s*
2Ti 4: 2 be prepared in *s* and out of *s*;

SEASONED* (SEASON)
Col 4: 6 full of grace, *s* with salt,

SEASONS (SEASON)
Ge 1:14 signs to mark *s* and days and years,
Gal 4:10 and months and *s* and years!

SEAT (SEATED SEATS)
Ps 1: 1 or sit in the *s* of mockers.
Pr 31:23 where he takes his *s*
Da 7: 9 and the Ancient of Days took his *s*.
Lk 14: 9 say to you, 'Give this man your *s*.'
2Co 5:10 before the judgment *s* of Christ,

SEATED (SEAT)
Ps 47: 8 God is *s* on his holy throne.
Isa 6: 1 I saw the Lord *s* on a throne,
Lk 22:69 of Man will be *s* at the right hand
Eph 1:20 and *s* him at his right hand
2: 6 and *s* us with him in the heavenly
Col 3: 1 where Christ is *s* at the right hand
Rev 14:14 *s* on the cloud was one "like a son
20:11 white throne and him who was *s*

SEATS (SEAT)
Lk 11:43 you love the most important *s*

SECLUSION*
Lk 1:24 and for five months remained in *s*.

SECRET (SECRETLY SECRETS)
Dt 29:29 The *s* things belong
Jdg 16: 6 Tell me the *s* of your great strength
Ps 90: 8 our *s* sins in the light
139:15 when I was made in the *s* place.
Pr 11:13 but a trustworthy man keeps a *s*.
21:14 A gift given in *s* soothes anger,
Jer 23:24 Can anyone hide in *s* places
Mt 6: 4 so that your giving may be in *s*.
6:18 who sees what is done in *s*,
Mk 4:11 "The *s* of the kingdom
1Co 2: 7 No, we speak of God's *s* wisdom,
4: 1 entrusted with the *s* things of God.
2Co 4: 2 we have renounced *s* and shameful
Eph 5:12 what the disobedient do in *s*.
Php 4:12 I have learned the *s*

SECRETLY (SECRET)
2Pe 2: 1 They will *s* introduce destructive
Jude : 4 about long ago have *s* slipped

SECRETS (SECRET)
Ps 44:21 since he knows the *s* of the heart?
Ro 2:16 day when God will judge men's *s*
1Co 14:25 the *s* of his heart will be laid bare.
Rev 2:24 Satan's so-called deep *s* (I will not

SECURE (SECURITY)
Dt 33:12 beloved of the LORD rest *s* in him,
Ps 16: 5 you have made my lot *s*.
16: 9 my body also will rest *s*,
112: 8 His heart is *s*, he will have no fear;
Pr 14:26 fears the LORD has a *s* fortress,
Heb 6:19 an anchor for the soul, firm and *s*.
2Pe 3:17 and fall from your *s* position.

SECURITY (SECURE)
Job 31:24 or said to pure gold, 'You are my *s*,'

SEED (SEEDS SEEDTIME)
Ge 1:11 on the land that bear fruit with *s*
Isa 55:10 so that it yields *s* for the sower
Mt 13: 3 "A farmer went out to sow his *s*.
13:31 of heaven is like a mustard *s*,
17:20 have faith as small as a mustard *s*,
Lk 8:11 of the parable: The *s* is the word
1Co 3: 6 I planted the *s*, Apollos watered it,
2Co 9:10 he who supplies *s* to the sower
Gal 3:29 then you are Abraham's *s*,
1Pe 1:23 not of perishable *s*,
1Jn 3: 9 because God's *s* remains in him;

SEEDS (SEED)
Jn 12:24 But if it dies, it produces many *s*.
Gal 3:16 Scripture does not say "and to *s*,"

SEEDTIME* (SEED)
Ge 8:22 *s* and harvest,

SEEK (SEEKING SEEKS SELF-SEEKING SOUGHT)
Lev 19:18 Do not *s* revenge or bear a grudge
Dt 4:29 if from there you *s* the LORD your
1Ki 22: 5 "First *s* the counsel of the LORD."
1Ch 28: 9 If you *s* him, he will be found
2Ch 7:14 themselves and pray and *s* my face
15: 2 If you *s* him, he will be found
Ps 34:10 those who *s* the LORD lack no
105: 3 of those who *s* the LORD rejoice.
105: 4 *s* his face always.
119: 2 and *s* him with all their heart.
119:10 I *s* you with all my heart;
119:176 *S* your servant,
Pr 8:17 and those who *s* me find me.
18:15 the ears of the wise *s* it out.
25:27 is it honorable to *s* one's own honor
28: 5 those who *s* the LORD understand
Isa 55: 6 *S* the LORD while he may be
65: 1 found by those who did not *s* me.
Jer 29:13 You will *s* me and find me
Hos 10:12 for it is time to *s* the LORD,
Am 5: 4 "*S* me and live;
Zep 2: 3 *S* the LORD, all you humble
Mt 6:33 But *s* first his kingdom

Mt 7: 7 and it will be given to you; *s*
Lk 12:31 *s* his kingdom, and these things will
19:10 For the Son of Man came to *s*
Jn 5:30 for I *s* not to please myself
Ro 10:20 found by those who did not *s* me;
1Co 7:27 you married? Do not *s* a divorce.
10:24 Nobody should *s* his own good,
Heb 11: 6 rewards those who earnestly *s* him.
1Pe 3:11 he must *s* peace and pursue it.

SEEKING (SEEK)
2Ch 30:19 who sets his heart on *s* God—
Pr 20:18 Make plans by *s* advice;
Mal 3: 1 the Lord you are *s* will come
Jn 8:50 I am not *s* glory for myself;
1Co 10:33 For I am not *s* my own good

SEEKS (SEEK)
Pr 11:27 He who *s* good finds good will,
Mt 7: 8 he who *s* finds; and to him who
Jn 4:23 the kind of worshipers the Father *s*.
Ro 3:11 no one who *s* God.

SEER
1Sa 9: 9 of today used to be called a *s*.)

SELF-CONTROL* (CONTROL)
Pr 25:28 is a man who lacks *s*.
Ac 24:25 *s* and the judgment to come,
1Co 7: 5 you because of your lack of *s*.
Gal 5:23 faithfulness, gentleness and *s*.
2Ti 3: 3 slanderous, without *s*, brutal,
2Pe 1: 6 and to knowledge, *s*; and to *s*,

SELF-CONTROLLED* (CONTROL)
1Th 5: 6 are asleep, but let us be alert and *s*.
5: 8 let us be *s*, putting on faith and love
1Ti 3: 2 *s*, respectable, hospitable,
Tit 1: 8 who is *s*, upright, holy
2: 2 worthy of respect, *s*, and sound
2: 5 to be *s* and pure, to be busy at home
2: 6 encourage the young men to be *s*.
2:12 to live *s*, upright and godly lives
1Pe 1:13 prepare your minds for action; be *s*;
4: 7 and *s* so that you can pray.
5: 8 Be *s* and alert.

SELF-DISCIPLINE* (DISCIPLINE)
2Ti 1: 7 a spirit of power, of love and of *s*.

SELF-INDULGENCE*
Mt 23:25 inside they are full of greed and *s*.
Jas 5: 5 lived on earth in luxury and *s*.

SELF-SEEKING* (SEEK)
Ro 2: 8 But for those who are *s*
1Co 13: 5 it is not *s*, it is not easily angered,

SELFISH*
Ps 119:36 and not toward *s* gain.
Pr 18: 1 An unfriendly man pursues *s* ends;
Gal 5:20 fits of rage, *s* ambition, dissensions,
Php 1:17 preach Christ out of *s* ambition,
2: 3 Do nothing out of *s* ambition
Jas 3:14 and *s* ambition in your hearts,
3:16 you have envy and *s* ambition,

SELL (SELLING SELLS SOLD)
Ge 25:31 "First *s* me your birthright."
Mk 10:21 *s* everything you have
Rev 13:17 or *s* unless he had the mark,

SELLING (SELL)
Lk 17:28 buying and *s*, planting and building

SELLS (SELL)
Pr 31:24 makes linen garments and *s* them,

SEND (SENDING SENDS SENT)
Ps 43: 3 *S* forth your light and your truth,
Isa 6: 8 *S* me!" He said, "Go and tell this
Mal 3: 1 "See, I will *s* my messenger,
Mt 9:38 to *s* out workers into his harvest
24:31 And he will *s* his angels
Mk 1: 2 I will *s* my messenger ahead of you,
Lk 20:13 I will *s* my son, whom I love;
Jn 3:17 For God did not *s* his Son
16: 7 but if I go, I will *s* him to you.
1Co 1:17 For Christ did not *s* me to baptize,

SENDING (SEND)
Mt 10:16 I am *s* you out like sheep
Jn 20:21 Father has sent me, I am *s* you."
Ro 8: 3 God did by *s* his own Son

SENDS (SEND)
Ps 57: 3 God *s* his love and his faithfulness.

SENNACHERIB
Assyrian king whose siege of Jerusalem was overthrown by the LORD following prayer of Hezekiah and Isaiah (2Ki 18:13–19:37; 2Ch 32:1–21; Isa 36–37).

SENSES*
Lk 15:17 "When he came to his *s*, he said,
1Co 15:34 Come back to your *s* as you ought,
2Ti 2:26 and that they will come to their *s*

SENSITIVITY*
Eph 4:19 Having lost all *s*, they have given

SENSUAL* (SENSUALITY)
Col 2:23 value in restraining *s* indulgence.
1Ti 5:11 For when their *s* desires overcome

SENSUALITY* (SENSUAL)
Eph 4:19 have given themselves over to *s*

SENT (SEND)
Ex 3:14 to the Israelites: 'I AM has *s* me
Isa 55:11 achieve the purpose for which I *s* it.
61: 1 He has *s* me to bind up
Jer 28: 9 as one truly *s* by the LORD only
Mt 10:40 me receives the one who *s* me.
Mk 6: 7 he *s* them out two by two
Lk 4:18 He has *s* me to proclaim freedom
9: 2 and he *s* them out to preach
10:16 rejects me rejects him who *s* me."
Jn 1: 6 There came a man who was *s*
4:34 "is to do the will of him who *s* me
5:24 believes him who *s* me has eternal
8:16 I stand with the Father, who *s* me.
9: 4 must do the work of him who *s* me.
16: 5 "Now I am going to him who *s* me,
17: 3 and Jesus Christ, whom you have *s*.
17:18 As you *s* me into the world,
20:21 As the Father has *s* me, I am
Ro 10:15 can they preach unless they are *s*?
Gal 4: 4 God *s* his Son, born of a woman,
1Jn 4:10 but that he loved us and *s* his Son

SENTENCE
2Co 1: 9 in our hearts we felt the *s* of death.

SEPARATE (SEPARATED SEPARATES SEPARATION)
Mt 19: 6 has joined together, let man not *s*."
Ro 8:35 Who shall *s* us from the love
1Co 7:10 wife must not *s* from her husband.
2Co 6:17 and be *s*, says the Lord.
Eph 2:12 at that time you were *s* from Christ,

SEPARATED (SEPARATE)
Isa 59: 2 But your iniquities have *s*
Eph 4:18 in their understanding and *s*

SEPARATES (SEPARATE)
Pr 16:28 and a gossip *s* close friends.
17: 9 repeats the matter *s* close friends.
Mt 25:32 as a shepherd *s* the sheep

SEPARATION (SEPARATE)
Nu 6: 2 a vow of *s* to the LORD

SERAPHS*
Isa 6: 2 Above him were *s*, each
6: 6 Then one of the *s* flew to me

SERIOUSNESS*
Tit 2: 7 *s* and soundness of speech that

SERPENT (SERPENT'S)
Ge 3: 1 the *s* was more crafty than any
Isa 27: 1 Leviathan the coiling *s*;
Rev 12: 9 that ancient *s* called the devil
20: 2 that ancient *s*, who is the devil,

SERPENT'S (SERPENT)
2Co 11: 3 Eve was deceived by the *s* cunning,

SERVANT (SERVANTS)
Ex 14:31 trust in him and in Moses his *s*.
21: 2 "If you buy a Hebrew *s*, he is
1Sa 3:10 "Speak, for your *s* is listening."
2Sa 7:19 the future of the house of your *s*.
1Ki 20:40 While your *s* was busy here
Job 1: 8 "Have you considered my *s* Job?
Ps 19:11 By them is your *s* warned;
19:13 Keep your *s* also from willful sins;
31:16 Let your face shine on your *s*;
89: 3 I have sworn to David my *s*,
Pr 14:35 A king delights in a wise *s*,
17: 2 wise *s* will rule over a disgraceful
22: 7 and the borrower is *s* to the lender.
31:15 and portions for her *s* girls.
Isa 41: 8 "But you, O Israel, my *s*,
49: 3 He said to me, "You are my *s*,
53:11 my righteous *s* will justify
Zec 3: 8 going to bring my *s*, the Branch.
Mal 1: 6 his father, and a *s* his master.
Mt 8:13 his *s* was healed at that very hour.
20:26 great among you must be your *s*,
24:45 Who then is the faithful and wise *s*,
25:21 'Well done, good and faithful *s*!
Lk 1:38 I am the Lord's *s*," Mary answered.
16:13 "No *s* can serve two masters.
Jn 12:26 and where I am, my *s* also will be.
Ro 1: 1 a *s* of Christ Jesus, called
13: 4 For he is God's *s* to do you good.
Php 2: 7 taking the very nature of a *s*,
Col 1:23 of which I, Paul, have become a *s*.
2Ti 2:24 And the Lord's *s* must not quarrel;

SERVANTS (SERVANT)
Lev 25:55 for the Israelites belong to me as *s*.
2Ki 17:13 to you through my *s* the prophets."
Ezr 5:11 "We are the *s* of the God of heaven
Ps 34:22 The LORD redeems his *s*;
103:21 you his *s* who do his will.
104: 4 flames of fire his *s*.
Isa 44:26 who carries out the words of his *s*
65: 8 so will I do in behalf of my *s*;
65:13 my *s* will drink,
Lk 17:10 should say, 'We are unworthy *s*;
Jn 15:15 longer call you *s*, because a servant
Ro 13: 6 for the authorities are God's *s*,
1Co 3: 5 And what is Paul? Only *s*,
Heb 1: 7 his *s* flames of fire."

SERVE (SERVED SERVES SERVICE SERVING)
Dt 10:12 to *s* the LORD your God
11:13 and to *s* him with all your heart
13: 4 *s* him and hold fast to him.
28:47 you did not *s* the LORD your
Jos 22: 5 and to *s* him with all your heart
24:15 this day whom you will *s*,
24:18 We too will *s* the LORD,
1Sa 7: 3 to the LORD and *s* him only,
12:20 but *s* the LORD with all your heart
12:24 *s* him faithfully with all your heart;
2Ch 19: 9 "You must *s* faithfully
Job 36:11 If they obey and *s* him,
Ps 2:11 *S* the LORD with fear
Da 3:17 the God we *s* is able to save us

Mt 4:10 Lord your God, and *s* him only.' "
6:24 "No one can *s* two masters.
20:28 but to *s*, and to give his life
Ro 12: 7 If it is serving, let him *s*;
Gal 5:13 rather, *s* one another in love.
Eph 6: 7 *S* wholeheartedly,
1Ti 6: 2 they are to *s* them even better,
Heb 9:14 so that we may *s* the living God!
1Pe 4:10 gift he has received to *s* others,
5: 2 greedy for money, but eager to *s*;
Rev 5:10 kingdom and priests to *s* our God,

SERVED (SERVE)
Mt 20:28 Son of Man did not come to be *s*,
Jn 12: 2 Martha *s*, while Lazarus was
Ac 17:25 And he is not *s* by human hands,
Ro 1:25 and *s* created things rather
1Ti 3:13 Those who have *s* well gain

SERVES (SERVE)
Lk 22:26 one who rules like the one who *s*.
22:27 But I am among you as one who *s*.
Jn 12:26 Whoever *s* me must follow me;
Ro 14:18 because anyone who *s* Christ
1Pe 4:11 If anyone *s*, he should do it

SERVICE (SERVE)
Lk 9:62 fit for *s* in the kingdom
12:35 "Be dressed ready for *s*
Ro 15:17 in Christ Jesus in my *s* to God.
1Co 12: 5 There are different kinds of *s*,
16:15 themselves to the *s* of the saints.
2Co 9:12 This *s* that you perform is not only
Eph 4:12 God's people for works of *s*,
Rev 2:19 and faith, your *s* and perseverance,

SERVING (SERVE)
Jos 24:15 if *s* the LORD seems undesirable
2Ch 12: 8 learn the difference between *s* me
Ro 12: 7 If it is *s*, let him serve;
12:11 your spiritual fervor, *s* the Lord.
16:18 people are not *s* our Lord Christ,
Eph 6: 7 as if you were *s* the Lord, not men,
Col 3:24 It is the Lord Christ you are *s*.
2Ti 2: 4 No one *s* as a soldier gets involved

SETH
Ge 4:25 birth to a son and named him *S*,

SETTLE
Mt 5:25 "*S* matters quickly
2Th 3:12 in the Lord Jesus Christ to *s* down

SEVEN (SEVENS SEVENTH)
Ge 7: 2 Take with you *s* of every kind
Jos 6: 4 march around the city *s* times,
1Ki 19:18 Yet I reserve *s* thousand in Israel—
Pr 6:16 *s* that are detestable to him:
24:16 a righteous man falls *s* times,
Isa 4: 1 In that day *s* women
Da 9:25 comes, there will be *s* 'sevens,'
Mt 18:21 Up to *s* times?" Jesus answered,
Lk 11:26 takes *s* other spirits more wicked
Ro 11: 4 for myself *s* thousand who have not
Rev 1: 4 To the *s* churches in the province
6: 1 opened the first of the *s* seals.
8: 2 and to them were given *s* trumpets.
10: 4 And when the *s* thunders spoke,
15: 7 to the *s* angels *s* golden bowls filled

SEVENS* (SEVEN)
Da 9:24 "Seventy '*s*' are decreed
9:25 will be seven '*s*,' and sixty-two '*s*.'
9:26 the sixty-two '*s*,' the Anointed

SEVENTH (SEVEN)
Ge 2: 2 By the *s* day God had finished
Ex 20:10 but the *s* day is a Sabbath
23:11 but during the *s* year let the land lie
23:12 but on the *s* day do not work,
Heb 4: 4 "And on the *s* day God rested

SEVERE
2Co 8: 2 Out of the most *s* trial, their
1Th 1: 6 of the Lord; in spite of *s* suffering,

SEWED (SEWS)
Ge 3: 7 so they *s* fig leaves together

SEWS (SEWED)
Mt 9:16 No one *s* a patch of unshrunk cloth

SEXUAL (SEXUALLY)
Ex 22:19 "Anyone who has *s* relations
Lev 18: 6 relative to have *s* relations.
18: 7 father by having *s* relations
18:20 Do not have *s* relations with
Mt 15:19 murder, adultery, *s* immorality,
Ac 15:20 by idols, from *s* immorality,
1Co 5: 1 reported that there is *s* immorality
6:13 body is not meant for *s* immorality,
6:18 Flee from *s* immorality.
10: 8 should not commit *s* immorality,
2Co 12:21 *s* sin and debauchery
Gal 5:19 *s* immorality, impurity
Eph 5: 3 even a hint of *s* immorality,
Col 3: 5 *s* immorality, impurity, lust,
1Th 4: 3 that you should avoid *s* immorality

SEXUALLY (SEXUAL)
1Co 5: 9 to associate with *s* immoral people
6: 9 Neither the *s* immoral nor idolaters
6:18 he who sins *s* sins against his own
Heb 12:16 See that no one is *s* immoral,
13: 4 the adulterer and all the *s* immoral.
Rev 21: 8 the murderers, the *s* immoral,

SHADE
Ps 121: 5 the LORD is your *s*
Isa 25: 4 and a *s* from the heat.

SHADOW
Ps 17: 8 hide me in the *s* of your wings
23: 4 through the valley of the *s* of death,
36: 7 find refuge in the *s* of your wings.
91: 1 will rest in the *s* of the Almighty.
Isa 51:16 covered you with the *s* of my hand
Col 2:17 These are a *s* of the things that
Heb 8: 5 and *s* of what is in heaven.
10: 1 The law is only a *s*

SHADRACH
Hebrew exiled to Babylon; name changed from Hananiah (Da 1:6–7). Refused defilement by food (Da 1:8–20). Refused to worship idol (Da 3:1–18); saved from furnace (Da 3:19–30).

SHAKE (SHAKEN SHAKING)
Ps 64: 8 all who see them will *s* their heads
99: 1 let the earth *s*.
Hag 2: 6 I will once more *s* the heavens
Heb 12:26 "Once more I will *s* not only

SHAKEN (SHAKE)
Ps 16: 8 I will not be *s*.
30: 6 "I will never be *s*."
62: 2 he is my fortress, I will never be *s*.
112: 6 Surely he will never be *s*;
Isa 54:10 Though the mountains be *s*
Mt 24:29 and the heavenly bodies will be *s*.'
Lk 6:38 *s* together and running over,
Ac 2:25 I will not be *s*.
Heb 12:27 that what cannot be *s* may remain.

SHAKING* (SHAKE)
Ps 22: 7 they hurl insults, *s* their heads:
Mt 27:39 insults at him, *s* their heads
Mk 15:29 *s* their heads and saying, "So!

SHALLUM
King of Israel (2Ki 15:10–16).

SHAME (ASHAMED SHAMED SHAMEFUL)
Ps 25: 3 will ever be put to *s*,
34: 5 their faces are never covered with *s*
69: 6 not be put to *s* because of me,
Pr 13:18 discipline comes to poverty and *s*,
18:13 that is his folly and his *s*.
Jer 8: 9 The wise will be put to *s*;
8:12 No, they have no *s* at all;
Ro 9:33 trusts in him will never be put to *s*."
10:11 trusts in him will never be put to *s*."
1Co 1:27 things of the world to *s* the wise;
Heb 12: 2 endured the cross, scorning its *s*,

SHAMED (SHAME)
Jer 10:14 every goldsmith is *s* by his idols.
Joel 2:26 never again will my people be *s*.

SHAMEFUL (SHAME)
2Co 4: 2 have renounced secret and *s* ways;
2Pe 2: 2 Many will follow their *s* ways
Rev 21:27 nor will anyone who does what is *s*

SHAMGAR
Judge; killed 600 Philistines (Jdg 3:31).

SHAPE (SHAPES SHAPING)
Job 38:14 The earth takes *s* like clay

SHAPES (SHAPE)
Isa 44:10 Who *s* a god and casts an idol,

SHAPING (SHAPE)
Jer 18: 4 the pot he was *s* from the clay was

SHARE (SHARED SHARERS SHARES SHARING)
Ge 21:10 that slave woman's son will never *s*
Lev 19:17 frankly so you will not *s* in his guilt.
Dt 10: 9 That is why the Levites have no *s*
1Sa 30:24 All will *s* alike."
Eze 18:20 The son will not *s* the guilt
Mt 25:21 and *s* your master's happiness!'
Lk 3:11 "The man with two tunics should *s*
Ro 8:17 if indeed we *s* in his sufferings
12:13 *S* with God's people who are
2Co 1: 7 as you *s* in our sufferings,
Gal 4:30 the slave woman's son will never *s*
6: 6 in the word must *s* all good things
Eph 4:28 something to *s* with those in need.
Col 1:12 you to *s* in the inheritance
2Th 2:14 that you might *s* in the glory
1Ti 5:22 and do not *s* in the sins of others.
6:18 and to be generous and willing to *s*.
2Ti 2: 6 the first to receive a *s* of the crops.
Heb 12:10 that we may *s* in his holiness.
13:16 to do good and to *s* with others,
Rev 22:19 from him his *s* in the tree of life

SHARED (SHARE)
Ps 41: 9 he who *s* my bread,
Ac 4:32 but they *s* everything they had.
Heb 2:14 he too *s* in their humanity so that

SHARERS* (SHARE)
Eph 3: 6 and *s* together in the promise

SHARES (SHARE)
Pr 22: 9 for he *s* his food with the poor.
Jn 13:18 'He who *s* my bread has lifted up

SHARING (SHARE)
1Co 9:10 so in the hope of *s* in the harvest.
2Co 9:13 for your generosity in *s* with them
Php 3:10 the fellowship of *s* in his sufferings,
Phm : 6 you may be active in *s* your faith,

SHARON
SS 2: 1 I am a rose of *S*,

SHARP (SHARPENED SHARPENS SHARPER)
Pr 5: 4 *s* as a double-edged sword.
Isa 5:28 Their arrows are *s*,
Rev 1:16 came a *s* double-edged sword.

Rev 19:15 Out of his mouth comes a *s* sword

SHARPENED (SHARP)
Eze 21: 9 *s* and polished—

SHARPENS* (SHARP)
Pr 27:17 As iron *s* iron,
27:17 so one man *s* another.

SHARPER* (SHARP)
Heb 4:12 *S* than any double-edged sword,

SHATTER (SHATTERED SHATTERS)
Jer 51:20 with you I *s* nations,

SHATTERED (SHATTER)
1Sa 2:10 who oppose the LORD will be *s.*
Job 16:12 All was well with me, but he *s* me;
17:11 days have passed, my plans are *s,*
Ecc 12: 6 before the pitcher is *s* at the spring,

SHATTERS (SHATTER)
Ps 46: 9 he breaks the bow and *s* the spear,

SHAVED
Jdg 16:17 my head were *s,* my strength would
1Co 11: 5 it is just as though her head were *s.*

SHEAF (SHEAVES)
Lev 23:11 is to wave the *s* before the LORD

SHEARER* (SHEARERS)
Ac 8:32 and as a lamb before the *s* is silent,

SHEARERS (SHEARER)
Isa 53: 7 and as a sheep before her *s* is silent,

SHEAVES (SHEAF)
Ge 37: 7 while your *s* gathered around mine
Ps 126: 6 carrying *s* with him.

SHEBA
1. Benjamite who rebelled against David (2Sa 20).
2. See QUEEN.

SHECHEM
1. Raped Jacob's daughter Dinah; killed by Simeon and Levi (Ge 34).
2. City where Joshua renewed the covenant (Jos 24).

SHED (SHEDDING SHEDS)
Ge 9: 6 by man shall his blood be *s;*
Pr 6:17 hands that *s* innocent blood,
Ro 3:15 "Their feet are swift to *s* blood;
Col 1:20 through his blood, *s* on the cross.

SHEDDING (SHED)
Heb 9:22 without the *s* of blood there is no

SHEDS (SHED)
Ge 9: 6 "Whoever *s* the blood of man,

SHEEP (SHEEP'S SHEEPSKINS)
Nu 27:17 LORD's people will not be like *s*
Dt 17: 1 a *s* that has any defect or flaw in it,
1Sa 15:14 "What then is this bleating of *s*
Ps 44:22 we are considered as *s*
78:52 led them like *s* through the desert.
100: 3 we are his people, the *s*
119:176 I have strayed like a lost *s.*
SS 4: 2 teeth are like a flock of *s* just shorn,
Isa 53: 6 We all, like *s,* have gone astray,
53: 7 as a *s* before her shearers is silent,
Jer 50: 6 "My people have been lost *s;*
Eze 34:11 I myself will search for my *s*
Zec 13: 7 and the *s* will be scattered,
Mt 9:36 helpless, like *s* without a shepherd.
10:16 I am sending you out like *s*
12:11 "If any of you has a *s* and it falls
18:13 he is happier about that one *s*
25:32 as a shepherd separates the *s*
Jn 10: 1 man who does not enter the *s* pen
10: 3 He calls his own *s* by name
10: 7 the truth, I am the gate for the *s.*
10:15 and I lay down my life for the *s.*
10:27 My *s* listen to my voice; I know
21:17 Jesus said, "Feed my *s.*
1Pe 2:25 For you were like *s* going astray,

SHEEP'S* (SHEEP)
Mt 7:15 They come to you in *s* clothing,

SHEEPSKINS* (SHEEP)
Heb 11:37 They went about in *s* and goatskins

SHEKEL
Ex 30:13 This half *s* is an offering

SHELTER
Ps 27: 5 me in the *s* of his tabernacle
31:20 In the *s* of your presence you hide
55: 8 I would hurry to my place of *s,*
61: 4 take refuge in the *s* of your wings.
91: 1 in the *s* of the Most High
Ecc 7:12 Wisdom is a *s*
Isa 4: 6 It will be a *s* and shade
25: 4 a *s* from the storm
32: 2 Each man will be like a *s*
58: 7 the poor wanderer with *s*—

SHEM
Son of Noah (Ge 5:32; 6:10). Blessed (Ge 9:26). Descendants (Ge 10:21–31; 11:10–32).

SHEPHERD (SHEPHERDS)
Ge 48:15 the God who has been my *s*
49:24 because of the *S,* the Rock of Israel
Nu 27:17 will not be like sheep without a *s.*"
2Sa 7: 7 commanded to *s* my people Israel,
1Ki 22:17 on the hills like sheep without a *s,*
Ps 23: 1 LORD is my *s,* I shall not be in want.
28: 9 be their *s* and carry them forever.
80: 1 Hear us, O *S* of Israel,
Isa 40:11 He tends his flock like a *s:*
Jer 31:10 will watch over his flock like a *s.'*
Eze 34: 5 scattered because there was no *s,*
34:12 As a *s* looks after his scattered
Zec 11: 9 and said, "I will not be your *s.*
11:17 "Woe to the worthless *s,*
13: 7 "Strike the *s,*
Mt 2: 6 who will be the *s* of my people
9:36 and helpless, like sheep without a *s.*
26:31 " 'I will strike the *s,*
Jn 10:11 The good *s* lays down his life
10:14 "I am the good *s;* I know my sheep
10:16 there shall be one flock and one *s.*
Heb 13:20 that great *S* of the sheep, equip you
1Pe 5: 4 And when the Chief *S* appears,
Rev 7:17 of the throne will be their *s;*

SHEPHERDS (SHEPHERD)
Jer 23: 1 "Woe to the *s* who are destroying
50: 6 their *s* have led them astray
Eze 34: 2 prophesy against the *s* of Israel;
Lk 2: 8 there were *s* living out in the fields
Ac 20:28 Be *s* of the church of God,
1Pe 5: 2 Be *s* of God's flock that is
Jude :12 *s* who feed only themselves.

SHIBBOLETH*
Jdg 12: 6 No," they said, "All right, say *'S.'* "

SHIELD (SHIELDED SHIELDS)
Ge 15: 1 I am your *s,*
2Sa 22: 3 my *s* and the horn of my salvation.
22:36 You give me your *s* of victory;
Ps 3: 3 But you are a *s* around me,
5:12 with your favor as with a *s.*
7:10 My *s* is God Most High,
18: 2 He is my *s* and the horn
28: 7 LORD is my strength and my *s;*
33:20 he is our help and our *s.*
84:11 For the LORD God is a sun and *s;*
Ps 91: 4 his faithfulness will be your *s*
115: 9 he is their help and *s.*
119:114 You are my refuge and my *s;*
144: 2 my *s,* in whom I take refuge,
Pr 2: 7 he is a *s* to those whose walk is
30: 5 he is a *s* to those who take refuge
Eph 6:16 to all this, take up the *s* of faith,

SHIELDED (SHIELD)
1Pe 1: 5 through faith are *s* by God's power

SHIELDS (SHIELD)
Dt 33:12 for he *s* him all day long,

SHIFTLESS*
Pr 19:15 and the *s* man goes hungry.

SHIMEI
Cursed David (2Sa 16:5–14); spared (2Sa 19:16–23). Killed by Solomon (1Ki 2:8–9, 36–46).

SHINE (SHINES SHINING SHONE)
Nu 6:25 the LORD make his face *s*
Job 33:30 that the light of life may *s* on him.
Ps 4: 6 Let the light of your face *s* upon us,
37: 6 make your righteousness *s* like
67: 1 and make his face *s* upon us; *Selah*
80: 1 between the cherubim, *s* forth
118:27 and he has made his light *s* upon us.
Isa 60: 1 "Arise, *s,* for your light has come,
Da 12: 3 are wise will *s* like the brightness
Mt 5:16 let your light *s* before men,
13:43 the righteous will *s* like the sun
2Co 4: 6 made his light *s* in our hearts
Eph 5:14 and Christ will *s* on you."
Php 2:15 in which you *s* like stars

SHINES (SHINE)
Ps 50: 2 God *s* forth.
Pr 13: 9 The light of the righteous *s* brightly
Jn 1: 5 The light *s* in the darkness,

SHINING (SHINE)
Pr 4:18 *s* ever brighter till the full light
2Pe 1:19 as to a light *s* in a dark place,
Rev 1:16 His face was like the sun *s*

SHIPS
Pr 31:14 She is like the merchant *s,*

SHIPWRECKED*
2Co 11:25 I was stoned, three times I was *s,*
1Ti 1:19 and so have *s* their faith.

SHISHAK
1Ki 14:25 *S* king of Egypt attacked Jerusalem
2Ch 12: 2 *S* king of Egypt attacked Jerusalem

SHOCKING*
Jer 5:30 "A horrible and *s* thing

SHONE (SHINE)
Mt 17: 2 His face *s* like the sun,
Lk 2: 9 glory of the Lord *s* around them,
Rev 21:11 It *s* with the glory of God,

SHOOT
Isa 53: 2 up before him like a tender *s,*
Ro 11:17 and you, though a wild olive *s,*

SHORE
Lk 5: 3 asked him to put out a little from *s.*

SHORT (SHORTENED)
Nu 11:23 "Is the LORD's arm too *s?*
Isa 50: 2 Was my arm too *s* to ransom you?
59: 1 of the LORD is not too *s* to save,
Mt 24:22 If those days had not been cut *s,*
Ro 3:23 and fall *s* of the glory of God,
1Co 7:29 brothers, is that the time is *s.*
Heb 4: 1 of you be found to have fallen *s* of it
Rev 20: 3 he must be set free for a *s* time.

SHORTENED (SHORT)
Mt 24:22 of the elect those days will be *s.*

SHOULDER (SHOULDERS)
Zep 3: 9 and serve him *s* to *s.*

SHOULDERS (SHOULDER)
Dt 33:12 LORD loves rests between his *s."*
Isa 9: 6 and the government will be on his *s*
Lk 15: 5 he joyfully puts it on his *s*

SHOUT (SHOUTED)
Ps 47: 1 *s* to God with cries of joy.
66: 1 *S* with joy to God, all the earth!
95: 1 let us *s* aloud to the Rock
98: 4 *S* for joy to the LORD, all the earth
100: 1 *S* for joy to the LORD, all the earth
Isa 12: 6 *S* aloud and sing for joy, people
26:19 wake up and *s* for joy.
35: 6 the mute tongue *s* for joy.
40: 9 lift up your voice with a *s,*
42: 2 He will not *s* or cry out,
44:23 *s* aloud, O earth beneath.
54: 1 burst into song, *s* for joy,
Zec 9: 9 *S,* Daughter of Jerusalem!

SHOUTED (SHOUT)
Job 38: 7 and all the angels *s* for joy?

SHOW (SHOWED)
Ex 18:20 and *s* them the way to live
33:18 Moses said, "Now *s* me your glory
2Sa 22:26 the faithful you *s* yourself faithful,
1Ki 2: 2 "So be strong, *s* yourself a man,
Ps 17: 7 *S* the wonder of your great love,
25: 4 *S* me your ways, O LORD,
39: 4 "*S* me, O LORD, my life's end
85: 7 *S* us your unfailing love, O LORD,
143: 8 *S* me the way I should go,
Pr 23: 4 have the wisdom to *s* restraint.
SS 2:14 *s* me your face,
Isa 5:16 the holy God will *s* himself holy
30:18 he rises to *s* you compassion.
Eze 28:25 I will *s* myself holy among them
Joel 2:30 I will *s* wonders in the heavens
Zec 7: 9 *s* mercy and compassion
Ac 2:19 I will *s* wonders in the heaven
10:34 it is that God does not *s* favoritism
1Co 12:31 now I will *s* you the most excellent
Eph 2: 7 ages he might *s* the incomparable
Tit 2: 7 In your teaching *s* integrity,
Jas 2:18 I will *s* you my faith by what I do.
Jude :23 to others *s* mercy, mixed with fear

SHOWED (SHOW)
1Ki 3: 3 Solomon *s* his love for the LORD
Lk 24:40 he *s* them his hands and feet.
1Jn 4: 9 This is how God *s* his love

SHOWERS
Eze 34:26 in season; there will be *s* of blessing
Hos 10:12 and *s* righteousness on you.

SHREWD
2Sa 22:27 to the crooked you show yourself *s.*
Mt 10:16 Therefore be as *s* as snakes and

SHRINK (SHRINKS)
Heb 10:39 But we are not of those who *s* back

SHRINKS* (SHRINK)
Heb 10:38 And if he *s* back,

SHRIVEL
Isa 64: 6 we all *s* up like a leaf,

SHUDDER
Eze 32:10 and their kings will *s* with horror

SHUHITE
Job 2:11 Bildad the *S* and Zophar

SHUN* (SHUNS)
Job 28:28 and to *s* evil is understanding.' "
Pr 3: 7 fear the LORD and *s* evil.

SHUNS (SHUN)
Job 1: 8 a man who fears God and *s* evil."
Pr 14:16 man fears the LORD and *s* evil,

SHUT
Ge 7:16 Then the LORD *s* him in.
Isa 22:22 what he opens no one can *s,*
60:11 they will never be *s,* day or night,
Da 6:22 and he *s* the mouths of the lions.
Heb 11:33 who *s* the mouths of lions,
Rev 3: 7 no one can *s,* and what he shuts
21:25 On no day will its gates ever be *s,*

SICK (SICKNESS)
Pr 13:12 Hope deferred makes the heart *s,*
Eze 34: 4 or healed the *s* or bound up
Mt 9:12 who need a doctor, but the *s.*
10: 8 Heal the *s,* raise the dead, cleanse
25:36 I was *s* and you looked after me,
1Co 11:30 many among you are weak and *s,*
Jas 5:14 of you *s?* He should call the elders

SICKBED* (BED)
Ps 41: 3 LORD will sustain him on his *s*

SICKLE
Joel 3:13 Swing the *s,*
Rev 14:14 gold on his head and a sharp *s*

SICKNESS (SICK)
Mt 4:23 and healing every disease and *s*

SIDE (SIDES)
Ps 91: 7 A thousand may fall at your *s,*
124: 1 If the LORD had not been on our *s*
Jn 18:37 Everyone on the *s* of truth listens
20:20 he showed them his hands and *s.*
2Ti 4:17 But the Lord stood at my *s*
Heb 10:33 at other times you stood *s* by *s*

SIDES (SIDE)
Nu 33:55 in your eyes and thorns in your *s.*

SIFT
Lk 22:31 Satan has asked to *s* you as wheat.

SIGHING
Isa 35:10 and sorrow and *s* will flee away.

SIGHT
Ps 51: 4 and done what is evil in your *s,*
90: 4 For a thousand years in your *s*
116:15 Precious in the *s* of the LORD
Pr 3: 4 in the *s* of God and man.
Mt 11: 5 The blind receive *s,* the lame walk,
Ac 4:19 right in God's *s* to obey you rather
1Co 3:19 this world is foolishness in God's *s.*
2Co 5: 7 We live by faith, not by *s.*
1Pe 3: 4 which is of great worth in God's *s.*

SIGN (SIGNS)
Ge 9:12 "This is the *s* of the covenant I am
17:11 and it will be the *s* of the covenant
Isa 7:14 the Lord himself will give you a *s:*
55:13 for an everlasting *s,*
Eze 20:12 I gave them my Sabbaths as a *s*
Mt 12:38 to see a miraculous *s* from you."
24: 3 what will be the *s* of your coming
24:30 "At that time the *s* of the Son
Lk 2:12 This will be a *s* to you: You will
11:29 It asks for a miraculous *s,*
Ro 4:11 he received the *s* of circumcision,
1Co 11:10 to have a *s* of authority on her head
14:22 are a *s,* not for believers

SIGNS (SIGN)
Ge 1:14 let them serve as *s* to mark seasons
Ps 78:43 day he displayed his miraculous *s*
105:27 They performed his miraculous *s*
Da 6:27 he performs *s* and wonders
Mt 24:24 and perform great *s* and miracles
Mk 16:17 these *s* will accompany those who
Jn 3: 2 perform the miraculous *s* you are
20:30 Jesus did many other miraculous *s*
Ac 2:19 and *s* on the earth below,
1Co 1:22 Jews demand miraculous *s*
2Co 12:12 *s,* wonders and miracles—
2Th 2: 9 *s* and wonders, and in every sort

SIHON
Nu 21:21 to say to *S* king of the Amorites:
Ps 136:19 *S* king of the Amorites

SILAS*

Prophet (Ac 15:22–32); co-worker with Paul on second missionary journey (Ac 16–18; 2Co 1:19). Co-writer with Paul (1Th 1:1; 2Th 1:1); Peter (1Pe 5:12).

SILENCE (SILENCED SILENT)
1Pe 2:15 good you should *s* the ignorant talk
Rev 8: 1 there was *s* in heaven

SILENCED (SILENCE)
Ro 3:19 so that every mouth may be *s*
Tit 1:11 They must be *s,* because they are

SILENT (SILENCE)
Est 4:14 For if you remain *s* at this time,
Ps 30:12 to you and not be *s.*
32: 3 When I kept *s,*
39: 2 But when I was *s* and still,
Pr 17:28 a fool is thought wise if he keeps *s,*
Ecc 3: 7 a time to be *s* and a time to speak,
Isa 53: 7 as a sheep before her shearers is *s,*
62: 1 For Zion's sake I will not keep *s,*
Hab 2:20 let all the earth be *s* before him."
Ac 8:32 and as a lamb before the shearer is *s*
1Co 14:34 women should remain *s*
1Ti 2:12 over a man; she must be *s.*

SILVER
Ps 12: 6 like *s* refined in a furnace of clay,
66:10 you refined us like *s.*
Pr 2: 4 and if you look for it as for *s*
3:14 for she is more profitable than *s*
8:10 Choose my instruction instead of *s,*
22: 1 to be esteemed is better than *s*
25: 4 Remove the dross from the *s,*
25:11 is like apples of gold in settings of *s.*
Isa 48:10 I have refined you, though not as *s;*
Eze 22:18 They are but the dross of *s.*
Da 2:32 its chest and arms of *s,* its belly
Hag 2: 8 'The *s* is mine and the gold is mine,'
Zec 13: 9 I will refine them like *s*
Ac 3: 6 Peter said, "*S* or gold I do not have,
1Co 3:12 *s,* costly stones, wood, hay or straw
1Pe 1:18 not with perishable things such as *s*

SILVERSMITH
Ac 19:24 A *s* named Demetrius, who made

SIMEON

Son of Jacob by Leah (Ge 29:33; 35:23; 1Ch 2:1). With Levi killed Shechem for rape of Dinah (Ge 34:25–29). Held hostage by Joseph in Egypt (Ge 42:24–43:23). Tribe of blessed (Ge 49:5–7), numbered (Nu 1:23; 26:14), allotted land (Jos 19:1–9; Eze 48:24), 12,000 from (Rev 7:7).

SIMON

1. See PETER.

2. Apostle, called the Zealot (Mt 10:4; Mk 3:18; Lk 6:15; Ac 1:13).

3. Samaritan sorcerer (Ac 8:9–24).

SIMPLE
Ps 19: 7 making wise the *s.*
119:130 it gives understanding to the *s.*
Pr 8: 5 You who are *s,* gain prudence;

Pr 14:15 A *s* man believes anything,

SIMPLEHEARTED* (HEART)

Ps 116: 6 The LORD protects the *s*;

SIN (SINFUL SINNED SINNER SINNERS SINNING SINS)

Ge 4: 7 *s* is crouching at your door;
Ex 32:32 please forgive their *s*— but if not,
Nu 5: 7 and must confess the *s* he has
32:23 be sure that your *s* will find you
Dt 24:16 each is to die for his own *s*.
1Sa 12:23 it from me that I should *s*
15:23 For rebellion is like the *s*
1Ki 8:46 for there is no one who does not *s*
2Ch 7:14 and will forgive their *s* and will heal
Job 1:22 Job did not *s* by charging God
Ps 4: 4 In your anger do not *s*;
17: 3 resolved that my mouth will not *s*.
32: 2 whose *s* the LORD does not count
32: 5 Then I acknowledged my *s* to you
36: 2 too much to detect or hate his *s*.
38:18 I am troubled by my *s*.
39: 1 and keep my tongue from *s*;
51: 2 and cleanse me from my *s*.
66:18 If I had cherished *s* in my heart,
119:11 that I might not *s* against you.
119:133 let no *s* rule over me.
Pr 5:22 the cords of his *s* hold him fast.
10:19 words are many, *s* is not absent,
14: 9 Fools mock at making amends for *s*
16: 6 faithfulness *s* is atoned for;
17:19 He who loves a quarrel loves *s*;
20: 9 I am clean and without *s*"?
Isa 3: 9 they parade their *s* like Sodom;
6: 7 is taken away and your *s* atoned
64: 5 But when we continued to *s*
Jer 31:30 everyone will die for his own *s*;
Eze 3:18 that wicked man will die for his *s*,
18:26 his righteousness and commits *s*,
33: 8 that wicked man will die for his *s*,
Am 4: 4 "Go to Bethel and *s*;
Mic 6: 7 of my body for the *s* of my soul?
7:18 who pardons *s* and forgives
Zec 3: 4 "See, I have taken away your *s*,
Mt 18: 6 little ones who believe in me to *s*,
Mk 3:29 he is guilty of an eternal *s*."
9:43 If your hand causes you to *s*,
Lk 17: 1 people to *s* are bound to come,
Jn 1:29 who takes away the *s* of the world!
8: 7 "If any one of you is without *s*,
8:34 everyone who sins is a slave to *s*.
8:46 Can any of you prove me guilty of *s*
Ro 2:12 All who *s* apart from the law will
5:12 as *s* entered the world
5:20 where *s* increased, grace increased
6: 2 By no means! We died to *s*;
6:11 count yourselves dead to *s*
6:14 For *s* shall not be your master,
6:23 For the wages of *s* is death,
7: 7 I would not have known what *s* was
7:25 sinful nature a slave to the law of *s*.
14:23 that does not come from faith is *s*.
1Co 8:12 When you *s* against your brothers
15:56 The sting of death is *s*,
2Co 5:21 God made him who had no *s* to be *s*
Gal 6: 1 if someone is caught in a *s*,
1Ti 5:20 Those who *s* are to be rebuked
Heb 4:15 just as we are—yet was without *s*.
9:26 to do away with *s* by the sacrifice
11:25 the pleasures of *s* for a short time.
12: 1 and the *s* that so easily entangles,
Jas 1:15 it gives birth to *s*; and *s*,
1Pe 2:22 "He committed no *s*,
1Jn 1: 7 his Son, purifies us from all *s*.
1: 8 If we claim to be without *s*,
2: 1 But if anybody does *s*, we have one
3: 4 in fact, *s* is lawlessness.
3: 5 And in him is no *s*.
3: 6 No one who continues to *s* has
3: 9 born of God will continue to *s*,
5:16 There is a *s* that leads to death.
5:17 All wrongdoing is *s*, and there is *s*
5:18 born of God does not continue to *s*;

SINAI

Ex 19:20 descended to the top of Mount *S*
31:18 speaking to Moses on Mount *S*,
Ps 68:17 from *S* into his sanctuary.

SINCERE* (SINCERITY)

Da 11:34 many who are not *s* will join them.
Ac 2:46 ate together with glad and *s* hearts,
Ro 12: 9 Love must be *s*.
2Co 6: 6 in the Holy Spirit and in *s* love;
11: 3 somehow be led astray from your *s*
1Ti 1: 5 a good conscience and a *s* faith.
3: 8 *s*, not indulging in much wine,
2Ti 1: 5 have been reminded of your *s* faith,
Heb 10:22 near to God with a *s* heart
Jas 3:17 and good fruit, impartial and *s*.
1Pe 1:22 the truth so that you have *s* love

SINCERITY* (SINCERE)

1Co 5: 8 bread without yeast, the bread of *s*
2Co 1:12 in the holiness and *s* that are
2:17 speak before God with *s*,
8: 8 but I want to test the *s* of your love
Eph 6: 5 and with *s* of heart, just
Col 3:22 but with *s* of heart and reverence

SINFUL (SIN)

Ps 51: 5 Surely I was *s* at birth,
51: 5 *s* from the time my mother
Lk 5: 8 from me, Lord; I am a *s* man!"
Ro 7: 5 we were controlled by the *s* nature,
7:18 lives in me, that is, in my *s* nature.
7:25 but in the *s* nature a slave to the law
8: 3 Son in the likeness of *s* man
8: 4 not live according to the *s* nature
8: 7 the *s* mind is hostile to God.
8: 8 by the *s* nature cannot please God.
8: 9 are controlled not by the *s* nature
8:13 if you live according to the *s* nature
13:14 to gratify the desires of the *s* nature
1Co 5: 5 so that the *s* nature may be
Gal 5:13 freedom to indulge the *s* nature;
5:16 gratify the desires of the *s* nature.
5:19 The acts of the *s* nature are obvious
5:24 Jesus have crucified the *s* nature
6: 8 sows to please his *s* nature,
Col 2:11 in the putting off of the *s* nature,
Heb 3:12 brothers, that none of you has a *s*,
1Pe 2:11 abstain from *s* desires, which war
1Jn 3: 8 He who does what is *s* is

SING (SANG SINGER SINGING SINGS SONG SONGS SUNG)

Ex 15: 1 "I will *s* to the LORD,
Ps 5:11 let them ever *s* for joy.
13: 6 I will *s* to the LORD,
30: 4 *S* to the LORD, you saints of his;
33: 1 *S* joyfully to the LORD, you
47: 6 *S* praises to God, *s* praises;
57: 7 I will *s* and make music,
59:16 But I will *s* of your strength,
63: 7 I *s* in the shadow of your wings.
66: 2 *S* to the glory of his name;
89: 1 I will *s* of the LORD's great love
95: 1 Come, let us *s* for joy to the LORD
96: 1 *S* to the LORD a new song;
98: 1 *S* to the LORD a new song,
101: 1 I will *s* of your love and justice;
108: 1 I will *s* and make music
137: 3 "*S* us one of the songs of Zion!"
147: 1 is to *s* praises to our God,
149: 1 *S* to the LORD a new song,
Isa 54: 1 "*S*, O barren woman,
1Co 14:15 also pray with my mind; I will *s*
Eph 5:19 *S* and make music in your heart
Col 3:16 and as you *s* psalms, hymns
Jas 5:13 Is anyone happy? Let him *s* songs

SINGER* (SING)

2Sa 23: 1 Israel's *s* of songs:

SINGING (SING)

Ps 63: 5 with *s* lips my mouth will praise
68: 6 he leads forth the prisoners with *s*;
98: 5 with the harp and the sound of *s*,
Isa 35:10 They will enter Zion with *s*;
Zep 3:17 he will rejoice over you with *s*."
Ac 16:25 Silas were praying and *s* hymns
Rev 5:13 on the sea, and all that is in them, *s*:

SINGLE

Ex 23:29 I will not drive them out in a *s* year,
Mt 6:27 you by worrying can add a *s* hour
Gal 5:14 law is summed up in a *s* command:

SINGS (SING)

Eze 33:32 more than one who *s* love songs

SINNED (SIN)

Lev 5: 5 confess in what way he has *s*
1Sa 15:24 Then Saul said to Samuel, "I have *s*
2Sa 12:13 "I have *s* against the LORD."
24:10 I have *s* greatly in what I have done
2Ch 6:37 'We have *s*, we have done wrong
Job 1: 5 "Perhaps my children have *s*
33:27 'I *s*, and perverted what was right,
Ps 51: 4 Against you, you only, have I *s*
Jer 2:35 because you say, 'I have not *s*.'
14:20 we have indeed *s* against you.
Da 9: 5 we have *s* and done wrong.
Mic 7: 9 Because I have *s* against him,
Mt 27: 4 "I have *s*," he said,
Lk 15:18 I have *s* against heaven
Ro 3:23 for all have *s* and fall short
5:12 all *s*— for before the law was given,
2Pe 2: 4 did not spare angels when they *s*,
1Jn 1:10 claim we have not *s*, we make him

SINNER (SIN)

Ecc 9:18 but one *s* destroys much good.
Lk 15: 7 in heaven over one *s* who repents
18:13 'God, have mercy on me, a *s*.'
1Co 14:24 convinced by all that he is a *s*
Jas 5:20 Whoever turns a *s* from the error
1Pe 4:18 become of the ungodly and the *s*?"

SINNERS (SIN)

Ps 1: 1 or stand in the way of *s*
37:38 But all *s* will be destroyed;
Pr 1:10 My son, if *s* entice you,
23:17 Do not let your heart envy *s*,
Mt 9:13 come to call the righteous, but *s*."
Ro 5: 8 While we were still *s*, Christ died
Gal 2:17 evident that we ourselves are *s*,
1Ti 1:15 came into the world to save *s*—
Heb 7:26 set apart from *s*, exalted

SINNING (SIN)

Ex 20:20 be with you to keep you from *s*."
1Co 15:34 stop *s*; for there are some who are
Heb 10:26 If we deliberately keep on *s*
1Jn 3: 6 No one who lives in him keeps on *s*
3: 9 go on *s*, because he has been born

SINS (SIN)

Lev 5: 1 " 'If a person *s* because he does not
16:30 you will be clean from all your *s*.
26:40 " 'But if they will confess their *s*
Nu 15:30 " 'But anyone who *s* defiantly,
1Sa 2:25 If a man *s* against another man,
2Ki 14: 6 each is to die for his own *s*."
Ezr 9: 6 our *s* are higher than our heads
9:13 less than our *s* have deserved
Ps 19:13 your servant also from willful *s*;
32: 1 whose *s* are covered.
51: 9 Hide your face from my *s*
79: 9 deliver us and forgive our *s*
85: 2 and covered all their *s*.
103: 3 who forgives all your *s*
103:10 does not treat us as our *s* deserve

Ps 130: 3 O LORD, kept a record of *s*,
Pr 14:21 He who despises his neighbor *s*,
28:13 who conceals his *s* does not
29:22 one commits many *s*.
Ecc 7:20 who does what is right and never *s*.
Isa 1:18 "Though your *s* are like scarlet,
38:17 you have put all my *s*
43:25 and remembers your *s* no more.
59: 2 your *s* have hidden his face
64: 6 like the wind our *s* sweep us away.
Jer 31:34 and will remember their *s* no more
La 3:39 complain when punished for his *s*?
Eze 18: 4 soul who *s* is the one who will die.
33:10 Our offenses and *s* weigh us down,
36:33 day I cleanse you from all your *s*,
Hos 14: 1 Your *s* have been your downfall!
Mt 1:21 he will save his people from their *s*
6:15 if you do not forgive men their *s*,
9: 6 authority on earth to forgive *s*....."
18:15 "If your brother *s* against you,
26:28 for many for the forgiveness of *s*.
Lk 5:24 authority on earth to forgive *s*....."
11: 4 Forgive us our *s*,
17: 3 "If your brother *s*, rebuke him,
Jn 8:24 you will indeed die in your *s*."
20:23 If you forgive anyone his *s*,
Ac 2:38 for the forgiveness of your *s*.
3:19 so that your *s* may be wiped out,
10:43 forgiveness of *s* through his name."
22:16 be baptized and wash your *s* away,
26:18 they may receive forgiveness of *s*
Ro 4: 7 whose *s* are covered.
4:25 delivered over to death for our *s*
1Co 15: 3 died for our *s* according
2Co 5:19 not counting men's *s* against them.
Gal 1: 4 himself for our *s* to rescue us
Eph 2: 1 dead in your transgressions and *s*,
Col 2:13 us all our *s*, having canceled
1Ti 5:22 and do not share in the *s* of others.
Heb 1: 3 he had provided purification for *s*,
2:17 atonement for the *s* of the people.
7:27 He sacrificed for their *s* once for all
8:12 and will remember their *s* no more
9:28 to take away the *s* of many people;
10: 4 of bulls and goats to take away *s*.
10:12 for all time one sacrifice for *s*,
10:26 of the truth, no sacrifice for *s* is left,
Jas 4:17 ought to do and doesn't do it, *s*.
5:16 Therefore confess your *s*
5:20 and cover over a multitude of *s*.
1Pe 2:24 He himself bore our *s* in his body
3:18 For Christ died for *s* once for all,
4: 8 love covers over a multitude of *s*.
1Jn 1: 9 If we confess our *s*, he is faithful
2: 2 He is the atoning sacrifice for our *s*,
3: 5 so that he might take away our *s*.
4:10 as an atoning sacrifice for our *s*.
Rev 1: 5 has freed us from our *s* by his blood

SISERA
Jdg 4: 2 The commander of his army was *S*,
5:26 She struck *S*, she crushed his head,

SISTER (SISTERS)
Lev 18: 9 have sexual relations with your *s*,
Mk 3:35 does God's will is my brother and *s*

SISTERS (SISTER)
Mt 19:29 or brothers or *s* or father or mother
1Ti 5: 2 as *s*, with absolute purity.

SIT (SAT SITS SITTING)
Dt 6: 7 them when you *s* at home
1Ki 8:25 fail to have a man to *s* before me
Ps 1: 1 or *s* in the seat of mockers.
26: 5 and refuse to *s* with the wicked.
80: 1 you who *s* enthroned
110: 1 "*S* at my right hand
139: 2 You know when I *s* and when I rise
SS 2: 3 I delight to *s* in his shade,
Isa 16: 5 in faithfulness a man will *s* on it—
Mic 4: 4 Every man will *s* under his own
Mt 20:23 to *s* at my right or left is not for me
22:44 "*S* at my right hand
Lk 22:30 in my kingdom and *s* on thrones,
Heb 1:13 "*S* at my right hand
Rev 3:21 right to *s* with me on my throne,

SITS (SIT)
Ps 99: 1 *s* enthroned between the cherubim,
Isa 40:22 He *s* enthroned above the circle
Mt 19:28 of Man *s* on his glorious throne,
Rev 4: 9 thanks to him who *s* on the throne

SITTING (SIT)
Est 2:19 Mordecai was *s* at the king's gate.
Mt 26:64 the Son of Man *s* at the right hand
Rev 4: 2 in heaven with someone *s* on it.

SITUATION (SITUATIONS)
1Co 7:24 remain in the *s* God called him
Php 4:12 of being content in any and every *s*,

SITUATIONS* (SITUATION)
2Ti 4: 5 head in all *s*, endure hardship,

SKIES (SKY)
Ps 19: 1 the *s* proclaim the work
71:19 Your righteousness reaches to the *s*
108: 4 your faithfulness reaches to the *s*.

SKILL (SKILLED SKILLFUL)
Ps 137: 5 may my right hand forget ›its *s*‹.
Ecc 10:10 but *s* will bring success.

SKILLED (SKILL)
Pr 22:29 Do you see a man *s* in his work?

SKILLFUL (SKILL)
Ps 45: 1 my tongue is the pen of a *s* writer.
78:72 with *s* hands he led them.

SKIN (SKINS)
Job 19:20 with only the *s* of my teeth.
19:26 And after my *s* has been destroyed,
Jer 13:23 Can the Ethiopian change his *s*

SKINS (SKIN)
Ex 25: 5 ram *s* dyed red and hides
Lk 5:37 the new wine will burst the *s*,

SKULL
Mt 27:33 (which means The Place of the *S*).

SKY (SKIES)
Ge 1: 8 God called the expanse "*s*."
Pr 30:19 the way of an eagle in the *s*,
Isa 34: 4 and the *s* rolled up like a scroll;
Jer 33:22 stars of the *s* and as measureless
Mt 24:29 the stars will fall from the *s*,
24:30 coming on the clouds of the *s*,
Rev 20:11 Earth and *s* fled from his presence,

SLACK*
Pr 18: 9 One who is *s* in his work

SLAIN (SLAY)
1Sa 18: 7 "Saul has *s* his thousands,
Eze 37: 9 into these *s*, that they may live.' "
Rev 5: 6 as if it had been *s*, standing
5:12 "Worthy is the Lamb, who was *s*,
6: 9 the souls of those who had been *s*

SLANDER (SLANDERED SLANDERER SLANDERERS SLANDEROUS)
Lev 19:16 " 'Do not go about spreading *s*
Ps 15: 3 and has no *s* on his tongue,
Pr 10:18 and whoever spreads *s* is a fool.
2Co 12:20 outbursts of anger, factions, *s*,
Eph 4:31 rage and anger, brawling and *s*,
1Ti 5:14 the enemy no opportunity for *s*.
Tit 3: 2 to *s* no one, to be peaceable
1Pe 3:16 in Christ may be ashamed of their *s*
2Pe 2:10 afraid to *s* celestial beings;

SLANDERED (SLANDER)
1Co 4:13 when we are *s*, we answer kindly.

SLANDERER (SLANDER)
1Co 5:11 an idolater or a *s*, a drunkard

SLANDERERS (SLANDER)
Ro 1:30 They are gossips, *s*, God-haters,
1Co 6:10 nor the greedy nor drunkards nor *s*
Tit 2: 3 not to be *s* or addicted

SLANDEROUS (SLANDER)
2Ti 3: 3 unforgiving, *s*, without self-control
2Pe 2:11 do not bring *s* accusations

SLAUGHTER (SLAUGHTERED)
Isa 53: 7 he was led like a lamb to the *s*,
Jer 11:19 been like a gentle lamb led to the *s*;
Ac 8:32 "He was led like a sheep to the *s*,

SLAUGHTERED (SLAUGHTER)
Ps 44:22 we are considered as sheep to be *s*.
Ro 8:36 we are considered as sheep to be *s*

SLAVE (ENSLAVED SLAVERY SLAVES)
Ge 21:10 "Get rid of that *s* woman
Mt 20:27 wants to be first must be your *s*—
Jn 8:34 everyone who sins is a *s* to sin.
Ro 7:14 I am unspiritual, sold as a *s* to sin.
1Co 7:21 Were you a *s* when you were called
12:13 whether Jews or Greeks, *s* or free
Gal 3:28 *s* nor free, male nor female,
4: 7 So you are no longer a *s*, but a son;
4:30 Get rid of the *s* woman and her son
Col 3:11 barbarian, Scythian, *s* or free,
1Ti 1:10 for *s* traders and liars and perjurers
Phm :16 no longer as a *s*, but better than a *s*,
2Pe 2:19 a man is a *s* to whatever has

SLAVERY (SLAVE)
Ex 2:23 The Israelites groaned in their *s*
Ro 6:19 parts of your body in *s* to impurity
Gal 4: 3 were in *s* under the basic principles
1Ti 6: 1 of *s* should consider their masters

SLAVES (SLAVE)
Ps 123: 2 As the eyes of *s* look to the hand
Ecc 10: 7 I have seen *s* on horseback,
Ro 6: 6 that we should no longer be *s* to sin
6:16 you are *s* to sin, which leads
6:22 and have become *s* to God,
Gal 2: 4 in Christ Jesus and to make us *s*.
4: 8 you were *s* to those who
Eph 6: 5 *S*, obey your earthly masters
Col 3:22 *S*, obey your earthly masters
4: 1 provide your *s* with what is right
Tit 2: 9 Teach *s* to be subject

SLAY (SLAIN)
Job 13:15 Though he *s* me, yet will I hope

SLEEP (ASLEEP SLEEPER SLEEPING SLEEPS)
Ge 2:21 the man to fall into a deep *s*;
15:12 Abram fell into a deep *s*,
28:11 it under his head and lay down to *s*.
Ps 4: 8 I will lie down and *s* in peace,
121: 4 will neither slumber nor *s*.
127: 2 for he grants *s* to those he loves.
Pr 6: 9 When will you get up from your *s*?
Ecc 5:12 The *s* of a laborer is sweet,
1Co 15:51 We will not all *s*, but we will all be
1Th 5: 7 For those who *s*, *s* at night,

SLEEPER (SLEEP)
Eph 5:14 "Wake up, O *s*,

SLEEPING (SLEEP)
Mk 13:36 suddenly, do not let him find you *s*.

SLEEPLESS*
2Co 6: 5 in hard work, *s* nights and hunger;

SLEEPS (SLEEP)
Pr 10: 5 he who *s* during harvest is

SLIMY
Ps 40: 2 He lifted me out of the *s* pit,

SLING
1Sa 17:50 over the Philistine with a *s*

SLIP (SLIPPING)
Dt 4: 9 let them *s* from your heart as long
Ps 121: 3 He will not let your foot *s*—

SLIPPING (SLIP)
Ps 66: 9 and kept our feet from *s.*

SLOW
Ex 34: 6 and gracious God, *s* to anger,
Jas 1:19 *s* to speak and *s* to become angry,
2Pe 3: 9 The Lord is not *s* in keeping his

SLUGGARD
Pr 6: 6 Go to the ant, you *s;*
13: 4 The *s* craves and gets nothing,
20: 4 A *s* does not plow in season;
26:15 The *s* buries his hand in the dish;

SLUMBER
Ps 121: 3 he who watches over you will not *s;*
Pr 6:10 A little sleep, a little *s,*
Ro 13:11 for you to wake up from your *s,*

SLUR
Ps 15: 3 and casts no *s* on his fellow man,

SMELL
Ecc 10: 1 As dead flies give perfume a bad *s,*
2Co 2:16 To the one we are the *s* of death;

SMITTEN
Isa 53: 4 *s* by him, and afflicted.

SMOKE
Ex 19:18 Mount Sinai was covered with *s,*
Ps 104:32 touches the mountains, and they *s.*
Isa 6: 4 and the temple was filled with *s.*
Joel 2:30 blood and fire and billows of *s.*
Ac 2:19 blood and fire and billows of *s.*
Rev 15: 8 filled with *s* from the glory

SMYRNA
Rev 2: 8 the angel of the church in *S* write:

SNAKE (SNAKES)
Nu 21: 8 "Make a *s* and put it up on a pole;
Pr 23:32 In the end it bites like a *s*
Jn 3:14 Moses lifted up the *s* in the desert,

SNAKES (SNAKE)
Mt 10:16 as shrewd as *s* and as innocent
Mk 16:18 they will pick up *s* with their hands;

SNARE (ENSNARE ENSNARED SNARED)
Dt 7:16 for that will be a *s* to you.
Ps 69:22 before them become a *s;*
91: 3 from the fowler's *s*
Pr 29:25 Fear of man will prove to be a *s,*
Ro 11: 9 "May their table become a *s*

SNARED (SNARE)
Pr 3:26 will keep your foot from being *s.*

SNATCH
Jn 10:28 no one can *s* them out of my hand.
Jude :23 *s* others from the fire and save

SNOUT
Pr 11:22 Like a gold ring in a pig's *s*

SNOW
Ps 51: 7 and I will be whiter than *s.*
Isa 1:18 they shall be as white as *s;*

SNUFF (SNUFFED)
Isa 42: 3 a smoldering wick he will not *s* out.
Mt 12:20 a smoldering wick he will not *s* out,

SNUFFED (SNUFF)
Pr 13: 9 but the lamp of the wicked is *s* out.

SOAP
Mal 3: 2 a refiner's fire or a launderer's *s.*

SOAR (SOARED)
Isa 40:31 They will *s* on wings like eagles;

SOARED (SOAR)
2Sa 22:11 he *s* on the wings of the wind.

SOBER
Ro 12: 3 think of yourself with *s* judgment,

SODOM
Ge 13:12 and pitched his tents near *S.*
19:24 rained down burning sulfur on *S*
Isa 1: 9 we would have become like *S,*
Lk 10:12 on that day for *S* than for that town
Ro 9:29 we would have become like *S,*
Rev 11: 8 which is figuratively called *S*

SOIL
Ge 4: 2 kept flocks, and Cain worked the *s.*
Mt 13:23 on good *s* is the man who hears

SOLD (SELL)
1Ki 21:25 who *s* himself to do evil in the eyes
Mt 10:29 Are not two sparrows *s* for a penny
13:44 then in his joy went and *s* all he had
Ro 7:14 I am unspiritual, *s* as a slave to sin.

SOLDIER
1Co 9: 7 as a *s* at his own expense?
2Ti 2: 3 with us like a good *s* of Christ Jesus

SOLE
Dt 28:65 place for the *s* of your foot.
Isa 1: 6 From the *s* of your foot to the top

SOLID
2Ti 2:19 God's *s* foundation stands firm,
Heb 5:12 You need milk, not *s* food!

SOLOMON
Son of David by Bathsheba; king of Judah (2Sa 12:24; 1Ch 3:5, 10). Appointed king by David (1Ki 1); adversaries Adonijah, Joab, Shimei killed by Benaiah (1Ki 2). Asked for wisdom (1Ki 3; 2Ch 1). Judged between two prostitutes (1Ki 3:16–28). Built temple (1Ki 5–7; 2Ch 2–5); prayer of dedication (1Ki 8; 2Ch 6). Visited by Queen of Sheba (1Ki 10; 2Ch 9). Wives turned his heart from God (1Ki 11:1–13). Jeroboam rebelled against (1Ki 11:26–40). Death (1Ki 11:41–43; 2Ch 9:29–31).
Proverbs of (1Ki 4:32; Pr 1:1; 10:1; 25:1); psalms of (Ps 72; 127); song of (SS 1:1).

SON (SONS SONSHIP)
Ge 17:19 your wife Sarah will bear you a *s,*
21:10 rid of that slave woman and her *s,*
22: 2 "Take your *s,* your only *s,* Isaac,
Ex 11: 5 Every firstborn *s* in Egypt will die,
Dt 1:31 father carries his *s,* all the way you
6:20 In the future, when your *s* asks you,
8: 5 as a man disciplines his *s,*
21:18 rebellious *s* who does not obey his
2Sa 7:14 be his father, and he will be my *s.*
1Ki 3:20 and put her dead *s* by my breast.
Ps 2: 7 He said to me, "You are my *S;*
2:12 Kiss the *S,* lest he be angry
8: 4 the *s* of man that you care for him?
Pr 3:12 as a father the *s* he delights in.
6:20 My *s,* keep your father's
10: 1 A wise *s* brings joy to his father,
13:24 He who spares the rod hates his *s,*
29:17 Discipline your *s,* and he will give
Isa 7:14 with child and will give birth to a *s,*
Eze 18:20 The *s* will not share the guilt
Da 3:25 the fourth looks like a *s* of the gods
7:13 before me was one like a *s* of man,
Hos 11: 1 and out of Egypt I called my *s.*
Am 7:14 neither a prophet nor a prophet's *s,*
Mt 1: 1 of Jesus Christ the *s* of David,
1:21 She will give birth to a *s,*
2:15 "Out of Egypt I called my *s.*"
3:17 "This is my *S,* whom I love;
4: 3 "If you are the *S* of God, tell these
8:20 but the *S* of Man has no place
11:27 one knows the *S* except the Father,
12: 8 For the *S* of Man is Lord
12:32 a word against the *S* of Man will be
12:40 so the *S* of Man will be three days
13:41 *S* of Man will send out his angels,
13:55 "Isn't this the carpenter's *s?*
14:33 "Truly you are the *S* of God."
16:16 "You are the Christ, the *S*
16:27 For the *S* of Man is going to come
17: 5 "This is my *S,* whom I love;
19:28 when the *S* of Man sits
20:18 and the *S* of Man will be betrayed
20:28 as the *S* of Man did not come
21: 9 "Hosanna to the *S* of David!"
22:42 Whose *s* is he?" "The *s* of David,"
24:27 so will be the coming of the *S*
24:30 They will see the *S* of Man coming
24:44 the *S* of Man will come at an hour
25:31 "When the *S* of Man comes
26:63 if you are the Christ, the *S* of God."
27:54 "Surely he was the *S* of God!"
28:19 and of the *S* and of the Holy Spirit,
Mk 1:11 "You are my *S,* whom I love;
2:28 So the *S* of Man is Lord
8:38 the *S* of Man will be ashamed
9: 7 "This is my *S,* whom I love.
10:45 even the *S* of Man did not come
13:32 nor the *S,* but only the Father.
14:62 you will see the *S* of Man sitting
Lk 1:32 and will be called the *S*
2: 7 she gave birth to her firstborn, a *s.*
3:22 "You are my *S,* whom I love;
9:35 This is my *S,* whom I have chosen;
9:58 but the *S* of Man has no place
12: 8 the *S* of Man will also acknowledge
15:20 he ran to his *s,* threw his arms
18: 8 when the *S* of Man comes,
18:31 written by the prophets about the *S*
19:10 For the *S* of Man came to seek
Jn 1:34 I testify that this is the *S* of God."
3:14 so the *S* of Man must be lifted up,
3:16 that he gave his one and only *S,*
3:36 believes in the *S* has eternal life,
5:19 the *S* can do nothing by himself;
6:40 is that everyone who looks to the *S*
11: 4 so that God's *S* may be glorified
17: 1 Glorify your *S,* that your *S* may
Ac 7:56 and the *S* of Man standing
13:33 " 'You are my *S;*
Ro 1: 4 with power to be the *S* of God
5:10 to him through the death of his *S,*
8: 3 did by sending his own *S*
8:29 conformed to the likeness of his *S,*
8:32 He who did not spare his own *S,*
1Co 15:28 then the *S* himself will be made
Gal 2:20 I live by faith in the *S* of God,
4: 4 God sent his *S,* born of a woman,
4:30 rid of the slave woman and her *s,*
1Th 1:10 and to wait for his *S* from heaven,
Heb 1: 2 days he has spoken to us by his *S,*
1: 5 "You are my *S;*
2: 6 the *s* of man that you care for him?
4:14 Jesus the *S* of God, let us hold
5: 5 "You are my *S;*
7:28 appointed the *S,* who has been
10:29 punished who has trampled the *S*
12: 6 everyone he accepts as a *s.*"
2Pe 1:17 saying, "This is my *S,* whom I love;

Job 33: 4 The *S* of God has made me;
Ps 31: 5 Into your hands I commit my *s;*
34:18 saves those who are crushed in *s.*
51:10 and renew a steadfast *s* within me.
51:11 or take your Holy *S* from me.
51:17 sacrifices of God are a broken *s;*
106:33 rebelled against the *S* of God,
139: 7 Where can I go from your *S?*
143:10 may your good *S*
Isa 11: 2 The *S* of the LORD will rest
30: 1 an alliance, but not by my *S,*
32:15 till the *S* is poured upon us
44: 3 I will pour out my *S*
57:15 him who is contrite and lowly in *s,*
61: 1 The *S* of the Sovereign LORD is
63:10 and grieved his Holy *S.*
Eze 11:19 an undivided heart and put a new *s*
13: 3 prophets who follow their own *s*
36:26 you a new heart and put a new *s*
Da 4: 8 and the *s* of the holy gods is in him
Joel 2:28 I will pour out my *S* on all people.
Zec 4: 6 but by my *S,'* says the LORD
Mt 1:18 to be with child through the Holy *S*
3:11 will baptize you with the Holy *S*
3:16 he saw the *S* of God descending
4: 1 led by the *S* into the desert
5: 3 saying: "Blessed are the poor in *s,*
10:20 but the *S* of your Father speaking
12:31 against the *S* will not be forgiven.
26:41 *s* is willing, but the body is weak."
28:19 and of the Son and of the Holy *S,*
Mk 1: 8 he will baptize you with the Holy *S*
Lk 1:35 "The Holy *S* will come upon you,
1:80 child grew and became strong in *s;*
3:16 will baptize you with the Holy *S*
4:18 "The *S* of the Lord is on me,
11:13 Father in heaven give the Holy *S*
23:46 into your hands I commit my *s."*
Jn 1:33 who will baptize with the Holy *S.'*
3: 5 a man is born of water and the *S,*
4:24 God is *s,* and his worshipers must
6:63 The *S* gives life; the flesh counts
7:39 Up to that time the *S* had not been
14:26 But the Counselor, the Holy *S,*
16:13 But when he, the *S* of truth, comes,
20:22 and said, "Receive the Holy *S.*
Ac 1: 5 will be baptized with the Holy *S."*
1: 8 when the Holy *S* comes on you;
2: 4 of them were filled with the Holy *S*
2:17 I will pour out my *S* on all people.
2:38 will receive the gift of the Holy *S.*
4:31 they were all filled with the Holy *S*
5: 3 that you have lied to the Holy *S*
6: 3 who are known to be full of the *S*
8:15 that they might receive the Holy *S,*
9:17 and be filled with the Holy *S."*
11:16 will be baptized with the Holy *S.'*
13: 2 and fasting, the Holy *S* said,
19: 2 "Did you receive the Holy *S*
Ro 8: 4 nature but according to the *S.*
8: 5 set on what the *S* desires.
8: 9 And if anyone does not have the *S*
8:13 but if by the *S* you put
8:16 The *S* himself testifies
8:23 who have the firstfruits of the *S,*
8:26 the *S* helps us in our weakness.
1Co 2:10 God has revealed it to us by his *S.*
2:14 man without the *S* does not accept
5: 3 present, I am with you in *s.*
6:19 body is a temple of the Holy *S,*
12:13 baptized by one *S* into one body—
2Co 1:22 and put his *S* in our hearts
3: 3 but with the *S* of the living God,
3: 6 the letter kills, but the *S* gives life.
3:17 Now the Lord is the *S,*
5: 5 and has given us the *S* as a deposit,
7: 1 that contaminates body and *s,*
Gal 3: 2 Did you receive the *S*
5:16 by the *S,* and you will not gratify
5:22 But the fruit of the *S* is love, joy,
Gal 5:25 let us keep in step with the *S.*
6: 8 from the *S* will reap eternal life.
Eph 1:13 with a seal, the promised Holy *S,*
2:22 in which God lives by his *S.*
4: 4 There is one body and one *S*—
4:30 do not grieve the Holy *S* of God,
5:18 Instead, be filled with the *S.*
6:17 of salvation and the sword of the *S,*
Php 2: 2 being one in *s* and purpose.
1Th 5:23 May your whole *s,* soul
2Th 2:13 the sanctifying work of the *S*
1Ti 3:16 was vindicated by the *S,*
2Ti 1: 7 For God did not give us a *s*
Heb 2: 4 of the Holy *S* distributed according
4:12 even to dividing soul and *s,*
10:29 and who has insulted the *S* of grace
1Pe 3: 4 beauty of a gentle and quiet *s,*
2Pe 1:21 carried along by the Holy *S.*
1Jn 3:24 We know it by the *S* he gave us.
4: 1 Dear friends, do not believe every *s*
4:13 because he has given us of his *S.*
Jude :20 holy faith and pray in the Holy *S.*
Rev 2: 7 let him hear what the *S* says

SPIRIT'S* (SPIRIT)
1Co 2: 4 a demonstration of the *S* power,
1Th 5:19 not put out the *S* fire; do not treat

SPIRITS (SPIRIT)
1Co 12:10 to another distinguishing between *s,*
14:32 The *s* of prophets are subject
1Jn 4: 1 test the *s* to see whether they are

SPIRITUAL (SPIRIT)
Ro 12: 1 to God—this is your *s* act of worship.
12:11 but keep your *s* fervor, serving
1Co 2:13 expressing *s* truths in *s* words.
3: 1 I could not address you as *s* but
12: 1 Now about *s* gifts, brothers,
14: 1 of love and eagerly desire *s* gifts,
15:44 a natural body, it is raised a *s* body.
Gal 6: 1 you who are *s* should restore him
Eph 1: 3 with every *s* blessing in Christ.
5:19 with psalms, hymns and *s* songs.
6:12 and against the *s* forces of evil
1Pe 2: 2 newborn babies, crave pure *s* milk,
2: 5 are being built into a *s* house

SPIRITUALLY (SPIRIT)
1Co 2:14 because they are *s* discerned.

SPIT
Mt 27:30 They *s* on him, and took the staff
Rev 3:16 I am about to *s* you out

SPLENDOR
1Ch 16:29 the LORD in the *s* of his holiness.
29:11 the glory and the majesty and the *s,*
Job 37:22 of the north he comes in golden *s;*
Ps 29: 2 in the *s* of his holiness.
45: 3 clothe yourself with *s* and majesty.
96: 6 *S* and majesty are before him;
96: 9 in the *s* of his holiness;
104: 1 you are clothed with *s* and majesty.
145: 5 of the glorious *s* of your majesty,
145:12 and the glorious *s* of your kingdom.
148:13 his *s* is above the earth
Pr 4: 9 and present you with a crown of *s."*
16:31 Gray hair is a crown of *s;*
20:29 gray hair the *s* of the old.
Isa 55: 5 for he has endowed you with *s."*
60:21 for the display of my *s.*
61: 3 the LORD for the display of his *s.*
63: 1 Who is this, robed in *s,*
Hab 3: 4 His *s* was like the sunrise;
Mt 6:29 in all his *s* was dressed like one
Lk 9:31 appeared in glorious *s,* talking
2Th 2: 8 and destroy by the *s* of his coming.

SPOIL (SPOILS)
Ps 119:162 like one who finds great *s.*

SPOILS (SPOIL)
Isa 53:12 he will divide the *s* with the strong,
Jn 6:27 Do not work for food that *s,*

SPONTANEOUS*
Phm :14 so that any favor you do will be *s*

SPOTLESS
2Pe 3:14 make every effort to be found *s,*

SPOTS (SPOTTED)
Jer 13:23 or the leopard its *s?*

SPOTTED (SPOTS)
Ge 30:32 and every *s* or speckled goat.

SPREAD (SPREADING SPREADS)
Ps 78:19 "Can God *s* a table in the desert?
Ac 6: 7 So the word of God *s.*
12:24 of God continued to increase and *s.*
13:49 of the Lord *s* through the whole
19:20 the word of the Lord *s* widely
2Th 3: 1 message of the Lord may *s* rapidly

SPREADING (SPREAD)
Pr 29: 5 is *s* a net for his feet.
1Th 3: 2 God's fellow worker in *s* the gospel

SPREADS (SPREAD)
Pr 10:18 and whoever *s* slander is a fool.

SPRING (SPRINGS WELLSPRING)
Jer 2:13 the *s* of living water,
Jn 4:14 in him a *s* of water welling up
Jas 3:12 can a salt *s* produce fresh water.

SPRINGS (SPRING)
2Pe 2:17 These men are *s* without water

SPRINKLE (SPRINKLED SPRINKLING)
Lev 16:14 and with his finger *s* it on the front

SPRINKLED (SPRINKLE)
Heb 10:22 having our hearts *s* to cleanse us

SPRINKLING (SPRINKLE)
1Pe 1: 2 to Jesus Christ and *s* by his blood:

SPROUT
Pr 23: 5 for they will surely *s* wings
Jer 33:15 I will make a righteous Branch *s*

SPUR*
Heb 10:24 how we may *s* one another

SPURNS*
Pr 15: 5 A fool *s* his father's discipline,

SPY
Gal 2: 4 ranks to *s* on the freedom we have

SQUANDERED (SQUANDERS)
Lk 15:13 there *s* his wealth in wild living.

SQUANDERS* (SQUANDERED)
Pr 29: 3 of prostitutes *s* his wealth.

SQUARE
Rev 21:16 The city was laid out like a *s,*

STABILITY*
Pr 29: 4 By justice a king gives a country *s,*

STAFF
Ge 49:10 the ruler's *s* from between his feet,
Ex 7:12 Aaron's *s* swallowed up their staffs.
Nu 17: 6 and Aaron's *s* was among them.
Ps 23: 4 your rod and your *s,*

STAIN (STAINED)
Eph 5:27 without *s* or wrinkle or any other

STAINED (STAIN)
Isa 63: 1 with his garments *s* crimson?

STAKES
Isa 54: 2 strengthen your *s*.

STAND (STANDING STANDS STOOD)
Ex 14:13 *S* firm and you will see
Jos 10:12 "O sun, *s* still over Gibeon,
2Ch 20:17 *s* firm and see the deliverance
Job 19:25 in the end he will *s* upon the earth.
Ps 1: 1 or *s* in the way of sinners
1: 5 Therefore the wicked will not *s*
24: 3 Who may *s* in his holy place?
33:11 of the LORD *s* firm forever,
40: 2 and gave me a firm place to *s*.
76: 7 Who can *s* before you
93: 5 Your statutes *s* firm;
119:120 I *s* in awe of your laws.
130: 3 O Lord, who could *s*?
Ecc 5: 7 Therefore *s* in awe of God.
Isa 7: 9 If you do not *s* firm in your faith,
29:23 will *s* in awe of the God of Israel.
Eze 22:30 *s* before me in the gap on behalf
Hab 3: 2 I *s* in awe of your deeds, O LORD.
Zec 14: 4 On that day his feet will *s*
Mal 3: 2 Who can *s* when he appears?
Mt 12:25 divided against itself will not *s*.
Ro 14: 4 for the Lord is able to make him *s*.
14:10 we will all *s* before God's judgment
1Co 10:13 out so that you can *s* up under it.
15:58 Therefore, my dear brothers, *s* firm
16:13 Be on your guard; *s* firm in the faith
Gal 5: 1 *S* firm, then, and do not let
Eph 6:14 *S* firm then, with the belt
2Th 2:15 *s* firm and hold to the teachings we
Jas 5: 8 You too, be patient and *s* firm,
Rev 3:20 Here I am! I *s* at the door

STANDING (STAND)
Ex 3: 5 where you are *s* is holy ground."
Jos 5:15 the place where you are *s* is holy."
Ru 2: 1 a man of *s*, whose name was Boaz.
4:11 May you have *s* in Ephrathah
Lk 21:19 By *s* firm you will gain life.
1Ti 3:13 have served well gain an excellent *s*
1Pe 5: 9 Resist him, *s* firm in the faith,

STANDS (STAND)
Ps 89: 2 that your love *s* firm forever,
119:89 it *s* firm in the heavens.
Pr 12: 7 the house of the righteous *s* firm.
Isa 40: 8 but the word of our God *s* forever."
Mt 10:22 but he who *s* firm to the end will be
2Ti 2:19 God's solid foundation *s* firm,
1Pe 1:25 but the word of the Lord *s* forever

STAR (STARS)
Nu 24:17 A *s* will come out of Jacob;
Isa 14:12 O morning *s*, son of the dawn!
Mt 2: 2 We saw his *s* in the east
2Pe 1:19 the morning *s* rises in your hearts.
Rev 2:28 I will also give him the morning *s*.
22:16 and the bright Morning *S*."

STARS (STAR)
Ge 1:16 He also made the *s*.
Job 38: 7 while the morning *s* sang together
Da 12: 3 like the *s* for ever and ever.
Php 2:15 in which you shine like *s*

STATURE
1Sa 2:26 boy Samuel continued to grow in *s*
Lk 2:52 And Jesus grew in wisdom and *s*,

STATUTES
Ps 19: 7 *s* of the LORD are trustworthy,
93: 5 Your *s* stand firm;
119: 2 Blessed are they who keep his *s*
119:14 I rejoice in following your *s*
119:24 Your *s* are my delight;
119:36 Turn my heart toward your *s*
119:99 for I meditate on your *s*.
119:111 Your *s* are my heritage forever;
Ps 119:125 that I may understand your *s*.
119:129 Your *s* are wonderful;
119:138 The *s* you have laid
119:152 Long ago I learned from your *s*
119:167 I obey your *s*,

STEADFAST*
Ps 51:10 and renew a *s* spirit within me.
57: 7 My heart is *s*, O God,
57: 7 my heart is *s*;
108: 1 My heart is *s*, O God;
111: 8 They are *s* for ever and ever,
112: 7 his heart is *s*, trusting in the LORD
119: 5 Oh, that my ways were *s*
Isa 26: 3 him whose mind is *s*,
1Pe 5:10 and make you strong, firm and *s*.

STEADY
Isa 35: 3 *s* the knees that give way;

STEAL (STOLEN)
Ex 20:15 "You shall not *s*.
Lev 19:11 " 'Do not *s*.
Dt 5:19 "You shall not *s*.
Mt 19:18 do not *s*, do not give false
Ro 13: 9 "Do not *s*," "Do not covet,"
Eph 4:28 has been stealing must *s* no longer,

STEP (FOOTSTEPS STEPS)
Job 34:21 he sees their every *s*.
Gal 5:25 let us keep in *s* with the Spirit.

STEPHEN
Deacon (Ac 6:5). Arrested (Ac 6:8–15). Speech
to Sanhedrin (Ac 7). Stoned (Ac 7:54–60; 22:20).

STEPS (STEP)
Ps 37:23 he makes his *s* firm;
Pr 14:15 prudent man gives thought to his *s*.
16: 9 but the LORD determines his *s*.
20:24 A man's *s* are directed
Jer 10:23 it is not for man to direct his *s*.
1Pe 2:21 that you should follow in his *s*.

STERN (STERNNESS)
Pr 15:10 *S* discipline awaits him who leaves

STERNNESS* (STERN)
Ro 11:22 and *s* of God: *s* to those who fell,

STICKS
Pr 18:24 there is a friend who *s* closer

STIFF-NECKED (NECK)
Ex 34: 9 Although this is a *s* people,
Pr 29: 1 A man who remains *s*

STILL
Jos 10:13 So the sun stood *s*,
Ps 37: 7 Be *s* before the LORD
46:10 "Be *s*, and know that I am God;
89: 9 its waves mount up, you *s* them.
Zec 2:13 Be *s* before the LORD, all mankind
Mk 4:39 said to the waves, "Quiet! Be *s*!"

STIMULATE*
2Pe 3: 1 as reminders to *s* you

STING
1Co 15:55 Where, O death, is your *s*?"

STINGY
Pr 28:22 A *s* man is eager to get rich

STIRRED (STIRS)
Ps 45: 1 My heart is *s* by a noble theme

STIRS (STIRRED)
Pr 6:19 and a man who *s* up dissension
10:12 Hatred *s* up dissension,
15: 1 but a harsh word *s* up anger.
15:18 hot-tempered man *s* up dissension,
16:28 A perverse man *s* up dissension,
Pr 28:25 A greedy man *s* up dissension,
29:22 An angry man *s* up dissension,

STOLEN (STEAL)
Lev 6: 4 he must return what he has *s*
SS 4: 9 You have *s* my heart, my sister,

STOMACH
1Co 6:13 Food for the *s* and the *s* for food"—
Php 3:19 their god is their *s*, and their glory

STONE (CAPSTONE CORNERSTONE MILLSTONE STONED STONES)
Ex 24: 4 set up twelve *s* pillars representing
28:10 on one *s* and the remaining six
34: 1 "Chisel out two *s* tablets like
Dt 4:13 then wrote them on two *s* tablets.
19:14 your neighbor's boundary *s* set up
1Sa 17:50 the Philistine with a sling and a *s*;
Ps 91:12 will not strike your foot against a *s*.
118:22 The *s* the builders rejected
Pr 22:28 not move an ancient boundary *s*
Isa 8:14 a *s* that causes men to stumble
28:16 "See, I lay a *s* in Zion,
Eze 11:19 remove from them their heart of *s*
36:26 remove from you your heart of *s*
Mt 7: 9 will give him a *s*? Or if he asks
21:42 " 'The *s* the builders rejected
24: 2 not one *s* here will be left
Mk 16: 3 "Who will roll the *s* away
Lk 4: 3 tell this *s* to become bread."
Jn 8: 7 the first to throw a *s* at her."
Ac 4:11 " 'the *s* you builders rejected,
Ro 9:32 stumbled over the "stumbling *s*."
2Co 3: 3 not on tablets of *s* but on tablets
1Pe 2: 6 "See, I lay a *s* in Zion,
Rev 2:17 also give him a white *s*

STONED (STONE)
2Co 11:25 once I was *s*, three times I was
Heb 11:37 They were *s*; they were sawed

STONES (STONE)
Ex 28:21 are to be twelve *s*, one for each
Jos 4: 3 to take up twelve *s* from the middle
1Sa 17:40 chose five smooth *s*
Mt 3: 9 out of these *s* God can raise up
1Co 3:12 silver, costly *s*, wood, hay or straw,
1Pe 2: 5 also, like living *s*, are being built

STOOD (STAND)
Jos 10:13 So the sun *s* still,
Lk 22:28 You are those who have *s* by me
2Ti 4:17 But the Lord *s* at my side
Jas 1:12 because when he has *s* the test,

STOOP (STOOPS)
2Sa 22:36 you *s* down to make me great.

STOOPS (STOOP)
Ps 113: 6 who *s* down to look

STOP
Job 37:14 *s* and consider God's wonders.
Isa 1:13 *S* bringing meaningless offerings!
1:16 *S* doing wrong,
2:22 *S* trusting in man,
Jer 32:40 I will never *s* doing good to them,
Mk 9:39 "Do not *s* him," Jesus said.
Jn 6:43 "*S* grumbling among yourselves,"
7:24 *S* judging by mere appearances,
20:27 *S* doubting and believe."
Ro 14:13 Therefore let us *s* passing judgment
1Co 14:20 Brothers, *s* thinking like children.

STORE (STORED)
Pr 2: 1 and *s* up my commands within you,
7: 1 and *s* up my commands within you.
10:14 Wise men *s* up knowledge,
Isa 33: 6 a rich *s* of salvation and wisdom
Mt 6:19 not *s* up for yourselves treasures
6:26 or reap or *s* away in barns,

2Ti 4: 8 Now there is in *s* for me the crown

STORED (STORE)
Lk 6:45 out of the good *s* up in his heart,
Col 1: 5 from the hope that is *s* up for you

STOREHOUSE (HOUSE)
Mal 3:10 Bring the whole tithe into the *s*,

STORIES*
2Pe 1:16 did not follow cleverly invented *s*
2: 3 you with *s* they have made up.

STORM
Job 38: 1 LORD answered Job out of the *s*.
Ps 107:29 He stilled the *s* to a whisper;
Lk 8:24 the *s* subsided, and all was calm.

STOUTHEARTED* (HEART)
Ps 138: 3 you made me bold and *s*.

STRAIGHT
Ps 27:11 lead me in a *s* path
107: 7 He led them by a *s* way
Pr 2:13 who leave the *s* paths
3: 6 and he will make your paths *s*.
4:11 and lead you along *s* paths.
4:25 Let your eyes look *s* ahead,
11: 5 of the blameless makes a *s* way
15:21 of understanding keeps a *s* course.
Isa 40: 3 make *s* in the wilderness
Mt 3: 3 make *s* paths for him.' "
Jn 1:23 'Make *s* the way for the Lord.' "
2Pe 2:15 They have left the *s* way

STRAIN (STRAINING)
Mt 23:24 You *s* out a gnat but swallow

STRAINING (STRAIN)
Php 3:13 and *s* toward what is ahead,

STRANGE (STRANGER STRANGERS)
Isa 28:11 with foreign lips and *s* tongues
1Co 14:21 "Through men of *s* tongues
1Pe 4: 4 They think it *s* that you do not

STRANGER (STRANGE)
Ps 119:19 I am a *s* on earth;
Mt 25:35 I was a *s* and you invited me in,
Jn 10: 5 But they will never follow a *s*;

STRANGERS (STRANGE)
Heb 13: 2 Do not forget to entertain *s*,
1Pe 2:11 as aliens and *s* in the world,

STRAW
Isa 11: 7 and the lion will eat *s* like the ox.
1Co 3:12 silver, costly stones, wood, hay or *s*

STRAYED (STRAYS)
Ps 119:176 I have *s* like a lost sheep.
Jer 31:19 After I *s*,

STRAYS (STRAYED)
Pr 21:16 A man who *s* from the path
Eze 34:16 for the lost and bring back the *s*.

STREAM (STREAMS)
Am 5:24 righteousness like a never-failing *s*!

STREAMS (STREAM)
Ps 1: 3 He is like a tree planted by *s*
46: 4 is a river whose *s* make glad
Ecc 1: 7 All *s* flow into the sea,
Jn 7:38 *s* of living water will flow

STREET
Mt 6: 5 on the *s* corners to be seen by men.
22: 9 Go to the *s* corners and invite
Rev 21:21 The great *s* of the city was of pure gold,

STRENGTH (STRONG)
Ex 15: 2 The LORD is my *s* and my song;
Dt 4:37 by his Presence and his great *s*,
6: 5 all your soul and with all your *s*.
Jdg 16:15 told me the secret of your great *s*."
2Sa 22:33 It is God who arms me with *s*
2Ki 23:25 with all his soul and with all his *s*,
1Ch 16:11 Look to the LORD and his *s*;
16:28 ascribe to the LORD glory and *s*,
29:12 In your hands are *s* and power
Ne 8:10 for the joy of the LORD is your *s*."
Ps 18: 1 I love you, O LORD, my *s*.
21:13 Be exalted, O LORD, in your *s*;
28: 7 The LORD is my *s* and my shield;
29:11 The LORD gives *s* to his people;
33:16 no warrior escapes by his great *s*.
46: 1 God is our refuge and *s*,
59:17 O my *S*, I sing praise to you;
65: 6 having armed yourself with *s*,
73:26 but God is the *s* of my heart
84: 5 Blessed are those whose *s* is in you,
96: 7 ascribe to the LORD glory and *s*.
105: 4 Look to the LORD and his *s*;
118:14 The LORD is my *s* and my song;
147:10 not in the *s* of the horse,
Pr 24: 5 a man of knowledge increases *s*;
30:25 Ants are creatures of little *s*,
Isa 12: 2 the LORD, is my *s* and my song;
31: 1 and in the great *s* of their horsemen
40:26 of his great power and mighty *s*,
40:31 will renew their *s*.
63: 1 forward in the greatness of his *s*?
Jer 9:23 or the strong man boast of his *s*
Mic 5: 4 flock in the *s* of the LORD,
Hab 3:19 The Sovereign LORD is my *s*;
Mk 12:30 all your mind and with all your *s*.
1Co 1:25 of God is stronger than man's *s*.
Eph 1:19 is like the working of his mighty *s*,
Php 4:13 through him who gives me *s*.
Heb 11:34 whose weakness was turned to *s*;
1Pe 4:11 it with the *s* God provides,

STRENGTHEN (STRONG)
2Ch 16: 9 to *s* those whose hearts are fully
Ps 119:28 *s* me according to your word.
Isa 35: 3 *S* the feeble hands,
41:10 I will *s* you and help you;
Lk 22:32 have turned back, *s* your brothers."
Eph 3:16 of his glorious riches he may *s* you
1Th 3:13 May he *s* your hearts
2Th 2:17 and *s* you in every good deed
Heb 12:12 *s* your feeble arms and weak knees.

STRENGTHENED (STRONG)
Col 1:11 being *s* with all power according
Heb 13: 9 good for our hearts to be *s* by grace,

STRENGTHENING (STRONG)
1Co 14:26 done for the *s* of the church.

STRETCHES
Ps 104: 2 he *s* out the heavens like a tent

STRICKEN (STRIKE)
Isa 53: 8 of my people he was *s*.

STRICT
1Co 9:25 in the games goes into *s* training.

STRIFE (STRIVE)
Pr 17: 1 than a house full of feasting, with *s*.
20: 3 It is to a man's honor to avoid *s*,
22:10 out the mocker, and out goes *s*;
30:33 so stirring up anger produces *s*."
1Ti 6: 4 *s*, malicious talk, evil suspicions

STRIKE (STRIKES STROKE)
Ge 3:15 and you will *s* his heel."
Zec 13: 7 "*S* the shepherd,
Mt 4: 6 so that you will not *s* your foot
26:31 " 'I will *s* the shepherd,

STRIKES (STRIKE)
Mt 5:39 If someone *s* you on the right

STRIPS
Lk 2:12 You will find a baby wrapped in *s*
Jn 20: 5 in at the *s* of linen lying there

STRIVE* (STRIFE)
Ac 24:16 I *s* always to keep my conscience
1Ti 4:10 (and for this we labor and *s*),

STROKE (STRIKE)
Mt 5:18 the smallest letter, not the least *s*

STRONG (STRENGTH STRENGTHEN STRENGTHENED STRENGTHENING STRONGER)
Dt 3:24 your greatness and your *s* hand.
31: 6 Be *s* and courageous.
Jos 1: 6 "Be *s* and courageous,
Jdg 5:21 March on, my soul; be *s*!
2Sa 10:12 Be *s* and let us fight bravely
1Ki 2: 2 "So be *s*, show yourself a man,
1Ch 28:20 "Be *s* and courageous,
2Ch 32: 7 them with these words: "Be *s*
Ps 24: 8 The LORD *s* and mighty,
31: 2 a *s* fortress to save me.
62:11 that you, O God, are *s*,
Pr 18:10 The name of the LORD is a *s* tower
31:17 her arms are *s* for her tasks.
Ecc 9:11 or the battle to the *s*,
SS 8: 6 for love is as *s* as death,
Isa 35: 4 "Be *s*, do not fear;
53:12 he will divide the spoils with the *s*,
Jer 9:23 or the *s* man boast of his strength
50:34 Yet their Redeemer is *s*;
Hag 2: 4 Be *s*, all you people of the land,'
Mt 12:29 can anyone enter a *s* man's house
Lk 2:40 And the child grew and became *s*;
Ro 15: 1 We who are *s* ought to bear
1Co 1: 8 He will keep you *s* to the end,
1:27 things of the world to shame the *s*.
16:13 in the faith; be men of courage; be *s*
2Co 12:10 For when I am weak, then I am *s*.
Eph 6:10 be *s* in the Lord and in his mighty
2Ti 2: 1 be *s* in the grace that is
1Pe 5:10 restore you and make you *s*,

STRONGER (STRONG)
Dt 4:38 before you nations greater and *s*
1Co 1:25 of God is *s* than man's strength.

STRONGHOLD (STRONGHOLDS)
2Sa 22: 3 He is my *s*, my refuge and my
Ps 9: 9 a *s* in times of trouble.
18: 2 the horn of my salvation, my *s*.
27: 1 The LORD is the *s* of my life—
144: 2 my *s* and my deliverer,

STRONGHOLDS (STRONGHOLD)
Zep 3: 6 their *s* are demolished.
2Co 10: 4 have divine power to demolish *s*.

STRUGGLE (STRUGGLED STRUGGLING)
Ro 15:30 me in my *s* by praying to God
Eph 6:12 For our *s* is not against flesh
Heb 12: 4 In your *s* against sin, you have not

STRUGGLED (STRUGGLE)
Ge 32:28 because you have *s* with God

STRUGGLING* (STRUGGLE)
Col 1:29 To this end I labor, *s*
2: 1 to know how much I am *s* for you

STUDENT (STUDY)
Mt 10:24 "A *s* is not above his teacher,

STUDY (STUDENT)
Ezr 7:10 Ezra had devoted himself to the *s*
Ecc 12:12 and much *s* wearies the body.
Jn 5:39 You diligently *s* the Scriptures

Ps 19: 9 The ordinances of the LORD are *s*
132:11 a *s* oath that he will not revoke:
Pr 27:23 Be *s* you know the condition
Isa 28:16 cornerstone for a *s* foundation;
Eph 5: 5 of this you can be *s*: No immoral,
Heb 11: 1 faith is being *s* of what we hope for
2Pe 1:10 to make your calling and election *s*.

SURFACE
2Co 10: 7 You are looking only on the *s*

SURPASS* (SURPASSED SURPASSES SURPASSING)
Pr 31:29 but you *s* them all."

SURPASSED* (SURPASS)
Jn 1:15 'He who comes after me has *s* me
1:30 man who comes after me has *s* me

SURPASSES* (SURPASS)
Pr 8:19 what I yield *s* choice silver.
Mt 5:20 unless your righteousness *s* that
Eph 3:19 to know this love that *s* knowledge

SURPASSING* (SURPASS)
Ps 150: 2 praise him for his *s* greatness.
2Co 3:10 in comparison with the *s* glory.
9:14 of the *s* grace God has given you.
Php 3: 8 the *s* greatness of knowing Christ

SURPRISE (SURPRISED)
1Th 5: 4 that this day should *s* you like

SURPRISED (SURPRISE)
1Pe 4:12 do not be *s* at the painful trial you
1Jn 3:13 Do not be *s*, my brothers,

SURRENDER
1Co 13: 3 and *s* my body to the flames,

SURROUND (SURROUNDED SURROUNDS)
Ps 5:12 you *s* them with your favor
32: 7 and *s* me with songs of deliverance.
89: 7 awesome than all who *s* him.
125: 2 As the mountains *s* Jerusalem,
Jer 31:22 a woman will *s* a man."

SURROUNDED (SURROUND)
Heb 12: 1 since we are *s* by such a great cloud

SURROUNDS* (SURROUND)
Ps 32:10 *s* the man who trusts in him.
89: 8 and your faithfulness *s* you.
125: 2 so the LORD *s* his people

SUSA
Ezr 4: 9 and Babylon, the Elamites of *S*,
Ne 1: 1 while I was in the citadel of *S*,

SUSPENDS*
Job 26: 7 he *s* the earth over nothing.

SUSPICIONS*
1Ti 6: 4 evil *s* and constant friction

SUSTAIN (SUSTAINING SUSTAINS)
Ps 55:22 and he will *s* you;
Isa 46: 4 I am he, I am he who will *s* you.

SUSTAINING* (SUSTAIN)
Heb 1: 3 *s* all things by his powerful word.

SUSTAINS (SUSTAIN)
Ps 18:35 and your right hand *s* me;
146: 9 and *s* the fatherless and the widow,
147: 6 The LORD *s* the humble
Isa 50: 4 to know the word that *s* the weary.

SWALLOW (SWALLOWED)
Isa 25: 8 he will *s* up death forever.
Jnh 1:17 provided a great fish to *s* Jonah,
Mt 23:24 You strain out a gnat but *s* a camel.

SWALLOWED (SWALLOW)
1Co 15:54 "Death has been *s* up in victory."
2Co 5: 4 so that what is mortal may be *s* up

SWAYED
Mt 11: 7 A reed *s* by the wind? If not,
22:16 You aren't *s* by men, because you
2Ti 3: 6 are *s* by all kinds of evil desires,

SWEAR (SWORE SWORN)
Lev 19:12 " 'Do not *s* falsely by my name
Ps 24: 4 or *s* by what is false.
Isa 45:23 by me every tongue will *s*.
Mt 5:34 Do not *s* at all: either by heaven,
Jas 5:12 Above all, my brothers, do not *s*—

SWEAT*
Ge 3:19 By the *s* of your brow
Lk 22:44 his *s* was like drops of blood falling

SWEET (SWEETER SWEETNESS)
Job 20:12 "Though evil is *s* in his mouth
Ps 119:103 How *s* are your words
Pr 9:17 "Stolen water is *s*;
13:19 A longing fulfilled is *s* to the soul,
16:24 *s* to the soul and healing
20:17 by fraud tastes *s* to a man,
24:14 also that wisdom is *s* to your soul;
Ecc 5:12 The sleep of a laborer is *s*,
Isa 5:20 and *s* for bitter.
Eze 3: 3 it tasted as *s* as honey in my mouth.
Rev 10:10 It tasted as *s* as honey in my mouth

SWEETER (SWEET)
Ps 19:10 they are *s* than honey,
119:103 *s* than honey to my mouth!

SWEETNESS* (SWEET)
SS 4:11 Your lips drop *s* as the honeycomb,
5:16 His mouth is *s* itself;

SWEPT
Mt 12:44 finds the house unoccupied, *s* clean

SWERVE*
Pr 4: 5 do not forget my words or *s*
4:27 Do not *s* to the right or the left;

SWIFT
Pr 1:16 they are *s* to shed blood.
Ecc 9:11 The race is not to the *s*
Isa 59: 7 they are *s* to shed innocent blood.
Ro 3:15 "Their feet are *s* to shed blood;
2Pe 2: 1 bringing *s* destruction

SWINDLER* (SWINDLERS)
1Co 5:11 or a slanderer, a drunkard or a *s*.

SWINDLERS* (SWINDLER)
1Co 5:10 or the greedy and *s*, or idolaters.
6:10 *s* will inherit the kingdom of God.

SWORD (SWORDS)
Ge 3:24 and a flaming *s* flashing back
Dt 32:41 when I sharpen my flashing *s*
Jos 5:13 of him with a drawn *s* in his hand.
1Sa 17:45 "You come against me with *s*
17:47 here will know that it is not by *s*
31: 4 so Saul took his own *s* and fell on it.
2Sa 12:10 therefore, the *s* will never depart
Ps 44: 6 my *s* does not bring me victory;
45: 3 Gird your *s* upon your side,
Pr 12:18 Reckless words pierce like a *s*,
Isa 2: 4 Nation will not take up *s*
Mic 4: 3 Nation will not take up *s*
Mt 10:34 come to bring peace, but a *s*.
26:52 all who draw the *s* will die by the *s*.
Lk 2:35 a *s* will pierce your own soul too."
Ro 13: 4 for he does not bear the *s*
Eph 6:17 of salvation and the *s* of the Spirit,
Heb 4:12 Sharper than any double-edged *s*,
Rev 1:16 came a sharp double-edged *s*.
Rev 19:15 Out of his mouth comes a sharp *s*

SWORDS (SWORD)
Ps 64: 3 who sharpen their tongues like *s*
Isa 2: 4 They will beat their *s*
Joel 3:10 Beat your plowshares into *s*

SWORE (SWEAR)
Heb 6:13 for him to swear by, he *s* by himself

SWORN (SWEAR)
Ps 110: 4 The LORD has *s*
Eze 20:42 the land I had *s* with uplifted hand
Heb 7:21 "The Lord has *s*

SYCAMORE-FIG (FIG)
Am 7:14 and I also took care of *s* trees.
Lk 19: 4 and climbed a *s* tree to see him,

SYMBOLIZES*
1Pe 3:21 this water *s* baptism that now saves

SYMPATHETIC* (SYMPATHY)
1Pe 3: 8 in harmony with one another; be *s*,

SYMPATHIZED* (SYMPATHY)
Heb 10:34 You *s* with those in prison

SYMPATHY (SYMPATHETIC SYMPATHIZED)
Ps 69:20 I looked for *s*, but there was none,

SYNAGOGUE
Lk 4:16 the Sabbath day he went into the *s*,
Ac 17: 2 custom was, Paul went into the *s*,

TABERNACLE (TABERNACLES)
Ex 40:34 the glory of the LORD filled the *t*.
Heb 8: 2 the true *t* set up by the Lord,
9:11 and more perfect *t* that is not
9:21 sprinkled with the blood both the *t*
Rev 15: 5 that is, the *t* of the Testimony,

TABERNACLES (TABERNACLE)
Lev 23:34 the LORD's Feast of *T* begins,
Dt 16:16 Feast of Weeks and the Feast of *T*.
Zec 14:16 and to celebrate the Feast of *T*.

TABLE (TABLES)
Ex 25:23 "Make a *t* of acacia wood—
Ps 23: 5 You prepare a *t* before me

TABLES (TABLE)
Jn 2:15 changers and overturned their *t*.
Ac 6: 2 word of God in order to wait on *t*.

TABLET (TABLETS)
Pr 3: 3 write them on the *t* of your heart.
7: 3 write them on the *t* of your heart.

TABLETS (TABLET)
Ex 31:18 he gave him the two *t*
Dt 10: 5 and put the *t* in the ark I had made,
2Co 3: 3 not on *t* of stone but on *t*

TAKE (TAKEN TAKES TAKING TOOK)
Ge 15: 7 land to *t* possession of it."
22:17 Your descendants will *t* possession
Ex 3: 5 "*T* off your sandals,
21:23 you are to *t* life for life, eye for eye,
22:22 "Do not *t* advantage of a widow
Lev 10:17 given to you to *t* away the guilt
25:14 do not *t* advantage of each other.
Nu 13:30 and *t* possession of the land,
Dt 1: 8 and *t* possession of the land that
12:32 do not add to it or *t* away from it.
31:26 "*T* this Book of the Law
1Sa 8:11 He will *t* your sons and make them
1Ch 17:13 I will never *t* my love away
Job 23:10 But he knows the way that I *t*;
Ps 2:12 Blessed are all who *t* refuge in him.
25:18 and *t* away all my sins.
27:14 be strong and *t* heart

Ps 31:24 Be strong and *t* heart,
49:17 for he will *t* nothing with him
51:11 or *t* your Holy Spirit from me.
73:24 afterward you will *t* me into glory.
118: 8 It is better to *t* refuge in the LORD
Pr 22:23 for the LORD will *t* up their case
Isa 62: 4 for the LORD will *t* delight in you,
Eze 3:10 and *t* to heart all the words I speak
33:11 I *t* no pleasure in the death
Mt 10:38 anyone who does not *t* his cross
11:29 *T* my yoke upon you and learn
16:24 deny himself and *t* up his cross
26:26 saying, "*T* and eat; this is my body
Mk 14:36 *T* this cup from me.
1Ti 6:12 *T* hold of the eternal life

TAKEN (TAKE)
Ge 2:23 for she was *t* out of man."
Lev 6: 4 must return what he has stolen or *t*
Nu 8:16 I have *t* them as my own in place
19: 3 it is to be *t* outside the camp
Ecc 3:14 added to it and nothing *t* from it.
Isa 6: 7 your guilt is *t* away and your sin
Zec 3: 4 "See, I have *t* away your sin,
Mt 13:12 even what he has will be *t* from him
24:40 one will be *t* and the other left.
26:39 may this cup be *t* from me.
Mk 16:19 he was *t* up into heaven
Ac 1: 9 he was *t* up before their very eyes,
Ro 5:13 But sin is not *t* into account
1Ti 3:16 was *t* up in glory.

TAKES (TAKE)
1Ki 20:11 should not boast like one who *t* it
Ps 5: 4 You are not a God who *t* pleasure
34: 8 blessed is the man who *t* refuge
Lk 6:30 and if anyone *t* what belongs to you
Jn 1:29 who *t* away the sin of the world!
10:18 No one *t* it from me, but I lay it
Rev 22:19 And if anyone *t* words away

TAKING (TAKE)
Ac 15:14 by *t* from the Gentiles a people
Php 2: 7 *t* the very nature of a servant,

TALENT
Mt 25:15 to another one *t*, each according

TALES*
1Ti 4: 7 with godless myths and old wives' *t*

TALL
1Sa 17: 4 He was over nine feet *t*.
1Ch 11:23 who was seven and a half feet *t*.

TAMAR
1. Wife of Judah's sons Er and Onan (Ge 38:1–10). Tricked Judah into fathering children when he refused her his third son (Ge 38:11–30).
2. Daughter of David, raped by Amnon (2Sa 13).

TAMBOURINE
Ps 150: 4 praise him with *t* and dancing,

TAME* (TAMED)
Jas 3: 8 but no man can *t* the tongue.

TAMED* (TAME)
Jas 3: 7 the sea are being *t* and have been *t*

TARSHISH
Jnh 1: 3 from the LORD and headed for *T*.

TARSUS
Ac 9:11 ask for a man from *T* named Saul,

TASK (TASKS)
1Ch 29: 1 The *t* is great, because this palatial
Mk 13:34 each with his assigned *t*,
Ac 20:24 complete the *t* the Lord Jesus has
1Co 3: 5 the Lord has assigned to each his *t*.
2Co 2:16 And who is equal to such a *t*?
1Ti 3: 1 an overseer, he desires a noble *t*.

TASKS (TASK)
Pr 31:17 her arms are strong for her *t*.

TASTE (TASTED TASTY)
Ps 34: 8 *T* and see that the LORD is good;
119:103 sweet are your words to my *t*,
Pr 24:13 from the comb is sweet to your *t*.
SS 2: 3 and his fruit is sweet to my *t*.
Col 2:21 Do not *t*! Do not touch!"?
Heb 2: 9 the grace of God he might *t* death

TASTED (TASTE)
Eze 3: 3 it *t* as sweet as honey in my mouth.
1Pe 2: 3 now that you have *t* that the Lord
Rev 10:10 It *t* as sweet as honey in my mouth,

TASTY (TASTE)
Ge 27: 4 Prepare me the kind of *t* food I like

TATTOO*
Lev 19:28 or put *t* marks on yourselves.

TAUGHT (TEACH)
1Ki 4:33 He also *t* about animals and birds,
2Ki 17:28 *t* them how to worship the LORD.
2Ch 17: 9 They *t* throughout Judah,
Ps 119:102 for you yourself have *t* me.
Pr 4: 4 he *t* me and said,
31: 1 an oracle his mother *t* him:
Isa 29:13 is made up only of rules *t* by men.
50: 4 ear to listen like one being *t*.
Mt 7:29 he *t* as one who had authority,
15: 9 their teachings are but rules *t*
Lk 4:15 He *t* in their synagogues,
Ac 20:20 have *t* you publicly and from house
1Co 2:13 but in words *t* by the Spirit,
Gal 1:12 nor was I *t* it; rather, I received it
1Ti 1:20 to Satan to be *t* not to blaspheme.
1Jn 2:27 just as it has *t* you, remain in him.

TAX (TAXES)
Mt 11:19 a friend of *t* collectors and "sinners
17:24 of the two-drachma *t* came to Peter

TAXES (TAX)
Mt 22:17 Is it right to pay *t* to Caesar or not
Ro 13: 7 If you owe *t*, pay *t*; if revenue,

TEACH (TAUGHT TEACHER TEACHERS TEACHES TEACHING TEACHINGS)
Ex 4:12 and will *t* you what to say."
18:20 *T* them the decrees and laws,
33:13 *t* me your ways so I may know you
Lev 10:11 and you must *t* the Israelites all
Dt 4: 9 *T* them to your children
6: 1 me to *t* you to observe
8: 3 to *t* you that man does not live
11:19 *T* them to your children, talking
1Sa 12:23 I will *t* you the way that is good
1Ki 8:36 *T* them the right way to live,
Job 12: 7 ask the animals, and they will *t* you
Ps 32: 8 *t* you in the way you should go;
34:11 I will *t* you the fear of the LORD.
51:13 I will *t* transgressors your ways,
78: 5 forefathers to *t* their children,
90:12 *T* us to number our days aright,
119:33 *T* me, O LORD, to follow your
143:10 *T* me to do your will,
Pr 9: 9 *t* a righteous man and he will add
Jer 31:34 No longer will a man *t* his neighbor
Mic 4: 2 He will *t* us his ways,
Lk 11: 1 said to him, "Lord, *t* us to pray,
12:12 for the Holy Spirit will *t* you
Jn 14:26 will *t* you all things and will remind
Ro 2:21 who *t* others, do you not *t* yourself?
15: 4 in the past was written to *t* us,
1Ti 2:12 I do not permit a woman to *t*
3: 2 respectable, hospitable, able to *t*,
2Ti 2: 2 also be qualified to *t* others.
2Ti 2:24 kind to everyone, able to *t*,
Tit 2: 1 You must *t* what is in accord
2:15 then, are the things you should *t*.
Heb 8:11 No longer will a man *t* his neighbor
Jas 3: 1 know that we who *t* will be judged
1Jn 2:27 you do not need anyone to *t* you.

TEACHER (TEACH)
Ecc 1: 1 The words of the *T*, son of David,
Mt 10:24 "A student is not above his *t*,
13:52 "Therefore every *t*
23:10 Nor are you to be called '*t*,'
Lk 6:40 A student is not above his *t*,
Jn 3: 2 we know you are a *t* who has come
13:14 and *T*, have washed your feet,

TEACHERS (TEACH)
Ps 119:99 I have more insight than all my *t*,
Pr 5:13 I would not obey my *t*
Lk 20:46 "Beware of the *t* of the law.
1Co 12:28 third *t*, then workers of miracles,
Eph 4:11 and some to be pastors and *t*,
2Ti 4: 3 around them a great number of *t*
Heb 5:12 by this time you ought to be *t*,
Jas 3: 1 of you should presume to be *t*,
2Pe 2: 1 as there will be false *t* among you.

TEACHES (TEACH)
Ps 25: 9 and *t* them his way.
94:10 Does he who *t* man lack
Pr 15:33 of the LORD *t* a man wisdom,
Isa 48:17 who *t* you what is best for you,
Mt 5:19 *t* these commands will be called
1Ti 6: 3 If anyone *t* false doctrines
Tit 2:12 It *t* us to say "No" to ungodliness
1Jn 2:27 his anointing *t* you about all things

TEACHING (TEACH)
Ezr 7:10 to *t* its decrees and laws in Israel.
Pr 1: 8 and do not forsake your mother's *t*.
3: 1 My son, do not forget my *t*,
6:23 this *t* is a light,
Mt 28:20 *t* them to obey everything I have
Jn 7:17 whether my *t* comes from God or
8:31 to my *t*, you are really my disciples.
14:23 loves me, he will obey my *t*.
Ac 2:42 themselves to the apostles' *t*
Ro 12: 7 let him serve; if it is *t*, let him teach;
Eph 4:14 and there by every wind of *t*
2Th 3: 6 to the *t* you received from us.
1Ti 4:13 of Scripture, to preaching and to *t*.
5:17 whose work is preaching and *t*.
6: 3 Lord Jesus Christ and to godly *t*,
2Ti 3:16 is God-breathed and is useful for *t*,
Tit 1:11 by *t* things they ought not
2: 7 In your *t* show integrity,
Heb 5:13 with the *t* about righteousness.
2Jn : 9 and does not continue in the *t*

TEACHINGS (TEACH)
Pr 7: 2 guard my *t* as the apple of your eye.
2Th 2:15 hold to the *t* we passed on to you,
Heb 6: 1 leave the elementary *t* about Christ

TEAR (TEARS)
Rev 7:17 God will wipe away every *t*
21: 4 He will wipe every *t*

TEARS (TEAR)
Ps 126: 5 Those who sow in *t*
Isa 25: 8 LORD will wipe away the *t*
Jer 31:16 and your eyes from *t*,
50: 4 in *t* to seek the LORD their God.
Lk 7:38 she began to wet his feet with her *t*.
2Co 2: 4 anguish of heart and with many *t*,
Php 3:18 and now say again even with *t*,

TEETH (TOOTH)
Job 19:20 with only the skin of my *t*.
Ps 35:16 they gnashed their *t* at me.
Jer 31:29 and the children's *t* are set on edge
Mt 8:12 will be weeping and gnashing of *t*."

TEMPER (EVEN-TEMPERED HOT-TEMPERED ILL-TEMPERED QUICK-TEMPERED)
Pr 16:32 a man who controls his *t*

TEMPERANCE see SELF-CONTROL

TEMPERATE*
1Ti 3: 2 *t*, self-controlled, respectable,
3:11 not malicious talkers but *t*
Tit 2: 2 Teach the older men to be *t*,

TEMPEST
Ps 50: 3 and around him a *t* rages.
55: 8 far from the *t* and storm."

TEMPLE (TEMPLES)
1Ki 6: 1 began to build the *t* of the LORD.
6:38 the *t* was finished in all its details
8:10 the cloud filled the *t* of the LORD.
8:27 How much less this *t* I have built!
2Ch 36:19 They set fire to God's *t*
36:23 me to build a *t* for him at Jerusalem
Ezr 6:14 finished building the *t* according
Ps 27: 4 and to seek him in his *t*.
Isa 6: 1 and the train of his robe filled the *t*.
Eze 10: 4 cloud filled the *t*, and the court was
43: 4 glory of the LORD entered the *t*
Hab 2:20 But the LORD is in his holy *t*;
Mt 12: 6 that one greater than the *t* is here.
26:61 'I am able to destroy the *t* of God
27:51 of the *t* was torn in two from top
Lk 21: 5 about how the *t* was adorned
Jn 2:14 In the *t* courts he found men selling
1Co 3:16 that you yourselves are God's *t*
6:19 you not know that your body is a *t*
2Co 6:16 For we are the *t* of the living God.
Rev 21:22 I did not see a *t* in the city,

TEMPLES (TEMPLE)
Ac 17:24 does not live in *t* built by hands.

TEMPORARY
2Co 4:18 what is seen is *t*, but what is unseen

TEMPT* (TEMPTATION TEMPTED TEMPTER TEMPTING)
1Co 7: 5 again so that Satan will not *t* you
Jas 1:13 does he *t* anyone; but each one is

TEMPTATION* (TEMPT)
Mt 6:13 And lead us not into *t*,
26:41 pray so that you will not fall into *t*.
Mk 14:38 pray so that you will not fall into *t*.
Lk 11: 4 And lead us not into *t*.'"
22:40 "Pray that you will not fall into *t*."
22:46 pray so that you will not fall into *t*
1Co 10:13 No *t* has seized you except what is
1Ti 6: 9 want to get rich fall into *t*

TEMPTED* (TEMPT)
Mt 4: 1 into the desert to be *t* by the devil.
Mk 1:13 was in the desert forty days, being *t*
Lk 4: 2 for forty days he was *t* by the devil.
1Co 10:13 But when you are *t*, he will
10:13 he will not let you be *t*
Gal 6: 1 yourself, or you also may be *t*.
1Th 3: 5 way the tempter might have *t* you
Heb 2:18 able to help those who are being *t*.
2:18 he himself suffered when he was *t*,
4:15 but we have one who has been *t*
Jas 1:13 For God cannot be *t* by evil,
1:13 When *t*, no one should say,
1:14 each one is *t* when, by his own evil

TEMPTER* (TEMPT)
Mt 4: 3 The *t* came to him and said,
1Th 3: 5 some way the *t* might have

TEMPTING* (TEMPT)
Lk 4:13 the devil had finished all this *t*,
Jas 1:13 no one should say, "God is *t* me."

TEN (TENTH TITHE TITHES)
Ex 34:28 covenant—the *T* Commandments.
Lev 26: 8 of you will chase *t* thousand,
Dt 4:13 covenant, the *T* Commandments,
10: 4 The *T* Commandments he had
Ps 91: 7 *t* thousand at your right hand,
Da 7:24 *t* horns are *t* kings who will come
Mt 25: 1 will be like *t* virgins who took
25:28 it to the one who has the *t* talents.
Lk 15: 8 suppose a woman has *t* silver coins
Rev 12: 3 and *t* horns and seven crowns

TENANTS
Mt 21:34 servants to the *t* to collect his fruit.

TEND
Jer 23: 2 to the shepherds who *t* my people:
Eze 34:14 I will *t* them in a good pasture,

TENDERNESS*
Isa 63:15 Your *t* and compassion are
Php 2: 1 fellowship with the Spirit, if any *t*

TENT (TENTMAKER TENTS)
Ex 27:21 In the *T* of Meeting,
40: 2 "Set up the tabernacle, the *T*
Isa 54: 2 "Enlarge the place of your *t*,
2Co 5: 1 that if the earthly *t* we live
2Pe 1:13 as long as I live in the *t* of this body,

TENTH (TEN)
Ge 14:20 Abram gave him a *t* of everything.
Nu 18:26 you must present a *t* of that tithe
Dt 14:22 Be sure to set aside a *t*
1Sa 8:15 He will take a *t* of your grain
Lk 11:42 you give God a *t* of your mint,
18:12 I fast twice a week and give a *t*
Heb 7: 4 patriarch Abraham gave him a *t*

TENTMAKER* (TENT)
Ac 18: 3 and because he was a *t* as they were

TENTS (TENT)
Ge 13:12 and pitched his *t* near Sodom.
Ps 84:10 than dwell in the *t* of the wicked.

TERAH
Ge 11:31 *T* took his son Abram, his

TERRIBLE (TERROR)
2Ti 3: 1 There will be *t* times

TERRIFIED (TERROR)
Dt 7:21 Do not be *t* by them,
20: 3 do not be *t* or give way to panic
Ps 90: 7 and *t* by your indignation.
Mt 14:26 walking on the lake, they were *t*.
17: 6 they fell facedown to the ground, *t*.
27:54 they were *t*, and exclaimed,
Mk 4:41 They were *t* and asked each other,

TERRIFYING (TERROR)
Heb 12:21 The sight was so *t* that Moses said,

TERRITORY
2Co 10:16 done in another man's *t*.

TERROR (TERRIBLE TERRIFIED TERRIFYING)
Dt 2:25 very day I will begin to put the *t*
28:67 of the *t* that will fill your hearts
Job 9:34 so that his *t* would frighten me no
Ps 91: 5 You will not fear the *t* of night,
Pr 21:15 but *t* to evildoers.
Isa 13: 8 *T* will seize them,
24:17 *T* and pit and snare await you,
51:13 live in constant *t* every day
54:14 *T* will be far removed;
Lk 21:26 Men will faint from *t*, apprehensive
Ro 13: 3 For rulers hold no *t*

TEST (TESTED TESTING TESTS)
Dt 6:16 Do not *t* the LORD your God
Jdg 3: 1 to *t* all those Israelites who had not
1Ki 10: 1 came to *t* him with hard questions.
1Ch 29:17 that you *t* the heart and are pleased
Ps 26: 2 *T* me, O LORD, and try me,
78:18 They willfully put God to the *t*
106:14 wasteland they put God to the *t*.
139:23 *t* me and know my anxious
Jer 11:20 and *t* the heart and mind,
Lk 4:12 put the Lord your God to the *t*.'"
Ac 5: 9 How could you agree to *t* the Spirit
Ro 12: 2 Then you will be able to *t*
1Co 3:13 and the fire will *t* the quality
10: 9 We should not *t* the Lord,
2Co 13: 5 unless, of course, you fail the *t*?
1Th 5:21 *T* everything.
Jas 1:12 because when he has stood the *t*,
1Jn 4: 1 *t* the spirits to see whether they are

TESTED (TEST)
Ge 22: 1 Some time later God *t* Abraham.
Job 23:10 when he has *t* me, I will come forth
34:36 that Job might be *t* to the utmost
Ps 66:10 For you, O God, *t* us;
Pr 27:21 man is *t* by the praise he receives.
Isa 28:16 a *t* stone,
48:10 I have *t* you in the furnace
1Ti 3:10 They must first be *t*; and then
Heb 11:17 By faith Abraham, when God *t* him

TESTIFIES (TESTIFY)
Jn 5:32 There is another who *t* in my favor,
Ro 8:16 The Spirit himself *t*

TESTIFY (TESTIFIES TESTIMONY)
Pr 24:28 Do not *t* against your neighbor
Jn 1: 7 a witness to *t* concerning that light,
1:34 and I *t* that this is the Son of God."
5:39 are the Scriptures that *t* about me,
7: 7 because I *t* that what it does is evil.
15:26 he will *t* about me. And you
Ac 4:33 continued to *t* to the resurrection
10:43 All the prophets *t* about him that
2Ti 1: 8 ashamed to *t* about our Lord,
1Jn 4:14 *t* that the Father has sent his Son
5: 7 For there are three that *t*: the Spirit

TESTIMONY (TESTIFY)
Ex 20:16 "You shall not give false *t*
31:18 gave him the two tablets of the *T*,
Nu 35:30 only on the *t* of witnesses.
Dt 19:18 giving false *t* against his brother,
Pr 12:17 A truthful witness gives honest *t*,
Isa 8:20 and to the *t*! If they do not speak
Mt 15:19 sexual immorality, theft, false *t*,
24:14 preached in the whole world as a *t*
Lk 18:20 not give false *t*, honor your father
Jn 2:25 He did not need man's *t* about man
21:24 We know that his *t* is true.
1Jn 5: 9 but God's *t* is greater because it is
Rev 12:11 and by the word of their *t*;

TESTING (TEST)
Lk 8:13 but in the time of *t* they fall away.
Heb 3: 8 during the time of *t* in the desert,
Jas 1: 3 because you know that the *t*

TESTS (TEST)
Pr 17: 3 but the LORD *t* the heart.
1Th 2: 4 but God, who *t* our hearts.

THADDAEUS
Apostle (Mt 10:3; Mk 3:18); probably also known as Judas son of James (Lk 6:16; Ac 1:13).

THANK (THANKFUL THANKFULNESS THANKS THANKSGIVING)
Php 1: 3 I *t* my God every time I remember
1Th 3: 9 How can we *t* God enough for you

THANKFUL (THANK)
Col 3:15 And be *t*.
Heb 12:28 let us be *t*, and so worship God

Ecc 3: 1 There is a *t* for everything,
8: 5 wise heart will know the proper *t*
Da 7:25 to him for a *t*, times and half a *t*.
12: 7 "It will be for a *t*, times and half a *t*.
Hos 10:12 for it is *t* to seek the LORD,
Jn 2: 4 Jesus replied, "My *t* has not yet
17: 1 prayed: "Father, the *t* has come.
Ro 9: 9 "At the appointed *t* I will return,
13:11 understanding the present *t*.
1Co 7:29 brothers, is that the *t* is short.
2Co 6: 2 now is the *t* of God's favor,
2Ti 1: 9 Jesus before the beginning of *t*,
Tit 1: 2 promised before the beginning of *t*,
Heb 9:28 and he will appear a second *t*,
10:12 for all *t* one sacrifice for sins,
1Pe 4:17 For it is *t* for judgment to begin

TIMES (TIME)
Ps 9: 9 a stronghold in *t* of trouble.
31:15 My *t* are in your hands;
62: 8 Trust in him at all *t*, O people;
Pr 17:17 A friend loves at all *t*,
Isa 46:10 from ancient *t*, what is still to come
Am 5:13 for the *t* are evil.
Mt 16: 3 cannot interpret the signs of the *t*.
18:21 how many *t* shall I forgive my
Ac 1: 7 "It is not for you to know the *t*
Rev 12:14 *t* and half a time, out

TIMID (TIMIDITY)
1Th 5:14 encourage the *t*, help the weak,

TIMIDITY* (TIMID)
2Ti 1: 7 For God did not give us a spirit of *t*

TIMOTHY
Believer from Lystra (Ac 16:1). Joined Paul on second missionary journey (Ac 16–20). Sent to settle problems at Corinth (1Co 4:17; 16:10). Led church at Ephesus (1Ti 1:3). Co-writer with Paul (1Th 1:1; 2Th 1:1; Phm 1).

TIP
Job 33: 2 my words are on the *t* of my tongue

TIRE (TIRED)
2Th 3:13 never *t* of doing what is right.

TIRED (TIRE)
Ex 17:12 When Moses' hands grew *t*,
Isa 40:28 He will not grow *t* or weary,

TITHE (TEN)
Lev 27:30 " 'A *t* of everything from the land,
Dt 12:17 eat in your own towns the *t*
Mal 3:10 the whole *t* into the storehouse,

TITHES (TEN)
Nu 18:21 give to the Levites all the *t* in Israel
Mal 3: 8 'How do we rob you?' "In *t*

TITUS*
Gentile co-worker of Paul (Gal 2:1–3; 2Ti 4:10); sent to Corinth (2Co 2:13; 7–8; 12:18), Crete (Tit 1:4–5).

TODAY
Ps 2: 7 *t* I have become your Father.
95: 7 *T*, if you hear his voice,
Mt 6:11 Give us *t* our daily bread.
Lk 2:11 *T* in the town of David a Savior has
23:43 *t* you will be with me in paradise."
Ac 13:33 *t* I have become your Father.'
Heb 1: 5 *t* I have become your Father"?
3: 7 "*T*, if you hear his voice,
3:13 daily, as long as it is called *T*,
5: 5 *t* I have become your Father."
13: 8 Christ is the same yesterday and *t*

TOIL (TOILED TOILING)
Ge 3:17 through painful *t* you will eat of it

TOILED (TOIL)
2Co 11:27 and *t* and have often gone

TOILING (TOIL)
2Th 3: 8 *t* so that we would not be a burden

TOLERANCE* (TOLERATE)
Ro 2: 4 for the riches of his kindness, *t*

TOLERATE (TOLERANCE)
Hab 1:13 you cannot *t* wrong.
Rev 2: 2 that you cannot *t* wicked men,

TOMB
Mt 27:65 make the *t* as secure as you know
Lk 24: 2 the stone rolled away from the *t*,

TOMORROW
Pr 27: 1 Do not boast about *t*,
Isa 22:13 "for *t* we die!"
Mt 6:34 Therefore do not worry about *t*,
1Co 15:32 for *t* we die."
Jas 4:13 "Today or *t* we will go to this

TONGUE (TONGUES)
Ex 4:10 I am slow of speech and *t*."
Job 33: 2 my words are on the tip of my *t*.
Ps 5: 9 with their *t* they speak deceit.
34:13 keep your *t* from evil
37:30 and his *t* speaks what is just.
39: 1 and keep my *t* from sin;
51:14 my *t* will sing of your righteousness
52: 4 O you deceitful *t*!
71:24 My *t* will tell of your righteous acts
119:172 May my *t* sing of your word,
137: 6 May my *t* cling to the roof
139: 4 Before a word is on my *t*
Pr 6:17 a lying *t*,
10:19 but he who holds his *t* is wise.
12:18 but the *t* of the wise brings healing.
15: 4 The *t* that brings healing is a tree
17:20 he whose *t* is deceitful falls
21:23 He who guards his mouth and his *t*
25:15 and a gentle *t* can break a bone.
26:28 A lying *t* hates those it hurts,
28:23 than he who has a flattering *t*.
31:26 and faithful instruction is on her *t*.
SS 4:11 milk and honey are under your *t*.
Isa 32: 4 and the stammering *t* will be fluent
45:23 by me every *t* will swear.
50: 4 has given me an instructed *t*,
59: 3 and your *t* mutters wicked things.
Lk 16:24 of his finger in water and cool my *t*,
Ro 14:11 every *t* will confess to God.' "
1Co 14: 2 speaks in a *t* does not speak to men
14: 4 He who speaks in a *t* edifies himself
14: 9 intelligible words with your *t*,
14:13 in a *t* should pray that he may
14:19 than ten thousand words in a *t*.
14:26 revelation, a *t* or an interpretation.
14:27 If anyone speaks in a *t*, two—
Php 2:11 every *t* confess that Jesus Christ is
Jas 1:26 does not keep a tight rein on his *t*,
3: 5 Likewise the *t* is a small part
3: 8 but no man can tame the *t*.
1Jn 3:18 or *t* but with actions and in truth.

TONGUES (TONGUE)
Ps 12: 4 "We will triumph with our *t*;
126: 2 our *t* with songs of joy.
Isa 28:11 with foreign lips and strange *t*
66:18 and gather all nations and *t*,
Jer 23:31 the prophets who wag their own *t*
Mk 16:17 in new *t*; they will pick up snakes
Ac 2: 3 to be *t* of fire that separated
2: 4 and began to speak in other *t*
10:46 For they heard them speaking in *t*
19: 6 and they spoke in *t* and prophesied
Ro 3:13 their *t* practice deceit."
1Co 12:10 still another the interpretation of *t*.
12:28 speaking in different kinds of *t*.
1Co 12:30 Do all speak in *t*? Do all interpret?
13: 1 If I speak in the *t* of men
13: 8 where there are *t*, they will be
14: 5 greater than one who speaks in *t*,
14:18 speak in *t* more than all of you.
14:21 "Through men of strange *t*
14:39 and do not forbid speaking in *t*.

TOOK (TAKE)
Isa 53: 4 Surely he *t* up our infirmities
Mt 8:17 "He *t* up our infirmities
26:26 they were eating, Jesus *t* bread,
26:27 Then he *t* the cup, gave thanks
1Co 11:23 the night he was betrayed, *t* bread,
11:25 after supper he *t* the cup, saying,
Php 3:12 for which Christ Jesus *t* hold of me.

TOOTH (TEETH)
Ex 21:24 eye for eye, *t* for *t*, hand for hand,
Mt 5:38 'Eye for eye, and *t* for *t*.'

TOP
Dt 28:13 you will always be at the *t*,
Isa 1: 6 of your foot to the *t* of your head
Mt 27:51 torn in two from *t* to bottom.

TORMENT (TORMENTED TORMENTORS)
Lk 16:28 also come to this place of *t*.'
2Co 12: 7 a messenger of Satan, to *t* me.

TORMENTED (TORMENT)
Rev 20:10 They will be *t* day and night

TORMENTORS (TORMENT)
Ps 137: 3 our *t* demanded songs of joy;

TORN
Gal 4:15 you would have *t* out your eyes
Php 1:23 I do not know! I am *t*

TORTURED*
Mt 18:34 turned him over to the jailers to be *t*,
Heb 11:35 Others were *t* and refused

TOSSED (TOSSING)
Eph 4:14 *t* back and forth by the waves,
Jas 1: 6 of the sea, blown and *t* by the wind.

TOSSING (TOSSED)
Isa 57:20 But the wicked are like the *t* sea,

TOUCH (TOUCHED TOUCHES)
Ge 3: 3 you must not *t* it, or you will die.' "
Ex 19:12 go up the mountain or *t* the foot
Ps 105:15 "Do not *t* my anointed ones;
Mt 9:21 If I only *t* his cloak, I will be healed
Lk 18:15 babies to Jesus to have him *t* them.
24:39 It is I myself! *T* me and see;
2Co 6:17 *T* no unclean thing,
Col 2:21 Do not taste! Do not *t*!"?

TOUCHED (TOUCH)
1Sa 10:26 men whose hearts God had *t*.
Isa 6: 7 With it he *t* my mouth and said,
Mt 14:36 and all who *t* him were healed.
Lk 8:45 "Who *t* me?" Jesus asked.
1Jn 1: 1 looked at and our hands have *t*—

TOUCHES (TOUCH)
Ex 19:12 Whoever *t* the mountain shall
Zec 2: 8 for whoever *t* you *t* the apple

TOWER
Ge 11: 4 with a *t* that reaches to the heavens
Pr 18:10 of the LORD is a strong *t*;

TOWN (TOWNS)
Mt 2:23 and lived in a *t* called Nazareth.

TOWNS (TOWN)
Nu 35: 2 to give the Levites *t* to live
35:15 These six *t* will be a place of refuge
Jer 11:13 as many gods as you have *t*,

Mt 9:35 Jesus went through all the *t*

TRACING*
Ro 11:33 and his paths beyond *t* out!

TRACK
Job 14:16 but not keep *t* of my sin.

TRADERS (TRADING)
1Ti 1:10 for slave *t* and liars and perjurers—

TRADING (TRADERS)
1Ki 10:22 The king had a fleet of *t* ships at sea
Pr 31:18 She sees that her *t* is profitable,

TRADITION (TRADITIONS)
Mt 15: 2 "Why do your disciples break the *t*
15: 6 word of God for the sake of your *t*.
Mk 7:13 by your *t* that you have handed
Col 2: 8 which depends on human *t*

TRADITIONS (TRADITION)
Mk 7: 8 are holding on to the *t* of men."
Gal 1:14 zealous for the *t* of my fathers.

TRAIL
1Ti 5:24 the sins of others *t* behind them.

TRAIN* (TRAINED TRAINING)
Ps 68:18 you led captives in your *t*;
Pr 22: 6 *T* a child in the way he should go,
Isa 2: 4 nor will they *t* for war anymore.
6: 1 the *t* of his robe filled the temple.
Mic 4: 3 nor will they *t* for war anymore.
Eph 4: 8 he led captives in his *t*
1Ti 4: 7 rather, *t* yourself to be godly.
Tit 2: 4 they can *t* the younger women

TRAINED (TRAIN)
Lk 6:40 everyone who is fully *t* will be like
Ac 22: 3 Under Gamaliel I was thoroughly *t*
2Co 11: 6 I may not be a *t* speaker,
Heb 5:14 by constant use have *t* themselves
12:11 for those who have been *t* by it.

TRAINING* (TRAIN)
1Co 9:25 in the games goes into strict *t*.
Eph 6: 4 up in the *t* and instruction
1Ti 4: 8 For physical *t* is of some value,
2Ti 3:16 correcting and *t* in righteousness,

TRAITOR (TRAITORS)
Lk 6:16 and Judas Iscariot, who became a *t*.
Jn 18: 5 Judas the *t* was standing there

TRAITORS (TRAITOR)
Ps 59: 5 show no mercy to wicked *t*.

TRAMPLE (TRAMPLED)
Joel 3:13 Come, *t* the grapes,
Am 2: 7 They *t* on the heads of the poor
5:11 You *t* on the poor
8: 4 Hear this, you who *t* the needy
Mt 7: 6 they may *t* them under their feet,
Lk 10:19 I have given you authority to *t*

TRAMPLED (TRAMPLE)
Isa 63: 6 I *t* the nations in my anger;
Lk 21:24 Jerusalem will be *t*
Heb 10:29 to be punished who has *t* the Son
Rev 14:20 They were *t* in the winepress

TRANCE*
Ac 10:10 was being prepared, he fell into a *t*.
11: 5 and in a *t* I saw a vision.
22:17 into a *t* and saw the Lord speaking.

TRANQUILLITY*
Ecc 4: 6 Better one handful with *t*

TRANSACTIONS*
Ru 4: 7 method of legalizing *t* in Israel.)

TRANSCENDS*
Php 4: 7 which *t* all understanding,

TRANSFIGURED*
Mt 17: 2 There he was *t* before them.
Mk 9: 2 There he was *t* before them.

TRANSFORM* (TRANSFORMED)
Php 3:21 will *t* our lowly bodies

TRANSFORMED (TRANSFORM)
Ro 12: 2 be *t* by the renewing of your mind.
2Co 3:18 are being *t* into his likeness

TRANSGRESSED* (TRANSGRESSION)
Da 9:11 All Israel has *t* your law

TRANSGRESSION* (TRANSGRESSED TRANSGRESSIONS TRANSGRESSORS)
Ps 19:13 innocent of great *t*.
Isa 53: 8 for the *t* of my people he was
Da 9:24 and your holy city to finish *t*,
Mic 1: 5 All this is because of Jacob's *t*,
1: 5 What is Jacob's *t*?
3: 8 to declare to Jacob his *t*,
6: 7 Shall I offer my firstborn for my *t*,
7:18 who pardons sin and forgives the *t*
Ro 4:15 where there is no law there is no *t*.
11:11 Rather, because of their *t*,
11:12 if their *t* means riches for the world

TRANSGRESSIONS* (TRANSGRESSION)
Ps 32: 1 whose *t* are forgiven,
32: 5 my *t* to the LORD"—
39: 8 Save me from all my *t*;
51: 1 blot out my *t*.
51: 3 For I know my *t*,
65: 3 you forgave our *t*.
103:12 so far has he removed our *t* from us
Isa 43:25 your *t*, for my own sake,
50: 1 of your *t* your mother was sent
53: 5 But he was pierced for our *t*,
Mic 1:13 for the *t* of Israel
Ro 4: 7 whose *t* are forgiven,
Gal 3:19 because of *t* until the Seed to whom
Eph 2: 1 you were dead in your *t* and sins,
2: 5 even when we were dead in *t*—

TRANSGRESSORS* (TRANSGRESSION)
Ps 51:13 Then I will teach *t* your ways,
Isa 53:12 and made intercession for the *t*.
53:12 and was numbered with the *t*.
Lk 22:37 'And he was numbered with the *t*';

TRAP (TRAPPED TRAPS)
Ps 69:22 may it become retribution and a *t*.
Pr 20:25 a *t* for a man to dedicate something
28:10 will fall into his own *t*,
Isa 8:14 a *t* and a snare.
Mt 22:15 and laid plans to *t* him in his words.
Lk 21:34 close on you unexpectedly like a *t*.
Ro 11: 9 their table become a snare and a *t*,
1Ti 3: 7 into disgrace and into the devil's *t*.
6: 9 and a *t* and into many foolish
2Ti 2:26 and escape from the *t* of the devil,

TRAPPED (TRAP)
Pr 6: 2 if you have been *t* by what you said
12:13 An evil man is *t* by his sinful talk,

TRAPS (TRAP)
Jos 23:13 they will become snares and *t*
La 4:20 was caught in their *t*.

TRAVEL (TRAVELER)
Pr 4:15 Avoid it, do not *t* on it;
Mt 23:15 You *t* over land and sea

TRAVELER (TRAVEL)
Job 31:32 door was always open to the *t*—
Jer 14: 8 like a *t* who stays only a night?

TREACHEROUS (TREACHERY)
Ps 25: 3 who are *t* without excuse.
2Ti 3: 4 not lovers of the good, *t*, rash,

TREACHERY (TREACHEROUS)
Isa 59:13 rebellion and *t* against the LORD,

TREAD (TREADING TREADS)
Ps 91:13 You will *t* upon the lion

TREADING (TREAD)
Dt 25: 4 an ox while it is *t* out the grain.
1Co 9: 9 an ox while it is *t* out the grain."
1Ti 5:18 the ox while it is *t* out the grain,"

TREADS (TREAD)
Rev 19:15 He *t* the winepress of the fury

TREASURE (TREASURED TREASURES TREASURY)
Pr 2: 4 and search for it as for hidden *t*,
Isa 33: 6 of the LORD is the key to this *t*.
Mt 6:21 For where your *t* is, there your
13:44 of heaven is like *t* hidden in a field.
Lk 12:33 a *t* in heaven that will not be
2Co 4: 7 But we have this *t* in jars of clay
1Ti 6:19 In this way they will lay up *t*

TREASURED (TREASURE)
Ex 19: 5 you will be my *t* possession.
Dt 7: 6 to be his people, his *t* possession.
26:18 his *t* possession as he promised,
Job 23:12 I have *t* the words
Mal 3:17 when I make up my *t* possession.
Lk 2:19 But Mary *t* up all these things
2:51 But his mother *t* all these things

TREASURES (TREASURE)
1Ch 29: 3 my God I now give my personal *t*
Pr 10: 2 Ill-gotten *t* are of no value,
Mt 6:19 up for yourselves *t* on earth,
13:52 out of his storeroom new *t*
Col 2: 3 in whom are hidden all the *t*
Heb 11:26 of greater value than the *t* of Egypt,

TREASURY (TREASURE)
Mk 12:43 more into the *t* than all the others.

TREAT (TREATED TREATING TREATMENT)
Lev 22: 2 sons to *t* with respect the sacred
Ps 103:10 he does not *t* us as our sins deserve
Mt 18:17 *t* him as you would a pagan
18:35 my heavenly Father will *t* each
Eph 6: 9 *t* your slaves in the same way.
1Th 5:20 do not *t* prophecies with contempt.
1Ti 5: 1 *T* younger men as brothers,
1Pe 3: 7 and *t* them with respect

TREATED (TREAT)
Lev 19:34 The alien living with you must be *t*
25:40 He is to be *t* as a hired worker
1Sa 24:17 "You have *t* me well, but I have
Heb 10:29 who has *t* as an unholy thing

TREATING (TREAT)
Ge 18:25 *t* the righteous and the wicked
Heb 12: 7 as discipline; God is *t* you as sons.

TREATMENT (TREAT)
Col 2:23 and their harsh *t* of the body,

TREATY
Ex 34:12 not to make a *t* with those who live
Dt 7: 2 Make no *t* with them, and show
23: 6 Do not seek a *t* of friendship with them

TREE (TREES)
Ge 2: 9 and the *t* of the knowledge of good
2: 9 of the garden were the *t* of life
Dt 21:23 hung on a *t* is under God's curse.
2Sa 18: 9 Absalom's head got caught in the *t*.

1Ki 14:23 and under every spreading *t*.
Ps 1: 3 He is like a *t* planted by streams
52: 8 But I am like an olive *t*
92:12 righteous will flourish like a palm *t*,
Pr 3:18 She is a *t* of life to those who
11:30 of the righteous is a *t* of life,
27:18 He who tends a fig *t* will eat its fruit
Isa 65:22 For as the days of a *t*,
Jer 17: 8 He will be like a *t* planted
Eze 17:24 I the LORD bring down the tall *t*
Da 4:10 before me stood a *t* in the middle
Mic 4: 4 and under his own fig *t*,
Zec 3:10 to sit under his vine and fig *t*,'
Mt 3:10 every *t* that does not produce good
12:33 for a *t* is recognized by its fruit.
Lk 19: 4 climbed a sycamore-fig *t* to see him
Ac 5:30 killed by hanging him on a *t*.
Ro 11:24 be grafted into their own olive *t*!
Gal 3:13 is everyone who is hung on a *t*."
Jas 3:12 My brothers, can a fig *t* bear olives,
1Pe 2:24 sins in his body on the *t*,
Rev 2: 7 the right to eat from the *t* of life,
22: 2 side of the river stood the *t* of life,
22:14 they may have the right to the *t*
22:19 from him his share in the *t* of life

TREES (TREE)
Jdg 9: 8 One day the *t* went out
Ps 96:12 Then all the *t* of the forest will sing
Isa 55:12 and all the *t* of the field
Mt 3:10 The ax is already at the root of the *t*
Mk 8:24 they look like *t* walking around."
Jude :12 autumn *t*, without fruit

TREMBLE (TREMBLED TREMBLES TREMBLING)
Ex 15:14 The nations will hear and *t*;
1Ch 16:30 *T* before him, all the earth!
Ps 114: 7 *T*, O earth, at the presence
Jer 5:22 "Should you not *t* in my presence?
Eze 38:20 of the earth will *t* at my presence.
Joel 2: 1 Let all who live in the land *t*,
Hab 3: 6 he looked, and made the nations *t*.

TREMBLED (TREMBLE)
Ex 19:16 Everyone in the camp *t*.
20:18 in smoke, they *t* with fear.
2Sa 22: 8 "The earth *t* and quaked,
Ac 7:32 Moses *t* with fear and did not dare

TREMBLES (TREMBLE)
Ps 97: 4 the earth sees and *t*.
104:32 he who looks at the earth, and it *t*,
Isa 66: 2 and *t* at my word.
Jer 10:10 When he is angry, the earth *t*;
Na 1: 5 The earth *t* at his presence,

TREMBLING (TREMBLE)
Ps 2:11 and rejoice with *t*.
Da 10:10 set me *t* on my hands and knees.
Php 2:12 out your salvation with fear and *t*,
Heb 12:21 terrifying that Moses said, "I am *t*

TRESPASS* (TRESPASSES)
Ro 5:15 But the gift is not like the *t*.
5:15 died by the *t* of the one man,
5:17 For if, by the *t* of the one man,
5:18 result of one *t* was condemnation
5:20 added so that the *t* might increase.

TRESPASSES* (TRESPASS)
Ro 5:16 but the gift followed many *t*

TRIAL (TRIALS)
Ps 37:33 condemned when brought to *t*.
Mk 13:11 you are arrested and brought to *t*,
2Co 8: 2 most severe *t*, their overflowing
Jas 1:12 is the man who perseveres under *t*,
1Pe 4:12 at the painful *t* you are suffering,
Rev 3:10 you from the hour of *t* that is going

TRIALS* (TRIAL)
Dt 7:19 saw with your own eyes the great *t*,
29: 3 own eyes you saw those great *t*,
Lk 22:28 who have stood by me in my *t*.
1Th 3: 3 one would be unsettled by these *t*.
2Th 1: 4 the persecutions and *t* you are
Jas 1: 2 whenever you face *t* of many kinds,
1Pe 1: 6 had to suffer grief in all kinds of *t*.
2Pe 2: 9 how to rescue godly men from *t*

TRIBE (HALF-TRIBE TRIBES)
Heb 7:13 no one from that *t* has ever served
Rev 5: 5 See, the Lion of the *t* of Judah,
5: 9 God from every *t* and language
11: 9 men from every people, *t*,
14: 6 to every nation, *t*, language

TRIBES (TRIBE)
Ge 49:28 All these are the twelve *t* of Israel,
Mt 19:28 judging the twelve *t* of Israel.

TRIBULATION*
Rev 7:14 who have come out of the great *t*;

TRICKERY*
Ac 13:10 full of all kinds of deceit and *t*.
2Co 12:16 fellow that I am, I caught you by *t*!

TRIED (TRY)
Ps 73:16 When I *t* to understand all this,
95: 9 where your fathers tested and *t* me,
Heb 3: 9 where your fathers tested and *t* me

TRIES (TRY)
Lk 17:33 Whoever *t* to keep his life will lose

TRIMMED
Mt 25: 7 virgins woke up and *t* their lamps.

TRIUMPH (TRIUMPHAL TRIUMPHED TRIUMPHING TRIUMPHS)
Ps 25: 2 nor let my enemies *t* over me.
54: 7 my eyes have looked in *t*
112: 8 in the end he will look in *t*
118: 7 I will look in *t* on my enemies.
Pr 28:12 When the righteous *t*, there is great
Isa 42:13 and will *t* over his enemies.

TRIUMPHAL* (TRIUMPH)
Isa 60:11 their kings led in *t* procession.
2Co 2:14 us in *t* procession in Christ

TRIUMPHED (TRIUMPH)
Rev 5: 5 of Judah, the Root of David, has *t*.

TRIUMPHING* (TRIUMPH)
Col 2:15 of them, *t* over them by the cross.

TRIUMPHS* (TRIUMPH)
Jas 2:13 Mercy *t* over judgment! What

TROUBLE (TROUBLED TROUBLES)
Ge 41:51 God has made me forget all my *t*
Jos 7:25 Why have you brought this *t* on us?
Job 2:10 good from God, and not *t*?"
5: 7 Yet man is born to *t*
14: 1 is of few days and full of *t*.
42:11 him over all the *t* the LORD had
Ps 7:14 conceives *t* gives birth
7:16 The *t* he causes recoils on himself;
9: 9 a stronghold in times of *t*.
10:14 But you, O God, do see *t* and grief;
22:11 for *t* is near
27: 5 For in the day of *t*
32: 7 you will protect me from *t*
37:39 he is their stronghold in time of *t*.
41: 1 LORD delivers him in times of *t*.
46: 1 an ever-present help in *t*.
50:15 and call upon me in the day of *t*;
59:16 my refuge in times of *t*.
66:14 spoke when I was in *t*.
86: 7 In the day of my *t* I will call to you,
Ps 91:15 I will be with him in *t*,
107: 6 to the LORD in their *t*,
107:13 they cried to the LORD in their *t*,
116: 3 I was overcome by *t* and sorrow.
119:143 *T* and distress have come upon me,
138: 7 Though I walk in the midst of *t*,
143:11 righteousness, bring me out of *t*.
Pr 11: 8 righteous man is rescued from *t*,
11:17 a cruel man brings *t* on himself
11:29 He who brings *t* on his family will
12:13 but a righteous man escapes *t*.
12:21 but the wicked have their fill of *t*.
15:27 A greedy man brings *t* to his family
19:23 one rests content, untouched by *t*.
22: 8 He who sows wickedness reaps *t*,
24:10 If you falter in times of *t*,
25:19 on the unfaithful in times of *t*.
28:14 he who hardens his heart falls into *t*
Jer 30: 7 It will be a time of *t* for Jacob,
Na 1: 7 a refuge in times of *t*.
Zep 1:15 a day of *t* and ruin,
Mt 6:34 Each day has enough *t* of its own.
13:21 When *t* or persecution comes
Jn 16:33 In this world you will have *t*.
Ro 8:35 Shall *t* or hardship or persecution
2Co 1: 4 those in any *t* with the comfort we
2Th 1: 6 *t* to those who *t* you
Jas 5:13 one of you in *t*? He should pray.

TROUBLED (TROUBLE)
Ps 38:18 I am *t* by my sin.
Isa 38:14 I am *t*; O Lord, come to my aid!"
Mk 14:33 began to be deeply distressed and *t*.
Jn 14: 1 "Do not let your hearts be *t*.
14:27 Do not let your hearts be *t*
2Th 1: 7 and give relief to you who are *t*,

TROUBLES (TROUBLE)
Ps 34: 6 he saved him out of all his *t*.
34:17 he delivers them from all their *t*.
34:19 A righteous man may have many *t*,
40:12 For *t* without number surround me
54: 7 he has delivered me from all my *t*,
1Co 7:28 those who marry will face many *t*
2Co 1: 4 who comforts us in all our *t*,
4:17 and momentary *t* are achieving
6: 4 in *t*, hardships and distresses;
7: 4 in all our *t* my joy knows no bounds
Php 4:14 good of you to share in my *t*.

TRUE (TRUTH)
Nu 11:23 not what I say will come *t* for you."
12: 7 this is not *t* of my servant Moses;
Dt 18:22 does not take place or come *t*,
Jos 23:15 of the LORD your God has come *t*
1Sa 9: 6 and everything he says comes *t*.
1Ki 10: 6 and your wisdom is *t*.
2Ch 6:17 your servant David come *t*.
15: 3 was without the *t* God,
Ps 33: 4 of the LORD is right and *t*;
119:142 and your law is *t*.
119:151 and all your commands are *t*.
119:160 All your words are *t*;
Pr 8: 7 My mouth speaks what is *t*,
22:21 teaching you *t* and reliable words,
Jer 10:10 But the LORD is the *t* God;
28: 9 only if his prediction comes *t*."
Eze 33:33 "When all this comes *t*—
Lk 16:11 who will trust you with *t* riches?
Jn 1: 9 The *t* light that gives light
4:23 when the *t* worshipers will worship
6:32 Father who gives you the *t* bread
7:28 on my own, but he who sent me is *t*
15: 1 "I am the *t* vine, and my Father is
17: 3 the only *t* God, and Jesus Christ,
19:35 testimony, and his testimony is *t*.
21:24 We know that his testimony is *t*.
Ac 10:34 "I now realize how *t* it is that God
11:23 all to remain *t* to the Lord
14:22 them to remain *t* to the faith.
17:11 day to see if what Paul said was *t*.

Ro 3: 4 Let God be *t*, and every man a liar.
Php 4: 8 whatever is *t*, whatever is noble,
1Jn 2: 8 and the *t* light is already shining.
5:20 He is the *t* God and eternal life.
Rev 19: 9 "These are the *t* words of God."
22: 6 These words are trustworthy and *t*.

TRUMPET (TRUMPETS)
Isa 27:13 And in that day a great *t* will sound
Eze 33: 5 Since he heard the sound of the *t*
Zec 9:14 Sovereign LORD will sound the *t*;
Mt 24:31 send his angels with a loud *t* call,
1Co 14: 8 if the *t* does not sound a clear call,
15:52 For the *t* will sound, the dead will
1Th 4:16 and with the *t* call of God,
Rev 8: 7 The first angel sounded his *t*,

TRUMPETS (TRUMPET)
Jdg 7:19 They blew their *t* and broke the jars
Rev 8: 2 and to them were given seven *t*.

TRUST* (ENTRUST ENTRUSTED TRUSTED TRUSTFULLY TRUSTING TRUSTS TRUSTWORTHY)
Ex 14:31 put their *t* in him and in Moses his
19: 9 and will always put their *t* in you."
Nu 20:12 "Because you did not *t*
Dt 1:32 you did not *t* in the LORD your
9:23 You did not *t* him or obey him.
28:52 walls in which you *t* fall down.
Jdg 11:20 did not *t* Israel to pass
2Ki 17:14 who did not *t* in the LORD their
18:30 to *t* in the LORD when he says,
1Ch 9:22 to their positions of *t* by David
Job 4:18 If God places no *t* in his servants,
15:15 If God places no *t* in his holy ones,
31:24 "If I have put my *t* in gold
39:12 Can you *t* him to bring
Ps 4: 5 and *t* in the LORD.
9:10 Those who know your name will *t*
13: 5 But I *t* in your unfailing love;
20: 7 Some *t* in chariots and some
20: 7 we *t* in the name of the LORD our
22: 4 In you our fathers put their *t*;
22: 9 you made me *t* in you
25: 2 I lift up my soul; in you I *t*,
31: 6 I *t* in the LORD.
31:14 But I *t* in you, O LORD;
33:21 for we *t* in his holy name.
37: 3 *T* in the LORD and do good;
37: 5 *t* in him and he will do this:
40: 3 and put their *t* in the LORD.
40: 4 who makes the LORD his *t*,
44: 6 I do not *t* in my bow,
49: 6 those who *t* in their wealth
49:13 of those who *t* in themselves,
52: 8 I *t* in God's unfailing love
55:23 But as for me, I *t* in you.
56: 3 I will *t* in you.
56: 4 in God I *t*; I will not be afraid.
56:11 in God I *t*; I will not be afraid.
62: 8 *T* in him at all times, O people;
62:10 Do not *t* in extortion
78: 7 Then they would put their *t* in God
78:22 or *t* in his deliverance.
91: 2 my God, in whom I *t*."
115: 8 and so will all who *t* in them.
115: 9 O house of Israel, *t* in the LORD—
115:10 O house of Aaron, *t* in the LORD
115:11 You who fear him, *t* in the LORD
118: 8 than to *t* in man.
118: 9 than to *t* in princes.
119:42 for I *t* in your word.
125: 1 Those who *t* in the LORD are like
135:18 and so will all who *t* in them.
143: 8 for I have put my *t* in you.
146: 3 Do not put your *t* in princes,
Pr 3: 5 *T* in the LORD with all your heart
21:22 the stronghold in which they *t*.
22:19 So that your *t* may be in the LORD
Isa 8:17 I will put my *t* in him.
Isa 12: 2 I will *t* and not be afraid.
26: 4 *T* in the LORD forever,
30:15 in quietness and *t* is your strength,
31: 1 who *t* in the multitude
36:15 to *t* in the LORD when he says,
42:17 But those who *t* in idols,
50:10 *t* in the name of the LORD
Jer 2:37 LORD has rejected those you *t*;
5:17 the fortified cities in which you *t*.
7: 4 Do not *t* in deceptive words
7:14 the temple you *t* in, the place I gave
9: 4 do not *t* your brothers.
12: 6 Do not *t* them,
28:15 you have persuaded this nation to *t*
39:18 you *t* in me, declares the LORD.'"
48: 7 Since you *t* in your deeds
49: 4 you *t* in your riches and say,
49:11 Your widows too can *t* in me."
Mic 7: 5 Do not *t* a neighbor;
Na 1: 7 He cares for those who *t* in him,
Zep 3: 2 She does not *t* in the LORD,
3:12 who *t* in the name of the LORD.
Lk 16:11 who will *t* you with true riches?
Jn 12:36 Put your *t* in the light
14: 1 *T* in God; *t* also in me.
Ac 14:23 Lord, in whom they had put their *t*.
Ro 15:13 you with all joy and peace as you *t*
1Co 4: 2 been given a *t* must prove faithful.
9:17 discharging the *t* committed
2Co 13: 6 I *t* that you will discover that we
Heb 2:13 "I will put my *t* in him."

TRUSTED* (TRUST)
1Sa 27:12 Achish *t* David and said to himself,
2Ki 18: 5 Hezekiah *t* in the LORD, the God
1Ch 5:20 their prayers, because they *t*
Job 12:20 He silences the lips of *t* advisers
Ps 5: 9 from their mouth can be *t*;
22: 4 they *t* and you delivered them.
22: 5 in you they *t* and were not
26: 1 I have *t* in the LORD
41: 9 Even my close friend, whom I *t*,
52: 7 but *t* in his great wealth
Isa 20: 5 Those who *t* in Cush and boasted
25: 9 This is the LORD, we *t* in him;
25: 9 we *t* in him, and he saved us.
47:10 You have *t* in your wickedness
Jer 13:25 and *t* in false gods.
38:22 those *t* friends of yours.
48:13 ashamed when they *t* in Bethel.
Eze 16:15 " 'But you *t* in your beauty
Da 3:28 They *t* in him and defied the king's
6:23 because he had *t* in his God.
Lk 11:22 the armor in which the man *t*
16:10 *t* with very little can also be *t*
Ac 12:20 a *t* personal servant of the king,
Tit 2:10 but to show that they can be fully *t*,
3: 8 so that those who have *t*

TRUSTFULLY* (TRUST)
Pr 3:29 who lives *t* near you.

TRUSTING* (TRUST)
Job 15:31 by *t* what is worthless,
Ps 112: 7 his heart is steadfast, *t*
Isa 2:22 Stop *t* in man,
Jer 7: 8 you are *t* in deceptive words that

TRUSTS* (TRUST)
Job 8:14 What he *t* in is fragile;
Ps 21: 7 For the king *t* in the LORD;
22: 8 "He *t* in the LORD;
28: 7 my heart *t* in him, and I am helped.
32:10 surrounds the man who *t* in him.
84:12 blessed is the man who *t* in you.
86: 2 who *t* in you.
Pr 11:28 Whoever *t* in his riches will fall,
16:20 blessed is he who *t* in the LORD.
28:25 he who *t* in the LORD will prosper.
28:26 He who *t* in himself is a fool,
29:25 whoever *t* in the LORD is kept safe
Isa 26: 3 because he *t* in you.
28:16 one who *t* will never be dismayed.
Jer 17: 5 "Cursed is the one who *t* in man,
17: 7 blessed is the man who *t*
Eze 33:13 but then he *t* in his righteousness
Hab 2:18 For he who makes it *t*
Mt 27:43 He *t* in God.
Ro 4: 5 but *t* God who justifies the wicked,
9:33 one who *t* in him will never be put
10:11 "Anyone who *t* in him will never
1Co 13: 7 always protects, always *t*,
1Pe 2: 6 and the one who *t* in him

TRUSTWORTHY* (TRUST)
Ex 18:21 *t* men who hate dishonest gain—
2Sa 7:28 you are God! Your words are *t*,
Ne 13:13 these men were considered *t*.
Ps 19: 7 The statutes of the LORD are *t*,
111: 7 all his precepts are *t*.
119:86 All your commands are *t*;
119:138 they are fully *t*.
Pr 11:13 but a *t* man keeps a secret.
13:17 but a *t* envoy brings healing.
25:13 is a *t* messenger to those who send
Da 2:45 and the interpretation is *t*."
6: 4 he was *t* and neither corrupt
Lk 16:11 So if you have not been *t*
16:12 And if you have not been *t*
19:17 'Because you have been *t*
1Co 7:25 one who by the Lord's mercy is *t*.
1Ti 1:15 Here is a *t* saying that deserves full
3: 1 Here is a *t* saying: If anyone sets his
3:11 but temperate and *t* in everything.
4: 9 This is a *t* saying that deserves full
2Ti 2:11 Here is a *t* saying:
Tit 1: 9 must hold firmly to the *t* message
3: 8 This is a *t* saying.
Rev 21: 5 for these words are *t* and true."
22: 6 "These words are *t* and true.

TRUTH* (TRUE TRUTHFUL TRUTHFULNESS TRUTHS)
Ge 42:16 tested to see if you are telling the *t*.
1Ki 17:24 LORD from your mouth is the *t*."
22:16 the *t* in the name of the LORD?"
2Ch 18:15 the *t* in the name of the LORD?"
Ps 15: 2 who speaks the *t* from his heart
25: 5 guide me in your *t* and teach me,
26: 3 and I walk continually in your *t*.
31: 5 redeem me, O LORD, the God of *t*
40:10 do not conceal your love and your *t*
40:11 your *t* always protect me.
43: 3 Send forth your light and your *t*,
45: 4 victoriously in behalf of *t*, humility
51: 6 Surely you desire *t*
52: 3 than speaking the *t*.
86:11 and I will walk in your *t*;
96:13 and the peoples in his *t*.
119:30 I have chosen the way of *t*;
119:43 of *t* from my mouth,
145:18 to all who call on him in *t*.
Pr 16:13 they value a man who speaks the *t*.
23:23 Buy the *t* and do not sell it;
Isa 45:19 I, the LORD, speak the *t*;
48: 1 but not in *t* or righteousness—
59:14 *t* has stumbled in the streets,
59:15 *T* is nowhere to be found,
65:16 will do so by the God of *t*;
65:16 will swear by the God of *t*.
Jer 5: 1 who deals honestly and seeks the *t*,
5: 3 do not your eyes look for *t*?
7:28 *T* has perished; it has vanished
9: 3 it is not by *t*
9: 5 and no one speaks the *t*.
26:15 for in *t* the LORD has sent me
Da 8:12 and *t* was thrown to the ground.
9:13 and giving attention to your *t*.
10:21 what is written in the Book of *T*.
11: 2 "Now then, I tell you the *t*:
Am 5:10 and despise him who tells the *t*.
Zec 8: 3 will be called the City of *T*,

Zec 8:16 are to do: Speak the *t* to each other,
8:19 Therefore love *t* and peace."
Mt 5:18 I tell you the *t*, until heaven
5:26 I tell you the *t*, you will not get out
6: 2 I tell you the *t*, they have received
6: 5 I tell you the *t*, they have received
6:16 I tell you the *t*, they have received
8:10 "I tell you the *t*, I have not found
10:15 I tell you the *t*, it will be more
10:23 I tell you the *t*, you will not finish
10:42 I tell you the *t*, he will certainly not
11:11 I tell you the *t*: Among those born
13:17 For I tell you the *t*, many prophets
16:28 I tell you the *t*, some who are
17:20 I tell you the *t*, if you have faith
18: 3 And he said: "I tell you the *t*,
18:13 And if he finds it, I tell you the *t*,
18:18 "I tell you the *t*, whatever you bind
19:23 to his disciples, "I tell you the *t*,
19:28 "I tell you the *t*, at the renewal
21:21 Jesus replied, "I tell you the *t*,
21:31 Jesus said to them, "I tell you the *t*,
22:16 of God in accordance with the *t*.
23:36 I tell you the *t*, all this will come
24: 2 "I tell you the *t*, not one stone here
24:34 I tell you the *t*, this generation will
24:47 I tell you the *t*, he will put him
25:12 'I tell you the *t*, I don't know you.'
25:40 The King will reply, 'I tell you the *t*
25:45 "He will reply, 'I tell you the *t*,
26:13 tell you the *t*, wherever this gospel
26:21 "I tell you the *t*, one
26:34 "I tell you the *t*," Jesus answered,
Mk 3:28 I tell you the *t*, all the sins
5:33 with fear, told him the whole *t*.
8:12 I tell you the *t*, no sign will be given
9: 1 he said to them, "I tell you the *t*,
9:41 I tell you the *t*, anyone who gives
10:15 I tell you the *t*, anyone who will not
10:29 "I tell you the *t*," Jesus replied,
11:23 "I tell you the *t*, if anyone says
12:14 of God in accordance with the *t*.
12:43 Jesus said, "I tell you the *t*,
13:30 I tell you the *t*, this generation will
14: 9 I tell you the *t*, wherever the gospel
14:18 "I tell you the *t*, one
14:25 "I tell you the *t*, I will not drink
14:30 "I tell you the *t*," Jesus answered,
Lk 4:24 "I tell you the *t*," he continued,
9:27 I tell you the *t*, some who are
12:37 I tell you the *t*, he will dress himself
12:44 I tell you the *t*, he will put him
18:17 I tell you the *t*, anyone who will not
18:29 I tell you the *t*," Jesus said to them,
20:21 of God in accordance with the *t*.
21: 3 "I tell you the *t*," he said, "this
21:32 tell you the *t*, this generation will
23:43 answered him, "I tell you the *t*,
Jn 1:14 from the Father, full of grace and *t*.
1:17 and *t* came through Jesus Christ.
1:51 "I tell you the *t*, you shall see
3: 3 "I tell you the *t*, no one can see
3: 5 Jesus answered, "I tell you the *t*,
3:11 I tell you the *t*, we speak
3:21 But whoever lives by the *t* comes
4:23 worship the Father in spirit and *t*,
4:24 must worship in spirit and in *t*."
5:19 "I tell you the *t*, the Son can do
5:24 "I tell you the *t*, whoever hears my
5:25 I tell you the *t*, a time is coming
5:33 and he has testified to the *t*.
6:26 "I tell you the *t*, you are looking
6:32 Jesus said to them, "I tell you the *t*,
6:47 I tell you the *t*, he who believes has
6:53 Jesus said to them, "I tell you the *t*,
7:18 the one who sent him is a man of *t*;
8:32 Then you will know the *t*,
8:32 and the *t* will set you free."
8:34 Jesus replied, "I tell you the *t*,
8:40 who has told you the *t* that I heard
Jn 8:44 to the *t*, for there is no *t* in him.
8:45 I tell the *t*, you do not believe me!
8:46 I am telling the *t*, why don't you
8:51 I tell you the *t*, if anyone keeps my
8:58 "I tell you the *t*," Jesus answered,
10: 1 "I tell you the *t*, the man who does
10: 7 "I tell you the *t*, I am the gate
12:24 I tell you the *t*, unless a kernel
13:16 I tell you the *t*, no servant is greater
13:20 tell you the *t*, whoever accepts
13:21 "I tell you the *t*, one of you is going
13:38 I tell you the *t*, before the rooster
14: 6 I am the way and the *t* and the life.
14:12 I tell you the *t*, anyone who has
14:17 with you forever—the Spirit of *t*.
15:26 the Spirit of *t* who goes out
16: 7 But I tell you the *t*: It is
16:13 But when he, the Spirit of *t*, comes,
16:13 comes, he will guide you into all *t*.
16:20 I tell you the *t*, you will weep
16:23 I tell you the *t*, my Father will give
17:17 them by the *t*; your word is *t*.
18:23 if I spoke the *t*, why did you strike
18:37 into the world, to testify to the *t*.
18:37 on the side of *t* listens to me."
18:38 "What is *t*?" Pilate asked.
19:35 He knows that he tells the *t*,
21:18 I tell you the *t*, when you were
Ac 20:30 and distort the *t* in order
21:24 everybody will know there is no *t*
21:34 commander could not get at the *t*
24: 8 able to learn the *t* about all these
28:25 "The Holy Spirit spoke the *t*
Ro 1:18 of men who suppress the *t*
1:25 They exchanged the *t* of God
2: 2 who do such things is based on *t*.
2: 8 who reject the *t* and follow evil,
2:20 embodiment of knowledge and *t*—
9: 1 I speak the *t* in Christ—I am not
15: 8 of the Jews on behalf of God's *t*,
1Co 5: 8 the bread of sincerity and *t*.
13: 6 in evil but rejoices with the *t*.
2Co 4: 2 setting forth the *t* plainly we
11:10 As surely as the *t* of Christ is in me,
12: 6 because I would be speaking the *t*.
13: 8 against the *t*, but only for the *t*.
Gal 2: 5 so that the *t* of the gospel might
2:14 in line with the *t* of the gospel,
4:16 enemy by telling you the *t*?
5: 7 and kept you from obeying the *t*?
Eph 1:13 when you heard the word of *t*,
4:15 Instead, speaking the *t* in love,
4:21 him in accordance with the *t* that is
5: 9 and *t*) and find out what pleases
6:14 with the belt of *t* buckled
Col 1: 5 heard about in the word of *t*,
1: 6 understood God's grace in all its *t*.
2Th 2:10 because they refused to love the *t*
2:12 who have not believed the *t*
2:13 and through belief in the *t*.
1Ti 2: 4 to come to a knowledge of the *t*.
2: 7 I am telling the *t*, I am not lying—
3:15 the pillar and foundation of the *t*.
4: 3 who believe and who know the *t*.
6: 5 who have been robbed of the *t*
2Ti 2:15 correctly handles the word of *t*.
2:18 have wandered away from the *t*.
2:25 them to a knowledge of the *t*,
3: 7 never able to acknowledge the *t*.
3: 8 so also these men oppose the *t*—
4: 4 will turn their ears away from the *t*
Tit 1: 1 the knowledge of the *t* that leads
1:14 of those who reject the *t*.
Heb 10:26 received the knowledge of the *t*,
Jas 1:18 birth through the word of *t*,
3:14 do not boast about it or deny the *t*.
5:19 of you should wander from the *t*
1Pe 1:22 by obeying the *t* so that you have
2Pe 1:12 established in the *t* you now have.
2: 2 the way of *t* into disrepute.
1Jn 1: 6 we lie and do not live by the *t*.
1: 8 deceive ourselves and the *t* is not
2: 4 commands is a liar, and the *t* is not
2: 8 its *t* is seen in him and you,
2:20 and all of you know the *t*.
2:21 because no lie comes from the *t*.
2:21 because you do not know the *t*,
3:18 or tongue but with actions and in *t*.
3:19 we know that we belong to the *t*,
4: 6 is how we recognize the Spirit of *t*
5: 6 testifies, because the Spirit is the *t*.
2Jn : 1 whom I love in the *t*—
: 2 who know the *t*— because of the *t*,
: 3 will be with us in *t* and love.
: 4 of your children walking in the *t*,
3Jn : 1 friend Gaius, whom I love in the *t*.
: 3 how you continue to walk in the *t*.
: 3 tell about your faithfulness to the *t*
: 4 my children are walking in the *t*.
: 8 we may work together for the *t*.
:12 everyone—and even by the *t* itself.

TRUTHFUL* (TRUTH)
Pr 12:17 A *t* witness gives honest testimony,
12:19 *T* lips endure forever,
12:22 but he delights in men who are *t*.
14: 5 A *t* witness does not deceive,
14:25 A *t* witness saves lives,
Jer 4: 2 and if in a *t*, just and righteous way
Jn 3:33 it has certified that God is *t*.
2Co 6: 7 in *t* speech and in the power

TRUTHFULNESS* (TRUTH)
Ro 3: 7 "If my falsehood enhances God's *t*

TRUTHS* (TRUTH)
1Co 2:13 expressing spiritual *t*
1Ti 3: 9 hold of the deep *t* of the faith
4: 6 brought up in the *t* of the faith
Heb 5:12 to teach you the elementary *t*

TRY (TRIED TRIES TRYING)
Ps 26: 2 Test me, O LORD, and *t* me,
Isa 7:13 enough to *t* the patience of men?
Lk 12:58 *t* hard to be reconciled to him
13:24 will *t* to enter and will not be able
1Co 10:33 even as I *t* to please everybody
14:12 *t* to excel in gifts that build up
2Co 5:11 is to fear the Lord, we *t*
1Th 5:15 always *t* to be kind to each other
Tit 2: 9 to *t* to please them, not to talk back

TRYING (TRY)
2Co 5:12 We are not *t* to commend ourselves
Gal 1:10 If I were still *t* to please men,
1Th 2: 4 We are not *t* to please men but God
1Pe 1:11 *t* to find out the time
1Jn 2:26 things to you about those who are *t*

TUMORS
1Sa 5: 6 them and afflicted them with *t*.

TUNE
1Co 14: 7 anyone know what *t* is being

TUNIC (TUNICS)
Lk 6:29 do not stop him from taking your *t*.

TUNICS (TUNIC)
Lk 3:11 "The man with two *t* should share

TURMOIL
Ps 65: 7 and the *t* of the nations.
Pr 15:16 than great wealth with *t*.

TURN (TURNED TURNING TURNS)
Ex 32:12 *T* from your fierce anger; relent
Nu 32:15 If you *t* away from following him,
Dt 5:32 do not *t* aside to the right
28:14 Do not *t* aside from any
30:10 and *t* to the LORD your God
Jos 1: 7 do not *t* from it to the right

Pr 4: 5 Get wisdom, get *u;*
4: 7 Though it cost all you have, get *u.*
7: 4 and call *u* your kinsman;
9:10 knowledge of the Holy One is *u.*
10:23 but a man of *u* delights in wisdom.
11:12 but a man of *u* holds his tongue.
14:29 A patient man has great *u,*
15:21 a man of *u* keeps a straight course.
15:32 whoever heeds correction gains *u.*
16:16 to choose *u* rather than silver!
16:22 *U* is a fountain of life
17:27 and a man of *u* is even-tempered.
18: 2 A fool finds no pleasure in *u*
19: 8 he who cherishes *u* prospers.
20: 5 but a man of *u* draws them out.
23:23 get wisdom, discipline and *u.*
Isa 11: 2 the Spirit of wisdom and of *u,*
40:28 and his *u* no one can fathom.
56:11 They are shepherds who lack *u;*
Jer 3:15 you with knowledge and *u.*
10:12 stretched out the heavens by his *u.*
Da 5:12 a keen mind and knowledge and *u,*
10:12 that you set your mind to gain *u*
Hos 4:11 which take away the *u*
Mk 4:12 and ever hearing but never *u;*
12:33 with all your *u* and with all your
Lk 2:47 who heard him was amazed at his *u*
2Co 6: 6 in purity, *u,* patience and kindness;
Eph 1: 8 on us with all wisdom and *u.*
Php 4: 7 of God, which transcends all *u,*
Col 1: 9 through all spiritual wisdom and *u.*
2: 2 have the full riches of complete *u,*
1Jn 5:20 God has come and has given us *u,*

UNDERSTANDS (UNDERSTAND)
1Ch 28: 9 and *u* every motive
Jer 9:24 that he *u* and knows me,
Mt 13:23 man who hears the word and *u* it.
Ro 3:11 there is no one who *u,*
1Ti 6: 4 he is conceited and *u* nothing.

UNDERSTOOD (UNDERSTAND)
Ne 8:12 they now *u* the words that had
Ps 73:17 then I *u* their final destiny.
Isa 40:13 Who has *u* the mind of the LORD,
40:21 Have you not *u* since the earth was
Jn 1: 5 but the darkness has not *u* it.
Ro 1:20 being *u* from what has been made,

UNDESIRABLE*
Jos 24:15 But if serving the LORD seems *u*

UNDIVIDED*
1Ch 12:33 to help David with *u* loyalty—
Ps 86:11 give me an *u* heart,
Eze 11:19 I will give them an *u* heart
1Co 7:35 way in *u* devotion to the Lord.

UNDOING
Pr 18: 7 A fool's mouth is his *u,*

UNDYING*
Eph 6:24 Lord Jesus Christ with an *u* love.

UNEQUALED*
Mt 24:21 *u* from the beginning of the world
Mk 13:19 of distress *u* from the beginning,

UNFADING*
1Pe 3: 4 the *u* beauty of a gentle

UNFAILING*
Ex 15:13 "In your *u* love you will lead
1Sa 20:14 But show me *u* kindness like that
2Sa 22:51 he shows *u* kindness
Ps 6: 4 save me because of your *u* love.
13: 5 But I trust in your *u* love;
18:50 he shows *u* kindness
21: 7 through the *u* love
31:16 save me in your *u* love.
32:10 but the LORD's *u* love
33: 5 the earth is full of his *u* love.
Ps 33:18 those whose hope is in his *u* love,
33:22 May your *u* love rest upon us,
36: 7 How priceless is your *u* love!
44:26 redeem us because of your *u* love.
48: 9 we meditate on your *u* love.
51: 1 according to your *u* love;
52: 8 I trust in God's *u* love
77: 8 Has his *u* love vanished forever?
85: 7 Show us your *u* love, O LORD,
90:14 in the morning with your *u* love,
107: 8 thanks to the LORD for his *u* love
107:15 thanks to the LORD for his *u* love
107:21 to the LORD for his *u* love
107:31 to the LORD for his *u* love
119:41 May your *u* love come to me,
119:76 May your *u* love be my comfort,
130: 7 for with the LORD is *u* love
143: 8 bring me word of your *u* love,
143:12 In your *u* love, silence my enemies;
147:11 who put their hope in his *u* love.
Pr 19:22 What a man desires is *u* love;
20: 6 Many a man claims to have *u* love,
Isa 54:10 yet my *u* love for you will not be
La 3:32 so great is his *u* love.
Hos 10:12 reap the fruit of *u* love,

UNFAITHFUL (UNFAITHFULNESS)
Lev 6: 2 is *u* to the LORD by deceiving his
Nu 5: 6 and so is *u* to the LORD,
1Ch 10:13 because he was *u* to the LORD;
Pr 11: 6 the *u* are trapped by evil desires.
13: 2 the *u* have a craving for violence.
13:15 but the way of the *u* is hard.
22:12 but he frustrates the words of the *u.*
23:28 and multiplies the *u* among men.
25:19 is reliance on the *u* in times
Jer 3:20 But like a woman *u* to her husband,

UNFAITHFULNESS (UNFAITHFUL)
1Ch 9: 1 to Babylon because of their *u.*
Mt 5:32 except for marital *u,* causes her
19: 9 for marital *u,* and marries another

UNFIT*
Tit 1:16 and *u* for doing anything good.

UNFOLDING
Ps 119:130 the *u* of your words gives light;

UNFORGIVING*
2Ti 3: 3 unholy, without love, *u,* slanderous

UNFRIENDLY*
Pr 18: 1 An *u* man pursues selfish ends;

UNFRUITFUL
1Co 14:14 my spirit prays, but my mind is *u.*

UNGODLINESS (UNGODLY)
Tit 2:12 It teaches us to say "No" to *u*

UNGODLY (UNGODLINESS)
Ro 5: 6 powerless, Christ died for the *u.*
1Ti 1: 9 the *u* and sinful, the unholy
2Ti 2:16 in it will become more and more *u.*
2Pe 2: 6 of what is going to happen to the *u;*
Jude :15 and to convict all the *u*

UNGRATEFUL*
Lk 6:35 he is kind to the *u* and wicked.
2Ti 3: 2 disobedient to their parents, *u,*

UNHOLY*
1Ti 1: 9 and sinful, the *u* and irreligious;
2Ti 3: 2 ungrateful, *u,* without love,
Heb 10:29 as an *u* thing the blood

UNINTENTIONALLY
Lev 4: 2 'When anyone sins *u* and does
Nu 15:22 " 'Now if you *u* fail to keep any
Dt 4:42 flee if he had *u* killed his neighbor

UNIT
1Co 12:12 body is a *u,* though it is made up

UNITE (UNITED UNITY)
1Co 6:15 and *u* them with a prostitute?

UNITED (UNITE)
Ge 2:24 and mother and be *u* to his wife,
Mt 19: 5 and mother and be *u* to his wife,
Ro 6: 5 If we have been *u* with him like this
Eph 5:31 and mother and be *u* to his wife,
Php 2: 1 from being *u* with Christ,
Col 2: 2 encouraged in heart and *u* in love,

UNITY* (UNITE)
2Ch 30:12 the people to give them *u* of mind
Ps 133: 1 is when brothers live together in *u!*
Jn 17:23 May they be brought to complete *u*
Ro 15: 5 a spirit of *u* among yourselves
Eph 4: 3 effort to keep the *u* of the Spirit
4:13 up until we all reach *u* in the faith
Col 3:14 them all together in perfect *u.*

UNIVERSE*
1Co 4: 9 made a spectacle to the whole *u,*
Eph 4:10 in order to fill the whole *u.)*
Php 2:15 which you shine like stars in the *u*
Heb 1: 2 and through whom he made the *u.*
11: 3 understand that the *u* was formed

UNJUST
Ro 3: 5 That God is *u* in bringing his wrath
9:14 What then shall we say? Is God *u?*
1Pe 2:19 up under the pain of *u* suffering

UNKNOWN
Ac 17:23 TO AN *U* GOD.

UNLEAVENED
Ex 12:17 "Celebrate the Feast of *U* Bread,
Dt 16:16 at the Feast of *U* Bread, the Feast

UNLIMITED*
1Ti 1:16 Jesus might display his *u* patience

UNLOVED
Pr 30:23 an *u* woman who is married,

UNMARRIED
1Co 7: 8 It is good for them to stay *u,*
7:27 Are you *u?* Do not look for a wife.
7:32 An *u* man is concerned about

UNPLOWED
Ex 23:11 the seventh year let the land lie *u*
Hos 10:12 and break up your *u* ground;

UNPRODUCTIVE
Tit 3:14 necessities and not live *u* lives.
2Pe 1: 8 and *u* in your knowledge

UNPROFITABLE
Tit 3: 9 because these are *u* and useless.

UNPUNISHED
Ex 34: 7 Yet he does not leave the guilty *u;*
Pr 6:29 no one who touches her will go *u.*
11:21 of this: The wicked will not go *u,*
19: 5 A false witness will not go *u,*

UNQUENCHABLE
Lk 3:17 he will burn up the chaff with *u* fire

UNREPENTANT*
Ro 2: 5 stubbornness and your *u* heart,

UNRIGHTEOUS*
Zep 3: 5 yet the *u* know no shame.
Mt 5:45 rain on the righteous and the *u.*
1Pe 3:18 the righteous for the *u,* to bring you
2Pe 2: 9 and to hold the *u* for the day

UNSEARCHABLE
Ro 11:33 How *u* his judgments,
Eph 3: 8 preach to the Gentiles the *u* riches

UNSEEN*
Mt 6: 6 and pray to your Father, who is *u.*
6:18 who is *u;* and your Father,
2Co 4:18 on what is seen, but on what is *u.*
4:18 temporary, but what is *u* is eternal.

UNSETTLED*
1Th 3: 3 so that no one would be *u*
2Th 2: 2 not to become easily *u*

UNSHRUNK
Mt 9:16 patch of *u* cloth on an old garment,

UNSPIRITUAL*
Ro 7:14 but I am *u,* sold as a slave to sin.
Col 2:18 and his *u* mind puffs him up
Jas 3:15 down from heaven but is earthly, *u,*

UNSTABLE*
Jas 1: 8 he is a double-minded man, *u*
2Pe 2:14 they seduce the *u;* they are experts
3:16 ignorant and *u* people distort,

UNTHINKABLE*
Job 34:12 It is *u* that God would do wrong,

UNTIE
Mk 1: 7 worthy to stoop down and *u.*
Lk 13:15 each of you on the Sabbath *u* his ox

UNVEILED*
2Co 3:18 with *u* faces all reflect the Lord's

UNWHOLESOME*
Eph 4:29 Do not let any *u* talk come out

UNWISE
Eph 5:15 how you live—not as *u* but as wise,

UNWORTHY*
Ge 32:10 I am *u* of all the kindness
Job 40: 4 "I am *u*— how can I reply to you?
Lk 17:10 should say, 'We are *u* servants;
1Co 11:27 Lord in an *u* manner will be guilty

UPHOLD (UPHOLDS)
Isa 41:10 I will *u* you with my righteous right
Ro 3:31 Not at all! Rather, we *u* the law.

UPHOLDS* (UPHOLD)
Ps 37:17 but the LORD *u* the righteous.
37:24 for the LORD *u* him with his hand.
63: 8 your right hand *u* me.
140:12 and *u* the cause of the needy.
145:14 The LORD *u* all those who fall
146: 7 He *u* the cause of the oppressed

UPRIGHT
Dt 32: 4 *u* and just is he.
Job 1: 1 This man was blameless and *u;*
Ps 7:10 who saves the *u* in heart.
11: 7 *u* men will see his face.
25: 8 Good and *u* is the LORD;
33: 1 it is fitting for the *u* to praise him.
64:10 let all the *u* in heart praise him!
92:15 proclaiming, "The LORD is *u;*
97:11 and joy on the *u* in heart.
119: 7 I will praise you with an *u* heart
Pr 2: 7 He holds victory in store for the *u,*
3:32 but takes the *u* into his confidence.
14: 2 whose walk is *u* fears the LORD,
15: 8 but the prayer of the *u* pleases him.
21:29 an *u* man gives thought to his ways.
Isa 26: 7 O *u* One, you make the way
Tit 1: 8 who is self-controlled, *u,* holy
2:12 *u* and godly lives in this present

UPROOTED
Dt 28:63 You will be *u* from the land you are
Jer 31:40 The city will never again be *u*
Jude :12 without fruit and *u*— twice dead.

UPSET
Lk 10:41 are worried and *u* about many

URIAH
Hittite husband of Bathsheba, killed by David's order (2Sa 11).

USEFUL
Eph 4:28 doing something *u*
2Ti 2:21 *u* to the Master and prepared
3:16 Scripture is God-breathed and is *u*
Phm :11 now he has become *u* both to you

USELESS
1Co 15:14 our preaching is *u*
Tit 3: 9 these are unprofitable and *u.*
Phm :11 Formerly he was *u* to you,
Heb 7:18 *u* (for the law made nothing perfect
Jas 2:20 faith without deeds is *u?*

USURY
Ne 5:10 But let the exacting of *u* stop!
Ps 15: 5 who lends his money without *u*

UTMOST
Job 34:36 that Job might be tested to the *u*

UTTER (UTTERS)
Ps 78: 2 I will *u* hidden things, things from of old—
Mt 13:35 I will *u* things hidden

UTTERS (UTTER)
1Co 14: 2 he *u* mysteries with his spirit.

UZZIAH
Son of Amaziah; king of Judah also known as Azariah (2Ki 15:1–7; 1Ch 6:24; 2Ch 26). Struck with leprosy because of pride (2Ch 26:16–23).

VAIN
Ps 33:17 A horse is a *v* hope for deliverance;
73:13 in *v* have I kept my heart pure;
127: 1 its builders labor in *v.*
Isa 65:23 They will not toil in *v*
1Co 15: 2 Otherwise, you have believed in *v.*
15:58 labor in the Lord is not in *v.*
2Co 6: 1 not to receive God's grace in *v.*
Gal 2: 2 running or had run my race in *v.*

VALIANT
1Sa 10:26 by *v* men whose hearts God had

VALID
Jn 8:14 my own behalf, my testimony is *v,*

VALLEY (VALLEYS)
Ps 23: 4 walk through the *v* of the shadow
Isa 40: 4 Every *v* shall be raised up,
Joel 3:14 multitudes in the *v* of decision!

VALLEYS (VALLEY)
SS 2: 1 a lily of the *v.*

VALUABLE (VALUE)
Lk 12:24 And how much more *v* you are

VALUE (VALUABLE VALUED)
Lev 27: 3 set the *v* of a male between the ages
Pr 16:13 they *v* a man who speaks the truth.
31:11 and lacks nothing of *v.*
Mt 13:46 When he found one of great *v,*
1Ti 4: 8 For physical training is of some *v,*
Heb 11:26 as of greater *v* than the treasures

VALUED (VALUE)
Lk 16:15 What is highly *v* among men is

VANISHES
Jas 4:14 appears for a little while and then *v.*

VASHTI*
Queen of Persia replaced by Esther (Est 1–2).

VAST
Ge 2: 1 completed in all their *v* array.
Dt 1:19 of the Amorites through all that *v*
8:15 He led you through the *v*
Ps 139:17 How *v* is the sum of them!

VEGETABLES
Pr 15:17 of *v* where there is love
Ro 14: 2 whose faith is weak, eats only *v.*

VEIL
Ex 34:33 to them, he put a *v* over his face.
2Co 3:14 for to this day the same *v* remains

VENGEANCE (AVENGE AVENGER AVENGES AVENGING REVENGE)
Nu 31: 3 to carry out the LORD's *v* on them
Isa 34: 8 For the LORD has a day of *v,*
Na 1: 2 The LORD takes *v* on his foes

VERDICT
Jn 3:19 This is the *v:* Light has come

VICTOR'S* (VICTORY)
2Ti 2: 5 he does not receive the *v* crown

VICTORIES* (VICTORY)
2Sa 22:51 He gives his king great *v;*
Ps 18:50 He gives his king great *v;*
21: 1 great is his joy in the *v* you give!
21: 5 Through the *v* you gave, his glory is
44: 4 who decrees *v* for Jacob.

VICTORIOUS (VICTORY)
Ps 20: 5 for joy when you are *v*

VICTORIOUSLY* (VICTORY)
Ps 45: 4 In your majesty ride forth *v*

VICTORY (VICTOR'S VICTORIES VICTORIOUS VICTORIOUSLY)
2Sa 8: 6 gave David *v* wherever he
Ps 44: 6 my sword does not bring me *v;*
60:12 With God we will gain the *v,*
129: 2 they have not gained the *v* over me.
Pr 11:14 but many advisers make *v* sure.
1Co 15:54 "Death has been swallowed up in *v*
15:57 He gives us the *v* through our Lord
1Jn 5: 4 This is the *v* that has overcome

VIEW
Pr 5:21 are in full *v* of the LORD,
2Ti 4: 1 and in *v* of his appearing

VILLAGE
Mk 6: 6 went around teaching from *v* to *v.*

VINDICATED (VINDICATION)
Job 13:18 I know I will be *v.*
1Ti 3:16 was *v* by the Spirit,

VINDICATION (VINDICATED)
Ps 24: 5 and *v* from God his Savior.

VINE (VINEYARD)
Ps 128: 3 Your wife will be like a fruitful *v*
Isa 36:16 one of you will eat from his own *v*
Jnh 4: 6 Jonah was very happy about the *v.*
Jn 15: 1 "I am the true *v,* and my Father is

VINEGAR
Pr 10:26 As *v* to the teeth and smoke
Mk 15:36 filled a sponge with wine *v,*

VINEYARD (VINE)
1Ki 21: 1 an incident involving a *v* belonging
Pr 31:16 out of her earnings she plants a *v.*
SS 1: 6 my own *v* I have neglected.
Isa 5: 1 My loved one had a *v*
1Co 9: 7 Who plants a *v* and does not eat

VIOLATION
Heb 2: 2 every *v* and disobedience received

VIOLENCE (VIOLENT)
Ge 6:11 in God's sight and was full of *v*.
Isa 53: 9 though he had done no *v*,
60:18 No longer will *v* be heard
Eze 45: 9 Give up your *v* and oppression
Joel 3:19 of *v* done to the people of Judah,
Jnh 3: 8 give up their evil ways and their *v*.

VIOLENT (VIOLENCE)
Eze 18:10 "Suppose he has a *v* son, who sheds
1Ti 1:13 and a persecutor and a *v* man,
3: 3 not *v* but gentle, not quarrelsome,
Tit 1: 7 not *v*, not pursuing dishonest gain.

VIPERS
Ps 140: 3 the poison of *v* is on their lips.
Lk 3: 7 "You brood of *v*! Who warned you
Ro 3:13 "The poison of *v* is on their lips."

VIRGIN (VIRGINS)
Dt 22:15 shall bring proof that she was a *v*
Isa 7:14 The *v* will be with child
Mt 1:23 "The *v* will be with child
Lk 1:34 I am a *v*?" The angel answered,
2Co 11: 2 that I might present you as a pure *v*

VIRGINS (VIRGIN)
Mt 25: 1 will be like ten *v* who took their
1Co 7:25 Now about *v*: I have no command

VIRTUES*
Col 3:14 And over all these *v* put on love,

VISIBLE
Eph 5:13 exposed by the light becomes *v*,
Col 1:16 and on earth, *v* and invisible,

VISION (VISIONS)
Da 9:24 to seal up *v* and prophecy
Ac 26:19 disobedient to the *v* from heaven.

VISIONS (VISION)
Nu 12: 6 I reveal myself to him in *v*,
Joel 2:28 your young men will see *v*.
Ac 2:17 your young men will see *v*,

VOICE
Dt 30:20 listen to his *v*, and hold fast to him.
1Sa 15:22 as in obeying the *v* of the LORD?
Job 40: 9 and can your *v* thunder like his?
Ps 19: 4 Their *v* goes out into all the earth,
29: 3 The *v* of the LORD is
66:19 and heard my *v* in prayer.
95: 7 Today, if you hear his *v*,
Pr 8: 1 Does not understanding raise her *v*
Isa 30:21 your ears will hear a *v* behind you,
40: 3 A *v* of one calling:
Mk 1: 3 "a *v* of one calling in the desert,
Jn 5:28 are in their graves will hear his *v*
10: 3 and the sheep listen to his *v*.
Ro 10:18 "Their *v* has gone out
Heb 3: 7 "Today, if you hear his *v*,
Rev 3:20 If anyone hears my *v* and opens

VOMIT
Lev 18:28 it will *v* you out as it vomited out
Pr 26:11 As a dog returns to its *v*,
2Pe 2:22 "A dog returns to its *v*," and,

VOW (VOWS)
Nu 6: 2 a *v* of separation to the LORD
30: 2 When a man makes a *v*
Jdg 11:30 Jephthah made a *v* to the LORD:

VOWS (VOW)
Ps 116:14 I will fulfill my *v* to the LORD
Pr 20:25 and only later to consider his *v*.

VULTURES
Mt 24:28 is a carcass, there the *v* will gather.

WAGE (WAGES WAGING)
2Co 10: 3 we do not *w* war as the world does.

WAGES (WAGE)
Mal 3: 5 who defraud laborers of their *w*,
Lk 10: 7 for the worker deserves his *w*.
Ro 4: 4 his *w* are not credited to him
6:23 For the *w* of sin is death,
1Ti 5:18 and "The worker deserves his *w*."

WAGING (WAGE)
Ro 7:23 *w* war against the law of my mind

WAILING
Ps 30:11 You turned my *w* into dancing;

WAIST
2Ki 1: 8 and with a leather belt around his *w*."
Mt 3: 4 he had a leather belt around his *w*.

WAIT (AWAITS WAITED WAITING WAITS)
Ps 27:14 *W* for the LORD;
130: 5 I *w* for the LORD, my soul waits,
Isa 30:18 Blessed are all who *w* for him!
Ac 1: 4 *w* for the gift my Father promised,
Ro 8:23 as we *w* eagerly for our adoption
1Th 1:10 and to *w* for his Son from heaven,
Tit 2:13 while we *w* for the blessed hope—

WAITED (WAIT)
Ps 40: 1 I *w* patiently for the LORD;

WAITING (WAIT)
Heb 9:28 to those who are *w* for him.

WAITS (WAIT)
Ro 8:19 creation *w* in eager expectation

WAKE (AWAKE WAKENS)
Eph 5:14 "*W* up, O sleeper,

WAKENS* (WAKE)
Isa 50: 4 He *w* me morning by morning,
50: 4 *w* my ear to listen like one being

WALK (WALKED WALKING WALKS)
Lev 26:12 I will *w* among you and be your
Dt 5:33 *W* in all the way that the LORD
6: 7 and when you *w* along the road,
10:12 to *w* in all his ways, to love him,
11:19 and when you *w* along the road,
11:22 to *w* in all his ways and to hold fast
26:17 and that you will *w* in his ways,
Jos 22: 5 to *w* in all his ways,
Ps 1: 1 who does not *w* in the counsel
15: 2 He whose *w* is blameless
23: 4 Even though I *w*
84:11 from those whose *w* is blameless.
89:15 who *w* in the light of your presence
119:45 I will *w* about in freedom,
Pr 4:12 When you *w*, your steps will not be
6:22 When you *w*, they will guide you;
Isa 2: 3 so that we may *w* in his paths."
2: 5 let us *w* in the light of the LORD.
30:21 saying, "This is the way; *w* in it."
40:31 they will *w* and not be faint.
57: 2 Those who *w* uprightly
Jer 6:16 ask where the good way is, and *w*
Da 4:37 And those who *w* in pride he is able
Am 3: 3 Do two *w* together
Mic 4: 5 All the nations may *w*
6: 8 and to *w* humbly with your God.
Mk 2: 9 'Get up, take your mat and *w*'?
Jn 8:12 Whoever follows me will never *w*
1Jn 1: 6 with him yet *w* in the darkness,
1: 7 But if we *w* in the light,
2Jn : 6 his command is that you *w* in love.

WALKED (WALK)
Ge 5:24 Enoch *w* with God; then he was no
Jos 14: 9 which your feet have *w* will be your
Mt 14:29 *w* on the water and came toward Jesus.

WALKING (WALK)
1Ki 3: 3 love for the LORD by *w* according
Da 3:25 I see four men *w* around in the fire,
2Jn : 4 of your children *w* in the truth,

WALKS (WALK)
Pr 10: 9 The man of integrity *w* securely,
13:20 He who *w* with the wise grows wise
Isa 33:15 He who *w* righteously
Jn 11: 9 A man who *w* by day will not

WALL (WALLS)
Jos 6:20 *w* collapsed; so every man charged
Ne 2:17 let us rebuild the *w* of Jerusalem,
Eph 2:14 the dividing *w* of hostility,
Rev 21:12 It had a great, high *w*

WALLOWING
2Pe 2:22 back to her *w* in the mud."

WALLS (WALL)
Isa 58:12 be called Repairer of Broken *W*,
60:18 but you will call your *w* Salvation
Heb 11:30 By faith the *w* of Jericho fell,

WANDER (WANDERED)
Nu 32:13 he made them *w* in the desert forty
Jas 5:19 one of you should *w* from the truth

WANDERED (WANDER)
Eze 34: 6 My sheep *w* over all the mountains
Mt 18:12 go to look for the one that *w* off?
1Ti 6:10 have *w* from the faith and pierced
2Ti 2:18 who have *w* away from the truth.

WANT (WANTED WANTING WANTS)
1Sa 8:19 "We *w* a king over us.
Mt 19:21 Jesus answered, "If you *w*
Lk 19:14 'We don't *w* this man to be our king
Ro 7:15 For what I *w* to do I do not do,
13: 3 Do you *w* to be free from fear
2Co 12:14 what I *w* is not your possessions
Php 3:10 I *w* to know Christ and the power

WANTED (WANT)
1Co 12:18 of them, just as he *w* them to be.
Heb 6:17 Because God *w* to make

WANTING (WANT)
Da 5:27 weighed on the scales and found *w*.
2Pe 3: 9 with you, not *w* anyone to perish,

WANTS (WANT)
Mt 5:42 from the one who *w* to borrow
20:26 whoever *w* to become great
Mk 8:35 For whoever *w* to save his life will
10:43 whoever *w* to become great
Ro 9:18 he hardens whom he *w* to harden.
1Ti 2: 4 who *w* all men to be saved
1Pe 5: 2 you are willing, as God *w* you to be;

WAR (WARRIOR WARS)
Jos 11:23 Then the land had rest from *w*.
1Sa 15:18 make *w* on them until you have
Ps 68:30 the nations who delight in *w*.
120: 7 but when I speak, they are for *w*.
144: 1 who trains my hands for *w*,
Isa 2: 4 nor will they train for *w* anymore.
Da 9:26 *W* will continue until the end,
Ro 7:23 waging *w* against the law
2Co 10: 3 we do not wage *w* as the world does
1Pe 2:11 which *w* against your soul.
Rev 12: 7 And there was *w* in heaven.
19:11 With justice he judges and makes *w*

WARN* (WARNED WARNING WARNINGS)
Ex 19:21 *w* the people so they do not force
Nu 24:14 let me *w* you of what this people
1Sa 8: 9 but *w* them solemnly and let them
1Ki 2:42 swear by the LORD and *w* you,
2Ch 19:10 you are to *w* them not to sin
Ps 81: 8 O my people, and I will *w* you—

Jer 42:19 I *w* you today that you made a fatal
Eze 3:18 and you do not *w* him or speak out
3:19 But if you do *w* the wicked man
3:20 Since you did not *w* him, he will die
3:21 if you do *w* the righteous man not
33: 3 blows the trumpet to *w* the people,
33: 6 blow the trumpet to *w* the people
33: 9 if you do *w* the wicked man to turn
Lk 16:28 Let him *w* them, so that they will
Ac 4:17 we must *w* these men
1Co 4:14 but to *w* you, as my dear children.
Gal 5:21 I *w* you, as I did before, that those
1Th 5:14 brothers, *w* those who are idle,
2Th 3:15 an enemy, but *w* him as a brother.
2Ti 2:14 *W* them before God
Tit 3:10 and then *w* him a second time.
3:10 *W* a divisive person once,
Rev 22:18 I *w* everyone who hears the words

WARNED (WARN)
2Ki 17:13 The LORD *w* Israel and Judah
Ps 19:11 By them is your servant *w;*
Jer 22:21 I *w* you when you felt secure,
Mt 3: 7 Who *w* you to flee
1Th 4: 6 have already told you and *w* you.
Heb 11: 7 when *w* about things not yet seen,
12:25 they refused him who *w* them

WARNING (WARN)
Jer 6: 8 Take *w,* O Jerusalem,
1Ti 5:20 so that the others may take *w.*

WARNINGS (WARN)
1Co 10:11 and were written down as *w* for us,

WARRIOR (WAR)
Ex 15: 3 The LORD is a *w;*
1Ch 28: 3 you are a *w* and have shed blood.'
Pr 16:32 Better a patient man than a *w,*

WARS (WAR)
Ps 46: 9 He makes *w* cease to the ends
Mt 24: 6 You will hear of *w* and rumors of *w,*

WASH (WASHED WASHING)
Ps 51: 7 *w* me, and I will be whiter
Jer 4:14 *w* the evil from your heart
Jn 13: 5 and began to *w* his disciples' feet,
Ac 22:16 be baptized and *w* your sins away,
Jas 4: 8 *W* your hands, you sinners,
Rev 22:14 Blessed are those who *w* their robes

WASHED (WASH)
Ps 73:13 in vain have I *w* my hands
1Co 6:11 you were *w,* you were sanctified,
Heb 10:22 and having our bodies *w*
2Pe 2:22 and, "A sow that is *w* goes back
Rev 7:14 they have *w* their robes

WASHING (WASH)
Eph 5:26 cleansing her by the *w* with water
1Ti 5:10 showing hospitality, *w* the feet
Tit 3: 5 us through the *w* of rebirth

WASTED (WASTING)
Jn 6:12 Let nothing be *w."*

WASTING (WASTED)
2Co 4:16 Though outwardly we are *w* away,

WATCH (WATCHER WATCHES WATCHING WATCHMAN)
Ge 31:49 "May the LORD keep *w*
Ps 90: 4 or like a *w* in the night.
141: 3 keep *w* over the door of my lips.
Pr 4: 6 love her, and she will *w* over you.
6:22 when you sleep, they will *w*
Jer 31:10 will *w* over his flock like a shepherd
Mic 7: 7 I *w* in hope for the LORD,
Mt 24:42 "Therefore keep *w,* because you do
26:41 *W* and pray so that you will not fall
Mk 13:35 "Therefore keep *w* because you do
Lk 2: 8 keeping *w* over their flocks at night
1Ti 4:16 *W* your life and doctrine closely.
Heb 13:17 They keep *w* over you

WATCHER* (WATCH)
Job 7:20 O *w* of men?

WATCHES* (WATCH)
Nu 19: 5 While he *w,* the heifer is
Job 24:15 The eye of the adulterer *w* for dusk;
Ps 1: 6 For the LORD *w* over the way
33:14 from his dwelling place he *w*
63: 6 of you through the *w* of the night.
119:148 through the *w* of the night,
121: 3 he who *w* over you will not slumber
121: 4 indeed, he who *w* over Israel
121: 5 The LORD *w* over you—
127: 1 Unless the LORD *w* over the city,
145:20 LORD *w* over all who love him,
146: 9 The LORD *w* over the alien
Pr 31:27 She *w* over the affairs
Ecc 11: 4 Whoever *w* the wind will not plant;
La 2:19 as the *w* of the night begin;
4:16 he no longer *w* over them.

WATCHING (WATCH)
Lk 12:37 whose master finds them *w*

WATCHMAN (WATCH)
Eze 3:17 I have made you a *w* for the house
33: 6 but I will hold the *w* accountable

WATER (WATERED WATERING WATERS WELL-WATERED)
Ex 7:20 all the *w* was changed into blood.
17: 1 but there was no *w* for the people
Nu 20: 2 there was no *w* for the community,
Ps 1: 3 like a tree planted by streams of *w,*
22:14 I am poured out like *w,*
42: 1 As the deer pants for streams of *w,*
Pr 25:21 if he is thirsty, give him *w* to drink.
Isa 12: 3 With joy you will draw *w*
30:20 of adversity and the *w* of affliction,
32: 2 like streams of *w* in the desert
49:10 and lead them beside springs of *w.*
Jer 2:13 broken cisterns that cannot hold *w.*
17: 8 will be like a tree planted by the *w*
31: 9 I will lead them beside streams of *w*
Eze 36:25 I will sprinkle clean *w* on you,
Zec 14: 8 On that day living *w* will flow out
Mt 14:29 walked on the *w* and came toward Jesus.
Mk 9:41 anyone who gives you a cup of *w*
Lk 5: 4 to Simon, "Put out into deep *w,*
Jn 3: 5 unless he is born of *w* and the Spirit.
4:10 he would have given you living *w."*
7:38 streams of living *w* will flow
Eph 5:26 washing with *w* through the word,
Heb 10:22 our bodies washed with pure *w.*
1Pe 3:21 this *w* symbolizes baptism that now
2Pe 2:17 These men are springs without *w*
1Jn 5: 6 This is the one who came by *w*
5: 6 come by *w* only, but by *w*
5: 8 the Spirit, the *w* and the blood;
Rev 7:17 to springs of living *w.*
21: 6 cost from the spring of the *w* of life.

WATERED (WATER)
1Co 3: 6 I planted the seed, Apollos *w* it,

WATERING (WATER)
Isa 55:10 it without *w* the earth

WATERS (WATER)
Ps 23: 2 he leads me beside quiet *w,*
Ecc 11: 1 Cast your bread upon the *w,*
SS 8: 7 Many *w* cannot quench love;
Isa 11: 9 as the *w* cover the sea.
43: 2 When you pass through the *w,*
55: 1 come to the *w;*
58:11 like a spring whose *w* never fail.
Hab 2:14 as the *w* cover the sea.
1Co 3: 7 plants nor he who *w* is anything,

WAVE (WAVES)
Lev 23:11 He is to *w* the sheaf
Jas 1: 6 he who doubts is like a *w* of the sea,

WAVER*
1Ki 18:21 "How long will you *w*
Ro 4:20 Yet he did not *w* through unbelief

WAVES (WAVE)
Isa 57:20 whose *w* cast up mire and mud.
Mt 8:27 Even the winds and the *w* obey him
Eph 4:14 tossed back and forth by the *w,*

WAY (WAYS)
Ex 13:21 of cloud to guide them on their *w*
18:20 and show them the *w* to live
Dt 1:33 to show you the *w* you should go.
32: 6 Is this the *w* you repay the LORD,
1Sa 12:23 I will teach you the *w* that is good
2Sa 22:31 "As for God, his *w* is perfect;
1Ki 8:23 wholeheartedly in your *w.*
8:36 Teach them the right *w* to live,
Job 23:10 But he knows the *w* that I take;
Ps 1: 1 or stand in the *w* of sinners
32: 8 teach you in the *w* you should go;
37: 5 Commit your *w* to the LORD;
86:11 Teach me your *w,* O LORD,
119: 9 can a young man keep his *w* pure?
139:24 See if there is any offensive *w* in me
Pr 4:11 I guide you in the *w* of wisdom
12:15 The *w* of a fool seems right to him,
14:12 There is a *w* that seems right
16:17 he who guards his *w* guards his life.
19: 2 nor to be hasty and miss the *w.*
22: 6 Train a child in the *w* he should go,
30:19 and the *w* of a man with a maiden.
Isa 30:21 saying, "This is the *w;* walk in it."
35: 8 it will be called the *W* of Holiness.
40: 3 the *w* for the LORD;
48:17 you in the *w* you should go.
53: 6 each of us has turned to his own *w;*
55: 7 Let the wicked forsake his *w*
Jer 5:31 and my people love it this *w.*
Mal 3: 1 who will prepare the *w* before me.
Mt 3: 3 'Prepare the *w* for the Lord,
Lk 7:27 who will prepare your *w* before you
Jn 14: 6 "I am the *w* and the truth
Ac 1:11 in the same *w* you have seen him go
9: 2 any there who belonged to the *W,*
24:14 of the *W,* which they call a sect.
1Co 10:13 also provide a *w* out so that you can
12:31 will show you the most excellent *w.*
14: 1 Follow the *w* of love and eagerly
Col 1:10 and may please him in every *w:*
Tit 2:10 that in every *w* they will make
Heb 4:15 who has been tempted in every *w,*
9: 8 was showing by this that the *w*
10:20 and living *w* opened for us
13:18 desire to live honorably in every *w.*

WAYS (WAY)
Ex 33:13 teach me your *w* so I may know
Dt 10:12 to walk in all his *w,* to love him,
26:17 and that you will walk in his *w,*
30:16 in his *w,* and to keep his commands
32: 4 and all his *w* are just.
Jos 22: 5 in all his *w,* to obey his commands,
2Ch 11:17 walking in the *w* of David
Job 34:21 "His eyes are on the *w* of men;
Ps 25: 4 Show me your *w,* O LORD,
25:10 All the *w* of the LORD are loving
37: 7 fret when men succeed in their *w,*
51:13 I will teach transgressors your *w,*
77:13 Your *w,* O God, are holy.
119:59 I have considered my *w*
139: 3 you are familiar with all my *w.*
145:17 The LORD is righteous in all his *w*
Pr 3: 6 in all your *w* acknowledge him,
4:26 and take only *w* that are firm.

Pr 5:21 For a man's *w* are in full view
16: 2 All a man's *w* seem innocent
16: 7 When a man's *w* are pleasing
Isa 2: 3 He will teach us his *w*,
55: 8 neither are your *w* my *w*,"
Eze 28:15 You were blameless in your *w*
33: 8 out to dissuade him from his *w*,
Hos 14: 9 The *w* of the LORD are right;
Ro 1:30 they invent *w* of doing evil;
Jas 3: 2 We all stumble in many *w*.

WEAK (WEAKER WEAKNESS WEAKNESSES)
Ps 41: 1 is he who has regard for the *w*;
72:13 He will take pity on the *w*
82: 3 Defend the cause of the *w*
Eze 34: 4 You have not strengthened the *w*
Mt 26:41 spirit is willing, but the body is *w*."
Ac 20:35 of hard work we must help the *w*,
Ro 14: 1 Accept him whose faith is *w*,
15: 1 to bear with the failings of the *w*
1Co 1:27 God chose the *w* things
8: 9 become a stumbling block to the *w*.
9:22 To the *w* I became *w*, to win the *w*.
11:30 That is why many among you are *w*
2Co 12:10 For when I am *w*, then I am strong.
1Th 5:14 help the *w*, be patient
Heb 12:12 your feeble arms and *w* knees.

WEAK-WILLED (WILL)
2Ti 3: 6 and gain control over *w* women,

WEAKER* (WEAK)
2Sa 3: 1 the house of Saul grew *w* and *w*.
1Co 12:22 seem to be *w* are indispensable,
1Pe 3: 7 them with respect as the *w* partner

WEAKNESS* (WEAK)
La 1: 6 in *w* they have fled
Ro 8:26 the Spirit helps us in our *w*.
1Co 1:25 and the *w* of God is stronger
2: 3 I came to you in *w* and fear,
15:43 it is sown in *w*, it is raised in power;
2Co 11:30 boast of the things that show my *w*.
12: 9 for my power is made perfect in *w*
13: 4 he was crucified in *w*, yet he lives
Heb 5: 2 since he himself is subject to *w*.
11:34 whose *w* was turned to strength;

WEAKNESSES* (WEAK)
2Co 12: 5 about myself, except about my *w*.
12: 9 all the more gladly about my *w*,
12:10 I delight in *w*, in insults,
Heb 4:15 unable to sympathize with our *w*,

WEALTH
Dt 8:18 gives you the ability to produce *w*,
2Ch 1:11 and you have not asked for *w*,
Ps 39: 6 he heaps up *w*, not knowing who
Pr 3: 9 Honor the LORD with your *w*,
10: 4 but diligent hands bring *w*.
11: 4 *W* is worthless in the day of wrath,
13: 7 to be poor, yet has great *w*.
15:16 than great *w* with turmoil.
22: 4 bring *w* and honor and life.
Ecc 5:10 whoever loves *w* is never satisfied
5:13 *w* hoarded to the harm of its owner,
SS 8: 7 all the *w* of his house for love,
Mt 13:22 and the deceitfulness of *w* choke it,
Mk 10:22 away sad, because he had great *w*.
12:44 They all gave out of their *w*; but she
Lk 15:13 and there squandered his *w*
1Ti 6:17 nor to put their hope in *w*,
Jas 5: 2 Your *w* has rotted, and moths have
5: 3 You have hoarded *w*

WEAPON (WEAPONS)
Ne 4:17 work with one hand and held a *w*

WEAPONS (WEAPON)
Ecc 9:18 Wisdom is better than *w* of war,
2Co 6: 7 with *w* of righteousness
2Co 10: 4 The *w* we fight with are not

WEAR (WEARING)
Dt 8: 4 Your clothes did not *w* out
22: 5 nor a man *w* women's clothing,
Ps 102:26 they will all *w* out like a garment.
Pr 23: 4 Do not *w* yourself out to get rich;
Isa 51: 6 the earth will *w* out like a garment
Heb 1:11 they will all *w* out like a garment.
Rev 3:18 and white clothes to *w*,

WEARIES (WEARY)
Ecc 12:12 and much study *w* the body.

WEARING (WEAR)
Jn 19: 5 When Jesus came out *w* the crown
Jas 2: 3 attention to the man *w* fine clothes
1Pe 3: 3 as braided hair and the *w*
Rev 7: 9 They were *w* white robes

WEARY (WEARIES)
Isa 40:28 He will not grow tired or *w*,
40:31 they will run and not grow *w*,
50: 4 know the word that sustains the *w*.
Mt 11:28 all you who are *w* and burdened,
Gal 6: 9 Let us not become *w* in doing good,
Heb 12: 3 so that you will not grow *w*
Rev 2: 3 my name, and have not grown *w*.

WEDDING
Mt 22:11 who was not wearing *w* clothes.
Rev 19: 7 For the *w* of the Lamb has come,

WEEDS
Mt 13:25 and sowed *w* among the wheat,

WEEK
Mt 28: 1 at dawn on the first day of the *w*,
1Co 16: 2 On the first day of every *w*,

WEEP (WEEPING WEPT)
Ecc 3: 4 a time to *w* and a time to laugh,
Lk 6:21 Blessed are you who *w* now,
23:28 *w* for yourselves and for your

WEEPING (WEEP)
Ps 30: 5 *w* may remain for a night,
126: 6 He who goes out *w*,
Jer 31:15 Rachel *w* for her children
Mt 2:18 Rachel *w* for her children
8:12 where there will be *w* and gnashing

WEIGH (OUTWEIGHS WEIGHED WEIGHS WEIGHTIER WEIGHTS)
1Co 14:29 others should *w* carefully what is

WEIGHED (WEIGH)
Job 28:15 nor can its price be *w* in silver.
Da 5:27 You have been *w* on the scales
Lk 21:34 or your hearts will be *w*

WEIGHS (WEIGH)
Pr 12:25 An anxious heart *w* a man down,
15:28 of the righteous *w* its answers,
21: 2 but the LORD *w* the heart.
24:12 not he who *w* the heart perceive

WEIGHTIER* (WEIGH)
Jn 5:36 "I have testimony *w* than that

WEIGHTS (WEIGH)
Lev 19:36 Use honest scales and honest *w*,
Dt 25:13 Do not have two differing *w*
Pr 11: 1 but accurate *w* are his delight.

WELCOME (WELCOMES)
Mk 9:37 welcomes me does not *w* me
2Pe 1:11 and you will receive a rich *w*

WELCOMES (WELCOME)
Mt 18: 5 whoever *w* a little child like this
2Jn :11 Anyone who *w* him shares

WELL (WELLED WELLING WELLS)
Mt 15:31 crippled made *w*, the lame walking
Lk 14: 5 falls into a *w* on the Sabbath day,
17:19 your faith has made you *w*."
Jas 5:15 in faith will make the sick person *w*

WELL-WATERED (WATER)
Isa 58:11 You will be like a *w* garden,

WELLED* (WELL)
2Co 8: 2 and their extreme poverty *w* up

WELLING* (WELL)
Jn 4:14 of water *w* up to eternal life."

WELLS (WELL)
Isa 12: 3 from the *w* of salvation.

WELLSPRING* (SPRING)
Pr 4:23 for it is the *w* of life.

WEPT (WEEP)
Ps 137: 1 of Babylon we sat and *w*
Lk 22:62 And he went outside and *w* bitterly
Jn 11:35 Jesus *w*.

WEST
Ps 103:12 as far as the east is from the *w*,
107: 3 from east and *w*, from north

WHEAT
Mt 3:12 gathering his *w* into the barn
13:25 and sowed weeds among the *w*,
Lk 22:31 Satan has asked to sift you as *w*.
Jn 12:24 a kernel of *w* falls to the ground

WHEELS
Eze 1:16 appearance and structure of the *w*:

WHIRLWIND (WIND)
2Ki 2: 1 to take Elijah up to heaven in a *w*,
Hos 8: 7 and reap the *w*.
Na 1: 3 His way is in the *w* and the storm,

WHISPER (WHISPERED)
1Ki 19:12 And after the fire came a gentle *w*.
Job 26:14 how faint the *w* we hear of him!
Ps 107:29 He stilled the storm to a *w*;

WHISPERED (WHISPER)
Mt 10:27 speak in the daylight; what is *w*

WHITE (WHITER)
Isa 1:18 they shall be as *w* as snow;
Da 7: 9 His clothing was as *w* as snow;
7: 9 the hair of his head was *w* like wool
Mt 28: 3 and his clothes were *w* as snow.
Rev 1:14 hair were *w* like wool, as *w* as snow,
3: 4 dressed in *w*, for they are worthy.
6: 2 and there before me was a *w* horse!
7:13 "These in *w* robes—who are they,
19:11 and there before me was a *w* horse,
20:11 Then I saw a great *w* throne

WHITER (WHITE)
Ps 51: 7 and I will be *w* than snow.

WHOLE
Ge 1:29 plant on the face of the *w* earth
2: 6 and watered the *w* surface
11: 1 Now the *w* world had one language
Ex 12:47 The *w* community
19: 5 Although the *w* earth is mine,
Lev 16:17 and the *w* community of Israel.
Nu 14:21 of the LORD fills the *w* earth,
32:13 until the *w* generation
Dt 13:16 *w* burnt offering to the LORD your
19: 8 gives you the *w* land he promised
Jos 2: 3 come to spy out the *w* land."
1Sa 1:28 For his *w* life he will be given
17:46 the *w* world will know that there is
1Ki 10:24 The *w* world sought audience
2Ki 21: 8 and will keep the *w* Law that my

Ps 72:19 may the *w* earth be filled
Pr 4:22 and health to a man's *w* body.
8:31 rejoicing in his *w* world
Ecc 12:13 for this is the *w* duty of man.
Isa 1: 5 Your *w* head is injured,
6: 3 the *w* earth is full of his glory."
14:26 plan determined for the *w* world;
Eze 34: 6 were scattered over the *w* earth,
37:11 these bones are the *w* house
Da 2:35 mountain and filled the *w* earth.
Zep 1:18 the *w* world will be consumed,
Zec 14: 9 will be king over the *w* earth.
Mal 3:10 the *w* tithe into the storehouse,
Mt 5:29 than for your *w* body to be thrown
6:22 your *w* body will be full of light.
16:26 for a man if he gains the *w* world,
24:14 will be preached in the *w* world
Lk 21:35 live on the face of the *w* earth.
Jn 12:19 Look how the *w* world has gone
13:10 to wash his feet; his *w* body is clean
21:25 the *w* world would not have room
Ac 17:26 they should inhabit the *w* earth;
20:27 proclaim to you the *w* will of God.
Ro 1: 9 whom I serve with my *w* heart
3:19 and the *w* world held accountable
8:22 know that the *w* creation has been
1Co 4: 9 made a spectacle to the *w* universe,
12:17 If the *w* body were an ear,
Gal 3:22 declares that the *w* world is
5: 3 obligated to obey the *w* law.
Eph 4:10 in order to fill the *w* universe.)
4:13 attaining to the *w* measure
1Th 5:23 May your *w* spirit, soul
Jas 2:10 For whoever keeps the *w* law
1Jn 2: 2 but also for the sins of the *w* world.
Rev 3:10 going to come upon the *w* world

WHOLEHEARTED* (HEART)
2Ki 20: 3 you faithfully and with *w* devotion
1Ch 28: 9 and serve him with *w* devotion
29:19 my son Solomon the *w* devotion
Isa 38: 3 you faithfully and with *w* devotion

WHOLEHEARTEDLY* (HEART)
Nu 14:24 a different spirit and follows me *w*,
32:11 they have not followed me *w*,
32:12 for they followed the LORD *w*.'
Dt 1:36 because he followed the LORD *w*
Jos 14: 8 followed the LORD my God *w*.
14: 9 followed the LORD my God *w*.'
14:14 the LORD, the God of Israel, *w*.
1Ki 8:23 with your servants who continue *w*
1Ch 29: 9 for they had given freely and *w*
2Ch 6:14 with your servants who continue *w*
15:15 oath because they had sworn it *w*.
19: 9 and *w* in the fear of the LORD.
25: 2 in the eyes of the LORD, but not *w*
31:21 he sought his God and worked *w*.
Ro 6:17 you *w* obeyed the form of teaching
Eph 6: 7 Serve *w*, as if you were serving

WHOLESOME*
2Ki 2:22 And the water has remained *w*
2Pe 3: 1 to stimulate you to *w* thinking.

WICK
Isa 42: 3 a smoldering *w* he will not snuff out
Mt 12:20 a smoldering *w* he will not snuff out

WICKED (WICKEDNESS)
Ge 13:13 Now the men of Sodom were *w*
39: 9 How then could I do such a *w* thing
Ex 23: 1 Do not help a *w* man
Nu 14:35 things to this whole *w* community,
Dt 15: 9 not to harbor this *w* thought:
Jdg 19:22 some of the *w* men
1Sa 2:12 Eli's sons were *w* men; they had no
15:18 completely destroy those *w* people,
25:17 He is such a *w* man that no one can
2Sa 13:12 in Israel! Don't do this *w* thing.
2Ki 17:11 They did *w* things that provoked
2Ch 7:14 and turn from their *w* ways,
19: 2 "Should you help the *w*
Ne 13:17 "What is this *w* thing you are doing
Ps 1: 1 walk in the counsel of the *w*
1: 5 Therefore the *w* will not stand
7: 9 to an end the violence of the *w*
10:13 Why does the *w* man revile God?
11: 5 the *w* and those who love violence
12: 8 The *w* freely strut about
26: 5 and refuse to sit with the *w*.
32:10 Many are the woes of the *w*,
36: 1 concerning the sinfulness of the *w*:
37:13 but the Lord laughs at the *w*,
49: 5 when *w* deceivers surround me—
50:16 But to the *w*, God says:
58: 3 Even from birth the *w* go astray;
73: 3 when I saw the prosperity of the *w*.
82: 2 and show partiality to the *w*? *Selah*
112:10 the longings of the *w* will come
119:61 Though the *w* bind me with ropes,
119:155 Salvation is far from the *w*,
140: 8 do not grant the *w* their desires,
141:10 Let the *w* fall into their own nets,
146: 9 but he frustrates the ways of the *w*.
Pr 2:12 you from the ways of *w* men,
4:14 Do not set foot on the path of the *w*
6:18 a heart that devises *w* schemes,
9: 7 whoever rebukes a *w* man incurs
10:20 the heart of the *w* is of little value.
10:28 the hopes of the *w* come to nothing
11: 5 *w* are brought down by their own
11:10 when the *w* perish, there are shouts
11:21 The *w* will not go unpunished,
12: 5 but the advice of the *w* is deceitful.
12:10 the kindest acts of the *w* are cruel.
14:19 the *w* at the gates of the righteous.
15: 3 keeping watch on the *w*
15:26 detests the thoughts of the *w*,
21:10 The *w* man craves evil;
21:29 A *w* man puts up a bold front,
28: 1 *w* man flees though no one pursues,
28: 4 who forsake the law praise the *w*,
29: 7 but the *w* have no such concern.
29:16 When the *w* thrive, so does sin,
29:27 the *w* detest the upright.
Isa 11: 4 breath of his lips he will slay the *w*.
13:11 the *w* for their sins.
26:10 Though grace is shown to the *w*,
48:22 says the LORD, "for the *w*."
53: 9 He was assigned a grave with the *w*
55: 7 Let the *w* forsake his way
57:20 But the *w* are like the tossing sea,
Jer 35:15 of you must turn from your *w* ways
Eze 3:18 that *w* man will die for his sin,
13:22 you encouraged the *w* not to turn
14: 7 and puts a *w* stumbling block
18:21 "But if a *w* man turns away
18:23 pleasure in the death of the *w*?
21:25 " 'O profane and *w* prince of Israel,
33: 8 When I say to the *w*, 'O *w* man,
33:11 pleasure in the death of the *w*,
33:14 to the *w* man, 'You will surely die,'
33:19 And if a *w* man turns away
Da 12:10 but the *w* will continue to be *w*.
Mt 12:39 *w* and adulterous generation asks
12:45 be with this *w* generation."
12:45 with it seven other spirits more *w*
Lk 6:35 he is kind to the ungrateful and *w*.
Ac 2:23 and you, with the help of *w* men,
Ro 4: 5 but trusts God who justifies the *w*,
1Co 5:13 "Expel the *w* man from among you
6: 9 not know that the *w* will not inherit
Rev 2: 2 that you cannot tolerate *w* men,

WICKEDNESS (WICKED)
Ge 6: 5 The LORD saw how great man's *w*
Ex 34: 7 and forgiving *w*, rebellion and sin.
Lev 16:21 and confess over it all the *w*
19:29 to prostitution and be filled with *w*.
Dt 9: 4 it is on account of the *w*
Ne 9: 2 and confessed their sins and the *w*
Ps 45: 7 You love righteousness and hate *w*;
92:15 he is my Rock, and there is no *w*
Pr 13: 6 but *w* overthrows the sinner.
Jer 3: 2 land with your prostitution and *w*.
8: 6 No one repents of his *w*,
14:20 O LORD, we acknowledge our *w*
Eze 18:20 the *w* of the wicked will be charged
28:15 created till *w* was found in you.
33:19 wicked man turns away from his *w*
Da 4:27 and your *w* by being kind
9:24 to atone for *w*, to bring
Jnh 1: 2 its *w* has come up before me."
Mt 24:12 Because of the increase of *w*,
Lk 11:39 inside you are full of greed and *w*.
Ac 1:18 (With the reward he got for his *w*,
Ro 1:18 who suppress the truth by their *w*,
1Co 5: 8 the yeast of malice and *w*,
2Co 6:14 what do righteousness and *w* have
2Ti 2:19 of the Lord must turn away from *w*
Tit 2:14 for us to redeem us from all *w*
Heb 1: 9 loved righteousness and hated *w*;
8:12 For I will forgive their *w*
2Pe 2:15 who loved the wages of *w*.

WIDE
Ps 81:10 Open *w* your mouth and I will fill it
Isa 54: 2 stretch your tent curtains *w*,
Mt 7:13 For *w* is the gate and broad is
2Co 6:13 my children—open *w* your hearts
Eph 3:18 to grasp how *w* and long and high

WIDOW (WIDOWS)
Ex 22:22 "Do not take advantage of a *w*
Dt 10:18 cause of the fatherless and the *w*,
Ps 146: 9 sustains the fatherless and the *w*,
Isa 1:17 plead the case of the *w*.
Lk 21: 2 saw a poor *w* put in two very small
1Ti 5: 4 But if a *w* has children

WIDOWS (WIDOW)
Ps 68: 5 to the fatherless, a defender of *w*,
Ac 6: 1 their *w* were being overlooked
1Co 7: 8 to the unmarried and the *w* I say:
1Ti 5: 3 to those *w* who are really
Jas 1:27 look after orphans and *w*

WIFE (WIVES WIVES')
Ge 2:24 and mother and be united to his *w*,
19:26 But Lot's *w* looked back,
24:67 she became his *w*, and he loved her;
Ex 20:17 shall not covet your neighbor's *w*,
Lev 20:10 adultery with another man's *w*—
Dt 5:21 shall not covet your neighbor's *w*.
24: 5 happiness to the *w* he has married.
Ru 4:13 took Ruth and she became his *w*.
Pr 5:18 in the *w* of your youth.
12: 4 *w* of noble character is her
18:22 He who finds a *w* finds what is
19:13 quarrelsome *w* is like a constant
31:10 *w* of noble character who can find?
Hos 1: 2 take to yourself an adulterous *w*
Mal 2:14 the witness between you and the *w*
Mt 1:20 to take Mary home as your *w*,
19: 3 for a man to divorce his *w* for any
Lk 17:32 Remember Lot's *w*! Whoever tries
18:29 or *w* or brothers or parents
1Co 7: 2 each man should have his own *w*,
7:33 how he can please his *w*—
Eph 5:23 the husband is the head of the *w*
5:33 must love his *w* as he loves himself,
1Ti 3: 2 husband of but one *w*, temperate,
Rev 21: 9 I will show you the bride, the *w*

WILD
Ge 1:25 God made the *w* animals according
8: 1 Noah and all the *w* animals
Lk 15:13 squandered his wealth in *w* living.
Ro 11:17 and you, though a *w* olive shoot,

WILL (WEAK-WILLED WILLFUL WILLING WILLINGNESS)
Ps 40: 8 I desire to do your *w,* O my God;
143:10 Teach me to do your *w,*
Isa 53:10 Yet it was the LORD'S *w*
Mt 6:10 your *w* be done
7:21 who does the *w* of my Father
10:29 apart from the *w* of your Father.
12:50 does the *w* of my Father
26:39 Yet not as I *w,* but as you *w."*
26:42 I drink it, may your *w* be done."
Jn 6:38 but to do the *w* of him who sent me.
7:17 If anyone chooses to do God's *w,*
Ac 20:27 to you the whole *w* of God.
Ro 12: 2 and approve what God's *w* is—
1Co 7:37 but has control over his own *w,*
Eph 5:17 understand what the Lord's *w* is.
Php 2:13 for it is God who works in you to *w*
1Th 4: 3 God's *w* that you should be sanctified:
5:18 for this is God's *w* for you
2Ti 2:26 has taken them captive to do his *w.*
Heb 2: 4 distributed according to his *w.*
9:16 In the case of a *w,* it is necessary
10: 7 I have come to do your *w,* O God
13:21 everything good for doing his *w,*
Jas 4:15 "If it is the Lord's *w,*
1Pe 3:17 It is better, if it is God's *w,*
4: 2 but rather for the *w* of God.
2Pe 1:21 never had its origin in the *w*
1Jn 5:14 we ask anything according to his *w,*
Rev 4:11 and by your *w* they were created

WILLFUL (WILL)
Ps 19:13 Keep your servant also from *w* sins;

WILLING (WILL)
1Ch 28: 9 devotion and with a *w* mind,
29: 5 who is *w* to consecrate himself
Ps 51:12 grant me a *w* spirit, to sustain me.
Da 3:28 were *w* to give up their lives rather
Mt 18:14 Father in heaven is not *w* that any
23:37 her wings, but you were not *w.*
26:41 The spirit is *w,* but the body is weak
1Ti 6:18 and to be generous and *w* to share.
1Pe 5: 2 but because you are *w,*

WILLINGNESS* (WILL)
2Co 8:11 so that your eager *w*
8:12 For if the *w* is there, the gift is

WIN (WINS WON)
1Co 9:19 myself a slave to everyone, to *w*
Php 3:14 on toward the goal to *w* the prize
1Th 4:12 your daily life may *w* the respect

WIND (WHIRLWIND WINDS)
Ps 1: 4 that the *w* blows away.
Ecc 2:11 meaningless, a chasing after the *w;*
Hos 8: 7 "They sow the *w*
Mk 4:41 Even the *w* and the waves obey
Jn 3: 8 The *w* blows wherever it pleases.
Eph 4:14 and there by every *w* of teaching
Jas 1: 6 blown and tossed by the *w.*

WINDOW
Jos 2:21 she tied the scarlet cord in the *w.*
Ac 20: 9 in a *w* was a young man named
2Co 11:33 in a basket from a *w* in the wall

WINDS (WIND)
Ps 104: 4 He makes *w* his messengers,
Mt 24:31 gather his elect from the four *w,*
Heb 1: 7 "He makes his angels *w,*

WINE
Ps 104:15 *w* that gladdens the heart of man,
Pr 20: 1 *W* is a mocker and beer a brawler;
23:20 join those who drink too much *w*
23:31 Do not gaze at *w* when it is red,
31: 6 *w* to those who are in anguish;
SS 1: 2 your love is more delightful than *w.*
Isa 28: 7 And these also stagger from *w*
55: 1 Come, buy *w* and milk
Mt 9:17 Neither do men pour new *w*
Lk 23:36 They offered him *w* vinegar
Jn 2: 3 When the *w* was gone, Jesus'
Ro 14:21 not to eat meat or drink *w*
Eph 5:18 on *w,* which leads to debauchery.
1Ti 5:23 a little *w* because of your stomach
Rev 16:19 with the *w* of the fury of his wrath.

WINEPRESS
Isa 63: 2 like those of one treading the *w?*
Rev 19:15 He treads the *w* of the fury

WINESKINS
Mt 9:17 do men pour new wine into old *w.*

WINGS
Ex 19: 4 and how I carried you on eagles' *w*
Ru 2:12 under whose *w* you have come
Ps 17: 8 hide me in the shadow of your *w*
91: 4 under his *w* you will find refuge;
Isa 6: 2 him were seraphs, each with six *w:*
40:31 They will soar on *w* like eagles;
Eze 1: 6 of them had four faces and four *w.*
Zec 5: 9 in their *w!* They had *w* like those
Mal 4: 2 rise with healing in its *w.*
Lk 13:34 hen gathers her chicks under her *w,*
Rev 4: 8 the four living creatures had six *w*

WINS (WIN)
Pr 11:30 and he who *w* souls is wise.

WINTER
Mk 13:18 that this will not take place in *w,*

WIPE (WIPED)
Isa 25: 8 The Sovereign LORD will *w* away
Rev 7:17 God will *w* away every tear
21: 4 He will *w* every tear

WIPED (WIPE)
Lk 7:38 Then she *w* them with her hair,
Ac 3:19 so that your sins may be *w* out,

WISDOM (WISE)
Ge 3: 6 and also desirable for gaining *w,*
1Ki 4:29 God gave Solomon *w* and very
2Ch 1:10 Give me *w* and knowledge,
Ps 51: 6 you teach me *w* in the inmost place
111:10 of the LORD is the beginning of *w;*
Pr 2: 6 For the LORD gives *w,*
3:13 Blessed is the man who finds *w,*
4: 7 *W* is supreme; therefore get
8:11 for *w* is more precious than rubies,
11: 2 but with humility comes *w.*
13:10 *w* is found in those who take advice
23:23 get *w,* discipline and understanding
29: 3 A man who loves *w* brings joy
29:15 The rod of correction imparts *w,*
31:26 She speaks with *w,*
Isa 11: 2 Spirit of *w* and of understanding,
28:29 in counsel and magnificent in *w.*
Jer 10:12 he founded the world by his *w*
Mic 6: 9 and to fear your name is *w*—
Mt 11:19 But *w* is proved right by her actions
Lk 2:52 And Jesus grew in *w* and stature,
Ac 6: 3 known to be full of the Spirit and *w.*
Ro 11:33 the depth of the riches of the *w*
1Co 1:17 not with words of human *w,*
1:30 who has become for us *w* from God
12: 8 through the Spirit the message of *w*
Eph 1:17 may give you the Spirit of *w*
Col 2: 3 are hidden all the treasures of *w*
2:23 indeed have an appearance of *w,*
Jas 1: 5 of you lacks *w,* he should ask God,
3:13 in the humility that comes from *w.*
Rev 5:12 and wealth and *w* and strength

WISE (WISDOM WISER)
1Ki 3:12 give you a *w* and discerning heart,
Job 5:13 He catches the *w* in their craftiness
Ps 19: 7 making *w* the simple.
Pr 3: 7 Do not be *w* in your own eyes;
9: 8 rebuke a *w* man and he will love
10: 1 A *w* son brings joy to his father,
11:30 and he who wins souls is *w.*
13: 1 A *w* son heeds his father's
13:20 He who walks with the *w* grows *w,*
16:23 A *w* man's heart guides his mouth,
17:28 Even a fool is thought *w*
Ecc 9:17 The quiet words of the *w* are more
Jer 9:23 "Let not the *w* man boast
Eze 28: 6 " 'Because you think you are *w,*
Da 2:21 He gives wisdom to the *w*
12: 3 Those who are *w* will shine like
Mt 11:25 hidden these things from the *w*
25: 2 them were foolish and five were *w.*
1Co 1:19 I will destroy the wisdom of the *w;*
1:27 things of the world to shame the *w;*
3:19 He catches the *w* in their craftiness
Eph 5:15 but as *w,* making the most
2Ti 3:15 able to make you *w* for salvation
Jas 3:13 Who is *w* and understanding

WISER (WISE)
Pr 9: 9 a wise man and he will be *w* still;
1Co 1:25 of God is *w* than man's wisdom,

WISH (WISHES)
Jn 15: 7 ask whatever you *w,* and it will be
Ro 9: 3 For I could *w* that I myself were
Rev 3:15 I *w* you were either one

WISHES (WISH)
Rev 22:17 let him come; and whoever *w,*

WITCHCRAFT
Dt 18:10 engages in *w,* or casts spells,
Gal 5:20 idolatry and *w;* hatred, discord,

WITHDREW
Lk 5:16 But Jesus often *w* to lonely places

WITHER (WITHERS)
Ps 1: 3 and whose leaf does not *w.*
37:19 In times of disaster they will not *w;*

WITHERS (WITHER)
Isa 40: 7 The grass *w* and the flowers fall,
1Pe 1:24 the grass *w* and the flowers fall,

WITHHELD (WITHHOLD)
Ge 22:12 you have not *w* from me your son,

WITHHOLD (WITHHELD WITHHOLDS)
Ps 84:11 no good thing does he *w*
Pr 23:13 Do not *w* discipline from a child;

WITHHOLDS (WITHHOLD)
Dt 27:19 "Cursed is the man who *w* justice

WITNESS (EYEWITNESSES WITNESSES)
Pr 12:17 truthful *w* gives honest testimony,
19: 9 A false *w* will not go unpunished,
Jn 1: 8 he came only as a *w* to the light.

WITNESSES (WITNESS)
Dt 19:15 by the testimony of two or three *w.*
Mt 18:16 by the testimony of two or three *w.'*
Ac 1: 8 and you will be my *w* in Jerusalem,

WIVES (WIFE)
Eph 5:22 *W,* submit to your husbands
5:25 love your *w,* just as Christ loved
1Pe 3: 1 words by the behavior of their *w,*

WIVES' (WIFE)
1Ti 4: 7 with godless myths and old *w* tales

WOE
Isa 6: 5 "*W* to me!" I cried.
Eze 34: 2 *W* to the shepherds
Mt 18: 7 "*W* to the world
23:13 "*W* to you, teachers of the law

Jer 48:10 lax in doing the LORD's *w!*
Mt 20: 1 to hire men to *w* in his vineyard.
Jn 6:27 Do not *w* for food that spoils,
9: 4 we must do the *w* of him who sent
Ac 13: 2 for the *w* to which I have called
1Co 3:13 test the quality of each man's *w.*
4:12 We *w* hard with our own hands.
Eph 4:16 up in love, as each part does its *w.*
Php 1: 6 that he who began a good *w*
2:12 continue to *w* out your salvation
Col 3:23 Whatever you do, *w* at it
1Th 4:11 and to *w* with your hands,
5:12 to respect those who *w* hard
2Th 3:10 If a man will not *w,* he shall not eat
2Ti 3:17 equipped for every good *w.*
Heb 6:10 he will not forget your *w*
2Jn :11 him shares in his wicked *w.*
3Jn : 8 men so that we may *w* together

WORKED (WORK)
1Co 15:10 No, I *w* harder than all of them—
2Th 3: 8 On the contrary, we *w* night

WORKER (WORK)
Lk 10: 7 for the *w* deserves his wages.
1Ti 5:18 and "The *w* deserves his wages."

WORKERS (WORK)
Mt 9:37 is plentiful but the *w* are few.
1Co 3: 9 For we are God's fellow *w;*

WORKING (WORK)
Col 3:23 as *w* for the Lord, not for men,

WORKMAN (WORK)
2Ti 2:15 a *w* who does not need

WORKMANSHIP* (WORK)
Eph 2:10 For we are God's *w,* created

WORKS (WORK)
Ps 66: 5 how awesome his *w* in man's behalf
145: 6 of the power of your awesome *w,*
Pr 8:22 As the first of his *w,*
31:31 let her *w* bring her praise
Ro 4: 2 in fact, Abraham was justified by *w*
8:28 in all things God *w* for the good
Eph 2: 9 not by *w,* so that no one can boast.
4:12 to prepare God's people for *w*

WORLD (WORLDLY)
Ps 9: 8 He will judge the *w*
50:12 for the *w* is mine, and all that is in it
96:13 He will judge the *w*
Pr 8:23 before the *w* began.
Isa 13:11 I will punish the *w* for its evil,
Zep 1:18 the whole *w* will be consumed,
Mt 5:14 "You are the light of the *w.*
16:26 for a man if he gains the whole *w,*
Mk 16:15 into all the *w* and preach the good
Jn 1:29 who takes away the sin of the *w!*
3:16 so loved the *w* that he gave his one
8:12 he said, "I am the light of the *w.*
15:19 As it is, you do not belong to the *w,*
16:33 In this *w* you will have trouble.
17: 5 had with you before the *w* began.
17:14 not of the *w* any more than I am
18:36 "My kingdom is not of this *w.*
Ac 17:24 "The God who made the *w*
Ro 3:19 and the whole *w* held accountable
10:18 their words to the ends of the *w.*"
1Co 1:27 things of the *w* to shame the strong.
3:19 the wisdom of this *w* is foolishness
6: 2 that the saints will judge the *w?*
2Co 5:19 that God was reconciling the *w*
10: 3 For though we live in the *w,*
1Ti 6: 7 For we brought nothing into the *w,*
Heb 11:38 the *w* was not worthy of them.
Jas 2: 5 poor in the eyes of the *w* to be rich
4: 4 with the *w* is hatred toward God?
1Pe 1:20 before the creation of the *w,*
1Jn 2: 2 but also for the sins of the whole *w.*
2:15 not love the *w* or anything in the *w.*
5: 4 born of God overcomes the *w.*
Rev 13: 8 slain from the creation of the *w.*

WORLDLY (WORLD)
1Co 3: 1 address you as spiritual but as *w*—
Tit 2:12 to ungodliness and *w* passions,

WORM
Mk 9:48 " 'their *w* does not die,

WORRY (WORRYING)
Mt 6:25 I tell you, do not *w* about your life,
10:19 do not *w* about what to say

WORRYING (WORRY)
Mt 6:27 of you by *w* can add a single hour

WORSHIP (WORSHIPED WORSHIPS)
Jos 22:27 that we will *w* the LORD
2Ki 17:36 arm, is the one you must *w.*
1Ch 16:29 *w* the LORD in the splendor
Ps 95: 6 Come, let us bow down in *w,*
100: 2 *w* the LORD with gladness;
Zec 14:17 up to Jerusalem to *w* the King,
Mt 2: 2 and have come to *w* him."
4: 9 "if you will bow down and *w* me."
Jn 4:24 and his worshipers must *w* in spirit
Ro 12: 1 to God—this is your spiritual act of *w.*
Heb 10: 1 perfect those who draw near to *w.*

WORSHIPED (WORSHIP)
2Ch 29:30 and bowed their heads and *w.*
Mt 28: 9 clasped his feet and *w* him.

WORSHIPS (WORSHIP)
Isa 44:15 But he also fashions a god and *w* it;

WORTH (WORTHY)
Job 28:13 Man does not comprehend its *w;*
Pr 31:10 She is *w* far more than rubies.
Mt 10:31 are *w* more than many sparrows.
Ro 8:18 sufferings are not *w* comparing
1Pe 1: 7 of greater *w* than gold,
3: 4 which is of great *w* in God's sight.

WORTHLESS
Pr 11: 4 Wealth is *w* in the day of wrath,
Jas 1:26 himself and his religion is *w.*

WORTHY (WORTH)
1Ch 16:25 For great is the LORD and most *w*
Mt 10:37 more than me is not *w* of me;
Lk 15:19 I am no longer *w* to be called your
Eph 4: 1 to live a life *w* of the calling you
Php 1:27 in a manner *w* of the gospel
Col 1:10 in order that you may live a life *w*
1Ti 3: 8 are to be men *w* of respect, sincere,
Heb 3: 3 Jesus has been found *w*
3Jn : 6 on their way in a manner *w* of God.
Rev 5: 2 "Who is *w* to break the seals

WOUND (WOUNDS)
1Co 8:12 and *w* their weak conscience,

WOUNDS (WOUND)
Pr 27: 6 *w* from a friend can be trusted
Isa 53: 5 and by his *w* we are healed.
Zec 13: 6 'What are these *w* on your body?'
1Pe 2:24 by his *w* you have been healed.

WRAPS
Ps 104: 2 He *w* himself in light

WRATH
2Ch 36:16 scoffed at his prophets until the *w*
Ps 2: 5 and terrifies them in his *w,* saying,
76:10 Surely your *w* against men brings
Pr 15: 1 A gentle answer turns away *w,*
Isa 13:13 at the *w* of the LORD Almighty,
51:17 the cup of his *w,*
Jer 25:15 filled with the wine of my *w*
Eze 5:13 my *w* against them will subside,
20: 8 So I said I would pour out my *w*
Am 1: 3 I will not turn back ›my *w*‹.
Na 1: 2 maintains his *w* against his enemies
Zep 1:15 That day will be a day of *w,*
Jn 3:36 for God's *w* remains on him."
Ro 1:18 The *w* of God is being revealed
2: 5 you are storing up *w*
5: 9 saved from God's *w* through him!
9:22 choosing to show his *w*
1Th 5: 9 God did not appoint us to suffer *w*
Rev 6:16 and from the *w* of the Lamb!
19:15 the fury of the *w* of God Almighty.

WRESTLED
Ge 32:24 and a man *w* with him till daybreak

WRITE (WRITER WRITING WRITTEN WROTE)
Dt 6: 9 *W* them on the doorframes
10: 2 I will *w* on the tablets the words
Pr 7: 3 *w* them on the tablet of your heart.
Jer 31:33 and *w* it on their hearts.
Heb 8:10 and *w* them on their hearts.
Rev 3:12 I will also *w* on him my new name.

WRITER* (WRITE)
Ps 45: 1 my tongue is the pen of a skillful *w.*

WRITING (WRITE)
1Co 14:37 him acknowledge that what I am *w*

WRITTEN (WRITE)
Dt 28:58 which are *w* in this book,
Jos 1: 8 careful to do everything *w* in it.
23: 6 to obey all that is *w* in the Book
Ps 40: 7 it is *w* about me in the scroll.
Da 12: 1 everyone whose name is found *w*
Mal 3:16 A scroll of remembrance was *w*
Lk 10:20 but rejoice that your names are *w*
24:44 must be fulfilled that is *w* about me
Jn 20:31 these are *w* that you may believe
21:25 for the books that would be *w.*
Ro 2:15 of the law are *w* on their hearts,
1Co 4: 6 "Do not go beyond what is *w.*"
10:11 as examples and were *w* down
2Co 3: 3 *w* not with ink but with the Spirit
Col 2:14 having canceled the *w* code,
Heb 10: 7 it is *w* about me in the scroll—
12:23 whose names are *w* in heaven.
Rev 21:27 but only those whose names are *w*

WRONG (WRONGDOING WRONGED WRONGS)
Ex 23: 2 Do not follow the crowd in doing *w*
Nu 5: 7 must make full restitution for his *w,*
Dt 32: 4 A faithful God who does no *w,*
Job 34:12 unthinkable that God would do *w,*
Ps 5: 5 you hate all who do *w.*
Gal 2:11 to his face, because he was clearly in the *w.*
1Th 5:15 that nobody pays back *w* for *w,*

WRONGDOING (WRONG)
Job 1:22 sin by charging God with *w.*
1Jn 5:17 All *w* is sin, and there is sin that

WRONGED (WRONG)
1Co 6: 7 not rather be *w?* Why not rather

WRONGS (WRONG)
Pr 10:12 but love covers over all *w.*
1Co 13: 5 angered, it keeps no record of *w.*

WROTE (WRITE)
Ex 34:28 And he *w* on the tablets the words
Jn 5:46 for he *w* about me.
8: 8 down and *w* on the ground.

XERXES
King of Persia, husband of Esther. Deposed Vashti; replaced her with Esther (Est 1–2). Sealed

Haman's edict to annihilate the Jews (Est 3). Received Esther without having called her (Est 5:1–8). Honored Mordecai (Est 6). Hanged Haman (Est 7). Issued edict allowing Jews to defend themselves (Est 8). Exalted Mordecai (Est 8:1–2, 15; 9:4; 10).

YEAR (YEARS)
Ex 34:23 Three times a *y* all your men are
Lev 16:34 to be made once a *y* for all the sins
25: 4 But in the seventh *y* the land is
25:11 The fiftieth *y* shall be a jubilee
Heb 10: 1 repeated endlessly *y* after *y,*

YEARS (YEAR)
Ge 1:14 to mark seasons and days and *y,*
Ex 12:40 lived in Egypt was 430 *y.*
16:35 The Israelites ate manna forty *y,*
Job 36:26 of his *y* is past finding out.
Ps 90: 4 For a thousand *y* in your sight
90:10 The length of our days is seventy *y*
Pr 3: 2 they will prolong your life many *y*
Lk 3:23 Jesus himself was about thirty *y* old
2Pe 3: 8 the Lord a day is like a thousand *y,*
Rev 20: 2 and bound him for a thousand *y.*

YEAST
Ex 12:15 are to eat bread made without *y.*
Mt 16: 6 guard against the *y* of the Pharisees
1Co 5: 6 you know that a little *y* works

YESTERDAY
Heb 13: 8 Jesus Christ is the same *y*

YOKE (YOKED)
1Ki 12: 4 and the heavy *y* he put on us,
Mt 11:29 Take my *y* upon you and learn
Gal 5: 1 be burdened again by a *y*

YOKED (YOKE)
2Co 6:14 Do not be *y* together

YOUNG (YOUNGER YOUTH)
2Ch 10:14 he followed the advice of the *y* men
Ps 37:25 I was *y* and now I am old,
119: 9 How can a *y* man keep his way
Pr 20:29 The glory of *y* men is their strength
Isa 40:11 he gently leads those that have *y.*
Joel 2:28 your *y* men will see visions.
Ac 2:17 your *y* men will see visions,
7:58 at the feet of a *y* man named Saul.
1Ti 4:12 down on you because you are *y,*
Tit 2: 6 encourage the *y* men
1Pe 5: 5 *Y* men, in the same way be
1Jn 2:13 I write to you, *y* men,

YOUNGER (YOUNG)
1Ti 5: 1 Treat *y* men as brothers, older
Tit 2: 4 Then they can train the *y* women

YOUTH (YOUNG)
Ps 103: 5 so that your *y* is renewed like
Ecc 12: 1 Creator in the days of your *y,*
2Ti 2:22 Flee the evil desires of *y,*

ZACCHAEUS
Lk 19: 2 A man was there by the name of *Z;*

ZEAL (ZEALOUS)
Ps 69: 9 for *z* for your house consumes me,
Pr 19: 2 to have *z* without knowledge,
Isa 59:17 and wrapped himself in *z*
Jn 2:17 "*Z* for your house will consume me
Ro 10: 2 their *z* is not based on knowledge.
12:11 Never be lacking in *z,*

ZEALOUS (ZEAL)
Nu 25:13 he was *z* for the honor of his God
Pr 23:17 always be *z* for the fear
Eze 39:25 and I will be *z* for my holy name.
Gal 4:18 fine to be *z,* provided the purpose is

ZEBULUN

Son of Jacob by Leah (Ge 30:20; 35:23; 1Ch 2:1). Tribe of blessed (Ge 49:13; Dt 33:18–19), numbered (Nu 1:31; 26:27), allotted land (Jos 19:10–16; Eze 48:26), failed to fully possess (Jdg 1:30), supported Deborah (Jdg 4:6–10; 5:14, 18), David (1Ch 12:33), 12,000 from (Rev 7:8).

ZECHARIAH

1. Son of Jeroboam II; king of Israel (2Ki 15:8–12).

2. Post-exilic prophet who encouraged rebuilding of temple (Ezr 5:1; 6:14; Zec 1:1).

3. Father of John the Baptist (Lk 1:13; 3:2).

ZEDEKIAH

1. False prophet (1Ki 22:11–24; 2Ch 18:10–23).

2. Mattaniah, son of Josiah (1Ch 3:15), made king of Judah by Nebuchadnezzar (2Ki 24:17–25:7; 2Ch 36:10–14; Jer 37–39; 52:1–11).

ZEPHANIAH

Prophet; descendant of Hezekiah (Zep 1:1).

ZERUBBABEL

Descendant of David (1Ch 3:19; Mt 1:3). Led return from exile (Ezr 2:2; Ne 7:7). Governor of Israel; helped rebuild altar and temple (Ezr 3; Hag 1–2; Zec 4).

ZILPAH

Servant of Leah, mother of Jacob's sons Gad and Asher (Ge 30:9–12; 35:26, 46:16–18).

ZIMRI

King of Israel (1Ki 16:9–20).

ZION
2Sa 5: 7 David captured the fortress of *Z,*
Ps 2: 6 King on *Z,* my holy hill."
9:11 to the LORD, enthroned in *Z;*
74: 2 Mount *Z,* where you dwelt.
87: 2 the LORD loves the gates of *Z*
102:13 and have compassion on *Z,*
137: 3 "Sing us one of the songs of *Z!*"
Isa 2: 3 The law will go out from *Z,*
28:16 "See, I lay a stone in *Z,*
51:11 They will enter *Z* with singing;
52: 8 When the LORD returns to *Z,*
Jer 50: 5 They will ask the way to *Z*
Joel 3:21 The LORD dwells in *Z!*
Am 6: 1 to you who are complacent in *Z,*
Mic 4: 2 The law will go out from *Z,*
Zec 9: 9 Rejoice greatly, O Daughter of *Z!*
Ro 9:33 I lay in *Z* a stone that causes men
11:26 "The deliverer will come from *Z;*
Heb 12:22 But you have come to Mount *Z,*
Rev 14: 1 standing on Mount *Z,*

ZIPPORAH*

Daughter of Reuel; wife of Moses (Ex 2:21–22; 4:20–26; 18:1–6).

ZOPHAR

One of Job's friends (Job 11; 20).

THE FRUIT *of the* SPIRIT BIBLE

Dr. Calvin Miller, General Editor

Project management and editorial by Shari TeSlaa

*Editorial assistance by Natalie Block,
Donna Huisjen, Carol Ochs and Julie Zahm*

Production management by Phil Herich

Art direction by Jamie DeBruyn

Cover design by Curt Diepenhorst

*Interior design by Mark Veldheer,
Byron Center, MI*

*Interior proofreading by Peachtree Editorial
and Proofreading Service,
Peachtree City, GA*

*Literary agency Alive Communications,
Colorado Springs, CO*

*Interior typesetting by The Livingstone Corporation,
Carol Stream, IL*

*Back matter typesetting by Blue Heron Bookcraft,
Battle Ground, WA*

Cover photo by Photographic Concepts

Guarantee

Zondervan Publishing House guarantees leather Bibles unconditionally against manufacturing defects for a lifetime and hardcover, softcover and Leather Look™ Bibles for four years. This guarantee does not apply to normal wear. Contact Zondervan Customer Service, 800-727-1309, for replacement instructions.

Care

We suggest loosening the binding of your new Bible by gently pressing on a small section of pages at a time from the center. To ensure against breakage of the spine, it is best not to bend the cover backward around the spine or to carry study notes, church bulletins, pens, etc., inside the cover. Because a felt-tipped marker will "bleed" through the pages, we recommend use of a ballpoint pen or pencil to underline favorite passages. Your Bible should not be exposed to excessive heat, cold or humidity. Protecting the gold or silver edges of the paper from moisture will avoid spotting, streaking or fading.